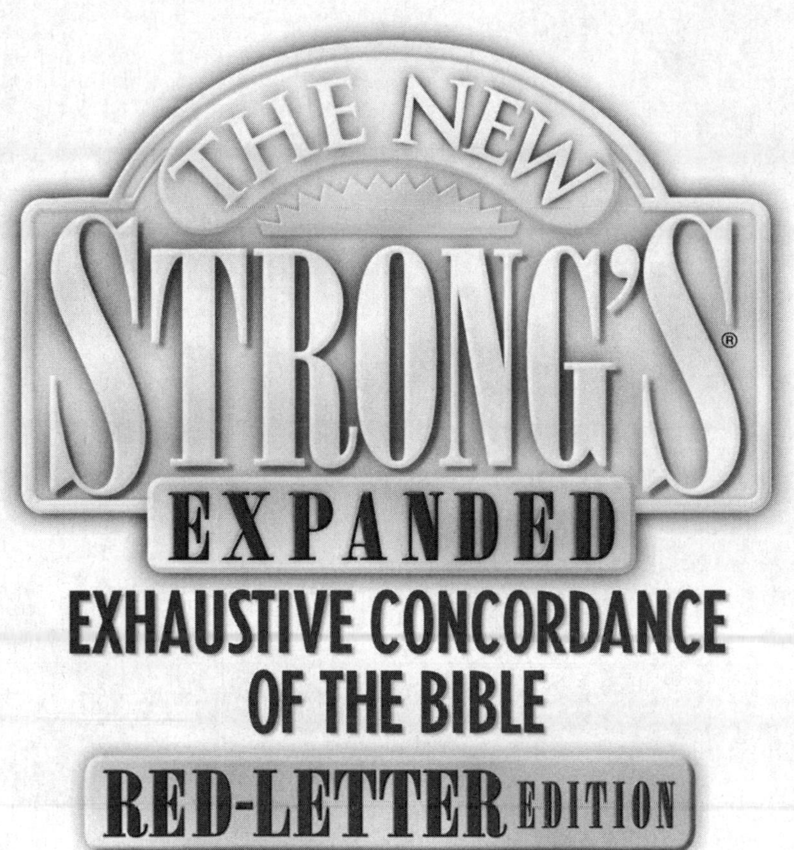
THE NEW
STRONG'S®
EXPANDED
EXHAUSTIVE CONCORDANCE
OF THE BIBLE
RED-LETTER EDITION

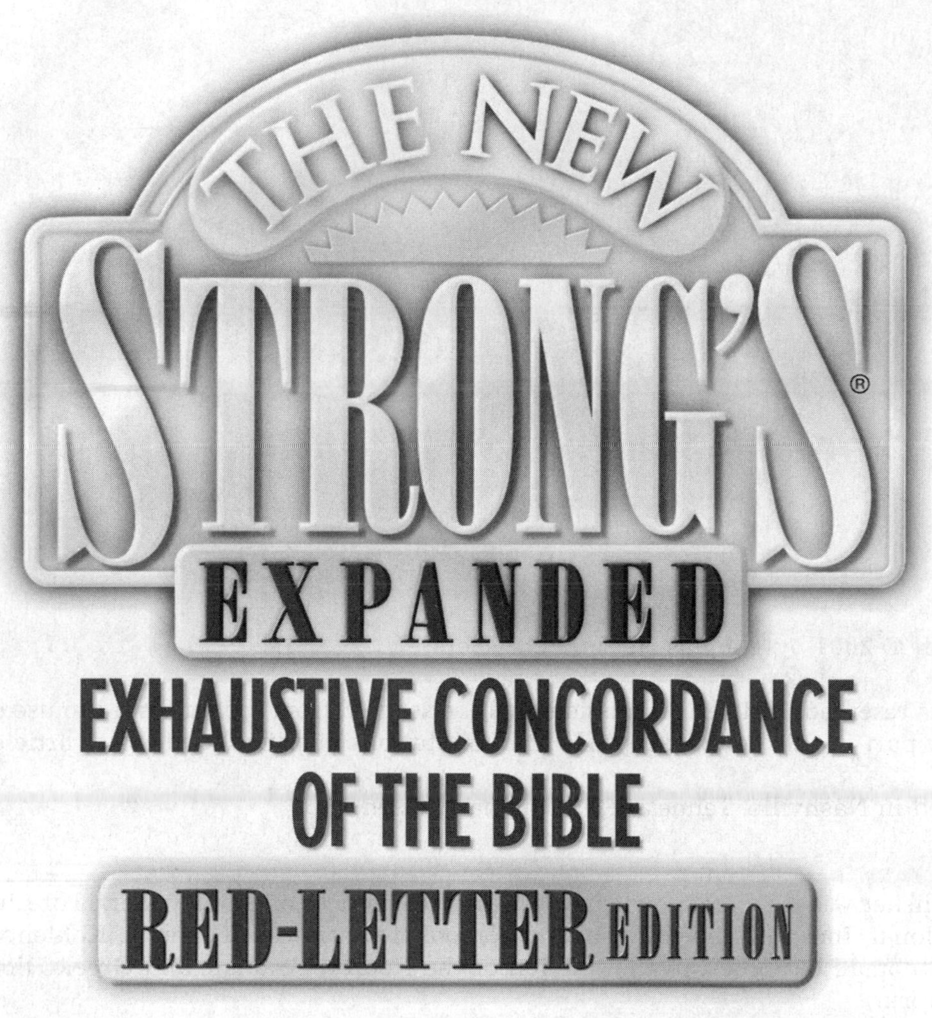

The New Strong's Expanded Exhaustive Concordance of the Bible

Red-Letter Edition

James Strong, LL.D., S.T.D.

Dictionaries include contributions by

John R. Kohlenberger, III

THOMAS NELSON PUBLISHERS

Nashville

Published in Nashville, Tennessee, by Thomas Nelson, Inc.

The Publisher wishes to acknowledge the editorial services of Stanley Morris of Linguatech International, Inc., and the editorial and composition services of John R. Kohlenberger, III and Multnomah Graphics, in the revision of the Hebrew/Aramaic and Greek Dictionaries in this work.

All Scripture references are from the King James Version of the Bible.

The Hebraica and Graeca fonts used to print the Hebrew/Aramaic and Greek Dictionaries are available from Linguist's Software, Inc., P.O. Box 580, Edmonds, WA 98020–0580, tel. (206) 775-1130.

Library of Congress Cataloging-in-Publication Data

Strong, James, 1822–1894.
The new Strong's expanded exhaustive concordance of the Bible / James Strong—Red letter ed.
p. cm.
Rev. ed. of: The new Strong's exhaustive concordance of the Bible. © 1990.
ISBN 0-7852-4539-1 (hc)—ISBN 0-7852-4540-5 (ss)
1. Bible—Concordances, English. 2. Hebrew language—Dictionaries—English. 3. Bible—Indexes. 4. Greek language, Biblical—Dictionaries—English. I. Strong, James, 1822–1894. New Strong's exhaustive concordance of the Bible II. Title.

BS425.S845 2001
220.5'2033—dc21 2001032651

Printed in the United States of America
5 6 7 — 06 05 04 03

PUBLISHER'S PREFACE

For over 100 years, Dr. James Strong's monumental work, *Strong's Exhaustive Concordance of the Bible,* has been the most widely used Bible concordance ever compiled. Originally assembled without the aid of computers or other electronic devices and based on the King James Version of the Bible, *Strong's* has stood the test of time. It has confirmed Dr. Strong's vision for a complete, simple, and accurate concordance that would become "a permanent standard for purposes of reference."

With the publication of *The New Strong's® Exhaustive Concordance of the Bible* in 1984, Thomas Nelson Publishers sought to extend the vision and influence of the original with new typesetting and enhanced features. These included placing Strong's Hebrew and Greek numbers next to the Scripture location for easy reference, adding a more complete numbering system, and cross-referencing proper names so the book could be used with translations other than the King James Version.

Building on this lofty tradition, Thomas Nelson has again added even more significant new features. These additions in *The New Strong's® Expanded Exhaustive Concordance of the Bible* include the following:

- The words of Christ, along with the context lines, are in red type. Since many readers of the Bible use a red-letter edition of the Bible, it seemed wise to incorporate this feature in the new concordance. This allows for easy transition from the Bible to the concordance and quicker location of words in the concordance.
- The most extensive addition is the expansion of the Hebrew and Greek dictionaries. Enlarging the dictionaries to three times their former size by incorporating the best of *Vine's Complete Expository Dictionary of Old and New Testament Words* allows for more thorough and accurate word studies. This enables the user to appreciate all the various shades of meaning. The enhanced word study material also comes from standard dictionaries such as *Brown-Driver-Briggs Hebrew and English Lexicon, Bauer-Arndt-Gingrich-Danker,* and the *Theological Wordbook of the Old Testament.*
- Computer-generated text assures the highest accuracy.
- Frequency counts for all the Hebrew/Aramaic and Greek words and the English words have been added. The main concordance provides the number of times a particular English word appears in the King James Version. This number occurs after the English word and within curly brackets {}. The dictionaries also contain the number of times the original Hebrew/Aramaic or Greek word is used in either the Hebrew Old Testament or the Greek New Testament. In addition, it gives the number of times the King James Version translators used a particular English word. For more information about this feature, see "How to Use the Hebrew and Aramaic Dictionary" and "How to Use the Greek Dictionary," which appear before the respective dictionaries. These sections were composed by John R. Kohlenberger, III.
- A listing of synonyms distinguishes the nuances of the words used in the original. These appear within the enhanced definitions in the dictionaries.
- Also appearing within the enhanced definitions are cross-references to other leading word study dictionaries. This feature directs users to more information when a more advanced word study is desired.

Many features of the 1984 edition are also included in this new red-letter, expanded edition. These include the following:

- Proper names are defined, and those referring to more than one person have their occurrences grouped accordingly.
- Proper names also include variant spellings so Strong's can be used with other Bible translations, including NASB, RSV, NIV, TEV, and NKJV.
- It is truly exhaustive—every word and every reference in the King James Version is indexed.
- The exclusive Fan-Tab™ Thumb-Index Reference System provides quick access.
- Scripture references are listed next to Strong's reference numbers for accurate information.

Additional features from the 1990 edition include:

- Topical Index to the Bible
- Harmony of the Gospels
- Teachings and Illustrations of Christ
- The Parables of Jesus Christ
- The Miracles of Jesus Christ
- Prophecies of the Messiah Fulfilled in Jesus Christ
- The Laws of the Bible
- Old Testament Chronology
- Prayers of the Bible
- The Jewish Calendar/Jewish Feasts
- Monies and Weights/New Testament Monies
- Measures of Length/Dry Measures/Liquid Measures

With the publication of *The New Strong's® Expanded Exhaustive Concordance of the Bible,* this classic reference tool now provides the user with much more information. Word studies can now be conducted with precision and accuracy. In short, it retains the best of previous editions while incorporating even more features in order to make this the concordance of choice.

The Publisher wishes to thank Robert P. Kendall for providing the expanded definitions contained in the dictionaries.

Thomas Nelson issues this new concordance with the prayer that it will continue to serve generations of Bible students for the 21st century and beyond.

INSTRUCTIONS TO THE READER

The New Strong's® Expanded Exhaustive Concordance of the Bible—Red-Letter Edition enables the reader to locate any Scripture passage in the King James Version, as well as every Hebrew or Greek word behind the English words. The most direct way of using these features is as follows:

1. Beginning with the word you are researching, find that word in the Main Concordance, which lists every occurrence of every word in the Bible. If you are looking for a specific occurrence of that word, you should read the context lines until you find the reference.

2. Each context line has three segments. From left to right, they are: The text of the Scripture in which the reference word appears; the reference to the book, chapter, and verse where it may be found; and a reference number to the Hebrew and Greek dictionaries at the back of the concordance. If the reference number is set in Italic type (such as this: *2614*) you should look for it in the Greek Dictionary. Otherwise, it appears in the Hebrew/Aramaic Dictionary. If no number appears, the word may have been supplied by the translators to clarify the meaning, even though no specific Hebrew or Greek word was used to express it.

ABBREVIATIONS

Old Testament

Gen ....Genesis
Ex ....Exodus
Lev ....Leviticus
Num ....Numbers
Deut ....Deuteronomy
Josh ....Joshua
Judg............Judges
Ruth ....Ruth
1Sa ....1 Samuel
2Sa ....2 Samuel
1Kin ....1 Kings
2Kin ....2 Kings
1Chr ....1 Chronicles
2Chr ....2 Chronicles
Ezr ....Ezra
Neh ....Nehemiah
Est ....Esther
Job ....Job
Ps ....Psalms
Prov............Proverbs
Eccl ....Ecclesiastes
Song ....Song of Solomon
Is ....Isaiah
Jer ....Jeremiah
Lam ....Lamentations
Eze ....Ezekiel
Dan ....Daniel
Hos ....Hosea
Joel ....Joel
Amos ....Amos
Obad ....Obadiah
Jonah ....Jonah
Mic ....Micah
Nah ....Nahum
Hab ....Habakkuk
Zeph ....Zephaniah
Hag ....Haggai
Zec ....Zechariah
Mal ....Malachi

New Testament

Mt ....Matthew
Mk ....Mark
Lk ....Luke
Jn ....John
Acts ....Acts
Rom ....Romans
1Cor ....1 Corinthians
2Cor ....2 Corinthians
Gal ....Galatians
Eph ....Ephesians
Phil ....Philippians
Col ....Colossians
1Th ....1 Thessalonians
2Th ....2 Thessalonians
1Ti ....1 Timothy
2Ti ....2 Timothy
Titus ....Titus
Philem ......Philemon
Heb ....Hebrews
Jas ....James
1Pet ....1 Peter
2Pet ....2 Peter
1Jn ....1 John
2Jn ....2 John
3Jn ....3 John
Jude............Jude
Rev ....Revelation

MAIN CONCORDANCE

MAIN CONCORDANCE

A

A See APPENDIX.

AARON *(a'-ur-un)* {319} See AARON'S, AARONITES.
First High Priest of Israel; brother of Moses.

Is not *A* the Levite thy brother	Ex 4:14	175
And the LORD said to *A*, Go into	Ex 4:27	175
Moses told *A* all the words of the	Ex 4:28	175
A went and gathered together all	Ex 4:29	175
A spake all the words which the	Ex 4:30	175
A went in, and told Pharaoh, Thus	Ex 5:1	175
them, Wherefore do ye, Moses and *A*	Ex 5:4	175
And they met Moses and *A*, who stood	Ex 5:20	175
LORD spake unto Moses and unto *A*	Ex 6:13	175
and she bare him *A* and Moses	Ex 6:20	175
A took him Elisheba, daughter of	Ex 6:23	175
These are that *A* and Moses, to	Ex 6:26	175
these are that Moses and *A*	Ex 6:27	175
A thy brother shall be thy	Ex 7:1	175
A thy brother shall speak unto	Ex 7:2	175
A did as the LORD commanded them,	Ex 7:6	175
A fourscore and three years old,	Ex 7:7	175
LORD spake unto Moses and unto *A*	Ex 7:8	175
then thou shalt say unto *A*	Ex 7:9	175
A went in unto Pharaoh, and they	Ex 7:10	175
A cast down his rod before	Ex 7:10	175
LORD spake unto Moses, Say unto *A*	Ex 7:19	175
A did so, as the LORD commanded	Ex 7:20	175
LORD spake unto Moses, Say unto *A*	Ex 8:5	175
A stretched out his hand over the	Ex 8:6	175
Pharaoh called for Moses and *A*	Ex 8:8	175
Moses and *A* went out from Pharaoh	Ex 8:12	175
LORD said unto Moses, Say unto *A*	Ex 8:16	175
for *A* stretched out his hand with	Ex 8:17	175
Pharaoh called for Moses and for *A*	Ex 8:25	175
LORD said unto Moses and unto *A*	Ex 9:8	175
sent, and called for Moses and *A*	Ex 9:27	175
A came in unto Pharaoh, and said	Ex 10:3	175
A were brought again unto Pharaoh	Ex 10:8	175
called for Moses and *A* in haste	Ex 10:16	175
A did all these wonders before	Ex 11:10	175
A in the land of Egypt, saying,	Ex 12:1	175
LORD had commanded Moses and *A*	Ex 12:28	175
A by night, and said, Rise up, and	Ex 12:31	175
And the LORD said unto Moses and *A*	Ex 12:43	175
the LORD commanded Moses and *A*	Ex 12:50	175
the prophetess, the sister of *A*	Ex 15:20	175
Moses and *A* in the wilderness	Ex 16:2	175
A said unto all the children of	Ex 16:6	175
And Moses spake unto *A*, Say unto	Ex 16:9	175
as *A* spake unto the whole	Ex 16:10	175
And Moses said unto *A*, Take a pot,	Ex 16:33	175
so *A* laid it up before the	Ex 16:34	175
and Moses, *A*, and Hur went up to	Ex 17:10	175
and *A* and Hur stayed up his hands,	Ex 17:12	175
A came, and all the elders of	Ex 18:12	175
come up, thou, and *A* with thee	Ex 19:24	175
Come up unto the LORD, thou, and *A*	Ex 24:1	175
Then went up Moses, and *A*, Nadab,	Ex 24:9	175
and, behold, *A* and Hur are with you	Ex 24:14	175
which is before the testimony, *A*	Ex 27:21	175
take thou unto thee *A* thy brother	Ex 28:1	175
me in the priest's office, even *A*	Ex 28:1	175
for *A* thy brother for glory	Ex 28:2	175
holy garments for *A* thy brother	Ex 28:4	175
A shall bear their names before	Ex 28:12	175
A shall bear the names of the	Ex 28:29	175
A shall bear the judgment of the	Ex 28:30	175
And it shall be upon *A* to minister	Ex 28:35	175
that *A* may bear the iniquity of	Ex 28:38	175
shalt put them upon *A* thy brother	Ex 28:41	175
And they shall be upon *A*, and upon	Ex 28:43	175
And *A* and his sons thou shalt bring	Ex 29:4	175
garments, and put upon *A* the coat	Ex 29:5	175
shalt gird them with girdles, *A*	Ex 29:9	175
and thou shalt consecrate *A*	Ex 29:9	175
and *A* and his sons shall put their	Ex 29:10	175
and *A* and his sons shall put their	Ex 29:15	175
and *A* and his sons shall put their	Ex 29:19	175
the tip of the right ear of *A*	Ex 29:20	175
oil, and sprinkle it upon *A*	Ex 29:21	175
shalt put all in the hands of *A*	Ex 29:24	175
even of that which is for *A*	Ex 29:27	175
the holy garments of *A* shall be	Ex 29:29	175
And *A* and his sons shall eat the	Ex 29:32	175
And thus shalt thou do unto *A*	Ex 29:35	175
I will sanctify also both *A*	Ex 29:44	175
A shall burn thereon sweet	Ex 30:7	175
when *A* lighteth the lamps at even	Ex 30:8	175
A shall make an atonement upon	Ex 30:10	175
For *A* and his sons shall wash	Ex 30:19	175
And thou shalt anoint *A* and his	Ex 30:30	175
holy garments for *A* the priest	Ex 31:10	175
themselves together unto *A*	Ex 32:1	175
A said unto them, Break off the	Ex 32:2	175
ears, and brought them unto *A*	Ex 32:3	175
when *A* saw it, he built an altar	Ex 32:5	175
A made proclamation, and said, To	Ex 32:5	175
And Moses said unto *A*, What did	Ex 32:21	175
A said, Let not the anger of my	Ex 32:22	175
(for *A* had made them naked unto	Ex 32:25	175
they made the calf, which *A* made	Ex 32:35	175
And when *A* and all the children of	Ex 34:30	175
and *A* and all the rulers of the	Ex 34:31	175
holy garments for *A* the priest	Ex 35:19	175
of Ithamar, son to *A* the priest	Ex 38:21	175
and made the holy garments for *A*	Ex 39:1	175
of fine linen of woven work for *A*	Ex 39:27	175
holy garments for *A* the priest	Ex 39:41	175
And thou shalt bring *A* and his sons	Ex 40:12	175
put upon *A* the holy garments	Ex 40:13	175
And Moses and *A* and his sons	Ex 40:31	175
the sons of *A* the priest shall	Lev 1:7	175
the sons of *A* shall sprinkle the	Lev 3:13	175
Command *A* and his sons, saying,	Lev 6:9	175
the sons of *A* shall offer it	Lev 6:14	175
And the remainder thereof shall *A*	Lev 6:16	175
the children of *A* shall eat of it	Lev 6:18	175
This is the offering of *A*	Lev 6:20	175
Speak unto *A* and to his sons,	Lev 6:25	175
dry, shall all the sons of *A* have	Lev 7:10	175
He among the sons of *A*, that	Lev 7:33	175
have given them unto *A* the priest	Lev 7:34	175
the portion of the anointing of *A*	Lev 7:35	175
Take *A* and his sons with him, and	Lev 8:2	175
And Moses brought *A* and his sons,	Lev 8:6	175
and *A* and his sons laid their hands	Lev 8:14	175
and *A* and his sons laid their hands	Lev 8:18	175
and *A* and his sons laid their hands	Lev 8:22	175
the altar, and sprinkled it upon *A*	Lev 8:30	175
and sanctified *A*, and his garments,	Lev 8:30	175
And Moses said unto *A* and to his	Lev 8:31	175
as I commanded, saying, *A*	Lev 8:31	175
So *A* and his sons did all things	Lev 8:36	175
eighth day, that Moses called *A*	Lev 9:1	175
And he said unto *A*, Take thee a	Lev 9:2	175
And Moses said unto *A*, Go unto the	Lev 9:7	175
A therefore went unto the altar,	Lev 9:8	175
the sons of *A* brought the blood	Lev 9:9	175
the right shoulder *A* waved for a	Lev 9:21	175
A lifted up his hand toward the	Lev 9:22	175
A went into the tabernacle of the	Lev 9:23	175
And Nadab and Abihu, the sons of *A*	Lev 10:1	175
Then Moses said unto *A*, This is	Lev 10:3	175
And *A* held his peace	Lev 10:3	175
the sons of Uzziel the uncle of *A*	Lev 10:4	175
And Moses said unto *A*, and unto	Lev 10:6	175
And the LORD spake unto *A*, saying,	Lev 10:8	175
And Moses spake unto *A*, and unto	Lev 10:12	175
the sons of *A* which were left	Lev 10:16	175
A said unto Moses, Behold, this	Lev 10:19	175
the LORD spake unto Moses and to *A*	Lev 11:1	175
the LORD spake unto Moses and *A*	Lev 13:1	175
be brought unto *A* the priest	Lev 13:2	175
LORD spake unto Moses and unto *A*	Lev 14:33	175
the LORD spake unto Moses and to *A*	Lev 15:1	175
the death of the two sons of *A*	Lev 16:1	175
Speak unto *A* thy brother, that he	Lev 16:2	175
Thus shall *A* come into the holy	Lev 16:3	175
A shall offer his bullock of the	Lev 16:6	175
A shall cast lots upon the two	Lev 16:8	175
A shall bring the goat upon which	Lev 16:9	175
A shall bring the bullock of the	Lev 16:11	175
A shall lay both his hands upon	Lev 16:21	175
A shall come into the tabernacle	Lev 16:23	175
Speak unto *A*, and unto his sons,	Lev 17:2	175
unto the priests the sons of *A*	Lev 21:1	175
Speak unto *A*, saying, Whosoever	Lev 21:17	175
A the priest shall come nigh to	Lev 21:21	175
And Moses told it unto *A*, and to	Lev 21:24	175
Speak unto *A* and to his sons, that	Lev 22:2	175
of the seed of *A* is a leper	Lev 22:4	175
Speak unto *A*, and to his sons, and	Lev 22:18	175
shall *A* order it from the evening	Lev 24:3	175
A shall number them by their	Num 1:3	175
A took these men which are	Num 1:17	175
A numbered, and the princes of	Num 1:44	175
LORD spake unto Moses and unto *A*	Num 2:1	175
also are the generations of *A*	Num 3:1	175
are the names of the sons of *A*	Num 3:2	175
are the names of the sons of *A*	Num 3:3	175
in the sight of *A* their father	Num 3:4	175
present them before *A* the priest	Num 3:6	175
shalt give the Levites unto *A*	Num 3:9	175
And thou shalt appoint *A* and his	Num 3:10	175
Eleazar the son of *A* the priest	Num 3:32	175
eastward, shall be Moses, and *A*	Num 3:38	175
A numbered at the commandment of	Num 3:39	175
of them is to be redeemed, unto *A*	Num 3:48	175
of them that were redeemed unto *A*	Num 3:51	175
LORD spake unto Moses and unto *A*	Num 4:1	175
A shall come, and his sons, and	Num 4:5	175
And when *A* and his sons have made	Num 4:15	175
office of Eleazar the son of *A*	Num 4:16	175
LORD spake unto Moses and unto *A*	Num 4:17	175
A and his sons shall go in, and	Num 4:19	175
At the appointment of *A* and his	Num 4:27	175
Ithamar the son of *A* the priest	Num 4:28	175
Ithamar the son of *A* the priest	Num 4:33	175
And Moses and *A* and the chief of the	Num 4:34	175
A did number according to the	Num 4:37	175
A did number according to the	Num 4:41	175
A numbered according to the word	Num 4:45	175
of the Levites, whom Moses and *A*	Num 4:46	175
Speak unto *A* and unto his sons,	Num 6:23	175
Ithamar the son of *A* the priest	Num 7:8	175
Speak unto *A*, and say unto him,	Num 8:2	175
And *A* did so	Num 8:3	175
A shall offer the Levites before	Num 8:11	175
shalt set the Levites before *A*	Num 8:13	175
given the Levites as a gift to *A*	Num 8:19	175
And Moses, and *A*, and all the	Num 8:20	175
A offered them as an offering	Num 8:21	175
A made an atonement for them to	Num 8:21	175
of the congregation before *A*	Num 8:22	175
Moses and before *A* on that day	Num 9:6	175
And the sons of *A*, the priests,	Num 10:8	175
A spake against Moses because of	Num 12:1	175
suddenly unto Moses, and unto *A*	Num 12:4	175
of the tabernacle, and called *A*	Num 12:5	175
A looked upon Miriam, and, behold,	Num 12:10	175
A said unto Moses, Alas, my lord,	Num 12:11	175
went and came to Moses, and to *A*	Num 13:26	175
against Moses and against *A*	Num 14:2	175
A fell on their faces before all	Num 14:5	175
LORD spake unto Moses and unto *A*	Num 14:26	175
brought him unto Moses and *A*	Num 15:33	175
against Moses and against *A*	Num 16:3	175
and what is *A*, that ye murmur	Num 16:11	175
the LORD, thou, and they, and *A*	Num 16:16	175
thou also, and *A*, each of you his	Num 16:17	175
the congregation with Moses and *A*	Num 16:18	175
LORD spake unto Moses and unto *A*	Num 16:20	175
Eleazar the son of *A* the priest	Num 16:37	175
which is not of the seed of *A*	Num 16:40	175
against Moses and against *A*	Num 16:41	175
against Moses and against *A*	Num 16:42	175
A came before the tabernacle of	Num 16:43	175
And Moses said unto *A*, Take a	Num 16:46	175
A took as Moses commanded, and ran	Num 16:47	175
A returned unto Moses unto the	Num 16:50	175
the rod of *A* was among their rods	Num 17:6	175
the rod of *A* for the house of	Num 17:8	175
And the LORD said unto *A*, Thou and	Num 18:1	175
And the LORD spake unto *A*, Behold,	Num 18:8	175
And the LORD spake unto *A*, Thou	Num 18:20	175
heave offering to *A* the priest	Num 18:28	175
LORD spake unto Moses and unto *A*	Num 19:1	175
against Moses and against *A*	Num 20:2	175
A went from the presence of the	Num 20:6	175
A thy brother, and speak ye unto	Num 20:8	175
A gathered the congregation	Num 20:10	175
the LORD spake unto Moses and *A*	Num 20:12	175
A in mount Hor, by the coast of	Num 20:23	175
A shall be gathered unto his	Num 20:24	175
Take *A* and Eleazar his son, and	Num 20:25	175
strip *A* of his garments, and put	Num 20:26	175
A shall be gathered unto his	Num 20:26	175
Moses stripped *A* of his garments,	Num 20:28	175
A died there in the top of the	Num 20:28	175
congregation saw that *A* was dead	Num 20:29	175
they mourned for *A* thirty days	Num 20:29	175
Eleazar, the son of *A* the priest	Num 25:7	175
Eleazar, the son of *A* the priest	Num 25:11	175
Eleazar the son of *A* the priest	Num 26:1	175
against *A* in the company of Korah	Num 26:9	175
bare unto Amram *A* and Moses	Num 26:59	175
unto *A* was born Nadab, and Abihu,	Num 26:60	175
A the priest numbered, when they	Num 26:64	175
as *A* thy brother was gathered	Num 27:13	175
under the hand of Moses and *A*	Num 33:1	175
A the priest went up into mount	Num 33:38	175
A was an hundred and twenty and	Num 33:39	175
with *A* to have destroyed him	Deut 9:20	175
I prayed for *A* also the same time	Deut 9:20	175
there *A* died, and there he was	Deut 10:6	175
as *A* thy brother died in mount	Deut 32:50	175
and the children of *A* the priest	Josh 21:4	175

Which the children of *A*, being of ... Josh 21:10 175
of *A* the priest Hebron with her ... Josh 21:13 175
the cities of the children of *A* ... Josh 21:19 175
I sent Moses also and *A*, and I ... Josh 24:5 175
And Eleazar the son of *A* died ... Josh 24:33 175
the son of Eleazar, the son of *A* ... Judg 20:28 175
the LORD that advanced Moses and *A* ... 1Sa 12:6 175
then the LORD sent Moses and *A* ... 1Sa 12:8 175
A, and Moses, and Miriam ... 1Chr 6:3 175
The sons also of *A* ... 1Chr 6:3 175
But *A* and his sons offered upon ... 1Chr 6:49 175
And these are the sons of *A* ... 1Chr 6:50 175
in their coasts, of the sons of *A* ... 1Chr 6:54 175
to the sons of *A* they gave the ... 1Chr 6:57 175
David assembled the children of *A* ... 1Chr 15:4 175
sons of Amram; *A* and Moses ... 1Chr 23:13 175
A was separated, that he should ... 1Chr 23:13 175
was to wait on the sons of *A* for ... 1Chr 23:28 175
of the sons of *A* their brethren ... 1Chr 23:32 175
the divisions of the sons of *A* ... 1Chr 24:1 175
The sons of *A*; Nadab, and Abihu ... 1Chr 24:1 175
under *A* their father, as the LORD ... 1Chr 24:19 175
their brethren the sons of *A* in ... 1Chr 24:31 175
of the LORD, the sons of *A* ... 2Chr 13:9 175
unto the LORD, are the sons of *A* ... 2Chr 13:10 175
but to the priests the sons of *A* ... 2Chr 26:18 175
the priests the sons of *A* to ... 2Chr 29:21 175
Also of the sons of *A* the priests ... 2Chr 31:19 175
of *A* were busied in offering of ... 2Chr 35:14 175
and for the priests the sons of *A* ... 2Chr 35:14 175
the son of *A* the chief priest ... Ezr 7:5 175
the priest the son of *A* shall be ... Neh 10:38 175
them unto the children of *A* ... Neh 12:47 175
a flock by the hand of Moses and *A* ... Ps 77:20 175
A among his priests, and Samuel ... Ps 99:6 175
and *A* whom he had chosen ... Ps 105:26 175
camp, and *A* the saint of the LORD ... Ps 106:16 175
O house of *A*, trust in the LORD ... Ps 115:10 175
he will bless the house of *A* ... Ps 115:12 175
Let the house of *A* now say ... Ps 118:3 175
bless the LORD, O house of *A* ... Ps 135:19 175
and I sent before thee Moses, *A* ... Mic 6:4 175
wife was of the daughters of *A* ... Lk 1:5 *2*
Saying unto *A*, Make us gods to go ... Acts 7:40 *2*
that is called of God, as was *A* ... Heb 5:4 *2*
be called after the order of *A* ... Heb 7:11 *2*

AARONITES *(a'-ur-un-ites)* {2} *Priests; Aaron's descendants.*
Jehoiada was the leader of the *A* ... 1Chr 12:27 175
of the *A*, Zadok ... 1Chr 27:17 175

AARON'S *(a'-ur-uns)* {31}
Eleazar *A* son took him one of the ... Ex 6:25 175
but *A* rod swallowed up their rods ... Ex 7:12 175
Abihu, Eleazar and Ithamar, *A* sons ... Ex 28:1 175
that they may make *A* garments to ... Ex 28:3 175
and they shall be upon *A* heart ... Ex 28:30 175
And it shall be upon *A* forehead ... Ex 28:38 175
for *A* sons thou shalt make coats ... Ex 28:40 175
of the ram of *A* consecration ... Ex 29:26 175
And it shall be *A* and his sons' by ... Ex 29:28 175
A sons, shall bring the blood, and ... Lev 1:5 175
A sons, shall lay the parts, the ... Lev 1:8 175
A sons, shall sprinkle his blood ... Lev 1:11 175
bring it to *A* sons the priests ... Lev 2:2 175
of the meat offerings shall be *A* ... Lev 2:3 175
of the meat offering shall be *A* ... Lev 2:10 175
A sons the priests shall sprinkle ... Lev 3:2 175
A sons shall burn it on the altar ... Lev 3:5 175
A sons shall sprinkle the blood ... Lev 3:8 175
but the breast shall be *A* ... Lev 7:31 175
of the anointing oil upon *A* head ... Lev 8:12 175
And Moses brought *A* sons, and put ... Lev 8:13 175
it upon the tip of *A* right ear ... Lev 8:23 175
And he brought *A* sons, and Moses ... Lev 8:24 175
And he put all upon *A* hands ... Lev 8:27 175
A sons presented unto him the ... Lev 9:12 175
A sons presented unto him the ... Lev 9:18 175
And it shall be *A* and his sons' ... Lev 24:9 175
thou shalt write *A* name upon the ... Num 17:3 175
Bring *A* rod again before the ... Num 17:10 175
down upon the beard, even *A* beard ... Ps 133:2 175
A rod that budded, and the tables ... Heb 9:4 *2*

ABADDON *(ab-ad'-dun)* {1} *Angel of the Abyss.*
name in the Hebrew tongue is *A* ... Rev 9:11 *3*

ABAGTHA *(ab-ag'-thah)* {1} *Servant of King Ahaseurus.*
Biztha, Harbona, Bigtha, and *A* ... Est 1:10 5

ABANA *(ab-ay'-nah)* {1} *A river in Syria.*
Are not *A* and Pharpar, rivers of ... 2Kin 5:12 71

ABANAH See ABANA.

ABARIM *(ab'-ar-im)* {4} See IJE-ABARIM. *A mountain range in Moab.*
Get thee up into this mount *A* ... Num 27:12 5682
and pitched in the mountains of *A* ... Num 33:47 5682
departed from the mountains of *A* ... Num 33:48 5682
Get thee up into this mountain *A* ... Deut 32:49 5682

ABASE {4}
every one that is proud, and *a* him ... Job 40:11 8213
nor *a* himself for the noise of ... Is 31:4 6031
is low, and *a* him that is high ... Eze 21:26 8213
walk in pride he is able to *a* ... Dan 4:37 8214

ABASED {4}
shall exalt himself shall be *a* ... Mt 23:12 *5013*
exalteth himself shall be *a* ... Lk 14:11 *5013*
that exalteth himself shall be *a* ... Lk 18:14 *5013*
I know both how to be *a*, and I ... Phil 4:12 *5013*

ABASING {1}
Have I committed an offence in *a* ... 2Cor 11:7 *5013*

ABATED {6}
and fifty days the waters were *a* ... Gen 8:3 2637
to see if the waters were *a* from ... Gen 8:8 7043
waters were *a* from off the earth ... Gen 8:11 7043
it shall be *a* from thy estimation ... Lev 27:18 1639
not dim, nor his natural force *a* ... Deut 34:7 5127
Then their anger was *a* toward him ... Judg 8:3 7503

ABBA *(ab'-bah)* {3} *Aramaic for "Father."*
And he said, *A*, Father, all things ... Mk 14:36 *5*
of adoption, whereby we cry, *A* ... Rom 8:15 *5*
Son into your hearts, crying, *A* ... Gal 4:6 *5*

ABDA *(ab'-dah)* {2}
1. Father of Adoniram.
Adoniram the son of *A* was over ... 1Kin 4:6 5653
2. A chief Levite after the exile.
A the son of Shammua, the son of ... Neh 11:17 5653

ABDEEL *(ab'-de-el)* {1} *Father of Shelemiah.*
Azriel, and Shelemiah the son of *A* ... Jer 36:26 5655

ABDI *(ab'-di)* {3}
1. Levite grandfather of Ethan.
the son of Kishi, the son of *A* ... 1Chr 6:44 5660
sons of Merari, Kish the son of *A* ... 2Chr 29:12 5660
2. Married a foreigner while in exile.
Zechariah, and Jehiel, and *A* ... Ezr 10:26 5660

ABDIEL *(ab'-de-el)* {1} *Son of Guni.*
Ahi the son of *A*, the son of Guni ... 1Chr 5:15 5661

ABDON *(ab'-dun)* {8}
1. Levitical city in Asher.
her suburbs, *A* with her suburbs, ... Josh 21:30 5658
suburbs, and *A* with her suburbs, ... 1Chr 6:74 5658
2. A judge of Israel.
after him *A* the son of Hillel, a ... Judg 12:13 5658
And *A* the son of Hillel the ... Judg 12:15 5658
3. A Benjamite in Jerusalem.
And *A*, and Zichri, and Hanan, ... 1Chr 8:23 5658
4. Son of Jehiel.
And his firstborn son *A*, and Zur, ... 1Chr 8:30 5658
And his firstborn son *A*, then Zur, ... 1Chr 9:36 5658
5. Son of Micah.
A the son of Micah, and Shaphan ... 2Chr 34:20 5658

ABED-NEGO *(ab-ed'-ne-go)* {15} *A companion of Daniel in captivity.*
and to Azariah, of *A* ... Dan 1:7 5664
and he set Shadrach, Meshach, and *A* ... Dan 2:49 5665
Babylon, Shadrach, Meshach, and *A* ... Dan 3:12 5665
to bring Shadrach, Meshach, and *A* ... Dan 3:13 5665
true, O Shadrach, Meshach, and *A* ... Dan 3:14 5665
Shadrach, Meshach, and *A*, answered ... Dan 3:16 5665
against Shadrach, Meshach, and *A* ... Dan 3:19 5665
to bind Shadrach, Meshach, and *A* ... Dan 3:20 5665
took up Shadrach, Meshach, and *A* ... Dan 3:22 5665
men, Shadrach, Meshach, and *A* ... Dan 3:23 5665
and said, Shadrach, Meshach, and *A* ... Dan 3:26 5665
Then Shadrach, Meshach, and *A* ... Dan 3:26 5665
God of Shadrach, Meshach, and *A* ... Dan 3:28 5665
God of Shadrach, Meshach, and *A* ... Dan 3:29 5665
promoted Shadrach, Meshach, and *A* ... Dan 3:30 5665

ABEL *(a'-bel)* {16}
1. Second son of Adam.
And she again bare his brother *A* ... Gen 4:2 1893
A was a keeper of sheep, but Cain ... Gen 4:2 1893
And *A*, he also brought of the ... Gen 4:4 1893
And the LORD had respect unto *A* ... Gen 4:4 1893
And Cain talked with *A* his brother ... Gen 4:8 1893
rose up against *A* his brother ... Gen 4:8 1893
unto Cain, Where is *A* thy brother ... Gen 4:9 1893
me another seed instead of *A* ... Gen 4:25 1893
from the blood of righteous *A* ... Mt 23:35 *6*
From the blood of *A* unto the ... Lk 11:51 *6*
By faith *A* offered unto God a ... Heb 11:4 *6*
better things than that of *A* ... Heb 12:24 *6*
2. Great stone near Beth-shemesh.
even unto the great stone of *A* ... 1Sa 6:18 59
3. A city in Naphtali.
all the tribes of Israel unto *A* ... 2Sa 20:14 62
besieged him in *A* of Beth-maachah ... 2Sa 20:15 62
shall surely ask counsel at *A* ... 2Sa 20:18 59

ABEL ACACIA GROVE See ABEL-SHITTIM.

ABEL BETH MAACAH See BETH-MAACHAH.

ABEL-BETH-MAACHAH *(a'-bel-beth-ma'-a-kah)* {2} *A city in northern Israel.*
and smote Ijon, and Dan, and *A* ... 1Kin 15:20 62
of Assyria, and took Ijon, and *A* ... 2Kin 15:29 62

ABEL-MAIM *(a'-bel-ma'-im)* {1} *Another name for Abel-beth-maachah.*
and they smote Ijon, and Dan, and *A* ... 2Chr 16:4 66

ABEL-MEHOLAH *(a'-bel-me-ho'-lah)* {3} *A city in Issachar.*
Zererath, and to the border of *A* ... Judg 7:22 65
Jezreel, from Beth-shean to *A* ... 1Kin 4:12 65
Elisha the son of Shaphat of *A* ... 1Kin 19:16 65

ABEL-MIZRAIM *(a'-bel-miz'-ra-im)* {1} *A place east of the Jordan River.*
the name of it was called *A* ... Gen 50:11 67

ABEL-SHITTIM *(a'-bel-shit'-tim)* {1} *A place in Moab.*
even unto *A* in the plains of Moab ... Num 33:49 63

ABEZ *(a'-bez)* {1} *A place in Issachar.*
And Rabbith, and Kishion, and *A* ... Josh 19:20 77

ABHOR {19}
and my soul shall not *a* you ... Lev 26:11 1602
or if your soul *a* my judgments ... Lev 26:15 1602
idols, and my soul shall *a* you ... Lev 26:30 1602
them away, neither will I *a* them ... Lev 26:44 1602
it, and thou shalt utterly *a* it ... Deut 7:26 8581
Thou shalt not *a* an Edomite ... Deut 23:7 8581
thou shalt not *a* an Egyptian ... Deut 23:7 8581
people Israel utterly to *a* him ... 1Sa 27:12 887
and mine own clothes shall *a* me ... Job 9:31 8581
They *a* me, they flee far from me, ... Job 30:10 8581
Wherefore I *a* myself, and repent ... Job 42:6 3988
the LORD will *a* the bloody ... Ps 5:6 8581
I hate and *a* lying ... Ps 119:163 8581
people curse, nations shall *a* him ... Prov 24:24 2194
Do not *a* us, for thy name's sake, ... Jer 14:21 5006
gate, and they *a* him that speaketh ... Amos 5:10 8581
I *a* the excellency of Jacob, and ... Amos 6:8 8374
that *a* judgment, and pervert all ... Mic 3:9 8581
A that which is evil ... Rom 12:9 *655*

ABHORRED {16}
to be *a* in the eyes of Pharaoh ... Ex 5:21 887
things, and therefore I *a* them ... Lev 20:23 6973
because their soul *a* my statutes ... Lev 26:43 1602
he *a* them, because of the ... Deut 32:19 5006
for men *a* the offering of the ... 1Sa 2:17 5006
that thou art *a* of thy father ... 2Sa 16:21 887
he *a* Israel, and reigned over ... 1Kin 11:25 6973
All my inward friends *a* me ... Job 19:19 8581
For he hath not despised nor *a* ... Ps 22:24 8262
he was wroth, and greatly *a* Israel ... Ps 78:59 3988
But thou hast cast off and *a* ... Ps 89:38 3988
insomuch that he *a* his own ... Ps 106:40 8581
he that is *a* of the LORD shall ... Prov 22:14 2194
he hath *a* his sanctuary, he hath ... Lam 2:7 5010
and hast made thy beauty to be *a* ... Eze 16:25 8581
them, and their soul also *a* me ... Zec 11:8 973

ABHORREST {2}
the land that thou *a* shall be ... Is 7:16 6973
thou that *a* idols, dost thou ... Rom 2:22 *948*

ABHORRETH {5}
So that his life *a* bread, and his ... Job 33:20 2092
the covetous, whom the LORD *a* ... Ps 10:3 5006
he *a* not evil ... Ps 36:4 3988
Their soul *a* all manner of meat ... Ps 107:18 8581
to him whom the nation *a* ... Is 49:7 8581

ABHORRING {1}
they shall be an *a* unto all flesh ... Is 66:24 1860

ABI *(a'-bi)* {1} See ABI-ABLON, ABI-EZER. *Mother of King Hezekiah.*
His mother's name also was *A* ... 2Kin 18:2 21

ABIA *(ab-i'-ah)* {4} See ABIAH, ABIJAH, ABIJAM.
1. A son of Rehoboam.
Rehoboam, *A* his son, Asa his son, ... 1Chr 3:10 29
and Roboam begat *A* ... Mt 1:7 *7*
and *A* begat Asa ... Mt 1:7 *7*
2. A priest.
Zacharias, of the course of *A* ... Lk 1:5 *7*

ABIAH *(ab-i'-ah)* {4} See ABIA.
1. A son of Samuel.
and the name of his second, *A* ... 1Sa 8:2 29
the firstborn Vashni, and *A* ... 1Chr 6:28 29
2. Mother of Ashur.
then *A* Hezron's wife bare him ... 1Chr 2:24 29
3. Son of Becher.
and Omri, and Jerimoth, and *A* ... 1Chr 7:8 29

ABI-ALBON *(ab'-i-al'-bun)* {1} *A "mighty man" of David.*
A the Arbathite, Azmaveth the ... 2Sa 23:31 45

ABIASAPH *(ab-i'-as-af)* {1} See EBIASAPH. *A son of Korah.*
Assir, and Elkanah, and *A* ... Ex 6:24 23

ABIATHAR *(ab-i'-uth-ur)* {30} See ABITHAR'S. *High Priest during David's reign.*
the son of Ahitub, named *A* ... 1Sa 22:20 54
A shewed David that Saul had ... 1Sa 22:21 54
And David said unto *A*, I knew it ... 1Sa 22:22 54
when *A* the son of Ahimelech fled ... 1Sa 23:6 54
and he said to *A* the priest ... 1Sa 23:9 54
And David said to *A* the priest ... 1Sa 30:7 54
A brought thither the ephod to ... 1Sa 30:7 54
Ahitub, and Ahimelech the son of *A* ... 2Sa 8:17 54
A went up, until all the people ... 2Sa 15:24 54
thy son, and Jonathan the son of *A* ... 2Sa 15:27 54
A carried the ark of God again to ... 2Sa 15:29 54
with thee Zadok and *A* the priests ... 2Sa 15:35 54
tell it to Zadok and *A* the priests ... 2Sa 15:35 54
to *A* the priests, Thus and thus ... 2Sa 17:15 54
to *A* the priests, saying, Speak ... 2Sa 19:11 54
and Zadok and *A* were the priests ... 2Sa 20:25 54
of Zeruiah, and with *A* the priest ... 1Kin 1:7 54
A the priest, and Joab the captain ... 1Kin 1:19 54
of the host, and *A* the priest ... 1Kin 1:25 54
the son of *A* the priest came ... 1Kin 1:42 54
for *A* the priest, and for Joab the ... 1Kin 2:22 54
unto *A* the priest said the king, ... 1Kin 2:26 54
So Solomon thrust out *A* from ... 1Kin 2:27 54
did the king put in the room of *A* ... 1Kin 2:35 54
and Zadok and *A* were the priests ... 1Kin 4:4 54
A the priests, and for the Levites ... 1Chr 15:11 54
Ahitub, and Abimelech the son of *A* ... 1Chr 18:16 54
priest, and Ahimelech the son of *A* ... 1Chr 24:6 54
Jehoiada the son of Benaiah, and *A* ... 1Chr 27:34 54
in the days of *A* the high priest ... Mk 2:26 *8*

ABIATHAR'S *(ab-i'-uth-urs)* {1}
Zadok's son, and Jonathan *A* son 2Sa 15:36 54

ABIB *(a'-bib)* {6} See TEL-ABIB. *First month of the Hebrew year.*
day came ye out in the month *A* Ex 13:4 24
the time appointed of the month *A* Ex 23:15 24
thee, in the time of the month *A* Ex 34:18 24
for in the month *A* thou camest Ex 34:18 24
Observe the month of *A*, and keep Deut 16:1 24
for in the month of *A* the LORD Deut 16:1 24

ABIDA *(ab'-id-ah)* {1} See ABIDAH. *A son of Midian.*
Ephah, and Epher, and Henoch, and *A* 1Chr 1:33 28

ABIDAH *(ab'-id-ah)* {1} See ABIDA. *Same as Abida.*
Ephah, and Epher, and Hanoch, and *A* Gen 25:4 28

ABIDAN *(ab'-id-an)* {5} *Son of Gideoni.*
A the son of Gideoni Num 1:11 27
shall be *A* the son of Gideoni Num 2:22 27
On the ninth day *A* the son of Num 7:60 27
offering of *A* the son of Gideoni Num 7:65 27
Benjamin was *A* the son of Gideoni Num 10:24 27

ABIDE {84}
but we will *a* in the street all Gen 19:2 3885
young men, *A* ye here with the ass Gen 22:5 3427
Let the damsel *a* with us a few Gen 24:55 3427
a with me Gen 29:19 3427
let thy servant *a* instead of the Gen 44:33 3427
a ye every man in his place, let Ex 16:29 3427
Therefore shall ye *a* at the door Lev 8:35 3427
a with thee all night until the Lev 19:13 3885
earth, and they *a* over against me Num 22:5 3427
do ye *a* without the camp seven Num 31:19 2583
Every thing that may *a* the fire Num 31:23 935
he shall *a* in it unto the death Num 35:25 3427
shall *a* in your cities which I Deut 3:19 3427
Judah shall *a* in their coast on Josh 18:5 5975
the house of Joseph shall *a* in Josh 18:5 5975
but *a* here fast by my maidens Ruth 2:8 1692
the LORD, and there *a* for ever 1Sa 1:22 3427
God of Israel shall not *a* with us 1Sa 5:7 3427
a in a secret place, and hide 1Sa 19:2 3427
unto David, *A* not in the hold 1Sa 22:5 3427
A thou with me, fear not 1Sa 22:23 3427
made also to *a* at the brook Besor 1Sa 30:21 3427
and Israel, and Judah, *a* in tents 2Sa 11:11 3427
to thy place, and *a* with the king 2Sa 15:19 3427
will I be, and with him will I *a* 2Sa 16:18 3427
place for thee to *a* in for ever 1Kin 8:13 3427
a now at home 2Chr 25:19 3427
that ye *a* in the siege in 2Chr 32:10 3427
nor *a* in the paths thereof Job 24:13 3427
a in the covert to lie in wait Job 38:40 3427
to serve thee, or *a* by thy crib Job 39:9 3885
who shall *a* in thy tabernacle Ps 15:1 1481
I will *a* in thy tabernacle for Ps 61:4 1481
He shall *a* before God for ever Ps 61:7 3427
shall *a* under the shadow of the Ps 91:1 3885
her feet *a* not in her house Prov 7:11 7931
he that hath it shall *a* satisfied Prov 19:23 3885
for that shall *a* with him of his Eccl 8:15 3867
not be able to *a* his indignation Jer 10:10 3557
If ye will still *a* in this land Jer 42:10 3427
the LORD, no man shall *a* there Jer 49:18 3427
there shall no man *a* there Jer 49:33 3427
so shall no man *a* there, neither Jer 50:40 3427
Thou shalt *a* for me many days Hos 3:3 3427
shall *a* many days without a king Hos 3:4 3427
the sword shall *a* on his cities Hos 11:6 2342
and who can *a* it Joel 2:11 3557
and they shall *a* Mic 5:4 3427
who can *a* in the fierceness of Nah 1:6 6965
But who may *a* the day of his Mal 3:2 3557
there *a* till ye go thence Mt 10:11 *3306*
there *a* till ye depart from that Mk 6:10 *3306*
house ye enter into, there *a* Lk 9:4 *3306*
for to day I must *a* at thy house Lk 19:5 *3306*
him, saying, *A* with us Lk 24:29 *3306*
on me should not *a* in darkness Jn 12:46 *3306*
that he may *a* with you for ever Jn 14:16 *3306*
A in me, and I in you Jn 15:4 *3306*
itself, except it *a* in the vine Jn 15:4 *3306*
no more can ye, except ye *a* in me Jn 15:4 *3306*
If a man *a* not in me, he is cast Jn 15:6 *3306*
If ye *a* in me, and my words *a* Jn 15:7 *3306*
a in me, and my words *a* in you Jn 15:7 *3306*
ye shall *a* in my love Jn 15:10 *3306*
commandments, and *a* in his love Jn 15:10 *3306*
it pleased Silas to *a* there still Acts 15:34 *1961*
come into my house, and *a* there Acts 16:15 *3306*
that bonds and afflictions *a* me Acts 20:23 *3306*
Except these *a* in the ship Acts 27:31 *3306*
if they *a* not still in unbelief, Rom 11:23 *1961*
If any man's work *a* which he hath 1Cor 3:14 *3306*
good for them if they *a* even as I 1Cor 7:8 *3306*
Let every man *a* in the same 1Cor 7:20 *3306*
he is called, therein *a* with God 1Cor 7:24 *3306*
But she is happier if she so *a* 1Cor 7:40 *3306*
And it may be that I will *a* 1Cor 16:6 *3887*
Nevertheless to *a* in the flesh is Phil 1:24 *1961*
confidence, I know that I shall *a* Phil 1:25 *3306*
thee to *a* still at Ephesus 1Ti 1:3 *4357*
Let that therefore *a* in you 1Jn 2:24 *3306*
taught you, ye shall *a* in him 1Jn 2:27 *3306*
And now, little children, *a* in him 1Jn 2:28 *3306*

ABIDETH {30}
all that *a* not the fire ye shall Num 31:23 935
king, Behold, he *a* at Jerusalem 2Sa 16:3 3427
a on the rock, upon the crag of Job 39:28 3885
man being in honour *a* not Ps 49:12 3885
them, even he that *a* of old Ps 55:19 3427
established the earth, and it *a* Ps 119:90 5975
cannot be removed, but *a* for ever Ps 125:1 3427
reproof of life *a* among the wise Prov 15:31 3885
but the earth *a* for ever Eccl 1:4 5975
He that *a* in this city shall die Jer 21:9 3427
but the wrath of God *a* on him Jn 3:36 *3306*
the servant *a* not in the house Jn 8:35 *3306*
but the Son *a* ever Jn 8:35 *3306*
the ground and die, it *a* alone Jn 12:24 *3306*
of the law that Christ *a* for ever Jn 12:34 *3306*
He that *a* in me, and I in him, the Jn 15:5 *3306*
now *a* faith, hope, charity, these 1Cor 13:13 *3306*
we believe not, yet he *a* faithful 2Ti 2:13 *3306*
a a priest continually Heb 7:3 *3306*
God, which liveth and *a* for ever 1Pet 1:23 *3306*
He that saith he *a* in him ought 1Jn 2:6 *3306*
loveth his brother *a* in the light 1Jn 2:10 *3306*
and the word of God *a* in you 1Jn 2:14 *3306*
doeth the will of God *a* for ever 1Jn 2:17 *3306*
ye have received of him *a* in you 1Jn 2:27 *3306*
Whosoever *a* in him sinneth not 1Jn 3:6 *3306*
loveth not his brother *a* in death 1Jn 3:14 *3306*
And hereby we know that he *a* in us 1Jn 3:24 *3306*
a not in the doctrine of Christ, 2Jn 9 *3306*
He that *a* in the doctrine of 2Jn 9 *3306*

ABIDING {9}
he saw Israel *a* in his tents Num 24:2 7931
a with her in the chamber Judg 16:9 3427
liers in wait *a* in the chamber Judg 16:12 3427
driven me out this day from *a* in 1Sa 26:19 5596
as a shadow, and there is none *a* 1Chr 29:15 4723
country shepherds *a* in the field Lk 2:8 *63*
And ye have not his word *a* in you Jn 5:38 *3306*
were in that city *a* certain days Acts 16:12 *1304*
hath eternal life *a* in him 1Jn 3:15 *3306*

ABIEL *(a'-be-el)* {3}
1. Grandfather of King Saul.
whose name was Kish, the son of *A* 1Sa 9:1 22
father of Abner was the son of *A* 1Sa 14:51 22
2. A "mighty man" of David.
brooks of Gaash, *A* the Arbathite, 1Chr 11:32 22

ABI-EZER *(ab-i-e'-zur)* {2} See ABIEZRITE, JEEZER.
1. A descendant of Manasseh.
and *A* was gathered after him Judg 6:34 44
better than the vintage of *A* Judg 8:2 44

ABIEZER {5}
for the children of *A*, and for the Josh 17:2 44
A the Anethothite, Mebunnai the 2Sa 23:27 44
Hammoleketh bare Ishod, and *A* 1Chr 7:18 44
the Tekoite, *A* the Antothite, 1Chr 11:28 44
ninth month was *A* the Anetothite 1Chr 27:12 44

ABI-EZRITE *(ab-i-ez'-rite)* {1} See ABI-EZRITES. *A descendant of Abiezer.*
that pertained unto Joash the *A* Judg 6:11 33

ABI-EZRITES *(ab-i-ez'-rites)* {2}
day it is yet in Ophrah of the *A* Judg 6:24 33
his father, in Ophrah of the *A* Judg 8:32 33

ABIGAIL *(ab'-e-gul)* {17}
1. A wife of David.
and the name of his wife *A* 1Sa 25:3 26
But one of the young men told *A* 1Sa 25:14 26
Then *A* made haste, and took two 1Sa 25:18 26
when *A* saw David, she hasted, and 1Sa 25:23 26
And David said to *A*, Blessed be 1Sa 25:32 26
And *A* came to Nabal 1Sa 25:36 26
And David sent and communed with *A* 1Sa 25:39 26
of David were come to *A* to Carmel 1Sa 25:40 26
A hasted, and arose, and rode upon 1Sa 25:42 26
A the Carmelitess, Nabal's wife 1Sa 27:3 26
A the wife of Nabal the Carmelite 1Sa 30:5 26
A Nabal's wife the Carmelite 2Sa 2:2 26
of *A* the wife of Nabal the 2Sa 3:3 26
Daniel, of *A* the Carmelitess 1Chr 3:1 26
2. Mother of Amosa.
that went in to *A* the daughter of 2Sa 17:25 26
Whose sisters were Zeruiah, and *A* 1Chr 2:16 26
And *A* bare Amasa 1Chr 2:17 26

ABIHAIL *(ab-e-ha'-il)* {6}
1. Head of Levital family of Merari.
of Merari was Zuriel the son of *A* Num 3:35 32
2. Wife of Abishur.
name of the wife of Abishur was *A* 1Chr 2:29 32
3. Chief of a family of Gad.
the children of *A* the son of Huri 1Chr 5:14 32
4. Descendant of Eliab.
A the daughter of Eliab the son 2Chr 11:18 32
5. Father of Esther.
the daughter of *A* the uncle of Est 2:15 32
the queen, the daughter of *A* Est 9:29 32

ABIHU *(a-bi'-hew)* {12} *A son of Aaron.*
and she bare him Nadab, and *A* Ex 6:23 30
LORD, thou, and Aaron, Nadab, and *A* Ex 24:1 30
up Moses, and Aaron, Nadab, and *A* Ex 24:9 30
office, even Aaron, Nadab and *A* Ex 28:1 30
And Nadab and *A*, the sons of Aaron, Lev 10:1 30
Nadab the firstborn, and *A* Num 3:2 30
A died before the LORD, when they Num 3:4 30
unto Aaron was born Nadab, and *A* Num 26:60 30
A died, when they offered strange Num 26:61 30
Nadab, and *A*, Eleazar, and Ithamar 1Chr 6:3 30
Nadab, and *A*, Eleazar, and Ithamar 1Chr 24:1 30
A died before their father, and 1Chr 24:2 30

ABIHUD *(a-bi'-hud)* {1} *A son of Bela.*
Bela were, Addar, and Gera, and *A* 1Chr 8:3 31

ABIJAH *(a-bi'-jah)* {20} See ABIA, ABIJAM.
1. A son of Jeroboam I.
At that time *A* the son of 1Kin 14:1 29
2. A priest during David's reign.
to Hakkoz, the eighth to *A* 1Chr 24:10 29
3. A son of Rehoboam.
which bare him *A*, and Attai, and 2Chr 11:20 29
Rehoboam made *A* the son of 2Chr 11:22 29
A his son reigned in his stead 2Chr 12:16 29
began *A* to reign over Judah 2Chr 13:1 29
And there was war between *A* 2Chr 13:2 29
A set the battle in array with an 2Chr 13:3 29
A stood up upon mount Zemaraim, 2Chr 13:4 29
Jeroboam and all Israel before *A* 2Chr 13:15 29
And *A* and his people slew them with 2Chr 13:17 29
A pursued after Jeroboam, and took 2Chr 13:19 29
strength again in the days of *A* 2Chr 13:20 29
But *A* waxed mighty, and married 2Chr 13:21 29
And the rest of the acts of *A* 2Chr 13:22 29
So *A* slept with his fathers, and 2Chr 14:1 29
4. Mother of King Hezekiah.
And his mother's name was *A* 2Chr 29:1 29
5. A priest in Nehemiah's time.
Meshullam, *A*, Mijamin, Neh 10:7 29
6. A priest who returned from Exile under Zerubbabel.
Iddo, Ginnetho, *A*, Neh 12:4 29
Of *A*, Zichri Neh 12:17 29

ABIJAM *(a-bi'-jum)* {05} *Son and successor of King Rehoboam.*
A his son reigned in his stead 1Kin 14:31 38
son of Nebat reigned *A* over Judah 1Kin 15:1 38
Now the rest of the acts of *A* 1Kin 15:7 38
And there was war between *A* 1Kin 15:7 38
And *A* slept with his fathers 1Kin 15:8 38

ABILENE *(ab-i-le'-ne)* {1} *A Roman tetrarchy in northern Palestine.*
and Lysanias the tetrarch of *A* Lk 3:1 *9*

ABILITY {7}
according to his *a* that vowed Lev 27:8 5381
They gave after their *a* unto the Ezr 2:69 3581
We after our *a* have redeemed our Neh 5:8 1767
such as had *a* in them to stand in Dan 1:4 3581
man according to his several *a* Mt 25:15 *1411*
every man according to his *a* Acts 11:29 *2141*
it as of the *a* which God giveth 1Pet 4:11 *2479*

ABIMAEL *(a-bim'-ah-el)* {2} *A son of Joktan in Arabia.*
And Obal, and *A*, and Sheba, Gen 10:28 39
And Ebal, and *A*, and Sheba, 1Chr 1:22 39

ABIMELECH *(a-bim'-e-lek)* {65} See ABIMELECH'S.
1. Philistine king in Abraham's time.
A king of Gerar sent, and took Gen 20:2 40
But God came to *A* in a dream by Gen 20:3 40
But *A* had not come near her Gen 20:4 40
Therefore *A* rose early in the Gen 20:8 40
Then *A* called Abraham, and said Gen 20:9 40
A said unto Abraham, What sawest Gen 20:10 40
A took sheep, and oxen, and Gen 20:14 40
A said, Behold, my land is before Gen 20:15 40
and God healed *A*, and his wife, and Gen 20:17 40
all the wombs of the house of *A* Gen 20:18 40
came to pass at that time, that *A* Gen 21:22 40
Abraham reproved *A* because of a Gen 21:25 40
A said, I wot not who hath done Gen 21:26 40
and oxen, and gave them unto *A* Gen 21:27 40
A said unto Abraham, What mean Gen 21:29 40
then *A* rose up, and Phichol the Gen 21:32 40
Isaac went unto *A* king of the Gen 26:1 40
that *A* king of the Philistines Gen 26:8 40
A called Isaac, and said, Behold, Gen 26:9 40
A said, What is this thou hast Gen 26:10 40
A charged all his people, saying, Gen 26:11 40
A said unto Isaac, Go from us Gen 26:16 40
Then *A* went to him from Gerar, and Gen 26:26 40
2. Son of Gideon.
him a son, whose name he called *A* Judg 8:31 40
A the son of Jerubbaal went to Judg 9:1 40
their hearts inclined to follow *A* Judg 9:3 40
wherewith *A* hired vain and light Judg 9:4 40
of Millo, and went, and made *A* king Judg 9:6 40
in that ye have made *A* king Judg 9:16 40
upon one stone, and have made *A* Judg 9:18 40
this day, then rejoice ye in *A* Judg 9:19 40
if not, let fire come out from *A* Judg 9:20 40
the house of Millo, and devour *A* Judg 9:20 40
there, for fear of *A* his brother Judg 9:21 40
When *A* had reigned three years Judg 9:22 40
God sent an evil spirit between *A* Judg 9:23 40
dealt treacherously with *A* Judg 9:23 40
be laid upon *A* their brother Judg 9:24 40
and it was told *A* Judg 9:25 40
and did eat and drink, and cursed *A* Judg 9:27 40
the son of Ebed said, Who is *A* Judg 9:28 40
then would I remove *A* Judg 9:29 40
And he said to *A*, Increase thine Judg 9:29 40
he sent messengers unto *A* privily Judg 9:31 40
A rose up, and all the people that Judg 9:34 40
A rose up, and the people that Judg 9:35 40
wherewith thou saidst, Who is *A* Judg 9:38 40
men of Shechem, and fought with *A* Judg 9:39 40
A chased him, and he fled before Judg 9:40 40
And *A* dwelt at Arumah Judg 9:41 40
and they told *A* Judg 9:42 40
And *A*, and the company that was Judg 9:44 40
A fought against the city all Judg 9:45 40

And it was told *A*, that all the ... Judg 9:47 40
A gat him up to mount Zalmon, he... Judg 9:48 40
A took an axe in his hand, and cut... Judg 9:48 40
man his bough, and followed *A*... Judg 9:49 40
Then went *A* to Thebez, and ... Judg 9:50 40
A came unto the tower, and fought... Judg 9:52 40
men of Israel saw that *A* was dead... Judg 9:55 40
God rendered the wickedness of *A*... Judg 9:56 40
after *A* there arose to defend ... Judg 10:1 40
Who smote *A* the son of ... 2Sa 11:21 40
3. Son of Abiathar the High Priest.
A the son of Abiathar, were the ... 1Chr 18:16 40
4. Used in title of Psalm 34.
he changed his behaviour before *A*... Ps 34:*t* 40

ABIMELECH'S *(a-bim'-e-leks)* {2}
which *A* servants had violently ... Gen 21:25 40
piece of a millstone upon *A* head... Judg 9:53 40

ABINADAB *(a-bin'-ah-dab)* {13}
1. A Levite of Kirjath-jearim.
into the house of *A* in the hill ... 1Sa 7:1 41
the house of *A* that was in Gibeah... 2Sa 6:3 41
and Uzzah and Ahio, the sons of *A*... 2Sa 6:3 41
house of *A* which was at Gibeah... 2Sa 6:4 41
a new cart out of the house of *A*... 1Chr 13:7 41
2. A brother of David.
Then Jesse called *A*, and made him ... 1Sa 16:8 41
first born, and next unto him *A*... 1Sa 17:13 41
A the second, and Shimma the third ... 1Chr 2:13 41
3. A son of King Saul.
Philistines slew Jonathan, and *A* ... 1Sa 31:2 41
Jonathan, and Malchi-shua, and *A* ... 1Chr 8:33 41
Jonathan, and Malchi-shua, and *A* ... 1Chr 9:39 41
Philistines slew Jonathan, and *A* ... 1Chr 10:2 41
4. Father of an officer of Solomon.
The son of *A*, in all the region... 1Kin 4:11 41

ABINOAM *(a-bin'-o-am)* {4} *Father of Barak.*
son of *A* out of Kedesh-naphtali... Judg 4:6 42
of *A* was gone up to mount Tabor ... Judg 4:12 42
and Barak the son of *A* on that day... Judg 5:1 42
captivity captive, thou son of *A* ... Judg 5:12 42

ABIRAM *(a-bi'-rum)* {11}
1. A conspirator against Moses.
the son of Levi, and Dathan and *A*... Num 16:1 48
And Moses sent to call Dathan and *A*... Num 16:12 48
tabernacle of Korah, Dathan, and *A*... Num 16:24 48
rose up and went unto Dathan and *A*... Num 16:25 48
tabernacle of Korah, Dathan, and *A*... Num 16:27 48
A came out, and stood in the door... Num 16:27 48
Nemuel, and Dathan, and *A*... Num 26:9 48
This is that Dathan and *A*, which... Num 26:9 48
And what he did unto Dathan and *A*... Deut 11:6 48
and covered the company of *A* ... Ps 106:17 48
2. Son of Hiel the Bethelite.
thereof in *A* his firstborn ... 1Kin 16:34 48

ABISHAG *(ab'-e-shag)* {5} *An attendant of David.*
found *A* a Shunammite, and brought... 1Kin 1:3 49
A the Shunammite ministered unto... 1Kin 1:15 49
that he give me *A* the Shunammite... 1Kin 2:17 49
Let *A* the Shunammite be given to ... 1Kin 2:21 49
And why dost thou ask *A* the... 1Kin 2:22 49

ABISHAI *(ab'-e-shahee)* {25} *David's nephew.*
to *A* the son of Zeruiah, brother ... 1Sa 26:6 52
A said, I will go down with thee... 1Sa 26:6 52
A came to the people by night ... 1Sa 26:7 52
Then said *A* to David, God hath ... 1Sa 26:8 52
And David said to *A*, Destroy him... 1Sa 26:9 52
sons of Zeruiah there, Joab, and *A*... 2Sa 2:18 52
also and *A* pursued after Abner... 2Sa 2:24 52
A his brother slew Abner, because... 2Sa 3:30 52
into the hand of *A* his brother ... 2Sa 10:10 52
then fled they also before *A* ... 2Sa 10:14 52
Then said *A* the son of Zeruiah... 2Sa 16:9 52
And David said to *A*, and to all his ... 2Sa 16:11 52
the hand of *A* the son of Zeruiah... 2Sa 18:2 52
And the king commanded Joab and *A*... 2Sa 18:5 52
the king charged thee and *A* ... 2Sa 18:12 52
But *A* the son of Zeruiah answered ... 2Sa 19:21 52
And David said to *A*, Now shall... 2Sa 20:6 52
A his brother pursued after Sheba... 2Sa 20:10 52
But *A* the son of Zeruiah... 2Sa 21:17 52
And *A*, the brother of Joab, the... 2Sa 23:18 52
A, and Joab, and Asahel, three... 1Chr 2:16 52
A the brother of Joab, he was... 1Chr 11:20 52
A the son Zeruiah slew of the ... 1Chr 18:12 52
unto the hand of *A* his brother ... 1Chr 19:11 52
fled before *A* his brother ... 1Chr 19:15 52

ABISHALOM *(a-bish'-ah-lum)* {2} See ABSALOM. *Father of Maachah.*
was Maachah, the daughter of *A* ... 1Kin 15:2 53
was Maachah, the daughter of *A* ... 1Kin 15:10 53

ABISHUA *(a-bish'-u-ah)* {5}
1. Son of Phinehas.
begat Phinehas, Phinehas begat *A*... 1Chr 6:4 50
A begat Bukki, and Bukki begat... 1Chr 6:5 50
son, Phinehas his son, *A* his son,... 1Chr 6:50 50
The son of *A*, the son of Phinehas... Ezr 7:5 50
And *A*, and Naaman, and Ahoah, ... 1Chr 8:4 50

ABISHUR *(ab'-e-shur)* {2} *A son of Shammai.*
Nadab, and *A*... 1Chr 2:28 51
name of the wife of *A* was Abihail... 1Chr 2:29 51

ABITAL *(ab'-e-tal)* {2} *A wife of David.*
fifth, Shephatiah the son of *A*... 2Sa 3:4 37
The fifth, Shephatiah of *A* ... 1Chr 3:3 37

ABITUB *(ab'-e-tub)* {1} *Son of Shahareim.*
And of Hushim he begat *A*, and... 1Chr 8:11 36

ABIUD *(a-bi'-ud)* {2} *A descendant of Zerubbabel; ancestor of Jesus.*
And Zorobabel begat *A* ... Mt 1:13 *10*
and *A* begat Eliakim ... Mt 1:13 *10*

ABJECTS {1}
the *a* gathered themselves ... Ps 35:15 5222

ABLE {160}
the land was not *a* to bear them ... Gen 13:6 5375
if thou be *a* to number them ... Gen 15:5 3201
me and the children be *a* to endure... Gen 33:14 7272
one cannot be *a* to see the earth... Ex 10:5 3201
thou art not *a* to perform it... Ex 18:18 3201
out of all the people *a* men... Ex 18:21 2428
then thou shalt be *a* to endure ... Ex 18:23 3201
Moses chose *a* men out of all... Ex 18:25 2428
Moses was not *a* to enter into the ... Ex 40:35 3201
if he be not *a* to bring a lamb,... Lev 5:7 5060,1767
But if he be not *a* to bring two... Lev 5:11 5381
if she be not *a* to bring a lamb,... Lev 12:8 4672,1767
pigeons, such as he is *a* to get ... Lev 14:22 5381
Even such as he is *a* to get ... Lev 14:31 5381
whose hand is not *a* to get that... Lev 14:32 5381
himself be *a* to redeem it... Lev 25:26 5381
But if he be not *a* to restore it... Lev 25:28 4672,1767
or if he be *a*, he may redeem ... Lev 25:49 5381
all that are *a* to go forth to war ... Num 1:3 3318
all that were *a* to go forth to... Num 1:20 3318
all that were *a* to go forth to... Num 1:22 3318
all that were *a* to go forth to... Num 1:24 3318
all that were *a* to go forth to... Num 1:26 3318
all that were *a* to go forth to... Num 1:28 3318
all that were *a* to go forth to... Num 1:30 3318
all that were *a* to go forth to... Num 1:32 3318
all that were *a* to go forth to... Num 1:34 3318
all that were *a* to go forth to... Num 1:36 3318
all that were *a* to go forth to... Num 1:38 3318
all that were *a* to go forth to... Num 1:40 3318
all that were *a* to go forth to... Num 1:42 3318
all that were *a* to go forth to... Num 1:45 3318
I am not *a* to bear all this... Num 11:14 3201
for we are well *a* to overcome it... Num 13:30 3201
We be not *a* to go up against the... Num 13:31 3201
Because the LORD was not *a* to ... Num 14:16 3201
I shall be *a* to overcome them ... Num 22:11 3201
am I not *a* indeed to promote thee... Num 22:37 3201
all that are *a* to go to war in ... Num 26:2 3318
I am not *a* to bear you myself... Deut 1:9 3201
no man be *a* to stand before thee... Deut 7:24 3320
Because the LORD was not *a* to ... Deut 9:28 3201
no man be *a* to stand before you ... Deut 11:25 3320
that thou art not *a* to carry it... Deut 14:24 3201
Every man shall give as he is *a* ... Deut 16:17 4979,3027
There shall not any man be *a* to... Josh 1:5 3320
then I shall be *a* to drive them ... Josh 14:12
no man hath been *a* to stand... Josh 23:9 5975
what was I *a* to do in comparison ... Judg 8:3 3201
Who is *a* to stand before this... 1Sa 6:20 3201
If he be *a* to fight with me, and ... 1Sa 17:9 3201
Thou art not *a* to go against this... 1Sa 17:33 3201
for who is *a* to judge this thy so... 1Kin 3:9 3201
were not *a* utterly to destroy ... 1Kin 9:21 3201
all that were *a* to put on armour... 2Kin 3:21 2296
if thou be *a* on thy part to set ... 2Kin 18:23 3201
for he shall not be *a* to deliver ... 2Kin 18:29 3201
men *a* to bear buckler and sword,... 1Chr 5:18 5375
very *a* men for the work of the... 1Chr 9:13 2428
a men for strength for the ... 1Chr 26:8 2428
that we should be *a* to offer so ... 1Chr 29:14 6113,3581
But who is *a* to build him an... 2Chr 2:6 6113,3581
a to receive the burnt offerings ... 2Chr 7:7 3201
so that none is *a* to withstand... 2Chr 20:6
they were not *a* to go to Tarshish... 2Chr 20:37 6113
a to go forth to war, that could ... 2Chr 25:5
The LORD is *a* to give thee much... 2Chr 25:9
a to deliver their lands out of... 2Chr 32:13 3201
that your God should be *a* to ... 2Chr 32:14 3201
a to deliver his people out of... 2Chr 32:15 3201
we are not *a* to stand without, ... Ezr 10:13 3581
we are not *a* to build the wall ... Neh 4:10 3201
who then is *a* to stand before me ... Job 41:10
them that they were not *a* to rise... Ps 18:38 3201
which they are not *a* to perform... Ps 21:11 3201
down, and shall not be *a* to rise... Ps 36:12 3201
me, so that I am not *a* to look up ... Ps 40:12 3201
but who is *a* to stand before envy ... Prov 27:4
yet shall he not be *a* to find it... Eccl 8:17 3201
if thou be *a* on thy part to set ... Is 36:8 3201
he shall not be *a* to deliver you ... Is 36:14 3201
thou shalt not be *a* to put it off... Is 47:11 3201
so be thou shalt be *a* to profit... Is 47:12 3201
not be *a* to abide his indignation ... Jer 10:10 3201
they shall not be *a* to escape ... Jer 11:11 3201
he shall not be *a* to hide himself... Jer 49:10 3201
from whom I am not *a* to rise up ... Lam 1:14 3201
their gold shall not be *a* to ... Eze 7:19 3201
a to live for his righteousness... Eze 33:12 3201
lambs as he shall be *a* to give... Eze 46:5 4991,3027
to the lambs as he is *a* to give ... Eze 46:11 4991,3027
Art thou *a* to make known unto me... Dan 2:26 3546
our God whom we serve is *a* to ... Dan 3:17 3202
not *a* to make known unto me the... Dan 4:18 3202
but thou art *a* ... Dan 4:18 3546
walk in pride he is *a* to abase ... Dan 4:37 3202
a to deliver thee from the lions ... Dan 6:20 3202
the land is not *a* to bear all his ... Amos 7:10 3201
a to deliver them in the day of... Zeph 1:18 3201
that God is *a* of these stones to... Mt 3:9 *1410*
Believe ye that I am *a* to do this ... Mt 9:28 *1410*
but are not *a* to kill the soul ... Mt 10:28 *1410*
which is *a* to destroy both soul ... Mt 10:28 *1410*
He that is *a* to receive it, let ... Mt 19:12 *1410*
Are ye *a* to drink of the cup that ... Mt 20:22 *1410*
They say unto him, We are *a* ... Mt 20:22 *1410*
no man was *a* to answer him a word... Mt 22:46 *1410*
I am *a* to destroy the temple of... Mt 26:61 *1410*
them, as they were *a* to hear it... Mk 4:33 *1410*
not *a* to speak, until the day ... Lk 1:20 *1410*
That God is *a* of these stones to... Lk 3:8 *1410*
If ye then be not *a* to do that ... Lk 12:26 *1410*
to enter in, and shall not be *a* ... Lk 13:24 *2480*
is not *a* to finish it, all that ... Lk 14:29 *2480*
to build, and was not *a* to finish ... Lk 14:30 *2480*
consulteth whether he be *a* with ... Lk 14:31 *1415*
not be *a* to gainsay nor resist ... Lk 21:15 *1410*
no man is *a* to pluck them out of ... Jn 10:29 *1410*
now they were not *a* to draw it ... Jn 21:6 *2480*
they were not *a* to resist the... Acts 6:10 *2480*
our fathers nor we were *a* to bear... Acts 15:10 *2480*
which is *a* to build you up, and to ... Acts 20:32 *1410*
said he, which among you are *a* ... Acts 25:5 *1415*
he was *a* also to perform ... Rom 4:21 *1415*
shall be *a* to separate us from ... Rom 8:39 *1410*
for God is *a* to graff them in ... Rom 11:23 *1415*
for God is *a* to make him stand... Rom 14:4 *1415*
a also to admonish one another ... Rom 15:14 *1410*
hitherto ye were not *a* to bear it ... 1Cor 3:2 *1410*
neither yet now are ye *a*... 1Cor 3:2 *1410*
not one that shall be *a* to judge... 1Cor 6:5 *1410*
to be tempted above that ye are *a* ... 1Cor 10:13 *1410*
that ye may be *a* to bear it ... 1Cor 10:13 *1410*
that we may be *a* to comfort them ... 2Cor 1:4 *1410*
Who also hath made us *a* ministers ... 2Cor 3:6 *2427*
God is *a* to make all grace abound... 2Cor 9:8 *1415*
May be *a* to comprehend with all... Eph 3:18 *1840*
Now unto him that is *a* to do ... Eph 3:20 *1410*
that ye may be *a* to stand against ... Eph 6:11 *1410*
that ye may be *a* to withstand in ... Eph 6:13 *1410*
wherewith ye shall be *a* to quench... Eph 6:16 *1410*
to the working whereby he is *a* ... Phil 3:21 *1410*
am persuaded that he is *a* to keep ... 2Ti 1:12 *1415*
who shall be *a* to teach others... 2Ti 2:2 *2425*
never *a* to come to the knowledge... 2Ti 3:7 *1410*
which are *a* to make thee wise ... 2Ti 3:15 *1410*
that he may be *a* by sound ... Titus 1:9 *1415*
he is *a* to succour them that are... Heb 2:18 *1410*
that was *a* to save him from death... Heb 5:7 *1410*
Wherefore he is *a* also to save ... Heb 7:25 *1410*
that God was *a* to raise him up... Heb 11:19 *1415*
which is *a* to save your souls... Jas 1:21 *1410*
a also to bridle the whole body... Jas 3:2 *1415*
who is *a* to save and to destroy ... Jas 4:12 *1410*
a after my decease to have these... 2Pet 1:15 *2192*
Now unto him that is *a* to keep... Jude 24 *1410*
was *a* to open the book, neither ... Rev 5:3 *1410*
and who shall be *a* to stand ... Rev 6:17 *1410*
who is *a* to make war with him... Rev 13:4 *1410*
no man was *a* to enter into the... Rev 15:8 *1410*

ABNER *(ab'-nur)* {62} See ABNER'S. *King Saul's military commander.*
of the captain of his host was *A*... 1Sa 14:50 74
Ner the father of *A* was the son ... 1Sa 14:51 74
the Philistine, he said unto *A*... 1Sa 17:55 74
the captain of the host, *A*... 1Sa 17:55 74
A said, As thy soul liveth, O... 1Sa 17:55 74
A took him, and brought him before... 1Sa 17:57 74
A sat by Saul's side, and David's... 1Sa 20:25 74
A the son of Ner, the captain of... 1Sa 26:5 74
but *A* and the people lay round ... 1Sa 26:7 74
to *A* the son of Ner, saying, ... 1Sa 26:14 74
Answerest thou not, *A*... 1Sa 26:14 74
Then *A* answered and said, Who art ... 1Sa 26:14 74
And David said to *A*, Art not thou... 1Sa 26:15 74
But *A* the son of Ner, captain of ... 2Sa 2:8 74
A the son of Ner, and the servants ... 2Sa 2:12 74
A said to Joab, Let the young men... 2Sa 2:14 74
A was beaten, and the men of... 2Sa 2:17 74
And Asahel pursued after *A*... 2Sa 2:19 74
nor to the left from following *A*... 2Sa 2:19 74
Then *A* looked behind him, and said ... 2Sa 2:20 74
A said to him, Turn thee aside to... 2Sa 2:21 74
A said again to Asahel, Turn thee... 2Sa 2:22 74
wherefore *A* with the hinder end ... 2Sa 2:23 74
also and Abishai pursued after *A* ... 2Sa 2:24 74
themselves together after *A*... 2Sa 2:25 74
Then *A* called to Joab, and said, ... 2Sa 2:26 74
And *A* and his men walked all that ... 2Sa 2:29 74
And Joab returned from following *A* ... 2Sa 2:30 74
that *A* made himself strong for ... 2Sa 3:6 74
and Ish-bosheth said to *A*, ... 2Sa 3:7 74
Then was *A* very wroth for the... 2Sa 3:8 74
So do God to *A*, and more also, ... 2Sa 3:9 74
could not answer *A* a word again... 2Sa 3:11 74
A sent messengers to David on his... 2Sa 3:12 74
Then said *A* unto him, Go, return ... 2Sa 3:16 74
A had communication with the... 2Sa 3:17 74
A also spake in the ears of ... 2Sa 3:19 74
A went also to speak in the ears ... 2Sa 3:19 74
So *A* came to David to Hebron, and ... 2Sa 3:20 74
And David made *A* and the men that ... 2Sa 3:20 74
A said unto David, I will arise ... 2Sa 3:21 74
And David sent *A* away... 2Sa 3:21 74
but *A* was not with David in... 2Sa 3:22 74

A the son of Ner came to the king 2Sa 3:23 74
behold, A came unto the 2Sa 3:24 74
Thou knowest A the son of Ner, ... 2Sa 3:25 74
David, he sent messengers after A 2Sa 3:26 74
when A was returned to Hebron, ... 2Sa 3:27 74
the blood of A the son of Ner 2Sa 3:28 74
and Abishai his brother slew A 2Sa 3:30 74
with sackcloth, and mourn before A 2Sa 3:31 74
And they buried A in Hebron 2Sa 3:32 74
voice, and wept at the grave of A 2Sa 3:32 74
And the king lamented over A 2Sa 3:33 74
and said, Died A as a fool dieth 2Sa 3:33 74
the king to slay A the son of Ner 2Sa 3:37 74
heard that A was dead in Hebron 2Sa 4:1 74
in the sepulchre of A in Hebron 2Sa 4:12 74
unto A the son of Ner, and unto 1Kin 2:5 74
A the son of Ner, captain of the 1Kin 2:32 74
A the son of Ner, and Joab the son 1Chr 26:28 74
of Benjamin, Jaasiel the son of A 1Chr 27:21 74

ABNER'S *(ab'-nurs)* {1}

of A men, so that three hundred 2Sa 2:31 74

ABOARD {1}

over unto Phenicia, we went a .... Acts 21:2 *1910*

ABODE {69}

he a with him the space of a .... Gen 29:14 3427
But his bow a in strength .... Gen 49:24 3427
of the LORD a upon mount Sinai .... Ex 24:16 7931
because the cloud a thereon .... Ex 40:35 7931
and in the place where the cloud a .... Num 9:17 7931
as long as the cloud a upon the .... Num 9:18 7931
of the LORD they a in their tents .... Num 9:20 2583
when the cloud a from even unto .... Num 9:21 1961
of Israel a in their tents .... Num 9:22 2583
and a at Hazeroth .... Num 11:35 1961
and the people a in Kadesh .... Num 20:1 3427
the princes of Moab a with Balaam .... Num 22:8 3427
Israel a in Shittim, and the .... Num 25:1 3427
So ye a in Kadesh many days, ... Deut 1:46 3427
unto the days that ye a there .... Deut 1:46 3427
So we a in the valley over .... Deut 3:29 3427
then I a in the mount forty days .... Deut 9:9 3427
a there three days, until the .... Josh 2:22 3427
that they a in their places in .... Josh 5:8 3427
a between Beth-el and Ai, on the .... Josh 8:9 3427
Gilead a beyond Jordan .... Judg 5:17 7931
sea shore, and a in his breaches .... Judg 5:17 7931
and Israel a in Kadesh .... Judg 11:17 3427
and he a with him three days .... Judg 19:4 3427
a in the rock Rimmon four months .... Judg 20:47 3427
a there till even before God, and .... Judg 21:2 3427
So the woman a, and gave her son 1Sa 1:23 3427
while the ark a in Kirjath-jearim 1Sa 7:2 3427
them, a in Gibeah of Benjamin 1Sa 13:16 3427
(now Saul a in Gibeah under a 1Sa 22:6 3427
David a in the wilderness in 1Sa 23:14 3427
David a in the wood, and Jonathan 1Sa 23:18 3427
a in the wilderness of Maon 1Sa 23:25 3427
two hundred a by the stuff 1Sa 25:13 3427
But David a in the wilderness, and 1Sa 26:3 3427
for two hundred a behind, which 1Sa 30:10 5975
David had a two days in Ziklag 2Sa 1:1 3427
So Uriah a in Jerusalem that day, ... 2Sa 11:12 3427
vow while I a at Geshur in Syria 2Sa 15:8 3427
him up into a loft, where he a 1Kin 17:19 3427
But I know thy a, and thy going 2Kin 19:27 3427
there a we in tents three days .... Ezr 8:15 2583
Jerusalem, and a there three days .... Ezr 8:32 3427
But I know thy a, and thy going .... Is 37:28 3427
So Jeremiah a in the court of the .... Jer 38:28 3427
And while they a in Galilee .... Mt 17:22 *390*
Mary a with her about three .... Lk 1:56 *3306*
neither a in any house, but in .... Lk 8:27 *3306*
a in the mount that is called the .... Lk 21:37 *835*
like a dove, and it a upon him .... Jn 1:32 *3306*
he dwelt, and a with him that day .... Jn 1:39 *3306*
and he a there two days .... Jn 4:40 *3306*
unto them, he a still in Galilee .... Jn 7:9 *3306*
a not in the truth, because there .... Jn 8:44 *2476*
and there he a .... Jn 10:40 *3306*
he a two days still in the same .... Jn 11:6 *3306*
unto him, and make our a with him .... Jn 14:23 *3438*
where a both Peter, and James, and .... Acts 1:13 *2650*
Judaea to Caesarea, and there a .... Acts 12:19 *1304*
Long time therefore a they .... Acts 14:3 *1304*
there they a long time with the .... Acts 14:28 *1304*
Silas and Timotheus a there still .... Acts 17:14 *5278*
he a with them, and wrought .... Acts 18:3 *3306*
And there a three months .... Acts 20:3 *4160*
where we a seven days .... Acts 20:6 *1304*
brethren, and a with them one day .... Acts 21:7 *3306*
of the seven; and a with him .... Acts 21:8 *3306*
Peter, and a with him fifteen days .... Gal 1:18 *1961*
Erastus a at Corinth 2Ti 4:20 *3306*

ABODEST {1}

Why a thou among the sheepfolds, ... Judg 5:16 3427

ABOLISH {1}

And the idols he shall utterly a .... Is 2:18 2498

ABOLISHED {5}

my righteousness shall not be a .... Is 51:6 2865
cut down, and your works may be a .... Eze 6:6 4229
to the end of that which is a 2Cor 3:13 *2673*
Having a in his flesh the enmity, ... Eph 2:15 *2673*
Jesus Christ, who hath a death 2Ti 1:10 *2673*

ABOMINABLE {23}

or any a unclean thing, and eat of .... Lev 7:21 8263
a with any creeping thing that .... Lev 11:43 8262
not any one of these a customs .... Lev 18:30 8441
at all on the third day, it is a .... Lev 19:7 6292
not make your souls a by beast .... Lev 20:25 8262
Thou shalt not eat any a thing .... Deut 14:3 8441
for the king's word was a to Joab 1Chr 21:6 8581
put away the a idols out of all 2Chr 15:8 8251
How much more a and filthy is man, ... Job 15:16 8581
corrupt, they have done a works .... Ps 14:1 8581
are they, and have done a iniquity .... Ps 53:1 8581
out of thy grave like an a branch .... Is 14:19 8581
broth of a things is in their .... Is 65:4 6292
of their detestable and a things .... Jer 16:18 8441
do not this a thing that I hate .... Jer 44:4 8441
neither came there a flesh into .... Eze 4:14 6292
a beasts, and all the idols of the .... Eze 8:10 8263
hast committed more a than they .... Eze 16:52 8581
and the scant measure that is a .... Mic 6:10 2194
I will cast a filth upon thee, and 1Nah 3:6 8251
in works they deny him, being a .... Titus 1:16 *947*
banquetings, and a idolatries 1Pet 4:3 *111*
fearful, and unbelieving, and the a .... Rev 21:8 *948*

ABOMINABLY {1}

he did very a in following idols, ... 1Kin 21:26 8581

ABOMINATION {76}

for that is an a unto the .... Gen 43:32 8441
is an a unto the Egyptians .... Gen 46:34 8441
for we shall sacrifice the a of .... Ex 8:26 8441
shall we sacrifice the a of the .... Ex 8:26 8441
it shall be an a, and the soul .... Lev 7:18 6292
they shall be an a unto you .... Lev 11:10 8263
They shall be even an a unto you .... Lev 11:11 8263
ye shall have their carcases in a .... Lev 11:11 8262
that shall be an a unto you .... Lev 11:12 8263
shall have in a among the fowls .... Lev 11:13 8262
shall not be eaten, they are an a .... Lev 11:13 8263
all four, shall be an a unto you .... Lev 11:20 8263
four feet, shall be an a unto you .... Lev 11:23 8263
upon the earth shall be an a .... Lev 11:41 8263
for they are an a .... Lev 11:42 8263
with womankind: it is a .... Lev 18:22 8441
both of them have committed an a .... Lev 20:13 8441
for it is an a to the LORD thy .... Deut 7:25 8441
thou bring an a into thine house .... Deut 7:26 8441
for every a to the LORD, which he .... Deut 12:31 8441
that such a is wrought among you .... Deut 13:14 8441
for that is an a unto the LORD .... Deut 17:1 8441
that such a is wrought in Israel .... Deut 17:4 8441
things are an a unto the LORD .... Deut 18:12 8441
do so are a unto the LORD thy God .... Deut 22:5 8441
these are a unto the LORD thy God .... Deut 23:18 8441
for that is a before the LORD .... Deut 24:4 8441
are an a unto the LORD thy God .... Deut 25:16 8441
an a unto the LORD, the work of .... Deut 27:15 8441
was had in a with the Philistines 1Sa 13:4 887
Milcom the a of the Ammonites 1Kin 11:5 8251
the a of Moab, in the hill that 1Kin 11:7 8251
the a of the children of Ammon 1Kin 11:7 8251
Ashtoreth the a of the Zidonians 2Kin 23:13 8251
for Chemosh the a of the Moabites 2Kin 23:13 8251
for Milcom the a of the children 2Kin 23:13 8441
thou hast made me an a unto them .... Ps 88:8 8441
For the froward is a to the LORD .... Prov 3:32 8441
yea, seven are an a unto him .... Prov 6:16 8441
and wickedness is an a to my lips .... Prov 8:7 8441
A false balance is a to the LORD .... Prov 11:1 8441
a froward heart are a to the LORD .... Prov 11:20 8441
Lying lips are a to the LORD .... Prov 12:22 8441
but it is a to fools to depart .... Prov 13:19 8441
of the wicked is an a to the LORD .... Prov 15:8 8441
the wicked is an a unto the LORD .... Prov 15:9 8441
the wicked are an a to the LORD .... Prov 15:26 8441
in heart is an a to the LORD .... Prov 16:5 8441
It is an a to kings to commit .... Prov 16:12 8441
even they both are a to the LORD .... Prov 17:15 8441
of them are alike a to the LORD .... Prov 20:10 8441
weights are an a unto the LORD .... Prov 20:23 8441
The sacrifice of the wicked is a .... Prov 21:27 8441
and the scorner is an a to men .... Prov 24:9 8441
law, even his prayer shall be a .... Prov 28:9 8441
An unjust man is an a to the just .... Prov 29:27 8441
in the way is a to the wicked .... Prov 29:27 8441
incense is an a unto me .... Is 1:13 8441
an a is he that chooseth you .... Is 41:24 8441
I make the residue thereof an a .... Is 44:19 8441
eating swine's flesh, and the a .... Is 66:17 8263
land, and made mine heritage an a .... Jer 2:7 8441
ashamed when they had committed a .... Jer 6:15 8441
ashamed when they had committed a .... Jer 8:12 8441
mind, that they should do this a .... Jer 32:35 8441
haughty, and committed a before me .... Eze 16:50 8441
to the idols, hath committed a .... Eze 18:12 8441
one hath committed a with his .... Eze 22:11 8441
stand upon your sword, ye work a .... Eze 33:26 8441
place the a that maketh desolate .... Dan 11:31 8251
the a that maketh desolate set up .... Dan 12:11 8251
an a is committed in Israel and in .... Mal 2:11 8441
shall see the a of desolation .... Mt 24:15 *946*
ye shall see the a of desolation .... Mk 13:14 *946*
men is a in the sight of God .... Lk 16:15 *946*
neither whatsoever worketh a .... Rev 21:27 *946*

ABOMINATIONS {76}

shall not commit any of these a .... Lev 18:26 8441
(For all these a have the men of .... Lev 18:27 8441
shall commit any of these a .... Lev 18:29 8441
do after the a of those nations .... Deut 18:9 8441
because of these a the LORD thy .... Deut 18:12 8441
you not to do after all their a .... Deut 20:18 8441
And ye have seen their a, and their .... Deut 29:17 8251
with a provoked they him to anger .... Deut 32:16 8441
a of the nations which the LORD 1Kin 14:24 8441
according to the a of the heathen 2Kin 16:3 8441
after the a of the heathen, whom 2Kin 21:2 8441
king of Judah hath done these a 2Kin 21:11 8441
all the a that were spied in the 2Kin 23:24 8251
after the a of the heathen whom 2Chr 28:3 8441
like unto the a of the heathen, ... 2Chr 33:2 8441
Josiah took away all the a out of 2Chr 34:33 8441
his a which he did, and that which 2Chr 36:8 8441
after all the a of the heathen 2Chr 36:14 8441
lands, doing according to their a .... Ezr 9:1 8441
people of the lands, with their a .... Ezr 9:11 8441
with the people of these a .... Ezr 9:14 8441
there are seven a in his heart .... Prov 26:25 8441
their soul delighteth in their a .... Is 66:3 8251
put away thine a out of my sight .... Jer 4:1 8251
are delivered to do all these a .... Jer 7:10 8441
they have set their a in the .... Jer 7:30 8251
thine a on the hills in the .... Jer 13:27 8251
But they set their a in the house .... Jer 32:34 8251
because of the a which ye have .... Jer 44:22 8441
the like, because of all thine a .... Eze 5:9 8441
things, and with all thine a .... Eze 5:11 8441
have committed in all their a .... Eze 6:9 8441
Alas for all the evil a of the .... Eze 6:11 8441
recompense upon thee all thine a .... Eze 7:3 8441
thine a shall be in the midst of .... Eze 7:4 8441
recompense thee for all thine a .... Eze 7:8 8441
thine a that are in the midst of .... Eze 7:9 8441
they made the images of their a .... Eze 7:20 8441
even the great a that the house .... Eze 8:6 8441
and thou shalt see greater a .... Eze 8:6 8441
the wicked a that they do here .... Eze 8:9 8441
shalt see greater a that they do .... Eze 8:13 8441
shalt see greater a than these .... Eze 8:15 8441
the a which they commit here .... Eze 8:17 8441
that cry for all the a that be .... Eze 9:4 8441
all the a thereof from thence .... Eze 11:18 8441
detestable things and their a .... Eze 11:21 8441
a among the heathen whither they .... Eze 12:16 8441
away your faces from all your a .... Eze 14:6 8441
cause Jerusalem to know her a .... Eze 16:2 8441
And in all thine a and thy .... Eze 16:22 8441
and with all the idols of thy a .... Eze 16:36 8441
this lewdness above all thine a .... Eze 16:43 8441
ways, nor done after their a .... Eze 16:47 8441
multiplied thine a more than they .... Eze 16:51 8441
all thine a which thou hast done .... Eze 16:51 8441
borne thy lewdness and thine a .... Eze 16:58 8441
he hath done all these a .... Eze 18:13 8441
the a that the wicked man doeth .... Eze 18:24 8441
to know the a of their fathers .... Eze 20:4 8441
away every man the a of his eyes .... Eze 20:7 8251
man cast away the a of their eyes .... Eze 20:8 8251
commit ye whoredom after their a .... Eze 20:30 8251
thou shalt shew her all her a .... Eze 22:2 8441
yea, declare unto them their a .... Eze 23:36 8441
their a which they have committed .... Eze 33:29 8441
for your iniquities and for your a .... Eze 36:31 8441
their a that they have committed .... Eze 43:8 8441
let it suffice you of all your a .... Eze 44:6 8441
my covenant because of all your a .... Eze 44:7 8441
their a which they have committed .... Eze 44:13 8441
for the overspreading of a he .... Dan 9:27 8251
their a were according as they .... Hos 9:10 8251
his a from between his teeth .... Zec 9:7 8251
golden cup in her hand full of a .... Rev 17:4 *946*
AND A OF THE EARTH .... Rev 17:5 *946*

ABOUND {19}

man shall a with blessings .... Prov 28:20 7227
And because iniquity shall a .... Mt 24:12 *4129*
entered, that the offence might a .... Rom 5:20 *4121*
abounded, grace did much more a .... Rom 5:20 *5248*
continue in sin, that grace may a .... Rom 6:1 *4121*
believing, that ye may a in hope .... Rom 15:13 *4052*
the sufferings of Christ a in us 2Cor 1:5 *4052*
as ye a in every thing, in faith, ... 2Cor 8:7 *4052*
see that ye a in this grace also 2Cor 8:7 *4052*
to make all grace a toward you 2Cor 9:8 *4052*
things, may a to every good work 2Cor 9:8 *4052*
that your love may a yet more .... Phil 1:9 *4052*
to be abased, and I know how to a .... Phil 4:12 *4052*
full and to be hungry, both to a .... Phil 4:12 *4052*
fruit that may a to your account .... Phil 4:17 *4121*
But I have all, and a .... Phil 4:18 *4052*
a in love one toward another, and 1Th 3:12 *4052*
to please God, so ye would a more 1Th 4:1 *4052*
if these things be in you, and a 2Pet 1:8 *4121*

ABOUNDED {5}

a through my lie unto his glory .... Rom 3:7 *4052*
Jesus Christ, hath a unto many .... Rom 5:15 *4052*
But where sin a, grace did much .... Rom 5:20 *4121*
their deep poverty a unto the 2Cor 8:2 *4052*
Wherein he hath a toward us in .... Eph 1:8 *4052*

ABOUNDETH {3}

a furious man a in transgression .... Prov 29:22 7227
our consolation also a by Christ 2Cor 1:5 *4052*
of you all toward each other a 2Th 1:3 *4121*

ABOUNDING {3}
were no fountains *a* with water .... Prov 8:24 3513
always *a* in the work of the Lord, ... 1Cor 15:58 *4052*
a therein with thanksgiving .... Col 2:7 *4052*

ABOUT See APPENDIX.

ABOVE See APPENDIX.

ABRAHAM *(a'-bra-ham)* {231} See ABRAHAM'S, ABRAM. *Father of the nation of Israel.*
Abram, but thy name shall be *A* .... Gen 17:5 85
And God said unto *A*, Thou shalt .... Gen 17:9 85
And God said unto *A*, As for Sarai .... Gen 17:15 85
Then *A* fell upon his face, and .... Gen 17:17 85
A said unto God, O that Ishmael .... Gen 17:18 85
with him, and God went up from *A* .... Gen 17:22 85
A took Ishmael his son, and all.............. Gen 17:23 85
A was ninety years old and nine, ... Gen 17:24 85
selfsame day was *A* circumcised .... Gen 17:26 85
A hastened into the tent unto .... Gen 18:6 85
A ran unto the herd, and fetcht a .... Gen 18:7 85
Now *A* and Sarah were old and well ...... Gen 18:11 85
And the LORD said unto *A*, ... Gen 18:13 85
A went with them to bring them on........ Gen 18:16 85
Shall I hide from *A* that thing .... Gen 18:17 85
Seeing that *A* shall surely become .... Gen 18:18 85
A that which he hath spoken of.............. Gen 18:19 85
but *A* stood yet before the LORD .... Gen 18:22 85
A drew near, and said, Wilt thou .... Gen 18:23 85
A answered and said, Behold now, I ...... Gen 18:27 85
as he had left communing with *A* .... Gen 18:33 85
A returned unto his place....................... Gen 18:33 85
A gat up early in the morning to............ Gen 19:27 85
the plain, that God remembered *A* .... Gen 19:29 85
A journeyed from thence toward............ Gen 20:1 85
A said of Sarah his wife, She is .... Gen 20:2 85
Then Abimelech called *A*, and said......... Gen 20:9 85
And Abimelech said unto *A*, What.......... Gen 20:10 85
A said, Because I thought, Surely .... Gen 20:11 85
and gave them unto *A*, and restored .... Gen 20:14 85
So *A* prayed unto God .... Gen 20:17 85
bare *A* a son in his old age, at.............. Gen 21:2 85
A called the name of his son that........... Gen 21:3 85
A circumcised his son Isaac being........... Gen 21:4 85
A was an hundred years old, when .... Gen 21:5 85
said, Who would have said unto *A*............ Gen 21:7 85
A made a great feast the same day .... Gen 21:8 85
which she had born unto *A* .... Gen 21:9 85
Wherefore she said unto *A* .... Gen 21:10 85
And God said unto *A*, Let it not be .... Gen 21:12 85
A rose up early in the morning, ... Gen 21:14 85
captain of his host spake unto *A*............. Gen 21:22 85
And *A* said, I will swear......................... Gen 21:24 85
A reproved Abimelech because of a .... Gen 21:25 85
A took sheep and oxen, and gave............ Gen 21:27 85
A set seven ewe lambs of the.................. Gen 21:28 85
And Abimelech said unto *A*, What........... Gen 21:29 85
A planted a grove in Beer-sheba, ... Gen 21:33
A sojourned in the Philistines' .... Gen 21:34 85
things, that God did tempt *A* .... Gen 22:1 85
and said unto him, *A*............................... Gen 22:1 85
A rose up early in the morning, ... Gen 22:3 85
third day *A* lifted up his eyes .... Gen 22:4 85
A said unto his young men, Abide .... Gen 22:5 85
A took the wood of the burnt................. Gen 22:6 85
And Isaac spake unto *A* his father .... Gen 22:7 85
A said, My son, God will provide............. Gen 22:8 85
A built an altar there, and laid .... Gen 22:9 85
A stretched forth his hand, and .... Gen 22:10 85
of heaven, and said, *A*, *A*....................... Gen 22:11 85
A lifted up his eyes, and looked, ... Gen 22:13 85
A went and took the ram, and .... Gen 22:13 85
A called the name of that place .... Gen 22:14 85
A out of heaven the second time .... Gen 22:15 85
So *A* returned unto his young men, ... Gen 22:19 85
and *A* dwelt at Beer-sheba .... Gen 22:19 85
these things, that it was told *A* .... Gen 22:20 85
A came to mourn for Sarah, and to .... Gen 23:2 85
A stood up from before his dead, ... Gen 23:3 85
the children of Heth answered *A* .... Gen 23:5 85
A stood up, and bowed himself to............ Gen 23:7 85
Ephron the Hittite answered *A* in .... Gen 23:10 85
A bowed down himself before the............ Gen 23:12 85
And Ephron answered *A*, saying unto....... Gen 23:14 85
And *A* hearkened unto Ephron .... Gen 23:16 85
A weighed to Ephron the silver, ... Gen 23:16 85
Unto *A* for a possession in the .... Gen 23:18 85
A buried Sarah his wife in the................. Gen 23:19 85
were made sure unto *A* for a .... Gen 23:20 85
A was old, and well stricken in.............. Gen 24:1 85
LORD had blessed *A* in all things .... Gen 24:1 85
A said unto his eldest servant of............ Gen 24:2 85
A said unto him, Beware thou that......... Gen 24:6 85
under the thigh of *A* his master .... Gen 24:9 85
said, O LORD God of my master *A* .... Gen 24:12 85
and shew kindness unto my master *A*..... Gen 24:12 85
be the LORD God of my master *A* .... Gen 24:27 85
said, O LORD God of my master *A* .... Gen 24:42 85
the LORD God of my master *A* .... Gen 24:48 85
Then again *A* took a wife, and her......... Gen 25:1 85
A gave all that he had unto Isaac .... Gen 25:5 85
of the concubines, which *A* had .... Gen 25:6 85
A gave gifts, and sent them away............ Gen 25:6 85
Then *A* gave up the ghost, and died......... Gen 25:8 85
The field which *A* purchased of .... Gen 25:10 85
there was *A* buried, and Sarah his.......... Gen 25:10 85
came to pass after the death of *A* .... Gen 25:11 85
Sarah's handmaid, bare unto *A*.............. Gen 25:12 85
A begat Isaac... Gen 25:19 85
famine that was in the days of *A* .... Gen 26:1 85
which I sware unto *A* thy father .... Gen 26:3 85
Because that *A* obeyed my voice, ... Gen 26:5 85
in the days of *A* his father...................... Gen 26:15 85
in the days of *A* his father...................... Gen 26:18 85
stopped them after the death of *A* .... Gen 26:18 85
I am the God of *A* thy father.................. Gen 26:24 85
And give thee the blessing of *A*.............. Gen 28:4 85
a stranger, which God gave unto *A* .... Gen 28:4 85
I am the LORD God of *A* thy father .... Gen 28:13 85
God of my father, the God of *A*.............. Gen 31:42 85
The God of *A*, and the God of Nahor...... Gen 31:53 85
Jacob said, O God of my father *A* .... Gen 32:9 85
And the land which I gave *A* .... Gen 35:12 85
Arbah, which is Hebron, where *A* .... Gen 35:27 85
God, before whom my fathers *A* .... Gen 48:15 85
them, and the name of my fathers *A*...... Gen 48:16 85
which *A* bought with the field of............ Gen 49:30 85
There they buried *A* and Sarah his......... Gen 49:31 85
which *A* bought with the field for .... Gen 50:13 85
unto the land which he sware to *A* .... Gen 50:24 85
remembered his covenant with *A*............. Ex 2:24 85
God of thy father, the God of *A*............. Ex 3:6 85
God of your fathers, the God of *A* .... Ex 3:15 85
God of your fathers, the God of *A* .... Ex 3:16 85
of their fathers, the God of *A*................ Ex 4:5 85
And I appeared unto *A*, unto Isaac, ... Ex 6:3 85
which I did swear to give it to *A*............ Ex 6:8 85
Remember *A*, Isaac, and Israel, thy.......... Ex 32:13 85
the land which I sware unto *A* .... Ex 33:1 85
covenant with *A* will I remember............ Lev 26:42 85
see the land which I sware unto *A* .... Num 32:11 85
LORD sware unto your fathers, *A* .... Deut 1:8 85
he sware unto thy fathers, to *A*.............. Deut 6:10 85
LORD sware unto thy fathers, *A* .... Deut 9:5 85
Remember thy servants, *A*, Isaac, ... Deut 9:27 85
hath sworn unto thy fathers, to *A* .... Deut 29:13 85
LORD sware unto thy fathers, to *A* .... Deut 30:20 85
is the land which I sware unto *A* .... Deut 34:4 85
time, even Terah, the father of *A* .... Josh 24:2 85
I took your father *A* from the................. Josh 24:3 85
came near, and said, LORD God of *A*...... 1Kin 18:36 85
because of his covenant with *A*.............. 2Kin 13:23 85
Abram; the same is *A* 1Chr 1:27 85
The sons of *A*; Isaac, and........................ 1Chr 1:28 85
And *A* begat Isaac 1Chr 1:34 85
the covenant which he made with *A*........ 1Chr 16:16 85
O LORD God of *A*, Isaac, and of 1Chr 29:18 85
the seed of *A* thy friend for ever 2Chr 20:7 85
turn again unto the LORD God of *A* 2Chr 30:6 85
and gavest him the name of *A*............... Neh 9:7 85
even the people of the God of *A*............. Ps 47:9 85
O ye seed of *A* his servant .... Ps 105:6 85
Which covenant he made with *A*.............. Ps 105:9 85
holy promise, and *A* his servant .... Ps 105:42 85
saith the LORD, who redeemed *A* .... Is 29:22 85
chosen, the seed of *A* my friend .... Is 41:8 85
Look unto *A* your father, and unto .... Is 51:2 85
though *A* be ignorant of us, and .... Is 63:16 85
to be rulers over the seed of *A* .... Jer 33:26 85
A was one, and he inherited the............. Eze 33:24 85
truth to Jacob, and the mercy to *A* .... Mic 7:20 85
the son of David, the son of *A*............... Mt 1:1 *11*
A begat Isaac.. Mt 1:2 *11*
from *A* to David are fourteen .... Mt 1:17 *11*
We have *A* to our father .... Mt 3:9 *11*
to raise up children unto *A* .... Mt 3:9 *11*
and west, and shall sit down with *A* .... Mt 8:11 *11*
I am the God of *A*, and the God of .... Mt 22:32 *11*
him, saying, I am the God of *A* .... Mk 12:26 *11*
As he spake to our fathers, to *A*............ Lk 1:55 *11*
which he sware to our father *A*............. Lk 1:73 *11*
We have *A* to our father .... Lk 3:8 *11*
to raise up children unto *A* .... Lk 3:8 *11*
of Isaac, which was the son of *A*............. Lk 3:34 *11*
this woman, being a daughter of *A* .... Lk 13:16 *11*
of teeth, when ye shall see *A* .... Lk 13:28 *11*
seeth *A* afar off, and Lazarus in............. Lk 16:23 *11*
And he cried and said, Father *A* .... Lk 16:24 *11*
But *A* said, Son, remember that............. Lk 16:25 *11*
A saith unto him, They have Moses .... Lk 16:29 *11*
And he said, Nay, father *A* .... Lk 16:30 *11*
as he also is a son of *A* .... Lk 19:9 *11*
he calleth the Lord the God of *A* .... Lk 20:37 *11*
and said unto him, *A* is our father.......... Jn 8:39 *11*
ye would do the works of *A* .... Jn 8:39 *11*
of God: this did not *A* .... Jn 8:40 *11*
A is dead, and the prophets .... Jn 8:52 *11*
thou greater than our father *A*............... Jn 8:53 *11*
Your father *A* rejoiced to see my .... Jn 8:56 *11*
years old, and hast thou seen *A* .... Jn 8:57 *11*
I say unto you, Before *A* was.................. Jn 8:58 *11*
The God of *A*, and of Isaac, and of .... Acts 3:13 *11*
with our fathers, saying unto *A* .... Acts 3:25 *11*
glory appeared unto our father *A* .... Acts 7:2 *11*
so *A* begat Isaac, and circumcised .... Acts 7:8
laid in the sepulchre that *A*.................... Acts 7:16 *11*
nigh, which God had sworn to *A* .... Acts 7:17 *11*
God of thy fathers, the God of *A* .... Acts 7:32 *11*
children of the stock of *A* .... Acts 13:26 *11*
we say then that *A* our father .... Rom 4:1 *11*
For if *A* were justified by works,............. Rom 4:2 *11*
A believed God, and it was counted .... Rom 4:3 *11*
reckoned to *A* for righteousness .... Rom 4:9 *11*
of that faith of our father *A* .... Rom 4:12 *11*
heir of the world, was not to *A* .... Rom 4:13 *11*
also which is of the faith of *A* .... Rom 4:16 *11*
because they are the seed of *A* .... Rom 9:7 *11*
am an Israelite, of the seed of *A* .... Rom 11:1 *11*
Are they the seed of *A*.......................... 2Cor 11:22 *11*
Even as *A* believed God, and it was......... Gal 3:6 *11*
the same are the children of *A* .... Gal 3:7 *11*
preached before the gospel unto *A* .... Gal 3:8 *11*
faith are blessed with faithful *A* .... Gal 3:9 *11*
That the blessing of *A* might come .... Gal 3:14 *11*
Now to *A* and his seed were the............. Gal 3:16 *11*
but God gave it to *A* by promise .... Gal 3:18 *11*
that *A* had two sons, the one by a........... Gal 4:22 *11*
but he took on him the seed of *A*............ Heb 2:16 *11*
For when God made promise to *A*............ Heb 6:13 *11*
who met *A* returning from the .... Heb 7:1 *11*
To whom also *A* gave a tenth part........... Heb 7:2 *11*
A gave the tenth of the spoils................ Heb 7:4 *11*
they come out of the loins of *A* .... Heb 7:5 *11*
from them received tithes of *A*.............. Heb 7:6 *11*
tithes, payed tithes in *A* .... Heb 7:9 *11*
By faith *A*, when he was called to .... Heb 11:8 *11*
By faith *A*, when he was tried,............... Heb 11:17 *11*
Was not *A* our father justified by........... Jas 2:21 *11*
A believed God, and it was imputed....... Jas 2:23 *11*
Even as Sarah obeyed *A*, calling............. 1Pet 3:6 *11*

ABRAHAM'S *(a'-bra-hams)* {19}
male among the men of *A* house .... Gen 17:23 85
because of Sarah *A* wife........................ Gen 20:18 85
in *A* sight because of his son................... Gen 21:11 85
did bear to Nahor, *A* brother.................. Gen 22:23 85
A brother, with her pitcher upon .... Gen 24:15 85
And he said, I am *A* servant................... Gen 24:34 85
when *A* servant heard their words,......... Gen 24:52 85
nurse, and *A* servant, and his men......... Gen 24:59 85
years of *A* life which he lived................. Gen 25:7 85
A son, whom Hagar the Egyptian, ... Gen 25:12 85
the generations of Isaac, *A* son .... Gen 25:19 85
thy seed for my servant *A* sake .... Gen 26:24 85
the daughter of Ishmael *A* son .... Gen 28:9 85
the sons of Keturah, *A* concubine 1Chr 1:32 85
by the angels into *A* bosom .... Lk 16:22 *11*
They answered him, We be *A* seed .... Jn 8:33 *11*
I know that ye are *A* seed .... Jn 8:37 *11*
unto them, If ye were *A* children............ Jn 8:39 *11*
be Christ's, then are ye *A* seed .... Gal 3:29 *11*

ABRAM *(a'-brum)* {54} See ABRAHAM, ABRAM'S. *Abraham's original name.*
lived seventy years, and begat *A* .... Gen 11:26 87
Terah begat *A*, Nahor, and Haran........... Gen 11:27 87
And *A* and Nahor took them wives......... Gen 11:29 87
And Terah took *A* his son, and Lot......... Gen 11:31 87
Now the LORD had said unto *A*............... Gen 12:1 87
So *A* departed, as the LORD had .... Gen 12:4 87
A was seventy and five years old .... Gen 12:4 87
A took Sarai his wife, and Lot his........... Gen 12:5 87
A passed through the land unto.............. Gen 12:6 87
And the LORD appeared unto *A* .... Gen 12:7 87
A journeyed, going on still .... Gen 12:9 87
A went down into Egypt to sojourn .... Gen 12:10 87
when *A* was come into Egypt, the............ Gen 12:14 87
he entreated *A* well for her sake .... Gen 12:16 87
And Pharaoh called *A*, and said,............. Gen 12:18 87
A went up out of Egypt, he, and .... Gen 13:1 87
A was very rich in cattle, in .... Gen 13:2 87
there *A* called on the name of the........... Gen 13:4 87
And Lot also, which went with *A* .... Gen 13:5 87
A said unto Lot, Let there be no .... Gen 13:8 87
A dwelled in the land of Canaan,............ Gen 13:12 87
And the LORD said unto *A*, after............. Gen 13:14 87
Then *A* removed his tent, and came......... Gen 13:18 87
had escaped, and told *A* the Hebrew ...... Gen 14:13 87
and these were confederate with *A*......... Gen 14:13 87
when *A* heard that his brother was......... Gen 14:14 87
Blessed be *A* of the most high God .... Gen 14:19 87
And the king of Sodom said unto *A*......... Gen 14:21 87
A said to the king of Sodom, I .... Gen 14:22 87
shouldest say, I have made *A* rich .... Gen 14:23 87
the LORD came unto *A* in a vision............ Gen 15:1 87
in a vision, saying, Fear not, *A*.............. Gen 15:1 87
A said, Lord GOD, what wilt thou .... Gen 15:2 87
A said, Behold, to me thou hast .... Gen 15:3 87
the carcases, *A* drove them away .... Gen 15:11 87
down, a deep sleep fell upon *A* .... Gen 15:12 87
And he said unto *A*, Know of a .... Gen 15:13 87
the LORD made a covenant with *A*.......... Gen 15:18 87
And Sarai said unto *A*, Behold now,........ Gen 16:2 87
A hearkened to the voice of Sarai .... Gen 16:2 87
after *A* had dwelt ten years in................ Gen 16:3 87
to her husband *A* to be his wife.............. Gen 16:3 87
And Sarai said unto *A*, My wrong be...... Gen 16:5 87
But *A* said unto Sarai, Behold,.............. Gen 16:6 87
And Hagar bare *A* a son......................... Gen 16:15 87
A called his son's name, which.............. Gen 16:15 87
A was fourscore and six years old,.......... Gen 16:16 87
old, when Hagar bare Ishmael to *A* .... Gen 16:16 87
when *A* was ninety years old and .... Gen 17:1 87
and nine, the LORD appeared to *A* .... Gen 17:1 87
And *A* fell on his face............................. Gen 17:3 87
thy name any more be called *A* .... Gen 17:5 87
A; the same is Abraham 1Chr 1:27 87
LORD the God, who didst choose *A* .... Neh 9:7 87

ABRAM'S *(a'-brums)* {7}
the name of *A* wife was Sarai .... Gen 11:29 87
daughter in law, his son *A* wife.............. Gen 11:31 87
plagues because of Sarai *A* wife .... Gen 12:17 87
between the herdmen of *A* cattle .... Gen 13:7 87
A brother's son, who dwelt in................ Gen 14:12 87
Now Sarai *A* wife bare him no................ Gen 16:1 87
Sarai *A* wife took Hagar her maid.......... Gen 16:3 87

ABROAD {80}
of the Canaanites spread *a* ... Gen 10:18 5310
lest we be scattered *a* upon the ... Gen 11:4 6527
So the LORD scattered them *a* from ... Gen 11:8 6527
did the LORD scatter them *a* upon ... Gen 11:9 6527
And he brought him forth *a* ... Gen 15:5 2351
they had brought them forth *a* ... Gen 19:17 2351
thou shalt spread *a* to the west ... Gen 28:14 6555
a throughout all the land of ... Ex 5:12 6527
I will spread *a* my hands unto the ... Ex 9:29 6566
spread *a* his hands unto the LORD ... Ex 9:33 6566
of the flesh *a* out of the house ... Ex 12:46 2351
walk *a* upon his staff, then shall ... Ex 21:19 2351
he spread *a* the tent over the ... Ex 40:19 6566
scab spread much *a* in the skin ... Lev 13:7 6581
a leprosy break out *a* in the skin ... Lev 13:12 6524
if it spread much *a* in the skin ... Lev 13:22 6581
it be spread much *a* in the skin ... Lev 13:27 6581
shall tarry *a* out of his tent ... Lev 14:8 2351
she be born at home, or born *a* ... Lev 18:9 2351
they spread them all *a* for ... Num 11:32 7849
shall he go *a* out of the camp ... Deut 23:10 2351
whither thou shalt go forth *a* ... Deut 23:12 2351
be, when thou wilt ease thyself *a* ... Deut 23:13 2351
Thou shalt stand *a*, and the man to ... Deut 24:11 2351
bring out the pledge *a* unto thee ... Deut 24:11 2351
her young, spreadeth *a* her wings ... Deut 32:11 6566
thirty daughters, whom he sent *a* ... Judg 12:9 2351
daughters from *a* for his sons ... Judg 12:9 2351
out both of them, he and Samuel, *a* ... 1Sa 9:26 2351
they were spread *a* upon all the ... 1Sa 30:16 5203
the street, and did spread them *a* ... 2Sa 22:43 7554
walkest *a* any whither, that thou ... 1Kin 2:42
borrow thee vessels *a* of all thy ... 2Kin 4:3 2351
let us send *a* unto our brethren ... 1Chr 13:2 6555
spread themselves *a* in the valley ... 1Chr 14:13 6584
his name spread *a* even to the ... 2Chr 26:8
And his name spread far *a* ... 2Chr 26:15 7350
to carry it out *a* into the brook ... 2Chr 29:16 2351
as soon as the commandment came *a* ... 2Chr 31:5 6555
scatter you *a* among the nations ... Neh 1:8 6327
queen shall come *a* unto all women ... Est 1:17 3318
is a certain people scattered *a* ... Est 3:8 6340
lion's whelps are scattered *a* ... Job 4:11 6504
He wandereth *a* for bread, saying, ... Job 15:23 5074
Cast *a* the rage of thy wrath ... Job 40:11 6327
when he goeth *a*, he telleth it ... Ps 41:6 2351
thine arrows also went *a* ... Ps 77:17 1980
Let thy fountains be dispersed *a* ... Prov 5:16 2351
scattereth *a* the inhabitants ... Is 24:1 6327
doth he not cast *a* the fitches ... Is 28:25 6327
that spreadeth *a* the earth by ... Is 44:24 7554
pour it out upon the children *a* ... Jer 6:11 2351
a the sword bereaveth, at home ... Lam 1:20 2351
till ye have scattered them *a* ... Eze 34:21 2351
prosperity shall yet be spread *a* ... Zec 1:17 6527
for I have spread you *a* as the ... Zec 2:6 6566
hereof went *a* into all that land ... Mt 9:26 *1831*
spread *a* his fame in all that ... Mt 9:31 *1310*
they fainted, and were scattered *a* ... Mt 9:36 *4496*
not with me scattereth *a* ... Mt 12:30 *4650*
of the flock shall be scattered *a* ... Mt 26:31 *1287*
immediately his fame spread *a* ... Mk 1:28 *1831*
to blaze *a* the matter, insomuch ... Mk 1:45 *1310*
secret, but that it should come *a* ... Mk 4:22 *1519,5318*
(for his name was spread *a* ... Mk 6:14 *1519,1096*
all these sayings were noised *a* ... Lk 1:65 *1255*
they made known *a* the saying ... Lk 2:17 *1232*
more went there a fame *a* of him ... Lk 5:15 *1330*
shall not be known and come *a* ... Lk 8:17 *1519,5318*
of God that were scattered *a* ... Jn 11:52 *1287*
this saying *a* among the brethren ... Jn 21:23 *1831*
Now when this was noised *a* ... Acts 2:6 *1096,5456*
they were all scattered *a* ... Acts 8:1 *1289*
they that were scattered *a* went ... Acts 8:4 *1289*
Now they which were scattered *a* ... Acts 11:19 *1289*
a in our hearts by the Holy Ghost ... Rom 5:5 *1632*
obedience is come *a* unto all men ... Rom 16:19 *864*
is written, He hath dispersed *a* ... 2Cor 9:9 *4650*
faith to God-ward is spread *a* ... 1Th 1:8 *1831*
tribes which are scattered *a* ... Jas 1:1 *1290*

ABRONAH See EBRONAH.

ABSALOM *(ab'-sal-um)* {105} *A son of David.*
A the son of Maacah the daughter ... 2Sa 3:3 53
that *A* the son of David had a ... 2Sa 13:1 53
A her brother said unto her, Hath ... 2Sa 13:20 53
A spake unto his brother Amnon ... 2Sa 13:22 53
for *A* hated Amnon, because he had ... 2Sa 13:22 53
that *A* had sheepshearers in ... 2Sa 13:23 53
A invited all the king's sons ... 2Sa 13:23 53
A came to the king, and said, ... 2Sa 13:24 53
And the king said to *A*, Nay, my ... 2Sa 13:25 53
Then said *A*, If not, I pray thee, ... 2Sa 13:26 53
But *A* pressed him, that he let ... 2Sa 13:27 53
Now *A* had commanded his servants, ... 2Sa 13:28 53
the servants of *A* did unto Amnon ... 2Sa 13:29 53
did unto Amnon as *A* had commanded ... 2Sa 13:29 53
A hath slain all the king's sons, ... 2Sa 13:30 53
for by the appointment of *A* this ... 2Sa 13:32 53
But *A* fled. ... 2Sa 13:34 53
But *A* fled, and went to Talmai, ... 2Sa 13:37 53
So *A* fled, and went to Geshur, and ... 2Sa 13:38 53
David longed to go forth unto *A* ... 2Sa 13:39 53
the king's heart was toward *A* ... 2Sa 14:1 53
bring the young man *A* again ... 2Sa 14:21 53
Geshur, and brought *A* to Jerusalem ... 2Sa 14:23 53
So *A* returned to his own house, ... 2Sa 14:24 53
much praised as *A* for his beauty ... 2Sa 14:25 53
unto *A* there were born three sons ... 2Sa 14:27 53
So *A* dwelt two full years in ... 2Sa 14:28 53
Therefore *A* sent for Joab, to ... 2Sa 14:29 53
came to *A* unto his house, and said ... 2Sa 14:31 53
A answered Joab, Behold, I sent ... 2Sa 14:32 53
and when he had called for *A* ... 2Sa 14:33 53
and the king kissed *A* ... 2Sa 14:33 53
that *A* prepared him chariots and ... 2Sa 15:1 53
A rose up early, and stood beside ... 2Sa 15:2 53
then *A* called unto him, and said, ... 2Sa 15:2 53
A said unto him, See, thy matters ... 2Sa 15:3 53
A said moreover, Oh that I were ... 2Sa 15:4 53
on this manner did *A* to all ... 2Sa 15:6 53
so *A* stole the hearts of the men ... 2Sa 15:6 53
that *A* said unto the king, I pray ... 2Sa 15:7 53
But *A* sent spies throughout all ... 2Sa 15:10 53
shall say, *A* reigneth in Hebron ... 2Sa 15:10 53
with *A* went two hundred men out ... 2Sa 15:11 53
A sent for Ahithophel the ... 2Sa 15:12 53
increased continually with *A* ... 2Sa 15:12 53
of the men of Israel are after *A* ... 2Sa 15:13 53
we shall not else escape from *A* ... 2Sa 15:14 53
is among the conspirators with *A* ... 2Sa 15:31 53
return to the city, and say unto *A* ... 2Sa 15:34 53
city, and *A* came into Jerusalem ... 2Sa 15:37 53
into the hand of *A* thy son ... 2Sa 16:8 53
And *A*, and all the people the men ... 2Sa 16:15 53
David's friend, was come unto *A* ... 2Sa 16:16 53
A, that Hushai said unto *A* ... 2Sa 16:16 53
A said to Hushai, Is this thy ... 2Sa 16:17 53
And Hushai said unto *A*, Nay ... 2Sa 16:18 53
Then said *A* to Ahithophel, Give ... 2Sa 16:20 53
And Ahithophel said unto *A* ... 2Sa 16:21 53
So they spread *A* a tent upon the ... 2Sa 16:22 53
A went in unto his father's ... 2Sa 16:22 53
both with David and with *A* ... 2Sa 16:23 53
Moreover Ahithophel said unto *A* ... 2Sa 17:1 53
And the saying pleased *A* well ... 2Sa 17:4 53
Then said *A*, Call now Hushai the ... 2Sa 17:5 53
And when Hushai was come to *A* ... 2Sa 17:6 53
A spake unto him, saying, ... 2Sa 17:6 53
And Hushai said unto *A*, The ... 2Sa 17:7 53
among the people that follow *A* ... 2Sa 17:9 53
And *A* and all the men of Israel ... 2Sa 17:14 53
the LORD might bring evil upon *A* ... 2Sa 17:14 53
and thus did Ahithophel counsel *A* ... 2Sa 17:15 53
a lad saw them, and told *A* ... 2Sa 17:18 53
A passed over Jordan, he and all ... 2Sa 17:24 53
A made Amasa captain of the host ... 2Sa 17:25 53
A pitched in the land of Gilead ... 2Sa 17:26 53
with the young man, even with *A* ... 2Sa 18:5 53
the captains charge concerning *A* ... 2Sa 18:5 53
A met the servants of David ... 2Sa 18:9 53
A rode upon a mule, and the mule ... 2Sa 18:9 53
Behold, I saw *A* hanged in an oak ... 2Sa 18:10 53
that none touch the young man *A* ... 2Sa 18:12 53
them through the heart of *A* ... 2Sa 18:14 53
armour compassed about and smote *A* ... 2Sa 18:15 53
And they took *A*, and cast him into ... 2Sa 18:17 53
Now *A* in his lifetime had taken ... 2Sa 18:18 53
said, Is the young man *A* safe ... 2Sa 18:29 53
Cushi, Is the young man *A* safe ... 2Sa 18:32 53
my son *A*, my son, my son *A* ... 2Sa 18:33 53
God I had died for thee, O *A* ... 2Sa 18:33 53
king weepeth and mourneth for *A* ... 2Sa 19:1 53
loud voice, O my son *A*, O *A* ... 2Sa 19:4 53
that if *A* had lived, and all we ... 2Sa 19:6 53
he is fled out of the land for *A* ... 2Sa 19:9 53
And *A*, whom we anointed over us, ... 2Sa 19:10 53
Bichri do us more harm than did *A* ... 2Sa 20:6 53
and his mother bare him after *A* ... 1Kin 1:6 53
I fled because of *A* thy brother ... 1Kin 2:7 53
though he turned not after *A* ... 1Kin 2:28 53
A the son of Maachah the daughter ... 1Chr 3:2 53
he took Maachah the daughter of *A* ... 2Chr 11:20 53
daughter of *A* above all his wives ... 2Chr 11:21 53
when he fled from *A* his son ... Ps 3:*t* 53

ABSALOM'S *(ab'-sal-ums)* {5}
I love Tamar, my brother *A* sister ... 2Sa 13:4 53
desolate in her brother *A* house ... 2Sa 13:20 53
A servants set the field on fire ... 2Sa 14:30 53
when *A* servants came to the woman ... 2Sa 17:20 53
is called unto this day, *A* place ... 2Sa 18:18 53

ABSENCE {2}
them in the *a* of the multitude ... Lk 22:6 *817*
only, but now much more in my *a* ... Phil 2:12 *666*

ABSENT {11}
when we are *a* one from another ... Gen 31:49 5641
as *a* in body, but present in ... 1Cor 5:3 *548*
the body, we are *a* from the Lord ... 2Cor 5:6 *553*
rather to be *a* from the body ... 2Cor 5:8 *553*
that, whether present or *a* ... 2Cor 5:9 *553*
but being *a* am bold toward you ... 2Cor 10:1 *548*
in word by letters when we are *a* ... 2Cor 10:11 *548*
being *a* now I write to them which ... 2Cor 13:2 *548*
I write these things being *a* ... 2Cor 13:10 *548*
I come and see you, or else be *a* ... Phil 1:27 *548*
For though I be *a* in the flesh ... Col 2:5 *548*

ABSTAIN {6}
that they *a* from pollutions of ... Acts 15:20 *567*
That ye *a* from meats offered to ... Acts 15:29 *567*
that ye should *a* from fornication ... 1Th 4:3 *567*
A from all appearance of evil ... 1Th 5:22 *567*
and commanding to *a* from meats ... 1Ti 4:3 *567*
a from fleshly lusts, which war ... 1Pet 2:11 *567*

ABSTINENCE {1}
But after long *a* Paul stood forth ... Acts 27:21 *776*

ABUNDANCE {68}
of heart, for the *a* of all things ... Deut 28:47 7230
shall suck of the *a* of the seas ... Deut 33:19 8228
for out of the *a* of my complaint ... 1Sa 1:16 7230
the spoil of the city in great *a* ... 2Sa 12:30 7235
oxen and fat cattle and sheep in *a* ... 1Kin 1:19 7230
oxen and fat cattle and sheep in *a* ... 1Kin 1:25 7230
there came no more such *a* of ... 1Kin 10:10 7230
trees that are in the vale, for *a* ... 1Kin 10:27 7230
for there is a sound of *a* of rain ... 1Kin 18:41 1995
David prepared iron in *a* for the ... 1Chr 22:3 7230
brass in *a* without weight ... 1Chr 22:3 7230
Also cedar trees in *a* ... 1Chr 22:4 369,4557
for it is in *a* ... 1Chr 22:14 7230
there are workmen with thee in *a* ... 1Chr 22:15 7230
stones, and marble stones in *a* ... 1Chr 29:2 7230
sacrifices in *a* for all Israel ... 1Chr 29:21 7230
trees that are in the vale for *a* ... 2Chr 1:15 7230
Even to prepare me timber in *a* ... 2Chr 2:9 7230
made all these vessels in great *a* ... 2Chr 4:18 7230
that bare spices, and gold in *a* ... 2Chr 9:1 7230
of gold, and of spices great *a* ... 2Chr 9:9 7230
that are in the low plains in *a* ... 2Chr 9:27 7230
and he gave them victual in *a* ... 2Chr 11:23 7230
carried away sheep and camels in *a* ... 2Chr 14:15 7230
fell to him out of Israel in *a* ... 2Chr 15:9 7230
and he had riches and honour in *a* ... 2Chr 17:5 7230
had riches and honour in *a* ... 2Chr 18:1 7230
killed sheep and oxen for him in *a* ... 2Chr 18:2 7230
they found among them in *a* both ... 2Chr 20:25 7230
by day, and gathered money in *a* ... 2Chr 24:11 7230
the burnt offerings were in *a* ... 2Chr 29:35 7230
in *a* the firstfruits of corn ... 2Chr 31:5 7235
and made darts and shields in *a* ... 2Chr 32:5 7230
of flocks and herds in *a* ... 2Chr 32:29 7230
oliveyards, and fruit trees in *a* ... Neh 9:25 7230
from another,) and royal wine in *a* ... Est 1:7 7227
and *a* of waters cover thee ... Job 22:11 8229
he giveth meat in *a* ... Job 36:31 4342
that *a* of waters may cover thee ... Job 38:34 8229
themselves in the *a* of peace ... Ps 37:11 7230
trusted in the *a* of his riches ... Ps 52:7 7230
a of peace so long as the moon ... Ps 72:7 7230
land brought forth frogs in *a* ... Ps 105:30 8317
he that loveth *a* with increase ... Eccl 5:10 1995
but the *a* of the rich will not ... Eccl 5:12 7647
for the *a* of milk that they shall ... Is 7:22 7230
Therefore the *a* they have gotten, ... Is 15:7 3502
and for the great *a* of thine ... Is 47:9 6109
because the *a* of the sea shall be ... Is 60:5 1995
delighted with the *a* of her glory ... Is 66:11 2123
reveal unto them the *a* of peace ... Jer 33:6 6283
a of idleness was in her and in ... Eze 16:49 7962
By reason of the *a* of his horses ... Eze 26:10 8229
and silver, and apparel, in great *a* ... Zec 14:14 7230
for out of the *a* of the heart the ... Mt 12:34 *4051*
be given, and he shall have more *a* ... Mt 13:12 *4052*
be given, and he shall have *a* ... Mt 25:29 *4052*
all they did cast in of their *a* ... Mk 12:44 *4052*
for of the *a* of the heart his ... Lk 6:45 *4051*
in the *a* of the things which he ... Lk 12:15 *4052*
For all these have of their *a* ... Lk 21:4 *4052*
they which receive *a* of grace ... Rom 5:17 *4050*
of affliction the *a* of their joy ... 2Cor 8:2 *4050*
that now at this time your *a* may ... 2Cor 8:14 *4051*
that their *a* also may be a supply ... 2Cor 8:14 *4051*
a which is administered by us ... 2Cor 8:20 *100*
through the *a* of the revelations ... 2Cor 12:7 *5236*
through the *a* of her delicacies ... Rev 18:3 *1411*

ABUNDANT {13}
and *a* in goodness and truth, ... Ex 34:6 7227
be as this day, and much more *a* ... Is 56:12 1419
a in treasures, thine end is come ... Jer 51:13 7227
these we bestow more *a* honour ... 1Cor 12:23 *4055*
parts have more *a* comeliness ... 1Cor 12:23 *4055*
having given more *a* honour to ... 1Cor 12:24 *4055*
that the *a* grace might through ... 2Cor 4:15 *4121*
affection is more *a* toward you ... 2Cor 7:15 *4056*
the saints, but is *a* also by many ... 2Cor 9:12 *4052*
in labours more *a*, in stripes ... 2Cor 11:23 *4056*
a in Jesus Christ for me by my ... Phil 1:26 *4052*
Lord was exceeding *a* with faith ... 1Ti 1:14 *5250*
which according to his *a* mercy ... 1Pet 1:3 *4183*

ABUNDANTLY {32}
Let the waters bring forth *a* the ... Gen 1:20 8317
which the waters brought forth *a* ... Gen 1:21 8317
they may breed *a* in the earth ... Gen 8:17 8317
bring forth *a* in the earth, and ... Gen 9:7 8317
were fruitful, and increased *a* ... Ex 1:7 8317
river shall bring forth frogs *a* ... Ex 8:3 8317
and the water came out *a*, and the ... Num 20:11 7227
wine, and oil, and oxen, and sheep *a* ... 1Chr 12:40 7230
David prepared *a* before his death ... 1Chr 22:5 7230
saying, Thou hast shed blood *a* ... 1Chr 22:8 7230
of all things brought they in *a* ... 2Chr 31:5 7230
into whose hand God bringeth *a* ... Job 12:6
do drop and distil upon man *a* ... Job 36:28 7227
They shall be *a* satisfied with ... Ps 36:8 7301
waterest the ridges thereof *a* ... Ps 65:10 7301
I will *a* bless her provision ... Ps 132:15 1288
They shall *a* utter the memory of ... Ps 145:7 5042
drink, yea, drink *a*, O beloved ... Song 5:1 7937
every one shall howl, weeping *a* ... Is 15:3 3381
It shall blossom *a*, and rejoice ... Is 35:2 6524
to our God, for he will *a* pardon ... Is 55:7 7235

and that they might have it more a ... Jn 10:10 4053
I laboured more a than they all ... 1Cor 15:10 4054
the world, and more a to you-ward ... 2Cor 1:12 4056
love which I have more a unto you ... 2Cor 2:4 4056
by you according to our rule a ... 2Cor 10:15 1519,4050
though the more a I love you ... 2Cor 12:15 4056
that is able to do exceeding a ... Eph 3:20 1537,4053
endeavoured the more a to see ... 1Th 2:17 4056
Which he shed on us a through ... Titus 3:6 4146
willing more a to shew unto the ... Heb 6:17 4054
shall be ministered unto you a ... 2Pet 1:11 4146

ABUSE {3}
and thrust me through, and a me ... 1Sa 31:4 5953
these uncircumcised come and a me ... 1Chr 10:4 5953
that I a not my power in the ... 1Cor 9:18 2710

ABUSED {1}
a her all the night until the ... Judg 19:25 5953

ABUSERS {1}
nor a of themselves with mankind, ... 1Cor 6:9 733

ABUSING {1}
that use this world, as not a it ... 1Cor 7:31 2710

ACBOR See ACHBOR.

ACCAD *(ak'-kad)* {1} *A city of Shinar.*
kingdom was Babel, and Erech, and A ... Gen 10:10 390

ACCEPT {25}
peradventure he will a of me ... Gen 32:20 5375
the owner of it shall a thereof ... Ex 22:11 3947
they then a of the punishment of ... Lev 26:41 7521
they shall a of the punishment of ... Lev 26:43 7521
and a the work of his hands ... Deut 33:11 7521
against me, let him a an offering ... 1Sa 26:19 7306
the king, The LORD thy God a thee ... 2Sa 24:23 7521
Will ye a his person ... Job 13:8 5375
you, if ye do secretly a persons ... Job 13:10 5375
a any man's person, neither let ... Job 32:21 5375
for him will I a ... Job 42:8 5375
and a thy burnt sacrifice ... Ps 20:3 1878
a the persons of the wicked ... Ps 82:2 5375
A, I beseech thee, the freewill ... Ps 119:108 7521
It is not good to a the person of ... Prov 18:5 5375
the LORD doth not a them ... Jer 14:10 7521
and an oblation, I will not a them ... Jer 14:12 7521
there will I a them, and there ... Eze 20:40 7521
I will a you with your sweet ... Eze 20:41 7521
and I will a you, saith the Lord ... Eze 43:27 7521
meat offerings, I will not a them ... Amos 5:22 7521
with thee, or a thy person ... Mal 1:8 5375
neither will I a an offering at ... Mal 1:10 7521
should I a this of your hand ... Mal 1:13 7521
We a it always, and in all places, ... Acts 24:3 588

ACCEPTABLE {23}
for it shall not be a for you ... Lev 22:20 7522
let him be a to his brethren, and ... Deut 33:24 7522
be a in thy sight, O LORD, my ... Ps 19:14 7522
unto thee, O LORD, in an a time ... Ps 69:13 7522
of the righteous know what is a ... Prov 10:32 7522
judgment is more a to the LORD ... Prov 21:3 977
sought to find out a words ... Eccl 12:10 2656
In an a time have I heard thee, ... Is 49:8 7522
a fast, and an a day to the LORD ... Is 58:5 7522
To proclaim the a year of the ... Is 61:2 7522
your burnt offerings are not a ... Jer 6:20 7522
let my counsel be a unto thee ... Dan 4:27 8232
To preach the a year of the Lord ... Lk 4:19 1184
a unto God, which is your ... Rom 12:1 2101
may prove what is that good, and a ... Rom 12:2 2101
things serveth Christ is a to God ... Rom 14:18 2101
up of the Gentiles might be a ... Rom 15:16 2144
Proving what is a unto the Lord ... Eph 5:10 2101
of a sweet smell, a sacrifice a ... Phil 4:18 1184
a in the sight of God our Saviour ... 1Ti 2:3 587
for that is good and a before God ... 1Ti 5:4 587
a to God by Jesus Christ ... 1Pet 2:5 2144
it patiently, this is a with God ... 1Pet 2:20 5485

ACCEPTABLY {1}
we may serve God a with reverence ... Heb 12:28 2102

ACCEPTANCE {1}
come up with a on mine altar ... Is 60:7 7522

ACCEPTATION {2}
saying, and worthy of all a ... 1Ti 1:15 594
saying and worthy of all a ... 1Ti 4:9 594

ACCEPTED {29}
doest well, shalt thou not be a ... Gen 4:7 7613
I have a thee concerning this ... Gen 19:21 5375
they may be a before the LORD ... Ex 28:38 7522
it shall be a for him to make ... Lev 1:4 7521
the third day, it shall not be a ... Lev 7:18 7521
should it have been a in the ... Lev 10:19 3190
it shall not be a ... Lev 19:7 7521
it shall be perfect to be a ... Lev 22:21 7522
but for a vow it shall not be a ... Lev 22:23 7521
they shall not be a for you ... Lev 22:25 7521
thenceforth it shall be a for an ... Lev 22:27 7521
before the LORD, to be a for you ... Lev 23:11 7522
he was a in the sight of all the ... 1Sa 18:5 3190
thy voice, and have a thy person ... 1Sa 25:35 5375
a of the multitude of his ... Est 10:3 7521
the LORD also a Job ... Job 42:9 5375
shall be a upon mine altar ... Is 56:7 7522
I pray thee, be a before thee ... Jer 37:20 5307
our supplication be a before thee ... Jer 42:2 5307
No prophet is a in his own ... Lk 4:24 1184
righteousness, is a with him ... Acts 10:35 1184
Jerusalem may be a of the saints ... Rom 15:31 2144
or absent, we may be a of him ... 2Cor 5:9 2101
I have heard thee in a time a ... 2Cor 6:2 1184
behold, now is the a time ... 2Cor 6:2 2144
it is a according to that a man ... 2Cor 8:12 2144
For indeed he a the exhortation ... 2Cor 8:17 1209
gospel, which ye have not a ... 2Cor 11:4 1209
he hath made us a in the beloved ... Eph 1:6 5487

ACCEPTEST {1}
neither a thou the person of any, ... Lk 20:21 2983

ACCEPTETH {4}
How much less to him that a not ... Job 34:19 5375
for God now a thy works ... Eccl 9:7 7521
but the LORD a them not ... Hos 8:13 7521
God a no man's person ... Gal 2:6 2983

ACCEPTING {1}
were tortured, not a deliverance ... Heb 11:35 4327

ACCESS {3}
By whom also we have a by faith ... Rom 5:2 4318
For through him we both have a by ... Eph 2:18 4318
a with confidence by the faith of ... Eph 3:12 4318

ACCHO *(ak'-ko)* {1} *A coastal city in Asher.*
drive out the inhabitants of A ... Judg 1:31 5910

ACCO See ACCHO.

ACCOMPANIED {4}
certain brethren from Joppa a him ... Acts 10:23 4905
these six brethren a me ... Acts 11:12 2064,4862
there a him into Asia Sopater of ... Acts 20:4 4902
And they a him unto the ship ... Acts 20:38 4311

ACCOMPANY {1}
you, and things that a salvation ... Heb 6:9 2192

ACCOMPANYING {1}
was at Gibeah, a the ark of God ... 2Sa 6:4 5973

ACCOMPLISH {13}
unto the LORD to a his vow ... Lev 22:21 6381
and thou shalt a my desire ... 1Kin 5:9 6213
that he may rest, till he shall a ... Job 14:6 7521
they a a diligent search ... Ps 64:6 8552
but it shall a that which I ... Is 55:11 6213
ye will surely a your vows ... Jer 44:25 6965
thus will I a my fury upon them ... Eze 6:12 3615
thee, and a mine anger upon thee ... Eze 7:8 3615
Thus will I a my wrath upon the ... Eze 13:15 3615
to a my anger against them in the ... Eze 20:8 3615
to a my anger against them in the ... Eze 20:21 3615
that he would a seventy years in ... Dan 9:2 4390
which he should a at Jerusalem ... Lk 9:31 4137

ACCOMPLISHED {26}
the mouth of Jeremiah might be a ... 2Chr 36:22 3615
the days of their purifications a ... Est 2:12 4390
It shall be a before his time, and ... Job 15:32 4390
The desire a is sweet to the soul ... Prov 13:19 1961
unto her, that her warfare is a ... Is 40:2 4390
to pass, when seventy years are a ... Jer 25:12 4390
and of your dispersions are a ... Jer 25:34 4390
be a at Babylon I will visit you ... Jer 29:10 4390
they shall be a in that day ... Jer 39:16
The LORD hath a his fury ... Lam 4:11 3615
punishment of thine iniquity is a ... Lam 4:22 8552
And when thou hast a them, lie ... Eze 4:6 3615
Thus shall mine anger be a ... Eze 5:13 3615
when I have a my fury in them ... Eze 5:13 3615
prosper till the indignation be a ... Dan 11:36 3615
when he shall have a to scatter ... Dan 12:7 3615
days of his ministration were a ... Lk 1:23 4130
the days were a that she should ... Lk 2:6 4130
when eight days were a for the ... Lk 2:21 4130
to the law of Moses were a ... Lk 2:22 4130
how am I straitened till it be a ... Lk 12:50 5055
the Son of man shall be a ... Lk 18:31 5055
is written must yet be a in me ... Lk 22:37 5055
that all things were now a ... Jn 19:28 5055
And when we had a those days ... Acts 21:5 1822
a in your brethren that are in ... 1Pet 5:9 2005

ACCOMPLISHING {1}
tabernacle, a the service of God ... Heb 9:6 2005

ACCOMPLISHMENT {1}
to signify the a of the days of ... Acts 21:26 1604

ACCORD {16}
a of thy harvest thou shalt not ... Lev 25:5 5599
Joshua and with Israel, with one a ... Josh 9:2 6310
continued with one a in prayer ... Acts 1:14 3661
were all with one a in one place ... Acts 2:1 3661
daily with one a in the temple ... Acts 2:46 3661
up their voice to God with one a ... Acts 4:24 3661
all with one a in Solomon's porch ... Acts 5:12 3661
ears, and ran upon him with one a ... Acts 7:57 3661
the people with one a gave heed ... Acts 8:6 3661
which opened to them of his own a ... Acts 12:10 844
but they came with one a to him ... Acts 12:20 3661
us, being assembled with one a ... Acts 15:25 3661
with one a against Paul, and ... Acts 18:12 3661
with one a into the theatre ... Acts 19:29 3661
of his own a he went unto you ... 2Cor 8:17 830
the same love, being of one a ... Phil 2:2 4861

ACCORDING See APPENDIX.

ACCORDINGLY {1}
a he will repay, fury to his ... Is 59:18 5922

ACCOUNT {17}
of every one that passeth the a ... 2Kin 12:4
was the number put in the a of ... 1Chr 27:24 4557
to the number of their a by the ... 2Chr 26:11 6486
for he giveth not a of any of his ... Job 33:13 6030
of man, that thou makest a of him ... Ps 144:3 2803
one by one, to find out the a ... Eccl 7:27 2808
they shall give a thereof in the ... Mt 12:36 3056
would take a of his servants ... Mt 18:23 3056
give an a of thy stewardship ... Lk 16:2 3056
may give an a of this concourse ... Acts 19:40 3056
us shall give a of himself to God ... Rom 14:12 3056
Let a man so a of us, as of the ... 1Cor 4:1 3049
fruit that may abound to your a ... Phil 4:17 3056
thee ought, put that on mine a ... Philem 18 1677
souls, as they that must give a ... Heb 13:17 3056
Who shall give a to him that is ... 1Pet 4:5 3056
a that the longsuffering of our ... 2Pet 3:15 2233

ACCOUNTED {12}
Which also were a giants, as the ... Deut 2:11 2803
(That also was a a land of giants ... Deut 2:20 2803
it was nothing a of in the days ... 1Kin 10:21 2803
it was not any thing a of in the ... 2Chr 9:20 2803
it shall be a to the Lord for a ... Ps 22:30 5608
for wherein is he to be a of ... Is 2:22 2803
are a to rule over the Gentiles ... Mk 10:42 1380
But they which shall be a worthy ... Lk 20:35 2661
that ye may be a worthy to escape ... Lk 21:36 2661
of them should be a the greatest ... Lk 22:24 1380
we are a as sheep for the ... Rom 8:36 3049
it was a to him for righteousness ... Gal 3:6 3049

ACCOUNTING {1}
A that God was able to raise him ... Heb 11:19 3049

ACCOUNTS {1}
princes might give a unto them ... Dan 6:2 2941

ACCURSED {20}
for he that is hanged is a of God ... Deut 21:23 7045
And the city shall be a, even it, ... Josh 6:17 2764
keep yourselves from the a thing ... Josh 6:18 2764
lest ye make yourselves a ... Josh 6:18 2763
when ye take of the a thing ... Josh 6:18 2764
a trespass in the a thing ... Josh 7:1 2764
of Judah, took of the a thing ... Josh 7:1 2764
have even taken of the a thing ... Josh 7:11 2764
enemies, because they were a ... Josh 7:12 2764
ye destroy the a from among you ... Josh 7:12 2764
There is an a thing in the midst ... Josh 7:13 2764
away the a thing from among you ... Josh 7:13 2764
a thing shall be burnt with fire ... Josh 7:15 2764
commit a trespass in the a thing ... Josh 22:20 2764
who transgressed in the thing a ... 1Chr 2:7 2764
an hundred years old shall be a ... Is 65:20 7043
a from Christ for my brethren ... Rom 9:3 331
the Spirit of God calleth Jesus a ... 1Cor 12:3 331
preached unto you, let him be a ... Gal 1:8 331
ye have received, let him be a ... Gal 1:9 331

ACCUSATION {10}
wrote they unto him an a against ... Ezr 4:6 7855
up over his head his a written ... Mt 27:37 156
of his a was written over ... Mk 15:26 156
they might find an a against him ... Lk 6:7 2724
any thing from any man by false a ... Lk 19:8 4811
What a bring ye against this man ... Jn 18:29 2724
they brought none a of such ... Acts 25:18 156
Against an elder receive not an a ... 1Ti 5:19 2724
bring not railing a against them ... 2Pet 2:11 2920
not bring against him a railing a ... Jude 9 2920

ACCUSE {16}
A not a servant unto his master, ... Prov 30:10 3960
that they might a him ... Mt 12:10 2723
that they might a him ... Mk 3:2 2723
to no man, neither a any falsely ... Lk 3:14 4811
his mouth, that they might a him ... Lk 11:54 2722
And they began to a him, saying, ... Lk 23:2 2722
those things whereof ye a him ... Lk 23:14 2722
that I will a you to the Father ... Jn 5:45 2722
that they might have to a him ... Jn 8:6 2722
forth, Tertullus began to a him ... Acts 24:2 2722
these things, whereof we a him ... Acts 24:8 2722
the things whereof they now a me ... Acts 24:13 2722
a this man, if there be any ... Acts 25:5 2722
these things whereof these a me ... Acts 25:11 2722
I had ought to a my nation of ... Acts 28:19 2722
a your good conversation in ... 1Pet 3:16 1908

ACCUSED {14}
came near, and a the Jews ... Dan 3:8 399,7170
those men which had a Daniel ... Dan 6:24 399,7170
when he was a of the chief ... Mt 27:12 2723
the chief priests a him of many ... Mk 15:3 2723
the same was a unto him that he ... Lk 16:1 1225
scribes stood and vehemently a him ... Lk 23:10 2722
wherefore he was a of the Jews ... Acts 22:30 2722
the cause wherefore they a him ... Acts 23:28 1458
Whom I perceived to be a of ... Acts 23:29 1458
before that he which is a have ... Acts 25:16 2722
things whereof I am a of the Jews ... Acts 26:2 1458
king Agrippa, I am a of the Jews ... Acts 26:7 1458
children not a of riot or unruly ... Titus 1:6 1722,2724
which a them before our God day ... Rev 12:10 2722

ACCUSER {1}
for the a of our brethren is cast ... Rev 12:10 2723

ACCUSERS {8}
Woman, where are those thine a ... Jn 8:10 2723
gave commandment to his a also to ... Acts 23:30 2723
when thine a are also come ... Acts 23:35 2723
Commanding his a to come unto ... Acts 24:8 2723
accused have the a face to face ... Acts 25:16 2723
Against whom when the a stood up ... Acts 25:18 2723
affection, trucebreakers, false a ... 2Ti 3:3 1228
as becometh holiness, not false a ... Titus 2:3 1228

ACCUSETH {1}
there is one that *a* you, even ... Jn 5:45 *2723*

ACCUSING {1}
a or else excusing one another ... Rom 2:15 *2722*

ACCUSTOMED {1}
do good, that are *a* to do evil ... Jer 13:23 3928

ACELDAMA *(as-el'-dam-ah)* {1} *A burial ground bought with Judas' betrayal money.*
called in their proper tongue, *A* ... Acts 1:19 *184*

ACHAIA *(ak-ah'-yah)* {11} *Roman province in Greece.*
when Gallio was the deputy of *A* ... Acts 18:12 *882*
he was disposed to pass into *A* ... Acts 18:27 *882*
had passed through Macedonia and *A* ... Acts 19:21 *882*
A to make a certain contribution ... Rom 15:26 *882*
the firstfruits of *A* unto Christ ... Rom 16:5 *882*
that it is the firstfruits of *A* ... 1Cor 16:15 *882*
all the saints which are in all *A* ... 2Cor 1:1 *882*
that *A* was ready a year ago ... 2Cor 9:2 *882*
this boasting in the regions of *A* ... 2Cor 11:10 *882*
that believe in Macedonia and *A* ... 1Th 1:7 *882*
Lord not only in Macedonia and *A* ... 1Th 1:8 *882*

ACHAICUS *(ak-ah'-yah-cus)* {2} *A Corinthian who visited Paul in Philippi.*
of Stephanas and Fortunatus and *A* ... 1Cor 16:17 *883*
by Stephanus, and Fortunatus, and *A* ... 1Cor s

ACHAN *(a'-kan)* {6} See ACHAR. *Soldier under Joshua executed for disobedience.*
for *A*, the son of Carmi, the son ... Josh 7:1 5912
and *A*, the son of Carmi, the son ... Josh 7:18 5912
And Joshua said unto *A*, My son, ... Josh 7:19 5912
A answered Joshua, and said, ... Josh 7:20 5912
took *A* the son of Zerah, and the ... Josh 7:24 5912
Did not *A* the son of Zerah commit ... Josh 22:20 5912

ACHAR *(a'-kar)* {1} See ACHAN. *A form of Achan.*
A, the troubler of Israel, who ... 1Chr 2:7 5917

ACHAZ *(a'-kaz)* {2} See AHAZ. *The Greek form of Ahaz.*
and Joatham begat *A* ... Mt 1:9 *881*
and *A* begat Ezekias ... Mt 1:9 *881*

ACHBOR *(ak'-bor)* {7}
1. Father of an Edomite king.
the son of *A* reigned in his stead ... Gen 36:38 5907
And Baal-hanan the son of *A* died ... Gen 36:39 5907
the son of *A* reigned in his stead ... 1Chr 1:49 5907
2. A messenger of Josiah to Huldah.
A the son of Michaiah, and Shaphan ... 2Kin 22:12 5907
the priest, and Ahikam, and *A* ... 2Kin 22:14 5907
3. Father of Elnathan.
namely, Elnathan the son of *A* ... Jer 26:22 5907
and Elnathan the son of *A* ... Jer 36:12 5907

ACHIM *(a'-kim)* {2} *Son of Sadoc; ancestor of Jesus.*
and Sadoc begat *A* ... Mt 1:14 *885*
and *A* begat Eliud ... Mt 1:14 *885*

ACHISH *(a'-kish)* {21}
1. A king of Gath who aided David.
went to *A* the king of Gath ... 1Sa 21:10 397
the servants of *A* said unto him ... 1Sa 21:11 397
sore afraid of *A* the king of Gath ... 1Sa 21:12 397
Then said *A* unto his servants, Lo ... 1Sa 21:14 397
men that were with him unto *A* ... 1Sa 27:2 397
And David dwelt with *A* at Gath ... 1Sa 27:3 397
And David said unto *A*, If I have ... 1Sa 27:5 397
Then *A* gave him Ziklag that day ... 1Sa 27:6 397
and returned, and came to *A* ... 1Sa 27:9 397
A said, Whither have ye made a ... 1Sa 27:10 397
A believed David, saying, He hath ... 1Sa 27:12 397
A said unto David, Know thou ... 1Sa 28:1 397
And David said to *A*, Surely thou ... 1Sa 28:2 397
A said to David, Therefore will I ... 1Sa 28:2 397
passed on in the rereward with *A* ... 1Sa 29:2 397
A said unto the princes of the ... 1Sa 29:3 397
Then *A* called David, and said unto ... 1Sa 29:6 397
And David said unto *A*, But what ... 1Sa 29:8 397
A answered and said to David, I ... 1Sa 29:9 397
2. A king of Gath during Solomon's reign.
of Shimei ran away unto *A* son of ... 1Kin 2:39 397
went to Gath to *A* to seek his ... 1Kin 2:40 397

ACHMETHA *(ak'-meth-ah)* {1} *A city in Media.*
And there was found at *A*, in the ... Ezr 6:2 307

ACHOR *(a'-kor)* {5} *A valley near Jericho.*
brought them unto the valley of *A* ... Josh 7:24 5911
place was called, The valley of *A* ... Josh 7:26 5911
toward Debir from the valley of *A* ... Josh 15:7 5911
the valley of *A* a place for the ... Is 65:10 5911
the valley of *A* for a door of ... Hos 2:15 5911

ACHSA *(ak'-sah)* {1} See ACHSAH. *Daughter of Caleb.*
and the daughter of Caleb was *A* ... 1Chr 2:49 5915

ACHSAH *(ak'-sah)* {4} See ACHSA. *A form of Achsa.*
to him will I give *A* my daughter ... Josh 15:16 5915
he gave him *A* his daughter to ... Josh 15:17 5915
to him will I give *A* my daughter ... Judg 1:12 5919
he gave him *A* his daughter to ... Judg 1:13 5919

ACHSHAPH *(ak'-shaf)* {3} *A Phoenician city in Asher.*
of Shimron, and to the king of *A* ... Josh 11:1 407
the king of *A*, one ... Josh 12:20 407
Helkath, and Hali, and Beten, and *A* ... Josh 19:25 407

ACHZIB *(ak'-zib)* {4} See CHEZIB.
1. A town in western Judah.
And Keilah, and *A*, and Mareshah ... Josh 15:44 392
the houses of *A* shall be a lie to ... Mic 1:14 392
2. A coastal city in Asher.
at the sea from the coast to *A* ... Josh 19:29 392
of Zidon, nor of Ahlab, nor of *A* ... Judg 1:31 392

ACKNOWLEDGE {6}
But he shall *a* the son of the ... Deut 21:17 5234
neither did he *a* his brethren ... Deut 33:9 5234
For I *a* my transgressions ... Ps 51:3 3045
In all thy ways *a* him, and he ... Prov 3:6 3045
and, ye that are near, *a* my might ... Is 33:13 3045
all that see them shall *a* them ... Is 61:9 5234
of us, and Israel *a* us not ... Is 63:16 5234
Only *a* thine iniquity, that thou ... Jer 3:13 3045
We *a*, O LORD, our wickedness, and ... Jer 14:20 3045
so will I *a* them that are carried ... Jer 24:5 5234
a strange god, whom he shall *a* ... Dan 11:39 5234
till they *a* their offence, and ... Hos 5:15
let him *a* that the things that I ... 1Cor 14:37 *1921*
therefore *a* ye them that are such ... 1Cor 16:18 *1921*
unto you, than what ye read or *a* ... 2Cor 1:13 *1921*
trust ye shall *a* even to the end ... 2Cor 1:13 *1921*

ACKNOWLEDGED {3}
And Judah *a* them, and said, She ... Gen 38:26 5234
I *a* my sin unto thee, and mine ... Ps 32:5 3045
As also ye have *a* us in part ... 2Cor 1:14 *1922*

ACKNOWLEDGEMENT {1}
to the *a* of the mystery of God, ... Col 2:2 *1922*

ACKNOWLEDGETH {1}
{ but } he that *a* the Son hath ... 1Jn 2:23

ACKNOWLEDGING {3}
repentance to the *a* of the truth ... 2Ti 2:25 *1922*
the *a* of the truth which is after ... Titus 1:1 *1922*
may become effectual by the *a* of ... Philem 6 *1922*

ACQUAINT {1}
A now thyself with him, and be at ... Job 22:21 5532

ACQUAINTANCE {11}
it to them, every man of his *a* ... 2Kin 12:5 4378
receive no more money of your *a* ... 2Kin 12:7 4378
mine *a* are verily estranged from ... Job 19:13 3045
that had been of his *a* before ... Job 42:11 3045
neighbours, and a fear to mine *a* ... Ps 31:11 3045
mine equal, my guide, and mine *a* ... Ps 55:13 3045
hast put away mine *a* far from me ... Ps 88:8 3045
from me, and mine *a* into darkness ... Ps 88:18 3045
him among their kinsfolk and *a* ... Lk 2:44 *1110*
And all his *a*, and the women that ... Lk 23:49 *1110*
a to minister or come unto him ... Acts 24:23 *2398*

ACQUAINTED {2}
down, and art *a* with all my ways ... Ps 139:3 5532
a man of sorrows, and *a* with grief ... Is 53:3 3045

ACQUAINTING {1}
yet *a* mine heart with wisdom ... Eccl 2:3 5090

ACQUIT {2}
thou wilt not *a* me from mine ... Job 10:14 5352
and will not at all *a* the wicked ... Nah 1:3 5352

ACRE {1}
as it were an half *a* of land ... 1Sa 14:14 4618

ACRES {1}
ten *a* of vineyard shall yield one ... Is 5:10 6776

ACSAH See ACHSA.

ACSHAPH See ACHSHAPH.

ACT {4}
to pass his *a*, his strange *a* ... Is 28:21 5556
the *a* of violence is in their ... Is 59:6 6467
taken in adultery, in the very *a* ... Jn 8:4 *1888*

ACTIONS {1}
and by him *a* are weighed ... 1Sa 2:3 5949

ACTIVITY {1}
knowest any men of *a* among them ... Gen 47:6 2428

ACTS {66}
And his miracles, and his *a* ... Deut 11:3 4640
great *a* of the LORD which he did ... Deut 11:7 4640
the righteous *a* of the LORD ... Judg 5:11
even the righteous *a* toward the ... Judg 5:11
all the righteous *a* of the LORD ... 1Sa 12:7
of Kabzeel, who had done many *a* ... 2Sa 23:20 6467
I heard in mine own land of thy *a* ... 1Kin 10:6 1697
And the rest of the *a* of Solomon ... 1Kin 11:41 1697
in the book of the *a* of Solomon ... 1Kin 11:41 1697
And the rest of the *a* of Jeroboam ... 1Kin 14:19 1697
Now the rest of the *a* of Rehoboam ... 1Kin 14:29 1697
Now the rest of the *a* of Abijam ... 1Kin 15:7 1697
The rest of all the *a* of Asa ... 1Kin 15:23 1697
Now the rest of the *a* of Nadab ... 1Kin 15:31 1697
Now the rest of the *a* of Baasha ... 1Kin 16:5 1697
Now the rest of the *a* of Elah ... 1Kin 16:14 1697
Now the rest of the *a* of Zimri ... 1Kin 16:20 1697
Now the rest of the *a* of Omri ... 1Kin 16:27 1697
Now the rest of the *a* of Ahab ... 1Kin 22:39 1697
the rest of the *a* of Jehoshaphat ... 1Kin 22:45 1697
Now the rest of the *a* of Ahaziah ... 2Kin 1:18 1697
And the rest of the *a* of Joram ... 2Kin 8:23 1697
Now the rest of the *a* of Jehu ... 2Kin 10:34 1697
And the rest of the *a* of Joash ... 2Kin 12:19 1697
Now the rest of the *a* of Jehoahaz ... 2Kin 13:8 1697
And the rest of the *a* of Joash ... 2Kin 13:12 1697
Now the rest of the *a* of Jehoash ... 2Kin 14:15 1697
And the rest of the *a* of Amaziah ... 2Kin 14:18 1697
Now the rest of the *a* of Jeroboam ... 2Kin 14:28 1697
And the rest of the *a* of Azariah ... 2Kin 15:6 1697
And the rest of the *a* of Zachariah ... 2Kin 15:11 1697
And the rest of the *a* of Shallum ... 2Kin 15:15 1697
And the rest of the *a* of Menahem ... 2Kin 15:21 1697
And the rest of the *a* of Pekahiah ... 2Kin 15:26 1697
And the rest of the *a* of Pekah ... 2Kin 15:31 1697
Now the rest of the *a* of Jotham ... 2Kin 15:36 1697
Now the rest of the *a* of Ahaz ... 2Kin 16:19 1697
And the rest of the *a* of Hezekiah ... 2Kin 20:20 1697
Now the rest of the *a* of Manasseh ... 2Kin 21:17 1697
Now the rest of the *a* of Amon ... 2Kin 21:25 1697
the *a* that he had done in Beth-el ... 2Kin 23:19 4640
Now the rest of the *a* of Josiah ... 2Kin 23:28 1697
the rest of the *a* of Jehoiakim ... 2Kin 24:5 1697
of Kabzeel, who had done many *a* ... 1Chr 11:22 6467
Now the *a* of David the king, ... 1Chr 29:29 1697
heard in mine own land of thine *a* ... 2Chr 9:5 1697
Now the rest of the *a* of Solomon ... 2Chr 9:29 1697
Now the *a* of Rehoboam, first and ... 2Chr 12:15 1697
And the rest of the *a* of Abijah ... 2Chr 13:22 1697
the *a* of Asa, first and last, lo, ... 2Chr 16:11 1697
the rest of the *a* of Jehoshaphat ... 2Chr 20:34 1697
Now the rest of the *a* of Amaziah ... 2Chr 25:26 1697
Now the rest of the *a* of Uzziah ... 2Chr 26:22 1697
Now the rest of the *a* of Jotham ... 2Chr 27:7 1697
Now the rest of his *a* and of all ... 2Chr 28:26 1697
Now the rest of the *a* of Hezekiah ... 2Chr 32:32 1697
Now the rest of the *a* of Manasseh ... 2Chr 33:18 1697
Now the rest of the *a* of Josiah ... 2Chr 35:26 1697
the rest of the *a* of Jehoiakim ... 2Chr 36:8 1697
all the *a* of his power and of his ... Est 10:2 4640
his *a* unto the children of Israel ... Ps 103:7 5949
utter the mighty *a* of the LORD ... Ps 106:2
and shall declare thy mighty *a* ... Ps 145:4
of the might of thy terrible *a* ... Ps 145:6
to the sons of men his mighty *a* ... Ps 145:12
Praise him for his mighty *a* ... Ps 150:2

ACZIB See ACHZIB.

ADADAH *(ad'-ad-ah)* {1} *A city in southern Judah.*
And Kinah, and Dimonah, and *A* ... Josh 15:22 5735

ADAH *(a'-dah)* {8}
1. A wife of Lemech.
the name of the one was *A* ... Gen 4:19 5711
And *A* bare Jabal ... Gen 4:20 5711
And Lamech said unto his wives, *A* ... Gen 4:23 5711
2. A wife of Esau.
A the daughter of Elon the ... Gen 36:2 5711
And *A* bare to Esau Eliphaz ... Gen 36:4 5711
the son of *A* the wife of Esau ... Gen 36:10 5711
were the sons of *A* Esau's wife ... Gen 36:12 5711
these were the sons of *A* ... Gen 36:16 5711

ADAIAH *(ad-a-i'-yah)* {9}
1. Grandfather of King Josiah.
the daughter of *A* of Boscath ... 2Kin 22:1 5718
2. A Levite descendant of Gershon.
the son of Zerah, the son of *A* ... 1Chr 6:41 5718
3. A son of Shimhi.
And *A*, and Beraiah, and Shimrath, ... 1Chr 8:21 5718
4. A Levite of Jerusalem.
A the son of Jeroham, the son of ... 1Chr 9:12 5718
5. Father of Maaseiah.
of Obed, and Maaseiah the son of *A* ... 2Chr 23:1 5718
6. Married a foreign wife in Exile.
Meshullam, Malluch, and *A*, Jashub, ... Ezr 10:29 5718
7. Married a foreign wife in Exile.
And Shelemiah, and Nathan, and *A* ... Ezr 10:39 5718
8. A descendant of Pharez.
the son of Hazaiah, the son of *A* ... Neh 11:5 5718
9. An Aaronite Levite.
A the son of Jeroham, the son of ... Neh 11:12 5718

ADALIA *(ad-al-i'-yah)* {1} *A son of Haman.*
And Poratha, and *A*, and Aridatha, ... Est 9:8 118

ADAM *(ad'-um)* {30} See ADAM'S.
1. First man created by God.
brought them unto *A* to see what ... Gen 2:19 120
whatsoever *A* called every living ... Gen 2:19 120
A gave names to all cattle, and to ... Gen 2:20 120
but for *A* there was not found an ... Gen 2:20 120
a deep sleep to fall upon *A* ... Gen 2:21 121
A said, This is now bone of my ... Gen 2:23 120
and *A* and his wife hid themselves ... Gen 3:8 120
And the LORD God called unto *A* ... Gen 3:9 120
unto *A* he said, Because thou hast ... Gen 3:17 121
A called his wife's name Eve ... Gen 3:20 120
Unto *A* also and to his wife did ... Gen 3:21 120
And *A* knew Eve his wife ... Gen 4:1 120
And *A* knew his wife again ... Gen 4:25 120
the book of the generations of *A* ... Gen 5:1 120
them, and called their name *A* ... Gen 5:2 120
A lived an hundred and thirty ... Gen 5:3 121
the days of *A* after he had ... Gen 5:4 121
all the days that *A* lived were ... Gen 5:5 121
when he separated the sons of *A* ... Deut 32:8 120
A, Sheth, Enosh, ... 1Chr 1:1 121
I covered my transgressions as *A* ... Job 31:33 121
of Seth, which was the son of *A* ... Lk 3:38 *76*
death reigned from *A* to Moses ... Rom 5:14 *76*
For as in *A* all die, even so in ... 1Cor 15:22 *76*
The first man *A* was made a living ... 1Cor 15:45 *76*
the last *A* was made a quickening ... 1Cor 15:45 *76*
For *A* was first formed, then Eve ... 1Ti 2:13 *76*
A was not deceived, but the woman ... 1Ti 2:14 *76*
And Enoch also, the seventh from *A* ... Jude 14 *76*
2. A town in Manasseh.
an heap very far from the city *A* ... Josh 3:16 121

ADAMAH *(ad'-am-ah)* {1} *A walled city in Naphtali.*
And *A*, and Ramah, and Hazor, ... Josh 19:36 128

ADAMANT {2}
As an *a* harder than flint have I ... Eze 3:9 8068
made their hearts as an *a* stone ... Zec 7:12 8068

ADAMI *(ad'-am-i)* {1} *A variant of Adamah.*
from Allon to Zaanannim, and *A* ... Josh 19:33 129

ADAMI NEKEB See NEKEB.

ADAM'S *(ad'-ums)* {1}
the similitude of A transgression ... Rom 5:14 *76*

ADAR *(a'-dar)* {10} See ADDAR, ATAROTH-ADAR.
1. A city in southern Judah.
along to Hezron, and went up to A ... Josh 15:3 146
2. Twelfth month of the Hebrew year.
on the third day of the month A ... Ezr 6:15 144
month, that is, the month A ... Est 3:7 143
month, which is the month A ... Est 3:13 143
month, which is the month A ... Est 8:12 143
month, that is, the month A ... Est 9:1 143
day also of the month A, and slew ... Est 9:15 143
the thirteenth day of the month A ... Est 9:17 143
of the month A a day of gladness ... Est 9:19 143
the fourteenth day of the month A ... Est 9:21 143

ADBEEL *(ad'-be-el)* {2} *Son of Ishmael.*
and Kedar, and A, and Mibsam, ... Gen 25:13 110
then Kedar, and A, and Mibsam, ... 1Chr 1:29 110

ADD {33}
The LORD shall a to me another ... Gen 30:24 3254
shall a the fifth part thereto, ... Lev 5:16 3254
shall a the fifth part more ... Lev 6:5 3254
then he shall a a fifth part ... Lev 27:13 3254
then he shall a the fifth part of ... Lev 27:15 3254
then he shall a the fifth part of ... Lev 27:19 3254
shall a a fifth part of it ... Lev 27:27 3254
he shall a thereto the fifth part ... Lev 27:31 3254
a unto it the fifth part thereof, ... Num 5:7 3254
and to them ye shall a forty ... Num 35:6 5414
Ye shall not a unto the word ... Deut 4:2 3254
thou shalt not a thereto, nor ... Deut 12:32 3254
then shalt thou a three cities ... Deut 19:9 3254
to a drunkenness to thirst ... Deut 29:19 5595
LORD thy God a unto the people ... 2Sa 24:3 3254
heavy yoke, I will a to your yoke ... 1Kin 12:11 3254
heavy, and I will a to your yoke ... 1Kin 12:14 3254
I will a unto thy days fifteen ... 2Kin 20:6 3254
and thou mayest a thereto ... 1Chr 22:14 3254
yoke heavy, but I will a thereto ... 2Chr 10:14 3254
ye intend to a more to our sins ... 2Chr 28:13 3254
A iniquity unto their iniquity ... Ps 69:27 5414
and peace, shall they a to thee ... Prov 3:2 3254
A thou not unto his words, lest ... Prov 30:6 3254
a ye year to year ... Is 29:1 5595
that they may a sin to sin ... Is 30:1 5595
I will a unto thy days fifteen ... Is 38:5 3254
can a one cubit unto his stature ... Mt 6:27 *4369*
can a to his stature one cubit ... Lk 12:25 *4369*
supposing to a affliction to my ... Phil 1:16 *2018*
diligence, a to your faith virtue ... 2Pet 1:5 *2023*
If any man shall a unto these ... Rev 22:18 *2007*
God shall a unto him the plagues ... Rev 22:18 *2007*

ADDAN *(ad'-dan)* {1} *Home of some Exiles in Babylon.*
Tel-melah, Tel-harsa, Cherub, A ... Ezr 2:59 135

ADDAR *(ad'-dar)* {1} See ADAR, ATAROTH-ADDAR. *Son of Bela.*
And the sons of Bela were, A ... 1Chr 8:3 146

ADDED {15}
and he a no more ... Deut 5:22 3254
for we have a unto all our sins ... 1Sa 12:19 3254
there were a besides unto them ... Jer 36:32 3254
for the LORD hath a grief to my ... Jer 45:3 3254
excellent majesty was a unto me ... Dan 4:36 3255
these things shall be a unto you ... Mt 6:33 *4369*
A yet this above all, that he ... Lk 3:20 *4369*
these things shall be a unto you ... Lk 12:31 *4369*
as they heard these things, he a ... Lk 19:11 *4369*
the same day there were a unto ... Acts 2:41 *4369*
the Lord a to the church daily ... Acts 2:47 *4369*
were the more a to the Lord ... Acts 5:14 *4369*
much people was a unto the Lord ... Acts 11:24 *4369*
in conference a nothing to me ... Gal 2:6 *4323*
It was a because of ... Gal 3:19 *4369*

ADDER {4}
an a in the path, that biteth the ... Gen 49:17 8207
the deaf a that stoppeth her ear ... Ps 58:4 6620
shalt tread upon the lion and a ... Ps 91:13 6620
a serpent, and stingeth like an a ... Prov 23:32 6848

ADDERS' {1}
a poison is under their lips ... Ps 140:3 5919

ADDETH {4}
For he a rebellion unto his sin, ... Job 34:37 3254
rich, and he a no sorrow with it ... Prov 10:22 3254
mouth, and a learning to his lips ... Prov 16:23 3254
no man disannulleth, or a thereto ... Gal 3:15 *1928*

ADDI *(ad'-di)* {1} *Son of Cozam; ancestor of Jesus.*
of Melchi, which was the son of A ... Lk 3:28 *78*

ADDICTED {1}
that they have a themselves to ... 1Cor 16:15 *5021*

ADDITION {1}
molten, at the side of every a ... 1Kin 7:30 3914

ADDITIONS {2}
were certain a made of thin work ... 1Kin 7:29 3914
of every one, and a round about ... 1Kin 7:36 3914

ADDON *(ad'-don)* {1} *A form of Addan.*
Tel-melah, Tel-haresha, Cherub, A ... Neh 7:61 114

ADER *(a'-dur)* {1} *A son of Beriah.*
And Zebadiah, and Arad, and A ... 1Chr 8:15 5738

ADIEL *(a'-de-el)* {3}
1. A descendant of Simeon.
and Jeshohaiah, and Asaiah, and A ... 1Chr 4:36 5717
2. Father of Massiai.
and Maasiai the son of A, the son ... 1Chr 9:12 5717
3. Father of Azmaveth.
was Azmaveth the son of A ... 1Chr 27:25 5717

ADIN *(a'-din)* {4}
1. Family who returned from exile.
The children of A, four hundred ... Ezr 2:15 5720
The children of A, six hundred ... Neh 7:20 5720
2. Family who sealed the covenant with Nehemiah.
Adonijah, Bigvai, A, ... Neh 10:16 5720
3. An exilic family with Ezra.
Of the sons also of A ... Ezr 8:6 5720

ADINA *(ad'-in-ah)* {1} *A "mighty man" of David.*
A the son of Shiza the Reubenite, ... 1Chr 11:42 5721

ADINO *(ad'-in-o)* {1} *A "mighty man" of David.*
the same was A the Eznite ... 2Sa 23:8 5722

ADITHAIM *(ad-ith-a'-im)* {1} *A city in the plain of Judah.*
Sharaim, and A, and Gederah, and ... Josh 15:36 5723

ADJURE {5}
How many times shall I a thee ... 1Kin 22:16 7650
How many times shall I a thee ... 2Chr 18:15 7650
I a thee by the living God, that ... Mt 26:63 *1844*
I a thee by God, that thou ... Mk 5:7 *3726*
We a you by Jesus whom Paul ... Acts 19:13 *3726*

ADJURED {2}
Joshua a them at that time, ... Josh 6:26 7650
for Saul had a the people ... 1Sa 14:24 422

ADLAI *(ad'-la-i)* {1} *Father of Shapat.*
valleys was Shaphat the son of A ... 1Chr 27:29 5724

ADMAH *(ad'-mah)* {5} *A city destroyed with Sodom and Gomorrah.*
unto Sodom, and Gomorrah, and A ... Gen 10:19 126
of Gomorrah, Shinab king of A ... Gen 14:2 126
of Gomorrah, and the king of A ... Gen 14:8 126
of Sodom, and Gomorrah, A, and ... Deut 29:23 126
how shall I make thee as A ... Hos 11:8 126

ADMATHA *(ad'-math-ah)* {1} *A prince of Persia.*
unto him was Carshena, Shethar, A ... Est 1:14 133

ADMINISTERED {2}
which is a by us to the glory of ... 2Cor 8:19 *1247*
this abundance which is a by us ... 2Cor 8:20 *1247*

ADMINISTRATION {1}
For the a of this service not ... 2Cor 9:12 *1248*

ADMINISTRATIONS {1}
And there are differences of a ... 1Cor 12:5 *1248*

ADMIRATION {2}
persons in a because of advantage ... Jude 16 *2296*
saw her, I wondered with great a ... Rev 17:6 *2295*

ADMIRED {1}
to be a in all them that believe ... 2Th 1:10 *2296*

ADMONISH {3}
able also to a one another ... Rom 15:14 *3560*
over you in the Lord, and a you ... 1Th 5:12 *3560*
an enemy, but a him as a brother ... 2Th 3:15 *3560*

ADMONISHED {5}
king, who will no more be a ... Eccl 4:13 2094
further, by these, my son, be a ... Eccl 12:12 2094
that I have a you this day ... Jer 42:19 5749
was now already past, Paul a them ... Acts 27:9 *3867*
as Moses was a of God when he was ... Heb 8:5 *5537*

ADMONISHING {1}
a one another in psalms and hymns ... Col 3:16 *3560*

ADMONITION {3}
and they are written for our a ... 1Cor 10:11 *3559*
in the nurture and a of the Lord ... Eph 6:4 *3559*
the first and second a reject ... Titus 3:10 *3559*

ADNA *(ad'-nah)* {2} See ADNAH.
1. Married a foreigner while in exile.
A, and Chelal, Benaiah, Maaseiah, ... Ezr 10:30 5733
2. A priest during Joiakim's reign.
Of Harim, A ... Neh 12:15 5733

ADNAH *(ad'-nah)* {2} See ADNA.
1. A captain in David's army.
there fell to him of Manasseh, A ... 1Chr 12:20 5734
2. A commander in Jehoshaphat's army.
A the chief, and with him mighty ... 2Chr 17:14 5734

ADO {1}
unto them, Why make ye this a ... Mk 5:39 *2350*

ADONI-BEZEK *(ad'-on-i-be'-zek)* {3} *A lord of a Canaanite city.*
And they found A in Bezek ... Judg 1:5 137
But A fled ... Judg 1:6 137
A said, Threescore and ten kings, ... Judg 1:7 137

ADONIJAH *(ad-on-i'-jah)* {26} See TOB-ADONIJAH.
1. A son of David.
the fourth, A the son of Haggith ... 2Sa 3:4 138
Then A the son of Haggith exalted ... 1Kin 1:5 138
and they following A helped him ... 1Kin 1:7 138
to David, were not with A ... 1Kin 1:8 138
A slew sheep and oxen and fat ... 1Kin 1:9 138
Hast thou not heard that A the ... 1Kin 1:11 138
why then doth A reign ... 1Kin 1:13 138
And now, behold, A reigneth ... 1Kin 1:18 138
A shall reign after me, and he ... 1Kin 1:24 138
him, and say, God save king A ... 1Kin 1:25 138
And A and all the guests that were ... 1Kin 1:41 138
and A said unto him, Come in ... 1Kin 1:42 138
And Jonathan answered and said to A ... 1Kin 1:43 138
that were with A were afraid ... 1Kin 1:49 138
A feared because of Solomon, and ... 1Kin 1:50 138
Behold, A feareth king Solomon ... 1Kin 1:51 138
A the son of Haggith came to ... 1Kin 2:13 138
Solomon, to speak unto him for A ... 1Kin 2:19 138
be given to A thy brother to wife ... 1Kin 2:21 138
ask Abishag the Shunammite for A ... 1Kin 2:22 138
if A have not spoken this word ... 1Kin 2:23 138
A shall be put to death this day ... 1Kin 2:24 138
for Joab had turned after A ... 1Kin 2:28 138
the fourth, A the son of Haggith ... 1Chr 3:2 138
2. A Levite under King Jehoshaphat.
Shemiramoth, and Jehonathan, and A ... 2Chr 17:8 138
3. A clan leader who sealed the covenant with Nehemiah.
A, Bigvai, Adin, ... Neh 10:16 138

ADONIKAM *(ad-on-i'-kam)* {3} *A family in exile.*
The children of A, six hundred ... Ezr 2:13 140
And of the last sons of A, whose ... Ezr 8:13 140
The children of A, six hundred ... Neh 7:18 140

ADONIRAM *(ad-on-i'-ram)* {2} See ADORAM. *A tribute officer under Solomon.*
A the son of Abda was over the ... 1Kin 4:6 141
and A was over the levy ... 1Kin 5:14 141

ADONI-ZEDEK *(ad'-on-i-ze'-dek)* {2} *Canaanite king slain by Joshua.*
when A king of Jerusalem had ... Josh 10:1 139
Wherefore A king of Jerusalem ... Josh 10:3 139

ADOPTION {5}
ye have received the Spirit of a ... Rom 8:15 *5206*
ourselves, waiting for the a ... Rom 8:23 *5206*
to whom pertaineth the a, and the ... Rom 9:4 *5206*
we might receive the a of sons ... Gal 4:5 *5206*
predestinated us unto the a of ... Eph 1:5 *5206*

ADORAIM *(ad-o-ra'-im)* {1} *A city built by Rehoboam.*
And A, and Lachish, and Azekah, ... 2Chr 11:9 115

ADORAM *(ad-o'-ram)* {2} See ADONIRAM.
1. A tribute officer under David.
And A was over the tribute ... 2Sa 20:24 151
2. A tribute officer under Solomon.
Then king Rehoboam sent A ... 1Kin 12:18 151

ADORN {2}
that women a themselves in modest ... 1Ti 2:9 *2885*
that they may a the doctrine of ... Titus 2:10 *2885*

ADORNED {4}
shalt again be a with thy tabrets ... Jer 31:4 5710
how it was a with goodly stones ... Lk 21:5 *2885*
a themselves, being in subjection ... 1Pet 3:5 *2885*
as a bride a for her husband ... Rev 21:2 *2885*

ADORNETH {1}
as a bride a herself with her ... Is 61:10 5710

ADORNING {2}
Whose a let it not be that ... 1Pet 3:3 *2889*
outward a of plaiting the hair ... 1Pet 3:3 *2889*

ADRAMMELECH *(a-dram'-mel-ek)* {3}
1. A god of the Avites.
burnt their children in fire to A ... 2Kin 17:31 152
2. A son of Sennacherib.
house of Nisroch his god, that A ... 2Kin 19:37 152
house of Nisroch his god, that A ... Is 37:38 152

ADRAMYTTIAN See ADRAMYTTIUM.

ADRAMYTTIUM *(a-dram-mit'-te-um)* {1} *A seaport of Mysia in Asia Minor.*
And entering into a ship of A ... Acts 27:2 *98*

ADRIA *(a'-dre-ah)* {1} *The Adriatic Sea.*
as we were driven up and down in A ... Acts 27:27 *99*

ADRIATIC See ADRIA.

ADRIEL *(a'-dre-el)* {2} *Husband of Merab, Saul's daughter.*
unto A the Meholathite to wife ... 1Sa 18:19 5741
whom she brought up for A the son ... 2Sa 21:8 5741

ADULLAM *(a-dul'-lam)* {8} See ADULLAMITE.
1. A city south of Jerusalem.
the king of A, one ... Josh 12:15 5725
Jarmuth, and A, and Socoh, and Azekah, ... Josh 15:35 5725
And Beth-zur, and Shoco, and A ... 2Chr 11:7 5725
Zanoah, A, and in their villages, ... Neh 11:30 5725
he shall come unto A the glory of ... Mic 1:15 5725
2. A large cave near the city of Adullam.
thence, and escaped to the cave A ... 1Sa 22:1 5725
harvest time unto the cave of A ... 2Sa 23:13 5725
rock to David, into the cave of A ... 1Chr 11:15 5725

ADULLAMITE *(a-dul'-lam-ite)* {3} *A native of Adullam.*
and turned in to a certain A ... Gen 38:1 5726
he and his friend Hirah the A ... Gen 38:12 5726
by the hand of his friend the A ... Gen 38:20 5726

ADULTERER {3}
with his neighbour's wife, the a ... Lev 20:10 5003
The eye also of the a waiteth for ... Job 24:15 5003
the sorceress, the seed of the a ... Is 57:3 5003

ADULTERERS {9}
him, and hast been partaker with a ... Ps 50:18 5003
for they be all a, an assembly of ... Jer 9:2 5003
For the land is full of a ... Jer 23:10 5003
They are all a, as an oven heated ... Hos 7:4 5003
the sorcerers, and against the a ... Mal 3:5 5003
men are, extortioners, unjust, a ... Lk 18:11 *3432*
fornicators, nor idolaters, nor a ... 1Cor 6:9 *3432*
whoremongers and a God will judge ... Heb 13:4 *3432*
Ye a and adulteresses, know ye not ... Jas 4:4 *3432*

ADULTERESS {5}
the *a* shall surely be put to ...... Lev 20:10 5003
the *a* will hunt for the precious ...... Prov 6:26 802,376
beloved of her friend, yet an *a* ...... Hos 3:1 5003
man, she shall be called an *a* ...... Rom 7:3 *3428*
so that she is no *a*, though she ...... Rom 7:3 *3428*

ADULTERESSES {3}
judge them after the manner of *a* ...... Eze 23:45 5003
because they are *a*, and blood is ...... Eze 23:45 5003
Ye adulterers and *a*, know ye not ...... Jas 4:4 *3428*

ADULTERIES {5}
I have seen thine *a*, and thy ...... Jer 13:27 5004
said I unto her that was old in *a* ...... Eze 23:43 5004
her *a* from between her breasts ...... Hos 2:2 5005
proceed evil thoughts, murders, *a* ...... Mt 15:19 *3430*
of men, proceed evil thoughts, *a* ...... Mk 7:21 *3430*

ADULTEROUS {4}
Such is the way of an *a* woman ...... Prov 30:20 5003
a generation seeketh after a sign ...... Mt 12:39 *3428*
a generation seeketh after a sign ...... Mt 16:4 *3428*
of me and of my words in this *a* ...... Mk 8:38 *3428*

ADULTERY {40}
Thou shalt not commit *a* ...... Ex 20:14 5003
a with another man's wife ...... Lev 20:10 5003
even he that committeth *a* with ...... Lev 20:10 5003
Neither shalt thou commit *a* ...... Deut 5:18 5003
committeth *a* with a woman lacketh ...... Prov 6:32 5003
committed *a* I had put her away ...... Jer 3:8 5003
committed *a* with stones and with ...... Jer 3:9 5003
the full, they then committed *a* ...... Jer 5:7 5003
ye steal, murder, and commit *a* ...... Jer 7:9 5003
they commit *a*, and walk in lies ...... Jer 23:14 5003
have committed *a* with their ...... Jer 29:23 5003
But as a wife that committeth *a* ...... Eze 16:32 5003
That they have committed *a* ...... Eze 23:37 5003
their idols have they committed *a* ...... Eze 23:37 5003
and stealing, and committing *a* ...... Hos 4:2 5003
and your spouses shall commit *a* ...... Hos 4:13 5003
your spouses when they commit *a* ...... Hos 4:14 5003
old time, Thou shalt not commit *a* ...... Mt 5:27 *3431*
a with her already in his heart ...... Mt 5:28 *3431*
causeth her to commit *a* ...... Mt 5:32 *3429*
her that is divorced committeth *a* ...... Mt 5:32 *3429*
shall marry another, committeth *a* ...... Mt 19:9 *3429*
which is put away doth commit *a* ...... Mt 19:9 *3429*
murder, Thou shalt not commit *a* ...... Mt 19:18 *3431*
another, committeth *a* against her ...... Mk 10:11 *3429*
to another, she committeth *a* ...... Mk 10:12 *3429*
the commandments, Do not commit *a* ...... Mk 10:19 *3431*
and marrieth another, committeth *a* ...... Lk 16:18 *3431*
from her husband committeth *a* ...... Lk 16:18 *3431*
the commandments, Do not commit *a* ...... Lk 18:20 *3431*
unto him a woman taken in *a* ...... Jn 8:3 *3430*
Master, this woman was taken in *a* ...... Jn 8:4 *3431*
sayest a man should not commit *a* ...... Rom 2:22 *3431*
dost thou commit *a*? ...... Rom 2:22 *3431*
For this, Thou shalt not commit *a* ...... Rom 13:9 *3431*
A, fornication, uncleanness, ... Gal 5:19 *3430*
For he that said, Do not commit *a* ...... Jas 2:11 *3431*
Now if thou commit no *a*, yet if ...... Jas 2:11 *3431*
Having eyes full of *a*, and that 2Pet 2:14 *3428*
them that commit *a* with her into ...... Rev 2:22 *3431*

ADUMMIM *(a-dum'-mim)* {2}
that is before the going up to *A* ...... Josh 15:7 131
is over against the going up of *A* ...... Josh 18:17 131

ADVANCED {4}
It is the LORD that *a* Moses 1Sa 12:6 6213
a him, and set his seat above all ...... Est 3:1 5375
how he had *a* him above the ...... Est 5:11 5375
whereunto the king *a* him ...... Est 10:2 1431

ADVANTAGE {4}
What *a* will it be unto thee ...... Job 35:3 5532
What *a* then hath the Jew ...... Rom 3:1 *4053*
Lest Satan should get an *a* of us 2Cor 2:11 *4122*
in admiration because of *a* ...... Jude 16 *5622*

ADVANTAGED {1}
For what is a man *a*, if he gain ...... Lk 9:25 *5623*

ADVANTAGETH {1}
what *a* it me, if the dead rise 1Cor 15:32 *3786*

ADVENTURE {2}
which would not *a* to set the sole ...... Deut 28:56 5254
not *a* himself into the theatre ...... Acts 19:31 *1325*

ADVENTURED {1}
a his life far, and delivered you ...... Judg 9:17 7993

ADVERSARIES {36}
and an adversary unto thine *a* ...... Ex 23:22 6696
lest their *a* should behave ...... Deut 32:27 6862
and will render vengeance to his *a* ...... Deut 32:43 6862
Art thou for us, or for our *a* ...... Josh 5:13 6862
The *a* of the LORD shall be broken 1Sa 2:10 7378
ye should this day be *a* unto me 2Sa 19:22 7854
Now when the *a* of Judah and ...... Ezr 4:1 6862
our *a* said, They shall not know, ... Neh 4:11 6862
render evil for good are mine *a* ...... Ps 38:20 7853
mine *a* are all before thee ...... Ps 69:19 6887
and consumed that are *a* to my soul ...... Ps 71:13 7853
and turned my hand against their *a* ...... Ps 81:14 6862
set up the right hand of his *a* ...... Ps 89:42 6862
For my love they are my *a* ...... Ps 109:4 7853
reward of mine *a* from the LORD ...... Ps 109:20 7853
Let mine *a* be clothed with shame, ... Ps 109:29 7853
Ah, I will ease me of mine *a* ...... Is 1:24 6862
set up the *a* of Rezin against him ...... Is 9:11 6862
the *a* of Judah shall be cut off ...... Is 11:13 6887
he will repay, fury to his *a* ...... Is 59:18 6862
our *a* have trodden down thy ...... Is 63:18 6862
to make thy name known to thine *a* ...... Is 64:2 6862
and all thine *a*, every one of them ...... Jer 30:16 6862
that he may avenge him of his *a* ...... Jer 46:10 6862
and their *a* said, We offend not, ... Jer 50:7 6862
Her *a* are the chief, her enemies ...... Lam 1:5 6862
the *a* saw her, and did mock at her ...... Lam 1:7 6862
that his *a* should be round about ...... Lam 1:17 6862
hath set up the horn of thine *a* ...... Lam 2:17 6862
shall be lifted up upon thine *a* ...... Mic 5:9 6862
LORD will take vengeance on his *a* ...... Nah 1:2 6862
things, all his *a* were ashamed ...... Lk 13:17 *480*
which all your *a* shall not be ...... Lk 21:15 *480*
unto me, and there are many *a* 1Cor 16:9 *480*
And in nothing terrified by your *a* ...... Phil 1:28 *480*
which shall devour the *a* ...... Heb 10:27 *5227*

ADVERSARY {22}
an *a* unto thine adversaries ...... Ex 23:22 6887
in the way for an *a* against him ...... Num 22:22 7854
her *a* also provoked her sore, for 1Sa 1:6 6869
in the battle he be an *a* to us 1Sa 29:4 7854
is neither *a* nor evil occurrent 1Kin 5:4 7854
LORD stirred up an *a* unto Solomon 1Kin 11:14 7854
And God stirred him up another *a* 1Kin 11:23 7854
he was an *a* to Israel all the 1Kin 11:25 7854
And Esther said, The *a* and enemy is ...... Est 7:6 6862
that mine *a* had written a book ...... Job 31:35 376,7379
how long shall the *a* reproach ...... Ps 74:10 6862
who is mine *a*? ...... Is 50:8 1166,4941
The *a* hath spread out his hand ...... Lam 1:10 6862
stood with his right hand as an *a* ...... Lam 2:4 6862
not have believed that the *a* ...... Lam 4:12 6862
An *a* there shall be even round ...... Amos 3:11 6862
Agree with thine *a* quickly ...... Mt 5:25 *476*
lest at any time the *a* deliver ...... Mt 5:25 *476*
with thine *a* to the magistrate ...... Lk 12:58 *476*
him, saying, Avenge me of mine *a* ...... Lk 18:3 *476*
to the *a* to speak reproachfully 1Ti 5:14 *480*
because your *a* the devil, as a 1Pet 5:8 *476*

ADVERSITIES {2}
saved you out of all your *a* 1Sa 10:19 7451
thou hast known my soul in *a* ...... Ps 31:7 6869

ADVERSITY {10}
redeemed my soul out of all *a* 2Sa 4:9 6869
for God did vex them with all *a* 2Chr 15:6 6869
for I shall never be in *a* ...... Ps 10:6 7451
But in mine *a* they rejoiced, and ...... Ps 35:15 6761
give him rest from the days of *a* ...... Ps 94:13 7451
times, and a brother is born for *a* ...... Prov 17:17 6869
If thou faint in the day of *a* ...... Prov 24:10 6869
but in the day of *a* consider ...... Eccl 7:14 7451
the Lord give you the bread of *a* ...... Is 30:20 6862
and them which suffer *a*, as being ...... Heb 13:3 *2558*

ADVERTISE {2}
I will *a* thee what this people ...... Num 24:14 3289
And I thought to *a* thee, saying, ... Ruth 4:4 1540,241

ADVICE {9}
consider of it, take *a*, and speak ...... Judg 19:30 5779
give here your *a* and counsel ...... Judg 20:7 1697
And blessed be thy *a*, and blessed 1Sa 25:33 2940
that our *a* should not be first 2Sa 19:43 1697
What *a* give ye that we may return 2Chr 10:9 3289
them after the *a* of the young men 2Chr 10:14 6098
Then Amaziah king of Judah took *a* 2Chr 25:17 3289
and with good *a* make war ...... Prov 20:18 8458
And herein I give my *a* 2Cor 8:10 *1106*

ADVISE {3}
now *a*, and see what answer I shall 2Sa 24:13 3045
How do ye *a* that I may answer 1Kin 12:6 3289
Now therefore *a* thyself what word 1Chr 21:12 7200

ADVISED {2}
but with the well *a* is wisdom ...... Prov 13:10 3289
the more part *a* to depart thence ...... Acts 27:12 *1012,5087*

ADVISEMENT {1}
Philistines upon *a* sent him away 1Chr 12:19 6098

ADVOCATE {1}
we have an *a* with the Father, ... 1Jn 2:1 *3875*

AENEAS *(e'-ne-as)* {2} *A paralytic healed by Peter.*
he found a certain man named *A* ...... Acts 9:33 *132*
And Peter said unto him, *A* ...... Acts 9:34 *132*

AENON *(e'-non)* {1} *A place in the valley of Shechem.*
was baptizing in *A* near to Salim ...... Jn 3:23 *137*

AFAR See APPENDIX.

AFFAIRS {8}
to God, and *a* of the king 1Chr 26:32 1697
will guide his *a* with discretion ...... Ps 112:5 1697
over the *a* of the province of ...... Dan 2:49 5673
the *a* of the province of Babylon ...... Dan 3:12 5673
But that ye also may know my *a* ...... Eph 6:21 *2596*
purpose, that ye might know our *a* ...... Eph 6:22 *4012*
be absent, I may hear of your *a* ...... Phil 1:27 *4012*
himself with the *a* of this life 2Ti 2:4 *4230*

AFFECT {2}
They zealously *a* you, but not ...... Gal 4:17 *2206*
exclude you, that ye might *a* them ...... Gal 4:17 *2206*

AFFECTED {2}
minds evil *a* against the brethren ...... Acts 14:2 *2559*
a always in a good thing, and not ...... Gal 4:18 *2206*

AFFECTETH {1}
Mine eye *a* mine heart because of ...... Lam 3:51 5953

AFFECTION {6}
because I have set my *a* to the 1Chr 29:3 7521
without natural *a*, implacable, ... Rom 1:31 *794*
his inward *a* is more abundant 2Cor 7:15 *4698*
Set your *a* on things above, not ...... Col 3:2 *5426*
uncleanness, inordinate *a* ...... Col 3:5 *3806*
Without natural *a*, trucebreakers, ... 2Ti 3:3 *794*

AFFECTIONATELY {1}
So being *a* desirous of you, we 1Th 2:8 *2442*

AFFECTIONED {1}
Be kindly *a* one to another with ...... Rom 12:10 *5387*

AFFECTIONS {2}
God gave them up unto vile *a* ...... Rom 1:26 *3806*
crucified the flesh with the *a* ...... Gal 5:24 *3804*

AFFINITY {3}
Solomon made *a* with Pharaoh king 1Kin 3:1 2859
abundance, and joined *a* with Ahab 2Chr 18:1 2859
join in *a* with the people of ...... Ezr 9:14 2859

AFFIRM {3}
as some *a* that we say,) Let us do ...... Rom 3:8 *5346*
what they say, nor whereof they *a* 1Ti 1:7 *1226*
I will that thou *a* constantly ...... Titus 3:8 *1226*

AFFIRMED {3}
hour after another confidently *a* ...... Lk 22:59 *1340*
But she constantly *a* that it was ...... Acts 12:15 *1340*
was dead, whom Paul *a* to be alive ...... Acts 25:19 *5335*

AFFLICT {36}
they shall *a* them four hundred ...... Gen 15:13 6031
If thou shalt *a* my daughters ...... Gen 31:50 6031
to *a* them with their burdens ...... Ex 1:11 6031
Ye shall not *a* any widow, or ...... Ex 22:22 6031
If thou *a* them in any wise, and ...... Ex 22:23 6031
ye shall *a* your souls, and do no ...... Lev 16:29 6031
ye shall *a* your souls, by a ...... Lev 16:31 6031
ye shall *a* your souls, and offer ...... Lev 23:27 6031
of rest, and ye shall *a* your souls ...... Lev 23:32 6031
a Asshur, and shall *a* Eber ...... Num 24:24 6031
and ye shall *a* your souls ...... Num 29:7 6031
every binding oath to *a* the soul ...... Num 30:13 6031
that we may bind him to *a* him ...... Judg 16:5 6031
thou mightest be bound to *a* thee ...... Judg 16:6 6031
and she began to *a* him, and his ...... Judg 16:19 6031
of wickedness *a* them any more 2Sa 7:10 6031
I will for this *a* the seed of 1Kin 11:39 6031
their sin, when thou dost *a* them 2Chr 6:26 6031
that we might *a* ourselves before ...... Ezr 8:21 6031
he will not *a* ...... Job 37:23 6031
how thou didst *a* the people ...... Ps 44:2 7489
a them, even he that abideth of ...... Ps 55:19 6031
nor the son of wickedness *a* him ...... Ps 89:22 6031
O LORD, and *a* thine heritage ...... Ps 94:5 6031
destroy all them that *a* my soul ...... Ps 143:12 6887
a her by the way of the sea ...... Is 9:1 3513
into the hand of them that *a* thee ...... Is 51:23 3013
a day for a man to *a* his soul ...... Is 58:5 6031
hold thy peace, and *a* us very sore ...... Is 64:12 6031
down, and to destroy, and to *a* ...... Jer 31:28 7489
For he doth not *a* willingly nor ...... Lam 3:33 6031
they *a* the just, they take a ...... Amos 5:12 6887
they shall *a* you from the ...... Amos 6:14 3905
thee, I will *a* thee no more ...... Nah 1:12 6031
time I will undo all that *a* thee ...... Zeph 3:19 6031

AFFLICTED {55}
But the more they *a* them, the ...... Ex 1:12 6031
shall not be *a* in that same day ...... Lev 23:29 6031
Wherefore hast thou *a* thy servant ...... Num 11:11 7489
a us, and laid upon us hard ...... Deut 26:6 6031
me, and the Almighty hath *a* me ...... Ruth 1:21 7489
the *a* people thou wilt save 2Sa 22:28 6041
because thou hast been *a* in all 1Kin 2:26 6031
in all wherein my father was *a* 1Kin 2:26 6031
a them, and delivered them into 2Kin 17:20 6031
To him that is *a* pity should be ...... Job 6:14 4523
a me, they have also let loose ...... Job 30:11 6031
and he heareth the cry of the *a* ...... Job 34:28 6041
For thou wilt save the *a* people ...... Ps 18:27 6041
abhorred the affliction of the *a* ...... Ps 22:24 6041
for I am desolate and *a* ...... Ps 25:16 6041
do justice to the *a* and needy ...... Ps 82:3 6041
thou hast *a* me with all thy waves ...... Ps 88:7 6031
I am *a* and ready to die from my ...... Ps 88:15 6041
the days wherein thou hast *a* us ...... Ps 90:15 6031
A Prayer of the *a*, when he is ...... Ps 102:*t* 6041
of their iniquities, are *a* ...... Ps 107:17 6031
I was greatly *a* ...... Ps 116:10 6031
Before I was *a* I went astray ...... Ps 119:67 6031
is good for me that I have been *a* ...... Ps 119:71 6031
thou in faithfulness hast *a* me ...... Ps 119:75 6031
I am *a* very much ...... Ps 119:107 6031
time have they *a* me from my youth ...... Ps 129:1 6887
time have they *a* me from my youth ...... Ps 129:2 6887
will maintain the cause of the *a* ...... Ps 140:12 6041
All the days of the *a* are evil ...... Prov 15:15 6041
neither oppress the *a* in the gate ...... Prov 22:22 6041
hateth those that are *a* by it ...... Prov 26:28 1790
the judgment of any of the *a* ...... Prov 31:5 6040
he lightly *a* the land of Zebulun ...... Is 9:1 7043
and will have mercy upon his *a* ...... Is 49:13 6041
Therefore hear now this, thou *a* ...... Is 51:21 6041
stricken, smitten of God, and *a* ...... Is 53:4 6031
He was oppressed, and he was *a* ...... Is 53:7 6031
O thou *a*, tossed with tempest, and ...... Is 54:11 6041
wherefore have we *a* our soul ...... Is 58:3 6031
the hungry, and satisfy the *a* soul ...... Is 58:10 6031
The sons also of them that *a* thee ...... Is 60:14 6031

In all their affliction he was *a*........ Is 63:9 6862
priests sigh, her virgins are *a*........ Lam 1:4 3013
for the LORD hath *a* her for the........ Lam 1:5 3013
wherewith the LORD hath *a* me in........ Lam 1:12 3013
driven out, and her that I have *a*........ Mic 4:6 7489
Though I have *a* thee, I will........ Nah 1:12 6031
leave in the midst of thee an *a*........ Zeph 3:12 6041
shall they deliver you up to be *a*........ Mt 24:9 *2347*
And whether we be *a*, it is for........ 2Cor 1:6 *2346*
feet, if she have relieved the *a*........ 1Ti 5:10 *2346*
being destitute, *a*, tormented........ Heb 11:37 *2346*
Be *a*, and mourn, and weep........ Jas 4:9 *5003*
Is any among you *a*........ Jas 5:13 *2553*

AFFLICTEST {1}
from their sin, when thou *a* them........ 1Kin 8:35 6031

AFFLICTION {75}
because the LORD hath heard thy *a*........ Gen 16:11 6040
the LORD hath looked upon my *a*........ Gen 29:32 6040
God hath seen mine *a* and the........ Gen 31:42 6040
be fruitful in the land of my *a*........ Gen 41:52 6040
I have surely seen the *a* of my........ Ex 3:7 6040
a of Egypt unto the land of the........ Ex 3:17 6040
that he had looked upon their *a*........ Ex 4:31 6040
therewith, even the bread of *a*........ Deut 16:3 6040
our voice, and looked on our *a*........ Deut 26:7 6040
look on the *a* of thine handmaid........ 1Sa 1:11 6040
that the LORD will look on mine *a*........ 2Sa 16:12 6040
bread of *a* and with water of *a*........ 1Kin 22:27 3905
For the LORD saw the *a* of Israel........ 2Kin 14:26 6040
bread of *a* and with water of *a*........ 2Chr 18:26 3905
house,) and cry unto thee in our *a*........ 2Chr 20:9 6869
And when he was in *a*, he besought........ 2Chr 33:12 6887
in the province are in great *a*........ Neh 1:3 7451
didst see the *a* of our fathers in........ Neh 9:9 6040
Although *a* cometh not forth of........ Job 5:6 205
therefore see thou mine *a*........ Job 10:15 6040
the days of *a* have taken hold........ Job 30:16 6040
the days of *a* prevented me........ Job 30:27 6040
and be holden in cords of *a*........ Job 36:8 6040
He delivereth the poor in his *a*........ Job 36:15 6040
hast thou chosen rather than *a*........ Job 36:21 6040
abhorred the *a* of the afflicted........ Ps 22:24 6039
Look upon mine *a* and my pain........ Ps 25:18 6040
thy face, and forgettest our *a*........ Ps 44:24 6040
thou laidst *a* upon our loins........ Ps 66:11 4157
Mine eye mourneth by reason of *a*........ Ps 88:9 6040
Nevertheless he regarded their *a*........ Ps 106:44 6862
shadow of death, being bound in *a*........ Ps 107:10 6040
brought low through oppression, *a*........ Ps 107:39 7451
he the poor on high from *a*........ Ps 107:41 6040
This is my comfort in my *a*........ Ps 119:50 6040
then have perished in mine *a*........ Ps 119:92 6040
Consider mine *a*, and deliver me........ Ps 119:153 6040
of adversity, and the water of *a*........ Is 30:20 3905
chosen thee in the furnace of *a*........ Is 48:10 6040
In all their *a* he was afflicted,........ Is 63:9 6869
publisheth *a* from mount Ephraim........ Jer 4:15 205
time of evil and in the time of *a*........ Jer 15:11 6869
and my refuge in the day of *a*........ Jer 16:19 6869
Why criest thou for thine *a*........ Jer 30:15 7667
to come, and his *a* hasteth fast........ Jer 48:16 7451
gone into captivity because of *a*........ Lam 1:3 6040
remembered in the days of her *a*........ Lam 1:7 6040
O LORD, behold my *a*........ Lam 1:9 6040
seen *a* by the rod of his wrath........ Lam 3:1 6040
Remembering mine *a* and my misery,........ Lam 3:19 6040
in their *a* they will seek me........ Hos 5:15 6862
not grieved for the *a* of Joseph........ Amos 6:6 7667
not have looked on their *a* in the........ Obad 13 7451
by reason of mine *a* unto the LORD........ Jonah 2:2 6869
a shall not rise up the second........ Nah 1:9 6869
I saw the tents of Cushan in *a*........ Hab 3:7 205
and they helped forward the *a*........ Zec 1:15 7451
out or came in because of the *a*........ Zec 8:10 6862
shall pass through the sea with *a*........ Zec 10:11 6869
when *a* or persecution ariseth for........ Mk 4:17 *2347*
For in those days shall be *a*........ Mk 13:19 *2347*
of Egypt and Chanaan, and great *a*........ Acts 7:11 *2347*
I have seen the *a* of my people........ Acts 7:34 *2561*
For out of much *a* and anguish of........ 2Cor 2:4 *2347*
For our light *a*, which is but for........ 2Cor 4:17 *2347*
of *a* the abundance of their joy........ 2Cor 8:2 *2347*
supposing to add *a* to my bonds........ Phil 1:16 *2347*
that ye did communicate with my *a*........ Phil 4:14 *2347*
received the word in much *a*........ 1Th 1:6 *2347*
comforted over you in all our *a*........ 1Th 3:7 *2347*
suffer *a* with the people of God........ Heb 11:25 *4797*
fatherless and widows in their *a*........ Jas 1:27 *2347*
for an example of suffering *a*........ Jas 5:10 *2552*

AFFLICTIONS {13}
Many are the *a* of the righteous........ Ps 34:19 7451
remember David, and all his *a*........ Ps 132:1 6031
And delivered him out of all his *a*........ Acts 7:10 *2347*
saying that bonds and *a* abide me........ Acts 20:23 *2347*
of God, in much patience, in *a*........ 2Cor 6:4 *2347*
a of Christ in my flesh for his........ Col 1:24 *2347*
no man should be moved by these *a*........ 1Th 3:3 *2347*
but be thou partaker of the *a* of........ 2Ti 1:8 *4777*
Persecutions, *a*, which came unto........ 2Ti 3:11 *3804*
thou in all things, endure *a*........ 2Ti 4:5 *2553*
ye endured a great fight of *a*........ Heb 10:32 *3804*
both by reproaches and *a*........ Heb 10:33 *2347*
knowing that the same *a* are........ 1Pet 5:9 *3804*

AFFORDING {1}
be full, *a* all manner of store........ Ps 144:13 6329

AFFRIGHT {1}
to *a* them, and to trouble them........ 2Chr 32:18 3372

AFFRIGHTED {9}
Thou shalt not be *a* at them........ Deut 7:21 6206
as they that went before were *a*........ Job 18:20 270,8178
He mocketh at fear, and is not *a*........ Job 39:22 2865
My heart panted, fearfulness *a* me........ Is 21:4 1204
fire, and the men of war are *a*........ Jer 51:32 926
and they were *a*........ Mk 16:5 *1568*
And he saith unto them, Be not *a*........ Mk 16:6 *1568*
But they were terrified and *a*........ Lk 24:37 *1719*
and the remnant were *a*, and gave........ Rev 11:13 *1719*

AFOOT {2}
ran *a* thither out of all cities,........ Mk 6:33 *3979*
minding himself to go *a*........ Acts 20:13 *3978*

AFORE {7}
a Isaiah was gone out into the........ 2Kin 20:4 3808
which withereth *a* it groweth up........ Ps 129:6 6924
For *a* the harvest, when the bud........ Is 18:5 6440
a he that was escaped came........ Eze 33:22 6440
(Which he had promised *a* by his........ Rom 1:2 *4279*
which he had *a* prepared unto........ Rom 9:23 *4282*
(as I wrote *a* in few words,........ Eph 3:3 *4270*

AFOREHAND {1}
she is come *a* to anoint my body........ Mk 14:8 *4301*

AFORETIME {7}
where *a* they laid the meat........ Neh 13:5 6440
and *a* I was as a tabret........ Job 17:6 6440
My people went down *a* into Egypt........ Is 52:4 7223
Their children also shall be as *a*........ Jer 30:20 6924
before his God, as he did *a*........ Dan 6:10 4481,6928,1836
Pharisees him that *a* was blind........ Jn 9:13 *4218*
a were written for our learning........ Rom 15:4 *4270*

AFRAID {193}
voice in the garden, and I was *a*........ Gen 3:10 3372
for she was *a*........ Gen 18:15 3372
and the men were sore *a*........ Gen 20:8 3372
And he was *a*, and said, How........ Gen 28:17 3372
and said to Laban, Because I was *a*........ Gen 31:31 3372
Then Jacob was greatly *a* and........ Gen 32:7 3372
heart failed them, and they were *a*........ Gen 42:28 2729
the bundles of money, they were *a*........ Gen 42:35 3372
And the men were *a*, because they........ Gen 43:18 3372
for he was *a* to look upon God........ Ex 3:6 3372
and they were sore *a*........ Ex 14:10 3372
The people shall hear, and be *a*........ Ex 15:14 7264
they were *a* to come nigh him........ Ex 34:30 3372
down, and none shall make you *a*........ Lev 26:6 2729
wherefore then were ye not *a* to........ Num 12:8 3372
And Moab was sore *a* of the people........ Num 22:3 1481
ye shall not be *a* of the face of........ Deut 1:17 1481
Dread not, neither be *a* of them........ Deut 1:29 3372
and they shall be *a* of you........ Deut 2:4 3372
for ye were *a* by reason of the........ Deut 5:5 3372
Thou shalt not be *a* of them........ Deut 7:18 3372
all the people of whom thou art *a*........ Deut 7:19 3373
For I was *a* of the anger and hot........ Deut 9:19 3025
thou shalt not be *a* of him........ Deut 18:22 1481
more than thou, be not *a* of them........ Deut 20:1 3372
and they shall be *a* of thee........ Deut 28:10 3372
of Egypt, which thou wast *a* of........ Deut 28:60 3025
fear not, nor be *a* of them........ Deut 31:6 6206
be not *a*, neither be thou........ Josh 1:9 6206
therefore we were sore *a* of our........ Josh 9:24 3372
Joshua, Be not *a* because of them........ Josh 11:6 3372
saying, Whosoever is fearful and *a*........ Judg 7:3 2730
at midnight, that the man was *a*........ Ruth 3:8 2729
And the Philistines were *a*........ 1Sa 4:7 3372
they were *a* of the Philistines........ 1Sa 7:7 3372
they were dismayed, and greatly *a*........ 1Sa 17:11 3372
fled from him, and were sore *a*........ 1Sa 17:24 3372
And Saul was *a* of David, because........ 1Sa 18:12 3372
very wisely, he was *a* of him........ 1Sa 18:15 1481
Saul was yet the more *a* of David........ 1Sa 18:29 3372
Ahimelech was *a* at the meeting of........ 1Sa 21:1 2729
was sore *a* of Achish the king of........ 1Sa 21:12 3372
Behold, we be *a* here in Judah........ 1Sa 23:3 3373
host of the Philistines, he was *a*........ 1Sa 28:5 3372
the king said unto her, Be not *a*........ 1Sa 28:13 3372
along on the earth, and was sore *a*........ 1Sa 28:20 3372
for he was sore *a*........ 1Sa 31:4 3372
How wast thou not *a* to stretch........ 2Sa 1:14 3372
David was *a* of the LORD that day,........ 2Sa 6:9 3372
because the people have made me *a*........ 2Sa 14:15 3372
weak handed, and will make him *a*........ 2Sa 17:2 2729
floods of ungodly men made me *a*........ 2Sa 22:5 1204
they shall be *a* out of their........ 2Sa 22:46 2296
that were with Adonijah were *a*........ 1Kin 1:49 2729
be not *a* of him........ 2Kin 1:15 3372
But they were exceedingly *a*........ 2Kin 10:4 3372
Be not *a* of the words which thou........ 2Kin 19:6 3372
for they were *a* of the Chaldees........ 2Kin 25:26 3372
for he was sore *a*........ 1Chr 10:4 3372
David was *a* of God that day,........ 1Chr 13:12 3372
for he was *a* because of the sword........ 1Chr 21:30 1204
Be not *a* nor dismayed by reason........ 2Chr 20:15 3372
be not *a* nor dismayed for the........ 2Chr 32:7 3372
Then I was very sore *a*,........ Neh 2:2 3372
the people, Be not ye *a* of them........ Neh 4:14 3372
For they all made us *a*, saying,........ Neh 6:9 3372
was he hired, that I should be *a*........ Neh 6:13 3372
Then Haman was *a* before the king........ Est 7:6 1204
that which I was *a* of is come........ Job 3:25 3025
neither shalt thou be *a* of........ Job 5:21 3372
neither shalt thou be *a* of the........ Job 5:22 3372
ye see my casting down, and are *a*........ Job 6:21 3372
I am *a* of all my sorrows, I know........ Job 9:28 3025
down, and none shall make thee *a*........ Job 11:19 2729
not his excellency make you *a*........ Job 13:11 1204
and let not thy dread make me *a*........ Job 13:21 1204
and anguish shall make him *a*........ Job 15:24 1204
shall make him *a* on every side........ Job 18:11 1204
Be ye *a* of the sword........ Job 19:29 1481
Even when I remember I am *a*........ Job 21:6 926
when I consider, I am *a* of him........ Job 23:15 6342
wherefore I was *a*, and durst not........ Job 32:6 2119
my terror shall not make thee *a*........ Job 33:7 1204
thou make him *a* as a grasshopper........ Job 39:20 7493
up himself, the mighty are *a*........ Job 41:25 1481
I will not be *a* of ten thousands........ Ps 3:6 3372
floods of ungodly men made me *a*........ Ps 18:4 1204
be *a* out of their close places........ Ps 18:45 2727
of whom shall I be *a*........ Ps 27:1 6342
Be not thou *a* when one is made........ Ps 49:16 3372
What time I am *a*, I will trust in........ Ps 56:3 3372
I will not be *a* what man can do........ Ps 56:11 3372
parts are *a* at thy tokens........ Ps 65:8 3372
they were *a*........ Ps 77:16 2342
make them *a* with thy storm........ Ps 83:15 926
Thou shalt not be *a* for the........ Ps 91:5 3372
He shall not be *a* of evil tidings........ Ps 112:7 3372
is established, he shall not be *a*........ Ps 112:8 3372
and I am *a* of thy judgments........ Ps 119:120 3372
liest down, thou shalt not be *a*........ Prov 3:24 6342
Be not *a* of sudden fear, neither........ Prov 3:25 3372
She is not *a* of the snow for her........ Prov 31:21 3372
shall be *a* of that which is high........ Eccl 12:5 3372
fear ye their fear, nor be *a*........ Is 8:12 6206
in Zion, be not *a* of the Assyrian........ Is 10:24 3372
Ramah is *a*........ Is 10:29 2729
I will trust, and not be *a*........ Is 12:2 6342
And they shall be *a*........ Is 13:8 926
down, and none shall make them *a*........ Is 17:2 2729
and it shall be *a* and fear because........ Is 19:16 2729
thereof shall be *a* in himself........ Is 19:17 6342
And they shall be *a* and ashamed of........ Is 20:5 2865
he will not be *a* of their voice........ Is 31:4 2865
princes shall be *a* of the ensign........ Is 31:9 2865
The sinners in Zion are *a*........ Is 33:14 6342
Be not *a* of the words that thou........ Is 37:6 3372
lift it up, be not *a*........ Is 40:9 3372
the ends of the earth were *a*........ Is 41:5 2729
Fear ye not, neither be *a*........ Is 44:8 7297
of men, neither be ye *a* of their........ Is 51:7 2865
that thou shouldest be *a* of a man........ Is 51:12 3372
whom hast thou been *a* or feared........ Is 57:11 1672
Be not *a* of their faces........ Jer 1:8 3372
at this, and be horribly *a*........ Jer 2:12 8175
Be not *a* of them........ Jer 10:5 3372
when Urijah heard it, he was *a*........ Jer 26:21 3372
quiet, and none shall make him *a*........ Jer 30:10 2729
the words, they were *a* both one........ Jer 36:16 6342
Yet they were not *a*, nor rent........ Jer 36:24 6342
I am *a* of the Jews that are........ Jer 38:19 1672
of the men of whom thou art *a*........ Jer 39:17 3025
for they were *a* of them, because........ Jer 41:18 3372
Be not *a* of the king of Babylon,........ Jer 42:11 3372
of whom ye are *a*........ Jer 42:11 3373
be not *a* of him, saith the LORD........ Jer 42:11 3372
and the famine, whereof ye were *a*........ Jer 42:16 1672
at ease, and none shall make him *a*........ Jer 46:27 2729
be not *a* of them........ Eze 2:6 3372
neither be *a* of their words,........ Eze 2:6 3372
be not *a* of their words, nor be........ Eze 2:6 3372
and their kings shall be sore *a*........ Eze 27:35 8175
to make the careless Ethiopians *a*........ Eze 30:9 2729
shall be horribly *a* for thee........ Eze 32:10 8175
safely, and none shall make them *a*........ Eze 34:28 2729
their land, and none made them *a*........ Eze 39:26 2729
I saw a dream which made me *a*........ Dan 4:5 1763
and when he came, I was *a*, and fell........ Dan 8:17 1204
Be not *a*, ye beasts of the field........ Joel 2:22 3372
the city, and the people not be *a*........ Amos 3:6 2729
Then the mariners were *a*, and........ Jonah 1:5 3372
Then were the men exceedingly *a*........ Jonah 1:10 3372
and none shall make them *a*........ Mic 4:4 2729
they shall be *a* of the LORD our........ Mic 7:17 6342
lion's whelp, and none made them *a*........ Nah 2:11 2729
of beasts, which made them *a*........ Hab 2:17 2865
I have heard thy speech, and was *a*........ Hab 3:2 3372
down, and none shall make them *a*........ Zeph 3:13 2729
me, and was *a* before my name........ Mal 2:5 2865
Herod, he was *a* to go thither........ Mt 2:22 *5399*
be not *a*........ Mt 14:27 *5399*
saw the wind boisterous, he was *a*........ Mt 14:30 *5399*
on their face, and were sore *a*........ Mt 17:6 *5399*
them, and said, Arise, and be not *a*........ Mt 17:7 *5399*
And I was *a*, and went and hid thy........ Mt 25:25 *5399*
said Jesus unto them, Be not *a*........ Mt 28:10 *5399*
and they were *a*........ Mk 5:15 *5399*
ruler of the synagogue, Be not *a*........ Mk 5:36 *5399*
be not *a*........ Mk 6:50 *5399*
for they were sore *a*........ Mk 9:6 *1630*
that saying, and were *a* to ask him........ Mk 9:32 *5399*
and as they followed, they were *a*........ Mk 10:32 *5399*
thing to any man for they were *a*........ Mk 16:8 *5399*
and they were sore *a*........ Lk 2:9 *5399*
And they being *a* wondered, saying........ Lk 8:25 *5399*
and they were *a*........ Lk 8:35 *5399*
Be not *a* of them that kill the........ Lk 12:4 *5399*
And as they were *a*, and bowed down........ Lk 24:5 *1719*
and they were *a*........ Jn 6:19 *5399*
be not *a*........ Jn 6:20 *5399*
be troubled, neither let it be *a*........ Jn 14:27 *1168*

that saying, he was the more *a* ... Jn 19:8 *5399*
but they were all *a* of him ... Acts 9:26 *5399*
when he looked on him, he was *a* ... Acts 10:4 *1719*
the night by a vision, Be not *a* ... Acts 18:9 *5399*
saw indeed the light, and were *a* ... Acts 22:9 *1719*
and the chief captain also was *a* ... Acts 22:29 *5399*
thou then not be *a* of the power ... Rom 13:3 *5399*
thou do that which is evil, be *a* ... Rom 13:4 *5399*
I am *a* of you, lest I have ... Gal 4:11 *5399*
they were not *a* of the king's ... Heb 11:23 *5399*
are not *a* with any amazement ... 1Pet 3:6 *5399*
be not *a* of their terror, neither ... 1Pet 3:14 *5399*
they are not *a* to speak evil of ... 2Pet 2:10 *5141*

AFRESH {1}
to themselves the Son of God *a* ... Heb 6:6 *388*

AFTER See APPENDIX.

AFTERNOON {1}
And they tarried until *a*, and they .. Judg 19:8 5186,3117

AFTERWARD See APPENDIX.

AFTERWARDS {13}
a she bare a daughter, and called ... Gen 30:21 310
a he will let you go hence ... Ex 11:1 310,3651
a the hand of all the people ... Deut 13:9 314
a they eat that be bidden ... 1Sa 9:13 310,3651
mark, and *a* we will speak ... Job 18:2 310
but *a* his mouth shall be filled ... Prov 20:17 310
and *a* build thine house ... Prov 24:27 310
He that rebuketh a man *a* shall ... Prov 28:23 310
a wise man keepeth it in till *a* ... Prov 29:11 268
A the spirit took me up, and ... Eze 11:24
but thou shalt follow me *a* ... Jn 13:36 *5305*
A I came into the regions of ... Gal 1:21 *1899*
faith which should *a* be revealed ... Gal 3:23

AGABUS *(ag'-ab-us)* {2} *A Christian prophet.*
stood up one of them named *A* ... Acts 11:28 *13*
Judaea a certain prophet, named *A* ... Acts 21:10 *13*

AGAG *(a'-gag)* {8} See AGAGITE. *A king of Amalek during Exodus.*
his king shall be higher than *A* ... Num 24:7 90
he took *A* the king of the ... 1Sa 15:8 90
But Saul and the people spared *A* ... 1Sa 15:9 90
have brought *A* the king of Amalek ... 1Sa 15:20 90
Bring ye hither to me *A* the king ... 1Sa 15:32 90
A came unto him delicately ... 1Sa 15:32 90
A said, Surely the bitterness of ... 1Sa 15:32 90
Samuel hewed *A* in pieces before ... 1Sa 15:33 90

AGAGITE *(ag'-ag-ite)* {5} *A member of an Amalekite tribe.*
Haman the son of Hammedatha the *A* ... Est 3:1 91
Haman the son of Hammedatha the *A* ... Est 3:10 91
away the mischief of Haman the *A* ... Est 8:3 91
Haman the son of Hammedatha the *A* ... Est 8:5 91
the son of Hammedatha, the *A* ... Est 9:24 91

AGAIN See APPENDIX.

AGAINST See APPENDIX.

AGAR *(a'-gar)* {02} See HAGAR. *Greek form of Hagar.*
gendereth to bondage, which is *A* ... Gal 4:24 *28*
For this *A* is mount Sinai in ... Gal 4:25 *28*

AGATE {3}
And the third row a ligure, an *a* ... Ex 28:19 7618
And the third row, a ligure, an *a* ... Ex 39:12 7618
and fine linen, and coral, and *a* ... Eze 27:16 3539

AGATES {1}
And I will make thy windows of *a* ... Is 54:12 3539

AGE {42}
shalt be buried in a good old *a* ... Gen 15:15 7872
were old and well stricken in *a* ... Gen 18:11 3117
bare Abraham a son in his old *a* ... Gen 21:2
have born him a son in his old *a* ... Gen 21:7
was old, and well stricken in *a* ... Gen 24:1 3117
ghost, and died in a good old *a* ... Gen 25:8 7872
he was the son of his old *a* ... Gen 37:3
old man, and a child of his old *a* ... Gen 44:20
so the whole *a* of Jacob was an ... Gen 47:28 3117
the eyes of Israel were dim for *a* ... Gen 48:10 2207
from the *a* of fifty years they ... Num 8:25 1121
Joshua waxed old and stricken in *a* ... Josh 23:1 3117
them, I am old and stricken in *a* ... Josh 23:2 3117
son of Joash died in a good old *a* ... Judg 8:32 7872
and a nourisher of thine old *a* ... Ruth 4:15 7872
die in the flower of their *a* ... 1Sa 2:33 582
eyes were set by reason of his *a* ... 1Kin 14:4Ez7869
in the time of his old *a* he was ... 1Kin 15:23
from the *a* of thirty years ... 1Chr 23:3 1121
from the *a* of twenty years and ... 1Chr 23:24 1121
And he died in a good old *a* ... 1Chr 29:28 7872
man, or him that stooped for *a* ... 2Chr 36:17 3485
come to thy grave in a full *a* ... Job 5:26 3624
I pray thee, of the former *a* ... Job 8:8 1755
thine *a* shall be clearer than the ... Job 11:17 2465
in whom old *a* was perished ... Job 30:2 3624
mine *a* is as nothing before thee ... Ps 39:5 2465
me not off in the time of old *a* ... Ps 71:9
still bring forth fruit in old *a* ... Ps 92:14 7872
Mine *a* is departed, and is removed ... Is 38:12 1755
And even to your old *a* I am he ... Is 46:4 2209
his staff in his hand for very *a* ... Zec 8:4 3117
she was of the *a* of twelve years ... Mk 5:42
also conceived a son in her old *a* ... Lk 1:36
she was of a great *a*, and had ... Lk 2:36 *2250*
to be about thirty years of *a* ... Lk 3:23
daughter, about twelve years of *a* ... Lk 8:42 *2244*
he is of *a* ... Jn 9:21 *2244*
said his parents, He is of *a* ... Jn 9:23 *2244*
if she pass the flower of her *a* ... 1Cor 7:36 *5230*
to them that are of full *a* ... Heb 5:14 *5046*
of a child when she was past *a* ... Heb 11:11 *2244*

AGED {09}
Now Barzillai was a very *a* man ... 2Sa 19:32 2204
away the understanding of the *a* ... Job 12:20 2205
both the grayheaded and very *a* men ... Job 15:10 3453
and the *a* arose, and stood up ... Job 29:8 2205
neither do the *a* understand ... Job 32:9 2205
the *a* with him that is full of ... Jer 6:11 2205
That the *a* men be sober, grave, ... Titus 2:2 *4246*
The *a* women likewise, that they ... Titus 2:3 *4247*
being such an one as Paul the *a* ... Philem 9 *4246*

AGEE *(ag'-ee)* {1} *Father of a "mighty man" of David.*
Shammah the son of *A* the Hararite ... 2Sa 23:11 89

AGES {4}
That in the *a* to come he might ... Eph 2:7 *165*
Which in other *a* was not made ... Eph 3:5 *1074*
by Christ Jesus throughout all *a* ... Eph 3:21 *1074*
which hath been hid from *a* ... Col 1:26 *165*

AGO See APPENDIX.

AGONE {1}
because three days *a* I fell sick ... 1Sa 30:13

AGONY {1}
being in an *a* he prayed more ... Lk 22:44 *74*

AGREE {7}
A with thine adversary quickly, ... Mt 5:25 *2132*
That if two of you shall *a* on ... Mt 18:19 *4856*
didst not thou *a* with me for a ... Mt 20:13 *4856*
so did their witness *a* together ... Mk 14:59 *2470*
to this *a* the words of the ... Acts 15:15 *4856*
and these three *a* in one ... 1Jn 5:8 *1526*
to fulfil his will, and to *a* ... Rev 17:17 *4160,3391,1106*

AGREED {8}
walk together, except they be *a* ... Amos 3:3 3259
when he had *a* with the labourers ... Mt 20:2 *4856*
but their witness *a* not together ... Mk 14:56 *2470*
for the Jews had *a* already ... Jn 9:22 *4934*
How is it that ye have *a* together ... Acts 5:9 *4856*
And to him they *a* ... Acts 5:40 *3982*
The Jews have *a* to desire thee ... Acts 23:20 *4934*
when they *a* not among themselves, ... Acts 28:25 *800*

AGREEMENT {6}
Make an *a* with me by a present, ... 2Kin 18:31
death, and with hell are we at *a* ... Is 28:15 2374
your *a* with hell shall not stand ... Is 28:18 2380
Make an *a* with me by a present, ... Is 36:16
king of the north to make an *a* ... Dan 11:6 4339
what *a* hath the temple of God ... 2Cor 6:16 *4783*

AGREETH {2}
and thy speech *a* thereto ... Mk 14:70 *3662*
out of the new *a* not with the old ... Lk 5:36 *4856*

AGRIPPA *(ag-rip'-pah)* {12} *Great-grandson of Herod the Great.*
And after certain days king *A* ... Acts 25:13 *67*
Then *A* said unto Festus, I would ... Acts 25:22 *67*
when *A* was come, and Bernice, with ... Acts 25:23 *67*
And Festus said, King *A*, and all ... Acts 25:24 *67*
specially before thee, O king *A* ... Acts 25:26 *67*
Then *A* said unto Paul, Thou art ... Acts 26:1 *67*
I think myself happy, king *A* ... Acts 26:2 *67*
For which hope's sake, king *A* ... Acts 26:7 *67*
Whereupon, O king *A*, I was not ... Acts 26:19 *67*
King *A*, believest thou the ... Acts 26:27 *67*
Then *A* said unto Paul, Almost ... Acts 26:28 *67*
Then said *A* unto Festus, This man ... Acts 26:32 *67*

AGROUND {1}
two seas met, they ran the ship *a* ... Acts 27:41 *2027*

AGUE {1}
consumption, and the burning *a* ... Lev 26:16 6920

AGUR *(a'-gur)* {1} *Son of Jakeh.*
The words of *A* the son of Jakeh, ... Prov 30:1 94

AH See APPENDIX.

AHA See APPENDIX.

AHAB *(a'-hab)* {92} See AHAB'S.
1. A king of Israel.
A his son reigned in his stead ... 1Kin 16:28 256
A the son of Omri to reign over ... 1Kin 16:29 256
A the son of Omri reigned over ... 1Kin 16:29 256
A the son of Omri did evil in the ... 1Kin 16:30 256
And *A* made a grove ... 1Kin 16:33 256
A did more to provoke the LORD ... 1Kin 16:33 256
of Gilead, said unto *A*, As the ... 1Kin 17:1 256
saying, Go, shew thyself unto *A* ... 1Kin 18:1 256
went to shew himself unto *A* ... 1Kin 18:2 256
A called Obadiah, which was the ... 1Kin 18:3 256
A said unto Obadiah, Go into the ... 1Kin 18:5 256
A went one way by himself, and ... 1Kin 18:6 256
thy servant into the hand of *A* ... 1Kin 18:9 256
and so when I come and tell *A* ... 1Kin 18:12 256
So Obadiah went to meet *A* ... 1Kin 18:16 256
and *A* went to meet Elijah ... 1Kin 18:16 256
when *A* saw Elijah, that *A* said ... 1Kin 18:17 256
So *A* sent unto all the children ... 1Kin 18:20 256
And Elijah said unto *A*, Get thee ... 1Kin 18:41 256
So *A* went up to eat and to drink ... 1Kin 18:42 256
And he said, Go up, say unto *A* ... 1Kin 18:44 256
A rode, and went to Jezreel ... 1Kin 18:45 256
ran before *A* to the entrance of ... 1Kin 18:46 256
A told Jezebel all that Elijah ... 1Kin 19:1 256
he sent messengers to *A* king of ... 1Kin 20:2 256
a prophet unto *A* king of Israel ... 1Kin 20:13 256
And *A* said, By whom ... 1Kin 20:14 256
Then said *A*, I will send thee ... 1Kin 20:34
the palace of *A* king of Samaria ... 1Kin 21:1 256
A spake unto Naboth, saying, Give ... 1Kin 21:2 256
And Naboth said to *A*, The LORD ... 1Kin 21:3 256
A came into his house heavy and ... 1Kin 21:4 256
was dead, that Jezebel said to *A* ... 1Kin 21:15 256
when *A* heard that Naboth was dead ... 1Kin 21:16 256
that *A* rose up to go down to the ... 1Kin 21:16 256
go down to meet *A* king of Israel ... 1Kin 21:18 256
A said to Elijah, Hast thou found ... 1Kin 21:20 256
will cut off from *A* him that ... 1Kin 21:21 256
Him that dieth of *A* in the city ... 1Kin 21:24 256
But there was none like unto *A* ... 1Kin 21:25 256
when *A* heard those words, that he ... 1Kin 21:27 256
Seest thou how *A* humbleth himself ... 1Kin 21:29 256
LORD said, Who shall persuade *A* ... 1Kin 22:20 256
Now the rest of the acts of *A* ... 1Kin 22:39 256
So *A* slept with his fathers ... 1Kin 22:40 256
fourth year of *A* king of Israel ... 1Kin 22:41 256
the son of *A* unto Jehoshaphat ... 1Kin 22:49 256
Ahaziah the son of *A* began to ... 1Kin 22:51 256
Israel after the death of *A* ... 2Kin 1:1 256
Now Jehoram the son of *A* began to ... 2Kin 3:1 256
when *A* was dead, that the king of ... 2Kin 3:5 256
Joram the son of *A* king of Israel ... 2Kin 8:16 256
of Israel, as did the house of *A* ... 2Kin 8:18 256
the daughter of *A* was his wife ... 2Kin 8:18 256
year of Joram the son of *A* king ... 2Kin 8:25 256
in the way of the house of *A* ... 2Kin 8:27 256
the LORD, as did the house of *A* ... 2Kin 8:27 256
the son in law of the house of *A* ... 2Kin 8:27 256
he went with Joram the son of *A* ... 2Kin 8:28 256
see Joram the son of *A* in Jezreel ... 2Kin 8:29 256
smite the house of *A* thy master ... 2Kin 9:7 256
the whole house of *A* shall perish ... 2Kin 9:8 256
I will cut off from *A* him that ... 2Kin 9:8 256
I will make the house of *A* like ... 2Kin 9:9 256
rode together after *A* his father ... 2Kin 9:25 256
year of Joram the son of *A* began ... 2Kin 9:29 256
A had seventy sons in Samaria ... 2Kin 10:1 256
spake concerning the house of *A* ... 2Kin 10:10 256
of the house of *A* in Jezreel ... 2Kin 10:11 256
that remained unto *A* in Samaria ... 2Kin 10:17 256
unto them, *A* served Baal a little ... 2Kin 10:18 256
hast done unto the house of *A* ... 2Kin 10:30 256
a grove, as did *A* king of Israel ... 2Kin 21:3 256
and the plummet of the house of *A* ... 2Kin 21:13 256
and joined affinity with *A* ... 2Chr 18:1 256
he went down to *A* to Samaria ... 2Chr 18:2 256
A killed sheep and oxen for him in ... 2Chr 18:2 256
A king of Israel said unto ... 2Chr 18:3 256
Who shall entice *A* king of Israel ... 2Chr 18:19 256
like as did the house of *A* ... 2Chr 21:6 256
he had the daughter of *A* to wife ... 2Chr 21:6 256
the whoredoms of the house of *A* ... 2Chr 21:13 256
in the ways of the house of *A* ... 2Chr 22:3 256
of the LORD like the house of *A* ... 2Chr 22:4 256
went with Jehoram the son of *A* ... 2Chr 22:5 256
Jehoram the son of *A* at Jezreel ... 2Chr 22:6 256
to cut off the house of *A* ... 2Chr 22:7 256
judgment upon the house of *A* ... 2Chr 22:8 256
all the works of the house of *A* ... Mic 6:16 256
2. A false prophet during the Exile.
of *A* the son of Kolaiah, and of ... Jer 29:21 256
make thee like Zedekiah and like *A* ... Jer 29:22 256

AHAB'S *(a'-habs)* {2}
So she wrote letters in *A* name ... 1Kin 21:8 256
them that brought up *A* children ... 2Kin 10:1 256

AHARAH *(a-har'-ah)* {1} See AHER, AHIRAM, EHI. *Third son of Benjamin.*
the second, and *A* the third, ... 1Chr 8:1 315

AHARHEL *(a-har'-hel)* {1} *A descendant of Judah.*
the families of *A* the son of ... 1Chr 4:8 316

AHASAI *(a-ha'-sa-i)* {1} *Family of returned exiles.*
the son of Azareel, the son of *A* ... Neh 11:13 273

AHASBAI *(a-has'-ba-i)* {1} *Father of a "mighty man" of David.*
Eliphelet the son of *A*, the son ... 2Sa 23:34 308

AHASUERUS *(a-has-u-e'-rus)* {30} See AHASUERUS'.
1. A Persian king, Cambyses.
And in the reign of *A*, in the ... Ezr 4:6 325
2. Father of Darius the Mede.
first year of Darius the son of *A* ... Dan 9:1 325
3. A king of Persia, Xerxes.
it came to pass in the days of *A* ... Est 1:1 325
(this is *A* which reigned from ... Est 1:1 325
when the king *A* sat on the throne ... Est 1:2 325
house which belonged to king *A* ... Est 1:9 325
in the presence of *A* the king ... Est 1:10 325
of the king *A* by the chamberlains ... Est 1:15 325
all the provinces of the king *A* ... Est 1:16 325
The king *A* commanded Vashti the ... Est 1:17 325
Vashti come no more before king *A* ... Est 1:19 325
the wrath of king *A* was appeased ... Est 2:1 325
turn was come to go in to king *A* ... Est 2:12 325
A into his house royal in the ... Est 2:16 325
sought to lay hand on the king *A* ... Est 2:21 325
king *A* promote Haman the son of ... Est 3:1 325
throughout the whole kingdom of *A* ... Est 3:6 325
in the twelfth year of king *A* ... Est 3:7 325
And Haman said unto king *A* ... Est 3:8 325
the name of king *A* was it written ... Est 3:12 325
sought to lay hand on the king *A* ... Est 6:2 325
Then the king *A* answered and said ... Est 7:5 325

On that day did the king A give ... Est 8:1 325
Then the king A said unto Esther ... Est 8:7 325
in all the provinces of king A ... Est 8:12 325
all the provinces of the king A ... Est 9:2 325
all the provinces of the king A ... Est 9:20 325
provinces of the kingdom of A ... Est 9:30 325
the king A laid a tribute upon ... Est 10:1 325
the Jew was next unto king A ... Est 10:3 325

AHASUERUS' (*a-has-u-e'-rus*) {1} *Refers to Ahasuerus 3.*
And he wrote in the king A name ... Est 8:10 325

AHAVA (*a-ha'-vah*) {3} See IVA. *A river of Babylon.*
to the river than runneth to A ... Ezr 8:15 163
a fast there, at the river of A ... Ezr 8:21 163
we departed from the river of A ... Ezr 8:31 163

AHAZ (*a'-haz*) {42} See ACHAZ.
1. A king of Judah.
A his son reigned in his stead ... 2Kin 15:38 271
of Pekah the son of Remaliah A ... 2Kin 16:1 271
Twenty years old was A when he ... 2Kin 16:2 271
and they besieged A, but could not ... 2Kin 16:5 271
So A sent messengers to ... 2Kin 16:7 271
A took the silver and gold that ... 2Kin 16:8 271
king A went to Damascus to meet ... 2Kin 16:10 271
king A sent to Urijah the priest ... 2Kin 16:10 271
king A had sent from Damascus ... 2Kin 16:11 271
against king A came from Damascus ... 2Kin 16:11 271
king A commanded Urijah the ... 2Kin 16:15 271
to all that king A commanded ... 2Kin 16:16 271
king A cut off the borders of the ... 2Kin 16:17 271
of the acts of A which he did ... 2Kin 16:19 271
A slept with his fathers, and was ... 2Kin 16:20 271
In the twelfth year of A king of ... 2Kin 17:1 271
that Hezekiah the son of A king ... 2Kin 18:1 271
it had gone down in the dial of A ... 2Kin 20:11 271
the top of the upper chamber of A ... 2Kin 23:12 271
A his son, Hezekiah his son, ... 1Chr 3:13 271
A his son reigned in his stead ... 2Chr 27:9 271
A was twenty years old when he ... 2Chr 28:1 271
At that time did king A send unto ... 2Chr 28:16 271
low because of A king of Israel ... 2Chr 28:19 271
For A took away a portion out of ... 2Chr 28:21 271
this is that king A ... 2Chr 28:22 271
A gathered together the vessels ... 2Chr 28:24 271
A slept with his fathers, and they ... 2Chr 28:27 271
which king A in his reign did ... 2Chr 29:19 271
in the days of Uzziah, Jotham, A ... Is 1:1 271
the days of A the son of Jotham ... Is 7:1 271
Isaiah, Go forth now to meet A ... Is 7:3 271
the LORD spake again unto A ... Is 7:10 271
But A said, I will not ask, ... Is 7:12 271
that king A died was this burden ... Is 14:28 271
is gone down in the sun dial of A ... Is 38:8 271
in the days of Uzziah, Jotham, A ... Hos 1:1 271
in the days of Jotham, A, and ... Mic 1:1 271
2. A Benjaminite and relative of Saul.
Pithon, and Melech, and Tarea, and A ... 1Chr 8:35 271
And A begat Jehoadah ... 1Chr 8:36 271
and Melech, and Tahrea, and A ... 1Chr 9:41 271
And A begat Jarah ... 1Chr 9:42 271

AHAZIAH (*a-haz-i'-ah*) {37} See AZARIAH, JEHOAHAZ.
1. A king of Israel.
A his son reigned in his stead ... 1Kin 22:40 274
Then said A the son of Ahab unto ... 1Kin 22:49 274
A the son of Ahab began to reign ... 1Kin 22:51 274
A fell down through a lattice in ... 2Kin 1:2 274
of the acts of A which he did ... 2Kin 1:18 274
A his son, Joash his son, ... 1Chr 3:11 274
himself with A king of Israel ... 2Chr 20:35 274
thou hast joined thyself with A ... 2Chr 20:37 274
2. Son and successor of King Jehoram of Judah.
A his son reigned in his stead ... 2Kin 8:24 274
did A the son of Jehoram king of ... 2Kin 8:25 274
twenty years old was A when he ... 2Kin 8:26 274
A the son of Jehoram king of ... 2Kin 8:29 274
A king of Judah was come down to ... 2Kin 9:16 274
A king of Judah went out, each in ... 2Kin 9:21 274
his hands, and fled, and said to A ... 2Kin 9:23 274
There is treachery, O A ... 2Kin 9:23 274
But when A the king of Judah saw ... 2Kin 9:27 274
Ahab began A to reign over Judah ... 2Kin 9:29 274
the brethren of A king of Judah ... 2Kin 10:13 274
We are the brethren of A ... 2Kin 10:13 274
of A saw that her son was dead ... 2Kin 11:1 274
of king Joram, sister of A ... 2Kin 11:2 274
took Joash the son of A ... 2Kin 11:2 274
Jehoshaphat, and Jehoram, and A ... 2Kin 12:18 274
year of Joash the son of A king ... 2Kin 13:1 274
the son of Jehoash the son of A ... 2Kin 14:13 274
A his youngest son king in his ... 2Chr 22:1 274
So A the son of Jehoram king of ... 2Chr 22:1 274
two years old was A when he began ... 2Chr 22:2 274
the destruction of A was of God ... 2Chr 22:7 274
and the sons of the brethren of A ... 2Chr 22:8 274
that ministered to A ... 2Chr 22:8 274
And he sought A ... 2Chr 22:9 274
So the house of A had no power to ... 2Chr 22:9 274
of A saw that her son was dead ... 2Chr 22:10 274
the king, took Joash the son of A ... 2Chr 22:11 274
(for she was the sister of A ... 2Chr 22:11 274

AHBAN (*ah'-ban*) {1} *A descendant of Pharez.*
was Abihail, and she bare him A ... 1Chr 2:29 257

AHER (*a'-hur*) {1} See AHARAH. *A descendant of Benjamin.*
of Ir, and Hushim, the sons of A ... 1Chr 7:12 313

AHI (*a'-hi*) {2}
1. A son of Abdiel.
A the son of Abdiel, the son of ... 1Chr 5:15 277
2. A chief of the Asherites.
A, and Rohgah, Jehubbah, and Aram ... 1Chr 7:34 277

AHIAH (*a-hi'-ah*) {4} See AHIJAH.
1. Grandson of Phinehas.
And A, the son of Ahitub, ... 1Sa 14:3 281
And Saul said unto A, Bring hither ... 1Sa 14:18 281
2. A scribe of Solomon.
Elihoreph and A, the sons of ... 1Kin 4:3 281
3. A descendant of Benjamin.
And Naaman, and A, and Gera, he ... 1Chr 8:7 281

AHIAM (*a-hi'-am*) {2} *Son of Shahar.*
A the son of Sharar the Hararite, ... 2Sa 23:33 279
A the son of Sacar the Hararite, ... 1Chr 11:35 279

AHIAN (*a-hi'-an*) {1}
And the sons of Shemidah were, A ... 1Chr 7:19 291

AHIEZER (*a-hi-e'-zer*) {6}
1. One who numbered the people.
A the son of Ammishaddai ... Num 1:12 295
shall be A the son of Ammishaddai ... Num 2:25 295
On the tenth day A the son of ... Num 7:66 295
of A the son of Ammishaddai ... Num 7:71 295
over his host was A the son of ... Num 10:25 295
2. A chief of the Benjamites.
The chief was A, then Joash, the ... 1Chr 12:3 295

AHIHUD (*a-hi'-hud*) {2}
1. A prince of Asher.
of Asher, A the son of Shelomi ... Num 34:27 282
2. A Benjamite of the Ehud family.
removed them, and begat Uzza, and A ... 1Chr 8:7 284

AHIJAH (*a-hi'-jah*) {20} See AHIAH, AHIMELECH.
1. A prophet during the reigns of Solomon and Rehoboam.
that the prophet A the Shilonite ... 1Kin 11:29 281
A caught the new garment that was ... 1Kin 11:30 281
which the LORD spake by A the ... 1Kin 12:15 281
there is A the prophet, which ... 1Kin 14:2 281
Shiloh, and came to the house of A ... 1Kin 14:4 281
But A could not see ... 1Kin 14:4 281
And the LORD said unto A, Behold, ... 1Kin 14:5 281
when A heard the sound of her ... 1Kin 14:6 281
hand of his servant A the prophet ... 1Kin 14:18 281
by his servant A the Shilonite ... 1Kin 15:29 281
the prophecy of A the Shilonite ... 2Chr 9:29 281
A the Shilonite to Jeroboam the ... 2Chr 10:15 281
2. Father of Baasha.
And Baasha the son of A, of the ... 1Kin 15:27 281
of A to reign over all Israel in ... 1Kin 15:33 281
the house of Baasha the son of A ... 1Kin 21:22 281
the house of Baasha the son of A ... 2Kin 9:9 281
3. Son of Jerahmeel.
Bunah, and Oren, and Ozem, and A ... 1Chr 2:25 281
4. A "mighty man" of David.
the Mecherathite, A the Pelonite, ... 1Chr 11:36 281
5. A treasury official under David.
A was over the treasures of the ... 1Chr 26:20 281
6. A Levite who renewed the covenant.
And A, Hanan, Anan, ... Neh 10:26 281

AHIKAM (*a-hi'-kam*) {20} *An officer in Josiah's court.*
A the son of Shaphan, and Achbor ... 2Kin 22:12 296
So Hilkiah the priest, and A ... 2Kin 22:14 296
he made Gedaliah the son of A ... 2Kin 25:22 296
A the son of Shaphan, and Abdon ... 2Chr 34:20 296
Nevertheless the hand of A the ... Jer 26:24 296
the son of A the son of Shaphan ... Jer 39:14 296
the son of A the son of Shaphan ... Jer 40:5 296
Gedaliah the son of A to Mizpah ... Jer 40:6 296
the son of A governor in the land ... Jer 40:7 296
Gedaliah the son of A the son of ... Jer 40:9 296
the son of A the son of Shaphan ... Jer 40:11 296
the son of A believed them not ... Jer 40:14 296
But Gedaliah the son of A said ... Jer 40:16 296
Gedaliah the son of A to Mizpah ... Jer 41:1 296
smote Gedaliah the son of A the ... Jer 41:2 296
Come to Gedaliah the son of A ... Jer 41:6 296
to Gedaliah the son of A ... Jer 41:10 296
had slain Gedaliah the son of A ... Jer 41:16 296
had slain Gedaliah the son of A ... Jer 41:18 296
the son of A the son of Shaphan ... Jer 43:6 296

AHILUD (*a-hi'-lud*) {5} *Father of a recorder under David and Solomon.*
the son of A was recorder ... 2Sa 8:16 286
the son of A was recorder ... 2Sa 20:24 286
Jehoshaphat the son of A, the ... 1Kin 4:3 286
Baana the son of A ... 1Kin 4:12 286
and Jehoshaphat the son of A ... 1Chr 18:15 286

AHIMAAZ (*a-him'-a-az*) {15}
1. Father of Ahinoam.
was Ahinoam, the daughter of A ... 1Sa 14:50 290
2. Son of Zadok.
A thy son, and Jonathan the son of ... 2Sa 15:27 290
A Zadok's son, and Jonathan ... 2Sa 15:36 290
Jonathan and A stayed by En-rogel ... 2Sa 17:17 290
the house, they said, Where is A ... 2Sa 17:20 290
Then said A the son of Zadok, Let ... 2Sa 18:19 290
Then said A the son of Zadok yet ... 2Sa 18:22 290
Then A ran by the way of the ... 2Sa 18:23 290
the running of A the son of Zadok ... 2Sa 18:27 290
A called, and said unto the king, ... 2Sa 18:28 290
A answered, When Joab sent the ... 2Sa 18:29 290
begat Zadok, and Zadok begat A ... 1Chr 6:8 290
A begat Azariah, and Azariah begat ... 1Chr 6:9 290
Zadok his son, A his son ... 1Chr 6:53 290
3. An officer of Solomon.
A was in Naphtali ... 1Kin 4:15 290

AHIMAN (*a-hi'-man*) {4}
1. A giant of Anak.
where A, Sheshai, and Talmai, the ... Num 13:22 289
three sons of Anak, Sheshai, and A ... Josh 15:14 289
and they slew Sheshai, and A ... Judg 1:10 289
2. A Levite Temple servant.
and Akkub, and Talmon, and A ... 1Chr 9:17 289

AHIMELECH (*a-him'-el-ek*) {16}
1. A priest.
came David to Nob to A the priest ... 1Sa 21:1 288
A was afraid at the meeting of ... 1Sa 21:1 288
And David said unto A the priest ... 1Sa 21:2 288
And David said unto A, And is there ... 1Sa 21:8 288
to Nob, to A the son of Ahitub ... 1Sa 22:9 288
king sent to call A the priest ... 1Sa 22:11 288
Then A answered the king, and said ... 1Sa 22:14 288
said, Thou shalt surely die, A ... 1Sa 22:16 288
the sons of A the son of Ahitub ... 1Sa 22:20 288
son of A fled to David to Keilah ... 1Sa 23:6 288
A the son of Abiathar, were the ... 2Sa 8:17 288
A of the sons of Ithamar, ... 1Chr 24:3 288
A the son of Abiathar, and before ... 1Chr 24:6 288
of David the king, and Zadok, and A ... 1Chr 24:31 288
David is come to the house of A ... Ps 52:*t* 288
2. A Hittite officer.
said to A the Hittite, and to ... 1Sa 26:6 288

AHIMELECH'S (*a-him'-el-eks*) {1} *Refers to Ahimelech 1.*
A son, I pray thee, bring me ... 1Sa 30:7 288

AHIMOTH {1}
Amasai, and A ... 1Chr 6:25 287

AHINADAB (*a-hin'-ad-ab*) {1} *A son of Iddo.*
A the son of Iddo had Mahanaim ... 1Kin 4:14 292

AHINOAM (*a-hin'-o-am*) {7}
1. A wife of King Saul.
And the name of Saul's wife was A ... 1Sa 14:50 293
2. A wife of David.
David also took A of Jezreel ... 1Sa 25:43 293
A the Jezreelitess, and Abigail ... 1Sa 27:3 293
A the Jezreelitess, and Abigail ... 1Sa 30:5 293
A the Jezreelitess, and Abigail ... 2Sa 2:2 293
was Amnon, of A the Jezreelitess ... 2Sa 3:2 293
Amnon, of A the Jezreelitess ... 1Chr 3:1 293

AHIO (*a-hi'-o*) {6}
1. A son of Abinadab.
and Uzzah and A, the sons of ... 2Sa 6:3 283
and A went before the ark ... 2Sa 6:4 283
and Uzza and A drave the cart ... 1Chr 13:7 283
2. A son of Beriah the Benjamite.
And A, Shashak, and Jeremoth, ... 1Chr 8:14 283
3. A son of Jehiel.
And Gedor, and A, and Zacher ... 1Chr 8:31 283
And Gedor, and A, and Zechariah, and ... 1Chr 9:37 283

AHIRA (*a-hi'-rah*) {5} *A chief of Naphtali.*
A the son of Enan ... Num 1:15 299
shall be A the son of Enan ... Num 2:29 299
the twelfth day A the son of Enan ... Num 7:78 299
the offering of A the son of Enan ... Num 7:83 299
of Naphtali was A the son of Enan ... Num 10:27 299

AHIRAM (*a-hi'-rum*) {1} See AHARAH, AHIRAMITES. *A descendant of Benjamin.*
of A, the family of the ... Num 26:38 297

AHIRAMITES (*a-hi'-rum-ites*) {1} *Descendants of Ahiram.*
of Ahiram, the family of the A ... Num 26:38 298

AHISAMACH (*a-his'-am-ak*) {3} *Father of Aholiab.*
with him Aholiab, the son of A ... Ex 31:6 294
both he, and Aholiab, the son of A ... Ex 35:34 294
And with him was Aholiab, son of A ... Ex 38:23 294

AHISHAHAR (*a-hish'-a-har*) {1} *A son of Bilhan.*
and Zethan, and Tharshish, and A ... 1Chr 7:10 300

AHISHAR (*a-hi'-shar*) {1} *Governor of the palace under Solomon.*
And A was over the household ... 1Kin 4:6 301

AHITHOPHEL (*a-hith'-o-fel*) {20} *A counsellor of David.*
Absalom sent for A the Gilonite ... 2Sa 15:12 302
A is among the conspirators with ... 2Sa 15:31 302
the counsel of A into foolishness ... 2Sa 15:31 302
for me defeat the counsel of A ... 2Sa 15:34 302
came to Jerusalem, and A with him ... 2Sa 16:15 302
Then said Absalom to A, Give ... 2Sa 16:20 302
A said unto Absalom, Go in unto ... 2Sa 16:21 302
And the counsel of A, which he ... 2Sa 16:23 302
the counsel of A both with David ... 2Sa 16:23 302
Moreover A said unto Absalom, Let ... 2Sa 17:1 302
A hath spoken after this manner ... 2Sa 17:6 302
The counsel that A hath given is ... 2Sa 17:7 302
is better than the counsel of A ... 2Sa 17:14 302
to defeat the good counsel of A ... 2Sa 17:14 302
thus did A counsel Absalom and the ... 2Sa 17:15 302
for thus hath A counselled ... 2Sa 17:21 302
when A saw that his counsel was ... 2Sa 17:23 302
Eliam the son of A the Gilonite ... 2Sa 23:34 302
A was the king's counsellor ... 1Chr 27:33 302
after A was Jehoiada the son of ... 1Chr 27:34 302

AHITUB (*a-hi'-tub*) {15}
1. The son of Phinehas.
And Ahiah, the son of A, ... 1Sa 14:3 285
to Nob, to Ahimelech the son of A ... 1Sa 22:9 285
the priest, the son of A, and all ... 1Sa 22:11 285

said, Hear now, thou son of A 1Sa 22:12 285
sons of Ahimelech the son of A 1Sa 22:20 285
2. Father of the high priest during David's reign.
And Zadok the son of A, and 2Sa 8:17 285
begat Amariah, and Amariah begat A 1Chr 6:7 285
A begat Zadok, and Zadok begat 1Chr 6:8 285
son, Amariah his son, A his son, ... 1Chr 6:52 285
And Zadok the son of A, and 1Chr 18:16 285
the son of Zadok, the son of A .... Ezr 7:2 285
3. A priest seven generations later than Ahitub 2.
begat Amariah, and Amariah begat A 1Chr 6:11 285
A begat Zadok, and Zadok begat 1Chr 6:12 285
4. A priest in Nehemiah's time.
the son of Meraioth, the son of A 1Chr 9:11 285
the son of Meraioth, the son of A .... Neh 11:11 285

AHLAB *(ah'-lab)* {1} *A city of Asher.*
inhabitants of Zidon, nor of A .... Judg 1:31 303

AHLAI *(ah'-lahee)* {2}
1. A daughter of Sheshan.
And the children of Sheshan; A 1Chr 2:31 304
2. Father of a "mighty man" of David.
the Hittite, Zabad the son of A 1Chr 11:41 304

AHOAH *(a-ho'-ah)* {1} See AHOHITE. *The son of Bela.*
And Abishua, and Naaman, and A 1Chr 8:4 265

AHOHITE *(a-ho'-hite)* {5}
1. A descendant of Ahoah.
Zalmon the A, Maharai the 2Sa 23:28 266
Eleazar the son of Dodo, the A 1Chr 11:12 266
the Hushathite, Ilai the A 1Chr 11:29 266
the second month was Dodai an A 1Chr 27:4 266
2. A rendering of "son of Ahohi."
Eleazar the son of Dodo the A 2Sa 23:9 1121,266

AHOLAH *(a-ho'-lah)* {5} *A name for Samaria and the Ten Tribes.*
names of them were A the elder .... Eze 23:4 170
Samaria is A, and Jerusalem .... Eze 23:4 170
A played the harlot when she was .... Eze 23:5 170
Son of man, wilt thou judge A .... Eze 23:36 170
so went they in unto A and unto .... Eze 23:44 170

AHOLIAB *(a-ho'-lee-ab)* {5} *A Danite craftsman.*
behold, I have given with him A .... Ex 31:6 171
that he may teach, both he, and A .... Ex 35:34 171
Then wrought Bezaleel and A .... Ex 36:1 171
And Moses called Bezaleel and A .... Ex 36:2 171
And with him was A, son of .... Ex 38:23 171

AHOLIBAH *(a-hol'-ib-ah)* {6} *A name for Jerusalem and Judah.*
Aholah the elder, and A her sister .... Eze 23:4 172
Samaria is Aholah, and Jerusalem A .... Eze 23:4 172
And when her sister A saw this .... Eze 23:11 172
Therefore, O A, thus saith the .... Eze 23:22 172
man, wilt thou judge Aholah and A .... Eze 23:36 172
they in unto Aholah and unto A .... Eze 23:44 172

AHOLIBAMAH *(a-hol'-ib-a'-mah)* {8}
1. A wife of Esau.
A the daughter of Anah the .... Gen 36:2 173
A bare Jeush, and Jaalam, and Korah .... Gen 36:5 173
And these were the sons of A .... Gen 36:14 173
are the sons of A Esau's wife .... Gen 36:18 173
came of A the daughter of Anah .... Gen 36:18 173
Dishon, and A the daughter of Anah .... Gen 36:25 173
2. A chief from Esau.
Duke A, duke Elah, duke Pinon, ... Gen 36:41 173
Duke A, duke Elah, duke Pinon, ... 1Chr 1:52 173

AHUMAI *(a-hoo'-mahee)* {1} *Grandson of Shobal.*
and Jahath begat A, and Lahad 1Chr 4:2 267

AHUZAM *(a-hoo'-zam)* {1} *A son of Ashur.*
And Naarah bare him A, and Hepher, ... 1Chr 4:6 275

AHUZZAM See AHUZAM.

AHUZZATH *(a-huz'-zath)* {1} *A friend of Ahimilech the Philistine king.*
A one of his friends, and Phichol .... Gen 26:26 276

AHZAI See AHASAI.

AI *(a'-i)* {36} See AIATH, AIJA, HAI. *A city near Bethel in Benjamin.*
Joshua sent men from Jericho to A .... Josh 7:2 5857
And the men went up and viewed A .... Josh 7:2 5857
thousand men go up and smite A .... Josh 7:3 5857
and they fled before the men of A .... Josh 7:4 5857
the men of A smote of them about .... Josh 7:5 5857
with thee, and arise, go up to A .... Josh 8:1 5857
given into thy hand the king of A .... Josh 8:1 5857
And thou shalt do to A and her king .... Josh 8:2 5857
people of war, to go up against A .... Josh 8:3 5857
and A, on the west side of A .... Josh 8:9 5857
of Israel, before the people to A .... Josh 8:10 5857
and pitched on the north side of A .... Josh 8:11 5857
was a valley between them and A .... Josh 8:11 5857
in ambush between Beth-el and A .... Josh 8:12 5857
pass, when the king of A saw it .... Josh 8:14 5857
all the people that were in A .... Josh 8:16 5892
not a man left in A or Beth-el .... Josh 8:17 5857
that is in thy hand toward A .... Josh 8:18 5857
when the men of A looked behind .... Josh 8:20 5857
again, and slew the men of A .... Josh 8:21 5857
the king of A they took alive, and .... Josh 8:23 5857
the inhabitants of A in the field .... Josh 8:24 5857
the Israelites returned unto A .... Josh 8:24 5857
thousand, even all the men of A .... Josh 8:25 5857
all the inhabitants of A .... Josh 8:26 5857
And Joshua burnt A, and made it an .... Josh 8:28 5857
the king of A he hanged on a tree .... Josh 8:29 5857
had done unto Jericho and to A .... Josh 9:3 5857
had heard how Joshua had taken A .... Josh 10:1 5857
and her king, so he had done to A .... Josh 10:1 5857
and because it was greater than A .... Josh 10:2 5857
the king of A, which is beside .... Josh 12:9 5857
The men of Beth-el and A, two .... Ezr 2:28 5857
The men of Beth-el and A, an .... Neh 7:32 5857
Howl, O Heshbon, for A is spoiled .... Jer 49:3 5857

AIAH *(a-i'-ah)* {5} See AJAH.
1. A son of Zibeon the Horite.
A, and Anah 1Chr 1:40 345
2. The father of Saul's concubine.
was Rizpah, the daughter of A 2Sa 3:7 345
sons of Rizpah the daughter of A 2Sa 21:8 345
the daughter of A took sackcloth 2Sa 21:10 345
what Rizpah the daughter of A 2Sa 21:11 345

AIATH *(a-i'-ath)* {1} See AI. *A form of Ai.*
He is come to A, he is passed to .... Is 10:28 5857

AIDED {1}
which a him in the killing of his ..... Judg 9:24 2388,3027

AIJA *(a-i'-jah)* {1} See AI. *A form of Ai.*
from Geba dwelt at Michmash, and A .... Neh 11:31 5857

AIJALON *(a-ij'-el-on)* {7} See AJALON.
1. A Levitical city in Dan.
A with her suburbs, Gath-rimmon .... Josh 21:24 357
would dwell in mount Heres in A .... Judg 1:35 357
2. A place in Zebulun.
was buried in A in the country of .... Judg 12:12 357
3. A town between Benjamin and Judah.
that day from Michmash to A 1Sa 14:31 357
fathers of the inhabitants of A 1Chr 8:13 357
And Zorah, and A, and Hebron, which ... 2Chr 11:10 357
4. A Levitical city in Ephraim.
And A with her suburbs, and 1Chr 6:69 357

AIJELETH *(a-ij'-el-eth)* {1} *A musical notation.*
the chief Musician upon A Shahar .... Ps 22:t 365

AILED {1}
What a thee, O thou sea, that .... Ps 114:5

AILETH {7}
and said unto her, What a thee .... Gen 21:17
and said unto Micah, What a thee .... Judg 18:23
that ye say unto me, What a thee .... Judg 18:24
What a the people that they weep 1Sa 11:5
king said unto her, What a thee 2Sa 14:5
king said unto her, What a thee 2Kin 6:28
What a thee now, that thou art .... Is 22:1

AIN *(ah'-yin)* {5} See EN.
1. A place between Riblah and the Sea of Chinnereth.
to Riblah, on the east side of A .... Num 34:11 5871
2. A Levitical city in Simeon.
And Lebaoth, and Shilhim, and A .... Josh 15:32 5871
A, Remmon, and Ether, and Ashan .... Josh 19:7 5871
A with her suburbs, and Juttah .... Josh 21:16 5871
their villages were, Etam, and A 1Chr 4:32 5871

AIR {39}
sea, and over the fowl of the a .... Gen 1:26 8064
sea, and over the fowl of the a .... Gen 1:28 8064
earth, and to every fowl of the a .... Gen 1:30 8064
the field, and every fowl of the a .... Gen 2:19 8064
cattle, and to the fowl of the a .... Gen 2:20 8064
thing, and the fowls of the a .... Gen 6:7 8064
Of fowls also of the a by sevens .... Gen 7:3 8064
and upon every fowl of the a .... Gen 9:2 8064
winged fowl that flieth in the a .... Deut 4:17 8064
be meat unto all fowls of the a .... Deut 28:26 8064
thy flesh unto the fowls of the a 1Sa 17:44 8064
this day unto the fowls of the a 1Sa 17:46 8064
of the a to rest on them by day 2Sa 21:10 8064
shall the fowls of the a eat 1Kin 14:11 8064
shall the fowls of the a eat 1Kin 16:4 8064
shall the fowls of the a eat 1Kin 21:24 8064
and the fowls of the a, and they .... Job 12:7 8064
close from the fowls of the a .... Job 28:21 8064
that no a can come between them .... Job 41:16 7307
The fowl of the a, and the fish of .... Ps 8:8 8064
The way of an eagle in the a .... Prov 30:19 8064
for a bird of the a shall carry .... Eccl 10:20 8064
Behold the fowls of the a .... Mt 6:26 3772
and the birds of the a have nests .... Mt 8:20 3772
so that the birds of the a come .... Mt 13:32 3772
side, and the fowls of the a came .... Mk 4:4 3772
so that the fowls of the a may .... Mk 4:32 3772
and the fowls of the a devoured it .... Lk 8:5 3772
and birds of the a have nests .... Lk 9:58 3772
the fowls of the a lodged in the .... Lk 13:19 3772
things, and fowls of the a .... Acts 10:12 3772
things, and fowls of the a .... Acts 11:6 3772
clothes, and threw dust into the a .... Acts 22:23 109
I, not as one that beateth the a 1Cor 9:26 109
for ye shall speak into the a 1Cor 14:9 109
the prince of the power of the a .... Eph 2:2 109
clouds, to meet the Lord in the a 1Th 4:17 109
the a were darkened by reason of .... Rev 9:2 109
poured out his vial into the a .... Rev 16:17 109

AJAH *(a'-jah)* {1} See AIAH. *A son of Zibeon the Horite.*
both A, and Anah .... Gen 36:24 345

AJALON *(aj'-a-lon)* {3} See AIJALON.
1. A valley of Dan.
and thou, Moon, in the valley of A .... Josh 10:12 357
2. A Levitical city in Dan.
And Shaalabbin, and A, and Jethlah, ... Josh 19:42 357
3. A town between Benjamin and Judah.
and had taken Beth-shemesh, and A 2Chr 28:18 357

AKAN *(a'-kan)* {1} See JAAKAN, JAKAN. *A son of Ezer.*
Bilhan, and Zaavan, and A .... Gen 36:27 6130

AKEL DAMA See ACELDAMA.

AKKAD See ACCAD.

AKKUB *(ak'-kub)* {8}
1. A descendant of David.
and Eliashib, and Pelaiah, and A 1Chr 3:24 6126
2. A Levitical gatekeeper.
the porters were, Shallum, and A 1Chr 9:17 6126
Moreover the porters, A, Talmon, ... Neh 11:19 6126
Obadiah, Meshullam, Talmon, A .... Neh 12:25 6126
3. A family of Levitical porters.
of Talmon, the children of A .... Ezr 2:42 6126
of Talmon, the children of A .... Neh 7:45 6126
4. A family of returned exiles.
of Hagabah, the children of A .... Ezr 2:45 6126
5. A priest in Ezra's time.
and Bani, and Sherebiah, Jamin, A .... Neh 8:7 6126

AKRABBIM *(ac-rab'-bim)* {2} See MAALE-ACRABBIM. *An ascent south of the Dead Sea.*
from the south to the ascent of A .... Num 34:4 6137
was from the going up to A .... Judg 1:36 6137

ALABASTER {3}
a box of very precious ointment .... Mt 26:7 *211*
an a box of ointment of spikenard .... Mk 14:3 *211*
brought an a box of ointment, ... Lk 7:37 *211*

ALAMETH *(al'-am-eth)* {1} *A son of Becher.*
and Abiah, and Anathoth, and A 1Chr 7:8 5964

ALAMMELECH *(a-lam'-mel-ek)* {1} *A town in Asher.*
And A, and Amad, and Misheal .... Josh 19:26 487

ALAMOTH *(al'-am-oth)* {2} *A musical notation.*
and Benaiah, with psalteries on A 1Chr 15:20 5961
the sons of Korah, A Song upon A .... Ps 46:t 5961

ALARM {10}
When ye blow an a, then the camps .... Num 10:5 8643
When ye blow an a the second time .... Num 10:6 8643
blow an a for their journeys .... Num 10:6 8643
blow, but ye shall not sound an a .... Num 10:7 7321
shall blow an a with the trumpets .... Num 10:9 7321
trumpets to cry a against you 2Chr 13:12 7321
of the trumpet, the a of war .... Jer 4:19 8643
that I will cause an a of war to .... Jer 49:2 8643
sound an a in my holy mountain .... Joel 2:1 7321
a against the fenced cities, and .... Zeph 1:16 8643

ALAS See APPENDIX.

ALBEIT {2}
a I have not spoken .... Eze 13:7
a I do not say to thee how thou .... Philem 19 *2443*

ALEMETH *(al-e'-meth)* {3}
1. A Levitical city in Benjamin.
A with her suburbs, and Anathoth 1Chr 6:60 5964
2. A descendant of Jonathan.
and Jehoadah begat A, and Azmaveth, ... 1Chr 8:36 5964
Jarah begat A, and Azmaveth, and 1Chr 9:42 5964

ALEXANDER *(al-ex-an'-dur)* {6}
1. Son of Simeon who bore Jesus' cross.
of the country, the father of A .... Mk 15:21 *223*
2. A Christian leader in Jerusalem.
and Caiaphas, and John, and A .... Acts 4:6 *223*
3. A participant in the Ephesian riot.
they drew A out of the multitude, ... Acts 19:33 *223*
A beckoned with the hand, and .... Acts 19:33 *223*
4. An opponent of Paul.
Of whom is Hymenaeus and A 1Ti 1:20
A the coppersmith did me much 2Ti 4:14 *223*

ALEXANDRIA *(al-ex-an'-dree-ah)* {3} See ALEXANDRIANS. *A city in Egypt.*
Jew named Apollos, born at A .... Acts 18:24 *221*
a ship of A sailing into Italy .... Acts 27:6 *221*
months we departed in a ship of A .... Acts 28:11 *221*

ALEXANDRIAN See ALEXANDRIA.

ALEXANDRIANS *(al-ex-an'-dree-uns)* {1} *Residents of Alexandria.*
Libertines, and Cyrenians, and A .... Acts 6:9 *221*

ALGUM {3}
trees, and a trees, out of Lebanon 2Chr 2:8 418
gold from Ophir, brought a trees 2Chr 9:10 418
the king made of the a trees 2Chr 9:11 418

ALIAH *(a-li'-ah)* {1} See ALVAH. *A chief of Edom.*
duke Timnah, duke A, duke Jetheth 1Chr 1:51 5933

ALIAN *(a-li'-un)* {1} See ALVAN. *A son of Shobal.*
A, and Manahath, and Ebal, Shephi, ... 1Chr 1:40 5935

ALIEN {5}
I have been an a in a strange .... Ex 18:3 1616
or thou mayest sell it unto an a .... Deut 14:21 5237
I am an a in their sight .... Job 19:15 5237
an a unto my mother's children .... Ps 69:8 5237
the sons of the a shall be your .... Is 61:5 5236

ALIENATE {1}
nor a the firstfruits of the land .... Eze 48:14 5674

ALIENATED {7}
them, and her mind was a from them ..... Eze 23:17 3363
then my mind was a from her .... Eze 23:18 3363
as my mind was a from her sister .... Eze 23:18 5361
thee, from whom thy mind is a .... Eze 23:22 5361
of them from whom thy mind is a .... Eze 23:28 5361
being a from the life of God .... Eph 4:18 *526*
And you, that were sometime a .... Col 1:21 *526*

ALIENS {3}
to strangers, our houses to a .... Lam 5:2 5237
being a from the commonwealth of .... Eph 2:12 *526*
to flight the armies of the a .... Heb 11:34 *245*

ALIKE See APPENDIX.

ALIVE {88}
the ark, to keep them *a* with thee ... Gen 6:19 2421
come unto thee, to keep them *a* ... Gen 6:20 2421
to keep seed *a* upon the face of ... Gen 7:3 2421
and Noah only remained *a*, and they ... Gen 7:23
me, but they will save thee *a* ... Gen 12:12 2421
saying, Is your father yet *a* ... Gen 43:7 2416
Is he yet *a* ... Gen 43:27 2416
is in good health, he is yet *a* ... Gen 43:28 2416
told him, saying, Joseph is yet *a* ... Gen 45:26 2416
Joseph my son is yet *a* ... Gen 45:28 2416
thy face, because thou art yet *a* ... Gen 46:30 2416
this day, to save much people *a* ... Gen 50:20 2421
but saved the men children *a* ... Ex 1:17 2421
and have saved the men children *a* ... Ex 1:18 2421
and every daughter ye shall save *a* ... Ex 1:22 2421
and see whether they be yet *a* ... Ex 4:18 2416
be certainly found in his hand *a* ... Ex 22:4
sons of Aaron which were left *a* ... Lev 10:16
is to be cleansed two birds *a* ... Lev 14:4 2416
be presented *a* before the LORD ... Lev 16:10 2416
upon them that are left *a* of you ... Lev 26:36
went down *a* into the pit, and the ... Num 16:33 2416
until there was none left him *a* ... Num 21:35 8300
I had slain thee, and saved her *a* ... Num 22:33 2421
Have ye saved all the women *a* ... Num 31:15 2421
with him, keep *a* for yourselves ... Num 31:18 2421
are *a* every one of you this day ... Deut 4:4 2416
who are all of us here *a* this day ... Deut 5:3 2416
that he might preserve us *a* ... Deut 6:24 2421
thou shalt save *a* nothing that ... Deut 20:16 2421
while I am yet *a* with you this ... Deut 31:27 2416
I kill, and I make *a* ... Deut 32:39 2421
And that ye will save *a* my father ... Josh 2:13 2421
Joshua saved Rahab the harlot *a* ... Josh 6:25 2421
And the king of Ai they took *a* ... Josh 8:23 2416
behold, the LORD hath kept me *a* ... Josh 14:10 2421
liveth, if ye had saved them *a* ... Judg 8:19 2421
a of the women of Jabesh-gilead ... Judg 21:14 2421
The LORD killeth, and maketh *a* ... 1Sa 2:6 2421
Agag the king of the Amalekites *a* ... 1Sa 15:8 2416
and left neither man nor woman *a* ... 1Sa 27:9 2421
saved neither man nor woman *a* ... 1Sa 27:11 2421
and with one full line to keep *a* ... 2Sa 8:2 2421
Behold, while the child was yet *a* ... 2Sa 12:18 2416
for the child, while it was *a* ... 2Sa 12:21 2416
said, While the child was yet *a* ... 2Sa 12:22 2416
while he was yet *a* in the midst ... 2Sa 18:14 2416
to save the horses and mules *a* ... 1Kin 18:5 2421
come out for peace, take them *a* ... 1Kin 20:18 2416
be come out for war, take them *a* ... 1Kin 20:18 2416
And he said, Is he yet *a* ... 1Kin 20:32 2416
for Naboth is not *a*, but dead ... 1Kin 21:15 2416
Am I God, to kill and to make *a* ... 2Kin 5:7 2421
if they save us *a*, we shall live ... 2Kin 7:4 2421
the city, we shall catch them *a* ... 2Kin 7:12 2416
And he said, Take them *a* ... 2Kin 10:14 2416
And they took them *a*, and slew them ... 2Kin 10:14 2416
other ten thousand left *a* did the ... 2Chr 25:12 2416
and none can keep *a* his own soul ... Ps 22:29 2421
thou hast kept me *a*, that I ... Ps 30:3 2421
and to keep them *a* in famine ... Ps 33:19 2421
will preserve him, and keep him *a* ... Ps 41:2 2421
us swallow them up *a* as the grave ... Prov 1:12 2416
than the living which are yet *a* ... Eccl 4:2 2416
children, I will preserve them *a* ... Jer 49:11 2421
is sold, although they were yet *a* ... Eze 7:13 2416
the souls *a* that come unto you ... Eze 13:18 2421
to save the souls *a* that should ... Eze 13:19 2421
right, he shall save his soul *a* ... Eze 18:27 2421
and whom he would he kept *a* ... Dan 5:19 2418
deceiver said, while he was yet *a* ... Mt 27:63 *2198*
when they had heard that he was *a* ... Mk 16:11 *2198*
my son was dead, and is *a* again ... Lk 15:24 *326*
brother was dead, and is *a* again ... Lk 15:32 *326*
angels, which said that he was *a* ... Lk 24:23 *2198*
a after his passion by many ... Acts 1:3 *2198*
saints and widows, presented her *a* ... Acts 9:41 *2198*
And they brought the young man *a* ... Acts 20:12 *2198*
dead, whom Paul affirmed to be *a* ... Acts 25:19 *2198*
but *a* unto God through Jesus ... Rom 6:11 *2198*
as those that are *a* from the dead ... Rom 6:13 *2198*
For I was *a* without the law once ... Rom 7:9 *2198*
so in Christ shall all be made *a* ... 1Cor 15:22 *2227*
of the Lord, that we which are *a* ... 1Th 4:15 *2198*
Then we which are *a* and remain ... 1Th 4:17 *2198*
I am *a* for evermore, Amen ... Rev 1:18 *2198*
the last, which was dead, and is *a* ... Rev 2:8 *2198*
These both were cast *a* into a ... Rev 19:20 *2198*

ALL See APPENDIX.

ALLAMMELECH See ALAMMELECH.

ALLEGING {1}
Opening and *a*, that Christ must ... Acts 17:3 *3908*

ALLEGORY {1}
Which things are an *a* ... Gal 4:24 *238*

ALLELUIA *(al-le-loo'-yah)* {4} *Greek form of Hallelujah.*
much people in heaven, saying, *A* ... Rev 19:1 *239*
And again they said, *A* ... Rev 19:3 *239*
saying, Amen; *A* ... Rev 19:4 *239*
of mighty thunderings, saying, *A* ... Rev 19:6 *239*

ALLIED {1}
of our God, was *a* unto Tobiah ... Neh 13:4 7138

ALLON *(al'-lon)* {2} See ALLON-BACHUTH, ELON.
1. A city in Naphtali.
from *A* to Zaanannim, and Adami, ... Josh 19:33 438
2. A chief of a Simeonite family.
the son of Shiphi, the son of *A* ... 1Chr 4:37 438

ALLON-BACHUTH *(al'-lon-bak'-ooth)* {1} *A place near Bethel.*
and the name of it was called *A* ... Gen 35:8 439

ALLOW {3}
ye *a* the deeds of your fathers ... Lk 11:48 *4909*
God, which they themselves also *a* ... Acts 24:15 *4327*
For that which I do I *a* not ... Rom 7:15 *1097*

ALLOWANCE {2}
his *a* was a continual *a* ... 2Kin 25:30 737

ALLOWED {1}
But as we were *a* of God to be put ... 1Th 2:4 *1381*

ALLOWETH {1}
himself in that thing which he *a* ... Rom 14:22 *1381*

ALLURE {2}
Therefore, behold, I will *a* her ... Hos 2:14 6601
they *a* through the lusts of the ... 2Pet 2:18 *1185*

ALMIGHTY {57} *A term for God meaning sufficient or all-powerful.*
and said unto him, I am the *A* God ... Gen 17:1 7706
God *A* bless thee, and make thee ... Gen 28:3 7706
And God said unto him, I am God *A* ... Gen 35:11 7706
God *A* give you mercy before the ... Gen 43:14 7706
God *A* appeared unto me at Luz in ... Gen 48:3 7706
and by the *A*, who shall bless thee ... Gen 49:25 7706
unto Jacob, by the name of God *A* ... Ex 6:3 7706
which saw the vision of the *A* ... Num 24:4 7706
which saw the vision of the *A* ... Num 24:16 7706
for the *A* hath dealt very ... Ruth 1:20 7706
me, and the *A* hath afflicted me ... Ruth 1:21 7706
not thou the chastening of the *A* ... Job 5:17 7706
the arrows of the *A* are within me ... Job 6:4 7706
he forsaketh the fear of the *A* ... Job 6:14 7706
or doth the *A* pervert justice ... Job 8:3 7706
and make thy supplication to the *A* ... Job 8:5 7706
find out the *A* unto perfection ... Job 11:7 7706
Surely I would speak to the *A* ... Job 13:3 7706
himself against the *A* ... Job 15:25 7706
What is the *A*, that we should ... Job 21:15 7706
shall drink of the wrath of the *A* ... Job 21:20 7706
Is it any pleasure to the *A* ... Job 22:3 7706
and what can the *A* do for them ... Job 22:17 7706
If thou return to the *A*, thou ... Job 22:23 7706
the *A* shall be thy defence, and ... Job 22:25 7706
thou have thy delight in the *A* ... Job 22:26 7706
heart soft, and the *A* troubleth me ... Job 23:16 7706
times are not hidden from the *A* ... Job 24:1 7706
and the *A*, who hath vexed my soul ... Job 27:2 7706
Will he delight himself in the *A* ... Job 27:10 7706
is with the *A* will I not conceal ... Job 27:11 7706
which they shall receive of the *A* ... Job 27:13 7706
When the *A* was yet with me, when ... Job 29:5 7706
inheritance of the *A* from on high ... Job 31:2 7706
that the *A* would answer me, and ... Job 31:35 7706
the inspiration of the *A* giveth ... Job 32:8 7706
the breath of the *A* hath given me ... Job 33:4 7706
and from the *A*, that he should ... Job 34:10 7706
will the *A* pervert judgment ... Job 34:12 7706
neither will the *A* regard it ... Job 35:13 7706
Touching the *A*, we cannot find ... Job 37:23 7706
with the *A* instruct him ... Job 40:2 7706
When the *A* scattered kings in it ... Ps 68:14 7706
abide under the shadow of the *A* ... Ps 91:1 7706
come as a destruction from the *A* ... Is 13:6 7706
waters, as the voice of the *A* ... Eze 1:24 7706
as the voice of the *A* God when he ... Eze 10:5 7706
from the *A* shall it come ... Joel 1:15 7706
and daughters, saith the Lord *A* ... 2Cor 6:18 *3841*
was, and which is to come, the *A* ... Rev 1:8 *3841*
Holy, holy, holy, Lord God *A* ... Rev 4:8 *3841*
We give thee thanks, O Lord God *A* ... Rev 11:17 *3841*
are thy works, Lord God *A* ... Rev 15:3 *3841*
altar say, Even so, Lord God *A* ... Rev 16:7 *3841*
battle of that great day of God *A* ... Rev 16:14 *3841*
the fierceness and wrath of *A* God ... Rev 19:15 *3841*
for the Lord God *A* and the Lamb ... Rev 21:22 *3841*

ALMODAD *(al-mo'-dad)* {2} *A descendant of Shem.*
And Joktan begat *A*, and Sheleph, and ... Gen 10:26 486
And Joktan begat *A*, and Sheleph, and ... 1Chr 1:20 486

ALMON *(al'-mon)* {1} *A Levitical town in Benjamin.*
suburbs, and *A* with her suburbs ... Josh 21:18 5960

ALMOND {2}
the *a* tree shall flourish, and the ... Eccl 12:5 8247
I said, I see a rod of an *a* tree ... Jer 1:11 8247

ALMON-DIBLATHAIM *(al'-mon-dib-lath-a'-im)* {2} *An encampment of Israel in the Wilderness.*
from Dibon-gad, and encamped in *A* ... Num 33:46 5963
And they removed from *A*, and ... Num 33:47 5963

ALMONDS {8}
spices, and myrrh, nuts, and *a* ... Gen 43:11 8247
Three bowls made like unto *a* ... Ex 25:33 8246
made like *a* in the other branch ... Ex 25:33 8246
be four bowls made like unto *a* ... Ex 25:34 8246
the fashion of *a* in one branch ... Ex 37:19 8246
made like *a* in another branch ... Ex 37:19 8246
were four bowls made like *a* ... Ex 37:20 8246
and bloomed blossoms, and yielded *a* ... Num 17:8 8247

ALMOST See APPENDIX.

ALMS {13}
that ye do not your *a* before men ... Mt 6:1 *1654*
Therefore when thou doest thine *a* ... Mt 6:2 *1654*
But when thou doest *a*, let not ... Mt 6:3 *1654*
That thine *a* may be in secret ... Mt 6:4 *1654*
But rather give *a* of such things ... Lk 11:41 *1654*
Sell that ye have, and give *a* ... Lk 12:33 *1654*
to ask *a* of them that entered ... Acts 3:2 *1654*
to go into the temple asked an *a* ... Acts 3:3 *1654*
a at the Beautiful gate of the ... Acts 3:10 *1654*
which gave much *a* to the people ... Acts 10:2 *1654*
thine *a* are come up for a ... Acts 10:4 *1654*
thine *a* are had in remembrance in ... Acts 10:31 *1654*
I came to bring *a* to my nation ... Acts 24:17 *1654*

ALMSDEEDS {1}
of good works and *a* which she did ... Acts 9:36 *1654*

ALMUG {3}
Ophir great plenty of *a* trees ... 1Kin 10:11 484
the king made of the *a* trees ... 1Kin 10:12 484
there came no such *a* trees ... 1Kin 10:12 484

ALOES {5}
as the trees of lign *a* which the ... Num 24:6 174
thy garments smell of myrrh, and *a* ... Ps 45:8 174
perfumed my bed with myrrh, *a* ... Prov 7:17 174
myrrh and *a*, with all the chief ... Song 4:14 174
brought a mixture of myrrh and *a* ... Jn 19:39 *250*

ALONE See APPENDIX.

ALONG See APPENDIX.

ALOOF {1}
my friends stand *a* from my sore ... Ps 38:11 5048

ALOTH *(a'-loth)* {1} See BEALOTH. *A region near Asher.*
of Hushai was in Asher and in *A* ... 1Kin 4:16 1175

ALOUD {20}
And he wept *a* ... Gen 45:2 5414,854,6963
mocked them, and said, Cry *a* ... 1Kin 18:27 6963,1419
And they cried *a*, and cut ... 1Kin 18:28 1419,3605
and many shouted *a* for joy ... Ezr 3:12 7311,1419
I cry *a*, but there is no judgment ... Job 19:7 7768
shall sing *a* of thy righteousness ... Ps 51:14 7442
and at noon, will I pray, and cry *a* ... Ps 55:17 1993
I will sing *a* of thy mercy in the ... Ps 59:16 7442
Sing *a* unto God our strength ... Ps 81:1 7442
her saints shall shout *a* for joy ... Ps 132:16 7442
let them sing *a* upon their beds ... Ps 149:5 7442
they shall cry *a* from the sea ... Is 24:14 6670
forth into singing, and cry *a* ... Is 54:1 6670
Cry *a*, spare not, lift up thy ... Is 58:1 1627
Then an herald cried *a*, To you it ... Dan 3:4 2429
He cried *a*, and said thus, Hew ... Dan 4:14 2429
The king cried *a* to bring in the ... Dan 5:7 2429
cry *a* at Beth-aven, after thee, O ... Hos 5:8 7321
Now why dost thou cry out *a* ... Mic 4:9 7452
the multitude crying *a* began to ... Mk 15:8 *310*

ALPHA *(al'-fah)* {4} *First letter of Greek alphabet.*
I am *A* and Omega, the beginning ... Rev 1:8 *1*
Saying, I am *A* and Omega, the ... Rev 1:11 *1*
I am *A* and Omega, the beginning ... Rev 21:6 *1*
I am *A* and Omega, the beginning ... Rev 22:13 *1*

ALPHAEUS *(al-fe'-us)* {5} See CLEOPAS.
1. Father of the apostle James.
James the son of *A*, and Lebbaeus, ... Mt 10:3 *256*
and Thomas, and James the son of *A* ... Mk 3:18 *256*
and Thomas, James the son of *A* ... Lk 6:15 *256*
and Matthew, James the son of *A* ... Acts 1:13 *256*
2. Father of the apostle Levi.
he saw Levi the son of *A* sitting ... Mk 2:14 *256*

ALREADY See APPENDIX.

ALSO See APPENDIX.

ALTAR {378}
Noah builded an *a* unto the LORD ... Gen 8:20 4196
offered burnt offerings on the *a* ... Gen 8:20 4196
builded he an *a* unto the LORD ... Gen 12:7 4196
he builded an *a* unto the LORD ... Gen 12:8 4196
Unto the place of the *a*, which he ... Gen 13:4 4196
and built there an *a* unto the LORD ... Gen 13:18 4196
and Abraham built an *a* there ... Gen 22:9 4196
laid him on the *a* upon the wood ... Gen 22:9 4196
And he builded an *a* there, and ... Gen 26:25 4196
And he erected there an *a*, and ... Gen 33:20 4196
and make there an *a* unto God ... Gen 35:1 4196
I will make there an *a* unto God ... Gen 35:3 4196
And he built there an *a*, and called ... Gen 35:7 4196
And Moses built an *a*, and called ... Ex 17:15 4196
An *a* of earth thou shalt make ... Ex 20:24 4196
thou wilt make me an *a* of stone ... Ex 20:25 4196
thou go up by steps unto mine *a* ... Ex 20:26 4196
thou shalt take him from mine *a* ... Ex 21:14 4196
builded an *a* under the hill, and ... Ex 24:4 4196
the blood he sprinkled on the *a* ... Ex 24:6 4196
shalt make an *a* of shittim wood ... Ex 27:1 4196
the *a* shall be foursquare ... Ex 27:1 4196
the compass of the *a* beneath ... Ex 27:5 4196
may be even to the midst of the *a* ... Ex 27:5 4196
thou shalt make staves for the *a* ... Ex 27:6 4196
be upon the two sides of the *a* ... Ex 27:7 4196
a to minister in the holy place ... Ex 28:43 4196
horns of the *a* with thy finger ... Ex 29:12 4196
blood beside the bottom of the *a* ... Ex 29:12 4196
them, and burn them upon the *a* ... Ex 29:13 4196
it round about upon the *a* ... Ex 29:16 4196
burn the whole ram upon the *a* ... Ex 29:18 4196
the blood upon the *a* round about ... Ex 29:20 4196
of the blood that is upon the *a* ... Ex 29:21 4196
burn them upon the *a* for a burnt ... Ex 29:25 4196

and thou shalt cleanse the *a* Ex 29:36 4196
shalt make an atonement for the *a* Ex 29:37 4196
and it shall be an *a* most holy Ex 29:37 4196
toucheth the *a* shall be holy Ex 29:37 4196
which thou shalt offer upon the *a* Ex 29:38 4196
of the congregation, and the *a* Ex 29:44 4196
thou shalt make an *a* to burn Ex 30:1 4196
of the congregation and the *a* Ex 30:18 4196
come near to the *a* to minister Ex 30:20 4196
his vessels, and the *a* of incense, Ex 30:27 4196
the *a* of burnt offering with all Ex 30:28 4196
furniture, and the *a* of incense, Ex 31:8 4196
the *a* of burnt offering with all Ex 31:9 4196
saw it, he built an *a* before it Ex 32:5 4196
And the incense *a*, and his staves, Ex 35:15 4196
The *a* of burnt offering, with his Ex 35:16 4196
the incense *a* of shittim wood Ex 37:25 4196
he made the *a* of burnt offering Ex 38:1 4196
he made all the vessels of the *a* Ex 38:3 4196
he made for the *a* a brasen grate Ex 38:4 4196
the rings on the sides of the *a* Ex 38:7 4196
he made the *a* hollow with boards Ex 38:7
the congregation, and the brasen *a* Ex 38:30 4196
it, and all the vessels of the *a* Ex 38:30 4196
And the golden *a*, and the anointing Ex 39:38 4196
The brasen *a*, and his grate of Ex 39:39 4196
thou shalt set the *a* of gold for Ex 40:5 4196
thou shalt set the *a* of the burnt Ex 40:6 4196
tent of the congregation and the *a* Ex 40:7 4196
the *a* of the burnt offering Ex 40:10 4196
his vessels, and sanctify the *a* Ex 40:10 4196
and it shall be an *a* most holy Ex 40:10 4196
he put the golden *a* in the tent Ex 40:26 4196
he put the *a* of burnt offering by Ex 40:29 4196
tent of the congregation and the *a* Ex 40:30 4196
and when they came near unto the *a* Ex 40:32 4196
about the tabernacle and the *a* Ex 40:33 4196
the *a* that is by the door of the Lev 1:5 4196
priest shall put fire upon the *a* Lev 1:7 4196
on the fire which is upon the *a* Lev 1:8 4196
priest shall burn all on the *a* Lev 1:9 4196
the *a* northward before the LORD Lev 1:11 4196
his blood round about upon the *a* Lev 1:11 4196
on the fire which is upon the *a* Lev 1:12 4196
it all, and burn it upon the *a* Lev 1:13 4196
priest shall bring it unto the *a* Lev 1:15 4196
off his head, and burn it on the *a* Lev 1:15 4196
be wrung out at the side of the *a* Lev 1:15 4196
it beside the *a* on the east part Lev 1:16 4196
priest shall burn it upon the *a* Lev 1:17 4196
the memorial of it upon the *a* Lev 2:2 4196
he shall bring it unto the *a* Lev 2:8 4196
and shall burn it upon the *a* Lev 2:9 4196
burnt on the *a* for a sweet savour Lev 2:12 4196
the blood upon the *a* round about Lev 3:2 4196
on the *a* upon the burnt sacrifice Lev 3:5 4196
thereof round about upon the *a* Lev 3:8 4196
priest shall burn it upon the *a* Lev 3:11 4196
thereof upon the *a* round about Lev 3:13 4196
priest shall burn them upon the *a* Lev 3:16 4196
the *a* of sweet incense before the Lev 4:7 4196
of the *a* of the burnt offering Lev 4:7 4196
upon the *a* of the burnt offering Lev 4:10 4196
of the *a* which is before the LORD Lev 4:18 4196
of the *a* of the burnt offering Lev 4:18 4196
from him, and burn it upon the *a* Lev 4:19 4196
horns of the *a* of burnt offering Lev 4:25 4196
bottom of the *a* of burnt offering Lev 4:25 4196
shall burn all his fat upon the *a* Lev 4:26 4196
horns of the *a* of burnt offering Lev 4:30 4196
thereof at the bottom of the *a* Lev 4:30 4196
the *a* for a sweet savour unto the Lev 4:31 4196
horns of the *a* of burnt offering Lev 4:34 4196
thereof at the bottom of the *a* Lev 4:34 4196
priest shall burn them upon the *a* Lev 4:35 4196
offering upon the side of the *a* Lev 5:9 4196
wrung out at the bottom of the *a* Lev 5:9 4196
thereof, and burn it on the *a* Lev 5:12 4196
the *a* all night unto the morning Lev 6:9 4196
the fire of the *a* shall be Lev 6:9 4196
with the burnt offering on the *a* Lev 6:10 4196
and he shall put them beside the *a* Lev 6:10 4196
the fire upon the *a* shall be Lev 6:12 4196
shall ever be burning upon the *a* Lev 6:13 4196
it before the LORD, before the *a* Lev 6:14 4196
it upon the *a* for a sweet savour Lev 6:15 4196
sprinkle round about upon the *a* Lev 7:2 4196
a for an offering made by fire Lev 7:5 4196
shall burn the fat upon the *a* Lev 7:31 4196
thereof upon the *a* seven times Lev 8:11 4196
seven times, and anointed the *a* Lev 8:11 4196
the *a* round about with his finger Lev 8:15 4196
his finger, and purified the *a* Lev 8:15 4196
the blood at the bottom of the *a* Lev 8:15 4196
and Moses burned it upon the *a* Lev 8:16 4196
the blood upon the *a* round about Lev 8:19 4196
burnt the whole ram upon the *a* Lev 8:21 4196
the blood upon the *a* round about Lev 8:24 4196
burnt them on the *a* upon the Lev 8:28 4196
of the blood which was upon the *a* Lev 8:30 4196
said unto Aaron, Go unto the *a* Lev 9:7 4196
Aaron therefore went unto the *a* Lev 9:8 4196
and put it upon the horns of the *a* Lev 9:9 4196
the blood at the bottom of the *a* Lev 9:9 4196
sin offering, he burnt upon the *a* Lev 9:10 4196
sprinkled round about upon the *a* Lev 9:12 4196
and he burnt them upon the *a* Lev 9:13 4196
upon the burnt offering on the *a* Lev 9:14 4196

thereof, and burnt it upon the *a* Lev 9:17 4196
sprinkled upon the *a* round about Lev 9:18 4196
and he burnt the fat upon the *a* Lev 9:20 4196
consumed upon the *a* the burnt Lev 9:24 4196
it without leaven beside the *a* Lev 10:12 4196
and the meat offering upon the *a* Lev 14:20 4196
from off the *a* before the LORD Lev 16:12 4196
the *a* that is before the LORD Lev 16:18 4196
the horns of the *a* round about Lev 16:18 4196
of the congregation, and the *a* Lev 16:20 4196
offering shall he burn upon the *a* Lev 16:25 4196
of the congregation, and for the *a* Lev 16:33 4196
sprinkle the blood upon the *a* of Lev 17:6 4196
a to make an atonement for your Lev 17:11 4196
vail, nor come nigh unto the *a* Lev 21:23 4196
of them upon the *a* unto the LORD Lev 22:22 4196
by the *a* round about, and the Num 3:26 4196
upon the golden *a* they shall Num 4:11 4196
take away the ashes from the *a* Num 4:13 4196
basons, all the vessels of the *a* Num 4:14 4196
by the *a* round about, and their Num 4:26 4196
the LORD, and offer it upon the *a* Num 5:25 4196
thereof, and burn it upon the *a* Num 5:26 4196
instruments thereof, both the *a* Num 7:1 4196
offered for dedicating of the *a* Num 7:10 4196
their offering before the *a* Num 7:10 4196
day, for the dedicating of the *a* Num 7:11 4196
This was the dedication of the *a* Num 7:84 4196
This was the dedication of the *a* Num 7:88 4196
plates for a covering of the *a* Num 16:38 4196
plates for a covering of the *a* Num 16:39 4196
put fire therein from off the *a* Num 16:46 4196
vessels of the sanctuary and the *a* Num 18:3 4196
sanctuary, and the charge of the *a* Num 18:5 4196
office for every thing of the *a* Num 18:7 4196
sprinkle their blood upon the *a* Num 18:17 4196
offered on every *a* a bullock Num 23:2 4196
offered upon every *a* a bullock Num 23:4 4196
a bullock and a ram on every *a* Num 23:14 4196
a bullock and a ram on every *a* Num 23:30 4196
upon the *a* of the LORD thy God Deut 12:27 4196
upon the *a* of the LORD thy God Deut 12:27 4196
unto the *a* of the LORD thy God Deut 16:21 4196
before the *a* of the LORD thy God Deut 26:4 4196
there shalt thou build an *a* Deut 27:5 4196
the LORD thy God, an *a* of stones Deut 27:5 4196
Thou shalt build the *a* of the Deut 27:6 4196
burnt sacrifice upon thine *a* Deut 33:10 4196
Then Joshua built an *a* unto the Josh 8:30 4196
an *a* of whole stones, over which Josh 8:31 4196
for the *a* of the LORD, even unto Josh 9:27 4196
a by Jordan, a great *a* Josh 22:10 4196
a over against the land of Canaan Josh 22:11 4196
in that ye have builded you an *a* Josh 22:16 4196
an *a* beside the *a* of the LORD Josh 22:19 4196
That we have built us an *a* to Josh 22:23 4196
us now prepare to build us an *a* Josh 22:26 4196
the pattern of the *a* of the LORD Josh 22:28 4196
to build an *a* for burnt offerings Josh 22:29 4196
beside the *a* of the LORD our God Josh 22:29 4196
children of Gad called the *a* Ed Josh 22:34 4196
built an *a* there unto the LORD Judg 6:24 4196
throw down the *a* of Baal that thy Judg 6:25 4196
build an *a* unto the LORD thy God Judg 6:26 4196
the *a* of Baal was cast down, and Judg 6:28 4196
offered upon the *a* that was built Judg 6:28 4196
he hath cast down the *a* of Baal Judg 6:30 4196
because one hath cast down his *a* Judg 6:31 4196
because he hath thrown down his *a* Judg 6:32 4196
up toward heaven from off the *a* Judg 13:20 4196
ascended in the flame of the *a* Judg 13:20 4196
rose early, and built there an *a* Judg 21:4 4196
my priest, to offer upon mine *a* 1Sa 2:28 4196
I shall not cut off from mine *a* 1Sa 2:33 4196
there he built an *a* unto the LORD 1Sa 7:17 4196
And Saul built an *a* unto the LORD 1Sa 14:35 4196
the same was the first *a* that he 1Sa 14:35 4196
rear an *a* unto the LORD in the 2Sa 24:18 4196
to build an *a* unto the LORD, that 2Sa 24:21 4196
built there an *a* unto the LORD 2Sa 24:25 4196
caught hold on the horns of the *a* 1Kin 1:50 4196
caught hold on the horns of the *a* 1Kin 1:51 4196
they brought him down from the *a* 1Kin 1:53 4196
caught hold on the horns of the *a* 1Kin 2:28 4196
and, behold, he is by the *a* 1Kin 2:29 4196
did Solomon offer upon that *a* 1Kin 3:4 4196
so covered the *a* which was of 1Kin 6:20 4196
also the whole *a* that was by the 1Kin 6:22 4196
the *a* of gold, and the table of 1Kin 7:48 4196
Solomon stood before the *a* of the 1Kin 8:22 4196
come before thine *a* in this house 1Kin 8:31 4196
from before the *a* of the LORD 1Kin 8:54 4196
because the brasen *a* that was 1Kin 8:64 4196
peace offerings upon the *a* which 1Kin 9:25 4196
the *a* that was before the LORD 1Kin 9:25 4196
Judah, and he offered upon the *a* 1Kin 12:32 4196
So he offered upon the *a* which he 1Kin 12:33 4196
and he offered upon the *a*, and 1Kin 12:33 4196
stood by the *a* to burn incense 1Kin 13:1 4196
he cried against the *a* in the 1Kin 13:2 4196
of the LORD, and said, O *a*, *a*, 1Kin 13:2 4196
the *a* shall be rent, and the ashes 1Kin 13:3 4196
cried against the *a* in Beth-el 1Kin 13:4 4196
he put forth his hand from the *a* 1Kin 13:4 4196
The *a* also was rent 1Kin 13:5 4196
the ashes poured out from the *a* 1Kin 13:5 4196
the LORD against the *a* in Beth-el 1Kin 13:32 4196
he reared up an *a* for Baal in the 1Kin 16:32 4196

leaped upon the *a* which was made 1Kin 18:26 4196
he repaired the *a* of the LORD 1Kin 18:30 4196
an *a* in the name of the LORD 1Kin 18:32 4196
and he made a trench about the *a* 1Kin 18:32 4196
the water ran round about the *a* 1Kin 18:35 4196
of the temple, along by the *a* 2Kin 11:11 4196
lid of it, and set it beside the *a* 2Kin 12:9 4196
saw an *a* that was at Damascus 2Kin 16:10 4196
the priest the fashion of the *a* 2Kin 16:10 4196
Urijah the priest built an *a* 2Kin 16:11 4196
from Damascus, the king saw the *a* 2Kin 16:12 4196
and the king approached to the *a* 2Kin 16:12 4196
his peace offerings, upon the *a* 2Kin 16:13 4196
And he brought also the brasen *a* 2Kin 16:14 4196
of the house, from between the *a* 2Kin 16:14 4196
put it on the north side of the *a* 2Kin 16:14 4196
Upon the great *a* burn the morning 2Kin 16:15 4196
the brasen *a* shall be for me to 2Kin 16:15 4196
before this *a* in Jerusalem 2Kin 18:22 4196
to the *a* of the LORD in Jerusalem 2Kin 23:9 4196
Moreover the *a* that was at 2Kin 23:15 4196
to sin, had made, both that *a* 2Kin 23:15 4196
and burned them upon the *a* 2Kin 23:16 4196
done against the *a* of Beth-el 2Kin 23:17 4196
upon the *a* of the burnt offering 1Chr 6:49 4196
on the *a* of incense, and were 1Chr 6:49 4196
upon the *a* of the burnt offering 1Chr 16:40 4196
set up an *a* unto the LORD in the 1Chr 21:18 4196
that I may build an *a* therein 1Chr 21:22 4196
built there an *a* unto the LORD 1Chr 21:26 4196
fire upon the *a* of burnt offering 1Chr 21:26 4196
the *a* of the burnt offering, were 1Chr 21:29 4196
this is the *a* of the burnt 1Chr 22:1 4196
for the *a* of incense refined gold 1Chr 28:18 4196
Moreover the brasen *a*, that 2Chr 1:5 4196
to the brasen *a* before the LORD 2Chr 1:6 4196
Moreover he made an *a* of brass 2Chr 4:1 4196
house of God, the golden *a* also 2Chr 4:19 4196
stood at the east end of the *a* 2Chr 5:12 4196
he stood before the *a* of the LORD 2Chr 6:12 4196
come before thine *a* in this house 2Chr 6:22 4196
because the brasen *a* which 2Chr 7:7 4196
dedication of the *a* seven days 2Chr 7:9 4196
the LORD on the *a* of the LORD 2Chr 8:12 4196
and renewed the *a* of the LORD 2Chr 15:8 4196
of the temple, along by the *a* 2Chr 23:10 4196
incense upon the *a* of incense 2Chr 26:16 4196
LORD, from beside the incense *a* 2Chr 26:19 4196
the *a* of burnt offering, with all 2Chr 29:18 4196
they are before the *a* of the LORD 2Chr 29:19 4196
offer them on the *a* of the LORD 2Chr 29:21 4196
blood, and sprinkled it on the *a* 2Chr 29:22 4196
sprinkled the blood upon the *a* 2Chr 29:22 4196
sprinkled the blood upon the *a* 2Chr 29:22 4196
with their blood upon the *a* 2Chr 29:24 4196
the burnt offering upon the *a* 2Chr 29:27 4196
Ye shall worship before one *a* 2Chr 32:12 4196
And he repaired the *a* of the LORD 2Chr 33:16 4196
offerings upon the *a* of the LORD 2Chr 35:16 4196
builded the *a* of the God of Ezr 3:2 4196
they set the *a* upon his bases Ezr 3:3 4196
offer them upon the *a* of the Ezr 7:17 4056
to burn upon the *a* of the LORD Neh 10:34 4196
so will I compass thine *a* Ps 26:6 4196
Then will I go unto the *a* of God Ps 43:4 4196
they offer bullocks upon thine *a* Ps 51:19 4196
even unto the horns of the *a* Ps 118:27 4196
with the tongs from off the *a* Is 6:6 4196
In that day shall there be an *a* Is 19:19 4196
a as chalkstones that are beaten Is 27:9 4196
Ye shall worship before this *a* Is 36:7 4196
shall be accepted upon mine *a* Is 56:7 4196
come up with acceptance on mine *a* Is 60:7 4196
The Lord hath cast off his *a* Lam 2:7 4196
northward at the gate of the *a* Eze 8:5 4196
LORD, between the porch and the *a* Eze 8:16 4196
in, and stood beside the brasen *a* Eze 9:2 4196
keepers of the charge of the *a* Eze 40:46 4196
the *a* that was before the house Eze 40:47 4196
The *a* of wood was three cubits Eze 41:22 4196
of the *a* after the cubits Eze 43:13 4196
be the higher place of the *a* Eze 43:13 4196
So the *a* shall be four cubits Eze 43:15 741
and from the *a* and upward shall be Eze 43:15 741
the *a* shall be twelve cubits long Eze 43:16 741
a in the day when they shall make Eze 43:18 4196
and they shall cleanse the *a* Eze 43:22 4196
Seven days shall they purge the *a* Eze 43:26 4196
your burnt offerings upon the *a* Eze 43:27 4196
corners of the settle of the *a* Eze 45:19 4196
house, at the south side of the *a* Eze 47:1 4196
howl, ye ministers of the *a* Joel 1:13 4196
weep between the porch and the *a* Joel 2:17 4196
clothes laid to pledge by every *a* Amos 2:8 4196
horns of the *a* shall be cut off Amos 3:14 4196
saw the Lord standing upon the *a* Amos 9:1 4196
bowls, and as the corners of the *a* Zec 9:15 4196
be like the bowls before the *a* Zec 14:20 4196
offer polluted bread upon mine *a* Mal 1:7 4196
kindle fire on mine *a* for nought Mal 1:10 4196
covering the *a* of the LORD with Mal 2:13 4196
if thou bring thy gift to the *a* Mt 5:23 *2379*
Leave there thy gift before the *a* Mt 5:24 *2379*
Whosoever shall swear by the *a* Mt 23:18 *2379*
or the *a* that sanctifieth the Mt 23:19 *2379*
therefore shall swear by the *a* Mt 23:20 *2379*
slew between the temple and the *a* Mt 23:35 *2379*
right side of the *a* of incense Lk 1:11 *2379*

which perished between the a Lk 11:51 2379
devotions, I found an a with this Acts 17:23 1041
a are partakers with the a 1Cor 9:13 2379
the sacrifices partakers of the a 1Cor 10:18 2379
no man gave attendance at the a Heb 7:13 2379
We have an a, whereof they have Heb 13:10 2379
offered Isaac his son upon the a Jas 2:21 2379
I saw under the a the souls of Rev 6:9 2379
angel came and stood at the a Rev 8:3 2379
a which was before the throne Rev 8:3 2379
and filled it with fire of the a Rev 8:5 2379
the golden a which is before God Rev 9:13 2379
the temple of God, and the a Rev 11:1 2379
another angel came out from the a Rev 14:18 2379
I heard another out of the a say Rev 16:7 2379

ALTARS {55}
But ye shall destroy their a Ex 34:13 4196
and the candlestick, and the a Num 3:31 4196
unto Balak, Build me here seven a Num 23:1 4196
unto him, I have prepared seven a Num 23:4 4196
top of Pisgah, and built seven a Num 23:14 4196
unto Balak, Build me here seven a Num 23:29 4196
ye shall destroy their a, and Deut 7:5 4196
And ye shall overthrow their a Deut 12:3 4196
ye shall throw down their a Judg 2:2 4196
thy covenant, thrown down thine a 1Kin 19:10 4196
thy covenant, thrown down thine a 1Kin 19:14 4196
his a and his images brake they in 2Kin 11:18 4196
the priest of Baal before the a 2Kin 11:18 4196
whose a Hezekiah hath taken away, 2Kin 18:22 4196
and he reared up a for Baal 2Kin 21:3 4196
he built a in the house of the 2Kin 21:4 4196
he built a for all the host of 2Kin 21:5 4196
the a that were on the top of the 2Kin 23:12 4196
the a which Manasseh had made in 2Kin 23:12 4196
places that were there upon the a 2Kin 23:20 4196
away the a of the strange gods 2Chr 14:3 4196
and brake it down, and brake his a 2Chr 23:17 4196
the priest of Baal before the a 2Chr 23:17 4196
he made him a in every corner of 2Chr 28:24 4196
took away the a that were in 2Chr 30:14 4196
all the a for incense took they 2Chr 30:14
the a out of all Judah and 2Chr 31:1 4196
away his high places and his a 2Chr 32:12 4196
and he reared up a for Baalim 2Chr 33:3 4196
Also he built a in the house of 2Chr 33:4 4196
he built a for all the host of 2Chr 33:5 4196
all the a that he had built in 2Chr 33:15 4196
they brake down the a of Baalim 2Chr 34:4 4196
bones of the priests upon their a 2Chr 34:5 4196
And when he had broken down the a 2Chr 34:7 4196
may lay her young, even thine a Ps 84:3 4196
And he shall not look to the a Is 17:8 4196
whose a Hezekiah hath taken away, Is 36:7 4196
burneth incense upon a of brick Is 65:3
set up a to that shameful thing Jer 11:13 4196
even a to burn incense unto Baal Jer 11:13 4196
and upon the horns of your a Jer 17:1 4196
their children remember their a Jer 17:2 4196
your a shall be desolate, and your Eze 6:4 4196
your bones round about your a Eze 6:5 4196
that your a may be laid waste and Eze 6:6 4196
their idols round about their a Eze 6:13 4196
Ephraim hath made many a to sin Hos 8:11 4196
a shall be unto him to sin Hos 8:11 4196
his fruit he hath increased the a Hos 10:1 4196
he shall break down their a Hos 10:2 4196
thistle shall come up on their a Hos 10:8 4196
their a are as heaps in the Hos 12:11 4196
will also visit the a of Beth-el Amos 3:14 4196
prophets, and digged down thine a Rom 11:3 2379

ALTASCHITH {4}
To the chief Musician, A, Michtam Ps 57:t 516
To the chief Musician, A, Michtam Ps 58:t 516
To the chief Musician, A, Michtam Ps 59:t 516
To the chief Musician, A, A Psalm Ps 75:t 516

AL-TASHHETH See ALTASCHITH.

ALTER {4}
He shall not a it, nor change it, Lev 27:10 2498
that whosoever shall a this word Ezr 6:11 8133
that shall put to their hand to a Ezr 6:12 8133
nor a the thing that is gone out Ps 89:34 8138

ALTERED {2}
and the Medes, that it be not a Est 1:19 5674
fashion of his countenance was a Lk 9:29 1096,2087

ALTERETH {2}
Medes and Persians, which a not Dan 6:8 5709
Medes and Persians, which a not Dan 6:12 5709

ALTHOUGH See APPENDIX.

ALTOGETHER See APPENDIX.

ALUSH *(a'-lush)* {2} *An Israelite encampment during the Exodus.*
from Dophkah, and encamped in A Num 33:13 442
And they removed from A, and Num 33:14 442

ALVAH *(al'-vah)* {1} See ALIAH. *An Edomite chief.*
duke Timnah, duke A, duke Jetheth Gen 36:40 5933

ALVAN *(al'-van)* {1} See ALIAN. *A son of Shobal the Horite.*
A, and Manahath, and Ebal, Shepho, Gen 36:23 5935

ALWAY {23}
the table shewbread before me a Ex 25:30 8548
So it was a Num 9:16 8548
and his commandments, a Deut 11:1 3605,3117
be only oppressed and crushed a Deut 28:33 3605,3117
son shall eat bread a at my table 2Sa 9:10 8548
a light a before me in Jerusalem 1Kin 11:36 3605,3117
him to give him a a light 2Kin 8:19 3605,3117
I would not live a Job 7:16 5769
needy shall not a be forgotten Ps 9:18 5331
heart to perform thy statutes a Ps 119:112 5769
Happy is the man that feareth a Prov 28:14 8548
and, lo, I am with you a, even Mt 28:20 3956,2250
but your time is a ready Jn 7:6 3842
to the people, and prayed to God a Acts 10:2 1275
not see, and bow down their back a Rom 11:10 1275
For we which live are a delivered 2Cor 4:11 104
As sorrowful, yet a rejoicing 2Cor 6:10 104
Rejoice in the Lord a Phil 4:4 104
Let your speech be a with grace Col 4:6 104
be saved, to fill up their sins a 1Th 2:16 104
to give thanks a to God for you 2Th 2:13 104
said, The Cretians are a liars Titus 1:12 104
They do a err in their heart Heb 3:10 104

ALWAYS {62}
shall not a strive with man Gen 6:3 5769
to cause the lamp to burn a Ex 27:20 8548
it shall be a upon his forehead, Ex 28:38 8548
keep all my commandments a Deut 5:29 3605,3117
the LORD our God, for our good a Deut 6:24 3605,3117
of the LORD thy God are a upon it Deut 11:12 8548
learn to fear the LORD thy God a Deut 14:23 3605,3117
Be ye mindful a of his covenant 1Chr 16:15 5769
good unto me, but a evil 2Chr 18:7 3605,3117
will he a call upon God Job 27:10 3605,6256
Great men are not a wise Job 32:9
His ways are a grievous Ps 10:5 3605,6256
I have set the LORD a before me Ps 16:8 8548
He will not a chide Ps 103:9 5331
be thou ravished a with her love Prov 5:19 8548
delight, rejoicing a before him Prov 8:30 3605,6256
Let thy garments be a white Eccl 9:8 3605,6256
ever, neither will I be a wroth Is 57:16 5331
and her womb to be a great with me Jer 20:17 5769
Israel, which have been a waste Eze 38:8 8548
a behold the face of my Father Mt 18:10 1223,3956
For ye have the poor a with you Mt 26:11 3842
but me ye have not a Mt 26:11 3842
And a, night and day, he was in the Mk 5:5 1275
For ye have the poor with you a Mk 14:7 3842
but me ye have not a Mk 14:7 3842
end, that men ought a to pray Lk 18:1 3842
ye therefore, and pray a Lk 21:36 1722,3956,2540
for I do a those things that Jn 8:29 3842
And I knew that thou hearest me a Jn 11:42 3842
For the poor a ye have with you Jn 12:8 3842
but me ye have not a Jn 12:8 3842
temple, whither the Jews a resort Jn 18:20 3842
the Lord a before my face Acts 2:25 1223,3956
ye do a resist the Holy Ghost Acts 7:51 104
We accept it a, and in all places, Acts 24:3 3839
to have a a conscience void of Acts 24:16 1275
mention of you a in my prayers Rom 1:9 3842
I thank my God a on your behalf 1Cor 1:4 3842
a abounding in the work of the 1Cor 15:58 3842
which a causeth us to triumph in 2Cor 2:14 3842
A bearing about in the body the 2Cor 4:10 3842
Therefore we are a confident 2Cor 5:6 3842
a having all sufficiency in all 2Cor 9:8 3842
affected a in a good thing Gal 4:18 3842
Giving thanks a for all things Eph 5:20 3842
Praying a with all prayer and Eph 6:18 1722,3956,2540
A in every prayer of mine for you Phil 1:4 3842
but that with all boldness, as a Phil 1:20 3842
my beloved, as ye have a obeyed Phil 2:12 3842
Jesus Christ, praying a for you Col 1:3 3842
a labouring fervently for you in Col 4:12 3842
give thanks to God a for you all 1Th 1:2 3842
ye have good remembrance of us a 1Th 3:6 3842
are bound to thank God a for you 2Th 1:3 3842
Wherefore also we pray a for you 2Th 1:11 3842
give you peace a by all means 2Th 3:16 1223,3956
mention of thee a in my prayers Philem 4 3842
the priests went a into the first Heb 9:6 1275
be ready a to give an answer to 1Pet 3:15 104
not be negligent to put you a in 2Pet 1:12 104
these things a in remembrance 2Pet 1:15 1539

AM See APPENDIX.

AMAD *(a'-mad)* {1} *A town on the border of Asher.*
And Alammelech, and A, and Misheal Josh 19:26 6008

AMAL *(a'-mal)* {1} *A descendant of Asher.*
and Imna, and Shelesh, and A 1Chr 7:35 6000

AMALEK *(am'-al-ek)* {24} See AMALEKITE.
1. The son of Eliphaz.
and she bare to Eliphaz A Gen 36:12 6002
Duke Korah, duke Gatam, and duke A Gen 36:16 6002
and Gatam, Kenaz, and Timna, and A 1Chr 1:36 6002
2. Descendants of Amalek.
Then came A, and fought with Ex 17:8 6002
out men, and go out, fight with A Ex 17:9 6002
had said to him, and fought with A Ex 17:10 6002
he let down his hand, A prevailed Ex 17:11 6002
And Joshua discomfited A and his Ex 17:13 6002
of A from under heaven Ex 17:14 6002
the LORD will have war with A Ex 17:16 6002
And when he looked on A, he took Num 24:20 6002
A was the first of the nations Num 24:20 6002
Remember what A did unto thee by Deut 25:17 6002
of A from under heaven Deut 25:19 6002
him the children of Ammon and A Judg 3:13 6002
there a root of them against A Judg 5:14 6002
that which A did to Israel 1Sa 15:2 6002
Now go and smite A, and utterly 1Sa 15:3 6002
And Saul came to a city of A 1Sa 15:5 6002
have brought Agag the king of A 1Sa 15:20 6002
his fierce wrath upon A, 1Sa 28:18 6002
and of the Philistines, and of A 2Sa 8:12 6002
from the Philistinesand, from A 1Chr 18:11 6002
Gebal, and Ammon, and A Ps 83:7 6002

AMALEKITE *(am'-al-ek-ite)* {3} See AMALEKITES. *A descendant of Amalek.*
man of Egypt, servant to an A 1Sa 30:13 6003
And I answered him, I am an A 2Sa 1:8 6003
I am the son of a stranger, an A 2Sa 1:13 6003

AMALEKITES *(am'-al-ek-ites)* {24}
and smote all the country of the A Gen 14:7 6003
The A dwell in the land of the Num 13:29 6003
(Now the A and the Canaanites Num 14:25 6003
For the A and the Canaanites are Num 14:43 6003
Then the A came down, and the Num 14:45 6003
the Midianites came up, and the A Judg 6:3 6003
Then all the Midianites and the A Judg 6:33 6003
And the Midianites and the A Judg 7:12 6003
The Zidonians also, and the A Judg 10:12 6003
of Ephraim, in the mount of the A Judg 12:15 6003
gathered an host, and smote the A 1Sa 14:48 6003
get you down from among the A 1Sa 15:6 6003
Kenites departed from among the A 1Sa 15:6 6003
Saul smote the A from Havilah 1Sa 15:7 6003
took Agag the king of the A alive 1Sa 15:8 6003
They have brought them from the A 1Sa 15:15 6003
utterly destroy the sinners the A 1Sa 15:18 6003
and have utterly destroyed the A 1Sa 15:20 6003
to me Agag the king of the A 1Sa 15:32 6003
and the Gezrites, and the A 1Sa 27:8 6003
that the A had invaded the south, 1Sa 30:1 6003
all that the A had carried away 1Sa 30:18 6003
from the slaughter of the A 2Sa 1:1 6003
rest of the A that were escaped 1Chr 4:43 6003

AMAM *(a'-mam)* {1} *A city near Shema and Moladah.*
A, and Shema, and Moladah, Josh 15:26 538

AMANA *(am-a'-nah)* {1} *A city in southern Judah.*
look from the top of A, from the Song 4:8 549

AMARIAH *(am-a-ri'-ah)* {15}
1. A descendant of Aaron.
begat A, and A begat Ahitub, 1Chr 6:7 568
A his son, Ahitub his son, 1Chr 6:52 568
The son of A, the son of Azariah, Ezr 7:3 568
2. A High Priest during Solomon's reign.
begat Amariah, and A begat Ahitub, 1Chr 6:11 568
3. A descendant of Kohath.
A the second, Jahaziel the third, 1Chr 23:19 568
A the second, Jahaziel the third, 1Chr 24:23 568
4. Chief priest during Jehoshaphat's reign.
A the chief priest is over you in 2Chr 19:11 568
5. A Levite in Hezekiah's time.
and Jeshua, and Shemaiah, A 2Chr 31:15 568
6. Married a foreign wife in exile.
Shallum, A, and Joseph Ezr 10:42 568
7. A priest who sealed the covenant with Nehemiah.
Pashur, A, Malchijah, Neh 10:3 568
A, Malluch, Hattush, Neh 12:2 568
of A, Jehohanan Neh 12:13 568
8. A descendant of Judah.
son of Zechariah, the son of A Neh 11:4 568
9. An ancestor of Zephaniah the prophet.
the son of Gedaliah, the son of A Zeph 1:1 568

AMASA *(am'-a-sah)* {16}
1. David's nephew.
Absalom made A captain of the 2Sa 17:25 6021
which A was a man's son, whose 2Sa 17:25 6021
And say ye to A, Art thou not of 2Sa 19:13 6021
Then said the king to A, Assemble 2Sa 20:4 6021
So A went to assemble the men of 2Sa 20:5 6021
is in Gibeon, A went before them 2Sa 20:8 6021
And Joab said to A, Art thou in 2Sa 20:9 6021
And Joab took A, by the beard with 2Sa 20:9 6021
But A took no heed to the sword 2Sa 20:10 6021
A wallowed in blood in the midst 2Sa 20:12 6021
he removed A out of the highway 2Sa 20:12 6021
unto A the son of Jether, whom he 1Kin 2:5 6021
A the son of Jether, captain of 1Kin 2:32 6021
And Abigail bare A 1Chr 2:17 6021
the father of A was Jether the 1Chr 2:17 6021
2. An Ephraimite who opposed the slavery of the Jews.
A the son of Hadlai, stood up 2Chr 28:12 6021

AMASAI *(am'-as-ahee)* {5}
l. A descendant of Kohath.
A, and Ahimoth 1Chr 6:25 6022
the son of Mahath, the son of A 1Chr 6:35 6022
arose, Mahath the son of A 2Chr 29:12 6022
2. A captain in David's army.
Then the spirit came upon A 1Chr 12:18 6022
3. A Levite who helped relocate the Ark.
Jehoshaphat, and Nethaneel, and A 1Chr 15:24 6022

AMASHAI *(am'-ash-ahee)* {1} *A priest of the Emmer family.*
A the son of Azareel, the son of Neh 11:13 6023

AMASHSAI See AMASHI.

AMASIAH *(am-a-si'-ah)* {1} *Chief captain of Jehoshaphat's army.*
next him was A the son of Zichri, 2Chr 17:16 6007

AMAZED {21}
Then the dukes of Edom shall be a Ex 15:15 926
again, the men of Benjamin were a Judg 20:41 926

They were a, they answered no ... Job 32:15 2865
they shall be a one at another ... Is 13:8 8539
I will make many people a at thee ... Eze 32:10 8074
And all the people were a, and said ... Mt 12:23 1839
heard it, they were exceedingly a ... Mt 19:25 1605
And they were all a, insomuch that ... Mk 1:27 2284
insomuch that they were all a ... Mk 2:12 1839
they were sore a in themselves ... Mk 6:51 1839
they beheld him, were greatly a ... Mk 9:15 1568
and they were a ... Mk 10:32 2284
and John, and began to be sore a ... Mk 14:33 1568
for they trembled and were a ... Mk 16:8 1611
And when they saw him, they were a ... Lk 2:48 1605
And they were all a, and spake ... Lk 4:36 1096,2285
And they were all a, and they ... Lk 5:26 1611,2983
they were all a at the mighty ... Lk 9:43 1605
And they were all a and marvelled, ... Acts 2:7 1839
And they were all a, and were in ... Acts 2:12 1839
But all that heard him were a ... Acts 9:21 1839

AMAZEMENT {2}
a at that which had happened unto ... Acts 3:10 1611
and are not afraid with any a ... 1Pet 3:6 4423

AMAZIAH *(am-a-zi'-ah)* {40}
1. Son and successor of King Joash of Judah.
A his son reigned in his stead ... 2Kin 12:21 558
he fought against A king of Judah ... 2Kin 13:12 558
A the son of Joash king of Judah ... 2Kin 14:1 558
Then A sent messengers to Jehoash ... 2Kin 14:8 558
of Israel sent to A king of Judah ... 2Kin 14:9 558
But A would not hear ... 2Kin 14:11 558
A king of Judah looked one ... 2Kin 14:11 558
of Israel took A king of Judah ... 2Kin 14:13 558
he fought with A king of Judah ... 2Kin 14:15 558
A the son of Joash king of Judah ... 2Kin 14:17 558
And the rest of the acts of A ... 2Kin 14:18 558
him king instead of his father A ... 2Kin 14:21 558
In the fifteenth year of A the ... 2Kin 14:23 558
son of A king of Judah to reign ... 2Kin 15:1 558
to all that his father A had done ... 2Kin 15:3 558
A his son, Azariah his son, ... 1Chr 3:12 558
A his son reigned in his stead ... 2Chr 24:27 558
A was twenty and five years old ... 2Chr 25:1 558
Moreover A gathered Judah ... 2Chr 25:5 558
A said to the man of God, But ... 2Chr 25:9 558
Then A separated them, to wit, ... 2Chr 25:10 558
A strengthened himself, and led ... 2Chr 25:11 558
of the army which A sent back ... 2Chr 25:13 558
after that A was come from the ... 2Chr 25:14 558
of the LORD was kindled against A ... 2Chr 25:15 558
Then A king of Judah took advice, ... 2Chr 25:17 558
of Israel sent to A king of Judah ... 2Chr 25:18 558
But A would not hear ... 2Chr 25:20 558
A king of Judah, at Beth-shemesh, ... 2Chr 25:21 558
of Israel took A king of Judah ... 2Chr 25:23 558
A the son of Joash king of Judah ... 2Chr 25:25 558
Now the rest of the acts of A ... 2Chr 25:26 558
Now after the time that A did ... 2Chr 25:27 558
king in the room of his father A ... 2Chr 26:1 558
to all that his father A did ... 2Chr 26:4 558
2. A Simeonite.
Jamlech, and Joshah the son of A ... 1Chr 4:34 558
3. A Levite from the Merari family.
son of Hashabiah, the son of A ... 1Chr 6:45 558
4. Priest of the idols at Bethel.
Then A the priest of Beth-el sent ... Amos 7:10 558
Also A said unto Amos, O thou ... Amos 7:12 558
Then answered Amos, and said to A ... Amos 7:14 558

AMBASSADOR {4}
but a faithful a is health ... Prov 13:17 6735
an a is sent unto the heathen, ... Jer 49:14 6735
an a is sent among the heathen, ... Obad 1 6735
For which I am an a in bonds ... Eph 6:20 4243

AMBASSADORS {8}
and made as if they had been a ... Josh 9:4 6735
the a of the princes of Babylon ... 2Chr 32:31 3887
But he sent a to him, saying, ... 2Chr 35:21 4397
That sendeth a by the sea ... Is 18:2 6735
at Zoan, and his a came to Hanes ... Is 30:4 4397
the a of peace shall weep ... Is 33:7 4397
him in sending his a into Egypt ... Eze 17:15 4397
Now then we are a for Christ ... 2Cor 5:20 4243

AMBASSAGE {1}
a great way off, he sendeth an a ... Lk 14:32 4242

AMBER {3}
midst thereof as the colour of a ... Eze 1:4 2830
And I saw as the colour of a ... Eze 1:27 2830
of brightness, as the colour of a ... Eze 8:2 2830

AMBUSH {7}
lay thee an a for the city behind ... Josh 8:2 693
Then ye shall rise up from the a ... Josh 8:7 693
and they went to lie in a, and ... Josh 8:9 693
them to lie in a between Beth-el ... Josh 8:12 693
in a against him behind the city ... Josh 8:14 693
the a arose quickly out of their ... Josh 8:19 693
saw that the a had taken the city ... Josh 8:21 693

AMBUSHES {1}
up the watchmen, prepare the a ... Jer 51:12 693

AMBUSHMENT {2}
But Jeroboam caused an a to come ... 2Chr 13:13 3993
Judah, and the a was behind them ... 2Chr 13:13 3993

AMBUSHMENTS {1}
the LORD set a against the ... 2Chr 20:22 693

AMEN {78}
1. A term meaning "so be it."
And the woman shall say, A, a ... Num 5:22 543
the people shall answer and say, A ... Deut 27:15 543
and all the people shall say, A ... Deut 27:16 543
And all the people shall say, A ... Deut 27:17 543
And all the people shall say, A ... Deut 27:18 543
And all the people shall say, A ... Deut 27:19 543
And all the people shall say, A ... Deut 27:20 543
And all the people shall say, A ... Deut 27:21 543
And all the people shall say, A ... Deut 27:22 543
And all the people shall say, A ... Deut 27:23 543
And all the people shall say, A ... Deut 27:24 543
And all the people shall say, A ... Deut 27:25 543
And all the people shall say, A ... Deut 27:26 543
answered the king, and said, A ... 1Kin 1:36 543
And all the people said, A ... 1Chr 16:36 543
And all the congregation said, A ... Neh 5:13 543
all the people answered, A, A ... Neh 8:6 543
A, and A ... Ps 41:13 543
A, and A ... Ps 72:19 543
A, and A ... Ps 89:52 543
and let all the people say, A ... Ps 106:48 543
Even the prophet Jeremiah said, A ... Jer 28:6 543
and the glory, for ever. A ... Mt 6:13 281
the end of the world. A ... Mt 28:20 281
with signs following. A ... Mk 16:20 281
praising and blessing God. A ... Lk 24:53 281
that should be written. A ... Jn 21:25 281
who is blessed for ever. A ... Rom 1:25 281
God blessed for ever. A ... Rom 9:5 281
to whom be glory for ever. A ... Rom 11:36 281
peace be with you all. A ... Rom 15:33 281
Jesus Christ be with you. A ... Rom 16:20 281
Jesus Christ be with you all. A ... Rom 16:24 281
through Jesus Christ for ever. A ... Rom 16:27 281
say A at thy giving of thanks ... 1Cor 14:16 281
with you all in Christ Jesus. A ... 1Cor 16:24 281
God in him are yea, and in him A ... 2Cor 1:20 281
Holy Ghost, be with you all. A ... 2Cor 13:14 281
be glory for ever and ever. A ... Gal 1:5 281
Christ be with your spirit. A ... Gal 6:18 281
all ages, world without end. A ... Eph 3:21 281
Lord Jesus Christ in sincerity. A ... Eph 6:24 281
be glory for ever and ever. A ... Phil 4:20 281
Jesus Christ be with you all. A ... Phil 4:23 281
Grace be with you. A ... Col 4:18 281
Jesus Christ be with you. A ... 1Th 5:28 281
Jesus Christ be with you all. A ... 2Th 3:18 281
glory for ever and ever. A ... 1Ti 1:17 281
honour and power everlasting. A ... 1Ti 6:16 281
Grace be with thee. A ... 1Ti 6:21 281
be glory for ever and ever. A ... 2Ti 4:18 281
Grace be with you. A ... 2Ti 4:22 281
Grace be with you all. A ... Titus 3:15 281
Christ be with your spirit. A ... Philem 25 281
be glory for ever and ever. A ... Heb 13:21 281
Grace be with you all. A ... Heb 13:25 281
dominion for ever and ever. A ... 1Pet 4:11 281
dominion for ever and ever. A ... 1Pet 5:11 281
all that are in Christ Jesus. A ... 1Pet 5:14 281
glory both now and for ever. A ... 2Pet 3:18 281
keep yourselves from idols. A ... 1Jn 5:21 281
thy elect sister greet thee. A ... 2Jn 13 281
power, both now and ever. A ... Jude 25 281
dominion for ever and ever. A ... Rev 1:6 281
Even so, A ... Rev 1:7 281
I am alive for evermore, A ... Rev 1:18 281
And the four beasts said, A ... Rev 5:14 281
Saying, A: Blessing, and glory ... Rev 7:12 281
our God for ever and ever. A ... Rev 7:12 281
sat on the throne, saying, A; ... Rev 19:4 281
Surely I come quickly. A ... Rev 22:20 281
Jesus Christ be with you all. A ... Rev 22:21 281
2. A title of Christ.
These things saith the A, the ... Rev 3:14 281

AMEND {6}
LORD, to repair and a the house ... 2Chr 34:10 2388
A your ways and your doings, and I ... Jer 7:3 3190
For if ye throughly a your ways ... Jer 7:5 3190
Therefore now a your ways ... Jer 26:13 3190
a your doings, and go not after ... Jer 35:15 3190
the hour when he began to a ... Jn 4:52 2192,2866

AMENDS {1}
he shall make a for the harm that ... Lev 5:16 7999

AMERCE {1}
they shall a him in an hundred ... Deut 22:19 6064

AMETHYST {3}
row a ligure, an agate, and an a ... Ex 28:19 306
row, a ligure, an agate, and an a ... Ex 39:12 306
the twelfth, an a ... Rev 21:20 271

AMI *(a'-mi)* {1} *A family of returned exiles.*
of Zebaim, the children of A ... Ezr 2:57 532

AMIABLE {1}
How a are thy tabernacles, O LORD ... Ps 84:1 3039

AMINADAB *(a-min'-a-dab)* {3} See AMMINADAB. *Son of Aram; ancestor of Jesus.*
And Aram begat A ... Mt 1:4 284
and A begat Naasson ... Mt 1:4 284
Which was the son of A, which was ... Lk 3:33 284

AMISS {4}
We have sinned, we have done a ... 2Chr 6:37 5753
which speak any thing a against ... Dan 3:29 7955
but this man hath done nothing a ... Lk 23:41 824
and receive not, because ye ask a ... Jas 4:3 2560

AMITTAI *(a-mit'-tahee)* {2} *Father of Jonah.*
his servant Jonah, the son of A ... 2Kin 14:25 573
LORD came unto Jonah the son of A ... Jonah 1:1 573

AMMAH *(am'-mah)* {1} See METHEG-AMMAH. *A hill near Gibeon.*
they were come to the hill of A ... 2Sa 2:24 522

AMMI *(am'-mi)* {1} See AMMI-NADIB, BEN-AMMI, LO-AMMI. *A name given to Israel by Hosea meaning "my people."*
Say ye unto your brethren, A ... Hos 2:1 5971

AMMIEL *(am'-me-el)* {6} See ELIAM.
1. A spy for Moses.
of Dan, A the son of Gemalli ... Num 13:12 5988
2. A Manassehite of Lodebar.
the house of Machir, the son of A ... 2Sa 9:4 5988
the house of Machir, the son of A ... 2Sa 9:5 5988
Machir the son of A of Lo-debar ... 2Sa 17:27 5988
3. Father of a wife of David.
of Bath-shua the daughter of A ... 1Chr 3:5 5988
4. A Levite Tabernacle servant.
A the sixth, Issachar the seventh ... 1Chr 26:5 5988

AMMIHUD *(am-mi'-hud)* {10}
1. Father of Elishama.
Elishama the son of A ... Num 1:10 5989
shall be Elishama the son of A ... Num 2:18 5989
seventh day Elishama the son of A ... Num 7:48 5989
offering of Elishama the son of A ... Num 7:53 5989
host was Elishama the son of A ... Num 10:22 5989
A his son, Elishama his son, ... 1Chr 7:26 5989
2. A Simeonite.
of Simeon, Shemuel the son of A ... Num 34:20 5989
3. A Naphtalite.
of Naphtali, Pedahel the son of A ... Num 34:28 5989
4. Father of the king of Geshur.
and went to Talmai, the son of A ... 2Sa 13:37 5989
5. A son of Omri.
Uthai the son of A, the son of ... 1Chr 9:4 5989

AMMINADAB *(am-min'-a-dab)* {13} See AMINADAB, AMMI-NADIB.
1. Aaron's father-in-law.
took him Elisheba, daughter of A ... Ex 6:23 5992
2. A prince of Judah.
Nahshon the son of A ... Num 1:7 5992
Nahshon the son of A shall be ... Num 2:3 5992
day was Nahshon the son of A ... Num 7:12 5992
offering of Nahshon the son of A ... Num 7:17 5992
his host was Nahshon the son of A ... Num 10:14 5992
Hezron begat Ram, and Ram begat A ... Ruth 4:19 5992
A begat Nahshon, and Nahshon begat ... Ruth 4:20 5992
And Ram begat A ... 1Chr 2:10 5992
A begat Nahshon, prince of the ... 1Chr 2:10 5992
3. A son of Kohath.
A his son, Korah his son, Assir ... 1Chr 6:22 5992
4. A Levite who relocated the Ark.
A the chief, and his brethren an ... 1Chr 15:10 5992
and Joel, Shemaiah, and Eliel, and A ... 1Chr 15:11 5992

AMMI-NADIB {1}
made me like the chariots of A ... Song 6:12 5993

AMMISHADDAI *(am-mi-shad'-dahee)* {5} *Father of the chief of the tribe of Dan.*
Ahiezer the son of A ... Num 1:12 5996
Dan shall be Ahiezer the son of A ... Num 2:25 5996
tenth day Ahiezer the son of A ... Num 7:66 5996
offering of Ahiezer the son of A ... Num 7:71 5996
his host was Ahiezer the son of A ... Num 10:25 5996

AMMIZABAD *(am-miz'-a-bad)* {1} *Son of a captain of David.*
and in his course was A his son ... 1Chr 27:6 5990

AMMON *(am'-mon)* {91} *Territory in Jordan.*
the children of A unto this day ... Gen 19:38 5983
even unto the children of A ... Num 21:24 5983
of the children of A was strong ... Num 21:24 5983
over against the children of A ... Deut 2:19 5983
the children of A any possession ... Deut 2:19 5983
the children of A thou camest not ... Deut 2:37 5983
in Rabbath of the children of A ... Deut 3:11 5983
the border of the children of A ... Deut 3:16 5983
the border of the children of A ... Josh 12:2 5983
the border of the children of A ... Josh 13:10 5983
the land of the children of A ... Josh 13:25 5983
unto him the children of A ... Judg 3:13 5983
and the gods of the children of A ... Judg 10:6 5983
the hands of the children of A ... Judg 10:7 5983
Moreover the children of A passed ... Judg 10:9 5983
Amorites, from the children of A ... Judg 10:11 5983
Then the children of A were ... Judg 10:17 5983
fight against the children of A ... Judg 10:18 5983
that the children of A made war ... Judg 11:4 5983
of A made war against Israel ... Judg 11:5 5983
may fight with the children of A ... Judg 11:6 5983
fight against the children of A ... Judg 11:8 5983
fight against the children of A ... Judg 11:9 5983
the king of the children of A ... Judg 11:12 5983
the king of the children of A ... Judg 11:13 5983
the king of the children of A ... Judg 11:14 5983
nor the land of the children of A ... Judg 11:15 5983
of Israel and the children of A ... Judg 11:27 5983
the king of the children of A ... Judg 11:28 5983
over unto the children of A ... Judg 11:29 5983
the children of A into mine hands ... Judg 11:30 5983
in peace from the children of A ... Judg 11:31 5983
of A to fight against them ... Judg 11:32 5983
Thus the children of A were ... Judg 11:33 5983
even of the children of A ... Judg 11:36 5983
fight against the children of A ... Judg 12:1 5983

strife with the children of A ... Judg 12:2 5983
over against the children of A ... Judg 12:3 5983
children of A came against you ... 1Sa 12:12 5983
and against the children of A ... 1Sa 14:47 5983
of Moab, and of the children of A ... 2Sa 8:12 5983
king of the children of A died ... 2Sa 10:1 5983
the land of the children of A ... 2Sa 10:2 5983
of A said unto Hanun their lord ... 2Sa 10:3 5983
when the children of A saw that ... 2Sa 10:6 5983
David, the children of A sent ... 2Sa 10:6 5983
And the children of A came out ... 2Sa 10:8 5983
array against the children of A ... 2Sa 10:10 5983
of A be too strong for thee ... 2Sa 10:11 5983
when the children of A saw that ... 2Sa 10:14 5983
returned from the children of A ... 2Sa 10:14 5983
help the children of A any more ... 2Sa 10:19 5983
they destroyed the children of A ... 2Sa 11:1 5983
the sword of the children of A ... 2Sa 12:9 5983
Rabbah of the children of A ... 2Sa 12:26 5983
the cities of the children of A ... 2Sa 12:31 5983
of Rabbah of the children of A ... 2Sa 17:27 5983
abomination of the children of A ... 1Kin 11:7 5983
the god of the children of A ... 1Kin 11:33 5983
abomination of the children of A ... 2Kin 23:13 5983
and bands of the children of A ... 2Kin 24:2 5983
Moab, and from the children of A ... 1Chr 18:11 5983
king of the children of A died ... 1Chr 19:1 5983
of the children of A to Hanun ... 1Chr 19:2 5983
the children of A said to Hanun ... 1Chr 19:3 5983
when the children of A saw that ... 1Chr 19:6 5983
the children of A sent a thousand ... 1Chr 19:6 5983
the children of A gathered ... 1Chr 19:7 5983
And the children of A came out ... 1Chr 19:9 5983
array against the children of A ... 1Chr 19:11 5983
of A be too strong for thee ... 1Chr 19:12 5983
when the children of A saw that ... 1Chr 19:15 5983
help the children of A any more ... 1Chr 19:19 5983
the country of the children of A ... 1Chr 20:1 5983
the cities of the children of A ... 1Chr 20:3 5983
of Moab, and the children of A ... 2Chr 20:1 5983
And now, behold, the children of A ... 2Chr 20:10 5983
against the children of A ... 2Chr 20:22 5983
For the children of A and Moab ... 2Chr 20:23 5983
the children of A gave him the ... 2Chr 27:5 5983
the children of A pay unto him ... 2Chr 27:5 5983
had married wives of Ashdod, of A ... Neh 13:23 5983
Gebal, and A, and Amalek ... Ps 83:7 5983
the children of A shall obey them ... Is 11:14 5983
and Edom, and the children of A ... Jer 9:26 5983
and Moab, and the children of A ... Jer 25:21 5983
captivity of the children of A ... Jer 49:6 5983
and the chief of the children of A ... Dan 11:41 5983
of the children of A, and for four ... Amos 1:13 5983
revilings of the children of A ... Zeph 2:8 5983
and the children of A as Gomorrah ... Zeph 2:9 5983

AMMONITE *(am'-mon-ite)* {9} See AMMONITES, AMMONITESS. *A descendant of Ammon.*
An A or Moabite shall not enter ... Deut 23:3 5984
Then Nahash the A came up ... 1Sa 11:1 5984
Nahash the A answered them, On ... 1Sa 11:2 5984
Zelek the A, Nahari the ... 2Sa 23:37 5984
Zelek the A, Naharai the ... 1Chr 11:39 5984
and Tobiah the servant, the A ... Neh 2:10 5984
and Tobiah the servant, the A ... Neh 2:19 5984
Now Tobiah the A was by him ... Neh 4:3 5984
was found written, that the A ... Neh 13:1 5984

AMMONITES *(am'-mon-ites)* {23}
the A call them Zamzummims ... Deut 2:20 5984
slew the A until the heat of the ... 1Sa 11:11 5984
Pharaoh, women of the Moabites, A ... 1Kin 11:1 5984
Milcom the abomination of the A ... 1Kin 11:5 5984
and with them other beside the A ... 2Chr 20:1 5984
the A gave gifts to Uzziah ... 2Chr 26:8 5984
also with the king of the A ... 2Chr 27:5 5984
Perizzites, the Jebusites, the A ... Ezr 9:1 5984
Tobiah, and the Arabians, and the A ... Neh 4:7 5984
of Moab, and to the king of the A ... Jer 27:3 5984
that were in Moab, and among the A ... Jer 40:11 5984
that Baalis the king of the A ... Jer 40:14 5984
and departed to go over to the A ... Jer 41:10 5984
with eight men, and went to the A ... Jer 41:15 5984
Concerning The A, thus saith the ... Jer 49:1 5984
to be heard in Rabbah of the A ... Jer 49:2 5984
may come to Rabbah of the A ... Eze 21:20 1121,5984
the Lord GOD concerning the A ... Eze 21:28 1121,5984
man, set thy face against the A ... Eze 25:2 1121,5984
say unto the A, Hear the word ... Eze 25:3 1121,5984
the A a couchingplace for flocks ... Eze 25:5 1121,5984
the men of the east with the A ... Eze 25:10 1121,5984
the A may not be remembered ... Eze 25:10 1121,5984

AMMONITESS *(am'-mon-i-tess)* {4}
his mother's name was Naamah an A ... 1Kin 14:21 5984
his mother's name was Naamah an A ... 1Kin 14:31 5984
his mother's name was Naamah an A ... 2Chr 12:13 5984
Zabad the son of Shimeath an A ... 2Chr 24:26 5984

AMNON *(am'-non)* {25} See AMNON'S.
1. A son of David.
and his firstborn was A, of ... 2Sa 3:2 550
A the son of David loved her ... 2Sa 13:1 550
A was so vexed, that he fell sick ... 2Sa 13:2 550
A thought it hard for him to do ... 2Sa 13:2 550
But A had a friend, whose name ... 2Sa 13:3 550
A said unto him, I love Tamar, my ... 2Sa 13:4 550
So A lay down, and made himself ... 2Sa 13:6 550
A said unto the king, I pray thee ... 2Sa 13:6 550
A said, Have out all men from me ... 2Sa 13:9 550
A said unto Tamar, Bring the meat ... 2Sa 13:10 550
into the chamber to A her brother ... 2Sa 13:10 550
Then A hated her exceedingly ... 2Sa 13:15 550
A said unto her, Arise, be gone ... 2Sa 13:15 550
Hath A thy brother been with thee ... 2Sa 13:20 550
brother A neither good nor bad ... 2Sa 13:22 550
for Absalom hated A, because he ... 2Sa 13:22 550
thee, let my brother A go with us ... 2Sa 13:26 550
pressed him, that he let A ... 2Sa 13:27 550
and when I say unto you, Smite A ... 2Sa 13:28 550
unto A as Absalom had commanded ... 2Sa 13:29 550
for A only is dead ... 2Sa 13:32 550
for A only is dead ... 2Sa 13:33 550
for he was comforted concerning A ... 2Sa 13:39 550
the firstborn A, of Ahinoam the ... 1Chr 3:1 550
2. A son of Shimon.
And the sons of Shimon were, A ... 1Chr 4:20 550

AMNON'S *(am'-nons)* {3} *Refers to Amnon 1.*
Go now to thy brother A house ... 2Sa 13:7 550
Tamar went to her brother A house ... 2Sa 13:8 550
Mark ye now when A heart is merry ... 2Sa 13:28 550

AMOK *(a'-mok)* {2} *A priest who returned from exile under Zerubbabel.*
Sallu, A, Hilkiah, Jedaiah ... Neh 12:7 5987
of A, Eber ... Neh 12:20 5987

AMON *(a'-mon)* {19}
1. A governor of Samaria.
carry him back unto A the ... 1Kin 22:26 526
carry him back to A the governor ... 2Chr 18:25 526
2. Son and successor of King Manasseh of Judah.
A his son reigned in his stead ... 2Kin 21:18 526
A was twenty and two years old ... 2Kin 21:19 526
the servants of A conspired ... 2Kin 21:23 526
that had conspired against king A ... 2Kin 21:24 526
of the acts of A which he did ... 2Kin 21:25 526
A his son, Josiah his son ... 1Chr 3:14 526
A his son reigned in his stead ... 2Chr 33:20 526
A was two and twenty years old ... 2Chr 33:21 526
for A sacrificed unto all the ... 2Chr 33:22 526
but A trespassed more and more ... 2Chr 33:23 526
that had conspired against king A ... 2Chr 33:25 526
Josiah the son of A king of Judah ... Jer 1:2 526
Josiah the son of A king of Judah ... Jer 25:3 526
the days of Josiah the son of A ... Zeph 1:1 526
and Manasses begat A ... Mt 1:10 *300*
and A begat Josias ... Mt 1:10 *300*
3. A descendant of Solomon who returned from the Exile under Zerubbabel.
of Zebaim, the children of A ... Neh 7:59 526

AMONG See APPENDIX.

AMONGST {2}
God a the trees of the garden ... Gen 3:8 8432
of a buryingplace a you ... Gen 23:9 8432

AMORITE *(am'-o-rite)* {14} *A descendant of Canaan, Ham's son.*
And the Jebusite, and the A ... Gen 10:16 567
dwelt in the plain of Mamre the A ... Gen 14:13 567
the hand of the A with my sword ... Gen 48:22 567
drive out the Canaanite, the A ... Ex 33:2 567
I drive out before thee the A ... Ex 34:11 567
the A which was in it ... Num 32:39 567
given into thine hand Sihon the A ... Deut 2:24 567
Lebanon, the Hittite, and the A ... Josh 9:1 567
east and on the west, and to the A ... Josh 11:3 567
The Jebusite also, and the A ... 1Chr 1:14 567
thy father was an A, and thy ... Eze 16:3 567
an Hittite, and your father an A ... Eze 16:45 567
Yet destroyed I the A before them ... Amos 2:9 567
to possess the land of the A ... Amos 2:10 567

AMORITES *(am'-o-rites)* {73}
of the Amalekites, and also the A ... Gen 14:7 567
iniquity of the A is not yet full ... Gen 15:16 567
And the A, and the Canaanites, and ... Gen 15:21 567
and the Hittites, and the A ... Ex 3:8 567
and the Hittites, and the A ... Ex 3:17 567
and the Hittites, and the A ... Ex 13:5 567
thee, and bring thee in unto the A ... Ex 23:23 567
and the Jebusites, and the A ... Num 13:29 567
cometh out of the coasts of the A ... Num 21:13 567
of Moab, between Moab and the A ... Num 21:13 567
unto Sihon king of the A, saying, ... Num 21:21 567
dwelt in all the cities of the A ... Num 21:25 567
city of Sihon the king of the A ... Num 21:26 567
unto Sihon king of the A ... Num 21:29 567
Israel dwelt in the land of the A ... Num 21:31 567
drove out the A that were there ... Num 21:32 567
didst unto Sihon king of the A ... Num 21:34 567
all that Israel had done to the A ... Num 22:2 567
kingdom of Sihon king of the A ... Num 32:33 567
had slain Sihon the king of the A ... Deut 1:4 567
and go to the mount of the A ... Deut 1:7 567
the way of the mountain of the A ... Deut 1:19 567
come unto the mountain of the A ... Deut 1:20 567
deliver us into the hand of the A ... Deut 1:27 567
And the A, which dwelt in that ... Deut 1:44 567
didst unto Sihon king of the A ... Deut 3:2 567
hand of the two kings of the A ... Deut 3:8 567
and the A call it Shenir ... Deut 3:9 567
the land of Sihon king of the A ... Deut 4:46 567
of Bashan, two kings of the A ... Deut 4:47 567
and the Girgashites, and the A ... Deut 7:1 567
namely, the Hittites, and the A ... Deut 20:17 567
to Sihon and to Og, kings of the A ... Deut 31:4 567
did unto the two kings of the A ... Josh 2:10 567
and the Girgashites, and the A ... Josh 3:10 567
pass, when all the kings of the A ... Josh 5:1 567
deliver us into the hand of the A ... Josh 7:7 567
he did to the two kings of the A ... Josh 9:10 567
Therefore the five kings of the A ... Josh 10:5 567
for all the kings of the A that ... Josh 10:6 567
A before the children of Israel ... Josh 10:12 567
Sihon king of the A, who dwelt in ... Josh 12:2 567
the Hittites, the A, and the ... Josh 12:8 567
Aphek, to the borders of the A ... Josh 13:4 567
the cities of Sihon king of the A ... Josh 13:10 567
kingdom of Sihon king of the A ... Josh 13:21 567
you into the land of the A ... Josh 24:8 567
Jericho fought against you, the A ... Josh 24:11 567
you, even the two kings of the A ... Josh 24:12 567
the flood, or the gods of the A ... Josh 24:15 567
even the A which dwelt in the ... Josh 24:18 567
the A forced the children of Dan ... Judg 1:34 567
But the A would dwell in mount ... Judg 1:35 567
the coast of the A was from the ... Judg 1:36 567
the Canaanites, Hittites, and A ... Judg 3:5 567
fear not the gods of the A ... Judg 6:10 567
side Jordan in the land of the A ... Judg 10:8 567
from the Egyptians, and from the A ... Judg 10:11 567
unto Sihon king of the A, the ... Judg 11:19 567
possessed all the land of the A ... Judg 11:21 567
possessed all the coasts of the A ... Judg 11:22 567
A from before his people Israel ... Judg 11:23 567
was peace between Israel and the A ... 1Sa 7:14 567
but of the remnant of the A ... 2Sa 21:2 567
country of Sihon king of the A ... 1Kin 4:19 567
people that were left of the A ... 1Kin 9:20 567
to all things as did the A ... 1Kin 21:26 567
wickedly above all that the A did ... 2Kin 21:11 567
left of the Hittites, and the A ... 2Chr 8:7 567
Moabites, the Egyptians, and the A ... Ezr 9:1 567
Canaanites, the Hittites, the A ... Neh 9:8 567
Sihon king of the A, and Og king ... Ps 135:11 567
Sihon king of the A ... Ps 136:19 567

AMOS *(a'-mos)* {8}
1. A prophet during the reign of Uzziah.
The words of A, who was among the ... Amos 1:1 5986
And the LORD said unto me, A ... Amos 7:8 5986
A hath conspired against thee in ... Amos 7:10 5986
For thus A saith, Jeroboam shall ... Amos 7:11 5986
Also Amaziah said unto A, O thou ... Amos 7:12 5986
Then answered A, and said to ... Amos 7:14 5986
And he said, A, what seest thou ... Amos 8:2 5986
2. Son of Naum; an ancestor of Jesus.
which was the son of A, which ... Lk 3:25 *301*

AMOUNTING {1}
gold, a to six hundred talents ... 2Chr 3:8

AMOZ *(a'-moz)* {13} *Father of Isaiah.*
Isaiah the prophet the son of A ... 2Kin 19:2 531
the son of A sent to Hezekiah ... 2Kin 19:20 531
Isaiah the son of A came to him ... 2Kin 20:1 531
Isaiah the prophet, the son of A ... 2Chr 26:22 531
the prophet Isaiah the son of A ... 2Chr 32:20 531
Isaiah the prophet, the son of A ... 2Chr 32:32 531
The vision of Isaiah the son of A ... Is 1:1 531
the son of A saw concerning Judah ... Is 2:1 531
which Isaiah the son of A did see ... Is 13:1 531
the LORD by Isaiah the son of A ... Is 20:2 531
Isaiah the prophet the son of A ... Is 37:2 531
the son of A sent unto Hezekiah ... Is 37:21 531
the son of A came unto him ... Is 38:1 531

AMPHIPOLIS *(am-fip'-o-lis)* {1} *A city in Macedonia.*
when they had passed through A ... Acts 17:1 *295*

AMPLIAS *(am'-ple-as)* {1} *A Christian acquaintance of Paul's.*
Greet A my beloved in the Lord ... Rom 16:8 *291*

AMRAM *(am'-ram)* {14} See AMRAMITES, AMRAM'S, HEMDAN.
1. Father of Moses and Aaron.
A, and Izhar, and Hebron, and Uzziel ... Ex 6:18 6019
A took him Jochebed his father's ... Ex 6:20 6019
of the life of A were an hundred ... Ex 6:20 6019
A, and Izehar, Hebron, and Uzziel ... Num 3:19 6019
And Kohath begat A ... Num 26:58 6019
and she bare unto A Aaron and Moses ... Num 26:59 6019
A, Izhar, and Hebron, and Uzziel ... 1Chr 6:2 6019
And the children of A ... 1Chr 6:3 6019
And the sons of Kohath were, A ... 1Chr 6:18 6019
A, Izhar, Hebron, and Uzziel, four ... 1Chr 23:12 6019
The sons of A ... 1Chr 23:13 6019
Of the sons of A ... 1Chr 24:20 6019
2. Married a foreign wife in Exile.
Maadai, A, and Uel, ... Ezr 10:34 6019
3. A son of Dishon.
A, and Eshban, and Ithran, and ... 1Chr 1:41 2566

AMRAMITES *(am'-ram-ites)* {2} *Descendants of Amram 1.*
of Kohath was the family of the A ... Num 3:27 6020
Of the A, and the Izharites, the ... 1Chr 26:23 6020

AMRAM'S *(am'-rams)* {1}
the name of A wife was Jochebed, ... Num 26:59 6019

AMRAPHEL *(am'-raf-el)* {2} *King of Shinar in Abraham's time.*
in the days of A king of Shinar ... Gen 14:1 569
A king of Shinar, and Arioch king ... Gen 14:9 569

AMZI *(am'-zi)* {2}
1. A son of Merari.
The son of A, the son of Bani, ... 1Chr 6:46 557
2. Ancestor of Adaiah.
the son of Pelaliah, the son of A ... Neh 11:12 557

AN See APPENDIX.
ANAB *(a'-nab)* {2} *A Canaanite city.*
from Hebron, from Debir, from A Josh 11:21 6024
And A, and Eshtemoh, and Anim, Josh 15:50 6024
ANAH *(a'-nah)* {12}
1. A daughter of Zibeon.
of A the daughter of Zibeon the Gen 36:2 6034
the daughter of A the daughter of Gen 36:14 6034
of Aholibamah the daughter of A Gen 36:18 6034
And the children of A were these Gen 36:25 6034
and Aholibamah the daughter of A Gen 36:25 6034
2. A son of Seir.
Lotan, and Shobal, and Zibeon, and A... Gen 36:20 6034
duke Shobal, duke Zibeon, duke A Gen 36:29 6034
Lotan, and Shobal, and Zibeon, and A... 1Chr 1:38 6034
3. A son of Zibeon.
both Ajah, and A Gen 36:24 6034
this was that A that found the Gen 36:24 6034
Aiah, and A 1Chr 1:40 6034
The sons of A 1Chr 1:41 6034
ANAHARATH *(an-a-ha'-rath)* {1} *A town in Issachar.*
And Haphraim, and Shihon, and A Josh 19:19 588
ANAIAH *(an-a-i'-ah)* {2}
1. A priest who assisted Ezra.
stood Mattithiah, and Shema, and A Neh 8:4 6043
2. A Jew who sealed the covenant.
Pelatiah, Hanan, A, Neh 10:22 6043
ANAK *(a'-nak)* {9} See ANAKIMS. *The son of Arba.*
and Talmai, the children of A Num 13:22 6061
we saw the children of A there Num 13:28 6061
we saw the giants, the sons of A Num 13:33 6061
stand before the children of A Deut 9:2 6061
the city of Arba the father of A Josh 15:13 6061
drove thence the three sons of A Josh 15:14 6061
and Talmai, the children of A Josh 15:14 6061
the city of Arba the father of A Josh 21:11 6061
thence the three sons of A Judg 1:20 6061
ANAKIM See ANAKIMS.
ANAKIMS *(an'-ak-ims)* {9} *Descendants of Anak.*
have seen the sons of the A there Deut 1:28 6062
great, and many, and tall, as the A Deut 2:10 6062
were accounted giants, as the A Deut 2:11 6062
great, and many, and tall, as the A Deut 2:21 6062
and tall, the children of the A Deut 9:2 6062
cut off the A from the mountains, Josh 11:21 6062
There was none of the A left in Josh 11:22 6062
in that day how the A were there Josh 14:12 6062
Arba was a great man among the A Josh 14:15 6062
ANAKITES See ANAKIMS.
ANAMIM *(an'-am-im)* {2} *A people of northern Egypt.*
And Mizraim begat Ludim, and A Gen 10:13 6047
And Mizraim begat Ludim, and A 1Chr 1:11 6047
ANAMITES See ANAMIM.
ANAMMELECH *(a-nam'-mel-ek)* {1} *A god of the Babylonians.*
in fire to Adrammelech and A 2Kin 17:31 6048
ANAN *(a'-nan)* {1} *An Israelite who sealed the covenant under Nehemiah.*
And Ahijah, Hanan, A, Neh 10:26 6052
ANANI *(an-a'-ni)* {1} *A son of Elioneai.*
and Johanan, and Dalaiah, and A 1Chr 3:24 6054
ANANIAH *(an-an-i'-ah)* {2} See ANANIAS.
1. Grandfather of Azariah.
the son of A by his house Neh 3:23 6055
2. A town in Benjamin.
And at Anathoth, Nob, A, Neh 11:32 6055
ANANIAS *(an-an-i'-as)* {11} See ANANIAH.
1. A Christian who tried to deceive the apostles.
But a certain man named A Acts 5:1 367
But Peter said, A, why hath Satan Acts 5:3 367
A hearing these words fell down, Acts 5:5 367
2. A Christian who aided Paul.
disciple at Damascus, named A Acts 9:10 367
him said the Lord in a vision, A Acts 9:10 367
a vision a man named A coming in Acts 9:12 367
Then A answered, Lord, I have Acts 9:13 367
A went his way, and entered into Acts 9:17 367
And one A, a devout man according Acts 22:12 367
3. The High Priest who interrogated Paul.
the high priest A commanded them Acts 23:2 367
after five days A the high priest Acts 24:1 367
ANATH *(a'-nath)* {2} See BETH-ANATH. *Father of Shamgar the judge.*
him was Shamgar the son of A Judg 3:31 6067
the days of Shamgar the son of A Judg 5:6 6067
ANATHEMA *(a-nath'-em-ah)* {1} *Greek word for "accursed."*
Christ, let him be A Maranatha 1Cor 16:22 331
ANATHOTH *(an'-a-thoth)* {16} See ANETOTHITE.
1. A Levitical city in Benjamin.
A with her suburbs, and Almon with Josh 21:18 6068
said the king, Get thee to A 1Kin 2:26 6068
suburbs, and A with her suburbs 1Chr 6:60 6068
The men of A, an hundred twenty Ezr 2:23 6068
The men of A, an hundred twenty Neh 7:27 6068
And at A, Nob, Ananiah, Neh 11:32 6068
to be heard unto Laish, O poor A Is 10:30 6068
were in A in the land of Benjamin Jer 1:1 6068
saith the LORD of the men of A Jer 11:21 6068
will bring evil upon the men of A Jer 11:23 6068
thou not reproved Jeremiah of A Jer 29:27 6068
Buy thee my field that is in A Jer 32:7 6068
field, I pray thee, that is in A Jer 32:8 6068
my uncle's son, that was in A Jer 32:9 6068
2. A son of Becher.
Omri, and Jerimoth, and Abiah, and A... 1Chr 7:8 6068
3. An Israelite who sealed the covenant under Nehemiah.
Hariph, A, Nebai, Neh 10:19 6068
ANATHOTHITE See ANTOTHITE.
ANCESTORS {1}
remember the covenant of their a Lev 26:45 7223
ANCHOR {1}
hope we have as an a of the soul Heb 6:19 45
ANCHORS {3}
they cast four a out of the stern Acts 27:29 45
have cast a out of the foreship Acts 27:30
And when they had taken up the a Acts 27:40 45
ANCIENT {26}
chief things of the a mountains Deut 33:15 6924
that a river, the river Kishon Judg 5:21 6917
of a times that I have formed it 2Kin 19:25 6924
And these are a things 1Chr 4:22 6267
of the fathers, who were a men Ezr 3:12 2204
With the a is wisdom Job 12:12 3453
days of old, the years of a times Ps 77:5 5769
Remove not the a landmark Prov 22:28 5769
prophet, and the prudent, and the a Is 3:2 2204
himself proudly against the a Is 3:5 2204
The a and honourable, he is the Is 9:15 2204
of the wise, the son of a kings Is 19:11 6924
whose antiquity is of a days Is 23:7 6924
of a times, that I have formed it Is 37:26 6924
since I appointed the a people Is 44:7 5769
hath declared this from a time Is 45:21 6924
from a times the things that are Is 46:10 6924
upon the a hast thou very heavily Is 47:6 2204
awake, as in the a days, in the Is 51:9 6924
mighty nation, it is an a nation Jer 5:15 5769
in their ways from the a paths Jer 18:15 5769
Then they began at the a men Eze 9:6 2204
even the a high places are ours Eze 36:2 5769
the A of days did sit, whose Dan 7:9 6268
heaven, and came to the A of days Dan 7:13 6268
Until the A of days came, and Dan 7:22 6268
ANCIENTS {10}
As saith the proverb of the a 1Sa 24:13 6931
I understand more than the a Ps 119:100 2204
judgment with the a of his people Is 3:14 2204
and before his a gloriously Is 24:23 2204
take of the a of the people Jer 19:1 2204
and of the a of the priests Jer 19:1 2204
the priest, and counsel from the a Eze 7:26 2204
of the a of the house of Israel Eze 8:11 2204
hast thou seen what the a of the Eze 8:12 2204
The a of Gebal and the wise men Eze 27:9 2204
ANCLE {1}
a bones received strength Acts 3:7 4974
ANCLES {1}
the waters were to the a Eze 47:3 657
AND See APPENDIX.
ANDREW *(an'-drew)* {13} *One of the twelve disciples.*
A his brother, casting a net into Mt 4:18 406
is called Peter, and A his brother Mt 10:2 406
A his brother casting a net into Mk 1:16 406
into the house of Simon and A Mk 1:29 406
And A, and Philip, and Bartholomew, Mk 3:18 406
and John and A asked him privately, Mk 13:3 406
A his brother, James and John, Lk 6:14 406
speak, and followed him, was A Jn 1:40 406
was of Bethsaida, the city of A Jn 1:44 406
One of his disciples, A, Simon Jn 6:8 406
Philip cometh and telleth A Jn 12:22 406
and again A and Philip tell Jesus Jn 12:22 406
Peter, and James, and John, and A Acts 1:13 406
ANDRONICUS *(an-dro-ni'-cus)* {1} *A relative of Paul.*
Salute A and Junia, my kinsmen, and Rom 16:7 408
ANEM *(a'-nem)* {1} See EN-GANNIM. *A Levitical city in Issachar.*
suburbs, and A with her suburbs 1Chr 6:73 6046
ANER *(a'-nur)* {3}
1. An ally of Abraham.
of Eshcol, and brother of A Gen 14:13 6063
of the men which went with me, A Gen 14:24 6063
2. A Levitical city in Manasseh.
A with her suburbs, and Bileam 1Chr 6:70 6063
ANETHOTHITE *(an'-e-thoth-ite)* {1} See ANETOTHITE. *A native of Anathoth.*
Abiezer the A, Mebunnai the 2Sa 23:27 6069
ANETOTHITE *(an'-e-toth-ite)* {1} See ANETHOTHITE, ANTOTHITE. *Same as Anethothite.*
the ninth month was Abiezer the A 1Chr 27:12 6069
ANGEL {201}
the a of the LORD found her by a Gen 16:7 4397
the a of the LORD said unto her, Gen 16:9 4397
the a of the LORD said unto her, Gen 16:10 4397
the a of the LORD said unto her, Gen 16:11 4397
the a of God called to Hagar out Gen 21:17 4397
the a of the LORD called unto him Gen 22:11 4397
the a of the LORD called unto Gen 22:15 4397
he shall send his a before thee Gen 24:7 4397
I walk, will send his a with thee Gen 24:40 4397
the a of God spake unto me in a Gen 31:11 4397
The a which redeemed me from all Gen 48:16 4397
the a of the LORD appeared unto Ex 3:2 4397
the a of God, which went before Ex 14:19 4397
I send an A before thee, to keep Ex 23:20 4397
For mine A shall go before thee, Ex 23:23 4397
mine A shall go before thee Ex 32:34 4397
And I will send an a before thee Ex 33:2 4397
he heard our voice, and sent an a Num 20:16 4397
the a of the LORD stood in the Num 22:22 4397
the ass saw the a of the LORD Num 22:23 4397
But the a of the LORD stood in a Num 22:24 4397
the ass saw the a of the LORD Num 22:25 4397
the a of the LORD went further, Num 22:26 4397
the ass saw the a of the LORD Num 22:27 4397
he saw the a of the LORD standing Num 22:31 4397
the a of the LORD said unto him, Num 22:32 4397
said unto the a of the LORD Num 22:34 4397
the a of the LORD said unto Num 22:35 4397
an a of the LORD came up from Judg 2:1 4397
when the a of the LORD spake Judg 2:4 4397
said the a of the LORD, curse ye Judg 5:23 4397
And there came an a of the LORD Judg 6:11 4397
the a of the LORD appeared unto Judg 6:12 4397
the a of God said unto him, Take Judg 6:20 4397
Then the a of the LORD put forth Judg 6:21 4397
Then the a of the LORD departed Judg 6:21 4397
that he was an a of the LORD Judg 6:22 4397
an a of the LORD face to face Judg 6:22 4397
the a of the LORD appeared unto Judg 13:3 4397
the countenance of an a of God Judg 13:6 4397
the a of God came again unto the Judg 13:9 4397
the a of the LORD said unto Judg 13:13 4397
said unto the a of the LORD Judg 13:15 4397
the a of the LORD said unto Judg 13:16 4397
not that he was an a of the LORD Judg 13:16 4397
said unto the a of the LORD Judg 13:17 4397
the a of the LORD said unto him, Judg 13:18 4397
and the a did wonderously Judg 13:19
that the a of the LORD ascended Judg 13:20 4397
But the a of the LORD did no more Judg 13:21 4397
knew that he was an a of the LORD Judg 13:21 4397
good in my sight, as an a of God 1Sa 29:9
for as an a of God, so is my lord 2Sa 14:17 4397
to the wisdom of an a of God 2Sa 14:20 4397
lord the king is as an a of God 2Sa 19:27 4397
when the a stretched out his hand 2Sa 24:16 4397
said to the a that destroyed the 2Sa 24:16 4397
the a of the LORD was by the 2Sa 24:16 4397
saw the a that smote the people 2Sa 24:17 4397
an a spake unto me by the word of 1Kin 13:18 4397
then an a touched him, and said 1Kin 19:5 4397
the a of the LORD came again the 1Kin 19:7 4397
But the a of the LORD said to 2Kin 1:3 4397
the a of the LORD said unto 2Kin 1:15 4397
that the a of the LORD went out, 2Kin 19:35 4397
the a of the LORD destroying 1Chr 21:12 4397
God sent an a unto Jerusalem to 1Chr 21:15 4397
said to the a that destroyed, It 1Chr 21:15 4397
the a of the LORD stood by the 1Chr 21:15 4397
saw the a of the LORD stand 1Chr 21:16 4397
Then the a of the LORD commanded 1Chr 21:18 4397
Ornan turned back, and saw the a 1Chr 21:20 4397
And the LORD commanded the a 1Chr 21:27 4397
of the sword of the a of the LORD 1Chr 21:30 4397
And the LORD sent an a, which cut 2Chr 32:21 4397
The a of the LORD encampeth round Ps 34:7 4397
let the a of the LORD chase them Ps 35:5 4397
let the a of the LORD persecute Ps 35:6 4397
neither say thou before the a Eccl 5:6 4397
Then the a of the LORD went forth Is 37:36 4397
the a of his presence saved them Is 63:9 4397
and Abed-nego, who hath sent his a Dan 3:28 4398
My God hath sent his a, and hath Dan 6:22 4398
Yea, he had power over the a Hos 12:4 4397
the a that talked with me said Zec 1:9 4397
they answered the a of the LORD Zec 1:11 4397
Then the a of the LORD answered Zec 1:12 4397
the LORD answered the a that Zec 1:13 4397
So the a that communed with me Zec 1:14 4397
I said unto the a that talked Zec 1:19 4397
the a that talked with me went Zec 2:3 4397
another a went out to meet him, Zec 2:3 4397
standing before the a of the LORD Zec 3:1 4397
garments, and stood before the a Zec 3:3 4397
the a of the LORD stood by Zec 3:5 4397
the a of the LORD protested unto Zec 3:6 4397
the a that talked with me came Zec 4:1 4397
spake to the a that talked with Zec 4:4 4397
Then the a that talked with me Zec 4:5 4397
Then the a that talked with me Zec 5:5 4397
Then said I to the a that talked Zec 5:10 4397
said unto the a that talked with Zec 6:4 4397
the a answered and said unto me, Zec 6:5 4397
as the a of the LORD before them Zec 12:8 4397
the a of the Lord appeared unto Mt 1:20 32
the a of the Lord had bidden him Mt 1:24 32
the a of the Lord appeareth to Mt 2:13 32
an a of the Lord appeareth in a Mt 2:19 32
for the a of the Lord descended Mt 28:2 32
the a answered and said unto the Mt 28:5 32
there appeared unto him an a of Lk 1:11 32
But the a said unto him, Fear not Lk 1:13 32
And Zacharias said unto the a Lk 1:18 32
the a answering said unto him, I Lk 1:19 32
in the sixth month the a Gabriel Lk 1:26 32
the a came in unto her, and said, Lk 1:28 32
the a said unto her, Fear not, Lk 1:30 32
Then said Mary unto the a Lk 1:34 32
the a answered and said unto her, Lk 1:35 32
And the a departed from her Lk 1:38 32

the *a* of the Lord came upon them, Lk 2:9 32
the *a* said unto them, Fear not Lk 2:10 32
the *a* a multitude of the heavenly Lk 2:13 32
which was so named of the *a* Lk 2:21 32
there appeared an *a* unto him from Lk 22:43 32
For an *a* went down at a certain Jn 5:4 32
others said, An *a* spake to him Jn 12:29 32
But the *a* of the Lord by night Acts 5:19 32
as it had been the face of an *a* Acts 6:15 32
a of the Lord in a flame of fire Acts 7:30 32
a which appeared to him in the Acts 7:35 32
in the wilderness with the *a* Acts 7:38 32
the *a* of the Lord spake unto Acts 8:26 32
day an *a* of God coming in to him Acts 10:3 32
when the *a* which spake unto Acts 10:7 32
was warned from God by an holy *a* Acts 10:22 32
how he had seen an *a* in his house Acts 11:13 32
the *a* of the Lord came upon him, Acts 12:7 32
the *a* said unto him, Gird thyself Acts 12:8 32
was true which was done by the *a* Acts 12:9 32
forthwith the *a* departed from him Acts 12:10 32
that the Lord hath sent his *a* Acts 12:11 32
Then said they, It is his *a* Acts 12:15
immediately the *a* of the Lord Acts 12:23 32
is no resurrection, neither *a* Acts 23:8 32
spirit or an *a* hath spoken to him Acts 23:9 32
by me this night the *a* of God Acts 27:23 32
is transformed into an *a* of light 2Cor 11:14 32
or an *a* from heaven, preach any Gal 1:8 32
but received me as an *a* of God Gal 4:14 32
signified it by his *a* unto his Rev 1:1 32
Unto the *a* of the church of Rev 2:1 32
unto the *a* of the church in Rev 2:8 32
to the *a* of the church in Rev 2:12 32
unto the *a* of the church in Rev 2:18 32
unto the *a* of the church in Rev 3:1 32
to the *a* of the church in Rev 3:7 32
unto the *a* of the church of the Rev 3:14 32
I saw a strong *a* proclaiming with Rev 5:2 32
I saw another *a* ascending from Rev 7:2 32
And another *a* came and stood at the Rev 8:3 32
the *a* took the censer, and filled Rev 8:5 32
The first *a* sounded, and there Rev 8:7 32
And the second *a* sounded, and as it Rev 8:8 32
And the third *a* sounded, and there Rev 8:10 32
And the fourth *a* sounded, and the Rev 8:12 32
heard an *a* flying through the Rev 8:13 32
And the fifth *a* sounded, and I saw Rev 9:1 32
which is the *a* of the bottomless Rev 9:11 32
And the sixth *a* sounded, and I Rev 9:13 32
Saying to the sixth *a* which had Rev 9:14 32
I saw another mighty *a* come down Rev 10:1 32
the *a* which I saw stand upon the Rev 10:5 32
of the voice of the seventh *a* Rev 10:7 32
is open in the hand of the *a* Rev 10:8 32
And I went unto the *a*, and said Rev 10:9 32
the *a* stood, saying, Rise, and Rev 11:1 32
And the seventh *a* sounded Rev 11:15 32
I saw another *a* fly in the midst Rev 14:6 32
And there followed another *a* Rev 14:8 32
the third *a* followed them, saying Rev 14:9 32
another *a* came out of the temple, Rev 14:15 32
another *a* came out of the temple Rev 14:17 32
another *a* came out from the altar Rev 14:18 32
the *a* thrust in his sickle into Rev 14:19 32
the second *a* poured out his vial Rev 16:3 32
the third *a* poured out his vial Rev 16:4 32
I heard the *a* of the waters say, Rev 16:5 32
the fourth *a* poured out his vial Rev 16:8 32
the fifth *a* poured out his vial Rev 16:10 32
the sixth *a* poured out his vial Rev 16:12 32
the seventh *a* poured out his vial Rev 16:17 32
the *a* said unto me, Wherefore Rev 17:7 32
another *a* come down from heaven Rev 18:1 32
a mighty *a* took up a stone like a Rev 18:21 32
I saw an *a* standing in the sun Rev 19:17 32
I saw an *a* come down from heaven, Rev 20:1 32
of a man, that is, of the *a* Rev 21:17 32
a to shew unto his servants the Rev 22:6 32
a which shewed me these things Rev 22:8 32
I Jesus have sent mine *a* to Rev 22:16 32

ANGEL'S {2}

up before God out of the *a* hand Rev 8:4 32
the little book out of the *a* hand Rev 10:10 32

ANGELS {93}

there came two *a* to Sodom at even Gen 19:1 4397
then the *a* hastened Lot, saying, Gen 19:15 4397
behold the *a* of God ascending and Gen 28:12 4397
his way, and the *a* of God met him Gen 32:1 4397
his *a* he charged with folly Job 4:18 4397
him a little lower than the *a* Ps 8:5 430
thousand, even thousands of *a* Ps 68:17 8136
by sending evil *a* among them Ps 78:49 4397
shall give his *a* charge over thee Ps 91:11 4397
Bless the LORD, ye his *a*, that Ps 103:20 4397
Who maketh his *a* spirits Ps 104:4 4397
Praise ye him, all his *a* Ps 148:2 4397
He shall give his *a* charge Mt 4:6 32
a came and ministered unto him Mt 4:11 32
and the reapers are the *a* Mt 13:39 32
Son of man shall send forth his *a* Mt 13:41 32
the *a* shall come forth, and sever Mt 13:49 32
glory of his Father with his *a* Mt 16:27 32
That in heaven their *a* do always Mt 18:10 32
but are as the *a* of God in heaven Mt 22:30 32
he shall send his *a* with a great Mt 24:31 32
not the *a* of heaven, but my Mt 24:36 32
glory, and all the holy *a* with him Mt 25:31 32
prepared for the devil and his *a* Mt 25:41 32
me more than twelve legions of *a* Mt 26:53 32
the *a* ministered unto him Mk 1:13 32
of his Father with the holy *a* Mk 8:38 32
but are as the *a* which are in Mk 12:25 32
And then shall he send his *a* Mk 13:27 32
not the *a* which are in heaven, Mk 13:32 32
as the *a* were gone away from them Lk 2:15 32
shall give his *a* charge over thee Lk 4:10 32
in his Father's, and of the holy *a* Lk 9:26 32
also confess before the *a* of God Lk 12:8 32
be denied before the *a* of God Lk 12:9 32
the *a* of God over one sinner that Lk 15:10 32
was carried by the *a* into Lk 16:22 32
for they are equal unto the *a* Lk 20:36 2465
they had also seen a vision of *a* Lk 24:23 32
the *a* of God ascending and Jn 1:51 32
seeth two *a* in white sitting, the Jn 20:12 32
the law by the disposition of *a* Acts 7:53 32
neither death, nor life, nor *a* Rom 8:38 32
spectacle unto the world, and to *a* 1Cor 4:9 32
Know ye not that we shall judge *a* 1Cor 6:3 32
on her head because of the *a* 1Cor 11:10 32
with the tongues of men and of *a* 1Cor 13:1 32
it was ordained by *a* in the hand Gal 3:19 32
humility and worshipping of *a* Col 2:18 32
from heaven with his mighty *a* 2Th 1:7 32
in the Spirit, seen of *a*, 1Ti 3:16 32
Lord Jesus Christ, and the elect *a* 1Ti 5:21 32
made so much better than the *a* Heb 1:4 32
of the *a* said he at any time Heb 1:5 32
let all the *a* of God worship him Heb 1:6 32
of the *a* he saith Heb 1:7 32
Who maketh his *a* spirits Heb 1:7 32
But to which of the *a* said he at Heb 1:13 32
the word spoken by *a* was stedfast Heb 2:2 32
For unto the *a* hath he not put in Heb 2:5 32
him a little lower than the *a* Heb 2:7 32
the *a* for the suffering of death Heb 2:9 32
took not on him the nature of *a* Heb 2:16 32
and to an innumerable company of *a* Heb 12:22 32
some have entertained *a* unawares Heb 13:2 32
which things the *a* desire to look 1Pet 1:12 32
a and authorities and powers being 1Pet 3:22 32
God spared not the *a* that sinned 2Pet 2:4 32
Whereas *a*, which are greater in 2Pet 2:11 32
the *a* which kept not their first Jude 6 32
are the *a* of the seven churches Rev 1:20 32
before my Father, and before his *a* Rev 3:5 32
of many *a* round about the throne Rev 5:11 32
after these things I saw four *a* Rev 7:1 32
with a loud voice to the four *a* Rev 7:2 32
all the *a* stood round about the Rev 7:11 32
I saw the seven *a* which stood Rev 8:2 32
the seven *a* which had the seven Rev 8:6 32
of the trumpet of the three *a* Rev 8:13 32
Loose the four *a* which are bound Rev 9:14 32
the four *a* were loosed, which Rev 9:15 32
his *a* fought against the dragon Rev 12:7 32
and the dragon fought and his *a* Rev 12:7 32
his *a* were cast out with him Rev 12:9 32
in the presence of the holy *a* Rev 14:10 32
seven *a* having the seven last Rev 15:1 32
the seven *a* came out of the Rev 15:6 32
a seven golden vials full of the Rev 15:7 32
of the seven *a* were fulfilled Rev 15:8 32
the temple saying to the seven *a* Rev 16:1 32
seven *a* which had the seven vials Rev 17:1 32
came unto me one of the seven *a* Rev 21:9 32
gates, and at the gates twelve *a* Rev 21:12 32

ANGELS' {1}

Man did eat *a* food Ps 78:25 47

ANGER {234}

brother's *a* turn away from thee Gen 27:45 639
Jacob's *a* was kindled against Gen 30:2 639
let not thine *a* burn against thy Gen 44:18 639
for in their *a* they slew a man, Gen 49:6 639
Cursed be their *a*, for it was Gen 49:7 639
the *a* of the LORD was kindled Ex 4:14 639
out from Pharaoh in a great *a* Ex 11:8 639
Moses' *a* waxed hot, and he cast Ex 32:19 639
Let not the *a* of my lord wax hot Ex 32:22 639
and his *a* was kindled Num 11:1 639
the *a* of the LORD was kindled Num 11:10 639
the *a* of the LORD was kindled Num 12:9 639
God's *a* was kindled because he Num 22:22 639
Balaam's *a* was kindled, and he Num 22:27 639
Balak's *a* was kindled against Num 24:10 639
the *a* of the LORD was kindled Num 25:3 639
that the fierce *a* of the LORD may Num 25:4 639
the LORD's *a* was kindled the same Num 32:10 639
the LORD's *a* was kindled against Num 32:13 639
a of the LORD toward Israel Num 32:14 639
LORD thy God, to provoke him to *a* Deut 4:25 3707
a of the LORD thy God be kindled Deut 6:15 639
so will the *a* of the LORD be Deut 7:4 639
of the LORD, to provoke him to *a* Deut 9:18 3707
For I was afraid of the *a* Deut 9:19 639
turn from the fierceness of his *a* Deut 13:17 639
him, but then the *a* of the LORD Deut 29:20 639
which the LORD overthrew in his *a* Deut 29:23 639
meaneth the heat of this great *a* Deut 29:24 639
the *a* of the LORD was kindled Deut 29:27 639
them out of their land in *a* Deut 29:28 639
Then my *a* shall be kindled Deut 31:17 639
to provoke him to *a* through the Deut 31:29 3707
provoked they him to *a* Deut 32:16 3707
me to *a* with their vanities Deut 32:21 3707
them to *a* with a foolish nation Deut 32:21
For a fire is kindled in mine *a* Deut 32:22 639
the *a* of the LORD was kindled Josh 7:1 639
from the fierceness of his *a* Josh 7:26 639
then shall the *a* of the LORD be Josh 23:16 639
them, and provoked the LORD to *a* Judg 2:12 3707
the *a* of the LORD was hot against Judg 2:14 639
the *a* of the LORD was hot against Judg 2:20 639
Therefore the *a* of the LORD was Judg 3:8 639
Let not thine *a* be hot against me Judg 6:39 639
Then their *a* was abated toward Judg 8:3 7307
son of Ebed, his *a* was kindled Judg 9:30 639
the *a* of the LORD was hot against Judg 10:7 639
his *a* was kindled, and he went up Judg 14:19 639
his *a* was kindled greatly 1Sa 11:6 639
Eliab's *a* was kindled against 1Sa 17:28 639
Then Saul's *a* was kindled against 1Sa 20:30 639
arose from the table in fierce *a* 1Sa 20:34 639
the *a* of the LORD was kindled 2Sa 6:7 639
David's *a* was greatly kindled 2Sa 12:5 639
again the *a* of the LORD was 2Sa 24:1 639
molten images, to provoke me to *a* 1Kin 14:9 3707
groves, provoking the LORD to *a* 1Kin 14:15 3707
the LORD God of Israel to *a* 1Kin 15:30 3707
provoke me to *a* with their sins 1Kin 16:2 3707
in provoking him to *a* with the 1Kin 16:7 3707
Israel to *a* with their vanities 1Kin 16:13 3707
Israel to *a* with their vanities 1Kin 16:26 3707
the LORD God of Israel to *a* than 1Kin 16:33 3707
thou hast provoked me to *a* 1Kin 21:22 3707
provoked to *a* the LORD God of 1Kin 22:53 3707
the *a* of the LORD was kindled 2Kin 13:3 639
things to provoke the LORD to *a* 2Kin 17:11 3707
of the LORD, to provoke him to *a* 2Kin 17:17 3707
of the LORD, to provoke him to *a* 2Kin 21:6 3707
sight, and have provoked me to *a* 2Kin 21:15 3707
to *a* with all the works of their 2Kin 22:17 3707
had made to provoke the LORD to *a* 2Kin 23:19 3707
wherewith his *a* was kindled 2Kin 23:26 639
For through the *a* of the LORD it 2Kin 24:20 639
the *a* of the LORD was kindled 1Chr 13:10 639
wherefore their *a* was greatly 2Chr 25:10 639
and they returned home in great *a* 2Chr 25:10 639
Wherefore the *a* of the LORD was 2Chr 25:15 639
provoked to *a* the LORD God of his 2Chr 28:25 3707
of the LORD, to provoke him to *a* 2Chr 33:6 3707
to *a* with all the works of their 2Chr 34:25 3707
thee to *a* before the builders Neh 4:5 3707
gracious and merciful, slow to *a* Neh 9:17 639
wroth, and his *a* burned in him Est 1:12 2534
which overturneth them in his *a* Job 9:5 639
If God will not withdraw his *a* Job 9:13 639
He teareth himself in his *a* Job 18:4 639
God distributeth sorrows in his *a* Job 21:17 639
not so, he hath visited in his *a* Job 35:15 639
O lord, rebuke me not in thine *a* Ps 6:1 639
Arise, O LORD, in thine *a* Ps 7:6 639
fiery oven in the time of thine *a* Ps 21:9 6440
put not thy servant away in *a* Ps 27:9 639
For his *a* endureth but a moment Ps 30:5 639
Cease from *a*, and forsake wrath Ps 37:8 639
in my flesh because of thine *a* Ps 38:3 2195
in thine *a* cast down the people, Ps 56:7 639
let thy wrathful *a* take hold of Ps 69:24 639
why doth thine *a* smoke against Ps 74:1 639
hath he in *a* shut up his tender Ps 77:9 639
a also came up against Israel Ps 78:21 639
many a time turned he his *a* away Ps 78:38 639
upon them the fierceness of his *a* Ps 78:49 639
He made a way to his *a* Ps 78:50 639
him to *a* with their high places Ps 78:58 3707
from the fierceness of thine *a* Ps 85:3 639
cause thine *a* toward us to cease Ps 85:4 3708
out thine *a* to all generations Ps 85:5 639
For we are consumed by thine *a* Ps 90:7 639
Who knoweth the power of thine *a* Ps 90:11 639
merciful and gracious, slow to *a* Ps 103:8 639
will he keep his *a* for ever Ps 103:9 639
him to *a* with their inventions Ps 106:29 3707
slow to *a*, and of great mercy Ps 145:8 639
but grievous words stir up *a* Prov 15:1 639
is slow to *a* appeaseth strife Prov 15:18 639
He that is slow to *a* is better Prov 16:32 639
of a man deferreth his *a* Prov 19:11 639
whoso provoketh him to *a* sinneth Prov 20:2 5674
A gift in secret pacifieth *a* Prov 21:14 639
and the rod of his *a* shall fail Prov 22:8 5678
is cruel, and *a* is outrageous Prov 27:4 639
for *a* resteth in the bosom of Eccl 7:9 3708
the Holy One of Israel unto *a* Is 1:4 5006
Therefore is the *a* of the LORD Is 5:25 639
For all this his *a* is not turned Is 5:25 639
for the fierce *a* of Rezin with Is 7:4 639
For all this his *a* is not turned Is 9:12 639
For all this his *a* is not turned Is 9:17 639
For all this his *a* is not turned Is 9:21 639
For all this his *a* is not turned Is 10:4 639
O Assyrian, the rod of mine *a* Is 10:5 639
mine *a* in their destruction Is 10:25 639
thine *a* is turned away, and thou Is 12:1 639
called my mighty ones for mine *a* Is 13:3 639
cruel both with wrath and fierce *a* Is 13:9 639
and in the day of his fierce *a* Is 13:13 639
he that ruled the nations in *a* Is 14:6 639
from far, burning with his *a* Is 30:27 639
with the indignation of his *a* Is 30:30 639

poured upon him the fury of his *a* ... Is 42:25 639
name's sake will I defer mine *a* ... Is 48:9 639
for I will tread them in mine *a* ... Is 63:3 639
tread down the people in mine *a* ... Is 63:6 639
me to *a* continually to my face ... Is 65:3 3707
to render his *a* with fury ... Is 66:15 639
surely his *a* shall turn from me ... Jer 2:35 639
Will he reserve his *a* for ever ... Jer 3:5
not cause mine *a* to fall upon you ... Jer 3:12 6440
and I will not keep *a* for ever ... Jer 3:12
for the fierce *a* of the LORD is ... Jer 4:8 639
of the LORD, and by his fierce *a* ... Jer 4:26 639
that they may provoke me to *a* ... Jer 7:18 3707
Do they provoke me to *a* ... Jer 7:19 3707
Behold, mine *a* and my fury shall ... Jer 7:20 639
me to *a* with their graven images ... Jer 8:19 3707
not in thine *a*, lest thou bring ... Jer 10:24 639
themselves to provoke me to *a* in ... Jer 11:17 3707
of the fierce *a* of the LORD ... Jer 12:13 639
for a fire is kindled in mine *a* ... Jer 15:14 639
ye have kindled a fire in mine *a* ... Jer 17:4 639
with them in the time of thine *a* ... Jer 18:23 639
and with a strong arm, even in *a* ... Jer 21:5 639
The *a* of the LORD shall not ... Jer 23:20 639
provoke me not to *a* with the ... Jer 25:6 3707
that ye might provoke me to *a* ... Jer 25:7 3707
of the fierce *a* of the LORD ... Jer 25:37 639
and because of his fierce *a* ... Jer 25:38 639
The fierce *a* of the LORD shall ... Jer 30:24 639
other gods, to provoke me to *a* ... Jer 32:29 3707
to *a* with the work of their hands ... Jer 32:30 3707
to me as a provocation of mine *a* ... Jer 32:31 639
they have done to provoke me to *a* ... Jer 32:32 3707
I have driven them in mine *a* ... Jer 32:37 639
men, whom I have slain in mine *a* ... Jer 33:5 639
for great is the *a* and the fury ... Jer 36:7 639
As mine *a* and my fury hath been ... Jer 42:18 639
have committed to provoke me to *a* ... Jer 44:3 3707
mine *a* was poured forth, and was ... Jer 44:6 639
evil upon them, even my fierce *a* ... Jer 49:37 639
from the fierce *a* of the LORD ... Jer 51:45 639
For through the *a* of the LORD it ... Jer 52:3 639
me in the day of his fierce *a* ... Lam 1:12 639
of Zion with a cloud in his *a* ... Lam 2:1 639
his footstool in the day of his *a* ... Lam 2:1 639
fierce *a* all the horn of Israel ... Lam 2:3 639
the indignation of his *a* the king ... Lam 2:6 639
slain them in the day of thine *a* ... Lam 2:21 639
a none escaped nor remained ... Lam 2:22 639
Thou hast covered with *a*, and ... Lam 3:43 639
destroy them in *a* from under the ... Lam 3:66 639
he hath poured out his fierce *a* ... Lam 4:11 639
The *a* of the LORD hath divided ... Lam 4:16 6440
Thus shall mine *a* be accomplished ... Eze 5:13 639
execute judgments in thee in *a* ... Eze 5:15 639
and I will send mine *a* upon thee ... Eze 7:3 639
and accomplish mine *a* upon thee ... Eze 7:8 639
have returned to provoke me to *a* ... Eze 8:17 3707
an overflowing shower in mine *a* ... Eze 13:13 639
thy whoredoms, to provoke me to *a* ... Eze 16:26 3707
to accomplish my *a* against them ... Eze 20:8 639
to accomplish my *a* against them ... Eze 20:21 639
so will I gather you in mine *a* ... Eze 22:20 639
do in Edom according to mine *a* ... Eze 25:14 639
will even do according to thine *a* ... Eze 35:11 639
I have consumed them in mine *a* ... Eze 43:8 639
I beseech thee, let thine *a* ... Dan 9:16 639
shall be destroyed, neither in *a* ... Dan 11:20 639
mine *a* is kindled against them ... Hos 8:5 639
execute the fierceness of mine *a* ... Hos 11:9 639
provoked him to *a* most bitterly ... Hos 12:14 3707
I gave thee a king in mine *a* ... Hos 13:11 639
for mine *a* is turned away from ... Hos 14:4 639
gracious and merciful, slow to *a* ... Joel 2:13 639
his *a* did tear perpetually, and he ... Amos 1:11 639
and turn away from his fierce *a* ... Jonah 3:9 639
God, and merciful, slow to *a* ... Jonah 4:2 639
And I will execute vengeance in *a* ... Mic 5:15 639
he retaineth not his *a* for ever ... Mic 7:18 639
The LORD is slow to *a*, and great ... Nah 1:3 639
abide in the fierceness of his *a* ... Nah 1:6 639
was thine *a* against the rivers ... Hab 3:8 639
didst thresh the heathen in *a* ... Hab 3:12 639
before the fierce *a* of the LORD ... Zeph 2:2 639
day of the LORD's *a* come upon you ... Zeph 2:2 639
be hid in the day of the LORD's *a* ... Zeph 2:3 639
indignation, even all my fierce *a* ... Zeph 3:8 639
Mine *a* was kindled against the ... Zec 10:3 639
looked round about on them with *a* ... Mk 3:5 *3709*
by a foolish nation I will *a* you ... Rom 10:19 *3949*
all bitterness, and wrath, and *a* ... Eph 4:31 *3709*
a, wrath, malice, blasphemy, ... Col 3:8 *3709*
provoke not your children to *a* ... Col 3:21

ANGERED {1}
They *a* him also at the waters of ... Ps 106:32 7107

ANGLE {2}
all they that cast *a* into the ... Is 19:8 2443
take up all of them with the *a* ... Hab 1:15 2443

ANGRY {44}
him, Oh let not the LORD be *a* ... Gen 18:30 2734
he said, Oh let not the Lord be *a* ... Gen 18:32 2734
nor *a* with yourselves, that ye ... Gen 45:5 2734
he was *a* with Eleazar and Ithamar, ... Lev 10:16 7107
Also the LORD was *a* with me for ... Deut 1:37 599
LORD was *a* with me for your sakes ... Deut 4:21 599
so that the LORD was *a* with you ... Deut 9:8 599
the LORD was very *a* with Aaron to ... Deut 9:20 599
lest *a* fellows run upon thee, ... Judg 18:25 4751,5315
then be ye *a* for this matter ... 2Sa 19:42 2734
thou be *a* with them, and deliver ... 1Kin 8:46 599
And the LORD was *a* with Solomon ... 1Kin 11:9 599
the LORD was very *a* with Israel ... 2Kin 17:18 599
thou be *a* with them, and deliver ... 2Chr 6:36 599
wouldest not thou be *a* with us ... Ezr 9:14 599
I was very *a* when I heard their ... Neh 5:6 2734
Kiss the Son, lest he be *a* ... Ps 2:12 599
God is *a* with the wicked every ... Ps 7:11 2194
in thy sight when once thou art *a* ... Ps 76:7 639
wilt thou be *a* for ever ... Ps 79:5 599
how long wilt thou be *a* against ... Ps 80:4 6225
Wilt thou be *a* with us for ever ... Ps 85:5 599
He that is soon *a* dealeth ... Prov 14:17 639
with a contentious and an *a* woman ... Prov 21:19 3708
Make no friendship with an *a* man ... Prov 22:24 639
so doth an *a* countenance a ... Prov 25:23 2194
An *a* man stirreth up strife, and a ... Prov 29:22 639
should God be *a* at thy voice ... Eccl 5:6 7107
not hasty in thy spirit to be *a* ... Eccl 7:9 3707
mother's children were *a* with me ... Song 1:6 2734
though thou wast *a* with me ... Is 12:1 599
be quiet, and will be no more *a* ... Eze 16:42 3707
For this cause the king was *a* ... Dan 2:12 1149
exceedingly, and he was very *a* ... Jonah 4:1 2734
the LORD, Doest thou well to be *a* ... Jonah 4:4 2734
thou well to be *a* for the gourd ... Jonah 4:9 2734
And he said, I do well to be *a* ... Jonah 4:9 2734
That whosoever is *a* with his ... Mt 5:22 *3710*
house being *a* said to his servant ... Lk 14:21 *3710*
And he was *a*, and would not go in ... Lk 15:28 *3710*
are ye *a* at me, because I have ... Jn 7:23 *5520*
Be ye *a*, and sin not ... Eph 4:26 *3710*
not selfwilled, not soon *a* ... Titus 1:7 *3711*
And the nations were *a*, and thy ... Rev 11:18 *3710*

ANGUISH {17}
in that we saw the *a* of his soul ... Gen 42:21 6869
not unto Moses for *a* of spirit ... Ex 6:9 7115
and be in *a* because of thee ... Deut 2:25 2342
for *a* is come upon me, because my ... 2Sa 1:9 7661
will speak in the *a* of my spirit ... Job 7:11 6862
and *a* shall make him afraid ... Job 15:24 4691
and *a* have taken hold on me ... Ps 119:143 4689
distress and *a* cometh upon you ... Prov 1:27 6695
trouble and darkness, dimness of *a* ... Is 8:22 6695
into the land of trouble and *a* ... Is 30:6 6695
the *a* as of her that bringeth ... Jer 4:31 6869
a hath taken hold of us, and pain, ... Jer 6:24 6869
a and sorrows have taken her, as a ... Jer 49:24 6869
a took hold of him, and pangs as ... Jer 50:43 6869
she remembereth no more the *a* ... Jn 16:21 *2347*
Tribulation and *a*, upon every soul ... Rom 2:9 *4730*
a of heart I wrote unto you with ... 2Cor 2:4 *4928*

ANIAM *(a'-ne-am)* {1} *A son of Shemida.*
Ahian, and Shechem, and Likhi, and *A* ... 1Chr 7:19 593

ANIM *(a'-nim)* {1} *A city in Judah.*
And Anab, and Eshtemoh, and *A* ... Josh 15:50 6044

ANISE {1}
for ye pay tithe of mint and *a* ... Mt 23:23 *432*

ANNA *(an'-nah)* {1} *A prophetess.*
And there was one *A*, a prophetess, ... Lk 2:36 *451*

ANNAS *(an'-nas)* {4} *A High Priest during Jesus' ministry.*
A and Caiaphas being the high ... Lk 3:2 *452*
And led him away to *A* first ... Jn 18:13 *452*
Now *A* had sent him bound unto ... Jn 18:24 *452*
A the high priest, and Caiaphas, ... Acts 4:6 *452*

ANOINT {35}
and shalt *a* them, and consecrate ... Ex 28:41 4886
pour it upon his head, and *a* him ... Ex 29:7 4886
for it, and thou shalt *a* it ... Ex 29:36 4886
thou shalt *a* the tabernacle of ... Ex 30:26 4886
And thou shalt *a* Aaron and his sons ... Ex 30:30 4886
a the tabernacle, and all that is ... Ex 40:9 4886
thou shalt *a* the altar of the ... Ex 40:10 4886
And thou shalt *a* the laver ... Ex 40:11 4886
and *a* him, and sanctify him ... Ex 40:13 4886
And thou shalt *a* them ... Ex 40:15 4886
as thou didst *a* their father ... Ex 40:15 4886
And the priest, whom he shall *a* ... Lev 16:32 4886
but thou shalt not *a* thyself with ... Deut 28:40 5480
on a time to *a* a king over them ... Judg 9:8 4886
If in truth ye *a* me king over you ... Judg 9:15 4886
a thee, and put thy raiment upon ... Ruth 3:3 5480
thou shalt *a* him to be captain ... 1Sa 9:16 4886
The LORD sent me to *a* thee to be ... 1Sa 15:1 4886
thou shalt *a* unto me him whom I ... 1Sa 16:3 4886
And the LORD said, Arise, *a* him ... 1Sa 16:12 4886
a not thyself with oil, but be as ... 2Sa 14:2 5480
Nathan the prophet *a* him there ... 1Kin 1:34 4886
a Hazael to be king over Syria ... 1Kin 19:15 4886
thou *a* to be king over Israel ... 1Kin 19:16 4886
thou *a* to be prophet in thy room ... 1Kin 19:16 4886
ye princes, and *a* the shield ... Is 21:5 4886
prophecy, and to *a* the most Holy ... Dan 9:24 4886
neither did I *a* myself at all ... Dan 10:3 5480
a themselves with the chief ... Amos 6:6 4886
thou shalt not *a* thee with oil ... Mic 6:15 5480
a thine head, and wash thy face ... Mt 6:17 *218*
to *a* my body to the burying ... Mk 14:8 *3462*
that they might come and *a* him ... Mk 16:1 *218*
My head with oil thou didst not *a* ... Lk 7:46 *218*
a thine eyes with eyesalve, that ... Rev 3:18 *1472*

ANOINTED {98}
and wafers unleavened *a* with oil ... Ex 29:2 4886
to be *a* therein, and to be ... Ex 29:29 4888
or unleavened wafers *a* with oil ... Lev 2:4 4886
If the priest that is *a* do sin ... Lev 4:3 4899
the priest that is *a* shall take ... Lev 4:5 4899
the priest that is *a* shall bring ... Lev 4:16 4899
the LORD in the day when he is *a* ... Lev 6:20 4886
is *a* in his stead shall offer it ... Lev 6:22 4899
and unleavened wafers *a* with oil ... Lev 7:12 4886
Israel, in the day that he *a* them ... Lev 7:36 4886
a the tabernacle and all that was ... Lev 8:10 4886
a the altar and all his vessels, ... Lev 8:11 4886
head, and *a* him, to sanctify him ... Lev 8:12 4886
Aaron, the priests which were *a* ... Num 3:3 4886
of unleavened bread *a* with oil ... Num 6:15 4886
up the tabernacle, and had *a* it ... Num 7:1 4886
had *a* them, and sanctified them ... Num 7:1 4886
altar in the day that it was *a* ... Num 7:10 4886
altar, in the day when it was *a* ... Num 7:84 4886
of the altar, after that it was *a* ... Num 7:88 4886
which was *a* with the holy oil ... Num 35:25 4886
king, and exalt the horn of his *a* ... 1Sa 2:10 4899
shall walk before mine *a* for ever ... 1Sa 2:35 4899
a thee to be captain over his ... 1Sa 10:1 4886
before the LORD, and before his *a* ... 1Sa 12:3 4899
his *a* is witness this day, that ... 1Sa 12:5 4899
the LORD *a* thee king over Israel ... 1Sa 15:17 4886
Surely the LORD's *a* is before him ... 1Sa 16:6 4899
a him in the midst of his ... 1Sa 16:13 4886
unto my master, the LORD's *a* ... 1Sa 24:6 4899
seeing he is the *a* of the LORD ... 1Sa 24:6 4899
for he is the LORD's *a* ... 1Sa 24:10 4899
his hand against the LORD's *a* ... 1Sa 26:9 4899
mine hand against the LORD's *a* ... 1Sa 26:11 4899
kept your master, the LORD's *a* ... 1Sa 26:16 4899
mine hand against the LORD's *a* ... 1Sa 26:23 4899
hand to destroy the LORD's *a* ... 2Sa 1:14 4899
saying, I have slain the LORD's *a* ... 2Sa 1:16 4899
though he had not been *a* with oil ... 2Sa 1:21 4899
there they *a* David king over the ... 2Sa 2:4 4886
of Judah have *a* me king over them ... 2Sa 2:7 4886
I am this day weak, though *a* king ... 2Sa 3:39 4886
they *a* David king over Israel ... 2Sa 5:3 4886
they had *a* David king over Israel ... 2Sa 5:17 4886
I *a* thee king over Israel, and I ... 2Sa 12:7 4886
a himself, and changed his apparel ... 2Sa 12:20 5480
And Absalom, whom we *a* over us ... 2Sa 19:10 4886
because he cursed the LORD's *a* ... 2Sa 19:21 4899
and sheweth mercy to his *a* ... 2Sa 22:51 4899
the *a* of the God of Jacob, and the ... 2Sa 23:1 4899
of the tabernacle, and *a* Solomon ... 1Kin 1:39 4886
prophet have *a* him king in Gihon ... 1Kin 1:45 4886
had *a* him king in the room of his ... 1Kin 5:1 4886
I have *a* thee king over Israel ... 2Kin 9:3 4886
I have *a* thee king over the ... 2Kin 9:6 4886
I have *a* thee king over Israel ... 2Kin 9:12 4886
and they made him king, and *a* him ... 2Kin 11:12 4886
a him, and made him king in his ... 2Kin 23:30 4886
they *a* David king over Israel, ... 1Chr 11:3 4886
David was *a* king over all Israel ... 1Chr 14:8 4886
Saying, Touch not mine *a*, and do ... 1Chr 16:22 4899
a him unto the LORD to be the ... 1Chr 29:22 4886
turn not away the face of thine *a* ... 2Chr 6:42 4899
whom the LORD had *a* to cut off ... 2Chr 22:7 4886
And Jehoiada and his sons *a* him ... 2Chr 23:11 4886
a them, and carried all the feeble ... 2Chr 28:15 4886
the LORD, and against his *a* ... Ps 2:2 4899
and sheweth mercy to his *a* ... Ps 18:50 4899
know I that the LORD saveth his *a* ... Ps 20:6 4899
is the saving strength of his *a* ... Ps 28:8 4899
hath *a* thee with the oil of ... Ps 45:7 4886
and look upon the face of thine *a* ... Ps 84:9 4899
with my holy oil have I *a* him ... Ps 89:20 4886
thou hast been wroth with thine *a* ... Ps 89:38 4899
the footsteps of thine *a* ... Ps 89:51 4899
I shall be *a* with fresh oil ... Ps 92:10 1101
Saying, Touch not mine *a*, and do ... Ps 105:15 4899
turn not away the face of thine *a* ... Ps 132:10 4899
I have ordained a lamp for mine *a* ... Ps 132:17 4899
Thus saith the LORD to his *a* ... Is 45:1 4899
because the LORD hath *a* me to ... Is 61:1 4886
the *a* of the LORD, was taken in ... Lam 4:20 4899
from thee, and I *a* thee with oil ... Eze 16:9 5480
Thou art the *a* cherub that ... Eze 28:14 4473
even for salvation with thine *a* ... Hab 3:13 4899
These are the two *a* ones ... Zec 4:14 1121,3323
a with oil many that were sick, ... Mk 6:13 *218*
because he hath *a* me to preach ... Lk 4:18 *5548*
feet, and *a* them with the ointment ... Lk 7:38 *218*
but this woman hath *a* my feet ... Lk 7:46 *218*
he *a* the eyes of the blind man ... Jn 9:6 *2025,1909*
a mine eyes, and said unto me, Go ... Jn 9:11 *2025*
which *a* the Lord with ointment ... Jn 11:2 *218*
a the feet of Jesus, and wiped his ... Jn 12:3 *218*
child Jesus, whom thou hast *a* ... Acts 4:27 *5548*
How God *a* Jesus of Nazareth with ... Acts 10:38 *5548*
with you in Christ, and hath *a* us ... 2Cor 1:21 *5548*
hath *a* thee with the oil of ... Heb 1:9 *5548*

ANOINTEDST {1}
Beth-el, where thou *a* the pillar ... Gen 31:13 4886

ANOINTEST {1}
thou *a* my head with oil ... Ps 23:5 1878

ANOINTING {28}
for the light, spices for *a* oil ... Ex 25:6 4888
Then shalt thou take the *a* oil ... Ex 29:7 4888
upon the altar, and of the *a* oil ... Ex 29:21 4888

it shall be an holy *a* oil ... Ex 30:25 4888
This shall be an holy *a* oil unto ... Ex 30:31 4888
And the *a* oil, and sweet incense ... Ex 31:11 4888
the light, and spices for *a* oil ... Ex 35:8 4888
and his staves, and the *a* oil ... Ex 35:15 4888
for the light, and for the *a* oil ... Ex 35:28 4888
And he made the holy *a* oil ... Ex 37:29 4888
And the golden altar, and the *a* oil ... Ex 39:38 4888
And thou shalt take the *a* oil ... Ex 40:9 4888
for their *a* shall surely be an ... Ex 40:15 4888
is the portion of the *a* of Aaron ... Lev 7:35 4888
of the *a* of his sons, out of the ... Lev 7:35 4888
and the garments, and the *a* oil ... Lev 8:2 4888
And Moses took the *a* oil, and ... Lev 8:10 4888
he poured of the *a* oil upon ... Lev 8:12 4888
And Moses took of the *a* oil ... Lev 8:30 4888
for the *a* oil of the LORD is upon ... Lev 10:7 4888
whose head the *a* oil was poured ... Lev 21:10 4888
for the crown of the *a* oil of his ... Lev 21:12 4888
daily meat offering, and the *a* oil ... Num 4:16 4888
I given them by reason of the *a* ... Num 18:8 4888
be destroyed because of the *a* ... Is 10:27 8081
a him with oil in the name of the ... Jas 5:14 *218*
But the *a* which ye have received ... 1Jn 2:27 *5545*
but as the same *a* teacheth you of ... 1Jn 2:27 *5545*

ANON {2}
word, and *a* with joy receiveth it ... Mt 13:20 *2117*
fever, and *a* they tell him of her ... Mk 1:30 *2112*

ANOTHER See APPENDIX.

ANOTHER'S See APPENDIX.

ANSWER See APPENDIX.

ANSWERABLE {1}
a to the hangings of the court ... Ex 38:18 5980

ANSWERED See APPENDIX.

ANSWEREDST {2}
Thou *a* them, O LORD our God ... Ps 99:8 6030
In the day when I cried thou *a* me ... Ps 138:3 6030

ANSWEREST {6}
of Ner, saying, *A* thou not, Abner ... 1Sa 26:14 6030
what emboldeneth thee that thou *a* ... Job 16:3 6030
and said unto him, *A* thou nothing ... Mt 26:62 *611*
Jesus, saying, *A* thou nothing ... Mk 14:60 *611*
him again, saying, *A* thou nothing ... Mk 15:4 *611*
A thou the high priest so ... Jn 18:22 *611*

ANSWERETH {13}
a me no more, neither by prophets ... 1Sa 28:15 6030
and the God that *a* by fire ... 1Kin 18:24 6030
who calleth upon God, and he *a* him ... Job 12:4 6030
He that *a* a matter before he ... Prov 18:13 7725
but the rich *a* roughly ... Prov 18:23 6030
As in water face *a* to face ... Prov 27:19
because God *a* him in the joy of ... Eccl 5:20 6030
but money *a* all things ... Eccl 10:19 6030
And Peter *a* and saith unto him, ... Mk 8:29 *611*
He *a* him, and saith, O faithless ... Mk 9:19 *611*
But Jesus *a* again, and saith unto ... Mk 10:24 *611*
He *a* and saith unto them, He that ... Lk 3:11 *611*
a to Jerusalem which now is, and ... Gal 4:25 *4960*

ANSWERING See APPENDIX.

ANSWERS See APPENDIX.

ANT {1}
Go to the *a*, thou sluggard ... Prov 6:6 5244

ANTHOTHIJAH See ANTOTHIJAH.

ANTICHRIST {4}
ye have heard that *a* shall come ... 1Jn 2:18 *500*
He is *a*, that denieth the Father ... 1Jn 2:22 *500*
and this is that spirit of *a* ... 1Jn 4:3 *500*
This is a deceiver and an *a* ... 2Jn 7 *500*

ANTICHRISTS {1}
come, even now are there many *a* ... 1Jn 2:18 *500*

ANTIOCH *(an'-te-ok)* {19}
1. A city in Syria.
and Nicolas a proselyte of *A* ... Acts 6:5 *491*
far as Phenice, and Cyprus, and *A* ... Acts 11:19 *490*
which, when they were come to *A* ... Acts 11:20 *490*
that he should go as far as *A* ... Acts 11:22 *490*
found him, he brought him unto *A* ... Acts 11:26 *490*
were called Christians first in *A* ... Acts 11:26 *490*
prophets from Jerusalem unto *A* ... Acts 11:27 *490*
that was at *A* certain prophets ... Acts 13:1 *490*
And thence sailed to *A*, from ... Acts 14:26 *490*
their own company to *A* with Paul ... Acts 15:22 *490*
which are of the Gentiles in *A* ... Acts 15:23 *490*
were dismissed, they came to *A* ... Acts 15:30 *490*
also and Barnabas continued in *A* ... Acts 15:35 *490*
the church, he went down to *A* ... Acts 18:22 *490*
But when Peter was come to *A* ... Gal 2:11 *490*
2. A city in Pisidia.
Perga, they came to *A* in Pisidia ... Acts 13:14 *490*
came thither certain Jews from *A* ... Acts 14:19 *490*
to Lystra, and to Iconium, and *A* ... Acts 14:21 *490*
which came unto me at *A*, at ... 2Ti 3:11 *490*

ANTIPAS *(an'-tip-as)* {1} *A Christian martyr.*
wherein *A* was my faithful martyr ... Rev 2:13 *493*

ANTIPATRIS *(an-tip'-at-ris)* {1} *A city in northern Palestine.*
and brought him by night to *A* ... Acts 23:31 *494*

ANTIQUITY {1}
whose *a* is of ancient days ... Is 23:7 6927

ANTOTHIJAH *(an-to-thi'-jah)* {1} *Son of Shashak.*
And Hananiah, and Elam, and *A* ... 1Chr 8:24 6070

ANTOTHITE *(an'-to-thite)* {2} See ANETOTHITE. *A native of Anathoth.*
Ikkesh the Tekoite, Abiezer the *A* ... 1Chr 11:28 6069
and Berachah, and Jehu the *A* ... 1Chr 12:3 6069

ANTS {1}
The *a* are a people not strong, ... Prov 30:25 5244

ANUB *(a'-nub)* {1} *A descendant of Judah.*
And Coz begat *A*, and Zobebah, and ... 1Chr 4:8 6036

ANVIL {1}
the hammer him that smote the *a* ... Is 41:7 6471

ANY See APPENDIX.

APACE {3}
And he came *a*, and drew near ... 2Sa 18:25
Kings of armies did flee *a* ... Ps 68:12
are beaten down, and are fled *a* ... Jer 46:5

APART See APPENDIX.

APELLES *(a-pel'-leze)* {1} *A Christian acquaintance of Paul.*
Salute *A* approved in Christ ... Rom 16:10 *559*

APES {2}
gold, and silver, ivory, and *a* ... 1Kin 10:22 6971
gold, and silver, ivory, and *a* ... 2Chr 9:21 6971

APHARSACHITES *(a-far'-sak-ites)* {2} See APHARSATHCHITES. *An Assyrian tribe.*
and his companions the *A*, which ... Ezr 5:6 671
and your companions the *A* ... Ezr 6:6 671

APHARSATHCHITES *(a-far'-sath-kites)* {1} See APHARSACHITES, APHARSITES. *Same as Apharsachites.*
the Dinaites, the *A*, the ... Ezr 4:9 671

APHARSITES *(a-far'-sites)* {1} See APHARSATHCHITES. *Same as Apharsachites*
the Tarpelites, the *A*, the ... Ezr 4:9 670

APHEK *(a'-fek)* {8} See APHIK.
1. A Canaanite city.
The king of *A*, one ... Josh 12:18 663
and the Philistines pitched in *A* ... 1Sa 4:1 663
together all their armies to *A* ... 1Sa 29:1 663
2. A city in Asher.
is beside the Sidonians, unto *A* ... Josh 13:4 663
Ummah also, and *A*, and Rehob ... Josh 19:30 663
3. Place where Ahab defeated Benhadad.
the Syrians, and went up to *A* ... 1Kin 20:26 663
But the rest fled to *A*, into the ... 1Kin 20:30 663
thou shalt smite the Syrians in *A* ... 2Kin 13:17 663

APHEKAH *(af-e'-kah)* {1} *A city in Judah.*
And Janum, and Beth-tappuah, and *A* ... Josh 15:53 664

APHIAH *(af-i'-ah)* {1} *An ancestor of Saul.*
son of Bechorath, the son of *A* ... 1Sa 9:1 647

APHIK *(a'-fik)* {1} See APHEK. *Same as Aphek 2.*
Achzib, nor of Helbah, nor of *A* ... Judg 1:31 663

APHRAH *(af'-rah)* {1} See BETH-LEAPHRAH, OPHRAH. *A city in Benjamin.*
in the house of *A* roll thyself in ... Mic 1:10 1036

APHSES *(af'-seze)* {1} *A Levite chief.*
to Hezir, the eighteenth to *A* ... 1Chr 24:15 6483

APIECE {8}
take five shekels *a* by the poll ... Num 3:47
incense, weighing ten shekels *a* ... Num 7:86
of their princes gave him a rod *a* ... Num 17:6
brass, of eighteen cubits high *a* ... 1Kin 7:15 5982,259
Every one had four faces *a* ... Eze 10:21 259
And the doors had two leaves *a* ... Eze 41:24
neither have two coats *a* ... Lk 9:3 *303*
containing two or three firkins *a* ... Jn 2:6 *303*

APOLLONIA *(ap-ol-lo'-ne-ah)* {1} *A city in Macedonia.*
passed through Amphipolis and *A* ... Acts 17:1 *624*

APOLLOS *(ap-ol'-los)* {10} *A Christian Jew from Alexandria.*
And a certain Jew named *A*, born at ... Acts 18:24 *625*
while *A* was at Corinth, Paul ... Acts 19:1 *625*
and I of *A* ... 1Cor 1:12 *625*
and another, I am of *A* ... 1Cor 3:4 *625*
Who then is Paul, and who is *A* ... 1Cor 3:5 *625*
I have planted, *A* watered ... 1Cor 3:6 *625*
Whether Paul, or *A*, or Cephas, or ... 1Cor 3:22 *625*
to myself and to *A* for your sakes ... 1Cor 4:6 *625*
As touching our brother *A* ... 1Cor 16:12 *625*
A on their journey diligently, ... Titus 3:13 *625*

APOLLYON *(ap-ol'-le-on)* {1} *The angel of the Abyss.*
the Greek tongue hath his name *A* ... Rev 9:11 *623*

APOSTLE {19}
Jesus Christ, called to be an *a* ... Rom 1:1 *652*
as I am the *a* of the Gentiles ... Rom 11:13 *652*
called to be an *a* of Jesus Christ ... 1Cor 1:1 *652*
Am I not an *a* ... 1Cor 9:1 *652*
If I be not an *a* unto others ... 1Cor 9:2 *652*
am not meet to be called an *a* ... 1Cor 15:9 *652*
an *a* of Jesus Christ by the will ... 2Cor 1:1 *652*
Truly the signs of an *a* were ... 2Cor 12:12 *652*
Paul, an *a*, (not of men, neither ... Gal 1:1 *652*
an *a* of Jesus Christ by the will ... Eph 1:1 *652*
an *a* of Jesus Christ by the will ... Col 1:1 *652*
an *a* of Jesus Christ by the ... 1Ti 1:1 *652*
I am ordained a preacher, and an *a* ... 1Ti 2:7 *652*
an *a* of Jesus Christ by the will ... 2Ti 1:1 *652*
am appointed a preacher, and an *a* ... 2Ti 1:11 *652*
an *a* of Jesus Christ, according ... Titus 1:1 *652*
heavenly calling, consider the *A* ... Heb 3:1 *652*
an *a* of Jesus Christ, to the ... 1Pet 1:1 *652*
an *a* of Jesus Christ, to them ... 2Pet 1:1 *652*

APOSTLES {55}
names of the twelve *a* are these ... Mt 10:2 *652*
the *a* gathered themselves ... Mk 6:30 *652*
twelve, whom also he named *a* ... Lk 6:13 *652*
And the *a*, when they were returned ... Lk 9:10 *652*
I will send them prophets and *a* ... Lk 11:49 *652*
the *a* said unto the Lord, ... Lk 17:5 *652*
down, and the twelve *a* with him ... Lk 22:14 *652*
told these things unto the *a* ... Lk 24:10 *652*
unto the *a* whom he had chosen ... Acts 1:2 *652*
he was numbered with the eleven *a* ... Acts 1:26 *652*
Peter and to the rest of the *a* ... Acts 2:37 *652*
and signs were done by the *a* ... Acts 2:43 *652*
with great power gave the *a* ... Acts 4:33 *652*
who by the *a* was surnamed ... Acts 4:36 *652*
hands of the *a* were many signs ... Acts 5:12 *652*
And laid their hands on the *a* ... Acts 5:18 *652*
Peter and the other *a* answered ... Acts 5:29 *652*
to put the *a* forth a little space ... Acts 5:34 *652*
and when they had called the *a* ... Acts 5:40 *652*
Whom they set before the *a* ... Acts 6:6 *652*
Judaea and Samaria, except the *a* ... Acts 8:1 *652*
Now when the *a* which were at ... Acts 8:14 *652*
took him, and brought him to the *a* ... Acts 9:27 *652*
And the *a* and brethren that were in ... Acts 11:1 *652*
with the Jews, and part with the *a* ... Acts 14:4 *652*
Which when the *a*, Barnabas and ... Acts 14:14 *652*
go up to Jerusalem unto the *a* ... Acts 15:2 *652*
of the church, and of the *a* ... Acts 15:4 *652*
And the *a* and elders came together ... Acts 15:6 *652*
Then pleased it the *a* and elders, ... Acts 15:22 *652*
The *a* and elders and brethren send ... Acts 15:23 *652*
from the brethren unto the *a* ... Acts 15:33
keep, that were ordained of the *a* ... Acts 16:4 *652*
who are of note among the *a* ... Rom 16:7 *652*
God hath set forth us the *a* last ... 1Cor 4:9 *652*
a wife, as well as other *a* ... 1Cor 9:5 *652*
set some in the church, first *a* ... 1Cor 12:28 *652*
Are all *a*? ... 1Cor 12:29 *652*
then of all the *a* ... 1Cor 15:7 *652*
For I am the least of the *a* ... 1Cor 15:9 *652*
a whit behind the very chiefest *a* ... 2Cor 11:5 *652*
For such are false *a*, deceitful ... 2Cor 11:13 *652*
themselves into the *a* of Christ ... 2Cor 11:13 *5570*
am I behind the very chiefest *a* ... 2Cor 12:11 *652*
to them which were *a* before me ... Gal 1:17 *652*
But other of the *a* saw I none ... Gal 1:19 *652*
upon the foundation of the *a* ... Eph 2:20 *652*
is now revealed unto his holy *a* ... Eph 3:5 *652*
And he gave some, *a* ... Eph 4:11 *652*
burdensome, as the *a* of Christ ... 1Th 2:6 *652*
of us the *a* of the Lord and ... 2Pet 3:2 *652*
of the *a* of our Lord Jesus Christ ... Jude 17 *652*
tried them which say they are *a* ... Rev 2:2 *652*
her, thou heaven, and ye holy *a* ... Rev 18:20 *652*
names of the twelve *a* of the Lamb ... Rev 21:14 *652*

APOSTLES' {5}
stedfastly in the *a* doctrine ... Acts 2:42 *652*
And laid them down at the *a* feet ... Acts 4:35 *652*
money, and laid it at the *a* feet ... Acts 4:37 *652*
part, and laid it at the *a* feet ... Acts 5:2 *652*
that through laying on of the *a* ... Acts 8:18 *652*

APOSTLESHIP {4}
take part of this ministry and *a* ... Acts 1:25 *651*
whom we have received grace and *a* ... Rom 1:5 *651*
seal of mine *a* are ye in the Lord ... 1Cor 9:2 *651*
to the *a* of the circumcision ... Gal 2:8 *651*

APOTHECARIES {1}
Hananiah the son of one of the *a* ... Neh 3:8 7543

APOTHECARIES' {1}
of spices prepared by the *a* art ... 2Chr 16:14 4842

APOTHECARY {4}
compound after the art of the *a* ... Ex 30:25 7543
confection after the art of the *a* ... Ex 30:35 7543
according to the work of the *a* ... Ex 37:29 7543
a to send forth a stinking savour ... Eccl 10:1 7543

APPAIM *(ap'-pa-im)* {2} *A son of Nadab.*
Seled, and *A* ... 1Chr 2:30 649
And the sons of *A* ... 1Chr 2:31 649

APPAREL {28}
by the year, and a suit of *a* ... Judg 17:10 899
asses, and the camels, and the *a* ... 1Sa 27:9 899
on ornaments of gold upon your *a* ... 2Sa 1:24 3830
himself, and changed his *a* ... 2Sa 12:20 8071
mourner, and put on now mourning *a* ... 2Sa 14:2 899
of his ministers, and their *a* ... 1Kin 10:5 4403
of his ministers, and their *a* ... 2Chr 9:4 4403
his cupbearers also, and their *a* ... 2Chr 9:4 4403
priests in their *a* with trumpets ... Ezr 3:10 3847
that Esther put on her royal *a* ... Est 5:1
Let the royal *a* be brought which ... Est 6:8 3830
And let this *a* and horse be ... Est 6:9 3830
Haman, Make haste, and take the *a* ... Est 6:10 3830
Then took Haman the *a* and the ... Est 6:11 3830
of the king in royal *a* of blue ... Est 8:15 3830
The changeable suits of *a* ... Is 3:22 4254
our own bread, and wear our own *a* ... Is 4:1 8071
this that is glorious in his *a* ... Is 63:1 3830
Wherefore art thou red in thine *a* ... Is 63:2 3830
work, and in chests of rich *a* ... Eze 27:24 1264
as are clothed with strange *a* ... Zeph 1:8 4403
together, gold, and silver, and *a* ... Zec 14:14 899
two men stood by them in white *a* ... Acts 1:10 *2066*
set day Herod, arrayed in royal *a* ... Acts 12:21 *2066*
no man's silver, or gold, or *a* ... Acts 20:33 *2441*

adorn themselves in modest *a* ... 1Ti 2:9 *2689*
man with a gold ring, in goodly *a* ... Jas 2:2 *2066*
of gold, or of putting on of *a* ... 1Pet 3:3 *2440*

APPARELLED {2}
daughters that were virgins *a* ... 2Sa 13:18 3847
they which are gorgeously *a* ... Lk 7:25 *2441*

APPARENTLY {1}
I speak mouth to mouth, even *a* ... Num 12:8 4758

APPEAL {2}
I *a* unto Caesar ... Acts 25:11 *1941*
was constrained to *a* unto Caesar ... Acts 28:19 *1941*

APPEALED {4}
answered, Hast thou *a* unto Caesar ... Acts 25:12 *1941*
But when Paul had *a* to be ... Acts 25:21 *1941*
he himself hath *a* to Augustus ... Acts 25:25 *1941*
if he had not *a* unto Caesar ... Acts 26:32 *1941*

APPEAR {54}
one place, and let the dry land *a* ... Gen 1:9 7200
made the white *a* which was in the ... Gen 30:37 4286
none shall *a* before me empty ... Ex 23:15 7200
males shall *a* before the Lord GOD ... Ex 23:17 7200
none shall *a* before me empty ... Ex 34:20 7200
children *a* before the Lord GOD ... Ex 34:23 7200
when thou shalt go up to *a* before ... Ex 34:24 7200
to day the LORD will *a* unto you ... Lev 9:4 7200
of the LORD shall *a* unto you ... Lev 9:6 7200
if it *a* still in the garment ... Lev 13:57 7200
for I will *a* in the cloud upon ... Lev 16:2 7200
in a year shall all thy males *a* ... Deut 16:16 7200
they shall not *a* before the LORD ... Deut 16:16 7200
When all Israel is come to *a* ... Deut 31:11 7200
the LORD did no more *a* to Manoah ... Judg 13:21 7200
that he may *a* before the LORD, and ... 1Sa 1:22 7200
Did I plainly *a* unto the house of ... 1Sa 2:27 1540
that night did God *a* unto Solomon ... 2Chr 1:7 7200
when shall I come and *a* before God ... Ps 42:2 7200
Let thy work *a* unto thy servants ... Ps 90:16 7200
up Zion, he shall *a* in his glory ... Ps 102:16 7200
The flowers *a* on the earth ... Song 2:12 7200
goats, that *a* from mount Gilead ... Song 4:1 1570
flock of goats that *a* from Gilead ... Song 6:5 1570
whether the tender grape *a* ... Song 7:12 6524
When ye come to *a* before me ... Is 1:12 7200
but he shall *a* to your joy ... Is 66:5 7200
thy face, that thy shame may *a* ... Jer 13:26 7200
in all your doings your sins do *a* ... Eze 21:24 7200
that they may *a* unto men to fast ... Mt 6:16 *5316*
That thou *a* not unto men to fast ... Mt 6:18 *5316*
which indeed *a* beautiful outward ... Mt 23:27 *5316*
outwardly *a* righteous unto men ... Mt 23:28 *5316*
then shall *a* the sign of the Son ... Mt 24:30 *5316*
for ye are as graves which *a* not ... Lk 11:44 *82*
of God should immediately *a* ... Lk 19:11 *398*
priests and all their council to *a* ... Acts 22:30 *2064*
in the which I will *a* unto thee ... Acts 26:16 *3700*
But sin, that it might *a* sin ... Rom 7:13 *5316*
For we must all *a* before the ... 2Cor 5:10 *5319*
the sight of God might *a* unto you ... 2Cor 7:12 *5319*
not that we should *a* approved ... 2Cor 13:7 *5316*
Christ, who is our life, shall *a* ... Col 3:4 *5319*
shall ye also *a* with him in glory ... Col 3:4 *5319*
that thy profiting may *a* to all ... 1Ti 4:15 *5318,5600*
now to *a* in the presence of God ... Heb 9:24 *1718*
he *a* the second time without sin ... Heb 9:28 *3700*
not made of things which do *a* ... Heb 11:3 *5316*
shall the ungodly and the sinner *a* ... 1Pet 4:18 *5316*
when the chief Shepherd shall *a* ... 1Pet 5:4 *5319*
that, when he shall *a*, we may ... 1Jn 2:28 *5319*
it doth not yet *a* what we shall ... 1Jn 3:2 *5319*
but we know that, when he shall *a* ... 1Jn 3:2 *5319*
shame of thy nakedness do not *a* ... Rev 3:18 *5319*

APPEARANCE {38}
as it were the *a* of fire, until ... Num 9:15 4758
by day, and the *a* of fire by night ... Num 9:16 4758
for man looketh on the outward *a* ... 1Sa 16:7 5869
And this was their *a* ... Eze 1:5 4758
their *a* was like burning coals of ... Eze 1:13 4758
and like the *a* of lamps ... Eze 1:13 4758
returned as the *a* of a flash of ... Eze 1:14 4758
The *a* of the wheels and their work ... Eze 1:16 4758
and their *a* and their work was as ... Eze 1:16 4758
as the *a* of a sapphire stone ... Eze 1:26 4758
as the *a* of a man above upon it ... Eze 1:26 4758
as the *a* of fire round about ... Eze 1:27 4758
from the *a* of his loins even ... Eze 1:27 4758
from the *a* of his loins even ... Eze 1:27 4758
I saw as it were the *a* of fire ... Eze 1:27 4758
As the *a* of the bow that is in ... Eze 1:28 4758
so was the *a* of the brightness ... Eze 1:28 4758
This was the *a* of the likeness of ... Eze 1:28 4758
and lo a likeness as the *a* of fire ... Eze 8:2 4758
from the *a* of his loins even ... Eze 8:2 4758
as the *a* of brightness, as the ... Eze 8:2 4758
as the *a* of the likeness of a ... Eze 10:1 4758
as for their *a*, the wheels was as the ... Eze 10:9 4758
whose *a* was like the *a* ... Eze 40:3 4758
the *a* of the one as the *a* ... Eze 41:21 4758
the *a* of the chambers which were ... Eze 42:11 4758
it was according to the *a* of the ... Eze 43:3 4758
stood before me as the *a* of a man ... Dan 8:15 4758
and his face as the *a* of lightning ... Dan 10:6 4758
me one like the *a* of a man ... Dan 10:18 4758
a of them is as the *a* of horses ... Joel 2:4 4758
Judge not according to the *a* ... Jn 7:24 *3799*
to answer them which glory in *a* ... 2Cor 5:12 *4383*
on things after the outward *a* ... 2Cor 10:7 *4383*
Abstain from all *a* of evil ... 1Th 5:22 *1491*

APPEARANCES {2}
And as for their *a*, they four had ... Eze 10:10 4758
by the river of Chebar, their *a* ... Eze 10:22 4758

APPEARED {70}
the LORD *a* unto Abram, and said ... Gen 12:7 7200
unto the LORD, who *a* unto him ... Gen 12:7 7200
old and nine, the LORD *a* to Abram ... Gen 17:1 7200
the LORD *a* unto him in the plains ... Gen 18:1 7200
And the LORD *a* unto him, and said ... Gen 26:2 7200
the LORD *a* unto him the same ... Gen 26:24 7200
that *a* unto thee when thou ... Gen 35:1 7200
because there God *a* unto him ... Gen 35:7 1540
God *a* unto Jacob again, when he ... Gen 35:9 7200
God Almighty *a* unto me at Luz in ... Gen 48:3 7200
the angel of the LORD *a* unto him ... Ex 3:2 7200
a unto me, saying, I have surely ... Ex 3:16 7200
The LORD hath not *a* unto thee ... Ex 4:1 7200
God of Jacob, hath *a* unto thee ... Ex 4:5 7200
I *a* unto Abraham, unto Isaac, and ... Ex 6:3 7200
his strength when the morning *a* ... Ex 14:27 6437
glory of the LORD *a* in the cloud ... Ex 16:10 7200
of the LORD *a* unto all the people ... Lev 9:23 7200
the glory of the LORD *a* in the ... Num 14:10 7200
the glory of the LORD *a* unto all ... Num 16:19 7200
it, and the glory of the LORD *a* ... Num 16:42 7200
the glory of the LORD *a* unto them ... Num 20:6 7200
the LORD *a* in the tabernacle in a ... Deut 31:15 7200
the angel of the LORD *a* unto him ... Judg 6:12 7200
of the LORD *a* unto the woman ... Judg 13:3 7200
Behold, the man hath *a* unto me ... Judg 13:10 7200
the LORD *a* again in Shiloh ... 1Sa 3:21 7200
And the channels of the sea *a* ... 2Sa 22:16 7200
In Gibeon the LORD *a* to Solomon ... 1Kin 3:5 7200
That the LORD *a* to Solomon the ... 1Kin 9:2 7200
as he had *a* unto him at Gibeon ... 1Kin 9:2 7200
which had *a* unto him twice ... 1Kin 11:9 7200
there *a* a chariot of fire, and ... 2Kin 2:11
where the LORD *a* unto David his ... 2Chr 3:1 7200
the LORD *a* to Solomon by night ... 2Chr 7:12 7200
of the morning till the stars *a* ... Neh 4:21 3318
The LORD hath *a* of old unto me ... Jer 31:3 7200
a over them as it were a sapphire ... Eze 10:1 7200
there *a* in the cherubims the form ... Eze 10:8 7200
she *a* in her height with the ... Eze 19:11 7200
days their countenances *a* fairer ... Dan 1:15 7200
Belshazzar a vision *a* unto me ... Dan 8:1 7200
after that which *a* unto me at the ... Dan 8:1 7200
of the Lord *a* unto him in a dream ... Mt 1:20 *5316*
diligently what time the star *a* ... Mt 2:7 *5316*
fruit, then *a* the tares also ... Mt 13:26 *5316*
there *a* unto them Moses and Elias ... Mt 17:3 *3700*
the holy city, and *a* unto many ... Mt 27:53 *1718*
there *a* unto them Elias with ... Mk 9:4 *3700*
he *a* first to Mary Magdalene, out ... Mk 16:9 *5316*
After that he *a* in another form ... Mk 16:12 *5319*
Afterward he *a* unto the eleven as ... Mk 16:14 *5319*
there *a* unto him an angel of the ... Lk 1:11 *3700*
And of some, that Elias had *a* ... Lk 9:8 *5316*
Who *a* in glory, and spake of his ... Lk 9:31 *3700*
there *a* an angel unto him from ... Lk 22:43 *3700*
risen indeed, and hath *a* to Simon ... Lk 24:34 *3700*
there *a* unto them cloven tongues ... Acts 2:3 *3700*
The God of glory *a* unto our ... Acts 7:2 *3700*
there *a* to him in the wilderness ... Acts 7:30 *3700*
angel which *a* to him in the bush ... Acts 7:35 *3700*
that *a* unto thee in the way as ... Acts 9:17 *3700*
a vision *a* to Paul in the night ... Acts 16:9 *3700*
for I have *a* unto thee for this ... Acts 26:16 *3700*
sun nor stars in many days *a* ... Acts 27:20 *2014*
salvation hath *a* to all men ... Titus 2:11 *2014*
of God our Saviour toward man *a* ... Titus 3:4 *2014*
hath he *a* to put away sin by the ... Heb 9:26 *5319*
there *a* a great wonder in heaven ... Rev 12:1 *3700*
there *a* another wonder in heaven ... Rev 12:3 *3700*

APPEARETH {10}
But when raw flesh *a* in him ... Lev 13:14 7200
as the leprosy *a* in the skin of ... Lev 13:43 4758
him into thy hand, as *a* this day ... Deut 2:30
one of them in Zion *a* before God ... Ps 84:7 7200
The hay *a*, and the tender grass ... Prov 27:25 1540
for evil *a* out of the north, and ... Jer 6:1 8259
and who shall stand when he *a* ... Mal 3:2 7200
the Lord *a* to Joseph in a dream ... Mt 2:13 *5316*
an angel of the Lord *a* in a dream ... Mt 2:19 *5316*
that *a* for a little time, and then ... Jas 4:14 *5316*

APPEARING {6}
until the *a* of our Lord Jesus ... 1Ti 6:14 *2015*
the *a* of our Saviour Jesus Christ ... 2Ti 1:10 *2015*
the quick and the dead at his *a* ... 2Ti 4:1 *2015*
all them also that love his *a* ... 2Ti 4:8 *2015*
the glorious *a* of the great God ... Titus 2:13 *2015*
glory at the *a* of Jesus Christ ... 1Pet 1:7 *602*

APPEASE {1}
I will *a* him with the present ... Gen 32:20 3722,6440

APPEASED {2}
the wrath of king Ahasuerus was *a* ... Est 2:1 7918
the townclerk had *a* the people ... Acts 19:35 *2687*

APPEASETH {1}
he that is slow to anger *a* strife ... Prov 15:18 8252

APPERTAIN {2}
up, with all that *a* unto them ... Num 16:30
for to thee doth it *a* ... Jer 10:7 2969

APPERTAINED {3}
and all the men that *a* unto Korah ... Num 16:32
They, and all that *a* to them ... Num 16:33
the palace which *a* to the house ... Neh 2:8

APPERTAINETH {2}
and give it unto him to whom it *a* ... Lev 6:5
It *a* not unto thee, Uzziah, to ... 2Chr 26:18

APPETITE {4}
or fill the *a* of the young lions ... Job 38:39 2416
if thou be a man given to *a* ... Prov 23:2 5315
mouth, and yet the *a* is not filled ... Eccl 6:7 5315
he is faint, and his soul hath *a* ... Is 29:8 8264

APPHIA *(af'-fee-ah)* {1} *A Christian acquaintance of Paul.*
And to our beloved *A*, and Archippus ... Philem 2 *682*

APPII *(ap'-pe-i)* {1} *A place south of Rome.*
came to meet us as far as *A* forum ... Acts 28:15 *675*

APPIUS See APPII.

APPLE {8}
he kept him as the *a* of his eye ... Deut 32:10 380
Keep me as the *a* of the eye ... Ps 17:8 380,1323
and my law as the *a* of thine eye ... Prov 7:2 380
As the *a* tree among the trees of ... Song 2:3 8598
I raised thee up under the *a* tree ... Song 8:5 8598
let not the *a* of thine eye cease ... Lam 2:18 1323
the *a* tree, even all the trees of ... Joel 1:12 8598
you toucheth the *a* of his eye ... Zec 2:8 892

APPLES {3}
A word fitly spoken is like *a* of ... Prov 25:11 8598
with flagons, comfort me with *a* ... Song 2:5 8598
and the smell of thy nose like *a* ... Song 7:8 8598

APPLIED {3}
I *a* mine heart to know, and to ... Eccl 7:25 5437
a my heart unto every work that ... Eccl 8:9 5414
When I *a* mine heart to know ... Eccl 8:16 5414

APPLY {4}
that we may *a* our hearts unto ... Ps 90:12 935
a thine heart to understanding ... Prov 2:2 5186
a thine heart unto my knowledge ... Prov 22:17 7896
A thine heart unto instruction ... Prov 23:12 935

APPOINT {41}
A me thy wages, and I will give it ... Gen 30:28 5344
let him *a* officers over the land ... Gen 41:34 6485
then I will *a* thee a place ... Ex 21:13 7760
shalt *a* it for the service of the ... Ex 30:16 5414
I will even *a* over you terror ... Lev 26:16 6485
But thou shalt *a* the Levites over ... Num 1:50 6485
And thou shalt *a* Aaron and his sons ... Num 3:10 6485
a them every one to his service ... Num 4:19 7760
ye shall *a* unto them in charge ... Num 4:27 6485
refuge, which ye shall *a* for the ... Num 35:6 5414
Then ye shall *a* you cities to be ... Num 35:11 7136
A out for you cities of refuge ... Josh 20:2 5414
a them for himself, for his ... 1Sa 8:11 7760
he will *a* him captains over ... 1Sa 8:12 7760
to *a* me ruler over the people of ... 2Sa 6:21 6680
Moreover I will *a* a place for my ... 2Sa 7:10 7760
my lord the king shall *a* ... 2Sa 15:15 977
to all that thou shalt *a* ... 1Kin 5:6 559
the place that thou shalt *a* me ... 1Kin 5:9 7971
to *a* their brethren to be the ... 1Chr 15:16 5975
a watches of the inhabitants of ... Neh 7:3 5975
let the king *a* officers in all ... Est 2:3 6485
thou wouldest *a* me a set time ... Job 14:13 7896
salvation will God *a* for walls ... Is 26:1 7896
To *a* unto them that mourn in Zion ... Is 61:3 7760
I will *a* over them four kinds ... Jer 15:3 6485
chosen man, that I may *a* over her ... Jer 49:19 6485
and who will *a* me the time ... Jer 49:19 3259
chosen man, that I may *a* over her ... Jer 50:44 6485
and who will *a* me the time ... Jer 50:44 3259
a a captain against her ... Jer 51:27 6485
a thee two ways, that the sword ... Eze 21:19 7760
A a way, that the sword may come ... Eze 21:20 7760
to *a* captains, to open the mouth ... Eze 21:22 7760
to *a* battering rams against the ... Eze 21:22 7760
ye shall *a* the possession of the ... Eze 45:6 5414
a themselves one head, and they ... Hos 1:11 7760
a him his portion with the ... Mt 24:51 *5087*
will *a* him his portion with the ... Lk 12:46 *5087*
I *a* unto you a kingdom, as my ... Lk 22:29 *1303*
whom we may *a* over this business ... Acts 6:3 *2525*

APPOINTED {126}
hath *a* me another seed instead of ... Gen 4:25 7896
At the time *a* I will return unto ... Gen 18:14 4150
thou hast *a* for thy servant Isaac ... Gen 24:14 3198
hath *a* out for my master's son ... Gen 24:44 3198
the LORD *a* a set time, saying, To ... Ex 9:5 7760
in the time *a* of the month Abib ... Ex 23:15 4150
keep the passover at his *a* season ... Num 9:2 4150
ye shall keep it in his *a* season ... Num 9:3 4150
a season among the children of ... Num 9:7 4150
of the LORD in his *a* season ... Num 9:13 4150
he and all his people, at a time *a* ... Josh 8:14 4150
they *a* Kedesh in Galilee in mount ... Josh 20:7 6942
These were the cities *a* for all ... Josh 20:9 4152
six hundred men *a* with weapons of ... Judg 18:11 2296
the six hundred men *a* with their ... Judg 18:16 2296
that were *a* with weapons of war ... Judg 18:17 2296
Now there was an *a* sign between ... Judg 20:38 4150
to the set time that Samuel had *a* ... 1Sa 13:8
thou camest not within the days *a* ... 1Sa 13:11 4150
and Samuel standing as *a* over them ... 1Sa 19:20 5324
field at the time *a* with David ... 1Sa 20:35 4150

I have *a* my servants to such and ... 1Sa 21:2 3045
shall have *a* thee ruler over ... 1Sa 25:30 6680
his place which thou hast *a* him ... 1Sa 29:4 6485
For the LORD had *a* to defeat the ... 2Sa 17:14 6680
the set time which he had *a* him ... 2Sa 20:5 3259
the morning even to the time *a* ... 2Sa 24:15 4150
I have *a* him to be ruler over ... 1Kin 1:35 6680
a him victuals, and gave him land ... 1Kin 11:18 559
the third day, as the king had *a* ... 1Kin 12:12 1696
man whom I *a* to utter destruction ... 1Kin 20:42 2764
the king *a* the lord on whose hand ... 2Kin 7:17 6485
So the king *a* unto her a certain ... 2Kin 8:6 5414
Jehu *a* fourscore men without, and ... 2Kin 10:24 7760
the priest *a* officers over the ... 2Kin 11:18 7760
the king of Assyria *a* unto ... 2Kin 18:14 7760
a unto all manner of service of ... 1Chr 6:48 5414
were *a* for all the work of the ... 1Chr 6:49
were *a* to oversee the vessels ... 1Chr 9:29 4487
So the Levites *a* Heman the son of ... 1Chr 15:17 5975
were *a* to sound with cymbals of ... 1Chr 15:19
he *a* certain of the Levites to ... 1Chr 16:4 5414
And he *a*, according to the order ... 2Chr 8:14 5975
he *a* singers unto the LORD, and ... 2Chr 20:21 5975
Also Jehoiada *a* the offices of ... 2Chr 23:18 7760
Hezekiah *a* the courses of the ... 2Chr 31:2 5975
He *a* also the king's portion of ... 2Chr 31:3
which I have *a* for your fathers ... 2Chr 33:8 5975
and they that the king had *a* ... 2Chr 34:22
a the Levites, from twenty years ... Ezr 3:8 5975
the princes had *a* for the service ... Ezr 8:20 5414
in our cities come at *a* times ... Ezr 10:14 2163
from the time that I was *a* to be ... Neh 5:14 6680
thou hast also *a* prophets to ... Neh 6:7 5975
the singers and the Levites were *a* ... Neh 7:1 6485
in their rebellion *a* a captain to ... Neh 9:17 5414
at times *a* year by year, to burn ... Neh 10:34 2163
a two great companies of them ... Neh 12:31 5975
at that time were some *a* over the ... Neh 12:44 6485
a the wards of the priests and the ... Neh 13:30 5975
for the wood offering, at times *a* ... Neh 13:31 2163
for so the king had *a* to all the ... Est 1:8 3245
the keeper of the women, *a* ... Est 2:15 559
whom he had *a* to attend upon her, ... Est 4:5 5975
to their *a* time every year ... Est 9:27
days of Purim in their times *a* ... Est 9:31
Is there not an *a* time to man ... Job 7:1 6635
and wearisome nights are *a* to me ... Job 7:3 4487
thou hast *a* his bounds that he ... Job 14:5 6213
the days of my *a* time will I wait ... Job 14:14 6635
the heritage *a* unto him by God ... Job 20:29 561
the thing that is *a* for me ... Job 23:14 2706
to the house *a* for all living ... Job 30:23 4150
given us like sheep *a* for meat ... Ps 44:11
a a law in Israel, which he ... Ps 78:5 7760
thou those that are *a* to die ... Ps 79:11 1121
in the new moon, in the time *a* ... Ps 81:3 3677
loose those that are *a* to death ... Ps 102:20 1121
He *a* the moon for seasons ... Ps 104:19 6213
and will come home at the day *a* ... Prov 7:20 3677
when he *a* the foundations of the ... Prov 8:29 2710
all such as are *a* to destruction ... Prov 31:8 1121
your *a* feasts my soul hateth ... Is 1:14 4150
shall be alone in his *a* times ... Is 14:31 4151
the *a* barley and the rie in their ... Is 28:25 5567
since I *a* the ancient people ... Is 44:7 7760
us the *a* weeks of the harvest ... Jer 5:24 2708
in the heaven knoweth her *a* times ... Jer 8:7 4150
if I have not *a* the ordinances of ... Jer 33:25 7760
he hath passed the time *a* ... Jer 46:17 4150
there hath he *a* it ... Jer 47:7 3259
I have *a* thee each day for a year ... Eze 4:6 5414
which have *a* my land into their ... Eze 36:5 5414
it in the *a* place of the house ... Eze 43:21 4662
the king *a* them a daily provision ... Dan 1:5 4487
who hath *a* your meat and your ... Dan 1:10 4487
for at the time *a* the end shall ... Dan 8:19 4150
was true, but the time *a* was long ... Dan 10:1 6635
the end shall be at the time *a* ... Dan 11:27 4150
At the time *a* he shall return, and ... Dan 11:29 4150
because it is yet for a time *a* ... Dan 11:35 4150
hear ye the rod, and who hath *a* it ... Mic 6:9 3259
the vision is yet for an *a* time ... Hab 2:3 4150
disciples did as Jesus had *a* them ... Mt 26:19 *4929*
potter's field, as the Lord *a* me ... Mt 27:10 *4929*
a mountain where Jesus had *a* them ... Mt 28:16 *5021*
no more than that which is *a* you ... Lk 3:13 *1299*
the Lord *a* other seventy also ... Lk 10:1 *322*
as my Father hath *a* unto me ... Lk 22:29 *1303*
And they *a* two, Joseph called ... Acts 1:23 *1476*
in the wilderness, as he had *a* ... Acts 7:44 *1299*
determined the times before *a* ... Acts 17:26 *4384*
Because he hath *a* a day, in the ... Acts 17:31 *2476*
for so had he *a*, minding himself ... Acts 20:13 *1299*
things which are *a* for thee to do ... Acts 22:10 *5021*
And when they had *a* him a day ... Acts 28:23 *5021*
last, as it were *a* to death ... 1Cor 4:9 *1935*
until the time *a* of the father ... Gal 4:2 *4287*
know that we are *a* thereunto ... 1Th 3:3 *2749*
For God hath not *a* us to wrath ... 1Th 5:9 *5087*
Whereunto I am *a* a preacher ... 2Ti 1:11 *5087*
in every city, as I had *a* thee ... Titus 1:5 *1299*
whom he hath *a* heir of all things ... Heb 1:2 *5081*
was faithful to him that *a* him ... Heb 3:2 *4160*
as it is *a* unto men once to die, ... Heb 9:27 *606*
whereunto also they were *a* ... 1Pet 2:8 *5087*

APPOINTETH {1}
that he *a* over it whomsoever he ... Dan 5:21 6966

APPOINTMENT {4}
At the *a* of Aaron and his sons ... Num 4:27 6310
for by the *a* of Absalom this hath ... 2Sa 13:32 6310
according to the *a* of the priests ... Ezr 6:9 3883
for they had made an *a* together ... Job 2:11 3259

APPREHEND {2}
with a garrison, desirous to *a* me ... 2Cor 11:32 *4084*
if that I may *a* that for which ... Phil 3:12 *2638*

APPREHENDED {3}
And when he had *a* him, he put him ... Acts 12:4 *4084*
which also I am *a* of Christ Jesus ... Phil 3:12 *2638*
I count not myself to have *a* ... Phil 3:13 *2638*

APPROACH {19}
None of you shall *a* to any that ... Lev 18:6 7126
thou shalt not *a* to his wife ... Lev 18:14 7126
Also thou shalt not *a* unto a ... Lev 18:19 7126
if a woman *a* unto any beast, and ... Lev 20:16 7126
let him not *a* to offer the bread ... Lev 21:17 7126
hath a blemish, he shall not *a* ... Lev 21:18 7126
when they *a* unto the most holy ... Num 4:19 5066
battle, that the priest shall *a* ... Deut 20:2 5066
ye *a* this day unto battle against ... Deut 20:3 7126
thy days *a* that thou must die ... Deut 31:14 7126
are with me, will *a* unto the city ... Josh 8:5 7126
can make his sword to *a* unto him ... Job 40:19 5066
and causest to *a* unto thee ... Ps 65:4 7126
draw near, and he shall *a* unto me ... Jer 30:21 5066
engaged his heart to *a* unto me ... Jer 30:21 5066
where the priests that *a* unto the ... Eze 42:13 7138
shall *a* to those things which are ... Eze 42:14 7126
which *a* unto me, to minister unto ... Eze 43:19 7126
the light which no man can *a* unto ... 1Ti 6:16 *676*

APPROACHED {2}
Wherefore *a* ye so nigh unto the ... 2Sa 11:20 5066
the king *a* to the altar, and ... 2Kin 16:12 7126

APPROACHETH {1}
faileth not, where no thief *a* ... Lk 12:33 *1448*

APPROACHING {2}
they take delight in *a* to God ... Is 58:2 7132
the more, as ye see the day *a* ... Heb 10:25 *1448*

APPROVE {3}
their posterity *a* their sayings ... Ps 49:13 7520
ye shall *a* by your letters ... 1Cor 16:3 *1381*
That ye may *a* things that are ... Phil 1:10 *1381*

APPROVED {8}
a man *a* of God among you by ... Acts 2:22 *584*
is acceptable to God, and *a* of men ... Rom 14:18 *1384*
Salute Apelles *a* in Christ ... Rom 16:10 *1384*
that they which are *a* may be made ... 1Cor 11:19 *1384*
In all things ye have *a* ... 2Cor 7:11 *4921*
he that commendeth himself is *a* ... 2Cor 10:18 *1384*
not that we should appear *a* ... 2Cor 13:7 *1384*
Study to shew thyself *a* unto God ... 2Ti 2:15 *1384*

APPROVEST {1}
a the things that are more ... Rom 2:18 *1381*

APPROVETH {1}
man in his cause, the Lord *a* not ... Lam 3:36 7200

APPROVING {1}
But in all things *a* ourselves as ... 2Cor 6:4 *4921*

APRONS {2}
together, and made themselves *a* ... Gen 3:7 2290
unto the sick handkerchiefs or *a* ... Acts 19:12 *4612*

APT {4}
a for war, even them the king of ... 2Kin 24:16 6213
of them that were *a* to the war ... 1Chr 7:40
given to hospitality, *a* to teach ... 1Ti 3:2 *1317*
all men, *a* to teach, patient, ... 2Ti 2:24 *1317*

AQUILA *(ac'-quil-ah)* {6} *A Christian acquaintance of Paul.*
And found a certain Jew named *A* ... Acts 18:2 *207*
Syria, and with him Priscilla and *A* ... Acts 18:18 *207*
whom when *A* and Priscilla had ... Acts 18:26 *207*
A my helpers in Christ Jesus ... Rom 16:3 *207*
A and Priscilla salute you much in ... 1Cor 16:19 *207*
Salute Prisca and *A*, and the ... 2Ti 4:19 *207*

AR *(ar)* {6} *The capital of Moab.*
goeth down to the dwelling of *A* ... Num 21:15 6144
it hath consumed *A* of Moab ... Num 21:28 6144
because I have given *A* unto the ... Deut 2:9 6144
Thou art to pass over through *A* ... Deut 2:18 6144
and the Moabites which dwell in *A* ... Deut 2:29 6144
Because in the night *A* of Moab is ... Is 15:1 6144

ARA *(a'-rah)* {1} *A son of Jether.*
Jephunneh, and Pispah, and *A* ... 1Chr 7:38 690

ARAB *(a'-rab)* {1} See ARBITE. *A city in Judah.*
A, and Dumah, and Eshean, ... Josh 15:52 694

ARABAH *(ar'-ab-ah)* {2} See BETH-ARABAH. *The Jordan Valley.*
the side over against *A* northward ... Josh 18:18 6160
and went down unto *A* ... Josh 18:18 6160

ARABIA *(a-ra'-be-ah)* {8} *The northern part of the Arabian peninsula.*
and of all the kings of *A* ... 1Kin 10:15 6152
And all the kings of *A* and ... 2Chr 9:14 6152
The burden upon *A* ... Is 21:13 6152
In the forest in *A* shall ye lodge ... Is 21:13 6152
And all the kings of *A*, and all the ... Jer 25:24 6152
A, and all the princes of Kedar, ... Eze 27:21 6152
but I went into *A*, and returned ... Gal 1:17 *688*
For this Agar is mount Sinai in *A* ... Gal 4:25 *688*

ARABIAN *(a-ra'-be-un)* {4} See ARABIANS. *An inhabitant of Arabia.*
the Ammonite, and Geshem the *A* ... Neh 2:19 6163
and Tobiah, and Geshem the *A* ... Neh 6:1 6163
shall the *A* pitch tent there ... Is 13:20 6153
as the *A* in the wilderness ... Jer 3:2 6163

ARABIANS *(a-ra'-be-uns)* {6}
the *A* brought him flocks, seven ... 2Chr 17:11 6163
of the Philistines, and of the *A* ... 2Chr 21:16 6163
A to the camp had slain all the ... 2Chr 22:1 6163
against the *A* that dwelt in ... 2Chr 26:7 6163
Sanballat, and Tobiah, and the *A* ... Neh 4:7 6163
Cretes and *A*, we do hear them ... Acts 2:11 *690*

ARABS See ARABIANS.

ARAD *(a'-rad)* {5}
1. A Canaanite king.
when king *A* the Canaanite, which ... Num 21:1 6166
king *A* the Canaanite, which dwelt ... Num 33:40 6166
2. A district in Judah.
the king of *A*, one ... Josh 12:14 6166
which lieth in the south of *A* ... Judg 1:16 6166
3. A son of Beriah.
And Zebadiah, and *A*, and Ader, ... 1Chr 8:15 6166

ARAH *(a'-rah)* {4}
1. A son of Ulla.
A, and Haniel, and Rezia ... 1Chr 7:39 733
2. A family of exiles who returned under Zerubbabel.
The children of *A*, seven hundred ... Ezr 2:5 733
The children of *A*, six hundred ... Neh 7:10 733
3. Grandfather of Tobiah's wife.
in law of Shechaniah the son of *A* ... Neh 6:18 733

ARAM *(a'-ram)* {10} See ARAMITESS, ARAM-NAHARAIM, ARAM-ZOBAH, BETH-ARAM, PADAN-ARAM, SYRIA.
1. The son of Shem.
and Arphaxad, and Lud, and *A* ... Gen 10:22 758
And the children of *A* ... Gen 10:23 758
and Arphaxad, and Lud, and *A* ... 1Chr 1:17 758
2. The son of Kemuel.
and Kemuel the father of *A* ... Gen 22:21 758
3. Another name for Syria.
of Moab hath brought me from *A* ... Num 23:7 758
4. A district of Canaan.
And he took Geshur, and *A*, with the ... 1Chr 2:23 758
5. The son of Shamer.
Ahi, and Rohgah, Jehubbah, and *A* ... 1Chr 7:34 758
and Esrom begat *A* ... Mt 1:3 *689*
And *A* begat Aminadab ... Mt 1:4 *689*
Aminadab, which was the son of *A* ... Lk 3:33 *689*

ARAMEAN See ARAMITESS.

ARAMITESS *(a'-ram-i-tes)* {1} See SYRIAN. *Manasseh's concubine.*
(but his concubine the *A* bare ... 1Chr 7:14 761

ARAM-NAHARAIM *(a'-ram-na-ha-ra'-im)* {1} See MESOPOTAMIA. *The area between the Tigris and Euphrates rivers.*
when he strove with *A* and with ... Ps 60:*t* 763

ARAM-ZOBAH *(a'-ram-zo'-bah)* {1} *The area between the Orontes and Euphrates rivers.*
with Aram-naharaim and with *A* ... Ps 60:*t* 760

ARAN *(a'-ran)* {2} See BETH-ARAN. *The son of Seir the Horite.*
of Dishan are these; Uz, and *A* ... Gen 36:28 765
sons of Dishan; Uz, and *A* ... 1Chr 1:42 765

ARARAT *(ar'-ar-at)* {2} See ARMENIA. *A district in Armenia.*
month, upon the mountains of *A* ... Gen 8:4 780
against her the kingdoms of *A* ... Jer 51:27 780

ARAUNAH *(a-raw'-nah)* {9} See ORNAN. *A Jebusite.*
threshingplace of *A* the Jebusite ... 2Sa 24:16 728
threshingfloor of *A* the Jebusite ... 2Sa 24:18 728
A looked, and saw the king and his ... 2Sa 24:20 728
A went out, and bowed himself ... 2Sa 24:20 728
A said, Wherefore is my lord the ... 2Sa 24:21 728
A said unto David, Let my lord ... 2Sa 24:22 728
All these things did *A*, as a king ... 2Sa 24:23 728
A said unto the king, The LORD ... 2Sa 24:23 728
And the king said unto *A*, Nay ... 2Sa 24:24 728

ARBA *(ar'-bah)* {2} See ARBAH, ARBATHITE, ARBITE, KIRJATH-ABBA. *Father of Anakim.*
even the city of *A* the father of ... Josh 15:13 704
the city of *A* the father of Anak ... Josh 21:11 704

ARBAH *(ar'-bah)* {1} See ARBA. *Another name for Hebron.*
unto Mamre, unto the city of *A* ... Gen 35:27 704

ARBATHITE *(ar'-bath-ite)* {2} *A native of Arbah.*
Abi-albon the *A*, Azmaveth the ... 2Sa 23:31 6164
the brooks of Gaash, Abiel the *A* ... 1Chr 11:32 6164

ARBITE *(ar'-bite)* {1} *A native of Arab.*
the Carmelite, Paarai the *A* ... 2Sa 23:35 701

ARCHANGEL {2}
a shout, with the voice of the *a* ... 1Th 4:16 *743*
Yet Michael the *a*, when ... Jude 9 *743*

ARCHELAUS *(ar-ke-la'-us)* {1} *A son of Herod the Great.*
But when he heard that *A* did ... Mt 2:22 *745*

ARCHER {2}
in the wilderness, and became an *a* ... Gen 21:20 7198
bendeth let the *a* bend his bow ... Jer 51:3 1869

ARCHERS {12}
The *a* have sorely grieved him Gen 49:23 1167,2671
a in the places of drawing water Judg 5:11 2686
Saul, and the *a* hit him 1Sa 31:3 3384,376,7198
and he was sore wounded of the *a* 1Sa 31:3 3384
were mighty men of valour, *a* 1Chr 8:40 1869,7198
the *a* hit him 1Chr 10:3 3384,7198
and he was wounded of the *a* 1Chr 10:3 3384
the *a* shot at king Josiah 2Chr 35:23 3384
His *a* compass me round about, he Job 16:13 7228
And the residue of the number of *a* Is 21:17 7198
together, they are bound by the *a* Is 22:3 7198
together the *a* against Babylon Jer 50:29 7228

ARCHES {15}
round about, and likewise to the *a* Eze 40:16 361
the *a* thereof were after the Eze 40:21 361
And their windows, and their *a* Eze 40:22 361
the *a* thereof were before them Eze 40:22 361
the *a* thereof according to these Eze 40:24 361
in the *a* thereof round about, Eze 40:25 361
the *a* thereof were before them Eze 40:26 361
the *a* thereof, according to these Eze 40:29 361
in the *a* thereof round about Eze 40:29 361
the *a* round about were five and Eze 40:30 361
the *a* thereof were toward the Eze 40:31 361
the *a* thereof, were according to Eze 40:33 361
in the *a* thereof round about Eze 40:33 361
the *a* thereof were toward the Eze 40:34 361
the *a* thereof, and the windows to Eze 40:36 361

ARCHEVITES *(ar'-ke-vites)* {1} *Chaldean settlers in Samaria.*
Tarpelites, the Apharsites, the *A* Ezr 4:9 756

ARCHI *(ar'-kee)* {1} See ARCHITE. *A border city of Ephraim.*
unto the borders of *A* to Ataroth Josh 16:2 757

ARCHIPPUS *(ar-kip'-pus)* {2} *A Christian acquaintance of Paul.*
And say to *A*, Take heed to the Col 4:17 *751*
A our fellowsoldier, and to the Philem 2 *751*

ARCHITE *(ar'-kite)* {5} See ARCHI. *A friend of David.*
Hushai the *A* came to meet him 2Sa 15:32 757
came to pass, when Hushai the *A* 2Sa 16:16 757
Call now Hushai the *A* also 2Sa 17:5 757
The counsel of Hushai the *A* is 2Sa 17:14 757
Hushai the *A* was the king's 1Chr 27:33 757

ARCHITES See ARCHI.

ARCTURUS *(ark-tu'-rus)* {2} *Another name for "the Great Bear."*
Which maketh *A*, Orion, and Job 9:9 5906
canst thou guide *A* with his sons Job 38:32 5906

ARD *(ard)* {3} See ARDITES.
1. A son of Benjamin.
Rosh, Muppim, and Huppim, and *A* Gen 46:21 714
2. A son of Bela.
And the sons of Bela were *A* Num 26:40 714
of *A*, the family of the Ardites Num 26:40 714

ARDITES *(ar'-dites)* {1} *Descendants of Bela.*
of Ard, the family of the *A* Num 26:40 716

ARDON *(ar'-don)* {1} *A son of Caleb.*
Jesher, and Shobab, and *A* 1Chr 2:18 715

ARE See APPENDIX.

ARELI *(a-re'-li)* {2} See ARELITES. *A son of Gad.*
and Ezbon, Eri, and Arodi, and *A* Gen 46:16 692
of *A*, the family of the Arelites Num 26:17 692

ARELITES *(a-re'-lites)* {1} See ARELI. *Descendants of Areli.*
of Areli, the family of the *A* Num 26:17 692

AREOPAGITE *(a-re-op'-a-jite)* {1} *A title of Dionysius.*
the which was Dionysius the *A* Acts 17:34 *698*

AREOPAGUS *(a-re-op'-a-gus)* {1} See AREOPAGITE, MARS'. *A plaza in Athens.*
took him, and brought him unto *A* Acts 17:19 *697*

ARETAS *(ar'-e-tas)* {1} *A north Arabian ruler.*
A the king kept the city of the 2Cor 11:32 *702*

ARGOB *(ar'-gob)* {5}
1. A district of Og in Bashan.
cities, all the region of *A* Deut 3:4 709
all the region of *A*, with all Deut 3:13 709
took all the country of *A* unto Deut 3:14 709
also pertained the region of *A* 1Kin 4:13 709
2. An official of King Pekah of Israel.
of the king's house, with *A* 2Kin 15:25 709

ARGUING {1}
but what doth your *a* reprove Job 6:25 3198

ARGUMENTS {1}
him, and fill my mouth with *a* Job 23:4 8433

ARIDAI *(a-rid'-a-i)* {1} *A son of Haman.*
And Parmashta, and Arisai, and *A* Est 9:9 742

ARIDATHA *(a-rid'-a-thah)* {1} *A son of Haman.*
And Poratha, and Adalia, and *A* Est 9:8 743

ARIEH *(a-ri'-eh)* {1} *A companion of Argob.*
the king's house, with Argob and *A* 2Kin 15:25 745

ARIEL *(a'-re-el)* {5} See JERUSALEM.
1. An emissary of Ezra.
Then sent I for Eliezer, for *A* Ezr 8:16 740
2. A name for Jerusalem.
Woe to Ariel, to *A*, the city Is 29:1 740
Yet I will distress *A*, and there Is 29:2 740
and it shall be unto me as *A* Is 29:2 740
the nations that fight against *A* Is 29:7 740

ARIGHT {5}
a will I shew the salvation of Ps 50:23
that set not their heart *a* Ps 78:8 3559
of the wise useth knowledge *a* Prov 15:2 3190
the cup, when it moveth itself *a* Prov 23:31 4339
and heard, but they spake not *a* Jer 8:6 3651

ARIMATHAEA *(ar-im-ath-e'-ah)* {4} *Another name for Ramah.*
come, there came a rich man of *A* Mt 27:57 *707*
Joseph of *A*, an honourable Mk 15:43 *707*
he was of *A*, a city of the Jews Lk 23:51 *707*
And after this Joseph of *A* Jn 19:38 *707*

ARIMATHEA See ARIMATHAEA.

ARIOCH *(a'-re-ok)* {7}
1. King of Ellasar in Assyria.
A king of Ellasar, Chedorlaomer Gen 14:1 746
of Shinar, and *A* king of Ellasar Gen 14:9 746
2. Captain of Nebuchadnezzar's guard.
wisdom to *A* the captain of the Dan 2:14 746
said to *A* the king's captain, Why Dan 2:15 746
Then *A* made the thing known to Dan 2:15 746
Therefore Daniel went in unto *A* Dan 2:24 746
Then *A* brought in Daniel before Dan 2:25 746

ARISAI *(a-ris'-a-i)* {1} *A son of Haman.*
Parmashta, and Arisai, and Aridai, and Est 9:9 747

ARISE {149}
A, walk through the land in the Gen 13:17 6965
angels hastened Lot, saying, *A* Gen 19:15 6965
A, lift up the lad, and hold him Gen 21:18 6965
a, I pray thee, sit and eat of my Gen 27:19 6965
unto his father, Let my father *a* Gen 27:31 6965
and *a*, flee thou to Laban my Gen 27:43 6965
A, go to Padan-aram, to the house Gen 28:2 6965
now *a*, get thee out from this Gen 31:13 6965
And God said unto Jacob, *A* Gen 35:1 6965
And let us *a*, and go up to Beth-el Gen 35:3 6965
there shall *a* after them seven Gen 41:30 6965
the lad with me, and we will *a* Gen 43:8 6965
Take also your brother, and *a* Gen 43:13 6965
And the LORD said unto me, *A* Deut 9:12 6965
And the LORD said unto me, *A* Deut 10:11 6965
If there *a* among you a prophet, Deut 13:1 6965
If there *a* a matter too hard for Deut 17:8 6965
then shalt thou *a*, and get thee up Deut 17:8 6965
now therefore *a*, go over this Josh 1:2 6965
the people of war with thee, and *a* Josh 8:1 6965
a, Barak, and lead thy captivity Judg 5:12 6965
that the LORD said unto him, *A* Judg 7:9 6965
the host of Israel, and said, *A* Judg 7:15 6965
And they said, *A*, that we may go Judg 18:9 6965
to *a* up out of the city with a Judg 20:40 5927
of the servants with thee, and *a* 1Sa 9:3 6965
And the LORD said, *A*, anoint him 1Sa 16:12 6965
the LORD answered him and said, *A* 1Sa 23:4 6965
to Joab, Let the young men now *a* 2Sa 2:14 6965
And Joab said, Let them *a* 2Sa 2:14 6965
Abner said unto David, I will *a* 2Sa 3:21 6965
if so be that the king's wrath *a* 2Sa 11:20 5927
And Amnon said unto her, *A* 2Sa 13:15 6965
were with him at Jerusalem, *A* 2Sa 15:14 6965
twelve thousand men, and I will *a* 2Sa 17:1 6965
king David, and said unto David, *A* 2Sa 17:21 6965
Now therefore *a*, go forth, and 2Sa 19:7 6965
them, that they could not *a* 2Sa 22:39 6965
thee shall any *a* like unto thee 1Kin 3:12 6965
And Jeroboam said to his wife, *A* 1Kin 14:2 6965
A thou therefore, get thee to 1Kin 14:12 6965
A, get thee to Zarephath, which 1Kin 17:9 6965
touched him, and said unto him, *A* 1Kin 19:5 6965
time, and touched him, and said, *A* 1Kin 19:7 6965
a, and eat bread, and let thine 1Kin 21:7 6965
that Jezebel said to Ahab, *A* 1Kin 21:15 6965
A, go down to meet Ahab king of 1Kin 21:18 6965
said to Elijah the Tishbite, *A* 2Kin 1:3 6965
had restored to life, saying, *A* 2Kin 8:1 6965
make him *a* up from among his 2Kin 9:2 6965
A therefore, and be doing, and the 1Chr 22:16 6965
a therefore, and build ye the 1Chr 22:19 6965
Now therefore *a*, O LORD God, into 2Chr 6:41 6965
A; for this matter belongeth Ezr 10:4 6965
therefore we his servants will *a* Neh 2:20 6965
Thus shall there *a* too much Est 1:18
deliverance *a* to the Jews from Est 4:14 5975
I lie down, I say, When shall I *a* Job 7:4 6965
and upon whom doth not his light *a* Job 25:3 6965
A, O LORD Ps 3:7 6965
A, O LORD, in thine anger, lift Ps 7:6 6965
A, O LORD Ps 9:19 6965
A, O LORD Ps 10:12 6965
of the needy, now will I *a* Ps 12:5 6965
A, O LORD, disappoint him, cast Ps 17:13 6965
a, cast us not off for ever Ps 44:23 6974
A for our help, and redeem us for Ps 44:26 6965
Let God *a*, let his enemies be Ps 68:1 6965
A, O God, plead thine own cause Ps 74:22 6965
who should *a* and declare them to Ps 78:6 6965
A, O God, judge the earth Ps 82:8 6965
shall the dead *a* and praise thee Ps 88:10 6965
when the waves thereof *a*, thou Ps 89:9 7721
Thou shalt *a*, and have mercy upon Ps 102:13 6965
when they *a*, let them be ashamed Ps 109:28 6965
A, O LORD, into thy rest Ps 132:8 6965
when wilt thou *a* out of thy sleep Prov 6:9 6965
Her children *a* up, and call her Prov 31:28 6965
A, my love, my fair one, and come Song 2:13 6965
a, ye princes, and anoint the Is 21:5 6965
a, pass over to Chittim Is 23:12 6965
with my dead body shall they *a* Is 26:19 6965
but will *a* against the house of Is 31:2 6965
of rulers, Kings shall see and *a* Is 49:7 6965
a, and sit down, O Jerusalem Is 52:2 6965
A, shine; Is 60:1 6965
but the LORD shall *a* upon thee Is 60:2 2224
therefore gird up thy loins, and *a* Jer 1:17 6965
of their trouble they will say, *A* Jer 2:27 6965
let them *a*, if they can save thee Jer 2:28 6965
a, and let us go up at noon Jer 6:4 6965
A, and let us go by night, and let Jer 6:5 6965
Shall they fall, and not *a* Jer 8:4 6965
which is upon thy loins, and *a* Jer 13:4 6965
that the LORD said unto me, *A* Jer 13:6 6965
A, and go down to the potter's Jer 18:2 6965
A ye, and let us go up to Zion Jer 31:6 6965
and they said, *A*, and let us go Jer 46:16 6965
A ye, go up to Kedar, and spoil Jer 49:28 6965
A, get you up unto the wealthy Jer 49:31 6965
A, cry out in the night Lam 2:19 6965
and he said unto me, *A*, go forth Eze 3:22 6965
after thee shall *a* another Dan 2:39 6965
and they said thus unto it, *A* Dan 7:5 6966
which shall *a* out of the earth Dan 7:17 6966
are ten kings that shall *a* Dan 7:24 6966
shall a tumult *a* among thy people Hos 10:14 6965
by whom shall Jacob *a* Amos 7:2 6965
by whom shall Jacob *a* Amos 7:5 6965
A ye, and let us rise up against Obad 1 6965
A, go to Nineveh, that great city Jonah 1:2 6965
a, call upon thy God, if so be Jonah 1:6 6965
A, go unto Nineveh, that great Jonah 3:2 6965
came to pass, when the sun did *a* Jonah 4:8 2224
A ye, and depart Mic 2:10 6965
A and thresh, O daughter of Zion Mic 4:13 6965
A, contend thou before the Mic 6:1 6965
when I fall, I shall *a* Mic 7:8 6965
to the dumb stone, *A*, it shall Hab 2:19 5782
a with healing in his wings Mal 4:2 2224
to Joseph in a dream, saying, *A* Mt 2:13 *1453*
Saying, *A*, and take the young Mt 2:20 *1453*
or to say, *A*, and walk Mt 9:5 *1453*
he to the sick of the palsy,) *A* Mt 9:6 *1453*
came and touched them, and said, *A* Mt 17:7 *1453*
For there shall *a* false Christs Mt 24:24 *1453*
or to say, *A*, and take up thy bed, Mk 2:9 *1453*
I say unto thee, *A*, and take up Mk 2:11 *1453*
Damsel, I say unto thee, *a* Mk 5:41 *1453*
of the palsy,) I say unto thee, *A* Lk 5:24 *1453*
Young man, I say unto thee, *A* Lk 7:14 *1453*
hand, and called, saying, Maid, *a* Lk 8:54 *1453*
I will *a* and go to my father, and Lk 15:18 *450*
And he said unto him, *A*, go thy Lk 17:19 *450*
why do thoughts *a* in your hearts Lk 24:38 *305*
A, let us go hence Jn 14:31 *1453*
Lord spake unto Philip, saying, *A* Acts 8:26 *450*
And the Lord said unto him, *A* Acts 9:6 *450*
And the Lord said unto him, *A* Acts 9:11 *450*
a, and make thy bed Acts 9:34 *450*
him to the body said, Tabitha, *a* Acts 9:40 *450*
A therefore, and get thee down, and Acts 10:20 *450*
I heard a voice saying unto me, *A* Acts 11:7 *450*
him up, saying, *A* up quickly Acts 12:7 *450*
of your own selves shall men *a* Acts 20:30 *450*
And the Lord said unto me, *A* Acts 22:10 *450*
a, and be baptized, and wash away Acts 22:16 *450*
a from the dead, and Christ shall Eph 5:14 *450*
the day star *a* in your hearts 2Pet 1:19 *393*

ARISETH {11}
there *a* a little cloud out of the 1Kin 18:44 5927
The sun *a*, they gather themselves Ps 104:22 2224
there *a* light in the darkness Ps 112:4 2224
The sun also *a*, and the sun goeth Eccl 1:5 2224
when he *a* to shake terribly the Is 2:19 6965
when he *a* to shake terribly the Is 2:21 6965
but when the sun *a* they flee away Nah 3:17 2224
persecution *a* because of the word Mt 13:21 *1096*
persecution *a* for the word's sake Mk 4:17 *1096*
for out of Galilee *a* no prophet Jn 7:52 *1453*
there *a* another priest, Heb 7:15 *450*

ARISING {1}
the king *a* from the banquet of Est 7:7 6965

ARISTARCHUS *(ar-is-tar'-cus)* {5} *A companion of Paul.*
and having caught Gaius and *A* Acts 19:29 *708*
and of the Thessalonians, *A* Acts 20:4 *708*
one *A*, a Macedonian of Acts 27:2 *708*
A my fellowprisoner saluteth you, Col 4:10 *708*
Marcus, *A*, Demas, Lucas, my Philem 24 *708*

ARISTOBULUS See ARISTOBULUS'.

ARISTOBULUS' *(a-rus-to-bu'-luz)* {1} *A Christian acquaintance of Paul.*
them which are of *A* household Rom 16:10 *711*

ARK {230}
Make thee an *a* of gopher wood Gen 6:14 8392
rooms shalt thou make in the *a* Gen 6:14 8392
The length of the *a* shall be Gen 6:15 8392
A window shalt thou make to the *a* Gen 6:16 8392
the door of the *a* shalt thou set Gen 6:16 8392
and thou shalt come into the *a* Gen 6:18 8392
sort shalt thou bring into the *a* Gen 6:19 8392
thou and all thy house into the *a* Gen 7:1 8392
sons' wives with him, into the *a* Gen 7:7 8392
two and two unto Noah into the *a* Gen 7:9 8392
of his sons with them, into the *a* Gen 7:13 8392

they went in unto Noah into the *a* Gen 7:15 8392
increased, and bare up the *a* Gen 7:17 8392
the *a* went upon the face of the Gen 7:18 8392
they that were with him in the *a* Gen 7:23 8392
cattle that was with him in the *a* Gen 8:1 8392
the *a* rested in the seventh month Gen 8:4 8392
window of the *a* which he had made Gen 8:6 8392
she returned unto him into the *a* Gen 8:9 8392
pulled her in unto him into the *a* Gen 8:9 8392
sent forth the dove out of the *a* Gen 8:10 8392
removed the covering of the *a* Gen 8:13 8392
Go forth of the *a*, thou, and thy Gen 8:16 8392
kinds, went forth out of the *a* Gen 8:19 8392
from all that go out of the *a* Gen 9:10 8392
of Noah, that went forth of the *a* Gen 9:18 8392
took for him an *a* of bulrushes Ex 2:3 8392
she saw the *a* among the flags Ex 2:5 8392
shall make an *a* of shittim wood Ex 25:10 727
the rings by the sides of the *a* Ex 25:14 727
that the *a* may be borne with them Ex 25:14 727
shall be in the rings of the *a* Ex 25:15 727
thou shalt put into the *a* the Ex 25:16 727
the mercy seat above upon the *a* Ex 25:21 727
in the *a* thou shalt put the Ex 25:21 727
are upon the *a* of the testimony Ex 25:22 727
the vail the *a* of the testimony Ex 26:33 727
put the mercy seat upon the *a* of Ex 26:34 727
that is by the *a* of the testimony Ex 30:6 727
and the *a* of the testimony, Ex 30:26 727
the *a* of the testimony, and the Ex 31:7 727
The *a*, and the staves thereof, Ex 35:12 727
made the *a* of shittim wood Ex 37:1 727
sides of the *a*, to bear the *a* Ex 37:5 727
The *a* of the testimony, and the Ex 39:35 727
therein the *a* of the testimony Ex 40:3 727
cover the *a* with the vail Ex 40:3 727
before the *a* of the testimony Ex 40:5 727
and put the testimony into the *a* Ex 40:20 727
and set the staves on the *a* Ex 40:20 727
the mercy seat above upon the *a* Ex 40:20 727
he brought the *a* into the Ex 40:21 727
covered the *a* of the testimony Ex 40:21 727
mercy seat, which is upon the *a* Lev 16:2 727
And their charge shall be the *a* Num 3:31 727
cover the *a* of testimony with it Num 4:5 727
that was upon the *a* of testimony Num 7:89 727
the *a* of the covenant of the LORD Num 10:33 727
when the *a* set forward, that Num 10:35 727
nevertheless the *a* of the Num 14:44 727
mount, and make thee an *a* of wood Deut 10:1 727
and thou shalt put them in the *a* Deut 10:2 727
I made an *a* of shittim wood, and Deut 10:3 727
tables in the *a* which I had made Deut 10:5 727
to bear the *a* of the covenant of Deut 10:8 727
which bare the *a* of the covenant Deut 31:9 727
which bare the *a* of the covenant Deut 31:25 727
put it in the side of the *a* of Deut 31:26 727
When ye see the *a* of the covenant Josh 3:3 727
Take up the *a* of the covenant, and Josh 3:6 727
took up the *a* of the covenant Josh 3:6 727
that bear the *a* of the covenant Josh 3:8 727
the *a* of the covenant of the Lord Josh 3:11 727
that bear the *a* of the LORD Josh 3:13 727
the priests bearing the *a* of the Josh 3:14 727
bare the *a* were come unto Jordan Josh 3:15 727
of the priests that bare the *a* Josh 3:15 727
the priests that bare the *a* of Josh 3:17 727
Pass over before the *a* of the Josh 4:5 727
the *a* of the covenant of the LORD Josh 4:7 727
bare the *a* of the covenant stood Josh 4:9 727
a stood in the midst of Jordan Josh 4:10 727
that the *a* of the LORD passed Josh 4:11 727
that bear the *a* of the testimony Josh 4:16 727
the *a* of the covenant of the LORD Josh 4:18 727
a seven trumpets of rams' horns Josh 6:4 727
Take up the *a* of the covenant, and Josh 6:6 727
horns before the *a* of the LORD Josh 6:6 727
pass on before the *a* of the LORD Josh 6:7 727
the *a* of the covenant of the LORD Josh 6:8 727
and the rereward came after the *a* Josh 6:9 727
So the *a* of the LORD compassed Josh 6:11 727
priests took up the *a* of the LORD Josh 6:12 727
of rams' horns before the *a* of Josh 6:13 727
came after the *a* of the LORD Josh 6:13 727
a of the LORD until the eventide Josh 7:6 727
judges, stood on this side the *a* Josh 8:33 727
which bare the *a* of the covenant Josh 8:33 727
(for the *a* of the covenant of God Judg 20:27 727
where the *a* of God was, and Samuel 1Sa 3:3 727
Let us fetch the *a* of the 1Sa 4:3 727
might bring from thence the *a* of 1Sa 4:4 727
were there with the *a* of the 1Sa 4:4 727
when the *a* of the covenant of the 1Sa 4:5 727
they understood that the *a* of the 1Sa 4:6 727
And the *a* of God was taken 1Sa 4:11 727
heart trembled for the *a* of God 1Sa 4:13 727
dead, and the *a* of God is taken 1Sa 4:17 727
he made mention of the *a* of God 1Sa 4:18 727
that the *a* of God was taken 1Sa 4:19 727
because the *a* of God was taken, 1Sa 4:21 727
for the *a* of God is taken 1Sa 4:22 727
the Philistines took the *a* of God 1Sa 5:1 727
the Philistines took the *a* of God 1Sa 5:2 727
earth before the *a* of the LORD 1Sa 5:3 727
ground before the *a* of the LORD 1Sa 5:4 727
The *a* of the God of Israel shall 1Sa 5:7 727
with the *a* of the God of Israel 1Sa 5:8 727
Let the *a* of the God of Israel be 1Sa 5:8 727
they carried the *a* of the God of 1Sa 5:8 727
they sent the *a* of God to Ekron 1Sa 5:10 727
as the *a* of God came to Ekron, 1Sa 5:10 727
the *a* of the God of Israel to us 1Sa 5:10 727
Send away the *a* of the God of 1Sa 5:11 727
the *a* of the LORD was in the 1Sa 6:1 727
shall we do to the *a* of the LORD 1Sa 6:2 727
If ye send away the *a* of the God 1Sa 6:3 727
take the *a* of the LORD, and lay it 1Sa 6:8 727
they laid the *a* of the LORD upon 1Sa 6:11 727
up their eyes, and saw the *a* 1Sa 6:13 727
took down the *a* of the LORD 1Sa 6:15 727
they set down the *a* of the LORD 1Sa 6:18 727
had looked into the *a* of the LORD 1Sa 6:19 727
brought again the *a* of the LORD 1Sa 6:21 727
and brought up the *a* of the LORD 1Sa 7:1 727
his son to keep the *a* of the LORD 1Sa 7:1 727
to pass, while the *a* abode in 1Sa 7:2 727
Ahiah, Bring hither the *a* of God 1Sa 14:18 727
For the *a* of God was at that time 1Sa 14:18 727
bring up from thence the *a* of God 2Sa 6:2 727
they set the *a* of God upon a new 2Sa 6:3 727
Gibeah, accompanying the *a* of God 2Sa 6:4 727
and Ahio went before the *a* 2Sa 6:4 727
forth his hand to the *a* of God 2Sa 6:6 727
and there he died by the *a* of God 2Sa 6:7 727
How shall the *a* of the LORD come 2Sa 6:9 727
a of the LORD unto him into the 2Sa 6:10 727
the *a* of the LORD continued in 2Sa 6:11 727
unto him, because of the *a* of God 2Sa 6:12 727
brought up the *a* of God from the 2Sa 6:12 727
that when they that bare the *a* of 2Sa 6:13 727
the *a* of the LORD with shouting 2Sa 6:15 727
as the *a* of the LORD came into 2Sa 6:16 727
they brought in the *a* of the LORD 2Sa 6:17 727
but the *a* of God dwelleth within 2Sa 7:2 727
And Uriah said unto David, The *a* 2Sa 11:11 727
bearing the *a* of the covenant of 2Sa 15:24 727
and they set down the *a* of God 2Sa 15:24 727
Carry back the *a* of God into the 2Sa 15:25 727
Abiathar carried the *a* of God 2Sa 15:29 727
because thou barest the *a* of the 1Kin 2:26 727
stood before the *a* of the 1Kin 3:15 727
to set there the *a* of the 1Kin 6:19 727
that they might bring up the *a* of 1Kin 8:1 727
and the priests took up the *a* 1Kin 8:3 727
they brought up the *a* of the LORD 1Kin 8:4 727
him, were with him before the *a* 1Kin 8:5 727
the priests brought in the *a* of 1Kin 8:6 727
two wings over the place of the *a* 1Kin 8:7 727
and the cherubims covered the *a* 1Kin 8:7 727
There was nothing in the *a* save 1Kin 8:9 727
have set there a place for the *a* 1Kin 8:21 727
LORD, after that the *a* had rest 1Chr 6:31 727
again the *a* of our God to us 1Chr 13:3 727
to bring the *a* of God from 1Chr 13:5 727
up thence the *a* of God the LORD 1Chr 13:6 727
they carried the *a* of God in a 1Chr 13:7 727
put forth his hand to hold the *a* 1Chr 13:9 727
because he put his hand to the *a* 1Chr 13:10 727
I bring the *a* of God home to me 1Chr 13:12 727
So David brought not the *a* home 1Chr 13:13 727
the *a* of God remained with the 1Chr 13:14 727
prepared a place for the *a* of God 1Chr 15:1 727
the *a* of God but the Levites 1Chr 15:2 727
LORD chosen to carry the *a* of God 1Chr 15:2 727
to bring up the *a* of the LORD 1Chr 15:3 727
that ye may bring up the *a* of the 1Chr 15:12 727
the *a* of the LORD God of Israel 1Chr 15:14 727
of the Levites bare the *a* of God 1Chr 15:15 727
were doorkeepers for the *a* 1Chr 15:23 727
the trumpets before the *a* of God 1Chr 15:24 727
Jehiah were doorkeepers for the *a* 1Chr 15:24 727
went to bring up the *a* of the 1Chr 15:25 727
the Levites that bare the *a* of 1Chr 15:26 727
all the Levites that bare the *a* 1Chr 15:27 727
the *a* of the covenant of the LORD 1Chr 15:28 727
as the *a* of the covenant of the 1Chr 15:29 727
So they brought the *a* of God 1Chr 16:1 727
minister before the *a* of the LORD 1Chr 16:4 727
the *a* of the covenant of God 1Chr 16:6 727
the *a* of the covenant of the LORD 1Chr 16:37 727
minister before the *a* continually 1Chr 16:37 727
but the *a* of the covenant of the 1Chr 17:1 727
to bring the *a* of the covenant of 1Chr 22:19 727
the *a* of the covenant of the LORD 1Chr 28:2 727
covered the *a* of the covenant of 1Chr 28:18 727
But the *a* of God had David 2Chr 1:4 727
to bring up the *a* of the covenant 2Chr 5:2 727
and the Levites took up the *a* 2Chr 5:4 727
And they brought up the *a*, and the 2Chr 5:5 727
assembled unto him before the *a* 2Chr 5:6 727
the priests brought in the *a* of 2Chr 5:7 727
wings over the place of the *a* 2Chr 5:8 727
and the cherubims covered the *a* 2Chr 5:8 727
they drew out the staves of the *a* 2Chr 5:9 727
seen from the *a* before the oracle 2Chr 5:9
There was nothing in the *a* save 2Chr 5:10 727
And in it have I put the *a* 2Chr 6:11 727
thou, and the *a* of thy strength 2Chr 6:41 727
whereunto the *a* of the LORD hath 2Chr 8:11 727
Put the holy *a* in the house which 2Chr 35:3 727
thou, and the *a* of thy strength Ps 132:8 727
The *a* of the covenant of the LORD Jer 3:16 727
day that Noe entered into the *a* Mt 24:38 *2787*
day that Noe entered into the *a* Lk 17:27 *2787*
the *a* of the covenant overlaid Heb 9:4 *2787*
prepared an *a* to the saving of Heb 11:7 *2787*
while the *a* was a preparing, 1Pet 3:20 *2787*
his temple the *a* of his testament Rev 11:19 *2787*

ARKITE *(ar'-kite)* {2} *A tribe descended from Canaan.*
And the Hivite, and the *A*, and the Gen 10:17 6208
And the Hivite, and the *A*, and the 1Chr 1:15 6208

ARKITES See ARCHI.

ARM {67}
redeem you with a stretched out *a* Ex 6:6 2220
by the greatness of thine *a* they Ex 15:16 2220
A some of yourselves unto the war Num 31:3 2502
hand, and by a stretched out *a* Deut 4:34 2220
hand and by a stretched out *a* Deut 5:15 2220
hand, and the stretched out *a* Deut 7:19 2220
power and by thy stretched out *a* Deut 9:29 2220
hand, and his stretched out *a* Deut 11:2 2220
hand, and with an outstretched *a* Deut 26:8 2220
teareth the *a* with the crown of Deut 33:20 2220
come, that I will cut off thine *a* 1Sa 2:31 2220
the *a* of thy father's house, that 1Sa 2:31 2220
and the bracelet that was on his *a* 2Sa 1:10 2220
hand, and of thy stretched out *a* 1Kin 8:42 2220
great power and a stretched out *a* 2Kin 17:36 2220
hand, and thy stretched out *a* 2Chr 6:32 2220
With his is an *a* of flesh 2Chr 32:8 2220
how savest thou the *a* that hath Job 26:2 2220
Then let mine *a* fall from my Job 31:22 3802
mine *a* be broken from the bone Job 31:22 248
by reason of the *a* of the mighty Job 35:9 2220
the high *a* shall be broken Job 38:15 2220
Hast thou an *a* like God Job 40:9 2220
Break thou the *a* of the wicked Ps 10:15 2220
neither did their own *a* save them Ps 44:3 2220
but thy right hand, and thine *a* Ps 44:3 2220
with thine *a* redeemed thy people Ps 77:15 2220
thine enemies with thy strong *a* Ps 89:10 2220
Thou hast a mighty *a* Ps 89:13 2220
mine *a* also shall strengthen him Ps 89:21 2220
his right hand, and his holy *a* Ps 98:1 2220
hand, and with a stretched out *a* Ps 136:12 2220
heart, as a seal upon thine *a* Song 8:6 2220
every man the flesh of his own *a* Is 9:20 2220
and reapeth the ears with his *a* Is 17:5 2220
shew the lighting down of his *a* Is 30:30 2220
be thou their *a* every morning Is 33:2 2220
hand, and his *a* shall rule for him Is 40:10 2220
shall gather the lambs with his *a* Is 40:11 2220
his *a* shall be on the Chaldeans Is 48:14 2220
on mine *a* shall they trust Is 51:5 2220
put on strength, O *a* of the LORD Is 51:9 2220
LORD hath made bare his holy *a* in Is 52:10 2220
to whom is the *a* of the LORD Is 53:1 2220
therefore his *a* brought salvation Is 59:16 2220
by the *a* of his strength, Surely Is 62:8 2220
therefore mine own *a* brought Is 63:5 2220
hand of Moses with his glorious *a* Is 63:12 2220
in man, and maketh flesh his *a* Jer 17:5 2220
hand and with a strong *a*, even in Jer 21:5 2220
power and by my outstretched *a* Jer 27:5 2220
great power and stretched out *a* Jer 32:17 2220
hand, and with a stretched out *a* Jer 32:21 248
his *a* is broken, saith the LORD Jer 48:25 2220
thine *a* shall be uncovered, and Eze 4:7 2220
hand, and with a stretched out *a* Eze 20:33 2220
hand, and with a stretched out *a* Eze 20:34 2220
I have broken the *a* of Pharaoh Eze 30:21 2220
and they that were his *a*, that Eze 31:17 2220
not retain the power of the *a* Dan 11:6 2220
neither shall he stand, nor his *a* Dan 11:6 2220
the sword shall be upon his *a* Zec 11:17 2220
his *a* shall be clean dried up, and Zec 11:17 2220
hath shewed strength with his *a* Lk 1:51 *1023*
to whom hath the *a* of the Lord Jn 12:38 *1023*
with an high *a* brought he them Acts 13:17 *1023*
a yourselves likewise with the 1Pet 4:1 *3695*

ARMAGEDDON *(ar-mag-ed'-don)* {1} *Scene of the last great battle of time.*
called in the Hebrew tongue *A* Rev 16:16 *717*

ARMED {30}
he *a* his trained servants, born Gen 14:14 7324
tribe, twelve thousand *a* for war Num 31:5 2502
a before the children of Israel Num 32:17 2502
if ye will go *a* before the LORD Num 32:20 2502
will go all of you *a* over Jordan Num 32:21 2502
pass over, every man *a* for war Num 32:27 2502
Jordan, every man *a* to battle Num 32:29 2502
will not pass over with you *a* Num 32:30 2502
We will pass over *a* before the Num 32:32 2502
ye shall pass over *a* before your Deut 3:18 2502
shall pass before your brethren *a* Josh 1:14 2571
passed over *a* before the children Josh 4:12 2571
let him that is *a* pass on before Josh 6:7 2502
the *a* men went before the priests Josh 6:9 2502
the *a* men went before them Josh 6:13 2502
the *a* men that were in the host Judg 7:11 2571
he was *a* with a coat of mail 1Sa 17:5 3847
Saul *a* David with his armour, and 1Sa 17:38 3847
also he *a* him with a coat of mail 1Sa 17:38 3847
They were *a* with bows, and could 1Chr 12:2 5401
that were ready *a* to the war 1Chr 12:23 2502
eight hundred, ready *a* to the war 1Chr 12:24 2502
with him *a* men with bow and shield 2Chr 17:17 5401
So the *a* men left the captives and 2Chr 28:14 2502
he goeth on to meet the *a* men Job 39:21 5402
The children of Ephraim, being *a* Ps 78:9 5401
and thy want as an *a* man Prov 6:11 4043
and thy want as an *a* man Prov 24:34 4043

therefore the *a* soldiers of Moab ... Is 15:4 2502
When a strong man *a* keepeth his ... Lk 11:21 *2528*

ARMENIA *(ar-me'-ne-ah)* {2} *A region between the lower ends of the Black and Caspian seas.*
they escaped into the land of *A* ... 2Kin 19:37 780
they escaped into the land of *A* ... Is 37:38 780

ARMHOLES {2}
under thine *a* under the cords ... Jer 38:12 679,3027
women that sew pillows to all *a* ... Eze 13:18 679,3027

ARMIES {43}
of Egypt according to their *a* ... Ex 6:26 6635
upon Egypt, and bring forth mine *a* ... Ex 7:4 6635
day have I brought your *a* out of ... Ex 12:17 6635
of the land of Egypt by their *a* ... Ex 12:51 6635
shall number them by their *a* ... Num 1:3 6635
of Judah pitch throughout their *a* ... Num 2:3 6635
four hundred, throughout their *a* ... Num 2:9 6635
of Reuben according to their *a* ... Num 2:10 6635
and fifty, throughout their *a* ... Num 2:16 6635
of Ephraim according to their *a* ... Num 2:18 6635
and an hundred, throughout their *a* ... Num 2:24 6635
be on the north side by their *a* ... Num 2:25 6635
of Judah according to their *a* ... Num 10:14 6635
set forward according to their *a* ... Num 10:18 6635
set forward according to their *a* ... Num 10:22 6635
of Israel according to their *a* ... Num 10:28 6635
their *a* under the hand of Moses ... Num 33:1 6635
of the *a* to lead the people ... Deut 20:9 6635
together their *a* to battle ... 1Sa 17:1 4264
and cried unto the *a* of Israel ... 1Sa 17:8 4634
I defy the *a* of Israel this day ... 1Sa 17:10 4634
out of the *a* of the Philistines, ... 1Sa 17:23 4630
defy the *a* of the living God ... 1Sa 17:26 4634
defied the *a* of the living God ... 1Sa 17:36 4634
hosts, the God of the *a* of Israel ... 1Sa 17:45 4634
against the *a* of the Philistines ... 1Sa 23:3 4634
their *a* together for warfare ... 1Sa 28:1 4264
together all their *a* to Aphek ... 1Sa 29:1 4264
And when all the captains of the *a* ... 2Kin 25:23 2428
great, and the captains of the *a* ... 2Kin 25:26 2428
the valiant men of the *a* were ... 1Chr 11:26 2428
sent the captains of his *a* ... 2Chr 16:4 2428
Is there any number of his *a* ... Job 25:3 1416
and goest not forth with our *a* ... Ps 44:9 6635
which didst not go out with our *a* ... Ps 60:10 6635
Kings of *a* did flee apace ... Ps 68:12 6635
As it were the company of two *a* ... Song 6:13 4264
and his fury upon all their *a* ... Is 34:2 6635
and he sent forth his *a*, and ... Mt 22:7 *4753*
see Jerusalem compassed with *a* ... Lk 21:20 *4760*
to flight the *a* of the aliens ... Heb 11:34 *3925*
the *a* which were in heaven ... Rev 19:14 *4753*
kings of the earth, and their *a* ... Rev 19:19 *4753*

ARMONI *(ar-mo'-ni)* {1} *A son of King Saul.*
Aiah, whom she bare unto Saul, *A* ... 2Sa 21:8 764

ARMOUR {24}
the young man that bare his *a* ... 1Sa 14:1 3627
to the young man that bare his *a* ... 1Sa 14:6 3627
And Saul armed David with his *a* ... 1Sa 17:38 4055
David girded his sword upon his *a* ... 1Sa 17:39 4055
but he put his *a* in his tent ... 1Sa 17:54 3627
his head, and stripped off his *a* ... 1Sa 31:9 3627
they put his *a* in the house of ... 1Sa 31:10 3627
the young men, and take thee his *a* ... 2Sa 2:21 2488
bare Joab's *a* compassed about ... 2Sa 18:15 3627
of gold, and garments, and *a* ... 1Kin 10:25 5402
and they washed his *a* ... 1Kin 22:38 2185
all that were able to put on *a* ... 2Kin 3:21 2290
horses, a fenced city also, and *a* ... 2Kin 10:2 5402
and all the house of his *a* ... 2Kin 20:13 3627
him, they took his head, and his *a* ... 1Chr 10:9 3627
they put his *a* in the house of ... 1Chr 10:10 3627
the *a* of the house of the forest ... Is 22:8 5402
and all the house of his *a* ... Is 39:2 3627
them clothed with all sorts of *a* ... Eze 38:4 3627
him all his *a* wherein he trusted ... Lk 11:22 *3833*
and let us put on the *a* of light ... Rom 13:12 *3696*
by the *a* of righteousness on the ... 2Cor 6:7 *3696*
Put on the whole *a* of God ... Eph 6:11 *3833*
take unto you the whole *a* of God ... Eph 6:13 *3833*

ARMOURBEARER {18}
unto the young man his *a* ... Judg 9:54 5375,3627
his *a* said unto him, Do all that ... 1Sa 14:7 5375,3627
answered Jonathan and his *a* ... 1Sa 14:12 5375,3627
And Jonathan said unto his *a* ... 1Sa 14:12 5375,3627
upon his feet, and his *a* after him ... 1Sa 14:13 5375,3627
and his *a* slew after him ... 1Sa 14:13 5375,3627
a made, was about twenty men, ... 1Sa 14:14 5375,3627
Jonathan and his *a* were not there .. 1Sa 14:17 5375,3627
and he became his *a* ... 1Sa 16:21 5375,3627
Then said Saul unto his *a* ... 1Sa 31:4 5375,3627
But his *a* would not ... 1Sa 31:4 5375,3627
his *a* saw that Saul was dead ... 1Sa 31:5 5375,3627
and his three sons, and his *a* ... 1Sa 31:6 5375,3627
a to Joab the son of Zeruiah, ... 2Sa 23:37 5375,3627
said Saul to his *a*, Draw thy ... 1Chr 10:4 5375,3627
But his *a* would not ... 1Chr 10:4 5375,3627
his *a* saw that Saul was dead ... 1Chr 10:5 5375,3627
the *a* of Joab the son of Zeruiah, ... 1Chr 11:39 5375,3627

ARMOURY {3}
the *a* at the turning of the wall ... Neh 3:19 5402
tower of David builded for an *a* ... Song 4:4 8530
The LORD hath opened his *a* ... Jer 50:25 214

ARMS {29}
the *a* of his hands were made ... Gen 49:24 2220
underneath are the everlasting *a* ... Deut 33:27 2220
the cords that were upon his *a* ... Judg 15:14 2220
them from off his *a* like a thread ... Judg 16:12 2220
bow of steel is broken by mine *a* ... 2Sa 22:35 2220
and smote Jehoram between his *a* ... 2Kin 9:24 2220
the *a* of the fatherless have been ... Job 22:9 2220
bow of steel is broken by mine *a* ... Ps 18:34 2220
For the *a* of the wicked shall be ... Ps 37:17 2220
strength, and strengtheneth her *a* ... Prov 31:17 2220
it with the strength of his *a* ... Is 44:12 2220
shall bring thy sons in their *a* ... Is 49:22 2684
mine *a* shall judge the people ... Is 51:5 2220
and I will tear them from your *a* ... Eze 13:20 2220
of Egypt, and will break his *a* ... Eze 30:22 2220
I will strengthen the *a* of the ... Eze 30:24 2220
but I will break Pharaoh's *a* ... Eze 30:24 2220
the *a* of the king of Babylon ... Eze 30:25 2220
the *a* of Pharaoh shall fall down ... Eze 30:25 2220
his *a* of silver, his belly and his ... Dan 2:32 1672
eyes as lamps of fire, and his *a* ... Dan 10:6 2220
the *a* of the south shall not ... Dan 11:15 2220
with the *a* of a flood shall they ... Dan 11:22 2220
a shall stand on his part, and ... Dan 11:31 2220
bound and strengthened their *a* ... Hos 7:15 2220
to go, taking them by their *a* ... Hos 11:3 2220
and when he had taken him in his *a* ... Mk 9:36 *1723*
And he took them up in his *a* ... Mk 10:16 *1723*
Then took he him up in his *a* ... Lk 2:28 *43*

ARMY {84}
the chief captain of his *a* ... Gen 26:26 6635
and his horsemen, and his *a* ... Ex 14:9 2428
what he did unto the *a* of Egypt ... Deut 11:4 2428
Sisera, the captain of Jabin's *a* ... Judg 4:7 6635
we should give bread unto thine *a* ... Judg 8:6 6635
to Abimelech, Increase thine *a* ... Judg 9:29 6635
they slew of the *a* in the field ... 1Sa 4:2 4634
a man of Benjamin out of the *a* ... 1Sa 4:12 4634
I am he that came out of the *a* ... 1Sa 4:16 4634
and I fled to day out of the *a* ... 1Sa 4:16 4634
battle in array, *a* against *a* ... 1Sa 17:21 4634
battle in array, *a* against *a* ... 1Sa 17:21 2428
the carriage, and ran into the *a* ... 1Sa 17:22 4634
run toward the *a* to meet the ... 1Sa 17:48 4634
the *a* which followed them ... 1Kin 20:19 2428
And number thee an *a* ... 1Kin 20:25 2428
like the *a* that thou hast lost, ... 1Kin 20:25 2428
the *a* of the Chaldees pursued ... 2Kin 25:5 2428
all his *a* were scattered from him ... 2Kin 25:5 2428
all the *a* of the Chaldees, that ... 2Kin 25:10 2428
Joab led forth the power of the *a* ... 1Chr 20:1 6635
general of the king's *a* was Joab ... 1Chr 27:34 6635
with an *a* of valiant men of war ... 2Chr 13:3 2428
Asa had an *a* of men that bare ... 2Chr 14:8 2428
as they went out before the *a* ... 2Chr 20:21 2502
For the *a* of the Syrians came ... 2Chr 24:24 2428
let not the *a* of Israel go with ... 2Chr 25:7 6635
I have given to the *a* of Israel ... 2Chr 25:9 1416
the *a* that was come to him out of ... 2Chr 25:10 1416
of the *a* which Amaziah sent back ... 2Chr 25:13 1416
And under their hand was an *a* ... 2Chr 26:13 2426,6635
king had sent captains of the *a* ... Neh 2:9 2428
the *a* of Samaria, and said, What ... Neh 4:2 2428
and dwelt as a king in the *a* ... Job 29:25 1416
terrible as an *a* with banners ... Song 6:4
and terrible as an *a* with banners ... Song 6:10
unto king Hezekiah with a great *a* ... Is 36:2 2426
forth the chariot and horse, the *a* ... Is 43:17 2428
of Babylon's *a* besieged Jerusalem ... Jer 32:2 2428
king of Babylon, and all his *a* ... Jer 34:1 2428
a fought against Jerusalem ... Jer 34:7 2428
hand of the king of Babylon's *a* ... Jer 34:21 2428
fear of the *a* of the Chaldeans ... Jer 35:11 2428
for fear of the *a* of the Syrians ... Jer 35:11 2428
Then Pharaoh's *a* was come forth ... Jer 37:5 2428
Behold, Pharaoh's *a*, which is ... Jer 37:7 2428
a of the Chaldeans that fight ... Jer 37:10 2428
that when the *a* of the Chaldeans ... Jer 37:11 2428
Jerusalem for fear of Pharaoh's *a* ... Jer 37:11 2428
hand of the king of Babylon's *a* ... Jer 38:3 2428
all his *a* against Jerusalem, and ... Jer 39:1 2428
Chaldeans' *a* pursued after them ... Jer 39:5 2428
against the *a* of Pharaoh-necho ... Jer 46:2 2428
for they shall march with an *a* ... Jer 46:22 2428
of Babylon came, he and all his *a* ... Jer 52:4 2428
But the *a* of the Chaldeans ... Jer 52:8 2428
all his *a* was scattered from him ... Jer 52:8 2428
all the *a* of the Chaldeans, that ... Jer 52:14 2428
shall Pharaoh with his mighty *a* ... Eze 17:17 2428
of Lud and of Phut were in thine *a* ... Eze 27:10 2428
The men of Arvad with thine *a* ... Eze 27:11 2428
his *a* to serve a great service ... Eze 29:18 2428
yet had he no wages, nor his *a* ... Eze 29:18 2428
it shall be the wages for his *a* ... Eze 29:19 2428
all his *a* slain by the sword, ... Eze 32:31 2428
their feet, an exceeding great *a* ... Eze 37:10 2428
bring thee forth, and all thine *a* ... Eze 38:4 2428
a great company, and a mighty *a* ... Eze 38:15 2428
were in his *a* to bind Shadrach ... Dan 3:20 2429
to his will in the *a* of heaven ... Dan 4:35 2429
which shall come with an *a* ... Dan 11:7 2428
certain years with a great *a* ... Dan 11:13 2428
king of the south with a great *a* ... Dan 11:25 2428
with a very great and mighty *a* ... Dan 11:25 2428
him, and his *a* shall overflow ... Dan 11:26 2428
utter his voice before his *a* ... Joel 2:11 2428
far off from you the northern *a* ... Joel 2:20
my great *a* which I sent among you ... Joel 2:25 2428
about mine house because of the *a* ... Zec 9:8 4675
then came I with an *a*, and rescued ... Acts 23:27 *4753*
the number of the *a* of the ... Rev 9:16 *4753*
on the horse, and against his *a* ... Rev 19:19 *4753*

ARNAN *(ar'-nan)* {1} *Descendants of David.*
sons of Rephaiah, the sons of *A* ... 1Chr 3:21 770

ARNON *(ar'-non)* {25} *A river in southern Canaan.*
and pitched on the other side of *A* ... Num 21:13 769
for *A* is the border of Moab, ... Num 21:13 769
Red sea, and in the brooks of *A* ... Num 21:14 769
his land from *A* unto Jabbok ... Num 21:24 769
land out of his hand, even unto *A* ... Num 21:26 769
the lords of the high places of *A* ... Num 21:28 769
Moab, which is in the border of *A* ... Num 22:36 769
journey, and pass over the river *A* ... Deut 2:24 769
is by the brink of the river of *A* ... Deut 2:36 769
the river of *A* unto mount Hermon ... Deut 3:8 769
Aroer, which is by the river *A* ... Deut 3:12 769
unto the river *A* half the valley ... Deut 3:16 769
is by the bank of the river *A* ... Deut 4:48 769
from the river *A* unto mount ... Josh 12:1 769
is upon the bank of the river *A* ... Josh 12:2 769
is upon the bank of the river *A* ... Josh 13:9 769
is on the bank of the river *A* ... Josh 13:16 769
from *A* even unto Jabbok, and unto ... Judg 11:13 769
and pitched on the other side of *A* ... Judg 11:18 769
for *A* was the border of Moab ... Judg 11:18 769
from *A* even unto Jabbok, and from ... Judg 11:22 769
that be along by the coasts of *A* ... Judg 11:26 769
Aroer, which is by the river *A* ... 2Kin 10:33 769
Moab shall be at the fords of *A* ... Is 16:2 769
tell ye it in *A*, that Moab is ... Jer 48:20 769

AROD *(a'-rod)* {1} See ARODITES. *A son of Gad.*
Of *A*, the family of the Arodites ... Num 26:17 720

ARODI *(ar'-o-di)* {1} See ARODITES. *Descendants of Arod.*
Haggi, Shuni, and Ezbon, Eri, and *A* ... Gen 46:16 722

ARODITES *(a'-ro-dites)* {1} *Same as Arodi.*
Of Arod, the family of the *A* ... Num 26:17 722

AROER *(ar'-o-ur)* {16}
1. A city in the valley of Jabbok.
Gad built Dibon, and Ataroth, and *A* ... Num 32:34 6177
unto *A* that is before Rabbah ... Josh 13:25 6177
over Jordan, and pitched in *A* ... 2Sa 24:5 6177
The cities of *A* are forsaken ... Is 17:2 6177
2. An Amorite city.
From *A*, which is by the brink of ... Deut 2:36 6177
we possessed at that time, from *A* ... Deut 3:12 6177
From *A*, which is by the bank of ... Deut 4:48 6177
dwelt in Heshbon, and ruled from *A* ... Josh 12:2 6177
From *A*, that is upon the bank of ... Josh 13:9 6177
And their coast was from *A* ... Josh 13:16 6177
in Heshbon and her towns, and in *A* ... Judg 11:26 6177
And he smote them from *A*, even ... Judg 11:33 6177
and the Manassites, from *A* ... 2Kin 10:33 6177
the son of Joel, who dwelt in *A* ... 1Chr 5:8 6177
O inhabitant of *A*, stand by the ... Jer 48:19 6177
3. A city in southern Judah.
And to them which were in *A* ... 1Sa 30:28 6177

AROERITE *(ar'-o-ur-ite)* {1} *A native of Aroer.*
Jehiel the sons of Hothan the *A* ... 1Chr 11:44 6200

AROSE {173}
And when the morning *a*, then the ... Gen 19:15 5927
when she lay down, nor when she *a* ... Gen 19:33 6965
and the younger *a*, and lay with him ... Gen 19:35 6965
when she lay down, nor when she *a* ... Gen 19:35 6965
and he *a*, and went to Mesopotamia, ... Gen 24:10 6965
And Rebekah *a*, and her damsels, and ... Gen 24:61 6965
in the field, and, lo, my sheaf *a* ... Gen 37:7 6965
And she *a*, and went away, and laid ... Gen 38:19 6965
Now there *a* up a new king over ... Ex 1:8 6965
there *a* not a prophet since in ... Deut 34:10 6965
So Joshua *a*, and all the people of ... Josh 8:3 6965
the ambush *a* quickly out of their ... Josh 8:19 6965
And the men *a*, and went away ... Josh 18:8 6965
son of Zippor, king of Moab, *a* ... Josh 24:9 6965
there *a* another generation after ... Judg 2:10 6965
And he *a* out of his seat ... Judg 3:20 6965
And Deborah *a*, and went with Barak ... Judg 4:9 6965
in Israel, until that I Deborah *a* ... Judg 5:7 6965
that I *a* a mother in Israel ... Judg 5:7 6965
the city *a* early in the morning ... Judg 6:28 7925
And Gideon *a*, and slew Zebah and ... Judg 8:21 6965
after Abimelech there *a* to defend ... Judg 10:1 6965
And after him *a* Jair, a Gileadite, ... Judg 10:3 6965
And Manoah *a*, and went after his ... Judg 13:11 6965
a at midnight, and took the doors ... Judg 16:3 6965
And her husband *a*, and went after ... Judg 19:3 6965
when they *a* early in the morning, ... Judg 19:5 7925
he *a* early in the morning on the ... Judg 19:8 7925
And all the people *a* as one man ... Judg 20:8 6965
And the children of Israel *a* ... Judg 20:18 6965
Then she *a* with her daughters in ... Ruth 1:6 6965
And Samuel *a* and went to Eli, and ... 1Sa 3:6 6965
And he *a* and went to Eli, and said, ... 1Sa 3:8 6965
of Ashdod *a* early on the morrow ... 1Sa 5:3 7925
when they *a* early on the morrow ... 1Sa 5:4 7925
And they *a* early ... 1Sa 9:26 7925
And Saul *a*, and they went out both ... 1Sa 9:26 6965
And Samuel *a*, and gat him up from ... 1Sa 13:15 6965
when he *a* against me, I caught ... 1Sa 17:35 6965
to pass, when the Philistine *a* ... 1Sa 17:48 6965
the men of Israel and of Judah *a* ... 1Sa 17:52 6965

Wherefore David *a* and went, he and 1Sa 18:27 6965
and Jonathan *a*, and Abner sat by 1Sa 20:25 6965
So Jonathan *a* from the table in............. 1Sa 20:34 6965
David *a* out of a place toward the.......... 1Sa 20:41 6965
And he *a* and departed.......................... 1Sa 20:42 6965
And David *a*, and fled that day for......... 1Sa 21:10 6965
which were about six hundred, *a*........... 1Sa 23:13 6965
And Jonathan Saul's son *a*, and went 1Sa 23:16 6965
And they *a*, and went to Ziph before...... 1Sa 23:24 6965
Then David *a*, and cut off the 1Sa 24:4 6965
David also *a* afterward, and went 1Sa 24:8 6965
And David *a*, and went down to the 1Sa 25:1 6965
And she *a*, and bowed herself on her...... 1Sa 25:41 6965
And Abigail hasted, and *a*, and rode 1Sa 25:42 6965
Then Saul *a*, and went down to the 1Sa 26:2 6965
And David *a*, and came to the place 1Sa 26:5 6965
And David *a*, and he passed over............ 1Sa 27:2 6965
So he *a* from the earth, and sat.............. 1Sa 28:23 6965
All the valiant men *a*, and went............. 1Sa 31:12 6965
Then there *a* and went over by............... 2Sa 2:15 6965
And David *a*, and went with all the......... 2Sa 6:2 6965
that David *a* from off his bed, and.......... 2Sa 11:2 6965
And the elders of his house *a*................ 2Sa 12:17 6965
Then David *a* from the earth, and........... 2Sa 12:20 6965
Then all the king's sons *a*...................... 2Sa 13:29 6965
Then the king *a*, and tare his 2Sa 13:31 6965
So Joab *a* and went to Geshur, and......... 2Sa 14:23 6965
Then Joab *a*, and came to Absalom......... 2Sa 14:31 6965
So he *a*, and went to Hebron.................. 2Sa 15:9 6965
Then David *a*, and all the people 2Sa 17:22 6965
he saddled his ass, and *a*....................... 2Sa 17:23 6965
Then the king *a*, and sat in the 2Sa 19:8 6965
He *a*, and smote the Philistines.............. 2Sa 23:10 6965
feared because of Solomon, and *a*.......... 1Kin 1:50 6965
And Shimei *a*, and saddled his ass,........ 1Kin 2:40 6965
she *a* at midnight, and took my son........ 1Kin 3:20 6965
he *a* from before the altar of the............ 1Kin 8:54 6965
they *a* out of Midian, and came to 1Kin 11:18 6965
And Jeroboam *a*, and fled into Egypt 1Kin 11:40 6965
And Jeroboam's wife did so, and *a*.......... 1Kin 14:4 6965
And Jeroboam's wife *a*, and departed 1Kin 14:17 6965
So he *a* and went to Zarephath.............. 1Kin 17:10 6965
And when he saw that, he *a*................... 1Kin 19:3 6965
And he *a*, and did eat and drink, and..... 1Kin 19:8 6965
Then he *a*, and went after Elijah,.......... 1Kin 19:21 6965
And he *a*, and went down with him........ 2Kin 1:15 6965
And he *a*, and followed her 2Kin 4:30 6965
Wherefore they *a* and fled in the............ 2Kin 7:7 6965
the king *a* in the night, and said............ 2Kin 7:12 6965
And the woman *a*, and did after the........ 2Kin 8:2 6965
And he *a*, and went into the house......... 2Kin 9:6 6965
And he *a* and departed, and came to 2Kin 10:12 6965
saw that her son was dead, she *a*........... 2Kin 11:1 6965
And his servants *a*, and made a 2Kin 12:20 6965
when they *a* early in the morning, ... 2Kin 19:35 7925
neither after him *a* there any 2Kin 23:25 6965
and the captains of the armies, *a*........... 2Kin 25:26 6965
They *a*, all the valiant men, and............. 1Chr 10:12 6965
that there *a* war at Gezer with............... 1Chr 20:4 5975
saw that her son was dead, she *a* 2Chr 22:10 6965
Then the Levites *a*, Mahath the 2Chr 29:12 6965
And they *a* and took away the altars 2Chr 30:14 6965
Then the priests the Levites *a*................ 2Chr 30:27 6965
of the LORD *a* against his people........... 2Chr 36:16 5927
I *a* up from my heaviness .... Ezr 9:5 6965
Then *a* Ezra, and made the chief .... Ezr 10:5 6965
I *a* in the night, I and some few .... Neh 2:12 6965
So Esther *a*, and stood before the .... Est 8:4 6965
Then Job *a*, and rent his mantle,............ Job 1:20 6965
I *a*, and they spake against me............... Job 19:18 6965
and the aged *a*, and stood up .... Job 29:8 6965
When God *a* to judgment, to save .... Ps 76:9 6965
hasteth to his place where he *a*.............. Eccl 1:5 2224
when they *a* early in the morning, ... Is 37:36 2224
Then *a* Ishmael the son of .... Jer 41:2 6965
Then I *a*, and went forth into the............ Eze 3:23 6965
Then the king *a* very early in the .... Dan 6:19 6966
So Jonah *a*, and went unto Nineveh,....... Jonah 3:3 6965
he *a* from his throne, and he laid........... Jonah 3:6 6965
When he *a*, he took the young................ Mt 2:14 *1453*
And he *a*, and took the young child .... Mt 2:21 *1453*
and she *a*, and ministered unto them...... Mt 8:15 *1453*
there *a* a great tempest in the .... Mt 8:24 *1096*
Then he *a*, and rebuked the winds .... Mt 8:26 *1453*
And he *a*, and departed to his house....... Mt 9:7 *1453*
And he *a*, and followed him .... Mt 9:9 *450*
And Jesus *a*, and followed him, and........ Mt 9:19 *1453*
her by the hand, and the maid *a* .... Mt 9:25 *1453*
Then all those virgins *a*, and.................. Mt 25:7 *1453*
And the high priest *a*, and said.............. Mt 26:62 *450*
of the saints which slept *a*.................... Mt 27:52 *1453*
And immediately he *a*, took up the......... Mk 2:12 *1453*
And he *a* and followed him .... Mk 2:14 *450*
there *a* a great storm of wind, and.......... Mk 4:37 *1096*
And he *a*, and rebuked the wind, and..... Mk 4:39 *1326*
And straightway the damsel *a*................ Mk 5:42 *450*
And from thence he *a*, and went into...... Mk 7:24 *450*
and he *a* .... Mk 9:27 *450*
he *a* from thence, and cometh into.......... Mk 10:1 *450*
there *a* certain, and bare false................ Mk 14:57 *450*
Mary *a* in those days, and went.............. Lk 1:39 *450*
he *a* out of the synagogue, and.............. Lk 4:38 *450*
and immediately she *a* and..................... Lk 4:39 *450*
And he *a* and stood forth .... Lk 6:8 *450*
and when the flood *a*, the stream........... Lk 6:48 *1096*
Then he *a*, and rebuked the wind and .... Lk 8:24 *1453*
came again, and she *a* straightway .... Lk 8:55 *450*
Then there *a* a reasoning among .... Lk 9:46 *1525*
there *a* a mighty famine in that .... Lk 15:14 *1096*
And he *a*, and came to his father........... Lk 15:20 *450*
And the whole multitude of them *a* .... Lk 23:1 *450*
Then *a* Peter, and ran unto the.............. Lk 24:12 *450*
Then there *a* a question between .... Jn 3:25 *1096*
the sea *a* by reason of a great............... Jn 6:18 *1326*
she *a* quickly, and came unto him .... Jn 11:29 *1453*
And the young men *a*, wound him up, ... Acts 5:6 *450*
there *a* a murmuring of the.................... Acts 6:1 *1096*
Then there *a* certain of the.................... Acts 6:9 *450*
Till another king *a*, which knew .... Acts 7:18 *450*
And he *a* and went .... Acts 8:27 *450*
And Saul *a* from the earth .... Acts 9:8 *1453*
he received sight forthwith, and *a*.......... Acts 9:18 *450*
And he *a* immediately .... Acts 9:34 *450*
Then Peter *a* and went with them .... Acts 9:39 *450*
upon the persecution that *a* about .... Acts 11:19 *1096*
the same time there *a* no small .... Acts 19:23 *1096*
there *a* a dissension between the............ Acts 23:7 *1096*
And there *a* a great cry......................... Acts 23:9 *1096*
were of the Pharisees' part *a*................. Acts 23:9 *450*
when there *a* a great dissension, ... Acts 23:10 *1096*
But not long after there *a*..................... Acts 27:14 *906*
there *a* a smoke out of the pit, ... Rev 9:2 *305*

ARPAD *(ar'-pad)* {4} *A city near Hamath.*
are the gods of Hamath, and of *A* 2Kin 18:34 774
king of Hamath, and the king of *A* 2Kin 19:13 774
is not Hamath as *A*................................ Is 10:9 774
Hamath is confounded, and *A*.................. Jer 49:23 774

ARPHAD *(ar'-fad)* {2} See ARPAD. *Same as Arpad.*
Where are the gods of Hamath and *A*..... Is 36:19 774
king of Hamath, and the king of *A* .... Is 37:13 774

ARPHAXAD {10}
Elam, and Asshur, and *A*, and Lud,........ Gen 10:22 775
And *A* begat Salah .... Gen 10:24 775
begat *A* two years after the flood............ Gen 11:10 775
he begat *A* five hundred years................ Gen 11:11 775
A lived five and thirty years, and............ Gen 11:12 775
A lived after he begat Salah four .... Gen 11:13 775
Elam, and Asshur, and *A*, and Lud,........ 1Chr 1:17 775
A begat Shelah, and Shelah begat 1Chr 1:18 775
Shem, *A*, Shelah,.................................... 1Chr 1:24 775
of Cainan, which was the son of *A*.......... Lk 3:36 *742*

ARRAY {34}
a to fight against them at Gibeah........... Judg 20:20 6186
set their battle again in *a* in.................. Judg 20:22 6186
put themselves in *a* the first day............ Judg 20:22 6186
themselves in *a* against Gibeah.............. Judg 20:30 6186
put themselves in *a* at Baal-tamar.......... Judg 20:33 6186
themselves in *a* against Israel 1Sa 4:2 6186
set the battle in *a* against the................. 1Sa 17:2 6186
come out to set your battle in *a* 1Sa 17:8 6186
had put the battle in *a*, army 1Sa 17:21 6186
put the battle in *a* at the 2Sa 10:8 6186
put them in *a* against the Syrians 2Sa 10:9 6186
that he might put them in *a* 2Sa 10:10 6186
set themselves in *a* against David 2Sa 10:17 6186
his servants, Set yourselves in *a*............. 1Kin 20:12
themselves in *a* against the city 1Kin 20:12
put the battle in *a* before the 1Chr 19:9 6186
put them in *a* against the Syrians 1Chr 19:10 6186
they set themselves in *a* against............. 1Chr 19:11 6186
set the battle in *a* against them.............. 1Chr 19:17 6186
battle in *a* against the Syrians 1Chr 19:17 6186
Abijah set the battle in *a* with 2Chr 13:3 631
a against him with eight hundred........... 2Chr 13:3 6186
they set the battle in *a* in the 2Chr 14:10 6186
that they may *a* the man withal.............. Est 6:9 3847
do set themselves in *a* against me .... Job 6:4 6186
a thyself with glory and beauty .... Job 40:10 3847
set themselves in *a* at the gate .... Is 22:7 7896
set in *a* as men for war against .... Jer 6:23 6186
he shall *a* himself with the land.............. Jer 43:12 5844
set themselves in *a* against her.............. Jer 50:9 6186
Put yourselves in *a* against..................... Jer 50:14 6186
upon horses, every one put in *a*.............. Jer 50:42 6186
a strong people set in battle *a*................ Joel 2:5 6186
or gold, or pearls, or costly *a*................. 1Ti 2:9 *2441*

ARRAYED {11}
a him in vestures of fine linen,............... Gen 41:42 3847
being *a* in white linen, having................. 2Chr 5:12 3847
a them, and shod them, and gave............ 2Chr 28:15 3847
a Mordecai, and brought him on............. Est 6:11 3847
glory was not *a* like one of these............ Mt 6:29 *4016*
glory was not *a* like one of these............ Lk 12:27 *4016*
a him in a gorgeous robe, and sent .... Lk 23:11 *4016*
a in royal apparel, sat upon his.............. Acts 12:21 *1746*
these which are *a* in white robes .... Rev 7:13 *4016*
And the woman was *a* in purple .... Rev 17:4 *4016*
she should be *a* in fine linen .... Rev 19:8 *4016*

ARRIVED {2}
they *a* at the country of the.................... Lk 8:26 *2668*
and the next day we *a* at Samos .... Acts 20:15 *3846*

ARROGANCY {2}
let not *a* come out of your mouth............ 1Sa 2:3 6277
pride, and *a*, and the evil way, and .... Prov 8:13 1347
I will cause the *a* of the proud .... Is 13:11 1347
proud) his loftiness, and his *a* .... Jer 48:29 1347

ARROW {16}
lad ran, he shot an *a* beyond him............ 1Sa 20:36 2678
of the *a* which Jonathan had shot 1Sa 20:37 2678
and said, Is not the *a* beyond thee 1Sa 20:37 2678
the *a* went out at his heart, and............. 2Kin 9:24 2678
The *a* of the LORD's deliverance, ... 2Kin 13:17 2671
the *a* of deliverance from Syria 2Kin 13:17 2671
this city, nor shoot an *a* there................. 2Kin 19:32 2671
The *a* cannot make him flee .... Job 41:28 1121,7198
ready their *a* upon the string.................. Ps 11:2 2671
God shall shoot at them with an *a*.......... Ps 64:7 2671
nor for the *a* that flieth by day................ Ps 91:5 2671
a maul, and a sword, and a sharp *a* .... Prov 25:18 2671
this city, nor shoot an *a* there................. Is 37:33 2671
Their tongue is as an *a* shot out.............. Jer 9:8 2671
and set me as a mark for the *a*................ Lam 3:12 2671
his *a* shall go forth as the .... Zec 9:14 2671

ARROWS {41}
and pierce them through with his *a* .... Num 24:8 2671
I will spend mine *a* upon them................ Deut 32:23 2671
will make mine *a* drunk with blood........ Deut 32:42 2671
I will shoot three *a* on the side.............. 1Sa 20:20 2671
a lad, saying, Go, find out the *a* 1Sa 20:21 2671
the *a* are on this side of thee, ... 1Sa 20:21 2671
Behold, the *a* are beyond thee 1Sa 20:22 2671
find out now the *a* which I shoot 1Sa 20:36 2671
Jonathan's lad gathered up the *a* 1Sa 20:38 2678
And he sent out *a*, and scattered............. 2Sa 22:15 2671
said unto him, Take bow and *a* 2Kin 13:15 2671
And he took unto him bow and *a*............ 2Kin 13:15 2671
And he said, Take the *a*......................... 2Kin 13:18 2671
shooting *a* out of a bow, even of............. 1Chr 12:2 2671
and upon the bulwarks, to shoot *a*.......... 2Chr 26:15 2671
For the *a* of the Almighty are.................. Job 6:4 2671
he ordaineth his *a* against the................. Ps 7:13 2671
Yea, he sent out his *a*, and..................... Ps 18:14 2671
thou shalt make ready thine *a*................ Ps 21:12
For thine *a* stick fast in me, and .... Ps 38:2 2671
Thine *a* are sharp in the heart of .... Ps 45:5 2671
men, whose teeth are spears and *a*.......... Ps 57:4 2671
he bendeth his bow to shoot his *a*........... Ps 58:7 2671
bend their bows to shoot their *a* .... Ps 64:3 2671
There brake he the *a* of the bow .... Ps 76:3 7565
thine *a* also went abroad .... Ps 77:17 2687
Sharp *a* of the mighty, with coals .... Ps 120:4 2671
As *a* are in the hand of a mighty.............. Ps 127:4 2671
shoot out thine *a*, and destroy................. Ps 144:6 2671
mad man who casteth firebrands, *a*........ Prov 26:18 2671
Whose *a* are sharp, and all their .... Is 5:28 2671
With *a* and with bows shall men............. Is 7:24 2671
their *a* shall be as of a mighty................. Jer 50:9 2671
the bow, shoot at her, spare no *a*............ Jer 50:14 2671
Make bright the *a*................................... Jer 51:11 1121
He hath caused the *a* of his.................... Lam 3:13 2671
upon them the evil *a* of famine .... Eze 5:16 2671
he made his *a* bright, he........................ Eze 21:21 2671
will cause thine *a* to fall out of .... Eze 39:3 2671
the bucklers, the bows and the *a*............. Eze 39:9 2671
at the light of thine *a* they went .... Hab 3:11 2671

ART See APPENDIX.

ARTAXERXES *(ar-tax-erx'-ees)* {14} See ARTAXERXES'.
1. A Persian king known as Longimanus.
And in the days of *A* wrote Bishlam .... Ezr 4:7 783
companions, unto *A* king of Persia .... Ezr 4:7 783
to *A* the king in this sort .... Ezr 4:8 783
unto him, even unto *A* the king............... Ezr 4:11 783
2. A Persian king known as Cambyses.
and Darius, and *A* king of Persia .... Ezr 6:14 783
3. A Persian king known as Darius.
in the reign of *A* king of Persia .... Ezr 7:1 783
in the seventh year of *A* the king............ Ezr 7:7 783
king *A* gave unto Ezra the priest .... Ezr 7:11 783
A, king of kings, unto Ezra the................ Ezr 7:12 783
even I *A* the king, do make a.................. Ezr 7:21 783
in the reign of *A* the king........................ Ezr 8:1 783
the twentieth year of *A* the king............. Neh 2:1 783
and thirtieth year of *A* the king.............. Neh 5:14 783
thirtieth year of *A* king of....................... Neh 13:6 783

ARTAXERXES' *(ar-tax-erx'-eez)* {1} *Refers to Artaxerxes 1.*
Now when the copy of king *A*.................. Ezr 4:23 783

ARTEMAS *(ar'-te-mas)* {1} *A companion of Paul.*
When I shall send *A* unto thee .... Titus 3:12 *734*

ARTEMIS See DIANA.

ARTIFICER {2}
an instructer of every *a* in brass .... Gen 4:22 2794
the counsellor, and the cunning *a* .... Is 3:3 2796

ARTIFICERS {2}
work to be made by the hands of *a*......... 1Chr 29:5 2796
Even to the *a* and builders gave............. 2Chr 34:11 2796

ARTILLERY {1}
Jonathan gave his *a* unto his lad............ 1Sa 20:40 3627

ARTS {1}
a brought their books together............... Acts 19:19 *4021*

ARUBBOTH See ARUBOTH.

ARUBOTH *(ar'-u-both)* {1} *A district of Solomon's rule.*
The son of Hesed, in *A* 1Kin 4:10 700

ARUMAH *(a-ru'-mah)* {1} *A place in Ephraim.*
And Abimelech dwelt at *A* .... Judg 9:41 725

ARVAD *(ar'-vad)* {2} See ARVADITE. *An island near Zidon.*
of Zidon and *A* were thy mariners.......... Eze 27:8 719
The men of *A* with thine army were .... Eze 27:11 719

ARVADITE *(ar'-vad-ite)* {2} *Descendants of Canaan.*
And the *A*, and the Zemarite, and the .... Gen 10:18 721
And the *A*, and the Zemarite, and the 1Chr 1:16 721

ARVADITES See ARVADITE.

ARZA *(ar'-zah)* {1} *A steward of King Elah of Israel.*
himself drunk in the house of *A* ... 1Kin 16:9 777

AS See APPENDIX.

ASA *(a'-sah)* {59} See ASA'S.
1. A king of Judah.
A his son reigned in his stead ... 1Kin 15:8 609
of Israel reigned *A* over Judah ... 1Kin 15:9 609
A did that which was right in the ... 1Kin 15:11 609
A destroyed her idol, and burnt it ... 1Kin 15:13 609
And there was war between *A* ... 1Kin 15:16 609
out or come in to *A* king of Judah ... 1Kin 15:17 609
Then *A* took all the silver and the ... 1Kin 15:18 609
king *A* sent them to Ben-hadad, ... 1Kin 15:18 609
Ben-hadad hearkened unto king *A* ... 1Kin 15:20 609
Then king *A* made a proclamation ... 1Kin 15:22 609
king *A* built with them Geba of ... 1Kin 15:22 609
The rest of all the acts of *A* ... 1Kin 15:23 609
A slept with his fathers, and was ... 1Kin 15:24 609
second year of *A* king of Judah ... 1Kin 15:25 609
Even in the third year of *A* king ... 1Kin 15:28 609
And there was war between *A* ... 1Kin 15:32 609
In the third year of *A* king of ... 1Kin 15:33 609
sixth year of *A* king of Judah ... 1Kin 16:8 609
seventh year of *A* king of Judah ... 1Kin 16:10 609
seventh year of *A* king of Judah ... 1Kin 16:15 609
first year of *A* king of Judah ... 1Kin 16:23 609
eighth year of *A* king of Judah ... 1Kin 16:29 609
Jehoshaphat the son of *A* began to ... 1Kin 22:41 609
in all the ways of *A* his father ... 1Kin 22:43 609
in the days of his father *A* ... 1Kin 22:46 609
A his son, Jehoshaphat his son, ... 1Chr 3:10 609
A his son reigned in his stead ... 2Chr 14:1 609
A did that which was good and ... 2Chr 14:2 609
A had an army of men that bare ... 2Chr 14:8 609
Then *A* went out against him, and ... 2Chr 14:10 609
A cried unto the LORD his God, and ... 2Chr 14:11 609
smote the Ethiopians before *A* ... 2Chr 14:12 609
And *A* and the people that were with ... 2Chr 14:13 609
And he went out to meet *A*, and said ... 2Chr 15:2 609
and said unto him, Hear ye me, *A* ... 2Chr 15:2 609
when *A* heard these words, and the ... 2Chr 15:8 609
fifteenth year of the reign of *A* ... 2Chr 15:10 609
Maachah the mother of *A* the king ... 2Chr 15:16 609
A cut down her idol, and stamped ... 2Chr 15:16 609
of *A* was perfect all his days ... 2Chr 15:17 609
thirtieth year of the reign of *A* ... 2Chr 15:19 609
A Baasha king of Israel came up ... 2Chr 16:1 609
out or come in to *A* king of Judah ... 2Chr 16:1 609
Then *A* brought out silver and gold ... 2Chr 16:2 609
Ben-hadad hearkened unto king *A* ... 2Chr 16:4 609
Then *A* the king took all Judah ... 2Chr 16:6 609
the seer came to *A* king of Judah ... 2Chr 16:7 609
Then *A* was wroth with the seer, ... 2Chr 16:10 609
A oppressed some of the people ... 2Chr 16:10 609
And, behold, the acts of *A* ... 2Chr 16:11 609
A in the thirty and ninth year of ... 2Chr 16:12 609
A slept with his fathers, and died ... 2Chr 16:13 609
which *A* his father had taken ... 2Chr 17:2 609
walked in the way of *A* his father ... 2Chr 20:32 609
in the ways of *A* king of Judah ... 2Chr 21:12 609
was it which *A* the king had made ... Jer 41:9 609
and Abia begat *A* ... Mt 1:7 *760*
And *A* begat Josaphat ... Mt 1:8 *760*
2. Chief of a Levite family.
and Berechiah the son of *A* ... 1Chr 9:16 609

ASAHEL *(as'-a-hel)* {18}
1. The son of Zeruiah, David's sister.
there, Joab, and Abishai, and *A* ... 2Sa 2:18 760
A was as light of foot as a wild ... 2Sa 2:18 6214
And *A* pursued after Abner ... 2Sa 2:19 6214
behind him, and said, Art thou *A* ... 2Sa 2:20 6214
But *A* would not turn aside from ... 2Sa 2:21 6214
And Abner said again to *A*, Turn ... 2Sa 2:22 6214
to the place where *A* fell down ... 2Sa 2:23 6214
servants nineteen men and *A* ... 2Sa 2:30 6214
And they took up *A*, and buried him ... 2Sa 2:32 6214
for the blood of *A* his brother ... 2Sa 3:27 6214
brother *A* at Gibeon in the battle ... 2Sa 3:30 6214
A the brother of Joab was one of ... 2Sa 23:24 6214
Abishai, and Joab, and *A*, three ... 1Chr 2:16 6214
A the brother of Joab, Elhanan ... 1Chr 11:26 6214
month was *A* the brother of Joab ... 1Chr 27:7 6214
2. A Levite teacher.
and Nethaniah, and Zebadiah, and *A* ... 2Chr 17:8 6214
3. A Levite officer.
and Azaziah, and Nahath, and *A* ... 2Chr 31:13 6214
4. Father of Jonathan.
Only Jonathan the son of *A* ... Ezr 10:15 6214

ASAHIAH *(as-a-hi'-ah)* {2} See ASAIAH. *An officer of King Josiah.*
A a servant of the king's, saying ... 2Kin 22:12 6222
and Achbor, and Shaphan, and *A* ... 2Kin 22:14 6222

ASAIAH *(as-a'-yah)* {6}
1. A descendant of Simeon.
and Jaakobah, and Jeshohaiah, and *A* ... 1Chr 4:36 6222
2. A descendant of Libni.
son, Haggiah his son, *A* his son ... 1Chr 6:30 6222
3. A Shilonite of Jerusalem.
A the firstborn, and his sons ... 1Chr 9:5 6222
4. A descendant of Merari.
A the chief, and his brethren two ... 1Chr 15:6 6222
and for the Levites, for Uriel, *A* ... 1Chr 15:11 6222
5. Same as Asahiah.
A a servant of the king's, saying ... 2Chr 34:20 6222

ASAPH *(a'-saf)* {44} See ASAPH'S.
1. Father of Joah.
and Joah the son of *A* the recorder ... 2Kin 18:18 623
and Joah the son of *A* the recorder ... 2Kin 18:37 623
the scribe, and Joah, the son of *A* ... Is 36:22 623
2. A musician of David and Solomon.
And his brother *A*, who stood on ... 1Chr 6:39 623
even *A* the son of Berachiah, the ... 1Chr 6:39 623
brethren, *A* the son of Berechiah ... 1Chr 15:17 623
So the singers, Heman, *A*, and ... 1Chr 15:19 623
A the chief, and next to him ... 1Chr 16:5 623
but *A* made a sound with cymbals ... 1Chr 16:5 623
thank the LORD into the hand of *A* ... 1Chr 16:7 623
ark of the covenant of the LORD *A* ... 1Chr 16:37 623
to the service of the sons of *A* ... 1Chr 25:1 623
Of the sons of *A* ... 1Chr 25:2 623
of Asaph under the hands of *A* ... 1Chr 25:2 623
to the king's order to *A*, ... 1Chr 25:6 623
lot came forth for *A* to Joseph ... 1Chr 25:9 623
the singers, all of them of *A* ... 2Chr 5:12 623
a Levite of the sons of *A* ... 2Chr 20:14 623
and of the sons of *A* ... 2Chr 29:13 623
words of David, and of *A* the seer ... 2Chr 29:30 623
the sons of *A* were in their place ... 2Chr 35:15 623
to the commandment of David, and *A* ... 2Chr 35:15 623
the children of *A*, an hundred ... Ezr 2:41 623
the sons of *A* with cymbals ... Ezr 3:10 623
the children of *A*, an hundred ... Neh 7:44 623
the son of Zabdi, the son of *A* ... Neh 11:17 623
Of the sons of *A*, the singers ... Neh 11:22 623
the son of Zaccur, the son of *A* ... Neh 12:35 623
A of old there were chief of the ... Neh 12:46 623
A Psalm of *A* ... Ps 50:*t* 623
A Psalm of *A* ... Ps 73:*t* 623
Maschil of *A* ... Ps 74:*t* 623
Altaschith, A Psalm or Song of *A* ... Ps 75:*t* 623
on Neginoth, A Psalm or Song of *A* ... Ps 76:*t* 623
to Jeduthun, A Psalm of *A* ... Ps 77:*t* 623
Maschil of *A* ... Ps 78:*t* 623
A Psalm of *A* ... Ps 79:*t* 623
Shoshannim-Eduth, A Psalm of *A* ... Ps 80:*t* 623
upon Gittith, A Psalm of *A* ... Ps 81:*t* 623
A Psalm of *A* ... Ps 82:*t* 623
A Song or Psalm of *A* ... Ps 83:*t* 623
3. A Levite family in post-exilic Jerusalem.
the son of Zichri, the son of *A* ... 1Chr 9:15 623
4. Descendants of Merari.
the son of Kore, of the sons of *A* ... 1Chr 26:1 623
5. A Persian official.
a letter unto *A* the keeper of the ... Neh 2:8 623

ASAPH'S *(a'-safs)* {1} *Refers to Asaph 1.*
and Joah, *A* son, the recorder ... Is 36:3 623

ASAREEL *(a-sar'-e-el)* {1} *A son of Jehaleleel.*
Ziph, and Ziphah, Tiria, and *A* ... 1Chr 4:16 840

ASARELAH *(as-a-re'-lah)* {1} See JESHARELAH. *A son of a musician of David.*
and Joseph, and Nethaniah, and *A* ... 1Chr 25:2 841

ASA'S *(a'-sahz)* {1} *Refers to Asa 1.*
nevertheless *A* heart was perfect ... 1Kin 15:14 609

ASCEND {13}
the people shall *a* up every man ... Josh 6:5 5927
Who shall *a* into the hill of the ... Ps 24:3 5927
He causeth the vapours to *a* from ... Ps 135:7 5927
If I *a* up into heaven, thou art ... Ps 139:8 5927
I will *a* into heaven, I will ... Is 14:13 5927
I will *a* above the heights of the ... Is 14:14 5927
he causeth the vapors to *a* from ... Jer 10:13 5927
he causeth the vapors to *a* from ... Jer 51:16 5927
Thou shalt *a* and come like a storm ... Eze 38:9 5927
of man *a* up where he was before ... Jn 6:62 *305*
I *a* unto my Father, and your ... Jn 20:17 *305*
heart, Who shall *a* into heaven ... Rom 10:6 *305*
shall *a* out of the bottomless pit ... Rev 17:8 *305*

ASCENDED {19}
the smoke thereof *a* as the smoke ... Ex 19:18 5927
they *a* by the south, and came unto ... Num 13:22 5927
smoke of the city *a* up to heaven ... Josh 8:20 5927
and that the smoke of the city *a* ... Josh 8:21 5927
So Joshua *a* from Gilgal, he, and ... Josh 10:7 5927
a up on the south side unto ... Josh 15:3 5927
LORD *a* in the flame of the altar ... Judg 13:20 5927
flame of the city *a* up to heaven ... Judg 20:40 5927
Thou hast *a* on high, thou hast ... Ps 68:18 5927
Who hath *a* up into heaven, or ... Prov 30:4 5927
no man hath *a* up to heaven, but ... Jn 3:13 *305*
for I am not yet *a* to my Father ... Jn 20:17 *305*
David is not *a* into the heavens ... Acts 2:34 *305*
after three days he *a* from ... Acts 25:1 *305*
When he *a* up on high, he led ... Eph 4:8 *305*
(Now that he *a*, what is it but ... Eph 4:9 *305*
that *a* up far above all heavens ... Eph 4:10 *305*
a up before God out of the ... Rev 8:4 *305*
they *a* up to heaven in a cloud ... Rev 11:12 *305*

ASCENDETH {2}
the beast that *a* out of the ... Rev 11:7 *305*
of their torment *a* up for ever ... Rev 14:11 *305*

ASCENDING {5}
and behold the angels of God *a* ... Gen 28:12 5927
I saw gods *a* out of the earth ... 1Sa 28:13 5927
he went before, *a* up to Jerusalem ... Lk 19:28 *305*
open, and the angels of God *a* ... Jn 1:51 *305*
saw another angel *a* from the east ... Rev 7:2 *305*

ASCENT {4}
the south to the *a* of Akrabbim ... Num 34:4 4608
went up by the *a* of mount Olivet ... 2Sa 15:30 4608
his *a* by which he went up unto ... 1Kin 10:5 5930
his *a* by which he went up into ... 2Chr 9:4 5944

ASCRIBE {3}
a ye greatness unto our God ... Deut 32:3 3051
will *a* righteousness to my Maker ... Job 36:3 5414
A ye strength unto God ... Ps 68:34 5414

ASCRIBED {2}
They have *a* unto David ten ... 1Sa 18:8 5414
to me they have *a* but thousands ... 1Sa 18:8 5414

ASENATH *(as'-e-nath)* {3} *A great-grandson of Solomon.*
he gave him to wife *A* the ... Gen 41:45 621
came, which *A* the daughter of ... Gen 41:50 621
Ephraim, which *A* the daughter of ... Gen 46:20 621

ASER *(a'-sur)* {2} See ASHER. *Greek form of Asher.*
of Phanuel, of the tribe of *A* ... Lk 2:36 *768*
Of the tribe of *A* were sealed ... Rev 7:6 *768*

ASH {1}
he planteth an *a*, and the rain ... Is 44:14 766

ASHAMED {122}
man and his wife, and were not *a* ... Gen 2:25 954
should she not be *a* seven days ... Num 12:14 3637
And they tarried till they were *a* ... Judg 3:25 954
because the men were greatly *a* ... 2Sa 10:5 3637
as people being *a* steal away when ... 2Sa 19:3 3637
when they urged him till he was *a* ... 2Kin 2:17 954
stedfastly, until he was *a* ... 2Kin 8:11 954
for the men were greatly *a* ... 1Chr 19:5 3637
the priests and the Levites were *a* ... 2Chr 30:15 3637
For I was *a* to require of the ... Ezr 8:22 954
And said, O my God, I am *a* ... Ezr 9:6 954
they came thither, and were *a* ... Job 6:20 2659
mockest, shall no man make thee *a* ... Job 11:3 3637
ye are not *a* that ye make ... Job 19:3 954
Let all mine enemies be *a* ... Ps 6:10 954
let them return and be *a* suddenly ... Ps 6:10 954
let me not be *a*, let not mine ... Ps 25:2 954
let none that wait on thee be *a* ... Ps 25:3 954
let them be *a* which transgress ... Ps 25:3 954
let me not be *a* ... Ps 25:20 954
let me never be *a* ... Ps 31:1 954
Let me not be *a*, O LORD ... Ps 31:17 954
let the wicked be *a*, and let them ... Ps 31:17 954
and their faces were not *a* ... Ps 34:5 2659
Let them be *a* and brought to ... Ps 35:26 954
shall not be *a* in the evil time ... Ps 37:19 954
Let them be *a* and confounded ... Ps 40:14 954
GOD of hosts, be *a* for my sake ... Ps 69:6 954
Let them be *a* and confounded that ... Ps 70:2 954
O let not the oppressed return *a* ... Ps 74:21 3637
which hate me may see it, and be *a* ... Ps 86:17 954
when they arise, let them be *a* ... Ps 109:28 954
Then shall I not be *a*, when I ... Ps 119:6 954
before kings, and will not be *a* ... Ps 119:46 954
Let the proud be *a* ... Ps 119:78 954
that I be not *a* ... Ps 119:80 954
and let me not be *a* of my hope ... Ps 119:116 954
they shall not be *a*, but they ... Ps 127:5 954
but she that maketh *a* is as ... Prov 12:4 954
For they shall be *a* of the oaks ... Is 1:29 954
a of Ethiopia their expectation, ... Is 20:5 954
Be thou *a*, O Zidon ... Is 23:4 954
shall be confounded, and the sun *a* ... Is 24:23 954
be *a* for their envy at the people ... Is 26:11 954
Jacob, Jacob shall not now be *a* ... Is 29:22 954
They were all *a* of a people that ... Is 30:5 954
Lebanon is *a* and hewn down ... Is 33:9 2659
incensed against thee shall be *a* ... Is 41:11 954
back, they shall be greatly *a* ... Is 42:17 954
that they may be *a* ... Is 44:9 954
all his fellows shall be *a* ... Is 44:11 954
fear, and they shall be *a* together ... Is 44:11 954
They shall be *a*, and also ... Is 45:16 954
ye shall not be *a* nor confounded ... Is 45:17 954
incensed against him shall be *a* ... Is 45:24 954
shall not be *a* that wait for me ... Is 49:23 954
and I know that I shall not be *a* ... Is 50:7 954
for thou shalt not be *a* ... Is 54:4 954
shall rejoice, but ye shall be *a* ... Is 65:13 954
to your joy, and they shall be *a* ... Is 66:5 954
As the thief is *a* when he is ... Jer 2:26 1322
so is the house of Israel *a* ... Jer 2:26 954
thou also shalt be *a* of Egypt ... Jer 2:36 954
as thou wast *a* of Assyria ... Jer 2:36 954
forehead, thou refusedst to be *a* ... Jer 3:3 3637
Were they *a* when they had ... Jer 6:15 954
nay, they were not at all *a* ... Jer 6:15 954
The wise men are *a*, they are ... Jer 8:9 954
Were they *a* when they had ... Jer 8:12 954
nay, they were not at all *a* ... Jer 8:12 954
they shall be *a* of your revenues ... Jer 12:13 954
they were *a* and confounded, and ... Jer 14:3 954
in the earth, the plowmen were *a* ... Jer 14:4 954
she hath been *a* and confounded ... Jer 15:9 954
all that forsake thee shall be *a* ... Jer 17:13 954
they shall be greatly *a* ... Jer 20:11 954
surely then shalt thou be *a* ... Jer 22:22 954
I was *a*, yea, even confounded, ... Jer 31:19 954
And Moab shall be *a* of Chemosh ... Jer 48:13 954
as the house of Israel was *a* of ... Jer 48:13 954
she that bare you shall be *a* ... Jer 50:12 2659
which are *a* of thy lewd way ... Eze 16:27 3637
shalt remember thy ways, and be *a* ... Eze 16:61 3637
terror they are *a* of their might ... Eze 32:30 954
be *a* and confounded for your own ... Eze 36:32 954
that they may be *a* of their ... Eze 43:10 3637

if they be *a* of all that they ... Eze 43:11 3637
they shall be *a* because of their ... Hos 4:19 954
Israel shall be *a* of his own ... Hos 10:6 954
Be ye *a*, O ye husbandmen ... Joel 1:11 954
and my people shall never be *a* ... Joel 2:26 954
and my people shall never be *a* ... Joel 2:27 954
Then shall the seers be *a* ... Mic 3:7 954
thou not be *a* for all thy doings ... Zeph 3:11 954
for her expectation shall be *a* ... Zec 9:5 954
be *a* every one of his vision ... Zec 13:4 954
therefore shall be *a* of me ... Mk 8:38 *1870*
also shall the Son of man be *a* ... Mk 8:38 *1870*
For whosoever shall be *a* of me ... Lk 9:26 *1870*
of him shall the Son of man be *a* ... Lk 9:26 *1870*
all his adversaries were *a* ... Lk 13:17 *2617*
to beg I am *a* ... Lk 16:3 *153*
For I am not *a* of the gospel of ... Rom 1:16 *1870*
And hope maketh not *a* ... Rom 5:5 *2617*
those things whereof ye are now *a* ... Rom 6:21 *1870*
believeth on him shall not be *a* ... Rom 9:33 *2617*
believeth on him shall not be *a* ... Rom 10:11 *2617*
thing to him of you, I am not *a* ... 2Cor 7:14 *2617*
ye) should be *a* in this same ... 2Cor 9:4 *2617*
destruction, I should not be *a* ... 2Cor 10:8 *153*
that in nothing I shall be *a* ... Phil 1:20 *153*
with him, that he may be *a* ... 2Th 3:14 *1788*
Be not thou therefore *a* of the ... 2Ti 1:8 *1870*
nevertheless I am not *a* ... 2Ti 1:12 *1870*
me, and was not *a* of my chain ... 2Ti 1:16 *1870*
workman that needeth not to be *a* ... 2Ti 2:15 *422*
is of the contrary part may be *a* ... Titus 2:8 *1788*
he is not *a* to call them brethren ... Heb 2:11 *1870*
wherefore God is not *a* to be ... Heb 11:16 *1870*
they may be *a* that falsely accuse ... 1Pet 3:16 *2617*
as a Christian, let him not be *a* ... 1Pet 4:16 *153*
not be *a* before him at his coming ... 1Jn 2:28 *153*

ASHAN *(a'-shan)* {4} See CHOR-ASHAN. *A Levitical city in Judah.*
Libnah, and Ether, and *A*, ... Josh 15:42 6228
Ain, Remmon, and Ether, and *A* ... Josh 19:7 6228
and Ain, Rimmon, and Tochen, and *A* ... 1Chr 4:32 6228
and *A* with her suburbs, and ... 1Chr 6:59 6228

ASHARELAH See ASARELAH.

ASHBEA *(ash'-be-ah)* {1} *Descendants of Shelah.*
fine linen, of the house of *A* ... 1Chr 4:21 791

ASHBEL *(ash'-bel)* {3} See ASHBELITES. *A son of Benjamin.*
were Belah, and Becher, and *A* ... Gen 46:21 788
of *A*, the family of the ... Num 26:38 788
A the second, and Aharah the third ... 1Chr 8:1 788

ASHBELITES *(ash'-bel-ites)* {1} *Descendants of Ashbel.*
of Ashbel, the family of the *A* ... Num 26:38 789

ASHCHENAZ *(ash'-ke-naz)* {2} See ASHKENAZ.
1. A son of Gomer.
A, and Riphath, and Togarmah ... 1Chr 1:6 813
2. A tribe near Armenia.
kingdoms of Ararat, Minni, and *A* ... Jer 51:27 813

ASHDOD *(ash'-dod)* {21} See ASHDODITES, AZOTUS. *A Philistine city.*
only in Gaza, in Gath, and in *A* ... Josh 11:22 795
unto the sea, all that lay near *A* ... Josh 15:46 795
A with her towns and her villages, ... Josh 15:47 795
brought it from Eben-ezer unto *A* ... 1Sa 5:1 795
when they of *A* arose early on the ... 1Sa 5:3 795
of Dagon in *A* unto this day ... 1Sa 5:5 795
the LORD was heavy upon them of *A* ... 1Sa 5:6 795
smote them with emerods, even *A* ... 1Sa 5:6 795
when the men of *A* saw that it was ... 1Sa 5:7 795
for *A* one, for Gaza one, for ... 1Sa 6:17 795
wall of Jabneh, and the wall of *A* ... 2Chr 26:6 795
and built cities about *A* ... 2Chr 26:6 795
Jews that had married wives of *A* ... Neh 13:23 795
spake half in the speech of *A* ... Neh 13:24 795
the year that Tartan came unto *A* ... Is 20:1 795
sent him,) and fought against *A* ... Is 20:1 795
and Ekron, and the remnant of *A* ... Jer 25:20 795
cut off the inhabitant from *A* ... Amos 1:8 795
Publish in the palaces at *A* ... Amos 3:9 795
shall drive out *A* at the noonday ... Zeph 2:4 795
And a bastard shall dwell in *A* ... Zec 9:6 795

ASHDODITES *(ash'-dod-ites)* {1} See ASHDOTHITES. *Inhabitants of Ashdod.*
and the Ammonites, and the *A* ... Neh 4:7 796

ASHDOTHITES *(ash'-doth-ites)* {1} See ASHDODITES. *Same as Ashdodites.*
the Gazathites, and the *A*, the ... Josh 13:3 796

ASHDOTH-PISGAH *(ash'-doth-piz'-gah)* {3} *The eastern slope of Mt. Pisgah.*
the salt sea, under *A* eastward ... Deut 3:17 798,6449
and from the south, under *A* ... Josh 12:3 798,6449
And Beth-peor, and *A*, and ... Josh 13:20 798,6449

ASHER *(ash'-ur)* {43} See ASER, ASHERITES.
1. A son of Jacob by Zilpah.
and she called his name *A* ... Gen 30:13 836
Gad, and *A*: these are the sons ... Gen 35:26 836
And the sons of *A* ... Gen 46:17 836
Out of *A* his bread shall be fat, ... Gen 49:20 836
Dan, and Naphtali, Gad, and *A* ... Ex 1:4 836
of the daughter of *A* was Sarah ... Num 26:46 836
and Benjamin, Naphtali, Gad, and *A* ... 1Chr 2:2 836
The sons of *A*; Imnah, and Isuah ... 1Chr 7:30 836
All these were the children of *A* ... 1Chr 7:40 836
2. A tribe descended from Asher 1.
Of *A* ... Num 1:13 836
Of the children of *A*, by their ... Num 1:40 836
of them, even of the tribe of *A* ... Num 1:41 836
by him shall be the tribe of *A* ... Num 2:27 836
of *A* shall be Pagiel the son of ... Num 2:27 836
prince of the children of *A* ... Num 7:72 836
of *A* was Pagiel the son of Ocran ... Num 10:26 836
Of the tribe of *A*, Sethur the son ... Num 13:13 836
Of the children of *A* after their ... Num 26:44 836
of *A* according to those that were ... Num 26:47 836
of the tribe of the children of *A* ... Num 34:27 836
Reuben, Gad, and *A*, and Zebulun, ... Deut 27:13 836
of *A* he said, Let Asher be ... Deut 33:24 836
of *A* according to their families ... Josh 19:24 836
of *A* according to their families ... Josh 19:31 836
reacheth to *A* on the west side, ... Josh 19:34 836
and out of the tribe of *A* ... Josh 21:6 836
And out of the tribe of *A*, Mishal ... Josh 21:30 836
Neither did *A* drive out the ... Judg 1:31 836
A continued on the sea shore, and ... Judg 5:17 836
and he sent messengers unto *A* ... Judg 6:35 836
out of Naphtali, and out of *A* ... Judg 7:23 836
and out of the tribe of *A* ... 1Chr 6:62 836
And out of the tribe of *A* ... 1Chr 6:74 836
And of *A*, such as went forth to ... 1Chr 12:36 836
Nevertheless divers of *A* and ... 2Chr 30:11 836
the west side, a portion for *A* ... Eze 48:2 836
And by the border of *A*, from the ... Eze 48:3 836
one gate of Gad, one gate of *A* ... Eze 48:34 836
3. A town in Manasseh.
Manasseh was from *A* to Michmethah ... Josh 17:7 836
met together in *A* on the north ... Josh 17:10 836
in *A* Beth-shean and her towns ... Josh 17:11 836
Baanah the son of Hushai was in *A* ... 1Kin 4:16 836

ASHERITES *(ash'-ur-ites)* {1} *Same as Asher 2.*
But the *A* dwelt among the ... Judg 1:32 843

ASHES {43}
the Lord, which am but dust and *a* ... Gen 18:27 665
you handfuls of *a* of the furnace ... Ex 9:8 6368
they took *a* of the furnace, and ... Ex 9:10 6368
make his pans to receive his *a* ... Ex 27:3 1878
east part, by the place of the *a* ... Lev 1:16 1880
where the *a* are poured out, and ... Lev 4:12 1880
where the *a* are poured out shall ... Lev 4:12 1880
take up the *a* which the fire hath ... Lev 6:10 1880
carry forth the *a* without the ... Lev 6:11 1880
take away the *a* from the altar ... Num 4:13 1878
gather up the *a* of the heifer ... Num 19:9 665
he that gathereth the *a* of the ... Num 19:10 665
of the *a* of the burnt heifer of ... Num 19:17 6083
Tamar put *a* on her head, and rent ... 2Sa 13:19 665
the *a* that are upon it shall be ... 1Kin 13:3 1880
the *a* poured out from the altar, ... 1Kin 13:5 1880
himself with *a* upon his face ... 1Kin 20:38 665
took the *a* away from his face ... 1Kin 20:41 665
carried the *a* of them unto ... 2Kin 23:4 6083
and put on sackcloth with *a* ... Est 4:1 665
and many lay in sackcloth and *a* ... Est 4:3 665
and he sat down among the *a* ... Job 2:8 665
Your remembrances are like unto *a* ... Job 13:12 665
and I am become like dust and *a* ... Job 30:19 665
myself, and repent in dust and *a* ... Job 42:6 665
For I have eaten *a* like bread ... Ps 102:9 665
scattereth the hoar frost like *a* ... Ps 147:16 665
He feedeth on *a* ... Is 44:20 665
spread sackcloth and *a* under him ... Is 58:5 665
to give unto them beauty for *a* ... Is 61:3 665
sackcloth, and wallow thyself in *a* ... Jer 6:26 665
and wallow yourselves in the *a* ... Jer 25:34
of the dead bodies, and of the *a* ... Jer 31:40 1880
stones, he hath covered me with *a* ... Lam 3:16 665
shall wallow themselves in the *a* ... Eze 27:30 665
I will bring thee to *a* upon the ... Eze 28:18 665
with fasting, and sackcloth, and *a* ... Dan 9:3 665
him with sackcloth, and sat in *a* ... Jonah 3:6 665
for they shall be *a* under the ... Mal 4:3 665
long ago in sackcloth and *a* ... Mt 11:21 *4700*
sitting in sackcloth and *a* ... Lk 10:13 *4700*
the *a* of an heifer sprinkling the ... Heb 9:13 *4700*
Gomorrah into *a* condemned them ... 2Pet 2:6 *5077*

ASHHUR See ASHUR.

ASHIMA *(ash'-im-ah)* {1} *An idol of Hamath.*
and the men of Hamath made *A* ... 2Kin 17:30 807

ASHKELON *(ash'-ke-lon)* {9} See ASKELON, ESHKALONITES. *A Philistine city.*
upon him, and he went down to *A* ... Judg 14:19 831
the land of the Philistines, and *A* ... Jer 25:20 831
A is cut off with the remnant of ... Jer 47:5 831
hath given it a charge against *A* ... Jer 47:7 831
that holdeth the sceptre from *A* ... Amos 1:8 831
be forsaken, and *A* a desolation ... Zeph 2:4 831
in the houses of *A* shall they lie ... Zeph 2:7 831
A shall see it, and fear ... Zec 9:5 831
Gaza, and *A* shall not be inhabited ... Zec 9:5 831

ASHKENAZ *(ash'-ke-naz)* {1} See ASHCHENAZ. *A son of Gomer.*
A, and Riphath, and Togarmah ... Gen 10:3 813

ASHNAH *(ash'-nah)* {2}
1. A town in Judah near Dan.
valley, Eshtaol, and Zoreah, and *A* ... Josh 15:33 823
2. A town in Judah on the plains.
And Jiphtah, and *A*, and Nezib, ... Josh 15:43 823

ASHPENAZ *(ash'-pe-naz)* {1} *A prince of the eunuchs under Nebuchadnezzar.*
the king spake unto *A* the master ... Dan 1:3 828

ASHRIEL *(ash'-re-el)* {1} See ASRIEL. *A grandson of Manasseh.*
A, whom she bare ... 1Chr 7:14 845

ASHTAROTH *(ash'-ta-roth)* {11} See ASHTERATHITE, ASHTEROTH, ASTORETH, ASTAROTH, BEESHTERAH.
1. A god of the Philistines, Phoenicians, and Zidonians.
the LORD, and served Baal and *A* ... Judg 2:13 6252
the LORD, and served Baalim, and *A* ... Judg 10:6 6252
A from among you, and prepare your ... 1Sa 7:3 6252
Israel did put away Baalim and *A* ... 1Sa 7:4 6252
LORD, and have served Baalim and *A* ... 1Sa 12:10 6252
put his armour in the house of *A* ... 1Sa 31:10 6252
2. A city in Bashan.
Og king of Bashan, which was at *A* ... Josh 9:10 6252
of the giants, that dwelt at *A* ... Josh 12:4 6252
Og in Bashan, which reigned in *A* ... Josh 13:12 6252
And half Gilead, and *A*, and Edrei, ... Josh 13:31 6252
3. A Levitical city in Manasseh.
suburbs, and *A* with her suburbs ... 1Chr 6:71 6252

ASHTERATHITE *(ash'-ter-a-thite)* {1} *Family name of Uzziah.*
Uzzia the *A*, Shama and Jehiel the ... 1Chr 11:44 6254

ASHTEROTH *(ash'-te-roth)* {1} *A city in Og.*
smote the Rephaims in *A* Karnaim ... Gen 14:5 6255

ASHTEROTH-KARNAIM See ASHTEROTH.

ASHTORETH *(ash'-to-reth)* {3} See ASHTAROTH. *Same as Ashtaroth 1.*
For Solomon went after *A* the ... 1Kin 11:5 6252
have worshipped *A* the goddess of ... 1Kin 11:33 6252
for *A* the abomination of the ... 2Kin 23:13 6252

ASHUR *(ash'-ur)* {2} See ASHURITES, ASSHUR, ASSUR, ASSYRIA. *A son of Hezvon.*
bare him *A* the father of Tekoa ... 1Chr 2:24 804
A the father of Tekoa had two ... 1Chr 4:5 804

ASHURBANIPAL See ASNAPPER.

ASHURITES *(ash'-ur-ites)* {2} See ASSHURIM. *A tribe in the plain of Esdraelon.*
king over Gilead, and over the *A* ... 2Sa 2:9 843
the company of the *A* have made ... Eze 27:6 843

ASHVATH *(ash'-vath)* {1} *A descendant of Asher.*
Pasach, and Bimhal, and *A* ... 1Chr 7:33 6220

ASIA *(a'-she-ah)* {21}
1. A Roman province.
and Cappadocia, in Pontus, and *A* ... Acts 2:9 *773*
and of them of Cilicia and of *A* ... Acts 6:9 *773*
Ghost to preach the word in *A* ... Acts 16:6 *773*
in *A* heard the word of the Lord ... Acts 19:10 *773*
himself stayed in *A* for a season ... Acts 19:22 *773*
And certain of the chief of *A* ... Acts 19:31 *775*
him into *A* Sopater of Berea ... Acts 20:4 *773*
and of *A*, Tychicus and Trophimus ... Acts 20:4 *773*
he would not spend the time in *A* ... Acts 20:16 *773*
the first day that I came into *A* ... Acts 20:18 *773*
The churches of *A* salute you ... 1Cor 16:19 *773*
our trouble which came to us in *A* ... 2Cor 1:8 *773*
are in *A* be turned away from me ... 2Ti 1:15 *773*
Pontus, Galatia, Cappadocia, *A* ... 1Pet 1:1 *773*
the seven churches which are in *A* ... Rev 1:4 *773*
the seven churches which are in *A* ... Rev 1:11 *773*
2. Another name for Asia Minor.
but almost throughout all *A* ... Acts 19:26 *773*
should be destroyed, whom all *A* ... Acts 19:27 *773*
ended, the Jews which were of *A* ... Acts 21:27 *773*
Whereupon certain Jews from *A* ... Acts 24:18 *773*
to sail by the coasts of *A* ... Acts 27:2 *773*

ASIDE See APPENDIX.

ASIEL *(a'-se'-el)* {1} *Grandfather of Jeha.*
the son of Seraiah, the son of *A* ... 1Chr 4:35 6221

ASK {109}
it that thou dost *a* after my name ... Gen 32:29 7592
A me never so much dowry and gift, ... Gen 34:12 7235
who shall *a* counsel for him after ... Num 27:21 7592
For *a* now of the days that are ... Deut 4:32 7592
a from the one side of heaven ... Deut 4:32
and make search, and *a* diligently ... Deut 13:14 7592
a thy father, and he will shew ... Deut 32:7 7592
that when your children *a* their ... Josh 4:6 7592
When your children shall *a* their ... Josh 4:21 7592
him to *a* of her father a field ... Josh 15:18 7592
him to *a* of her father a field ... Judg 1:14 7592
A counsel, we pray thee, of God, ... Judg 18:5 7592
sins this evil, to *a* us a king ... 1Sa 12:19 7592
A thy young men, and they will ... 1Sa 25:8 7592
Wherefore then dost thou *a* of me ... 1Sa 28:16 7592
the thing that I shall *a* thee ... 2Sa 14:18 7592
shall surely *a* counsel at Abel ... 2Sa 20:18 7592
now I *a* one petition of thee, ... 1Kin 2:16 7592
said unto her, *A* on, my mother ... 1Kin 2:20 7592
why dost thou *a* Abishag the ... 1Kin 2:22 7592
a for him the kingdom also ... 1Kin 2:22 7592
said, *A* what I shall give thee ... 1Kin 3:5 7592
to *a* a thing of thee for her son ... 1Kin 14:5 1875
A what I shall do for thee, ... 2Kin 2:9 7592
him, *A* what I shall give thee ... 2Chr 1:7 7592
together, to *a* help of the LORD ... 2Chr 20:4 1245
But *a* now the beasts, and they ... Job 12:7 7592
A of me, and I shall give thee the ... Ps 2:8 7592
A thee a sign of the LORD thy God ... Is 7:11 7592
a it either in the depth, or in ... Is 7:11 7592
But Ahaz said, I will not *a* ... Is 7:12 7592

A me of things to come concerning ... Is 45:11 7592
they a of me the ordinances of ... Is 58:2 7592
a for the old paths, where is the ... Jer 6:16 7592
go aside to a how thou doest ... Jer 15:5 7592
A ye now among the heathen, who ... Jer 18:13 7592
or a priest, shall a thee ... Jer 23:33 7592
A ye now, and see whether a man ... Jer 30:6 7592
Jeremiah, I will a thee a thing ... Jer 38:14 7592
a him that fleeth, and her that ... Jer 48:19 7592
They shall a the way to Zion with ... Jer 50:5 7592
the young children a bread ... Lam 4:4 7592
that whosoever shall a a petition ... Dan 6:7 1156
that every man that shall a a ... Dan 6:12 1156
My people a counsel at their ... Hos 4:12 7592
A now the priests concerning the ... Hag 2:11 7592
A ye of the LORD rain in the time ... Zec 10:1 7592
ye have need of, before ye a him ... Mt 6:8 *154*
A, and it shall be given you ... Mt 7:7 *154*
of you, whom if his son a bread ... Mt 7:9 *154*
Or if he a a fish, will he give ... Mt 7:10 *154*
good things to them that a him ... Mt 7:11 *154*
give her whatsoever she would a ... Mt 14:7 *154*
any thing that they shall a ... Mt 18:19 *154*
and said, Ye know not what ye a ... Mt 20:22 *154*
whatsoever ye shall a in prayer ... Mt 21:22 *154*
I also will a you one thing, ... Mt 21:24 *2065*
forth a him any more questions ... Mt 22:46 *1905*
that they should a Barabbas ... Mt 27:20 *154*
A of me whatsoever thou wilt, and ... Mk 6:22 *154*
Whatsoever thou shalt a of me ... Mk 6:23 *154*
unto her mother, What shall I a ... Mk 6:24 *154*
saying, and were afraid to a him ... Mk 9:32 *1905*
unto them, Ye know not what ye a ... Mk 10:38 *154*
I will also a of you one question ... Mk 11:29 *1905*
that durst a him any question ... Mk 12:34 *1905*
unto them, I will a you one thing ... Lk 6:9 *1905*
away thy goods a them not again ... Lk 6:30 *523*
they feared to a him of that ... Lk 9:45 *2065*
And I say unto you, A, and it shall ... Lk 11:9 *154*
If a son shall a bread of any of ... Lk 11:11 *154*
or if he a a fish, will he for a ... Lk 11:11
Or if he shall a an egg, will he ... Lk 11:12 *154*
Holy Spirit to them that a him ... Lk 11:13 *154*
much, of him they will a the more ... Lk 12:48 *154*
And if any man a you, Why do ye ... Lk 19:31 *2065*
I will also a you one thing ... Lk 20:3 *2065*
not a him any question at all ... Lk 20:40 *1905*
And if I also a you, ye will not ... Lk 22:68 *2065*
Levites from Jerusalem to a him ... Jn 1:19 *2065*
a him: he shall speak ... Jn 9:21 *2065*
He is of age; a him ... Jn 9:23 *2065*
whatsoever thou wilt a of God ... Jn 11:22 *154*
that he should a who it should be ... Jn 13:24 *4441*
whatsoever ye shall a in my name ... Jn 14:13 *154*
If ye shall a any thing in my ... Jn 14:14 *154*
ye shall a what ye will, and it ... Jn 15:7 *154*
shall a of the Father in my name ... Jn 15:16 *154*
that they were desirous to a him ... Jn 16:19 *2065*
in that day ye shall a me nothing ... Jn 16:23 *2065*
Whatsoever ye shall a the Father ... Jn 16:23 *154*
a, and ye shall receive, that your ... Jn 16:24 *154*
At that day ye shall a in my name ... Jn 16:26 *154*
not that any man should a thee ... Jn 16:30 *2065*
a them which heard me, what I ... Jn 18:21 *1905*
none of the disciples durst a him ... Jn 21:12 *1833*
to a alms of them that entered ... Acts 3:2 *154*
I a therefore for what intent ye ... Acts 10:29 *4441*
let them a their husbands at home ... 1Cor 14:35 *1905*
above all that we a or think ... Eph 3:20 *154*
you lack wisdom, let him a of God ... Jas 1:5 *154*
But let him a in faith, nothing ... Jas 1:6 *154*
yet ye have not, because ye a not ... Jas 4:2 *154*
Ye a, and receive not ... Jas 4:3 *154*
because ye a amiss ... Jas 4:3 *154*
And whatsoever we a, we receive of ... 1Jn 3:22 *154*
if we a any thing according to ... 1Jn 5:14 *154*
that he hear us, whatsoever we a ... 1Jn 5:15 *154*
is not unto death, he shall a ... 1Jn 5:16 *154*

ASKED {119}
I a her, and said, Whose daughter ... Gen 24:47 7592
of the place a him of his wife ... Gen 26:7 7592
And Jacob a him, and said, Tell me, ... Gen 32:29 7592
and the man a him, saying, What ... Gen 37:15 7592
Then he a the men of that place, ... Gen 38:21 7592
he a Pharaoh's officers that were ... Gen 40:7 7592
The man a us straitly of our ... Gen 43:7 7592
he a them of their welfare, and ... Gen 43:27 7592
My lord a his servants, saying, ... Gen 44:19 7592
they a each other of their ... Ex 18:7 7592
a not counsel at the mouth of the ... Josh 9:14 7592
they gave him the city which he a ... Josh 19:50 7592
the children of Israel a the LORD ... Judg 1:1 7592
He a water, and she gave him milk ... Judg 5:25 7592
And when they enquired and a ... Judg 6:29 1245
but I a him not whence he was, ... Judg 13:6 7592
a counsel of God, and said, Which ... Judg 20:18 7592
a counsel of the LORD, saying, ... Judg 20:23 7592
petition that thou hast a of him ... 1Sa 1:17 7592
Because I have a him of the LORD ... 1Sa 1:20 7592
me my petition which I a of him ... 1Sa 1:27 7592
the people that a of him a king ... 1Sa 8:10 7592
Saul a counsel of God, Shall I go ... 1Sa 14:37 7592
and he a and said, Where are Samuel ... 1Sa 19:22 7592
David earnestly a leave of me ... 1Sa 20:6 7592
David earnestly a leave of me to ... 1Sa 20:28 7592
that Solomon had a this thing ... 1Kin 3:10 7592
Because thou hast a this thing ... 1Kin 3:11 7592
hast not a for thyself long life ... 1Kin 3:11 7592
neither hast a riches for thyself ... 1Kin 3:11 7592
nor hast a the life of thine ... 1Kin 3:11 7592
but hast a for thyself ... 1Kin 3:11 7592
thee that which thou hast not a ... 1Kin 3:13 7592
all her desire, whatsoever she a ... 1Kin 10:13 7592
he said, Thou hast a a hard thing ... 2Kin 2:10 7592
And when the king a the woman ... 2Kin 8:6 7592
heart, and thou hast not a riches ... 2Chr 1:11 7592
neither yet hast a long life ... 2Chr 1:11 7592
but hast a wisdom and knowledge ... 2Chr 1:11 7592
all her desire, whatsoever she a ... 2Chr 9:12 7592
Then a we those elders, and said ... Ezr 5:9 7593
We a their names also, to certify ... Ezr 5:10 7593
I a them concerning the Jews that ... Neh 1:2 7592
Have ye not a them that go by the ... Job 21:29 7592
He a life of thee, and thou gavest ... Ps 21:4 7592
The people a, and he brought ... Ps 105:40 7592
Egypt, and have not a at my mouth ... Is 30:2 7592
when I a of them, could answer a ... Is 41:28 7592
sought of them that a not for me ... Is 65:1 7592
they a Baruch, saying, Tell us ... Jer 36:17 7592
the king a him secretly in his ... Jer 37:17 7592
princes unto Jeremiah, and a him ... Jer 38:27 7592
that a such things at any ... Dan 2:10 7593
a him the truth of all this ... Dan 7:16 1156
And they a him, saying, Is it ... Mt 12:10 *1905*
he a his disciples, saying, Whom ... Mt 16:13 *2065*
And his disciples a him, saying, ... Mt 17:10 *1905*
is no resurrection, and a him, ... Mt 22:23 *1905*
a him a question, tempting him, ... Mt 22:35 *1905*
gathered together, Jesus a them ... Mt 22:41 *1905*
and the governor a him, saying, ... Mt 27:11 *1905*
the twelve a of him the parable ... Mk 4:10 *2065*
he a him, What is thy name ... Mk 5:9 *1905*
with haste unto the king, and a ... Mk 6:25 *154*
the Pharisees and scribes a him ... Mk 7:5 *1905*
his disciples a him concerning ... Mk 7:17 *1905*
he a them, How many loaves have ... Mk 8:5 *1905*
him, he a him if he saw ought ... Mk 8:23 *1905*
and by the way he a his disciples ... Mk 8:27 *1905*
And they a him, saying, Why say ... Mk 9:11 *1905*
he a the scribes, What question ... Mk 9:16 *1905*
he a his father, How long is it ... Mk 9:21 *1905*
his disciples a him privately ... Mk 9:28 *1905*
and being in the house he a them ... Mk 9:33 *1905*
a him, Is it lawful for a man to ... Mk 10:2 *1905*
in the house his disciples a him ... Mk 10:10 *1905*
a him, Good Master, what shall I ... Mk 10:17 *1905*
and they a him, saying, ... Mk 12:18 *1905*
a him, Which is the first ... Mk 12:28 *1905*
John and Andrew a him privately, ... Mk 13:3 *1905*
a Jesus, saying, Answerest thou ... Mk 14:60 *1905*
Again the high priest a him ... Mk 14:61 *1905*
And Pilate a him, Art thou the ... Mk 15:2 *1905*
Pilate a him again, saying, ... Mk 15:4 *1905*
he a him whether he had been any ... Mk 15:44 *1905*
he a for a writing table, and ... Lk 1:63 *154*
And the people a him, saying, What ... Lk 3:10 *1905*
And his disciples a him, saying, ... Lk 8:9 *1905*
And Jesus a him, saying, What is ... Lk 8:30 *1905*
he a them, saying, Whom say the ... Lk 9:18 *1905*
a what these things meant ... Lk 15:26 *4441*
And a certain ruler a him, saying, ... Lk 18:18 *1905*
pass by, he a what it meant ... Lk 18:36 *4441*
when he was come near, he a him, ... Lk 18:40 *1905*
And they a him, saying, Master, we ... Lk 20:21 *1905*
and they a him, ... Lk 20:27 *1905*
And they a him, saying, Master, ... Lk 21:7 *1905*
a him, saying, Prophesy, who is ... Lk 22:64 *1905*
And Pilate a him, saying, Art thou ... Lk 23:3 *1905*
he a whether the man were a ... Lk 23:6 *1905*
And they a him, What then ... Jn 1:21 *2065*
And they a him, and said unto him, ... Jn 1:25 *2065*
thou wouldest have a of him ... Jn 4:10 *154*
Then a they him, What man is that ... Jn 5:12 *2065*
And his disciples a him, saying, ... Jn 9:2 *2065*
a him how he had received his ... Jn 9:15 *2065*
And they a them, saying, Is this ... Jn 9:19 *2065*
Hitherto have ye a nothing in my ... Jn 16:24 *154*
Then a he them again, Whom seek ... Jn 18:7 *1905*
The high priest then a Jesus of ... Jn 18:19 *2065*
they a of him, saying, Lord, wilt ... Acts 1:6 *1905*
to go into the temple a an alms ... Acts 3:3 *2065*
had set them in the midst, they a ... Acts 4:7 *4441*
and the high priest a them ... Acts 5:27 *1905*
a whether Simon, which was ... Acts 10:18 *4441*
a him, What is that thou hast to ... Acts 23:19 *2065*
he a of what province he was ... Acts 23:34 *1905*
I a him whether he would go to ... Acts 25:20 *3004*
unto them that a not after me ... Rom 10:20 *1905*

ASKELON *(as'-ke-lon)* {3} See ASHKELON. *A Philistine city.*
A with the coast thereof, and ... Judg 1:18 831
one, for Gaza one, for A one ... 1Sa 6:17 831
it not in the streets of A ... 2Sa 1:20 831

ASKEST {3}
Why a thou thus after my name, ... Judg 13:18 7592
a drink of me, which am a woman ... Jn 4:9 *154*
Why a thou me? ... Jn 18:21 *1905*

ASKETH {11}
a thee, saying, Whose art thou ... Gen 32:17 7592
thy son a thee in time to come ... Ex 13:14 7592
when thy son a thee in time to ... Deut 6:20 7592
hands earnestly, the prince a ... Mic 7:3 7592
and the judge a for a reward ... Mic 7:3 7592
Give to him that a thee, and from ... Mt 5:42 *154*
For every one that a receiveth ... Mt 7:8 *154*
Give to every man that a of thee ... Lk 6:30 *154*
For every one that a receiveth ... Lk 11:10 *154*
and none of you a me, Whither ... Jn 16:5 *2065*
an answer to every man that a you ... 1Pet 3:15 *154*

ASKING {7}
of the LORD, in a you a king ... 1Sa 12:17 7592
also for a counsel of one that ... 1Chr 10:13 7592
heart by a meat for their lust ... Ps 78:18 7592
hearing them, and a them questions ... Lk 2:46 1905
So when they continued a him ... Jn 8:7 2065
a no question for conscience sake ... 1Cor 10:25 350
a no question for conscience sake ... 1Cor 10:27 350

ASLEEP {16}
for he was fast a and weary ... Judg 4:21 7290
for they were all a ... 1Sa 26:12 3463
lips of those that are a to speak ... Song 7:9 3463
and he lay, and was fast a ... Jonah 1:5 7290
but he was a ... Mt 8:24 *2518*
the disciples, and findeth them a ... Mt 26:40 *2518*
And he came and found them a again ... Mt 26:43 *2518*
part of the ship, a on a pillow ... Mk 4:38 *2518*
returned, he found them a again ... Mk 14:40 *2518*
But as they sailed he fell a ... Lk 8:23 *879*
when he had said this, he fell a ... Acts 7:60 *2837*
present, but some are fallen a ... 1Cor 15:6 *2837*
fallen a in Christ are perished ... 1Cor 15:18 *2837*
concerning them which are a ... 1Th 4:13 *2837*
not prevent them which are a ... 1Th 4:15 *2837*
for since the fathers fell a ... 2Pet 3:4 *2837*

ASNAH *(as'-nah)* {1} *A family of exiles.*
The children of A, the children ... Ezr 2:50 619

ASNAPPER *(as-nap'-pur)* {1} *An Assyrian king.*
noble A brought over, and set in ... Ezr 4:10 620

ASP {1}
shall play on the hole of the a ... Is 11:8 6620

ASPATHA *(as'-pa-thah)* {1} *A son of Haman.*
and Dalphon, and A ... Est 9:7 630

ASPS {4}
dragons, and the cruel venom of a ... Deut 32:33 6620
it is the gall of a within him ... Job 20:14 6620
He shall suck the poison of a ... Job 20:16 6620
the poison of a is under their ... Rom 3:13 *785*

ASRIEL *(as'-re-el)* {2} See ASHRIEL, ASRIELITES. *A grandson of Manasseh.*
And of A, the family of the ... Num 26:31 844
Helek, and for the children of A ... Josh 17:2 844

ASRIELITES *(as'-re-el-ites)* {1} *Descendants of Asriel.*
And of Asriel, the family of the A ... Num 26:31 845

ASS {86}
in the morning, and saddled his a ... Gen 22:3 2543
men, Abide ye here with the a ... Gen 22:5 2543
give his a provender in the inn ... Gen 42:27 2543
clothes, and laded every man his a ... Gen 44:13 2543
Issachar is a strong a couching ... Gen 49:14 2543
his sons, and set them upon an a ... Ex 4:20 2543
every firstling of an a thou ... Ex 13:13 2543
nor his ox, nor his a, nor any ... Ex 20:17 2543
an ox or an a fall therein ... Ex 21:33 2543
alive, whether it be ox, or a ... Ex 22:4 2543
whether it be for ox, for a ... Ex 22:9 2543
deliver unto his neighbour an a ... Ex 22:10 2543
enemy's ox or his a going astray ... Ex 23:4 2543
If thou see the a of him that ... Ex 23:5 2543
thine a may rest, and the son of ... Ex 23:12 2543
But the firstling of an a thou ... Ex 34:20 2543
I have not taken one a from them ... Num 16:15 2543
in the morning, and saddled his a ... Num 22:21 860
Now he was riding upon his a ... Num 22:22 860
the a saw the angel of the LORD ... Num 22:23 860
the a turned aside out of the way ... Num 22:23 860
and Balaam smote the a, to turn ... Num 22:23 860
when the a saw the angel of the ... Num 22:25 860
when the a saw the angel of the ... Num 22:27 860
and he smote the a with a staff ... Num 22:27 860
LORD opened the mouth of the a ... Num 22:28 860
And Balaam said unto the a ... Num 22:29 860
the a said unto Balaam ... Num 22:30 860
Am not I thine a, ... Num 22:30 860
smitten thine a these three times ... Num 22:32 860
the a saw me, and turned from me ... Num 22:33 860
nor thine ox, nor thine a ... Deut 5:14 2543
his maidservant, his ox, or his a ... Deut 5:21 2543
manner shalt thou do with his a ... Deut 22:3 2543
shalt not see thy brother's a or ... Deut 22:4 2543
plow with an ox and an a together ... Deut 22:10 2543
thine a shall be violently taken ... Deut 28:31 2543
and old, and ox, and sheep, and a ... Josh 6:21 2543
and she lighted off her a ... Josh 15:18 2543
and she lighted from off her a ... Judg 1:14 2543
neither sheep, nor ox, nor a ... Judg 6:4 2543
sons that rode on thirty a colts ... Judg 10:4 5895
rode on threescore and ten a colts ... Judg 12:14 5895
And he found a new jawbone of an a ... Judg 15:15 2543
said, With the jawbone of an a ... Judg 15:16 2543
with the jaw of an a have I slain ... Judg 15:16 2543
the man took her up upon an a ... Judg 19:28 2543
or whose a have I taken ... 1Sa 12:3 2543
suckling, ox and sheep, camel and a ... 1Sa 15:3 2543
Jesse took an a laden with bread, ... 1Sa 16:20 2543
it was so, as she rode on the a ... 1Sa 25:20 2543
she hasted, and lighted off the a ... 1Sa 25:23 2543
and arose, and rode upon an a ... 1Sa 25:42 2543
not followed, he saddled his a ... 2Sa 17:23 2543

said, I will saddle me an *a* ... 2Sa 19:26 2543
And Shimei arose, and saddled his *a* ... 1Kin 2:40 2543
unto his sons, Saddle me the *a* ... 1Kin 13:13 2543
So they saddled him the *a* ... 1Kin 13:13 2543
that he saddled for him the *a* ... 1Kin 13:23 2543
the *a* stood by it, the lion also ... 1Kin 13:24 2543
his sons, saying, Saddle me the *a* ... 1Kin 13:27 2543
carcase cast in the way, and the *a* ... 1Kin 13:28 2543
eaten the carcase, nor torn the *a* ... 1Kin 13:28 2543
man of God, and laid it upon the *a* ... 1Kin 13:29 2543
Then she saddled an *a*, and said to ... 2Kin 4:24 860
Doth the wild *a* bray when he hath ... Job 6:5 6501
away the *a* of the fatherless ... Job 24:3 2543
Who hath sent out the wild *a* free ... Job 39:5 5601
loosed the bands of the wild *a* ... Job 39:5 6171
for the horse, a bridle for the *a* ... Prov 26:3 2543
owner, and the *a* his master's crib ... Is 1:3 2543
the feet of the ox and the *a* ... Is 32:20 2543
A wild *a* used to the wilderness, ... Jer 2:24 6501
be buried with the burial of an *a* ... Jer 22:19 2543
a wild *a* alone by himself ... Hos 8:9 6501
lowly, and riding upon an *a* ... Zec 9:9 2543
and upon a colt the foal of an *a* ... Zec 9:9 860
mule, of the camel, and of the *a* ... Zec 14:15 2543
ye shall find an *a* tied, and a ... Mt 21:2 *3688*
thee, meek, and sitting upon an *a* ... Mt 21:5 *3688*
and a colt the foal of an *a* ... Mt 21:5 *5268*
And brought the *a*, and the colt, and ... Mt 21:7 *3688*
his ox or his *a* from the stall ... Lk 13:15 *3688*
an *a* or an ox fallen into a pit ... Lk 14:5 *3688*
when he had found a young *a* ... Jn 12:14 *3678*
the dumb *a* speaking with man's ... 2Pet 2:16 *5268*

ASSAULT {2}
and province that would *a* them ... Est 8:11 6696
when there was an *a* made both of ... Acts 14:5 *3730*

ASSAULTED {1}
a the house of Jason, and sought ... Acts 17:5 *2186*

ASSAY {1}
If we *a* to commune with thee, ... Job 4:2 5254

ASSAYED {4}
Or hath God *a* to go and take him a ... Deut 4:34 5254
upon his armour, and he *a* to go ... 1Sa 17:39 2974
he *a* to join himself to the ... Acts 9:26 *3987*
they *a* to go into Bithynia ... Acts 16:7 *3985*

ASSAYING {1}
Egyptians *a* to do were drowned ... Heb 11:29 *3984,2983*

ASSEMBLE {20}
them, all the assembly shall *a* ... Num 10:3 3259
A me the men of Judah within ... 2Sa 20:4 2199
Amasa went to *a* the men of Judah ... 2Sa 20:5 2199
shall *a* the outcasts of Israel, ... Is 11:12 622
A yourselves and come ... Is 45:20 6908
All ye, *a* yourselves, and hear ... Is 48:14 6908
A yourselves, and let us go into ... Jer 4:5 622
a yourselves, and let us enter ... Jer 8:14 622
a all the beasts of the field, ... Jer 12:9 622
I will *a* them into the midst of ... Jer 21:4 622
a you out of the countries where ... Eze 11:17 622
the field, *A* yourselves, and come ... Eze 39:17 6908
shall *a* a multitude of great ... Dan 11:10 622
they *a* themselves for corn and ... Hos 7:14 1481
a the elders, gather the children ... Joel 2:16 6908
A yourselves, and come, all ye ... Joel 3:11 5789
A yourselves upon the mountains ... Amos 3:9 622
I will surely *a*, O Jacob, all of ... Mic 2:12 622
will I *a* her that halteth, and I ... Mic 4:6 622
that I may *a* the kingdoms, to ... Zeph 3:8 6908

ASSEMBLED {36}
which *a* at the door of the ... Ex 38:8 6638
they *a* all the congregation ... Num 1:18 6950
of Israel *a* together at Shiloh ... Josh 18:1 6950
of Israel *a* themselves together ... Judg 10:17 622
they lay with the women that *a* at ... 1Sa 2:22 6633
that were with him *a* themselves ... 1Sa 14:20 2199
Then Solomon *a* the elders of ... 1Kin 8:1 6950
And all the men of Israel *a* ... 1Kin 8:2 6950
of Israel, that were *a* unto him ... 1Kin 8:5 3259
he *a* all the house of Judah, with ... 1Kin 12:21 6950
David *a* the children of Aaron, and ... 1Chr 15:4 662
David *a* all the princes of Israel ... 1Chr 28:1 6950
Then Solomon *a* the elders of ... 2Chr 5:2 6950
a themselves unto the king in the ... 2Chr 5:3 6950
of Israel that were *a* unto him ... 2Chr 5:6 3259
And on the fourth day they *a* ... 2Chr 20:26 6950
there *a* at Jerusalem much people ... 2Chr 30:13 622
Then were *a* unto me every one ... Ezr 9:4 622
there *a* unto him out of Israel a ... Ezr 10:1 6908
of Israel were *a* with fasting ... Neh 9:1 622
the Jews that were at Shushan *a* ... Est 9:18 6950
For, lo, the kings were *a* ... Ps 48:4 3259
together, and let the people be *a* ... Is 43:9
a themselves by troops in the ... Jer 5:7 1413
thy company that are *a* unto thee ... Eze 38:7 6950
princes *a* together to the king ... Dan 6:6 7284
Then these men *a*, and found Daniel ... Dan 6:11 7284
Then these men *a* unto the king ... Dan 6:15 7284
Then *a* together the chief priests ... Mt 26:3 *4863*
the scribes and the elders were *a* ... Mt 26:57 *4863*
when they were *a* with the elders, ... Mt 28:12 *4863*
with him were *a* all the chief ... Mk 14:53 *4905*
were *a* for fear of the Jews ... Jn 20:19 *4863*
being *a* together with them, ... Acts 1:4 *4871*
shaken where they were *a* together ... Acts 4:31 *4863*
to pass, that a whole year they *a* ... Acts 11:26 *4863*
being *a* with one accord, to send ... Acts 15:25 *1096*

ASSEMBLIES {6}
the *a* of violent men have sought ... Ps 86:14 5712
fastened by the masters of *a* ... Eccl 12:11 627
and sabbaths, the calling of *a* ... Is 1:13 4744
of mount Zion, and upon her *a* ... Is 4:5 4744
laws and my statutes in all mine *a* ... Eze 44:24 4150
I will not smell in your solemn *a* ... Amos 5:21 6116

ASSEMBLING {2}
the lookingglasses of the women *a* ... Ex 38:8 6633
Not forsaking the *a* of ourselves ... Heb 10:25 *1997*

ASSEMBLY {49}
unto their *a*, mine honour, be not ... Gen 49:6 6951
the whole *a* of the congregation ... Ex 12:6 6951
to kill this whole *a* with hunger ... Ex 16:3 6951
be hid from the eyes of the *a* ... Lev 4:13 6951
the *a* was gathered together unto ... Lev 8:4 5712
it is a solemn *a* ... Lev 23:36 6116
whole *a* of the children of Israel ... Num 8:9 5712
use them for the calling of the *a* ... Num 10:2 5712
them, all the *a* shall assemble ... Num 10:3 5712
the *a* of the congregation of the ... Num 14:5 6951
hundred and fifty princes of the *a* ... Num 16:2 5712
went from the presence of the *a* ... Num 20:6 6951
and gather thou the *a* together ... Num 20:8 5712
day ye shall have a solemn *a* ... Num 29:35 6116
the LORD spake unto all your *a* in ... Deut 5:22 6951
of the fire in the day of the *a* ... Deut 9:10 6951
of the fire in the day of the *a* ... Deut 10:4 6951
be a solemn *a* to the LORD thy God ... Deut 16:8 6116
God in Horeb in the day of the *a* ... Deut 18:16 6951
in the *a* of the people of God ... Judg 20:2 6951
camp from Jabesh-gilead to the *a* ... Judg 21:8 6951
all this *a* shall know that the ... 1Sa 17:47 6951
Proclaim a solemn *a* for Baal ... 2Kin 10:20 6116
eighth day they made a solemn *a* ... 2Chr 7:9 6116
the whole *a* took counsel to keep ... 2Chr 30:23 6951
And I set a great *a* against them ... Neh 5:7 6952
on the eighth day was a solemn *a* ... Neh 8:18 6116
the *a* of the wicked have inclosed ... Ps 22:16 5712
be feared in the *a* of the saints ... Ps 89:7 5475
praise him in the *a* of the elders ... Ps 107:32 4186
in the *a* of the upright, and in ... Ps 111:1 5475
midst of the congregation and *a* ... Prov 5:14 5712
upon the *a* of young men together ... Jer 6:11 5475
an *a* of treacherous men ... Jer 9:2 6116
I sat not in the *a* of the mockers ... Jer 15:17 5475
spake to all the *a* of the people ... Jer 26:17 6951
to come up against Babylon an *a* ... Jer 50:9 6951
he hath called an *a* against me to ... Lam 1:15 4150
destroyed his places of the *a* ... Lam 2:6 4150
not be in the *a* of my people ... Eze 13:9 5475
with an *a* of people, which shall ... Eze 23:24 6951
ye a fast, call a solemn *a* ... Joel 1:14 6116
sanctify a fast, call a solemn *a* ... Joel 2:15 6116
are sorrowful for the solemn *a* ... Zeph 3:18 4150
for the *a* was confused ... Acts 19:32 *1577*
shall be determined in a lawful *a* ... Acts 19:39 *1577*
thus spoken, he dismissed the *a* ... Acts 19:41 *1577*
To the general *a* and church of the ... Heb 12:23 *3831*
your *a* a man with a gold ring ... Jas 2:2 *4864*

ASSENT {1}
good to the king with one *a* ... 2Chr 18:12 6310

ASSENTED {1}
And the Jews also *a*, saying that ... Acts 24:9 *4934*

ASSES {64}
and he had sheep, and oxen, and he *a* ... Gen 12:16 2543
and maidservants, and she *a* ... Gen 12:16 860
and maidservants, and camels, and *a* ... Gen 24:35 2543
and menservants, and camels, and *a* ... Gen 30:43 2543
And I have oxen, and *a*, flocks, and ... Gen 32:5 2543
kine, and ten bulls, twenty she *a* ... Gen 32:15 860
sheep, and their oxen, and their *a* ... Gen 34:28 2543
as he fed the *a* of Zibeon his ... Gen 36:24 2543
they laded their *a* with the corn ... Gen 42:26 2543
and take us for bondmen, and our *a* ... Gen 43:18 2543
and he gave their *a* provender ... Gen 43:24 2543
were sent away, they and their *a* ... Gen 44:3 2543
ten *a* laden with the good things ... Gen 45:23 860
ten she *a* laden with corn and ... Gen 45:23 2543
cattle of the herds, and for the *a* ... Gen 47:17 2543
upon the horses, upon the *a* ... Ex 9:3 2543
and of the beeves, and of the *a* ... Num 31:28 2543
persons, of the beeves, of the *a* ... Num 31:30 2543
And threescore and one thousand *a* ... Num 31:34 2543
the *a* were thirty thousand and ... Num 31:39 2543
And thirty thousand *a* and five ... Num 31:45 2543
daughters, and his oxen, and his *a* ... Josh 7:24 2543
and took old sacks upon their *a* ... Josh 9:4 2543
Speak, ye that ride on white *a* ... Judg 5:10 860
with him, and a couple of *a* ... Judg 19:3 2543
there were with him two *a* saddled ... Judg 19:10 2543
both straw and provender for our *a* ... Judg 19:19 2543
and gave provender unto the *a* ... Judg 19:21 2543
goodliest young men, and your *a* ... 1Sa 8:16 2543
the *a* of Kish Saul's father were ... 1Sa 9:3 860
thee, and arise, go seek the *a* ... 1Sa 9:3 860
my father leave caring for the *a* ... 1Sa 9:5 860
as for thine *a* that were lost ... 1Sa 9:20 860
The *a* which thou wentest to seek ... 1Sa 10:2 860
hath left the care of the *a* ... 1Sa 10:2 860
And he said, To seek the *a* ... 1Sa 10:14 860
us plainly that the *a* were found ... 1Sa 10:16 860
and sucklings, and oxen, and *a* ... 1Sa 22:19 2543
cakes of figs, and laid them on *a* ... 1Sa 25:18 2543
the sheep, and the oxen, and the *a* ... 1Sa 27:9 2543
him, with a couple of *a* saddled ... 2Sa 16:1 2543
The *a* be for the king's household ... 2Sa 16:2 2543
of the young men, and one of the *a* ... 2Kin 4:22 860
and their horses, and their *a* ... 2Kin 7:7 2543
a tied, and the tents as they were ... 2Kin 7:10 2543
of *a* two thousand, and of men an ... 1Chr 5:21 2543
and Naphtali, brought bread on *a* ... 1Chr 12:40 2543
over the *a* was Jehdeiah the ... 1Chr 27:30 860
all the feeble of them upon *a* ... 2Chr 28:15 2543
their *a*, six thousand seven ... Ezr 2:67 2543
seven hundred and twenty *a* ... Neh 7:69 2543
bringing in sheaves, and lading *a* ... Neh 13:15 2543
of oxen, and five hundred she *a* ... Job 1:3 860
the *a* feeding beside them ... Job 1:14 860
as wild *a* in the desert, go they ... Job 24:5 6501
yoke of oxen, and a thousand she *a* ... Job 42:12 860
the wild *a* quench their thirst ... Ps 104:11 6501
of horsemen, a chariot of *a* ... Is 21:7 2543
upon the shoulders of young *a* ... Is 30:6 5895
the young *a* that ear the ground ... Is 30:24 5895
dens for ever, a joy of wild *a* ... Is 32:14 6501
the wild *a* did stand in the high ... Jer 14:6 6501
whose flesh is as the flesh of *a* ... Eze 23:20 2543
his dwelling was with the wild *a* ... Dan 5:21 6167

ASSHUR *(ash'-ur)* {8} See ASHUR, ASSUR, ASSYRIA.
1. The builder of Nineveh.
Out of that land went forth *A* ... Gen 10:11 804
2. A son of Shem.
Elam, and *A*, and Arphaxad, and Lud, ... Gen 10:22 804
Elam, and *A*, and Arphaxad, and Lud, ... 1Chr 1:17 804
3. Another name for Assyria.
until *A* shall carry thee away ... Num 24:22 804
of Chittim, and shall afflict *A* ... Num 24:24 804
Eden, the merchants of Sheba, *A* ... Eze 27:23 804
A is there and all her company ... Eze 32:22 804
A shall not save us ... Hos 14:3 804

ASSHURIM *(ash'-u-rim)* {1} See ASHURITES. *Descendants of Dedan.*
And the sons of Dedan were *A* ... Gen 25:3 805

ASSHURITES See ASSHURIM.

ASSIGNED {3}
had a portion *a* them of Pharaoh ... Gen 47:22
they *a* Bezer in the wilderness ... Josh 20:8 5414
that he *a* Uriah unto a place ... 2Sa 11:16 5414

ASSIR *(as'-sur)* {5}
1. A son of Korah.
A, and Elkanah, and Abiasaph ... Ex 6:24 617
son, Korah his son, *A* his son, ... 1Chr 6:22 617
2. A son of Ebiasaph.
Ebiasaph his son, and *A* his son, ... 1Chr 6:23 617
The son of Tahath, the son of *A* ... 1Chr 6:37 617
3. A son of Jeconiah.
A, Salathiel his son, ... 1Chr 3:17 617

ASSIST {1}
that ye *a* her in whatsoever ... Rom 16:2 *3936*

ASSOCIATE {1}
A yourselves, O ye people, and ye ... Is 8:9 7489

ASSOS *(as'-sos)* {2} *A seaport of Mysia in Asia Minor.*
before to ship, and sailed unto *A* ... Acts 20:13 *789*
And when he met with us at *A* ... Acts 20:14 *789*

ASS'S {4}
his *a* colt unto the choice vine ... Gen 49:11 860
until an *a* head was sold for ... 2Kin 6:25 2543
man be born like a wild *a* colt ... Job 11:12 6501
King cometh, sitting on an *a* colt ... Jn 12:15 *3688*

ASSUR *(As'-sur)* {2} See ASSHUR. *Same as Asshur 3.*
the days of Esar-haddon king of *A* ... Ezr 4:2 804
A also is joined with them ... Ps 83:8 804

ASSURANCE {7}
and shalt have none *a* of thy life ... Deut 28:66 539
quietness and *a* for ever ... Is 32:17 983
he hath given *a* unto all men ... Acts 17:31 *4102*
of the full *a* of understanding ... Col 2:2 *4136*
in the Holy Ghost, and in much *a* ... 1Th 1:5 *4136*
the full *a* of hope unto the end ... Heb 6:11 *4136*
a true heart in full *a* of faith ... Heb 10:22 *4136*

ASSURE {1}
shall *a* our hearts before him ... 1Jn 3:19 *3983*

ASSURED {3}
unto it, and it shall be *a* to him ... Lev 27:19 6966
give you *a* peace in this place ... Jer 14:13 571
hast learned and hast been *a* of ... 2Ti 3:14 *4104*

ASSUREDLY {9}
said unto David, Know thou *a* ... 1Sa 28:1 3045
A Solomon thy son shall reign ... 1Kin 1:13 3588
A Solomon thy son shall reign ... 1Kin 1:17 3588
A Solomon thy son shall reign ... 1Kin 1:30 3588
this land *a* with my whole heart ... Jer 32:41 571
If thou wilt *a* go forth unto the ... Jer 38:17 3318
drink of the cup have *a* drunken ... Jer 49:12 8354
all the house of Israel know *a* ... Acts 2:36 *806*
a gathering that the Lord had ... Acts 16:10 *4822*

ASSWAGE {1}
of my lips should *a* your grief ... Job 16:5 2820

ASSWAGED {2}
over the earth, and the waters *a* ... Gen 8:1 7918
Though I speak, my grief is not *a* ... Job 16:6 2820

ASSYRIA *(as-sir'-e-ah)* {118} See ASSHUR, ASSYRIAN. *A Mesopotamian empire.*
which goeth toward the east of *A* ... Gen 2:14 804
Egypt, as thou goest toward *A* ... Gen 25:18 804
Pul the king of *A* came against ... 2Kin 15:19 804
silver, to give to the king of *A* ... 2Kin 15:20 804

So the king of *A* turned back 2Kin 15:20 804
came Tiglath-pileser king of *A* 2Kin 15:29 804
and carried them captive to *A* 2Kin 15:29 804
to Tiglath-pileser king of *A* 2Kin 16:7 804
it for a present to the king of *A* 2Kin 16:8 804
the king of *A* hearkened unto him 2Kin 16:9 804
for the king of *A* went up against 2Kin 16:9 804
to meet Tiglath-pileser king of *A* 2Kin 16:10 804
of the LORD for the king of *A* 2Kin 16:18 804
him came up Shalmaneser king of *A* 2Kin 17:3 804
the king of *A* found conspiracy in 2Kin 17:4 804
no present to the king of *A* 2Kin 17:4 804
the king of *A* shut him up 2Kin 17:4 804
Then the king of *A* came up 2Kin 17:5 804
Hoshea the king of *A* took Samaria 2Kin 17:6 804
and carried Israel away into *A* 2Kin 17:6 804
their own land to *A* unto this day 2Kin 17:23 804
the king of *A* brought men from 2Kin 17:24 804
they spake to the king of *A* 2Kin 17:26 804
Then the king of *A* commanded 2Kin 17:27 804
he rebelled against the king of *A* 2Kin 18:7 804
king of *A* came up against Samaria 2Kin 18:9 804
the king of *A* did carry away 2Kin 18:11 804
did carry away Israel unto *A* 2Kin 18:11 804
did Sennacherib king of *A* come up 2Kin 18:13 804
sent to the king of *A* to Lachish 2Kin 18:14 804
the king of *A* appointed unto 2Kin 18:14 804
and gave it to the king of *A* 2Kin 18:16 804
And the king of *A* sent Tartan 2Kin 18:17 804
the great king, the king of *A* 2Kin 18:19 804
pledges to my lord the king of *A* 2Kin 18:23 804
of the great king, the king of *A* 2Kin 18:28 804
into the hand of the king of *A* 2Kin 18:30 804
for thus saith the king of *A* 2Kin 18:31 804
out of the hand of the king of *A* 2Kin 18:33 804
whom the king of *A* his master 2Kin 19:4 804
the king of *A* have blasphemed me 2Kin 19:6 804
found the king of *A* warring 2Kin 19:8 804
into the hand of the king of *A* 2Kin 19:10 804
kings of *A* have done to all lands 2Kin 19:11 804
the kings of *A* have destroyed the 2Kin 19:17 804
king of *A* I have heard 2Kin 19:20 804
the LORD concerning the king of *A* 2Kin 19:32 804
So Sennacherib king of *A* departed 2Kin 19:36 804
out of the hand of the king of *A* 2Kin 20:6 804
king of *A* to the river Euphrates 2Kin 23:29 804
king of *A* carried away captive 1Chr 5:6 804
up the spirit of Pul king of *A* 1Chr 5:26 804
of Tilgath-pilneser king of *A* 1Chr 5:26 804
unto the kings of *A* to help him 2Chr 28:16 804
king of *A* came unto him, and 2Chr 28:20 804
and gave it unto the king of *A* 2Chr 28:21 804
out of the hand of the kings of *A* 2Chr 30:6 804
Sennacherib king of *A* came 2Chr 32:1 804
Why should the kings of *A* come 2Chr 32:4 804
nor dismayed for the king of *A* 2Chr 32:7 804
this did Sennacherib king of *A* 2Chr 32:9 804
Thus saith Sennacherib king of *A* 2Chr 32:10 804
out of the hand of the king of *A* 2Chr 32:11 804
in the camp of the king of *A* 2Chr 32:21 804
hand of Sennacherib the king of *A* 2Chr 32:22 804
of the host of the king of *A* 2Chr 33:11 804
heart of the king of *A* unto them ..... Ezr 6:22 804
of the kings of *A* unto this day ..... Neh 9:32 804
even the king of *A* ..... Is 7:17 804
the bee that is in the land of *A* ..... Is 7:18 804
the river, by the king of *A* ..... Is 7:20 804
taken away before the king of *A* ..... Is 8:4 804
and many, even the king of *A* ..... Is 8:7 804
the stout heart of the king of *A* ..... Is 10:12 804
which shall be left, from *A* ..... Is 11:11 804
which shall be left, from *A* ..... Is 11:16 804
be a highway out of Egypt to *A* ..... Is 19:23 804
Egypt, and the Egyptian into *A* ..... Is 19:23 804
be the third with Egypt and with *A* ..... Is 19:24 804
A the work of my hands, and Israel ..... Is 19:25 804
Sargon the king of *A* sent him ..... Is 20:1 804
So shall the king of *A* lead away ..... Is 20:4 804
be delivered from the king of *A* ..... Is 20:6 804
ready to perish in the land of *A* ..... Is 27:13 804
king of *A* came up against all the ..... Is 36:1 804
the king of *A* sent Rabshakeh from ..... Is 36:2 804
the great king, the king of *A* ..... Is 36:4 804
thee, to my master the king of *A* ..... Is 36:8 804
of the great king, the king of *A* ..... Is 36:13 804
into the hand of the king of *A* ..... Is 36:15 804
for thus saith the king of *A* ..... Is 36:16 804
out of the hand of the king of *A* ..... Is 36:18 804
whom the king of *A* his master ..... Is 37:4 804
the king of *A* have blasphemed me ..... Is 37:6 804
found the king of *A* warring ..... Is 37:8 804
into the hand of the king of *A* ..... Is 37:10 804
of *A* have done to all lands by ..... Is 37:11 804
the kings of *A* have laid waste ..... Is 37:18 804
me against Sennacherib king of *A* ..... Is 37:21 804
the LORD concerning the king of *A* ..... Is 37:33 804
So Sennacherib king of *A* departed ..... Is 37:37 804
out of the hand of the king of *A* ..... Is 38:6 804
hast thou to do in the way of *A* ..... Jer 2:18 804
Egypt, as thou wast ashamed of *A* ..... Jer 2:36 804
the king of *A* hath devoured him ..... Jer 50:17 804
as I have punished the king of *A* ..... Jer 50:18 804
that were the chosen men of *A* ..... Eze 23:7 804
they call to Egypt, they go to *A* ..... Hos 7:11 804
For they are gone up to *A* ..... Hos 8:9 804
shall eat unclean things in *A* ..... Hos 9:3 804
A for a present to king Jareb ..... Hos 10:6 804
and as a dove out of the land of *A* ..... Hos 11:11 804
the land of *A* with the sword ..... Mic 5:6 804
he shall come even to thee from *A* ..... Mic 7:12 804
shepherds slumber, O king of *A* ..... Nah 3:18 804
against the north, and destroy *A* ..... Zeph 2:13 804
of Egypt, and gather them out of *A* ..... Zec 10:10 804
the pride of *A* shall be brought ..... Zec 10:11 804

ASSYRIAN *(as-sir'-e'-un)* {13} See ASSYRIANS. *An inhabitant of Assyria.*
O *A*, the rod of mine anger, and ..... Is 10:5 804
in Zion, be not afraid of the *A* ..... Is 10:24 804
I will break the *A* in my land ..... Is 14:25 804
the *A* shall come into Egypt, and ..... Is 19:23 804
til the *A* founded it for them ..... Is 23:13 804
LORD shall the *A* be beaten down ..... Is 30:31 804
Then shall the *A* fall with the ..... Is 31:8 804
the *A* oppressed them without ..... Is 52:4 804
the *A* was a cedar in Lebanon with ..... Eze 31:3 804
wound, then went Ephraim to the *A* ..... Hos 5:13 804
but the *A* shall be his king, ... Hos 11:5 804
when the *A* shall come into our ..... Mic 5:5 804
shall he deliver us from the *A* ..... Mic 5:6 804

ASSYRIANS *(as-sir'-e-uns)* {10}
of the *A* an hundred fourscore 2Kin 19:35 804
Egyptians shall serve with the *A* ..... Is 19:23 804
in the camp of the *A* an hundred ..... Is 37:36 804
to the Egyptians, and to the *A* ..... Lam 5:6 804
played the whore also with the *A* ..... Eze 16:28 804
lovers, on the *A* her neighbours, ... Eze 23:5 804
lovers, into the hand of the *A* ..... Eze 23:9 804
doted upon the *A* her neighbours ..... Eze 23:12 804
and Koa, and all the *A* with them ..... Eze 23:23 804
do make a covenant with the *A* ..... Hos 12:1 804

ASTAROTH *(as'-ta-roth)* {1} See ASHTAROTH. *A city in Bashan.*
Bashan, which dwelt at *A* in Edrei ..... Deut 1:4 6252

ASTONIED {10}
and of my beard, and sat down *a* ..... Ezr 9:3 8074
I sat *a* until the evening ..... Ezr 9:4 8074
Upright men shall be *a* at this ..... Job 17:8 8074
after him shall be *a* at his day ..... Job 18:20 8074
As many were *a* at thee ..... Is 52:14 8074
Why shouldest thou be as a man *a* ..... Jer 14:9 1724
be *a* one with another, and consume ..... Eze 4:17 8074
Nebuchadnezzar the king was *a* ..... Dan 3:24 8429
was *a* for one hour, and his ..... Dan 4:19 8075
in him, and his lords were *a* ..... Dan 5:9 7672

ASTONISHED {34}
dwell therein shall be *a* at it ..... Lev 26:32 8074
one that passeth by it shall be *a* 1Kin 9:8 8074
Mark me, and be *a*, and lay your ..... Job 21:5 8074
tremble, and are *a* at his reproof ..... Job 26:11 8539
Be *a*, O ye heavens, at this, and ..... Jer 2:12 8074
and the priests shall be *a* ..... Jer 4:9 8074
that passeth thereby shall be *a* ..... Jer 18:16 8074
that passeth thereby shall be *a* ..... Jer 19:8 8074
one that goeth by it shall be *a* ..... Jer 49:17 8074
that goeth by Babylon shall be *a* ..... Jer 50:13 8074
remained there *a* among them seven ..... Eze 3:15 8074
at every moment, and be *a* at thee ..... Eze 26:16 8074
of the isles shall be *a* at thee ..... Eze 27:35 8074
the people shall be *a* at thee ..... Eze 28:19 8074
I was *a* at the vision, but none ..... Dan 8:27 8074
the people were *a* at his doctrine ..... Mt 7:28 1605
insomuch that they were *a* ..... Mt 13:54 1605
they were *a* at his doctrine ..... Mt 22:33 1605
they were *a* at his doctrine ..... Mk 1:22 1605
And they were *a* with a great ..... Mk 5:42 1839
and many hearing him were *a* ..... Mk 6:2 1605
And were beyond measure *a*, saying, ... Mk 7:37 1605
the disciples were *a* at his words ..... Mk 10:24 2284
they were *a* out of measure, ... Mk 10:26 1605
the people was *a* at his doctrine ..... Mk 11:18 1605
him were *a* at his understanding ..... Lk 2:47 1839
they were *a* at his doctrine ..... Lk 4:32 1605
For he was *a*, and all that were ..... Lk 5:9 4023,2285
And her parents were *a* ..... Lk 8:56 1839
also of our company made us *a* ..... Lk 24:22 1839
a said, Lord, what wilt thou have ..... Acts 9:6 2284
which believed were *a*, as many as ..... Acts 10:45 1839
the door, and saw him, they were *a* ..... Acts 12:16 1839
being *a* at the doctrine of the ..... Acts 13:12 1605

ASTONISHMENT {21}
and blindness, and *a* of heart ..... Deut 28:28 8541
And thou shalt become an *a* ..... Deut 28:37 8047
shall be an *a* to every one that 2Chr 7:21 8074
delivered them to trouble, to *a* 2Chr 29:8 8047
made us to drink the wine of *a* ..... Ps 60:3 8653
a hath taken hold on me ..... Jer 8:21 8047
destroy them, and make them an *a* ..... Jer 25:9 8047
shall be a desolation, and an *a* ..... Jer 25:11 8047
to make them a desolation, an *a* ..... Jer 25:18 8047
the earth, to be a curse, and an *a* ..... Jer 29:18 8047
shall be an execration, and an *a* ..... Jer 42:18 8047
shall be an execration, and an *a* ..... Jer 44:12 8047
your land a desolation, and an *a* ..... Jer 44:22 8047
dwelling place for dragons, an *a* ..... Jer 51:37 8047
become an *a* among the nations ..... Jer 51:41 8047
drink water by measure, and with *a* ..... Eze 4:16 8078
an *a* unto the nations that are ..... Eze 5:15 8047
and drink their water with *a* ..... Eze 12:19 8078
and sorrow, with the cup of *a* ..... Eze 23:33 8047
I will smite every horse with *a* ..... Zec 12:4 8541
were astonished with a great *a* ..... Mk 5:42 1611

ASTRAY {22}
enemy's ox or his ass going *a* ..... Ex 23:4 8582
brother's ox or his sheep go *a* ..... Deut 22:1 5080
they go *a* as soon as they be born ..... Ps 58:3 8582
Before I was afflicted I went *a* ..... Ps 119:67 7683
I have gone *a* like a lost sheep ..... Ps 119:176 8582
of his folly he shall go *a* ..... Prov 5:23 7686
her ways, go not *a* in her paths ..... Prov 7:25 8582
righteous to go *a* in an evil way ..... Prov 28:10 7686
All we like sheep have gone *a* ..... Is 53:6 8582
have caused them to go *a*, they ..... Jer 50:6 8582
Israel may go no more *a* from me ..... Eze 14:11 8582
far from me, when Israel went *a* ..... Eze 44:10 8582
which went *a* away from me after ..... Eze 44:10 8582
children of Israel went *a* from me ..... Eze 44:15 8582
which went not *a* when the ..... Eze 48:11 8582
the children of Israel went *a* ..... Eze 48:11 8582
as the Levites went *a* ..... Eze 48:11 8582
sheep, and one of them be gone *a* ..... Mt 18:12 4105
and seeketh that which is gone *a* ..... Mt 18:12 4105
ninety and nine which went not *a* ..... Mt 18:13 4105
For ye were as sheep going *a* 1Pet 2:25 4105
the right way, and are gone *a* 2Pet 2:15 4105

ASTROLOGER {1}
such things at any magician, or *a* ..... Dan 2:10 826

ASTROLOGERS {8}
Let now the *a*, the stargazers, ... Is 47:13 1895,8064
a that were in all his realm ..... Dan 1:20 825
to call the magicians, and the *a* ..... Dan 2:2 825
cannot the wise men, the *a* ..... Dan 2:27 826
Then came in the magicians, the *a* ..... Dan 4:7 826
cried aloud to bring in the *a* ..... Dan 5:7 826
made master of the magicians, *a* ..... Dan 5:11 826
And now the wise men, the *a* ..... Dan 5:15 826

ASUNDER {21}
but shall not divide it *a* ..... Lev 1:17
neck, but shall not divide it *a* ..... Lev 5:8
clave *a* that was under them ..... Num 16:31
of fire, and parted them both *a* 2Kin 2:11 996
at ease, but he hath broken me *a* ..... Job 16:12
about, he cleaveth my reins *a* ..... Job 16:13
Let us break their bands *a* ..... Ps 2:3
he hath cut *a* the cords of the ..... Ps 129:4
of the whole earth cut in *a* ..... Jer 50:23
great pain, and No shall be rent *a* ..... Eze 30:16
he beheld, and drove *a* the nations ..... Hab 3:6
staff, even Beauty, and cut it *a* ..... Zec 11:10
Then I cut *a* mine other staff, ... Zec 11:14
together, let not man put *a* ..... Mt 19:6 5563
And shall cut him *a*, and appoint ..... Mt 24:51 1371
chains had been plucked *a* by him ..... Mk 5:4 1288
together, let not man put *a* ..... Mk 10:9 5563
he burst *a* in the midst, and all ..... Acts 1:18 2997
departed *a* one from the other ..... Acts 15:39 673
even to the dividing *a* of soul ..... Heb 4:12
were stoned, they were sawn *a* ..... Heb 11:37 4249

ASUPPIM {2} *Storage for temple gods.*
and to his sons the house of *A* 1Chr 26:15 624
four a day, and toward *A* two 1Chr 26:17 624

ASYNCRITUS *(a-sin'-cri-tus)* {1} *A Christian acquaintance of Paul.*
Salute *A*, Phlegon, Hermas, ... Rom 16:14 799

AT See APPENDIX.

ATAD *(a'-tad)* {2} See ABEL-MIZRAIM. *A place east of the Jordan.*
came to the threshingfloor of *A* ..... Gen 50:10 329
the mourning in the floor of *A* ..... Gen 50:11 329

ATARAH *(at'-a-rah)* {1} *A wife of Jerahmeel.*
another wife, whose name was *A* 1Chr 2:26 5851

ATAROTH *(at'-a-roth)* {5} See ATAROTH-ADAR, ATROTH.
1. *A city east of the Jordan.*
A, and Dibon, and Jazer, and Nimrah, ... Num 32:3 5852
children of Gad built Dibon, and *A* ..... Num 32:34 5852
2. *A city in Ephraim.*
unto the borders of Archi to *A* ..... Josh 16:2 5852
And it went down from Janohah to *A* ..... Josh 16:7 5852
3. *A city in Judah.*
and the Netophathites, *A*, the 1Chr 2:54 5852

ATAROTH-ADAR *(at'-a-roth-a'-dar)* {1} See ATAROTH-ADDAR. *A city on the border of Benjamin.*
and the border descended to *A* ..... Josh 18:13 5853

ATAROTH-ADDAR *(at'-a-roth-ad'-dar)* {1} See ATAROTH-ADAR. *Same as Ataroth-adar.*
on the east side was *A*, unto ..... Josh 16:5 5853

ATE {3}
a the sacrifices of the dead ..... Ps 106:28 398
I *a* no pleasant bread, neither ..... Dan 10:3 398
of the angel's hand, and *a* it up ..... Rev 10:10 2719

ATER *(a'-tur)* {5}
1. *An ancestor of an exiled family.*
The children of *A* of Hezekiah ..... Ezr 2:16 333
The children of *A* of Hezekiah ..... Neh 7:21 333
2. *An exiled family who returned under Zerubbabel.*
of Shallum, the children of *A* ..... Ezr 2:42 333
of Shallum, the children of *A* ..... Neh 7:45 333
3. *An Israelite who sealed the covenant with Nehemiah.*
A, Hizkijah, Azzur, ... Neh 10:17 333

ATHACH *(a'-thak)* {1} *A city in Judah.*
and to them which were in *A* 1Sa 30:30 6269

ATHAIAH *(ath-a-i'-ah)* {1} *A son of Uzziah*
A the son of Uzziah, the son of ..... Neh 11:4 6265

ATHALIAH *(ath-a-li'-ah)* {17}
1. Daughter of Jezebel.
And his mother's name was *A* ... 2Kin 8:26 6271
when *A* the mother of Ahaziah saw ... 2Kin 11:1 6271
nurse, in the bedchamber from *A* ... 2Kin 11:2 6271
A did reign over the land ... 2Kin 11:3 6271
when *A* heard the noise of the ... 2Kin 11:13 6271
A rent her clothes, and cried, ... 2Kin 11:14 6271
they slew *A* with the sword beside ... 2Kin 11:20 6271
also was *A* the daughter of Omri ... 2Chr 22:2 6271
But when *A* the mother of Ahaziah ... 2Chr 22:10 6271
of Ahaziah,) hid him from *A* ... 2Chr 22:11 6271
and *A* reigned over the land ... 2Chr 22:12 6271
Now when *A* heard the noise of the ... 2Chr 23:12 6271
Then *A* rent her clothes, and said, ... 2Chr 23:13 6271
they had slain *A* with the sword ... 2Chr 23:21 6271
For the sons of *A*, that wicked ... 2Chr 24:7 6271
2. A son of Jeroham.
and Shehariah, and *A* ... 1Chr 8:26 6271
3. Father of Jeshiah.
Jeshaiah the son of *A*, and with ... Ezr 8:7 6271

ATHENIANS *(a-the'-ne-uns)* {1} *Citizens of Athens*
(For all the *A* and strangers which ... Acts 17:21 *117*

ATHENS *(ath'-ens)* {7} See ATHENIANS. *A city in Greece.*
conducted Paul brought him unto *A* ... Acts 17:15 *116*
while Paul waited for them at *A* ... Acts 17:16 *116*
Mars' hill, and said, Ye men of *A* ... Acts 17:22 *117*
these things Paul departed from *A* ... Acts 18:1 *116*
it good to be left at *A* alone ... 1Th 3:1 *116*
Thessalonians was written from *A* ... 1Th *s* *116*
Thessalonians was written from *A* ... 2Th *s* *116*

ATHIRST {5}
And he was sore *a*, and called on ... Judg 15:18 6770
and when thou art *a*, go unto the ... Ruth 2:9 6770
when saw we thee an hungred, or *a* ... Mt 25:44 *1372*
I will give unto him that is *a* of ... Rev 21:6 *1372*
And let him that is *a* come ... Rev 22:17 *1372*

ATHLAI *(ath'-lahee)* {1} *Married a foreign wife in exile.*
Jehohanan, Hananiah, Zabbai, and *A* ... Ezr 10:28 6270

ATONEMENT {81}
things wherewith the *a* was made ... Ex 29:33 3722
bullock for a sin offering for *a* ... Ex 29:36 3725
when thou hast made an *a* for it ... Ex 29:36 3722
shalt make an *a* for the altar ... Ex 29:37 3722
Aaron shall make an *a* upon the ... Ex 30:10 3722
he make *a* upon it throughout your ... Ex 30:10 3722
to make an *a* for your souls ... Ex 30:15 3722
thou shalt take the *a* money of ... Ex 30:16 3725
to make an *a* for your souls ... Ex 30:16 3722
I shall make an *a* for your sin ... Ex 32:30 3722
for him to make *a* for him ... Lev 1:4 3722
priest shall make an *a* for them ... Lev 4:20 3722
the priest shall make an *a* for ... Lev 4:26 3722
priest shall make an *a* for him ... Lev 4:31 3722
an *a* for his sin that he hath ... Lev 4:35 3722
the priest shall make an *a* for ... Lev 5:6 3722
the priest shall make an *a* for ... Lev 5:10 3722
the priest shall make an *a* for ... Lev 5:13 3722
the priest shall make an *a* for ... Lev 5:16 3722
make an *a* for him concerning his ... Lev 5:18 3722
make an *a* for him before the LORD ... Lev 6:7 3722
the priest that maketh *a* ... Lev 7:7 3722
to do, to make an *a* for you ... Lev 8:34 3722
make an *a* for thyself, and for the ... Lev 9:7 3722
the people, and make an *a* for them ... Lev 9:7 3722
to make *a* for them before the ... Lev 10:17 3722
the LORD, and make an *a* for her ... Lev 12:7 3722
priest shall make an *a* for her ... Lev 12:8 3722
make an *a* for him before the LORD ... Lev 14:18 3722
make an *a* for him that is to be ... Lev 14:19 3722
priest shall make an *a* for him ... Lev 14:20 3722
to be waved, to make an *a* for him ... Lev 14:21 3722
to make an *a* for him before the ... Lev 14:29 3722
the priest shall make an *a* for ... Lev 14:31 3722
and make an *a* for the house ... Lev 14:53 3722
the priest shall make an *a* for ... Lev 15:15 3722
the priest shall make an *a* for ... Lev 15:30 3722
make an *a* for himself, and for his ... Lev 16:6 3722
the LORD, to make an *a* with him ... Lev 16:10 3722
and shall make an *a* for himself ... Lev 16:11 3722
he shall make an *a* for the holy ... Lev 16:16 3722
in to make an *a* in the holy place ... Lev 16:17 3722
and have made an *a* for himself ... Lev 16:17 3722
the LORD, and make an *a* for it ... Lev 16:18 3722
make an *a* for himself, and for the ... Lev 16:24 3722
in to make *a* in the holy place ... Lev 16:27 3722
the priest make an *a* for you ... Lev 16:30 3722
father's stead, shall make the *a* ... Lev 16:32 3722
he shall make an *a* for the holy ... Lev 16:33 3722
he shall make an *a* for the ... Lev 16:33 3722
shall make an *a* for the priests ... Lev 16:33 3722
to make an *a* for the children of ... Lev 16:34 3722
altar to make an *a* for your souls ... Lev 17:11 3722
that maketh an *a* for the soul ... Lev 17:11 3722
the priest shall make an *a* for ... Lev 19:22 3722
month there shall be a day of *a* ... Lev 23:27 3725
for it is a day of *a* ... Lev 23:28 3725
to make an *a* for you before the ... Lev 23:28 3722
in the day of *a* shall ye make the ... Lev 25:9 3725
beside the ram of the *a* ... Num 5:8 3725
whereby an *a* shall be made for ... Num 5:8 3722
offering, and make an *a* for him ... Num 6:11 3722
to make an *a* for the Levites ... Num 8:12 3722
to make an *a* for the children of ... Num 8:19 3722
Aaron made an *a* for them to ... Num 8:21 3722
the priest shall make an *a* for ... Num 15:25 3722
the priest shall make an *a* for ... Num 15:28 3722
the LORD, to make an *a* for him ... Num 15:28 3722
and make an *a* for them ... Num 16:46 3722
and made an *a* for the people ... Num 16:47 3722
made an *a* for the children of ... Num 25:13 3722
offering, to make an *a* for you ... Num 28:22 3722
the goats, to make an *a* for you ... Num 28:30 3722
offering, to make an *a* for you ... Num 29:5 3722
beside the sin offering of *a* ... Num 29:11 3725
to make an *a* for our souls before ... Num 31:50 3722
and wherewith shall I make the *a* ... 2Sa 21:3 3722
holy, and to make an *a* for Israel ... 1Chr 6:49 3722
to make an *a* for all Israel ... 2Chr 29:24 3722
offerings to make an *a* for Israel ... Neh 10:33 3722
whom we have now received the *a* ... Rom 5:11 *2643*

ATONEMENTS {1}
blood of the sin offering of *a* ... Ex 30:10 3725

ATROTH *(a'-troth)* {1} See ATAROTH. *A city in Gad.*
And *A*, Shophan, and Jaazer, and ... Num 32:35 5855

ATROTH BETH JOAB See ATROTH.

ATTAI *(at'-tahee)* {4}
1. A grandson of Sheshan.
and she bare him *A* ... 1Chr 2:35 6262
A begat Nathan, and Nathan begat ... 1Chr 2:36 6262
2. A Gadite in David's army.
A the sixth, Eliel the seventh, ... 1Chr 12:11 6262
3. A son of Rehoboam.
which bare him Abijah, and *A* ... 2Chr 11:20 6262

ATTAIN {6}
it is high, I cannot *a* unto it ... Ps 139:6
shall *a* unto wise counsels ... Prov 1:5 7069
as his hand shall *a* unto, and an ... Eze 46:7 5381
it be ere they *a* to innocency ... Hos 8:5 3201
any means they might *a* to Phenice ... Acts 27:12 *2658*
If by any means I might *a* unto ... Phil 3:11 *2658*

ATTAINED {10}
have not *a* unto the days of the ... Gen 47:9 5381
howbeit he *a* not unto the first ... 2Sa 23:19 935
but he *a* not to the first three ... 2Sa 23:23 935
howbeit he *a* not to the first ... 1Chr 11:21 935
but *a* not to the first three ... 1Chr 11:25 935
have *a* to righteousness, even the ... Rom 9:30 *2638*
hath not *a* to the law of ... Rom 9:31 *5348*
Not as though I had already *a* ... Phil 3:12 *2983*
whereto we have already *a* ... Phil 3:16 *5348*
doctrine, whereunto thou hast *a* ... 1Ti 4:6 *3877*

ATTALIA *(at-ta-li'-ah)* {1} *A seaport near Perga.*
in Perga, they went down into *A* ... Acts 14:25 *825*

ATTEND {11}
he had appointed to *a* upon her ... Est 4:5 6440
a unto my cry, give ear unto my ... Ps 17:1 7181
A unto me, and hear me ... Ps 55:2 7181
a unto my prayer ... Ps 61:1 7181
and *a* to the voice of my ... Ps 86:6 7181
A unto my cry ... Ps 142:6 7181
and *a* to know understanding ... Prov 4:1 7181
My son, *a* to my words ... Prov 4:20 7181
a unto my wisdom, and bow thine ... Prov 5:1 7181
a to the words of my mouth ... Prov 7:24 7181
that ye may *a* upon the Lord ... 1Cor 7:35 *2145*

ATTENDANCE {4}
the *a* of his ministers, and their ... 1Kin 10:5 4612
the *a* of his ministers, and their ... 2Chr 9:4 4612
give *a* to reading, to exhortation ... 1Ti 4:13 *4337*
which no man gave *a* at the altar ... Heb 7:13 *4337*

ATTENDED {3}
I *a* unto you, and, behold, there ... Job 32:12 995
he hath *a* to the voice of my ... Ps 66:19 7181
that she *a* unto the things which ... Acts 16:14 *4337*

ATTENDING {1}
a continually upon this very ... Rom 13:6 *4343*

ATTENT {2}
let thine ears be *a* unto the ... 2Chr 6:40 7183
mine ears *a* unto the prayer that ... 2Chr 7:15 7183

ATTENTIVE {5}
Let thine ear now be *a*, and thine ... Neh 1:6 7183
let now thine ear be *a* to the ... Neh 1:11 7183
were *a* unto the book of the law ... Neh 8:3
let thine ears be *a* to the voice ... Ps 130:2 7183
people were very *a* to hear him ... Lk 19:48 *1582*

ATTENTIVELY {1}
Hear *a* the noise of his voice, and ... Job 37:2 8085

ATTIRE {3}
a woman with the *a* of an harlot ... Prov 7:10 7897
her ornaments, or a bride her *a* ... Jer 2:32 7196
in dyed *a* upon their heads ... Eze 23:15 2871

ATTIRED {1}
the linen mitre shall he be *a* ... Lev 16:4 6801

AUDIENCE {12}
in the *a* of the children of Heth ... Gen 23:10 241
the *a* of the people of the land ... Gen 23:13 241
in the *a* of the sons of Heth ... Gen 23:16 241
read in the *a* of the people ... Ex 24:7 241
I pray thee, speak in thine *a* ... 1Sa 25:24 241
in the *a* of our God, keep and seek ... 1Chr 28:8 241
of Moses in the *a* of the people ... Neh 13:1 241
sayings in the *a* of the people ... Lk 7:1 *189*
Then in the *a* of all the people ... Lk 20:45 *191*
and ye that fear God, give *a* ... Acts 13:16 *191*
gave *a* to Barnabas and Paul, ... Acts 15:12 *191*
they gave him *a* unto this word, ... Acts 22:22 *191*

AUGMENT {1}
to *a* yet the fierce anger of the ... Num 32:14 5595

AUGUSTAN See AUGUSTUS.

AUGUSTUS *(aw-gus'-tus)* {3} See AUGUSTUS', CAESAR. *An emperor of Rome.*
went out a decree from Caesar *A* ... Lk 2:1 *828*
be reserved unto the hearing of *A* ... Acts 25:21 *828*
he himself hath appealed to *A* ... Acts 25:25 *828*

AUGUSTUS' *(aw-gus'-tus)* {1}
Julius, a centurion of *A* band ... Acts 27:1 *828*

AUL {2}
bore his ear through with an *a* ... Ex 21:6 4836
Then thou shalt take an *a* ... Deut 15:17 4836

AUNT {1}
she is thine *a* ... Lev 18:14 1733

AUSTERE {2}
thee, because thou art an *a* man ... Lk 19:21 *840*
Thou knewest that I was an *a* man ... Lk 19:22 *840*

AUTHOR {3}
For God is not the *a* of confusion ... 1Cor 14:33
he became the *a* of eternal ... Heb 5:9 *159*
Looking unto Jesus the *a* and ... Heb 12:2 *747*

AUTHORITIES {1}
angels and *a* and powers being made ... 1Pet 3:22 *1849*

AUTHORITY {37}
the Jew, wrote with all *a* ... Est 9:29 8633
When the righteous are in *a* ... Prov 29:2 7235
he taught them as one having *a* ... Mt 7:29 *1849*
For I am a man under *a*, having ... Mt 8:9 *1849*
are great exercise *a* upon them ... Mt 20:25 *2715*
By what *a* doest thou these things ... Mt 21:23 *1849*
and who gave thee this *a* ... Mt 21:23 *1849*
you by what *a* I do these things ... Mt 21:24 *1849*
I you by what *a* I do these things ... Mt 21:27 *1849*
he taught them as one that had *a* ... Mk 1:22 *1849*
for with *a* commandeth he even the ... Mk 1:27 *1849*
great ones exercise *a* upon them ... Mk 10:42 *2715*
By what *a* doest thou these things ... Mk 11:28 *1849*
thee this *a* to do these things ... Mk 11:28 *1849*
you by what *a* I do these things ... Mk 11:29 *1849*
you by what *a* I do these things ... Mk 11:33 *1849*
gave *a* to his servants, and to ... Mk 13:34 *1849*
for with *a* and power he commandeth ... Lk 4:36 *1849*
For I also am a man set under *a* ... Lk 7:8 *1849*
a over all devils, and to cure ... Lk 9:1 *1849*
have thou *a* over ten cities ... Lk 19:17 *1849*
by what *a* doest thou these things ... Lk 20:2 *1849*
who is he that gave thee this *a* ... Lk 20:2 *1849*
I you by what *a* I do these things ... Lk 20:8 *1849*
the power and *a* of the governor ... Lk 20:20 *1849*
they that exercise *a* upon them ... Lk 22:25 *1850*
hath given him *a* to execute ... Jn 5:27 *1849*
an eunuch of great *a* under ... Acts 8:27 *1413*
here he hath *a* from the chief ... Acts 9:14 *1849*
having received *a* from the chief ... Acts 26:10 *1849*
as I went to Damascus with *a* ... Acts 26:12 *1849*
have put down all rule and all *a* ... 1Cor 15:24 *1849*
boast somewhat more of our *a* ... 2Cor 10:8 *1849*
kings, and for all that are in *a* ... 1Ti 2:2 *5247*
nor to usurp *a* over the man ... 1Ti 2:12 *831*
and exhort, and rebuke with all *a* ... Titus 2:15 *2003*
power, and his seat, and great *a* ... Rev 13:2 *1849*

AVA *(a'-vah)* {1} See IVAH. *An area near Babylon.*
and from Cuthah, and from *A* ... 2Kin 17:24 5755

AVAILETH {4}
Yet all this *a* me nothing ... Est 5:13 7737
neither circumcision *a* any thing ... Gal 5:6 *2480*
neither circumcision *a* any thing ... Gal 6:15 *2480*
prayer of a righteous man *a* much ... Jas 5:16 *2480*

AVEN See BETH-AVEN.{3} *Another name for Heliopolis, in Egypt.*
The young men of *A* and of ... Eze 30:17 206
The high places also of *A* ... Hos 10:8 206
inhabitant from the plain of *A* ... Amos 1:5 206

AVENGE {17}
Thou shalt not *a*, nor bear any ... Lev 19:18 5358
that shall *a* the quarrel of my ... Lev 26:25 5358
A the children of Israel of the ... Num 31:2 5358,5360
and *a* the LORD of Midian ... Num 31:3 5414,5360
for he will *a* the blood of his ... Deut 32:43 5358
and thee, and the LORD *a* me of thee ... 1Sa 24:12 5358
that I may *a* the blood of my ... 2Kin 9:7 5358
to *a* themselves on their enemies ... Est 8:13 5358
and *a* me of mine enemies ... Is 1:24 5358
that he may *a* him of his ... Jer 46:10 5358
I will *a* the blood of Jezreel ... Hos 1:4 6485
saying, *A* me of mine adversary ... Lk 18:3 *1556*
widow troubleth me, I will *a* her ... Lk 18:5 *1556*
shall not God *a* his own elect ... Lk 18:7 *4160,3588,1557*
that he will *a* them speedily ... Lk 18:8 *4160,3588,1557*
a not yourselves, but rather give ... Rom 12:19 *1556*
a our blood on them that dwell on ... Rev 6:10 *1556*

AVENGED {16}
If Cain shall be *a* sevenfold ... Gen 4:24 5358
until the people had *a* themselves ... Josh 10:13 5358
done this, yet will I be *a* of you ... Judg 15:7 5358
that I may be at once *a* of the ... Judg 16:28 5358
that I may be *a* on mine enemies ... 1Sa 14:24 5358
to be *a* of the king's enemies ... 1Sa 18:25 5358
or that my lord hath *a* himself ... 1Sa 25:31 3467
LORD hath *a* my lord the king ... 2Sa 4:8 5414,5360
LORD hath *a* him of his enemies ... 2Sa 18:19 8199
for the LORD hath *a* thee this day ... 2Sa 18:31 8199

shall not my soul be *a* on such a ... Jer 5:9 5358
shall not my soul be *a* on such a ... Jer 5:29 5358
shall not my soul be *a* on such a ... Jer 9:9 5358
a him that was oppressed, and ... Acts 7:24
for God hath *a* you on her ... Rev 18:20 *2919,3588,2917*
hath *a* the blood of his servants ... Rev 19:2 *1556*

AVENGER {9}
you cities for refuge from the *a* ... Num 35:12 1350
Lest the *a* of the blood pursue ... Deut 19:6 1350
into the hand of the *a* of blood ... Deut 19:12 1350
your refuge from the *a* of blood ... Josh 20:3 1350
if the *a* of blood pursue after ... Josh 20:5 1350
die by the hand of the *a* of blood ... Josh 20:9 1350
mightest still the enemy and the *a* ... Ps 8:2 5358
by reason of the enemy and *a* ... Ps 44:16 5358
the Lord is the *a* of all such ... 1Th 4:6 *1558*

AVENGETH {2}
It is God that *a* me, and that ... 2Sa 22:48 5414,5360
It is God that *a* me, and subdueth ... Ps 18:47 5414,5360

AVENGING {3}
ye the LORD for the *a* of Israel ... Judg 5:2 6544,6546
from *a* thyself with thine own ... 1Sa 25:26 3467
from *a* myself with mine own hand ... 1Sa 25:33 3467

AVERSE {1}
by securely as men *a* from war ... Mic 2:8 7725

AVIM *(a'-vim)* {1} See AVIMS, AVITES. *A city near Bethel.*
And A, and Parah, and Ophrah, ... Josh 18:23 5761

AVIMS *(a'-vims)* {1} See AVIM. *A Canaanite tribe.*
the A which dwelt in Hazerim, ... Deut 2:23 5757

AVITES *(a'-vites)* {2} See AVIM.
1. Same as Avims.
and the Ekronites; also the A ... Josh 13:3 5757
2. A tribe moved to Samaria.
the A made Nibhaz and Tartak, and ... 2Kin 17:31 5757

AVITH *(a'-vith)* {2} *Capital of Edom.*
and the name of his city was A ... Gen 36:35 5762
and the name of his city was A ... 1Chr 1:46 5762

AVOID {5}
A it, pass not by it, turn from ... Prov 4:15 6544
and *a* them ... Rom 16:17 *1578*
to *a* fornication, let every man ... 1Cor 7:2 *1223*
foolish and unlearned questions *a* ... 2Ti 2:23 *3868*
But *a* foolish questions, and ... Titus 3:9 *4026*

AVOIDED {1}
David *a* out of his presence twice ... 1Sa 18:11 5437

AVOIDING {2}
A this, that no man should blame ... 2Cor 8:20 *4724*
a profane and vain babblings, and ... 1Ti 6:20 *1624*

AVOUCHED {2}
Thou hast *a* the LORD this day to ... Deut 26:17 559
the LORD hath *a* thee this day to ... Deut 26:18 559

AVVA See AVA.

AVVIM See AVITES.

AWAIT {1}
But their laying *a* was known of ... Acts 9:24 *1917*

AWAKE {42}
A, *a*, Deborah ... Judg 5:12 5782
a, *a*, utter a song ... Judg 5:12 5782
surely now he would *a* for thee ... Job 8:6 5782
be no more, they shall not *a* ... Job 14:12 6974
a for me to the judgment that ... Ps 7:6 5782
I shall be satisfied, when I *a* ... Ps 17:15 6974
a to my judgment, even unto my ... Ps 35:23 6974
A, why sleepest thou, O Lord ... Ps 44:23 5782
A up, my glory ... Ps 57:8 5782
a, psaltery and harp ... Ps 57:8 5782
I myself will *a* early ... Ps 57:8 5782
a to help me, and behold ... Ps 59:4 5782
a to visit all the heathen ... Ps 59:5 6974
A, psaltery and harp ... Ps 108:2 5782
I myself will *a* early ... Ps 108:2 5782
when I *a*, I am still with thee ... Ps 139:18 6974
when shall I *a* ... Prov 23:35 6974
nor *a* my love, till he please ... Song 2:7 5782
nor *a* my love, till he please ... Song 3:5 5782
A, O north wind ... Song 4:16 5782
nor *a* my love, until he please ... Song 8:4 5782
A and sing, ye that dwell in dust ... Is 26:19 6974
A, *a*, put on strength, O arm ... Is 51:9 5782
a, as in the ancient days, in the ... Is 51:9 5782
A, *a*, stand up, O Jerusalem, ... Is 51:17 5782
A, *a*; put on thy strength ... Is 52:1 5782
in the dust of the earth shall *a* ... Dan 12:2 6974
A, ye drunkards, and weep ... Joel 1:5 6974
a that shall vex thee, and thou ... Hab 2:7 6974
him that saith to the wood, A ... Hab 2:19 6974
A, O sword, against my shepherd, ... Zec 13:7 5782
and they *a* him, and say unto him, ... Mk 4:38 *1326*
and when they were *a*, they saw his ... Lk 9:32 *1235*
that I may *a* him out of sleep ... Jn 11:11 *1852*
it is high time to *a* out of sleep ... Rom 13:11 *1453*
A to righteousness, and sin not ... 1Cor 15:34 *1594*
A thou that sleepest, and arise ... Eph 5:14 *1453*

AWAKED {8}
Jacob *a* out of his sleep, and he ... Gen 28:16 3364
he *a* out of his sleep, and went ... Judg 16:14 3364
saw it, nor knew it, neither *a* ... 1Sa 26:12 6974
he sleepeth, and must be *a* ... 1Kin 18:27 3364
him, saying, The child is not *a* ... 2Kin 4:31 6974
I *a*; for the LORD sustained me ... Ps 3:5 6974
Then the Lord *a* as one out of ... Ps 78:65 3364
Upon this I *a*, and beheld ... Jer 31:26 6974

AWAKEST {2}
so, O Lord, when thou *a*, thou ... Ps 73:20 5782
and when thou *a*, it shall talk ... Prov 6:22 6974

AWAKETH {3}
As a dream when one *a* ... Ps 73:20 6974
but he *a*, and his soul is empty ... Is 29:8 6974
but he *a*, and, behold, he is faint ... Is 29:8 6974

AWAKING {1}
of the prison *a* out of his sleep ... Acts 16:27 *1096,1853*

AWARE {5}
Or ever I was *a*, my soul made me ... Song 6:12 3045
O Babylon, and thou wast not *a* ... Jer 50:24 3045
and in an hour that he is not *a* of ... Mt 24:50 *1097*
walk over them are not *a* of them ... Lk 11:44 *1492*
and at an hour when he is not *a* ... Lk 12:46 *1097*

AWAY See APPENDIX.

AWE {3}
Stand in *a*, and sin not ... Ps 4:4 7264
of the world stand in *a* of him ... Ps 33:8 1481
heart standeth in *a* of thy word ... Ps 119:161 6342

AWOKE {8}
Noah *a* from his wine, and knew ... Gen 9:24 3364
So Pharaoh *a* ... Gen 41:4 3364
And Pharaoh *a*, and, behold, it was ... Gen 41:7 3364
So I *a* ... Gen 41:21 3364
he *a* out of his sleep, and said, I ... Judg 16:20 3364
And Solomon *a* ... 1Kin 3:15 3364
a him, saying, Lord, save us ... Mt 8:25 *1453*
a him, saying, Master, master, we ... Lk 8:24 *1326*

AX {7}
by forcing an *a* against them ... Deut 20:19 1631
share, and his coulter, and his *a* ... 1Sa 13:20 7134
the *a* head fell into the water ... 2Kin 6:5 1270
Shall the *a* boast itself against ... Is 10:15 1631
hands of the workman, with the *a* ... Jer 10:3 4621
Thou art my battle *a* and weapons ... Jer 51:20 4601
now also the *a* is laid unto the ... Mt 3:10 *513*

AXE {4}
with the *a* to cut down the tree ... Deut 19:5 1631
Abimelech took an *a* in his hand ... Judg 9:48 7134
there was neither hammer nor *a* ... 1Kin 6:7 1631
now also the *a* is laid unto the ... Lk 3:9 *513*

AXES {7}
and for the forks, and for the *a* ... 1Sa 13:21 7134
under *a* of iron, and made them ... 2Sa 12:31 4037
with harrows of iron, and with *a* ... 1Chr 20:3 4050
lifted up *a* upon the thick trees ... Ps 74:5 7134
work thereof at once with *a* ... Ps 74:6 3781
army, and come against her with *a* ... Jer 46:22 7134
with his *a* he shall break down ... Eze 26:9 2719

AXLETREES {2}
the *a* of the wheels were joined ... 1Kin 7:32 3027
their *a*, and their naves, and their ... 1Kin 7:33 3027

AZAL *(a'-zal)* {1} *A place near Jerusalem.*
the mountains shall reach unto A ... Zec 14:5 682

AZALIAH *(az-a-li'-ah)* {2} *Father of Shaphan.*
king sent Shaphan the son of A ... 2Kin 22:3 683
he sent Shaphan the son of A ... 2Chr 34:8 683

AZANIAH *(az-a-ni'-ah)* {1} *Father of Jeshua.*
both Jeshua the son of A, Binnui ... Neh 10:9 245

AZARAEL *(a-zar'-a-el)* {1} See AZAREEL. *A priest from the Immer family.*
And his brethren, Shemaiah, and A ... Neh 12:36 5832

AZAREEL *(a-zar'-e-el)* {5} See AZARAEL.
1. A Korahite in David's army.
Elkanah, and Jesiah, and A, and ... 1Chr 12:6 5832
2. A priest during David's time.
The eleventh to A, he, his sons, ... 1Chr 25:18 5832
3. A Danite prince during David's time.
Of Dan, A the son of Jeroham ... 1Chr 27:22 5832
4. Married a foreign wife in exile.
A, and Shelemiah, Shemariah, ... Ezr 10:41 5832
5. Same as Azarael.
and Amashai the son of A, the son ... Neh 11:13 5832

AZAREL See AZAREEL.

AZARIAH *(az-a-ri'-ah)* {48} See AHAZIAH.
1. A descendant of Zadok.
A the son of Zadok the priest, ... 1Kin 4:2 5838
2. Captain of Solomon's guard.
A the son of Nathan was over the ... 1Kin 4:5 5838
3. A king of Judah.
And all the people of Judah took A ... 2Kin 14:21 5838
Jeroboam king of Israel began A ... 2Kin 15:1 5838
And the rest of the acts of A ... 2Kin 15:6 5838
So A slept with his fathers ... 2Kin 15:7 5838
eighth year of A king of Judah ... 2Kin 15:8 5838
thirtieth year of A king of Judah ... 2Kin 15:17 5838
In the fiftieth year of A king of ... 2Kin 15:23 5838
fiftieth year of A king of Judah ... 2Kin 15:27 5838
A his son, Jotham his son, ... 1Chr 3:12 5838
4. A descendant of Judah.
the sons of Ethan; A ... 1Chr 2:8 5838
5. A descendant of Jerahmeel.
Obed begat Jehu, and Jehu begat A ... 1Chr 2:38 5838
A begat Helez, and Helez begat ... 1Chr 2:39 5838
6. A son of Ahimaaz.
And Ahimaaz begat A, and Azariah ... 1Chr 6:9 5838
7. Grandson of Ahimaah.
And Johanan begat A, (he it is ... 1Chr 6:10 5838
A begat Amariah, and Amariah begat ... 1Chr 6:11 5838
8. A son of Hilkiah.
begat Hilkiah, and Hilkiah begat A ... 1Chr 6:13 5838
A begat Seraiah, and Seraiah begat ... 1Chr 6:14 5838
A the son of Hilkiah, the son of ... 1Chr 9:11 5838
the son of Seraiah, the son of A ... Ezr 7:1 5838
9. A descendant of Kohath.
the son of Joel, the son of A ... 1Chr 6:36 5838
10. A prophet sent to King Asa.
God came upon A the son of Oded ... 2Chr 15:1 5838
11. A son of King Jehoshaphat.
the sons of Jehoshaphat, A ... 2Chr 21:2 5838
12. A brother of King Jehoram.
and Jehiel, and Zechariah, and A ... 2Chr 21:2 5838
13. A son of King Jehoram.
A the son of Jehoram king of ... 2Chr 22:6 5838
14. A conspirator with Joash.
A the son of Jeroham, and Ishmael ... 2Chr 23:1 5838
15. Another conspirator with Joash.
A the son of Obed, and Maaseiah ... 2Chr 23:1 5838
16. A High Priest.
A the priest went in after him, ... 2Chr 26:17 5838
A the chief priest, and all the ... 2Chr 26:20 5838
17. A chief of Ephraim.
A the son of Johanan, Berechiah ... 2Chr 28:12 5838
18. Father of Joel.
of Amasai, and Joel the son of A ... 2Chr 29:12 5838
19. Helped cleanse the Temple.
Abdi, and A the son of Jehalelel ... 2Chr 29:12 5838
20. A chief priest.
A the chief priest of the house ... 2Chr 31:10 5838
A the ruler of the house of God ... 2Chr 31:13 5838
21. Great-grandfather of Zadok.
The son of Amariah, the son of A ... Ezr 7:3 5838
22. A repairer of the Jerusalem walls.
After him repaired A the son of ... Neh 3:23 5838
from the house of A unto the ... Neh 3:24 5838
23. An exile with Zerubbabel.
Zerubbabel, Jeshua, Nehemiah, A ... Neh 7:7 5838
24. A priest with Ezra.
Hodijah, Maaseiah, Kelita, A ... Neh 8:7 5838
25. A priest who renewed the covenant.
Seraiah, A, Jeremiah, ... Neh 10:2 5838
26. A prince of Judah.
And A, Ezra, and Meshullam, ... Neh 12:33 5838
27. The son of Hoshaiah.
Then spake A the son of Hoshaiah, ... Jer 43:2 5838
28. A companion of Daniel.
Daniel, Hananiah, Mishael, and A ... Dan 1:6 5838
and to A, of Abed-nego ... Dan 1:7 5838
Daniel, Hananiah, Mishael, and A ... Dan 1:11 5838
Daniel, Hananiah, Mishael, and A ... Dan 1:19 5838
known to Hananiah, Mishael, and A ... Dan 2:17 5839

AZARYAHU See AZARIAH.

AZAZ *(a'-zaz)* {1} *Father of Bela.*
And Bela the son of A, the son of ... 1Chr 5:8 5811

AZAZIAH *(az-a-zi'-ah)* {2}
1. A Levite who relocated the Ark.
and Obed-edom, and Jeiel, and A ... 1Chr 15:21 5812
2. Father of Hoshea.
of Ephraim, Hoshea the son of A ... 1Chr 27:20 5812
3. A Levite during Hezekiah's reign.
And Jehiel, and A, and Nahath, and ... 2Chr 31:13 5812

AZBUK *(az'-buk)* {1} *Father of Nehemiah.*
repaired Nehemiah the son of A ... Neh 3:16 5802

AZEKAH *(a-ze'-kah)* {7} *A town in Judah.*
to Beth-horon, and smote them to A ... Josh 10:10 5825
from heaven upon them unto A ... Josh 10:11 5825
Jarmuth, and Adullam, Socoh, and A ... Josh 15:35 5825
and pitched between Shochoh and A ... 1Sa 17:1 5825
And Adoraim, and Lachish, and A ... 2Chr 11:9 5825
and the fields thereof, at A ... Neh 11:30 5825
against Lachish, and against A ... Jer 34:7 5825

AZEL *(a'-zel)* {6} See JAAZIEL. *A descendant of King Saul.*
son, Eleasah his son, A his son ... 1Chr 8:37 682
A had six sons, whose names are ... 1Chr 8:38 682
All these were the sons of A ... 1Chr 8:38 682
son, Eleasah his son, A his son ... 1Chr 9:43 682
A had six sons, whose names are ... 1Chr 9:44 682
these were the sons of A ... 1Chr 9:44 682

AZEM *(a'-zem)* {2} See EZEM. *A city in Judah.*
Baalah, and Iim, and A, ... Josh 15:29 6107
And Hazar-shual, and Balah, and A ... Josh 19:3 6107

AZGAD *(az'-gad)* {4}
1. A family of exiles.
The children of A, a thousand two ... Ezr 2:12 5803
The children of A, two thousand ... Neh 7:17 5803
2. An exile with Ezra.
And of the sons of A ... Ezr 8:12 5803
3. A family who sealed the covenant.
Bunni, A, Bebai, ... Neh 10:15 5803

AZIEL *(a'-ze-el)* {1} *A Levite who relocated the Ark.*
And Zechariah, and A, and ... 1Chr 15:20 5815

AZIZA *(a-zi'-zah)* {1} *Married a foreigner in exile.*
and Jeremoth, and Zabad, and A ... Ezr 10:27 5819

AZMAVETH *(az-ma'-veth)* {8} See BETH-AZMAVETH.
1. A "mighty man" of David.
the Arbathite, A the Barhumite, ... 2Sa 23:31 5820
A the Baharumite, Eliahba the ... 1Chr 11:33 5820

2. A descendant of Jonathan.
and Jehoadah begat Alemeth, and *A* 1Chr 8:36 5820
and Jarah begat Alemeth, and *A*............ 1Chr 9:42 5820
3. Father of Jeziel and Pelet.
Jeziel, and Pelet, the sons of *A*.............. 1Chr 12:3 5820
4. A village on the border of Judah.
The children of *A*, forty and two............ Ezr 2:24 5820
and out of the fields of Geba and *A*........ Neh 12:29 5820
5. A treasurer of David.
treasures was *A* the son of Adiel............ 1Chr 27:25 5820

AZMON *(az'-mon)* {3} See HESHMON. *A place in southern Canaan.*
to Hazar-addar, and pass on to *A* .... Num 34:4 6111
from *A* unto the river of Egypt .... Num 34:5 6111
From thence it passed toward *A*.............. Josh 15:4 6111

AZNOTH-TABOR *(az'-noth-ta'-bor)* {1} *Hills on the border of Naphtali.*
the coast turneth westward to *A*............ Josh 19:34 243

AZOR *(a'-zor)* {2} *Great-grandson of Zorobabel.*
and Eliakim begat *A* .... Mt 1:13 *107*
And *A* begat Sadoc................................ Mt 1:14 *107*

AZOTUS *(a-zo'-tus)* {1} See ASHDOD. *Greek form of Ashdod.*
But Philip was found at *A*...................... Acts 8:40 *108*

AZRIEL *(az'-re-el)* {3}
1. Chief of a family of Manasseh.
Epher, and Ishi, and Eliel, and *A*........... 1Chr 5:24 5837
2. Father of Jerimoth
Naphtali, Jerimoth the son of *A*............. 1Chr 27:19 5837
3. Father of Seraiah.
and Seraiah the son of *A*, and................ Jer 36:26 5837

AZRIKAM *(az'-ri-kam)* {6}
1. A son of Neariah.
Elioenai, and Hezekiah, and *A*............... 1Chr 3:23 5840
2. A son of Azel.
sons, whose names are these, *A*.............. 1Chr 8:38 5840
sons, whose names are these, *A*.............. 1Chr 9:44 5840
3. A descendant of Merari.
the son of Hasshub, the son of *A*............ 1Chr 9:14 5840
the son of Hashub, the son of *A* .... Neh 11:15 5840
4. Governor of the house of King Ahaz.
A the governor of the house, and 2Chr 28:7 5840

AZUBAH *(a-zu'-bah)* {4}
1. Mother of King Jehoshaphat.
his mother's name was *A* the................... 1Kin 22:42 5806
his mother's name was *A* the................... 2Chr 20:31 5806
2. Wife of Caleb.
begat children of *A* his wife.................... 1Chr 2:18 5806
when *A* was dead, Caleb took unto......... 1Chr 2:19 5806

AZUR *(a'-zur)* {2} See AZZUR.
1. Father of Hananiah.
Hananiah the son of *A* the prophet......... Jer 28:1 5809
2. Father of Jaazaniah.
whom I saw Jaazaniah the son of *A*........ 5809

AZZAH *(az'-zah)* {3} See GAZA. *A Philistine city.*
dwelt in Hazerim, even unto *A*............... Deut 2:23 5804
the river, from Tiphsah even to *A*............ 1Kin 4:24 5804
Philistines, and Ashkelon, and *A* .... Jer 25:20 5804

AZZAN *(az'-zan)* {1} *A prince of Issachar.*
of Issachar, Paltiel the son of *A*.............. Num 34:26 5821

AZZUR *(az'-zur)* {1} *An Israelite who sealed the covenant under Nehemiah.*
Ater, Hizkijah, *A*,.................................... Neh 10:17 5809

B

BAAL *(ba'-al)* {63} See BAAL-BERITH, BAALE, BAAL-GAD, BAAL-HAMON, BAAL-HANAN, BAAL-HAZOR, BAAL-HERMON, BAALIM, BAAL-MEON, BAAL-PEOR, BAAL-PERAZIM, BAAL-SHALISHA, BAAL-TAMAR.
1. Chief god of the Canaanites.
him up into the high places of *B*............ Num 22:41 1168
forsook the LORD, and served *B* .... Judg 2:13 1168
altar of *B* that thy father hath .... Judg 6:25 1168
the altar of *B* was cast down, and........... Judg 6:28 1168
he hath cast down the altar of *B*............. Judg 6:30 1168
against him, Will ye plead for *B* .... Judg 6:31 1168
Let *B* plead against him, because .... Judg 6:32 1168
Zidonians, and went and served *B*.......... 1Kin 16:31 1168
altar for *B* in the house of *B*................. 1Kin 16:32 1168
and the prophets of *B* four hundred 1Kin 18:19 1168
but if *B*, then follow him....................... 1Kin 18:21 1168
said unto the prophets of *B*.................... 1Kin 18:25 1168
called on the name of *B* from................. 1Kin 18:26 1168
even until noon, saying, O *B* 1Kin 18:26 1168
unto them, Take the prophets of *B*.......... 1Kin 18:40 1168
knees which have not bowed unto *B*....... 1Kin 19:18 1168
For he served *B*, and worshipped 1Kin 22:53 1168
of *B* that his father had made................. 2Kin 3:2 1168
unto them, Ahab served *B* a little........... 2Kin 10:18 1168
unto me all the prophets of *B* 2Kin 10:19 1168
have a great sacrifice to do to *B* 2Kin 10:19 1168
destroy the worshippers of *B* 2Kin 10:19 1168
Proclaim a solemn assembly for *B* 2Kin 10:20 1168
and all the worshippers of *B* came 2Kin 10:21 1168
And they came into the house of *B*......... 2Kin 10:21 1168
the house of *B* was full from one 2Kin 10:21 1168
for all the worshippers of *B*.................... 2Kin 10:22 1168
of Rechab, into the house of *B* 2Kin 10:23 1168
and said unto the worshippers of *B*........ 2Kin 10:23 1168
but the worshippers of *B* only................. 2Kin 10:23 1168
to the city of the house of *B*.................. 2Kin 10:25 1168
the images out of the house of *B*............. 2Kin 10:26 1168
And they brake down the image of *B* 2Kin 10:27 1168
and brake down the house of *B* 2Kin 10:27 1168
Jehu destroyed *B* out of Israel................. 2Kin 10:28 1168
the land went into the house of *B*........... 2Kin 11:18 1168
the priest of *B* before the altars 2Kin 11:18 1168
the host of heaven, and served *B*............. 2Kin 17:16 1168
and he reared up altars for *B*.................. 2Kin 21:3 1168
the vessels that were made for *B* 2Kin 23:4 1168
also that burned incense unto *B* 2Kin 23:5 1168
the people went to the house of *B*.......... 2Chr 23:17 1168
the priest of *B* before the altars 2Chr 23:17 1168
and the prophets prophesied by *B* .... Jer 2:8 1168
falsely, and burn incense unto *B* .... Jer 7:9 1168
altars to burn incense unto *B*.................. Jer 11:13 1168
anger in offering incense unto *B*............. Jer 11:17 1168
taught my people to swear by *B*............. Jer 12:16 1168
built also the high places of *B* .... Jer 19:5 1168
fire for burnt offerings unto *B* .... Jer 19:5 1168
they prophesied in *B*, and caused .... Jer 23:13 1168
have forgotten my name for *B*................. Jer 23:27 1168
they have offered incense unto *B* .... Jer 32:29 1168
they built the high places of *B*............... Jer 32:35 1168
gold, which they prepared for *B* .... Hos 2:8 1168
but when he offended in *B*...................... Hos 13:1 1168
the remnant of *B* from this place .... Zeph 1:4 1168
bowed the knee to the image of *B*........... Rom 11:4 *896*
2. A city in Simeon.
about the same cities, unto *B*.................. 1Chr 4:33 1168
3. A descendant of Reuben.
son, Reaia his son, *B* his son,.................. 1Chr 5:5 1168
4. A descendant of Benjamin.
son Abdon, and Zur, and Kish, and *B*..... 1Chr 8:30 1168
Abdon, then Zur, and Kish, and *B* 1Chr 9:36 1168

BAALAH *(ba'-al-ah)* {5} See BAALE, BALEH, BILHAH, KIRJATH-BAAL.
1. A city in Judah.
and the border was drawn to *B*............... Josh 15:9 1173
from *B* westward unto mount Seir.......... Josh 15:10 1173
B, and Iim, and Azem............................. Josh 15:29 1173
went up, and all Israel, to *B*.................... 1Chr 13:6 1173
2. A hill in Judah.
and passed along to mount *B*.................. Josh 15:11 1173

BAALATH *(ba'-al-ath)* {3} See BAALATH-BEER. *A town in Dan.*
And Eltekeh, and Gibbethon, and *B*....... Josh 19:44 1191
And *B*, and Tadmor in the wilderness 1Kin 9:18 1191
And *B*, and all the store cities................ 2Chr 8:6 1191

BAALATH-BEER *(ba'-al-ath-be'-ur)* {1} *A city in Simeon.*
round about these cities to *B* .... Josh 19:8 1192

BAAL-BERITH *(ba'-al-be'-rith)* {2} *An idol.*
after Baalim, and made *B* their god........ Judg 8:33 1170
of silver out of the house of *B*................ Judg 9:4 1170

BAALE *(ba'-al-eh)* {1} *A form of Baalah.*
were with him from *B* of Judah 2Sa 6:2 1184

BAALE-JUDAH See BAALE.

BAAL-GAD *(ba'-al-gad')* {3} *A Canaanite city.*
even unto *B* in the valley of .... Josh 11:17 1171
from *B* in the valley of Lebanon .... Josh 12:7 1171
from *B* under mount Hermon unto .... Josh 13:5 1171

BAAL-HAMON *(ba'-al-ha'-mon)* {1} *A place near Samaria.*
Solomon had a vineyard at *B*.................. Song 8:11 1174

BAAL-HANAN *(ba'-al-ha'-nan)* {5}
1. A king of Edom.
B the son of Achbor reigned in .... Gen 36:38 1177
B the son of Achbor died, and .... Gen 36:39 1177
B the son of Achbor reigned in 1Chr 1:49 1177
when *B* was dead, Hadad reigned in....... 1Chr 1:50 1177
2. A superintendent for David.
the low plains was *B* the Gederite 1Chr 27:28 1177

BAAL-HAZOR *(ba'-al-ha'-zor)* {1} See HAZOR. *A place near Ephraim.*
Absalom had sheepshearers in *B* 2Sa 13:23 1178

BAAL-HERMON *(ba'-al-her'-mon)* {2} *A city near Mt. Hermon.*
from mount *B* unto the entering in......... Judg 3:3 1179
they increased from Bashan unto *B*......... 1Chr 5:23 1179

BAALI *(ba'-al-i)* {1} *A rejected title of God.*
and shalt call me no more *B* .... Hos 2:16 1180

BAALIM *(ba'-al-im)* {18} See BAAL. *Plural of Baal.*
sight of the LORD, and served *B*............. Judg 2:11 1168
the LORD their God, and served *B* .... Judg 3:7 1168
again, and went a whoring after *B* .... Judg 8:33 1168
sight of the LORD, and served *B* .... Judg 10:6 1168
our God, and also served *B* .... Judg 10:10 1168
children of Israel did put away *B* 1Sa 7:4 1168
the LORD, and have served *B*................. 1Sa 12:10 1168
the LORD, and thou hast followed *B* 1Kin 18:18 1168
David, and sought not unto *B*................ 2Chr 17:3 1168
the LORD did they bestow upon *B*.......... 2Chr 24:7 1168
and made also molten images for *B*........ 2Chr 28:2 1168
and he reared up altars for *B*.................. 2Chr 33:3 1168
the altars of *B* in his presence................ 2Chr 34:4 1168
polluted, I have not gone after *B* .... Jer 2:23 1168
of their own heart, and after *B* .... Jer 9:14 1168
will visit upon her the days of *B*............. Hos 2:13 1168
the names of *B* out of her mouth .... Hos 2:17 1168
they sacrificed unto *B*, and burned......... Hos 11:2 1168

BAALIS *(ba'-al-is)* {1} *A king of the Ammonites.*
Dost thou certainly know that *B*............. Jer 40:14 1185

BAAL-MEON *(ba'-al-me'-on)* {3} See BETH-BAAL-MEON. *A Reubenite town.*
And Nebo, and *B*, (their names being ..... Num 32:38 1186
in Aroer, even unto Nebo and *B*............. 1Chr 5:8 1186
of the country, Beth-jeshimoth, *B*........... Eze 25:9 1186

BAAL-PEOR *(ba'-al-pe'-or)* {6} See PEOR. *A Moabite idol.*
And Israel joined himself unto *B*........... Num 25:3 1187
his men that were joined unto *B*............. Num 25:5 1187
what the LORD did because of *B*.............. Deut 4:3 1187
for all the men that followed *B*............... Deut 4:3 1187
joined themselves also unto *B*................. Ps 106:28 1187
but they went to *B*, and separated.......... Hos 9:10 1187

BAAL-PERAZIM *(ba'-al-per'-a-zim)* {4} *A place near the valley of Rephaim.*
And David came to *B*, and David 2Sa 5:20 1188
called the name of that place *B* 2Sa 5:20 1188
So they came up to *B* 1Chr 14:11 1188
called the name of that place *B* 1Chr 14:11 1188

BAAL'S *(ba'-als)* {1}
but *B* prophets are four hundred............. 1Kin 18:22 1168

BAAL-SHALISHA *(ba'-al-shal'-i-shah)* {1} *A place in Ephraim.*
And there came a man from *B* 2Kin 4:42 1190

BAAL-TAMAR *(ba'-al-ta'-mar)* {1} *A place in Benjamin.*
and put themselves in array at *B* .... Judg 20:33 1193

BAAL-ZEBUB *(ba'-al-ze'-bub)* {4} See BEELZEBUB. *A Philistine idol.*
enquire of *B* the god of Ekron 2Kin 1:2 1176
to enquire of *B* the god of Ekron 2Kin 1:3 1176
to enquire of *B* the god of Ekron 2Kin 1:6 1176
to enquire of *B* the god of Ekron 2Kin 1:16 1176

BAAL-ZEPHON *(ba'-al-ze'-fon)* {3} *A place near the Red Sea crossing.*
Migdol and the sea, over against *B* .... Ex 14:2 1189
sea, beside Pi-hahiroth, before *B* .... Ex 14:9 1189
Pi-hahiroth, which is before *B*................ Num 33:7 1189

BAANA *(ba'-an-ah)* {2} See BAANAH.
1. An officer in Solomon's army.
B the son of Ahilud 1Kin 4:12 1195
2. Father of Zadok.
them repaired Zadok the son of *B* .... Neh 3:4 1195

BAANAH *(ba'-an-ah)* {10} See BAANA.
1. A captain in Ishbosheth's army.
the name of the one was *B* 2Sa 4:2 1195
the Beerothite, Rechab and *B* 2Sa 4:5 1195
Rechab and *B* his brother escaped.......... 2Sa 4:6 1195
B his brother, the sons of Rimmon.......... 2Sa 4:9 1195
2. Father of Heleb.
Heleb the son of *B*, a 2Sa 23:29 1195
the son of *B* the Netophathite................ 1Chr 11:30 1195
3. An officer in Solomon's army.
B the son of Hushai was in Asher........... 1Kin 4:16 1195
4. An exile who returned with Zerubbabel.
Bilshan, Mizpar, Bigvai, Rehum, *B* .... Ezr 2:2 1195
Mispereth, Bigvai, Nehum, *B* .... Neh 7:7 1195
Malluch, Harim, *B*.................................. Neh 10:27 1195

BAARA *(ba'-ar-ah)* {1} *A wife of Shaharaim.*
Hushim and *B* were his wives 1Chr 8:8 1199

BAASEIAH *(ba-as-i'-ah)* {1} *A Gersonite Levite.*
The son of Michael, the son of *B*............ 1Chr 6:40 1202

BAASHA *(ba'-ash-ah)* {28} *A king of Israel.*
B king of Israel all their days 1Kin 15:16 1201
B king of Israel went up against............. 1Kin 15:17 1201
thy league with *B* king of Israel............. 1Kin 15:19 1201
when *B* heard thereof, that he 1Kin 15:21 1201
thereof, wherewith *B* had builded 1Kin 15:22 1201
B the son of Ahijah, of the house........... 1Kin 15:27 1201
B smote him at Gibbethon, which 1Kin 15:27 1201
Asa king of Judah did *B* slay him........... 1Kin 15:28 1201
B king of Israel all their days 1Kin 15:32 1201
B the son of Ahijah to reign over........... 1Kin 15:33 1201
Jehu the son of Hanani against *B* 1Kin 16:1 1201
will take away the posterity of *B* 1Kin 16:3 1201
Him that dieth of *B* in the city 1Kin 16:4 1201
Now the rest of the acts of *B* 1Kin 16:5 1201
So *B* slept with his fathers, and.............. 1Kin 16:6 1201
the word of the LORD against *B* 1Kin 16:7 1201
B to reign over Israel in Tirzah 1Kin 16:8 1201
that he slew all the house of *B*............... 1Kin 16:11 1201
Zimri destroy all the house of *B* 1Kin 16:12 1201
against *B* by Jehu the prophet 1Kin 16:12 1201
For all the sins of *B*, and the.................. 1Kin 16:13 1201
the house of *B* the son of Ahijah............. 1Kin 21:22 1201

the house of *B* the son of Ahijah ... 2Kin 9:9 1201
year of the reign of Asa *B* king ... 2Chr 16:1 1201
thy league with *B* king of Israel ... 2Chr 16:3 1201
when *B* heard it, that he left off ... 2Chr 16:5 1201
thereof, wherewith *B* was building ... 2Chr 16:6 1201
made for fear of *B* king of Israel ... Jer 41:9 1201

BABBLER {2}
and a *b* is no better ... Eccl 10:11 1167,3956
some said, What will this *b* say ... Acts 17:18 *4691*

BABBLING {1}
who hath *b* ... Prov 23:29 7879

BABBLINGS {2}
trust, avoiding profane and vain *b* ... 1Ti 6:20 *2757*
But shun profane and vain *b* ... 2Ti 2:16 *2757*

BABE {6}
and, behold, the *b* wept ... Ex 2:6 5288
of Mary, the *b* leaped in her womb ... Lk 1:41 *1025*
the *b* leaped in my womb for joy ... Lk 1:44 *1025*
Ye shall find the *b* wrapped in ... Lk 2:12 *1025*
and the *b* lying in a manger ... Lk 2:16 *1025*
for he is a *b* ... Heb 5:13 *3516*

BABEL *(ba'-bel)* {2} See BABYLON. *A city in the plain of Shinar.*
beginning of his kingdom was *B* ... Gen 10:10 894
is the name of it called *B* ... Gen 11:9 894

BABES {9}
Out of the mouth of *b* and ... Ps 8:2 5768
of their substance to their *b* ... Ps 17:14 5768
and *b* shall rule over them ... Is 3:4 8586
and hast revealed them unto *b* ... Mt 11:25 *3516*
never read, Out of the mouth of *b* ... Mt 21:16 *3516*
and hast revealed them unto *b* ... Lk 10:21 *3516*
of the foolish, a teacher of *b* ... Rom 2:20 *3516*
carnal, even as unto *b* in Christ ... 1Cor 3:1 *3516*
As newborn *b*, desire the sincere ... 1Pet 2:2 *1025*

BABYLON *(bab'-il-un)* {286} See BABEL, BABYLONIANS, BABYLONISH, BABYLON'S, CHALDEA, SHESHACH. *Capital of the Babylonian Empire; located on the Euphrates River.*
of Assyria brought men from *B* ... 2Kin 17:24 894
the men of *B* made Succoth-benoth, ... 2Kin 17:30 894
the son of Baladan, king of *B* ... 2Kin 20:12 894
from a far country, even from *B* ... 2Kin 20:14 894
this day, shall be carried into *B* ... 2Kin 20:17 894
in the palace of the king of *B* ... 2Kin 20:18 894
Nebuchadnezzar king of *B* came up ... 2Kin 24:1 894
for the king of *B* had taken from ... 2Kin 24:7 894
of *B* came up against Jerusalem ... 2Kin 24:10 894
king of *B* came against the city ... 2Kin 24:11 894
Judah went out to the king of *B* ... 2Kin 24:12 894
the king of *B* took him in the ... 2Kin 24:12 894
he carried away Jehoiachin to *B* ... 2Kin 24:15 894
captivity from Jerusalem to *B* ... 2Kin 24:15 894
of *B* brought captive to *B* ... 2Kin 24:16 894
the king of *B* made Mattaniah his ... 2Kin 24:17 894
rebelled against the king of *B* ... 2Kin 24:20 894
Nebuchadnezzar king of *B* came ... 2Kin 25:1 894
him up to the king of *B* to Riblah ... 2Kin 25:6 894
of brass, and carried him to *B* ... 2Kin 25:7 894
of king Nebuchadnezzar king of *B* ... 2Kin 25:8 894
guard, a servant of the king of *B* ... 2Kin 25:8 894
that fell away to the king of *B* ... 2Kin 25:11 894
and carried the brass of them to *B* ... 2Kin 25:13 894
them to the king of *B* to Riblah ... 2Kin 25:20 894
And the king of *B* smote them ... 2Kin 25:21 894
Nebuchadnezzar king of *B* had left ... 2Kin 25:22 894
heard that the king of *B* had made ... 2Kin 25:23 894
the land, and serve the king of *B* ... 2Kin 25:24 894
that Evil-merodach king of *B* in ... 2Kin 25:27 894
the kings that were with him in *B* ... 2Kin 25:28 894
away to *B* for their transgression ... 1Chr 9:1 894
ambassadors of the princes of *B* ... 2Chr 32:31 894
with fetters, and carried him to *B* ... 2Chr 33:11 894
came up Nebuchadnezzar king of *B* ... 2Chr 36:6 894
him in fetters, to carry him to *B* ... 2Chr 36:6 894
of the house of the LORD to *B* ... 2Chr 36:7 894
and put them in his temple at *B* ... 2Chr 36:7 894
sent, and brought him to *B* ... 2Chr 36:10 894
all these he brought to *B* ... 2Chr 36:18 894
the sword carried he away to *B* ... 2Chr 36:20 894
brought up from *B* unto Jerusalem ... Ezr 1:11 894
B had carried away unto *B* ... Ezr 2:1 894
of Nebuchadnezzar the king of *B* ... Ezr 5:12 895
and carried the people away into *B* ... Ezr 5:12 895
of *B* the same king Cyrus made a ... Ezr 5:13 895
brought them into the temple of *B* ... Ezr 5:14 895
king take out of the temple of *B* ... Ezr 5:14 895
house, which is there at *B* ... Ezr 5:17 895
the treasures were laid up in *B* ... Ezr 6:1 895
at Jerusalem, and brought unto *B* ... Ezr 6:5 895
This Ezra went up from *B* ... Ezr 7:6 894
month began he to go up from *B* ... Ezr 7:9 894
find in all the province of *B* ... Ezr 7:16 895
them that went up with me from *B* ... Ezr 8:1 894
the king of *B* had carried away ... Neh 7:6 894
king of *B* came I unto the king ... Neh 13:6 894
the king of *B* had carried away ... Est 2:6 894
Rahab and *B* to them that know me ... Ps 87:4 894
By the rivers of *B*, there we sat ... Ps 137:1 894
O daughter of *B*, who art to be ... Ps 137:8 894
The burden of *B*, which Isaiah the ... Is 13:1 894
And *B*, the glory of kingdoms, the ... Is 13:19 894
proverb against the king of *B* ... Is 14:4 894
hosts, and cut off from *B* the name ... Is 14:22 894
and said, *B* is fallen, is fallen ... Is 21:9 894
the son of Baladan, king of *B* ... Is 39:1 894
far country unto me, even from *B* ... Is 39:3 894
this day, shall be carried to *B* ... Is 39:6 894
in the palace of the king of *B* ... Is 39:7 894
For your sake I have sent to *B* ... Is 43:14 894
the dust, O virgin daughter of *B* ... Is 47:1 894
he will do his pleasure on *B* ... Is 48:14 894
Go ye forth of *B*, flee ye from ... Is 48:20 894
into the hand of the king of *B* ... Jer 20:4 894
shall carry them captive into *B* ... Jer 20:4 894
and take them, and carry them to *B* ... Jer 20:5 894
and thou shalt come to *B*, and there ... Jer 20:6 894
king of *B* maketh war against us ... Jer 21:2 894
ye fight against the king of *B* ... Jer 21:4 894
hand of Nebuchadrezzar king of *B* ... Jer 21:7 894
into the hand of the king of *B* ... Jer 21:10 894
hand of Nebuchadrezzar king of *B* ... Jer 22:25 894
of *B* had carried away captive ... Jer 24:1 894
and had brought them to *B* ... Jer 24:1 894
year of Nebuchadrezzar king of *B* ... Jer 25:1 894
and Nebuchadrezzar the king of *B* ... Jer 25:9 894
serve the king of *B* seventy years ... Jer 25:11 894
that I will punish the king of *B* ... Jer 25:12 894
of Nebuchadnezzar the king of *B* ... Jer 27:6 894
same Nebuchadnezzar the king of *B* ... Jer 27:8 894
under the yoke of the king of *B* ... Jer 27:8 894
Ye shall not serve the king of *B* ... Jer 27:9 894
under the yoke of the king of *B* ... Jer 27:11 894
under the yoke of the king of *B* ... Jer 27:12 894
that will not serve the king of *B* ... Jer 27:13 894
Ye shall not serve the king of *B* ... Jer 27:14 894
shortly be brought again from *B* ... Jer 27:16 894
serve the king of *B*, and live ... Jer 27:17 894
and at Jerusalem, go not to *B* ... Jer 27:18 894
Nebuchadnezzar king of *B* took not ... Jer 27:20 894
king of Judah from Jerusalem to *B* ... Jer 27:20 894
They shall be carried to *B* ... Jer 27:22 894
broken the yoke of the king of *B* ... Jer 28:2 894
of *B* took away from this place ... Jer 28:3 894
this place, and carried them to *B* ... Jer 28:3 894
of Judah, that went into *B* ... Jer 28:4 894
break the yoke of the king of *B* ... Jer 28:4 894
captive, from *B* into this place ... Jer 28:6 894
of *B* from the neck of all nations ... Jer 28:11 894
serve Nebuchadnezzar king of *B* ... Jer 28:14 894
away captive from Jerusalem to *B* ... Jer 29:1 894
king of Judah sent unto *B* to ... Jer 29:3 894
Nebuchadnezzar king of *B*) saying ... Jer 29:3 894
away from Jerusalem unto *B* ... Jer 29:4 894
at *B* I will visit you, and perform ... Jer 29:10 894
hath raised us up prophets in *B* ... Jer 29:15 894
I have sent from Jerusalem to *B* ... Jer 29:20 894
hand of Nebuchadrezzar king of *B* ... Jer 29:21 894
captivity of Judah which are in *B* ... Jer 29:22 894
whom the king of *B* roasted in the ... Jer 29:22 894
therefore he sent unto us in *B* ... Jer 29:28 894
into the hand of the king of *B* ... Jer 32:3 894
into the hand of the king of *B* ... Jer 32:4 894
And he shall lead Zedekiah to *B* ... Jer 32:5 894
hand of Nebuchadrezzar king of *B* ... Jer 32:28 894
of the king of *B* by the sword ... Jer 32:36 894
when Nebuchadnezzar king of *B* ... Jer 34:1 894
into the hand of the king of *B* ... Jer 34:2 894
behold the eyes of the king of *B* ... Jer 34:3 894
to mouth, and thou shalt go to *B* ... Jer 34:3 894
king of *B* came up into the land ... Jer 35:11 894
The king of *B* shall certainly ... Jer 36:29 894
whom Nebuchadrezzar king of *B* ... Jer 37:1 894
into the hand of the king of *B* ... Jer 37:17 894
The king of *B* shall not come ... Jer 37:19 894
by the hand of the king of *B* ... Jer 38:23 894
came Nebuchadrezzar king of *B* ... Jer 39:1 894
princes of the king of *B* came in ... Jer 39:3 894
of the princes of the king of *B* ... Jer 39:3 894
up to Nebuchadnezzar king of *B* to ... Jer 39:5 894
Then the king of *B* slew the sons ... Jer 39:6 894
also the king of *B* slew all the ... Jer 39:6 894
with chains, to carry him to *B* ... Jer 39:7 894
B the remnant of the people that ... Jer 39:9 894
Now Nebuchadrezzar king of *B* gave ... Jer 39:11 894
were carried away captive unto *B* ... Jer 40:1 894
unto thee to come with me into *B* ... Jer 40:4 894
unto thee to come with me into *B* ... Jer 40:4 894
whom the king of *B* hath made ... Jer 40:5 894
heard that the king of *B* had made ... Jer 40:7 894
not carried away captive to *B* ... Jer 40:7 894
the land, and serve the king of *B* ... Jer 40:9 894
heard that the king of *B* had left ... Jer 40:11 894
whom the king of *B* had made ... Jer 41:2 894
whom the king of *B* made governor ... Jer 41:18 894
Be not afraid of the king of *B* ... Jer 42:11 894
and carry us away captives into *B* ... Jer 43:3 894
take Nebuchadrezzar the king of *B* ... Jer 43:10 894
hand of Nebuchadrezzar king of *B* ... Jer 44:30 894
of *B* smote in the fourth year of ... Jer 46:2 894
king of *B* should come and smite ... Jer 46:13 894
hand of Nebuchadrezzar king of *B* ... Jer 46:26 894
king of *B* shall smite, thus saith ... Jer 49:28 894
for Nebuchadrezzar king of *B* hath ... Jer 49:30 894
that the LORD spake against *B* ... Jer 50:1 894
B is taken, Bel is confounded, ... Jer 50:2 894
Remove out of the midst of *B* ... Jer 50:8 894
cause to come up against *B* an ... Jer 50:9 894
goeth by *B* shall be astonished ... Jer 50:13 894
in array against *B* round about ... Jer 50:14 894
Cut off the sower from *B*, and him ... Jer 50:16 894
king of *B* hath broken his bones ... Jer 50:17 894
I will punish the king of *B* ... Jer 50:18 894
how is *B* become a desolation ... Jer 50:23 894
thee, and thou art also taken, O *B* ... Jer 50:24 894
and escape out of the land of *B* ... Jer 50:28 894
together the archers against *B* ... Jer 50:29 894
and disquiet the inhabitants of *B* ... Jer 50:34 894
and upon the inhabitants of *B* ... Jer 50:35 894
against thee, O daughter of *B* ... Jer 50:42 894
The king of *B* hath heard the ... Jer 50:43 894
that he hath taken against *B* ... Jer 50:45 894
taking of *B* the earth is moved ... Jer 50:46 894
Behold, I will raise up against *B* ... Jer 51:1 894
And will send unto *B* fanners ... Jer 51:2 894
Flee out of the midst of *B* ... Jer 51:6 894
B hath been a golden cup in the ... Jer 51:7 894
B is suddenly fallen and destroyed ... Jer 51:8 894
We would have healed *B*, but she ... Jer 51:9 894
for his device is against *B* ... Jer 51:11 894
the standard upon the walls of *B* ... Jer 51:12 894
against the inhabitants of *B* ... Jer 51:12 894
And I will render unto *B* and to all ... Jer 51:24 894
LORD shall be performed against *B* ... Jer 51:29 894
to make the land of *B* a ... Jer 51:29 894
The mighty men of *B* have forborn ... Jer 51:30 894
to shew the king of *B* that his ... Jer 51:31 894
The daughter of *B* is like a ... Jer 51:33 894
the king of *B* hath devoured me ... Jer 51:34 894
to me and to my flesh be upon *B* ... Jer 51:35 894
B shall become heaps, a dwelling ... Jer 51:37 894
how is *B* become an astonishment ... Jer 51:41 894
The sea is come up upon *B* ... Jer 51:42 894
And I will punish Bel in *B* ... Jer 51:44 894
yea, the wall of *B* shall fall ... Jer 51:44 894
upon the graven images of *B* ... Jer 51:47 894
that is therein, shall sing for *B* ... Jer 51:48 894
As *B* hath caused the slain of ... Jer 51:49 894
so at *B* shall fall the slain of ... Jer 51:49 894
Though *B* should mount up to ... Jer 51:53 894
A sound of a cry cometh from *B* ... Jer 51:54 894
Because the LORD hath spoiled *B* ... Jer 51:55 894
is come upon her, even upon *B* ... Jer 51:56 894
The broad walls of *B* shall be ... Jer 51:58 894
B in the fourth year of his reign ... Jer 51:59 894
the evil that should come upon *B* ... Jer 51:60 894
words that are written against *B* ... Jer 51:60 894
to Seraiah, When thou comest to *B* ... Jer 51:61 894
thou shalt say, Thus shall *B* sink ... Jer 51:64 894
rebelled against the king of *B* ... Jer 52:3 894
Nebuchadrezzar king of *B* came ... Jer 52:4 894
B to Riblah in the land of Hamath ... Jer 52:9 894
the king of *B* slew the sons of ... Jer 52:10 894
the king of *B* bound him in chains ... Jer 52:11 894
and carried him to *B* ... Jer 52:11 894
year of Nebuchadrezzar king of *B* ... Jer 52:12 894
guard, which served the king of *B* ... Jer 52:12 894
away, that fell to the king of *B* ... Jer 52:15 894
all the brass of them to *B* ... Jer 52:17 894
them to the king of *B* to Riblah ... Jer 52:26 894
And the king of *B* smote them ... Jer 52:27 894
that Evil-merodach king of *B* in ... Jer 52:31 894
the kings that were with him in *B* ... Jer 52:32 894
diet given him of the king of *B* ... Jer 52:34 894
I will bring him to *B* to the land ... Eze 12:13 894
Behold, the king of *B* is come to ... Eze 17:12 894
and led them with him to *B* ... Eze 17:12 894
in the midst of *B* he shall die ... Eze 17:16 894
snare, and I will bring him to *B* ... Eze 17:20 894
and brought him to the king of *B* ... Eze 19:9 894
sword of the king of *B* may come ... Eze 21:19 894
For the king of *B* stood at the ... Eze 21:21 894
the king of *B* set himself against ... Eze 24:2 894
Tyrus Nebuchadrezzar king of *B* ... Eze 26:7 894
Nebuchadrezzar king of *B* caused ... Eze 29:18 894
unto Nebuchadrezzar king of *B* ... Eze 29:19 894
hand of Nebuchadrezzar king of *B* ... Eze 30:10 894
the arms of the king of *B* ... Eze 30:24 894
the arms of the king of *B* ... Eze 30:25 894
into the hand of the king of *B* ... Eze 30:25 894
king of *B* shall come upon thee ... Eze 32:11 894
king of *B* unto Jerusalem, and ... Dan 1:1 894
to destroy all the wise men of *B* ... Dan 2:12 895
forth to slay the wise men of *B* ... Dan 2:14 895
the rest of the wise men of *B* ... Dan 2:18 895
to destroy the wise men of *B* ... Dan 2:24 895
Destroy not the wise men of *B* ... Dan 2:24 895
over the whole province of *B* ... Dan 2:48 895
over all the wise men of *B* ... Dan 2:48 895
the affairs of the province of *B* ... Dan 2:49 895
of Dura, in the province of *B* ... Dan 3:1 895
the affairs of the province of *B* ... Dan 3:12 895
Abed-nego, in the province of *B* ... Dan 3:30 895
all the wise men of *B* before me ... Dan 4:6 895
in the palace of the kingdom of *B* ... Dan 4:29 895
and said, Is not this great *B* ... Dan 4:30 895
and said to the wise men of *B* ... Dan 5:7 895
king of *B* Daniel had a dream ... Dan 7:1 895
field, and thou shalt go even to *B* ... Mic 4:10 894
dwellest with the daughter of *B* ... Zec 2:7 894
of Jedaiah, which are come from *B* ... Zec 6:10 894
time they were carried away to *B* ... Mt 1:11 *897*
And after they were brought to *B* ... Mt 1:12 *897*
into *B* are fourteen generations ... Mt 1:17 *897*
into *B* unto Christ are fourteen ... Mt 1:17 *897*
and I will carry you away beyond *B* ... Acts 7:43 *897*
The church that is at *B*, elected ... 1Pet 5:13 *897*
B is fallen, is fallen, that ... Rev 14:8 *897*
great *B* came in remembrance ... Rev 16:19 *897*
B THE GREAT, THE MOTHER OF ... Rev 17:5 *897*
B the great is fallen, is fallen, ... Rev 18:2 *897*

Alas, alas that great city *B* ... Rev 18:10 *897*
that great city *B* be thrown down ... Rev 18:21 *897*

BABYLONIA See BABYLONISH.

BABYLONIAN See CHALDEANS'.

BABYLONIANS *(bab-il-o'-ne-ans)* {4} See CHALDEANS. *Inhabitants of Babylonia.*
Apharsites, the Archevites, the *B* ... Ezr 4:9 896
the manner of the *B* of Chaldea ... Eze 23:15 1121,894
the *B* came to her into the bed of ... Eze 23:17 1121,894
The *B*, and all the Chaldeans, ... Eze 23:23 1121,894

BABYLONISH *(bab-il-o'-nish)* {1} See BABYLONIANS.
the spoils a goodly *B* garment ... Josh 7:21 8152

BABYLON'S *(bab'-il-ons)* {8}
For then the king of *B* army ... Jer 32:2 894
When the king of *B* army fought ... Jer 34:7 894
the hand of the king of *B* army ... Jer 34:21 894
the hand of the king of *B* army ... Jer 38:3 894
forth unto the king of *B* princes ... Jer 38:17 894
go forth to the king of *B* princes ... Jer 38:18 894
forth to the king of *B* princes ... Jer 38:22 894
and all the king of *B* princes ... Jer 39:13 894

BACA *(ba'-cah)* {1} *A valley near Jerusalem.*
the valley of *B* make it a well ... Ps 84:6 1056

BACHRITES *(bak'-rites)* {1} *Descendants of Becher.*
of Becher, the family of the *B* ... Num 26:35 1076

BACK See APPENDIX.

BACKBITERS {1}
B, haters of God, despiteful, ... Rom 1:30 *2637*

BACKBITETH {1}
He that *b* not with his tongue, ... Ps 15:3 7270

BACKBITING {1}
an angry countenance a *b* tongue ... Prov 25:23 5643

BACKBITINGS {1}
envyings, wraths, strifes, *b* ... 2Cor 12:20 *2636*

BACKBONE {1}
shall he take off hard by the *b* ... Lev 3:9 6096

BACKS {8}
enemies turn their *b* unto thee ... Ex 23:27 6203
their *b* before their enemies ... Josh 7:8 6203
but turned their *b* before their ... Josh 7:12 6203
Therefore they turned their *b* ... Judg 20:42
of the LORD, and turned their *b* ... 2Chr 29:6 6203
and cast thy law behind their *b* ... Neh 9:26 1458
with their *b* toward the temple of ... Eze 8:16 268
And their whole body, and their *b* ... Eze 10:12 1354

BACKSIDE {3}
the flock to the *b* of the desert ... Ex 3:1 310
hang over the *b* of the tabernacle ... Ex 26:12 268
a book written within and on the *b* ... Rev 5:1 *3693*

BACKSLIDER {1}
The *b* in heart shall be filled ... Prov 14:14 5472

BACKSLIDING {12}
that which *b* Israel hath done ... Jer 3:6 4878
b Israel committed adultery I had ... Jer 3:8 4878
The *b* Israel hath justified ... Jer 3:11 4878
thou *b* Israel, saith the LORD ... Jer 3:12 4878
O *b* children, saith the LORD ... Jer 3:14 7726
ye *b* children, and I will heal ... Jer 3:22 7726
slidden back by a perpetual *b* ... Jer 8:5 4878
thou go about, O thou *b* daughter ... Jer 31:22 7728
thy flowing valley, O *b* daughter ... Jer 49:4 7728
Israel slideth back as a *b* heifer ... Hos 4:16 5637
my people are bent to *b* from me ... Hos 11:7 4878
I will heal their *b*, I will love ... Hos 14:4 4878

BACKSLIDINGS {4}
thee, and thy *b* shall reprove thee ... Jer 2:19 4878
children, and I will heal your *b* ... Jer 3:22 4878
many, and their *b* are increased ... Jer 5:6 4878
for our *b* are many ... Jer 14:7 4878

BACKWARD {18}
both their shoulders, and went *b* ... Gen 9:23 322
and their faces were *b*, and they ... Gen 9:23 322
so that his rider shall fall *b* ... Gen 49:17 268
seat *b* by the side of the gate ... 1Sa 4:18 322
the shadow return *b* ten degrees ... 2Kin 20:10 322
brought the shadow ten degrees *b* ... 2Kin 20:11 322
and *b*, but I cannot perceive him ... Job 23:8 268
let them be driven *b* and put to ... Ps 40:14 268
let them be turned *b*, and put to ... Ps 70:2 268
unto anger, they are gone away *b* ... Is 1:4 268
that they might go, and fall *b* ... Is 28:13 268
sun dial of Ahaz, ten degrees *b* ... Is 38:8 322
that turneth wise men *b*, and ... Is 44:25 268
And judgment is turned away *b* ... Is 59:14 268
of their evil heart, and went *b* ... Jer 7:24 268
saith the LORD, thou art gone *b* ... Jer 15:6 268
yea, she sigheth, and turneth *b* ... Lam 1:8 268
I am he, they went *b* ... Jn 18:6 *1519,3588,3694*

BAD {18}
cannot speak unto thee *b* or good ... Gen 24:50 7451
not to Jacob either good or *b* ... Gen 31:24 7451
not to Jacob either good or *b* ... Gen 31:29 7451
good for a *b*, or a *b* for a good ... Lev 27:10 7451
value it, whether it be good or *b* ... Lev 27:12 7451
it, whether it be good or *b* ... Lev 27:14 7451
search whether it be good or *b* ... Lev 27:33 7451
dwell in, whether it be good or *b* ... Num 13:19 7451
either good or *b* of mine own mind ... Num 24:13 7451
brother Amnon neither good nor *b* ... 2Sa 13:22 7451
the king to discern good and *b* ... 2Sa 14:17 7451
I may discern between good and *b* ... 1Kin 3:9 7451
the *b* city, and have set up the ... Ezr 4:12 873
not be eaten, they were so *b* ... Jer 24:2 7451
into vessels, but cast the *b* away ... Mt 13:48 *4550*
all as many as they found, both *b* ... Mt 22:10 *4190*
done, whether it be good or *b* ... 2Cor 5:10 *2556*

BADE {18}
And the man did as Joseph *b* ... Gen 43:17 559
up till the morning, as Moses *b* ... Ex 16:24 6680
b stone them with stones ... Num 14:10 559
did unto them as the LORD *b* him ... Josh 11:9 559
all that her mother in law *b* her ... Ruth 3:6 6680
and some *b* me kill thee ... 1Sa 24:10 559
(Also he *b* them teach the ... 2Sa 1:18 559
for thy servant Joab, he *b* me ... 2Sa 14:19 6680
on the third day, as the king *b* ... 2Chr 10:12 1696
Then Esther *b* them return ... Est 4:15 559
understood they how that he *b* ... Mt 16:12 *2036*
And he that *b* thee and him come and ... Lk 14:9 *2564*
that when he that *b* thee cometh ... Lk 14:10 *2564*
said he also to him that *b* him ... Lk 14:12 *2564*
made a great supper, and *b* many ... Lk 14:16 *2564*
the Spirit *b* me go with them, ... Acts 11:12 *2036*
But *b* them farewell, saying, I ... Acts 18:21 *657*
b that he should be examined by ... Acts 22:24 *2036*

BADEST {1}
have done according as thou *b* me ... Gen 27:19 1696

BADGERS' {14}
b skins, and shittim wood, ... Ex 25:5 8476
and a covering above of *b* skins ... Ex 26:14 8476
b skins, and shittim wood, ... Ex 35:7 8476
of rams, and *b* skins, brought them ... Ex 35:23 8476
a covering of *b* skins above that ... Ex 36:19 8476
red, and the covering of *b* skins ... Ex 39:34 8476
thereon the covering of *b* skins ... Num 4:6 8476
same with a covering of *b* skins ... Num 4:8 8476
within a covering of *b* skins ... Num 4:10 8476
it with a covering of *b* skins ... Num 4:11 8476
them with a covering of *b* skins ... Num 4:12 8476
upon it a covering of *b* skins ... Num 4:14 8476
the covering of the *b* skins that ... Num 4:25 8476
work, and shod thee with *b* skin ... Eze 16:10 8476

BADNESS {1}
in all the land of Egypt for *b* ... Gen 41:19 7455

BAG {11}
not have in thy *b* divers weights ... Deut 25:13 3599
in a shepherd's *b* which he had ... 1Sa 17:40 3627
And David put his hand in his *b* ... 1Sa 17:49 3627
transgression is sealed up in a *b* ... Job 14:17 6872
He hath taken a *b* of money with ... Prov 7:20 6872
the weights of the *b* are his work ... Prov 16:11 3599
They lavish gold out of the *b* ... Is 46:6 3599
with the *b* of deceitful weights ... Mic 6:11 3599
to put it into a *b* with holes ... Hag 1:6 6872
he was a thief, and had the *b* ... Jn 12:6 *1101*
thought, because Judas had the *b* ... Jn 13:29 *1101*

BAGS {3}
two talents of silver in two *b* ... 2Kin 5:23 2754
came up, and they put up in *b* ... 2Kin 12:10 6696
yourselves *b* which wax not old ... Lk 12:33 *905*

BAHARUMITE *(ba-ha'-rum-ite)* {1} See BARHUMITE. *Inhabitants of Bahurim.*
Azmaveth the *B*, Eliahba the ... 1Chr 11:33 978

BAHURIM *(ba-hu'-rim)* {5} See BAHARUMITE. *A village near Jerusalem.*
her along weeping behind her to *B* ... 2Sa 3:16 980
And when king David came to *B* ... 2Sa 16:5 980
and came to a man's house in *B* ... 2Sa 17:18 980
Gera, a Benjamite, which was of *B* ... 2Sa 19:16 980
the son of Gera, a Benjamite of *B* ... 1Kin 2:8 980

BAJITH *(ba'-jith)* {1} *A temple in Moab.*
He is gone up to *B*, and to Dibon, ... Is 15:2 1006

BAKBAKKAR *(bak-bak'-kar)* {1} *A Levite who returned from exile.*
And *B*, Heresh, and Galal, and ... 1Chr 9:15 1230

BAKBUK *(bak'-buk)* {2} *A family who returned from exile.*
The children of *B*, the children ... Ezr 2:51 1227
The children of *B*, the children ... Neh 7:53 1227

BAKBUKIAH *(bak-buk-i'-ah)* {3} *A Levite exile who resettled in Jerusalem.*
B the second among his brethren, ... Neh 11:17 1229
Also *B* and Unni, their brethren, ... Neh 12:9 1229
Mattaniah, and *B*, Obadiah, ... Neh 12:25 1229

BAKE {9}
did *b* unleavened bread, and they ... Gen 19:3 644
b that which ye will *b* to day, ... Ex 16:23 644
flour, and *b* twelve cakes thereof ... Lev 24:5 644
ten women shall *b* your bread in ... Lev 26:26 644
did *b* unleavened bread thereof ... 1Sa 28:24 644
in his sight, and did *b* the cakes ... 2Sa 13:8 1310
thou shalt *b* it with dung that ... Eze 4:12 5746
where they shall *b* the meat ... Eze 46:20 644

BAKED {4}
they *b* unleavened cakes of the ... Ex 12:39 644
b it in pans, and made cakes of it ... Num 11:8 1310
and for that which is *b* in the pan ... 1Chr 23:29
also I have *b* bread upon the ... Is 44:19 644

BAKEMEATS {1}
of all manner of *b* for Pharaoh . Gen 40:17 3978,4639,644

BAKEN {9}
of a meat offering *b* in the oven ... Lev 2:4 644
be a meat offering *b* in a pan ... Lev 2:5
meat offering *b* in the frying pan ... Lev 2:7
It shall not be *b* with leaven ... Lev 6:17 644
and when it is *b*, thou shalt bring ... Lev 6:21 7246
the *b* pieces of the meat offering ... Lev 6:21 8601
offering that is *b* in the oven ... Lev 7:9 644
they shall be *b* with leaven ... Lev 23:17 644
there was a cake *b* on the coals ... 1Kin 19:6

BAKER {8}
his *b* had offended their lord the ... Gen 40:1 644
the *b* of the king of Egypt, which ... Gen 40:5 644
When the chief *b* saw that the ... Gen 40:16 644
of the chief *b* among his servants ... Gen 40:20 644
But he hanged the chief *b* ... Gen 40:22 644
house, both me and the chief *b* ... Gen 41:10 644
as an oven heated by the *b* ... Hos 7:4 644
their *b* sleepeth all the night ... Hos 7:6 644

BAKERS {2}
and against the chief of the *b* ... Gen 40:2 644
and to be cooks, and to be *b* ... 1Sa 8:13 644

BAKERS' {1}
of bread out of the *b* street ... Jer 37:21 644

BAKETH {1}
yea, he kindleth it, and *b* bread ... Is 44:15 644

BALAAM *(ba'-la-am)* {60} See BALAAM'S. *Son of Beor.*
unto *B* the son of Beor to Pethor ... Num 22:5 1109
and they came unto *B*, and spake ... Num 22:7 1109
the princes of Moab abode with *B* ... Num 22:8 1109
And God came unto *B*, and said, What ... Num 22:9 1109
B said unto God, Balak the son of ... Num 22:10 1109
And God said unto *B*, Thou shalt ... Num 22:12 1109
B rose up in the morning, and said ... Num 22:13 1109
B refuseth to come with us ... Num 22:14 1109
And they came to *B*, and said to him ... Num 22:16 1109
B answered and said unto the ... Num 22:18 1109
And God came unto *B* at night ... Num 22:20 1109
B rose up in the morning, and ... Num 22:21 1109
B smote the ass, to turn her into ... Num 22:23 1109
the LORD, she fell down under *B* ... Num 22:27 1109
of the ass, and she said unto *B* ... Num 22:28 1109
B said unto the ass, Because thou ... Num 22:29 1109
And the ass said unto *B*, Am not I ... Num 22:30 1109
the LORD opened the eyes of *B* ... Num 22:31 1109
B said unto the angel of the LORD ... Num 22:34 1109
the angel of the LORD said unto *B* ... Num 22:35 1109
So *B* went with the princes of ... Num 22:35 1109
when Balak heard that *B* was come ... Num 22:36 1109
And Balak said unto *B*, Did I not ... Num 22:37 1109
B said unto Balak, Lo, I am come ... Num 22:38 1109
B went with Balak, and they came ... Num 22:39 1109
oxen and sheep, and sent to *B* ... Num 22:40 1109
on the morrow, that Balak took *B* ... Num 22:41 1109
B said unto Balak, Build me here ... Num 23:1 1109
And Balak did as *B* had spoken ... Num 23:2 1109
B offered on every altar a ... Num 23:2 1109
B said unto Balak, Stand by thy ... Num 23:3 1109
And God met *B* ... Num 23:4 1109
And Balak said unto *B*, What hast ... Num 23:11 1109
And the LORD met *B*, and put a word ... Num 23:16 1109
And Balak said unto *B*, Neither ... Num 23:25 1109
But *B* answered and said unto Balak ... Num 23:26 1109
And Balak said unto *B*, Come, I ... Num 23:27 1109
Balak brought *B* unto the top of ... Num 23:28 1109
B said unto Balak, Build me here ... Num 23:29 1109
And Balak did as *B* had said ... Num 23:30 1109
when *B* saw that it pleased the ... Num 24:1 1109
B lifted up his eyes, and he saw ... Num 24:2 1109
B the son of Beor hath said, and ... Num 24:3 1109
anger was kindled against *B* ... Num 24:10 1109
and Balak said unto *B*, I called ... Num 24:10 1109
B said unto Balak, Spake I not ... Num 24:12 1109
B the son of Beor hath said, and ... Num 24:15 1109
B rose up, and went and returned to ... Num 24:25 1109
B also the son of Beor they slew ... Num 31:8 1109
Israel, through the counsel of *B* ... Num 31:16 1109
B the son of Beor of Pethor of ... Deut 23:4 1109
thy God would not hearken unto *B* ... Deut 23:5 1109
B also the son of Beor, the ... Josh 13:22 1109
called *B* the son of Beor to curse ... Josh 24:9 1109
But I would not hearken unto *B* ... Josh 24:10 1109
but hired *B* against them, that he ... Neh 13:2 1109
what *B* the son of Beor answered ... Mic 6:5 1109
the way of *B* the son of Bosor ... 2Pet 2:15 *903*
after the error of *B* for reward ... Jude 11 *903*
them that hold the doctrine of *B* ... Rev 2:14 *903*

BALAAM'S {3}
crushed *B* foot against the wall ... Num 22:25 1109
B anger was kindled, and he smote ... Num 22:27 1109
And the LORD put a word in *B* mouth ... Num 23:5 1109

BALAC *(ba'-lak)* {1} See BALAK. *Greek form of Balak.*
of Balaam, who taught *B* to cast a ... Rev 2:14 *904*

BALADAN *(bal'-adan)* {2} See BERODACH-BALADAN, MERODACH-BALADAN. *Father of a Babylonian king.*
Berodach-baladan, the son of *B* ... 2Kin 20:12 1081
Merodach-baladan, the son of *B* ... Is 39:1 1081

BALAH *(ba'-lah)* {1} See BAALAH. *A city in Simeon.*
And Hazar-shual, and Balah, and Azem, ... Josh 19:3 1088

BALAK *(ba'-lak)* {42} See BALAC, BALAK'S. *A king of Moab.*
B the son of Zippor saw all that ... Num 22:2 1111
B the son of Zippor was king of ... Num 22:4 1111
and spake unto him the words of *B* ... Num 22:7 1111
B the son of Zippor, king of Moab ... Num 22:10 1111
and said unto the princes of *B* ... Num 22:13 1111
Moab rose up, and they went unto *B* ... Num 22:14 1111
B sent yet again princes, more, ... Num 22:15 1111

Thus saith B the son of Zippor, Num 22:16 1111
and said unto the servants of B Num 22:18 1111
If B would give me his house full Num 22:18 1111
Balaam went with the princes of B Num 22:35 1111
when B heard that Balaam was come Num 22:36 1111
B said unto Balaam, Did I not Num 22:37 1111
And Balaam said unto B, Lo, I am Num 22:38 1111
And Balaam went with B, and they Num 22:39 1111
B offered oxen and sheep, and sent Num 22:40 1111
that B took Balaam, and brought Num 22:41 1111
And Balaam said unto B, Build me Num 23:1 1111
B did as Balaam had spoken Num 23:2 1111
and B and Balaam offered on every Num 23:2 1111
And Balaam said unto B, Stand by Num 23:3 1111
mouth, and said, Return unto B Num 23:5 1111
B the king of Moab hath brought Num 23:7 1111
B said unto Balaam, What hast Num 23:11 1111
B said unto him, Come, I pray Num 23:13 1111
And he said unto B, Stand here by Num 23:15 1111
mouth, and said, Go again unto B Num 23:16 1111
B said unto him, What hath the Num 23:17 1111
his parable, and said, Rise up, B Num 23:18 1111
B said unto Balaam, Neither curse Num 23:25 1111
Balaam answered and said unto B Num 23:26 1111
B said unto Balaam, Come, I pray Num 23:27 1111
B brought Balaam unto the top of Num 23:28 1111
And Balaam said unto B, Build me Num 23:29 1111
B did as Balaam had said, and Num 23:30 1111
B said unto Balaam, I called thee Num 24:10 1111
And Balaam said unto B, Spake I Num 24:12 1111
If B would give me his house full Num 24:13 1111
and B also went his way Num 24:25 1111
Then B the son of Zippor, king of Josh 24:9 1111
better than B the son of Zippor Judg 11:25 1111
remember now what B king of Moab Mic 6:5 1111

BALAK'S *(ba'-laks)* {1}
B anger was kindled against Num 24:10 1111

BALANCE {8}
Let me be weighed in an even b Job 31:6 3976
to be laid in the b, they are Ps 62:9 3976
A false b is abomination to the Prov 11:1 3976
A just weight and b are the LORD'S Prov 16:11 3976
and a false b is not good Prov 20:23 3976
in scales, and the hills in a b Is 40:12 3976
as the small dust of the b Is 40:15 3976
the bag, and weigh silver in the b Is 46:6 7070

BALANCES {10}
Just b, just weights, a just Lev 19:36 3976
calamity laid in the b together Job 6:2 3976
and weighed him the money in the b Jer 32:10 3976
then take thee b to weigh Eze 5:1 3976
Ye shall have just b, and a just Eze 45:10 3976
Thou art weighed in the b Dan 5:27 3977
the b of deceit are in his hand Hos 12:7 3976
and falsifying the b by deceit Amos 8:5 3976
count them pure with the wicked b Mic 6:11 3976
him had a pair of b in his hand Rev 6:5

BALANCINGS {1}
thou know the b of the clouds Job 37:16 4657

BALD {16}
the b locust after his kind, and Lev 11:22 5556
is fallen off his head, he is b Lev 13:40 7142
toward his face, he is forehead b Lev 13:41 1371
And if there be in the b head Lev 13:42 7146
or b forehead, a white reddish Lev 13:42 1372
his b head, or his b forehead Lev 13:42 1372
b head, or in his b forehead Lev 13:43 1372
said unto him, Go up, thou b head 2Kin 2:23 7142
go up, thou b head 2Kin 2:23 7142
nor make themselves b for them Jer 16:6 7139
For every head shall be b Jer 48:37 7144
themselves utterly b for thee Eze 27:31 7139
every head was made b, and every Eze 29:18 7139
Make thee b, and poll thee for thy Mic 1:16 7139

BALDNESS {9}
shall not make b upon their head Lev 21:5 7144
nor make any b between your eyes Deut 14:1 7144
and instead of well set hair b Is 3:24 7144
on all their heads shall be b Is 15:2 7144
weeping, and to mourning, and to b Is 22:12 7144
B is come upon Gaza Jer 47:5 7144
faces, and b upon all their heads Eze 7:18 7144
all loins, and b upon every head Amos 8:10 7144
enlarge thy b as the eagle Mic 1:16 7144

BALL {1}
toss thee like a b into a large Is 22:18 1754

BALM {6}
their camels bearing spicery and b Gen 37:25 6875
the man a present, a little b Gen 43:11 6875
Is there no b in Gilead Jer 8:22 6875
Go up into Gilead, and take b Jer 46:11 6875
take b for her pain, if so be she Jer 51:8 6875
and Pannag, and honey, and oil, and b Eze 27:17 6875

BAMAH *(ba'-mah)* {1} See BAMOTH. *Places where Israel sacrificed to idols.*
thereof is called B unto this day Eze 20:29 1117

BAMOTH *(ba'-moth)* {2} See BAMOTH-BAAL. *A city on the Arnon River.*
and from Nahaliel to B Num 21:19 1120
from B in the valley, that is in Num 21:20 1120

BAMOTH-BAAL *(ba'-moth-ba'-al)* {1} *A Moabite town.*
Dibon, and B, and Beth-baal-meon, Josh 13:17 1120

BAND {19}
with a b round about the hole, Ex 39:23 8193
and there went with him a b of men 1Sa 10:26 2428
him, and became captain over a b 1Kin 11:24 1416
behold, they spied a b of men 2Kin 13:21 1416
and made them captains of the b 1Chr 12:18 1416
David against the b of the rovers 1Chr 12:21 1416
for the b of men that came with 2Chr 22:1 1416
of the king a b of soldiers Ezr 8:22 2428
unicorn with his b in the furrow Job 39:10 5688
the earth, even with a b of iron Dan 4:15 613
the earth, even with a b of iron Dan 4:23 613
unto him the whole b of soldiers Mt 27:27 *4686*
and they call together the whole b Mk 15:16 *4686*
then, having received a b of men Jn 18:3 *4686*
Then the b and the captain and Jn 18:12 *4686*
of the b called the Italian b Acts 10:1 *4686*
unto the chief captain of the b Acts 21:31 *4686*
a centurion of Augustus' b Acts 27:1 *4686*

BANDED {1}
certain of the Jews b together Acts 23:12 *4160,4963*

BANDS {46}
herds, and the camels, into two b Gen 32:7 4264
and now I am become two b Gen 32:10 4264
I have broken the b of your yoke Lev 26:13 4133
his b loosed from off his hands Judg 15:14 612
two men that were captains of b 2Sa 4:2 1416
So the b of Syria came no more 2Kin 6:23 1416
the b of the Moabites invaded the 2Kin 13:20 1416
Pharaoh-nechoh put him in b at 2Kin 23:33 631
against him b of the Chaldees 2Kin 24:2 1416
b of the Syrians, and b of the 2Kin 24:2 1416
b of the children of Ammon, and 2Kin 24:2 1416
were b of soldiers for war, six 1Chr 7:4 1416
b that were ready armed to the 1Chr 12:23 7218
men, that went out to war by b 2Chr 26:11 1416
The Chaldeans made out three b Job 1:17 7218
Pleiades, or loose the b of Orion Job 38:31 4189
hath loosed the b of the wild ass Job 39:5 4147
Let us break their b asunder Ps 2:3 4147
For there are no b in their death Ps 73:4 2784
death, and brake their b in sunder Ps 107:14 4147
The b of the wicked have robbed Ps 119:61 2256
go they forth all of them by b Prov 30:27 2683
snares and nets, and her hands as b Eccl 7:26 612
lest your b be made strong Is 28:22 4147
thyself from the b of thy neck Is 52:2 4147
to loose the b of wickedness, to Is 58:6 2784
broken thy yoke, and burst thy b Jer 2:20 4147
they shall put b upon thee Eze 3:25 5688
behold, I will lay b upon thee Eze 4:8 5688
him to help him, and all his b Eze 12:14 102
all his b shall fall by the sword Eze 17:21 102
I have broken the b of their yoke Eze 34:27 4133
Gomer, and all his b Eze 38:6 102
the north quarters, and all his b Eze 38:6 102
the land, thou, and all thy b Eze 38:9 102
will rain upon him, and upon his b Eze 38:22 102
of Israel, thou, and all thy b Eze 39:4 102
cords of a man, with b of love Hos 11:4 5688
Beauty, and the other I called B Zec 11:7 2256
asunder mine other staff, even B Zec 11:14 2256
and he brake the b, and was driven Lk 8:29 *1199*
and every one's b were loosed Acts 16:26 *1199*
Jews, he loosed him from his b Acts 22:30 *1199*
the sea, and loosed the rudder b Acts 27:40 *2202*
b having nourishment ministered, Col 2:19 *4886*

BANI *(ba'-ni)* {15}
1. A "mighty man" of David.
of Nathan of Zobah, B the Gadite, 2Sa 23:36 1137
2. A Levite descendant of Merari.
The son of Amzi, the son of B 1Chr 6:46 1137
3. A descendant of Pharez.
the son of Imri, the son of B 1Chr 9:4 1137
4. A family of exiles.
The children of B, six hundred Ezr 2:10 1137
And of the sons of B Ezr 10:29 1137
5. Father whose sons married foreign wives.
Of the sons of B Ezr 10:34 1137
6. A Jewish descendant of a foreign woman.
And B, and Binnui, Shimei, Ezr 10:38 1137
7. Father of Rehum.
the Levites, Rehum the son of B Neh 3:17 1137
Also Jeshua, and B, and Sherebiah, Neh 8:7 1137
of the Levites, Jeshua, and B Neh 9:4 1137
Levites, Jeshua, and Kadmiel, B Neh 9:5 1137
8. A priest who assisted Ezra.
Shebaniah, Bunni, Sherebiah, B Neh 9:4 1137
Hodijah, B, Beninu Neh 10:13 1137
9. An Israelite who renewed the covenant under Nehemiah.
Pahath-moab, Elam, Zatthu, B Neh 10:14 1137
10. A family of exiles.
Jerusalem was Uzzi the son of B Neh 11:22 1137

BANISHED {2}
doth not fetch home again his b 2Sa 14:13 5080
that his b be not expelled from 2Sa 14:14 5080

BANISHMENT {2}
whether it be unto death, or to b Ezr 7:26 8331
thee false burdens and causes of b Lam 2:14 4065

BANK {14}
I stood upon the b of the river Gen 41:17 8193
which is by the b of the river Deut 4:48 8193
which is upon the b of the river Josh 12:2 8193
that is upon the b of the river Josh 13:9 8193
that is on the b of the river Josh 13:16 8193
they cast up a b against the city 2Sa 20:15 5550
back, and stood by the b of Jordan 2Kin 2:13 8193
shield, nor cast a b against it 2Kin 19:32 5550
shields, nor cast a b against it Is 37:33 5550
at the b of the river were very Eze 47:7 8193
by the river upon the b thereof Eze 47:12 8193
this side of the b of the river Dan 12:5 8193
that side of the b of the river Dan 12:5 8193
not thou my money into the b Lk 19:23 *5132*

BANKS {5}
all his b all the time of harvest Josh 3:15 1415
place, and flowed over all his b Josh 4:18 1415
when it had overflown all his b 1Chr 12:15 1428
channels, and go over all his b Is 8:7 1415
man's voice between the b of Ulai Dan 8:16

BANNER {3}
Thou hast given a b to them that Ps 60:4 5251
house, and his b over me was love Song 2:4 1714
Lift ye up a b upon the high Is 13:2 5251

BANNERS {3}
of our God we will set up our b Ps 20:5 1713
terrible as an army with b Song 6:4 1713
and terrible as an army with b Song 6:10 1713

BANQUET {14}
b that I have prepared for him Est 5:4 4960
Haman came to the b that Esther Est 5:5 4960
said unto Esther at the b of wine Est 5:6 4960
Haman come to the b that I shall Est 5:8 4960
the b that she had prepared but Est 5:12 4960
merrily with the king unto the b Est 5:14 4960
the b that Esther had prepared Est 6:14 4960
Haman came to b with Esther the Est 7:1 8354
the second day at the b of wine Est 7:2 4960
the king arising from the b of Est 7:7 4960
into the place of the b of wine Est 7:8 4960
the companions make a b of him Job 41:6 3738
his lords, came into the b house Dan 5:10 4961
the b of them that stretched Amos 6:7 4797

BANQUETING {1}
He brought me to the b house Song 2:4 3196

BANQUETINGS {1}
excess of wine, revellings, b 1Pet 4:3 *4224*

BAPTISM {22}
and Sadducees come to his b Mt 3:7 *908*
the b that I am baptized with Mt 20:22 *908*
be baptized with the b that I am Mt 20:23 *908*
The b of John, whence was it Mt 21:25 *908*
preach the b of repentance for Mk 1:4 *908*
be baptized with the b that I am Mk 10:38 *908*
with the b that I am baptized Mk 10:39 *908*
The b of John, was it from heaven Mk 11:30 *908*
preaching the b of repentance for Lk 3:3 *908*
being baptized with the b of John Lk 7:29 *908*
But I have a b to be baptized Lk 12:50 *908*
The b of John, was it from heaven Lk 20:4 *908*
Beginning from the b of John Acts 1:22 *908*
after the b which John preached Acts 10:37 *908*
preached before his coming the b Acts 13:24 *908*
Lord, knowing only the b of John Acts 18:25 *908*
And they said, Unto John's b Acts 19:3 *908*
baptized with the b of repentance Acts 19:4 *908*
buried with him by b into death Rom 6:4 *908*
One Lord, one faith, one b Eph 4:5 *908*
Buried with him in b, wherein Col 2:12 *908*
b doth also now save us (not the 1Pet 3:21 *908*

BAPTISMS {1}
Of the doctrine of b, and of Heb 6:2 *909*

BAPTIST *(bap'-tist)* {14} See BAPTIST'S. *John, the fore-runner of Jesus.*
In those days came John the B Mt 3:1 *910*
risen a greater than John the B Mt 11:11 *910*
from the days of John the B until Mt 11:12 *910*
his servants, This is John the B Mt 14:2 *910*
Some say that thou art John the B Mt 16:14 *910*
he spake unto them of John the B Mt 17:13 *910*
That John the B was risen from Mk 6:14 *907*
she said, The head of John the B Mk 6:24 *910*
a charger the head of John the B Mk 6:25 *910*
And they answered, John the B Mk 8:28 *910*
John B hath sent us unto thee, Lk 7:20 *910*
a greater prophet than John the B Lk 7:28 *910*
For John the B came neither Lk 7:33 *910*
They answering said, John the B Lk 9:19 *910*

BAPTIST'S *(bap'-tists)* {1}
me here John B head in a charger Mt 14:8 *910*

BAPTIZE {9}
I indeed b you with water unto Mt 3:11 *907*
he shall b you with the Holy Mt 3:11 *907*
John did b in the wilderness, and Mk 1:4 *907*
but he shall b you with the Holy Mk 1:8 *907*
I indeed b you with water Lk 3:16 *907*
he shall b you with the Holy Lk 3:16 *907*
them, saying, I b with water Jn 1:26 *907*
he that sent me to b with water Jn 1:33 *907*
For Christ sent me not to b 1Cor 1:17 *907*

BAPTIZED {61}
And were b of him in Jordan, Mt 3:6 *907*
Jordan unto John, to be b of him Mt 3:13 *907*
I have need to be b of thee Mt 3:14 *907*
And Jesus, when he was b, went up Mt 3:16 *907*
b with the baptism that I am b Mt 20:22 *907*
b with the baptism that I am b Mt 20:23 *907*
were all b of him in the river of Mk 1:5 *907*
I indeed have b you with water Mk 1:8 *907*

and was *b* of John in Jordan ... Mk 1:9 *907*
b with the baptism that I am *b* ... Mk 10:38 *907*
am *b* withal shall ye be *b* ... Mk 10:39 *907*
believeth and is *b* shall be saved ... Mk 16:16 *907*
that came forth to be *b* of him ... Lk 3:7 *907*
Then came also publicans to be *b* ... Lk 3:12 *907*
Now when all the people were *b* ... Lk 3:21 *907*
to pass, that Jesus also being *b* ... Lk 3:21 *907*
being *b* with the baptism of John ... Lk 7:29 *907*
themselves, being not *b* of him ... Lk 7:30 *907*
But I have a baptism to be *b* with ... Lk 12:50 *907*
there he tarried with them, and *b* ... Jn 3:22 *907*
and they came, and were *b* ... Jn 3:23 *907*
b more disciples than John, ... Jn 4:1 *907*
(Though Jesus himself *b* not ... Jn 4:2 *907*
the place where John at first *b* ... Jn 10:40 *907*
For John truly *b* with water ... Acts 1:5 *907*
but ye shall be *b* with the Holy ... Acts 1:5 *907*
be *b* every one of you in the name ... Acts 2:38 *907*
gladly received his word were *b* ... Acts 2:41 *907*
name of Jesus Christ, they were *b* ... Acts 8:12 *907*
and when he was *b*, he continued ... Acts 8:13 *907*
only they were *b* in the name of ... Acts 8:16 *907*
what doth hinder me to be *b* ... Acts 8:36 *907*
and he *b* him ... Acts 8:38 *907*
forthwith, and arose, and was *b* ... Acts 9:18 *907*
water, that these should not be *b* ... Acts 10:47 *907*
to be *b* in the name of the Lord ... Acts 10:48 *907*
he said, John indeed *b* with water ... Acts 11:16 *907*
but ye shall be *b* with the Holy ... Acts 11:16 *907*
And when she was *b*, and her ... Acts 16:15 *907*
and was *b*, he and all his, ... Acts 16:33 *907*
hearing believed, and were *b* ... Acts 18:8 *907*
them, Unto what then were ye *b* ... Acts 19:3 *907*
John verily *b* with the baptism of ... Acts 19:4 *907*
they were *b* in the name of the ... Acts 19:5 *907*
arise, and be *b*, and wash away thy ... Acts 22:16 *907*
that so many of us as were *b* into ... Rom 6:3 *907*
Christ were *b* into his death ... Rom 6:3 *907*
or were ye *b* in the name of Paul ... 1Cor 1:13 *907*
I thank God that I *b* none of you ... 1Cor 1:14 *907*
say that I had *b* in mine own name ... 1Cor 1:15 *907*
I *b* also the household of ... 1Cor 1:16 *907*
I know not whether I *b* any other ... 1Cor 1:16 *907*
were all *b* into Moses in the ... 1Cor 10:2 *907*
Spirit are we all *b* into one body ... 1Cor 12:13 *907*
they do which are *b* for the dead ... 1Cor 15:29 *907*
why are they then *b* for the dead ... 1Cor 15:29 *907*
b into Christ have put on Christ ... Gal 3:27 *907*

BAPTIZEST {1}
Why *b* thou then, if thou be not ... Jn 1:25 *907*

BAPTIZETH {2}
is he which *b* with the Holy Ghost ... Jn 1:33 *907*
witness, behold, the same *b* ... Jn 3:26 *907*

BAPTIZING {4}
b them in the name of the Father, ... Mt 28:19 *907*
beyond Jordan, where John was *b* ... Jn 1:28 *907*
therefore am I come *b* with water ... Jn 1:31 *907*
John also was *b* in Aenon near to ... Jn 3:23 *907*

BAR {7}
the middle *b* in the midst of the ... Ex 26:28 1280
he made the middle *b* to shoot ... Ex 36:33 1280
skins, and shall put it upon a *b* ... Num 4:10 4132
skins, and shall put them on a *b* ... Num 4:12 4132
posts, and went away with them, *b* ... Judg 16:3 1280
them shut the doors, and *b* them ... Neh 7:3 270
will break also the *b* of Damascus ... Amos 1:5 1280

BARABBAS *(ba-rab'-bas)* {11} *A criminal released instead of Jesus.*
then a notable prisoner, called *B* ... Mt 27:16 *912*
B, or Jesus which is called ... Mt 27:17 *912*
multitude that they should ask *B* ... Mt 27:20 *912*
They said, *B* ... Mt 27:21 *912*
Then released he *B* unto them ... Mt 27:26 *912*
And there was one named *B*, which ... Mk 15:7 *912*
should rather release *B* unto them ... Mk 15:11 *912*
people, released *B* unto them, and ... Mk 15:15 *912*
this man, and release unto us *B* ... Lk 23:18 *912*
saying, Not this man, but *B* ... Jn 18:40 *912*
Now *B* was a robber ... Jn 18:40 *912*

BARACHEL *(bar'-ak-el)* {2} *Father of Elihu.*
of Elihu the son of *B* the Buzite ... Job 32:2 1292
Elihu the son of *B* the Buzite ... Job 32:6 1292

BARACHIAH See BARACHIAS.

BARACHIAS *(bar'-ak-i'-as)* {1} *Father of Zachariah.*
the blood of Zacharias son of *B* ... Mt 23:35 *914*

BARAK *(ba'-rak)* {14} *A captain in Deborah's army.*
called *B* the son of Abinoam out ... Judg 4:6 1301
B said unto her, If thou wilt go ... Judg 4:8 1301
arose, and went with *B* to Kedesh ... Judg 4:9 1301
B called Zebulun and Naphtali to ... Judg 4:10 1301
they shewed Sisera that *B* the son ... Judg 4:12 1301
And Deborah said unto *B*, Up ... Judg 4:14 1301
So *B* went down from mount Tabor, ... Judg 4:14 1301
the edge of the sword before *B* ... Judg 4:15 1301
But *B* pursued after the chariots, ... Judg 4:16 1301
as *B* pursued Sisera, Jael came ... Judg 4:22 1301
B the son of Abinoam on that day, ... Judg 5:1 1301
arise, *B*, and lead thy captivity ... Judg 5:12 1301
even Issachar, and also *B* ... Judg 5:15 1301
me to tell of Gedeon, and of *B* ... Heb 11:32 *913*

BARAKEL See BARACHEL.

BARBARIAN {3}
be unto him that speaketh a *b* ... 1Cor 14:11 *915*
speaketh shall be a *b* unto me ... 1Cor 14:11 *915*
nor uncircumcision, *B*, Scythian, ... Col 3:11 *915*

BARBARIANS {2}
when the *b* saw the venomous beast ... Acts 28:4 *915*
both to the Greeks, and to the *B* ... Rom 1:14 *915*

BARBAROUS {1}
the *b* people shewed us no little ... Acts 28:2 *915*

BARBED {1}
thou fill his skin with *b* irons ... Job 41:7 7905

BARBER'S {1}
sharp knife, take thee a *b* razor ... Eze 5:1 1532

BARE {186}
b Cain, and said, I have gotten a ... Gen 4:1 3205
she again *b* his brother Abel ... Gen 4:2 3205
and she conceived, and *b* Enoch ... Gen 4:17 3205
And Adah *b* Jabal ... Gen 4:20 3205
she also *b* Tubal-cain, an ... Gen 4:22 3205
she *b* a son, and called his name ... Gen 4:25 3205
they *b* children to them, the same ... Gen 6:4 3205
b up the ark, and it was lift up ... Gen 7:17 5375
Abram's wife *b* him no children ... Gen 16:1 3205
And Hagar *b* Abram a son ... Gen 16:15 3205
his son's name, which Hagar *b* ... Gen 16:15 3205
when Hagar *b* Ishmael to Abram ... Gen 16:16 3205
And the firstborn *b* a son, and ... Gen 19:37 3205
And the younger, she also *b* a son ... Gen 19:38 3205
and they *b* children ... Gen 20:17 3205
b Abraham a son in his old age, ... Gen 21:2 3205
unto him, whom Sarah *b* to him ... Gen 21:3 3205
she *b* also Tebah, and Gaham, and ... Gen 22:24 3205
of Milcah, which she *b* unto Nahor ... Gen 24:24 3205
Sarah my master's wife *b* a son to ... Gen 24:36 3205
son, whom Milcah *b* unto him ... Gen 24:47 3205
she *b* him Zimran, and Jokshan, and ... Gen 25:2 3205
Sarah's handmaid, *b* unto Abraham ... Gen 25:12 3205
years old when she *b* them ... Gen 25:26 3205
b a son, and she called his name ... Gen 29:32 3205
she conceived again, and *b* a son ... Gen 29:33 3205
she conceived again, and *b* a son ... Gen 29:34 3205
she conceived again, and *b* a son ... Gen 29:35 3205
saw that she *b* Jacob no children ... Gen 30:1 3205
conceived, and *b* Jacob a son ... Gen 30:5 3205
again, and *b* Jacob a second son ... Gen 30:7 3205
Zilpah Leah's maid *b* Jacob a son ... Gen 30:10 3205
Leah's maid *b* Jacob a second son ... Gen 30:12 3205
and *b* Jacob the fifth son ... Gen 30:17 3205
again, and *b* Jacob the sixth son ... Gen 30:19 3205
And afterwards she *b* a daughter ... Gen 30:21 3205
And she conceived, and *b* a son ... Gen 30:23 3205
then all the cattle *b* speckled ... Gen 31:8 3205
then *b* all the cattle ringstraked ... Gen 31:8 3205
I *b* the loss of it ... Gen 31:39 2398
which she *b* unto Jacob, went out ... Gen 34:1 3205
And Adah *b* to Esau Eliphaz ... Gen 36:4 3205
and Bashemath *b* Reuel ... Gen 36:4 3205
And Aholibamah *b* Jeush, and Jaalam, ... Gen 36:5 3205
and she *b* to Eliphaz Amalek ... Gen 36:12 3205
she *b* to Esau Jeush, and Jaalam, ... Gen 36:14 3205
And she conceived, and *b* a son ... Gen 38:3 3205
she conceived again, and *b* a son ... Gen 38:4 3205
yet again conceived, and *b* a son ... Gen 38:5 3205
he was at Chezib, when she *b* him ... Gen 38:5 3205
priest of On *b* unto him ... Gen 41:50 3205
know that my wife *b* me two sons ... Gen 44:27 3205
which she *b* unto Jacob in ... Gen 46:15 3205
these she *b* unto Jacob, even ... Gen 46:18 3205
priest of On *b* unto him ... Gen 46:20 3205
and she *b* these unto Jacob ... Gen 46:25 3205
the woman conceived, and *b* a son ... Ex 2:2 3205
she *b* him a son, and he called his ... Ex 2:22 3205
and she *b* him Aaron and Moses ... Ex 6:20 3205
she *b* him Nadab, and Abihu, ... Ex 6:23 3205
and she *b* him Phinehas ... Ex 6:25 3205
how I *b* you on eagles' wings, and ... Ex 19:4 5375
shall be rent, and his head *b* ... Lev 13:45 6544
whether it be *b* within or without ... Lev 13:55 7146
they *b* it between two upon a ... Num 13:23 5375
whom her mother *b* to Levi in ... Num 26:59 3205
she *b* unto Amram Aaron and Moses, ... Num 26:59 3205
how that the LORD thy God *b* thee ... Deut 1:31 5375
which *b* the ark of the covenant ... Deut 31:9 5375
which *b* the ark of the covenant ... Deut 31:25 5375
as they that *b* the ark were come ... Josh 3:15 5375
the feet of the priests that *b* ... Josh 3:15 5375
the priests that *b* the ark of the ... Josh 3:17 5375
b the ark of the covenant stood ... Josh 4:9 5375
For the priests which *b* the ark ... Josh 4:10 5375
when the priests that *b* the ark ... Josh 4:18 5375
which *b* the ark of the covenant ... Josh 8:33 5375
the people that *b* the present ... Judg 3:18 5375
she also *b* him a son, whose name ... Judg 8:31 3205
And Gilead's wife *b* him sons ... Judg 11:2 3205
and his wife was barren, and *b* not ... Judg 13:2 3205
And the woman *b* a son, and called ... Judg 13:24 3205
Pharez, whom Tamar *b* unto Judah ... Ruth 4:12 3205
her conception, and she *b* a son ... Ruth 4:13 3205
had conceived, that she *b* a son ... 1Sa 1:20 3205
b three sons and two daughters ... 1Sa 2:21 3205
the young man that *b* his armour ... 1Sa 14:1 5375
the young man that *b* his armour ... 1Sa 14:6 5375
the man that *b* the shield went ... 1Sa 17:41 5375
that when they that *b* the ark of ... 2Sa 6:13 5375
became his wife, and *b* him a son ... 2Sa 11:27 3205
that Uriah's wife *b* unto David ... 2Sa 12:15 3205
she *b* a son, and he called his ... 2Sa 12:24 3205
ten young men that *b* Joab's ... 2Sa 18:15 5375
whom she *b* unto Saul, Armoni and ... 2Sa 21:8 3205
his mother *b* him after Absalom ... 1Kin 1:6
and ten thousand that *b* burdens ... 1Kin 5:15 5375
which *b* rule over the people that ... 1Kin 9:23 7287
train, with camels that *b* spices ... 1Kin 10:2 5375
Tahpenes *b* him Genubath his son ... 1Kin 11:20 3205
the LORD, that the guard *b* them ... 1Kin 14:28 5375
b a son at that season that ... 2Kin 4:17 3205
and they *b* them before him ... 2Kin 5:23 5375
she *b* Zimran, and Jokshan, and ... 1Chr 1:32 3205
his daughter in law *b* him Pharez ... 1Chr 2:4 3205
And Abigail *b* Amasa ... 1Chr 2:17 3205
unto him Ephrath, which *b* him Hur ... 1Chr 2:19 3205
and she *b* him Segub ... 1Chr 2:21 3205
then Abiah Hezron's wife *b* him ... 1Chr 2:24 3205
she *b* him Ahban, and Molid ... 1Chr 2:29 3205
and she *b* him Attai ... 1Chr 2:35 3205
b Haran, and Moza, and Gazez ... 1Chr 2:46 3205
concubine, *b* Sheber, and Tirhanah ... 1Chr 2:48 3205
She *b* also Shaaph the father of ... 1Chr 2:49 3205
Naarah *b* him Ahuzam, and Hepher, ... 1Chr 4:6 3205
Because I *b* him with sorrow ... 1Chr 4:9 3205
she *b* Miriam, and Shammai, and ... 1Chr 4:17 2029
his wife Jehudijah *b* Jered the ... 1Chr 4:18 3205
Ashriel, whom she *b* ... 1Chr 7:14 3205
b Machir the father of Gilead ... 1Chr 7:14 3205
the wife of Machir *b* a son ... 1Chr 7:16 3205
And his sister Hammoleketh *b* Ishod ... 1Chr 7:18 3205
b a son, and he called his name ... 1Chr 7:23 3205
children of Judah that *b* shield ... 1Chr 12:24 5375
b the ark of God upon their ... 1Chr 15:15 5375
God helped the Levites that *b* the ... 1Chr 15:26 5375
and all the Levites that *b* the ark ... 1Chr 15:27 5375
that *b* rule over the people ... 2Chr 8:10 7287
company, and camels that *b* spices ... 2Chr 9:1 5375
Which *b* him children ... 2Chr 11:19 3205
which *b* him Abijah, and Attai, and ... 2Chr 11:20 3205
had an army of men that *b* targets ... 2Chr 14:8 5375
that *b* shields and drew bows, two ... 2Chr 14:8 5375
the wall, and they that *b* burdens ... Neh 4:17 5375
even their servants *b* rule over ... Neh 5:15 7980
and bitterness to her that *b* him ... Prov 17:25 3205
she that *b* thee shall rejoice ... Prov 23:25 3205
the choice one of her that *b* her ... Song 6:9 3205
brought thee forth that *b* thee ... Song 8:5 3205
and she conceived, and *b* a son ... Is 8:3 3205
Elam *b* the quiver with chariots ... Is 22:6 5375
strip you, and make you *b*, and gird ... Is 32:11 6209
make *b* the leg, uncover the thigh ... Is 47:2 2834
father, and unto Sarah that *b* you ... Is 51:2 2342
The LORD hath made *b* his holy arm ... Is 52:10 2834
he *b* the sin of many, and made ... Is 53:12 5375
he *b* them, and carried them all ... Is 63:9 5190
discovered, and thy heels made *b* ... Jer 13:22 2554
their mothers that *b* them ... Jer 16:3 3205
wherein my mother *b* me be blessed ... Jer 20:14 3205
out, and thy mother that *b* thee ... Jer 22:26 3205
But I have made Esau *b*, I have ... Jer 49:10 2834
she that *b* you shall be ashamed ... Jer 50:12 3205
I *b* it upon my shoulder in their ... Eze 12:7 5375
whereas thou wast naked and *b* ... Eze 16:7 6181
youth, when thou wast naked and *b* ... Eze 16:22 6181
jewels, and leave thee naked and *b* ... Eze 16:39 6181
the sceptres of them that *b* rule ... Eze 19:11 4910
and they were mine, and they *b* sons ... Eze 23:4 3205
and shall leave thee naked and *b* ... Eze 23:29 6181
their sons, whom they *b* unto me ... Eze 23:37 3205
which conceived, and *b* him a son ... Hos 1:3 3205
conceived again, and *b* a daughter ... Hos 1:6 3205
she conceived, and *b* a son ... Hos 1:8 3205
he hath made it clean *b*, and cast ... Joel 1:7 2834
infirmities, and *b* our sicknesses ... Mt 8:17 *941*
For many *b* false witness against ... Mk 14:56 *5576*
b false witness against him, ... Mk 14:57 *5576*
all *b* him witness, and wondered at ... Lk 4:22 *3140*
they that *b* him stood still ... Lk 7:14 *941*
up, and *b* fruit an hundredfold ... Lk 8:8 *4160*
Blessed is the womb that *b* thee ... Lk 11:27 *941*
barren, and the wombs that never *b* ... Lk 23:29 *1080*
John *b* witness of him, and cried, ... Jn 1:15 *3140*
John *b* record, saying, I saw the ... Jn 1:32 *3140*
b record that this is the Son of ... Jn 1:34 *3140*
And they *b* it ... Jn 2:8 *5342*
he *b* witness unto the truth ... Jn 5:33 *3140*
bag, and *b* what was put therein ... Jn 12:6 *941*
him from the dead, *b* record ... Jn 12:17 *3140*
And he that saw it *b* record ... Jn 19:35 *3140*
b them witness, giving them the ... Acts 15:8 *3140*
but *b* grain, it may chance of ... 1Cor 15:37 *1131*
Who his own self *b* our sins in ... 1Pet 2:24 *399*
Who *b* record of the word of God, ... Rev 1:2 *3140*
which *b* twelve manner of fruits, ... Rev 22:2 *4160*

BAREFOOT {4}
his head covered, and he went *b* ... 2Sa 15:30 3182
And he did so, walking naked and *b* ... Is 20:2 3182
b three years for a sign and ... Is 20:3 3182
young and old, naked and *b* ... Is 20:4 3182

BAREST {3}
because thou *b* the ark of the ... 1Kin 2:26 5375
thou never *b* rule over them ... Is 63:19 4910
Jordan, to whom thou *b* witness ... Jn 3:26 *3140*

BARHUMITE *(bar'-hu-mite)* {1} See BAHARUMITE. *A form of Baharumite.*
the Arbathite, Azmaveth the *B* ... 2Sa 23:31 1273

BARIAH *(ba-ri'-ah)* {1} *Grandson of Shechaniah.*
Hattush, and Igeal, and *B*, and 1Chr 3:22 1282

BAR-JESUS *(bar-je'-sus)* {1} See ELYMAS. *Another name of Elymas.*
prophet, a Jew, whose name was *B*......... Acts 13:6 *919*

BAR-JONA *(bar-jo'-nah)* {1} See SIMON. *Another name of Simon Peter.*
him, Blessed art thou, Simon *B* .... Mt 16:17 *920*

BAR-JONAH See BAR-JONA.

BARK {1}
are all dumb dogs, they cannot *b*........... Is 56:10 5024

BARKED {1}
my vine waste, and *b* my fig tree............. Joel 1:7 7111

BARKOS *(bar'-cos)* {2} *A family who returned from the exile.*
The children of *B*, the children .... Ezr 2:53 1302
The children of *B*, the children .... Neh 7:55 1302

BARLEY {37}
And the flax and the *b* was smitten .... Ex 9:31 8184
for the *b* was in the ear, and the............. Ex 9:31 8184
a homer of *b* seed shall be valued .... Lev 27:16 8184
tenth part of an ephah of *b* meal............ Num 5:15 8184
A land of wheat, and *b*, and vines,.......... Deut 8:8 8184
a cake of *b* bread tumbled into .... Judg 7:13 8184
in the beginning of *b* harvest .... Ruth 1:22 8184
and it was about an ephah of *b*.............. Ruth 2:17 8184
glean unto the end of *b* harvest.............. Ruth 2:23 8184
he winnoweth *b* to night in the............... Ruth 3:2 8184
it, he measured six measures of *b* .... Ruth 3:15 8184
six measures of *b* gave he me .... Ruth 3:17 8184
is near mine, and he hath *b* there............ 2Sa 14:30 8184
earthen vessels, and wheat, and *b*........... 2Sa 17:28 8184
in the beginning of *b* harvest 2Sa 21:9 8184
B also and straw for the horses and......... 1Kin 4:28 8184
firstfruits, twenty loaves of *b* 2Kin 4:42 8184
and two measures of *b* for a shekel 2Kin 7:1 8184
and two measures of *b* for a shekel.......... 2Kin 7:16 8184
Two measures of *b* for a shekel............... 2Kin 7:18 8184
was a parcel of ground full of *b*............. 1Chr 11:13 8184
and twenty thousand measures of *b*........ 2Chr 2:10 8184
Now therefore the wheat, and the *b*......... 2Chr 2:15 8184
of wheat, and ten thousand of *b*............. 2Chr 27:5 8184
of wheat, and cockle instead of *b*........... Job 31:40 8184
wheat and the appointed *b* and the .... Is 28:25 8184
in the field, of wheat, and of *b*............. Jer 41:8 8184
thou also unto thee wheat, and *b*............ Eze 4:9 8184
And thou shalt eat it as *b* cakes .... Eze 4:12 8184
among my people for handfuls of *b*.......... Eze 13:19 8184
part of an ephah of an homer of *b* .... Eze 45:13 8184
of *b*, and an half homer of *b*................ Hos 3:2 8184
for the wheat and for the *b* .... Joel 1:11 8184
here, which hath five *b* loaves................ Jn 6:9 *2916*
fragments of the five *b* loaves................ Jn 6:13 *2916*
three measures of *b* for a penny .... Rev 6:6 *2915*

BARN {4}
thy seed, and gather it into thy *b* .... Job 39:12 1637
Is the seed yet in the *b*........................ Hag 2:19 4035
but gather the wheat into my *b* .... Mt 13:30 *596*
neither have storehouse nor *b* .... Lk 12:24 *596*

BARNABAS *(bar'-na-bas)* {29} See JOSES. *A companion of Paul.*
by the apostles was surnamed *B*............. Acts 4:36 *921*
But *B* took him, and brought him to........ Acts 9:27 *921*
and they sent forth *B*, that he .... Acts 11:22 *921*
Then departed *B* to Tarsus..................... Acts 11:25 *921*
to the elders by the hands of *B* .... Acts 11:30 *921*
And *B* and Saul returned from .... Acts 12:25 *921*
as *B*, and Simeon that was called .... Acts 13:1 *921*
Holy Ghost said, Separate me *B* .... Acts 13:2 *921*
who called for *B* and Saul, and............... Acts 13:7 *921*
proselytes followed Paul and *B*.............. Acts 13:43 *921*
B waxed bold, and said, It was.............. Acts 13:46 *921*
persecution against Paul and *B* .... Acts 13:50 *921*
And they called *B*, Jupiter .... Acts 14:12 *921*
Which when the apostles, *B*................... Acts 14:14 *921*
day he departed with *B* to Derbe............. Acts 14:20 *921*
B had no small dissension and................ Acts 15:2 *921*
they determined that Paul and *B* .... Acts 15:2 *921*
silence, and gave audience to *B* .... Acts 15:12 *921*
company to Antioch with Paul and *B*..... Acts 15:22 *921*
men unto you with our beloved *B*........... Acts 15:25 *921*
B continued in Antioch, teaching........... Acts 15:35 *921*
some days after Paul said unto *B*........... Acts 15:36 *921*
B determined to take with them .... Acts 15:37 *921*
so *B* took Mark, and sailed unto............. Acts 15:39 *921*
Or I only and *B*, have not we power........ 1Cor 9:6 *921*
went up again to Jerusalem with *B*.......... Gal 2:1 *921*
B the right hands of fellowship .... Gal 2:9 *921*
insomuch that *B* also was carried........... Gal 2:13 *921*
you, and Marcus, sister's son to *B*.......... Col 4:10 *921*

BARNFLOOR {1}
out of the *b*, or out of the 2Kin 6:27 1637

BARNS {4}
So shall thy *b* be filled with.................... Prov 3:10 618
desolate, the *b* are broken down.............. Joel 1:17 4460
do they reap, nor gather into *b*.............. Mt 6:26 *596*
I will pull down my *b*, and build............ Lk 12:18 *596*

BARREL {3}
but an handful of meal in a *b*................ 1Kin 17:12 3537
The *b* of meal shall not waste,................ 1Kin 17:14 3537
the *b* of meal wasted not, neither........... 1Kin 17:16 3537

BARRELS {1}
Fill four *b* with water, and pour............. 1Kin 18:33 3537

BARREN {23}
But Sarai was *b* .... Gen 11:30 6135
for his wife, because she was *b* .... Gen 25:21 6135
but Rachel was *b* .... Gen 29:31 6135
cast their young, nor be *b*...................... Ex 23:26 6135
not be male or female *b* among you .... Deut 7:14 6135
and his wife was *b*, and bare not............. Judg 13:2 6135
unto her, Behold now, thou art *b*............ Judg 13:3 6135
so that the *b* hath born seven.................. 1Sa 2:5 6135
water is naught, and the ground *b*.......... 2Kin 2:19 7921
thence any more death or *b* land............ 2Kin 2:21 7921
entreateth the *b* that beareth not .... Job 24:21 6135
and the *b* land his dwellings .... Job 39:6 4420
He maketh the *b* woman to keep.............. Ps 113:9 6135
and the *b* womb .... Prov 30:16 6115
twins, and none is *b* among them............ Song 4:2 7909
and there is not one *b* among them......... Song 6:6 7909
Sing, O *b*, thou that didst not................. Is 54:1 6135
and will drive him into a land *b*.............. Joel 2:20 6723
because that Elisabeth was *b* .... Lk 1:7 *4722*
month with her, who was called *b*........... Lk 1:36 *4722*
they shall say, Blessed are the *b* .... Lk 23:29 *4722*
Rejoice, thou *b* that bearest not .... Gal 4:27 *4722*
you that ye shall neither be *b*................ 2Pet 1:8 *692*

BARRENNESS {1}
A fruitful land into *b*, for the.................. Ps 107:34 4420

BARS {38}
thou shalt make *b* of shittim wood.......... Ex 26:26 1280
five *b* for the boards of the..................... Ex 26:27 1280
five *b* for the boards of the side .... Ex 26:27 1280
of gold for places for the *b* .... Ex 26:29 1280
shalt overlay the *b* with gold.................. Ex 26:29 1280
his taches, and his boards, his *b*............. Ex 35:11 1280
he made *b* of shittim wood...................... Ex 36:31 1280
five *b* for the boards of the..................... Ex 36:32 1280
five *b* for the boards of the..................... Ex 36:32 1280
b, and overlaid the *b* with gold .... Ex 36:34 1280
his taches, his boards, his *b*................... Ex 39:33 1280
thereof, and put in the *b* thereof .... Ex 40:18 1280
the *b* thereof, and the pillars.................. Num 3:36 1280
the *b* thereof, and the pillars.................. Num 4:31 1280
with high walls, gates, and *b*................. Deut 3:5 1280
into a town that hath gates and *b* 1Sa 23:7 1280
cities with walls and brasen *b*................ 1Kin 4:13 1280
cities, with walls, gates, and *b* 2Chr 8:5 1280
walls, and towers, gates, and *b*.............. 2Chr 14:7 1280
locks thereof, and the *b* thereof.............. Neh 3:3 1280
locks thereof, and the *b* thereof.............. Neh 3:6 1280
the *b* thereof, and a thousand .... Neh 3:13 1280
locks thereof, and the *b* thereof.............. Neh 3:14 1280
the *b* thereof, and the wall of the............ Neh 3:15 1280
shall go down to the *b* of the pit .... Job 17:16 905
for it my decreed place, and set *b* .... Job 38:10 1280
his bones are like *b* of iron .... Job 40:18 4800
cut the *b* of iron in sunder..................... Ps 107:16 1280
strengthened the *b* of thy gates .... Ps 147:13 1280
are like the *b* of a castle .... Prov 18:19 1280
and cut in sunder the *b* of iron................ Is 45:2 1280
which have neither gates nor *b* .... Jer 49:31 1280
her *b* are broken .... Jer 51:30 1280
he hath destroyed and broken her *b*........ Lam 2:9 1280
and having neither *b* nor gates................ Eze 38:11 1280
the earth with her *b* was about me .... Jonah 2:6 1280
the fire shall devour thy *b* .... Nah 3:13 1280

BARSABAS *(bar'-sab-as)* {2} See JOSEPH, JUDAS, JUSTUS.
1. The successor of Judas as apostle.
appointed two, Joseph called *B*.............. Acts 1:23 *923*
2. A disciple sent to Antioch with Silas.
namely, Judas surnamed *B*, and .... Acts 15:22 *923*

BARSABBAS See BARSABAS.

BARTHOLOMEW *(bar-thol'-o-mew)* {4} See NATHANAEL. *One of Jesus' twelve disciples.*
Philip, and *B*; Thomas, and..................... Mt 10:3 *918*
And Andrew, and Philip, and *B* .... Mk 3:18 *918*
James and John, Philip and *B*................. Lk 6:14 *918*
and Andrew, Philip, and Thomas, *B* .... Acts 1:13 *918*

BARTIMAEUS *(bar-ti-me'-us)* {1} *A blind beggar.*
a great number of people, blind *B* .... Mk 10:46 *924*

BARUCH *(ba'-rook)* {26}
1. A son of Zabbai.
After him *B* the son of Zabbai................. Neh 3:20 1263
Daniel, Ginnethon, *B*,........................... Neh 10:6 1263
2. A descendant of Perez.
And Maaseiah the son of *B*, the son........ Neh 11:5 1263
3. The scribe of Jeremiah.
purchase unto *B* the son of Neriah .... Jer 32:12 1263
I charged *B* before them, saying,............ Jer 32:13 1263
purchase unto *B* the son of Neriah .... Jer 32:16 1263
called *B* the son of Neriah .... Jer 36:4 1263
B wrote from the mouth of .... Jer 36:4 1263
And Jeremiah commanded *B*, saying, ... Jer 36:5 1263
B the son of Neriah did according........... Jer 36:8 1263
Then read *B* in the book the words.......... Jer 36:10 1263
when *B* read the book in the ears .... Jer 36:13 1263
the son of Cushi, unto *B*........................ Jer 36:14 1263
So *B* the son of Neriah took the.............. Jer 36:14 1263
So *B* read it in their ears........................ Jer 36:15 1263
both one and other, and said unto *B*....... Jer 36:16 1263
And they asked *B*, saying, Tell us .... Jer 36:17 1263
Then *B* answered them, He .... Jer 36:18 1263
Then said the princes unto *B* .... Jer 36:19 1263
to take *B* the scribe and Jeremiah........... Jer 36:26 1263
the words which *B* wrote at the.............. Jer 36:27 1263
roll, and gave it to *B* the scribe.............. Jer 36:32 1263
But *B* the son of Neriah setteth .... Jer 43:3 1263
prophet, and *B* the son of Neriah............ Jer 43:6 1263
spake unto *B* the son of Neriah............... Jer 45:1 1263
the God of Israel, unto thee, O *B* .... Jer 45:2 1263

BARZILLAI *(bar-zil'-la-i)* {12}
1. A friend of David.
B the Gileadite of Rogelim,...................... 2Sa 17:27 1271
B the Gileadite came down from 2Sa 19:31 1271
Now *B* was a very aged man, even............ 2Sa 19:32 1271
And the king said unto *B*, Come 2Sa 19:33 1271
B said unto the king, How long 2Sa 19:34 1271
was come over, the king kissed *B*........... 2Sa 19:39 1271
unto the sons of *B* the Gileadite 1Kin 2:7 1271
of Koz, the children of *B* .... Ezr 2:61 1271
the daughters of *B* the Gileadite.............. Ezr 2:61 1271
of Koz, the children of *B*......................... Neh 7:63 1271
of *B* the Gileadite to wife......................... Neh 7:63 1271
2. Husband of Merab.
the son of *B* the Meholathite.................... 2Sa 21:8 1271

BASE {18}
will be *b* in mine own sight...................... 2Sa 6:22 8217
cubits was the length of one *b*................. 1Kin 7:27 4350
the ledges there was a *b* above 1Kin 7:29 3653
every *b* had four brasen wheels,.............. 1Kin 7:30 4350
was round after the work of the *b*........... 1Kin 7:31 3653
the wheels were joined to the *b*.............. 1Kin 7:32 4350
to the four corners of one *b* 1Kin 7:34 4350
were of the very *b* itself.......................... 1Kin 7:34 4350
in the top of the *b* was there a 1Kin 7:35 4350
on the top of the *b* the ledges.................. 1Kin 7:35 4350
of fools, yea, children of *b* men .... Job 30:8 1097,8034
the *b* against the honourable................... Is 3:5 7034
That the kingdom might be *b*.................. Eze 17:14 8217
they shall be there a *b* kingdom............... Eze 29:14 8217
and set there upon her own *b*................. Zec 5:11 4369
and *b* before all the people,..................... Mal 2:9 8217
b things of the world, and things 1Cor 1:28 *36*
who in presence am *b* among you 2Cor 10:1 *5011*

BASEMATH See BASMATH.

BASER {1}
lewd fellows of the *b* sort .... Acts 17:5 *60*

BASES {16}
And he made ten *b* of brass.................... 1Kin 7:27 4350
the work of the *b* was on this................. 1Kin 7:28 4350
this manner he made the ten *b*............... 1Kin 7:37 4350
every one of the ten *b* one laver 1Kin 7:38 4350
he put five *b* on the right side 1Kin 7:39 4350
ten *b*, and ten lavers on the *b* 1Kin 7:43 4350
Ahaz cut off the borders of the *b* 2Kin 16:17 4350
the house of the LORD, and the *b* 2Kin 25:13 4350
the *b* which Solomon had made for 2Kin 25:16 4350
b, and lavers made he upon the *b*........... 2Chr 4:14 4350
And they set the altar upon his *b*........... Ezr 3:3 4350
the sea, and concerning the *b*................. Jer 27:19 4369
the house of the LORD, and the *b* .... Jer 52:17 4350
bulls that were under the *b* .... Jer 52:20 4350

BASEST {2}
It shall be the *b* of the kingdoms .... Eze 29:15 8217
setteth up over it the *b* of men .... Dan 4:17 8215

BASHAN *(ba'-shan)* {59} See BASHAN-HAVOTH-JAIR. *Kingdom of King Og.*
turned and went up by the way of *B* .... Num 21:33 1316
Og the king of *B* went out against .... Num 21:33 1316
and the kingdom of Og king of *B*............ Num 32:33 1316
in Heshbon, and Og the king of *B*........... Deut 1:4 1316
turned, and went up the way to *B* .... Deut 3:1 1316
Og the king of *B* came out against.......... Deut 3:1 1316
our hands Og also, the king of *B* .... Deut 3:3 1316
of Argob, the kingdom of Og in *B*........... Deut 3:4 1316
plain, and all Gilead, and all *B*.............. Deut 3:10 1316
cities of the kingdom of Og in *B*............ Deut 3:10 1316
For only Og king of *B* remained of.......... Deut 3:11 1316
And the rest of Gilead, and all *B* .... Deut 3:13 1316
the region of Argob, with all *B* .... Deut 3:13 1316
and Golan in *B*, of the Manassites........... Deut 4:43 1316
land, and the land of Og king of *B* .... Deut 4:47 1316
of Heshbon, and Og the king of *B*........... Deut 29:7 1316
lambs, and rams of the breed of *B*.......... Deut 32:14 1316
he shall leap from *B*............................. Deut 33:22 1316
of Heshbon, and to Og king of *B* .... Josh 9:10 1316
And the coast of Og king of *B*................. Josh 12:4 1316
Hermon, and in Salcah, and in all *B* .... Josh 12:5 1316
Hermon, and all *B* unto Salcah............... Josh 13:11 1316
All the kingdom of Og in *B*.................... Josh 13:12 1316
coast was from Mahanaim, all *B*............. Josh 13:30 1316
all the kingdom of Og king of *B* .... Josh 13:30 1316
the towns of Jair, which are in *B* .... Josh 13:30 1316
cities of the kingdom of Og in *B*............ Josh 13:31 1316
war, therefore he had Gilead and *B*......... Josh 17:1 1316
beside the land of Gilead and *B*.............. Josh 17:5 1316
Golan in *B* out of the tribe of .... Josh 20:8 1316
the half tribe of Manasseh in *B* .... Josh 21:6 1316
gave Golan in *B* with her suburbs .... Josh 21:27 1316
Moses had given possession in *B*............ Josh 22:7 1316
region of Argob, which is in *B* 1Kin 4:13 1316
the Amorites, and of Og king of *B*.......... 1Kin 4:19 1316
the river Arnon, even Gilead and *B* 2Kin 10:33 1316
in the land of *B* unto Salchah................. 1Chr 5:11 1316
next, and Jaanai, and Shaphat in *B*........ 1Chr 5:12 1316
And they dwelt in Gilead in *B* 1Chr 5:16 1316
increased from *B* unto Baal-hermon........ 1Chr 5:23 1316
out of the tribe of Manasseh in *B* 1Chr 6:62 1316
Golan in *B* with her suburbs, and............ 1Chr 6:71 1316
and the land of Og king of *B* .... Neh 9:22 1316
strong bulls of *B* have beset me .... Ps 22:12 1316

hill of God is as the hill of *B* ... Ps 68:15 1316
an high hill as the hill of *B* ... Ps 68:15 1316
said, I will bring again from *B* ... Ps 68:22 1316
of the Amorites, and Og king of *B* ... Ps 135:11 1316
And Og the king of *B* ... Ps 136:20 1316
up, and upon all the oaks of *B* ... Is 2:13 1316
and *B* and Carmel shake off their ... Is 33:9 1316
and lift up thy voice in *B* ... Jer 22:20 1316
and he shall feed on Carmel and *B* ... Jer 50:19 1316
Of the oaks of *B* have they made ... Eze 27:6 1316
all of them fatlings of *B* ... Eze 39:18 1316
Hear this word, ye kine of *B* ... Amos 4:1 1316
let them feed in *B* and Gilead, as ... Mic 7:14 1316
B languisheth, and Carmel, and the ... Nah 1:4 1316
howl, O ye oaks of *B* ... Zec 11:2 1316

BASHAN-HAVOTH-JAIR *(ba'-shan-ha'-voth-ja'-ur)* {1} *Same as Argob.*
them after his own name, *B* ... Deut 3:14 1316,2334

BASHEMATH *(bash'-e-math)* {6} See BASMATH.
1. Daughter of Elon the Hittite.
B the daughter of Elon the ... Gen 26:34 1315
2. Daughter of Ishmael.
B Ishmael's daughter, sister of ... Gen 36:3 1315
and *B* bare Reuel ... Gen 36:4 1315
the son of *B* the wife of Esau ... Gen 36:10 1315
were the sons of *B* Esau's wife ... Gen 36:13 1315
are the sons of *B* Esau's wife ... Gen 36:17 1315

BASKET {23}
in the uppermost *b* there was of ... Gen 40:17 5536
them out of the *b* upon my head ... Gen 40:17 5536
b, and bring them in the *b* ... Ex 29:3 5536
one wafer out of the *b* of the ... Ex 29:23 5536
and the bread that is in the *b* ... Ex 29:32 5536
rams, and a *b* of unleavened bread ... Lev 8:2 5536
out of the *b* of unleavened bread, ... Lev 8:26 5536
that is in the *b* of consecrations ... Lev 8:31 5536
a *b* of unleavened bread, cakes of ... Num 6:15 5536
with the *b* of unleavened bread ... Num 6:17 5536
one unleavened cake out of the *b* ... Num 6:19 5536
thee, and shalt put it in a *b* ... Deut 26:2 2935
take the *b* out of thine hand ... Deut 26:4 2935
Blessed shall be thy *b* and thy ... Deut 28:5 2935
Cursed shall be thy *b* and thy ... Deut 28:17 2935
the flesh he put in a *b*, and he ... Judg 6:19 5536
One *b* had very good figs, even ... Jer 24:2 1731
the other *b* had very naughty figs ... Jer 24:2 1731
behold a *b* of summer fruit ... Amos 8:1 3619
And I said, A *b* of summer fruit ... Amos 8:2 3619
let him down by the wall in a *b* ... Acts 9:25 *4711*
through a window in a *b* was I let ... 2Cor 11:33 *4553*

BASKETS {15}
I had three white *b* on my head ... Gen 40:16 5536
The three *b* are three days ... Gen 40:18 5536
persons, and put their heads in *b* ... 2Kin 10:7 1731
as a grapegatherer into the *b* ... Jer 6:9 5552
two *b* of figs were set before the ... Jer 24:1 1736
that remained twelve *b* full ... Mt 14:20 *2894*
meat that was left seven *b* full ... Mt 15:37 *4711*
and how many *b* ye took up ... Mt 16:9 *2894*
and how many *b* ye took up ... Mt 16:10 *4711*
they took up twelve *b* full of the ... Mk 6:43 *2894*
broken meat that was left seven *b* ... Mk 8:8 *4711*
how many *b* full of fragments took ... Mk 8:19 *2894*
how many *b* full of fragments took ... Mk 8:20 *4711*
that remained to them twelve *b* ... Lk 9:17 *2894*
and filled twelve *b* with the ... Jn 6:13 *2894*

BASMATH *(bas'-math)* {1} See BASHEMATH. *A daughter of Solomon.*
he also took *B* the daughter of ... 1Kin 4:15 1315

BASON {5}
it in the blood that is in the *b* ... Ex 12:22 5592
with the blood that is in the *b* ... Ex 12:22 5592
gave gold by weight for every *b* ... 1Chr 28:17 3713
by weight for every *b* of silver ... 1Chr 28:17 3713
that he poureth water into a *b* ... Jn 13:5 *3537*

BASONS {18}
half of the blood, and put it in *b* ... Ex 24:6 101
ashes, and his shovels, and his *b* ... Ex 27:3 4219
pots, and the shovels, and the *b* ... Ex 38:3 4219
and the shovels, and the *b* ... Num 4:14 4219
Brought beds, and *b*, and earthen ... 2Sa 17:28 5592
lavers, and the shovels, and the *b* ... 1Kin 7:40 4219
pots, and the shovels, and the *b* ... 1Kin 7:45 4219
bowls, and the snuffers, and the *b* ... 1Kin 7:50 4219
LORD bowls of silver, snuffers, *b* ... 2Kin 12:13 4219
for the golden *b* he gave gold by ... 1Chr 28:17 3713
And he made an hundred *b* of gold ... 2Chr 4:8 4219
pots, and the shovels, and the *b* ... 2Chr 4:11 4219
And the snuffers, and the *b* ... 2Chr 4:22 4219
Thirty *b* of gold, silver *b* ... Ezr 1:10 3713
Also twenty *b* of gold, of a ... Ezr 8:27 3713
a thousand drams of gold, fifty *b* ... Neh 7:70 4219
And the *b*, and the firepans, and the ... Jer 52:19 5592

BASTARD {2}
A *b* shall not enter into the ... Deut 23:2 4464
a *b* shall dwell in Ashdod, and I ... Zec 9:6 4464

BASTARDS {1}
all are partakers, then are ye *b* ... Heb 12:8 *3541*

BAT {2}
kind, and the lapwing, and the *b* ... Lev 11:19 5847
kind, and the lapwing, and the *b* ... Deut 14:18 5847

BATH {6}
of vineyard shall yield one *b* ... Is 5:10 1324
and a just ephah, and a just *b* ... Eze 45:10 1324
the *b* shall be of one measure, ... Eze 45:11 1324
that the *b* may contain the tenth ... Eze 45:11 1324
the *b* of oil, ye shall offer the ... Eze 45:14 1324
tenth part of a *b* out of the cor ... Eze 45:14 1324

BATHE {18}
b himself in water, and be unclean ... Lev 15:5 7364
b himself in water, and be unclean ... Lev 15:6 7364
b himself in water, and be unclean ... Lev 15:7 7364
b himself in water, and be unclean ... Lev 15:8 7364
b himself in water, and be unclean ... Lev 15:10 7364
b himself in water, and be unclean ... Lev 15:11 7364
b his flesh in running water, and ... Lev 15:13 7364
they shall both *b* themselves in ... Lev 15:18 7364
b himself in water, and be unclean ... Lev 15:21 7364
b himself in water, and be unclean ... Lev 15:22 7364
b himself in water, and be unclean ... Lev 15:27 7364
and *b* his flesh in water, and ... Lev 16:26 7364
and *b* his flesh in water, and ... Lev 16:28 7364
b himself in water, and be unclean ... Lev 17:15 7364
he wash them not, nor *b* his flesh ... Lev 17:16 7364
he shall *b* his flesh in water, and ... Num 19:7 7364
b his flesh in water, and shall be ... Num 19:8 7364
b himself in water, and shall be ... Num 19:19 7364

BATHED {1}
For my sword shall be *b* in heaven ... Is 34:5 7301

BATH-RABBIM *(bath-rab'-bim)* {1} *A gate at Heshbon.*
in Heshbon, by the gate of *B* ... Song 7:4 1337

BATHS {9}
it contained two thousand *b* ... 1Kin 7:26 1324
one laver contained forty *b* ... 1Kin 7:38 1324
and twenty thousand *b* of wine ... 2Chr 2:10 1324
and twenty thousand *b* of oil ... 2Chr 2:10 1324
received and held three thousand *b* ... 2Chr 4:5 1324
wheat, and to an hundred *b* of wine ... Ezr 7:22 1325
and to an hundred *b* of oil ... Ezr 7:22 1324
cor, which is an homer of ten *b* ... Eze 45:14 1324
for ten *b* are an homer ... Eze 45:14 1324

BATH-SHEBA *(bath-she'-bah)* {11} See BATH-SHUA. *A wife of David.*
And one said, Is not this *B* ... 2Sa 11:3 1339
And David comforted *B* his wife ... 2Sa 12:24 1339
unto *B* the mother of Solomon ... 1Kin 1:11 1339
B went in unto the king into the ... 1Kin 1:15 1339
B bowed, and did obeisance unto ... 1Kin 1:16 1339
David answered and said, Call me *B* ... 1Kin 1:28 1339
Then *B* bowed with her face to the ... 1Kin 1:31 1339
came to *B* the mother of Solomon ... 1Kin 2:13 1339
And *B* said, Well ... 1Kin 2:18 1339
B therefore went unto king ... 1Kin 2:19 1339
him, after he had gone in to *B* ... Ps 51:*t* 1339

BATH-SHUA *(bath'-shu-ah)* {1} See BATH-SHEBA. *A form of Bath-sheba.*
of *B* the daughter of Ammiel ... 1Chr 3:5 1340

BATS {1}
worship, to the moles and to the *b* ... Is 2:20 5847

BATTERED {1}
that were with Joab *b* the wall ... 2Sa 20:15 7843

BATTERING {2}
set *b* rams against it round about ... Eze 4:2
to appoint *b* rams against the ... Eze 21:22

BATTLE {170}
they joined *b* with them in the ... Gen 14:8 4421
all his people, to the *b* at Edrei ... Num 21:33 4421
which came from the *b* ... Num 31:14 6635,4421
men of war which went to the *b* ... Num 31:21 4421
war upon them, who went out to *b* ... Num 31:27 6635
men of war which went out to *b* ... Num 31:28 6635
for war, before the LORD to *b* ... Num 32:27 4421
over Jordan, every man armed to *b* ... Num 32:29 4421
neither contend with them in *b* ... Deut 2:9 4421
it, and contend with him in *b* ... Deut 2:24 4421
and all his people, to *b* at Edrei ... Deut 3:1 4421
out to *b* against thine enemies ... Deut 20:1 4421
when ye are come nigh unto the *b* ... Deut 20:2 4421
day unto *b* against your enemies ... Deut 20:3 4421
his house, lest he die in the *b* ... Deut 20:5 4421
his house, lest he die in the *b* ... Deut 20:6 4421
his house, lest he die in the *b* ... Deut 20:7 4421
came out against us unto *b* ... Deut 29:7 4421
over before the LORD unto *b* ... Josh 4:13 4421
city went out against Israel to *b* ... Josh 8:14 4421
all other they took in *b* ... Josh 11:19 4421
should come against Israel in *b* ... Josh 11:20 4421
intend to go up against them in *b* ... Josh 22:33 6635
from *b* before the sun was up ... Judg 8:13 4421
to go out to *b* against the ... Judg 20:14 4421
to the *b* against the children of ... Judg 20:18 4421
went out to *b* against Benjamin ... Judg 20:20 4421
set their *b* again in array in the ... Judg 20:22 4421
Shall I go up again to *b* against ... Judg 20:23 4421
out to *b* against the children of ... Judg 20:28 4421
of all Israel, and the *b* was sore ... Judg 20:34 4421
men of Israel retired in the *b* ... Judg 20:39 4421
down before us, as in the first *b* ... Judg 20:39 4421
but the *b* overtook them ... Judg 20:42 4421
out against the Philistines to *b* ... 1Sa 4:1 4421
and when they joined *b*, Israel was ... 1Sa 4:2 4421
drew near to *b* against Israel ... 1Sa 7:10 4421
it came to pass in the day of *b* ... 1Sa 13:22 4421
themselves, and they came to the *b* ... 1Sa 14:20 4421
followed hard after them in the *b* ... 1Sa 14:22 4421
the *b* passed over unto Beth-aven ... 1Sa 14:23 4421
together their armies to *b* ... 1Sa 17:1 4421
set the *b* in array against the ... 1Sa 17:2 4421
come out to set your *b* in array ... 1Sa 17:8 4421
went and followed Saul to the *b* ... 1Sa 17:13 4421
the *b* were Eliab the first born ... 1Sa 17:13 4421
the fight, and shouted for the *b* ... 1Sa 17:20 4421
had put the *b* in array, army ... 1Sa 17:21
down that thou mightest see the *b* ... 1Sa 17:28 4421
for the *b* is the LORD's, and he ... 1Sa 17:47 4421
or he shall descend into *b* ... 1Sa 26:10 4421
thou shalt go out with me to *b* ... 1Sa 28:1 4264
let him not go down with us to *b* ... 1Sa 29:4 4421
lest in the *b* he be an adversary ... 1Sa 29:4 4421
shall not go up with us to the *b* ... 1Sa 29:9 4421
part is that goeth down to the *b* ... 1Sa 30:24 4421
the *b* went sore against Saul, and ... 1Sa 31:3 4421
the people are fled from the *b* ... 2Sa 1:4 4421
fallen in the midst of the *b* ... 2Sa 1:25 4421
there was a very sore *b* that day ... 2Sa 2:17 4421
brother Asahel at Gibeon in the *b* ... 2Sa 3:30 4421
put the *b* in array at the ... 2Sa 10:8 4221
of the *b* was against him before ... 2Sa 10:9 4421
unto the *b* against the Syrians ... 2Sa 10:13 4421
the time when kings go forth to *b* ... 2Sa 11:1
in the forefront of the hottest *b* ... 2Sa 11:15 4421
make thy *b* more strong against ... 2Sa 11:25 4421
that thou go to *b* in thine own ... 2Sa 17:11 7128
the *b* was in the wood of Ephraim ... 2Sa 18:6 4421
For the *b* was there scattered ... 2Sa 18:8 4421
steal away when they flee in *b* ... 2Sa 19:3 4421
we anointed over us, is dead in *b* ... 2Sa 19:10 4421
shalt go no more out with us to *b* ... 2Sa 21:17 4421
that there was again a *b* with the ... 2Sa 21:18 4421
there was again a *b* in Gob with ... 2Sa 21:19 4421
And there was yet a *b* in Gath ... 2Sa 21:20 4421
hast girded me with strength to *b* ... 2Sa 22:40 4421
were there gathered together to *b* ... 2Sa 23:9 4421
go out to *b* against their enemy ... 1Kin 8:44 4421
he said, Who shall order the *b* ... 1Kin 20:14 4421
the seventh day the *b* was joined ... 1Kin 20:29 4421
went out into the midst of the *b* ... 1Kin 20:39 4421
go with me to *b* to Ramoth-gilead ... 1Kin 22:4 4421
I go against Ramoth-gilead to *b* ... 1Kin 22:6 4421
we go against Ramoth-gilead to *b* ... 1Kin 22:15 4421
myself, and enter into the *b* ... 1Kin 22:30 4421
himself, and went into the *b* ... 1Kin 22:30 4421
And the *b* increased that day ... 1Kin 22:35 4421
thou go with me against Moab to *b* ... 2Kin 3:7 4421
that the *b* was too sore for him ... 2Kin 3:26 4421
for they cried to God in the *b* ... 1Chr 5:20 4421
fit to go out for war and *b* ... 1Chr 7:11 4421
to *b* was twenty and six thousand ... 1Chr 7:40 4421
the *b* went sore against Saul, and ... 1Chr 10:3 4421
were gathered together to *b* ... 1Chr 11:13 4421
and men of war fit for the *b* ... 1Chr 12:8 4421
the Philistines against Saul to *b* ... 1Chr 12:19 4421
Zebulun, such as went forth to *b* ... 1Chr 12:33 6635
of Asher, such as went forth to *b* ... 1Chr 12:36 6635
of instruments of war for the *b* ... 1Chr 12:37 4421
that then thou shalt go out to *b* ... 1Chr 14:15 4421
from their cities, and came to *b* ... 1Chr 19:7 4421
put the *b* in array before the ... 1Chr 19:9 4421
the *b* was set against him before ... 1Chr 19:10 4421
before the Syrians unto the *b* ... 1Chr 19:14 4421
set the *b* in array against them ... 1Chr 19:17
So when David had put the *b* in ... 1Chr 19:17 4421
the time that kings go out to *b* ... 1Chr 20:1
Abijah set the *b* in array with an ... 2Chr 13:3 4421
Jeroboam also set the *b* in array ... 2Chr 13:3 4421
the *b* was before and behind ... 2Chr 13:14 4421
they set the *b* in array in the ... 2Chr 14:10 4421
Shall we go to Ramoth-gilead to *b* ... 2Chr 18:5 4421
shall we go to Ramoth-gilead to *b* ... 2Chr 18:14 4421
myself, and will go to the *b* ... 2Chr 18:29 4421
and they went to the *b* ... 2Chr 18:29 4421
And the *b* increased that day ... 2Chr 18:34 4421
came against Jehoshaphat to *b* ... 2Chr 20:1 4421
for the *b* is not yours, but God's ... 2Chr 20:15 4421
shall not need to fight in this *b* ... 2Chr 20:17
go, do it, be strong for the *b* ... 2Chr 25:8 4421
they should not go with him to *b* ... 2Chr 25:13 4421
him, as a king ready to the *b* ... Job 15:24 3593
of trouble, against the day of *b* ... Job 38:23 7128
and he smelleth the *b* afar off ... Job 39:25 4421
hand upon him, remember the *b* ... Job 41:8 4421
me with strength unto the *b* ... Ps 18:39 4421
and mighty, the LORD mighty in *b* ... Ps 24:8 4421
from the *b* that was against me ... Ps 55:18 7128
shield, and the sword, and the *b* ... Ps 76:3 4421
bows, turned back in the day of *b* ... Ps 78:9 7128
not made him to stand in the *b* ... Ps 89:43 4421
covered my head in the day of *b* ... Ps 140:7 5402
is prepared against the day of *b* ... Prov 21:31 4421
nor the *b* to the strong, neither ... Eccl 9:11 4421
For every *b* of the warrior is ... Is 9:5 5430
hosts mustereth the host of the *b* ... Is 13:4 4421
with the sword, nor dead in *b* ... Is 22:2 4421
briers and thorns against me in *b* ... Is 27:4 4421
them that turn the *b* to the gate ... Is 28:6 4421
his anger, and the strength of *b* ... Is 42:25 4421
as the horse rusheth into the *b* ... Jer 8:6 4421
men be slain by the sword in *b* ... Jer 18:21 4421
and shield, and draw near to *b* ... Jer 46:3 4421
against her, and rise up to the *b* ... Jer 49:14 4421
A sound of *b* is in the land, and ... Jer 50:22 4421
put in array, like a man to the *b* ... Jer 50:42 4421
Thou art my *b* ax and weapons of ... Jer 51:20 4661
but none goeth to the *b* ... Eze 7:14 4421
in the *b* in the day of the LORD ... Eze 13:5 4421
neither in anger, nor in *b* ... Dan 11:20 4421

stirred up to *b* with a very great ... Dan 11:25 4421
by bow, nor by sword, nor by *b* ... Hos 1:7 4421
the *b* out of the earth, and will ... Hos 2:18 4421
the *b* in Gibeah against the ... Hos 10:9 4421
Beth-arbel in the day of *b* ... Hos 10:14 4421
as a strong people set in *b* array ... Joel 2:5 4421
with shouting in the day of *b* ... Amos 1:14 4421
let us rise up against her in *b* ... Obad 1 4421
the *b* bow shall be cut off ... Zec 9:10 4421
them as his goodly horse in the *b* ... Zec 10:3 4421
the nail, out of him the *b* bow ... Zec 10:4 4421
the mire of the streets in the *b* ... Zec 10:5 4421
nations against Jerusalem to *b* ... Zec 14:2 4421
as when he fought in the day of *b* ... Zec 14:3 7128
shall prepare himself to the *b* ... 1Cor 14:8 *4171*
like unto horses prepared unto *b* ... Rev 9:7 *4171*
of many horses running to *b* ... Rev 9:9 *4171*
to gather them to the *b* of that ... Rev 16:14 *4171*
to gather them together to *b* ... Rev 20:8 *4171*

BATTLEMENT {1}
thou shalt make a *b* for thy roof ... Deut 22:8 4624

BATTLEMENTS {1}
take away her *b* ... Jer 5:10 5189

BATTLES {6}
go out before us, and fight our *b* ... 1Sa 8:20 4421
for me, and fight the LORD's *b* ... 1Sa 18:17 4421
lord fighteth the *b* of the LORD ... 1Sa 25:28 4421
Out of the spoils won in *b* did ... 1Chr 26:27 4421
God to help us, and to fight our *b* ... 2Chr 32:8 4421
in *b* of shaking will he fight ... Is 30:32 4421

BAVAI *(bav'-a-i)* {1} *A descendant of Henadad.*
B the son of Henadad, the ruler ... Neh 3:18 942

BAVVAI See BAVAI.

BAY {6}
from the *b* that looketh southward ... Josh 15:2 3956
the *b* of the sea at the uttermost ... Josh 15:5 3956
b of the salt sea at the south ... Josh 18:19 3956
himself like a green *b* tree ... Ps 37:35 249
chariot grisled and *b* horses ... Zec 6:3 554
the *b* went forth, and sought to go ... Zec 6:7 554

BAZLITH *(baz'-lith)* {1} See BAZLUTH. *A family who returned from exile.*
The children of *B*, the children ... Neh 7:54 1213

BAZLUTH *(baz'-luth)* {1} See BAZLITH. *A form of Bazlith.*
The children of *B*, the children ... Ezr 2:52 1213

BDELLIUM {2}
there is *b* and the onyx stone ... Gen 2:12 916
colour thereof as the colour of *b* ... Num 11:7 916

BE See APPENDIX.

BEACON {1}
till ye be left as a *b* upon the ... Is 30:17 8650

BEALIAH *(be-a-li'-ah)* {1} *A warrior in David's army.*
Eluzai, and Jerimoth, and *B*, ... 1Chr 12:5 1183

BEALOTH *(be'-a-loth)* {1} See ALOTH. *A city in Judah.*
Ziph, and Telem, and *B*, ... Josh 15:24 1175

BEAM {15}
went away with the pin of the *b* ... Judg 16:14 708
his spear was like a weaver's *b* ... 1Sa 17:7 4500
whose spear was like a weaver's *b* ... 2Sa 21:19 4500
the thick *b* were before them ... 1Kin 7:6 5646
and take thence every man a *b* ... 2Kin 6:2 6982
But as one was felling a *b* ... 2Kin 6:5 6982
was a spear like a weaver's *b* ... 1Chr 11:23 4500
spear staff was like a weaver's *b* ... 1Chr 20:5 4500
the *b* out of the timber shall ... Hab 2:11 3714
but considerest not the *b* that is ... Mt 7:3 *1385*
behold, a *b* is in thine own eye ... Mt 7:4 *1385*
first cast out the *b* out of thine ... Mt 7:5 *1385*
but perceivest not the *b* that is ... Lk 6:41 *1385*
the *b* that is in thine own eye ... Lk 6:42 *1385*
cast out first the *b* out of thine ... Lk 6:42 *1385*

BEAMS {12}
that the *b* should not be fastened ... 1Kin 6:6
and covered the house with *b* ... 1Kin 6:9 1356
hewed stone, and a row of cedar *b* ... 1Kin 6:36 3773
with cedar *b* upon the pillars ... 1Kin 7:2 3773
with cedar above upon the *b* ... 1Kin 7:3 6763
hewed stones, and a row of cedar *b* ... 1Kin 7:12 3773
He overlaid also the house, the *b* ... 2Chr 3:7 6982
b for the gates of the palace ... Neh 2:8 7136
who also laid the *b* thereof ... Neh 3:3 7136
they laid the *b* thereof, and set ... Neh 3:6 7136
Who layeth the *b* of his chambers ... Ps 104:3 7136
The *b* of our house are cedar, and ... Song 1:17 6982

BEANS {2}
and flour, and parched corn, and *b* ... 2Sa 17:28 6321
unto thee wheat, and barley, and *b* ... Eze 4:9 6321

BEAR {215}
is greater than I can *b* ... Gen 4:13 5375
the land was not able to *b* them ... Gen 13:6 5375
art with child, and shalt *b* a son ... Gen 16:11 3205
that is ninety years old, *b* ... Gen 17:17 3205
wife shall *b* thee a son indeed ... Gen 17:19 3205
which Sarah shall *b* unto thee at ... Gen 17:21 3205
Shall I of a surety *b* a child ... Gen 18:13 3205
these eight Milcah did *b* to Nahor ... Gen 22:23 3205
she shall *b* upon my knees, that I ... Gen 30:3 3205
b them because of their cattle ... Gen 36:7 5375
then let me *b* the blame for ever ... Gen 43:9 2398
then I shall *b* the blame to my ... Gen 44:32 2398
and bowed his shoulder to *b* ... Gen 49:15 5445
they shall *b* the burden with thee ... Ex 18:22 5375
Thou shalt not *b* false witness ... Ex 20:16 6030
of the staves to *b* the table ... Ex 25:27 5375
two sides of the altar, to *b* it ... Ex 27:7 5375
Aaron shall *b* their names before ... Ex 28:12 5375
Aaron shall *b* the names of the ... Ex 28:29 5375
Aaron shall *b* the judgment of the ... Ex 28:30 5375
that Aaron may *b* the iniquity of ... Ex 28:38 5375
that they *b* not iniquity, and die ... Ex 28:43 5375
for the staves to *b* it withal ... Ex 30:4 5375
sides of the ark, to *b* the ark ... Ex 37:5 5375
for the staves to *b* the table ... Ex 37:14 5375
them with gold, to *b* the table ... Ex 37:15 5375
for the staves to *b* it withal ... Ex 37:27 5375
of the altar, to *b* it withal ... Ex 38:7 5375
it, then he shall *b* his iniquity ... Lev 5:1 5375
guilty, and shall *b* his iniquity ... Lev 5:17 5375
eateth of it shall *b* his iniquity ... Lev 7:18 5375
it you to *b* the iniquity of the ... Lev 10:17 5375
But if she *b* a maid child, then ... Lev 12:5 3205
the goat shall *b* upon him all ... Lev 16:22 5375
then he shall *b* his iniquity ... Lev 17:16 5375
eateth it shall *b* his iniquity ... Lev 19:8 5375
nor *b* any grudge against the ... Lev 19:18 5201
he shall *b* his iniquity ... Lev 20:17 5375
they shall *b* their iniquity ... Lev 20:19 5375
they shall *b* their sin ... Lev 20:20 5375
lest they *b* sin for it, and die ... Lev 22:9 5375
Or suffer them to *b* the iniquity ... Lev 22:16 5375
curseth his God shall *b* his sin ... Lev 24:15 5375
they shall *b* the tabernacle, and ... Num 1:50 5375
sons of Kohath shall come to *b* it ... Num 4:15 5375
they shall *b* the curtains of the ... Num 4:25 5375
this woman shall *b* her iniquity ... Num 5:31 5375
should *b* upon their shoulders ... Num 7:9 5375
season, that man shall *b* his sin ... Num 9:13 5375
I am not able to *b* all this ... Num 11:14 5375
they shall *b* the burden of the ... Num 11:17 5375
that thou *b* it not thyself alone ... Num 11:17 5375
How long shall I *b* with this evil ... Num 14:27
b your whoredoms, until your ... Num 14:33 5375
shall ye *b* your iniquities, even ... Num 14:34 5375
b the iniquity of the sanctuary ... Num 18:1 5375
thy sons with thee shall *b* the ... Num 18:1 5375
the congregation, lest they *b* sin ... Num 18:22 5375
they shall *b* their iniquity ... Num 18:23 5375
ye shall *b* no sin by reason of it ... Num 18:32 5375
then he shall *b* her iniquity ... Num 30:15 5375
am not able to *b* you myself alone ... Deut 1:9 5375
I myself alone *b* your cumbrance ... Deut 1:12 5375
thee, as a man doth *b* his son ... Deut 1:31 5375
Neither shalt thou *b* false ... Deut 5:20 6030
to *b* the ark of the covenant of ... Deut 10:8 5375
her children which she shall *b* ... Deut 28:57 3205
that *b* the ark of the covenant ... Josh 3:8 5375
that *b* the ark of the LORD ... Josh 3:13 5375
that *b* the ark of the testimony ... Josh 4:16 5375
seven priests shall *b* before the ... Josh 6:4 5375
let seven priests *b* seven ... Josh 6:6 5375
thou shalt conceive, and *b* a son ... Judg 13:3 3205
thou shalt conceive, and *b* a son ... Judg 13:5 3205
thou shalt conceive, and *b* a son ... Judg 13:7 3205
to night, and should also *b* sons ... Ruth 1:12 3205
and there came a lion, and a *b* ... 1Sa 17:34 1677
slew both the lion and the *b* ... 1Sa 17:36 1677
lion, and out of the paw of the *b* ... 1Sa 17:37 1677
as a *b* robbed of her whelps in ... 2Sa 17:8 1677
b the king tidings, how that the ... 2Sa 18:19 1319
Thou shalt not *b* tidings this day ... 2Sa 18:20 1319
but thou shalt *b* tidings another ... 2Sa 18:20 1319
this day thou shalt *b* no tidings ... 2Sa 18:20 1319
it was not my son, which I did *b* ... 1Kin 3:21 3205
to *b* witness against him, saying, ... 1Kin 21:10 5749
which thou puttest on me will I *b* ... 2Kin 18:14 5375
root downward, and *b* fruit upward ... 2Kin 19:30 6213
men, men able to *b* buckler ... 1Chr 5:18 5375
and ten thousand men to *b* burdens ... 2Chr 2:2 5445
should *b* rule in his own house ... Est 1:22 8323
I *b* up the pillars of it ... Ps 75:3 8505
how I do *b* in my bosom the ... Ps 89:50 5375
They shall *b* thee up in their ... Ps 91:12 5375
scornest, thou alone shalt *b* it ... Prov 9:12 5375
hand of the diligent shall *b* rule ... Prov 12:24 4910
Let a *b* robbed of her whelps meet ... Prov 17:12 1677
but a wounded spirit who can *b* ... Prov 18:14 5375
As a roaring lion, and a ranging *b* ... Prov 28:15 1677
and for four which it cannot *b* ... Prov 30:21 5375
whereof every one *b* twins ... Song 4:2 8382
I am weary to *b* them ... Is 1:14 5375
b a son, and shall call his name ... Is 7:14 3205
And the cow and the *b* shall feed ... Is 11:7 1677
root downward, and *b* fruit upward ... Is 37:31 6213
I have made, and I will *b* ... Is 46:4 5375
They *b* him upon the shoulder, ... Is 46:7 5375
that *b* the vessels of the LORD ... Is 52:11 5375
for he shall *b* their iniquities ... Is 53:11 5445
O barren, thou that didst not *b* ... Is 54:1 5375
the priests *b* rule by their means ... Jer 5:31 7287
this is a grief, and I must *b* it ... Jer 10:19 5375
b no burden on the sabbath day, ... Jer 17:21 5375
not to *b* a burden, even entering ... Jer 17:27 5375
to husbands, that they may *b* sons ... Jer 29:6 3205
because I did *b* the reproach of ... Jer 31:19 5375
that the LORD could no longer *b* ... Jer 44:22 5375
was unto me as a *b* lying in wait ... Lam 3:10 1677
that he *b* the yoke in his youth ... Lam 3:27 5375
it thou shalt *b* their iniquity ... Eze 4:4 5375
so shalt thou *b* the iniquity of ... Eze 4:5 5375
thou shalt *b* the iniquity of the ... Eze 4:6 5375
thou *b* it upon thy shoulders ... Eze 12:6 5375
shall *b* upon his shoulder in the ... Eze 12:12 5375
they shall *b* the punishment of ... Eze 14:10 5375
b thine own shame for thy sins ... Eze 16:52 5375
b thy shame, in that thou hast ... Eze 16:52 5375
thou mayest *b* thine own shame ... Eze 16:54 5375
and that it might *b* fruit ... Eze 17:8 5375
b fruit, and be a goodly cedar ... Eze 17:23 6213
doth not the son *b* the iniquity ... Eze 18:19 5375
The son shall not *b* the iniquity ... Eze 18:20 5375
father *b* the iniquity of the son ... Eze 18:20 5375
therefore *b* thou also thy ... Eze 23:35 5375
ye shall *b* the sins of your idols ... Eze 23:49 5375
b their shame with them that go ... Eze 32:30 5375
neither *b* the shame of the ... Eze 34:29 5375
you, they shall *b* their shame ... Eze 36:7 5375
neither shalt thou *b* the reproach ... Eze 36:15 5375
they shall even *b* their iniquity ... Eze 44:10 5375
they shall *b* their iniquity ... Eze 44:12 5375
but they shall *b* their shame ... Eze 44:13 5375
that they *b* them not out into the ... Eze 46:20 3318
which shall *b* rule over all the ... Dan 2:39 7981
beast, a second, like to a *b* ... Dan 7:5 1678
dried up, they shall *b* no fruit ... Hos 9:16 6213
I will meet them as a *b* that is ... Hos 13:8 1677
flee from a lion, and a *b* met him ... Amos 5:19 1677
is not able to *b* all his words ... Amos 7:10 3557
therefore ye shall *b* the reproach ... Mic 6:16 5375
I will *b* the indignation of the ... Mic 7:9 5375
all they that *b* silver are cut ... Zeph 1:11 5187
If one *b* holy flesh in the skirt ... Hag 2:12 5375
me, Whither do these *b* the ephah ... Zec 5:10 3212
he shall *b* the glory, and shall ... Zec 6:13 5375
whose shoes I am not worthy to *b* ... Mt 3:11 *941*
their hands they shall *b* thee up ... Mt 4:6 *142*
Thou shalt not *b* false witness ... Mt 19:18 *5576*
him they compelled to *b* his cross ... Mt 27:32 *142*
Do not *b* false witness, Defraud ... Mk 10:19 *5576*
and Rufus, to *b* his cross ... Mk 15:21 *142*
wife Elisabeth shall *b* thee a son ... Lk 1:13 *1080*
their hands they shall *b* thee up ... Lk 4:11 *142*
Truly ye *b* witness that ye allow ... Lk 11:48 *3140*
And if it *b* fruit, well ... Lk 13:9 *4160*
And whosoever doth not *b* his cross, ... Lk 14:27 *941*
though he *b* long with them ... Lk 18:7 *3114*
Do not *b* false witness, Honour ... Lk 18:20 *5576*
that he might *b* it after Jesus ... Lk 23:26 *5342*
to *b* witness of the Light, that ... Jn 1:7 *3140*
but was sent to *b* witness of that ... Jn 1:8 *3140*
b unto the governor of the feast ... Jn 2:8 *5342*
Ye yourselves *b* me witness ... Jn 3:28 *3140*
If I *b* witness of myself, my ... Jn 5:31 *3140*
b witness of me, that the Father ... Jn 5:36 *3140*
Though I *b* record of myself, yet ... Jn 8:14 *3140*
I am one that *b* witness of myself ... Jn 8:18 *3140*
name, they *b* witness of me ... Jn 10:25 *3140*
branch cannot *b* fruit of itself ... Jn 15:4 *5342*
glorified, that ye *b* much fruit ... Jn 15:8 *5342*
And ye also shall *b* witness ... Jn 15:27 *3140*
you, but ye cannot *b* them now ... Jn 16:12 *941*
evil, *b* witness of the evil ... Jn 18:23 *3140*
that I should *b* witness unto the ... Jn 18:37 *3140*
to *b* my name before the Gentiles, ... Acts 9:15 *941*
our fathers nor we were able to *b* ... Acts 15:10 *941*
would that I should *b* with you ... Acts 18:14 *430*
the high priest doth *b* me witness ... Acts 22:5 *3140*
so must thou *b* witness also at ... Acts 23:11 *3140*
could not *b* up into the wind, we ... Acts 27:15 *503*
For I *b* them record that they ... Rom 10:2 *3140*
Thou shalt not *b* false witness ... Rom 13:9 *5576*
to *b* the infirmities of the weak ... Rom 15:1 *941*
hitherto ye were not able to *b* it ... 1Cor 3:2
that ye may be able to *b* it ... 1Cor 10:13 *5297*
we shall also *b* the image of the ... 1Cor 15:49 *5409*
I *b* record, yea, and beyond their ... 2Cor 8:3 *3140*
Would to God ye could *b* with me a ... 2Cor 11:1 *430*
and indeed *b* with me ... 2Cor 11:1 *430*
ye might well *b* with him ... 2Cor 11:4 *430*
for I *b* you record, that, if it ... Gal 4:15 *3140*
you shall *b* his judgment, ... Gal 5:10 *941*
B ye one another's burdens, and so ... Gal 6:2 *941*
every man shall *b* his own burden ... Gal 6:5 *941*
for I *b* in my body the marks of ... Gal 6:17 *941*
For I *b* him record, that he hath ... Col 4:13 *3140*
b children, guide the house, give ... 1Ti 5:14 *5041*
offered to *b* the sins of many ... Heb 9:28 *399*
my brethren, *b* olive berries ... Jas 3:12 *4160*
b witness, and shew unto you that ... 1Jn 1:2 *3140*
are three that *b* record in heaven ... 1Jn 5:7 *3140*
are three that *b* witness in earth ... 1Jn 5:8 *3140*
yea, and we also *b* record ... 3Jn 12
how thou canst not *b* them which ... Rev 2:2 *941*
his feet were as the feet of a *b* ... Rev 13:2 *715*

BEARD {16}
a plague upon the head or the *b* ... Lev 13:29 2206
even a leprosy upon the head or *b* ... Lev 13:30 2206
his hair off his head and his *b* ... Lev 14:9 2206
thou mar the corners of thy *b* ... Lev 19:27 2206
shave off the corner of their *b* ... Lev 21:5 2206
against me, I caught him by his *b* ... 1Sa 17:35 2206
his spittle fall down upon his *b* ... 1Sa 21:13 2206
his feet, nor trimmed his *b* ... 2Sa 19:24 8222
by the *b* with the right hand to ... 2Sa 20:9 2206
the hair of my head and of my *b* ... Ezr 9:3 2206
upon the *b*, even Aaron's *b* ... Ps 133:2 2206
and it shall also consume the *b* ... Is 7:20 2206

be baldness, and every *b* cut off ... Is 15:2 ... 2206
shall be bald, and every *b* clipped ... Jer 48:37 ... 2206
upon thine head and upon thy *b* ... Eze 5:1 ... 2206

BEARDS {4}
off the one half of their *b* ... 2Sa 10:4 ... 2206
at Jericho until your *b* be grown ... 2Sa 10:5 ... 2206
at Jericho until your *b* be grown ... 1Chr 19:5 ... 2206
men, having their *b* shaven ... Jer 41:5 ... 2206

BEARERS {3}
of them to be *b* of burdens ... 2Chr 2:18 ... 5449
they were over the *b* of burdens ... 2Chr 34:13 ... 5449
The strength of the *b* of burdens ... Neh 4:10 ... 5449

BEAREST {5}
now, thou art barren, and *b* not ... Judg 13:3 ... 3205
that thou *b* unto thy people ... Ps 106:4
him, Thou *b* record of thyself ... Jn 8:13 ... *3140*
thou *b* not the root, but the root ... Rom 11:18 ... *941*
Rejoice, thou barren that *b* not ... Gal 4:27 ... *5088*

BEARETH {25}
whosoever *b* ought of the carcase ... Lev 11:25 ... 5375
he that *b* the carcase of them ... Lev 11:28 ... 5375
he also that *b* the carcase of it ... Lev 11:40 ... 5375
he that *b* any of those things ... Lev 15:10 ... 5375
father *b* the sucking child ... Num 11:12 ... 5375
b shall succeed in the name of ... Deut 25:6 ... 3205
be among you a root that *b* gall ... Deut 29:18 ... 6509
that it is not sown, nor *b* ... Deut 29:23 ... 6779
taketh them, *b* them on her wings ... Deut 32:11 ... 5375
up in me *b* witness to my face ... Job 16:8 ... 6030
entreateth the barren that *b* not ... Job 24:21 ... 3205
A man that *b* false witness ... Prov 25:18 ... 6030
but when the wicked *b* rule ... Prov 29:2 ... 4910
whereof every one *b* twins ... Song 6:6 ... 8382
spring, for the tree *b* her fruit ... Joel 2:22 ... 5375
which also *b* fruit, and bringeth ... Mt 13:23 ... *2592*
is another that *b* witness of me ... Jn 5:32 ... *3140*
that sent me *b* witness of me ... Jn 8:18 ... *3140*
Every branch in me that *b* not ... Jn 15:2 ... *5342*
and every branch that *b* fruit ... Jn 15:2 ... *5342*
The Spirit itself *b* witness with ... Rom 8:16 ... *4828*
for he *b* not the sword in vain ... Rom 13:4 ... *5409*
B all things, believeth all ... 1Cor 13:7 ... *4722*
But that which *b* thorns and briers ... Heb 6:8 ... *1627*
it is the Spirit that *b* witness ... 1Jn 5:6 ... *3140*

BEARING {22}
have given you every herb *b* seed ... Gen 1:29 ... 2232
LORD hath restrained me from *b* ... Gen 16:2 ... 3205
his name Judah; and left *b* ... Gen 29:35 ... 3205
When Leah saw that she had left *b* ... Gen 30:9 ... 3205
with their camels *b* spicery ... Gen 37:25 ... 5375
set forward, *b* the tabernacle ... Num 10:17 ... 5375
set forward, *b* the sanctuary ... Num 10:21 ... 5375
and the priests the Levites *b* it ... Josh 3:3 ... 5375
the priests *b* the ark of the ... Josh 3:14 ... 5375
that the seven priests *b* the ... Josh 6:8 ... 5375
seven priests *b* seven trumpets of ... Josh 6:13 ... 5375
one *b* a shield went before him ... 1Sa 17:7 ... 5375
b the ark of the covenant of God ... 2Sa 15:24 ... 5375
b precious seed, shall doubtless ... Ps 126:6 ... 5375
you a man *b* a pitcher of water ... Mk 14:13 ... *941*
meet you, *b* a pitcher of water ... Lk 22:10 ... *941*
he *b* his cross went forth into a ... Jn 19:17 ... *941*
their conscience also *b* witness ... Rom 2:15 ... *4828*
my conscience also *b* me witness ... Rom 9:1 ... *4828*
Always *b* about in the body the ... 2Cor 4:10 ... *4064*
God also *b* them witness, both ... Heb 2:4 ... *4901*
without the camp, *b* his reproach ... Heb 13:13 ... *5342*

BEARS {2}
forth two she *b* out of the wood ... 2Kin 2:24 ... 1677
We roar all like *b*, and mourn sore ... Is 59:11 ... 1677

BEAST {182}
b of the earth after his kind ... Gen 1:24 ... 2416
God made the *b* of the earth after ... Gen 1:25 ... 2416
to every *b* of the earth, and to ... Gen 1:30 ... 2416
God formed every *b* of the field ... Gen 2:19 ... 2416
air, and to every *b* of the field ... Gen 2:20 ... 2416
was more subtil than any *b* of the ... Gen 3:1 ... 2416
above every *b* of the field ... Gen 3:14 ... 2416
both man, and *b*, and the creeping ... Gen 6:7 ... 929
Of every clean *b* thou shalt take ... Gen 7:2 ... 929
every *b* after his kind, and all ... Gen 7:14 ... 2416
of fowl, and of cattle, and of *b* ... Gen 7:21 ... 2416
Every *b*, every creeping thing, and ... Gen 8:19 ... 2416
and took of every clean *b*, and of ... Gen 8:20 ... 929
be upon every *b* of the earth ... Gen 9:2 ... 2416
hand of every *b* will I require it ... Gen 9:5 ... 2416
of every *b* of the earth with you ... Gen 9:10 ... 2416
the ark, to every *b* of the earth ... Gen 9:10 ... 2416
every *b* of theirs be ours ... Gen 34:23 ... 929
Some evil *b* hath devoured him ... Gen 37:20 ... 2416
an evil *b* hath devoured him ... Gen 37:33 ... 2416
and it became lice in man, and in *b* ... Ex 8:17 ... 929
were lice upon man, and upon *b* ... Ex 8:18 ... 929
with blains upon man, and upon *b* ... Ex 9:9 ... 929
with blains upon man, and upon *b* ... Ex 9:10 ... 929
b which shall be found in the ... Ex 9:19 ... 929
of Egypt, upon man, and upon *b* ... Ex 9:22 ... 929
was in the field, both man and *b* ... Ex 9:25 ... 929
move his tongue, against man or *b* ... Ex 11:7 ... 929
the land of Egypt, both man and *b* ... Ex 12:12 ... 929
of Israel, both of man and of *b* ... Ex 13:2 ... 929
cometh of a *b* which thou hast ... Ex 13:12 ... 929
of man, and the firstborn of *b* ... Ex 13:15 ... 929
whether it be *b* or man, it shall ... Ex 19:13 ... 929
and the dead *b* shall be his ... Ex 21:34 ... 929
be eaten, and shall put in his *b* ... Ex 22:5 ... 1165
or an ox, or a sheep, or any *b* ... Ex 22:10 ... 929
Whosoever lieth with a *b* shall ... Ex 22:19 ... 929
the *b* of the field multiply ... Ex 23:29 ... 2416
it be a carcase of an unclean *b* ... Lev 5:2 ... 2416
of man, or any unclean *b*, or any ... Lev 7:21 ... 929
the fat of the *b* that dieth of ... Lev 7:24 ... 5038
whosoever eateth the fat of the *b* ... Lev 7:25 ... 929
whether it be of fowl or of *b* ... Lev 7:26 ... 929
The carcases of every *b* which ... Lev 11:26 ... 929
And if any *b*, of which ye may eat ... Lev 11:39 ... 929
between the *b* that may be eaten ... Lev 11:47 ... 2416
the *b* that may not be eaten ... Lev 11:47 ... 2416
catcheth any *b* or fowl that may ... Lev 17:13 ... 2416
any *b* to defile thyself therewith ... Lev 18:23 ... 929
before a *b* to lie down thereto ... Lev 18:23 ... 929
And if a man lie with a *b*, he ... Lev 20:15 ... 929
and ye shall slay the *b* ... Lev 20:15 ... 929
And if a woman approach unto any *b* ... Lev 20:16 ... 929
shalt kill the woman, and the *b* ... Lev 20:16 ... 929
make your souls abominable by *b* ... Lev 20:25 ... 929
he that killeth a *b* shall make it ... Lev 24:18 ... 5315,929
shall make it good; *b* for *b* ... Lev 24:18 ... 5315
shall make it good; *b* for *b* ... Lev 24:18 ... 929
And he that killeth a *b*, he shall ... Lev 24:21 ... 929
for the *b* that are in thy land ... Lev 25:7 ... 2416
And if it be a *b*, whereof men ... Lev 27:9 ... 929
shall at all change *b* for *b* ... Lev 27:10 ... 929
And if it be any unclean *b* ... Lev 27:11 ... 929
present the *b* before the priest ... Lev 27:11 ... 929
And if it be of an unclean *b* ... Lev 27:27 ... 929
that he hath, both of man and *b* ... Lev 27:28 ... 929
in Israel, both man and *b* ... Num 3:13 ... 929
of Israel are mine, both man and *b* ... Num 8:17 ... 929
was taken, both of man and of *b* ... Num 31:26 ... 929
of fifty, both of man and of *b* ... Num 31:47 ... 929
The likeness of any *b* that is on ... Deut 4:17 ... 929
every *b* that parteth the hoof, and ... Deut 14:6 ... 929
that lieth with any manner of *b* ... Deut 27:21 ... 929
the men of every city, as the *b* ... Judg 20:48 ... 929
by a wild *b* that was in Lebanon ... 2Kin 14:9 ... 2416
by a wild *b* that was in Lebanon ... 2Chr 25:18 ... 2416
neither was there any *b* with me ... Neh 2:12 ... 929
save the *b* that I rode upon ... Neh 2:12 ... 929
the *b* that was under me to pass ... Neh 2:14 ... 929
or that the wild *b* may break them ... Job 39:15 ... 2416
O LORD, thou preservest man and *b* ... Ps 36:6 ... 929
For every *b* of the forest is mine ... Ps 50:10 ... 2416
I was as a *b* before thee ... Ps 73:22 ... 929
the wild *b* of the field doth ... Ps 80:13 ... 2123
drink to every *b* of the field ... Ps 104:11 ... 2416
of Egypt, both of man and *b* ... Ps 135:8 ... 929
He giveth to the *b* his food ... Ps 147:9 ... 929
man regardeth the life of his *b* ... Prov 12:10 ... 929
man hath no preeminence above a *b* ... Eccl 3:19 ... 929
the spirit of the *b* that goeth ... Eccl 3:21 ... 929
nor any ravenous *b* shall go up ... Is 35:9 ... 2416
The *b* of the field shall honour ... Is 43:20 ... 2416
they are a burden to the weary *b* ... Is 46:1
As a *b* goeth down into the valley ... Is 63:14 ... 929
this place, upon man, and upon *b* ... Jer 7:20 ... 929
of the heavens and the *b* are fled ... Jer 9:10 ... 929
of this city, both man and *b* ... Jer 21:6 ... 929
the *b* that are upon the ground ... Jer 27:5 ... 929
of man, and with the seed of *b* ... Jer 31:27 ... 929
It is desolate without man or *b* ... Jer 32:43 ... 929
desolate without man and without *b* ... Jer 33:10 ... 929
without inhabitant, and without *b* ... Jer 33:10 ... 929
desolate without man and without *b* ... Jer 33:12 ... 929
to cease from thence man and *b* ... Jer 36:29 ... 929
they shall depart, both man and *b* ... Jer 50:3 ... 929
remain in it, neither man nor *b* ... Jer 51:62 ... 929
and will cut off man and *b* from it ... Eze 14:13 ... 929
that I cut off man and *b* from it ... Eze 14:17 ... 929
to cut off from it man and *b* ... Eze 14:19 ... 929
and the famine, and the noisome *b* ... Eze 14:21 ... 2416
to cut off from it man and *b* ... Eze 14:21 ... 929
and will cut off man and *b* from it ... Eze 25:13 ... 929
and cut off man and *b* out of thee ... Eze 29:8 ... 929
nor foot of *b* shall pass through ... Eze 29:11 ... 929
meat to every *b* of the field ... Eze 34:8 ... 2416
neither shall the *b* of the land ... Eze 34:28 ... 2416
I will multiply upon you man and *b* ... Eze 36:11 ... 929
to every *b* of the field, Assemble ... Eze 39:17 ... 2416
or torn, whether it be fowl or *b* ... Eze 44:31 ... 929
And behold another *b*, a second ... Dan 7:5 ... 2423
the *b* had also four heads ... Dan 7:6 ... 2423
visions, and behold a fourth *b* ... Dan 7:7 ... 2423
beheld even till the *b* was slain ... Dan 7:11 ... 2423
know the truth of the fourth *b* ... Dan 7:19 ... 2423
The fourth *b* shall be the fourth ... Dan 7:23 ... 2423
the wild *b* shall tear them ... Hos 13:8 ... 2416
saying, Let neither man nor *b* ... Jonah 3:7 ... 929
b be covered with sackcloth, and ... Jonah 3:8 ... 929
bind the chariot to the swift *b* ... Mic 1:13 ... 7409
I will consume man and *b* ... Zeph 1:3 ... 929
hire for man, nor any hire for *b* ... Zec 8:10 ... 929
and wine, and set him on his own *b* ... Lk 10:34 ... *2934*
the venomous *b* hang on his hand ... Acts 28:4 ... *2342*
he shook off the *b* into the fire ... Acts 28:5 ... *2342*
if so much as a *b* touch the ... Heb 12:20 ... *2342*
the first *b* was like a lion, and ... Rev 4:7 ... *2226*
the second *b* like a calf ... Rev 4:7 ... *2226*
the third *b* had a face as a man ... Rev 4:7 ... *2226*
the fourth *b* was like a flying ... Rev 4:7 ... *2226*
seal, I heard the second *b* say ... Rev 6:3 ... *2226*
seal, I heard the third *b* say ... Rev 6:5 ... *2226*
the voice of the fourth *b* say ... Rev 6:7 ... *2226*
the *b* that ascendeth out of the ... Rev 11:7 ... *2342*
saw a *b* rise up out of the sea ... Rev 13:1 ... *2342*
the *b* which I saw was like unto a ... Rev 13:2 ... *2342*
the world wondered after the *b* ... Rev 13:3 ... *2342*
which gave power unto the *b* ... Rev 13:4 ... *2342*
and they worshipped the *b* ... Rev 13:4 ... *2342*
saying, Who is like unto the *b* ... Rev 13:4 ... *2342*
I beheld another *b* coming up out ... Rev 13:11 ... *2342*
power of the first *b* before him ... Rev 13:12 ... *2342*
therein to worship the first *b* ... Rev 13:12 ... *2342*
power to do in the sight of the *b* ... Rev 13:14 ... *2342*
should make an image to the *b* ... Rev 13:14 ... *2342*
give life unto the image of the *b* ... Rev 13:15 ... *2342*
image of the *b* should both speak ... Rev 13:15 ... *2342*
image of the *b* should be killed ... Rev 13:15 ... *2342*
the mark, or the name of the *b* ... Rev 13:17 ... *2342*
count the number of the *b* ... Rev 13:18 ... *2342*
voice, If any man worship the *b* ... Rev 14:9 ... *2342*
day nor night, who worship the *b* ... Rev 14:11 ... *2342*
had gotten the victory over the *b* ... Rev 15:2 ... *2342*
men which had the mark of the *b* ... Rev 16:2 ... *2342*
his vial upon the seat of the *b* ... Rev 16:10 ... *2342*
and out of the mouth of the *b* ... Rev 16:13 ... *2342*
sit upon a scarlet coloured *b* ... Rev 17:3 ... *2342*
of the *b* that carrieth her, which ... Rev 17:7 ... *2342*
The *b* that thou sawest was, and is ... Rev 17:8 ... *2342*
when they behold the *b* that was ... Rev 17:8 ... *2342*
the *b* that was, and is not, even ... Rev 17:11 ... *2342*
as kings one hour with the *b* ... Rev 17:12 ... *2342*
power and strength unto the *b* ... Rev 17:13 ... *2342*
which thou sawest upon the *b* ... Rev 17:16 ... *2342*
and give their kingdom unto the *b* ... Rev 17:17 ... *2342*
And I saw the *b*, and the kings of ... Rev 19:19 ... *2342*
the *b* was taken, and with him the ... Rev 19:20 ... *2342*
had received the mark of the *b* ... Rev 19:20 ... *2342*
and which had not worshipped the *b* ... Rev 20:4 ... *2342*
of fire and brimstone, where the *b* ... Rev 20:10 ... *2342*

BEAST'S {1}
let a *b* heart be given unto him ... Dan 4:16 ... 2423

BEASTS {157}
of *b* that are not clean by two ... Gen 7:2 ... 929
Of clean *b*, and of *b* that are ... Gen 7:8 ... 929
That which was torn of *b* I ... Gen 31:39 ... 2966
and his cattle, and all his *b* ... Gen 36:6 ... 929
lade your *b*, and go, get you unto ... Gen 45:17 ... 1165
and all the firstborn of *b* ... Ex 11:5 ... 929
that is torn of *b* in the field ... Ex 22:31 ... 2966
what they leave the *b* of the ... Ex 23:11 ... 2416
fat of that which is torn with *b* ... Lev 7:24 ... 2966
These are the *b* which ye shall ... Lev 11:2 ... 2416
all the *b* that are on the earth ... Lev 11:2 ... 929
and cheweth the cud, among the *b* ... Lev 11:3 ... 929
manner of *b* that go on all four ... Lev 11:27 ... 2416
This is the law of the *b*, and of ... Lev 11:46 ... 929
or that which was torn with *b* ... Lev 17:15 ... 2966
put difference between clean *b* ... Lev 20:25 ... 929
of itself, or is torn with *b* ... Lev 22:8 ... 2966
I will rid evil *b* out of the land ... Lev 26:6 ... 2416
I will also send wild *b* among you ... Lev 26:22 ... 2416
Only the firstling of the *b* ... Lev 27:26 ... 929
LORD, whether it be of men or *b* ... Num 18:15 ... 929
of unclean *b* shalt thou redeem ... Num 18:15 ... 929
the congregation and their *b* drink ... Num 20:8 ... 1165
drank, and their *b* also ... Num 20:11 ... 1165
all the prey, both of men and of *b* ... Num 31:11 ... 929
of the flocks, of all manner of *b* ... Num 31:30 ... 929
their goods, and for all their *b* ... Num 35:3 ... 2416
lest the *b* of the field increase ... Deut 7:22 ... 2416
These are the *b* which ye shall ... Deut 14:4 ... 929
and cheweth the cud among the *b* ... Deut 14:6 ... 929
unto the *b* of the earth, and no ... Deut 28:26 ... 929
send the teeth of *b* upon them ... Deut 32:24 ... 929
the air, and to the *b* of the field ... 1Sa 17:44 ... 929
to the wild *b* of the earth ... 1Sa 17:46 ... 2416
nor the *b* of the field by night ... 2Sa 21:10 ... 2416
he spake also of *b*, and of fowl ... 1Kin 4:33 ... 929
alive, that we lose not all the *b* ... 1Kin 18:5 ... 929
ye, and your cattle, and your *b* ... 2Kin 3:17 ... 929
and stalls for all manner of *b* ... 2Chr 32:28 ... 929
gold, and with goods, and with *b* ... Ezr 1:4 ... 929
with gold, with goods, and with *b* ... Ezr 1:6 ... 929
be afraid of the *b* of the earth ... Job 5:22 ... 2416
the *b* of the field shall be at ... Job 5:23 ... 2416
But ask now the *b*, and they shall ... Job 12:7 ... 929
Wherefore are we counted as *b* ... Job 18:3 ... 929
us more than the *b* of the earth ... Job 35:11 ... 929
Then the *b* go into dens, and ... Job 37:8 ... 2416
where all the *b* of the field play ... Job 40:20 ... 2416
oxen, yea, and the *b* of the field ... Ps 8:7 ... 929
he is like the *b* that perish ... Ps 49:12 ... 929
not, is like the *b* that perish ... Ps 49:20 ... 929
the wild *b* of the field are mine ... Ps 50:11 ... 2123
saints unto the *b* of the earth ... Ps 79:2 ... 2416
wherein all the *b* of the forest ... Ps 104:20 ... 2416
both small and great *b* ... Ps 104:25 ... 2416
B, and all cattle ... Ps 148:10 ... 2416
She hath killed her *b* ... Prov 9:2 ... 2874
A lion which is strongest among *b* ... Prov 30:30 ... 929
see that they themselves are *b* ... Eccl 3:18 ... 929
the sons of men befalleth *b* ... Eccl 3:19 ... 929
of rams, and the fat of fed *b* ... Is 1:11 ... 4806
But wild *b* of the desert shall ... Is 13:21 ... 6728
the wild *b* of the islands shall ... Is 13:22 ... 338
and to the *b* of the earth ... Is 18:6 ... 929
all the *b* of the earth shall ... Is 18:6 ... 929
The burden of the *b* of the south ... Is 30:6 ... 929
The wild *b* of the desert shall ... Is 34:14 ... 6728

with the wild b of the island Is 34:14 338
nor the b thereof sufficient for Is 40:16 2416
their idols were upon the b Is 46:1 2416
All ye b of the field, come to Is 56:9 2416
yea, all ye b in the forest Is 56:9 2416
and upon mules, and upon swift b Is 66:20 3753
heaven, and for the b of the earth Jer 7:33 929
the b are consumed, and the birds Jer 12:4 929
assemble all the b of the field Jer 12:9 2416
the b of the earth, to devour and Jer 15:3 929
heaven, and for the b of the earth Jer 16:4 929
heaven, and for the b of the earth Jer 19:7 929
the b of the field have I given Jer 27:6 2416
given him the b of the field also Jer 28:14 2416
heaven, and to the b of the earth Jer 34:20 929
Therefore the wild b of the Jer 50:39 6728
wild b of the islands shall dwell Jer 50:39 338
I send upon you famine and evil b Eze 5:17 2416
creeping things, and abominable b Eze 8:10 929
If I cause noisome b to pass Eze 14:15 2416
may pass through because of the b Eze 14:15 2416
for meat to the b of the field Eze 29:5 2416
b of the field bring forth their Eze 31:6 2416
all the b of the field shall be Eze 31:13 2416
I will fill the b of the whole Eze 32:4 2416
I will destroy also all the b Eze 32:13 929
nor the hoofs of b trouble them Eze 32:13 929
I give to the b to be devoured Eze 33:27 2416
meat to all the b of the field Eze 34:5 2416
will cause the evil b to cease Eze 34:25 2416
the b of the field, and all Eze 38:20 2416
to the b of the field to be Eze 39:4 2416
the b of the field and the fowls Dan 2:38 2423
the b of the field had shadow Dan 4:12 2423
let the b get away from under it, Dan 4:14 2423
the b in the grass of the earth Dan 4:15 2423
under which the b of the field Dan 4:21 2423
be with the b of the field Dan 4:23 2423
shall be with the b of the field Dan 4:25 2423
shall be with the b of the field Dan 4:32 2423
and his heart was made like the b Dan 5:21 2423
four great b came up from the sea Dan 7:3 2423
all the b that were before it Dan 7:7 2423
As concerning the rest of the b Dan 7:12 2423
These great b, which are four, Dan 7:17 2423
so that no b might stand before Dan 8:4 2416
the b of the field shall eat them Hos 2:12 2416
for them with the b of the field Hos 2:18 2416
with the b of the field, and with Hos 4:3 2416
How do the b groan Joel 1:18 929
The b of the field cry also unto Joel 1:20 929
Be not afraid, ye b of the field Joel 2:22 929
the peace offerings of your fat b Amos 5:22 4806
a lion among the b of the forest Mic 5:8 929
cover thee, and the spoil of b Hab 2:17 929
of her, all the b of the nations Zeph 2:14 2416
a place for b to lie down in Zeph 2:15 2416
of all the b that shall be in Zec 14:15 929
and was with the wild b Mk 1:13 2342
have ye offered to me slain b Acts 7:42 4968
of fourfooted b of the earth Acts 10:12 5074
b of the earth, and wild b Acts 10:12 2342
b of the earth, and wild b Acts 11:6 2342
And provide them b, that they may Acts 23:24 2934
man, and to birds, and fourfooted b Rom 1:23 5074
I have fought with b at Ephesus 1Cor 15:32 2341
flesh of men, another flesh of b 1Cor 15:39 2934
Cretians are alway liars, evil b Titus 1:12 2342
For the bodies of those b Heb 13:11 2226
For every kind of b, and of birds, Jas 3:7 2342
But these, as natural brute b 2Pet 2:12 2226
they know naturally, as brute b Jude 10 2226
were four b full of eyes before Rev 4:6 2226
the four b had each of them six Rev 4:8 2226
And when those b give glory Rev 4:9 2226
of the throne and of the four b Rev 5:6 2226
he had taken the book, the four b Rev 5:8 2226
round about the throne and the b Rev 5:11 2226
And the four b said, Amen Rev 5:14 2226
thunder, one of the four b saying Rev 6:1 2226
in the midst of the four b say Rev 6:6 2226
death, and with the b of the earth Rev 6:8 2342
and about the elders and the four b Rev 7:11 2226
the throne, and before the four b Rev 14:3 2226
one of the four b gave unto the Rev 15:7 2226
and fine flour, and wheat, and b Rev 18:13 2934
elders and the four b fell down and Rev 19:4 2226

BEAT {36}
thou shalt b some of it very Ex 30:36 7833
they did b the gold into thin Ex 39:3 7554
or b it in a mortar, and baked it Num 11:8 1743
b him above these with many Deut 25:3 5221
he b down the tower of Penuel, and Judg 8:17 5422
b down the city, and sowed it with Judg 9:45 5422
b at the door, and spake to the Judg 19:22 1849
b out that she had gleaned Ruth 2:17 2251
Then did I b them as small as the 2Sa 22:43 7833
they b down the cities, and on 2Kin 3:25 2040
Three times did Joash b him 2Kin 13:25 5221
of the LORD, did the king b down 2Kin 23:12 5422
Then did I b them small as the Ps 18:42 7833
I will b down his foes before his Ps 89:23 3807
Thou shalt b him with the rod, and Prov 23:14 5221
they shall b their swords into Is 2:4 3807
ye that ye b my people to pieces Is 3:15 1792
that the LORD shall b off from Is 27:12 2251
b them small, and shalt make the Is 41:15 1854
B your plowshares into swords, and Joel 3:10 3807
the sun b upon the head of Jonah, Jonah 4:8 5221
they shall b their swords into Mic 4:3 3807
thou shalt b in pieces many Mic 4:13 1854
winds blew, and b upon that house Mt 7:25 4363
winds blew, and b upon that house Mt 7:27 4350
b one, and killed another, and Mt 21:35 1194
the waves b into the ship, so Mk 4:37 1911
b him, and sent him away empty Mk 12:3 1194
the stream b vehemently upon that Lk 6:48 4366
which the stream did b vehemently Lk 6:49 4366
shall begin to b the menservants Lk 12:45 5180
but the husbandmen b him, and sent Lk 20:10 1194
they b him also, and entreated him Lk 20:11 1194
clothes, and commanded to b them Acts 16:22 4463
b him before the judgment seat Acts 18:17 5180
b in every synagogue them that Acts 22:19 1194

BEATEN {40}
had set over them, were b Ex 5:14 5221
and, behold, thy servants are b Ex 5:16 5221
of b work shalt thou make them, Ex 25:18 4749
of b work shall the candlestick Ex 25:31 4749
shall be one b work of pure gold Ex 25:36 4749
pure oil olive b for the light Ex 27:20 3795
fourth part of an hin of b oil Ex 29:40 3795
b out of one piece made he them, Ex 37:7 4749
of b work made he the candlestick Ex 37:17 4749
of it was one b work of pure gold Ex 37:22 4749
even corn b out of full ears Lev 2:14 1643
part of the b corn thereof, and Lev 2:16 1643
full of sweet incense b small Lev 16:12 1851
pure oil olive b for the light Lev 24:2 3795
of the candlestick was of b gold Num 8:4 4749
the flowers thereof, was b work Num 8:4 4749
fourth part of an hin of b oil Num 28:5 3795
the wicked man be worthy to be b Deut 25:2 5221
down, and to be b before his face, Deut 25:2 5221
as if they were b before them Josh 8:15 5060
and Abner was b, and the men of 2Sa 2:17 5062
two hundred targets of b gold 1Kin 10:16 7820
three hundred shields of b gold 1Kin 10:17 7820
thousand measures of b wheat 2Chr 2:10 4347
two hundred targets of b gold 2Chr 9:15 7820
six hundred shekels of b gold 2Chr 9:15 7820
hundred shields made he of b gold 2Chr 9:16 7820
had b the graven images into 2Chr 34:7 3807
they have b me, and I felt it not Prov 23:35 1986
chalkstones that are b in sunder Is 27:9 5310
fitches are b out with a staff Is 28:27 2251
LORD shall the Assyrian be b down Is 30:31 2865
and their mighty ones are b down Jer 46:5 3807
thereof shall be b to pieces Mic 1:7 3807
in the synagogues ye shall be b Mk 13:9 1194
shall be b with many stripes Lk 12:47 1194
shall be b with few stripes Lk 12:48 1194
b them, they commanded that they Acts 5:40 1194
They have b us openly uncondemned Acts 16:37 1194
Thrice was I b with rods, once 2Cor 11:25 4463

BEATEST {2}
When thou b thine olive tree, Deut 24:20 2251
for if thou b him with the rod, Prov 23:13 5221

BEATETH {1}
I, not as one that b the air 1Cor 9:26 1194

BEATING {3}
they went on b down one another 1Sa 14:16 1986
b some, and killing some Mk 12:5 1194
the soldiers, they left b of Paul Acts 21:32 5180

BEAUTIES {1}
in the b of holiness from the Ps 110:3 1926

BEAUTIFUL {23}
Rachel was b and well favoured Gen 29:17 3303,8389
among the captives a b woman Deut 21:11 3303,8389
and withal of a b countenance 1Sa 16:12 3303
and of a b countenance 1Sa 25:3 3303
the woman was very b to look upon 2Sa 11:2 2896
and the maid was fair and b Est 2:7 2896,4758
B for situation, the joy of the Ps 48:2 3303
made every thing b in his time Eccl 3:11 3303
Thou art b, O my love, as Tirzah, Song 6:4 3303
How b are thy feet with shoes, O Song 7:1 3303
shall the branch of the LORD be b Is 4:2 6643
put on thy b garments, O Is 52:1 8597
How b upon the mountains are the Is 52:7 4998
our b house, where our fathers Is 64:11 8597
that was given thee, thy b flock Jer 13:20 8597
strong staff broken, and the b rod Jer 48:17 8597
a b crown upon thine head Eze 16:12 8597
and thou wast exceeding b, and thou Eze 16:13 3303
b crowns upon their heads Eze 23:42 8597
which indeed appear b outward Mt 23:27 5611
of the temple which is called B Acts 3:2 5611
alms at the B gate of the temple Acts 3:10 5611
How b are the feet of them that Rom 10:15 5611

BEAUTIFY {3}
to b the house of the LORD which Ezr 7:27 6286
he will b the meek with salvation Ps 149:4 6286
to b the place of my sanctuary Is 60:13 6286

BEAUTY {49}
thy brother for glory and for b Ex 28:2 8597
make for them, for glory and for b Ex 28:40 8597
The b of Israel is slain upon thy 2Sa 1:19 6643
much praised as Absalom for his b 2Sa 14:25 3308
the LORD in the b of holiness 1Chr 16:29 1927
house with precious stones for b 2Chr 3:6 8597
should praise the b of holiness 2Chr 20:21 1927
the people and the princes her b Est 1:11 3308
and array thyself with glory and b Job 40:10 1926
life, to behold the b of the LORD Ps 27:4 5278
the LORD in the b of holiness Ps 29:2 1927
thou makest his b to consume away Ps 39:11 2530
the king greatly desire thy b Ps 45:11 3308
their b shall consume in the Ps 49:14 6736
Out of Zion, the perfection of b Ps 50:2 3308
let the b of the LORD our God be Ps 90:17 5278
and b are in his sanctuary Ps 96:6 8597
the LORD in the b of holiness Ps 96:9 1927
not after her b in thine heart Prov 6:25 3308
the b of old men is the grey head Prov 20:29 1926
Favour is deceitful, and b is vain Prov 31:30 3308
and burning instead of b Is 3:24 3308
the b of the Chaldees' excellency Is 13:19 8597
whose glorious b is a fading Is 28:1 8597
And the glorious b, which is on Is 28:4 8597
of glory, and for a diadem of b Is 28:5 8597
eyes shall see the king in his b Is 33:17 3308
man, according to the b of a man Is 44:13 8597
there is no b that we should Is 53:2 4758
to give unto them b for ashes Is 61:3 6287
of Zion all her b is departed Lam 1:6 1926
unto the earth the b of Israel Lam 2:1 8597
that men call The perfection of b Lam 2:15 3308
As for the b of his ornament, he Eze 7:20 6643
forth among the heathen for thy b Eze 16:14 3308
thou didst trust in thine own b Eze 16:15 3308
hast made thy b to be abhorred, Eze 16:25 3308
thou hast said, I am of perfect b Eze 27:3 3308
thy builders have perfected thy b Eze 27:4 3308
they have made thy b perfect Eze 27:11 3308
against the b of thy wisdom Eze 28:7 3308
full of wisdom, and perfect in b Eze 28:12 3308
was lifted up because of thy b Eze 28:17 3308
of God was like unto him in his b Eze 31:8 3308
Whom dost thou pass in b Eze 32:19 5276
his b shall be as the olive tree, Hos 14:6 1935
goodness, and how great is his b Zec 9:17 3308
the one I called B, and the other Zec 11:7 5278
And I took my staff, even B Zec 11:10 5278

BEBAI *(beb'-a-i)* {6}
1. Father of returned exiles.
The children of B, six hundred Ezr 2:11 893
The children of B, six hundred Neh 7:16 893
2. Father of returned exiles with Ezra.
And of the sons of B Ezr 8:11 893
Zechariah the son of B, and with Ezr 8:11 893
Of the sons also of B Ezr 10:28 893
3. One who sealed the covenant.
Bunni, Azgad, B, Neh 10:15 893

BECAME See APPENDIX.

BECAMEST {2}
and thou, LORD, b their God 1Chr 17:22 1961
the Lord GOD, and thou b mine Eze 16:8 1961

BECAUSE See APPENDIX.

BECHER *(be'-ker)* {5} See BACHRITES.
1. A son of Benjamin.
sons of Benjamin were Belah, and B Gen 46:21 1071
Bela, and B, and Jediael, three 1Chr 7:6 1071
And the sons of B 1Chr 7:8 1071
All these are the sons of B 1Chr 7:8 1071
2. A son of Ephraim.
of B, the family of the Bachrites Num 26:35 1071

BECHERITES See BACHRITES.

BECHORATH *(be-ko'-rath)* {1} *An ancestor of King Saul.*
the son of Zeror, the son of B 1Sa 9:1 1064

BECKONED {6}
for he b unto them, and remained Lk 1:22 1269
they b unto their partners, which Lk 5:7 2656
Simon Peter therefore b to him Jn 13:24 3506
Alexander b with the hand, and Acts 19:33 2678
b with the hand unto the people Acts 21:40 2678
governor had b unto him to speak Acts 24:10 3506

BECKONING {2}
b unto them with the hand to hold Acts 12:17 2678
b with his hand said, Men of Acts 13:16 2678

BECOME See APPENDIX.

BECOMETH {15}
holiness b thine house, O LORD, Ps 93:5 4998
He b poor that dealeth with a Prov 10:4
Excellent speech b not a fool Prov 17:7 5000
b surety in the presence of his Prov 17:18 6148
is born in his kingdom b poor Eccl 4:14
for thus it b us to fulfil all Mt 3:15 4241
the word, and he b unfruitful Mt 13:22 1096
b a tree, so that the birds of Mt 13:32 1096
the word, and it b unfruitful Mk 4:19 1096
b greater than all herbs, and Mk 4:32 1096
as b saints, and that ye assist Rom 16:2 516
once named among you, as b saints Eph 5:3 4241
be as it b the gospel of Christ Phil 1:27 516
But (which b women professing 1Ti 2:10 516
be in behaviour as b holiness Titus 2:3 2412

BECORATH See BECHORATH.

BED {90}
himself, and sat upon the b Gen 48:2 4296
thou wentest up to thy father's b Gen 49:4 4904
gathered up his feet into the b Gen 49:33 4296
thy bedchamber, and upon thy b Ex 8:3 4296
and he die not, but keepeth his b Ex 21:18 4904
Every b, whereon he lieth that Lev 15:4 4904

his *b* shall wash his clothes ... Lev 15:5 4904
her *b* shall wash his clothes ... Lev 15:21 4904
And if it be on her *b*, or on any ... Lev 15:23 4904
all the *b* whereon he lieth shall ... Lev 15:24 4904
Every *b* whereon she lieth all the ... Lev 15:26 4904
her as the *b* of her separation ... Lev 15:26 4904
an image, and laid it in the *b* ... 1Sa 19:13 4296
Bring him up to me in the *b* ... 1Sa 19:15 4296
there was an image in the *b* ... 1Sa 19:16 4296
from the earth, and sat upon the *b* ... 1Sa 28:23 4296
who lay on a *b* at noon ... 2Sa 4:5 4904
he lay on his *b* in his bedchamber ... 2Sa 4:7 4296
in his own house upon his *b* ... 2Sa 4:11 4904
that David arose from off his *b* ... 2Sa 11:2 4904
b with the servants of his lord ... 2Sa 11:13 4904
unto him, Lay thee down on thy *b* ... 2Sa 13:5 4904
the king bowed himself upon the *b* ... 1Kin 1:47 4904
abode, and laid him upon his own *b* ... 1Kin 17:19 4296
And he laid him down upon his *b* ... 1Kin 21:4 4296
that *b* on which thou art gone up ... 2Kin 1:4 4296
that *b* on which thou art gone up ... 2Kin 1:6 4296
that *b* on which thou art gone up ... 2Kin 1:16 4296
and let us set for him there a *b* ... 2Kin 4:10 4296
laid him on the *b* of the man of ... 2Kin 4:21 4296
was dead, and laid upon his *b* ... 2Kin 4:32 4296
as he defiled his father's *b* ... 1Chr 5:1 3326
laid him in the *b* which was ... 2Chr 16:14 4904
the priest, and slew him on his *b* ... 2Chr 24:25 4296
upon the *b* whereon Esther was ... Est 7:8 4296
My *b* shall comfort me, my couch ... Job 7:13 6210
I have made my *b* in the darkness ... Job 17:13 3326
men, in slumberings upon the *b* ... Job 33:15 4904
also with pain upon his *b* ... Job 33:19 4904
with your own heart upon your *b* ... Ps 4:4 4904
all the night make I my *b* to swim ... Ps 6:6 4296
He deviseth mischief upon his *b* ... Ps 36:4 4904
him upon the *b* of languishing ... Ps 41:3 6210
make all his *b* in his sickness ... Ps 41:3 4904
When I remember thee upon my *b* ... Ps 63:6 3326
of my house, nor go up into my *b* ... Ps 132:3 6210,3326
if I make my *b* in hell, behold, ... Ps 139:8 3331
I have decked my *b* with coverings ... Prov 7:16 6210
I have perfumed my *b* with myrrh ... Prov 7:17 4904
take away thy *b* from under thee ... Prov 22:27 4904
so doth the slothful upon his *b* ... Prov 26:14 4296
also our *b* is green ... Song 1:16 6210
By night on my *b* I sought him ... Song 3:1 4904
Behold his *b*, which is Solomon's ... Song 3:7 4296
His cheeks are as a *b* of spices ... Song 5:13 6170
For the *b* is shorter than that a ... Is 28:20 4702
high mountain hast thou set thy *b* ... Is 57:7 4904
thou hast enlarged thy *b*, and made ... Is 57:8 4904
thou lovedst their *b* where thou ... Is 57:8 4904
came to her into the *b* of love ... Eze 23:17 4904
And satest upon a stately *b* ... Eze 23:41 4296
They have set her a *b* in the ... Eze 32:25 4904
visions of thy head upon thy *b* ... Dan 2:28 4903
came into thy mind upon thy *b* ... Dan 2:29 4903
afraid, and the thoughts upon my *b* ... Dan 4:5 4903
the visions of mine head in my *b* ... Dan 4:10 4903
the visions of my head upon my *b* ... Dan 4:13 4903
and visions of his head upon his *b* ... Dan 7:1 4903
in Samaria in the corner of a *b* ... Amos 3:12 4296
sick of the palsy, lying on a *b* ... Mt 9:2 *2825*
the palsy,) Arise, take up thy *b* ... Mt 9:6 *2825*
they let down the *b* wherein the ... Mk 2:4 *2895*
to say, Arise, and take up thy *b* ... Mk 2:9 *2895*
thee, Arise, and take up thy *b* ... Mk 2:11 *2895*
he arose, took up the *b*, and went ... Mk 2:12 *2895*
put under a bushel, or under a *b* ... Mk 4:21 *2825*
and her daughter laid upon the *b* ... Mk 7:30 *2825*
men brought in a *b* a man which ... Lk 5:18 *2825*
a vessel, or putteth it under a *b* ... Lk 8:16 *2825*
and my children are with me in *b* ... Lk 11:7 *2845*
there shall be two men in one *b* ... Lk 17:34 *2825*
unto him, Rise, take up thy *b* ... Jn 5:8 *2895*
was made whole, and took up his *b* ... Jn 5:9 *2895*
lawful for thee to carry thy *b* ... Jn 5:10 *2895*
same said unto me, Take up thy *b* ... Jn 5:11 *2895*
said unto thee, Take up thy *b* ... Jn 5:12 *2895*
which had kept his *b* eight years ... Acts 9:33 *2895*
arise, and make thy *b* ... Acts 9:34 *4766*
in all, and the *b* undefiled ... Heb 13:4 *2845*
Behold, I will cast her into a *b* ... Rev 2:22 *2825*

BEDAD *(be'-dad)* {2} *Father of Hadad.*
died, and Hadad the son of *B* ... Gen 36:35 911
was dead, Hadad the son of *B* ... 1Chr 1:46 911

BEDAN *(be'-dan)* {2}
1. A judge of Israel.
And the LORD sent Jerubbaal, and *B* ... 1Sa 12:11 917
2. A descendant of Manasseh.
And the sons of Ulam; *B* ... 1Chr 7:17 917

BEDCHAMBER {6}
into thine house, and into thy *b* ... Ex 8:3 2315,4904
house, he lay on his bed in his *b* ... 2Sa 4:7 2315,4904
words that thou speakest in thy *b* ... 2Kin 6:12 2315,4904
in the *b* from Athaliah, so that ... 2Kin 11:2 2315,4296
and put him and his nurse in a *b* ... 2Chr 22:11 2315,4296
and curse not the rich in thy *b* ... Eccl 10:20 2315,4296

BEDEIAH *(be-de'-yah)* {1} *Married a foreign wife in exile.*
Benaiah, *B*, Chelluh, ... Ezr 10:35 912

BED'S {1}
bowed himself upon the *b* head ... Gen 47:31 4296

BEDS {10}
Brought *b*, and basons, and earthen ... 2Sa 17:28 4904
the *b* were of gold and silver, ... Est 1:6 4296
let them sing aloud upon their *b* ... Ps 149:5 4904
to the *b* of spices, to feed in ... Song 6:2 6170
they shall rest in their *b* ... Is 57:2 4904
when they howled upon their *b* ... Hos 7:14 4904
That lie upon *b* of ivory, and ... Amos 6:4 4296
and work evil upon their *b* ... Mic 2:1 4904
about in *b* those that were sick ... Mk 6:55 *2895*
the streets, and laid them on *b* ... Acts 5:15 *2825*

BEDSTEAD {2}
his *b* was a *b* of iron ... Deut 3:11 6210

BEE {1}
for the *b* that is in the land of ... Is 7:18 1682

BEELIADA *(be-e-li'-ad-ah)* {1} *A son of David.*
And Elishama, and *B*, and Eliphalet ... 1Chr 14:7 1182

BEELZEBUB *(be-el'-ze-bub)* {7} See BAAL-ZEBUB. *Chief of evil spirits.*
called the master of the house *B* ... Mt 10:25 *954*
but by *B* the prince of the devils ... Mt 12:24 *954*
if I by *B* cast out devils, by ... Mt 12:27 *954*
from Jerusalem said, He hath *B* ... Mk 3:22 *954*
through *B* the chief of the devils ... Lk 11:15 *954*
that I cast out devils through *B* ... Lk 11:18 *954*
if I by *B* cast out devils, by ... Lk 11:19 *954*

BEELZEBULL See BEELZEBUB.

BEEN See APPENDIX.

BEER *(be'-ur)* {2} See BAALITH-BEER, BEER-ELIM, BEER-LAHAI-ROI, BEER-SHEBA.
1. An Israelite post beyond the Arnon River.
And from thence they went to *B* ... Num 21:16 876
2. A town in Judah.
ran away, and fled, and went to *B* ... Judg 9:21 876

BEERA *(be-e'-rah)* {1} *Son of Zophah.*
and Shilshah, and Ithran, and *B* ... 1Chr 7:37 878

BEERAH *(be-e'-rah)* {1} *A Reubenite prince.*
B his son, whom Tilgath-pilneser ... 1Chr 5:6 880

BEER-ELIM *(be'-ur-e'-lim)* {1} *A well in Moab.*
and the howling thereof unto *B* ... Is 15:8 879

BEERI *(be-e'-ri)* {2}
1. Father of Judith.
the daughter of *B* the Hittite ... Gen 26:34 882
2. Father of Hosea.
came unto Hosea, the son of *B* ... Hos 1:1 882

BEER-LAHAI-ROI *(be'-ur-la'-hahe-ro'-e)* {1} *A well.*
Wherefore the well was called *B* ... Gen 16:14 883

BEEROTH *(be-e'-roth)* {6} See BEROTHITE.
1. An Israelite encampment during the Exodus.
B of the children of Jaakan to ... Deut 10:6 881
2. A Hivite city in Canaan.
were Gibeon, and Chephirah, and *B* ... Josh 9:17 881
Gibeon, and Ramah, and *B*, ... Josh 18:25 881
(for *B* also was reckoned to ... 2Sa 4:2 881
of Kirjath-arim, Chephirah, and *B* ... Ezr 2:25 881
Kirjath-jearim, Chephirah, and *B* ... Neh 7:29 881

BEEROTHITE *(be-er'-o-thite)* {4} See BEEROTHITES, BEROTHITE. *An inhabitant of Beeroth.*
Rechab, the sons of Rimmon a *B* ... 2Sa 4:2 886
And the sons of Rimmon the *B* ... 2Sa 4:5 886
brother, the sons of Rimmon the *B* ... 2Sa 4:9 886
Zelek the Ammonite, Nahari the *B* ... 2Sa 23:37 886

BEEROTHITES *(be-er'-o-thites)* {1}
the *B* fled to Gittaim, and were ... 2Sa 4:3 886

BEER-SHEBA *(be-ur'-she-bah)* {34} *A Canaanite city.*
wandered in the wilderness of *B* ... Gen 21:14 884
Wherefore he called that place *B* ... Gen 21:31 884
Thus they made a covenant at *B* ... Gen 21:32 884
And Abraham planted a grove in *B* ... Gen 21:33 884
rose up and went together to *B* ... Gen 22:19 884
and Abraham dwelt at *B* ... Gen 22:19 884
And he went up from thence to *B* ... Gen 26:23 884
of the city is *B* unto this day ... Gen 26:33 884
And Jacob went out from *B*, and went ... Gen 28:10 884
all that he had, and came to *B* ... Gen 46:1 884
And Jacob rose up from *B* ... Gen 46:5 884
And Hazar-shual, and *B*, and ... Josh 15:28 884
they had in their inheritance *B* ... Josh 19:2 884
as one man, from Dan even to *B* ... Judg 20:1 884
even to *B* knew that Samuel was ... 1Sa 3:20 884
they were judges in *B* ... 1Sa 8:2 884
and over Judah, from Dan even to *B* ... 2Sa 3:10 884
unto thee, from Dan even to *B* ... 2Sa 17:11 884
of Israel, from Dan even to *B* ... 2Sa 24:2 884
to the south of Judah, even to *B* ... 2Sa 24:7 884
even to *B* seventy thousand men ... 2Sa 24:15 884
his fig tree, from Dan even to *B* ... 1Kin 4:25 884
went for his life, and came to *B* ... 1Kin 19:3 884
his mother's name was Zibiah of *B* ... 2Kin 12:1 884
burned incense, from Geba to *B* ... 2Kin 23:8 884
And they dwelt at *B*, and Moladah, ... 1Chr 4:28 884
number Israel from *B* even to Dan ... 1Chr 21:2 884
people from *B* to mount Ephraim ... 2Chr 19:4 884
name also was Zibiah of *B* ... 2Chr 24:1 884
from *B* even to Dan, that they ... 2Chr 30:5 884
And at Hazar-shual, and at *B* ... Neh 11:27 884
they dwelt from *B* unto the valley ... Neh 11:30 884
into Gilgal, and pass not to *B* ... Amos 5:5 884
and, The manner of *B* liveth ... Amos 8:14 884

BEES {3}
you, and chased you, as *b* do ... Deut 1:44 1682
behold, there was a swarm of *b* ... Judg 14:8 1682
They compassed me about like *b* ... Ps 118:12 1682

BE-ESHTARAH See BEESH-TERAH.

BEESH-TERAH *(be-esh'-te-rah)* {1} See ASHTAROTH. *A Levitical city in Manasseh.*
and *B* with her suburbs ... Josh 21:27 1203

BEETLE {1}
the *b* after his kind, and the ... Lev 11:22 2728

BEEVES {7}
a male without blemish, of the *b* ... Lev 22:19 1241
a freewill offering in *b* or sheep ... Lev 22:21 1241
both of the persons, and of the *b* ... Num 31:28 1241
fifty, of the persons, of the *b* ... Num 31:30 1241
threescore and twelve thousand *b* ... Num 31:33 1241
the *b* were thirty and six thousand ... Num 31:38 1241
And thirty and six thousand *b* ... Num 31:44 1241

BEFALL {9}
Lest peradventure mischief *b* him ... Gen 42:4 7122
if mischief *b* him by the way in ... Gen 42:38 7122
also from me, and mischief *b* him ... Gen 44:29 7136
shall *b* you in the last days ... Gen 49:1 7122
evils and troubles shall *b* them ... Deut 31:17 4672
evil will *b* you in the latter ... Deut 31:29 7122
There shall no evil *b* thee ... Ps 91:10 579
b thy people in the latter days ... Dan 10:14 7136
the things that shall *b* me there ... Acts 20:22 *4876*

BEFALLEN {7}
and such things have *b* me ... Lev 10:19 7122
all the travel that hath *b* us ... Num 20:14 4672
many evils and troubles are *b* them ... Deut 31:21 4672
us, why then is all this *b* us ... Judg 6:13 4672
he thought, Something hath *b* him ... 1Sa 20:26 4745
every thing that had *b* him ... Est 6:13 7136
what was *b* to the possessed of ... Mt 8:33 *4876*

BEFALLETH {3}
b the sons of men *b* beasts ... Eccl 3:19 4745
even one thing *b* them ... Eccl 3:19 4745

BEFELL {5}
and told him all that *b* unto them ... Gen 42:29 7136
told him all things that *b* them ... Josh 2:23 4672
thee than all the evil that *b* ... 2Sa 19:7 935
that saw it told them how it *b* to ... Mk 5:16 *1096*
which *b* me by the lying in wait ... Acts 20:19 *4819*

BEFORE See APPENDIX.

BEFOREHAND See APPENDIX.

BEFORETIME {11}
The Horims also dwelt in Seir *b* ... Deut 2:12 6440
for Hazor *b* was the head of all ... Josh 11:10 6440
unwittingly, and hated him not *b* ... Josh 20:5 8543,8032
(*B* in Israel, when a man went to ... 1Sa 9:9 6440
a Prophet was *b* called a Seer ... 1Sa 9:9 6440
when all that knew him *b* saw that ... 1Sa 10:11 865,832
afflict them any more, as *b* ... 2Sa 7:10 7223
Israel dwelt in their tents, as *b* ... 2Kin 13:5 8543,8032
Now I had not been *b* sad in his ... Neh 2:1
and *b*, that we may say, He is ... Is 41:26 6440
which *b* in the same city used ... Acts 8:9 *4391*

BEG {3}
be continually vagabonds, and *b* ... Ps 109:10 7592
therefore shall he *b* in harvest ... Prov 20:4 7592
to *b* I am ashamed ... Lk 16:3 *1871*

BEGAN See APPENDIX.

BEGAT {225}
and Irad *b* Mehujael ... Gen 4:18 3205
and Mehujael *b* Methusael ... Gen 4:18 3205
and Methusael *b* Lamech ... Gen 4:18 3205
b a son in his own likeness, ... Gen 5:3 3205
and he *b* sons and daughters ... Gen 5:4 3205
hundred and five years, and *b* Enos ... Gen 5:6 3205
after he *b* Enos eight hundred ... Gen 5:7 3205
years, and *b* sons and daughters ... Gen 5:7 3205
lived ninety years, and *b* Cainan ... Gen 5:9 3205
Enos lived after he *b* Cainan ... Gen 5:10 3205
years, and *b* sons and daughters ... Gen 5:10 3205
seventy years, and *b* Mahalaleel ... Gen 5:12 3205
And Cainan lived after he *b* ... Gen 5:13 3205
years, and *b* sons and daughters ... Gen 5:13 3205
sixty and five years, and *b* Jared ... Gen 5:15 3205
after he *b* Jared eight hundred ... Gen 5:16 3205
years, and *b* sons and daughters ... Gen 5:16 3205
sixty and two years, and he *b* Enoch ... Gen 5:18 3205
Jared lived after he *b* Enoch ... Gen 5:19 3205
years, and *b* sons and daughters ... Gen 5:19 3205
and five years, and *b* Methuselah ... Gen 5:21 3205
b Methuselah three hundred years ... Gen 5:22 3205
and *b* sons and daughters ... Gen 5:22 3205
and seven years, and *b* Lamech ... Gen 5:25 3205
Methuselah lived after he *b* ... Gen 5:26 3205
two years, and *b* sons and daughters ... Gen 5:26 3205
eighty and two years, and *b* a son ... Gen 5:28 3205
Lamech lived after he *b* Noah five ... Gen 5:30 3205
years, and *b* sons and daughters ... Gen 5:30 3205
and Noah *b* Shem, Ham, and Japheth ... Gen 5:32 3205
Noah *b* three sons, Shem, Ham, and ... Gen 6:10 3205
And Cush *b* Nimrod ... Gen 10:8 3205
And Mizraim *b* Ludim, and Anamim, ... Gen 10:13 3205
Canaan *b* Sidon his firstborn, and ... Gen 10:15 3205
And Arphaxad *b* Salah ... Gen 10:24 3205
and Salah *b* Eber ... Gen 10:24 3205
Joktan *b* Almodad, and Sheleph, and ... Gen 10:26 3205
b Arphaxad two years after the ... Gen 11:10 3205

Shem lived after he *b* Arphaxad ... Gen 11:11 3205
years, and *b* sons and daughters ... Gen 11:11 3205
five and thirty years, and *b* Salah ... Gen 11:12 3205
after he *b* Salah four hundred ... Gen 11:13 3205
years, and *b* sons and daughters ... Gen 11:13 3205
lived thirty years, and *b* Eber ... Gen 11:14 3205
after he *b* Eber four hundred ... Gen 11:15 3205
years, and *b* sons and daughters ... Gen 11:15 3205
four and thirty years, and *b* Peleg ... Gen 11:16 3205
after he *b* Peleg four hundred ... Gen 11:17 3205
years, and *b* sons and daughters ... Gen 11:17 3205
lived thirty years, and *b* Reu ... Gen 11:18 3205
lived after he *b* Reu two hundred ... Gen 11:19 3205
years, and *b* sons and daughters ... Gen 11:19 3205
two and thirty years, and *b* Serug ... Gen 11:20 3205
after he *b* Serug two hundred ... Gen 11:21 3205
years, and *b* sons and daughters ... Gen 11:21 3205
lived thirty years, and *b* Nahor ... Gen 11:22 3205
Serug lived after he *b* Nahor two ... Gen 11:23 3205
years, and *b* sons and daughters ... Gen 11:23 3205
nine and twenty years, and *b* Terah ... Gen 11:24 3205
lived after he *b* Terah an hundred ... Gen 11:25 3205
years, and *b* sons and daughters ... Gen 11:25 3205
and *b* Abram, Nahor, and Haran ... Gen 11:26 3205
Terah *b* Abram, Nahor, and Haran ... Gen 11:27 3205
and Haran *b* Lot ... Gen 11:27 3205
And Bethuel *b* Rebekah ... Gen 22:23 3205
And Jokshan *b* Sheba, and Dedan ... Gen 25:3 3205
Abraham *b* Isaac ... Gen 25:19 3205
which they *b* in your land ... Lev 25:45 3205
and Machir *b* Gilead ... Num 26:29 3205
And Kohath *b* Amram ... Num 26:58 3205
Of the Rock that *b* thee thou art ... Deut 32:18 3205
and Gilead *b* Jephthah ... Judg 11:1 3205
Pharez *b* Hezron, ... Ruth 4:18 3205
And Hezron *b* Ram ... Ruth 4:19 3205
and Ram *b* Amminadab ... Ruth 4:19 3205
And Amminadab *b* Nahshon, and ... Ruth 4:20 3205
Nahshon, and Nahshon *b* Salmon ... Ruth 4:20 3205
Salmon *b* Boaz, and Boaz *b* Obed ... Ruth 4:21 3205
Obed *b* Jesse ... Ruth 4:22 3205
and Jesse *b* David ... Ruth 4:22 3205
And Cush *b* Nimrod ... 1Chr 1:10 3205
And Mizraim *b* Ludim, and Anamim, ... 1Chr 1:11 3205
Canaan *b* Zidon his firstborn, and ... 1Chr 1:13 3205
And Arphaxad *b* Shelah ... 1Chr 1:18 3205
and Shelah *b* Eber ... 1Chr 1:18 3205
Joktan *b* Almodad, and Sheleph, and ... 1Chr 1:20 3205
And Abraham *b* Isaac ... 1Chr 1:34 3205
And Ram *b* Amminadab ... 1Chr 2:10 3205
and Amminadab *b* Nahshon, prince of ... 1Chr 2:10 3205
And Nahshon *b* Salma ... 1Chr 2:11 3205
and Salma *b* Boaz ... 1Chr 2:11 3205
Boaz *b* Obed, and Obed *b* Jesse, ... 1Chr 2:12 3205
Jesse *b* his firstborn Eliab, and ... 1Chr 2:13 3205
Caleb the son of Hezron *b* ... 1Chr 2:18 3205
Hur *b* Uri, and Uri *b* Bezaleel ... 1Chr 2:20 3205
And Segub *b* Jair, who had three and ... 1Chr 2:22 3205
Attai *b* Nathan ... 1Chr 2:36 3205
and Nathan *b* Zabad ... 1Chr 2:36 3205
Zabad *b* Ephlal ... 1Chr 2:37 3205
Ephlal *b* Obed ... 1Chr 2:37 3205
And Obed *b* Jehu ... 1Chr 2:38 3205
and Jehu *b* Azariah ... 1Chr 2:38 3205
And Azariah *b* Helez ... 1Chr 2:39 3205
and Helez *b* Eleasah ... 1Chr 2:39 3205
And Eleasah *b* Sisamai ... 1Chr 2:40 3205
and Sisamai *b* Shallum ... 1Chr 2:40 3205
Shallum *b* Jekamiah ... 1Chr 2:41 3205
and Jekamiah *b* Elishama ... 1Chr 2:41 3205
And Shema *b* Raham, the father of ... 1Chr 2:44 3205
and Rekem *b* Shammai ... 1Chr 2:44 3205
and Haran *b* Gazez ... 1Chr 2:46 3205
Reaiah the son of Shobal *b* Jahath ... 1Chr 4:2 3205
and Jahath *b* Ahumai, and Lahad ... 1Chr 4:2 3205
Coz *b* Anub, and Zobebah, and the ... 1Chr 4:8 3205
the brother of Shuah *b* Mehir ... 1Chr 4:11 3205
Eshton *b* Beth-rapha, and Paseah, ... 1Chr 4:12 3205
And Meonothai *b* Ophrah ... 1Chr 4:14 3205
and Seraiah *b* Joab, the father of ... 1Chr 4:14 3205
Eleazar *b* Phinehas ... 1Chr 6:4 3205
Phinehas *b* Abishua ... 1Chr 6:4 3205
And Abishua *b* Bukki ... 1Chr 6:5 3205
and Bukki *b* Uzzi ... 1Chr 6:5 3205
And Uzzi *b* Zerahiah ... 1Chr 6:6 3205
and Zerahiah *b* Meraioth ... 1Chr 6:6 3205
Meraioth *b* Amariah ... 1Chr 6:7 3205
and Amariah *b* Ahitub ... 1Chr 6:7 3205
And Ahitub *b* Zadok ... 1Chr 6:8 3205
and Zadok *b* Ahimaaz ... 1Chr 6:8 3205
And Ahimaaz *b* Azariah ... 1Chr 6:9 3205
and Azariah *b* Johanan ... 1Chr 6:9 3205
And Johanan *b* Azariah, (he it is ... 1Chr 6:10 3205
And Azariah *b* Amariah ... 1Chr 6:11 3205
and Amariah *b* Ahitub ... 1Chr 6:11 3205
And Ahitub *b* Zadok ... 1Chr 6:12 3205
and Zadok *b* Shallum ... 1Chr 6:12 3205
And Shallum *b* Hilkiah ... 1Chr 6:13 3205
and Hilkiah *b* Azariah ... 1Chr 6:13 3205
And Azariah *b* Seraiah ... 1Chr 6:14 3205
and Seraiah *b* Jehozadak ... 1Chr 6:14 3205
Heber *b* Japhlet, and Shomer, and ... 1Chr 7:32 3205
Now Benjamin *b* Bela his firstborn ... 1Chr 8:1 3205
them, and *b* Uzza, and Ahihud ... 1Chr 8:7 3205
Shaharaim *b* children in the ... 1Chr 8:8 3205
he *b* of Hodesh his wife, Jobab, ... 1Chr 8:9 3205
And of Hushim he *b* Abitub, and ... 1Chr 8:11 3205
And Mikloth *b* Shimeah ... 1Chr 8:32 3205
And Ner *b* Kish, and Kish *b* Saul ... 1Chr 8:33 3205
Saul *b* Jonathan, and Malchi-shua, ... 1Chr 8:33 3205
and Merib-baal *b* Micah ... 1Chr 8:34 3205
And Ahaz *b* Jehoadah ... 1Chr 8:36 3205
and Jehoadah *b* Alemeth, and ... 1Chr 8:36 3205
and Zimri *b* Moza, ... 1Chr 8:36 3205
And Moza *b* Binea ... 1Chr 8:37 3205
And Mikloth *b* Shimeam ... 1Chr 9:38 3205
And Ner *b* Kish ... 1Chr 9:39 3205
and Kish *b* Saul ... 1Chr 9:39 3205
Saul *b* Jonathan, and Malchi-shua, ... 1Chr 9:39 3205
and Merib-baal *b* Micah ... 1Chr 9:40 3205
And Ahaz *b* Jarah ... 1Chr 9:42 3205
Jarah *b* Alemeth, and Azmaveth, and ... 1Chr 9:42 3205
and Zimri *b* Moza ... 1Chr 9:42 3205
And Moza *b* Binea ... 1Chr 9:43 3205
David *b* more sons and daughters ... 1Chr 14:3 3205
b twenty and eight sons, and ... 2Chr 11:21 3205
b twenty and two sons, and sixteen ... 2Chr 13:21 3205
and he *b* sons and daughters ... 2Chr 24:3 3205
Jeshua *b* Joiakim ... Neh 12:10 3205
Joiakim also *b* Eliashib ... Neh 12:10 3205
and Eliashib *b* Joiada ... Neh 12:10 3205
Joiada *b* Jonathan ... Neh 12:11 3205
and Jonathan *b* Jaddua ... Neh 12:11 3205
unto thy father that *b* thee ... Prov 23:22 3205
fathers that *b* them in this land ... Jer 16:3 3205
brought her, and he that *b* her ... Dan 11:6 3205
his mother that *b* him shall say ... Zec 13:3 3205
his mother that *b* him shall ... Zec 13:3 3205
Abraham *b* Isaac ... Mt 1:2 *1080*
and Isaac *b* Jacob ... Mt 1:2 *1080*
and Jacob *b* Judas and his brethren ... Mt 1:2 *1080*
Judas *b* Phares and Zara of Thamar ... Mt 1:3 *1080*
and Phares *b* Esrom ... Mt 1:3 *1080*
and Esrom *b* Aram ... Mt 1:3 *1080*
And Aram *b* Aminadab ... Mt 1:4 *1080*
and Aminadab *b* Naasson ... Mt 1:4 *1080*
and Naasson *b* Salmon ... Mt 1:4 *1080*
And Salmon *b* Booz of Rachab ... Mt 1:5 *1080*
and Booz *b* Obed of Ruth ... Mt 1:5 *1080*
and Obed *b* Jesse ... Mt 1:5 *1080*
And Jesse *b* David the king ... Mt 1:6 *1080*
David the king *b* Solomon of her ... Mt 1:6 *1080*
And Solomon *b* Roboam ... Mt 1:7 *1080*
and Roboam *b* Abia ... Mt 1:7 *1080*
and Abia *b* Asa ... Mt 1:7 *1080*
And Asa *b* Josaphat ... Mt 1:8 *1080*
and Josaphat *b* Joram ... Mt 1:8 *1080*
and Joram *b* Ozias ... Mt 1:8 *1080*
And Ozias *b* Joatham ... Mt 1:9 *1080*
and Joatham *b* Achaz ... Mt 1:9 *1080*
and Achaz *b* Ezekias ... Mt 1:9 *1080*
And Ezekias *b* Manasses ... Mt 1:10 *1080*
and Manasses *b* Amon ... Mt 1:10 *1080*
and Amon *b* Josias ... Mt 1:10 *1080*
Josias *b* Jechonias and his ... Mt 1:11 *1080*
to Babylon, Jechonias *b* Salathiel ... Mt 1:12 *1080*
and Salathiel *b* Zorobabel ... Mt 1:12 *1080*
And Zorobabel *b* Abiud ... Mt 1:13 *1080*
and Abiud *b* Eliakim ... Mt 1:13 *1080*
and Eliakim *b* Azor ... Mt 1:13 *1080*
And Azor *b* Sadoc ... Mt 1:14 *1080*
and Sadoc *b* Achim ... Mt 1:14 *1080*
and Achim *b* Eliud ... Mt 1:14 *1080*
And Eliud *b* Eleazar ... Mt 1:15 *1080*
and Eleazar *b* Matthan ... Mt 1:15 *1080*
and Matthan *b* Jacob ... Mt 1:15 *1080*
Jacob *b* Joseph the husband of ... Mt 1:16 *1080*
and so Abraham *b* Isaac, and ... Acts 7:8 *1080*
and Isaac *b* Jacob ... Acts 7:8
Jacob *b* the twelve patriarchs ... Acts 7:8 *1080*
of Madian, where he *b* two sons ... Acts 7:29 *1080*
Of his own will *b* he us with the ... Jas 1:18 *616*
that *b* loveth him also that is ... 1Jn 5:1 *1080*

BEGET {10}
twelve princes shall he *b* ... Gen 17:20 3205
When thou shalt *b* children ... Deut 4:25 3205
Thou shalt *b* sons and daughters, ... Deut 28:41 3205
from thee, which thou shalt *b* ... 2Kin 20:18 3205
If a man *b* an hundred children, ... Eccl 6:3 3205
from thee, which thou shall *b* ... Is 39:7 3205
ye wives, and *b* sons and daughters ... Jer 29:6 3205
If he *b* a son that is a robber, a ... Eze 18:10 3205
Now, lo, if he *b* a son, that ... Eze 18:14 3205
which shall *b* children among you ... Eze 47:22 3205

BEGETTEST {2}
issue, which thou *b* after them ... Gen 48:6 3205
unto his father, What *b* thou ... Is 45:10 3205

BEGETTETH {3}
He that *b* a fool doeth it to his ... Prov 17:21 3205
he that *b* a wise child shall have ... Prov 23:24 3205
he *b* a son, and there is nothing ... Eccl 5:14 3205

BEGGAR {3}
lifteth up the *b* from the ... 1Sa 2:8 34
was a certain *b* named Lazarus ... Lk 16:20 *4434*
it came to pass, that the *b* died ... Lk 16:22 *4434*

BEGGARLY {1}
b elements, whereunto ye desire ... Gal 4:9 *4434*

BEGGED {3}
to Pilate, and *b* the body of Jesus ... Mt 27:58 *154*
Pilate, and *b* the body of Jesus ... Lk 23:52 *154*
Is not this he that sat and *b* ... Jn 9:8 *4319*

BEGGING {3}
forsaken, nor his seed *b* bread ... Ps 37:25 1245
sat by the highway side *b* ... Mk 10:46 *4319*
blind man sat by the way side *b* ... Lk 18:35 *4319*

BEGIN See APPENDIX.

BEGINNEST {1}
weeks from such time as thou *b* to ... Deut 16:9 2490

BEGINNING See APPENDIX.

BEGINNINGS {4}
in the *b* of your months, ye shall ... Num 10:10 7218
in the *b* of your months ye shall ... Num 28:11 7218
do better unto you than at your *b* ... Eze 36:11 7221
these are the *b* of sorrows ... Mk 13:8 *746*

BEGOTTEN {24}
b Seth were eight hundred years ... Gen 5:4 3205
b of thy father, she is thy ... Lev 18:11 4138
have I *b* them, that thou ... Num 11:12 3205
The children that are *b* of them ... Deut 23:8 3205
and ten sons of his body *b* ... Judg 8:30 3318
or who hath *b* the drops of dew ... Job 38:28 3205
this day have I *b* thee ... Ps 2:7 3205
thine heart, Who hath *b* me these ... Is 49:21 3205
for they have *b* strange children ... Hos 5:7 3205
as of the only *b* of the Father ... Jn 1:14 *3439*
the only *b* Son, which is in the ... Jn 1:18 *3439*
that he gave his only *b* Son ... Jn 3:16 *3439*
the name of the only *b* Son of God ... Jn 3:18 *3439*
my Son, this day have I *b* thee ... Acts 13:33 *1080*
I have *b* you through the gospel ... 1Cor 4:15 *1080*
whom I have *b* in my bonds ... Philem 10 *1080*
my Son, this day have I *b* thee ... Heb 1:5 *1080*
art my Son, to day have I *b* thee ... Heb 5:5 *1080*
offered up his only *b* son ... Heb 11:17 *3439*
to his abundant mercy hath *b* us ... 1Pet 1:3 *313*
his only *b* Son into the world ... 1Jn 4:9 *3439*
loveth him also that is *b* of him ... 1Jn 5:1 *1080*
but he that is *b* of God keepeth ... 1Jn 5:18 *1080*
the first *b* of the dead, and the ... Rev 1:5 *4416*

BEGUILE {2}
lest any man should *b* you with ... Col 2:4 *3884*
Let no man *b* you of your reward ... Col 2:18 *2603*

BEGUILED {5}
the woman said, The serpent *b* me ... Gen 3:13 5377
wherefore then hast thou *b* me ... Gen 29:25 7411
wherewith they have *b* you in the ... Num 25:18 5230
saying, Wherefore have ye *b* us ... Josh 9:22 7411
as the serpent *b* Eve through his ... 2Cor 11:3 *1818*

BEGUILING {1}
b unstable souls ... 2Pet 2:14 *1185*

BEGUN See APPENDIX.

BEHALF {13}
the *b* of the children of Israel ... Ex 27:21 854
sent messengers to David on his *b* ... 2Sa 3:12 8478
to shew himself strong in the *b* ... 2Chr 16:9 5973
I have yet to speak on God's *b* ... Job 36:2
own *b* shall cause the reproach ... Dan 11:18
I am glad therefore on your *b* ... Rom 16:19 *1909*
I thank my God always on your *b* ... 1Cor 1:4 *4012*
may be given by many on our *b* ... 2Cor 1:11 *5228*
you occasion to glory on our *b* ... 2Cor 5:12 *5228*
and of our boasting on your *b* ... 2Cor 8:24 *5228*
you should be in vain in this *b* ... 2Cor 9:3 *3313*
it is given in the *b* of Christ ... Phil 1:29 *5228*
but let him glorify God on this *b* ... 1Pet 4:16 *3313*

BEHAVE {6}
should *b* themselves strangely ... Deut 32:27 5234
let us *b* ourselves valiantly for ... 1Chr 19:13 2388
I will *b* myself wisely in a ... Ps 101:2 7919
the child shall *b* himself proudly ... Is 3:5 7292
Doth not *b* itself unseemly, ... 1Cor 13:5 *807*
know how thou oughtest to *b* ... 1Ti 3:15 *390*

BEHAVED {9}
sent him, and *b* himself wisely ... 1Sa 18:5 7919
David *b* himself wisely in all his ... 1Sa 18:14 7919
saw that he *b* himself very wisely ... 1Sa 18:15 7919
that David *b* himself more wisely ... 1Sa 18:30 7919
I *b* myself as though he had been ... Ps 35:14 1980
Surely I have *b* and quieted myself ... Ps 131:2 7737
as they have *b* themselves ill in ... Mic 3:4 7489
unblameably we *b* ourselves among ... 1Th 2:10 *1096*
for we *b* not ourselves disorderly ... 2Th 3:7 *812*

BEHAVETH {1}
he *b* himself uncomely toward his ... 1Cor 7:36 *807*

BEHAVIOUR {4}
And he changed his *b* before them ... 1Sa 21:13 2940
he changed his *b* before Abimelech ... Ps 34:*t* 2940
wife, vigilant, sober, of good *b* ... 1Ti 3:2 *2887*
that they be in *b* as becometh ... Titus 2:3 *2688*

BEHEADED {7}
heifer that is *b* in the valley ... Deut 21:6 6202
b him, and took his head, and ... 2Sa 4:7 5493,7218
he sent, and *b* John in the prison ... Mt 14:10 *607*
he said, It is John, whom I *b* ... Mk 6:16 *607*
he went and *b* him in the prison, ... Mk 6:27 *607*
And Herod said, John have I *b* ... Lk 9:9 *607*
were *b* for the witness of Jesus ... Rev 20:4 *3990*

BEHELD {53}
the Egyptians *b* the woman that ... Gen 12:14 7200
b all the plain of Jordan, that ... Gen 13:10 7200
all the land of the plain, and *b* ... Gen 19:28 7200
Jacob *b* the countenance of Laban, ... Gen 31:2 7200
Israel *b* Joseph's sons, and said, ... Gen 48:8 7200
when he *b* the serpent of brass, ... Num 21:9 5027

He hath not *b* iniquity in Jacob, Num 23:21 5027
that *b* while Samson made sport Judg 16:27 7200
David *b* the place where Saul lay, 1Sa 26:5 7200
as he was destroying, the LORD *b* 1Chr 21:15 7200
If I *b* the sun when it shined, or Job 31:26 7200
I *b* the transgressors, and was Ps 119:158 7200
I looked on my right hand, and *b* Ps 142:4 7200
b among the simple ones, I Prov 7:7 7200
Then I *b* all the work of God, Eccl 8:17 7200
For I *b*, and there was no man Is 41:28 7200
I *b* the earth, and, lo, it was Jer 4:23 7200
I *b* the mountains, and, lo, they Jer 4:24 7200
I *b*, and, lo, there was no man, and Jer 4:25 7200
I *b*, and, lo, the fruitful place Jer 4:26 7200
Upon this I awaked, and *b* Jer 31:26 7200
Now as I *b* the living creatures, Eze 1:15 7200
Then I *b*, and lo a likeness as the Eze 8:2 7200
And when I *b*, lo, the sinews and Eze 37:8 7200
I *b* till the wings thereof were Dan 7:4 2370,934
After this I *b*, and lo another, Dan 7:6 2370,934
I *b* till the thrones were cast Dan 7:9 2370,934
I *b* then because of the voice of Dan 7:11 2370,934
I *b* even till the beast was slain Dan 7:11 2370,934
I *b*, and the same horn made war Dan 7:21 2370,934
he *b*, and drove asunder the Hab 3:6 7200
But Jesus *b* them, and said unto Mt 19:26 *1689*
all the people, when they *b* him Mk 9:15 *1492*
b how the people cast money into Mk 12:41 *2334*
of Joses *b* where he was laid Mk 15:47 *2334*
I *b* Satan as lightning fall from Lk 10:18 *2334*
he *b* the city, and wept over it, Lk 19:41 *1492*
he *b* them, and said, What is this Lk 20:17 *1689*
But a certain maid *b* him as he Lk 22:56 *1492*
b the sepulchre, and how his body Lk 23:55 *2300*
he *b* the linen clothes laid by Lk 24:12 *991*
we *b* his glory, the glory as of Jn 1:14 *2300*
And when Jesus *b* him, he said, Jn 1:42 *1689*
spoken these things, while they *b* Acts 1:9 *991*
b your devotions, I found an Acts 17:23 *333*
And I *b*, and, lo, in the midst of Rev 5:6 *1492*
And I *b*, and I heard the voice of Rev 5:11 *1492*
And I *b*, and lo a black horse Rev 6:5 *1492*
I *b* when he had opened the sixth Rev 6:12 *1492*
After this I *b*, and, lo, a great Rev 7:9 *1492*
And I *b*, and heard an angel flying Rev 8:13 *1492*
and their enemies *b* them Rev 11:12 *2334*
I *b* another beast coming up out Rev 13:11 *1492*

BEHEMOTH {1}
Behold now *b*, which I made with Job 40:15 930

BEHIND See APPENDIX.

BEHOLD {1327}
And God said, *B*, I have given you Gen 1:29 2009
thing that he had made, and, *b* Gen 1:31 2009
And the LORD God said, *B*, the man Gen 3:22 2005
B, thou hast driven me out this Gen 4:14 2005
God looked upon the earth, and, *b* Gen 6:12 2009
and, *b*, I will destroy them with Gen 6:13 2005
And, *b*, I, even I, do bring a Gen 6:17 2005
of the ark, and looked, and, *b* Gen 8:13 2009
And I, *b*, I establish my covenant Gen 9:9 2005
And the LORD said, *B*, the people Gen 11:6 2005
B now, I know that thou art a Gen 12:11 2009
now therefore *b* thy wife, take Gen 12:19 2009
And Abram said, *B*, to me thou hast Gen 15:3 2005
And, *b*, the word of the LORD came Gen 15:4 2009
b a smoking furnace, and a burning Gen 15:17 2009
B now, the LORD hath restrained Gen 16:2 2009
But Abram said unto Sarai, *B* Gen 16:6 2009
of the LORD said unto her, *B* Gen 16:11 2009
b, it is between Kadesh and Bered Gen 16:14 2009
As for me, *b*, my covenant is with Gen 17:4 2009
B, I have blessed him, and will Gen 17:20 2009
And he said, *B*, in the tent Gen 18:9 2009
B now, I have taken upon me to Gen 18:27 2009
B now, I have taken upon me to Gen 18:31 2009
B now, my lords, turn in, I pray Gen 19:2 2009
B now, I have two daughters which Gen 19:8 2009
B now, thy servant hath found Gen 19:19 2009
B now, this city is near to flee Gen 19:20 2009
said unto the younger, *B*, I lay Gen 19:34 2005
dream by night, and said to him, *B* Gen 20:3 2009
And Abimelech said, *B*, my land is Gen 20:15 2009
And unto Sarah he said, *B*, I have Gen 20:16 2009
b, he is to thee a covering of Gen 20:16 2009
and he said, *B*, here I am Gen 22:1 2009
he said, *B* the fire and the wood Gen 22:7 2009
b behind him a ram caught in a Gen 22:13 2009
it was told Abraham, saying, *B* Gen 22:20 2009
B, I stand here by the well of Gen 24:13 2009
he had done speaking, that, *b* Gen 24:15 2009
and, *b*, he stood by the camels at Gen 24:30 2009
B, I stand by the well of water Gen 24:43 2009
done speaking in mine heart, *b* Gen 24:45 2009
B, Rebekah is before thee, take Gen 24:51 2009
lifted up his eyes, and saw, and, *b* Gen 24:63 2009
to be delivered were fulfilled, *b* Gen 25:24 2009
And Esau said, *B*, I am at the Gen 25:32 2009
out at a window, and saw, and, *b* Gen 26:8 2009
called Isaac, and said, *B*, of a Gen 26:9 2009
and he said unto him, *B*, here am I Gen 27:1 2009
B now, I am old, I know not the Gen 27:2 2009
unto Jacob her son, saying, *B* Gen 27:6 2009
said to Rebekah his mother, *B* Gen 27:11 2005
and, *b*, now he hath taken away my Gen 27:36 2009
answered and said unto Esau, *B* Gen 27:37 2005
answered and said unto him, *B* Gen 27:39 2009
younger son, and said unto him, *B* Gen 27:42 2009
b a ladder set up on the earth, Gen 28:12 2009
b the angels of God ascending and Gen 28:12 2009
And, *b*, the LORD stood above it, Gen 28:13 2009
And, *b*, I am with thee, and will Gen 28:15 2009
b a well in the field, and, lo, Gen 29:2 2009
and, *b*, Rachel his daughter cometh Gen 29:6 2009
to pass, that in the morning, *b* Gen 29:25 2009
B my maid Bilhah, go in unto her Gen 30:3 2009
And Laban said, *B*, I would it Gen 30:34 2005
the countenance of Laban, and, *b* Gen 31:2 2009
eyes, and saw in a dream, and, *b* Gen 31:10 2009
B this heap, and *b* this Gen 31:51 2009
and, *b*, also he is behind us Gen 32:18 2009
And say ye moreover, *B*, thy Gen 32:20 2009
up his eyes, and looked, and, *b* Gen 33:1 2009
for the land, *b*, it is large Gen 34:21 2009
For, *b*, we were binding sheaves Gen 37:7 2009
and, *b*, your sheaves stood round Gen 37:7 2009
told it his brethren, and said, *B* Gen 37:9 2009
and, *b*, the sun and the moon and the Gen 37:9 2009
And a certain man found him, and, *b* Gen 37:15 2009
And they said one to another, *B* Gen 37:19 2009
up their eyes and looked, and, *b* Gen 37:25 2009
and, *b*, Joseph was not in the pit Gen 37:29 2009
B thy father in law goeth up to Gen 38:13 2009
b, I sent this kid, and thou hast Gen 38:23 2009
and also, *b*, she is with child by Gen 38:24 2009
the time of her travail, that, *b* Gen 38:27 2009
as he drew back his hand, that, *b* Gen 38:29 2009
and said unto his master's wife, *B* Gen 39:8 2005
and looked upon them, and, *b* Gen 40:6 2009
and said to him, In my dream, *b* Gen 40:9 2009
I also was in my dream, and, *b* Gen 40:16 2009
and, *b*, he stood by the river Gen 41:1 2009
And, *b*, there came up out of the Gen 41:2 2009
And, *b*, seven other kine came up Gen 41:3 2009
and, *b*, seven ears of corn came up Gen 41:5 2009
And, *b*, seven thin ears and blasted Gen 41:6 2009
And Pharaoh awoke, and, *b*, it was a Gen 41:7 2009
said unto Joseph, In my dream, *b* Gen 41:17 2005
And, *b*, there came up out of the Gen 41:18 2009
And, *b*, seven other kine came up Gen 41:19 2009
And I saw in my dream, and, *b* Gen 41:22 2009
And, *b*, seven ears, withered, thin Gen 41:23 2009
B, there come seven years of Gen 41:29 2009
And he said, *B*, I have heard that Gen 42:2 2009
and, *b*, the youngest is this day Gen 42:13 2009
therefore, *b*, also his blood is Gen 42:22 2009
for, *b*, it was in his sack's Gen 42:27 2009
they emptied their sacks, that, *b* Gen 42:35 2009
that we opened our sacks, and, *b* Gen 43:21 2009
B, the money, which we found in Gen 44:8 2005
b, we are my lord's servants, Gen 44:16 2009
And, *b*, your eyes see, and the eyes Gen 45:12 2009
and, *b*, they are in the land of Gen 47:1 2009
Joseph said unto the people, *B* Gen 47:23 2009
things, that one told Joseph, *B* Gen 48:1 2009
And one told Jacob, and said, *B* Gen 48:2 2009
And said unto me, *B*, I will make Gen 48:4 2005
And Israel said unto Joseph, *B* Gen 48:21 2009
and they said, *B*, we be thy Gen 50:18 2009
And he said unto his people, *B* Ex 1:9 2009
and, *b*, the babe wept Ex 2:6 2009
he went out the second day, *b* Ex 2:13 2009
and he looked, and, *b*, the bush Ex 3:2 2009
Now therefore, *b*, the cry of the Ex 3:9 2009
And Moses said unto God, *B* Ex 3:13 2009
And Moses answered and said, But, *b* Ex 4:1 2005
and when he took it out, *b* Ex 4:6 2009
it out of his bosom, and, *b* Ex 4:7 2009
And also, *b*, he cometh forth to Ex 4:14 2009
if thou refuse to let him go, *b* Ex 4:23 2009
And Pharaoh said, *B*, the people of Ex 5:5 2005
and, *b*, thy servants are beaten Ex 5:16 2009
spake before the LORD, saying, *B* Ex 6:12 2005
And Moses said before the LORD, *B* Ex 6:30 2005
and, *b*, hitherto thou wouldest not Ex 7:16 2009
b, I will smite with the rod that Ex 7:17 2009
if thou refuse to let them go, *b* Ex 8:2 2009
thou wilt not let my people go, *b* Ex 8:21 2005
And Moses said, *B*, I go out from Ex 8:29 2009
B, the hand of the LORD is upon Ex 9:3 2009
And Pharaoh sent, and, *b*, there was Ex 9:7 2009
B, to morrow about this time I Ex 9:18 2005
refuse to let my people go, *b* Ex 10:4 2005
lifted up their eyes, and, *b* Ex 14:10 2009
And I, *b*, I will harden the hearts Ex 14:17 2005
Then said the LORD unto Moses, *B* Ex 16:4 2005
toward the wilderness, and, *b* Ex 16:10 2009
the dew that lay was gone up, *b* Ex 16:14 2009
B, I will stand before thee there Ex 17:6 2005
B, I send an Angel before thee, Ex 23:20 2009
B the blood of the covenant, Ex 24:8 2009
and, *b*, Aaron and Hur are with you Ex 24:14 2009
And I, *b*, I have given with him Ex 31:6 2009
I have seen this people, and, *b* Ex 32:9 2009
b, mine Angel shall go before Ex 32:34 2009
And the LORD said, *B*, there is a Ex 33:21 2009
And he said, *B*, I make a covenant Ex 34:10 2009
b, I drive out before thee the Ex 34:11 2005
children of Israel saw Moses, *b* Ex 34:30 2009
did look upon all the work, and, *b* Ex 39:43 2009
goat of the sin offering, and, *b* Lev 10:16 2009
B, the blood of it was not Lev 10:18 2005
And Aaron said unto Moses, *B* Lev 10:19 2005
and, *b*, if the plague in his sight Lev 13:5 2009
and, *b*, if the plague be somewhat Lev 13:6 2009
And if the priest see that, *b* Lev 13:8 2009
and, *b*, if the rising be white in Lev 13:10 2009
and, *b*, if the leprosy have Lev 13:13 2009
and, *b*, if the plague be turned Lev 13:17 2009
if, when the priest seeth it, *b* Lev 13:20 2009
if the priest look on it, and, *b* Lev 13:21 2009
and, *b*, if the hair in the bright Lev 13:25 2009
if the priest look on it, and, *b* Lev 13:26 2009
and, *b*, if it be in sight deeper Lev 13:30 2009
on the plague of the scall, and, *b* Lev 13:31 2009
and, *b*, if the scall spread not, Lev 13:32 2009
and, *b*, if the scall be not spread Lev 13:34 2009
and, *b*, if the scall be spread in Lev 13:36 2009
and, *b*, if the bright spots in the Lev 13:39 2009
and, *b*, if the rising of the sore Lev 13:43 2009
if the priest shall look, and, *b* Lev 13:53 2009
and, *b*, if the plague have not Lev 13:55 2009
And if the priest look, and, *b* Lev 13:56 2009
and the priest shall look, and, *b* Lev 14:3 2009
shall look on the plague, and, *b* Lev 14:37 2009
and, *b*, if the plague be spread in Lev 14:39 2009
priest shall come and look, and, *b* Lev 14:44 2009
come in, and look upon it, and, *b* Lev 14:48 2009
b, we shall not sow, nor gather Lev 25:20 2005
And I, *b*, I have taken the Levites Num 3:12 2009
similitude of the LORD shall he *b* Num 12:8 5027
and, *b*, Miriam became leprous, Num 12:10 2009
Aaron looked upon Miriam, and, *b* Num 12:10 2009
and, *b*, the cloud covered it, and Num 16:42 2009
and, *b*, the plague was begun among Num 16:47 2009
and, *b*, the rod of Aaron for the Num 17:8 2009
spake unto Moses, saying, *B* Num 17:12 2005
And I, *b*, I have taken your Num 18:6 2009
And the LORD spake unto Aaron, *B* Num 18:8 2009
And, *b*, I have given the children Num 18:21 2009
and, *b*, we are in Kadesh, a city Num 20:16 2009
people, to call him, saying, *B* Num 22:5 2009
b, they cover the face of the Num 22:5 2009
B, there is a people come out of Num 22:11 2009
b, I went out to withstand thee, Num 22:32 2009
him, and from the hills I *b* him Num 23:9 7789
thee to curse mine enemies, and, *b* Num 23:11 2009
And when he came to him, *b* Num 23:17 2009
B, I have received commandment to Num 23:20 2009
B, the people shall rise up as a Num 23:24 2005
thee to curse mine enemies, and, *b* Num 24:10 2009
And now, *b*, I go unto my people Num 24:14 2005
I shall *b* him, but not nigh Num 24:17 7789
And, *b*, one of the children of Num 25:6 2009
Wherefore say, *B*, I give unto him Num 25:12 2005
B, these caused the children of Num 31:16 2005
and the land of Gilead, that, *b* Num 32:1 2009
And, *b*, ye are risen up in your Num 32:14 2009
But if ye will not do so, *b* Num 32:23 2009
B, I have set the land before you Deut 1:8 7200
God hath multiplied you, and, *b* Deut 1:10 2009
B, the LORD thy God hath set the Deut 1:21 7200
b, I have given into thine hand Deut 2:24 7200
And the LORD said unto me, *B* Deut 2:31 7200
b, his bedstead was a bedstead of Deut 3:11 2009
eastward, and *b* it with thine eyes Deut 3:27 7200
B, I have taught you statutes and Deut 4:5 7200
And ye said, *B*, the LORD our God Deut 5:24 2005
I have seen this people, and, *b* Deut 9:13 2009
And I looked, and, *b*, ye had sinned Deut 9:16 2009
B, the heaven and the heaven of Deut 10:14 2005
B, I set before you this day a Deut 11:26 7200
and, *b*, if it be truth, and the Deut 13:14 2009
it, and enquired diligently, and, *b* Deut 17:4 2009
and, *b*, if the witness be a false Deut 19:18 2009
And now, *b*, I have brought the Deut 26:10 2009
And the LORD said unto Moses, *B* Deut 31:14 2005
And the LORD said unto Moses, *B* Deut 31:16 2009
b, while I am yet alive with you Deut 31:27 2005
b the land of Canaan, which I Deut 32:49 7200
the king of Jericho, saying, *B* Josh 2:2 2009
B, when we come into the land, Josh 2:18 2009
B, the ark of the covenant of the Josh 3:11 2009
up his eyes and looked, and, *b* Josh 5:13 2009
and, *b*, they are hid in the earth Josh 7:21 2009
and, *b*, it was hid in his tent, and Josh 7:22 2009
And he commanded them, saying, *B* Josh 8:4 7200
behind them, they saw, and, *b* Josh 8:20 2009
but now, *b*, it is dry, and it is Josh 9:12 2009
and, *b*, they be rent Josh 9:13 2009
And now, *b*, we are in thine hand Josh 9:25 2005
And now, *b*, the LORD hath kept me Josh 14:10 2009
children of Israel heard say, *B* Josh 22:11 2009
B the pattern of the altar of the Josh 22:28 7200
B, I have divided unto you by lot Josh 23:4 7200
And, *b*, this day I am going the Josh 23:14 2009
said unto all the people, *B* Josh 24:27 2009
b, I have delivered the land into Judg 1:2 2009
and when they saw that, *b*, the Judg 3:24 2009
and, *b*, he opened not the doors of Judg 3:25 2009
and, *b*, their lord was fallen down Judg 3:25 2009
And, *b*, as Barak pursued Sisera, Judg 4:22 2009
And when he came into her tent, *b* Judg 4:22 2009
b, my family is poor in Manasseh, Judg 6:15 2009
arose early in the morning, *b* Judg 6:28 2009
B, I will put a fleece of wool in Judg 6:37 2009
And when Gideon was come, *b* Judg 7:13 2009
dream unto his fellow, and said, *B* Judg 7:13 2009
and, *b*, when I come to the outside Judg 7:17 2009
B Zebah and Zalmunna, with whom ye Judg 8:15 2009
unto Abimelech privily, saying, *B* Judg 9:31 2009
and, *b*, they fortify the city Judg 9:31 2009
and, *b*, when he and the people that Judg 9:33 2009
the people, he said to Zebul, *B* Judg 9:36 2009

in the field, and looked, and, *b*	Judg 9:43	2009
to Mizpeh unto his house, and, *b*	Judg 11:34	2009
B now, thou art barren, and	Judg 13:3	2009
But he said unto me, *B*, thou	Judg 13:7	2009
her husband, and said unto him, *B*	Judg 13:10	2009
and, *b*, a young lion roared	Judg 14:5	2009
and, *b*, there was a swarm of bees	Judg 14:8	2009
And he said unto her, *B*, I have	Judg 14:16	2009
And Delilah said unto Samson, *B*	Judg 16:10	2009
spakest of also in mine ears, *b*	Judg 17:2	2009
for we have seen the land, and, *b*	Judg 18:9	2009
b, it is behind Kirjath-jearim	Judg 18:12	2009
damsel's father, said unto him, *B*	Judg 19:9	2009
b, the day groweth to an end,	Judg 19:9	2009
And, *b*, there came an old man from	Judg 19:16	2009
were making their hearts merry, *b*	Judg 19:22	2009
B, here is my daughter a maiden,	Judg 19:24	2009
and, *b*, the woman his concubine	Judg 19:27	2009
B, ye are all children of Israel	Judg 20:7	2009
looked behind them, and, *b*	Judg 20:40	2009
And, *b*, there came none to the	Judg 21:8	2009
the people were numbered, and, *b*	Judg 21:9	2009
Then they said, *B*, there is a	Judg 21:19	2009
And see, and, *b*, if the daughters	Judg 21:21	2009
And she said, *B*, thy sister in law	Ruth 1:15	2009
And, *b*, Boaz came from Beth-lehem,	Ruth 2:4	2009
B, he winnoweth barley to night	Ruth 3:2	2009
and, *b*, a woman lay at his feet	Ruth 3:8	2009
and, *b*, the kinsman of whom Boaz	Ruth 4:1	2009
B, the days come, that I will cut	1Sa 2:31	2009
And the LORD said to Samuel, *B*	1Sa 3:11	2009
arose early on the morrow, *b*	1Sa 5:3	2009
early on the morrow morning, *b*	1Sa 5:4	2009
And said unto him, *B*, thou art old	1Sa 8:5	2009
B now, there is in this city a	1Sa 9:6	2009
said Saul to his servant, But, *b*	1Sa 9:7	2009
answered Saul again, and said, *B*	1Sa 9:8	2009
b, he is before you	1Sa 9:12	2009
they were come into the city, *b*	1Sa 9:14	2009
B the man whom I spake to thee of	1Sa 9:17	2009
Samuel said, *B* that which is left	1Sa 9:24	2009
and, *b*, I will come down unto thee	1Sa 10:8	2009
they came thither to the hill, *b*	1Sa 10:10	2009
knew him beforetime saw that, *b*	1Sa 10:11	2009
And the LORD answered, *B*, he hath	1Sa 10:22	2009
And, *b*, Saul came after the herd	1Sa 11:5	2009
And Samuel said unto all Israel, *B*	1Sa 12:1	2009
And now, *b*, the king walketh	1Sa 12:2	2009
and, *b*, my sons are with you	1Sa 12:2	2009
B, here I am	1Sa 12:3	2009
Now therefore *b* the king whom ye	1Sa 12:13	2009
and, *b*, the LORD hath set a king	1Sa 12:13	2009
of offering the burnt offering, *b*	1Sa 13:10	2009
b, I am with thee according to	1Sa 14:7	2005
Then said Jonathan, *B*, we will	1Sa 14:8	2009
and the Philistines said, *B*	1Sa 14:11	2009
and, *b*, the multitude melted away,	1Sa 14:16	2009
And when they had numbered, *b*	1Sa 14:17	2009
and, *b*, every man's sword was	1Sa 14:20	2009
people were come into the wood, *b*	1Sa 14:26	2009
Then they told Saul, saying, *B*	1Sa 14:33	2009
Saul came to Carmel, and, *b*	1Sa 15:12	2009
B, to obey is better than	1Sa 15:22	2009
remaineth yet the youngest, and, *b*	1Sa 16:11	2009
B now, an evil spirit from God	1Sa 16:15	2009
one of the servants, and said, *B*	1Sa 16:18	2009
And as he talked with them, *b*	1Sa 17:23	2009
B my elder daughter Merab, her	1Sa 18:17	2009
with David secretly, and say, *B*	1Sa 18:22	2009
the messengers were come in, *b*	1Sa 19:16	2009
And it was told Saul, saying, *B*	1Sa 19:19	2009
And one said, *B*, they be at Naioth	1Sa 19:22	2009
b, my father will do nothing	1Sa 20:2	2009
And David said unto Jonathan, *B*	1Sa 20:5	2009
any time, or the third day, and, *b*	1Sa 20:12	2009
And, *b*, I will send a lad, saying,	1Sa 20:21	2009
I expressly say unto the lad, *B*	1Sa 20:21	2009
I say thus unto the young man, *B*	1Sa 20:22	2009
which thou and I have spoken of, *b*	1Sa 20:23	2009
slewest in the valley of Elah, *b*	1Sa 21:9	2009
Then they told David, saying, *B*	1Sa 23:1	2009
And David's men said unto him, *B*	1Sa 23:3	2009
that it was told him, saying, *B*	1Sa 24:1	2009
B the day of which the LORD said	1Sa 24:4	2009
which the LORD said unto thee, *B*	1Sa 24:4	2009
thou men's words, saying, *B*	1Sa 24:9	2009
B, this day thine eyes have seen	1Sa 24:10	2009
And now, *b*, I know well that thou	1Sa 24:20	2009
Abigail, Nabal's wife, saying, *B*	1Sa 25:14	2009
b, I come after you	1Sa 25:19	2005
by the covert of the hill, and, *b*	1Sa 25:20	2009
and, *b*, he held a feast in his	1Sa 25:36	2009
her face to the earth, and said, *B*	1Sa 25:41	2009
and, *b*, Saul lay sleeping within	1Sa 26:7	2009
b, I have played the fool, and	1Sa 26:21	2009
and said, *B* the king's spear	1Sa 26:22	2009
And, *b*, as thy life was much set	1Sa 26:24	2009
And his servants said to him, *B*	1Sa 28:7	2009
And the woman said unto him, *B*	1Sa 28:9	2009
troubled, and said unto him, *B*	1Sa 28:21	2009
his men came to the city, and, *b*	1Sa 30:3	2009
when he had brought him down, *b*	1Sa 30:16	2009
B a present for you of the spoil	1Sa 30:26	2009
to pass on the third day, that, *b*	2Sa 1:2	2009
by chance upon mount Gilboa, *b*	2Sa 1:6	2009
b, it is written in the book of	2Sa 1:18	2009
Make thy league with me, and, *b*	2Sa 3:12	2009
And, *b*, the servants of David and	2Sa 3:22	2009
b, Abner came unto thee	2Sa 3:24	2009
B the head of Ish-bosheth the son	2Sa 4:8	2009
When one told me, saying, *B*	2Sa 4:10	2009
unto Hebron, and spake, saying, *B*	2Sa 5:1	2005
And Ziba said unto the king, *B*	2Sa 9:4	2009
And he answered, *B* thy servant	2Sa 9:6	2009
Thus saith the LORD, *B*, I will	2Sa 12:11	2005
for they said, *B*, while the child	2Sa 12:18	2009
and said, *B* now, thy servant hath	2Sa 13:24	2009
up his eyes, and looked, and, *b*	2Sa 13:34	2009
And Jonadab said unto the king, *B*	2Sa 13:35	2009
made an end of speaking, that, *b*	2Sa 13:36	2009
And, *b*, the whole family is risen	2Sa 14:7	2009
B now, I have done this thing	2Sa 14:21	2009
And Absalom answered Joab, *B*	2Sa 14:32	2009
servants said unto the king, *B*	2Sa 15:15	2009
b, here am I, let him do to me as	2Sa 15:26	2005
mount, where he worshipped God, *b*	2Sa 15:32	2009
B, they have there with them	2Sa 15:36	2009
past the top of the hill, *b*	2Sa 16:1	2009
And Ziba said unto the king, *B*	2Sa 16:3	2009
Then said the king to Ziba, *B*	2Sa 16:4	2009
king David came to Bahurim, *b*	2Sa 16:5	2009
and, *b*, thou art taken in thy	2Sa 16:8	2009
and to all his servants, *B*	2Sa 16:11	2009
B, he is hid now in some pit, or	2Sa 17:9	2009
saw it, and told Joab, and said, *B*	2Sa 18:10	2009
unto the man that told him, And, *b*	2Sa 18:11	2009
looked, and *b* a man running alone	2Sa 18:24	2009
B another man running alone	2Sa 18:26	2009
And, *b*, Cushi came	2Sa 18:31	2009
And it was told Joab, *B*, the king	2Sa 19:1	2009
unto all the people, saying, *B*	2Sa 19:8	2009
therefore, *b*, I am come the first	2Sa 19:20	2009
But *b* thy servant Chimham	2Sa 19:37	2009
And, *b*, all the men of Israel came	2Sa 19:41	2009
And the woman said unto Joab, *B*	2Sa 20:21	2009
b, here be oxen for burnt	2Sa 24:22	7200
B, while thou yet talkest there	1Kin 1:14	2009
And now, *b*, Adonijah reigneth	1Kin 1:18	2009
saying, *B* Nathan the prophet	1Kin 1:23	2009
and, *b*, they eat and drink before	1Kin 1:25	2009
And while he yet spake, *b*,	1Kin 1:42	2009
And it was told Solomon, saying, *B*	1Kin 1:51	2009
And, *b*, thou hast with thee Shimei	1Kin 2:8	2009
and, *b*, he is by the altar	1Kin 2:29	2009
And they told Shimei, saying, *B*	1Kin 2:39	2009
B, I have done according to thy	1Kin 3:12	2009
and, *b*, it was a dream	1Kin 3:15	2009
morning to give my child suck, *b*	1Kin 3:21	2009
considered it in the morning, *b*	1Kin 3:21	2009
And, *b*, I purpose to build an	1Kin 5:5	2005
b, the heaven and heaven of	1Kin 8:27	2009
and, *b*, the half was not told me	1Kin 10:7	2009
hast thou lacked with me, that, *b*	1Kin 11:22	2009
the LORD, the God of Israel, *B*	1Kin 11:31	2005
b thy gods, O Israel, which	1Kin 12:28	2009
And, *b*, there came a man of God	1Kin 13:1	2009
B, a child shall be born unto the	1Kin 13:2	2009
B, the altar shall be rent, and	1Kin 13:3	2009
And, *b*, men passed by, and saw the	1Kin 13:25	2009
b, there is Ahijah the prophet,	1Kin 14:2	2009
And the LORD said unto Ahijah, *B*	1Kin 14:5	2009
Therefore, *b*, I will bring evil	1Kin 14:10	2005
he warred, and how he reigned, *b*	1Kin 14:19	2009
b, I have sent unto thee a	1Kin 15:19	2009
B, I will take away the posterity	1Kin 16:3	2005
b, I have commanded a widow woman	1Kin 17:9	2009
came to the gate of the city, *b*	1Kin 17:10	2009
and, *b*, I am gathering two sticks,	1Kin 17:12	2005
And as Obadiah was in the way, *b*	1Kin 18:7	2009
go, tell thy lord, *B*, Elijah is	1Kin 18:8	2009
thou sayest, Go, tell thy lord, *B*	1Kin 18:11	2009
thou sayest, Go, tell thy lord, *B*	1Kin 18:14	2009
the seventh time, that he said, *B*	1Kin 18:44	2009
and slept under a juniper tree, *b*	1Kin 19:5	2009
And he looked, and, *b*, there was a	1Kin 19:6	2009
and, *b*, the word of the LORD came	1Kin 19:9	2009
And, *b*, the LORD passed by, and a	1Kin 19:11	2009
And, *b*, there came a voice unto	1Kin 19:13	2009
And, *b*, there came a prophet unto	1Kin 20:13	2009
b, I will deliver it into thine	1Kin 20:13	2005
B now, we have heard that the	1Kin 20:31	2009
obeyed the voice of the LORD, *b*	1Kin 20:36	2009
and, *b*, a man turned aside, and	1Kin 20:39	2009
b, he is in the vineyard of	1Kin 21:18	2009
B, I will bring evil upon thee,	1Kin 21:21	2005
B now, the words of the prophets	1Kin 22:13	2009
Now therefore, *b*, the LORD hath	1Kin 22:23	2009
And Micaiah said, *B*, thou shalt	1Kin 22:25	2009
and, *b*, he sat on the top of an	2Kin 1:9	2009
B, there came fire down from	2Kin 1:14	2009
still went on, and talked, that, *b*	2Kin 2:11	2009
B now, there be with thy servants	2Kin 2:16	2009
of the city said unto Elisha, *B*	2Kin 2:19	2009
offering was offered, that, *b*	2Kin 3:20	2009
B now, I perceive that this is an	2Kin 4:9	2009
unto him, Say now unto her, *B*	2Kin 4:13	2009
he said to Gehazi his servant, *B*	2Kin 4:25	2009
Elisha was come into the house, *b*	2Kin 4:32	2009
this letter is come unto thee, *b*	2Kin 5:6	2009
wroth, and went away, and said, *B*	2Kin 5:11	2009
and he said, *B*, now I know that	2Kin 5:15	2009
of Elisha the man of God, said, *B*	2Kin 5:20	2009
My master hath sent me, saying, *B*	2Kin 5:22	2009
B now, the place where we dwell	2Kin 6:1	2009
And it was told him, saying, *B*	2Kin 6:13	2009
was risen early, and gone forth, *b*	2Kin 6:15	2009
and, *b*, the mountain was full of	2Kin 6:17	2009
and, *b*, they were in the midst of	2Kin 6:20	2009
and, *b*, they besieged it, until an	2Kin 6:25	2009
wall, and the people looked, and, *b*	2Kin 6:30	2009
while he yet talked with them, *b*	2Kin 6:33	2009
and he said, *B*, this evil is of	2Kin 6:33	2009
the man of God, and said, *B*	2Kin 7:2	2009
And he said, *B*, thou shalt see it	2Kin 7:2	2009
part of the camp of Syria, *b*	2Kin 7:5	2009
to the camp of the Syrians, and, *b*	2Kin 7:10	2009
which are left in the city, (*b*	2Kin 7:13	2009
b, I say, they are even as all	2Kin 7:13	2009
the man of God, and said, Now, *b*	2Kin 7:19	2009
And he said, *B*, thou shalt see it	2Kin 7:19	2009
a dead body to life, that, *b*	2Kin 8:5	2009
And when he came, *b*, the captains	2Kin 9:5	2009
exceedingly afraid, and said, *B*	2Kin 10:4	2009
b, I conspired against my master,	2Kin 10:9	2009
And when she looked, *b*, the king	2Kin 11:14	2009
they were burying a man, that, *b*	2Kin 13:21	2009
rest of the acts of Zachariah, *b*	2Kin 15:11	2009
his conspiracy which he made, *b*	2Kin 15:15	2009
Pekahiah, and all that he did, *b*	2Kin 15:26	2009
of Pekah, and all that he did, *b*	2Kin 15:31	2009
hath sent lions among them, and, *b*	2Kin 17:26	2009
Now, *b*, thou trustest upon the	2Kin 18:21	2009
B, I will send a blast upon him,	2Kin 19:7	2005
of Tirhakah king of Ethiopia, *B*	2Kin 19:9	2009
B, thou hast heard what the kings	2Kin 19:11	2009
arose early in the morning, *b*	2Kin 19:35	2009
b, I will heal thee	2Kin 20:5	2005
B, the days come, that all that	2Kin 20:17	2009
saith the LORD God of Israel, *B*	2Kin 21:12	2009
Thus saith the LORD, *B*, I will	2Kin 22:16	2005
B therefore, I will gather thee	2Kin 22:20	2005
and, *b*, they were written in the	1Chr 9:1	2009
to David unto Hebron, saying, *B*	1Chr 11:1	2009
B, he was honourable among the	1Chr 11:25	2009
B, a son shall be born to thee,	1Chr 22:9	2009
Now, *b*, in my trouble I have	1Chr 22:14	2009
And, *b*, the courses of the priests	1Chr 28:21	2009
David the king, first and last, *b*	1Chr 29:29	2009
B, I build an house to the name	2Chr 2:4	2009
and, *b*, my servants shall be with	2Chr 2:8	2009
And, *b*, I will give to thy	2Chr 2:10	2009
b, heaven and the heaven of	2Chr 6:18	2009
and, *b*, the one half of the	2Chr 9:6	2009
And, *b*, God himself is with us for	2Chr 13:12	2009
And when Judah looked back, *b*	2Chr 13:14	2009
b, I have sent thee silver and	2Chr 16:3	2009
And, *b*, the acts of Asa, first and	2Chr 16:11	2009
Micaiah spake to him, saying, *B*	2Chr 18:12	2009
Now therefore, *b*, the LORD hath	2Chr 18:22	2009
And Micaiah said, *B*, thou shalt	2Chr 18:24	2009
And, *b*, Amariah the chief priest	2Chr 19:11	2009
and, *b*, they be in Hazazon-tamar,	2Chr 20:2	2009
And now, *b*, the children of Ammon	2Chr 20:10	2009
B, I say, how they reward us, to	2Chr 20:11	2009
b, they come up by the cliff of	2Chr 20:16	2009
looked unto the multitude, and, *b*	2Chr 20:24	2009
of Jehoshaphat, first and last, *b*	2Chr 20:34	2009
B, with a great plague will the	2Chr 21:14	2009
And he said unto them, *B*, the	2Chr 23:3	2009
And she looked, and, *b*, the king	2Chr 23:13	2009
repairing of the house of God, *b*	2Chr 24:27	2009
acts of Amaziah, first and last, *b*	2Chr 25:26	2009
priests, looked upon him, and, *b*	2Chr 26:20	2009
to Samaria, and said unto them, *B*	2Chr 28:9	2009
of all his ways, first and last, *b*	2Chr 28:26	2009
we prepared and sanctified, and, *b*	2Chr 29:19	2009
of Hezekiah, and his goodness, *b*	2Chr 32:32	2009
name of the LORD God of Israel, *b*	2Chr 33:18	2009
b, they are written among the	2Chr 33:19	2009
Thus saith the LORD, *B*, I will	2Chr 34:24	2005
B, I will gather thee to thy	2Chr 34:28	2005
and, *b*, they are written in the	2Chr 35:25	2009
And his deeds, first and last, *b*	2Chr 35:27	2009
and that which was found in him, *b*	2Chr 36:8	2009
b, we are before thee in our	Ezr 9:15	2005
B, we are servants this day, and	Neh 9:36	2009
thereof and the good thereof, *b*	Neh 9:36	2009
king's servants said unto him, *B*	Est 6:5	2009
B also, the gallows fifty cubits	Est 7:9	2009
queen and to Mordecai the Jew, *B*	Est 8:7	2009
And the LORD said unto Satan, *B*	Job 1:12	2009
And, *b*, there came a great wind	Job 1:19	2009
And the LORD said unto Satan, *B*	Job 2:6	2009
B, thou hast instructed many, and	Job 4:3	2009
B, he put no trust in his	Job 4:18	2005
B, happy is the man whom God	Job 5:17	2009
B, this is the joy of his way, and	Job 8:19	2005
B, God will not cast away a	Job 8:20	2005
B, he taketh away, who can hinder	Job 9:12	2005
B, he breaketh down, and it cannot	Job 12:14	2005
B, he withholdeth the waters, and	Job 12:15	2005
B now, I have ordered my cause	Job 13:18	2009
B, he putteth no trust in his	Job 15:15	2005
Also now, *b*, my witness is in	Job 16:19	2009
B, I cry out of wrong, but I am	Job 19:7	2005
for myself, and mine eyes shall *b*	Job 19:27	7200
shall his place any more *b* him	Job 20:9	7789
B, I know your thoughts, and the	Job 21:27	2005
b the height of the stars, how	Job 22:12	7200
B, I go forward, but he is not	Job 23:8	2005
he doth work, but I cannot *b* him	Job 23:9	2372
B, as wild asses in the desert,	Job 24:5	2005
B even to the moon, and it shineth	Job 25:5	2005
B, all ye yourselves have seen it	Job 27:12	2005

And unto man he said, *B*, the fear	Job 28:28	2005
b, my desire is, that the	Job 31:35	2005
B, I waited for your words	Job 32:11	2005
Yea, I attended unto you, and, *b*	Job 32:12	2009
B, my belly is as wine which hath	Job 32:19	2009
B, now I have opened my mouth, my	Job 33:2	2009
B, I am according to thy wish in	Job 33:6	2005
B, my terror shall not make thee	Job 33:7	2009
B, he findeth occasions against	Job 33:10	2005
B, in this thou art not just	Job 33:12	2005
his face, who then can *b* him	Job 34:29	7789
b the clouds which are higher	Job 35:5	7789
B, God is mighty, and despiseth	Job 36:5	2005
B, God exalteth by his power	Job 36:22	2005
magnify his work, which men *b*	Job 36:24	7891
man may *b* it afar off	Job 36:25	5027
B, God is great, and we know him	Job 36:26	2005
B, he spreadeth his light upon it	Job 36:30	2005
the prey, and her eyes *b* afar off	Job 39:29	5027
B, I am vile	Job 40:4	2005
b every one that is proud, and	Job 40:11	7200
B now behemoth, which I made with	Job 40:15	2009
B, he drinketh up a river, and	Job 40:23	2005
B, the hope of him is in vain	Job 41:9	2005
B, he travaileth with iniquity,	Ps 7:14	2009
his eyes *b*, his eyelids try, the	Ps 11:4	2372
countenance doth *b* the upright	Ps 11:7	2372
let thine eyes *b* the things that	Ps 17:2	2372
As for me, I will *b* thy face in	Ps 17:15	2372
to *b* the beauty of the LORD, and	Ps 27:4	2372
B, the eye of the LORD is upon	Ps 33:18	2009
the perfect man, and *b* the upright	Ps 37:37	7200
B, thou hast made my days as an	Ps 39:5	2009
b the works of the LORD, what	Ps 46:8	2372
B, I was shapen in iniquity	Ps 51:5	2005
B, thou desirest truth in the	Ps 51:6	2005
B, God is mine helper	Ps 54:4	2009
awake to help me, and *b*	Ps 59:4	7200
B, they belch out with their	Ps 59:7	2009
his eyes *b* the nations	Ps 66:7	6822
B, these are the ungodly, who	Ps 73:12	2009
b, I should offend against the	Ps 73:15	2009
B, he smote the rock, that the	Ps 78:20	2005
look down from heaven, and *b*	Ps 80:14	7200
B, O God our shield, and look upon	Ps 84:9	7200
b Philistia, and Tyre, with	Ps 87:4	2009
Only with thine eyes shalt thou *b*	Ps 91:8	5027
heaven did the LORD *b* the earth	Ps 102:19	5027
Who humbleth himself to *b* the	Ps 113:6	7200
that I may *b* wondrous things out	Ps 119:18	5027
B, I have longed after thy	Ps 119:40	2009
B, he that keepeth Israel shall	Ps 121:4	2009
B, as the eyes of servants look	Ps 123:2	2009
B, that thus shall the man be	Ps 128:4	2009
B, how good and how pleasant it is	Ps 133:1	2009
B, bless ye the LORD, all ye	Ps 134:1	2009
if I make my bed in hell, *b*	Ps 139:8	2009
b, I will pour out my spirit unto	Prov 1:23	2009
And, *b*, there met him a woman with	Prov 7:10	2009
B, the righteous shall be	Prov 11:31	2005
Thine eyes shall *b* strange women	Prov 23:33	7200
If thou sayest, *B*, we knew it not	Prov 24:12	2005
and, *b*, all is vanity and vexation	Eccl 1:14	2009
and, *b*, this also is vanity	Eccl 2:1	2009
and, *b*, all was vanity and vexation	Eccl 2:11	2009
And I turned myself to *b* wisdom	Eccl 2:12	7200
b the tears of such as were	Eccl 4:1	2009
B that which I have seen	Eccl 5:18	2009
B, this have I found, saith the	Eccl 7:27	7200
it is for the eyes to *b* the sun	Eccl 11:7	7200
B, thou art fair, my love	Song 1:15	2009
b, thou art fair	Song 1:15	2009
B, thou art fair, my beloved, yea	Song 1:16	2009
b, he cometh leaping upon the	Song 2:8	2009
b, he standeth behind our wall,	Song 2:9	2009
B his bed, which is Solomon's	Song 3:7	2009
b king Solomon with the crown	Song 3:11	7200
B, thou art fair, my love	Song 4:1	2009
b, thou art fair	Song 4:1	2009
For, *b*, the Lord, the LORD of	Is 3:1	2009
for judgment, but *b* oppression	Is 5:7	2009
for righteousness, but *b* a cry	Is 5:7	2009
and, *b*, they shall come with speed	Is 5:26	2009
b darkness and sorrow, and the	Is 5:30	2009
B, a virgin shall conceive, and	Is 7:14	2009
Now therefore, *b*, the Lord	Is 8:7	2009
B, I and the children whom the	Is 8:18	2009
b trouble and darkness, dimness of	Is 8:22	2009
B, the Lord, the LORD of hosts,	Is 10:33	2009
B, God is my salvation	Is 12:2	2009
B, the day of the LORD cometh,	Is 13:9	2009
B, I will stir up the Medes	Is 13:17	2005
B, Damascus is taken away from	Is 17:1	2009
And *b* at eveningtide trouble	Is 17:14	2009
B, the LORD rideth upon a swift	Is 19:1	2009
isle shall say in that day, *B*	Is 20:6	2009
And, *b*, here cometh a chariot of	Is 21:9	2009
b joy and gladness, slaying oxen,	Is 22:13	2009
B, the LORD will carry thee away	Is 22:17	2009
B the land of the Chaldeans	Is 23:13	2005
B, the LORD maketh the earth	Is 24:1	2009
will not *b* the majesty of the	Is 26:10	7200
For, *b*, the LORD cometh out of	Is 26:21	2009
B, the Lord hath a mighty and	Is 28:2	2009
thus saith the Lord GOD, *B*	Is 28:16	2005
an hungry man dreameth, and, *b*	Is 29:8	2009
a thirsty man dreameth, and, *b*	Is 29:8	2009
but he awaketh, and, *b*, he is	Is 29:8	2009
Therefore, *b*, I will proceed to	Is 29:14	2005
B, the name of the LORD cometh	Is 30:27	2009
B, a king shall reign in	Is 32:1	2005
B, their valiant ones shall cry	Is 33:7	2005
they shall *b* the land that is	Is 33:17	7200
b, it shall come down upon Idumea	Is 34:5	2009
b, your God will come with	Is 35:4	2009
B, I will send a blast upon him,	Is 37:7	2005
B, thou hast heard what the kings	Is 37:11	2009
arose early in the morning, *b*	Is 37:36	2009
b, I will add unto thy days	Is 38:5	2005
B, I will bring again the shadow	Is 38:8	2005
I shall *b* man no more with the	Is 38:11	7200
B, for peace I had great	Is 38:17	2009
B, the days come, that all that	Is 39:6	2009
the cities of Judah, *B* your God	Is 40:9	2009
B, the Lord GOD will come with	Is 40:10	2009
b, his reward is with him, and his	Is 40:10	2009
B, the nations are as a drop of a	Is 40:15	2005
b, he taketh up the isles as a	Is 40:15	2005
b who hath created these things,	Is 40:26	7200
B, all they that were incensed	Is 41:11	2005
B, I will make thee a new sharp	Is 41:15	2009
may be dismayed, and *b* it together	Is 41:23	7200
B, ye are of nothing, and your	Is 41:24	2005
shall say to Zion, *B*, *b* them	Is 41:27	2009
B, they are all vanity	Is 41:29	2005
B my servant, whom I uphold	Is 42:1	2005
B, the former things are come to	Is 42:9	2009
B, I will do a new thing	Is 43:19	2005
B, all his fellows shall be	Is 44:11	2005
B, they shall be as stubble	Is 47:14	2009
lest thou shouldest say, *B*	Is 48:7	2009
B, I have refined thee, but not	Is 48:10	2009
B, these shall come from far	Is 49:12	2009
B, I have graven thee upon the	Is 49:16	2005
up thine eyes round about, and *b*	Is 49:18	7200
B, I was left alone	Is 49:21	2005
Thus saith the Lord GOD, *B*	Is 49:22	2009
B, for your iniquities have ye	Is 50:1	2005
b, at my rebuke I dry up the sea,	Is 50:2	2005
B, the Lord GOD will help me	Is 50:9	2005
B, all ye that kindle a fire,	Is 50:11	2005
the cause of his people, *B*	Is 51:22	2009
b, it is I	Is 52:6	2009
B, my servant shall deal	Is 52:13	2009
with tempest, and not comforted, *b*	Is 54:11	2009
B, they shall surely gather	Is 54:15	2005
B, I have created the smith that	Is 54:16	2005
B, I have given him for a witness	Is 55:4	2005
B, thou shalt call a nation that	Is 55:5	2005
neither let the eunuch say, *B*	Is 56:3	2005
B, in the day of your fast ye	Is 58:3	2005
B, ye fast for strife and debate,	Is 58:4	2005
B, the LORD's hand is not	Is 59:1	2005
wait for light, but *b* obscurity	Is 59:9	2009
For, *b*, the darkness shall cover	Is 60:2	2009
B, the LORD hath proclaimed unto	Is 62:11	2009
Say ye to the daughter of Zion, *B*	Is 62:11	2009
b, his reward is with him, and his	Is 62:11	2009
b from the habitation of thy	Is 63:15	7200
b, thou art wroth	Is 64:5	2005
b, see, we beseech thee, we are	Is 64:9	2005
B me, *b* me, unto a nation	Is 65:1	2009
b me, unto a nation that was not	Is 65:1	2009
B, it is written before me	Is 65:6	2009
thus saith the Lord GOD, *B*	Is 65:13	2009
b, my servants shall drink, but	Is 65:13	2009
b, my servants shall rejoice, but	Is 65:13	2009
B, my servants shall sing for joy	Is 65:14	2009
For, *b*, I create new heavens and a	Is 65:17	2005
for, *b*, I create Jerusalem a	Is 65:18	2005
For thus saith the LORD, *B*	Is 66:12	2005
For, *b*, the LORD will come with	Is 66:15	2009
b, I cannot speak	Jer 1:6	2009
And the LORD said unto me, *B*	Jer 1:9	2009
For, *b*, I have made thee this day	Jer 1:18	2009
B, I will plead with thee,	Jer 2:35	2005
B, thou hast spoken and done evil	Jer 3:5	2009
B, we come unto thee	Jer 3:22	2005
B, he shall come up as clouds, and	Jer 4:13	2009
b, publish against Jerusalem,	Jer 4:16	2009
Because ye speak this word, *b*	Jer 5:14	2005
b, their ear is uncircumcised, and	Jer 6:10	2009
b, the word of the LORD is unto	Jer 6:10	2009
b, I will bring evil upon this	Jer 6:19	2009
Therefore thus saith the LORD, *B*	Jer 6:21	2005
Thus saith the LORD, *B*, a people	Jer 6:22	2009
B, ye trust in lying words, that	Jer 7:8	2009
B, even I have seen it, saith the	Jer 7:11	2009
B, mine anger and my fury shall be	Jer 7:20	2009
Therefore, *b*, the days come,	Jer 7:32	2009
a time of health, and *b* trouble	Jer 8:15	2009
For, *b*, I will send serpents,	Jer 8:17	2005
B the voice of the cry of the	Jer 8:19	2009
thus saith the LORD of hosts, *B*	Jer 9:7	2005
B, I will feed them, even this	Jer 9:15	2005
B, the days come, saith the LORD,	Jer 9:25	2009
For thus saith the LORD, *B*	Jer 10:18	2009
B, the noise of the bruit is come	Jer 10:22	2009
Therefore thus saith the LORD, *B*	Jer 11:11	2009
thus saith the LORD of hosts, *B*	Jer 11:22	2005
B, I will pluck them out of their	Jer 12:14	2005
and, *b*, the girdle was marred, it	Jer 13:7	2009
unto them, Thus saith the LORD, *B*	Jer 13:13	2005
b them that come from the north	Jer 13:20	7200
b, the prophets say unto them, Ye	Jer 14:13	2009
then *b* the slain with the sword	Jer 14:18	2009
then *b* them that are sick with	Jer 14:18	2009
the time of healing, and *b* trouble	Jer 14:19	2009
B, I will cause to cease out of	Jer 16:9	2005
for, *b*, ye walk every one after	Jer 16:12	2009
Therefore, *b*, the days come,	Jer 16:14	2009
B, I will send for many fishers,	Jer 16:16	2005
Therefore, *b*, I will this once	Jer 16:21	2005
B, they say unto me, Where is the	Jer 17:15	2009
down to the potter's house, and, *b*	Jer 18:3	2009
B, as the clay is in the potter's	Jer 18:6	2009
B, I frame evil against you, and	Jer 18:11	2009
B, I will bring evil upon this	Jer 19:3	2005
Therefore, *b*, the days come,	Jer 19:6	2009
B, I will bring upon this city and	Jer 19:15	2005
For thus saith the LORD, *B*	Jer 20:4	2005
enemies, and thine eyes shall *b* it	Jer 20:4	7200
B, I will turn back the weapons	Jer 21:4	2005
B, I set before you the way of	Jer 21:8	2005
B, I am against thee, O	Jer 21:13	2005
b, I will visit upon you the evil	Jer 23:2	2005
B, the days come, saith the LORD,	Jer 23:5	2009
Therefore, *b*, the days come,	Jer 23:7	2009
B, I will feed them with wormwood	Jer 23:15	2005
B, a whirlwind of the LORD is	Jer 23:19	2009
Therefore, *b*, I am against the	Jer 23:30	2005
B, I am against the prophets,	Jer 23:31	2005
B, I am against them that	Jer 23:32	2005
Therefore, *b*, I, even I, will	Jer 23:39	2005
The LORD shewed me, and, *b*	Jer 24:1	2009
B, I will send and take all the	Jer 25:9	2005
Thus saith the LORD of hosts, *B*	Jer 25:32	2009
As for me, *b*, I am in your hand	Jer 26:14	2005
that prophesy unto you, saying, *B*	Jer 27:16	2009
B, I will cast thee from off the	Jer 28:16	2005
B, I will send upon them the	Jer 29:17	2005
B, I will deliver them into the	Jer 29:21	2009
B, I will punish Shemaiah the	Jer 29:32	2005
neither shall he *b* the good that	Jer 29:32	7200
B, I will bring again the	Jer 30:18	2005
B, the whirlwind of the LORD	Jer 30:23	2009
B, I will bring them from the	Jer 31:8	2005
B, the days come, saith the LORD,	Jer 31:27	2009
B, the days come, saith the LORD,	Jer 31:31	2009
B, the days come, saith the LORD,	Jer 31:38	2009
and say, Thus saith the LORD, *B*	Jer 32:3	2005
and his eyes shall *b* his eyes	Jer 32:4	7200
B, Hanameel the son of Shallum	Jer 32:7	2009
b, thou hast made the heaven and	Jer 32:17	2009
B the mounts, they are come unto	Jer 32:24	2009
and, *b*, thou seest it	Jer 32:24	2009
B, I am the LORD, the God of all	Jer 32:27	2009
B, I will give this city into the	Jer 32:28	2005
B, I will gather them out of all	Jer 32:37	2005
B, I will bring it health and cure	Jer 33:6	2005
B, the days come, saith the LORD,	Jer 33:14	2009
B, I will give this city into the	Jer 34:2	2005
thine eyes shall *b* the eyes of	Jer 34:3	7200
b, I proclaim a liberty for you,	Jer 34:17	2005
B, I will command, saith the LORD	Jer 34:22	2005
B, I will bring upon Judah and	Jer 35:17	2005
B, Pharaoh's army, which is come	Jer 37:7	2005
Then Zedekiah the king said, *B*	Jer 38:5	2009
And, *b*, all the women that are	Jer 38:22	2009
B, I will bring my words upon	Jer 39:16	2005
And now, *b*, I loose thee this day	Jer 40:4	2009
b, all the land is before thee	Jer 40:4	7200
As for me, *b*, I will dwell at	Jer 40:10	2005
of many, as thine eyes do *b* us	Jer 42:2	7200
b, I will pray unto the LORD your	Jer 42:4	2005
B, I will send and take	Jer 43:10	2005
and, *b*, this day they are a	Jer 44:2	2009
B, I will set my face against you	Jer 44:11	2005
B, I have sworn by my great name,	Jer 44:26	2005
B, I will watch over them for	Jer 44:27	2005
B, I will give Pharaoh-hophra	Jer 44:30	2005
B, that which I have built will I	Jer 45:4	2009
for, *b*, I will bring evil upon	Jer 45:5	2005
B, I will punish the multitude of	Jer 46:25	2005
for, *b*, I will save thee from	Jer 46:27	2005
B, waters rise up out of the	Jer 47:2	2009
Therefore, *b*, the days come,	Jer 48:12	2009
B, he shall fly as an eagle, and	Jer 48:40	2009
Therefore, *b*, the days come,	Jer 49:2	2009
B, I will bring a fear upon thee,	Jer 49:5	2005
B, they whose judgment was not to	Jer 49:12	2009
B, he shall come up like a lion	Jer 49:19	2009
B, he shall come up and fly as the	Jer 49:22	2009
B, I will break the bow of Elam,	Jer 49:35	2005
b, the hindermost of the nations	Jer 50:12	2009
B, I will punish the king of	Jer 50:18	2005
B, I am against thee, O thou most	Jer 50:31	2005
B, a people shall come from the	Jer 50:41	2009
B, he shall come up like a lion	Jer 50:44	2009
B, I will raise up against	Jer 51:1	2005
B, I am against thee, O	Jer 51:25	2005
B, I will plead thy cause, and	Jer 51:36	2005
Therefore, *b*, the days come, that	Jer 51:47	2009
Wherefore, *b*, the days come,	Jer 51:52	2009
O LORD, *b* my affliction	Lam 1:9	7200
b, and see if there be any sorrow	Lam 1:12	5027
you, all people, and *b* my sorrow	Lam 1:18	7200
B, O LORD	Lam 1:20	7200
B, O LORD, and consider to whom	Lam 2:20	7200
LORD look down, and *b* from heaven	Lam 3:50	7200
B their sitting down, and their	Lam 3:63	5027
consider, and *b* our reproach	Lam 5:1	7200
And I looked, and, *b*, a whirlwind	Eze 1:4	2009
b one wheel upon the earth by the	Eze 1:15	2009

And when I looked, *b*, an hand was	Eze 2:9	2009
B, I have made thy face strong	Eze 3:8	2009
and, *b*, the glory of the LORD	Eze 3:23	2009
But thou, O son of man, *b*	Eze 3:25	2009
And, *b*, I will lay bands upon thee	Eze 4:8	2009
b, my soul hath not been polluted	Eze 4:14	2009
he said unto me, Son of man, *b*	Eze 4:16	2005
B, I, even I, am against thee, and	Eze 5:8	2005
B, I, even I, will bring a sword	Eze 6:3	2005
An evil, an only evil, *b*, is come	Eze 7:5	2009
b, it is come	Eze 7:6	2009
B the day, *b*, it is come	Eze 7:10	2009
And, *b*, the glory of the God of	Eze 8:4	2009
b northward at the gate of the	Eze 8:5	2009
I looked, *b* a hole in the wall	Eze 8:7	2009
had digged in the wall, *b* a door	Eze 8:8	2009
b the wicked abominations that	Eze 8:9	7200
b every form of creeping things,	Eze 8:10	2009
and, *b*, there sat women weeping	Eze 8:14	2009
court of the LORD's house, and, *b*	Eze 8:16	2009
And, *b*, six men came from the way	Eze 9:2	2009
And, *b*, the man clothed with linen	Eze 9:11	2009
Then I looked, and, *b*, in the	Eze 10:1	2009
looked, *b* the four wheels by the	Eze 10:9	2009
b at the door of the gate five and	Eze 11:1	2009
Son of man, *b*, they of the house	Eze 12:27	2009
and seen lies, therefore, *b*	Eze 13:8	2005
B, I am against your pillows,	Eze 13:20	2005
Yet, *b*, therein shall be left a	Eze 14:22	2009
b, they shall come forth unto you	Eze 14:22	2009
B, it is cast into the fire for	Eze 15:4	2009
B, when it was whole, it was meet	Eze 15:5	2009
by thee, and looked upon thee, *b*	Eze 16:8	2009
B, therefore I have stretched out	Eze 16:27	2009
B, therefore I will gather all	Eze 16:37	2005
b, therefore I also will	Eze 16:43	1887
B, every one that useth proverbs	Eze 16:44	2009
B, this was the iniquity of thy	Eze 16:49	2009
and, *b*, this vine did bend her	Eze 17:7	2009
Yea, *b*, being planted, shall it	Eze 17:10	2009
tell them, *B*, the king of Babylon	Eze 17:12	2009
B, all souls are mine	Eze 18:4	2005
B, I will kindle a fire in thee,	Eze 20:47	2005
B, I am against thee, and will	Eze 21:3	2005
b, it cometh, and shall be brought	Eze 21:7	2009
B, the princes of Israel, every	Eze 22:6	2009
B, therefore I have smitten mine	Eze 22:13	2009
ye are all become dross, *b*	Eze 22:19	2005
B, I will raise up thy lovers	Eze 23:22	2005
B, I will deliver thee into the	Eze 23:28	2005
Son of man, *b*, I take away from	Eze 24:16	2005
B, I will profane my sanctuary,	Eze 24:21	2005
B, therefore I will deliver thee	Eze 25:4	2005
B, therefore I will stretch out	Eze 25:7	2005
that Moab and Seir do say, *B*	Eze 25:8	2009
Therefore, *b*, I will open the	Eze 25:9	2005
B, I will stretch out mine hand	Eze 25:16	2005
B, I am against thee, O Tyrus, and	Eze 26:3	2005
B, I will bring upon Tyrus	Eze 26:7	2005
B, thou art wiser than Daniel	Eze 28:3	2009
B, therefore I will bring	Eze 28:7	2005
kings, that they may *b* thee	Eze 28:17	7200
the sight of all them that *b* thee	Eze 28:18	7200
B, I am against thee, O Zidon	Eze 28:22	2005
B, I am against thee, Pharaoh	Eze 29:3	2005
B, I will bring a sword upon thee	Eze 29:8	2005
B, therefore I am against thee,	Eze 29:10	2005
B, I will give the land of Egypt	Eze 29:19	2005
B, I am against Pharaoh king of	Eze 30:22	2005
B, the Assyrian was a cedar in	Eze 31:3	2009
B, I am against the shepherds	Eze 34:10	2005
B, I, even I, will both search my	Eze 34:11	2005
B, I judge between cattle and	Eze 34:17	2005
B, I, even I, will judge between	Eze 34:20	2005
B, O mount Seir, I am against	Eze 35:3	2005
B, I have spoken in my jealousy	Eze 36:6	2005
For, *b*, I am for you, and I will	Eze 36:9	2005
and, *b*, there were very many in	Eze 37:2	2009
B, I will cause breath to enter	Eze 37:5	2009
b a shaking, and the bones came	Eze 37:7	2009
b, they say, Our bones are dried,	Eze 37:11	2009
B, O my people, I will open your	Eze 37:12	2009
B, I will take the stick of	Eze 37:19	2009
B, I will take the children of	Eze 37:21	2009
B, I am against thee, O Gog, the	Eze 38:3	2005
B, I am against thee, O Gog, the	Eze 39:1	2005
B, it is come, and it is done,	Eze 39:8	2009
And he brought me thither, and, *b*	Eze 40:3	2009
b with thine eyes, and hear with	Eze 40:4	7200
b a wall on the outside of the	Eze 40:5	2009
b a gate toward the south	Eze 40:24	2009
And, *b*, the glory of the God of	Eze 43:2	2009
and, *b*, the glory of the LORD	Eze 43:5	2009
B, this is the law of the house	Eze 43:12	2009
and I looked, and, *b*, the glory of	Eze 44:4	2009
b with thine eyes, and hear with	Eze 44:5	7200
and, *b*, there was a place on the	Eze 46:19	2009
and, *b*, in every corner of the	Eze 46:21	2009
and, *b*, waters issued out from	Eze 47:1	2009
and, *b*, there ran out waters on	Eze 47:2	2009
Now when I had returned, *b*	Eze 47:7	2009
king, sawest, and *b* a great image	Dan 2:31	431
b a tree in the midst of the	Dan 4:10	431
of my head upon my bed, and, *b*	Dan 4:13	431
saw in my vision by night, and, *b*	Dan 7:2	718
b another beast, a second, like	Dan 7:5	718
b a fourth beast, dreadful and	Dan 7:7	718
I considered the horns, and, *b*	Dan 7:8	431
and, *b*, in this horn were eyes	Dan 7:8	431
I saw in the night visions, and, *b*	Dan 7:13	718
up mine eyes, and saw, and, *b*	Dan 8:3	2009
And as I was considering, *b*	Dan 8:5	2009
sought for the meaning, then, *b*	Dan 8:15	2009
And he said, *B*, I will make thee	Dan 8:19	2005
b our desolations, and the city	Dan 9:18	7200
b a certain man clothed in linen,	Dan 10:5	2009
And, *b*, an hand touched me, which	Dan 10:10	2009
And, *b*, one like the similitude of	Dan 10:16	2009
B, there shall stand up yet three	Dan 11:2	2009
Then I Daniel looked, and, *b*	Dan 12:5	2009
Therefore, *b*, I will hedge up thy	Hos 2:6	2005
Therefore, *b*, I will allure her,	Hos 2:14	2009
answer and say unto his people, *B*	Joel 2:19	2005
For, *b*, in those days, and in that	Joel 3:1	2009
B, I will raise them out of the	Joel 3:7	2005
B, I am pressed under you, as a	Amos 2:13	2009
b the great tumults in the midst	Amos 3:9	7200
For, *b*, the LORD commandeth, and	Amos 6:11	2009
But, *b*, I will raise up against	Amos 6:14	2005
and, *b*, he formed grasshoppers in	Amos 7:1	2009
and, *b*, the Lord GOD called to	Amos 7:4	2009
and, *b*, the Lord stood upon a wall	Amos 7:7	2009
Then said the Lord, *B*, I will set	Amos 7:8	2005
b a basket of summer fruit	Amos 8:1	2009
B, the days come, saith the Lord	Amos 8:11	2009
B, the eyes of the Lord GOD are	Amos 9:8	2009
B, the days come, saith the LORD,	Amos 9:13	2009
B, I have made thee small among	Obad 2	2009
For, *b*, the LORD cometh forth out	Mic 1:3	2009
B, against this family do I	Mic 2:3	2005
I shall *b* his righteousness	Mic 7:9	7200
mine eyes shall *b* her	Mic 7:10	7200
B upon the mountains the feet of	Nah 1:15	2209
B, I am against thee, saith the	Nah 2:13	2205
B, I am against thee, saith the	Nah 3:5	2205
B, thy people in the midst of	Nah 3:13	2009
and cause me to *b* grievance	Hab 1:3	5027
B ye among the heathen, and regard	Hab 1:5	7200
art of purer eyes than to *b* evil	Hab 1:13	7200
B, his soul which is lifted up is	Hab 2:4	2009
B, is it not of the LORD of hosts	Hab 2:13	2009
B, it is laid over with gold and	Hab 2:19	2009
B, at that time I will undo all	Zeph 3:19	2005
b a man riding upon a red horse,	Zec 1:8	2009
and fro through the earth, and, *b*	Zec 1:11	2009
eyes, and saw, and *b* four horns	Zec 1:18	2009
b a man with a measuring line in	Zec 2:1	2009
And, *b*, the angel that talked with	Zec 2:3	2009
For, *b*, I will shake mine hand	Zec 2:9	2005
And unto him he said, *B*, I have	Zec 3:4	7200
for, *b*, I will bring forth my	Zec 3:8	2005
For *b* the stone that I have laid	Zec 3:9	2009
b, I will engrave the graving	Zec 3:9	2005
b a candlestick all of gold, with	Zec 4:2	2005
and looked, and *b* a flying roll	Zec 5:1	2009
And, *b*, there was lifted up a	Zec 5:7	2009
I up mine eyes, and looked, and, *b*	Zec 5:9	2009
up mine eyes, and looked, and, *b*	Zec 6:1	2009
me, and spake unto me, saying, *B*	Zec 6:8	7200
B the man whose name is The	Zec 6:12	2009
B, I will save my people from the	Zec 8:7	2005
B, the Lord will cast her out, and	Zec 9:4	2009
b, thy King cometh unto thee	Zec 9:9	2009
B, I will make Jerusalem a cup of	Zec 12:2	2009
B, the day of the LORD cometh, and	Zec 14:1	2009
Ye said also, *B*, what a weariness	Mal 1:13	2009
B, I will corrupt your seed, and	Mal 2:3	2005
B, I will send my messenger, and	Mal 3:1	2005
b, he shall come, saith the LORD	Mal 3:1	2009
For, *b*, the day cometh, that	Mal 4:1	2009
B, I will send you Elijah the	Mal 4:5	2009
he thought on these things, *b*	Mt 1:20	*2400*
B, a virgin shall be with child,	Mt 1:23	*2400*
in the days of Herod the king, *b*	Mt 2:1	*2400*
And when they were departed, *b*	Mt 2:13	*2400*
But when Herod was dead, *b*	Mt 2:19	*2400*
Then the devil leaveth him, and, *b*	Mt 4:11	*2400*
B the fowls of the air	Mt 6:26	*1689*
and, *b*, a beam is in thine own eye	Mt 7:4	*2400*
And, *b*, there came a leper and	Mt 8:2	*2400*
And, *b*, there arose a great	Mt 8:24	*2400*
And, *b*, they cried out, saying,	Mt 8:29	*2400*
and, *b*, the whole herd of swine	Mt 8:32	*2400*
And, *b*, the whole city came out to	Mt 8:34	*2400*
And, *b*, they brought to him a man	Mt 9:2	*2400*
And, *b*, certain of the scribes	Mt 9:3	*2400*
Jesus sat at meat in the house, *b*	Mt 9:10	*2400*
spake these things unto them, *b*	Mt 9:18	*2400*
And, *b*, a woman, which was	Mt 9:20	*2400*
As they went out, *b*, they brought	Mt 9:32	*2400*
B, I send you forth as sheep in	Mt 10:16	*2400*
b, they that wear soft clothing	Mt 11:8	*2400*
is he, of whom it is written, *B*	Mt 11:10	*2400*
say, *B* a man gluttonous, and a	Mt 11:19	*2400*
saw it, they said unto him, *B*	Mt 12:2	*2400*
And, *b*, there was a man which had	Mt 12:10	*2400*
B my servant, whom I have chosen	Mt 12:18	*2400*
and, *b*, a greater than Jonas is	Mt 12:41	*2400*
and, *b*, a greater than Solomon is	Mt 12:42	*2400*
he yet talked to the people, *b*	Mt 12:46	*2400*
Then one said unto him, *B*	Mt 12:47	*2400*
B my mother and my brethren	Mt 12:49	*2400*
unto them in parables, saying, *B*	Mt 13:3	*2400*
And, *b*, a woman of Canaan came out	Mt 15:22	*2400*
And, *b*, there appeared unto them	Mt 17:3	*2400*
While he yet spake, *b*, a bright	Mt 17:5	*2400*
b a voice out of the cloud, which	Mt 17:5	*2400*
heaven their angels do always *b*	Mt 18:10	*991*
And, *b*, one came and said unto him,	Mt 19:16	*2400*
Peter and said unto him, *B*	Mt 19:27	*2400*
B, we go up to Jerusalem	Mt 20:18	*2400*
And, *b*, two blind men sitting by	Mt 20:30	*2400*
Tell ye the daughter of Sion, *B*	Mt 21:5	*2400*
Tell them which are bidden, *B*	Mt 22:4	*2400*
Wherefore, *b*, I send unto you	Mt 23:34	*2400*
B, your house is left unto you	Mt 23:38	*2400*
B, I have told you before	Mt 24:25	*2400*
if they shall say unto you, *B*	Mt 24:26	*2400*
b, he is in the secret chambers	Mt 24:26	*2400*
midnight there was a cry made, *B*	Mt 25:6	*2400*
b, I have gained beside them five	Mt 25:20	*2396*
b, I have gained two other	Mt 25:22	*2396*
b, the hour is at hand, and the	Mt 26:45	*2400*
b, he is at hand that doth betray	Mt 26:46	*2400*
And, *b*, one of them which were	Mt 26:51	*2400*
b, now ye have heard his	Mt 26:65	*2396*
And, *b*, the veil of the temple was	Mt 27:51	*2400*
And, *b*, there was a great	Mt 28:2	*2400*
and, *b*, he goeth before you into	Mt 28:7	*2400*
went to tell his disciples, *b*	Mt 28:9	*2400*
Now when they were going, *b*	Mt 28:11	*2400*
it is written in the prophets, *B*	Mk 1:2	*2400*
And the Pharisees said unto him, *B*	Mk 2:24	*2396*
him, and they said unto him, *B*	Mk 3:32	*2396*
B my mother and my brethren	Mk 3:34	*2396*
B, there went out a sower to sow	Mk 4:3	*2400*
And, *b*, there cometh one of the	Mk 5:22	*2400*
Saying, *B*, we go up to Jerusalem	Mk 10:33	*2400*
saith unto him, Master, *b*	Mk 11:21	*2396*
b, I have foretold you all things	Mk 13:23	*2400*
b, the Son of man is betrayed	Mk 14:41	*2400*
b how many things they witness	Mk 15:4	*2396*
by, when they heard it said, *B*	Mk 15:35	*2400*
b the place where they laid him	Mk 16:6	*2396*
And, *b*, thou shalt be dumb, and not	Lk 1:20	*2400*
And, *b*, thou shalt conceive in thy	Lk 1:31	*2400*
And, *b*, thy cousin Elisabeth, she	Lk 1:36	*2400*
B the handmaid of the Lord	Lk 1:38	*2400*
for, *b*, from henceforth all	Lk 1:48	*2400*
for, *b*, I bring you good tidings	Lk 2:10	*2400*
And, *b*, there was a man in	Lk 2:25	*2400*
and said unto Mary his mother, *B*	Lk 2:34	*2400*
b, thy father and I have sought	Lk 2:48	*2400*
city, *b* a man full of leprosy	Lk 5:12	*2400*
And, *b*, men brought in a bed a man	Lk 5:18	*2400*
for, *b*, your reward is great in	Lk 6:23	*2400*
nigh to the gate of the city, *b*	Lk 7:12	*2400*
B, they which are gorgeously	Lk 7:25	*2400*
is he, of whom it is written, *B*	Lk 7:27	*2400*
ye say, *B* a gluttonous man, and a	Lk 7:34	*2400*
And, *b*, a woman in the city, which	Lk 7:37	*2400*
And, *b*, there came a man named	Lk 8:41	*2400*
And, *b*, there talked with him two	Lk 9:30	*2400*
And, *b*, a man of the company cried	Lk 9:38	*2400*
b, I send you forth as lambs	Lk 10:3	*2400*
B, I give unto you power to tread	Lk 10:19	*2400*
And, *b*, a certain lawyer stood up,	Lk 10:25	*2400*
and, *b*, a greater than Solomon is	Lk 11:31	*2400*
and, *b*, a greater than Jonas is	Lk 11:32	*2400*
and, *b*, all things are clean unto	Lk 11:41	*2400*
the dresser of his vineyard, *B*	Lk 13:7	*2400*
And, *b*, there was a woman which	Lk 13:11	*2400*
And, *b*, there are last which shall	Lk 13:30	*2400*
them, Go ye, and tell that fox, *B*	Lk 13:32	*2400*
B, your house is left unto you	Lk 13:35	*2400*
And, *b*, there was a certain man	Lk 14:2	*2400*
all that *b* it begin to mock him,	Lk 14:29	*2334*
for, *b*, the kingdom of God is	Lk 17:21	*2400*
the twelve, and said unto them, *B*	Lk 18:31	*2400*
And, *b*, there was a man named	Lk 19:2	*2400*
B, Lord, the half of my goods I	Lk 19:8	*2400*
And another came, saying, Lord, *b*	Lk 19:20	*2400*
As for these things which ye *b*	Lk 21:6	*2334*
B the fig tree, and all the trees	Lk 21:29	*1492*
And he said unto them, *B*, when ye	Lk 22:10	*2400*
But, *b*, the hand of him that	Lk 22:21	*2400*
And the Lord said, Simon, Simon, *b*	Lk 22:31	*2400*
And they said, Lord, *b*, here are	Lk 22:38	*2400*
b a multitude, and he that was	Lk 22:47	*2400*
and, *b*, I, having examined him	Lk 23:14	*2400*
For, *b*, the days are coming, in	Lk 23:29	*2400*
And, *b*, there was a man named	Lk 23:50	*2400*
were much perplexed thereabout, *b*	Lk 24:4	*2400*
And, *b*, two of them went that same	Lk 24:13	*2400*
B my hands and my feet, that it is	Lk 24:39	*1492*
And, *b*, I send the promise of my	Lk 24:49	*2400*
B the Lamb of God, which taketh	Jn 1:29	*2396*
he saith, *B* the Lamb of God	Jn 1:36	*2396*
B an Israelite indeed, in whom is	Jn 1:47	*2396*
to whom thou barest witness, *b*	Jn 3:26	*2396*
b, I say unto you, Lift up your	Jn 4:35	*2400*
the temple, and said unto him, *B*	Jn 5:14	*2396*
sent unto him, saying, Lord, *b*	Jn 11:3	*2396*
said the Jews, *B* how he loved him	Jn 11:36	*2396*
b, thy King cometh, sitting on an	Jn 12:15	*2400*
b, the world is gone after him	Jn 12:19	*2396*
B, the hour cometh, yea, is now	Jn 16:32	*2400*
that they may *b* my glory, which	Jn 17:24	*2334*
b, they know what I said	Jn 18:21	*2396*
again, and saith unto them, *B*	Jn 19:4	*2396*
Pilate saith unto them, *B* the man	Jn 19:5	*2396*
saith unto the Jews, *B* your King	Jn 19:14	*2396*
unto his mother, Woman, *b* thy son	Jn 19:26	*2400*
he to the disciple, *B* thy mother	Jn 19:27	*2400*

hither thy finger, and b my hands	Jn 20:27	2396
toward heaven as he went up, b	Acts 1:10	2400
saying one to another, B	Acts 2:7	2400
now, Lord, b their threatenings	Acts 4:29	1896
b, the feet of them which have	Acts 5:9	2400
came one and told them, saying, B	Acts 5:25	2400
and, b, ye have filled Jerusalem	Acts 5:28	2400
and as he drew near to b it	Acts 7:31	2657
Moses trembled, and durst not b	Acts 7:32	2657
And said, B, I see the heavens	Acts 7:56	2400
and, b, a man of Ethiopia, an	Acts 8:27	2400
And he said, B, I am here, Lord	Acts 9:10	2400
for, b, he prayeth,	Acts 9:11	2400
which he had seen should mean, b	Acts 10:17	2400
the Spirit said unto him, B	Acts 10:19	2400
and said, B, I am he whom ye seek	Acts 10:21	2400
hour I prayed in my house, and, b	Acts 10:30	2400
And, b, immediately there were	Acts 11:11	2400
And, b, the angel of the Lord came	Acts 12:7	2400
And now, b, the hand of the Lord	Acts 13:11	2400
But, b, there cometh one after me	Acts 13:25	2400
B, ye despisers, and wonder, and	Acts 13:41	1492
and, b, a certain disciple was	Acts 16:1	2400
And now, b, I go bound in the	Acts 20:22	2400
And now, b, I know that ye all,	Acts 20:25	2400
B, thou art called a Jew, and	Rom 2:17	2396
As it is written, B, I lay in	Rom 9:33	2400
B therefore the goodness and	Rom 11:22	1492
B Israel after the flesh	1Cor 10:18	991
B, I shew you a mystery	1Cor 15:51	2400
of Israel could not stedfastly b	2Cor 3:7	816
b, all things are become new	2Cor 5:17	2400
b, now is the accepted time	2Cor 6:2	2400
b, now is the day of salvation	2Cor 6:2	2400
as dying, and, b, we live	2Cor 6:9	2400
For b this selfsame thing, that	2Cor 7:11	2400
B, the third time I am ready to	2Cor 12:14	2400
things which I write unto you, b	Gal 1:20	2400
B, I Paul say unto you, that if	Gal 5:2	2396
B I and the children which God	Heb 2:13	2400
fault with them, he saith, B	Heb 8:8	2400
B, we put bits in the horses'	Jas 3:3	2400
B also the ships, which though	Jas 3:4	2400
B, how great a matter a little	Jas 3:5	2400
B, the hire of the labourers who	Jas 5:4	2400
B, the husbandman waiteth for the	Jas 5:7	2400
b, the judge standeth before the	Jas 5:9	2400
B, we count them happy which	Jas 5:11	2400
is contained in the scripture, B	1Pet 2:6	2400
good works, which they shall b	1Pet 2:12	2029
While they b your chaste	1Pet 3:2	2029
B, what manner of love the Father	1Jn 3:1	1492
prophesied of these, saying, B	Jude 14	2400
B, he cometh with clouds	Rev 1:7	2400
and, b, I am alive for evermore,	Rev 1:18	2400
b, the devil shall cast some of	Rev 2:10	2400
B, I will cast her into a bed, and	Rev 2:22	2400
B, I have set before thee an open	Rev 3:8	2400
B, I will make them of the	Rev 3:9	2400
b, I will make them to come and	Rev 3:9	2400
B, I come quickly	Rev 3:11	2400
B, I stand at the door, and knock	Rev 3:20	2400
After this I looked, and, b	Rev 4:1	2400
and, b, a throne was set in heaven	Rev 4:2	2400
b, the Lion of the tribe of Juda,	Rev 5:5	2400
And I saw, and b a white horse	Rev 6:2	2400
And I looked, and b a pale horse	Rev 6:8	2400
and, b, there come two woes more	Rev 9:12	2400
and, b, the third woe cometh	Rev 11:14	2400
b a great red dragon, having	Rev 12:3	2400
b a white cloud, and upon the	Rev 14:14	2400
And after that I looked, and, b	Rev 15:5	2400
B, I come as a thief	Rev 16:15	2400
when they b the beast that was,	Rev 17:8	991
heaven opened, and b a white horse	Rev 19:11	2400
voice out of heaven saying, B	Rev 21:3	2400
that sat upon the throne said, B	Rev 21:5	2400
B, I come quickly	Rev 22:7	2400
And, b, I come quickly	Rev 22:12	2400

BEHOLDEST {4}

for thou b mischief and spite, to	Ps 10:14	5027
why b thou the mote that is in	Mt 7:3	991
why b thou the mote that is in	Lk 6:41	991
when thou thyself b not the beam	Lk 6:42	991

BEHOLDETH {15}

he b not the way of the vineyards	Job 24:18	6437
He b all high things	Job 41:34	7200
he b all the sons of men	Ps 33:13	7200
For he b himself, and goeth his	Jas 1:24	2657

BEHOLDING {15}

Turn away mine eyes from b vanity	Ps 119:37	7200
place, b the evil and the good	Prov 15:3	6822
saving the b of them with their	Eccl 5:11	7200
many women were there b afar off	Mt 27:55	2334
Then Jesus b him loved him, and	Mk 10:21	1689
And the people stood b	Lk 23:35	2334
b the things which were done,	Lk 23:48	2334
stood afar off, b these things	Lk 23:49	3708
b the man which was healed	Acts 4:14	991
b the miracles and signs which	Acts 8:13	2334
who stedfastly b him, and	Acts 14:9	816
earnestly b the council, said,	Acts 23:1	816
with open face b as in a glass	2Cor 3:18	2734
b your order, and the stedfastness	Col 2:5	991
he is like unto a man b his	Jas 1:23	2657

BEHOVED {2}

thus it b Christ to suffer, and to	Lk 24:46	1163
Wherefore in all things it b him	Heb 2:17	3784

BEING See APPENDIX.

BEKAH {1}

A b for every man, that is, half	Ex 38:26	1235

BEKERITE See BACHRITES.

BEL *(bel)* {3} See BAAL. *A Babylonian god.*

B boweth down, Nebo stoopeth,	Is 46:1	1078
B is confounded, Merodach is	Jer 50:2	1078
And I will punish B in Babylon	Jer 51:44	1078

BELA *(be'-lah)* {13} See BELAH, BELAITES.

1. Another name for Zoar.

king of Zeboiim, and the king of B	Gen 14:2	1106
the king of B (the same is Zoar	Gen 14:8	1106

2. An Edomite king.

B the son of Beor reigned in Edom	Gen 36:32	1106
B died, and Jobab the son of Zerah	Gen 36:33	1106
B the son of Beor	1Chr 1:43	1106
when B was dead, Jobab the son of	1Chr 1:44	1106

3. A son of Benjamin.

of B, the family of the Belaites	Num 26:38	1106
And the sons of B were Ard	Num 26:40	1106
B, and Becher, and Jediael, three	1Chr 7:6	1106
And the sons of B	1Chr 7:7	1106
Benjamin begat B his firstborn	1Chr 8:1	1106
And the sons of B were, Addar, and	1Chr 8:3	1106

4. A son of Azaz the Reubenite.

B the son of Azaz, the son of	1Chr 5:8	1106

BELAH *(be'-lah)* {1} See BELA. *A form of Bela.*

And the sons of Benjamin were B	Gen 46:21	1106

BELAITES *(be'-lah-ites)* {1} *Descendants of Bela.*

of Bela, the family of the B	Num 26:38	1108

BELCH {1}

they b out with their mouth	Ps 59:7	5042

BELIAL *(be'-le-al)* {17} *A title for a "worthless person."*

Certain men, the children of B	Deut 13:13	1100
of the city, certain sons of B	Judg 19:22	1100
us the men, the children of B	Judg 20:13	1100
handmaid for a daughter of B	1Sa 1:16	1100
the sons of Eli were sons of B	1Sa 2:12	1100
But the children of B said	1Sa 10:27	1100
for he is such a son of B	1Sa 25:17	1100
I pray thee, regard this man of B	1Sa 25:25	1100
all the wicked men and men of B	1Sa 30:22	1100
thou bloody man, and thou man of B	2Sa 16:7	1100
happened to be there a man of B	2Sa 20:1	1100
But the sons of B shall be all of	2Sa 23:6	1100
And set two men, sons of B	1Kin 21:10	1100
came in two men, children of B	1Kin 21:13	1100
the men of B witnessed against	1Kin 21:13	1100
him vain men, the children of B	2Chr 13:7	1100
what concord hath Christ with B	2Cor 6:15	955

BELIED {1}

They have b the LORD, and said, It	Jer 5:12	3584

BELIEF {1}

of the Spirit and b of the truth	2Th 2:13	4102

BELIEVE {143}

But, behold, they will not b me	Ex 4:1	539
That they may b that the LORD God	Ex 4:5	539
to pass, if they will not b thee	Ex 4:8	539
that they will b the voice of the	Ex 4:8	539
if they will not b also these two	Ex 4:9	539
with thee, and b thee for ever	Ex 19:9	539
how long will it be ere they b me	Num 14:11	539
ye did not b the LORD your God	Deut 1:32	539
that did not b in the LORD their	2Kin 17:14	539
B in the LORD your God, so shall	2Chr 20:20	539
b his prophets, so shall ye	2Chr 20:20	539
on this manner, neither yet b him	2Chr 32:15	539
yet would I not b that he had	Job 9:16	539
Wilt thou b him, that he will	Job 39:12	539
When he speaketh fair, b him not	Prov 26:25	539
If ye will not b, surely ye shall	Is 7:9	539
b me, and understand that I am he	Is 43:10	539
b them not, though they speak	Jer 12:6	539
in your days, which ye will not b	Hab 1:5	539
B ye that I am able to do this	Mt 9:28	4100
these little ones which b in me	Mt 18:6	4100
us, Why did ye not then b him	Mt 21:25	4100
afterward, that ye might b him	Mt 21:32	4100
b it not	Mt 24:23	4100
b it not	Mt 24:26	4100
from the cross, and we will b him	Mt 27:42	4100
repent ye, and b the gospel	Mk 1:15	4100,1722
synagogue, Be not afraid, only b	Mk 5:36	4100
said unto him, If thou canst b	Mk 9:23	4100
and said with tears, Lord, I b	Mk 9:24	4100
of these little ones that b in me	Mk 9:42	4100
but shall b that those things	Mk 11:23	4100
b that ye receive them, and ye	Mk 11:24	4100
say, Why then did ye not b him	Mk 11:31	4100
b him not	Mk 13:21	4100
the cross, that we may see and b	Mk 15:32	4100
signs shall follow them that b	Mk 16:17	4100
their hearts, lest they should b	Lk 8:12	4100
have no root, which for a while b	Lk 8:13	4100
b only, and she shall be made	Lk 8:50	4100
If I tell you, ye will not b	Lk 22:67	4100
slow of heart to b all that the	Lk 24:25	4100,1909
that all men through him might b	Jn 1:7	4100
even to them that b on his name	Jn 1:12	4100
and ye b not, how shall ye b	Jn 3:12	4100
b me, the hour cometh, when ye	Jn 4:21	4100
And said unto the woman, Now we b	Jn 4:42	4100
signs and wonders, ye will not b	Jn 4:48	4100
whom he hath sent, him ye b not	Jn 5:38	4100
How can ye b, which receive	Jn 5:44	4100
But if ye b not his writings	Jn 5:47	4100
how shall ye b my words	Jn 5:47	4100
that ye b on him whom he hath	Jn 6:29	4100
then, that we may see, and b thee	Jn 6:30	4100
ye also have seen me, and b not	Jn 6:36	4100
there are some of you that b not	Jn 6:64	4100
And we b and are sure that thou art	Jn 6:69	4100
neither did his brethren b in him	Jn 7:5	4100
which they that b on him should	Jn 7:39	4100
for if ye b not that I am he, ye	Jn 8:24	4100
I tell you the truth, ye b me not	Jn 8:45	4100
say the truth, why do ye not b me	Jn 8:46	4100
the Jews did not b concerning him	Jn 9:18	4100
Dost thou b on the Son of God	Jn 9:35	4100
he, Lord, that I might b on him	Jn 9:36	4100
And he said, Lord, I b	Jn 9:38	4100
But ye b not, because ye are not	Jn 10:26	4100
the works of my Father, b me not	Jn 10:37	4100
ye b not me, b the works	Jn 10:38	4100
that ye may know, and b, that the	Jn 10:38	4100
not there, to the intent ye may b	Jn 11:15	4100
I b that thou art the Christ, the	Jn 11:27	4100
thee, that, if thou wouldest b	Jn 11:40	4100
that they may b that thou hast	Jn 11:42	4100
thus alone, all men will b on him	Jn 11:48	4100
b in the light, that ye may be	Jn 12:36	4100
Therefore they could not b	Jn 12:39	4100
words, and b not, I judge him not	Jn 12:47	4100
to pass, ye may b that I am he	Jn 13:19	4100
ye b in God, b also in me	Jn 14:1	4100
B me that I am in the Father, and	Jn 14:11	4100
or else b me for the very works'	Jn 14:11	4100
it is come to pass, ye might b	Jn 14:29	4100
Of sin, because they b not on me	Jn 16:9	4100
by this we b that thou camest	Jn 16:30	4100
answered them, Do ye now b	Jn 16:31	4100
shall b on me through their word	Jn 17:20	4100
that the world may b that thou	Jn 17:21	4100
he saith true, that ye might b	Jn 19:35	4100
hand into his side, I will not b	Jn 20:25	4100
that ye might b that Jesus is the	Jn 20:31	4100
I b that Jesus Christ is the Son	Acts 8:37	4100
by him all that b are justified	Acts 13:39	4100
work which ye shall in no wise b	Acts 13:41	4100
hear the word of the gospel, and b	Acts 15:7	4100
But we b that through the grace	Acts 15:11	4100
B on the Lord Jesus Christ, and	Acts 16:31	4100
that they should b on him which	Acts 19:4	4100
of Jews there are which b	Acts 21:20	4100
As touching the Gentiles which b	Acts 21:25	4100
for I b God, that it shall be	Acts 27:25	4100
For what if some did not b	Rom 3:3	569
unto all and upon all them that b	Rom 3:22	4100
be the father of all them that b	Rom 4:11	4100
if we b on him that raised up	Rom 4:24	4100
we b that we shall also live with	Rom 6:8	4100
shalt b in thine heart that God	Rom 10:9	4100
how shall they b in him of whom	Rom 10:14	4100
from them that do not b in Judaea	Rom 15:31	544
of preaching to save them that b	1Cor 1:21	4100
If any of them that b not bid you	1Cor 10:27	571
and I partly b it	1Cor 11:18	4100
for a sign, not to them that b	1Cor 14:22	4100
but to them that b not	1Cor 14:22	571
serveth not for them that b	1Cor 14:22	571
but for them which b	1Cor 14:22	4100
the minds of them which b not	2Cor 4:4	571
we also b, and therefore speak	2Cor 4:13	4100
might be given to them that b	Gal 3:22	4100
of his power to us-ward who b	Eph 1:19	4100
of Christ, not only to b on him	Phil 1:29	4100
to all that b in Macedonia	1Th 1:7	4100
ourselves among you that b	1Th 2:10	4100
worketh also in you that b	1Th 2:13	4100
For if we b that Jesus died and	1Th 4:14	4100
b (because our testimony among	2Th 1:10	4100
that they should b a lie	2Th 2:11	4100
b on him to life everlasting	1Ti 1:16	4100
with thanksgiving of them which b	1Ti 4:3	4103
men, specially of those that b	1Ti 4:10	4103
If we b not, yet he abideth	2Ti 2:13	569
but of them that b to the saving	Heb 10:39	4102
cometh to God must b that he is	Heb 11:6	4100
the devils also b, and tremble	Jas 2:19	4100
Who by him do b in God, that	1Pet 1:21	4100
therefore which b he is precious	1Pet 2:7	4100
That we should b on the name of	1Jn 3:23	4100
b not every spirit, but try the	1Jn 4:1	4100
have I written unto you that b on	1Jn 5:13	4100
that ye may b on the name of the	1Jn 5:13	4100

BELIEVED {116}

And he b in the LORD	Gen 15:6	539
heart fainted, for he b them not	Gen 45:26	539
And the people b	Ex 4:31	539
b the LORD, and his servant Moses	Ex 14:31	539
and Aaron, Because ye b me not	Num 20:12	539
ye b him not, nor hearkened to	Deut 9:23	539
And Achish b David, saying, He	1Sa 27:12	539
Howbeit I b not the words, until	1Kin 10:7	539
Howbeit I b not their words,	2Chr 9:6	539
I laughed on them, they b it not	Job 29:24	539
unless I had b to see the	Ps 27:13	539
Because they b not in God	Ps 78:22	539

b not for his wondrous works — Ps 78:32 — 539
Then *b* they his words — Ps 106:12 — 539
land, they *b* not his word — Ps 106:24 — 539
I *b*, therefore have I spoken — Ps 116:10 — 539
for I have *b* thy commandments — Ps 119:66 — 539
Who hath *b* our report — Is 53:1 — 539
the son of Ahikam *b* them not — Jer 40:14 — 539
would not have *b* that the — Lam 4:12 — 539
upon him, because he *b* in his God — Dan 6:23 — 540
So the people of Nineveh *b* God — Jonah 3:5 — 539
and as thou hast *b*, so be it done — Mt 8:13 — *4100*
of righteousness, and ye *b* him not — Mt 21:32 — *4100*
publicans and the harlots *b* him — Mt 21:32 — *4100*
and had been seen of her, *b* not — Mk 16:11 — *569*
neither *b* they them — Mk 16:13 — *4100*
because they *b* not them which had — Mk 16:14 — *4100*
which are most surely *b* among us — Lk 1:1 — *4135*
And blessed is she that *b* — Lk 1:45 — *4100*
will say, Why then *b* ye him not — Lk 20:5 — *4100*
as idle tales, and they *b* them not — Lk 24:11 — *569*
And while they yet *b* not for joy — Lk 24:41 — *569*
and his disciples *b* on him — Jn 2:11 — *4100*
they *b* the scripture, and the word — Jn 2:22 — *4100*
many *b* in his name, when they saw — Jn 2:23 — *4100*
because he hath not *b* in the name — Jn 3:18 — *4100*
b on him for the saying of the — Jn 4:39 — *4100*
many more *b* because of his own — Jn 4:41 — *4100*
the man *b* the word that Jesus had — Jn 4:50 — *4100*
and himself *b*, and his whole house — Jn 4:53 — *4100*
b Moses, ye would have *b* me — Jn 5:46 — *4100*
who they were that *b* not, and who — Jn 6:64 — *4100*
And many of the people *b* on him — Jn 7:31 — *4100*
or of the Pharisees *b* on him — Jn 7:48 — *4100*
spake these words, many *b* on him — Jn 8:30 — *4100*
to those Jews which *b* on him — Jn 8:31 — *4100*
them, I told you, and ye *b* not — Jn 10:25 — *4100*
And many *b* on him there — Jn 10:42 — *4100*
things which Jesus did, *b* on him — Jn 11:45 — *4100*
the Jews went away, and *b* on Jesus — Jn 12:11 — *4100*
them, yet they *b* not on him — Jn 12:37 — *4100*
Lord, who hath *b* our report — Jn 12:38 — *4100*
chief rulers also many *b* on him — Jn 12:42 — *4100*
have *b* that I came out from God — Jn 16:27 — *4100*
they have *b* that thou didst send — Jn 17:8 — *4100*
to the sepulchre, and he saw, and *b* — Jn 20:8 — *4100*
thou hast seen me, thou hast *b* — Jn 20:29 — *4100*
that have not seen, and yet have *b* — Jn 20:29 — *4100*
all that *b* were together, and had — Acts 2:44 — *4100*
of them which heard the word *b* — Acts 4:4 — *4100*
of them that *b* were of one heart — Acts 4:32 — *4100*
But when they *b* Philip preaching — Acts 8:12 — *4100*
Then Simon himself *b* also — Acts 8:13 — *4100*
b not that he was a disciple — Acts 9:26 — *4100*
and many *b* in the Lord — Acts 9:42 — *4100*
which *b* were astonished, as many — Acts 10:45 — *4103*
who *b* on the Lord Jesus Christ — Acts 11:17 — *4100*
and a great number *b*, and turned — Acts 11:21 — *4100*
when he saw what was done, *b* — Acts 13:12 — *4100*
were ordained to eternal life *b* — Acts 13:48 — *4100*
the Jews and also of the Greeks *b* — Acts 14:1 — *4100*
them to the Lord, on whom they *b* — Acts 14:23 — *4100*
the sect of the Pharisees which *b* — Acts 15:5 — *4100*
woman, which was a Jewess, and *b* — Acts 16:1 — *4103*
And some of them *b*, and consorted — Acts 17:4 — *3982*
But the Jews which *b* not, moved — Acts 17:5 — *544*
Therefore many of them *b* — Acts 17:12 — *4100*
certain men clave unto him, and *b* — Acts 17:34 — *4100*
b on the Lord with all his house — Acts 18:8 — *4100*
many of the Corinthians hearing *b* — Acts 18:8 — *4100*
much which had *b* through grace — Acts 18:27 — *4100*
the Holy Ghost since ye *b* — Acts 19:2 — *4100*
b not, but spake evil of that way — Acts 19:9 — *544*
And many that *b* came, and confessed — Acts 19:18 — *4100*
synagogue them that *b* on thee — Acts 22:19 — *4100*
the centurion *b* the master — Acts 27:11 — *3982*
some *b* the things which were — Acts 28:24 — *3982*
which were spoken, and some *b* not — Acts 28:24
b God, and it was counted — Rom 4:3 — *569,4100*
nations,) before him whom he *b* — Rom 4:17 — *4100*
Who against hope *b* in hope — Rom 4:18 — *4100*
on him in whom they have not *b* — Rom 10:14 — *4100*
Lord, who hath *b* our report — Rom 10:16 — *4100*
ye in times past have not *b* God — Rom 11:30 — *544*
Even so have these also now not *b* — Rom 11:31 — *544*
salvation nearer than when we *b* — Rom 13:11 — *4100*
but ministers by whom ye *b* — 1Cor 3:5 — *4100*
you, unless ye have *b* in vain — 1Cor 15:2 — *4100*
or they, so we preach, and so ye *b* — 1Cor 15:11 — *4100*
according as it is written, I *b* — 2Cor 4:13 — *4100*
even we have *b* in Jesus Christ — Gal 2:16 — *4100*
Even as Abraham *b* God, and it was — Gal 3:6 — *4100*
in whom also after that ye *b* — Eph 1:13 — *4100*
among you was *b*) in that day — 2Th 1:10 — *4100*
be damned who *b* not the truth — 2Th 2:12 — *4100*
b on in the world, received up — 1Ti 3:16 — *4100*
for I know whom I have *b*, and am — 2Ti 1:12 — *4100*
that they which have *b* in God — Titus 3:8 — *4100*
his rest, but to them that *b* not — Heb 3:18 — *544*
For we which have *b* do enter into — Heb 4:3 — *4100*
perished not with them that *b* not — Heb 11:31 — *544*
which saith, Abraham *b* God — Jas 2:23 — *4100*
b the love that God hath to us — 1Jn 4:16 — *4100*
destroyed them that *b* not — Jude 5 — *4100*

BELIEVERS {2}
b were the more added to the Lord — Acts 5:14 — *4100*
but be thou an example of the *b* — 1Ti 4:12 — *4103*

BELIEVEST {8}
because thou *b* not my words — Lk 1:20 — *4100*
thee under the fig tree, *b* thou — Jn 1:50 — *4100*
B thou this — Jn 11:26 — *4100*
B thou not that I am in the — Jn 14:10 — *4100*
If thou *b* with all thine heart — Acts 8:37 — *4100*
King Agrippa, *b* thou the prophets — Acts 26:27 — *4100*
I know that thou *b* — Acts 26:27 — *4100*
Thou *b* that there is one God — Jas 2:19 — *4100*

BELIEVETH {45}
He *b* not that he shall return out — Job 15:22 — 539
neither *b* he that it is the sound — Job 39:24 — 539
The simple *b* every word — Prov 14:15 — 539
he that *b* shall not make haste — Is 28:16 — 539
things are possible to him that *b* — Mk 9:23 — *4100*
He that *b* and is baptized shall be — Mk 16:16 — *4100*
but he that *b* not shall be damned — Mk 16:16 — *569*
That whosoever *b* in him should — Jn 3:15 — *4100*
that whosoever *b* in him should — Jn 3:16 — *4100*
He that *b* on him is not condemned — Jn 3:18 — *4100*
but he that *b* not is condemned — Jn 3:18 — *4100*
He that *b* on the Son hath — Jn 3:36 — *4100*
he that *b* not the Son shall not — Jn 3:36 — *544*
b on him that sent me, hath — Jn 5:24 — *4100*
he that *b* on me shall never — Jn 6:35 — *4100*
b on him, may have everlasting — Jn 6:40 — *4100*
He that *b* on me hath everlasting — Jn 6:47 — *4100*
He that *b* on me, as the scripture — Jn 7:38 — *4100*
he that *b* in me, though he were — Jn 11:25 — *4100*
liveth and *b* in me shall never die — Jn 11:26 — *4100*
cried and said, He that *b* on me — Jn 12:44 — *4100*
b not on me, but on him that sent — Jn 12:44 — *4100*
that whosoever *b* on me should not — Jn 12:46 — *4100*
I say unto you, He that *b* on me — Jn 14:12 — *4100*
b in him shall receive remission — Acts 10:43 — *4100*
salvation to every one that *b* — Rom 1:16 — *4100*
justifier of him which *b* in Jesus — Rom 3:26 — *1537,4102*
but *b* on him that justifieth the — Rom 4:5 — *4100*
whosoever *b* on him shall not be — Rom 9:33 — *4100*
righteousness to every one that *b* — Rom 10:4 — *4100*
heart man *b* unto righteousness — Rom 10:10 — *4100*
Whosoever *b* on him shall not be — Rom 10:11 — *4100*
For one *b* that he may eat all — Rom 14:2 — *4100*
brother hath a wife that *b* not — 1Cor 7:12 — *571*
which hath an husband that *b* not — 1Cor 7:13 — *571*
b all things, hopeth all things — 1Cor 13:7 — *4100*
and there come in one that *b* not — 1Cor 14:24 — *571*
hath he that *b* with an infidel — 2Cor 6:15 — *4103*
man or woman that *b* have widows — 1Ti 5:16 — *4103*
he that *b* on him shall not be — 1Pet 2:6 — *4100*
Whosoever *b* that Jesus is the — 1Jn 5:1 — *4100*
but he that *b* that Jesus is the — 1Jn 5:5 — *4100*
He that *b* on the Son of God hath — 1Jn 5:10 — *4100*
he that *b* not God hath made him a — 1Jn 5:10 — *4100*
because he *b* not the record that — 1Jn 5:10 — *4100*

BELIEVING {8}
ye shall ask in prayer, *b* — Mt 21:22 — *4100*
and be not faithless, but *b* — Jn 20:27 — *4103*
that *b* ye might have life through — Jn 20:31 — *4100*
b in God with all his house — Acts 16:34 — *4100*
b all things which are written in — Acts 24:14 — *4100*
you with all joy and peace in *b* — Rom 15:13 — *4100*
And they that have *b* masters — 1Ti 6:2 — *4103*
though now ye see him not, yet *b* — 1Pet 1:8 — *4100*

BELL {4}
A golden *b* and a pomegranate — Ex 28:34 — 6472
and a pomegranate, a golden *b* — Ex 28:34 — 6472
A *b* and a pomegranate, a *b* and a — Ex 39:26 — 6472

BELLIES {1}
alway liars, evil beasts, slow *b* — Titus 1:12 — *1064*

BELLOW {1}
heifer at grass, and *b* as bulls — Jer 50:11 — 6670

BELLOWS {1}
The *b* are burned, the lead is — Jer 6:29 — 4647

BELLS {4}
b of gold between them round — Ex 28:33 — 6472
they made *b* of pure gold — Ex 39:25 — 6472
and put the *b* between the — Ex 39:25 — 6472
there be upon the *b* of the horses — Zec 14:20 — 4698

BELLY {12}
upon thy *b* shalt thou go, and dust — Gen 3:14 — 1512
Whatsoever goeth upon the *b* — Lev 11:42 — 1512
thigh to rot, and thy *b* to swell — Num 5:21 — 990
bowels, to make thy *b* to swell — Num 5:22 — 990
her *b* shall swell, and her thigh — Num 5:27 — 990
and the woman through her *b* — Num 25:8 — 6897
thigh, and thrust it into his *b* — Judg 3:21 — 990
not draw the dagger out of his *b* — Judg 3:22 — 990
over against the *b* which was by — 1Kin 7:20 — 990
ghost when I came out of the *b* — Job 3:11 — 990
fill his *b* with the east wind — Job 15:2 — 990
and their *b* prepareth deceit — Job 15:35 — 990
God shall cast them out of his *b* — Job 20:15 — 990
shall not feel quietness in his *b* — Job 20:20 — 990
When he is about to fill his *b* — Job 20:23 — 990
my *b* is as wine which hath no — Job 32:19 — 990
force is in the navel of his *b* — Job 40:16 — 990
whose *b* thou fillest with thy hid — Ps 17:14 — 990
art my God from my mother's *b* — Ps 22:10 — 990
with grief, yea, my soul and my *b* — Ps 31:9 — 990
our *b* cleaveth unto the earth — Ps 44:25 — 990
but the *b* of the wicked shall — Prov 13:25 — 990
into the innermost parts of the *b* — Prov 18:8 — 990
A man's *b* shall be satisfied with — Prov 18:20 — 990
all the inward parts of the *b* — Prov 20:27 — 990
stripes the inward parts of the *b* — Prov 20:30 — 990
into the innermost parts of the *b* — Prov 26:22 — 990
his *b* is as bright ivory overlaid — Song 5:14 — 4578
thy *b* is like an heap of wheat — Song 7:2 — 990
which are borne by me from the *b* — Is 46:3 — 990
formed thee in the *b* I knew thee — Jer 1:5 — 990
filled his *b* with my delicates — Jer 51:34 — 3770
Son of man, cause thy *b* to eat — Eze 3:3 — 990
and his arms of silver, his *b* — Dan 2:32 — 4577
Jonah was in the *b* of the fish — Jonah 1:17 — 4578
LORD his God out of the fish's *b* — Jonah 2:1 — 4578
out of the *b* of hell cried I, and — Jonah 2:2 — 990
When I heard, my *b* trembled — Hab 3:16 — 990
and three nights in the whale's *b* — Mt 12:40 — *2836*
in at the mouth goeth into the *b* — Mt 15:17 — *2836*
into his heart, but into the *b* — Mk 7:19 — *2836*
b with the husks that the swine — Lk 15:16 — *2836*
out of his *b* shall flow rivers of — Jn 7:38 — *2836*
Jesus Christ, but their own *b* — Rom 16:18 — *2836*
Meats for the *b*, and the *b* for — 1Cor 6:13 — *2836*
destruction, whose God is their *b* — Phil 3:19 — *2836*
and it shall make thy *b* bitter — Rev 10:9 — *2836*
I had eaten it, my *b* was bitter — Rev 10:10 — *2836*

BELONG {12}
Do not interpretations *b* to God — Gen 40:8
the possession of the land did *b* — Lev 27:24
and over all things that *b* to it — Num 1:50
The secret things *b* unto the LORD — Deut 29:29
which are revealed *b* unto us — Deut 29:29
shields of the earth *b* unto God — Ps 47:9
unto GOD the Lord *b* the issues — Ps 68:20
These things also *b* to the wise — Prov 24:23
To the Lord our God *b* mercies — Dan 9:9
my name, because ye *b* to Christ — Mk 9:41 — *1510*
the things which *b* unto thy peace — Lk 19:42
for the things that *b* to the Lord — 1Cor 7:32

BELONGED {12}
on the border of Manasseh *b* to — Josh 17:8
of the herdmen that *b* to Saul — 1Sa 21:7
the mighty men which *b* to David — 1Kin 1:8
which *b* to the Philistines — 1Kin 15:27
which *b* to the Philistines — 1Kin 16:15
which *b* to Judah, for Israel, are — 2Kin 14:28
All these *b* to the sons of Machir — 1Chr 2:23
which *b* to Judah, to bring up — 1Chr 13:6
the burial which *b* to the kings — 2Chr 26:23
house which *b* to king Ahasuerus — Est 1:9
with such things as *b* to her — Est 2:9 — 4490
he *b* unto Herod's jurisdiction — Lk 23:7 — *1510*

BELONGEST {1}
said unto him, To whom *b* thou — 1Sa 30:13

BELONGETH {20}
This is it that *b* unto the — Num 8:24
To me *b* vengeance, and recompence — Deut 32:35
by Gibeah, which *b* to Benjamin — Judg 19:14
into Gibeah that *b* to Benjamin — Judg 20:4
which *b* to Judah, and pitched — 1Sa 17:1
upon the coast which *b* to Judah — 1Sa 30:14
which *b* to Zidon, and dwell there — 1Kin 17:9
which *b* to Judah, and left his — 1Kin 19:3
at Beth-shemesh, which *b* to Judah — 2Kin 14:11
at Beth-shemesh, which *b* to Judah — 2Chr 25:21
for this matter *b* unto thee — Ezr 10:4
Salvation *b* unto the LORD — Ps 3:8
that power *b* unto God — Ps 62:11
Also unto thee, O Lord, *b* mercy — Ps 62:12
O LORD God, to whom vengeance *b* — Ps 94:1
O God, to whom vengeance *b* — Ps 94:1
O Lord, righteousness *b* unto thee — Dan 9:7
to us *b* confusion of face, to our — Dan 9:8
But strong meat *b* to them that — Heb 5:14 — *1510*
hath said, Vengeance *b* unto me — Heb 10:30

BELONGING {5}
the service of the sanctuary *b* — Num 7:9
a part of the field *b* unto Boaz — Ruth 2:3
Philistines *b* to the five lords — 1Sa 6:18
meddleth with strife *b* not to him — Prov 26:17
b to the city called Bethsaida — Lk 9:10

BELOVED {111}
If a man have two wives, one *b* — Deut 21:15 — 157
born him children, both the *b* — Deut 21:15 — 157
he may not make the son of the *b* — Deut 21:16 — 157
The *b* of the LORD shall dwell in — Deut 33:12 — 3039
who was *b* of his God, and God made — Neh 13:26 — 157
That thy *b* may be delivered — Ps 60:5 — 3039
That thy *b* may be delivered — Ps 108:6 — 3039
for so he giveth his *b* sleep — Ps 127:2 — 3039
only *b* in the sight of my mother — Prov 4:3
My *b* is unto me as a cluster of — Song 1:14 — 1730
Behold, thou art fair, my *b* — Song 1:16 — 157
so is my *b* among the sons — Song 2:3 — 1730
The voice of my *b* — Song 2:8 — 1730
My *b* is like a roe or a young — Song 2:9 — 1730
My *b* spake, and said unto me, Rise — Song 2:10 — 1730
My *b* is mine, and I am his — Song 2:16 — 1730
the shadows flee away, turn, my *b* — Song 2:17 — 1730
Let my *b* come into his garden, and — Song 4:16 — 1730
drink, yea, drink abundantly, O *b* — Song 5:1 — 1730
the voice of my *b* that knocketh — Song 5:2 — 1730
My *b* put in his hand by the hole — Song 5:4 — 1730
I rose up to open to my *b* — Song 5:5 — 1730
I opened to my *b* — Song 5:6 — 1730
but my *b* had withdrawn himself — Song 5:6 — 1730
of Jerusalem, if ye find my *b* — Song 5:8 — 1730
thy *b* more than another *b* — Song 5:9 — 1730
thy *b* more than another *b* — Song 5:9 — 1730

My *b* is white and ruddy, the Song 5:10 1730
This is my *b*, and this is my Song 5:16 1730
Whither is thy *b* gone, O thou Song 6:1 1730
whither is thy *b* turned aside Song 6:1 1730
My *b* is gone down into his garden Song 6:2 1730
am my beloved's, and my *b* is mine Song 6:3 1730
mouth like the best wine for my *b* Song 7:9 1730
Come, my *b*, let us go forth into Song 7:11 1730
I have laid up for thee, O my *b* Song 7:13 1730
wilderness, leaning upon her *b* Song 8:5 1730
Make haste, my *b*, and be thou like Song 8:14 1730
of my *b* touching his vineyard Is 5:1 1730
What hath my *b* to do in mine Jer 11:15 3039
I have given the dearly *b* of my Jer 12:7 3033
for thou art greatly *b* Dan 9:23 2530
me, O Daniel, a man greatly *b* Dan 10:11 2530
And said, O man greatly *b*, fear Dan 10:19 2530
love a woman *b* of her friend, yet Hos 3:1 157
even the *b* fruit of their womb Hos 9:16 4261
heaven, saying, This is my *b* Son Mt 3:17 *27*
my *b*, in whom my soul is well Mt 12:18 *27*
which said, This is my *b* Son Mt 17:5 *27*
heaven, saying, Thou art my *b* Son Mk 1:11 *27*
cloud, saying, This is my *b* Son Mk 9:7 *27*
which said, Thou art my *b* Son Lk 3:22 *27*
cloud, saying, This is my *b* Son Lk 9:35 *27*
I will send my *b* son Lk 20:13 *27*
men unto you with our *b* Barnabas Acts 15:25 *27*
b of God, called to be saints Rom 1:7 *27*
and her *b*, which was not *b* Rom 9:25 *27*
they are *b* for the fathers' sakes Rom 11:28 *27*
Dearly *b*, avenge not yourselves, Rom 12:19 *27*
Greet Amplias my *b* in the Lord Rom 16:8 *27*
helper in Christ, and Stachys my *b* Rom 16:9 *27*
Salute the *b* Persis, which Rom 16:12 *27*
but as my *b* sons I warn you 1Cor 4:14 *27*
you Timotheus, who is my *b* son 1Cor 4:17 *27*
Wherefore, my dearly *b*, flee from 1Cor 10:14 *27*
my *b* brethren, be ye stedfast, 1Cor 15:58 *27*
therefore these promises dearly *b* 2Cor 7:1 *27*
but we do all things, dearly *b* 2Cor 12:19 *27*
he hath made us accepted in the *b* Eph 1:6 *25*
a *b* brother and faithful minister Eph 6:21 *27*
Wherefore, my *b*, as ye have Phil 2:12 *27*
Therefore, my brethren dearly *b* Phil 4:1 *27*
fast in the Lord, my dearly *b* Phil 4:1 *27*
as the elect of God, holy and *b* Col 3:12 *25*
unto you, who is a *b* brother Col 4:7 *27*
b brother, who is one of you Col 4:9 *27*
the *b* physician, and Demas, greet Col 4:14 *27*
Knowing, brethren *b*, your 1Th 1:4 *25*
brethren *b* of the Lord, because 2Th 2:13 *25*
because they are faithful and *b* 1Ti 6:2 *27*
To Timothy, my dearly *b* son 2Ti 1:2 *27*
unto Philemon our dearly *b* Philem 1 *27*
And to our *b* Apphia, and Archippus Philem 2 *27*
but above a servant, a brother *b* Philem 16 *27*
But, *b*, we are persuaded better Heb 6:9 *27*
Do not err, my *b* brethren Jas 1:16 *27*
my *b* brethren, let every man be Jas 1:19 *27*
my *b* brethren, Hath not God Jas 2:5 *27*
Dearly *b*, I beseech you as 1Pet 2:11 *27*
B, think it not strange 1Pet 4:12 *27*
excellent glory, This is my *b* Son 2Pet 1:17 *27*
This second epistle, *b*, I now 2Pet 3:1 *27*
But, *b*, be not ignorant of this 2Pet 3:8 *27*
Wherefore, *b*, seeing that ye look 2Pet 3:14 *27*
even as our *b* brother Paul also 2Pet 3:15 *27*
Ye therefore, *b*, seeing ye know 2Pet 3:17 *27*
B, now are we the sons of God, and 1Jn 3:2 *27*
B, if our heart condemn us not, 1Jn 3:21 *27*
B, believe not every spirit, but 1Jn 4:1 *27*
B, let us love one another 1Jn 4:7 *27*
B, if God so loved us, we ought 1Jn 4:11 *27*
B, I wish above all things that 3Jn 2 *27*
B, thou doest faithfully 3Jn 5 *27*
B, follow not that which is evil, 3Jn 11 *27*
B, when I gave all diligence to Jude 3 *27*
But, *b*, remember ye the words Jude 17 *27*
But ye, *b*, building up yourselves Jude 20 *27*
the saints about, and the *b* city Rev 20:9 *25*

BELOVED'S {2}
I am my *b*, and my beloved is mine Song 6:3 1730
I am my *b*, and his desire is Song 7:10 1730

BELSHAZZAR *(bel-shaz'-ar)* {8} *A Babylonian king.*
B the king made a great feast to Dan 5:1 1113
B, whiles he tasted the wine, Dan 5:2 1113
Then was king *B* greatly troubled, Dan 5:9 1113
And thou his son, O *B*, hast not Dan 5:22 1113
Then commanded *B*, and they clothed Dan 5:29 1113
In that night was *B* the king of Dan 5:30 1113
In the first year of *B* king of Dan 7:1 1113
king *B* a vision appeared unto me Dan 8:1 1113

BELTESHAZZAR *(bel-te-shaz'-ar)* {10} See DANIEL.
The Babylonian name given to Daniel.
he gave unto Daniel the name of *B* Dan 1:7 1095
said to Daniel, whose name was *B* Dan 2:26 1096
in before me, whose name was *B* Dan 4:8 1096
O *B*, master of the magicians, Dan 4:9 1096
Now thou, O *B*, declare the Dan 4:18 1096
Then Daniel, whose name was *B* Dan 4:19 1096
The king spake, and said, *B* Dan 4:19 1096
B answered and said, My lord, the Dan 4:19 1096
Daniel, whom the king named *B* Dan 5:12 1096
Daniel, whose name was called *B* Dan 10:1 1095

BEMOAN {5}
or who shall *b* thee Jer 15:5 5110
neither go to lament nor *b* them Jer 16:5 5110
not for the dead, neither *b* him Jer 22:10 5110
All ye that are about him, *b* him Jer 48:17 5110
who will *b* her Nah 3:7 5110

BEMOANED {1}
and they *b* him, and comforted him Job 42:11 5110

BEMOANING {1}
heard Ephraim *b* himself thus Jer 31:18 5110

BEN *(ben)* {1} *A Levite.*
the second degree, Zechariah, *B* 1Chr 15:18 1122

BENAIAH *(ben-ay'-ah)* {42}
1. An officer of David.
B the son of Jehoiada was over 2Sa 8:18 1141
B the son of Jehoiada was over 2Sa 20:23 1141
B the son of Jehoiada, the son of 2Sa 23:20 1141
These things did *B* the son of 2Sa 23:22 1141
B the son of Jehoiada, and Nathan 1Kin 1:8 1141
But Nathan the prophet, and *B* 1Kin 1:10 1141
B the son of Jehoiada, and thy 1Kin 1:26 1141
prophet, and *B* the son of Jehoiada 1Kin 1:32 1141
B the son of Jehoiada answered 1Kin 1:36 1141
B the son of Jehoiada, and the 1Kin 1:38 1141
B the son of Jehoiada, and the 1Kin 1:44 1141
the hand of *B* the son of Jehoiada 1Kin 2:25 1141
Then Solomon sent *B* the son of 1Kin 2:29 1141
B came to the tabernacle of the 1Kin 2:30 1141
B brought the king word again, 1Kin 2:30 1141
So *B* the son of Jehoiada went up, 1Kin 2:34 1141
the king put *B* the son of 1Kin 2:35 1141
commanded *B* the son of Jehoiada 1Kin 2:46 1141
B the son of Jehoiada was over 1Kin 4:4 1141
B the son of Jehoiada, the son of 1Chr 11:22 1141
These things did *B* the son of 1Chr 11:24 1141
B the son of Jehoiada was over 1Chr 18:17 1141
month was *B* the son of Jehoiada 1Chr 27:5 1141
This is that *B*, who was mighty 1Chr 27:6 1141
2. A "mighty man" of David.
B the Pirathonite, Hiddai of the 2Sa 23:30 1141
of Benjamin, *B* the Pirathonite, 1Chr 11:31 1141
month was *B* the Pirathonite 1Chr 27:14 1141
3. A Simeonite family chief.
and Adiel, and Jesimiel, and *B* 1Chr 4:36 1141
4. A priest of David.
and Jehiel, and Unni, Eliab, and *B* 1Chr 15:18 1141
Unni, and Eliab, and Maaseiah, and *B* 1Chr 15:20 1141
and Amasai, and Zechariah, and *B* 1Chr 15:24 1141
and Mattithiah, and Eliab, and *B* 1Chr 16:5 1141
B also and Jahaziel the priests 1Chr 16:6 1141
5. Father of Jehoida.
was Jehoiada the son of *B* 1Chr 27:34 1141
6. Grandfather of Jehaziel.
son of Zechariah, the son of *B* 2Chr 20:14 1141
7. A Levite during Hezekiah's reign.
and Ismachiah, and Mahath, and *B* 2Chr 31:13 1141
8. A descendant of Parosh.
and Eleazar, and Malchijah, and *B* Ezr 10:25 1141
9. A son of Pahath-moab.
Adna, and Chelal, *B*, Maaseiah, Ezr 10:30 1141
10. A son of Bani.
B, Bedeiah, Chelluh, Ezr 10:35 1141
11. A son of Nebo.
Zabad, Zebina, Jadau, and Joel, *B* Ezr 10:43 1141
12. Father of Pelatiah.
of Azur, and Pelatiah the son of *B* Eze 11:1 1141
that Pelatiah the son of *B* died Eze 11:13 1141

BEN-AMMI *(ben-am'-mi)* {1} *A son of Lot.*
bare a son, and called his name *B* Gen 19:38 1151

BENCHES {1}
have made thy *b* of ivory, brought Eze 27:6 7175

BEND {8}
For, lo, the wicked *b* their bow Ps 11:2 1869
b their bows to shoot their Ps 64:3 1869
they *b* their tongues like their Jer 9:3 1869
Lydians, that handle and *b* the bow Jer 46:9 1869
all ye that *b* the bow, shoot at Jer 50:14 1869
all ye that *b* the bow, camp Jer 50:29 1869
bendeth let the archer *b* his bow Jer 51:3 1869
this vine did *b* her roots toward Eze 17:7 3719

BEN DEKER See DEKAR.

BENDETH {2}
when he *b* his bow to shoot his Ps 58:7 1869
Against him that *b* let the archer Jer 51:3 1869

BENDING {1}
thee shall come *b* unto thee Is 60:14 7817

BENEATH See APPENDIX.

BENE BARAK See BENE-BERAK.

BENE-BERAK *(be'-ne-be'-rak)* {1} *A city in Dan.*
And Jehud, and *B*, and Gath-rimmon, Josh 19:45 1138

BENEFACTORS {1}
authority upon them are called *b* Lk 22:25 *2110*

BENEFIT {5}
according to the *b* done unto him 2Chr 32:25 1576
wherewith I said I would *b* them Jer 18:10 3190
that ye might have a second *b* 2Cor 1:15 *5485*
and beloved, partakers of the *b* 1Ti 6:2 *2108*
that thy *b* should not be as it Philem 14 *18*

BENEFITS {3}
Lord, who daily loadeth us with *b* Ps 68:19
my soul, and forget not all his *b* Ps 103:2 1576
the LORD for all his *b* toward me Ps 116:12 8408

BENE JAAKAN See BENE-JAAKAN.

BENE-JAAKAN *(be'-ne-ja'-a-kan)* {2} *Namesake of several wells.*
from Moseroth, and pitched in *B* Num 33:31 1142
And they removed from *B*, and Num 33:32 1142

BENEVOLENCE {1}
render unto the wife due *b* 1Cor 7:3 *2133*

BEN-HADAD *(ben'-ha-dad)* {27}
1. A Syrian king, son of Tabrimon.
and king Asa sent them to *B* 1Kin 15:18 1131
So *B* hearkened unto king Asa, and 1Kin 15:20 1131
sent to *B* king of Syria, that 2Chr 16:2 1130
B hearkened unto king Asa, and 2Chr 16:4 1130
2. A Syrian king during Ahab's reign.
B the king of Syria gathered all 1Kin 20:1 1131
and said unto him, Thus saith *B* 1Kin 20:2 1131
again, and said, Thus speaketh *B* 1Kin 20:5 1131
he said unto the messengers of *B* 1Kin 20:9 1131
B sent unto him, and said, The 1Kin 20:10 1131
when *B* heard this message, as he 1Kin 20:12
But *B* was drinking himself drunk 1Kin 20:16 1130
B sent out, and they told him, 1Kin 20:17 1130
B the king of Syria escaped on an 1Kin 20:20 1130
that *B* numbered the Syrians, and 1Kin 20:26 1130
B fled, and came into the city, 1Kin 20:30 1130
and said, Thy servant *B* saith 1Kin 20:32 1130
and they said, Thy brother *B* 1Kin 20:33 1130
Then *B* came forth to him 1Kin 20:33 1130
B said unto him, The cities, 1Kin 20:34
that *B* king of Syria gathered all 2Kin 6:24 1130
B the king of Syria was sick 2Kin 8:7 1130
Thy son *B* king of Syria hath sent 2Kin 8:9 1130
3. A Syrian king, son of Hazael.
into the hand of *B* the son of 2Kin 13:3 1130
B his son reigned in his stead 2Kin 13:24 1130
of *B* the son of Hazael the cities 2Kin 13:25 1130
shall devour the palaces of *B* Amos 1:4 1130
4. A title for all the Syrian kings.
it shall consume the palaces of *B* Jer 49:27 1130

BEN-HAIL *(ben-ha'-il)* {1} *A prince of Judah.*
he sent to his princes, even to *B* 2Chr 17:7 1134

BEN-HANAN *(ben-ha'-nan)* {1} *A son of Shimon.*
Shimon were, Amnon, and Rinnah, *B* 1Chr 4:20 1135

BENINU *(ben'-i-nu)* {1} *A Levite who renewed the covenant.*
Hodijah, Bani, *B* Neh 10:13 1148

BENJAMIN *(ben'-ja-min)* {162} See BENJAMIN'S, BENJAMITE.
1. Youngest son of Jacob.
but his father called him *B* Gen 35:18 1144
Joseph, and *B* Gen 35:24 1144
But *B*, Joseph's brother, Jacob Gen 42:4 1144
is not, and ye will take *B* away Gen 42:36 1144
away your other brother, and *B* Gen 43:14 1144
double money in their hand, and *B* Gen 43:15 1144
And when Joseph saw *B* with them Gen 43:16 1144
up his eyes, and saw his brother *B* Gen 43:29 1144
see, and the eyes of my brother *B* Gen 45:12 1144
and *B* wept upon his neck Gen 45:14 1144
but to *B* he gave three hundred Gen 45:22 1144
Joseph, and *B* Gen 46:19 1144
And the sons of *B* were Belah Gen 46:21 1144
Issachar, Zebulun, and *B*, Ex 1:3 1144
Dan, Joseph, and *B*, Naphtali, Gad, 1Chr 2:2 1144
The sons of *B* 1Chr 7:6 1144
Now *B* begat Bela his firstborn, 1Chr 8:1 1144
2. One of the twelve tribes comprising Israel.
B shall ravin as a wolf: Gen 49:27 1144
Of *B* Num 1:11 1144
Of the children of *B*, by their Num 1:36 1144
of them, even of the tribe of *B* Num 1:37 1144
Then the tribe of *B* Num 2:22 1144
of *B* shall be Abidan the son of Num 2:22 1144
prince of the children of *B* Num 7:60 1144
B was Abidan the son of Gideoni Num 10:24 1144
Of the tribe of *B*, Palti the son Num 13:9 1144
The sons of *B* after their Num 26:38 1144
sons of *B* after their families Num 26:41 1144
Of the tribe of *B*, Elidad the son Num 34:21 1144
and Issachar, and Joseph, and *B* Deut 27:12 1144
of *B* he said, The beloved of the Deut 33:12 1144
of *B* came up according to their Josh 18:11 1144
inheritance of the children of *B* Josh 18:20 1144
of *B* according to their families Josh 18:21 1144
of *B* according to their families Josh 18:28 1144
Simeon, and out of the tribe of *B* Josh 21:4 1144
And out of the tribe of *B*, Gibeon Josh 21:17 1144
the children of *B* did not drive Judg 1:21 1144
of *B* in Jerusalem unto this day Judg 1:21 1144
after thee, *B*, among thy people Judg 5:14 1144
also against Judah, and against *B* Judg 10:9 1144
by Gibeah, which belongeth to *B* Judg 19:14 1144
(Now the children of *B* heard that Judg 20:3 1144
into Gibeah that belongeth to *B* Judg 20:4 1144
do, when they come to Gibeah of *B* Judg 20:10 1144
men through all the tribe of *B* Judg 20:12 1144
But the children of *B* would not Judg 20:13 1144
But the children of *B* gathered Judg 20:14 1144
the children of *B* were numbered Judg 20:15 1144
And the men of Israel, beside *B* Judg 20:17 1144
battle against the children of *B* Judg 20:18 1144
went out to battle against *B* Judg 20:20 1144
the children of *B* came forth out Judg 20:21 1144
the children of *B* my brother Judg 20:23 1144
the children of *B* the second day Judg 20:24 1144

B went forth against them out of Judg 20:25 1144
the children of *B* my brother Judg 20:28 1144
children of *B* on the third day Judg 20:30 1144
the children of *B* went out Judg 20:31 1144
And the children of *B* said Judg 20:32 1144
And the LORD smote *B* before Israel Judg 20:35 1144
So the children of *B* saw that Judg 20:36 1144
B began to smite and kill of the Judg 20:39 1144
again, the men of *B* were amazed Judg 20:41 1144
there fell of *B* eighteen thousand Judg 20:44 1144
fell that day of *B* were twenty Judg 20:46 1144
again upon the children of *B* Judg 20:48 1144
give his daughter unto *B* to wife Judg 21:1 1144
repented them for *B* their brother Judg 21:6 1144
to speak to the children of *B* Judg 21:13 1144
B came again at that time Judg 21:14 1144
And the people repented them for *B* Judg 21:15 1144
the women are destroyed out of *B* Judg 21:16 1144
for them that be escaped of *B* Judg 21:17 1144
be he that giveth a wife to *B* Judg 21:18 1144
they commanded the children of *B* Judg 21:20 1144
of Shiloh, and go to the land of *B* Judg 21:21 1144
And the children of *B* did so Judg 21:23 1144
ran a man of *B* out of the army 1Sa 4:12 1144
Now there was a man of *B*, whose 1Sa 9:1 1144
thee a man out of the land of *B* 1Sa 9:16 1144
the families of the tribe of *B* 1Sa 9:21 1144
in the border of *B* at Zelzah 1Sa 10:2 1144
near, the tribe of *B* was taken 1Sa 10:20 1144
B to come near by their families 1Sa 10:21 1144
were with Jonathan in Gibeah of *B* 1Sa 13:2 1144
up from Gilgal unto Gibeah of *B* 1Sa 13:15 1144
with them, abode in Gibeah of *B* 1Sa 13:16 1144
of Saul in Gibeah of *B* looked 1Sa 14:16 1144
and over Ephraim, and over *B* 2Sa 2:9 1144
went over by number twelve of *B* 2Sa 2:15 1144
the children of *B* gathered 2Sa 2:25 1144
of David had smitten of *B* 2Sa 2:31 1144
Abner also spake in the ears of *B* 2Sa 3:19 1144
good to the whole house of *B* 2Sa 3:19 1144
Beerothite, of the children of *B* 2Sa 4:2 1144
Beeroth also was reckoned to *B* 2Sa 4:2 1144
were a thousand men of *B* with him 2Sa 19:17 1144
they in the country of *B* in Zelah 2Sa 21:14 1144
of Gibeah of the children of *B* 2Sa 23:29 1144
Shimei the son of Elah, in *B* 1Kin 4:18 1144
of Judah, with the tribe of *B* 1Kin 12:21 1144
unto all the house of Judah and *B* 1Kin 12:23 1144
Asa built with them Geba of *B* 1Kin 15:22 1144
And out of the tribe of *B* 1Chr 6:60 1144
of the tribe of the children of *B* 1Chr 6:65 1144
All these are of the sons of *B* 1Chr 8:40 1144
of Judah, and of the children of *B* 1Chr 9:3 1144
And of the sons of *B* 1Chr 9:7 1144
pertained to the children of *B* 1Chr 11:31 1144
bow, even of Saul's brethren of *B* 1Chr 12:2 1144
there came of the children of *B* 1Chr 12:16 1144
And of the children of *B*, the 1Chr 12:29 1144
B counted he not among them 1Chr 21:6 1144
of *B*, Jaasiel the son of Abner 1Chr 27:21 1144
B an hundred and fourscore 2Chr 11:1 1144
and to all Israel in Judah and *B* 2Chr 11:3 1144
in Judah and in *B* fenced cities 2Chr 11:10 1144
having Judah and *B* on his side 2Chr 11:12 1144
all the countries of Judah and *B* 2Chr 11:23 1144
and out of *B*, that bare shields and 2Chr 14:8 1144
ye me, Asa, and all Judah and *B* 2Chr 15:2 1144
out of all the land of Judah and *B* 2Chr 15:8 1144
And he gathered all Judah and *B* 2Chr 15:9 1144
And of *B* 2Chr 17:17 1144
throughout all Judah and *B* 2Chr 25:5 1144
the altars out of all Judah and *B* 2Chr 31:1 1144
of Israel, and of all Judah and *B* 2Chr 34:9 1144
in Jerusalem and *B* to stand to it 2Chr 34:32 1144
of the fathers of Judah and *B* Ezr 1:5 1144
B heard that the children of the Ezr 4:1 1144
B gathered themselves together Ezr 10:9 1144
of Judah, and of the children of *B* Neh 11:4 1144
And these are the sons of *B* Neh 11:7 1144
The children also of *B* from Geba Neh 11:31 1144
were divisions in Judah, and in *B* Neh 11:36 1144
There is little *B* with their Ps 68:27 1144
Before Ephraim and *B* and Manasseh Ps 80:2 1144
were in Anathoth in the land of *B* Jer 1:1 1144
O ye children of *B*, gather Jer 6:1 1144
Jerusalem, and from the land of *B* Jer 17:26 1144
which is in the country of *B* Jer 32:8 1144
take witnesses in the land of *B* Jer 32:44 1144
of the south, and in the land of *B* Jer 33:13 1144
to go into the land of *B*, to Jer 37:12 1144
of Judah and the border of *B* Eze 48:22 1144
west side, *B* shall have a portion Eze 48:23 1144
And by the border of *B*, from the Eze 48:24 1144
one gate of Joseph, one gate of *B* Eze 48:32 1144
at Beth-aven, after thee, O *B* Hos 5:8 1144
and *B* shall possess Gilead Obad 19 1144
of Cis, a man of the tribe of *B* Acts 13:21 *953*
of Abraham, of the tribe of *B* Rom 11:1 *953*
of Israel, of the tribe of *B* Phil 3:5 *953*
Of the tribe of *B* were sealed Rev 7:8 *953*
3. Great-grandson of Benjamin 1.
Jeush, and *B*, and Ehud, and 1Chr 7:10 1144
4. A descendant of Harim.
B, Malluch, and Shemariah Ezr 10:32 1144
5. A repairer of the Jerusalem wall.
After him repaired *B* and Hashub Neh 3:23 1144
6. Purified the Jerusalem wall.
Judah, and *B*, and Shemaiah, and Neh 12:34 1144
7. A gate of Jerusalem.
that were in the high gate of *B* Jer 20:2 1144
And when he was in the gate of *B* Jer 37:13 1144
then sitting in the gate of *B* Jer 38:7 1144

BENJAMIN'S *(ben'-ja-mins)* {4}
1. Refers to Benjamin 1.
but *B* mess was five times so much Gen 43:34 1144
and the cup was found in *B* sack Gen 44:12 1144
he fell upon his brother *B* neck Gen 45:14 1144
2. Refers to Benjamin 7.
from *B* gate unto the place of the Zec 14:10 1144

BENJAMITE *(ben'-ja-mite)* {9} See BENJAMITES. *A descendant of Benjamin.*
Ehud the son of Gera, a *B* Judg 3:15 1145
Bechorath, the son of Aphiah, a *B* 1Sa 9:1 1145
answered and said, Am not I a *B* 1Sa 9:21 1145
much more now may this *B* do it 2Sa 16:11 1145
And Shimei the son of Gera, a *B* 2Sa 19:16 1145
was Sheba, the son of Bichri, a *B* 2Sa 20:1 1145
a *B* of Bahurim, which cursed me 1Kin 2:8 1145
of Shimei, the son of Kish, a *B* Est 2:5 1145
the words of Cush the *B* Ps 7:*t* 1145

BENJAMITES *(ben'-ja-mites)* {8}
but the men of the place were *B* Judg 19:16 1145
of the *B* that day twenty and five Judg 20:35 1145
men of Israel gave place to the *B* Judg 20:36 1145
the *B* looked behind them, and, Judg 20:40 1145
they inclosed the *B* round about Judg 20:43 1145
passed through the land of the *B* 1Sa 9:4 1145
stood about him, Hear now, ye *B* 1Sa 22:7 1145
Abiezer the Anetothite, of the *B* 1Chr 27:12 1145

BENO *(be'-no)* {2} *A descendant of Merari.*
sons of Jaaziah; *B* 1Chr 24:26 1121
B, and Shoham, and Zaccur, and Ibri 1Chr 24:27 1121

BEN-ONI *(ben-o'-ni)* {1} *Rachel's second son.*
died) that she called his name *B* Gen 35:18 1126

BENT {8}
he hath *b* his bow, and made it Ps 7:12 1869
have *b* their bow, to cast down Ps 37:14 1869
are sharp, and all their bows *b* Is 5:28 1869
drawn sword, and from the *b* bow Is 21:15 1869
He hath *b* his bow like an enemy Lam 2:4 1869
He hath *b* his bow, and set me as a Lam 3:12 1869
my people are *b* to backsliding Hos 11:7 8511
When I have *b* Judah for me, Zec 9:13 1869

BEN-ZOHETH *(ben-zo'-heth)* {1} *A descendant of Caleb.*
sons of Ishi were, Zoheth, and *B* 1Chr 4:20 1132

BEON *(be'-on)* {1} *A place east of the Jordan River.*
and Shebam, and Nebo, and *B* Num 32:3 1194

BEOR *(be'-or)* {10}
1. Father of Bela.
Bela the son of *B* reigned in Edom Gen 36:32 1160
Bela the son of *B* 1Chr 1:43 1160
2. Father of Balaam.
Balaam the son of *B* to Pethor Num 22:5 1160
Balaam the son of *B* hath said Num 24:3 1160
Balaam the son of *B* hath said Num 24:15 1160
Balaam also the son of *B* they Num 31:8 1160
son of *B* of Pethor of Mesopotamia Deut 23:4 1160
Balaam also the son of *B*, the Josh 13:22 1160
Balaam the son of *B* to curse you Josh 24:9 1160
what Balaam the son of *B* answered Mic 6:5 1160

BERA *(be'-rah)* {1} *King of Sodom.*
made war with *B* king of Sodom Gen 14:2 1298

BERACAH See BERACHAH.

BERACHAH *(ber'-a-kah)* {3}
1. A Benjamite warrior in David's army.
and *B*, and Jehu the Antothite, 1Chr 12:3 1294
2. A valley in Judah.
themselves in the valley of *B* 2Chr 20:26 1294
place was called, The valley of *B* 2Chr 20:26 1294

BERACHIAH *(ber-a-ki'-ah)* {1} See BERECHIAH. *Father of Asaph.*
hand, even Asaph the son of *B* 1Chr 6:39 1296

BERAIAH *(ber-a-i'-ah)* {1} *A son of Shimhi.*
And Adaiah, and *B*, and Shimrath, the 1Chr 8:21 1256

BERAKIAH See BERACHIAH.

BEREA *(be-re'-a)* {3} *A city in Macedonia.*
Paul and Silas by night unto *B* Acts 17:10 *960*
of God was preached of Paul at *B* Acts 17:13 *960*
him into Asia Sopater of *B* Acts 20:4 *960*

BEREAVE {6}
do I labour, and *b* my soul of good Eccl 4:8 2637
I will *b* them of children, I will Jer 15:7 7921
evil beasts, and they shall *b* thee Eze 5:17 7921
no more henceforth *b* them of men Eze 36:12 7921
neither *b* thy nations any more, Eze 36:14 3782,(7921)
their children, yet will I *b* them Hos 9:12 7921

BEREAVED {6}
Me have ye *b* of my children Gen 42:36 7921
b of my children, I am *b* Gen 43:14 7921
wives be *b* of their children Jer 18:21 7909
up men, and hast *b* thy nations Eze 36:13 7921
as a bear that is *b* of her whelps Hos 13:8 7909

BEREAVETH {1}
abroad the sword *b*, at home there Lam 1:20 7921

BERECHIAH *(ber-e-ki'-ah)* {10} See BERACHIAH.
1. A descendant of King Jehoiakim.
And Hashubah, and Ohel, and *B* 1Chr 3:20 1296
2. Same as Berachiah.
his brethren, Asaph the son of *B* 1Chr 15:17 1296
3. A Levite near Jerusalem.
B the son of Asa, the son of 1Chr 9:16 1296
4. A Levite doorkeeper.
And *B* and Elkanah were doorkeepers 1Chr 15:23 1296
5. An Ephraimite.
B the son of Meshillemoth, and 2Chr 28:12 1296
6. Father of Meshullam.
repaired Meshullam the son of *B* Neh 3:4 1296
son of *B* over against his chamber Neh 3:30 1296
of Meshullam the son of *B* Neh 6:18 1296
7. Father of Zechariah.
LORD unto Zechariah, the son of *B* Zec 1:1 1296
LORD unto Zechariah, the son of *B* Zec 1:7 1296

BERED *(be'-red)* {2}
1. A place in southern Canaan.
behold, it is between Kadesh and *B* Gen 16:14 1260
2. An Ephraimite.
B his son, and Tahath his son, and 1Chr 7:20 1260

BEREKIAH See BERECHIAH.

BERI *(be'-ri)* {1} See BERITES. *Son of Zophah.*
and Harnepher, and Shual, and *B* 1Chr 7:36 1275

BERIAH *(be-ri'-ah)* {11} See BERIITES.
1. A son of Asher.
Jimnah, and Ishuah, and Isui, and *B* Gen 46:17 1283
and the sons of *B* Gen 46:17 1283
of *B*, the family of the Beriites Num 26:44 1283
Of the sons of *B* Num 26:45 1283
Imnah, and Isuah, and Ishuai, and *B* 1Chr 7:30 1283
And the sons of *B* 1Chr 7:31 1283
2. A son of Ephraim.
a son, and he called his name *B* 1Chr 7:23 1283
3. A son of Elpaal.
B also, and Shema, who were heads 1Chr 8:13 1283
and Ispah, and Joha, the sons of *B* 1Chr 8:16 1283
4. A Levite.
Jahath, Zina, and Jeush, and *B* 1Chr 23:10 1283
but Jeush and *B* had not many sons 1Chr 23:11 1283

BERIITES *(be-ri'-ites)* {1} *Descendants of Beriah 1.*
of Beriah, the family of the *B* Num 26:44 1284

BERITES *(be'-rites)* {1} *Descendants of Beri.*
and to Beth-maachah, and all the *B* 2Sa 20:14 1276

BERITH *(be'-rith)* {1} See BAAL-BERITH. *Idol at Shechem.*
an hold of the house of the god *B* Judg 9:46 1286

BERNICE *(bur-ni'-see)* {3} *Daughter of Herod Agrippa.*
B came unto Caesarea to salute Acts 25:13 *959*
when Agrippa was come, and *B* Acts 25:23 *959*
rose up, and the governor, and *B* Acts 26:30 *959*

BERODACH-BALADAN *(ber-o'-dak-bal'-a-dan)* {1} See MERODACH-BALADAN. *A king of Babylon.*
At that time *B*, the son of 2Kin 20:12 1255

BEROEA See BEREA.

BEROTHAH *(ber-o'-thah)* {1} See BEROTHAI, BEROTHITE. *A city near Hamath.*
Hamath, *B*, Sibraim, which is Eze 47:16 1268

BEROTHAI *(ber'-o-thahee)* {1} See BEROTHAH. *A city of Hadadezer.*
And from Betah, and from *B*, cities 2Sa 8:8 1268

BEROTHITE *(be'-ro-thite)* {1} See BEEROTHITE. *A native of Beeroth.*
Zelek the Ammonite, Naharai the *B* 1Chr 11:39 1307

BERRIES {2}
two or three *b* in the top of the Is 17:6 1620
tree, my brethren, bear olive *b* Jas 3:12 *1636*

BERYL {8}
And the fourth row a *b*, and an onyx Ex 28:20 8658
And the fourth row, a *b*, an onyx, Ex 39:13 8658
are as gold rings set with the *b* Song 5:14 8658
was like unto the colour of a *b* Eze 1:16 8658
was as the colour of a *b* stone Eze 10:9 8658
topaz, and the diamond, the *b* Eze 28:13 8658
His body also was like the *b* Dan 10:6 8658
the eighth, *b* Rev 21:20 *969*

BESAI *(be'-sahee)* {2} *A family of exiles.*
of Paseah, the children of *B* Ezr 2:49 1153
The children of *B*, the children Neh 7:52 1153

BESEECH {68}
we *b* thee, three days' journey Ex 3:18 4994
I *b* thee, shew me thy glory Ex 33:18 4994
I *b* thee, lay not the sin upon us Num 12:11 4994
Heal her now, O God, I *b* thee Num 12:13 4994
I *b* thee, let the power of my Num 14:17 4994
I *b* thee, the iniquity of this Num 14:19 4994
I *b* thee, tell thy servant 1Sa 23:11 4994
I *b* thee, and his servants go with 2Sa 13:24 4994
I humbly *b* thee that I may find 2Sa 16:4
I *b* thee, O LORD, take away the 2Sa 24:10 4994
I *b* thee, save thou us out of his 2Kin 19:19 4994
I *b* thee, O LORD, remember now 2Kin 20:3 577
I *b* thee, do away the iniquity of 1Chr 21:8 4994
I *b* thee, thine eyes be open, and 2Chr 6:40 4994
I *b* thee, O LORD God of heaven, Neh 1:5 577
I *b* thee, the word that thou Neh 1:8 4994
I *b* thee, let now thine ear be Neh 1:11 577
I *b* thee, that thou hast made me Job 10:9 4994
I *b* thee, and I will speak Job 42:4 4994
we *b* thee, O God of hosts Ps 80:14 4994
I *b* thee, deliver my soul Ps 116:4 577
Save now, I *b* thee, O LORD Ps 118:25 577
I *b* thee, send now prosperity Ps 118:25 577

I *b* thee, the freewill offerings ... Ps 119:108 4994
I *b* thee, how I have walked ... Is 38:3 577
we *b* thee, we are all thy people ... Is 64:9 4994
We *b* thee, let this man be put to ... Jer 38:4 4994
I *b* thee, the voice of the LORD, ... Jer 38:20 4994
we *b* thee, our supplication be ... Jer 42:2 4994
thy servants, I *b* thee, ten days ... Dan 1:12 4994
I *b* thee, let thine anger and thy ... Dan 9:16 4994
O Lord GOD, forgive, I *b* thee ... Amos 7:2 4994
I, O Lord GOD, cease, I *b* thee ... Amos 7:5 4994
We *b* thee, O LORD, we *b* ... Jonah 1:14 577
I *b* thee, my life from me ... Jonah 4:3 4994
b God that he will be gracious ... Mal 1:9 2470,6440
they *b* him to put his hand upon ... Mk 7:32 *3870*
I *b* thee, torment me not ... Lk 8:28 *1189*
I *b* thee, look upon my son ... Lk 9:38 *1189*
I *b* thee, suffer me to speak unto ... Acts 21:39 *1189*
wherefore I *b* thee to hear me ... Acts 26:3 *1189*
I *b* you therefore, brethren, by ... Rom 12:1 *3870*
Now I *b* you, brethren, for the ... Rom 15:30 *3870*
Now I *b* you, brethren, mark them ... Rom 16:17 *3870*
Now I *b* you, brethren, by the ... 1Cor 1:10 *3870*
Wherefore I *b* you, be ye ... 1Cor 4:16 *3870*
I *b* you, brethren, (ye know the ... 1Cor 16:15 *3870*
Wherefore I *b* you that ye would ... 2Cor 2:8 *3870*
as though God did *b* you by us ... 2Cor 5:20 *3870*
b you also that ye receive not ... 2Cor 6:1 *3870*
Now I Paul myself *b* you by the ... 2Cor 10:1 *3870*
But I *b* you, that I may not be ... 2Cor 10:2 *1189*
Brethren, I *b* you, be as I am ... Gal 4:12 *1189*
b you that ye walk worthy of the ... Eph 4:1 *3870*
I *b* Euodias, and *b* Syntyche, ... Phil 4:2 *3870*
b Syntyche, that they be of the ... Phil 4:2 *3870*
Furthermore then we *b* you ... 1Th 4:1 *2065*
but we *b* you, brethren, that ye ... 1Th 4:10 *3870*
we *b* you, brethren, to know them ... 1Th 5:12 *2065*
Now we *b* you, brethren, by the ... 2Th 2:1 *2065*
for love's sake I rather *b* thee ... Philem 9 *3870*
I *b* thee for my son Onesimus, ... Philem 10 *3870*
But I *b* you the rather to do this ... Heb 13:19 *3870*
I *b* you, brethren, suffer the ... Heb 13:22 *3870*
I *b* you as strangers and pilgrims, ... 1Pet 2:11 *3870*
And now I *b* thee, lady, not as ... 2Jn 5 *2065*

BESEECHING {3}
came unto him a centurion, *b* him, ... Mt 8:5 *3870*
b him, and kneeling down to him, ... Mk 1:40 *3870*
b him that he would come and heal ... Lk 7:3 *2065*

BESET {6}
b the house round about, and beat ... Judg 19:22 5437
b the house round about upon me ... Judg 20:5 5437
bulls of Bashan have *b* me round ... Ps 22:12 3803
Thou hast *b* me behind and before, ... Ps 139:5 6696
own doings have *b* them about ... Hos 7:2 5437
the sin which doth so easily *b* us ... Heb 12:1 *2139*

BESIDE See APPENDIX.

BESIDES See APPENDIX.

BESIEGE {11}
thee, then thou shalt *b* it ... Deut 20:12 6696
When thou shalt *b* a city a long ... Deut 20:19 6696
he shall *b* thee in all thy gates, ... Deut 28:52 6887
he shall *b* thee in all thy gates, ... Deut 28:52 6887
to Keilah, to *b* David and his men ... 1Sa 23:8 6696
if their enemy *b* them in the land ... 1Kin 8:37 6887
city, and his servants did *b* it ... 2Kin 24:11 6696
if their enemies *b* them in the ... 2Chr 6:28 6696
b, O Media ... Is 21:2 6696
which *b* you without the walls, and ... Jer 21:4 6696
to the Chaldeans that *b* you ... Jer 21:9 6696

BESIEGED {23}
children of Ammon, and *b* Rabbah ... 2Sa 11:1 6696
b him in Abel of Beth-maachah, and ... 2Sa 20:15 6696
Israel with him, and they *b* Tirzah ... 1Kin 16:17 6696
b Samaria, and warred against it ... 1Kin 20:1 6696
host, and went up, and *b* Samaria ... 2Kin 6:24 6696
and, behold, they *b* it, until an ... 2Kin 6:25 6696
and they *b* Ahaz, but could not ... 2Kin 16:5 6696
to Samaria, and *b* it three years ... 2Kin 17:5 6696
came up against Samaria, and *b* it ... 2Kin 18:9 6696
up all the rivers of *b* places ... 2Kin 19:24 4693
Jerusalem, and the city was *b* ... 2Kin 24:10 935,4692
the city was *b* unto the eleventh ... 2Kin 25:2 935,4692
of Ammon, and came and *b* Rabbah ... 1Chr 20:1 6696
b it, and built great bulwarks ... Eccl 9:14 6696
garden of cucumbers, as a *b* city ... Is 1:8 5341
up all the rivers of the *b* places ... Is 37:25 4693
of Babylon's army *b* Jerusalem ... Jer 32:2 6696
when the Chaldeans that *b* ... Jer 37:5 6696
against Jerusalem, and they *b* it ... Jer 39:1 6696
So the city was *b* unto the ... Jer 52:5 935,4692
face against it, and it shall be *b* ... Eze 4:3 4692
is *b* shall die by the famine ... Eze 6:12 5341
Babylon unto Jerusalem, and *b* it ... Dan 1:1 6696

BESODEIAH *(bes-o-di'-ah)* {1} *A repairer of Jerusalem's walls.*
Paseah, and Meshullam the son of *B* ... Neh 3:6 1152

BESOM {1}
it with the *b* of destruction ... Is 14:23 4292

BESOR *(be'-sor)* {3} *A brook in southern Judah.*
with him, and came to the brook *B* ... 1Sa 30:9 1308
could not go over the brook *B* ... 1Sa 30:10 1308
made also to abide at the brook *B* ... 1Sa 30:21 1308

BESOUGHT {44}
anguish of his soul, when he *b* us ... Gen 42:21 2603
Moses *b* the LORD his God, and said ... Ex 32:11 2470
I *b* the LORD at that time, saying ... Deut 3:23 2603
David therefore *b* God for the ... 2Sa 12:16 1245
And the man of God *b* the LORD ... 1Kin 13:6 2470
b him, and said unto him, O man of ... 2Kin 1:13 2603
And Jehoahaz *b* the LORD, and the ... 2Kin 13:4 2470
he *b* the LORD his God, and humbled ... 2Chr 33:12 2470
we fasted and *b* our God for this ... Ezr 8:23 1245
b him with tears to put away the ... Est 8:3 2603
b the LORD, and the LORD repented ... Jer 26:19 2470
So the devils *b* him, saying, If ... Mt 8:31 *3870*
they *b* him that he would depart ... Mt 8:34 *3870*
b him that they might only touch ... Mt 14:36 *3870*
b him, saying, Send her away ... Mt 15:23 *2065*
b him, saying, Have patience with ... Mt 18:29 *3870*
he *b* him much that he would not ... Mk 5:10 *3870*
And all the devils *b* him, saying, ... Mk 5:12 *3870*
b him greatly, saying, My little ... Mk 5:23 *3870*
b him that they might touch if it ... Mk 6:56 *3870*
she *b* him that he would cast ... Mk 7:26 *2065*
unto him, and *b* him to touch him ... Mk 8:22 *3870*
and they *b* him for her ... Lk 4:38 *2065*
b him, saying, Lord, if thou wilt ... Lk 5:12 *1189*
they *b* him instantly, saying, ... Lk 7:4 *3870*
they *b* him that he would not ... Lk 8:31 *3870*
they *b* him that he would suffer ... Lk 8:32 *3870*
about *b* him to depart from them ... Lk 8:37 *2065*
b him that he might be with him ... Lk 8:38 *1189*
b him that he would come into his ... Lk 8:41 *3870*
I *b* thy disciples to cast him out ... Lk 9:40 *1189*
a certain Pharisee *b* him to dine ... Lk 11:37 *2065*
they *b* him that he would tarry ... Jn 4:40 *2065*
b him that he would come down, and ... Jn 4:47 *2065*
b Pilate that their legs might ... Jn 19:31 *2065*
b Pilate that he might take away ... Jn 19:38 *2065*
the Gentiles *b* that these words ... Acts 13:42 *3870*
and her household, she *b* us ... Acts 16:15 *3870*
b them, and brought them out, and ... Acts 16:39 *3870*
b him not to go up to Jerusalem ... Acts 21:12 *3870*
him against Paul, and *b* him, ... Acts 25:2 *3870*
Paul *b* them all to take meat, ... Acts 27:33 *3870*
this thing I *b* the Lord thrice ... 2Cor 12:8 *3870*
As I *b* thee to abide still at ... 1Ti 1:3 *3870*

BEST {25}
take of the *b* fruits in the land ... Gen 43:11 2173
in the *b* of the land make thy ... Gen 47:6 4315
in the *b* of the land, in the land ... Gen 47:11 4315
of the *b* of his own field ... Ex 22:5 4315
of the *b* of his own vineyard, ... Ex 22:5 4315
All the *b* of the oil ... Num 18:12 2459
all the *b* of the wine, and of the ... Num 18:12 2459
of the LORD, of all the *b* thereof ... Num 18:29 2459
have heaved the *b* thereof from it ... Num 18:30 2459
have heaved from it the *b* of it ... Num 18:32 2459
them marry to whom they think *b* ... Num 36:6 2896
thy gates, where it liketh him *b* ... Deut 23:16 2896
oliveyards, even the *b* of them ... 1Sa 8:14 2896
the *b* of the sheep, and of the ... 1Sa 15:9 4315
people spared the *b* of the sheep ... 1Sa 15:15 4315
What seemeth you *b* I will do ... 2Sa 18:4 3190
and overlaid it with the *b* gold ... 1Kin 10:18 6338
Look even out the *b* and meetest of ... 2Kin 10:3 2896
her maids unto the *b* place of the ... Est 2:9 2896
verily every man at his *b* state ... Ps 39:5 5324
like the *b* wine for my beloved ... Song 7:9 2896
b of Lebanon, all that drink ... Eze 31:16 2896
The *b* of them is as a brier ... Mic 7:4 2896
servants, Bring forth the *b* robe ... Lk 15:22 *4413*
But covet earnestly the *b* gifts ... 1Cor 12:31 *2909*

BESTEAD {1}
shall pass through it, hardly *b* ... Is 8:21

BESTIR {1}
that then thou shalt *b* thyself ... 2Sa 5:24 2782

BESTOW {9}
that he may *b* upon you a blessing ... Ex 32:29 5414
thou shalt *b* that money for ... Deut 14:26 5414
the LORD did they *b* upon Baalim ... 2Chr 24:7 6213
thou shalt have occasion to *b* ... Ezr 7:20 5415
b it out of the king's treasure ... Ezr 7:20 5415
have no room where to *b* my fruits ... Lk 12:17 *4863*
there will I *b* all my fruits and ... Lk 12:18 *4863*
upon these we *b* more abundant ... 1Cor 12:23 *4060*
though I *b* all my goods to feed ... 1Cor 13:3 *5595*

BESTOWED {14}
whom he *b* in the cities for ... 1Kin 10:26 3240
hand, and *b* them in the house ... 2Kin 5:24 6485
the money to be *b* on workmen ... 2Kin 12:15 5414
b upon him such royal majesty as ... 1Chr 29:25 5414
whom he *b* in the chariot cities, ... 2Chr 9:25 3240
to all that the LORD hath *b* on us ... Is 63:7 1580
which he hath *b* on them according ... Is 63:7 1580
reap that whereon ye *b* no labour ... Jn 4:38 *2872*
Mary, who *b* much labour on us ... Rom 16:6 *2872*
his grace which was *b* upon me was ... 1Cor 15:10
that for the gift *b* upon us by ... 2Cor 1:11
b on the churches of Macedonia ... 2Cor 8:1 *1325*
lest I have *b* upon you labour in ... Gal 4:11 *2872*
of love the Father hath *b* upon us ... 1Jn 3:1 *1325*

BETAH *(be'-tah)* {1} *A city of Hadadezer.*
And from *B*, and from Berothai, ... 2Sa 8:8 984

BETEN *(be'-ten)* {1} *A city in Asher.*
border was Helkath, and Hali, and *B* ... Josh 19:25 991

BETHABARA *(beth-ab'-ar-ah)* {1} See BETHBARAH. *A place east of the Jordan River.*
were done in *B* beyond Jordan ... Jn 1:28 *962*

BETH ACACIA See BETH-SHITTAH.

BETH-ANATH *(beth'-a-nath)* {3} *A city in Naphtali.*
Iron, and Migdal-el, Horem, and *B* ... Josh 19:38 1043
nor the inhabitants of *B* ... Judg 1:33 1043
of *B* became tributaries unto them ... Judg 1:33 1043

BETH-ANOTH *(beth'-a-noth)* {1} *A city in Judah.*
And Maarath, and *B*, and Eltekon ... Josh 15:59 1042

BETHANY *(beth'-a-ny)* {11} *A village near Jerusalem.*
and went out of the city into *B* ... Mt 21:17 *963*
Now when Jesus was in *B*, in the ... Mt 26:6 *963*
to Jerusalem, unto Bethphage and *B* ... Mk 11:1 *963*
went out unto *B* with the twelve ... Mk 11:11 *963*
when they were come from *B* ... Mk 11:12 *963*
being in *B* in the house of Simon ... Mk 14:3 *963*
was come nigh to Bethphage and *B* ... Lk 19:29 *963*
And he led them out as far as to *B* ... Lk 24:50 *963*
man was sick, named Lazarus, of *B* ... Jn 11:1 *963*
Now *B* was nigh unto Jerusalem, ... Jn 11:18 *963*
before the passover came to *B* ... Jn 12:1 *963*

BETH APHRAH See APHRAH.

BETH-ARABAH *(beth-ar'-ab-ah)* {3} *A city of the Arabah.*
and passed along by the north of *B* ... Josh 15:6 1026
In the wilderness, *B*, Middin, and ... Josh 15:61 1026
And *B*, and Zemaraim, and Beth-el, ... Josh 18:22 1026

BETH-ARAM *(beth'-a-ram)* {1} *A city in Gad.*
And in the valley, *B*, and ... Josh 13:27 1027

BETH-ARBEL *(beth-ar'-bel)* {1} *A city destroyed by the Assyrians.*
as Shalman spoiled *B* in the day ... Hos 10:14 1009

BETH ASHBEA See ASHBEA.

BETH-AVEN *(beth-a'-ven)* {7} *A town in Benjamin.*
Jericho to Ai, which is beside *B* ... Josh 7:2 1007
were at the wilderness of *B* ... Josh 18:12 1007
in Michmash, eastward from *B* ... 1Sa 13:5 1007
and the battle passed over unto *B* ... 1Sa 14:23 1007
Gilgal, neither go ye up to *B* ... Hos 4:15 1007
cry aloud at *B*, after thee, O ... Hos 5:8 1007
fear because of the calves of *B* ... Hos 10:5 1007

BETH-AZMAVETH *(beth-az'-maveth)* {1} See AZMAVETH. *A village in Judah.*
The men of *B*, forty and two ... Neh 7:28 1041

BETH-BAAL-MEON *(beth-ba'-al-me'-on)* {1} *A Moabite town.*
Dibon, and Bamoth-baal, and *B* ... Josh 13:17 1010

BETH-BARAH *(beth-ba'-rah)* {2} See BETHABARA. *A place in Gad.*
before them the waters unto *B* ... Judg 7:24 1012
and took the waters unto *B* ... Judg 7:24 1012

BETH-BIREI *(beth-bir'-e-i)* {1} See BETH-LEBAOTH. *A town in Simeon.*
and Hazar-susim, and at *B*, and at ... 1Chr 4:31 1011

BETH BIRI See BETH-BIREI.

BETH-CAR *(beth'-car)* {1} *A Philistine stronghold in Judah.*
them, until they came under *B* ... 1Sa 7:11 1033

BETH-DAGON *(beth-da'-gon)* {2}
1. A town in Judah.
And Gederoth, *B*, and Naamah, and ... Josh 15:41 1016
2. A town in Asher.
turneth toward the sunrising to *B* ... Josh 19:27 1016

BETH-DIBLATHAIM *(beth-dib-lath-a'-im)* {1} *A Moabite town.*
Dibon, and upon Nebo, and upon *B* ... Jer 48:22 1015

BETH-EL {66}
unto a mountain on the east of *B* ... Gen 12:8 1008
having *B* on the west, and Hai on ... Gen 12:8 1008
journeys from the south even to *B* ... Gen 13:3 1008
been at the beginning, between *B* ... Gen 13:3 1008
called the name of that place *B* ... Gen 28:19 1008
I am the God of *B*, where thou ... Gen 31:13 1008
unto Jacob, Arise, go up to *B* ... Gen 35:1 1008
And let us arise, and go up to *B* ... Gen 35:3 1008
in the land of Canaan, that is, *B* ... Gen 35:6 1008
was buried beneath *B* under an oak ... Gen 35:8 1008
place where God spake with him, *B* ... Gen 35:15 1008
And they journeyed from *B* ... Gen 35:16 1008
Beth-aven, on the east side of *B* ... Josh 7:2 1008
lie in ambush, and abode between *B* ... Josh 8:9 1008
them to lie in ambush between *B* ... Josh 8:12 1008
was not a man left in Ai or *B* ... Josh 8:17 1008
the king of Ai, which is beside *B* ... Josh 12:9 1008
the king of *B*, one ... Josh 12:16 1008
from Jericho throughout mount *B* ... Josh 16:1 1008
And goeth out from *B* to Luz ... Josh 16:2 1008
to the side of Luz, which is *B* ... Josh 18:13 1008
Beth-arabah, and Zemaraim, and *B* ... Josh 18:22 1008
they also went up against *B* ... Judg 1:22 1008
house of Joseph sent to descry *B* ... Judg 1:23 1008
Ramah and *B* in mount Ephraim ... Judg 4:5 1008
which is on the north side of *B* ... Judg 21:19 1008
that goeth up from *B* to Shechem ... Judg 21:19 1008
from year to year in circuit to *B* ... 1Sa 7:16 1008
three men going up to God to *B* ... 1Sa 10:3 1008
Saul in Michmash and in mount *B* ... 1Sa 13:2 1008
To them which were in *B*, and to ... 1Sa 30:27 1008
And he set the one in *B*, and the ... 1Kin 12:29 1008
So did he in *B*, sacrificing unto ... 1Kin 12:32 1008
he placed in *B* the priests of the ... 1Kin 12:32 1008
the altar which he had made in *B* ... 1Kin 12:33 1008
by the word of the LORD unto *B* ... 1Kin 13:1 1008
had cried against the altar in *B* ... 1Kin 13:4 1008
not by the way that he came to *B* ... 1Kin 13:10 1008

there dwelt an old prophet in *B* ... 1Kin 13:11 1008
man of God had done that day in *B* ... 1Kin 13:11 1008
the LORD against the altar in *B* ... 1Kin 13:32 1008
for the LORD hath sent me to *B* ... 2Kin 2:2 1008
So they went down to *B* ... 2Kin 2:2 1008
were at *B* came forth to Elisha ... 2Kin 2:3 1008
And he went up from thence unto *B* ... 2Kin 2:23 1008
the golden calves that were in *B* ... 2Kin 10:29 1008
from Samaria came and dwelt in *B* ... 2Kin 17:28 1008
carried the ashes of them unto *B* ... 2Kin 23:4 1008
Moreover the altar that was at *B* ... 2Kin 23:15 1008
hast done against the altar of *B* ... 2Kin 23:17 1008
the acts that he had done in *B* ... 2Kin 23:19 1008
and habitations were, *B* and the ... 1Chr 7:28 1008
B with the towns thereof, and ... 2Chr 13:19 1008
The men of *B* and Ai, two hundred ... Ezr 2:28 1008
The men of *B* and Ai, an hundred ... Neh 7:32 1008
dwelt at Michmash, and Aija, and *B* ... Neh 11:31 1008
was ashamed of *B* their confidence ... Jer 48:13 1008
So shall *B* do unto you because of ... Hos 10:15 1008
he found him in *B*, and there he ... Hos 12:4 1008
I will also visit the altars of *B* ... Amos 3:14 1008
Come to *B*, and transgress ... Amos 4:4 1008
But seek not *B*, nor enter into ... Amos 5:5 1008
and *B* shall come to nought ... Amos 5:5 1008
there be none to quench it in *B* ... Amos 5:6 1008
Then Amaziah the priest of *B* sent ... Amos 7:10 1008
prophesy not again any more at *B* ... Amos 7:13 1008

BETH-ELITE *(beth'-el-ite)* {1} *A native of Beth-el.*
days did Hiel the *B* build Jericho ... 1Kin 16:34 1017

BETH-EMEK *(beth-e'-mek)* {1} *A town in Asher.*
toward the north side of *B* ... Josh 19:27 1025

BETHER *(be'-thur)* {1} *A district in the Jordan valley.*
hart upon the mountains of *B* ... Song 2:17 1336

BETHESDA *(beth-ez'-dah)* {1} *A pool in Jerusalem.*
is called in the Hebrew tongue *B* ... Jn 5:2 *964*

BETH-EZEL *(beth-e'-zel)* {1} *A city in Judah.*
not forth in the mourning of *B* ... Mic 1:11 1018

BETH-GADER *(beth-ga'-der)* {1} See GEDER. *A descendant of Caleb.*
Hareph the father of *B* ... 1Chr 2:51 1013

BETH-GAMUL *(beth-ga'-mul)* {1} *A Moabite town.*
And upon Kiriathaim, and upon *B* ... Jer 48:23 1014

BETH-HACCEREM *(beth-hak'-se-rem)* {2} *A town in Judah.*
of Rechab, the ruler of part of *B* ... Neh 3:14 1021
and set up a sign of fire in *B* ... Jer 6:1 1021

BETH HAKKEREM See BETH-HACCEREM.

BETH-HARAN *(beth-ha'-ran)* {1} See ELON-BETH-HARAN. *A city in Gad.*
And Beth-nimrah, and *B*, fenced ... Num 32:36 1028

BETH-HOGLA *(beth-hog'-lah)* {1} See BETH-HOGLAH. *A city in Benjamin.*
And the border went up to *B* ... Josh 15:6 1031

BETH HOGLAH See BETH-HOGLA.

BETH-HOGLAH *(beth-hog'-lah)* {2} See BETH-HOGLAH. *Same as Beth-hogla.*
along to the side of *B* northward ... Josh 18:19 1031
their families were Jericho, and *B* ... Josh 18:21 1031

BETH-HORON *(beth-ho'-ron)* {14} *Two cities in Ephraim, near Benjamin.*
along the way that goeth up to *B* ... Josh 10:10 1032
and were in the going down to *B* ... Josh 10:11 1032
unto the coast of *B* the nether ... Josh 16:3 1032
Ataroth-addar, unto *B* the upper ... Josh 16:5 1032
on the south side of the nether *B* ... Josh 18:13 1032
that lieth before *B* southward ... Josh 18:14 1032
suburbs, and *B* with her suburbs ... Josh 21:22 1032
company turned the way to *B* ... 1Sa 13:18 1032
built Gezer, and *B* the nether ... 1Kin 9:17 1032
suburbs, and *B* with her suburbs ... 1Chr 6:68 1032
who built *B* the nether, and the ... 1Chr 7:24 1032
Also he built *B* the upper ... 2Chr 8:5 1032
B the nether, fenced cities, with ... 2Chr 8:5 1032
Judah, from Samaria even unto *B* ... 2Chr 25:13 1032

BETHINK {2}
if they shall *b* themselves in ... 1Kin 8:47 7725,413,3820
Yet if they *b* themselves in the .. 2Chr 6:37 7725,413,3820

BETH JESHIMOTH See JESIMOTH.

BETH-JESHIMOTH *(beth-jesh'-im-oth)* {3} See BETH-JESIMOTH. *Same as Beth-jesimoth.*
sea on the east, the way to *B* ... Josh 12:3 1020
and Ashdoth-pisgah, and *B* ... Josh 13:20 1020
the glory of the country, *B* ... Eze 25:9 1020

BETH-JESIMOTH *(beth-jes'-im-oth)* {1} See BETH-JESHIMOTH. *A Moabite city.*
from *B* even unto Abel-shittim in ... Num 33:49 1020

BETH-LE-APHRAH See APHRAH.

BETH-LEBAOTH *(beth-leb'-a-oth)* {1} See BETH-BISEI. *A town in Simeon.*
And *B*, and Sharuhen ... Josh 19:6 1034

BETH-LEHEM *(beth'-le-hem)* {24} See BETH-LEHEMITE, BETH-LEHEM-JUDAH.
1. A city in Judah.
in the way to Ephrath, which is *B* ... Gen 35:19 1035
the same is *B* ... Gen 48:7 1035
two went until they came to *B* ... Ruth 1:19 1035
to pass, when they were come to *B* ... Ruth 1:19 1035
they came to *B* in the beginning ... Ruth 1:22 1035
And, behold, Boaz came from *B* ... Ruth 2:4 1035
in Ephratah, and be famous in *B* ... Ruth 4:11 1035
the LORD spake, and came to *B* ... 1Sa 16:4 1035
to feed his father's sheep at *B* ... 1Sa 17:15 1035
that he might run to *B* his city ... 1Sa 20:6 1035
asked leave of me to go to *B* ... 1Sa 20:28 1035
of his father, which was in *B* ... 2Sa 2:32 1035
of the Philistines was then in *B* ... 2Sa 23:14 1035
of the water of the well of *B* ... 2Sa 23:15 1035
drew water out of the well of *B* ... 2Sa 23:16 1035
Elhanan the son of Dodo of *B* ... 2Sa 23:24 1035
garrison was then at *B* ... 1Chr 11:16 1035
of the water of the well of *B* ... 1Chr 11:17 1035
drew water out of the well of *B* ... 1Chr 11:18 1035
Elhanan the son of Dodo of *B* ... 1Chr 11:26 1035
He built even *B*, and Etam, and ... 2Chr 11:6 1035
The children of *B*, an hundred ... Ezr 2:21 1035
The men of *B* and Netophah, an ... Neh 7:26 1035
B Ephratah, though thou be little ... Mic 5:2 1035
2. A town in Zebulun.
and Shimron, and Idalah, and *B* ... Josh 19:15 1035
3. A town in Ephraim.
him Ibzan of *B* judged Israel ... Judg 12:8 1035
died Ibzan, and was buried at *B* ... Judg 12:10 1035
4. A descendant of Caleb.
Salma the father of *B*, Hareph the ... 1Chr 2:51 1035
B, and the Netophathites, Ataroth, ... 1Chr 2:54 1035
of Ephratah, the father of *B* ... 1Chr 4:4 1035

BETHLEHEM {15} *A town in Judea.*
of Chimham, which is by *B* ... Jer 41:17 1035
Now when Jesus was born in *B* of ... Mt 2:1 *965*
said unto him, In *B* of Judaea ... Mt 2:5 *965*
And thou *B*, in the land of Juda ... Mt 2:6 *965*
And he sent them to *B*, and said, Go ... Mt 2:8 *965*
all the children that were in *B* ... Mt 2:16 *965*
city of David, which is called *B* ... Lk 2:4 *965*
Let us now go even unto *B* ... Lk 2:15 *965*
of David, and out of the town of *B* ... Jn 7:42 *965*

BETH-LEHEMITE *(beth'-le-hem-ite)* {4} *A native of Bethlehem.*
I will send thee to Jesse the *B* ... 1Sa 16:1 1022
I have seen a son of Jesse the *B* ... 1Sa 16:18 1022
son of thy servant Jesse the *B* ... 1Sa 17:58 1022
the son of Jaare-oregim, a *B* ... 2Sa 21:19 1022

BETH-LEHEM-JUDAH *(beth'-le-hem-ju'-dah)* {10} *Same as Beth-lehem 1.*
out of *B* of the family of Judah ... Judg 17:7 1035
departed out of the city from *B* ... Judg 17:8 1035
said unto him, I am a Levite of *B* ... Judg 17:9 1035
took to him a concubine out of *B* ... Judg 19:1 1035
him unto her father's house to *B* ... Judg 19:2 1035
We are passing from *B* toward the ... Judg 19:18 1035
and I went to *B*, but I am now ... Judg 19:18 1035
a certain man of *B* went to ... Ruth 1:1 1035
and Chilion, Ephrathites of *B* ... Ruth 1:2 1035
the son of that Ephrathite of *B* ... 1Sa 17:12 1035

BETH MAACAH {2}

BETH-MAACHAH *(beth-ma'-a-kah)* {2} See ABEL-BETH-MAACHAH. *A city in Manasseh.*
of Israel unto Abel, and to *B* ... 2Sa 20:14 1038
came and besieged him in Abel of *B* ... 2Sa 20:15 1038

BETH-MARCABOTH *(beth-mar'-cab-oth)* {2} *A city in Judah.*
And Ziklag, and *B*, and Hazar-susah, ... Josh 19:5 1024
And at *B*, and Hazar-susim, and at ... 1Chr 4:31 1024

BETH-MEON *(beth-me'-on)* {1} See BETH-BAAL-MEON. *A Moabite city.*
and upon Beth-gamul, and upon *B* ... Jer 48:23 1010

BETH-NIMRAH *(beth-nim'-rah)* {2} See NIMRAH. *A city in Gad.*
And *B*, and Beth-haran, fenced ... Num 32:36 1039
And in the valley, Beth-aram, and *B* ... Josh 13:27 1039

BETH OPHRAH See APHRAH.

BETH-PALET *(beth-pa'-let)* {1} See BETH-PELET. *A town in Judah.*
Hazar-gaddah, and Heshmon, and *B* ... Josh 15:27 1046

BETH-PAZZEZ *(beth-paz'-zez)* {1} *A town in Issachar.*
and En-haddah, and *B* ... Josh 19:21 1048

BETH PELET See BETH-PALET.

BETH-PEOR *(beth-pe'-or)* {4} *A Moabite city.*
in the valley over against *B* ... Deut 3:29 1047
in the valley over against *B* ... Deut 4:46 1047
the land of Moab, over against *B* ... Deut 34:6 1047
And *B*, and Ashdoth-pisgah, and ... Josh 13:20 1047

BETHPHAGE *(beth'-fa-je)* {3} *A village near Jerusalem.*
unto Jerusalem, and were come to *B* ... Mt 21:1 *967*
came nigh to Jerusalem, unto *B* ... Mk 11:1 *967*
pass, when he was come nigh to *B* ... Lk 19:29 *967*

BETH-PHELET *(beth'-fe-let)* {1} See BETH-PALET. *A town in Judah.*
at Jeshua, and at Moladah, and at *B* ... Neh 11:26 1046

BETH-RAPHA *(beth'-ra-fah)* {1} *Son of Eshton.*
And Eshton begat *B*, and Paseah, and ... 1Chr 4:12 1051

BETH-REHOB *(beth'-re-hob)* {2} *A place in northern Canaan.*
was in the valley that lieth by *B* ... Judg 18:28 1050
sent and hired the Syrians of *B* ... 2Sa 10:6 1050

BETHSAIDA *(beth-sa'-dah)* {7}
1. A city in Galilee.
woe unto thee, *B* ... Mt 11:21 *966*
to the other side before unto *B* ... Mk 6:45 *966*
woe unto thee, *B* ... Lk 10:13 *966*
Now Philip was of *B*, the city of ... Jn 1:44 *966*
Philip, which was of *B* of Galilee ... Jn 12:21 *966*
2. A place east of Lake Gennesareth.
And he cometh to *B* ... Mk 8:22 *966*
belonging to the city called *B* ... Lk 9:10 *966*

BETH SHAN See BETH-SHEAN.

BETH-SHAN *(beth'-shan)* {3} See BETH-SHEAN. *A city in Manasseh.*
his body to the wall of *B* ... 1Sa 31:10 1052
of his sons from the wall of *B* ... 1Sa 31:12 1052
stolen them from the street of *B* ... 2Sa 21:12 1052

BETH-SHEAN *(beth-she'-an)* {6} See BETH-SHAN. *Same as Beth-shan.*
had in Issachar and in Asher *B* ... Josh 17:11 1052
of iron, both they who are of *B* ... Josh 17:16 1052
drive out the inhabitants of *B* ... Judg 1:27 1052
Taanach and Megiddo, and all *B* ... 1Kin 4:12 1052
from *B* to Abel-meholah, even unto ... 1Kin 4:12 1052
of the children of Manasseh, *B* ... 1Chr 7:29 1052

BETH SHEMESH See SHEMESH.

BETH-SHEMESH *(beth'-she-mesh)* {21} See BETH-SHEMITE.
1. A town in Judah.
the north side, and went down to *B* ... Josh 15:10 1053
suburbs, and *B* with her suburbs ... Josh 21:16 1053
by the way of his own coast to *B* ... 1Sa 6:9 1053
the straight way to the way of *B* ... 1Sa 6:12 1053
after them unto the border of *B* ... 1Sa 6:12 1053
they of *B* were reaping their ... 1Sa 6:13 1053
the men of *B* offered burnt ... 1Sa 6:15 1053
And he smote the men of *B*, because ... 1Sa 6:19 1053
And the men of *B* said, Who is able ... 1Sa 6:20 1053
in Makaz, and in Shaalbim, and *B* ... 1Kin 4:9 1053
one another in the face at *B* ... 2Kin 14:11 1053
Jehoash the son of Ahaziah, at *B* ... 2Kin 14:13 1053
suburbs, and *B* with her suburbs ... 1Chr 6:59 1053
he and Amaziah king of Judah, at *B* ... 2Chr 25:21 1053
Joash, the son of Jehoahaz, at *B* ... 2Chr 25:23 1053
south of Judah, and had taken *B* ... 2Chr 28:18 1053
2. A city in Issachar.
to Tabor, and Shahazimah, and *B* ... Josh 19:22 1053
3. A city in Naphtali.
Horem, and Beth-anath, and *B* ... Josh 19:38 1053
drive out the inhabitants of *B* ... Judg 1:33 1053
nevertheless the inhabitants of *B* ... Judg 1:33 1053
4. A temple in Egypt.
shall break also the images of *B* ... Jer 43:13 1053

BETH-SHEMITE *(beth'-shem-ite)* {2} *An inhabitant of Beth-shemesh.*
into the field of Joshua, a *B* ... 1Sa 6:14 1030
day in the field of Joshua, the *B* ... 1Sa 6:18 1030

BETH-SHITTAH *(beth-shit'-tah)* {1} *A place in the Jordan valley.*
and the host fled to *B* in Zererath ... Judg 7:22 1029

BETH-TAPPUAH *(beth-tap'-pu-ah)* {1} *A city in Judah.*
And Janum, and *B*, and Aphekah, ... Josh 15:53 1054

BETHUEL *(beth-u'-el)* {10} See BETHUL.
1. Son of Nahor.
and Pildash, and Jidlaph, and *B* ... Gen 22:22 1328
And *B* begat Rebekah ... Gen 22:23 1328
came out, who was born to *B* ... Gen 24:15 1328
daughter of *B* the son of Milcah ... Gen 24:24 1328
And she said, The daughter of *B* ... Gen 24:47 1328
B answered and said, The thing ... Gen 24:50 1328
the daughter of *B* the Syrian of ... Gen 25:20 1328
to the house of *B* thy mother's ... Gen 28:2 1328
son of *B* the Syrian, the brother ... Gen 28:5 1328
2. A town in Simeon.
And at *B*, and at Hormah, and at ... 1Chr 4:30 1328

BETHUL *(beth'-ul)* {1} See BETHUEL. *A city in Simeon.*
And Eltolad, and *B*, and Hormah, ... Josh 19:4 1329

BETHZATHA See BETHESDA.

BETHZOR See BETH-ZUR.

BETH-ZUR *(beth'-zur)* {4}
1. A town in Judah.
Halhul, *B*, and Gedor, ... Josh 15:58 1049
And *B*, and Shoco, and Adullam, ... 2Chr 11:7 1049
the ruler of the half part of *B* ... Neh 3:16 1049
2. A descendant of Caleb.
and Maon was the father of *B* ... 1Chr 2:45 1049

BETIMES {5}
they rose up *b* in the morning, and ... Gen 26:31 7925
by his messengers, rising up *b* ... 2Chr 36:15 7925
If thou wouldest seek unto God *b* ... Job 8:5 7836
rising *b* for a prey ... Job 24:5 7836
that loveth him chasteneth him *b* ... Prov 13:24 7836

BETONIM *(bet'-o-nim)* {1} *A town in Gad.*
Heshbon unto Ramath-mizpeh, and *B* ... Josh 13:26 993

BETRAY {18}
be come to *b* me to mine enemies ... 1Chr 12:17 7411
shall *b* one another, and shall ... Mt 24:10 *3860*
he sought opportunity to *b* him ... Mt 26:16 *3860*
you, that one of you shall *b* me ... Mt 26:21 *3860*
in the dish, the same shall *b* me ... Mt 26:23 *3860*
he is at hand that doth *b* me ... Mt 26:46 *3860*
shall *b* the brother to death ... Mk 13:12 *3860*
chief priests, to *b* him unto them ... Mk 14:10 *3860*
how he might conveniently *b* him ... Mk 14:11 *3860*
which eateth with me shall *b* me ... Mk 14:18 *3860*
how he might *b* him unto them ... Lk 22:4 *3860*
sought opportunity to *b* him unto ... Lk 22:6 *3860*
believed not, and who should *b* him ... Jn 6:64 *3860*
for he it was that should *b* him ... Jn 6:71 *3860*
Simon's son, which should *b* him ... Jn 12:4 *3860*
Iscariot, Simon's son, to *b* him ... Jn 13:2 *3860*

For he knew who should *b* him ... Jn 13:11 *3860*
you, that one of you shall *b* me ... Jn 13:21 *3860*

BETRAYED {18}
and Judas Iscariot, who also *b* him ... Mt 10:4 *3860*
shall be *b* into the hands of men ... Mt 17:22 *3860*
shall be *b* unto the chief priests ... Mt 20:18 *3860*
Son of man is *b* to be crucified ... Mt 26:2 *3860*
man by whom the Son of man is *b* ... Mt 26:24 *3860*
Then Judas, which *b* him, answered ... Mt 26:25 *3860*
the Son of man is *b* into the ... Mt 26:45 *3860*
Now he that *b* him gave them a ... Mt 26:48 *3860*
that I have *b* the innocent blood ... Mt 27:4 *3860*
Judas Iscariot, which also *b* him ... Mk 3:19 *3860*
man by whom the Son of man is *b* ... Mk 14:21 *3860*
the Son of man is *b* into the ... Mk 14:41 *3860*
he that *b* him had given them a ... Mk 14:44 *3860*
ye shall be *b* both by parents, and ... Lk 21:16 *3860*
woe unto that man by whom he is *b* ... Lk 22:22 *3860*
And Judas also, which *b* him ... Jn 18:2 *3860*
And Judas also, which *b* him ... Jn 18:5 *3860*
in which he was *b* took bread ... 1Cor 11:23 *3860*

BETRAYERS {1}
of whom ye have been now the *b* ... Acts 7:52 *4273*

BETRAYEST {1}
b thou the Son of man with a kiss ... Lk 22:48 *3860*

BETRAYETH {4}
Then Judas, which had *b* him ... Mt 27:3
lo, he that *b* me is at hand ... Mk 14:42 *3860*
the hand of him that *b* me is with ... Lk 22:21 *3860*
Lord, which is he that *b* thee ... Jn 21:20 *3860*

BETROTH {4}
Thou shalt *b* a wife, and another ... Deut 28:30 781
I will *b* thee unto me for ever ... Hos 2:19 781
yea, I will *b* thee unto me in ... Hos 2:19 781
I will even *b* thee unto me in ... Hos 2:20 781

BETROTHED {9}
who hath *b* her to himself, then ... Ex 21:8 3259
if he have *b* her unto his son, he ... Ex 21:9 3259
a man entice a maid that is not *b* ... Ex 22:16 781
b to an husband, and not at all ... Lev 19:20 2778
man is there that hath *b* a wife ... Deut 20:7 781
is a virgin be *b* unto an husband ... Deut 22:23 781
man find a *b* damsel in the field ... Deut 22:25 781
the *b* damsel cried, and there was ... Deut 22:27 781
that is a virgin, which is not *b* ... Deut 22:28 781

BETTER See APPENDIX.

BETTERED {1}
that she had, and was nothing *b* ... Mk 5:26 *5623*

BETWEEN See APPENDIX.

BETWIXT {16}
be a token of the covenant *b* me ... Gen 17:11 996
what is that *b* me and thee ... Gen 23:15 996
now an oath *b* us, even *b* us ... Gen 26:28 996
set three days' journey *b* himself ... Gen 30:36 996
that they may judge *b* us both ... Gen 31:37 996
see, God is witness *b* me and thee ... Gen 31:50 996
pillar, which I have cast *b* me ... Gen 31:51 996
God of their father, judge *b* us ... Gen 31:53 996
before me, and put a space *b* drove ... Gen 32:16 996
Neither is there any daysman *b* us ... Job 9:33 996
shine by the cloud that cometh *b* ... Job 36:32 6293
shall lie all night *b* my breasts ... Song 1:13 996
I pray you, *b* me and my vineyard ... Is 5:3 996
by the gate *b* the two walls ... Jer 39:4 996
For I am in a strait *b* two ... Phil 1:23 *1537*

BEULAH *(be-u'-lah)* {1} *A name of restored Israel.*
called Hephzi-bah, and thy land *B* ... Is 62:4 1166

BEWAIL {6}
b the burning which the LORD hath ... Lev 10:6 1058
b her father and her mother a full ... Deut 21:13 1058
b my virginity, I and my fellows ... Judg 11:37 1058
Therefore I will *b* with the ... Is 16:9 1058
that I shall *b* many which have ... 2Cor 12:21 *3996*
deliciously with her, shall *b* her ... Rev 18:9 *2799*

BEWAILED {3}
and *b* her virginity upon the ... Judg 11:38 1058
And all wept, and *b* her ... Lk 8:52 *2875*
people, and of women, which also *b* ... Lk 23:27 *2875*

BEWAILETH {1}
that *b* herself, that spreadeth ... Jer 4:31 3306

BEWARE {28}
B thou that thou bring not my son ... Gen 24:6 8104
B of him, and obey his voice, ... Ex 23:21 8104
Then *b* lest thou forget the LORD, ... Deut 6:12 8104
B that thou forget not the LORD ... Deut 8:11 8104
B that there be not a thought in ... Deut 15:9 8104
Now therefore *b*, I pray thee, and ... Judg 13:4 8104
I said unto the woman let her *b* ... Judg 13:13 8104
B that none touch the young man ... 2Sa 18:12 8104
B that thou pass not such a place ... 2Kin 6:9 8104
b lest he take thee away with his ... Job 36:18
a scorner, and the simple will *b* ... Prov 19:25 6191
B lest Hezekiah persuade you, ... Is 36:18
B of false prophets, which come ... Mt 7:15 *4337*
But *b* of men ... Mt 10:17 *4337*
b of the leaven of the Pharisees ... Mt 16:6 *4337*
that ye should *b* of the leaven of ... Mt 16:11 *4337*
them not *b* of the leaven of bread ... Mt 16:12 *4337*
b of the leaven of the Pharisees, ... Mk 8:15 *991*
B of the scribes, which love to ... Mk 12:38 *991*
B ye of the leaven of the ... Lk 12:1 *4337*
Take heed, and *b* of covetousness ... Lk 12:15 *5442*
B of the scribes, which desire to ... Lk 20:46 *4337*
B therefore, lest that come upon ... Acts 13:40 *991*
B of dogs, *b* of evil workers ... Phil 3:2 *991*
b of the concision ... Phil 3:2 *991*
B lest any man spoil you through ... Col 2:8 *991*
b lest ye also, being led away ... 2Pet 3:17 *5442*

BEWITCHED {3}
b the people of Samaria, giving ... Acts 8:9 *1839*
time he had *b* them with sorceries ... Acts 8:11 *1839*
foolish Galatians, who hath *b* you ... Gal 3:1 *940*

BEWRAY {1}
b not him that wandereth ... Is 16:3 1540

BEWRAYETH {3}
of his right hand, which *b* itself ... Prov 27:16 7121
he heareth cursing, and *b* it not ... Prov 29:24 5046
for thy speech *b* thee ... Mt 26:73 *1212,4160*

BEYOND See APPENDIX.

BEZAI *(be'-zahee)* {3}
1. A family of exiles.
The children of *B*, three hundred ... Ezr 2:17 1209
The children of *B*, three hundred ... Neh 7:23 1209
2. A family who renewed the covenant.
Hodijah, Hashum, *B*, ... Neh 10:18 1209

BEZALEEL *(be-zal'-e-el)* {9}
1. A craftsman.
called by name *B* the son of Uri ... Ex 31:2 1212
called by name *B* the son of Uri ... Ex 35:30 1212
Then wrought *B* and Aholiab, and ... Ex 36:1 1212
And Moses called *B* and Aholiab, and ... Ex 36:2 1212
B made the ark of shittim wood ... Ex 37:1 1212
B the son of Uri, the son of Hur, ... Ex 38:22 1212
And Hur begat Uri, and Uri begat *B* ... 1Chr 2:20 1212
that *B* the son of Uri, the son of ... 2Chr 1:5 1212
2. Married a foreign wife in exile.
Benaiah, Maaseiah, Mattaniah, *B* ... Ezr 10:30 1212

BEZALEL See BEZALEEL.

BEZEK *(be'-zek)* {3} See ADONI-BEZEK. *A place in the Jordan valley.*
of them in *B* ten thousand men ... Judg 1:4 966
And they found Adoni-bezek in *B* ... Judg 1:5 966
And when he numbered them in *B* ... 1Sa 11:8 966

BEZER *(be'-zer)* {5}
1. A city of refuge.
B in the wilderness, in the plain ... Deut 4:43 1221
they assigned *B* in the wilderness ... Josh 20:8 1221
B with her suburbs, and Jahazah ... Josh 21:36 1221
B in the wilderness with her ... 1Chr 6:78 1221
2. A son of Liph.
B, and Hod, and Shamma, ... 1Chr 7:37 1221

BICHRI *(bik'-ri)* {8} *Father of Sheba.*
name was Sheba, the son of *B* ... 2Sa 20:1 1075
and followed Sheba the son of *B* ... 2Sa 20:2 1075
son of *B* do us more harm than did ... 2Sa 20:6 1075
pursue after Sheba the son of *B* ... 2Sa 20:7 1075
pursued after Sheba the son of *B* ... 2Sa 20:10 1075
pursue after Sheba the son of *B* ... 2Sa 20:13 1075
Sheba the son of *B* by name ... 2Sa 20:21 1075
the head of Sheba the son of *B* ... 2Sa 20:22 1075

BICHRITES See BERITES.

BICRI See BICHRI.

BID {17}
b them that they make them ... Num 15:38 559
until the day I *b* you shout ... Josh 6:10 559
B the servant pass on before us, ... 1Sa 9:27 559
ere thou *b* the people return from ... 2Sa 2:26 559
riding for me, except I *b* thee ... 2Kin 4:24 559
if the prophet had *b* thee do some ... 2Kin 5:13 1696
will do all that thou shalt *b* us ... 2Kin 10:5 559
it the preaching that I *b* thee ... Jonah 3:2 1696
a sacrifice, he hath *b* his guests ... Zeph 1:7 6942
b me come unto thee on the water ... Mt 14:28 *2753*
ye shall find, *b* to the marriage ... Mt 22:9 *2564*
whatsoever they *b* you observe ... Mt 23:3 *2036*
let me first go *b* them farewell ... Lk 9:61 *657*
b her therefore that she help me ... Lk 10:40 *2036*
lest they also *b* thee again ... Lk 14:12 *479*
that believe not *b* you to a feast ... 1Cor 10:27 *2564*
house, neither *b* him God speed ... 2Jn 10 *3004*

BIDDEN {14}
and afterwards they eat that be *b* ... 1Sa 9:13 7121
place among them that were *b* ... 1Sa 9:22 7121
for the LORD hath *b* him ... 2Sa 16:11 559
the angel of the Lord had *b* him ... Mt 1:24 *4367*
them that were *b* to the wedding ... Mt 22:3 *2564*
saying, Tell them which are *b* ... Mt 22:4 *2564*
they which were *b* were not worthy ... Mt 22:8 *2564*
Pharisee which had *b* him saw it ... Lk 7:39 *2564*
a parable to those which were *b* ... Lk 14:7 *2564*
When thou art *b* of any man to a ... Lk 14:8 *2564*
man than thou be *b* of him ... Lk 14:8 *2564*
But when thou art *b*, go and sit ... Lk 14:10 *2564*
time to say to them that were *b* ... Lk 14:17 *2564*
were *b* shall taste of my supper ... Lk 14:24 *2564*

BIDDETH {1}
For he that *b* him God speed is ... 2Jn 11 *3004*

BIDDING {1}
son in law, and goeth at thy *b* ... 1Sa 22:14 4928

BIDKAR *(bid'-kar)* {1} *A captain of Jehu.*
Then said Jehu to *B* his captain ... 2Kin 9:25 920

BIER {2}
king David himself followed the *b* ... 2Sa 3:31 4296
And he came and touched the *b* ... Lk 7:14 *4673*

BIGTHA *(big'-thah)* {1} *A servant of Ahasuerus.*
Mehuman, Biztha, Harbona, *B* ... Est 1:10 903

BIGTHAN *(big'-than)* {1} See BIGTHANA. *A conspirator against Ahasuerus.*
two of the king's chamberlains, *B* ... Est 2:21 904

BIGTHANA *(big'-than-ah)* {1} See BIGTHAN. *Same as Bigthan.*
that Mordecai had told of *B* ... Est 6:2 904

BIGVAI *(big'-vahee)* {6}
1. A family chief with Zerubbabel.
Mordecai, Bilshan, Mizpar, *B* ... Ezr 2:2 902
Mordecai, Bilshan, Mispereth, *B* ... Neh 7:7 902
2. A family of exiles with Zerubbabel.
The children of *B*, two thousand ... Ezr 2:14 902
The children of *B*, two thousand ... Neh 7:19 902
3. A family of exiles with Ezra.
Of the sons also of *B* ... Ezr 8:14 902
4. A family who renewed the covenant.
Adonijah, *B*, Adin, ... Neh 10:16 902

BILDAD *(bil'-dad)* {5} *A friend of Job.*
B the Shuhite, and Zophar the ... Job 2:11 1085
Then answered *B* the Shuhite ... Job 8:1 1085
Then answered *B* the Shuhite ... Job 18:1 1085
Then answered *B* the Shuhite ... Job 25:1 1085
B the Shuhite and Zophar the ... Job 42:9 1085

BILEAM *(bil'-e-am)* {1} See IBLEAM. *A Levitical city in Manasseh.*
B with her suburbs, for the ... 1Chr 6:70 1109

BILGAH *(bil'-gah)* {3}
1. A priest during David's time.
The fifteenth to *B*, the sixteenth ... 1Chr 24:14 1083
2. A priest with Zerubbabel.
Miamin, Maadiah, *B*, ... Neh 12:5 1083
Of *B*, Shammua ... Neh 12:18 1083

BILGAI *(bil'-gahee)* {1} *A priest with Zerubbabel.*
Maaziah, *B*, Shemaiah ... Neh 10:8 1084

BILHAH *(bil'-hah)* {11} See BALAH.
1. Mother of Dan and Naphtali.
B his handmaid to be her maid ... Gen 29:29 1090
And she said, Behold my maid *B* ... Gen 30:3 1090
she gave him *B* her handmaid to ... Gen 30:4 1090
B conceived, and bare Jacob a son ... Gen 30:5 1090
B Rachel's maid conceived again, ... Gen 30:7 1090
lay with *B* his father's concubine ... Gen 35:22 1090
And the sons of *B*, Rachel's ... Gen 35:25 1090
and the lad was with the sons of *B* ... Gen 37:2 1090
These are the sons of *B*, which ... Gen 46:25 1090
Jezer, and Shallum, the sons of *B* ... 1Chr 7:13 1090
2. A town in Simeon.
And at *B*, and at Ezem, and at Tolad, ... 1Chr 4:29 1090

BILHAN *(bil'-han)* {4}
1. Son of Ezer.
B, and Zaavan, and Akan ... Gen 36:27 1092
B, and Zavan, and Jakan ... 1Chr 1:42 1092
2. Son of Jediael.
also of Jediael; *B* ... 1Chr 7:10 1092
and the sons of *B* ... 1Chr 7:10 1092

BILL {7}
him write her a *b* of divorcement ... Deut 24:1 5612
write her a *b* of divorcement, and ... Deut 24:3 5612
Where is the *b* of your mother's ... Is 50:1 5612
away, and given her a *b* of divorce ... Jer 3:8 5612
to write a *b* of divorcement ... Mk 10:4 *975*
And he said unto him, Take thy *b* ... Lk 16:6 *1121*
And he said unto him, Take thy *b* ... Lk 16:7 *1121*

BILLOWS {2}
waves and thy *b* are gone over me ... Ps 42:7 1530
all thy *b* and thy waves passed ... Jonah 2:3 4867

BILSHAN *(bil'-shan)* {2} *A Jewish prince with Zerubbabel.*
Seraiah, Reelaiah, Mordecai, *B* ... Ezr 2:2 1114
Raamiah, Nahamani, Mordecai, *B* ... Neh 7:7 1114

BIMHAL *(bim'-hal)* {1} *A son of Japlet.*
Pasach, and *B*, and Ashvath ... 1Chr 7:33 1118

BIND {49}
they shall *b* the breastplate by ... Ex 28:28 7405
they did *b* the breastplate by his ... Ex 39:21 7405
or swear an oath to *b* his soul ... Num 30:2 631
b herself by a bond, being in her ... Num 30:3 631
thou shalt *b* them for a sign upon ... Deut 6:8 7194
b them for a sign upon your hand, ... Deut 11:18 7194
b up the money in thine hand, and ... Deut 14:25 6887
thou shalt *b* this line of scarlet ... Josh 2:18 7194
To *b* Samson are we come up, to do ... Judg 15:10 631
him, We are come down to *b* thee ... Judg 15:12 631
but we will *b* thee fast, and ... Judg 15:13 631
that we may *b* him to afflict him ... Judg 16:5 631
If they *b* me with seven green ... Judg 16:7 631
If they *b* me fast with new ropes ... Judg 16:11 631
and *b* it as a crown to me ... Job 31:36 6029
Canst thou *b* the sweet influences ... Job 38:31 7194
Canst thou *b* the unicorn with his ... Job 39:10 7194
and *b* their faces in secret ... Job 40:13 2280
or wilt thou *b* him for thy ... Job 41:5 7194
To *b* his princes at his pleasure ... Ps 105:22 631
b the sacrifice with cords, even ... Ps 118:27 631
To *b* their kings with chains, and ... Ps 149:8 631
b them about thy neck ... Prov 3:3 7194
B them continually upon thine ... Prov 6:21 7194
B them upon thy fingers, write ... Prov 7:3 7194
B up the testimony, seal the law ... Is 8:16 6887
b them on thee, as a bride doeth ... Is 49:18 7194
he hath sent me to *b* up the ... Is 61:1 2280

that thou shalt *b* a stone to it ... Jer 51:63 7164
shall *b* thee with them, and thou ... Eze 3:25 631
number, and *b* them in thy skirts ... Eze 5:3 6887
b the tire of thine head upon ... Eze 24:17 2280
healed, to put a roller to *b* it ... Eze 30:21 2280
will *b* up that which was broken, ... Eze 34:16 2280
were in his army to *b* Shadrach ... Dan 3:20 3729
hath smitten, and he will *b* us up ... Hos 6:1 2280
when they shall *b* themselves in ... Hos 10:10 631
b the chariot to the swift beast ... Mic 1:13 7573
except he first *b* the strong man ... Mt 12:29 *1210*
b them in bundles to burn them ... Mt 13:30 *1210*
whatsoever thou shalt *b* on earth ... Mt 16:19 *1210*
Whatsoever ye shall *b* on earth ... Mt 18:18 *1210*
B him hand and foot, and take him ... Mt 22:13 *1210*
For they *b* heavy burdens and ... Mt 23:4 *1195*
he will first *b* the strong man ... Mk 3:27 *1210*
and no man could *b* him, no, not ... Mk 5:3 *1210*
to *b* all that call on thy name ... Acts 9:14 *1210*
Gird thyself, and *b* on thy sandals ... Acts 12:8 *5265*
So shall the Jews at Jerusalem *b* ... Acts 21:11 *1210*

BINDETH {9}
For he maketh sore, and *b* up ... Job 5:18 2280
He *b* up the waters in his thick ... Job 26:8 6887
He *b* the floods from overflowing ... Job 28:11 2280
it *b* me about as the collar of my ... Job 30:18 247
they cry not when he *b* them ... Job 36:13 631
nor he that *b* sheaves his bosom ... Ps 129:7 6014
in heart, and *b* up their wounds ... Ps 147:3 2280
As he that *b* a stone in a sling, ... Prov 26:8 6887
in the day that the LORD *b* up the ... Is 30:26 2280

BINDING {5}
we were *b* sheaves in the field, ... Gen 37:7 481
B his foal unto the vine, and his ... Gen 49:11 681
it shall have a *b* of woven work ... Ex 28:32 8193
every *b* oath to afflict the soul, ... Num 30:13 632
this way unto the death, *b* ... Acts 22:4 *1195*

BINEA *(bin'-e-ah)* {2} *A son of Moza.*
And Moza begat *B* ... 1Chr 8:37 1150
And Moza begat *B* ... 1Chr 9:43 1150

BINNUI *(bin'-nu-ee)* {7}
1. A Levite who returned from exile.
Jeshua, and Noadiah the son of *B* ... Ezr 8:33 1131
2. A descendant of Pahath-moab.
Mattaniah, Bezaleel, and *B* ... Ezr 10:30 1131
3. A descendant of Bani.
And Bani, and *B*, Shimei, ... Ezr 10:38 1131
4. A descendant of Henadad.
After him repaired *B* the son of ... Neh 3:24 1131
B of the sons of Henadad, Kadmiel ... Neh 10:9 1131
5. A family who returned from exile.
The children of *B*, six hundred ... Neh 7:15 1131
6. A Levite with Zerubbabel.
Jeshua, *B*, Kadmiel, Sherebiah, ... Neh 12:8 1131

BIRD {28}
his kind, every *b* of every sort ... Gen 7:14 6833
As for the living *b*, he shall ... Lev 14:6 6833
the living *b* in the blood of the ... Lev 14:6 6833
of the *b* that was killed over the ... Lev 14:6 6833
shall let the living *b* loose into ... Lev 14:7 6833
and the scarlet, and the living *b* ... Lev 14:51 6833
them in the blood of the slain *b* ... Lev 14:51 6833
the house with the blood of the *b* ... Lev 14:52 6833
water, and with the living *b* ... Lev 14:52 6833
b out of the city into the open ... Lev 14:53 6833
thou play with him as with a *b* ... Job 41:5 6833
Flee as a *b* to your mountain ... Ps 11:1 6833
Our soul is escaped as a *b* out of ... Ps 124:7 6833
is spread in the sight of any *b* ... Prov 1:17 1167,3671
as a *b* from the hand of the ... Prov 6:5 6833
as a *b* hasteth to the snare, and ... Prov 7:23 6833
As the *b* by wandering, as the ... Prov 26:2 6833
As a *b* that wandereth from her ... Prov 27:8 6833
for a *b* of the air shall carry ... Eccl 10:20 5775
rise up at the voice of the *b* ... Eccl 12:4 6833
as a wandering *b* cast out of the ... Is 16:2 5775
a ravenous *b* from the east ... Is 46:11 5861
is unto me as a speckled *b* ... Jer 12:9 5861
enemies chased me sore, like a *b* ... Lam 3:52 6833
glory shall fly away like a *b* ... Hos 9:11 5775
shall tremble as a *b* out of Egypt ... Hos 11:11 6833
Can a *b* fall in a snare upon the ... Amos 3:5 6833
of every unclean and hateful *b* ... Rev 18:2 *3732*

BIRD'S {1}
If a *b* nest chance to be before ... Deut 22:6 6833

BIRDS {24}
but the *b* divided he not ... Gen 15:10 6833
the *b* did eat them out of the ... Gen 40:17 5775
the *b* shall eat thy flesh from ... Gen 40:19 5775
is to be cleansed two *b* alive ... Lev 14:4 6833
shall command that one of the *b* ... Lev 14:5 6833
take to cleanse the house two *b* ... Lev 14:49 6833
the *b* in an earthen vessel over ... Lev 14:50 6833
Of all clean *b* ye shall eat ... Deut 14:11 6833
suffered neither the *b* of the air ... 2Sa 21:10 5775
Where the *b* make their nests ... Ps 104:17 6833
as the *b* that are caught in the ... Eccl 9:12 6833
time of the singing of *b* is come ... Song 2:12
As *b* flying, so will the LORD of ... Is 31:5 6833
all the *b* of the heavens were ... Jer 4:25 5775
As a cage is full of *b*, so are ... Jer 5:27 5775
the beasts are consumed, and the *b* ... Jer 12:4 5775
the *b* round about are against her ... Jer 12:9 5861
unto the ravenous *b* of every sort ... Eze 39:4 6833
the *b* of the air have nests ... Mt 8:20 *4071*
so that the *b* of the air come and ... Mt 13:32 *4071*
holes, and *b* of the air have nests ... Lk 9:58 *4071*
like to corruptible man, and to *b* ... Rom 1:23 *4071*
of fishes, and another of *b* ... 1Cor 15:39 *4421*
For every kind of beasts, and of *b* ... Jas 3:7 *4071*

BIRDS' {1}
and his nails like *b* claws ... Dan 4:33 6853

BIRSHA *(bur'-shah)* {1} *A king of Gomorrah.*
with *B* king of Gomorrah, Shinab ... Gen 14:2 1306

BIRTH {15}
other stone, according to their *b* ... Ex 28:10 8435
the children are come to the *b* ... 2Kin 19:3 4866
hidden untimely *b* I had not been ... Job 3:16 5309
like the untimely *b* of a woman ... Ps 58:8 5309
that an untimely *b* is better than ... Eccl 6:3 5309
of death than the day of one's *b* ... Eccl 7:1 3205
the children are come to the *b* ... Is 37:3 4866
Shall I bring to the *b*, and not ... Is 66:9 7665
Thy *b* and thy nativity is of the ... Eze 16:3 4351
fly away like a bird, from the *b* ... Hos 9:11 3205
Now the *b* of Jesus Christ was on ... Mt 1:18 *1083*
and many shall rejoice at his *b* ... Lk 1:14 *1083*
a man which was blind from his *b* ... Jn 9:1 *1079*
of whom I travail in *b* again ... Gal 4:19 *5605*
with child cried, travailing in *b* ... Rev 12:2 *5605*

BIRTHDAY {3}
third day, which was Pharaoh's *b* ... Gen 40:20 3117,3205
But when Herod's *b* was kept ... Mt 14:6 *1077*
that Herod on his *b* made a supper ... Mk 6:21 *1077*

BIRTHRIGHT {10}
said, Sell me this day thy *b* ... Gen 25:31 1062
what profit shall this *b* do to me ... Gen 25:32 1062
and he sold his *b* unto Jacob ... Gen 25:33 1062
thus Esau despised his *b* ... Gen 25:34 1062
he took away my *b* ... Gen 27:36 1062
the firstborn according to his *b* ... Gen 43:33 1062
his *b* was given unto the sons of ... 1Chr 5:1 1062
is not to be reckoned after the *b* ... 1Chr 5:1 1062
but the *b* was Joseph's ... 1Chr 5:2 1062
for one morsel of meat sold his *b* ... Heb 12:16 *4415*

BIRZAITH See BIRZAVITH.

BIRZAVITH *(bur'-za-vith)* {1} *A descendant of Asher.*
Malchiel, who is the father of *B* ... 1Chr 7:31 1269

BISHLAM *(bish'-lam)* {1} *A commissioner of Artaxerxes.*
in the days of Artaxerxes wrote *B* ... Ezr 4:7 1312

BISHOP {6}
If a man desire the office of a *b* ... 1Ti 3:1 *1984*
A *b* then must be blameless, the ... 1Ti 3:2 *1985*
ordained the first *b* of the ... 2Ti *s* *1985*
For a *b* must be blameless, as the ... Titus 1:7 *1985*
ordained the first *b* of the ... Titus *s* *1985*
the Shepherd and *B* of your souls ... 1Pet 2:25 *1985*

BISHOPRICK {1}
and his *b* let another take ... Acts 1:20 *1984*

BISHOPS {1}
which are at Philippi, with the *b* ... Phil 1:1 *1985*

BIT {3}
the people, and they *b* the people ... Num 21:6 5391
mouth must be held in with *b* ... Ps 32:9 4964
on the wall, and a serpent *b* him ... Amos 5:19 5391

BITE {7}
an hedge, a serpent shall *b* him ... Eccl 10:8 5391
will *b* without enchantment ... Eccl 10:11 5391
be charmed, and they shall *b* you ... Jer 8:17 5391
the serpent, and he shall *b* them ... Amos 9:3 5391
that *b* with their teeth, and cry, ... Mic 3:5 5391
up suddenly that shall *b* thee ... Hab 2:7 5391
But if ye *b* and devour one another ... Gal 5:15 *1143*

BITETH {2}
that *b* the horse heels, so that ... Gen 49:17 5391
At the last it *b* like a serpent ... Prov 23:32 5391

BITHIA See BITHIAH.

BITHIAH *(bith-i'-ah)* {1} *Daughter of Pharaoh.*
these are the sons of *B* the ... 1Chr 4:18 1332

BITHRON *(bith'-ron)* {1} *A district in Arabah.*
Jordan, and went through all *B* ... 2Sa 2:29 1338

BITHYNIA *(bith-in'-e-ah)* {2} *A Roman province in Asia Minor.*
Mysia, they assayed to go into *B* ... Acts 16:7 *978*
Galatia, Cappadocia, Asia, and *B* ... 1Pet 1:1 *978*

BITS {1}
we put *b* in the horses' mouths, ... Jas 3:3 *5469*

BITTEN {2}
to pass, that every one that is *b* ... Num 21:8 5391
that if a serpent had *b* any man ... Num 21:9 5391

BITTER {38}
with a great and exceeding *b* cry ... Gen 27:34 4751
their lives *b* with hard bondage ... Ex 1:14 4843
with *b* herbs they shall eat it ... Ex 12:8 4844
waters of Marah, for they were *b* ... Ex 15:23 4751
shall have in his hand the *b* ... Num 5:18 4751
be thou free from this *b* water ... Num 5:19 4751
blot them out with the *b* water ... Num 5:23 4751
b water that causeth the curse ... Num 5:24 4751
shall enter into her, and become *b* ... Num 5:24 4751
shall enter into her, and become *b* ... Num 5:27 4751
with unleavened bread and *b* herbs ... Num 9:11 4844
heat, and with *b* destruction ... Deut 32:24 4815
of gall, their clusters are *b* ... Deut 32:32 4846
of Israel, that it was very *b* ... 2Kin 14:26 4784
and cried with a loud and a *b* cry ... Est 4:1 4751
and life unto the *b* in soul ... Job 3:20 4751
For thou writest *b* things against ... Job 13:26 4846
Even to day is my complaint *b* ... Job 23:2 4805
shoot their arrows, even *b* words ... Ps 64:3 4751
But her end is *b* as wormwood ... Prov 5:4 4751
soul every *b* thing is sweet ... Prov 27:7 4751
I find more *b* than death the ... Eccl 7:26 4751
b for sweet, and sweet for *b* ... Is 5:20 4751
shall be *b* to them that drink it ... Is 24:9 4843
see that it is an evil thing and *b* ... Jer 2:19 4751
thy wickedness, because it is *b* ... Jer 4:18 4751
an only son, most *b* lamentation ... Jer 6:26 8563
Ramah, lamentation, and *b* weeping ... Jer 31:15 8563
bitterness of heart and *b* wailing ... Eze 27:31 4751
and the end thereof as a *b* day ... Amos 8:10 4751
I raise up the Chaldeans, that *b* ... Hab 1:6 4751
wives, and be not *b* against them ... Col 3:19 *4087*
the same place sweet water and *b* ... Jas 3:11 *4089*
But if ye have *b* envying and ... Jas 3:14 *4089*
waters, because they were made *b* ... Rev 8:11 *4087*
and it shall make thy belly *b* ... Rev 10:9 *4087*
as I had eaten it, my belly was *b* ... Rev 10:10 *4087*

BITTERLY {9}
curse ye *b* the inhabitants ... Judg 5:23 779
hath dealt very *b* with me ... Ruth 1:20 4843
I will weep *b*, labour not to ... Is 22:4 4843
ambassadors of peace shall weep *b* ... Is 33:7 4751
against thee, and shall cry *b* ... Eze 27:30 4751
provoked him to anger most *b* ... Hos 12:14 8563
the mighty man shall cry there *b* ... Zeph 1:14 4751
And he went out, and wept *b* ... Mt 26:75 *4090*
And Peter went out, and wept *b* ... Lk 22:62 *4090*

BITTERN {3}
make it a possession for the *b* ... Is 14:23 7090
and the *b* shall possess it ... Is 34:11 7090
the *b* shall lodge in the upper ... Zeph 2:14 7090

BITTERNESS {22}
And she was in *b* of soul, and ... 1Sa 1:10 4751
Surely the *b* of death is past ... 1Sa 15:32 4751
it will be *b* in the latter end ... 2Sa 2:26 4751
will complain in the *b* of my soul ... Job 7:11 4751
my breath, but filleth me with *b* ... Job 9:18 4472
I will speak in the *b* of my soul ... Job 10:1 4751
dieth in the *b* of his soul ... Job 21:25 4751
The heart knoweth his own *b* ... Prov 14:10 4751
father, and *b* to her that bare him ... Prov 17:25 4470
all my years in the *b* of my soul ... Is 38:15 4751
Behold, for peace I had great *b* ... Is 38:17 4843
are afflicted, and she is in *b* ... Lam 1:4 4843
He hath filled me with *b*, he hath ... Lam 3:15 4844
and took me away, and I went in *b* ... Eze 3:14 4751
with *b* sigh before their eyes ... Eze 21:6 4814
weep for thee with *b* of heart ... Eze 27:31 4751
son, and shall be in *b* for him ... Zec 12:10 4843
that is in *b* for his firstborn ... Zec 12:10 4843
that thou art in the gall of *b* ... Acts 8:23 *4088*
mouth is full of cursing and *b* ... Rom 3:14 *4088*
Let all *b*, and wrath, and anger, and ... Eph 4:31 *4088*
lest any root of *b* springing up ... Heb 12:15 *4088*

BIZIOTHIAH See BIZJOTHJAH.

BIZJOTHJAH *(biz-joth'-jah)* {1} *A town in Judah.*
Hazar-shual, and Beer-sheba, and *B* ... Josh 15:28 964

BIZTHA *(biz'-thah)* {1} *An eunuch of Ahasuerus.*
wine, he commanded Mehuman, *B* ... Est 1:10 968

BLACK {18}
and that there is no *b* hair in it ... Lev 13:31 7838
that there is *b* hair grown up ... Lev 13:37 7838
that the heaven was *b* with clouds ... 1Kin 18:45 6937
of red, and blue, and white, and *b* ... Est 1:6 5508
My skin is *b* upon me, and my bones ... Job 30:30 7835
in the evening, in the *b* ... Prov 7:9 380
I am *b*, but comely, O ye ... Song 1:5 7838
Look not upon me, because I am *b* ... Song 1:6 7840
locks are bushy, and *b* as a raven ... Song 5:11 7838
mourn, and the heavens above be *b* ... Jer 4:28 6937
I am *b* ... Jer 8:21 6937
they are *b* unto the ground ... Jer 14:2 6937
Our skin was *b* like an oven ... Lam 5:10 3648
and in the second chariot *b* horses ... Zec 6:2 7838
The *b* horses which are therein go ... Zec 6:6 7838
not make one hair white or *b* ... Mt 5:36 *3189*
And I beheld, and lo a *b* horse ... Rev 6:5 *3189*
the sun became *b* as sackcloth of ... Rev 6:12 *3189*

BLACKER {1}
Their visage is *b* than a coal ... Lam 4:8 2821

BLACKISH {1}
Which are *b* by reason of the ice, ... Job 6:16 6937

BLACKNESS {6}
let the *b* of the day terrify it ... Job 3:5 3650
I clothe the heavens with *b* ... Is 50:3 6940
all faces shall gather *b* ... Joel 2:6 6289
and the faces of them all gather *b* ... Nah 2:10 6289
that burned with fire, nor unto *b* ... Heb 12:18 *1105*
the *b* of darkness for ever ... Jude 13 *2217*

BLADE {5}
the haft also went in after the *b* ... Judg 3:22 3851
and the fat closed upon the *b* ... Judg 3:22 3851
mine arm fall from my shoulder *b* ... Job 31:22 7929
But when the *b* was sprung up, and ... Mt 13:26 *5528*
first the *b*, then the ear, after ... Mk 4:28 *5528*

BLAINS {2}
breaking forth with *b* upon man ... Ex 9:9 76
breaking forth with *b* upon man ... Ex 9:10 76

BLAME {4}
then let me bear the b for ever ... Gen 43:9 2398
bear the b to my father for ever ... Gen 44:32 2398
that no man should b us in this ... 2Cor 8:20 *3469*
without b before him in love ... Eph 1:4 *299*

BLAMED {2}
thing, that the ministry be not b ... 2Cor 6:3 *3469*
the face, because he was to be b ... Gal 2:11 *2607*

BLAMELESS {15}
and ye shall be b ... Gen 44:10 5355
We will be b of this thine oath ... Josh 2:17 5355
Now shall I be more b than the ... Judg 15:3 5352
profane the sabbath, and are b ... Mt 12:5 *338*
and ordinances of the Lord b ... Lk 1:6 *273*
that ye may be b in the day of ... 1Cor 1:8 *410*
That ye may be b and harmless, the ... Phil 2:15 *273*
which is in the law, b ... Phil 3:6 *273*
body be preserved b unto the ... 1Th 5:23 *274*
A bishop then must be b, the ... 1Ti 3:2 *423*
office of a deacon, being found b ... 1Ti 3:10 *410*
in charge, that they may be b ... 1Ti 5:7 *423*
If any be b, the husband of one ... Titus 1:6 *410*
For a bishop must be b, as the ... Titus 1:7 *410*
him in peace, without spot, and b ... 2Pet 3:14 *298*

BLASPHEME {10}
to the enemies of the LORD to b ... 2Sa 12:14 5006
him, saying, Thou didst b God ... 1Kin 21:10 1288
people, saying, Naboth did b God ... 1Kin 21:13 1288
shall the enemy b thy name for ... Ps 74:10 5006
wherewith soever they shall b ... Mk 3:28 *987*
But he that shall b against the ... Mk 3:29 *987*
synagogue, and compelled them to b ... Acts 26:11 *987*
that they may learn not to b ... 1Ti 1:20 *987*
Do not they b that worthy name by ... Jas 2:7 *987*
to b his name, and his tabernacle, ... Rev 13:6 *987*

BLASPHEMED {16}
son b the name of the LORD ... Lev 24:11 5344
of the king of Assyria have b me ... 2Kin 19:6 1442
Whom hast thou reproached and b ... 2Kin 19:22 1442
foolish people have b thy name ... Ps 74:18 5006
of the king of Assyria have b me ... Is 37:6 1442
Whom hast thou reproached and b ... Is 37:23 1442
name continually every day is b ... Is 52:5 5006
mountains, and b me upon the hills ... Is 65:7 2778
in this your fathers have b me ... Eze 20:27 1442
they opposed themselves, and b ... Acts 18:6 *987*
For the name of God is b among ... Rom 2:24 *987*
of God and his doctrine be not b ... 1Ti 6:1 *987*
that the word of God be not b ... Titus 2:5 *987*
b the name of God, which hath ... Rev 16:9 *987*
b the God of heaven because of ... Rev 16:11 *987*
men b God because of the plague ... Rev 16:21 *987*

BLASPHEMER {1}
Who was before a b, and a ... 1Ti 1:13 *989*

BLASPHEMERS {2}
nor yet b of your goddess ... Acts 19:37 *987*
covetous, boasters, proud, b ... 2Ti 3:2 *989*

BLASPHEMEST {1}
and sent into the world, Thou b ... Jn 10:36 *987*

BLASPHEMETH {5}
he that b the name of the LORD, ... Lev 24:16 5344
when he b the name of the LORD, ... Lev 24:16 5344
of him that reproacheth and b ... Ps 44:16 1442
within themselves, This man b ... Mt 9:3 *987*
but unto him that b against the ... Lk 12:10 *987*

BLASPHEMIES {6}
that I have heard all thy b which ... Eze 35:12 5007
thefts, false witness, b ... Mt 15:19 *988*
Why doth this man thus speak b ... Mk 2:7 *988*
b wherewith soever they shall ... Mk 3:28 *988*
Who is this which speaketh b ... Lk 5:21 *988*
mouth speaking great things and b ... Rev 13:5 *988*

BLASPHEMING {1}
by Paul, contradicting and b ... Acts 13:45 *987*

BLASPHEMOUS {2}
him speak b words against Moses ... Acts 6:11 *989*
b words against this holy place ... Acts 6:13 *989*

BLASPHEMOUSLY {1}
many other things b spake they ... Lk 22:65 *987*

BLASPHEMY {14}
of trouble, and of rebuke, and b ... 2Kin 19:3 5007
of trouble, and of rebuke, and of b ... Is 37:3 5007
b shall be forgiven unto men ... Mt 12:31 *988*
but the b against the Holy Ghost ... Mt 12:31 *988*
clothes, saying, He hath spoken b ... Mt 26:65 *987*
behold, now ye have heard his b ... Mt 26:65 *988*
lasciviousness, an evil eye, b ... Mk 7:22 *988*
Ye have heard the b ... Mk 14:64 *988*
stone thee not; but for b ... Jn 10:33 *988*
anger, wrath, malice, b, filthy ... Col 3:8 *988*
I know the b of them which say ... Rev 2:9 *988*
and upon his heads the name of b ... Rev 13:1 *988*
opened his mouth in b against God ... Rev 13:6 *988*
beast, full of names of b ... Rev 17:3 *988*

BLAST {8}
with the b of thy nostrils the ... Ex 15:8 7307
make a long b with the ram's horn ... Josh 6:5
at the b of the breath of his ... 2Sa 22:16 5397
Behold, I will send a b upon him ... 2Kin 19:7 7307
By the b of God they perish, and ... Job 4:9 5397
at the b of the breath of thy ... Ps 18:15 5397
when the b of the terrible ones ... Is 25:4 7307
Behold, I will send a b upon him ... Is 37:7 7307

BLASTED {5}
b with the east wind sprung up ... Gen 41:6 7710
b with the east wind, sprung up ... Gen 41:23 7710
the seven empty ears b with the ... Gen 41:27 7710
as corn b before it be grown up ... 2Kin 19:26 7711
as corn b before it be grown up ... Is 37:27 7709

BLASTING {5}
and with the sword, and with b ... Deut 28:22 7711
famine, if there be pestilence, b ... 1Kin 8:37 7711
be pestilence, if there be b ... 2Chr 6:28 7711
I have smitten you with b ... Amos 4:9 7711
I smote you with b and with mildew ... Hag 2:17 7711

BLASTUS *(blas'-tus)* {1} *A servant of Herod Agrippa I.*
him, and, having made B the king's ... Acts 12:20 *986*

BLAZE {1}
to b abroad the matter, insomuch ... Mk 1:45 *1310*

BLEATING {1}
What meaneth then this b of the ... 1Sa 15:14 6963

BLEATINGS {1}
to hear the b of the flocks ... Judg 5:16 8292

BLEMISH {63}
Your lamb shall be without b ... Ex 12:5 8549
bullock, and two rams without b ... Ex 29:1 8549
let him offer a male without b ... Lev 1:3 8549
shall bring it a male without b ... Lev 1:10 8549
it without b before the LORD ... Lev 3:1 8549
he shall offer it without b ... Lev 3:6 8549
without b unto the LORD for a sin ... Lev 4:3 8549
of the goats, a male without b ... Lev 4:23 8549
of the goats, a female without b ... Lev 4:28 8549
shall bring it a female without b ... Lev 4:32 8549
a ram without b out of the flocks ... Lev 5:15 8549
a ram without b out of the flock ... Lev 5:18 8549
a ram without b out of the flock, ... Lev 6:6 8549
for a burnt offering, without b ... Lev 9:2 8549
both of the first year, without b ... Lev 9:3 8549
shall take two he lambs without b ... Lev 14:10 8549
lamb of the first year without b ... Lev 14:10 8549
their generations that hath any b ... Lev 21:17 3971
man he be that hath a b, he shall ... Lev 21:18 3971
or that hath a b in his eye ... Lev 21:20 8400
No man that hath a b of the seed ... Lev 21:21 3971
he hath a b ... Lev 21:21 3971
the altar, because he hath a b ... Lev 21:23 3971
at your own will a male without b ... Lev 22:19 8549
But whatsoever hath a b, that ... Lev 22:20 3971
there shall be no b therein ... Lev 22:21 3971
the sheaf an he lamb without b of ... Lev 23:12 8549
lambs without b of the first year ... Lev 23:18 8549
a man cause a b in his neighbour ... Lev 24:19 3971
as he hath caused a b in a man ... Lev 24:20 3971
without b for a burnt offering ... Num 6:14 8549
year without b for a sin offering ... Num 6:14 8549
one ram without b for peace ... Num 6:14 8549
without spot, wherein is no b ... Num 19:2 3971
they shall be unto you without b ... Num 28:19 8549
they shall be unto you without b) ... Num 28:31 8549
lambs of the first year without b ... Num 29:2 8549
they shall be unto you without b ... Num 29:8 8549
they shall be without b ... Num 29:13 8549
lambs of the first year without b ... Num 29:20 8549
lambs of the first year without b ... Num 29:23 8549
lambs of the first year without b ... Num 29:29 8549
lambs of the first year without b ... Num 29:32 8549
lambs of the first year without b ... Num 29:36 8549
And if there be any b therein ... Deut 15:21 3971
lame, or blind, or have any ill b ... Deut 15:21 3971
bullock, or sheep, wherein is b ... Deut 17:1 3971
of his head there was no b in him ... 2Sa 14:25 3971
without b for a sin offering ... Eze 43:22 8549
offer a young bullock without b ... Eze 43:23 8549
a ram out of the flock without b ... Eze 43:23 8549
a ram out of the flock, without b ... Eze 43:25 8549
take a young bullock without b ... Eze 45:18 8549
seven rams without b daily the ... Eze 45:23 8549
day shall be six lambs without b ... Eze 46:4 8549
b, and a ram without b ... Eze 46:4 8549
be a young bullock without b ... Eze 46:6 8549
they shall be without b ... Eze 46:6 8549
lamb of the first year without b ... Eze 46:13 8549
Children in whom was no b ... Dan 1:4 3971
it should be holy and without b ... Eph 5:27 *299*
of Christ, as of a lamb without b ... 1Pet 1:19 *299*

BLEMISHES {2}
is in them, and b be in them ... Lev 22:25 3971
Spots they are and b, sporting ... 2Pet 2:13 *3470*

BLESS {127}
a great nation, and I will b thee ... Gen 12:2 1288
And I will b them that b thee ... Gen 12:3 1288
And I will b her, and give thee a ... Gen 17:16 1288
yea, I will b her, and she shall ... Gen 17:16 1288
That in blessing I will b thee ... Gen 22:17 1288
will be with thee, and will b thee ... Gen 26:3 1288
I am with thee, and will b thee ... Gen 26:24 1288
that my soul may b thee before I ... Gen 27:4 1288
b thee before the LORD before my ... Gen 27:7 1288
that he may b thee before his ... Gen 27:10 1288
venison, that thy soul may b me ... Gen 27:19 1288
venison, that my soul may b thee ... Gen 27:25 1288
venison, that thy soul may b me ... Gen 27:31 1288
B me, even me also, O my father ... Gen 27:34 1288
b me, even me also, O my father ... Gen 27:38 1288
And God Almighty b thee, and make ... Gen 28:3 1288
not let thee go, except thou b me ... Gen 32:26 1288
thee, unto me, and I will b them ... Gen 48:9 1288
me from all evil, b the lads ... Gen 48:16 1288
saying, In thee shall Israel b ... Gen 48:20 1288
who shall b thee with blessings ... Gen 49:25 1288
and b me also ... Ex 12:32 1288
come unto thee, and I will b thee ... Ex 20:24 1288
he shall b thy bread, and thy ... Ex 23:25 1288
On this wise ye shall b the ... Num 6:23 1288
The LORD b thee, and keep thee ... Num 6:24 1288
and I will b them ... Num 6:27 1288
I have received commandment to b ... Num 23:20 1288
them at all, nor b them at all ... Num 23:25 1288
it pleased the LORD to b Israel ... Num 24:1 1288
b you, as he hath promised you ... Deut 1:11 1288
thee, and b thee, and multiply thee ... Deut 7:13 1288
he will also b the fruit of thy ... Deut 7:13 1288
then thou shalt b the LORD thy ... Deut 8:10 1288
to b in his name, unto this day ... Deut 10:8 1288
that the LORD thy God may b thee ... Deut 14:29 1288
for the LORD shall greatly b thee ... Deut 15:4 1288
God shall b thee in all thy works ... Deut 15:10 1288
the LORD thy God shall b thee in ... Deut 15:18 1288
b thee in all thine increase ... Deut 16:15 1288
to b in the name of the LORD ... Deut 21:5 1288
that the LORD thy God may b thee ... Deut 23:20 1288
in his own raiment, and b thee ... Deut 24:13 1288
that the LORD thy God may b thee ... Deut 24:19 1288
b thy people Israel, and the land ... Deut 26:15 1288
mount Gerizim to b the people ... Deut 27:12 1288
he shall b thee in the land which ... Deut 28:8 1288
to b all the work of thine hand ... Deut 28:12 1288
that he b himself in his heart, ... Deut 29:19 1288
the LORD thy God shall b thee in ... Deut 30:16 1288
B, LORD, his substance, and accept ... Deut 33:11 1288
that they should b the people of ... Josh 8:33 1288
B ye the LORD ... Judg 5:9 1288
answered him, The LORD b thee ... Ruth 2:4 1288
because he doth b the sacrifice ... 1Sa 9:13 1288
David returned to b his household ... 2Sa 6:20 1288
to b the house of thy servant ... 2Sa 7:29 1288
to b him, because he had fought ... 2Sa 8:10 1288
that ye may b the inheritance of ... 2Sa 21:3 1288
came to b our lord king David ... 1Kin 1:47 1288
Oh that thou wouldest b me indeed ... 1Chr 4:10 1288
and David returned to b his house ... 1Chr 16:43 1288
to b the house of thy servant ... 1Chr 17:27 1288
to b in his name for ever ... 1Chr 23:13 1288
Now b the LORD your God ... 1Chr 29:20 1288
b the LORD your God for ever and ... Neh 9:5 1288
thou, LORD, wilt b the righteous ... Ps 5:12 1288
I will b the LORD, who hath given ... Ps 16:7 1288
congregations will I b the LORD ... Ps 26:12 1288
people, and b thine inheritance ... Ps 28:9 1288
the LORD will b his people with ... Ps 29:11 1288
I will b the LORD at all times ... Ps 34:1 1288
they b with their mouth, but they ... Ps 62:4 1288
Thus will I b thee while I live ... Ps 63:4 1288
O b our God, ye people, and make ... Ps 66:8 1288
God be merciful unto us, and b us ... Ps 67:1 1288
God, even our own God, shall b us ... Ps 67:6 1288
God shall b us ... Ps 67:7 1288
B ye God in the congregations, ... Ps 68:26 1288
Sing unto the LORD, b his name ... Ps 96:2 1288
thankful unto him, and b his name ... Ps 100:4 1288
B the LORD, O my soul ... Ps 103:1 1288
is within me, b his holy name ... Ps 103:1
B the LORD, O my soul, and forget ... Ps 103:2 1288
B the LORD, ye his angels, that ... Ps 103:20 1288
B ye the LORD, all ye his hosts ... Ps 103:21 1288
B the LORD, all his works in all ... Ps 103:22 1288
b the LORD, O my soul ... Ps 103:22 1288
B the LORD, O my soul ... Ps 104:1 1288
B thou the LORD, O my soul ... Ps 104:35 1288
Let them curse, but b thou ... Ps 109:28 1288
he will b us ... Ps 115:12 1288
he will b the house of Israel ... Ps 115:12 1288
he will b the house of Aaron ... Ps 115:12 1288
He will b them that fear the LORD ... Ps 115:13 1288
But we will b the LORD from this ... Ps 115:18 1288
The LORD shall b thee out of Zion ... Ps 128:5 1288
we b you in the name of the LORD ... Ps 129:8 1288
I will abundantly b her provision ... Ps 132:15 1288
b ye the LORD, all ye servants of ... Ps 134:1 1288
in the sanctuary, and b the LORD ... Ps 134:2 1288
and earth b thee out of Zion ... Ps 134:3 1288
B the LORD, O house of Israel ... Ps 135:19 1288
b the LORD, O house of Aaron ... Ps 135:19 1288
B the LORD, O house of Levi ... Ps 135:20 1288
ye that fear the LORD, b the LORD ... Ps 135:20 1288
I will b thy name for ever and ... Ps 145:1 1288
Every day will I b thee ... Ps 145:2 1288
and thy saints shall b thee ... Ps 145:10 1288
let all flesh b his holy name for ... Ps 145:21 1288
and doth not b their mother ... Prov 30:11 1288
Whom the LORD of hosts shall b ... Is 19:25 1288
himself in the earth shall b ... Is 65:16 1288
nations shall b themselves in him ... Jer 4:2 1288
The LORD b thee, O habitation of ... Jer 31:23 1288
from this day will I b you ... Hag 2:19 1288
b them that curse you, do good to ... Mt 5:44 *2127*
B them that curse you, and pray ... Lk 6:28 *2127*
his Son Jesus, sent him to b you ... Acts 3:26 *2127*
B them which persecute you ... Rom 12:14 *2127*
b, and curse not ... Rom 12:14 *2127*
being reviled, we b ... 1Cor 4:12 *2127*
The cup of blessing which we b ... 1Cor 10:16 *2127*
when thou shalt b with the spirit ... 1Cor 14:16 *2127*
Surely blessing I will b thee ... Heb 6:14 *2127*
Therewith b we God, even the ... Jas 3:9 *2127*

BLESSED {302}
God *b* them, saying, Be fruitful, Gen 1:22 1288
God *b* them, and God said unto them Gen 1:28 1288
God *b* the seventh day, and Gen 2:3 1288
b them, and called their name Adam Gen 5:2 1288
God *b* Noah and his sons, and said Gen 9:1 1288
B be the LORD God of Shem Gen 9:26 1288
all families of the earth be *b* Gen 12:3 1288
he *b* him, and said Gen 14:19 1288
B be Abram of the most high God, Gen 14:19 1288
b be the most high God, which Gen 14:20 1288
Behold, I have *b* him, and will Gen 17:20 1288
of the earth shall be *b* in him Gen 18:18 1288
all the nations of the earth be *b* Gen 22:18 1288
the LORD had *b* Abraham in all Gen 24:1 1288
B be the LORD God of my master Gen 24:27 1288
said, Come in, thou *b* of the LORD Gen 24:31 1288
the LORD hath *b* my master greatly Gen 24:35 1288
b the LORD God of my master Gen 24:48 1288
they *b* Rebekah, and said unto her, Gen 24:60 1288
Abraham, that God *b* his son Isaac Gen 25:11 1288
all the nations of the earth be *b* Gen 26:4 1288
and the LORD *b* him Gen 26:12 1288
thou art now the *b* of the LORD Gen 26:29 1288
so he *b* him Gen 27:23 1288
b him, and said, See, the smell of Gen 27:27 1288
of a field which the LORD hath *b* Gen 27:27 1288
b be he that blesseth thee Gen 27:29 1288
before thou camest, and have *b* him Gen 27:33 1288
yea, and he shall be *b* Gen 27:33 1288
wherewith his father *b* him Gen 27:41 1288
b him, and charged him, and said Gen 28:1 1288
Esau saw that Isaac had *b* Jacob Gen 28:6 1288
that as he *b* him he gave him a Gen 28:6 1288
the families of the earth be *b* Gen 28:14 1288
for the daughters will call me *b* Gen 30:13 833
the LORD hath *b* me for thy sake Gen 30:27 1288
the LORD hath *b* thee since my Gen 30:30 1288
sons and his daughters, and *b* them Gen 31:55 1288
And he *b* him there Gen 32:29 1288
came out of Padan-aram, and *b* him Gen 35:9 1288
that the LORD *b* the Egyptian's Gen 39:5 1288
and Jacob *b* Pharaoh Gen 47:7 1288
Jacob *b* Pharaoh, and went out from Gen 47:10 1288
in the land of Canaan, and *b* me, Gen 48:3 1288
he *b* Joseph, and said, God, before Gen 48:15 1288
he *b* them that day, saying, In Gen 48:20 1288
father spake unto them, and *b* them Gen 49:28 1288
to his blessing he *b* them Gen 49:28 1288
B be the LORD, who hath delivered Ex 18:10 1288
the LORD *b* the sabbath day Ex 20:11 1288
and Moses *b* them Ex 39:43 1288
b them, and came down from Lev 9:22 1288
and came out, and *b* the people Lev 9:23 1288
that he whom thou blessest is *b* Num 22:6 1288
for they are *b* Num 22:12 1288
thou hast *b* them altogether Num 23:11 1288
and he hath *b* Num 23:20 1288
B is he that blesseth thee, and Num 24:9 1288
thou hast altogether *b* them these Num 24:10 1288
For the LORD thy God hath *b* thee Deut 2:7 1288
Thou shalt be *b* above all people Deut 7:14 1288
the LORD thy God hath *b* thee Deut 12:7 1288
when the LORD thy God hath *b* thee Deut 14:24 1288
b thee thou shalt give unto him Deut 15:14 1288
as the LORD thy God hath *b* thee Deut 16:10 1288
B shalt thou be in the city, and Deut 28:3 1288
b shalt thou be in the field Deut 28:3 1288
B shall be the fruit of thy body, Deut 28:4 1288
B shall be thy basket and thy Deut 28:5 1288
B shalt thou be when thou comest Deut 28:6 1288
b shalt thou be when thou goest Deut 28:6 1288
b the children of Israel before Deut 33:1 1288
B of the LORD be his land, for Deut 33:13 1288
B be he that enlargeth Gad Deut 33:20 1288
Let Asher be *b* with children Deut 33:24 1288
And Joshua *b* him, and gave unto Josh 14:13 1288
as the LORD hath *b* me hitherto Josh 17:14 1288
So Joshua *b* them, and sent them Josh 22:6 1288
unto their tents, then he *b* them Josh 22:7 1288
and the children of Israel *b* God Josh 22:33 1288
therefore he *b* you still Josh 24:10 1288
B above women shall Jael the wife Judg 5:24 1288
b shall she be above women in the Judg 5:24 1288
the child grew, and the LORD *b* him Judg 13:24 1288
B be thou of the LORD, my son Judg 17:2 1288
b be he that did take knowledge Ruth 2:19 1288
B be he of the LORD, who hath not Ruth 2:20 1288
B be thou of the LORD, my Ruth 3:10 1288
B be the LORD, which hath not Ruth 4:14 1288
Eli *b* Elkanah and his wife, and 1Sa 2:20 1288
unto him, *B* be thou of the LORD 1Sa 15:13 1288
And Saul said, *B* be ye of the LORD 1Sa 23:21 1288
B be the LORD God of Israel, 1Sa 25:32 1288
b be thy advice, and *b* be 1Sa 25:33 1288
B be the LORD, that hath pleaded 1Sa 25:39 1288
to David, *B* be thou, my son David 1Sa 26:25 1288
B be ye of the LORD, that ye have 2Sa 2:5 1288
the LORD *b* Obed-edom, and all his 2Sa 6:11 1288
The LORD hath *b* the house of 2Sa 6:12 1288
he *b* the people in the name of 2Sa 6:18 1288
of thy servant be *b* for ever 2Sa 7:29 1288
he would not go, but *b* him 2Sa 13:25 1288
B be the LORD thy God, which hath 2Sa 18:28 1288
king kissed Barzillai, and *b* him 2Sa 19:39 1288
and *b* be my rock 2Sa 22:47 1288
B be the LORD God of Israel, 1Kin 1:48 1288
And king Solomon shall be *b* 1Kin 2:45 1288
B be the LORD this day, which 1Kin 5:7 1288
b all the congregation of Israel 1Kin 8:14 1288
B be the LORD God of Israel, 1Kin 8:15 1288
b all the congregation of Israel 1Kin 8:55 1288
B be the LORD, that hath given 1Kin 8:56 1288
they *b* the king, and went unto 1Kin 8:66 1288
B be the LORD thy God, which 1Kin 10:9 1288
the LORD *b* the house of Obed-edom 1Chr 13:14 1288
he *b* the people in the name of 1Chr 16:2 1288
B be the LORD God of Israel for 1Chr 16:36 1288
O LORD, and it shall be *b* for ever 1Chr 17:27 1288
for God *b* him 1Chr 26:5 1288
Wherefore David *b* the LORD before 1Chr 29:10 1288
B be thou, LORD God of Israel our 1Chr 29:10 1288
all the congregation *b* the LORD 1Chr 29:20 1288
B be the LORD God of Israel, that 2Chr 2:12 1288
b the whole congregation of 2Chr 6:3 1288
B be the LORD God of Israel, who 2Chr 6:4 1288
B be the LORD thy God, which 2Chr 9:8 1288
for there they *b* the LORD 2Chr 20:26 1288
the Levites arose and *b* the people 2Chr 30:27 1288
they *b* the LORD, and his people 2Chr 31:8 1288
for the LORD hath *b* his people 2Chr 31:10 1288
B be the LORD God of our fathers, Ezr 7:27 1288
Ezra *b* the LORD, the great God Neh 8:6 1288
b be thy glorious name, which is Neh 9:5 1288
the people *b* all the men, that Neh 11:2 1288
thou hast *b* the work of his hands Job 1:10 1288
b be the name of the LORD Job 1:21 1288
the ear heard me, then it *b* me Job 29:11 833
If his loins have not *b* me Job 31:20 1288
So the LORD *b* the latter end of Job 42:12 1288
B is the man that walketh not in Ps 1:1 835
B are all they that put their Ps 2:12 835
and *b* be my rock Ps 18:46 1288
hast made him most *b* for ever Ps 21:6 1293
B be the LORD, because he hath Ps 28:6 1288
B be the LORD Ps 31:21 1288
B is he whose transgression is Ps 32:1 835
B is the man unto whom the LORD Ps 32:2 835
B is the nation whose God is the Ps 33:12 835
b is the man that trusteth in him Ps 34:8 835
For such as be *b* of him shall Ps 37:22 1288
and his seed is *b* Ps 37:26 1293
B is that man that maketh the Ps 40:4 835
B is he that considereth the poor Ps 41:1 835
he shall be *b* upon the earth Ps 41:2 833
B be the LORD God of Israel from Ps 41:13 1288
God hath *b* thee for ever Ps 45:2 1288
while he lived he *b* his soul Ps 49:18 1288
B is the man whom thou choosest, Ps 65:4 835
B be God, which hath not turned Ps 66:20 1288
B be the Lord, who daily loadeth Ps 68:19 1288
B be God Ps 68:35 1288
and men shall be *b* in him Ps 72:17 1288
all nations shall call him *b* Ps 72:17 833
B be the LORD God, the God of Ps 72:18 1288
b be his glorious name for ever Ps 72:19 1288
B are they that dwell in thy Ps 84:4 835
B is the man whose strength is in Ps 84:5 835
b is the man that trusteth in Ps 84:12 835
B is the people that know the Ps 89:15 835
B be the LORD for evermore Ps 89:52 1288
B is the man whom thou chastenest Ps 94:12 835
B are they that keep judgment, and Ps 106:3 835
B be the LORD God of Israel from Ps 106:48 1288
B is the man that feareth the Ps 112:1 835
of the upright shall be *b* Ps 112:2 1288
B be the name of the LORD from Ps 113:2 1288
Ye are *b* of the LORD which made Ps 115:15 1288
B be he that cometh in the name Ps 118:26 1288
we have *b* you out of the house of Ps 118:26 1288
B are the undefiled in the way, Ps 119:1 835
B are they that keep his Ps 119:2 835
B art thou, O LORD Ps 119:12 1288
B be the LORD, who hath not given Ps 124:6 1288
B is every one that feareth the Ps 128:1 835
man be *b* that feareth the LORD Ps 128:4 1288
B be the LORD out of Zion, which Ps 135:21 1288
B be the LORD my strength, which Ps 144:1 1288
he hath *b* thy children within Ps 147:13 1288
Let thy fountain be *b* Prov 5:18 1288
for *b* are they that keep my ways Prov 8:32 835
B is the man that heareth me, Prov 8:34 835
The memory of the just is *b* Prov 10:7 1293
his children are *b* after him Prov 20:7 835
the end thereof shall not be *b* Prov 20:21 1288
hath a bountiful eye shall be *b* Prov 22:9 1288
children arise up, and call her *b* Prov 31:28 833
B art thou, O land, when thy king Eccl 10:17 835
The daughters saw her, and *b* her Song 6:9 833
B be Egypt my people, and Assyria Is 19:25 1288
b are all they that wait for him Is 30:18 835
B are ye that sow beside all Is 32:20 835
alone, and *b* him, and increased him Is 51:2 1288
B is the man that doeth this, and Is 56:2 835
the seed which the LORD hath *b* Is 61:9 1288
are the seed of the *b* of the LORD Is 65:23 1288
incense, as if he *b* an idol Is 66:3 1288
B is the man that trusteth in the Jer 17:7 1288
wherein my mother bare me be *b* Jer 20:14 1288
B be the glory of the LORD from Eze 3:12 1288
Then Daniel *b* the God of heaven Dan 2:19 1289
B be the name of God for ever and Dan 2:20 1289
B be the God of Shadrach, Meshach Dan 3:28 1289
I *b* the most High, and I praised Dan 4:34 1289
B is he that waiteth, and cometh Dan 12:12 835
that sell them say, *B* be the LORD Zec 11:5 1288
And all nations shall call you *b* Mal 3:12 833
B are the poor in spirit Mt 5:3 *3107*
B are they that mourn Mt 5:4 *3107*
B are the meek Mt 5:5 *3107*
B are they which do hunger and Mt 5:6 *3107*
B are the merciful Mt 5:7 *3107*
B are the pure in heart Mt 5:8 *3107*
B are the peacemakers Mt 5:9 *3107*
B are they which are persecuted Mt 5:10 *3107*
B are ye, when men shall revile Mt 5:11 *3107*
b is he, whosoever shall not be Mt 11:6 *3107*
But *b* are your eyes, for they see Mt 13:16 *3107*
and looking up to heaven, he *b* Mt 14:19 *2127*
B art thou, Simon Bar-jona Mt 16:17 *3107*
B is he that cometh in the name Mt 21:9 *2127*
B is he that cometh in the name Mt 23:39 *2127*
B is that servant, whom his lord Mt 24:46 *3107*
ye *b* of my Father, inherit the Mt 25:34 *2127*
b it, and brake it, and gave it to Mt 26:26 *2127*
he looked up to heaven, and *b* Mk 6:41 *2127*
and he *b*, and commanded to set them Mk 8:7 *2127*
his hands upon them, and *b* them Mk 10:16 *2127*
B is he that cometh in the name Mk 11:9 *2127*
B be the kingdom of our father Mk 11:10 *2127*
did eat, Jesus took bread, and *b* Mk 14:22 *2127*
thou the Christ, the Son of the *B* Mk 14:61 *2128*
b art thou among women Lk 1:28 *2127*
B art thou among women, and Lk 1:42 *2127*
b is the fruit of thy womb Lk 1:42 *2127*
And *b* is she that believed Lk 1:45 *3107*
all generations shall call me *b* Lk 1:48 *3106*
B be the Lord God of Israel Lk 1:68 *2128*
in his arms, and *b* God, and said, Lk 2:28 *2127*
And Simeon *b* them, and said unto Lk 2:34 *2127*
disciples, and said, *B* be ye poor Lk 6:20 *3107*
B are ye that hunger now Lk 6:21 *3107*
B are ye that weep now Lk 6:21 *3107*
B are ye, when men shall hate you Lk 6:22 *3107*
b is he, whosoever shall not be Lk 7:23 *3107*
he *b* them, and brake, and gave to Lk 9:16 *2127*
B are the eyes which see the Lk 10:23 *3107*
B is the womb that bare thee, and Lk 11:27 *3107*
b are they that hear the word of Lk 11:28 *3107*
B are those servants, whom the Lk 12:37 *3107*
them so, *b* are those servants Lk 12:38 *3107*
B is that servant, whom his lord Lk 12:43 *3107*
B is he that cometh in the name Lk 13:35 *2127*
And thou shalt be *b* Lk 14:14 *3107*
B is he that shall eat bread in Lk 14:15 *3107*
B be the King that cometh in the Lk 19:38 *2127*
B are the barren, and the wombs Lk 23:29 *3107*
b it, and brake, and gave to them Lk 24:30 *2127*
he lifted up his hands, and *b* them Lk 24:50 *2127*
it came to pass, while he *b* them Lk 24:51 *2127*
B is the King of Israel that Jn 12:13 *2127*
b are they that have not seen, and Jn 20:29 *3107*
the kindreds of the earth be *b* Acts 3:25 *1757*
It is more *b* to give than to Acts 20:35 *3107*
the Creator, who is *b* for ever Rom 1:25 *2128*
B are they whose iniquities are Rom 4:7 *3107*
B is the man to whom the Lord Rom 4:8 *3107*
who is over all, God *b* for ever Rom 9:5 *2128*
B be God, even the Father of our 2Cor 1:3 *2128*
which is *b* for evermore, knoweth 2Cor 11:31 *2128*
In thee shall all nations be *b* Gal 3:8 *1757*
faith are *b* with faithful Abraham Gal 3:9 *2127*
B be the God and Father of our Eph 1:3 *2128*
who hath *b* us with all spiritual Eph 1:3 *2127*
the glorious gospel of the *b* God 1Ti 1:11 *3107*
times he shall shew, who is the *b* 1Ti 6:15 *3107*
Looking for that *b* hope, and the Titus 2:13 *3107*
slaughter of the kings, and *b* him Heb 7:1 *2127*
b him that had the promises Heb 7:6 *2127*
the less is *b* of the better Heb 7:7 *2127*
By faith Isaac *b* Jacob and Esau Heb 11:20 *2127*
b both the sons of Joseph Heb 11:21 *2127*
B is the man that endureth Jas 1:12 *3107*
this man shall be *b* in his deed Jas 1:25 *3107*
B be the God and Father of our 1Pet 1:3 *2128*
B is he that readeth, and they Rev 1:3 *3107*
B are the dead which die in the Rev 14:13 *3107*
B is he that watcheth, and keepeth Rev 16:15 *3107*
B are they which are called unto Rev 19:9 *3107*
B and holy is he that hath part in Rev 20:6 *3107*
b is he that keepeth the sayings Rev 22:7 *3107*
B are they that do his Rev 22:14 *3107*

BLESSEDNESS {3}
also describeth the *b* of the man Rom 4:6 *3108*
Cometh this *b* then upon the Rom 4:9 *3108*
Where is then the *b* ye spake of Gal 4:15 *3108*

BLESSEST {3}
that he whom thou *b* is blessed Num 22:6 1288
for thou *b*, O LORD, and it shall 1Chr 17:27 1288
thou *b* the springing thereof Ps 65:10 1288

BLESSETH {8}
and blessed be he that *b* thee Gen 27:29 1288
Blessed is he that *b* thee Num 24:9 1288
For the LORD thy God *b* thee Deut 15:6 1288
b the covetous, whom the LORD Ps 10:3 1288
He *b* them also, so that they are Ps 107:38 1288
but he *b* the habitation of the Prov 3:33 1288
He that *b* his friend with a loud Prov 27:14 1288
That he who *b* himself in the Is 65:16 1288

BLESSING {67}
and thou shalt be a *b* Gen 12:2 1293
That in *b* I will bless thee, and Gen 22:17 1288

bring a curse upon me, and not a *b* ... Gen 27:12 1293
Isaac had made an end of *b* Jacob ... Gen 27:30 1293
and hath taken away thy *b* ... Gen 27:35 1293
now he hath taken away my *b* ... Gen 27:36 1293
Hast thou not reserved a *b* for me ... Gen 27:36 1293
his father, Hast thou but one *b* ... Gen 27:38 1293
b wherewith his father blessed ... Gen 27:41 1293
And give thee the *b* of Abraham ... Gen 28:4 1293
my *b* that is brought to thee ... Gen 33:11 1293
the *b* of the LORD was upon all ... Gen 39:5 1293
to his *b* he blessed them ... Gen 49:28 1293
may bestow upon you a *b* this day ... Ex 32:29 1293
Then I will command my *b* upon you ... Lev 25:21 1293
I set before you this day a *b* ... Deut 11:26 1293
A *b*, if ye obey the commandments ... Deut 11:27 1293
put the *b* upon mount Gerizim ... Deut 11:29 1293
according to the *b* of the LORD ... Deut 12:15 1293
according to the *b* of the LORD ... Deut 16:17 1293
the curse into a *b* unto thee ... Deut 23:5 1293
The LORD shall command the *b* upon ... Deut 28:8 1293
things are come upon thee, the *b* ... Deut 30:1 1293
set before you life and death, *b* ... Deut 30:19 1293
And this is the *b*, wherewith Moses ... Deut 33:1 1293
And this is the *b* of Judah ... Deut 33:7
let the *b* come upon the head of ... Deut 33:16
and full with the *b* of the LORD ... Deut 33:23 1293
Who answered, Give me a *b* ... Josh 15:19 1293
And she said unto him, Give me a *b* ... Judg 1:15 1293
now this *b* which thine handmaid ... 1Sa 25:27 1293
with thy *b* let the house of thy ... 2Sa 7:29 1293
thee, take a *b* of thy servant ... 2Kin 5:15 1293
which is exalted above all *b* ... Neh 9:5 1293
our God turned the curse into a *b* ... Neh 13:2 1293
The *b* of him that was ready to ... Job 29:13 1293
thy *b* is upon thy people ... Ps 3:8 1293
shall receive the *b* from the LORD ... Ps 24:5 1293
as he delighted not in *b*, so let ... Ps 109:17 1293
The *b* of the LORD be upon you ... Ps 129:8 1293
there the LORD commanded the *b* ... Ps 133:3 1293
The *b* of the LORD, it maketh rich ... Prov 10:22 1293
By the *b* of the upright the city ... Prov 11:11 1293
but *b* shall be upon the head of ... Prov 11:26 1293
a good *b* shall come upon them ... Prov 24:25 1293
even a *b* in the midst of the land ... Is 19:24 1293
my *b* upon thine offspring ... Is 44:3 1293
for a *b* is in it ... Is 65:8 1293
places round about my hill a *b* ... Eze 34:26 1293
there shall be showers of *b* ... Eze 34:26 1293
that he may cause the *b* to rest ... Eze 44:30 1293
repent, and leave a *b* behind him ... Joel 2:14 1293
I save you, and ye shall be a *b* ... Zec 8:13 1293
of heaven, and pour you out a *b* ... Mal 3:10 1293
in the temple, praising and *b* God ... Lk 24:53 *2127*
of the *b* of the gospel of Christ ... Rom 15:29 *2129*
The cup of *b* which we bless, is ... 1Cor 10:16 *2129*
That the *b* of Abraham might come ... Gal 3:14 *2129*
is dressed, receiveth *b* from God ... Heb 6:7 *2129*
Surely *b* I will bless thee, and ... Heb 6:14 *2129*
he would have inherited the *b* ... Heb 12:17 *2129*
of the same mouth proceedeth *b* ... Jas 3:10 *2129*
but contrariwise *b* ... 1Pet 3:9 *2129*
that ye should inherit a *b* ... 1Pet 3:9 *2129*
and honour, and glory, and *b* ... Rev 5:12 *2129*
are in them, heard I saying, *B* ... Rev 5:13 *2129*
B, and glory, and wisdom, and ... Rev 7:12 *2129*

BLESSINGS {12}
bless thee with *b* of heaven above ... Gen 49:25 1293
b of the deep that lieth under, ... Gen 49:25 1293
b of the breasts, and of the womb ... Gen 49:25 1293
The *b* of thy father have ... Gen 49:26 1293
the *b* of my progenitors unto the ... Gen 49:26 1293
all these *b* shall come on thee, ... Deut 28:2 1293
all the words of the law, the *b* ... Josh 8:34 1293
him with the *b* of goodness ... Ps 21:3 1293
B are upon the head of the just ... Prov 10:6 1293
faithful man shall abound with *b* ... Prov 28:20 1293
upon you, and I will curse your *b* ... Mal 2:2 1293
b in heavenly places in Christ ... Eph 1:3 *2129*

BLEW {23}
the LORD, and *b* with the trumpets ... Josh 6:8 8628
priests that *b* with the trumpets ... Josh 6:9 8628
and *b* with the trumpets ... Josh 6:13 8628
when the priests *b* with the ... Josh 6:16 8628
the priests *b* with the trumpets ... Josh 6:20 8628
that he *b* a trumpet in the ... Judg 3:27 8628
upon Gideon, and he *b* a trumpet ... Judg 6:34 8628
they *b* the trumpets, and brake the ... Judg 7:19 8628
three companies *b* the trumpets ... Judg 7:20 8628
the three hundred *b* the trumpets ... Judg 7:22 8628
Saul *b* the trumpet throughout all ... 1Sa 13:3 8628
So Joab *b* a trumpet, and all the ... 2Sa 2:28 8628
Joab *b* the trumpet, and the people ... 2Sa 18:16 8628
he *b* a trumpet, and said, We have ... 2Sa 20:1 8628
he *b* a trumpet, and they retired ... 2Sa 20:22 8628
And they *b* the trumpet ... 1Kin 1:39 8628
b with trumpets, saying, Jehu is ... 2Kin 9:13 8628
land rejoiced, and *b* with trumpets ... 2Kin 11:14 8628
the floods came, and the winds *b* ... Mt 7:25 *4154*
the floods came, and the winds *b* ... Mt 7:27 *4154*
by reason of a great wind that *b* ... Jn 6:18 *4154*
And when the south wind *b* softly ... Acts 27:13 *5285*
and after one day the south wind *b* ... Acts 28:13 *1920*

BLIND {86}
or deaf, or the seeing, or the *b* ... Ex 4:11 5787
put a stumblingblock before the *b* ... Lev 19:14 5787
a *b* man, or a lame, or he that ... Lev 21:18 5787
B, or broken, or maimed, or ... Lev 22:22 5788
therein, as if it be lame, or *b* ... Deut 15:21 5787
for a gift doth *b* the eyes of the ... Deut 16:19 5786
the *b* to wander out of the way ... Deut 27:18 5787
as the *b* gropeth in darkness, and ... Deut 28:29 5787
bribe to *b* mine eyes therewith ... 1Sa 12:3 5956
Except thou take away the *b* ... 2Sa 5:6 5787
Jebusites, and the lame and the *b* ... 2Sa 5:8 5787
Wherefore they said, The *b* ... 2Sa 5:8 5787
I was eyes to the *b*, and feet was ... Job 29:15 5787
LORD openeth the eyes of the *b* ... Ps 146:8 5787
the eyes of the *b* shall see out ... Is 29:18 5787
the eyes of the *b* shall be opened ... Is 35:5 5787
To open the *b* eyes, to bring out ... Is 42:7 5787
I will bring the *b* by a way that ... Is 42:16 5787
and look, ye *b*, that ye may see ... Is 42:18 5787
Who is *b*, but my servant ... Is 42:19 5787
who is *b* as he that is perfect, ... Is 42:19 5787
and *b* as the LORD's servant ... Is 42:19 5787
Bring forth the *b* people that ... Is 43:8 5787
His watchmen are *b* ... Is 56:10 5787
We grope for the wall like the *b* ... Is 59:10 5787
of the earth, and with them the *b* ... Jer 31:8 5787
wandered as *b* men in the streets ... Lam 4:14 5787
that they shall walk like *b* men ... Zeph 1:17 5787
if ye offer the *b* for sacrifice ... Mal 1:8 5787
two *b* men followed him, crying, ... Mt 9:27 *5185*
the house, the *b* men came to him ... Mt 9:28 *5185*
The *b* receive their sight, and the ... Mt 11:5 *5185*
him one possessed with a devil, *b* ... Mt 12:22 *5185*
healed him, insomuch that the *b* ... Mt 12:22 *5185*
they be *b* leaders of the *b* ... Mt 15:14 *5185*
they be *b* leaders of the *b* ... Mt 15:14 *5185*
if the *b* lead the *b*, both ... Mt 15:14 *5185*
And if the *b* lead the *b* ... Mt 15:14 *5185*
with them those that were lame, *b* ... Mt 15:30 *5185*
the lame to walk, and the *b* to see ... Mt 15:31 *5185*
two *b* men sitting by the way side ... Mt 20:30 *5185*
And the *b* and the lame came to him ... Mt 21:14 *5185*
ye *b* guides, which say, Whosoever ... Mt 23:16 *5185*
Ye fools and *b*: ... Mt 23:17 *5185*
Ye fools and *b*: ... Mt 23:19 *5185*
Ye *b* guides, which strain at a ... Mt 23:24 *5185*
Thou *b* Pharisee, cleanse first ... Mt 23:26 *5185*
and they bring a *b* man unto him ... Mk 8:22 *5185*
he took the *b* man by the hand, and ... Mk 8:23 *5185*
b Bartimaeus, the son of Timaeus, ... Mk 10:46 *5185*
And they call the *b* man, saying ... Mk 10:49 *5185*
The *b* man said unto him, Lord, ... Mk 10:51 *5185*
and recovering of sight to the *b* ... Lk 4:18 *5185*
them, Can the *b* lead the *b* ... Lk 6:39 *5185*
many that were *b* he gave sight ... Lk 7:21 *5185*
how that the *b* see, the lame walk ... Lk 7:22 *5185*
poor, the maimed, the lame, the *b* ... Lk 14:13 *5185*
the maimed, and the halt, and the *b* ... Lk 14:21 *5185*
a certain *b* man sat by the way ... Lk 18:35 *5185*
multitude of impotent folk, of *b* ... Jn 5:3 *5185*
a man which was *b* from his birth ... Jn 9:1 *5185*
his parents, that he was born *b* ... Jn 9:2 *5185*
eyes of the *b* man with the clay ... Jn 9:6 *5185*
before had seen him that he was *b* ... Jn 9:8 *5185*
him that aforetime was *b* ... Jn 9:13 *5185*
They say unto the *b* man again ... Jn 9:17 *5185*
him, that he had been *b*, and ... Jn 9:18 *5185*
your son, who ye say was born *b* ... Jn 9:19 *5185*
is our son, and that he was born *b* ... Jn 9:20 *5185*
called they the man that was *b* ... Jn 9:24 *5185*
I know, that, whereas I was *b* ... Jn 9:25 *5185*
the eyes of one that was born *b* ... Jn 9:32 *5185*
they which see might be made *b* ... Jn 9:39 *5185*
and said unto him, Are we *b* also ... Jn 9:40 *5185*
said unto them, If ye were *b* ... Jn 9:41 *5185*
a devil open the eyes of the *b* ... Jn 10:21 *5185*
which opened the eyes of the *b* ... Jn 11:37 *5185*
is upon thee, and thou shalt be *b* ... Acts 13:11 *5185*
thou thyself art a guide of the *b* ... Rom 2:19 *5185*
he that lacketh these things is *b* ... 2Pet 1:9 *5185*
and miserable, and poor, and *b* ... Rev 3:17 *5185*

BLINDED {5}
He hath *b* their eyes, and hardened ... Jn 12:40 *5186*
obtained it, and the rest were *b* ... Rom 11:7 *4456*
But their minds were *b* ... 2Cor 3:14 *4456*
b the minds of them which believe ... 2Cor 4:4 *5186*
that darkness hath *b* his eyes ... 1Jn 2:11 *5186*

BLINDETH {1}
for the gift *b* the wise, and ... Ex 23:8 5786

BLINDFOLDED {1}
And when they had *b* him, they ... Lk 22:64 *4028*

BLINDNESS {7}
at the door of the house with *b* ... Gen 19:11 5575
smite thee with madness, and *b* ... Deut 28:28 5788
this people, I pray thee, with *b* ... 2Kin 6:18 5575
he smote them with *b* according to ... 2Kin 6:18 5575
every horse of the people with *b* ... Zec 12:4 5788
that *b* in part is happened to ... Rom 11:25 *4457*
because of the *b* of their heart ... Eph 4:18 *4457*

BLOOD {447}
the voice of thy brother's *b* ... Gen 4:10 1818
thy brother's *b* from thy hand ... Gen 4:11 1818
thereof, which is the *b* thereof ... Gen 9:4 1818
surely your *b* of your lives will ... Gen 9:5 1818
Whoso sheddeth man's *b*, ... Gen 9:6 1818
by man shall his *b* be shed ... Gen 9:6 1818
Reuben said unto them, Shed no *b* ... Gen 37:22 1818
our brother, and conceal his *b* ... Gen 37:26 1818
and dipped the coat in the *b* ... Gen 37:31 1818
behold, also his *b* is required ... Gen 42:22 1818
and his clothes in the *b* of grapes ... Gen 49:11 1818
shall become *b* upon the dry land ... Ex 4:9 1818
and they shall be turned to *b* ... Ex 7:17 1818
of water, that they may become *b* ... Ex 7:19 1818
that there may be *b* throughout ... Ex 7:19 1818
in the river were turned to *b* ... Ex 7:20 1818
there was *b* throughout all the ... Ex 7:21 1818
And they shall take of the *b* ... Ex 12:7 1818
the *b* shall be to you for a token ... Ex 12:13 1818
and when I see the *b*, I will pass ... Ex 12:13 1818
dip it in the *b* that is in the ... Ex 12:22 1818
with the *b* that is in the bason ... Ex 12:22 1818
he seeth the *b* upon the lintel ... Ex 12:23 1818
there shall no *b* be shed for him ... Ex 22:2 1818
there shall be *b* shed for him ... Ex 22:3 1818
Thou shalt not offer the *b* of my ... Ex 23:18 1818
And Moses took half of the *b* ... Ex 24:6 1818
half of the *b* he sprinkled on the ... Ex 24:6 1818
And Moses took the *b*, and sprinkled ... Ex 24:8 1818
Behold the *b* of the covenant, ... Ex 24:8 1818
take of the *b* of the bullock ... Ex 29:12 1818
pour all the *b* beside the bottom ... Ex 29:12 1818
the ram, and thou shalt take his *b* ... Ex 29:16 1818
kill the ram, and take of his *b* ... Ex 29:20 1818
sprinkle the *b* upon the altar ... Ex 29:20 1818
of the *b* that is upon the altar ... Ex 29:21 1818
with the *b* of the sin offering of ... Ex 30:10 1818
Thou shalt not offer the *b* of my ... Ex 34:25 1818
Aaron's sons, shall bring the *b* ... Lev 1:5 1818
sprinkle the *b* round about upon ... Lev 1:5 1818
shall sprinkle his *b* round about ... Lev 1:11 1818
the *b* thereof shall be wrung out ... Lev 1:15 1818
the *b* upon the altar round about ... Lev 3:2 1818
b thereof round about upon the ... Lev 3:8 1818
of Aaron shall sprinkle the *b* ... Lev 3:13 1818
that ye eat neither fat nor *b* ... Lev 3:17 1818
shall take of the bullock's *b* ... Lev 4:5 1818
shall dip his finger in the *b* ... Lev 4:6 1818
sprinkle of the *b* seven times ... Lev 4:6 1818
priest shall put some of the *b* ... Lev 4:7 1818
shall pour all the *b* of the ... Lev 4:7 1818
b to the tabernacle of the ... Lev 4:16 1818
dip his finger in some of the *b* ... Lev 4:17 1818
he shall put some of the *b* upon ... Lev 4:18 1818
shall pour out all the *b* at the ... Lev 4:18 1818
b of the sin offering with his ... Lev 4:25 1818
shall pour out his *b* at the ... Lev 4:25 1818
of the *b* thereof with his finger ... Lev 4:30 1818
shall pour out all the *b* thereof ... Lev 4:30 1818
b of the sin offering with his ... Lev 4:34 1818
shall pour out all the *b* thereof ... Lev 4:34 1818
he shall sprinkle of the *b* of the ... Lev 5:9 1818
the rest of the *b* shall be wrung ... Lev 5:9 1818
of the *b* thereof upon any garment ... Lev 6:27 1818
whereof any of the *b* is brought ... Lev 6:30 1818
the *b* thereof shall he sprinkle ... Lev 7:2 1818
the *b* of the peace offerings ... Lev 7:14 1818
ye shall eat no manner of *b* ... Lev 7:26 1818
it be that eateth any manner of *b* ... Lev 7:27 1818
that offereth the *b* of the peace ... Lev 7:33 1818
and Moses took the *b*, and put it ... Lev 8:15 1818
poured the *b* at the bottom of the ... Lev 8:15 1818
Moses sprinkled the *b* upon the ... Lev 8:19 1818
and Moses took of the *b* of it ... Lev 8:23 1818
Moses put of the *b* upon the tip ... Lev 8:24 1818
Moses sprinkled the *b* upon the ... Lev 8:24 1818
of the *b* which was upon the altar ... Lev 8:30 1818
of Aaron brought the *b* unto him ... Lev 9:9 1818
and he dipped his finger in the *b* ... Lev 9:9 1818
poured out the *b* at the bottom of ... Lev 9:9 1818
sons presented unto him the *b* ... Lev 9:12 1818
sons presented unto him the *b* ... Lev 9:18 1818
the *b* of it was not brought in ... Lev 10:18 1818
in the *b* of her purifying three ... Lev 12:4 1818
she shall continue in the *b* of ... Lev 12:5 1818
cleansed from the issue of her *b* ... Lev 12:7 1818
the living bird in the *b* of the ... Lev 14:6 1818
of the *b* of the trespass offering ... Lev 14:14 1818
upon the *b* of the trespass ... Lev 14:17 1818
of the *b* of the trespass offering ... Lev 14:25 1818
upon the place of the *b* of the ... Lev 14:28 1818
dip them in the *b* of the slain ... Lev 14:51 1818
the house with the *b* of the bird ... Lev 14:52 1818
and her issue in her flesh be *b* ... Lev 15:19 1818
b many days out of the time of ... Lev 15:25 1818
take of the *b* of the bullock ... Lev 16:14 1818
the *b* with his finger seven times ... Lev 16:14 1818
bring his *b* within the vail, and ... Lev 16:15 1818
do with that *b* as he did with the ... Lev 16:15 1818
he did with the *b* of the bullock ... Lev 16:15 1818
take of the *b* of the bullock ... Lev 16:18 1818
of the *b* of the goat, and put it ... Lev 16:18 1818
he shall sprinkle of the *b* upon ... Lev 16:19 1818
whose *b* was brought in to make ... Lev 16:27 1818
b shall be imputed unto that man ... Lev 17:4 1818
he hath shed *b* ... Lev 17:4 1818
b upon the altar of the LORD at ... Lev 17:6 1818
you, that eateth any manner of *b* ... Lev 17:10 1818
against that soul that eateth *b* ... Lev 17:10 1818
the life of the flesh is in the *b* ... Lev 17:11 1818
for it is the *b* that maketh an ... Lev 17:11 1818
No soul of you shall eat *b* ... Lev 17:12 1818
that sojourneth among you eat *b* ... Lev 17:12 1818
shall even pour out the *b* thereof ... Lev 17:13 1818
the *b* of it is for the life ... Lev 17:14 1818
Ye shall eat the *b* of no manner ... Lev 17:14 1818
of all flesh is the *b* thereof ... Lev 17:14 1818
against the *b* of thy neighbour ... Lev 19:16 1818

not eat any thing with the *b* .... Lev 19:26 1818
his *b* shall be upon him .... Lev 20:9 1818
their *b* shall be upon them .... Lev 20:11 1818
their *b* shall be upon them .... Lev 20:12 1818
their *b* shall be upon them .... Lev 20:13 1818
their *b* shall be upon them .... Lev 20:16 1818
uncovered the fountain of her *b* .... Lev 20:18 1818
their *b* shall be upon them .... Lev 20:27 1818
sprinkle their *b* upon the altar .... Num 18:17 1818
take of her *b* with his finger .... Num 19:4 1818
sprinkle of her *b* directly before .... Num 19:4 1818
her skin, and her flesh, and her *b* .... Num 19:5 1818
prey, and drink the *b* of the slain .... Num 23:24 1818
The revenger of *b* himself shall .... Num 35:19 1818
the revenger of *b* shall slay the .... Num 35:21 1818
the revenger of *b* according to .... Num 35:24 1818
of the hand of the revenger of *b* .... Num 35:25 1818
the revenger of *b* find him .... Num 35:27 1818
the revenger of *b* kill the slayer .... Num 35:27 1818
he shall not be guilty of *b* .... Num 35:27 1818
for *b* it defileth the land .... Num 35:33 1818
of the *b* that is shed therein .... Num 35:33 1818
but by the *b* of him that shed it .... Num 35:33 1818
Only ye shall not eat the *b* .... Deut 12:16 1818
be sure that thou eat not the *b* .... Deut 12:23 1818
for the *b* is the life .... Deut 12:23 1818
offerings, the flesh and the *b* .... Deut 12:27 1818
the *b* of thy sacrifices shall be .... Deut 12:27 1818
thou shalt not eat the *b* thereof .... Deut 15:23 1818
in judgment, between *b* and *b* .... Deut 17:8 1818
of the *b* pursue the slayer .... Deut 19:6 1818
That innocent *b* be not shed in .... Deut 19:10 1818
inheritance, and so *b* be upon thee .... Deut 19:10 1818
into the hand of the avenger of *b* .... Deut 19:12 1818
guilt of innocent *b* from Israel .... Deut 19:13 1818
Our hands have not shed this *b* .... Deut 21:7 1818
lay not innocent *b* unto thy .... Deut 21:8 1818
the *b* shall be forgiven them .... Deut 21:8 1818
of innocent *b* from among you .... Deut 21:9 1818
thou bring not *b* upon thine house .... Deut 22:8 1818
drink the pure *b* of the grape .... Deut 32:14 1818
make mine arrows drunk with *b* .... Deut 32:42 1818
and that with the *b* of the slain .... Deut 32:42 1818
will avenge the *b* of his servants .... Deut 32:43 1818
his *b* shall be upon his head, and .... Josh 2:19 1818
his *b* shall be on our head, if .... Josh 2:19 1818
your refuge from the avenger of *b* .... Josh 20:3 1818
the avenger of *b* pursue after him .... Josh 20:5 1818
by the hand of the avenger of *b* .... Josh 20:9 1818
their *b* be laid upon Abimelech .... Judg 9:24 1818
people did eat them with the *b* 1Sa 14:32 1818
LORD, in that they eat with the *b* 1Sa 14:33 1818
the LORD in eating with the *b* 1Sa 14:34 1818
wilt thou sin against innocent *b* 1Sa 19:5 1818
thee from coming to shed *b* 1Sa 25:26 1818
that thou hast shed *b* causeless 1Sa 25:31 1818
me this day from coming to shed *b* 1Sa 25:33 1818
let not my *b* fall to the earth 1Sa 26:20 1818
unto him, Thy *b* be upon thy head 2Sa 1:16 1818
From the *b* of the slain, from the 2Sa 1:22 1818
for the *b* of Asahel his brother 2Sa 3:27 1818
the *b* of Abner the son of Ner 2Sa 3:28 1818
now require his *b* of your hand 2Sa 4:11 1818
of *b* to destroy any more, lest 2Sa 14:11 1818
all the *b* of the house of Saul 2Sa 16:8 1818
Amasa wallowed in *b* in the midst 2Sa 20:12 1818
is not this the *b* of the men that 2Sa 23:17 1818
shed the *b* of war in peace, and 1Kin 2:5 1818
put the *b* of war upon his girdle 1Kin 2:5 1818
thou down to the grave with *b* 1Kin 2:9 1818
mayest take away the innocent *b* 1Kin 2:31 1818
return his *b* upon his own head 1Kin 2:32 1818
Their *b* shall therefore return 1Kin 2:33 1818
thy *b* shall be upon thine own 1Kin 2:37 1818
till the *b* gushed out upon them 1Kin 18:28 1818
b of Naboth shall dogs lick thy 1Kin 21:19 1818
of Naboth shall dogs lick thy *b* 1Kin 21:19 1818
the *b* ran out of the wound into 1Kin 22:35 1818
and the dogs licked up his *b* 1Kin 22:38 1818
on the other side as red as *b* 2Kin 3:22 1818
And they said, This is *b* 2Kin 3:23 1818
that I may avenge the *b* of my 2Kin 9:7 1818
the *b* of all the servants of the 2Kin 9:7 1818
seen yesterday the *b* of Naboth 2Kin 9:26 1818
the *b* of his sons, saith the LORD 2Kin 9:26 1818
some of her *b* was sprinkled on 2Kin 9:33 1818
sprinkled the *b* of his peace 2Kin 16:13 1818
all the *b* of the burnt offering 2Kin 16:15 1818
all the *b* of the sacrifice 2Kin 16:15 1818
shed innocent *b* very much 2Kin 21:16 1818
for the innocent *b* that he shed 2Kin 24:4 1818
filled Jerusalem with innocent *b* 2Kin 24:4 1818
shall I drink the *b* of these men 1Chr 11:19 1818
Thou hast shed *b* abundantly 1Chr 22:8 1818
much *b* upon the earth in my sight 1Chr 22:8 1818
been a man of war, and hast shed *b* 1Chr 28:3 1818
their cities, between *b* and *b* 2Chr 19:10 1818
the *b* of the sons of Jehoiada the 2Chr 24:25 1818
and the priests received the *b* 2Chr 29:22 1818
sprinkled the *b* upon the altar 2Chr 29:22 1818
sprinkled the *b* upon the altar 2Chr 29:22 1818
with their *b* upon the altar 2Chr 29:24 1818
the priests sprinkled the *b* 2Chr 30:16 1818
sprinkled the *b* from their hands 2Chr 35:11
O earth, cover not thou my *b* .... Job 16:18 1818
Her young ones also suck up *b* .... Job 39:30 1818
When he maketh inquisition for *b* .... Ps 9:12 1818
offerings of *b* will I not offer .... Ps 16:4 1818

What profit is there in my *b* .... Ps 30:9 1818
of bulls, or drink the *b* of goats .... Ps 50:13 1818
his feet in the *b* of the wicked .... Ps 58:10 1818
dipped in the *b* of thine enemies .... Ps 68:23 1818
shall their *b* be in his sight .... Ps 72:14 1818
And had turned their rivers into *b* .... Ps 78:44 1818
Their *b* have they shed like water .... Ps 79:3 1818
b of thy servants which is shed .... Ps 79:10 1818
and condemn the innocent *b* .... Ps 94:21 1818
He turned their waters into *b* .... Ps 105:29 1818
And shed innocent *b* .... Ps 106:38 1818
even the *b* of their sons and of .... Ps 106:38 1818
and the land was polluted with *b* .... Ps 106:38 1818
with us, let us lay wait for *b* .... Prov 1:11 1818
to evil, and make haste to shed *b* .... Prov 1:16 1818
And they lay wait for their own *b* .... Prov 1:18 1818
and hands that shed innocent *b* .... Prov 6:17 1818
wicked are to lie in wait for *b* .... Prov 12:6 1818
man that doeth violence to the *b* .... Prov 28:17 1818
of the nose bringeth forth *b* .... Prov 30:33 1818
delight not in the *b* of bullocks .... Is 1:11 1818
your hands are full of *b* .... Is 1:15 1818
shall have purged the *b* of .... Is 4:4 1818
noise, and garments rolled in *b* .... Is 9:5 1818
of Dimon shall be full of *b* .... Is 15:9 1818
earth also shall disclose her *b* .... Is 26:21 1818
his ears from hearing of *b* .... Is 33:15 1818
shall be melted with their *b* .... Is 34:3 1818
of the LORD is filled with *b* .... Is 34:6 1818
fatness, and with the *b* of lambs .... Is 34:6 1818
their land shall be soaked with *b* .... Is 34:7 1818
shall be drunken with their own *b* .... Is 49:26 1818
For your hands are defiled with *b* .... Is 59:3 1818
make haste to shed innocent *b* .... Is 59:7 1818
their *b* shall be sprinkled upon .... Is 63:3 5332
as if he offered swine's *b* .... Is 66:3 1818
the *b* of the souls of the poor .... Jer 2:34 1818
shed not innocent *b* in this place .... Jer 7:6 1818
pour out their *b* by the force of .... Jer 18:21
place with the *b* of innocents .... Jer 19:4 1818
shed innocent *b* in this place .... Jer 22:3 1818
and for to shed innocent *b* .... Jer 22:17 1818
bring innocent *b* upon yourselves .... Jer 26:15 1818
and made drunk with their *b* .... Jer 46:10 1818
keepeth back his sword from *b* .... Jer 48:10 1818
my *b* upon the inhabitants of .... Jer 51:35 1818
that have shed the *b* of the just .... Lam 4:13 1818
have polluted themselves with *b* .... Lam 4:14 1818
but his *b* will I require at thine .... Eze 3:18 1818
but his *b* will I require at thine .... Eze 3:20 1818
b shall pass through thee .... Eze 5:17 1818
great, and the land is full of *b* .... Eze 9:9 1818
and pour out my fury upon it in *b* .... Eze 14:19 1818
saw thee polluted in thine own *b* .... Eze 16:6 1818
unto thee when thou wast in thy *b* .... Eze 16:6 1818
unto thee when thou wast in thy *b* .... Eze 16:6 1818
washed away thy *b* from thee .... Eze 16:9 1818
bare, and wast polluted in thy *b* .... Eze 16:22 1818
by the *b* of thy children, which .... Eze 16:36 1818
wedlock and shed *b* are judged .... Eze 16:38 1818
and I will give thee *b* in fury .... Eze 16:38 1818
that is a robber, a shedder of *b* .... Eze 18:10 1818
his *b* shall be upon him .... Eze 18:13 1818
mother is like a vine in thy *b* .... Eze 19:10 1818
thy *b* shall be in the midst of .... Eze 21:32 1818
The city sheddeth *b* in the midst .... Eze 22:3 1818
in thy *b* that thou hast shed .... Eze 22:4 1818
in thee to their power to shed *b* .... Eze 22:6 1818
men that carry tales to shed *b* .... Eze 22:9 1818
have they taken gifts to shed *b* .... Eze 22:12 1818
at thy *b* which hath been in the .... Eze 22:13 1818
ravening the prey, to shed *b* .... Eze 22:27 1818
b is in their hands, and with .... Eze 23:37 1818
the manner of women that shed *b* .... Eze 23:45 1818
and *b* is in their hands .... Eze 23:45 1818
For her *b* is in the midst of her .... Eze 24:7 1818
I have set her *b* upon the top of .... Eze 24:8 1818
pestilence, and *b* into her street .... Eze 28:23 1818
I will also water with thy *b* the .... Eze 32:6 1818
his *b* shall be upon his own head .... Eze 33:4 1818
his *b* shall be upon him .... Eze 33:5 1818
but his *b* will I require at the .... Eze 33:6 1818
but his *b* will I require at thine .... Eze 33:8 1818
Ye eat with the *b*, and lift up .... Eze 33:25 1818
eyes toward your idols, and shed *b* .... Eze 33:25 1818
hast shed the *b* of the children .... Eze 35:5
b, and *b* shall pursue thee .... Eze 35:6 1818
b, even *b* shall pursue thee .... Eze 35:6 1818
my fury upon them for the *b* that .... Eze 36:18 1818
him with pestilence and with *b* .... Eze 38:22 1818
that ye may eat flesh, and drink *b* .... Eze 39:17 1818
drink the *b* of the princes of the .... Eze 39:18 1818
drink *b* till ye be drunken, of my .... Eze 39:19 1818
thereon, and to sprinkle *b* thereon .... Eze 43:18 1818
thou shalt take of the *b* thereof .... Eze 43:20 1818
offer my bread, the fat and the *b* .... Eze 44:7 1818
to offer unto me the fat and the *b* .... Eze 44:15 1818
take of the *b* of the sin offering .... Eze 45:19 1818
I will avenge the *b* of Jezreel .... Hos 1:4 1818
break out, and *b* toucheth *b* .... Hos 4:2 1818
iniquity, and is polluted with *b* .... Hos 6:8 1818
shall he leave his *b* upon him .... Hos 12:14 1818
in the heavens and in the earth, *b* .... Joel 2:30 1818
into darkness, and the moon into *b* .... Joel 2:31 1818
shed innocent *b* in their land .... Joel 3:19 1818
their *b* that I have not cleansed .... Joel 3:21 1818
and lay not upon us innocent *b* .... Jonah 1:14 1818
They build up Zion with *b* .... Mic 3:10 1818

they all lie in wait for *b* .... Mic 7:2 1818
because of men's *b*, and for the .... Hab 2:8 1818
him that buildeth a town with *b* .... Hab 2:12 1818
them afraid, because of men's *b* .... Hab 2:17 1818
their *b* shall be poured out as .... Zeph 1:17 1818
take away his *b* out of his mouth .... Zec 9:7 1818
by the *b* of thy covenant I have .... Zec 9:11 1818
with an issue of *b* twelve years .... Mt 9:20 *131*
b hath not revealed it unto thee .... Mt 16:17 *129*
them in the *b* of the prophets .... Mt 23:30 *129*
righteous *b* shed upon the earth .... Mt 23:35 *129*
b of righteous Abel unto the *b* .... Mt 23:35 *129*
For this is my *b* of the new .... Mt 26:28 *129*
I have betrayed the innocent *b* .... Mt 27:4 *129*
because it is the price of *b* .... Mt 27:6 *129*
field was called, The field of *b* .... Mt 27:8 *129*
of the *b* of this just person .... Mt 27:24 *129*
His *b* be on us, and on our .... Mt 27:25 *129*
had an issue of *b* twelve years .... Mk 5:25 *129*
fountain of her *b* was dried up .... Mk 5:29 *129*
This is my *b* of the new testament .... Mk 14:24 *129*
having an issue of *b* twelve years .... Lk 8:43 *129*
her issue of *b* stanched .... Lk 8:44 *129*
That the *b* of all the prophets .... Lk 11:50 *129*
From the *b* of Abel unto the *b* .... Lk 11:51 *129*
whose *b* Pilate had mingled with .... Lk 13:1 *129*
cup is the new testament in my *b* .... Lk 22:20 *129*
of *b* falling down to the ground .... Lk 22:44 *129*
Which were born, not of *b* .... Jn 1:13 *129*
of the Son of man, and drink his *b* .... Jn 6:53 *129*
eateth my flesh, and drinketh my *b* .... Jn 6:54 *129*
indeed, and my *b* is drink indeed .... Jn 6:55 *129*
eateth my flesh, and drinketh my *b* .... Jn 6:56 *129*
and forthwith came there out *b* .... Jn 19:34 *129*
that is to say, The field of *b* .... Acts 1:19 *129*
b, and fire, and vapour of smoke .... Acts 2:19 *129*
into darkness, and the moon into *b* .... Acts 2:20 *129*
to bring this man's *b* upon us .... Acts 5:28 *129*
from things strangled, and from *b* .... Acts 15:20 *129*
meats offered to idols, and from *b* .... Acts 15:29 *129*
hath made of one *b* all nations of .... Acts 17:26 *129*
Your *b* be upon your own heads .... Acts 18:6 *129*
I am pure from the *b* of all men .... Acts 20:26 *129*
he hath purchased with his own *b* .... Acts 20:28 *129*
offered to idols, and from *b* .... Acts 21:25 *129*
when the *b* of thy martyr Stephen .... Acts 22:20 *129*
Their feet are swift to shed *b* .... Rom 3:15 *129*
through faith in his *b*, to .... Rom 3:25 *129*
being now justified by his *b* .... Rom 5:9 *129*
the communion of the *b* of Christ 1Cor 10:16 *129*
cup is the new testament in my *b* 1Cor 11:25 *129*
of the body and *b* of the Lord 1Cor 11:27 *129*
b cannot inherit the kingdom of 1Cor 15:50 *129*
I conferred not with flesh and *b* .... Gal 1:16 *129*
we have redemption through his *b* .... Eph 1:7 *129*
are made nigh by the *b* of Christ .... Eph 2:13 *129*
we wrestle not against flesh and *b* .... Eph 6:12 *129*
we have redemption through his *b* .... Col 1:14 *129*
peace through the *b* of his cross .... Col 1:20 *129*
are partakers of flesh and *b* .... Heb 2:14 *129*
once every year, not without *b* .... Heb 9:7 *129*
Neither by the *b* of goats .... Heb 9:12 *129*
but by his own *b* he entered in .... Heb 9:12 *129*
For if the *b* of bulls and of goats .... Heb 9:13 *129*
much more shall the *b* of Christ .... Heb 9:14 *129*
testament was dedicated without *b* .... Heb 9:18 *129*
the law, he took the *b* of calves .... Heb 9:19 *129*
This is the *b* of the testament .... Heb 9:20 *129*
with *b* both the tabernacle .... Heb 9:21 *129*
are by the law purged with *b* .... Heb 9:22 *129*
shedding of *b* is no remission .... Heb 9:22 *130*
place every year with *b* of others .... Heb 9:25 *129*
not possible that the *b* of bulls .... Heb 10:4 *129*
the holiest by the *b* of Jesus .... Heb 10:19 *129*
counted the *b* of the covenant .... Heb 10:29 *129*
passover, and the sprinkling of *b* .... Heb 11:28 *129*
Ye have not yet resisted unto *b* .... Heb 12:4 *129*
to the *b* of sprinkling, that .... Heb 12:24 *129*
whose *b* is brought into the .... Heb 13:11 *129*
the people with his own *b* .... Heb 13:12 *129*
through the *b* of the everlasting .... Heb 13:20 *129*
of the *b* of Jesus Christ 1Pet 1:2 *129*
But with the precious *b* of Christ 1Pet 1:19 *129*
the *b* of Jesus Christ his Son 1Jn 1:7 *129*
is he that came by water and *b* 1Jn 5:6 *129*
by water only, but by water and *b* 1Jn 5:6 *129*
spirit, and the water, and the *b* 1Jn 5:8 *129*
us from our sins in his own *b* .... Rev 1:5 *129*
God by thy *b* out of every kindred .... Rev 5:9 *129*
avenge our *b* on them that dwell .... Rev 6:10 *129*
of hair, and the moon became as *b* .... Rev 6:12 *129*
them white in the *b* of the Lamb .... Rev 7:14 *129*
hail and fire mingled with *b* .... Rev 8:7 *129*
third part of the sea became *b* .... Rev 8:8 *129*
over waters to turn them to *b* .... Rev 11:6 *129*
overcame him by the *b* of the Lamb .... Rev 12:11 *129*
b came out of the winepress, even .... Rev 14:20 *129*
it became as the *b* of a dead man .... Rev 16:3 *129*
and they became *b* .... Rev 16:4 *129*
they have shed the *b* of saints .... Rev 16:6 *129*
thou hast given them *b* to drink .... Rev 16:6 *129*
drunken with the *b* of the saints .... Rev 17:6 *129*
with the *b* of the martyrs of .... Rev 17:6 *129*
her was found the *b* of prophets .... Rev 18:24 *129*
hath avenged the *b* of his .... Rev 19:2 *129*
with a vesture dipped in *b* .... Rev 19:13 *129*

BLOODGUILTINESS {1}
Deliver me from *b*, O God, thou ... Ps 51:14 1818

BLOODTHIRSTY {1}
The *b* hate the upright ... Prov 29:10 582,1818

BLOODY {16}
Surely a *b* husband art thou to me ... Ex 4:25 1818
A *b* husband thou art, because of ... Ex 4:26 1818
Come out, come out, thou *b* man ... 2Sa 16:7 1818
because thou art a *b* man ... 2Sa 16:8 1818
is for Saul, and for his *b* house ... 2Sa 21:1 1818
the LORD will abhor the *b* ... Ps 5:6 1818
sinners, nor my life with *b* men ... Ps 26:9 1818
b and deceitful men shall not live ... Ps 55:23 1818
iniquity, and save me from *b* men ... Ps 59:2 1818
from me therefore, ye *b* men ... Ps 139:19 1818
for the land is full of *b* crimes ... Eze 7:23 1818
judge, wilt thou judge the *b* city ... Eze 22:2 1818
Woe to the *b* city, to the pot ... Eze 24:6 1818
Woe to the *b* city ... Eze 24:9 1818
Woe to the *b* city ... Nah 3:1 1818
sick of a fever and of a *b* flux ... Acts 28:8 *1420*

BLOOMED {1}
b blossoms, and yielded almonds ... Num 17:8 6692

BLOSSOM {6}
rod, whom I shall choose, shall *b* ... Num 17:5 6524
their *b* shall go up as dust ... Is 5:24 6525
Israel shall *b* and bud, and fill ... Is 27:6 6692
shall rejoice, and *b* as the rose ... Is 35:1 6524
It shall *b* abundantly, and rejoice ... Is 35:2 6524
Although the fig tree shall not *b* ... Hab 3:17 6524

BLOSSOMED {1}
the rod hath *b*, pride hath budded ... Eze 7:10 6692

BLOSSOMS {2}
it budded, and her *b* shot forth ... Gen 40:10 5322
brought forth buds, and bloomed *b* ... Num 17:8 6731

BLOT {13}
b me, I pray thee, out of thy ... Ex 32:32 4229
him will I *b* out of my book ... Ex 32:33 4229
he shall *b* them out with the ... Num 5:23 4229
b out their name from under ... Deut 9:14 4229
that thou shalt *b* out the ... Deut 25:19 4229
the LORD shall *b* out his name ... Deut 29:20 4229
b out the name of Israel from ... 2Kin 14:27 4229
if any *b* hath cleaved to mine ... Job 31:7 3971
mercies *b* out my transgressions ... Ps 51:1 4229
b out all mine iniquities ... Ps 51:9 4229
a wicked man getteth himself a *b* ... Prov 9:7 3971
neither *b* out their sin from thy ... Jer 18:23 4229
I will not *b* out his name out of ... Rev 3:5 *1813*

BLOTTED {6}
sin be *b* out from before thee ... Neh 4:5 4229
Let them be *b* out of the book of ... Ps 69:28 4229
following let their name be *b* out ... Ps 109:13 4229
the sin of his mother be *b* out ... Ps 109:14 4229
I have *b* out, as a thick cloud, ... Is 44:22 4229
that your sins may be *b* out ... Acts 3:19 *1813*

BLOTTETH {2}
I, even I, am he that *b* out thy ... Is 43:25 4229

BLOTTING {1}
B out the handwriting of ... Col 2:14 *1813*

BLOW {39}
Thou didst *b* with thy wind, the ... Ex 15:10 5398
And when they shall *b* with them ... Num 10:3 8628
if they *b* but with one trumpet, ... Num 10:4 8628
When ye *b* an alarm, then the ... Num 10:5 8628
When ye *b* an alarm the second ... Num 10:6 8628
they shall *b* an alarm for their ... Num 10:6 8628
be gathered together, ye shall *b* ... Num 10:7 8628
shall *b* with the trumpets ... Num 10:8 8628
then ye shall *b* an alarm with the ... Num 10:9 7321
ye shall *b* with the trumpets over ... Num 10:10 8628
and the trumpets to *b* in his hand ... Num 31:6 8643
priests shall *b* with the trumpets ... Josh 6:4 8628
When I *b* with a trumpet, I and all ... Judg 7:18 8628
then *b* ye the trumpets also on ... Judg 7:18 8628
in their right hands to *b* withal ... Judg 7:20 8628
b ye with the trumpet, and say, ... 1Kin 1:34 8628
did *b* with the trumpets before ... 1Chr 15:24 2690
consumed by the *b* of thine hand ... Ps 39:10 8409
an east wind to *b* in the heaven ... Ps 78:26 5265
B up the trumpet in the new moon, ... Ps 81:3 8628
he causeth his wind to *b*, and the ... Ps 147:18 5380
b upon my garden, that the spices ... Song 4:16 6315
and he shall also *b* upon them ... Is 40:24 5398
B ye the trumpet in the land ... Jer 4:5 8628
b the trumpet in Tekoa, and set up ... Jer 6:1 8628
breach, with a very grievous *b* ... Jer 14:17 4347
b the trumpet among the nations, ... Jer 51:27 8628
I will *b* against thee in the fire ... Eze 21:31 6315
to *b* the fire upon it, to melt it ... Eze 22:20 5301
b upon you in the fire of my ... Eze 22:21 5301
he *b* the trumpet, and warn the ... Eze 33:3 8628
b not the trumpet, and the people ... Eze 33:6 8628
B ye the cornet in Gibeah, and the ... Hos 5:8 8628
B ye the trumpet in Zion, and ... Joel 2:1 8628
B the trumpet in Zion, sanctify a ... Joel 2:15 8628
brought it home, I did *b* upon it ... Hag 1:9 5301
the Lord GOD shall *b* the trumpet ... Zec 9:14 8628
And when ye see the south wind *b* ... Lk 12:55 *4154*
wind should not *b* on the earth ... Rev 7:1 *4154*

BLOWETH {4}
when he *b* a trumpet, hear ye ... Is 18:3 8628
the spirit of the LORD *b* upon it ... Is 40:7 5380
that *b* the coals in the fire ... Is 54:16 5301
The wind *b* where it listeth, and ... Jn 3:8 *4154*

BLOWING {4}
a memorial of *b* of trumpets ... Lev 23:24 8643
it is a day of *b* the trumpets ... Num 29:1 8643
going on, and *b* with the trumpets ... Josh 6:9 8628
going on, and *b* with the trumpets ... Josh 6:13 8628

BLOWN {4}
a fire not *b* shall consume him ... Job 20:26 5301
that the great trumpet shall be *b* ... Is 27:13 8628
They have *b* the trumpet, even to ... Eze 7:14 8628
Shall a trumpet be *b* in the city ... Amos 3:6 8628

BLUE {50}
And *b*, and purple, and scarlet, and ... Ex 25:4 8504
of fine twined linen, and *b* ... Ex 26:1 8504
of *b* upon the edge of the one ... Ex 26:4 8504
And thou shalt make a vail of *b* ... Ex 26:31 8504
for the door of the tent, of *b* ... Ex 26:36 8504
an hanging of twenty cubits, of *b* ... Ex 27:16 8504
And they shall take gold, and *b* ... Ex 28:5 8504
make the ephod of gold, of *b* ... Ex 28:6 8504
even of gold, of *b*, and purple, and ... Ex 28:8 8504
of gold, of *b*, and of purple, and ... Ex 28:15 8504
of the ephod with a lace of *b* ... Ex 28:28 8504
the robe of the ephod all of *b* ... Ex 28:31 8504
thou shalt make pomegranates of *b* ... Ex 28:33 8504
And thou shalt put it on a *b* lace ... Ex 28:37 8504
And *b*, and purple, and scarlet, and ... Ex 35:6 8504
every man, with whom was found *b* ... Ex 35:23 8504
which they had spun, both of *b* ... Ex 35:25 8504
and of the embroiderer, in *b* ... Ex 35:35 8504
of fine twined linen, and *b* ... Ex 36:8 8504
he made loops of *b* on the edge of ... Ex 36:11 8504
And he made a vail of *b*, and purple ... Ex 36:35 8504
for the tabernacle door of *b* ... Ex 36:37 8504
of the court was needlework, of *b* ... Ex 38:18 8504
workman, and an embroiderer in *b* ... Ex 38:23 8504
And of the *b*, and purple, and ... Ex 39:1 8504
And he made the ephod of gold, *b* ... Ex 39:2 8504
into wires, to work it in the *b* ... Ex 39:3 8504
of gold, *b*, and purple, and scarlet ... Ex 39:5 8504
of gold, *b*, and purple, and scarlet ... Ex 39:8 8504
of the ephod with a lace of *b* ... Ex 39:21 8504
the ephod of woven work, all of *b* ... Ex 39:22 8504
of the robe pomegranates of *b* ... Ex 39:24 8504
girdle of fine twined linen, and *b* ... Ex 39:29 8504
And they tied unto it a lace of *b* ... Ex 39:31 8504
over it a cloth wholly of *b* ... Num 4:6 8504
they shall spread a cloth of *b* ... Num 4:7 8504
And they shall take a cloth of *b* ... Num 4:9 8504
they shall spread a cloth of *b* ... Num 4:11 8504
and put them in a cloth of *b* ... Num 4:12 8504
of the borders a ribband of *b* ... Num 15:38 8504
and in purple, and crimson, and *b* ... 2Chr 2:7 8504
and in timber, in purple, in *b* ... 2Chr 2:14 8504
And he made the vail of *b*, and ... 2Chr 3:14 8504
Where were white, green, and *b* ... Est 1:6 8504
upon a pavement of red, and *b* ... Est 1:6 8504
of the king in royal apparel of *b* ... Est 8:15 8504
b and purple is their clothing ... Jer 10:9 8504
Which were clothed with *b* ... Eze 23:6 8504
b and purple from the isles of ... Eze 27:7 8504
in *b* clothes, and broidered work, ... Eze 27:24 8504

BLUENESS {1}
The *b* of a wound cleanseth away ... Prov 20:30 2250

BLUNT {1}
If the iron be *b*, and he do not ... Eccl 10:10 6949

BLUSH {3}
b to lift up my face to thee, my ... Ezr 9:6 3637
all ashamed, neither could they *b* ... Jer 6:15 3637
all ashamed, neither could they *b* ... Jer 8:12 3637

BOANERGES *(bo-an-er'-jees)* {1} *Surname of James and John, the sons of Zebedee.*
and he surnamed them *B*, which is, ... Mk 3:17 *993*

BOAR {1}
The *b* out of the wood doth waste ... Ps 80:13 2386

BOARD {17}
cubits shall be the length of a *b* ... Ex 26:16 7175
shall be the breadth of one *b* ... Ex 26:16 7175
tenons shall there be in one *b* ... Ex 26:17 7175
under one *b* for his two tenons ... Ex 26:19 7175
another *b* for his two tenons ... Ex 26:19 7175
two sockets under one *b* ... Ex 26:21 7175
and two sockets under another *b* ... Ex 26:21 7175
two sockets under one *b* ... Ex 26:25 7175
and two sockets under another *b* ... Ex 26:25 7175
The length of a *b* was ten cubits ... Ex 36:21 7175
and the breadth of a *b* one cubit ... Ex 36:21 7175
One *b* had two tenons, equally ... Ex 36:22 7175
under one *b* for his two tenons ... Ex 36:24 7175
another *b* for his two tenons ... Ex 36:24 7175
two sockets under one *b* ... Ex 36:26 7175
and two sockets under another *b* ... Ex 36:26 7175
silver, under every *b* two sockets ... Ex 36:30 7175

BOARDS {41}
thou shalt make *b* for the ... Ex 26:15 7175
for all the *b* of the tabernacle ... Ex 26:17 7175
make the *b* for the tabernacle ... Ex 26:18 7175
twenty *b* on the south side ... Ex 26:18 7175
of silver under the twenty *b* ... Ex 26:19 7175
side there shall be twenty *b* ... Ex 26:20 7175
westward thou shalt make six *b* ... Ex 26:22 7175
two *b* shalt thou make for the ... Ex 26:23 7175
And they shall be eight *b*, and ... Ex 26:25 7175
five for the *b* of the one side of ... Ex 26:26 7175
five bars for the *b* of the other ... Ex 26:27 7175
five bars for the *b* of the side ... Ex 26:27 7175
the *b* shall reach from end to end ... Ex 26:28 7175
shalt overlay the *b* with gold ... Ex 26:29 7175
Hollow with *b* shalt thou make it ... Ex 27:8 3871
covering, his taches, and his *b* ... Ex 35:11 7175
he made *b* for the tabernacle of ... Ex 36:20 7175
for all the *b* of the tabernacle ... Ex 36:22 7175
he made *b* for the tabernacle ... Ex 36:23 7175
twenty *b* for the south side ... Ex 36:23 7175
silver he made under the twenty *b* ... Ex 36:24 7175
north corner, he made twenty *b* ... Ex 36:25 7175
tabernacle westward he made six *b* ... Ex 36:27 7175
two *b* made he for the corners of ... Ex 36:28 7175
And there were eight *b* ... Ex 36:30 7175
five for the *b* of the one side of ... Ex 36:31 7175
five bars for the *b* of the other ... Ex 36:32 7175
five bars for the *b* of the ... Ex 36:32 7175
b from the one end to the other ... Ex 36:33 7175
And he overlaid the *b* with gold ... Ex 36:34 7175
he made the altar hollow with *b* ... Ex 38:7 3871
his furniture, his taches, his *b* ... Ex 39:33 7175
sockets, and set up the *b* thereof ... Ex 40:18 7175
shall be the *b* of the tabernacle ... Num 3:36 7175
the *b* of the tabernacle, and the ... Num 4:31 7175
house with beams and *b* of cedar ... 1Kin 6:9 7713
the house within with *b* of cedar ... 1Kin 6:15 6763
and the walls with *b* of cedar ... 1Kin 6:16 6763
will inclose her with *b* of cedar ... Song 8:9 3871
thy ship *b* of fir trees of Senir ... Eze 27:5 3871
And the rest, some on *b*, and some ... Acts 27:44 *4548*

BOAST {20}
b himself as he that putteth it ... 1Kin 20:11 1984
thine heart lifteth thee up to *b* ... 2Chr 25:19 3513
soul shall make her *b* in the LORD ... Ps 34:2 1984
In God we *b* all the day long, and ... Ps 44:8 1984
b themselves in the multitude of ... Ps 49:6 1984
workers of iniquity *b* themselves ... Ps 94:4 559
that *b* themselves of idols ... Ps 97:7 1984
B not thyself of to morrow ... Prov 27:1 1984
Shall the ax *b* itself against him ... Is 10:15 6286
their glory shall ye *b* yourselves ... Is 61:6 3235
the law, and makest thy *b* of God ... Rom 2:17 *2744*
Thou that makest thy *b* of the law ... Rom 2:23 *2744*
B not against the branches ... Rom 11:18 *2620*
But if thou *b*, thou bearest not ... Rom 11:18
for which I *b* of you to them of ... 2Cor 9:2 *2744*
For though I should *b* somewhat ... 2Cor 10:8 *2744*
But we will not *b* of things ... 2Cor 10:13 *2744*
not to *b* in another man's line of ... 2Cor 10:16 *2744*
that I may *b* myself a little ... 2Cor 11:16 *2744*
of works, lest any man should *b* ... Eph 2:9 *2744*

BOASTED {2}
your mouth ye have *b* against me ... Eze 35:13 1431
For if I have *b* any thing to him ... 2Cor 7:14 *2744*

BOASTERS {2}
of God, despiteful, proud, *b* ... Rom 1:30 *213*
of their own selves, covetous, *b* ... 2Ti 3:2 *213*

BOASTEST {1}
Why *b* thou thyself in mischief, O ... Ps 52:1 1984

BOASTETH {4}
For the wicked *b* of his heart's ... Ps 10:3 1984
he is gone his way, then he *b* ... Prov 20:14 1984
Whoso *b* himself of a false gift ... Prov 25:14 1984
little member, and *b* great things ... Jas 3:5 *3166*

BOASTING {9}
Theudas, *b* himself to be somebody ... Acts 5:36 *3004*
Where is *b* then ... Rom 3:27 *2746*
to you in truth, even so our *b* ... 2Cor 7:14 *2746*
love, and of our *b* on your behalf ... 2Cor 8:24 *2746*
lest our *b* of you should be in ... 2Cor 9:3 *2745*
ashamed in this same confident *b* ... 2Cor 9:4 *2746*
Not *b* of things without our ... 2Cor 10:15 *2744*
this *b* in the regions of Achaia ... 2Cor 11:10 *2746*
in this confidence of *b* ... 2Cor 11:17 *2746*

BOASTINGS {1}
But now ye rejoice in your *b* ... Jas 4:16 *212*

BOAT {6}
there went over a ferry *b* to ... 2Sa 19:18 5679
that there was none other *b* there ... Jn 6:22 *4142*
not with his disciples into the *b* ... Jn 6:22 *4142*
we had much work to come by the *b* ... Acts 27:16 *4627*
had let down the *b* into the sea ... Acts 27:30 *4627*
cut off the ropes of the *b* ... Acts 27:32 *4627*

BOATS {1}
(Howbeit there came other *b* from ... Jn 6:23 *4142*

BOAZ *(bo'-az)* {24} See BOOZ.
1. Husband of Ruth.
and his name was *B* ... Ruth 2:1 1162
of the field belonging unto *B* ... Ruth 2:3 1162
B came from Beth-lehem, and said ... Ruth 2:4 1162
Then said *B* unto his servant that ... Ruth 2:5 1162
Then said *B* unto Ruth, Hearest ... Ruth 2:8 1162
B answered and said unto her, It ... Ruth 2:11 1162
B said unto her, At mealtime come ... Ruth 2:14 1162
B commanded his young men, saying ... Ruth 2:15 1162
with whom I wrought to day is *B* ... Ruth 2:19 1162
B to glean unto the end of barley ... Ruth 2:23 1162
now is not *B* of our kindred, with ... Ruth 3:2 1162
when *B* had eaten and drunk, and his ... Ruth 3:7 1162
Then went *B* up to the gate, and ... Ruth 4:1 1162
kinsman of whom *B* spake came by ... Ruth 4:1 1162
Then said *B*, What day thou buyest ... Ruth 4:5 1162

Therefore the kinsman said unto *B*... Ruth 4:8 1162
B said unto the elders, and unto... Ruth 4:9 1162
So *B* took Ruth, and she was his... Ruth 4:13 1162
And Salmon begat *B*... Ruth 4:21 1162
and *B* begat Obed... Ruth 4:21 1162
begat Salma, and Salma begat *B*... 1Chr 2:11 1162
B begat Obed, and Obed begat Jesse... 1Chr 2:12 1162
2. *A pillar in Solomon's Temple.*
and called the name thereof *B*... 1Kin 7:21 1162
and the name of that on the left *B*... 2Chr 3:17 1162

BOCHERU *(bok'-er-u)* {2} *A relative of Saul.*
whose names are these, Azrikam, *B*... 1Chr 8:38 1074
whose names are these, Azrikam, *B*... 1Chr 9:44 1074

BOCHIM *(bo'-kim)* {2} *A place near Gilgal.*
the LORD came up from Gilgal to *B*... Judg 2:1 1066
called the name of that place *B*... Judg 2:5 1066

BODIES {35}
the sight of my lord, but our *b*... Gen 47:18 1472
the *b* of his sons from the wall... 1Sa 31:12 1472
the *b* of his sons, and brought... 1Chr 10:12 1480
they were dead *b* fallen to the... 2Chr 20:24 6297
both riches with the dead *b*... 2Chr 20:25 6297
they have dominion over our *b*... Neh 9:37 1472
ashes, your *b* to *b* of clay... Job 13:12 1354
ashes, your *b* to *b* of clay... Job 13:12 1472
The dead *b* of thy servants have... Ps 79:2 5038
fill the places with the dead *b*... Ps 110:6 1472
And the whole valley of the dead *b*... Jer 31:40 6297
fill them with the dead *b* of men... Jer 33:5 6297
their dead *b* shall be for meat... Jer 34:20 5038
cast all the dead *b* of the men... Jer 41:9 6297
another, and two covered their *b*... Eze 1:11 1472
covered on that side, their *b*... Eze 1:23 1472
upon whose *b* the fire had no... Dan 3:27 1655
king's word, and yielded their *b*... Dan 3:28 1655
be many dead *b* in every place... Amos 8:3 6297
many *b* of the saints which slept... Mt 27:52 *4983*
that the *b* should not remain upon... Jn 19:31 *4983*
their own *b* between themselves... Rom 1:24 *4983*
b by his Spirit that dwelleth in... Rom 8:11 *4983*
present your *b* a living sacrifice... Rom 12:1 *4983*
Know ye not that your *b* are the... 1Cor 6:15 *4983*
There are also celestial *b*... 1Cor 15:40 *4983*
and *b* terrestrial... 1Cor 15:40 *4983*
love their wives as their own *b*... Eph 5:28 *4983*
our *b* washed with pure water... Heb 10:22 *4983*
For the *b* of those beasts, whose... Heb 13:11 *4983*
their dead *b* shall lie in the... Rev 11:8 *4430*
shall see their dead *b* three days... Rev 11:9 *4430*
their dead *b* to be put in graves... Rev 11:9 *4430*

BODILY {4}
in a *b* shape like a dove upon him... Lk 3:22 *4984*
but his *b* presence is weak, and... 2Cor 10:10 *4983*
all the fulness of the Godhead *b*... Col 2:9 *4985*
For *b* exercise profiteth little... 1Ti 4:8 *4984*

BODY {174}
as it were the *b* of heaven in his... Ex 24:10 6106
shall he go in to any dead *b*... Lev 21:11 5315
LORD he shall come at no dead *b*... Num 6:6 5315
defiled by the dead *b* of a man... Num 9:6 5315
defiled by the dead *b* of a man... Num 9:7 5315
be unclean by reason of a dead *b*... Num 9:10 5315
He that toucheth the dead *b* of... Num 19:11 5315
dead *b* of any man that is dead... Num 19:13 5315
in the open fields, or a dead *b*... Num 19:16 5315
His *b* shall not remain all night... Deut 21:23 5038
shall be the fruit of thy *b*... Deut 28:4 990
in goods, in the fruit of thy *b*... Deut 28:11 990
shall be the fruit of thy *b*... Deut 28:18 990
eat the fruit of thine own *b*... Deut 28:53 990
thine hand, in the fruit of thy *b*... Deut 30:9 990
and ten sons of his *b* begotten... Judg 8:30 3409
they fastened his *b* to the wall... 1Sa 31:10 1472
all night, and took the *b* of Saul... 1Sa 31:12 1472
he had restored a dead *b* to life... 2Kin 8:5
men, and took away the *b* of Saul... 1Chr 10:12 1480
the children's sake of mine own *b*... Job 19:17 990
my skin worms destroy this *b*... Job 19:26
is drawn, and cometh out of the *b*... Job 20:25 1465
Of the fruit of thy *b* will I set... Ps 132:11 990
thy flesh and thy *b* are consumed... Prov 5:11 7607
fruitful field, both soul and *b*... Is 10:18 1320
with my dead *b* shall they arise... Is 26:19 5038
hast laid thy *b* as the ground... Is 51:23 1460
cast his dead *b* into the graves... Jer 26:23 5038
his dead *b* shall be cast out in... Jer 36:30 5038
were more ruddy in *b* than rubies... Lam 4:7 6106
And their whole *b*, and their backs... Eze 10:12 1320
his *b* was wet with the dew of... Dan 4:33 1655
his *b* was wet with the dew of... Dan 5:21 1655
his *b* destroyed, and given to the... Dan 7:11 1655
in my spirit in the midst of my *b*... Dan 7:15 5085
His *b* also was like the beryl, and... Dan 10:6 1472
the fruit of my *b* for the sin of... Mic 6:7 990
by a dead *b* touch any of these... Hag 2:13 5315
not that thy whole *b* should be... Mt 5:29 *4983*
not that thy whole *b* should be... Mt 5:30 *4983*
The light of the *b* is the eye... Mt 6:22 *4983*
thy whole *b* shall be full of... Mt 6:22 *4983*
thy whole *b* shall be full of... Mt 6:23 *4983*
nor yet for your *b*, what ye shall... Mt 6:25 *4983*
than meat, and the *b* than raiment... Mt 6:25 *4983*
And fear not them which kill the *b*... Mt 10:28 *4983*
to destroy both soul and *b* in hell... Mt 10:28 *4983*
disciples came, and took up the *b*... Mt 14:12 *4983*
hath poured this ointment on my *b*... Mt 26:12 *4983*
this is my *b*... Mt 26:26 *4983*
Pilate, and begged the *b* of Jesus... Mt 27:58 *4983*
commanded the *b* to be delivered... Mt 27:58 *4983*
And when Joseph had taken the *b*... Mt 27:59 *4983*
she felt in her *b* that she was... Mk 5:29 *4983*
to anoint my *b* to the burying... Mk 14:8 *4983*
this is my *b*... Mk 14:22 *4983*
cloth cast about his naked *b*... Mk 14:51 *4983*
Pilate, and craved the *b* of Jesus... Mk 15:43 *4983*
he gave the *b* to Joseph... Mk 15:45 *4983*
The light of the *b* is the eye... Lk 11:34 *4983*
thy whole *b* also is full of light... Lk 11:34 *4983*
thy *b* also is full of darkness... Lk 11:34 *4983*
If thy whole *b* therefore be full... Lk 11:36 *4983*
afraid of them that kill the *b*... Lk 12:4 *4983*
neither for the *b*, what ye shall... Lk 12:22 *4983*
the *b* is more than raiment... Lk 12:23 *4983*
unto them, Wheresoever the *b* is... Lk 17:37 *4983*
This is my *b* which is given for... Lk 22:19 *4983*
Pilate, and begged the *b* of Jesus... Lk 23:52 *4983*
sepulchre, and how his *b* was laid... Lk 23:55 *4983*
found not the *b* of the Lord Jesus... Lk 24:3 *4983*
And when they found not his *b*... Lk 24:23 *4983*
he spake of the temple of his *b*... Jn 2:21 *4983*
he might take away the *b* of Jesus... Jn 19:38 *4983*
therefore, and took the *b* of Jesus... Jn 19:38 *4983*
Then took they the *b* of Jesus... Jn 19:40 *4983*
where the *b* of Jesus had lain... Jn 20:12 *4983*
and turning him to the *b* said... Acts 9:40 *4983*
So that from his *b* were brought... Acts 19:12 *5559*
considered not his own *b* now dead... Rom 4:19 *4983*
that the *b* of sin might be... Rom 6:6 *4983*
therefore reign in your mortal *b*... Rom 6:12 *4983*
to the law by the *b* of Christ... Rom 7:4 *4983*
me from the *b* of this death... Rom 7:24 *4983*
the *b* is dead because of sin... Rom 8:10 *4983*
do mortify the deeds of the *b*... Rom 8:13 *4983*
to wit, the redemption of our *b*... Rom 8:23 *4983*
as we have many members in one *b*... Rom 12:4 *4983*
are one *b* in Christ, and every one... Rom 12:5 *4983*
For I verily, as absent in *b*... 1Cor 5:3 *4983*
Now the *b* is not for fornication... 1Cor 6:13 *4983*
and the Lord for the *b*... 1Cor 6:13 *4983*
is joined to an harlot is one *b*... 1Cor 6:16 *4983*
that a man doeth is without the *b*... 1Cor 6:18 *4983*
sinneth against his own *b*... 1Cor 6:18 *4983*
know ye not that your *b* is the... 1Cor 6:19 *4983*
therefore glorify God in your *b*... 1Cor 6:20 *4983*
wife hath not power of her own *b*... 1Cor 7:4 *4983*
hath not power of his own *b*... 1Cor 7:4 *4983*
that she may be holy both in *b*... 1Cor 7:34 *4983*
But I keep under my *b*, and bring... 1Cor 9:27 *4983*
the communion of the *b* of Christ... 1Cor 10:16 *4983*
many are one bread, and one *b*... 1Cor 10:17 *4983*
this is my *b*, which is broken for... 1Cor 11:24 *4983*
shall be guilty of the *b*... 1Cor 11:27 *4983*
not discerning the Lord's *b*... 1Cor 11:29 *4983*
For as the *b* is one, and hath many... 1Cor 12:12 *4983*
one *b*, being many, are one *b*... 1Cor 12:12 *4983*
are we all baptized into one *b*... 1Cor 12:13 *4983*
For the *b* is not one member, but... 1Cor 12:14 *4983*
not the hand, I am not of the *b*... 1Cor 12:15 *4983*
is it therefore not of the *b*... 1Cor 12:15 *4983*
am not the eye, I am not of the *b*... 1Cor 12:16 *4983*
is it therefore not of the *b*... 1Cor 12:16 *4983*
If the whole *b* were an eye... 1Cor 12:17 *4983*
every one of them in the *b*... 1Cor 12:18 *4983*
all one member, where were the *b*... 1Cor 12:19 *4983*
they many members, yet but one *b*... 1Cor 12:20 *4983*
much more those members of the *b*... 1Cor 12:22 *4983*
And those members of the *b*... 1Cor 12:23 *4983*
God hath tempered the *b* together... 1Cor 12:24 *4983*
should be no schism in the *b*... 1Cor 12:25 *4983*
Now ye are the *b* of Christ... 1Cor 12:27 *4983*
though I give my *b* to be burned... 1Cor 13:3 *4983*
and with what *b* do they come... 1Cor 15:35 *4983*
sowest not that *b* that shall be... 1Cor 15:37 *4983*
But God giveth it a *b* as it hath... 1Cor 15:38 *4983*
him, and to every seed his own *b*... 1Cor 15:38 *4983*
It is sown a natural *b*... 1Cor 15:44 *4983*
it is raised a spiritual *b*... 1Cor 15:44 *4983*
There is a natural *b*... 1Cor 15:44 *4983*
and there is a spiritual *b*... 1Cor 15:44 *4983*
the *b* the dying of the Lord Jesus... 2Cor 4:10 *4983*
might be made manifest in our *b*... 2Cor 4:10 *4983*
whilst we are at home in the *b*... 2Cor 5:6 *4983*
rather to be absent from the *b*... 2Cor 5:8 *4983*
receive the things done in his *b*... 2Cor 5:10 *4983*
years ago, (whether in the *b*... 2Cor 12:2 *4983*
or whether out of the *b*, I cannot... 2Cor 12:2 *4983*
in the *b*, or out of the *b*... 2Cor 12:3 *4983*
for I bear in my *b* the marks of... Gal 6:17 *4983*
Which is his *b*, the fulness of... Eph 1:23 *4983*
unto God in one *b* by the cross... Eph 2:16 *4983*
be fellowheirs, and of the same *b*... Eph 3:6 *4954*
There is one *b*, and one Spirit... Eph 4:4 *4983*
the edifying of the *b* of Christ... Eph 4:12 *4983*
From whom the whole *b* fitly... Eph 4:16 *4983*
maketh increase of the *b* unto the... Eph 4:16 *4983*
and he is the saviour of the *b*... Eph 5:23 *4983*
For we are members of his *b*... Eph 5:30 *4983*
Christ shall be magnified in my *b*... Phil 1:20 *4983*
Who shall change our vile *b*... Phil 3:21 *4983*
like unto his glorious *b*... Phil 3:21 *4983*
And he is the head of the *b*... Col 1:18 *4983*
In the *b* of his flesh through... Col 1:22 *4983*
in putting off the *b* of the sins... Col 2:11 *4983*
but the *b* is of Christ... Col 2:17 *4983*
from which all the *b* by joints... Col 2:19 *4983*
humility, and neglecting of the *b*... Col 2:23 *4983*
which also ye are called in one *b*... Col 3:15 *4983*
b be preserved blameless unto the... 1Th 5:23 *4983*
but a *b* hast thou prepared me... Heb 10:5 *4983*
through the offering of the *b* of... Heb 10:10 *4983*
as being yourselves also in the *b*... Heb 13:3 *4983*
things which are needful to the *b*... Jas 2:16 *4983*
For as the *b* without the spirit... Jas 2:26 *4983*
able also to bridle the whole *b*... Jas 3:2 *4983*
and we turn about their whole *b*... Jas 3:3 *4983*
that it defileth the whole *b*... Jas 3:6 *4983*
our sins in his own *b* on the tree... 1Pet 2:24 *4983*
he disputed about the *b* of Moses... Jude 9 *4983*

BODY'S {1}
Christ in my flesh for his *b* sake... Col 1:24 *4983*

BOHAN *(bo'-han)* {2} *A namesake of a border stone.*
the stone of *B* the son of Reuben... Josh 15:6 932
the stone of *B* the son of Reuben... Josh 18:17 932

BOIL {16}
shall be a *b* breaking forth with... Ex 9:9 7822
it became a *b* breaking forth with... Ex 9:10 7822
for the *b* was upon the magicians... Ex 9:11 7822
B the flesh at the door of the... Lev 8:31 1310
even in the skin thereof, was a *b*... Lev 13:18 7822
in the place of the *b* there be a... Lev 13:19 7822
of leprosy broken out of the *b*... Lev 13:20 7822
and spread not, it is a burning *b*... Lev 13:23 7822
And they took and laid it on the *b*... 2Kin 20:7 7822
maketh the deep to *b* like a pot... Job 41:31 7570
lay it for a plaister upon the *b*... Is 38:21 7822
the fire causeth the waters to *b*... Is 64:2 1158
bones under it, and make it *b* well... Eze 24:5 7570
shall *b* the trespass offering... Eze 46:20 1310
are the places of them that *b*... Eze 46:24 1310
b the sacrifice of the people... Eze 46:24 1310

BOILED {3}
them, and *b* their flesh with the... 1Kin 19:21 1310
So we *b* my son, and did eat him... 2Kin 6:29 1310
My bowels *b*, and rested not... Job 30:27 7570

BOILING {1}
it was made with *b* places under... Eze 46:23 4018

BOILS {2}
before Moses because of the *b*... Ex 9:11 7822
smote Job with sore *b* from the... Job 2:7 7822

BOISTEROUS {1}
But when he saw the wind *b*... Mt 14:30 *2478*

BOKERU See BOCHERU.

BOKIM See BOCHIM.

BOLD {11}
but the righteous are *b* as a lion... Prov 28:1 982
Then Paul and Barnabas waxed *b*... Acts 13:46 *3955*
But Esaias is very *b*, and saith, I... Rom 10:20 *662*
but being absent am *b* toward you... 2Cor 10:1 *2292*
that I may not be *b* when I am... 2Cor 10:2 *2292*
I think to be *b* against some... 2Cor 10:2 *5111*
Howbeit whereinsoever any is *b*... 2Cor 11:21 *5111*
(I speak foolishly,) I am *b* also... 2Cor 11:21 *5111*
are much more *b* to speak the word... Phil 1:14 *5111*
we were *b* in our God to speak... 1Th 2:2 *3955*
though I might be much *b* in... Philem 8 *3954*

BOLDLY {13}
sword, and came upon the city *b*... Gen 34:25 983
went in *b* unto Pilate, and craved... Mk 15:43 *5111*
But, lo, he speaketh *b*, and they... Jn 7:26 *3954*
how he had preached *b* at Damascus... Acts 9:27 *3955*
he spake *b* in the name of the... Acts 9:29 *3955*
abode they speaking *b* in the Lord... Acts 14:3 *3955*
began to speak *b* in the synagogue... Acts 18:26 *3955*
spake *b* for the space of three... Acts 19:8 *3955*
the more *b* unto you in some sort... Rom 15:15 *5112*
me, that I may open my mouth *b*... Eph 6:19 *3954*
that therein I may speak *b*... Eph 6:20 *3955*
Let us therefore come *b* unto the... Heb 4:16 *3954*
So that we may *b* say, The Lord is... Heb 13:6 *2292*

BOLDNESS {10}
the *b* of his face shall be... Eccl 8:1 5797
Now when they saw the *b* of Peter... Acts 4:13 *3954*
that with all *b* they may speak... Acts 4:29 *3954*
they spake the word of God with *b*... Acts 4:31 *3954*
Great is my *b* of speech toward... 2Cor 7:4 *3954*
In whom we have *b* and access with... Eph 3:12 *3954*
be ashamed, but that with all *b*... Phil 1:20 *3954*
great *b* in the faith which is in... 1Ti 3:13 *3954*
b to enter into the holiest by... Heb 10:19 *3954*
that we may have *b* in the day of... 1Jn 4:17 *3954*

BOLLED {1}
was in the ear, and the flax was *b*... Ex 9:31 1392

BOLSTER {6}
a pillow of goats' hair for his *b*... 1Sa 19:13 4763
a pillow of goats' hair for his *b*... 1Sa 19:16 4763
stuck in the ground at his *b*... 1Sa 26:7 4763
now the spear that is at his *b*... 1Sa 26:11 4763
the cruse of water from Saul's *b*... 1Sa 26:12 4763
cruse of water that was at his *b*... 1Sa 26:16 4763

BOLT {1}
from me, and *b* the door after her... 2Sa 13:17 5274

BOLTED {1}
her out, and *b* the door after her... 2Sa 13:18 5274

BOND {19}
an oath to bind his soul with a *b*... Num 30:2 632
the LORD, and bind herself by a *b*... Num 30:3 632

her *b* wherewith she hath bound Num 30:4 632
every *b* wherewith she hath bound Num 30:4 632
her soul by a *b* with an oath Num 30:10 632
every *b* wherewith she bound her Num 30:11 632
or concerning the *b* of her soul Num 30:12 632
He looseth the *b* of kings Job 12:18 4148
you into the *b* of the covenant Eze 20:37 4562
from this *b* on the sabbath day Lk 13:16 *1199*
and in the *b* of iniquity Acts 8:23 *4886*
Gentiles, whether we be *b* or free 1Cor 12:13 *1401*
there is neither *b* nor free Gal 3:28 *1401*
of the Spirit in the *b* of peace Eph 4:3 *4886*
the Lord, whether he be *b* or free Eph 6:8 *1401*
Barbarian, Scythian, *b* nor free Col 3:11 *1401*
which is the *b* of perfectness Col 3:14 *4886*
and great, rich and poor, free and *b* Rev 13:16 *1401*
flesh of all men, both free and *b* Rev 19:18 *1401*

BONDAGE {39}
their lives bitter with hard *b* Ex 1:14 5656
Israel sighed by reason of the *b* Ex 2:23 5656
up unto God by reason of the *b* Ex 2:23 5656
whom the Egyptians keep in *b* Ex 6:5 5647
and I will rid you out of their *b* Ex 6:6 5656
anguish of spirit, and for cruel *b* Ex 6:9 5656
from Egypt, out of the house of *b* Ex 13:3 5650
from Egypt, from the house of *b* Ex 13:14 5650
of Egypt, out of the house of *b* Ex 20:2 5650
of Egypt, from the house of *b* Deut 5:6 5650
of Egypt, from the house of *b* Deut 6:12 5650
of Egypt, from the house of *b* Deut 8:14 5650
you out of the house of *b* Deut 13:5 5650
of Egypt, from the house of *b* Deut 13:10 5650
us, and laid upon us hard *b* Deut 26:6 5656
of Egypt, from the house of *b* Josh 24:17 5650
you forth out of the house of *b* Judg 6:8 5650
us a little reviving in our *b* Ezr 9:8 5659
God hath not forsaken us in our *b* Ezr 9:9 5659
and, lo, we bring into *b* our sons Neh 5:5 3533
are brought unto *b* already Neh 5:5 3533
because the *b* was heavy upon this Neh 5:18 5656
a captain to return to their *b* Neh 9:17 5659
from the hard *b* wherein thou wast Is 14:3 5656
and were never in *b* to any man Jn 8:33 *1398*
they should bring them into *b* Acts 7:6 *1402*
they shall be in *b* will I judge Acts 7:7 *1398*
the spirit of *b* again to fear Rom 8:15 *1397*
shall be delivered from the *b* of Rom 8:21 *1397*
is not under *b* in such cases 1Cor 7:15 *1402*
suffer, if a man bring you into *b* 2Cor 11:20 *2615*
that they might bring us into *b* Gal 2:4 *2615*
were in *b* under the elements of Gal 4:3 *1402*
ye desire again to be in *b* Gal 4:9 *1398*
mount Sinai, which gendereth to *b* Gal 4:24 *1397*
is in *b* with her children Gal 4:25 *1398*
again with the yoke of *b* Gal 5:1 *1397*
all their lifetime subject to *b* Heb 2:15 *1397*
of the same is he brought in *b* 2Pet 2:19 *1402*

BONDMAID {2}
with a woman, that is a *b* Lev 19:20 8198
had two sons, the one by a *b* Gal 4:22 *3814*

BONDMAIDS {2}
Both thy bondmen, and thy *b* Lev 25:44 519
of them shall ye buy bondmen and *b* Lev 25:44 519

BONDMAN {6}
instead of the lad a *b* to my lord Gen 44:33 5650
wast a *b* in the land of Egypt Deut 15:15 5650
that thou wast a *b* in Egypt Deut 16:12 5650
that thou wast a *b* in Egypt Deut 24:18 5650
wast a *b* in the land of Egypt Deut 24:22 5650
and the mighty men, and every *b* Rev 6:15 *1401*

BONDMEN {17}
and fall upon us, and take us for *b* Gen 43:18 5650
and we also will be my lord's *b* Gen 44:9 5650
they shall not be sold as *b* Lev 25:42 5650
Both thy *b*, and thy bondmaids, Lev 25:44 5650
of them shall ye buy *b* and Lev 25:44 5650
they shall be your *b* for ever Lev 25:46 5647
that ye should not be their *b* Lev 26:13 5650
son, We were Pharaoh's *b* in Egypt Deut 6:21 5650
you out of the house of *b* Deut 7:8 5650
be sold unto your enemies for *b* Deut 28:68 5650
none of you be freed from being *b* Josh 9:23 5650
of Israel did Solomon make no *b* 1Kin 9:22 5650
take unto him my two sons to be *b* 2Kin 4:1 5650
of Judah and Jerusalem for *b* 2Chr 28:10 5650
For we were *b* Ezr 9:9 5650
But if we had been sold for *b* Est 7:4 5650
of Egypt, out of the house of *b* Jer 34:13 5650

BONDS {26}
or of her *b* wherewith she hath Num 30:5 632
her *b* wherewith she bound her Num 30:7 632
all her vows, or all her *b* Num 30:14 632
thou hast loosed my *b* Ps 116:16 4147
broken the yoke, and burst the *b* Jer 5:5 4147
Make thee *b* and yokes, and put them Jer 27:2 4147
off thy neck, and will burst thy *b* Jer 30:8 4147
and will burst thy *b* in sunder Nah 1:13 4147
in every city, saying that *b* Acts 20:23 *1199*
charge worthy of death or of *b* Acts 23:29 *1199*
a certain man left in *b* by Felix Acts 25:14 *1198*
such as I am, except these *b* Acts 26:29 *1199*
nothing worthy of death or of *b* Acts 26:31 *1199*
For which I am an ambassador in *b* Eph 6:20 *254*
inasmuch as both in my *b*, and in Phil 1:7 *1199*
So that my *b* in Christ are Phil 1:13 *1199*
Lord, waxing confident by my *b* Phil 1:14 *1199*
to add affliction to my *b* Phil 1:16 *1199*
Christ, for which I am also in *b* Col 4:3 *1210*
Remember my *b* Col 4:18 *1199*
as an evil doer, even unto *b* 2Ti 2:9 *1199*
whom I have begotten in my *b* Philem 10 *1199*
unto me in the *b* of the gospel Philem 13 *1199*
ye had compassion of me in my *b* Heb 10:34 *1199*
and scourgings, yea, moreover of *b* Heb 11:36 *1199*
Remember them that are in *b* Heb 13:3 *1198*

BONDSERVANT {1}
not compel him to serve as a *b* Lev 25:39 5656,5650

BONDSERVICE {1}
levy a tribute of *b* unto this day 1Kin 9:21 5647

BONDWOMAN {8}
unto Abraham, Cast out this *b* Gen 21:10 519
for the son of this *b* shall not Gen 21:10 519
of the lad, and because of thy *b* Gen 21:12 519
son of the *b* will I make a nation Gen 21:13 519
But he who was of the *b* was born Gal 4:23 *3814*
Cast out the *b* and her son Gal 4:30 *3814*
for the son of the *b* shall not be Gal 4:30 *3814*
we are not children of the *b* Gal 4:31 *3814*

BONDWOMEN {3}
your enemies for bondmen and *b* Deut 28:68 8198
for bondmen and *b* unto you 2Chr 28:10 8198
we had been sold for bondmen and *b* Est 7:4 8198

BONE {19}
said, This is now *b* of my bones Gen 2:23 6106
said to him, Surely thou art my *b* Gen 29:14 6106
shall ye break a *b* thereof Ex 12:46 6106
morning, nor break any *b* of it Num 9:12 6106
or a *b* of a man, or a grave, Num 19:16 6106
and upon him that touched a *b* Num 19:18 6106
remember also that I am your *b* Judg 9:2 6106
saying, Behold, we are thy *b* 2Sa 5:1 6106
ye to Amasa, Art thou not of my *b* 2Sa 19:13 6106
saying, Behold, we are thy *b* 1Chr 11:1 6106
thine hand now, and touch his *b* Job 2:5 6106
My *b* cleaveth to my skin and to my Job 19:20 6106
and mine arm be broken from the *b* Job 31:22 7070
all mine enemies upon the cheek *b* Ps 3:7
and a soft tongue breaketh the *b* Prov 25:15 1634
came together, *b* to his *b* Eze 37:7 6106
land, when any seeth a man's *b* Eze 39:15 6106
A *b* of him shall not be broken Jn 19:36 *3747*

BONES {99}
said, This is now bone of my *b* Gen 2:23 6106
ye shall carry up my *b* from hence Gen 50:25 6106
Moses took the *b* of Joseph with Ex 13:19 6106
carry up my *b* away hence with you Ex 13:19 6106
enemies, and shall break their *b* Num 24:8 6106
the *b* of Joseph, which the Josh 24:32 6106
divided her, together with her *b* Judg 19:29 6106
And they took their *b*, and buried 1Sa 31:13 6106
Ye are my brethren, ye are my *b* 2Sa 19:12 6106
David went and took the *b* of Saul 2Sa 21:12 6106
the *b* of Jonathan his son from 2Sa 21:12 6106
up from thence the *b* of Saul 2Sa 21:13 6106
the *b* of Jonathan his son 2Sa 21:13 6106
they gathered the *b* of them that 2Sa 21:13 6106
the *b* of Saul and Jonathan his son 2Sa 21:14 6106
men's *b* shall be burnt upon thee 1Kin 13:2 6106
lay my *b* beside his *b* 1Kin 13:31 6106
down, and touched the *b* of Elisha 2Kin 13:21 6106
their places with the *b* of men 2Kin 23:14 6106
took the *b* out of the sepulchres, 2Kin 23:16 6106
let no man move his *b* 2Kin 23:18 6106
So they let his *b* alone 2Kin 23:18 6106
with the *b* of the prophet that 2Kin 23:18 6106
and burned men's *b* upon them 2Kin 23:20 6106
buried their *b* under the oak in 1Chr 10:12 6106
he burnt the *b* of the priests 2Chr 34:5 6106
which made all my *b* to shake Job 4:14 6106
flesh, and hast fenced me with *b* Job 10:11 6106
His *b* are full of the sin of his Job 20:11 6106
his *b* are moistened with marrow Job 21:24 6106
My *b* are pierced in me in the Job 30:17 6106
my *b* are burned with heat Job 30:30 6106
of his *b* with strong pain Job 33:19 6106
his *b* that were not seen stick Job 33:21 6106
His *b* are as strong pieces of Job 40:18 6106
his *b* are like bars of iron Job 40:18 1634
for my *b* are vexed Ps 6:2 6106
all my *b* are out of joint Ps 22:14 6106
I may tell all my *b* Ps 22:17 6106
iniquity, and my *b* are consumed Ps 31:10 6106
my *b* waxed old through my roaring Ps 32:3 6106
He keepeth all his *b* Ps 34:20 6106
All my *b* shall say, LORD, who is Ps 35:10 6106
rest in my *b* because of my sin Ps 38:3 6106
As with a sword in my *b*, mine Ps 42:10 6106
that the *b* which thou hast broken Ps 51:8 6106
for God hath scattered the *b* of Ps 53:5 6106
my *b* are burned as an hearth Ps 102:3 6106
groaning my *b* cleave to my skin Ps 102:5 6106
water, and like oil into his *b* Ps 109:18 6106
Our *b* are scattered at the Ps 141:7 6106
to thy navel, and marrow to thy *b* Prov 3:8 6106
ashamed is as rottenness in his *b* Prov 12:4 6106
but envy the rottenness of the *b* Prov 14:30 6106
and a good report maketh the *b* fat Prov 15:30 6106
to the soul, and health to the *b* Prov 16:24 6106
but a broken spirit drieth the *b* Prov 17:22 1634
nor how the *b* do grow in the womb Eccl 11:5 6106
a lion, so will he break all my *b* Is 38:13 6106
in drought, and make fat thy *b* Is 58:11 6106
your *b* shall flourish like an Is 66:14 6106
out the *b* of the kings of Judah Jer 8:1 6106
the *b* of his princes, and the Jer 8:1 6106
the *b* of the priests, and the Jer 8:1 6106
the *b* of the prophets, and the Jer 8:1 6106
the *b* of the inhabitants of Jer 8:1 6106
as a burning fire shut up in my *b* Jer 20:9 6106
all my *b* shake Jer 23:9 6106
king of Babylon hath broken his *b* Jer 50:17 6106
above hath he sent fire into my *b* Lam 1:13 6106
he hath broken my *b* Lam 3:4 6106
their skin cleaveth to their *b* Lam 4:8 6106
I will scatter your *b* round about Eze 6:5 6106
fill it with the choice *b* Eze 24:4 6106
and burn also the *b* under it Eze 24:5 6106
them seethe the *b* of it therein Eze 24:5 6106
it well, and let the *b* be burned Eze 24:10 6106
iniquities shall be upon their *b* Eze 32:27 6106
of the valley which was full of *b* Eze 37:1 6106
me, Son of man, can these *b* live Eze 37:3 6106
unto me, Prophesy upon these *b* Eze 37:4 6106
and say unto them, O ye dry *b* Eze 37:4 6106
saith the Lord GOD unto these *b* Eze 37:5 6106
the *b* came together, bone to his Eze 37:7 6106
these *b* are the whole house of Eze 37:11 6106
Our *b* are dried, and our hope is Eze 37:11 6106
brake all their *b* in pieces or Dan 6:24 1635
because he burned the *b* of the Amos 2:1 6106
bring out the *b* out of the house Amos 6:10 6106
and their flesh from off their *b* Mic 3:2 6106
and they break their *b*, and chop Mic 3:3 6106
rottenness entered into my *b* Hab 3:16 6106
gnaw not the *b* till the morrow Zeph 3:3 1633
are within full of dead men's *b* Mt 23:27 *3747*
for a spirit hath not flesh and *b* Lk 24:39 *3747*
ancle *b* received strength Acts 3:7 *4974*
body, of his flesh, and of his *b* Eph 5:30 *3747*
gave commandment concerning his *b* Heb 11:22 *3747*

BONNETS {6}
b shalt thou make for them, for Ex 28:40 4021
and his sons, and put the *b* on them Ex 29:9 4021
goodly *b* of fine linen, and linen Ex 39:28 4021
with girdles, and put *b* upon them Lev 8:13 4021
The *b*, and the ornaments of the Is 3:20 6287
have linen *b* upon their heads Eze 44:18 6287

BOOK {188}
This is the *b* of the generations Gen 5:1 5612
Write this for a memorial in a *b* Ex 17:14 5612
he took the *b* of the covenant, and Ex 24:7 5612
out of thy *b* which thou hast Ex 32:32 5612
me, him will I blot out of my *b* Ex 32:33 5612
shall write these curses in a *b* Num 5:23 5612
in the *b* of the wars of the LORD Num 21:14 5612
him a copy of this law in a *b* out Deut 17:18 5612
law that are written in this *b* Deut 28:58 5612
not written in the *b* of this law Deut 28:61 5612
in this *b* shall lie upon him Deut 29:20 5612
are written in this *b* of the law Deut 29:21 5612
curses that are written in this *b* Deut 29:27 5612
are written in this *b* of the law Deut 30:10 5612
the words of this law in a *b* Deut 31:24 5612
Take this *b* of the law, and put it Deut 31:26 5612
This *b* of the law shall not Josh 1:8 5612
in the *b* of the law of Moses Josh 8:31 5612
is written in the *b* of the law Josh 8:34 5612
this written in the *b* of Jasher Josh 10:13 5612
by cities into seven parts in a *b* Josh 18:9 5612
in the *b* of the law of Moses Josh 23:6 5612
words in the *b* of the law of God Josh 24:26 5612
the kingdom, and wrote it in a *b* 1Sa 10:25 5612
it is written in the *b* of Jasher 2Sa 1:18 5612
in the *b* of the acts of Solomon 1Kin 11:41 5612
they are written in the *b* of the 1Kin 14:19 5612
are they not written in the *b* of 1Kin 14:29 5612
are they not written in the *b* of 1Kin 15:7 5612
are they not written in the *b* of 1Kin 15:23 5612
are they not written in the *b* of 1Kin 15:31 5612
are they not written in the *b* of 1Kin 16:5 5612
are they not written in the *b* of 1Kin 16:14 5612
are they not written in the *b* of 1Kin 16:20 5612
are they not written in the *b* of 1Kin 16:27 5612
are they not written in the *b* of 1Kin 22:39 5612
are they not written in the *b* of 1Kin 22:45 5612
are they not written in the *b* of 2Kin 1:18 5612
are they not written in the *b* of 2Kin 8:23 5612
are they not written in the *b* of 2Kin 10:34 5612
are they not written in the *b* of 2Kin 12:19 5612
are they not written in the *b* of 2Kin 13:8 5612
are they not written in the *b* of 2Kin 13:12 5612
in the *b* of the law of Moses 2Kin 14:6 5612
are they not written in the *b* of 2Kin 14:15 5612
are they not written in the *b* of 2Kin 14:18 5612
are they not written in the *b* of 2Kin 14:28 5612
are they not written in the *b* of 2Kin 15:6 5612
they are written in the *b* of the 2Kin 15:11 5612
they are written in the *b* of the 2Kin 15:15 5612
are they not written in the *b* of 2Kin 15:21 5612
they are written in the *b* of the 2Kin 15:26 5612
they are written in the *b* of the 2Kin 15:31 5612
are they not written in the *b* of 2Kin 15:36 5612
are they not written in the *b* of 2Kin 16:19 5612
are they not written in the *b* of 2Kin 20:20 5612
are they not written in the *b* of 2Kin 21:17 5612
b of the chronicles of the kings 2Kin 21:25 5612
I have found the *b* of the law in 2Kin 22:8 5612
And Hilkiah gave the *b* to Shaphan 2Kin 22:8 5612
the priest hath delivered me a *b* 2Kin 22:10 5612

the words of the *b* of the law 2Kin 22:11 5612
the words of this *b* that is found 2Kin 22:13 5612
unto the words of this *b*, to do 2Kin 22:13 5612
even all the words of the *b* which 2Kin 22:16 5612
b of the covenant which was found 2Kin 23:2 5612
that were written in this *b* 2Kin 23:3 5612
written in the *b* of this covenant 2Kin 23:21 5612
b that Hilkiah the priest found 2Kin 23:24 5612
are they not written in the *b* of 2Kin 23:28 5612
are they not written in the *b* of 2Kin 24:5 5612
in the *b* of the kings of Israel 1Chr 9:1 5612
in the *b* of Samuel the seer 1Chr 29:29 1697
in the *b* of Nathan the prophet, 1Chr 29:29 1697
in the *b* of Gad the seer, 1Chr 29:29 1697
in the *b* of Nathan the prophet 2Chr 9:29 1697
in the *b* of Shemaiah the prophet 2Chr 12:15 1697
in the *b* of the kings of Judah 2Chr 16:11 5612
had the *b* of the law of the LORD 2Chr 17:9 5612
they are written in the *b* of Jehu 2Chr 20:34 1697
in the *b* of the kings of Israel 2Chr 20:34 5612
the story of the *b* of the kings 2Chr 24:27 5612
in the law in the *b* of Moses 2Chr 25:4 5612
in the *b* of the kings of Judah 2Chr 25:26 5612
in the *b* of the kings of Israel 2Chr 27:7 5612
in the *b* of the kings of Judah 2Chr 28:26 5612
in the *b* of the kings of Judah and 2Chr 32:32 5612
in the *b* of the kings of Israel 2Chr 33:18 1697
Hilkiah the priest found a *b* of 2Chr 34:14 5612
I have found the *b* of the law in 2Chr 34:15 5612
delivered the *b* to Shaphan 2Chr 34:15 5612
Shaphan carried the *b* to the king 2Chr 34:16 5612
the priest hath given me a *b* 2Chr 34:18 5612
the words of the *b* that is found 2Chr 34:21 5612
all that is written in this *b* 2Chr 34:21 5612
curses that are written in the *b* 2Chr 34:24 5612
b of the covenant that was found 2Chr 34:30 5612
which are written in this *b* 2Chr 34:31 5612
it is written in the *b* of Moses 2Chr 35:12 5612
in the *b* of the kings of Israel 2Chr 35:27 5612
in the *b* of the kings of Israel 2Chr 36:8 5612
b of the records of thy fathers Ezr 4:15 5609
thou find in the *b* of the records Ezr 4:15 5609
it is written in the *b* of Moses Ezr 6:18 5609
bring the *b* of the law of Moses Neh 8:1 5612
attentive unto the *b* of the law Neh 8:3 5612
Ezra opened the *b* in the sight of Neh 8:5 5612
So they read in the *b* in the law Neh 8:8 5612
he read in the *b* of the law of Neh 8:18 5612
read in the *b* of the law of the Neh 9:3 5612
in the *b* of the chronicles Neh 12:23 5612
On that day they read in the *b* of Neh 13:1 5612
it was written in the *b* of the Est 2:23 5612
he commanded to bring the *b* of Est 6:1 5612
and it was written in the *b* Est 9:32 5612
are they not written in the *b* of Est 10:2 5612
oh that they were printed in a *b* Job 19:23 5612
mine adversary had written a *b* Job 31:35 5612
of the *b* it is written of me Ps 40:7 5612
are they not in thy *b* Ps 56:8 5612
out of the *b* of the living Ps 69:28 5612
in thy *b* all my members were Ps 139:16 5612
the words of a *b* that is sealed Is 29:11 5612
the *b* is delivered to him that is Is 29:12 5612
the deaf hear the words of the *b* Is 29:18 5612
in a table, and note it in a *b* Is 30:8 5612
Seek ye out of the *b* of the LORD Is 34:16 5612
all that is written in this *b* Jer 25:13 5612
I have spoken unto thee in a *b* Jer 30:2 5612
subscribed the *b* of the purchase Jer 32:12 5612
Take thee a roll of a *b*, and write Jer 36:2 5612
unto him, upon a roll of a *b* Jer 36:4 5612
reading in the *b* the words of the Jer 36:8 5612
Then read Baruch in the *b* the Jer 36:10 5612
had heard out of the *b* all the Jer 36:11 5612
when Baruch read the *b* in the Jer 36:13 5612
and I wrote them with ink in the *b* Jer 36:18 5612
b which Jehoiakim king of Judah Jer 36:32 5612
in a *b* at the mouth of Jeremiah Jer 45:1 5612
So Jeremiah wrote in a *b* all the Jer 51:60 5612
made an end of reading this *b* Jer 51:63 5612
and, lo, a roll of a *b* was therein Eze 2:9 5612
shall be found written in the *b* Dan 12:1 5612
shut up the words, and seal the *b* Dan 12:4 5612
The *b* of the vision of Nahum the Nah 1:1 5612
a *b* of remembrance was written Mal 3:16 5612
The *b* of the generation of Jesus Mt 1:1 *976*
ye not read in the *b* of Moses Mk 12:26 *976*
As it is written in the *b* of the Lk 3:4 *976*
him the *b* of the prophet Esaias Lk 4:17 *975*
And when he had opened the *b* Lk 4:17 *975*
And he closed the *b*, and he gave it Lk 4:20 *975*
himself saith in the *b* of Psalms Lk 20:42 *976*
which are not written in this *b* Jn 20:30 *975*
it is written in the *b* of Psalms Acts 1:20 *976*
written in the *b* of the prophets Acts 7:42 *976*
in the *b* of the law to do them Gal 3:10 *975*
whose names are in the *b* of life Phil 4:3 *976*
hyssop, and sprinkled both the *b* Heb 9:19 *975*
of the *b* it is written of me Heb 10:7 *975*
and, What thou seest, write in a *b* Rev 1:11 *975*
out his name out of the *b* of life Rev 3:5 *976*
on the throne a *b* written within Rev 5:1 *975*
Who is worthy to open the *b* Rev 5:2 *975*
the earth, was able to open the *b* Rev 5:3 *975*
worthy to open and to read the *b* Rev 5:4 *975*
hath prevailed to open the *b* Rev 5:5 *975*
took the *b* out of the right hand Rev 5:7 *975*
And when he had taken the *b* Rev 5:8 *975*
Thou art worthy to take the *b* Rev 5:9 *975*
had in his hand a little *b* open Rev 10:2 *974*
take the little *b* which is open Rev 10:8 *974*
unto him, Give me the little *b* Rev 10:9 *974*
I took the little *b* out of the Rev 10:10 *974*
names are not written in the *b* of Rev 13:8 *976*
names were not written in the *b* Rev 17:8 *976*
another *b* was opened Rev 20:12 *976*
which is the *b* of life Rev 20:12 *976*
was not found written in the *b* of Rev 20:15 *976*
written in the Lamb's *b* of life Rev 21:27 *975*
sayings of the prophecy of this *b* Rev 22:7 *975*
which keep the sayings of this *b* Rev 22:9 *975*
sayings of the prophecy of this *b* Rev 22:10 *975*
words of the prophecy of this *b* Rev 22:18 *975*
that are written in this *b* Rev 22:18 *975*
words of the *b* of this prophecy Rev 22:19 *976*
his part out of the *b* of life Rev 22:19 *976*
which are written in this *b* Rev 22:19 *975*

BOOKS {8}

of making many *b* there is no end Eccl 12:12 5612
was set, and the *b* were opened Dan 7:10 5609
by *b* the number of the years Dan 9:2 5612
the *b* that should be written Jn 21:25 *975*
arts brought their *b* together Acts 19:19 *976*
comest, bring with thee, and the *b* 2Ti 4:13 *975*
and the *b* were opened Rev 20:12 *975*
which were written in the *b* Rev 20:12 *975*

BOOTH {2}

as a *b* that the keeper maketh Job 27:18 5521
the city, and there made him a *b* Jonah 4:5 5521

BOOTHS {9}

house, and made *b* for his cattle Gen 33:17 5521
Ye shall dwell in *b* seven days Lev 23:42 5521
Israelites born shall dwell in *b* Lev 23:42 5521
children of Israel to dwell in *b* Lev 23:43 5521
of Israel should dwell in *b* in Neh 8:14 5521
of thick trees, to make *b* Neh 8:15 5521
them, and made themselves *b* Neh 8:16 5521
made *b*, and sat under the *b* Neh 8:17 5521

BOOTIES {1}

and thou shalt be for *b* unto them Hab 2:7 4933

BOOTY {3}

And the *b*, being the rest of the Num 31:32 4455
And their camels shall be a *b* Jer 49:32 957
their goods shall become a *b* Zeph 1:13 4953

BOOZ *(bo'-oz)* {3} See BOAZ. *Greek form of Boaz.*

And Salmon begat *B* of Rachab Mt 1:5 *1003*
and *B* begat Obed of Ruth Mt 1:5 *1003*
of Obed, which was the son of *B* Lk 3:32 *1003*

BOR ASHAN See CHOR-ASHAN.

BORDER {158}

the *b* of the Canaanites was from Gen 10:19 1366
his *b* shall be unto Zidon Gen 49:13 3411
the mount, or touch the *b* of it Ex 19:12 7097
thou shalt make unto it a *b* of an Ex 25:25 4526
to the *b* thereof round about Ex 25:25 4526
Over against the *b* shall the Ex 25:27 4526
the breastplate in the *b* thereof Ex 28:26 8193
Also he made thereunto a *b* of an Ex 37:12 4526
for the *b* thereof round about Ex 37:12 4526
Over against the *b* were the rings Ex 37:14 4526
the breastplate, upon the *b* of it Ex 39:19 8193
a city in the uttermost of thy *b* Num 20:16 1366
give Israel passage through his *b* Num 20:21 1366
for Arnon is the *b* of Moab Num 21:13 1366
Ar, and lieth upon the *b* of Moab Num 21:15 1366
Israel to pass through his *b* Num 21:23 1366
for the *b* of the children of Num 21:24 1366
Moab, which is in the *b* of Arnon Num 22:36 1366
in Ije-abarim, in the *b* of Moab Num 33:44 1366
your south *b* shall be the outmost Num 34:3 1366
your *b* shall turn from the south Num 34:4 1366
the *b* shall fetch a compass from Num 34:5 1366
And as for the western *b*, ye shall Num 34:6 1366
even have the great sea for a *b* Num 34:6 1366
this shall be your west *b* Num 34:6 1366
And this shall be your north *b* Num 34:7 1366
b unto the entrance of Hamath Num 34:8 1366
forth of the *b* shall be to Zedad Num 34:8 1366
the *b* shall go on to Ziphron, and Num 34:9 1366
this shall be your north *b* Num 34:9 1366
east *b* from Hazar-enan to Shepham Num 34:10 1366
the *b* shall descend, and shall Num 34:11 1366
the *b* shall go down to Jordan, and Num 34:12 1366
the *b* of the city of his refuge Num 35:26 1366
the *b* even unto the river Jabbok, Deut 3:16 1366
which is the *b* of the children of Deut 3:16 1366
LORD thy God shall enlarge thy *b* Deut 12:20 1366
Gilgal, in the east *b* of Jericho Josh 4:19 7097
which is the *b* of the children of Josh 12:2 1366
unto the *b* of the Geshurites and Josh 12:5 1366
the *b* of Sihon king of Heshbon Josh 12:5 1366
unto the *b* of the children of Josh 13:10 1366
the *b* of the Geshurites and Josh 13:11 1366
the *b* of the children of Reuben Josh 13:23 1366
was Jordan, and the *b* thereof Josh 13:23 1366
from Mahanaim unto the *b* of Debir Josh 13:26 1366
king of Heshbon, Jordan and his *b* Josh 13:27 1366
even to the *b* of Edom the Josh 15:1 1366
their south *b* was from the shore Josh 15:2 1366
the east *b* was the salt sea, even Josh 15:5 1366
their *b* in the north quarter was Josh 15:5 1366
the *b* went up to Beth-hogla, and Josh 15:6 1366
the *b* went up to the stone of Josh 15:6 1366
the *b* went up toward Debir from Josh 15:7 1366
the *b* passed toward the waters of Josh 15:7 1366
the *b* went up by the valley of Josh 15:8 1366
the *b* went up to the top of the Josh 15:8 1366
the *b* was drawn from the top of Josh 15:9 1366
the *b* was drawn to Baalah, which Josh 15:9 1366
the *b* compassed from Baalah Josh 15:10 1366
the *b* went out unto the side of Josh 15:11 1366
the *b* was drawn to Shicron, and Josh 15:11 1366
out of the *b* were at the sea Josh 15:11 1366
the west *b* was to the great sea Josh 15:12 1366
the great sea, and the *b* thereof Josh 15:47 1366
the *b* of the children of Ephraim Josh 16:5 1366
even the *b* of their inheritance Josh 16:5 1366
the *b* went out toward the sea to Josh 16:6 1366
the *b* went about eastward unto Josh 16:6 1366
The *b* went out from Tappuah Josh 16:8 1366
the *b* went along on the right Josh 17:7 1366
but Tappuah on the *b* of Manasseh Josh 17:8 1366
Manasseh's, and the sea is his *b* Josh 17:10 1366
their *b* on the north side was Josh 18:12 1366
the *b* went up to the side of Josh 18:12 1366
the *b* went over from thence Josh 18:13 1366
the *b* descended to Ataroth-adar, Josh 18:13 1366
the *b* was drawn thence, and Josh 18:14 1366
the *b* went out on the west, and Josh 18:15 1366
the *b* came down to the end of the Josh 18:16 1366
the *b* passed along to the side of Josh 18:19 1366
the outgoings of the *b* were at Josh 18:19 1366
Jordan was the *b* of it on the Josh 18:20 1379
the *b* of their inheritance was Josh 19:10 1366
their *b* went up toward the sea, Josh 19:11 1366
unto the *b* of Chisloth-tabor Josh 19:12 1366
the *b* compasseth it on the north Josh 19:14 1366
their *b* was toward Jezreel, and Josh 19:18 1366
of their *b* were at Jordan Josh 19:22 1366
their *b* was Helkath, and Hali, and Josh 19:25 1366
Rakkon, with the *b* before Japho Josh 19:46 1366
hath made Jordan a *b* between us Josh 22:25 1366
in the *b* of his inheritance in Josh 24:30 1366
in the *b* of his inheritance in Judg 2:9 1366
to the *b* of Abel-meholah, unto Judg 7:22 8193
but came not within the *b* of Moab Judg 11:18 1366
for Arnon was the *b* of Moab Judg 11:18 1366
them unto the *b* of Beth-shemesh 1Sa 6:12 1366
in the *b* of Benjamin at Zelzah 1Sa 10:2 1366
turned to the way of the *b* that 1Sa 13:18 1366
his *b* at the river Euphrates 2Sa 8:3 3027
and unto the *b* of Egypt 1Kin 4:21 1366
and upward, and stood in the *b* 2Kin 3:21 1366
Philistines, and to the *b* of Egypt 2Chr 9:26 1366
them to the *b* of his sanctuary Ps 78:54 1366
will establish the *b* of the widow Prov 15:25 1366
a pillar at the *b* thereof to the Is 19:19 1366
enter into the height of his *b* Is 37:24 7093
shall come again to their own *b* Jer 31:17 1366
against her from the utmost *b* Jer 50:26 7093
will judge you in the *b* of Israel Eze 11:10 1366
will judge you in the *b* of Israel Eze 11:11 1366
Syene even unto the *b* of Ethiopia Eze 29:10 1366
the *b* thereof by the edge thereof Eze 43:13 1366
the *b* about it shall be half a Eze 43:17 1366
settle, and upon the *b* round about Eze 43:20 1366
the west *b* unto the east *b* Eze 45:7 1366
This shall be the *b*, whereby ye Eze 47:13 1366
this shall be the *b* of the land Eze 47:15 1366
is between the *b* of Damascus Eze 47:16 1366
of Damascus and the *b* of Hamath Eze 47:16 1366
the *b* from the sea shall be Eze 47:17 1366
the *b* of Damascus, and the north Eze 47:17 1366
northward, and the *b* of Hamath Eze 47:17 1366
from the *b* unto the east sea Eze 47:18 1366
shall be the great sea from the *b* Eze 47:20 1366
the *b* of Damascus northward, to Eze 48:1 1366
And by the *b* of Dan, from the east Eze 48:2 1366
by the *b* of Asher, from the east Eze 48:3 1366
by the *b* of Naphtali, from the Eze 48:4 1366
by the *b* of Manasseh, from the Eze 48:5 1366
by the *b* of Ephraim, from the Eze 48:6 1366
by the *b* of Reuben, from the east Eze 48:7 1366
by the *b* of Judah, from the east Eze 48:8 1366
most holy by the *b* of the Levites Eze 48:12 1366
over against the *b* of the priests Eze 48:13 1366
of the oblation toward the east *b* Eze 48:21 1366
twenty thousand toward the west *b* Eze 48:21 1366
prince's, between the *b* of Judah Eze 48:22 1366
the *b* of Benjamin, shall be for Eze 48:22 1366
by the *b* of Benjamin, from the Eze 48:24 1366
by the *b* of Simeon, from the east Eze 48:25 1366
by the *b* of Issachar, from the Eze 48:26 1366
by the *b* of Zebulun, from the Eze 48:27 1366
And by the *b* of Gad, at the south Eze 48:28 1366
the *b* shall be even from Tamar Eze 48:28 1366
remove them far from their *b* Joel 3:6 1366
that they might enlarge their *b* Amos 1:13 1366
their *b* greater than your *b* Amos 6:2 1366
have brought thee even to the *b* Obad 7 1366
themselves against their *b* Zeph 2:8 1366
And Hamath also shall *b* thereby Zec 9:2 1379
The *b* of wickedness, and, The Mal 1:4 1366
be magnified from the *b* of Israel Mal 1:5 1366
it were but the *b* of his garment Mk 6:56 *2899*
touched the *b* of his garment Lk 8:44 *2899*

BORDERS {43}

were in all the *b* round about Gen 23:17 1366
to cities from one end of the *b* Gen 47:21 1366
I will smite all thy *b* with frogs Ex 8:2 1366

unto the *b* of the land of Canaan ... Ex 16:35 7097
before thee, and enlarge thy *b* ... Ex 34:24 1366
b of their garments throughout ... Num 15:38 3671
fringe of the *b* a ribband of blue ... Num 15:38 3671
left, until we have passed thy *b* ... Num 20:17 1366
high way, until we be past thy *b* ... Num 21:22 1366
the *b* of the city of his refuge ... Num 35:27 1366
in the *b* of Dor on the west, ... Josh 11:2 5299
all the *b* of the Philistines, and ... Josh 13:2 1552
Egypt, even unto the *b* of Ekron ... Josh 13:3 1366
Aphek, to the *b* of the Amorites ... Josh 13:4 1366
unto the *b* of Archi to Ataroth ... Josh 16:2 1366
they came unto the *b* of Jordan ... Josh 22:10 1552
in the *b* of Jordan, at the ... Josh 22:11 1552
they had *b*, and the *b* were ... 1Kin 7:28 4526
on the *b* that were between the ... 1Kin 7:29 4526
of it were gravings with their *b* ... 1Kin 7:31 4526
under the *b* were four wheels ... 1Kin 7:32 4526
the *b* thereof were of the same ... 1Kin 7:35 4526
on the *b* thereof, he graved ... 1Kin 7:36 4526
Ahaz cut off the *b* of the bases ... 2Kin 16:17 4526
the *b* thereof, from the tower of ... 2Kin 18:8 1366
enter into the lodgings of his *b* ... 2Kin 19:23 7093
suburbs of Sharon, upon their *b* ... 1Chr 5:16 8444
by the *b* of the children of ... 1Chr 7:29 3027
hast set all the *b* of the earth ... Ps 74:17 1367
He maketh peace in thy *b*, and ... Ps 147:14 1366
We will make thee *b* of gold with ... Song 1:11 8447
is gone round about the *b* of Moab ... Is 15:8 1366
all thy *b* of pleasant stones ... Is 54:12 1366
nor destruction within thy *b* ... Is 60:18 1366
all thy sins, even in all thy *b* ... Jer 15:13 1366
for sin, throughout all thy *b* ... Jer 17:3 1366
Thy *b* are in the midst of the ... Eze 27:4 1366
in all the *b* thereof round about ... Eze 45:1 1366
and when he treadeth within our *b* ... Mic 5:6 1366
in the *b* of Zabulon and Nephthalim ... Mt 4:13 *3725*
enlarge the *b* of their garments, ... Mt 23:5 *2899*
arose, and went into the *b* of Tyre ... Mk 7:24 *3181*

BORE {2}
his master shall *b* his ear ... Ex 21:6 7527
or *b* his jaw through with a thorn ... Job 41:2 5344

BORED {1}
b a hole in the lid of it, and set ... 2Kin 12:9 5344

BORN {155}
And unto Enoch was *b* Irad ... Gen 4:18 3205
to him also there was *b* a son ... Gen 4:26 3205
and daughters were *b* unto them ... Gen 6:1 3205
them were sons *b* after the flood ... Gen 10:1 3205
even to him were children *b* ... Gen 10:21 3205
And unto Eber were *b* two sons ... Gen 10:25 3205
b in his own house, three hundred ... Gen 14:14 3211
one *b* in my house is mine heir ... Gen 15:3 1121
he that is *b* in the house, or ... Gen 17:12 3211
He that is *b* in thy house, and he ... Gen 17:13 3211
Shall a child be *b* unto him that ... Gen 17:17 3205
and all that were *b* in his house ... Gen 17:23 3211
b in the house, and bought with ... Gen 17:27 3211
of his son that was *b* unto him ... Gen 21:3 3205
when his son Isaac was *b* unto him ... Gen 21:5 3205
for I have *b* him a son in his old ... Gen 21:7 3205
which she had *b* unto Abraham ... Gen 21:9 3205
she hath also *b* children unto thy ... Gen 22:20 3205
who was *b* to Bethuel, son of ... Gen 24:15 3205
because I have *b* him three sons ... Gen 29:34 3205
me, because I have *b* him six sons ... Gen 30:20 3205
to pass, when Rachel had *b* Joseph ... Gen 30:25 3205
their children which they have *b* ... Gen 31:43 3205
which were *b* to him in Padan-aram ... Gen 35:26 3205
which were *b* unto him in the land ... Gen 36:5 3205
unto Joseph were *b* two sons ... Gen 41:50 3205
the land of Egypt were *b* Manasseh ... Gen 46:20 3205
of Rachel, which were *b* to Jacob ... Gen 46:22 3205
which were *b* him in Egypt, were ... Gen 46:27 3205
which were *b* unto thee in the ... Gen 48:5 3205
Every son that is *b* ye shall cast ... Ex 1:22 3209
be a stranger, or *b* in the land ... Ex 12:19 249
be as one that is *b* in the land ... Ex 12:48 249
she have *b* him sons or daughters ... Ex 21:4 3205
conceived seed, and *b* a man child ... Lev 12:2 3205
that hath *b* a male or a female ... Lev 12:7 3205
mother, whether she be *b* at home ... Lev 18:9 4138
or *b* abroad, even their nakedness ... Lev 18:9 4138
be unto you as one *b* among you ... Lev 19:34 249
he that is *b* in his house ... Lev 22:11 3211
b shall dwell in booths ... Lev 23:42 249
as he that is *b* in the land ... Lev 24:16 249
and for him that was *b* in the land ... Num 9:14 249
All that are *b* of the country ... Num 15:13 249
both for him that is *b* among the ... Num 15:29 249
whether he be *b* in the land ... Num 15:30 249
And unto Aaron was *b* Nadab ... Num 26:60 3205
they have *b* him children, both ... Deut 21:15 3205
but all the people that were *b* in ... Josh 5:5 3209
as he that was *b* among them ... Josh 8:33 249
do unto the child that shall be *b* ... Judg 13:8 3205
father, who was *b* unto Israel ... Judg 18:29 3205
thee than seven sons, hath *b* him ... Ruth 4:15 3205
saying, There is a son *b* to Naomi ... Ruth 4:17 3205
so that the barren hath *b* seven ... 1Sa 2:5 3205
for thou hast *b* a son ... 1Sa 4:20 3205
the battle were Eliab the first *b* ... 1Sa 17:13 3205
unto David were sons *b* in Hebron ... 2Sa 3:2 3205
These were *b* to David in Hebron ... 2Sa 3:5 3205
yet sons and daughters *b* to David ... 2Sa 5:13 3205
that were *b* unto him in Jerusalem ... 2Sa 5:14 3209
the child also that is *b* unto ... 2Sa 12:14 3209
Absalom there were *b* three sons ... 2Sa 14:27 3205
he also was *b* to the giant ... 2Sa 21:20 3205
These four were *b* to the giant in ... 2Sa 21:22 3205
a child shall be *b* unto the house ... 1Kin 13:2 3205
And unto Eber were *b* two sons ... 1Chr 1:19 3205
which three were *b* unto him of ... 1Chr 2:3 3205
of Hezron, that were *b* unto him ... 1Chr 2:9 3205
which were *b* unto him in Hebron ... 1Chr 3:1 3205
These six were *b* unto him in ... 1Chr 3:4 3205
And these were *b* unto him in ... 1Chr 3:5 3205
that were *b* in that land slew ... 1Chr 7:21 3205
These were *b* unto the giant in ... 1Chr 20:8 3205
Behold, a son shall be *b* to thee ... 1Chr 22:9 3205
unto Shemaiah his son were sons *b* ... 1Chr 26:6 3205
wives, and such as are *b* of them ... Ezr 10:3 3205
there were *b* unto him seven sons ... Job 1:2 3205
the day perish wherein I was *b* ... Job 3:3 3205
Yet man is *b* unto trouble, as the ... Job 5:7 3205
though man be *b* like a wild ass's ... Job 11:12 3205
Man that is *b* of a woman is of ... Job 14:1 3205
Art thou the first man that was *b* ... Job 15:7 3205
and he which is *b* of a woman ... Job 15:14 3205
he be clean that is *b* of a woman ... Job 25:4 3205
thou it, because thou wast then *b* ... Job 38:21 3205
unto a people that shall be *b* ... Ps 22:31 3205
go astray as soon as they be *b* ... Ps 58:3 990
the children which should be *b* ... Ps 78:6 3205
this man was *b* there ... Ps 87:4 3205
This and that man was *b* in her ... Ps 87:5 3205
people, that this man was *b* there ... Ps 87:6 3205
a brother is *b* for adversity ... Prov 17:17 3205
and had servants *b* in my house ... Eccl 2:7 1121
A time to be *b*, and a time to die ... Eccl 3:2 3205
whereas also he that is *b* in his ... Eccl 4:14 3205
For unto us a child is *b*, unto us ... Is 9:6 3205
or shall a nation be *b* at once ... Is 66:8 3205
that are *b* in this place, and ... Jer 16:3 3205
Cursed be the day wherein I was *b* ... Jer 20:14 3205
A man child is *b* unto thee ... Jer 20:15 3205
country, where ye were not *b* ... Jer 22:26 3205
in the day thou wast *b* thy navel ... Eze 16:4 3205
in the day that thou wast *b* ... Eze 16:5 3205
you as *b* in the country among the ... Eze 47:22 249
her as in the day that she was *b* ... Hos 2:3 3205
of Mary, of whom was *b* Jesus ... Mt 1:16 *1080*
Now when Jesus was *b* in Bethlehem ... Mt 2:1 *1080*
is he that is *b* King of the Jews ... Mt 2:2 *5088*
of them where Christ should be *b* ... Mt 2:4 *1080*
Among them that are *b* of women ... Mt 11:11 *1084*
which were so *b* from their ... Mt 19:12 *1080*
for that man if he had not been *b* ... Mt 26:24 *1080*
that man if he had never been *b* ... Mk 14:21 *1080*
that holy thing which shall be *b* ... Lk 1:35 *1080*
For unto you is *b* this day in the ... Lk 2:11 *5088*
Among those that are *b* of women ... Lk 7:28 *1084*
Which were *b*, not of blood, nor ... Jn 1:13 *1080*
thee, Except a man be *b* again ... Jn 3:3 *1080*
How can a man be *b* when he is old ... Jn 3:4 *1080*
into his mother's womb, and be *b* ... Jn 3:4 *1080*
thee, Except a man be *b* of water ... Jn 3:5 *1080*
That which is *b* of the flesh is ... Jn 3:6 *1080*
that which is *b* of the Spirit is ... Jn 3:6 *1080*
unto thee, Ye must be *b* again ... Jn 3:7 *1080*
every one that is *b* of the Spirit ... Jn 3:8 *1080*
We be not *b* of fornication ... Jn 8:41 *1080*
his parents, that he was *b* blind ... Jn 9:2 *1080*
your son, who ye say was *b* blind ... Jn 9:19 *1080*
our son, and that he was *b* blind ... Jn 9:20 *1080*
the eyes of one that was *b* blind ... Jn 9:32 *1080*
Thou wast altogether *b* in sins ... Jn 9:34 *1080*
that a man is *b* into the world ... Jn 16:21 *1080*
To this end was I *b*, and for this ... Jn 18:37 *1080*
our own tongue, wherein we were *b* ... Acts 2:8 *1080*
In which time Moses was *b* ... Acts 7:20 *1080*
b in Pontus, lately come from ... Acts 18:2 *1085*
b at Alexandria, an eloquent man, ... Acts 18:24 *1085*
b in Tarsus, a city in Cilicia, ... Acts 22:3 *1080*
And Paul said, But I was free *b* ... Acts 22:28 *1080*
(For the children being not yet *b* ... Rom 9:11 *1080*
as of one *b* out of due time ... 1Cor 15:8 *1626*
bondwoman was *b* after the flesh ... Gal 4:23 *1080*
But as then he that was *b* after ... Gal 4:29 *1080*
him that was *b* after the Spirit ... Gal 4:29
By faith Moses, when he was *b* ... Heb 11:23 *1080*
Being *b* again, not of corruptible ... 1Pet 1:23 *313*
doeth righteousness is *b* of him ... 1Jn 2:29 *1080*
Whosoever is *b* of God doth not ... 1Jn 3:9 *1080*
sin, because he is *b* of God ... 1Jn 3:9 *1080*
every one that loveth is *b* of God ... 1Jn 4:7 *1080*
Jesus is the Christ is *b* of God ... 1Jn 5:1 *1080*
For whatsoever is *b* of God ... 1Jn 5:4 *1080*
whosoever is *b* of God sinneth not ... 1Jn 5:18 *1080*
her child as soon as it was *b* ... Rev 12:4 *5088*

BORNE {31}
that the ark may be *b* with them ... Ex 25:14 5375
that the table may be *b* with them ... Ex 25:28 5375
stood, and on which it was *b* up ... Judg 16:29 5564
I have *b* chastisement, I will not ... Job 34:31 5375
then I could have *b* it ... Ps 55:12 5375
for thy sake I have *b* reproach ... Ps 69:7 5375
which are *b* by me from the belly, ... Is 46:3 6006
Surely he hath *b* our griefs ... Is 53:4 5375
ye shall be *b* upon her sides, and ... Is 66:12 5375
they must needs be *b*, because ... Jer 10:5 5375
She that hath *b* seven languisheth ... Jer 15:9 3205
that thou hast *b* me a man of ... Jer 15:10 3205
because he hath *b* it upon him ... Lam 3:28 5190
we have *b* their iniquities ... Lam 5:7 5445
whom thou hast *b* unto me ... Eze 16:20 3205
Thou hast *b* thy lewdness and thine ... Eze 16:58 5375
yet have they *b* their shame with ... Eze 32:24 5375
yet have they *b* their shame with ... Eze 32:25 5375
because ye have *b* the shame of ... Eze 36:6 5375
that they have *b* their shame ... Eze 39:26 5375
But ye have *b* the tabernacle of ... Amos 5:26 5375
unto us, which have *b* the burden ... Mt 20:12 *941*
heavy burdens and grievous to be *b* ... Mt 23:4 *1418*
of the palsy, which was *b* of four ... Mk 2:3 *142*
men with burdens grievous to be *b* ... Lk 11:46 *1418*
sent me, hath *b* witness of me ... Jn 5:37
Sir, if thou have *b* him hence ... Jn 20:15 *941*
that he was *b* of the soldiers for ... Acts 21:35 *941*
as we have *b* the image of the ... 1Cor 15:49 *5409*
Which have *b* witness of thy ... 3Jn 6
And hast *b*, and hast patience, and ... Rev 2:3 *941*

BORROW {8}
woman shall *b* of her neighbour ... Ex 3:22 7592
let every man *b* of his neighbour, ... Ex 11:2 7592
if a man *b* ought of his neighbour ... Ex 22:14 7592
nations, but thou shalt not *b* ... Deut 15:6 5670
many nations, and thou shalt not *b* ... Deut 28:12 3867
b thee vessels abroad of all thy ... 2Kin 4:3 7592
b not a few ... 2Kin 4:3
from him that would *b* of thee ... Mt 5:42 *1155*

BORROWED {3}
they *b* of the Egyptians jewels of ... Ex 12:35 7592
for it was *b* ... 2Kin 6:5 7592
We have *b* money for the king's ... Neh 5:4 3867

BORROWER {2}
the *b* is servant to the lender ... Prov 22:7 3867
as with the lender, so with the *b* ... Is 24:2 3867

BORROWETH {1}
The wicked *b*, and payeth not again ... Ps 37:21 3867

BORSHAN See CHOR-ASHAN.

BOSCATH *(bos'-cath)* {1} See BOSKETH. *A city in Judah.*
the daughter of Adaiah of *B* ... 2Kin 22:1 1218

BOSOM {41}
I have given my maid into thy *b* ... Gen 16:5 2436
Put now thine hand into thy *b* ... Ex 4:6 2436
And he put his hand into his *b* ... Ex 4:6 2436
Put thine hand into thy *b* again ... Ex 4:7 2436
he put his hand into his *b* again ... Ex 4:7 2436
and plucked it out of his *b* ... Ex 4:7 2436
say unto me, Carry them in thy *b* ... Num 11:12 2436
daughter, or the wife of thy *b* ... Deut 13:6 2436
and toward the wife of his *b* ... Deut 28:54 2436
evil toward the husband of her *b* ... Deut 28:56 2436
the child, and laid it in her *b* ... Ruth 4:16 2436
of his own cup, and lay in his *b* ... 2Sa 12:3 2436
and thy master's wives into thy *b* ... 2Sa 12:8 2436
him, and let her lie in thy *b* ... 1Kin 1:2 2436
slept, and laid it in her *b* ... 1Kin 3:20 2436
and laid her dead child in my *b* ... 1Kin 3:20 2436
And he took him out of her *b* ... 1Kin 17:19 2436
by hiding mine iniquity in my *b* ... Job 31:33 2243
prayer returned into mine own *b* ... Ps 35:13 2436
pluck it out of thy *b* ... Ps 74:11 2436
into their *b* their reproach ... Ps 79:12 2436
how I do bear in my *b* the ... Ps 89:50 2436
nor he that bindeth sheaves his *b* ... Ps 129:7 2683
embrace the *b* of a stranger ... Prov 5:20 2436
Can a man take fire in his *b* ... Prov 6:27 2436
man taketh a gift out of the *b* to ... Prov 17:23 2436
man hideth his hand in his *b* ... Prov 19:24 6747
and a reward in the *b* strong wrath ... Prov 21:14 2436
slothful hideth his hand in his *b* ... Prov 26:15 6747
anger resteth in the *b* of fools ... Eccl 7:9 2436
his arm, and carry them in his *b* ... Is 40:11 2436
even recompense into their *b* ... Is 65:6 2436
their former work into their *b* ... Is 65:7 2436
of the fathers into the *b* of ... Jer 32:18 2436
poured out into their mothers' *b* ... Lam 2:12 2436
from her that lieth in thy *b* ... Mic 7:5 2436
over, shall men give into your *b* ... Lk 6:38 *2859*
by the angels into Abraham's *b* ... Lk 16:22 *2859*
afar off, and Lazarus in his *b* ... Lk 16:23 *2859*
which is in the *b* of the Father ... Jn 1:18 *2859*
on Jesus' *b* one of his disciples ... Jn 13:23 *2859*

BOSOR *(bo'-sor)* {1} *Greek form of Besor.*
the way of Balaam the son of *B* ... 2Pet 2:15 *1007*

BOSSES {1}
upon the thick *b* of his bucklers ... Job 15:26 1354

BOTCH {2}
smite thee with the *b* of Egypt ... Deut 28:27 7822
with a sore *b* that cannot be ... Deut 28:35 7822

BOTH See APPENDIX.

BOTTLE {15}
a *b* of water, and gave it unto ... Gen 21:14 2573
And the water was spent in the *b* ... Gen 21:15 2573
went, and filled the *b* with water ... Gen 21:19 2573
And she opened a *b* of milk ... Judg 4:19 4997
a *b* of wine, and brought him unto ... 1Sa 1:24 5035
and another carrying a *b* of wine ... 1Sa 10:3 5035
a *b* of wine, and a kid, and sent ... 1Sa 16:20 4997
of summer fruits, and a *b* of wine ... 2Sa 16:1 5035
put thou my tears into thy *b* ... Ps 56:8 4997
I am become like a *b* in the smoke ... Ps 119:83 4997
Every *b* shall be filled with wine ... Jer 13:12 5035
every *b* shall be filled with wine ... Jer 13:12 5035
Go and get a potter's earthen *b* ... Jer 19:1 1228

Then shalt thou break the *b* in .... Jer 19:10 1228
drink, that puttest thy *b* to him .... Hab 2:15 2573

BOTTLES {19}
sacks upon their asses, and wine *b* .... Josh 9:4 4997
these *b* of wine, which we filled, ... Josh 9:13 4997
two *b* of wine, and five sheep 1Sa 25:18 5035
it is ready to burst like new *b* .... Job 32:19 178
or who can stay the *b* of heaven .... Job 38:37 5035
his vessels, and break their *b* .... Jer 48:12 5035
have made him sick with *b* of wine .... Hos 7:5 2573
do men put new wine into old *b* .... Mt 9:17 *779*
else the *b* break, and the wine .... Mt 9:17 *779*
wine runneth out, and the *b* perish .... Mt 9:17 *779*
but they put new wine into new *b* .... Mt 9:17 *779*
man putteth new wine into old *b* .... Mk 2:22 *779*
the new wine doth burst the *b* .... Mk 2:22 *779*
spilled, and the *b* will be marred .... Mk 2:22 *779*
new wine must be put into new *b* .... Mk 2:22 *779*
man putteth new wine into old *b* .... Lk 5:37 *779*
the new wine will burst the *b* .... Lk 5:37 *779*
be spilled, and the *b* shall perish .... Lk 5:37 *779*
new wine must be put into new *b* .... Lk 5:38 *779*

BOTTOM {20}
they sank into the *b* as a stone .... Ex 15:5 4688
blood beside the *b* of the altar .... Ex 29:12 3247
the *b* of the altar of the burnt .... Lev 4:7 3247
the *b* of the altar of the burnt .... Lev 4:18 3247
b of the altar of burnt offering .... Lev 4:25 3247
thereof at the *b* of the altar .... Lev 4:30 3247
thereof at the *b* of the altar .... Lev 4:34 3247
wrung out at the *b* of the altar .... Lev 5:9 3247
the blood at the *b* of the altar .... Lev 8:15 3247
the blood at the *b* of the altar .... Lev 9:9 3247
it, and covereth the *b* of the sea .... Job 36:30 8328
the *b* thereof of gold, the .... Song 3:10 7507
even the *b* shall be a cubit, and .... Eze 43:13 2436
from the *b* upon the ground even .... Eze 43:14 2436
the *b* thereof shall be a cubit .... Eze 43:17 3247
they came at the *b* of the den .... Dan 6:24 773
from my sight in the *b* of the sea .... Amos 9:3 7172
myrtle trees that were in the *b* .... Zec 1:8 4699
in twain from the top to the *b* .... Mt 27:51 *2736*
in twain from the top to the *b* .... Mk 15:38 *2736*

BOTTOMLESS {7}
was given the key of the *b* pit .... Rev 9:1 *12*
And he opened the *b* pit .... Rev 9:2 *12*
which is the angel of the *b* pit .... Rev 9:11 *12*
b pit shall make war against them .... Rev 11:7 *12*
and shall ascend out of the *b* pit .... Rev 17:8 *12*
having the key of the *b* pit .... Rev 20:1 *12*
And cast him into the *b* pit .... Rev 20:3 *12*

BOTTOMS {1}
down to the *b* of the mountains .... Jonah 2:6 7095

BOUGH {7}
Joseph is a fruitful *b* .... Gen 49:22 1121
even a fruitful *b* by a well .... Gen 49:22 1121
cut down a *b* from the trees, and .... Judg 9:48 7754
likewise cut down every man his *b* .... Judg 9:49 7754
shall lop the *b* with terror .... Is 10:33 6288
in the top of the uppermost *b* .... Is 17:6 534
strong cities be as a forsaken *b* .... Is 17:9 2793

BOUGHS {18}
first day the *b* of goodly trees .... Lev 23:40 6529
the *b* of thick trees, and willows .... Lev 23:40 6057
shalt not go over the *b* again .... Deut 24:20 6288
under the thick *b* of a great oak 2Sa 18:9 7730
bring forth *b* like a plant .... Job 14:9 7105
the *b* thereof were like the .... Ps 80:10 6057
She sent out her *b* unto the sea .... Ps 80:11 7105
I will take hold of the *b* thereof .... Song 7:8 5577
When the *b* thereof are withered, ... Is 27:11 7105
and it shall bring forth *b* .... Eze 17:23 6057
and his top was among the thick *b* .... Eze 31:3 5688
his *b* were multiplied, and his .... Eze 31:5 5634
heaven made their nests in his *b* .... Eze 31:6 5589
the fir trees were not like his *b* .... Eze 31:8 5589
shot up his top among the thick *b* .... Eze 31:10 5688
his *b* are broken by all the .... Eze 31:12 6288
up their top among the thick *b* .... Eze 31:14 5688
the heaven dwelt in the *b* thereof .... Dan 4:12 6056

BOUGHT {44}
or *b* with money of any stranger, ... Gen 17:12 4736
he that is *b* with thy money, must .... Gen 17:13 4736
all that were *b* with his money, ... Gen 17:23 4736
b with money of the stranger, ... Gen 17:27 4736
he *b* a parcel of a field, where .... Gen 33:19 7069
b him of the hands of the .... Gen 39:1 7069
Canaan, for the corn which they *b* .... Gen 47:14 7666
Joseph *b* all the land of Egypt .... Gen 47:20 7069
the land of the priests *b* he not .... Gen 47:22 7069
I have *b* you this day and your .... Gen 47:23 7069
which Abraham *b* with the field of .... Gen 49:30 7069
which Abraham *b* with the field .... Gen 50:13 7069
man's servant that is *b* for money .... Ex 12:44 4736
b it until the year of jubile .... Lev 25:28 7069
for ever to him that *b* it .... Lev 25:30 7069
b him from the year that he was .... Lev 25:50 7069
of the money that he was *b* for .... Lev 25:51 4736
the LORD a field which he hath *b* .... Lev 27:22 4736
return unto him of whom it was *b* .... Lev 27:24 7069
he thy father that hath *b* thee .... Deut 32:6 7069
a parcel of ground which Jacob *b* .... Josh 24:32 7069
that I have *b* all that was .... Ruth 4:9 7069
little ewe lamb, which he had *b* 2Sa 12:3 7069
So David *b* the threshingfloor and 2Sa 24:24 7069
he *b* the hill Samaria of Shemer 1Kin 16:24 7069
this wall, neither *b* we any land .... Neh 5:16 7069
Thou hast *b* me no sweet cane with .... Is 43:24 7069
I *b* the field of Hanameel my .... Jer 32:9 7069
And fields shall be *b* in this land .... Jer 32:43 7069
So I *b* her to me for fifteen .... Hos 3:2 3739
and sold all that he had, and *b* it .... Mt 13:46 *59*
b in the temple, and overthrew the .... Mt 21:12 *59*
b with them the potter's field, ... Mt 27:7 *59*
b in the temple, and overthrew the .... Mk 11:15 *59*
he *b* fine linen, and took him down .... Mk 15:46 *59*
had *b* sweet spices, that they .... Mk 16:1 *59*
I have *b* a piece of ground, and I .... Lk 14:18 *59*
I have *b* five yoke of oxen, and I .... Lk 14:19 *59*
they did eat, they drank, they *b* .... Lk 17:28 *59*
that sold therein, and them that *b* .... Lk 19:45 *59*
in the sepulchre that Abraham *b* .... Acts 7:16 *5608*
For ye are *b* with a price 1Cor 6:20 *59*
Ye are *b* with a price 1Cor 7:23 *59*
even denying the Lord that *b* them 2Pet 2:1 *59*

BOUND {104}
b Isaac his son, and laid him on .... Gen 22:9 6123
b upon his hand a scarlet thread, ... Gen 38:28 7194
where the king's prisoners were *b* .... Gen 39:20 631
the place where Joseph was *b* .... Gen 40:3 631
which were *b* in the prison .... Gen 40:5 631
be *b* in the house of your prison .... Gen 42:19 631
and *b* him before their eyes .... Gen 42:24 631
life is *b* up in the lad's life .... Gen 44:30 7194
utmost *b* of the everlasting hills .... Gen 49:26 8379
their kneadingtroughs being *b* up .... Ex 12:34 6887
ephod, and *b* it unto him therewith .... Lev 8:7 640
which hath no covering *b* upon it .... Num 19:15 6616
wherewith she hath *b* her soul .... Num 30:4 631
she hath *b* her soul shall stand .... Num 30:4 631
wherewith she hath *b* her soul .... Num 30:5 631
lips, wherewith she *b* her soul .... Num 30:6 631
she *b* her soul shall stand .... Num 30:7 631
lips, wherewith she *b* her soul .... Num 30:8 631
wherewith they have *b* their souls .... Num 30:9 631
or *b* her soul by a bond with an .... Num 30:10 631
she *b* her soul shall stand .... Num 30:11 631
she *b* the scarlet line in the .... Josh 2:21 7194
bottles, old, and rent, and *b* up .... Josh 9:4 6887
they *b* him with two new cords, and .... Judg 15:13 631
mightest be *b* to afflict thee .... Judg 16:6 631
dried, and she *b* him with them .... Judg 16:8 631
wherewith thou mightest be *b* .... Judg 16:10 631
b him therewith, and said unto him .... Judg 16:12 631
me wherewith thou mightest be *b* .... Judg 16:13 631
b him with fetters of brass .... Judg 16:21 631
the soul of my lord shall be *b* in 1Sa 25:29 6887
Thy hands were not *b*, nor thy 2Sa 3:34 631
b two talents of silver in two 2Kin 5:23 6887
shut him up, and *b* him in prison 2Kin 17:4 631
b him with fetters of brass, and 2Kin 25:7 631
b him with fetters, and carried 2Chr 33:11 631
b him in fetters, to carry him to 2Chr 36:6 631
And if they be *b* in fetters .... Job 36:8 631
take it to the *b* thereof, and that .... Job 38:20 1366
out those which are *b* with chains .... Ps 68:6 615
Thou hast set a *b* that they may .... Ps 104:9 1366
being *b* in affliction and iron .... Ps 107:10 615
Foolishness is *b* in the heart of .... Prov 22:15 7194
who hath *b* the waters in a .... Prov 30:4 6887
not been closed, neither *b* up .... Is 1:6 2280
they are *b* by the archers .... Is 22:3 631
are found in thee are *b* together .... Is 22:3 631
of the prison to them that are *b* .... Is 61:1 631
the *b* of the sea by a perpetual .... Jer 5:22 1366
cause, that thou mayest be *b* up .... Jer 30:13 4205
b him with chains, to carry him .... Jer 39:7 631
when he had taken him being *b* in .... Jer 40:1 631
king of Babylon *b* him in chains .... Jer 52:11 631
transgressions is *b* by his hand .... Lam 1:14 8244
b with cords, and made of cedar, ... Eze 27:24 2280
it shall not be *b* up to be healed .... Eze 30:21 2280
neither have ye *b* up that which .... Eze 34:4 2280
these men were *b* in their coats .... Dan 3:21 3729
fell down *b* into the midst of the .... Dan 3:23 3729
Did not we cast three men *b* into .... Dan 3:24 3729
The wind hath *b* her up in her .... Hos 4:19 6887
were like them that remove the *b* .... Hos 5:10 1366
Though I have *b* and strengthened .... Hos 7:15 3256
The iniquity of Ephraim is *b* up .... Hos 13:12 6887
her great men were *b* in chains .... Nah 3:10 7576
b him, and put him in prison for .... Mt 14:3 *1210*
on earth shall be *b* in heaven .... Mt 16:19 *1210*
on earth shall be *b* in heaven .... Mt 18:18 *1210*
And when they had *b* him, they led .... Mt 27:2 *1210*
he had been often *b* with fetters .... Mk 5:4 *1210*
b him in prison for Herodias' .... Mk 6:17 *1210*
b Jesus, and carried him away, and .... Mk 15:1 *1210*
which lay *b* with them that had .... Mk 15:7 *1210*
and he was kept *b* with chains .... Lk 8:29 *1196*
b up his wounds, pouring in oil .... Lk 10:34 *2611*
of Abraham, whom Satan hath *b* .... Lk 13:16 *1210*
b hand and foot with graveclothes .... Jn 11:44 *1210*
his face was *b* about with a .... Jn 11:44 *4019*
of the Jews took Jesus, and *b* him, ... Jn 18:12 *1210*
Now Annas had sent him *b* unto .... Jn 18:24 *1210*
might bring them *b* unto Jerusalem .... Acts 9:2 *1210*
them *b* unto the chief priests .... Acts 9:21 *1210*
two soldiers, *b* with two chains .... Acts 12:6 *1210*
I go *b* in the spirit unto .... Acts 20:22 *1210*
b his own hands and feet, and said, ... Acts 21:11 *1210*
for I am ready not to be *b* only .... Acts 21:13 *1210*
him to be *b* with two chains .... Acts 21:33 *1210*
which were there *b* unto Jerusalem .... Acts 22:5 *1210*
as they *b* him with thongs, Paul .... Acts 22:25 *4385*
a Roman, and because he had *b* him .... Acts 22:29 *1210*
b themselves under a curse, ... Acts 23:12 *332*
We have *b* ourselves under a great .... Acts 23:14 *332*
which have *b* themselves with an .... Acts 23:21 *332*
the Jews a pleasure, left Paul *b* .... Acts 24:27 *1210*
of Israel I am *b* with this chain .... Acts 28:20 *4029*
is *b* by the law to her husband so .... Rom 7:2 *1210*
Art thou *b* unto a wife 1Cor 7:27 *1210*
The wife is *b* by the law as long 1Cor 7:39 *1210*
We are *b* to thank God always for 2Th 1:3 *3784*
But we are *b* to give thanks alway 2Th 2:13 *3784*
but the word of God is not *b* 2Ti 2:9 *1210*
that are in bonds, as *b* with them .... Heb 13:3 *4887*
b in the great river Euphrates .... Rev 9:14 *1210*
Satan, and *b* him a thousand years, ... Rev 20:2 *1210*

BOUNDS {8}
thou shalt set *b* unto the people .... Ex 19:12 1379
Set *b* about the mount, and .... Ex 19:23 1379
I will set thy *b* from the Red sea .... Ex 23:31 1366
he set the *b* of the people .... Deut 32:8 1367
his *b* that he cannot pass .... Job 14:5 2706
hath compassed the waters with *b* .... Job 26:10 2706
have removed the *b* of the people .... Is 10:13 1367
the *b* of their habitation .... Acts 17:26 *3734*

BOUNTIFUL {2}
He that hath a *b* eye shall be .... Prov 22:9 2896
nor the churl said to be *b* .... Is 32:5 7771

BOUNTIFULLY {6}
because he hath dealt *b* with me .... Ps 13:6 1580
the LORD hath dealt *b* with thee .... Ps 116:7 1580
Deal *b* with thy servant, that I .... Ps 119:17 1580
for thou shalt deal *b* with me .... Ps 142:7 1580
soweth *b* shall reap also *b* 2Cor 9:6 *2129*

BOUNTIFULNESS {1}
enriched in every thing to all *b* 2Cor 9:11 *572*

BOUNTY {3}
Solomon gave her of his royal *b* 1Kin 10:13 3027
you, and make up beforehand your *b* 2Cor 9:5 *2129*
might be ready, as a matter of *b* 2Cor 9:5 *2129*

BOW See also WORSHIP.
I do set my *b* in the cloud, and it .... Gen 9:13 7198
that the *b* shall be seen in the .... Gen 9:14 7198
the *b* shall be in the cloud .... Gen 9:16 7198
thy weapons, thy quiver and thy *b* .... Gen 27:3 7198
thee, and nations *b* down to thee .... Gen 27:29 7812
thy mother's sons *b* down to thee .... Gen 27:29 7812
thy brethren indeed come to *b* .... Gen 37:10 7812
they cried before him, *B* the knee .... Gen 41:43 86
with my sword and with my *b* .... Gen 48:22 7198
children shall *b* down before thee .... Gen 49:8 7812
But his *b* abode in strength, and .... Gen 49:24 7198
b down themselves unto me, saying .... Ex 11:8 7812
Thou shalt not *b* down thyself to .... Ex 20:5 7812
Thou shalt not *b* down to their .... Ex 23:24 7812
in your land, to *b* down unto it .... Lev 26:1 7812
Thou shalt not *b* down thyself .... Deut 5:9 7812
nor *b* yourselves unto them .... Josh 23:7 7812
with thy sword, nor with thy *b* .... Josh 24:12 7198
them, and to *b* down unto them .... Judg 2:19 7812
even to his sword, and to his *b* 1Sa 18:4 7198
of Judah the use of the *b* 2Sa 1:18 7198
the *b* of Jonathan turned not back 2Sa 1:22 7198
so that a *b* of steel is broken by 2Sa 22:35 7198
certain man drew a *b* at a venture 1Kin 22:34 7198
I *b* myself in the house of Rimmon 2Kin 5:18 7812
when I *b* down myself in the house 2Kin 5:18 7812
with thy sword and with thy *b* 2Kin 6:22 7198
Jehu drew a *b* with his full 2Kin 9:24 7198
And Elisha said unto him, Take *b* 2Kin 13:15 7198
And he took unto him *b* and arrows 2Kin 13:15 7198
Israel, Put thine hand upon the *b* 2Kin 13:16 7198
nor *b* yourselves to them, nor 2Kin 17:35 7812
b down thine ear, and hear 2Kin 19:16 5186
and sword, and to shoot with *b* 1Chr 5:18 7198
and shooting arrows out of a *b* 1Chr 12:2 7198
and with him armed men with *b* 2Chr 17:17 7198
certain man drew a *b* at a venture 2Chr 18:33 7198
the *b* of steel shall strike him .... Job 20:24 7198
my *b* was renewed in my hand .... Job 29:20 7198
let others *b* down upon her .... Job 31:10 3766
They *b* themselves, they bring .... Job 39:3 3766
he hath bent his *b*, and made it .... Ps 7:12 7198
For, lo, the wicked bend their *b* .... Ps 11:2 7198
so that a *b* of steel is broken by .... Ps 18:34 7198
to the dust shall *b* before him .... Ps 22:29 3766
B down thine ear to me .... Ps 31:2 5186
the sword, and have bent their *b* .... Ps 37:14 7198
For I will not trust in my *b* .... Ps 44:6 7198
he breaketh the *b*, and cutteth the .... Ps 46:9 7198
bendeth his *b* to shoot his arrows .... Ps 58:7
the wilderness shall *b* before him .... Ps 72:9 3766
brake he the arrows of the *b* .... Ps 76:3 7198
turned aside like a deceitful *b* .... Ps 78:57 7198
B down thine ear, O LORD, hear me .... Ps 86:1 5186
O come, let us worship and *b* down .... Ps 95:6 3766
B thy heavens, O LORD, and come .... Ps 144:5 5186
b thine ear to my understanding .... Prov 5:1 5186
The evil *b* before the good .... Prov 14:19 7817
B down thine ear, and hear the .... Prov 22:17 5186
the strong men shall *b* themselves .... Eccl 12:3 5791
Without me they shall *b* down .... Is 10:4 3766
drawn sword, and from the bent *b* .... Is 21:15 7198
and as driven stubble to his *b* .... Is 41:2 7198

That unto me every knee shall *b* Is 45:23 3766
They stoop, they *b* down together Is 46:2 3766
they shall *b* down to thee with Is 49:23 7812
B down, that we may go over Is 51:23 7812
is it to *b* down his head as a Is 58:5 3721
they that despised thee shall *b* Is 60:14 7812
ye shall all *b* down to the Is 65:12 3766
Pul, and Lud, that draw the *b* Is 66:19 7198
They shall lay hold on *b* and spear Jer 6:23 7198
tongues like their *b* for lies Jer 9:3 7198
that handle and bend the *b* Jer 46:9 7198
I will break the *b* of Elam Jer 49:35 7198
all ye that bend the *b*, shoot at Jer 50:14 7198
all ye that bend the *b*, camp Jer 50:29 7198
They shall hold the *b* and the Jer 50:42 7198
bendeth let the archer bend his *b* Jer 51:3 7198
He hath bent his *b* like an enemy Lam 2:4 7198
He hath bent his *b*, and set me as Lam 3:12 7198
As the appearance of the *b* that Eze 1:28 7198
I will smite thy *b* out of thy Eze 39:3 7198
that I will break the *b* of Israel Hos 1:5 7198
God, and will not save them by *b* Hos 1:7 7198
and I will break the *b* and the Hos 2:18 7198
they are like a deceitful *b* Hos 7:16 7198
he stand that handleth the *b* Amos 2:15 7198
b myself before the high God Mic 6:6 3721
the perpetual hills did *b* Hab 3:6 7817
Thy *b* was made quite naked, Hab 3:9 7198
the battle *b* shall be cut off Zec 9:10 7198
filled the *b* with Ephraim, and Zec 9:13 7198
the nail, out of him the battle *b* Zec 10:4 7198
see, and *b* down their back alway Rom 11:10 *4781*
Lord, every knee shall *b* to me Rom 14:11 *2578*
For this cause I *b* my knees unto Eph 3:14 *2578*
name of Jesus every knee should *b* Phil 2:10 *2578*
and he that sat on him had a *b* Rev 6:2 *5115*

BOWED {78}
b himself toward the ground, Gen 18:2 7812
he *b* himself with his face toward Gen 19:1 7812
b himself to the people of the Gen 23:7 7812
Abraham *b* down himself before the Gen 23:12 7812
the man *b* down his head, and Gen 24:26 6915
I *b* down my head, and worshipped Gen 24:48 6915
b himself to the ground seven Gen 33:3 7812
children, and they *b* themselves Gen 33:6 7812
came near, and *b* themselves Gen 33:7 7812
and Rachel, and they *b* themselves Gen 33:7 7812
b down themselves before him with Gen 42:6 7812
b themselves to him to the earth Gen 43:26 7812
they *b* down their heads, and made Gen 43:28 6915
Israel *b* himself upon the bed's Gen 47:31 7812
he *b* himself with his face to the Gen 48:12 7812
b his shoulder to bear, and became Gen 49:15 5186
then they *b* their heads and Ex 4:31 6915
And the people *b* the head and Ex 12:27 6915
b his head toward the earth, and Ex 34:8 6915
he *b* down his head, and fell flat Num 22:31 6915
did eat, and *b* down to their gods Num 25:2 7812
gods, and *b* yourselves to them Josh 23:16 7812
b themselves unto them, and Judg 2:12 7812
gods, and *b* themselves unto them Judg 2:17 7812
At her feet he *b*, he fell, he lay Judg 5:27 3766
at her feet he *b*, he fell Judg 5:27 3766
where he *b*, there he fell down Judg 5:27 3766
b down upon their knees to drink Judg 7:6 3766
he *b* himself with all his might Judg 16:30 5186
b herself to the ground, and said Ruth 2:10 7812
she *b* herself and travailed 1Sa 4:19 3766
ground, and *b* himself three times 1Sa 20:41 7812
face to the earth, and *b* himself 1Sa 24:8 7812
face, and *b* herself to the ground, 1Sa 25:23 7812
b herself on her face to the 1Sa 25:41 7812
face to the ground, and *b* himself 1Sa 28:14 7812
he *b* himself, and said, What is 2Sa 9:8 7812
b himself, and thanked the king 2Sa 14:22 7812
b himself on his face to the 2Sa 14:33 7812
Cushi *b* himself unto Joab, and ran 2Sa 18:21 7812
he *b* the heart of all the men of 2Sa 19:14 5186
He *b* the heavens also, and came 2Sa 22:10 5186
b himself before the king on his 2Sa 24:20 7812
And Bath-sheba *b*, and did obeisance 1Kin 1:16 6915
he *b* himself before the king with 1Kin 1:23 7812
Then Bath-sheba *b* with her face 1Kin 1:31 6915
the king *b* himself upon the bed 1Kin 1:47 7812
b himself to king Solomon 1Kin 1:53 7812
b himself unto her, and sat down 1Kin 2:19 7812
knees which have not *b* unto Baal 1Kin 19:18 3766
b themselves to the ground before 2Kin 2:15 7812
b herself to the ground, and took 2Kin 4:37 7812
b himself to David with his face 1Chr 21:21 7812
b down their heads, and worshipped 1Chr 29:20 6915
they *b* themselves with their 2Chr 7:3 7812
Jehoshaphat *b* his head with his 2Chr 20:18 6915
b down himself before them, and 2Chr 25:14 7812
present with him *b* themselves 2Chr 29:29 3766
they *b* their heads and worshipped 2Chr 29:30 6915
they *b* their heads, and worshipped Neh 8:6 6915
that were in the king's gate, *b* Est 3:2 3766
But Mordecai *b* not, nor did him Est 3:2 3766
Haman saw that Mordecai *b* not Est 3:5 3766
He *b* the heavens also, and came Ps 18:9 5186
I *b* down heavily, as one that Ps 35:14 7817
I am *b* down greatly Ps 38:6 7817
For our soul is *b* down to the Ps 44:25 7743
my soul is *b* down Ps 57:6 3721
up all those that be *b* down Ps 145:14 3721
LORD raiseth them that are *b* down Ps 146:8 3721
of men shall be *b* down, and the Is 2:11 7817
loftiness of man shall be *b* down Is 2:17 7817
I was *b* down at the hearing of it Is 21:3 5791
they *b* the knee before him, and Mt 27:29 *1120*
was *b* together, and could in no Lk 13:11 *4794*
b down their faces to the earth, Lk 24:5 *2827*
he *b* his head, and gave up the Jn 19:30 *2827*
who have not *b* the knee to the Rom 11:4 *2578*

BOWELS {39}
thine own *b* shall be thine heir Gen 15:4 4578
shall be separated from thy *b* Gen 25:23 4578
for his *b* did yearn upon his Gen 43:30 7358
the curse shall go into thy *b* Num 5:22 4578
which shall proceed out of thy *b* 2Sa 7:12 4578
my son, which came forth of my *b* 2Sa 16:11 4578
shed out his *b* to the ground, and 2Sa 20:10 4578
for her *b* yearned upon her son, 1Kin 3:26 7358
sickness by disease of thy *b* 2Chr 21:15 4578
until thy *b* fall out by reason of 2Chr 21:15 4578
his *b* with an incurable disease 2Chr 21:18 4578
his *b* fell out by reason of his 2Chr 21:19 4578
b slew him there with the sword 2Chr 32:21 4578
Yet his meat in his *b* is turned Job 20:14 4578
My *b* boiled, and rested not Job 30:27 4578
it is melted in the midst of my *b* Ps 22:14 4578
that took me out of my mother's *b* Ps 71:6 4578
let it come into his *b* like water Ps 109:18 7130
door, and my *b* were moved for him Song 5:4 4578
Wherefore my *b* shall sound like Is 16:11 4578
the offspring of thy *b* like the Is 48:19 4578
from the *b* of my mother hath he Is 49:1 4578
strength, the sounding of thy *b* Is 63:15 4578
My *b*, my *b* Jer 4:19 4578
therefore my *b* are troubled for Jer 31:20 4578
my *b* are troubled Lam 1:20 4578
my *b* are troubled, my liver is Lam 2:11 4578
fill thy *b* with this roll that I Eze 3:3 4578
their souls, neither fill their *b* Eze 7:19 4578
midst, and all his *b* gushed out Acts 1:18 *4698*
ye are straitened in your own *b* 2Cor 6:12 *4698*
you all in the *b* of Jesus Christ Phil 1:8 *4698*
of the Spirit, if any *b* and Phil 2:1 *4698*
beloved, *b* of mercies, kindness, Col 3:12 *4698*
because the *b* of the saints are Philem 7 *4698*
receive him, that is, mine own *b* Philem 12 *4698*
refresh my *b* in the Lord Philem 20 *4698*
shutteth up his *b* of compassion 1Jn 3:17 *4698*

BOWETH {3}
likewise every one that *b* down Judg 7:5 3766
And the mean man *b* down, and the Is 2:9 7817
Bel *b* down, Nebo stoopeth, their Is 46:1 3766

BOWING {4}
the LORD, *b* himself to the earth Gen 24:52
their eyes *b* down to the earth Ps 17:11 5186
as a *b* wall shall ye be, and as a Ps 62:3 5186
b their knees worshipped him Mk 15:19 *5087*

BOWL {17}
one silver *b* of seventy shekels, Num 7:13 4219
one silver *b* of seventy shekels, Num 7:19 4219
one silver *b* of seventy shekels, Num 7:25 4219
one silver *b* of seventy shekels, Num 7:31 4219
one silver *b* of seventy shekels, Num 7:37 4219
a silver *b* of seventy shekels, Num 7:43 4219
one silver *b* of seventy shekels, Num 7:49 4219
one silver *b* of seventy shekels, Num 7:55 4219
one silver *b* of seventy shekels, Num 7:61 4219
one silver *b* of seventy shekels, Num 7:67 4219
one silver *b* of seventy shekels, Num 7:73 4219
one silver *b* of seventy shekels, Num 7:79 4219
and thirty shekels, each *b* seventy Num 7:85 4219
of the fleece, a *b* full of water Judg 6:38 5602
loosed, or the golden *b* be broken Eccl 12:6 1543
with a *b* upon the top of it, and Zec 4:2 1543
one upon the right side of the *b* Zec 4:3 1543

BOWLS {24}
b thereof, to cover withal Ex 25:29 4518
his shaft, and his branches, his *b* Ex 25:31 1375
Three *b* made like unto almonds, Ex 25:33 1375
three *b* made like almonds in the Ex 25:33 1375
be four *b* made like unto almonds Ex 25:34 1375
dishes, and his spoons, and his *b* Ex 37:16 4518
his shaft, and his branch, his *b* Ex 37:17 1375
Three *b* made after the fashion of Ex 37:19 1375
three *b* made like almonds in Ex 37:19 1375
were four *b* made like almonds Ex 37:20 1375
dishes, and the spoons, and the *b* Num 4:7 4518
of silver, twelve silver *b* Num 7:84 4219
the two *b* of the chapiters that 1Kin 7:41 1543
to cover the two *b* of the 1Kin 7:41 1543
to cover the two *b* of the 1Kin 7:42 1543
And the *b*, and the snuffers, and the 1Kin 7:50 5592
the house of the LORD *b* of silver 2Kin 12:13 5592
And the firepans, and the *b* 2Kin 25:15 4219
gold for the fleshhooks, and the *b* 1Chr 28:17 4219
and the snuffers, and the *b* Jer 52:18 4219
basons, and the firepans, and the *b* Jer 52:19 4219
That drink wine in *b*, and anoint Amos 6:6 4219
and they shall be filled like *b* Zec 9:15 4219
be like the *b* before the altar Zec 14:20 4219

BOWMEN {1}
the noise of the horsemen and *b* Jer 4:29 7411,7198

BOWS {14}
The *b* of the mighty men are 1Sa 2:4 7198
They were armed with *b*, and could 1Chr 12:2 7198
that bare shields and drew *b* 2Chr 14:8 7198
and helmets, and habergeons, and *b* 2Chr 26:14 7198
swords, their spears, and their *b* Neh 4:13 7198
the spears, the shields, and the *b* Neh 4:16 7198
heart, and their *b* shall be broken Ps 37:15 7198
bend their *b* to shoot their Ps 64:3
being armed, and carrying *b* Ps 78:9 7198
are sharp, and all their *b* bent Is 5:28 7198
with *b* shall men come thither Is 7:24 7198
Their *b* also shall dash the young Is 13:18 7198
every one of their *b* is broken Jer 51:56 7198
shields and the bucklers, the *b* Eze 39:9 7198

BOWSHOT {1}
a good way off, as it were a *b* Gen 21:16 2909,7198

BOX {8}
take this *b* of oil in thine hand, 2Kin 9:1 6378
Then take the *b* of oil, and pour 2Kin 9:3 6378
the pine, and the *b* tree together Is 41:19 8391
the *b* together, to beautify the Is 60:13 8391
b of very precious ointment Mt 26:7 *211*
a woman having an alabaster *b* of Mk 14:3 *211*
and she brake the *b*, and poured it Mk 14:3 *211*
an alabaster *b* of ointment Lk 7:37 *211*

BOY {1}
have given a *b* for an harlot, and Joel 3:3 3206

BOYS {2}
And the *b* grew Gen 25:27 5288
of the city shall be full of *b* Zec 8:5 3206

BOZEZ *(bo'-zez)* {1} *A rock near Michmash.*
and the name of the one was *B* 1Sa 14:4 949

BOZKATH *(boz'-kath)* {1} *A city in Judah.*
Lachish, and *B*, and Eglon, Josh 15:39 1218

BOZRAH *(boz'-rah)* {9}
1. The capital city of Edom.
Zerah of *B* reigned in his stead Gen 36:33 1224
Zerah of *B* reigned in his stead 1Chr 1:44 1224
the LORD hath a sacrifice in *B* Is 34:6 1224
Edom, with dyed garments from *B* Is 63:1 1224
that *B* shall become a desolation, Jer 49:13 1224
eagle, and spread his wings over *B* Jer 49:22 1224
shall devour the palaces of *B* Amos 1:12 1224
them together as the sheep of *B* Mic 2:12 1224
2. A place in Moab.
And upon Kerioth, and upon *B* Jer 48:24 1224

BRACELET {1}
the *b* that was on his arm, and 2Sa 1:10 685

BRACELETS {10}
two *b* for her hands of ten Gen 24:22 6781
b upon his sister's hands, and Gen 24:30 6781
her face, and the *b* upon her hands Gen 24:47 6781
And she said, Thy signet, and thy *b* Gen 38:18 6616
whose are these, the signet, and *b* Gen 38:25 6616
willing hearted, and brought *b* Ex 35:22 2397
of jewels of gold, chains, and *b* Num 31:50 6781
The chains, and the *b*, and the Is 3:19 8285
I put *b* upon thy hands, and a Eze 16:11 6781
which put *b* upon their hands, and Eze 23:42 6781

BRAKE {73}
b every tree of the field Ex 9:25 7665
all the people *b* off the golden Ex 32:3 6561
and *b* them beneath the mount Ex 32:19 7665
hands, and *b* them before your eyes Deut 9:17 7665
b the pitchers that were in their Judg 7:19 5310
b the pitchers, and held the lamps Judg 7:20 7665
head, and all to *b* his skull Judg 9:53 7533
he *b* the withs, as a thread of Judg 16:9 5423
he *b* them from off his arms like Judg 16:12 5423
side of the gate, and his neck *b* 1Sa 4:18 7665
the three mighty men *b* through 2Sa 23:16 1234
b in pieces the rocks before the 1Kin 19:11 7665
they *b* down the image of Baal, and 2Kin 10:27 5422
b down the house of Baal, and made 2Kin 10:27 5422
the house of Baal, and *b* it down 2Kin 11:18 5422
his images *b* they in pieces 2Kin 11:18 7665
b down the wall of Jerusalem from 2Kin 14:13 6555
b the images, and cut down the 2Kin 18:4 7665
b in pieces the brasen serpent 2Kin 18:4 3807
he *b* down the houses of the 2Kin 23:7 5422
b down the high places of the 2Kin 23:8 5422
b them down from thence, and cast 2Kin 23:12 7323
he *b* in pieces the images, and cut 2Kin 23:14 7665
altar and the high place he *b* down 2Kin 23:15 5422
b down the walls of Jerusalem 2Kin 25:10 5422
the three *b* through the host of 1Chr 11:18 1234
b down the images, and cut down 2Chr 14:3 7665
b into it, and carried away all 2Chr 21:17 1234
b it down, and *b* his altars and 2Chr 23:17 5422
b down the wall of Jerusalem from 2Chr 25:23 6555
b down the wall of Gath, and the 2Chr 26:6 6555
b the images in pieces, and cut 2Chr 31:1 7665
they *b* down the altars of Baalim 2Chr 34:4 5422
he *b* in pieces, and made dust of 2Chr 34:4 7665
b down the wall of Jerusalem, and 2Chr 36:19 5422
I *b* the jaws of the wicked, and Job 29:17 7665
sea with doors, when it *b* forth Job 38:8 1518
b up for it my decreed place, and Job 38:10 7665
There *b* he the arrows of the bow, Ps 76:3 7665
he *b* the whole staff of bread Ps 105:16 7665
b the trees of their coasts Ps 105:33 7665
the plague *b* in upon them Ps 106:29 6555
death, and *b* their bands in sunder Ps 107:14 5423
prophet Jeremiah's neck, and *b* it Jer 28:10 7665
which my covenant they *b*, Jer 31:32 6565
b down the walls of Jerusalem Jer 39:8 5422
b down all the walls of Jerusalem Jer 52:14 5422

of the LORD, the Chaldeans *b* .... Jer 52:17 7665
despised, and whose covenant he *b* .... Eze 17:16 6565
troubled, and his sleep *b* from him .... Dan 2:1 1961
iron and clay, and *b* them to pieces .... Dan 2:34 1855
that it *b* in pieces the iron, the .... Dan 2:45 1855
b all their bones in pieces or .... Dan 6:24 1855
b in pieces, and stamped the .... Dan 7:7 1855
b in pieces, and stamped the .... Dan 7:19 1855
smote the ram, and *b* his two horns .... Dan 8:7 7665
up to heaven, he blessed, and *b* .... Mt 14:19 *2806*
b them, and gave to his disciples, ... Mt 15:36 *2806*
b it, and gave it to the disciples .... Mt 26:26 *2806*
b the loaves, and gave them to his .... Mk 6:41 *2622*
loaves, and gave thanks, and *b* .... Mk 8:6 *2806*
When I *b* the five loaves among .... Mk 8:19 *2806*
she *b* the box, and poured it on .... Mk 14:3 *4937*
b it and gave to them, and said, ... Mk 14:22 *2806*
and their net *b* .... Lk 5:6 *1284*
he *b* the bands, and was driven of .... Lk 8:29 *1284*
to heaven, he blessed them, and *b* .... Lk 9:16 *2622*
b it, and gave unto them, saying, ... Lk 22:19 *2806*
took bread, and blessed it, and *b* .... Lk 24:30 *2806*
b the legs of the first, and of .... Jn 19:32 *2608*
dead already, they *b* not his legs .... Jn 19:33 *2608*
when he had given thanks, he *b* it 1Cor 11:24 *2806*

BRAKEST {5}
in the first tables, which thou *b* .... Ex 34:1 7665
in the first tables which thou *b* .... Deut 10:2 7665
thou *b* the heads of the dragons .... Ps 74:13 7665
Thou *b* the heads of leviathan in .... Ps 74:14 7533
they leaned upon thee, thou *b* .... Eze 29:7 7665

BRAMBLE {4}
said all the trees unto the *b* .... Judg 9:14 329
the *b* said unto the trees, If in .... Judg 9:15 329
not, let fire come out of the *b* .... Judg 9:15 329
nor of a *b* bush gather they .... Lk 6:44 *942*

BRAMBLES {1}
b in the fortresses thereof .... Is 34:13 2336

BRANCH {37}
with a knop and a flower in one *b* .... Ex 25:33 7070
made like almonds in the other *b* .... Ex 25:33 7070
his shaft, and his *b*, his bowls, ... Ex 37:17 7070
the fashion of almonds in one *b* .... Ex 37:19 7070
made like almonds in another *b* .... Ex 37:19 7070
cut down from thence a *b* with one .... Num 13:23 2156
his *b* shooteth forth in his .... Job 8:16 3127
that the tender *b* thereof will .... Job 14:7
time, and his *b* shall not be green .... Job 15:32 3712
and above shall his *b* be cut off .... Job 18:16 7105
the dew lay all night upon my *b* .... Job 29:19 7105
the *b* that thou madest strong for .... Ps 80:15 1121
righteous shall flourish as a *b* .... Prov 11:28 5929
In that day shall the *b* of the .... Is 4:2 6780
off from Israel head and tail, *b* .... Is 9:14 3712
a *B* shall grow out of his roots .... Is 11:1 5342
of thy grave like an abominable *b* .... Is 14:19 5342
forsaken bough, and an uppermost *b* .... Is 17:9 534
head or tail, *b* or rush, may do .... Is 19:15 3712
the *b* of the terrible ones shall .... Is 25:5 2158
the *b* of my planting, the work of .... Is 60:21 5342
raise unto David a righteous *B* .... Jer 23:5 6780
that time, will I cause the *B* of .... Jer 33:15 6780
they put the *b* to their nose .... Eze 8:17 2156
or than a *b* which is among the .... Eze 15:2 2156
took the highest *b* of the cedar .... Eze 17:3 6788
the highest *b* of the high cedar .... Eze 17:22 6788
But out of a *b* of her roots shall .... Dan 11:7 5342
will bring forth my servant the *B* .... Zec 3:8 6780
the man whose name is The *B* .... Zec 6:12 6780
leave them neither root nor *b* .... Mal 4:1 6057
When his *b* is yet tender, and .... Mt 24:32 *2798*
When her *b* is yet tender, and .... Mk 13:28 *2798*
Every *b* in me that beareth not .... Jn 15:2 *2814*
every *b* that beareth fruit, he .... Jn 15:2
As the *b* cannot bear fruit of .... Jn 15:4 *2814*
in me, he is cast forth as a *b* .... Jn 15:6 *2814*

BRANCHES {75}
And in the vine were three *b* .... Gen 40:10 8299
The three *b* are three days .... Gen 40:12 8299
whose *b* run over the wall .... Gen 49:22 1121
his shaft, and his *b*, his bowls, ... Ex 25:31 7070
six *b* shall come out of the sides .... Ex 25:32 7070
three *b* of the candlestick out of .... Ex 25:32 7070
three *b* of the candlestick out of .... Ex 25:32 7070
so in the six *b* that come out of .... Ex 25:33 7070
be a knop under two *b* of the same .... Ex 25:35 7070
and a knop under two *b* of the same .... Ex 25:35 7070
and a knop under two *b* of the same .... Ex 25:35 7070
according to the six *b* that .... Ex 25:35 7070
their *b* shall be of the same .... Ex 25:36 7070
six *b* going out of the sides .... Ex 37:18 7070
three *b* of the candlestick out of .... Ex 37:18 7070
three *b* of the candlestick out of .... Ex 37:18 7070
so throughout the six *b* going out .... Ex 37:19 7070
And a knop under two *b* of the same .... Ex 37:21 7070
and a knop under two *b* of the same .... Ex 37:21 7070
and a knop under two *b* of the same .... Ex 37:21 7070
to the six *b* going out of it .... Ex 37:21 7070
knops and their *b* were of the same .... Ex 37:22 7070
b of palm trees, and the boughs of .... Lev 23:40 3709
fetch olive *b*, and pine *b* .... Neh 8:15 5929
and myrtle *b*, and palm *b* .... Neh 8:15 5929
b of thick trees, to make booths, ... Neh 8:15 5929
the flame shall dry up his *b* .... Job 15:30 3127
the sea, and her *b* unto the river .... Ps 80:11 3127
which sing among the *b* .... Ps 104:12 6073
her *b* are stretched out, they are .... Is 16:8 7976
in the outmost fruitful *b* thereof .... Is 17:6 5585
and take away and cut down the *b* .... Is 18:5 5189
down, and consume the *b* thereof .... Is 27:10 5585
it, and the *b* of it are broken .... Jer 11:16 1808
whose *b* turned toward him, and the .... Eze 17:6 1808
became a vine, and brought forth *b* .... Eze 17:6 905
and shot forth her *b* toward him .... Eze 17:7 1808
that it might bring forth *b* .... Eze 17:8 6057
in the shadow of the *b* thereof .... Eze 17:23 1808
full of *b* by reason of many .... Eze 19:10 6058
was exalted among the thick *b* .... Eze 19:11 5688
with the multitude of her *b* .... Eze 19:11 1808
is gone out of a rod of her *b* .... Eze 19:14 905
a cedar in Lebanon with fair *b* .... Eze 31:3 6057
his *b* became long because of the .... Eze 31:5 6288
under his *b* did all the beasts of .... Eze 31:6 6288
greatness, in the length of his *b* .... Eze 31:7 1808
chesnut trees were not like his *b* .... Eze 31:8 6288
fair by the multitude of his *b* .... Eze 31:9 1808
all the valleys his *b* are fallen .... Eze 31:12 1808
of the field shall be upon his *b* .... Eze 31:13 6288
ye shall shoot forth your *b* .... Eze 36:8 6057
down the tree, and cut off his *b* .... Dan 4:14 6056
under it, and the fowls from his *b* .... Dan 4:14 6056
upon whose *b* the fowls of the .... Dan 4:21 6056
cities, and shall consume his *b* .... Hos 11:6 905
His *b* shall spread, and his beauty .... Hos 14:6 3127
the *b* thereof are made white .... Joel 1:7 8299
them out, and marred their vine *b* .... Nah 2:2 2156
What be these two olive *b* which .... Zec 4:12 7641
come and lodge in the *b* thereof .... Mt 13:32 *2798*
others cut down *b* from the trees .... Mt 21:8 *2798*
herbs, and shooteth out great *b* .... Mk 4:32 *2798*
others cut down *b* off the trees .... Mk 11:8 *4746*
of the air lodged in the *b* of it .... Lk 13:19 *2798*
Took *b* of palm trees, and went .... Jn 12:13 *902*
I am the vine, ye are the *b* .... Jn 15:5 *2814*
if the root be holy, so are the *b* .... Rom 11:16 *2798*
And if some of the *b* be broken off .... Rom 11:17 *2798*
Boast not against the *b* .... Rom 11:18 *2798*
The *b* were broken off, that I .... Rom 11:19 *2798*
if God spared not the natural *b* .... Rom 11:21 *2798*
these, which be the natural *b* .... Rom 11:24

BRAND {1}
is not this a *b* plucked out of .... Zec 3:2 181

BRANDISH {1}
when I shall *b* my sword before .... Eze 32:10 5774

BRANDS {1}
And when he had set the *b* on fire .... Judg 15:5 3940

BRASEN {29}
four *b* rings in the four corners .... Ex 27:4 5178
burnt offering, with his *b* grate .... Ex 35:16 5178
he made for the altar a *b* grate .... Ex 38:4 5178
twenty, and their *b* sockets twenty .... Ex 38:10 5178
the *b* altar, and the *b* grate .... Ex 38:30 5178
The *b* altar, and his grate of .... Ex 39:39 5178
and if it be sodden in a *b* pot .... Lev 6:28 5178
the priest took the *b* censers .... Num 16:39 5178
great cities with walls and *b* bars 1Kin 4:13 5178
And every base had four *b* wheels 1Kin 7:30 5178
because the *b* altar that was 1Kin 8:64 5178
made in their stead *b* shields 1Kin 14:27 5178
And he brought also the *b* altar 2Kin 16:14 5178
the *b* altar shall be for me to 2Kin 16:15 5178
off the *b* oxen that were under it 2Kin 16:17 5178
brake in pieces the *b* serpent 2Kin 18:4 5178
the *b* sea that was in the house 2Kin 25:13 5178
wherewith Solomon made the *b* sea 1Chr 18:8 5178
Moreover the *b* altar, that 2Chr 1:5 5178
to the *b* altar before the LORD 2Chr 1:6 5178
For Solomon had made a *b* scaffold 2Chr 6:13 5178
because the *b* altar which Solomon 2Chr 7:7 5178
b walls against the whole land, ... Jer 1:18 5178
unto this people a fenced *b* wall .... Jer 15:20 5178
the *b* sea that was in the house .... Jer 52:17 5178
twelve *b* bulls that were under .... Jer 52:20 5178
in, and stood beside the *b* altar .... Eze 9:2 5178
and pots, *b* vessels, and of tables .... Mk 7:4 *5473*

BRASS {126}
of every artificer in *b* and iron .... Gen 4:22 5178
gold, and silver, and *b*, ... Ex 25:3 5178
thou shalt make fifty taches of *b* .... Ex 26:11 5178
cast five sockets of *b* for them .... Ex 26:37 5178
and thou shalt overlay it with *b* .... Ex 27:2 5178
thereof thou shalt make of *b* .... Ex 27:3 5178
for it a grate of network of *b* .... Ex 27:4 5178
wood, and overlay them with *b* .... Ex 27:6 5178
twenty sockets shall be of *b* .... Ex 27:10 5178
and their twenty sockets of *b* .... Ex 27:11 5178
of silver, and their sockets of *b* .... Ex 27:17 5178
linen, and their sockets of *b* .... Ex 27:18 5178
pins of the court, shall be of *b* .... Ex 27:19 5178
Thou shalt also make a laver of *b* .... Ex 30:18 5178
and his foot also of *b* .... Ex 30:18 5178
in gold, and in silver, and in *b* .... Ex 31:4 5178
gold, and silver, and *b*, ... Ex 35:5 5178
b brought the LORD's offering .... Ex 35:24 5178
in gold, and in silver, and in *b* .... Ex 35:32 5178
he made fifty taches of *b* to .... Ex 36:18 5178
but their five sockets were of *b* .... Ex 36:38 5178
and he overlaid it with *b* .... Ex 38:2 5178
the vessels thereof made he of *b* .... Ex 38:3 5178
the four ends of the grate of *b* .... Ex 38:5 5178
wood, and overlaid them with *b* .... Ex 38:6 5178
And he made the laver of *b* .... Ex 38:8 5178
and the foot of it of *b* .... Ex 38:8 5178
and their sockets of *b* twenty .... Ex 38:11 5178
sockets for the pillars were of *b* .... Ex 38:17 5178
four, and their sockets of *b* four .... Ex 38:19 5178
the court round about, were of *b* .... Ex 38:20 5178
the *b* of the offering was seventy .... Ex 38:29 5178
brasen altar, and his grate of *b* .... Ex 39:39 5178
as iron, and your earth as *b* .... Lev 26:19 5154
And Moses made a serpent of *b* .... Num 21:9 5178
when he beheld the serpent of *b* .... Num 21:9 5178
the gold, and the silver, the *b* .... Num 31:22 5178
of whose hills thou mayest dig *b* .... Deut 8:9 5178
that is over thy head shall be *b* .... Deut 28:23 5178
Thy shoes shall be iron and *b* .... Deut 33:25 5178
silver, and gold, and vessels of *b* .... Josh 6:19 5178
and the gold, and the vessels of *b* .... Josh 6:24 5178
silver, and with gold, and with *b* .... Josh 22:8 5178
and bound him with fetters of *b* .... Judg 16:21 5178
had an helmet of *b* upon his head 1Sa 17:5 5178
was five thousand shekels of *b* 1Sa 17:5 5178
he had greaves of *b* upon his legs 1Sa 17:6 5178
a target of *b* between his 1Sa 17:6 5178
put an helmet of *b* upon his head 1Sa 17:38 5178
king David took exceeding much *b* 2Sa 8:8 5178
vessels of gold, and vessels of *b* 2Sa 8:10 5178
hundred shekels of *b* in weight 2Sa 21:16 5178
was a man of Tyre, a worker in *b* 1Kin 7:14 5178
and cunning to work all works in *b* 1Kin 7:14 5178
For he cast two pillars of *b* 1Kin 7:15 5178
he made two chapiters of molten *b* 1Kin 7:16 5178
And he made ten bases of *b* 1Kin 7:27 5178
brasen wheels, and plates of *b* 1Kin 7:30 5178
Then made he ten lavers of *b* 1Kin 7:38 5178
of the LORD, were of bright *b* 1Kin 7:45 5178
was the weight of the *b* found out 1Kin 7:47 5178
and bound him with fetters of *b* 2Kin 25:7 5178
the pillars of *b* that were in the 2Kin 25:13 5178
carried the *b* of them to Babylon 2Kin 25:13 5178
all the vessels of *b* wherewith 2Kin 25:14 5178
the *b* of all these vessels was 2Kin 25:16 5178
and the chapiter upon it was *b* 2Kin 25:17 5178
chapiter round about, all of *b* 2Kin 25:17 5178
to sound with cymbals of *b* 1Chr 15:19 5178
brought David very much *b* 1Chr 18:8 5178
the pillars, and the vessels of *b* 1Chr 18:8 5178
of vessels of gold and silver and *b* 1Chr 18:10 5178
b in abundance without weight 1Chr 22:3 5178
and of *b* and iron without weight 1Chr 22:14 5178
Of the gold, the silver, and the *b* 1Chr 22:16 5178
and the *b* for things of *b* 1Chr 29:2 5178
of *b* eighteen thousand talents, ... 1Chr 29:7 5178
in gold, and in silver, and in *b* 2Chr 2:7 5178
work in gold, and in silver, in *b* 2Chr 2:14 5178
Moreover he made an altar of *b* 2Chr 4:1 5178
overlaid the doors of them with *b* 2Chr 4:9 5178
the house of the LORD of bright *b* 2Chr 4:16 5178
for the weight of the *b* could not 2Chr 4:18 5178
king Rehoboam made shields of *b* 2Chr 12:10 5178
b to mend the house of the LORD 2Chr 24:12 5178
or is my flesh of *b* .... Job 6:12 5153
b is molten out of the stone .... Job 28:2 5154
bones are as strong pieces of *b* .... Job 40:18 5154
as straw, and *b* as rotten wood .... Job 41:27 5154
For he hath broken the gates of *b* .... Ps 107:16 5178
break in pieces the gates of *b* .... Is 45:2 5154
is an iron sinew, and thy brow *b* .... Is 48:4 5154
For *b* I will bring gold, and for .... Is 60:17 5178
will bring silver, and for wood *b* .... Is 60:17 5178
they are *b* and iron .... Jer 6:28 5178
Also the pillars of *b* that were .... Jer 52:17 5178
carried all the *b* of them to .... Jer 52:17 5178
all the vessels of *b* wherewith .... Jer 52:18 5178
the *b* of all these vessels was .... Jer 52:20 5178
And a chapiter of *b* was upon it .... Jer 52:22 5178
chapiters round about, all of *b* .... Jer 52:22 5178
like the colour of burnished *b* .... Eze 1:7 5178
all they are *b*, and tin, and iron, ... Eze 22:18 5178
As they gather silver, and *b* .... Eze 22:20 5178
that the *b* of it may be hot, and .... Eze 24:11 5178
vessels of *b* in thy market .... Eze 27:13 5178
was like the appearance of *b* .... Eze 40:3 5178
his belly and his thighs of *b* .... Dan 2:32 5174
was the iron, the clay, the *b* .... Dan 2:35 5174
and another third kingdom of *b* .... Dan 2:39 5174
brake in pieces the iron, the *b* .... Dan 2:45 5174
even with a band of iron and *b* .... Dan 4:15 5174
even with a band of iron and *b* .... Dan 4:23 5174
gods of gold, and of silver, of *b* .... Dan 5:4 5174
the gods of silver, and gold, of *b* .... Dan 5:23 5174
were of iron, and his nails of *b* .... Dan 7:19 5174
feet like in colour to polished *b* .... Dan 10:6 5178
iron, and I will make thy hoofs *b* .... Mic 4:13 5154
the mountains were mountains of *b* .... Zec 6:1 5178
nor silver, nor *b* in your purses, ... Mt 10:9 *5475*
I am become as sounding *b* 1Cor 13:1 *5475*
And his feet like unto fine *b* .... Rev 1:15 *5474*
fire, and his feet are like fine *b* .... Rev 2:18 *5474*
and idols of gold, and silver, and *b* .... Rev 9:20 *5470*
of most precious wood, and of *b* .... Rev 18:12 *5475*

BRAVERY {1}
the *b* of their tinkling ornaments .... Is 3:18 8597

BRAWLER {1}
but patient, not a *b*, not 1Ti 3:3 *269*

BRAWLERS {1}
speak evil of no man, to be no *b* .... Titus 3:2 *269*

BRAWLING {2}
the housetop, than with a *b* woman ... Prov 21:9 4090
the housetop, than with a *b* woman ... Prov 25:24 4090

BRAY {2}
Doth the wild ass *b* when he hath ... Job 6:5 5101
Though thou shouldest *b* a fool in ... Prov 27:22 3806

BRAYED {1}
Among the bushes they *b* ... Job 30:7 5101

BREACH {22}
this *b* be upon thee ... Gen 38:29 6556
B for *b*, eye for eye, tooth ... Lev 24:20 7667
and ye shall know my *b* of promise ... Num 14:34 8569
made a *b* in the tribes of Israel ... Judg 21:15 6556
before me, as the *b* of waters ... 2Sa 5:20 6556
the LORD had made a *b* upon Uzzah ... 2Sa 6:8 6556
wheresoever any *b* shall be found ... 2Kin 12:5 919
the LORD had made a *b* upon Uzza ... 1Chr 13:11 6556
the LORD our God made a *b* upon us ... 1Chr 15:13 6555
that there was no *b* left therein ... Neh 6:1 6556
He breaketh me with *b* upon *b* ... Job 16:14 6556
chosen stood before him in the *b* ... Ps 106:23 6556
therein is a *b* in the spirit ... Prov 15:4 7667
let us make a *b* therein for us, ... Is 7:6 1234
be to you as a *b* ready to fall ... Is 30:13 6556
bindeth up the *b* of his people ... Is 30:26 7667
be called, The repairer of the *b* ... Is 58:12 6556
people is broken with a great *b* ... Jer 14:17 7667
for thy *b* is great like the sea ... Lam 2:13 7667
into a city wherein is made a *b* ... Eze 26:10 1234

BREACHES {15}
the sea shore, and abode in his *b* ... Judg 5:17 4664
repaired the *b* of the city of ... 1Kin 11:27 6556
them repair the *b* of the house ... 2Kin 12:5 919
not repaired the *b* of the house ... 2Kin 12:6 919
repair ye not the *b* of the house ... 2Kin 12:7 919
deliver it for the *b* of the house ... 2Kin 12:7 919
to repair the *b* of the house ... 2Kin 12:8 919
the *b* of the house of the LORD ... 2Kin 12:12 919
to repair the *b* of the house ... 2Kin 22:5 919
that the *b* began to be stopped, ... Neh 4:7 6555
heal the *b* thereof ... Ps 60:2 7667
also the *b* of the city of David ... Is 22:9 1233
And ye shall go out at the *b* ... Amos 4:3 6556
will smite the great house with *b* ... Amos 6:11 7447
fallen, and close up the *b* thereof ... Amos 9:11 6556

BREAD {360}
of thy face shalt thou eat *b* ... Gen 3:19 3899
king of Salem brought forth *b* ... Gen 14:18 3899
And I will fetch a morsel of *b* ... Gen 18:5 3899
a feast, and did bake unleavened *b* ... Gen 19:3
early in the morning, and took *b* ... Gen 21:14 3899
Then Jacob gave Esau *b* and pottage ... Gen 25:34 3899
gave the savoury meat and the *b* ... Gen 27:17 3899
I go, and will give me *b* to eat ... Gen 28:20 3899
and called his brethren to eat *b* ... Gen 31:54 3899
and they did eat *b*, and tarried all ... Gen 31:54 3899
And they sat down to eat *b* ... Gen 37:25 3899
save the *b* which he did eat ... Gen 39:6 3899
all the land of Egypt there was *b* ... Gen 41:54 3899
the people cried to Pharaoh for *b* ... Gen 41:55 3899
that they should eat *b* there ... Gen 43:25 3899
himself, and said, Set on *b* ... Gen 43:31 3899
might not eat *b* with the Hebrews ... Gen 43:32 3899
she asses laden with corn and *b* ... Gen 45:23 3899
his father's household, with *b* ... Gen 47:12 3899
there was no *b* in all the land ... Gen 47:13 3899
unto Joseph, and said, Give us *b* ... Gen 47:15 3899
Joseph gave them *b* in exchange ... Gen 47:17 3899
he fed them with *b* for all their ... Gen 47:17 3899
buy us and our land for *b*, and we ... Gen 47:19 3899
Out of Asher his *b* shall be fat ... Gen 49:20 3899
call him, that he may eat *b* ... Ex 2:20 3899
roast with fire, and unleavened *b* ... Ex 12:8
days shall ye eat unleavened *b* ... Ex 12:15
b from the first day until the ... Ex 12:15
observe the feast of unleavened *b* ... Ex 12:17
even, ye shall eat unleavened *b* ... Ex 12:18
shall ye eat unleavened *b* ... Ex 12:20
shall no leavened *b* be eaten ... Ex 13:3
days thou shalt eat unleavened *b* ... Ex 13:6
Unleavened *b* shall be eaten seven ... Ex 13:7
no leavened *b* be seen with thee ... Ex 13:7
and when we did eat *b* to the full ... Ex 16:3 3899
I will rain *b* from heaven for you ... Ex 16:4 3899
and in the morning *b* to the full ... Ex 16:8 3899
morning ye shall be filled with *b* ... Ex 16:12 3899
This is the *b* which the LORD hath ... Ex 16:15 3899
day they gathered twice as much *b* ... Ex 16:22 3899
the sixth day the *b* of two days ... Ex 16:29 3899
that they may see the *b* wherewith ... Ex 16:32 3899
to eat *b* with Moses' father in ... Ex 18:12 3899
keep the feast of unleavened *b* ... Ex 23:15
shalt eat unleavened *b* seven days ... Ex 23:15
of my sacrifice with leavened *b* ... Ex 23:18
your God, and he shall bless thy *b* ... Ex 23:25 3899
And unleavened *b*, and cakes ... Ex 29:2 3899
one loaf of *b*, and one cake of oiled ... Ex 29:23 3899
b that is before the LORD ... Ex 29:23
the *b* that is in the basket, by ... Ex 29:32 3899
of the consecrations, or of the *b* ... Ex 29:34 3899
of unleavened *b* shalt thou keep ... Ex 34:18
days thou shalt eat unleavened *b* ... Ex 34:18
he did neither eat *b*, nor drink ... Ex 34:28 3899
he set the *b* in order upon it ... Ex 40:23 3899
with unleavened *b* shall it be ... Lev 6:16
leavened *b* with the sacrifice of ... Lev 7:13 3899
rams, and a basket of unleavened *b* ... Lev 8:2
out of the basket of unleavened *b* ... Lev 8:26
cake, and a cake of oiled *b* ... Lev 8:26
there eat it with the *b* that is ... Lev 8:31 3899
of the *b* shall ye burn with fire ... Lev 8:32 3899
the *b* of their God, they do offer ... Lev 21:6 3899
for he offereth the *b* of thy God ... Lev 21:8 3899
to offer the *b* of his God ... Lev 21:17 3899
nigh to offer the *b* of his God ... Lev 21:21 3899
He shall eat the *b* of his God ... Lev 21:22 3899
hand shall ye offer the *b* of your ... Lev 22:25 3899
of unleavened *b* unto the LORD ... Lev 23:6
days ye must eat unleavened *b* ... Lev 23:6
And ye shall eat neither *b* ... Lev 23:14 3899
ye shall offer with the *b* seven ... Lev 23:18 3899
b of the first fruits for a wave ... Lev 23:20 3899
it may be on the *b* for a memorial ... Lev 24:7 3899
ye shall eat your *b* to the full ... Lev 26:5 3899
I have broken the staff of your *b* ... Lev 26:26 3899
shall bake your *b* in one oven ... Lev 26:26 3899
you your *b* again by weight ... Lev 26:26 3899
the continual *b* shall be thereon ... Num 4:7 3899
And a basket of unleavened *b* ... Num 6:15
of unleavened *b* anointed with oil ... Num 6:15
with the basket of unleavened *b* ... Num 6:17
it, and eat it with unleavened *b* ... Num 9:11
for they are *b* for us ... Num 14:9 3899
when ye eat of the *b* of the land ... Num 15:19 3899
for there is no *b*, neither is ... Num 21:5 3899
and our soul loatheth this light *b* ... Num 21:5 3899
my *b* for my sacrifices made by ... Num 28:2 3899
days shall unleavened *b* be eaten ... Num 28:17
that man doth not live by *b* only ... Deut 8:3 3899
shalt eat *b* without scarceness ... Deut 8:9 3899
neither did eat *b* nor drink water ... Deut 9:9 3899
I did neither eat *b*, nor drink ... Deut 9:18 3899
shalt eat no leavened *b* with it ... Deut 16:3
thou eat unleavened *b* therewith ... Deut 16:3
even the *b* of affliction ... Deut 16:3 3899
there shall be no leavened *b* seen ... Deut 16:4
days thou shalt eat unleavened *b* ... Deut 16:8
in the feast of unleavened *b* ... Deut 16:16
Because they met you not with *b* ... Deut 23:4 3899
Ye have not eaten *b*, neither have ... Deut 29:6 3899
all the *b* of their provision was ... Josh 9:5 3899
This our *b* we took hot for our ... Josh 9:12 3899
a cake of barley *b* tumbled into ... Judg 7:13 3899
loaves of *b* unto the people that ... Judg 8:5 3899
we should give *b* unto thine army ... Judg 8:6 3899
that we should give *b* unto thy ... Judg 8:15 3899
me, I will not eat of thy *b* ... Judg 13:16 3899
thine heart with a morsel of *b* ... Judg 19:5 3899
and there is *b* and wine also for me ... Judg 19:19 3899
his people in giving them *b* ... Ruth 1:6 3899
come thou hither, and eat of the *b* ... Ruth 2:14 3899
have hired out themselves for *b* ... 1Sa 2:5 3899
piece of silver and a morsel of *b* ... 1Sa 2:36 3899
that I may eat a piece of *b* ... 1Sa 2:36 3899
for the *b* is spent in our vessels ... 1Sa 9:7 3899
carrying three loaves of *b* ... 1Sa 10:3 3899
and give thee two loaves of *b* ... 1Sa 10:4 3899
And Jesse took an ass laden with *b* ... 1Sa 16:20 3899
me five loaves of *b* in mine hand ... 1Sa 21:3 3899
is no common *b* under mine hand ... 1Sa 21:4 3899
but there is hallowed *b* ... 1Sa 21:4 3899
the *b* is in a manner common, yea, ... 1Sa 21:5
So the priest gave him hallowed *b* ... 1Sa 21:6
for there was no *b* there but the ... 1Sa 21:6 3899
to put hot *b* in the day when it ... 1Sa 21:6 3899
in that thou hast given him *b* ... 1Sa 22:13 3899
Shall I then take my *b*, and my ... 1Sa 25:11 3899
for he had eaten no *b* all the day ... 1Sa 28:20 3899
me set a morsel of *b* before thee ... 1Sa 28:22 3899
and did bake unleavened *b* thereof ... 1Sa 28:24
him to David, and gave him *b* ... 1Sa 30:11 3899
for he had eaten no *b*, nor drunk ... 1Sa 30:12 3899
on the sword, or that lacketh *b* ... 2Sa 3:29 3899
to me, and more also, if I taste *b* ... 2Sa 3:35 3899
as men, to every one a cake of *b* ... 2Sa 6:19 3899
thou shalt eat *b* at my table ... 2Sa 9:7 3899
son shall eat *b* alway at my table ... 2Sa 9:10 3899
neither did he eat *b* with them ... 2Sa 12:17 3899
they set *b* before him, and he did ... 2Sa 12:20 3899
dead, thou didst rise and eat *b* ... 2Sa 12:21 3899
upon them two hundred loaves of *b* ... 2Sa 16:1 3899
and the *b* and summer fruit for the ... 2Sa 16:2 3899
neither will I eat *b* nor drink ... 1Kin 13:8 3899
of the LORD, saying, Eat no *b* ... 1Kin 13:9 3899
him, Come home with me, and eat *b* ... 1Kin 13:15 3899
neither will I eat *b* nor drink ... 1Kin 13:16 3899
Thou shalt eat no *b* nor drink ... 1Kin 13:17 3899
thine house, that he may eat *b* ... 1Kin 13:18 3899
did eat *b* in his house, and drank ... 1Kin 13:19 3899
But camest back, and hast eaten *b* ... 1Kin 13:22 3899
LORD did say to thee, Eat no *b* ... 1Kin 13:22 3899
to pass, after he had eaten *b* ... 1Kin 13:23 3899
And the ravens brought him *b* ... 1Kin 17:6 3899
and flesh in the morning, and *b* ... 1Kin 17:6 3899
a morsel of *b* in thine hand ... 1Kin 17:11 3899
in a cave, and fed them with *b* ... 1Kin 18:4 3899
in a cave, and fed them with *b* ... 1Kin 18:13 3899
away his face, and would eat no *b* ... 1Kin 21:4 3899
so sad, that thou eatest no *b* ... 1Kin 21:5 3899
arise, and eat *b*, and let thine ... 1Kin 21:7 3899
and feed him with *b* of affliction ... 1Kin 22:27 3899
and she constrained him to eat *b* ... 2Kin 4:8 3899
by, he turned in thither to eat *b* ... 2Kin 4:8 3899
man of God *b* of the firstfruits ... 2Kin 4:42 3899
set *b* and water before them, that ... 2Kin 6:22 3899
land of corn and wine, a land of *b* ... 2Kin 18:32 3899
unleavened *b* among their brethren ... 2Kin 23:9
there was no *b* for the people of ... 2Kin 25:3 3899
he did eat *b* continually before ... 2Kin 25:29 3899
brought *b* on asses, and on camels, ... 1Chr 12:40 3899
woman, to every one a loaf of *b* ... 1Chr 16:3 3899
even in the feast of unleavened *b* ... 2Chr 8:13
and feed him with *b* of affliction ... 2Chr 18:26 3899
unleavened *b* in the second month ... 2Chr 30:13
kept the feast of unleavened *b* ... 2Chr 30:21
feast of unleavened *b* seven days ... 2Chr 35:17
unleavened *b* seven days with joy ... Ezr 6:22
he came thither, he did eat no *b* ... Ezr 10:6 3899
not eaten the *b* of the governor ... Neh 5:14 3899
people, and had taken of them *b* ... Neh 5:15 3899
not I the *b* of the governor ... Neh 5:18 3899
gavest them *b* from heaven for ... Neh 9:15 3899
not the children of Israel with *b* ... Neh 13:2 3899
He wandereth abroad for *b* ... Job 15:23 3899
hast withholden *b* from the hungry ... Job 22:7 3899
shall not be satisfied with *b* ... Job 27:14 3899
for the earth, out of it cometh *b* ... Job 28:5 3899
So that his life abhorreth *b* ... Job 33:20 3899
did eat *b* with him in his house ... Job 42:11 3899
eat up my people as they eat *b* ... Ps 14:4 3899
forsaken, nor his seed begging *b* ... Ps 37:25 3899
I trusted, which did eat of my *b* ... Ps 41:9 3899
eat up my people as they eat *b* ... Ps 53:4 3899
can he give *b* also ... Ps 78:20 3899
feedest them with the *b* of tears ... Ps 80:5 3899
so that I forget to eat my *b* ... Ps 102:4 3899
For I have eaten ashes like *b* ... Ps 102:9 3899
b which strengtheneth man's heart ... Ps 104:15 3899
he brake the whole staff of *b* ... Ps 105:16 3899
them with the *b* of heaven ... Ps 105:40 3899
let them seek their *b* also out of ... Ps 109:10
up late, to eat the *b* of sorrows ... Ps 127:2 3899
I will satisfy her poor with *b* ... Ps 132:15 3899
For they eat the *b* of wickedness ... Prov 4:17 3899
a man is brought to a piece of *b* ... Prov 6:26 3899
Come, eat of my *b*, and drink of ... Prov 9:5 3899
b eaten in secret is pleasant ... Prov 9:17 3899
honoureth himself, and lacketh *b* ... Prov 12:9 3899
land shall be satisfied with *b* ... Prov 12:11 3899
and thou shalt be satisfied with *b* ... Prov 20:13 3899
B of deceit is sweet to a man ... Prov 20:17 3899
he giveth of his *b* to the poor ... Prov 22:9 3899
Eat thou not the *b* of him that ... Prov 23:6 3899
be hungry, give him *b* to eat ... Prov 25:21 3899
his land shall have plenty of *b* ... Prov 28:19 3899
for for a piece of *b* that man ... Prov 28:21 3899
and eateth not the *b* of idleness ... Prov 31:27 3899
eat thy *b* with joy, and drink thy ... Eccl 9:7 3899
strong, neither yet *b* to the wise ... Eccl 9:11 3899
Cast thy *b* upon the waters ... Eccl 11:1 3899
and the staff, the whole stay of *b* ... Is 3:1 3899
house is neither *b* nor clothing ... Is 3:7 3899
saying, We will eat our own *b* ... Is 4:1 3899
with their *b* him that fled ... Is 21:14 3899
B corn is bruised ... Is 28:28 3899
Lord give you the *b* of adversity ... Is 30:20 3899
b of the increase of the earth, ... Is 30:23 3899
b shall be given him ... Is 33:16 3899
land of corn and wine, a land of *b* ... Is 36:17 3899
yea, he kindleth it, and baketh *b* ... Is 44:15 3899
also I have baked *b* upon the ... Is 44:19 3899
pit, nor that his *b* should fail ... Is 51:14 3899
money for that which is not *b* ... Is 55:2 3899
to the sower, and *b* to the eater ... Is 55:10 3899
not to deal thy *b* to the hungry ... Is 58:7 3899
eat up thine harvest, and thy *b* ... Jer 5:17 3899
of *b* out of the bakers' street ... Jer 37:21 3899
until all the *b* in the city were ... Jer 37:21 3899
there is no more *b* in the city ... Jer 38:9 3899
they did eat *b* together in Mizpah ... Jer 41:1 3899
the trumpet, nor have hunger of *b* ... Jer 42:14 3899
so that there was no *b* for the ... Jer 52:6 3899
he did continually eat *b* before ... Jer 52:33 3899
All her people sigh, they seek *b* ... Lam 1:11 3899
the young children ask *b*, and no ... Lam 4:4 3899
Assyrians, to be satisfied with *b* ... Lam 5:6 3899
We gat our *b* with the peril of ... Lam 5:9 3899
vessel, and make thee *b* thereof ... Eze 4:9 3899
defiled *b* among the Gentiles ... Eze 4:13 3899
shalt prepare thy *b* therewith ... Eze 4:15 3899
break the staff of *b* in Jerusalem ... Eze 4:16 3899
and they shall eat *b* by weight ... Eze 4:16 3899
That they may want *b* and water, and ... Eze 4:17 3899
and will break your staff of *b* ... Eze 5:16 3899
eat thy *b* with quaking, and drink ... Eze 12:18 3899
eat their *b* with carefulness ... Eze 12:19 3899
of barley and for pieces of *b* ... Eze 13:19 3899
break the staff of the *b* thereof ... Eze 14:13 3899
sister Sodom, pride, fulness of *b* ... Eze 16:49 3899
hath given his *b* to the hungry ... Eze 18:7 3899
hath given his *b* to the hungry ... Eze 18:16 3899
thy lips, and eat not the *b* of men ... Eze 24:17 3899
your lips, nor eat the *b* of men ... Eze 24:22 3899
in it to eat *b* before the LORD ... Eze 44:3 3899
even my house, when ye offer my *b* ... Eze 44:7 3899
unleavened *b* shall be eaten ... Eze 45:21
I ate no pleasant *b*, neither came ... Dan 10:3 3899
my lovers, that give me my *b* ... Hos 2:5 3899
be unto them as the *b* of mourners ... Hos 9:4 3899
for their *b* for their soul shall ... Hos 9:4 3899
want of *b* in all your places ... Amos 4:6 3899
the land of Judah, and there eat *b* ... Amos 7:12 3899

in the land, not a famine of *b* … Amos 8:11 3899
they that eat thy *b* have laid a … Obad 7 3899
and with his skirt do touch *b* … Hag 2:12 3899
offer polluted *b* upon mine altar … Mal 1:7 3899
that these stones be made *b* … Mt 4:3 *740*
Man shall not live by *b* alone … Mt 4:4 *740*
Give us this day our daily *b* … Mt 6:11 *740*
of you, whom if his son ask *b* … Mt 7:9 *740*
not their hands when they eat *b* … Mt 15:2 *740*
not meet to take the children's *b* … Mt 15:26 *740*
have so much *b* in the wilderness … Mt 15:33 *740*
they had forgotten to take *b* … Mt 16:5 *740*
It is because we have taken no *b* … Mt 16:7 *740*
because ye have brought no *b* … Mt 16:8 *740*
spake it not to you concerning *b* … Mt 16:11 *740*
not beware of the leaven of *b* … Mt 16:12 *740*
b the disciples came to Jesus … Mt 26:17
as they were eating, Jesus took *b* … Mt 26:26 *740*
they could not so much as eat *b* … Mk 3:20 *740*
no scrip, no *b*, no money in their … Mk 6:8 *740*
the villages, and buy themselves *b* … Mk 6:36 *740*
buy two hundred pennyworth of *b* … Mk 6:37 *740*
his disciples eat *b* with defiled … Mk 7:2 *740*
but eat *b* with unwashen hands … Mk 7:5 *740*
not meet to take the children's *b* … Mk 7:27 *740*
men with *b* here in the wilderness … Mk 8:4 *740*
disciples had forgotten to take *b* … Mk 8:14 *740*
It is because we have no *b* … Mk 8:16 *740*
reason ye, because ye have no *b* … Mk 8:17 *740*
the passover, and of unleavened *b* … Mk 14:1
And the first day of unleavened *b* … Mk 14:12
And as they did eat, Jesus took *b* … Mk 14:22 *740*
this stone that it be made *b* … Lk 4:3 *740*
man shall not live by *b* alone … Lk 4:4 *740*
eating *b* nor drinking wine … Lk 7:33 *740*
staves, nor scrip, neither *b* … Lk 9:3 *740*
Give us day by day our daily *b* … Lk 11:3 *740*
If a son shall ask *b* of any of … Lk 11:11 *740*
to eat *b* on the sabbath day … Lk 14:1 *740*
shall eat *b* in the kingdom of God … Lk 14:15 *740*
of my father's have *b* enough … Lk 15:17 *740*
feast of unleavened *b* drew nigh … Lk 22:1
Then came the day of unleavened *b* … Lk 22:7
And he took *b*, and gave thanks, and … Lk 22:19 *740*
sat at meat with them, he took *b* … Lk 24:30 *740*
known of them in breaking of *b* … Lk 24:35 *740*
Philip, Whence shall we buy *b* … Jn 6:5 *740*
Two hundred pennyworth of *b* is … Jn 6:7 *740*
the place where they did eat *b* … Jn 6:23 *740*
He gave them *b* from heaven to eat … Jn 6:31 *740*
gave you not that *b* from heaven … Jn 6:32 *740*
giveth you the true *b* from heaven … Jn 6:32 *740*
For the *b* of God is he which … Jn 6:33 *740*
Lord, evermore give us this *b* … Jn 6:34 *740*
unto them, I am the *b* of life … Jn 6:35 *740*
I am the *b* which came down from … Jn 6:41 *740*
I am that *b* of life … Jn 6:48 *740*
This is the *b* which cometh down … Jn 6:50 *740*
I am the living *b* which came down … Jn 6:51 *740*
if any man eat of this *b*, he … Jn 6:51 *740*
the *b* that I will give is my … Jn 6:51 *740*
This is that *b* which came down … Jn 6:58 *740*
of this *b* shall live for ever … Jn 6:58 *740*
He that eateth *b* with me hath … Jn 13:18 *740*
there, and fish laid thereon, and *b* … Jn 21:9 *740*
Jesus then cometh, and taketh *b* … Jn 21:13 *740*
fellowship, and in breaking of *b* … Acts 2:42 *740*
breaking *b* from house to house, … Acts 2:46 *740*
were the days of unleavened *b* … Acts 12:3
after the days of unleavened *b* … Acts 20:6
came together to break *b*, Paul … Acts 20:7 *740*
come up again, and had broken *b* … Acts 20:11 *740*
he had thus spoken, he took *b* … Acts 27:35 *740*
the unleavened *b* of sincerity … 1Cor 5:8
The *b* which we break, is it not … 1Cor 10:16 *740*
For we being many are one *b* … 1Cor 10:17 *740*
are all partakers of that one *b* … 1Cor 10:17 *740*
in which he was betrayed took *b* … 1Cor 11:23 *740*
For as often as ye eat this *b* … 1Cor 11:26 *740*
whosoever shall eat this *b* … 1Cor 11:27 *740*
and so let him eat of that *b* … 1Cor 11:28 *740*
both minister *b* for your food … 2Cor 9:10 *740*
did we eat any man's *b* for nought … 2Th 3:8 *740*
they work, and eat their own *b* … 2Th 3:12 *740*

BREADTH {88}

the *b* of it fifty cubits, and the … Gen 6:15 7341
length of it and in the *b* of it … Gen 13:17 7341
a cubit and a half the *b* thereof … Ex 25:10 7341
a cubit and a half the *b* thereof … Ex 25:17 7341
thereof, and a cubit the *b* thereof … Ex 25:23 7341
a border of an hand *b* round about … Ex 25:25 2948
the *b* of one curtain four cubits … Ex 26:2 7341
the *b* of one curtain four cubits … Ex 26:8 7341
half shall be the *b* of one board … Ex 26:16 7341
for the *b* of the court on the … Ex 27:12 7341
the *b* of the court on the east … Ex 27:13 7341
the *b* fifty every where, and the … Ex 27:18 7341
and a span shall be the *b* thereof … Ex 28:16 7341
thereof, and a cubit the *b* thereof … Ex 30:2 7341
the *b* of one curtain four cubits … Ex 36:9 7341
cubits was the *b* of one curtain … Ex 36:15 7341
the *b* of a board one cubit and a … Ex 36:21 7341
and a cubit and a half the *b* of it … Ex 37:1 7341
one cubit and a half the *b* thereof … Ex 37:6 7341
thereof, and a cubit the *b* thereof … Ex 37:10 7341
a cubit, and the *b* of it a cubit … Ex 37:25 7341
and five cubits the *b* thereof … Ex 38:1 7341
height in the *b* was five cubits … Ex 38:18 7341
thereof, and a span the *b* thereof … Ex 39:9 7341
and four cubits the *b* of it … Deut 3:11 7341
could sling stones at an hair *b* … Judg 20:16
the *b* thereof twenty cubits, and … 1Kin 6:2 7341
according to the *b* of the house … 1Kin 6:3 7341
ten cubits was the *b* thereof … 1Kin 6:3 7341
in length, and twenty cubits in *b* … 1Kin 6:20 7341
the *b* thereof fifty cubits, and … 1Kin 7:2 7341
the *b* thereof thirty cubits … 1Kin 7:6 7341
And it was an hand *b* thick … 1Kin 7:26 2947
and four cubits the *b* thereof … 1Kin 7:27 7341
cubits, and the *b* twenty cubits … 2Chr 3:3 7341
according to the *b* of the house … 2Chr 3:4 7341
according to the *b* of the house … 2Chr 3:8 7341
the *b* thereof twenty cubits … 2Chr 3:8 7341
and twenty cubits the *b* thereof … 2Chr 4:1 7341
the *b* thereof threescore cubits … Ezr 6:3 6613
the *b* of the waters is straitened … Job 37:10 7341
thou perceived the *b* of the earth … Job 38:18 7338
shall fill the *b* of thy land … Is 8:8 7341
long by the cubit and an hand *b* … Eze 40:5 2948
he measured the *b* of the building … Eze 40:5 7341
he measured the *b* of the entry of … Eze 40:11 7341
the *b* was five and twenty cubits, … Eze 40:13 7341
Then he measured the *b* from the … Eze 40:19 7341
length thereof, and the *b* thereof … Eze 40:20 7341
the *b* five and twenty cubits … Eze 40:21 7341
the *b* five and twenty cubits … Eze 40:25 7341
the *b* five and twenty cubits … Eze 40:36 7341
the *b* of the gate was three … Eze 40:48 7341
cubits, and the *b* eleven cubits … Eze 40:49 7341
which was the *b* of the tabernacle … Eze 41:1 7341
the *b* of the door was ten cubits … Eze 41:2 7341
and the *b*, twenty cubits … Eze 41:2 7341
the *b* of the door, seven cubits … Eze 41:3 7341
and the *b*, twenty cubits, before … Eze 41:4 7341
the *b* of every side chamber, four … Eze 41:5 7341
therefore the *b* of the house was … Eze 41:7 7341
the *b* of the place that was left … Eze 41:11 7341
Also the *b* of the face of the … Eze 41:14 7341
door, and the *b* was fifty cubits … Eze 42:2 7341
was a walk of ten cubits *b* inward … Eze 42:4 7341
The cubit is a cubit and an hand *b* … Eze 43:13 2948
the *b* a cubit, and the border … Eze 43:13 7341
be two cubits, and the *b* one cubit … Eze 43:14 7341
four cubits, and the *b* one cubit … Eze 43:14 7341
the *b* shall be ten thousand … Eze 45:1 7341
in length, with five hundred in *b* … Eze 45:2 7341
and the *b* of ten thousand … Eze 45:3 7341
length, and the ten thousand of *b* … Eze 45:5 7341
and twenty thousand reeds in *b* … Eze 48:8 7341
length, and of ten thousand in *b* … Eze 48:9 7341
toward the west ten thousand in *b* … Eze 48:10 7341
toward the east ten thousand in *b* … Eze 48:10 7341
in length, and ten thousand in *b* … Eze 48:13 7341
thousand, and the *b* ten thousand … Eze 48:13 7341
that are left in the *b* over … Eze 48:15 7341
and the *b* thereof six cubits … Dan 3:1 6613
march through the *b* of the land … Hab 1:6 4800
to see what is the *b* thereof … Zec 2:2 7341
and the *b* thereof ten cubits … Zec 5:2 7341
with all saints what is the *b* … Eph 3:18 *4114*
went up on the *b* of the earth … Rev 20:9 *4114*
the length is as large as the *b* … Rev 21:16 *4114*
The length and the *b* and the height … Rev 21:16 *4114*

BREAK {140}

Lot, and came near to *b* the door … Gen 19:9 7665
that thou shalt *b* his yoke from … Gen 27:40 6561
neither shall ye *b* a bone thereof … Ex 12:46 7665
it, then thou shalt *b* his neck … Ex 13:13 6202
lest they *b* through unto the LORD … Ex 19:21 2040
lest the LORD *b* forth upon them … Ex 19:22 6555
the people *b* through to come up … Ex 19:24 2040
lest he *b* forth upon them … Ex 19:24 6555
If fire *b* out, and catch in thorns … Ex 22:6 3318
quite *b* down their images … Ex 23:24 7665
B off the golden earrings, which … Ex 32:2 6561
hath any gold, let them *b* it off … Ex 32:24 6561
b their images, and cut down their … Ex 34:13 7665
not, then shalt thou *b* his neck … Ex 34:20 6202
and ye shall *b* it … Lev 11:33 7665
if a leprosy *b* out abroad in the … Lev 13:12 6524
b out in the house, after that he … Lev 14:43 6524
he shall *b* down the house, the … Lev 14:45 5422
but that ye *b* my covenant … Lev 26:15 6565
I will *b* the pride of your power … Lev 26:19 7665
to *b* my covenant with them … Lev 26:44 6565
the morning, nor *b* any bone of it … Num 9:12 7665
shall *b* their bones, and pierce … Num 24:8 1633
he shall not *b* his word, he shall … Num 30:2 2490
b down their images, and cut down … Deut 7:5 7665
b their pillars, and burn their … Deut 12:3 7665
b my covenant which I have made … Deut 31:16 6565
and provoke me, and *b* my covenant … Deut 31:20 6565
I will never *b* my covenant with … Judg 2:1 6565
peace, I will *b* down this tower … Judg 8:9 5422
many servants now a days that *b* … 1Sa 25:10 6555
they came to Hebron at *b* of day … 2Sa 2:32 215
b thy league with Baasha king of … 1Kin 15:19 6565
to *b* through even unto the king … 2Kin 3:26 1234
did the Chaldees *b* in pieces … 2Kin 25:13 7665
b thy league with Baasha king of … 2Chr 16:3 6565
Should we again *b* thy … Ezr 9:14 6565
he shall even *b* down their stone … Neh 4:3 6565
Wilt thou *b* a leaf driven to and … Job 13:25 6206
b me in pieces with words … Job 19:2 1792
He shall *b* in pieces mighty men … Job 34:24 7489
or that the wild beast may *b* them … Job 39:15 1758
Let us *b* their bands asunder, and … Ps 2:3 5423
Thou shalt *b* them with a rod of … Ps 2:9 7489
B thou the arm of the wicked and … Ps 10:15 7665
B their teeth, O God, in their … Ps 58:6 2040
b out the great teeth of the … Ps 58:6 5422
shall *b* in pieces the oppressor … Ps 72:4 1792
But now they *b* down the carved … Ps 74:6 1986
If they *b* my statutes, and keep … Ps 89:31 2490
My covenant will I not *b*, nor … Ps 89:34 2490
They *b* in pieces thy people, O … Ps 94:5 1792
oil, which shall not *b* my head … Ps 141:5 5106
a time to *b* down, and a time to … Eccl 3:3 6555
Until the day *b*, and the shadows … Song 2:17 6315
Until the day *b*, and the shadows … Song 4:6 6315
b down the wall thereof, and it … Is 5:5 6555
they *b* forth into singing … Is 14:7 6476
That I will *b* the Assyrian in my … Is 14:25 7665
b the clods of his ground … Is 28:24 7702
nor *b* it with the wheel of his … Is 28:28 2000
he shall *b* it as the breaking of … Is 30:14 7665
the wilderness shall waters *b* out … Is 35:6 1234
so will he *b* all my bones … Is 38:13 7665
A bruised reed shall he not *b* … Is 42:3 7665
b forth into singing, ye … Is 44:23 6476
I will *b* in pieces the gates of … Is 45:2 7665
b forth into singing, O mountains … Is 49:13 6476
B forth into joy, sing together, … Is 52:9 6476
b forth into singing, and cry … Is 54:1 6476
For thou shalt *b* forth on the … Is 54:3 6555
the hills shall *b* forth before … Is 55:12 6476
go free, and that ye *b* every yoke … Is 58:6 5423
thy light *b* forth as the morning … Is 58:8 1234
b forth upon all the inhabitants … Jer 1:14 6605
B up your fallow ground, and sow … Jer 4:3 5214
b not thy covenant with us … Jer 14:21 6565
Shall iron *b* the northern iron and … Jer 15:12 7489
Then shalt thou *b* the bottle in … Jer 19:10 7665
Even so will I *b* this people … Jer 19:11 7665
for I will *b* the yoke of the king … Jer 28:4 7665
Even so will I *b* the yoke of the … Jer 28:11 7665
that I will *b* his yoke from off … Jer 30:8 7665
to *b* down, and to throw down, and … Jer 31:28 5422
If ye can *b* my covenant of the … Jer 33:20 6565
He shall *b* also the images of … Jer 43:13 7665
which I have built will I *b* down … Jer 45:4 2040
his vessels, and *b* their bottles … Jer 48:12 5310
I will *b* the bow of Elam, the … Jer 49:35 7665
for with thee will I *b* in pieces … Jer 51:20 5310
with thee will I *b* in pieces the … Jer 51:21 5310
with thee will I *b* in pieces the … Jer 51:21 5310
thee also will I *b* in pieces man … Jer 51:22 5310
with thee will I *b* in pieces old … Jer 51:22 5310
with thee will I *b* in pieces the … Jer 51:22 5310
I will also *b* in pieces with thee … Jer 51:23 5310
with thee will I *b* in pieces the … Jer 51:23 5310
with thee will I *b* in pieces … Jer 51:23 5310
I will *b* the staff of bread in … Eze 4:16 7665
will *b* your staff of bread … Eze 5:16 7665
So will I *b* down the wall that ye … Eze 13:14 2040
will *b* the staff of the bread … Eze 14:13 7665
thee, as women that *b* wedlock … Eze 16:38 5003
shall *b* down thy high places … Eze 16:39 5422
or shall he *b* the covenant, and be … Eze 17:15 6565
thou shalt *b* the sherds thereof, … Eze 23:34 1633
of Tyrus, and *b* down her towers … Eze 26:4 2040
axes he shall *b* down thy towers … Eze 26:9 5422
they shall *b* down thy walls, and … Eze 26:12 2040
of thee by thy hand, thou didst *b* … Eze 29:7 7533
when I shall *b* there the yokes of … Eze 30:18 7665
will *b* his arms, the strong, and … Eze 30:22 7665
but I will *b* Pharaoh's arms, and … Eze 30:24 7665
shall it *b* in pieces and bruise … Dan 2:40 1854
people, but it shall *b* in pieces … Dan 2:44 1854
b off thy sins by righteousness, … Dan 4:27 6562
tread it down, and *b* it in pieces … Dan 7:23 1854
that I will *b* the bow of Israel … Hos 1:5 7665
I will *b* the bow and the sword and … Hos 2:18 7665
committing adultery, they *b* out … Hos 4:2 6555
he shall *b* down their altars, he … Hos 10:2 6202
plow, and Jacob shall *b* his clods … Hos 10:11 7702
b up your fallow ground … Hos 10:12 5214
and they shall not *b* their ranks … Joel 2:7 5670
I will *b* also the bar of Damascus … Amos 1:5 7665
lest he *b* out like fire in the … Amos 5:6 6743
they *b* their bones, and chop them … Mic 3:3 6746
For now will I *b* his yoke from … Nah 1:13 7665
that I might *b* my covenant which … Zec 11:10 6565
that I might *b* the brotherhood … Zec 11:14 6565
Whosoever therefore shall *b* one … Mt 5:19 *3089*
and where thieves *b* through … Mt 6:19 *1358*
do not *b* through nor steal … Mt 6:20 *1358*
else the bottles *b*, and the wine … Mt 9:17 *4486*
A bruised reed shall he not *b* … Mt 12:20 *2608*
came together to *b* bread, Paul … Acts 20:7 *2806*
a long while, even till *b* of day … Acts 20:11 *827*
ye to weep and to *b* mine heart … Acts 21:13 *4919*
The bread which we *b*, is it not … 1Cor 10:16 *2806*
b forth and cry, thou that … Gal 4:27 *4486*

BREAKER {2}

The *b* is come up before them … Mic 2:13 6555
but if thou be a *b* of the law … Rom 2:25 *3848*

BREAKEST {1}

Thou *b* the ships of Tarshish with … Ps 48:7 7665

BREAKETH {17}
he said, Let me go, for the day *b* Gen 32:26 5927
For he *b* me with a tempest, and Job 9:17 7779
he *b* down, and it cannot be built Job 12:14 2040
He *b* me with breach upon breach, Job 16:14 6555
The flood *b* out from the Job 28:4 6555
voice of the LORD *b* the cedars Ps 29:5 7665
the LORD *b* the cedars of Lebanon Ps 29:5 7665
he *b* the bow, and cutteth the Ps 46:9 7665
My soul *b* for the longing that it Ps 119:20 1638
and a soft tongue *b* the bone Prov 25:15 7665
whoso *b* an hedge, a serpent shall Eccl 10:8 6555
is crushed *b* out into a viper Is 59:5 1234
as one *b* a potter's vessel, that Jer 19:11 7665
hammer that *b* the rock in pieces Jer 23:29 6327
bread, and no man *b* it unto them Lam 4:4 6566
forasmuch as iron *b* in pieces Dan 2:40 1855
and as iron that *b* all these Dan 2:40 7940

BREAKING {18}
with him until the *b* of the day Gen 32:24 5927
shall be a boil *b* forth with Ex 9:9 6524
it became a boil *b* forth with Ex 9:10 6524
If a thief be found *b* up, and be Ex 22:2 4290
hand like the *b* forth of waters 1Chr 14:11 6556
upon me as a wide *b* in of waters Job 30:14 6556
that there be no *b* in, nor going Ps 144:14 6556
b down the walls, and of crying to Is 22:5 6979
whose *b* cometh suddenly at an Is 30:13 7667
he shall break it as the *b* of the Is 30:14 7667
the oath in *b* the covenant Eze 16:59 6565
the oath by *b* the covenant Eze 17:18 6565
of man, with the *b* of thy loins Eze 21:6 7670
place of the *b* forth of children Hos 13:13 4866
was known of them in *b* of bread Lk 24:35 *2800*
in *b* of bread, and in prayers Acts 2:42 *2800*
b bread from house to house, did Acts 2:46 *2806*
through *b* the law dishonourest Rom 2:23 *3847*

BREAKINGS {1}
by reason of *b* they purify Job 41:25 7667

BREAST {18}
thou shalt take the *b* of the ram Ex 29:26 2373
the *b* of the wave offering Ex 29:27 2373
made by fire, the fat with the *b* Lev 7:30 2373
that the *b* may be waved for a Lev 7:30 2373
but the *b* shall be Aaron's and his Lev 7:31 2373
For the wave *b* and the heave Lev 7:34 2373
And Moses took the *b*, and waved it Lev 8:29 2373
And the wave *b* and heave shoulder Lev 10:14 2373
the wave *b* shall they bring with Lev 10:15 2373
for the priest, with the wave *b* Num 6:20 2373
shall be thine, as the wave *b* Num 18:18 2373
pluck the fatherless from the *b* Job 24:9 7699
and shalt suck the *b* of kings Is 60:16 7699
the sea monsters draw out the *b* Lam 4:3 7699
head was of fine gold, his *b* Dan 2:32 2306
unto heaven, but smote upon his *b* Lk 18:13 *4738*
lying on Jesus' *b* saith unto him Jn 13:25 *4738*
also leaned on his *b* at supper Jn 21:20 *4738*

BREASTPLATE {28}
be set in the ephod, and in the *b* Ex 25:7 2833
a *b*, and an ephod, and a robe, and a Ex 28:4 2833
thou shalt make the *b* of judgment Ex 28:15 2833
thou shalt make upon the *b* chains Ex 28:22 2833
make upon the *b* two rings of gold Ex 28:23 2833
rings on the two ends of the *b* Ex 28:23 2833
which are on the ends of the *b* Ex 28:24 2833
of the *b* in the border thereof Ex 28:26 2833
they shall bind the *b* by the Ex 28:28 2833
that the *b* be not loosed from the Ex 28:28 2833
the *b* of judgment upon his heart Ex 28:29 2833
put in the *b* of judgment the Urim Ex 28:30 2833
the ephod, and the ephod, and the *b* Ex 29:5 2833
set for the ephod, and for the *b* Ex 35:9 2833
set, for the ephod, and for the *b* Ex 35:27 2833
he made the *b* of cunning work, Ex 39:8 2833
they made the *b* double Ex 39:9 2833
upon the *b* chains at the ends Ex 39:15 2833
rings in the two ends of the *b* Ex 39:16 2833
two rings on the ends of the *b* Ex 39:17 2833
put them on the two ends of the *b* Ex 39:19 2833
they did bind the *b* by his rings Ex 39:21 2833
that the *b* might not be loosed Ex 39:21 2833
And he put the *b* upon him Lev 8:8 2833
also he put in the *b* the Urim Lev 8:8 2833
he put on righteousness as a *b* Is 59:17 8302
having on the *b* of righteousness Eph 6:14 *2382*
sober, putting on the *b* of faith 1Th 5:8 *2382*

BREASTPLATES {3}
And they had *b* Rev 9:9 *2382*
as it were *b* of iron Rev 9:9 *2382*
having *b* of fire, and of jacinth, Rev 9:17 *2382*

BREASTS {27}
lieth under, blessings of the *b* Gen 49:25 7699
And they put the fat upon the *b* Lev 9:20 2373
And the *b* and the right shoulder Lev 9:21 2373
or why the *b* that I should suck Job 3:12 7699
His *b* are full of milk, and his Job 21:24 5845
when I was upon my mother's *b* Ps 22:9 7699
let her *b* satisfy thee at all Prov 5:19 1717
shall lie all night betwixt my *b* Song 1:13 7699
Thy two *b* are like two young roes Song 4:5 7699
Thy two *b* are like two young roes Song 7:3 7699
thy *b* to clusters of grapes Song 7:7 7699
now also thy *b* shall be as Song 7:8 7699
that sucked the *b* of my mother Song 8:1 7699
a little sister, and she hath no *b* Song 8:8 7699
I am a wall, and my *b* like towers Song 8:10 7699
the milk, and drawn from the *b* Is 28:9 7699
with the *b* of her consolations Is 66:11 7699
thy *b* are fashioned, and thine Eze 16:7 7699
there were their *b* pressed Eze 23:3 7699
bruised the *b* of her virginity Eze 23:8 1717
thereof, and pluck off thine own *b* Eze 23:34 7699
her adulteries from between her *b* Hos 2:2 7699
them a miscarrying womb and dry *b* Hos 9:14 7699
and those that suck the *b* Joel 2:16 7699
of doves, tabering upon their *b* Nah 2:7 3824
which were done, smote their *b* Lk 23:48 *4738*
having their *b* girded with golden Rev 15:6 *4738*

BREATH {42}
into his nostrils the *b* of life Gen 2:7 5397
flesh, wherein is the *b* of life Gen 6:17 7307
flesh, wherein is the *b* of life Gen 7:15 7307
whose nostrils was the *b* of life Gen 7:22 5397
blast of the *b* of his nostrils 2Sa 22:16 7307
that there was no *b* left in him 1Kin 17:17 5397
by the *b* of his nostrils are they Job 4:9 7307
will not suffer me to take my *b* Job 9:18 7307
thing, and the *b* of all mankind Job 12:10 7307
by the *b* of his mouth shall he go Job 15:30 7307
My *b* is corrupt, my days are Job 17:1 7307
My *b* is strange to my wife, Job 19:17 7307
All the while my *b* is in me Job 27:3 5397
the *b* of the Almighty hath given Job 33:4 5397
unto himself his spirit and his *b* Job 34:14 5397
By the *b* of God frost is given Job 37:10 5397
His *b* kindleth coals, and a flame Job 41:21 5315
blast of the *b* of thy nostrils Ps 18:15 7307
of them by the *b* of his mouth Ps 33:6 7307
thou takest away their *b*, they Ps 104:29 7307
is there any *b* in their mouths Ps 135:17 7307
His *b* goeth forth, he returneth Ps 146:4 7307
thing that hath *b* praise the LORD Ps 150:6 5397
yea, they have all one *b* Eccl 3:19 7307
whose *b* is in his nostrils Is 2:22 5397
with the *b* of his lips shall he Is 11:4 7307
And his *b*, as an overflowing Is 30:28 7307
the *b* of the LORD, like a stream Is 30:33 5397
your *b*, as fire, shall devour you Is 33:11 7307
he that giveth *b* unto the people Is 42:5 5397
and there is no *b* in them Jer 10:14 7307
and there is no *b* in them Jer 51:17 7307
The *b* of our nostrils, the Lam 4:20 7307
I will cause *b* to enter into you, Eze 37:5 7307
put *b* in you, and ye shall live Eze 37:6 7307
but there was no *b* in them Eze 37:8 7307
Come from the four winds, O *b* Eze 37:9 7307
the *b* came into them, and they Eze 37:10 7307
and the God in whose hand thy *b* is Dan 5:23 5396
me, neither is there *b* left in me Dan 10:17 5397
there is no *b* at all in the midst Hab 2:19 7307
he giveth to all life, and *b* Acts 17:25 *4157*

BREATHE {4}
there was not any left to *b* Josh 11:11 5397
them, neither left they any to *b* Josh 11:14 5397
me, and such as *b* out cruelty Ps 27:12 3307
b upon these slain, that they may Eze 37:9 5301

BREATHED {4}
b into his nostrils the breath of Gen 2:7 5301
but utterly destroyed all that *b* Josh 10:40 5397
left not to Jeroboam any that *b* 1Kin 15:29 5397
he *b* on them, and saith unto them, Jn 20:22 *1720*

BREATHETH {1}
shalt save alive nothing that *b* Deut 20:16 5397

BREATHING {2}
hide not thine ear at my *b* Lam 3:56 7309
yet *b* out threatenings and Acts 9:1 *1709*

BRED {1}
morning, and it *b* worms, and stank Ex 16:20 7311

BREECHES {5}
linen *b* to cover their nakedness Ex 28:42 4370
linen *b* of fine twined linen, Ex 39:28 4370
his linen *b* shall he put upon his Lev 6:10 4370
have the linen *b* upon his flesh Lev 16:4 4370
have linen *b* upon their loins Eze 44:18 4370

BREED {2}
that they may *b* abundantly in the Gen 8:17 8317
lambs, and rams of the *b* of Bashan Deut 32:14 1121

BREEDING {1}
even the *b* of nettles, and Zeph 2:9 4476

BRETHREN {562}
father, and told his two *b* without Gen 9:22 251
servants shall he be unto his *b* Gen 9:25 251
for we be *b* Gen 13:8 251
in the presence of all his *b* Gen 16:12 251
And said, I pray you, *b*, do not so Gen 19:7 251
me to the house of my master's *b* Gen 24:27 251
died in the presence of all his *b* Gen 25:18 251
be lord over thy *b*, and let thy Gen 27:29 251
all his *b* have I given to him for Gen 27:37 251
And Jacob said unto them, My *b* Gen 29:4 251
And he took his *b* with him Gen 31:23 251
Laban with his *b* pitched in the Gen 31:25 251
before our *b* discern thou what is Gen 31:32 251
here before my *b* and thy *b* Gen 31:37 251
And Jacob said unto his *b*, Gather Gen 31:46 251
called his *b* to eat bread Gen 31:54 251
unto her father and unto her *b* Gen 34:11 251
Jacob, Simeon and Levi, Dinah's *b* Gen 34:25 251
was feeding the flock with his *b* Gen 37:2 251
when his *b* saw that their father Gen 37:4 251
loved him more than all his *b* Gen 37:4 251
a dream, and he told it his *b* Gen 37:5 251
his *b* said to him, Shalt thou Gen 37:8 251
another dream, and told it his *b* Gen 37:9 251
it to his father, and to his *b* Gen 37:10 251
thy *b* indeed come to bow down Gen 37:10 251
And his *b* envied him Gen 37:11 251
his *b* went to feed their father's Gen 37:12 251
Do not thy *b* feed the flock in Gen 37:13 251
see whether it be well with thy *b* Gen 37:14 251
And he said, I seek my *b* Gen 37:16 251
And Joseph went after his *b* Gen 37:17 251
when Joseph was come unto his *b* Gen 37:23 251
And Judah said unto his *b*, What Gen 37:26 251
And his *b* were content Gen 37:27 251
And he returned unto his *b* Gen 37:30 251
that Judah went down from his *b* Gen 38:1 251
he die also, as his *b* did Gen 38:11 251
Joseph's ten *b* went down to buy Gen 42:3 251
Jacob sent not with his *b* Gen 42:4 251
and Joseph's *b* came, and bowed down Gen 42:6 251
And Joseph saw his *b*, and he knew Gen 42:7 251
And Joseph knew his *b*, but they Gen 42:8 251
said, Thy servants are twelve *b* Gen 42:13 251
let one of your *b* be bound in the Gen 42:19 251
And he said unto his *b*, My money Gen 42:28 251
We be twelve *b*, sons of our Gen 42:32 251
leave one of your *b* here with me Gen 42:33 251
his *b* came to Joseph's house Gen 44:14 251
and let the lad go up with his *b* Gen 44:33 251
made himself known unto his *b* Gen 45:1 251
And Joseph said unto his *b* Gen 45:3 251
his *b* could not answer him Gen 45:3 251
And Joseph said unto his *b* Gen 45:4 251
Moreover he kissed all his *b* Gen 45:15 251
after that his *b* talked with him Gen 45:15 251
saying, Joseph's *b* are come Gen 45:16 251
said unto Joseph, Say unto thy *b* Gen 45:17 251
So he sent his *b* away, and they Gen 45:24 251
And Joseph said unto his *b* Gen 46:31 251
Pharaoh, and say unto him, My *b* Gen 46:31 251
and said, My father and my *b* Gen 47:1 251
And he took some of his *b*, even Gen 47:2 251
And Pharaoh said unto his *b* Gen 47:3 251
and thy *b* are come unto thee Gen 47:5 251
make thy father and *b* to dwell Gen 47:6 251
Joseph placed his father and his *b* Gen 47:11 251
nourished his father, and his *b* Gen 47:12 251
of their *b* in their inheritance Gen 48:6 251
to thee one portion above thy *b* Gen 48:22 251
Simeon and Levi are *b* Gen 49:5 251
art he whom thy *b* shall praise Gen 49:8 251
him that was separate from his *b* Gen 49:26 251
all the house of Joseph, and his *b* Gen 50:8 251
returned into Egypt, he, and his *b* Gen 50:14 251
when Joseph's *b* saw that their Gen 50:15 251
thee now, the trespass of thy *b* Gen 50:17 251
his *b* also went and fell down Gen 50:18 251
And Joseph said unto his *b* Gen 50:24 251
And Joseph died, and all his *b* Ex 1:6 251
that he went out unto his *b* Ex 2:11 251
smiting an Hebrew, one of his *b* Ex 2:11 251
return unto my *b* which are in Ex 4:18 251
carry your *b* from before the Lev 10:4 251
but let your *b*, the whole house Lev 10:6 251
is the high priest among his *b* Lev 21:10 251
but over your *b* the children of Lev 25:46 251
one of his *b* may redeem him Lev 25:48 251
their *b* in the tabernacle of the Num 8:26 251
all thy *b* the sons of Levi with Num 16:10 251
thy *b* also of the tribe of Levi, Num 18:2 251
I have taken your *b* the Levites Num 18:6 251
when our *b* died before the LORD Num 20:3 251
brought unto his *b* a Midianitish Num 25:6 251
among the *b* of our father Num 27:4 251
among their father's *b* Num 27:7 251
give his inheritance unto his *b* Num 27:9 251
And if he have no *b*, then ye shall Num 27:10 251
inheritance unto his father's *b* Num 27:10 251
And if his father have no *b* Num 27:11 251
of Reuben, Shall your *b* go to war Num 32:6 251
Hear the causes between your *b* Deut 1:16 251
our *b* have discouraged our heart, Deut 1:28 251
of your *b* the children of Esau Deut 2:4 251
from our *b* the children of Esau Deut 2:8 251
your *b* the children of Israel Deut 3:18 251
LORD have given rest unto your *b* Deut 3:20 251
part nor inheritance with his *b* Deut 10:9 251
you a poor man of one of thy *b* Deut 15:7 251
one from among thy *b* shalt thou Deut 17:15 251
be not lifted up above his *b* Deut 17:20 251
have no inheritance among their *b* Deut 18:2 251
as all his *b* the Levites do, Deut 18:7 251
from the midst of thee, of thy *b* Deut 18:15 251
up a Prophet from among their *b* Deut 18:18 251
his *b* of the children of Israel Deut 24:7 251
and needy, whether he be of thy *b* Deut 24:14 251
If *b* dwell together, and one of Deut 25:5 251
neither did he acknowledge his *b* Deut 33:9 251
him that was separated from his *b* Deut 33:16 251
let him be acceptable to his *b* Deut 33:24 251
ye shall pass before your *b* armed Josh 1:14 251
the LORD have given your *b* rest Josh 1:15 251
my father, and my mother, and my *b* Josh 2:13 251
father, and thy mother, and thy *b* Josh 2:18 251
father, and her mother, and her *b* Josh 6:23 251
Nevertheless my *b* that went up Josh 14:8 251

us an inheritance among our *b* ... Josh 17:4 251
among the *b* of their father ... Josh 17:4 251
Ye have not left your *b* these ... Josh 22:3 251
God hath given rest unto your *b* ... Josh 22:4 251
b on this side Jordan westward ... Josh 22:7 251
spoil of your enemies with your *b* ... Josh 22:8 251
And he said, They were my *b* ... Judg 8:19 251
to Shechem unto his mother's *b* ... Judg 9:1 251
his mother's *b* spake of him in ... Judg 9:3 251
slew his *b* the sons of Jerubbaal, ... Judg 9:5 251
aided him in the killing of his *b* ... Judg 9:24 251
the son of Ebed came with his *b* ... Judg 9:26 251
Ebed and his *b* be come to Shechem ... Judg 9:31 251
and Zebul thrust out Gaal and his *b* ... Judg 9:41 251
father, in slaying his seventy *b* ... Judg 9:56 251
Then Jephthah fled from his *b* ... Judg 11:3 251
among the daughters of thy *b* ... Judg 14:3 251
Then his *b* and all the house of ... Judg 16:31 251
they came unto their *b* to Zorah ... Judg 18:8 251
their *b* said unto them, What say ... Judg 18:8 251
of Laish, and said unto their *b* ... Judg 18:14 251
and said unto them, Nay, my *b* ... Judg 19:23 251
of their *b* the children of Israel ... Judg 20:13 251
their *b* come unto us to complain ... Judg 21:22 251
be not cut off from among his *b* ... Ruth 4:10 251
him in the midst of his *b* ... 1Sa 16:13 251
Take now for thy *b* an ephah of ... 1Sa 17:17 251
and run to the camp to thy *b* ... 1Sa 17:17 251
thousand, and look how thy *b* fare ... 1Sa 17:18 251
army, and came and saluted his *b* ... 1Sa 17:22 251
away, I pray thee, and see my *b* ... 1Sa 20:29 251
and when his *b* and all his father's ... 1Sa 22:1 251
David, Ye shall not do so, my *b* ... 1Sa 30:23 251
return from following their *b* ... 2Sa 2:26 251
of Saul thy father, to his *b* ... 2Sa 3:8 251
return thou, and take back thy *b* ... 2Sa 15:20 251
Ye are my *b*, ye are my bones and ... 2Sa 19:12 251
Why have our *b* the men of Judah ... 2Sa 19:41 251
called all his *b* the king's sons, ... 1Kin 1:9 251
your *b* the children of Israel ... 1Kin 12:24 251
him arise up from among his *b* ... 2Kin 9:2 251
Jehu met with the *b* of Ahaziah ... 2Kin 10:13 251
answered, We are the *b* of Ahaziah ... 2Kin 10:13 251
unleavened bread among their *b* ... 2Kin 23:9 251
was more honourable than his *b* ... 1Chr 4:9 251
but his *b* had not many children, ... 1Chr 4:27 251
For Judah prevailed above his *b* ... 1Chr 5:2 251
his *b* by their families, when the ... 1Chr 5:7 251
their *b* of the house of their ... 1Chr 5:13 251
their *b* the sons of Merari stood ... 1Chr 6:44 251
Their *b* also the Levites were ... 1Chr 6:48 251
their *b* among all the families of ... 1Chr 7:5 251
his *b* came to comfort him ... 1Chr 7:22 251
dwelt with their *b* in Jerusalem ... 1Chr 8:32 251
Jeuel, and their *b*, six hundred and ... 1Chr 9:6 251
And their *b*, according to their ... 1Chr 9:9 251
And their *b*, heads of the house of ... 1Chr 9:13 251
and Talmon, and Ahiman, and their *b* ... 1Chr 9:17 251
the son of Korah, and his *b* ... 1Chr 9:19 251
And their *b*, which were in their ... 1Chr 9:25 251
And other of their *b*, of the sons ... 1Chr 9:32 251
dwelt with their *b* at Jerusalem ... 1Chr 9:38 251
over against their *b* ... 1Chr 9:38 251
bow, even of Saul's *b* of Benjamin ... 1Chr 12:2 251
all their *b* were at their ... 1Chr 12:32 251
for their *b* had prepared for them ... 1Chr 12:39 251
abroad unto our *b* every where ... 1Chr 13:2 251
his *b* an hundred and twenty ... 1Chr 15:5 251
his *b* two hundred and twenty ... 1Chr 15:6 251
his *b* an hundred and thirty ... 1Chr 15:7 251
the chief, and his *b* two hundred ... 1Chr 15:8 251
the chief, and his *b* fourscore ... 1Chr 15:9 251
his *b* an hundred and twelve ... 1Chr 15:10 251
yourselves, both ye and your *b* ... 1Chr 15:12 251
their *b* to be the singers with ... 1Chr 15:16 251
and of his *b*, Asaph the son of ... 1Chr 15:17 251
and of the sons of Merari their *b* ... 1Chr 15:17 251
with them their *b* of the second ... 1Chr 15:18 251
into the hand of Asaph and his *b* ... 1Chr 16:7 251
of the LORD Asaph and his *b* ... 1Chr 16:37 251
And Obed-edom with their *b* ... 1Chr 16:38 251
his *b* the priests, before the ... 1Chr 16:39 251
their *b* the sons of Kish took ... 1Chr 23:22 251
of the sons of Aaron their *b* ... 1Chr 23:32 251
their *b* the sons of Aaron in the ... 1Chr 24:31 251
over against their younger *b* ... 1Chr 24:31 251
with their *b* that were instructed ... 1Chr 25:7 251
to Gedaliah, who with his *b* ... 1Chr 25:9 251
to Zaccur, he, his sons, and his *b* ... 1Chr 25:10 251
to Izri, he, his sons, and his *b* ... 1Chr 25:11 251
Nethaniah, he, his sons, and his *b* ... 1Chr 25:12 251
Bukkiah, he, his sons, and his *b* ... 1Chr 25:13 251
he, his sons, and his *b*, were ... 1Chr 25:14 251
Jeshaiah, he, his sons, and his *b* ... 1Chr 25:15 251
Mattaniah, he, his sons, and his *b* ... 1Chr 25:16 251
to Shimei, he, his sons, and his *b* ... 1Chr 25:17 251
Azareel, he, his sons, and his *b* ... 1Chr 25:18 251
Hashabiah, he, his sons, and his *b* ... 1Chr 25:19 251
Shubael, he, his sons, and his *b* ... 1Chr 25:20 251
he, his sons, and his *b*, were ... 1Chr 25:21 251
Jeremoth, he, his sons, and his *b* ... 1Chr 25:22 251
Hananiah, he, his sons, and his *b* ... 1Chr 25:23 251
he, his sons, and his *b*, were ... 1Chr 25:24 251
to Hanani, he, his sons, and his *b* ... 1Chr 25:25 251
Mallothi, he, his sons, and his *b* ... 1Chr 25:26 251
Eliathah, he, his sons, and his *b* ... 1Chr 25:27 251
to Hothir, he, his sons, and his *b* ... 1Chr 25:28 251
Giddalti, he, his sons, and his *b* ... 1Chr 25:29 251

Mahazioth, he, his sons, and his *b* ... 1Chr 25:30 251
he, his sons, and his *b*, were ... 1Chr 25:31 251
whose *b* were strong men, Elihu, ... 1Chr 26:7 251
they and their sons and their *b* ... 1Chr 26:8 251
And Meshelemiah had sons and *b* ... 1Chr 26:9 251
sons and *b* of Hosah were thirteen ... 1Chr 26:11 251
And his *b* by Eliezer ... 1Chr 26:25 251
his *b* were over all the treasures ... 1Chr 26:26 251
hand of Shelomith, and of his *b* ... 1Chr 26:28 251
Hebronites, Hashabiah and his *b* ... 1Chr 26:30 251
And his *b*, men of valour, were two ... 1Chr 26:32 251
Elihu, one of the *b* of David ... 1Chr 27:18 251
his feet, and said, Hear me, my *b* ... 1Chr 28:2 251
with their sons and their *b* ... 2Chr 5:12 251
go up, nor fight against your *b* ... 2Chr 11:4 251
chief, to be ruler among his *b* ... 2Chr 11:22 251
shall come to you of your *b* that ... 2Chr 19:10 251
come upon you, and upon your *b* ... 2Chr 19:10 251
he had *b* the sons of Jehoshaphat, ... 2Chr 21:2 251
slew all his *b* with the sword, and ... 2Chr 21:4 251
also hast slain thy *b* of thy ... 2Chr 21:13 251
and the sons of the *b* of Ahaziah ... 2Chr 22:8 251
of their *b* two hundred thousand ... 2Chr 28:8 251
ye have taken captive of your *b* ... 2Chr 28:11 251
city of palm trees, to their *b* ... 2Chr 28:15 251
And they gathered their *b*, and ... 2Chr 29:15 251
wherefore their *b* the Levites did ... 2Chr 29:34 251
like your fathers, and like your *b* ... 2Chr 30:7 251
turn again unto the LORD, your *b* ... 2Chr 30:9 251
to give to their *b* by courses ... 2Chr 31:15 251
the fathers of your *b* the people ... 2Chr 35:5 251
yourselves, and prepare your *b* ... 2Chr 35:6 251
and Shemaiah and Nethaneel, his *b* ... 2Chr 35:9 251
for their *b* the Levites prepared ... 2Chr 35:15 251
his *b* the priests, and Zerubbabel ... Ezr 3:2 251
the son of Shealtiel, and his *b* ... Ezr 3:2 251
remnant of their *b* the priests ... Ezr 3:8 251
Jeshua with his sons and his *b* ... Ezr 3:9 251
their sons and their *b* the Levites ... Ezr 3:9 251
for their *b* the priests, and for ... Ezr 6:20 251
seem good to thee, and to thy *b* ... Ezr 7:18 252
to his *b* the Nethinims, at the ... Ezr 8:17 251
Sherebiah, with his sons and his *b* ... Ezr 8:18 251
of the sons of Merari, his *b* ... Ezr 8:19 251
and ten of their *b* with them ... Ezr 8:24 251
the son of Jozadak, and his *b* ... Ezr 10:18 251
That Hanani, one of my *b*, came, ... Neh 1:2 251
rose up with his *b* the priests ... Neh 3:1 251
After him repaired their *b* ... Neh 3:18 251
And he spake before his *b* and the ... Neh 4:2 251
and terrible, and fight for your *b* ... Neh 4:14 251
So neither I, nor my *b*, nor my ... Neh 4:23 251
wives against their *b* the Jews ... Neh 5:1 251
flesh is as the flesh of our *b* ... Neh 5:5 251
have redeemed our *b* the Jews ... Neh 5:8 251
and will ye even sell your *b* ... Neh 5:8 251
I likewise, and my *b*, and my ... Neh 5:10 251
my *b* have not eaten the bread of ... Neh 5:14 251
And their *b*, Shebaniah, Hodijah, ... Neh 10:10 251
They clave to their *b*, their ... Neh 10:29 251
their *b* that did the work of the ... Neh 11:12 251
And his *b*, chief of the fathers, ... Neh 11:13 251
And their *b*, mighty men of valour, ... Neh 11:14 251
Bakbukiah the second among his *b* ... Neh 11:17 251
their *b* that kept the gates, were ... Neh 11:19 251
of their *b* in the days of Jeshua ... Neh 12:7 251
the thanksgiving, he and his *b* ... Neh 12:8 251
Also Bakbukiah and Unni, their *b* ... Neh 12:9 251
with their *b* over against them, ... Neh 12:24 251
And his *b*, Shemaiah, and Azarael, ... Neh 12:36 251
was to distribute unto their *b* ... Neh 13:13 251
of the multitude of his *b* ... Est 10:3 251
My *b* have dealt deceitfully as a ... Job 6:15 251
He hath put my *b* far from me ... Job 19:13 251
came there unto him all his *b* ... Job 42:11 251
them inheritance among their *b* ... Job 42:15 251
I will declare thy name unto my *b* ... Ps 22:22 251
I am become a stranger unto my *b* ... Ps 69:8 251
For my *b* and companions' sakes, I ... Ps 122:8 251
how pleasant it is for *b* to dwell ... Ps 133:1 251
and he that soweth discord among *b* ... Prov 6:19 251
of the inheritance among the *b* ... Prov 17:2 251
All the *b* of the poor do hate him ... Prov 19:7 251
Your *b* that hated you, that cast ... Is 66:5 251
they shall bring all your *b* for ... Is 66:20 251
as I have cast out all your *b* ... Jer 7:15 251
For even thy *b*, and the house of ... Jer 12:6 251
of your *b* that are not gone forth ... Jer 29:16 251
the son of Habaziniah, and his *b* ... Jer 35:3 251
and slew them not among their *b* ... Jer 41:8 251
his seed is spoiled, and his *b* ... Jer 49:10 251
of man, thy *b*, even thy *b* ... Eze 11:15 251
Say ye unto your *b*, Ammi ... Hos 2:1 251
Though he be fruitful among his *b* ... Hos 13:15 251
then the remnant of his *b* shall ... Mic 5:3 251
and Jacob begat Judas and his *b* ... Mt 1:2 *80*
Josias begat Jechonias and his *b* ... Mt 1:11 *80*
by the sea of Galilee, saw two *b* ... Mt 4:18 *80*
from thence, he saw other two *b* ... Mt 4:21 *80*
And if ye salute your *b* only ... Mt 5:47 *80*
his *b* stood without, desiring to ... Mt 12:46 *80*
thy *b* stand without, desiring to ... Mt 12:47 *80*
and who are my *b* ... Mt 12:48 *80*
and said, Behold my mother and my *b* ... Mt 12:49 *80*
and his *b*, James, and Joses, and ... Mt 13:55 *80*
that hath forsaken houses, or *b* ... Mt 19:29 *80*
indignation against the two *b* ... Mt 20:24 *80*
Now there were with us seven *b* ... Mt 22:25 *80*

and all ye are *b* ... Mt 23:8 *80*
one of the least of these my *b* ... Mt 25:40 *80*
go tell my *b* that they go into ... Mt 28:10 *80*
There came then his *b* and his ... Mk 3:31 *80*
thy *b* without seek for thee ... Mk 3:32 *80*
saying, Who is my mother, or my *b* ... Mk 3:33 *80*
and said, Behold my mother and my *b* ... Mk 3:34 *80*
no man that hath left house, or *b* ... Mk 10:29 *80*
now in this time, houses, and *b* ... Mk 10:30 *80*
Now there were seven *b* ... Mk 12:20 *80*
came to him his mother and his *b* ... Lk 8:19 *80*
thy *b* stand without, desiring to ... Lk 8:20 *80*
my *b* are these which hear the ... Lk 8:21 *80*
call not thy friends, nor thy *b* ... Lk 14:12 *80*
and wife, and children, and *b* ... Lk 14:26 *80*
For I have five *b* ... Lk 16:28 *80*
hath left house, or parents, or *b* ... Lk 18:29 *80*
There were therefore seven *b* ... Lk 20:29 *80*
be betrayed both by parents, and *b* ... Lk 21:16 *80*
art converted, strengthen thy *b* ... Lk 22:32 *80*
he, and his mother, and his *b* ... Jn 2:12 *80*
His *b* therefore said unto him, ... Jn 7:3 *80*
neither did his *b* believe in him ... Jn 7:5 *80*
But when his *b* were gone up ... Jn 7:10 *80*
but go to my *b*, and say unto them, ... Jn 20:17 *80*
this saying abroad among the *b* ... Jn 21:23 *80*
mother of Jesus, and with his *b* ... Acts 1:14 *80*
Men and *b*, this scripture must ... Acts 1:16 *80*
Men and *b*, let me freely speak ... Acts 2:29 *80*
rest of the apostles, Men and *b* ... Acts 2:37 *80*
And now, *b*, I wot that through ... Acts 3:17 *80*
God raise up unto you of your *b* ... Acts 3:22 *80*
Wherefore, *b*, look ye out among ... Acts 6:3 *80*
And he said, Men, *b*, and fathers, ... Acts 7:2 *80*
Joseph was made known to his *b* ... Acts 7:13 *80*
his *b* the children of Israel ... Acts 7:23 *80*
For he supposed his *b* would have ... Acts 7:25 *80*
one again, saying, Sirs, ye are *b* ... Acts 7:26 *80*
God raise up unto you of your *b* ... Acts 7:37 *80*
Which when the *b* knew, they ... Acts 9:30 *80*
certain *b* from Joppa accompanied ... Acts 10:23 *80*
b that were in Judaea heard that ... Acts 11:1 *80*
these six *b* accompanied me ... Acts 11:12 *80*
unto the *b* which dwelt in Judaea ... Acts 11:29 *80*
things unto James, and to the *b* ... Acts 12:17 *80*
unto them, saying, Ye men and *b* ... Acts 13:15 *80*
Men and *b*, children of the stock ... Acts 13:26 *80*
unto you therefore, men and *b* ... Acts 13:38 *80*
minds evil affected against the *b* ... Acts 14:2 *80*
down from Judaea taught the *b* ... Acts 15:1 *80*
caused great joy unto all the *b* ... Acts 15:3 *80*
up, and said unto them, Men and *b* ... Acts 15:7 *80*
James answered, saying, Men and *b* ... Acts 15:13 *80*
and Silas, chief men among the *b* ... Acts 15:22 *80*
b send greeting unto the *b* ... Acts 15:23 *80*
exhorted the *b* with many words, ... Acts 15:32 *80*
from the *b* unto the apostles ... Acts 15:33 *80*
visit our *b* in every city where ... Acts 15:36 *80*
by the *b* unto the grace of God ... Acts 15:40 *80*
of by the *b* that were at Lystra ... Acts 16:2 *80*
and when they had seen the *b* ... Acts 16:40 *80*
certain *b* unto the rulers of the ... Acts 17:6 *80*
the *b* immediately sent away Paul ... Acts 17:10 *80*
then immediately the *b* sent away ... Acts 17:14 *80*
and then took his leave of the *b* ... Acts 18:18 *80*
the *b* wrote, exhorting the ... Acts 18:27 *80*
And now, *b*, I commend you to God, ... Acts 20:32 *80*
to Ptolemais, and saluted the *b* ... Acts 21:7 *80*
the *b* received us gladly ... Acts 21:17 *80*
Men, *b*, and fathers, hear ye my ... Acts 22:1 *80*
I received letters unto the *b* ... Acts 22:5 *80*
the council, said, Men and *b* ... Acts 23:1 *80*
Then said Paul, I wist not, *b* ... Acts 23:5 *80*
out in the council, Men and *b* ... Acts 23:6 *80*
Where we found *b*, and were desired ... Acts 28:14 *80*
when the *b* heard of us, they came ... Acts 28:15 *80*
he said unto them, Men and *b* ... Acts 28:17 *80*
neither any of the *b* that came ... Acts 28:21 *80*
I would not have you ignorant, *b* ... Rom 1:13 *80*
Know ye not, *b*, (for I speak to ... Rom 7:1 *80*
Wherefore, my *b*, ye also are ... Rom 7:4 *80*
Therefore, *b*, we are debtors, not ... Rom 8:12 *80*
be the firstborn among many *b* ... Rom 8:29 *80*
accursed from Christ for my *b* ... Rom 9:3 *80*
B, my heart's desire and prayer to ... Rom 10:1 *80*
For I would not, *b*, that ye ... Rom 11:25 *80*
I beseech you therefore, *b* ... Rom 12:1 *80*
also am persuaded of you, my *b* ... Rom 15:14 *80*
Nevertheless, *b*, I have written ... Rom 15:15 *80*
Now I beseech you, *b*, for the ... Rom 15:30 *80*
the *b* which are with them ... Rom 16:14 *80*
Now I beseech you, *b*, mark them ... Rom 16:17 *80*
Now I beseech you, *b*, by the name ... 1Cor 1:10 *80*
declared unto me of you, my *b* ... 1Cor 1:11 *80*
For ye see your calling, *b* ... 1Cor 1:26 *80*
And I, *b*, when I came to you, came ... 1Cor 2:1 *80*
And I, *b*, could not speak unto you ... 1Cor 3:1 *80*
And these things, *b*, I have in a ... 1Cor 4:6 *80*
be able to judge between his *b* ... 1Cor 6:5 *80*
wrong, and defraud, and that your *b* ... 1Cor 6:8 *80*
B, let every man, wherein he is ... 1Cor 7:24 *80*
But this I say, *b*, the time is ... 1Cor 7:29 *80*
But when ye sin so against the *b* ... 1Cor 8:12 *80*
as the *b* of the Lord, and Cephas ... 1Cor 9:5 *80*
Moreover, *b*, I would not that ye ... 1Cor 10:1 *80*
Now I praise you, *b*, that ye ... 1Cor 11:2 *80*
Wherefore, my *b*, when ye come ... 1Cor 11:33 *80*
Now concerning spiritual gifts, *b* ... 1Cor 12:1 *80*

Now, *b*, if I come unto you 1Cor 14:6 *80*
B, be not children in 1Cor 14:20 *80*
How is it then, *b* 1Cor 14:26 *80*
Wherefore, *b*, covet to prophesy, 1Cor 14:39 *80*
Moreover, *b*, I declare unto you 1Cor 15:1 *80*
of above five hundred *b* at once 1Cor 15:6 *80*
Now this I say, *b*, that flesh and 1Cor 15:50 *80*
Therefore, my beloved *b*, be ye 1Cor 15:58 *80*
for I look for him with the *b* 1Cor 16:11 *80*
him to come unto you with the *b* 1Cor 16:12 *80*
I beseech you, *b*, (ye know the 1Cor 16:15 *80*
All the *b* greet you 1Cor 16:20 *80*
For we would not, *b*, have you 2Cor 1:8 *80*
Moreover, *b*, we do you to wit of 2Cor 8:1 *80*
or our *b* be enquired of, they are 2Cor 8:23 *80*
Yet have I sent the *b*, lest our 2Cor 9:3 *80*
it necessary to exhort the *b* 2Cor 9:5 *80*
the *b* which came from Macedonia 2Cor 11:9 *80*
the sea, in perils among false *b* 2Cor 11:26 *5569*
Finally, *b*, farewell 2Cor 13:11 *80*
all the *b* which are with me, unto Gal 1:2 *80*
But I certify you, *b*, that the Gal 1:11 *80*
of false *b* unawares brought in Gal 2:4 *5569*
B, I speak after the manner of Gal 3:15 *80*
B, I beseech you, be as I am Gal 4:12 *80*
Now we, *b*, as Isaac was, are the Gal 4:28 *80*
So then, *b*, we are not children Gal 4:31 *80*
And I, *b*, if I yet preach Gal 5:11 *80*
For, *b*, ye have been called unto Gal 5:13 *80*
B, if a man be overtaken in a Gal 6:1 *80*
B, the grace of our Lord Jesus Gal 6:18 *80*
Finally, my *b*, be strong in the Eph 6:10 *80*
Peace be to the *b*, and love with Eph 6:23 *80*
I would ye should understand, *b* Phil 1:12 *80*
And many of the *b* in the Lord Phil 1:14 *80*
Finally, my *b*, rejoice in the Phil 3:1 *80*
B, I count not myself to have Phil 3:13 *80*
B, be followers together of me, Phil 3:17 *80*
my *b* dearly beloved and longed for Phil 4:1 *80*
Finally, *b*, whatsoever things are Phil 4:8 *80*
The *b* which are with me greet you Phil 4:21 *80*
faithful *b* in Christ which are at Col 1:2 *80*
Salute the *b* which are in Col 4:15 *80*
b beloved, your election of God 1Th 1:4 *80*
For yourselves, *b*, know our 1Th 2:1 *80*
For ye remember, *b*, our labour and 1Th 2:9 *80*
For ye, *b*, became followers of 1Th 2:14 *80*
But we, *b*, being taken from you 1Th 2:17 *80*
Therefore, *b*, we were comforted 1Th 3:7 *80*
then we beseech you, *b*, and exhort 1Th 4:1 *80*
the *b* which are in all Macedonia 1Th 4:10 *80*
but we beseech you, *b*, that ye 1Th 4:10 *80*
not have you to be ignorant, *b* 1Th 4:13 *80*
of the times and the seasons, *b* 1Th 5:1 *80*
But ye, *b*, are not in darkness, 1Th 5:4 *80*
And we beseech you, *b*, to know 1Th 5:12 *80*
Now we exhort you, *b*, warn them 1Th 5:14 *80*
B, pray for us 1Th 5:25 *80*
Greet all the *b* with an holy kiss 1Th 5:26 *80*
be read unto all the holy *b* 1Th 5:27 *80*
to thank God always for you, *b* 2Th 1:3 *80*
Now we beseech you, *b*, by the 2Th 2:1 *80*
b beloved of the Lord, because 2Th 2:13 *80*
Therefore, *b*, stand fast, and hold 2Th 2:15 *80*
Finally, *b*, pray for us, that the 2Th 3:1 *80*
Now we command you, *b*, in the 2Th 3:6 *80*
But ye, *b*, be not weary in well 2Th 3:13 *80*
If thou put the *b* in remembrance 1Ti 4:6 *80*
and the younger men as *b* 1Ti 5:1 *80*
despise them, because they are *b* 1Ti 6:2 *80*
Linus, and Claudia, and all the *b* 2Ti 4:21 *80*
he is not ashamed to call them *b* Heb 2:11 *80*
I will declare thy name unto my *b* Heb 2:12 *80*
him to be made like unto his *b* Heb 2:17 *80*
Wherefore, holy *b*, partakers of Heb 3:1 *80*
Take heed, *b*, lest there be in Heb 3:12 *80*
to the law, that is, of their *b* Heb 7:5 *80*
Having therefore, *b*, boldness to Heb 10:19 *80*
And I beseech you, *b*, suffer the Heb 13:22 *80*
My *b*, count it all joy when ye Jas 1:2 *80*
Do not err, my beloved *b* Jas 1:16 *80*
Wherefore, my beloved *b*, let Jas 1:19 *80*
My *b*, have not the faith of our Jas 2:1 *80*
Hearken, my beloved *b*, Hath not Jas 2:5 *80*
What doth it profit, my *b* Jas 2:14 *80*
My *b*, be not many masters, Jas 3:1 *80*
My *b*, these things ought not so Jas 3:10 *80*
Can the fig tree, my *b*, bear Jas 3:12 *80*
Speak not evil one of another, *b* Jas 4:11 *80*
Be patient therefore, *b*, unto the Jas 5:7 *80*
Grudge not one against another, *b* Jas 5:9 *80*
Take, my *b*, the prophets, who Jas 5:10 *80*
But above all things, my *b* Jas 5:12 *80*
B, if any of you do err from the Jas 5:19 *80*
unto unfeigned love of the *b* 1Pet 1:22 *5360*
one of another, love as *b* 1Pet 3:8 *5361*
in your *b* that are in the world 1Pet 5:9 *81*
Wherefore the rather, *b*, give 2Pet 1:10 *80*
B, I write no new commandment 1Jn 2:7 *80*
Marvel not, my *b*, if the world 1Jn 3:13 *80*
unto life, because we love the *b* 1Jn 3:14 *80*
to lay down our lives for the *b* 1Jn 3:16 *80*
rejoiced greatly, when the *b* came 3Jn 3 *80*
whatsoever thou doest to the *b* 3Jn 5 *80*
doth he himself receive the *b* 3Jn 10 *80*
fellowservants also and their *b* Rev 6:11 *80*
the accuser of our *b* is cast down Rev 12:10 *80*
of thy *b* that have the testimony Rev 19:10 *80*
of thy *b* the prophets, and of them Rev 22:9 *80*

BRETHREN'S {1}
lest his *b* heart faint as well as Deut 20:8 251

BRIBE {2}
b to blind mine eyes therewith 1Sa 12:3 3724
afflict the just, they take a *b* Amos 5:12 3724

BRIBERY {1}
consume the tabernacles of *b* Job 15:34 7810

BRIBES {3}
aside after lucre, and took *b* 1Sa 8:3 7810
and their right hand is full of *b* Ps 26:10 7810
his hands from holding of *b* Is 33:15 7810

BRICK {7}
to another, Go to, let us make *b* Gen 11:3 3835
they had *b* for stone, and slime Gen 11:3 3843
hard bondage, in morter, and in *b* Ex 1:14 3843
give the people straw to make *b* Ex 5:7 3835
task in making *b* both yesterday Ex 5:14 3835
and they say to us, Make *b* Ex 5:16 3843
burneth incense upon altars of *b* Is 65:3 3843

BRICKKILN {3}
and made them pass through the *b* 2Sa 12:31 4404
and hide them in the clay in the *b* Jer 43:9 4404
the morter, make strong the *b* Nah 3:14 4404

BRICKS {4}
And the tale of the *b*, which they Ex 5:8 3843
shall ye deliver the tale of *b* Ex 5:18 3843
from your *b* of your daily task Ex 5:19 3843
The *b* are fallen down, but we Is 9:10 3843

BRIDE {14}
bind them on thee, as a *b* doeth Is 49:18 3618
as a *b* adorneth herself with her Is 61:10 3618
bridegroom rejoiceth over the *b* Is 62:5 3618
her ornaments, or a *b* her attire Jer 2:32 3618
bridegroom, and the voice of the *b* Jer 7:34 3618
bridegroom, and the voice of the *b* Jer 16:9 3618
bridegroom, and the voice of the *b* Jer 25:10 3618
bridegroom, and the voice of the *b* Jer 33:11 3618
and the *b* out of her closet Joel 2:16 3618
He that hath the *b* is the Jn 3:29 *3565*
of the *b* shall be heard no more Rev 18:23 *3565*
prepared as a *b* adorned for her Rev 21:2 *3565*
hither, I will shew thee the *b* Rev 21:9 *3565*
And the Spirit and the *b* say Rev 22:17 *3565*

BRIDECHAMBER {3}
Can the children of the *b* mourn Mt 9:15 *3567*
Can the children of the *b* fast Mk 2:19 *3567*
make the children of the *b* fast Lk 5:34 *3567*

BRIDEGROOM {23}
Which is as a *b* coming out of his Ps 19:5 2860
as a *b* decketh himself with Is 61:10 2860
as the *b* rejoiceth over the bride Is 62:5 2860
of gladness, the voice of the *b* Jer 7:34 2860
of gladness, the voice of the *b* Jer 16:9 2860
of gladness, the voice of the *b* Jer 25:10 2860
of gladness, the voice of the *b* Jer 33:11 2860
let the *b* go forth of his chamber Joel 2:16 2860
as long as the *b* is with them Mt 9:15 *3566*
when the *b* shall be taken from Mt 9:15 *3566*
and went forth to meet the *b* Mt 25:1 *3566*
While the *b* tarried, they all Mt 25:5 *3566*
a cry made, Behold, the *b* cometh Mt 25:6 *3566*
they went to buy, the *b* came Mt 25:10 *3566*
fast, while the *b* is with them Mk 2:19 *3566*
long as they have the *b* with them Mk 2:19 *3566*
when the *b* shall be taken away Mk 2:20 *3566*
fast, while the *b* is with them Lk 5:34 *3566*
when the *b* shall be taken away Lk 5:35 *3566*
of the feast called the *b* Jn 2:9 *3566*
He that hath the bride is the *b* Jn 3:29 *3566*
but the friend of the *b*, which Jn 3:29 *3566*
and the voice of the *b* and of the Rev 18:23 *3566*

BRIDEGROOM'S {1}
greatly because of the *b* voice Jn 3:29 *3566*

BRIDLE {9}
my *b* in thy lips, and I will turn 2Kin 19:28 4964
also let loose the *b* before me Job 30:11 7448
can come to him with his double *b* Job 41:13 7448
must be held in with bit and *b* Ps 32:9 7448
I will keep my mouth with a *b* Ps 39:1 4269
a *b* for the ass, and a rod for the Prov 26:3 4964
there shall be a *b* in the jaws of Is 30:28 7448
my *b* in thy lips, and I will turn Is 37:29 4964
able also to *b* the whole body Jas 3:2 *5469*

BRIDLES {1}
winepress, even unto the horse *b* Rev 14:20 *5469*

BRIDLETH {1}
b not his tongue, but deceiveth Jas 1:26 *5468*

BRIEFLY {2}
it is *b* comprehended in this Rom 13:9 *346*
as I suppose, I have written *b* 1Pet 5:12 *1223,3641*

BRIER {3}
instead of the *b* shall come up Is 55:13 5636
b unto the house of Israel Eze 28:24 5544
The best of them is as a *b* Mic 7:4 2312

BRIERS {12}
of the wilderness and with *b* Judg 8:7 1303
and thorns of the wilderness and *b* Judg 8:16 1303
but there shall come up *b* Is 5:6 8068
it shall even be for *b* and thorns Is 7:23 8068
all the land shall become *b* Is 7:24 8068
not come thither the fear of *b* Is 7:25 8068
it shall devour the *b* and thorns, Is 9:18 8068
his thorns and his *b* in one day Is 10:17 8068
who would set the *b* and thorns Is 27:4 8068
people shall come up thorns and *b* Is 32:13 8068
afraid of their words, though *b* Eze 2:6 5621
b is rejected, and is nigh unto Heb 6:8 *5146*

BRIGANDINE {1}
that lifteth himself up in his *b* Jer 51:3 5630

BRIGANDINES {1}
the spears, and put on the *b* Jer 46:4 5630

BRIGHT {29}
or *b* spot, and it be in the skin Lev 13:2 934
If the *b* spot be white in the Lev 13:4 934
be a white rising, or a *b* spot Lev 13:19 934
But if the *b* spot stay in his Lev 13:23 934
that burneth have a white *b* spot Lev 13:24 934
if the hair in the *b* spot be Lev 13:25 934
be no white hair in the *b* spot Lev 13:26 934
if the *b* spot stay in his place, Lev 13:28 934
b spots, even white *b* spots Lev 13:38 934
if the *b* spots in the skin of Lev 13:39 934
and for a scab, and for a *b* spot Lev 14:56 934
of the LORD, were of *b* brass 1Kin 7:45 4803
the house of the LORD of *b* brass 2Chr 4:16 4838
he scattereth his *b* cloud Job 37:11 216
now men see not the *b* light which Job 37:21 925
his belly is as *b* ivory overlaid Song 5:14 6247
Make *b* the arrows Jer 51:11 1305
and the fire was *b*, and out of the Eze 1:13 5051
it is made *b*, it is wrapped up Eze 21:15 1300
he made his arrows *b*, he Eze 21:21 7043
b iron, cassia, and calamus, were Eze 27:19 6219
All the *b* lights of heaven will I Eze 32:8 3974
lifteth up both the *b* sword Nah 3:3 3851
so the LORD shall make *b* clouds Zec 10:1 2385
a *b* cloud overshadowed them Mt 17:5 *5460*
as when the *b* shining of a candle Lk 11:36 *796*
man stood before me in *b* clothing Acts 10:30 *2986*
the offspring of David, and the *b* Rev 22:16 *2986*

BRIGHTNESS {22}
Through the *b* before him were 2Sa 22:13 5051
shined, or the moon walking in *b* Job 31:26 3368
At the *b* that was before him his Ps 18:12 5051
for *b*, but we walk in darkness Is 59:9 5054
kings to the *b* of thy rising Is 60:3 5051
neither for *b* shall the moon give Is 60:19 5051
thereof go forth as *b*, and the Is 62:1 5051
a *b* was about it, and out of the Eze 1:4 5051
of fire, and it had *b* round about Eze 1:27 5051
appearance of the *b* round about Eze 1:28 5051
upward, as the appearance of *b* Eze 8:2 2096
full of the *b* of the LORD's glory Eze 10:4 5051
and they shall defile thy *b* Eze 28:7 3314
thy wisdom by reason of thy *b* Eze 28:17 3314
whose *b* was excellent, stood Dan 2:31 2122
mine honour and *b* returned unto me Dan 4:36 2122
shine as the *b* of the firmament Dan 12:3 2096
even very dark, and no *b* in it Amos 5:20 5051
And his *b* was as the light Hab 3:4 5051
above the *b* of the sun, shining Acts 26:13 *2987*
destroy with the *b* of his coming 2Th 2:8 *2015*
Who being the *b* of his glory Heb 1:3 *541*

BRIM {10}
were dipped in the *b* of the water Josh 3:15 7097
from the one *b* to the other 1Kin 7:23 8193
under the *b* of it round about 1Kin 7:24 8193
the *b* thereof was wrought like 1Kin 7:26 8193
was wrought like the *b* of a cup 1Kin 7:26 8193
sea of ten cubits from *b* to *b* 2Chr 4:2 8193
the *b* of it like the work of the 2Chr 4:5 8193
like the work of the *b* of a cup 2Chr 4:5 8193
And they filled them up to the *b* Jn 2:7 *507*

BRIMSTONE {15}
upon Sodom and upon Gomorrah *b* Gen 19:24 1614
that the whole land thereof is *b* Deut 29:23 1614
b shall be scattered upon his Job 18:15 1614
he shall rain snares, fire and *b* Ps 11:6 1614
of the LORD, like a stream of *b* Is 30:33 1614
pitch, and the dust thereof into *b* Is 34:9 1614
and great hailstones, fire, and *b* Eze 38:22 1614
b from heaven, and destroyed them Lk 17:29 *2303*
of fire, and of jacinth, and *b* Rev 9:17 *2306*
mouths issued fire and smoke and *b* Rev 9:17 *2303*
and by the smoke, and by the *b* Rev 9:18 *2303*
b in the presence of the holy Rev 14:10 *2303*
a lake of fire burning with *b* Rev 19:20 *2303*
cast into the lake of fire and *b* Rev 20:10 *2303*
lake which burneth with fire and *b* Rev 21:8 *2303*

BRING See APPENDIX.

BRINGERS {1}
the *b* up of the children, sent to 2Kin 10:5 539

BRINGEST {5}
a valiant man, and *b* good tidings 1Kin 1:42 1319
b me into judgment with thee Job 14:3 935
that *b* good tidings, get thee up Is 40:9 1319
that *b* good tidings, lift up thy Is 40:9 1319
For thou *b* certain strange things Acts 17:20 *1533*

BRINGETH See APPENDIX.

BRINGING See APPENDIX.

BRINK {6}
kine upon the *b* of the river Gen 41:3 8193
it in the flags by the river's *b* Ex 2:3 8193
by the river's *b* against he come Ex 7:15 8193

which is by the b of the river of ... Deut 2:36 8193
to the b of the water of Jordan ... Josh 3:8 7097
to return to the b of the river ... Eze 47:6 8193

BROAD {36}
cubits long, and five cubits b ... Ex 27:1 7341
let them make them b plates for a ... Num 16:38 7555
they were made b plates for a ... Num 16:39 7554
chamber was five cubits b ... 1Kin 6:6 7341
and the middle was six cubits b ... 1Kin 6:6 7341
and the third was seven cubits b ... 1Kin 6:6 7341
cubits long, and five cubits b ... 2Chr 6:13 7341
Jerusalem unto the b wall ... Neh 3:8 7342
the furnaces even unto the b wall ... Neh 12:38 7342
out of the strait into a b place ... Job 36:16 7338
thy commandment is exceeding b ... Ps 119:96 7342
in the b ways I will seek him ... Song 3:2 7339
be unto us a place of b rivers ... Is 33:21 7338,3027
seek in the b places thereof, if ... Jer 5:1 7339
The b walls of Babylon shall be ... Jer 51:58 7342
of the gate, which was one reed b ... Eze 40:6 7341
of the gate, which was one reed b ... Eze 40:6 7341
was one reed long, and one reed b ... Eze 40:7 7341
long, and five and twenty cubits b ... Eze 40:29 7341
cubits long, and five cubits b ... Eze 40:30 7341
long, and five and twenty cubits b ... Eze 40:33 7341
long, and a cubit and an half b ... Eze 40:42 7341
And within were hooks, an hand b ... Eze 40:43
long, and an hundred cubits b ... Eze 40:47 7341
six cubits b on the one side, and ... Eze 41:1 7341
six cubits b on the other side, ... Eze 41:1 7341
the west was seventy cubits b ... Eze 41:12 7341
as long as they, and as b as they ... Eze 42:11 7342
reeds long, and five hundred b ... Eze 42:20 7341
be twelve cubits long, twelve b ... Eze 43:16 7341
fourteen b in the four squares ... Eze 43:17 7341
of the city five thousand b ... Eze 45:6 7341
of forty cubits long and thirty b ... Eze 46:22 7341
one against another in the b ways ... Nah 2:4 7339
b is the way, that leadeth to ... Mt 7:13 2149
they make b their phylacteries, ... Mt 23:5 4115

BROADER {1}
than the earth, and b than the sea ... Job 11:9 7342

BROIDED {1}
not with b hair, or gold, or ... 1Ti 2:9 4117

BROIDERED {8}
a b coat, a mitre, and a girdle ... Ex 28:4 8665
I clothed thee also with b work ... Eze 16:10 7553
of fine linen, and silk, and b work ... Eze 16:13 7553
And tookest thy b garments ... Eze 16:18 7553
and put off their b garments ... Eze 26:16 7553
Fine linen with b work from Egypt ... Eze 27:7 7553
b work, and fine linen, and coral, ... Eze 27:16 7553
b work, and in chests of rich ... Eze 27:24 7553

BROILED {1}
they gave him a piece of a b fish ... Lk 24:42 3702

BROKEN {186}
fountains of the great deep b up ... Gen 7:11 1234
he hath b my covenant ... Gen 17:14 6565
she said, How hast thou b forth ... Gen 38:29 6555
wherein it is sodden shall be b ... Lev 6:28 7665
for pots, they shall be b down ... Lev 11:35 5422
of leprosy b out of the boil ... Lev 13:20 6524
it is a leprosy b out of the ... Lev 13:25 6524
which hath the issue, shall be b ... Lev 15:12 7665
or scabbed, or hath his stones b ... Lev 21:20 4790
Blind, or b, or maimed, or having ... Lev 22:22 7665
is bruised, or crushed, or b ... Lev 22:24 5423
I have b the bands of your yoke, ... Lev 26:13 7665
when I have b the staff of your ... Lev 26:26 7665
hath b his commandment, that soul ... Num 15:31 6565
Then were the horsehoofs b by the ... Judg 5:22 1986
as a thread of tow is b when it ... Judg 16:9 5423
The bows of the mighty men are b ... 1Sa 2:4 2844
of the LORD shall be b to pieces ... 1Sa 2:10 2865
The LORD hath b forth upon mine ... 2Sa 5:20 6555
a bow of steel is b by mine arms ... 2Sa 22:35 5181
altar of the LORD that was b down ... 1Kin 18:30 2040
the ships were b at Ezion-geber ... 1Kin 22:48 7665
the house, that it be not b down ... 2Kin 11:6 4535
And the city was b up, and all the ... 2Kin 25:4 1234
God hath b in upon mine enemies ... 1Chr 14:11 6555
the LORD hath b thy works ... 2Chr 20:37 6555
And the ships were b, that they ... 2Chr 20:37 7665
had b up the house of God ... 2Chr 24:7 6555
that they all were b in pieces ... 2Chr 25:12 1234
built up all the wall that was b ... 2Chr 32:5 6555
Hezekiah his father had b down ... 2Chr 33:3 5422
when he had b down the altars and ... 2Chr 34:7 5422
wall of Jerusalem also is b down ... Neh 1:3 6555
of Jerusalem, which were b down ... Neh 2:13 6555
teeth of the young lions, are b ... Job 4:10 5421
my skin is b, and become loathsome ... Job 7:5 7280
at ease, but he hath b me asunder ... Job 16:12 6565
are past, my purposes are b off ... Job 17:11 5423
of the fatherless have been b ... Job 22:9 1792
wickedness shall be b as a tree ... Job 24:20 7665
mine arm be b from the bone ... Job 31:22 7665
and the high arm shall be b ... Job 38:15 7665
thou hast b the teeth of the ... Ps 3:7 7665
a bow of steel is b by mine arms ... Ps 18:34 5181
I am like a b vessel ... Ps 31:12 6
unto them that are of a b heart ... Ps 34:18 7665
not one of them is b ... Ps 34:20 7665
heart, and their bows shall be b ... Ps 37:15 7665
the arms of the wicked shall be b ... Ps 37:17 7665
I am feeble and sore b ... Ps 38:8 1794
Though thou hast sore b us in the ... Ps 44:19 1794
which thou hast b may rejoice ... Ps 51:8 1794
sacrifices of God are a b spirit ... Ps 51:17 7665
a b and a contrite heart, O God, ... Ps 51:17 7665
he hath b his covenant ... Ps 55:20 2490
thou hast b it ... Ps 60:2 6480
Reproach hath b my heart ... Ps 69:20 7665
hast thou then b down her hedges ... Ps 80:12 6555
Thou hast b Rahab in pieces, as ... Ps 89:10 1792
Thou hast b down all his hedges ... Ps 89:40 6555
For he hath b the gates of brass, ... Ps 107:16 7665
he might even slay the b in heart ... Ps 109:16 5218
the snare is b, and we are escaped ... Ps 124:7 7665
He healeth the b in heart ... Ps 147:3 7665
his knowledge the depths are b up ... Prov 3:20 1234
shall he be b without remedy ... Prov 6:15 7665
of the heart the spirit is b ... Prov 15:13 5218
but a b spirit drieth the bones ... Prov 17:22 5218
the stone wall thereof was b down ... Prov 24:31 2040
time of trouble is like a b tooth ... Prov 25:19 7465
is like a city that is b down ... Prov 25:28 6555
a threefold cord is not quickly b ... Eccl 4:12 5423
loosed, or the golden bowl be b ... Eccl 12:6 7533
the pitcher be b at the fountain ... Eccl 12:6 7665
or the wheel b at the cistern ... Eccl 12:6 7533
the latchet of their shoes be b ... Is 5:27 5423
and five years shall Ephraim be b ... Is 7:8 2844
and ye shall be b in pieces ... Is 8:9 2844
and ye shall be b in pieces ... Is 8:9 2844
and ye shall be b in pieces ... Is 8:9 2844
shall stumble, and fall, and be b ... Is 8:15 7665
For thou hast b the yoke of his ... Is 9:4 2865
The LORD hath b the staff of the ... Is 14:5 7665
rod of him that smote thee is b ... Is 14:29 7665
have b down the principal plants ... Is 16:8 1986
they shall be b in the purposes ... Is 19:10 1792
gods he hath b unto the ground ... Is 21:9 7665
the houses have ye b down to ... Is 22:10 5422
b the everlasting covenant ... Is 24:5 6565
The city of confusion is b down ... Is 24:10 7665
The earth is utterly b down ... Is 24:19 7489
are withered, they shall be b off ... Is 27:11 7665
go, and fall backward, and be b ... Is 28:13 7665
vessel that is b in pieces ... Is 30:14 3807
he hath b the covenant, he hath ... Is 33:8 6565
any of the cords thereof be b ... Is 33:20 5423
in the staff of this b reed ... Is 36:6 7533
b cisterns, that can hold no ... Jer 2:13 7665
Tahapanes have b the crown of thy ... Jer 2:16 7462
For of old time I have b thy yoke ... Jer 2:20 7665
b down at the presence of the ... Jer 4:26 5422
these have altogether b the yoke ... Jer 5:5 7665
is spoiled, and all my cords are b ... Jer 10:20 5423
the house of Judah have b my ... Jer 11:10 6565
it, and the branches of it are b ... Jer 11:16 7489
people is b with a great breach ... Jer 14:17 7665
this man Coniah a despised b idol ... Jer 22:28 5310
me is b because of the prophets ... Jer 23:9 7665
I have b the yoke of the king of ... Jer 28:2 7665
b the yoke from off the neck of ... Jer 28:12 7665
Thou hast b the yokes of wood ... Jer 28:13 7665
be b with David my servant ... Jer 33:21 6565
b up from Jerusalem for fear of ... Jer 37:11 5927
of the month, the city was b up ... Jer 39:2 1234
say, How is the strong staff b ... Jer 48:17 7665
for it is b down ... Jer 48:20 2865
Moab is cut off, and his arm is b ... Jer 48:25 7665
for I have b Moab like a vessel ... Jer 48:38 7665
howl, saying, How is it b down ... Jer 48:39 2865
Merodach is b in pieces ... Jer 50:2 2844
her images are b in pieces ... Jer 50:2 2865
king of Babylon hath b his bones ... Jer 50:17 6105
whole earth cut in asunder and b ... Jer 50:23 7665
her bars are b ... Jer 51:30 7665
every one of their bows is b ... Jer 51:56 2865
of Babylon shall be utterly b ... Jer 51:58 6209
Then the city was b up, and all ... Jer 52:7 1234
he hath destroyed and b her bars ... Lam 2:9 7665
he hath b my bones ... Lam 3:4 7665
He hath also b my teeth with ... Lam 3:16 1638
and your images shall be b ... Eze 6:4 7665
desolate, and your idols may be b ... Eze 6:6 7665
because I am b with their whorish ... Eze 6:9 7665
and my covenant that he hath b ... Eze 17:19 6331
her strong rods were b and ... Eze 19:12 6561
she is b that was the gates of ... Eze 26:2 7665
the east wind hath b thee in the ... Eze 27:26 7665
be b by the seas in the depths of ... Eze 27:34 7665
her foundations shall be b down ... Eze 30:4 2040
I have b the arm of Pharaoh king ... Eze 30:21 7665
the strong, and that which was b ... Eze 30:22 7665
his boughs are b by all the ... Eze 31:12 7665
thou shalt be b in the midst of ... Eze 32:28 7665
have ye bound up that which was b ... Eze 34:4 7665
and will bind up that which was b ... Eze 34:16 7665
when I have b the bands of their ... Eze 34:27 7665
they have b my covenant because ... Eze 44:7 6565
b to pieces together, and became ... Dan 2:35 1854
be partly strong, and partly b ... Dan 2:42 8406
was strong, the great horn was b ... Dan 8:8 7665
Now that being b, whereas four ... Dan 8:22 7665
but he shall be b without hand ... Dan 8:25 7665
stand up, his kingdom shall be b ... Dan 11:4 7665
from before him, and shall be b ... Dan 11:22 7665
b in judgment, because he ... Hos 5:11 7533
of Samaria shall be b in pieces ... Hos 8:6 7616
desolate, the barns are b down ... Joel 1:17 2040
so that the ship was like to be b ... Jonah 1:4 7665
they have b up, and have passed ... Mic 2:13 6555
And it was b in that day ... Zec 11:11 6565
one, nor heal that that is b ... Zec 11:16 7665
they took up of the b meat that ... Mt 15:37 2801
fall on this stone shall be b ... Mt 21:44 4917
suffered his house to be b up ... Mt 24:43 1358
and when they had b it up, they ... Mk 2:4 1846
him, and the fetters b in pieces ... Mk 5:4 4937
they took up of the b meat that ... Mk 8:8 2801
his house to be b through ... Lk 12:39 1358
fall upon that stone shall be b ... Lk 20:18 4917
he not only had b the sabbath ... Jn 5:18 3089
the law of Moses should not be b ... Jn 7:23 3089
and the scripture cannot be b ... Jn 10:35 3089
Pilate that their legs might be b ... Jn 19:31 2608
A bone of him shall not be b ... Jn 19:36 4937
so many, yet was not the net b ... Jn 21:11 4977
when the congregation was b up ... Acts 13:43 3089
had b bread, and eaten, and talked ... Acts 20:11 2806
and when he had b it, he began to ... Acts 27:35 2806
but the hinder part was b with ... Acts 27:41 3089
some on b pieces of the ship ... Acts 27:44
if some of the branches be b off ... Rom 11:17 1575
say then, The branches were b off ... Rom 11:19 1575
of unbelief they were b off ... Rom 11:20 1575
is my body, which is b for you ... 1Cor 11:24 2806
hath b down the middle wall of ... Eph 2:14 3089
potter shall they be b to shivers ... Rev 2:27 4937

BROKENFOOTED {1}
Or a man that is b, or ... Lev 21:19 7667,7272

BROKENHANDED {1}
a man that is brokenfooted, or b ... Lev 21:19 7667,3027

BROKENHEARTED {2}
he hath sent me to bind up the b ... Is 61:1 7665,3820
he hath sent me to heal the b ... Lk 4:18 4937,2588

BROOD {1}
doth gather her b under her wings ... Lk 13:34 3555

BROOK {39}
them, and sent them over the b ... Gen 32:23 5158
thick trees, and willows of the b ... Lev 23:40 5158
And they came unto the b of Eshcol ... Num 13:23 5158
The place was called the b Eshcol ... Num 13:24 5158
I, and get you over the b Zered ... Deut 2:13 5158
And we went over the b Zered ... Deut 2:13 5158
we were come over the b Zered ... Deut 2:14 5158
cast the dust thereof into the b ... Deut 9:21 5158
five smooth stones out of the b ... 1Sa 17:40 5158
with him, and came to the b Besor ... 1Sa 30:9 5158
could not go over the b Besor ... 1Sa 30:10 5158
made also to abide at the b Besor ... 1Sa 30:21 5158
himself passed over the b Kidron ... 2Sa 15:23 5158
They be gone over the b of water ... 2Sa 17:20 4323
out, and passest over the b Kidron ... 1Kin 2:37 5158
idol, and burnt it by the b Kidron ... 1Kin 15:13 5158
and hide thyself by the b Cherith ... 1Kin 17:3 5158
that thou shalt drink of the b ... 1Kin 17:4 5158
he went and dwelt by the b Cherith ... 1Kin 17:5 5158
and he drank of the b ... 1Kin 17:6 5158
a while, that the b dried up ... 1Kin 17:7 5158
brought them down to the b Kishon ... 1Kin 18:40 5158
Jerusalem, unto the b Kidron ... 2Kin 23:6 5158
and burned it at the b Kidron ... 2Kin 23:6 5158
dust of them into the b Kidron ... 2Kin 23:12 5158
it, and burnt it at the b Kidron ... 2Chr 15:16 5158
find them at the end of the b ... 2Chr 20:16 5158
it out abroad into the b Kidron ... 2Chr 29:16 5158
and cast them into the b Kidron ... 2Chr 30:14 5158
the b that ran through the midst ... 2Chr 32:4 5158
went I up in the night by the b ... Neh 2:15 5158
have dealt deceitfully as a b ... Job 6:15 5158
of the b compass him about ... Job 40:22 5158
as to Jabin, at the b of Kison ... Ps 83:9 5158
shall drink of the b in the way ... Ps 110:7 5158
of wisdom as a flowing b ... Prov 18:4 5158
away to the b of the willows ... Is 15:7 5158
the fields unto the b of Kidron ... Jer 31:40 5158
his disciples over the b Cedron ... Jn 18:1 5493

BROOKS {15}
Red sea, and in the b of Arnon, ... Num 21:14 5158
at the stream of the b that goeth ... Num 21:15 5158
a good land, a land of b of water ... Deut 8:7 5158
Hiddai of the b of Gaash ... 2Sa 23:30 5158
fountains of water, and unto all b ... 1Kin 18:5 5158
Hurai of the b of Gaash, Abiel ... 1Chr 11:32 5158
as the stream of b they pass away ... Job 6:15 5158
floods, the b of honey and butter ... Job 20:17 5158
of Ophir as the stones of the b ... Job 22:24 5158
hart panteth after the water b ... Ps 42:1 650
the b of defence shall be emptied ... Is 19:6 2975
the b, by the mouth of the b ... Is 19:7 2975
and every thing sown by the b ... Is 19:7 2975
angle into the b shall lament ... Is 19:8 2975

BROTH {3}
basket, and he put the b in a pot ... Judg 6:19 4839
upon this rock, and pour out the b ... Judg 6:20 4839
b of abominable things is in ... Is 65:4 6564

BROTHER {370}
And she again bare his b Abel ... Gen 4:2 251
And Cain talked with Abel his b ... Gen 4:8 251
Cain rose up against Abel his b ... Gen 4:8 251
unto Cain, Where is Abel thy b ... Gen 4:9 251
at the hand of every man's b will ... Gen 9:5 251
the b of Japheth the elder, even ... Gen 10:21 251
b of Eshcol, and b of Aner ... Gen 14:13 251
b of Eshcol, and b of Aner ... Gen 14:13 251

that his *b* was taken captive	Gen 14:14	251
and also brought again his *b* Lot	Gen 14:16	251
even she herself said, He is my *b*	Gen 20:5	251
shall come, say of me, He is my *b*	Gen 20:13	251
I have given thy *b* a thousand	Gen 20:16	251
born children unto thy *b* Nahor	Gen 22:20	251
Huz his firstborn, and Buz his *b*	Gen 22:21	251
did bear to Nahor, Abraham's *b*	Gen 22:23	251
the wife of Nahor, Abraham's *b*	Gen 24:15	251
And Rebekah had a *b*, and his name	Gen 24:29	251
he gave also to her *b* and to her	Gen 24:53	251
And her *b* and her mother said, Let	Gen 24:55	251
And after that came his *b* out	Gen 25:26	251
thy father speak unto Esau thy *b*	Gen 27:6	251
Esau my *b* is a hairy man, and I am	Gen 27:11	251
were hairy, as his *b* Esau's hands	Gen 27:23	251
that Esau his *b* came in from his	Gen 27:30	251
Thy *b* came with subtilty, and hath	Gen 27:35	251
thou live, and shalt serve thy *b*	Gen 27:40	251
then will I slay my *b* Jacob	Gen 27:41	251
thy *b* Esau, as touching thee	Gen 27:42	251
flee thou to Laban my *b* to Haran	Gen 27:43	251
daughters of Laban thy mother's *b*	Gen 28:2	251
the *b* of Rebekah, Jacob's and	Gen 28:5	251
daughter of Laban his mother's *b*	Gen 29:10	251
the sheep of Laban his mother's *b*	Gen 29:10	251
the flock of Laban his mother's *b*	Gen 29:10	251
Rachel that he was her father's *b*	Gen 29:12	251
unto Jacob, Because thou art my *b*	Gen 29:15	251
Esau his *b* unto the land of Seir	Gen 32:3	251
saying, We came to thy *b* Esau	Gen 32:6	251
pray thee, from the hand of my *b*	Gen 32:11	251
his hand a present for Esau his *b*	Gen 32:13	251
When Esau my *b* meeteth thee	Gen 32:17	251
until he came near to his *b*	Gen 33:3	251
And Esau said, I have enough, my *b*	Gen 33:9	251
from the face of Esau thy *b*	Gen 35:1	251
he fled from the face of his *b*	Gen 35:7	251
from the face of his *b* Jacob	Gen 36:6	251
profit is it if we slay our *b*	Gen 37:26	251
for he is our *b* and our flesh	Gen 37:27	251
her, and raise up seed to thy *b*	Gen 38:8	251
that he should give seed to his *b*	Gen 38:9	251
that, behold, his *b* came out	Gen 38:29	251
And afterward came out his *b*	Gen 38:30	251
But Benjamin, Joseph's *b*, Jacob	Gen 42:4	251
your youngest *b* come hither	Gen 42:15	251
of you, and let him fetch your *b*	Gen 42:16	251
But bring your youngest *b* unto me	Gen 42:20	251
verily guilty concerning our *b*	Gen 42:21	251
And bring your youngest *b* unto me	Gen 42:34	251
so will I deliver you your *b*	Gen 42:34	251
for his *b* is dead, and he is left	Gen 42:38	251
face, except your *b* be with you	Gen 43:3	251
If thou wilt send our *b* with us	Gen 43:4	251
face, except your *b* be with you	Gen 43:5	251
the man whether ye had yet a *b*	Gen 43:6	251
have ye another *b*	Gen 43:7	251
he would say, Bring your *b* down	Gen 43:7	251
Take also your *b*, and arise, go	Gen 43:13	251
he may send away your other *b*	Gen 43:14	251
saw his *b* Benjamin, his mother's	Gen 43:29	251
and said, Is this your younger *b*	Gen 43:29	251
his bowels did yearn upon his *b*	Gen 43:30	251
saying, Have ye a father, or a *b*	Gen 44:19	251
his *b* is dead, and he alone is	Gen 44:20	251
youngest *b* come down with you	Gen 44:23	251
if our youngest *b* be with us	Gen 44:26	251
except our youngest *b* be with us	Gen 44:26	251
And he said, I am Joseph your *b*	Gen 45:4	251
see, and the eyes of my *b* Benjamin	Gen 45:12	251
fell upon his *b* Benjamin's neck	Gen 45:14	251
but truly his younger *b* shall be	Gen 48:19	251
Is not Aaron the Levite thy *b*	Ex 4:14	251
Aaron thy *b* shall be thy prophet	Ex 7:1	251
Aaron thy *b* shall speak unto	Ex 7:2	251
take thou unto thee Aaron thy *b*	Ex 28:1	251
for Aaron thy *b* for glory	Ex 28:2	251
holy garments for Aaron thy *b*	Ex 28:4	251
shalt put them upon Aaron thy *b*	Ex 28:41	251
the camp, and slay every man his *b*	Ex 32:27	251
man upon his son, and upon his *b*	Ex 32:29	251
Moses, Speak unto Aaron thy *b*	Lev 16:2	251
the nakedness of thy father's *b*	Lev 18:14	251
not hate thy *b* in thine heart	Lev 19:17	251
and for his daughter, and for his *b*	Lev 21:2	251
If thy *b* be waxen poor, and hath	Lev 25:25	251
he redeem that which his *b* sold	Lev 25:25	251
if thy *b* be waxen poor, and fallen	Lev 25:35	251
that thy *b* may live with thee	Lev 25:36	251
if thy *b* that dwelleth by thee be	Lev 25:39	251
thy *b* that dwelleth by him wax	Lev 25:47	251
or for his mother, for his *b*	Num 6:7	251
together, thou, and Aaron thy *b*	Num 20:8	251
of Edom, Thus saith thy *b* Israel	Num 20:14	251
as Aaron thy *b* was gathered	Num 27:13	251
our *b* unto his daughters	Num 36:2	251
between every man and his *b*	Deut 1:16	251
If thy *b*, the son of thy mother,	Deut 13:6	251
it of his neighbour, or of his *b*	Deut 15:2	251
thy *b* thine hand shall release	Deut 15:3	251
shut thine hand from thy poor *b*	Deut 15:7	251
eye be evil against thy poor *b*	Deut 15:9	251
open thine hand wide unto thy *b*	Deut 15:11	251
And if thy *b*, an Hebrew man, or an	Deut 15:12	251
over thee, which is not thy *b*	Deut 17:15	251
testified falsely against his *b*	Deut 19:18	251
thought to have done unto his *b*	Deut 19:19	251
case bring them again unto thy *b*	Deut 22:1	251
if thy *b* be not nigh unto thee,	Deut 22:2	251
thee until thy *b* seek after it	Deut 22:2	251
for he is thy *b*	Deut 23:7	251
not lend upon usury to thy *b*	Deut 23:19	251
but unto thy *b* thou shalt not	Deut 23:20	251
thou dost lend thy *b* any thing	Deut 24:10	7453
then thy *b* should seem vile unto	Deut 25:3	251
her husband's *b* shall go in unto	Deut 25:5	2993
duty of an husband's *b* unto her	Deut 25:5	2992
the name of his *b* which is dead	Deut 25:6	251
My husband's *b* refuseth to raise	Deut 25:7	2993
up unto his *b* a name in Israel	Deut 25:7	251
the duty of my husband's *b*	Deut 25:7	2992
eye shall be evil toward his *b*	Deut 28:54	251
as Aaron thy *b* died in mount Hor,	Deut 32:50	251
of Kenaz, the *b* of Caleb, took it	Josh 15:17	251
And Judah said unto Simeon his *b*	Judg 1:3	251
son of Kenaz, Caleb's younger *b*	Judg 1:13	251
And Judah went with Simeon his *b*	Judg 1:17	251
son of Kenaz, Caleb's younger *b*	Judg 3:9	251
for they said, He is our *b*	Judg 9:3	251
of Shechem, because he is your *b*	Judg 9:18	251
for fear of Abimelech his *b*	Judg 9:21	251
be laid upon Abimelech their *b*	Judg 9:24	251
the children of Benjamin my *b*	Judg 20:23	251
the children of Benjamin my *b*	Judg 20:28	251
them for Benjamin their *b*	Judg 21:6	251
land, which was our *b* Elimelech's	Ruth 4:3	251
the son of Ahitub, I-chabod's *b*	1Sa 14:3	251
Eliab his eldest *b* heard when he	1Sa 17:28	251
and my *b*, he hath commanded me to	1Sa 20:29	251
b to Joab, saying, Who will go	1Sa 26:6	251
for thee, my *b* Jonathan	2Sa 1:26	251
I hold up my face to Joab thy *b*	2Sa 2:22	251
up every one from following his *b*	2Sa 2:27	251
for the blood of Asahel his *b*	2Sa 3:27	251
Joab and Abishai his *b* slew Abner	2Sa 3:30	251
because he had slain their *b*	2Sa 3:30	251
Rechab and Baanah his *b* escaped	2Sa 4:6	251
answered Rechab and Baanah his *b*	2Sa 4:9	251
into the hand of Abishai his *b*	2Sa 10:10	251
the son of Shimeah David's *b*	2Sa 13:3	251
love Tamar, my *b* Absalom's sister	2Sa 13:4	251
Go now to thy *b* Amnon's house	2Sa 13:7	251
Tamar went to her *b* Amnon's house	2Sa 13:8	251
into the chamber to Amnon her *b*	2Sa 13:10	251
And she answered him, Nay, my *b*	2Sa 13:12	251
Absalom her *b* said unto her	2Sa 13:20	251
Hath Amnon thy *b* been with thee	2Sa 13:20	251
he is thy *b*	2Sa 13:20	251
desolate in her *b* Absalom's house	2Sa 13:20	251
Absalom spake unto his *b* Amnon	2Sa 13:22	
let my *b* Amnon go with us	2Sa 13:26	251
the son of Shimeah David's *b*	2Sa 13:32	251
Deliver him that smote his *b*	2Sa 14:7	251
the life of his *b* whom he slew	2Sa 14:7	251
the son of Zeruiah, Joab's *b*	2Sa 18:2	251
Amasa, Art thou in health, my *b*	2Sa 20:9	251
Abishai his *b* pursued after Sheba	2Sa 20:10	251
slew the *b* of Goliath the Gittite	2Sa 21:19	
Shimeah the *b* of David slew him	2Sa 21:21	251
the *b* of Joab, the son of Zeruiah	2Sa 23:18	251
Asahel the *b* of Joab was one of	2Sa 23:24	251
the mighty men, and Solomon his *b*	1Kin 1:10	251
I fled because of Absalom thy *b*	1Kin 2:7	251
given to Adonijah thy *b* to wife	1Kin 2:21	251
for he is mine elder *b*	1Kin 2:22	251
which thou hast given me, my *b*	1Kin 9:13	251
over him, saying, Alas, my *b*	1Kin 13:30	251
he is my *b*	1Kin 20:32	251
and they said, Thy *b* Ben-hadad	1Kin 20:33	251
his father's *b* king in his stead	2Kin 24:17	251
the sons of Jada the *b* of Shammai	1Chr 2:32	251
of Caleb the *b* of Jerahmeel were	1Chr 2:42	251
Chelub the *b* of Shuah begat Mehir	1Chr 4:11	251
his *b* Asaph, who stood on his	1Chr 6:39	251
and the name of his *b* was Sheresh	1Chr 7:16	251
And the sons of his *b* Helem	1Chr 7:35	251
And the sons of Eshek his *b* were	1Chr 8:39	251
And Abishai the *b* of Joab, he was	1Chr 11:20	251
armies were, Asahel the *b* of Joab	1Chr 11:26	251
Joel the *b* of Nathan, Mibhar the	1Chr 11:38	251
the son of Shimri, and Joha his *b*	1Chr 11:45	251
unto the hand of Abishai his *b*	1Chr 19:11	251
fled before Abishai his *b*	1Chr 19:15	251
the *b* of Goliath the Gittite	1Chr 20:5	251
son of Shimea David's *b* slew him	1Chr 20:7	251
The *b* of Michah was Isshiah	1Chr 24:25	1730
Zetham, and Joel his *b*, which were	1Chr 26:22	251
month was Asahel the *b* of Joab	1Chr 27:7	251
Shimei his *b* was the next	2Chr 31:12	251
hand of Cononiah and Shimei his *b*	2Chr 31:13	251
Eliakim his *b* king over Judah	2Chr 36:4	251
And Necho took Jehoahaz his *b*	2Chr 36:4	251
Zedekiah his *b* king over Judah	2Chr 36:10	251
exact usury, every one of his *b*	Neh 5:7	251
That I gave my *b* Hanani, and	Neh 7:2	251
a pledge from thy *b* for nought	Job 22:6	251
I am a *b* to dragons, and a	Job 30:29	251
though he had been my friend or *b*	Ps 35:14	251
can by any means redeem his *b*	Ps 49:7	251
sittest and speakest against thy *b*	Ps 50:20	251
a *b* is born for adversity	Prov 17:17	251
b to him that is a great waster	Prov 18:9	251
A *b* offended is harder to be won	Prov 18:19	251
that sticketh closer than a *b*	Prov 18:24	251
that is near than a *b* far off	Prov 27:10	251
yea, he hath neither child nor *b*	Eccl 4:8	251
O that thou wert as my *b*, that	Song 8:1	251
his *b* of the house of his father	Is 3:6	251
no man shall spare his *b*	Is 9:19	251
fight every one against his *b*	Is 19:2	251
and every one said to his *b*	Is 41:6	251
and trust ye not in any *b*	Jer 9:4	251
for every *b* will utterly supplant	Jer 9:4	251
lament for him, saying, Ah my *b*	Jer 22:18	251
neighbour, and every one to his *b*	Jer 23:35	251
his neighbour, and every man his *b*	Jer 31:34	251
of them, to wit, of a Jew his *b*	Jer 34:9	251
ye go every man his *b* an Hebrew	Jer 34:14	251
liberty, every one to his *b*	Jer 34:17	251
spoiled his *b* by violence	Eze 18:18	251
to another, every one to his *b*	Eze 33:30	251
sword shall be against his *b*	Eze 38:21	251
for son, or for daughter, for *b*	Eze 44:25	251
He took his *b* by the heel in the	Hos 12:3	251
did pursue his *b* with the sword	Amos 1:11	251
b Jacob shame shall cover thee	Obad 10	251
thy *b* in the day that he became a	Obad 12	251
hunt every man his *b* with a net	Mic 7:2	251
every one by the sword of his *b*	Hag 2:22	251
and compassions every man to his *b*	Zec 7:9	251
evil against his *b* in your heart	Zec 7:10	251
Was not Esau Jacob's *b*	Mal 1:2	251
every man against his *b*, by	Mal 2:10	251
called Peter, and Andrew his *b*	Mt 4:18	*80*
the son of Zebedee, and John his *b*	Mt 4:21	*80*
his *b* without a cause shall be in	Mt 5:22	*80*
and whosoever shall say to his *b*	Mt 5:22	*80*
thy *b* hath ought against thee	Mt 5:23	*80*
first be reconciled to thy *b*	Mt 5:24	*80*
Or how wilt thou say to thy *b*	Mt 7:4	*80*
is called Peter, and Andrew his *b*	Mt 10:2	*80*
the son of Zebedee, and John his *b*	Mt 10:2	*80*
b shall deliver up the *b* to death	Mt 10:21	*80*
is in heaven, the same is my *b*	Mt 12:50	*80*
sake, his *b* Philip's wife	Mt 14:3	*80*
Peter, James, and John his *b*	Mt 17:1	*80*
Moreover if thy *b* shall trespass	Mt 18:15	*80*
hear thee, thou hast gained thy *b*	Mt 18:15	*80*
how oft shall my *b* sin against me	Mt 18:21	*80*
every one his *b* their trespasses	Mt 18:35	*80*
his *b* shall marry his wife	Mt 22:24	*80*
and raise up seed unto his *b*	Mt 22:24	*80*
issue, left his wife unto his *b*	Mt 22:25	*80*
Andrew his *b* casting a net into	Mk 1:16	*80*
the son of Zebedee, and John his *b*	Mk 1:19	*80*
Zebedee, and John the *b* of James	Mk 3:17	*80*
the will of God, the same is my *b*	Mk 3:35	*80*
and James, and John the *b* of James	Mk 5:37	*80*
the *b* of James, and Joses, and of	Mk 6:3	*80*
sake, his *b* Philip's wife	Mk 6:17	*80*
wrote unto us, If a man's *b* die	Mk 12:19	*80*
that his *b* should take his wife,	Mk 12:19	*80*
and raise up seed unto his *b*	Mk 12:19	*80*
b shall betray the *b* to death	Mk 13:12	*80*
his *b* Philip tetrarch of Ituraea	Lk 3:1	*80*
for Herodias his *b* Philip's wife	Lk 3:19	*80*
named Peter,) and Andrew his *b*	Lk 6:14	*80*
And Judas the *b* of James, and Judas	Lk 6:16	
canst thou say to thy *b*, *B*	Lk 6:42	*80*
unto him, Master, speak to my *b*	Lk 12:13	*80*
he said unto him, Thy *b* is come	Lk 15:27	*80*
for this thy *b* was dead, and is	Lk 15:32	*80*
If thy *b* trespass against thee,	Lk 17:3	*80*
wrote unto us, If any man's *b* die	Lk 20:28	*80*
that his *b* should take his wife,	Lk 20:28	*80*
wife, and raise up seed unto his *b*	Lk 20:28	*80*
him, was Andrew, Simon Peter's *b*	Jn 1:40	*80*
He first findeth his own *b* Simon	Jn 1:41	*80*
Andrew, Simon Peter's *b*, saith	Jn 6:8	*80*
hair, whose *b* Lazarus was sick	Jn 11:2	*80*
comfort them concerning their *b*	Jn 11:19	*80*
been here, my *b* had not died	Jn 11:21	*80*
unto her, Thy *b* shall rise again	Jn 11:23	*80*
been here, my *b* had not died	Jn 11:32	*80*
Zelotes, and Judas the *b* of James	Acts 1:13	
B Saul, the Lord, even Jesus,	Acts 9:17	*80*
he killed James the *b* of John	Acts 12:2	*80*
and said unto him, Thou seest, *b*	Acts 21:20	*80*
B Saul, receive thy sight	Acts 22:13	*80*
But why dost thou judge thy *b*	Rom 14:10	*80*
why dost thou set at nought thy *b*	Rom 14:10	*80*
But if thy *b* be grieved with thy	Rom 14:15	*80*
any thing whereby thy *b* stumbleth	Rom 14:21	*80*
city saluteth you, and Quartus a *b*	Rom 16:23	*80*
will of God, and Sosthenes our *b*	1Cor 1:1	*80*
is called a *b* be a fornicator	1Cor 5:11	*80*
But *b* goeth to law with *b*,	1Cor 6:6	*80*
If any *b* hath a wife that	1Cor 7:12	*80*
A *b* or a sister is not under	1Cor 7:15	*80*
knowledge shall the weak *b* perish	1Cor 8:11	*80*
if meat make my *b* to offend	1Cor 8:13	*80*
lest I make my *b* to offend	1Cor 8:13	*80*
As touching our *b* Apollos	1Cor 16:12	*80*
the will of God, and Timothy our *b*	2Cor 1:1	*80*
because I found not Titus my *b*	2Cor 2:13	*80*
And we have sent with him the *b*	2Cor 8:18	*80*
And we have sent with them our *b*	2Cor 8:22	*80*
Titus, and with him I sent a *b*	2Cor 12:18	*80*
I none, save James the Lord's *b*	Gal 1:19	*80*
how I do, Tychicus, a beloved *b*	Eph 6:21	*80*
to send to you Epaphroditus, my *b*	Phil 2:25	*80*
will of God, and Timotheus our *b*	Col 1:1	*80*
unto you, who is a beloved *b*	Col 4:7	*80*

Onesimus, a faithful and beloved *b* ... Col 4:9 *80*
And sent Timotheus, our *b*, and ... 1Th 3:2 *80*
defraud his *b* in any matter ... 1Th 4:6 *80*
every *b* that walketh disorderly ... 2Th 3:6 *80*
an enemy, but admonish him as a *b* ... 2Th 3:15 *80*
of Jesus Christ, and Timothy our *b* ... Philem 1 *80*
saints are refreshed by thee, *b* ... Philem 7 *80*
a *b* beloved, specially to me, but ... Philem 16 *80*
Yea, *b*, let me have joy of thee ... Philem 20 *80*
his neighbour, and every man his *b* ... Heb 8:11 *80*
Know ye that our *b* Timothy is set ... Heb 13:23 *80*
Let the *b* of low degree rejoice ... Jas 1:9 *80*
If a *b* or sister be naked, and ... Jas 2:15 *80*
He that speaketh evil of his *b* ... Jas 4:11 *80*
of his *b*, and judgeth his *b* ... Jas 4:11 *80*
Silvanus, a faithful *b* unto you ... 1Pet 5:12 *80*
even as our beloved *b* Paul also ... 2Pet 3:15 *80*
is in the light, and hateth his *b* ... 1Jn 2:9 *80*
He that loveth his *b* abideth in ... 1Jn 2:10 *80*
that hateth his *b* is in darkness ... 1Jn 2:11 *80*
neither he that loveth not his *b* ... 1Jn 3:10 *80*
of that wicked one, and slew his *b* ... 1Jn 3:12 *80*
loveth not his *b* abideth in death ... 1Jn 3:14 *80*
hateth his *b* is a murderer ... 1Jn 3:15 *80*
good, and seeth his *b* have need ... 1Jn 3:17 *80*
say, I love God, and hateth his *b* ... 1Jn 4:20 *80*
not his *b* whom he hath seen ... 1Jn 4:20 *80*
he who loveth God love his *b* also ... 1Jn 4:21 *80*
If any man see his *b* sin a sin ... 1Jn 5:16 *80*
b of James, to them that are ... Jude 1 *80*
I John, who also am your *b* ... Rev 1:9 *80*

BROTHERHOOD {2}
I might break the *b* between Judah ... Zec 11:14 264
Love the *b* ... 1Pet 2:17 *81*

BROTHERLY {6}
and remembered not the *b* covenant ... Amos 1:9 251
one to another with *b* love ... Rom 12:10 *5360*
But as touching *b* love ye need ... 1Th 4:9 *5360*
Let *b* love continue ... Heb 13:1 *5360*
And to godliness *b* kindness ... 2Pet 1:7 *5360*
and to *b* kindness charity ... 2Pet 1:7 *5360*

BROTHER'S {35}
Am I my *b* keeper ... Gen 4:9 251
the voice of thy *b* blood crieth ... Gen 4:10 251
receive thy *b* blood from thy hand ... Gen 4:11 251
And his *b* name was Jubal ... Gen 4:21 251
and his *b* name was Joktan ... Gen 10:25 251
Sarai his wife, and Lot his *b* son ... Gen 12:5 251
And they took Lot, Abram's *b* son ... Gen 14:12 251
master's *b* daughter unto his son ... Gen 24:48 251
until thy *b* fury turn away ... Gen 27:44 251
Until thy *b* anger turn away from ... Gen 27:45 251
unto Onan, Go in unto thy *b* wife ... Gen 38:8 251
when he went in unto his *b* wife ... Gen 38:9 251
the nakedness of thy *b* wife ... Lev 18:16 251
it is thy *b* nakedness ... Lev 18:16 251
And if a man shall take his *b* wife ... Lev 20:21 251
he hath uncovered his *b* nakedness ... Lev 20:21 251
Thou shalt not see thy *b* ox or ... Deut 22:1 251
and with all lost things of thy *b* ... Deut 22:3 251
Thou shalt not see thy *b* ass or ... Deut 22:4 251
man like not to take his *b* wife ... Deut 25:7 2994
then let his *b* wife go up to the ... Deut 25:7 2994
Then shall his *b* wife come unto ... Deut 25:9 2994
will not build up his *b* house ... Deut 25:9 251
turned about, and is become my *b* ... 1Kin 2:15 251
and his *b* name was Joktan ... 1Chr 1:19 251
wine in their eldest *b* house ... Job 1:13 251
wine in their eldest *b* house ... Job 1:18 251
neither go into thy *b* house in ... Prov 27:10 251
the mote that is in thy *b* eye ... Mt 7:3 *80*
out the mote out of thy *b* eye ... Mt 7:5 *80*
for thee to have thy *b* wife ... Mk 6:18 *80*
the mote that is in thy *b* eye ... Lk 6:41 *80*
out the mote that is in thy *b* eye ... Lk 6:42 *80*
an occasion to fall in his *b* way ... Rom 14:13 *80*
were evil, and his *b* righteous ... 1Jn 3:12 *80*

BROTHERS' {1}
unto their father's *b* sons ... Num 36:11 1730

BROUGHT See APPENDIX.

BROUGHTEST See APPENDIX.

BROW {2}
is an iron sinew, and thy *b* brass ... Is 48:4 4696
led him unto the *b* of the hill ... Lk 4:29 *3790*

BROWN {4}
all the *b* cattle among the sheep, ... Gen 30:32 2345
b among the sheep, that shall be ... Gen 30:33 2345
all the *b* among the sheep, and ... Gen 30:35 2345
all the *b* in the flock of Laban ... Gen 30:40 2345

BRUISE {8}
it shall *b* thy head, and thou ... Gen 3:15 7779
head, and thou shalt *b* his heel ... Gen 3:15 7779
nor *b* it with his horsemen ... Is 28:28 1854
Yet it pleased the LORD to *b* him ... Is 53:10 1792
Thy *b* is incurable, and thy wound ... Jer 30:12 7667
shall it break in pieces and *b* ... Dan 2:40 7490
There is no healing of thy *b* ... Nah 3:19 7667
the God of peace shall *b* Satan ... Rom 16:20 *4937*

BRUISED {9}
unto the LORD that which is *b* ... Lev 22:24 4600
upon the staff of this *b* reed ... 2Kin 18:21 7533
Bread corn is *b* ... Is 28:28 1854
A *b* reed shall he not break, and ... Is 42:3 7533
he was *b* for our iniquities ... Is 53:5 1792
there they *b* the teats of their ... Eze 23:3 6213
they *b* the breasts of her ... Eze 23:8 6213
A *b* reed shall he not break, and ... Mt 12:20 *4937*
to set at liberty them that are *b* ... Lk 4:18 *2352*

BRUISES {1}
but wounds, and *b*, and putrifying ... Is 1:6 2250

BRUISING {2}
in *b* thy teats by the Egyptians ... Eze 23:21 6213
b him hardly departeth from him ... Lk 9:39 *4937*

BRUIT {2}
the noise of the *b* is come ... Jer 10:22 8052
all that hear the *b* of thee shall ... Nah 3:19 8088

BRUTE {2}
But these, as natural *b* beasts ... 2Pet 2:12 *249*
as *b* beasts, in those things they ... Jude 10 *249*

BRUTISH {11}
the *b* person perish, and leave ... Ps 49:10 1197
A *b* man knoweth not ... Ps 92:6 1197
Understand, ye *b* among the people ... Ps 94:8 1197
but he that hateth reproof is *b* ... Prov 12:1 1197
Surely I am more *b* than any man ... Prov 30:2 1197
of Pharaoh is become *b* ... Is 19:11 1197
But they are altogether *b* ... Jer 10:8 1197
Every man is *b* in his knowledge ... Jer 10:14 1197
For the pastors are become *b* ... Jer 10:21 1197
Every man is *b* by his knowledge ... Jer 51:17 1197
thee into the hand of *b* men ... Eze 21:31 1197

BUCKET {1}
the nations are as a drop of a *b* ... Is 40:15 1805

BUCKETS {1}
shall pour the water out of his *b* ... Num 24:7 1805

BUCKLER {11}
he is a *b* to all them that trust ... 2Sa 22:31 4043
valiant men, men able to bear *b* ... 1Chr 5:18 4043
that could handle shield and *b* ... 1Chr 12:8 7420
my *b*, and the horn of my salvation ... Ps 18:2 4043
he is a *b* to all those that trust ... Ps 18:30 4043
Take hold of shield and *b*, and ... Ps 35:2 6793
truth shall be thy shield and *b* ... Ps 91:4 5507
he is a *b* to them that walk ... Prov 2:7 4043
Order ye the *b* and shield, and draw ... Jer 46:3 4043
which shall set against thee *b* ... Eze 23:24 6793
lift up the *b* against thee ... Eze 26:8 6793

BUCKLERS {5}
captains of hundreds spears, and *b* ... 2Chr 23:9 4043
upon the thick bosses of his *b* ... Job 15:26 4043
whereon there hang a thousand *b* ... Song 4:4 4043
even a great company with *b* ... Eze 38:4 6793
both the shields and the *b* ... Eze 39:9 6793

BUD {11}
the scent of water it will *b* ... Job 14:9 6524
to cause the *b* of the tender herb ... Job 38:27 4161
I make the horn of David to *b* ... Ps 132:17 6779
and the pomegranates *b* forth ... Song 7:12 5132
when the *b* is perfect, and the ... Is 18:5 6525
Israel shall blossom and *b* ... Is 27:6 6524
and maketh it bring forth and *b* ... Is 55:10 6779
as the earth bringeth forth her *b* ... Is 61:11 6779
to multiply as the *b* of the field ... Eze 16:7 6779
of the house of Israel to *b* forth ... Eze 29:21 6779
the *b* shall yield no meal ... Hos 8:7 6779

BUDDED {5}
and it was as though it *b*, and her ... Gen 40:10 6524
Aaron for the house of Levi was *b* ... Num 17:8 6524
flourished, and the pomegranates *b* ... Song 6:11 5132
rod hath blossomed, pride hath *b* ... Eze 7:10 6524
had manna, and Aaron's rod that *b* ... Heb 9:4 *985*

BUDS {1}
was budded, and brought forth *b* ... Num 17:8 6525

BUFFET {2}
to *b* him, and to say unto him, ... Mk 14:65 *2852*
the messenger of Satan to *b* me ... 2Cor 12:7 *2852*

BUFFETED {3}
they spit in his face, and *b* him ... Mt 26:67 *2852*
and thirst, and are naked, and are *b* ... 1Cor 4:11 *2852*
when ye be *b* for your faults, ye ... 1Pet 2:20 *2852*

BUILD {163}
let us *b* us a city and a tower, ... Gen 11:4 1129
and they left off to *b* the city ... Gen 11:8 1129
thou shalt not *b* it of hewn stone ... Ex 20:25 1129
B me here seven altars, and ... Num 23:1 1129
B me here seven altars, and ... Num 23:29 1129
We will *b* sheepfolds here for our ... Num 32:16 1129
B you cities for your little ones ... Num 32:24 1129
thou shalt *b* bulwarks against the ... Deut 20:20 1129
will not *b* up his brother's house ... Deut 25:9 1129
there shalt thou *b* an altar unto ... Deut 27:5 1129
Thou shalt *b* the altar of the ... Deut 27:6 1129
thou shalt *b* an house, and thou ... Deut 28:30 1129
us now prepare to *b* us an altar ... Josh 22:26 1129
to *b* an altar for burnt offerings ... Josh 22:29 1129
b an altar unto the LORD thy God ... Judg 6:26 1129
which two did *b* the house of ... Ruth 4:11 1129
I will *b* him a sure house ... 1Sa 2:35 1129
Shalt thou *b* me an house for me ... 2Sa 7:5 1129
Why *b* ye not me an house of cedar ... 2Sa 7:7 1129
He shall *b* an house for my name, ... 2Sa 7:13 1129
saying, I will *b* thee an house ... 2Sa 7:27 1129
to *b* an altar unto the LORD, that ... 2Sa 24:21 1129
B thee an house in Jerusalem, and ... 1Kin 2:36 1129
b an house unto the name of the ... 1Kin 5:3 1129
I purpose to *b* an house unto the ... 1Kin 5:5 1129
he shall *b* an house unto my name ... 1Kin 5:5 1129
timber and stones to *b* the house ... 1Kin 5:18 1129
that he began to *b* the house of ... 1Kin 6:1 1129
tribes of Israel to *b* an house ... 1Kin 8:16 1129
to *b* an house for the name of the ... 1Kin 8:17 1129
heart to *b* an house unto my name ... 1Kin 8:18 1129
thou shalt not *b* the house ... 1Kin 8:19 1129
he shall *b* the house unto my name ... 1Kin 8:19 1129
for to *b* the house of the LORD, ... 1Kin 9:15 1129
Solomon desired to *b* in Jerusalem ... 1Kin 9:19 1129
then did he *b* Millo ... 1Kin 9:24 1129
Then did Solomon *b* an high place ... 1Kin 11:7 1129
b thee a sure house, as I built ... 1Kin 11:38 1129
did Hiel the Beth-elite *b* Jericho ... 1Kin 16:34 1129
and carpenters, to *b* him an house ... 1Chr 14:1 1129
Thou shalt not *b* me an house to ... 1Chr 17:4 1129
the LORD will *b* thee an house ... 1Chr 17:10 1129
He shall *b* me an house, and I will ... 1Chr 17:12 1129
that thou wilt *b* him an house ... 1Chr 17:25 1129
that I may *b* an altar therein ... 1Chr 21:22 1129
stones to *b* the house of God ... 1Chr 22:2 1129
charged him to *b* an house for the ... 1Chr 22:6 1129
it was in my mind to *b* an house ... 1Chr 22:7 1129
thou shalt not *b* an house unto my ... 1Chr 22:8 1129
He shall *b* an house for my name ... 1Chr 22:10 1129
b the house of the LORD thy God, ... 1Chr 22:11 1129
b ye the sanctuary of the LORD ... 1Chr 22:19 1129
I had in mine heart to *b* an house ... 1Chr 28:2 1129
Thou shalt not *b* an house for my ... 1Chr 28:3 1129
thy son, he shall *b* my house ... 1Chr 28:6 1129
to *b* an house for the sanctuary ... 1Chr 28:10 1129
to *b* thee an house for thine holy ... 1Chr 29:16 1129
to *b* the palace, for the which I ... 1Chr 29:19 1129
Solomon determined to *b* an house ... 2Chr 2:1 1129
didst send him cedars to *b* him an ... 2Chr 2:3 1129
I *b* an house to the name of the ... 2Chr 2:4 1129
And the house which I *b* is great ... 2Chr 2:5 1129
But who is able to *b* him an house ... 2Chr 2:6 1129
that I should *b* him an house ... 2Chr 2:6 1129
to *b* shall be wonderful great ... 2Chr 2:9 1129
that might *b* an house for the ... 2Chr 2:12 1129
Then Solomon began to *b* the house ... 2Chr 3:1 1129
he began to *b* in the second day ... 2Chr 3:2 1129
tribes of Israel to *b* an house in ... 2Chr 6:5 1129
to *b* an house for the name of the ... 2Chr 6:7 1129
heart to *b* an house for my name ... 2Chr 6:8 1129
thou shalt not *b* the house ... 2Chr 6:9 1129
he shall *b* the house for my name ... 2Chr 6:9 1129
Solomon desired to *b* in Jerusalem ... 2Chr 8:6 1129
Let us *b* these cities, and make ... 2Chr 14:7 1129
son of David king of Israel did *b* ... 2Chr 35:3 1129
he hath charged me to *b* him an ... 2Chr 36:23 1129
he hath charged me to *b* him an ... Ezr 1:2 1129
b the house of the LORD God of ... Ezr 1:3 1129
to go up to *b* the house of the ... Ezr 1:5 1129
said unto them, Let us *b* with you ... Ezr 4:2 1129
us to *b* an house unto our God ... Ezr 4:3 1129
b unto the LORD God of Israel ... Ezr 4:3 1129
began to *b* the house of God which ... Ezr 5:2 1124
commanded you to *b* this house ... Ezr 5:3 1124
Who commanded you to *b* this house ... Ezr 5:9 1124
b the house that was builded ... Ezr 5:11 1124
a decree to *b* this house of God ... Ezr 5:13 1124
was made of Cyrus the king to *b* ... Ezr 5:17 1124
the elders of the Jews *b* this ... Ezr 6:7 1124
sepulchres, that I may *b* it ... Neh 2:5 1129
let us *b* up the wall of Jerusalem ... Neh 2:17 1129
And they said, Let us rise up and *b* ... Neh 2:18 1129
we his servants will arise and *b* ... Neh 2:20 1129
gate did the sons of Hassenaah *b* ... Neh 3:3 1129
he said, Even that which they *b* ... Neh 4:3 1129
we are not able to *b* the wall ... Neh 4:10 1129
destroy them, and not *b* them up ... Ps 28:5 1129
b thou the walls of Jerusalem ... Ps 51:18 1129
will *b* the cities of Judah ... Ps 69:35 1129
ever, and *b* up thy throne to all ... Ps 89:4 1129
When the LORD shall *b* up Zion ... Ps 102:16 1129
Except the LORD *b* the house ... Ps 127:1 1129
they labour in vain that *b* it ... Ps 127:1 1129
The LORD doth *b* up Jerusalem ... Ps 147:2 1129
and afterwards *b* thine house ... Prov 24:27 1129
to break down, and a time to *b* up ... Eccl 3:3 1129
we will *b* upon her a palace of ... Song 8:9 1129
but we will *b* with hewn stones ... Is 9:10 1129
he shall *b* my city, and he shall ... Is 45:13 1129
thee shall *b* the old waste places ... Is 58:12 1129
of strangers shall *b* up thy walls ... Is 60:10 1129
they shall *b* the old wastes, they ... Is 61:4 1129
And they shall *b* houses, and ... Is 65:21 1129
They shall not *b*, and another ... Is 65:22 1129
is the house that ye *b* unto me ... Is 66:1 1129
destroy, and to throw down, to *b* ... Jer 1:10 1129
and concerning a kingdom, to *b* ... Jer 18:9 1129
I will *b* me a wide house and large ... Jer 22:14 1129
and I will *b* them, and not pull ... Jer 24:6 1129
B ye houses, and dwell in them ... Jer 29:5 1129
b ye houses, and dwell in them ... Jer 29:28 1129
Again I will *b* thee, and thou ... Jer 31:4 1129
so will I watch over them, to *b* ... Jer 31:28 1129
Israel to return, and will *b* them ... Jer 33:7 1129
Neither shall ye *b* house, nor sow ... Jer 35:7 1129
Nor to *b* houses for us to dwell ... Jer 35:9 1129
in this land, then will I *b* you ... Jer 42:10 1129
b a fort against it, and cast a ... Eze 4:2 1129
let us *b* houses ... Eze 11:3 1129
to cast a mount, and to *b* a fort ... Eze 21:22 1129
and shall *b* houses, and plant ... Eze 28:26 1129
I the LORD *b* the ruined places ... Eze 36:36 1129
to *b* Jerusalem unto the Messiah ... Dan 9:25 1129

I will *b* it as in the days of old .... Amos 9:11 1129
they shall *b* the waste cities, and .... Amos 9:14 1129
They *b* up Zion with blood, and .... Mic 3:10 1129
they shall also *b* houses, but not .... Zeph 1:13 1129
and bring wood, and *b* the house .... Hag 1:8 1129
To *b* it an house in the land of .... Zec 5:11 1129
he shall *b* the temple of the LORD .... Zec 6:12 1129
Even he shall *b* the temple of the .... Zec 6:13 1129
b in the temple of the LORD, and .... Zec 6:15 1129
Tyrus did *b* herself a strong hold .... Zec 9:3 1129
return and *b* the desolate places .... Mal 1:4 1129
the LORD of hosts, They shall *b* .... Mal 1:4 1129
upon this rock I will *b* my church .... Mt 16:18 *3618*
because ye *b* the tombs of the .... Mt 23:29 *3618*
of God, and to *b* it in three days .... Mt 26:61 *3618*
within three days I will *b* .... Mk 14:58 *3618*
Woe unto you! for ye *b* the .... Lk 11:47 *3618*
them, and ye *b* their sepulchres .... Lk 11:48 *3618*
pull down my barns, and *b* greater .... Lk 12:18 *3618*
of you, intending to *b* a tower .... Lk 14:28 *3618*
Saying, This man began to *b* .... Lk 14:30 *3618*
what house will ye *b* me .... Acts 7:49 *3618*
will *b* again the tabernacle of .... Acts 15:16 *456*
I will *b* again the ruins thereof, ... Acts 15:16 *456*
grace, which is able to *b* you up .... Acts 20:32 *2026*
lest I should *b* upon another .... Rom 15:20 *3618*
Now if any man *b* upon this 1Cor 3:12 *2026*
For if I *b* again the things which .... Gal 2:18 *3618*

BUILDED {50}
he *b* a city, and called the name .... Gen 4:17 1129
Noah *b* an altar unto the LORD .... Gen 8:20 1129
b Nineveh, and the city Rehoboth, ... Gen 10:11 1129
which the children of men *b* .... Gen 11:5 1129
there *b* he an altar unto the LORD .... Gen 12:7 1129
there he *b* an altar unto the LORD .... Gen 12:8 1129
he *b* an altar there, and called .... Gen 26:25 1129
b an altar under the hill, and .... Ex 24:4 1129
unto the cities which they *b* .... Num 32:38 1129
in that ye have *b* you an altar .... Josh 22:16 1129
less this house that I have *b* 1Kin 8:27 1129
that this house, which I have *b* 1Kin 8:43 1129
thereof, wherewith Baasha had *b* 1Kin 15:22 1129
b for Ashtoreth the abomination 2Kin 23:13 1129
the house that is to be *b* for the 1Chr 22:5 1129
b the altar of the God of Israel, ... Ezr 3:2 1129
the children of the captivity *b* .... Ezr 4:1 1129
the king, that, if this city be *b* .... Ezr 4:13 1124
that, if this city be *b* again .... Ezr 4:16 1124
cease, and that this city be not *b* .... Ezr 4:21 1124
which is *b* with great stones, and .... Ezr 5:8 1124
that was *b* these many years ago .... Ezr 5:11 1124
which a great king of Israel *b* .... Ezr 5:11 1124
house of God be *b* in his place .... Ezr 5:15 1124
at Jerusalem, Let the house be *b* .... Ezr 6:3 1124
And the elders of the Jews *b* .... Ezr 6:14 1124
And they *b*, and finished it, ... Ezr 6:14 1124
priests, and they *b* the sheep gate .... Neh 3:1 1129
next unto him *b* the men of .... Neh 3:2 1129
next to them *b* Zaccur the son of .... Neh 3:2 1129
heard that we *b* the wall, he was .... Neh 4:1 1129
They which *b* on the wall, and they .... Neh 4:17 1129
sword girded by his side, and so *b* .... Neh 4:18 1129
heard that I had *b* the wall .... Neh 6:1 1129
therein, and the houses were not *b* .... Neh 7:4 1129
for the singers had *b* them .... Neh 12:29 1129
away an house which he *b* not .... Job 20:19 1129
Jerusalem is *b* as a city that is .... Ps 122:3 1129
Wisdom hath *b* her house, she hath .... Prov 9:1 1129
Through wisdom is an house *b* .... Prov 24:3 1129
I *b* me houses .... Eccl 2:4 1129
tower of David *b* for an armoury .... Song 4:4 1129
city shall be *b* upon her own heap .... Jer 30:18 1129
He hath *b* against me, and .... Lam 3:5 1129
and the wastes shall be *b* .... Eze 36:10 1129
cities, and the wastes shall be *b* .... Eze 36:33 1129
they sold, they planted, they *b* .... Lk 17:28 *3618*
In whom ye also are *b* together .... Eph 2:22 *4925*
inasmuch as he who hath *b* the .... Heb 3:3 *2680*
For every house is *b* by some man .... Heb 3:4 *2680*

BUILDEDST {1}
goodly cities, which thou *b* not .... Deut 6:10 1129

BUILDER {1}
which hath foundations, whose *b* .... Heb 11:10 *5079*

BUILDERS {15}
Solomon's *b* and Hiram's *b* 1Kin 5:18 1129
it out to the carpenters and *b* 2Kin 12:11 1129
Unto carpenters, and *b*, and masons, ... 2Kin 22:6 1129
b gave they it, to buy hewn stone 2Chr 34:11 1129
when the *b* laid the foundation of .... Ezr 3:10 1129
thee to anger before the *b* .... Neh 4:5 1129
For the *b*, every one had his .... Neh 4:18 1129
The stone which the *b* refused is .... Ps 118:22 1129
thy *b* have perfected thy beauty .... Eze 27:4 1129
The stone which the *b* rejected .... Mt 21:42 *3618*
The stone which the *b* rejected is .... Mk 12:10 *3618*
The stone which the *b* rejected .... Lk 20:17 *3618*
which was set at nought of you *b* .... Acts 4:11 *3618*
the stone which the *b* disallowed 1Pet 2:7 *3618*

BUILDEST {5}
When thou *b* a new house, then .... Deut 22:8 1129
for which cause thou *b* the wall .... Neh 6:6 1129
In that thou *b* thine eminent .... Eze 16:31 1129
b it in three days, save thyself .... Mt 27:40 *3618*
temple, and *b* it in three days, ... Mk 15:29 *3618*

BUILDETH {9}
riseth up and *b* this city Jericho .... Josh 6:26 1129
He *b* his house as a moth, and as a .... Job 27:18 1129
Every wise woman *b* her house .... Prov 14:1 1129
Woe unto him that *b* his house by .... Jer 22:13 1129
forgotten his Maker, and *b* temples .... Hos 8:14 1129
It is he that *b* his stories in .... Amos 9:6 1129
Woe to him that *b* a town with .... Hab 2:12 1129
foundation, and another *b* thereon 1Cor 3:10 *2026*
man take heed how he *b* thereupon 1Cor 3:10 *2026*

BUILDING {37}
in *b* you an altar beside the .... Josh 22:19 1129
made an end of *b* his own house 1Kin 3:1 1129
And the house, when it was in *b* 1Kin 6:7 1129
in the house, while it was in *b* 1Kin 6:7 1129
this house which thou art in *b* 1Kin 6:12 1129
So was he seven years in *b* it 1Kin 6:38 1129
But Solomon was *b* his own house 1Kin 7:1 1129
the *b* of the house of the LORD 1Kin 9:1 1129
that he left off *b* of Ramah 1Kin 15:21 1129
God, and had made ready for the *b* 1Chr 28:2 1129
for the *b* of the house of God 2Chr 3:3 1129
it, that he left off *b* of Ramah 2Chr 16:5 1129
thereof, wherewith Baasha was *b* 2Chr 16:6 1129
of Judah, and troubled them in *b* .... Ezr 4:4 1129
b the rebellious and the bad city, ... Ezr 4:12 1124
names of the men that make this *b* .... Ezr 5:4 1147
even until now hath it been in *b* .... Ezr 5:16 1124
for the *b* of this house of God .... Ezr 6:8 1124
much slothfulness the *b* decayeth .... Eccl 10:18 4746
b forts, to cut off many persons .... Eze 17:17 1129
he measured the breadth of the *b* .... Eze 40:5 1146
Now the *b* that was before the .... Eze 41:12 1146
the wall of the *b* was five cubits .... Eze 41:12 1146
and the separate place, and the *b* .... Eze 41:13 1140
he measured the length of the *b* .... Eze 41:15 1146
was before the *b* toward the north .... Eze 42:1 1146
and than the middlemost of the *b* .... Eze 42:5 1146
therefore the *b* was straitened .... Eze 42:6
place, and over against the *b* .... Eze 42:10 1146
there was a row of *b* round about .... Eze 46:23
and six years was this temple in *b* .... Jn 2:20 *3618*
God's husbandry, ye are God's *b* 1Cor 3:9 *3619*
dissolved, we have a *b* of God 2Cor 5:1 *3619*
In whom all the *b* fitly framed .... Eph 2:21 *3619*
that is to say, not of this *b* .... Heb 9:11 *2937*
b up yourselves on your most holy .... Jude 20 *2026*
the *b* of the wall of it was of .... Rev 21:18 *1739*

BUILDINGS {3}
to shew him the *b* of the temple .... Mt 24:1 *3619*
of stones and what *b* are here .... Mk 13:1 *3619*
him, Seest thou these great *b* .... Mk 13:2 *3619*

BUILT {169}
b there an altar unto the LORD .... Gen 13:18 1129
Abraham *b* an altar there, and laid .... Gen 22:9 1129
b him an house, and made booths .... Gen 33:17 1129
he *b* there an altar, and called .... Gen 35:7 1129
they *b* for Pharaoh treasure .... Ex 1:11 1129
Moses *b* an altar, and called the .... Ex 17:15 1129
saw it, he *b* an altar before it .... Ex 32:5 1129
(Now Hebron was *b* seven years .... Num 13:22 1129
let the city of Sihon be *b* .... Num 21:27 1129
b seven altars, and offered a .... Num 23:14 1129
And the children of Gad *b* Dibon .... Num 32:34 1129
the children of Reuben *b* Heshbon .... Num 32:37 1129
hast *b* goodly houses, and dwelt .... Deut 8:12 1129
it shall not be *b* again .... Deut 13:16 1129
is there that hath *b* a new house .... Deut 20:5 1129
Then Joshua *b* an altar unto the .... Josh 8:30 1129
he *b* the city, and dwelt therein .... Josh 19:50 1129
b there an altar by Jordan .... Josh 22:10 1129
b an altar over against the land .... Josh 22:11 1129
That we have *b* us an altar to .... Josh 22:23 1129
labour, and cities which ye *b* not .... Josh 24:13 1129
b a city, and called the name .... Judg 1:26 1129
Then Gideon *b* an altar there unto .... Judg 6:24 1129
offered upon the altar that was *b* .... Judg 6:28 1129
they *b* a city, and dwelt therein .... Judg 18:28 1129
b there an altar, and offered .... Judg 21:4 1129
there he *b* an altar unto the LORD 1Sa 7:17 1129
Saul *b* an altar unto the LORD 1Sa 14:35 1129
altar that he *b* unto the LORD 1Sa 14:35 1129
David *b* round about from Millo and 2Sa 5:9 1129
and they *b* David an house 2Sa 5:11 1129
David *b* there an altar unto the 2Sa 24:25 1129
house *b* unto the name of the LORD 1Kin 3:2 1129
which king Solomon *b* for the LORD 1Kin 6:2 1129
house he *b* chambers round about 1Kin 6:5 1129
was *b* of stone made ready before 1Kin 6:7 1129
So he *b* the house, and finished it 1Kin 6:9 1129
then he *b* chambers against all 1Kin 6:10 1129
So Solomon *b* the house, and 1Kin 6:14 1129
he *b* the walls of the house 1Kin 6:15 1129
he *b* twenty cubits on the sides 1Kin 6:16 1129
he even *b* them for it within, ... 1Kin 6:16 1129
he *b* the inner court with three 1Kin 6:36 1129
He *b* also the house of the forest 1Kin 7:2 1129
I have surely *b* thee an house to 1Kin 8:13 1129
have *b* an house for the name of 1Kin 8:20 1129
house that I have *b* for thy name 1Kin 8:44 1129
house which I have *b* for thy name 1Kin 8:48 1129
this house, which thou hast *b* 1Kin 9:3 1129
when Solomon had *b* the two houses 1Kin 9:10 1129
And Solomon *b* Gezer, and Beth-horon 1Kin 9:17 1129
house which Solomon had *b* for her 1Kin 9:24 1129
altar which he *b* unto the LORD 1Kin 9:25 1129
and the house that he had *b* 1Kin 10:4 1129
Solomon *b* Millo, and repaired the 1Kin 11:27 1129
as I *b* for David, and will give 1Kin 11:38 1129
Then Jeroboam *b* Shechem in mount 1Kin 12:25 1129
went out from thence, and *b* Penuel 1Kin 12:25 1129
For they also *b* them high places, ... 1Kin 14:23 1129
b Ramah, that he might not suffer 1Kin 15:17 1129
king Asa *b* with them Geba of 1Kin 15:22 1129
he did, and the cities which he *b* 1Kin 15:23 1129
b on the hill, and called the name 1Kin 16:24 1129
the name of the city which he *b* 1Kin 16:24 1129
Baal, which he had *b* in Samaria 1Kin 16:32 1129
with the stones he *b* an altar in 1Kin 18:32 1129
made, and all the cities that he *b* 1Kin 22:39 1129
He *b* Elath, and restored it to 2Kin 14:22 1129
He *b* the higher gate of the house 2Kin 15:35 1129
Urijah the priest *b* an altar 2Kin 16:11 1129
that they had *b* in the house 2Kin 16:18 1129
they *b* them high places in all 2Kin 17:9 1129
For he *b* up again the high places 2Kin 21:3 1129
he *b* altars in the house of the 2Kin 21:4 1129
he *b* altars for all the host of 2Kin 21:5 1129
they *b* forts against it round 2Kin 25:1 1129
that Solomon *b* in Jerusalem 1Chr 6:10 1129
until Solomon had *b* the house of 1Chr 6:32 1129
who *b* Beth-horon the nether, and 1Chr 7:24 1129
and Misham, and Shamed, who *b* Ono 1Chr 8:12 1129
he *b* the city round about, even 1Chr 11:8 1129
Why have ye not *b* me an house of 1Chr 17:6 1129
David *b* there an altar unto the 1Chr 21:26 1129
to be *b* to the name of the LORD 1Chr 22:19 1129
But I have *b* an house of 2Chr 6:2 1129
have *b* the house for the name of 2Chr 6:10 1129
less this house which I have *b* 2Chr 6:18 1129
I have *b* is called by thy name 2Chr 6:33 1129
house which I have *b* for thy name 2Chr 6:34 1129
house which I have *b* for thy name 2Chr 6:38 1129
wherein Solomon had *b* the house 2Chr 8:1 1129
to Solomon, Solomon *b* them 2Chr 8:2 1129
he *b* Tadmor in the wilderness, and 2Chr 8:4 1129
cities, which he *b* in Hamath 2Chr 8:4 1129
Also he *b* Beth-horon the upper, ... 2Chr 8:5 1129
the house that he had *b* for her 2Chr 8:11 1129
which he had *b* before the porch, ... 2Chr 8:12 1129
and the house that he had *b* 2Chr 9:3 1129
b cities for defence in Judah 2Chr 11:5 1129
He *b* even Beth-lehem, and Etam, and 2Chr 11:6 1129
he *b* fenced cities in Judah 2Chr 14:6 1129
So they *b* and prospered 2Chr 14:7 1129
b Ramah, to the intent that he 2Chr 16:1 1129
he *b* therewith Geba and Mizpah 2Chr 16:6 1129
he *b* in Judah castles, and cities 2Chr 17:12 1129
have *b* thee a sanctuary therein 2Chr 20:8 1129
He *b* Eloth, and restored it to 2Chr 26:2 1129
b cities about Ashdod, and among 2Chr 26:6 1129
Moreover Uzziah *b* towers in 2Chr 26:9 1129
Also he *b* towers in the desert, ... 2Chr 26:10 1129
He *b* the high gate of the house 2Chr 27:3 1129
and on the wall of Ophel he *b* much 2Chr 27:3 1129
Moreover he *b* cities in the 2Chr 27:4 1129
and in the forests he *b* castles 2Chr 27:4 1129
b up all the wall that was broken 2Chr 32:5 1129
For he *b* again the high places 2Chr 33:3 1129
Also he *b* altars in the house of 2Chr 33:4 1129
he *b* altars for all the host of 2Chr 33:5 1129
Now after this he *b* a wall 2Chr 33:14 1129
all the altars that he had *b* in 2Chr 33:15 1129
places wherein he *b* high places 2Chr 33:19 1129
they *b* it, and set up the doors .... Neh 3:13 1129
he *b* it, and set up the doors .... Neh 3:14 1129
he *b* it, and covered it, and set up .... Neh 3:15 1129
So *b* we the wall .... Neh 4:6 1129
came to pass, when the wall was *b* .... Neh 7:1 1129
which *b* desolate places for .... Job 3:14 1129
down, and it cannot be *b* again .... Job 12:14 1129
the Almighty, thou shalt be *b* up .... Job 22:23 1129
he *b* his sanctuary like high .... Ps 78:69 1129
Mercy shall be *b* up for ever .... Ps 89:2 1129
b great bulwarks against it .... Eccl 9:14 1129
b a tower in the midst of it, and .... Is 5:2 1129
it shall never be *b* .... Is 25:2 1129
cities of Judah, Ye shall be *b* .... Is 44:26 1129
to Jerusalem, Thou shalt be *b* .... Is 44:28 1129
they have *b* the high places of .... Jer 7:31 1129
then shall they be *b* in the midst .... Jer 12:16 1129
They have *b* also the high places .... Jer 19:5 1129
build thee, and thou shalt be *b* .... Jer 31:4 1129
that the city shall be *b* to the .... Jer 31:38 1129
that they *b* it even unto this day .... Jer 32:31 1129
they *b* the high places of Baal, ... Jer 32:35 1129
which I have *b* will I break down .... Jer 45:4 1129
b forts against it round about .... Jer 52:4 1129
one *b* up a wall, and, lo, others .... Eze 13:10 1129
That thou hast also *b* unto thee .... Eze 16:24 1129
Thou hast *b* thy high place at .... Eze 16:25 1129
thou shalt be *b* no more .... Eze 26:14 1129
that I have *b* for the house of .... Dan 4:30 1124
the street shall be *b* again .... Dan 9:25 1129
ye have *b* houses of hewn stone, ... Amos 5:11 1129
day that thy walls are to be *b* .... Mic 7:11 1129
that the LORD's house should be *b* .... Hag 1:2 1129
my house shall be *b* in it .... Zec 1:16 1129
laid, that the temple might be *b* .... Zec 8:9 1129
which *b* his house upon a rock .... Mt 7:24 *3618*
which *b* his house upon the sand .... Mt 7:26 *3618*
b a tower, and let it out to .... Mt 21:33 *3618*
b a tower, and let it out to .... Mk 12:1 *3618*
the hill whereon their city was *b* .... Lk 4:29 *3618*
He is like a man which *b* an house .... Lk 6:48 *3618*

b an house upon the earth Lk 6:49 *3618*
and he hath *b* us a synagogue Lk 7:5 *3618*
But Solomon *b* him an house Acts 7:47 *3618*
abide which he hath *b* thereupon 1Cor 3:14 *2026*
are *b* upon the foundation of the Eph 2:20 *2026*
b up in him, and stablished in the Col 2:7 *2026*
but he that *b* all things is God Heb 3:4 *2680*
are *b* up a spiritual house, an 1Pet 2:5 *3618*

BUKKI *(buk'-ki)* {5}
1. A high priest.
And Abishua begat *B* 1Chr 6:5 1231
and *B* begat Uzzi 1Chr 6:5 1231
B his son, Uzzi his son, Zerahiah 1Chr 6:51 1231
the son of Uzzi, the son of *B* Ezr 7:4 1231
2. A Danite prince.
of Dan, *B* the son of Jogli Num 34:22 1231

BUKKIAH *(buk-ki'-ah)* {2} *A Levite musician.*
B, Mattaniah, Uzziel, Shebuel, and 1Chr 25:4 1232
The sixth to *B*, he, his sons, and 1Chr 25:13 1232

BUL *(bul)* {1} *Eighth month of the Hebrew year.*
the eleventh year, in the month *B* 1Kin 6:38 945

BULL {2}
Their *b* gendereth, and faileth not Job 21:10 7794
the streets, as a wild *b* in a net Is 51:20 8377

BULLOCK {104}
Take one young *b*, and two rams Ex 29:1 6499
them in the basket, with the *b* Ex 29:3 6499
thou shalt cause a *b* to be Ex 29:10 6499
hands upon the head of the *b* Ex 29:10 6499
shalt kill the *b* before the LORD Ex 29:11 6499
shalt take of the blood of the *b* Ex 29:12 6499
But the flesh of the *b*, and his Ex 29:14 6499
day a *b* for a sin offering for Ex 29:36 6499
shall kill the *b* before the LORD Lev 1:5 1121,1241
a young *b* without blemish unto Lev 4:3 6499
he shall bring the *b* unto the Lev 4:4 6499
kill the *b* before the LORD Lev 4:4 6499
b at the bottom of the altar of Lev 4:7 6499
fat of the *b* for the sin offering Lev 4:8 6499
the *b* of the sacrifice of peace Lev 4:10 7794
And the skin of the *b*, and all his Lev 4:11 6499
Even the whole *b* shall he carry Lev 4:12 6499
shall offer a young *b* for the sin Lev 4:14 6499
the head of the *b* before the LORD Lev 4:15 6499
the *b* shall be killed before the Lev 4:15 6499
he shall do with the *b* as he did Lev 4:20 6499
did with the *b* for a sin offering Lev 4:20 6499
forth the *b* without the camp Lev 4:21 6499
burn him as he burned the first *b* Lev 4:21 6499
a *b* for the sin offering, and two Lev 8:2 6499
he brought the *b* for the sin Lev 8:14 6499
of the *b* for the sin offering Lev 8:14 6499
But the *b*, and his hide, his flesh Lev 8:17 6499
Also a *b* and a ram for peace Lev 9:4 7794
He slew also the *b* and the ram for Lev 9:18 7794
And the fat of the *b* and of the ram Lev 9:19 7794
with a young *b* for a sin offering Lev 16:3 6499
offer his *b* of the sin offering Lev 16:6 6499
bring the *b* of the sin offering Lev 16:11 6499
shall kill the *b* of the sin Lev 16:11 6499
shall take of the blood of the *b* Lev 16:14 6499
as he did with the blood of the *b* Lev 16:15 6499
shall take of the blood of the *b* Lev 16:18 6499
the *b* for the sin offering, and Lev 16:27 6499
Either a *b* or a lamb that hath Lev 22:23 7794
When a *b*, or a sheep, or a goat, Lev 22:27 7794
of the first year, and one young *b* Lev 23:18 6499
One young *b*, one ram, one lamb of Num 7:15 6499
One young *b*, one ram, one lamb of Num 7:21 6499
One young *b*, one ram, one lamb of Num 7:27 6499
One young *b*, one ram, one lamb of Num 7:33 6499
One young *b*, one ram, one lamb of Num 7:39 6499
One young *b*, one ram, one lamb of Num 7:45 6499
One young *b*, one ram, one lamb of Num 7:51 6499
One young *b*, one ram, one lamb of Num 7:57 6499
One young *b*, one ram, one lamb of Num 7:63 6499
One young *b*, one ram, one lamb of Num 7:69 6499
One young *b*, one ram, one lamb of Num 7:75 6499
One young *b*, one ram, one lamb of Num 7:81 6499
a young *b* with his meat offering Num 8:8 6499
another young *b* shalt thou take Num 8:8 6499
a *b* for a burnt offering, or for Num 15:8 1121,1241
Then shall he bring with a *b* a Num 15:9 1121,1241
Thus shall it be done for one *b* Num 15:11 7794
one young *b* for a burnt offering Num 15:24 6499
Balaam offered on every altar a *b* Num 23:2 6499
have offered upon every altar a *b* Num 23:4 6499
seven altars, and offered a *b* Num 23:14 6499
Balaam had said, and offered a *b* Num 23:30 6499
mingled with oil, for one *b* Num 28:12 6499
be half an hin of wine unto a *b* Num 28:14 6499
deals shall ye offer for a *b* Num 28:20 6499
oil, three tenth deals unto one *b* Num 28:28 6499
one young *b*, one ram, and seven Num 29:2 6499
oil, three tenth deals for a *b* Num 29:3 6499
one young *b*, one ram, and seven Num 29:8 6499
oil, three tenth deals to a *b* Num 29:9 6499
every *b* of the thirteen bullocks Num 29:14 6499
one *b*, one ram, seven lambs of Num 29:36 6499
their drink offerings for the *b* Num 29:37 6499
work with the firstling of thy *b* Deut 15:19 7794
unto the LORD thy God any *b* Deut 17:1 7794
is like the firstling of his *b* Deut 33:17 7794
him, Take thy father's young *b* Judg 6:25 6499
even the second *b* of seven years Judg 6:25 6499
place, and take the second *b* Judg 6:26 6499
the second *b* was offered upon the Judg 6:28 6499
And they slew a *b*, and brought the 1Sa 1:25 6499
them choose one *b* for themselves 1Kin 18:23 6499
and I will dress the other *b* 1Kin 18:23 6499
Choose you one *b* for yourselves 1Kin 18:25 6499
they took the *b* which was given 1Kin 18:26 6499
cut the *b* in pieces, and laid him 1Kin 18:33 6499
consecrate himself with a young *b* 2Chr 13:9 6499
I will take no *b* out of thy house Ps 50:9 6499
than an ox or *b* that hath horns Ps 69:31 6499
lion shall eat straw like the *b* Is 65:25 1241
as a *b* unaccustomed to the yoke Jer 31:18 5695
a young *b* for a sin offering Eze 43:19 6499
Thou shalt take the *b* also of the Eze 43:21 6499
as they did cleanse it with the *b* Eze 43:22 6499
offer a young *b* without blemish Eze 43:23 6499
they shall also prepare a young *b* Eze 43:25 6499
take a young *b* without blemish Eze 45:18 6499
the land a *b* for a sin offering Eze 45:22 6499
meat offering of an ephah for a *b* Eze 45:24 6499
be a young *b* without blemish Eze 46:6 6499
a meat offering, an ephah for a *b* Eze 46:7 6499
offering shall be an ephah to a *b* Eze 46:11 6499

BULLOCK'S {3}
lay his hand upon the *b* head Lev 4:4 6499
shall take of the *b* blood Lev 4:5 6499
b blood to the tabernacle of the Lev 4:16 6499

BULLOCKS {45}
the burnt offering were twelve *b* Num 7:87 6499
offerings were twenty and four *b* Num 7:88 6499
hands upon the heads of the *b* Num 8:12 6499
and prepare me here seven *b* Num 23:29 6499
two young *b*, and one ram, and seven Num 28:11 6499
two young *b*, and one ram, and seven Num 28:19 6499
two young *b*, one ram, seven lambs Num 28:27 6499
thirteen young *b*, two rams, and Num 29:13 6499
every bullock of the thirteen *b* Num 29:14 6499
day ye shall offer twelve young *b* Num 29:17 6499
their drink offerings for the *b* Num 29:18 6499
And on the third day eleven *b* Num 29:20 6499
their drink offerings for the *b* Num 29:21 6499
And on the fourth day ten *b* Num 29:23 6499
their drink offerings for the *b* Num 29:24 6499
And on the fifth day nine *b* Num 29:26 6499
their drink offerings for the *b* Num 29:27 6499
And on the sixth day eight *b* Num 29:29 6499
their drink offerings for the *b* Num 29:30 6499
And on the seventh day seven *b* Num 29:32 6499
their drink offerings for the *b* Num 29:33 6499
him up with her, with three *b* 1Sa 1:24 6499
Let them therefore give us two *b* 1Kin 18:23 6499
LORD, that they offered seven *b* 1Chr 15:26 6499
after that day, even a thousand *b* 1Chr 29:21 6499
And they brought seven *b*, and seven 2Chr 29:21 6499
So they killed the *b*, and the 2Chr 29:22 1241
brought, was threescore and ten *b* 2Chr 29:32 1241
to the congregation a thousand *b* 2Chr 30:24 6499
to the congregation a thousand *b* 2Chr 30:24 6499
thousand, and three thousand *b* 2Chr 35:7 1241
they have need of, both young *b* Ezr 6:9 8450
of this house of God an hundred *b* Ezr 6:17 8450
buy speedily with this money *b* Ezr 7:17 8450
twelve *b* for all Israel, ninety Ezr 8:35 6499
take unto you now seven *b* Job 42:8 6499
they offer *b* upon thine altar Ps 51:19 6499
I will offer *b* with goats Ps 66:15 1241
I delight not in the blood of *b* Is 1:11 6499
them, and the *b* with the bulls Is 34:7 6499
in the midst of her like fatted *b* Jer 46:21 5695
Slay all her *b* Jer 50:27 6499
rams, of lambs, and of goats, of *b* Eze 39:18 6499
offering to the LORD, seven *b* Eze 45:23 6499
they sacrifice *b* in Gilgal Hos 12:11 7794

BULLS {10}
their colts, forty kine, and ten *b* Gen 32:15 6499
Many *b* have compassed me Ps 22:12 6499
strong *b* of Bashan have beset me Ps 22:12
Will I eat the flesh of *b* Ps 50:13 47
spearmen, the multitude of the *b* Ps 68:30 47
them, and the bullocks with the *b* Is 34:7 47
heifer at grass, and bellow as *b* Jer 50:11 47
twelve brasen *b* that were under Jer 52:20 1241
For if the blood of *b* and of goats Heb 9:13 *5022*
not possible that the blood of *b* Heb 10:4 *5022*

BULRUSH {1}
is it to bow down his head as a *b* Is 58:5 100

BULRUSHES {2}
him, she took for him an ark of *b* Ex 2:3 1573
in vessels of *b* upon the waters Is 18:2 1573

BULWARKS {5}
thou shalt build *b* against the Deut 20:20 4692
to be on the towers and upon the *b* 2Chr 26:15 6438
Mark ye well her *b*, consider her Ps 48:13 2430
it, and built great *b* against it Eccl 9:14 4685
will God appoint for walls and *b* Is 26:1 2426

BUNAH *(boo'-nah)* {2} *Son of Jerahmeel.*
were, Ram the firstborn, and *B* 1Chr 2:25 946

BUNCH {1}
And ye shall take a *b* of hyssop Ex 12:22 92

BUNCHES {3}
bread, and an hundred *b* of raisins 2Sa 16:1 6778
b of raisins, and wine, and oil, and 1Chr 12:40 6778
treasures upon the *b* of camels Is 30:6 1707

BUNDLE {4}
every man's *b* of money was in his Gen 42:35 6872
b of life with the LORD thy God 1Sa 25:29 6872
A *b* of myrrh is my wellbeloved Song 1:13 6872
Paul had gathered a *b* of sticks Acts 28:3 *4128*

BUNDLES {2}
their father saw the *b* of money Gen 42:35 6872
and bind them in *b* to burn them Mt 13:30 *1197*

BUNNI *(bun'-ni)* {3}
1. A Levite with Ezra.
and Bani, Kadmiel, Shebaniah, *B* Neh 9:4 1137
2. Father of Hashabiah.
son of Hashabiah, the son of *B* Neh 11:15 1137
3. A family who renewed the covenant.
B, Azgad, Bebai, Neh 10:15 1137

BURDEN {69}
they shall bear the *b* with thee Ex 18:22
hateth thee lying under his *b* Ex 23:5 4853
These things are the *b* of the Num 4:15 4853
one to his service and to his *b* Num 4:19 4853
And this is the charge of their *b* Num 4:31 4853
of the charge of their *b* Num 4:32 4853
the service of the *b* in the Num 4:47 4853
service, and according to his *b* Num 4:49 4853
that thou layest the *b* of all Num 11:11 4853
they shall bear the *b* of the Num 11:17 4853
bear your cumbrance, and your *b* Deut 1:12 4853
then thou shalt be a *b* unto me 2Sa 15:33 4853
be yet a *b* unto my lord the king 2Sa 19:35 4853
thy servant two mules' *b* of earth 2Kin 5:17 4853
of Damascus, forty camels' *b* 2Kin 8:9 4853
the LORD laid this *b* upon him 2Kin 9:25 4853
it shall not be a *b* upon your 2Chr 35:3 4853
that there should no *b* be brought Neh 13:19 4853
thee, so that I am a *b* to myself Job 7:20 4853
as an heavy *b* they are too heavy Ps 38:4 4853
Cast thy *b* upon the LORD, and he Ps 55:22 3053
I removed his shoulder from the *b* Ps 81:6 5449
and the grasshopper shall be a *b* Eccl 12:5 5445
hast broken the yoke of his *b* Is 9:4 5448
that his *b* shall be taken away Is 10:27 5448
The *b* of Babylon, which Isaiah Is 13:1 4853
his *b* depart from off their Is 14:25 5448
that king Ahaz died was this *b* Is 14:28 4853
The *b* of Moab Is 15:1 4853
The *b* of Damascus Is 17:1 4853
The *b* of Egypt Is 19:1 4853
The *b* of the desert of the sea Is 21:1 4853
The *b* of Dumah Is 21:11 4853
The *b* upon Arabia Is 21:13 4853
The *b* of the valley of vision Is 22:1 4853
the *b* that was upon it shall be Is 22:25 4853
The *b* of Tyre Is 23:1 4853
The *b* of the beasts of the south Is 30:6 4853
anger, and the *b* thereof is heavy Is 30:27 4858
they are a *b* to the weary beast Is 46:1 4853
they could not deliver the *b* Is 46:2 4853
bear no *b* on the sabbath day, nor Jer 17:21 4853
Neither carry forth a *b* out of Jer 17:22 4853
to bring in no *b* through the Jer 17:24 4853
sabbath day, and not to bear a *b* Jer 17:27 4853
saying, What is the *b* of the LORD Jer 23:33 4853
shalt then say unto them, What *b* Jer 23:33 4853
The *b* of the LORD, I will even Jer 23:34 4853
the *b* of the LORD shall ye Jer 23:36 4853
every man's word shall be his *b* Jer 23:36 4853
since ye say, The *b* of the LORD Jer 23:38 4853
The *b* of the LORD, and I have sent Jer 23:38 4853
shall not say, The *b* of the LORD Jer 23:38 4853
This *b* concerneth the prince in Eze 12:10 4853
for the *b* of the king of princes Hos 8:10 4853
The *b* of Nineveh Nah 1:1 4853
The *b* which Habakkuk the prophet Hab 1:1 4853
whom the reproach of it was a *b* Zeph 3:18 4864
The *b* of the word of the LORD in Zec 9:1 4853
The *b* of the word of the LORD for Zec 12:1 4853
all that *b* themselves with it Zec 12:3 6006
The *b* of the word of the LORD to Mal 1:1 4853
my yoke is easy, and my *b* is light Mt 11:30 *5413*
unto us, which have borne the *b* Mt 20:12 *922*
to lay upon you no greater *b* than Acts 15:28 *922*
the ship was to unlade her *b* Acts 21:3 *1117*
But be it so, I did not *b* you 2Cor 12:16 *2599*
every man shall bear his own *b* Gal 6:5 *5413*
I will put upon you none other *b* Rev 2:24 *922*

BURDENED {2}
this tabernacle do groan, being *b* 2Cor 5:4 *916*
that other men be eased, and ye *b* 2Cor 8:13 *2347*

BURDENS {25}
ass couching down between two *b* Gen 49:14 4942
to afflict them with their *b* Ex 1:11 5450
brethren, and looked on their *b* Ex 2:11 5450
get you unto your *b* Ex 5:4 5450
and ye make them rest from their *b* Ex 5:5 5450
from under the *b* of the Egyptians Ex 6:6 5450
from under the *b* of the Egyptians Ex 6:7 5450
Gershonites, to serve, and for *b* Num 4:24 4853
the Gershonites, in all their *b* Num 4:27 4853
unto them in charge all their *b* Num 4:27 4853
and ten thousand that bare *b* 1Kin 5:15 5449
and ten thousand men to bear *b* 2Chr 2:2 5449
of them to be bearers of *b* 2Chr 2:18 5449
greatness of the *b* laid upon him 2Chr 24:27 4853
they were over the bearers of *b* 2Chr 34:13 5449
of the bearers of *b* is decayed Neh 4:10 5449
on the wall, and they that bare *b* Neh 4:17 5447

and figs, and all manner of *b*	Neh 13:15	4853
wickedness, to undo the heavy *b*	Is 58:6	92
but have seen for thee false *b*	Lam 2:14	4864
and ye take from him *b* of wheat	Amos 5:11	4864
For they bind heavy *b* and grievous	Mt 23:4	*5413*
men with *b* grievous to be borne	Lk 11:46	*5413*
the *b* with one of your fingers	Lk 11:46	*5413*
Bear ye one another's *b*, and so	Gal 6:2	*922*

BURDENSOME {5}

a *b* stone for all people	Zec 12:3	4614
kept myself from being *b* unto you	2Cor 11:9	*4*
be that I myself was not *b* to you	2Cor 12:13	*2655*
and I will not be *b* to you	2Cor 12:14	*2655*
when we might have been *b*	1Th 2:6	*1722,922*

BURIAL {6}

the *b* which belonged to the kings	2Chr 26:23	6900
good, and also that he have no *b*	Eccl 6:3	6900
not be joined with them in *b*	Is 14:20	6900
be buried with the *b* of an ass	Jer 22:19	6900
on my body, she did it for my *b*	Mt 26:12	*1779*
men carried Stephen to his *b*	Acts 8:2	

BURIED {106}

thou shalt be *b* in a good old age	Gen 15:15	6912
Abraham *b* Sarah his wife in the	Gen 23:19	6912
Ishmael *b* him in the cave of	Gen 25:9	6912
there was Abraham *b*, and Sarah his	Gen 25:10	6912
she was *b* beneath Beth-el under	Gen 35:8	6912
was *b* in the way to Ephrath,	Gen 35:19	6912
and his sons Esau and Jacob *b* him	Gen 35:29	6912
I *b* her there in the way of	Gen 48:7	6912
There they *b* Abraham and Sarah his	Gen 49:31	6912
there they *b* Isaac and Rebekah his	Gen 49:31	6912
and there I *b* Leah	Gen 49:31	6912
b him in the cave of the field of	Gen 50:13	6912
father, after he had *b* his father	Gen 50:14	6912
because there they *b* the people	Num 11:34	6912
Miriam died there, and was *b* there	Num 20:1	6912
For the Egyptians *b* all their	Num 33:4	6912
Aaron died, and there he was *b*	Deut 10:6	6912
he *b* him in a valley in the land	Deut 34:6	6912
they *b* him in the border of his	Josh 24:30	6912
b they in Shechem, in a parcel of	Josh 24:32	6912
they *b* him in a hill that	Josh 24:33	6912
they *b* him in the border of his	Judg 2:9	6912
was *b* in the sepulchre of Joash	Judg 8:32	6912
and died, and was *b* in Shamir	Judg 10:2	6912
And Jair died, and was *b* in Camon	Judg 10:5	6912
was *b* in one of the cities of	Judg 12:7	6912
Ibzan, and was *b* at Beth-lehem	Judg 12:10	6912
was *b* in Aijalon in the country	Judg 12:12	6912
was *b* in Pirathon in the land of	Judg 12:15	6912
b him between Zorah and Eshtaol in	Judg 16:31	6912
will I die, and there will I be *b*	Ruth 1:17	6912
b him in his house at Ramah	1Sa 25:1	6912
b him in Ramah, even in his own	1Sa 28:3	6912
b them under a tree at Jabesh, and	1Sa 31:13	6912
were they that *b* Saul	2Sa 2:4	6912
even unto Saul, and have *b* him	2Sa 2:5	6912
b him in the sepulchre of his	2Sa 2:32	6912
And they *b* Abner in Hebron	2Sa 3:32	6912
b it in the sepulchre of Abner in	2Sa 4:12	6912
was *b* in the sepulchre of his	2Sa 17:23	6912
be *b* by the grave of my father and	2Sa 19:37	
Jonathan his son *b* they in the	2Sa 21:14	6912
was *b* in the city of David	1Kin 2:10	6912
he was *b* in his own house in the	1Kin 2:34	6912
was *b* in the city of David his	1Kin 11:43	6912
came to pass, after he had *b* him	1Kin 13:31	6912
wherein the man of God is *b*	1Kin 13:31	6912
And they *b* him	1Kin 14:18	6912
was *b* with his fathers in the	1Kin 14:31	6912
they *b* him in the city of David	1Kin 15:8	6912
was *b* with his fathers in the	1Kin 15:24	6912
his fathers, and was *b* in Tirzah	1Kin 16:6	6912
his fathers, and was *b* in Samaria	1Kin 16:28	6912
they *b* the king in Samaria	1Kin 22:37	6912
was *b* with his fathers in the	1Kin 22:50	6912
was *b* with his fathers in the	2Kin 8:24	6912
b him in his sepulchre with his	2Kin 9:28	6912
and they *b* him in Samaria	2Kin 10:35	6912
they *b* him with his fathers in	2Kin 12:21	6912
and they *b* him in Samaria	2Kin 13:9	6912
Joash was *b* in Samaria with the	2Kin 13:13	6912
And Elisha died, and they *b* him	2Kin 13:20	6912
was *b* in Samaria with the kings	2Kin 14:16	6912
he was *b* at Jerusalem with his	2Kin 14:20	6912
they *b* him with his fathers in	2Kin 15:7	6912
was *b* with his fathers in the	2Kin 15:38	6912
was *b* with his fathers in the	2Kin 16:20	6912
was *b* in the garden of his own	2Kin 21:18	6912
he was *b* in his sepulchre in the	2Kin 21:26	6912
b him in his own sepulchre	2Kin 23:30	6912
b their bones under the oak in	1Chr 10:12	6912
he was *b* in the city of David his	2Chr 9:31	6912
was *b* in the city of David	2Chr 12:16	6912
they *b* him in the city of David	2Chr 14:1	6912
they *b* him in his own sepulchres,	2Chr 16:14	6912
was *b* with his fathers in the	2Chr 21:1	6912
Howbeit they *b* him in the city of	2Chr 21:20	6912
they had slain him, they *b* him	2Chr 22:9	6912
they *b* him in the city of David	2Chr 24:16	6912
they *b* him in the city of David,	2Chr 24:25	6912
but they *b* him not in the	2Chr 24:25	6912
b him with his fathers in the	2Chr 25:28	6912
they *b* him with his fathers in	2Chr 26:23	6912
they *b* him in the city of David	2Chr 27:9	6912
they *b* him in the city, even in	2Chr 28:27	6912
they *b* him in the chiefest of the	2Chr 32:33	6912
they *b* him in his own house	2Chr 33:20	6912
was *b* in one of the sepulchres of	2Chr 35:24	6912
remain of him shall be *b* in death	Job 27:15	6912
And so I saw the wicked *b*, who had	Eccl 8:10	6912
shall not be gathered, nor be *b*	Jer 8:2	6912
neither shall they be *b*	Jer 16:4	6912
they shall not be *b*, neither	Jer 16:6	6912
shalt die, and shalt be *b* there	Jer 20:6	6912
He shall be *b* with the burial of	Jer 22:19	6912
lamented, neither gathered, nor *b*	Jer 25:33	6912
till the buriers have *b* it in the	Eze 39:15	6912
b it, and went and told Jesus	Mt 14:12	*2290*
the rich man also died, and was *b*	Lk 16:22	*2290*
David, that he is both dead and *b*	Acts 2:29	*2290*
up, and carried him out, and *b* him	Acts 5:6	*2290*
b thy husband are at the door	Acts 5:9	*2290*
her forth, *b* her by her husband	Acts 5:10	*2290*
Therefore we are *b* with him by	Rom 6:4	*4916*
And that he was *b*, and that he rose	1Cor 15:4	*2290*
B with him in baptism, wherein	Col 2:12	*4916*

BURIERS {1}

till the *b* have buried it in the	Eze 39:15	6912

BURN {138}

make brick, and *b* them throughly	Gen 11:3	8313
thine anger *b* against thy servant	Gen 44:18	2734
the morning ye shall *b* with fire	Ex 12:10	8313
to cause the lamp to *b* always	Ex 27:20	5927
them, and *b* them upon the altar	Ex 29:13	6999
shalt thou *b* with fire without	Ex 29:14	8313
thou shalt *b* the whole ram upon	Ex 29:18	6999
b them upon the altar for a burnt	Ex 29:25	6999
then thou shalt *b* the remainder	Ex 29:34	8313
make an altar to *b* incense upon	Ex 30:1	4729
Aaron shall *b* thereon sweet	Ex 30:7	6999
he shall *b* incense upon it	Ex 30:7	6999
he shall *b* incense upon it, a	Ex 30:8	6999
to *b* offering made by fire unto	Ex 30:20	6999
priest shall *b* all on the altar	Lev 1:9	6999
it all, and *b* it upon the altar	Lev 1:13	6999
his head, and *b* it on the altar	Lev 1:15	6999
the priest shall *b* it upon the	Lev 1:17	6999
the priest shall *b* the memorial	Lev 2:2	6999
shall *b* it upon the altar	Lev 2:9	6999
for ye shall *b* no leaven, nor any	Lev 2:11	6999
the priest shall *b* the memorial	Lev 2:16	6999
Aaron's sons shall *b* it on the	Lev 3:5	6999
the priest shall *b* it upon the	Lev 3:11	6999
the priest shall *b* them upon the	Lev 3:16	6999
the priest shall *b* them upon the	Lev 4:10	6999
b him on the wood with fire	Lev 4:12	8313
from him, and *b* it upon the altar	Lev 4:19	6999
b him as he burned the first	Lev 4:21	8313
he shall *b* all his fat upon the	Lev 4:26	6999
the priest shall *b* it upon the	Lev 4:31	6999
the priest shall *b* them upon the	Lev 4:35	6999
b it on the altar, according to	Lev 5:12	6999
the priest shall *b* wood on it	Lev 6:12	1197
he shall *b* thereon the fat of the	Lev 6:12	6999
shall *b* it upon the altar for a	Lev 6:15	6999
the priest shall *b* them upon the	Lev 7:5	6999
the priest shall *b* the fat upon	Lev 7:31	6999
of the bread shall ye *b* with fire	Lev 8:32	8313
He shall therefore *b* that garment	Lev 13:52	8313
thou shalt *b* it in the fire	Lev 13:55	8313
thou shalt *b* that wherein the	Lev 13:57	8313
shall he *b* upon the altar	Lev 16:25	6999
they shall *b* in the fire their	Lev 16:27	8313
b the fat for a sweet savour unto	Lev 17:6	6999
cause the lamps to *b* continually	Lev 24:2	5927
b it upon the altar, and afterward	Num 5:26	6999
shalt *b* their fat for an offering	Num 18:17	6999
one shall *b* the heifer in his	Num 19:5	8313
blood, with her dung, shall he *b*	Num 19:5	8313
(for the mountain did *b* with fire	Deut 5:23	1197
b their graven images with fire	Deut 7:5	8313
their gods shall ye *b* with fire	Deut 7:25	8313
and *b* their groves with fire	Deut 12:3	8313
shalt *b* with fire the city, and	Deut 13:16	8313
shall *b* unto the lowest hell, and	Deut 32:22	3344
b their chariots with fire	Josh 11:6	8313
that did Joshua *b*	Josh 11:13	8313
of the tower to *b* it with fire	Judg 9:52	8313
we will *b* thine house upon thee	Judg 12:1	8313
us the riddle, lest we *b* thee	Judg 14:15	8313
not fail to *b* the fat presently	1Sa 2:16	6999
to *b* incense, to wear an ephod	1Sa 2:28	6999
stood by the altar to *b* incense	1Kin 13:1	6999
places that *b* incense upon thee	1Kin 13:2	6999
Upon the great altar *b* the	2Kin 16:15	6999
of Israel did *b* incense to it	2Kin 18:4	6999
b incense in the high places in	2Kin 23:5	6999
to *b* incense before the LORD, to	1Chr 23:13	6999
to *b* before him sweet incense, and	2Chr 2:4	6999
save only to *b* sacrifice before	2Chr 2:6	6999
that they should *b* after the	2Chr 4:20	1197
they *b* unto the LORD every	2Chr 13:11	6999
lamps thereof, to *b* every evening	2Chr 13:11	1197
to *b* incense upon the altar of	2Chr 26:16	6999
to *b* incense unto the LORD, but	2Chr 26:18	6999
that are consecrated to *b* incense	2Chr 26:18	6999
a censer in his hand to *b* incense	2Chr 26:19	6999
to *b* incense unto other gods	2Chr 28:25	6999
minister unto him, and *b* incense	2Chr 29:11	6999
one altar, and *b* incense upon it	2Chr 32:12	6999
to *b* upon the altar of the LORD	Neh 10:34	1197
shall thy jealousy *b* like fire	Ps 79:5	1197
shall thy wrath *b* like fire	Ps 89:46	1197
and they shall both *b* together	Is 1:31	1197
and it shall *b* and devour his	Is 10:17	1197
them, I would *b* them together	Is 27:4	6702
And Lebanon is not sufficient to *b*	Is 40:16	1197
Then shall it be for a man to *b*	Is 44:15	1197
the fire shall *b* them	Is 47:14	8313
b that none can quench it because	Jer 4:4	1197
b incense unto Baal, and walk	Jer 7:9	6999
and it shall *b*, and shall not be	Jer 7:20	1197
Hinnom, to *b* their sons and their	Jer 7:31	8313
even altars to *b* incense unto	Jer 11:13	6999
anger, which shall *b* upon you	Jer 15:14	3344
anger, which shall *b* for ever	Jer 17:4	3344
to *b* their sons with fire for	Jer 19:5	8313
and he shall *b* it with fire	Jer 21:10	8313
b that none can quench it,	Jer 21:12	1197
b it with the houses, upon whose	Jer 32:29	8313
and he shall *b* it with fire	Jer 34:2	8313
so shall they *b* odours for thee	Jer 34:5	8313
and take it, and *b* it with fire	Jer 34:22	8313
king that he would not *b* the roll	Jer 36:25	8313
and take it, and *b* it with fire	Jer 37:8	8313
tent, and *b* this city with fire	Jer 37:10	8313
they shall *b* it with fire, and	Jer 38:18	8313
and he shall *b* them, and carry them	Jer 43:12	8313
Egyptians shall he *b* with fire	Jer 43:13	8313
in that they went to *b* incense	Jer 44:3	6999
to *b* no incense unto other gods	Jer 44:5	6999
to *b* incense unto the queen of	Jer 44:17	6999
But since we left off to *b*	Jer 44:18	6999
to *b* incense to the queen of	Jer 44:25	6999
Thou shalt *b* with fire a third	Eze 5:2	1197
the fire, and *b* them in the fire	Eze 5:4	8313
they shall *b* thine houses with	Eze 16:41	8313
b up their houses with fire	Eze 23:47	8313
b also the bones under it, and	Eze 24:5	1754
brass of it may be hot, and may *b*	Eze 24:11	2787
b the weapons, both the shields	Eze 39:9	5400
they shall *b* them with fire seven	Eze 39:9	1197
for they shall *b* the weapons with	Eze 39:10	1197
he shall *b* it in the appointed	Eze 43:21	8313
b incense upon the hills, under	Hos 4:13	6999
I will *b* her chariots in the	Nah 2:13	1197
b incense unto their drag	Hab 1:16	6999
cometh, that shall *b* as an oven	Mal 4:1	1197
day that cometh shall *b* them up	Mal 4:1	3857
but he will *b* up the chaff with	Mt 3:12	*2618*
and bind them in bundles to *b* them	Mt 13:30	*2618*
his lot was to *b* incense when he	Lk 1:9	*2370*
but the chaff he will *b* with fire	Lk 3:17	*2618*
Did not our heart *b* within us	Lk 24:32	*2545*
it is better to marry than to *b*	1Cor 7:9	*4448*
who is offended, and I *b* not	2Cor 11:29	*4448*
eat her flesh, and *b* her with fire	Rev 17:16	*2618*

BURNED {98}

the bush *b* with fire, and the bush	Ex 3:2	1197
burn him as he *b* the first	Lev 4:21	8313
Moses *b* it upon the altar	Lev 8:16	6999
the mountain *b* with fire unto the	Deut 4:11	1197
mount, and the mount *b* with fire	Deut 9:15	1197
b them with fire, after they had	Josh 7:25	8313
Israel *b* none of them, save Hazor	Josh 11:13	8313
smitten Ziklag, and *b* it with fire	1Sa 30:1	8313
and, behold, it was *b* with fire	1Sa 30:3	8313
and we *b* Ziklag with fire	1Sa 30:14	8313
and David and his men *b* them	2Sa 5:21	5375
they shall be utterly *b* with fire	2Sa 23:7	8313
of the house of Baal, and *b* them	2Kin 10:26	8313
b incense still in the high	2Kin 15:35	6999
have *b* incense unto other gods,	2Kin 22:17	6999
he *b* them without Jerusalem in	2Kin 23:4	8313
them also that *b* incense unto	2Kin 23:5	6999
b it at the brook Kidron, and	2Kin 23:6	8313
where the priests had *b* incense	2Kin 23:8	6999
b the chariots of the sun with	2Kin 23:11	8313
b the high place, and stamped it	2Kin 23:15	8313
small to powder, and *b* the grove	2Kin 23:15	8313
b them upon the altar, and	2Kin 23:16	8313
b men's bones upon them, and	2Kin 23:20	8313
and they were *b* with fire	1Chr 14:12	8313
them, and *b* incense unto them	2Chr 25:14	6999
have not *b* incense nor offered	2Chr 29:7	6999
have *b* incense unto other gods,	2Chr 34:25	6999
the gates thereof are *b* with fire	Neh 1:3	3341
the gates thereof are *b* with fire	Neh 2:17	3341
heaps of the rubbish which are *b*	Neh 4:2	8313
very wroth, and his anger *b* in him	Est 1:12	1197
hath *b* up the sheep, and the	Job 1:16	1197
me, and my bones are *b* with heat	Job 30:30	2787
while I was musing the fire *b*	Ps 39:3	1197
they have *b* up all the synagogues	Ps 74:8	8313
It is *b* with fire, it is cut down	Ps 80:16	8313
and my bones are *b* as an hearth	Ps 102:3	2787
the flame *b* up the wicked	Ps 106:18	3857
bosom, and his clothes not be *b*	Prov 6:27	8313
hot coals, and his feet not be *b*	Prov 6:28	3554
your cities are *b* with fire	Is 1:7	8313
inhabitants of the earth are *b*	Is 24:6	2787
up shall they be *b* in the fire	Is 33:12	3341
it *b* him, yet he laid it not to	Is 42:25	1197
the fire, thou shalt not be *b*	Is 43:2	3554
I have *b* part of it in the fire	Is 44:19	8314
praised thee, is *b* up with fire	Is 64:11	8316
which have *b* incense upon the	Is 65:7	6999
have *b* incense unto other gods,	Jer 1:16	6999
his cities are *b* without	Jer 2:15	3341

The bellows are b, the lead is ... Jer 6:29 2787
because they are b up, so that ... Jer 9:10 3341
is b up like a wilderness, that ... Jer 9:12 3341
they have b incense to vanity, and ... Jer 18:15 6999
have b incense in it unto other ... Jer 19:4 6999
upon whose roofs they have b ... Jer 19:13 6999
that the king had b the roll ... Jer 36:27 8313
the king of Judah hath b ... Jer 36:28 8313
Thou hast b this roll, saying, ... Jer 36:29 8313
king of Judah had b in the fire ... Jer 36:32 8313
city shall not be b with fire ... Jer 38:17 8313
cause this city to be b with fire ... Jer 38:23 8313
the Chaldeans b the king's house, ... Jer 39:8 8313
had b incense unto other gods ... Jer 44:15 6999
when we b incense to the queen of ... Jer 44:19 6999
The incense that ye b in the ... Jer 44:21 6999
Because ye have b incense ... Jer 44:23 6999
daughters shall be b with fire ... Jer 49:2 3341
they have b her dwellingplaces ... Jer 51:30 3341
the reeds they have b with fire ... Jer 51:32 8313
high gates shall be b with fire ... Jer 51:58 3341
b the house of the LORD, and the ... Jer 52:13 8313
of the great men, b he with fire ... Jer 52:13 8313
he b against Jacob like a flaming ... Lam 2:3 1197
of it, and the midst of it is b ... Eze 15:4 2787
fire hath devoured it, and it is b ... Eze 15:5 2787
to the north shall be b therein ... Eze 20:47 6866
it well, and let the bones be b ... Eze 24:10 2787
wherein she b incense to them, and ... Hos 2:13 6999
b incense to graven images ... Hos 11:2 6999
the flame hath b all the trees of ... Joel 1:19 3857
because he b the bones of the ... Amos 2:1 8313
thereof shall be b with the fire ... Mic 1:7 8313
the earth is b at his presence, ... Nah 1:5 5375
are gathered and b in the fire ... Mt 13:40 2618
murderers, and b up their city ... Mt 22:7 1714
them into the fire, and they are b ... Jn 15:6 2545
and b them before all men ... Acts 19:19 2618
b in their lust one toward ... Rom 1:27 1572
If any man's work shall be b ... 1Cor 3:15 2618
and though I give my body to be b ... 1Cor 13:3 2545
whose end is to be b ... Heb 6:8 2740
that b with fire, nor unto ... Heb 12:18 2545
for sin, are b without the camp ... Heb 13:11 2618
that are therein shall be b up ... 2Pet 3:10 2618
as if they b in a furnace ... Rev 1:15 4448
she shall be utterly b with fire ... Rev 18:8 2618

BURNETH {18}
the quick flesh that b have a ... Lev 13:24 4348
he that b them shall wash his ... Lev 16:28 8313
he that b her shall wash his ... Num 19:8 8313
he b the chariot in the fire ... Ps 46:9 8313
As the fire b a wood, and as the ... Ps 83:14 1197
b up his enemies round about ... Ps 97:3 3857
For wickedness b as the fire ... Is 9:18 1197
He b part thereof in the fire ... Is 44:16 8313
thereof as a lamp that b ... Is 62:1 1197
As when the melting fire b ... Is 64:2 6919
b incense upon altars of brick ... Is 65:3 6999
nose, a fire that b all the day ... Is 65:5 3344
he that b incense, as if he ... Is 66:3 2142
him that b incense to his gods ... Jer 48:35 6999
morning it b as a flaming fire ... Hos 7:6 1197
and behind them a flame b ... Joel 2:3 3857
take him up, and he that b him ... Amos 6:10 5635
in the lake which b with fire ... Rev 21:8 2545

BURNING {64}
a b lamp that passed between ... Gen 15:17 784
B for b, wound for wound, ... Ex 21:25 3555
B for b, wound for wound, ... Ex 21:25 3345
because of the b upon the altar ... Lev 6:9 4169
of the altar shall be b in it ... Lev 6:9 3344
upon the altar shall be b in it ... Lev 6:12 3344
shall ever be b upon the altar ... Lev 6:13 3344
bewail the b which the LORD hath ... Lev 10:6 8316
and spread not, it is a b boil ... Lev 13:23 6867
the skin whereof there is a hot b ... Lev 13:24 4348
is a leprosy broken out of the b ... Lev 13:25 4348
it is a rising of the b, and the ... Lev 13:28 4348
it is an inflammation of the b ... Lev 13:28 4348
of b coals of fire from off the ... Lev 16:12 784
the b ague, that shall consume ... Lev 26:16 6920
take up the censers out of the b ... Num 16:37 8316
the midst of the b of the heifer ... Num 19:6 8316
and with an extreme b, and with ... Deut 28:22 2746
is brimstone, and salt, and b ... Deut 29:23 8316
hunger, and devoured with b heat ... Deut 32:24
they made a very great b for him ... 2Chr 16:14 8316
And his people made no b for him ... 2Chr 21:19 8316
like the b of his fathers ... 2Chr 21:19 8316
Out of his mouth go b lamps ... Job 41:19 3940
Let b coals fall upon them ... Ps 140:10 784
in his lips there is as a b fire ... Prov 16:27 6867
As coals are to b coals, and wood ... Prov 26:21 1513
B lips and a wicked heart are like ... Prov 26:23 1814
and b instead of beauty ... Is 3:24 3587
judgment, and by the spirit of b ... Is 4:4 1197
but this shall be with b and fuel ... Is 9:5 8316
a b like ... Is 10:16 3350
the b of a fire ... Is 10:16 3345
b with his anger, and the burden ... Is 30:27 1197
land thereof shall become b pitch ... Is 34:9 1197
as a b fire shut up in my bones ... Jer 20:9 1197
a fire on the hearth b before him ... Jer 36:22 1197
b incense unto other gods in the ... Jer 44:8 6999
was like b coals of fire, and like ... Eze 1:13 1197
the midst of a b fiery furnace ... Dan 3:6 3345
the midst of a b fiery furnace ... Dan 3:11 3345
the midst of a b fiery furnace ... Dan 3:15 3345
us from the b fiery furnace ... Dan 3:17 3345
them into the b fiery furnace ... Dan 3:20 3345
the midst of the b fiery furnace ... Dan 3:21 3345
the midst of the b fiery furnace ... Dan 3:23 3345
the mouth of the b fiery furnace ... Dan 3:26 3345
flame, and his wheels as b fire ... Dan 7:9 1815
and given to the b flame ... Dan 7:11 3346
a firebrand plucked out of the b ... Amos 4:11 8316
b coals went forth at his feet ... Hab 3:5 7565
be girded about, and your lights b ... Lk 12:35 2545
He was a b and a shining light ... Jn 5:35 2545
is no sooner risen with a b heat ... Jas 1:11 2742
lamps of fire b before the throne ... Rev 4:5 2545
as it were a great mountain b ... Rev 8:8 2545
b as it were a lamp, and it fell ... Rev 8:10 2545
they shall see the smoke of her b ... Rev 18:9 4451
when they saw the smoke of her b ... Rev 18:18 4451
a lake of fire b with brimstone ... Rev 19:20 2545

BURNINGS {3}
people shall be as the b of lime ... Is 33:12 4955
us shall dwell with everlasting b ... Is 33:14 4168
with the b of thy fathers, the ... Jer 34:5 4955

BURNISHED {1}
like the colour of b brass ... Eze 1:7 7044

BURNT {368}
offered b offerings on the altar ... Gen 8:20 5930
offer him there for a b offering ... Gen 22:2 5930
clave the wood for the b offering ... Gen 22:3 5930
took the wood of the b offering ... Gen 22:6 5930
is the lamb for a b offering ... Gen 22:7 5930
himself a lamb for a b offering ... Gen 22:8 5930
offered him up for a b offering ... Gen 22:13 5930
Bring her forth, and let her be b ... Gen 38:24 8313
sight, why the bush is not b ... Ex 3:3 1197
and b offerings, that we may ... Ex 10:25 5930
took a b offering and sacrifices ... Ex 18:12 5930
sacrifice thereon thy b offerings ... Ex 20:24 5930
Israel, which offered b offerings ... Ex 24:5 5930
it is a b offering unto the LORD ... Ex 29:18 5930
upon the altar for a b offering ... Ex 29:25 5930
b offering throughout your ... Ex 29:42 5930
nor b sacrifice, nor meat ... Ex 30:9 5930
the altar of b offering with all ... Ex 30:28 5930
the altar of b offering with all ... Ex 31:9 5930
offered b offerings, and brought ... Ex 32:6 5930
b it in the fire, and ground it to ... Ex 32:20 8313
The altar of b offering, with his ... Ex 35:16 5930
he made the altar of b offering ... Ex 38:1 5930
b offering before the door of the ... Ex 40:6 5930
the altar of the b offering ... Ex 40:10 5930
he b sweet incense thereon ... Ex 40:27 6999
he put the altar of b offering by ... Ex 40:29 5930
and offered upon it the b offering ... Ex 40:29 5930
If his offering be a b sacrifice ... Lev 1:3 5930
upon the head of the b offering ... Lev 1:4 5930
And he shall flay the b offering ... Lev 1:6 5930
to be a b sacrifice, an offering ... Lev 1:9 5930
of the goats, for a b sacrifice ... Lev 1:10 5930
it is a b sacrifice, an offering ... Lev 1:13 5930
if the b sacrifice for his ... Lev 1:14 5930
it is a b sacrifice, an offering ... Lev 1:17 5930
but they shall not be b on the ... Lev 2:12 5927
on the altar upon the b sacrifice ... Lev 3:5 5930
of the altar of the b offering ... Lev 4:7 5930
upon the altar of the b offering ... Lev 4:10 5930
are poured out shall he be b ... Lev 4:12 8313
of the altar of the b offering ... Lev 4:18 5930
the b offering before the LORD ... Lev 4:24 5930
horns of the altar of b offering ... Lev 4:25 5930
bottom of the altar of b offering ... Lev 4:25 5930
in the place of the b offering ... Lev 4:29 5930
horns of the altar of b offering ... Lev 4:30 5930
where they kill the b offering ... Lev 4:33 5930
horns of the altar of b offering ... Lev 4:34 5930
and the other for a b offering ... Lev 5:7 5930
offer the second for a b offering ... Lev 5:10 5930
This is the law of the b offering ... Lev 6:9 5930
It is the b offering, because of ... Lev 6:9 5930
with the b offering on the altar ... Lev 6:10 5930
lay the b offering in order upon ... Lev 6:12 6999
it shall be wholly b ... Lev 6:22 6999
for the priest shall be wholly b ... Lev 6:23
In the place where the b offering ... Lev 6:25 5930
it shall be b in the fire ... Lev 6:30 8313
b offering shall they kill the ... Lev 7:2 5930
offereth any man's b offering ... Lev 7:8 5930
b offering which he hath offered ... Lev 7:8 5930
third day shall be b with fire ... Lev 7:17 8313
it shall be b with fire ... Lev 7:19 8313
This is the law of the b offering ... Lev 7:37 5930
he b with fire without the camp ... Lev 8:17 8313
the ram for the b offering ... Lev 8:18 5930
Moses b the head, and the pieces, ... Lev 8:20 6999
Moses b the whole ram upon the ... Lev 8:21 6999
it was a b sacrifice for a sweet ... Lev 8:21 5930
b them on the altar upon the ... Lev 8:28 6999
on the altar upon the b offering ... Lev 8:28 5930
and a ram for a b offering ... Lev 9:2 5930
without blemish, for a b offering ... Lev 9:3 5930
thy b offering, and make an ... Lev 9:7 5930
sin offering, he b upon the altar ... Lev 9:10 5930
the hide he b with fire without ... Lev 9:11 8313
And he slew the b offering ... Lev 9:12 5930
presented the b offering unto him ... Lev 9:13 5930
and he b them upon the altar ... Lev 9:13 6999
b them upon ... Lev 9:14 6999
upon the b offering on ... Lev 9:14 5930
And he brought the b offering ... Lev 9:16 5930
b it upon the altar ... Lev 9:17 6999
beside the b sacrifice of the ... Lev 9:17 5930
he b the fat upon the altar ... Lev 9:20 6999
and the b offering, and peace ... Lev 9:22 5930
upon the altar the b offering ... Lev 9:24 5930
offering, and, behold, it was b ... Lev 10:16 8313
their b offering before the LORD ... Lev 10:19 5930
the first year for a b offering ... Lev 12:6 5930
the one for the b offering ... Lev 12:8 5930
it shall be b in the fire ... Lev 13:52 8313
the b offering, in the holy place ... Lev 14:13 5930
he shall kill the b offering ... Lev 14:19 5930
priest shall offer the b offering ... Lev 14:20 5930
and the other a b offering ... Lev 14:22 5930
and the other for a b offering ... Lev 14:31 5930
and the other for a b offering ... Lev 15:15 5930
and the other for a b offering ... Lev 15:30 5930
and a ram for a b offering ... Lev 16:3 5930
and one ram for a b offering ... Lev 16:5 5930
forth, and offer his b offering ... Lev 16:24 5930
the b offering of the people, and ... Lev 16:24 5930
that offereth a b offering or ... Lev 17:8 5930
day, it shall be b in the fire ... Lev 19:6 8313
they shall be b with fire ... Lev 20:14 8313
she shall be b with fire ... Lev 21:9 8313
unto the LORD for a b offering ... Lev 22:18 5930
for a b offering unto the LORD ... Lev 23:12 5930
they shall be for a b offering ... Lev 23:18 5930
a b offering, and a meat offering, ... Lev 23:37 5930
and the other for a b offering ... Num 6:11 5930
without blemish for a b offering ... Num 6:14 5930
sin offering, and his b offering ... Num 6:16 5930
the first year, for a b offering ... Num 7:15 5930
the first year, for a b offering ... Num 7:21 5930
the first year, for a b offering ... Num 7:27 5930
the first year, for a b offering ... Num 7:33 5930
the first year, for a b offering ... Num 7:39 5930
the first year, for a b offering ... Num 7:45 5930
the first year, for a b offering ... Num 7:51 5930
the first year, for a b offering ... Num 7:57 5930
the first year, for a b offering ... Num 7:63 5930
the first year, for a b offering ... Num 7:69 5930
the first year, for a b offering ... Num 7:75 5930
the first year, for a b offering ... Num 7:81 5930
All the oxen for the b offering ... Num 7:87 5930
and the other for a b offering ... Num 8:12 5930
trumpets over your b offerings ... Num 10:10 5930
the fire of the LORD b among them ... Num 11:1 1197
the fire of the LORD b among them ... Num 11:3 1197
a b offering, or a sacrifice in ... Num 15:3 5930
with the b offering or sacrifice ... Num 15:5 5930
a bullock for a b offering ... Num 15:8 5930
young bullock for a b offering ... Num 15:24 5930
they that were b had offered ... Num 16:39 8313
b heifer of purification for sin ... Num 19:17 8316
Balak, Stand by thy b offering ... Num 23:3 5930
lo, he stood by his b sacrifice ... Num 23:6 5930
Stand here by thy b offering ... Num 23:15 5930
he stood by his b offering ... Num 23:17 5930
day, for a continual b offering ... Num 28:3 5930
It is a continual b offering ... Num 28:6 5930
This is the b offering of every ... Num 28:10 5930
beside the continual b offering ... Num 28:10 5930
offer a b offering unto the LORD ... Num 28:11 5930
for a b offering of a sweet ... Num 28:13 5930
this is the b offering of every ... Num 28:14 5930
beside the continual b offering ... Num 28:15 5930
for a b offering unto the LORD ... Num 28:19 5930
the b offering in the morning ... Num 28:23 5930
is for a continual b offering ... Num 28:23 5930
beside the continual b offering ... Num 28:24 5930
But ye shall offer the b offering ... Num 28:27 5930
beside the continual b offering ... Num 28:31 5930
ye shall offer a b offering for a ... Num 29:2 5930
Beside the b offering of the ... Num 29:6 5930
offering, and the daily b offering ... Num 29:6 5930
But ye shall offer a b offering ... Num 29:8 5930
and the continual b offering ... Num 29:11 5930
And ye shall offer a b offering ... Num 29:13 5930
beside the continual b offering ... Num 29:16 5930
beside the continual b offering ... Num 29:19 5930
beside the continual b offering ... Num 29:22 5930
beside the continual b offering ... Num 29:25 5930
beside the continual b offering ... Num 29:28 5930
beside the continual b offering ... Num 29:31 5930
beside the continual b offering ... Num 29:34 5930
But ye shall offer a b offering ... Num 29:36 5930
beside the continual b offering ... Num 29:38 5930
for your b offerings, and for your ... Num 29:39 5930
they b all their cities wherein ... Num 31:10 8313
b it with fire, and stamped it, and ... Deut 9:21 8313
ye shall bring your b offerings ... Deut 12:6 5930
your b offerings, and your ... Deut 12:11 5930
b offerings in every place that ... Deut 12:13 5930
thou shalt offer thy b offerings ... Deut 12:14 5930
thou shalt offer thy b offerings ... Deut 12:27 5930
have b in the fire to their gods ... Deut 12:31 8313
thou shalt offer b offerings ... Deut 27:6 5930
They shall be b with hunger ... Deut 32:24 4198
whole b sacrifice upon thine ... Deut 33:10 3632
they b the city with fire, and all ... Josh 6:24 8313
thing shall be b with fire ... Josh 7:15 8313
And Joshua b Ai, and made it an ... Josh 8:28 8313
they offered thereon b offerings ... Josh 8:31 5930
b their chariots with fire ... Josh 11:9 8313

and he *b* Hazor with fire — Josh 11:11 — 8313
or if to offer thereon *b* offering — Josh 22:23 — 5930
not for *b* offering, nor for — Josh 22:26 — 5930
before him with our *b* offerings — Josh 22:27 — 5930
not for *b* offerings, nor for — Josh 22:28 — 5930
to build an altar for *b* offerings — Josh 22:29 — 5930
offer a *b* sacrifice with the wood — Judg 6:26 — 5930
will offer it up for a *b* offering — Judg 11:31 — 5930
if thou wilt offer a *b* offering — Judg 13:16 — 5930
not have received a *b* offering — Judg 13:23 — 5930
b up both the shocks, and also the — Judg 15:5 — 1197
b her and her father with fire — Judg 15:6 — 8313
as flax that was *b* with fire — Judg 15:14 — 1197
sword, and *b* the city with fire — Judg 18:27 — 8313
offered *b* offerings and peace — Judg 20:26 — 5930
offered *b* offerings and peace — Judg 21:4 — 5930
Also before they *b* the fat — 1Sa 2:15 — 6999
offered the kine a *b* offering — 1Sa 6:14 — 5930
Beth-shemesh offered *b* offerings — 1Sa 6:15 — 5930
offered it for a *b* offering — 1Sa 7:9 — 5930
was offering up the *b* offering — 1Sa 7:10 — 5930
to offer *b* offerings, and to — 1Sa 10:8 — 5930
Bring hither a *b* offering to me — 1Sa 13:9 — 5930
And he offered the *b* offering — 1Sa 13:9 — 5930
an end of offering the *b* offering — 1Sa 13:10 — 5930
and offered a *b* offering — 1Sa 13:12 — 5930
as great delight in *b* offerings — 1Sa 15:22 — 5930
came to Jabesh, and *b* them there — 1Sa 31:12 — 8313
and David offered *b* offerings — 2Sa 6:17 — 5930
an end of offering *b* offerings — 2Sa 6:18 — 5930
here be oxen for *b* sacrifice — 2Sa 24:22 — 5930
neither will I offer *b* offerings — 2Sa 24:24 — 5930
offered *b* offerings and peace — 2Sa 24:25 — 5930
and *b* incense in high places — 1Kin 3:3 — 6999
a thousand *b* offerings did — 1Kin 3:4 — 5930
LORD, and offered up *b* offerings — 1Kin 3:15 — 5930
for there he offered *b* offerings — 1Kin 8:64 — 5930
little to receive the *b* offerings — 1Kin 8:64 — 5930
b it with fire, and slain the — 1Kin 9:16 — 8313
did Solomon offer *b* offerings — 1Kin 9:25 — 5930
he *b* incense upon the altar that — 1Kin 9:25 — 6999
which *b* incense and sacrificed — 1Kin 11:8 — 6999
upon the altar, and *b* incense — 1Kin 12:33 — 6999
men's bones shall be *b* upon thee — 1Kin 13:2 — 8313
idol, and *b* it by the brook Kidron — 1Kin 15:13 — 8313
b the king's house over him with — 1Kin 16:18 — 8313
and pour it on the *b* sacrifice — 1Kin 18:33 — 5930
fell, and consumed the *b* sacrifice — 1Kin 18:38 — 5930
b incense yet in the high places — 1Kin 22:43 — 6999
b up the two captains of the — 2Kin 1:14 — 398
offered him for a *b* offering upon — 2Kin 3:27 — 5930
b offering nor sacrifice unto — 2Kin 5:17 — 5930
b offerings, Jehu appointed — 2Kin 10:24 — 5930
an end of offering the *b* offering — 2Kin 10:25 — 5930
b incense in the high places — 2Kin 12:3 — 6999
b incense on the high places — 2Kin 14:4 — 6999
b incense still on the high — 2Kin 15:4 — 6999
b incense in the high places, and — 2Kin 16:4 — 6999
And he *b* his *b* offering — 2Kin 16:13 — 6999
altar burn the morning *b* offering — 2Kin 16:15 — 5930
and the king's *b* sacrifice — 2Kin 16:15 — 5930
with the *b* offering of all the — 2Kin 16:15 — 5930
all the blood of the *b* offering — 2Kin 16:15 — 5930
there they *b* incense in all the — 2Kin 17:11 — 6999
the Sepharvites *b* their children — 2Kin 17:31 — 8313
he *b* the house of the LORD, and — 2Kin 25:9 — 8313
great man's house *b* he with fire — 2Kin 25:9 — 8313
upon the altar of the *b* offering — 1Chr 6:49 — 5930
and they offered *b* sacrifices — 1Chr 16:1 — 5930
end of offering the *b* offerings — 1Chr 16:2 — 5930
To offer *b* offerings unto the — 1Chr 16:40 — 5930
b offering continually morning — 1Chr 16:40 — 5930
the oxen also for *b* offerings — 1Chr 21:23 — 5930
nor offer *b* offerings without — 1Chr 21:24 — 5930
offered *b* offerings and peace — 1Chr 21:26 — 5930
fire upon the altar of *b* offering — 1Chr 21:26 — 5930
and the altar of the *b* offering — 1Chr 21:29 — 5930
of the *b* offering for Israel — 1Chr 22:1 — 5930
to offer all *b* sacrifices unto — 1Chr 23:31 — 5930
offered *b* offerings unto the LORD — 1Chr 29:21 — 5930
a thousand *b* offerings upon it — 2Chr 1:6 — 5930
for the *b* offerings morning and — 2Chr 2:4 — 5930
b offering they washed in them — 2Chr 4:6 — 5930
and consumed the *b* offering — 2Chr 7:1 — 5930
for there he offered *b* offerings — 2Chr 7:7 — 5930
able to receive the *b* offerings — 2Chr 7:7 — 5930
Then Solomon offered *b* offerings — 2Chr 8:12 — 5930
and every evening *b* sacrifices — 2Chr 13:11 — 5930
it, and *b* it at the brook Kidron — 2Chr 15:16 — 8313
to offer the *b* offerings of the — 2Chr 23:18 — 5930
they offered *b* offerings in the — 2Chr 24:14 — 5930
Moreover he *b* incense in the — 2Chr 28:3 — 6999
b his children in the fire, after — 2Chr 28:3 — 1197
b incense in the high places, and — 2Chr 28:4 — 6999
b offerings in the holy place — 2Chr 29:7 — 5930
LORD, and the altar of *b* offering — 2Chr 29:18 — 5930
commanded that the *b* offering — 2Chr 29:24 — 5930
the *b* offering upon the altar — 2Chr 29:27 — 5930
when the *b* offering began, the — 2Chr 29:27 — 5930
until the *b* offering was finished — 2Chr 29:28 — 5930
were of a free heart *b* offerings — 2Chr 29:31 — 5930
And the number of the *b* offerings — 2Chr 29:32 — 5930
were for a *b* offering to the LORD — 2Chr 29:32 — 5930
not flay all the *b* offerings — 2Chr 29:34 — 5930
also the *b* offerings were in — 2Chr 29:35 — 5930
offerings for every *b* offering — 2Chr 29:35 — 5930
brought in the *b* offerings into — 2Chr 30:15 — 5930
and Levites for *b* offerings — 2Chr 31:2 — 5930
his substance for the *b* offerings — 2Chr 31:3 — 5930
evening *b* offerings, and the *b* — 2Chr 31:3 — 5930
he *b* the bones of the priests — 2Chr 34:5 — 8313
And they removed the *b* offerings — 2Chr 35:12 — 5930
busied in offering of *b* offerings — 2Chr 35:14 — 5930
to offer *b* offerings upon the — 2Chr 35:16 — 5930
they *b* the house of God, and brake — 2Chr 36:19 — 8313
b all the palaces thereof with — 2Chr 36:19 — 8313
to offer *b* offerings thereon, as — Ezr 3:2 — 5930
they offered *b* offerings thereon — Ezr 3:3 — 5930
even *b* offerings morning and — Ezr 3:3 — 5930
offered the daily *b* offerings by — Ezr 3:4 — 5930
offered the continual *b* offering — Ezr 3:5 — 5930
offer *b* offerings unto the LORD — Ezr 3:6 — 5930
for the *b* offerings of the God of — Ezr 6:9 — 5928
offered *b* offerings unto the God — Ezr 8:35 — 5930
all this was a *b* offering unto — Ezr 8:35 — 5930
and for the continual *b* offering — Neh 10:33 — 5930
offered *b* offerings according to — Job 1:5 — 5930
up for yourselves a *b* offering — Job 42:8 — 5930
and accept thy *b* sacrifice — Ps 20:3 — 5930
b offering and sin offering hast — Ps 40:6 — 5930
thy sacrifices or thy *b* offerings — Ps 50:8 — 5930
thou delightest not in *b* offering — Ps 51:16 — 5930
b offering and whole *b* offering — Ps 51:19 — 5930
into thy house with *b* offerings — Ps 66:13 — 5930
thee *b* sacrifices of fatlings — Ps 66:15 — 5930
I am full of the *b* offerings of — Is 1:11 — 5930
sufficient for a *b* offering — Is 40:16 — 5930
small cattle of thy *b* offerings — Is 43:23 — 5930
their *b* offerings and their — Is 56:7 — 5930
I hate robbery for *b* offering — Is 61:8 — 5930
your *b* offerings are not — Jer 6:20 — 5930
Put your *b* offerings unto your — Jer 7:21 — 5930
concerning *b* offerings or — Jer 7:22 — 5930
and when they offer *b* offering — Jer 14:12 — 5930
south, bringing *b* offerings, and — Jer 17:26 — 5930
fire for *b* offerings unto Baal — Jer 19:5 — 5930
before me to offer *b* offerings — Jer 33:18 — 5930
and will make thee a *b* mountain — Jer 51:25 — 8316
where they washed the *b* offering — Eze 40:38 — 5930
to slay thereon the *b* offering — Eze 40:39 — 5930
of hewn stone for the *b* offering — Eze 40:42 — 5930
they slew the *b* offering and the — Eze 40:42 — 5930
to offer *b* offerings thereon, and — Eze 43:18 — 5930
up for a *b* offering unto the LORD — Eze 43:24 — 5930
your *b* offerings upon the altar — Eze 43:27 — 5930
they shall slay the *b* offering — Eze 44:11 — 5930
for a *b* offering, and for peace — Eze 45:15 — 5930
prince's part to give *b* offerings — Eze 45:17 — 5930
the *b* offering, and the peace — Eze 45:17 — 5930
prepare a *b* offering to the LORD — Eze 45:23 — 5930
according to the *b* offering — Eze 45:25 — 5930
shall prepare his *b* offering — Eze 46:2 — 5930
the *b* offering that the prince — Eze 46:4 — 5930
shall prepare a voluntary *b* — Eze 46:12 — 5930
he shall prepare his *b* offering — Eze 46:12 — 5930
Thou shalt daily prepare a *b* — Eze 46:13 — 5930
for a continual *b* offering — Eze 46:15 — 5930
of God more than *b* offerings — Hos 6:6 — 5930
Though ye offer me *b* offerings — Amos 5:22 — 5930
come before him with *b* offerings — Mic 6:6 — 5930
more than all whole *b* offerings — Mk 12:33 — *3646*
In *b* offerings and sacrifices for — Heb 10:6 — *3646*
b offerings and offering for sin — Heb 10:8 — *3646*
the third part of trees was *b* up — Rev 8:7 — *2618*
and all green grass was *b* up — Rev 8:7 — *2618*

BURST {9}
it is ready to *b* like new bottles — Job 32:19 — 1234
presses shall *b* out with new wine — Prov 3:10 — 6555
broken thy yoke, and *b* thy bands — Jer 2:20 — 5423
broken the yoke, and *b* the bonds — Jer 5:5 — 5423
will *b* thy bonds, and strangers — Jer 30:8 — 5423
will *b* thy bonds in sunder — Nah 1:13 — 5423
the new wine doth *b* the bottles — Mk 2:22 — *4486*
the new wine will *b* the bottles — Lk 5:37 — *4486*
he *b* asunder in the midst, and all — Acts 1:18 — *2997*

BURSTING {1}
b of it a sherd to take fire from — Is 30:14 — 4386

BURY {39}
that I may *b* my dead out of my — Gen 23:4 — 6912
of our sepulchres *b* thy dead — Gen 23:6 — 6912
but that thou mayest *b* thy dead — Gen 23:6 — 6912
should *b* my dead out of my sight — Gen 23:8 — 6912
b thy dead — Gen 23:11 — 6912
of me, and I will *b* my dead there — Gen 23:13 — 6912
b therefore thy dead — Gen 23:15 — 6912
b me not, I pray thee, in Egypt — Gen 47:29 — 6912
b me in their buryingplace — Gen 47:30 — 6912
b me with my fathers in the cave — Gen 49:29 — 6912
of Canaan, there shalt thou *b* me — Gen 50:5 — 6912
b my father, and I will come again — Gen 50:5 — 6912
b thy father, according as he — Gen 50:6 — 6912
And Joseph went up to *b* his father — Gen 50:7 — 6912
went up with him to *b* his father — Gen 50:14 — 6912
shalt in any wise *b* him that day — Deut 21:23 — 6912
said, and fall upon him, and *b* him — 1Kin 2:31 — 6912
host was gone up to *b* the slain — 1Kin 11:15 — 6912
to the city, to mourn and to *b* him — 1Kin 13:29 — 6912
then *b* me in the sepulchre — 1Kin 13:31 — 6912
shall mourn for him, and *b* him — 1Kin 14:13 — 6912
and there shall be none to *b* her — 2Kin 9:10 — 6912
now this cursed woman, and *b* her — 2Kin 9:34 — 6912
And they went to *b* her — 2Kin 9:35 — 6912
and there was none to *b* them — Ps 79:3 — 6912
for they shall *b* in Tophet — Jer 7:32 — 6912
and they shall have none to *b* them — Jer 14:16 — 6912
they shall *b* them in Tophet — Jer 19:11 — 6912
till there be no place to *b* — Jer 19:11 — 6912
and there shall they *b* Gog — Eze 39:11 — 6912
people of the land shall *b* them — Eze 39:13 — 6912
passing through the land to *b* — Eze 39:14 — 6912
them up, Memphis shall *b* them — Hos 9:6 — 6912
me first to go and *b* my father — Mt 8:21 — *2290*
and let the dead *b* their dead — Mt 8:22 — *2290*
potter's field, to *b* strangers in — Mt 27:7 — *5027*
me first to go and *b* my father — Lk 9:59 — *2290*
him, Let the dead *b* their dead — Lk 9:60 — *2290*
as the manner of the Jews is to *b* — Jn 19:40 — *1779*

BURYING {4}
to pass, as they were *b* a man — 2Kin 13:21 — 6912
the house of Israel be *b* of them — Eze 39:12 — 6912
to anoint my body to the *b* — Mk 14:8 — *1780*
day of my *b* hath she kept this — Jn 12:7 — *1780*

BURYINGPLACE {7}
me a possession of a *b* with you — Gen 23:4 — 6913
a possession of a *b* amongst you — Gen 23:9 — 6913
of a *b* by the sons of Heth — Gen 23:20 — 6913
of Egypt, and bury me in their *b* — Gen 47:30 — 6913
Hittite for a possession of a *b* — Gen 49:30 — 6913
of a *b* of Ephron the Hittite — Gen 50:13 — 6913
Eshtaol in the *b* of Manoah his — Judg 16:31 — 6913

BUSH {11}
of fire out of the midst of a *b* — Ex 3:2 — 5572
the *b* burned with fire — Ex 3:2 — 5572
and the *b* was not consumed — Ex 3:2 — 5572
sight, why the *b* is not burnt — Ex 3:3 — 5572
him out of the midst of the *b* — Ex 3:4 — 5572
will of him that dwelt in the *b* — Deut 33:16 — 5572
how in the *b* God spake unto him — Mk 12:26 — *942*
nor of a bramble *b* gather they — Lk 6:44 — *942*
even Moses shewed at the *b* — Lk 20:37 — *942*
Lord in a flame of fire in a *b* — Acts 7:30 — *942*
which appeared to him in the *b* — Acts 7:35 — *942*

BUSHEL {3}
a candle, and put it under a *b* — Mt 5:15 — *3426*
brought to be put under a *b* — Mk 4:21 — *3426*
a secret place, neither under a *b* — Lk 11:33 — *3426*

BUSHES {3}
Who cut up mallows by the *b* — Job 30:4 — 7880
Among the *b* they brayed — Job 30:7 — 7880
and upon all thorns, and upon all *b* — Is 7:19 — 5097

BUSHY {1}
most fine gold, his locks are *b* — Song 5:11 — 8534

BUSIED {1}
b in offering of burnt offerings — 2Chr 35:14

BUSINESS {29}
went into the house to do his *b* — Gen 39:11 — 4399
shall he be charged with any *b* — Deut 24:5 — 1697
yours, if ye utter not this our *b* — Josh 2:14 — 1697
And if thou utter this our *b* — Josh 2:20 — 1697
and had no *b* with any man — Judg 18:7 — 1697
they had no *b* with any man — Judg 18:28 — 1697
thyself when the *b* was in hand — 1Sa 20:19 — 4639
The king hath commanded me a *b* — 1Sa 21:2 — 1697
of the *b* whereabout I send thee — 1Sa 21:2 — 1697
the king's *b* required haste — 1Sa 21:8 — 1697
for the outward *b* over Israel — 1Chr 26:29 — 4399
westward in all the *b* of the LORD — 1Chr 26:30 — 4399
and the Levites wait upon their *b* — 2Chr 13:10 — 4399
he had much *b* in the cities of — 2Chr 17:13 — 4399
Howbeit in the *b* of the — 2Chr 32:31
the outward *b* of the house of God — Neh 11:16 — 4399
over the *b* of the house of God — Neh 11:22 — 4399
the Levites, every one in his *b* — Neh 13:30 — 4399
that have the charge of the *b* — Est 3:9 — 4399
that do *b* in great waters — Ps 107:23 — 4399
thou a man diligent in his *b* — Prov 22:29 — 4399
cometh through the multitude of *b* — Eccl 5:3 — 6045
to see the *b* that is done upon — Eccl 8:16 — 6045
I rose up, and did the king's *b* — Dan 8:27 — 4399
I must be about my Father's *b* — Lk 2:49
whom we may appoint over this *b* — Acts 6:3 — *5532*
Not slothful in *b* — Rom 12:11 — *4710*
whatsoever *b* she hath need of you — Rom 16:2 — *4229*
to be quiet, and to do your own *b* — 1Th 4:11 — *2398*

BUSY {1}
And as thy servant was *b* here — 1Kin 20:40 — 6213

BUSYBODIES {2}
working not at all, but are *b* — 2Th 3:11 — *4020*
only idle, but tattlers also and *b* — 1Ti 5:13 — *4021*

BUSYBODY {1}
or as a *b* in other men's matters — 1Pet 4:15 — *244*

BUT See APPENDIX.

BUTLER {8}
that the *b* of the king of Egypt — Gen 40:1 — 4945
of his dream, the *b* and the baker — Gen 40:5 — 4945
the chief *b* told his dream to — Gen 40:9 — 4945
manner when thou wast his *b* — Gen 40:13 — 4945
lifted up the head of the chief *b* — Gen 40:20 — 4945
he restored the chief *b* unto his — Gen 40:21 — 4945
not the chief *b* remember Joseph — Gen 40:23 — 4945
spake the chief *b* unto Pharaoh — Gen 41:9 — 4945

BUTLERS {1}
against the chief of the *b* — Gen 40:2 — 4945

BUTLERSHIP {1}
the chief butler unto his b again ... Gen 40:21 4945

BUTTER {11}
And he took b, and milk, and the ... Gen 18:8 2529
B of kine, and milk of sheep, with ... Deut 32:14 2529
brought forth b in a lordly dish ... Judg 5:25 2529
And honey, and b, and sheep, and ... 2Sa 17:29 2529
floods, the brooks of honey and b ... Job 20:17 2529
When I washed my steps with b ... Job 29:6 2529
of his mouth were smoother than b ... Ps 55:21 4260
churning of milk bringeth forth b ... Prov 30:33 2529
B and honey shall he eat, that he ... Is 7:15 2529
they shall give, he shall eat b ... Is 7:22 2529
for b and honey shall every one ... Is 7:22 2529

BUTTOCKS {3}
in the middle, even to their b ... 2Sa 10:4 8357
in the midst hard by their b ... 1Chr 19:4 4667
even with their b uncovered ... Is 20:4 8357

BUY {56}
Egypt to Joseph for to b corn ... Gen 41:57 7666
thither, and b for us from thence ... Gen 42:2 7666
went down to b corn in Egypt ... Gen 42:3 7666
to b corn among those that came ... Gen 42:5 7666
From the land of Canaan to b food ... Gen 42:7 7666
but to b food are thy servants ... Gen 42:10 7666
Go again, b us a little food ... Gen 43:2 7666
we will go down and b thee food ... Gen 43:4 7666
down at the first time to b food ... Gen 43:20 7666
down in our hands to b food ... Gen 43:22 7666
Go again, and b us a little food ... Gen 44:25 7666
b us and our land for bread, and we ... Gen 47:19 7069
If thou b an Hebrew servant, six ... Ex 21:2 7069
But if the priest b any soul with ... Lev 22:11 7069
thou shalt b of thy neighbour ... Lev 25:15 7069
of them shall ye b bondmen ... Lev 25:44 7069
among you, of them shall ye b ... Lev 25:45 7069
Ye shall b meat of them for money ... Deut 2:6 7666
ye shall also b water of them for ... Deut 2:6 3739
bondwomen, and no man shall b you ... Deut 28:68 7069
B it before the inhabitants, and ... Ruth 4:4 7069
thou must b it also of Ruth the ... Ruth 4:5 7069
said unto Boaz, B it for thee ... Ruth 4:8 7069
To b the threshingfloor of thee, ... 2Sa 24:21 7069
but I will surely b it of thee at ... 2Sa 24:24 7069
to b timber and hewed stone to ... 2Kin 12:12 7069
to b timber and hewn stone to ... 2Kin 22:6 7069
but I will verily b it for the ... 1Chr 21:24 7069
to b hewn stone, and timber for ... 2Chr 34:11 7069
That thou mayest b speedily with ... Ezr 7:17 7066
and houses, that we might b corn ... Neh 5:3 3947
that we would not b it of them on ... Neh 10:31 3947
B the truth, and sell it not ... Prov 23:23 7069
come ye, b, and eat ... Is 55:1 7666
b wine and milk without money and ... Is 55:1 7666
B thee my field that is in ... Jer 32:7 7069
of redemption is thine to b it ... Jer 32:7 7069
B my field, I pray thee, that is ... Jer 32:8 7069
b it for thyself ... Jer 32:8 7069
B thee the field for money, and ... Jer 32:25 7069
Men shall b fields for money, and ... Jer 32:44 7069
That we may b the poor for silver ... Amos 8:6 7069
and b themselves victuals ... Mt 14:15 59
that sell, and b for yourselves ... Mt 25:9 59
And while they went to b, the ... Mt 25:10 59
villages, and b themselves bread ... Mk 6:36 59
b two hundred pennyworth of bread ... Mk 6:37 59
b meat for all this people ... Lk 9:13 59
him sell his garment, and b one ... Lk 22:36 59
gone away unto the city to b meat ... Jn 4:8 59
Philip, Whence shall we b bread ... Jn 6:5 59
B those things that we have need ... Jn 13:29 59
and they that b, as though they ... 1Cor 7:30 59
and continue there a year, and b ... Jas 4:13 1710
I counsel thee to b of me gold ... Rev 3:18 59
And that no man might b or sell ... Rev 13:17 59

BUYER {3}
naught, it is naught, saith the b ... Prov 20:14 7069
as with the b, so with the seller ... Is 24:2 7069
let not the b rejoice, nor the ... Eze 7:12 7069

BUYEST {2}
or b ought of thy neighbour's ... Lev 25:14 7069
What day thou b the field of the ... Ruth 4:5 7069

BUYETH {3}
She considereth a field, and b it ... Prov 31:16 3947
all that he hath, and b that field ... Mt 13:44 59
for no man b their merchandise ... Rev 18:11 59

BUZ *(buz)* {3}
1. Son of Nahor.
B his brother, and Kemuel the ... Gen 22:21 938
2. A Gadite.
the son of Jahdo, the son of B ... 1Chr 5:14 938
3. A tribe in northern Arabia.
Dedan, and Tema, and B, and all that ... Jer 25:23 938

BUZI *(boo'-zi)* {1} See BUZITE. *Father of Ezekiel.*
Ezekiel the priest, the son of B ... Eze 1:3 941

BUZITE *(boo'-zite)* {2} *A member of Buz 3.*
Elihu the son of Barachel the B ... Job 32:2 940
son of Barachel the B answered ... Job 32:6 940

BY See APPENDIX.

BYWAYS {1}
the travellers walked through b ... Judg 5:6 734,6128

BYWORD {6}
astonishment, a proverb, and a b ... Deut 28:37 8148
a proverb and a b among all people ... 1Kin 9:7 8148
proverb and a b among all nations ... 2Chr 7:20 8148
made me also a b of the people ... Job 17:6 4914
I their song, yea, I am their b ... Job 30:9 4405
Thou makest us a b among the ... Ps 44:14 4912

C

CAB {1}
the fourth part of a c of dove's ... 2Kin 6:25 6894

CABBON *(cab'-bon)* {1} *A town in Judah.*
And C, and Lahmam, and Kithlish, ... Josh 15:40 3522

CABINS {1}
into the dungeon, and into the c ... Jer 37:16 2588

CABUL *(ca'-bul)* {2} *A town in Asher.*
goeth out to C on the left hand, ... Josh 19:27 3521
them the land of C unto this day ... 1Kin 9:13 3521

CAESAR *(se'-zur)* {21} See CAESAR'S. *Title for the Roman Emperor.*
it lawful to give tribute unto C ... Mt 22:17 2541
Render therefore unto C the ... Mt 22:21 2541
Is it lawful to give tribute to C ... Mk 12:14 2541
Render to C the things that are ... Mk 12:17 2541
went out a decree from C Augustus ... Lk 2:1 2541
year of the reign of Tiberius C ... Lk 3:1 2541
for us to give tribute unto C ... Lk 20:22 2541
Render therefore unto C the ... Lk 20:25 2541
forbidding to give tribute to C ... Lk 23:2 2541
himself a king speaketh against C ... Jn 19:12 2541
answered, We have no king but C ... Jn 19:15 2541
to pass in the days of Claudius C ... Acts 11:28 2541
do contrary to the decrees of C ... Acts 17:7 2541
the temple, nor yet against C ... Acts 25:8 2541
I appeal unto C ... Acts 25:11 2541
Hast thou appealed unto C ... Acts 25:12 2541
unto C shalt thou go ... Acts 25:12 2541
kept till I might send him to C ... Acts 25:21 2541
if he had not appealed unto C ... Acts 26:32 2541
thou must be brought before C ... Acts 27:24 2541
was constrained to appeal unto C ... Acts 28:19 2541

CAESAREA *(ses-a-re'-ah)* {17}
1. A town north of Galilee.
into the coasts of C Philippi ... Mt 16:13 2542
into the towns of C Philippi ... Mk 8:27 2542
2. A Judean Mediterranean port.
all the cities, till he came to C ... Acts 8:40 2542
knew, they brought him down to C ... Acts 9:30 2542
certain man in C called Cornelius ... Acts 10:1 2542
morrow after they entered into C ... Acts 10:24 2542
where I was, sent from C unto me ... Acts 11:11 2542
And he went down from Judaea to C ... Acts 12:19 2542
And when he had landed at C ... Acts 18:22 2542
company departed, and came unto C ... Acts 21:8 2542
certain of the disciples of C ... Acts 21:16 2542
two hundred soldiers to go to C ... Acts 23:23 2542
Who, when they came to C, and ... Acts 23:33 2542
he ascended from C to Jerusalem ... Acts 25:1 2542
that Paul should be kept at C ... Acts 25:4 2542
ten days, he went down unto C ... Acts 25:6 2542
came unto C to salute Festus ... Acts 25:13 2542

CAESAR'S *(se'-zurs)* {9}
They say unto him, C ... Mt 22:21 2541
Caesar the things which are C ... Mt 22:21 2541
And they said unto him, C ... Mk 12:16 2541
to Caesar the things that are C ... Mk 12:17 2541
They answered and said, C ... Lk 20:24 2541
unto Caesar the things which be C ... Lk 20:25 2541
man go, thou art not C friend ... Jn 19:12 2541
I stand at C judgment seat, where ... Acts 25:10 2541
they that are of C household ... Phil 4:22 2541

CAGE {2}
As a c is full of birds, so are ... Jer 5:27 3619
a c of every unclean and hateful ... Rev 18:2 5438

CAIAPHAS *(cah'-ya-fus)* {9} *A High Priest during Jesus' time.*
the high priest, who was called C ... Mt 26:3 2533
led him away to C the high priest ... Mt 26:57 2533
C being the high priests, the ... Lk 3:2 2533
And one of them, named C, being ... Jn 11:49 2533
for he was father in law to C ... Jn 18:13 2533
Now C was he, which gave counsel ... Jn 18:14 2533
him bound unto C the high priest ... Jn 18:24 2533
Then led they Jesus from C unto ... Jn 18:28 2533
And Annas the high priest, and C ... Acts 4:6 2533

CAIN {20} See TUBAL-CAIN.
1. Eldest son of Adam and Eve.
and she conceived, and bare C ... Gen 4:1 7014
but C was a tiller of the ground ... Gen 4:2 7014
that C brought of the fruit of ... Gen 4:3 7014
But unto C and to his offering he ... Gen 4:5 7014
And C was very wroth, and his ... Gen 4:5 7014
And the LORD said unto C, Why art ... Gen 4:6 7014
C talked with Abel his brother ... Gen 4:8 7014
that C rose up against Abel his ... Gen 4:8 7014
And the LORD said unto C, Where is ... Gen 4:9 7014
And C said unto the LORD, My ... Gen 4:13 7014
Therefore whosoever slayeth C ... Gen 4:15 7014
And the LORD set a mark upon C ... Gen 4:15 7014
C went out from the presence of ... Gen 4:16 7014
And C knew his wife ... Gen 4:17 7014
If C shall be avenged sevenfold, ... Gen 4:24 7014
seed instead of Abel, whom C slew ... Gen 4:25 7014
a more excellent sacrifice than C ... Heb 11:4 2535
Not as C, who was of that wicked ... 1Jn 3:12 2535
they have gone in the way of C ... Jude 11 2535
2. A town in Judah.
C, Gibeah, and Timnah ... Josh 15:57 7014

CAINAN *(ca'-nun)* {7} See KENAN. *Son of Enos.*
lived ninety years, and begat C ... Gen 5:9 7018
after he begat C eight hundred ... Gen 5:10 7018
C lived seventy years, and begat ... Gen 5:12 7018
C lived after he begat Mahalaleel ... Gen 5:13 7018
all the days of C were nine ... Gen 5:14 7018
Which was the son of C, which was ... Lk 3:36 2536
Maleleel, which was the son of C ... Lk 3:37 2536

CAKE {13}
one c of oiled bread, and one ... Ex 29:23 2471
LORD, he took one unleavened c ... Lev 8:26 2471
a c of oiled bread, and one wafer, ... Lev 8:26 2471
two tenth deals shall be in one c ... Lev 24:5 2471
one unleavened c out of the ... Num 6:19 2471
Ye shall offer up a c of the ... Num 15:20 2471
a c of barley bread tumbled into ... Judg 7:13 6742
gave him a piece of a c of figs ... 1Sa 30:12 1690
as men, to every one a c of bread ... 2Sa 6:19 2471
thy God liveth, I have not a c ... 1Kin 17:12 4580
make me thereof a little c first ... 1Kin 17:13 5692
there was a c baken on the coals, ... 1Kin 19:6 5692
Ephraim is a c not turned ... Hos 7:8 5692

CAKES {25}
it, and make c upon the hearth ... Gen 18:6 5692
they baked unleavened c of the ... Ex 12:39 5692
c unleavened tempered with oil, ... Ex 29:2 2471
it shall be unleavened c of fine ... Lev 2:4 2471
unleavened c mingled with oil ... Lev 7:12 2471
c mingled with oil, of fine flour ... Lev 7:12 2471
Besides the c, he shall offer for ... Lev 7:13 2471
flour, and bake twelve c thereof ... Lev 24:5 2471
c of fine flour mingled with oil, ... Num 6:15 2471
baked it in pans, and made c of it ... Num 11:8 5692
after the passover, unleavened c ... Josh 5:11 4682
unleavened c of an ephah of flour ... Judg 6:19 4682
the flesh and the unleavened c ... Judg 6:20 4682
the flesh and the unleavened c ... Judg 6:21 4682
the flesh and the unleavened c ... Judg 6:21 2471
raisins, and two hundred c of figs ... 1Sa 25:18 1690
make me a couple of c in my sight ... 2Sa 13:6 3834
made c in his sight, and did bake ... 2Sa 13:8 3823
in his sight, and did bake the c ... 2Sa 13:8 3834
Tamar took the c which she had ... 2Sa 13:10 3834
c of figs, and bunches of raisins, ... 1Chr 12:40 1690
offering, and for the unleavened c ... 1Chr 23:29 7550
to make c to the queen of heaven, ... Jer 7:18 3561
did we make her c to worship her ... Jer 44:19 3561
And thou shalt eat it as barley c ... Eze 4:12 5692

CALAH *(ca'-lah)* {3} *An Assyrian city.*
and the city Rehoboth, and C ... Gen 10:11 3625
And Resen between Nineveh and C ... Gen 10:12 3625

CALAMITIES {3}
refuge, until these c be overpast ... Ps 57:1 1942
prayer also shall be in their c ... Ps 141:5 7451
he that is glad at c shall not be ... Prov 17:5 343

CALAMITY {19}
for the day of their c is at hand ... Deut 32:35 343
prevented me in the day of my c ... 2Sa 22:19 343
my c laid in the balances ... Job 6:2 1942
my path, they set forward my c ... Job 30:13 1942
prevented me in the day of my c ... Ps 18:18 343
I also will laugh at your c ... Prov 1:26 343
shall his c come suddenly ... Prov 6:15 343
son is the c of his father ... Prov 19:13 1942
For their c shall rise suddenly ... Prov 24:22 343
house in the day of thy c ... Prov 27:10 343
the face, in the day of their c ... Jer 18:17 343
day of their c was come upon them ... Jer 46:21 343
The c of Moab is near to come, and ... Jer 48:16 343
will bring the c of Esau upon him ... Jer 49:8 343
I will bring their c from all ... Jer 49:32 343
the sword in the time of their c ... Eze 35:5 343
my people in the day of their c ... Obad 13 343
affliction in the day of their c ... Obad 13 343
substance in the day of their c ... Obad 13 343

CALAMUS {3}
of sweet c two hundred and fifty ... Ex 30:23 7070
c and cinnamon, with all trees of ... Song 4:14 7070
bright iron, cassia, and c ... Eze 27:19 7070

CALCOL *(cal'-col)* {1} See CHALCOL. *A son of Zerah.*
Zimri, and Ethan, and Heman, and C ... 1Chr 2:6 3633

CALDRON {6}
it into the pan, or kettle, or c ... 1Sa 2:14 7037
as out of a seething pot or c ... Job 41:20 100
this city is the c, and we be the ... Eze 11:3 5518
the flesh, and this city is the c ... Eze 11:7 5518
This city shall not be your c ... Eze 11:11 5518
the pot, and as flesh within the c ... Mic 3:3 7037

CALDRONS {3}
sod they in pots, and in c ... 2Chr 35:13 1731
The c also, and the shovels, and ... Jer 52:18 5518
firepans, and the bowls, and the c ... Jer 52:19 5518

CALEB *(ca'-leb)* {32} See CALEB'S, CALEB-EPHRATAH, CHELUBAI.
1. A son of Jephunneh.
of Judah, C the son of Jephunneh ... Num 13:6 3612
C stilled the people before Moses ... Num 13:30 3612
C the son of Jephunneh, which ... Num 14:6 3612
But my servant C, because he had ... Num 14:24 3612
save C the son of Jephunneh, and ... Num 14:30 3612
C the son of Jephunneh, which ... Num 14:38 3612
save C the son of Jephunneh, and ... Num 26:65 3612
Save C the son of Jephunneh the ... Num 32:12 3612
of Judah, C the son of Jephunneh ... Num 34:19 3612
Save C the son of Jephunneh ... Deut 1:36 3612
C the son of Jephunneh the ... Josh 14:6 3612
gave unto C the son of Jephunneh ... Josh 14:13 3612
of C the son of Jephunneh the ... Josh 14:14 3612
unto C the son of Jephunneh he ... Josh 15:13 3612
C drove thence the three sons of ... Josh 15:14 3612
And C said, He that smiteth ... Josh 15:16 3612
son of Kenaz, the brother of C ... Josh 15:17 3612
C said unto her, What wouldest ... Josh 15:18 3612
gave they to C the son of ... Josh 21:12 3612
And C said, He that smiteth ... Judg 1:12 3612
C said unto her, What wilt thou ... Judg 1:14 3612
C gave her the upper springs and ... Judg 1:15 3612
And they gave Hebron unto C ... Judg 1:20 3612
and he was of the house of C ... 1Sa 25:3 3612
to Judah, and upon the south of C ... 1Sa 30:14 3612
and the daughter of C was Achsa ... 1Chr 2:49 3612
And the sons of C the son of ... 1Chr 4:15 3612
they gave to C the son of ... 1Chr 6:56 3612
2. A son of Hezron.
C the son of Hezron begat ... 1Chr 2:18 3612
C took unto him Ephrath, which ... 1Chr 2:19 3612
Now the sons of C the brother of ... 1Chr 2:42 3612
3. A son of Hur.
were the sons of C the son of Hur ... 1Chr 2:50 3612

CALEB-EPHRATAH *(ca'-leb-ef'-ra-tah)* {1} *The place where Hezron died.*
after that Hezron was dead in C ... 1Chr 2:24 3613

CALEB-EPHRATHAH See CALEB-EPHRATAH.

CALEB'S *(ca'-lebs)* {4} *Refers to Caleb 1.*
C younger brother, took it ... Judg 1:13 3612
son of Kenaz, C younger brother ... Judg 3:9 3612
C concubine, bare Haran, and Moza, ... 1Chr 2:46 3612
C concubine, bare Sheber, and ... 1Chr 2:48 3612

CALF {29}
the herd, and fetcht a c tender ... Gen 18:7 1121,1241
the c which he had dressed, and ... Gen 18:8 1121,1241
after he had made it a molten c ... Ex 32:4 5695
they have made them a molten c ... Ex 32:8 5695
unto the camp, that he saw the c ... Ex 32:19 5695
he took the c which they had made ... Ex 32:20 5695
fire, and there came out this c ... Ex 32:24 5695
people, because they made the c ... Ex 32:35 5695
Take thee a young c for a sin ... Lev 9:2 5695
and a c and a lamb, both of the ... Lev 9:3 5695
slew the c of the sin offering, ... Lev 9:8 5695
God, and had made you a molten c ... Deut 9:16 5695
the c which ye had made, and burnt ... Deut 9:21 5695
woman had a fat c in the house ... 1Sa 28:24 5695
they had made them a molten c ... Neh 9:18 5695
cow calveth, and casteth not her c ... Job 21:10
maketh them also to skip like a c ... Ps 29:6 5695
They made a c in Horeb, and ... Ps 106:19 5695
and the c and the young lion and the ... Is 11:6 5695
there shall the c feed, and there ... Is 27:10 5695
me, when they cut the c in twain ... Jer 34:18 5695
passed between the parts of the c ... Jer 34:19 5695
Thy c, O Samaria, hath cast thee ... Hos 8:5 5695
but the c of Samaria shall be ... Hos 8:6 5695
And bring hither the fatted c ... Lk 15:23 *3448*
father hath killed the fatted c ... Lk 15:27 *3448*
hast killed for him the fatted c ... Lk 15:30 *3448*
they made a c in those days, and ... Acts 7:41 *3447*
and the second beast like a c ... Rev 4:7 *3448*

CALF'S {1}
was like the sole of a c foot ... Eze 1:7 5695

CALKERS {2}
men thereof were in thee thy c ... Eze 27:9 2388,919
mariners, and thy pilots, thy c ... Eze 27:27 2388,919

CALL {196}
Adam to see what he would c them ... Gen 2:19 7121
then began men to c upon the name ... Gen 4:26 7121
son, and shalt c his name Ishmael ... Gen 16:11 7121
thou shalt not c her name Sarai ... Gen 17:15 7121
thou shalt c his name Isaac ... Gen 17:19 7121
We will c the damsel, and enquire ... Gen 24:57 7121
the daughters will c me blessed ... Gen 30:13 833
to pass, when Pharaoh shall c you ... Gen 46:33 7121
c to thee a nurse of the Hebrew ... Ex 2:7 7121
c him, that he may eat bread ... Ex 2:20 7121
one c thee, and thou eat of his ... Ex 34:15 7121
And Moses sent to c Dathan ... Num 16:12 7121
to c him, saying, Behold, there ... Num 22:5 7121
him, If the men come to c thee ... Num 22:20 7121
send unto thee to c thee ... Num 22:37 7121
but the Moabites c them Emims ... Deut 2:11 7121
the Ammonites c them Zamzummims ... Deut 2:20 7121
Hermon the Sidonians c Sirion ... Deut 3:9 7121
and the Amorites c it Shenir ... Deut 3:9 7121
all things that we c upon him for ... Deut 4:7 7121
I c heaven and earth to witness ... Deut 4:26 5749
elders of his city shall c him ... Deut 25:8 7121
thou shalt c them to mind among ... Deut 30:1 7725
I c heaven and earth to record ... Deut 30:19 5749
c Joshua, and present yourselves ... Deut 31:14 7121
c heaven and earth to record ... Deut 31:28 5749
They shall c the people unto the ... Deut 33:19 7121
didst not c us to go with thee ... Judg 12:1 7121
C for Samson, that he may make us ... Judg 16:25 7121
and to c peaceably unto them ... Judg 21:13 7121
C me not Naomi, c me Mara ... Ruth 1:20 7121
why then c ye me Naomi, seeing ... Ruth 1:21 7121
for thou didst c me ... 1Sa 3:6 7121
for thou didst c me ... 1Sa 3:8 7121
and it shall be, if he c thee ... 1Sa 3:9 7121
I will c unto the LORD, and he ... 1Sa 12:17 7121
c Jesse to the sacrifice, and I ... 1Sa 16:3 7121
sent to c Ahimelech the priest ... 1Sa 22:11 7121
C now Hushai the Archite also, and ... 2Sa 17:5 7121
I will c on the LORD, who is ... 2Sa 22:4 7121
answered and said, C me Bath-sheba ... 1Kin 1:28 7121
C me Zadok the priest, and Nathan ... 1Kin 1:32 7121
in all that they c for unto thee ... 1Kin 8:52 7121
me to c my sin to remembrance ... 1Kin 17:18 2142
c ye on the name of your gods, and ... 1Kin 18:24 7121
I will c on the name of the LORD ... 1Kin 18:24 7121
c on the name of your gods, but ... 1Kin 18:25 7121
gone to c Micaiah spake unto him ... 1Kin 22:13 7121
his servant, C this Shunammite ... 2Kin 4:12 7121
And he said, C her ... 2Kin 4:15 7121
and said, C this Shunammite ... 2Kin 4:36 7121
c on the name of the LORD his God ... 2Kin 5:11 7121
Now therefore c unto me all the ... 2Kin 10:19 7121
c upon his name, make known his ... 1Chr 16:8 7121
went to c Micaiah spake to him ... 2Chr 18:12 7121
C now, if there be any that will ... Job 5:1 7121
Then c thou, and I will answer ... Job 13:22 7121
Thou shalt c, and I will answer ... Job 14:15 7121
will he always c upon God ... Job 27:10 7121
Hear me when I c, O God of my ... Ps 4:1 7121
LORD will hear when I c unto him ... Ps 4:3 7121
eat bread, and c not upon the LORD ... Ps 14:4 7121
I will c upon the LORD, who is ... Ps 18:3 7121
let the king hear us when we c ... Ps 20:9 7121
they c their lands after their ... Ps 49:11 7121
He shall c to the heavens from ... Ps 50:4 7121
c upon me in the day of trouble ... Ps 50:15 7121
As for me, I will c upon God ... Ps 55:16 7121
all nations shall c him blessed ... Ps 72:17 833
I c to remembrance my song in the ... Ps 77:6 2142
us, and we will c upon thy name ... Ps 80:18 7121
unto all them that c upon thee ... Ps 86:5 7121
of my trouble I will c upon thee ... Ps 86:7 7121
He shall c upon me, and I will ... Ps 91:15 7121
among them that c upon his name ... Ps 99:6 7121
in the day when I c answer me ... Ps 102:2 7121
c upon his name ... Ps 105:1 7121
therefore will I c upon him as ... Ps 116:2 7121
c upon the name of the LORD ... Ps 116:13 7121
will c upon the name of the LORD ... Ps 116:17 7121
unto all them that c upon him ... Ps 145:18 7121
to all that c upon him in truth ... Ps 145:18 7121
Then shall they c upon me ... Prov 1:28 7121
c understanding thy kinswoman ... Prov 7:4 7121
Unto you, O men, I c ... Prov 8:4 7121
To c passengers who go right on ... Prov 9:15 7121
arise up, and c her blessed ... Prov 31:28 833
Woe unto them that c evil good ... Is 5:20 559
shall c his name Immanuel ... Is 7:14 7121
C his name Maher-shalal-hash-baz ... Is 8:3 7121
c upon his name, declare his ... Is 12:4 7121
Lord GOD of hosts c to weeping ... Is 22:12 7121
that I will c my servant Eliakim ... Is 22:20 7121
will not c back his words ... Is 31:2 5493
They shall c the nobles thereof ... Is 34:12 7121
the sun shall he c upon my name ... Is 41:25 7121
another shall c himself by the ... Is 44:5 7121
And who, as I, shall c, and shall ... Is 44:7 7121
which c thee by thy name, am the ... Is 45:3 7121
For they c themselves of the holy ... Is 48:2 7121
when I c unto them, they stand up ... Is 48:13 7121
thou shalt c a nation that thou ... Is 55:5 7121
c ye upon him while he is near ... Is 55:6 7121
wilt thou c this a fast, and an ... Is 58:5 7121
Then shalt thou c, and the LORD ... Is 58:9 7121
c the sabbath a delight, the holy ... Is 58:13 7121
and they shall c thee, The city of ... Is 60:14 7121
but thou shalt c thy walls ... Is 60:18 7121
shall c you the Ministers of our ... Is 61:6 7121
And they shall c them, The holy ... Is 62:12 7121
c his servants by another name ... Is 65:15 7121
come to pass, that before they c ... Is 65:24 7121
I will c all the families of the ... Jer 1:15 7121
At that time they shall c ... Jer 3:17 7121
and I said, Thou shalt c me ... Jer 3:19 7121
Reprobate silver shall men c them ... Jer 6:30 7121
thou shalt also c unto them ... Jer 7:27 7121
c for the mourning women, that ... Jer 9:17 7121
families that c not on thy name ... Jer 10:25 7121
for I will c for a sword upon all ... Jer 25:29 7121
Then shall ye c upon me, and ye ... Jer 29:12 7121
C unto me, and I will answer thee, ... Jer 33:3 7121
C together the archers against ... Jer 50:29 8085
c together against her the ... Jer 51:27 8085
men c The perfection of beauty ... Lam 2:15 559
but he will c to remembrance the ... Eze 21:23 2142
I will c for the corn, and will ... Eze 36:29 7121
I will c for a sword against him ... Eze 38:21 7121
they shall c it The valley of ... Eze 39:11 7121
king commanded to c the magicians ... Dan 2:2 7121
said unto him, C his name Jezreel ... Hos 1:4 7121
unto him, C her name Lo-ruhamah ... Hos 1:6 7121
Then said God, C his name Lo-ammi ... Hos 1:9 7121
LORD, that thou shalt c me Ishi ... Hos 2:16 7121
and shalt c me no more Baali ... Hos 2:16 7121
they c to Egypt, they go to ... Hos 7:11 7121
c a solemn assembly, gather the ... Joel 1:14 7121
a fast, c a solemn assembly ... Joel 2:15 7121
that whosoever shall c on the ... Joel 2:32 7121
the remnant whom the LORD shall c ... Joel 2:32 7121
they shall c the husbandman to ... Amos 5:16 7121
c upon thy God, if so be that God ... Jonah 1:6 7121
that they may all c upon the name ... Zeph 3:9 7121
hosts, shall ye c every man his ... Zec 3:10 7121
they shall c on my name, and I ... Zec 13:9 7121
and they shall c them, The border ... Mal 1:4 7121
all nations shall c you blessed ... Mal 3:12 833
And now we c the proud happy ... Mal 3:15 833
thou shalt c his name JESUS ... Mt 1:21 *2564*
they shall c his name Emmanuel, ... Mt 1:23 *2564*
I am not come to c the righteous ... Mt 9:13 *2564*
they c them of his household ... Mt 10:25 *2564*
C the labourers, and give them ... Mt 20:8 *2564*
sent forth his servants to c them ... Mt 22:3 *2564*
doth David in spirit c him Lord ... Mt 22:43 *2564*
If David then c him Lord ... Mt 22:45 *2564*
c no man your father upon the ... Mt 23:9 *2564*
I came not to c the righteous ... Mk 2:17 *2564*
they c the blind man, saying unto ... Mk 10:49 *5455*
whom ye c the King of the Jews ... Mk 15:12 *3004*
they c together the whole band ... Mk 15:16 *4779*
thou shalt c his name John ... Lk 1:13 *2564*
a son, and shalt c his name JESUS ... Lk 1:31 *2564*
generations shall c me blessed ... Lk 1:48 *3106*
I came not to c the righteous ... Lk 5:32 *2564*
why c ye me, Lord, Lord, and do ... Lk 6:46 *2564*
c not thy friends, nor thy ... Lk 14:12 *5455*
c the poor, the maimed, the lame, ... Lk 14:13 *2564*
c thy husband, and come hither ... Jn 4:16 *5455*
Ye c me Master and Lord ... Jn 13:13 *5455*
Henceforth I c you not servants ... Jn 15:15 *3004*
that whosoever shall c on the ... Acts 2:21 *1941*
many as the Lord our God shall c ... Acts 2:39 *4341*
to bind all that c on thy name ... Acts 9:14 *1941*
c for one Simon, whose surname is ... Acts 10:5 *3343*
cleansed, that c not thou common ... Acts 10:15 *2840*
not c any man common or unclean ... Acts 10:28 *3004*
c hither Simon, whose surname is ... Acts 10:32 *3333*
cleansed, that c not thou common ... Acts 11:9 *2840*
c for Simon, whose surname is ... Acts 11:13 *3343*
took upon them to c over them ... Acts 19:13 *3687*
after the way which they c heresy ... Acts 24:14 *3004*
season, I will c for thee ... Acts 24:25 *3333*
I will c them my people, which ... Rom 9:25 *2564*
is rich unto all that c upon him ... Rom 10:12 *1941*
For whosoever shall c upon the ... Rom 10:13 *1941*
How then shall they c on him in ... Rom 10:14 *1941*
with all that in every place c ... 1Cor 1:2 *1941*
Moreover I c God for a record ... 2Cor 1:23 *1941*
When I c to remembrance the ... 2Ti 1:5 *2983*
with them that c on the Lord out ... 2Ti 2:22 *1941*
is not ashamed to c them brethren ... Heb 2:11 *2564*
But c to remembrance the former ... Heb 10:32 *363*
let him c for the elders of the ... Jas 5:14 *4341*
if ye c on the Father, who ... 1Pet 1:17 *1941*

CALLED {624}
God c the light Day, and the ... Gen 1:5 7121
Day, and the darkness he c Night ... Gen 1:5 7121
God c the firmament Heaven ... Gen 1:8 7121
And God c the dry land Earth ... Gen 1:10 7121
together of the waters c he Seas ... Gen 1:10 7121
whatsoever Adam c every living ... Gen 2:19 7121
she shall be c Woman, because she ... Gen 2:23 7121
And the LORD God c unto Adam ... Gen 3:9 7121
Adam c his wife's name Eve ... Gen 3:20 7121
c the name of the city, after the ... Gen 4:17 7121
bare a son, and c his name Seth ... Gen 4:25 7121
and he c his name Enos ... Gen 4:26 7121
c their name Adam, in the day ... Gen 5:2 7121
and c his name Seth ... Gen 5:3 7121
he c his name Noah, saying, This ... Gen 5:29 7121
is the name of it c Babel ... Gen 11:9 7121
c upon the name of the LORD ... Gen 12:8 7121
And Pharaoh c Abram, and said, ... Gen 12:18 7121
there Abram c on the name of the ... Gen 13:4 7121
she c the name of the LORD that ... Gen 16:13 7121
the well was c Beer-lahai-roi ... Gen 16:14 7121
Abram c his son's name, which ... Gen 16:15 7121
thy name any more be c Abram ... Gen 17:5 7121
they c unto Lot, and said unto him ... Gen 19:5 7121
the name of the city was c Zoar ... Gen 19:22 7121
bare a son, and c his name Moab ... Gen 19:37 7121
a son, and c his name Ben-ammi ... Gen 19:38 7121
c all his servants, and told all ... Gen 20:8 7121
Then Abimelech c Abraham, and said ... Gen 20:9 7121
Abraham c the name of his son ... Gen 21:3 7121
for in Isaac shall thy seed be c ... Gen 21:12 7121

C

the angel of God c to Hagar out	Gen 21:17	7121
Wherefore he c that place	Gen 21:31	7121
c there on the name of the LORD,	Gen 21:33	7121
the angel of the LORD c unto him	Gen 22:11	7121
Abraham c the name of that place	Gen 22:14	7121
the angel of the LORD c unto	Gen 22:15	7121
they c Rebekah, and said unto her,	Gen 24:58	7121
and they c his name Esau	Gen 25:25	7121
and his name was c Jacob	Gen 25:26	7121
therefore was his name c Edom	Gen 25:30	7121
And Abimelech c Isaac, and said,	Gen 26:9	7121
he c their names after the names	Gen 26:18	7121
by which his father had c them	Gen 26:18	7121
he c the name of the well Esek	Gen 26:20	7121
he c the name of it Sitnah	Gen 26:21	7121
he c the name of it Rehoboth	Gen 26:22	7121
c upon the name of the LORD, and	Gen 26:25	7121
And he c it Shebah	Gen 26:33	7121
he c Esau his eldest son, and said	Gen 27:1	7121
c Jacob her younger son, and said	Gen 27:42	7121
And Isaac c Jacob, and blessed him,	Gen 28:1	7121
he c the name of that place	Gen 28:19	7121
that city was c Luz at the first	Gen 28:19	
a son, and she c his name Reuben	Gen 29:32	7121
and she c his name Simeon	Gen 29:33	7121
therefore was his name c Levi	Gen 29:34	7121
therefore she c his name Judah	Gen 29:35	7121
therefore c she his name Dan	Gen 30:6	7121
and she c his name Naphtali	Gen 30:8	7121
and she c his name Gad	Gen 30:11	7121
and she c his name Asher	Gen 30:13	7121
and she c his name Issachar	Gen 30:18	7121
and she c his name Zebulun	Gen 30:20	7121
a daughter, and c her name Dinah	Gen 30:21	7121
And she c his name Joseph	Gen 30:24	7121
c Rachel and Leah to the field	Gen 31:4	7121
Laban c it Jegar-sahadutha	Gen 31:47	7121
but Jacob c it Galeed	Gen 31:47	7121
was the name of it c Galeed	Gen 31:48	7121
c his brethren to eat bread	Gen 31:54	7121
he c the name of that place	Gen 32:2	7121
Thy name shall be c no more Jacob	Gen 32:28	559
Jacob c the name of the place	Gen 32:30	7121
name of the place is c Succoth	Gen 33:17	7121
an altar, and c it El-elohe-Israel	Gen 33:20	7121
altar, and c the place El-beth-el	Gen 35:7	7121
name of it was c Allon-bachuth	Gen 35:8	7121
shall not be c any more Jacob	Gen 35:10	7121
and he c his name Israel	Gen 35:10	7121
Jacob c the name of the place	Gen 35:15	7121
died) that she c his name Ben-oni	Gen 35:18	7121
but his father c him Benjamin	Gen 35:18	7121
and he c his name Er	Gen 38:3	7121
and she c his name Onan	Gen 38:4	7121
and c his name Shelah	Gen 38:5	7121
therefore his name was c Pharez	Gen 38:29	7121
and his name was c Zarah	Gen 38:30	7121
That she c unto the men of her	Gen 39:14	7121
c for all the magicians of Egypt,	Gen 41:8	7121
c Joseph, and they brought him	Gen 41:14	7121
And Pharaoh c Joseph's name	Gen 41:45	7121
And Joseph c the name of the	Gen 41:51	7121
name of the second c he Ephraim	Gen 41:52	7121
he c his son Joseph, and said unto	Gen 47:29	7121
shall be c after the name of	Gen 48:6	7121
Jacob c unto his sons, and said,	Gen 49:1	7121
the name of it was c Abel-mizraim	Gen 50:11	7121
king of Egypt c for the midwives	Ex 1:18	7121
maid went and c the child's mother	Ex 2:8	7121
And she c his name Moses	Ex 2:10	7121
a son, and he c his name Gershom	Ex 2:22	7121
God c unto him out of the midst	Ex 3:4	7121
Then Pharaoh also c the wise men	Ex 7:11	7121
Then Pharaoh c for Moses and Aaron	Ex 8:8	7121
Pharaoh c for Moses and for Aaron,	Ex 8:25	7121
c for Moses and Aaron, and said	Ex 9:27	7121
Then Pharaoh c for Moses and Aaron	Ex 10:16	7121
Pharaoh c unto Moses, and said, Go	Ex 10:24	7121
Then Moses c for all the elders	Ex 12:21	7121
he c for Moses and Aaron by night,	Ex 12:31	7121
the name of it was c Marah	Ex 15:23	7121
the house of Israel c the name	Ex 16:31	7121
he c the name of the place Massah	Ex 17:7	7121
c the name of it Jehovah-nissi	Ex 17:15	7121
the LORD c unto him out of the	Ex 19:3	7121
c for the elders of the people,	Ex 19:7	7121
the LORD c Moses up to the top of	Ex 19:20	7121
the seventh day he c unto Moses	Ex 24:16	7121
I have c by name Bezaleel the son	Ex 31:2	7121
c it the Tabernacle of the	Ex 33:7	7121
And Moses c unto them	Ex 34:31	7121
the LORD hath c by name Bezaleel	Ex 35:30	7121
Moses c Bezaleel and Aholiab, and	Ex 36:2	7121
the LORD c unto Moses, and spake	Lev 1:1	7121
eighth day, that Moses c Aaron	Lev 9:1	7121
Moses c Mishael and Elzaphan, and	Lev 10:4	7121
he c the name of the place	Num 11:3	7121
he c the name of that place	Num 11:34	7121
tabernacle, and c Aaron and Miriam	Num 12:5	7121
Moses c Oshea the son of Nun	Num 13:16	7121
The place was c the brook Eshcol,	Num 13:24	7121
he c the name of the place Hormah	Num 21:3	7121
I c thee to curse mine enemies,	Num 24:10	7121
they c the people unto the	Num 25:2	7121
thereof, and c them Havoth-jair	Num 32:41	7121
c it Nobah, after his own name	Num 32:42	7121
which was c the land of giants	Deut 3:13	7121
c them after his own name,	Deut 3:14	7121

Moses c all Israel, and said unto	Deut 5:1	7121
because it is c the LORD's	Deut 15:2	7121
And his name shall be c in Israel	Deut 25:10	7121
art c by the name of the LORD	Deut 28:10	7121
Moses c unto all Israel, and said	Deut 29:2	7121
Moses c unto Joshua, and said unto	Deut 31:7	7121
Then Joshua c the twelve men,	Josh 4:4	7121
place is c Gilgal unto this day	Josh 5:9	7121
the son of Nun c the priests	Josh 6:6	7121
the name of that place was c	Josh 7:26	7121
c together to pursue after them	Josh 8:16	2199
Joshua c for them, and he spake	Josh 9:22	7121
that Joshua c for all the men of	Josh 10:24	7121
c Leshem, Dan, after the name of	Josh 19:47	7121
Then Joshua c the Reubenites, and	Josh 22:1	7121
children of Gad c the altar Ed	Josh 22:34	7121
Joshua c for all Israel, and for	Josh 23:2	7121
c for the elders of Israel, and	Josh 24:1	7121
c Balaam the son of Beor to curse	Josh 24:9	7121
the name of the city was c Hormah	Judg 1:17	7121
a city, and c the name thereof Luz	Judg 1:26	7121
they c the name of that place	Judg 2:5	7121
c Barak the son of Abinoam out of	Judg 4:6	7121
Barak c Zebulun and Naphtali to	Judg 4:10	2199
the LORD, and c it Jehovah-shalom	Judg 6:24	7121
on that day he c him Jerubbaal	Judg 6:32	7121
a son, whose name he c Abimelech	Judg 8:31	7760
Then he c hastily unto the young	Judg 9:54	7121
which are c Havoth-jair unto this	Judg 10:4	7121
and when I c you, ye delivered me	Judg 12:2	2199
bare a son, and c his name Samson	Judg 13:24	7121
have ye c us to take that we have	Judg 14:15	7121
hand, and c that place Ramath-lehi	Judg 15:17	7121
c on the LORD, and said, Thou hast	Judg 15:18	7121
wherefore he c the name thereof	Judg 15:19	7121
sent and c for the lords of the	Judg 16:18	7121
she c for a man, and she caused	Judg 16:19	7121
they c for Samson out of the	Judg 16:25	7121
Samson c unto the LORD, and said,	Judg 16:28	7121
wherefore they c that place	Judg 18:12	7121
they c the name of the city Dan,	Judg 18:29	7121
and they c his name Obed	Ruth 4:17	7121
c his name Samuel, saying,	1Sa 1:20	7121
That the LORD c Samuel	1Sa 3:4	7121
And he said, I c not	1Sa 3:5	7121
the LORD c yet again, Samuel	1Sa 3:6	7121
And he answered, I c not, my son	1Sa 3:6	7121
the LORD c Samuel again the third	1Sa 3:8	7121
that the LORD had c the child	1Sa 3:8	7121
c as at other times, Samuel,	1Sa 3:10	7121
Then Eli c Samuel, and said,	1Sa 3:16	7121
the Philistines c for the priests	1Sa 6:2	7121
c the name of it Eben-ezer,	1Sa 7:12	7121
for he that is now c a Prophet	1Sa 9:9	
a Prophet was beforetime c a Seer	1Sa 9:9	7121
that Samuel c Saul to the top of	1Sa 9:26	7121
Samuel c the people together unto	1Sa 10:17	6817
So Samuel c unto the LORD	1Sa 12:18	7121
the people were c together after	1Sa 13:4	6817
sons, and c them to the sacrifice	1Sa 16:5	7121
Then Jesse c Abinadab, and made	1Sa 16:8	7121
And Jonathan c David, and Jonathan	1Sa 19:7	7121
Saul c all the people together to	1Sa 23:8	8085
therefore they c that place	1Sa 23:28	7121
therefore I have c thee, that	1Sa 28:15	7121
Then Achish c David, and said unto	1Sa 29:6	7121
him, he saw me, and c unto me	2Sa 1:7	7121
David c one of the young men, and	2Sa 1:15	7121
that place was c Helkath-hazzurim	2Sa 2:16	7121
Then Abner c to Joab, and said,	2Sa 2:26	7121
fort, and c it the city of David	2Sa 5:9	7121
Therefore he c the name of that	2Sa 5:20	7121
whose name is c by the name of	2Sa 6:2	7121
he c the name of the place	2Sa 6:8	7121
when they had c him unto David,	2Sa 9:2	7121
Then the king c to Ziba, Saul's	2Sa 9:9	7121
And when David had c him, he did	2Sa 11:13	7121
a son, and he c his name Solomon	2Sa 12:24	7121
he c his name Jedidiah, because	2Sa 12:25	7121
city, and it be c after my name	2Sa 12:28	7121
Then he c his servant that	2Sa 13:17	7121
and when he had c for Absalom	2Sa 14:33	7121
judgment, then Absalom c unto him	2Sa 15:2	7121
men out of Jerusalem, that were c	2Sa 15:11	7121
he c the pillar after his own	2Sa 18:18	7121
it is c unto this day, Absalom's	2Sa 18:18	7121
the watchman c unto the porter,	2Sa 18:26	7121
And Ahimaaz c, and said unto the	2Sa 18:28	7121
the king c the Gibeonites, and	2Sa 21:2	7121
In my distress I c upon the LORD	2Sa 22:7	7121
c all his brethren the king's	1Kin 1:9	7121
and Solomon his brother, he c not	1Kin 1:10	7121
hath c all the sons of the king,	1Kin 1:19	7121
Solomon thy servant hath he not c	1Kin 1:19	7121
hath c all the king's sons, and	1Kin 1:25	7121
servant Solomon, hath he not c	1Kin 1:26	7121
c for Shimei, and said unto him,	1Kin 2:36	7121
c for Shimei, and said unto him,	1Kin 2:42	7121
c the name thereof Jachin	1Kin 7:21	7121
and c the name thereof Boaz	1Kin 7:21	7121
I have builded, is c by thy name	1Kin 8:43	7121
he c them the land of Cabul unto	1Kin 9:13	7121
That they sent and c him	1Kin 12:3	7121
c him unto the congregation, and	1Kin 12:20	7121
c the name of the city which he	1Kin 16:24	7121
he c to her, and said, Fetch me, I	1Kin 17:10	7121
he c to her, and said, Bring me, I	1Kin 17:11	7121
Ahab c Obadiah, which was the	1Kin 18:3	7121

c on the name of Baal from	1Kin 18:26	7121
Then the king of Israel c all the	1Kin 20:7	7121
the king of Israel c an officer	1Kin 22:9	7121
that the LORD hath c these three	2Kin 3:10	7121
for the LORD hath c these three	2Kin 3:13	7121
And when he had c her, she stood	2Kin 4:12	7121
And when he had c her, she stood	2Kin 4:15	7121
she c unto her husband, and said,	2Kin 4:22	7121
he c Gehazi, and said, Call this	2Kin 4:36	7121
So he c her	2Kin 4:36	7121
he c his servants, and said unto	2Kin 6:11	7121
c unto the porter of the city	2Kin 7:10	7121
And he c the porters	2Kin 7:11	7121
for the LORD hath c for a famine	2Kin 8:1	7121
Elisha the prophet c one of the	2Kin 9:1	7121
Then king Jehoash c for Jehoiada	2Kin 12:7	7121
c the name of it Joktheel unto	2Kin 14:7	7121
and he c it Nehushtan	2Kin 18:4	7121
And when they had c to the king	2Kin 18:18	7121
his mother c his name Jabez,	1Chr 4:9	7121
Jabez c on the God of Israel,	1Chr 4:10	7121
which are c by their names	1Chr 6:65	7121
a son, and she c his name Peresh	1Chr 7:16	7121
he c his name Beriah, because it	1Chr 7:23	7121
therefore they c it the city of	1Chr 11:7	7121
cherubims, whose name is c on it	1Chr 13:6	7121
place is c Perez-uzza to this day	1Chr 13:11	7121
therefore they c the name of that	1Chr 14:11	7121
David c for Zadok and Abiathar the	1Chr 15:11	7121
offerings, and c upon the LORD	1Chr 21:26	7121
Then he c for Solomon his son, and	1Chr 22:6	7121
c the name of that on the right	2Chr 3:17	7121
I have built is c by thy name	2Chr 6:33	7121
which are c by my name, shall	2Chr 7:14	7121
And they sent and c him	2Chr 10:3	7121
the king of Israel c for one of	2Chr 18:8	7121
the name of the same place was c	2Chr 20:26	7121
the king c for Jehoiada the chief	2Chr 24:6	7121
and was c after their name	Ezr 2:61	7121
Then I c the priests, and took an	Neh 5:12	7121
wife, and was c after their name	Neh 7:63	7121
her, and that she were c by name	Est 2:14	7121
c on the thirteenth day of the	Est 3:12	7121
Then c Esther for Hatach, one of	Est 4:5	7121
the inner court, who is not c	Est 4:11	7121
but I have not been c to come in	Est 4:11	7121
c for his friends, and Zeresh his	Est 5:10	935
Then were the king's scribes c at	Est 8:9	7121
Wherefore they c these days Purim	Est 9:26	7121
c for their three sisters to eat	Job 1:4	7121
If I had c, and he had answered me	Job 9:16	7121
I c my servant, and he gave me no	Job 19:16	7121
he c the name of the first,	Job 42:14	7121
I have c upon thee, for thou wilt	Ps 17:6	7121
In my distress I c upon the LORD	Ps 18:6	7121
for I have c upon thee	Ps 31:17	7121
c the earth from the rising of	Ps 50:1	7121
they have not c upon God	Ps 53:4	7121
that have not c upon thy name	Ps 79:6	7121
I have c daily upon thee, I have	Ps 88:9	7121
they c upon the LORD, and he	Ps 99:6	7121
Moreover he c for a famine upon	Ps 105:16	7121
Then c I upon the name of the	Ps 116:4	7121
I c upon the LORD in distress	Ps 118:5	7121
Because I have c, and ye refused	Prov 1:24	7121
wise in heart shall be c prudent	Prov 16:21	7121
shall be c a mischievous person	Prov 24:8	7121
I c him, but he gave me no answer	Song 5:6	7121
afterward thou shalt be c	Is 1:26	7121
only let us be c by thy name	Is 4:1	7121
in Jerusalem, shall be c holy	Is 4:3	559
and his name shall be c Wonderful	Is 9:6	7121
I have also c my mighty ones for	Is 13:3	7121
one shall be c, The city of	Is 19:18	559
shepherds is c forth against him	Is 31:4	7121
person shall be no more c liberal	Is 32:5	7121
it shall be c The way of holiness	Is 35:8	7121
c him to his foot, gave the	Is 41:2	7121
c thee from the chief men thereof	Is 41:9	7121
I the LORD have c thee in	Is 42:6	7121
I have c thee by thy name	Is 43:1	7121
every one that is c by my name	Is 43:7	7121
But thou hast not c upon me	Is 43:22	7121
I have even c thee by thy name	Is 45:4	7121
thou shalt no more be c tender	Is 47:1	7121
for thou shalt no more be c	Is 47:5	7121
which are c by the name of Israel	Is 48:1	7121
wast c a transgressor from the	Is 48:8	7121
unto me, O Jacob and Israel, my c	Is 48:12	7121
yea, I have c him	Is 48:15	7121
The LORD hath c me from the womb	Is 49:1	7121
when I c, was there none to	Is 50:2	7121
for I c him alone, and blessed him	Is 51:2	7121
of the whole earth shall he be c	Is 54:5	7121
For the LORD hath c thee as a	Is 54:6	7121
for mine house shall be c an	Is 56:7	7121
and thou shalt be c, The repairer	Is 58:12	7121
that they might be c trees of	Is 61:3	7121
and thou shalt be c by a new name	Is 62:2	7121
but thou shalt be c Hephzi-bah	Is 62:4	7121
and thou shalt be c, Sought out, A	Is 62:12	7121
they were not c by thy name	Is 63:19	7121
nation that was not c by my name	Is 65:1	7121
because when I c, ye did not	Is 65:12	7121
because when I c, none did answer	Is 66:4	7121
which is c by my name, and say, We	Jer 7:10	7121
which is c by my name, become a	Jer 7:11	7121
I c you, but ye answered not	Jer 7:13	7121

which is c by my name, wherein ye Jer 7:14 7121
the house which is c by my name Jer 7:30 7121
that it shall no more be c Tophet Jer 7:32 559
The LORD c thy name, A green Jer 11:16 7121
they have c a multitude after Jer 12:6 7121
of us, and we are c by thy name Jer 14:9 7121
for I am c by thy name, O LORD Jer 15:16 7121
place shall no more be c Tophet Jer 19:6 7121
LORD hath not c thy name Pashur Jer 20:3 7121
is his name whereby he shall be c Jer 23:6 7121
on the city which is c by my name Jer 25:29 7121
because they c thee an Outcast, Jer 30:17 7121
which is c by my name, to defile Jer 32:34 7121
the name wherewith she shall be c Jer 33:16 7121
the house which is c by my name Jer 34:15 7121
I have c unto them, but they have Jer 35:17 7121
Then Jeremiah c Baruch the son of Jer 36:4 7121
Then c he Johanan the son of Jer 42:8 7121
he hath c an assembly against me Lam 1:15 7121
I c for my lovers, but they Lam 1:19 7121
bring the day that thou hast c Lam 1:21 7121
Thou hast c as in a solemn day my Lam 2:22 7121
I c upon thy name, O LORD, out of Lam 3:55 7121
in the day that I c upon thee Lam 3:57 7121
he c to the man clothed with Eze 9:3 7121
thereof is c Bamah unto this day Eze 20:29 7121
now let Daniel be c, and he will Dan 5:12 7123
the banks of Ulai, which c Dan 8:16 7121
the city which is c by thy name Dan 9:18 7121
and thy people are c by thy name Dan 9:19 7121
whose name was c Belteshazzar Dan 10:1 7121
him, and c my son out of Egypt Hos 11:1 7121
As they c them, so they went from Hos 11:2 7121
though they c them to the most Hos 11:7 7121
the Lord GOD c to contend by fire Amos 7:4 7121
which are c by my name, saith the Amos 9:12 7121
I c for a drought upon the land, Hag 1:11 7121
shall be c a city of truth Zec 8:3 7121
two staves; the one I c Beauty Zec 11:7 7121
Beauty, and the other I c Bands Zec 11:7 7121
was born Jesus, who is c Christ Mt 1:16 *3004*
and he c his name JESUS Mt 1:25 *2564*
he had privily c the wise men Mt 2:7 *2564*
Out of Egypt have I c my son Mt 2:15 *2564*
and dwelt in a city c Nazareth Mt 2:23 *3004*
He shall be c a Nazarene Mt 2:23 *2564*
saw two brethren, Simon c Peter Mt 4:18 *3004*
and he c them Mt 4:21 *2564*
for they shall be c the children Mt 5:9 *2564*
he shall be c the least in the Mt 5:19 *2564*
the same shall be c great in the Mt 5:19 *2564*
when he had c unto him his twelve Mt 10:1 *4341*
The first, Simon, who is c Peter Mt 10:2 *3004*
If they have c the master of the Mt 10:25 *2564*
is not his mother c Mary Mt 13:55 *3004*
he c the multitude, and said unto Mt 15:10 *4341*
Then Jesus c his disciples unto Mt 15:32 *4341*
Jesus c a little child unto him, Mt 18:2 *4341*
his lord, after that he had c him Mt 18:32 *4341*
for many be c, but few chosen Mt 20:16 *2822*
But Jesus c them unto him, and Mt 20:25 *4341*
c them, and said, What will ye Mt 20:32 *5455*
My house shall be c the house of Mt 21:13 *2564*
For many are c, but few are Mt 22:14 *2822*
to be c of men, Rabbi, Rabbi Mt 23:7 *2564*
But be not ye c Rabbi Mt 23:8 *2564*
Neither be ye c masters Mt 23:10 *2564*
who c his own servants, and Mt 25:14 *2564*
high priest, who was c Caiaphas, Mt 26:3 *3004*
c Judas Iscariot, went unto the Mt 26:14 *3004*
them unto a place c Gethsemane Mt 26:36 *3004*
Wherefore that field was c Mt 27:8 *2564*
a notable prisoner, c Barabbas Mt 27:16 *3004*
or Jesus which is c Christ Mt 27:17 *3004*
then with Jesus which is c Christ Mt 27:22 *3004*
were come unto a place c Golgotha Mt 27:33 *3004*
And straightway he c them Mk 1:20 *2564*
he c them unto him, and said unto Mk 3:23 *4341*
he c unto him the twelve, and Mk 6:7 *4341*
when he had c all the people unto Mk 7:14 *4341*
Jesus c his disciples unto him, Mk 8:1 *4341*
when he had c the people unto him Mk 8:34 *4341*
c the twelve, and saith unto them, Mk 9:35 *5455*
But Jesus c them to him, and saith Mk 10:42 *4341*
still, and commanded him to be c Mk 10:49 *5455*
My house shall be c of all Mk 11:17 *2564*
he c unto him his disciples, and Mk 12:43 *4341*
Peter c to mind the word that Mk 14:72 *363*
away into the hall, c Praetorium Mk 15:16 *3739,2076*
shall be c the Son of the Highest Lk 1:32 *2564*
of thee shall be c the Son of God Lk 1:35 *2564*
month with her, who was c barren Lk 1:36 *2564*
they c him Zacharias, after the Lk 1:59 *2564*
but he shall be c John Lk 1:60 *2564*
kindred that is c by this name Lk 1:61 *2564*
father, how he would have him c Lk 1:62 *2564*
shalt be c the prophet of the Lk 1:76 *2564*
of David, which is c Bethlehem Lk 2:4 *2564*
the child, his name was c JESUS Lk 2:21 *2564*
womb shall be c holy to the Lord Lk 2:23 *2564*
he c unto him his disciples Lk 6:13 *4377*
of Alphaeus, and Simon c Zelotes, Lk 6:15 *2564*
that he went into a city c Nain Lk 7:11 *2564*
Mary c Magdalene, out of whom Lk 8:2 *2564*
and took her by the hand, and c Lk 8:54 *5455*
Then he c his twelve disciples Lk 9:1 *4779*
belonging to the city c Bethsaida Lk 9:10 *2564*
And she had a sister c Mary Lk 10:39 *2564*
he c her to him, and said unto her Lk 13:12 *4377*
am no more worthy to be c thy son Lk 15:19 *2564*
am no more worthy to be c thy son Lk 15:21 *2564*
he c one of the servants, and Lk 15:26 *4341*
he c him, and said unto him, How Lk 16:2 *5455*
So he c every one of his lord's Lk 16:5 *4341*
But Jesus c them unto him, and Lk 18:16 *4341*
he c his ten servants, and Lk 19:13 *2564*
these servants to be c unto him Lk 19:15 *5455*
at the mount c the mount of Lk 19:29 *2564*
that is c the mount of Olives Lk 21:37 *2564*
nigh, which is c the Passover Lk 22:1 *3004*
upon them are c benefactors Lk 22:25 *2564*
multitude, and he that was c Judas Lk 22:47 *3004*
when he had c together the chief Lk 23:13 *4779*
to the place, which is c Calvary Lk 23:33 *2564*
same day to a village c Emmaus Lk 24:13 *3686*
thou shalt be c Cephas, which is Jn 1:42 *2564*
him, Before that Philip c thee Jn 1:48 *5455*
And both Jesus was c, and his Jn 2:2 *2564*
of the feast c the bridegroom Jn 2:9 *5455*
of Samaria, which is c Sychar Jn 4:5 *3004*
Messias cometh, which is c Christ Jn 4:25 *3044*
which is c in the Hebrew tongue Jn 5:2 *1951*
A man that is c Jesus made clay, Jn 9:11 *3004*
until they c the parents of him Jn 9:18 *5455*
Then again c they the man that Jn 9:24 *5455*
If he c them gods, unto whom the Jn 10:35 *2036*
said Thomas, which is c Didymus Jn 11:16 *3004*
c Mary her sister secretly, Jn 11:28 *5455*
wilderness, into a city c Ephraim Jn 11:54 *3004*
he c Lazarus out of his grave Jn 12:17 *5455*
but I have c you friends Jn 15:15 *2046*
c Jesus, and said unto him, Art Jn 18:33 *5455*
in a place that is c the Pavement Jn 19:13 *3004*
a place c the place of a skull Jn 19:17 *3004*
which is c in the Hebrew Golgotha Jn 19:17 *3004*
c Didymus, was not with them when Jn 20:24 *3004*
Thomas c Didymus, and Nathanael of Jn 21:2 *3004*
Jerusalem from the mount c Olivet Acts 1:12 *2564*
field is c in their proper tongue Acts 1:19 *2564*
Joseph c Barsabas, who was Acts 1:23 *2564*
the temple which is c Beautiful Acts 3:2 *3004*
in the porch that is c Solomon's Acts 3:11 *2564*
And they c them, and commanded Acts 4:18 *2564*
c the council together, and all Acts 5:21 *4779*
and when they had c the apostles Acts 5:40 *4341*
Then the twelve c the multitude Acts 6:2 *4341*
which is c the synagogue of the Acts 6:9 *3004*
c his father Jacob to him, and all Acts 7:14 *3333*
c Simon, which beforetime in the Acts 8:9 *3686*
the street which is c Straight Acts 9:11 *2564*
the house of Judas for one c Saul Acts 9:11 *3686*
which c on this name in Jerusalem Acts 9:21 *1941*
by interpretation is c Dorcas Acts 9:36 *3004*
up, and when he had c the saints Acts 9:41 *5455*
man in Caesarea c Cornelius Acts 10:1 *3686*
of the band c the Italian band Acts 10:1 *2564*
he c two of his household Acts 10:7 *5455*
And c, and asked whether Simon, Acts 10:18 *5455*
Then c he them in, and lodged them Acts 10:23 *1528*
had c together his kinsmen and Acts 10:24 *4779*
the disciples were c Christians Acts 11:26 *5537*
and Simeon that was c Niger Acts 13:1 *2564*
the work whereunto I have c them Acts 13:2 *4341*
who c for Barnabas and Saul, and Acts 13:7 *4341*
Then Saul, (who also is c Paul Acts 13:9
And they c Barnabas, Jupiter Acts 14:12 *2564*
Gentiles, upon whom my name is c Acts 15:17 *1941*
had c us for to preach the gospel Acts 16:10 *4341*
Then he c for a light, and sprang Acts 16:29 *154*
Whom he c together with the Acts 19:25 *4867*
be c in question for this day's Acts 19:40 *1458*
Paul c unto him the disciples, and Acts 20:1 *4341*
c the elders of the church Acts 20:17 *3333*
of the dead I am c in question Acts 23:6 *2919*
Then Paul c one of the centurions Acts 23:17 *4341*
Paul the prisoner c me unto him Acts 23:18 *4341*
he c unto him two centurions, Acts 23:23 *4341*
And when he was c forth, Tertullus Acts 24:2 *2564*
am c in question by you this day Acts 24:21 *2919*
place which is c The fair havens Acts 27:8 *2564*
a tempestuous wind, c Euroclydon Acts 27:14 *2564*
certain island which is c Clauda Acts 27:16 *2564*
knew that the island was c Melita Acts 28:1 *2564*
that after three days Paul c the Acts 28:17 *4779*
cause therefore have I c for you Acts 28:20 *3870*
c to be an apostle, separated Rom 1:1 *2822*
are ye also the c of Jesus Christ Rom 1:6 *2822*
beloved of God, c to be saints Rom 1:7 *2822*
Behold, thou art c a Jew, and Rom 2:17 *2028*
she shall be c an adulteress Rom 7:3 *5537*
to them who are the c according Rom 8:28 *2822*
did predestinate, them he also c Rom 8:30 *2564*
and whom he c, them he also Rom 8:30 *2564*
but, In Isaac shall thy seed be c Rom 9:7 *2564*
Even us, whom he hath c, not of Rom 9:24 *2564*
there shall they be c the Rom 9:26 *2564*
c to be an apostle of Jesus 1Cor 1:1 *2822*
c to be saints, with all that in 1Cor 1:2 *2822*
by whom ye were c unto the 1Cor 1:9 *2564*
But unto them which are c 1Cor 1:24 *2822*
mighty, not many noble, are c 1Cor 1:26
if any man that is c a brother be 1Cor 5:11 *3687*
but God hath c us to peace 1Cor 7:15 *2564*
man, as the Lord hath c every one 1Cor 7:17 *2564*
Is any man c being circumcised 1Cor 7:18 *2564*
Is any c in uncircumcision 1Cor 7:18 *2564*
the same calling wherein he was c 1Cor 7:20 *2564*
Art thou c being a servant 1Cor 7:21 *2564*
For he that is c in the Lord 1Cor 7:22 *2564*
likewise also he that is c 1Cor 7:22 *2564*
let every man, wherein he is c 1Cor 7:24 *2564*
though there be that are c gods 1Cor 8:5 *3004*
am not meet to be c an apostle 1Cor 15:9 *2564*
c you into the grace of Christ Gal 1:6 *2564*
womb, and c me by his grace, Gal 1:15 *2564*
ye have been c unto liberty Gal 5:13 *2564*
who are c Uncircumcision by that Eph 2:11 *3004*
c the Circumcision in the flesh Eph 2:11 *3004*
the vocation wherewith ye are c Eph 4:1 *2564*
even as ye are c in one hope of Eph 4:4 *2564*
which also ye are c in one body Col 3:15 *2564*
And Jesus, which is c Justus Col 4:11 *3004*
who hath c you unto his kingdom 1Th 2:12 *2564*
For God hath not c us unto 1Th 4:7 *2564*
himself above all that is c 2Th 2:4 *3004*
Whereunto he c you by our gospel, 2Th 2:14 *2564*
life, whereunto thou art also c 1Ti 6:12 *2564*
of science falsely so c 1Ti 6:20 *5581*
c us with an holy calling, not 2Ti 1:9 *2564*
daily, while it is c To day Heb 3:13 *2564*
himself, but he that is c of God Heb 5:4 *2564*
C of God an high priest after the Heb 5:10 *4316*
not be c after the order of Aaron Heb 7:11 *3004*
which is c the sanctuary Heb 9:2 *3004*
which is c the Holiest of all Heb 9:3 *3004*
they which are c might receive Heb 9:15 *2564*
when he was c to go out into a Heb 11:8 *2564*
is not ashamed to be c their God Heb 11:16 *1941*
That in Isaac shall thy seed be c Heb 11:18 *2564*
refused to be c the son of Heb 11:24 *3004*
worthy name by the which ye are c Jas 2:7 *1941*
he was c the Friend of God Jas 2:23 *2564*
as he which hath c you is holy 1Pet 1:15 *2564*
the praises of him who hath c you 1Pet 2:9 *2564*
For even hereunto were ye c 1Pet 2:21 *2564*
knowing that ye are thereunto c 1Pet 3:9 *2564*
who hath c us unto his eternal 1Pet 5:10 *2564*
of him that hath c us to glory 2Pet 1:3 *2564*
we should be c the sons of God 1Jn 3:1 *2564*
preserved in Jesus Christ, and c Jude 1 *2822*
was in the isle that is c Patmos Rev 1:9 *2564*
name of the star is c Wormwood Rev 8:11 *3004*
which spiritually is c Sodom Rev 11:8 *2564*
c the Devil, and Satan, which Rev 12:9 *2564*
them together into a place c in Rev 16:16 *2564*
and they that are with him are c Rev 17:14 *2822*
Blessed are they which are c unto Rev 19:9 *2564*
that sat upon him was c Faithful Rev 19:11 *2564*
his name is c The Word of God Rev 19:13 *2564*

CALLEDST {4}

us thus, that thou c us not Judg 8:1 7121
for thou c me 1Sa 3:5 7121
Thou c in trouble, and I delivered Ps 81:7 7121
Thus thou c to remembrance the Eze 23:21 6485

CALLEST {3}

said unto him, Why c thou me good Mt 19:17 *3004*
said unto him, Why c thou me good Mk 10:18 *3004*
said unto him, Why c thou me good Lk 18:19 *3004*

CALLETH {30}

that the stranger c to thee for 1Kin 8:43 7121
that the stranger c to thee for 2Chr 6:33 7121
who c upon God, and he answereth Job 12:4 7121
Deep c unto deep at the noise of Ps 42:7 7121
he c them all by their names Ps 147:4 7121
and his mouth c for strokes Prov 18:6 7121
He c to me out of Seir, Watchman, Is 21:11 7121
he c them all by names by the Is 40:26 7121
None c for justice, nor any Is 59:4 7121
is none that c upon thy name Is 64:7 7121
is none among them that c unto me Hos 7:7 7121
that c for the waters of the sea, Amos 5:8 7121
he that c for the waters of the Amos 9:6 7121
that, said, This man c for Elias Mt 27:47 *5455*
and c unto him whom he would Mk 3:13 *4341*
he c thee Mk 10:49 *5455*
therefore himself c him Lord Mk 12:37 *3004*
heard it said, Behold, he c Elias Mk 15:35 *5455*
he c together his friends and Lk 15:6 *4779*
it, she c her friends and her Lk 15:9 *4779*
when he c the Lord the God of Lk 20:37 *3004*
David therefore c him Lord Lk 20:44 *2564*
he c his own sheep by name, and Jn 10:3 *2564*
The Master is come, and c for thee Jn 11:28 *5455*
c those things which be not as Rom 4:17 *2564*
not of works, but of him that c Rom 9:11 *2564*
Spirit of God c Jesus accursed 1Cor 12:3 *3004*
cometh not of him that c you Gal 5:8 *2564*
Faithful is he that c you 1Th 5:24 *2564*
which c herself a prophetess, to Rev 2:20 *3004*

CALLING {24}

them for the c of the assembly Num 10:2 4744
the c of assemblies, I cannot Is 1:13 7121
c the generations from the Is 41:4 7121
C a ravenous bird from the east, Is 46:11 7121
in c to remembrance the days of Eze 23:19 2142
markets, and c unto their fellows, Mt 11:16 *4377*
without, sent unto him, c him Mk 3:31 *5455*
Peter c to remembrance saith unto Mk 11:21 *363*
c unto him the centurion, he Mk 15:44 *4341*
John c unto him two of his Lk 7:19 *4341*
c one to another, and saying, We Lk 7:32 *4377*
c upon God, and saying, Lord Jesus Acts 7:59 *1941*

c on the name of the Lord ... Acts 22:16 *1941*
c of God are without repentance ... Rom 11:29 *2821*
For ye see your c, brethren, how ... 1Cor 1:26 *2821*
the same c wherein he was called ... 1Cor 7:20 *2821*
know what is the hope of his c ... Eph 1:18 *2821*
are called in one hope of your c ... Eph 4:4 *2821*
the high c of God in Christ Jesus ... Phil 3:14 *2821*
would count you worthy of this c ... 2Th 1:11 *2821*
us, and called us with an holy c ... 2Ti 1:9 *2821*
partakers of the heavenly c ... Heb 3:1 *2821*
Sarah obeyed Abraham, c him lord ... 1Pet 3:6 *2564*
give diligence to make your c ... 2Pet 1:10 *2821*

CALM {6}
He maketh the storm a c, so that ... Ps 107:29 1827
that the sea may be c unto us ... Jonah 1:11 8367
so shall the sea be c unto you ... Jonah 1:12 8367
and there was a great c ... Mt 8:26 *1055*
ceased, and there was a great c ... Mk 4:39 *1055*
and they ceased, and there was a c ... Lk 8:24 *1055*

CALNEH *(cal'-neh)* {2} See CALNO, CANNEH. *A center of Babylonian worship.*
Babel, and Erech, and Accad, and C ... Gen 10:10 3641
Pass ye unto C, and see ... Amos 6:2 3641

CALNO *(cal'-no)* {1} See CALNEH. *Same as Calneh.*
Is not C as Carchemish ... Is 10:9 3641

CALVARY {1}
to the place, which is called C ... Lk 23:33 *2898*

CALVE {2}
thou mark when the hinds do c ... Job 39:1 2342
of the LORD maketh the hinds to c ... Ps 29:9 2342

CALVED {1}
Yea, the hind also c in the field ... Jer 14:5 3205

CALVES {18}
bring their c home from them ... 1Sa 6:7 1121
cart, and shut up their c at home ... 1Sa 6:10 1121
and took sheep, and oxen, and c ... 1Sa 14:32 1121,1241
counsel, and made two c of gold ... 1Kin 12:28 5695
unto the c that he had made ... 1Kin 12:32 5695
the golden c that were in Beth-el ... 2Kin 10:29 5695
them molten images, even two c ... 2Kin 17:16 5695
for the c which he had made ... 2Chr 11:15 5695
and there are with you golden c ... 2Chr 13:8 5695
with the c of the people, till ... Ps 68:30 5695
because of the c of Beth-aven ... Hos 10:5 5697
the men that sacrifice kiss the c ... Hos 13:2 5697
will we render the c of our lips ... Hos 14:2 6499
the c out of the midst of the ... Amos 6:4 5695
offerings, with c of a year old ... Mic 6:6 5695
grow up as c of the stall ... Mal 4:2 5695
by the blood of goats and c ... Heb 9:12 *3448*
the law, he took the blood of c ... Heb 9:19 *3448*

CALVETH {1}
their cow c, and casteth not her ... Job 21:10 6403

CAME See APPENDIX.

CAMEL {9}
saw Isaac, she lighted off the c ... Gen 24:64 1581
as the c, because he cheweth the ... Lev 11:4 1581
as the c, and the hare, and the ... Deut 14:7 1581
and suckling, ox and sheep, c ... 1Sa 15:3 1581
the horse, of the mule, of the c ... Zec 14:15 1581
It is easier for a c to go ... Mt 19:24 *2574*
strain at a gnat, and swallow a c ... Mt 23:24 *2574*
It is easier for a c to go ... Mk 10:25 *2574*
For it is easier for a c to go ... Lk 18:25 *2574*

CAMEL'S {3}
and put them in the c furniture ... Gen 31:34 1581
John had his raiment of c hair ... Mt 3:4 *2574*
And John was clothed with c hair ... Mk 1:6 *2574*

CAMELS {47}
maidservants, and she asses, and c ... Gen 12:16 1581
ten c of the c of his master ... Gen 24:10 1581
he made his c to kneel down ... Gen 24:11 1581
and I will give thy c drink also ... Gen 24:14 1581
I will draw water for thy c also ... Gen 24:19 1581
draw water, and drew for all his c ... Gen 24:20 1581
as the c had done drinking, that ... Gen 24:22 1581
he stood by the c at the well ... Gen 24:30 1581
the house, and room for the c ... Gen 24:31 1581
and he ungirded his c ... Gen 24:32 1581
gave straw and provender for the c ... Gen 24:32 1581
and maidservants, and c, and asses ... Gen 24:35 1581
and I will also draw for thy c ... Gen 24:44 1581
and I will give thy c drink also ... Gen 24:46 1581
and she made the c drink also ... Gen 24:46 1581
damsels, and they rode upon the c ... Gen 24:61 1581
and, behold, the c were coming ... Gen 24:63 1581
and menservants, and c, and asses ... Gen 30:43 1581
set his sons and his wives upon c ... Gen 31:17 1581
and the flocks, and herds, and the c ... Gen 32:7 1581
Thirty milch c with their colts, ... Gen 32:15 1581
with their c bearing spicery ... Gen 37:25 1581
upon the asses, upon the c ... Ex 9:3 1581
their c were without number ... Judg 6:5 1581
their c were without number, as ... Judg 7:12 1581
the oxen, and the asses, and the c ... 1Sa 27:9 1581
young men, which rode upon c ... 1Sa 30:17 1581
with c that bare spices, and very ... 1Kin 10:2 1581
of their c fifty thousand, and of ... 1Chr 5:21 1581
brought bread on asses, and on c ... 1Chr 12:40 1581
Over the c also was Obil the ... 1Chr 27:30 1581
c that bare spices, and gold in ... 2Chr 9:1 1581
c in abundance, and returned to ... 2Chr 14:15 1581
Their c, four hundred thirty and ... Ezr 2:67 1581
Their c, four hundred thirty and ... Neh 7:69 1581
horseback, and riders on mules, c ... Est 8:10 327
c went out, being hastened and ... Est 8:14 327
sheep, and three thousand c ... Job 1:3 1581
three bands, and fell upon the c ... Job 1:17 1581
thousand sheep, and six thousand c ... Job 42:12 1581
of asses, and a chariot of c ... Is 21:7 1581
treasures upon the bunches of c ... Is 30:6 1581
multitude of c shall cover thee ... Is 60:6 1581
and all their vessels, and their c ... Jer 49:29 1581
their c shall be a booty, and the ... Jer 49:32 1581
I will make Rabbah a stable for c ... Eze 25:5 1581

CAMELS' {3}
that were on their c necks ... Judg 8:21 1581
that were about their c necks ... Judg 8:26 1581
forty c burden, and came and stood ... 2Kin 8:9 1581

CAMEST See APPENDIX.

CAMON *(ca'-mon)* {1} *A town in Gilead.*
And Jair died, and was buried in C ... Judg 10:5 7056

CAMP {136}
which went before the c of Israel ... Ex 14:19 4264
between the c of the Egyptians ... Ex 14:20 4264
the Egyptians and the c of Israel ... Ex 14:20 4264
quails came up, and covered the c ... Ex 16:13 4264
people that was in the c trembled ... Ex 19:16 4264
out of the c to meet with God ... Ex 19:17 4264
thou burn with fire without the c ... Ex 29:14 4264
There is a noise of war in the c ... Ex 32:17 4264
soon as he came nigh unto the c ... Ex 32:19 4264
Moses stood in the gate of the c ... Ex 32:26 4264
gate to gate throughout the c ... Ex 32:27 4264
the c, afar off from the c ... Ex 33:7 4264
which was without the c ... Ex 33:7 4264
And he turned again into the c ... Ex 33:11 4264
to be proclaimed throughout the c ... Ex 36:6 4264
without the c unto a clean place ... Lev 4:12 4264
forth the bullock without the c ... Lev 4:21 4264
without the c unto a clean place ... Lev 6:11 4264
he burnt with fire without the c ... Lev 8:17 4264
he burnt with fire without the c ... Lev 9:11 4264
before the sanctuary out of the c ... Lev 10:4 4264
them in their coats out of the c ... Lev 10:5 4264
without the c shall his ... Lev 13:46 4264
shall go forth out of the c ... Lev 14:3 4264
that he shall come into the c ... Lev 14:8 4264
and afterward come into the c ... Lev 16:26 4264
one carry forth without the c ... Lev 16:27 4264
he shall come into the c ... Lev 16:28 4264
an ox, or lamb, or goat, in the c ... Lev 17:3 4264
or that killeth it out of the c ... Lev 17:3 4264
Israel strove together in the c ... Lev 24:10 4264
that hath cursed without the c ... Lev 24:14 4264
him that had cursed out of the c ... Lev 24:23 4264
tents, every man by his own c ... Num 1:52 4264
they of the standard of the c of ... Num 2:3 4264
in the c of Judah were an hundred ... Num 2:9 4264
c of Reuben according to their ... Num 2:10 4264
the c of Reuben were an hundred ... Num 2:16 4264
shall set forward with the c of ... Num 2:17 4264
the Levites in the midst of the c ... Num 2:17 4264
shall be the standard of the c of ... Num 2:18 4264
the c of Ephraim were an hundred ... Num 2:24 4264
The standard of the c of Dan ... Num 2:25 4264
they that were numbered in the c ... Num 2:31 4264
when the c setteth forward, Aaron ... Num 4:5 4264
as the c is to set forward ... Num 4:15 4264
they put out of the c every leper ... Num 5:2 4264
without the c shall ye put them ... Num 5:3 4264
so, and put them out without the c ... Num 5:4 4264
of the c of the children of Judah ... Num 10:14 4264
the standard of the c of Reuben ... Num 10:18 4264
the standard of the c of the ... Num 10:22 4264
the standard of the c of the ... Num 10:25 4264
day, when they went out of the c ... Num 10:34 4264
in the uttermost parts of the c ... Num 11:1 4264
dew fell upon the c in the night ... Num 11:9 4264
remained two of the men in the c ... Num 11:26 4264
and they prophesied in the c ... Num 11:26 4264
and Medad do prophesy in the c ... Num 11:27 4264
And Moses gat him into the c ... Num 11:30 4264
sea, and let them fall by the c ... Num 11:31 4264
the other side, round about the c ... Num 11:31 4264
for themselves round about the c ... Num 11:32 4264
be shut out from the c seven days ... Num 12:14 4264
shut out from the c seven days ... Num 12:15 4264
Moses, departed not out of the c ... Num 14:44 4264
him with stones without the c ... Num 15:35 4264
brought him without the c ... Num 15:36 4264
may bring her forth without the c ... Num 19:3 4264
he shall come into the c, and the ... Num 19:7 4264
up without the c in a clean place ... Num 19:9 4264
unto the c at the plains of Moab, ... Num 31:12 4264
forth to meet them without the c ... Num 31:13 4264
ye abide without the c seven days ... Num 31:19 4264
ye shall come into the c ... Num 31:24 4264
shall he go abroad out of the c ... Deut 23:10 4264
he shall not come within the c ... Deut 23:10 4264
he shall come into the c again ... Deut 23:11 4264
have a place also without the c ... Deut 23:12 4264
God walketh in the midst of thy c ... Deut 23:14 4264
therefore shall thy c be holy ... Deut 23:14 4264
and thy stranger that is in thy c ... Deut 29:11 4264
abode in their places in the c ... Josh 5:8 4264
into the c, and lodged in the c ... Josh 6:11 4264
city once, and returned into the c ... Josh 6:14 4264
make the c of Israel a curse, and ... Josh 6:18 4264
left them without the c of Israel ... Josh 6:23 4264
to Joshua unto the c at Gilgal ... Josh 9:6 4264
unto Joshua to the c to Gilgal ... Josh 10:6 4264
with him, unto the c to Gilgal ... Josh 10:15 4264
c to Joshua at Makkedah in peace ... Josh 10:21 4264
with him, unto the c to Gilgal ... Josh 10:43 4264
I come to the outside of the c ... Judg 7:17 4264
also on every side of all the c ... Judg 7:18 4264
came unto the outside of the c in ... Judg 7:19 4264
in his place round about the c ... Judg 7:21 4264
in the c of Dan between Zorah ... Judg 13:25 4264
there came none to the c from ... Judg 21:8 4264
brought them unto the c to Shiloh ... Judg 21:12 4264
the people were come into the c ... 1Sa 4:3 4264
of the LORD came into the c ... 1Sa 4:5 4264
shout in the c of the Hebrews ... 1Sa 4:6 4264
of the LORD was come into the c ... 1Sa 4:6 4264
they said, God is come into the c ... 1Sa 4:7 4264
the c of the Philistines in three ... 1Sa 13:17 4264
went up with them into the c from ... 1Sa 14:21 4264
out of the c of the Philistines ... 1Sa 17:4 4264
run to the c to thy brethren ... 1Sa 17:17 4264
go down with me to Saul to the c ... 1Sa 26:6 4264
a man came out of the c from Saul ... 2Sa 1:2 4264
Out of the c of Israel am I ... 2Sa 1:3 4264
over Israel that day in the c ... 1Kin 16:16 4264
when they came to the c of Israel ... 2Kin 3:24 4264
and such a place shall be my c ... 2Kin 6:8 8466
to go unto the c of the Syrians ... 2Kin 7:5 4264
uttermost part of the c of Syria ... 2Kin 7:5 4264
even the c as it was, and fled for ... 2Kin 7:7 4264
to the uttermost part of the c ... 2Kin 7:8 4264
We came to the c of the Syrians ... 2Kin 7:10 4264
are they gone out of the c to ... 2Kin 7:12 4264
smote in the c of the Assyrians ... 2Kin 19:35 4264
to the c had slain all the eldest ... 2Chr 22:1 4264
captains in the c of the king of ... 2Chr 32:21 4264
it fall in the midst of their c ... Ps 78:28 4264
They envied Moses also in the c ... Ps 106:16 4264
I will c against thee round about ... Is 29:3 2583
smote in the c of the Assyrians ... Is 37:36 4264
the bow, c against it round about ... Jer 50:29 2583
set the c also against it, and set ... Eze 4:2 4264
for his c is very great ... Joel 2:11 4264
which c in the hedges in the cold ... Nah 3:17 2583
for sin, are burned without the c ... Heb 13:11 *3925*
therefore unto him without the c ... Heb 13:13 *3925*
compassed the c of the saints ... Rev 20:9 *3925*

CAMPED {1}
there Israel c before the mount ... Ex 19:2 2583

CAMPHIRE {2}
is unto me as a cluster of c in ... Song 1:14 3724
c, with spikenard, ... Song 4:13 3724

CAMPS {7}
c throughout their hosts were six ... Num 2:32 4264
that they defile not their c ... Num 5:3 4264
and for the journeying of the c ... Num 10:2 4264
then the c that lie on the east ... Num 10:5 4264
then the c that lie on the south ... Num 10:6 4264
all the c throughout their hosts ... Num 10:25 4264
c to come up unto your nostrils ... Amos 4:10 4264

CAN See APPENDIX.

CANA *(ca'-nah)* {4} *A village in Galilee.*
was a marriage in C of Galilee ... Jn 2:1 *2580*
did Jesus in C of Galilee ... Jn 2:11 *2580*
came again into C of Galilee ... Jn 4:46 *2580*
and Nathanael of C in Galilee ... Jn 21:2 *2580*

CANAAN *(ca'-na-an)* {91} See CANAANITE.
1. *Son of Ham.*
and Ham is the father of C ... Gen 9:18 3667
And Ham, the father of C, saw the ... Gen 9:22 3667
And he said, Cursed be C ... Gen 9:25 3667
and C shall be his servant ... Gen 9:26 3667
and C shall be his servant ... Gen 9:27 3667
Cush, and Mizraim, and Phut, and C ... Gen 10:6 3667
C begat Sidon his firstborn, and ... Gen 10:15 3667
Cush, and Mizraim, Put, and C ... 1Chr 1:8 3667
C begat Zidon his firstborn, and ... 1Chr 1:13 3667
2. *Place where Canaanites dwell.*
to go into the land of C ... Gen 11:31 3667
forth to go into the land of C ... Gen 12:5 3667
and into the land of C they came ... Gen 12:5 3667
Abram dwelled in the land of C ... Gen 13:12 3667
dwelt ten years in the land of C ... Gen 16:3 3667
art a stranger, all the land of C ... Gen 17:8 3667
same is Hebron in the land of C ... Gen 23:2 3667
same is Hebron in the land of C ... Gen 23:19 3667
take a wife of the daughters of C ... Gen 28:1 3667
take a wife of the daughters of C ... Gen 28:6 3667
of C pleased not Isaac his father ... Gen 28:8 3667
Isaac his father in the land of C ... Gen 31:18 3667
which is in the land of C ... Gen 33:18 3667
to Luz, which is in the land of C ... Gen 35:6 3667
his wives of the daughters of C ... Gen 36:2 3667
born unto him in the land of C ... Gen 36:5 3667
which he had got in the land of C ... Gen 36:6 3667
was a stranger, in the land of C ... Gen 37:1 3667
the famine was in the land of C ... Gen 42:5 3667
From the land of C to buy food ... Gen 42:7 3667
sons of one man in the land of C ... Gen 42:13 3667
their father unto the land of C ... Gen 42:29 3667
with our father in the land of C ... Gen 42:32 3667
unto thee out of the land of C ... Gen 44:8 3667
and go, get you unto the land of C ... Gen 45:17 3667
came into the land of C unto ... Gen 45:25 3667
they had gotten in the land of C ... Gen 46:6 3667
Er and Onan died in the land of C ... Gen 46:12 3667

which were in the land of *C* ..... Gen 46:31 3667
are come out of the land of *C* ..... Gen 47:1 3667
famine is sore in the land of *C* ..... Gen 47:4 3667
all the land of *C* fainted by ..... Gen 47:13 3667
of Egypt, and in the land of *C* ..... Gen 47:14 3667
of Egypt, and in the land of *C* ..... Gen 47:15 3667
unto me at Luz in the land of *C* ..... Gen 48:3 3667
by me in the land of *C* in the way ..... Gen 48:7 3667
is before Mamre, in the land of *C* ..... Gen 49:30 3667
digged for me in the land of *C* ..... Gen 50:5 3667
carried him into the land of *C* ..... Gen 50:13 3667
them, to give them the land of *C* ..... Ex 6:4 3667
inhabitants of *C* shall melt away ..... Ex 15:15 3667
unto the borders of the land of *C* ..... Ex 16:35 3667
ye be come into the land of *C* ..... Lev 14:34 3667
after the doings of the land of *C* ..... Lev 18:3 3667
Egypt, to give you the land of *C* ..... Lev 25:38 3667
they may search the land of *C* ..... Num 13:2 3667
them to spy out the land of *C* ..... Num 13:17 3667
Er and Onan died in the land of *C* ..... Num 26:19 3667
among you in the land of *C* ..... Num 32:30 3667
the LORD into the land of *C* ..... Num 32:32 3667
in the south in the land of *C* ..... Num 33:40 3667
over Jordan into the land of *C* ..... Num 33:51 3667
When ye come into the land of *C* ..... Num 34:2 3667
even the land of *C* with the ..... Num 34:2 3667
of Israel in the land of *C* ..... Num 34:29 3667
over Jordan into the land of *C* ..... Num 35:10 3667
shall ye give in the land of *C* ..... Num 35:14 3667
and behold the land of *C*, which I ..... Deut 32:49 3667
fruit of the land of *C* that year ..... Josh 5:12 3667
Israel inherited in the land of *C* ..... Josh 14:1 3667
them at Shiloh in the land of *C* ..... Josh 21:2 3667
Shiloh, which is in the land of *C* ..... Josh 22:9 3667
Jordan, that are in the land of *C* ..... Josh 22:10 3667
altar over against the land of *C* ..... Josh 22:11 3667
of Gilead, unto the land of *C* ..... Josh 22:32 3667
him throughout all the land of *C* ..... Josh 24:3 3667
had not known all the wars of *C* ..... Judg 3:1 3667
into the hand of Jabin king of *C* ..... Judg 4:2 3667
C before the children of Israel ..... Judg 4:23 3667
against Jabin the king of *C* ..... Judg 4:24 3667
had destroyed Jabin king of *C* ..... Judg 4:24 3667
then fought the kings of *C* in ..... Judg 5:19 3667
Shiloh, which is in the land of *C* ..... Judg 21:12 3667
thee will I give the land of *C* 1Chr 16:18 3667
thee will I give the land of *C* ..... Ps 105:11 3667
sacrificed unto the idols of *C* ..... Ps 106:38 3667
Bashan, and all the kingdoms of *C* ..... Ps 135:11 3667
of Egypt speak the language of *C* ..... Is 19:18 3667
thy nativity is of the land of *C* ..... Eze 16:3 3667
in the land of *C* unto Chaldea ..... Eze 16:29 3667
O *C*, the land of the Philistines, ... Zeph 2:5 3667
a woman of *C* came out of the same ..... Mt 15:22 *5478*

CANAANITE *(ca'-na-an-ite)* {14} See CANAANITES, CANAANITESS, CANAANITISH, ZELOTES. *Descendants of Canaan.*
the *C* was then in the land ..... Gen 12:6 3669
and the *C* and the Perizzite dwelled ..... Gen 13:7 3669
there a daughter of a certain *C* ..... Gen 38:2 3669
shall drive out the Hivite, the *C* ..... Ex 23:28 3669
and I will drive out the *C* ..... Ex 33:2 3669
before thee the Amorite, and the *C* ..... Ex 34:11 3669
And when king Arad the *C*, which ..... Num 21:1 3669
And king Arad the *C*, which dwelt ..... Num 33:40 3669
Hittite, and the Amorite, the *C* ..... Josh 9:1 3669
to the *C* on the east and on the ..... Josh 11:3 3669
which is counted to the *C* ..... Josh 13:3 3669
the *C* in the house of the LORD of ..... Zec 14:21 3669
Simon the *C*, and Judas Iscariot, ... Mt 10:4 *2581*
and Thaddaeus, and Simon the *C* ..... Mk 3:18 *2581*

CANAANITES *(ca'-na-an-ites)* {55}
families of the *C* spread abroad ..... Gen 10:18 3669
border of the *C* was from Sidon ..... Gen 10:19 3669
And the Amorites, and the *C* ..... Gen 15:21 3669
my son of the daughters of the *C* ..... Gen 24:3 3669
my son of the daughters of the *C* ..... Gen 24:37 3669
of the land, among the *C* and the ..... Gen 34:30 3669
inhabitants of the land, the *C* ..... Gen 50:11 3669
unto the place of the *C*, and the ..... Ex 3:8 3669
of Egypt unto the land of the *C* ..... Ex 3:17 3669
bring thee into the land of the *C* ..... Ex 13:5 3669
bring thee into the land of the *C* ..... Ex 13:11 3669
and the Perizzites, and the *C* ..... Ex 23:23 3669
the *C* dwell by the sea, and by the ..... Num 13:29 3669
the *C* dwelt in the valley ..... Num 14:25 3669
the *C* are there before you, and ye ..... Num 14:43 3669
the *C* which dwelt in that hill, ... Num 14:45 3669
of Israel, and delivered up the *C* ..... Num 21:3 3669
sea side, to the land of the *C* ..... Deut 1:7 3669
and the Amorites, and the *C* ..... Deut 7:1 3669
goeth down, in the land of the *C* ..... Deut 11:30 3669
Hittites, and the Amorites, the *C* ..... Deut 20:17 3669
drive out from before you the *C* ..... Josh 3:10 3669
and all the kings of the *C* ..... Josh 5:1 3669
For the *C* and all the inhabitants ..... Josh 7:9 3669
Hittites, the Amorites, and the *C* ..... Josh 12:8 3669
the south, all the land of the *C* ..... Josh 13:4 3669
not out the *C* that dwelt in Gezer ..... Josh 16:10 3669
but the *C* dwell among the ..... Josh 16:10 3669
but the *C* would dwell in that ..... Josh 17:12 3669
that they put the *C* to tribute ..... Josh 17:13 3669
all the *C* that dwell in the land ..... Josh 17:16 3669
for thou shalt drive out the *C* ..... Josh 17:18 3669
and the Perizzites, and the *C* ..... Josh 24:11 3669
go up for us against the *C* first ..... Judg 1:1 3669
that we may fight against the *C* ..... Judg 1:3 3669
and the LORD delivered the *C* ..... Judg 1:4 3669
against him, and they slew the *C* ..... Judg 1:5 3669
went down to fight against the *C* ..... Judg 1:9 3669
the *C* that dwelt in Hebron ..... Judg 1:10 3669
they slew the *C* that inhabited ..... Judg 1:17 3669
but the *C* would dwell in that ..... Judg 1:27 3669
that they put the *C* to tribute ..... Judg 1:28 3669
out the *C* that dwelt in Gezer ..... Judg 1:29 3669
but the *C* dwelt in Gezer among ..... Judg 1:29 3669
but the *C* dwelt among them, and ..... Judg 1:30 3669
the Asherites dwelt among the *C* ..... Judg 1:32 3669
but he dwelt among the *C*, the ..... Judg 1:33 3669
of the Philistines, and all the *C* ..... Judg 3:3 3669
of Israel dwelt among the *C* ..... Judg 3:5 3669
of the Hivites, and of the *C* 2Sa 24:7 3669
slain the *C* that dwelt in the 1Kin 9:16 3669
their abominations, even of the *C* ..... Ezr 9:1 3669
him to give the land of the *C* ..... Neh 9:8 3669
inhabitants of the land, the *C* ..... Neh 9:24 3669
shall possess that of the *C* ..... Obad 20 3669

CANAANITESS *(ca'-na-an-ite-ess)* {1}
him of the daughter of Shua the *C* 1Chr 2:3 3669

CANAANITISH *(ca'-na-an-i-tish)* {2}
and Shaul the son of a *C* woman ..... Gen 46:10 3669
and Shaul the son of a *C* woman ..... Ex 6:15 3669

CANDACE *(can'-da-see)* {1} *Name for a dynasty of Ethiopian queens.*
under *C* queen of the Ethiopians ..... Acts 8:27 *2582*

CANDLE {16}
his *c* shall be put out with him ..... Job 18:6 5216
How oft is the *c* of the wicked ..... Job 21:17 5216
When his *c* shined upon my head, ... Job 29:3 5216
For thou wilt light my *c* ..... Ps 18:28 5216
of man is the *c* of the LORD ..... Prov 20:27 5216
the *c* of the wicked shall be put ..... Prov 24:20 5216
her *c* goeth not out by night ..... Prov 31:18 5216
millstones, and the light of the *c* ..... Jer 25:10 5216
Neither do men light a *c*, and put ..... Mt 5:15 *3088*
Is a *c* brought to be put under a ..... Mk 4:21 *3088*
No man, when he hath lighted a *c* ..... Lk 8:16 *3088*
No man, when he hath lighted a *c* ..... Lk 11:33 *3088*
of a *c* doth give thee light ..... Lk 11:36 *3088*
one piece, doth not light a *c* ..... Lk 15:8 *3088*
the light of a *c* shall shine no ..... Rev 18:23 *3088*
and they need no *c*, neither light ..... Rev 22:5 *3088*

CANDLES {1}
I will search Jerusalem with *c* ..... Zeph 1:12 5216

CANDLESTICK {41}
thou shalt make a *c* of pure gold ..... Ex 25:31 4501
beaten work shall the *c* be made ..... Ex 25:31 4501
of the *c* out of the one side ..... Ex 25:32 4501
of the *c* out of the other side ..... Ex 25:32 4501
branches that come out of the *c* ..... Ex 25:33 4501
in the *c* shall be four bowls made ..... Ex 25:34 4501
that proceed out of the *c* ..... Ex 25:35 4501
the *c* over against the table on ..... Ex 26:35 4501
and all his vessels, and the *c* ..... Ex 30:27 4501
the pure *c* with all his furniture ..... Ex 31:8 4501
The *c* also for the light, and his ..... Ex 35:14 4501
he made the *c* of pure gold ..... Ex 37:17 4501
of beaten work made he the *c* ..... Ex 37:17 4501
three branches of the *c* out of ..... Ex 37:18 4501
three branches of the *c* out of ..... Ex 37:18 4501
six branches going out of the *c* ..... Ex 37:19 4501
in the *c* were four bowls made ..... Ex 37:20 4501
The pure *c*, with the lamps ..... Ex 39:37 4501
and thou shalt bring in the *c* ..... Ex 40:4 4501
he put the *c* in the tent of the ..... Ex 40:24 4501
c before the LORD continually ..... Lev 24:4 4501
the ark, and the table, and the *c* ..... Num 3:31 4501
cover the *c* of the light, and his ..... Num 4:9 4501
give light over against the *c* ..... Num 8:2 4501
lamps thereof over against the *c* ..... Num 8:3 4501
this work of the *c* was of beaten ..... Num 8:4 4501
shewed Moses, so he made the *c* ..... Num 8:4 4501
and a table, and a stool, and a *c* 2Kin 4:10 4501
of gold, by weight for every *c* 1Chr 28:15 4501
silver by weight, both for the *c* 1Chr 28:15 4501
according to the use of every *c* 1Chr 28:15 4501
the *c* of gold with the lamps 2Chr 13:11 4501
wrote over against the *c* upon the ..... Dan 5:5 5043
behold a *c* all of gold, with a ..... Zec 4:2 4501
upon the right side of the *c* ..... Zec 4:11 4501
put it under a bushel, but on a *c* ..... Mt 5:15 *3087*
and not to be set on a *c* ..... Mk 4:21 *3087*
but setteth it on a *c*, that they ..... Lk 8:16 *3087*
under a bushel, but on a *c* ..... Lk 11:33 *3087*
the first, wherein was the *c* ..... Heb 9:2 *3087*
will remove thy *c* out of his ..... Rev 2:5 *3087*

CANDLESTICKS {12}
the *c* of pure gold, five on the 1Kin 7:49 4501
Even the weight for the *c* of gold 1Chr 28:15 4501
for the *c* of silver by weight, ... 1Chr 28:15 4501
he made ten *c* of gold according 2Chr 4:7 4501
Moreover the *c* with their lamps, ... 2Chr 4:20 4501
bowls, and the caldrons, and the *c* ..... Jer 52:19 4501
turned, I saw seven golden *c* ..... Rev 1:12 *3087*
in the midst of the seven *c* one ..... Rev 1:13 *3087*
right hand, and the seven golden *c* ..... Rev 1:20 *3087*
the seven *c* which thou sawest are ..... Rev 1:20 *3087*
the midst of the seven golden *c* ..... Rev 2:1 *3087*
the two *c* standing before the God ..... Rev 11:4 *3087*

CANE {2}
bought me no sweet *c* with money ..... Is 43:24 7070
the sweet *c* from a far country ..... Jer 6:20 7070

CANKER {1}
their word will eat as doth a *c* 2Ti 2:17 *1044*

CANKERED {1}
Your gold and silver is *c* ..... Jas 5:3 *2728*

CANKERWORM {6}
locust hath left hath the *c* eaten ..... Joel 1:4 3218
that which the *c* hath left hath ..... Joel 1:4 3218
that the locust hath eaten, the *c* ..... Joel 2:25 3218
it shall eat thee up like the *c* ..... Nah 3:15 3218
make thyself many as the *c* ..... Nah 3:15 3218
the *c* spoileth, and fleeth away ..... Nah 3:16 3218

CANNEH *(can'-neh)* {1} See CALNEH. *A place in southern Arabia.*
Haran, and *C*, and Eden, the ..... Eze 27:23 3656

CANNOT See APPENDIX.

CANST See APPENDIX.

CAPERNAUM *(ca-pur'-na-um)* {16} *A city in Galilee.*
Nazareth, he came and dwelt in *C* ..... Mt 4:13 *2584*
And when Jesus was entered into *C* ..... Mt 8:5 *2584*
And thou, *C*, which art exalted ..... Mt 11:23 *2584*
And when they were come to *C* ..... Mt 17:24 *2584*
And they went into *C* ..... Mk 1:21 *2584*
he entered into *C* after some days ..... Mk 2:1 *2584*
And he came to *C* ..... Mk 9:33 *2584*
we have heard done in *C*, do also ..... Lk 4:23 *2584*
And came down to *C*, a city of ..... Lk 4:31 *2584*
of the people, he entered into *C* ..... Lk 7:1 *2584*
And thou, *C*, which art exalted to ..... Lk 10:15 *2584*
After this he went down to *C* ..... Jn 2:12 *2584*
nobleman, whose son was sick at *C* ..... Jn 4:46 *2584*
and went over the sea toward *C* ..... Jn 6:17 *2584*
also took shipping, and came to *C* ..... Jn 6:24 *2584*
the synagogue, as he taught in *C* ..... Jn 6:59 *2584*

CAPHTHORIM *(caf'-tho-rim)* {1} See CAPHTORIM. *People of Caphtor.*
whom came the Philistines,) and *C* 1Chr 1:12 3732

CAPHTOR *(caf'-tor)* {3} See CAPHTORIM. *Original land of the Philistines.*
which came forth out of *C* ..... Deut 2:23 3731
the remnant of the country of *C* ..... Jer 47:4 3731
and the Philistines from *C* ..... Amos 9:7 3731

CAPHTORIM *(caf'-to-rim)* {1} See CAPHTHORIM, CAPHTORIMS. *Same as Caphthorim.*
out of whom came Philistim,) and *C* ..... Gen 10:14 3732

CAPHTORIMS *(caf'-to-rims)* {1} See CAPHTORIM.
Hazerim, even unto Azzah, the *C* ..... Deut 2:23 3732

CAPHTORITES See CAPHTORIMS.

CAPPADOCIA *(cap-pa-do'-she-ah)* {2} *A Roman province in Asia Minor.*
Mesopotamia, and in Judaea, and *C* ..... Acts 2:9 *2587*
throughout Pontus, Galatia, *C* 1Pet 1:1 *2587*

CAPTAIN {139}
Phichol the chief *c* of his host ..... Gen 21:22 8269
Phichol the chief *c* of his host ..... Gen 21:32 8269
Phichol the chief *c* of his army ..... Gen 26:26 8269
of Pharaoh's, and *c* of the guard ..... Gen 37:36 8269
c of the guard, an Egyptian, ... Gen 39:1 8269
the house of the *c* of the guard ..... Gen 40:3 8269
the *c* of the guard charged Joseph ..... Gen 40:4 8269
in the *c* of the guard's house ..... Gen 41:10 8269
servant to the *c* of the guard ..... Gen 41:12 8269
be *c* of the children of Judah ..... Num 2:3 5387
the son of Zuar shall be *c* of the ..... Num 2:5 5387
be *c* of the children of Zebulun ..... Num 2:7 5387
the *c* of the children of Reuben ..... Num 2:10 5387
the *c* of the children of Simeon ..... Num 2:12 5387
the *c* of the sons of Gad shall be ..... Num 2:14 5387
the *c* of the sons of Ephraim ..... Num 2:18 5387
the *c* of the children of Manasseh ..... Num 2:20 5387
the *c* of the sons of Benjamin ..... Num 2:22 5387
the *c* of the children of Dan ..... Num 2:25 5387
the *c* of the children of Asher ..... Num 2:27 5387
the *c* of the children of Naphtali ..... Num 2:29 5387
one to another, Let us make a *c* ..... Num 14:4 7218
but as *c* of the host of the LORD ..... Josh 5:14 8269
the *c* of the LORD's host said ..... Josh 5:15 8269
the *c* of whose host was Sisera, ... Judg 4:2 8269
the *c* of Jabin's army, with his ..... Judg 4:7 8269
unto Jephthah, Come, and be our *c* ..... Judg 11:6 7101
made him head and *c* over them ..... Judg 11:11 7101
him to be *c* over my people Israel 1Sa 9:16 5057
thee to be *c* over his inheritance 1Sa 10:1 5057
c of the host of Hazor, and into 1Sa 12:9 8269
him to be *c* over his people 1Sa 13:14 5057
the name of the *c* of his host was 1Sa 14:50 8269
unto the *c* of their thousand 1Sa 17:18 8269
the *c* of the host, Abner, whose 1Sa 17:55 8269
made him his *c* over a thousand 1Sa 18:13 8269
and he became a *c* over them 1Sa 22:2 8269
the son of Ner, the *c* of his host 1Sa 26:5 8269
of Ner, *c* of Saul's host, took 2Sa 2:8 8269
and thou shalt be a *c* over Israel 2Sa 5:2 5057
soul, he shall be chief and *c* 2Sa 5:8
Shobach the *c* of the host of 2Sa 10:16 8269
smote Shobach the *c* of their host 2Sa 10:18 8269
Absalom made Amasa *c* of the host 2Sa 17:25 5921
if thou be not *c* of the host 2Sa 19:13 8269
therefore he was their *c* 2Sa 23:19 8269
said to Joab the *c* of the host 2Sa 24:2 8269
priest, and Joab the *c* of the host 1Kin 1:19 8269
c of the host of Israel, and Amasa 1Kin 2:32 8269
of Jether, *c* of the host of Judah 1Kin 2:32 8269
Joab the *c* of the host was gone 1Kin 11:15 8269
that Joab the *c* of the host was 1Kin 11:21 8269

Context	Reference	Number
became *c* over a band, when David	1Kin 11:24	8269
c of half his chariots, conspired	1Kin 16:9	8269
the *c* of the host, king over	1Kin 16:16	8269
him a *c* of fifty with his fifty	2Kin 1:9	8269
and said to the *c* of fifty	2Kin 1:10	8269
another *c* of fifty with his fifty	2Kin 1:11	8269
he sent again a *c* of the third	2Kin 1:13	8269
the third *c* of fifty went up, and	2Kin 1:13	8269
the king, or to the *c* of the host	2Kin 4:13	8269
c of the host of the king of	2Kin 5:1	8269
I have an errand to thee, O *c*	2Kin 9:5	8269
And he said, To thee, O *c*	2Kin 9:5	8269
Then said Jehu to Bidkar his *c*	2Kin 9:25	7991
a *c* of his, conspired against him	2Kin 15:25	7991
one *c* of the least of my master's	2Kin 18:24	6346
tell Hezekiah the *c* of my people	2Kin 20:5	5057
c of the guard, a servant of the	2Kin 25:8	7227
that were with the *c* of the guard	2Kin 25:10	7227
did Nebuzar-adan the *c* of the	2Kin 25:11	7227
But the *c* of the guard left of	2Kin 25:12	7227
the *c* of the guard took away	2Kin 25:15	7227
the *c* of the guard took Seraiah	2Kin 25:18	7227
Nebuzar-adan *c* of the guard took	2Kin 25:20	7227
first shall be chief and *c*	1Chr 11:6	8269
for he was their *c*	1Chr 11:21	8269
a *c* of the Reubenites, and thirty	1Chr 11:42	7218
Shophach the *c* of the host of	1Chr 19:16	8269
killed Shophach the *c* of the host	1Chr 19:18	8269
The third *c* of the host for the	1Chr 27:5	8269
The fourth *c* for the fourth month	1Chr 27:7	
The fifth *c* for the fifth month	1Chr 27:8	8269
The sixth *c* for the sixth month	1Chr 27:9	
The seventh *c* for the seventh	1Chr 27:10	
The eighth *c* for the eighth month	1Chr 27:11	
The ninth *c* for the ninth month	1Chr 27:12	
The tenth *c* for the tenth month	1Chr 27:13	
The eleventh *c* for the eleventh	1Chr 27:14	
The twelfth *c* for the twelfth	1Chr 27:15	
God himself is with us for our *c*	2Chr 13:12	7218
next to him was Jehohanan the *c*	2Chr 17:15	8269
a *c* to return to their bondage	Neh 9:17	7218
The *c* of fifty, and the honourable	Is 3:3	8269
one *c* of the least of my master's	Is 36:9	6346
a *c* of the ward was there, whose	Jer 37:13	1167
Then Nebuzar-adan the *c* of the	Jer 39:9	7227
But Nebuzar-adan the *c* of the	Jer 39:10	
Nebuzar-adan the *c* of the guard	Jer 39:11	7227
the *c* of the guard sent, and	Jer 39:13	7227
the *c* of the guard had let him go	Jer 40:1	7227
the *c* of the guard took Jeremiah,	Jer 40:2	7227
So the *c* of the guard gave him	Jer 40:5	7227
whom Nebuzar-adan the *c* of the	Jer 41:10	7227
the *c* of the guard had left with	Jer 43:6	7227
appoint a *c* against her	Jer 51:27	2951
c of the guard, which served the	Jer 52:12	7227
that were with the *c* of the guard	Jer 52:14	7227
Then Nebuzar-adan the *c* of the	Jer 52:15	7227
But Nebuzar-adan the *c* of the	Jer 52:16	7227
took the *c* of the guard away	Jer 52:19	7227
the *c* of the guard took Seraiah	Jer 52:24	7227
So Nebuzar-adan the *c* of the	Jer 52:26	7227
the *c* of the guard carried away	Jer 52:30	7227
Arioch the *c* of the king's guard	Dan 2:14	7229
and said to Arioch the king's *c*	Dan 2:15	7990
Then the band and the *c* and	Jn 18:12	*5506*
the *c* of the temple, and the	Acts 4:1	*4755*
the *c* of the temple and the chief	Acts 5:24	*4755*
Then went the *c* with the officers	Acts 5:26	*4755*
came unto the chief *c* of the band	Acts 21:31	*5506*
and when they saw the chief *c*	Acts 21:32	*5506*
Then the chief *c* came near	Acts 21:33	*5506*
castle, he said unto the chief *c*	Acts 21:37	*5506*
The chief *c* commanded him to be	Acts 22:24	*5506*
that, he went and told the chief *c*	Acts 22:26	*5506*
Then the chief *c* came, and said	Acts 22:27	*5506*
And the chief *c* answered, With a	Acts 22:28	*5506*
the chief *c* also was afraid,	Acts 22:29	*5506*
a great dissension, the chief *c*	Acts 23:10	*5506*
council signify to the chief *c*	Acts 23:15	*5506*
this young man unto the chief *c*	Acts 23:17	*5506*
and brought him to the chief *c*	Acts 23:18	*5506*
Then the chief *c* took him by the	Acts 23:19	*5506*
So the chief *c* then let the young	Acts 23:22	*5506*
But the chief *c* Lysias came upon	Acts 24:7	*5506*
the chief *c* shall come down	Acts 24:22	*5506*
prisoners to the *c* of the guard	Acts 28:16	*4759*
to make the *c* of their salvation	Heb 2:10	*747*

CAPTAINS {124}

Context	Reference	Number
and *c* over every one of them	Ex 14:7	7991
his chosen *c* also are drowned in	Ex 15:4	7991
with the *c* over thousands, and	Num 31:14	8269
c over hundreds, which came from	Num 31:14	8269
the *c* of thousands, and *c*	Num 31:48	8269
c of hundreds, came near unto	Num 31:48	8269
of the *c* of thousands, and of the	Num 31:52	8269
of the *c* of hundreds, was sixteen	Num 31:52	8269
the gold of the *c* of thousands	Num 31:54	8269
c over thousands, and *c*	Deut 1:15	8269
c over hundreds, and *c* over	Deut 1:15	8269
c over fifties, and *c* over	Deut 1:15	8269
c over tens, and officers among	Deut 1:15	8269
that they shall make *c* of the	Deut 20:9	8269
your *c* of your tribes, your	Deut 29:10	7218
said unto the *c* of the men of war	Josh 10:24	7101
will appoint him *c* over thousands	1Sa 8:12	8269
over thousands, and *c* over fifties	1Sa 8:12	8269
and make you all *c* of thousands	1Sa 22:7	8269
of thousands, and *c* of hundreds	1Sa 22:7	8269
had two men that were *c* of bands	2Sa 4:2	8269
set *c* of thousands and *c* of	2Sa 18:1	8269
and *c* of hundreds over them	2Sa 18:1	8269
the *c* charge concerning Absalom	2Sa 18:5	8269
in the seat, chief among the *c*	2Sa 23:8	7991
and against the *c* of the host	2Sa 24:4	8269
the *c* of the host went out from	2Sa 24:4	8269
the *c* of the host, and Abiathar	1Kin 1:25	8269
the two *c* of the hosts of Israel	1Kin 2:5	8269
and his princes, and his *c*	1Kin 9:22	7991
sent the *c* of the hosts which he	1Kin 15:20	8269
place, and put *c* in their rooms	1Kin 20:24	6346
two *c* that had rule over his	1Kin 22:31	8269
when the *c* of the chariots saw	1Kin 22:32	8269
when the *c* of the chariots	1Kin 22:33	8269
burnt up the two *c* of the former	2Kin 1:14	8269
about, and the *c* of the chariots	2Kin 8:21	8269
the *c* of the host were sitting	2Kin 9:5	8269
said to the guard and to the *c*	2Kin 10:25	7991
the *c* cast them out, and went to	2Kin 10:25	7991
rulers over hundreds, with the *c*	2Kin 11:4	3746
the *c* over the hundreds did	2Kin 11:9	8269
to the *c* over hundreds did the	2Kin 11:10	8269
commanded the *c* of the hundreds	2Kin 11:15	8269
rulers over hundreds, and the *c*	2Kin 11:19	3746
when all the *c* of the armies,	2Kin 25:23	8269
the *c* of the armies, arose, and	2Kin 25:26	8269
Seir, having for their *c* Pelatiah	1Chr 4:42	7218
a Hachmonite, the chief of the *c*	1Chr 11:11	7991
Now three of the thirty *c* went	1Chr 11:15	7218
of the sons of Gad, *c* of the host	1Chr 12:14	7218
Amasai, who was chief of the *c*	1Chr 12:18	7991
them, and made them *c* of the band	1Chr 12:18	7218
c of the thousands that were of	1Chr 12:20	7218
of valour, and were *c* in the host	1Chr 12:21	8269
father's house twenty and two *c*	1Chr 12:28	8269
And of Naphtali a thousand *c*	1Chr 12:34	8269
consulted with the *c* of thousands	1Chr 13:1	8269
the *c* over thousands, went to	1Chr 15:25	8269
the *c* of the host separated to	1Chr 25:1	8269
the *c* over thousands and hundreds,	1Chr 26:26	8269
the *c* of the host, had dedicated	1Chr 26:26	8269
c of thousands and hundreds, and	1Chr 27:1	8269
Perez was the chief of all the *c*	1Chr 27:3	8269
the *c* of the companies that	1Chr 28:1	8269
the *c* over the thousands, and	1Chr 28:1	8269
c over the hundreds, and the	1Chr 28:1	8269
the *c* of thousands and of hundreds	1Chr 29:6	8269
to the *c* of thousands and of	2Chr 1:2	8269
men of war, and chief of his *c*	2Chr 8:9	7991
c of his chariots and horsemen	2Chr 8:9	8269
put *c* in them, and store of	2Chr 11:11	5057
sent the *c* of his armies against	2Chr 16:4	8269
Of Judah, the *c* of thousands	2Chr 17:14	8269
c of the chariots that were with	2Chr 18:30	8269
when the *c* of the chariots saw	2Chr 18:31	8269
when the *c* of the chariots	2Chr 18:32	8269
him in, and the *c* of the chariots	2Chr 21:9	8269
took the *c* of hundreds, Azariah	2Chr 23:1	8269
to the *c* of hundreds spears	2Chr 23:9	8269
the priest brought out the *c* of	2Chr 23:14	8269
And he took the *c* of hundreds	2Chr 23:20	8269
made them *c* over thousands, and	2Chr 25:5	8269
c over hundreds, according to the	2Chr 25:5	8269
of Hananiah, one of the king's *c*	2Chr 26:11	8269
he set *c* of war over the people,	2Chr 32:6	8269
c in the camp of the king of	2Chr 32:21	8269
the *c* of the host of the king of	2Chr 33:11	8269
put *c* of war in all the fenced	2Chr 33:14	8269
the king had sent *c* of the army	Neh 2:9	8269
afar off, the thunder of the *c*	Job 39:25	8269
for thou hast taught them to be *c*	Jer 13:21	441
Now when all the *c* of the forces	Jer 40:7	8269
all the *c* of the forces that were	Jer 40:13	8269
all the *c* of the forces that were	Jer 41:11	8269
all the *c* of the forces that were	Jer 41:13	8269
all the *c* of the forces that were	Jer 41:16	8269
Then all the *c* of the forces, and	Jer 42:1	8269
all the *c* of the forces which	Jer 42:8	8269
all the *c* of the forces, and all	Jer 43:4	8269
all the *c* of the forces, took all	Jer 43:5	8269
thee will I break in pieces *c*	Jer 51:23	6346
the *c* thereof, and all the rulers	Jer 51:28	6346
princes, and her wise men, her *c*	Jer 51:57	6346
for Jerusalem, to appoint *c*	Eze 21:22	3733
Which were clothed with blue, *c*	Eze 23:6	6346
the Assyrians her neighbours, *c*	Eze 23:12	6346
of them desirable young men, *c*	Eze 23:23	6346
princes, the governors, and the *c*	Dan 3:2	6347
the princes, the governors, and *c*	Dan 3:3	6347
And the princes, governors, and *c*	Dan 3:27	6347
the counsellors, and the *c*	Dan 6:7	6347
thy *c* as the great grasshoppers,	Nah 3:17	2951
a supper to his lords, high *c*	Mk 6:21	*5506*
with the chief priests and *c*	Lk 22:4	*4755*
c of the temple, and the elders,	Lk 22:52	*4755*
of hearing, with the chief *c*	Acts 25:23	*5506*
and the rich men, and the chief *c*	Rev 6:15	*5506*
flesh of kings, and the flesh of *c*	Rev 19:18	*5506*

CAPTIVE {60}

Context	Reference	Number
that his brother was taken *c*	Gen 14:14	7617
ones, and their wives took they *c*	Gen 34:29	7617
of the *c* that was in the dungeon	Ex 12:29	7628
Asshur shall carry thee away *c*	Num 24:22	7617
hands, and thou hast taken them *c*	Deut 21:10	7617
Barak, and lead thy captivity *c*	Judg 5:12	7617
enemies, which led them away *c*	1Kin 8:48	7617
before them who carried them *c*	1Kin 8:50	7617
had brought away *c* out of the	2Kin 5:2	7617
thou hast taken *c* with thy sword	2Kin 6:22	7617
and carried them *c* to Assyria	2Kin 15:29	1540
carried the people of it *c* to Kir	2Kin 16:9	1540
of Babylon brought *c* to Babylon	2Kin 24:16	1473
king of Assyria carried away *c*	1Chr 5:6	1540
land whither they are carried *c*	2Chr 6:37	7617
children of Judah carry away *c*	2Chr 25:12	7617
c of their brethren two hundred	2Chr 28:8	7617
ye have taken *c* of your brethren	2Chr 28:11	7617
before them that lead them *c*	2Chr 30:9	7617
high, thou hast led captivity *c*	Ps 68:18	7617
us away *c* required of us a song	Ps 137:3	7617
my children, and am desolate, a *c*	Is 49:21	1473
mighty, or the lawful *c* delivered	Is 49:24	7628
The *c* exile hasteneth that he may	Is 51:14	6808
of thy neck, O *c* daughter of Zion	Is 52:2	7628
of Jerusalem *c* in the fifth month	Jer 1:3	1540
LORD's flock is carried away *c*	Jer 13:17	7617
shall be carried away *c* all of it	Jer 13:19	1540
it shall be wholly carried away *c*	Jer 13:19	1540
shall carry them *c* into Babylon	Jer 20:4	1540
place whither they have led him *c*	Jer 22:12	1540
of Babylon had carried away *c*	Jer 24:1	1540
that are carried away *c* of Judah	Jer 24:5	1546
when he carried away *c* Jeconiah	Jer 27:20	1540
and all that is carried away *c*	Jer 28:6	1473
away *c* from Jerusalem to Babylon	Jer 29:1	1473
I caused you to be carried away *c*	Jer 29:14	1540
of the guard carried away *c* into	Jer 39:9	1540
were carried away *c* of Jerusalem	Jer 40:1	1546
were carried away *c* unto Babylon	Jer 40:1	1540
not carried away *c* to Babylon	Jer 40:7	1540
Then Ishmael carried away *c* all	Jer 41:10	7617
of Nethaniah carried them away *c*	Jer 41:10	7617
away *c* from Mizpah cast about	Jer 41:14	7617
of the guard carried away *c*	Jer 52:15	1540
away *c* out of his own land	Jer 52:27	1540
Nebuchadrezzar carried away *c*	Jer 52:28	1540
c from Jerusalem eight hundred	Jer 52:29	1540
of the guard carried away *c* of	Jer 52:30	1540
away *c* the whole captivity	Amos 1:6	1540
Therefore now shall they go *c*	Amos 6:7	1540
c with the first that go *c*	Amos 6:7	1540
led away *c* out of their own land	Amos 7:11	1540
carried away *c* his forces	Obad 11	7617
And Huzzab shall be led away *c*	Nah 2:7	1540
be led away *c* into all nations	Lk 21:24	*163*
up on high, he led captivity *c*	Eph 4:8	*162*
who are taken *c* by him at his	2Ti 2:26	*2221*
lead *c* silly women laden with	2Ti 3:6	*162*

CAPTIVES {45}

Context	Reference	Number
as *c* taken with the sword	Gen 31:26	7617
took all the women of Midian *c*	Num 31:9	7617
And they brought the *c*, and the	Num 31:12	7628
your *c* on the third day, and on	Num 31:19	7628
seest among the *c* a beautiful	Deut 21:11	7633
blood of the slain and of the *c*	Deut 32:42	7633
And had taken the women *c*, that	1Sa 30:2	7617
and their daughters, were taken *c*	1Sa 30:3	7617
And David's two wives were taken *c*	1Sa 30:5	7617
away *c* unto the land of the enemy	1Kin 8:46	7617
land whither they were carried *c*	1Kin 8:47	7617
land of them that carried them *c*	1Kin 8:47	7617
of valour, even ten thousand *c*	2Kin 24:14	1540
they carry them away *c* unto a	2Chr 6:36	7617
whither they have carried them *c*	2Chr 6:38	7617
away a great multitude of them *c*	2Chr 28:5	7633
therefore, and deliver the *c* again	2Chr 28:11	7633
shall not bring in the *c* hither	2Chr 28:13	7633
So the armed men left the *c*	2Chr 28:14	7633
by name rose up, and took the *c*	2Chr 28:15	7633
smitten Judah, and carried away *c*	2Chr 28:17	7628
of all those that carried them *c*	Ps 106:46	7617
and they shall take them *c*	Is 14:2	7617
them *c*, whose *c* they were	Is 14:2	7617
prisoners, and the Ethiopians *c*	Is 20:4	1546
my city, and he shall let go my *c*	Is 45:13	1546
Even the *c* of the mighty shall be	Is 49:25	7628
to proclaim liberty to the *c*	Is 61:1	7628
of Judah, with all the *c* of Judah	Jer 28:4	1546
elders which were carried away *c*	Jer 29:1	1473
unto all that are carried away *c*	Jer 29:4	1473
caused you to be carried away *c*	Jer 29:7	1540
and carry us away *c* into Babylon	Jer 43:3	1540
burn them, and carry them away *c*	Jer 43:12	7617
for thy sons are taken *c*, and thy	Jer 48:46	7628
c, and thy daughters *c*	Jer 48:46	7633
that took them *c* held them fast	Jer 50:33	7617
as I was among the *c* by the river	Eze 1:1	1473
whither they shall be carried *c*	Eze 6:9	7617
of thy *c* in the midst of them	Eze 16:53	7628
found a man of the *c* of Judah	Dan 2:25	1123,1547
shall also carry *c* into Egypt	Dan 11:8	7628
to preach deliverance to the *c*	Lk 4:18	*164*

CAPTIVITY {129}

Context	Reference	Number
into *c* unto Sihon king of the	Num 21:29	7628
the raiment of her *c* from off her	Deut 21:13	7633
for they shall go into *c*	Deut 28:41	7628
the LORD thy God will turn thy *c*	Deut 30:3	7622
Barak, and lead thy *c* captive	Judg 5:12	7628
the day of the *c* of the land	Judg 18:30	1546
those carried he into *c* from	2Kin 24:15	1473
thirtieth year of the *c* of	2Kin 25:27	1546
dwelt in their steads until the *c*	1Chr 5:22	1473

And Jehozadak went into c, when ... 1Chr 6:15
unto thee in the land of their c ... 2Chr 6:37 7633
their soul in the land of their c ... 2Chr 6:38 7633
and our wives are in c for this ... 2Chr 29:9 7628
the c that were brought up from ... Ezr 1:11 1473
that went up out of the c ... Ezr 2:1 7628
come out of the c unto Jerusalem ... Ezr 3:8 7628
the c builded the temple unto the ... Ezr 4:1 1473
the rest of the children of the c ... Ezr 6:16 1547
the children of the c kept the ... Ezr 6:19 1473
for all the children of the c ... Ezr 6:20 1473
which were come again out of c ... Ezr 6:21 1473
which were come out of the c ... Ezr 8:35 7628
of the lands, to the sword, to c ... Ezr 9:7 7628
unto all the children of the c ... Ezr 10:7 1473
And the children of the c did so ... Ezr 10:16 1473
escaped, which were left of the c ... Neh 1:2 7628
c there in the province are in ... Neh 1:3 7628
them for a prey in the land of c ... Neh 4:4 7633
that went up out of the c ... Neh 7:6 7628
again out of the c made booths ... Neh 8:17 7628
the c which had been carried away ... Est 2:6 1473
And the LORD turned the c of Job ... Job 42:10 7622
bringeth back the c of his people ... Ps 14:7 7622
bringeth back the c of his people ... Ps 53:6 7622
on high, thou hast led c captive ... Ps 68:18 7628
And delivered his strength into c ... Ps 78:61 7628
hast brought back the c of Jacob ... Ps 85:1 7622
LORD turned again the c of Zion ... Ps 126:1 7622
Turn again our c, O LORD, as the ... Ps 126:4 7622
my people are gone into c ... Is 5:13 1540
carry thee away with a mighty c ... Is 22:17 2925
but themselves are gone into c ... Is 46:2 7628
are for the c, to the c ... Jer 15:2 7628
in thine house shall go into c ... Jer 20:6 7628
and thy lovers shall go into c ... Jer 22:22 7628
and I will turn away your c ... Jer 29:14 7622
not gone forth with you into c ... Jer 29:16 1473
word of the LORD, all ye of the c ... Jer 29:20 1473
c of Judah which are in Babylon ... Jer 29:22 1546
Babylon, saying, This c is long ... Jer 29:28
Send to all them of the c ... Jer 29:31 1473
again the c of my people Israel ... Jer 30:3 7622
thy seed from the land of their c ... Jer 30:10 7628
one of them, shall go into c ... Jer 30:16 7633
again the c of Jacob's tents ... Jer 30:18 7622
when I shall bring again their c ... Jer 31:23 7622
I will cause their c to return ... Jer 32:44 7622
And I will cause the c of Judah ... Jer 33:7 7622
the c of Israel to return, and ... Jer 33:7 7622
cause to return the c of the land ... Jer 33:11 7622
I will cause their c to return ... Jer 33:26 7622
and such as are for c to c ... Jer 43:11 7628
and such as are for c to c ... Jer 43:11 7628
furnish thyself to go into c ... Jer 46:19 1473
thy seed from the land of their c ... Jer 46:27 7633
go forth into c with his priests ... Jer 48:7 1473
neither hath he gone into c ... Jer 48:11 1473
the c of Moab in the latter days ... Jer 48:47 7622
for their king shall go into c ... Jer 49:3 1473
I will bring again the c of the ... Jer 49:6 7622
I will bring again the c of Elam ... Jer 49:39 7622
thirtieth year of the c of ... Jer 52:31 1546
Judah is gone into c because of ... Lam 1:3 1540
are gone into c before the enemy ... Lam 1:5 7628
and my young men are gone into c ... Lam 1:18 7628
iniquity, to turn away thy c ... Lam 2:14 7622
no more carry thee away into c ... Lam 4:22 1540
fifth year of king Jehoiachin's c ... Eze 1:2 1546
And go, get thee to them of the c ... Eze 3:11 1473
came to them of the c at Tel-abib ... Eze 3:15 1473
into Chaldea, to them of the c ... Eze 11:24 1473
c all the things that the LORD ... Eze 11:25 1473
as they that go forth into c ... Eze 12:4 1473
my stuff by day, as stuff for c ... Eze 12:7 1473
they shall remove and go into c ... Eze 12:11 7628
When I shall bring again their c ... Eze 16:53 7622
the c of Sodom and her daughters, ... Eze 16:53 7622
the c of Samaria and her daughters ... Eze 16:53 7622
then will I bring again the c of ... Eze 16:53 7622
of Judah, when they went into c ... Eze 25:3 1473
I will bring again the c of Egypt ... Eze 29:14 7622
and these cities shall go into c ... Eze 30:17 7628
and her daughters shall go into c ... Eze 30:18 7628
pass in the twelfth year of our c ... Eze 33:21 1546
went into c for their iniquity ... Eze 39:23 1540
will I bring again the c of Jacob ... Eze 39:25 7622
be led into c among the heathen ... Eze 39:28 1473
five and twentieth year of our c ... Eze 40:1 1546
of the children of the c of Judah ... Dan 5:13 1547
of the children of the c of Judah ... Dan 6:13 1547
by the sword, and by flame, by c ... Dan 11:33 7628
I returned the c of my people ... Hos 6:11 7622
shall bring again the c of Judah ... Joel 3:1 7622
of Syria shall go into c unto Kir ... Amos 1:5 1540
carried away captive the whole c ... Amos 1:6 1546
delivered up the whole c to Edom ... Amos 1:9 1546
And their king shall go into c ... Amos 1:15 1473
for Gilgal shall surely go into c ... Amos 5:5 1540
you to go into c beyond Damascus ... Amos 5:27 1540
go into c forth of his land ... Amos 7:17 1540
though they go into c before ... Amos 9:4 7628
the c of my people of Israel ... Amos 9:14 7622
the c of this host of the ... Obad 20 1546
the c of Jerusalem, which is in ... Obad 20 1546
they are gone into c from thee ... Mic 1:16 1540
she carried away, she went into c ... Nah 3:10 7628
shall gather the c as the sand ... Hab 1:9 7628

visit them, and turn away their c ... Zeph 2:7 7622
turn back your c before your eyes ... Zeph 3:20 7622
Take of them of the c, even of ... Zec 6:10 1473
of the city shall go forth into c ... Zec 14:2 1473
bringing me into c to the law of ... Rom 7:23 *163*
bringing into c every thought to ... 2Cor 10:5 *163*
he led c captive, and gave gifts ... Eph 4:8 *161*
into c shall go into c ... Rev 13:10 *161*

CARBUNCLE {3}
be a sardius, a topaz, and a c ... Ex 28:17 1304
was a sardius, a topaz, and a c ... Ex 39:10 1304
sapphire, the emerald, and the c ... Eze 28:13 1304

CARBUNCLES {1}
of agates, and thy gates of c ... Is 54:12 68,688

CARCAS *(car'-cas)* {1} *A servant of King Ahasuerus.*
Bigtha, and Abagtha, Zethar, and C ... Est 1:10 3752

CARCASE {34}
whether it be a c of an unclean ... Lev 5:2 5038
or a c of unclean cattle, or the ... Lev 5:2 5038
or the c of unclean creeping ... Lev 5:2 5038
their c shall ye not touch ... Lev 11:8 5038
whosoever toucheth the c of them ... Lev 11:24 5038
c of them shall wash his clothes ... Lev 11:25 5038
whoso toucheth their c shall be ... Lev 11:27 5038
he that beareth the c of them ... Lev 11:28 5038
their c falleth shall be unclean ... Lev 11:35 5038
toucheth their c shall be unclean ... Lev 11:36 5038
if any part of their c fall upon ... Lev 11:37 5038
any part of their c fall thereon ... Lev 11:38 5038
he that toucheth the c thereof ... Lev 11:39 5038
he that eateth of the c of it ... Lev 11:40 5038
he also that beareth the c of it ... Lev 11:40 5038
flesh, nor touch their dead c ... Deut 14:8 5038
thy c shall be meat unto all ... Deut 28:26 5038
take his c down from the tree ... Josh 8:29 5038
aside to see the c of the lion ... Judg 14:8 4658
and honey in the c of the lion ... Judg 14:8 1472
honey out of the c of the lion ... Judg 14:9 1472
thy c shall not come unto the ... 1Kin 13:22 5038
his c was cast in the way, and the ... 1Kin 13:24 5038
it, the lion also stood by the c ... 1Kin 13:24 5038
saw the c cast in the way ... 1Kin 13:25 5038
and the lion standing by the c ... 1Kin 13:25 5038
found his c cast in the way, and ... 1Kin 13:28 5038
ass and the lion standing by the c ... 1Kin 13:28 5038
the lion had not eaten the c ... 1Kin 13:28 5038
took up the c of the man of God ... 1Kin 13:29 5038
he laid his c in his own grave ... 1Kin 13:30 5038
the c of Jezebel shall be as dung ... 2Kin 9:37 5038
as a c trodden under feet ... Is 14:19 6297
For wheresoever the c is, there ... Mt 24:28 *4430*

CARCASES {22}
the fowls came down upon the c ... Gen 15:11 6297
shall have their c in abomination ... Lev 11:11 5038
The c of every beast which ... Lev 11:26 5038
cast your c upon the c of ... Lev 26:30 6297
Your c shall fall in this ... Num 14:29 6297
But as for you, your c, they ... Num 14:32 6297
until your c be wasted in the ... Num 14:33 6297
I will give the c of the host of ... 1Sa 17:46 6297
their c were torn in the midst of ... Is 5:25 5038
shall come up out of their c ... Is 34:3 6297
look upon the c of the men that ... Is 66:24 6297
the c of this people shall be ... Jer 7:33 5038
Even the c of men shall fall as ... Jer 9:22 5038
their c shall be meat for the ... Jer 16:4 5038
with the c of their detestable ... Jer 16:18 5038
their c will I give to be meat ... Jer 19:7 5038
I will lay the dead c of the ... Eze 6:5 6297
nor by the c of their kings in ... Eze 43:7 6297
the c of their kings, far from me ... Eze 43:9 6297
of slain, and a great number of c ... Nah 3:3 6297
whose c fell in the wilderness ... Heb 3:17 *2966*

CARCHEMISH *(car'-ke-mish)* {2} See CHARCHEMISH. *A city on the Euphrates River.*
Is not Calno as C ... Is 10:9 3751
was by the river Euphrates in C ... Jer 46:2 3751

CARE {20}
hath left the c of the asses ... 1Sa 10:2 1697
flee away, they will not c for us ... 2Sa 18:3 7760,3820
of us die, will they c for us ... 2Sa 18:3 7760,3820
careful for us with all this c ... 2Kin 4:13 2731
nation, that dwelleth without c ... Jer 49:31 983
eat bread by weight, and with c ... Eze 4:16 1674
the c of this world, and the ... Mt 13:22 *3308*
him to an inn, and took c of him ... Lk 10:34 *1959*
and said unto him, Take c of him ... Lk 10:35 *1959*
dost thou not c that my sister ... Lk 10:40 *3199*
c not for it ... 1Cor 7:21 *3199*
Doth God take c for oxen ... 1Cor 9:9 *3199*
have the same c one for another ... 1Cor 12:25 *3309*
but that our c for you in the ... 2Cor 7:12 *4710*
which put the same earnest c into ... 2Cor 8:16 *4710*
the c of all the churches ... 2Cor 11:28 *3308*
will naturally c for your state ... Phil 2:20 *3309*
that now at the last your c of me ... Phil 4:10 *5426*
how shall he take c of the church ... 1Ti 3:5 *1959*
Casting all your c upon him ... 1Pet 5:7 *3308*

CAREAH *(ca-re'-ah)* {1} See KAREAH. *Father of Johanan.*
and Johanan the son of C, and ... 2Kin 25:23 7143

CARED {3}
no man c for my soul ... Ps 142:4 1875
not that he c for the poor ... Jn 12:6 *3199*
Gallio c for none of those things ... Acts 18:17 *3199*

CAREFUL {7}
thou hast been c for us with all ... 2Kin 4:13 2729
shall not be c in the year of ... Jer 17:8 1672
we are not c to answer thee in ... Dan 3:16 2818
her, Martha, Martha, thou art c ... Lk 10:41 *3309*
Be c for nothing ... Phil 4:6 *3309*
wherein ye were also c, but ye ... Phil 4:10 *5426*
might be c to maintain good works ... Titus 3:8 *5431*

CAREFULLY {4}
Only if thou c hearken unto the ... Deut 15:5 8085
of Maroth waited c for good ... Mic 1:12 2470
I sent him therefore the more c ... Phil 2:28 *4708*
though he sought it c with tears ... Heb 12:17 *1567*

CAREFULNESS {4}
water with trembling and with c ... Eze 12:18 1674
They shall eat their bread with c ... Eze 12:19 1674
But I would have you without c ... 1Cor 7:32 *275*
what c it wrought in you, yea, ... 2Cor 7:11 *4710*

CARELESS {5}
were therein, how they dwelt c ... Judg 18:7 983
hear my voice, ye c daughters ... Is 32:9 982
shall ye be troubled, ye c women ... Is 32:10 982
be troubled, ye c ones ... Is 32:11 982
to make the c Ethiopians afraid ... Eze 30:9 983

CARELESSLY {3}
to pleasures, that dwellest c ... Is 47:8 983
them that dwell c in the isles ... Eze 39:6 983
the rejoicing city that dwelt c ... Zeph 2:15 983

CARES {3}
the c of this world, and the ... Mk 4:19 *3303*
go forth, and are choked with c ... Lk 8:14 *3303*
c of this life, and so that day ... Lk 21:34 *3303*

CAREST {3}
neither c thou for any man ... Mt 22:16 *3199*
c thou not that we perish ... Mk 4:38 *3199*
thou art true, and c for no man ... Mk 12:14 *3199*

CARETH {7}
land which the LORD thy God c for ... Deut 11:12 1875
hireling, and c not for the sheep ... Jn 10:13 *3199*
He that is unmarried c for the ... 1Cor 7:32 *3309*
But he that is married c for the ... 1Cor 7:33 *3309*
The unmarried woman c for the ... 1Cor 7:34 *3309*
but she that is married c for the ... 1Cor 7:34 *3309*
for he c for you ... 1Pet 5:7 *3199*

CARING {1}
my father leave c for the asses ... 1Sa 9:5

CARKAS See CARCAS.

CARMEL *(car'-mel)* {26} See CARMELITE.
1. A mountain range in Canaan.
the king of Jokneam of C, one ... Josh 12:22 3760
and reacheth to C westward ... Josh 19:26 3760
Samuel, saying, Saul came to C ... 1Sa 15:12 3760
to me all Israel unto mount C ... 1Kin 18:19 3760
prophets together unto mount C ... 1Kin 18:20 3760
And Elijah went up to the top of C ... 1Kin 18:42 3760
And he went from thence to mount C ... 2Kin 2:25 3760
unto the man of God to mount C ... 2Kin 4:25 3760
and into the forest of his C ... 2Kin 19:23 3760
in the mountains, and in C ... 2Chr 26:10 3760
Thine head upon thee is like C ... Song 7:5 3760
and C shake off their fruits ... Is 33:9 3760
unto it, the excellency of C ... Is 35:2 3760
border, and the forest of his C ... Is 37:24 3760
as C by the sea, so shall he come ... Jer 46:18 3760
habitation, and he shall feed on C ... Jer 50:19 3760
the top of C shall wither ... Amos 1:2 3760
hide themselves in the top of C ... Amos 9:3 3760
in the wood, in the midst of C ... Mic 7:14 3760
Bashan languisheth, and C, and the ... Nah 1:4 3760
2. A town in Judah.
Maon, C, and Ziph, and Juttah, ... Josh 15:55 3760
Maon, whose possessions were in C ... 1Sa 25:2 3760
and he was shearing his sheep in C ... 1Sa 25:2 3760
the young men, Get you up to C ... 1Sa 25:5 3760
all the while they were in C ... 1Sa 25:7 3760
David were come to Abigail to C ... 1Sa 25:40 3760

CARMELITE *(car'-mel-ite)* {5} See CARMELITESS. *An inhabitant of Carmel 2.*
Abigail the wife of Nabal the C ... 1Sa 30:5 3761
and Abigail Nabal's wife the C ... 2Sa 2:2 3761
Abigail the wife of Nabal the C ... 2Sa 3:3 3761
Hezrai the C, Paarai the Arbite, ... 2Sa 23:35 3761
Hezro the C, Naarai the son of ... 1Chr 11:37 3761

CARMELITESS *(car'-mel-i-tess)* {2}
Jezreelitess, and Abigail the C ... 1Sa 27:3 3762
second Daniel, of Abigail the C ... 1Chr 3:1 3762

CARMI *(car'-mi)* {8} See CARMITES.
1. Father of Achan.
for Achan, the son of C, the son ... Josh 7:1 3756
and Achan, the son of C, the son ... Josh 7:18 3756
And the sons of C ... 1Chr 2:7 3756
Pharez, Hezron, and C, and Hur, and ... 1Chr 4:1 3756
2. A son of Reuben.
and Phallu, and Hezron, and C ... Gen 46:9 3756
Hanoch, and Pallu, Hezron, and C ... Ex 6:14 3756
of C, the family of the Carmites ... Num 26:6 3756
Hanoch, and Pallu, Hezron, and C ... 1Chr 5:3 3756

CARMITES *(car'-mites)* {1} *Descendants of Carmi 2.*
of Carmi, the family of the C ... Num 26:6 3757

CARNAL {11}
but I am c, sold under sin ... Rom 7:14 *4559*
Because the c mind is enmity ... Rom 8:7 *4561*
to minister unto them in c things ... Rom 15:27 *4559*

as unto spiritual, but as unto c ... 1Cor 3:1 4559
For ye are yet c ... 1Cor 3:3 4559
and divisions, are ye not c ... 1Cor 3:3 4559
are ye not c? ... 1Cor 3:4 4559
if we shall reap your c things ... 1Cor 9:11 4559
weapons of our warfare are not c ... 2Cor 10:4 4559
after the law of a c commandment ... Heb 7:16 4559
c ordinances, imposed on them ... Heb 9:10 4561

CARNALLY {4}
lie c with thy neighbour's wife ... Lev 18:20 7903,2233
whosoever lieth c with a woman ... Lev 19:20 7902,2233
a man lie with her c, and it be ... Num 5:13 7902,2233
For to be c minded is death ... Rom 8:6 4561

CARPENTER {3}
So the c encouraged the goldsmith ... Is 41:7 2796
The c stretcheth out his rule ... Is 44:13 2796,6086
Is not this the c, the son of ... Mk 6:3 5045

CARPENTER'S {1}
Is not this the c son ... Mt 13:55 5045

CARPENTERS {9}
to David, and cedar trees, and c ... 2Sa 5:11 2796,6086
and they laid it out to the c ... 2Kin 12:11 6086
Unto c, and builders, and masons, ... 2Kin 22:6 2796
of cedars, with masons and c ... 1Chr 14:1 2796,6086
c to repair the house of the LORD ... 2Chr 24:12 2796
also unto the masons, and to the c ... Ezr 3:7 2796
the princes of Judah, with the c ... Jer 24:1 2796
of Judah and Jerusalem, and the c ... Jer 29:2 2796
And the LORD shewed me four c ... Zec 1:20 2796

CARPUS *(car'-pus)* {1} *A friend of Paul.*
cloke that I left at Troas with C ... 2Ti 4:13 2591

CARRIAGE {3}
the cattle and the c before them ... Judg 18:21 3520
David left his c in the hand of ... 1Sa 17:22 3627
the hand of the keeper of the c ... 1Sa 17:22 3627

CARRIAGES {3}
at Michmash he hath laid up his c ... Is 10:28 3627
your c were heavy loaden ... Is 46:1 5385
after those days we took up our c ... Acts 21:15 643

CARRIED {145}
he c away all his cattle, and all ... Gen 31:18 5090
c away my daughters, as captives ... Gen 31:26 5090
of Israel c Jacob their father ... Gen 46:5 5375
For his sons c him into the land ... Gen 50:13 5375
c them in their coats out of the ... Lev 10:5 5375
c them over with them unto the ... Josh 4:8 5674
c them up to the top of an hill ... Judg 16:3 5927
of Israel be c about unto Gath ... 1Sa 5:8 5437
they c the ark of the God of ... 1Sa 5:8 5437
that, after they had c it about ... 1Sa 5:9 5437
but c them away, and went on their ... 1Sa 30:2 5090
that the Amalekites had c away ... 1Sa 30:18 3947
but David c it aside into the ... 2Sa 6:10 5186
Abiathar c the ark of God again ... 2Sa 15:29 7725
land whither they were c captives ... 1Kin 8:47 7617
land of them that c them captives ... 1Kin 8:47 7617
before them who c them captive ... 1Kin 8:50 7617
c him up into a loft, where he ... 1Kin 17:19 5927
Then they c him forth out of the ... 1Kin 21:13 3318
c thence silver, and gold, and ... 2Kin 7:8 5375
c thence also, and went and hid it ... 2Kin 7:8 5375
his servants c him in a chariot ... 2Kin 9:28 7392
c them captive to Assyria ... 2Kin 15:29 1540
c the people of it captive to Kir ... 2Kin 16:9 1540
c Israel away into Assyria, and ... 2Kin 17:6 1540
whom the LORD c away before them ... 2Kin 17:11 1540
So was Israel c away out of their ... 2Kin 17:23 1540
they had c away from Samaria came ... 2Kin 17:28 1540
whom they c away from thence ... 2Kin 17:33 1540
this day, shall be c into Babylon ... 2Kin 20:17 5375
c the ashes of them unto Beth-el ... 2Kin 23:4 5375
his servants c him in a chariot ... 2Kin 23:30 7392
he c out thence all the treasures ... 2Kin 24:13 3318
he c away all Jerusalem, and all ... 2Kin 24:14 1540
he c away Jehoiachin to Babylon, ... 2Kin 24:15 1540
those c he into captivity from ... 2Kin 24:15 1980
of brass, and c him to Babylon ... 2Kin 25:7 935
c the brass of them to Babylon ... 2Kin 25:13 5375
So Judah was c away out of their ... 2Kin 25:21 1540
king of Assyria c away captive ... 1Chr 5:6 1540
and he c them away, even the ... 1Chr 5:26 1540
when the LORD c away Judah ... 1Chr 6:15 1540
who were c away to Babylon for ... 1Chr 9:1 1540
they c the ark of God in a new ... 1Chr 13:7 7392
but c it aside into the house of ... 1Chr 13:13 5186
land whither they are c captive ... 2Chr 6:37 7617
whither they have c them captives ... 2Chr 6:38 7617
he c away also the shields of ... 2Chr 12:9 3947
they c away very much spoil ... 2Chr 14:13 5375
c away sheep and camels in ... 2Chr 14:15 7617
they c away the stones of Ramah, ... 2Chr 16:6 5375
c away all the substance that was ... 2Chr 21:17 7617
it, and c it to his place again ... 2Chr 24:11 7725
c away a great multitude of them ... 2Chr 28:5 7617
the children of Israel c away ... 2Chr 28:8 7617
c all the feeble of them upon ... 2Chr 28:15 5095
smitten Judah, and c away captives ... 2Chr 28:17 7617
with fetters, and c him to Babylon ... 2Chr 33:11 3212
Shaphan c the book to the king, ... 2Chr 34:16 935
his brother, and c him to Egypt ... 2Chr 36:4 935
Nebuchadnezzar also c of the ... 2Chr 36:7 935
the sword c he away to Babylon ... 2Chr 36:20 1473
of those which had been c away ... Ezr 2:1 1540
Babylon had c away unto Babylon ... Ezr 2:1 1540
c the people away into Babylon ... Ezr 5:12 1541

of those that had been c away ... Ezr 8:35 1473
of those that had been c away ... Ezr 9:4 1473
of them that had been c away ... Ezr 10:6 1473
of those that had been c away ... Ezr 10:8 1473
of those that had been c away ... Neh 7:6 1473
the king of Babylon had c away ... Neh 7:6 1540
Who had been c away from ... Est 2:6 1540
been c away with Jeconiah king of ... Est 2:6 1540
the king of Babylon had c away ... Est 2:6 1540
have c them away, yea, and slain ... Job 1:17 3947
of the froward is c headlong ... Job 5:13 4116
I should have been c from the ... Job 10:19 2986
though the mountains be c into ... Ps 46:2 4131
of all those that c them captives ... Ps 106:46 7617
For there they that c us away ... Ps 137:3 7617
this day, shall be c to Babylon ... Is 39:6 5375
which are c from the womb ... Is 46:3 5375
shall be c upon their shoulders ... Is 49:22 5375
our griefs, and c our sorrows ... Is 53:4 5445
c them all the days of old ... Is 63:9 5375
LORD's flock is c away captive ... Jer 13:17 7617
Judah shall be c away captive all ... Jer 13:19 1540
it shall be wholly c away captive ... Jer 13:19 1540
king of Babylon had c away ... Jer 24:1 1540
that are c away captive of Judah ... Jer 24:5 1546
when he c away captive Jeconiah ... Jer 27:20 1546
They shall be c to Babylon ... Jer 27:22 935
this place, and c them to Babylon ... Jer 28:3 935
all that is c away captive, from ... Jer 28:6 1473
elders which were c away captives ... Jer 29:1 1473
c away captive from Jerusalem to ... Jer 29:1 1540
unto all that are c away captives ... Jer 29:4 1473
to be c away from Jerusalem unto ... Jer 29:4 1540
caused you to be c away captives ... Jer 29:7 1540
I caused you to be c away captive ... Jer 29:14 1540
the captain of the guard c away ... Jer 39:9 1540
were c away captive of Jerusalem ... Jer 40:1 1546
which were c away captive unto ... Jer 40:1 1540
of them that were not c away ... Jer 40:7 1540
Then Ishmael c away captive all ... Jer 41:10 7617
of Nethaniah c them away captive ... Jer 41:10 7617
c away captive from Mizpah cast ... Jer 41:14 7617
c him up unto the king of Babylon ... Jer 52:9 5927
c him to Babylon, and put him in ... Jer 52:11 935
the captain of the guard c away ... Jer 52:15 1540
c all the brass of them to ... Jer 52:17 5375
Thus Judah was c away captive out ... Jer 52:27 1540
Nebuchadrezzar c away captive ... Jer 52:28 1540
year of Nebuchadrezzar he c away ... Jer 52:29
the captain of the guard c away ... Jer 52:30 1540
whither they shall be c captives ... Eze 6:9 7617
c it into a land of traffick ... Eze 17:4 935
c me out in the spirit of the ... Eze 37:1 3318
which he c into the land of ... Dan 1:2 935
the wind c them away, that no ... Dan 2:35 5376
It shall be also c unto Assyria ... Hos 10:6 2986
Assyrians, and oil is c into Egypt ... Hos 12:1 2986
have c into your temples my ... Joel 3:5 935
because they c away captive the ... Amos 1:6 1540
c away captive his forces ... Obad 11 7617
Yet was she c away, she went into ... Nah 3:10 1473
time they were c away to Babylon ... Mt 1:11 3350
c him away, and delivered him to ... Mk 15:1 667
there was a dead man c out ... Lk 7:12 1580
died, and was c by the angels into ... Lk 16:22 667
from them, and c up into heaven ... Lk 24:51 339
lame from his mother's womb was c ... Acts 3:2 941
up, and c him out, and buried him ... Acts 5:6 1627
were c over into Sychem, and laid ... Acts 7:16 3346
devout men c Stephen to his ... Acts 8:2 4792
him to be c into the castle ... Acts 21:34 71
c away unto these dumb idols, ... 1Cor 12:2 520
c away with their dissimulation ... Gal 2:13 4879
c about with every wind of ... Eph 4:14 4064
Be not c about with divers and ... Heb 13:9 4064
clouds that are c with a tempest ... 2Pet 2:17 1643
without water, c about of winds ... Jude 12 4064
her to be c away of the flood ... Rev 12:15 4216
So he c me away in the spirit ... Rev 17:3 667
he c me away in the spirit to a ... Rev 21:10 667

CARRIEST {1}
Thou c them away as with a flood ... Ps 90:5 2229

CARRIETH {3}
and as chaff that the storm c away ... Job 21:18 1589
The east wind c him away, and he ... Job 27:21 5375
woman, and of the beast that c her ... Rev 17:7 941

CARRY {90}
going to c it down to Egypt ... Gen 37:25 3381
c corn for the famine of your ... Gen 42:19 935
c down the man a present, a ... Gen 43:11 3381
sacks, c it again in your hand ... Gen 43:12 7725
with food, as much as they can c ... Gen 44:1 5375
which Joseph had sent to c him ... Gen 45:27 5375
which Pharaoh had sent to c him ... Gen 46:5 5375
thou shalt c me out of Egypt, and ... Gen 47:30 5375
ye shall c up my bones from hence ... Gen 50:25 5927
thou shalt not c forth ought of ... Ex 12:46 3318
ye shall c up my bones away hence ... Ex 13:19 5927
to c us forth out of Egypt ... Ex 14:11 3318
go not with me, c us not up hence ... Ex 33:15 5927
c forth without the camp unto a ... Lev 4:12 3318
he shall c forth the bullock ... Lev 4:21 3318
c forth the ashes without the ... Lev 6:11 3318
c your brethren from before the ... Lev 10:4 5375
he shall c them forth out of the ... Lev 14:45 3318
shall one c forth without the ... Lev 16:27 3318
C them in thy bosom, as a nursing ... Num 11:12 5375

Asshur shall c thee away captive ... Num 24:22 7617
so that thou art not able to c it ... Deut 14:24 5375
Thou shalt c much seed out into ... Deut 28:38 3318
ye shall c them over with you, and ... Josh 4:3 5674
c these ten cheeses unto the ... 1Sa 17:18 935
unto him, Go, c them to the city ... 1Sa 20:40 935
C back the ark of God into the ... 2Sa 15:25 7725
to c over the king's household ... 2Sa 19:18 5674
so that they c them away captives ... 1Kin 8:46 7617
shall c thee whither I know not ... 1Kin 18:12 5375
then c him out, and stone him, ... 1Kin 21:10 3318
c him back unto Amon the governor ... 1Kin 22:26 7725
hand, and c me out of the host ... 1Kin 22:34 3318
to a lad, C him to his mother ... 2Kin 4:19 5375
c him to an inner chamber ... 2Kin 9:2 935
C thither one of the priests whom ... 2Kin 17:27 1980
the king of Assyria did c away ... 2Kin 18:11 1540
the captain of the guard c away ... 2Kin 25:11 1540
to c tidings unto their idols, and ... 1Chr 10:9 1319
None ought to c the ark of God ... 1Chr 15:2 5375
LORD chosen to c the ark of God ... 1Chr 15:2 5375
shall no more c the tabernacle ... 1Chr 23:26 5375
thou shalt c it up to Jerusalem ... 2Chr 2:16 5927
they c them away captives unto a ... 2Chr 6:36 7617
c him back to Amon the governor ... 2Chr 18:25 7725
that thou mayest c me out of the ... 2Chr 18:33 3318
more than they could c away ... 2Chr 20:25 4853
children of Judah c away captive ... 2Chr 25:12 7617
c forth the filthiness out of the ... 2Chr 29:5 3318
to c it out abroad into the brook ... 2Chr 29:16 3318
in fetters, to c him to Babylon ... 2Chr 36:6 3212
c them into the temple that is in ... Ezr 5:15 5182
to c the silver and gold, which ... Ezr 7:15 2987
Why doth thine heart c thee away ... Job 15:12 3947
he dieth he shall c nothing away ... Ps 49:17 3947
which he may c away in his hand ... Eccl 5:15 3212
bird of the air shall c the voice ... Eccl 10:20 3212
shall c it away safe, and none ... Is 5:29 6403
shall they c away to the brook of ... Is 15:7 5375
the LORD will c thee away with a ... Is 22:17 2904
her own feet shall c her afar off ... Is 23:7 2986
they will c their riches upon the ... Is 30:6 5375
c them in his bosom, and shall ... Is 40:11 5375
and the wind shall c them away ... Is 41:16 5375
even to hoar hairs will I c you ... Is 46:4 5445
even I will c, and will deliver ... Is 46:4 5445
him upon the shoulder, they c him ... Is 46:7 5445
the wind shall c them all away ... Is 57:13 5375
Neither c forth a burden out of ... Jer 17:22 3318
he shall c them captive into ... Jer 20:4 1540
take them, and c them to Babylon ... Jer 20:5 935
with chains, to c him to Babylon ... Jer 39:7 935
that he should c him home ... Jer 39:14 3318
c us away captives into Babylon ... Jer 43:3 1540
them, and c them away captives ... Jer 43:12 7617
he will no more c thee away into ... Lam 4:22 1540
in their sight, and c out thereby ... Eze 12:5 3318
c it forth in the twilight ... Eze 12:6 3318
through the wall to c out thereby ... Eze 12:12 3318
men that c tales to shed blood ... Eze 22:9 7400
to c away silver and gold, to take ... Eze 38:13 5375
shall also c captives into Egypt ... Dan 11:8 935
began to c about in beds those ... Mk 6:55 4046
c any vessel through the temple ... Mk 11:16 1308
C neither purse, nor scrip, nor ... Lk 10:4 941
not lawful for thee to c thy bed ... Jn 5:10 142
c thee whither thou wouldest not ... Jn 21:18 5342
at the door, and shall c thee out ... Acts 5:9 1627
I will c you away beyond Babylon ... Acts 7:43 3351
is certain we can c nothing out ... 1Ti 6:7 1627

CARRYING {8}
one c three kids, and another ... 1Sa 10:3 5375
another c three loaves of bread, ... 1Sa 10:3 5375
another c a bottle of wine ... 1Sa 10:3 5375
c bows, turned back in the day of ... Ps 78:9 7411
unto the c away of Jerusalem ... Jer 1:3 1540
from David until the c away into ... Mt 1:17 3350
from the c away into Babylon unto ... Mt 1:17 3350
c her forth, buried her by her ... Acts 5:10 1627

CARSHENA *(car-she'-nah)* {1} *A Persian prince.*
And the next unto him was C ... Est 1:14 3771

CART {15}
Now therefore make a new c ... 1Sa 6:7 5600
no yoke, and tie the kine to the c ... 1Sa 6:7 5699
of the LORD, and lay it upon the c ... 1Sa 6:8 5699
milch kine, and tied them to the c ... 1Sa 6:10 5699
the ark of the LORD upon the c ... 1Sa 6:11 5699
the c came into the field of ... 1Sa 6:14 5699
and they clave the wood of the c ... 1Sa 6:14 5699
set the ark of God upon a new c ... 2Sa 6:3 5699
sons of Abinadab, drave the new c ... 2Sa 6:3 5699
c out of the house of Abinadab ... 1Chr 13:7 5699
and Uzza and Ahio drave the c ... 1Chr 13:7 5699
and sin as it were with a c rope ... Is 5:18 5699
neither is a c wheel turned about ... Is 28:27 5699
break it with the wheel of his c ... Is 28:28 5699
as a c is pressed that is full of ... Amos 2:13 5699

CARVED {13}
house, and fetched the c image ... Judg 18:18 6459
the house within was c with knops ... 1Kin 6:18 4734
he c all the walls of the house ... 1Kin 6:29 7049
about with c figures of cherubims ... 1Kin 6:29 6603
he c upon them carvings of ... 1Kin 6:32 7049
he c thereon cherubims and palm ... 1Kin 6:35 7049
with gold fitted upon the c work ... 1Kin 6:35 2707
And he set a c image, the idol ... 2Chr 33:7 6459

the *c* images which Manasseh his 2Chr 33:22 6456
the *c* images, and the molten 2Chr 34:3 6456
the *c* images, and the molten 2Chr 34:4 6456
But now they break down the *c* Ps 74:6 6603
with *c* works, with fine linen of Prov 7:16 2405

CARVING {2}
in *c* of timber, to work in all Ex 31:5 2799
in *c* of wood, to make any manner Ex 35:33 2799

CARVINGS {1}
carved upon them *c* of cherubims 1Kin 6:32 4734

CASE {8}
did see that they were in evil *c* Ex 5:19
this is the *c* of the slayer, Deut 19:4 1697
thou shalt in any *c* bring them Deut 22:1 7725
In any *c* thou shalt deliver him Deut 24:13 7725
that people, that is in such a *c* Ps 144:15 3602
ye shall in no *c* enter into the Mt 5:20 *3364*
If the *c* of the man be so with Mt 19:10 *156*
been now a long time in that *c* Jn 5:6

CASEMENT {1}
of my house I looked through my *c* Prov 7:6 822

CASES {1}
is not under bondage in such *c* 1Cor 7:15

CASIPHIA *(cas-if'-e-ah)* {2} *A place in Syria.*
Iddo the chief at the place *C* Ezr 8:17 3703
the Nethinims, at the place *C* Ezr 8:17 3703

CASLUHIM *(cas'-loo-him)* {2} *Descendants of Mizraim.*
And Pathrusim, and *C*, (out of whom Gen 10:14 3695
And Pathrusim, and *C*, (of whom came 1Chr 1:12 3695

CASLUHITES See CASLUHIM.

CASSIA {3}
of *c* five hundred shekels, after Ex 30:24 6916
smell of myrrh, and aloes, and *c* Ps 45:8 7102
bright iron, *c*, and calamus, were Eze 27:19 6916

CAST {501}
C out this bondwoman and her son Gen 21:10 1644
she *c* the child under one of the Gen 21:15 7993
she goats have not *c* their young Gen 31:38 7921
pillar, which I have *c* betwixt me Gen 31:51 3384
c him into some pit, and we will Gen 37:20 7993
but *c* him into this pit that is Gen 37:22 7993
took him, and *c* him into a pit Gen 37:24 7993
wife *c* her eyes upon Joseph Gen 39:7 5375
is born ye shall *c* into the river Ex 1:22 7993
And he said, *C* it on the ground Ex 4:3 7993
he *c* it on the ground, and it Ex 4:3 7993
c it at his feet, and said, Surely Ex 4:25 5060
c it before Pharaoh, and it shall Ex 7:9 7993
Aaron *c* down his rod before Ex 7:10 7993
For they *c* down every man his rod Ex 7:12 7993
and *c* them into the Red sea Ex 10:19 8628
his host hath he *c* into the sea Ex 15:4 3384
when he had *c* into the waters Ex 15:25 7993
ye shall *c* it to the dogs Ex 22:31 7993
There shall nothing *c* their young Ex 23:26 7921
thou shalt *c* four rings of gold Ex 25:12 3332
thou shalt *c* five sockets of Ex 26:37 3332
he *c* the tables out of his hands, Ex 32:19 7993
then I *c* it into the fire, and Ex 32:24 7993
For I will *c* out the nations Ex 34:24 3423
he *c* for them four sockets of Ex 36:36 3332
he *c* for it four rings of gold, Ex 37:3 3332
he *c* for it four rings of gold, Ex 37:13 3332
he *c* four rings for the four ends Ex 38:5 3332
c the sockets of the sanctuary Ex 38:27 3332
c it beside the altar on the east Lev 1:16 7993
they shall *c* them into an unclean Lev 14:40 7993
Aaron shall *c* lots upon the two Lev 16:8 5414
defiled which I *c* out before you Lev 18:24 7971
nation, which I *c* out before you Lev 20:23 7971
c your carcases upon the carcases Lev 26:30 5414
enemies, I will not *c* them away Lev 26:44 3988
c it into the midst of the Num 19:6 7993
or have *c* upon him any thing Num 35:22 7993
c it upon him, that he die, and Num 35:23 5307
To *c* out all thine enemies from Deut 6:19 1920
hath *c* out many nations before Deut 7:1 5390
hath *c* them out from before thee Deut 9:4 1920
c them out of my two hands, and Deut 9:17 7993
I *c* the dust thereof into the Deut 9:21 7993
for thine olive shall *c* his fruit Deut 28:40 5394
c them into another land, as it Deut 29:28 7993
c it at the entering of the gate Josh 8:29 7993
that the LORD *c* down great stones Josh 10:11 7993
c them into the cave wherein they Josh 10:27 7993
did Moses smite, and *c* them out Josh 13:12 3423
that I may *c* lots for you here Josh 18:6 3384
that I may here *c* lots for you Josh 18:8 7993
Joshua *c* lots for them in Shiloh Josh 18:10 7993
the altar of Baal was *c* down Judg 6:28 5422
because he hath *c* down the altar Judg 6:30 5422
because one hath *c* down his altar Judg 6:31 5422
did *c* therein every man the Judg 8:25 7993
a certain woman *c* a piece of a Judg 9:53 7993
that he *c* away the jawbone out of Judg 15:17 7993
C lots between me and Jonathan my 1Sa 14:42 5307
And Saul *c* the javelin 1Sa 18:11 2904
Saul *c* a javelin at him to smite 1Sa 20:33 2904
of the mighty is vilely *c* away 2Sa 1:21 1602
did not a woman *c* a piece of a 2Sa 11:21 7993
he *c* stones at David, and at all 2Sa 16:6 5619
and threw stones at him, and *c* dust 2Sa 16:13 6080
c him into a great pit in the 2Sa 18:17 7993
c a cloth upon him, when he saw 2Sa 20:12 7993
they *c* up a bank against the city 2Sa 20:15 8210
of Bichri, and *c* it out to Joab 2Sa 20:22 7993
For he *c* two pillars of brass, of 1Kin 7:15 6696
c in two rows, when it was *c* 1Kin 7:24 3333
of Jordan did the king *c* them 1Kin 7:46 3332
my name, will I *c* out of my sight 1Kin 9:7 7971
and his carcase was *c* in the way 1Kin 13:24 7993
and saw the carcase *c* in the way 1Kin 13:25 7993
and found his carcase *c* in the way 1Kin 13:28 7993
hast *c* me behind thy back 1Kin 14:9 7993
LORD *c* out before the children of 1Kin 14:24 3423
he *c* himself down upon the earth, 1Kin 18:42 1457
by him, and *c* his mantle upon him 1Kin 19:19 7993
whom the LORD *c* out before the 1Kin 21:26 3423
c him upon some mountain, or into 2Kin 2:16 7993
c the salt in there, and said, 2Kin 2:21 7993
of land *c* every man his stone 2Kin 3:25 7993
And he *c* it into the pot 2Kin 4:41 7993
down a stick, and *c* it in thither 2Kin 6:6 7993
Syrians had *c* away in their haste 2Kin 7:15 7993
c him in the portion of the field 2Kin 9:25 7993
c him into the plat of ground, 2Kin 9:26 7993
guard and the captains *c* them out 2Kin 10:25 7993
they *c* the man into the sepulchre 2Kin 13:21 7993
neither *c* he them from his 2Kin 13:23 7993
whom the LORD *c* out from before 2Kin 16:3 3423
whom the LORD *c* out from before 2Kin 17:8 3423
until he had *c* them out of his 2Kin 17:20 7993
have *c* their gods into the fire 2Kin 19:18 5414
shield, nor *c* a bank against it 2Kin 19:32 8210
whom the LORD *c* out before the 2Kin 21:2 3423
c the powder thereof upon the 2Kin 23:6 7993
c the dust of them into the brook 2Kin 23:12 7993
will *c* off this city Jerusalem 2Kin 23:27 3988
until he had *c* them out from his 2Kin 24:20 7993
These likewise *c* lots over 1Chr 24:31 5307
And they *c* lots, ward against ward 1Chr 25:8 5307
And they *c* lots, as well the small 1Chr 26:13 5307
a wise counsellor, they *c* lots 1Chr 26:14 5307
he will *c* thee off for ever 1Chr 28:9 2186
Two rows of oxen were *c* 2Chr 4:3 3332
when it was *c* 2Chr 4:3 4166
of Jordan did the king *c* them 2Chr 4:17 3332
will I *c* out of my sight, and will 2Chr 7:20 7993
his sons had *c* them off from 2Chr 11:14 2186
Have ye not *c* out the priests of 2Chr 13:9 5080
to come to *c* us out of thy 2Chr 20:11 1644
c into the chest, until they had 2Chr 24:10 7993
hath power to help, and to *c* down 2Chr 25:8 3782
c them down from the top of the 2Chr 25:12 7993
and bows, and slings to *c* stones 2Chr 26:14
had *c* out before the children of 2Chr 28:3 3423
did *c* away in his transgression 2Chr 29:19 2186
c them into the brook Kidron 2Chr 30:14 7993
whom the LORD had *c* out before 2Chr 33:2 3423
and *c* them out of the city 2Chr 33:15 7993
though there were of you *c* out Neh 1:9 5080
they were much *c* down in their Neh 6:16 5307
c thy law behind their backs, and Neh 9:26 7993
we *c* the lots among the priests, Neh 10:34 5307
rest of the people also *c* lots Neh 11:1 5307
therefore I *c* forth all the Neh 13:8 7993
of king Ahasuerus, they *c* Pur Est 3:7 5307
to destroy them, and had *c* Pur Est 9:24 5307
he have *c* them away for their Job 8:4 7971
God will not *c* away a perfect man Job 8:20 3988
shall *c* off his flower as the Job 15:33 7993
his own counsel shall *c* him down Job 18:7 7993
For he is *c* into a net by his own Job 18:8 7971
God shall *c* them out of his belly Job 20:15 3423
God shall *c* the fury of his wrath Job 20:23 7971
When men are *c* down, then thou Job 22:29 8213
For God shall *c* upon him, and not Job 27:22 7993
of my countenance they *c* not down Job 29:24 5307
He hath *c* me into the mire, and I Job 30:19 3384
ones, they *c* out their sorrows Job 39:3 7971
C abroad the rage of thy wrath Job 40:11 6327
shall not one be *c* down even at Job 41:9 2904
c away their cords from us Ps 2:3 7993
c them out in the multitude of Ps 5:10 5080
LORD, disappoint him, *c* him down Ps 17:13 3766
I did *c* them out as the dirt in Ps 18:42 7324
I was *c* upon thee from the womb Ps 22:10 7993
them, and *c* lots upon my vesture Ps 22:18 5307
they are *c* down, and shall not be Ps 36:12 1760
to *c* down the poor and needy, and Ps 37:14 5307
he shall not be utterly *c* down Ps 37:24 2904
Why art thou *c* down, O my soul Ps 42:5 7817
my soul is *c* down within me Ps 42:6 7817
Why art thou *c* down, O my soul Ps 42:11 7817
why dost thou *c* me off Ps 43:2 2186
Why art thou *c* down, O my soul Ps 43:5 7817
afflict the people, and *c* them out Ps 44:2 7971
But thou hast *c* off, and put us to Ps 44:9 2186
arise, *c* us not off for ever Ps 44:23 2186
C me not away from thy presence Ps 51:11 7993
for they *c* iniquity upon me, and Ps 55:3 4131
C thy burden upon the LORD, and he Ps 55:22 7993
in thine anger *c* down the people, Ps 56:7 3381
O God, thou hast *c* us off Ps 60:1 2186
over Edom will I *c* out my shoe Ps 60:8 7993
thou, O God, which hadst *c* us off Ps 60:10 2186
They only consult to *c* him down Ps 62:4 5080
C me not off in the time of old Ps 71:9 7993
why hast thou *c* us off for ever Ps 74:1 2186
They have *c* fire into thy Ps 74:7 7971
horse are *c* into a dead sleep Ps 76:6 7290
Will the Lord *c* off for ever Ps 77:7 2186
He *c* upon them the fierceness of Ps 78:49 7971
He *c* out the heathen also before Ps 78:55 1644
thou hast *c* out the heathen, and Ps 80:8 1644
But thou hast *c* off and abhorred, Ps 89:38 2186
c his throne down to the ground Ps 89:44 4048
LORD will not *c* off his people Ps 94:14 5203
hast lifted me up, and *c* me down Ps 102:10 7993
over Edom will I *c* out my shoe Ps 108:9 7993
thou, O God, who hast *c* us off Ps 108:11 2186
let them be *c* into the fire Ps 140:10 5307
C forth lightning, and scatter Ps 144:6 1299
C in thy lot among us Prov 1:14 5307
For she hath *c* down many wounded Prov 7:26 5307
The lot is *c* into the lap Prov 16:33 2904
C out the scorner, and contention Prov 22:10 1644
A time to *c* away stones, and a Eccl 3:5 7993
time to keep, and a time to *c* away Eccl 3:6 7993
C thy bread upon the waters Eccl 11:1 7971
a man shall *c* his idols of silver Is 2:20 7993
because they have *c* away the law Is 5:24 3988
in them, when they *c* their leaves Is 6:13 7995
But thou art *c* out of thy grave Is 14:19 7993
wandering bird *c* out of the nest Is 16:2 7971
all they that *c* angle into the Is 19:8 7993
of the covering *c* over all people Is 25:7 3874
and the earth shall *c* out the dead Is 26:19 5307
shall *c* down to the earth with Is 28:2 3240
doth he not *c* abroad the fitches, Is 28:25 6327
c in the principal wheat and the Is 28:25 7760
thou shalt *c* them away as a Is 30:22 2219
shall *c* away his idols of silver Is 31:7 3988
Their slain also shall be *c* out Is 34:3 7993
he hath *c* the lot for them, and Is 34:17 5307
have *c* their gods into the fire Is 37:19 5414
shields, nor *c* a bank against it Is 37:33 8210
for thou hast *c* all my sins Is 38:17 7993
chosen thee, and not *c* thee away Is 41:9 3988
C ye up, *c* ye up, prepare the Is 57:14 5549
rest, whose waters *c* up mire Is 57:20 1644
poor that are *c* out to thy house Is 58:7 4788
c up, *c* up the highways Is 62:10 5549
that *c* you out for my name's sake Is 66:5 5077
c a mount against Jerusalem Jer 6:6 8210
I visit them they shall be *c* down Jer 6:15 3782
I will *c* you out of my sight, as Jer 7:15 7993
as I have *c* out all your brethren Jer 7:15 7993
and *c* it away, and take up a Jer 7:29 7993
visitation they shall be *c* down Jer 8:12 3782
our dwellings have *c* us out Jer 9:19 7993
to whom they prophesy shall be *c* Jer 14:16 7993
c them out of my sight, and let Jer 15:1 7971
Therefore will I *c* you out of Jer 16:13 2904
walk in paths, in a way not *c* up Jer 18:15 5549
cedars, and *c* them into the fire Jer 22:7 5307
c forth beyond the gates of Jer 22:19 7993
I will *c* thee out, and thy mother Jer 22:26 2904
wherefore are they *c* out, he and Jer 22:28 7993
are *c* into a land which they know Jer 22:28 2904
and *c* you out of my presence Jer 23:39
c his dead body into the graves Jer 26:23 7993
I will *c* thee from off the face Jer 28:16 7971
I will also *c* off all the seed of Jer 31:37 3988
chosen, he hath even *c* them off Jer 33:24 3988
Then will I *c* away the seed of Jer 33:26 3988
c it into the fire that was on Jer 36:23 7933
his dead body shall be *c* out in Jer 36:30 7933
c him into the dungeon of Jer 38:6 7933
whom they have *c* into the dungeon Jer 38:9 7933
and took thence old *c* clouts Jer 38:11 5499
Put now these old *c* clouts Jer 38:12 5499
c them into the midst of the pit, Jer 41:7
c all the dead bodies of the men Jer 41:9 7993
away captive from Mizpah *c* about Jer 41:14 5437
c her up as heaps, and destroy her Jer 50:26 5549
my delicates, he hath *c* me out Jer 51:34 1740
c it into the midst of Euphrates Jer 51:63 7993
till he had *c* them out from his Jer 52:3 7993
c down from heaven unto the earth Lam 2:1 7993
The Lord hath *c* off his altar Lam 2:7 2186
they have *c* up dust upon their Lam 2:10 5927
the Lord will not *c* off for ever Lam 3:31 2186
the dungeon, and *c* a stone upon me Lam 3:53 3034
it, and *c* a mount against it Eze 4:2 8210
c them into the midst of the fire Eze 5:4 7993
I will *c* down your slain men Eze 6:4 5307
They shall *c* their silver in the Eze 7:19 7993
Although I have *c* them far off Eze 11:16 7368
it is *c* into the fire for fuel Eze 15:4 5414
but thou wast *c* out in the open Eze 16:5 7993
C away from you all your Eze 18:31 7993
she was *c* down to the ground, and Eze 19:12 7993
them, *C* ye away every man the Eze 20:7 7993
they did not every man *c* away the Eze 20:8 7993
to *c* a mount, and to build a fort Eze 21:22 8210
c me behind thy back, therefore Eze 23:35 7998
c a mount against thee, and lift Eze 26:8 8210
shall *c* up dust upon their heads, Eze 27:30 5927
therefore I will *c* thee as Eze 28:16 2490
I will *c* thee to the ground, I Eze 28:17 7993
when I *c* him down to hell with Eze 31:16 3381
I will *c* thee forth upon the open Eze 32:4 2904
c them down, even her, and the Eze 32:18 3381
minds, to *c* it out for a prey Eze 36:5 4054
priests shall *c* salt upon them Eze 43:24 7993
shall the same hour be *c* into the Dan 3:6 7412
that he should be *c* into the Dan 3:11 7412
ye shall be *c* the same hour into Dan 3:15 7412
to *c* them into the burning fiery Dan 3:20 7412

were *c* into the midst of the ... Dan 3:21 7412
Did not we *c* three men bound into ... Dan 3:24 7412
he shall be *c* into the den of ... Dan 6:7 7412
shall be *c* into the den of lions ... Dan 6:12 7412
c him into the den of lions ... Dan 6:16 7412
they *c* them into the den of lions ... Dan 6:24 7412
till the thrones were *c* down ... Dan 7:9 7412
but he *c* him down to the ground, ... Dan 8:7 7993
it *c* down some of the host and of ... Dan 8:10 5307
place of his sanctuary was *c* down ... Dan 8:11 7993
it *c* down the truth to the ground ... Dan 8:12 7993
and he shall *c* down many ten ... Dan 11:12 5307
c up a mount, and take the most ... Dan 11:15 8210
Israel hath *c* off the thing that ... Hos 8:3 2186
calf, O Samaria, hath *c* thee off ... Hos 8:5 2186
My God will *c* them away, because ... Hos 9:17 3988
c forth his roots as Lebanon ... Hos 14:5 5221
made it clean bare, and *c* it away ... Joel 1:7 7993
they have *c* lots for my people ... Joel 3:3 3032
did *c* off all pity, and his anger ... Amos 1:11 7843
ye shall *c* them into the palace, ... Amos 4:3 7993
they shall *c* them forth with ... Amos 8:3 7993
and it shall be *c* out and drowned, ... Amos 8:8 1644
c lots upon Jerusalem, even thou ... Obad 11 3032
c forth the wares that were in ... Jonah 1:5 2904
fellow, Come, and let us *c* lots ... Jonah 1:7 5307
So they *c* lots, and the lot fell ... Jonah 1:7 5307
me up, and *c* me forth into the sea ... Jonah 1:12 2904
and *c* him forth into the sea ... Jonah 1:15 2904
For thou hadst *c* me into the deep ... Jonah 2:3 7993
I said, I am *c* out of thy sight ... Jonah 2:4 1644
that shall *c* a cord by lot in the ... Mic 2:5 7993
c out from their pleasant houses ... Mic 2:9 1644
her that was *c* far off a strong ... Mic 4:7 1972
thou wilt *c* all their sins into ... Mic 7:19 7993
I will *c* abominable filth upon ... Nah 3:6 7993
they *c* lots for her honourable ... Nah 3:10 3032
he hath *c* out thine enemy ... Zeph 3:15 6437
to *c* out the horns of the ... Zec 1:21 3034
he *c* it into the midst of the ... Zec 5:8 7993
he *c* the weight of lead upon the ... Zec 5:8 7993
Behold, the Lord will *c* her out ... Zec 9:4 3423
be as though I had not *c* them off ... Zec 10:6 2186
unto me, *C* it unto the potter ... Zec 11:13 7993
c them to the potter in the house ... Zec 11:13 7993
neither shall your vine *c* her ... Mal 3:11 7921
is hewn down, and *c* into the fire ... Mt 3:10 *906*
be the Son of God, *c* thyself down ... Mt 4:6 *906*
heard that John was *c* into prison ... Mt 4:12 *3860*
good for nothing, but to be *c* out ... Mt 5:13 *906*
officer, and thou be *c* into prison ... Mt 5:25 *906*
pluck it out, and *c* it from thee ... Mt 5:29 *906*
whole body should be *c* into hell ... Mt 5:29 *906*
cut it off, and *c* it from thee ... Mt 5:30 *906*
whole body should be *c* into hell ... Mt 5:30 *906*
to morrow is *c* into the oven, ... Mt 6:30 *906*
first *c* out the beam out of thine ... Mt 7:5 *1544*
to *c* out the mote out of thy ... Mt 7:5 *1544*
neither *c* ye your pearls before ... Mt 7:6 *906*
is hewn down, and *c* into the fire ... Mt 7:19 *906*
and in thy name have *c* out devils ... Mt 7:22 *1544*
be *c* out into outer darkness ... Mt 8:12 *1544*
he *c* out the spirits with his ... Mt 8:16 *1544*
him, saying, If thou *c* us out ... Mt 8:31 *1544*
And when the devil was *c* out ... Mt 9:33 1544
to *c* them out, and to heal all ... Mt 10:1 1544
raise the dead, *c* out devils ... Mt 10:8 *1544*
This fellow doth not *c* out devils ... Mt 12:24 *1544*
if Satan *c* out Satan, he is ... Mt 12:26 *1544*
And if I by Beelzebub *c* out devils ... Mt 12:27 *1544*
whom do your children *c* them out ... Mt 12:27 *1544*
But if I *c* out devils by the ... Mt 12:28 *1544*
shall *c* them into a furnace of ... Mt 13:42 *906*
that was *c* into the sea, and ... Mt 13:47 *906*
into vessels, but *c* the bad away ... Mt 13:48 *906*
shall *c* them into the furnace of ... Mt 13:50 *906*
is *c* out into the draught ... Mt 15:17 *1544*
bread, and to *c* it to dogs ... Mt 15:26 *906*
c them down at Jesus' feet ... Mt 15:30 *4496*
said, Why could not we *c* him out ... Mt 17:19 *1544*
c an hook, and take up the fish ... Mt 17:27 *906*
cut them off, and *c* them from thee ... Mt 18:8 *906*
to be *c* into everlasting fire ... Mt 18:8 *906*
pluck it out, and *c* it from thee ... Mt 18:9 *906*
two eyes to be *c* into hell fire ... Mt 18:9 *906*
c him into prison, till he should ... Mt 18:30 *906*
c out all them that sold and ... Mt 21:12 *1544*
and be thou *c* into the sea ... Mt 21:21 *906*
c him out of the vineyard, and ... Mt 21:39 *1544*
c him into outer darkness ... Mt 22:13 *1544*
c ye the unprofitable servant ... Mt 25:30 *1544*
he *c* down the pieces of silver in ... Mt 27:5 *4496*
upon my vesture did they *c* lots ... Mt 27:35 *906*
with him, *c* the same in his teeth ... Mt 27:44 *3679*
diseases, and *c* out many devils ... Mk 1:34 *1544*
all Galilee, and *c* out devils ... Mk 1:39 *1544*
sicknesses, and to *c* out devils ... Mk 3:15 *1544*
How can Satan *c* out Satan ... Mk 3:23 *1544*
as if a man should *c* seed into ... Mk 4:26 *906*
they *c* out many devils, and ... Mk 6:13 *1544*
c forth the devil out of her ... Mk 7:26 *1544*
bread, and to *c* it unto the dogs ... Mk 7:27 *906*
that they should *c* him out ... Mk 9:18 *1544*
ofttimes it hath *c* him into the ... Mk 9:22 *906*
Why could not we *c* him out ... Mk 9:28 *1544*
neck, and he were *c* into the sea ... Mk 9:42 *906*
having two feet to be *c* into hell ... Mk 9:45 *906*
two eyes to be *c* into hell fire ... Mk 9:47 *906*

Jesus, and *c* their garments on him ... Mk 11:7 *1911*
began to *c* out them that sold and ... Mk 11:15 *1544*
and be thou *c* into the sea ... Mk 11:23 *906*
and at him they *c* stones, and ... Mk 12:4 *3036*
c him out of the vineyard ... Mk 12:8 *1544*
beheld how the people *c* money ... Mk 12:41 *906*
and many that were rich *c* in much ... Mk 12:41 *906*
this poor widow hath *c* more in ... Mk 12:43 *906*
which have *c* into the treasury ... Mk 12:43 *906*
For all they did *c* in of their ... Mk 12:44 *906*
want did *c* in all that she had ... Mk 12:44 *906*
cloth *c* about his naked body ... Mk 14:51 *4016*
out of whom he had *c* seven devils ... Mk 16:9 *1544*
my name shall they *c* out devils ... Mk 16:17 *1544*
c in her mind what manner of ... Lk 1:29 *1260*
is hewn down, and *c* into the fire ... Lk 3:9 *906*
c thyself down from hence ... Lk 4:9 *906*
that they might *c* him down ... Lk 4:29 *2630*
c out your name as evil, for the ... Lk 6:22 *1544*
c out first the beam out of thine ... Lk 6:42 *1544*
and lose himself, or be *c* away ... Lk 9:25 *2210*
thy disciples to *c* him out ... Lk 9:40 *1544*
because ye say that I *c* out ... Lk 11:18 *1544*
And if I by Beelzebub *c* out devils ... Lk 11:19 *1544*
by whom do your sons *c* them out ... Lk 11:19 *1544*
the finger of God *c* out devils ... Lk 11:20 *1544*
killed hath power to *c* into hell ... Lk 12:5 *1685*
to morrow is *c* into the oven ... Lk 12:28 *906*
the officer *c* thee into prison ... Lk 12:58 *906*
a man took, and *c* into his garden ... Lk 13:19 *906*
I *c* out devils, and I do cures to ... Lk 13:32 *1544*
but men *c* it out ... Lk 14:35 *906*
he *c* into the sea, than that he ... Lk 17:2 *4406*
they *c* their garments upon the ... Lk 19:35 *1977*
shall *c* a trench about thee ... Lk 19:43 *4016*
began to *c* out them that sold ... Lk 19:45 *1544*
wounded him also, and *c* him out ... Lk 20:12 *1544*
So they *c* him out of the vineyard ... Lk 20:15 *1544*
hath *c* in more than they all ... Lk 21:3 *906*
c in unto the offerings of God ... Lk 21:4 *906*
but she of her penury hath *c* in ... Lk 21:4 *906*
from them about a stone's *c* ... Lk 22:41 *1000*
and for murder, was *c* into prison ... Lk 23:19 *906*
murder was *c* into prison, whom ... Lk 23:25 *906*
parted his raiment, and *c* lots ... Lk 23:34 *906*
John was not yet *c* into prison ... Jn 3:24 *906*
to me I will in no wise *c* out ... Jn 6:37 *1544*
let him first *c* a stone at her ... Jn 8:7 *906*
took they up stones to *c* at him ... Jn 8:59 *906*
And they *c* him out ... Jn 9:34 *1544*
heard that they had *c* him out ... Jn 9:35 *1544*
the prince of this world be *c* out ... Jn 12:31 *1544*
he is *c* forth as a branch, and is ... Jn 15:6 *906*
c them into the fire, and they are ... Jn 15:6 *906*
but *c* lots for it, whose it shall ... Jn 19:24 *2975*
and for my vesture they did *c* lots ... Jn 19:24 *906*
C the net on the right side of ... Jn 21:6 *906*
They *c* therefore, and now they ... Jn 21:6 *906*
did *c* himself into the sea ... Jn 21:7 *906*
so that they *c* out their young ... Acts 7:19 *4160,1570*
And when he was *c* out, Pharaoh's ... Acts 7:21 *1620*
c him out of the city, and stoned ... Acts 7:58 *1544*
C thy garment about thee, and ... Acts 12:8 *4016*
they *c* them into prison, charging ... Acts 16:23 *906*
Romans, and have *c* us into prison ... Acts 16:37 *906*
c off their clothes, and threw ... Acts 22:23 *4496*
the third day we *c* out with our ... Acts 27:19 *4496*
Howbeit we must be *c* upon a ... Acts 27:26 *1601*
they *c* four anchors out of the ... Acts 27:29 *4496*
as though they would have *c* ... Acts 27:30 *1614*
c out the wheat into the sea ... Acts 27:38 *1544*
they which could swim should *c* ... Acts 27:43 *641*
Hath God *c* away his people ... Rom 11:1 *683*
God hath not *c* away his people ... Rom 11:2 *683*
let us therefore *c* off the works ... Rom 13:12 *656*
not that I may *c* a snare upon you ... 1Cor 7:35 *1911*
c down, but not destroyed ... 2Cor 4:9 *2598*
comforteth those that are *c* down ... 2Cor 7:6 *5011*
C out the bondwoman and her son ... Gal 4:30 *1544*
because they have *c* off their ... 1Ti 5:12 *114*
C not away therefore your ... Heb 10:35 *577*
but *c* them down to hell, and ... 2Pet 2:4 *5020*
the devil shall *c* some of you ... Rev 2:10 *906*
Balaam, who taught Balac to *c* a ... Rev 2:14 *906*
I will *c* her into a bed, and them ... Rev 2:22 *906*
c their crowns before the throne, ... Rev 4:10 *906*
the altar, and *c* it into the earth ... Rev 8:5 *906*
they were *c* upon the earth ... Rev 8:7 *906*
with fire was *c* into the sea ... Rev 8:8 *906*
and did *c* them to the earth ... Rev 12:4 *906*
And the great dragon was *c* out ... Rev 12:9 *906*
he was *c* out into the earth, and ... Rev 12:9 *906*
and his angels were *c* out with him ... Rev 12:9 *906*
accuser of our brethren is *c* down ... Rev 12:10 *2598*
saw that he was *c* unto the earth ... Rev 12:13 *906*
the serpent *c* out of his mouth ... Rev 12:15 *906*
the dragon *c* out of his mouth ... Rev 12:16 *906*
c it into the great winepress of ... Rev 14:19 *906*
they *c* dust on their heads, and ... Rev 18:19 *906*
c it into the sea, saying, Thus ... Rev 18:21 *906*
These both were *c* alive into a ... Rev 19:20 *1544*
c him into the bottomless pit, and ... Rev 20:3 *906*
them was *c* into the lake of fire ... Rev 20:10 *906*
hell were *c* into the lake of fire ... Rev 20:14 *906*
life was *c* into the lake of fire ... Rev 20:15 *906*

CASTAWAY {1}
to others, I myself should be a *c* ... 1Cor 9:27 *96*

CASTEDST {1}
thou *c* them down into destruction ... Ps 73:18 5307

CASTEST {3}
thou *c* off fear, and restrainest ... Job 15:4 6565
and *c* my words behind thee ... Ps 50:17 7993
LORD, why *c* thou off my soul ... Ps 88:14 2186

CASTETH {16}
cow calveth, and *c* not her calf ... Job 21:10 7921
he *c* the wicked down to the ... Ps 147:6 8213
He *c* forth his ice like morsels ... Ps 147:17 7993
but he *c* away the substance of ... Prov 10:3 1920
Slothfulness *c* into a deep sleep ... Prov 19:15 5307
c down the strength of the ... Prov 21:22 3381
As a mad man who *c* firebrands ... Prov 26:18 3384
with gold, and *c* silver chains ... Is 40:19 6884
As a fountain *c* out her waters, ... Jer 6:7 6979
so she *c* out her wickedness ... Jer 6:7 6979
He *c* out devils through the ... Mt 9:34 *1544*
of the devils *c* he out devils ... Mk 3:22 *1544*
He *c* out devils through Beelzebub ... Lk 11:15 *1544*
but perfect love *c* out fear ... 1Jn 4:18 *906*
and *c* them out of the church ... 3Jn 10 *1544*
as a fig tree *c* her untimely figs ... Rev 6:13 *906*

CASTING {21}
c them down to the ground ... 2Sa 8:2 7901
all of them had one *c*, one ... 1Kin 7:37 4165
c himself down before the house ... Ezr 10:1 5307
ye see my *c* down, and are afraid ... Job 6:21 2866
they have defiled by *c* down the ... Ps 74:7
his crown by *c* it to the ground ... Ps 89:39
by *c* up mounts, and building forts ... Eze 17:17 8210
thy *c* down shall be in the midst ... Mic 6:14 3445
his brother, *c* a net into the sea ... Mt 4:18 *906*
and parted his garments, *c* lots ... Mt 27:35 *906*
his brother *c* a net into the sea ... Mk 1:16 *906*
we saw one *c* out devils in thy ... Mk 9:38 *1544*
c away his garment, rose, and came ... Mk 10:50 *577*
c lots upon them, what every man ... Mk 15:24 *906*
we saw one *c* out devils in thy ... Lk 9:49 *1544*
he was *c* out a devil, and it was ... Lk 11:14 *1544*
saw the rich men *c* their gifts ... Lk 21:1 *906*
poor widow *c* in thither two mites ... Lk 21:2 *906*
For if the *c* away of them be the ... Rom 11:15 *580*
C down imaginations, and every ... 2Cor 10:5 *2507*
C all your care upon him ... 1Pet 5:7 *1977*

CASTLE {9}
David took the *c* of Zion, which ... 1Chr 11:5 4686
And David dwelt in the *c* ... 1Chr 11:7 4679
are like the bars of a *c* ... Prov 18:19 759
him to be carried into the *c* ... Acts 21:34 *3925*
as Paul was to be led into the *c* ... Acts 21:37 *3925*
him to be brought into the *c* ... Acts 22:24 *3925*
them, and to bring him into the *c* ... Acts 23:10 *3925*
he went and entered into the *c* ... Acts 23:16 *3925*
go with him, and returned to the *c* ... Acts 23:32 *3925*

CASTLES {6}
by their towns, and by their *c* ... Gen 25:16 2918
they dwelt, and all their goodly *c* ... Num 31:10 2918
their *c* in their coasts, of the ... 1Chr 6:54 2918
and in the villages, and in the *c* ... 1Chr 27:25 4026
and he built in Judah *c*, and cities ... 2Chr 17:12 1003
and in the forests he built *c* ... 2Chr 27:4 1003

CASTOR *(cas'-tor)* {1} *Patron god of sailors.*
in the isle, whose sign was *C* ... Acts 28:11 *1359*

CATCH {15}
c in thorns, so that the stacks ... Ex 22:6 4672
c you every man his wife of the ... Judg 21:21 2414
from him, and did hastily *c* it ... 1Kin 20:33 2480
we shall *c* them alive, and get ... 2Kin 7:12 8610
he lieth in wait to *c* the poor ... Ps 10:9 2414
he doth *c* the poor, when he ... Ps 10:9 2414
net that he hath hid *c* himself ... Ps 35:8 3920
extortioner *c* all that he hath ... Ps 109:11 5367
they set a trap, they *c* men ... Jer 5:26 3920
lion, and it learned to *c* the prey ... Eze 19:3 2963
lion, and learned to *c* the prey ... Eze 19:6 2963
they *c* them in their net, and ... Hab 1:15 1641
Herodians, to *c* him in his words ... Mk 12:13 *64*
from henceforth thou shalt *c* men ... Lk 5:10 *2221*
seeking to *c* something out of his ... Lk 11:54 *2340*

CATCHETH {3}
c any beast or fowl that may be ... Lev 17:13 6679
c away that which was sown in his ... Mt 13:19 *726*
and the wolf *c* them, and scattereth ... Jn 10:12 *726*

CATERPILLAR {5}
mildew, locust, or if there be *c* ... 1Kin 8:37 2625
also their increase unto the *c* ... Ps 78:46 2625
like the gathering of the *c* ... Is 33:4 2625
hath left hath the *c* eaten ... Joel 1:4 2625
eaten, the cankerworm, and the *c* ... Joel 2:25 2625

CATERPILLARS {4}
or mildew, locusts, or *c* ... 2Chr 6:28 2625
spake, and the locusts came, and *c* ... Ps 105:34 3218
fill thee with men, as with *c* ... Jer 51:14 3218
horses to come up as the rough *c* ... Jer 51:27 3218

CATTLE {153}
living creature after his kind, *c* ... Gen 1:24 929
c after their kind, and every ... Gen 1:25 929
fowl of the air, and over the *c* ... Gen 1:26 929
And Adam gave names to all *c* ... Gen 2:20 929
this, thou art cursed above all *c* ... Gen 3:14 929
in tents, and of such as have *c* ... Gen 4:20 4735
of *c* after their kind, of every ... Gen 6:20 929
all the *c* after their kind, and ... Gen 7:14 929

the earth, both of fowl, and of c Gen 7:21 929
of the ground, both man, and of c Gen 7:23 929
all the c that was with him in Gen 8:1 929
all flesh, both of fowl, and of c Gen 8:17 929
with you, of the fowl, of the c Gen 9:10 929
And Abram was very rich in c Gen 13:2 4735
c and the herdmen of Lot's c Gen 13:7 4735
the c should be gathered together Gen 29:7 4735
thee, and how thy c was with me Gen 30:29 4735
all the speckled and spotted c Gen 30:32 7716
all the brown c among the sheep, Gen 30:32 7716
and brought forth c ringstraked Gen 30:39 6629
and put them not unto Laban's c Gen 30:40 6629
the stronger c did conceive Gen 30:41 6629
the eyes of the c in the gutters Gen 30:41 6629
But when the c were feeble Gen 30:42 6629
exceedingly, and had much c Gen 30:43 6629
then all the c bare speckled Gen 31:8 6629
then bare all the c ringstraked Gen 31:8 6629
taken away the c of your father Gen 31:9 4735
at the time that the c conceived Gen 31:10 6629
upon the c were ringstraked Gen 31:10 6629
leap upon the c are ringstraked Gen 31:12 6629
And he carried away all his c Gen 31:18 4735
the c of his getting, which he Gen 31:18 4735
daughters, and six years for thy c Gen 31:41 6629
these c are my c, and all Gen 31:43 6629
according as the c that goeth Gen 33:14 4399
house, and made booths for his c Gen 33:17 4735
sons were with his c in the field Gen 34:5 4735
Shall not their c and their Gen 34:23 4735
persons of his house, and his c Gen 36:6 4735
not bear them because of their c Gen 36:7 4735
And they took their c, and their Gen 46:6 4735
their trade hath been to feed c Gen 46:32 4735
c from our youth even until now Gen 46:34 4735
then make them rulers over my c Gen 47:6 4735
And Joseph said, Give your c Gen 47:16 4735
and I will give you for your c Gen 47:16 4735
they brought their c unto Joseph Gen 47:17 4735
for the c of the herds, and for Gen 47:17 4735
for all their c for that year Gen 47:17 4735
my lord also hath our herds of c Gen 47:18 929
upon thy c which is in the field Ex 9:3 4735
sever between the c of Israel Ex 9:4 4735
of Israel and the c of Egypt Ex 9:4 4735
and all the c of Egypt died Ex 9:6 4735
but of the c of the children of Ex 9:6 4735
of the c of the Israelites dead Ex 9:7 4735
therefore now, and gather thy c Ex 9:19 4735
his c flee into the houses Ex 9:20 4735
servants and his c in the field Ex 9:21 4735
Our c also shall go with us Ex 10:26 4735
and all the firstborn of c Ex 12:29 929
and herds, even very much c Ex 12:38 4735
our children and our c with thirst Ex 17:3 4735
nor thy maidservant, nor thy c Ex 20:10 929
and every firstling among thy c Ex 34:19 4735
bring your offering of the c Lev 1:2 929
beast, or a carcase of unclean c Lev 5:2 929
Thou shalt not let thy c gender Lev 19:19 929
And for thy c, and for the beast Lev 25:7 929
your children, and destroy your c Lev 26:22 929
the c of the Levites instead of Num 3:41 929
the c of the children of Israel Num 3:41 929
the c of the Levites instead of Num 3:45 929
of the Levites instead of their c Num 3:45 926
that we and our c should die there Num 20:4 1165
my c drink of thy water, then I Num 20:19 4735
and took the spoil of all their c Num 31:9 929
had a very great multitude of c Num 32:1 4735
the place was a place for c Num 32:1 4735
c, and thy servants have c Num 32:4 4735
build sheepfolds here for our c Num 32:16 4735
wives, our flocks, and all our c Num 32:26 929
of them shall be for their c Num 35:3 929
Only the c we took for a prey Deut 2:35 929
But all the c, and the spoil of Deut 3:7 929
and your little ones, and your c Deut 3:19 4735
(for I know that ye have much c Deut 3:19 4735
nor thine ass, nor any of thy c Deut 5:14 929
barren among you, or among your c Deut 7:14 929
grass in thy fields for thy c Deut 11:15 929
the c thereof, with the edge of Deut 13:15 929
and the little ones, and the c Deut 20:14 929
thy ground, and the fruit of thy c Deut 28:4 929
body, and in the fruit of thy c Deut 28:11 929
he shall eat the fruit of thy c Deut 28:51 929
body, and in the fruit of thy c Deut 30:9 929
your little ones, and your c Josh 1:14 4735
the c thereof, shall ye take for Josh 8:2 929
Only the c and the spoil of that Josh 8:27 929
spoil of these cities, and the c Josh 11:14 929
with their suburbs for their c Josh 14:4 4735
the suburbs thereof for our c Josh 21:2 929
your tents, and with very much c Josh 22:8 4735
For they came up with their c Judg 6:5 4735
and put the little ones and the c Judg 18:21 4735
and brought away their c, and 1Sa 23:5 4735
they drave before those other c 1Sa 30:20 4735
fat c by the stone of Zoheleth, 1Kin 1:9 4806
And he hath slain oxen and fat c 1Kin 1:19 4806
day, and hath slain oxen and fat c 1Kin 1:25 4806
for the c that followed them 2Kin 3:9 929
ye may drink, both ye, and your c 2Kin 3:17 4735
because their c were multiplied 1Chr 5:9 4735
And they took away their c 1Chr 5:21 929
came down to take away their c 1Chr 7:21 929
They smote also the tents of c 2Chr 14:15 929
for he had much c, both in the 2Chr 26:10 929
thousand and six hundred small c 2Chr 35:8
offerings five thousand small c 2Chr 35:9
over our bodies, and over our c Neh 9:37 929
of our sons, and of our c, as it Neh 10:36 929
the c also concerning the vapour Job 36:33 4735
the c upon a thousand hills Ps 50:10 929
gave up their c also to the hail Ps 78:48 1165
the grass to grow for the c Ps 104:14 929
suffereth not their c to decrease Ps 107:38 929
Beasts, and all c Ps 148:10 929
small c above all that were in Eccl 2:7 4735
and for the treading of lesser c Is 7:25 7716
in that day shall thy c feed in Is 30:23 4735
small c of thy burnt offerings Is 43:23 7716
upon the beasts, and upon the c Is 46:1 929
can men hear the voice of the c Jer 9:10 4735
the multitude of their c a spoil Jer 49:32 4734
I judge between c and c Eze 34:17 7716
fat c and between the lean c Eze 34:20 7716
I will judge between c and c Eze 34:22 7716
the nations, which have gotten c Eze 38:12 4735
silver and gold, to take away c Eze 38:13 4735
the herds of c are perplexed, Joel 1:18 1241
and also much c Jonah 4:11 929
forth, and upon men, and upon c Hag 1:11 929
the multitude of men and c therein Zec 2:4 929
taught me to keep c from my youth Zec 13:5 7069
a servant plowing or feeding c Lk 17:7 *4165*
and his children, and his c Jn 4:12 *2353*

CAUDA See CLAUDA.

CAUGHT {37}
behold behind him a ram c in a Gen 22:13 270
she c him by his garment, saying, Gen 39:12 8610
c it, and it became a rod in his Ex 4:4 2388
prey which the men of war had c Num 31:32 962
c him, and cut off his thumbs and Judg 1:6 270
c a young man of the men of Judg 8:14 3920
c three hundred foxes, and took Judg 15:4 3920
of them that danced, whom they c Judg 21:23 1497
I c him by his beard, and smote 1Sa 17:35 2388
they c every one his fellow by 2Sa 2:16 2388
his head c hold of the oak, and he 2Sa 18:9 2388
c hold on the horns of the altar 1Kin 1:50 2388
he hath c hold on the horns of 1Kin 1:51 270
c hold on the horns of the altar 1Kin 2:28 2388
Ahijah c the new garment that was 1Kin 11:30 8610
the hill, she c him by the feet 2Kin 4:27 2388
and they c him, (for he was hid in 2Chr 22:9 3920
So she c him, and kissed him, and Prov 7:13 2388
the birds that are c in the snare Eccl 9:12 270
thou art found, and also c Jer 50:24 8610
c him, and said unto him, O thou Mt 14:31 *1949*
And they c him, and cast him out of Mt 21:39 *2983*
And they c him, and beat him, and Mk 12:3 *2983*
For oftentimes it had c him Lk 8:29 *4884*
and that night they c nothing Jn 21:3 *4084*
of the fish which ye have now c Jn 21:10 *4084*
c him, and brought him to the Acts 6:12 *4884*
Spirit of the Lord c away Philip Acts 8:39 *726*
their gains was gone, they c Paul Acts 16:19 *1949*
and having c Gaius and Aristarchus, Acts 19:29 *4884*
the Jews c me in the temple Acts 26:21 *4815*
And when the ship was c, and could Acts 27:15 *4884*
such an one c up to the third 2Cor 12:2 *726*
How that he was c up into 2Cor 12:4 *726*
being crafty, I c you with guile 2Cor 12:16 *2983*
remain shall be c up together 1Th 4:17 *726*
and her child was c up unto God Rev 12:5 *726*

CAUL {12}
the c that is above the liver, and Ex 29:13 3508
the c above the liver, and the two Ex 29:22 3508
the c above the liver, with the Lev 3:4 3508
the c above the liver, with the Lev 3:10 3508
the c above the liver, with the Lev 3:15 3508
the c above the liver, with the Lev 4:9 3508
the c that is above the liver, Lev 7:4 3508
the c above the liver, and the two Lev 8:16 3508
the c above the liver, and the two Lev 8:25 3508
the c above the liver of the sin Lev 9:10 3508
kidneys, and the c above the liver Lev 9:19 3508
will rend the c of their heart, Hos 13:8 5458

CAULS {1}
about their feet, and their c Is 3:18 7636

CAUSE {328}
I will c it to rain upon the Gen 7:4
C every man to go out from me Gen 45:1
c frogs to come up upon the land Ex 8:5
for this c have I raised thee up Ex 9:16 5668
morrow about this time I will c Ex 9:18
shall c him to be thoroughly Ex 21:19
If a man shall c a field or Ex 22:5
the c of both parties shall come Ex 22:9 1697
neither shalt thou speak in a c Ex 23:2 7379
countenance a poor man in his c Ex 23:3 7379
the judgment of thy poor in his c Ex 23:6 7379
to c the lamp to burn always Ex 27:20
thou shalt c a bullock to be Ex 29:10
he shall c the house to be Lev 14:41
daughter, to c her to be a whore Lev 19:29
the light, to c the lamps to burn Lev 24:2
if a man c a blemish in his Lev 24:19 5414
Then shalt thou c the trumpet of Lev 25:9
the eyes, and c sorrow of heart Lev 26:16
he shall c the woman to drink the Num 5:24
afterward shall c the woman to Num 5:26
will c him to come near unto him Num 16:5
will he c to come near unto him Num 16:5
For which c both thou and all thy Num 16:11 3651
brought their c before the LORD Num 27:5 4941
thou shalt c the inheritance of Num 27:7
then ye shall c his inheritance Num 27:8
c the strong wine to be poured Num 28:7
any person to c him to die Num 35:30
the c that is too hard for you, Deut 1:17 1697
for he shall c Israel to inherit Deut 1:38
he shall c them to inherit the Deut 3:28
to c his name to dwell there Deut 12:11
nor c the people to return to Deut 17:16
thou shalt not c the land to sin, Deut 24:4
the judge shall c him to lie down Deut 25:2
The LORD shall c thine enemies Deut 28:7 5414
The LORD shall c thee to be Deut 28:25 5414
thou shalt c them to inherit it Deut 31:7
this is the c why Joshua did Josh 5:4 1697
shall declare his c in the ears Josh 20:4 1697
nor c to swear by them, neither Josh 23:7
Is there not a c? 1Sa 17:29 1697
blood, to slay David without a c 1Sa 19:5 2600
me and thee, and see, and plead my c 1Sa 24:15 7379
that hath pleaded the c of my 1Sa 25:39 7379
snare for my life, to c me to die 1Sa 28:9
when all the people came to c 2Sa 3:35
whither shall I c my shame to go 2Sa 13:13
she said unto him, There is no c 2Sa 13:16 182
any suit or c might come unto me 2Sa 15:4 4941
c Solomon my son to ride upon 1Kin 1:33
will c them to be discharged 1Kin 5:9
laid upon him to c him to swear 1Kin 8:31
supplication, and maintain their c 1Kin 8:45 4941
place, and maintain their c 1Kin 8:49 4941
he maintain the c of his servant 1Kin 8:59 4941
the c of his people Israel at all 1Kin 8:59 4941
this was the c that he lifted up 1Kin 11:27 1697
for the c was from the LORD, that 1Kin 12:15 5438
I will c him to fall by the sword 2Kin 19:7
why will he be a c of trespass to 1Chr 21:3
supplication, and maintain their c 2Chr 6:35 4941
and maintain their c, and forgive 2Chr 6:39 4941
for the c was of God, that the 2Chr 10:15 5252
what c soever shall come to you 2Chr 19:10 7379
for this c Hezekiah the king, and 2Chr 32:20
for which c was this city Ezr 4:15
to c these men to cease, and that Ezr 4:21
they could not c them to cease Ezr 5:5
slay them, and c the work to cease Neh 4:11
for which c thou buildest the Neh 6:6
him did outlandish women c to sin Neh 13:26
to c to perish, all Jews, both Est 3:13
C Haman to make haste, that he Est 5:5
to c to perish, all the power of Est 8:11
him, to destroy him without c Job 2:3 2600
and unto God would I commit my c Job 5:8 1700
c me to understand wherein I have Job 6:24
multiplieth my wounds without c Job 9:17 2600
Behold now, I have ordered my c Job 13:18 4941
do my thoughts c me to answer Job 20:2
I would order my c before him Job 23:4 4941
They c the naked to lodge without Job 24:7
They c him to go naked without Job 24:10
the c which I knew not I searched Job 29:16 7379
If I did despise the c of my Job 31:13 4941
c every man to find according to Job 34:11
So that they c the cry of the Job 34:28
To c it to rain on the earth, Job 38:26
to c the bud of the tender herb Job 38:27
him that without c is mine enemy Ps 7:4 7387
hast maintained my right and my c Ps 9:4 1779
thou wilt c thine ear to hear Ps 10:17
which transgress without c Ps 25:3 7387
Plead my c, O LORD, with them Ps 35:1 7378
For without c have they hid for Ps 35:7 2600
which without c they have digged Ps 35:7 2600
the eye that hate me without a c Ps 35:19 2600
to my judgment, even unto my c Ps 35:23 7379
glad, that favour my righteous c Ps 35:27 6664
plead my c against an ungodly Ps 43:1 7379
c his face to shine upon us Ps 67:1
They that hate me without a c are Ps 69:4 2600
righteousness, and c me to escape Ps 71:2
Arise, O God, plead thine own c Ps 74:22 7379
Thou didst c judgment to be heard Ps 76:8
O God, and c thy face to shine Ps 80:3
of hosts, and c thy face to shine Ps 80:7
didst c it to take deep root, and Ps 80:9
God of hosts, c thy face to shine Ps 80:19
c thine anger toward us to cease Ps 85:4
and fought against me without a c Ps 109:3 2600
perversely with me without a c Ps 119:78 8267
Plead my c, and deliver me Ps 119:154 7379
have persecuted me without a c Ps 119:161 2600
maintain the c of the afflicted Ps 140:12 1779
C me to hear thy lovingkindness Ps 143:8
c me to know the way wherein I Ps 143:8
for the innocent without c Prov 1:11 2600
Strive not with a man without c Prov 3:30 2600
unless they c some to fall Prov 4:16
That I may c those that love me Prov 8:21
first in his own c seemeth just Prov 18:17 7379
For the LORD will plead their c Prov 22:23 7379
he shall plead their c with thee Prov 23:11 7379
who hath wounds without c Prov 23:29 2600
against thy neighbour without c Prov 24:28 2600

Debate thy *c* with thy neighbour ... Prov 25:9 7379
considereth the *c* of the poor ... Prov 29:7 1779
thy mouth for the dumb in the *c* ... Prov 31:8 1779
plead the *c* of the poor and needy ... Prov 31:9 1777
Therefore I went about to *c* my ... Eccl 2:20
thy mouth to *c* thy flesh to sin ... Eccl 5:6
What is the *c* that the former ... Eccl 7:10 1961
Dead flies *c* the ointment of the ... Eccl 10:1
I would *c* thee to drink of spiced ... Song 8:2
c me to hear it ... Song 8:13
neither doth the *c* of the widow ... Is 1:23 7379
which lead thee *c* thee to err ... Is 3:12
of this people *c* them to err ... Is 9:16
c it to be heard unto Laish, O ... Is 10:30
shall not *c* her light to shine ... Is 13:10
I will *c* the arrogancy of the ... Is 13:11
He shall *c* them that come of ... Is 27:6
ye may *c* the weary to rest ... Is 28:12
c the Holy One of Israel to cease ... Is 30:11
the LORD shall *c* his glorious ... Is 30:30
he will *c* the drink of the ... Is 32:6
I will *c* him to fall by the sword ... Is 37:7
Produce your *c*, saith the LORD ... Is 41:21 7379
nor *c* his voice to be heard in ... Is 42:2
to *c* to inherit the desolate ... Is 49:8
that pleadeth the *c* of his people ... Is 51:22 7378
Assyrian oppressed them without *c* ... Is 52:4 657
I will *c* thee to ride upon the ... Is 58:14
the Lord GOD will *c* righteousness ... Is 61:11
birth, and not *c* to bring forth ... Is 66:9
shall I *c* to bring forth, and shut ... Is 66:9
I will not *c* mine anger to fall ... Jer 3:12
they judge not the *c* ... Jer 5:28 1779
the *c* of the fatherless, yet they ... Jer 5:28 1779
I will *c* you to dwell in this ... Jer 7:3
Then will I *c* you to dwell in ... Jer 7:7
Then will I *c* to cease from the ... Jer 7:34
unto thee have I revealed my *c* ... Jer 11:20 7379
your God, before he *c* darkness ... Jer 13:16
of the Gentiles that can *c* rain ... Jer 14:22
I will *c* them to be removed into ... Jer 15:4 5414
verily I will *c* the enemy to ... Jer 15:11
I will *c* to cease out of this ... Jer 16:9
I will this once *c* them to know ... Jer 16:21
I will *c* them to know mine hand ... Jer 16:21
I will *c* thee to serve thine ... Jer 17:4
there I will *c* thee to hear my ... Jer 18:2
I will *c* them to fall by the ... Jer 19:7
I will *c* them to eat the flesh of ... Jer 19:9
for unto thee have I opened my *c* ... Jer 20:12 7379
He judged the *c* of the poor ... Jer 22:16 1779
Which think to *c* my people to ... Jer 23:27
c my people to err by their lies, ... Jer 23:32
c all the nations, to whom I send ... Jer 25:15
dreams which ye *c* to be dreamed ... Jer 29:8
I will *c* them to return to the ... Jer 30:3
There is none to plead thy *c* ... Jer 30:13 1779
I will *c* him to draw near, and he ... Jer 30:21
when I went to *c* him to rest ... Jer 31:2
I will *c* them to walk by the ... Jer 31:9
Hinnom, to *c* their sons and their ... Jer 32:35 4616
abomination, to *c* Judah to sin ... Jer 32:35
I will *c* them to dwell safely ... Jer 32:37
for I will *c* their captivity to ... Jer 32:44
I will *c* the captivity of Judah ... Jer 33:7
For I will *c* to return the ... Jer 33:11
that time, will I *c* the Branch of ... Jer 33:15
for I will *c* their captivity to ... Jer 33:26
c them to return to this city ... Jer 34:22
shall *c* to cease from thence man ... Jer 36:29
that thou *c* me not to return to ... Jer 37:20
thou shalt *c* this city to be ... Jer 38:23
that he would not *c* me to return ... Jer 38:26
c you to return to your own land ... Jer 42:12
that shall *c* him to wander, and ... Jer 48:12
Moreover I will *c* to cease in ... Jer 48:35
that I will *c* an alarm of war to ... Jer 49:2
For I will *c* Elam to be dismayed ... Jer 49:37
c to come up against Babylon an ... Jer 50:9
he shall throughly plead their *c* ... Jer 50:34 7379
c the horses to come up as the ... Jer 51:27
Behold, I will plead thy *c* ... Jer 51:36 7379
But though he *c* grief, yet will ... Lam 3:32
To subvert a man in his *c* ... Lam 3:36 7379
me sore, like a bird, without *c* ... Lam 3:52 2600
judge thou my *c* ... Lam 3:59 4941
c thy belly to eat, and fill thy ... Eze 3:3
c it to pass upon thine head and ... Eze 5:1
I will *c* my fury to rest upon ... Eze 5:13
C them that have charge over the ... Eze 9:1
If I *c* noisome beasts to pass ... Eze 14:15
c all that I have done in it ... Eze 14:23 2600
of man, *c* Jerusalem to know her ... Eze 16:2
delivered them to *c* them to pass ... Eze 16:21
I will *c* thee to cease from ... Eze 16:41
c them to know the abominations ... Eze 20:4
I will *c* you to pass under the ... Eze 20:37
and I will *c* my fury to rest ... Eze 21:17
Shall I *c* it to return into his ... Eze 21:30
Thus will I *c* lewdness to cease ... Eze 23:48
That it might *c* fury to come up ... Eze 24:8
to *c* thee to hear it with thine ... Eze 24:26 2045
I will *c* thee to perish out of ... Eze 25:7
will *c* many nations to come up ... Eze 26:3
I will *c* the noise of thy songs ... Eze 26:13
which *c* their terror to be on all ... Eze 26:17 5414
shall *c* their voice to be heard ... Eze 27:30

I will *c* the fish of thy rivers ... Eze 29:4
will *c* them to return into the ... Eze 29:14
In that day will I *c* the horn of ... Eze 29:21
I will *c* their images to cease ... Eze 30:13
I will *c* the sword to fall out of ... Eze 30:22
will *c* all the fowls of the ... Eze 32:4
will I *c* thy multitude to fall ... Eze 32:12
c their rivers to run like oil, ... Eze 32:14
c them to cease from feeding the ... Eze 34:10
I will *c* them to lie down, saith ... Eze 34:15
will *c* the evil beasts to cease ... Eze 34:25
I will *c* the shower to come down ... Eze 34:26
I will *c* men to walk upon you, ... Eze 36:12
Neither will I *c* men to hear in ... Eze 36:15
neither shalt thou *c* thy nations ... Eze 36:15
c you to walk in my statutes, and ... Eze 36:27 6213
also *c* you to dwell in the cities ... Eze 36:33
I will *c* breath to enter into you ... Eze 37:5
c you to come up out of your ... Eze 37:12
will *c* thee to come up from the ... Eze 39:2
will *c* thine arrows to fall out ... Eze 39:3
c them to discern between the ... Eze 44:23
that he may *c* the blessing to ... Eze 44:30
For this *c* the king was angry and ... Dan 2:12 1836
his policy also he shall *c* craft ... Dan 8:25
c thy face to shine upon thy ... Dan 9:17
the week he shall *c* the sacrifice ... Dan 9:27
c the reproach offered by him to ... Dan 11:18
he shall *c* it to turn upon him ... Dan 11:18
he shall *c* them to rule over many ... Dan 11:39
will *c* to cease the kingdom of ... Hos 1:4
I will also *c* all her mirth to ... Hos 2:11
he will *c* to come down for you ... Joel 2:23
thither *c* thy mighty ones to come ... Joel 3:11
Therefore will I *c* you to go into ... Amos 5:27
c the seat of violence to come ... Amos 6:3
that I will *c* the sun to go down ... Amos 8:9
for whose *c* this evil is upon us ... Jonah 1:7 7945
for whose *c* this evil is upon us ... Jonah 1:8 834
against him, until he plead my *c* ... Mic 7:9 7379
and *c* me to behold grievance ... Hab 1:3
I will *c* the remnant of this ... Zec 8:12
also I will *c* the prophets and the ... Zec 13:2
a *c* shall be in danger of the ... Mt 5:22 *1500*
saving for the *c* of fornication ... Mt 5:32 *3056*
c them to be put to death ... Mt 10:21 *2289*
to put away his wife for every *c* ... Mt 19:3 *156*
For this *c* shall a man leave ... Mt 19:5 *1752*
For this *c* shall a man leave his ... Mk 10:7 *1752*
shall *c* them to be put to death ... Mk 13:12 *2289*
for what *c* she had touched him ... Lk 8:47 *156*
shall they *c* to be put to death ... Lk 21:16 *2289*
I have found no *c* of death in him ... Lk 23:22 *158*
For this *c* the people also met ... Jn 12:18 *1223*
but for this *c* came I unto this ... Jn 12:27 *1223*
law, They hated me without a *c* ... Jn 15:25 *1432*
for this *c* came I into the world, ... Jn 18:37
what is the *c* wherefore ye are ... Acts 10:21 *156*
they found no *c* of death in him ... Acts 13:28 *156*
there being no *c* whereby we may ... Acts 19:40 *158*
the *c* wherefore they accused him ... Acts 23:28 *156*
declared Paul's *c* unto the king ... Acts 25:14 *156*
there was no *c* of death in me ... Acts 28:18 *156*
For this *c* therefore have I ... Acts 28:20 *156*
For this *c* God gave them up unto ... Rom 1:26 *1223*
For for this *c* pay ye tribute ... Rom 13:6 *1223*
For this *c* I will confess to thee ... Rom 15:9 *1223*
For which *c* also I have been much ... Rom 15:22 *1352*
mark them which *c* divisions ... Rom 16:17 *4160*
For this *c* have I sent unto you ... 1Cor 4:17 *1223*
For this *c* ought the woman to ... 1Cor 11:10 *1223*
For this *c* many are weak and ... 1Cor 11:30 *1223*
For which *c* we faint not ... 2Cor 4:16 *1352*
we be sober, it is for your *c* ... 2Cor 5:13
I did it not for his *c* that had ... 2Cor 7:12 *1752*
nor for his *c* that suffered wrong ... 2Cor 7:12 *1752*
For this *c* I Paul, the prisoner ... Eph 3:1 *5484*
For this *c* I bow my knees unto ... Eph 3:14 *5484*
For this *c* shall a man leave his ... Eph 5:31 *873*
For the same *c* also do ye joy, and ... Phil 2:18 *846*
For this *c* we also, since the day ... Col 1:9 *5124*
c that it be read also in the ... Col 4:16 *4160*
For this *c* also thank we God ... 1Th 2:13 *1223*
For this *c*, when I could no ... 1Th 3:5 *1223*
for this *c* God shall send them ... 2Th 2:11 *1223*
for this *c* I obtained mercy ... 1Ti 1:16 *1223*
For the which *c* I also suffer ... 2Ti 1:12 *156*
For this *c* left I thee in Crete, ... Titus 1:5 *5484*
for which *c* he is not ashamed to ... Heb 2:11 *156*
for this *c* he is the mediator of ... Heb 9:15 *1223*
For for this *c* was the gospel ... 1Pet 4:6 *5124*
that he might *c* her to be carried ... Rev 12:15 *4160*
c that as many as would not ... Rev 13:15 *4160*

CAUSED {94}

for the LORD God had not *c* it to ... Gen 2:5
the LORD God *c* a deep sleep to ... Gen 2:21
when God *c* me to wander from my ... Gen 20:13
For God hath *c* me to be fruitful ... Gen 41:52
the LORD *c* the sea to go back by ... Ex 14:21
they *c* it to be proclaimed ... Ex 36:6
as he hath *c* a blemish in a man, ... Lev 24:20 5414
these *c* the children of Israel, ... Num 31:16 1961
I have *c* thee to see it with ... Deut 34:4
she *c* him to shave off the seven ... Judg 16:19
when Samuel had *c* all the tribes ... 1Sa 10:20
When he had *c* the tribe of ... 1Sa 10:21

Jonathan *c* David to swear again, ... 1Sa 20:17
have *c* thee to rest from all ... 2Sa 7:11
c Solomon to ride upon king ... 1Kin 1:38
they have *c* him to ride upon the ... 1Kin 1:44
c a seat to be set for the king's ... 1Kin 2:19
he *c* him to come up into the ... 1Kin 20:33
they *c* their sons and their ... 2Kin 17:17
c the children of Israel to dwell ... 2Chr 8:2
But Jeroboam *c* an ambushment to ... 2Chr 13:13
c the inhabitants of Jerusalem to ... 2Chr 21:11
he *c* his children to pass through ... 2Chr 33:6
he *c* all that were present in ... 2Chr 34:32
the God that hath *c* his name to ... Ezr 6:12
c the people to understand the ... Neh 8:7
c them to understand the reading ... Neh 8:8
he *c* the gallows to be made ... Est 5:14
I *c* the widow's heart to sing for ... Job 29:13
or have *c* the eyes of the widow ... Job 31:16
or have *c* the owners thereof to ... Job 31:39
c the light of his cloud to shine ... Job 37:15
c the dayspring to know his place ... Job 38:12
Thou hast *c* men to ride over our ... Ps 66:12
sea, and *c* them to pass through ... Ps 78:13
c waters to run down like rivers ... Ps 78:16
He *c* an east wind to blow in the ... Ps 78:26
upon which thou hast *c* me to hope ... Ps 119:49
fair speech she *c* him to yield ... Prov 7:21
they have *c* Egypt to err in every ... Is 19:14
I have not *c* thee to serve with ... Is 43:23
he *c* the waters to flow out of ... Is 48:21
Spirit of the LORD *c* him to rest ... Is 63:14
c my people Israel to inherit ... Jer 12:14
so have I *c* to cleave unto me the ... Jer 13:11
I have *c* him to fall upon it ... Jer 15:8
they have *c* them to stumble in ... Jer 18:15
c my people Israel to err ... Jer 23:13
had *c* my people to hear my words, ... Jer 23:22
whom I have *c* to be carried away ... Jer 29:4
of the city whither I have *c* you ... Jer 29:7
again into the place whence I *c* ... Jer 29:14
he *c* you to trust in a lie ... Jer 29:31
therefore thou hast *c* all this ... Jer 32:23
c the servants and the handmaids, ... Jer 34:11
c every man his servant, and every ... Jer 34:16
ones have *c* a cry to be heard ... Jer 48:4
I have *c* wine to fail from the ... Jer 48:33
have *c* them to go astray, they ... Jer 50:6
As Babylon hath *c* the slain of ... Jer 51:49
the LORD hath *c* the solemn feasts ... Lam 2:6
he hath *c* thine enemy to rejoice ... Lam 2:17
He hath *c* the arrows of his ... Lam 3:13
and he *c* me to eat that roll ... Eze 3:2
I have *c* thee to multiply as the ... Eze 16:7 5414
Wherefore I *c* them to go forth ... Eze 20:10
in that they *c* to pass through ... Eze 20:26
thou hast *c* thy days to draw near ... Eze 22:4
have also *c* their sons, whom they ... Eze 23:37
till I have *c* my fury to rest ... Eze 24:13
c his army to serve a great ... Eze 29:18
down to the grave I *c* a mourning ... Eze 31:15
I *c* Lebanon to mourn for him, and ... Eze 31:15
which *c* terror in the land of the ... Eze 32:23 5414
which *c* their terror in the land ... Eze 32:24 5414
though their terror was *c* in the ... Eze 32:25 5414
though they *c* their terror in the ... Eze 32:26 5414
For I have *c* my terror in the ... Eze 32:32 5414
c me to pass by them round about ... Eze 37:2
which *c* them to be led into ... Eze 39:28
c the house of Israel to fall ... Eze 44:12 1961
c me to pass by the four corners ... Eze 46:21
c me to return to the brink of ... Eze 47:6 1980
being *c* to fly swiftly, touched ... Dan 9:21
of whoredoms hath *c* them to err ... Hos 4:12
their lies *c* them to err, after ... Amos 2:4
I *c* it to rain upon one city, and ... Amos 4:7
c it not to rain upon another ... Amos 4:7
he *c* it to be proclaimed and ... Jonah 3:7
I have *c* thine iniquity to pass ... Zec 3:4
ye have *c* many to stumble at the ... Mal 2:8
have *c* that even this man should ... Jn 11:37 *4160*
they *c* great joy unto all the ... Acts 15:3 *4160*
But if any have *c* grief, he hath ... 2Cor 2:5 *3076*

CAUSELESS {2}

that thou hast shed blood *c* ... 1Sa 25:31 2600
so the curse *c* shall not come ... Prov 26:2 2600

CAUSES {7}

thou mayest bring the *c* unto God ... Ex 18:19 1697
the hard *c* they brought unto ... Ex 18:26 1697
Hear the *c* between your brethren, ... Deut 1:16
when for all the *c* whereby ... Jer 3:8 182
false burdens and *c* of banishment ... Lam 2:14
hast pleaded the *c* of my soul ... Lam 3:58 7379
For these *c* the Jews caught me in ... Acts 26:21 *1752*

CAUSEST {2}

thou *c* me to ride upon it, and ... Job 30:22
c to approach unto thee, that he ... Ps 65:4

CAUSETH {32}

the bitter water that *c* the curse ... Num 5:18
bitter water that *c* the curse ... Num 5:19
this water that *c* the curse shall ... Num 5:22
the bitter water that *c* the curse ... Num 5:24
the water that *c* the curse shall ... Num 5:24
that the water that *c* the curse ... Num 5:27
c them to wander in a wilderness ... Job 12:24
my understanding *c* me to answer ... Job 20:3

He c it to come, whether for .... Job 37:13
He c the grass to grow for the .... Ps 104:14
and c them to wander in the .... Ps 107:40
He c the vapours to ascend from .... Ps 135:7
he c his wind to blow, and the .... Ps 147:18
in harvest is a son that c shame .... Prov 10:5
winketh with the eye c sorrow .... Prov 10:10 5414
wrath is against him that c shame .... Prov 14:35
have rule over a son that c shame .... Prov 17:2
The lot c contentions to cease, ... Prov 18:18
his mother, is a son that c shame .... Prov 19:26
that c to err from the words of .... Prov 19:27
Whoso c the righteous to go .... Prov 28:10
as the garden c the things that .... Is 61:11
the fire c the waters to boil, to .... Is 64:2
he c the vapors to ascend from .... Jer 10:13
he c the vapors to ascend from .... Jer 51:16
as the sea c his waves to come up .... Eze 26:3
with any thing that c sweat .... Eze 44:18 3154
c her to commit adultery .... Mt 5:32 *4160*
which always c us to triumph in 2Cor 2:14 *2358*
which c through us thanksgiving 2Cor 9:11 *2716*
c the earth and them which dwell .... Rev 13:12 *4160*
he c all, both small and great, ... Rev 13:16 *4160*

CAUSEWAY {2}
by the c of the going up, ward 1Chr 26:16 4546
At Parbar westward, four at the c 1Chr 26:18 4546

CAUSING {4}
c the lips of those that are .... Song 7:9
jaws of the people, c them to err .... Is 30:28
in c you to return to this place .... Jer 29:10
c their flocks to lie down .... Jer 33:12

CAVE {33}
and he dwelt in a c, he and his two .... Gen 19:30 4631
he may give me the c of Machpelah .... Gen 23:9 4631
the c that is therein, I give it .... Gen 23:11 4631
the c which was therein, and all .... Gen 23:17 4631
the c of the field of Machpelah .... Gen 23:19 4631
the c that is therein, were made .... Gen 23:20 4631
buried him in the c of Machpelah .... Gen 25:9 4631
c that is in the field of Ephron .... Gen 49:29 4631
In the c that is in the field of .... Gen 49:30 4631
of the c that is therein was from .... Gen 49:32 4631
buried him in the c of the field .... Gen 50:13 4631
hid themselves in a c at Makkedah .... Josh 10:16 4631
are found hid in a c at Makkedah .... Josh 10:17 4631
stones upon the mouth of the c .... Josh 10:18 4631
Joshua, Open the mouth of the c .... Josh 10:22 4631
five kings unto me out of the c .... Josh 10:22 4631
five kings unto him out of the c .... Josh 10:23 4631
cast them into the c wherein they .... Josh 10:27 4631
and escaped to the c Adullam 1Sa 22:1 4631
by the way, where was a c 1Sa 24:3 4631
remained in the sides of the c 1Sa 24:3 4631
But Saul rose up out of the c 1Sa 24:7 4631
afterward, and went out of the c 1Sa 24:8 4631
to day into mine hand in the c 1Sa 24:10 4631
time unto the c of Adullam 2Sa 23:13 4631
and hid them by fifty in a c 1Kin 18:4 4631
LORD's prophets by fifty in a c 1Kin 18:13 4631
And he came thither unto a c 1Kin 19:9 4631
stood in the entering in of the c 1Kin 19:13 4631
to David, into the c of Adullam 1Chr 11:15 4631
when he fled from Saul in the c .... Ps 57:*t* 4631
A Prayer when he was in the c .... Ps 142:*t* 4631
It was a c, and a stone lay upon .... Jn 11:38 *4693*

CAVE'S {1}
laid great stones in the c mouth .... Josh 10:27 4631

CAVES {6}
which are in the mountains, and c .... Judg 6:2 4631
people did hide themselves in c 1Sa 13:6 4631
in c of the earth, and in the .... Job 30:6 2356
into the c of the earth, for fear .... Is 2:19 4247
in the c shall die of the .... Eze 33:27 4631
and in dens and c of the earth .... Heb 11:38 *3692*

CEASE {70}
and day and night shall not c .... Gen 8:22 7673
and the thunder shall c, neither .... Ex 9:29 2308
shall c waiting upon the service .... Num 8:25 7725
they prophesied, and did not c .... Num 11:25 3254
I will make to c from me the .... Num 17:5 7918
shall never c out of the land .... Deut 15:11 2308
of them to c from among men .... Deut 32:26 7673
children c from fearing the LORD .... Josh 22:25 7673
of you, and after that I will c .... Judg 15:7 2308
Benjamin my brother, or shall I c .... Judg 20:28 2308
C not to cry unto the LORD our 1Sa 7:8 2790
of Ramah, and let his work c 2Chr 16:5 7673
to cause these men to c, and that .... Ezr 4:21 989
Jews, and made them to c by force .... Ezr 4:23 989
they could not cause them to c .... Ezr 5:5 989
slay them, and cause the work to c .... Neh 4:11 7673
why should the work c, whilst I .... Neh 6:3 7673
There the wicked c from troubling .... Job 3:17 2308
c then, and let me alone, that I .... Job 10:20 2308
tender branch thereof will not c .... Job 14:7 2308
C from anger, and forsake wrath .... Ps 37:8 7503
He maketh wars to c unto the end .... Ps 46:9 7673
cause thine anger toward us to c .... Ps 85:4 6565
Thou hast made his glory to c .... Ps 89:44 7673
The lot causeth contentions to c .... Prov 18:18 7673
C, my son, to hear the .... Prov 19:27 2308
honour for a man to c from strife .... Prov 20:3 7647
yea, strife and reproach shall c .... Prov 22:10 7673
c from thine own wisdom .... Prov 23:4 2308
the grinders c because they are .... Eccl 12:3 988
c to do evil .... Is 1:16 2308
C ye from man, whose breath is in .... Is 2:22 2308
while, and the indignation shall c .... Is 10:25 3615
the arrogancy of the proud to c .... Is 13:11 7673
made their vintage shouting to c .... Is 16:10 7673
also shall c from Ephraim .... Is 17:3 7673
sighing thereof have I made to c .... Is 21:2 7673
One of Israel to c from before us .... Is 30:11 7673
when thou shalt c to spoil .... Is 33:1 8552
Then will I cause to c from the .... Jer 7:34 7673
night and day, and let them not c .... Jer 14:17 1820
I will cause to c out of this .... Jer 16:9 7673
neither shall c from yielding .... Jer 17:8 4185
c from being a nation before me .... Jer 31:36 7673
shall cause to c from thence man .... Jer 36:29 7673
I will cause to c in Moab .... Jer 48:35 7673
let not the apple of thine eye c .... Lam 2:18 1826
and your idols may be broken and c .... Eze 6:6 7673
make the pomp of the strong to c .... Eze 7:24 7673
I will make this proverb to c .... Eze 12:23 7673
I will cause thee to c from .... Eze 16:41 7673
make thy lewdness to c from thee .... Eze 23:27 7673
lewdness to c out of the land .... Eze 23:48 7673
cause the noise of thy songs to c .... Eze 26:13 7673
c by the hand of Nebuchadrezzar .... Eze 30:10 7673
their images to c out of Noph .... Eze 30:13 7673
of her strength shall c in her .... Eze 30:18 7673
the pomp of her strength shall c .... Eze 33:28 7673
cause them to c from feeding the .... Eze 34:10 7673
evil beasts to c out of the land .... Eze 34:25 7673
sacrifice and the oblation to c .... Dan 9:27 7673
the reproach offered by him to c .... Dan 11:18 7673
will cause to c the kingdom of .... Hos 1:4 7673
also cause all her mirth to c .... Hos 2:11 7673
Then said I, O Lord GOD, c .... Amos 7:5 2308
wilt thou not c to pervert the .... Acts 13:10 *3973*
there be tongues, they shall c 1Cor 13:8 *3973*
C not to give thanks for you .... Eph 1:16 *3973*
do not c to pray for you, and to .... Col 1:9 *3973*
and that cannot c from sin 2Pet 2:14 *180*

CEASED {33}
it c to be with Sarah after the .... Gen 18:11 2308
and the thunders and hail c .... Ex 9:33 2308
the hail and the thunders were c .... Ex 9:34 2308
the manna c on the morrow after .... Josh 5:12 7673
they c not from their own doings .... Judg 2:19 5307
The inhabitants of the villages c .... Judg 5:7 2308
they c in Israel, until that I .... Judg 5:7 2308
and they that were hungry c 1Sa 2:5 2308
words in the name of David, and c 1Sa 25:9 5117
Then c the work of the house of .... Ezr 4:24 989
So it c unto the second year of .... Ezr 4:24 1934,989
these three men c to answer Job .... Job 32:1 7673
they did tear me, and c not .... Ps 35:15 1826
sore ran in the night, and c not .... Ps 77:2 6313
and say, How hath the oppressor c .... Is 14:4 7673
the golden city c .... Is 14:4 7673
The elders have c from the gate .... Lam 5:14 7673
The joy of our heart is c .... Lam 5:15 7673
the sea c from her raging .... Jonah 1:15 5975
come into the ship, the wind c .... Mt 14:32 *2869*
And the wind c, and there was a .... Mk 4:39 *2869*
and the wind c .... Mk 6:51 *2869*
in hath not c to kiss my feet .... Lk 7:45 *1257*
and they c, and there was a calm .... Lk 8:24 *3973*
in a certain place, when he c .... Lk 11:1 *3973*
they c not to teach and preach .... Acts 5:42 *3973*
And after the uproar was c .... Acts 20:1 *3973*
I c not to warn every one night .... Acts 20:31 *3973*
he would not be persuaded, we c .... Acts 21:14 *2270*
is the offence of the cross c .... Gal 5:11 *2673*
he also hath c from his own works .... Heb 4:10 *2664*
they not have c to be offered .... Heb 10:2 *3973*
in the flesh hath c from sin 1Pet 4:1 *3973*

CEASETH {10}
for the godly man c .... Ps 12:1 1584
is precious, and it c for ever .... Ps 49:8 2308
is no talebearer, the strife c .... Prov 26:20 8367
is at an end, the spoiler c .... Is 16:4 3615
The mirth of tabrets c, the noise .... Is 24:8 7673
endeth, the joy of the harp c .... Is 24:8 7673
lie waste, the wayfaring man c .... Is 33:8 7673
c not, without any intermission .... Lam 3:49 1820
who c from raising after he hath .... Hos 7:4 7673
said, This man c not to speak .... Acts 6:13 *3973*

CEASING {7}
the LORD in c to pray for you 1Sa 12:23 2308
but prayer was made without c of .... Acts 12:5 *1618*
that without c I make mention of .... Rom 1:9 *89*
without c your work of faith 1Th 1:3 *89*
cause also thank we God without c 1Th 2:13 *89*
Pray without c 1Th 5:17 *89*
that without c I have remembrance 2Ti 1:3 *83*

CEDAR {51}
c wood, and scarlet, and hyssop .... Lev 14:4 730
the c wood, and the scarlet, and .... Lev 14:6 730
c wood, and scarlet, and hyssop .... Lev 14:49 730
And he shall take the c wood .... Lev 14:51 730
living bird, and with the c wood .... Lev 14:52 730
And the priest shall take c wood .... Num 19:6 730
as c trees beside the waters .... Num 24:6 730
c trees, and carpenters, and masons 2Sa 5:11 730
See now, I dwell in an house of c 2Sa 7:2 730
Why build ye not me an house of c 2Sa 7:7 730
from the c tree that is in 1Kin 4:33 730
hew me c trees out of Lebanon 1Kin 5:6 730
thy desire concerning timber of c 1Kin 5:8 730
So Hiram gave Solomon c trees 1Kin 5:10 730
house with beams and boards of c 1Kin 6:9 730
on the house with timber of c 1Kin 6:10 730
the house within with boards of c 1Kin 6:15 730
and the walls with boards of c 1Kin 6:16 730
the c of the house within was 1Kin 6:18 730
all was c 1Kin 6:18 730
covered the altar which was of c 1Kin 6:20 730
hewed stone, and a row of c beams 1Kin 6:36 730
upon four rows of c pillars 1Kin 7:2 730
with c beams upon the pillars 1Kin 7:2 730
it was covered with c above upon 1Kin 7:3 730
it was covered with c from one 1Kin 7:7 730
hewed stones, and a row of c beams 1Kin 7:12 730
furnished Solomon with c trees 1Kin 9:11 730
sent to the c that was in Lebanon 2Kin 14:9 730
cut down the tall c trees thereof 2Kin 19:23 730
Also c trees in abundance 1Chr 22:4 730
Tyre brought much c wood to David 1Chr 22:4 730
c trees made he as the sycomore 2Chr 1:15 730
Send me also c trees, fir trees, ... 2Chr 2:8 730
c trees made he as the sycomore 2Chr 9:27 730
sent to the c that was in Lebanon 2Chr 25:18 730
to bring c trees from Lebanon to .... Ezr 3:7 730
He moveth his tail like a c .... Job 40:17 730
he shall grow like a c in Lebanon .... Ps 92:12 730
The beams of our house are c .... Song 1:17 730
will inclose her with boards of c .... Song 8:9 730
plant in the wilderness the c .... Is 41:19 730
and it is cieled with c, and .... Jer 22:14 730
because thou closest thyself in c .... Jer 22:15 730
took the highest branch of the c .... Eze 17:3 730
the highest branch of the high c .... Eze 17:22 730
and bear fruit, and be a goodly c .... Eze 17:23 730
bound with cords, and made of c .... Eze 27:24 729
the Assyrian was a c in Lebanon .... Eze 31:3 730
for he shall uncover the c work .... Zeph 2:14 731
for the c is fallen .... Zec 11:2 730

CEDARS {24}
and devour the c of Lebanon .... Judg 9:15 730
measures of hewed stones, and c 1Kin 7:11 730
c made he to be as the sycomore 1Kin 10:27 730
to David, and timber of c, with 1Chr 14:1 730
Lo, I dwell in an house of c 1Chr 17:1 730
ye not built me an house of c 1Chr 17:6 730
didst send him c to build him an 2Chr 2:3 730
voice of the LORD breaketh the c .... Ps 29:5 730
LORD breaketh the c of Lebanon .... Ps 29:5 730
thereof were like the goodly c .... Ps 80:10 730
the c of Lebanon, which he hath .... Ps 104:16 730
fruitful trees, and all c .... Ps 148:9 730
is as Lebanon, excellent as the c .... Song 5:15 730
And upon all the c of Lebanon .... Is 2:13 730
but we will change them into c .... Is 9:10 730
the c of Lebanon, saying, Since .... Is 14:8 730
will cut down the tall c thereof .... Is 37:24 730
He heweth him down c, and taketh .... Is 44:14 730
they shall cut down thy choice c .... Jer 22:7 730
that makest thy nest in the c .... Jer 22:23 730
they have taken c from Lebanon to .... Eze 27:5 730
The c in the garden of God could .... Eze 31:8 730
was like the height of the c .... Amos 2:9 730
that the fire may devour thy c .... Zec 11:1 730

CEDRON *(se'-drun)* {1} See KIDRON. *Same as Kidron.*
his disciples over the brook C .... Jn 18:1 *2748*

CEILED {4}
greater house he c with fir tree 2Chr 3:5 2645
it is c with cedar, and painted .... Jer 22:14 5603
c with wood round about, and from .... Eze 41:16 7824
O ye, to dwell in your c houses .... Hag 1:4 5603

CEILING {1}
the house, and the walls of the c 1Kin 6:15 5604

CELEBRATE {3}
even, shall ye c your sabbath .... Lev 23:32 7673
ye shall c it in the seventh .... Lev 23:41 2278
praise thee, death can not c thee .... Is 38:18 1984

CELESTIAL {2}
There are also c bodies, and 1Cor 15:40 *2032*
but the glory of the c is one 1Cor 15:40 *2032*

CELLARS {2}
wine c was Zabdi the Shiphmite 1Chr 27:27 214
over the c of oil was Joash 1Chr 27:28 214

CENCHREA *(sen'-kre-ah)* {3} *Harbor city for Corinth.*
having shorn his head in C .... Acts 18:18 *2747*
of the church which is at C .... Rom 16:1 *2747*
Phebe servant of the church at C .... Rom *s*

CENCHREAE See CENCHREA.

CENSER {12}
Aaron, took either of them his c .... Lev 10:1 4289
he shall take a c full of burning .... Lev 16:12 4289
And take every man his c, and put .... Num 16:17 4289
before the LORD every man his c .... Num 16:17 4289
also, and Aaron, each of you his c .... Num 16:17 4289
And they took every man his c .... Num 16:18 4289
Moses said unto Aaron, Take a c .... Num 16:46 4289
had a c in his hand to burn 2Chr 26:19 4730
with every man his c in his hand .... Eze 8:11 4730
Which had the golden c, and the .... Heb 9:4 *2369*
at the altar, having a golden c .... Rev 8:3 *3031*
And the angel took the c, and .... Rev 8:5 *3031*

CENSERS {8}
minister about it, even the c ... Num 4:14 4289
Take you c, Korah, and all his ... Num 16:6 4289
censer, two hundred and fifty c ... Num 16:17 4289
take up the c out of the burning ... Num 16:37 4289
The c of these sinners against ... Num 16:38 4289
the priest took the brasen c ... Num 16:39 4289
the spoons, and the c of pure gold ... 1Kin 7:50 4289
basons, and the spoons, and the c ... 2Chr 4:22 4289

CENTURION {20}
there came unto him a c, ... Mt 8:5 *1543*
The c answered and said, Lord, I ... Mt 8:8 *1543*
And Jesus said unto the c, Go thy ... Mt 8:13 *1543*
Now when the c, and they that were ... Mt 27:54 *1543*
And when the c, which stood over ... Mk 15:39 *2760*
and calling unto him the c ... Mk 15:44 *2760*
And when he knew it of the c ... Mk 15:45 *2760*
the c sent friends to him, saying ... Lk 7:6 *1543*
Now when the c saw what was done, ... Lk 23:47 *1543*
a c of the band called the ... Acts 10:1 *1543*
And they said, Cornelius the c ... Acts 10:22 *1543*
said unto the c that stood by ... Acts 22:25 *1543*
When the c heard that, he went and ... Acts 22:26 *1543*
And he commanded a c to keep Paul ... Acts 24:23 *1543*
Julius, a c of Augustus' band ... Acts 27:1 *1543*
there the c found a ship of ... Acts 27:6 *1543*
Nevertheless the c believed the ... Acts 27:11 *1543*
Paul said to the c and to the ... Acts 27:31 *1543*
But the c, willing to save Paul, ... Acts 27:43 *1543*
the c delivered the prisoners to ... Acts 28:16 *1543*

CENTURION'S {1}
And a certain c servant, who was ... Lk 7:2 *1543*

CENTURIONS {3}
immediately took soldiers and c ... Acts 21:32 *1543*
Paul called one of the c unto him ... Acts 23:17 *1543*
And he called unto him two c ... Acts 23:23 *1543*

CEPHAS *(se'-fas)* {6} See PETER. *Name given to Simon Peter.*
thou shalt be called C, which is ... Jn 1:42 *2786*
and I of C ... 1Cor 1:12 *2786*
Whether Paul, or Apollos, or C ... 1Cor 3:22 *2786*
as the brethren of the Lord, and C ... 1Cor 9:5 *2786*
And that he was seen of C, then of ... 1Cor 15:5 *2786*
And when James, C, and John, who ... Gal 2:9 *2786*

CEREMONIES {1}
and according to all the c thereof ... Num 9:3 4941

CERTAIN {196}
And he lighted upon a c place ... Gen 28:11
a c man found him, and, behold, he ... Gen 37:15
and turned in to a c Adullamite ... Gen 38:1 376
there a daughter of a c Canaanite ... Gen 38:2 376
gather a c rate every day, that I ... Ex 16:4 1697
And there were c men, who were ... Num 9:6
with c of the children of Israel, ... Num 16:2 582
C men, the children of Belial, ... Deut 13:13
if it be truth, and the thing c ... Deut 13:14 3559
it be true, and the thing c ... Deut 17:4 3559
to his fault, by a c number ... Deut 25:2
a c woman cast a piece of a ... Judg 9:53 259
there was a c man of Zorah, of ... Judg 13:2 259
that there was a c Levite ... Judg 19:1 376
c sons of Belial, beset the house ... Judg 19:22 582
a c man of Beth-lehem-judah went ... Ruth 1:1
Now there was a c man of ... 1Sa 1:1 259
Now a c man of the servants of ... 1Sa 21:7
a c man saw it, and told Joab, and ... 2Sa 18:10 259
thou shalt know for c that thou ... 1Kin 2:37 3045
unto thee, saying, Know for a c ... 1Kin 2:42 3045
oxen were c additions made of ... 1Kin 7:29
c Edomites of his father's ... 1Kin 11:17 582
a c man of the sons of the ... 1Kin 20:35 259
a c man drew a bow at a venture, ... 1Kin 22:34
Now there cried a c woman of the ... 2Kin 4:1 259
appointed unto her a c officer ... 2Kin 8:6 259
c of them had the charge of the ... 1Chr 9:28
he appointed c of the Levites to ... 1Chr 16:4
Then there went c, and told David ... 1Chr 19:5
Even after a c rate every day, ... 2Chr 8:13 1697
after c years he went down to ... 2Chr 18:2
a c man drew a bow at a venture, ... 2Chr 18:33
Then c of the heads of the ... 2Chr 28:12 592
with c chief of the fathers, ... Ezr 10:16 592
came, he and c men of Judah ... Neh 1:2
down and wept, and mourned c days ... Neh 1:4
at Jerusalem dwelt c of the ... Neh 11:4
that a c portion should be for ... Neh 11:23
c of the priests' sons with ... Neh 12:35
after c days obtained I leave of ... Neh 13:6
smote c of them, and plucked off ... Neh 13:25 582
the palace there was a c Jew ... Est 2:5 376
There is a c people scattered ... Est 3:8 259
But know ye for c, that if ye put ... Jer 26:15 3045
Then rose up c of the elders of ... Jer 26:17 582
c men with him into Egypt ... Jer 26:22
That there came c from Shechem ... Jer 41:5 582
c of the poor of the people ... Jer 52:15
c of the poor of the land for ... Jer 52:16
Then came c of the elders of ... Eze 14:1 582
that c of the elders of Israel ... Eze 20:1 582
that he should bring c of the ... Dan 1:3
and the dream is c, and the ... Dan 2:45 3330
that time c Chaldeans came near ... Dan 3:8 1400
There are c Jews whom thou hast ... Dan 3:12 1400
unto that c saint which spake ... Dan 8:13 6422
fainted, and was sick c days ... Dan 8:27
behold a c man clothed in linen, ... Dan 10:5 259
after c years with a great army ... Dan 11:13 6256
a c scribe came, and said unto him ... Mt 8:19 *1520*
c of the scribes said within ... Mt 9:3 *5100*
behold, there came a c ruler ... Mt 9:18
Then c of the scribes and of the ... Mt 12:38 *5100*
there came to him a c man ... Mt 17:14
of heaven likened unto a c king ... Mt 18:23 *444*
desiring a c thing of him ... Mt 20:20 *5100*
A c man had two sons ... Mt 21:28
There was a c householder ... Mt 21:33 *444,5100*
of heaven is like unto a c king ... Mt 22:2 *444*
But there were c of the scribes ... Mk 2:6 *5100*
a c woman, which had an issue of ... Mk 5:25 *5100*
synagogue's house c which said ... Mk 5:35
c of the scribes, which came from ... Mk 7:1 *5100*
For a c woman, whose young ... Mk 7:25
c of them that stood there said ... Mk 11:5 *5100*
A c man planted a vineyard, and ... Mk 12:1
send unto him c of the Pharisees ... Mk 12:13 *5100*
And there came a c poor widow ... Mk 12:42 *1520*
there followed him a c young man ... Mk 14:51 *5100*
And there arose c, and bare false ... Mk 14:57 *5100*
a c priest named Zacharias, of ... Lk 1:5 *5100*
to pass, when he was in a c city ... Lk 5:12 *1520*
And it came to pass on a c day ... Lk 5:17 *1520*
c of the Pharisees said unto them ... Lk 6:2 *5100*
a c centurion's servant, who was ... Lk 7:2 *5100*
There was a c creditor which had ... Lk 7:41 *5100*
c women, which had been healed of ... Lk 8:2 *5100*
it was told him by c which said ... Lk 8:20
Now it came to pass on a c day ... Lk 8:22 *1520*
met him out of the city a c man ... Lk 8:27 *5100*
a c man said unto him, Lord, I ... Lk 9:57 *5100*
a c lawyer stood up, and tempted ... Lk 10:25 *5100*
A c man went down from Jerusalem ... Lk 10:30 *5100*
came down a c priest that way ... Lk 10:31 *5100*
But a c Samaritan, as he ... Lk 10:33 *5100*
that he entered into a c village ... Lk 10:38 *5100*
a c woman named Martha received ... Lk 10:38 *5100*
as he was praying in a c place ... Lk 11:1 *5100*
a c woman of the company lifted ... Lk 11:27 *5100*
a c Pharisee besought him to dine ... Lk 11:37 *5100*
The ground of a c rich man ... Lk 12:16 *5100*
A c man had a fig tree planted in ... Lk 13:6 *5100*
day there came c of the Pharisees ... Lk 13:31 *5100*
there was a c man before him ... Lk 14:2 *5100*
A c man made a great supper, and ... Lk 14:16 *5100*
And he said, A c man had two sons ... Lk 15:11 *5100*
disciples, There was a c rich man ... Lk 16:1 *5100*
There was a c rich man, which was ... Lk 16:19 *5100*
there was a c beggar named ... Lk 16:20 *5100*
And as he entered into a c village ... Lk 17:12 *5100*
he spake this parable unto c ... Lk 18:9 *5100*
a c ruler asked him, saying, Good ... Lk 18:18 *5100*
a c blind man sat by the way side ... Lk 18:35 *5100*
A c nobleman went into a far ... Lk 19:12 *5100*
A c man planted a vineyard, and ... Lk 20:9 *5100*
came to him c of the Sadducees ... Lk 20:27 *5100*
Then c of the scribes answering ... Lk 20:39 *5100*
he saw also a c poor widow ... Lk 21:2 *5100*
But a c maid beheld him as he sat ... Lk 22:56 *5100*
(Who for a c sedition made in the ... Lk 23:19 *5100*
prepared, and c others with them ... Lk 24:1
c women also of our company made ... Lk 24:22 *5100*
c of them which were with us went ... Lk 24:24 *5100*
And there was a c nobleman ... Jn 4:46 *5100*
down at a c season into the pool ... Jn 5:4
a c man was there, which had an ... Jn 5:5 *5100*
Now a c man was sick, named ... Jn 11:1 *5100*
there were c Greeks among them ... Jn 12:20 *5100*
a c man lame from his mother's ... Acts 3:2 *5100*
But a c man named Ananias, with ... Acts 5:1 *5100*
privy to it, and brought a c part ... Acts 5:2 *5100*
there arose c of the synagogue ... Acts 6:9 *5100*
But there was a c man, called ... Acts 8:9 *5100*
way, they came unto a c water ... Acts 8:36 *5100*
there was a c disciple at ... Acts 9:10 *5100*
Then was Saul c days with the ... Acts 9:19 *5100*
he found a c man named Aeneas ... Acts 9:33 *5100*
Joppa a c disciple named Tabitha ... Acts 9:36 *5100*
There was a c man in Caesarea ... Acts 10:1 *5100*
a c vessel descending unto him, ... Acts 10:11 *5100*
c brethren from Joppa accompanied ... Acts 10:23 *5100*
prayed they him to tarry c days ... Acts 10:48 *5100*
A c vessel descend, as it had ... Acts 11:5 *5100*
his hands to vex c of the church ... Acts 12:1 *5100*
that was at Antioch c prophets ... Acts 13:1 *5100*
Paphos, they found a c sorcerer ... Acts 13:6 *5100*
there sat a c man at Lystra, ... Acts 14:8 *5100*
came thither c Jews from Antioch ... Acts 14:19
c men which came down from Judaea ... Acts 15:1 *5100*
c other of them, should go up to ... Acts 15:2 *5100*
But there rose up c of the sect ... Acts 15:5 *5100*
that c which went out from us ... Acts 15:24 *5100*
a c disciple was there, named ... Acts 16:1 *5100*
Timotheus, the son of a c woman ... Acts 16:1 *5100*
were in that city abiding c days ... Acts 16:12 *5100*
a c woman named Lydia, a seller ... Acts 16:14 *5100*
a c damsel possessed with a ... Acts 16:16 *5100*
took unto them c lewd fellows of ... Acts 17:5 *5100*
c brethren unto the rulers of the ... Acts 17:6 *5100*
Then c philosophers of the ... Acts 17:18 *5100*
For thou bringest c strange ... Acts 17:20 *5100*
as c also of your own poets have ... Acts 17:28 *5100*
Howbeit c men clave unto him, and ... Acts 17:34 *5100*
found a c Jew named Aquila, born ... Acts 18:2 *5100*
and entered into a c man's house ... Acts 18:7 *5100*
a c Jew named Apollos, born at ... Acts 18:24 *5100*
and finding c disciples, ... Acts 19:1 *5100*
Then c of the vagabond Jews, ... Acts 19:13 *5100*
For a c man named Demetrius, a ... Acts 19:24 *5100*
c of the chief of Asia, which ... Acts 19:31 *5100*
there sat in a window a c young ... Acts 20:9 *5100*
came down from Judaea a c prophet ... Acts 21:10 *5100*
There went with us also c of the ... Acts 21:16
c of the Jews banded together, and ... Acts 23:12 *5100*
for he hath a c thing to tell him ... Acts 23:17 *5100*
with a c orator named Tertullus, ... Acts 24:1 *5100*
Whereupon c Jews from Asia found ... Acts 24:18 *5100*
And after c days, when Felix came ... Acts 24:24 *5100*
after c days king Agrippa and ... Acts 25:13 *5100*
There is a c man left in bonds by ... Acts 25:14 *5100*
But had c questions against him ... Acts 25:19 *5100*
Of whom I have no c thing to ... Acts 25:26 *804*
c other prisoners unto one named ... Acts 27:1 *5100*
running under a c island which is ... Acts 27:16 *5100*
we must be cast upon a c island ... Acts 27:26 *5100*
discovered a c creek with a shore ... Acts 27:39 *5100*
Achaia to make a c contribution ... Rom 15:26 *5100*
have no c dwellingplace ... 1Cor 4:11 *790*
For before that c came from James ... Gal 2:12 *5100*
it is c we can carry nothing out ... 1Ti 6:7 *1212*
But one in a c place testified, ... Heb 2:6 *4225*
For he spake in a c place of the ... Heb 4:4 *4225*
Again, he limiteth a c day ... Heb 4:7 *5100*
But a c fearful looking for of ... Heb 10:27 *5100*
For there are c men crept in ... Jude 4 *5100*

CERTAINLY {31}
I will c return unto thee ... Gen 18:10
We saw c that the LORD was with ... Gen 26:28
could we c know that he would say ... Gen 43:7
that such a man as I can c divine ... Gen 44:15
will c requite us all the evil ... Gen 50:15
And he said, C I will be with thee ... Ex 3:12 3588
If the theft be c found in his ... Ex 22:4
he hath c trespassed against the ... Lev 5:19
congregation shall c stone him ... Lev 24:16
Because it was c told thy ... Josh 9:24
if ye can c declare it me within ... Judg 14:12
Thy father c knoweth that I have ... 1Sa 20:3
for if I knew c that evil were ... 1Sa 20:9
thy servant hath c heard that ... 1Sa 23:10
for the LORD will c make my lord ... 1Sa 25:28
even so will I c do this day ... 1Kin 1:30
unto him, Thou mayest c recover ... 2Kin 8:10
If thou c return in peace, then ... 2Chr 18:27
for riches c make themselves ... Prov 23:5
Lo, c in vain made he it ... Jer 8:8 403
Do we not c know that every ... Jer 13:12
Ye shall c drink ... Jer 25:28
The king of Babylon shall c come ... Jer 36:29
Dost thou c know that Baalis the ... Jer 40:14
know c that I have admonished you ... Jer 42:19
Now therefore know c that ye ... Jer 42:22
But we will c do whatsoever thing ... Jer 44:17
c this is the day that we looked ... Lam 2:16 389
and one shall c come, and overflow, ... Dan 11:10
shall c come after certain years ... Dan 11:13
C this was a righteous man ... Lk 23:47 *3689*

CERTAINTY {7}
Know for a c that the LORD your ... Josh 23:13
and come ye again to me with the c ... 1Sa 23:23 3559
know the c of the words of truth ... Prov 22:21 7189
I know of c that ye would gain ... Dan 2:8 3330
know the c of those things ... Lk 1:4 *803*
not know the c for the tumult ... Acts 21:34 *804*
c wherefore he was accused of the ... Acts 22:30 *804*

CERTIFIED {2}
have we sent and c the king ... Ezr 4:14 3064
Esther c the king thereof in ... Est 2:22 559

CERTIFY {5}
there come word from you to c me ... 2Sa 15:28 5046
We c the king that, if this city ... Ezr 4:16 3046
to c thee, that we might write ... Ezr 5:10 3046
Also we c you, that touching any ... Ezr 7:24 3046
But I c you, brethren, that the ... Gal 1:11 *1107*

CHAFED {1}
they be c in their minds, as a ... 2Sa 17:8 4751

CHAFF {14}
as c that the storm carrieth away ... Job 21:18 4671
but are like the c which the wind ... Ps 1:4 4671
Let them be as c before the wind ... Ps 35:5 4671
and the flame consumeth the c ... Is 5:24 2842
shall be chased as the c of the ... Is 17:13 4671
shall be as c that passeth away ... Is 29:5 4671
Ye shall conceive c, ye shall ... Is 33:11 2842
and shalt make the hills as c ... Is 41:15 4671
What is the c to the wheat ... Jer 23:28 8401
became like the c of the summer ... Dan 2:35 5784
as the c that is driven with the ... Hos 13:3 4671
before the day pass as the c ... Zeph 2:2 4671
up the c with unquenchable fire ... Mt 3:12 *892*
but the c he will burn with fire ... Lk 3:17 *892*

CHAIN {13}
put a gold c about his neck ... Gen 41:42 7242
work, and wreaths of c work ... 1Kin 7:17 8333
compasseth them about as a c ... Ps 73:6 6059
eyes, with one c of thy neck ... Song 4:9 6060
he hath made my c heavy ... Lam 3:7 5178
Make a c ... Eze 7:23 7659

thy hands, and a *c* on thy neck ... Eze 16:11 7242
have a *c* of gold about his neck, ... Dan 5:7 2002
have a *c* of gold about thy neck, ... Dan 5:16 2002
put a *c* of gold about his neck, ... Dan 5:29 2002
of Israel I am bound with this *c* ... Acts 28:20 *254*
me, and was not ashamed of my *c* ... 2Ti 1:16 *254*
pit and a great *c* in his hand ... Rev 20:1 *254*

CHAINS {37}
two *c* of pure gold at the ends ... Ex 28:14 8333
the wreathen *c* to the ouches ... Ex 28:14 8333
c at the ends of wreathen work of ... Ex 28:22 8337
c of gold in the two rings which ... Ex 28:24 5688
c thou shalt fasten in the two ... Ex 28:25
the breastplate *c* at the ends ... Ex 39:15 8333
they put the two wreathen *c* of ... Ex 39:17 5688
two ends of the two wreathen *c* ... Ex 39:18 5688
hath gotten, of jewels of gold, *c* ... Num 31:50 685
beside the *c* that were about ... Judg 8:26 6060
the *c* of gold before the oracle ... 1Kin 6:21 7569
and set thereon palm trees and *c* ... 2Chr 3:5 8333
And he made *c*, as in the oracle, ... 2Chr 3:16 8333
and put them on the *c* ... 2Chr 3:16 8333
out those which are bound with *c* ... Ps 68:6 3574
To bind their kings with *c* ... Ps 149:8 2131
thy head, and *c* about thy neck ... Prov 1:9 6060
jewels, thy neck with *c* of gold ... Song 1:10 2737
The *c*, and the bracelets, and the ... Is 3:19 5188
with gold, and casteth silver *c* ... Is 40:19 7569
in *c* they shall come over, and ... Is 45:14 2131
eyes, and bound him with *c* ... Jer 39:7 5178
in *c* among all that were carried ... Jer 40:1 246
the *c* which were upon thine hand ... Jer 40:4 246
king of Babylon bound him in *c* ... Jer 52:11 5178
they brought him with *c* unto the ... Eze 19:4 2397
And they put him in ward in *c* ... Eze 19:9 2397
all her great men were bound in *c* ... Nah 3:10 2131
could bind him, no, not with *c* ... Mk 5:3 *254*
often bound with fetters and *c* ... Mk 5:4 *254*
the *c* had been plucked asunder by ... Mk 5:4 *254*
and he was kept bound with *c* ... Lk 8:29 *254*
two soldiers, bound with two *c* ... Acts 12:6 *254*
his *c* fell off from his hands ... Acts 12:7 *254*
him to be bound with two *c* ... Acts 21:33 *254*
delivered them into *c* of darkness ... 2Pet 2:4 *4577*
c under darkness unto the ... Jude 6 *1199*

CHALCEDONY {1}
the third, a *c* ... Rev 21:19 *5472*

CHALCOL *(kal'-kol)* {1} See CALCOL. *Son of Mahol.*
the Ezrahite, and Heman, and *C* ... 1Kin 4:31 3633

CHALDAEANS *(kal-de'-uns)* {1} See CHALDEANS. *Inhabitants of southern Babylonia.*
came he out of the land of the *C* ... Acts 7:4 *5466*

CHALDEA *(kal-de'-ah)* {7} See BABYLON, CHALDEAN. *Southern portion of Babylonia.*
And *C* shall be a spoil ... Jer 50:10 3778
to all the inhabitants of *C* all ... Jer 51:24 3778
blood upon the inhabitants of *C* ... Jer 51:35 3778
by the Spirit of God into *C* ... Eze 11:24 3778
in the land of Canaan unto *C* ... Eze 16:29 3778
manner of the Babylonians of *C* ... Eze 23:15 3778
sent messengers unto them into *C* ... Eze 23:16 3778

CHALDEAN *(kal-de'-un)* {2} See BABYLONIAN, CHALDEANS, CHALDEANS'.
the king of Babylon, the *C* ... Ezr 5:12 3777
any magician, or astrologer, or *C* ... Dan 2:10 3777

CHALDEANS *(kal-de'-uns)* {65} See BABYLONIANS, CHALDAEANS, CHALDEANS', CHALDEES. *Same as Chaldaeans.*
The *C* made out three bands, and ... Job 1:17 3778
Behold the land of the *C* ... Is 23:13 3778
down all their nobles, and the *C* ... Is 43:14 3778
is no throne, O daughter of the *C* ... Is 47:1 3778
darkness, O daughter of the *C* ... Is 47:5 3778
and his arm shall be on the *C* ... Is 48:14 3778
of Babylon, flee ye from the *C* ... Is 48:20 3778
king of Babylon, and against the *C* ... Jer 21:4 3778
falleth to the *C* that besiege you ... Jer 21:9 3778
and into the hand of the *C* ... Jer 22:25 3778
the land of the *C* for their good ... Jer 24:5 3778
iniquity, and the land of the *C* ... Jer 25:12 3778
escape out of the hand of the *C* ... Jer 32:4 3778
though ye fight with the *C* ... Jer 32:5 3778
is given into the hand of the *C* ... Jer 32:24 3778
is given into the hand of the *C* ... Jer 32:25 3778
this city into the hand of the *C* ... Jer 32:28 3778
And the *C*, that fight against this ... Jer 32:29 3778
is given into the hand of the *C* ... Jer 32:43 3778
They come to fight with the *C* ... Jer 33:5 3778
for fear of the army of the *C* ... Jer 35:11 3778
and when the *C* that besieged ... Jer 37:5 3778
the *C* shall come again, and fight ... Jer 37:8 3778
The *C* shall surely depart from us ... Jer 37:9 3778
of the *C* that fight against you ... Jer 37:10 3778
that when the army of the *C* was ... Jer 37:11 3778
Thou fallest away to the *C* ... Jer 37:13 3778
I fall not away to the *C* ... Jer 37:14 3778
goeth forth to the *C* shall live ... Jer 38:2 3778
be given into the hand of the *C* ... Jer 38:18 3778
the Jews that are fallen to the *C* ... Jer 38:19 3778
wives and thy children to the *C* ... Jer 38:23 3778
the *C* burned the king's house, and ... Jer 39:8 3778
saying, Fear not to serve the *C* ... Jer 40:9 3778
dwell at Mizpah to serve the *C* ... Jer 40:10 3778
the *C* that were found there, and ... Jer 41:3 3778
Because of the *C* ... Jer 41:18 3778
deliver us into the hand of the *C* ... Jer 43:3 3778
of the *C* by Jeremiah the prophet ... Jer 50:1 3778
go forth out of the land of the *C* ... Jer 50:8 3778
GOD of hosts in the land of the *C* ... Jer 50:25 3778
A sword is upon the *C*, saith the ... Jer 50:35 3778
against the land of the *C* ... Jer 50:45 3778
shall fall in the land of the *C* ... Jer 51:4 3778
from the land of the *C* ... Jer 51:54 3778
(now the *C* were by the city round ... Jer 52:7 3778
But the army of the *C* pursued ... Jer 52:8 3779
And all the army of the *C*, that ... Jer 52:14 3779
the *C* brake, and carried all the ... Jer 52:17 3779
in the land of the *C* by the river ... Eze 1:3 3779
to Babylon to the land of the *C* ... Eze 12:13 3779
the images of the *C* pourtrayed ... Eze 23:14 3779
The Babylonians, and all the *C* ... Eze 23:23 3779
learning and the tongue of the *C* ... Dan 1:4 3779
and the sorcerers, and the *C* ... Dan 2:2 3779
Then spake the *C* to the king in ... Dan 2:4 3779
king answered and said to the *C* ... Dan 2:5 3779
The *C* answered before the king, ... Dan 2:10 3779
at that time certain *C* came near ... Dan 3:8 3779
magicians, the astrologers, the *C* ... Dan 4:7 3779
bring in the astrologers, the *C* ... Dan 5:7 3779
of the magicians, astrologers, *C* ... Dan 5:11 3779
the king of the *C* slain ... Dan 5:30 3779
made king over the realm of the *C* ... Dan 9:1 3778
For, lo, I raise up the *C* ... Hab 1:6 3778

CHALDEANS' *(kal-de'-uns)* {1}
But the *C* army pursued after them ... Jer 39:5 3778

CHALDEES *(kal'-dees)* {13} See CHALDEES'. *Same as Chaldeans.*
of his nativity, in Ur of the *C* ... Gen 11:28 3778
forth with them from Ur of the *C* ... Gen 11:31 3778
brought thee out of Ur of the *C* ... Gen 15:7 3778
sent against him bands of the *C* ... 2Kin 24:2 3778
(now the *C* were against the city ... 2Kin 25:4 3778
the army of the *C* pursued after ... 2Kin 25:5 3778
And all the army of the *C*, that ... 2Kin 25:10 3778
did the *C* break in pieces, and ... 2Kin 25:13 3778
not to be the servants of the *C* ... 2Kin 25:24 3778
the *C* that were with him at ... 2Kin 25:25 3778
for they were afraid of the *C* ... 2Kin 25:26 3778
upon them the king of the *C* ... 2Chr 36:17 3778
him forth out of Ur of the *C* ... Neh 9:7 3778

CHALDEES' *(kal'-dees)* {1} See CHALDEANS.
the beauty of the *C* excellency ... Is 13:19 3778

CHALKSTONES {1}
as *c* that are beaten in sunder ... Is 27:9 68,1615

CHALLENGETH {1}
thing, which another *c* to be his ... Ex 22:9 559

CHAMBER {52}
and he entered into his *c*, and wept ... Gen 43:30 2315
covereth his feet in his summer *c* ... Judg 3:24 2315
will go in to my wife into the *c* ... Judg 15:1 2315
wait, abiding with her in the *c* ... Judg 16:9 2315
liers in wait abiding in the *c* ... Judg 16:12 2315
Tamar, Bring the meat into the *c* ... 2Sa 13:10 2315
into the *c* to Amnon her brother ... 2Sa 13:10 2315
and went up to the *c* over the gate ... 2Sa 18:33 5944
went in unto the king into the *c* ... 1Kin 1:15 2315
The nethermost *c* was five cubits ... 1Kin 6:6 3326
The door for the middle *c* was in ... 1Kin 6:8 6763
winding stairs into the middle *c* ... 1Kin 6:8
them back into the guard *c* ... 1Kin 14:28 8372
down out of the *c* into the house ... 1Kin 17:23 5944
into the city, into an inner *c* ... 1Kin 20:30 2315
into an inner *c* to hide thyself ... 1Kin 22:25 2315
his upper *c* that was in Samaria ... 2Kin 1:2 5944
Let us make a little *c*, I pray ... 2Kin 4:10 5944
thither, and he turned into the *c* ... 2Kin 4:11 5944
and carry him to an inner *c* ... 2Kin 9:2 2315
by the *c* of Nathan-melech the ... 2Kin 23:11 3957
on the top of the upper *c* of Ahaz ... 2Kin 23:12 5944
them again into the guard *c* ... 2Chr 12:11 8372
into an inner *c* to hide thyself ... 2Chr 18:24 2315
went into the *c* of Johanan the ... Ezr 10:6 3957
of Berechiah over against his *c* ... Neh 3:30 5393
of the *c* of the house of our God ... Neh 13:4 3957
he had prepared for him a great *c* ... Neh 13:5 3957
in preparing him a *c* in the ... Neh 13:7 5393
stuff of Tobiah out of the *c* ... Neh 13:8 3957
a bridegroom coming out of his *c* ... Ps 19:5 2646
into the *c* of her that conceived ... Song 3:4 2315
into the *c* of the sons of Hanan, ... Jer 35:4 3957
which was by the *c* of the princes ... Jer 35:4 2315
which was above the *c* of Maaseiah ... Jer 35:4 3957
in the *c* of Gemariah the son of ... Jer 36:10 3957
king's house, into the scribe's *c* ... Jer 36:12 3957
in the *c* of Elishama the scribe ... Jer 36:20 3957
it out of Elishama the scribe's *c* ... Jer 36:21 3957
every little *c* was one reed long, ... Eze 40:7 8372
little *c* to the roof of another ... Eze 40:13 8372
And he said unto me, This *c* ... Eze 40:45 3957
the *c* whose prospect is toward ... Eze 40:46 3957
and the breadth of every side *c* ... Eze 41:5 6763
c to the highest by the midst ... Eze 41:7
which was for the side *c* without ... Eze 41:9 6763
he brought me into the *c* that was ... Eze 42:1 3957
open in his *c* toward Jerusalem ... Dan 6:10 5952
the bridegroom go forth of his *c* ... Joel 2:16 2315
they laid her in an upper *c* ... Acts 9:37 *5253*
they brought him into the upper *c* ... Acts 9:39 *5253*
were many lights in the upper *c* ... Acts 20:8 *5253*

CHAMBERING {1}
rioting and drunkenness, not in *c* ... Rom 13:13 *2845*

CHAMBERLAIN {6}
chamber of Nathan-melech the *c* ... 2Kin 23:11 5631
the custody of Hege the king's *c* ... Est 2:3 5631
of Shaashgaz, the king's *c* ... Est 2:14 5631
but what Hegai the king's *c* ... Est 2:15 5631
the king's *c* their friend ... Acts 12:20 *1909,3588,2846*
Erastus the *c* of the city ... Rom 16:23 *3623*

CHAMBERLAINS {9}
the seven *c* that served in the ... Est 1:10 5631
the king's commandment by his *c* ... Est 1:12 5631
of the king Ahasuerus by the *c* ... Est 1:15 5631
king's gate, two of the king's *c* ... Est 2:21 5631
her *c* came and told it her ... Est 4:4 5631
for Hatach, one of the king's *c* ... Est 4:5 5631
and Teresh, two of the king's *c* ... Est 6:2 5631
with him, came the king's *c* ... Est 6:14 5631
And Harbonah, one of the *c* ... Est 7:9 5631

CHAMBERS {67}
the house he built *c* round about ... 1Kin 6:5 3326
and he made *c* round about ... 1Kin 6:5 6763
then he built *c* against all the ... 1Kin 6:10 3326
set office, and were over the *c* ... 1Chr 9:26 3957
who remaining in the *c* were free ... 1Chr 9:33 3957
LORD, in the courts, and in the *c* ... 1Chr 23:28 3957
and of the upper *c* thereof ... 1Chr 28:11 5944
of all the *c* round about, of the ... 1Chr 28:12 3957
he overlaid the upper *c* with gold ... 2Chr 3:9 5944
c in the house of the LORD ... 2Chr 31:11 3957
in the *c* of the house of the LORD ... Ezr 8:29 3957
to the *c* of the house of our God ... Neh 10:37 3957
the house of our God, to the *c* ... Neh 10:38 3957
new wine, and the oil, unto the *c* ... Neh 10:39 3957
over the *c* for the treasures ... Neh 12:44 5393
commanded, and they cleansed the *c* ... Neh 13:9 3957
Pleiades, and the *c* of the south ... Job 9:9 2315
the beams of his *c* in the waters ... Ps 104:3 5944
He watereth the hills from his *c* ... Ps 104:13 5944
in the *c* of their kings ... Ps 105:30 2315
going down to the *c* of death ... Prov 7:27 2315
by knowledge shall the *c* be ... Prov 24:4 2315
king hath brought me into his *c* ... Song 1:4 2315
my people, enter thou into thy *c* ... Is 26:20 2315
and his *c* by wrong ... Jer 22:13 5944
build me a wide house and large *c* ... Jer 22:14 5944
of the LORD, into one of the *c* ... Jer 35:2 3957
every man in the *c* of his imagery ... Eze 8:12 2315
which entereth into their privy *c* ... Eze 21:14 2315
the little *c* were five cubits ... Eze 40:7 8372
the little *c* of the gate eastward ... Eze 40:10 8372
c was one cubit on this side ... Eze 40:12 8372
the little *c* were six cubits on ... Eze 40:12 8372
narrow windows to the little *c* ... Eze 40:16 8372
court, and, lo, there were *c* ... Eze 40:17 3957
thirty *c* were upon the pavement ... Eze 40:17 3957
the little *c* thereof were three ... Eze 40:21 8372
And the little *c* thereof, and the ... Eze 40:29 8372
And the little *c* thereof, and the ... Eze 40:33 8372
The little *c* thereof, the posts ... Eze 40:36 8372
And the *c* and the entries thereof ... Eze 40:38 3957
the *c* of the singers in the inner ... Eze 40:44 3957
the side *c* were three, one over ... Eze 41:6 6763
house for the side *c* round about ... Eze 41:6 6763
about still upward to the side *c* ... Eze 41:7 6763
the foundations of the side *c* ... Eze 41:8 6763
of the side *c* that were within ... Eze 41:9 6763
between the *c* was the wideness of ... Eze 41:10 3957
the doors of the side *c* were ... Eze 41:11 6763
and upon the side *c* of the house ... Eze 41:26 6763
before the *c* was a walk of ten ... Eze 42:4 3957
Now the upper *c* were shorter ... Eze 42:5 3957
was without over against the *c* ... Eze 42:7 3957
court on the forepart of the *c* ... Eze 42:7 3957
For the length of the *c* that were ... Eze 42:8 3957
from under these *c* was the entry ... Eze 42:9 3957
The *c* were in the thickness of ... Eze 42:10 3957
the *c* which were toward the north ... Eze 42:11 3957
according to the doors of the *c* ... Eze 42:12 3957
Then said he unto me, The north *c* ... Eze 42:13 3957
The north *c* and the south *c* ... Eze 42:13 3957
separate place, they be holy *c* ... Eze 42:13 3957
and lay them in the holy *c* ... Eze 44:19 3957
for a possession for twenty *c* ... Eze 45:5 3957
into the holy *c* of the priests, ... Eze 46:19 3957
behold, he is in the secret *c* ... Mt 24:26 *5009*

CHAMELEON {1}
And the ferret, and the *c*, and the ... Lev 11:30 3581

CHAMOIS {1}
pygarg, and the wild ox, and the *c* ... Deut 14:5 2169

CHAMPAIGN {1}
which dwell in the *c* over against ... Deut 11:30 6160

CHAMPION {3}
there went out a *c* out of the ... 1Sa 17:4 376,1143
them, behold, there came up the *c* .. 1Sa 17:23 376,1143
Philistines saw their *c* was dead ... 1Sa 17:51 1368

CHANAAN *(ka'-na-un)* {2} See CANAAN. *Greek form of Canaan.*
over all the land of Egypt and *C* ... Acts 7:11 *5477*
seven nations in the land of *C* ... Acts 13:19 *5477*

CHANCE {6}
If a bird's nest c to be before ... Deut 22:6 7122
it was a c that happened to us ... 1Sa 6:9 4745
As I happened by c upon mount ... 2Sa 1:6 7122
time and c happeneth to them all ... Eccl 9:11 6294
by c there came down a certain ... Lk 10:31 *4795*
it may c of wheat, or of some ... 1Cor 15:37 *5177*

CHANCELLOR {3}
Rehum the c and Shimshai the ... Ezr 4:8 1169,2942
Then wrote Rehum the c, and ... Ezr 4:9 1169,2942
an answer unto Rehum the c ... Ezr 4:17 1169,2942

CHANCETH {1}
uncleanness that c him by night ... Deut 23:10 4745

CHANGE {26}
and be clean, and c your garments ... Gen 35:2 2498
He shall not alter it, nor c it ... Lev 27:10 4171
he shall at all c beast for beast ... Lev 27:10 4171
or bad, neither shall he c it ... Lev 27:33 4171
if he c it at all, then both it ... Lev 27:33 4171
the c thereof shall be holy ... Lev 27:33 8545
sheets and thirty c of garments ... Judg 14:12 2487
sheets and thirty c of garments ... Judg 14:13 2487
gave c of garments unto them ... Judg 14:19 2487
time will I wait, till my c come ... Job 14:14 2487
They c the night into day ... Job 17:12 7760
as a vesture shalt thou c them ... Ps 102:26 2498
not with them that are given to c ... Prov 24:21 8138
but we will c them into cedars ... Is 9:10 2498
thou about so much to c thy way ... Jer 2:36 8138
Can the Ethiopian c his skin ... Jer 13:23 2015
most High, and think to c times ... Dan 7:25 8133
therefore will I c their glory ... Hos 4:7 4171
Then shall his mind c, and he ... Hab 1:11 2498
clothe thee with c of raiment ... Zec 3:4 4254
For I am the LORD, I c not ... Mal 3:6 8138
shall c the customs which Moses ... Acts 6:14 *236*
for even their women did c the ... Rom 1:26 *3337*
with you now, and to c my voice ... Gal 4:20 *236*
Who shall c our vile body, that ... Phil 3:21 *3345*
of necessity a c also of the law ... Heb 7:12 *3331*

CHANGEABLE {1}
The c suits of apparel, and the ... Is 3:22 4254

CHANGED {43}
me, and c my wages ten times ... Gen 31:7 2498
thou hast c my wages ten times ... Gen 31:41 2498
c his raiment, and came in unto ... Gen 41:14 2498
be c unto white, he shall come ... Lev 13:16 2015
the plague have not c his colour ... Lev 13:55 2015
Baal-meon, (their names being c ... Num 32:38 5437
he c his behaviour before them, ... 1Sa 21:13 8138
c his apparel, and came into the ... 2Sa 12:20 2498
stead, and c his name to Zedekiah ... 2Kin 24:17 5437
And c his prison garments ... 2Kin 25:29 8132
of my disease is my garment c ... Job 30:18 2664
when he c his behaviour before ... Ps 34:*t* 8138
change them, and they shall be c ... Ps 102:26 2498
Thus they c their glory into the ... Ps 106:20 4171
boldness of his face shall be c ... Eccl 8:1 8132
c the ordinance, broken the ... Is 24:5 2498
Hath a nation c their gods ... Jer 2:11 4171
but my people have c their glory ... Jer 2:11 4171
in him, and his scent is not c ... Jer 48:11 4171
And c his prison garments ... Jer 52:33 8138
how is the most fine gold c ... Lam 4:1 8132
she hath c my judgments into ... Eze 5:6 4171
before me, till the time be c ... Dan 2:9 8133
his visage was c against Shadrach ... Dan 3:19 8133
neither were their coats c ... Dan 3:27 8133
have c the king's word, and ... Dan 3:28 8133
Let his heart be c from man's ... Dan 4:16 8133
Then the king's countenance was c ... Dan 5:6 8133
and his countenance was c in him ... Dan 5:9 8133
nor let thy countenance be c ... Dan 5:10 8133
the writing, that it be not c ... Dan 6:8 8133
the king establisheth may be c ... Dan 6:15 8133
might not be c concerning Daniel ... Dan 6:17 8133
me, and my countenance c in me ... Dan 7:28 8133
he hath c the portion of my ... Mic 2:4 4171
they c their minds, and said that ... Acts 28:6 *3328*
c the glory of the uncorruptible ... Rom 1:23 *236*
Who c the truth of God into a lie ... Rom 1:25 *3337*
all sleep, but we shall all be c ... 1Cor 15:51 *236*
incorruptible, and we shall be c ... 1Cor 15:52 *236*
are c into the same image from ... 2Cor 3:18 *3339*
fold them up, and they shall be c ... Heb 1:12 *236*
For the priesthood being c ... Heb 7:12 *3346*

CHANGERS {1}
doves, and the c of money sitting ... Jn 2:14 *2773*

CHANGERS' {1}
and poured out the c money ... Jn 2:15 *2855*

CHANGES {7}
he gave each man c of raiment ... Gen 45:22 2487
of silver, and five c of raiment ... Gen 45:22 2487
of gold, and ten c of raiment ... 2Kin 5:5 2487
of silver, and two c of garments ... 2Kin 5:22 2487
with two c of garments, and laid ... 2Kin 5:23 2487
c and war are against me ... Job 10:17 2487
Because they have no c, therefore ... Ps 55:19 2487

CHANGEST {1}
thou c his countenance, and ... Job 14:20 8138

CHANGETH {2}
to his own hurt, and c not ... Ps 15:4 4171
he c the times and the seasons ... Dan 2:21 8133

CHANGING {1}
redeeming and concerning c ... Ruth 4:7 8545

CHANNEL {1}
LORD shall beat off from the c of ... Is 27:12 7641

CHANNELS {3}
the c of the sea appeared, the ... 2Sa 22:16 650
Then the c of waters were seen, ... Ps 18:15 650
he shall come up over all his c ... Is 8:7 650

CHANT {1}
That c to the sound of the viol, ... Amos 6:5 6527

CHAPEL {1}
for it is the king's c, and it is ... Amos 7:13 4720

CHAPITER {13}
of the one c was five cubits ... 1Kin 7:16 3805
of the other c was five cubits ... 1Kin 7:16 3805
seven for the one c ... 1Kin 7:17 3805
and seven for the other c ... 1Kin 7:17 3805
and so did he for the other c ... 1Kin 7:18 3805
rows round about upon the other c ... 1Kin 7:20 3805
And the mouth of it within the c ... 1Kin 7:31 3805
and the c upon it was brass ... 2Kin 25:17 3805
the height of the c three cubits ... 2Kin 25:17 3805
upon the c round about, all of ... 2Kin 25:17 3805
the c that was on the top of each ... 2Chr 3:15 6858
And a c of brass was upon it ... Jer 52:22 3805
height of one c was five cubits ... Jer 52:22 3805

CHAPITERS {16}
and he overlaid their c and their ... Ex 36:38 7218
overlaying of their c of silver ... Ex 38:17 7218
and the overlaying of their c ... Ex 38:19 7218
the pillars, and overlaid their c ... Ex 38:28 7218
he made two c of molten brass, to ... 1Kin 7:16 3805
for the c which were upon the top ... 1Kin 7:17 3805
to cover the c that were upon the ... 1Kin 7:18 3805
the c that were upon the top of ... 1Kin 7:19 3805
the c upon the two pillars had ... 1Kin 7:20 3805
the two bowls of the c that were ... 1Kin 7:41 3805
to cover the two bowls of the c ... 1Kin 7:41 3805
the c that were upon the pillars ... 1Kin 7:42 3805
the c which were on the top of ... 2Chr 4:12 3805
c which were on the top of the ... 2Chr 4:12 3805
the c which were upon the pillars ... 2Chr 4:13 3805
upon the c round about, all of ... Jer 52:22 3805

CHAPMEN {1}
that which c and merchants ... 2Chr 9:14 582,8846

CHAPT {1}
Because the ground is c, for ... Jer 14:4 2865

CHARASHIM *(car'-a-shim)* {1} *Place founded by Joab.*
the father of the valley of C ... 1Chr 4:14 2798

CHARCHEMISH *(car'-ke-mish)* {1} See CARCHEMISH. *Same as Carchemish.*
to fight against C by Euphrates ... 2Chr 35:20 3751

CHARGE {102}
obeyed my voice, and kept my c ... Gen 26:5 4931
as he blessed him he gave him a c ... Gen 28:6 6680
gave them a c unto the children ... Ex 6:13 6680
c the people, lest they break ... Ex 19:21 5749
keep the c of the LORD, that ye ... Lev 8:35 4931
the Levites shall keep the c of ... Num 1:53 4931
And they shall keep his c, and the ... Num 3:7 4931
the c of the whole congregation ... Num 3:7 4931
the c of the children of Israel, ... Num 3:8 4931
the c of the sons of Gershon in ... Num 3:25 4931
keeping the c of the sanctuary ... Num 3:28 4931
their c shall be the ark, and the ... Num 3:31 4931
that keep the c of the sanctuary ... Num 3:32 4931
c of the sons of Merari shall be ... Num 3:36 4931
keeping the c of the sanctuary ... Num 3:38 4931
the c of the children of Israel ... Num 3:38 4931
unto them in c all their burdens ... Num 4:27 4931
their c shall be under the hand ... Num 4:28 4931
this is the c of their burden, ... Num 4:31 4931
of the c of their burden ... Num 4:32 4931
the priest shall c her by an oath ... Num 5:19 7650
Then the priest shall c the woman ... Num 5:21 7650
the congregation, to keep the c ... Num 8:26 4931
unto the Levites touching their c ... Num 8:26 4931
of Israel kept the c of the LORD ... Num 9:19 4931
they kept the c of the LORD ... Num 9:23 4931
And they shall keep thy c, and the ... Num 18:3 4931
the c of all the tabernacle ... Num 18:3 4931
keep the c of the tabernacle of ... Num 18:4 4931
shall keep the c of the sanctuary ... Num 18:5 4931
sanctuary, and the c of the altar ... Num 18:5 4931
I also have given thee the c of ... Num 18:8 4931
give him a c in their sight ... Num 27:19 6680
hands upon him, and gave him a c ... Num 27:23 6680
Levites, which keep the c of the ... Num 31:30 4931
Levites, which kept the c of the ... Num 31:47 4931
men of war which are under our c ... Num 31:49 3027
But c Joshua, and encourage him, ... Deut 3:28 6680
the LORD thy God, and keep his c ... Deut 11:1 4931
unto thy people of Israel's c ... Deut 21:8 7130
that I may give him a c ... Deut 31:14 6680
he gave Joshua the son of Nun a c ... Deut 31:23 6680
but have kept the c of the ... Josh 22:3 4931
I will give c concerning thee ... 2Sa 14:8 6680
the captains c concerning Absalom ... 2Sa 18:5 6680
keep the c of the LORD thy God, ... 1Kin 2:3 4931
every man according to his c ... 1Kin 4:28 4941
all the c of the house of Joseph ... 1Kin 11:28 5447
leaned to have the c of the gate ... 2Kin 7:17 5921
because the c was upon them, and ... 1Chr 9:27 4931
certain of them had the c of the ... 1Chr 9:28 5921
give thee c concerning Israel, ... 1Chr 22:12 6680
the c of the tabernacle of the ... 1Chr 23:32 4931
the c of the holy place, and the ... 1Chr 23:32 4931
the c of the sons of Aaron their ... 1Chr 23:32 4931
for we keep the c of the LORD our ... 2Chr 13:11 4931
therefore the Levites had the c ... 2Chr 30:17 5921
of the palace, c over Jerusalem ... Neh 7:2 6680
to c ourselves yearly with the ... Neh 10:32 5414
that have the c of the business ... Est 3:9 6213
to c her that she should go in ... Est 4:8 6680
hath given him a c over the earth ... Job 34:13 6485
they laid to my c things that I ... Ps 35:11 7592
shall give his angels c over thee ... Ps 91:11 6680
I c you, O ye daughters of ... Song 2:7 7650
I c you, O ye daughters of ... Song 3:5 7650
I c you, O daughters of Jerusalem ... Song 5:8 7650
beloved, that thou dost so c us ... Song 5:9 7650
I c you, O daughters of Jerusalem ... Song 8:4 7650
of my wrath will I give him a c ... Is 10:6 6680
king of Babylon gave c concerning ... Jer 39:11 6680
given it a c against Ashkelon ... Jer 47:7 6680
which had the c of the men of war ... Jer 52:25 6496
Cause them that have c over the ... Eze 9:1 6486
the keepers of the c of the house ... Eze 40:45 4931
the keepers of the c of the altar ... Eze 40:46 4931
kept the c of mine holy things ... Eze 44:8 4931
but ye have set keepers of my c ... Eze 44:8 4931
having c at the gates of the ... Eze 44:11 6486
keepers of the c of the house ... Eze 44:14 4931
that kept the c of my sanctuary ... Eze 44:15 4931
unto me, and they shall keep my c ... Eze 44:16 4931
which have kept my c, which went ... Eze 48:11 4931
ways, and if thou wilt keep my c ... Zec 3:7 4931
give his angels c concerning thee ... Mt 4:6 *1781*
I c thee, come out of him, and ... Mk 9:25 *2004*
shall give his angels c over thee ... Lk 4:10 *1781*
Lord, lay not this sin to their c ... Acts 7:60 *2476*
who had the c of all her treasure ... Acts 8:27 *1909*
Who, having received such a c ... Acts 16:24 *3852*
his c worthy of death or of bonds ... Acts 23:29 *1462*
any thing to the c of God's elect ... Rom 8:33 *1458,2596*
the gospel of Christ without c ... 1Cor 9:18 *77*
I c you by the Lord that this ... 1Th 5:27 *3726*
that thou mightest c some that ... 1Ti 1:3 *3853*
This c I commit unto thee, son ... 1Ti 1:18 *3852*
And these things give in c ... 1Ti 5:7 *3853*
I c thee before God, and the Lord ... 1Ti 5:21 *1263*
I give thee c in the sight of God ... 1Ti 6:13 *3853*
C them that are rich in this ... 1Ti 6:17 *3853*
I c thee therefore before God, and ... 2Ti 4:1 *1263*
it may not be laid to their c ... 2Ti 4:16 *3049*

CHARGEABLE {5}
now go, lest we be c unto thee ... 2Sa 13:25 3513
before me were c unto the people ... Neh 5:15 3513
you, and wanted, I was c to no man ... 2Cor 11:9 *2655*
we would not be c unto any of you ... 1Th 2:9 *1912*
we might not be c to any of you ... 2Th 3:8 *1912*

CHARGED {51}
Abimelech c all his people, ... Gen 26:11 6680
c him, and said unto him, Thou ... Gen 28:1 6680
of the guard c Joseph with them ... Gen 40:4 6485
he c them, and said unto them, I ... Gen 49:29 6680
Pharaoh c all his people, saying, ... Ex 1:22 6680
I c your judges at that time, ... Deut 1:16 6680
shall he be c with any business ... Deut 24:5 5674,5921
Moses c the people the same day, ... Deut 27:11 6680
Joshua c them that went to ... Josh 18:8 6680
the servant of the LORD c you ... Josh 22:5 6680
have I not c the young men that ... Ruth 2:9 6680
father c the people with the oath ... 1Sa 14:27 7650
Thy father straitly c the people ... 1Sa 14:28 7650
c the messenger, saying, When ... 2Sa 11:19 6680
in our hearing the king c thee ... 2Sa 18:12 6680
he c Solomon his son, saying, ... 1Kin 2:1 6680
that I have c thee with ... 1Kin 2:43 6680
For so was it c me by the word of ... 1Kin 13:9 6680
whom the LORD had c them, that ... 2Kin 17:15 6680
c them, saying, Ye shall not fear ... 2Kin 17:35 6680
c him to build an house for the ... 1Chr 22:6 6680
judgments which the LORD c Moses ... 1Chr 22:13 6680
he c them, saying, Thus shall ye ... 2Chr 19:9 6680
he hath c me to build him an ... 2Chr 36:23 6485
he hath c me to build him an ... Ezr 1:2 6485
c that they should not be opened ... Neh 13:19 559
for Mordecai had c her that she ... Est 2:10 6680
as Mordecai had c her ... Est 2:20 6680
sinned not, nor c God foolishly ... Job 1:22 5414
and his angels he c with folly ... Job 4:18 7760
I c Baruch before them, saying, ... Jer 32:13 6680
father in all that he hath c us ... Jer 35:8 6680
and Jesus straitly c them, saying, ... Mt 9:30 *1690*
c them that they should not make ... Mt 12:16 *2008*
Then c he his disciples that they ... Mt 16:20 *1291*
from the mountain, Jesus c them ... Mt 17:9 *1781*
And he straitly c him, and ... Mk 1:43 *1690*
he straitly c them that they ... Mk 3:12 *2008*
he c them straitly that no man ... Mk 5:43 *1291*
he c them that they should tell ... Mk 7:36 *1291*
but the more he c them, so much ... Mk 7:36 *1291*
he c them, saying, Take heed, ... Mk 8:15 *1291*
he c them that they should tell ... Mk 8:30 *2008*
he c them that they should tell ... Mk 9:9 *1291*
many c him that he should hold ... Mk 10:48 *2008*
And he c him to tell no man ... Lk 5:14 *3853*

but he c them that they should ... Lk 8:56 *3853*
And he straitly c them, and ... Lk 9:21 *2008*
c him, See thou tell no man that ... Acts 23:22 *3853*
c every one of you, as a father ... 1Th 2:11 *3146*
them, and let not the church be c ... 1Ti 5:16 *916*

CHARGEDST {1}
for thou c us, saying, Set bounds ... Ex 19:23 5749

CHARGER {17}
And his offering was one silver c ... Num 7:13 7086
for his offering one silver c ... Num 7:19 7086
His offering was one silver c ... Num 7:25 7086
c of the weight of an hundred ... Num 7:31 7086
His offering was one silver c ... Num 7:37 7086
c of the weight of an hundred ... Num 7:43 7086
His offering was one silver c ... Num 7:49 7086
c of the weight of an hundred ... Num 7:55 7086
His offering was one silver c ... Num 7:61 7086
His offering was one silver c ... Num 7:67 7086
His offering was one silver c ... Num 7:73 7086
His offering was one silver c ... Num 7:79 7086
Each c of silver weighing an ... Num 7:85 7086
here John Baptist's head in a c ... Mt 14:8 *4094*
And his head was brought in a c ... Mt 14:11 *4094*
by in a c the head of John the ... Mk 6:25 *4094*
And brought his head in a c ... Mk 6:28 *4094*

CHARGERS {3}
twelve c of silver, twelve silver ... Num 7:84 7086
thirty c of gold, a thousand ... Ezr 1:9 105
of gold, a thousand c of silver ... Ezr 1:9 105

CHARGES {6}
and the Levites to their c ... 2Chr 8:14 4931
c according to their courses ... 2Chr 31:16 4931
in their c by their courses ... 2Chr 31:17 4931
And he set the priests in their c ... 2Chr 35:2 4931
be at c with them, that they may ... Acts 21:24 *1159*
a warfare any time at his own c ... 1Cor 9:7 *3800*

CHARGEST {1}
that thou c me to day with a ... 2Sa 3:8 6485

CHARGING {2}
c the jailer to keep them safely ... Acts 16:23 *3853*
c them before the Lord that they ... 2Ti 2:14 *1263*

CHARIOT {66}
ride in the second c which he had ... Gen 41:43 4818
And Joseph made ready his c ... Gen 46:29 4818
And he made ready his c, and took ... Ex 14:6 7393
And took off their c wheels ... Ex 14:25 4818
Sisera lighted down off his c ... Judg 4:15 4818
Why is his c so long in coming ... Judg 5:28 7393
and David houghed all the c horses ... 2Sa 8:4 7393
was like the work of a c wheel ... 1Kin 7:33 4818
a c came up and went out of Egypt ... 1Kin 10:29 4818
made speed to get him up to his c ... 1Kin 12:18 4818
up, say unto Ahab, Prepare thy c ... 1Kin 18:44
horse for horse, and c for c ... 1Kin 20:25 7393
horse for horse, and c for c ... 1Kin 20:25 7393
caused him to come up into the c ... 1Kin 20:33 4818
he said unto the driver of his c ... 1Kin 22:34 7395
up in his c against the Syrians ... 1Kin 22:35 4818
the wound into the midst of the c ... 1Kin 22:35 7393
one washed the c in the pool of ... 1Kin 22:38 7393
there appeared a c of fire ... 2Kin 2:11 7393
the c of Israel, and the horsemen ... 2Kin 2:12 7393
with his horses and with his c ... 2Kin 5:9 7393
down from the c to meet him ... 2Kin 5:21 4818
again from his c to meet thee ... 2Kin 5:26 4818
They took therefore two c horses ... 2Kin 7:14 7393
So Jehu rode in a c, and went to ... 2Kin 9:16
And his c was made ready ... 2Kin 9:21 7393
of Judah went out, each in his c ... 2Kin 9:21 7393
heart, and he sunk down in his c ... 2Kin 9:24 7393
and said, Smite him also in the c ... 2Kin 9:27 4818
carried him in a c to Jerusalem ... 2Kin 9:28
he took him up to him into the c ... 2Kin 10:15 4818
So they made him ride in his c ... 2Kin 10:16 7393
the c of Israel, and the horsemen ... 2Kin 13:14 7393
him in a c dead from Megiddo ... 2Kin 23:30
also houghed all the c horses ... 1Chr 18:4 7393
pattern of the c of the cherubims ... 1Chr 28:18 4818
which he placed in the c cities ... 2Chr 1:14 7393
a c for six hundred shekels of ... 2Chr 1:17 4818
Solomon had, and all the c cities ... 2Chr 8:6 7393
whom he bestowed in the c cities ... 2Chr 9:25 7393
made speed to get him up to his c ... 2Chr 10:18 4818
therefore he said to his c man ... 2Chr 18:33 7395
c against the Syrians until the ... 2Chr 18:34 4818
therefore took him out of that c ... 2Chr 35:24 4818
him in the second c that he had ... 2Chr 35:24 7393
he burneth the c in the fire ... Ps 46:9 5699
O God of Jacob, both the c ... Ps 76:6 7393
who maketh the clouds his c ... Ps 104:3 7398
a c of the wood of Lebanon ... Song 3:9 668
he saw a c with a couple of ... Is 21:7 7393
a c of asses, and a c of ... Is 21:7 7393
behold, here cometh a c of men ... Is 21:9 7393
Which bringeth forth the c ... Is 43:17 7393
thee will I break in pieces the c ... Jer 51:21 7393
bind the c to the swift beast ... Mic 1:13 4818
In the first c were red horses ... Zec 6:2 4818
and in the second c black horses ... Zec 6:2 4818
And in the third c white horses ... Zec 6:3 4818
and in the fourth c grisled ... Zec 6:3 4818
I will cut off the c from Ephraim ... Zec 9:10 7393
sitting in his c read Esaias the ... Acts 8:28 *716*
near, and join thyself to this c ... Acts 8:29 *716*
he commanded the c to stand still ... Acts 8:38 *716*

CHARIOTS {113}
And there went up with him both c ... Gen 50:9 7393
And he took six hundred chosen c ... Ex 14:7 7393
all the c of Egypt, and captains ... Ex 14:7 7393
c of Pharaoh, and his horsemen, and ... Ex 14:9 7393
and upon all his host, upon his c ... Ex 14:17 7393
honour upon Pharaoh, upon his c ... Ex 14:18 7393
even all Pharaoh's horses, his c ... Ex 14:23 7393
upon the Egyptians, upon their c ... Ex 14:26 7393
waters returned, and covered the c ... Ex 14:28 7393
Pharaoh's c and his host hath he ... Ex 15:4 4818
of Pharaoh went in with his c ... Ex 15:19 7393
unto their horses, and to their c ... Deut 11:4 7393
enemies, and seest horses, and c ... Deut 20:1 7393
with horses and c very many ... Josh 11:4 7393
horses, and burn their c with fire ... Josh 11:6 4818
and burnt their c with fire ... Josh 11:9 4818
land of the valley have c of iron ... Josh 17:16 7393
though they have iron c, and ... Josh 17:18 7393
pursued after your fathers with c ... Josh 24:6 7393
because they had c of iron ... Judg 1:19 7393
for he had nine hundred c of iron ... Judg 4:3 7393
of Jabin's army, with his c ... Judg 4:7 7393
gathered together all his c ... Judg 4:13 7393
even nine hundred c of iron ... Judg 4:13 7393
discomfited Sisera, and all his c ... Judg 4:15 7393
But Barak pursued after the c ... Judg 4:16 7393
Why tarry the wheels of his c ... Judg 5:28 4818
them for himself, for his c ... 1Sa 8:11 4818
and some shall run before his c ... 1Sa 8:11 4818
of war, and instruments of his c ... 1Sa 8:12 7393
with Israel, thirty thousand c ... 1Sa 13:5 7393
and, lo, the c and horsemen ... 2Sa 1:6 7393
David took from him a thousand c ... 2Sa 8:4
reserved of them for an hundred c ... 2Sa 8:4 7393
of seven hundred c of the Syrians ... 2Sa 10:18 7393
this, that Absalom prepared him c ... 2Sa 15:1 4818
and he prepared him c and horsemen, ... 1Kin 1:5 7393
stalls of horses for his c ... 1Kin 4:26 4817
Solomon had, and cities for his c ... 1Kin 9:19 7393
his captains, and rulers of his c ... 1Kin 9:22 7393
And Solomon gathered together c ... 1Kin 10:26 7393
had a thousand and four hundred c ... 1Kin 10:26 7393
he bestowed in the cities for c ... 1Kin 10:26 7393
Zimri, captain of half his c ... 1Kin 16:9 7393
kings with him, and horses, and c ... 1Kin 20:1 7393
out, and smote the horses and c ... 1Kin 20:21 7393
captains that had rule over his c ... 1Kin 22:31 7393
captains of the c saw Jehoshaphat ... 1Kin 22:32 7393
when the captains of the c ... 1Kin 22:33 7393
sent he thither horses, and c ... 2Kin 6:14 7393
the city both with horses and c ... 2Kin 6:15 7393
c of fire round about Elisha ... 2Kin 6:17 7393
the Syrians to hear a noise of c ... 2Kin 7:6 7393
to Zair, and all the c with him ... 2Kin 8:21 7393
about, and the captains of the c ... 2Kin 8:21 7393
with you, and there are with you c ... 2Kin 10:2 7393
but fifty horsemen, and ten c ... 2Kin 13:7 7393
and put thy trust on Egypt for c ... 2Kin 18:24 7393
With the multitude of my c I am ... 2Kin 19:23 7393
burned the c of the sun with fire ... 2Kin 23:11 4818
David took from him a thousand c ... 1Chr 18:4 7393
but reserved of them an hundred c ... 1Chr 18:4 7393
talents of silver to hire them c ... 1Chr 19:6 7393
hired thirty and two thousand c ... 1Chr 19:7 7393
thousand men which fought in c ... 1Chr 19:18 7393
Solomon gathered c and horsemen ... 2Chr 1:14 7393
had a thousand and four hundred c ... 2Chr 1:14 7393
captains, and captains of his c ... 2Chr 8:9 7393
thousand stalls for horses and c ... 2Chr 9:25 4818
With twelve hundred c, and ... 2Chr 12:3 7393
thousand, and three hundred c ... 2Chr 14:9 4818
a huge host, with very many c ... 2Chr 16:8 7393
of the c that were with him ... 2Chr 18:30 7393
captains of the c saw Jehoshaphat ... 2Chr 18:31 7393
when the captains of the c ... 2Chr 18:32 7393
princes, and all his c with him ... 2Chr 21:9 7393
him in, and the captains of the c ... 2Chr 21:9 7393
Some trust in c, and some in ... Ps 20:7 7393
The c of God are twenty thousand, ... Ps 68:17 7393
company of horses in Pharaoh's c ... Song 1:9 7393
made me like the c of Ammi-nadib ... Song 6:12 4818
is there any end of their c ... Is 2:7 4818
bare the quiver with c of men ... Is 22:6 7393
valleys shall be full of c ... Is 22:7 7393
there the c of thy glory shall be ... Is 22:18 4818
and stay on horses, and trust in c ... Is 31:1 7393
and put thy trust on Egypt for c ... Is 36:9 7393
By the multitude of my c am I ... Is 37:24 7393
with his c like a whirlwind, to ... Is 66:15 4818
all nations upon horses, and in c ... Is 66:20 7393
his c shall be as a whirlwind ... Jer 4:13 4818
the throne of David, riding in c ... Jer 17:25 7393
the throne of David, riding in c ... Jer 22:4 7393
and rage, ye c ... Jer 46:9 7393
horses, at the rushing of his c ... Jer 47:3 7393
their horses, and upon their c ... Jer 50:37 7393
shall come against thee with c ... Eze 23:24 2021
the north, with horses, and with c ... Eze 26:7 7393
and of the wheels, and of the c ... Eze 26:10 7393
in precious clothes for c ... Eze 27:20 7396
at my table with horses and c ... Eze 39:20 7393
him like a whirlwind, with c ... Dan 11:40 7393
Like the noise of c on the tops ... Joel 2:5 4818
of thee, and I will destroy thy c ... Mic 5:10 4818
the c shall be with flaming ... Nah 2:3 7393
The c shall rage in the streets, ... Nah 2:4 7393
and I will burn her c in the smoke ... Nah 2:13 7393
horses, and of the jumping c ... Nah 3:2 4818
horses and thy c of salvation ... Hab 3:8 4818
and I will overthrow the c ... Hag 2:22 4818
there came four c out from ... Zec 6:1 4818
of c of many horses running to ... Rev 9:9 *716*
beasts, and sheep, and horses, and c ... Rev 18:13 *4480*

CHARITABLY {1}
thy meat, now walkest thou not c ... Rom 14:15 *2596,26*

CHARITY {28}
puffeth up, but c edifieth ... 1Cor 8:1 *26*
men and of angels, and have not c ... 1Cor 13:1 *26*
remove mountains, and have not c ... 1Cor 13:2 *26*
body to be burned, and have not c ... 1Cor 13:3 *26*
C suffereth long, and is kind ... 1Cor 13:4 *26*
c envieth not ... 1Cor 13:4 *26*
c vaunteth not itself, is not ... 1Cor 13:4 *26*
C never faileth ... 1Cor 13:8 *26*
And now abideth faith, hope, c ... 1Cor 13:13 *26*
but the greatest of these is c ... 1Cor 13:13 *26*
Follow after c, and desire ... 1Cor 14:1 *26*
all your things be done with c ... 1Cor 16:14 *26*
above all these things put on c ... Col 3:14 *26*
good tidings of your faith and c ... 1Th 3:6 *26*
the c of every one of you all ... 2Th 1:3 *26*
is c out of a pure heart, and of a ... 1Ti 1:5 *26*
if they continue in faith and c ... 1Ti 2:15 *26*
in word, in conversation, in c ... 1Ti 4:12 *26*
follow righteousness, faith, c ... 2Ti 2:22 *26*
purpose, faith, longsuffering, c ... 2Ti 3:10 *26*
temperate, sound in faith, in c ... Titus 2:2 *26*
have fervent c among yourselves ... 1Pet 4:8 *26*
for c shall cover the multitude ... 1Pet 4:8 *26*
ye one another with a kiss of c ... 1Pet 5:14 *26*
and to brotherly kindness c ... 2Pet 1:7 *26*
of thy c before the church ... 3Jn 6 *26*
are spots in your feasts of c ... Jude 12 *26*
I know thy works, and c, and ... Rev 2:19 *26*

CHARMED {1}
among you, which will not be c ... Jer 8:17 3908

CHARMER {1}
Or a c, or a consulter with ... Deut 18:11 2266,2267

CHARMERS {2}
not hearken to the voice of c ... Ps 58:5 3907
seek to the idols, and to the c ... Is 19:3 328

CHARMING {1}
of charmers, c never so wisely ... Ps 58:5 2266,2267

CHARRAN *(car'-ran)* {2} See HARAN. *Greek form of Haran.*
Mesopotamia, before he dwelt in C ... Acts 7:2 *5488*
of the Chaldaeans, and dwelt in C ... Acts 7:4 *5488*

CHASE {6}
ye shall c your enemies, and they ... Lev 26:7 7291
And five of you shall c an hundred ... Lev 26:8 7291
of a shaken leaf shall c them ... Lev 26:36 7291
How should one c a thousand ... Deut 32:30 7291
One man of you shall c a thousand ... Josh 23:10 7291
let the angel of the LORD c them ... Ps 35:5 1760

CHASED {13}
c you, as bees do, and destroyed ... Deut 1:44 7291
for they c them from before the ... Josh 7:5 7291
wilderness wherein they c them ... Josh 8:24 7291
c them along the way that goeth ... Josh 10:10 7291
c them unto great Zidon, and unto ... Josh 11:8 7291
And Abimelech c him, and he fled ... Judg 9:40 7291
c them, and trode them down with ... Judg 20:43 7291
therefore I c him from me ... Neh 13:28 1272
darkness, and c out of the world ... Job 18:18 5074
he shall be c away as a vision of ... Job 20:8 5074
And it shall be as the c roe ... Is 13:14 5080
shall be c as the chaff of the ... Is 17:13 7291
Mine enemies c me sore, like a ... Lam 3:52 6679

CHASETH {1}
c away his mother, is a son that ... Prov 19:26 1272

CHASING {1}
from c after the Philistines ... 1Sa 17:53 1814

CHASTE {3}
you as a c virgin to Christ ... 2Cor 11:2 *53*
To be discreet, c, keepers at ... Titus 2:5 *53*
While they behold your c ... 1Pet 3:2 *53*

CHASTEN {6}
I will c him with the rod of men, ... 2Sa 7:14 3198
anger, neither c me in thy hot ... Ps 6:1 3256
neither c me in thy hot ... Ps 38:1 3256
C thy son while there is hope, and ... Prov 19:18 3256
to c thyself before thy God, thy ... Dan 10:12 6031
As many as I love, I rebuke and c ... Rev 3:19 *3811*

CHASTENED {8}
and that, when they have c him ... Deut 21:18 3256
He is c also with pain upon his ... Job 33:19 3198
c my soul with fasting, that was ... Ps 69:10
been plagued, and c every morning ... Ps 73:14 8433
The LORD hath c me sore ... Ps 118:18 3256
we are c of the Lord, that we ... 1Cor 11:32 *3811*
as c, and not killed ... 2Cor 6:9 *3811*
c us after their own pleasure ... Heb 12:10 *3811*

CHASTENEST {1}
Blessed is the man whom thou c ... Ps 94:12 3256

CHASTENETH {5}
heart, that, as a man c his son ... Deut 8:5 3256
son, so the LORD thy God c thee ... Deut 8:5 3256

he that loveth him c him betimes ... Prov 13:24 4148
For whom the Lord loveth he c ... Heb 12:6 *3811*
son is he whom the father c not ... Heb 12:7 *3811*

CHASTENING {6}
not thou the c of the Almighty ... Job 5:17 4148
despise not the c of the LORD ... Prov 3:11 4148
a prayer when thy c was upon them ... Is 26:16 4148
not thou the c of the Lord ... Heb 12:5 *3809*
If ye endure c, God dealeth with ... Heb 12:7 *3809*
Now no c for the present seemeth ... Heb 12:11 *3809*

CHASTISE {10}
will c you seven times for your ... Lev 26:28 3256
city shall take that man and c him ... Deut 22:18 3256
but I will c you with scorpions ... 1Kin 12:11 3256
but I will c you with scorpions ... 1Kin 12:14 3256
but I will c you with scorpions ... 2Chr 10:11
but I will c you with scorpions ... 2Chr 10:14
I will c them, as their ... Hos 7:12 3256
in my desire that I should c them ... Hos 10:10 3256
I will therefore c him, and ... Lk 23:16 *3811*
I will therefore c him, and let ... Lk 23:22 *3811*

CHASTISED {6}
my father hath c you with whips ... 1Kin 12:11 3256
my father also c you with whips ... 1Kin 12:14 3256
my father c you with whips, but I ... 2Chr 10:11 3256
my father c you with whips, but I ... 2Chr 10:14 3256
hast c me, and I was c ... Jer 31:18 3256

CHASTISEMENT {5}
seen the c of the LORD your God ... Deut 11:2 4148
be said unto God, I have borne c ... Job 34:31
the c of our peace was upon him ... Is 53:5 4148
with the c of a cruel one, for ... Jer 30:14 4148
But if ye be without c, whereof ... Heb 12:8 *3809*

CHASTISETH {1}
He that c the heathen, shall not ... Ps 94:10 3256

CHATTER {1}
a crane or a swallow, so did I c ... Is 38:14 6850

CHEBAR *(ke'-bar)* {8} *A river in Mesopotamia.*
the captives by the river of C ... Eze 1:1 3529
of the Chaldeans by the river C ... Eze 1:3 3529
that dwelt by the river of C ... Eze 3:15 3529
which I saw by the river of C ... Eze 3:23 3529
that I saw by the river of C ... Eze 10:15 3529
God of Israel by the river of C ... Eze 10:20 3529
which I saw by the river of C ... Eze 10:22 3529
vision that I saw by the river C ... Eze 43:3 3529

CHECK {1}
I have heard the c of my reproach ... Job 20:3 4148

CHECKER {1}
And nets of c work, and wreaths of ... 1Kin 7:17 7639

CHEDORLAOMER *(ke'-dor-la'-o-mer)* {5} *An Elamite king.*
C king of Elam, and Tidal king of ... Gen 14:1 3540
Twelve years they served C ... Gen 14:4 3540
And in the fourteenth year came C ... Gen 14:5 3540
With C the king of Elam, and with ... Gen 14:9 3540
return from the slaughter of C ... Gen 14:17 3540

CHEEK {9}
near, and smote Micaiah on the c ... 1Kin 22:24 3895
near, and smote Micaiah upon the c ... 2Chr 18:23 3895
me upon the c reproachfully ... Job 16:10 3895
all mine enemies upon the c bone ... Ps 3:7 3895
He giveth his c to him that ... Lam 3:30 3895
he hath the c teeth of a great ... Joel 1:6 4973
of Israel with a rod upon the c ... Mic 5:1 3895
shall smite thee on thy right c ... Mt 5:39 *4600*
on the one c offer also the other ... Lk 6:29 *4600*

CHEEKS {5}
priest the shoulder, and the two c ... Deut 18:3 3895
Thy c are comely with rows of ... Song 1:10 3895
His c are as a bed of spices, as ... Song 5:13 3895
my c to them that plucked off the ... Is 50:6 3895
night, and her tears are on her c ... Lam 1:2 3895

CHEER {10}
shall c up his wife which he hath ... Deut 24:5 8055
let thy heart c thee in the days ... Eccl 11:9 3190
Son, be of good c ... Mt 9:2 *2293*
unto them, saying, Be of good c ... Mt 14:27 *2293*
and saith unto them, Be of good c ... Mk 6:50 *2293*
but be of good c ... Jn 16:33 *2293*
by him, and said, Be of good c ... Acts 23:11 *2293*
now I exhort you to be of good c ... Acts 27:22 *2114*
Wherefore, sirs, be of good c ... Acts 27:25 *2114*
Then were they all of good c ... Acts 27:36 *2114*

CHEERETH {1}
I leave my wine, which c God ... Judg 9:13 8055

CHEERFUL {4}
heart maketh a c countenance ... Prov 15:13 3190
joy and gladness, and c feasts ... Zec 8:19 2896
corn shall make the young men c ... Zec 9:17 5107
for God loveth a c giver ... 2Cor 9:7 *2431*

CHEERFULLY {1}
I do the more c answer for myself ... Acts 24:10 *2115*

CHEERFULNESS {1}
he that sheweth mercy, with c ... Rom 12:8 *2432*

CHEESE {2}
c of kine, for David, and for the ... 2Sa 17:29 8194
out as milk, and curdled me like c ... Job 10:10 1385

CHEESES {1}
carry these ten c unto the ... 1Sa 17:18 2757,2461

CHELAL *(ke'-lal)* {1} *Married a foreign wife in exile.*
Adna, and C, Benaiah, Maaseiah, ... Ezr 10:30 3636

CHELLUH *(kel'-loo)* {1} *Married a foreign wife in exile.*
Benaiah, Bedeiah, C, ... Ezr 10:35 3622

CHELUB *(ke'-lub)* {2}
1. A descendant of Caleb.
C the brother of Shuah begat ... 1Chr 4:11 3620
2. Father of Ezri.
the ground was Ezri the son of C ... 1Chr 27:26 3620

CHELUBAI *(ke-loo'-bahee)* {1} *Son of Hezron.*
Jerahmeel, and Ram, and C ... 1Chr 2:9 3621

CHELUH See CHELLUH.

CHELUHI See CHELLUH.

CHEMARIMS *(kem'-a-rims)* {1} *Idolatrous priests of Judah.*
the name of the C with the ... Zeph 1:4 3649

CHEMOSH *(ke'-mosh)* {8} *A Moabite god.*
thou art undone, O people of C ... Num 21:29 3645
not thou possess that which C thy ... Judg 11:24 3645
Solomon build an high place for C ... 1Kin 11:7 3645
C the god of the Moabites, and ... 1Kin 11:33 3645
for C the abomination of the ... 2Kin 23:13 3645
C shall go forth into captivity ... Jer 48:7 3645
And Moab shall be ashamed of C ... Jer 48:13 3645
the people of C perisheth ... Jer 48:46 3645

CHENAANAH *(ke-na'-a-nah)* {5}
1. Father of Zedekiah.
Zedekiah the son of C made him ... 1Kin 22:11 3668
Zedekiah the son of C went near ... 1Kin 22:24 3668
Zedekiah the son of C had made ... 2Chr 18:10 3668
Zedekiah the son of C came near ... 2Chr 18:23 3668
2. Brother of Ehud.
Jeush, and Benjamin, and Ehud, and C .. 1Chr 7:10 3668

CHENANI *(ken'-a-ni)* {1} *A Levite helper of Ezra.*
Bunni, Sherebiah, Bani, and C ... Neh 9:4 3662

CHENANIAH *(ken-a-ni'-ah)* {3} See CONONIAH.
1. A chief Levite during David's reign.
And C, chief of the Levites, was ... 1Chr 15:22 3663
C the master of the song with the ... 1Chr 15:27 3663
2. An officer in David's army.
Of the Izharites, C and his sons ... 1Chr 26:29 3663

CHEPHAR-AMMONI See CHEPHAR-HAAMMONAI.

CHEPHAR-HAAMMONAI *(ke'-far-ha-am'-mo-nahee)* {1} *A town in Benjamin.*
And C, and Ophni, and Gaba ... Josh 18:24 3726

CHEPHIRAH *(ke-fi'-rah)* {4} *A Hittite village in Benjamin.*
their cities were Gibeon, and C ... Josh 9:17 3716
And Mizpeh, and C, and Mozah, ... Josh 18:26 3716
The children of Kirjath-arim, C ... Ezr 2:25 3716
The men of Kirjath-jearim, C ... Neh 7:29 3716

CHERAN *(ke'-ran)* {2} *Son of Dishon.*
and Eshban, and Ithran, and C ... Gen 36:26 3763
and Eshban, and Ithran, and C ... 1Chr 1:41 3763

CHERETHIMS *(ker'-e-thims)* {1} See CHERETHITES. *A Philistine tribe.*
and I will cut off the C, and ... Eze 25:16 3774

CHERETHITES *(ker'-e-thites)* {9} See CHERETHIMS.
1. Same as Cherethims.
invasion upon the south of the C ... 1Sa 30:14 3774
sea coast, the nation of the C ... Zeph 2:5 3774
2. Executioners and runners in David's army.
of Jehoiada was over both the C ... 2Sa 8:18 3774
and all the C, and all the ... 2Sa 15:18 3774
after him Joab's men, and the C ... 2Sa 20:7 3774
son of Jehoiada was over the C ... 2Sa 20:23 3774
the son of Jehoiada, and the C ... 1Kin 1:38 3746
the son of Jehoiada, and the C ... 1Kin 1:44 3774
son of Jehoiada was over the C ... 1Chr 18:17 3774

CHERISH {1}
before the king, and let her c him ... 1Kin 1:2 5532

CHERISHED {1}
c the king, and ministered to him ... 1Kin 1:4 5532

CHERISHETH {2}
c it, even as the Lord the church ... Eph 5:29 *2282*
even as a nurse c her children ... 1Th 2:7 *2282*

CHERITH *(ke'-rith)* {2} *A brook in Gilead.*
and hide thyself by the brook C ... 1Kin 17:3 3747
he went and dwelt by the brook C ... 1Kin 17:5 3747

CHERUB *(ke'-rub)* {30}
1. A winged celestial being.
make one c on the one end, and the ... Ex 25:19 3742
the other c on the other end ... Ex 25:19 3742
One c on the end on this side, and ... Ex 37:8 3742
another c on the other end on ... Ex 37:8 3742
And he rode upon a c, and did fly ... 2Sa 22:11 3742
cubits was the one wing of the c ... 1Kin 6:24 3742
cubits the other wing of the c ... 1Kin 6:24 3742
the other c was ten cubits ... 1Kin 6:25 3742
of the one c was ten cubits ... 1Kin 6:26 3742
and so was it of the other c ... 1Kin 6:26 3742
the wing of the other c touched ... 1Kin 6:27 3742
wing of the one c was five cubits ... 2Chr 3:11 3742
to the wing of the other c ... 2Chr 3:11 3742
of the other c was five cubits ... 2Chr 3:12 3742
to the wing of the other c ... 2Chr 3:12 3742
And he rode upon a c, and did fly ... Ps 18:10 3742
of Israel was gone up from the c ... Eze 9:3 3742
the wheels, even under the c ... Eze 10:2 3742
of the LORD went up from the c ... Eze 10:4 3742
one c stretched forth his hand ... Eze 10:7 3742
the cherubims, one wheel by one c ... Eze 10:9 3742
and another wheel by another c ... Eze 10:9 3742
first face was the face of a c ... Eze 10:14 3742
art the anointed c that covereth ... Eze 28:14 3742
I will destroy thee, O covering c ... Eze 28:16 3742
tree was between a c and a c ... Eze 41:18 3742
and every c had two faces ... Eze 41:18 3742
2. An exile who returned with Zerubbabel.
up from Tel-melah, Tel-harsa, C ... Ezr 2:59 3743
from Tel-melah, Tel-haresha, C ... Neh 7:61 3743

CHERUBIM {2}
the east of the garden of Eden C ... Gen 3:24 3742
the c shall stretch forth their ... Ex 25:20 3742

CHERUBIMS {62}
And thou shalt make two c of gold ... Ex 25:18 3742
the c on the two ends thereof ... Ex 25:19 3742
seat shall the faces of the c be ... Ex 25:20 3742
from between the two c which are ... Ex 25:22 3742
with c of cunning work shalt thou ... Ex 26:1 3742
with c shall it be made ... Ex 26:31 3742
with c of cunning work made he ... Ex 36:8 3742
with c made he it of cunning work ... Ex 36:35 3742
And he made two c of gold, beaten ... Ex 37:7 3742
he the c on the two ends thereof ... Ex 37:8 3742
the c spread out their wings on ... Ex 37:9 3742
seatward were the faces of the c ... Ex 37:9 3742
testimony, from between the two c ... Num 7:89 3742
which dwelleth between the c ... 1Sa 4:4 3742
hosts that dwelleth between the c ... 2Sa 6:2 3742
he made two c of olive tree ... 1Kin 6:23 3742
both the c were of one measure and ... 1Kin 6:25 3742
he set the c within the inner ... 1Kin 6:27 3742
forth the wings of the c, so that ... 1Kin 6:27 3742
And he overlaid the c with gold ... 1Kin 6:28 3742
about with carved figures of c ... 1Kin 6:29 3742
he carved upon them carvings of c ... 1Kin 6:32 3742
gold, and spread gold upon the c ... 1Kin 6:32 3742
And he carved thereon c and palm ... 1Kin 6:35 3742
the ledges were lions, oxen, and c ... 1Kin 7:29 3742
the borders thereof, he graved c ... 1Kin 7:36 3742
even under the wings of the c ... 1Kin 8:6 3742
For the c spread forth their two ... 1Kin 8:7 3742
the c covered the ark and the ... 1Kin 8:7 3742
which dwellest between the c ... 2Kin 19:15 3742
LORD, that dwelleth between the c ... 1Chr 13:6 3742
pattern of the chariot of the c ... 1Chr 28:18 3742
and graved c on the walls ... 2Chr 3:7 3742
house he made two c of image work ... 2Chr 3:10 3742
the wings of the c were twenty ... 2Chr 3:11 3742
The wings of these c spread ... 2Chr 3:13 3742
fine linen, and wrought c thereon ... 2Chr 3:14 3742
even under the wings of the c ... 2Chr 5:7 3742
For the c spread forth their ... 2Chr 5:8 3742
the c covered the ark and the ... 2Chr 5:8 3742
thou that dwellest between the c ... Ps 80:1 3742
he sitteth between the c ... Ps 99:1 3742
that dwellest between the c ... Is 37:16 3742
c there appeared over them as it ... Eze 10:1 3742
coals of fire from between the c ... Eze 10:2 3742
Now the c stood on the right side ... Eze 10:3 3742
the wheels, from between the c ... Eze 10:6 3742
c unto the fire that was between ... Eze 10:7 3742
the fire that was between the c ... Eze 10:7 3742
there appeared in the c the form ... Eze 10:8 3742
behold the four wheels by the c ... Eze 10:9 3742
And the c were lifted up ... Eze 10:15 3742
And when the c went, the wheels ... Eze 10:16 3742
when the c lifted up their wings ... Eze 10:16 3742
of the house, and stood over the c ... Eze 10:18 3742
the c lifted up their wings, and ... Eze 10:19 3742
and I knew that they were the c ... Eze 10:20 3742
Then did the c lift up their ... Eze 11:22 3742
And it was made with c and palm ... Eze 41:18 3742
ground unto above the door were c ... Eze 41:20 3742
on the doors of the temple, c ... Eze 41:25 3742
over it the c of glory shadowing ... Heb 9:5 *5502*

CHERUBIMS' {1}
the sound of the c wings was ... Eze 10:5 3742

CHESALON *(kes'-a-lon)* {1} *A landmark in Judah.*
side of mount Jearim, which is C ... Josh 15:10 3693

CHESED *(ke'-sed)* {1} *A son of Nahor.*
And C, and Hazo, and Pildash, and ... Gen 22:22 3777

CHESIL *(ke'-sil)* {1} *A Canaanite town.*
And Eltolad, and C, and Hormah ... Josh 15:30 3686

CHEST {6}
But Jehoiada the priest took a c ... 2Kin 12:9 727
there was much money in the c ... 2Kin 12:10 727
king's commandment they made a c ... 2Chr 24:8 727
and brought in, and cast into the c ... 2Chr 24:10 727
that at what time the c was ... 2Chr 24:11 727
officer came and emptied the c ... 2Chr 24:11 727

CHESTNUT {2}
poplar, and of the hazel and c tree ... Gen 30:37 6196
the c trees were not like his ... Eze 31:8 6196

CHESTS {1}
in c of rich apparel, bound with ... Eze 27:24 1595

CHESULLOTH *(ke-sul'-loth)* {1} See CHISLOTH-TABOR. *A town in Issachar.*
border was toward Jezreel, and C ... Josh 19:18 3694

CHEW {3}
ye not eat of them that c the cud ... Lev 11:4 5927
not eat of them that c the cud ... Deut 14:7 5927
for they c the cud, but divide ... Deut 14:7 5927

CHEWED {1}
between their teeth, ere it was *c* Num 11:33 3772

CHEWETH {8}
c the cud, among the beasts, that Lev 11:3 5927
the camel, because he *c* the cud Lev 11:4 5927
the coney, because he *c* the cud Lev 11:5 5927
And the hare, because he *c* the cud Lev 11:6 5927
yet he *c* not the cud Lev 11:7 1647
nor *c* the cud, are unclean unto Lev 11:26 5927
c the cud among the beasts, that Deut 14:6 5927
yet *c* not the cud, it is unclean Deut 14:8

CHEZIB *(ke'-zib)* {1} See ACHZIB, CHOZEBA. *A Canaanite village.*
and he was at *C*, when she bare him Gen 38:5 3580

CHICKENS {1}
gathereth her *c* under her wings Mt 23:37 3556

CHIDE {4}
the people did *c* with Moses Ex 17:2 7378
said unto them, Why *c* ye with me Ex 17:2 7378
they did *c* with him sharply Judg 8:1 7378
He will not always *c* Ps 103:9 7378

CHIDING {1}
because of the *c* of the children Ex 17:7 7379

CHIDON *(ki'-don)* {1} See NACHON. *Place where Uzzah died.*
came unto the threshingfloor of *C* 1Chr 13:9 3592

CHIEF {338}
Phichol the *c* captain of his host Gen 21:22
Phichol the *c* captain of his host Gen 21:32
Phichol the *c* captain of his army Gen 26:26
against the *c* of the butlers, and Gen 40:2 8269
against the *c* of the bakers Gen 40:2 8269
the *c* butler told his dream to Gen 40:9 8269
When the *c* baker saw that the Gen 40:16 8269
up the head of the *c* butler Gen 40:20 8269
of the *c* baker among his servants Gen 40:20 8269
he restored the *c* butler unto his Gen 40:21 8269
But he hanged the *c* baker Gen 40:22 8269
Yet did not the *c* butler remember Gen 40:23 8269
Then spake the *c* butler unto Gen 41:9 8269
house, both me and the *c* baker Gen 41:10 8269
being a *c* man among his people, Lev 21:4 1167
the *c* of the house of the father Num 3:24 5387
the *c* of the house of the father Num 3:30 5387
c over the *c* of the Levites Num 3:32 5387
the *c* of the house of the father Num 3:35 5387
the *c* of the congregation Num 4:34 5387
the *c* of Israel numbered, after Num 4:46 5387
a prince of a *c* house among the Num 25:14 1
people, and of a *c* house in Midian Num 25:15 1
the *c* fathers of the congregation Num 31:26 7218
the *c* fathers of the tribes of Num 32:28 7218
the *c* fathers of the families of Num 36:1 7218
the *c* fathers of the children of Num 36:1 7218
So I took the *c* of your tribes, Deut 1:15 7218
for the *c* things of the ancient Deut 33:15 7218
princes, of each *c* house a prince Josh 22:14 1
the *c* of all the people, even of Judg 20:2 6438
hither, all the *c* of the people 1Sa 14:38 6438
the *c* of the things which should 1Sa 15:21 7225
of David's soul, he shall be *c* 2Sa 5:8
and David's sons were *c* rulers 2Sa 8:18 3548
Jairite was a *c* ruler about David 2Sa 20:26 3548
in the seat, *c* among the captains 2Sa 23:8 7218
three of the thirty *c* went down 2Sa 23:13 7218
son of Zeruiah, was *c* among three 2Sa 23:18 7218
Beside the *c* of Solomon's 1Kin 5:16 8269
the *c* of the fathers of the 1Kin 8:1 5387
These were the *c* of the officers 1Kin 9:23 8269
the hands of the *c* of the guard 1Kin 14:27 8269
guard took Seraiah the *c* priest 2Kin 25:18 7218
and of him came the *c* ruler 1Chr 5:2 5059
was reckoned, were the *c*, Jeiel, 1Chr 5:7 7218
Joel the *c*, and Shapham the next, 1Chr 5:12 7218
c of the house of their fathers 1Chr 5:15 7218
all of them *c* men 1Chr 7:3 7218
men of valour, *c* of the princes 1Chr 7:40 7218
by their generations, *c* men 1Chr 8:28 7218
All these men were *c* of the 1Chr 9:9 7218
Shallum was the *c* 1Chr 9:17 7218
these Levites, the four *c* porters 1Chr 9:26 1368
c of the fathers of the Levites, 1Chr 9:33 7218
These *c* fathers of the Levites 1Chr 9:34 7218
fathers of the Levites were *c* 1Chr 9:34 7218
the Jebusites first shall be *c* 1Chr 11:6 7218
Zeruiah went first up, and was *c* 1Chr 11:6 7218
These also are the *c* of the 1Chr 11:10 7218
Hachmonite, the *c* of the captains 1Chr 11:11 7218
of Joab, he was *c* of the three 1Chr 11:20 7218
The *c* was Ahiezer, then Joash, 1Chr 12:3 7218
who was *c* of the captains, and he 1Chr 12:18 7218
Uriel the *c*, and his brethren an 1Chr 15:5 8269
Asaiah the *c*, and his brethren two 1Chr 15:6 8269
Joel the *c*, and his brethren an 1Chr 15:7 8269
Shemaiah the *c*, and his brethren 1Chr 15:8 8269
Eliel the *c*, and his brethren 1Chr 15:9 8269
Amminadab the *c*, and his brethren 1Chr 15:10 8269
Ye are the *c* of the fathers of 1Chr 15:12 7218
David spake to the *c* of the 1Chr 15:16 8269
c of the Levites, was for song 1Chr 15:22 8269
Asaph the *c*, and next to him 1Chr 16:5 7218
of David were *c* about the king 1Chr 18:17 7223
the *c* was Jehiel, and Zetham, and 1Chr 23:8 7218
These were the *c* of the fathers 1Chr 23:9 7218
And Jahath was the *c*, and Zizah the 1Chr 23:11 7218
of Gershom, Shebuel was the *c* 1Chr 23:16 7218
of Eliezer were, Rehabiah the *c* 1Chr 23:17 7218
Shelomith the *c* 1Chr 23:18 7218
even the *c* of the fathers, as 1Chr 23:24 7218
there were more *c* men found of 1Chr 24:4 7218
c men of the house of their 1Chr 24:4 7218
before the *c* of the fathers of 1Chr 24:6 7218
the *c* of the fathers of the 1Chr 24:31 7218
Simri the *c*, (for though he was 1Chr 26:10 7218
yet his father made him the *c* 1Chr 26:10 7218
the porters, even among the *c* men 1Chr 26:12 7218
c fathers, even of Laadan the 1Chr 26:21 7218
the *c* fathers, the captains over 1Chr 26:26 7218
the Hebronites was Jerijah the *c* 1Chr 26:31 7218
and seven hundred *c* fathers 1Chr 26:32 7218
the *c* fathers and captains of 1Chr 27:1 7218
the children of Perez was the *c* 1Chr 27:3 7218
the son of Jehoiada, a *c* priest 1Chr 27:5 7218
Then the *c* of the fathers and 1Chr 29:6 8269
the LORD to be the *c* governor 1Chr 29:22 5057
all Israel, the *c* of the fathers 2Chr 1:2 7218
the *c* of the fathers of the 2Chr 5:2 5387
c of his captains, and captains of 2Chr 8:9 8269
And these were the *c* of king 2Chr 8:10 8269
Abijah the son of Maachah the *c* 2Chr 11:22 7218
the hands of the *c* of the guard 2Chr 12:10 8269
Adnah the *c*, and with him mighty 2Chr 17:14 8269
of the *c* of the fathers of Israel 2Chr 19:8 7218
Amariah the *c* priest is over you 2Chr 19:11 7218
the *c* of the fathers of Israel, 2Chr 23:2 7218
king called for Jehoiada the *c* 2Chr 24:6 7218
The whole number of the *c* of the 2Chr 26:12 7218
And Azariah the *c* priest, and all 2Chr 26:20 7218
Azariah the *c* priest of the house 2Chr 31:10 7218
c of the Levites, gave unto the 2Chr 35:9 8269
Moreover all the *c* of the priests 2Chr 36:14 8269
Then rose up the *c* of the fathers Ezr 1:5 7218
some of the *c* of the fathers, Ezr 2:68 7218
c of the fathers, who were Ezr 3:12 7218
to the *c* of the fathers, and said Ezr 4:2 7218
the rest of the *c* of the fathers Ezr 4:3 7218
the men that were the *c* of them Ezr 5:10 7217
the son of Aaron the *c* priest Ezr 7:5 7218
of Israel *c* men to go up with me Ezr 7:28 7218
are now the *c* of their fathers Ezr 8:1 7218
and for Meshullam, *c* men Ezr 8:16 7218
Iddo the *c* at the place Casiphia Ezr 8:17 7218
twelve of the *c* of the priests Ezr 8:24 8269
them before the *c* of the priests Ezr 8:29 8269
c of the fathers of Israel, at Ezr 8:29 8269
hath been *c* in this trespass Ezr 9:2 7223
arose Ezra, and made the *c* priests Ezr 10:5 8269
with certain *c* of the fathers, Ezr 10:16 7218
some of the *c* of the fathers gave Neh 7:70 7218
some of the *c* of the fathers gave Neh 7:71 7218
the *c* of the fathers of all the Neh 8:13 7218
The *c* of the people Neh 10:14 7218
Now these are the *c* of the Neh 11:3 7218
c of the fathers, two hundred Neh 11:13 7218
of the *c* of the Levites, had the Neh 11:16 7218
These were the *c* of the priests Neh 12:7 7218
priests, the *c* of the fathers Neh 12:12 7218
were recorded *c* of the fathers Neh 12:22 7218
the *c* of the fathers, were Neh 12:23 7218
And the *c* of the Levites Neh 12:24 7218
old there were *c* of the singers Neh 12:46 7218
the *c* of the people of the earth Job 12:24 7218
I chose out their way, and sat *c* Job 29:25 7218
He is the *c* of the ways of God Job 40:19 7725
To the *c* Musician on Neginoth, A Ps 4:*t* 5329
To the *c* Musician upon Nehiloth, Ps 5:*t* 5329
To the *c* Musician on Neginoth Ps 6:*t* 5329
To the *c* Musician upon Gittith, A Ps 8:*t*
To the *c* Musician upon Ps 9:*t* 5329
To the *c* Musician, A Psalm of Ps 11:*t* 5329
To the *c* Musician upon Sheminith, Ps 12:*t* 5329
To the *c* Musician, A Psalm of Ps 13:*t* 5329
To the *c* Musician, A Psalm of Ps 14:*t* 5329
To the *c* Musician, A Psalm of Ps 18:*t* 5329
To the *c* Musician, A Psalm of Ps 19:*t* 5329
To the *c* Musician, A Psalm of Ps 20:*t* 5329
To the *c* Musician, A Psalm of Ps 21:*t* 5329
To the *c* Musician upon Aijeleth Ps 22:*t* 5329
To the *c* Musician, A Psalm of Ps 31:*t* 5329
To the *c* Musician, A Psalm of Ps 36:*t* 5329
To the *c* Musician, even to Ps 39:*t* 5329
To the *c* Musician, A Psalm of Ps 40:*t* 5329
To the *c* Musician, A Psalm of Ps 41:*t* 5329
To the *c* Musician, Maschil, for Ps 42:*t* 5329
To the *c* Musician for the sons of Ps 44:*t* 5329
To the *c* Musician upon Shoshannim Ps 45:*t* 5329
To the *c* Musician for the sons of Ps 46:*t* 5329
To the *c* Musician, A Psalm for Ps 47:*t* 5329
To the *c* Musician, A Psalm for Ps 49:*t* 5329
To the *c* Musician, A Psalm of Ps 51:*t* 5329
To the *c* Musician, Maschil, A Ps 52:*t* 5329
To the *c* Musician upon Mahalath, Ps 53:*t* 5329
To the *c* Musician on Neginoth, Ps 54:*t* 5329
To the *c* Musician on Neginoth, Ps 55:*t* 5329
To the *c* Musician upon Ps 56:*t* 5329
To the *c* Musician, Altaschith, Ps 57:*t* 5329
To the *c* Musician, Altaschith, Ps 58:*t* 5329
To the *c* Musician, Altaschith, Ps 59:*t* 5329
To the *c* Musician upon Ps 60:*t* 5329
To the *c* Musician upon Neginah, A Ps 61:*t* 5329
To the *c* Musician, to Jeduthun, A Ps 62:*t* 5329
To the *c* Musician, A Psalm of Ps 64:*t* 5329
To the *c* Musician, A Psalm and Ps 65:*t* 5329
To the *c* Musician, A Song or Ps 66:*t* 5329
To the *c* Musician on Neginoth, A Ps 67:*t* 5329
To the *c* Musician, A Psalm or Ps 68:*t* 5329
To the *c* Musician upon Shoshannim Ps 69:*t* 5329
To the *c* Musician, A Psalm of Ps 70:*t* 5329
To the *c* Musician, Altaschith, A Ps 75:*t* 5329
To the *c* Musician on Neginoth, A Ps 76:*t* 5329
To the *c* Musician, to Jeduthun, A Ps 77:*t* 5329
the *c* of their strength in the Ps 78:51 7225
To the *c* Musician upon Ps 80:*t* 5329
To the *c* Musician upon Gittith, A Ps 81:*t* 5329
To the *c* Musician upon Gittith, A Ps 84:*t* 5329
To the *c* Musician, A Psalm for Ps 85:*t* 5329
for the sons of Korah to the *c* Ps 88:*t* 5329
the *c* of all their strength Ps 105:36 7225
To the *c* Musician, A Psalm of Ps 109:*t* 5329
not Jerusalem above my *c* joy Ps 137:6 7218
To the *c* Musician, A Psalm of Ps 139:*t* 5329
To the *c* Musician, A Psalm of Ps 140:*t* 5329
She crieth in the *c* place of Prov 1:21 7218
a whisperer separateth *c* friends Prov 16:28 441
and aloes, with all the *c* spices Song 4:14 7218
even all the *c* ones of the earth Is 14:9 6260
thee from the *c* men thereof Is 41:9 678
to be captains, and as *c* over thee Jer 13:21 7218
who was also *c* governor in the Jer 20:1 5051
shout among the *c* of the nations Jer 31:7 7218
bow of Elam, the *c* of their might Jer 49:35 7225
guard took Seraiah the *c* priest Jer 52:24 7218
Her adversaries are the *c* Lam 1:5 7218
in thy fairs with *c* of all spices Eze 27:22 7218
the *c* prince of Meshech and Tubal, Eze 38:2 7218
the *c* prince of Meshech and Tubal Eze 38:3 7218
the *c* prince of Meshech and Tubal Eze 39:1 7218
c of the governors over all the Dan 2:48 7229
lo, Michael, one of the *c* princes Dan 10:13 7223
the *c* of the children of Ammon Dan 11:41 7225
which are named *c* of the nations Amos 6:1 7225
themselves with the *c* ointments Amos 6:6 7225
To the *c* singer on my stringed Hab 3:19 5329
he had gathered all the *c* priests Mt 2:4 749
c priests and scribes, and be Mt 16:21 749
be betrayed unto the *c* priests Mt 20:18 749
And whosoever will be *c* among you Mt 20:27 4413
And when the *c* priests and scribes Mt 21:15 749
the *c* priests and the elders of Mt 21:23 749
And when the *c* priests and Mt 21:45 749
the *c* seats in the synagogues, Mt 23:6 4410
assembled together the *c* priests Mt 26:3 749
Iscariot, went unto the *c* priests Mt 26:14 749
and staves, from the *c* priests Mt 26:47 749
Now the *c* priests, and elders, and Mt 26:59 749
was come, all the *c* priests Mt 27:1 749
pieces of silver to the *c* priests Mt 27:3 749
the *c* priests took the silver Mt 27:6 749
he was accused of the *c* priests Mt 27:12 749
But the *c* priests and elders Mt 27:20 749
Likewise also the *c* priests Mt 27:41 749
the *c* priests and Pharisees came Mt 27:62 749
shewed unto the *c* priests all the Mt 28:11 749
captains, and *c* estates of Galilee Mk 6:21 4413
of the *c* priests, and scribes, and Mk 8:31 749
be delivered unto the *c* priests Mk 10:33 749
c priests heard it, and sought how Mk 11:18 749
there come to him the *c* priests Mk 11:27 749
the *c* seats in the synagogues, and Mk 12:39 4410
the *c* priests and the scribes Mk 14:1 749
twelve, went unto the *c* priests Mk 14:10 749
and staves, from the *c* priest Mk 14:43 749
were assembled all the *c* priests Mk 14:53 749
the *c* priests and all the council Mk 14:55 749
the *c* priests held a consultation Mk 15:1 749
the *c* priests accused him of many Mk 15:3 749
For he knew that the *c* priests Mk 15:10 749
But the *c* priests moved the Mk 15:11 749
Likewise also the *c* priests Mk 15:31 749
c priests and scribes, and be slain Lk 9:22 749
Beelzebub the *c* of the devils Lk 11:15 758
into the house of one of the *c* Lk 14:1 758
how they chose out the *c* rooms Lk 14:7 4411
which was the *c* among the Lk 19:2 754
But the *c* priests and the scribes Lk 19:47 749
the *c* of the people sought to Lk 19:47 4413
the *c* priests and the scribes came Lk 20:1 749
the *c* priests and the scribes the Lk 20:19 749
and the *c* rooms at feasts Lk 20:46 4411
the *c* priests and scribes sought Lk 22:2 749
and communed with the *c* priests Lk 22:4 749
and he that is *c*, as he that doth Lk 22:26 2233
Jesus said unto the *c* priests Lk 22:52 749
the *c* priests and the scribes came Lk 22:66 749
Then said Pilate to the *c* priests Lk 23:4 749
the *c* priests and scribes stood and Lk 23:10 749
had called together the *c* priests Lk 23:13 749
of the *c* priests prevailed Lk 23:23 749
And how the *c* priests and our Lk 24:20 749
the *c* priests sent officers to Jn 7:32 749
the officers to the *c* priests Jn 7:45 749
Then gathered the *c* priests Jn 11:47 749
Now both the *c* priests and the Jn 11:57 749
But the *c* priests consulted that Jn 12:10 749
Nevertheless among the *c* rulers Jn 12:42 758
and officers from the *c* priests Jn 18:3 749
the *c* priests have delivered thee Jn 18:35 749

When the c priests therefore and ... Jn 19:6 749
The c priests answered, We have ... Jn 19:15 749
Then said the c priests of the ... Jn 19:21 749
reported all that the c priests ... Acts 4:23 749
the c priests heard these things, ... Acts 5:24 749
c priests to bind all that call ... Acts 9:14 749
them bound unto the c priests ... Acts 9:21 749
the c men of the city, and raised ... Acts 13:50 4413
because he was the c speaker ... Acts 14:12 2233
Silas, c men among the brethren ... Acts 15:22 2233
which is the c city of that part ... Acts 16:12 4413
and of the c women not a few ... Acts 17:4 4413
the c ruler of the synagogue, ... Acts 18:8 752
the c ruler of the synagogue, and ... Acts 18:17 752
c of the priests, which did so ... Acts 19:14 749
And certain of the c of Asia ... Acts 19:31 775
unto the c captain of the band ... Acts 21:31 5506
and when they saw the c captain ... Acts 21:32 5506
Then the c captain came near, and ... Acts 21:33 5506
he said unto the c captain ... Acts 21:37 5506
The c captain commanded him to be ... Acts 22:24 5506
he went and told the c captain ... Acts 22:26 5506
Then the c captain came, and said ... Acts 22:27 5506
the c captain answered, With a ... Acts 22:28 5506
the c captain also was afraid, ... Acts 22:29 5506
bands, and commanded the c priests ... Acts 22:30 749
the c captain, fearing lest Paul ... Acts 23:10 5506
And they came to the c priests ... Acts 23:14 749
c captain that he bring him down ... Acts 23:15 5506
this young man unto the c captain ... Acts 23:17 5506
and brought him to the c captain ... Acts 23:18 5506
Then the c captain took him by ... Acts 23:19 5506
So the c captain then let the ... Acts 23:22 5506
But the c captain Lysias came ... Acts 24:7 5506
When Lysias the c captain shall ... Acts 24:22 5506
the c of the Jews informed him ... Acts 25:2 4413
the c priests and the elders of ... Acts 25:15 749
of hearing, with the c captains ... Acts 25:23 5506
authority from the c priests ... Acts 26:10 749
and commission from the c priests ... Acts 26:12 749
of the c man of the island ... Acts 28:7 4413
called the c of the Jews together ... Acts 28:17 4413
himself being the c corner stone ... Eph 2:20 204
of whom I am c ... 1Ti 1:15 4413
I lay in Sion a c corner stone ... 1Pet 2:6 204
when the c Shepherd shall appear, ... 1Pet 5:4 750
the c captains, and the mighty men ... Rev 6:15 5506

CHIEFEST {9}
c of all the offerings of Israel ... 1Sa 2:29 7225
made them sit in the c place ... 1Sa 9:22 7218
the c of the herdmen that ... 1Sa 21:7 47
they buried him in the c of the ... 2Chr 32:33 4608
ruddy, the c among ten thousand ... Song 5:10 1713
And whosoever of you will be the c ... Mk 10:44 4413
a whit behind the very c apostles ... 2Cor 11:5 5228,3029
am I behind the very c apostles ... 2Cor 12:11 5228,3029
the c city of Phrygia Pacatiana ... 1Ti s 3390

CHIEFLY {3}
c, because that unto them were ... Rom 3:2 4412
c they that are of Caesar's ... Phil 4:22 3122
But c them that walk after the ... 2Pet 2:10 3122

CHILD {201}
she had no c ... Gen 11:30 2056
unto her, Behold, thou art with c ... Gen 16:11 2030
Every man c among you shall be ... Gen 17:10
every man c in your generations, ... Gen 17:12
the uncircumcised man c whose ... Gen 17:14
Shall a c be born unto him that ... Gen 17:17
Shall I of a surety bear a c ... Gen 18:13
of Lot with c by their father ... Gen 19:36 2029
the c grew, and was weaned ... Gen 21:8 3206
it on her shoulder, and the c ... Gen 21:14 3206
she cast the c under one of the ... Gen 21:15 3206
Let me not see the death of the c ... Gen 21:16 3206
brethren, and said, The c is not ... Gen 37:30 3206
behold, she is with c by whoredom ... Gen 38:24 2030
man, whose these are, am I with c ... Gen 38:25 2030
saying, Do not sin against the c ... Gen 42:22 3206
a c of his old age, a little one ... Gen 44:20 3206
saw him that he was a goodly c ... Ex 2:2
with pitch, and put the c therein ... Ex 2:3 3206
she had opened it, she saw the c ... Ex 2:6 3206
that she may nurse the c for thee ... Ex 2:7 3206
said unto her, Take this c away ... Ex 2:9 3206
And the woman took the c, and ... Ex 2:9 3206
the c grew, and she brought him ... Ex 2:10 3206
strive, and hurt a woman with c ... Ex 21:22 2030
any widow, or fatherless c ... Ex 22:22
conceived seed, and born a man c ... Lev 12:2
But if she bear a maid c, then ... Lev 12:5
widow, or divorced, and have no c ... Lev 22:13 2233
father beareth the sucking c ... Num 11:12
and one of them die, and have no c ... Deut 25:5 1121
and she was his only c ... Judg 11:34 3173
for the c shall be a Nazarite ... Judg 13:5 5288
for the c shall be a Nazarite to ... Judg 13:7 5288
do unto the c that shall be born ... Judg 13:8 5288
How shall we order the c, and how ... Judg 13:12 5288
the c grew, and the LORD blessed ... Judg 13:24 5288
And Naomi took the c, and laid it ... Ruth 4:16 3206
give unto thine handmaid a man c ... 1Sa 1:11 2233
not go up until the c be weaned ... 1Sa 1:22 5288
and the c was young ... 1Sa 1:24 5288
bullock, and brought the c to Eli ... 1Sa 1:25 5288
For this c I prayed ... 1Sa 1:27 5288
the c did minister unto the LORD ... 1Sa 2:11 5288
before the LORD, being a c ... 1Sa 2:18 5288
the c Samuel grew before the LORD ... 1Sa 2:21 5288
the c Samuel grew on, and was in ... 1Sa 2:26 5288
the c Samuel ministered unto the ... 1Sa 3:1 5288
that the LORD had called the c ... 1Sa 3:8 5288
law, Phinehas' wife, was with c ... 1Sa 4:19 2030
And she named the c I-chabod ... 1Sa 4:21 5288
no c unto the day of her death ... 2Sa 6:23 3206
told David, and said, I am with c ... 2Sa 11:5 2030
the c also that is born unto thee ... 2Sa 12:14 1121
the LORD struck the c that ... 2Sa 12:15 3206
therefore besought God for the c ... 2Sa 12:16 5288
the seventh day, that the c died ... 2Sa 12:18 3206
to tell him that the c was dead ... 2Sa 12:18 3206
while the c was yet alive, we ... 2Sa 12:18 3206
if we tell him that the c is dead ... 2Sa 12:18 3206
perceived that the c was dead ... 2Sa 12:19 3206
unto his servants, Is the c dead ... 2Sa 12:19 3206
thou didst fast and weep for the c ... 2Sa 12:21 3206
but when the c was dead, thou ... 2Sa 12:21 3206
While the c was yet alive, I ... 2Sa 12:22 3206
to me, that the c may live ... 2Sa 12:22 3206
and I am but a little c ... 1Kin 3:7 5288
I was delivered of a c with her ... 1Kin 3:17 3205
this woman's c died in the night ... 1Kin 3:19 1121
and laid her dead c in my bosom ... 1Kin 3:20 1121
in the morning to give my c suck ... 1Kin 3:21 1121
said, Divide the living c in two ... 1Kin 3:25 3206
the living c was unto the king ... 1Kin 3:26 1121
O my lord, give her the living c ... 1Kin 3:26 3205
and said, Give her the living c ... 1Kin 3:27 3205
Hadad being yet a little c ... 1Kin 11:17 5288
a c shall be born unto the house ... 1Kin 13:2 1121
thee what shall become of the c ... 1Kin 14:3 5288
into the city, the c shall die ... 1Kin 14:12 3206
threshold of the door, the c died ... 1Kin 14:17 5288
himself upon the c three times ... 1Kin 17:21 3206
the soul of the c came into him ... 1Kin 17:22 3206
And Elijah took the c, and brought ... 1Kin 17:23 3206
answered, Verily she hath no c ... 2Kin 4:14 1121
when the c was grown, it fell on ... 2Kin 4:18 3206
is it well with the c ... 2Kin 4:26 3206
my staff upon the face of the c ... 2Kin 4:29 5288
And the mother of the c said ... 2Kin 4:30 5288
the staff upon the face of the c ... 2Kin 4:31 5288
him, saying, The c is not awaked ... 2Kin 4:31 5288
the c was dead, and laid upon his ... 2Kin 4:32 5288
And he went up, and lay upon the c ... 2Kin 4:34 3206
he stretched himself upon the c ... 2Kin 4:34
and the flesh of the c waxed warm ... 2Kin 4:34 3206
the c sneezed seven times ... 2Kin 4:35 5288
and the c opened his eyes ... 2Kin 4:35 5288
like unto the flesh of a little c ... 2Kin 5:14 5288
and rip up their women with c ... 2Kin 8:12 2030
that were with c he ripped up ... 2Kin 15:16 2030
said, There is a man c conceived ... Job 3:3
as a c that is weaned of his ... Ps 131:2
my soul is even as a weaned c ... Ps 131:2
Even a c is known by his doings, ... Prov 20:11 5288
Train up a c in the way he should ... Prov 22:6 5288
is bound in the heart of a c ... Prov 22:15 5288
not correction from the c ... Prov 23:13 5288
a wise c shall have joy of him ... Prov 23:24
but a c left to himself bringeth ... Prov 29:15 5288
a c shall have him become his son ... Prov 29:21 5290
he hath neither c nor brother ... Eccl 4:8 1121
a wise c than an old and foolish ... Eccl 4:13 3206
with the second c that shall ... Eccl 4:15 3206
O land, when thy king is a c ... Eccl 10:16 5288
in the womb of her that is with c ... Eccl 11:5 4392
the c shall behave himself ... Is 3:5 5288
For before the c shall know to ... Is 7:16 5288
For before the c shall have ... Is 8:4 5288
For unto us a c is born, unto us ... Is 9:6 3206
be few, that a c may write them ... Is 10:19 5288
a little c shall lead them ... Is 11:6 5288
the sucking c shall play on the ... Is 11:8
the weaned c shall put his hand ... Is 11:8
Like as a woman with c, that ... Is 26:17 2030
We have been with c, we have been ... Is 26:18 2029
Can a woman forget her sucking c ... Is 49:15
that didst not travail with c ... Is 54:1
for the c shall die an hundred ... Is 65:20 5288
she was delivered of a man c ... Is 66:7
for I am a c ... Jer 1:6 5288
said unto me, Say not, I am a c ... Jer 1:7 5288
that bringeth forth her first c ... Jer 4:31
A man c is born unto thee ... Jer 20:15 1121
whether a man doth travail with c ... Jer 30:6 3205
and the lame, the woman with c ... Jer 31:8 2030
that travaileth with c together ... Jer 31:8 3205
is he a pleasant c ... Jer 31:20 3206
cut off from you man and woman, c ... Jer 44:7 5768
The tongue of the sucking c ... Lam 4:4
When Israel was a c, then I loved ... Hos 11:1 5288
their women with c shall be ... Hos 13:16 2030
up the women with c of Gilead ... Amos 1:13 2030
found with c of the Holy Ghost Mt 1:18 1722,1064,2192
a virgin shall be with c ... Mt 1:23 1722,1064,2192
search diligently for the young c ... Mt 2:8 3813
stood over where the young c was ... Mt 2:9 3813
they saw the young c with Mary ... Mt 2:11 3813
Arise, and take the young c ... Mt 2:13 3813
seek the young c to destroy him ... Mt 2:13 3813
he arose, he took the young c ... Mt 2:14 3813
Arise, and take the young c ... Mt 2:20 3813
And he arose, and took the young c ... Mt 2:21 3813
to death, and the father the c ... Mt 10:21 5043
the c was cured from that very ... Mt 17:18 3816
Jesus called a little c unto him ... Mt 18:2 3813
humble himself as this little c ... Mt 18:4 3813
little c in my name receiveth me ... Mt 18:5 3813
the c of hell than yourselves ... Mt 23:15 5207
woe unto them that are with c . Mt 24:19 1722,1064,2192
And he said, Of a c ... Mk 9:21 3812
the father of the c cried out ... Mk 9:24 3813
And he took a c, and set him in the ... Mk 9:36 3813
the kingdom of God as a little c ... Mk 10:15 3813
woe to them that are with c ... Mk 13:17 1722,1064,2192
And they had no c, because that ... Lk 1:7 5043
day they came to circumcise the c ... Lk 1:59 3813
What manner of c shall this be ... Lk 1:66 3813
And thou, c, shalt be called the ... Lk 1:76 3813
the c grew, and waxed strong in ... Lk 1:80 3813
espoused wife, being great with c ... Lk 2:5 1471
was told them concerning this c ... Lk 2:17 3813
for the circumcising of the c ... Lk 2:21 3813
parents brought in the c Jesus ... Lk 2:27 3813
this c is set for the fall and ... Lk 2:34
the c grew, and waxed strong in ... Lk 2:40 3813
the c Jesus tarried behind in ... Lk 2:43 3816
for he is mine only c ... Lk 9:38 3439
unclean spirit, and healed the c ... Lk 9:42 3816
thought of their heart, took a c ... Lk 9:47 3813
this c in my name receiveth me ... Lk 9:48 3813
c shall in no wise enter therein ... Lk 18:17 3813
woe unto them that are with c . Lk 21:23 1722,1064,2192
him, Sir, come down ere my c die ... Jn 4:49 3813
soon as she is delivered of the c ... Jn 16:21 3813
a truth against thy holy c Jesus ... Acts 4:27 3816
by the name of thy holy c Jesus ... Acts 4:30 3816
him, when as yet he had no c ... Acts 7:5 5043
thou c of the devil, thou enemy ... Acts 13:10 5207
I was a c, I spake as a c ... 1Cor 13:11 3516
I understood as a c ... 1Cor 13:11 3516
I thought as a c ... 1Cor 13:11 3516
the heir, as long as he is a c ... Gal 4:1 3516
travail upon a woman with c ... 1Th 5:3 1722,1064,2192
that from a c thou hast known the ... 2Ti 3:15 1025
was delivered of a c when she was ... Heb 11:11 5088
they saw he was a proper c ... Heb 11:23 3813
And she being with c cried ... Rev 12:2 1722,1064,2192
for to devour her c as soon as it ... Rev 12:4 5043
And she brought forth a man c ... Rev 12:5 5207
her c was caught up unto God, and ... Rev 12:5 5043
which brought forth the man c ... Rev 12:13

CHILDBEARING {1}
she shall be saved in c, if they ... 1Ti 2:15 5042

CHILDHOOD {2}
you from my c unto this day ... 1Sa 12:2 5271
for c and youth are vanity ... Eccl 11:10 3208

CHILDISH {1}
became a man, I put away c things ... 1Cor 13:11 3516

CHILDLESS {7}
wilt thou give me, seeing I go c ... Gen 15:2 6185
they shall die c ... Lev 20:20 6185
they shall be c ... Lev 20:21 6185
As thy sword hath made women c ... 1Sa 15:33 7921
shall thy mother be c among women ... 1Sa 15:33 7921
the LORD, Write ye this man c ... Jer 22:30 6185
took her to wife, and he died c ... Lk 20:30 815

CHILDREN {1804}
sorrow thou shalt bring forth c ... Gen 3:16 1121
of men, and they bare c to them ... Gen 6:4
the father of all the c of Eber ... Gen 10:21 1121
elder, even to him were c born ... Gen 10:21
The c of Shem ... Gen 10:22 1121
And the c of Aram ... Gen 10:23 1121
which the c of men builded ... Gen 11:5 1121
Sarai Abram's wife bare him no c ... Gen 16:1
may be that I may obtain c by her ... Gen 16:2 1129
him, that he will command his c ... Gen 18:19 1121
of the c of Ammon unto this day ... Gen 19:38 1121
and they bare c ... Gen 20:17
Sarah should have given c suck ... Gen 21:7 1121
she hath also born c unto thy ... Gen 22:20 1121
the c of Heth answered Abraham, ... Gen 23:5 1121
the land, even to the c of Heth ... Gen 23:7 1121
Ephron dwelt among the c of Heth ... Gen 23:10 1121
in the audience of the c of Heth ... Gen 23:10 1121
in the presence of the c of Heth ... Gen 23:18 1121
All these were the c of Keturah ... Gen 25:4 1121
the c struggled together within ... Gen 25:22 1121
saw that she bare Jacob no c ... Gen 30:1
and said unto Jacob, Give me c ... Gen 30:1 1121
that I may also have c by her ... Gen 30:3 1129
Give me my wives and my c, for ... Gen 30:26 3206
and these c are my c ... Gen 31:43 1121
or unto their c which they have ... Gen 31:43 1121
me, and the mother with the c ... Gen 32:11 1121
Therefore the c of Israel eat not ... Gen 32:32 1121
And he divided the c unto Leah ... Gen 33:1 3206
their c foremost, and Leah and her ... Gen 33:2 3206
her c after, and Rachel and Joseph ... Gen 33:2 3206
eyes, and saw the women and the c ... Gen 33:5 3206
The c which God hath graciously ... Gen 33:5 3206
came near, they and their c ... Gen 33:6 3206
And Leah also with her c came near ... Gen 33:7 3206
knoweth that the c are tender ... Gen 33:13 3206
the c be able to endure, until I ... Gen 33:14 3206
at the hand of the c of Hamor ... Gen 33:19 1121
the c of Seir in the land of Edom ... Gen 36:21 1121

the *c* of Lotan were Hori and Hemam ... Gen 36:22 1121
the *c* of Shobal were these ... Gen 36:23 1121
And these are the *c* of Zibeon ... Gen 36:24 1121
And the *c* of Anah were these ... Gen 36:25 1121
And these are the *c* of Dishon ... Gen 36:26 1121
The *c* of Ezer are these ... Gen 36:27 1121
The *c* of Dishan are these ... Gen 36:28 1121
any king over the *c* of Israel ... Gen 36:31 1121
loved Joseph more than all his *c* ... Gen 37:3 1121
them, Me have ye bereaved of my *c* ... Gen 42:36
If I be bereaved of my *c*, I am ... Gen 43:14
thy *c*, and thy children's *c* ... Gen 45:10 1121
And the *c* of Israel did so ... Gen 45:21 1121
are the names of the *c* of Israel ... Gen 46:8 1121
thy father's *c* shall bow down ... Gen 49:8 1121
is therein was from the *c* of Heth ... Gen 49:32 1121
Joseph saw Ephraim's *c* of the ... Gen 50:23 1121
the *c* also of Machir the son of ... Gen 50:23 1121
took an oath of the *c* of Israel ... Gen 50:25 1121
are the names of the *c* of Israel ... Ex 1:1 1121
the *c* of Israel were fruitful, and ... Ex 1:7 1121
the people of the *c* of Israel are ... Ex 1:9 1121
because of the *c* of Israel ... Ex 1:12 1121
the Egyptians made the *c* of ... Ex 1:13 1121
them, but saved the men *c* alive ... Ex 1:17 3206
and have saved the men *c* alive ... Ex 1:18 3206
This is one of the Hebrews' *c* ... Ex 2:6 3206
the *c* of Israel sighed by reason ... Ex 2:23 1121
God looked upon the *c* of Israel ... Ex 2:25 1121
the cry of the *c* of Israel is ... Ex 3:9 1121
the *c* of Israel out of Egypt ... Ex 3:10 1121
the *c* of Israel out of Egypt ... Ex 3:11 1121
when I come unto the *c* of Israel ... Ex 3:13 1121
thou say unto the *c* of Israel ... Ex 3:14 1121
thou say unto the *c* of Israel ... Ex 3:15 1121
all the elders of the *c* of Israel ... Ex 4:29 1121
LORD had visited the *c* of Israel ... Ex 4:31 1121
the officers of the *c* of Israel ... Ex 5:14 1121
officers of the *c* of Israel came ... Ex 5:15 1121
the officers of the *c* of Israel ... Ex 5:19 1121
the groaning of the *c* of Israel ... Ex 6:5 1121
say unto the *c* of Israel, I am ... Ex 6:6 1121
spake so unto the *c* of Israel ... Ex 6:9 1121
that he let the *c* of Israel go ... Ex 6:11 1121
Behold, the *c* of Israel have not ... Ex 6:12 1121
a charge unto the *c* of Israel ... Ex 6:13 1121
to bring the *c* of Israel out of ... Ex 6:13 1121
Bring out the *c* of Israel from ... Ex 6:26 1121
to bring out the *c* of Israel from ... Ex 6:27 1121
that he send the *c* of Israel out ... Ex 7:2 1121
and my people the *c* of Israel ... Ex 7:4 1121
bring out the *c* of Israel from ... Ex 7:5 1121
of the *c* of Israel died not one ... Ex 9:6 1121
where the *c* of Israel were, was ... Ex 9:26 1121
would he let the *c* of Israel go ... Ex 9:35 1121
would not let the *c* of Israel go ... Ex 10:20 1121
but all the *c* of Israel had light ... Ex 10:23 1121
But against any of the *c* of ... Ex 11:7 1121
c of Israel go out of his land ... Ex 11:10 1121
when your *c* shall say unto you, ... Ex 12:26 1121
of the *c* of Israel in Egypt ... Ex 12:27 1121
the *c* of Israel went away, and did ... Ex 12:28 1121
both ye and the *c* of Israel ... Ex 12:31 1121
the *c* of Israel did according to ... Ex 12:35 1121
the *c* of Israel journeyed from ... Ex 12:37 1121
on foot that were men, beside *c* ... Ex 12:37 2945
the sojourning of the *c* of Israel ... Ex 12:40 1121
c of Israel in their generations ... Ex 12:42 1121
Thus did all the *c* of Israel ... Ex 12:50 1121
that the LORD did bring the *c* of ... Ex 12:51 1121
the womb among the *c* of Israel ... Ex 13:2 1121
man among thy *c* shalt thou redeem ... Ex 13:13 1121
the firstborn of my *c* I redeem ... Ex 13:15 1121
the *c* of Israel went up harnessed ... Ex 13:18 1121
straitly sworn the *c* of Israel ... Ex 13:19 1121
Speak unto the *c* of Israel ... Ex 14:2 1121
will say of the *c* of Israel ... Ex 14:3 1121
he pursued after the *c* of Israel ... Ex 14:8 1121
the *c* of Israel went out with an ... Ex 14:8 1121
the *c* of Israel lifted up their ... Ex 14:10 1121
the *c* of Israel cried out unto ... Ex 14:10 1121
speak unto the *c* of Israel ... Ex 14:15 1121
the *c* of Israel shall go on dry ... Ex 14:16 1121
the *c* of Israel went into the ... Ex 14:22 1121
But the *c* of Israel walked upon ... Ex 14:29 1121
the *c* of Israel this song unto ... Ex 15:1 1121
but the *c* of Israel went on dry ... Ex 15:19 1121
of the *c* of Israel came unto the ... Ex 16:1 1121
the *c* of Israel murmured against ... Ex 16:2 1121
the *c* of Israel said unto them, ... Ex 16:3 1121
said unto all the *c* of Israel ... Ex 16:6 1121
congregation of the *c* of Israel ... Ex 16:9 1121
congregation of the *c* of Israel ... Ex 16:10 1121
the murmurings of the *c* of Israel ... Ex 16:12 1121
when the *c* of Israel saw it, they ... Ex 16:15 1121
the *c* of Israel did so, and ... Ex 16:17 1121
the *c* of Israel did eat manna ... Ex 16:35 1121
all the congregation of the *c* of ... Ex 17:1 1121
out of Egypt, to kill us and our *c* ... Ex 17:3 1121
of the chiding of the *c* of Israel ... Ex 17:7 1121
when the *c* of Israel were gone ... Ex 19:1 1121
of Jacob, and tell the *c* of Israel ... Ex 19:3 1121
shalt speak unto the *c* of Israel ... Ex 19:6 1121
fathers upon the *c* unto the third ... Ex 20:5 1121
shalt say unto the *c* of Israel ... Ex 20:22 1121
her *c* shall be her master's, and ... Ex 21:4 3206
love my master, my wife, and my *c* ... Ex 21:5 1121
be widows, and your *c* fatherless ... Ex 22:24 1121
sent young men of the *c* of Israel ... Ex 24:5 1121
upon the nobles of the *c* of ... Ex 24:11 1121
in the eyes of the *c* of Israel ... Ex 24:17 1121
Speak unto the *c* of Israel ... Ex 25:2 1121
commandment unto the *c* of Israel ... Ex 25:22 1121
shalt command the *c* of Israel ... Ex 27:20 1121
on the behalf of the *c* of Israel ... Ex 27:21 1121
him, from among the *c* of Israel ... Ex 28:1 1121
them the names of the *c* of Israel ... Ex 28:9 1121
with the names of the *c* of Israel ... Ex 28:11 1121
of memorial unto the *c* of Israel ... Ex 28:12 1121
with the names of the *c* of Israel ... Ex 28:21 1121
shall bear the names of the *c* of ... Ex 28:29 1121
shall bear the judgment of the *c* ... Ex 28:30 1121
which the *c* of Israel shall ... Ex 28:38 1121
for ever from the *c* of Israel ... Ex 29:28 1121
c of Israel of the sacrifice of ... Ex 29:28 1121
I will meet with the *c* of Israel ... Ex 29:43 1121
will dwell among the *c* of Israel ... Ex 29:45 1121
c of Israel after their number ... Ex 30:12 1121
money of the *c* of Israel, and ... Ex 30:16 1121
the *c* of Israel before the LORD ... Ex 30:16 1121
shalt speak unto the *c* of Israel ... Ex 30:31 1121
thou also unto the *c* of Israel ... Ex 31:13 1121
Wherefore the *c* of Israel shall ... Ex 31:16 1121
me and the *c* of Israel for ever ... Ex 31:17 1121
made the *c* of Israel drink of it ... Ex 32:20 1121
the *c* of Levi did according to ... Ex 32:28 1121
Moses, Say unto the *c* of Israel ... Ex 33:5 1121
And the *c* of Israel stripped ... Ex 33:6 1121
of the fathers upon the *c* ... Ex 34:7 1121
and upon the children's *c* ... Ex 34:7
men *c* appear before the Lord GOD ... Ex 34:23
all the *c* of Israel saw Moses, ... Ex 34:30 1121
afterward all the *c* of Israel ... Ex 34:32 1121
spake unto the *c* of Israel that ... Ex 34:34 1121
the *c* of Israel saw the face of ... Ex 34:35 1121
of the *c* of Israel together ... Ex 35:1 1121
congregation of the *c* of Israel ... Ex 35:4 1121
the *c* of Israel departed from the ... Ex 35:20 1121
The *c* of Israel brought a willing ... Ex 35:29 1121
Moses said unto the *c* of Israel ... Ex 35:30 1121
which the *c* of Israel had brought ... Ex 36:3 1121
with the names of the *c* of Israel ... Ex 39:6 1121
for a memorial to the *c* of Israel ... Ex 39:7 1121
to the names of the *c* of Israel ... Ex 39:14 1121
the *c* of Israel did according to ... Ex 39:32 1121
so the *c* of Israel made all the ... Ex 39:42 1121
the *c* of Israel went onward in ... Ex 40:36 1121
Speak unto the *c* of Israel ... Lev 1:2 1121
Speak unto the *c* of Israel ... Lev 4:2 1121
All the males among the *c* of ... Lev 6:18 1121
Speak unto the *c* of Israel ... Lev 7:23 1121
Speak unto the *c* of Israel ... Lev 7:29 1121
of the *c* of Israel from off the ... Lev 7:34 1121
ever from among the *c* of Israel ... Lev 7:34 1121
be given them of the *c* of Israel ... Lev 7:36 1121
the *c* of Israel to offer their ... Lev 7:38 1121
unto the *c* of Israel thou shalt ... Lev 9:3 1121
that ye may teach the *c* of Israel ... Lev 10:11 1121
offerings of the *c* of Israel ... Lev 10:14 1121
Speak unto the *c* of Israel ... Lev 11:2 1121
Speak unto the *c* of Israel ... Lev 12:2 1121
Speak unto the *c* of Israel ... Lev 15:2 1121
the *c* of Israel from their ... Lev 15:31 1121
c of Israel two kids of the goats ... Lev 16:5 1121
uncleanness of the *c* of Israel ... Lev 16:16 1121
uncleanness of the *c* of Israel ... Lev 16:19 1121
the iniquities of the *c* of Israel ... Lev 16:21 1121
c of Israel for all their sins ... Lev 16:34 1121
sons, and unto all the *c* of Israel ... Lev 17:2 1121
To the end that the *c* of Israel ... Lev 17:5 1121
I said unto the *c* of Israel ... Lev 17:12 1121
man there be of the *c* of Israel ... Lev 17:13 1121
I said unto the *c* of Israel ... Lev 17:14 1121
Speak unto the *c* of Israel ... Lev 18:2 1121
congregation of the *c* of Israel ... Lev 19:2 1121
against the *c* of thy people ... Lev 19:18 1121
thou shalt say to the *c* of Israel ... Lev 20:2 1121
he be of the *c* of Israel, or of ... Lev 20:2 1121
sons, and unto all the *c* of Israel ... Lev 21:24 1121
holy things of the *c* of Israel ... Lev 22:2 1121
which the *c* of Israel hallow unto ... Lev 22:3 1121
holy things of the *c* of Israel ... Lev 22:15 1121
sons, and unto all the *c* of Israel ... Lev 22:18 1121
be hallowed among the *c* of Israel ... Lev 22:32 1121
Speak unto the *c* of Israel ... Lev 23:2 1121
Speak unto the *c* of Israel ... Lev 23:10 1121
Speak unto the *c* of Israel ... Lev 23:24 1121
Speak unto the *c* of Israel ... Lev 23:34 1121
may know that I made the *c* of ... Lev 23:43 1121
Moses declared unto the *c* of ... Lev 23:44 1121
Command the *c* of Israel, that ... Lev 24:2 1121
being taken from the *c* of Israel ... Lev 24:8 1121
went out among the *c* of Israel ... Lev 24:10 1121
shalt speak unto the *c* of Israel ... Lev 24:15 1121
And Moses spake to the *c* of Israel ... Lev 24:23 1121
the *c* of Israel did as the LORD ... Lev 24:23 1121
Speak unto the *c* of Israel ... Lev 25:2 1121
possession among the *c* of Israel ... Lev 25:33 1121
his *c* with him, and shall return ... Lev 25:41 1121
Moreover of the *c* of the ... Lev 25:45 1121
inheritance for your *c* after you ... Lev 25:46 1121
your brethren the *c* of Israel ... Lev 25:46 1121
both he, and his *c* with him ... Lev 25:54 1121
For unto me the *c* of Israel are ... Lev 25:55 1121
which shall rob you of your *c* ... Lev 26:22 1121
the *c* of Israel in mount Sinai by ... Lev 26:46 1121
Speak unto the *c* of Israel ... Lev 27:2 1121
the *c* of Israel in mount Sinai ... Lev 27:34 1121
congregation of the *c* of Israel ... Num 1:2 1121
Of the *c* of Joseph ... Num 1:10 1121
the *c* of Reuben, Israel's eldest ... Num 1:20 1121
Of the *c* of Simeon, by their ... Num 1:22 1121
Of the *c* of Gad, by their ... Num 1:24 1121
Of the *c* of Judah, by their ... Num 1:26 1121
Of the *c* of Issachar, by their ... Num 1:28 1121
Of the *c* of Zebulun, by their ... Num 1:30 1121
Of the *c* of Joseph, namely, of ... Num 1:32 1121
of the *c* of Ephraim, by their ... Num 1:32 1121
Of the *c* of Manasseh, by their ... Num 1:34 1121
Of the *c* of Benjamin, by their ... Num 1:36 1121
Of the *c* of Dan, by their ... Num 1:38 1121
Of the *c* of Asher, by their ... Num 1:40 1121
Of the *c* of Naphtali, throughout ... Num 1:42 1121
were numbered of the *c* of Israel ... Num 1:45 1121
sum of them among the *c* of Israel ... Num 1:49 1121
the *c* of Israel shall pitch their ... Num 1:52 1121
congregation of the *c* of Israel ... Num 1:53 1121
the *c* of Israel did according to ... Num 1:54 1121
Every man of the *c* of Israel ... Num 2:2 1121
be captain of the *c* of Judah ... Num 2:3 1121
be captain of the *c* of Issachar ... Num 2:5 1121
be captain of the *c* of Zebulun ... Num 2:7 1121
the captain of the *c* of Reuben ... Num 2:10 1121
the captain of the *c* of Simeon ... Num 2:12 1121
the captain of the *c* of Manasseh ... Num 2:20 1121
the captain of the *c* of Dan shall ... Num 2:25 1121
the captain of the *c* of Asher ... Num 2:27 1121
the captain of the *c* of Naphtali ... Num 2:29 1121
which were numbered of the *c* of ... Num 2:32 1121
numbered among the *c* of Israel ... Num 2:33 1121
the *c* of Israel did according to ... Num 2:34 1121
of Sinai, and they had no *c* ... Num 3:4 1121
and the charge of the *c* of Israel ... Num 3:8 1121
unto him out of the *c* of Israel ... Num 3:9 1121
the Levites from among the *c* of ... Num 3:12 1121
the matrix among the *c* of Israel ... Num 3:12 1121
Number the *c* of Levi after the ... Num 3:15 1121
for the charge of the *c* of Israel ... Num 3:38 1121
the *c* of Israel from a month old ... Num 3:40 1121
firstborn among the *c* of Israel ... Num 3:41 1121
the cattle of the *c* of Israel ... Num 3:41 1121
firstborn among the *c* of Israel ... Num 3:42 1121
firstborn among the *c* of Israel ... Num 3:45 1121
the firstborn of the *c* of Israel ... Num 3:46 1121
Of the firstborn of the *c* of ... Num 3:50 1121
Command the *c* of Israel, that ... Num 5:2 1121
the *c* of Israel did so, and put ... Num 5:4 1121
Moses, so did the *c* of Israel ... Num 5:4 1121
Speak unto the *c* of Israel ... Num 5:6 1121
holy things of the *c* of Israel ... Num 5:9 1121
Speak unto the *c* of Israel ... Num 5:12 1121
Speak unto the *c* of Israel ... Num 6:2 1121
ye shall bless the *c* of Israel ... Num 6:23 1121
put my name upon the *c* of Israel ... Num 6:27 1121
Helon, prince of the *c* of Zebulun ... Num 7:24 1121
prince of the *c* of Reuben ... Num 7:30 1121
prince of the *c* of Simeon ... Num 7:36 1121
of Deuel, prince of the *c* of Gad ... Num 7:42 1121
prince of the *c* of Ephraim ... Num 7:48 1121
prince of the *c* of Manasseh ... Num 7:54 1121
prince of the *c* of Benjamin ... Num 7:60 1121
prince of the *c* of Dan, offered ... Num 7:66 1121
Ocran, prince of the *c* of Asher ... Num 7:72 1121
Enan, prince of the *c* of Naphtali ... Num 7:78 1121
from among the *c* of Israel ... Num 8:6 1121
of the *c* of Israel together ... Num 8:9 1121
the *c* of Israel shall put their ... Num 8:10 1121
an offering of the *c* of Israel ... Num 8:11 1121
from among the *c* of Israel ... Num 8:14 1121
me from among the *c* of Israel ... Num 8:16 1121
firstborn of all the *c* of Israel ... Num 8:16 1121
of the *c* of Israel are mine ... Num 8:17 1121
the firstborn of the *c* of Israel ... Num 8:18 1121
sons from among the *c* of Israel ... Num 8:19 1121
to do the service of the *c* of ... Num 8:19 1121
an atonement for the *c* of Israel ... Num 8:19 1121
no plague among the *c* of Israel ... Num 8:19 1121
when the *c* of Israel come nigh ... Num 8:19 1121
congregation of the *c* of Israel ... Num 8:20 1121
so did the *c* of Israel unto them ... Num 8:20 1121
Let the *c* of Israel also keep the ... Num 9:2 1121
Moses spake unto the *c* of Israel ... Num 9:4 1121
Moses, so did the *c* of Israel ... Num 9:5 1121
season among the *c* of Israel ... Num 9:7 1121
Speak unto the *c* of Israel ... Num 9:10 1121
that the *c* of Israel journeyed ... Num 9:17 1121
there the *c* of Israel pitched ... Num 9:17 1121
LORD the *c* of Israel journeyed ... Num 9:18 1121
then the *c* of Israel kept the ... Num 9:19 1121
the *c* of Israel abode in their ... Num 9:22 1121
the *c* of Israel took their ... Num 10:12 1121
the *c* of Judah according to their ... Num 10:14 1121
the host of the tribe of the *c* of ... Num 10:15 1121
the host of the tribe of the *c* of ... Num 10:16 1121
the host of the tribe of the *c* of ... Num 10:19 1121
the host of the tribe of the *c* of ... Num 10:20 1121
of the *c* of Ephraim set forward ... Num 10:22 1121
c of Manasseh was Gamaliel the ... Num 10:23 1121
the host of the tribe of the *c* of ... Num 10:24 1121
camp of the *c* of Dan set forward ... Num 10:25 1121
the host of the tribe of the *c* of ... Num 10:26 1121
the host of the tribe of the *c* of ... Num 10:27 1121
were the journeyings of the *c* of ... Num 10:28 1121
the *c* of Israel also wept again, ... Num 11:4 1121

which I give unto the c of Israel ... Num 13:2 1121
men were heads of the c of Israel ... Num 13:3 1121
and Talmai, the c of Anak, were ... Num 13:22 3211
c of Israel cut down from thence ... Num 13:24 1121
congregation of the c of Israel ... Num 13:26 1121
we saw the c of Anak there ... Num 13:28 3211
had searched unto the c of Israel ... Num 13:32 1121
all the c of Israel murmured ... Num 14:2 1121
wives and our c should be a prey ... Num 14:3 2945
congregation of the c of Israel ... Num 14:5 1121
the company of the c of Israel ... Num 14:7 1121
before all the c of Israel ... Num 14:10 1121
fathers upon the c unto the third ... Num 14:18 1121
the murmurings of the c of Israel ... Num 14:27 1121
your c shall wander in the ... Num 14:33 1121
sayings unto all the c of Israel ... Num 14:39 1121
Speak unto the c of Israel ... Num 15:2 1121
Speak unto the c of Israel ... Num 15:18 1121
congregation of the c of Israel ... Num 15:25 1121
congregation of the c of Israel ... Num 15:26 1121
is born among the c of Israel ... Num 15:29 1121
while the c of Israel were in the ... Num 15:32 1121
Speak unto the c of Israel ... Num 15:38 1121
with certain of the c of Israel ... Num 16:2 1121
and their sons, and their little c ... Num 16:27 2945
be a sign unto the c of Israel ... Num 16:38 1121
a memorial unto the c of Israel ... Num 16:40 1121
the c of Israel murmured against ... Num 16:41 1121
Speak unto the c of Israel ... Num 17:2 1121
the murmurings of the c of Israel ... Num 17:5 1121
Moses spake unto the c of Israel ... Num 17:6 1121
the LORD unto all the c of Israel ... Num 17:9 1121
the c of Israel spake unto Moses, ... Num 17:12 1121
any more upon the c of Israel ... Num 18:5 1121
from among the c of Israel ... Num 18:6 1121
things of the c of Israel ... Num 18:8 1121
wave offerings of the c of Israel ... Num 18:11 1121
which the c of Israel offer unto ... Num 18:19 1121
inheritance among the c of Israel ... Num 18:20 1121
I have given the c of Levi all ... Num 18:21 1121
Neither must the c of Israel ... Num 18:22 1121
that among the c of Israel they ... Num 18:23 1121
But the tithes of the c of Israel ... Num 18:24 1121
Among the c of Israel they shall ... Num 18:24 1121
When ye take of the c of Israel ... Num 18:26 1121
ye receive of the c of Israel ... Num 18:28 1121
holy things of the c of Israel ... Num 18:32 1121
Speak unto the c of Israel ... Num 19:2 1121
of the c of Israel for a water of ... Num 19:9 1121
it shall be unto the c of Israel ... Num 19:10 1121
Then came the c of Israel ... Num 20:1 1121
me in the eyes of the c of Israel ... Num 20:12 1121
because the c of Israel strove ... Num 20:13 1121
the c of Israel said unto him, We ... Num 20:19 1121
the c of Israel, even the whole ... Num 20:22 1121
I have given unto the c of Israel ... Num 20:24 1121
the c of Israel set forward, and ... Num 21:10 1121
Jabbok, even unto the c of Ammon ... Num 21:24 1121
of the c of Ammon was strong ... Num 21:24 1121
the c of Israel set forward, and ... Num 22:1 1121
because of the c of Israel ... Num 22:3 1121
the land of the c of his people ... Num 22:5 1121
and destroy all the c of Sheth ... Num 24:17 1121
one of the c of Israel came and ... Num 25:6 1121
congregation of the c of Israel ... Num 25:6 1121
was stayed from the c of Israel ... Num 25:8 1121
wrath away from the c of Israel ... Num 25:11 1121
that I consumed not the c of ... Num 25:11 1121
an atonement for the c of Israel ... Num 25:13 1121
congregation of the c of Israel ... Num 26:2 1121
the c of Israel, which went forth ... Num 26:4 1121
the c of Reuben ... Num 26:5 1121
the c of Korah died not ... Num 26:11 1121
The c of Gad after their families ... Num 26:15 1121
These are the families of the c ... Num 26:18 1121
Of the c of Asher after their ... Num 26:44 1121
the numbered of the c of Israel ... Num 26:51 1121
numbered among the c of Israel ... Num 26:62 1121
given them among the c of Israel ... Num 26:62 1121
who numbered the c of Israel in ... Num 26:63 1121
when they numbered the c of ... Num 26:64 1121
shalt speak unto the c of Israel ... Num 27:8 1121
it shall be unto the c of Israel ... Num 27:11 1121
I have given unto the c of Israel ... Num 27:12 1121
the c of Israel may be obedient ... Num 27:20 1121
all the c of Israel with him, ... Num 27:21 1121
Command the c of Israel, and say ... Num 28:2 1121
Moses told the c of Israel ... Num 29:40 1121
tribes concerning the c of Israel ... Num 30:1 1121
Avenge the c of Israel of the ... Num 31:2 1121
the c of Israel took all the ... Num 31:9 1121
congregation of the c of Israel ... Num 31:12 1121
these caused the c of Israel ... Num 31:16 1121
But all the women c, that have ... Num 31:18 2945
of the c of Israel's half, thou ... Num 31:30 1121
of the c of Israel's half, which ... Num 31:42 1121
Even of the c of Israel's half, ... Num 31:47 1121
for a memorial for the c of ... Num 31:54 1121
Now the c of Reuben and the ... Num 32:1 1121
the c of Gad had a very great ... Num 32:1 1121
The c of Gad and the c of ... Num 32:2 1121
And Moses said unto the c of Gad ... Num 32:6 1121
to the c of Reuben, Shall your ... Num 32:6 1121
c of Israel from going over into ... Num 32:7 1121
the heart of the c of Israel ... Num 32:9 1121
armed before the c of Israel ... Num 32:17 1121
until the c of Israel have ... Num 32:18 1121
the c of Gad and the c of ... Num 32:25 1121

of the tribes of the c of Israel ... Num 32:28 1121
said unto them, If the c of Gad ... Num 32:29 1121
the c of Reuben will pass with ... Num 32:29 1121
the c of Gad and the c of ... Num 32:31 1121
unto them, even to the c of Gad ... Num 32:33 1121
to the c of Reuben, and unto half ... Num 32:33 1121
the c of Gad built Dibon, and ... Num 32:34 1121
the c of Reuben built Heshbon, and ... Num 32:37 1121
the c of Machir the son of ... Num 32:39 1121
the journeys of the c of Israel ... Num 33:1 1121
morrow after the passover the c ... Num 33:3 1121
the c of Israel removed from ... Num 33:5 1121
c of Israel were come out of the ... Num 33:38 1121
of the coming of the c of Israel ... Num 33:40 1121
Speak unto the c of Israel ... Num 33:51 1121
Command the c of Israel, and say ... Num 34:2 1121
Moses commanded the c of Israel ... Num 34:13 1121
For the tribe of the c of Reuben ... Num 34:14 1121
the tribe of the c of Gad ... Num 34:14 1121
of the tribe of the c of Simeon ... Num 34:20 1121
of the tribe of the c of Dan ... Num 34:22 1121
The prince of the c of Joseph ... Num 34:23 1121
the tribe of the c of Manasseh ... Num 34:23 1121
of the tribe of the c of Ephraim ... Num 34:24 1121
of the tribe of the c of Zebulun ... Num 34:25 1121
of the tribe of the c of Issachar ... Num 34:26 1121
of the tribe of the c of Asher ... Num 34:27 1121
of the tribe of the c of Naphtali ... Num 34:28 1121
c of Israel in the land of Canaan ... Num 34:29 1121
Command the c of Israel, that ... Num 35:2 1121
the possession of the c of Israel ... Num 35:8 1121
Speak unto the c of Israel ... Num 35:10 1121
refuge, both for the c of Israel ... Num 35:15 1121
LORD dwell among the c of Israel ... Num 35:34 1121
the families of the c of Gilead ... Num 36:1 1121
chief fathers of the c of Israel ... Num 36:1 1121
by lot to the c of Israel ... Num 36:2 1121
other tribes of the c of Israel ... Num 36:3 1121
of the c of Israel shall be ... Num 36:4 1121
Moses commanded the c of Israel ... Num 36:5 1121
not the inheritance of the c of ... Num 36:7 1121
for every one of the c of Israel ... Num 36:7 1121
in any tribe of the c of Israel ... Num 36:8 1121
that the c of Israel may enjoy ... Num 36:8 1121
every one of the tribes of the c ... Num 36:9 1121
by the hand of Moses unto the c ... Num 36:13 1121
Moses spake unto the c of Israel ... Deut 1:3 1121
he hath trodden upon, and to his c ... Deut 1:36 1121
said should be a prey, and your c ... Deut 1:39 1121
of your brethren the c of Esau ... Deut 2:4 1121
from our brethren the c of Esau ... Deut 2:8 1121
the c of Lot for a possession ... Deut 2:9 1121
but the c of Esau succeeded them, ... Deut 2:12 1121
nigh over against the c of Ammon ... Deut 2:19 1121
of the c of Ammon any possession ... Deut 2:19 1121
the c of Lot for a possession ... Deut 2:19 1121
As he did to the c of Esau ... Deut 2:22 1121
(As the c of Esau which dwell in ... Deut 2:29 1121
of the c of Ammon thou camest not ... Deut 2:37 1121
destroying the men, women, and c ... Deut 3:6 2945
not in Rabbath of the c of Ammon ... Deut 3:11 1121
is the border of the c of Ammon ... Deut 3:16 1121
your brethren the c of Israel ... Deut 3:18 1121
and that they may teach their c ... Deut 4:10 1121
beget c, and children's c ... Deut 4:25 1121
with thy c after thee, and that ... Deut 4:40 1121
Moses set before the c of Israel ... Deut 4:44 1121
Moses spake unto the c of Israel ... Deut 4:45 1121
the c of Israel smote, after they ... Deut 4:46 1121
fathers upon the c unto the third ... Deut 5:9 1121
them, and with their c for ever ... Deut 5:29 1121
teach them diligently unto thy c ... Deut 6:7 1121
the c of the Anakims, whom thou ... Deut 9:2 1121
can stand before the c of Anak ... Deut 9:2 1121
the c of Israel took their ... Deut 10:6 1121
of the c of Jaakan to Mosera ... Deut 10:6 1121
with your c which have not known ... Deut 11:2 1121
And ye shall teach them your c ... Deut 11:19 1121
multiplied, and the days of your c ... Deut 11:21 1121
with thy c after thee, when thou ... Deut 12:25 1121
with thy c after thee for ever, ... Deut 12:28 1121
the c of Belial, are gone out ... Deut 13:13 1121
Ye are the c of the LORD your God ... Deut 14:1 1121
days in his kingdom, he, and his c ... Deut 17:20 1121
hated, and they have born him c ... Deut 21:15 1121
The c that are begotten of them ... Deut 23:8 1121
his brethren of the c of Israel ... Deut 24:7 1121
not be put to death for the c ... Deut 24:16 1121
neither shall the c be put to ... Deut 24:16 1121
of his c which he shall leave ... Deut 28:54 1121
flesh of his c which he shall eat ... Deut 28:55 1121
toward her c which she shall bear ... Deut 28:57 1121
Moses to make with the c of ... Deut 29:1 1121
c that shall rise up after you ... Deut 29:22 1121
to our c for ever, that we may do ... Deut 29:29 1121
thee this day, thou and thy c ... Deut 30:2 1121
together, men, and women, and c ... Deut 31:12 2945
And that their c, which have not ... Deut 31:13 1121
you, and teach it the c of Israel ... Deut 31:19 1121
for me against the c of Israel ... Deut 31:19 1121
day, and taught it the c of Israel ... Deut 31:22 1121
for thou shalt bring the c of ... Deut 31:23 1121
spot is not the spot of his c ... Deut 32:5 1121
to the number of the c of Israel ... Deut 32:8 1121
generation, c in whom is no faith ... Deut 32:20 1121
command your c to observe to do ... Deut 32:46 1121
which I give unto the c of Israel ... Deut 32:49 1121
the c of Israel at the waters of ... Deut 32:51 1121

in the midst of the c of Israel ... Deut 32:51 1121
land which I give the c of Israel ... Deut 32:52 1121
the c of Israel before his death ... Deut 33:1 1121
his brethren, nor knew his own c ... Deut 33:9 1121
said, Let Asher be blessed with c ... Deut 33:24 1121
the c of Israel wept for Moses in ... Deut 34:8 1121
the c of Israel hearkened unto ... Deut 34:9 1121
to them, even to the c of Israel ... Josh 1:2 1121
the c of Israel to search out the ... Josh 2:2 1121
all the c of Israel, and lodged ... Josh 3:1 1121
Joshua said unto the c of Israel ... Josh 3:9 1121
had prepared of the c of Israel ... Josh 4:4 1121
of the tribes of the c of Israel ... Josh 4:5 1121
that when your c ask their ... Josh 4:6 1121
unto the c of Israel for ever ... Josh 4:7 1121
the c of Israel did so as Joshua ... Josh 4:8 1121
of the tribes of the c of Israel ... Josh 4:8 1121
the c of Reuben, and the c ... Josh 4:12 1121
over armed before the c of Israel ... Josh 4:12 1121
And he spake unto the c of Israel ... Josh 4:21 1121
When your c shall ask their ... Josh 4:21 1121
Then ye shall let your c know ... Josh 4:22 1121
from before the c of Israel ... Josh 5:1 1121
more, because of the c of Israel ... Josh 5:1 1121
circumcise again the c of Israel ... Josh 5:2 1121
circumcised the c of Israel at ... Josh 5:3 1121
For the c of Israel walked forty ... Josh 5:6 1121
And their c, whom he raised up in ... Josh 5:7 1121
the c of Israel encamped in ... Josh 5:10 1121
neither had the c of Israel manna ... Josh 5:12 1121
up because of the c of Israel ... Josh 6:1 1121
But the c of Israel committed a ... Josh 7:1 1121
kindled against the c of Israel ... Josh 7:1 1121
Therefore the c of Israel could ... Josh 7:12 1121
and unto all the c of Israel ... Josh 7:23 1121
LORD commanded the c of Israel ... Josh 8:31 1121
the presence of the c of Israel ... Josh 8:32 1121
the c of Israel journeyed, and ... Josh 9:17 1121
the c of Israel smote them not, ... Josh 9:18 1121
of the hand of the c of Israel ... Josh 9:26 1121
Joshua and with the c of Israel ... Josh 10:4 1121
c of Israel slew with the sword ... Josh 10:11 1121
Amorites before the c of Israel ... Josh 10:12 1121
the c of Israel had made an end ... Josh 10:20 1121
against any of the c of Israel ... Josh 10:21 1121
the c of Israel took for a prey ... Josh 11:14 1121
made peace with the c of Israel ... Josh 11:19 1121
in the land of the c of Israel ... Josh 11:22 1121
which the c of Israel smote, and ... Josh 12:1 1121
is the border of the c of Ammon ... Josh 12:2 1121
the LORD and the c of Israel smite ... Josh 12:6 1121
the c of Israel smote on this ... Josh 12:7 1121
out from before the c of Israel ... Josh 13:6 1121
unto the border of the c of Ammon ... Josh 13:10 1121
Nevertheless the c of Israel ... Josh 13:13 1121
gave unto the tribe of the c of ... Josh 13:15 1121
did the c of Israel slay with the ... Josh 13:22 1121
the border of the c of Reuben was ... Josh 13:23 1121
c of Reuben after their families ... Josh 13:23 1121
even unto the c of Gad according ... Josh 13:24 1121
half the land of the c of Ammon ... Josh 13:25 1121
the c of Gad after their families ... Josh 13:28 1121
of the half tribe of the c of ... Josh 13:29 1121
were pertaining unto the c of ... Josh 13:31 1121
the c of Machir by their families ... Josh 13:31 1121
are the countries which the c of ... Josh 14:1 1121
of the tribes of the c of Israel ... Josh 14:1 1121
For the c of Joseph were two ... Josh 14:4 1121
so the c of Israel did, and they ... Josh 14:5 1121
Then the c of Judah came unto ... Josh 14:6 1121
while the c of Israel wandered in ... Josh 14:10
the c of Judah by their families ... Josh 15:1 1121
This is the coast of the c of ... Josh 15:12 1121
gave a part among the c of Judah ... Josh 15:13 1121
Ahiman, and Talmai, the c of Anak ... Josh 15:14 3211
the c of Judah according to their ... Josh 15:20 1121
cities of the tribe of the c of ... Josh 15:21 1121
the c of Judah could not drive ... Josh 15:63 1121
the Jebusites dwell with the c of ... Josh 15:63 1121
the lot of the c of Joseph fell ... Josh 16:1 1121
So the c of Joseph, Manasseh and ... Josh 16:4 1121
the border of the c of Ephraim ... Josh 16:5 1121
c of Ephraim by their families ... Josh 16:8 1121
the c of Ephraim were among the ... Josh 16:9 1121
inheritance of the c of Manasseh ... Josh 16:9 1121
c of Manasseh by their families ... Josh 17:2 1121
for the c of Abiezer ... Josh 17:2 1121
for the c of Helek ... Josh 17:2 1121
for the c of Asriel ... Josh 17:2 1121
for the c of Shechem ... Josh 17:2 1121
for the c of Hepher ... Josh 17:2 1121
and for the c of Shemida ... Josh 17:2 1121
these were the male c of Manasseh ... Josh 17:2 1121
belonged to the c of Ephraim ... Josh 17:8 1121
Yet the c of Manasseh could not ... Josh 17:12 1121
when the c of Israel were waxen ... Josh 17:13 1121
the c of Joseph spake unto Joshua ... Josh 17:14 1121
the c of Joseph said, The hill is ... Josh 17:16 1121
the whole congregation of the c ... Josh 18:1 1121
the c of Israel seven tribes ... Josh 18:2 1121
Joshua said unto the c of Israel ... Josh 18:3 1121
divided the land unto the c of ... Josh 18:10 1121
the lot of the tribe of the c of ... Josh 18:11 1121
came forth between the c of Judah ... Josh 18:11 1121
of Judah and the c of Joseph ... Josh 18:11 1121
a city of the c of Judah ... Josh 18:14 1121
inheritance of the c of Benjamin ... Josh 18:20 1121
c of Benjamin according to their ... Josh 18:21 1121

c of Benjamin according to their	Josh 18:28	1121
even for the tribe of the c of	Josh 19:1	1121
the inheritance of the c of Judah	Josh 19:1	1121
c of Simeon according to their	Josh 19:8	1121
Out of the portion of the c of	Josh 19:9	1121
inheritance of the c of Simeon	Josh 19:9	1121
for the part of the c of Judah	Josh 19:9	1121
therefore the c of Simeon had	Josh 19:9	1121
c of Zebulun according to their	Josh 19:10	1121
c of Zebulun according to their	Josh 19:16	1121
for the c of Issachar according	Josh 19:17	1121
c of Issachar according to their	Josh 19:23	1121
the c of Asher according to their	Josh 19:24	1121
the c of Asher according to their	Josh 19:31	1121
lot came out to the c of Naphtali	Josh 19:32	1121
even for the c of Naphtali	Josh 19:32	1121
c of Naphtali according to their	Josh 19:39	1121
the c of Dan according to their	Josh 19:40	1121
the coast of the c of Dan went	Josh 19:47	1121
therefore the c of Dan went up to	Josh 19:47	1121
the c of Dan according to their	Josh 19:48	1121
coasts, the c of Israel gave an	Josh 19:49	1121
of the tribes of the c of Israel	Josh 19:51	1121
Speak to the c of Israel, saying,	Josh 20:2	1121
appointed for all the c of Israel	Josh 20:9	1121
of the tribes of the c of Israel	Josh 21:1	1121
the c of Israel gave unto the	Josh 21:3	1121
the c of Aaron the priest, which	Josh 21:4	1121
the rest of the c of Kohath had	Josh 21:5	1121
the c of Gershon had by lot out	Josh 21:6	1121
The c of Merari by their families	Josh 21:7	1121
the c of Israel gave by lot unto	Josh 21:8	1121
of the tribe of the c of Judah	Josh 21:9	1121
of the tribe of the c of Simeon	Josh 21:9	1121
Which the c of Aaron, being of	Josh 21:10	1121
who were of the c of Levi	Josh 21:10	1121
Thus they gave to the c of Aaron	Josh 21:13	1121
All the cities of the c of Aaron	Josh 21:19	1121
the families of the c of Kohath	Josh 21:20	1121
which remained of the c of Kohath	Josh 21:20	1121
of the c of Kohath that remained	Josh 21:26	1121
unto the c of Gershon, of the	Josh 21:27	1121
the families of the c of Merari	Josh 21:34	1121
So all the cities for the c of	Josh 21:40	1121
of the c of Israel were forty	Josh 21:41	1121
the c of Reuben and the c	Josh 22:9	1121
departed from the c of Israel out	Josh 22:9	1121
the c of Reuben and the c	Josh 22:10	1121
the c of Israel heard say, Behold	Josh 22:11	1121
the c of Reuben and the c	Josh 22:11	1121
at the passage of the c of Israel	Josh 22:11	1121
when the c of Israel heard of it,	Josh 22:12	1121
c of Israel gathered themselves	Josh 22:12	1121
the c of Israel sent unto the	Josh 22:13	1121
Israel sent unto the c of Reuben	Josh 22:13	1121
and to the c of Gad	Josh 22:13	1121
And they came unto the c of Reuben	Josh 22:15	1121
and to the c of Gad	Josh 22:15	1121
Then the c of Reuben and the	Josh 22:21	1121
the c of Gad and the half tribe of	Josh 22:21	1121
c might speak unto our c	Josh 22:24	1121
ye c of Reuben and c of Gad	Josh 22:25	1121
so shall your c make our c	Josh 22:25	1121
your c may not say to our c	Josh 22:27	1121
the words that the c of Reuben	Josh 22:30	1121
the c of Gad and the c of	Josh 22:30	1121
c of Reuben, and to the c of Gad	Josh 22:31	1121
to the c of Manasseh, This day we	Josh 22:31	1121
now ye have delivered the c of	Josh 22:31	1121
returned from the c of Reuben	Josh 22:32	1121
and from the c of Gad	Josh 22:32	1121
to the c of Israel, and brought	Josh 22:32	1121
the thing pleased the c of Israel	Josh 22:33	1121
the c of Israel blessed God, and	Josh 22:33	1121
the land wherein the c of Reuben	Josh 22:33	1121
the c of Reuben and the c of	Josh 22:34	1121
his c went down into Egypt	Josh 24:4	1121
which the c of Israel brought up	Josh 24:32	1121
inheritance of the c of Joseph	Josh 24:32	1121
that the c of Israel asked the	Judg 1:1	1121
Now the c of Judah had fought	Judg 1:8	1121
afterward the c of Judah went	Judg 1:9	1121
the c of the Kenite, Moses'	Judg 1:16	1121
c of Judah into the wilderness of	Judg 1:16	1121
the c of Benjamin did not drive	Judg 1:21	1121
the Jebusites dwell with the c of	Judg 1:21	1121
the Amorites forced the c of Dan	Judg 1:34	1121
words unto all the c of Israel	Judg 2:4	1121
the c of Israel went every man	Judg 2:6	1121
the c of Israel did evil in the	Judg 2:11	1121
of the c of Israel might know	Judg 3:2	1121
the c of Israel dwelt among the	Judg 3:5	1121
the c of Israel did evil in the	Judg 3:7	1121
and the c of Israel served	Judg 3:8	1121
when the c of Israel cried unto	Judg 3:9	1121
up a deliverer to the c of Israel	Judg 3:9	1121
the c of Israel did evil again in	Judg 3:12	1121
gathered unto him the c of Ammon	Judg 3:13	1121
So the c of Israel served Eglon	Judg 3:14	1121
But when the c of Israel cried	Judg 3:15	1121
by him the c of Israel sent a	Judg 3:15	1121
the c of Israel went down with	Judg 3:27	1121
the c of Israel again did evil in	Judg 4:1	1121
the c of Israel cried unto the	Judg 4:3	1121
oppressed the c of Israel	Judg 4:3	1121
the c of Israel came up to her	Judg 4:5	1121
thousand men of the c of Naphtali	Judg 4:6	1121
Naphtali and of the c of Zebulun	Judg 4:6	1121
which was of the c of Hobab the	Judg 4:11	1121
of Canaan before the c of Israel	Judg 4:23	1121
the hand of the c of Israel	Judg 4:24	1121
the c of Israel did evil in the	Judg 6:1	1121
c of Israel made them the dens	Judg 6:2	1121
the c of the east, even they came	Judg 6:3	1121
the c of Israel cried unto the	Judg 6:6	1121
when the c of Israel cried unto	Judg 6:7	1121
a prophet unto the c of Israel	Judg 6:8	1121
the c of the east were gathered	Judg 6:33	1121
all the c of the east lay along	Judg 7:12	1121
the hosts of the c of the east	Judg 8:10	1121
one resembled the c of a king	Judg 8:18	1121
subdued before the c of Israel	Judg 8:28	1121
that the c of Israel turned again	Judg 8:33	1121
the c of Israel remembered not	Judg 8:34	1121
the c of Israel did evil again in	Judg 10:6	1121
and the gods of the c of Ammon	Judg 10:6	1121
into the hands of the c of Ammon	Judg 10:7	1121
and oppressed the c of Israel	Judg 10:8	1121
all the c of Israel that were on	Judg 10:8	1121
Moreover the c of Ammon passed	Judg 10:9	1121
the c of Israel cried unto the	Judg 10:10	1121
LORD said unto the c of Israel	Judg 10:11	1121
the Amorites, from the c of Ammon	Judg 10:11	1121
the c of Israel said unto the	Judg 10:15	1121
Then the c of Ammon were gathered	Judg 10:17	1121
the c of Israel assembled	Judg 10:17	1121
to fight against the c of Ammon	Judg 10:18	1121
that the c of Ammon made war	Judg 11:4	1121
that when the c of Ammon made war	Judg 11:5	1121
we may fight with the c of Ammon	Judg 11:6	1121
and fight against the c of Ammon	Judg 11:8	1121
to fight against the c of Ammon	Judg 11:9	1121
unto the king of the c of Ammon	Judg 11:12	1121
the king of the c of Ammon	Judg 11:13	1121
unto the king of the c of Ammon	Judg 11:14	1121
nor the land of the c of Ammon	Judg 11:15	1121
c of Israel and the c of Ammon	Judg 11:27	1121
Howbeit the king of the c of	Judg 11:28	1121
passed over unto the c of Ammon	Judg 11:29	1121
the c of Ammon into mine hands	Judg 11:30	1121
in peace from the c of Ammon	Judg 11:31	1121
Jephthah passed over unto the c	Judg 11:32	1121
Thus the c of Ammon were subdued	Judg 11:33	1121
subdued before the c of Israel	Judg 11:33	1121
enemies, even of the c of Ammon	Judg 11:36	1121
to fight against the c of Ammon	Judg 12:1	1121
great strife with the c of Ammon	Judg 12:2	1121
over against the c of Ammon	Judg 12:3	1121
the c of Israel did evil again in	Judg 13:1	1121
a riddle unto the c of my people	Judg 14:16	1121
the riddle to the c of her people	Judg 14:17	1121
the c of Dan sent of their family	Judg 18:2	1121
war, which were of the c of Dan	Judg 18:16	1121
and overtook the c of Dan	Judg 18:22	1121
And they cried unto the c of Dan	Judg 18:23	1121
the c of Dan said unto him, Let	Judg 18:25	1121
the c of Dan went their way	Judg 18:26	1121
the c of Dan set up the graven	Judg 18:30	1121
that is not of the c of Israel	Judg 19:12	1121
c of Israel came up out of the	Judg 19:30	1121
Then all the c of Israel went out	Judg 20:1	1121
(Now the c of Benjamin heard that	Judg 20:3	1121
the c of Israel were gone up to	Judg 20:3	1121
Then said the c of Israel	Judg 20:3	1121
Behold, ye are all c of Israel	Judg 20:7	1121
the c of Belial, which are in	Judg 20:13	1121
But the c of Benjamin would not	Judg 20:13	1121
of their brethren the c of Israel	Judg 20:13	1121
But the c of Benjamin gathered	Judg 20:14	1121
to battle against the c of Israel	Judg 20:14	1121
the c of Benjamin were numbered	Judg 20:15	1121
the c of Israel arose, and went up	Judg 20:18	1121
battle against the c of Benjamin	Judg 20:18	1121
the c of Israel rose up in the	Judg 20:19	1121
the c of Benjamin came forth out	Judg 20:21	1121
the c of Israel went up and wept	Judg 20:23	1121
the c of Benjamin my brother	Judg 20:23	1121
the c of Israel came near against	Judg 20:24	1121
the c of Benjamin the second day	Judg 20:24	1121
of the c of Israel again eighteen	Judg 20:25	1121
Then all the c of Israel, and all	Judg 20:26	1121
the c of Israel enquired of the	Judg 20:27	1121
the c of Benjamin my brother	Judg 20:28	1121
the c of Israel went up against	Judg 20:30	1121
c of Benjamin on the third day	Judg 20:30	1121
the c of Benjamin went out	Judg 20:31	1121
the c of Benjamin said, They are	Judg 20:32	1121
But the c of Israel said, Let us	Judg 20:32	1121
the c of Israel destroyed of the	Judg 20:35	1121
So the c of Benjamin saw that	Judg 20:36	1121
again upon the c of Benjamin	Judg 20:48	1121
the c of Israel said, Who is	Judg 21:5	1121
the c of Israel repented them for	Judg 21:6	1121
sword, with the women and the c	Judg 21:10	2945
sent some to speak to the c of	Judg 21:13	1121
for the c of Israel have sworn,	Judg 21:18	1121
they commanded the c of Benjamin	Judg 21:20	1121
the c of Benjamin did so, and took	Judg 21:23	1121
the c of Israel departed thence	Judg 21:24	1121
had c, but Hannah had no c	1Sa 1:2	3206
that hath many c is waxed feeble	1Sa 2:5	1121
made by fire of the c of Israel	1Sa 2:28	1121
Then the c of Israel did put away	1Sa 7:4	1121
Samuel judged the c of Israel in	1Sa 7:6	1121
the c of Israel were gathered	1Sa 7:7	1121
when the c of Israel heard it,	1Sa 7:7	1121
the c of Israel said to Samuel,	1Sa 7:8	1121
there was not among the c of	1Sa 9:2	1121
And said unto the c of Israel	1Sa 10:18	1121
But the c of Belial said, How	1Sa 10:27	1121
the c of Israel were three	1Sa 11:8	1121
the c of Ammon came against you	1Sa 12:12	1121
at that time with the c of Israel	1Sa 14:18	1121
Moab, and against the c of Ammon	1Sa 14:47	1121
kindness to all the c of Israel	1Sa 15:6	1121
unto Jesse, Are here all thy c	1Sa 16:11	5288
the c of Israel returned from	1Sa 17:53	1121
the sword, both men and women, c	1Sa 22:19	5768
but if they be the c of men	1Sa 26:19	1121
to every man his wife and his c	1Sa 30:22	1121
the c of Judah the use of the bow	2Sa 1:18	1121
the c of Benjamin gathered	2Sa 2:25	1121
Beerothite, of the c of Benjamin	2Sa 4:2	1121
up the c of Israel out of Egypt	2Sa 7:6	1121
I have walked with all the c of	2Sa 7:7	1121
neither shall the c of wickedness	2Sa 7:10	1121
with the stripes of the c of men	2Sa 7:14	1121
of the c of Ammon, and of the	2Sa 8:12	1121
the king of the c of Ammon died	2Sa 10:1	1121
into the land of the c of Ammon	2Sa 10:2	1121
the princes of the c of Ammon	2Sa 10:3	1121
when the c of Ammon saw that they	2Sa 10:6	1121
the c of Ammon sent and hired the	2Sa 10:6	1121
the c of Ammon came out, and put	2Sa 10:8	1121
in array against the c of Ammon	2Sa 10:10	1121
but if the c of Ammon be too	2Sa 10:11	1121
when the c of Ammon saw that the	2Sa 10:14	1121
Joab returned from the c of Ammon	2Sa 10:14	1121
to help the c of Ammon any more	2Sa 10:19	1121
and they destroyed the c of Ammon	2Sa 11:1	1121
together with him, and with his c	2Sa 12:3	1121
with the sword of the c of Ammon	2Sa 12:9	1121
against Rabbah of the c of Ammon	2Sa 12:26	1121
all the cities of the c of Ammon	2Sa 12:31	1121
of Rabbah of the c of Ammon	2Sa 17:27	1121
were not of the c of Israel	2Sa 21:2	1121
the c of Israel had sworn unto	2Sa 21:2	1121
in his zeal to the c of Israel	2Sa 21:2	1121
of Gibeah of the c of Benjamin	2Sa 23:29	1121
If thy c take heed to their way,	1Kin 2:4	1121
of all the c of the east country	1Kin 4:30	1121
eightieth year after the c of	1Kin 6:1	1121
will dwell among the c of Israel	1Kin 6:13	1121
of the fathers of the c of Israel	1Kin 8:1	1121
a covenant with the c of Israel	1Kin 8:9	1121
so that thy c take heed to their	1Kin 8:25	1121
the hearts of all the c of men	1Kin 8:39	1121
all the c of Israel dedicated the	1Kin 8:63	1121
from following me, ye or your c	1Kin 9:6	1121
which were not of the c of Israel	1Kin 9:20	1121
Their c that were left after them	1Kin 9:21	1121
whom the c of Israel also were	1Kin 9:21	1121
But of the c of Israel did	1Kin 9:22	1121
LORD said unto the c of Israel	1Kin 11:2	1121
the abomination of the c of Ammon	1Kin 11:7	1121
Milcom the god of the c of Ammon	1Kin 11:33	1121
But as for the c of Israel which	1Kin 12:17	1121
your brethren the c of Israel	1Kin 12:24	1121
a feast unto the c of Israel	1Kin 12:33	1121
cast out before the c of Israel	1Kin 14:24	1121
sent unto all the c of Israel	1Kin 18:20	1121
for the c of Israel have forsaken	1Kin 19:10	1121
because the c of Israel have	1Kin 19:14	1121
thy wives also and thy c, even the	1Kin 20:3	1121
thy gold, and thy wives, and thy c	1Kin 20:5	1121
unto me for my wives, and for my c	1Kin 20:7	1121
people, even all the c of Israel	1Kin 20:15	1121
the c of Israel were numbered, and	1Kin 20:27	1121
the c of Israel pitched before	1Kin 20:27	1121
the c of Israel slew of the	1Kin 20:29	1121
c of Belial, and sat before him	1Kin 21:13	1121
cast out before the c of Israel	1Kin 21:26	1121
forth little c out of the city	2Kin 2:23	5288
and tare forty and two c of them	2Kin 2:24	3206
and live thou and thy c of the rest	2Kin 4:7	1121
thou wilt do unto the c of Israel	2Kin 8:12	1121
the sword, and wilt dash their c	2Kin 8:12	6768
him alway a light, and to his c	2Kin 8:19	1121
one of the c of the prophets	2Kin 9:1	1121
to them that brought up Ahab's c	2Kin 10:1	
also, and the bringers up of the c	2Kin 10:5	
down to salute the c of the king	2Kin 10:13	1121
of the king and the c of the queen	2Kin 10:13	1121
thy c of the fourth generation	2Kin 10:30	1121
the c of Israel dwelt in their	2Kin 13:5	1121
But the c of the murderers he	2Kin 14:6	1121
not be put to death for the c	2Kin 14:6	1121
nor the c be put to death for the	2Kin 14:6	1121
out from before the c of Israel	2Kin 16:3	1121
that the c of Israel had sinned	2Kin 17:7	1121
out from before the c of Israel	2Kin 17:8	1121
the c of Israel did secretly	2Kin 17:9	1121
For the c of Israel walked in all	2Kin 17:22	1121
instead of the c of Israel	2Kin 17:24	1121
their c in fire to Adrammelech	2Kin 17:31	1121
the LORD commanded the c of Jacob	2Kin 17:34	1121
c, and their children's c	2Kin 17:41	1121
for unto those days the c of	2Kin 18:4	1121
for the c are come to the birth,	2Kin 19:3	1121
the c of Eden which were in	2Kin 19:12	1121
cast out before the c of Israel	2Kin 21:2	1121
destroyed before the c of Israel	2Kin 21:9	1121
the graves of the c of the people	2Kin 23:6	1121
in the valley of the c of Hinnom	2Kin 23:10	1121

the abomination of the *c* of Ammon 2Kin 23:13 1121
and bands of the *c* of Ammon 2Kin 24:2 1121
king reigned over the *c* of Israel............. 1Chr 1:43 1121
Nahshon, prince of the *c* of Judah 1Chr 2:10 1121
Hezron begat *c* of Azubah his wife......... 1Chr 2:18
but Seled died without *c* 1Chr 2:30 1121
And the *c* of Sheshan 1Chr 2:31 1121
and Jether died without *c*....................... 1Chr 2:32 1121
but his brethren had not many *c*............ 1Chr 4:27 1121
multiply, like to the *c* of Judah.............. 1Chr 4:27 1121
the *c* of Gad dwelt over against 1Chr 5:11 1121
These are the *c* of Abihail the 1Chr 5:14 1121
the *c* of the half tribe of........................ 1Chr 5:23 1121
And the *c* of Amram............................... 1Chr 6:3 1121
are they that waited with their *c* 1Chr 6:33 1121
the *c* of Israel gave to the..................... 1Chr 6:64 1121
of the tribe of the *c* of Judah.................. 1Chr 6:65 1121
of the tribe of the *c* of Simeon 1Chr 6:65 1121
of the tribe of the *c* of Benjamin............. 1Chr 6:65 1121
Unto the rest of the *c* of Merari 1Chr 6:77 1121
the *c* of Ir, and Hushim, the sons 1Chr 7:12 1121
the borders of the *c* of Manasseh 1Chr 7:29 1121
In these dwelt the *c* of Joseph 1Chr 7:29 1121
These are the *c* of Japhlet........................ 1Chr 7:33 1121
All these were the *c* of Asher 1Chr 7:40 1121
Shaharaim begat *c* in the country........... 1Chr 8:8
Jerusalem dwelt of the *c* of Judah........... 1Chr 9:3 1121
of the *c* of Benjamin 1Chr 9:3 1121
of the *c* of Ephraim, and Manasseh 1Chr 9:3 1121
of the *c* of Pharez the son of 1Chr 9:4 1121
in the companies of the *c* of Levi 1Chr 9:18 1121
their *c* had the oversight of the............. 1Chr 9:23 1121
pertained to the *c* of Benjamin................ 1Chr 11:31 1121
there came of the *c* of Benjamin 1Chr 12:16 1121
The *c* of Judah that bare shield.............. 1Chr 12:24 1121
Of the *c* of Simeon, mighty men of 1Chr 12:25 1121
Of the *c* of Levi four thousand and......... 1Chr 12:26 1121
of the *c* of Benjamin, the kindred 1Chr 12:29 1121
of the *c* of Ephraim twenty 1Chr 12:30 1121
of the *c* of Issachar, which were 1Chr 12:32 1121
his *c* which he had in Jerusalem 1Chr 14:4 3205
And David assembled the *c* of Aaron...... 1Chr 15:4 1121
the *c* of the Levites bare the ark 1Chr 15:15 1121
ye *c* of Jacob, his chosen ones 1Chr 16:13 1121
neither shall the *c* of wickedness 1Chr 17:9 1121
from Moab, and from the *c* of Ammon.... 1Chr 18:11 1121
the king of the *c* of Ammon died 1Chr 19:1 1121
land of the *c* of Ammon to Hanun 1Chr 19:2 1121
of the *c* of Ammon said to Hanun 1Chr 19:3 1121
when the *c* of Ammon saw that they....... 1Chr 19:6 1121
the *c* of Ammon sent a thousand............. 1Chr 19:6 1121
And the *c* of Ammon gathered 1Chr 19:7 1121
the *c* of Ammon came out, and put 1Chr 19:9 1121
in array against the *c* of Ammon............ 1Chr 19:11 1121
but if the *c* of Ammon be too 1Chr 19:12 1121
when the *c* of Ammon saw that the 1Chr 19:15 1121
help the *c* of Ammon any more 1Chr 19:19 1121
the country of the *c* of Ammon 1Chr 20:1 1121
all the cities of the *c* of Ammon............. 1Chr 20:3 1121
that was of the *c* of the giant 1Chr 20:4 3211
before their father, and had no *c*............ 1Chr 24:2 1121
of the *c* of Merari, had sons 1Chr 26:10 1121
Now the *c* of Israel after their................. 1Chr 27:1 1121
Of the *c* of Perez was the chief................ 1Chr 27:3 1121
the Pelonite, of the *c* of Ephraim 1Chr 27:10 1121
Pirathonite, of the *c* of Ephraim 1Chr 27:14 1121
Of the *c* of Ephraim, Hoshea the............. 1Chr 27:20 1121
for your *c* after you for ever 1Chr 28:8 1121
of the fathers of the *c* of Israel............... 2Chr 5:2 1121
a covenant with the *c* of Israel................ 2Chr 5:10 1121
that he made with the *c* of Israel 2Chr 6:11 1121
yet so that thy *c* take heed to 2Chr 6:16 1121
the hearts of the *c* of men........................ 2Chr 6:30 1121
when all the *c* of Israel saw how............. 2Chr 7:3 1121
caused the *c* of Israel to dwell................. 2Chr 8:2 1121
But of their *c*, who were left 2Chr 8:8 1121
whom the *c* of Israel consumed not 2Chr 8:8 1121
But of the *c* of Israel did 2Chr 8:9 1121
But as for the *c* of Israel that................. 2Chr 10:17 1121
the *c* of Israel stoned him with 2Chr 10:18 1121
Which bare him *c* 2Chr 11:19 1121
dispersed of all his *c* throughout............ 2Chr 11:23 1121
men, the *c* of Belial, and have 2Chr 13:7 1121
O *c* of Israel, fight ye not 2Chr 13:12 1121
the *c* of Israel fled before Judah............... 2Chr 13:16 1121
Thus the *c* of Israel were brought 2Chr 13:18 1121
the *c* of Judah prevailed, because 2Chr 13:18 1121
this also, that the *c* of Moab..................... 2Chr 20:1 1121
the *c* of Ammon, and with them................ 2Chr 20:1 1121
the *c* of Ammon and Moab and mount ... 2Chr 20:10 1121
ones, their wives, and their *c*................... 2Chr 20:13 1121
of the *c* of the Kohathites, and of 2Chr 20:19 1121
of the *c* of the Korhites, stood................. 2Chr 20:19 1121
against the *c* of Ammon, Moab, and 2Chr 20:22 1121
For the *c* of Ammon and Moab stood....... 2Chr 20:23 1121
LORD smite thy people, and thy *c*........... 2Chr 21:14 1121
But he slew not their *c*, but did 2Chr 25:4 1121
fathers shall not die for the *c*................. 2Chr 25:4 1121
neither shall the *c* die for the.................. 2Chr 25:4 1121
to wit, with all the *c* of Ephraim 2Chr 25:7 1121
smote of the *c* of Seir ten 2Chr 25:11 1121
the *c* of Judah carry away captive........... 2Chr 25:12 1121
brought the gods of the *c* of Seir............. 2Chr 25:14 1121
the *c* of Ammon gave him the same 2Chr 27:5 1121
So much did the *c* of Ammon pay 2Chr 27:5 1121
burnt his *c* in the fire, after.................... 2Chr 28:3 1121
cast out before the *c* of Israel.................. 2Chr 28:3 1121
the *c* of Israel carried away...................... 2Chr 28:8 1121
to keep under the *c* of Judah.................... 2Chr 28:10 1121
of the heads of the *c* of Ephraim............. 2Chr 28:12 1121
Ye *c* of Israel, turn again unto................ 2Chr 30:6 1121
your *c* shall find compassion.................. 2Chr 30:9 1121
the *c* of Israel that were present............. 2Chr 30:21 1121
Then all the *c* of Israel returned 2Chr 31:1 1121
the *c* of Israel brought in......................... 2Chr 31:5 1121
And concerning the *c* of Israel 2Chr 31:6 1121
cast out before the *c* of Israel.................. 2Chr 33:2 1121
he caused his *c* to pass through.............. 2Chr 33:6 1121
destroyed before the *c* of Israel 2Chr 33:9 1121
that pertained to the *c* of Israel 2Chr 34:33 1121
the *c* of Israel that were present............. 2Chr 35:17 1121
Now these are the *c* of the....................... Ezr 2:1 1121
The *c* of Parosh, two thousand an........... Ezr 2:3 1121
The *c* of Shephatiah, three .... Ezr 2:4 1121
The *c* of Arah, seven hundred .... Ezr 2:5 1121
The *c* of Pahath-moab .... Ezr 2:6 1121
of the *c* of Jeshua and Joab, two .... Ezr 2:6 1121
The *c* of Elam, a thousand two .... Ezr 2:7 1121
The *c* of Zattu, nine hundred .... Ezr 2:8 1121
The *c* of Zaccai, seven hundred and......... Ezr 2:9 1121
The *c* of Bani, six hundred forty .... Ezr 2:10 1121
The *c* of Bebai, six hundred .... Ezr 2:11 1121
The *c* of Azgad, a thousand two.............. Ezr 2:12 1121
The *c* of Adonikam, six hundred.............. Ezr 2:13 1121
The *c* of Bigvai, two thousand................. Ezr 2:14 1121
The *c* of Adin, four hundred fifty............. Ezr 2:15 1121
The *c* of Ater of Hezekiah, ninety........... Ezr 2:16 1121
The *c* of Bezai, three hundred .... Ezr 2:17 1121
The *c* of Jorah, an hundred and .... Ezr 2:18 1121
The *c* of Hashum, two hundred .... Ezr 2:19 1121
The *c* of Gibbar, ninety and five.............. Ezr 2:20 1121
The *c* of Beth-lehem, an hundred............. Ezr 2:21 1121
The *c* of Azmaveth, forty and two........... Ezr 2:24 1121
The *c* of Kirjath-arim, Chephirah, ... Ezr 2:25 1121
The *c* of Ramah and Gaba, six .... Ezr 2:26 1121
The *c* of Nebo, fifty and two .... Ezr 2:29 1121
The *c* of Magbish, an hundred.................. Ezr 2:30 1121
The *c* of the other Elam, a........................ Ezr 2:31 1121
The *c* of Harim, three hundred and.......... Ezr 2:32 1121
The *c* of Lod, Hadid, and Ono,.................. Ezr 2:33 1121
The *c* of Jericho, three hundred................ Ezr 2:34 1121
The *c* of Senaah, three thousand .... Ezr 2:35 1121
the *c* of Jedaiah, of the house of.............. Ezr 2:36 1121
The *c* of Immer, a thousand fifty............. Ezr 2:37 1121
The *c* of Pashur, a thousand two .... Ezr 2:38 1121
The *c* of Harim, a thousand and............... Ezr 2:39 1121
the *c* of Jeshua and Kadmiel .... Ezr 2:40 1121
of the *c* of Hodaviah, seventy and........... Ezr 2:40 1121
the *c* of Asaph, an hundred twenty......... Ezr 2:41 1121
The *c* of the porters .... Ezr 2:42 1121
the *c* of Shallum .... Ezr 2:42 1121
the *c* of Ater.. Ezr 2:42 1121
the *c* of Talmon.. Ezr 2:42 1121
the *c* of Akkub.. Ezr 2:42 1121
the *c* of Hatita .... Ezr 2:42 1121
the *c* of Shobai, in all an .... Ezr 2:42 1121
the *c* of Ziha .... Ezr 2:43 1121
the *c* of Hasupha .... Ezr 2:43 1121
the *c* of Tabbaoth...................................... Ezr 2:43 1121
The *c* of Keros .... Ezr 2:44 1121
the *c* of Siaha .... Ezr 2:44 1121
the *c* of Padon... Ezr 2:44 1121
The *c* of Lebanah....................................... Ezr 2:45 1121
the *c* of Hagabah .... Ezr 2:45 1121
the *c* of Akkub... Ezr 2:45 1121
The *c* of Hagab .... Ezr 2:46 1121
the *c* of Shalmai .... Ezr 2:46 1121
the *c* of Hanan... Ezr 2:46 1121
The *c* of Giddel.. Ezr 2:47 1121
the *c* of Gahar... Ezr 2:47 1121
the *c* of Reaiah.. Ezr 2:47 1121
The *c* of Rezin... Ezr 2:48 1121
the *c* of Nekoda .... Ezr 2:48 1121
the *c* of Gazzam.. Ezr 2:48 1121
The *c* of Uzza.. Ezr 2:49 1121
the *c* of Paseah.. Ezr 2:49 1121
the *c* of Besai .... Ezr 2:49 1121
The *c* of Asnah... Ezr 2:50 1121
the *c* of Mehunim .... Ezr 2:50 1121
the *c* of Nephusim .... Ezr 2:50 1121
The *c* of Bakbuk .... Ezr 2:51 1121
the *c* of Hakupha .... Ezr 2:51 1121
the *c* of Harhur.. Ezr 2:51 1121
The *c* of Bazluth .... Ezr 2:52 1121
the *c* of Mehida... Ezr 2:52 1121
the *c* of Harsha .... Ezr 2:52 1121
The *c* of Barkos... Ezr 2:53 1121
the *c* of Sisera... Ezr 2:53 1121
the *c* of Thamah.. Ezr 2:53 1121
The *c* of Neziah .... Ezr 2:54 1121
the *c* of Hatipha.. Ezr 2:54 1121
The *c* of Solomon's servants .... Ezr 2:55 1121
the *c* of Sotai .... Ezr 2:55 1121
the *c* of Sophereth .... Ezr 2:55 1121
the *c* of Peruda .... Ezr 2:55 1121
The *c* of Jaalah .... Ezr 2:56 1121
the *c* of Darkon.. Ezr 2:56 1121
the *c* of Giddel.. Ezr 2:56 1121
The *c* of Shephatiah .... Ezr 2:57 1121
the *c* of Hattil .... Ezr 2:57 1121
the *c* of Pochereth of Zebaim .... Ezr 2:57 1121
the *c* of Ami .... Ezr 2:57 1121
the *c* of Solomon's servants, were .... Ezr 2:58 1121
The *c* of Delaiah .... Ezr 2:60 1121
the *c* of Tobiah.. Ezr 2:60 1121
the *c* of Nekoda, six hundred .... Ezr 2:60 1121
And of the *c* of the priests....................... Ezr 2:61 1121
the *c* of Habaiah .... Ezr 2:61 1121
the *c* of Koz .... Ezr 2:61 1121
the *c* of Barzillai.. Ezr 2:61 1121
the *c* of Israel were in the......................... Ezr 3:1 1121
Benjamin heard that the *c* of the .... Ezr 4:1 1121
the *c* of Israel, the priests, and................ Ezr 6:16 1121
and the rest of the *c* of the .... Ezr 6:16 1121
the *c* of the captivity kept the................. Ezr 6:19 1121
for all the *c* of the captivity .... Ezr 6:20 1121
the *c* of Israel, which were come............. Ezr 6:21 1121
went up some of the *c* of Israel .... Ezr 7:7 1121
Also the *c* of those that had been............ Ezr 8:35 1121
an inheritance to your *c* for ever............ Ezr 9:12 1121
congregation of men and women and *c*... Ezr 10:1 3206
unto all the *c* of the captivity.................. Ezr 10:7 1121
the *c* of the captivity did so.................... Ezr 10:16 1121
them had wives by whom they had *c* ...... Ezr 10:44 1121
for the *c* of Israel thy servants,............... Neh 1:6 1121
the sins of the *c* of Israel .... Neh 1:6 1121
the welfare of the *c* of Israel .... Neh 2:10 1121
brethren, our *c* as their *c* .... Neh 5:5 1121
These are the *c* of the province, ... Neh 7:6 1121
The *c* of Parosh, two thousand an........... Neh 7:8 1121
The *c* of Shephatiah, three .... Neh 7:9 1121
The *c* of Arah, six hundred fifty .... Neh 7:10 1121
The *c* of Pahath-moab.............................. Neh 7:11 1121
of the *c* of Jeshua and Joab, two .... Neh 7:11 1121
The *c* of Elam, a thousand two .... Neh 7:12 1121
The *c* of Zattu, eight hundred .... Neh 7:13 1121
The *c* of Zaccai, seven hundred and......... Neh 7:14 1121
The *c* of Binnui, six hundred.................... Neh 7:15 1121
The *c* of Bebai, six hundred .... Neh 7:16 1121
The *c* of Azgad, two thousand.................. Neh 7:17 1121
The *c* of Adonikam, six hundred.............. Neh 7:18 1121
The *c* of Bigvai, two thousand.................. Neh 7:19 1121
The *c* of Adin, six hundred fifty.............. Neh 7:20 1121
The *c* of Ater of Hezekiah, ninety........... Neh 7:21 1121
The *c* of Hashum, three hundred............. Neh 7:22 1121
The *c* of Bezai, three hundred.................. Neh 7:23 1121
The *c* of Hariph, an hundred and............ Neh 7:24 1121
The *c* of Gibeon, ninety and five............. Neh 7:25 1121
The *c* of the other Elam, a....................... Neh 7:34 1121
The *c* of Harim, three hundred and .... Neh 7:35 1121
The *c* of Jericho, three hundred............... Neh 7:36 1121
The *c* of Lod, Hadid, and Ono,.................. Neh 7:37 1121
The *c* of Senaah, three thousand............. Neh 7:38 1121
the *c* of Jedaiah, of the house of.............. Neh 7:39 1121
The *c* of Immer, a thousand fifty............. Neh 7:40 1121
The *c* of Pashur, a thousand two .... Neh 7:41 1121
The *c* of Harim, a thousand and............... Neh 7:42 1121
the *c* of Jeshua, of Kadmiel, and.............. Neh 7:43 1121
of the *c* of Hodevah, seventy and .... Neh 7:43 1121
the *c* of Asaph, an hundred forty .... Neh 7:44 1121
the *c* of Shallum .... Neh 7:45 1121
the *c* of Ater.. Neh 7:45 1121
the *c* of Talmon.. Neh 7:45 1121
the *c* of Akkub.. Neh 7:45 1121
the *c* of Hatita .... Neh 7:45 1121
the *c* of Shobai, an hundred.................... Neh 7:45 1121
the *c* of Ziha .... Neh 7:46 1121
the *c* of Hashupha .... Neh 7:46 1121
the *c* of Tabbaoth...................................... Neh 7:46 1121
The *c* of Keros .... Neh 7:47 1121
c of Sia, the *c* of Padon, ... Neh 7:47 1121
The *c* of Lebana... Neh 7:48 1121
the *c* of Hagaba .... Neh 7:48 1121
the *c* of Shalmai .... Neh 7:48 1121
The *c* of Hanan.. Neh 7:49 1121
the *c* of Giddel.. Neh 7:49 1121
the *c* of Gahar... Neh 7:49 1121
The *c* of Reaiah... Neh 7:50 1121
the *c* of Rezin.. Neh 7:50 1121
the *c* of Nekoda .... Neh 7:50 1121
The *c* of Gazzam.. Neh 7:51 1121
the *c* of Uzza... Neh 7:51 1121
the *c* of Phaseah .... Neh 7:51 1121
The *c* of Besai .... Neh 7:52 1121
the *c* of Meunim... Neh 7:52 1121
the *c* of Nephishesim .... Neh 7:52 1121
The *c* of Bakbuk .... Neh 7:53 1121
the *c* of Hakupha....................................... Neh 7:53 1121
the *c* of Harhur.. Neh 7:53 1121
The *c* of Bazlith... Neh 7:54 1121
the *c* of Mehida... Neh 7:54 1121
the *c* of Harsha .... Neh 7:54 1121
The *c* of Barkos... Neh 7:55 1121
the *c* of Sisera... Neh 7:55 1121
the *c* of Tamah... Neh 7:55 1121
The *c* of Neziah .... Neh 7:56 1121
the *c* of Hatipha.. Neh 7:56 1121
The *c* of Solomon's servants .... Neh 7:57 1121
the *c* of Sotai .... Neh 7:57 1121
the *c* of Sophereth .... Neh 7:57 1121
the *c* of Perida .... Neh 7:57 1121
The *c* of Jaala .... Neh 7:58 1121
the *c* of Darkon.. Neh 7:58 1121
the *c* of Giddel.. Neh 7:58 1121
The *c* of Shephatiah .... Neh 7:59 1121
the *c* of Hattil .... Neh 7:59 1121
the *c* of Pochereth of Zebaim .... Neh 7:59 1121
the *c* of Amon .... Neh 7:59 1121
the *c* of Solomon's servants, were .... Neh 7:60 1121
The *c* of Delaiah .... Neh 7:62 1121
the *c* of Tobiah.. Neh 7:62 1121
the *c* of Nekoda, six hundred .... Neh 7:62 1121
the *c* of Habaiah .... Neh 7:63 1121
the *c* of Koz .... Neh 7:63 1121

C

the c of Barzillai, which took	Neh 7:63	1121
the c of Israel were in their	Neh 7:73	1121
that the c of Israel should dwell	Neh 8:14	1121
had not the c of Israel done so	Neh 8:17	1121
fourth day of this month the c of	Neh 9:1	1121
Their c also multipliedst thou as	Neh 9:23	1121
So the c went in and possessed the	Neh 9:24	1121
For the c of Israel and the	Neh 10:39	1121
the c of Levi shall bring the	Neh 10:39	1121
the c of Solomon's servants	Neh 11:3	1121
dwelt certain of the c of Judah	Neh 11:4	1121
and of the c of Benjamin	Neh 11:4	1121
Of the c of Judah	Neh 11:4	1121
of Mahalaleel, of the c of Perez	Neh 11:4	1121
of the c of Zerah the son of	Neh 11:24	1121
some of the c of Judah dwelt at	Neh 11:25	1121
The c also of Benjamin from Geba	Neh 11:31	1121
the wives also and the c rejoiced	Neh 12:43	3206
them unto the c of Aaron	Neh 12:47	1121
not the c of Israel with bread	Neh 13:2	1121
the sabbath unto the c of Judah	Neh 13:16	1121
their c spake half in the speech	Neh 13:24	1121
Jews, both young and old, little c	Est 3:13	2945
riches, and the multitude of his c	Est 5:11	1121
His c are far from safety, and	Job 5:4	1121
If thy c have sinned against him,	Job 8:4	1121
even the eyes of his c shall fail	Job 17:5	1121
Yea, young c despised me	Job 19:18	
His c shall seek to please the	Job 20:10	1121
like a flock, and their c dance	Job 21:11	3206
layeth up his iniquity for his c	Job 21:19	1121
food for them and for their c	Job 24:5	5288
If his c be multiplied, it is for	Job 27:14	1121
with me, when my c were about me	Job 29:5	5288
They were c of fools	Job 30:8	1121
yea, c of base men	Job 30:8	1121
is a king over all the c of pride	Job 41:34	1121
his eyelids try, the c of men	Ps 11:4	1121
fail from among the c of men	Ps 12:1	1121
from heaven upon the c of men	Ps 14:2	1121
they are full of c, and leave the	Ps 17:14	1121
seed from among the c of men	Ps 21:10	1121
Come, ye c, hearken unto me	Ps 34:11	1121
therefore the c of men put their	Ps 36:7	1121
Thou art fairer than the c of men	Ps 45:2	1121
of thy fathers shall be thy c	Ps 45:16	1121
from heaven upon the c of men	Ps 53:2	1121
in his doing toward the c of men	Ps 66:5	1121
and an alien unto my mother's c	Ps 69:8	1121
he shall save the c of the needy	Ps 72:4	1121
against the generation of thy c	Ps 73:15	1121
will not hide them from their c	Ps 78:4	1121
should make them known to their c	Ps 78:5	1121
even the c which should be born	Ps 78:6	1121
arise and declare them to their c	Ps 78:6	1121
The c of Ephraim, being armed, and	Ps 78:9	1121
all of you are c of the most High	Ps 82:6	1121
they have holpen the c of Lot	Ps 83:8	1121
If his c forsake my law, and walk	Ps 89:30	1121
and sayest, Return, ye c of men	Ps 90:3	1121
and thy glory unto their c	Ps 90:16	1121
The c of thy servants shall	Ps 102:28	1121
his acts unto the c of Israel	Ps 103:7	1121
Like as a father pitieth his c	Ps 103:13	1121
righteousness unto children's c	Ps 103:17	1121
servant, ye c of Jacob his chosen	Ps 105:6	1121
wonderful works to the c of men	Ps 107:8	1121
wonderful works to the c of men	Ps 107:15	1121
wonderful works to the c of men	Ps 107:21	1121
wonderful works to the c of men	Ps 107:31	1121
Let his c be fatherless, and his	Ps 109:9	1121
Let his c be continually	Ps 109:10	1121
be any to favour his fatherless c	Ps 109:12	
and to be a joyful mother of c	Ps 113:9	1121
you more and more, you and your c	Ps 115:14	1121
hath he given to the c of men	Ps 115:16	1121
c are an heritage of the LORD	Ps 127:3	1121
so are c of the youth	Ps 127:4	1121
thy c like olive plants round	Ps 128:3	1121
thou shalt see thy children's c	Ps 128:6	1121
If thy c will keep my covenant and	Ps 132:12	1121
their c shall also sit upon thy	Ps 132:12	1121
the c of Edom in the day of	Ps 137:7	1121
from the hand of strange c	Ps 144:7	1121
me from the hand of strange c	Ps 144:11	1121
he hath blessed thy c within thee	Ps 147:13	1121
old men, and c	Ps 148:12	5288
even of the c of Israel, a people	Ps 148:14	1121
let the c of Zion be joyful in	Ps 149:2	1121
Hear, ye c, the instruction of a	Prov 4:1	1121
Hear me now therefore, O ye c	Prov 5:7	1121
unto me now therefore, O ye c	Prov 7:24	1121
therefore hearken unto me, O ye c	Prov 8:32	1121
inheritance to his children's c	Prov 13:22	1121
his c shall have a place of	Prov 14:26	1121
then the hearts of the c of men	Prov 15:11	1121
Children's c are the crown of old	Prov 17:6	1121
the glory of c are their fathers	Prov 17:6	1121
his c are blessed after him	Prov 20:7	1121
Her c arise up, and call her	Prov 31:28	1121
If a man beget an hundred c	Eccl 6:3	
my mother's c were angry with me	Song 1:6	1121
I have nourished and brought up c	Is 1:2	1121
evildoers, c that are corrupters	Is 1:4	1121
themselves in the c of strangers	Is 2:6	3206
I will give c to be their princes	Is 3:4	5288
c are their oppressors, and women	Is 3:12	5768
the c whom the LORD hath given me	Is 8:18	3206
the c of Ammon shall obey them	Is 11:14	1121
Their c also shall be dashed to	Is 13:16	5768
their eye shall not spare c	Is 13:18	1121
his c for the iniquity of their	Is 14:21	1121
as the glory of the c of Israel	Is 17:3	1121
left because of the c of Israel	Is 17:9	1121
the mighty men of the c of Kedar	Is 21:17	1121
I travail not, nor bring forth c	Is 23:4	
one by one, O ye c of Israel	Is 27:12	1121
But when he seeth his c, the work	Is 29:23	3206
Woe to the rebellious c, saith	Is 30:1	1121
is a rebellious people, lying c	Is 30:9	1121
c that will not hear the law of	Is 30:9	1121
c of Israel have deeply revolted	Is 31:6	1121
for the c are come to the birth,	Is 37:3	1121
the c of Eden which were in	Is 37:12	1121
the father to the c shall make	Is 38:19	1121
shall I know the loss of c	Is 47:8	
moment in one day, the loss of c	Is 47:9	
Thy c shall make haste	Is 49:17	1121
The c which thou shalt have,	Is 49:20	1121
me these, seeing I have lost my c	Is 49:21	
with thee, and I will save thy c	Is 49:25	1121
for more are the c of the	Is 54:1	1121
than the c of the married wife	Is 54:1	1121
all thy c shall be taught of the	Is 54:13	1121
great shall be the peace of thy c	Is 54:13	1121
are ye not c of transgression, a	Is 57:4	3206
slaying the c in the valleys	Is 57:5	3206
my people, c that will not lie	Is 63:8	1121
she brought forth her c	Is 66:8	1121
as the c of Israel bring an	Is 66:20	1121
your children's c will I plead	Jer 2:9	1121
Also the c of Noph and Tahapanes	Jer 2:16	1121
In vain have I smitten your c	Jer 2:30	1121
Turn, O backsliding c, saith the	Jer 3:14	1121
How shall I put thee among the c	Jer 3:19	1121
supplications of the c of Israel	Jer 3:21	1121
Return, ye backsliding c, and I	Jer 3:22	1121
they are sottish c, and they have	Jer 4:22	1121
thy c have forsaken me, and sworn	Jer 5:7	1121
O ye c of Benjamin, gather	Jer 6:1	1121
pour it out upon the c abroad	Jer 6:11	5768
The c gather wood, and the fathers	Jer 7:18	1121
For the c of Judah have done evil	Jer 7:30	1121
to cut off the c from without	Jer 9:21	5768
the c of Ammon, and Moab, and all	Jer 9:26	1121
my c are gone forth of me, and	Jer 10:20	1121
I will bereave them of c, I will	Jer 15:7	
that brought up the c of Israel	Jer 16:14	1121
that brought up the c of Israel	Jer 16:15	1121
Whilst their c remember their	Jer 17:2	1121
the gate of the c of the people	Jer 17:19	1121
deliver up their c to the famine	Jer 18:21	1121
wives be bereaved of their c	Jer 18:21	
which brought up the c of Israel	Jer 23:7	1121
Edom, and Moab, and the c of Ammon	Jer 25:21	1121
Their c also shall be as	Jer 30:20	1121
Rahel weeping for her c refused	Jer 31:15	1121
refused to be comforted for her c	Jer 31:15	1121
that thy c shall come again to	Jer 31:17	1121
the bosom of their c after them	Jer 32:18	1121
For the c of Israel and the	Jer 32:30	1121
the c of Judah have only done	Jer 32:30	1121
for the c of Israel have only	Jer 32:30	1121
all the evil of the c of Israel	Jer 32:32	1121
of the c of Judah, which they	Jer 32:32	1121
of them, and of their c after them	Jer 32:39	1121
wives and thy c to the Chaldeans	Jer 38:23	1121
unto him men, and women, and c	Jer 40:7	2945
of war, and the women, and the c	Jer 41:16	2945
Even men, and women, and c, and the	Jer 43:6	2945
their c for feebleness of hands	Jer 47:3	1121
the captivity of the c of Ammon	Jer 49:6	1121
Leave thy fatherless c, I will	Jer 49:11	1121
the c of Israel shall come, they	Jer 50:4	1121
the c of Judah together, going and	Jer 50:4	1121
c of Israel and the c of Judah	Jer 50:33	1121
her c are gone into captivity	Lam 1:5	5768
my c are desolate, because the	Lam 1:16	1121
because the c and the sucklings	Lam 2:11	5768
him for the life of thy young c	Lam 2:19	
their fruit, and c of a span long	Lam 2:20	5768
willingly nor grieve the c of men	Lam 3:33	1121
the young c ask bread, and no man	Lam 4:4	5768
women have sodden their own c	Lam 4:10	3206
the c fell under the wood	Lam 5:13	5288
I send thee to the c of Israel	Eze 2:3	1121
For they are impudent c and	Eze 2:4	1121
unto the c of thy people, and	Eze 3:11	1121
Even thus shall the c of Israel	Eze 4:13	1121
c of Israel before their idols	Eze 6:5	1121
and young, both maids, and little c	Eze 9:6	2945
That thou hast slain my c	Eze 16:21	1121
and by the blood of thy c	Eze 16:36	1121
that lotheth her husband and her c	Eze 16:45	1121
lothed their husbands and their c	Eze 16:45	1121
unto their c in the wilderness	Eze 20:18	1121
the c rebelled against me	Eze 20:21	1121
had slain their c to their idols	Eze 23:39	1121
in the midst of the c of men	Eze 31:14	1121
speak to the c of thy people, and	Eze 33:2	1121
say unto the c of thy people, The	Eze 33:12	1121
Yet the c of thy people say, The	Eze 33:17	1121
the c of thy people still are	Eze 33:30	1121
hast shed the blood of the c of	Eze 35:5	1121
Judah, and for the c of Israel his	Eze 37:16	1121
when the c of thy people shall	Eze 37:18	1121
I will take the c of Israel from	Eze 37:21	1121
therein, even they, and their c	Eze 37:25	1121
and their children's c for ever	Eze 37:25	1121
midst of the c of Israel for ever	Eze 43:7	1121
that is among the c of Israel	Eze 44:9	1121
c of Israel went astray from me	Eze 44:15	1121
which shall beget c among you	Eze 47:22	1121
the country among the c of Israel	Eze 47:22	1121
when the c of Israel went astray	Eze 48:11	1121
bring certain of the c of Israel	Dan 1:3	1121
C in whom was no blemish, but	Dan 1:4	3206
these were of the c of Judah	Dan 1:6	1121
than the c which are of your sort	Dan 1:10	3206
the countenance of the c that eat	Dan 1:13	3206
c which did eat the portion of	Dan 1:15	3206
As for these four c, God gave	Dan 1:17	3206
And wheresoever the c of men dwell	Dan 2:38	1123
which art of the c of the	Dan 5:13	1123
Daniel, which is of the c of the	Dan 6:13	1123
the den of lions, them, their c	Dan 6:24	1123
and the chief of the c of Ammon	Dan 11:41	1121
standeth for the c of thy people	Dan 12:1	1121
of whoredoms and c of whoredoms	Hos 1:2	3206
Yet the number of the c of Israel	Hos 1:10	1121
Then shall the c of Judah	Hos 1:11	1121
the c of Israel be gathered	Hos 1:11	1121
I will not have mercy upon her c	Hos 2:4	1121
for they be the c of whoredoms	Hos 2:4	1121
the LORD toward the c of Israel	Hos 3:1	1121
For the c of Israel shall abide	Hos 3:4	1121
shall the c of Israel return	Hos 3:5	1121
word of the LORD, ye c of Israel	Hos 4:1	1121
thy God, I will also forget thy c	Hos 4:6	1121
for they have begotten strange c	Hos 5:7	1121
Though they bring up their c	Hos 9:12	1121
bring forth his c to the murderer	Hos 9:13	1121
c of iniquity did not overtake	Hos 10:9	1121
was dashed in pieces upon her c	Hos 10:14	1121
then the c shall tremble from the	Hos 11:10	1121
place of the breaking forth of c	Hos 13:13	1121
Tell ye your c of it	Joel 1:3	1121
let your c tell their c,	Joel 1:3	1121
and let your c tell their c	Joel 1:3	1121
assemble the elders, gather the c	Joel 2:16	5768
ye c of Zion, and rejoice in the	Joel 2:23	1121
The c also of Judah and the	Joel 3:6	1121
the c of Jerusalem have ye sold	Joel 3:6	1121
into the hand of the c of Judah	Joel 3:8	1121
the strength of the c of Israel	Joel 3:16	1121
violence against the c of Judah	Joel 3:19	1121
transgressions of the c of Ammon	Amos 1:13	1121
not even thus, O ye c of Israel	Amos 2:11	1121
O c of Israel, against the whole	Amos 3:1	1121
so shall the c of Israel be taken	Amos 3:12	1121
O ye c of Israel, saith the Lord	Amos 4:5	1121
Are ye not as c of the Ethiopians	Amos 9:7	1121
Ethiopians unto me, O c of Israel	Amos 9:7	1121
thou have rejoiced over the c of	Obad 12	1121
captivity of this host of the c	Obad 20	1121
and poll thee for thy delicate c	Mic 1:16	1121
from their c have ye taken away	Mic 2:9	5768
shall return unto the c of Israel	Mic 5:3	1121
her young c also were dashed in	Nah 3:10	5768
the princes, and the king's c	Zeph 1:8	1121
the revilings of the c of Ammon	Zeph 2:8	1121
the c of Ammon as Gomorrah, even	Zeph 2:9	1121
their c shall see it, and be glad	Zec 10:7	1121
and they shall live with their c	Zec 10:9	1121
the heart of the fathers to the c	Mal 4:6	1121
heart of the c to their fathers	Mal 4:6	1121
slew all the c that were in	Mt 2:16	*3816*
Rachel weeping for her c	Mt 2:18	*5043*
stones to raise up c unto Abraham	Mt 3:9	*5043*
they shall be called the c of God	Mt 5:9	*5207*
That ye may be the c of your	Mt 5:45	*5207*
to give good gifts unto your c	Mt 7:11	*5043*
But the c of the kingdom shall be	Mt 8:12	*5207*
Can the c of the bridechamber	Mt 9:15	*5207*
the c shall rise up against their	Mt 10:21	*5043*
It is like unto c sitting in the	Mt 11:16	*3808*
But wisdom is justified of her c	Mt 11:19	*5043*
by whom do your c cast them out	Mt 12:27	*5207*
seed are the c of the kingdom	Mt 13:38	*5207*
tares are the c of the wicked one	Mt 13:38	*5207*
thousand men, beside women and c	Mt 14:21	*3813*
thousand men, beside women and c	Mt 15:38	*3813*
of their own c, or of strangers	Mt 17:25	*5207*
unto him, Then are the c free	Mt 17:26	*5207*
converted, and become as little c	Mt 18:3	*3813*
him to be sold, and his wife, and c	Mt 18:25	*5043*
there brought unto him little c	Mt 19:13	*3813*
But Jesus said, Suffer little c	Mt 19:14	*3813*
father, or mother, or wife, or c	Mt 19:29	*5043*
of Zebedee's c with her sons	Mt 20:20	*5207*
the c crying in the temple, and	Mt 21:15	*3816*
said, If a man die, having no c	Mt 22:24	*5043*
that ye are the c of them which	Mt 23:31	*5207*
I have gathered thy c together	Mt 23:37	*5043*
whom they of the c of Israel did	Mt 27:9	*5207*
His blood be on us, and on our c	Mt 27:25	*5043*
and the mother of Zebedee's c	Mt 27:56	*5207*
Can the c of the bridechamber	Mk 2:19	*5207*
Let the c first be filled	Mk 7:27	*5043*
receive one of such c in my name	Mk 9:37	*3813*
And they brought young c to him	Mk 10:13	*3813*
the little c to come unto me	Mk 10:14	*3813*
again, and saith unto them, C	Mk 10:24	*5043*
father, or mother, or wife, or c	Mk 10:29	*5043*

and sisters, and mothers, and c .... Mk 10:30 *5043*
wife behind him, and leave no c .... Mk 12:19 *5043*
c shall rise up against their .... Mk 13:12 *5043*
many of the c of Israel shall he .... Lk 1:16 *5207*
hearts of the fathers to the c .... Lk 1:17 *5043*
stones to raise up c unto Abraham .... Lk 3:8 *5043*
them, Can ye make the c of the .... Lk 5:34 *5207*
ye shall be the c of the Highest .... Lk 6:35 *5207*
They are like unto c sitting in .... Lk 7:32 *3813*
wisdom is justified of all her c .... Lk 7:35 *5043*
shut, and my c are with me in bed .... Lk 11:7 *3813*
to give good gifts unto your c .... Lk 11:13 *5043*
I have gathered thy c together .... Lk 13:34 *5043*
father, and mother, and wife, and c .... Lk 14:26 *5043*
for the c of this world are in .... Lk 16:8 *5207*
wiser than the c of light .... Lk 16:8 *5207*
Suffer little c to come unto me, ... Lk 18:16 *3813*
or brethren, or wife, or c .... Lk 18:29 *5043*
the ground, and thy c within thee .... Lk 19:44 *5043*
a wife, and he die without c .... Lk 20:28 *815*
took a wife, and died without c .... Lk 20:29 *815*
and they left no c, and died .... Lk 20:31 *5043*
The c of this world marry, and are .... Lk 20:34 *5207*
and are the c of God, being the .... Lk 20:36 *5207*
being the c of the resurrection .... Lk 20:36 *5207*
for yourselves, and for your c .... Lk 23:28 *5043*
drank thereof himself, and his c .... Jn 4:12 *5207*
unto them, If ye were Abraham's c .... Jn 8:39 *5043*
the c of God that were scattered .... Jn 11:52 *5043*
that ye may be the c of light .... Jn 12:36 *5207*
Little c, yet a little while I am .... Jn 13:33 *5040*
Then Jesus saith unto them, C .... Jn 21:5 *3813*
promise is unto you, and to your c .... Acts 2:39 *5043*
Ye are the c of the prophets, and .... Acts 3:25 *5207*
all the senate of the c of Israel .... Acts 5:21 *5207*
that they cast out their young c .... Acts 7:19 *1025*
his brethren the c of Israel .... Acts 7:23 *5207*
which said unto the c of Israel .... Acts 7:37 *5207*
and kings, and the c of Israel .... Acts 9:15 *5207*
God sent unto the c of Israel .... Acts 10:36 *5207*
c of the stock of Abraham, and .... Acts 13:26 *5207*
the same unto us their c, in that .... Acts 13:33 *5043*
us on our way, with wives and c .... Acts 21:5 *5043*
ought not to circumcise their c .... Acts 21:21 *5043*
spirit, that we are the c of God .... Rom 8:16 *5043*
And if c, then heirs .... Rom 8:17 *5043*
glorious liberty of the c of God .... Rom 8:21 *5043*
seed of Abraham, are they all c .... Rom 9:7 *5043*
They which are the c of the flesh .... Rom 9:8 *5043*
these are not the c of God .... Rom 9:8 *5043*
but the c of the promise are .... Rom 9:8 *5043*
(For the c being not yet born, ... Rom 9:11
be called the c of the living God .... Rom 9:26 *5207*
Though the number of the c of .... Rom 9:27 *5207*
else were your c unclean 1Cor 7:14 *5043*
be not c in understanding 1Cor 14:20 *3813*
howbeit in malice be ye c 1Cor 14:20 *3515*
so that the c of Israel could not 2Cor 3:7 *5207*
that the c of Israel could not 2Cor 3:13 *5207*
the same, (I speak as unto my c 2Cor 6:13 *5043*
for the c ought not to lay up for 2Cor 12:14 *5043*
but the parents for the c 2Cor 12:14 *5043*
the same are the c of Abraham .... Gal 3:7 *5207*
For ye are all the c of God by .... Gal 3:26 *5207*
Even so we, when we were c .... Gal 4:3 *3516*
My little c, of whom I travail in .... Gal 4:19 *5040*
is, and is in bondage with her c .... Gal 4:25 *5043*
c than she which hath a husband .... Gal 4:27 *5043*
Isaac was, are the c of promise .... Gal 4:28 *5043*
we are not c of the bondwoman, ... Gal 4:31 *5043*
us unto the adoption of c by .... Eph 1:5 *5206*
worketh in the c of disobedience .... Eph 2:2 *5207*
and were by nature the c of wrath .... Eph 2:3 *5043*
That we henceforth be no more c .... Eph 4:14 *3516*
followers of God, as dear c .... Eph 5:1 *5043*
of God upon the c of disobedience .... Eph 5:6 *5207*
walk as c of light .... Eph 5:8 *5043*
C, obey your parents in the Lord .... Eph 6:1 *5043*
provoke not your c to wrath .... Eph 6:4 *5043*
cometh on the c of disobedience .... Col 3:6 *5207*
C, obey your parents in all .... Col 3:20 *5043*
provoke not your c to anger .... Col 3:21 *5043*
even as a nurse cherisheth her c 1Th 2:7 *5043*
of you, as a father doth his c 1Th 2:11 *5043*
c of light, and the c of the day 1Th 5:5 *5207*
having his c in subjection with 1Ti 3:4 *5043*
of one wife, ruling their c 1Ti 3:12 *5043*
if any widow have c or nephews 1Ti 5:4 *5043*
if she have brought up c, if she 1Ti 5:10 *5044*
the younger women marry, bear c 1Ti 5:14 *5041*
having faithful c not accused of .... Titus 1:6 *5043*
their husbands, to love their c .... Titus 2:4 *5388*
the c which God hath given me .... Heb 2:13 *3813*
Forasmuch then as the c are .... Heb 2:14 *3813*
the departing of the c of Israel .... Heb 11:22 *5027*
which speaketh unto you as unto c .... Heb 12:5 *5027*
As obedient c, not fashioning 1Pet 1:14 *5043*
with covetous practices; cursed c 2Pet 2:14 *5043*
My little c, these things write I 1Jn 2:1 *5040*
I write unto you, little c 1Jn 2:12 *5040*
I write unto you, little c 1Jn 2:13 *3813*
Little c, it is the last time 1Jn 2:18 *3813*
And now, little c, abide in him 1Jn 2:28 *5040*
Little c, let no man deceive you 1Jn 3:7 *5040*
In this the c of God are manifest 1Jn 3:10 *5043*
and the c of the devil 1Jn 3:10 *5043*
My little c, let us not love in 1Jn 3:18 *5040*
Ye are of God, little c, and have 1Jn 4:4 *5040*
we know that we love the c of God 1Jn 5:2 *5043*
Little c, keep yourselves from 1Jn 5:21 *5040*
unto the elect lady and her c 2Jn 1 *5043*
I found of thy c walking in truth 2Jn 4 *5043*
The c of thy elect sister greet 2Jn 13 *5043*
to hear that my c walk in truth 3Jn 4 *5043*
before the c of Israel, to eat .... Rev 2:14 *5207*
And I will kill her c with death .... Rev 2:23 *5043*
all the tribes of the c of Israel .... Rev 7:4 *5207*
twelve tribes of the c of Israel .... Rev 21:12 *5207*

CHILDREN'S See APPENDIX.

CHILD'S {4}
maid went and called the c mother .... Ex 2:8 3206
let this c soul come into him 1Kin 17:21 3206
flesh shall be fresher than a c .... Job 33:25 5290
which sought the young c life .... Mt 2:20 *3813*

CHILEAB *(kil'-e-ab)* {1} See DANIEL. *A son of David.*
And his second, C, of Abigail the 2Sa 3:3 3609

CHILION *(kil'-e-on)* {2} See CHILION'S. *A son of Elimelech.*
name of his two sons Mahlon and C .... Ruth 1:2 3630
and C died also both of them .... Ruth 1:5 3630

CHILION'S *(kil'-e-ons)* {1}
Elimelech's, and all that was C .... Ruth 4:9 3630

CHILMAD *(kil'-mad)* {1} *An area between Assyria and Arabia.*
merchants of Sheba, Asshur, and C .... Eze 27:23 3638

CHIMHAM *(kim'-ham)* {4} *A servant of David.*
But behold thy servant C 2Sa 19:37 3643
C shall go over with me, and I 2Sa 19:38 3643
to Gilgal, and C went on with him 2Sa 19:40 3643
and dwelt in the habitation of C .... Jer 41:17 3643

CHIMNEY {1}
and as the smoke out of the c .... Hos 13:3 699

CHINNERETH *(kin'-ne-reth)* {4} See CHINNEROTH, CINNEROTH, GENNESARET. *A district around the Sea of Galilee.*
the side of the sea of C eastward .... Num 34:11 3672
from C even unto the sea of the .... Deut 3:17 3672
sea of C on the other side Jordan .... Josh 13:27 3672
Zer, and Hammath, Rakkath, and C .... Josh 19:35 3672

CHINNEROTH *(kin'-ne-roth)* {2} See CHINNERETH. *Same as Chinnereth.*
and of the plains south of C .... Josh 11:2 3672
plain to the sea of C on the east .... Josh 12:3 3672

CHIOS *(ki'-os)* {1} *An island near Greece.*
came the next day over against C .... Acts 20:15 *5508*

CHISLEU *(kis'-lew)* {2} *Ninth month of the Hebrew year.*
And it came to pass in the month C .... Neh 1:1 3691
day of the ninth month, even in C .... Zec 7:1 3691

CHISLEV See CHISLEU.

CHISLON *(kis'-lon)* {1} *Father of Elidad.*
of Benjamin, Elidad the son of C .... Num 34:21 3692

CHISLOTH-TABOR *(kis'-loth-ta'-bor)* {1} See CHESULLOTH. *A city in Zebulon.*
sunrising unto the border of C .... Josh 19:12 3696

CHITTIM *(kit'-tim)* {6} See KITTIM. *Descendants of Javan.*
come from the coast of C .... Num 24:24 3794
from the land of C it is revealed .... Is 23:1 3794
arise, pass over to C .... Is 23:12 3794
For pass over the isles of C .... Jer 2:10 3794
brought out of the isles of C .... Eze 27:6 3794
For the ships of C shall come .... Dan 11:30 3794

CHIUN *(ki'-un)* {1} See REMPHAN. *Another name for the god Saturn.*
C your images, the star of your .... Amos 5:26 3594

CHLOE *(clo'-e)* {1} *A Christian acquaintance of Paul.*
them which are of the house of C 1Cor 1:11 *5514*

CHLOE'S See CHLOE.

CHODE {2}
Jacob was wroth, and c with Laban .... Gen 31:36 7378
And the people c with Moses .... Num 20:3 7378

CHOICE {21}
in the c of our sepulchres bury .... Gen 23:6 4005
and his ass's colt unto the c vine .... Gen 49:11 8321
all your c vows which ye vow unto .... Deut 12:11 4005
a c young man, and a goodly 1Sa 9:2 970
chose of all the c men of Israel 2Sa 10:9 977
fenced city, and every c city 2Kin 3:19 4005
and the c fir trees thereof 2Kin 19:23 4005
heads of their father's house, c 1Chr 7:40 1305
chose out of all the c of Israel 1Chr 19:10 970
them three hundred thousand c men 2Chr 25:5 970
daily was one ox and six c sheep .... Neh 5:18 1305
and knowledge rather than c gold .... Prov 8:10 977
and my revenue than c silver .... Prov 8:19 977
tongue of the just is as c silver .... Prov 10:20 977
she is the c one of her that bare .... Song 6:9 1249
and the c fir trees thereof .... Is 37:24 4005
they shall cut down thy c cedars .... Jer 22:7 4005
fill it with the c bones .... Eze 24:4 4005
Take the c of the flock, and burn .... Eze 24:5 4005
and all the trees of Eden, the c .... Eze 31:16 4005
while ago God made c among us .... Acts 15:7 *1586*

CHOICEST {2}
and planted it with the c vine .... Is 5:2 8321
that thy c valleys shall be full .... Is 22:7 4055

CHOKE {2}
c the word, and he becometh .... Mt 13:22 *4846*
c the word, and it becometh .... Mk 4:19 *4846*

CHOKED {6}
the thorns sprung up, and c them .... Mt 13:7 *638*
c it, and it yielded no fruit .... Mk 4:7 *4846*
and were c in the sea .... Mk 5:13 *4155*
thorns sprang up with it, and c it .... Lk 8:7 *638*
are c with cares and riches and .... Lk 8:14 *4846*
place into the lake, and were c .... Lk 8:33 *638*

C

CHOLER {2}
he was moved with c against him .... Dan 8:7 4843
the south shall be moved with c .... Dan 11:11 4843

CHOOSE {60}
C us out men, and go out, fight .... Ex 17:9 977
that the man whom the LORD doth c .... Num 16:7 977
the man's rod, whom I shall c .... Num 17:5 977
set his love upon you, nor c you .... Deut 7:7 977
c out of all your tribes to put .... Deut 12:5 977
c to cause his name to dwell .... Deut 12:11 977
LORD shall c in one of thy tribes .... Deut 12:14 977
which the LORD thy God shall c .... Deut 12:18 977
the place which the LORD shall c .... Deut 12:26 977
shall c to place his name there .... Deut 14:23 977
God shall c to set his name there .... Deut 14:24 977
which the LORD thy God shall c .... Deut 14:25 977
the place which the LORD shall c .... Deut 15:20 977
shall c to place his name there .... Deut 16:2 977
God shall c to place his name in .... Deut 16:6 977
which the LORD thy God shall c .... Deut 16:7 977
the place which the LORD shall c .... Deut 16:15 977
God in the place which he shall c .... Deut 16:16 977
which the LORD thy God shall c .... Deut 17:8 977
the LORD shall c shall shew thee .... Deut 17:10 977
whom the LORD thy God shall c .... Deut 17:15 977
the place which the LORD shall c .... Deut 18:6 977
he shall c in one of thy gates .... Deut 23:16 977
shall c to place his name there .... Deut 26:2 977
therefore c life, that both thou .... Deut 30:19 977
God in the place which he shall c .... Deut 31:11 977
in the place which he should c .... Josh 9:27 977
c you this day whom ye will serve .... Josh 24:15 977
did I c him out of all the tribes 1Sa 2:28 977
c you a man for you, and let him 1Sa 17:8 1262
and all the men of Israel, c 2Sa 16:18 977
Let me now c out twelve thousand 2Sa 17:1 977
of Saul, whom the LORD did c 2Sa 21:6 972
c thee one of them, that I may do 2Sa 24:12 977
the city which the LORD did c out 1Kin 14:21 977
let them c one bullock for 1Kin 18:23 977
C you one bullock for yourselves, ... 1Kin 18:25 977
c thee one of them, that I may do 1Chr 21:10 977
him, Thus saith the LORD, C thee 1Chr 21:11 6901
LORD the God, who didst c Abram .... Neh 9:7 977
c out my words to reason with him .... Job 9:14 977
Let us c to us judgment .... Job 34:4 977
thou refuse, or whether thou c .... Job 34:33 977
teach in the way that he shall c .... Ps 25:12 977
He shall c our inheritance for us .... Ps 47:4 977
did not c the fear of the LORD .... Prov 1:29 977
oppressor, and c none of his ways .... Prov 3:31 977
to refuse the evil, and c the good .... Is 7:15 977
c the good, the land that thou .... Is 7:16 977
on Jacob, and will yet c Israel .... Is 14:1 977
One of Israel, and he shall c thee .... Is 49:7 977
c the things that please me, and .... Is 56:4 977
did c that wherein I delighted .... Is 65:12 977
I also will c their delusions, and .... Is 66:4 977
c thou a place, c it at the .... Eze 21:19 1254
c it at the head of the way to .... Eze 21:19 1254
Zion, and shall yet c Jerusalem .... Zec 1:17 977
land, and shall c Jerusalem again .... Zec 2:12 977
yet what I shall c I wot not .... Phil 1:22 *138*

CHOOSEST {2}
thou c the tongue of the crafty .... Job 15:5 977
Blessed is the man whom thou c .... Ps 65:4 977

CHOOSETH {3}
So that my soul c strangling .... Job 7:15 977
c a tree that will not rot .... Is 40:20 977
an abomination is he that c you .... Is 41:24 977

CHOOSING {1}
C rather to suffer affliction .... Heb 11:25 *138*

CHOP {1}
c them in pieces, as for the pot, ... Mic 3:3 6566

CHOR-ASHAN *(cor-a'-shan)* {1} *A town in Judah.*
and to them which were in C 1Sa 30:30 3565

CHORAZIN *(co-ra'-zin)* {2} *A city near Capernaum.*
Woe unto thee, C .... Mt 11:21 *5523*
Woe unto thee, C .... Lk 10:13 *5523*

CHOSE {29}
them wives of all which they c .... Gen 6:2 977
Then Lot c him all the plain of .... Gen 13:11 977
Moses c able men out of all .... Ex 18:25 977
therefore he c their seed after .... Deut 4:37 977
he c their seed after them, even .... Deut 10:15 977
Joshua c out thirty thousand .... Josh 8:3 977
They c new gods .... Judg 5:8 977
Saul c him three thousand men of 1Sa 13:2 977
c him five smooth stones out of 1Sa 17:40 977
which c me before thy father, and 2Sa 6:21 977
he c of all the choice men of 2Sa 10:9 977
I c no city out of all the tribes 1Kin 8:16 977
but I c David to be over my 1Kin 8:16 977
David my servant's sake, whom I c 1Kin 11:34 977

he *c* out of all the choice of ... 1Chr 19:10 977
c me before all the house of my ... 1Chr 28:4 977
out of the land of Egypt I *c* no ... 2Chr 6:5 977
neither *c* I any man to be a ruler ... 2Chr 6:5 977
I *c* out their way, and sat chief, ... Job 29:25 977
c not the tribe of Ephraim ... Ps 78:67 977
But *c* the tribe of Judah, the ... Ps 78:68 977
He *c* David also his servant, and ... Ps 78:70 977
c that in which I delighted not ... Is 66:4 977
In the day when I *c* Israel ... Eze 20:5 977
and of them he *c* twelve, whom also ... Lk 6:13 *1586*
how they *c* out the chief rooms ... Lk 14:7 *1586*
they *c* Stephen, a man full of ... Acts 6:5 *1586*
people of Israel *c* our fathers ... Acts 13:17 *1586*
Paul *c* Silas, and departed, being ... Acts 15:40 *1951*

CHOSEN {123}

And he took six hundred *c* chariots ... Ex 14:7 970
his *c* captains also are drowned ... Ex 15:4 4005
even him whom he hath *c* will he ... Num 16:5 977
the LORD thy God hath *c* thee to ... Deut 7:6 977
which the LORD thy God hath *c* to ... Deut 12:21 977
the LORD hath *c* thee to be a ... Deut 14:2 977
hath *c* to place his name there ... Deut 16:11 977
hath *c* him out of all thy tribes ... Deut 18:5 977
God hath *c* to minister unto him ... Deut 21:5 977
that ye have *c* you the LORD ... Josh 24:22 977
cry unto the gods which ye have *c* ... Judg 10:14 977
were numbered seven hundred *c* men ... Judg 20:15 970
seven hundred *c* men lefthanded ... Judg 20:16 970
thousand *c* men out of all Israel ... Judg 20:34 970
king which ye shall have *c* you ... 1Sa 8:18 977
See ye him whom the LORD hath *c* ... 1Sa 10:24 977
behold the king whom ye have *c* ... 1Sa 12:13 977
Neither hath the LORD *c* this ... 1Sa 16:8 977
Neither hath the LORD *c* this ... 1Sa 16:9 977
Jesse, The LORD hath not *c* these ... 1Sa 16:10 977
do not I know that thou hast *c* ... 1Sa 20:30 977
thousand *c* men out of all Israel ... 1Sa 24:2 970
having three thousand *c* men of ... 1Sa 26:2 970
together all the *c* men of Israel ... 2Sa 6:1 970
of thy people which thou hast *c* ... 1Kin 3:8 977
toward the city which thou hast *c* ... 1Kin 8:44 977
the city which thou hast *c* ... 1Kin 8:48 977
Jerusalem's sake which I have *c* ... 1Kin 11:13 977
the city which I have *c* out of ... 1Kin 11:32 977
the city which I have *c* me to put ... 1Kin 11:36 977
and fourscore thousand *c* men ... 1Kin 12:21 970
which I have *c* out of all tribes ... 2Kin 21:7 977
city Jerusalem which I have *c* ... 2Kin 23:27 977
All these which were *c* to be ... 1Chr 9:22 1305
for them hath the LORD *c* to carry ... 1Chr 15:2 977
ye children of Jacob, his *c* ones ... 1Chr 16:13 972
Jeduthun, and the rest that were *c* ... 1Chr 16:41 1305
for he hath *c* Judah to be the ... 1Chr 28:4 977
he hath *c* Solomon my son to sit ... 1Chr 28:5 977
for I have *c* him to be my son, and ... 1Chr 28:6 977
for the LORD hath *c* thee to build ... 1Chr 28:10 977
my son, whom alone God hath *c* ... 1Chr 29:1 977
But I have *c* Jerusalem, that my ... 2Chr 6:6 977
have *c* David to be over my people ... 2Chr 6:6 977
this city which thou hast *c* ... 2Chr 6:34 977
toward the city which thou hast *c* ... 2Chr 6:38 977
have *c* this place to myself for ... 2Chr 7:12 977
For now have I *c* and sanctified ... 2Chr 7:16 977
and fourscore thousand *c* men ... 2Chr 11:1 970
the city which the LORD had *c* out ... 2Chr 12:13 977
even four hundred thousand *c* men ... 2Chr 13:3 970
with eight hundred thousand *c* men ... 2Chr 13:3 970
five hundred thousand *c* men ... 2Chr 13:17 970
for the LORD hath *c* you to stand ... 2Chr 29:11 970
which I have *c* before all the ... 2Chr 33:7 970
I have *c* to set my name there ... Neh 1:9 970
for this hast thou *c* rather than ... Job 36:21 970
he hath *c* for his own inheritance ... Ps 33:12 970
and smote down the *c* men of Israel ... Ps 78:31 970
I have made a covenant with my *c* ... Ps 89:3 972
exalted one *c* out of the people ... Ps 89:19 970
ye children of Jacob his *c* ... Ps 105:6 972
and Aaron whom he had *c* ... Ps 105:26 977
with joy, and his *c* with gladness ... Ps 105:43 972
That I may see the good of thy *c* ... Ps 106:5 972
had not Moses his *c* stood before ... Ps 106:23 972
I have *c* the way of truth ... Ps 119:30 977
for I have *c* thy precepts ... Ps 119:173 977
For the LORD hath *c* Zion ... Ps 132:13 977
For the LORD hath *c* Jacob unto ... Ps 135:4 977
rather to be *c* than silver ... Prov 16:16 977
rather to be *c* than great riches ... Prov 22:1 977
for the gardens that ye have *c* ... Is 1:29 977
my servant, Jacob whom I have *c* ... Is 41:8 977
I have *c* thee, and not cast thee ... Is 41:9 977
LORD, and my servant whom I have *c* ... Is 43:10 977
to give drink to my people, my *c* ... Is 43:20 972
and Israel, whom I have *c* ... Is 44:1 977
and thou, Jesurun, whom I have *c* ... Is 44:2 977
I have *c* thee in the furnace of ... Is 48:10 977
Is it such a fast that I have *c* ... Is 58:5 977
not this the fast that I have *c* ... Is 58:6 977
your name for a curse unto my *c* ... Is 65:15 972
they have *c* their own ways, and ... Is 66:3 977
death shall be *c* rather than life ... Jer 8:3 977
families which the LORD hath *c* ... Jer 33:24 977
his *c* young men are gone down to ... Jer 48:15 4005
and who is a *c* man, that I may ... Jer 49:19 970
and who is a *c* man, that I may ... Jer 50:44 970
that were the *c* men of Assyria ... Eze 23:7 4005
withstand, neither his *c* people ... Dan 11:15 4005
for I have *c* thee, saith the LORD ... Hag 2:23 977
that hath *c* Jerusalem rebuke thee ... Zec 3:2 977
Behold my servant, whom I have *c* ... Mt 12:18 *140*
for many be called, but few *c* ... Mt 20:16 *1588*
many are called, but few are *c* ... Mt 22:14 *1588*
the elect's sake, whom he hath *c* ... Mk 13:20 *1586*
Mary hath *c* that good part, which ... Lk 10:42 *1586*
if he be Christ, the *c* of God ... Lk 23:35 *1588*
them, Have not I *c* you twelve ... Jn 6:70 *1586*
I know whom I have *c* ... Jn 13:18 *1586*
not *c* me, but I have *c* you ... Jn 15:16 *1586*
but I have *c* you out of the world ... Jn 15:19 *1586*
unto the apostles whom he had *c* ... Acts 1:2 *1586*
whether of these two thou hast *c* ... Acts 1:24 *1586*
for he is a *c* vessel unto me, to ... Acts 9:15 *1589*
unto witnesses *c* before of God ... Acts 10:41 *4401*
to send *c* men of their own ... Acts 15:22 *1586*
to send *c* men unto you with our ... Acts 15:25 *1586*
God of our fathers hath *c* thee ... Acts 22:14 *4400*
Salute Rufus *c* in the Lord ... Rom 16:13 *1588*
But God hath *c* the foolish things ... 1Cor 1:27 *1586*
God hath *c* the weak things of the ... 1Cor 1:27 *1586*
which are despised, hath God *c* ... 1Cor 1:28 *1586*
but who was also *c* of the ... 2Cor 8:19 *5500*
According as he hath *c* us in him ... Eph 1:4 *1586*
c you to salvation through ... 2Th 2:13 *138*
who hath *c* him to be a soldier ... 2Ti 2:4 *4758*
Hath not God *c* the poor of this ... Jas 2:5 *1586*
but *c* of God, and precious, ... 1Pet 2:4 *1588*
But ye are a *c* generation ... 1Pet 2:9 *1588*
are with him are called, and *c* ... Rev 17:14 *1588*

CHOZEBA *(ko-ze'-bah)* {1} See CHEZIB. *A city in Judah.*

And Jokim, and the men of *C* ... 1Chr 4:22 3578

CHRIST *(krist)* {555} See ANTICHRIST, CHRISTIAN, CHRIST'S, CHRISTS, JESUS, MESSIAH. *A title of Jesus of Nazareth; Greek for Messiah.*

book of the generation of Jesus *C* ... Mt 1:1 *5547*
was born Jesus, who is called *C* ... Mt 1:16 *5547*
unto *C* are fourteen generations ... Mt 1:17 *5547*
birth of Jesus *C* was on this wise ... Mt 1:18 *5547*
of them where *C* should be born ... Mt 2:4 *5547*
in the prison the works of *C* ... Mt 11:2 *5547*
answered and said, Thou art the *C* ... Mt 16:16 *5547*
no man that he was Jesus the *C* ... Mt 16:20 *5547*
Saying, What think ye of *C* ... Mt 22:42 *5547*
for one is your Master, even *C* ... Mt 23:8 *5547*
for one is your Master, even *C* ... Mt 23:10 *5547*
come in my name, saying, I am *C* ... Mt 24:5 *5547*
shall say unto you, Lo, here is *C* ... Mt 24:23 *5547*
tell us whether thou be the *C* ... Mt 26:63 *5547*
Saying, Prophesy unto us, thou *C* ... Mt 26:68 *5547*
or Jesus which is called *C* ... Mt 27:17 *5547*
then with Jesus which is called *C* ... Mt 27:22 *5547*
of the gospel of Jesus *C*, the Son ... Mk 1:1 *5547*
and saith unto him, Thou art the *C* ... Mk 8:29 *5547*
my name, because ye belong to *C* ... Mk 9:41 *5547*
that *C* is the son of David ... Mk 12:35 *5547*
come in my name, saying, I am *C* ... Mk 13:6
shall say to you, Lo, here is *C* ... Mk 13:21 *5547*
and said unto him, Art thou the *C* ... Mk 14:61 *5547*
Let *C* the King of Israel descend ... Mk 15:32 *5547*
a Saviour, which is *C* the Lord ... Lk 2:11 *5547*
before he had seen the Lord's *C* ... Lk 2:26 *5547*
of John, whether he were the *C* ... Lk 3:15 *5547*
Thou art *C* the Son of God ... Lk 4:41 *5547*
for they knew that he was *C* ... Lk 4:41 *5547*
answering said, The *C* of God ... Lk 9:20 *5547*
say they that *C* is David's son ... Lk 20:41 *5547*
come in my name, saying, I am *C* ... Lk 21:8
Art thou the *C* ... Lk 22:67 *5547*
that he himself is *C* a King ... Lk 23:2 *5547*
let him save himself, if he be *C* ... Lk 23:35 *5547*
on him, saying, If thou be *C* ... Lk 23:39 *5547*
Ought not *C* to have suffered ... Lk 24:26 *5547*
and thus it behoved *C* to suffer ... Lk 24:46 *5547*
grace and truth came by Jesus *C* ... Jn 1:17 *5547*
but confessed, I am not the *C* ... Jn 1:20 *5547*
thou then, if thou be not that *C* ... Jn 1:25 *5547*
is, being interpreted, the *C* ... Jn 1:41 *5547*
that I said, I am not the *C* ... Jn 3:28 *5547*
Messias cometh, which is called *C* ... Jn 4:25 *5547*
is not this the *C* ... Jn 4:29 *5547*
and know that this is indeed the *C* ... Jn 4:42 *5547*
and are sure that thou art that *C* ... Jn 6:69 *5547*
indeed that this is the very *C* ... Jn 7:26 *5547*
but when *C* cometh, no man knoweth ... Jn 7:27 *5547*
When *C* cometh, will he do more ... Jn 7:31 *5547*
Others said, This is the *C* ... Jn 7:41 *5547*
Shall *C* come out of Galilee ... Jn 7:41 *5547*
That *C* cometh of the seed of ... Jn 7:42 *5547*
any man did confess that he was *C* ... Jn 9:22 *5547*
If thou be the *C*, tell us plainly ... Jn 10:24 *5547*
I believe that thou art the *C* ... Jn 11:27 *5547*
the law that *C* abideth for ever ... Jn 12:34 *5547*
the only true God, and Jesus *C* ... Jn 17:3 *5547*
might believe that Jesus is the *C* ... Jn 20:31 *5547*
he would raise up *C* to sit on his ... Acts 2:30 *5547*
spake of the resurrection of *C* ... Acts 2:31 *5547*
ye have crucified, both Lord and *C* ... Acts 2:36 *5547*
Jesus *C* for the remission of sins ... Acts 2:38 *5547*
of Jesus *C* of Nazareth rise up ... Acts 3:6 *5547*
that *C* should suffer, he hath so ... Acts 3:18 *5547*
And he shall send Jesus *C*, which ... Acts 3:20 *5547*
the name of Jesus *C* of Nazareth ... Acts 4:10 *5547*
the Lord, and against his *C* ... Acts 4:26 *5547*
not to teach and preach Jesus *C* ... Acts 5:42 *5547*
Samaria, and preached *C* unto them ... Acts 8:5 *5547*
of God, and the name of Jesus *C* ... Acts 8:12 *5547*
that Jesus *C* is the Son of God ... Acts 8:37 *5547*
he preached *C* in the synagogues ... Acts 9:20 *5547*
proving that this is very *C* ... Acts 9:22 *5547*
Jesus *C* maketh thee whole ... Acts 9:34 *5547*
preaching peace by Jesus *C* ... Acts 10:36 *5547*
who believed on the Lord Jesus *C* ... Acts 11:17 *5547*
Lord Jesus *C* we shall be saved ... Acts 15:11 *5547*
for the name of our Lord Jesus *C* ... Acts 15:26 *5547*
of Jesus *C* to come out of her ... Acts 16:18 *5547*
said, Believe on the Lord Jesus *C* ... Acts 16:31 *5547*
that *C* must needs have suffered, ... Acts 17:3 *5547*
whom I preach unto you, is *C* ... Acts 17:3 *5547*
to the Jews that Jesus was *C* ... Acts 18:5 *5547*
the scriptures that Jesus was *C* ... Acts 18:28 *5547*
after him, that is, on *C* Jesus ... Acts 19:4 *5547*
and faith toward our Lord Jesus *C* ... Acts 20:21 *5547*
him concerning the faith in *C* ... Acts 24:24 *5547*
That *C* should suffer, and that he ... Acts 26:23 *5547*
which concern the Lord Jesus *C* ... Acts 28:31 *5547*
Paul, a servant of Jesus *C* ... Rom 1:1 *5547*
his Son Jesus *C* our Lord, which ... Rom 1:3 *5547*
are ye also the called of Jesus *C* ... Rom 1:6 *5547*
our Father, and the Lord Jesus *C* ... Rom 1:7 *5547*
God through Jesus *C* for you all ... Rom 1:8 *5547*
am not ashamed of the gospel of *C* ... Rom 1:16 *5547*
by Jesus *C* according to my gospel ... Rom 2:16 *5547*
is by faith of Jesus *C* unto all ... Rom 3:22 *5547*
the redemption that is in *C* Jesus ... Rom 3:24 *5547*
with God through our Lord Jesus *C* ... Rom 5:1 *5547*
in due time *C* died for the ... Rom 5:6 *5547*
were yet sinners, *C* died for us ... Rom 5:8 *5547*
in God through our Lord Jesus *C* ... Rom 5:11 *5547*
which is by one man, Jesus *C* ... Rom 5:15 *5547*
reign in life by one, Jesus *C* ... Rom 5:17 *5547*
eternal life by Jesus *C* our Lord ... Rom 5:21 *5547*
C were baptized into his death ... Rom 6:3 *5547*
that like as *C* was raised up from ... Rom 6:4 *5547*
Now if we be dead with *C*, we ... Rom 6:8 *5547*
Knowing that *C* being raised from ... Rom 6:9 *5547*
unto God through Jesus *C* our Lord ... Rom 6:11 *5547*
life through Jesus *C* our Lord ... Rom 6:23 *5547*
dead to the law by the body of *C* ... Rom 7:4 *5547*
God through Jesus *C* our Lord ... Rom 7:25 *5547*
to them which are in *C* Jesus ... Rom 8:1 *5547*
in *C* Jesus hath made me free from ... Rom 8:2 *5547*
any man have not the Spirit of *C* ... Rom 8:9 *5547*
if *C* be in you, the body is dead ... Rom 8:10 *5547*
he that raised up *C* from the dead ... Rom 8:11 *5547*
of God, and joint-heirs with *C* ... Rom 8:17 *5477*
It is *C* that died, yea rather, ... Rom 8:34 *5547*
separate us from the love of *C* ... Rom 8:35 *5547*
which is in *C* Jesus our Lord ... Rom 8:39 *5547*
I say the truth in *C*, I lie not, ... Rom 9:1 *5547*
accursed from *C* for my brethren ... Rom 9:3 *5547*
as concerning the flesh *C* came ... Rom 9:5 *5547*
For *C* is the end of the law for ... Rom 10:4 *5547*
to bring *C* down from above ... Rom 10:6 *5547*
to bring up *C* again from the dead ... Rom 10:7 *5547*
we, being many, are one body in *C* ... Rom 12:5 *5547*
But put ye on the Lord Jesus *C* ... Rom 13:14 *5547*
For to this end *C* both died ... Rom 14:9 *5547*
before the judgment seat of *C* ... Rom 14:10 *5547*
with thy meat, for whom *C* died ... Rom 14:15 *5547*
serveth *C* is acceptable to God ... Rom 14:18 *5547*
For even *C* pleased not himself ... Rom 15:3 *5547*
another according to *C* Jesus ... Rom 15:5 *5547*
the Father of our Lord Jesus *C* ... Rom 15:6 *5547*
as *C* also received us to the ... Rom 15:7 *5547*
Now I say that Jesus *C* was a ... Rom 15:8 *5547*
of Jesus *C* to the Gentiles ... Rom 15:16 *5547*
I may glory through Jesus *C* in ... Rom 15:17 *5547*
which *C* hath not wrought by me ... Rom 15:18 *5547*
fully preached the gospel of *C* ... Rom 15:19 *5547*
the gospel, not where *C* was named ... Rom 15:20 *5547*
the blessing of the gospel of *C* ... Rom 15:29 *5547*
and Aquila my helpers in *C* Jesus ... Rom 16:3 *5547*
the firstfruits of Achaia unto *C* ... Rom 16:5 *5547*
who also were in *C* before me ... Rom 16:7 *5547*
Salute Urbane, our helper in *C* ... Rom 16:9 *5547*
Salute Apelles approved in *C* ... Rom 16:10 *5547*
The churches of *C* salute you ... Rom 16:16 *5547*
such serve not our Lord Jesus *C* ... Rom 16:18 *5547*
of our Lord Jesus *C* be with you ... Rom 16:20 *5547*
our Lord Jesus *C* be with you all ... Rom 16:24 *5547*
and the preaching of Jesus *C* ... Rom 16:25 *5547*
be glory through Jesus *C* for ever ... Rom 16:27 *5547*
Jesus *C* through the will of God ... 1Cor 1:1 *5547*
that are sanctified in *C* Jesus ... 1Cor 1:2 *5547*
upon the name of Jesus *C* our Lord ... 1Cor 1:2 *5547*
Father, and from the Lord Jesus *C* ... 1Cor 1:3 *5547*
God which is given you by Jesus *C* ... 1Cor 1:4 *5547*
of *C* was confirmed in you ... 1Cor 1:6 *5547*
the coming of our Lord Jesus *C* ... 1Cor 1:7 *5547*
in the day of our Lord Jesus *C* ... 1Cor 1:8 *5547*
of his Son Jesus *C* our Lord ... 1Cor 1:9 *5547*
by the name of our Lord Jesus *C* ... 1Cor 1:10 *5547*
and I of *C* ... 1Cor 1:12 *5547*
Is *C* divided? ... 1Cor 1:13 *5547*
For *C* sent me not to baptize, but ... 1Cor 1:17 *5547*
lest the cross of *C* should be ... 1Cor 1:17 *5547*
But we preach *C* crucified ... 1Cor 1:23 *5547*
C the power of God, and the wisdom ... 1Cor 1:24 *5547*
But of him are ye in *C* Jesus ... 1Cor 1:30 *5547*
any thing among you, save Jesus *C* ... 1Cor 2:2 *5547*
But we have the mind of *C* ... 1Cor 2:16 *5547*
carnal, even as unto babes in *C* ... 1Cor 3:1 *5547*

that is laid, which is Jesus *C* 1Cor 3:11 *5547*
and *C* is God's 1Cor 3:23 *5547*
of us, as of the ministers of *C* 1Cor 4:1 *5547*
sake, but ye are wise in *C* 1Cor 4:10 *5547*
ten thousand instructers in *C* 1Cor 4:15 *5547*
for in *C* Jesus I have begotten 1Cor 4:15 *5547*
of my ways which be in *C*, as I 1Cor 4:17 *5547*
In the name of our Lord Jesus *C* 1Cor 5:4 *5547*
the power of our Lord Jesus *C* 1Cor 5:4 *5547*
For even *C* our passover is 1Cor 5:7 *5547*
your bodies are the members of *C* 1Cor 6:15 *5547*
I then take the members of *C* 1Cor 6:15 *5547*
and one Lord Jesus *C*, by whom are 1Cor 8:6 *5547*
brother perish, for whom *C* died 1Cor 8:11 *5547*
weak conscience, ye sin against *C* 1Cor 8:12 *5547*
have I not seen Jesus *C* our Lord 1Cor 9:1 *5547*
we should hinder the gospel of *C* 1Cor 9:12 *5547*
the gospel of *C* without charge 1Cor 9:18 *5547*
to God, but under the law to *C* 1Cor 9:21 *5547*
and that Rock was *C* 1Cor 10:4 *5547*
Neither let us tempt *C*, as some 1Cor 10:9 *5547*
the communion of the blood of *C* 1Cor 10:16 *5547*
the communion of the body of *C* 1Cor 10:16 *5547*
of me, even as I also am of *C* 1Cor 11:1 *5547*
that the head of every man is *C* 1Cor 11:3 *5547*
and the head of *C* is God 1Cor 11:3 *5547*
so also is *C* 1Cor 12:12 *5547*
Now ye are the body of *C*, and 1Cor 12:27 *5547*
how that *C* died for our sins 1Cor 15:3 *5547*
Now if *C* be preached that he rose 1Cor 15:12 *5547*
of the dead, then is *C* not risen 1Cor 15:13 *5547*
if *C* be not risen, then is our 1Cor 15:14 *5547*
of God that he raised up *C* 1Cor 15:15 *5547*
rise not, then is not *C* raised 1Cor 15:16 *5547*
if *C* be not raised, your faith is 1Cor 15:17 *5547*
fallen asleep in *C* are perished 1Cor 15:18 *5547*
this life only we have hope in *C* 1Cor 15:19 *5547*
But now is *C* risen from the dead, 1Cor 15:20 *5547*
even so in *C* shall all be made 1Cor 15:22 *5547*
C the firstfruits 1Cor 15:23 *5547*
which I have in *C* Jesus our Lord 1Cor 15:31 *5547*
victory through our Lord Jesus *C* 1Cor 15:57 *5547*
any man love not the Lord Jesus *C* 1Cor 16:22 *5547*
of our Lord Jesus *C* be with you 1Cor 16:23 *5547*
love be with you all in *C* Jesus 1Cor 16:24 *5547*
of Jesus *C* by the will of God 2Cor 1:1 *5547*
Father, and from the Lord Jesus *C* 2Cor 1:2 *5547*
the Father of our Lord Jesus *C* 2Cor 1:3 *5547*
the sufferings of *C* abound in us 2Cor 1:5 *5547*
consolation also aboundeth by *C* 2Cor 1:5 *5547*
For the Son of God, Jesus *C* 2Cor 1:19 *5547*
stablisheth us with you in *C* 2Cor 1:21 *5547*
forgave I it in the person of *C* 2Cor 2:10 *5547*
always causeth us to triumph in *C* 2Cor 2:14 *5547*
are unto God a sweet savour of *C* 2Cor 2:15 *5547*
in the sight of God speak we in *C* 2Cor 2:17 *5547*
the epistle of *C* ministered by us 2Cor 3:3 *5547*
have we through *C* to God-ward 2Cor 3:4 *5547*
which vail is done away in *C* 2Cor 3:14 *5547*
light of the glorious gospel of *C* 2Cor 4:4 *5547*
ourselves, but *C* Jesus the Lord 2Cor 4:5 *5547*
of God in the face of Jesus *C* 2Cor 4:6 *5547*
before the judgment seat of *C* 2Cor 5:10 *5547*
For the love of *C* constraineth us 2Cor 5:14 *5547*
we have known *C* after the flesh 2Cor 5:16 *5547*
Therefore if any man be in *C* 2Cor 5:17 *5547*
us to himself by Jesus *C*, and hath 2Cor 5:18 *5547*
To wit, that God was in *C* 2Cor 5:19 *5547*
Now then we are ambassadors for *C* 2Cor 5:20 *5547*
what concord hath *C* with Belial 2Cor 6:15 *5547*
the grace of our Lord Jesus *C* 2Cor 8:9 *5547*
the churches, and the glory of *C* 2Cor 8:23 *5547*
subjection into the gospel of *C* 2Cor 9:13 *5547*
the meekness and gentleness of *C* 2Cor 10:1 *5547*
thought to the obedience of *C* 2Cor 10:5 *5547*
also in preaching the gospel of *C* 2Cor 10:14 *5547*
you as a chaste virgin to *C* 2Cor 11:2 *5547*
from the simplicity that is in *C* 2Cor 11:3 *5547*
As the truth of *C* is in me 2Cor 11:10 *5547*
themselves into the apostles of *C* 2Cor 11:13 *5547*
Are they ministers of *C* 2Cor 11:23 *5547*
God and Father of our Lord Jesus *C* 2Cor 11:31 *5547*
I knew a man in *C* above fourteen 2Cor 12:2 *5547*
the power of *C* may rest upon me 2Cor 12:9 *5547*
we speak before God in *C* 2Cor 12:19 *5547*
seek a proof of *C* speaking in me 2Cor 13:3 *5547*
how that Jesus *C* is in you 2Cor 13:5 *5547*
The grace of the Lord Jesus *C* 2Cor 13:14 *5547*
neither by man, but by Jesus *C* Gal 1:1 *5547*
Father, and from our Lord Jesus *C* Gal 1:3 *5547*
grace of *C* unto another gospel Gal 1:6 *5547*
and would pervert the gospel of *C* Gal 1:7 *5547*
I should not be the servant of *C* Gal 1:10 *5547*
but by the revelation of Jesus *C* Gal 1:12 *5547*
of Judaea which were in *C* Gal 1:22 *5547*
liberty which we have in *C* Jesus Gal 2:4 *5547*
law, but by the faith of Jesus *C* Gal 2:16 *5547*
even we have believed in Jesus *C* Gal 2:16 *5547*
be justified by the faith of *C* Gal 2:16 *5547*
we seek to be justified by *C* Gal 2:17 *5547*
is therefore *C* the minister of Gal 2:17 *5547*
I am crucified with *C* Gal 2:20 *5547*
yet not I, but *C* liveth in me Gal 2:20 *5547*
the law, then *C* is dead in vain Gal 2:21 *5547*
before whose eyes Jesus *C* hath Gal 3:1 *5547*
C hath redeemed us from the curse Gal 3:13 *5547*
on the Gentiles through Jesus *C* Gal 3:14 *5547*
one, And to thy seed, which is *C* Gal 3:16 *5547*
was confirmed before of God in *C* Gal 3:17 *5547*
C might be given to them that Gal 3:22 *5547*
schoolmaster to bring us unto *C* Gal 3:24 *5547*
of God by faith in *C* Jesus Gal 3:26 *5547*
baptized into *C* have put on *C* Gal 3:27 *5547*
for ye are all one in *C* Jesus Gal 3:28 *5547*
then an heir of God through *C* Gal 4:7 *5547*
an angel of God, even as *C* Jesus Gal 4:14 *5547*
again until *C* be formed in you Gal 4:19 *5547*
wherewith *C* hath made us free Gal 5:1 *5547*
C shall profit you nothing Gal 5:2 *5547*
C is become of no effect unto you Gal 5:4 *5547*
For in Jesus *C* neither Gal 5:6 *5547*
and so fulfil the law of *C* Gal 6:2 *5547*
persecution for the cross of *C* Gal 6:12 *5547*
in the cross of our Lord Jesus *C* Gal 6:14 *5547*
For in *C* Jesus neither Gal 6:15 *5547*
Lord Jesus *C* be with your spirit Gal 6:18 *5547*
of Jesus *C* by the will of God Eph 1:1 *5547*
and to the faithful in *C* Jesus Eph 1:1 *5547*
Father, and from the Lord Jesus *C* Eph 1:2 *5547*
God and Father of our Lord Jesus *C* Eph 1:3 *5547*
blessings in heavenly places in *C* Eph 1:3 *5547*
of children by Jesus *C* to himself Eph 1:5 *5547*
together in one all things in *C* Eph 1:10 *5547*
his glory, who first trusted in *C* Eph 1:12 *5547*
That the God of our Lord Jesus *C* Eph 1:17 *5547*
Which he wrought in *C*, when he Eph 1:20 *5547*
hath quickened us together with *C* Eph 2:5 *5547*
in heavenly places in *C* Jesus Eph 2:6 *5547*
toward us through *C* Jesus Eph 2:7 *5547*
created in *C* Jesus unto good Eph 2:10 *5547*
at that time ye were without *C* Eph 2:12 *5547*
But now in *C* Jesus ye who Eph 2:13 *5547*
are made nigh by the blood of *C* Eph 2:13 *5547*
Jesus *C* himself being the chief Eph 2:20 *5547*
of Jesus *C* for you Gentiles Eph 3:1 *5547*
my knowledge in the mystery of *C*) Eph 3:4 *5547*
of his promise in *C* by the gospel Eph 3:6 *5547*
the unsearchable riches of *C* Eph 3:8 *5547*
who created all things by Jesus *C* Eph 3:9 *5547*
he purposed in *C* Jesus our Lord Eph 3:11 *5547*
the Father of our Lord Jesus *C* Eph 3:14 *5547*
That *C* may dwell in your hearts Eph 3:17 *5547*
And to know the love of *C*, which Eph 3:19 *5547*
by *C* Jesus throughout all ages Eph 3:21 *5547*
to the measure of the gift of *C* Eph 4:7 *5547*
for the edifying of the body of *C* Eph 4:12 *5547*
the stature of the fulness of *C* Eph 4:13 *5547*
things, which is the head, even *C* Eph 4:15 *5547*
But ye have not so learned *C* Eph 4:20 *5547*
as *C* also hath loved us, and hath Eph 5:2 *5547*
inheritance in the kingdom of *C* Eph 5:5 *5547*
dead, and *C* shall give thee light Eph 5:14 *5547*
in the name of our Lord Jesus *C* Eph 5:20 *5547*
even as *C* is the head of the Eph 5:23 *5547*
as the church is subject unto *C* Eph 5:24 *5547*
even as *C* also loved the church, Eph 5:25 *5547*
but I speak concerning *C* and the Eph 5:32 *5547*
of your heart, as unto *C* Eph 6:5 *5547*
but as the servants of *C*, doing Eph 6:6 *5547*
the Father and the Lord Jesus *C* Eph 6:23 *5547*
our Lord Jesus *C* in sincerity Eph 6:24 *5547*
the servants of Jesus *C*, to all Phil 1:1 *5547*
to all the saints in *C* Jesus Phil 1:1 *5547*
Father, and from the Lord Jesus *C* Phil 1:2 *5547*
it until the day of Jesus *C* Phil 1:6 *5547*
you all in the bowels of Jesus *C* Phil 1:8 *5547*
without offence till the day of *C* Phil 1:10 *5547*
which are by Jesus *C*, unto the Phil 1:11 *5547*
So that my bonds in *C* are Phil 1:13 *5547*
Some indeed preach *C* even of envy Phil 1:15 *5547*
The one preach *C* of contention Phil 1:16 *5547*
or in truth, *C* is preached Phil 1:18 *5547*
supply of the Spirit of Jesus *C* Phil 1:19 *5547*
so now also *C* shall be magnified Phil 1:20 *5547*
For to me to live is *C*, and to die Phil 1:21 *5547*
desire to depart, and to be with *C* Phil 1:23 *5547*
C for me by my coming to you Phil 1:26 *5547*
be as it becometh the gospel of *C* Phil 1:27 *5547*
it is given in the behalf of *C* Phil 1:29 *5547*
be therefore any consolation in *C* Phil 2:1 *5547*
in you, which was also in *C* Jesus Phil 2:5 *5547*
confess that Jesus *C* is Lord Phil 2:11 *5547*
I may rejoice in the day of *C* Phil 2:16 *5547*
work of *C* he was nigh unto death Phil 2:30 *5547*
the spirit, and rejoice in *C* Jesus Phil 3:3 *5547*
to me, those I counted loss for *C* Phil 3:7 *5547*
the knowledge of *C* Jesus my Lord Phil 3:8 *5547*
them but dung, that I may win *C* Phil 3:8 *5547*
which is through the faith of *C* Phil 3:9 *5547*
also I am apprehended of *C* Jesus Phil 3:12 *5547*
high calling of God in *C* Jesus Phil 3:14 *5547*
are the enemies of the cross of *C* Phil 3:18 *5547*
for the Saviour, the Lord Jesus *C* Phil 3:20 *5547*
hearts and minds through *C* Jesus Phil 4:7 *5547*
through *C* which strengtheneth me Phil 4:13 *5547*
to his riches in glory by *C* Jesus Phil 4:19 *5547*
Salute every saint in *C* Jesus Phil 4:21 *5547*
our Lord Jesus *C* be with you all Phil 4:23 *5547*
of Jesus *C* by the will of God Col 1:1 *5547*
in *C* which are at Colosse Col 1:2 *5547*
our Father and the Lord Jesus *C* Col 1:2 *5547*
and the Father of our Lord Jesus *C* Col 1:3 *5547*
we heard of your faith in *C* Jesus Col 1:4 *5547*
for you a faithful minister of *C* Col 1:7 *5547*
C in my flesh for his body's sake Col 1:24 *5547*
which is *C* in you, the hope of Col 1:27 *5547*
every man perfect in *C* Jesus Col 1:28 *5547*
of God, and of the Father, and of *C* Col 2:2 *5547*
stedfastness of your faith in *C* Col 2:5 *5547*
received *C* Jesus the Lord Col 2:6 *5547*
of the world, and not after *C* Col 2:8 *5547*
flesh by the circumcision of *C* Col 2:11 *5547*
but the body is of *C* Col 2:17 *5547*
Wherefore if ye be dead with *C* Col 2:20 *5547*
If ye then be risen with *C* Col 3:1 *5547*
where *C* sitteth on the right hand Col 3:1 *5547*
and your life is hid with *C* in God Col 3:3 *5547*
When *C*, who is our life, shall Col 3:4 *5547*
but *C* is all, and in all Col 3:11 *5547*
even as *C* forgave you, so also do Col 3:13 *5547*
Let the word of *C* dwell in you Col 3:16 *5547*
for ye serve the Lord *C* Col 3:24 *5547*
to speak the mystery of *C* Col 4:3 *5547*
who is one of you, a servant of *C* Col 4:12 *5547*
the Father and in the Lord Jesus *C* 1Th 1:1 *5547*
our Father, and the Lord Jesus *C* 1Th 1:1 *5547*
of hope in our Lord Jesus *C* 1Th 1:3 *5547*
burdensome, as the apostles of *C* 1Th 2:6 *5547*
which in Judaea are in *C* Jesus 1Th 2:14 *5547*
of our Lord Jesus *C* at his coming 1Th 2:19 *5547*
fellowlabourer in the gospel of *C* 1Th 3:2 *5547*
our Father, and our Lord Jesus *C* 1Th 3:11 *5547*
Lord Jesus *C* with all his saints 1Th 3:13 *5547*
the dead in *C* shall rise first 1Th 4:16 *5547*
salvation by our Lord Jesus *C* 1Th 5:9 *5547*
of God in *C* Jesus concerning you 1Th 5:18 *5547*
the coming of our Lord Jesus *C* 1Th 5:23 *5547*
of our Lord Jesus *C* be with you 1Th 5:28 *5547*
our Father and the Lord Jesus *C* 2Th 1:1 *5547*
our Father and the Lord Jesus *C* 2Th 1:2 *5547*
the gospel of our Lord Jesus *C* 2Th 1:8 *5547*
Jesus *C* may be glorified in you 2Th 1:12 *5547*
of our God and the Lord Jesus *C* 2Th 1:12 *5547*
by the coming of our Lord Jesus *C* 2Th 2:1 *5547*
as that the day of *C* is at hand 2Th 2:2 *5547*
of the glory of our Lord Jesus *C* 2Th 2:14 *5547*
Now our Lord Jesus *C* himself 2Th 2:16 *5547*
and into the patient waiting for *C* 2Th 3:5 *5547*
in the name of our Lord Jesus *C* 2Th 3:6 *5547*
and exhort by our Lord Jesus *C* 2Th 3:12 *5547*
our Lord Jesus *C* be with you all 2Th 3:18 *5547*
an apostle of Jesus *C* by the 1Ti 1:1 *5547*
God our Saviour, and Lord Jesus *C* 1Ti 1:1 *5547*
our Father and Jesus *C* our Lord 1Ti 1:2 *5547*
I thank *C* Jesus our Lord, who 1Ti 1:12 *5547*
faith and love which is in *C* Jesus 1Ti 1:14 *5547*
that *C* Jesus came into the world 1Ti 1:15 *5547*
Jesus *C* might shew forth all 1Ti 1:16 *5547*
God and men, the man *C* Jesus 1Ti 2:5 *5547*
apostle, (I speak the truth in *C* 1Ti 2:7 *5547*
in the faith which is in *C* Jesus 1Ti 3:13 *5547*
be a good minister of Jesus *C* 1Ti 4:6 *5547*
begun to wax wanton against *C* 1Ti 5:11 *5547*
before God, and the Lord Jesus *C* 1Ti 5:21 *5547*
the words of our Lord Jesus *C* 1Ti 6:3 *5547*
all things, and before *C* Jesus 1Ti 6:13 *5547*
the appearing of our Lord Jesus *C* 1Ti 6:14 *5547*
of Jesus *C* by the will of God 2Ti 1:1 *5547*
of life which is in *C* Jesus 2Ti 1:1 *5547*
the Father and *C* Jesus our Lord 2Ti 1:2 *5547*
which was given us in *C* Jesus 2Ti 1:9 *5547*
appearing of our Saviour Jesus *C* 2Ti 1:10 *5547*
faith and love which is in *C* Jesus 2Ti 1:13 *5547*
in the grace that is in *C* Jesus 2Ti 2:1 *5547*
as a good soldier of Jesus *C* 2Ti 2:3 *5547*
Remember that Jesus *C* of the seed 2Ti 2:8 *5547*
is in *C* Jesus with eternal glory 2Ti 2:10 *5547*
name of *C* depart from iniquity 2Ti 2:19 *5547*
all that will live godly in *C* 2Ti 3:12 *5547*
through faith which is in *C* Jesus 2Ti 3:15 *5547*
before God, and the Lord Jesus *C* 2Ti 4:1 *5547*
The Lord Jesus *C* be with thy 2Ti 4:22 *5547*
of God, and an apostle of Jesus *C* Titus 1:1 *5547*
and the Lord Jesus *C* our Saviour Titus 1:4 *5547*
great God and our Saviour Jesus *C* Titus 2:13 *5547*
through Jesus *C* our Saviour Titus 3:6 *5547*
Paul, a prisoner of Jesus *C* Philem 1 *5547*
our Father and the Lord Jesus *C* Philem 3 *5547*
thing which is in you in *C* Jesus Philem 6 *5547*
in *C* to enjoin thee that which is Philem 8 *5547*
and now also a prisoner of Jesus *C* Philem 9 *5547*
my fellowprisoner in *C* Jesus Philem 23 *5547*
Lord Jesus *C* be with your spirit Philem 25 *5547*
Priest of our profession, *C* Jesus Heb 3:1 *5547*
But *C* as a son over his own house Heb 3:6 *5547*
For we are made partakers of *C* Heb 3:14 *5547*
So also *C* glorified not himself Heb 5:5 *5547*
principles of the doctrine of *C* Heb 6:1 *5547*
But *C* being come an high priest Heb 9:11 *5547*
much more shall the blood of *C* Heb 9:14 *5547*
For *C* is not entered into the Heb 9:24 *5547*
So *C* was once offered to bear the Heb 9:28 *5547*
the body of Jesus *C* once for all Heb 10:10 *5547*
of *C* greater riches than the Heb 11:26 *5547*
Jesus *C* the same yesterday, and to Heb 13:8 *5547*
in his sight, through Jesus *C* Heb 13:21 *5547*
of God and of the Lord Jesus *C* Jas 1:1 *5547*
not the faith of our Lord Jesus *C* Jas 2:1 *5547*
Peter, an apostle of Jesus *C* 1Pet 1:1 *5547*
of the blood of Jesus *C* 1Pet 1:2 *5547*
God and Father of our Lord Jesus *C* 1Pet 1:3 *5547*
of Jesus *C* from the dead, 1Pet 1:3 *5547*
glory at the appearing of Jesus *C* 1Pet 1:7 *5547*
manner of time the Spirit of *C* 1Pet 1:11 *5547*

beforehand the sufferings of C ... 1Pet 1:11 5547
you at the revelation of Jesus C ... 1Pet 1:13 5547
But with the precious blood of C ... 1Pet 1:19 5547
acceptable to God by Jesus C ... 1Pet 2:5 5547
because C also suffered for us, ... 1Pet 2:21 5547
your good conversation in C ... 1Pet 3:16 5547
For C also hath once suffered for ... 1Pet 3:18 5547
by the resurrection of Jesus C ... 1Pet 3:21 5547
Forasmuch then as C hath suffered ... 1Pet 4:1 5547
may be glorified through Jesus C ... 1Pet 4:11 5547
be reproached for the name of C ... 1Pet 4:14 5547
a witness of the sufferings of C ... 1Pet 5:1 5547
unto his eternal glory by C Jesus ... 1Pet 5:10 5547
with you all that are in C Jesus ... 1Pet 5:14 5547
servant and an apostle of Jesus C ... 2Pet 1:1 5547
of God and our Saviour Jesus C ... 2Pet 1:1 5547
the knowledge of our Lord Jesus C ... 2Pet 1:8 5547
of our Lord and Saviour Jesus C ... 2Pet 1:11 5547
our Lord Jesus C hath shewed me ... 2Pet 1:14 5547
and coming of our Lord Jesus C ... 2Pet 1:16 5547
of the Lord and Saviour Jesus C ... 2Pet 2:20 5547
of our Lord and Saviour Jesus C ... 2Pet 3:18 5547
Father, and with his Son Jesus C ... 1Jn 1:3 5547
the blood of Jesus C his Son ... 1Jn 1:7 5547
the Father, Jesus C the righteous ... 1Jn 2:1 5547
that denieth that Jesus is the C ... 1Jn 2:22 5547
on the name of his Son Jesus C ... 1Jn 3:23 5547
that confesseth that Jesus C is ... 1Jn 4:2 5547
C is come in the flesh is not of ... 1Jn 4:3 5547
Jesus is the C is born of God ... 1Jn 5:1 5547
by water and blood, even Jesus C ... 1Jn 5:6 5547
is true, even in his Son Jesus C ... 1Jn 5:20 5547
Father, and from the Lord Jesus C ... 2Jn 3 5547
that Jesus C is come in the flesh ... 2Jn 7 5547
abideth not in the doctrine of C ... 2Jn 9 5547
that abideth in the doctrine of C ... 2Jn 9 5547
Jude, the servant of Jesus C ... Jude 1 5547
Father, and preserved in Jesus C ... Jude 1 5547
Lord God, and our Lord Jesus C ... Jude 4 5547
the apostles of our Lord Jesus C ... Jude 17 5547
Lord Jesus C unto eternal life ... Jude 21 5547
The Revelation of Jesus C ... Rev 1:1 5547
and of the testimony of Jesus C ... Rev 1:2 5547
And from Jesus C, who is the ... Rev 1:5 5547
kingdom and patience of Jesus C ... Rev 1:9 5547
and for the testimony of Jesus C ... Rev 1:9 5547
kingdoms of our Lord, and of his C ... Rev 11:15 5547
of our God, and the power of his C ... Rev 12:10 5547
and have the testimony of Jesus C ... Rev 12:17 5547
reigned with C a thousand years ... Rev 20:4 5547
shall be priests of God and of C ... Rev 20:6 5547
our Lord Jesus C be with you all ... Rev 22:21 5547

CHRISTIAN *(kris'-tyan)* {2} See CHRISTIANS. *A follower of Jesus Christ.*
thou persuadest me to be a C ... Acts 26:28 5546
Yet if any man suffer as a C ... 1Pet 4:16 5546

CHRISTIANS *(kris'-tyans)* {1}
were called C first in Antioch ... Acts 11:26 5546

CHRIST'S *(krists)* {16}
for the Lord Jesus C sake ... Rom 15:30 5547
And ye are C ... 1Cor 3:23 5547
We are fools for C sake, but ye ... 1Cor 4:10 5547
called, being free, is C servant ... 1Cor 7:22 5547
they that are C at his coming ... 1Cor 15:23 5547
came to Troas to preach C gospel ... 2Cor 2:12 5547
we pray you in C stead, be ye ... 2Cor 5:20 5547
man trust to himself that he is C ... 2Cor 10:7 5547
he is C, even so are we C ... 2Cor 10:7 5547
in distresses for C sake ... 2Cor 12:10 5547
And if ye be C, then are ye ... Gal 3:29 5547
they that are C have crucified ... Gal 5:24 5547
even as God for C sake hath ... Eph 4:32 5547
not the things which are Jesus C ... Phil 2:21 5547
ye are partakers of C sufferings ... 1Pet 4:13 5547

CHRISTS *(krists)* {2}
For there shall arise false C ... Mt 24:24 5580
For false C and false prophets ... Mk 13:22 5580

CHRONICLES {38}
of the c of the kings of Israel ... 1Kin 14:19 1697,3117
of the c of the kings of Judah ... 1Kin 14:29 1697,3117
of the c of the kings of Judah ... 1Kin 15:7 1697,3117
of the c of the kings of Judah ... 1Kin 15:23 1697,3117
of the c of the kings of Israel ... 1Kin 15:31 1697,3117
of the c of the kings of Israel ... 1Kin 16:5 1697,3117
of the c of the kings of Israel ... 1Kin 16:14 1697,3117
of the c of the kings of Israel ... 1Kin 16:20 1697,3117
of the c of the kings of Israel ... 1Kin 16:27 1697,3117
of the c of the kings of Israel ... 1Kin 22:39 1697,3117
of the c of the kings of Judah ... 1Kin 22:45 1697,3117
of the c of the kings of Israel ... 2Kin 1:18 1697,3117
of the c of the kings of Judah ... 2Kin 8:23 1697,3117
of the c of the kings of Israel ... 2Kin 10:34 1697,3117
of the c of the kings of Judah ... 2Kin 12:19 1697,3117
of the c of the kings of Israel ... 2Kin 13:8 1697,3117
of the c of the kings of Israel ... 2Kin 13:12 1697,3117
of the c of the kings of Israel ... 2Kin 14:15 1697,3117
of the c of the kings of Judah ... 2Kin 14:18 1697,3117
of the c of the kings of Israel ... 2Kin 14:28 1697,3117
of the c of the kings of Judah ... 2Kin 15:6 1697,3117
of the c of the kings of Israel ... 2Kin 15:11 1697,3117
of the c of the kings of Israel ... 2Kin 15:15 1697,3117
of the c of the kings of Israel ... 2Kin 15:21 1697,3117
of the c of the kings of Israel ... 2Kin 15:26 1697,3117
of the c of the kings of Israel ... 2Kin 15:31 1697,3117
of the c of the kings of Judah ... 2Kin 15:36 1697,3117
of the c of the kings of Judah ... 2Kin 16:19 1697,3117
of the c of the kings of Judah ... 2Kin 20:20 1697,3117
of the c of the kings of Judah ... 2Kin 21:17 1697,3117
of the c of the kings of Judah ... 2Kin 21:25 1697,3117
of the c of the kings of Judah ... 2Kin 23:28 1697,3117
of the c of the kings of Judah ... 2Kin 24:5 1697,3117
account of the c of king David ... 1Chr 27:24 1697,3117
were written in the book of the c ... Neh 12:23 1697,3117
the book of the c before the king ... Est 2:23 1697,3117
the book of records of the c ... Est 6:1 1697,3117
of the c of the kings of Media ... Est 10:2 1697,3117

CHRYSOLITE {1}
the seventh, c ... Rev 21:20 5555

CHRYSOPRASUS {1}
the tenth, a c ... Rev 21:20 5556

CHUB *(cub)* {1} *Allies of Egypt.*
and all the mingled people, and C ... Eze 30:5 3552

CHUN *(kun)* {1} *A city in Aran-zobah.*
Likewise from Tibhath, and from C ... 1Chr 18:8 3560

CHURCH {80}
upon this rock I will build my c ... Mt 16:18 1577
to hear them, tell it unto the c ... Mt 18:17 1577
but if he neglect to hear the c ... Mt 18:17 1577
the Lord added to the c daily ... Acts 2:47 1577
And great fear came upon all the c ... Acts 5:11 1577
is he, that was in the c in the ... Acts 7:38 1577
the c which was at Jerusalem ... Acts 8:1 1577
for Saul, he made havock of the c ... Acts 8:3 1577
of the c which was in Jerusalem ... Acts 11:22 1577
assembled themselves with the c ... Acts 11:26 1577
his hands to vex certain of the c ... Acts 12:1 1577
ceasing of the c unto God for him ... Acts 12:5 1577
Now there were in the c that was ... Acts 13:1 1577
ordained them elders in every c ... Acts 14:23 1577
and had gathered the c together ... Acts 14:27 1577
brought on their way by the c ... Acts 15:3 1577
they were received of the c ... Acts 15:4 1577
and elders, with the whole c ... Acts 15:22 1577
and gone up, and saluted the c ... Acts 18:22 1577
and called the elders of the c ... Acts 20:17 1577
overseers, to feed the c of God ... Acts 20:28 1577
of the c which is at Cenchrea ... Rom 16:1 1577
Likewise greet the c that is in ... Rom 16:5 1577
mine host, and of the whole c ... Rom 16:23 1577
servant of the c at Cenchrea ... Rom *s* 1577
Unto the c of God which is at ... 1Cor 1:2 1577
as I teach every where in every c ... 1Cor 4:17 1577
who are least esteemed in the c ... 1Cor 6:4 1577
the Gentiles, nor to the c of God ... 1Cor 10:32 1577
when ye come together in the c ... 1Cor 11:18 1577
or despise ye the c of God ... 1Cor 11:22 1577
And God hath set some in the c ... 1Cor 12:28 1577
that prophesieth edifieth the c ... 1Cor 14:4 1577
that the c may receive edifying ... 1Cor 14:5 1577
excel to the edifying of the c ... 1Cor 14:12 1577
Yet in the c I had rather speak ... 1Cor 14:19 1577
If therefore the whole c be come ... 1Cor 14:23 1577
let him keep silence in the c ... 1Cor 14:28 1577
shame for women to speak in the c ... 1Cor 14:35 1577
because I persecuted the c of God ... 1Cor 15:9 1577
with the c that is in their house ... 1Cor 16:19 1577
unto the c of God which is at ... 2Cor 1:1 1577
measure I persecuted the c of God ... Gal 1:13 1577
the head over all things to the c ... Eph 1:22 1577
the c the manifold wisdom of God ... Eph 3:10 1577
Unto him be glory in the c by ... Eph 3:21 1577
as Christ is the head of the c ... Eph 5:23 1577
Therefore as the c is subject ... Eph 5:24 1577
even as Christ also loved the c ... Eph 5:25 1577
it to himself a glorious c ... Eph 5:27 1577
it, even as the Lord the c ... Eph 5:29 1577
speak concerning Christ and the c ... Eph 5:32 1577
zeal, persecuting the c ... Phil 3:6 1577
no c communicated with me as ... Phil 4:15 1577
he is the head of the body, the c ... Col 1:18 1577
his body's sake, which is the c ... Col 1:24 1577
the c which is in his house ... Col 4:15 1577
also in the c of the Laodiceans ... Col 4:16 1577
unto the c of the Thessalonians ... 1Th 1:1 1577
unto the c of the Thessalonians ... 2Th 1:1 1577
he take care of the c of God ... 1Ti 3:5 1577
which is the c of the living God, ... 1Ti 3:15 1577
them, and let not the c be charged ... 1Ti 5:16 1577
bishop of the c of the Ephesians ... 2Ti *s* 1577
bishop of the c of the Cretians ... Titus *s* 1577
and to the c in thy house ... Philem 2 1577
in the midst of the c will I sing ... Heb 2:12 1577
c of the firstborn, which are ... Heb 12:23 1577
him call for the elders of the c ... Jas 5:14 1577
The c that is at Babylon, elected ... 1Pet 5:13 1577
of thy charity before the c ... 3Jn 6 1577
I wrote unto the c ... 3Jn 9 1577
and casteth them out of the c ... 3Jn 10 1577
angel of the c of Ephesus write ... Rev 2:1 1577
angel of the c in Smyrna write ... Rev 2:8 1577
angel of the c in Pergamos write ... Rev 2:12 1577
angel of the c in Thyatira write ... Rev 2:18 1577
angel of the c in Sardis write ... Rev 3:1 1577
And to the angel of the c in ... Rev 3:7 1577
unto the angel of the c of the ... Rev 3:14 1577

CHURCHES {37}
Then had the c rest throughout ... Acts 9:31 1577
and Cilicia, confirming the c ... Acts 15:41 1577
so were the c established in the ... Acts 16:5 1577
which are neither robbers of c ... Acts 19:37 2417
also all the c of the Gentiles ... Rom 16:4 1577
The c of Christ salute you ... Rom 16:16 1577
And so ordain I in all c ... 1Cor 7:17 1577
such custom, neither the c of God ... 1Cor 11:16 1577
as in all c of the saints ... 1Cor 14:33 1577
your women keep silence in the c ... 1Cor 14:34 1577
given order to the c of Galatia ... 1Cor 16:1 1577
The c of Asia salute you ... 1Cor 16:19 1577
bestowed on the c of Macedonia ... 2Cor 8:1 1577
the gospel throughout all the c ... 2Cor 8:18 1577
the c to travel with us with this ... 2Cor 8:19 1577
they are the messengers of the c ... 2Cor 8:23 1577
shew ye to them, and before the c ... 2Cor 8:24 1577
I robbed other c, taking wages of ... 2Cor 11:8 1577
me daily, the care of all the c ... 2Cor 11:28 1577
ye were inferior to other c ... 2Cor 12:13 1577
with me, unto the c of Galatia ... Gal 1:2 1577
was unknown by face unto the c of ... Gal 1:22 1577
became followers of the c of God ... 1Th 2:14 1577
in the c of God for your patience ... 2Th 1:4 1577
to the seven c which are in Asia ... Rev 1:4 1577
the seven c which are in Asia ... Rev 1:11 1577
are the angels of the seven c ... Rev 1:20 1577
which thou sawest are the seven c ... Rev 1:20 1577
what the Spirit saith unto the c ... Rev 2:7 1577
what the Spirit saith unto the c ... Rev 2:11 1577
what the Spirit saith unto the c ... Rev 2:17 1577
all the c shall know that I am he ... Rev 2:23 1577
what the Spirit saith unto the c ... Rev 2:29 1577
what the Spirit saith unto the c ... Rev 3:6 1577
what the Spirit saith unto the c ... Rev 3:13 1577
what the Spirit saith unto the c ... Rev 3:22 1577
unto you these things in the c ... Rev 22:16 1577

CHURL {2}
nor the c said to be bountiful ... Is 32:5 3596
also of the c are evil ... Is 32:7 3596

CHURLISH {1}
but the man was c and evil in his ... 1Sa 25:3 7186

CHURNING {1}
Surely the c of milk bringeth ... Prov 30:33 4330

CHUSHAN-RISHATHAIM *(cu'-shan-rish-a-tha'-im)* {4} *A king of Mesopotamia.*
the hand of C king of Mesopotamia ... Judg 3:8 3573
of Israel served C eight years ... Judg 3:8 3573
the LORD delivered C king of ... Judg 3:10 3573
and his hand prevailed against C ... Judg 3:10 3573

CHUZA *(cu'-zah)* {1} *A steward of Herod Antipas.*
the wife of C Herod's steward ... Lk 8:3 5529

CILICIA *(sil-ish'-yah)* {8} *A Roman province in Asia Minor.*
and Alexandrians, and of them of C ... Acts 6:9 2791
Gentiles in Antioch and Syria and C ... Acts 15:23 2791
And he went through Syria and C ... Acts 15:41 2791
am a Jew of Tarsus, a city in C ... Acts 21:39 2791
Jew, born in Tarsus, a city in C ... Acts 22:3 2791
he understood that he was of C ... Acts 23:34 2791
we had sailed over the sea of C ... Acts 27:5 2791
into the regions of Syria and C ... Gal 1:21 2791

CINNAMON {4}
of sweet c half so much, even two ... Ex 30:23 7076
my bed with myrrh, aloes, and c ... Prov 7:17 7076
calamus and c, with all trees of ... Song 4:14 7076
And c, and odours, and ointments, and ... Rev 18:13 2792

CINNEROTH *(sin'-ne-roth)* {1} See CHINNEROTH. *Same as Chinneroth.*
and Abel-beth-maachah, and all C ... 1Kin 15:20 3672

CIRCLE {1}
sitteth upon the c of the earth ... Is 40:22 2329

CIRCUIT {3}
from year to year in c to Beth-el ... 1Sa 7:16 5437
and he walketh in the c of heaven ... Job 22:14 2329
his c unto the ends of it ... Ps 19:6 8622

CIRCUITS {1}
again according to his c ... Eccl 1:6 5439

CIRCUMCISE {10}
ye shall c the flesh of your ... Gen 17:11 5243
C therefore the foreskin of your ... Deut 10:16 4135
LORD thy God will c thine heart ... Deut 30:6 4135
c again the children of Israel ... Josh 5:2 4135
is the cause why Joshua did c ... Josh 5:4 4135
C yourselves to the LORD, and take ... Jer 4:4 4135
day they came to c the child ... Lk 1:59 4059
and ye on the sabbath day c a man ... Jn 7:22 4059
That it was needful to c them ... Acts 15:5 4059
ought not to c their children ... Acts 21:21 4059

CIRCUMCISED {39}
man child among you shall be c ... Gen 17:10 4135
days old shall be c among you ... Gen 17:12 4135
with thy money, must needs be c ... Gen 17:13 4135
flesh of his foreskin is not c ... Gen 17:14 4135
c the flesh of their foreskin in ... Gen 17:23 4135
when he was c in the flesh of his ... Gen 17:24 4135
when he was c in the flesh of his ... Gen 17:25 4135
In the selfsame day was Abraham c ... Gen 17:26 4135
of the stranger, were c with him ... Gen 17:27 4135
Abraham c his son Isaac being ... Gen 21:4 4135
be, that every male of you be c ... Gen 34:15 4135
will not hearken unto us, to be c ... Gen 34:17 4135
us be c, as they are c ... Gen 34:22 4135
and every male was c, all that ... Gen 34:24 4135
for money, when thou hast c him ... Ex 12:44 4135
the LORD, let all his males be c ... Ex 12:48 4135
flesh of his foreskin shall be c ... Lev 12:3 4135
c the children of Israel at the ... Josh 5:3 4135
the people that came out were c ... Josh 5:5 4135

out of Egypt, them they had not *c* .... Josh 5:5 4135
up in their stead, them Joshua *c* .... Josh 5:7 4135
they had not *c* them by the way .... Josh 5:7 4135
are *c* with the uncircumcised .... Jer 9:25 4135
Isaac, and *c* him the eighth day .... Acts 7:8 *4059*
Except ye be *c* after the manner .... Acts 15:1 *4059*
your souls, saying, Ye must be *c* .... Acts 15:24 *4059*
c him because of the Jews which .... Acts 16:3 *4059*
believe, though they be not *c* .... Rom 4:11 *203*
Is any man called being *c* 1Cor 7:18 *4059*
let him not be *c* 1Cor 7:18 *4059*
a Greek, was compelled to be *c* .... Gal 2:3 *4059*
say unto you, that if ye be *c* .... Gal 5:2 *4059*
again to every man that is *c* .... Gal 5:3 *4059*
flesh, they constrain you to be *c* .... Gal 6:12 *4059*
themselves who are *c* keep the law .... Gal 6:13 *4059*
but desire to have you *c*, that .... Gal 6:13 *4059*
C the eighth day, of the stock of .... Phil 3:5 *4061*
In whom also ye are *c* with the .... Col 2:11 *4059*

CIRCUMCISING {2}
they had done *c* all the people .... Josh 5:8 4135
for the *c* of the child, his name .... Lk 2:21 *4059*

CIRCUMCISION {36}
thou art, because of the *c* .... Ex 4:26 4139
Moses therefore gave unto you *c* .... Jn 7:22 *4061*
man on the sabbath day receive *c* .... Jn 7:23 *4061*
And he gave him the covenant of *c* .... Acts 7:8 *4061*
they of the *c* which believed were .... Acts 10:45 *4061*
were of the *c* contended with him .... Acts 11:2 *4061*
For *c* verily profiteth, if thou .... Rom 2:25 *4061*
thy *c* is made uncircumcision .... Rom 2:25 *4061*
uncircumcision be counted for *c* .... Rom 2:26 *4061*
c dost transgress the law .... Rom 2:27 *4061*
neither is that *c*, which is .... Rom 2:28 *4061*
c is that of the heart, in the .... Rom 2:29 *4061*
or what profit is there of *c* .... Rom 3:1 *4061*
shall justify the *c* by faith .... Rom 3:30 *4061*
blessedness then upon the *c* only .... Rom 4:9 *4061*
when he was in *c*, or in .... Rom 4:10 *4061*
Not in *c*, but in uncircumcision .... Rom 4:10 *4061*
And he received the sign of *c* .... Rom 4:11 *4061*
the father of *c* to them who are .... Rom 4:12 *4061*
to them who are not of the *c* only .... Rom 4:12 *4061*
of the *c* for the truth of God .... Rom 15:8 *4061*
C is nothing, and uncircumcision 1Cor 7:19 *4061*
gospel of the *c* was unto Peter .... Gal 2:7 *4061*
Peter to the apostleship of the *c* .... Gal 2:8 *4061*
the heathen, and they unto the *c* .... Gal 2:9 *4061*
fearing them which were of the *c* .... Gal 2:12 *4061*
neither *c* availeth any thing .... Gal 5:6 *4061*
And I, brethren, if I yet preach *c* .... Gal 5:11 *4061*
neither *c* availeth any thing .... Gal 6:15 *4061*
the *C* in the flesh made by hands .... Eph 2:11 *4061*
For we are the *c*, which worship .... Phil 3:3 *4061*
with the *c* made without hands .... Col 2:11 *4061*
of the flesh by the *c* of Christ .... Col 2:11 *4061*
c nor uncircumcision, Barbarian, ... Col 3:11 *4061*
called Justus, who are of the *c* .... Col 4:11 *4061*
specially they of the *c* .... Titus 1:10 *4061*

CIRCUMSPECT {1}
that I have said unto you be *c* .... Ex 23:13 8104

CIRCUMSPECTLY {1}
See then that ye walk *c*, not as .... Eph 5:15 *199*

CIS *(sis)* {1} See KISH. *Father of King Saul.*
gave unto them Saul the son of *C* .... Acts 13:21 *2797*

CISTERN {4}
ye every one the waters of his *c* 2Kin 18:31 953
Drink waters out of thine own *c* .... Prov 5:15 953
or the wheel broken at the *c* .... Eccl 12:6 953
every one the waters of his own *c* .... Is 36:16 953

CISTERNS {2}
hewed them out *c*, broken *c* .... Jer 2:13 877

CITIES See APPENDIX.

CITIZEN {2}
himself to a *c* of that country .... Lk 15:15 *4177*
in Cilicia, a *c* of no mean city .... Acts 21:39 *4177*

CITIZENS {1}
But his *c* hated him, and sent a .... Lk 19:14 *4177*

CITY {872}
and he builded a *c* .... Gen 4:17 5892
and called the name of the *c* .... Gen 4:17 5892
the *c* Rehoboth, and Calah, ... Gen 10:11 5892
the same is a great *c* .... Gen 10:12 5892
said, Go to, let us build us a *c* .... Gen 11:4 5892
the LORD came down to see the *c* .... Gen 11:5 5892
and they left off to build the *c* .... Gen 11:8 5892
be fifty righteous within the *c* .... Gen 18:24 5892
fifty righteous within the *c* .... Gen 18:26 5982
all the *c* for lack of five .... Gen 18:28 5892
they lay down, the men of the *c* .... Gen 19:4 5892
and whatsoever thou hast in the *c* .... Gen 19:12 5892
for the LORD will destroy this *c* .... Gen 19:14 5892
consumed in the iniquity of the *c* .... Gen 19:15 5892
forth, and set him without the *c* .... Gen 19:16 5892
this *c* is near to flee unto, and .... Gen 19:20 5892
that I will not overthrow this *c* .... Gen 19:21 5892
the name of the *c* was called Zoar .... Gen 19:22 5892
that went in at the gate of his *c* .... Gen 23:10 5892
that went in at the gate of his *c* .... Gen 23:18 5892
Mesopotamia, unto the *c* of Nahor .... Gen 24:10 5892
to kneel down without the *c* by a .... Gen 24:11 5892
of the *c* come out to draw water .... Gen 24:13 5892
therefore the name of the *c* is .... Gen 26:33 5892
but the name of that *c* was called .... Gen 28:19 5892
a *c* of Shechem, which is in the .... Gen 33:18 5892
and pitched his tent before the *c* .... Gen 33:18 5892
son came unto the gate of their *c* .... Gen 34:20 5892
communed with the men of their *c* .... Gen 34:20 5892
went out of the gate of his *c* .... Gen 34:24 5892
went out of the gate of his *c* .... Gen 34:24 5892
sword, and came upon the *c* boldly .... Gen 34:25 5892
upon the slain, and spoiled the *c* .... Gen 34:27 5892
asses, and that which was in the *c* .... Gen 34:28 5892
unto Mamre, unto the *c* of Arbah .... Gen 35:27 7151
and the name of his *c* was Dinhabah .... Gen 36:32 5892
and the name of his *c* was Avith .... Gen 36:35 5892
and the name of his *c* was Pau .... Gen 36:39 5892
which was round about every *c* .... Gen 41:48 5892
when they were gone out of the *c* .... Gen 44:4 5892
man his ass, and returned to the *c* .... Gen 44:13 5892
As soon as I am gone out of the *c* .... Ex 9:29 5892
went out of the *c* from Pharaoh .... Ex 9:33 5892
an unclean place without the *c* .... Lev 14:40 5892
the *c* into an unclean place .... Lev 14:41 5892
of the *c* into an unclean place .... Lev 14:45 5892
out of the *c* into the open fields .... Lev 14:53 5892
a dwelling house in a walled *c* .... Lev 25:29 5892
c shall be established for ever .... Lev 25:30 5892
the *c* of his possession, shall go .... Lev 25:33 5892
a *c* in the uttermost of thy .... Num 20:16 5892
For Heshbon was the *c* of Sihon .... Num 21:26 5892
let the *c* of Sihon be built and .... Num 21:27 5892
a flame from the *c* of Sihon .... Num 21:28 7151
out to meet him unto a *c* of Moab .... Num 22:36 5892
him that remaineth of the *c* .... Num 24:19 5892
reach from the wall of the *c* .... Num 35:4 5892
c on the east side two thousand .... Num 35:5 5892
the *c* shall be in the midst .... Num 35:5 5892
him to the *c* of his refuge .... Num 35:25 5892
the border of the *c* of his refuge .... Num 35:26 5892
borders of the *c* of his refuge .... Num 35:27 5892
c of his refuge until the death .... Num 35:28 5892
is fled to the *c* of his refuge .... Num 35:32 5892
and the little ones, of every *c* .... Deut 2:34 5892
from the *c* that is by the river, ... Deut 2:36 5892
was not one *c* too strong for us .... Deut 2:36 7151
there was not a *c* which we took .... Deut 3:4 7151
women, and children, of every *c* .... Deut 3:6 5892
the inhabitants of their *c* .... Deut 13:13 5892
that *c* with the edge of the sword .... Deut 13:15 5892
and shalt burn with fire the *c* .... Deut 13:16 5892
the elders of his *c* shall send .... Deut 19:12 5892
nigh unto a *c* to fight against it .... Deut 20:10 5892
cattle, and all that is in the *c* .... Deut 20:14 5892
shalt besiege a *c* a long time .... Deut 20:19 5892
the *c* that maketh war with thee .... Deut 20:20 5892
that the *c* which is next unto the .... Deut 21:3 5892
of that *c* shall take an heifer .... Deut 21:3 5892
the elders of that *c* shall bring .... Deut 21:4 5892
And all the elders of that *c* .... Deut 21:6 5892
him out unto the elders of his *c* .... Deut 21:19 5892
say unto the elders of his *c* .... Deut 21:20 5892
all the men of his *c* shall stone .... Deut 21:21 5892
the elders of the *c* in the gate .... Deut 22:15 5892
cloth before the elders of the *c* .... Deut 22:17 5892
the elders of that *c* shall take .... Deut 22:18 5892
the men of her *c* shall stone her .... Deut 22:21 5892
and a man find her in the *c* .... Deut 22:23 5892
both out unto the gate of that *c* .... Deut 22:24 5892
she cried not, being in the *c* .... Deut 22:24 5892
elders of his *c* shall call him .... Deut 25:8 5892
Blessed shalt thou be in the *c* .... Deut 28:3 5892
Cursed shalt thou be in the *c* .... Deut 28:16 5892
the *c* of palm trees, unto Zoar .... Deut 34:3 5892
an heap very far from the *c* Adam .... Josh 3:16 5892
And ye shall compass the *c* .... Josh 6:3 5892
war, and go round about the *c* once .... Josh 6:3 5892
shall compass the *c* seven times .... Josh 6:4 5892
the wall of the *c* shall fall down .... Josh 6:5 5892
people, Pass on, and compass the *c* .... Josh 6:7 5892
ark of the LORD compassed the *c* .... Josh 6:11 5892
day they compassed the *c* once .... Josh 6:14 5892
compassed the *c* after the same .... Josh 6:15 5892
they compassed the *c* seven times .... Josh 6:15 5892
for the LORD hath given you the *c* .... Josh 6:16 5892
the *c* shall be accursed, even it, ... Josh 6:17 5892
the people went up into the *c* .... Josh 6:20 5892
before him, and they took the *c* .... Josh 6:20 5892
destroyed all that was in the *c* .... Josh 6:21 5892
And they burnt the *c* with fire .... Josh 6:24 5892
up and buildeth this *c* Jericho .... Josh 6:26 5892
of Ai, and his people, and his *c* .... Josh 8:1 5892
an ambush for the *c* behind it .... Josh 8:2 5892
the *c*, even behind the *c* .... Josh 8:4 5892
go not very far from the *c* .... Josh 8:4 5892
with me, will approach unto the *c* .... Josh 8:5 5892
we have drawn them from the *c* .... Josh 8:6 5892
the ambush, and seize upon the *c* .... Josh 8:7 5892
be, when ye have taken the *c* .... Josh 8:8 5892
that ye shall set the *c* on fire .... Josh 8:8 5892
drew nigh, and came before the *c* .... Josh 8:11 5892
and Ai, on the west side of the *c* .... Josh 8:12 5892
that was on the north of the *c* .... Josh 8:13 5892
in wait on the west of the *c* .... Josh 8:13 5892
the men of the *c* went out against .... Josh 8:14 5892
ambush against him behind the *c* .... Josh 8:14 5892
and were drawn away from the *c* .... Josh 8:16 5892
and they left the *c* open, and .... Josh 8:17 5892
he had in his hand toward the *c* .... Josh 8:18 5892
and they entered into the *c* .... Josh 8:19 5892
and hasted and set the *c* on fire .... Josh 8:19 5892
the smoke of the *c* ascended up to .... Josh 8:20 5892
that the ambush had taken the *c* .... Josh 8:21 5892
that the smoke of the *c* ascended .... Josh 8:21 5892
issued out of the *c* against them .... Josh 8:22 5892
the spoil of that *c* Israel took .... Josh 8:27 5892
the entering of the gate of the *c* .... Josh 8:29 5892
because Gibeon was a great *c* .... Josh 10:2 5892
There was not a *c* that made peace .... Josh 11:19 5892
the *c* that is in the midst of the .... Josh 13:9 5892
the *c* that is in the midst of the .... Josh 13:16 5892
even the *c* of Arba the father of .... Josh 15:13 7151
father of Anak, which *c* is Hebron .... Josh 15:13
the *c* of Salt, and En-gedi .... Josh 15:62 5892
a *c* of the children of Judah .... Josh 18:14 5892
to Ramah, and to the strong *c* Tyre .... Josh 19:29 5892
gave him the *c* which he asked .... Josh 19:50 5892
and he built the *c*, and dwelt .... Josh 19:50 5892
the entering of the gate of the *c* .... Josh 20:4 5892
the ears of the elders of that *c* .... Josh 20:4 5892
take him into the *c* unto them .... Josh 20:4 5892
And he shall dwell in that *c* .... Josh 20:6 5892
return, and come unto his own *c* .... Josh 20:6 5892
unto the *c* from whence he fled .... Josh 20:6 5892
they gave them the *c* of Arba the .... Josh 21:11 7151
which *c* is Hebron, in the hill .... Josh 21:11
But the fields of the *c*, and the .... Josh 21:12 5892
to be a *c* of refuge for the .... Josh 21:13 5892
to be a *c* of refuge for the .... Josh 21:21 5892
to be a *c* of refuge for the .... Josh 21:27 5892
to be a *c* of refuge for the .... Josh 21:32 5892
to be a *c* of refuge for the .... Josh 21:38 5892
the sword, and set the *c* on fire .... Judg 1:8 5892
went up out of the *c* of palm .... Judg 1:16 5892
the name of the *c* was called .... Judg 1:17 5892
the name of the *c* before was Luz .... Judg 1:23 5892
saw a man come forth out of the *c* .... Judg 1:24 5892
thee, the entrance into the *c* .... Judg 1:24 5892
them the entrance into the *c* .... Judg 1:25 5892
they smote the *c* with the edge of .... Judg 1:25 5892
of the Hittites, and built a *c* .... Judg 1:26 5892
and possessed the *c* of palm trees .... Judg 3:13 5892
household, and the men of the *c* .... Judg 6:27 5892
when the men of the *c* arose early .... Judg 6:28 5892
the men of the *c* said unto Joash .... Judg 6:30 5892
And he took the elders of the *c* .... Judg 8:16 5892
Penuel, and slew the men of the *c* .... Judg 8:17 5892
ephod thereof, and put it in his *c* .... Judg 8:27 5892
when Zebul the ruler of the *c* .... Judg 9:30 5892
they fortify the *c* against thee .... Judg 9:31 5892
rise early, and set upon the *c* .... Judg 9:33 5892
the entering of the gate of the *c* .... Judg 9:35 5892
were come forth out of the *c* .... Judg 9:43 5892
the entering of the gate of the *c* .... Judg 9:44 5892
fought against the *c* all that day .... Judg 9:45 5892
and he took the *c*, and slew the .... Judg 9:45 5892
was therein, and beat down the *c* .... Judg 9:45 5892
was a strong tower within the *c* .... Judg 9:51 5892
and women, and all they of the *c* .... Judg 9:51 5892
the men of the *c* said unto him on .... Judg 14:18 5892
all night in the gate of the *c* .... Judg 16:2 5892
the doors of the gate of the *c* .... Judg 16:3 5892
of the *c* from Beth-lehem-judah to .... Judg 17:8 5892
sword, and burnt the *c* with fire .... Judg 18:27 5892
And they built a *c*, and dwelt .... Judg 18:28 5892
they called the name of the *c* Dan .... Judg 18:29 5892
of the *c* was Laish at the first .... Judg 18:29 5892
in into this *c* of the Jebusites .... Judg 19:11 5892
hither into the *c* of a stranger .... Judg 19:12 5892
sat him down in a street of the *c* .... Judg 19:15 5892
man in the street of the *c* .... Judg 19:17 5892
merry, behold, the men of the *c* .... Judg 19:22 5892
were gathered against the *c* .... Judg 20:11 5892
and were drawn away from the *c* .... Judg 20:31 5892
them from the *c* unto the highways .... Judg 20:32 5892
smote all the *c* with the edge of .... Judg 20:37 5892
with smoke rise up out of the *c* .... Judg 20:38 5892
of the *c* with a pillar of smoke .... Judg 20:40 5892
the flame of the *c* ascended up to .... Judg 20:40 5892
sword, as well the men of every *c* .... Judg 20:48 5892
that all the *c* was moved about .... Ruth 1:19 5892
took it up, and went into the *c* .... Ruth 2:18 5892
for all the *c* of my people doth .... Ruth 3:11 8179
and she went into the *c* .... Ruth 3:15 5892
ten men of the elders of the *c* .... Ruth 4:2 5892
up out of his *c* yearly to worship 1Sa 1:3 5892
And when the man came into the *c* 1Sa 4:13 5892
and told it, all the *c* cried out 1Sa 4:13 5892
of the LORD was against the *c* 1Sa 5:9 5892
and he smote the men of the *c* 1Sa 5:9 5892
destruction throughout all the *c* 1Sa 5:11 5892
the cry of the *c* went up to 1Sa 5:12 5892
Go ye every man unto his *c* 1Sa 8:22 5892
there is in this *c* a man of God 1Sa 9:6 5892
So they went unto the *c* where the 1Sa 9:10 5892
as they went up the hill to the *c* 1Sa 9:11 5892
now, for he came to day to the *c* 1Sa 9:12 5892
As soon as ye be come into the *c* 1Sa 9:13 5892
And they went up into the *c* 1Sa 9:14 5892
and when they were come into the *c* 1Sa 9:14 5892
from the high place into the *c* 1Sa 9:25 5892
going down to the end of the *c* 1Sa 9:27 5892
thou art come thither to the *c* 1Sa 10:5 5892
And Saul came to a *c* of Amalek 1Sa 15:5 5892
he might run to Beth-lehem his *c* 1Sa 20:6 5892
family hath a sacrifice in the *c* 1Sa 20:29 5892
unto him, Go, carry them to the *c* 1Sa 20:40 5892

and Jonathan went into the *c*	1Sa 20:42	5892
the *c* of the priests, smote he	1Sa 22:19	5892
to destroy the *c* for my sake	1Sa 23:10	5892
dwell in the royal *c* with thee	1Sa 27:5	5892
him in Ramah, even in his own *c*	1Sa 28:3	5892
So David and his men came to the *c*	1Sa 30:3	5892
the same is the *c* of David	2Sa 5:7	5892
fort, and called it the *c* of David	2Sa 5:9	5892
LORD unto him into the *c* of David	2Sa 6:10	5892
into the *c* of David with gladness	2Sa 6:12	5892
the LORD came into the *c* of David	2Sa 6:16	5892
unto thee, to search the *c*	2Sa 10:3	5892
Abishai, and entered into the *c*	2Sa 10:14	5892
to pass, when Joab observed the *c*	2Sa 11:16	5892
And the men of the *c* went out	2Sa 11:17	5892
nigh unto the *c* when ye did fight	2Sa 11:20	5892
battle more strong against the *c*	2Sa 11:25	5892
him, There were two men in one *c*	2Sa 12:1	5892
of Ammon, and took the royal *c*	2Sa 12:26	5892
and have taken the *c* of waters	2Sa 12:27	5892
together, and encamp against the *c*	2Sa 12:28	5892
lest I take the *c*, and it be	2Sa 12:28	5892
spoil of the *c* in great abundance	2Sa 12:30	5892
him, and said, Of what *c* art thou	2Sa 15:2	5892
David's counsellor, from his *c*	2Sa 15:12	5892
smite the *c* with the edge of the	2Sa 15:14	5892
had done passing out of the *c*	2Sa 15:24	5892
back the ark of God into the *c*	2Sa 15:25	5892
return into the *c* in peace	2Sa 15:27	5892
But if thou return to the *c*	2Sa 15:34	5892
David's friend came into the *c*	2Sa 15:37	5892
if he be gotten into a *c*	2Sa 17:13	5892
all Israel bring ropes to that *c*	2Sa 17:13	5892
not be seen to come into the *c*	2Sa 17:17	5892
him home to his house, to his *c*	2Sa 17:23	5892
that thou succour us out of the *c*	2Sa 18:3	5892
by stealth that day into the *c*	2Sa 19:3	5892
that I may die in mine own *c*	2Sa 19:37	5892
they cast up a bank against the *c*	2Sa 20:15	5892
cried a wise woman out of the *c*	2Sa 20:16	5892
thou seekest to destroy a *c*	2Sa 20:19	5892
only, and I will depart from the *c*	2Sa 20:21	5892
and they retired from the *c*	2Sa 20:22	5892
on the right side of the *c* that	2Sa 24:5	5892
noise of the *c* being in an uproar	1Kin 1:41	7151
so that the *c* rang again	1Kin 1:45	7151
and was buried in the *c* of David	1Kin 2:10	5892
brought her into the *c* of David	1Kin 3:1	5892
of the LORD out of the *c* of David	1Kin 8:1	5892
I chose no *c* out of all the	1Kin 8:16	5892
the *c* which thou hast chosen	1Kin 8:44	5892
the *c* which thou hast chosen, and	1Kin 8:48	5892
Canaanites that dwelt in the *c*	1Kin 9:16	5892
daughter came up out of the *c* of	1Kin 9:24	5892
of the *c* of David his father	1Kin 11:27	5892
the *c* which I have chosen out of	1Kin 11:32	5892
the *c* which I have chosen me to	1Kin 11:36	5892
was buried in the *c* of David his	1Kin 11:43	5892
told it in the *c* where the old	1Kin 13:25	5892
and the old prophet came to the *c*	1Kin 13:29	5892
in the *c* shall the dogs eat	1Kin 14:11	5892
and when thy feet enter into the *c*	1Kin 14:12	5892
the *c* which the LORD did choose	1Kin 14:21	5892
his fathers in the *c* of David	1Kin 14:31	5892
they buried him in the *c* of David	1Kin 15:8	5892
in the *c* of David his father	1Kin 15:24	5892
in the *c* shall the dogs eat	1Kin 16:4	5892
Zimri saw that the *c* was taken	1Kin 16:18	5892
the name of the *c* which he built	1Kin 16:24	5892
when he came to the gate of the *c*	1Kin 17:10	5892
to Ahab king of Israel into the *c*	1Kin 20:2	5892
themselves in array against the *c*	1Kin 20:12	5892
the provinces came out of the *c*	1Kin 20:19	5892
rest fled to Aphek, into the *c*	1Kin 20:30	5892
fled, and came into the *c*, into an	1Kin 20:30	5892
to the nobles that were in his *c*	1Kin 21:8	5892
And the men of his *c*, even the	1Kin 21:11	5892
who were the inhabitants in his *c*	1Kin 21:11	5892
carried him forth out of the *c*	1Kin 21:13	5892
Ahab in the *c* the dogs shall eat	1Kin 21:24	5892
unto Amon the governor of the *c*	1Kin 22:26	5892
sun, saying, Every man to his *c*	1Kin 22:36	5892
in the *c* of David his father	1Kin 22:50	5892
the men of the *c* said unto Elisha	2Kin 2:19	5892
situation of this *c* is pleasant	2Kin 2:19	5892
little children out of the *c*	2Kin 2:23	5892
And ye shall smite every fenced *c*	2Kin 3:19	5892
fenced *c*, and every choice *c*	2Kin 3:19	5892
night, and compassed the *c* about	2Kin 6:14	5892
compassed the *c* both with horses	2Kin 6:15	5892
the way, neither is this the *c*	2Kin 6:19	5892
we say, We will enter into the *c*	2Kin 7:4	5892
c, then the famine is in the *c*	2Kin 7:4	5892
called unto the porter of the *c*	2Kin 7:10	5892
When they come out of the *c*	2Kin 7:12	5892
them alive, and get into the *c*	2Kin 7:12	5892
remain, which are left in the *c*	2Kin 7:13	5892
his fathers in the *c* of David	2Kin 8:24	5892
the *c* to go to tell it in Jezreel	2Kin 9:15	5892
his fathers in the *c* of David	2Kin 9:28	5892
and horses, a fenced *c* also	2Kin 10:2	5892
house, and he that was over the *c*	2Kin 10:5	5892
were with the great men of the *c*	2Kin 10:6	5892
went to the *c* of the house of	2Kin 10:25	5892
rejoiced, and the *c* was in quiet	2Kin 11:20	5892
his fathers in the *c* of David	2Kin 12:21	5892
his fathers in the *c* of David	2Kin 14:20	5892
his fathers in the *c* of David	2Kin 15:7	5892
in the *c* of David his father	2Kin 15:38	5892
his fathers in the *c* of David	2Kin 16:20	5892
of the watchmen to the fenced *c*	2Kin 17:9	5892
of the watchmen to the fenced *c*	2Kin 18:8	5892
this *c* shall not be delivered	2Kin 18:30	5892
the king of the *c* of Sepharvaim	2Kin 19:13	5892
He shall not come into this *c*	2Kin 19:32	5892
and shall not come into this *c*	2Kin 19:33	5892
For I will defend this *c*, to save	2Kin 19:34	5892
this *c* out of the hand of the	2Kin 20:6	5892
defend this *c* for mine own sake	2Kin 20:6	5892
and brought water into the *c*	2Kin 20:20	5892
of Joshua the governor of the *c*	2Kin 23:8	5892
left hand at the gate of the *c*	2Kin 23:8	5892
And the men of the *c* told him	2Kin 23:17	5892
will cast off this *c* Jerusalem	2Kin 23:27	5892
Jerusalem, and the *c* was besieged	2Kin 24:10	5892
of Babylon came against the *c*	2Kin 24:11	5892
the *c* was besieged unto the	2Kin 25:2	5892
the famine prevailed in the *c*	2Kin 25:3	5892
the *c* was broken up, and all the	2Kin 25:4	5892
were against the *c* round about	2Kin 25:4	5892
people that were left in the *c*	2Kin 25:11	5892
out of the *c* he took an officer	2Kin 25:19	5892
which were found in the *c*	2Kin 25:19	5892
the land that were found in the *c*	2Kin 25:19	5892
and the name of his *c* was Dinhabah	1Chr 1:43	5892
and the name of his *c* was Avith	1Chr 1:46	5892
and the name of his *c* was Pai	1Chr 1:50	5892
But the fields of the *c*, and the	1Chr 6:56	5892
the *c* of refuge, and Libnah with	1Chr 6:57	
of Zion, which is the *c* of David	1Chr 11:5	5892
they called it the *c* of David	1Chr 11:7	5892
And he built the *c* round about	1Chr 11:8	5892
Joab repaired the rest of the *c*	1Chr 11:8	5892
home to himself to the *c* of David	1Chr 13:13	5892
made him houses in the *c* of David	1Chr 15:1	5892
the LORD came to the *c* of David	1Chr 15:29	5892
in array before the gate of the *c*	1Chr 19:9	5892
brother, and entered into the *c*	1Chr 19:15	5892
exceeding much spoil out of the *c*	1Chr 20:2	5892
of the LORD out of the *c* of David	2Chr 5:2	5892
c among all the tribes of Israel	2Chr 6:5	5892
this *c* which thou hast chosen	2Chr 6:34	5892
toward the *c* which thou hast	2Chr 6:38	5892
daughter of Pharaoh out of the *c*	2Chr 8:11	5892
in the *c* of David his father	2Chr 9:31	5892
in every several *c* he put shields	2Chr 11:12	5892
and Benjamin, unto every fenced *c*	2Chr 11:23	5892
the *c* which the LORD had chosen	2Chr 12:13	5892
and was buried in the *c* of David	2Chr 12:16	5892
they buried him in the *c* of David	2Chr 14:1	5892
destroyed of nation, and *c* of *c*	2Chr 15:6	5892
for himself in the *c* of David	2Chr 16:14	5892
to Amon the governor of the *c*	2Chr 18:25	5892
fenced cities of Judah, *c* by *c*	2Chr 19:5	5892
his fathers in the *c* of David	2Chr 21:1	5892
they buried him in the *c* of David	2Chr 21:20	5892
the *c* was quiet, after that they	2Chr 23:21	5892
they buried him in the *c* of David	2Chr 24:16	5892
they buried him in the *c* of David	2Chr 24:25	5892
his fathers in the *c* of Judah	2Chr 25:28	5892
they buried him in the *c* of David	2Chr 27:9	5892
the *c* of palm trees, to their	2Chr 28:15	5892
in every several *c* of Judah he	2Chr 28:25	5892
and they buried him in the *c*	2Chr 28:27	5892
and gathered the rulers of the *c*	2Chr 29:20	5892
the posts passed from *c* to *c*	2Chr 30:10	5892
their cities, in every several *c*	2Chr 31:19	5892
which were without the *c*	2Chr 32:3	5892
repaired Millo in the *c* of David	2Chr 32:5	5892
the street of the gate of the *c*	2Chr 32:6	5892
that they might take the *c*	2Chr 32:18	5892
the west side of the *c* of David	2Chr 32:30	5892
a wall without the *c* of David	2Chr 33:14	5892
and cast them out of the *c*	2Chr 33:15	5892
and Maaseiah the governor of the *c*	2Chr 34:8	5892
and Judah, every one unto his *c*	Ezr 2:1	5892
the rebellious and the bad *c*	Ezr 4:12	7149
if this *c* be builded, and the	Ezr 4:13	7149
that this *c* is a rebellious *c*	Ezr 4:15	7149
which cause was this *c* destroyed	Ezr 4:15	7149
if this *c* be builded again, and	Ezr 4:16	7149
that this *c* of old time hath made	Ezr 4:19	7149
that this *c* be not builded, until	Ezr 4:21	7179
with them the elders of every *c*	Ezr 10:14	5892
my countenance be sad, when the *c*	Neh 2:3	5892
unto the *c* of my fathers'	Neh 2:5	5892
house, and for the wall of the *c*	Neh 2:8	5892
that go down from the *c* of David	Neh 3:15	5892
Now the *c* was large and great	Neh 7:4	5892
and to Judah, every one unto his *c*	Neh 7:6	5892
to dwell in Jerusalem the holy *c*	Neh 11:1	5892
of Senuah was second over the *c*	Neh 11:9	5892
holy *c* were two hundred fourscore	Neh 11:18	5892
by the stairs of the *c* of David	Neh 12:37	5892
this evil upon us, and upon this *c*	Neh 13:18	5892
but the *c* Shushan was perplexed	Est 3:15	5892
went out into the midst of the *c*	Est 4:1	5892
Mordecai unto the street of the *c*	Est 4:6	5892
through the street of the *c*	Est 6:9	5892
through the street of the *c*	Est 6:11	5892
the Jews which were in every *c* to	Est 8:11	5892
the *c* of Shushan rejoiced and was	Est 8:15	5892
in every province, and in every *c*	Est 8:17	5892
every province, and every *c*	Est 9:28	5892
Men groan from out of the *c*	Job 24:12	5892
out to the gate through the *c*	Job 29:7	7176
scorneth the multitude of the *c*	Job 39:7	7151
marvellous kindness in a strong *c*	Ps 31:21	5892
shall make glad the *c* of God	Ps 46:4	5892
to be praised in the *c* of our God	Ps 48:1	5892
north, the *c* of the great King	Ps 48:2	7151
in the *c* of the LORD of hosts	Ps 48:8	5892
in the *c* of our God	Ps 48:8	5892
seen violence and strife in the *c*	Ps 55:9	5892
a dog, and go round about the *c*	Ps 59:6	5892
a dog, and go round about the *c*	Ps 59:14	5892
will bring me into the strong *c*	Ps 60:9	5892
they of the *c* shall flourish like	Ps 72:16	5892
are spoken of thee, O *c* of God	Ps 87:3	5892
doers from the *c* of the LORD	Ps 101:8	5892
they found no *c* to dwell in	Ps 107:4	5892
might go to a *c* of habitation	Ps 107:7	5892
may prepare a *c* for habitation	Ps 107:36	5892
will bring me into the strong *c*	Ps 108:10	5892
as a *c* that is compact together	Ps 122:3	5892
except the LORD keep the *c*	Ps 127:1	5892
in the *c* she uttereth her words,	Prov 1:21	5892
the gates, at the entry of the *c*	Prov 8:3	7176
upon the highest places of the *c*	Prov 9:3	7176
seat in the high places of the *c*	Prov 9:14	7176
rich man's wealth is his strong *c*	Prov 10:15	7151
the righteous, the *c* rejoiceth	Prov 11:10	7151
of the upright the *c* is exalted	Prov 11:11	7176
spirit than he that taketh a *c*	Prov 16:32	5892
rich man's wealth is his strong *c*	Prov 18:11	7151
harder to be won than a strong *c*	Prov 18:19	7151
man scaleth the *c* of the mighty	Prov 21:22	5892
is like a *c* that is broken down	Prov 25:28	5892
men bring a *c* into a snare	Prov 29:8	7151
ten mighty men which are in the *c*	Eccl 7:19	5892
in the *c* where they had so done	Eccl 8:10	5892
There was a little *c*, and few men	Eccl 9:14	5892
he by his wisdom delivered the *c*	Eccl 9:15	5892
he knoweth not how to go to the *c*	Eccl 10:15	5892
go about the *c* in the streets, and	Song 3:2	5892
that go about the *c* found me	Song 3:3	5892
that went about the *c* found me	Song 5:7	5892
of cucumbers, as a besieged *c*	Is 1:8	5892
the faithful *c* become an harlot	Is 1:21	7151
The *c* of righteousness, the	Is 1:26	5892
of righteousness, the faithful *c*	Is 1:26	7151
the golden *c* ceased	Is 14:4	4062
cry, O *c*	Is 14:31	5892
is taken away from being a *c*	Is 17:1	5892
c against *c*, and kingdom	Is 19:2	5892
be called, The *c* of destruction	Is 19:18	5892
art full of stirs, a tumultuous *c*	Is 22:2	5892
a joyous *c*: thy slain men	Is 22:2	7151
the breaches of the *c* of David	Is 22:9	5892
Is this your joyous *c*, whose	Is 23:7	
against Tyre, the crowning *c*	Is 23:8	
against the merchant *c*, to	Is 23:11	
Take an harp, go about the *c*	Is 23:16	5892
The *c* of confusion is broken down	Is 24:10	7151
In the *c* is left desolation, and	Is 24:12	5892
For thou hast made of a *c* an heap	Is 25:2	5892
of a defenced *c* a ruin	Is 25:2	7151
a palace of strangers to be no *c*	Is 25:2	5892
the *c* of the terrible nations	Is 25:3	7151
We have a strong *c*	Is 26:1	5892
the lofty *c*, he layeth it low	Is 26:5	7151
Yet the defenced *c* shall be	Is 27:10	5892
to Ariel, the *c* where David dwelt	Is 29:1	7151
the houses of joy in the joyous *c*	Is 32:13	7151
multitude of the *c* shall be left	Is 32:14	5892
the *c* shall be low in a low place	Is 32:19	5892
Zion, the *c* of our solemnities	Is 33:20	7151
this *c* shall not be delivered	Is 36:15	5892
the king of the *c* of Sepharvaim	Is 37:13	5892
He shall not come into this *c*	Is 37:33	5892
and shall not come into this *c*	Is 37:34	5892
For I will defend this *c* to save	Is 37:35	5892
this *c* out of the hand of the	Is 38:6	5892
and I will defend this *c*	Is 38:6	5892
he shall build my *c*, and he shall	Is 45:13	5892
call themselves of the holy *c*	Is 48:2	5892
garments, O Jerusalem, the holy *c*	Is 52:1	5892
The *c* of the LORD, The Zion of	Is 60:14	5892
Sought out, A *c* not forsaken	Is 62:12	5892
A voice of noise from the *c*	Is 66:6	5892
made thee this day a defenced *c*	Jer 1:18	5892
and I will take you one of a *c*	Jer 3:14	5892
The whole *c* shall flee for the	Jer 4:29	5892
every *c* shall be forsaken, and not	Jer 4:29	5892
this is the *c* to be visited	Jer 6:6	5892
the *c*, and those that dwell	Jer 8:16	5892
and if I enter into the *c*, then	Jer 14:18	5892
suddenly, and terrors upon the *c*	Jer 15:8	5892
of this *c* on the sabbath day	Jer 17:24	5892
into the gates of this *c* kings	Jer 17:25	5892
this *c* shall remain for ever	Jer 17:25	5892
And I will make this *c* desolate	Jer 19:8	5892
I break this people and this *c*	Jer 19:11	5892
and even make this *c* as Tophet	Jer 19:12	5892
Behold, I will bring upon this *c*	Jer 19:15	5892
all the strength of this *c*	Jer 20:5	5892
them into the midst of this *c*	Jer 21:4	5892
smite the inhabitants of this *c*	Jer 21:6	5892
in this *c* from the pestilence	Jer 21:7	5892
in this *c* shall die by the sword	Jer 21:9	5892

my face against this *c* for evil ... Jer 21:10 5892
many nations shall pass by this *c* ... Jer 22:8 5892
LORD done thus unto this great *c* ... Jer 22:8 5892
the *c* that I gave you and your ... Jer 23:39 5892
the *c* which is called by my name ... Jer 25:29 5892
will make this *c* a curse to all ... Jer 26:6 5892
this *c* shall be desolate without ... Jer 26:9 5892
he hath prophesied against this *c* ... Jer 26:11 5892
against this *c* all the words that ... Jer 26:12 5892
upon yourselves, and upon this *c* ... Jer 26:15 5892
who prophesied against this *c* ... Jer 26:20 5892
should this *c* be laid waste ... Jer 27:17 5892
the vessels that remain in this *c* ... Jer 27:19 5892
seek the peace of the *c* whither I ... Jer 29:7 5892
people that dwelleth in this *c* ... Jer 29:16 5892
the *c* shall be builded upon her ... Jer 30:18 5892
that the *c* shall be built to the ... Jer 31:38 5892
I will give this *c* into the hand ... Jer 32:3 5892
are come unto the *c* to take it ... Jer 32:24 5892
the *c* is given into the hand of ... Jer 32:24 5892
for the *c* is given into the hand ... Jer 32:25 5892
I will give this *c* into the hand ... Jer 32:28 5892
that fight against this *c* ... Jer 32:29 5892
shall come and set fire on this *c* ... Jer 32:29 5892
For this *c* hath been to me as a ... Jer 32:31 5892
God of Israel, concerning this *c* ... Jer 32:36 5892
concerning the houses of this *c* ... Jer 33:4 5892
I have hid my face from this *c* ... Jer 33:5 5892
I will give this *c* into the hand ... Jer 34:2 5892
and cause them to return to this *c* ... Jer 34:22 5892
again, and fight against this *c* ... Jer 37:8 5892
tent, and burn this *c* with fire ... Jer 37:10 5892
all the bread in the *c* were spent ... Jer 37:21 5892
in this *c* shall die by the sword ... Jer 38:2 5892
This *c* shall surely be given into ... Jer 38:3 5892
men of war that remain in this *c* ... Jer 38:4 5892
there is no more bread in the *c* ... Jer 38:9 5892
this *c* shall not be burned with ... Jer 38:17 5892
then shall this *c* be given into ... Jer 38:18 5892
thou shalt cause this *c* to be ... Jer 38:23 5892
of the month, the *c* was broken up ... Jer 39:2 5892
went forth out of the *c* by night ... Jer 39:4 5892
the people that remained in the *c* ... Jer 39:9 5892
my words upon this *c* for evil ... Jer 39:16 5892
they came into the midst of the *c* ... Jer 41:7 5892
I will destroy the *c* and the ... Jer 46:8 5892
the *c*, and them that dwell therein ... Jer 47:2 5892
every *c*, and no *c* shall escape ... Jer 48:8 5892
How is the *c* of praise not left, ... Jer 49:25 5892
praise not left, the *c* of my joy ... Jer 49:25 7151
that his *c* is taken at one end ... Jer 51:31 5892
So the *c* was besieged unto the ... Jer 52:5 5892
the famine was sore in the *c* ... Jer 52:6 5892
Then the *c* was broken up, and all ... Jer 52:7 5892
went forth out of the *c* by night ... Jer 52:7 5892
were by the *c* round about ... Jer 52:7 5892
the people that remained in the *c* ... Jer 52:15 5892
took also out of the *c* an eunuch ... Jer 52:25 5892
person, which were found in the *c* ... Jer 52:25 5892
were found in the midst of the *c* ... Jer 52:25 5892
How doth the *c* sit solitary ... Lam 1:1 5892
elders gave up the ghost in the *c* ... Lam 1:19 5892
swoon in the streets of the *c* ... Lam 2:11 7151
wounded in the streets of the *c* ... Lam 2:12 5892
Is this the *c* that men call The ... Lam 2:15 5892
of all the daughters of my *c* ... Lam 3:51 5892
thee, and pourtray upon it the *c* ... Eze 4:1 5892
of iron between thee and the *c* ... Eze 4:3 5892
third part in the midst of the *c* ... Eze 5:2 5892
and he that is in the *c*, famine and ... Eze 7:15 5892
the *c* is full of violence ... Eze 7:23 5892
charge over the *c* to draw near ... Eze 9:1 5892
Go through the midst of the *c* ... Eze 9:4 5892
Go ye after him through the *c* ... Eze 9:5 5892
they went forth, and slew in the *c* ... Eze 9:7 5892
the *c* full of perverseness ... Eze 9:9 5892
and scatter them over the *c* ... Eze 10:2 5892
and give wicked counsel in this *c* ... Eze 11:2 5892
this *c* is the caldron, and we be ... Eze 11:3
multiplied your slain in this *c* ... Eze 11:6 5892
flesh, and this *c* is the caldron ... Eze 11:7
This *c* shall not be your caldron, ... Eze 11:11
went up from the midst of the *c* ... Eze 11:23 5892
is on the east side of the *c* ... Eze 11:23 5892
he set it in a *c* of merchants ... Eze 17:4 5892
at the head of the way to the *c* ... Eze 21:19 5892
wilt thou judge the bloody *c* ... Eze 22:2 5892
The *c* sheddeth blood in the midst ... Eze 22:3 5892
Woe to the bloody *c*, to the pot ... Eze 24:6 5892
Woe to the bloody *c* ... Eze 24:9 5892
as men enter into a *c* wherein is ... Eze 26:10 5892
of seafaring men, the renowned *c* ... Eze 26:17 5892
I shall make thee a desolate *c* ... Eze 26:19 5892
What *c* is like Tyrus, like the ... Eze 27:32
unto me, saying, The *c* is smitten ... Eze 33:21 5892
name of the *c* shall be Hamonah ... Eze 39:16 5892
year after that the *c* was smitten ... Eze 40:1 5892
as the frame of a *c* on the south ... Eze 40:2 5892
saw when I came to destroy the *c* ... Eze 43:3 5892
of the *c* five thousand broad ... Eze 45:6 5892
and of the possession of the *c* ... Eze 45:7 5892
and before the possession of the *c* ... Eze 45:7 5892
be a profane place for the *c* ... Eze 48:15 5892
the *c* shall be in the midst ... Eze 48:15 5892
the suburbs of the *c* shall be ... Eze 48:17 5892
food unto them that serve the *c* ... Eze 48:18 5892
they that serve the *c* shall serve ... Eze 48:19 5892
with the possession of the *c* ... Eze 48:20 5892
and of the possession of the *c* ... Eze 48:21 5892
and from the possession of the *c* ... Eze 48:22 5892
out of the *c* on the north side ... Eze 48:30 5892
the gates of the *c* shall be after ... Eze 48:31 5892
the name of the *c* from that day ... Eze 48:35 5892
turned away from thy *c* Jerusalem ... Dan 9:16 5892
the *c* which is called by thy name ... Dan 9:18 5892
for thy *c* and thy people are ... Dan 9:19 5892
thy people and upon thy holy *c* ... Dan 9:24 5892
shall come shall destroy the *c* ... Dan 9:26 5892
Gilead is a *c* of them that work ... Hos 6:8 7151
and I will not enter into the *c* ... Hos 11:9 5892
They shall run to and fro in the *c* ... Joel 2:9 5892
Shall a trumpet be blown in the *c* ... Amos 3:6 5892
shall there be evil in a *c* ... Amos 3:6 5892
and I caused it to rain upon one *c* ... Amos 4:7 5892
it not to rain upon another *c* ... Amos 4:7 5892
three cities wandered unto one *c* ... Amos 4:8 5892
The *c* that went out by a thousand ... Amos 5:3 5892
up the *c* with all that is therein ... Amos 6:8 5892
wife shall be an harlot in the *c* ... Amos 7:17 5892
go to Nineveh, that great *c* ... Jonah 1:2 5892
go unto Nineveh, that great *c* ... Jonah 3:2 5892
great *c* of three days' journey ... Jonah 3:3 5892
enter into the *c* a day's journey ... Jonah 3:4 5892
So Jonah went out of the *c* ... Jonah 4:5 5892
and sat on the east side of the *c* ... Jonah 4:5 5892
see what would become of the *c* ... Jonah 4:5 5892
not I spare Nineveh, that great *c* ... Jonah 4:11 5892
shalt thou go forth out of the *c* ... Mic 4:10 7151
LORD's voice crieth unto the *c* ... Mic 6:9 5892
Woe to the bloody *c* ... Nah 3:1 5892
violence of the land, of the *c* ... Hab 2:8 7151
and stablisheth a *c* by iniquity ... Hab 2:12 7151
violence of the land, of the *c* ... Hab 2:17 7151
rejoicing *c* that dwelt carelessly ... Zeph 2:15 5892
and polluted, to the oppressing *c* ... Zeph 3:1 5892
shall be called a *c* of truth ... Zec 8:3 5892
the streets of the *c* shall be ... Zec 8:5 5892
of one *c* shall go to another ... Zec 8:21
the *c* shall be taken, and the ... Zec 14:2 5892
half of the *c* shall go forth into ... Zec 14:2 5892
shall not be cut off from the *c* ... Zec 14:2 5892
dwelt in a *c* called Nazareth ... Mt 2:23 *4172*
taketh him up into the holy *c* ... Mt 4:5 *4172*
A *c* that is set on an hill cannot ... Mt 5:14 *4172*
for it is the *c* of the great King ... Mt 5:35 *4172*
and went their ways into the *c* ... Mt 8:33 *4172*
the whole *c* came out to meet ... Mt 8:34 *4172*
over, and came into his own *c* ... Mt 9:1 *4172*
into any *c* of the Samaritans ... Mt 10:5 *4172*
into whatsoever *c* or town ye ... Mt 10:11 *4172*
ye depart out of that house or *c* ... Mt 10:14 *4172*
day of judgment, than for that *c* ... Mt 10:15 *4172*
when they persecute you in this *c* ... Mt 10:23 *4172*
every *c* or house divided against ... Mt 12:25 *4172*
all the *c* was moved, saying, Who ... Mt 21:10 *4172*
and went out of the *c* into Bethany ... Mt 21:17 *4172*
morning as he returned into the *c* ... Mt 21:18 *4172*
murderers, and burned up their *c* ... Mt 22:7 *4172*
and persecute them from *c* to *c* ... Mt 23:34 *4172*
Go into the *c* to such a man, and ... Mt 26:18 *4172*
and went into the holy *c*, and ... Mt 27:53 *4172*
some of the watch came into the *c* ... Mt 28:11 *4172*
all the *c* was gathered together ... Mk 1:33 *4172*
no more openly enter into the *c* ... Mk 1:45 *4172*
swine fled, and told it in the *c* ... Mk 5:14 *4172*
day of judgment, than for that *c* ... Mk 6:11 *4172*
was come, he went out of the *c* ... Mk 11:19 *4172*
saith unto them, Go ye into the *c* ... Mk 14:13 *4172*
went forth, and came into the *c* ... Mk 14:16 *4172*
sent from God unto a *c* of Galilee ... Lk 1:26 *4172*
with haste, into a *c* of Juda ... Lk 1:39 *4172*
taxed, every one into his own *c* ... Lk 2:3 *4172*
out of the *c* of Nazareth ... Lk 2:4 *4172*
into Judaea, unto the *c* of David ... Lk 2:4 *4172*
day in the *c* of David a Saviour ... Lk 2:11 *4172*
Galilee, to their own *c* Nazareth ... Lk 2:39 *4172*
a *c* of Sidon, unto a woman that ... Lk 4:26
up, and thrust him out of the *c* ... Lk 4:29 *4172*
hill whereon their *c* was built ... Lk 4:29 *4172*
a *c* of Galilee, and taught them on ... Lk 4:31 *4172*
pass, when he was in a certain *c* ... Lk 5:12 *4172*
that he went into a *c* called Nain ... Lk 7:11 *4172*
he came nigh to the gate of the *c* ... Lk 7:12 *4172*
much people of the *c* was with her ... Lk 7:12 *4172*
And, behold, a woman in the *c* ... Lk 7:37 *4172*
that he went throughout every *c* ... Lk 8:1 *4172*
were come to him out of every *c* ... Lk 8:4 *4172*
him out of the *c* a certain man ... Lk 8:27 *4172*
fled, and went and told it in the *c* ... Lk 8:34 *4172*
published throughout the whole *c* ... Lk 8:39 *4172*
you, when ye go out of that *c* ... Lk 9:5 *4172*
to the *c* called Bethsaida ... Lk 9:10 *4172*
two before his face into every *c* ... Lk 10:1 *4172*
And into whatsoever *c* ye enter ... Lk 10:8 *4172*
But into whatsoever *c* ye enter ... Lk 10:10 *4172*
Even the very dust of your *c* ... Lk 10:11 *4172*
day for Sodom, than for that *c* ... Lk 10:12 *4172*
the streets and lanes of the *c* ... Lk 14:21 *4172*
Saying, There was in a *c* a judge ... Lk 18:2 *4172*
And there was a widow in that *c* ... Lk 18:3 *4172*
he was come near, he beheld the *c* ... Lk 19:41 *4172*
when ye are entered into the *c* ... Lk 22:10 *4172*
a certain sedition made in the *c* ... Lk 23:19 *4172*
of Arimathaea, a *c* of the Jews ... Lk 23:51 *4172*
tarry ye in the *c* of Jerusalem ... Lk 24:49 *4172*
the *c* of Andrew and Peter ... Jn 1:44 *4172*
Then cometh he to a *c* of Samaria ... Jn 4:5 *4172*
gone away unto the *c* to buy meat ... Jn 4:8 *4172*
and went her way into the *c* ... Jn 4:28 *4172*
Then they went out of the *c* ... Jn 4:30 *4172*
c believed on him for the saying ... Jn 4:39 *4172*
into a *c* called Ephraim, and there ... Jn 11:54 *4172*
was crucified was nigh to the *c* ... Jn 19:20 *4172*
And cast him out of the *c*, and ... Acts 7:58 *4172*
went down to the *c* of Samaria ... Acts 8:5 *4172*
And there was great joy in that *c* ... Acts 8:8 *4172*
in the same *c* used sorcery ... Acts 8:9 *4172*
unto him, Arise, and go into the *c* ... Acts 9:6 *4172*
journey, and drew nigh unto the *c* ... Acts 10:9 *4172*
I was in the *c* of Joppa praying ... Acts 11:5 *4172*
iron gate that leadeth unto the *c* ... Acts 12:10 *4172*
day came almost the whole *c* ... Acts 13:44 *4172*
women, and the chief men of the *c* ... Acts 13:50 *4172*
multitude of the *c* was divided ... Acts 14:4 *4172*
Jupiter, which was before their *c* ... Acts 14:13 *4172*
Paul, drew him out of the *c* ... Acts 14:19 *4172*
he rose up, and came into the *c* ... Acts 14:20 *4172*
had preached the gospel to that *c* ... Acts 14:21 *4172*
in every *c* them that preach him ... Acts 15:21 *4172*
visit our brethren in every *c* ... Acts 15:36 *4172*
which is the chief *c* of that part ... Acts 16:12 *4172*
we were in that *c* abiding certain ... Acts 16:12 *4172*
went out of the *c* by a river side ... Acts 16:13 *4172*
of the *c* of Thyatira, which ... Acts 16:14 *4172*
do exceedingly trouble our *c* ... Acts 16:20 *4172*
them to depart out of the *c* ... Acts 16:39 *4172*
set all the *c* on an uproar, and ... Acts 17:5 *4172*
brethren unto the rulers of the *c* ... Acts 17:6 *4173*
the people and the rulers of the *c* ... Acts 17:8 *4173*
when he saw the *c* wholly given to ... Acts 17:16 *4172*
for I have much people in this *c* ... Acts 18:10 *4172*
the whole *c* was filled with ... Acts 19:29 *4172*
that the *c* of the Ephesians is a ... Acts 19:35 *4172*
Holy Ghost witnesseth in every *c* ... Acts 20:23 *4172*
till we were out of the *c* ... Acts 21:5 *4172*
in the *c* Trophimus an Ephesian ... Acts 21:29 *4172*
all the *c* was moved, and the ... Acts 21:30 *4172*
a Jew of Tarsus, a *c* in Cilicia ... Acts 21:39
a citizen of no mean *c* ... Acts 21:39 *4172*
born in Tarsus, a *c* ... Acts 22:3
yet brought up in this *c* at the ... Acts 22:3 *4172*
in the synagogues, nor in the *c* ... Acts 24:12 *4172*
and principal men of the *c* ... Acts 25:23 *4172*
we came to Myra, a *c* of Lycia ... Acts 27:5
nigh whereunto was the *c* of Lasea ... Acts 27:8 *4172*
chamberlain of the *c* saluteth you ... Rom 16:23 *4172*
the heathen, in perils in the *c* ... 2Cor 11:26 *4172*
the *c* of the Damascenes with a ... 2Cor 11:32 *4172*
a *c* of Macedonia, by Titus and ... 2Cor *s*
chiefest *c* of Phrygia Pacatiana ... 1Ti *s* *3390*
and ordain elders in every *c* ... Titus 1:5 *4172*
For he looked for a *c* which hath ... Heb 11:10 *4172*
for he hath prepared for them a *c* ... Heb 11:16 *4172*
unto the *c* of the living God, the ... Heb 12:22 *4172*
For here have we no continuing *c* ... Heb 13:14 *4172*
morrow we will go into such a *c* ... Jas 4:13 *4172*
and the name of the *c* of my God ... Rev 3:12 *4172*
the holy *c* shall they tread under ... Rev 11:2 *4172*
lie in the street of the great *c* ... Rev 11:8 *4172*
and the tenth part of the *c* fell ... Rev 11:13 *4172*
fallen, is fallen, that great *c* ... Rev 14:8 *4172*
was trodden without the *c* ... Rev 14:20 *4172*
the great *c* was divided into ... Rev 16:19 *4172*
which thou sawest is that great *c* ... Rev 17:18 *4172*
great *c* Babylon, that mighty *c* ... Rev 18:10 *4172*
saying, Alas, alas that great *c* ... Rev 18:16 *4172*
c is like unto this great *c* ... Rev 18:18 *4172*
saying, Alas, alas that great *c* ... Rev 18:19 *4172*
great *c* Babylon be thrown down ... Rev 18:21 *4172*
saints about, and the beloved *c* ... Rev 20:9 *4172*
And I John saw the holy *c*, new ... Rev 21:2 *4172*
and shewed me that great *c* ... Rev 21:10 *4172*
the wall of the *c* had twelve ... Rev 21:14 *4172*
a golden reed to measure the *c* ... Rev 21:15 *4172*
the *c* lieth foursquare, and the ... Rev 21:16 *4172*
he measured the *c* with the reed ... Rev 21:16 *4172*
the *c* was pure gold, like unto ... Rev 21:18 *4172*
c were garnished with all manner ... Rev 21:19 *4172*
the street of the *c* was pure gold ... Rev 21:21 *4172*
the *c* had no need of the sun, ... Rev 21:23 *4172*
in through the gates into the *c* ... Rev 22:14 *4172*
of life, and out of the holy *c* ... Rev 22:19 *4172*

CLAD {2}
he had *c* himself with a new ... 1Kin 11:29 3680
was *c* with zeal as a cloke ... Is 59:17 5844

CLAMOROUS {1}
A foolish woman is *c* ... Prov 9:13 1993

CLAMOUR {1}
and wrath, and anger, and *c* ... Eph 4:31 *2906*

CLAP {6}
Men shall *c* their hands at him, ... Job 27:23 5606
O *c* your hands, all ye people ... Ps 47:1 8628
Let the floods *c* their hands ... Ps 98:8 4222
of the field shall *c* their hands ... Is 55:12 4222
All that pass by *c* their hands at ... Lam 2:15 5606
thee shall *c* the hands over thee ... Nah 3:19 8628

CLAPPED {2}
they *c* their hands, and said, God ... 2Kin 11:12 5221
Because thou hast *c* thine hands ... Eze 25:6 4222

CLAPPETH {1}
he *c* his hands among us, and ... Job 34:37 5606

CLAUDA *(claw'-dah)* {1} *An island near Crete.*
certain island which is called *C* ... Acts 27:16 *2802*

CLAUDIA *(claw'-de-ah)* {1} *A Roman Christian.*
thee, and Pudens, and Linus, and *C* ... 2Ti 4:21 *2803*

CLAUDIUS *(claw'-de-us)* {3}
1. A Roman emperor.
to pass in the days of *C* Caesar ... Acts 11:28 *2804*
(because that *C* had commanded all ... Acts 18:2 *2804*
2. A Roman officer in Jerusalem.
C Lysias unto the most excellent ... Acts 23:26 *2804*

CLAVE {14}
c the wood for the burnt offering ... Gen 22:3 1234
his soul *c* unto Dinah the ... Gen 34:3 1692
that the ground *c* asunder that ... Num 16:31 1234
But God *c* an hollow place that ... Judg 15:19 1234
but Ruth *c* unto her ... Ruth 1:14 1692
they *c* the wood of the cart, and ... 1Sa 6:14 1234
men of Judah *c* unto their king ... 2Sa 20:2 1692
his hand *c* unto the sword ... 2Sa 23:10 1692
Solomon *c* unto these in love ... 1Kin 11:2 1692
For he *c* to the LORD, and departed ... 2Kin 18:6 1692
They *c* to their brethren, their ... Neh 10:29 2388
He *c* the rocks in the wilderness, ... Ps 78:15 1234
he *c* the rock also, and the waters ... Is 48:21 1234
Howbeit certain men *c* unto him ... Acts 17:34 *2853*

CLAWS {3}
and cleaveth the cleft into two *c* ... Deut 14:6 6541
and his nails like birds' *c* ... Dan 4:33
fat, and tear their *c* in pieces ... Zec 11:16 6541

CLAY {33}
in the *c* ground between Succoth ... 1Kin 7:46 4568
in the *c* ground between Succoth ... 2Chr 4:17 4568
in them that dwell in houses of *c* ... Job 4:19 2563
that thou hast made me as the *c* ... Job 10:9 2563
ashes, your bodies to bodies of *c* ... Job 13:12 2563
dust, and prepare raiment as the *c* ... Job 27:16 2563
I also am formed out of the *c* ... Job 33:6 2563
It is turned as *c* to the seal ... Job 38:14 2563
horrible pit, out of the miry *c* ... Ps 40:2 2916
be esteemed as the potter's *c* ... Is 29:16 2563
and as the potter treadeth *c* ... Is 41:25 2916
Shall the *c* say to him that ... Is 45:9 2563
we are the *c*, and thou our potter ... Is 64:8 2563
the vessel that he made of *c* was ... Jer 18:4 2563
as the *c* is in the potter's hand, ... Jer 18:6 2563
them in the *c* in the brickkiln ... Jer 43:9 4423
feet part of iron and part of *c* ... Dan 2:33 2635
his feet that were of iron and *c* ... Dan 2:34 2635
Then was the iron, the *c*, the ... Dan 2:35 2635
feet and toes, part of potters' *c* ... Dan 2:41 2635
sawest the iron mixed with miry *c* ... Dan 2:41 2635
were part of iron, and part of *c* ... Dan 2:42 2635
sawest iron mixed with miry *c* ... Dan 2:43 2635
even as iron is not mixed with *c* ... Dan 2:43 2635
pieces the iron, the brass, the *c* ... Dan 2:45 2635
go into *c*, and tread the morter, ... Nah 3:14 2916
that ladeth himself with thick *c* ... Hab 2:6 5671
made *c* of the spittle, and he ... Jn 9:6 *4081*
eyes of the blind man with the *c* ... Jn 9:6 *4081*
A man that is called Jesus made *c* ... Jn 9:11 *4081*
sabbath day when Jesus made the *c* ... Jn 9:14 *4081*
He put *c* upon mine eyes, and I ... Jn 9:15 *4081*
not the potter power over the *c* ... Rom 9:21 *4081*

CLEAN {133}
Of every *c* beast thou shalt take ... Gen 7:2 2889
of beasts that are not *c* by two ... Gen 7:2 2889
Of *c* beasts, and of beasts that ... Gen 7:8 2889
and of beasts that are not *c* ... Gen 7:8 2889
c beast, and of every *c* fowl ... Gen 8:20 2889
gods that are among you, and be *c* ... Gen 35:2 2891
without the camp unto a *c* place ... Lev 4:12 2889
without the camp unto a *c* place ... Lev 6:11 2889
all that be *c* shall eat thereof ... Lev 7:19 2889
unholy, and between unclean and *c* ... Lev 10:10 2889
shall ye eat in a *c* place ... Lev 10:14 2889
is plenty of water, shall be *c* ... Lev 11:36 2889
is to be sown, it shall be *c* ... Lev 11:37 2889
between the unclean and the *c* ... Lev 11:47 2889
for her, and she shall be *c* ... Lev 12:8 2891
the priest shall pronounce him *c* ... Lev 13:6 2891
shall wash his clothes, and be *c* ... Lev 13:6 2891
him *c* that hath the plague ... Lev 13:13 2891
he is *c* ... Lev 13:13 2889
him *c* that hath the plague ... Lev 13:17 2891
he is *c* ... Lev 13:17 2889
the priest shall pronounce him *c* ... Lev 13:23 2891
the priest shall pronounce him *c* ... Lev 13:28 2891
the priest shall pronounce him *c* ... Lev 13:34 2891
shall wash his clothes, and be *c* ... Lev 13:34 2891
the scall is healed, he is *c* ... Lev 13:37 2889
the priest shall pronounce him *c* ... Lev 13:37 2891
he is *c* ... Lev 13:39 2889
yet is he *c* ... Lev 13:40 2889
yet is he *c* ... Lev 13:41 2889
the second time, and shall be *c* ... Lev 13:58 2891
thing of skins, to pronounce it *c* ... Lev 13:59 2891
be cleansed two birds alive and *c* ... Lev 14:4 2889
times, and shall pronounce him *c* ... Lev 14:7 2891
in water, that he may be *c* ... Lev 14:8 2891
flesh in water, and he shall be *c* ... Lev 14:9 2891
the priest that maketh him *c* ... Lev 14:11 2891
the man that is to be made *c* ... Lev 14:11 2891
for him, and he shall be *c* ... Lev 14:20 2891
shall pronounce the house *c* ... Lev 14:48 2891
and it shall be *c* ... Lev 14:53 2891
it is unclean, and when it is *c* ... Lev 14:57 2889
the issue spit upon him that is *c* ... Lev 15:8 2889
in running water, and shall be *c* ... Lev 15:13 2891
and after that she shall be *c* ... Lev 15:28 2891
that ye may be *c* from all your ... Lev 16:30 2891
then shall he be *c* ... Lev 17:15 2891
put difference between *c* beasts ... Lev 20:25 2889
and between unclean fowls and *c* ... Lev 20:25 2889
of the holy things, until he be *c* ... Lev 22:4 2891
the sun is down, he shall be *c* ... Lev 22:7 2891
thou shalt not make *c* riddance of ... Lev 23:22
woman be not defiled, but be *c* ... Num 5:28 2889
clothes, and so make themselves *c* ... Num 8:7 2891
But the man that is *c*, and is not ... Num 9:13 2889
every one that is *c* in thy house ... Num 18:11 2889
every one that is *c* in thine ... Num 18:13 2889
a man that is *c* shall gather up ... Num 19:9 2889
up without the camp in a *c* place ... Num 19:9 2889
on the seventh day he shall be *c* ... Num 19:12 2891
the seventh day he shall not be *c* ... Num 19:12 2891
a *c* person shall take hyssop, and ... Num 19:18 2889
the *c* person shall sprinkle upon ... Num 19:19 2889
in water, and shall be *c* at even ... Num 19:19 2891
the fire, and it shall be *c* ... Num 31:23 2891
the seventh day, and ye shall be *c* ... Num 31:24 2891
the *c* may eat thereof, as of the ... Deut 12:15 2889
the *c* shall eat of them alike ... Deut 12:22 2889
Of all *c* birds ye shall eat ... Deut 14:11 2889
But of all *c* fowls ye may eat ... Deut 14:20 2889
the *c* person shall eat it alike, ... Deut 15:22 2889
that is not *c* by reason of ... Deut 23:10 2889
people were passed *c* over Jordan ... Josh 3:17 8552
people were *c* passed over Jordan ... Josh 4:1 8552
all the people were *c* passed over ... Josh 4:11 8552
hath befallen him, he is not *c* ... 1Sa 20:26 2889
surely he is not *c* ... 1Sa 20:26 2889
again to thee, and thou shalt be *c* ... 2Kin 5:10 2891
may I not wash in them, and be *c* ... 2Kin 5:12 2891
he saith to thee, Wash, and be *c* ... 2Kin 5:13 2891
of a little child, and he was *c* ... 2Kin 5:14 2891
for every one that was not *c* ... 2Chr 30:17 2889
and make my hands never so *c* ... Job 9:30 2141
is pure, and I am *c* in thine eyes ... Job 11:4 1249
Who can bring a *c* thing out of an ... Job 14:4 2889
What is man, that he should be *c* ... Job 15:14 2135
heavens are not *c* in his sight ... Job 15:15 2141
he that hath *c* hands shall be ... Job 17:9 2891
or how can he be *c* that is born ... Job 25:4 2135
I am *c* without transgression, I ... Job 33:9 2134
The fear of the LORD is *c* ... Ps 19:9 2889
He that hath *c* hands, and a pure ... Ps 24:4 5355
me with hyssop, and I shall be *c* ... Ps 51:7 2891
Create in me a *c* heart, O God ... Ps 51:10 2889
even to such as are of a *c* heart ... Ps 73:1 1249
Is his mercy *c* gone for ever ... Ps 77:8 656
Where no oxen are, the crib is *c* ... Prov 14:4 1249
of a man are *c* in his own eyes ... Prov 16:2 2134
can say, I have made my heart *c* ... Prov 20:9 2135
to the good and to the *c*, and to ... Eccl 9:2 2889
Wash you, make you *c* ... Is 1:16 2135
down, the earth is *c* dissolved ... Is 24:19 6565
so that there is no place *c* ... Is 28:8
the ground shall eat *c* provender ... Is 30:24 2548
be ye *c*, that bear the vessels of ... Is 52:11 1305
a *c* vessel into the house of the ... Is 66:20 2889
wilt thou not be made *c* ... Jer 13:27 2891
between the unclean and the *c* ... Eze 22:26 2889
will I sprinkle *c* water upon you ... Eze 36:25 2889
and ye shall be *c* ... Eze 36:25 2891
between the unclean and the *c* ... Eze 44:23 2889
he hath made it *c* bare, and cast ... Joel 1:7
his arm shall be *c* dried up ... Zec 11:17
thou wilt, thou canst make me *c* ... Mt 8:2
be thou *c* ... Mt 8:3
for ye make *c* the outside of the ... Mt 23:25
the outside of them may be *c* also ... Mt 23:26 *2513*
he wrapped it in a *c* linen cloth ... Mt 27:59 *2513*
thou wilt, thou canst make me *c* ... Mk 1:40 *2511*
be thou *c* ... Mk 1:41 *2511*
thou wilt, thou canst make me *c* ... Lk 5:12 *2511*
be thou *c* ... Lk 5:13 *2511*
make *c* the outside of the cup ... Lk 11:39 *2511*
behold, all things are *c* unto you ... Lk 11:41 *2513*
his feet, but is *c* every whit ... Jn 13:10 *2513*
and ye are *c*, but not all ... Jn 13:10 *2513*
said he, Ye are not all *c* ... Jn 13:11 *2513*
Now ye are *c* through the word ... Jn 15:3 *2513*
I am *c* ... Acts 18:6 *2513*
those that were *c* escaped from ... 2Pet 2:18 *3689*
be arrayed in fine linen, *c* ... Rev 19:8 *2513*
clothed in fine linen, white and *c* ... Rev 19:14 *2513*

CLEANNESS {5}
according to the *c* of my hands ... 2Sa 22:21 1252
according to my *c* in his eye ... 2Sa 22:25 1252
according to the *c* of my hands ... Ps 18:20 1252
according to the *c* of my hands in ... Ps 18:24 1252
I also have given you *c* of teeth ... Amos 4:6 5356

CLEANSE {33}
and thou shalt *c* the altar ... Ex 29:36 2398
he shall take to *c* the house two ... Lev 14:49 2398
he shall *c* the house with the ... Lev 14:52 2398
c it, and hallow it from the ... Lev 16:19 2891
to *c* you, that ye may be clean ... Lev 16:30 2891
the children of Israel, and *c* them ... Num 8:6 2891
thou do unto them, to *c* them ... Num 8:7 2891
and thou shalt *c* them, and offer ... Num 8:15 2891
an atonement for them to *c* them ... Num 8:21 2891
to *c* the house of the LORD ... 2Chr 29:15 2891
of the house of the LORD, to *c* it ... 2Chr 29:16 2891
that they should *c* themselves ... Neh 13:22 2891
c thou me from secret faults ... Ps 19:12 5352
iniquity, and *c* me from my sin ... Ps 51:2 2891
shall a young man *c* his way ... Ps 119:9 2135
my people, not to fan, nor to *c* ... Jer 4:11 1305
I will *c* them from all their ... Jer 33:8 2891
from all your idols, will I *c* you ... Eze 36:25 2891
they have sinned, and will *c* them ... Eze 37:23 2891
of them, that they may *c* the land ... Eze 39:12 2891
the face of the earth, to *c* it ... Eze 39:14 2891
Thus shall they *c* the land ... Eze 39:16 2891
thus shalt thou *c* and purge it ... Eze 43:20 2398
and they shall *c* the altar ... Eze 43:22 2398
as they did *c* it with the bullock ... Eze 43:22 2398
blemish, and *c* the sanctuary ... Eze 45:18 2398
For I will *c* their blood that I ... Joel 3:21 5352
c the lepers, raise the dead, ... Mt 10:8 *2511*
c first that which is within the ... Mt 23:26 *2511*
let us *c* ourselves from all ... 2Cor 7:1 *2511*
c it with the washing of water by ... Eph 5:26 *2511*
C your hands, ye sinners ... Jas 4:8 *2511*
to *c* us from all unrighteousness ... 1Jn 1:9 *2511*

CLEANSED {39}
so it shall be *c* ... Lev 11:32 2891
she shall be *c* from the issue of ... Lev 12:7 2891
that is to be *c* two birds alive ... Lev 14:4 2891
be *c* from the leprosy seven times ... Lev 14:7 2891
he that is to be *c* shall wash his ... Lev 14:8 2891
right ear of him that is to be *c* ... Lev 14:14 2891
right ear of him that is to be *c* ... Lev 14:17 2891
the head of him that is to be *c* ... Lev 14:18 2891
is to be *c* from his uncleanness ... Lev 14:19 2891
right ear of him that is to be *c* ... Lev 14:25 2891
right ear of him that is to be *c* ... Lev 14:28 2891
the head of him that is to be *c* ... Lev 14:29 2891
that is to be *c* before the LORD ... Lev 14:31 2891
hath an issue is *c* of his issue ... Lev 15:13 2891
But if she be *c* of her issue ... Lev 15:28 2891
the land cannot be *c* of the blood ... Num 35:33 3722
which we are not *c* until this day ... Josh 22:17 2891
We have *c* all the house of the ... 2Chr 29:18 2891
had not *c* themselves, yet did ... 2Chr 30:18 2891
though he be not *c* according to ... 2Chr 30:19
altars, and *c* Judah and Jerusalem ... 2Chr 34:5 2891
commanded, and they *c* the chambers ... Neh 13:9 2891
Thus *c* I them from all strangers, ... Neh 13:30 2891
I have, if I be *c* from my sin ... Job 35:3
Verily I have *c* my heart in vain, ... Ps 73:13 2135
Thou art the land that is not *c* ... Eze 22:24 2891
In the day that I shall have *c* ... Eze 36:33 2891
And after he is *c*, they shall ... Eze 44:26 2893
then shall the sanctuary be *c* ... Dan 8:14 6663
their blood that I have not *c* ... Joel 3:21 5352
And immediately his leprosy was *c* ... Mt 8:3 *2511*
the lame walk, the lepers are *c* ... Mt 11:5 *2511*
departed from him, and he was *c* ... Mk 1:42 *2511*
and none of them was *c*, saving ... Lk 4:27 *2511*
the lame walk, the lepers are *c* ... Lk 7:22 *2511*
that, as they went, they were *c* ... Lk 17:14 *2511*
said, Were there not ten *c* ... Lk 17:17 *2511*
the second time, What God hath *c* ... Acts 10:15 *2511*
from heaven, What God hath *c* ... Acts 11:9 *2511*

CLEANSETH {3}
but the wind passeth, and *c* them ... Job 37:21 2891
blueness of a wound *c* away evil ... Prov 20:30 8562
Christ his Son *c* us from all sin ... 1Jn 1:7 *2511*

CLEANSING {10}
been seen of the priest for his *c* ... Lev 13:7 2893
much in the skin after his *c* ... Lev 13:35 2893
of the leper in the day of his *c* ... Lev 14:2 2893
day for his *c* unto the priest ... Lev 14:23 2893
that which pertaineth to his *c* ... Lev 14:32 2893
to himself seven days for his *c* ... Lev 15:13 2893
his head in the day of his *c* ... Num 6:9 2893
thou hast made an end of *c* it ... Eze 43:23 2893
offer for thy *c* those things ... Mk 1:44 *2512*
to the priest, and offer for thy *c* ... Lk 5:14 *2512*

CLEAR {15}
thou shalt be *c* from this my oath ... Gen 24:8 5352
shalt thou be *c* from this my oath ... Gen 24:41 5352
one, thou shalt be *c* from my oath ... Gen 24:41 5355
or how shall we *c* ourselves ... Gen 44:16 6663
will by no means *c* the guilty ... Ex 34:7 5352
the earth by *c* shining after rain ... 2Sa 23:4
and be *c* when thou judgest ... Ps 51:4 2135
c as the sun, and terrible as an ... Song 6:10 1249
place like a *c* heat upon herbs ... Is 18:4 6703
darken the earth in the *c* day ... Amos 8:9 216
that the light shall not be *c* ... Zec 14:6 3368
yourselves to be *c* in this matter ... 2Cor 7:11 *53*
like a jasper stone, *c* as crystal ... Rev 21:11 *2929*
was pure gold, like unto *c* glass ... Rev 21:18 *2513*
c as crystal, proceeding out of ... Rev 22:1 *2986*

CLEARER {1}
age shall be *c* than the noonday ... Job 11:17 6965

CLEARING {2}
and by no means *c* the guilty ... Num 14:18 5352
what *c* of yourselves, yea, what ... 2Cor 7:11 *627*

CLEARLY {5}
my lips shall utter knowledge *c* ... Job 33:3 1305
then shalt thou see *c* to cast out ... Mt 7:5 *1227*
was restored, and saw every man *c* ... Mk 8:25 *5081*
then shalt thou see *c* to pull out ... Lk 6:42 *1227*
creation of the world are *c* seen ... Rom 1:20 *2529*

CLEARNESS {1}
were the body of heaven in his *c* ... Ex 24:10 2892

CLEAVE {30}
mother, and shall *c* unto his wife ... Gen 2:24 1692
he shall *c* it with the wings ... Lev 1:17 8156
But ye that did *c* unto the LORD ... Deut 4:4 1695
serve, and to him shalt thou *c* ... Deut 10:20 1692
in all his ways, and to *c* unto him ... Deut 11:22 1692
ye shall serve him, and *c* unto him ... Deut 13:4 1692
there shall *c* nought of the ... Deut 13:17 1692
make the pestilence *c* unto thee ... Deut 28:21 1692
and they shall *c* unto thee ... Deut 28:60 1692
and that thou mayest *c* unto him ... Deut 30:20 1692
to *c* unto him, and to serve him ... Josh 22:5 1692
But *c* unto the LORD your God, as ... Josh 23:8 1692
c unto the remnant of these ... Josh 23:12 1692
of Naaman shall *c* unto thee ... 2Kin 5:27 1692
the clods *c* fast together ... Job 38:38 1692
Thou didst *c* the fountain and the ... Ps 74:15 1234
it shall not *c* to me ... Ps 101:3 1692
my groaning my bones *c* to my skin ... Ps 102:5 1692
let my tongue *c* to the roof of my ... Ps 137:6 1692
they shall *c* to the house of ... Is 14:1 5596
so have I caused to *c* unto me the ... Jer 13:11 1692
I will make thy tongue *c* to the ... Eze 3:26 1692
they shall not *c* one to another ... Dan 2:43 1693
but many shall *c* to them with ... Dan 11:34 3867
Thou didst *c* the earth with ... Hab 3:9 1234
the mount of Olives shall *c* in ... Zec 14:4 1234
and mother, and shall *c* to his wife ... Mt 19:5 *4347*
and mother, and *c* to his wife ... Mk 10:7 *4347*
heart they would *c* unto the Lord ... Acts 11:23 *4347*
c to that which is good ... Rom 12:9 *2853*

CLEAVED {3}
Nevertheless he *c* unto the sins ... 2Kin 3:3 1692
their tongue *c* to the roof of ... Job 29:10 1692
if any blot hath *c* to mine hands ... Job 31:7 1692

CLEAVETH {13}
c the cleft into two claws, and ... Deut 14:6 8157
he *c* my reins asunder, and doth ... Job 16:13 6398
My bone *c* to my skin and to my ... Job 19:20 1692
and my tongue *c* to my jaws ... Ps 22:15 1692
say they, *c* fast unto him ... Ps 41:8 3332
our belly *c* unto the earth ... Ps 44:25 1692
My soul *c* unto the dust ... Ps 119:25 1692
cutteth and *c* wood upon the earth ... Ps 141:7 1234
and he that *c* wood shall be ... Eccl 10:9 1234
For as the girdle *c* to the loins ... Jer 13:11 1692
c to the roof of his mouth for ... Lam 4:4 1692
their skin *c* to their bones ... Lam 4:8 6821
dust of your city, which *c* on us ... Lk 10:11 *2853*

CLEFT {2}
cleaveth the *c* into two claws, and ... Deut 11:6 8156
him, and the valleys shall be *c* ... Mic 1:4 1234

CLEFTS {5}
that art in the *c* of the rock ... Song 2:14 2288
To go into the *c* of the rocks ... Is 2:21 5366
dwellest in the *c* of the rock ... Jer 49:16 2288
and the little house with *c* ... Amos 6:11 1233
dwellest in the *c* of the rock ... Obad 3 2288

CLEMENCY {1}
hear us of thy *c* a few words ... Acts 24:4 *1932*

CLEMENT *(clem'-ent)* {1} *A companion of Paul.*
me in the gospel, with *C* also ... Phil 4:3 *2815*

CLEOPAS *(cle'-o-pas)* {1} See ALPHAEUS, CLEOPHAS. *A disciple on Emmaus Road.*
the one of them, whose name was *C* ... Lk 24:18 *2810*

CLEOPHAS *(cle'-o-fas)* {1} See CLEOPAS. *Husband of Mary.*
sister, Mary the wife of *C* ... Jn 19:25 *2832*

CLIFF {1}
they come up by the *c* of Ziz ... 2Chr 20:16 4608

CLIFFS {1}
To dwell in the *c* of the valleys ... Job 30:6 6178

CLIFT {1}
will put thee in a *c* of the rock ... Ex 33:22 5366

CLIFTS {1}
valleys under the *c* of the rocks ... Is 57:5 5585

CLIMB {4}
thickets, and *c* up upon the rocks ... Jer 4:29 5927
they shall *c* the wall like men of ... Joel 2:7 5927
they shall *c* up upon the houses ... Joel 2:9 5927
though they *c* up to heaven, ... Amos 9:2 5927

CLIMBED {2}
Jonathan *c* up upon his hands and ... 1Sa 14:13 5927
c up into a sycomore tree to see ... Lk 19:4 *305*

CLIMBETH {1}
but *c* up some other way, the same ... Jn 10:1 *305*

CLIPPED {1}
shall be bald, and every beard *c* ... Jer 48:37 1639

CLODS {6}
clothed with worms and *c* of dust ... Job 7:5 1487
The *c* of the valley shall be ... Job 21:33 7263
the *c* cleave fast together ... Job 38:38 7263
break the *c* of his ground ... Is 28:24 7702
plow, and Jacob shall break his *c* ... Hos 10:11 7702
The seed is rotten under their *c* ... Joel 1:17 4053

CLOKE {7}
and was clad with zeal as a *c* ... Is 59:17 4598
thy coat, let him have thy *c* also ... Mt 5:40 *2440*
him that taketh away thy *c* forbid ... Lk 6:29 *2440*
now they have no *c* for their sin ... Jn 15:22 *4392*
ye know, nor a *c* of covetousness ... 1Th 2:5 *4392*
The *c* that I left at Troas with ... 2Ti 4:13 *5341*
liberty for a *c* of maliciousness ... 1Pet 2:16 *1942*

CLOPAS See CLEOPHAS.

CLOSE {11}
eyes of her husband, and be kept *c* ... Num 5:13 5956
be afraid out of their *c* places ... 2Sa 22:46 4526
while he yet kept himself *c* ... 1Chr 12:1 6113
kept *c* from the fowls of the air ... Job 28:21 5641
shut up together as with a *c* seal ... Job 41:15 6862
be afraid out of their *c* places ... Ps 18:45 4526
shall follow *c* after you there in ... Jer 42:16 1692
And I saw him come *c* unto the ram ... Dan 8:7 681
c up the breaches thereof ... Amos 9:11 1443
And they kept it *c*, and told no man ... Lk 9:36 *4601*
thence, they sailed *c* by Crete ... Acts 27:13 *788*

CLOSED {11}
c up the flesh instead thereof ... Gen 2:21 5462
For the LORD had fast *c* up all ... Gen 20:18 6113
the pit, and the earth *c* upon them ... Num 16:33 3680
the fat *c* upon the blade, so that ... Judg 3:22 5462
they have not been *c*, neither ... Is 1:6 2115
deep sleep, and hath *c* your eyes ... Is 29:10 6105
for the words are *c* up and sealed ... Dan 12:9 5640
the depth *c* me round about, the ... Jonah 2:5 5437
and their eyes they have *c* ... Mt 13:15 *2576*
he *c* the book, and he gave it ... Lk 4:20 *4428*
and their eyes have they *c* ... Acts 28:27 *2576*

CLOSER {1}
that sticketh *c* than a brother ... Prov 18:24

CLOSEST {1}
because thou *c* thyself in cedar ... Jer 22:15 8474

CLOSET {2}
and the bride out of her *c* ... Joel 2:16 2646
thou prayest, enter into thy *c* ... Mt 6:6 *5009*

CLOSETS {1}
in *c* shall be proclaimed upon the ... Lk 12:3 *5009*

CLOTH {18}
spread over it a *c* wholly of blue ... Num 4:6 899
they shall spread a *c* of blue ... Num 4:7 899
spread upon them a *c* of scarlet ... Num 4:8 899
And they shall take a *c* of blue ... Num 4:9 899
they shall spread a *c* of blue ... Num 4:11 899
and put them in a *c* of blue ... Num 4:12 899
and spread a purple *c* thereon ... Num 4:13 899
they shall spread the *c* before ... Deut 22:17 8071
bolster, and covered it with a *c* ... 1Sa 19:13 899
wrapped in a *c* behind the ephod ... 1Sa 21:9 8071
cast a *c* upon him, when he saw ... 2Sa 20:12 899
morrow, that he took a thick *c* ... 2Kin 8:15 4346
cast them away as a menstruous *c* ... Is 30:22
of new *c* unto an old garment ... Mt 9:16 *4470*
he wrapped it in a clean linen *c* ... Mt 27:59 *4616*
piece of new *c* on an old garment ... Mk 2:21 *4470*
having a linen *c* cast about his ... Mk 14:51 *4616*
And he left the linen *c*, and fled ... Mk 14:52 *4616*

CLOTHE {16}
his sons, and *c* them with coats ... Ex 40:14 3847
and she sent raiment to *c* Mordecai ... Est 4:4 3847
I will also *c* her priests with ... Ps 132:16 3847
His enemies will I *c* with shame ... Ps 132:18 3847
shall *c* a man with rags ... Prov 23:21 3847
I will *c* him with thy robe, and ... Is 22:21 3847
thou shalt surely *c* thee with ... Is 49:18 3847
I *c* the heavens with blackness, ... Is 50:3 3847
they shall *c* themselves with ... Eze 26:16 3847
ye *c* you with the wool, ye kill ... Eze 34:3 3847
ye *c* you, but there is none warm ... Hag 1:6 3847
I will *c* thee with change of ... Zec 3:4 3847
if God so *c* the grass of the ... Mt 6:30 *294*
shall he not much more *c* you ... Mt 6:30
If then God so *c* the grass ... Lk 12:28 *294*
how much more will he *c* you ... Lk 12:28

CLOTHED {73}
make coats of skins, and *c* them ... Gen 3:21 3847
c him with the robe, and put the ... Lev 8:7 3847
who *c* you in scarlet, with other ... 2Sa 1:24 3847
David was *c* with a robe of fine ... 1Chr 15:27 3736
who were *c* in sackcloth, fell ... 1Chr 21:16 3680
be *c* with salvation, and let thy ... 2Chr 6:41 3847
c in their robes, and they sat in ... 2Chr 18:9 3847
with the spoil *c* all that were ... 2Chr 28:15 3847
the king's gate *c* with sackcloth ... Est 4:2 3830
My flesh is *c* with worms and clods ... Job 7:5 3847
hate thee shall be *c* with shame ... Job 8:22 3847
Thou hast *c* me with skin and flesh ... Job 10:11 3847
put on righteousness, and it *c* me ... Job 29:14 3847
hast thou *c* his neck with thunder ... Job 39:19 3847
let them be *c* with shame and ... Ps 35:26 3847
The pastures are *c* with flocks ... Ps 65:13 3847
reigneth, he is *c* with majesty ... Ps 93:1 3847
the LORD is *c* with strength, ... Ps 93:1 3847
thou art *c* with honour and majesty ... Ps 104:1 3847
As he *c* himself with cursing like ... Ps 109:18 3847
mine adversaries be *c* with shame ... Ps 109:29 3847
priests be *c* with righteousness ... Ps 132:9 3847
her household are *c* with scarlet ... Prov 31:21 3847
for he hath *c* me with the ... Is 61:10 3847
prince shall be *c* with desolation ... Eze 7:27 3847
man among them was *c* with linen ... Eze 9:2 3847
he called to the man *c* with linen ... Eze 9:3 3847
the man *c* with linen, which had ... Eze 9:11 3847
spake unto the man *c* with linen ... Eze 10:2 3847
commanded the man *c* with linen ... Eze 10:6 3847
of him that was *c* with linen ... Eze 10:7 3847
I *c* thee also with broidered work ... Eze 16:10 3847
Which were *c* with blue, captains ... Eze 23:6 3847
rulers *c* most gorgeously, ... Eze 23:12 3847
all of them *c* with all sorts of ... Eze 38:4 3847
they shall be *c* with linen ... Eze 44:17 3847
shall be *c* with scarlet, and have ... Dan 5:7 3848
thou shalt be *c* with scarlet ... Dan 5:16 3848
they *c* Daniel with scarlet, and ... Dan 5:29 3848
behold a certain man *c* in linen ... Dan 10:5 3847
And one said to the man *c* in linen ... Dan 12:6 3847
And I heard the man *c* in linen ... Dan 12:7 3847
all such as are *c* with strange ... Zeph 1:8 3847
Now Joshua was *c* with filthy ... Zec 3:3 3847
his head, and *c* him with garments ... Zec 3:5 3847
or, Wherewithal shall we be *c* ... Mt 6:31 *4016*
A man *c* in soft raiment ... Mt 11:8 *294*
Naked, and ye *c* me ... Mt 25:36 *4016*
or naked, and *c* thee ... Mt 25:38 *4016*
naked, and ye *c* me not ... Mt 25:43 *4016*
John was *c* with camel's hair, and ... Mk 1:6 *1746*
and had the legion, sitting, and *c* ... Mk 5:15 *2439*
they *c* him with purple, and ... Mk 15:17 *1746*
c in a long white garment ... Mk 16:5 *4016*
A man *c* in soft raiment ... Lk 7:25 *294*
sitting at the feet of Jesus, *c* ... Lk 8:35 *2439*
rich man, which was *c* in purple ... Lk 16:19 *1737*
earnestly desiring to be *c* upon ... 2Cor 5:2 *1902*
If so be that being *c* we shall ... 2Cor 5:3 *1746*
but *c* upon, that mortality might ... 2Cor 5:4 *1902*
to another, and be *c* with humility ... 1Pet 5:5 *1463*
c with a garment down to the foot ... Rev 1:13 *1746*
same shall be *c* in white raiment ... Rev 3:5 *4016*
raiment, that thou mayest be *c* ... Rev 3:18 *4016*
sitting, *c* in white raiment ... Rev 4:4 *4016*
c with white robes, and palms in ... Rev 7:9 *4016*
down from heaven, *c* with a cloud ... Rev 10:1 *4016*
threescore days, *c* in sackcloth ... Rev 11:3 *4016*
a woman *c* with the sun, and the ... Rev 12:1 *4016*
c in pure and white linen, and ... Rev 15:6 *1746*
that was *c* in fine linen, and ... Rev 18:16 *4016*
he was *c* with a vesture dipped in ... Rev 19:13 *4016*
c in fine linen, white and clean ... Rev 19:14 *1746*

CLOTHES {101}
and he rent his *c* ... Gen 37:29 899
And Jacob rent his *c*, and put ... Gen 37:34 8071
Then they rent their *c*, and laded ... Gen 44:13 8071
his *c* in the blood of grapes ... Gen 49:11 5497
in their *c* upon their shoulders ... Ex 12:34 8071
morrow, and let them wash their *c* ... Ex 19:10 8071
and they washed their *c* ... Ex 19:14 8071
your heads, neither rend your *c* ... Lev 10:6 899
carcase of them shall wash his *c* ... Lev 11:25 899
carcase of them shall wash his *c* ... Lev 11:28 899
carcase of it shall wash his *c* ... Lev 11:40 899
carcase of it shall wash his *c* ... Lev 11:40 899
and he shall wash his *c*, and be ... Lev 13:6 899
and he shall wash his *c*, and be ... Lev 13:34 899
his *c* shall be rent, and his head ... Lev 13:45 899
to be cleansed shall wash his *c* ... Lev 14:8 899
and he shall wash his *c*, also he ... Lev 14:9 899
in the house shall wash his *c* ... Lev 14:47 899
in the house shall wash his *c* ... Lev 14:47 899
toucheth his bed shall wash his *c* ... Lev 15:5 899
hath the issue shall wash his *c* ... Lev 15:6 899
hath the issue shall wash his *c* ... Lev 15:7 899
then he shall wash his *c*, and ... Lev 15:8 899
of those things shall wash his *c* ... Lev 15:10 899
in water, he shall wash his *c* ... Lev 15:11 899
for his cleansing, and wash his *c* ... Lev 15:13 899
toucheth her bed shall wash his *c* ... Lev 15:21 899
she sat upon shall wash his *c* ... Lev 15:22 899
be unclean, and shall wash his *c* ... Lev 15:27 899
the scapegoat shall wash his *c* ... Lev 16:26 899
burneth them shall wash his *c* ... Lev 16:28 899
and shall put on the linen *c* ... Lev 16:32 899
he shall both wash his *c* ... Lev 17:15 899
uncover his head, nor rend his *c* ... Lev 21:10 899
flesh, and let them wash their *c* ... Num 8:7 899
purified, and they washed their *c* ... Num 8:21 899
searched the land, rent their *c* ... Num 14:6 899
Then the priest shall wash his *c* ... Num 19:7 899
her shall wash his *c* in water ... Num 19:8 899
of the heifer shall wash his *c* ... Num 19:10 899
purify himself, and wash his *c* ... Num 19:19 899
of separation shall wash his *c* ... Num 19:21 899
wash your *c* on the seventh day ... Num 31:24 899
your *c* are not waxen old upon you ... Deut 29:5 8008
And Joshua rent his *c*, and fell to ... Josh 7:6 8071
he saw her, that he rent his *c* ... Judg 11:35 899
the same day with his *c* rent ... 1Sa 4:12 4055
And he stript off his *c* also ... 1Sa 19:24 899
camp from Saul with his *c* rent ... 2Sa 1:2 899
Then David took hold on his *c* ... 2Sa 1:11 899
that were with him, Rend your *c* ... 2Sa 3:31 899
stood by with their *c* rent ... 2Sa 13:31 899
his beard, nor washed his *c* ... 2Sa 19:24 899
and they covered him with *c* ... 1Kin 1:1 899
those words, that he rent his *c* ... 1Kin 21:27 899
and he took hold of his own *c* ... 2Kin 2:12 899
the letter, that he rent his *c* ... 2Kin 5:7 899
the king of Israel had rent his *c* ... 2Kin 5:8 899
Wherefore hast thou rent thy *c* ... 2Kin 5:8 899
of the woman, that he rent his *c* ... 2Kin 6:30 899
and Athaliah rent her *c*, and cried, ... 2Kin 11:14 899
to Hezekiah with their *c* rent ... 2Kin 18:37 899
heard it, that he rent his *c* ... 2Kin 19:1 899

of the law, that he rent his c ... 2Kin 22:11 899
and a curse, and hast rent thy c ... 2Kin 22:19 899
Then Athaliah rent her c, and said ... 2Chr 23:13 899
of the law, that he rent his c ... 2Chr 34:19 899
before me, and didst rend thy c ... 2Chr 34:27 899
me, none of us put off our c ... Neh 4:23 899
their c waxed not old, and their ... Neh 9:21 8008
was done, Mordecai rent his c ... Est 4:1 899
mine own c shall abhor me ... Job 9:31 8008
his bosom, and his c not be burned ... Prov 6:27 899
to Hezekiah with their c rent ... Is 36:22 899
heard it, that he rent his c ... Is 37:1 899
beards shaven, and their c rent ... Jer 41:5 899
shall strip thee also of thy c ... Eze 16:39 899
also strip thee out of thy c ... Eze 23:26 899
in precious c for chariots ... Eze 27:20 899
in all sorts of things, in blue c ... Eze 27:24 1545
c laid to pledge by every altar ... Amos 2:8 899
the colt, and put on them their c ... Mt 21:7 *2440*
field return back to take his c ... Mt 24:18 *2440*
Then the high priest rent his c ... Mt 26:65 *2440*
said, If I may touch but his c ... Mk 5:28 *2440*
press, and said, Who touched my c ... Mk 5:30 *2440*
Then the high priest rent his c ... Mk 14:63 *5509*
from him, and put his own c on him ... Mk 15:20 *2440*
and wrapped him in swaddling c ... Lk 2:7 *4683*
the babe wrapped in swaddling c ... Lk 2:12 *4683*
devils long time, and ware no c ... Lk 8:27 *2440*
they spread their c in the way ... Lk 19:36 *2440*
the linen c laid by themselves ... Lk 24:12 *3608*
it in linen c with the spices ... Jn 19:40 *3608*
looking in, saw the linen c lying ... Jn 20:5 *3608*
and seeth the linen c lie ... Jn 20:6 *3608*
head, not lying with the linen c ... Jn 20:7 *3608*
their c at a young man's feet ... Acts 7:58 *2440*
Paul, heard of, they rent their c ... Acts 14:14 *2440*
the magistrates rent off their c ... Acts 16:22 *2440*
cried out, and cast off their c ... Acts 22:23 *2440*

CLOTHEST {1}
Though thou c thyself with ... Jer 4:30 3847

CLOTHING {19}
and stripped the naked of their c ... Job 22:6 899
the naked to lodge without c ... Job 24:7 3830
cause him to go naked without c ... Job 24:10 3830
seen any perish for want of c ... Job 31:19 3830
were sick, my c was sackcloth ... Ps 35:13 3830
her c is of wrought gold ... Ps 45:13 3830
The lambs are for thy c, and the ... Prov 27:26 3830
her c is silk and purple ... Prov 31:22 3830
Strength and honour are her c ... Prov 31:25 3830
his father, saying, Thou hast c ... Is 3:6 8071
my house is neither bread nor c ... Is 3:7 8071
sufficiently, and for durable c ... Is 23:18 4374
the garments of vengeance for c ... Is 59:17 8516
blue and purple is their c ... Jer 10:9 3830
which come to you in sheep's c ... Mt 7:15 *1742*
they that wear soft c are in ... Mt 11:8
which love to go in long c ... Mk 12:38 *4749*
a man stood before me in bright c ... Acts 10:30 *2066*
to him that weareth the gay c ... Jas 2:3 *2066*

CLOTHS {4}
the c of service, and the holy ... Ex 31:10 899
The c of service, to do service ... Ex 35:19 899
they made c of service, to do ... Ex 39:1 899
The c of service to do service in ... Ex 39:41 899

CLOUD {107}
I do set my bow in the c, and it ... Gen 9:13 6051
when I bring a c over the earth ... Gen 9:14 6051
the bow shall be seen in the c ... Gen 9:14 6051
And the bow shall be in the c ... Gen 9:16 6051
them by day in a pillar of a c ... Ex 13:21 6051
away the pillar of the c by day ... Ex 13:22 6051
the pillar of the c went from ... Ex 14:19 6051
and it was a c and darkness to them ... Ex 14:20 6051
the pillar of fire and of the c ... Ex 14:24 6051
of the LORD appeared in the c ... Ex 16:10 6051
Lo, I come unto thee in a thick c ... Ex 19:9 6051
a thick c upon the mount, and the ... Ex 19:16 6051
mount, and a c covered the mount ... Ex 24:15 6051
the c covered it six days ... Ex 24:16 6051
Moses out of the midst of the c ... Ex 24:16 6051
went into the midst of the c ... Ex 24:18 6051
And the LORD descended in the c ... Ex 34:5 6051
Then a c covered the tent of the ... Ex 40:34 6051
because the c abode thereon, and ... Ex 40:35 6051
when the c was taken up from over ... Ex 40:36 6051
But if the c were not taken up, ... Ex 40:37 6051
For the c of the LORD was upon ... Ex 40:38 6051
in the c upon the mercy seat ... Lev 16:2 6051
that the c of the incense may ... Lev 16:13 6051
up the c covered the tabernacle ... Num 9:15 6051
the c covered it by day, and the ... Num 9:16 6051
when the c was taken up from the ... Num 9:17 6051
and in the place where the c abode ... Num 9:17 6051
as long as the c abode upon the ... Num 9:18 6051
when the c tarried long upon the ... Num 9:19 6051
when the c was a few days upon ... Num 9:20 6051
when the c abode from even unto ... Num 9:21 6051
that the c was taken up in the ... Num 9:21 6051
by night that the c was taken up ... Num 9:21 6051
that the c tarried upon the ... Num 9:22 6051
that the c was taken up from off ... Num 10:11 6051
the c rested in the wilderness of ... Num 10:12 6051
the c of the LORD was upon them ... Num 10:34 6051
And the LORD came down in a c ... Num 11:25 6051
came down in the pillar of the c ... Num 12:5 6051
the c departed from off the ... Num 12:10 6051
that thy c standeth over them, and ... Num 14:14 6051
by daytime in a pillar of a c ... Num 14:14 6051
the c covered it, and the glory of ... Num 16:42 6051
ye should go, and in a c by day ... Deut 1:33 6051
the midst of the fire, of the c ... Deut 5:22 6051
the tabernacle in a pillar of a c ... Deut 31:15 6051
the pillar of the c stood over ... Deut 31:15 6051
that the c filled the house of ... 1Kin 8:10 6051
to minister because of the c ... 1Kin 8:11 6051
ariseth a little c out of the sea ... 1Kin 18:44 5645
the house was filled with a c ... 2Chr 5:13 6051
to minister by reason of the c ... 2Chr 5:14 6051
the pillar of the c departed not ... Neh 9:19 6051
let a c dwell upon it ... Job 3:5 6053
As the c is consumed and vanisheth ... Job 7:9 6051
can he judge through the dark c ... Job 22:13 6205
the c is not rent under them ... Job 26:8 6051
and spreadeth his c upon it ... Job 26:9 6051
and my welfare passeth away as a c ... Job 30:15 5645
by the c that cometh betwixt ... Job 36:32
watering he wearieth the thick c ... Job 37:11 5645
he scattereth his bright c ... Job 37:11 6051
the light of his c to shine ... Job 37:15 6051
When I made the c the garment ... Job 38:9 6051
daytime also he led them with a c ... Ps 78:14 6051
He spread a c for a covering ... Ps 105:39 6051
is as a c of the latter rain ... Prov 16:15 5645
Zion, and upon her assemblies, a c ... Is 4:5 6051
like a c of dew in the heat of ... Is 18:4 5645
the LORD rideth upon a swift c ... Is 19:1 5645
the heat with the shadow of a c ... Is 25:5 5645
I have blotted out, as a thick c ... Is 44:22 5645
thy transgressions, and, as a c ... Is 44:22 6051
Who are these that fly as a c ... Is 60:8 5645
of Zion with a c in his anger ... Lam 2:1 5743
hast covered thyself with a c ... Lam 3:44 6051
came out of the north, a great c ... Eze 1:4 6051
is in the c in the day of rain ... Eze 1:28 6051
a thick c of incense went up ... Eze 8:11 6051
the c filled the inner court ... Eze 10:3 6051
the house was filled with the c ... Eze 10:4 6051
a c shall cover her, and her ... Eze 30:18 6051
I will cover the sun with a c ... Eze 32:7 6051
be like a c to cover the land ... Eze 38:9 6051
Israel, as a c to cover the land ... Eze 38:16 6051
your goodness is as a morning c ... Hos 6:4 6051
they shall be as the morning c ... Hos 13:3 6051
a bright c overshadowed them ... Mt 17:5 *3507*
and behold a voice out of the c ... Mt 17:5 *3507*
there was a c that overshadowed ... Mk 9:7 *3507*
and a voice came out of the c ... Mk 9:7 *3507*
he thus spake, there came a c ... Lk 9:34 *3507*
feared as they entered into the c ... Lk 9:34 *3507*
there came a voice out of the c ... Lk 9:35 *3507*
When ye see a c rise out of the ... Lk 12:54 *3507*
of man coming in a c with power ... Lk 21:27 *3507*
a c received him out of their ... Acts 1:9 *3507*
all our fathers were under the c ... 1Cor 10:1 *3507*
all baptized unto Moses in the c ... 1Cor 10:2 *3507*
with so great a c of witnesses ... Heb 12:1 *3509*
from heaven, clothed with a c ... Rev 10:1 *3507*
they ascended up to heaven in a c ... Rev 11:12 *3507*
And I looked, and behold a white c ... Rev 14:14 *3507*
upon the c one sat like unto the ... Rev 14:14 *3507*
voice to him that sat on the c ... Rev 14:15 *3507*
he that sat on the c thrust in ... Rev 14:16 *3507*

CLOUDS {49}
midst of heaven, with darkness, c ... Deut 4:11 6051
dropped, the c also dropped water ... Judg 5:4 5645
waters, and thick c of the skies ... 2Sa 22:12 5645
riseth, even a morning without c ... 2Sa 23:4 5645
that the heaven was black with c ... 1Kin 18:45 5645
and his head reach unto the c ... Job 20:6 5645
Thick c are a covering to him, ... Job 22:14 5645
up the waters in his thick c ... Job 26:8 5645
behold the c which are higher ... Job 35:5 7834
Which the c do drop and distil ... Job 36:28 7834
the spreadings of the c, or the ... Job 36:29 5645
With c he covereth the light ... Job 36:32 3709
thou know the balancings of the c ... Job 37:16 5645
bright light which is in the c ... Job 37:21 7834
thou lift up thy voice to the c ... Job 38:34 5645
Who can number the c in wisdom ... Job 38:37 7834
waters and thick c of the skies ... Ps 18:11 5645
was before him his thick c passed ... Ps 18:12 5645
faithfulness reacheth unto the c ... Ps 36:5 7834
heavens, and thy truth unto the c ... Ps 57:10 7834
and his strength is in the c ... Ps 68:34 7834
The c poured out water ... Ps 77:17 5645
he had commanded the c from above ... Ps 78:23 7834
C and darkness are round about him ... Ps 97:2 6051
who maketh the c his chariot ... Ps 104:3 5645
and thy truth reacheth unto the c ... Ps 108:4 7834
Who covereth the heaven with c ... Ps 147:8 5645
up, and the c drop down the dew ... Prov 3:20 7834
When he established the c above ... Prov 8:28 7834
himself of a false gift is like c ... Prov 25:14 5387
If the c be full of rain, they ... Eccl 11:3 5645
regardeth the c shall not reap ... Eccl 11:4 5645
nor the c return after the rain ... Eccl 12:2 5645
I will also command the c that ... Is 5:6 5645
ascend above the heights of the c ... Is 14:14 5645
Behold, he shall come up as c ... Jer 4:13 6053
of man came with the c of heaven ... Dan 7:13 6050
and of gloominess, a day of c ... Joel 2:2 6051
the c are the dust of his feet ... Nah 1:3 6051
and gloominess, a day of c ... Zeph 1:15 6051
so the LORD shall make bright c ... Zec 10:1 2385
in the c of heaven with power ... Mt 24:30 *3507*
and coming in the c of heaven ... Mt 26:64 *3507*
coming in the c with great power ... Mk 13:26 *3507*
and coming in the c of heaven ... Mk 14:62 *3507*
up together with them in the c ... 1Th 4:17 *3507*
c that are carried with a tempest ... 2Pet 2:17 *3507*
c they are without water, carried ... Jude 12 *3507*
Behold, he cometh with c ... Rev 1:7 *3507*

CLOUDY {6}
the c pillar descended, and stood ... Ex 33:9 6051
all the people saw the c pillar ... Ex 33:10 6051
them in the day by a c pillar ... Neh 9:12 6051
spake unto them in the c pillar ... Ps 99:7 6051
day of the LORD is near, a c day ... Eze 30:3 6051
they have been scattered in the c ... Eze 34:12 6051

CLOUTED {1}
c upon their feet, and old ... Josh 9:5 2921

CLOUTS {2}
and took thence old cast c ... Jer 38:11 5499
Put now these old cast c ... Jer 38:12 5499

CLOVEN {2}
or of them that divide the c hoof ... Deut 14:7 8156
them c tongues like as of fire ... Acts 2:3 *1266*

CLOVENFOOTED {3}
parteth the hoof, and is c ... Lev 11:3 8156,8157,6541
he divide the hoof, and be c ... Lev 11:7 8156,8157,6541
divideth the hoof, and is not c ... Lev 11:26 8156,8157

CLUSTER {5}
a branch with one c of grapes ... Num 13:23 811
because of the c of grapes which ... Num 13:24 811
My beloved is unto me as a c of ... Song 1:14 811
As the new wine is found in the c ... Is 65:8 811
there is no c to eat ... Mic 7:1 811

CLUSTERS {7}
the c thereof brought forth ripe ... Gen 40:10 811
of gall, their c are bitter ... Deut 32:32 811
corn, and an hundred c of raisins ... 1Sa 25:18 6778
cake of figs, and two c of raisins ... 1Sa 30:12 6778
and thy breasts to c of grapes ... Song 7:7 811
breasts shall be as c of the vine ... Song 7:8 811
gather the c of the vine of the ... Rev 14:18 *1009*

CNIDUS *(ni'-dus)* {1} *A port town in southwestern Asia Minor.*
scarce were come over against C ... Acts 27:7 *2834*

COAL {4}
shall quench my c which is left ... 2Sa 14:7 1513
me, having a live c in his hand ... Is 6:6 7531
there shall not be a c to warm at ... Is 47:14 1513
Their visage is blacker than a c ... Lam 4:8 7815

COALS {28}
c of fire from off the altar ... Lev 16:12 1513
c were kindled by it ... 2Sa 22:9 1513
before him were c of fire kindled ... 2Sa 22:13 1513
there was a cake baken on the c ... 1Kin 19:6 7529
His breath kindleth c, and a flame ... Job 41:21 1513
c were kindled by it ... Ps 18:8 1513
passed, hail stones and c of fire ... Ps 18:12 1513
hail stones and c of fire ... Ps 18:13 1513
of the mighty, with c of juniper ... Ps 120:4 1513
Let burning c fall upon them ... Ps 140:10 1513
Can one go upon hot c, and his ... Prov 6:28 1513
For thou shalt heap c of fire ... Prov 25:22 1513
As c are to burning c, and ... Prov 26:21 6352
As c are to burning c ... Prov 26:21 1513
the c thereof are c of fire ... Song 8:6 7565
the tongs both worketh in the c ... Is 44:12 6352
baked bread upon the c thereof ... Is 44:19 1513
that bloweth the c in the fire ... Is 54:16 6352
was like burning c of fire ... Eze 1:13 1513
fill thine hand with c of fire ... Eze 10:2 1513
set it empty upon the c thereof ... Eze 24:11 1513
burning c went forth at his feet ... Hab 3:5 7565
there, who had made a fire of c ... Jn 18:18 *439*
land, they saw a fire of c there ... Jn 21:9 *439*
shalt heap c of fire on his head ... Rom 12:20 *440*

COAST {62}
I bring the locusts into thy c ... Ex 10:4 1366
by the sea, and by the c of Jordan ... Num 13:29 3027
by the c of the land of Edom, ... Num 20:23 1366
Arnon, which is in the utmost c ... Num 22:36 1366
come come from the c of Chittim ... Num 24:24 3027
of Zin along by the c of Edom ... Num 34:3 3027
c of the salt sea eastward ... Num 34:3 7097
the c shall go down from Shepham ... Num 34:11 1366
Ye are to pass through the c of ... Deut 2:4 1366
Ar, the c of Moab, this day ... Deut 2:18 1366
the c thereof, from Chinnereth ... Deut 3:17 1366
the uttermost sea shall your c be ... Deut 11:24 1366
with thee in all thy c seven days ... Deut 16:4 1366
if the LORD thy God enlarge thy c ... Deut 19:8 1366
down of the sun, shall be your c ... Josh 1:4 1366
the c of Og king of Bashan, which ... Josh 12:4 1366
The king of Dor in the c of Dor ... Josh 12:23 5299
their c was from Aroer, that is ... Josh 13:16 1366
their c was Jazer, and all the ... Josh 13:25 1366
their c was from Mahanaim, all ... Josh 13:30 1366
the uttermost part of the south c ... Josh 15:1 1366
out of that c were at the sea ... Josh 15:4 1366
this shall be your south c ... Josh 15:4 1366
the great sea, and the c thereof ... Josh 15:12 1366
This is the c of the children of ... Josh 15:12 1366
children of Judah toward the c of ... Josh 15:21 1366

westward to the *c* of Japhleti .... Josh 16:3 1366
unto the *c* of Beth-horon the .... Josh 16:3 1366
the *c* of Manasseh was from Asher .... Josh 17:7 1366
the *c* descended unto the river .... Josh 17:9 1366
the *c* of Manasseh also was on the .... Josh 17:9 1366
abide in their *c* on the south .... Josh 18:5 1366
the *c* of their lot came forth .... Josh 18:11 1366
this was the south *c* .... Josh 18:19 1366
the *c* reacheth to Tabor, and .... Josh 19:22 1366
then the *c* turneth to Ramah, and .... Josh 19:29 1366
and the *c* turneth to Hosah .... Josh 19:29 1366
at the sea from the *c* to Achzib .... Josh 19:29 2256
their *c* was from Heleph, from .... Josh 19:33 1366
then the *c* turneth westward to .... Josh 19:34 1366
the *c* of their inheritance was .... Josh 19:41 1366
the *c* of the children of Dan went .... Josh 19:47 1366
took Gaza with the *c* thereof .... Judg 1:18 1366
and Askelon with the *c* thereof .... Judg 1:18 1366
and Ekron with the *c* thereof .... Judg 1:18 1366
the *c* of the Amorites was from .... Judg 1:36 1366
not Israel to pass through his *c* .... Judg 11:20 1366
way of his own *c* to Beth-shemesh 1Sa 6:9 1366
came no more into the *c* of Israel 1Sa 7:13 1366
me any more in any *c* of Israel 1Sa 27:1 1366
upon the *c* which belongeth to 1Sa 30:14
He restored the *c* of Israel from 2Kin 14:25 1366
bless me indeed, and enlarge my *c* 1Chr 4:10 1366
destroy the remnant of the sea *c* .... Eze 25:16 2348
which is by the *c* of Hauran .... Eze 47:16 1366
to the *c* of the way of Hethlon .... Eze 48:1 3027
northward, to the *c* of Hamath .... Eze 48:1 3027
unto the inhabitants of the sea *c* .... Zeph 2:5 2256
the sea *c* shall be dwellings and .... Zeph 2:6 2256
the *c* shall be for the remnant of .... Zeph 2:7 2256
which is upon the sea *c*, in the .... Mt 4:13 *3864*
and from the sea *c* of Tyre .... Lk 6:17 *3882*

COASTS {51}
and rested in all the *c* of Egypt .... Ex 10:14 1366
one locust in all the *c* of Egypt .... Ex 10:19 1366
out of the *c* of the Amorites .... Num 21:13 1366
with the cities thereof in the *c* .... Num 32:33 1367
land of Canaan with the *c* thereof .... Num 34:2 1367
with the *c* thereof round about .... Num 34:12 1367
of Argob unto the *c* of Geshuri .... Deut 3:14 1366
divide the *c* of thy land, which .... Deut 19:3 1366
olive trees throughout all thy *c* .... Deut 28:40 1366
in all the *c* of the great sea .... Josh 9:1 2348
abide in their *c* on the north .... Josh 18:5 1366
by the *c* thereof round about, ... Josh 18:20 1367
land for inheritance by their *c* .... Josh 19:49 1367
all the *c* of the Amorites .... Judg 11:22 1366
that be along by the *c* of Arnon .... Judg 11:26 3027
family five men from their *c* .... Judg 18:2 7098
sent her into all the *c* of Israel .... Judg 19:29 1366
even Ashdod and the *c* thereof 1Sa 5:6 1366
the *c* thereof did Israel deliver 1Sa 7:14 1366
unto all the *c* of Israel 1Sa 11:3 1366
the *c* of Israel by the hands of 1Sa 11:7 1366
in any of the *c* of Israel 2Sa 21:5 1366
throughout all the *c* of Israel 1Kin 1:3 1366
smote them in all the *c* of Israel 2Kin 10:32 1366
the *c* thereof from Tirzah 2Kin 15:16 1366
their castles in their *c*, of the 1Chr 6:54 1366
c out of the tribe of Ephraim 1Chr 6:66 1366
throughout all the *c* of Israel 1Chr 21:12 1366
to him out of all their *c* 2Chr 11:13 1366
of flies, and lice in all their *c* .... Ps 105:31 1366
and brake the trees of their *c* .... Ps 105:33 1366
raised up from the *c* of the earth .... Jer 25:32 3411
them from the *c* of the earth .... Jer 31:8 3411
raised up from the *c* of the earth .... Jer 50:41 3411
of the land take a man of their *c* .... Eze 33:2 7097
Zidon, and all the *c* of Palestine .... Joel 3:4 1552
and in all the *c* thereof, from .... Mt 2:16 *3725*
he would depart out of their *c* .... Mt 8:34 *3725*
and departed into the *c* of Tyre .... Mt 15:21 *3313*
of Canaan came out of the same *c* .... Mt 15:22 *3725*
and came into the *c* of Magdala .... Mt 15:39 *3725*
into the *c* of Caesarea Philippi .... Mt 16:13 *3313*
came into the *c* of Judaea beyond .... Mt 19:1 *3725*
pray him to depart out of their *c* .... Mk 5:17 *3725*
departing from the *c* of Tyre .... Mk 7:31 *3725*
the midst of the *c* of Decapolis .... Mk 7:31 *3725*
cometh into the *c* of Judaea by .... Mk 10:1 *3725*
and expelled them out of their *c* .... Acts 13:50 *3725*
the upper *c* came to Ephesus .... Acts 19:1 *3313*
and throughout all the *c* of Judaea .... Acts 26:20 *5561*
meaning to sail by the *c* of Asia .... Acts 27:2 *5117*

COAT {25}
he made him a *c* of many colours .... Gen 37:3 3801
they stript Joseph out of his *c* .... Gen 37:23 3801
his *c* of many colours that was on .... Gen 37:23 3801
And they took Joseph's *c*, and .... Gen 37:31 3801
dipped the *c* in the blood .... Gen 37:31 3801
they sent the *c* of many colours, ... Gen 37:32 3801
whether it be thy son's *c* or no .... Gen 37:32 3801
it, and said, It is my son's *c* .... Gen 37:33 3801
and a robe, and a broidered *c* .... Ex 28:4 3801
embroider the *c* of fine linen .... Ex 28:39 3801
garments, and put upon Aaron the *c* .... Ex 29:5 3801
And he put upon him the *c*, and .... Lev 8:7 3801
He shall put on the holy linen *c* .... Lev 16:4 3801
his mother made him a little *c* 1Sa 2:19 4598
and he was armed with a *c* of mail 1Sa 17:5 8302
the weight of the *c* was five 1Sa 17:5 8302
he armed him with a *c* of mail 1Sa 17:38 8302
came to meet him with his *c* rent 2Sa 15:32 3801
me about as the collar of my *c* .... Job 30:18 3801
I have put off my *c* .... Song 5:3 3801
at the law, and take away thy *c* .... Mt 5:40 *5509*
forbid not to take thy *c* also .... Lk 6:29 *5509*
and also his *c* .... Jn 19:23 *5509*
now the *c* was without seam, woven .... Jn 19:23 *5509*
he girt his fisher's *c* unto him .... Jn 21:7 *1903*

COATS {14}
did the LORD God make *c* of skins .... Gen 3:21 3801
Aaron's sons thou shalt make *c* .... Ex 28:40 3801
his sons, and put *c* upon them .... Ex 29:8 3801
they made *c* of fine linen of .... Ex 39:27 3801
his sons, and clothe them with *c* .... Ex 40:14 3801
put *c* upon them, and girded them .... Lev 8:13 3801
them in their *c* out of the camp .... Lev 10:5 3801
these men were bound in their *c* .... Dan 3:21 5622
neither were their *c* changed .... Dan 3:27 5622
for your journey, neither two *c* .... Mt 10:10 *5509*
and not put on two *c* .... Mk 6:9 *5509*
unto them, He that hath two *c* .... Lk 3:11 *5509*
neither have two *c* apiece .... Lk 9:3 *5509*
by him weeping, and shewing the *c* .... Acts 9:39 *5509*

COCK {12}
this night, before the *c* crow .... Mt 26:34 *220*
And immediately the *c* crew .... Mt 26:74 *220*
said unto him, Before the *c* crow .... Mt 26:75 *220*
night, before the *c* crow twice .... Mk 14:30 *220*
and the *c* crew .... Mk 14:68 *220*
And the second time the *c* crew .... Mk 14:72 *220*
unto him, Before the *c* crow twice .... Mk 14:72 *220*
the *c* shall not crow this day, ... Lk 22:34 *220*
while he yet spake, the *c* crew .... Lk 22:60 *220*
said unto him, Before the *c* crow .... Lk 22:61 *220*
The *c* shall not crow, till thou .... Jn 13:38 *220*
and immediately the *c* crew .... Jn 18:27 *220*

COCKATRICE {1}
root shall come forth a *c* .... Is 14:29 6848

COCKATRICE'S {2}
shall put his hand on the *c* den .... Is 11:8 6848
They hatch *c* eggs, and weave the .... Is 59:5 6848

COCKATRICES {1}
behold, I will send serpents, *c* .... Jer 8:17 6848

COCKCROWING {1}
even, or at midnight, or at the *c* .... Mk 13:35 *219*

COCKLE {1}
of wheat, and *c* instead of barley .... Job 31:40 890

COFFER {3}
in a *c* by the side thereof 1Sa 6:8 712
the *c* with the mice of gold and 1Sa 6:11 712
the *c* that was with it, wherein 1Sa 6:15 712

COFFIN {1}
and he was put in a *c* in Egypt .... Gen 50:26 727

COGITATIONS {1}
my *c* much troubled me, and my .... Dan 7:28 7476

COLD {18}
seedtime and harvest, and *c* .... Gen 8:22 7120
they have no covering in the *c* .... Job 24:7 7135
and *c* out of the north .... Job 37:9 7135
who can stand before his *c* .... Ps 147:17 7135
will not plow by reason of the *c* .... Prov 20:4 2779
As the *c* of snow in the time of .... Prov 25:13 6793
away a garment in *c* weather .... Prov 25:20 7135
As *c* waters to a thirsty soul, so .... Prov 25:25 7119
or shall the *c* flowing waters .... Jer 18:14 7119
camp in the hedges in the *c* day .... Nah 3:17 7135
of *c* water only in the name of a .... Mt 10:42 *5593*
the love of many shall wax *c* .... Mt 24:12 *5594*
for it was *c* .... Jn 18:18 *5592*
present rain, and because of the *c* .... Acts 28:2 *5592*
thirst, in fastings often, in *c* 2Cor 11:27 *5592*
that thou art neither *c* nor hot .... Rev 3:15 *5593*
I would thou wert *c* or hot .... Rev 3:15 *5593*
lukewarm, and neither *c* nor hot .... Rev 3:16 *5593*

COLHOZEH *(col-ho'-zeh)* {2}
repaired Shallun the son of *C* .... Neh 3:15 3626
the son of Baruch, the son of *C* .... Neh 11:5 3626

COLLAR {1}
me about as the *c* of my coat .... Job 30:18 6310

COLLARS {1}
beside ornaments, and *c*, and purple .... Judg 8:26 5188

COLLECTION {3}
Judah and out of Jerusalem the *c* 2Chr 24:6 4864
to bring in to the LORD the *c* 2Chr 24:9 4864
concerning the *c* for the saints 1Cor 16:1 *3048*

COLLEGE {2}
she dwelt in Jerusalem in the *c* 2Kin 22:14 4932
she dwelt in Jerusalem in the *c* 2Chr 34:22 4932

COLLOPS {1}
maketh *c* of fat on his flanks .... Job 15:27 6371

COLONY {1}
of that part of Macedonia, and a *c* .... Acts 16:12 *2862*

COLORS {1}
I will lay thy stones with fair *c* .... Is 54:11 6320

COLOSSE *(co-los'-see)* {1} See COLOSSIANS. *A city in Phrygia.*
brethren in Christ which are at *C* .... Col 1:2 *2857*

COLOSSIANS *(co-los'-yans)* {1} *Residents of Colosse.*
from Rome to the *C* by Tychicus .... Col *s* *2858*

COLOUR {14}
the plague have not changed his *c* .... Lev 13:55 5869
the *c* thereof as the *c* of .... Num 11:7 5869
when it giveth his *c* in the cup .... Prov 23:31 5869
midst thereof as the *c* of amber .... Eze 1:4 5869
like the *c* of burnished brass .... Eze 1:7 5869
was like unto the *c* of a beryl .... Eze 1:16 5869
as the *c* of the terrible crystal .... Eze 1:22 5869
And I saw as the *c* of amber .... Eze 1:27 5869
of brightness, as the *c* of amber .... Eze 8:2 5869
was as the *c* of a beryl stone .... Eze 10:9 5869
his feet like in *c* to polished .... Dan 10:6 5869
under *c* as though they would have .... Acts 27:30 *4392*
arrayed in purple and scarlet *c* .... Rev 17:4

COLOURED {1}
woman sit upon a scarlet *c* beast .... Rev 17:3

COLOURS {11}
and he made him a coat of many *c* .... Gen 37:3 6446
coat of many *c* that was on him .... Gen 37:23 6446
And they sent the coat of many *c* .... Gen 37:32 6446
to Sisera a prey of divers *c* .... Judg 5:30 6648
a prey of divers *c* of needlework .... Judg 5:30 6648
of divers *c* of needlework on both .... Judg 5:30 6648
a garment of divers *c* upon her 2Sa 13:18 6446
of divers *c* that was on her 2Sa 13:19 6446
glistering stones, and of divers *c* 1Chr 29:2 7553
thy high places with divers *c* .... Eze 16:16 2921
of feathers, which had divers *c* .... Eze 17:3 7553

COLT {15}
his ass's *c* unto the choice vine .... Gen 49:11 1121
man be born like a wild ass's *c* .... Job 11:12 5895
upon a *c* the foal of an ass .... Zec 9:9 5895
find an ass tied, and a *c* with her .... Mt 21:2 *4454*
an ass, and a *c* the foal of an ass .... Mt 21:5 *4454*
And brought the ass, and the *c* .... Mt 21:7 *4454*
into it, ye shall find a *c* tied .... Mk 11:2 *4454*
found the *c* tied by the door .... Mk 11:4 *4454*
them, What do ye, loosing the *c* .... Mk 11:5 *4454*
And they brought the *c* to Jesus .... Mk 11:7 *4454*
entering ye shall find a *c* tied .... Lk 19:30 *4454*
And as they were loosing the *c* .... Lk 19:33 *4454*
unto them, Why loose ye the *c* .... Lk 19:33 *4454*
cast their garments upon the *c* .... Lk 19:35 *4454*
cometh, sitting on an ass's *c* .... Jn 12:15 *4454*

COLTS {3}
Thirty milch camels with their *c* .... Gen 32:15 1121
sons that rode on thirty ass *c* .... Judg 10:4 5895
rode on threescore and ten ass *c* .... Judg 12:14 5895

COME {1973}
and it shall *c* to pass, that every .... Gen 4:14 1961
end of all flesh is *c* before me .... Gen 6:13 935
thou shalt *c* into the ark, thou, ... Gen 6:18 935
of every sort shall *c* unto thee .... Gen 6:20 935
C thou and all thy house into the .... Gen 7:1 935
And it shall *c* to pass, when I .... Gen 9:14 935
when he was *c* near to enter into .... Gen 12:11 7126
Therefore it shall *c* to pass .... Gen 12:12 935
that, when Abram was *c* into Egypt .... Gen 12:14 935
but he that shall *c* forth out of .... Gen 15:4 3318
afterward shall they *c* out with .... Gen 15:14 3318
they shall *c* hither again .... Gen 15:16 7725
and kings shall *c* out of thee .... Gen 17:6 3318
are ye *c* to your servant .... Gen 18:5 5674
the cry of it, which is *c* unto me .... Gen 18:21 935
any thing till thou be *c* thither .... Gen 19:22 935
is not a man in the earth to *c* in .... Gen 19:31 935
C, let us make our father drink .... Gen 19:32 3212
But Abimelech had not *c* near her .... Gen 20:4 7126
at every place whither we shall *c* .... Gen 20:13 935
and worship, and *c* again to you .... Gen 22:5 7725
of the city *c* out to draw water .... Gen 24:13 3318
let it *c* to pass, that the damsel .... Gen 24:14 935
C in, thou blessed of the LORD .... Gen 24:31 935
and it shall *c* to pass, that when .... Gen 24:43 1961
unto them, Wherefore *c* ye to me .... Gen 26:27 935
C near, I pray thee, that I may .... Gen 27:21 5066
C near now, and kiss me, my son .... Gen 27:26 5066
it shall *c* to pass when thou .... Gen 27:40 1961
So that I *c* again to my father's .... Gen 28:21 7725
and said, Thou must *c* in unto me .... Gen 30:16 935
answer for me in time to *c* .... Gen 30:33 4279
when it shall *c* for my hire .... Gen 30:33 935
Now therefore *c* thou, let us make .... Gen 31:44 3212
If Esau *c* to the one company, and .... Gen 32:8 935
for I fear him, lest he will *c* .... Gen 32:11 935
until I *c* unto my lord unto Seir .... Gen 33:14 935
held his peace until they were *c* .... Gen 34:5 935
kings shall *c* out of thy loins .... Gen 35:11 3318
but a little way to *c* to Ephrath .... Gen 35:16 935
thy brethren indeed *c* to bow down .... Gen 37:10 935
c, and I will send thee unto them .... Gen 37:13 3212
C now therefore, and let us slay .... Gen 37:20 3212
when Joseph was *c* unto his .... Gen 37:23 935
C, and let us sell him to the .... Gen 37:27 3212
pray thee, let me *c* in unto thee .... Gen 38:16 935
me, that thou mayest *c* in unto me .... Gen 38:16 935
there *c* seven years of great .... Gen 41:29 935
food of those good years that *c* .... Gen 41:35 935
seven years of dearth began to *c* .... Gen 41:54 935
and he said unto them, Whence *c* ye .... Gen 42:7 935
nakedness of the land ye are *c* .... Gen 42:9 935
to buy food are thy servants *c* .... Gen 42:10 935
nakedness of the land ye are *c* .... Gen 42:12 935
your youngest brother *c* hither .... Gen 42:15 935
is this distress *c* upon us .... Gen 42:21 935
youngest brother *c* down with you .... Gen 44:23 3381
Now therefore when I *c* to thy .... Gen 44:30 935
It shall *c* to pass, when he seeth .... Gen 44:31 1961
evil that shall *c* on my father .... Gen 44:34 4672

C near to me, I pray you — Gen 45:4 — 5066
c down unto me, tarry not — Gen 45:9 — 3381
all that thou hast, c to poverty — Gen 45:11 — 3423
saying, Joseph's brethren are c — Gen 45:16 — 935
and your households, and c unto me — Gen 45:18 — 935
wives, and bring your father, and c — Gen 45:19 — 935
the land of Canaan, are c unto me — Gen 46:31 — 935
And it shall c to pass, when — Gen 46:33 — 1961
are c out of the land of Canaan — Gen 47:1 — 935
to sojourn in the land are we c — Gen 47:4 — 935
and thy brethren are c unto thee — Gen 47:5 — 935
it shall c to pass in the — Gen 47:24 — 1961
a little way to c unto Ephrath — Gen 48:7 — 935
c not thou into their secret — Gen 49:6 — 935
between his feet, until Shiloh c — Gen 49:10 — 935
bury my father, and I will c again — Gen 50:5 — 7725
C on, let us deal wisely with — Ex 1:10 — 3051
it c to pass, that, when there — Ex 1:10 — 1961
ere the midwives c in unto them — Ex 1:19 — 935
it that ye are c so soon to day — Ex 2:18 — 935
I am c down to deliver them out — Ex 3:8 — 3381
children of Israel is c unto me — Ex 3:9 — 935
C now therefore, and I will send — Ex 3:10 — 3212
when I c unto the children of — Ex 3:13 — 935
and thou shalt c, thou and the — Ex 3:18 — 935
and it shall c to pass, that, when — Ex 3:21 — 1961
And it shall c to pass, if they — Ex 4:8 — 1961
And it shall c to pass, if they — Ex 4:9 — 1961
by the river's brink against he c — Ex 7:15 — 7125
c into thine house, and into thy — Ex 8:3 — 935
the frogs shall c up both on thee — Ex 8:4 — 5927
cause frogs to c up upon the land — Ex 8:5 — 5927
the hail shall c down upon them — Ex 9:19 — 3381
that they may c up upon the land — Ex 10:12 — 5927
the LORD, until we c thither — Ex 10:26 — 935
thy servants shall c down unto me — Ex 11:8 — 3381
not suffer the destroyer to c in — Ex 12:23 — 935
And it shall c to pass — Ex 12:25 — 1961
when ye be c to the land which — Ex 12:25 — 935
And it shall c to pass, when your — Ex 12:26 — 1961
and then let him c near and keep — Ex 12:48 — 7126
thy son asketh thee in time to c — Ex 13:14 — 4279
that the waters may c again upon — Ex 14:26 — 7725
And it shall c to pass, that on — Ex 16:5 — 1961
of Israel, C near before the LORD — Ex 16:9 — 7126
there shall c water out of it, — Ex 17:6 — 3318
in law Jethro am c unto thee — Ex 18:6 — 935
that had c upon them by the way — Ex 18:8 — 4672
Because the people c unto me to — Ex 18:15 — 935
have a matter, they c unto me — Ex 18:16 — 935
were c to the desert of Sinai, and — Ex 19:2 — 935
I c unto thee in a thick cloud, — Ex 19:9 — 935
c down in the sight of all the — Ex 19:11 — 3381
they shall c up to the mount — Ex 19:13 — 5927
c not at your wives — Ex 19:15 — 5066
which c near to the LORD, — Ex 19:22 — 5066
people cannot c up to mount Sinai — Ex 19:23 — 5927
get thee down, and thou shalt c up — Ex 19:24 — 5927
through to c up unto the LORD — Ex 19:24 — 5927
for God is c to prove you, and — Ex 20:20 — 935
record my name I will c unto thee — Ex 20:24 — 935
But if a man c presumptuously — Ex 21:14 — 2102
parties shall c before the judges — Ex 22:9 — 935
and it shall c to pass, when he — Ex 22:27 — 1961
the people to whom thou shalt c — Ex 23:27 — 935
C up unto the LORD, thou, and — Ex 24:1 — 5927
Moses alone shall c near the LORD — Ex 24:2 — 5066
but they shall not c nigh — Ex 24:2 — 5066
C up to me into the mount, and be — Ex 24:12 — 5927
until we c again unto you — Ex 24:14 — 7725
to do, let him c unto them — Ex 24:14 — 5066
six branches shall c out of the — Ex 25:32 — 3318
that c out of the candlestick — Ex 25:33 — 3318
his sons, when they c in unto the — Ex 28:43 — 935
or when they c near unto the — Ex 28:43 — 5066
or when they c near to the altar — Ex 30:20 — 5066
to c down out of the mount — Ex 32:1 — 3381
let him c unto me — Ex 32:26
I will c up into the midst of — Ex 33:5 — 5927
And it shall c to pass, while my — Ex 33:22 — 1961
c up in the morning unto mount — Ex 34:2 — 5927
And no man shall c up with thee — Ex 34:3 — 5927
and they were afraid to c nigh him — Ex 34:30 — 5066
wise hearted among you shall c — Ex 35:10 — 935
up to c unto the work to do it — Ex 36:2 — 7126
hath sinned, c to his knowledge — Lev 4:23 — 3045
hath sinned, c to his knowledge — Lev 4:28 — 3045
sanctified in them that c nigh me — Lev 10:3 — 7138
C near, carry your brethren from — Lev 10:4 — 935
lest wrath c upon all the people — Lev 10:6 — 7107
nor c into the sanctuary, until — Lev 12:4 — 935
he shall c unto the priest — Lev 13:16 — 935
that he shall c into the camp — Lev 14:8 — 935
When ye be c into the land of — Lev 14:34 — 935
he that owneth the house shall c — Lev 14:35 — 935
the priest shall c again the — Lev 14:39 — 7725
And if the plague c again, and — Lev 14:43 — 7725
Then the priest shall c and look, — Lev 14:44 — 935
And if the priest shall c in — Lev 14:48 — 935
c before the LORD unto the door — Lev 15:14 — 935
that he c not at all times into — Lev 16:2 — 935
Thus shall Aaron c into the holy — Lev 16:3 — 935
in the holy place, until he c out — Lev 16:17 — 3318
Aaron shall c into the tabernacle — Lev 16:23 — 935
c forth, and offer his burnt — Lev 16:24 — 3318
afterward c into the camp — Lev 16:26 — 935
he shall c into the camp — Lev 16:28 — 935
of linen and woollen c upon thee — Lev 19:19 — 5927
And when ye shall c into the land — Lev 19:23 — 935
c nigh to offer the offerings of — Lev 21:21 — 5066
he shall not c nigh to offer the — Lev 21:21 — 5066
nor c nigh unto the altar, — Lev 21:23 — 5066
When ye be c into the land which — Lev 23:10 — 935
When ye c into the land which I — Lev 25:2 — 935
until her fruits c in ye shall — Lev 25:22 — 935
if any of his kin c to redeem it — Lev 25:25 — 935
were c out of the land of Egypt — Num 1:1 — 3318
setteth forward, Aaron shall c — Num 4:5 — 935
sons of Kohath shall c to bear it — Num 4:15 — 935
the spirit of jealousy c upon him — Num 5:14 — 5674
the spirit of jealousy c upon him — Num 5:14 — 5674
water, then it shall c to pass — Num 5:27 — 1961
shall no razor c upon his head — Num 6:5 — 5674
LORD he shall c at no dead body — Num 6:6 — 935
Israel c nigh unto the sanctuary — Num 8:19 — 5066
were c out of the land of Egypt — Num 9:1 — 3318
c thou with us, and we will do — Num 10:29 — 3212
And I will c down and talk with — Num 11:17 — 3381
until it c out at your nostrils, — Num 11:20 — 3318
shall c to pass unto thee or not — Num 11:23 — 7136
Miriam, C out ye three unto the — Num 12:4 — 3318
unto Rehob, as men c to Hamath — Num 13:21 — 935
of Anak, which c of the giants — Num 13:33 — 4480
ye shall not c into the land — Num 14:30 — 935
When ye be c into the land of — Num 15:2 — 935
When ye c into the land whither I — Num 15:18 — 935
will cause him to c near unto him — Num 16:5 — 7126
will he cause to c near unto him — Num 16:5 — 7126
which said, We will not c up — Num 16:12 — 5927
we will not c up — Num 16:14 — 5927
c near to offer incense before — Num 16:40 — 7126
And it shall c to pass, that the — Num 17:5 — 1961
only they shall not c nigh the — Num 18:3 — 7126
shall not c nigh unto you — Num 18:4 — 7126
c nigh the tabernacle of the — Num 18:22 — 7126
he shall c into the camp, and the — Num 19:7 — 935
all that c into the tent, and all — Num 19:14 — 935
ye made us to c up out of Egypt — Num 20:5 — 5927
lest I c out against thee with — Num 20:18 — 3318
and it shall c to pass, that every — Num 21:8 — 1961
C into Heshbon, let the city of — Num 21:27 — 935
is a people c out from Egypt — Num 22:5 — 3318
C now therefore, I pray thee, — Num 22:6 — 3212
there is a people c out of Egypt — Num 22:11 — 3318
c now, curse me them — Num 22:11 — 3212
Balaam refuseth to c with us — Num 22:14 — 1980
c therefore, I pray thee, curse — Num 22:17 — 3212
If the men c to call thee, rise — Num 22:20 — 935
Balak heard that Balaam was c — Num 22:36 — 935
unto Balak, Lo, I am c unto thee — Num 22:38 — 935
the LORD will c to meet me — Num 23:3 — 7136
C, curse me Jacob, and c — Num 23:7 — 3212
And Balak said unto him, C — Num 23:13 — 3212
And Balak said unto Balaam, C — Num 23:27 — 3212
c therefore, and I will advertise — Num 24:14 — 3212
there shall c a Star out of Jacob — Num 24:17 — 1869
Out of Jacob shall c he that — Num 24:19 — 3381
ships shall c from the coast — Num 24:24 — 4480
of Gilead c the family of the — Num 26:29
and at his word they shall c in — Num 27:21 — 935
ye shall c into the camp — Num 31:24 — 935
were c out of the land of Egypt — Num 33:38 — 3318
then it shall c to pass, that — Num 33:55 — 1961
Moreover it shall c to pass — Num 33:56 — 1961
When ye c into the land of Canaan — Num 34:2 — 935
When ye be c over Jordan into the — Num 35:10 — 5674
c without the border of the city — Num 35:26 — 3318
that he should c again to dwell — Num 35:32 — 7725
Ye are c unto the mountain of the — Deut 1:20 — 935
and into what cities we shall c — Deut 1:22 — 935
until we were c over the brook — Deut 2:14 — 5674
all these things are c upon thee — Deut 4:30 — 4672
after they were c forth out of — Deut 4:46 — 3318
thy son asketh thee in time to c — Deut 6:20 — 4279
Wherefore it shall c to pass — Deut 7:12 — 1961
c up unto me into the mount, and — Deut 10:1 — 5927
And it shall c to pass, if ye — Deut 11:13 — 1961
And it shall c to pass, when the — Deut 11:29 — 1961
ye seek, and thither thou shalt c — Deut 12:5 — 935
ye are not as yet c to the rest — Deut 12:9 — 935
the sign or the wonder c to pass — Deut 13:2 — 935
are within thy gates, shall c — Deut 14:29 — 935
males that c of thy herd and of — Deut 15:19 — 3205
thou shalt c unto the priests the — Deut 17:9 — 935
When thou art c unto the land — Deut 17:14 — 935
if a Levite c from any of thy — Deut 18:6 — 935
c with all the desire of his mind — Deut 18:6 — 935
When thou art c into the land — Deut 18:9 — 935
And it shall c to pass, that — Deut 18:19 — 1961
nor c to pass, that is the thing — Deut 18:22 — 935
when ye are c nigh unto the — Deut 20:2 — 7126
and thy judges shall c forth — Deut 21:2 — 3318
the sons of Levi shall c near — Deut 21:5 — 5506
he shall not c within the camp — Deut 23:10 — 935
he shall c into the camp again — Deut 23:11 — 935
it c to pass that she find no — Deut 24:1 — 1961
that ye were c forth out of Egypt — Deut 24:9 — 3318
they c unto judgment, that the — Deut 25:1 — 5066
Then shall his brother's wife c — Deut 25:9 — 5066
when ye were c forth out of Egypt — Deut 25:17 — 3318
when thou art c in unto the land — Deut 26:1 — 935
that I am c unto the country — Deut 26:3 — 935
people, when ye are c over Jordan — Deut 27:12 — 5674
And it shall c to pass, if thou — Deut 28:1 — 1961
these blessings shall c on thee — Deut 28:2 — 935
they shall c out against thee one — Deut 28:7 — 3318
But it shall c to pass, if thou — Deut 28:15 — 1961
these curses shall c upon thee — Deut 28:15 — 935
heaven shall it c down upon thee — Deut 28:24 — 3381
thou shalt c down very low — Deut 28:43 — 3381
these curses shall c upon thee — Deut 28:45 — 935
thy high and fenced walls c down — Deut 28:52 — 3381
And it shall c to pass, that as — Deut 28:63 — 1961
it c to pass, when he heareth the — Deut 29:19 — 1961
So that the generation to c of — Deut 29:22 — 314
that shall c from a far land — Deut 29:22 — 935
And it shall c to pass, when all — Deut 30:1 — 1961
all these things are c upon thee — Deut 30:1 — 935
I can no more go out and c in — Deut 31:2 — 935
When all Israel is c to appear — Deut 31:11 — 935
Are not these evils c upon us — Deut 31:17 — 4672
And it shall c to pass, when many — Deut 31:21 — 1961
that shall c upon them make haste — Deut 32:35 — 6264
let the blessing c upon the head — Deut 33:16 — 935
forth the men that are c to thee — Josh 2:3 — 935
for they be c to search out all — Josh 2:3 — 935
when we c into the land, thou — Josh 2:18 — 935
c not near unto it, that ye may — Josh 3:4 — 7126
When ye are c to the brink of the — Josh 3:8 — 935
C hither, and hear the words of — Josh 3:9 — 5066
And it shall c to pass, as soon as — Josh 3:13 — 1961
the waters that c down from above — Josh 3:13 — 3381
bare the ark were c unto Jordan — Josh 3:15 — 935
ask their fathers in time to c — Josh 4:6 — 4279
that they c up out of Jordan — Josh 4:16 — 5927
saying, C ye up out of Jordan — Josh 4:17 — 5927
c up out of the midst of Jordan — Josh 4:18 — 5927
ask their fathers in time to c — Josh 4:21 — 4279
the host of the LORD am I now c — Josh 5:14 — 935
And it shall c to pass, that when — Josh 6:5 — 1961
they shall c into the treasury of — Josh 6:19 — 935
shall c according to the families — Josh 7:14 — 7126
shall take shall c by households — Josh 7:14 — 7126
shall take shall c man by man — Josh 7:14 — 7126
and it shall c to pass, when they — Josh 8:5 — 1961
when they c out against us, as at — Josh 8:5 — 3318
(For they will c out after us) — Josh 8:6 — 3318
We be c from a far country — Josh 9:6 — 935
and from whence c ye — Josh 9:8 — 935
far country thy servants are c — Josh 9:9 — 935
C up unto me, and help me, that we — Josh 10:4 — 5927
c up to us quickly, and save us, — Josh 10:6 — 5927
C near, put your feet upon the — Josh 10:24 — 7126
that they should c against Israel — Josh 11:20 — 7122
war, both to go out, and to c in — Josh 14:11 — 935
and they shall c again to me — Josh 18:4 — 935
c again to me, that I may here — Josh 18:8 — 7725
c unto his own city, and unto his — Josh 20:6 — 935
In time to c your children might — Josh 22:24 — 4279
say to our children in time to c — Josh 22:27 — 4279
to our generations in time to c — Josh 22:28 — 4279
That ye c not among these nations — Josh 23:7 — 935
all are c to pass unto you, and — Josh 23:14 — 935
Therefore it shall c to pass — Josh 23:15 — 1961
as all good things are c upon you — Josh 23:15 — 935
C up with me into my lot, that we — Judg 1:3 — 5927
the spies saw a man c forth out — Judg 1:24 — 3318
them to c down to the valley — Judg 1:34 — 3381
And it came to pass, when he was c — Judg 3:27 — 935
it shall be, when any man doth c — Judg 4:20 — 935
to meet him, and said unto him, C — Judg 4:22 — 3212
the earth, till thou c unto Gaza — Judg 6:4 — 935
until I c unto thee, and bring — Judg 6:18 — 935
I will tarry until thou c again — Judg 6:18 — 7725
And when Gideon was c, behold, — Judg 7:13 — 935
when I c to the outside of the — Judg 7:17 — 935
C down against the Midianites, and — Judg 7:24 — 3381
When I c again in peace, I will — Judg 8:9 — 7725
tree, C thou, and reign over us — Judg 9:10 — 3212
vine, C thou, and reign over us — Judg 9:12 — 3212
bramble, C thou, and reign over us — Judg 9:14 — 3212
anoint me king over you, then c — Judg 9:15 — 935
let fire c out of the bramble, and — Judg 9:15 — 3318
let fire c out from Abimelech, and — Judg 9:20 — 3318
let fire c out from the men of — Judg 9:20 — 3318
and ten sons of Jerubbaal might c — Judg 9:24 — 935
Increase thine army, and c out — Judg 9:29 — 3318
and his brethren be c to Shechem — Judg 9:31 — 935
is with him c out against thee — Judg 9:33 — 3318
there c people down from the top — Judg 9:36 — 3381
See there c people down by the — Judg 9:37 — 3381
another company c along by the — Judg 9:37 — 935
the people were c forth out of — Judg 9:43 — 3318
And they said unto Jephthah, C — Judg 11:6 — 3212
why are ye c unto me now when ye — Judg 11:7 — 935
that thou art c against me to — Judg 11:12 — 935
even till thou c to Minnith — Judg 11:33 — 935
then are ye c up unto me this day — Judg 12:3 — 5927
and no razor shall c on his head — Judg 13:5 — 5927
thou didst send c again unto us — Judg 13:8 — 935
said, Now let thy words c to pass — Judg 13:12 — 935
that when thy sayings c to pass — Judg 13:17 — 935
Why are ye c up against us — Judg 15:10 — 5927
To bind Samson are we c up — Judg 15:10 — 5927
We are c down to bind thee, that — Judg 15:12 — 3381
saying, Samson is c hither — Judg 16:2 — 935
There hath not c a razor upon — Judg 16:17 — 5927
C up this once, for he hath — Judg 16:18 — 5927
ye shall c unto a people secure, — Judg 18:10 — 935
servant said unto his master, C — Judg 19:11 — 3212
And he said unto his servant, C — Judg 19:13 — 3212
this man is c into mine house — Judg 19:23 — 935
when he was c into his house, he — Judg 19:29 — 935
when they c to Gibeah of Benjamin — Judg 20:10 — 935

saw that evil was *c* upon them ... Judg 20:41 5060
why is this *c* to pass in Israel, ... Judg 21:3 1961
Shiloh *c* out to dance in dances ... Judg 21:21 3318
then *c* ye out of the vineyards, ... Judg 21:21 3318
brethren *c* unto us to complain ... Judg 21:22 935
when they were *c* to Beth-lehem ... Ruth 1:19 935
art *c* unto a people which thou ... Ruth 2:11 1980
whose wings thou art *c* to trust ... Ruth 2:12 935
her, At mealtime *c* thou hither ... Ruth 2:14 5060
that is *c* again out of the ... Ruth 4:3 7725
is *c* into thine house like Rachel ... Ruth 4:11 935
shall no razor *c* upon his head ... 1Sa 1:11 5927
when the time was *c* about after ... 1Sa 1:20 8622
not arrogancy *c* out of your mouth ... 1Sa 2:3 3318
Behold, the days *c*, that I will ... 1Sa 2:31 935
that shall *c* upon thy two sons, ... 1Sa 2:34 935
And it shall *c* to pass, that every ... 1Sa 2:36 1961
is left in thine house shall *c* ... 1Sa 2:36 935
the people were *c* into the camp ... 1Sa 4:3 935
of the LORD was *c* into the camp ... 1Sa 4:6 935
they said, God is *c* into the camp ... 1Sa 4:7 935
nor any that *c* into Dagon's house ... 1Sa 5:5 935
on which there hath *c* no yoke ... 1Sa 6:7 5927
c ye down, and fetch it up to you ... 1Sa 6:21 3381
when they were *c* to the land of ... 1Sa 9:5 935
his servant that was with him, *C* ... 1Sa 9:5 3212
enquire of God, thus he spake, *C* ... 1Sa 9:9 3212
c, let us go ... 1Sa 9:10 3212
As soon as ye be *c* into the city ... 1Sa 9:13 935
people will not eat until he *c* ... 1Sa 9:13 935
and when they were *c* into the city ... 1Sa 9:14 935
because their cry is *c* unto me ... 1Sa 9:16 935
when they were *c* down from the ... 1Sa 9:25 3381
thou shalt *c* to the plain of ... 1Sa 10:3 935
thou shalt *c* to the hill of God ... 1Sa 10:5 935
and it shall *c* to pass ... 1Sa 10:5 1961
when thou art *c* thither to the ... 1Sa 10:5 835
of the LORD will *c* upon thee ... 1Sa 10:6 6743
when these signs are *c* unto thee ... 1Sa 10:7 935
I will *c* down unto thee, to offer ... 1Sa 10:8 3381
till I *c* to thee, and shew thee ... 1Sa 10:8 935
that is *c* unto the son of Kish ... 1Sa 10:11 1961
the tribes of Israel to *c* near ... 1Sa 10:20 7126
to *c* near by their families ... 1Sa 10:21 7126
if the man should yet *c* thither ... 1Sa 10:22 935
to save us, we will *c* out to thee ... 1Sa 11:3 3318
To morrow we will *c* out unto you ... 1Sa 11:10 3318
Then said Samuel to the people, *C* ... 1Sa 11:14 3212
When Jacob was *c* into Egypt ... 1Sa 12:8 935
The Philistines will *c* down now ... 1Sa 13:12 3381
young man that bare his armour, *C* ... 1Sa 14:1 3212
young man that bare his armour, *C* ... 1Sa 14:6 3212
unto us, Tarry until we *c* to you ... 1Sa 14:9 5060
if they say thus, *C* up unto us ... 1Sa 14:10 5927
the Hebrews *c* forth out of the ... 1Sa 14:11 3318
C up to us, and we will shew you a ... 1Sa 14:12 5927
his armourbearer, *C* up after me ... 1Sa 14:12 5927
the people were *c* into the wood ... 1Sa 14:26 935
I am *c* to sacrifice to the LORD ... 1Sa 16:2 935
I am *c* to sacrifice unto the LORD ... 1Sa 16:5 935
c with me to the sacrifice ... 1Sa 16:5 935
it came to pass, when they were *c* ... 1Sa 16:6 935
not sit down till he *c* hither ... 1Sa 16:11 935
and it shall *c* to pass, when the ... 1Sa 16:16 1961
Why are ye *c* out to set your ... 1Sa 17:8 3318
for you, and let him *c* down to me ... 1Sa 17:8 3381
ye seen this man that is *c* up ... 1Sa 17:25 5927
surely to defy Israel is he *c* up ... 1Sa 17:25 5927
for thou art *c* down that thou ... 1Sa 17:28 3381
C to me, and I will give thy flesh ... 1Sa 17:44 3212
but I *c* to thee in the name of ... 1Sa 17:45 935
until thou *c* to the valley, and to ... 1Sa 17:52 935
And when the messengers were *c* in ... 1Sa 19:16 935
by my father to *c* upon thee ... 1Sa 20:9 935
And Jonathan said unto David, *C* ... 1Sa 20:11 3212
c to the place where thou didst ... 1Sa 20:19 935
then *c* thou ... 1Sa 20:21 935
and when the new moon was *c* ... 1Sa 20:24 1961
when the lad was *c* to the place ... 1Sa 20:37 935
shall this fellow *c* into my house ... 1Sa 21:15 935
c forth, and be with you, till I ... 1Sa 22:3 3318
how much more then if we *c* to ... 1Sa 23:3 3212
Saul that David was *c* to Keilah ... 1Sa 23:7 935
that Saul seeketh to *c* to Keilah ... 1Sa 23:10 935
will Saul *c* down, as thy servant ... 1Sa 23:11 3381
And the LORD said, He will *c* down ... 1Sa 23:11 3381
Saul was *c* out to seek his life ... 1Sa 23:15 3318
c down according to all the ... 1Sa 23:20 3381
the desire of thy soul to *c* down ... 1Sa 23:20 3381
c ye again to me with the ... 1Sa 23:23 7725
and it shall *c* to pass, if he be ... 1Sa 23:23 1961
Saul, saying, Haste thee, and *c* ... 1Sa 23:27 3212
whom is the king of Israel *c* out ... 1Sa 24:14 3318
for we *c* in a good day ... 1Sa 25:8 935
behold, I *c* after you ... 1Sa 25:19 935
And it shall *c* to pass, when the ... 1Sa 25:30 1961
c to meet me, surely there had ... 1Sa 25:34 935
David were *c* to Abigail to Carmel ... 1Sa 25:40 935
that Saul was *c* in very deed ... 1Sa 26:4 935
or his day shall *c* to die ... 1Sa 26:10 935
of Israel is *c* out to seek a flea ... 1Sa 26:20 3318
let one of the young men *c* over ... 1Sa 26:22 5674
servants that are *c* with thee ... 1Sa 29:10 935
his men were *c* to Ziklag on the ... 1Sa 30:1 935
lest these uncircumcised *c* ... 1Sa 31:4 935
for anguish is *c* upon me, because ... 2Sa 1:9 270
they were *c* to the hill of Ammah ... 2Sa 2:24 935
the host that was with him were *c* ... 2Sa 3:23 935
when Joab was *c* out from David, ... 2Sa 3:26 3318
lame, thou shalt not *c* in hither ... 2Sa 5:6 935
thinking, David cannot *c* in ... 2Sa 5:6 935
lame shall not *c* into the house ... 2Sa 5:8 935
after he was *c* from Hebron ... 2Sa 5:13 935
c upon them over against the ... 2Sa 5:23 935
from Geba until thou *c* to Gazer ... 2Sa 5:25 935
shall the ark of the LORD *c* to me ... 2Sa 6:9 935
house for a great while to *c* ... 2Sa 7:19 7350
was *c* unto David, he fell on his ... 2Sa 9:6 935
strong for thee, then I will *c* ... 2Sa 10:11 1980
And when Uriah was *c* unto him ... 2Sa 11:7 935
wayfaring man that was *c* unto him ... 2Sa 12:4 935
it for the man that was *c* to him ... 2Sa 12:4 935
pray thee, let my sister Tamar *c* ... 2Sa 13:5 935
and when the king was *c* to see him ... 2Sa 13:6 935
pray thee, let Tamar my sister *c* ... 2Sa 13:6 935
her, *C* lie with me, my sister ... 2Sa 13:11 935
king, Behold, the king's sons *c* ... 2Sa 13:35 935
c to the king, and speak on this ... 2Sa 14:3 935
Now therefore that I am *c* to ... 2Sa 14:15 935
but he would not *c* to him ... 2Sa 14:29 935
the second time, he would not *c* ... 2Sa 14:29 935
C hither, that I may send thee to ... 2Sa 14:32 935
say, Wherefore am I *c* from Geshur ... 2Sa 14:32 935
any suit or cause might *c* unto me ... 2Sa 15:4 935
until there *c* word from you to ... 2Sa 15:28 935
that when David was *c* to the top ... 2Sa 15:32 935
C out, *c* out, thou bloody man, ... 2Sa 16:7 3318
was *c* unto Absalom, that Hushai ... 2Sa 16:16 935
I will *c* upon him while he is ... 2Sa 17:2 935
And when Hushai was *c* to Absalom ... 2Sa 17:6 935
and it will *c* to pass, when some ... 2Sa 17:9 1961
So shall we *c* upon him in some ... 2Sa 17:12 935
not be seen to *c* into the city ... 2Sa 17:17 935
when David was *c* to Mahanaim ... 2Sa 17:27 935
of all Israel is *c* to the king ... 2Sa 19:11 935
the king, as he was *c* over Jordan ... 2Sa 19:18 5674
I am *c* the first this day of all ... 2Sa 19:20 935
when he was *c* to Jerusalem to ... 2Sa 19:25 935
as my lord the king is *c* again in ... 2Sa 19:30 935
C thou over with me, and I will ... 2Sa 19:33 5674
And when the king was *c* over ... 2Sa 19:39 5674
C near hither, that I may speak ... 2Sa 20:16 7126
when he was *c* near unto her, the ... 2Sa 20:17 7126
of famine *c* unto thee in thy land ... 2Sa 24:13 935
my lord the king *c* to his servant ... 2Sa 24:21 935
Now therefore *c*, let me, I pray ... 1Kin 1:12 3212
I also will *c* in after thee, and ... 1Kin 1:14 935
Otherwise it shall *c* to pass ... 1Kin 1:21 1961
when he was *c* in before the king, ... 1Kin 1:23 935
Then ye shall *c* up after him ... 1Kin 1:35 5927
that he may *c* ... 1Kin 1:35 935
and Adonijah said unto him, *C* in ... 1Kin 1:42 935
they are *c* up from thence ... 1Kin 1:45 5927
him, Thus saith the king, *C* forth ... 1Kin 2:30 3318
Jerusalem to Gath, and was *c* again ... 1Kin 2:41 7725
I know not how to go out or *c* in ... 1Kin 3:7 935
were *c* out of the land of Egypt ... 1Kin 6:1 3318
were *c* out of the holy place ... 1Kin 8:10 3318
shall *c* forth out of thy loins ... 1Kin 8:19 3318
the oath *c* before thine altar in ... 1Kin 8:31 935
when he shall *c* and pray toward ... 1Kin 8:42 935
and when she was *c* to Solomon ... 1Kin 10:2 935
neither shall they *c* in unto you ... 1Kin 11:2 935
for all Israel were *c* to Shechem ... 1Kin 12:1 935
three days, then *c* again to me ... 1Kin 12:5 7725
C to me again the third day ... 1Kin 12:12 7725
heard that Jeroboam was *c* again ... 1Kin 12:20 7725
when Rehoboam was *c* to Jerusalem ... 1Kin 12:21 935
C home with me, and refresh ... 1Kin 13:7 935
C home with me, and eat bread ... 1Kin 13:15 3212
thy carcase shall not *c* unto the ... 1Kin 13:22 935
Samaria, shall surely *c* to pass ... 1Kin 13:32 1961
C in, thou wife of Jeroboam ... 1Kin 14:6 935
of Jeroboam shall *c* to the grave ... 1Kin 14:13 935
out or *c* in to Asa king of Judah ... 1Kin 15:17 935
c and break thy league with Baasha ... 1Kin 15:19 3212
art thou *c* unto me to call my sin ... 1Kin 17:18 935
child's soul *c* into him again ... 1Kin 17:21 7725
And it shall *c* to pass, as soon as ... 1Kin 18:12 1961
and so when I *c* and tell Ahab, and ... 1Kin 18:12 935
all the people, *C* near unto me ... 1Kin 18:30 5066
And it shall *c* to pass, that him ... 1Kin 19:17 1961
There are men *c* out of Samaria ... 1Kin 20:17 3318
Whether they be *c* out for peace ... 1Kin 20:18 3318
or whether they be *c* out for war ... 1Kin 20:18 3318
of Syria will *c* up against thee ... 1Kin 20:22 5927
any thing would *c* from him ... 1Kin 20:33 4480
he caused him to *c* up into the ... 1Kin 20:33 5927
of affliction, until I *c* in peace ... 1Kin 22:27 935
Thou shalt not *c* down from that ... 2Kin 1:4 3381
therefore thou shalt not *c* down ... 2Kin 1:6 3381
God, the king hath said, *C* down ... 2Kin 1:9 3381
then let fire *c* down from heaven, ... 2Kin 1:10 3381
C down quickly ... 2Kin 1:11 3381
let fire *c* down from heaven, and ... 2Kin 1:12 3381
therefore thou shalt not *c* down ... 2Kin 1:16 3381
were *c* up to fight against them ... 2Kin 3:21 5927
the creditor is *c* to take unto ... 2Kin 4:1 935
And when thou art *c* in, thou shalt ... 2Kin 4:4 935
run to the man of God, and *c* again ... 2Kin 4:22 7725
when Elisha was *c* into the house ... 2Kin 4:32 935
And when she was *c* in unto him ... 2Kin 4:36 935
when this letter is *c* unto thee ... 2Kin 5:6 935
let him *c* now to me, and he shall ... 2Kin 5:8 935
thy flesh shall *c* again to thee ... 2Kin 5:10 7725
He will surely *c* out to me ... 2Kin 5:11 3318
even now there be *c* to me from ... 2Kin 5:22 935
thither the Syrians are *c* down ... 2Kin 6:9 5185
when they were *c* into Samaria ... 2Kin 6:20 935
Now therefore *c*, and let us fall ... 2Kin 7:4 3212
when they were *c* to the uttermost ... 2Kin 7:5 935
of the Egyptians, to *c* upon us ... 2Kin 7:6 935
some mischief will *c* upon us ... 2Kin 7:9 4672
now therefore *c*, that we may go ... 2Kin 7:9 3212
When they *c* out of the city, we ... 2Kin 7:12 3318
it shall also *c* upon the land ... 2Kin 8:1 935
The man of God is *c* hither ... 2Kin 8:7 935
of Judah was *c* down to see Joram ... 2Kin 9:16 3381
And when Jehu was *c* to Jezreel ... 2Kin 9:30 935
And when he was *c* in, he did eat ... 2Kin 9:34 935
c to me to Jezreel by to morrow ... 2Kin 10:6 935
C with me, and see my zeal for the ... 2Kin 10:16 3212
let none *c* forth ... 2Kin 10:25 3381
that were to *c* in on the sabbath ... 2Kin 11:9 935
Jehu, king of Israel, saying, *C* ... 2Kin 14:8 3212
c up, and save me out of the hand ... 2Kin 16:7 5927
when the king was *c* from Damascus ... 2Kin 16:12 935
c up against all the fenced ... 2Kin 18:13 5927
And when they were *c* up, they came ... 2Kin 18:17 5927
Am I now *c* up without the LORD ... 2Kin 18:25 5927
c out to me, and then eat ye every ... 2Kin 18:31 3318
Until I *c* and take you away to a ... 2Kin 18:32 935
the children are *c* to the birth ... 2Kin 19:3 935
he is *c* out to fight against thee ... 2Kin 19:9 3318
I am *c* up to the height of the ... 2Kin 19:23 5927
thy tumult is *c* up into mine ears ... 2Kin 19:28 5927
He shall not *c* into this city, ... 2Kin 19:32 935
nor *c* before it with shield, nor ... 2Kin 19:32 6923
shall not *c* into this city, saith ... 2Kin 19:33 935
They are *c* from a far country, ... 2Kin 20:14 935
Behold, the days *c*, that all that ... 2Kin 20:17 935
were to *c* after seven days from ... 1Chr 9:25 935
lest these uncircumcised *c* ... 1Chr 10:4 935
to David, Thou shalt not *c* hither ... 1Chr 11:5 935
If ye be *c* peaceably unto me to ... 1Chr 12:17 935
but if ye be *c* to betray me to ... 1Chr 12:17
were expressed by name, to *c* ... 1Chr 12:31 935
c upon them over against the ... 1Chr 14:14 935
an offering, and *c* before him ... 1Chr 16:29 935
And it shall *c* to pass, when thy ... 1Chr 17:11 1961
house for a great while to *c* ... 1Chr 17:17 7350
are not his servants *c* unto thee ... 1Chr 19:3 935
the kings that were *c* were by ... 1Chr 19:9 935
to *c* into the house of the LORD ... 1Chr 24:19 935
honour *c* of thee, and thou ... 1Chr 29:12 4480
for all things *c* of thee, and of ... 1Chr 29:14 4480
go out and *c* in before this people ... 2Chr 1:10 935
were *c* out of the holy place ... 2Chr 5:11 3318
shall *c* forth out of thy loins ... 2Chr 6:9 3318
the oath *c* before thine altar in ... 2Chr 6:22 935
but is *c* from a far country for ... 2Chr 6:32 935
if they *c* and pray in this house ... 2Chr 6:32 935
the ark of the LORD hath *c* ... 2Chr 8:11 935
and when she was *c* to Solomon ... 2Chr 9:1 935
all Israel *c* to make him king ... 2Chr 10:1 935
C again unto me after three days ... 2Chr 10:5 7725
C again to me on the third day ... 2Chr 10:12 7725
when Rehoboam was *c* to Jerusalem ... 2Chr 11:1 935
ambushment to *c* about behind them ... 2Chr 13:13 935
out or *c* in to Asa king of Judah ... 2Chr 16:1 935
And when he was *c* to the king ... 2Chr 18:14 935
what cause soever shall *c* to you ... 2Chr 19:10 935
the LORD, and so wrath *c* upon you ... 2Chr 19:10 1961
to *c* to cast us out of thy ... 2Chr 20:11 935
they *c* up by the cliff of Ziz ... 2Chr 20:16 5927
which were *c* against Judah ... 2Chr 20:22 935
for when he was *c*, he went out ... 2Chr 22:7 935
But let none *c* into the house of ... 2Chr 23:6 935
that were to *c* in on the sabbath ... 2Chr 23:8 935
when she was *c* to the entering of ... 2Chr 23:15 935
the army that was *c* to him out of ... 2Chr 25:10 935
after that Amaziah was *c* from the ... 2Chr 25:14 935
Jehu, king of Israel, saying, *C* ... 2Chr 25:17 3212
For again the Edomites had *c* ... 2Chr 28:17 935
c near and bring sacrifices and ... 2Chr 29:31 5066
that they should *c* to the house ... 2Chr 30:1 935
that they should *c* to keep the ... 2Chr 30:5 935
so that they shall *c* again into ... 2Chr 30:9 7725
saw that Sennacherib was *c* ... 2Chr 32:2 935
Why should the kings of Assyria *c* ... 2Chr 32:4 935
when he was *c* into the house of ... 2Chr 32:21 935
I *c* not against thee this day, ... 2Chr 35:21
And when the seventh month was *c* ... Ezr 3:1 5060
all they that were *c* out of the ... Ezr 3:8 935
thee to us are *c* unto Jerusalem ... Ezr 4:12 858
which were *c* again out of ... Ezr 6:21 7725
which were *c* out of the captivity ... Ezr 8:35 935
after all that is *c* upon us for ... Ezr 9:13 935
would not *c* within three days ... Ezr 10:8 935
our cities *c* at appointed times ... Ezr 10:14 935
me over till I *c* into Judah ... Neh 2:7 935
c a man to seek the welfare of ... Neh 2:10 935
c, and let us build up the wall of ... Neh 2:17 3212
all of them together to *c* ... Neh 4:8 935
till we *c* in the midst among them ... Neh 4:11 935
and Geshem sent unto me, saying, *C* ... Neh 6:2 3212
work, so that I cannot *c* down ... Neh 6:3 3381
I leave it, and *c* down to you ... Neh 6:3 3381
C now therefore, and let us take ... Neh 6:7 3212
for they will *c* to slay thee ... Neh 6:10 935
night will they *c* to slay thee ... Neh 6:10 935
congregation of them that were *c* ... Neh 8:17 7725
before thee, that hath *c* upon us ... Neh 9:32 4672
the Moabite should not *c* into the ... Neh 13:1 935

themselves, and that they should *c*	Neh 13:22	935
to *c* at the king's commandment by	Est 1:12	935
shall *c* abroad unto all women	Est 1:17	3318
That Vashti *c* no more before king	Est 1:19	935
was *c* to go in to king Ahasuerus	Est 2:12	5060
was *c* to go in unto the king, she	Est 2:15	5060
shall *c* unto the king into the	Est 4:11	935
c in unto the king these thirty	Est 4:11	935
who knoweth whether thou art *c* to	Est 4:14	5060
Haman *c* this day unto the banquet	Est 5:4	935
Haman *c* to the banquet that I	Est 5:8	935
man *c* in with the king unto the	Est 5:12	935
Now Haman was *c* into the outward	Est 6:4	935
And the king said, Let him *c* in	Est 6:5	935
evil that shall *c* unto my people	Est 8:6	4672
matter, and which had *c* unto them	Est 9:26	5060
all this evil that was *c* upon him	Job 2:11	935
together to *c* to mourn with him	Job 2:11	935
let it not *c* into the number of	Job 3:6	935
let no joyful voice *c* therein	Job 3:7	935
I greatly feared is *c* upon me	Job 3:25	857
I was afraid of is *c* unto me	Job 3:25	935
But now it is *c* upon thee	Job 4:5	935
Thou shalt *c* to thy grave in a	Job 5:26	935
to the grave shall *c* up no more	Job 7:9	5927
of the wicked shall *c* to nought	Job 8:22	369
we should *c* together in judgment	Job 9:32	935
speak, and let *c* on me what will	Job 13:13	5674
hypocrite shall not *c* before him	Job 13:16	935
will I wait, till my change *c*	Job 14:14	935
His sons *c* to honour, and he	Job 14:21	3513
the destroyer shall *c* upon him	Job 15:21	935
When a few years are *c*, then I	Job 16:22	857
you all, do ye return, and *c* now	Job 17:10	935
They that *c* after him shall be	Job 18:20	314
His troops *c* together, and raise	Job 19:12	935
of the wicked shall *c* upon him	Job 20:22	935
thereby good shall *c* unto thee	Job 22:21	935
that I might *c* even to his seat	Job 23:3	935
tried me, I shall *c* forth as gold	Job 23:10	3318
the day and night *c* to an end	Job 26:10	8503
the cry of the poor to *c* unto him	Job 34:28	935
He causeth it to *c*, whether for	Job 37:13	4672
And said, Hitherto shalt thou *c*	Job 38:11	935
or who can *c* to him with his	Job 41:13	935
that no air can *c* between them	Job 41:16	935
I will *c* into thy house in the	Ps 5:7	935
of the wicked *c* to an end	Ps 7:9	1584
shall *c* down upon his own pate	Ps 7:16	3381
destructions are *c* to a perpetual	Ps 9:6	8552
of Israel were *c* out of Zion	Ps 14:7	4480
Let my sentence *c* forth from thy	Ps 17:2	3318
They shall *c*, and shall declare	Ps 22:31	935
and the King of glory shall *c* in	Ps 24:7	935
and the King of glory shall *c* in	Ps 24:9	935
they shall not *c* nigh unto him	Ps 32:6	5060
lest they *c* near unto thee	Ps 32:9	7126
C, ye children, hearken unto me	Ps 34:11	3212
Let destruction *c* upon him at	Ps 35:8	935
the foot of pride *c* against me	Ps 36:11	935
Then said I, Lo, I *c*	Ps 40:7	935
if he *c* to see me, he speaketh	Ps 41:6	935
when shall I *c* and appear before	Ps 42:2	935
All this is *c* upon us	Ps 44:17	935
C, behold the works of the LORD,	Ps 46:8	3212
Our God shall *c*, and shall not	Ps 50:3	935
David is *c* to the house of	Ps 52:*t*	935
of Israel were *c* out of Zion	Ps 53:6	4480
and trembling are *c* upon me	Ps 55:5	935
unto thee shall all flesh *c*	Ps 65:2	935
C and see the works of God	Ps 66:5	3212
C and hear, all ye that fear God,	Ps 66:16	3212
Princes shall *c* out of Egypt	Ps 68:31	857
the waters are *c* in unto my soul	Ps 69:1	935
I am *c* into deep waters, where	Ps 69:2	935
and let them not *c* into thy	Ps 69:27	935
power to every one that is to *c*	Ps 71:18	935
He shall *c* down like rain upon	Ps 72:6	3381
to *c* the praises of the LORD	Ps 78:4	314
generation to *c* might know them	Ps 78:6	314
the heathen are *c* into thine	Ps 79:1	935
of the prisoner *c* before thee	Ps 79:11	935
stir up thy strength, and *c*	Ps 80:2	3212
They have said, *C*, and let us cut	Ps 83:4	3212
whom thou hast made shall *c*	Ps 86:9	935
Let my prayer *c* before thee	Ps 88:2	935
I am shut up, and I cannot *c* forth	Ps 88:8	3318
but it shall not *c* nigh thee	Ps 91:7	5066
any plague *c* nigh thy dwelling	Ps 91:10	7126
O *c*, let us sing unto the LORD	Ps 95:1	3212
Let us *c* before his presence with	Ps 95:2	6923
O *c*, let us worship and bow down	Ps 95:6	935
an offering, and *c* into his courts	Ps 96:8	935
c before his presence with	Ps 100:2	935
O when wilt thou *c* unto me	Ps 101:2	935
O LORD, and let my cry *c* unto thee	Ps 102:1	935
her, yea, the set time, is *c*	Ps 102:13	935
written for the generation to *c*	Ps 102:18	314
cursing, so let it *c* unto him	Ps 109:17	935
so let it *c* into his bowels like	Ps 109:18	935
Let thy mercies *c* also unto me	Ps 119:41	935
Let thy tender mercies *c* unto me	Ps 119:77	935
Let my cry *c* near before thee, O	Ps 119:169	7126
Let my supplication *c* before thee	Ps 119:170	935
shall doubtless *c* again with	Ps 126:6	935
Surely I will not *c* into the	Ps 132:3	935
thy heavens, O LORD, and *c* down	Ps 144:5	3381
C with us, let us lay wait for	Prov 1:11	3212
c again, and to morrow I will give	Prov 3:28	7725
c not nigh the door of her house	Prov 5:8	7126
when thou art *c* into the hand of	Prov 6:3	935
So shall thy poverty *c* as one	Prov 6:11	935
shall his calamity *c* suddenly	Prov 6:15	935
C, let us take our fill of love	Prov 7:18	3212
will *c* home at the day appointed	Prov 7:20	935
C, eat of my bread, and drink of	Prov 9:5	3212
the wicked, it shall *c* upon him	Prov 10:24	935
mischief, it shall *c* unto him	Prov 11:27	935
the just shall *c* out of trouble	Prov 12:13	3318
not sleep, lest thou *c* to poverty	Prov 20:13	3423
the rich, shall surely *c* to want	Prov 22:16	4270
and the glutton shall *c* to poverty	Prov 23:21	3423
a good blessing shall *c* upon them	Prov 24:25	935
So shall thy poverty *c* as one	Prov 24:34	935
there shall *c* forth a vessel for	Prov 25:4	3318
it be said unto thee, *C* up hither	Prov 25:7	5927
the curse causeless shall not *c*	Prov 26:2	935
not that poverty shall *c* upon him	Prov 28:22	935
and she shall rejoice in time to *c*	Prov 31:25	314
place from whence the rivers *c*	Eccl 1:7	1980
of things that are to *c* with	Eccl 1:11	314
with those that shall *c* after	Eccl 1:11	1961
I am *c* to great estate, and have	Eccl 1:16	1430
days to *c* shall all be forgotten	Eccl 2:16	935
they also that *c* after shall not	Eccl 4:16	314
God shall *c* forth of them all	Eccl 7:18	3318
saw the wicked buried, who had *c*	Eccl 8:10	935
All things *c* alike to all	Eccl 9:2	
youth, while the evil days *c* not	Eccl 12:1	935
my love, my fair one, and *c* away	Song 2:10	3212
time of the singing of birds is *c*	Song 2:12	5060
my love, my fair one, and *c* away	Song 2:13	3212
C with me from Lebanon, my spouse	Song 4:8	935
and *c*, thou south	Song 4:16	935
Let my beloved *c* into his garden,	Song 4:16	935
I am *c* into my garden, my sister,	Song 5:1	935
C, my beloved, let us go forth	Song 7:11	3212
When ye *c* to appear before me,	Is 1:12	935
C now, and let us reason together,	Is 1:18	3212
cause of the widow *c* unto them	Is 1:23	935
it shall *c* to pass in the last	Is 2:2	1961
C ye, and let us go up to the	Is 2:3	3212
c ye, and let us walk in the light	Is 2:5	3212
And it shall *c* to pass, that	Is 3:24	1961
And it shall *c* to pass, that he	Is 4:3	1961
but there shall *c* up briers	Is 5:6	5927
Holy One of Israel draw nigh and *c*	Is 5:19	935
they shall *c* with speed swiftly	Is 5:26	935
stand, neither shall it *c* to pass	Is 7:7	1961
house, days that have not *c*	Is 7:17	935
it shall *c* to pass in that day,	Is 7:18	1961
And they shall *c*, and shall rest	Is 7:19	935
it shall *c* to pass in that day,	Is 7:21	1961
And it shall *c* to pass, for the	Is 7:22	1961
it shall *c* to pass in that day,	Is 7:23	1961
and with bows shall men *c* thither	Is 7:24	935
there shall not *c* thither the	Is 7:25	935
he shall *c* up over all his	Is 8:7	5927
together, and it shall *c* to nought	Is 8:10	6565
and it shall *c* to pass, that when	Is 8:21	1961
desolation which shall *c* from far	Is 10:3	935
Wherefore it shall *c* to pass	Is 10:12	1961
it shall *c* to pass in that day,	Is 10:20	1961
it shall *c* to pass in that day,	Is 10:27	1961
He is *c* to Aiath, he is passed to	Is 10:28	935
there shall *c* forth a rod out of	Is 11:1	3318
it shall *c* to pass in that day,	Is 11:11	1961
They *c* from a far country, from	Is 13:5	935
it shall *c* as a destruction from	Is 13:6	935
and her time is near to *c*, and her	Is 13:22	935
it shall *c* to pass in the day	Is 14:3	1961
no feller is *c* up against us	Is 14:8	5927
thought, so shall it *c* to pass	Is 14:24	1961
root shall *c* forth a cockatrice	Is 14:29	3318
for there shall *c* from the north	Is 14:31	935
they are *c* even unto Jazer, they	Is 16:8	5060
And it shall *c* to pass, when it is	Is 16:12	1961
that he shall *c* to his sanctuary	Is 16:12	935
And in that day it shall *c* to pass	Is 17:4	1961
cloud, and shall *c* into Egypt	Is 19:1	935
the Assyrian shall *c* into Egypt	Is 19:23	935
enquire ye: return, *c*	Is 21:12	857
And it shall *c* to pass, that thy	Is 22:7	1961
it shall *c* to pass in that day,	Is 22:20	1961
it shall *c* to pass in that day,	Is 23:15	1961
it shall *c* to pass after the end	Is 23:17	1961
is shut up, that no man may *c* in	Is 24:10	935
And it shall *c* to pass, that he	Is 24:18	1961
it shall *c* to pass in that day,	Is 24:21	1961
C, my people, enter thou into thy	Is 26:20	3212
them that *c* of Jacob to take root	Is 27:6	935
the women *c*, and set them on fire	Is 27:11	935
it shall *c* to pass in that day,	Is 27:12	1961
it shall *c* to pass in that day,	Is 27:13	1961
they shall *c* which were ready to	Is 27:13	935
through, it shall not *c* unto us	Is 28:15	935
spirit shall *c* to understanding	Is 29:24	3045
anguish, from whence *c* the young	Is 30:6	
may be for the time to *c* for ever	Is 30:8	314
c into the mountain of the LORD	Is 30:29	935
so shall the LORD of hosts *c* down	Is 31:4	3381
fail, the gathering shall not *c*	Is 32:10	935
of my people shall *c* up thorns	Is 32:13	5927
C near, ye nations, to hear	Is 34:1	7126
and all things that *c* forth of it	Is 34:1	6631
their stink shall *c* up out of	Is 34:3	5927
it shall *c* down upon Idumea, and	Is 34:5	3381
unicorns shall *c* down with them	Is 34:7	3381
thorns shall *c* up in her palaces,	Is 34:13	5927
your God will *c* with vengeance,	Is 35:4	935
he will *c* and save you	Is 35:4	935
and *c* to Zion with songs and	Is 35:10	935
am I now *c* up without the LORD	Is 36:10	5927
me by a present, and *c* out to me	Is 36:16	3318
Until I *c* and take you away to a	Is 36:17	935
the children are *c* to the birth	Is 37:3	935
He is *c* forth to make war with	Is 37:9	3318
am I *c* up to the height of the	Is 37:24	5927
is *c* up into mine ears, therefore	Is 37:29	5927
is *c* up into mine ears, therefore	Is 37:29	5927
He shall not *c* into this city,	Is 37:33	935
nor *c* before it with shields, nor	Is 37:33	6923
shall not *c* into this city, saith	Is 37:34	935
They are *c* from a far country	Is 39:3	935
Behold, the days *c*, that all that	Is 39:6	935
Lord GOD will *c* with strong hand	Is 40:10	935
let them *c* near	Is 41:1	5066
let us *c* near together to	Is 41:1	7126
or declare us things for to *c*	Is 41:22	935
things that are to *c* hereafter	Is 41:23	857
one from the north, and he shall *c*	Is 41:25	857
he shall *c* upon princes as upon	Is 41:25	935
the former things are *c* to pass	Is 42:9	935
hearken and hear for the time to *c*	Is 42:23	268
that are coming, and shall *c*	Is 44:7	935
of things to *c* concerning my sons	Is 45:11	857
shall *c* over unto thee, and they	Is 45:14	5674
they shall *c* after thee	Is 45:14	3212
in chains they shall *c* over	Is 45:14	5674
Assemble yourselves and *c*	Is 45:20	935
even to him shall men *c*	Is 45:24	935
C down, and sit in the dust, O	Is 47:1	3381
But these two things shall *c* to	Is 47:9	935
they shall *c* upon thee in their	Is 47:9	935
Therefore shall evil *c* upon thee	Is 47:11	935
desolation shall *c* upon thee	Is 47:11	935
things that shall *c* upon thee	Is 47:13	935
are *c* forth out of the waters of	Is 48:1	3318
C ye near unto me, hear ye this	Is 48:16	7126
Behold, these shall *c* from far	Is 49:12	935
themselves together, and *c* to thee	Is 49:18	935
let him *c* near to me	Is 50:8	5066
and *c* with singing unto Zion	Is 51:11	935
These two things are *c* unto thee	Is 51:19	7122
c into thee the uncircumcised	Is 52:1	935
for it shall not *c* near thee	Is 54:14	7126
c ye to the waters, and he that	Is 55:1	3212
c ye, buy, and eat	Is 55:1	3212
yea, *c*, buy wine and milk without	Is 55:1	3212
Incline your ear, and *c* unto me	Is 55:3	3212
the thorn shall *c* up the fir tree	Is 55:13	5927
brier shall *c* up the myrtle tree	Is 55:13	5927
for my salvation is near to *c*	Is 56:1	935
c to devour, yea, all ye beasts	Is 56:9	857
C ye, say they, I will fetch wine	Is 56:12	857
is taken away from the evil to *c*	Is 57:1	
the enemy shall *c* in like a flood	Is 59:19	935
And the Redeemer shall *c* to Zion	Is 59:20	935
for thy light is *c*, and the glory	Is 60:1	935
the Gentiles shall *c* to thy light	Is 60:3	1980
together, they *c* to thee	Is 60:4	935
thy sons shall *c* from far	Is 60:4	935
of the Gentiles shall *c* unto thee	Is 60:5	935
all they from Sheba shall *c*	Is 60:6	935
they shall *c* up with acceptance	Is 60:7	5927
of Lebanon shall *c* unto thee	Is 60:13	935
thee shall *c* bending unto thee	Is 60:14	1980
and the year of my redeemed is *c*	Is 63:4	935
that thou wouldest *c* down	Is 64:1	3381
by thyself, *c* not near to me	Is 65:5	5066
be remembered, nor *c* into mind	Is 65:17	5927
And it shall *c* to pass, that	Is 65:24	1961
behold, the LORD will *c* with fire	Is 66:15	935
it shall *c*, that I will gather	Is 66:18	935
and they shall *c*, and see my glory	Is 66:18	935
And it shall *c* to pass, that from	Is 66:23	1961
shall all flesh *c* to worship	Is 66:23	935
and they shall *c*, and they shall	Jer 1:15	935
evil shall *c* upon them, saith the	Jer 2:3	935
we will *c* no more unto thee	Jer 2:31	935
And it shall *c* to pass, when ye be	Jer 3:16	1961
neither shall it *c* to mind	Jer 3:16	5927
they shall *c* together out of the	Jer 3:18	935
Behold, we *c* unto thee	Jer 3:22	857
lest my fury *c* forth like fire,	Jer 4:4	3318
The lion is *c* up from his thicket	Jer 4:7	5927
it shall *c* to pass at that day,	Jer 4:9	1961
from those places shall *c* unto me	Jer 4:12	935
he shall *c* up as clouds, and his	Jer 4:13	5927
that watchers *c* from a far	Jer 4:16	935
neither shall evil *c* upon us	Jer 5:12	935
And it shall *c* to pass, when ye	Jer 5:19	1961
their flocks shall *c* unto her	Jer 6:3	935
spoiler shall suddenly *c* upon us	Jer 6:26	935
And *c* and stand before me in this	Jer 7:10	935
Therefore, behold, the days *c*	Jer 7:32	935
for they are *c*, and have devoured	Jer 8:16	935
mourning women, that they may *c*	Jer 9:17	935
cunning women, that they may *c*	Jer 9:17	935
For death is *c* up into our	Jer 9:21	5927
Behold, the days *c*, saith the	Jer 9:25	935
the noise of the bruit is *c*	Jer 10:22	935
c ye, assemble all the beasts of	Jer 12:9	3212
beasts of the field, *c* to devour	Jer 12:9	857

The spoilers are *c* upon all high .... Jer 12:12 935
And it shall *c* to pass, after that .... Jer 12:15 1961
And it shall *c* to pass, if they .... Jer 12:16 1961
your principalities shall *c* down .... Jer 13:18 3381
behold them that *c* from the north .... Jer 13:20 935
Wherefore *c* these things upon me .... Jer 13:22 7122
And it shall *c* to pass, if they .... Jer 15:2 1961
And it shall *c* to pass, when thou .... Jer 16:10 1961
Therefore, behold, the days *c* .... Jer 16:14 935
the Gentiles shall *c* unto thee .... Jer 16:19 935
let it *c* now .... Jer 17:15 935
whereby the kings of Judah *c* in .... Jer 17:19 935
And it shall *c* to pass, if ye .... Jer 17:24 1961
they shall *c* from the cities of .... Jer 17:26 935
the cold flowing waters that *c* .... Jer 18:14
Then said they, *C*, and let us .... Jer 18:18 3212
C, and let us smite him with the .... Jer 18:18 3212
Therefore, behold, the days *c* .... Jer 19:6 935
and thou shalt *c* to Babylon .... Jer 20:6 935
Who shall *c* down against us .... Jer 21:13 5181
thou be when pangs *c* upon thee .... Jer 22:23 935
Behold, the days *c*, saith the .... Jer 23:5 935
Therefore, behold, the days *c* .... Jer 23:7 935
heart, No evil shall *c* upon you .... Jer 23:17 935
word of the LORD hath *c* unto me .... Jer 25:3 1961
And it shall *c* to pass, when .... Jer 25:12 1961
A noise shall *c* even to the ends .... Jer 25:31 935
which *c* to worship in the LORD's .... Jer 26:2 935
hand of the messengers which *c* to .... Jer 27:3 935
until the very time of his land *c* .... Jer 27:7 935
And it shall *c* to pass, that the .... Jer 27:8 1961
of the prophet shall *c* to pass .... Jer 28:9 935
For, lo, the days *c*, saith the .... Jer 30:3 935
For it shall *c* to pass in that .... Jer 30:8 1961
They shall *c* with weeping, and .... Jer 31:9 935
Therefore they shall *c* and sing in .... Jer 31:12 935
they shall *c* again from the land .... Jer 31:16 7725
that thy children shall *c* again .... Jer 31:17 7725
Behold, the days *c*, saith the .... Jer 31:27 935
And it shall *c* to pass, that like .... Jer 31:28 1961
Behold, the days *c*, saith the .... Jer 31:31 935
Behold, the days *c*, saith the .... Jer 31:38 935
thine uncle shall *c* unto thee .... Jer 32:7 935
all this evil to *c* upon them .... Jer 32:23 7122
they are *c* unto the city to take .... Jer 32:24 935
thou hast spoken is *c* to pass .... Jer 32:24 1961
fight against this city, shall *c* .... Jer 32:29 935
They *c* to fight with the .... Jer 33:5 935
Behold, the days *c*, saith the .... Jer 33:14 935
up into the land, that we said, *C* .... Jer 35:11 935
Judah that *c* out of their cities .... Jer 36:6 935
in the ears of the people, and *c* .... Jer 36:14 3212
king of Babylon shall certainly *c* .... Jer 36:29 935
army was *c* forth out of Egypt .... Jer 37:5 3318
which is *c* forth to help you .... Jer 37:7 3318
And the Chaldeans shall *c* again .... Jer 37:8 7725
Babylon shall not *c* against you .... Jer 37:19 935
they *c* unto thee, and say unto .... Jer 38:25 935
this thing is *c* upon you .... Jer 40:3 1961
to *c* with me into Babylon, *c* .... Jer 40:4 935
thee to *c* with me into Babylon .... Jer 40:4 935
Chaldeans, which will *c* unto us .... Jer 40:10 935
C to Gedaliah the son of Ahikam .... Jer 41:6 935
and it shall *c* to pass, that .... Jer 42:4 1961
Then it shall *c* to pass, that the .... Jer 42:16 1961
C up, ye horses .... Jer 46:9 5927
and let the mighty men *c* forth .... Jer 46:9 3318
king of Babylon should *c* and smite .... Jer 46:13 935
Carmel by the sea, so shall he *c* .... Jer 46:18 935
of their calamity was *c* upon them .... Jer 46:21 935
c against her with axes, as .... Jer 46:22 935
Baldness is *c* upon Gaza .... Jer 47:5 935
c, and let us cut it off from .... Jer 48:2 3212
spoiler shall *c* upon every city .... Jer 48:8 935
Therefore, behold, the days *c* .... Jer 48:12 935
The calamity of Moab is near to *c* .... Jer 48:16 935
c down from thy glory, and sit in .... Jer 48:18 3381
spoiler of Moab shall *c* upon thee .... Jer 48:18 5927
judgment is *c* upon the plain .... Jer 48:21 935
but a fire shall *c* forth out of .... Jer 48:45 3318
Therefore, behold, the days *c* .... Jer 49:2 935
saying, Who shall *c* unto me .... Jer 49:4 935
If grapegatherers *c* to thee .... Jer 49:9 935
c against her, and rise up to the .... Jer 49:14 935
he shall *c* up like a lion from .... Jer 49:19 5927
Behold, he shall *c* up and fly as .... Jer 49:22 5927
the outcasts of Elam shall not *c* .... Jer 49:36 935
But it shall *c* to pass in the .... Jer 49:39 1961
the children of Israel shall *c* .... Jer 50:4 935
faces thitherward, saying, *C* .... Jer 50:5 935
cause to *c* up against Babylon an .... Jer 50:9 5927
C against her from the utmost .... Jer 50:26 935
for their day is *c*, the time of .... Jer 50:27 935
for thy day is *c*, the time that I .... Jer 50:31 935
a people shall *c* from the north .... Jer 50:41 935
he shall *c* up like a lion from .... Jer 50:44 5927
c, and let us declare in Zion the .... Jer 51:10 935
in treasures, thine end is *c* .... Jer 51:13 935
cause the horses to *c* up as the .... Jer 51:27 5927
the time of her harvest shall *c* .... Jer 51:33 935
The sea is *c* up upon Babylon .... Jer 51:42 5927
a rumour shall both *c* one year .... Jer 51:46 935
in another year shall *c* a rumour .... Jer 51:46
Therefore, behold, the days *c* .... Jer 51:47 935
for the spoilers shall *c* unto her .... Jer 51:48 935
let Jerusalem *c* into your mind .... Jer 51:50 5927
for strangers are *c* into the .... Jer 51:51 935
Wherefore, behold, the days *c* .... Jer 51:52 935
from me shall spoilers *c* unto her .... Jer 51:53 935
Because the spoiler is *c* upon her .... Jer 51:56 935
evil that should *c* upon Babylon .... Jer 51:60 935
because none *c* to the solemn .... Lam 1:4 935
wreathed, and *c* up upon my neck .... Lam 1:14 5927
their wickedness *c* before thee .... Lam 1:22 935
Fear and a snare is *c* upon us .... Lam 3:47 1961
for our end is *c* .... Lam 4:18 935
O LORD, what is *c* upon us .... Lam 5:1 1961
for thereof shall a fire *c* forth .... Eze 5:4 3318
the end is *c* upon the four .... Eze 7:2 935
Now is the end *c* upon thee .... Eze 7:3
evil, an only evil, behold, is *c* .... Eze 7:5 935
An end is *c*, the end is *c* .... Eze 7:6 935
behold, it is *c* .... Eze 7:6 935
The morning is *c* unto thee .... Eze 7:7 935
the time is *c*, the day of trouble .... Eze 7:7 935
Behold the day, behold, it is *c* .... Eze 7:10 935
The time is *c*, the day draweth .... Eze 7:12 935
Mischief shall *c* upon mischief .... Eze 7:26 935
but *c* not near any man upon whom .... Eze 9:6 5066
the things that *c* into your mind .... Eze 11:5 4609
the countries where they shall *c* .... Eze 11:16 935
And they shall *c* thither, and they .... Eze 11:18 935
among the heathen whither they *c* .... Eze 12:16 935
I shall speak shall *c* to pass .... Eze 12:25 6213
he seeth is for many days to *c* .... Eze 12:27
the souls alive that *c* unto you .... Eze 13:18
they shall *c* forth unto you, and .... Eze 14:22 3318
thou art *c* to excellent ornaments .... Eze 16:7 935
the like things shall not *c* .... Eze 16:16 935
that they may *c* unto thee on .... Eze 16:33 935
king of Babylon is *c* to Jerusalem .... Eze 17:12 935
wife, neither hath *c* near to a .... Eze 18:6 7126
Are ye *c* to enquire of me .... Eze 20:3 935
of the king of Babylon may *c* .... Eze 21:19 935
both twain shall *c* forth out of .... Eze 21:19 3318
that the sword may *c* to Rabbath .... Eze 21:20 935
that ye are *c* to remembrance, ye .... Eze 21:24 2142
prince of Israel, whose day is *c* .... Eze 21:25 935
until he *c* whose right it is .... Eze 21:27 935
of the wicked, whose day is *c* .... Eze 21:29 935
midst of it, that her time may *c* .... Eze 22:3 935
art *c* even unto thy years .... Eze 22:4 935
they shall *c* against thee with .... Eze 23:24 935
have sent for men to *c* from far .... Eze 23:40 935
fury to *c* up to take vengeance .... Eze 24:8 5927
it shall *c* to pass, and I will do .... Eze 24:14 835
in that day shall *c* unto thee .... Eze 24:20 835
many nations to *c* up against thee .... Eze 26:3 5927
the sea causeth his waves to *c* up .... Eze 26:3 5927
shall *c* down from their thrones .... Eze 26:16 3381
shall *c* down from their ships .... Eze 27:29 3381
And the sword shall *c* upon Egypt .... Eze 30:4 935
pride of her power shall *c* down .... Eze 30:6 3381
and great pain shall *c* upon them .... Eze 30:9 1961
king of Babylon shall *c* upon thee .... Eze 32:11 935
seeth the sword *c* upon the land .... Eze 33:3 935
if the sword *c*, and take him away .... Eze 33:4 935
if the watchman see the sword *c* .... Eze 33:6 935
if the sword *c*, and take any .... Eze 33:6 935
one to his brother, saying, *C* .... Eze 33:30 935
they *c* unto thee as the people .... Eze 33:31 935
cometh to pass, (lo, it will *c* .... Eze 33:33 935
shower to *c* down in his season .... Eze 34:26 3381
for they are at hand to *c* .... Eze 36:8 935
C from the four winds, O breath .... Eze 37:9 935
cause you to *c* up out of your .... Eze 37:12 5927
c into the land that is brought .... Eze 38:8 935
c like a storm, thou shalt be .... Eze 38:9 935
It shall also *c* to pass, that at .... Eze 38:10 1961
time shall things *c* into thy mind .... Eze 38:10 5927
Art thou *c* to take a spoil .... Eze 38:13 935
thou shalt *c* from thy place out .... Eze 38:15 935
thou shalt *c* up against my people .... Eze 38:16 5927
it shall *c* to pass at the same .... Eze 38:18 1961
c against the land of Israel .... Eze 38:18 935
my fury shall *c* up in my face .... Eze 38:18 5927
will cause thee to *c* up from the .... Eze 39:2 5927
Behold, it is *c*, and it is done .... Eze 39:8 935
it shall *c* to pass in that day .... Eze 39:11 1961
field, Assemble yourselves, and *c* .... Eze 39:17 935
which *c* near to the LORD to .... Eze 40:46 7131
And they shall not *c* near unto me .... Eze 44:13 5066
nor to *c* near to any of my holy .... Eze 44:13 5066
they shall *c* near to me to .... Eze 44:15 7126
they shall *c* near to my table, to .... Eze 44:16 7126
And it shall *c* to pass, that when .... Eze 44:17 1961
and no wool shall *c* upon them .... Eze 44:17 5927
they shall *c* at no dead person to .... Eze 44:25 935
which shall *c* near to minister .... Eze 45:4 7131
the people of the land shall *c* .... Eze 46:9 935
And it shall *c* to pass, that every .... Eze 47:9 1961
whithersoever the rivers shall *c* .... Eze 47:9 935
these waters shall *c* thither .... Eze 47:9 935
And it shall *c* to pass, that the .... Eze 47:10 1961
till a man *c* over against Hamath .... Eze 47:20 935
And it shall *c* to pass, that ye .... Eze 47:22 1961
And it shall *c* to pass, that in .... Eze 47:23 1961
what should *c* to pass hereafter .... Dan 2:29 1934
to thee what shall *c* to pass .... Dan 2:29 1934
what shall *c* to pass hereafter .... Dan 2:45 1934
to *c* to the dedication of the .... Dan 3:2 858
high God, *c* forth .... Dan 3:26 5312
and *c* hither .... Dan 3:26 858
which is *c* upon my lord the king .... Dan 4:24 4291
I saw him *c* close unto the ram .... Dan 8:7 5060
transgressors are *c* to the full .... Dan 8:23 8552
Moses, all this evil is *c* upon us .... Dan 9:13 935
I am now *c* forth to give thee .... Dan 9:22 3318
forth, and I am *c* to shew thee .... Dan 9:23 935
shall *c* shall destroy the city .... Dan 9:26 935
heard, and I am *c* for thy words .... Dan 10:12 935
Now I am *c* to make thee .... Dan 10:14 935
thou wherefore I *c* unto thee .... Dan 10:20 935
lo, the prince of Grecia shall *c* .... Dan 10:20 935
c to the king of the north to .... Dan 11:6 935
which shall *c* with an army, and .... Dan 11:7 935
south shall *c* into his kingdom .... Dan 11:9 935
and one shall certainly *c*, and .... Dan 11:10 935
with choler, and shall *c* forth .... Dan 11:11 3318
shall certainly *c* after certain .... Dan 11:13 935
So the king of the north shall *c* .... Dan 11:15 935
but he shall *c* in peaceably .... Dan 11:21 935
for he shall *c* up, and shall .... Dan 11:23 5927
return, and *c* toward the south .... Dan 11:29 935
of Chittim shall *c* against him .... Dan 11:30 935
the king of the north shall *c* .... Dan 11:40 8175
yet he shall *c* to his end .... Dan 11:45 935
it shall *c* to pass at that day .... Hos 1:5 1961
and it shall *c* to pass, that in .... Hos 1:10 1961
they shall *c* up out of the land .... Hos 1:11 5927
it shall *c* to pass in that day, I .... Hos 2:21 1961
c not ye unto Gilgal, neither go .... Hos 4:15 935
C, and let us return unto the LORD .... Hos 6:1 3212
he shall *c* unto us as the rain .... Hos 6:3 935
He shall *c* as an eagle against .... Hos 8:1
not *c* into the house of the LORD .... Hos 9:4 935
The days of visitation are *c* .... Hos 9:7 935
the days of recompence are *c* .... Hos 9:7 935
the thistle shall *c* up on their .... Hos 10:8 5927
time to seek the LORD, till he *c* .... Hos 10:12 935
travailing woman shall *c* upon him .... Hos 13:13 935
brethren, an east wind shall *c* .... Hos 13:15 935
shall *c* up from the wilderness .... Hos 13:15 5927
For a nation is *c* up upon my land .... Joel 1:6 5927
c, lie all night in sackcloth, ye .... Joel 1:13 935
from the Almighty shall it *c* .... Joel 1:15 935
sea, and his stink shall *c* up .... Joel 2:20 5927
and his ill savour shall *c* up .... Joel 2:20 5927
he will cause to *c* down for you .... Joel 2:23 3381
it shall *c* to pass afterward .... Joel 2:28 1961
and the terrible day of the LORD *c* .... Joel 2:31 935
And it shall *c* to pass, that .... Joel 2:32 1961
let them *c* up .... Joel 3:9 5927
Assemble yourselves, and *c* .... Joel 3:11 935
cause thy mighty ones to *c* down .... Joel 3:11 5181
c up to the valley of Jehoshaphat .... Joel 3:12 5927
c, get you down .... Joel 3:13 935
it shall *c* to pass in that day .... Joel 3:18 1961
a fountain shall *c* forth of the .... Joel 3:18 3318
lo, the days shall *c* upon you .... Amos 4:2 935
C to Beth-el, and transgress .... Amos 4:4 935
camps to *c* up unto your nostrils .... Amos 4:10 5927
and Beth-el shall *c* to nought .... Amos 5:5 1961
shall *c* against the fortress .... Amos 5:9 935
the seat of violence to *c* near .... Amos 6:3 5066
And it shall *c* to pass, if there .... Amos 6:9 1961
The end is *c* upon my people of .... Amos 8:2 935
it shall *c* to pass in that day .... Amos 8:9 1961
Behold, the days *c*, saith the .... Amos 8:11 935
Behold, the days *c*, saith the .... Amos 9:13 935
saviours shall *c* up on mount Zion .... Obad 21 5927
wickedness is *c* up before me .... Jonah 1:2 5927
said every one to his fellow, *C* .... Jonah 1:7 3212
made it to *c* up over Jonah, that .... Jonah 4:6 5927
out of his place, and will *c* down .... Mic 1:3 3381
for it is *c* unto Judah .... Mic 1:9 935
he is *c* unto the gate of my .... Mic 1:9 5060
he shall *c* unto Adullam the glory .... Mic 1:15 935
The breaker is *c* up before them .... Mic 2:13 5927
none evil can *c* upon us .... Mic 3:11 935
the last days it shall *c* to pass .... Mic 4:1 1961
And many nations shall *c*, and say .... Mic 4:2 1980
C, and let us go up .... Mic 4:2 3212
of Zion, unto thee shall it *c* .... Mic 4:8 857
the kingdom shall *c* to the .... Mic 4:8 935
yet out of thee shall he *c* forth .... Mic 5:2 3318
Assyrian shall *c* into our land .... Mic 5:5 935
it shall *c* to pass in that day .... Mic 5:10 1961
shall I *c* before the LORD .... Mic 6:6 6923
shall I *c* before him with burnt .... Mic 6:6 6923
shall *c* even to thee from Assyria .... Mic 7:12 935
There is one *c* out of thee .... Nah 1:11 3318
in pieces is *c* up before thy face .... Nah 2:1 5927
And it shall *c* to pass, that all .... Nah 3:7 1961
their horsemen shall *c* from far .... Hab 1:8 935
They shall *c* all for violence .... Hab 1:9 935
because it will surely *c*, it will .... Hab 2:3 935
it shall *c* to pass in the day of .... Zeph 1:8 1961
it shall *c* to pass in that day .... Zeph 1:10 1961
it shall *c* to pass at that time .... Zeph 1:12 1961
anger of the LORD *c* upon you .... Zeph 2:2 935
of the LORD's anger *c* upon you .... Zeph 2:2 935
people say, The time is not *c* .... Hag 1:2 935
the desire of all nations shall *c* .... Hag 2:7 935
and their riders shall *c* down .... Hag 2:22 3381
Then said I, What *c* these to do .... Zec 1:21 935
but these are *c* to fray them .... Zec 1:21 935
c forth, and flee from the land of .... Zec 2:6
for, lo, I *c*, and I will dwell in .... Zec 2:10 935
which are *c* from Babylon, and *c* .... Zec 6:10 935
And they that are far off shall *c* .... Zec 6:15 935
And this shall *c* to pass, if ye .... Zec 6:15 1961
Therefore it is *c* to pass .... Zec 7:13 1961
And it shall *c* to pass, that as ye .... Zec 8:13 1961

C

It shall yet c to pass	Zec 8:20	1961
that there shall c people	Zec 8:20	935
strong nations shall c to seek	Zec 8:22	935
In those days it shall c to pass	Zec 8:23	1961
forest of the vintage is c down	Zec 11:2	3381
it shall c to pass in that day,	Zec 12:9	1961
nations that c against Jerusalem	Zec 12:9	935
it shall c to pass in that day,	Zec 13:2	1961
And it shall c to pass, that when	Zec 13:3	1961
it shall c to pass in that day,	Zec 13:4	1961
And it shall c to pass, that in	Zec 13:8	1961
and the LORD my God shall c	Zec 14:5	935
it shall c to pass in that day,	Zec 14:6	1961
but it shall c to pass, that at	Zec 14:7	1961
it shall c to pass in that day,	Zec 14:13	1961
And it shall c to pass, that every	Zec 14:16	1961
that whoso will not c up of all	Zec 14:17	5927
up, and c not, that have no rain	Zec 14:18	935
c not up to keep the feast of	Zec 14:18	5927
c not up to keep the feast of	Zec 14:19	5927
all they that sacrifice shall c	Zec 14:21	935
shall suddenly c to his temple	Mal 3:1	935
behold, he shall c, saith the	Mal 3:1	935
I will c near to you to judgment	Mal 3:5	7126
to their fathers, lest I c	Mal 4:6	935
the east, and are c to worship him	Mt 2:2	2064
out of thee shall c a Governor	Mt 2:6	1831
bring me word again, that I may c	Mt 2:8	2064
when they were c into the house	Mt 2:11	2064
Sadducees c to his baptism, he	Mt 3:7	2064
you to flee from the wrath to c	Mt 3:7	3195
that I am c to destroy the law	Mt 5:17	2064
I am not c to destroy, but to	Mt 5:17	2064
to thy brother, and then c	Mt 5:24	2064
shalt by no means c out thence	Mt 5:26	1831
Thy kingdom c	Mt 6:10	2064
which c to you in sheep's	Mt 7:15	2064
When he was c down from the	Mt 8:1	2597
And Jesus saith unto him, I will c	Mt 8:7	2064
thou shouldest c under my roof	Mt 8:8	1525
and to another, C, and he cometh	Mt 8:9	2064
That many shall c from the east	Mt 8:11	2240
when Jesus was c into Peter's	Mt 8:14	2064
When the even was c, they brought	Mt 8:16	1096
when he was c to the other side	Mt 8:28	2064
art thou c hither to torment us	Mt 8:29	2064
And when they were c out, they	Mt 8:32	1831
for I am not c to call the	Mt 9:13	2064
but the days will c, when the	Mt 9:15	2064
but c and lay thy hand upon her,	Mt 9:18	2064
when he was c into the house, the	Mt 9:28	2064
when ye c into an house, salute	Mt 10:12	1525
worthy, let your peace c upon it	Mt 10:13	2064
Israel, till the Son of man be c	Mt 10:23	2064
Think not that I am c to send	Mt 10:34	2064
For I am c to set a man at	Mt 10:35	2064
him, Art thou he that should c	Mt 11:3	2064
this is Elias, which was for to c	Mt 11:14	2064
C unto me, all ye that labour and	Mt 11:28	1205
the kingdom of God is c unto you	Mt 12:28	5348
world, neither in the world to c	Mt 12:32	3195
and when he is c, he findeth it	Mt 12:44	2064
so that the birds of the air c	Mt 13:32	2064
the angels shall c forth, and	Mt 13:49	1831
when he was c into his own	Mt 13:54	2064
and when the evening was c	Mt 14:23	1096
bid me c unto thee on the water	Mt 14:28	2064
And he said, C	Mt 14:29	2064
when Peter was c down out of the	Mt 14:29	2597
And when they were c into the ship	Mt 14:32	1684
the mouth c forth from the heart	Mt 15:18	1831
were c to the other side, they	Mt 16:5	2064
If any man will c after me	Mt 16:24	2064
For the Son of man shall c in the	Mt 16:27	2064
scribes that Elias must first c	Mt 17:10	2064
them, Elias truly shall first c	Mt 17:11	2064
unto you, That Elias is c already	Mt 17:12	2064
when they were c to the multitude	Mt 17:14	2064
And when they were c to Capernaum	Mt 17:24	2064
when he was c into the house,	Mt 17:25	1525
it must needs be that offences c	Mt 18:7	2064
For the Son of man is c to save	Mt 18:11	2064
and forbid them not, to c unto me	Mt 19:14	2064
and c and follow me	Mt 19:21	1204
So when even was c, the lord of	Mt 20:8	1096
were c to Bethphage, unto the	Mt 21:1	2064
when he was c into Jerusalem, all	Mt 21:10	1525
when he was c into the temple,	Mt 21:23	2064
c, let us kill him, and let us	Mt 21:38	1205
and they would not c	Mt 22:3	2064
c unto the marriage	Mt 22:4	1205
That upon you may c all the	Mt 23:35	2064
shall c upon this generation	Mt 23:36	2240
For many shall c in my name	Mt 24:5	2064
all these things must c to pass	Mt 24:6	1096
and then shall the end c	Mt 24:14	2240
which is on the housetop not c	Mt 24:17	2597
not what hour your Lord doth c	Mt 24:42	2064
in what watch the thief would c	Mt 24:43	2064
c in a day when he looketh not	Mt 24:50	2240
Son of man shall c in his glory	Mt 25:31	2064
unto them on his right hand, C	Mt 25:34	1205
Now when the even was c, he sat	Mt 26:20	1096
him, Friend, wherefore art thou c	Mt 26:50	3918
Are ye c out as against a thief	Mt 26:55	1831
When the morning was c, all the	Mt 27:1	1096
when they were c unto a place	Mt 27:33	2064
Son of God, c down from the cross	Mt 27:40	2597
let him now c down from the cross	Mt 27:42	2597
whether Elias will c to save him	Mt 27:49	2064
When the even was c, there came a	Mt 27:57	1096
lest his disciples c by night	Mt 27:64	2064
C, see the place where the Lord	Mt 28:6	1205
if this c to the governor's ears,	Mt 28:14	191
C ye after me, and I will make you	Mk 1:17	1205
art thou c to destroy us	Mk 1:24	2064
Hold thy peace, and c out of him	Mk 1:25	1831
when they were c out of the	Mk 1:29	1831
they c unto him, bringing one	Mk 2:3	2064
when they could not c nigh unto	Mk 2:4	4331
and they c and say unto him, Why do	Mk 2:18	2064
But the days will c, when the	Mk 2:20	2064
but that it should c abroad	Mk 4:22	2064
sickle, because the harvest is c	Mk 4:29	3936
the same day, when the even was c	Mk 4:35	1096
when he was c out of the ship,	Mk 5:2	1831
C out of the man, thou unclean	Mk 5:8	1831
they c to Jesus, and see him that	Mk 5:15	2064
when he was c into the ship, he	Mk 5:18	1684
I pray thee, c and lay thy hands	Mk 5:23	2064
And when he was c in, he saith	Mk 5:39	1525
And when the sabbath day was c	Mk 6:2	1096
And when a convenient day was c	Mk 6:21	1096
C ye yourselves apart into a	Mk 6:31	1205
And when even was c, the ship was	Mk 6:47	1096
when they were c out of the ship,	Mk 6:54	1831
when they c from the market,	Mk 7:4	
but the things which c out of him	Mk 7:15	1607
these evil things c from within	Mk 7:23	1607
And when she was c to her house	Mk 7:30	565
them, Whosoever will c after me	Mk 8:34	2064
the kingdom of God c with power	Mk 9:1	2064
scribes that Elias must first c	Mk 9:11	2064
unto you, That Elias is indeed c	Mk 9:13	2064
c out of him, and enter no more	Mk 9:25	1831
when he was c into the house, his	Mk 9:28	1525
This kind can c forth by nothing,	Mk 9:29	1831
the little children to c unto me	Mk 10:14	2064
and c, take up the cross, and	Mk 10:21	1204
and in the world to c eternal life	Mk 10:30	2064
c unto him, saying, Master, we	Mk 10:35	4365
things, and now the eventide was c	Mk 11:11	1511
when they were c from Bethany	Mk 11:12	1831
And they c to Jerusalem	Mk 11:15	2064
And when even was c, he went out	Mk 11:19	1096
which he saith shall c to pass	Mk 11:23	1096
they c again to Jerusalem	Mk 11:27	2064
there c to him the chief priests,	Mk 11:27	2064
c, let us kill him, and the	Mk 12:7	1205
he will c and destroy the	Mk 12:9	2064
And when they were c, they say	Mk 12:14	2064
Then c unto him the Sadducees,	Mk 12:18	2064
For many shall c in my name	Mk 13:6	2064
shall see these things c to pass	Mk 13:29	1096
she is c aforehand to anoint my	Mk 14:8	4301
it is enough, the hour is c	Mk 14:41	2064
And as soon as he was c, he goeth	Mk 14:45	2064
and said unto them, Are ye c out	Mk 14:48	1831
thyself, and c down from the cross	Mk 15:30	2597
And when the sixth hour was c	Mk 15:33	1096
Elias will c to take him down	Mk 15:36	2064
And now when the even was c	Mk 15:42	1096
sweet spices, that they might c	Mk 16:1	2064
The Holy Ghost shall c upon thee	Lk 1:35	1904
mother of my Lord should c to me	Lk 1:43	2064
see this thing which is c to pass	Lk 2:15	1096
you to flee from the wrath to c	Lk 3:7	3195
art thou c to destroy us	Lk 4:34	2064
Hold thy peace, and c out of him	Lk 4:35	1831
unclean spirits, and they c out	Lk 4:36	1831
other ship, that they should c	Lk 5:7	2064
which were c out of every town of	Lk 5:17	2064
But the days will c, when the	Lk 5:35	2064
beseeching him that he would c	Lk 7:3	2064
I myself worthy to c unto thee	Lk 7:7	2064
and to another, C, and he cometh	Lk 7:8	2064
saying, Art thou he that should c	Lk 7:19	2064
When the men were c unto him	Lk 7:20	3854
saying, Art thou he that should c	Lk 7:20	2064
The Son of man is c eating	Lk 7:34	2064
were c to him out of every city,	Lk 8:4	1975
shall not be known and c abroad	Lk 8:17	2064
could not c at him for the press	Lk 8:19	4940
spirit to c out of the man	Lk 8:29	1831
that he would c into his house	Lk 8:41	1525
all, If any man will c after me	Lk 9:23	2064
when he shall c in his own glory,	Lk 9:26	2064
when they were c down from the	Lk 9:37	2718
when the time was c that he	Lk 9:51	4845
fire to c down from heaven	Lk 9:54	2597
is not c to destroy men's lives	Lk 9:56	2064
place, whither he himself would c	Lk 10:1	2064
kingdom of God is c nigh unto you	Lk 10:9	1448
kingdom of God is c nigh unto you	Lk 10:11	1448
spendest more, when I c again	Lk 10:35	1880
Thy kingdom c	Lk 11:2	2064
of mine in his journey is c to me	Lk 11:6	3854
the kingdom of God is c upon you	Lk 11:20	5348
stronger than he shall c upon him	Lk 11:22	1904
that they which c in may see the	Lk 11:33	1531
will c forth and serve them	Lk 12:37	3928
if he shall c in the second watch	Lk 12:38	2064
or c in the third watch, and find	Lk 12:38	2064
known what hour the thief would c	Lk 12:39	2064
c in a day when he looketh not	Lk 12:46	2240
I am c to send fire on the earth	Lk 12:49	2064
Suppose ye that I am c to give	Lk 12:51	3854
these three years I c seeking	Lk 13:7	2064
in them therefore c and be healed,	Lk 13:14	2064
they shall c from the east, and	Lk 13:29	2240
until the time c when ye shall	Lk 13:35	2240
And he that bade thee and him c	Lk 14:9	2064
say to them that were bidden, C	Lk 14:17	2064
a wife, and therefore I cannot c	Lk 14:20	2064
and hedges, and compel them to c in	Lk 14:23	1525
If any man c to me, and hate not	Lk 14:26	2064
c after me, cannot be my disciple	Lk 14:27	2064
said unto him, Thy brother is c	Lk 15:27	2240
But as soon as this thy son was c	Lk 15:30	2064
to us, that would c from thence	Lk 16:26	
lest they also c into this place	Lk 16:28	2064
but that offences will c	Lk 17:1	2064
woe unto him, through whom they c	Lk 17:1	2064
when he is c from the field, Go	Lk 17:7	1525
when the kingdom of God should c	Lk 17:20	2064
the disciples, The days will c	Lk 17:22	2064
let him not c down to take it	Lk 17:31	2597
little children to c unto me	Lk 18:16	2064
and c, follow me	Lk 18:22	1204
time, and in the world to c life	Lk 18:30	2064
that as he was c nigh unto	Lk 18:35	1448
and when he was c near, he asked	Lk 18:40	1448
Zacchaeus, make haste, and c down	Lk 19:5	2597
day is salvation c to this house	Lk 19:9	1096
For the Son of man is c to seek	Lk 19:10	2064
said unto them, Occupy till I c	Lk 19:13	2064
when he was c nigh to Bethphage	Lk 19:29	1448
And when he was c nigh, even now	Lk 19:37	1448
And when he was c near, he beheld	Lk 19:41	1448
For the days shall c upon thee	Lk 19:43	2240
c, let us kill him, that the	Lk 20:14	1205
He shall c and destroy these	Lk 20:16	2064
which ye behold, the days will c	Lk 21:6	2064
when these things shall c to pass	Lk 21:7	1096
for many shall c in my name	Lk 21:8	2064
these things must first c to pass	Lk 21:9	1096
these things begin to c to pass	Lk 21:28	1096
ye see these things c to pass	Lk 21:31	1096
so that day c upon you unawares	Lk 21:34	2186
For as a snare shall it c on all	Lk 21:35	1904
these things that shall c to pass	Lk 21:36	1096
And when the hour was c, he sat	Lk 22:14	1096
until the kingdom of God shall c	Lk 22:18	2064
was c to his disciples, he found	Lk 22:45	2064
the elders, which were c to him	Lk 22:52	3854
Be ye c out	Lk 22:52	1831
And when they were c to the place	Lk 23:33	565
at that which was c to pass	Lk 24:12	1096
are c to pass there in these days	Lk 24:18	1096
therefore am I c baptizing with	Jn 1:31	2064
He saith unto them, C and see	Jn 1:39	2064
any good thing c out of Nazareth	Jn 1:46	1511
Philip saith unto him, C and see	Jn 1:46	2064
mine hour is not yet c	Jn 2:4	2240
thou art a teacher c from God	Jn 3:2	2064
that light is c into the world,	Jn 3:19	2064
baptizeth, and all men c to him	Jn 3:26	2064
not, neither c hither to draw	Jn 4:15	2064
Go, call thy husband, and c hither	Jn 4:16	2064
when he is c, he will tell us all	Jn 4:25	2064
C, see a man, which told me all	Jn 4:29	1205
the Samaritans were c unto him	Jn 4:40	2064
Then when he was c into Galilee	Jn 4:45	2064
was c out of Judaea into Galilee	Jn 4:47	2240
besought him that he would c down	Jn 4:47	2597
him, Sir, c down ere my child die	Jn 4:49	2597
when he was c out of Judaea into	Jn 4:54	2064
lest a worse thing c unto thee	Jn 5:14	1096
shall not c into condemnation	Jn 5:24	2064
And shall c forth	Jn 5:29	1607
And ye will not c to me, that ye	Jn 5:40	2064
I am c in my Father's name, and ye	Jn 5:43	2064
another shall c in his own name	Jn 5:43	2064
and saw a great company c unto him	Jn 6:5	2064
that should c into the world	Jn 6:14	2064
perceived that they would c	Jn 6:15	2064
And when even was now c, his	Jn 6:16	1096
dark, and Jesus was not c to them	Jn 6:17	2064
Father giveth me shall c to me	Jn 6:37	2240
No man can c to me, except the	Jn 6:44	2064
you, that no man can c unto me	Jn 6:65	2064
unto them, My time is not yet c	Jn 7:6	3918
for my time is not yet full c	Jn 7:8	4137
I am not c of myself, but he that	Jn 7:28	2064
because his hour was not yet c	Jn 7:30	2064
where I am, thither ye cannot c	Jn 7:34	2064
where I am, thither ye cannot c	Jn 7:36	2064
any man thirst, let him c unto me	Jn 7:37	2064
Shall Christ c out of Galilee	Jn 7:41	2064
but ye cannot tell whence I c	Jn 8:14	2064
for his hour was not yet c	Jn 8:20	2064
whither I go, ye cannot c	Jn 8:21	2064
saith, Whither I go, ye cannot c	Jn 8:22	2064
judgment I am c into this world	Jn 9:39	2064
I am c that they might have life,	Jn 10:10	2064
which should c into the world	Jn 11:27	2064
secretly, saying, The Master is c	Jn 11:28	3918
Jesus was not yet c into the town	Jn 11:30	2064
when Mary was c where Jesus was	Jn 11:32	2064
They said unto him, Lord, c	Jn 11:34	2064
a loud voice, Lazarus, c forth	Jn 11:43	1204
and the Romans shall c and take	Jn 11:48	2064
that he will not c to the feast	Jn 11:56	2064
people that were c to the feast	Jn 12:12	2064

Context	Reference	Strong's
them, saying, The hour is c	Jn 12:23	2064
light, lest darkness c upon you	Jn 12:35	2638
I am c a light into the world,	Jn 12:46	2064
c that he should depart out of	Jn 13:1	2064
hands, and that he was c from God	Jn 13:3	1831
c, that, when it is c to pass	Jn 13:19	1096
Jews, Whither I go, ye cannot c	Jn 13:33	2064
a place for you, I will c again	Jn 14:3	2064
I will c to you	Jn 14:18	2064
we will c unto him, and make our	Jn 14:23	2064
I go away, and c again unto you	Jn 14:28	2064
have told you before it c to pass	Jn 14:29	1096
that, when it is c to pass	Jn 14:29	1096
If I had not c and spoken unto	Jn 15:22	2064
But when the Comforter is c	Jn 15:26	2064
you, that when the time shall c	Jn 16:4	2064
the Comforter will not c unto you	Jn 16:7	2064
And when he is c, he will reprove	Jn 16:8	2064
he, the Spirit of truth, is c	Jn 16:13	2064
and he will shew you things to c	Jn 16:13	2064
sorrow, because her hour is c	Jn 16:21	2064
Father, and am c into the world	Jn 16:28	2064
the hour cometh, yea, is now c	Jn 16:32	2064
and said, Father, the hour is c	Jn 17:1	2064
are in the world, and I c to thee	Jn 17:11	2064
And now c I to thee	Jn 17:13	2064
all things that should c upon him	Jn 18:4	2064
But when the morning was now c	Jn 21:4	1096
soon then as they were c to land	Jn 21:9	576
Jesus saith unto them, C and dine	Jn 21:12	1205
If I will that he tarry till I c	Jn 21:22	2064
If I will that he tarry till I c	Jn 21:23	2064
they therefore were c together	Acts 1:6	4905
that the Holy Ghost is c upon you	Acts 1:8	1904
shall so c in like manner as ye	Acts 1:11	2064
And when they were c in, they went	Acts 1:13	1525
the day of Pentecost was fully c	Acts 2:1	4845
it shall c to pass in the last	Acts 2:17	1511
and notable day of the Lord c	Acts 2:20	2064
And it shall c to pass, that	Acts 2:21	1511
c from the presence of the Lord	Acts 3:19	2064
And it shall c to pass, that every	Acts 3:23	1511
be of men, it will c to nought	Acts 5:38	2647
c into the land which I shall	Acts 7:3	1204
and after that shall they c forth	Acts 7:7	1834
am c down to deliver them	Acts 7:34	2597
And now c, I will send thee into	Acts 7:34	1204
Who, when they were c down	Acts 8:15	2597
which ye have spoken c upon me	Acts 8:24	1904
had c to Jerusalem for to worship	Acts 8:27	2064
desired Philip that he would c up	Acts 8:31	305
when they were c up out of the	Acts 8:39	305
And when Saul was c to Jerusalem	Acts 9:26	3854
he would not delay to c to them	Acts 9:38	1330
When he was c, they brought him	Acts 9:39	3854
thine alms are c up for a	Acts 10:4	305
is the cause wherefore ye are c	Acts 10:21	3918
found many that were c together	Acts 10:27	4905
or c unto one of another nation	Acts 10:28	4334
hast well done that thou art c	Acts 10:33	3854
when Peter was c up to Jerusalem,	Acts 11:2	305
c unto the house where I was	Acts 11:11	2186
when they were c to Antioch	Acts 11:20	1525
And when Peter was c to himself	Acts 12:11	1096
therefore, lest that c upon you	Acts 13:40	1904
The gods are c down to us in the	Acts 14:11	2597
And when they were c, and had	Acts 14:27	3854
And when they were c to Jerusalem	Acts 15:4	3854
After they were c to Mysia	Acts 16:7	2064
C over into Macedonia, and help us	Acts 16:9	1224
c into my house, and abide there	Acts 16:15	1525
of Jesus Christ to c out of her	Acts 16:18	1831
but let them c themselves	Acts 16:37	2064
upside down are c hither also	Acts 17:6	3918
Timotheus for to c to him with	Acts 17:15	2064
lately c from Italy, with his	Acts 18:2	2064
Timotheus were c from Macedonia	Acts 18:5	2718
who, when he was c, helped them	Acts 18:27	3854
on him which should c after him	Acts 19:4	2064
wherefore they were c together	Acts 19:32	4905
When he therefore was c up again	Acts 20:11	305
And when they were c to him	Acts 20:18	3854
And when he was c unto us, he took	Acts 21:11	2064
And when we were c to Jerusalem	Acts 21:17	1096
multitude must needs c together	Acts 21:22	4905
they will hear that thou art c	Acts 21:22	2064
was c nigh unto Damascus about	Acts 22:6	1448
when I was c again to Jerusalem,	Acts 22:17	5290
and we, or ever he c near, are	Acts 23:15	1448
when thine accusers are also c	Acts 23:35	3854
his accusers to c unto thee	Acts 24:8	2064
the chief captain shall c down	Acts 24:22	2597
to minister or c unto him	Acts 24:23	4334
temperance, and judgment to c	Acts 24:25	1511
Festus was c into the province	Acts 25:1	1910
And when he was c, the Jews which	Acts 25:7	3854
when they were c hither, without	Acts 25:17	4905
on the morrow, when Agrippa was c	Acts 25:23	2064
God day and night, hope to c	Acts 26:7	2658
and Moses did say should c	Acts 26:22	1096
scarce were c over against Cnidus	Acts 27:7	1096
we had much work to c by the boat	Acts 27:16	1096
when the fourteenth night was c	Acts 27:27	1096
while, and saw no harm c to him	Acts 28:6	1096
and when they were c together	Acts 28:17	4905
by the will of God to c unto you	Rom 1:10	2064
I purposed to c unto you, (but	Rom 1:13	2064
Let us do evil, that good may c	Rom 3:8	2064
c short of the glory of God	Rom 3:23	5302
the figure of him that was to c	Rom 5:14	3195
things present, nor things to c	Rom 8:38	3195
of promise, At this time will I c	Rom 9:9	2064
And it shall c to pass, that in	Rom 9:26	1511
salvation is c unto the Gentiles	Rom 11:11	
fulness of the Gentiles be c in	Rom 11:25	1525
There shall c out of Sion the	Rom 11:26	2240
these many years to c unto you	Rom 15:23	2064
into Spain, I will c to you	Rom 15:24	2064
I will c by you into Spain	Rom 15:28	565
when I c unto you, I shall c	Rom 15:29	2064
That I may c unto you with joy by	Rom 15:32	2064
is c abroad unto all men	Rom 16:19	864
So that ye c behind in no gift	1Cor 1:7	5302
of this world, that c to nought	1Cor 2:6	2673
or things present, or things to c	1Cor 3:22	3195
before the time, until the Lord c	1Cor 4:5	2064
as though I would not c to you	1Cor 4:18	2064
But I will c to you shortly, if	1Cor 4:19	2064
shall I c unto you with a rod, or	1Cor 4:21	2064
c together again, that Satan	1Cor 7:5	4905
whom the ends of the world are c	1Cor 10:11	2658
that ye c together not for the	1Cor 11:17	4905
when ye c together in the church,	1Cor 11:18	4905
When ye c together therefore into	1Cor 11:20	4905
shew the Lord's death till he c	1Cor 11:26	2064
when ye c together to eat, tarry	1Cor 11:33	4905
that ye c not together unto	1Cor 11:34	4905
rest will I set in order when I c	1Cor 11:34	2064
when that which is perfect is c	1Cor 13:10	2064
if I c unto you speaking with	1Cor 14:6	2064
be c together into one place	1Cor 14:23	4905
there c in those that are	1Cor 14:23	1525
there c in one that believeth not	1Cor 14:24	1525
when ye c together, every one of	1Cor 14:26	4905
and with what body do they c	1Cor 15:35	2064
there be no gatherings when I c	1Cor 16:2	2064
And when I c, whomsoever ye shall	1Cor 16:3	3854
Now I will c unto you, when I	1Cor 16:5	2064
Now if Timotheus c, see that he	1Cor 16:10	2064
in peace, that he may c unto me	1Cor 16:11	2064
I greatly desired him to c unto	1Cor 16:12	2064
was not at all to c at this time	1Cor 16:12	2064
but he will c when he shall have	1Cor 16:12	2064
I was minded to c unto you before	2Cor 1:15	2064
to c again out of Macedonia unto	2Cor 1:16	2064
that I would not c again to you	2Cor 2:1	2064
Wherefore c out from among them,	2Cor 6:17	1831
when we were c into Macedonia,	2Cor 7:5	2064
if they of Macedonia c with me	2Cor 9:4	2064
for we are c as far as to you	2Cor 10:14	5348
I will c to visions and	2Cor 12:1	2064
third time I am ready to c to you	2Cor 12:14	2064
For I fear, lest, when I c	2Cor 12:20	2064
And lest, when I c again, my God	2Cor 12:21	2064
if I c again, I will not spare	2Cor 13:2	2064
But when Peter was c to Antioch	Gal 2:11	2064
but when they were c, he withdrew	Gal 2:12	2064
for if righteousness c by the law	Gal 2:21	
c on the Gentiles through Jesus	Gal 3:14	1096
till the seed should c to whom	Gal 3:19	2064
But after that faith is c	Gal 3:25	2064
the fulness of the time was c	Gal 4:4	2064
but also in that which is to c	Eph 1:21	3195
That in the ages to c he might	Eph 2:7	1904
Till we all c in the unity of the	Eph 4:13	2658
that whether I c and see you, or	Phil 1:27	2064
I also myself shall c shortly	Phil 2:24	2064
Which is c unto you, as it is in	Col 1:6	3918
Which are a shadow of things to c	Col 2:17	3195
if he c unto you, receive him	Col 4:10	2064
delivered us from the wrath to c	1Th 1:10	2064
for the wrath is c upon them to	1Th 2:16	5348
we would have c unto you, even I	1Th 2:18	2064
When he shall c to be glorified	2Th 1:10	2064
for that day shall not c	2Th 2:3	2064
except there c a falling away	2Th 2:3	2064
to c unto the knowledge of the	1Ti 2:4	2064
hoping to c unto thee shortly	1Ti 3:14	2064
now is, and of that which is to c	1Ti 4:8	3195
Till I c, give attendance to	1Ti 4:13	2064
foundation against the time to c	1Ti 6:19	3195
last days perilous times shall c	2Ti 3:1	1764
never able to c to the knowledge	2Ti 3:7	2064
For the time will c when they	2Ti 4:3	1511
diligence to c shortly unto me	2Ti 4:9	2064
thy diligence to c before winter	2Ti 4:21	2064
be diligent to c unto me to	Titus 3:12	2064
put in subjection the world to c	Heb 2:5	3195
you should seem to c short of it	Heb 4:1	5302
Let us therefore c boldly unto	Heb 4:16	4334
and the powers of the world to c	Heb 6:5	3195
though they c out of the loins of	Heb 7:5	1831
uttermost that c unto God by him	Heb 7:25	4334
he saith, Behold, the days c	Heb 8:8	2064
But Christ being c an high priest	Heb 9:11	3854
high priest of good things to c	Heb 9:11	3195
a shadow of good things to c	Heb 10:1	3195
I c (in the volume of the book it	Heb 10:7	2240
I c to do thy will, O God	Heb 10:9	2240
and he that shall c	Heb 10:37	2064
will c, and will not tarry	Heb 10:37	2240
and Esau concerning things to c	Heb 11:20	3195
Moses, when he was c to years	Heb 11:24	1096
For ye are not c unto the mount	Heb 12:18	4334
But ye are c unto mount Sion, and	Heb 12:22	4334
city, but we seek one to c	Heb 13:14	3195
if he c shortly, I will see you	Heb 13:23	2064
For if there c unto your assembly	Jas 2:2	1525
there c in also a poor man in	Jas 2:2	1525
From whence c wars and fightings	Jas 4:1	4159
c they not hence, even of your	Jas 4:1	1782
miseries that shall c upon you	Jas 5:1	1904
the grace that should c unto you	1Pet 1:10	
For the time is c that judgment	1Pet 4:17	
that there shall c in the last	2Pet 3:3	2064
that all should c to repentance	2Pet 3:9	5562
will c as a thief in the night	2Pet 3:10	2240
heard that antichrist shall c	1Jn 2:18	2064
is c in the flesh is of God	1Jn 4:2	2064
not that Jesus Christ is c in the	1Jn 4:3	2064
ye have heard that it should c	1Jn 4:3	2064
we know that the Son of God is c	1Jn 5:20	2240
Jesus Christ is c in the flesh	2Jn 7	2064
If there c any unto you, and bring	2Jn 10	2064
but I trust to c unto you	2Jn 12	2064
Wherefore, if I c, I will	3Jn 10	2064
which must shortly c to pass	Rev 1:1	1096
and which was, and which is to c	Rev 1:4	2064
and which was, and which is to c	Rev 1:8	2064
or else I will c unto thee	Rev 2:5	2064
or else I will c unto thee	Rev 2:16	2064
have already hold fast till I c	Rev 2:25	2240
I will c on thee as a thief, and	Rev 3:3	2240
know what hour I will c upon thee	Rev 3:3	2240
behold, I will make them to c	Rev 3:9	2240
which shall c upon all the world,	Rev 3:10	2064
Behold, I c quickly	Rev 3:11	2064
I will c in to him, and will sup	Rev 3:20	1525
C up hither, and I will shew thee	Rev 4:1	305
which was, and is, and is to c	Rev 4:8	2064
one of the four beasts saying, C	Rev 6:1	2064
I heard the second beast say, C	Rev 6:3	2064
I heard the third beast say, C	Rev 6:5	2064
voice of the fourth beast say, C	Rev 6:7	2064
the great day of his wrath is c	Rev 6:17	2064
there c two woes more hereafter	Rev 9:12	2064
mighty angel c down from heaven	Rev 10:1	2597
saying unto them, C up hither	Rev 11:12	305
which art, and wast, and art to c	Rev 11:17	2064
were angry, and thy wrath is c	Rev 11:18	2064
Now is c salvation, and strength,	Rev 12:10	1096
for the devil is c down unto you	Rev 12:12	2597
so that he maketh fire c down	Rev 13:13	2597
for the hour of his judgment is c	Rev 14:7	2064
for the time is c for thee to	Rev 14:15	2064
for all nations shall c and	Rev 15:4	2240
unclean spirits like frogs c out	Rev 16:13	
Behold, I c as a thief	Rev 16:15	2064
with me, saying unto me, C hither	Rev 17:1	1204
one is, and the other is not yet c	Rev 17:10	2064
another angel c down from heaven	Rev 18:1	2597
C out of her, my people, that ye	Rev 18:4	1831
shall her plagues c in one day	Rev 18:8	2240
for in one hour is thy judgment c	Rev 18:10	2064
so great riches is c to nought	Rev 18:17	2049
for the marriage of the Lamb is c	Rev 19:7	2064
fly in the midst of heaven, C	Rev 19:17	1205
I saw an angel c down from heaven	Rev 20:1	2597
C hither, I will shew thee the	Rev 21:9	1204
Behold, I c quickly	Rev 22:7	2064
And, behold, I c quickly	Rev 22:12	2064
And the Spirit and the bride say, C	Rev 22:17	2064
And let him that heareth say, C	Rev 22:17	2064
And let him that is athirst c	Rev 22:17	2064
things saith, Surely I c quickly	Rev 22:20	2064
Even so, c, Lord Jesus	Rev 22:20	2064

COMELINESS {5}

Context	Reference	Strong's
he hath no form nor c	Is 53:2	1926
for it was perfect through my c	Eze 16:14	1926
they set forth thy c	Eze 27:10	1926
for my c was turned in me into	Dan 10:8	1935
parts have more abundant c	1Cor 12:23	2157

COMELY {16}

Context	Reference	Strong's
a c person, and the LORD is with	1Sa 16:18	8389
his power, nor his c proportion	Job 41:12	2433
for praise is c for the upright	Ps 33:1	5000
and praise is c	Ps 147:1	5000
go well, yea, four are c in going	Prov 30:29	3190
c for one to eat and to drink, and	Eccl 5:18	3303
I am black, but c, O ye daughters	Song 1:5	5000
Thy cheeks are c with rows of	Song 1:10	4998
voice, and thy countenance is c	Song 2:14	5000
of scarlet, and thy speech is c	Song 4:3	5000
c as Jerusalem, terrible as an	Song 6:4	5000
c for them that are escaped of	Is 4:2	8597
the daughter of Zion to a c	Jer 6:2	5000
upon you, but for that which is c	1Cor 7:35	2158
is it c that a woman pray unto	1Cor 11:13	4241
For our c parts have no need	1Cor 12:24	2158

COMERS {1}

Context	Reference	Strong's
make the c thereunto perfect	Heb 10:1	4334

COMEST {29}

Context	Reference	Strong's
as thou c to Gerar, unto Gaza	Gen 10:19	935
of Egypt, as thou c unto Zoar	Gen 13:10	935
when thou c to my kindred	Gen 24:41	935
when thou c nigh over against the	Deut 2:19	7126
When thou c nigh unto a city to	Deut 20:10	7126
When thou c into thy neighbour's	Deut 23:24	935
When thou c into the standing	Deut 23:25	935
shalt thou be when thou c in	Deut 28:6	935
shalt thou be when thou c in	Deut 28:19	935

said unto him, Whence c thou ... Judg 17:9 935
that thou c with such a company ... Judg 18:23 2199
and whence c thou ... Judg 19:17 935
from Havilah until thou c to Shur ... 1Sa 15:7 935
coming, and said, C thou peaceably ... 1Sa 16:4 935
that thou c to me with staves ... 1Sa 17:43 935
Thou c to me with a sword, and ... 1Sa 17:45 935
said unto him, From whence c thou ... 2Sa 1:3 935
when thou c to see my face ... 2Sa 3:13 935
And she said, C thou peaceably ... 1Kin 2:13 935
and when thou c, anoint Hazael to ... 1Kin 19:15 935
said unto him, Whence c thou ... 2Kin 5:25 935
And when thou c thither, look out ... 2Kin 9:2 935
said unto Satan, Whence c thou ... Job 1:7 935
unto Satan, From whence c thou ... Job 2:2 935
When thou c to Babylon, and shalt ... Jer 51:61 935
and whence c thou ... Jonah 1:8 935
baptized of thee, and c thou to me ... Mt 3:14 *2064*
me when thou c into thy kingdom ... Lk 23:42 *2064*
at Troas with Carpus, when thou c ... 2Ti 4:13 *2064*

COMETH {282}

the virgin c forth to draw water ... Gen 24:43 3318
his daughter c with the sheep ... Gen 29:6 935
And Leah said, A troop c ... Gen 30:11 935
also he c to meet thee, and four ... Gen 32:6 1980
another, Behold, this dreamer c ... Gen 37:19 935
thy son Joseph c unto thee ... Gen 48:2 935
behold, he c forth to meet thee ... Ex 4:14 3318
lo, he c forth to the water ... Ex 8:20 3318
every firstling that c of a beast ... Ex 13:12 7698
before the LORD, and when he c out ... Ex 28:35 3318
when he c into the tabernacle of ... Ex 29:30 935
such water c shall be unclean ... Lev 11:34 935
the stranger that c nigh shall be ... Num 1:51 7131
the stranger that c nigh shall be ... Num 3:10 7131
the stranger that c nigh shall be ... Num 3:38 7131
the spirit of jealousy c upon him ... Num 5:30 5674
he c out of his mother's womb ... Num 12:12 3318
Whosoever c any thing near unto ... Num 17:13 7131
the stranger that c nigh shall be ... Num 18:7 7131
that c out of the coasts of the ... Num 21:13 3318
of whom c the family of the ... Num 26:5
beside that which c of the sale ... Deut 18:8 4480
it shall be, when evening c on ... Deut 23:11 6437
and cover that which c from thee ... Deut 23:13 6627
that c out from between her feet ... Deut 28:57 3318
that whatsoever c forth of the ... Judg 11:31 3318
of any thing that c of the vine ... Judg 13:14 3318
when it c among us, it may save ... 1Sa 4:3 935
that he saith c surely to pass ... 1Sa 9:6 935
Whosoever c not forth after Saul ... 1Sa 11:7 3318
Wherefore c not the son of Jesse ... 1Sa 20:27 935
Therefore he c not unto the ... 1Sa 20:29 935
whatsoever c to thine hand unto ... 1Sa 25:8 4672
And she said, An old man c up ... 1Sa 28:14 5927
and when thy father c to see thee ... 2Sa 13:5 935
good man, and c with good tidings ... 2Sa 18:27 935
but c out of a far country for ... 1Kin 8:41 935
the wife of Jeroboam c to ask a ... 1Kin 14:5 935
for it shall be, when she c in ... 1Kin 14:5 935
and it shall be, when he c to us ... 2Kin 4:10 935
look, when the messenger c ... 2Kin 6:32 935
came to them, but he c not again ... 2Kin 9:18 7725
even unto them, and c not again ... 2Kin 9:20 7725
as soon as this letter c to you ... 2Kin 10:2 935
he that c within the ranges, let ... 2Kin 11:8 935
as he goeth out and as he c in ... 2Kin 11:8 935
all the money that c into any ... 2Kin 12:4 5927
on the right side as one c into ... 2Kin 12:9 935
because he c to judge the earth ... 1Chr 16:33 935
thine holy name c of thine hand ... 1Chr 29:16 4480
so that whosoever c to consecrate ... 2Chr 13:9 935
There c a great multitude against ... 2Chr 20:2 935
If, when evil c upon us, as the ... 2Chr 20:9 935
great company that c against us ... 2Chr 20:12 935
whosoever else c into the house ... 2Chr 23:7 935
be ye with the king when he c in ... 2Chr 23:7 935
long for death, but it c not ... Job 3:21 369
For my sighing c before I eat ... Job 3:24 935
Although affliction c not forth ... Job 5:6 3318
afraid of destruction when it c ... Job 5:21 935
shock of corn c in in his season ... Job 5:26 5927
He c forth like a flower, and is ... Job 14:2 3318
the mountain falling c to nought ... Job 14:18 5034
It is drawn, and c out of the body ... Job 20:25 3318
sword c out of his gall ... Job 20:25 1980
how oft c their destruction upon ... Job 21:17 935
his cry when trouble c upon him ... Job 27:9 935
for the earth, out of it c bread ... Job 28:5 3318
Whence then c wisdom ... Job 28:20 935
shine by the cloud that c betwixt ... Job 36:32 6293
Out of the south c the whirlwind ... Job 37:9 935
Fair weather c out of the north ... Job 37:22 857
a night, but joy c in the morning ... Ps 30:5
from him c my salvation ... Ps 62:1
For promotion c neither from the ... Ps 75:6 4480
that passeth away, and c not again ... Ps 78:39 7725
for he c, for he c to judge ... Ps 96:13 935
for he c to judge the earth ... Ps 98:9 935
Blessed be he that c in the name ... Ps 118:26 935
the hills, from whence c my help ... Ps 121:1 935
My help c from the LORD, which ... Ps 121:2 4480
I will mock when your fear c ... Prov 1:26 935
When your fear c as desolation ... Prov 1:27 935
your destruction c as a whirlwind ... Prov 1:27 857
distress and anguish c upon you ... Prov 1:27 935
out of his mouth c knowledge ... Prov 2:6 4480
of the wicked, when it c ... Prov 3:25 935
When pride c, then c shame ... Prov 11:2 935
the wicked c in his stead ... Prov 11:8 935
man is loathsome, and c to shame ... Prov 13:5 2659
Only by pride c contention ... Prov 13:10 5414
heart sick, but when the desire c ... Prov 13:12 935
When the wicked c, then c ... Prov 18:3 935
but his neighbour c and searcheth ... Prov 18:17 935
man's judgment c from the LORD ... Prov 29:26 4480
away, and another generation c ... Eccl 1:4 935
the man do that c after the king ... Eccl 2:12 935
For out of prison he c to reign ... Eccl 4:14 3318
For a dream c through the ... Eccl 5:3 935
For he c in with vanity, and ... Eccl 6:4 935
All that c is vanity ... Eccl 11:8 935
he c leaping upon the mountains, ... Song 2:8 935
Who is this that c out of the ... Song 3:6 5927
Who is this that c up from the ... Song 8:5 5927
Behold, the day of the LORD c ... Is 13:9 935
so it c from the desert, from a ... Is 21:1 935
here c a chariot of men, with a ... Is 21:9 935
The watchman said, The morning c ... Is 21:12 857
he that c up out of the midst of ... Is 24:18 5927
the LORD c out of his place to ... Is 26:21 3318
This also c forth from the LORD ... Is 28:29 3318
whose breaking c suddenly at an ... Is 30:13 935
the name of the LORD c from far ... Is 30:27 935
earth, and that which c out of it ... Is 42:5 6631
For as the rain c down, and the ... Is 55:10 3381
of Zion, Behold, thy salvation c ... Is 62:11 935
Who is this that c from Edom ... Is 63:1 935
To what purpose c there to me ... Jer 6:20 935
a people c from the north country ... Jer 6:22 935
and shall not see when good c ... Jer 17:6 935
and shall not see when heat c ... Jer 17:8 935
c from the rock of the field ... Jer 18:14 4480
And when he c, he shall smite the ... Jer 43:11 935
Who is this that c up as a flood ... Jer 46:7 5927
fair heifer, but destruction c ... Jer 46:20 935
it c out of the north ... Jer 46:20 935
Because of the day that c to ... Jer 47:4 935
there c up a nation against her ... Jer 50:3 5927
A sound of a cry c from Babylon ... Jer 51:54 935
it c to pass, when the Lord ... Lam 3:37 1961
it with dung that c out of man ... Eze 4:12 6627
Destruction c; and they shall seek ... Eze 7:25 935
his face, and c to the prophet ... Eze 14:4 935
c according to the multitude of ... Eze 14:4 935
c to a prophet to enquire of him ... Eze 14:7 935
that which c into your mind shall ... Eze 20:32 5927
because it c: and every heart shall melt .. Eze 21:7 935
behold, it c, and shall be brought ... Eze 21:7 935
and when this c, ye shall know ... Eze 24:24 935
for, lo, it c ... Eze 30:9 935
word that c forth from the LORD ... Eze 33:30 3318
come unto thee as the people c ... Eze 33:31 935
And when this c to pass, (lo, it ... Eze 33:33 935
shall live whither the river c ... Eze 47:9 935
But he that c against him shall ... Dan 11:16 935
c to the thousand three hundred ... Dan 12:12 5060
and the thief c in, and the troop ... Hos 7:1 935
for the day of the LORD c ... Joel 2:1 935
the LORD c forth out of his place ... Mic 1:3 3318
when he c into our land, and when ... Mic 5:6 935
thy watchmen and thy visitation c ... Mic 7:4 935
when he c up unto the people, he ... Hab 3:16 5927
behold, thy King c unto thee ... Zec 9:9 935
Behold, the day of the LORD c ... Zec 14:1 935
For, behold, the day c, that ... Mal 4:1 935
the day that c shall burn them up ... Mal 4:1 935
but he that c after me is ... Mt 3:11 *2064*
Then c Jesus from Galilee to ... Mt 3:13 *3854*
is more than these c of evil ... Mt 5:37 *1511*
and to another, Come, and he c ... Mt 8:9 *2064*
then c the wicked one, and ... Mt 13:19 *2064*
but that which c out of the mouth ... Mt 15:11 *1607*
take up the fish that first c up ... Mt 17:27 *305*
to that man by whom the offence c ... Mt 18:7 *2064*
thy King c unto thee, meek, and ... Mt 21:5 *2064*
Blessed is he that c in the name ... Mt 21:9 *2064*
lord therefore of the vineyard c ... Mt 21:40 *2064*
Blessed is he that c in the name ... Mt 23:39 *2064*
the lightning c out of the east ... Mt 24:27 *1831*
as ye think not the Son of man c ... Mt 24:44 *2064*
when he c shall find so doing ... Mt 24:46 *2064*
made, Behold, the bridegroom c ... Mt 25:6 *2064*
the hour wherein the Son of man c ... Mt 25:13 *2064*
time the lord of those servants c ... Mt 25:19 *2064*
Then c Jesus with them unto a ... Mt 26:36 *2064*
he c unto the disciples, and ... Mt 26:40 *2064*
Then c he to his disciples, and ... Mt 26:45 *2064*
There c one mightier than I after ... Mk 1:7 *2064*
the multitude c together again, ... Mk 3:20 *4905*
Satan c immediately, and taketh ... Mk 4:15 *2064*
there c one of the rulers of the ... Mk 5:22 *2064*
he c to the house of the ruler of ... Mk 5:38 *2064*
watch of the night he c unto them ... Mk 6:48 *2064*
That which c out of the man, that ... Mk 7:20 *1607*
And he c to Bethsaida ... Mk 8:22 *2064*
when he c in the glory of his ... Mk 8:38 *2064*
told them, Elias verily c first ... Mk 9:12 *2064*
c into the coasts of Judaea by ... Mk 10:1 *2064*
Blessed is he that c in the name ... Mk 11:9 *2064*
that c in the name of the Lord ... Mk 11:10 *2064*
when the master of the house c ... Mk 13:35 *2064*
the evening he c with the twelve ... Mk 14:17 *2064*
And he c, and findeth them sleeping ... Mk 14:37 *2064*
he c the third time, and saith ... Mk 14:41 *2064*
c Judas, one of the twelve, and ... Mk 14:43 *3854*
there c one of the maids of the ... Mk 14:66 *2064*
but one mightier than I c ... Lk 3:16 *2064*
Whosoever c to me, and heareth my ... Lk 6:47 *2064*
and to another, Come, and he c ... Lk 7:8 *2064*
then c the devil, and taketh away ... Lk 8:12 *2064*
there c one from the ruler of the ... Lk 8:49 *2064*
And when he c, he findeth it swept ... Lk 11:25 *2064*
that when he c and knocketh, they ... Lk 12:36 *2064*
when he c shall find watching ... Lk 12:37 *2064*
for the Son of man c at an hour ... Lk 12:40 *2064*
when he c shall find so doing ... Lk 12:43 *2064*
ye say, There c a shower ... Lk 12:54 *2064*
and it c to pass ... Lk 12:55 *1096*
Blessed is he that c in the name ... Lk 13:35 *2064*
that when he that bade thee c ... Lk 14:10 *2064*
that c against him with twenty ... Lk 14:31 *2064*
And when he c home, he calleth ... Lk 15:6 *2064*
The kingdom of God c not with ... Lk 17:20 *2064*
when the Son of man c, shall he ... Lk 18:8 *2064*
that c in the name of the Lord ... Lk 19:38 *2064*
every man that c into the world ... Jn 1:9 *2064*
He that c after me is preferred ... Jn 1:15 *2064*
After me c a man which is ... Jn 1:30 *2064*
but canst not tell whence it c ... Jn 3:8 *2064*
neither c to the light, lest his ... Jn 3:20 *2064*
that doeth truth c to the light ... Jn 3:21 *2064*
He that c from above is above all ... Jn 3:31 *2064*
he that c from heaven is above ... Jn 3:31 *2064*
Then c he to a city of Samaria, ... Jn 4:5 *2064*
There c a woman of Samaria to ... Jn 4:7 *2064*
Woman, believe me, the hour c ... Jn 4:21 *2064*
But the hour c, and now is, when ... Jn 4:23 *2064*
unto him, I know that Messias c ... Jn 4:25 *2064*
four months, and then c harvest ... Jn 4:35 *2064*
the honour that c from God only ... Jn 5:44 *3844*
is he which c down from heaven ... Jn 6:33 *2597*
he that c to me shall never ... Jn 6:35 *2064*
him that c to me I will in no ... Jn 6:37 *2064*
learned of the Father, c unto me ... Jn 6:45 *2064*
bread which c down from heaven ... Jn 6:50 *2597*
but when Christ c, no man knoweth ... Jn 7:27 *2064*
on him, and said, When Christ c ... Jn 7:31 *2064*
That Christ c of the seed of ... Jn 7:42 *2064*
the night c, when no man can work ... Jn 9:4 *2064*
The thief c not, but for to steal ... Jn 10:10 *2064*
in himself c to the grave ... Jn 11:38 *2064*
that c in the name of the Lord ... Jn 12:13 *2064*
behold, thy King c, sitting on an ... Jn 12:15 *2064*
Philip c and telleth Andrew ... Jn 12:22 *2064*
Then c he to Simon Peter ... Jn 13:6 *2064*
no man c unto the Father, but by ... Jn 14:6 *2064*
for the prince of this world c ... Jn 14:30 *2064*
But this c to pass, that the word ... Jn 15:25
yea, the time c, that whosoever ... Jn 16:2 *2064*
but the time c, when I shall no ... Jn 16:25 *2064*
Behold, the hour c, yea, is now ... Jn 16:32 *2064*
c thither with lanterns and ... Jn 18:3 *2064*
the week c Mary Magdalene early ... Jn 20:1 *2064*
c to Simon Peter, and to the other ... Jn 20:2 *2064*
Then c Simon Peter following him, ... Jn 20:6 *2064*
Jesus then c, and taketh bread, and ... Jn 21:13 *2064*
who, when he c, shall speak unto ... Acts 10:32 *3854*
there c one after me, whose shoes ... Acts 13:25 *2064*
this feast that c in Jerusalem ... Acts 18:21 *2064*
C this blessedness then upon the ... Rom 4:9 *1909*
So then faith c by hearing ... Rom 10:17 *1537*
Then c the end, when he shall ... 1Cor 15:24
For if he that c preacheth ... 2Cor 11:4 *2064*
that which c upon me daily, the ... 2Cor 11:28 *1999*
This persuasion c not of him that ... Gal 5:8 *1537*
c the wrath of God upon the ... Eph 5:6 *2064*
things' sake the wrath of God c ... Col 3:6 *2064*
Lord so c as a thief in the night ... 1Th 5:2 *2064*
sudden destruction c upon them ... 1Th 5:3 *2186*
strifes of words, whereof c envy ... 1Ti 6:4 *1096*
in the rain that c oft upon it ... Heb 6:7 *2064*
when he c into the world, he ... Heb 10:5 *1525*
for he that c to God must believe ... Heb 11:6 *4334*
c down from the Father of lights, ... Jas 1:17 *2591*
the Lord c with ten thousands of ... Jude 14 *2064*
Behold, he c with clouds ... Rev 1:7 *2064*
which c down out of heaven from ... Rev 3:12 *2597*
behold, the third woe c quickly ... Rev 11:14 *2064*
and when he c, he must continue a ... Rev 17:10 *2064*

COMFORT {66}

This same shall c us concerning ... Gen 5:29 5162
of bread, and c ye your hearts ... Gen 18:5 5582
doth c himself, purposing to kill ... Gen 27:42 5162
his daughters rose up to c him ... Gen 37:35 5162
C thine heart with a morsel of ... Judg 19:5 5582
C thine heart, I pray thee ... Judg 19:8 5582
David sent to c him by the hand ... 2Sa 10:2 5162
and his brethren came to c him ... 1Chr 7:22 5162
David sent messengers to c him ... 1Chr 19:2 5162
of Ammon to Hanun, to c him ... 1Chr 19:2 5162
to mourn with him and to c him ... Job 2:11 5162
Then should I yet have c ... Job 6:10 5165
When I say, My bed shall c me ... Job 7:13 5162
off my heaviness, and c myself ... Job 9:27 1082
alone, that I may take c a little ... Job 10:20 1082
How then c ye me in vain, seeing ... Job 21:34 5162
thy rod and thy staff they c me ... Ps 23:4 5162
greatness, and c me on every side ... Ps 71:21 5162

This is my c in my affliction Ps 119:50 5162
thy merciful kindness be for my c Ps 119:76 5162
word, saying, When wilt thou c me Ps 119:82 5162
me with flagons, c me with apples Song 2:5 7502
weep bitterly, labour not to c me Is 22:4 5162
C ye, c ye my people, saith Is 40:1 5162
For the LORD shall c Zion Is 51:3 5162
he will c all her waste places Is 51:3 5162
by whom shall I c thee Is 51:19 5162
Should I receive c in these Is 57:6 5162
to c all that mourn Is 61:2 5162
comforteth, so will I c you Is 66:13 5162
When I would c myself against Jer 8:18 4010
mourning, to c them for the dead Jer 16:7 5162
mourning into joy, and will c them Jer 31:13 5162
her lovers she hath none to c her Lam 1:2 5162
hands, and there is none to c her Lam 1:17 5162
there is none to c me Lam 1:21 5162
equal to thee, that I may c thee Lam 2:13 5162
And they shall c you, when ye see Eze 14:23 5162
in that thou art a c unto them Eze 16:54 5162
and the LORD shall yet c Zion Zec 1:17 5162
they c in vain Zec 10:2 5162
he said, Daughter, be of good c Mt 9:22 2293
saying unto him, Be of good c Mk 10:49 2293
unto her, Daughter, be of good c Lk 8:48 2293
to c them concerning their Jn 11:19 3888
in the c of the Holy Ghost, were Acts 9:31 3874
c of the scriptures might have Rom 15:4 3874
edification, and exhortation, and c 1Cor 14:3 3889
of mercies, and the God of all c 2Cor 1:3 3874
that we may be able to c them 2Cor 1:4 3870
by the c wherewith we ourselves 2Cor 1:4 3874
c him, lest perhaps such a one 2Cor 2:7 3870
I am filled with c, I am 2Cor 7:4 3874
we were comforted in your c 2Cor 7:13 3874
Be perfect, be of good c, be of 2Cor 13:11 3870
and that he might c your hearts Eph 6:22 3870
Christ, if any c of love, if any Phil 2:1 3890
you, that I also may be of good c Phil 2:19 2174
your estate, and c your hearts Col 4:8 3870
God, which have been a c unto me Col 4:11 3931
to c you concerning your faith 1Th 3:2 3870
Wherefore c one another with 1Th 4:18 3870
Wherefore c yourselves together 1Th 5:11 3870
c the feebleminded, support the 1Th 5:14 3888
C your hearts, and stablish you in 2Th 2:17 3870

COMFORTABLE {2}
my lord the king shall now be c 2Sa 14:17 4496
me with good words and c words Zec 1:13 5150

COMFORTABLY {5}
speak c unto thy servants 2Sa 19:7 5921,3820
Hezekiah spake c unto all the 2Chr 30:22 5921,3820
city, and spake c to them, saying 2Chr 32:6 5921,3824
Speak ye c to Jerusalem, and cry Is 40:2 5921,3820
wilderness, and speak c unto her Hos 2:14 5921,3820

COMFORTED {36}
Isaac was c after his mother's Gen 24:67 5162
but he refused to be c Gen 37:35 5162
and Judah was c, and went up unto Gen 38:12 5162
he c them, and spake kindly unto Gen 50:21 5162
for that thou hast c me, and for Ruth 2:13 5162
David c Bath-sheba his wife, and 2Sa 12:24 5162
for he was c concerning Amnon 2Sa 13:39 5162
c him over all the evil that the Job 42:11 5162
my soul refused to be c Ps 77:2 5162
LORD, hast holpen me, and c me Ps 86:17 5162
and have c myself Ps 119:52 5162
for the LORD hath c his people Is 49:13 5162
for the LORD hath c his people Is 52:9 5162
tossed with tempest, and not c Is 54:11 5162
ye shall be c in Jerusalem Is 66:13 5162
refused to be c for her children Jer 31:15 5162
to rest upon them, and I will be c Eze 5:13 5162
ye shall be c concerning the evil Eze 14:22 5162
shall be c in the nether parts of Eze 31:16 5162
shall be c over all his multitude Eze 32:31 5162
her children, and would not be c Mt 2:18 3870
for they shall be c Mt 5:4 3870
but now he is c, and thou art Lk 16:25 3870
c her, when they saw Mary, that Jn 11:31 3888
seen the brethren, they c them Acts 16:40 3870
man alive, and were not a little c Acts 20:12 3870
that I may be c together with you Rom 1:12 4837
all may learn, and all may be c 1Cor 14:31 3870
we ourselves are c of God 2Cor 1:4 3870
or whether we be c, it is for 2Cor 1:6 3870
c us by the coming of Titus 2Cor 7:6 3870
wherewith he was c in you 2Cor 7:7 3870
we were c in your comfort 2Cor 7:13 3870
That their hearts might be c Col 2:2 3870
As ye know how we exhorted and c 1Th 2:11 3888
we were c over you in all our 1Th 3:7 3870

COMFORTEDST {1}
is turned away, and thou c me Is 12:1 5162

COMFORTER {8}
were oppressed, and they had no c Eccl 4:1 5162
but they had no c Eccl 4:1
she had no c Lam 1:9 5162
because the c that should relieve Lam 1:16 5162
and he shall give you another C Jn 14:16 3875
But the C, which is the Holy Jn 14:26 3875
But when the C is come, whom I Jn 15:26 3875
the C will not come unto you Jn 16:7 3875

COMFORTERS {5}
that he hath sent c unto thee 2Sa 10:3 5162
that he hath sent c unto thee 1Chr 19:3 5162
miserable c are ye all Job 16:2 5162
and for c, but I found none Ps 69:20 5162
whence shall I seek c for thee Nah 3:7 5162

COMFORTETH {5}
as one that c the mourners Job 29:25 5162
I, even I, am he that c you Is 51:12 5162
As one whom his mother c, so will Is 66:13 5162
Who c us in all our tribulation 2Cor 1:4 3870
that c those that are cast down 2Cor 7:6 3870

COMFORTLESS {1}
I will not leave you c Jn 14:18 3737

COMFORTS {2}
within me thy c delight my soul Ps 94:19 8575
restore c unto him and to his Is 57:18 5150

COMING {100}
and, behold, the camels were c Gen 24:63 935
LORD hath blessed thee since my c Gen 30:30 7272
thee, hinder thee from c unto me Num 22:16 1980
heard of the c of the children of Num 33:40 935
Why is his chariot so long in c Judg 5:28 935
meet a company of prophets c down 1Sa 10:5 3381
of the town trembled at his c 1Sa 16:4 7122
I saw the son of Jesse c to Nob 1Sa 22:9 935
thee from c to shed blood 1Sa 25:26 935
me this day from c to shed blood 1Sa 25:33 935
thy c in with me in the host is 1Sa 29:6 935
of thy c unto me unto this day 1Sa 29:6 935
to know thy going out and thy c in 2Sa 3:25 4126
his servants c on toward him 2Sa 24:20 5674
the son of Rechab c to meet him 2Kin 10:15 7125
the land at the c in of the year 2Kin 13:20 935
and thy going out, and thy c in 2Kin 19:27 935
Ahaziah was of God by c to Joram 2Chr 22:7 935
their c unto the house of God at Ezr 3:8 935
a bridegroom c out of his chamber Ps 19:5 3318
for he seeth that his day is c Ps 37:13 935
thy c in from this time forth, and Ps 121:8 935
city, at the c in at the doors Prov 8:3 3996
for thee to meet thee at thy c Is 14:9 935
shall hail, c down on the forest Is 32:19 3381
and thy going out, and thy c in Is 37:28 935
and the things that are c, and Is 44:7 857
observe the time of their c Jer 8:7 935
an holy one c down from heaven Dan 4:23 5182
According to the days of thy c Mic 7:15 3318
he had horns c out of his hand Hab 3:4 4480
who may abide the day of his c Mal 3:2 935
prophet before the c of the great Mal 4:5 935
c out of the tombs, exceeding Mt 8:28 1831
the Son of man c in his kingdom Mt 16:28 2064
what shall be the sign of thy c Mt 24:3 3952
so shall also the c of the Son of Mt 24:27 3952
c in the clouds of heaven with Mt 24:30 2064
so shall also the c of the Son of Mt 24:37 3952
so shall also the c of the Son of Mt 24:39 3952
his heart, My lord delayeth his c Mt 24:48 2064
then at my c I should have Mt 25:27 2064
c in the clouds of heaven Mt 26:64 2064
straightway c up out of the water Mk 1:10 305
for there were many c and going Mk 6:31 2064
shall they see the Son of man c Mk 13:26 2064
Lest c suddenly he find you Mk 13:36 2064
c in the clouds of heaven Mk 14:62 2064
c out of the country, the father Mk 15:21 2064
she c in that instant gave thanks Lk 2:38 2186
And as he was yet a c, the devil Lk 9:42 4334
his heart, My lord delayeth his c Lk 12:45 2064
by her continual c she weary me Lk 18:5 2064
that at my c I might have Lk 19:23 2064
things which are c on the earth Lk 21:26 1904
of man c in a cloud with power Lk 21:27 2064
c out of the country, and on him Lk 23:26 2064
For, behold, the days are c Lk 23:29 2064
c to him, and offering him vinegar Lk 23:36 4334
who c after me is preferred Jn 1:27 2064
day John seeth Jesus c unto him Jn 1:29 2064
Jesus saw Nathanael c to him Jn 1:47 2064
but while I am c, another Jn 5:7 2064
I say unto you, The hour is c Jn 5:25 2064
for the hour is c, in the which Jn 5:28 2064
sheep are not, seeth the wolf c Jn 10:12 2064
as she heard that Jesus was c Jn 11:20 2064
that Jesus was c to Jerusalem Jn 12:12 2064
before of the c of the Just One Acts 7:52 1660
a vision a man named Ananias c in Acts 9:12 1525
And he was with them c in and going Acts 9:28 1531
day an angel of God c in to him Acts 10:3 1525
And as Peter was c in, Cornelius Acts 10:25 1525
c the baptism of repentance to Acts 13:24 1529
who c thither went into the Acts 17:10 3854
And while the day was c on Acts 27:33 1096
been much hindered from c to you Rom 15:22 2064
waiting for the c of our Lord 1Cor 1:7 602
they that are Christ's at his c 1Cor 15:23 3952
I am glad of the c of Stephanas 1Cor 16:17 3952
comforted us by the c of Titus 2Cor 7:6 3952
And not by his c only, but by the 2Cor 7:7 3952
is the third time I am c to you 2Cor 13:1 2064
for me by my c to you again Phil 1:26 3952
of our Lord Jesus Christ at his c 1Th 2:19 3952
at the c of our Lord Jesus Christ 1Th 3:13 3952
remain unto the c of the Lord 1Th 4:15 3952
the c of our Lord Jesus Christ 1Th 5:23 3952
by the c of our Lord Jesus Christ 2Th 2:1 3952
with the brightness of his c 2Th 2:8 3952
whose c is after the working of 2Th 2:9 3952
brethren, unto the c of the Lord Jas 5:7 3952
for the c of the Lord draweth Jas 5:8 3952
To whom c, as unto a living stone 1Pet 2:4 4334
c of our Lord Jesus Christ, but 2Pet 1:16 3952
Where is the promise of his c 2Pet 3:4 3952
hasting unto the c of the day of 2Pet 3:12 3952
be ashamed before him at his c 1Jn 2:28 3952
beast c up out of the earth Rev 13:11 305
c down from God out of heaven Rev 21:2 2597

COMINGS {1}
the c in thereof, and all the Eze 43:11 4126

COMMAND {104}
him, that he will c his children Gen 18:19 6680
according to that which I c thee Gen 27:8 6680
Thy father did c before he died Gen 50:16 6680
shalt speak all that I c thee Ex 7:2 6680
LORD our God, as he shall c us Ex 8:27 559
God c thee so, then thou shalt be Ex 18:23 6680
thou shalt c the children of Ex 27:20 6680
thou that which I c thee this day Ex 34:11 6680
C Aaron and his sons, saying, This Lev 6:9 6680
Then the priest shall c that they Lev 13:54 6680
Then shall the priest c to take Lev 14:4 6680
the priest shall c that one of Lev 14:5 6680
Then the priest shall c that they Lev 14:36 6680
Then the priest shall c that they Lev 14:40 6680
C the children of Israel, that Lev 24:2 6680
Then I will c my blessing upon Lev 25:21 6680
C the children of Israel, that Num 5:2 6680
the LORD will c concerning you Num 9:8 6680
C the children of Israel, and say Num 28:2 6680
C the children of Israel, and say Num 34:2 6680
C the children of Israel, that Num 35:2 6680
c concerning the daughters of Num 36:6 6680
c thou the people, saying, Ye are Deut 2:4 6680
add unto the word which I c you Deut 4:2 6680
the LORD your God which I c you Deut 4:2 6680
which I c thee this day, that it Deut 4:40 6680
his commandments, which I c thee Deut 6:2 6680
which I c thee this day, shall be Deut 6:6 6680
which I c thee this day, to do Deut 7:11 6680
All the commandments which I c Deut 8:1 6680
statutes, which I c thee this day Deut 8:11 6680
which I c thee this day for thy Deut 10:13 6680
which I c you this day, that ye Deut 11:8 6680
which I c you this day, to love Deut 11:13 6680
these commandments which I c you Deut 11:22 6680
your God, which I c you this day Deut 11:27 6680
of the way which I c you this day Deut 11:28 6680
shall ye bring all that I c you Deut 12:11 6680
thou shalt do all that I c thee Deut 12:14 6680
all these words which I c thee Deut 12:28 6680
What thing soever I c you Deut 12:32 6680
which I c thee this day, to do Deut 13:18 6680
which I c thee this day Deut 15:5 6680
therefore I c thee, saying, Thou Deut 15:11 6680
therefore I c thee this thing to Deut 15:15 6680
unto them all that I shall c him Deut 18:18 6680
Wherefore I c thee, saying, Thou Deut 19:7 6680
which I c thee this day, to love Deut 19:9 6680
therefore I c thee to do this Deut 24:18 6680
therefore I c thee to do this Deut 24:22 6680
which I c you this day Deut 27:1 6680
which I c you this day, in mount Deut 27:4 6680
statutes, which I c thee this day Deut 27:10 6680
which I c thee this day, that the Deut 28:1 6680
The LORD shall c the blessing Deut 28:8 6680
which I c thee this day, to Deut 28:13 6680
the words which I c thee this day Deut 28:14 6680
statutes which I c thee this day Deut 28:15 6680
to all that I c thee this day Deut 30:2 6680
which I c thee this day Deut 30:8 6680
which I c thee this day, it is Deut 30:11 6680
In that I c thee this day to love Deut 30:16 6680
which ye shall c your children to Deut 32:46 6680
c the people, saying, Prepare you Josh 1:11 6680
thou shalt c the priests that Josh 3:8 6680
c ye them, saying, Take you hence Josh 4:3 6680
C the priests that bear the ark Josh 4:16 6680
servant, so did Moses c Joshua Josh 11:15 6680
Let our lord now c thy servants 1Sa 16:16 559
Now therefore c thou that they 1Kin 5:6 6680
hearken unto all that I c thee 1Kin 11:38 6680
or if I c the locusts to devour 2Chr 7:13 6680
Doth the eagle mount up at thy c Job 39:27 6310
Yet the LORD will c his Ps 42:8 6680
c deliverances for Jacob Ps 44:4 6680
I will also c the clouds that Is 5:6 6680
the work of my hands c ye me Is 45:11 6680
whatsoever I c thee thou shalt Jer 1:7 6680
speak unto them all that I c thee Jer 1:17 6680
according to all which I c you Jer 11:4 6680
all the words that I c thee to Jer 26:2 6680
c them to say unto their masters Jer 27:4 6680
Behold, I will c, saith the LORD Jer 34:22 6680
whom thou didst c that they Lam 1:10 6680
sea, thence will I c the serpent Amos 9:3 6680
thence will I c the sword Amos 9:4 6680
For, lo, I will c, and I will sift Amos 9:9 6680
c that these stones be made bread Mt 4:3 2036
Why did Moses then c to give a Mt 19:7 1781
C therefore that the sepulchre be Mt 27:64 2753

unto them, What did Moses c you........Mk 10:3 *1781*
c this stone that it be made...............Lk 4:3 *2036*
c them to go out into the deep ....Lk 8:31 *2004*
wilt thou that we c fire to come...........Lk 9:54 *2036*
if ye do whatsoever I c you...................Jn 15:14 *1781*
These things I c you, that ye ....Jn 15:17 *1781*
Did not we straitly c you that ye...........Acts 5:28 *3853*
to c them to keep the law of..................Acts 15:5 *3853*
I c thee in the name of Jesus ....Acts 16:18 *3853*
And unto the married I c, yet not 1Cor 7:10 *3853*
will do the things which we c you..........2Th 3:4 *3853*
Now we c you, brethren, in the 2Th 3:6 *3853*
Now them that are such we c.................2Th 3:12 *3853*
These things c and teach 1Ti 4:11 *3853*

COMMANDED {443}
And the LORD God c the man ....Gen 2:16 6680
whereof I c thee that thou......................Gen 3:11 6680
of the tree, of which I c thee ....Gen 3:17 6680
according to all that God c him ....Gen 6:22 6680
unto all that the LORD c him.................Gen 7:5 6680
and the female, as God had c Noah ....Gen 7:9 6680
of all flesh, as God had c him ....Gen 7:16 6680
Pharaoh c his men concerning him ....Gen 12:20 6680
eight days old, as God had c him ....Gen 21:4 6680
he c them, saying, Thus shall ye............Gen 32:4 6680
he c the foremost, saying, When............Gen 32:17 6680
so c he the second, and the third,...........Gen 32:19 6680
Then Joseph c to fill their sacks............Gen 42:25 6680
he c the steward of his house, ...Gen 44:1 6680
Now thou art c, this do ye......................Gen 45:19 6680
land of Rameses, as Pharaoh had c..........Gen 47:11 6680
Joseph c his servants the ....Gen 50:2 6680
unto him according as he c them ....Gen 50:12 6680
not as the king of Egypt c them.............Ex 1:17 1696
all the signs which he had c him............Ex 4:28 6680
Pharaoh c the same day the ....Ex 5:6 6680
and Aaron did as the LORD c them ....Ex 7:6 6680
and they did so as the LORD had c..........Ex 7:10 6680
and Aaron did so, as the LORD c ....Ex 7:20 6680
and did as the LORD had c Moses.............Ex 12:28 6680
as the LORD c Moses and Aaron, so.........Ex 12:50 6680
the thing which the LORD hath c ....Ex 16:16 6680
As the LORD c Moses, so Aaron...............Ex 16:34 6680
these words which the LORD c him ....Ex 19:7 6680
bread seven days, as I c thee ....Ex 23:15 6680
to all things which I have c thee ....Ex 29:35 6680
may make all that I have c thee ....Ex 31:6 6680
that I have c thee shall they do ....Ex 31:11 6680
out of the way which I c them.................Ex 32:8 6680
Sinai, as the LORD had c him...................Ex 34:4 6680
eat unleavened bread, as I c thee ....Ex 34:18 6680
of Israel that which he was c ....Ex 34:34 6680
the words which the LORD hath c ....Ex 35:1 6680
is the thing which the LORD c..................Ex 35:4 6680
and make all that the LORD hath c ....Ex 35:10 6680
which the LORD had c to be made............Ex 35:29 6680
to all that the LORD had c ....Ex 36:1 6680
work, which the LORD c to make ....Ex 36:5 6680
made all that the LORD c Moses..............Ex 38:22 6680
as the LORD c Moses................................Ex 39:1 6680
as the LORD c Moses................................Ex 39:5 6680
as the LORD c Moses................................Ex 39:7 6680
as the LORD c Moses................................Ex 39:21 6680
as the LORD c Moses................................Ex 39:26 6680
as the LORD c Moses................................Ex 39:29 6680
as the LORD c Moses................................Ex 39:31 6680
to all that the LORD c Moses ....Ex 39:32 6680
to all that the LORD c Moses ....Ex 39:42 6680
had done it as the LORD had c ....Ex 39:43 6680
to all that the LORD c him......................Ex 40:16 6680
as the LORD c Moses................................Ex 40:19 6680
as the LORD c Moses................................Ex 40:21 6680
as the LORD had c Moses..........................Ex 40:23 6680
as the LORD c Moses................................Ex 40:25 6680
as the LORD c Moses................................Ex 40:27 6680
as the LORD c Moses................................Ex 40:29 6680
as the LORD c Moses................................Ex 40:32 6680
Which the LORD c to be given them ....Lev 7:36 6680
Which the LORD c Moses in mount ....Lev 7:38 6680
in the day that he c the children ....Lev 7:38 6680
And Moses did as the LORD c him............Lev 8:4 6680
thing which the LORD c to be done ....Lev 8:5 6680
as the LORD c Moses................................Lev 8:9 6680
as the LORD c Moses................................Lev 8:13 6680
as the LORD c Moses................................Lev 8:17 6680
as the LORD c Moses................................Lev 8:21 6680
as the LORD c Moses................................Lev 8:29 6680
basket of consecrations, as I c.................Lev 8:31 6680
day, so the LORD hath c to do..................Lev 8:34 6680
for so I am c...Lev 8:35 6680
the LORD c by the hand of Moses.............Lev 8:36 6680
c before the tabernacle of the..................Lev 9:5 6680
the LORD c that ye should do ....Lev 9:6 6680
as the LORD c...Lev 9:7 6680
as the LORD c Moses................................Lev 9:10 6680
before the LORD; as Moses c....................Lev 9:21 6680
the LORD, which he c them not ....Lev 10:1 6680
for so I am c...Lev 10:13 6680
as the LORD hath c ....Lev 10:15 6680
it in the holy place, as I c.......................Lev 10:18 6680
And he did as the LORD c Moses.............Lev 16:34 6680
the thing which the LORD hath c ....Lev 17:2 6680
of Israel did as the LORD c Moses ....Lev 24:23 6680
which the LORD c Moses for the..............Lev 27:34 6680
As the LORD c Moses, so he.....................Num 1:19 6680
to all that the LORD c Moses ....Num 1:54 6680
as the LORD c Moses................................Num 2:33 6680
to all that the LORD c Moses ....Num 2:34 6680
the word of the LORD, as he was c ....Num 3:16 6680
Moses numbered, as the LORD c him........Num 3:42 6680
of the LORD, as the LORD c Moses.........Num 3:51 6680
of him, as the LORD c Moses...................Num 4:49 6680
candlestick, as the LORD c Moses...........Num 8:3 6680
unto all that the LORD c Moses ....Num 8:20 6680
as the LORD had c Moses.........................Num 8:22 6680
to all that the LORD c Moses ....Num 9:5 6680
hath c you by the hand of Moses.............Num 15:23 6680
the day that the LORD c Moses................Num 15:23 6680
as the LORD c Moses................................Num 15:36 6680
And Aaron took as Moses c, and ran ......Num 16:47 1696
as the LORD c him, so did he ....Num 17:11 6680
of the law which the LORD hath c...........Num 19:2 6680
from before the LORD, as he c him ....Num 20:9 6680
And Moses did as the LORD c..................Num 20:27 6680
as the LORD c Moses and the...................Num 26:4 6680
of judgment, as the LORD c Moses...........Num 27:11 6680
And Moses did as the LORD c him...........Num 27:22 6680
as the LORD c by the hand of ....Num 27:23 1696
to all that the LORD c Moses ....Num 29:40 6680
the thing which the LORD hath c ....Num 30:1 6680
statutes, which the LORD c Moses ....Num 30:16 6680
Midianites, as the LORD c Moses............Num 31:7 6680
of the law which the LORD c Moses ....Num 31:21 6680
priest did as the LORD c Moses ....Num 31:31 6680
the priest, as the LORD c Moses..............Num 31:41 6680
as the LORD c Moses................................Num 31:47 6680
them Moses c Eleazar the priest..............Num 32:28 6680
Moses c the children of Israel,.................Num 34:13 6680
which the LORD c to give unto the ....Num 34:13 6680
These are they whom the LORD c to.......Num 34:29 6680
The LORD c my lord to give the..............Num 36:2 6680
my lord was c by the LORD to give.........Num 36:2 6680
Moses c the children of Israel..................Num 36:5 6680
Even as the LORD c Moses, so did ....Num 36:10 6680
which the LORD c by the hand of.............Num 36:13 6680
I c you at that time all the ....Deut 1:18 6680
as the LORD our God c us........................Deut 1:19 6680
to all that the LORD our God c us ....Deut 1:41 6680
I c you at that time, saying, The.............Deut 3:18 6680
I c Joshua at that time, saying................Deut 3:21 6680
even as the LORD my God c me...............Deut 4:5 6680
which he c you to perform, even ....Deut 4:13 6680
the LORD c me at that time to ....Deut 4:14 6680
as the LORD thy God hath c thee............Deut 5:12 6680
therefore the LORD thy God c thee.........Deut 5:15 6680
as the LORD thy God hath c thee............Deut 5:16 6680
as the LORD your God hath c you ....Deut 5:32 6680
the LORD your God hath c you...............Deut 5:33 6680
the LORD your God c to teach you ....Deut 6:1 6680
statutes, which he hath c thee................Deut 6:17 6680
which the LORD our God hath c you......Deut 6:20 6680
the LORD c us to do all these.................Deut 6:24 6680
the LORD our God, as he hath c us.........Deut 6:25 6680
out of the way which I c them................Deut 9:12 6680
the way which the LORD had c you.........Deut 9:16 6680
there they be, as the LORD c me............Deut 10:5 6680
hath given thee, as I have c thee ....Deut 12:21 6680
LORD thy God c thee to walk in ....Deut 13:5 6680
of heaven, which I have not c.................Deut 17:3 6680
which I have not c him to speak ....Deut 18:20 6680
as the LORD thy God hath c thee............Deut 20:17 6680
as I c them, so ye shall observe ....Deut 24:8 6680
commandments which thou hast c me ....Deut 26:13 6680
to all that thou hast c me........................Deut 26:14 6680
hath c thee to do these statutes..............Deut 26:16 6680
the elders of Israel c the people ....Deut 27:1 6680
and his statutes which he c thee ....Deut 28:45 6680
which the LORD c Moses to make...........Deut 29:1 6680
commandments which I have c you..........Deut 31:5 6680
And Moses c them, saying, At the...........Deut 31:10 6680
That Moses c the Levites, which ....Deut 31:25 6680
from the way which I have c you ....Deut 31:29 6680
Moses c us a law, even the......................Deut 33:4 6680
him, and did as the LORD c Moses ....Deut 34:9 6680
which Moses my servant c thee...............Josh 1:7 6680
Have not I c thee ....Josh 1:9 6680
Then Joshua c the officers of the............Josh 1:10 6680
the servant of the LORD c you ....Josh 1:13 6680
they c the people, saying, When.............Josh 3:3 6680
of Israel did so as Joshua c......................Josh 4:8 6680
was finished that the LORD c ....Josh 4:10 6680
to all that Moses c Joshua ....Josh 4:10 6680
Joshua therefore c the priests..................Josh 4:17 6680
And Joshua had c the people....................Josh 6:10 6680
my covenant which I c them....................Josh 7:11 6680
he c them, saying, Behold, ye ....Josh 8:4 6680
See, I have c you ....Josh 8:8 6680
of the LORD which he c Joshua ....Josh 8:27 6680
Joshua c that they should take................Josh 8:29 6680
the LORD c the children of Israel...........Josh 8:31 6680
servant of the LORD had c before ....Josh 8:33 6680
not a word of all that Moses c.................Josh 8:35 6680
how that the LORD thy God c his............Josh 9:24 6680
down of the sun, that Joshua c.................Josh 10:27 6680
as the LORD God of Israel c.....................Josh 10:40 6680
Moses the servant of the LORD c ....Josh 11:12 6680
As the LORD c Moses his servant,...........Josh 11:15 6680
of all that the LORD c Moses ....Josh 11:15 6680
destroy them, as the LORD c Moses ....Josh 11:20 6680
an inheritance, as I have c thee..............Josh 13:6 6680
as the LORD c by the hand of ....Josh 14:2 6680
As the LORD c Moses, so the...................Josh 14:5 6680
The LORD c Moses to give us an.............Josh 17:4 6680
The LORD c by the hand of Moses...........Josh 21:2 6680
as the LORD c by the hand of ....Josh 21:8 6680
the servant of the LORD c you ....Josh 22:2 6680
my voice in all that I c you....................Josh 22:2 6680
the LORD your God, which he c you.......Josh 23:16 6680
covenant which I c their fathers ....Judg 2:20 6680
which he c their fathers by the ....Judg 3:4 6680
Hath not the LORD God of Israel c.........Judg 4:6 6680
all that I c her let her observe.................Judg 13:14 6680
c them, saying, Go and smite the ....Judg 21:10 6680
Therefore they c the children of..............Judg 21:20 6680
Boaz c his young men, saying, Let ....Ruth 2:15 6680
which I have c in my habitation..............1Sa 2:29 6680
the LORD thy God, which he c thee.........1Sa 13:13 6680
the LORD hath c him to be captain 1Sa 13:14 6680
kept that which the LORD c thee.............1Sa 13:14 6680
took, and went, as Jesse had c him 1Sa 17:20 6680
Saul c his servants, saying,.....................1Sa 18:22 6680
brother, he hath c me to be there 1Sa 20:29 6680
The king hath c me a business 1Sa 21:2 6680
send thee, and what I have c thee 1Sa 21:2 6680
David c his young men, and they 2Sa 4:12 6680
did so, as the LORD had c him.................2Sa 5:25 6680
whom I c to feed my people Israel 2Sa 7:7 6680
as since the time that I c judges..............2Sa 7:11 6680
lord the king hath c his servant 2Sa 9:11 6680
Now Absalom had c his servants 2Sa 13:28 6680
have not I c you 2Sa 13:28 6680
did unto Amnon as Absalom had c...........2Sa 13:29 6680
And the king c Joab and Abishai and.....2Sa 18:5 6680
performed all that the king c 2Sa 21:14 6680
of Gad, went up as the LORD c.................2Sa 24:19 6680
So the king c Benaiah the son of 1Kin 2:46 6680
And the king c, and they brought 1Kin 5:17 6680
judgments, which he c our fathers 1Kin 8:58 6680
to all that I have c thee 1Kin 9:4 6680
had c him concerning this thing,.............1Kin 11:10 6680
he kept not that which the LORD c..........1Kin 11:10 6680
my statutes, which I have c thee 1Kin 11:11 6680
which the LORD thy God c thee...............1Kin 13:21 6680
he c him all the days of his life...............1Kin 15:5 6680
I have c the ravens to feed thee...............1Kin 17:4 6680
I have c a widow woman there to 1Kin 17:9 6680
the king of Syria c his thirty 1Kin 22:31 6680
he c them, saying, This is the 2Kin 11:5 6680
things that Jehoiada the priest c..............2Kin 11:9 6680
But Jehoiada the priest c the...................2Kin 11:15 6680
law of Moses, wherein the LORD c 2Kin 14:6 6680
king Ahaz c Urijah the priest,..................2Kin 16:15 6680
according to all that king Ahaz c............2Kin 16:16 6680
the law which I c your fathers 2Kin 17:13 6680
Then the king of Assyria c 2Kin 17:27 6680
the LORD c the children of Jacob 2Kin 17:34 6680
which the LORD c Moses...........................2Kin 18:6 6680
Moses the servant of the LORD c 2Kin 18:12 6680
to all that I have c them 2Kin 21:8 6680
law that my servant Moses c them 2Kin 21:8 6680
the king c Hilkiah the priest, and 2Kin 22:12 6680
the king c Hilkiah the high 2Kin 23:4 6680
the king c all the people, saying..............2Kin 23:21 6680
Moses the servant of God had c 1Chr 6:49 6680
David therefore did as God c him 1Chr 14:16 6680
as Moses c according to the word 1Chr 15:15 6680
the word which he c to a thousand 1Chr 16:15 6680
of the LORD, which he c Israel................1Chr 16:40 6680
whom I c to feed my people, ...1Chr 17:6 6680
since the time that I c judges to 1Chr 17:10 6680
Is it not I that c the people to 1Chr 21:17 559
of the LORD c Gad to say to David..........1Chr 21:18 559
And the LORD c the angel.........................1Chr 21:27 559
David c to gather together the 1Chr 22:2 559
David also c all the princes of..................1Chr 22:17 6680
to the order c unto them,..........................1Chr 23:31
the LORD God of Israel had c him..........1Chr 24:19 6680
to all that I have c thee 2Chr 7:17 6680
for so had David the man of God c 2Chr 8:14 4687
c Judah to seek the LORD God of 2Chr 14:4 559
Now the king of Syria had c the 2Chr 18:30 6680
that Jehoiada the priest had c.................2Chr 23:8 6680
book of Moses, where the LORD c.............2Chr 25:4 6680
he c the priests the sons of 2Chr 29:21 559
for the king c that the burnt 2Chr 29:24 559
Hezekiah c to offer the burnt...................2Chr 29:27 559
the princes c the Levites to sing...............2Chr 29:30 559
Moreover he c the people that..................2Chr 31:4 559
Then Hezekiah c to prepare 2Chr 31:11 559
c Judah and Jerusalem, saying, Ye 2Chr 32:12 559
heed to do all that I have c them.............2Chr 33:8 6680
c Judah to serve the LORD God of............2Chr 33:16 559
And the king c Hilkiah, and Ahikam......2Chr 34:20 6680
for God c me to make haste 2Chr 35:21 559
the king of Persia hath c us......................Ezr 4:3 6680
I c, and search hath been made, ...Ezr 4:19 7761,2942
Who hath c you to build this...........Ezr 5:3 7761,2942
c you to build this house, and ....Ezr 5:9 7761,2942
Whatsoever is c by the God of.........Ezr 7:23 4480,2941
Which thou hast c by thy servants ....Ezr 9:11 6680
which the LORD had c to Israel ....Neh 8:1 6680
law which the LORD had c by Moses......Neh 8:14 6680
which was c to be given to the ....Neh 13:5 4687
Then I c, and they cleansed the...............Neh 13:9 559
I c that the gates should be shut ....Neh 13:19 559
I c the Levites that they should ....Neh 13:22 559
he c Mehuman, Biztha, Harbona,.............Est 1:10 559
The king Ahasuerus c Vashti the.............Est 1:17 559
the king had so c concerning him ....Est 3:2 6680
had c unto the king's lieutenants ....Est 3:12 6680

Then Mordecai c to answer Esther,	Est 4:13	559
to all that Esther had c him	Est 4:17	6680
he c to bring the book of records	Est 6:1	559
all that Mordecai c unto the Jews	Est 8:9	6680
the king c it so to be done	Est 9:14	559
he c by letters that his wicked	Est 9:25	559
Hast thou c the morning since thy	Job 38:12	6680
did according as the LORD c them	Job 42:9	1696
to the judgment that thou hast c	Ps 7:6	6680
he c, and it stood fast	Ps 33:9	6680
Thy God hath c thy strength	Ps 68:28	6680
which he c our fathers, that they	Ps 78:5	6680
Though he had c the clouds from	Ps 78:23	6680
the word which he c to a thousand	Ps 105:8	6680
concerning whom the LORD c them	Ps 106:34	559
he hath c his covenant for ever	Ps 111:9	6680
Thou hast c us to keep thy	Ps 119:4	6680
that thou hast c are righteous	Ps 119:138	6680
for there the LORD c the blessing	Ps 133:3	6680
for he c, and they were created	Ps 148:5	6680
I have c my sanctified ones, I	Is 13:3	6680
for my mouth it hath c, and his	Is 34:16	6680
and all their host have I c	Is 45:12	6680
and my molten image, hath c them	Is 48:5	6680
nor c them in the day that I	Jer 7:22	6680
But this thing c I them, saying,	Jer 7:23	6680
in all the ways that I have c you	Jer 7:23	6680
which I c them not, neither came	Jer 7:31	6680
Which I c your fathers in the day	Jer 11:4	6680
covenant, which I c them to do	Jer 11:8	6680
it by Euphrates, as the LORD c me	Jer 13:5	6680
which I c thee to hide there	Jer 13:6	6680
them not, neither have I c them	Jer 14:14	6680
sabbath day, as I c your fathers	Jer 17:22	6680
unto Baal, which I c not, nor	Jer 19:5	6680
yet I sent them not, nor c them	Jer 23:32	6680
had c him to speak unto all the	Jer 26:8	6680
my name, which I have not c them	Jer 29:23	6680
which I c them not, neither came	Jer 32:35	6680
the son of Rechab our father c us	Jer 35:6	6680
all that Jonadab our father c us	Jer 35:10	6680
that he c his sons not to drink	Jer 35:14	6680
of their father, which he c them	Jer 35:16	6680
unto all that he hath c you	Jer 35:18	6680
And Jeremiah c Baruch, saying, I	Jer 36:5	6680
that Jeremiah the prophet c him	Jer 36:8	6680
But the king c Jerahmeel the son	Jer 36:26	6680
Then Zedekiah the king c that	Jer 37:21	6680
Then the king c Ebed-melech the	Jer 38:10	6680
these words that the king had c	Jer 38:27	6680
to all that I have c thee	Jer 50:21	6680
c Seraiah the son of Neriah	Jer 51:59	6680
the LORD hath c concerning Jacob,	Lam 1:17	6680
that he had c in the days of old	Lam 2:17	6680
I have done as thou hast c me	Eze 9:11	6680
that when he had c the man	Eze 10:6	6680
And I did so as I was c	Eze 12:7	6680
I did in the morning as I was c	Eze 24:18	6680
So I prophesied as I was c	Eze 37:7	6680
So I prophesied as he c me	Eze 37:10	6680
Then the king c to call the	Dan 2:2	559
c to destroy all the wise men of	Dan 2:12	560
c that they should offer an	Dan 2:46	560
cried aloud, To you it is c	Dan 3:4	560
fury c to bring Shadrach, Meshach	Dan 3:13	560
c that they should heat the	Dan 3:19	560
he c the most mighty men that	Dan 3:20	560
whereas they c to leave the stump	Dan 4:26	560
c to bring the golden and silver	Dan 5:2	560
Then c Belshazzar, and they	Dan 5:29	560
Then the king c, and they brought	Dan 6:16	560
c that they should take Daniel up	Dan 6:23	560
And the king c, and they brought	Dan 6:24	560
c the prophets, saying, Prophesy	Amos 2:12	6680
which I c my servants the	Zec 1:6	6680
which I c unto him in Horeb for	Mal 4:4	6680
and offer the gift that Moses c	Mt 8:4	*4367*
c them, saying, Go not into the	Mt 10:5	*3853*
at meat, he c it to be given her	Mt 14:9	*2753*
he c the multitude to sit down on	Mt 14:19	*2753*
For God c, saying, Honour thy	Mt 15:4	*1781*
he c the multitude to sit down on	Mt 15:35	*2753*
his lord c him to be sold, and his	Mt 18:25	*2753*
went, and did as Jesus c them	Mt 21:6	*4367*
Then Pilate c the body to be	Mt 27:58	*2753*
things whatsoever I have c you	Mt 28:20	*1781*
those things which Moses c	Mk 1:44	*4367*
c that something should be given	Mk 5:43	*2036*
c them that they should take	Mk 6:8	*3853*
and c his head to be brought	Mk 6:27	*2004*
he c them to make all sit down by	Mk 6:39	*2004*
he c the people to sit down on	Mk 8:6	*3853*
c to set them also before them	Mk 8:7	*2036*
still, and c him to be called	Mk 10:49	*2036*
unto them even as Jesus had c	Mk 11:6	*1781*
work, and c the porter to watch	Mk 13:34	*1781*
cleansing, according as Moses c	Lk 5:14	*4367*
(For he had c the unclean spirit	Lk 8:29	*3853*
and he c to give her meat	Lk 8:55	*1299*
c them to tell no man that thing	Lk 9:21	*3853*
Lord, it is done as thou hast c	Lk 14:22	*2004*
he did the things that were c him	Lk 17:9	*1299*
all those things which are c you	Lk 17:10	*1299*
c him to be brought unto him	Lk 18:40	*2750*
then he c these servants to be	Lk 19:15	*2036*
Now Moses in the law c us	Jn 8:5	*1781*
c them that they should not	Acts 1:4	*3853*
But when they had c them to go	Acts 4:15	*2753*
c them not to speak at all nor	Acts 4:18	*3853*
c to put the apostles forth a	Acts 5:34	*2753*
they c that they should not speak	Acts 5:40	*3853*
he c the chariot to stand still	Acts 8:38	*2753*
all things that are c thee of God	Acts 10:33	*4367*
he c us to preach unto the people	Acts 10:42	*3853*
he c them to be baptized in the	Acts 10:48	*4367*
c that they should be put to	Acts 12:19	*2753*
For so hath the Lord c us	Acts 13:47	*1781*
their clothes, and c to beat them	Acts 16:22	*2753*
(because that Claudius had c all	Acts 18:2	*1299*
c him to be bound with two chains	Acts 21:33	*2753*
he c him to be carried into the	Acts 21:34	*2753*
The chief captain c him to be	Acts 22:24	*2753*
c the chief priests and all their	Acts 22:30	*2753*
the high priest Ananias c them	Acts 23:2	*2004*
c the soldiers to go down, and to	Acts 23:10	*2753*
the soldiers, as it was c them	Acts 23:31	*1299*
he c him to be kept in Herod's	Acts 23:35	*2753*
he c a centurion to keep Paul, and	Acts 24:23	*1299*
seat c Paul to be brought	Acts 25:6	*2753*
c the man to be brought forth	Acts 25:17	*2753*
I c him to be kept till I might	Acts 25:21	*2753*
c that they which could swim	Acts 27:43	*2753*
but they are c to be under	1Cor 14:34	
who c the light to shine out of	2Cor 4:6	*2036*
with your own hands, as we c you	1Th 4:11	*3853*
we were with you, this we c you	2Th 3:10	*3853*
could not endure that which was c	Heb 12:20	*1291*
it was c them that they should	Rev 9:4	*4483*

COMMANDEDST {4}

which thou c thy servant Moses	Neh 1:7	6680
that thou c thy servant Moses	Neh 1:8	6680
c them precepts, statutes, and	Neh 9:14	6680
of all that thou c them to do	Jer 32:23	6680

COMMANDER {1}

a leader and c to the people	Is 55:4	6680

COMMANDEST {3}

All that thou c us we will do	Josh 1:16	6680
thy words in all that thou c him	Josh 1:18	6680
c me to be smitten contrary to	Acts 23:3	*2753*

COMMANDETH {13}

is the thing which the LORD c	Ex 16:32	6680
Thy servants will do as my lord c	Num 32:25	6680
Which c the sun, and it riseth not	Job 9:7	559
c that they return from iniquity	Job 36:10	559
c it not to shine by the cloud	Job 36:32	6680
that they may do whatsoever he c	Job 37:12	6680
For he c, and raiseth the stormy	Ps 107:25	559
to pass, when the Lord c it not	Lam 3:37	6680
For, behold, the LORD c, and he	Amos 6:11	6680
for with authority c he even the	Mk 1:27	*2004*
power he c the unclean spirits,	Lk 4:36	*2004*
for he c even the winds and water,	Lk 8:25	*2004*
but now c all men every where to	Acts 17:30	*3853*

COMMANDING {4}

had made an end of c his sons	Gen 49:33	6680
an end of c his twelve disciples	Mt 11:1	*1299*
C his accusers to come unto thee	Acts 24:8	*2753*
c to abstain from meats, which	1Ti 4:3	

COMMANDMENT {177}

according to the c of Pharaoh	Gen 45:21	6310
according to the c of the LORD	Ex 17:1	6310
which I will give thee in c unto	Ex 25:22	6680
he gave them in c all that the	Ex 34:32	6680
And Moses gave c, and they caused	Ex 36:6	6680
according to the c of Moses	Ex 38:21	6310
numbered at the c of the LORD	Num 3:39	6310
the c of the LORD by the hand of	Num 4:37	6310
according to the c of the LORD	Num 4:41	6310
According to the c of the LORD	Num 4:49	6310
At the c of the LORD the children	Num 9:18	6310
at the c of the LORD they pitched	Num 9:18	6310
according to the c of the LORD	Num 9:20	6310
according to the c of the LORD	Num 9:20	6310
At the c of the LORD they rested	Num 9:23	6310
at the c of the LORD they	Num 9:23	6310
at the c of the LORD by the hand	Num 9:23	6310
the c of the LORD by the hand of	Num 10:13	6310
Moses by the c of the LORD sent	Num 13:3	6310
ye transgress the c of the LORD	Num 14:41	6310
of the LORD, and hath broken his c	Num 15:31	4687
I have received c to bless	Num 23:20	
go beyond the c of the LORD	Num 24:13	6310
against my c in the desert of Zin	Num 27:14	6310
journeys by the c of the LORD	Num 33:2	6310
mount Hor at the c of the LORD	Num 33:38	6310
LORD had given him in c unto them	Deut 1:3	6680
the c of the LORD your God	Deut 1:26	6310
against the c of the LORD	Deut 1:43	6310
the c of the LORD your God	Deut 9:23	6310
that he turn not aside from the c	Deut 17:20	4687
For this c which I command thee	Deut 30:11	4687
be that doth rebel against thy c	Josh 1:18	6310
according to the c of the LORD	Josh 8:8	1697
according to the c of the LORD to	Josh 15:13	6310
Therefore according to the c of	Josh 17:4	6310
at the c of the LORD, these	Josh 21:3	6310
of the c of the LORD your God	Josh 22:3	4687
take diligent heed to do the c	Josh 22:5	4687
not rebel against the c of the	1Sa 12:14	6310
rebel against the c of the LORD	1Sa 12:15	6310
kept the c of the LORD thy God	1Sa 13:13	4687
have performed the c of the LORD	1Sa 15:13	1697
transgressed the c of the LORD	1Sa 15:24	6310
thou despised the c of the LORD	2Sa 12:9	1697
the c that I have charged thee	1Kin 2:43	4687
hast not kept the c which the	1Kin 13:21	4687
c which the LORD commanded the	2Kin 17:34	4687
ordinances, and the law, and the c	2Kin 17:37	4687
for the king's c was, saying,	2Kin 18:36	4687
according to the c of Pharaoh	2Kin 23:35	6310
Surely at the c of the LORD came	2Kin 24:3	6310
their brethren were at their c	1Chr 12:32	6310
their gods there, David gave a c	1Chr 14:12	559
people will be wholly at thy c	1Chr 28:21	1697
according to the c of Moses	2Chr 8:13	4687
they departed not from the c of	2Chr 8:15	4687
and to do the law and the c	2Chr 14:4	4687
blood and blood, between law and c	2Chr 19:10	4687
according to the c of Moses the	2Chr 24:6	
at the king's c they made a chest	2Chr 24:8	559
stoned him with stones at the c	2Chr 24:21	4687
according to the c of the king	2Chr 29:15	4687
according to the c of David	2Chr 29:25	4687
for so was the c of the LORD by	2Chr 29:25	4687
and according to the c of the king	2Chr 30:6	4687
one heart to do the c of the king	2Chr 30:12	4687
And as soon as the c came abroad	2Chr 31:5	1697
at the c of Hezekiah the king, and	2Chr 31:13	4662
according to the king's c	2Chr 35:10	4687
according to the c of David	2Chr 35:15	4687
according to the c of king Josiah	2Chr 35:16	4687
Give ye now c to cause these men	Ezr 4:21	2942
until another c shall be given	Ezr 4:21	2941
according to the c of the God of	Ezr 6:14	2941
and according to the c of Cyrus	Ezr 6:14	2942
I sent them with c unto Iddo the	Ezr 8:17	3318
that tremble at the c of our God	Ezr 10:3	4687
was the king's c concerning them	Neh 11:23	4687
according to the c of David the	Neh 12:24	4687
according to the c of David	Neh 12:45	4687
the king's c by his chamberlains	Est 1:12	1697
she hath not performed the c of	Est 1:15	3982
let there go a royal c from him	Est 1:19	1697
came to pass, when the king's c	Est 2:8	1697
for Esther did the c of Mordecai	Est 2:20	3982
transgressest thou the king's c	Est 3:3	4687
a c to be given in every province	Est 3:14	1881
being hastened by the king's c	Est 3:15	1697
whithersoever the king's c	Est 4:3	1697
gave him a c to Mordecai, to know	Est 4:5	6680
and gave him c unto Mordecai	Est 4:10	6680
a c to be given in every province	Est 8:13	1881
and pressed on by the king's c	Est 8:14	1697
city, whithersoever the king's c	Est 8:17	1697
of the same, when the king's c	Est 9:1	1697
gone back from the c of his lips	Job 23:12	4687
the c of the LORD is pure,	Ps 19:8	4687
thou hast given c to save me	Ps 71:3	6680
but thy c is exceeding broad	Ps 119:96	4687
He sendeth forth his c upon earth	Ps 147:15	565
My son, keep thy father's c	Prov 6:20	4687
For the c is a lamp	Prov 6:23	4687
the waters should not pass his c	Prov 8:29	6310
feareth the c shall be rewarded	Prov 13:13	4687
He that keepeth the c keepeth his	Prov 19:16	4687
counsel thee to keep the king's c	Eccl 8:2	6310
Whoso keepeth the c shall feel no	Eccl 8:5	4687
the LORD hath given a c against	Is 23:11	6680
for the king's c was, saying,	Is 36:21	4687
none, but obey their father's c	Jer 35:14	4687
performed the c of their father	Jer 35:16	4687
the c of Jonadab your father	Jer 35:18	4687
for I have rebelled against his c	Lam 1:18	6310
because the king's c was urgent	Dan 3:22	4406
supplications the c came forth	Dan 9:23	1697
going forth of the c to restore	Dan 9:25	1697
he willingly walked after the c	Hos 5:11	6673
hath given a c concerning thee	Nah 1:14	6680
O ye priests, this c is for you	Mal 2:1	4687
that I have sent this c unto you	Mal 2:4	4687
he gave c to depart unto the	Mt 8:18	*2753*
the c of God by your tradition	Mt 15:3	*1785*
Thus have ye made the c of God of	Mt 15:6	*1785*
which is the great c in the law	Mt 22:36	*1785*
This is the first and great c	Mt 22:38	*1785*
For laying aside the c of God	Mk 7:8	*1785*
Full well ye reject the c of God	Mk 7:9	*1785*
him, Which is the first c of all	Mk 12:28	*1785*
this is the first c	Mk 12:30	*1785*
none other c greater than these	Mk 12:31	*1785*
transgressed I at any time thy c	Lk 15:29	*1785*
sabbath day according to the c	Lk 23:56	*1785*
This c have I received of my	Jn 10:18	*1785*
and the Pharisees had given a c	Jn 11:57	*1785*
which sent me, he gave me a c	Jn 12:49	*1785*
I know that his c is life	Jn 12:50	*1785*
A new c I give unto you, That ye	Jn 13:34	*1785*
and as the Father gave me c	Jn 14:31	*1781*
This is my c, That ye love one	Jn 15:12	*1785*
to whom we gave no such c	Acts 15:24	*1291*
and receiving a c unto Silas	Acts 17:15	*1785*
gave c to his accusers also to	Acts 23:30	*3853*
at Festus' c Paul was brought	Acts 25:23	*2753*
But sin, taking occasion by the c	Rom 7:8	*1785*
but when the c came, sin revived	Rom 7:9	*1785*
And the c, which was ordained to	Rom 7:10	*1785*
For sin, taking occasion by the c	Rom 7:11	*1785*
the c holy, and just, and good	Rom 7:12	*1785*
that sin by the c might become	Rom 7:13	*1785*

and if there be any other *c* Rom 13:9 *1785*
according to the *c* of the Rom 16:26 *2003*
this by permission, and not of *c* 1Cor 7:6 *2003*
virgins I have no *c* of the Lord 1Cor 7:25 *2003*
I speak not by *c*, but by occasion 2Cor 8:8 *2003*
which is the first *c* with promise Eph 6:2 *1785*
by the *c* of God our Saviour 1Ti 1:1 *2003*
Now the end of the *c* is charity 1Ti 1:5 *3852*
thou keep this *c* without spot 1Ti 6:14 *1785*
to the *c* of God our Saviour Titus 1:3 *2003*
have a *c* to take tithes of the Heb 7:5 *1785*
not after the law of a carnal *c* Heb 7:16 *1785*
c going before for the weakness Heb 7:18 *1785*
gave *c* concerning his bones Heb 11:22 *1781*
were not afraid of the king's *c* Heb 11:23 *1297*
the holy *c* delivered unto them 2Pet 2:21 *1785*
of the *c* of us the apostles of 2Pet 3:2 *1785*
I write no new *c* unto you 1Jn 2:7 *1785*
but an old *c* which ye had from 1Jn 2:7 *1785*
The old *c* is the word which ye 1Jn 2:7 *1785*
a new *c* I write unto you, which 1Jn 2:8 *1785*
And this is his *c*, That we should 1Jn 3:23 *1785*
love one another, as he gave us *c* 1Jn 3:23 *1785*
this *c* have we from him, That he 1Jn 4:21 *1785*
have received a *c* from the Father 2Jn 4 *1785*
though I wrote a new *c* unto thee 2Jn 5 *1785*
This is the *c*, That, as ye have 2Jn 6 *1785*

COMMANDMENTS {171}

my voice, and kept my charge, my *c* Gen 26:5 4687
sight, and wilt give ear to his *c* Ex 15:26 4687
How long refuse ye to keep my *c* Ex 16:28 4687
them that love me, and keep my *c* Ex 20:6 4687
a law, and *c* which I have written Ex 24:12 4687
words of the covenant, the ten *c* Ex 34:28 1697
ignorance against any of the *c* of Lev 4:2 4687
somewhat against any of the *c* of Lev 4:13 4687
ignorance against any of the *c* of Lev 4:22 4687
somewhat against any of the *c* of Lev 4:27 4687
to be done by the *c* of the LORD Lev 5:17 4687
Therefore shall ye keep my *c* Lev 22:31 4687
walk in my statutes, and keep my *c* Lev 26:3 4687
me, and will not do all these *c* Lev 26:14 4687
so that ye will not do all my *c* Lev 26:15 4687
These are the *c*, which the LORD Lev 27:34 4687
and not observed all these *c* Num 15:22 4687
and remember all the *c* of the LORD Num 15:39 4687
ye may remember, and do all my *c* Num 15:40 4687
These are the *c* and the judgments, Num 36:13 4687
that ye may keep the *c* of the Deut 4:2 4687
you to perform, even ten *c* Deut 4:13 1697
therefore his statutes, and his *c* Deut 4:40 4687
of them that love me and keep my *c* Deut 5:10 4687
fear me, and keep all my *c* always Deut 5:29 4687
I will speak unto thee all the *c* Deut 5:31 4687
Now these are the *c*, the statutes Deut 6:1 4687
to keep all his statutes and his *c* Deut 6:2 4687
keep the *c* of the LORD your God Deut 6:17 4687
these *c* before the LORD our God Deut 6:25 4687
him and keep his *c* to a thousand Deut 7:9 4687
Thou shalt therefore keep the *c* Deut 7:11 4687
All the *c* which I command thee Deut 8:1 4687
whether thou wouldest keep his *c* Deut 8:2 4687
keep the *c* of the LORD thy God Deut 8:6 4687
thy God, in not keeping his *c* Deut 8:11 4687
to the first writing, the ten *c* Deut 10:4 1697
To keep the *c* of the LORD Deut 10:13 4687
and his judgments, and his *c* Deut 11:1 4687
c which I command you this day Deut 11:8 4687
hearken diligently unto my *c* Deut 11:13 4687
all these *c* which I command you Deut 11:22 4687
if ye obey the *c* of the LORD your Deut 11:27 4687
obey the *c* of the LORD your God Deut 11:28 4687
God, and fear him, and keep his *c* Deut 13:4 4687
to keep all his *c* which I command Deut 13:18 4687
to observe to do all these *c* Deut 15:5 4687
shalt keep all these *c* to do them Deut 19:9 4687
according to all thy *c* which thou Deut 26:13 4687
I have not transgressed thy *c* Deut 26:13 4687
and to keep his statutes, and his *c* Deut 26:17 4687
thou shouldest keep all his *c* Deut 26:18 4687
Keep all the *c* which I command Deut 27:1 4687
of the LORD thy God, and do his *c* Deut 27:10 4687
to do all his *c* which I command Deut 28:1 4687
keep the *c* of the LORD thy God Deut 28:9 4687
unto the *c* of the LORD thy God Deut 28:13 4687
God, to observe to do all his *c* Deut 28:15 4687
the LORD thy God, to keep his *c* Deut 28:45 4687
do all his *c* which I command thee Deut 30:8 4687
the LORD thy God, to keep his *c* Deut 30:10 4687
in his ways, and to keep his *c* Deut 30:16 4687
the *c* which I have commanded you Deut 31:5 4687
in all his ways, and to keep his *c* Josh 22:5 4687
in, obeying the *c* of the LORD Judg 2:17 4687
hearken unto the *c* of the LORD Judg 3:4 4687
me, and hath not performed my *c* 1Sa 15:11 1697
to keep his statutes, and his *c* 1Kin 2:3 4687
ways, to keep my statutes and my *c* 1Kin 3:14 4687
keep all my *c* to walk in them 1Kin 6:12 4687
in all his ways, and to keep his *c* 1Kin 8:58 4687
in his statutes, and to keep his *c* 1Kin 8:61 4687
children, and will not keep my *c* 1Kin 9:6 4687
I chose, because he kept my *c* 1Kin 11:34 4687
to keep my statutes and my *c* 1Kin 11:38 4687
my servant David, who kept my *c* 1Kin 14:8 4687
have forsaken the *c* of the LORD 1Kin 18:18 4687
from your evil ways, and keep my *c* 2Kin 17:13 4687
they left all the *c* of the LORD 2Kin 17:16 4687
not the *c* of the LORD their God 2Kin 17:19 4687
following him, but kept his *c* 2Kin 18:6 4687
after the LORD, and to keep his *c* 2Kin 23:3 4687
if he be constant to do my *c* 1Chr 28:7 4687
seek for all the *c* of the LORD 1Chr 28:8 4687
a perfect heart, to keep thy *c* 1Chr 29:19 4687
and forsake my statutes and my *c* 2Chr 7:19 4687
of his father, and walked in his *c* 2Chr 17:4 4687
transgress ye the *c* of the LORD 2Chr 24:20 4687
God, and in the law, and in the *c* 2Chr 31:21 4687
after the LORD, and to keep his *c* 2Chr 34:31 4687
of the words of the *c* of the LORD Ezr 7:11 4687
for we have forsaken thy *c* Ezr 9:10 4687
Should we again break thy *c* Ezr 9:14 4687
that love him and observe his *c* Neh 1:5 4687
thee, and have not kept the *c* Neh 1:7 4687
if ye turn unto me, and keep my *c* Neh 1:9 4687
and true laws, good statutes and *c* Neh 9:13 4687
necks, and hearkened not to thy *c* Neh 9:16 4687
and hearkened not unto thy *c* Neh 9:29 4687
thy law, nor hearkened unto thy *c* Neh 9:34 4687
do all the *c* of the LORD our Lord Neh 10:29 4687
the works of God, but keep his *c* Ps 78:7 4687
my statutes, and keep not my *c* Ps 89:31 4687
that remember his *c* to do them Ps 103:18 6490
excel in strength, that do his *c* Ps 103:20 1697
all his *c* are sure Ps 111:7 6490
have all they that do his *c* Ps 111:10
that delighteth greatly in his *c* Ps 112:1 4687
I have respect unto all thy *c* Ps 119:6 4687
O let me not wander from thy *c* Ps 119:10 4687
hide not thy *c* from me Ps 119:19 4687
cursed, which do err from thy *c* Ps 119:21 4687
I will run the way of thy *c* Ps 119:32 4687
me to go in the path of thy *c* Ps 119:35 4687
And I will delight myself in thy *c* Ps 119:47 4687
also will I lift up unto thy *c* Ps 119:48 4687
and delayed not to keep thy *c* Ps 119:60 4687
for I have believed thy *c* Ps 119:66 4687
that I may learn thy *c* Ps 119:73 4687
All thy *c* are faithful Ps 119:86 4687
Thou through thy *c* hast made me Ps 119:98 4687
for I will keep the *c* of my God Ps 119:115 4687
Therefore I love thy *c* above gold Ps 119:127 4687
for I longed for thy *c* Ps 119:131 4687
yet thy *c* are my delights Ps 119:143 4687
and all thy *c* are truth Ps 119:151 4687
for thy salvation, and done thy *c* Ps 119:166 4687
for all thy *c* are righteousness Ps 119:172 4687
for I do not forget thy *c* Ps 119:176 4687
my words, and hide my *c* with thee Prov 2:1 4687
but let thine heart keep my *c* Prov 3:1 4687
keep my *c*, and live Prov 4:4 4687
words, and lay up my *c* with thee Prov 7:1 4687
Keep my *c*, and live Prov 7:2 4687
The wise in heart will receive *c* Prov 10:8 4687
Fear God, and keep his *c* Eccl 12:13 4687
that thou hadst hearkened to my *c* Is 48:18 4687
him, and to them that keep his *c* Dan 9:4 4687
the LORD, and have not kept his *c* Amos 2:4 2706
shall break one of these least *c* Mt 5:19 *1785*
for doctrines the *c* of men Mt 15:9 *1778*
wilt enter into life, keep the *c* Mt 19:17 *1785*
On these two *c* hang all the law Mt 22:40 *1785*
for doctrines the *c* of men Mk 7:7 *1778*
Thou knowest the *c*, Do not commit Mk 10:19 *1785*
him, The first of all the *c* is Mk 12:29 *1785*
before God, walking in all the *c* Lk 1:6 *1785*
Thou knowest the *c*, Do not commit Lk 18:20 *1785*
If ye love me, keep my *c* Jn 14:15 *1785*
He that hath my *c*, and keepeth Jn 14:21 *1785*
If ye keep my *c*, ye shall abide Jn 15:10 *1785*
even as I have kept my Father's *c* Jn 15:10 *1785*
the Holy Ghost had given *c* unto Acts 1:2 *1781*
but the keeping of the *c* of God 1Cor 7:19 *1785*
unto you are the *c* of the Lord 1Cor 14:37 *1785*
even the law of *c* contained in Eph 2:15 *1785*
after the *c* and doctrines of men Col 2:22 *1778*
(touching whom ye received *c* Col 4:10 *1785*
For ye know what *c* we gave you by 1Th 4:2 *3852*
c of men, that turn from the Titus 1:14 *1785*
we know him, if we keep his *c* 1Jn 2:3 *1785*
I know him, and keepeth not his *c* 1Jn 2:4 *1785*
of him, because we keep his *c* 1Jn 3:22 *1785*
keepeth his *c* dwelleth in him 1Jn 3:24 *1785*
when we love God, and keep his *c* 1Jn 5:2 *1785*
love of God, that we keep his *c* 1Jn 5:3 *1785*
and his *c* are not grievous 1Jn 5:3 *1785*
is love, that we walk after his *c* 2Jn 6 *1785*
her seed, which keep the *c* of God Rev 12:17 *1785*
are they that keep the *c* of God Rev 14:12 *1785*
Blessed are they that do his *c* Rev 22:14 *1785*

COMMEND {7}

into thy hands I *c* my spirit Lk 23:46 *3908*
I *c* you to God, and to the word of Acts 20:32 *3908*
c the righteousness of God Rom 3:5 *4921*
I *c* unto you Phebe our sister, Rom 16:1 *4921*
Do we begin again to *c* ourselves 2Cor 3:1 *4921*
For we *c* not ourselves again unto 2Cor 5:12 *4921*
with some that *c* themselves 2Cor 10:12 *4921*

COMMENDATION {2}

some others, epistles of *c* to you 2Cor 3:1 *4956*
to you, or letters of *c* from you 2Cor 3:1 *4956*

COMMENDED {6}

saw her, and *c* her before Pharaoh Gen 12:15 1984
A man shall be *c* according to his Prov 12:8 1984
Then I *c* mirth, because a man Eccl 8:15 7623
the lord *c* the unjust steward, Lk 16:8 *1867*
they *c* them to the Lord, on whom Acts 14:23 *3908*
for I ought to have been *c* of you 2Cor 12:11 *4921*

COMMENDETH {4}

But God *c* his love toward us, in Rom 5:8 *4921*
But meat *c* us not to God 1Cor 8:8 *3936*
For not he that *c* himself is 2Cor 10:18 *4921*
is approved, but whom the Lord *c* 2Cor 10:18 *4921*

COMMENDING {1}

truth *c* ourselves to every man's 2Cor 4:2 *4921*

COMMISSION {1}

c from the chief priests, Acts 26:12 *2011*

COMMISSIONS {1}

they delivered the king's *c* unto Ezr 8:36 1881

COMMIT {75}

Thou shalt not *c* adultery Ex 20:14 5003
If a soul *c* a trespass, and sin Lev 5:15 4603
c any of these things which are Lev 5:17 6213
c a trespass against the LORD, and Lev 6:2 4603
and shall not *c* any of these Lev 18:26 6213
For whosoever shall *c* any of Lev 18:29 6213
even the souls that *c* them shall Lev 18:29 6213
that ye *c* not any one of these Lev 18:30 6213
to *c* whoredom with Molech, from Lev 20:5 2181
When a man or woman shall *c* Num 5:6 6213
any sin that men *c*, to do Num 5:6
c a trespass against him, Num 5:12 4603
the people began to *c* whoredom Num 25:1 2181
to *c* trespass against the LORD in Num 31:16 4560
Neither shalt thou *c* adultery Deut 5:18 5003
shall henceforth *c* no more any Deut 19:20 6213
c a trespass in the accursed Josh 22:20 4603
If he *c* iniquity, I will chasten 2Sa 7:14 5753
of Jerusalem to *c* fornication 2Chr 21:11 2181
and unto God would I *c* my cause Job 5:8 7760
that he should *c* iniquity Job 34:10
Into thine hand I *c* my spirit Ps 31:5 6485
C thy way unto the LORD Ps 37:5 1556
C thy works unto the LORD, and thy Prov 16:3 1556
to kings to *c* wickedness Prov 16:12 6213
I will *c* thy government into his Is 22:21 5414
shall *c* fornication with all the Is 23:17 2181
c adultery, and swear falsely, and Jer 7:9 5003
and weary themselves to *c* iniquity Jer 9:5 5753
they *c* adultery, and walk in lies Jer 23:14 5003
c Jeremiah into the court of the Jer 37:21 6485
Wherefore *c* ye this great evil Jer 44:7 6213
and *c* iniquity, and I lay a Eze 3:20 6213
c the abominations which they *c* Eze 8:17 6213
didst *c* whoredom with them, Eze 16:17 2181
followeth thee to *c* whoredoms Eze 16:34 2181
thou shalt not *c* this lewdness Eze 16:43 6213
c ye whoredom after their Eze 20:30 2181
the midst of thee they *c* lewdness Eze 22:9 6213
Will they now *c* whoredoms with Eze 23:43 2181
and *c* iniquity, all his Eze 33:13 6213
they shall *c* whoredom, and shall Hos 4:10 2181
your daughters shall *c* whoredom Hos 4:13 2181
and your spouses shall *c* adultery Hos 4:13 5003
daughters when they *c* whoredom Hos 4:14 2181
your spouses when they *c* adultery Hos 4:14 5003
for they *c* lewdness Hos 6:9 6313
for they *c* falsehood Hos 7:1 6466
time, Thou shalt not *c* adultery Mt 5:27 *3431*
causeth her to *c* adultery Mt 5:32 *3429*
which is put away doth *c* adultery Mt 19:9 *3429*
murder, Thou shalt not *c* adultery Mt 19:18 *3431*
Do not *c* adultery, Do not kill, Mk 10:19 *3431*
did *c* things worthy of stripes, Lk 12:48 *4160*
who will *c* to your trust the true Lk 16:11 *4100*
Do not *c* adultery, Do not kill, Lk 18:20 *3431*
Jesus did not *c* himself unto them Jn 2:24 *4100*
that they which *c* such things are Rom 1:32 *4238*
against them which *c* such things Rom 2:2 *4238*
a man should not *c* adultery Rom 2:22 *3431*
dost thou *c* adultery Rom 2:22 *3431*
idols, dost thou *c* sacrilege Rom 2:22 *2416*
this, Thou shalt not *c* adultery Rom 13:9 *3431*
Neither let us *c* fornication 1Cor 10:8 *4203*
This charge I *c* unto thee 1Ti 1:18 *3908*
the same *c* thou to faithful men, 2Ti 2:2 *3908*
ye *c* sin, and are convinced of the Jas 2:9 *2038*
Do not *c* adultery, said also, Do Jas 2:11 *3431*
Now if thou *c* no adultery Jas 2:11 *3431*
according to the will of God *c* 1Pet 4:19 *3908*
is born of God doth not *c* sin 1Jn 3:9 *4160*
unto idols, and to *c* fornication Rev 2:14 *4203*
my servants to *c* fornication Rev 2:20 *4203*
them that *c* adultery with her Rev 2:22 *3431*

COMMITTED {92}

he hath *c* all that he hath to my Gen 39:8 5414
prison *c* to Joseph's hand all the Gen 39:22 5414
for his sin that he hath *c* Lev 4:35 2398
for his trespass, which he hath *c* Lev 5:7 2398
customs, which were *c* before you Lev 18:30 6213
of them have *c* an abomination Lev 20:13 6213
for they *c* all these things, and Lev 20:23 6213
if ought be *c* by ignorance Num 15:24 6213
which have *c* that wicked thing, Deut 17:5 6213
if a man have *c* a sin worthy of Deut 21:22 1961
c a trespass in the accursed Josh 7:1 4600
have *c* against the God of Israel Josh 22:16 4600
because ye have not *c* this Josh 22:31 4600
for they have *c* lewdness and folly Judg 20:6 6213

perversely, we have c wickedness 1Kin 8:47 7561
with their sins which they had c 1Kin 14:22 2398
c them unto the hands of the 1Kin 14:27 6485
which he c against the LORD 1Chr 10:13 4600
c them to the hands of the chief 2Chr 12:10 6485
All that was c to thy servants, ... 2Chr 34:16 5414
we have c iniquity, we have done .... Ps 106:6 5753
For my people have c two evils .... Jer 2:13 6213
whereby backsliding Israel c .... Jer 3:8 5003
c adultery with stones and with .... Jer 3:9 5003
to the full, they then c adultery .... Jer 5:7 5003
horrible thing is c in the land .... Jer 5:30 1961
when they had c abomination .... Jer 6:15 6213
when they had c abomination .... Jer 8:12 6213
have c against the LORD our God .... Jer 16:10 2398
they have c villany in Israel .... Jer 29:23 6213
have c adultery with their .... Jer 29:23 6213
c him unto Gedaliah the son of .... Jer 39:14 5414
had c unto him men, and women, and .... Jer 40:7 6485
the captain of the guard had c to .... Jer 41:10 6485
have c to provoke me to anger .... Jer 44:3 6213
which they have c in the land of .... Jer 44:9 6213
the abominations which ye have c .... Jer 44:22 6213
have c in all their abominations .... Eze 6:9 6213
because they have c a trespass .... Eze 15:8 4600
Thou hast also c fornication with .... Eze 16:26 2181
and c abomination before me .... Eze 16:50 6213
hath Samaria c half of thy sins .... Eze 16:51 2398
hast c more abominable than they .... Eze 16:52 8581
to the idols, hath c abomination, ... Eze 18:12 6213
from all his sins that he hath c .... Eze 18:21 6213
his transgressions that he hath c .... Eze 18:22 6213
his wickedness that he hath c .... Eze 18:27 6213
his transgressions that he hath c .... Eze 18:28 6213
in that they have c a trespass .... Eze 20:27 4600
for all your evils that ye have c .... Eze 20:43 6213
one hath c abomination with his .... Eze 22:11 6213
they c whoredoms in Egypt .... Eze 23:3 2181
they c whoredoms in their youth .... Eze 23:3 2181
Thus she c her whoredoms with .... Eze 23:7 5414
That they have c adultery .... Eze 23:37 5003
their idols have they c adultery .... Eze 23:37 5003
for his iniquity that he hath c .... Eze 33:13 6213
c shall be mentioned unto him .... Eze 33:16 2398
abominations which they have c .... Eze 33:29 6213
abominations that they have c .... Eze 43:8 6213
abominations which they have c .... Eze 44:13 6213
have c iniquity, and have done .... Dan 9:5 5753
the land hath c great whoredom .... Hos 1:2 2181
they have c whoredom continually .... Hos 4:18 2181
and an abomination is c in Israel .... Mal 2:11 6213
c adultery with her already in .... Mt 5:28 *3431*
with him, who had c murder in the .... Mk 15:7 *4160*
and to whom men have c much .... Lk 12:48 *3908*
but hath c all judgment unto the .... Jn 5:22 *1325*
men and women c them to prison .... Acts 8:3 *3860*
or have c any thing worthy of .... Acts 25:11 *4238*
he had c nothing worthy of death .... Acts 25:25 *4238*
they c themselves unto the sea, ... Acts 27:40 *1439*
though I have c nothing against .... Acts 28:17 *4160*
them were c the oracles of God .... Rom 3:2 *4100*
of the gospel is c unto me 1Cor 9:17 *4100*
fornication, as some of them c 1Cor 10:8 *4203*
hath c unto us the word of 2Cor 5:19 *5087*
Have I c an offence in abasing 2Cor 11:7 *4160*
lasciviousness which they have c 2Cor 12:21 *4238*
the uncircumcision was c unto me .... Gal 2:7 *4100*
God, which was c to my trust 1Ti 1:11 *4100*
keep that which is c to thy trust 1Ti 6:20 *3872*
have c unto him against that day 2Ti 1:12 *3866*
That good thing which was c unto 2Ti 1:14 *3872*
which is c unto me according to .... Titus 1:3 *4100*
and if he have c sins, they shall .... Jas 5:15 *4160*
but c himself to him that judgeth 1Pet 2:23 *3860*
deeds which they have ungodly c .... Jude 15 *764*
of the earth have c fornication .... Rev 17:2 *4203*
earth have c fornication with her .... Rev 18:3 *4203*
who have c fornication and lived .... Rev 18:9 *4203*

COMMITTEST {1}

thou c whoredom, and Israel is .... Hos 5:3 2181

COMMITTETH {19}

the man that c adultery with .... Lev 20:10 5003
even he that c adultery with his .... Lev 20:10 5003
the poor c himself unto thee .... Ps 10:14 5800
But whoso c adultery with a woman .... Prov 6:32 5003
that the house of Israel c here .... Eze 8:6 6213
But as a wife that c adultery .... Eze 16:32 5003
c iniquity, and doeth according to .... Eze 18:24 6213
c iniquity, and dieth in them .... Eze 18:26 6213
c iniquity, he shall even die .... Eze 33:18 6213
her that is divorced c adultery .... Mt 5:32 *3429*
shall marry another, c adultery .... Mt 19:9 *3429*
another, c adultery against her .... Mk 10:11 *3429*
to another, she c adultery .... Mk 10:12 *3429*
and marrieth another, c adultery .... Lk 16:18 *3431*
away from her husband c adultery .... Lk 16:18 *3431*
Whosoever c sin is the servant of .... Jn 8:34 *4160*
but he that c fornication sinneth 1Cor 6:18 *4203*
Whosoever c sin transgresseth 1Jn 3:4 *4160*
He that c sin is of the devil 1Jn 3:8 *4160*

COMMITTING {2}

of life, without c iniquity .... Eze 33:15 6213
c adultery, they break out, and .... Hos 4:2 5003

COMMODIOUS {1}

the haven was not c to winter in .... Acts 27:12 *428*

COMMON {21}

if any one of the c people sin .... Lev 4:27 776
men die the c death of all men .... Num 16:29
There is no c bread under mine 1Sa 21:4 2455
and the bread is in a manner c 1Sa 21:5 2455
the sun, and it is c among men .... Eccl 6:1 7227
into the graves of the c people .... Jer 26:23 1121
and shall eat them as c things .... Jer 31:5 2490
with the men of the c sort were .... Eze 23:42 7230
took Jesus into the c hall .... Mt 27:27 *4232*
the c people heard him gladly .... Mk 12:37 *4183*
together, and had all things c .... Acts 2:44 *2839*
but they had all things c .... Acts 4:32 *2839*
and put them in the c prison .... Acts 5:18 *1219*
any thing that is c or unclean .... Acts 10:14 *2839*
cleansed, that call not thou c .... Acts 10:15 *2840*
not call any man c or unclean .... Acts 10:28 *2839*
for nothing c or unclean hath at .... Acts 11:8 *2839*
cleansed, that call not thou c .... Acts 11:9 *2839*
taken you but such as is c to man 1Cor 10:13 *442*
mine own son after the c faith .... Titus 1:4 *2839*
write unto you of the c salvation .... Jude 3 *2839*

COMMONLY {2}

this saying is c reported among .... Mt 28:15 *1310*
It is reported c that there is 1Cor 5:1 *3654*

COMMONWEALTH {1}

being aliens from the c of Israel .... Eph 2:12 *4174*

COMMOTION {1}

a great c out of the north .... Jer 10:22 7494

COMMOTIONS {1}

when ye shall hear of wars and c .... Lk 21:9 *181*

COMMUNE {8}

went out unto Jacob to c with him .... Gen 34:6 1696
I will c with thee from above the .... Ex 25:22 1696
C with David secretly, and say, ... 1Sa 18:22 1696
I will c with my father of thee 1Sa 19:3 1696
If we assay to c with thee .... Job 4:2 1697
c with your own heart upon your .... Ps 4:4 559
they c of laying snares privily .... Ps 64:5 5608
I c with mine own heart .... Ps 77:6 7878

COMMUNED {18}

he c with them, saying, If it be .... Gen 23:8 1696
Hamor c with them, saying, The .... Gen 34:8 1696
c with the men of their city, ... Gen 34:20 1696
c with them, and took from them .... Gen 42:24 1696
they c with him at the door of .... Gen 43:19 1696
c with them, and with all the .... Judg 9:1 1696
Samuel c with Saul upon the top 1Sa 9:25 1696
c with Abigail, to take her to 1Sa 25:39 1696
she c with him of all that was in 1Kin 10:2 1696
and they c with her 2Kin 22:14 1696
she c with him of all that was in 2Chr 9:1 1696
I c with mine own heart, saying, ... Eccl 1:16 1696
And the king c with them .... Dan 1:19 1696
So the angel that c with me said .... Zec 1:14 1696
c one with another what they .... Lk 6:11 *1255*
c with the chief priests and .... Lk 22:4 *4814*
pass, that, while they c together .... Lk 24:15 *3656*
him the oftener, and c with him .... Acts 24:26 *3656*

COMMUNICATE {4}

c unto him that teacheth in all .... Gal 6:6 *2841*
that ye did c with my affliction .... Phil 4:14 *4790*
ready to distribute, willing to c 1Ti 6:18 *2843*
But to do good and to c forget not .... Heb 13:16 *2842*

COMMUNICATED {2}

c unto them that gospel which I .... Gal 2:2 *394*
no church c with me as concerning .... Phil 4:15 *2841*

COMMUNICATION {6}

Abner had c with the elders of 2Sa 3:17 1697
them, Ye know the man, and his c 2Kin 9:11 7879
But let your c be, Yea, yea .... Mt 5:37 *3056*
Let no corrupt c proceed out of .... Eph 4:29 *3056*
filthy c out of your mouth .... Col 3:8 *148*
That the c of thy faith may .... Philem 6 *2842*

COMMUNICATIONS {2}

What manner of c are these that .... Lk 24:17 *3056*
evil c corrupt good manners 1Cor 15:33 *3657*

COMMUNING {2}

as he had left c with Abraham .... Gen 18:33 1696
of c with him upon mount Sinai .... Ex 31:18 1696

COMMUNION {4}

is it not the c of the blood of 1Cor 10:16 *2842*
is it not the c of the body of 1Cor 10:16 *2842*
what c hath light with darkness 2Cor 6:14 *2842*
the c of the Holy Ghost, be with 2Cor 13:14 *2842*

COMPACT {1}

as a city that is c together .... Ps 122:3 2266

COMPACTED {1}

c by that which every joint .... Eph 4:16 *4822*

COMPANIED {1}

of these men which have c with us .... Acts 1:21 *4905*

COMPANIES {17}

three hundred men into three c .... Judg 7:16 7218
the three c blew the trumpets, and .... Judg 7:20 7218
wait against Shechem in four c .... Judg 9:34 7218
and divided them into three c .... Judg 9:43 7218
the two other c ran upon all the .... Judg 9:44 7218
Saul put the people in three c 1Sa 11:11 7218
of the Philistines in three c 1Sa 13:17 7218
And the Syrians had gone out by c 2Kin 5:2 1416
in the c of the children of Levi 1Chr 9:18 4264
the captains of the c that 1Chr 28:1 4256
appointed two great c of them .... Neh 12:31
So stood the two c of them that .... Neh 12:40
the c of Sheba waited for them .... Job 6:19 1979
O ye travelling c of Dedanim .... Is 21:13 736
criest, let thy c deliver thee .... Is 57:13
chariots, and with horsemen, and c .... Eze 26:7 6951
down by c upon the green grass .... Mk 6:39 *4849*

COMPANION {13}

his brother, and every man his c .... Ex 32:27 7453
Samson's wife was given to his c .... Judg 14:20 4828
therefore I gave her to thy c .... Judg 15:2 4828
his wife, and given her to his c .... Judg 15:6 4828
the Archite was the king's c 1Chr 27:33 7453
to dragons, and a c to owls .... Job 30:29 7453
I am a c of all them that fear .... Ps 119:63 2270
but a c of fools shall be .... Prov 13:20 7462
but he that is a c of riotous men .... Prov 28:7 7462
the same is the c of a destroyer .... Prov 28:24 2270
yet is she thy c, and the wife of .... Mal 2:14 2278
c in labour, and fellow soldier, ... Phil 2:25 *4904*
c in tribulation, and in the .... Rev 1:9 *4791*

COMPANIONS {21}

and she went with her c, and .... Judg 11:38 7464
brought thirty c to be with him .... Judg 14:11 4828
Tabeel, and the rest of their c .... Ezr 4:7 3675
scribe, and the rest of their c .... Ezr 4:9 3675
to the rest of their c that dwell .... Ezr 4:17 3675
Shimshai the scribe, and their c .... Ezr 4:23 3675
and Shethar-boznai, and their c .... Ezr 5:3 3675
his c the Apharsachites, which .... Ezr 5:6 3675
your c the Apharsachites, which .... Ezr 6:6 3675
river, Shethar-boznai, and their c .... Ezr 6:13 3675
answer thee, and thy c with thee .... Job 35:4 7453
Shall the c make a banquet of him .... Job 41:6 2271
the virgins her c that follow her .... Ps 45:14 7464
aside by the flocks of thy c .... Song 1:7 2270
the c hearken to thy voice .... Song 8:13 2270
are rebellious, and c of thieves .... Is 1:23 2270
for the children of Israel his c .... Eze 37:16 2270
for all the house of Israel his c .... Eze 37:16 2270
Mishael, and Azariah, his c .... Dan 2:17 2269
Paul's c in travel, they rushed .... Acts 19:29 *4898*
whilst ye became c of them that .... Heb 10:33 *2844*

COMPANIONS' {1}

c sakes, I will now say, Peace be .... Ps 122:8 7453

COMPANY {86}

said, If Esau come to the one c .... Gen 32:8 4264
then the other c which is left .... Gen 32:8 4264
lodged that night in the c .... Gen 32:21 4264
a c of nations shall be of thee, ... Gen 35:11 6951
a c of Ishmeelites came from .... Gen 37:25 736
and it was a very great c .... Gen 50:9 4264
they spake unto all the c of the .... Num 14:7 5712
unto Korah and unto all his c .... Num 16:5 5712
you censers, Korah, and all his c .... Num 16:6 5712
all thy c are gathered together .... Num 16:11 5712
all thy c before the LORD, thou, ... Num 16:16 5712
he be not as Korah, and as his c .... Num 16:40 5712
Now shall this c lick up all that .... Num 22:4 6951
against Aaron in the c of Korah .... Num 26:9 5712
with Korah, when that c died .... Num 26:10 5712
he was not in the c of them that .... Num 27:3 5712
the LORD in the c of Korah .... Num 27:3 5712
another c come along by the plain .... Judg 9:37 7218
the c that was with him, rushed .... Judg 9:44 7218
that thou comest with such a c .... Judg 18:23 2199
that thou shalt meet a c of 1Sa 10:5 2256
behold, a c of prophets met him 1Sa 10:10 2256
one c turned unto the way that 1Sa 13:17 7218
another c turned the way to 1Sa 13:18 7218
another c turned to the way of 1Sa 13:18 7218
when they saw the c of the 1Sa 19:20 3862
thou bring me down to this c 1Sa 30:15 1416
I will bring thee down to this c 1Sa 30:15 1416
delivered the c that came against 1Sa 30:23 1416
the man of God, he and all his c 2Kin 5:15 4264
he spied the c of Jehu as he came 2Kin 9:17 8229
and said, I see a c 2Kin 9:17 8229
at Jerusalem, with a very great c 2Chr 9:1 2428
great c that cometh against us 2Chr 20:12 1995
came with a small c of men 2Chr 24:24
the other c of them that gave .... Neh 12:38
thou hast made desolate all my c .... Job 16:7 5712
Which goeth in c with the workers .... Job 34:8 2274
walked unto the house of God in c .... Ps 55:14 7285
great was the c of those that .... Ps 68:11 6635
Rebuke the c of spearmen, the .... Ps 68:30 2416
and covered the c of Abiram .... Ps 106:17 5712
And a fire was kindled in their c .... Ps 106:18 5712
but he that keepeth c with .... Prov 29:3 7462
to a c of horses in Pharaoh's .... Song 1:9
As it were the c of two armies .... Song 6:13 4246
a great c shall return thither .... Jer 31:8 6951
also bring up a c against thee .... Eze 16:40 6951
great c make for him in the war, ... Eze 17:17 6951
I will bring up a c upon them .... Eze 23:46 6951
the c shall stone them with .... Eze 23:47 6951
the c of the Ashurites have made .... Eze 27:6 1323
in all thy c which is in the .... Eze 27:27 6951
all thy c in the midst of thee .... Eze 27:34 6951
over thee with a c of many people .... Eze 32:3 6951
Asshur is there and all her c .... Eze 32:22 6951
her c is round about her grave .... Eze 32:23 6951
even a great c with bucklers and .... Eze 38:4 6951
all thy c that are assembled unto .... Eze 38:7 6951

gathered thy *c* to take a prey... Eze 38:13 6951
riding upon horses, a great *c*... Eze 38:15 6951
so the *c* of priests murder in the... Hos 6:9 2267
him to have been in the *c*... Lk 2:44 *4923*
there was a great *c* of publicans... Lk 5:29 *3793*
the *c* of his disciples, and a... Lk 6:17 *3793*
shall separate you from their *c*... Lk 6:22
them sit down by fifties in a *c*... Lk 9:14 *2828*
behold, a man of the *c* cried out... Lk 9:38 *3793*
of the *c* lifted up her voice... Lk 11:27 *3793*
one of the *c* said unto him,... Lk 12:13 *3793*
followed him a great *c* of people... Lk 23:27 *4128*
also of our *c* made us astonished... Lk 24:22
saw a great *c* come unto him, he... Jn 6:5 *3793*
let go, they went to their own *c*... Acts 4:23 *2398*
a great *c* of the priests were... Acts 6:7 *3793*
for a man that is a Jew to keep *c*... Acts 10:28 *2853*
his *c* loosed from Paphos, they... Acts 13:13 *3588,4012*
their own *c* to Antioch with Paul... Acts 15:22
the baser sort, and gathered a *c*... Acts 17:5 *3792*
we that were of Paul's *c* departed... Acts 21:8 *4012*
I be somewhat filled with your *c*... Rom 15:24
epistle not to *c* with fornicators... 1Cor 5:9 *4874*
written unto you not to keep *c*... 1Cor 5:11 *4874*
have no *c* with him, that he may... 2Th 3:14 *4874*
and to an innumerable *c* of angels... Heb 12:22 *3461*
all the *c* in ships, and sailors,... Rev 18:17 *3658*

COMPARABLE {1}
c to fine gold, how are they... Lam 4:2 5577

COMPARE {4}
what likeness will ye *c* unto him... Is 40:18 6186
c me, that we may be like... Is 46:5 4911
what comparison shall we *c* it... Mk 4:30 *3846*
or *c* ourselves with some that... 2Cor 10:12 *4793*

COMPARED {5}
the heaven can be *c* unto the LORD... Ps 89:6 6186
desire are not to be *c* unto her... Prov 3:15 7737
be desired are not to be *c* to it... Prov 8:11 7737
I have *c* thee, O my love, to a... Song 1:9 1819
time are not worthy to be *c* with... Rom 8:18

COMPARING {2}
c spiritual things with spiritual... 1Cor 2:13 *4793*
c themselves among themselves,... 2Cor 10:12 *4793*

COMPARISON {4}
What have I done now in *c* of you... Judg 8:2
what was I able to do in *c* of you... Judg 8:3
your eyes in *c* of it as nothing... Hag 2:3 3644
or with what *c* shall we compare... Mk 4:30 *3850*

COMPASS {39}
under the *c* of the altar beneath... Ex 27:5 3749
grate of network under the *c*... Ex 38:4 3749
Red sea, to *c* the land of Edom... Num 21:4 5437
the border shall fetch a *c* from... Num 34:5 5437
And ye shall *c* the city, all ye... Josh 6:3 5437
ye shall *c* the city seven times... Josh 6:4 5437
c the city, and let him that is... Josh 6:7 5437
to Adar, and fetched a *c* to Karkaa... Josh 15:3 5437
but fetch a *c* behind them... 2Sa 5:23 5437
cubits did *c* either of them about... 1Kin 7:15 5437
cubits did *c* it round about... 1Kin 7:23 5437
a round *c* of half a cubit high... 1Kin 7:35 5439
they fetched a *c* of seven days'... 2Kin 3:9 5437
ye shall *c* the king round about,... 2Kin 11:8 5362
from brim to brim, round in *c*... 2Chr 4:2 5439
cubits did *c* it round about... 2Chr 4:2 5437
which did *c* it round about... 2Chr 4:3 5437
the Levites shall *c* the king... 2Chr 23:7 5362
His archers *c* me round about, he... Job 16:13 5437
willows of the brook *c* him about... Job 40:22 5437
wilt thou *c* him as with a shield... Ps 5:12 5849
of the people *c* thee about... Ps 7:7 5437
my deadly enemies, who *c* me about... Ps 17:9 5362
so will I *c* thine altar, O LORD... Ps 26:6 5437
thou shalt *c* me about with songs... Ps 32:7 5437
the LORD, mercy shall *c* him about... Ps 32:10 5437
of my heels shall *c* me about... Ps 49:5 5437
the head of those that *c* me about... Ps 140:9 4524
the righteous shall *c* me about... Ps 142:7 3803
when he set a *c* upon the face of... Prov 8:27 2329
and he marketh it out with the *c*... Is 44:13 4230
that *c* yourselves about with... Is 50:11 247
the earth, A woman shall *c* a man... Jer 31:22 5437
Gareb, and shall *c* about to Goath... Jer 31:39 5437
fillet of twelve cubits did *c* it... Jer 52:21 5437
wicked doth *c* about the righteous... Hab 1:4 3803
for ye *c* sea and land to make one... Mt 23:15 *4013*
c thee round, and keep thee in on... Lk 19:43 *4033*
And from thence we fetched a *c*... Acts 28:13 *4022*

COMPASSED {44}
c the house round, both old and... Gen 19:4 5437
we *c* mount Seir many days... Deut 2:1 5437
Ye have *c* this mountain long... Deut 2:3 5437
So the ark of the LORD *c* the city... Josh 6:11 5437
second day they *c* the city once... Josh 6:14 5437
c the city after the same manner... Josh 6:15 5437
day they *c* the city seven times... Josh 6:15 5437
the border *c* from Baalah westward... Josh 15:10 5437
c the corner of the sea southward... Josh 18:14 5437
c the land of Edom, and the land... Judg 11:18 5437
they *c* him in, and laid wait for... Judg 16:2 5437
for Saul and his men *c* David... 1Sa 23:26 5849
that bare Joab's armour *c* about... 2Sa 18:15 5437
When the waves of death *c* me... 2Sa 22:5 661
The sorrows of hell *c* me about... 2Sa 22:6 5437
by night, and *c* the city about... 2Kin 6:14 5362
an host *c* the city both with... 2Kin 6:15 5437
the Edomites which *c* him about... 2Kin 8:21 5437
Therefore they *c* about him to... 2Chr 18:31 5437
smote the Edomites which *c* him in... 2Chr 21:9 5437
c about Ophel, and raised it up a... 2Chr 33:14 5437
me, and hath *c* me with his net... Job 19:6 5362
He hath *c* the waters with bounds,... Job 26:10 2328
They have now *c* us in our steps... Ps 17:11 5437
The sorrows of death *c* me... Ps 18:4 661
The sorrows of hell *c* me about... Ps 18:5 5437
Many bulls have *c* me... Ps 22:12 5437
For dogs have *c* me... Ps 22:16 5437
innumerable evils have *c* me about... Ps 40:12 661
they *c* me about together... Ps 88:17 5362
They *c* me about also with words... Ps 109:3 5437
The sorrows of death *c* me... Ps 116:3 661
All nations *c* me about... Ps 118:10 5437
They *c* me about... Ps 118:11 5437
yea, they *c* me about... Ps 118:11 5437
They *c* me about like bees... Ps 118:12 5437
me, and *c* me with gall and travel... Lam 3:5 5362
and the floods *c* me about... Jonah 2:3 5437
The waters *c* me about, even to... Jonah 2:5 661
shall see Jerusalem *c* with armies... Lk 21:20 *2944*
himself also is *c* with infirmity... Heb 5:2 *4029*
after they were *c* about seven... Heb 11:30 *2944*
Wherefore seeing we also are *c*... Heb 12:1 *4029*
c the camp of the saints about,... Rev 20:9 *2944*

COMPASSEST {1}
Thou *c* my path and my lying down,... Ps 139:3 2219

COMPASSETH {5}
that is it which *c* the whole land... Gen 2:11 5437
the same is it that *c* the whole... Gen 2:13 5437
the border *c* it on the north side... Josh 19:14 5437
Therefore pride *c* them about as a... Ps 73:6 6059
Ephraim *c* me about with lies, and... Hos 11:12 5437

COMPASSING {3}
round about there were knops *c* it... 1Kin 7:24 5437
in a cubit, *c* the sea round about... 1Kin 7:24 5362
in a cubit, *c* the sea round about... 2Chr 4:3 5362

COMPASSION {41}
And she had *c* on him, and said,... Ex 2:6 2550
have *c* upon thee, and multiply... Deut 13:17 7355
have *c* upon thee, and will return... Deut 30:3 7355
for ye have *c* on me... 1Sa 23:21 2550
give them *c* before them who... 1Kin 8:50 7356
that they may have *c* on them... 1Kin 8:50 7355
had *c* on them, and had respect... 2Kin 13:23 7355
your children shall find *c* before... 2Chr 30:9 7356
because he had *c* on his people... 2Chr 36:15 2550
had no *c* upon young man or maiden... 2Chr 36:17 2550
But he, being full of *c*, forgave... Ps 78:38 7349
thou, O Lord, art a God full of *c*... Ps 86:15 7349
the LORD is gracious and full of *c*... Ps 111:4 7349
he is gracious, and full of *c*... Ps 112:4 7349
LORD is gracious, and full of *c*... Ps 145:8 7349
not have *c* on the son of her womb... Is 49:15 7355
have *c* on them, and will bring... Jer 12:15 7355
yet will he have *c* according to... Lam 3:32 7355
unto thee, to have *c* upon thee... Eze 16:5 2550
again, he will have *c* upon us... Mic 7:19 7355
he was moved with *c* on them... Mt 9:36 *4697*
and was moved with *c* toward them... Mt 14:14 *4697*
I have *c* on the multitude,... Mt 15:32 *4697*
of that servant was moved with *c*... Mt 18:27 *4697*
have had *c* on thy fellowservant... Mt 18:33 *1653*
So Jesus had *c* on them, and... Mt 20:34 *4697*
And Jesus, moved with *c*, put forth... Mk 1:41 *4697*
for thee, and hath had *c* on thee... Mk 5:19 *1653*
and was moved with *c* toward them... Mk 6:34 *4697*
I have *c* on the multitude,... Mk 8:2 *4697*
thing, have *c* on us, and help us... Mk 9:22 *4697*
the Lord saw her, he had *c* on her... Lk 7:13 *4697*
when he saw him, he had *c* on him... Lk 10:33 *4697*
off, his father saw him, and had *c*... Lk 15:20 *4697*
have *c* on whom I will have *c*... Rom 9:15 *3627*
Who can have *c* on the ignorant,... Heb 5:2 *3356*
For ye had *c* of me in my bonds,... Heb 10:34 *4834*
having *c* one of another, love as... 1Pet 3:8 *4835*
up his bowels of *c* from him... 1Jn 3:17
And of some have *c*, making a... Jude 22 *1653*

COMPASSIONS {2}
consumed, because his *c* fail not... Lam 3:22 7355
c every man to his brother... Zec 7:9 7356

COMPEL {5}
thou shalt not *c* him to serve as... Lev 25:39 5647
none did *c*... Est 1:8 597
whosoever shall *c* thee to go a... Mt 5:41 *29*
they *c* one Simon a Cyrenian, who... Mk 15:21 *29*
c them to come in, that my house... Lk 14:23 *315*

COMPELLED {6}
together with the woman, *c* him... 1Sa 28:23 6555
fornication, and *c* Judah thereto... 2Chr 21:11 5080
him they *c* to bear his cross... Mt 27:32 *29*
synagogue, and *c* them to blaspheme... Acts 26:11 *315*
ye have *c* me... 2Cor 12:11 *315*
a Greek, was *c* to be circumcised... Gal 2:3 *315*

COMPELLEST {1}
why *c* thou the Gentiles to live... Gal 2:14 *315*

COMPLAIN {4}
their brethren come unto us to *c*... Judg 21:22 7378
I will *c* in the bitterness of my... Job 7:11 7878
the furrows likewise thereof *c*... Job 31:38 1058
Wherefore doth a living man *c*... Lam 3:39 596

COMPLAINED {2}
And when the people *c*, it... Num 11:1 596
I *c*, and my spirit was overwhelmed... Ps 77:3 7878

COMPLAINERS {1}
These are murmurers, *c*, walking... Jude 16 *3202*

COMPLAINING {1}
that there be no *c* in our streets... Ps 144:14 6682

COMPLAINT {9}
for out of the abundance of my *c*... 1Sa 1:16 7878
me, my couch shall ease my *c*... Job 7:13 7878
If I say, I will forget my *c*... Job 9:27 7878
I will leave my *c* upon myself... Job 10:1 7878
As for me, is my *c* to man... Job 21:4 7878
Even to day is my *c* bitter... Job 23:2 7878
I mourn in my *c*, and make a noise... Ps 55:2 7878
poureth out his *c* before the LORD... Ps 102:*t* 7878
I poured out my *c* before him... Ps 142:2 7878

COMPLAINTS {1}
grievous *c* against Paul, which... Acts 25:7 *157*

COMPLETE {3}
seven sabbaths shall be *c*... Lev 23:15 8549
And ye are *c* in him, which is the... Col 2:10 *4137*
and *c* in all the will of God... Col 4:12 *4137*

COMPOSITION {2}
other like it, after the *c* of it... Ex 30:32 4971
according to the *c* thereof... Ex 30:37 4971

COMPOUND {1}
an ointment *c* after the art of... Ex 30:25 4842

COMPOUNDETH {1}
Whosoever *c* any like it, or... Ex 30:33 7543

COMPREHEND {2}
doeth he, which we cannot *c*... Job 37:5 3045
May be able to *c* with all saints... Eph 3:18 *2638*

COMPREHENDED {3}
c the dust of the earth in a... Is 40:12 3557
and the darkness *c* it not... Jn 1:5 *2638*
it is briefly *c* in this saying,... Rom 13:9 *346*

CONANIAH *(co-na-ni'-ah)* {1} See CONONIAH. *A chief Levite during Josiah's time.*
C also, and Shemaiah and Nethaneel,... 2Chr 35:9 3562

CONCEAL {6}
slay our brother, and *c* his blood... Gen 37:26 3680
spare, neither shalt thou *c* him... Deut 13:8 3680
is with the Almighty will I not *c*... Job 27:11 3582
I will not *c* his parts, nor his... Job 41:12 2790
is the glory of God to *c* a thing... Prov 25:2 5641
publish, and *c* not... Jer 50:2 3582

CONCEALED {2}
for I have not *c* the words of the... Job 6:10 3582
I have not *c* thy lovingkindness... Ps 40:10 3582

CONCEALETH {2}
of a faithful spirit *c* the matter... Prov 11:13 3680
A prudent man *c* knowledge... Prov 12:23 3680

CONCEIT {5}
and as an high wall in his own *c*... Prov 18:11 4906
lest he be wise in his own *c*... Prov 26:5 5869
thou a man wise in his own *c*... Prov 26:12 5869
sluggard is wiser in his own *c*... Prov 26:16 5869
The rich man is wise in his own *c*... Prov 28:11 5869

CONCEITS {2}
ye should be wise in your own *c*... Rom 11:25 *3844,1438*
Be not wise in your own *c*... Rom 12:16 *3844,1438*

CONCEIVE {14}
that they should *c* when they came... Gen 30:38 3179
the stronger cattle did *c*... Gen 30:41 3179
that they might *c* among the rods... Gen 30:41 3179
shall be free, and shall *c* seed... Num 5:28 2232
but thou shalt *c*, and bear a son... Judg 13:3 2030
For, lo, thou shalt *c*, and bear a... Judg 13:5 2030
unto me, Behold, thou shalt *c*... Judg 13:7 2030
They *c* mischief, and bring forth... Job 15:35 2029
and in sin did my mother *c* me... Ps 51:5 3179
Behold, a virgin shall *c*, and bear... Is 7:14 2030
Ye shall *c* chaff, ye shall bring... Is 33:11 2029
they *c* mischief, and bring forth... Is 59:4 2029
thou shalt *c* in thy womb, and... Lk 1:31 *4815*
received strength to *c* seed... Heb 11:11 *2602*

CONCEIVED {46}
and she *c*, and bare Cain, and said,... Gen 4:1 2030
and she *c*, and bare Enoch... Gen 4:17 2030
he went in unto Hagar, and she *c*... Gen 16:4 2030
and when she saw that she had *c*... Gen 16:4 2030
and when she saw that she had *c*... Gen 16:5 2030
For Sarah *c*, and bare Abraham a... Gen 21:2 2030
of him, and Rebekah his wife *c*... Gen 25:21 2030
And Leah *c*, and bare a son, and she... Gen 29:32 2030
she *c* again, and bare a son... Gen 29:33 2030
she *c* again, and bare a son... Gen 29:34 2030
she *c* again, and bare a son... Gen 29:35 2030
And Bilhah *c*, and bare Jacob a son... Gen 30:5 2030
And Bilhah Rachel's maid *c* again... Gen 30:7 2030
God hearkened unto Leah, and she *c*... Gen 30:17 2030
Leah *c* again, and bare Jacob the... Gen 30:19 2030
And she *c*, and bare a son... Gen 30:23 2030
the flocks *c* before the rods, and... Gen 30:39 3179
at the time that the cattle *c*... Gen 31:10 3179
And she *c*, and bare a son... Gen 38:3 2029
she *c* again, and bare a son... Gen 38:4 2030
And she yet again *c*, and bare a son... Gen 38:5 3254

came in unto her, and she *c* by him .... Gen 38:18 2030
And the woman *c*, and bare a son .... Ex 2:2 2030
saying, If a woman have *c* seed .... Lev 12:2 2232
Have I *c* all this people .... Num 11:12 2030
was come about after Hannah had *c* 1Sa 1:20 2030
visited Hannah, so that she *c* 1Sa 2:21 2030
And the woman *c*, and sent and told 2Sa 11:5 2030
And the woman *c*, and bare a son at 2Kin 4:17 2030
he went in to his wife, she *c* 1Chr 7:23 2030
was said, There is a man child *c* .... Job 3:3 2030
hath *c* mischief, and brought forth .... Ps 7:14 2030
into the chamber of her that *c* me .... Song 3:4 2030
and she *c*, and bare a son .... Is 8:3 2030
hath *c* a purpose against you .... Jer 49:30 2803
which *c*, and bare him a son .... Hos 1:3 2030
she *c* again, and bare a daughter .... Hos 1:6 2030
she had weaned Lo-ruhamah, she *c* .... Hos 1:8 2030
she that *c* them hath done .... Hos 2:5 2030
for that which is *c* in her is of .... Mt 1:20 *1080*
those days his wife Elisabeth *c* .... Lk 1:24 *4815*
she hath also *c* a son in her old .... Lk 1:36 *4815*
angel before he was *c* in the womb .... Lk 2:21 *4815*
why hast thou *c* this thing in .... Acts 5:4 *5087*
when Rebecca also had *c* by one ..... Rom 9:10 *2845,2192*
Then when lust hath *c*, it .... Jas 1:15 *4815*

CONCEIVING {1}
speaking oppression and revolt, *c* .... Is 59:13 2030

CONCEPTION {3}
multiply thy sorrow and thy *c* .... Gen 3:16 2032
in unto her, the LORD gave her *c* .... Ruth 4:13 2032
and from the womb, and from the *c* .... Hos 9:11 2032

CONCERN {2}
which *c* the Lord Jesus Christ .... Acts 28:31 *4012*
things which *c* mine infirmities 2Cor 11:30 *4012*

CONCERNETH {2}
LORD will perfect that which *c* me .... Ps 138:8 1157
This burden *c* the prince in .... Eze 12:10

CONCERNING See APPENDIX.

CONCISION {1}
of evil workers, beware of the *c* .... Phil 3:2 *2699*

CONCLUDE {1}
Therefore we *c* that a man is .... Rom 3:28 *3049*

CONCLUDED {3}
c that they observe no such thing .... Acts 21:25 *2919*
For God hath *c* them all in .... Rom 11:32 *4788*
scripture hath *c* all under sin .... Gal 3:22 *4788*

CONCLUSION {1}
Let us hear the *c* of the whole .... Eccl 12:13 5490

CONCORD {1}
what *c* hath Christ with Belial 2Cor 6:15 *4857*

CONCOURSE {2}
crieth in the chief place of *c* .... Prov 1:21 1993
we may give an account of this *c* .... Acts 19:40 *4963*

CONCUBINE {22}
And his *c*, whose name was Reumah, ... Gen 22:24 6370
and lay with Bilhah his father's *c* .... Gen 35:22 6370
Timna was *c* to Eliphaz Esau's son .... Gen 36:12 6370
his *c* that was in Shechem, she .... Judg 8:31 6370
who took to him a *c* out of .... Judg 19:1 6370
his *c* played the whore against .... Judg 19:2 6370
rose up to depart, he, and his *c* .... Judg 19:9 6370
saddled, his *c* also was with him .... Judg 19:10 6370
is my daughter a maiden, and his *c* .... Judg 19:24 6370
so the man took his *c*, and brought .... Judg 19:25 6370
the woman his *c* was fallen down .... Judg 19:27 6370
a knife, and laid hold on his *c* .... Judg 19:29 6370
belongeth to Benjamin, I and my *c* .... Judg 20:4 6370
my *c* have they forced, that she .... Judg 20:5 6370
And I took my *c*, and cut her in .... Judg 20:6 6370
And Saul had a *c*, whose name was 2Sa 3:7 6370
thou gone in unto my father's *c* 2Sa 3:7 6370
of Aiah, the *c* of Saul, had done 2Sa 21:11 6370
the sons of Keturah, Abraham's *c* 1Chr 1:32 6370
And Ephah, Caleb's *c*, bare Haran, ... 1Chr 2:46 6370
Maachah, Caleb's *c*, bare Sheber, ... 1Chr 2:48 6370
(but his *c* the Aramitess bare 1Chr 7:14 6370

CONCUBINES {17}
But unto the sons of the *c* .... Gen 25:6 6370
And David took him more *c* and wives 2Sa 5:13 6370
king left ten women, which were *c* 2Sa 15:16 6370
Go in unto thy father's *c* 2Sa 16:21 6370
went in unto his father's *c* in 2Sa 16:22 6370
thy wives, and the lives of thy *c* 2Sa 19:5 6370
the king took the ten women his *c* 2Sa 20:3 6370
princesses, and three hundred *c* 1Kin 11:3 6370
David, beside the sons of the *c* 1Chr 3:9 6370
above all his wives and his *c* 2Chr 11:21 6370
eighteen wives, and threescore *c* 2Chr 11:21 6370
chamberlain, which kept the *c* .... Est 2:14 6370
threescore queens, and fourscore *c* .... Song 6:8 6370
yea, the queens and the *c*, and they .... Song 6:9 6370
his princes, his wives, and his *c* .... Dan 5:2 3904
his princes, his wives, and his *c* .... Dan 5:3 3904
and thy lords, thy wives, and thy *c* .... Dan 5:23 3904

CONCUPISCENCE {3}
wrought in me all manner of *c* .... Rom 7:8 *1939*
inordinate affection, evil *c* .... Col 3:5 *1939*
Not in the lust of *c*, even as the 1Th 4:5 *1939*

CONDEMN {24}
and whom the judges shall *c* .... Ex 22:9 7561
the righteous, and *c* the wicked .... Deut 25:1 7561
myself, mine own mouth shall *c* me .... Job 9:20 7561
I will say unto God, Do not *c* me .... Job 10:2 7561
wilt thou *c* him that is most just .... Job 34:17 7561
wilt thou *c* me, that thou mayest .... Job 40:8 7561
nor *c* him when he is judged .... Ps 37:33 7561
and *c* the innocent blood .... Ps 94:21 7561
him from those that *c* his soul .... Ps 109:31 8199
a man of wicked devices will he *c* .... Prov 12:2 7561
who is he that shall *c* me .... Is 50:9 7561
thee in judgment thou shalt *c* .... Is 54:17 7561
this generation, and shall *c* it .... Mt 12:41 *2632*
this generation, and shall *c* it .... Mt 12:42 *2632*
they shall *c* him to death, ... Mt 20:18 *2632*
they shall *c* him to death, and .... Mk 10:33 *2632*
c not, and ye shall not be .... Lk 6:37 *2618*
men of this generation, and *c* them .... Lk 11:31 *2632*
this generation, and shall *c* it .... Lk 11:32 *2632*
Son into the world to *c* the world .... Jn 3:17 *2919*
unto her, Neither do I *c* thee .... Jn 8:11 *2632*
I speak not this to *c* you 2Cor 7:3 *2633*
For if our heart *c* us, God is 1Jn 3:20 *2607*
Beloved, if our heart *c* us not 1Jn 3:21 *2607*

CONDEMNATION {12}
seeing thou art in the same *c* .... Lk 23:40 *2917*
And this is the *c*, that light is .... Jn 3:19 *2920*
life, and shall not come into *c* .... Jn 5:24 *2920*
for the judgment was by one to *c* .... Rom 5:16 *2631*
judgment came upon all men to *c* .... Rom 5:18 *2631*
There is therefore now no *c* to .... Rom 8:1 *2631*
that ye come not together unto *c* 1Cor 11:34 *2917*
if the ministration of *c* be glory 2Cor 3:9 *2633*
he fall into the *c* of the devil 1Ti 3:6 *2917*
we shall receive the greater *c* .... Jas 3:1 *2917*
lest ye fall into *c* .... Jas 5:12 *5272*
before of old ordained to this *c* .... Jude 4 *2917*

CONDEMNED {21}
c the land in an hundred talents 2Chr 36:3 6064
found no answer, and yet had *c* Job .... Job 32:3 7561
he shall be judged, let him be *c* .... Ps 109:7 3318,7563
the *c* in the house of their god .... Amos 2:8 6064
ye would not have *c* the guiltless .... Mt 12:7 *2613*
and by thy words thou shalt be *c* .... Mt 12:37 *2613*
him, when he saw that he was *c* .... Mt 27:3 *2632*
they all *c* him to be guilty of .... Mk 14:64 *2632*
condemn not, and ye shall not be *c* .... Lk 6:37 *2613*
delivered him to be *c* to death .... Lk 24:20 *1519,2917*
He that believeth on him is not *c* .... Jn 3:18 *2919*
that believeth not is *c* already .... Jn 3:18 *2919*
hath no man *c* thee .... Jn 8:10 *2632*
and for sin, *c* sin in the flesh .... Rom 8:3 *2632*
we should not be *c* with the world 1Cor 11:32 *2632*
Sound speech, that cannot be *c* .... Titus 2:8 *176*
and sinneth, being *c* of himself .... Titus 3:11 *843*
by the which he *c* the world .... Heb 11:7 *2632*
Ye have *c* and killed the just .... Jas 5:6 *2613*
another, brethren, lest ye be *c* .... Jas 5:9 *2632*
Gomorrah into ashes *c* them with 2Pet 2:6 *2632*

CONDEMNEST {1}
judgest another, thou *c* thyself .... Rom 2:1 *2632*

CONDEMNETH {4}
Thine own mouth *c* thee, and not I .... Job 15:6 7561
he that *c* the just, even they .... Prov 17:15 7561
Who is he that *c* .... Rom 8:34 *2632*
Happy is he that *c* not himself in .... Rom 14:22 *4314*

CONDEMNING {2}
c the wicked, to bring his way 1Kin 8:32 7561
they have fulfilled them in *c* him .... Acts 13:27 *2919*

CONDESCEND {1}
but *c* to men of low estate .... Rom 12:16 *4879*

CONDITION {1}
On this *c* will I make a covenant 1Sa 11:2

CONDITIONS {1}
ambassage, and desireth *c* of peace .... Lk 14:32 *4314*

CONDUCT {3}
to *c* the king over Jordan 2Sa 19:15 5674
the king, to *c* him over Jordan 2Sa 19:31 7971
but *c* him forth in peace, that he 1Cor 16:11 *4311*

CONDUCTED {2}
the people of Judah *c* the king 2Sa 19:40 5674
they that *c* Paul brought him unto .... Acts 17:15 *2525*

CONDUIT {4}
stood by the *c* of the upper pool, ... 2Kin 18:17 8585
and how he made a pool, and a *c* 2Kin 20:20 8585
at the end of the *c* of the upper .... Is 7:3 8585
he stood by the *c* of the upper .... Is 36:2 8585

CONEY {2}
And the *c*, because he cheweth the .... Lev 11:5 8227
the camel, and the hare, and the *c* .... Deut 14:7 8227

CONFECTION {1}
perfume, a *c* after the art of the .... Ex 30:35 7545

CONFECTIONARIES {1}
will take your daughters to be *c* 1Sa 8:13 7543

CONFEDERACY {3}
Say ye not, A *c*, to all them to .... Is 8:12 7195
whom this people shall say, A *c* .... Is 8:12 7195
All the men of thy *c* have brought .... Obad 7 1285

CONFEDERATE {3}
and these were *c* with Abram .... Gen 14:13 1167,1285
they are *c* against thee .... Ps 83:5 1285,3772
saying, Syria is *c* with Ephraim .... Is 7:2 5117

CONFERENCE {1}
somewhat in *c* added nothing to me .... Gal 2:6 *4323*

CONFERRED {4}
he *c* with Joab the son of Zeruiah ... 1Kin 1:7 1961,1697
council, they *c* among themselves, ... Acts 4:15 *4820*
when he had *c* with the council, ... Acts 25:12 *4814*
immediately I *c* not with flesh and .... Gal 1:16 *4323*

CONFESS {28}
that he shall *c* that he hath .... Lev 5:5 3034
c over him all the iniquities of .... Lev 16:21 3034
If they shall *c* their iniquity, ... Lev 26:40 3034
Then they shall *c* their sin which .... Num 5:7 3034
c thy name, and pray, and make 1Kin 8:33 3034
c thy name, and turn from their 1Kin 8:35 3034
c thy name, and pray and make 2Chr 6:24 3034
c thy name, and turn from their 2Chr 6:26 3034
c the sins of the children of .... Neh 1:6 3034
Then will I also *c* unto thee that .... Job 40:14 3034
I will *c* my transgressions unto .... Ps 32:5 3034
therefore shall *c* me before men .... Mt 10:32 *3670*
him will I *c* also before my .... Mt 10:32 *3670*
Whosoever shall *c* me before men .... Lk 12:8 *3670*
also *c* before the angels of God .... Lk 12:8 *3670*
any man did *c* that he was Christ .... Jn 9:22 *3670*
the Pharisees they did not *c* him .... Jn 12:42 *3670*
but the Pharisees *c* both .... Acts 23:8 *3670*
But this I *c* unto thee, that .... Acts 24:14 *3670*
That if thou shalt *c* with thy .... Rom 10:9 *3670*
and every tongue shall *c* to God .... Rom 14:11 *1843*
For this cause I will *c* to thee .... Rom 15:9 *1843*
that every tongue should *c* that .... Phil 2:11 *1843*
C your faults one to another, and .... Jas 5:16 *1843*
If we *c* our sins, he is faithful 1Jn 1:9 *3670*
Whosoever shall *c* that Jesus is 1Jn 4:15 *3670*
who *c* not that Jesus Christ is 2Jn 7 *3670*
but I will *c* his name before my .... Rev 3:5 *1843*

CONFESSED {7}
Ezra had prayed, and when he had *c* .... Ezr 10:1 3034
c their sins, and the iniquities .... Neh 9:2 3034
and another fourth part they *c* .... Neh 9:3 3034
And he *c*, and denied not .... Jn 1:20 *3670*
but *c*, I am not the Christ .... Jn 1:20 *3670*
And many that believed came, and *c* ...... Acts 19:18 *1843*
c that they were strangers and .... Heb 11:13 *3670*

CONFESSETH {3}
but whoso *c* and forsaketh them .... Prov 28:13 3034
Every spirit that *c* that Jesus 1Jn 4:2 *3670*
every spirit that *c* not that 1Jn 4:3 *3670*

CONFESSING {3}
c my sin and the sin of my people .... Dan 9:20 3034
of him in Jordan, *c* their sins .... Mt 3:6 *1843*
the river of Jordan, *c* their sins .... Mk 1:5 *1843*

CONFESSION {6}
God of Israel, and make *c* unto him .... Josh 7:19 8426
making *c* to the LORD God of their 2Chr 30:22 3034
Now therefore make *c* unto the .... Ezr 10:11 8426
the LORD my God, and made my *c* .... Dan 9:4 3034
with the mouth *c* is made unto .... Rom 10:10 *3670*
Pontius Pilate witnessed a good *c* 1Ti 6:13 *3671*

CONFIDENCE {38}
men of Shechem put their *c* in him .... Judg 9:26 982
What *c* is this wherein thou 2Kin 18:19 986
Is not this thy fear, thy *c* .... Job 4:6 3690
His *c* shall be rooted out of his .... Job 18:14 4009
to the fine gold, Thou art my *c* .... Job 31:24 4009
who art the *c* of all the ends of .... Ps 65:5 4009
in the LORD than to put *c* in man .... Ps 118:8 982
the LORD than to put *c* in princes .... Ps 118:9 982
For the LORD shall be thy *c* .... Prov 3:26 3689
the fear of the LORD is strong *c* .... Prov 14:26 4009
the strength of the *c* thereof .... Prov 21:22 4009
C in an unfaithful man in time of .... Prov 25:19 4009
in *c* shall be your strength .... Is 30:15 985
What *c* is this wherein thou .... Is 36:4 986
was ashamed of Beth-el their *c* .... Jer 48:13 4009
yea, they shall dwell with *c* .... Eze 28:26 983
more the *c* of the house of Israel .... Eze 29:16 4009
a friend, put ye not *c* in a guide .... Mic 7:5 982
the Lord Jesus Christ, with all *c* .... Acts 28:31 *3954*
in this *c* I was minded to come 2Cor 1:15 *4006*
having *c* in you all, that my joy 2Cor 2:3 *3982*
I have *c* in you in all things 2Cor 7:16 *2292*
upon the great *c* which I have in 2Cor 8:22 *4006*
when I am present with that *c* 2Cor 10:2 *4006*
foolishly, in this *c* of boasting 2Cor 11:17 *5287*
I have *c* in you through the Lord, ... Gal 5:10 *3982*
access with *c* by the faith of him .... Eph 3:12 *4006*
And having this *c*, I know that I .... Phil 1:25 *3982*
Jesus, and have no *c* in the flesh .... Phil 3:3 *3982*
I might also have *c* in the flesh .... Phil 3:4 *4006*
we have *c* in the Lord touching 2Th 3:4 *3982*
Having *c* in thy obedience I wrote .... Philem 21 *3982*
are we, if we hold fast the *c* .... Heb 3:6 *3954*
of our *c* stedfast unto the end .... Heb 3:14 *5287*
Cast not away therefore your *c* .... Heb 10:35 *3954*
he shall appear, we may have *c* 1Jn 2:28 *3954*
us not, then have we *c* toward God 1Jn 3:21 *3954*
this is the *c* that we have in him 1Jn 5:14 *3954*

CONFIDENCES {1}
for the LORD hath rejected thy *c* .... Jer 2:37 4009

CONFIDENT {8}
against me, in this will I be *c* .... Ps 27:3 982
but the fool rageth, and is *c* .... Prov 14:16 982
art *c* that thou thyself art a .... Rom 2:19 *3982*
Therefore we are always *c* 2Cor 5:6 *2292*
We are *c*, I say, and willing 2Cor 5:8 *2292*

ashamed in this same c boasting 2Cor 9:4 5287
Being c of this very thing, that Phil 1:6 3982
waxing c by my bonds, are much Phil 1:14 3982

CONFIDENTLY {1}
one hour after another c affirmed Lk 22:59 1340

CONFIRM {13}
changing, for to c all things Ruth 4:7 6965
in after thee, and c thy words 1Kin 1:14 4390
him to c the kingdom in his hand 2Kin 15:19 2388
to c this second letter of Purim Est 9:29 6965
To c these days of Purim in their Est 9:31 6965
thou didst c thine inheritance Ps 68:9 3559
weak hands, and c the feeble knees Is 35:3 553
hope that they would c the word Eze 13:6 6965
he shall c the covenant with many Dan 9:27 1396
the Mede, even I, stood to c Dan 11:1 2388
to c the promises made unto the Rom 15:8 950
Who shall also c you unto the end 1Cor 1:8 950
ye would c your love toward him 2Cor 2:8 2964

CONFIRMATION {1}
c of the gospel, ye all are Phil 1:7 951
an oath for c is to them an end Heb 6:16 951

CONFIRMED {13}
For thou hast c to thyself thy 2Sa 7:24 3559
as the kingdom was c in his hand 2Kin 14:5 2388
LORD had c him king over Israel 1Chr 14:2 3559
hath c the same to Jacob for a 1Chr 16:17 5975
the decree of Esther c these Est 9:32 6965
c the same unto Jacob for a law, Ps 105:10 5975
he hath c his words, which he Dan 9:12 6965
with many words, and c them Acts 15:32 1991
testimony of Christ was c in you 1Cor 1:6 950
a man's covenant, yet if it be c Gal 3:15 2964
that was c before of God in Gal 3:17 4300
was c unto us by them that heard Heb 2:3 950
of his counsel, c it by an oath Heb 6:17 3315

CONFIRMETH {3}
he c them, because he held his Num 30:14 6965
Cursed be he that c not all the Deut 27:26 6965
That c the word of his servant, Is 44:26 6965

CONFIRMING {3}
c the word with signs following Mk 16:20 950
C the souls of the disciples, and Acts 14:22 1991
Syria and Cilicia, c the churches Acts 15:41 1991

CONFISCATION {1}
or to c of goods, or to Ezr 7:26 6065

CONFLICT {2}
Having the same c which ye saw in Phil 1:30 73
knew what great c I have for you Col 2:1 73

CONFORMABLE {1}
being made c unto his death Phil 3:10 4832

CONFORMED {2}
to be c to the image of his Son Rom 8:29 4832
And be not c to this world Rom 12:2 4964

CONFOUND {5}
there c their language, that they Gen 11:7 1101
because the LORD did there c the Gen 11:9 1101
lest I c thee before them Jer 1:17 2865
things of the world to c the wise 1Cor 1:27 2617
to c the things which are mighty 1Cor 1:27 2617

CONFOUNDED {50}
power, they were dismayed and c 2Kin 19:26 954
They were c because they had Job 6:20 954
trusted in thee, and were not c Ps 22:5 954
Let them be c and put to shame Ps 35:4 954
c together that seek after my Ps 40:14 2659
that seek thee be c for my sake Ps 69:6 3637
c that seek after my soul Ps 70:2 2659
Let them be c and consumed that Ps 71:13 954
for they are c, for they are Ps 71:24 954
Let them be c and troubled for Ps 83:17 954
C be all they that serve graven Ps 97:7 954
Let them all be c and turned back Ps 129:5 954
ye shall be c for the gardens Is 1:29 2659
that weave networks, shall be c Is 19:9 954
Then the moon shall be c, and the Is 24:23 2659
power, they were dismayed and c Is 37:27 954
thee shall be ashamed and c Is 41:11 3637
They shall be ashamed, and also c Is 45:16 3637
ashamed nor c world without end Is 45:17 3637
therefore shall I not be c Is 50:7 3637
neither be thou c Is 54:4 3637
we are greatly c, because we have Jer 9:19 954
every founder is c by the graven Jer 10:14 3001
they were ashamed and c, and Jer 14:3 3637
she hath been ashamed and c Jer 15:9 2659
Let them be c that persecute me, Jer 17:18 954
but let not me be c Jer 17:18 954
and c for all thy wickedness Jer 22:22 3637
I was ashamed, yea, even c Jer 31:19 3637
The daughter of Egypt shall be c Jer 46:24 3001
Kiriathaim is c and taken Jer 48:1 3001
Misgab is c and dismayed Jer 48:1 3001
Moab is c Jer 48:20 3001
Hamath is c, and Arpad Jer 49:23 954
say, Babylon is taken, Bel is c Jer 50:2 3001
her idols are c, her images are Jer 50:2 3001
Your mother shall be sore c Jer 50:12 954
every founder is c by the graven Jer 51:17 3001
and her whole land shall be c Jer 51:47 954
We are c, because we have heard Jer 51:51 954
yea, be thou c also, and bear thy Eze 16:52 954
mayest be c in all that thou hast Eze 16:54 3637
thou mayest remember, and be c Eze 16:63 954
c for your own ways, O house of Eze 36:32 3637
be ashamed, and the diviners c Mic 3:7 2659
see and be c at all their might Mic 7:16 954
the riders on horses shall be c Zec 10:5 3001
came together, and were c, because Acts 2:6 4797
c the Jews which dwelt at Acts 9:22 4797
believeth on him shall not be c 1Pet 2:6 2617

CONFUSED {2}
of the warrior is with c noise Is 9:5 7494
for the assembly was c Acts 19:32 4797

CONFUSION {26}
it is c Lev 18:23 8397
they have wrought c Lev 20:12 8397
the son of Jesse to thine own c 1Sa 20:30 1322
unto the c of thy mother's 1Sa 20:30 1322
to c of face, as it is this day Ezr 9:7 1322
I am full of c Job 10:15 7036
brought to c that devise my hurt Ps 35:4 2659
brought to c together that Ps 35:26 2659
My c is continually before me, and Ps 44:15 3639
be turned backward, and put to c Ps 70:2 3637
let me never be put to c Ps 71:1 954
cover themselves with their own c Ps 109:29 1322
The city of c is broken down Is 24:10 8414
in the shadow of Egypt your c Is 30:3 3639
stretch out upon it the line of c Is 34:11 8414
their molten images are wind and c Is 41:29 8414
they shall go to c together that Is 45:16 3639
for c they shall rejoice in their Is 61:7 3639
our shame, and our c covereth us Jer 3:25 3639
to the c of their own faces Jer 7:19 1322
their everlasting c shall never Jer 20:11 3639
unto thee, but unto us c of faces Dan 9:7 1322
O Lord, to us belongeth c of face Dan 9:8 1322
the whole city was filled with c Acts 19:29 4799
For God is not the author of c 1Cor 14:33 181
envying and strife is, there is c Jas 3:16 181

CONGEALED {1}
the depths were c in the heart of Ex 15:8 7087

CONGRATULATE {1}
to c him, because he had fought 1Chr 18:10 1288

CONGREGATION {364}
Speak ye unto all the c of Israel Ex 12:3 5712
the whole assembly of the c of Ex 12:6 5712
be cut off from the c of Israel Ex 12:19 5712
All the c of Israel shall keep it Ex 12:47 5712
all the c of the children of Ex 16:1 5712
the whole c of the children of Ex 16:2 5712
Say unto all the c of the Ex 16:9 5712
whole c of the children of Israel Ex 16:10 5712
and all the rulers of the c came Ex 16:22 5712
all the c of the children of Ex 17:1 5712
of the c without the veil Ex 27:21 4150
in unto the tabernacle of the c Ex 28:43 4150
door of the tabernacle of the c Ex 29:4 4150
before the tabernacle of the c Ex 29:10 4150
door of the tabernacle of the c Ex 29:11 4150
into the tabernacle of the c to Ex 29:30 4150
door of the tabernacle of the c Ex 29:32 4150
of the c before the LORD Ex 29:42 4150
sanctify the tabernacle of the c Ex 29:44 4150
of the tabernacle of the c Ex 30:16 4150
between the tabernacle of the c Ex 30:18 4150
go into the tabernacle of the c Ex 30:20 4150
the tabernacle of the c therewith Ex 30:26 4150
in the tabernacle of the c Ex 30:36 4150
The tabernacle of the c, and the Ex 31:7 4150
called it the Tabernacle of the c Ex 33:7 4150
out unto the tabernacle of the c Ex 33:7 4150
rulers of the c returned unto him Ex 34:31 5712
Moses gathered all the c of the Ex 35:1 5712
Moses spake unto all the c of the Ex 35:4 5712
all the c of the children of Ex 35:20 5712
work of the tabernacle of the c Ex 35:21 4150
door of the tabernacle of the c Ex 38:8 4150
of the c was an hundred talents Ex 38:25 5712
door of the tabernacle of the c Ex 38:30 4150
of the tent of the c finished Ex 39:32 4150
tabernacle, for the tent of the c Ex 39:40 4150
tabernacle of the tent of the c Ex 40:2 4150
tabernacle of the tent of the c Ex 40:6 4150
laver between the tent of the c Ex 40:7 4150
door of the tabernacle of the c Ex 40:12 4150
the table in the tent of the c Ex 40:22 4150
candlestick in the tent of the c Ex 40:24 4150
the tent of the c before the vail Ex 40:26 4150
tabernacle of the tent of the c Ex 40:29 4150
laver between the tent of the c Ex 40:30 4150
they went into the tent of the c Ex 40:32 4150
a cloud covered the tent of the c Ex 40:34 4150
to enter into the tent of the c Ex 40:35 4150
out of the tabernacle of the c Lev 1:1 4150
of the c before the LORD Lev 1:3 4150
door of the tabernacle of the c Lev 1:5 4150
door of the tabernacle of the c Lev 3:2 4150
it before the tabernacle of the c Lev 3:8 4150
it before the tabernacle of the c Lev 3:13 4150
of the c before the LORD Lev 4:4 4150
it to the tabernacle of the c Lev 4:5 4150
is in the tabernacle of the c Lev 4:7 4150
door of the tabernacle of the c Lev 4:7 4150
if the whole c of Israel sin Lev 4:13 5712
then the c shall offer a young Lev 4:14 6951
before the tabernacle of the c Lev 4:14 4150
the elders of the c shall lay Lev 4:15 5712
blood to the tabernacle of the c Lev 4:16 4150
is in the tabernacle of the c Lev 4:18 4150
door of the tabernacle of the c Lev 4:18 4150
it is a sin offering for the c Lev 4:21 6951
of the c they shall eat it Lev 6:16 4150
court of the tabernacle of the c Lev 6:26 4150
into the tabernacle of the c to Lev 6:30 4150
gather thou all the c together Lev 8:3 5712
door of the tabernacle of the c Lev 8:3 4150
door of the tabernacle of the c Lev 8:4 4150
And Moses said unto the c, This is Lev 8:5 5712
door of the tabernacle of the c Lev 8:31 4150
tabernacle of the c in seven days Lev 8:33 4150
of the tabernacle of the c day Lev 8:35 4150
before the tabernacle of the c Lev 9:5 4150
all the c drew near and stood Lev 9:5 5712
went into the tabernacle of the c Lev 9:23 4150
door of the tabernacle of the c Lev 10:7 4150
go into the tabernacle of the c Lev 10:9 4150
you to bear the iniquity of the c Lev 10:17 5712
door of the tabernacle of the c Lev 12:6 4150
door of the tabernacle of the c Lev 14:11 4150
door of the tabernacle of the c Lev 14:23 4150
door of the tabernacle of the c Lev 15:14 4150
door of the tabernacle of the c Lev 15:29 4150
he shall take of the c of the Lev 16:5 5712
door of the tabernacle of the c Lev 16:7 4150
he do for the tabernacle of the c Lev 16:16 4150
the c when he goeth in to make an Lev 16:17 4150
and for all the c of Israel Lev 16:17 6951
place, and the tabernacle of the c Lev 16:20 4150
come into the tabernacle of the c Lev 16:23 4150
for the tabernacle of the c Lev 16:33 4150
and for all the people of the c Lev 16:33 6951
door of the tabernacle of the c Lev 17:4 4150
door of the tabernacle of the c Lev 17:5 4150
door of the tabernacle of the c Lev 17:6 4150
door of the tabernacle of the c Lev 17:9 4150
Speak unto all the c of the Lev 19:2 5712
door of the tabernacle of the c Lev 19:21 4150
in the tabernacle of the c Lev 24:3 4150
head, and let all the c stone him Lev 24:14 5712
all the c shall certainly stone Lev 24:16 5712
Sinai, in the tabernacle of the c Num 1:1 4150
the c of the children of Israel Num 1:2 5712
These were the renowned of the c Num 1:16 5712
they assembled all the c together Num 1:18 5712
the c of the children of Israel Num 1:53 5712
of the c shall they pitch Num 2:2 4150
Then the tabernacle of the c Num 2:17 4150
the charge of the whole c before Num 3:7 5712
before the tabernacle of the c Num 3:7 4150
of the tabernacle of the c Num 3:8 4150
of the c shall be the tabernacle Num 3:25 4150
door of the tabernacle of the c Num 3:25 4150
the tabernacle of the c eastward Num 3:38 4150
work in the tabernacle of the c Num 4:3 4150
Kohath in the tabernacle of the c Num 4:4 4150
Kohath in the tabernacle of the c Num 4:15 4150
work in the tabernacle of the c Num 4:23 4150
and the tabernacle of the c Num 4:25 4150
door of the tabernacle of the c Num 4:25 4150
in the tabernacle of the c Num 4:28 4150
work of the tabernacle of the c Num 4:30 4150
in the tabernacle of the c Num 4:31 4150
in the tabernacle of the c Num 4:33 4150
the chief of the c numbered the Num 4:34 5712
work in the tabernacle of the c Num 4:35 4150
in the tabernacle of the c Num 4:37 4150
work in the tabernacle of the c Num 4:39 4150
in the tabernacle of the c Num 4:41 4150
work in the tabernacle of the c Num 4:43 4150
burden in the tabernacle of the c Num 4:47 4150
door of the tabernacle of the c Num 6:10 4150
door of the tabernacle of the c Num 6:13 4150
door of the tabernacle of the c Num 6:18 4150
of the tabernacle of the c Num 7:5 4150
of the c to speak with him Num 7:89 4150
before the tabernacle of the c Num 8:9 4150
of the tabernacle of the c Num 8:15 4150
Israel in the tabernacle of the c Num 8:19 4150
all the c of the children of Num 8:20 5712
tabernacle of the c before Aaron Num 8:22 4150
of the tabernacle of the c Num 8:24 4150
in the tabernacle of the c Num 8:26 4150
door of the tabernacle of the c Num 10:3 4150
But when the c is to be gathered Num 10:7 6951
them unto the tabernacle of the c Num 11:16 4150
unto the tabernacle of the c Num 12:4 4150
to all the c of the children of Num 13:26 5712
word unto them, and unto all the c Num 13:26 5712
all the c lifted up their voice, Num 14:1 5712
the whole c said unto them, Would Num 14:2 5712
the c of the children of Israel Num 14:5 5712
But all the c bade stone them Num 14:10 5712
in the tabernacle of the c before Num 14:10 4150
shall I bear with this evil c Num 14:27 5712
surely do it unto all this evil c Num 14:35 5712
made all the c to murmur against Num 14:36 5712
shall be both for you of the c Num 15:15 6951
without the knowledge of the c Num 15:24 5712
that all the c shall offer one Num 15:24 5712
the c of the children of Israel Num 15:25 5712
the c of the children of Israel Num 15:26 5712
Moses and Aaron, and unto all the c Num 15:33 5712
all the c shall stone him with Num 15:35

all the *c* brought him without the .... Num 15:36 5712
of the assembly, famous in the *c* .... Num 16:2 4150
you, seeing all the *c* are holy .... Num 16:3 5712
above the *c* of the LORD .... Num 16:3 6951
you from the *c* of Israel .... Num 16:9 5712
to stand before the *c* to minister .... Num 16:9 5712
tabernacle of the *c* with Moses .... Num 16:18 4150
Korah gathered all the *c* against .... Num 16:19 5712
door of the tabernacle of the *c* .... Num 16:19 4150
the LORD appeared unto all the *c* .... Num 16:19 5712
yourselves from among this *c* .... Num 16:21 5712
wilt thou be wroth with all the *c* .... Num 16:22 5712
Speak unto the *c*, saying, Get you .... Num 16:24 5712
And he spake unto the *c*, saying, ... Num 16:26 5712
and they perished from among the *c* .... Num 16:33 6951
the *c* of the children of Israel .... Num 16:41 5712
when the *c* was gathered against .... Num 16:42 5712
toward the tabernacle of the *c* .... Num 16:42 4150
before the tabernacle of the *c* .... Num 16:43 4150
Get you up from among this *c* .... Num 16:45 5712
incense, and go quickly unto the *c* .... Num 16:46 5712
and ran into the midst of the *c* .... Num 16:47 6951
door of the tabernacle of the *c* .... Num 16:50 4150
of the *c* before the testimony .... Num 17:4 4150
charge of the tabernacle of the *c* .... Num 18:4 4150
of the tabernacle of the *c* .... Num 18:6 4150
of the tabernacle of the *c* .... Num 18:21 4150
come nigh the tabernacle of the *c* .... Num 18:22 4150
of the tabernacle of the *c* .... Num 18:23 4150
in the tabernacle of the *c* .... Num 18:31 4150
tabernacle of the *c* seven times .... Num 19:4 4150
it shall be kept for the *c* of the .... Num 19:9 5712
shall be cut off from among the *c* .... Num 19:20 6951
of Israel, even the whole *c* .... Num 20:1 5712
And there was no water for the *c* .... Num 20:2 5712
up the *c* of the LORD into this .... Num 20:4 6951
door of the tabernacle of the *c* .... Num 20:6 4150
so thou shalt give the *c* and their .... Num 20:8 5712
Aaron gathered the *c* together .... Num 20:10 6951
the *c* drank, and their beasts also .... Num 20:11 5712
ye shall not bring this *c* into .... Num 20:12 6951
of Israel, even the whole *c* .... Num 20:22 5712
Hor in the sight of all the *c* .... Num 20:27 5712
when all the *c* saw that Aaron was .... Num 20:29 5712
in the sight of all the *c* of the .... Num 25:6 5712
door of the tabernacle of the *c* .... Num 25:6 4150
it, he rose up from among the *c* .... Num 25:7 5712
Take the sum of all the *c* of the .... Num 26:2 5712
which were famous in the *c* .... Num 26:9 5712
before the princes and all the *c* .... Num 27:2 5712
door of the tabernacle of the *c* .... Num 27:2 4150
of Zin, in the strife of the *c* .... Num 27:14 5712
all flesh, set a man over the *c* .... Num 27:16 5712
that the *c* of the LORD be not as .... Num 27:17 5712
the priest, and before all the *c* .... Num 27:19 5712
that all the *c* of the children of .... Num 27:20 5712
Israel with him, even all the *c* .... Num 27:21 5712
the priest, and before all the *c* .... Num 27:22 5712
unto the *c* of the children of .... Num 31:12 5712
and all the princes of the *c* .... Num 31:13 5712
a plague among the *c* of the LORD .... Num 31:16 5712
and the chief fathers of the *c* .... Num 31:26 5712
to battle, and between all the *c* .... Num 31:27 5712
the *c* was three hundred thousand .... Num 31:43 5712
it into the tabernacle of the *c* .... Num 31:54 4150
and unto the princes of the *c* .... Num 32:2 5712
LORD smote before the *c* of Israel .... Num 32:4 5712
he stand before the *c* in judgment .... Num 35:12 5712
Then the *c* shall judge between .... Num 35:24 5712
the *c* shall deliver the slayer .... Num 35:25 5712
the *c* shall restore him to the .... Num 35:25 5712
not enter into the *c* of the LORD .... Deut 23:1 6951
not enter into the *c* of the LORD .... Deut 23:2 6951
not enter into the *c* of the LORD .... Deut 23:2 6951
not enter into the *c* of the LORD .... Deut 23:3 6951
into the *c* of the LORD for ever .... Deut 23:3 6951
the *c* of the LORD in their third .... Deut 23:8 6951
in the tabernacle of the *c* .... Deut 31:14 4150
in the tabernacle of the *c* .... Deut 31:14 4150
the *c* of Israel the words of this .... Deut 31:30 4150
the inheritance of the *c* of Jacob .... Deut 33:4 6952
not before all the *c* of Israel .... Josh 8:35 6951
princes of the *c* sware unto them .... Josh 9:15 5712
because the princes of the *c* had .... Josh 9:18 5712
all the *c* murmured against the .... Josh 9:18 5712
the princes said unto all the *c* .... Josh 9:19 5712
drawers of water unto all the *c* .... Josh 9:21 5712
and drawers of water for the *c* .... Josh 9:27 5712
the whole *c* of the children of .... Josh 18:1 5712
up the tabernacle of the *c* there .... Josh 18:1 4150
door of the tabernacle of the *c* .... Josh 19:51 4150
stand before the *c* for judgment .... Josh 20:6 5712
until he stood before the *c* .... Josh 20:9 5712
the whole *c* of the children of .... Josh 22:12 5712
saith the whole *c* of the LORD .... Josh 22:16 5712
was a plague in the *c* of the LORD .... Josh 22:17 5712
wroth with the whole *c* of Israel .... Josh 22:18 5712
wrath fell on all the *c* of Israel .... Josh 22:20 5712
priest, and the princes of the *c* .... Josh 22:30 5712
the *c* was gathered together as .... Judg 20:1 5712
not up with the *c* unto the LORD .... Judg 21:5 6951
the *c* sent thither twelve .... Judg 21:10 5712
the whole *c* sent some to speak to .... Judg 21:13 5712
Then the elders of the *c* said .... Judg 21:16 5712
door of the tabernacle of the *c* 1Sa 2:22 4150
LORD, and the tabernacle of the *c* 1Kin 8:4 4150
all the *c* of Israel, that were 1Kin 8:5 5712
and blessed all the *c* of Israel 1Kin 8:14 6951
all the *c* of Israel stood 1Kin 8:14 6951
presence of all the *c* of Israel 1Kin 8:22 6951
blessed all the *c* of Israel with 1Kin 8:55 6951
and all Israel with him, a great *c* 1Kin 8:65 6951
all the *c* of Israel came, and 1Kin 12:3 6951
sent and called him unto the *c* 1Kin 12:20 5712
tabernacle of the *c* with singing 1Chr 6:32 4150
door of the tabernacle of the *c* 1Chr 9:21 4150
said unto all the *c* of Israel 1Chr 13:2 6951
all the *c* said that they would do 1Chr 13:4 6951
charge of the tabernacle of the *c* 1Chr 23:32 4150
of all Israel the *c* of the LORD 1Chr 28:8 6951
the king said unto all the *c* 1Chr 29:1 6951
blessed the LORD before all the *c* 1Chr 29:10 6951
And David said to all the *c* 1Chr 29:20 6951
all the *c* blessed the LORD God of 1Chr 29:20 6951
all the *c* with him, went to the 2Chr 1:3 6951
the tabernacle of the *c* of God 2Chr 1:3 4150
Solomon and the *c* sought unto it 2Chr 1:5 6951
was at the tabernacle of the *c* 2Chr 1:6 4150
before the tabernacle of the *c* 2Chr 1:13 4150
ark, and the tabernacle of the *c* 2Chr 5:5 4150
all the *c* of Israel that were 2Chr 5:6 5712
and blessed the whole *c* of Israel 2Chr 6:3 6951
all the *c* of Israel stood 2Chr 6:3 6951
presence of all the *c* of Israel 2Chr 6:12 6951
knees before all the *c* of Israel 2Chr 6:13 6951
Israel with him, a very great *c* 2Chr 7:8 6951
stood in the *c* of Judah and 2Chr 20:5 6951
of the LORD in the midst of the *c* 2Chr 20:14 6951
all the *c* made a covenant with 2Chr 23:3 6951
of the *c* of Israel, for the 2Chr 24:6 6951
before the princes and all the *c* 2Chr 28:14 6951
offering before the king and the *c* 2Chr 29:23 6951
all the *c* worshipped, and the 2Chr 29:28 6951
the *c* brought in sacrifices and 2Chr 29:31 6951
offerings, which the *c* brought 2Chr 29:32 6951
all the *c* in Jerusalem, to keep 2Chr 30:2 6951
pleased the king and all the *c* 2Chr 30:4 6951
the second month, a very great *c* 2Chr 30:13 6951
in the *c* that were not sanctified 2Chr 30:17 6951
give to the *c* a thousand bullocks 2Chr 30:24 6951
gave to the *c* a thousand bullocks 2Chr 30:24 6951
all the *c* of Judah, with the 2Chr 30:25 6951
all the *c* that came out of Israel 2Chr 30:25 6951
daughters, through all the *c* 2Chr 31:18 6951
The whole *c* together was forty and .... Ezr 2:64 6951
of Israel a very great *c* of men .... Ezr 10:1 6951
himself separated from the *c* of .... Ezr 10:8 6951
Then all the *c* answered and said .... Ezr 10:12 6951
now our rulers of all the *c* stand .... Ezr 10:14 6951
And all the *c* said, Amen, and .... Neh 5:13 6951
The whole *c* together was forty and .... Neh 7:66 6951
the law before the *c* both of men .... Neh 8:2 6951
all the *c* of them that were come .... Neh 8:17 6951
come into the *c* of God for ever .... Neh 13:1 6951
For the *c* of hypocrites shall be .... Job 15:34 5712
I stood up, and I cried in the *c* .... Job 30:28 6951
sinners in the *c* of the righteous .... Ps 1:5 5712
So shall the *c* of the people .... Ps 7:7 5712
midst of the *c* will I praise thee .... Ps 22:22 6951
shall be of thee in the great *c* .... Ps 22:25 6951
I have hated the *c* of evildoers .... Ps 26:5 6951
give thee thanks in the great *c* .... Ps 35:18 6951
righteousness in the great *c* .... Ps 40:9 6951
and thy truth from the great *c* .... Ps 40:10 6951
indeed speak righteousness, O *c* .... Ps 58:1 482
Thy *c* hath dwelt therein .... Ps 68:10 2416
Remember thy *c*, which thou hast .... Ps 74:2 5712
forget not the *c* of thy poor for .... Ps 74:19 2416
the *c* I will judge uprightly .... Ps 75:2 4150
standeth in the *c* of the mighty .... Ps 82:1 5712
also in the *c* of the saints .... Ps 89:5 6951
him also in the *c* of the people .... Ps 107:32 6951
of the upright, and in the *c* .... Ps 111:1 5712
and his praise in the *c* of saints .... Ps 149:1 6951
in all evil in the midst of the *c* .... Prov 5:14 6951
shall remain in the *c* of the dead .... Prov 21:16 6951
be shewed before the whole *c* .... Prov 26:26 6951
sit also upon the mount of the *c* .... Is 14:13 4150
hear, ye nations, and know, O *c* .... Jer 6:18 5712
their *c* shall be established .... Jer 30:20 5712
they should not enter into thy *c* .... Lam 1:10 6951
them, as their *c* hath heard .... Hos 7:12 5712
Gather the people, sanctify the *c* .... Joel 2:16 6951
cord by lot in the *c* of the LORD .... Mic 2:5 6951
Now when the *c* was broken up, ... Acts 13:43 *4865*

CONGREGATIONS {3}
in the *c* will I bless the LORD .... Ps 26:12 4721
Bless ye God in the *c*, even the .... Ps 68:26 4721
roar in the midst of thy *c* .... Ps 74:4 4150

CONIAH *(co-ni'-ah)* {3} See JEHOIACHIN. *Another name for Jehoiachin.*
though *C* the son of Jehoiakim .... Jer 22:24 3659
Is this man *C* a despised broken .... Jer 22:28 3659
instead of *C* the son of Jehoiakim .... Jer 37:1 3659

CONIES {2}
and the rocks for the *c* .... Ps 104:18 8226
The *c* are but a feeble folk, yet .... Prov 30:26 8226

CONONIAH *(co-no-ni'-ah)* {2} See CONANIAH. *A Levite during Hezekiah's time.*
over which *C* the Levite was ruler 2Chr 31:12 3562
overseers under the hand of *C* 2Chr 31:13 3562

CONQUER {1}
he went forth conquering, and to *c* .... Rev 6:2 *3528*

CONQUERING {1}
and he went forth *c*, and to conquer .... Rev 6:2 *3528*

CONQUERORS {1}
than *c* through him that loved us .... Rom 8:37 *5245*

CONSCIENCE {31}
being convicted by their own *c* .... Jn 8:9 *4893*
I have lived in all good *c* before .... Acts 23:1 *4893*
to have always a *c* void of .... Acts 24:16 *4893*
their *c* also bearing witness, and .... Rom 2:15 *4893*
my *c* also bearing me witness in .... Rom 9:1 *4893*
for wrath, but also for *c* sake .... Rom 13:5 *4893*
for some with *c* of the idol unto 1Cor 8:7 *4893*
their *c* being weak is defiled 1Cor 8:7 *4893*
shall not the *c* of him which is 1Cor 8:10 *4893*
brethren, and wound their weak *c* 1Cor 8:12 *4893*
asking no question for *c* sake 1Cor 10:25 *4893*
asking no question for *c* sake 1Cor 10:27 *4893*
that shewed it, and for *c* sake 1Cor 10:28 *4893*
C, I say, not thine own, but of 1Cor 10:29 *4893*
liberty judged of another man's *c* 1Cor 10:29 *4893*
is this, the testimony of our *c* 2Cor 1:12 *4893*
every man's *c* in the sight of God 2Cor 4:2 *4893*
of a pure heart, and of a good *c* 1Ti 1:5 *4893*
Holding faith, and a good *c* 1Ti 1:19 *4893*
mystery of the faith in a pure *c* 1Ti 3:9 *4893*
having their *c* seared with a hot 1Ti 4:2 *4893*
from my forefathers with pure *c* 2Ti 1:3 *4893*
even their mind and *c* is defiled .... Titus 1:15 *4893*
perfect, as pertaining to the *c* .... Heb 9:9 *4893*
purge your *c* from dead works to .... Heb 9:14 *4893*
should have had no more *c* of sins .... Heb 10:2 *4893*
hearts sprinkled from an evil *c* .... Heb 10:22 *4893*
for we trust we have a good *c* .... Heb 13:18 *4893*
if a man for *c* toward God endure 1Pet 2:19 *4893*
Having a good *c* 1Pet 3:16 *4893*
the answer of a good *c* toward God 1Pet 3:21 *4893*

CONSCIENCES {1}
also are made manifest in your *c* 2Cor 5:11 *4893*

CONSECRATE {14}
make Aaron's garments to *c* him .... Ex 28:3 6942
c them, and sanctify them, that .... Ex 28:41 4390,3027
shalt *c* Aaron and his sons .... Ex 29:9 4390,3027
the atonement was made, to *c* .... Ex 29:33 4390,3027
seven days shalt thou *c* them .... Ex 29:35 4390,3027
c them, that they may minister .... Ex 30:30 6942
C yourselves to day to the LORD, ... Ex 32:29 4390,3027
for seven days shall he *c* you .... Lev 8:33 4390,3027
whom he shall *c* to minister in .... Lev 16:32 4390,3027
he shall *c* unto the LORD the days .... Num 6:12 5144
who then is willing to *c* his 1Chr 29:5 4390,3027
so that whosoever cometh to *c* 2Chr 13:9 4390,3027
and they shall *c* themselves .... Eze 43:26 4390,3027
I will *c* their gain unto the LORD .... Mic 4:13 2763

CONSECRATED {14}
therein, and to be *c* in them .... Ex 29:29 4390,3027
that is *c* to put on the garments, ... Lev 21:10 4390,3027
whom he *c* to minister in the .... Num 3:3 4390,3027
and iron, are *c* unto the LORD .... Josh 6:19 6944
c one of his sons, who became .... Judg 17:5 4390,3027
And Micah *c* the Levite .... Judg 17:12 4390,3027
c him, and he became one of the 1Kin 13:33 4390,3027
that are *c* to burn incense 2Chr 26:18 6942
ye have *c* yourselves unto the 2Chr 29:31 4390,3027
the *c* things were six hundred 2Chr 29:33 6942
were *c* unto the LORD their God 2Chr 31:6 6942
feasts of the LORD that were *c* .... Ezr 3:5 6942
the Son, who is *c* for evermore .... Heb 7:28 *5048*
way, which he hath *c* for us .... Heb 10:20 *1457*

CONSECRATION {9}
for it is a ram of *c* .... Ex 29:22 4394
breast of the ram of Aaron's *c* .... Ex 29:26 4394
is heaved up, of the ram of the *c* .... Ex 29:27 4394
thou shalt take the ram of the *c* .... Ex 29:31 4394
the other ram, the ram of *c* .... Lev 8:22 4394
for of the ram of *c* it was Moses' .... Lev 8:29 4394
the days of your *c* be at an end .... Lev 8:33 4394
because the *c* of his God is upon .... Num 6:7 5145
he hath defiled the head of his *c* .... Num 6:9 5145

CONSECRATIONS {4}
And if ought of the flesh of the *c* .... Ex 29:34 4394
trespass offering, and of the *c* .... Lev 7:37 4394
they were *c* for a sweet savour .... Lev 8:28 4394
bread that is in the basket of *c* .... Lev 8:31 4394

CONSENT {15}
But in this will we *c* unto you .... Gen 34:15 225
Only herein will the men *c* unto .... Gen 34:22 225
only let us *c* unto them, and they .... Gen 34:23 225
Thou shalt not *c* unto him .... Deut 13:8 14
but he would not *c* .... Judg 11:17 14
and they came out with one *c* 1Sa 11:7 376
him, Hearken not unto him, nor *c* 1Kin 20:8 14
consulted together with one *c* .... Ps 83:5 3820
sinners entice thee, *c* thou not .... Prov 1:10 14
of priests murder in the way by *c* .... Hos 6:9 7926
the LORD, to serve him with one *c* .... Zeph 3:9 7926
they all with one *c* began to make .... Lk 14:18
I *c* unto the law that it is good .... Rom 7:16 *4852*
except it be with *c* for a time 1Cor 7:5 *4859*
c not to wholesome words, even 1Ti 6:3 *4334*

CONSENTED {4}
the priests *c* to receive no more 2Kin 12:8 225
So he *c* to them in this matter, ... Dan 1:14 8085
The same had not *c* to the counsel .... Lk 23:51 *4784*
longer time with them, he *c* not .... Acts 18:20 *1962*

CONSENTEDST {1}
a thief, then thou c with him ... Ps 50:18 7521

CONSENTING {2}
Saul was c unto his death ... Acts 8:1 *4909*
c unto his death, and kept the ... Acts 22:20 *4909*

CONSIDER {67}
c that this nation is thy people ... Ex 33:13 7200
Then the priest shall c ... Lev 13:13 7200
c it in thine heart, that the ... Deut 4:39 7725
Thou shalt also c in thine heart ... Deut 8:5 3045
c the years of many generations ... Deut 32:7 995
that they would c their latter ... Deut 32:29 995
now therefore c what ye have to ... Judg 18:14 3045
c of it, take advice, and speak ... Judg 19:30 7760
for c how great things he hath ... 1Sa 12:24 7200
know and c what thou wilt do ... 1Sa 25:17 7200
wherefore c, I pray you, and see ... 2Kin 5:7 3045
will he not then c it ... Job 11:11 995
when I c, I am afraid of him ... Job 23:15 995
would not c any of his ways ... Job 34:27 7919
c the wondrous works of God ... Job 37:14 995
c my meditation ... Ps 5:1 995
When I c thy heavens, the work of ... Ps 8:3 7200
c my trouble which I suffer of ... Ps 9:13 7200
C and hear me, O LORD my God ... Ps 13:3 5027
C mine enemies ... Ps 25:19 7200
thou shalt diligently c his place ... Ps 37:10 995
Hearken, O daughter, and c ... Ps 45:10 7200
well her bulwarks, c her palaces ... Ps 48:13 6448
Now c this, ye that forget God, ... Ps 50:22 995
they shall wisely c of his doing ... Ps 64:9 7919
but I will c thy testimonies ... Ps 119:95 995
C mine affliction, and deliver me ... Ps 119:153 7200
C how I love thy precepts ... Ps 119:159 7200
c her ways, and be wise ... Prov 6:6 7200
c diligently what is before thee ... Prov 23:1 995
he that pondereth the heart c it ... Prov 24:12 995
for they c not that they do evil ... Eccl 5:1 3045
C the work of God ... Eccl 7:13 7200
but in the day of adversity c ... Eccl 7:14 7200
not know, my people doth not c ... Is 1:3 995
neither c the operation of his ... Is 5:12 7200
c thee, saying, Is this the man ... Is 14:16 995
I will c in my dwelling place ... Is 18:4 5027
That they may see, and know, and c ... Is 41:20 7760
what they be, that we may c them .. Is 41:22 7760,3820
neither c the things of old ... Is 43:18 995
they had not heard shall they c ... Is 52:15 995
c diligently, and see if there be ... Jer 2:10 995
C ye, and call for the mourning ... Jer 9:17 995
days ye shall c it perfectly ... Jer 23:20 995
in the latter days ye shall c it ... Jer 30:24 995
see, O LORD, and c ... Lam 1:11 5027
c to whom thou hast done this ... Lam 2:20 5027
c, and behold our reproach ... Lam 5:1 5027
it may be they will c, though ... Eze 12:3 7200
the matter, and c the vision ... Dan 9:23 995
they c not in their hearts that I ... Hos 7:2 559
C your ways ... Hag 1:5 7760,3820,5921
C your ways ... Hag 1:7 7760,3820,5921
c from this day and upward, from ... Hag 2:15 7760,3820
C now from this day and upward, ... Hag 2:18 7760,3820
the LORD's temple was laid, c it ... Hag 2:18 7760,3820
C the lilies of the field, how ... Mt 6:28 *2648*
C the ravens ... Lk 12:24 *2657*
C the lilies how they grow ... Lk 12:27 *2657*
Nor c that it is expedient for us ... Jn 11:50 *1260*
together for to c of this matter ... Acts 15:6 *1492*
C what I say ... 2Ti 2:7 *3539*
c the Apostle and High Priest of ... Heb 3:1 *2657*
Now c how great this man was, ... Heb 7:4 *2334*
let us c one another to provoke ... Heb 10:24 *2657*
For c him that endured such ... Heb 12:3 *357*

CONSIDERED {16}
but when I had c it in the ... 1Kin 3:21 995
I have c the things which thou ... 1Kin 5:8 8085
Hast thou c my servant Job, that ... Job 1:8 7760,3820
Hast thou c my servant Job, that ... Job 2:3 7760,3820
for thou hast c my trouble ... Ps 31:7 7200
I have c the days of old, the ... Ps 77:5 2803
Then I saw, and c it well ... Prov 24:32 7896,3820
c all the oppressions that are ... Eccl 4:1 7200
I c all travail, and every right ... Eccl 4:4 7200
I c all the living which walk ... Eccl 4:15 7200
For all this I c in my heart even ... Eccl 9:1 5414
I c the horns, and, behold, there ... Dan 7:8 7920
For they c not the miracle of the ... Mk 6:52 *4920*
I had fastened mine eyes, I c ... Acts 11:6 *2657*
And when he had c the thing ... Acts 12:12 *4894*
he c not his own body now dead, ... Rom 4:19 *2657*

CONSIDEREST {2}
C thou not what this people have ... Jer 33:24 7200
but c not the beam that is in ... Mt 7:3 *2657*

CONSIDERETH {9}
he c all their works ... Ps 33:15 995
Blessed is he that c the poor ... Ps 41:1 7919
wisely c the house of the wicked ... Prov 21:12 7919
c not that poverty shall come ... Prov 28:22 3045
The righteous c the cause of the ... Prov 29:7 3045
She c a field, and buyeth it ... Prov 31:16 2161
none c in his heart, neither is ... Is 44:19 7725
sins which he hath done, and c ... Eze 18:14 7200
Because he c, and turneth away ... Eze 18:28 7200

CONSIDERING {4}
none c that the righteous is ... Is 57:1 995
And as I was c, behold, an he goat ... Dan 8:5 995
c thyself, lest thou also be ... Gal 6:1 *4648*
c the end of their conversation ... Heb 13:7 *333*

CONSIST {1}
things, and by him all things c ... Col 1:17 *4921*

CONSISTETH {1}
for a man's life c not in the ... Lk 12:15 *2076*

CONSOLATION {15}
of c to drink for their father or ... Jer 16:7 8575
waiting for the c of Israel ... Lk 2:25 *3874*
for ye have received your c ... Lk 6:24 *3874*
being interpreted, The son of c ... Acts 4:36 *3874*
had read, they rejoiced for the c ... Acts 15:31 *3874*
c grant you to be likeminded one ... Rom 15:5 *3874*
so our c also aboundeth by Christ ... 2Cor 1:5 *3874*
we be afflicted, it is for your c ... 2Cor 1:6 *3874*
we be comforted, it is for your c ... 2Cor 1:6 *3874*
so shall ye be also of the c ... 2Cor 1:7 *3874*
but by the c wherewith he was ... 2Cor 7:7 *3874*
be therefore any c in Christ ... Phil 2:1 *3874*
and hath given us everlasting c ... 2Th 2:16 *3874*
c in thy love, because the bowels ... Philem 7 *3874*
to lie, we might have a strong c ... Heb 6:18 *3874*

CONSOLATIONS {3}
Are the c of God small with thee ... Job 15:11 8575
my speech, and let this be your c ... Job 21:2 8575
with the breasts of her c ... Is 66:11 8575

CONSORTED {1}
believed, and c with Paul and Silas ... Acts 17:4 *4845*

CONSPIRACY {10}
And the c was strong ... 2Sa 15:12 7195
his servants arose, and made a c ... 2Kin 12:20 7195
Now they made a c against him in ... 2Kin 14:19 7195
his c which he made, behold, they ... 2Kin 15:15 7195
made a c against Pekah the son of ... 2Kin 15:30 7195
king of Assyria found c in Hoshea ... 2Kin 17:4 7195
made a c against him in Jerusalem ... 2Chr 25:27 7195
A c is found among the men of ... Jer 11:9 7195
There is a c of her prophets in ... Eze 22:25 7195
than forty which had made this c ... Acts 23:13 *4945*

CONSPIRATORS {1}
is among the c with Absalom ... 2Sa 15:31 7194

CONSPIRED {19}
they c against him to slay him ... Gen 37:18 5320
That all of you have c against me ... 1Sa 22:8 7194
him, Why have ye c against me ... 1Sa 22:13 7194
house of Issachar, c against him ... 1Kin 15:27 7194
c against him, as he was in ... 1Kin 16:9 7194
encamped heard say, Zimri hath c ... 1Kin 16:16 7194
the son of Nimshi c against Joram ... 2Kin 9:14 7194
I c against my master, and slew ... 2Kin 10:9 7194
the son of Jabesh c against him ... 2Kin 15:10 7194
c against him, and smote him in ... 2Kin 15:25 7194
servants of Amon c against him ... 2Kin 21:23 7194
them that had c against king Amon ... 2Kin 21:24 7194
they c against him, and stoned him ... 2Chr 24:21 7194
his own servants c against him ... 2Chr 24:25 7194
these are they that c against him ... 2Chr 24:26 7194
And his servants c against him ... 2Chr 33:24 7194
them that had c against king Amon ... 2Chr 33:25 7194
c all of them together to come and ... Neh 4:8 7194
Amos hath c against thee in the ... Amos 7:10 7194

CONSTANT {1}
if he be c to do my commandments ... 1Chr 28:7 2388

CONSTANTLY {3}
the man that heareth speaketh c ... Prov 21:28 5331
But she c affirmed that it was ... Acts 12:15 *1340*
things I will that thou affirm c ... Titus 3:8 *1226*

CONSTELLATIONS {1}
the c thereof shall not give ... Is 13:10 3685

CONSTRAIN {1}
they c you to be circumcised ... Gal 6:12 *315*

CONSTRAINED {6}
and she c him to eat bread ... 2Kin 4:8 2388
straightway Jesus c his disciples ... Mt 14:22 *315*
straightway he c his disciples to ... Mk 6:45 *315*
But they c him, saying, Abide ... Lk 24:29 *3849*
And she c us ... Acts 16:15 *3849*
I was c to appeal unto Caesar ... Acts 28:19 *315*

CONSTRAINETH {2}
the spirit within me c me ... Job 32:18 6693
For the love of Christ c us ... 2Cor 5:14 *4912*

CONSTRAINT {1}
the oversight thereof, not by c ... 1Pet 5:2 *317*

CONSULT {1}
They only c to cast him down from ... Ps 62:4 3289

CONSULTATION {1}
priests held a c with the elders ... Mk 15:1 *4824*

CONSULTED {13}
king Rehoboam c with the old men, ... 1Kin 12:6 3289
c with the young men that were ... 1Kin 12:8 3289
David c with the captains of ... 1Chr 13:1 3289
when he had c with the people, he ... 2Chr 20:21 3289
Then I c with myself, and I ... Neh 5:7 4427
c against thy hidden ones ... Ps 83:3 3289
For they have c together with one ... Ps 83:5 3289
he c with images, he looked in ... Eze 21:21 7592
have c together to establish a ... Dan 6:7 3272
now what Balak king of Moab c ... Mic 6:5 3289
Thou hast c shame to thy house by ... Hab 2:10 3289
c that they might take Jesus by ... Mt 26:4 *4823*
But the chief priests c that they ... Jn 12:10 *1011*

CONSULTER {1}
or a c with familiar spirits, or ... Deut 18:11 7592

CONSULTETH {1}
c whether he be able with ten ... Lk 14:31 *1011*

CONSUME {56}
and the famine shall c the land ... Gen 41:30 3615
them, and that I may c them ... Ex 32:10 3615
to c them from the face of the ... Ex 32:12 3615
lest I c thee in the way ... Ex 33:3 3615
of thee in a moment, and c thee ... Ex 33:5 3615
ague, that shall c the eyes ... Lev 26:16 3615
that I may c them in a moment ... Num 16:21 3615
that I may c them as in a moment ... Num 16:45 3615
for this great fire will c us ... Deut 5:25 398
thou shalt c all the people which ... Deut 7:16 398
thou mayest not c them at once ... Deut 7:22 3615
for the locust shall c it ... Deut 28:38 2628
of thy land shall the locust c ... Deut 28:42 3423
shall c the earth with her ... Deut 32:22 398
c you, after that he hath done ... Josh 24:20 3615
altar, shall be to c thine eyes ... 1Sa 2:33 3615
heaven, and c thee and thy fifty ... 2Kin 1:10 398
heaven, and c thee and thy fifty ... 2Kin 1:12 398
thou didst not utterly c them ... Neh 9:31 3615
to c them, and to destroy them ... Est 9:24 2000
fire shall c the tabernacles of ... Job 15:34 398
a fire not blown shall c him ... Job 20:26 398
Drought and heat c the snow waters ... Job 24:19 1497
they shall c ... Ps 37:20 3615
into smoke shall they c away ... Ps 37:20 3615
his beauty to c away like a moth ... Ps 39:11 4529
their beauty shall c in the grave ... Ps 49:14 1086
C them in wrath, c them, ... Ps 59:13 3615
their days did he c in vanity ... Ps 78:33 3615
and it shall also c the beard ... Is 7:20 5595
shall c the glory of his forest, ... Is 10:18 3615
down, and c the branches thereof ... Is 27:10 3615
I will surely c them, saith the ... Jer 8:13 5486
but I will c them by the sword, ... Jer 14:12 3615
it shall c the palaces of ... Jer 49:27 398
c away for their iniquity ... Eze 4:17 4743
hailstones in my fury to c it ... Eze 13:13 3615
them in the wilderness, to c them ... Eze 20:13 3615
to c because of the glittering ... Eze 21:28 398
will c thy filthiness out of thee ... Eze 22:15 8552
c the flesh, and spice it well, and ... Eze 24:10 8552
desolate, they are given us to c ... Eze 35:12 402
c all these kingdoms, and it shall ... Dan 2:44 5487
take away his dominion, to c ... Dan 7:26 8046
shall c his branches, and devour ... Hos 11:6 3615
I will utterly c all things from ... Zeph 1:2 5486
I will c man and beast ... Zeph 1:3 5486
I will c the fowls of the heaven, ... Zeph 1:3 5486
shall c it with the timber ... Zec 5:4 3615
Their flesh shall c away while ... Zec 14:12 4743
their eyes shall c away in their ... Zec 14:12 4743
their tongue shall c away in ... Zec 14:12 4743
c them, even as Elias did ... Lk 9:54 *355*
whom the Lord shall c with the ... 2Th 2:8 *355*
that ye may c it upon your lusts ... Jas 4:3 *1159*

CONSUMED {96}
lest thou be c in the iniquity of ... Gen 19:15 5595
to the mountain, lest thou be c ... Gen 19:17 5595
in the day the drought c me ... Gen 31:40 398
with fire, and the bush was not c ... Ex 3:2 398
wrath, which c them as stubble ... Ex 15:7 398
or the field, be c therewith ... Ex 22:6 398
the ashes which the fire hath c ... Lev 6:10 398
c upon the altar the burnt ... Lev 9:24 398
c them that were in the uttermost ... Num 11:1 398
half c when he cometh out of his ... Num 12:12 398
this wilderness they shall be c ... Num 14:35 8552
lest ye be c in all their sins ... Num 16:26 5595
c the two hundred and fifty men ... Num 16:35 398
shall we be c with dying ... Num 17:13 8552
it hath c Ar of Moab, and the ... Num 21:28 398
that I c not the children of ... Num 25:11 3615
in the sight of the LORD, was c ... Num 32:13 8552
among the host, until they were c ... Deut 2:15 8552
when all the men of war were c ... Deut 2:16 8552
until he have c thee from off the ... Deut 28:21 3615
which came out of Egypt, were c ... Josh 5:6 8552
of the sword, until they were c ... Josh 8:24 8552
great slaughter, till they were c ... Josh 10:20 8552
c the flesh and the unleavened ... Judg 6:21 398
still do wickedly, ye shall be c ... 1Sa 12:25 5595
against them until they be c ... 1Sa 15:18 3615
the king, The man that c us ... 2Sa 21:5 3615
not again until I had c them ... 2Sa 22:38 3615
And I have c them, and wounded them ... 2Sa 22:39 3615
c the burnt sacrifice, and the ... 1Kin 18:38 398
Syrians, until thou have c them ... 1Kin 22:11 3615
heaven, and c him and his fifty ... 2Kin 1:10 398
heaven, and c him and his fifty ... 2Kin 1:12 398
of the Israelites that are c ... 2Kin 7:13 8552
in Aphek, till thou have c them ... 2Kin 13:17 3615
Syria till thou hadst c it ... 2Kin 13:19 3615
c the burnt offering and the ... 2Chr 7:1 398
whom the children of Israel c not ... 2Chr 8:8 3615
shalt push Syria until they be c ... 2Chr 18:10 3615
with us till thou hadst c us ... Ezr 9:14 3615
the gates thereof are c with fire ... Neh 2:3 398
gates thereof were c with fire ... Neh 2:13 398
sheep, and the servants, and c them ... Job 1:16 398
breath of his nostrils are they c ... Job 4:9 3615

they are c out of their place ... Job 6:17 1846
As the cloud is c and vanisheth ... Job 7:9 3615
though my reins be c within me ... Job 19:27 3615
His flesh is c away, that it ... Job 33:21 3615
Mine eye is c because of grief ... Ps 6:7 6244
did I turn again till they were c ... Ps 18:37 3615
mine eye is c with grief, yea, my ... Ps 31:9 6244
mine iniquity, and my bones are c ... Ps 31:10 6244
I am c by the blow of thine hand ... Ps 39:10 3615
c that are adversaries to my soul ... Ps 71:13 3615
they are utterly c with terrors ... Ps 73:19 8552
The fire c their young men ... Ps 78:63 398
For we are c by thine anger, and ... Ps 90:7 3615
For my days are c like smoke ... Ps 102:3 3615
the sinners be c out of the earth ... Ps 104:35 8552
They had almost c me upon earth ... Ps 119:87 3615
My zeal hath c me, because mine ... Ps 119:139 6789
when thy flesh and thy body are c ... Prov 5:11 3615
that forsake the LORD shall be c ... Is 1:28 3615
oppressors are c out of the land ... Is 16:4 8552
to nought, and the scorner is c ... Is 29:20 3615
thy face from us, and hast c us ... Is 64:7 4127
and the mouse, shall be c together ... Is 66:17 5486
thou hast c them, but they have ... Jer 5:3 3615
burned, the lead is c of the fire ... Jer 6:29 8552
after them, till I have c them ... Jer 9:16 3615
him, and c him, and have made his ... Jer 10:25 3615
the beasts are c, and the birds ... Jer 12:4 5595
famine shall those prophets be c ... Jer 14:15 8552
and they shall be c by the sword ... Jer 16:4 3615
my days should be c with shame ... Jer 20:18 3615
till they be c from off the land ... Jer 24:10 8552
until I have c them by his hand ... Jer 27:8 8552
until all the roll was c in the ... Jer 36:23 8552
there, and they shall all be c ... Jer 44:12 8552
they shall even be c by the sword ... Jer 44:12 8552
have been c by the sword and by ... Jer 44:18 8552
of Egypt shall be c by the sword ... Jer 44:27 8552
after them, till I have c them ... Jer 49:37 3615
and brought up hath mine enemy c ... Lam 2:22 3615
LORD's mercies that we are not c ... Lam 3:22 8552
they be c in the midst of thee ... Eze 5:12 3615
ye shall be c in the midst ... Eze 13:14 3615
the fire c them ... Eze 19:12 398
I have c them with the fire of my ... Eze 22:31 3615
it, that the scum of it may be c ... Eze 24:11 8552
they shall be no more c with ... Eze 34:29 622
wherefore I have c them in mine ... Eze 43:8 398
shall the fruit thereof be c ... Eze 47:12 8552
which by his hand shall be c ... Dan 11:16 3615
ye sons of Jacob are not c ... Mal 3:6 3615
that ye be not c one of another ... Gal 5:15 *355*

CONSUMETH {4}
And he, as a rotten thing, c ... Job 13:28 1086
the remnant of them the fire c ... Job 22:20 398
is a fire that c to destruction ... Job 31:12 398
stubble, and the flame c the chaff ... Is 5:24 7503

CONSUMING {3}
For the LORD thy God is a c fire ... Deut 4:24 398
as a c fire he shall destroy them ... Deut 9:3 398
For our God is a c fire ... Heb 12:29 *2654*

CONSUMMATION {1}
it desolate, even until the c ... Dan 9:27 3617

CONSUMPTION {5}
even appoint over you terror, c ... Lev 26:16 7829
LORD shall smite thee with a c ... Deut 28:22 7829
the c decreed shall overflow with ... Is 10:22 3631
Lord GOD of hosts shall make a c ... Is 10:23 3617
from the Lord GOD of hosts a c ... Is 28:22 3617

CONTAIN {7}
heaven of heavens cannot c thee ... 1Kin 8:27 3557
as great as would c two measures ... 1Kin 18:32 1004
and heaven of heavens cannot c him ... 2Chr 2:6 3557
heaven of heavens cannot c thee ... 2Chr 6:18 3557
that the bath may c the tenth ... Eze 45:11 5375
not c the books that should be ... Jn 21:25 *5562*
But if they cannot c, let them ... 1Cor 7:9 *1467*

CONTAINED {5}
it c two thousand baths ... 1Kin 7:26 3557
one laver c forty baths ... 1Kin 7:38 3557
by nature the things c in the law ... Rom 2:14
of commandments c in ordinances ... Eph 2:15
also it is c in the scripture ... 1Pet 2:6 *4033*

CONTAINETH {1}
it c much ... Eze 23:32 3557

CONTAINING {1}
c two or three firkins apiece ... Jn 2:6 *5562*

CONTEMN {2}
Wherefore doth the wicked c God ... Ps 10:13 5006
what if the sword c even the rod ... Eze 21:13 3988

CONTEMNED {4}
In whose eyes a vile person is c ... Ps 15:4 959
c the counsel of the most High ... Ps 107:11 5006
for love, it would utterly be c ... Song 8:7 936
and the glory of Moab shall be c ... Is 16:14 7034

CONTEMNETH {1}
it c the rod of my son, as every ... Eze 21:10 3988

CONTEMPT {10}
Thus shall there arise too much c ... Est 1:18 963
He poureth c upon princes, and ... Job 12:21 937
or did the c of families terrify ... Job 31:34 937
He poureth c upon princes, and ... Ps 107:40 937
Remove from me reproach and c ... Ps 119:22 937
we are exceedingly filled with c ... Ps 123:3 937
ease, and with the c of the proud ... Ps 123:4 937
wicked cometh, then cometh also c ... Prov 18:3 937
glory, and to bring into c all the ... Is 23:9 7043
and some to shame and everlasting c ... Dan 12:2 1860

CONTEMPTIBLE {4}
say, The table of the LORD is c ... Mal 1:7 959
thereof, even his meat, is c ... Mal 1:12 959
Therefore have I also made you c ... Mal 2:9 959
presence is weak, and his speech c ... 2Cor 10:10 *1848*

CONTEMPTUOUSLY {1}
and c against the righteous ... Ps 31:18 937

CONTEND {14}
neither c with them in battle ... Deut 2:9 1624
it, and c with him in battle ... Deut 2:24 1624
If he will c with him, he cannot ... Job 9:3 7378
will ye c for God ... Job 13:8 7378
such as keep the law c with them ... Prov 28:4 1624
neither may he c with him that is ... Eccl 6:10 1777
for I will c with him that ... Is 49:25 7378
who will c with me ... Is 50:8 7378
For I will not c for ever ... Is 57:16 7378
then how canst thou c with horses ... Jer 12:5 8474
the voice of them that c with me ... Jer 18:19 3401
the Lord GOD called to c by fire ... Amos 7:4 7378
c thou before the mountains, and ... Mic 6:1 7378
c for the faith which was once ... Jude 3 *1864*

CONTENDED {6}
Then c I with the rulers, and said ... Neh 13:11 7378
Then I c with the nobles of Judah ... Neh 13:17 7378
I c with them, and cursed them, and ... Neh 13:25 7378
maidservant, when they c with me ... Job 31:13 7378
them, even them that c with thee ... Is 41:12 4695
of the circumcision c with him ... Acts 11:2 *1252*

CONTENDEST {1}
shew me wherefore thou c with me ... Job 10:2 7378

CONTENDETH {3}
Shall he that c with the Almighty ... Job 40:2 7378
If a wise man c with a foolish ... Prov 29:9 8199
contend with him that c with thee ... Is 49:25 3401

CONTENDING {1}
when c with the devil he disputed ... Jude 9 *1252*

CONTENT {16}
And his brethren were c ... Gen 37:27 8085
Moses was c to dwell with the man ... Ex 2:21 2974
Moses heard that, he was c ... Lev 10:20 3190,5869
would to God we had been c ... Josh 7:7 2974
the Levite was c to dwell with ... Judg 17:11 2974
had said unto the man, Be c ... Judg 19:6 2974
And Naaman said, Be c, take two ... 2Kin 5:23 2974
And one said, Be c, I pray thee, ... 2Kin 6:3 2974
Now therefore be c, look upon me ... Job 6:28 2974
neither will he rest c, though ... Prov 6:35 14
Pilate, willing to c the people ... Mk 15:15 *2425,3588,4160*
and be c with your wages ... Lk 3:14 *714*
state I am, therewith to be c ... Phil 4:11 *842*
and raiment let us be therewith c ... 1Ti 6:8 *714*
be c with such things as ye have ... Heb 13:5 *714*
not c therewith, neither doth he ... 3Jn 10 *714*

CONTENTION {9}
Only by pride cometh c ... Prov 13:10 4683
therefore leave off c, before it ... Prov 17:14 7379
A fool's lips enter into c ... Prov 18:6 7379
the scorner, and c shall go out ... Prov 22:10 4066
a man of c to the whole earth ... Jer 15:10 4066
are that raise up strife and c ... Hab 1:3 4066
the c was so sharp between them, ... Acts 15:39 *3948*
The one preach Christ of c ... Phil 1:16 *2052*
you the gospel of God with much c ... 1Th 2:2 *73*

CONTENTIONS {6}
The lot causeth c to cease ... Prov 18:18 4079
their c are like the bars of a ... Prov 18:19 4079
the c of a wife are a continual ... Prov 19:13 4079
who hath c ... Prov 23:29 4079
Chloe, that there are c among you ... 1Cor 1:11 *2054*
questions, and genealogies, and c ... Titus 3:9 *2054*

CONTENTIOUS {5}
in the wilderness, than with a c ... Prov 21:19 4066
so is a c man to kindle strife ... Prov 26:21 4066
rainy day and a c woman are alike ... Prov 27:15 4066
But unto them that are c, and do ... Rom 2:8 *1537,2052*
But if any man seem to be c ... 1Cor 11:16 *5380*

CONTENTMENT {1}
godliness with c is great gain ... 1Ti 6:6 *841*

CONTINUAL {33}
This shall be a c burnt offering ... Ex 29:42 8548
the c bread shall be thereon ... Num 4:7 8548
by day, for a c burnt offering ... Num 28:3 8548
It is a c burnt offering, which ... Num 28:6 8548
beside the c burnt offering, and ... Num 28:10 8548
beside the c burnt offering, and ... Num 28:15 8548
which is for a c burnt offering ... Num 28:23 8548
beside the c burnt offering ... Num 28:24 8548
them beside the c burnt offering ... Num 28:31 8548
the c burnt offering, and the meat ... Num 29:11 8548
beside the c burnt offering, his ... Num 29:16 8548
beside the c burnt offering, and ... Num 29:19 8548
beside the c burnt offering, and ... Num 29:22 8548
beside the c burnt offering, his ... Num 29:25 8548
beside the c burnt offering, and ... Num 29:28 8548
beside the c burnt offering, his ... Num 29:31 8548
beside the c burnt offering, his ... Num 29:34 8548
beside the c burnt offering, and ... Num 29:38 8548
his allowance was a c allowance ... 2Kin 25:30 8548
for the c shewbread, and for the ... 2Chr 2:4 8548
offered the c burnt offering ... Ezr 3:5 8548
for the c meat offering, and for ... Neh 10:33 8548
for the c burnt offering, of the ... Neh 10:33 8548
of a merry heart hath a c feast ... Prov 15:15 8548
of a wife are a c dropping ... Prov 19:13 2956
A c dropping in a very rainy day ... Prov 27:15 1115,5627
people in wrath with a c stroke ... Is 14:6
of Luhith c weeping shall go up ... Jer 48:5
there was a c diet given him of ... Jer 52:34 8548
sever out men of c employment ... Eze 39:14 8548
morning for a c burnt offering ... Eze 46:15 8548
by her c coming she weary me ... Lk 18:5 *1519,5056*
heaviness and c sorrow in my heart ... Rom 9:2 *88*

CONTINUALLY {81}
of his heart was only evil c ... Gen 6:5 3605,3117
returned from off the earth c ... Gen 8:3 1980,7725
the waters decreased c until the ... Gen 8:5 1980
for a memorial before the LORD c ... Ex 28:29 8548
upon his heart before the LORD c ... Ex 28:30 8548
of the first year day by day c ... Ex 29:38 8548
to cause the lamps to burn c ... Lev 24:2 8548
the morning before the LORD c ... Lev 24:3 8548
candlestick before the LORD c ... Lev 24:4 8548
set it in order before the LORD c ... Lev 24:8 8548
the ark of the LORD went on c ... Josh 6:13 1980
and Saul became David's enemy c .. 1Sa 18:29 3605,3117
shalt eat bread at my table c ... 2Sa 9:7 8548
for he did eat c at the king's ... 2Sa 9:13 8548
people increased c with Absalom ... 2Sa 15:12 1980
before me c in the room of Joab ... 2Sa 19:13 3605,3117
which stand c before thee ... 1Kin 10:8 8548
man of God, which passeth by us c ... 2Kin 4:9 8548
he did eat bread c before him all ... 2Kin 25:29 8548
the priests with trumpets c ... 1Chr 16:6 8548
and his strength, seek his face c ... 1Chr 16:11 8548
to minister before the ark c ... 1Chr 16:37 8548
of the burnt offering c morning ... 1Chr 16:40 8548
unto them, c before the LORD ... 1Chr 23:31 8548
which stand c before thee ... 2Chr 9:7 8548
Rehoboam and Jeroboam c ... 2Chr 12:15 3605,3117
LORD c all the days of Jehoiada ... 2Chr 24:14 8548
Thus did Job c ... Job 1:5 3605,3117
his praise shall c be in my mouth ... Ps 34:1 8548
yea, let them say c, Let the LORD ... Ps 35:27 8548
halt, and my sorrow is c before me ... Ps 38:17 8548
and thy truth c preserve me ... Ps 40:11 8544
such as love thy salvation say c ... Ps 40:16 8548
while they c say unto me, Where ... Ps 42:3 3605,3117
My confusion is c before me ... Ps 44:15 3605,3117
to have been c before me ... Ps 50:8 8548
the goodness of God endureth c ... Ps 52:1 3605,3117
melt away as waters which run c ... Ps 58:7
and make their loins c to shake ... Ps 69:23 8548
such as love thy salvation say c ... Ps 70:4 8548
whereunto I may c resort ... Ps 71:3 8548
my praise shall be c of thee ... Ps 71:6 8548
But I will hope c, and will yet ... Ps 71:14 8548
also shall be made for him c ... Ps 72:15 8548
Nevertheless I am c with thee ... Ps 73:23 8548
rise up against thee increaseth c ... Ps 74:23 8548
Let his children be c vagabonds ... Ps 109:10
Let them be before the LORD c ... Ps 109:15 8548
a girdle wherewith he is girded c ... Ps 109:19 8548
shall I keep thy law c for ever ... Ps 119:44 8548
My soul is c in my hand ... Ps 119:109 8548
have respect unto thy statutes c ... Ps 119:117 8548
c are they gathered together for ... Ps 140:2 3605,3117
his heart, he deviseth mischief c ... Prov 6:14 6256
Bind them c upon thine heart, and ... Prov 6:21 8548
it whirleth about c, and the wind ... Eccl 1:6
I stand c upon the watchtower in ... Is 21:8 8548
thy walls are c before me ... Is 49:16 8548
hast feared c every day because ... Is 51:13 8548
my name c every day is blasphemed ... Is 52:5 8548
And the LORD shall guide thee c ... Is 58:11 8548
thy gates shall be open c ... Is 60:11 8548
me to anger c to my face ... Is 65:3 8548
before me c is grief and wounds ... Jer 6:7 8548
offerings, and to do sacrifice c ... Jer 33:18 3605,3117
he did c eat bread before him all ... Jer 52:33 8548
a meat offering c by a perpetual ... Eze 46:14 8548
Thy God whom thou servest c ... Dan 6:16 8411
is thy God, whom thou servest c ... Dan 6:20 8411
they have committed whoredom c ... Hos 4:18
and judgment, and wait on thy God c ... Hos 12:6 8548
so shall all the heathen drink c ... Obad 16 8548
hath not thy wickedness passed c ... Nah 3:19 8548
not spare c to slay the nations ... Hab 1:17 8548
were c in the temple, praising and ... Lk 24:53 *1725*
will give ourselves c to prayer ... Acts 6:4 *4342*
of them that waited on him c ... Acts 10:7 *4342*
attending c upon this very thing ... Rom 13:6 *4342*
abideth a priest c ... Heb 7:3 *1519,1336*
year c make the comers thereunto ... Heb 10:1 *1519,1336*
the sacrifice of praise to God c ... Heb 13:15 *1275*

CONTINUANCE {5}
even great plagues, and of long c ... Deut 28:59 539
and sore sicknesses, and of long c ... Deut 28:59 539
which in c were fashioned, when ... Ps 139:16 3117
in those is c, and we shall be ... Is 64:5 5769
To them who by patient c in well ... Rom 2:7 *5281*

CONTINUE {38}
if he c a day or two, he shall ... Ex 21:21 5975
she shall then c in the blood of ... Lev 12:4 3427
she shall c in the blood of her ... Lev 12:5 3427
you c following the LORD your God ... 1Sa 12:14 1961

But now thy kingdom shall not c ... 1Sa 13:14 6965
that it may c for ever before ... 2Sa 7:29 1961
That the LORD may c his word ... 1Kin 2:4 6965
neither shall his substance c ... Job 15:29 6965
doth not mine eye c in their ... Job 17:2 3885
O c thy lovingkindness unto them ... Ps 36:10 4900
their houses shall c for ever ... Ps 49:11
children of thy servants shall c ... Ps 102:28 7931
They c this day according to ... Ps 119:91 5975
that c until night, till wine ... Is 5:11 309
vessel, that they may c many days ... Jer 32:14 5975
he shall c more years than the ... Dan 11:8 5975
because they c with me now three ... Mt 15:32 *4357*
If ye c in my word, then are ye ... Jn 8:31 *3306*
c ye in my love ... Jn 15:9 *3306*
persuaded them to c in the grace ... Acts 13:43 *1961*
exhorting them to c in the faith ... Acts 14:22 *1696*
I c unto this day, witnessing ... Acts 26:22 *2476*
Shall we c in sin, that grace may ... Rom 6:1 *1961*
if thou c in his goodness ... Rom 11:22 *1961*
of the gospel might c with you ... Gal 2:5 *1265*
abide and c with you all for your ... Phil 1:25 *4839*
If ye c in the faith grounded and ... Col 1:23 *1961*
C in prayer, and watch in the same ... Col 4:2 *4342*
if they c in faith and charity and ... 1Ti 2:15 *3306*
c in them ... 1Ti 4:16 *1961*
But c thou in the things which ... 2Ti 3:14 *3306*
suffered to c by reason of death ... Heb 7:23 *3887*
Let brotherly love c ... Heb 13:1 *3306*
c there a year, and buy and sell, ... Jas 4:13 *4160*
all things c as they were from ... 2Pet 3:4 *1265*
you, ye also shall c in the Son ... 1Jn 2:24 *3306*
was given unto him to c forty ... Rev 13:5 *4160*
cometh, he must c a short space ... Rev 17:10 *3306*

CONTINUED {29}
and they c a season in ward ... Gen 40:4 1961
Asher c on the sea shore, and ... Judg 5:17 3427
the country of Moab, and c there ... Ruth 1:2 1961
hath c even from the morning ... Ruth 2:7 5975
as she c praying before the LORD, ... 1Sa 1:12 7235
the ark of the LORD c in the ... 2Sa 6:11 3427
they c three years without war ... 1Kin 22:1 3427
all this c until the burnt ... 2Chr 29:28
also I c in the work of this wall ... Neh 5:16 2388
Moreover Job c his parable ... Job 27:1 3254
Moreover Job c his parable ... Job 29:1 3254
his name shall be c as long as ... Ps 72:17 5125
Daniel c even unto the first year ... Dan 1:21 1961
c all night in prayer to God ... Lk 6:12 *1273*
Ye are they which have c with me ... Lk 22:28 *1265*
they c there not many days ... Jn 2:12 *3306*
So when they c asking him ... Jn 8:7 *1961*
there c with his disciples ... Jn 11:54 *1304*
These all c with one accord in ... Acts 1:14 *4342*
And they c stedfastly in the ... Acts 2:42 *4342*
he c with Philip, and wondered, ... Acts 8:13 *4342*
But Peter c knocking ... Acts 12:16 *1961*
Barnabas c in Antioch, teaching ... Acts 15:35 *1304*
he c there a year and six months, ... Acts 18:11 *2523*
this c by the space of two years ... Acts 19:10 *1096*
c his speech until midnight ... Acts 20:7 *3905*
c fasting, having taken nothing ... Acts 27:33 *1300*
because they c not in my covenant ... Heb 8:9 *1696*
would no doubt have c with us ... 1Jn 2:19 *3306*

CONTINUETH {5}
fleeth also as a shadow, and c not ... Job 14:2 5975
Cursed is every one that c not in ... Gal 3:10 *1696*
c in supplications and prayers ... 1Ti 5:5 *4357*
But this man, because he c ever ... Heb 7:24 *3306*
c therein, he being not a ... Jas 1:25 *3887*

CONTINUING {4}
forth with fury, a c whirlwind ... Jer 30:23 1641
c daily with one accord in the ... Acts 2:46 *4342*
c instant in prayer ... Rom 12:12 *4342*
For here have we no c city ... Heb 13:14 *3306*

CONTRADICTING {1}
which were spoken by Paul, c ... Acts 13:45 *483*

CONTRADICTION {2}
without all c the less is blessed ... Heb 7:7 *485*
such c of sinners against himself ... Heb 12:3 *485*

CONTRARIWISE {3}
So that c ye ought rather to ... 2Cor 2:7 *5121*
But c, when they saw that the ... Gal 2:7 *5121*
but c blessing ... 1Pet 3:9 *5121*

CONTRARY {24}
And if ye walk c unto me, and will ... Lev 26:21 7147
things, but will walk c unto me ... Lev 26:23 7147
Then will I also walk c unto you ... Lev 26:24 7147
unto me, but walk c unto me ... Lev 26:27 7147
Then I will walk c unto you also ... Lev 26:28 7147
also they have walked c unto me ... Lev 26:40 7147
I also have walked c unto them ... Lev 26:41 7147
(though it was turned to the c ... Est 9:1
the c is in thee from other women ... Eze 16:34 2016
unto thee, therefore thou art c ... Eze 16:34 2016
for the wind was c ... Mt 14:24 *1727*
for the wind was c unto them ... Mk 6:48 *1727*
these all do c to the decrees of ... Acts 17:7 *561*
men to worship God c to the law ... Acts 18:13 *3844*
me to be smitten c to the law ... Acts 23:3 *3891*
things c to the name of Jesus of ... Acts 26:9 *1727*
Cyprus, because the winds were c ... Acts 27:4 *1727*
wert graffed c to nature into a ... Rom 11:24 *3844*
offences c to the doctrine which ... Rom 16:17 *3844*
these are c the one to the other ... Gal 5:17 *480*
was against us, which was c to us ... Col 2:14 *5227*
not God, and are c to all men ... 1Th 2:15 *1727*
thing that is c to sound doctrine ... 1Ti 1:10 *480*
is of the c part may be ashamed ... Titus 2:8 *1727*

CONTRIBUTION {1}
Achaia to make a certain c for ... Rom 15:26 *2842*

CONTRITE {5}
saveth such as be of a c spirit ... Ps 34:18 1793
a c heart, O God, thou wilt not ... Ps 51:17 1794
with him also that is of a c ... Is 57:15 1793
to revive the heart of the c ones ... Is 57:15 1792
of a c spirit, and trembleth at my ... Is 66:2 5223

CONTROVERSIES {1}
judgment of the LORD, and for c ... 2Chr 19:8 7379

CONTROVERSY {13}
matters of c within thy gates ... Deut 17:8 7379
the men, between whom the c is ... Deut 19:17 7379
and by their word shall every c ... Deut 21:5 7379
If there be a c between men ... Deut 25:1 7379
that when any man that had a c ... 2Sa 15:2 7379
of recompences for the c of Zion ... Is 34:8 7379
LORD hath a c with the nations ... Jer 25:31 7379
in c they shall stand in judgment ... Eze 44:24 7379
for the LORD hath a c with the ... Hos 4:1 7379
The LORD hath also a c with Judah ... Hos 12:2 7379
ye, O mountains, the LORD's c ... Mic 6:2 7379
the LORD hath a c with his people ... Mic 6:2 7379
without c great is the mystery of ... 1Ti 3:16 *3672*

CONVENIENT {9}
feed me with food c for me ... Prov 30:8 2706
c for thee to go, thither go ... Jer 40:4 3477
it seemeth c unto thee to go ... Jer 40:5 3477
when a c day was come, that Herod ... Mk 6:21 *2121*
when I have a c season, I will ... Acts 24:25 *2540*
do those things which are not c ... Rom 1:28 *2520*
come when he shall have c time ... 1Cor 16:12 *2119*
nor jesting, which are not c ... Eph 5:4 *433*
to enjoin thee that which is c ... Philem 8 *433*

CONVENIENTLY {1}
sought how he might c betray him ... Mk 14:11 *2122*

CONVERSANT {2}
strangers that were c among them ... Josh 8:35 1980
as long as we were c with them ... 1Sa 25:15 1980

CONVERSATION {20}
to slay such as be of upright c ... Ps 37:14 1870
his c aright will I shew the ... Ps 50:23 1870
we have had our c in the world ... 2Cor 1:12 *390*
For ye have heard of my c in time ... Gal 1:13 *391*
c in times past in the lusts of ... Eph 2:3 *390*
the former c the old man, which ... Eph 4:22 *391*
Only let your c be as it becometh ... Phil 1:27 *4176*
For our c is in heaven ... Phil 3:20 *4175*
of the believers, in word, in c ... 1Ti 4:12 *391*
Let your c be without ... Heb 13:5 *5158*
considering the end of their c ... Heb 13:7 *391*
good c his works with meekness of ... Jas 3:13 *391*
so be ye holy in all manner of c ... 1Pet 1:15 *391*
from your vain c received by ... 1Pet 1:18 *391*
Having your c honest among the ... 1Pet 2:12 *391*
word be won by the c of the wives ... 1Pet 3:1 *391*
your chaste c coupled with fear ... 1Pet 3:2 *391*
accuse your good c in Christ ... 1Pet 3:16 *391*
with the filthy c of the wicked ... 2Pet 2:7 *391*
ought ye to be in all holy c ... 2Pet 3:11 *391*

CONVERSION {1}
declaring the c of the Gentiles ... Acts 15:3 *1995*

CONVERT {2}
understand with their heart, and c ... Is 6:10 7725
err from the truth, and one c him ... Jas 5:19 *1994*

CONVERTED {9}
and sinners shall be c unto thee ... Ps 51:13 7725
of the sea shall be c unto thee ... Is 60:5 2015
with their heart, and should be c ... Mt 13:15 *1994*
I say unto you, Except ye be c ... Mt 18:3 *4762*
lest at any time they should be c ... Mk 4:12 *1994*
and when thou art c, strengthen ... Lk 22:32 *1994*
with their heart, and be c ... Jn 12:40 *1994*
Repent ye therefore, and be c ... Acts 3:19 *1994*
with their heart, and should be c ... Acts 28:27 *1994*

CONVERTETH {1}
that he which c the sinner from ... Jas 5:20 *1994*

CONVERTING {1}
the LORD is perfect, c the soul ... Ps 19:7 7725

CONVERTS {1}
and her c with righteousness ... Is 1:27 7725

CONVEY {2}
I will c them by sea in floats ... 1Kin 5:9 7760
that they may c me over till I ... Neh 2:7 5674

CONVEYED {1}
for Jesus had c himself away ... Jn 5:13 *1593*

CONVICTED {1}
being c by their own conscience, ... Jn 8:9 *1651*

CONVINCE {2}
to exhort and to c the gainsayers ... Titus 1:9 *1651*
to c all that are ungodly among ... Jude 15 *1827*

CONVINCED {4}
there was none of you that c Job ... Job 32:12 3198
For he mightily c the Jews ... Acts 18:28 *1246*
he is c of all, he is judged of ... 1Cor 14:24 *1651*
are c of the law as transgressors ... Jas 2:9 *1651*

CONVINCETH {1}
Which of you c me of sin ... Jn 8:46 *1651*

CONVOCATION {15}
day there shall be an holy c ... Ex 12:16 4744
there shall be an holy c to you ... Ex 12:16 4744
is the sabbath of rest, an holy c ... Lev 23:3 4744
first day ye shall have an holy c ... Lev 23:7 4744
in the seventh day is an holy c ... Lev 23:8 4744
that it may be an holy c unto you ... Lev 23:21 4744
of blowing of trumpets, an holy c ... Lev 23:24 4744
it shall be an holy c unto you ... Lev 23:27 4744
the first day shall be an holy c ... Lev 23:35 4744
day shall be an holy c unto you ... Lev 23:36 4744
the first day shall be an holy c ... Num 28:18 4744
day ye shall have an holy c ... Num 28:25 4744
be out, ye shall have an holy c ... Num 28:26 4744
month, ye shall have an holy c ... Num 29:1 4744
of this seventh month an holy c ... Num 29:7 4744

CONVOCATIONS {3}
ye shall proclaim to be holy c ... Lev 23:2 4744
feasts of the LORD, even holy c ... Lev 23:4 4744
ye shall proclaim to be holy c ... Lev 23:37 4744

COOK {2}
And Samuel said unto the c ... 1Sa 9:23 2876
the c took up the shoulder, and ... 1Sa 9:24 2876

COOKS {1}
to be confectionaries, and to be c ... 1Sa 8:13 2876

COOL {2}
in the garden in the c of the day ... Gen 3:8 7307
finger in water, and c my tongue ... Lk 16:24 *2711*

COOS *(co'-os)* {1} *An island near Cnidus.*
with a straight course unto C ... Acts 21:1 *2972*

COPIED {1}
of Hezekiah king of Judah c out ... Prov 25:1 6275

COPING {1}
from the foundation unto the c ... 1Kin 7:9 2947

COPPER {1}
and two vessels of fine c, ... Ezr 8:27 5178

COPPERSMITH {1}
Alexander the c did me much evil ... 2Ti 4:14 *5471*

COPULATION {3}
man's seed of c go out from him ... Lev 15:16 7902
skin, whereon is the seed of c ... Lev 15:17 7902
whom man shall lie with seed of c ... Lev 15:18 7902

COPY {9}
that he shall write him a c of ... Deut 17:18 4932
stones a c of the law of Moses ... Josh 8:32 4932
This is the c of the letter that ... Ezr 4:11 6573
Now when the c of king ... Ezr 4:23 6573
The c of the letter that Tatnai, ... Ezr 5:6 6573
Now this is the c of the letter ... Ezr 7:11 6573
The c of the writing for a ... Est 3:14 6572
Also he gave him the c of the ... Est 4:8 6572
The c of the writing for a ... Est 8:13 6572

COR {1}
tenth part of a bath out of the c ... Eze 45:14 3734

CORAL {2}
No mention shall be made of c ... Job 28:18 7215
work, and fine linen, and c ... Eze 27:16 7215

CORBAN *(cor'-ban)* {1} *A sacred gift.*
to his father or mother, It is C ... Mk 7:11 *2878*

CORD {6}
down by a c through the window ... Josh 2:15 2256
Because he hath loosed my c ... Job 30:11 3499
or his tongue with a c which thou ... Job 41:1 2256
a threefold c is not quickly ... Eccl 4:12 2339
Or ever the silver c be loosed ... Eccl 12:6 2256
have none that shall cast a c by ... Mic 2:5 2256

CORDS {26}
the pins of the court, and their c ... Ex 35:18 4340
hanging for the court gate, his c ... Ex 39:40 4340
the c of it for all the service ... Num 3:26 4340
and their pins, and their c ... Num 3:37 4340
the altar round about, and their c ... Num 4:26 4340
and their pins, and their c ... Num 4:32 4340
And they bound him with two new c ... Judg 15:13 5688
the c that were upon his arms ... Judg 15:14 5688
fastened with c of fine linen ... Est 1:6 2256
be holden in c of affliction ... Job 36:8 2256
and cast away their c from us ... Ps 2:3 5688
bind the sacrifice with c ... Ps 118:27 5688
cut asunder the c of the wicked ... Ps 129:4 5688
have hid a snare for me, and c ... Ps 140:5 2256
be holden with the c of his sins ... Prov 5:22 2256
draw iniquity with c of vanity ... Is 5:18 2256
any of the c thereof be broken ... Is 33:20 2256
spare not, lengthen thy c ... Is 54:2 4340
spoiled, and all my c are broken ... Jer 10:20 4340
and they let down Jeremiah with c ... Jer 38:6 2256
let them down by c into the ... Jer 38:11 2256
under thine armholes under the c ... Jer 38:12 2256
So they drew up Jeremiah with c ... Jer 38:13 2256
of rich apparel, bound with c ... Eze 27:24 2256
I drew them with c of a man ... Hos 11:4 2256
he had made a scourge of small c ... Jn 2:15 *4979*

CORE *(co'-ree)* {1} See KORAH. *Greek form of Korah.*
perished in the gainsaying of C ... Jude 11 *2879*

CORIANDER {2}
and it was like c seed, white ... Ex 16:31 1407
And the manna was as c seed ... Num 11:7 1407

CORINTH *(cor'-inth)* {6} See CORINTHIANS, CORINTHUS. *Capital of Achaia.*
from Athens, and came to *C* ... Acts 18:1 *2882*
that, while Apollos was at *C* ... Acts 19:1 *2882*
the church of God which is at *C* ... 1Cor 1:2 *2882*
the church of God which is at *C* ... 2Cor 1:1 *2882*
you I came not as yet unto *C* ... 2Cor 1:23 *2882*
Erastus abode at *C* ... 2Ti 4:20 *2882*

CORINTHIANS *(co-rin'-the-uns)* {4} *Residents of Corinth.*
many of the *C* hearing believed, ... Acts 18:8 *2881*
The first epistle to the *C* was ... 1Cor *s* *2881*
O ye *C*, our mouth is open unto ... 2Cor 6:11 *2881*
the *C* was written from Philippi ... 2Cor *s* *2881*

CORINTHUS *(co-rin'-thus)* {1} See CORINTH. *Same as Corinth.*
Written to the Romans from *C* ... Rom *s* *2882*

CORMORANT {4}
And the little owl, and the *c* ... Lev 11:17 7994
and the gier eagle, and the *c* ... Deut 14:17 7994
But the *c* and the bittern shall ... Is 34:11 6893
both the *c* and the bittern shall ... Zeph 2:14 6893

CORN {102}
of the earth, and plenty of *c* ... Gen 27:28 1715
and with *c* and wine have I ... Gen 27:37 1715
seven ears of *c* came up upon one ... Gen 41:5
lay up *c* under the hand of ... Gen 41:35 1250
Joseph gathered *c* as the sand of ... Gen 41:49 1250
into Egypt to Joseph for to buy *c* ... Gen 41:57
saw that there was *c* in Egypt ... Gen 42:1 7668
heard that there is *c* in Egypt ... Gen 42:2 7668
went down to buy *c* in Egypt ... Gen 42:3 1250
to buy *c* among those that came ... Gen 42:5
carry *c* for the famine of your ... Gen 42:19 7668
to fill their sacks with *c* ... Gen 42:25 1250
they laded their asses with the *c* ... Gen 42:26 7668
when they had eaten up the *c* ... Gen 43:2 7668
of the youngest, and his *c* money ... Gen 44:2 7688
and ten she asses laden with *c* ... Gen 45:23 1250
for the *c* which they bought ... Gen 47:14 7668
thorns, so that the stacks of *c* ... Ex 22:6
or the standing *c*, or the field ... Ex 22:6 7054
green ears of *c* dried by the fire ... Lev 2:14
even *c* beaten out of full ears ... Lev 2:14 1643
it, part of the beaten *c* thereof ... Lev 2:16 1643
eat neither bread, nor parched *c* ... Lev 23:14
were the *c* of the threshingfloor ... Num 18:27 1715
and the fruit of thy land, thy *c* ... Deut 7:13 1715
that thou mayest gather in thy *c* ... Deut 11:14 1715
thy gates the tithe of thy *c* ... Deut 12:17 1715
name there, the tithe of thy *c* ... Deut 14:23 1715
to put the sickle to the *c* ... Deut 16:9 7054
that thou hast gathered in thy *c* ... Deut 16:13 1637
The firstfruit also of thy *c* ... Deut 18:4 1715
the standing *c* of thy neighbour ... Deut 23:25 7054
unto thy neighbour's standing *c* ... Deut 23:25 7054
the ox when he treadeth out the *c* ... Deut 25:4
shall not leave thee either *c* ... Deut 28:51 1715
Jacob shall be upon a land of *c* ... Deut 33:28 1715
they did eat of the old *c* of the ... Josh 5:11 5669
parched *c* in the selfsame day ... Josh 5:11
eaten of the old *c* of the land ... Josh 5:12 5669
the standing *c* of the Philistines ... Judg 15:5 7054
shocks, and also the standing *c* ... Judg 15:5 7054
glean ears of *c* after him in ... Ruth 2:2
and he reached her parched *c* ... Ruth 2:14
down at the end of the heap of *c* ... Ruth 3:7 6194
an ephah of this parched *c* ... 1Sa 17:17
and five measures of parched *c* ... 1Sa 25:18
mouth, and spread ground *c* thereon ... 2Sa 17:19 7383
and barley, and flour, and parched *c* ... 2Sa 17:28
full ears of *c* in the husk ... 2Kin 4:42 3759
like your own land, a land of *c* ... 2Kin 18:32 1715
as *c* blasted before it be grown ... 2Kin 19:26
in abundance the firstfruits of *c* ... 2Chr 31:5 1715
also for the increase of *c* ... 2Chr 32:28 1715
therefore we take up *c* for them ... Neh 5:2 1715
and houses, that we might buy *c* ... Neh 5:3 1715
might exact of them money and *c* ... Neh 5:10 1715
part of the money, and of the *c* ... Neh 5:11 1715
shall bring the offering of the *c* ... Neh 10:39 1715
vessels, and the tithes of the *c* ... Neh 13:5 1715
all Judah the tithe of the *c* ... Neh 13:12 1715
like as a shock of *c* cometh in in ... Job 5:26
reap every one his *c* in the field ... Job 24:6 1098
off as the tops of the ears of *c* ... Job 24:24
good liking, they grow up with *c* ... Job 39:4 1250
than in the time that their *c* ... Ps 4:7 1715
thou preparest them *c*, when thou ... Ps 65:9 1715
also are covered over with *c* ... Ps 65:13 1250
of *c* in the earth upon the top of ... Ps 72:16 1250
had given them of the *c* of heaven ... Ps 78:24 1715
He that withholdeth *c*, the people ... Prov 11:26 1250
the harvestman gathereth the *c* ... Is 17:5 7054
threshing, and the *c* of my floor ... Is 21:10 1121
Bread *c* is bruised ... Is 28:28
like your own land, a land of *c* ... Is 36:17 1715
as *c* blasted before it be grown ... Is 37:27
c to be meat for thine enemies ... Is 62:8 1715
say to their mothers, Where is *c* ... Lam 2:12 1715
and I will call for the *c*, and will ... Eze 36:29 1715
did not know that I gave her *c* ... Hos 2:8 1715
take away my *c* in the time ... Hos 2:9 1715
And the earth shall hear the *c* ... Hos 2:22 1715
they assemble themselves for *c* ... Hos 7:14 1715
and loveth to tread out the *c* ... Hos 10:11
they shall revive as the *c* ... Hos 14:7 1715
for the *c* is wasted ... Joel 1:10 1715
for the *c* is withered ... Joel 1:17 1715
people, Behold, I will send you *c* ... Joel 2:19 1715
moon be gone, that we may sell *c* ... Amos 8:5 7668
like as *c* is sifted in a sieve, ... Amos 9:9
upon the mountains, and upon the *c* ... Hag 1:11 1715
c shall make the young men ... Zec 9:17 1715
on the sabbath day through the *c* ... Mt 12:1 *4702*
and began to pluck the ears of *c* ... Mt 12:1 *4719*
that he went through the *c* fields ... Mk 2:23 *4702*
they went, to pluck the ears of *c* ... Mk 2:23 *4719*
after that the full *c* in the ear ... Mk 4:28 *4621*
that he went through the *c* fields ... Lk 6:1 *4702*
disciples plucked the ears of *c* ... Lk 6:1 *4719*
Except a *c* of wheat fall into the ... Jn 12:24 *2848*
heard that there was *c* in Egypt ... Acts 7:12 *4621*
of the ox that treadeth out the *c* ... 1Cor 9:9
the ox that treadeth out the *c* ... 1Ti 5:18

CORNELIUS *(cor-ne'-le-us)* {10} *A Roman centurion converted by Peter.*
certain man in Caesarea called *C* ... Acts 10:1 *2883*
in to him, and saying unto him, *C* ... Acts 10:3 *2883*
which spake unto *C* was departed ... Acts 10:7 *2883*
C had made enquiry for Simon's ... Acts 10:17 *2883*
which were sent unto him from *C* ... Acts 10:21 *2883*
C the centurion, a just man, and ... Acts 10:22 *2883*
C waited for them, and had called ... Acts 10:24 *2883*
C met him, and fell down at his ... Acts 10:25 *2883*
C said, Four days ago I was ... Acts 10:30 *2883*
And said, *C*, thy prayer is heard, ... Acts 10:31 *2883*

CORNER {37}
which is toward the north *c* ... Ex 36:25 6285
shave off the *c* of their beard ... Lev 21:5 6285
compassed the *c* of the sea ... Josh 18:14 6285
from the right *c* of the temple to ... 2Kin 11:11 3802
to the left *c* of the temple ... 2Kin 11:11 3802
gate of Ephraim unto the *c* gate ... 2Kin 14:13 6438
the gate of Ephraim to the *c* gate ... 2Chr 25:23 6437
towers in Jerusalem at the *c* gate ... 2Chr 26:9 6438
altars in every *c* of Jerusalem ... 2Chr 28:24 6438
of the wall, even unto the *c* ... Neh 3:24 6438
and to the going up of the *c* ... Neh 3:31 6438
between the going up of the *c* ... Neh 3:32 6438
or who laid the *c* stone thereof ... Job 38:6 6438
is become the head stone of the *c* ... Ps 118:22 6438
our daughters may be as *c* stones ... Ps 144:12 2106
through the street near her *c* ... Prov 7:8 6438
and lieth in wait at every *c* ... Prov 7:12 6438
to dwell in a *c* of the housetop ... Prov 21:9 6438
to dwell in the *c* of the housetop ... Prov 25:24 6438
a tried stone, a precious *c* stone ... Is 28:16 6438
be removed into a *c* any more ... Is 30:20 3671
Hananeel unto the gate of the *c* ... Jer 31:38 6438
unto the *c* of the horse gate ... Jer 31:40 6438
and shall devour the *c* of Moab ... Jer 48:45 6285
not take of thee a stone for a *c* ... Jer 51:26 6438
in every *c* of the court there was ... Eze 46:21 4742
in Samaria in the *c* of a bed ... Amos 3:12 6285
Out of him came forth the *c* ... Zec 10:4 6438
the first gate, unto the *c* gate ... Zec 14:10 6434
same is become the head of the *c* ... Mt 21:42 *1137*
is become the head of the *c* ... Mk 12:10 *1137*
same is become the head of the *c* ... Lk 20:17 *1137*
which is become the head of the *c* ... Acts 4:11 *1137*
this thing was not done in a *c* ... Acts 26:26 *1137*
himself being the chief *c* stone ... Eph 2:20 *204*
I lay in Sion a chief *c* stone ... 1Pet 2:6 *204*
same is made the head of the *c* ... 1Pet 2:7 *1137*

CORNERS {39}
and put them in the four *c* thereof ... Ex 25:12 6471
four *c* that are on the four feet ... Ex 25:26 6285
c of the tabernacle in the two ... Ex 26:23 4742
they shall be for the two *c* ... Ex 26:24 4742
of it upon the four *c* thereof ... Ex 27:2 6438
rings in the four *c* thereof ... Ex 27:4 7098
crown of it, by the two *c* thereof ... Ex 30:4 6763
two boards made he for the *c* of ... Ex 36:28 4742
did to both of them in both the *c* ... Ex 36:29 4742
to be set by the four *c* of it ... Ex 37:3 6471
four *c* that were in the four feet ... Ex 37:13 6285
crown thereof, by the two *c* of it ... Ex 37:27 6763
horns thereof on the four *c* of it ... Ex 38:2 6438
wholly reap the *c* of thy field ... Lev 19:9 6285
not round the *c* of your heads ... Lev 19:27 6285
shalt thou mar the *c* of thy beard ... Lev 19:27 6285
c of thy field when thou reapest ... Lev 23:22 6285
and shall smite the *c* of Moab ... Num 24:17 6285
said, I would scatter them into *c* ... Deut 32:26 6284
and the four *c* thereof had ... 1Kin 7:30 6471
to the four *c* of one base ... 1Kin 7:34 6438
and didst divide them into *c* ... Neh 9:22 6285
and smote the four *c* of the house ... Job 1:19 6438
from the four *c* of the earth ... Is 11:12 3671
and all that are in the utmost *c* ... Jer 9:26 6285
and all that are in the utmost *c* ... Jer 25:23 6285
them that are in the utmost *c* ... Jer 49:32 6285
come upon the four *c* of the land ... Eze 7:2 3671
the *c* thereof, and the length ... Eze 41:22 4740
on the four *c* of the settle, and ... Eze 43:20 6438
upon the four *c* of the settle of ... Eze 45:19 6438
pass by the four *c* of the court ... Eze 46:21 4742
In the four *c* of the court there ... Eze 46:22 4742
these four *c* were of one measure ... Eze 46:22 7106
bowls, and as the *c* of the altar ... Zec 9:15 2106
in the *c* of the streets, that ... Mt 6:5 *1137*
a great sheet knit at the four *c* ... Acts 10:11 *746*
let down from heaven by four *c* ... Acts 11:5 *746*
on the four *c* of the earth ... Rev 7:1 *1137*

CORNET {7}
shouting, and with sound of the *c* ... 1Chr 15:28 7782
sound of *c* make a joyful noise ... Ps 98:6 7782
time ye hear the sound of the *c* ... Dan 3:5 7162
people heard the sound of the *c* ... Dan 3:7 7162
shall hear the sound of the *c* ... Dan 3:10 7162
time ye hear the sound of the *c* ... Dan 3:15 7162
Blow ye the *c* in Gibeah, and the ... Hos 5:8 7782

CORNETS {2}
and on timbrels, and on *c*, and on ... 2Sa 6:5 4517
and with trumpets, and with *c* ... 2Chr 15:14 7782

CORNFLOOR {1}
hast loved a reward upon every *c* ... Hos 9:1 1637,1715

CORPSE {1}
of it, they came and took up his *c* ... Mk 6:29 *4430*

CORPSES {4}
behold, they were all dead *c* ... 2Kin 19:35 6297
behold, they were all dead *c* ... Is 37:36 6297
and there is none end of their *c* ... Nah 3:3 1472
they stumble upon their *c* ... Nah 3:3 1472

CORRECT {7}
rebukes dost *c* man for iniquity ... Ps 39:11 3256
the heathen, shall not he *c* ... Ps 94:10 3198
C thy son, and he shall give thee ... Prov 29:17 3256
Thine own wickedness shall *c* thee ... Jer 2:19 3256
O LORD, *c* me, but with judgment ... Jer 10:24 3256
but I will *c* thee in measure, and ... Jer 30:11 3256
of thee, but *c* thee in measure ... Jer 46:28 3256

CORRECTED {2}
A servant will not be *c* by words ... Prov 29:19 3256
fathers of our flesh which *c* us ... Heb 12:9 *3810*

CORRECTETH {2}
happy is the man whom God *c* ... Job 5:17 3198
For whom the LORD loveth he *c* ... Prov 3:12 3198

CORRECTION {12}
causeth it to come, whether for *c* ... Job 37:13 7626
neither be weary of his *c* ... Prov 3:11 8433
as a fool to the *c* of the stocks ... Prov 7:22 4148
C is grievous unto him that ... Prov 15:10 4148
but the rod of *c* shall drive it ... Prov 22:15 4148
Withhold not *c* from the child ... Prov 23:13 4148
they received no *c* ... Jer 2:30 4148
they have refused to receive *c* ... Jer 5:3 4148
LORD their God, nor receiveth *c* ... Jer 7:28 4148
thou hast established them for *c* ... Hab 1:12 3198
she received not *c* ... Zeph 3:2 4148
for doctrine, for reproof, for *c* ... 2Ti 3:16 *1882*

CORRUPT {33}
The earth also was *c* before God ... Gen 6:11 7843
the earth, and, behold, it was *c* ... Gen 6:12 7843
Lest ye *c* yourselves, and make you ... Deut 4:16 7843
shall *c* yourselves, and make a ... Deut 4:25 7843
ye will utterly *c* yourselves ... Deut 31:29 7843
My breath is *c*, my days are ... Job 17:1 2254
They are *c*, they have done ... Ps 14:1 7843
are *c* because of my foolishness ... Ps 38:5 4743
C are they, and have done ... Ps 53:1 7843
They are *c*, and speak wickedly ... Ps 73:8 4167
troubled fountain, and a *c* spring ... Prov 25:26 7843
nor according to your *c* doings ... Eze 20:44 7843
she was more *c* in her inordinate ... Eze 23:11 7843
c words to speak before me, till ... Dan 2:9 7844
covenant shall he *c* by flatteries ... Dan 11:32 2610
unto the Lord a *c* thing ... Mal 1:14 7843
I will *c* your seed, and spread ... Mal 2:3 1605
earth, where moth and rust doth *c* ... Mt 6:19 *853*
neither moth nor rust doth *c* ... Mt 6:20 *853*
but a *c* tree bringeth forth evil ... Mt 7:17 *4550*
neither can a *c* tree bring forth ... Mt 7:18 *4550*
the tree *c*, and his fruit *c* ... Mt 12:33 *4550*
tree bringeth not forth *c* fruit ... Lk 6:43 *4550*
neither doth a *c* tree bring forth ... Lk 6:43 *4550*
communications *c* good manners ... 1Cor 15:33 *5351*
as many, which *c* the word of God ... 2Cor 2:17 *2585*
which is *c* according to the ... Eph 4:22 *5351*
Let no *c* communication proceed ... Eph 4:29 *4550*
disputings of men of *c* minds ... 1Ti 6:5 *1311*
men of *c* minds, reprobate ... 2Ti 3:8 *2704*
in those things they *c* themselves ... Jude 10 *5351*
which did *c* the earth with her ... Rev 19:2 *5351*

CORRUPTED {14}
for all flesh had *c* his way upon ... Gen 6:12 7843
the land was *c* by reason of the ... Ex 8:24 7843
land of Egypt, have *c* themselves ... Ex 32:7 7843
out of Egypt have *c* themselves ... Deut 9:12 7843
They have *c* themselves, their ... Deut 32:5 7843
c themselves more than their ... Judg 2:19 7843
thou wast *c* more than they in all ... Eze 16:47 7843
thou hast *c* thy wisdom by reason ... Eze 28:17 7843
They have deeply *c* themselves ... Hos 9:9 7843
rose early, and *c* all their doings ... Zeph 3:7 7843
ye have *c* the covenant of Levi, ... Mal 2:8 7843
wronged no man, we have *c* no man ... 2Cor 7:2 *5351*
so your minds should be *c* from ... 2Cor 11:3 *5351*
Your riches are *c*, and your ... Jas 5:2 *4595*

CORRUPTERS {2}
of evildoers, children that are *c* ... Is 1:4 7843
they are all *c* ... Jer 6:28 7843

CORRUPTETH {1}
thief approacheth, neither moth *c* ... Lk 12:33 *1311*

C

CORRUPTIBLE {7}
into an image made like to c man ... Rom 1:23 *5349*
they do it to obtain a c crown ... 1Cor 9:25 *5349*
For this c must put on ... 1Cor 15:53 *5349*
So when this c shall have put on ... 1Cor 15:54 *5349*
were not redeemed with c things ... 1Pet 1:18 *5349*
Being born again, not of c seed ... 1Pet 1:23 *5349*
the heart, in that which is not c ... 1Pet 3:4 *862*

CORRUPTING {1}
him the daughter of women, c her ... Dan 11:17 7843

CORRUPTION {21}
because their c is in them ... Lev 22:25 4893
the right hand of the mount of c ... 2Kin 23:13 4889
I have said to c, Thou art my ... Job 17:14 7845
suffer thine Holy One to see c ... Ps 16:10 7845
still live for ever, and not see c ... Ps 49:9 7845
delivered it from the pit of c ... Is 38:17 1097
was turned in me into c, and I ... Dan 10:8 4889
thou brought up my life from c ... Jonah 2:6 7845
suffer thine Holy One to see c ... Acts 2:27 *1312*
hell, neither his flesh did see c ... Acts 2:31 *1312*
dead, now no more to return to c ... Acts 13:34 *1312*
suffer thine Holy One to see c ... Acts 13:35 *1312*
laid unto his fathers, and saw c ... Acts 13:36 *1312*
whom God raised again, saw no c ... Acts 13:37 *1312*
of c into the glorious liberty of ... Rom 8:21 *5356*
It is sown in c ... 1Cor 15:42 *5356*
neither doth c inherit ... 1Cor 15:50 *5356*
flesh shall of the flesh reap c ... Gal 6:8 *5356*
having escaped the c that is in ... 2Pet 1:4 *5356*
utterly perish in their own c ... 2Pet 2:12 *5356*
themselves are the servants of c ... 2Pet 2:19 *5356*

CORRUPTLY {2}
And the people did yet c ... 2Chr 27:2 7843
We have dealt very c against thee ... Neh 1:7 2254

COSAM *(co'-sam)* {1} *Son of Elmodam; ancestor of Jesus*
of Addi, which was the son of C ... Lk 3:28 *2973*

COST {4}
we eaten at all of the king's c ... 2Sa 19:42
of that which doth c me nothing ... 2Sa 24:24 2600
offer burnt offerings without c ... 1Chr 21:24 2600
not down first, and counteth the c ... Lk 14:28 *1160*

COSTLINESS {1}
in the sea by reason of her c ... Rev 18:19 *5094*

COSTLY {6}
c stones, and hewed stones, to lay ... 1Kin 5:17 3368
All these were of c stones ... 1Kin 7:9 3368
And the foundation was of c stones ... 1Kin 7:10 3368
And above were c stones, after the ... 1Kin 7:11 3368
of ointment of spikenard, very c ... Jn 12:3 *4186*
or gold, or pearls, or c array ... 1Ti 2:9 *4185*

COTES {1}
manner of beasts, and c for flocks ... 2Chr 32:28 220

COTTAGE {2}
Zion is left as a c in a vineyard ... Is 1:8 5521
and shall be removed like a c ... Is 24:20 4412

COTTAGES {1}
c for shepherds, and folds for ... Zeph 2:6 3741

COUCH {7}
he went up to my c ... Gen 49:4 3326
my c shall ease my complaint ... Job 7:13 4904
When they c in their dens, and ... Job 38:40 7742
I water my c with my tears ... Ps 6:6 6210
of a bed, and in Damascus in a c ... Amos 3:12 6210
his c into the midst before Jesus ... Lk 5:19 *2826*
thee, Arise, and take up thy c ... Lk 5:24 *2826*

COUCHED {2}
he c as a lion, and as an old lion ... Gen 49:9 7257
He c, he lay down as a lion, and ... Num 24:9 3766

COUCHES {2}
stretch themselves upon their c ... Amos 6:4 6210
and laid them on beds and c ... Acts 5:15 *2895*

COUCHETH {1}
and for the deep that c beneath ... Deut 33:13 7257

COUCHING {1}
ass c down between two burdens ... Gen 49:14 7257

COUCHINGPLACE {1}
and the Ammonites a c for flocks ... Eze 25:5 4769

COULD See APPENDIX.

COULDEST {4}
and done evil things as thou c ... Jer 3:5 3201
them, and yet c not be satisfied ... Eze 16:28
c not thou watch one hour ... Mk 14:37 *2480*
Thou c have no power at all ... Jn 19:11

COULDST {1}
seeing thou c reveal this secret ... Dan 2:47 3202

COULTER {1}
every man his share, and his c ... 1Sa 13:20 855

COULTERS {1}
for the mattocks, and for the c ... 1Sa 13:21 855

COUNCIL {23}
the princes of Judah and their c ... Ps 68:27 7277
Raca, shall be in danger of the c ... Mt 5:22 *4892*
held a c against him, how they ... Mt 12:14 *4824*
priests, and elders, and all the c ... Mt 26:59 *4892*
all the c sought for witness ... Mk 14:55 *4892*
elders and scribes and the whole c ... Mk 15:1 *4892*
together, and led him into their c ... Lk 22:66 *4892*
priests and the Pharisees a c ... Jn 11:47 *4892*
them to go aside out of the c ... Acts 4:15 *4892*
him, and called the c together ... Acts 5:21 *4892*
them, they set them before the c ... Acts 5:27 *4892*
Then stood there up one in the c ... Acts 5:34 *4892*
from the presence of the c ... Acts 5:41 *4892*
him, and brought him to the c ... Acts 6:12 *4892*
And all that sat in the c, looking ... Acts 6:15 *4892*
priests and all their c to appear ... Acts 22:30 *4892*
Paul, earnestly beholding the c ... Acts 23:1 *4892*
Pharisees, he cried out in the c ... Acts 23:6 *4892*
Now therefore ye with the c ... Acts 23:15 *4892*
down Paul to morrow into the c ... Acts 23:20 *4892*
I brought him forth into their c ... Acts 23:28 *4892*
in me, while I stood before the c ... Acts 24:20 *4892*
when he had conferred with the c ... Acts 25:12 *4824*

COUNCILS {2}
they will deliver you up to the c ... Mt 10:17 *4891*
they shall deliver you up to c ... Mk 13:9 *4891*

COUNSEL {143}
unto my voice, I will give thee c ... Ex 18:19 3289
who shall ask c for him after the ... Num 27:21
Israel, through the c of Balaam ... Num 31:16 1697
For they are a nation void of c ... Deut 32:28 6098
asked not c at the mouth of the ... Josh 9:14
And they said unto him, Ask c ... Judg 18:5
give here your advice and c ... Judg 20:7 6098
asked c of God, and said, Which of ... Judg 20:18
asked c of the LORD, saying, ... Judg 20:23
And Saul asked c of God, Shall I ... 1Sa 14:37
turn the c of Ahithophel into ... 2Sa 15:31 6098
for me defeat the c of Ahithophel ... 2Sa 15:34 6098
Give c among you what we shall do ... 2Sa 16:20 6098
the c of Ahithophel, which he ... 2Sa 16:23 6098
so was all the c of Ahithophel ... 2Sa 16:23 6098
The c that Ahithophel hath given ... 2Sa 17:7 6098
Therefore I c that all Israel be ... 2Sa 17:11 3289
The c of Hushai the Archite is ... 2Sa 17:14 6098
better than the c of Ahithophel ... 2Sa 17:14 6098
defeat the good c of Ahithophel ... 2Sa 17:14 6098
and thus did Ahithophel c Absalom ... 2Sa 17:15 3289
saw that his c was not followed ... 2Sa 17:23 6098
They shall surely ask c at Abel ... 2Sa 20:18
let me, I pray thee, give thee c ... 1Kin 1:12 6098
he forsook the c of the old men ... 1Kin 12:8 6098
What c give ye that we may answer ... 1Kin 12:9 3289
old men's c that they gave him ... 1Kin 12:13 6098
them after the c of the young men ... 1Kin 12:14 6098
Whereupon the king took c ... 1Kin 12:28 3289
took c with his servants, saying, ... 2Kin 6:8 3289
are but vain words,) I have c ... 2Kin 18:20 6098
also for asking c of one that had ... 1Chr 10:13
king Rehoboam took c with the old ... 2Chr 10:6 3289
What c give ye me to return ... 2Chr 10:6 3289
But he forsook the c which the ... 2Chr 10:8 6098
took c with the young men that ... 2Chr 10:8 3289
forsook the c of the old men ... 2Chr 10:13 6098
He walked also after their c ... 2Chr 22:5 6098
Art thou made of the king's c ... 2Chr 25:16 3289
and hast not hearkened unto my c ... 2Chr 25:16 6098
For the king had taken c, and his ... 2Chr 30:2 3289
the whole assembly took c to keep ... 2Chr 30:23 3289
He took c with his princes and his ... 2Chr 32:3 3289
according to the c of my lord ... Ezr 10:3 6098
according to the c of the princes ... Ezr 10:8 6098
God had brought their c to nought ... Neh 4:15 6098
and let us take c together ... Neh 6:7 3289
the c of the froward is carried ... Job 5:13 6098
and shine upon the c of the wicked ... Job 10:3 6098
is wisdom and strength, he hath c ... Job 12:13 6098
his own c shall cast him down ... Job 18:7 6098
the c of the wicked is far from ... Job 21:16 6098
but the c of the wicked is far ... Job 22:18 6098
waited, and kept silence at my c ... Job 29:21 6098
c by words without knowledge ... Job 38:2 6098
that hideth c without knowledge ... Job 42:3 6098
not in the c of the ungodly ... Ps 1:1 6098
and the rulers take c together ... Ps 2:2 3245
long shall I take c in my soul ... Ps 13:2 6098
Ye have shamed the c of the poor ... Ps 14:6 6098
the LORD, who hath given me c ... Ps 16:7 3289
own heart, and fulfil all thy c ... Ps 20:4 6098
while they took c together ... Ps 31:13 3245
The LORD bringeth the c of the ... Ps 33:10 6098
The c of the LORD standeth for ... Ps 33:11 6098
We took sweet c together, and ... Ps 55:14 5475
from the secret c of the wicked ... Ps 64:2 5475
wait for my soul take c together ... Ps 71:10 3289
Thou shalt guide me with thy c ... Ps 73:24 6098
taken crafty c against thy people ... Ps 83:3 5475
they waited not for his c ... Ps 106:13 6098
they provoked him with their c ... Ps 106:43 6098
contemned the c of the most High ... Ps 107:11 6098
ye have set at nought all my c ... Prov 1:25 6098
They would none of my c ... Prov 1:30 6098
C is mine, and sound wisdom ... Prov 8:14 6098
Where no c is, the people fall ... Prov 11:14 8458
he that hearkeneth unto c is wise ... Prov 12:15 6098
Without c purposes are ... Prov 15:22 5475
Hear c, and receive instruction, ... Prov 19:20 6098
nevertheless the c of the LORD ... Prov 19:21 6098
C in the heart of man is like ... Prov 20:5 6098
Every purpose is established by c ... Prov 20:18 6098
nor c against the LORD ... Prov 21:30 6098
For by wise c thou shalt make thy ... Prov 24:6 8458
of a man's friend by hearty c ... Prov 27:9 6098
I c thee to keep the king's ... Eccl 8:2
let the c of the Holy One of ... Is 5:19 6098
have taken evil c against thee ... Is 7:5 3289
Take c together, and it shall come ... Is 8:10 6098
and understanding, the spirit of c ... Is 11:2 6098
Take c, execute judgment ... Is 16:3 6098
and I will destroy the c thereof ... Is 19:3 6098
the c of the wise counsellors of ... Is 19:11 6098
because of the c of the LORD of ... Is 19:17 6098
hath taken this c against Tyre ... Is 23:8 3289
of hosts, which is wonderful in c ... Is 28:29 6098
to hide their c from the LORD ... Is 29:15 6098
saith the LORD, that take c ... Is 30:1 6098
they are but vain words) I have c ... Is 36:5 6098
With whom took he c, and who ... Is 40:14 3289
and performeth the c of his ... Is 44:26 6098
yea, let them take c together ... Is 45:21 3289
My c shall stand, and I will do ... Is 46:10 6098
executeth my c from a far country ... Is 46:11 6098
nor c from the wise, nor the word ... Jer 18:18 6098
all their c against me to slay me ... Jer 18:23 6098
I will make void the c of Judah ... Jer 19:7 6098
hath stood in the c of the LORD ... Jer 23:18 5475
But if they had stood in my c ... Jer 23:22 5475
Great in c, and mighty in work ... Jer 32:19 6098
and if I give thee c, wilt thou ... Jer 38:15 3289
is c perished from the prudent ... Jer 49:7 6098
Therefore hear the c of the LORD ... Jer 49:20 6098
Babylon hath taken c against you ... Jer 49:30 6098
hear ye the c of the LORD ... Jer 50:45 6098
priest, and c from the ancients ... Eze 7:26 6098
give wicked c in this city ... Eze 11:2 6098
Then Daniel answered with c ... Dan 2:14 5843
let my c be acceptable unto thee, ... Dan 4:27 4431
My people ask c at their stocks, ... Hos 4:12
shall be ashamed of his own c ... Hos 10:6 6098
neither understand they his c ... Mic 4:12 6098
the c of peace shall be between ... Zec 6:13 6098
took c how they might entangle ... Mt 22:15 *4824*
elders of the people took c ... Mt 27:1 *4824*
And they took c, and bought with ... Mt 27:7 *4824*
with the elders, and had taken c ... Mt 28:12 *4824*
straightway took c with the ... Mk 3:6 *4824*
lawyers rejected the c of God ... Lk 7:30 *1012*
same had not consented to the c ... Lk 23:51 *1012*
took c together for to put him to ... Jn 11:53 *4823*
which gave c to the Jews, that it ... Jn 18:14 *4823*
delivered by the determinate c ... Acts 2:23 *1012*
thy c determined before to be ... Acts 4:28 *1012*
the heart, and took c to slay them ... Acts 5:33 *1011*
for if this c or this work be of ... Acts 5:38 *1012*
the Jews took c to kill him ... Acts 9:23 *4823*
declare unto you all the c of God ... Acts 20:27 *1012*
the soldiers' c was to kill the ... Acts 27:42 *1012*
after the c of his own will ... Eph 1:11 *1012*
promise the immutability of his c ... Heb 6:17 *1012*
I c thee to buy of me gold tried ... Rev 3:18 *4823*

COUNSELED {1}
How hast thou c him that hath no ... Job 26:3 3289

COUNSELLED {3}
which he c in those days, was as ... 2Sa 16:23 3289
and thus and thus have I c ... 2Sa 17:15 3289
hath Ahithophel c against you ... 2Sa 17:21 3289

COUNSELLOR {14}
the Gilonite, David's c, from his ... 2Sa 15:12 3289
for Zechariah his son, a wise c ... 1Chr 26:14 3289
Jonathan David's uncle was a c ... 1Chr 27:32 3289
And Ahithophel was the king's c ... 1Chr 27:33 3289
mother was his c to do wickedly ... 2Chr 22:3 3289
and the honourable man, and the c ... Is 3:3 3289
name shall be called Wonderful, C ... Is 9:6 3289
or being his c hath taught him ... Is 40:13 6098
among them, and there was no c ... Is 41:28 3289
is thy c perished? ... Mic 4:9 3289
evil against the LORD, a wicked c ... Nah 1:11 3289
of Arimathaea, an honourable c ... Mk 15:43 *1010*
there was a man named Joseph, a c ... Lk 23:50 *1010*
or who hath been his c ... Rom 11:34 *4825*

COUNSELLORS {21}
for they were his c after the ... 2Chr 22:4 3289
And hired c against them, to ... Ezr 4:5 3289
of the king, and of his seven c ... Ezr 7:14 3272
his c have freely offered unto ... Ezr 7:15 3272
unto me before the king, and his c ... Ezr 7:28 3289
our God, which the king, and his c ... Ezr 8:25 3289
c of the earth, which built ... Job 3:14 3289
He leadeth c away spoiled, and ... Job 12:17 3289
also are my delight, and my c ... Ps 119:24 6098
multitude of c there is safety ... Prov 11:14 3289
but to the c of peace is joy ... Prov 12:20 3289
of c they are established ... Prov 15:22 3289
in multitude of c there is safety ... Prov 24:6 3289
thy c as at the beginning ... Is 1:26 3289
the counsel of the wise c of ... Is 19:11 3289
the judges, the treasurers, the c ... Dan 3:2 1884
the judges, the treasurers, the c ... Dan 3:3 1884
and spake, and said unto his c ... Dan 3:24 1907
and captains, and the king's c ... Dan 3:27 1907
and my c and my lords sought unto ... Dan 4:36 1907
governors, and the princes, the c ... Dan 6:7 1907

COUNSELS {12}
it is turned round about by his c ... Job 37:12 8458
let them fall by their own c ... Ps 5:10 4156
and they walked in their own c ... Ps 81:12 4156
shall attain unto wise c ... Prov 1:5 8458
but the c of the wicked are ... Prov 12:5 8458
to thee excellent things in c ... Prov 22:20 4156
thy c of old are faithfulness and ... Is 25:1 6098
wearied in the multitude of thy c ... Is 47:13 6098
their ear, but walked in the c ... Jer 7:24 4156

them, because of their own *c* ... Hos 11:6 4156
of Ahab, and ye walk in their *c* ... Mic 6:16 4156
make manifest the *c* of the hearts ... 1Cor 4:5 *1012*

COUNT {26}
shall make your *c* for the lamb ... Ex 12:4 3699
then ye shall *c* the fruit thereof ... Lev 19:23
ye shall *c* unto you from the ... Lev 23:15 5608
Then let him *c* the years of the ... Lev 25:27 2803
jubile, then he shall *c* with him ... Lev 25:52 2803
Who can *c* the dust of Jacob, and ... Num 23:10 4487
C not thine handmaid for a ... 1Sa 1:16 5414
and my maids, *c* me for a stranger ... Job 19:15 2803
he see my ways, and *c* all my steps ... Job 31:4 5608
The LORD shall *c*, when he writeth ... Ps 87:6 5608
If I should *c* them, they are more ... Ps 139:18 5608
I *c* them mine enemies ... Ps 139:22 1961
Shall I *c* them pure with the ... Mic 6:11
neither *c* I my life dear unto ... Acts 20:24 *2192*
I *c* all things but loss for the ... Phil 3:8 *2233*
do *c* them but dung, that I may ... Phil 3:8 *2233*
Brethren, I *c* not myself to have ... Phil 3:13 *3049*
that our God would *c* you worthy ... 2Th 1:11 *515*
Yet *c* him not as an enemy, but ... 2Th 3:15 *2233*
servants as are under the yoke *c* ... 1Ti 6:1 *2233*
If thou *c* me therefore a partner, ... Philem 17 *2192*
c it all joy when ye fall into ... Jas 1:2 *2233*
we *c* them happy which endure ... Jas 5:11 *3106*
as they that *c* it pleasure to ... 2Pet 2:13 *2233*
promise, as some men *c* slackness ... 2Pet 3:9 *2233*
c the number of the beast ... Rev 13:18 *5585*

COUNTED {40}
he *c* it to him for righteousness ... Gen 15:6 2803
that shall be *c* stolen with me ... Gen 30:33
Are we not *c* of him strangers ... Gen 31:15 2803
of testimony, as it was *c* ... Ex 38:21 6485
be *c* as the fields of the country ... Lev 25:31 2803
then it shall be *c* unto the ... Num 18:30 2803
which is *c* to the Canaanite ... Josh 13:3 2803
son Solomon shall be *c* offenders ... 1Kin 1:21
be numbered nor *c* for multitude ... 1Kin 3:8 5608
Benjamin *c* he not among them ... 1Chr 21:6 6485
as they were *c* by number of names ... 1Chr 23:24 6485
for they were *c* faithful, and ... Neh 13:13 2803
Wherefore are we *c* as beasts ... Job 18:3 2803
Darts are *c* as stubble ... Job 41:29 2803
we are *c* as sheep for the ... Ps 44:22 2803
I am *c* with them that go down ... Ps 88:4 2803
And that was *c* unto him for ... Ps 106:31 2803
he holdeth his peace, is *c* wise ... Prov 17:28 2803
it shall be *c* a curse to him ... Prov 27:14 2803
hoofs shall be *c* like flint ... Is 5:28 2803
fruitful field be *c* for a forest ... Is 32:15 2803
where is he that *c* the towers ... Is 33:18 5608
are *c* as the small dust of the ... Is 40:15 2803
they are *c* to him less than ... Is 40:17 2803
but they were *c* as a strange ... Hos 8:12 2803
because they *c* him as a prophet ... Mt 14:5 *2192*
for all men *c* John, that he was a ... Mk 11:32 *2192*
rejoicing that they were *c* worthy ... Acts 5:41 *2661*
they *c* the price of them, and ... Acts 19:19 *4860*
be *c* for circumcision ... Rom 2:26 *3049*
God, and it was *c* unto him for ... Rom 4:3 *3049*
his faith is *c* for righteousness ... Rom 4:5 *3049*
of the promise are *c* for the seed ... Rom 9:8 *3049*
those I *c* loss for Christ ... Phil 3:7 *2233*
that ye may be *c* worthy of the ... 2Th 1:5 *2661*
me, for that he *c* me faithful ... 1Ti 1:12 *2233*
well be *c* worthy of double honour ... 1Ti 5:17 *515*
For this man was *c* worthy of more ... Heb 3:3 *515*
But he whose descent is not *c* ... Heb 7:6 *1075*
hath *c* the blood of the covenant, ... Heb 10:29 *2233*

COUNTENANCE {53}
was very wroth, and his *c* fell ... Gen 4:5 6440
and why is thy *c* fallen ... Gen 4:6 6440
And Jacob beheld the *c* of Laban ... Gen 31:2 6440
unto them, I see your father's *c* ... Gen 31:5 6440
Neither shalt thou *c* a poor man ... Ex 23:3 1921
The LORD lift up his *c* upon thee ... Num 6:26 6440
A nation of fierce *c*, which shall ... Deut 28:50 6440
his *c* was like the *c* of ... Judg 13:6 4758
did eat, and her *c* was no more sad ... 1Sa 1:18 6440
unto Samuel, Look not on his *c* ... 1Sa 16:7 4758
ruddy, and withal of a beautiful *c* ... 1Sa 16:12 5869
a youth, and ruddy, and of a fair *c* ... 1Sa 17:42 4758
and of a beautiful *c* ... 1Sa 25:3 8389
she was a woman of a fair *c* ... 2Sa 14:27 4758
And he settled his *c* stedfastly ... 2Kin 8:11 6440
said unto me, Why is thy *c* sad ... Neh 2:2 6440
why should not my *c* be sad ... Neh 2:3 6440
thou changest his *c*, and sendest ... Job 14:20 6440
the light of my *c* they cast not ... Job 29:24 6440
up the light of thy *c* upon us ... Ps 4:6 6440
through the pride of his *c* ... Ps 10:4 639
his *c* doth behold the upright ... Ps 11:7 6440
him exceeding glad with thy *c* ... Ps 21:6 6440
praise him for the help of his *c* ... Ps 42:5 6440
him, who is the health of my *c* ... Ps 42:11 6440
him, who is the health of my *c* ... Ps 43:5 6440
thine arm, and the light of thy *c* ... Ps 44:3 6440
perish at the rebuke of thy *c* ... Ps 80:16 6440
O LORD, in the light of thy *c* ... Ps 89:15 6440
secret sins in the light of thy *c* ... Ps 90:8 6440
A merry heart maketh a cheerful *c* ... Prov 15:13 6440
the light of the king's *c* is life ... Prov 16:15 6440
so doth an angry *c* a backbiting ... Prov 25:23 6440
sharpeneth the *c* of his friend ... Prov 27:17 6440
of the *c* the heart is made better ... Eccl 7:3 6440
of the stairs, let me see thy *c* ... Song 2:14 4758
is thy voice, and thy *c* is comely ... Song 2:14 4758
his *c* is as Lebanon, excellent as ... Song 5:15 4758
The shew of their *c* doth witness ... Is 3:9 6440
they shall be troubled in their *c* ... Eze 27:35 6440
the *c* of the children that eat of ... Dan 1:13 4758
Then the king's *c* was changed ... Dan 5:6 2122
his *c* was changed in him, and his ... Dan 5:9 2122
thee, nor let thy *c* be changed ... Dan 5:10 2122
me, and my *c* changed in me ... Dan 7:28 2122
to the full, a king of fierce *c* ... Dan 8:23 6440
as the hypocrites, of a sad *c* ... Mt 6:16 *4659*
His *c* was like lightning, and his ... Mt 28:3 *2397*
the fashion of his *c* was altered ... Lk 9:29 *4383*
make me full of joy with thy *c* ... Acts 2:28 *4383*
of Moses for the glory of his *c* ... 2Cor 3:7 *4383*
his *c* was as the sun shineth in ... Rev 1:16 *3799*

COUNTENANCES {2}
Then let our *c* be looked upon ... Dan 1:13 4758
ten days their *c* appeared fairer ... Dan 1:15 4758

COUNTERVAIL {1}
could not *c* the king's damage ... Est 7:4 7737

COUNTETH {3}
he *c* me unto him as one of his ... Job 19:11 2803
me, he *c* me for his enemy, ... Job 33:10 2803
c the cost, whether he have ... Lk 14:28 *5585*

COUNTING {1}
c one by one, to find out the ... Eccl 7:27

COUNTRIES {55}
after their tongues, in their *c* ... Gen 10:20 776
thy seed, I will give all these *c* ... Gen 26:3 776
give unto thy seed all these *c* ... Gen 26:4 776
all *c* came into Egypt to Joseph ... Gen 41:57 776
These are the *c* which Moses did ... Josh 13:32
these are the *c* which the ... Josh 14:1
and her towns, even three *c* ... Josh 17:11 5316
they among all the gods of the *c* ... 2Kin 18:35 776
fame and of glory throughout all *c* ... 1Chr 22:5 776
and over all the kingdoms of the *c* ... 1Chr 29:30 776
throughout all the *c* of Judah ... 2Chr 11:23 776
service of the kingdoms of the *c* ... 2Chr 12:8 776
upon all the inhabitants of the *c* ... 2Chr 15:5 776
on all the kingdoms of those *c* ... 2Chr 20:29 776
c that pertained to the children ... 2Chr 34:33 776
because of the people of those *c* ... Ezr 3:3 776
ruled over all *c* beyond the river ... Ezr 4:20
shall wound the heads over many *c* ... Ps 110:6 776
and give ear, all ye of far *c* ... Is 8:9 776
waste all the nations, and their *c* ... Is 37:18 776
all *c* whither I have driven them ... Jer 23:3 776
from all *c* whither I had driven ... Jer 23:8 776
prophesied both against many *c* ... Jer 28:8 776
I will gather them out of all *c* ... Jer 32:37 776
Edom, and that were in all the *c* ... Jer 40:11 776
c that are round about her ... Eze 5:5 776
the *c* that are round about her ... Eze 5:6 776
shall be scattered through the *c* ... Eze 6:8 776
I have scattered them among the *c* ... Eze 11:16 776
in the *c* where they shall come ... Eze 11:16 776
assemble you out of the *c* where ... Eze 11:17 776
and disperse them in the *c* ... Eze 12:15 776
and disperse them through the *c* ... Eze 20:23 776
heathen, as the families of the *c* ... Eze 20:32 776
of the *c* wherein ye are scattered ... Eze 20:34 776
gather you out of the *c* wherein ... Eze 20:41 776
heathen, and a mocking to all *c* ... Eze 22:4 776
and disperse thee in the *c* ... Eze 22:15 776
cause thee to perish out of the *c* ... Eze 25:7 776
midst of the *c* that are desolate ... Eze 29:12 776
will disperse them through the *c* ... Eze 29:12 776
midst of the *c* that are desolate ... Eze 30:7 776
will disperse them through the *c* ... Eze 30:23 776
and disperse them among the *c* ... Eze 30:26 776
into the *c* which thou hast not ... Eze 32:9 776
people, and gather them from the *c* ... Eze 34:13 776
these two *c* shall be mine, and we ... Eze 35:10 776
they were dispersed through the *c* ... Eze 36:19 776
and gather you out of all *c* ... Eze 36:24 776
through all the *c* whither thou ... Dan 9:7 776
and he shall enter into the *c* ... Dan 11:40 776
many *c* shall be overthrown ... Dan 11:41
forth his hand also upon the *c* ... Dan 11:42 776
they shall remember me in far *c* ... Zec 10:9
that are in the *c* enter thereinto ... Lk 21:21 *5561*

COUNTRY {179}
unto Abram, Get thee out of thy *c* ... Gen 12:1 776
smote all the *c* of the Amalekites ... Gen 14:7 7704
the smoke of the *c* went up as the ... Gen 19:28 776
from thence toward the south *c* ... Gen 20:1 776
But thou shalt go unto my *c* ... Gen 24:4 776
for he dwelt in the south *c* ... Gen 24:62 776
lived, eastward, unto the east *c* ... Gen 25:6 776
It must not be so done in our *c* ... Gen 29:26 4725
unto mine own place, and to my *c* ... Gen 30:25 776
the land of Seir, the *c* of Edom ... Gen 32:3 7704
saidst unto me, Return unto thy *c* ... Gen 32:9 776
Hamor the Hivite, prince of the *c* ... Gen 34:2 776
went into the *c* from the face of ... Gen 36:6 776
us, and took us for spies of the *c* ... Gen 42:30 776
And the man, the lord of the *c* ... Gen 42:33 776
land of Egypt, in the *c* of Goshen ... Gen 47:27 776
whether it be one of your own *c* ... Lev 16:29 249
whether it be one of your own *c* ... Lev 17:15 249
as for one of your own *c* ... Lev 24:22 249
be counted as the fields of the *c* ... Lev 25:31 776
All that are born of the *c* shall ... Num 15:13 249
pass, I pray thee, through thy *c* ... Num 20:17 776
valley, that is in the *c* of Moab ... Num 21:20 7704
Even the *c* which the LORD smote ... Num 32:4 776
the cities of the *c* round about ... Num 32:33 776
the *c* of Argob unto the coasts of ... Deut 3:14 2256
in the wilderness, in the plain *c* ... Deut 4:43 776
that I am come unto the *c* which ... Deut 26:3 776
of Israel to search out the *c* ... Josh 2:2 776
be come to search out all the *c* ... Josh 2:3 776
of the *c* do faint because of us ... Josh 2:24 776
two men that had spied out the *c* ... Josh 6:22 776
was noised throughout all the *c* ... Josh 6:27 776
them, saying, Go up and view the *c* ... Josh 7:2 776
Israel, We be come from a far *c* ... Josh 9:6 776
From a very far *c* thy servants ... Josh 9:9 776
inhabitants of our *c* spake to us ... Josh 9:11 776
smote all the *c* of the hills ... Josh 10:40 776
all the *c* of Goshen, even unto ... Josh 10:41 776
the hills, and all the south *c* ... Josh 11:16
the kings of the *c* which Joshua ... Josh 12:7 776
the wilderness, and in the south *c* ... Josh 12:8
of the hill *c* from Lebanon unto ... Josh 13:6
dukes of Sihon, dwelling in the *c* ... Josh 13:21 776
then get thee up to the wood *c* ... Josh 17:15
made an end of dividing the *c* ... Josh 19:51 776
is Hebron, in the hill *c* of Judah ... Josh 21:11
to go unto the *c* of Gilead ... Josh 22:9 776
the *c* was in quietness forty ... Judg 8:28 776
the inhabitants of that *c* ... Judg 11:21 776
in Aijalon in the *c* of Zebulun ... Judg 12:12 776
enemy, and the destroyer of our *c* ... Judg 16:24 776
went to spy out the *c* of Laish ... Judg 18:14 776
sent her throughout all the *c* of ... Judg 20:6 7704
went to sojourn in the *c* of Moab ... Ruth 1:1 7704
And they came into the *c* of Moab ... Ruth 1:2 7704
might return from the *c* of Moab ... Ruth 1:6 7704
for she had heard in the *c* of ... Ruth 1:6 7704
returned out of the *c* of Moab ... Ruth 1:22 7704
with Naomi out of the *c* of Moab ... Ruth 2:6 7704
come again out of the *c* of Moab ... Ruth 4:3 7704
the ark of the LORD was in the *c* ... 1Sa 6:1 7704
of *c* villages, even unto the ... 1Sa 6:18 6521
the camp from the *c* round about ... 1Sa 14:21
me a place in some town in the *c* ... 1Sa 27:5 7704
time that David dwelt in the *c* of ... 1Sa 27:7 7704
in the *c* of the Philistines ... 1Sa 27:11 7704
all the *c* wept with a loud voice, ... 2Sa 15:23 776
over the face of all the *c* ... 2Sa 18:8 776
in the *c* of Benjamin in Zelah ... 2Sa 21:14 776
son of Uri was in the *c* of Gilead ... 1Kin 4:19 776
in the *c* of Sihon king of the ... 1Kin 4:19 776
of all the children of the east *c* ... 1Kin 4:30
of a far *c* for thy name's sake ... 1Kin 8:41 776
she turned and went to her own *c* ... 1Kin 10:13 776
and of the governors of the *c* ... 1Kin 10:15 776
that I may go to mine own *c* ... 1Kin 11:21 776
thou seekest to go to thine own *c* ... 1Kin 11:22 776
but the Syrians filled the *c* ... 1Kin 20:27 776
city, and every man to his own *c* ... 1Kin 22:36 776
the *c* was filled with water ... 2Kin 3:20 776
the Moabites, even in their *c* ... 2Kin 3:24
their *c* out of mine hand, that ... 2Kin 18:35 776
said, They are come from a far *c* ... 2Kin 20:14 776
begat children in the *c* of Moab ... 1Chr 8:8 7704
wasted the *c* of the children of ... 1Chr 20:1 776
but is come from a far *c* for thy ... 2Chr 6:32 776
governors of the *c* brought gold ... 2Chr 9:14 776
much cattle, both in the low *c* ... 2Chr 26:10
invaded the cities of the low *c* ... 2Chr 28:18
to city through the *c* of Ephraim ... 2Chr 30:10 776
the plain *c* round about Jerusalem ... Neh 12:28
so is good news from a far *c* ... Prov 25:25 776
Your *c* is desolate, your cities ... Is 1:7 776
They come from a far *c*, from the ... Is 13:5 776
thee like a ball into a large *c* ... Is 22:18 776
are come from a far *c* unto me ... Is 39:3 776
executeth my counsel from a far *c* ... Is 46:11 776
I brought you into a plentiful *c* ... Jer 2:7 776
that watchers come from a far *c* ... Jer 4:16 776
and the sweet cane from a far *c* ... Jer 6:20 776
a people cometh from the north *c* ... Jer 6:22 776
of them that dwell in a far *c* ... Jer 8:19 776
commotion out of the north *c* ... Jer 10:22 776
no more, nor see his native *c* ... Jer 22:10 776
that bare thee, into another *c* ... Jer 22:26 776
of Israel out of the north *c* ... Jer 23:8 776
will bring them from the north *c* ... Jer 31:8 776
which is in the *c* of Benjamin ... Jer 32:8 776
in the *c* of Pathros, saying, ... Jer 44:1 776
north *c* by the river Euphrates ... Jer 46:10 776
the remnant of the *c* of Caphtor ... Jer 47:4 339
judgment is come upon the plain *c* ... Jer 48:21 776
of great nations from the north *c* ... Jer 50:9 776
us go every one into his own *c* ... Jer 51:9 776
out of the *c* where they sojourn ... Eze 20:38 776
into the *c* for the which I lifted ... Eze 20:42 776
his frontiers, the glory of the *c* ... Eze 25:9 776
the *c* shall be destitute of that ... Eze 32:15 776
all the inhabited places of the *c* ... Eze 34:13 776
issue out toward the east *c* ... Eze 47:8 1552
be unto you as born in the *c* ... Eze 47:22 249
And Jacob fled into the *c* of Syria ... Hos 12:12 7704
what is thy *c*? ... Jonah 1:8 776
my saying, when I was yet in my *c* ... Jonah 4:2 127
therein go forth into the north *c* ... Zec 6:6 776
go forth toward the south *c* ... Zec 6:6 776
c have quieted my spirit in the ... Zec 6:8 776
quieted my spirit in the north *c* ... Zec 6:8 776

C

east c, and from the west c ... Zec 8:7 776
into their own c another way ... Mt 2:12 5561
side into the c of the Gergesenes ... Mt 8:28 5561
abroad his fame in all that c ... Mt 9:31 1093
when he was come into his own c ... Mt 13:54 3968
without honour, save in his own c ... Mt 13:57 3968
out into all that c round about ... Mt 14:35 4066
husbandmen, and went into a far c ... Mt 21:33 589
as a man travelling into a far c ... Mt 25:14 589
into the c of the Gadarenes ... Mk 5:1 5561
not send them away out of the c ... Mk 5:10 5561
told it in the city, and in the c ... Mk 5:14 68
thence, and came into his own c ... Mk 6:1 3968
without honour, but in his own c ... Mk 6:4 3968
may go into the c round about ... Mk 6:36 68
into villages, or cities, or c ... Mk 6:56 68
husbandmen, and went into a far c ... Mk 12:1 589
passed by, coming out of the c ... Mk 15:21 68
they walked, and went into the c ... Mk 16:12 68
went into the hill c with haste ... Lk 1:39
all the hill c of Judaea ... Lk 1:65
And there were in the same c ... Lk 2:8 5561
came into all the c about Jordan ... Lk 3:3 4066
Capernaum, do also here in thy c ... Lk 4:23 3968
prophet is accepted in his own c ... Lk 4:24 3968
every place of the c round about ... Lk 4:37 4066
arrived at the c of the Gadarenes ... Lk 8:26 5561
told it in the city and in the c ... Lk 8:34 68
c of the Gadarenes round about ... Lk 8:37 4066
c round about, and lodge, and get ... Lk 9:12 68
and took his journey into a far c ... Lk 15:13 5561
himself to a citizen of that c ... Lk 15:15 5561
a far c to receive for himself a ... Lk 19:12 5561
went into a far c for a long time ... Lk 20:9 589
a Cyrenian, coming out of the c ... Lk 23:26 68
hath no honour in his own c ... Jn 4:44 3968
unto a c near to the wilderness ... Jn 11:54 5561
many went out of the c up to ... Jn 11:55 5561
a Levite, and of the c of Cyprus ... Acts 4:36 1085
unto him, Get thee out of thy c ... Acts 7:3 1093
because their c was nourished by ... Acts 12:20 5561
was nourished by the king's c ... Acts 12:20 5561
was with the deputy of the c ... Acts 13:7
and went over all the c of Galatia ... Acts 18:23 5561
that they drew near to some c ... Acts 27:27 5561
of promise, as in a strange c ... Heb 11:9
plainly that they seek a c ... Heb 11:14 3968
that c from whence they came out ... Heb 11:15
But now they desire a better c ... Heb 11:16

COUNTRYMEN {2}
robbers, in perils by mine own c ... 2Cor 11:26 1085
like things of your own c ... 1Th 2:14 4853

COUPLE {10}
c the curtains together with the ... Ex 26:6 2266
thou shalt c five curtains by ... Ex 26:9 2266
c the tent together, that it may ... Ex 26:11 2266
of brass to c the tent together ... Ex 36:18 2266
for it, to c it together ... Ex 39:4 2266
servant with him, and a c of asses ... Judg 19:3 6776
make me a c of cakes in my sight, ... 2Sa 13:6 8147
with a c of asses saddled, and ... 2Sa 16:1 6776
a chariot with a c of horsemen ... Is 21:7 6776
of men, with a c of horsemen ... Is 21:9 6776

COUPLED {12}
be c together one to another ... Ex 26:3 2266
shall be c one to another ... Ex 26:3 2266
they shall be c together beneath, ... Ex 26:24 8382
they shall be c together above ... Ex 26:24 8535
he c the five curtains one unto ... Ex 36:10 2266
curtains he c one unto another ... Ex 36:10 2266
c the curtains one unto another ... Ex 36:13 2266
he c five curtains by themselves, ... Ex 36:16 2266
And they were c beneath, and ... Ex 36:29 8382
c together at the head thereof, ... Ex 36:29 8535
the two edges was it c together ... Ex 39:4 2266
chaste conversation c with fear ... 1Pet 3:2

COUPLETH {2}
of the curtain which c the second ... Ex 26:10 2279
of the curtain which c the second ... Ex 36:17 2279

COUPLING {10}
from the selvedge in the c ... Ex 26:4 2279
curtain, in the c of the second ... Ex 26:4 4225
that is in the c of the second ... Ex 26:5 4225
curtain that is outmost in the c ... Ex 26:10 2279
over against the other c thereof ... Ex 28:27 4225
from the selvedge in the c ... Ex 36:11 4225
curtain, in the c of the second ... Ex 36:11 4225
which was in the c of the second ... Ex 36:12 4225
edge of the curtain in the c ... Ex 36:17 4225
over against the other c thereof ... Ex 39:20 4225

COUPLINGS {1}
buy hewn stone, and timber for c ... 2Chr 34:11 4226

COURAGE {20}
And be ye of good c, and bring of ... Num 13:20 2388
Be strong and of a good c, fear ... Deut 31:6 553
Israel, Be strong and of a good c ... Deut 31:7 553
and said, Be strong and of a good c ... Deut 31:23 553
Be strong and of a good c ... Josh 1:6 553
Be strong and of a good c ... Josh 1:9 553
only be strong and of a good c ... Josh 1:18 553
remain any more c in any man ... Josh 2:11 7307
dismayed, be strong and of good c ... Josh 10:25 553
Be of good c, and let us play the ... 2Sa 10:12 2388
Be of good c, and let us behave ... 1Chr 19:13 2388
be strong, and of good c ... 1Chr 22:13 553
his son, Be strong and of good c ... 1Chr 28:20 553
of Oded the prophet, he took c ... 2Chr 15:8 2388
be of good c, and do it ... Ezr 10:4 2388
be of good c, and he shall ... Ps 27:14 2388
Be of good c, and he shall ... Ps 31:24 2388
said to his brother, Be of good c ... Is 41:6 2388
his c against the king of the ... Dan 11:25 3824
saw, he thanked God, and took c ... Acts 28:15 2294

COURAGEOUS {5}
Only be thou strong and very c ... Josh 1:7 553
Be ye therefore very c to keep ... Josh 23:6 2388
be c, and be valiant ... 2Sa 13:28 2388
Be strong and c, be not afraid nor ... 2Chr 32:7 553
he that is c among the mighty ... Amos 2:16 533,3820

COURAGEOUSLY {1}
Deal c, and the LORD shall be with ... 2Chr 19:11 2388

COURSE {35}
of every c were twenty and four ... 1Chr 27:1 4256
Over the first c for the first ... 1Chr 27:2 4256
in his c were twenty and four ... 1Chr 27:2 4256
over the c of the second month ... 1Chr 27:4 4256
of his c was Mikloth also the ... 1Chr 27:4 4256
in his c likewise were twenty and ... 1Chr 27:4 4256
in his c were twenty and four ... 1Chr 27:5 4256
in his c was Ammizabad his son ... 1Chr 27:6 4256
in his c were twenty and four ... 1Chr 27:7 4256
in his c were twenty and four ... 1Chr 27:8 4256
in his c were twenty and four ... 1Chr 27:9 4256
in his c were twenty and four ... 1Chr 27:10 4256
in his c were twenty and four ... 1Chr 27:11 4256
in his c were twenty and four ... 1Chr 27:12 4256
in his c were twenty and four ... 1Chr 27:13 4256
in his c were twenty and four ... 1Chr 27:14 4256
in his c were twenty and four ... 1Chr 27:15 4256
that ministered to the king by c ... 1Chr 28:1 4256
and did not then wait by c ... 2Chr 5:11 4256
sang together by c in praising ... Ezr 3:11
of the earth are out of c ... Ps 82:5 4131
every one turned to his c ... Jer 8:6 4794
their c is evil, and their force ... Jer 23:10 4794
named Zacharias, of the c of Abia ... Lk 1:5 2183
before God in the order of his c ... Lk 1:8 2183
And as John fulfilled his c ... Acts 13:25 1408
with a straight c to Samothracia ... Acts 16:11 2113
that I might finish my c with joy ... Acts 20:24 1408
came with a straight c unto Coos ... Acts 21:1 4144
we had finished our c from Tyre ... Acts 21:7 4144
the most by three, and that by c ... 1Cor 14:27 3313
according to the c of this world ... Eph 2:2 165
word of the Lord may have free c ... 2Th 3:1 5143
good fight, I have finished my c ... 2Ti 4:7 1408
setteth on fire the c of nature ... Jas 3:6 5164

COURSES {18}
the stars in their c fought ... Judg 5:20 4546
ten thousand a month by c ... 1Kin 5:14 2487
into c among the sons of Levi ... 1Chr 23:6 4256
the king in any matter of the c ... 1Chr 27:1 4256
Also for the c of the priests and ... 1Chr 28:13 4256
the c of the priests and the ... 1Chr 28:21 4256
the c of the priests to their ... 2Chr 8:14 4256
also by their c at every gate ... 2Chr 8:14 4256
the priest dismissed not the c ... 2Chr 23:8 4256
appointed the c of the priests ... 2Chr 31:2 4256
and the Levites after their c ... 2Chr 31:2 4256
to give to their brethren by c ... 2Chr 31:15 4256
charges according to their c ... 2Chr 31:16 4256
in their charges by their c ... 2Chr 31:17 4256
of your fathers, after your c ... 2Chr 35:4 4256
place, and the Levites in their c ... 2Chr 35:10 4256
and the Levites in their c ... Ezr 6:18 4255
grass, as willows by the water c ... Is 44:4 2988

COURT {122}
make the c of the tabernacle ... Ex 27:9 2691
the c of fine twined linen of an ... Ex 27:9 2691
for the breadth of the c on the ... Ex 27:12 2691
the breadth of the c on the east ... Ex 27:13 2691
for the gate of the c shall be an ... Ex 27:16 2691
c shall be filleted with silver ... Ex 27:17 2691
The length of the c shall be an ... Ex 27:18 2691
thereof, and all the pins of the c ... Ex 27:19 2691
The hangings of the c, his ... Ex 35:17 2691
the hanging for the door of the c ... Ex 35:17 2691
tabernacle, and the pins of the c ... Ex 35:18 2691
And he made the c ... Ex 38:9 2691
the c were of fine twined linen ... Ex 38:9 2691
for the other side of the c gate ... Ex 38:15 2691
All the hangings of the c round ... Ex 38:16 2691
all the pillars of the c were ... Ex 38:17 2691
the gate of the c was needlework ... Ex 38:18 2691
to the hangings of the c ... Ex 38:18 2691
of the c round about, were of ... Ex 38:20 2691
the sockets of the c round about ... Ex 38:31 2691
and the sockets of the c gate ... Ex 38:31 2691
all the pins of the c round about ... Ex 38:31 2691
The hangings of the c, his ... Ex 39:40 2691
and the hanging for the c gate ... Ex 39:40 2691
shalt set up the c round about ... Ex 40:8 2691
hang up the hanging at the c gate ... Ex 40:8 2691
he reared up the c round about ... Ex 40:33 2691
set up the hanging of the c gate ... Ex 40:33 2691
in the c of the tabernacle of the ... Lev 6:16 2691
in the c of the tabernacle of the ... Lev 6:26 2691
And the hangings of the c, and the ... Num 3:26 2691
the curtain for the door of the c ... Num 3:26 2691
the pillars of the c round about ... Num 3:37 2691
And the hangings of the c, and the ... Num 4:26 2691
for the door of the gate of the c ... Num 4:26 2691
the pillars of the c round about ... Num 4:32 2691
which had a well in his c ... 2Sa 17:18 2691
he built the inner c with three ... 1Kin 6:36 2691
had another c within the porch ... 1Kin 7:8 2691
on the outside toward the great c ... 1Kin 7:9 2691
the great c round about was with ... 1Kin 7:12 2691
both for the inner c of the house ... 1Kin 7:12 2691
c that was before the house of ... 1Kin 8:64 2691
was gone out into the middle c ... 2Kin 20:4 5892
he made the c of the priests ... 2Chr 4:9 2691
great c, and doors for the c ... 2Chr 4:9 5835
had set it in the midst of the c ... 2Chr 6:13 5835
hallowed the middle of the c that ... 2Chr 7:7 2691
of the LORD, before the new c ... 2Chr 20:5 2691
in the c of the house of the LORD ... 2Chr 24:21 2691
the c of the house of the LORD ... 2Chr 29:16 2691
that was by the c of the prison ... Neh 3:25 2691
in the c of the garden of the ... Est 1:5 2691
before the c of the women's house ... Est 2:11 2691
unto the king into the inner c ... Est 4:11 2691
stood in the inner c of the ... Est 5:1 2691
the queen standing in the c ... Est 5:2 2691
And the king said, Who is in the c ... Est 6:4 2691
the outward c of the king's house ... Est 6:4 2691
Behold, Haman standeth in the c ... Est 6:5 2691
of dragons, and a c for owls ... Is 34:13 2681
he stood in the c of the LORD's ... Jer 19:14 2691
Stand in the c of the LORD's ... Jer 26:2 2691
shut up in the c of the prison ... Jer 32:2 2691
uncle's son came to me in the c ... Jer 32:8 2691
that sat in the c of the prison ... Jer 32:12 2691
shut up in the c of the prison ... Jer 33:1 2691
the scribe, in the higher c ... Jer 36:10 2691
went in to the king into the c ... Jer 36:20 2691
Jeremiah into the c of the prison ... Jer 37:21 2691
remained in the c of the prison ... Jer 37:21 2691
that was in the c of the prison ... Jer 38:6 2691
remained in the c of the prison ... Jer 38:13 2691
So Jeremiah abode in the c of the ... Jer 38:28 2691
out of the c of the prison ... Jer 39:14 2691
shut up in the c of the prison ... Jer 39:15 2691
brought me to the door of the c ... Eze 8:7 2691
the inner c of the LORD's house ... Eze 8:16 2691
and the cloud filled the inner c ... Eze 10:3 2691
the c was full of the brightness ... Eze 10:4 2691
was heard even to the outer c ... Eze 10:5 2691
of the c round about the gate ... Eze 40:14 2691
brought he me into the outward c ... Eze 40:17 2691
made for the c round about ... Eze 40:17 2691
forefront of the inner c without ... Eze 40:19 2691
the gate of the outward c that ... Eze 40:20 2691
the gate of the inner c was over ... Eze 40:23 2691
in the inner c toward the south ... Eze 40:27 2691
to the inner c by the south gate ... Eze 40:28 2691
thereof were toward the utter c ... Eze 40:31 2691
into the inner c toward the east ... Eze 40:32 2691
thereof were toward the outward c ... Eze 40:34 2691
thereof were toward the utter c ... Eze 40:37 2691
of the singers in the inner c ... Eze 40:44 2691
So he measured the c, an hundred ... Eze 40:47 2691
temple, and the porches of the c ... Eze 41:15 2691
brought me forth into the utter c ... Eze 42:1 2691
cubits which were for the inner c ... Eze 42:3 2691
which was for the utter c ... Eze 42:3 2691
toward the utter c on the ... Eze 42:7 2691
in the utter c was fifty cubits ... Eze 42:8 2691
goeth into them from the utter c ... Eze 42:9 2691
the wall of the c toward the east ... Eze 42:10 2691
the holy place into the utter c ... Eze 42:14 2691
and brought me into the inner c ... Eze 43:5 2691
in at the gates of the inner c ... Eze 44:17 2691
in the gates of the inner c ... Eze 44:17 2691
they go forth into the utter c ... Eze 44:19 2691
into the utter c to the people ... Eze 44:19 2691
when they enter into the inner c ... Eze 44:21 2691
the sanctuary, unto the inner c ... Eze 44:27 2691
posts of the gate of the inner c ... Eze 45:19 2691
The gate of the inner c that ... Eze 46:1 2691
them not out into the utter c ... Eze 46:20 2691
brought me forth into the utter c ... Eze 46:21 2691
pass by the four corners of the c ... Eze 46:21 2691
corner of the c there was a c ... Eze 46:21 2691
In the four corners of the c ... Eze 46:22 2691
chapel, and it is the king's c ... Amos 7:13 1004
But the c which is without the ... Rev 11:2 833

COURTEOUS {1}
as brethren, be pitiful, be c ... 1Pet 3:8 5391

COURTEOUSLY {2}
Julius c entreated Paul, and gave ... Acts 27:3 5364
us, and lodged us three days c ... Acts 28:7 5390

COURTS {25}
two c of the house of the LORD ... 2Kin 21:5 2691
two c of the house of the LORD ... 2Kin 23:12 2691
the house of the LORD, in the c ... 1Chr 23:28 2691
he shall build my house and my c ... 1Chr 28:6 2691
of the c of the house of the LORD ... 1Chr 28:12 2691
in the c of the house of the LORD ... 2Chr 23:5 2691
two c of the house of the LORD ... 2Chr 33:5 2691
roof of his house, and in their c ... Neh 8:16 2691
in the c of the house of God, and ... Neh 8:16 2691
in the c of the house of God ... Neh 13:7 2691
thee, that he may dwell in thy c ... Ps 65:4 2691
fainteth for the c of the LORD ... Ps 84:2 2691
For a day in thy c is better than ... Ps 84:10 2691
flourish in the c of our God ... Ps 92:13 2691
an offering, and come into his c ... Ps 96:8 2691

and into his c with praise Ps 100:4 2691
In the c of the LORD's house, in Ps 116:19 2691
in the c of the house of our God, Ps 135:2 2691
this at your hand, to tread my c Is 1:12 2691
drink it in the c of my holiness Is 62:9 2691
fill the c with the slain Eze 9:7 2691
pillars as the pillars of the c Eze 42:6 2691
c joined of forty cubits long Eze 46:22 2691
my house, and shalt also keep my c Zec 3:7 2691
live delicately, are in kings' c Lk 7:25

COUSIN {1}
thy c Elisabeth, she hath also Lk 1:36 *4773*

COUSINS {1}
her c heard how the Lord had Lk 1:58 *4773*

COVENANT {292}
with thee will I establish my c Gen 6:18 1285
behold, I establish my c with you Gen 9:9 1285
And I will establish my c with you Gen 9:11 1285
of the c which I make between me Gen 9:12 1285
be for a token of a c between me Gen 9:13 1285
And I will remember my c, which is Gen 9:15 1285
the everlasting c between God Gen 9:16 1285
Noah, This is the token of the c Gen 9:17 1285
day the LORD made a c with Abram Gen 15:18 1285
And I will make my c between me Gen 17:2 1285
my c is with thee, and thou shalt Gen 17:4 1285
I will establish my c between me Gen 17:7 1285
generations for an everlasting c Gen 17:7 1285
Thou shalt keep my c therefore Gen 17:9 1285
This is my c, which ye shall keep Gen 17:10 1285
be a token of the c betwixt me Gen 17:11 1285
my c shall be in your flesh for Gen 17:13 1285
your flesh for an everlasting c Gen 17:13 1285
he hath broken my c Gen 17:14 1285
I will establish my c with him Gen 17:19 1285
with him for an everlasting c Gen 17:19 1285
But my c will I establish with Gen 17:21 1285
and both of them made a c Gen 21:27 1285
Thus they made a c at Beer-sheba Gen 21:32 1285
and let us make a c with thee Gen 26:28 1285
come thou, let us make a c Gen 31:44 1285
God remembered his c with Abraham Ex 2:24 1285
also established my c with them Ex 6:4 1285
and I have remembered my c Ex 6:5 1285
my voice indeed, and keep my c Ex 19:5 1285
Thou shalt make no c with them Ex 23:32 1285
And he took the book of the c Ex 24:7 1285
said, Behold the blood of the c Ex 24:8 1285
generations, for a perpetual c Ex 31:16 1285
And he said, Behold, I make a c Ex 34:10 1285
lest thou make a c with the Ex 34:12 1285
Lest thou make a c with the Ex 34:15 1285
words I have made a c with thee Ex 34:27 1285
the tables the words of the c Ex 34:28 1285
thou suffer the salt of the c of Lev 2:13 1285
of Israel by an everlasting c Lev 24:8 1285
you, and establish my c with you Lev 26:9 1285
but that ye break my c Lev 26:15 1285
shall avenge the quarrel of my c Lev 26:25 1285
will I remember my c with Jacob Lev 26:42 1285
also my c with Isaac Lev 26:42 1285
also my c with Abraham will I Lev 26:42 1285
and to break my c with them Lev 26:44 1285
remember the c of their ancestors Lev 26:45 1285
the ark of the c of the LORD went Num 10:33 1285
the ark of the c of the LORD Num 14:44 1285
it is a c of salt for ever before Num 18:19 1285
I give unto him my c of peace Num 25:12 1285
even the c of an everlasting Num 25:13 1285
And he declared unto you his c Deut 4:13 1285
lest ye forget the c of the LORD Deut 4:23 1285
nor forget the c of thy fathers Deut 4:31 1285
our God made a c with us in Horeb Deut 5:2 1285
made not this c with our fathers Deut 5:3 1285
thou shalt make no c with them Deut 7:2 1285
the faithful God, which keepeth c Deut 7:9 1285
God shall keep unto thee the c Deut 7:12 1285
that he may establish his c which Deut 8:18 1285
even the tables of the c which Deut 9:9 1285
stone, even the tables of the c Deut 9:11 1285
of the c were in my two hands Deut 9:15 1285
bear the ark of the c of the LORD Deut 10:8 1285
thy God, in transgressing his c Deut 17:2 1285
These are the words of the c Deut 29:1 1285
beside the c which he made with Deut 29:1 1285
therefore the words of this c Deut 29:9 1285
into c with the LORD thy God Deut 29:12 1285
with you only do I make this c Deut 29:14 1285
to all the curses of the c that Deut 29:21 1285
the c of the LORD God of their Deut 29:25 1285
bare the ark of the c of the LORD Deut 31:9 1285
break my c which I have made with Deut 31:16 1285
and provoke me, and break my c Deut 31:20 1285
bare the ark of the c of the LORD Deut 31:25 1285
ark of the c of the LORD your God Deut 31:26 1285
observed thy word, and kept thy c Deut 33:9 1285
ark of the c of the LORD your God Josh 3:3 1285
saying, Take up the ark of the c Josh 3:6 1285
And they took up the ark of the c Josh 3:6 1285
that bear the ark of the c Josh 3:8 1285
the ark of the c of the Lord of Josh 3:11 1285
ark of the c before the people Josh 3:14 1285
that bare the ark of the c of the Josh 3:17 1285
the ark of the c of the LORD Josh 4:7 1285
which bare the ark of the c stood Josh 4:9 1285
that bare the ark of the c of the Josh 4:18 1285
them, Take up the ark of the c Josh 6:6 1285
the ark of the c of the LORD Josh 6:8 1285
my c which I commanded them Josh 7:11 1285
transgressed the c of the LORD Josh 7:15 1285
bare the ark of the c of the LORD Josh 8:33 1285
the c of the LORD your God Josh 23:16 1285
So Joshua made a c with the Josh 24:25 1285
I will never break my c with you Judg 2:1 1285
people hath transgressed my c Judg 2:20 1285
(for the ark of the c of God was Judg 20:27 1285
Let us fetch the ark of the c of 1Sa 4:3 1285
ark of the c of the LORD of hosts 1Sa 4:4 1285
with the ark of the c of God 1Sa 4:4 1285
when the ark of the c of the LORD 1Sa 4:5 1285
Make a c with us, and we will 1Sa 11:1 1285
will I make a c with you, that I 1Sa 11:2
Then Jonathan and David made a c 1Sa 18:3 1285
into a c of the LORD with thee 1Sa 20:8 1285
So Jonathan made a c with the 1Sa 20:16
they two made a c before the LORD 1Sa 23:18 1285
bearing the ark of the c of God 2Sa 15:24 1285
made with me an everlasting c 2Sa 23:5 1285
the ark of the c of the LORD 1Kin 3:15 1285
the ark of the c of the LORD 1Kin 6:19 1285
might bring up the ark of the c 1Kin 8:1 1285
brought in the ark of the c of 1Kin 8:6 1285
when the LORD made a c with the 1Kin 8:9 1285
ark, wherein is the c of the LORD 1Kin 8:21 1285
on earth beneath, who keepest c 1Kin 8:23 1285
thee, and thou hast not kept my c 1Kin 11:11 1285
of Israel have forsaken thy c 1Kin 19:10 1285
of Israel have forsaken thy c 1Kin 19:14 1285
I will send thee away with this c 1Kin 20:34 1285
So he made a c with him, and sent 1Kin 20:34 1285
made a c with them, and took an 2Kin 11:4 1285
Jehoiada made a c between the 2Kin 11:17 1285
because of his c with Abraham 2Kin 13:23 1285
his c that he made with their 2Kin 17:15 1285
With whom the LORD had made a c 2Kin 17:35 1285
the c that I have made with you 2Kin 17:38 1285
their God, but transgressed his c 2Kin 18:12 1285
the words of the book of the c 2Kin 23:2 1285
made a c before the LORD, to walk 2Kin 23:3 1285
to perform the words of this c 2Kin 23:3 1285
And all the people stood to the c 2Kin 23:3 1285
is written in the book of this c 2Kin 23:21 1285
David made a c with them in 1Chr 11:3 1285
c of the LORD out of the house of 1Chr 15:25 1285
bare the ark of the c of the LORD 1Chr 15:26 1285
the c of the LORD with shouting 1Chr 15:28 1285
as the ark of the c of the LORD 1Chr 15:29 1285
before the ark of the c of God 1Chr 16:6 1285
Be ye mindful always of his c 1Chr 16:15 1285
Even of the c which he made with 1Chr 16:16 1285
and to Israel for an everlasting c 1Chr 16:17 1285
ark of the c of the LORD Asaph 1Chr 16:37 1285
but the ark of the c of the LORD 1Chr 17:1 1285
the ark of the c of the LORD 1Chr 22:19 1285
for the ark of the c of the LORD 1Chr 28:2 1285
the ark of the c of the LORD 1Chr 28:18 1285
to bring up the ark of the c of 2Chr 5:2 1285
brought in the ark of the c of 2Chr 5:7 1285
when the LORD made a c with the 2Chr 5:10
ark, wherein is the c of the LORD 2Chr 6:11 1285
which keepest c, and shewest mercy 2Chr 6:14 1285
him and to his sons by a c of salt 2Chr 13:5 1285
they entered into a c to seek the 2Chr 15:12 1285
because of the c that he had made 2Chr 21:7 1285
son of Zichri, into c with him 2Chr 23:1 1285
all the congregation made a c 2Chr 23:3 1285
And Jehoiada made a c between him 2Chr 23:16 1285
a c with the LORD God of Israel 2Chr 29:10 1285
the words of the book of the c 2Chr 34:30 1285
made a c before the LORD, to walk 2Chr 34:31 1285
to perform the words of the c 2Chr 34:31 1285
did according to the c of God 2Chr 34:32 1285
Now therefore let us make a c Ezr 10:3 1285
and terrible God, that keepeth c Neh 1:5 1285
madest a c with him to give the Neh 9:8 1285
the terrible God, who keepest c Neh 9:32 1285
of all this we make a sure c Neh 9:38
the c of the priesthood, and of Neh 13:29 1285
I made a c with mine eyes Job 31:1 1285
Will he make a c with thee Job 41:4 1285
and truth unto such as keep his c Ps 25:10 1285
and he will shew them his c Ps 25:14 1285
have we dealt falsely in thy c Ps 44:17 1285
made a c with me by sacrifice Ps 50:5 1285
shouldest take my c in thy mouth Ps 50:16 1285
he hath broken his c Ps 55:20 1285
Have respect unto the c Ps 74:20 1285
They kept not the c of God Ps 78:10 1285
were they stedfast in his c Ps 78:37 1285
I have made a c with my chosen, I Ps 89:3 1285
my c shall stand fast with him Ps 89:28 1285
My c will I not break, nor alter Ps 89:34 1285
made void the c of thy servant Ps 89:39 1285
To such as keep his c, and to Ps 103:18 1285
He hath remembered his c for ever Ps 105:8 1285
Which c he made with Abraham, and Ps 105:9
and to Israel for an everlasting c Ps 105:10 1285
And he remembered for them his c Ps 106:45 1285
he will ever be mindful of his c Ps 111:5 1285
he hath commanded his c for ever Ps 111:9 1285
If thy children will keep my c Ps 132:12 1285
and forgetteth the c of her God Prov 2:17 1285
broken the everlasting c Is 24:5 1285
said, We have made a c with death Is 28:15 1285
your c with death shall be Is 28:18 1285
he hath broken the c, he hath Is 33:8 1285
give thee for a c of the people Is 42:6 1285
give thee for a c of the people Is 49:8 1285
neither shall the c of my peace Is 54:10 1285
make an everlasting c with you Is 55:3 1285
please me, and take hold of my c Is 56:4 1285
it, and taketh hold of my c Is 56:6 1285
bed, and made thee a c with them Is 57:8
As for me, this is my c with them Is 59:21 1285
make an everlasting c with them Is 61:8 1285
The ark of the c of the LORD Jer 3:16 1285
Hear ye the words of this c Jer 11:2 1285
obeyeth not the words of this c Jer 11:3 1285
Hear ye the words of this c Jer 11:6 1285
upon them all the words of this c Jer 11:8 1285
house of Judah have broken my c Jer 11:10 1285
remember, break not thy c with us Jer 14:21 1285
the c of the LORD their God Jer 22:9 1285
that I will make a new c with the Jer 31:31 1285
Not according to the c that I Jer 31:32 1285
which my c they brake, although I Jer 31:32 1285
But this shall be the c that I Jer 31:33 1285
make an everlasting c with them Jer 32:40 1285
If ye can break my c of the day Jer 33:20 1285
my c of the night, and that there Jer 33:20 1285
Then may also my c be broken with Jer 33:21 1285
If my c be not with day and night, Jer 33:25 1285
the king Zedekiah had made a c Jer 34:8 1285
which had entered into the c Jer 34:10 1285
I made a c with your fathers in Jer 34:13 1285
ye had made a c before me in the Jer 34:15 1285
men that have transgressed my c Jer 34:18 1285
c which they had made before me Jer 34:18 1285
to the LORD in a perpetual c that Jer 50:5 1285
and entered into a c with thee Eze 16:8 1285
the oath in breaking the c Eze 16:59 1285
my c with thee in the days of thy Eze 16:60 1285
unto thee an everlasting c Eze 16:60 1285
for daughters, but not by thy c Eze 16:61 1285
I will establish my c with thee Eze 16:62 1285
made a c with him, and hath taken Eze 17:13 1285
keeping of his c it might stand Eze 17:14 1285
or shall he break the c, and be Eze 17:15 1285
whose c he brake, even with him Eze 17:16 1285
the oath by breaking the c Eze 17:18 1285
my c that he hath broken, even it Eze 17:19 1285
bring you into the bond of the c Eze 20:37 1285
will make with them a c of peace Eze 34:25 1285
will make a c of peace with them Eze 37:26 1285
be an everlasting c with them Eze 37:26 1285
broken my c because of all your Eze 44:7 1285
and dreadful God, keeping the c Dan 9:4 1285
he shall confirm the c with many Dan 9:27 1285
yea, also the prince of the c Dan 11:22 1285
heart shall be against the holy c Dan 11:28 1285
indignation against the holy c Dan 11:30 1285
with them that forsake the holy c Dan 11:30 1285
c shall he corrupt by flatteries Dan 11:32 1285
in that day will I make a c for Hos 2:18 1285
like men have transgressed the c Hos 6:7 1285
they have transgressed my c Hos 8:1 1285
swearing falsely in making a c Hos 10:4 1285
they do make a c with the Hos 12:1 1285
and remembered not the brotherly c Amos 1:9 1285
by the blood of thy c I have sent Zec 9:11 1285
that I might break my c which I Zec 11:10 1285
that my c might be with Levi, Mal 2:4 1285
My c was with him of life and Mal 2:5 1285
ye have corrupted the c of Levi Mal 2:8 1285
by profaning the c of our fathers Mal 2:10 1285
companion, and the wife of thy c Mal 2:14 1285
even the messenger of the c Mal 3:1 1285
and to remember his holy c Lk 1:72 *1242*
of the c which God made with our Acts 3:25 *1242*
he gave him the c of circumcision Acts 7:8 *1242*
For this is my c unto them Rom 11:27 *1242*
Though it be but a man's c Gal 3:15 *1242*
And this I say, that the c Gal 3:17 *1242*
he is the mediator of a better c Heb 8:6 *1242*
For if that first c had been Heb 8:7
when I will make a new c with the Heb 8:8 *1242*
Not according to the c that I Heb 8:9 *1242*
they continued not in my c Heb 8:9 *1242*
For this is the c that I will Heb 8:10 *1242*
In that he saith, A new c Heb 8:13
Then verily the first c had also Heb 9:1
the ark of the c overlaid round Heb 9:4 *1242*
budded, and the tables of the c Heb 9:4 *1242*
This is the c that I will make Heb 10:16 *1242*
hath counted the blood of the c Heb 10:29 *1242*
Jesus the mediator of the new c Heb 12:24 *1242*
the blood of the everlasting c Heb 13:20 *1242*

COVENANTBREAKERS {1}
Without understanding, c, without Rom 1:31 *802*

COVENANTED {4}
according as I have c with David 2Chr 7:18 3772
I c with you when ye came out of Hag 2:5 3772
they c with him for thirty pieces Mt 26:15 *2476*
were glad, and c to give him money Lk 22:5 *4934*

COVENANTS {3}
adoption, and the glory, and the c Rom 9:4 *1242*
for these are the two c Gal 4:24 *1242*
strangers from the c of promise Eph 2:12 *1242*

COVER {72}
they shall c the face of the Ex 10:5 3680
man shall dig a pit, and not c it Ex 21:33 3680

C

and bowls thereof, to *c* withal Ex 25:29 5258
side and on that side, to *c* it Ex 26:13 3680
breeches to *c* their nakedness Ex 28:42 3680
will *c* thee with my hand while I Ex 33:22 5526
bowls, and his covers to *c* withal Ex 37:16 5258
and *c* the ark with the vail Ex 40:3 5526
the leprosy *c* all the skin of him Lev 13:12 3680
the cloud of the incense may *c* Lev 16:13 3680
blood thereof, and *c* it with dust Lev 17:13 3680
c the ark of testimony with it Num 4:5 3680
the bowls, and covers to *c* withal Num 4:7 5258
c the same with a covering of Num 4:8 3680
c the candlestick of the light, Num 4:9 3680
c it with a covering of badgers' Num 4:11 3680
c them with a covering of Num 4:12 3680
they *c* the face of the earth, and Num 22:5 3680
c that which cometh from thee Deut 23:13 3680
the LORD shall *c* him all the day Deut 33:12 2645
and Saul went in to *c* his feet 1Sa 24:3 5526
to *c* the chapiters that were upon 1Kin 7:18 3680
to *c* the two bowls of the 1Kin 7:41 3680
to *c* the two bowls of the 1Kin 7:42 3680
the two wreaths to *c* the two 2Chr 4:12 3680
to *c* the two pommels of the 2Chr 4:13 3680
c not their iniquity, and let not Neh 4:5 3680
c not thou my blood, and let my Job 16:18 3680
dust, and the worms shall *c* them Job 21:26 3680
and abundance of waters *c* thee Job 22:11 3680
abundance of waters may *c* thee Job 38:34 3680
The shady trees *c* him with their Job 40:22 5526
He shall *c* thee with his feathers Ps 91:4 5526
turn not again to *c* the earth Ps 104:9 3680
let them *c* themselves with their Ps 109:29 5844
Surely the darkness shall *c* me Ps 139:11 7779
mischief of their own lips *c* them Ps 140:9 3680
the LORD, as the waters *c* the sea Is 11:9 3680
under thee, and the worms *c* thee Is 14:11 4374
captivity, and will surely *c* thee Is 22:17 5844
and shall no more *c* her slain Is 26:21 3680
that *c* with a covering, but not Is 30:1 5258
seest the naked, that thou *c* him Is 58:7 3680
neither shall they *c* themselves Is 59:6 3680
the darkness shall *c* the earth Is 60:2 3680
multitude of camels shall *c* thee Is 60:6 3680
I will go up, and will *c* the earth Jer 46:8 3680
sackcloth, and horror shall *c* them Eze 7:18 3680
thou shalt *c* thy face, that thou Eze 12:6 3680
he shall *c* his face, that he see Eze 12:12 3680
the ground, to *c* it with dust Eze 24:7 3680
c not thy lips, and eat not the Eze 24:17 5844
ye shall not *c* your lips, nor eat Eze 24:22 5844
horses their dust shall *c* thee Eze 26:10 3680
and great waters shall *c* thee Eze 26:19 3680
as for her, a cloud shall *c* her Eze 30:18 3680
I will *c* the heaven, and make the Eze 32:7 3680
I will *c* the sun with a cloud, and Eze 32:7 3680
c you with skin, and put breath in Eze 37:6 7159
be like a cloud to *c* the land Eze 38:9 3680
Israel, as a cloud to *c* the land Eze 38:16 3680
my flax given to *c* her nakedness Hos 2:9 3680
shall say to the mountains, *C* us Hos 10:8 3680
brother Jacob shame shall *c* thee Obad 10 3680
yea, they shall all *c* their lips Mic 3:7 5844
shame shall *c* her which said unto Mic 7:10 3680
the LORD, as the waters *c* the sea Hab 2:14 3680
violence of Lebanon shall *c* thee Hab 2:17 3680
to *c* his face, and to buffet him, Mk 14:65 *4028*
and to the hills, *C* us Lk 23:30 *2572*
indeed ought not to *c* his head 1Cor 11:7 *2619*
for charity shall *c* the multitude 1Pet 4:8 *2572*

COVERED {105}

under the whole heaven, were *c* Gen 7:19 3680
and the mountains were *c* Gen 7:20 3680
c the nakedness of their father Gen 9:23 3680
she took a vail, and *c* herself Gen 24:65 3680
c her with a vail, and wrapped Gen 38:14 3680
because she had *c* her face Gen 38:15 3680
came up, and *c* the land of Egypt Ex 8:6 3680
For they *c* the face of the whole Ex 10:15 3680
c the chariots, and the horsemen, Ex 14:28 3680
The depths have *c* them Ex 15:5 3680
with thy wind, the sea *c* them Ex 15:10 3680
the quails came up, and *c* the camp Ex 16:13 3680
the mount, and a cloud *c* the mount Ex 24:15 3680
Sinai, and the cloud *c* it six days Ex 24:16 3680
c with their wings over the mercy Ex 37:9 5526
c the ark of the testimony Ex 40:21 5526
Then a cloud *c* the tent of the Ex 40:34 3680
the leprosy have *c* all his flesh Lev 13:13 3680
to see when the holy things are *c* Num 4:20 1104
six *c* wagons, and twelve oxen Num 7:3 6632
up the cloud *c* the tabernacle Num 9:15 3680
the cloud *c* it by day, and the Num 9:16 3680
and, behold, the cloud *c* it Num 16:42 3680
thick, thou art *c* with fatness Deut 32:15 3780
the sea upon them, and *c* them Josh 24:7 3680
the tent, she *c* him with a mantle Judg 4:18 3680
milk, and gave him drink, and *c* him Judg 4:19 3680
his bolster, and *c* it with a cloth 1Sa 19:13 3680
and he is *c* with a mantle 1Sa 28:14 5844
as he went up, and had his head *c* 2Sa 15:30 2645
was with him *c* every man his head 2Sa 15:30 2645
But the king *c* his face, and the 2Sa 19:4 3813
they *c* him with clothes, but he 1Kin 1:1 3680
c the house with beams and boards 1Kin 6:9 5603
he *c* them on the inside with wood 1Kin 6:15 6823
c the floor of the house with 1Kin 6:15 6823
so *c* the altar which was of cedar 1Kin 6:20 6823
c them with gold fitted upon the 1Kin 6:35 6823
it was *c* with cedar above upon 1Kin 7:3 5603
it was *c* with cedar from one side 1Kin 7:7 5603
ark, and the cherubims *c* the ark 1Kin 8:7 5526
c himself with sackcloth, and went 2Kin 19:1 3680
c with sackcloth, to Isaiah the 2Kin 19:2 3680
c the ark of the covenant of the 1Chr 28:18 5526
ark, and the cherubims *c* the ark 2Chr 5:8 3680
c it, and set up the doors thereof Neh 3:15 2926
mourning, and having his head *c* Est 6:12 2645
king's mouth, they *c* Haman's face Est 7:8 2645
neither hath he *c* the darkness Job 23:17 3680
If I *c* my transgressions as Adam, Job 31:33 3680
is forgiven, whose sin is *c* Ps 32:1 3680
and the shame of my face hath *c* me Ps 44:15 3680
c us with the shadow of death Ps 44:19 3680
valleys also are *c* over with corn Ps 65:13 5848
the wings of a dove *c* with silver Ps 68:13 2645
shame hath *c* my face Ps 69:7 3680
let them be *c* with reproach and Ps 71:13 5844
The hills were *c* with the shadow Ps 80:10 3680
thou hast *c* all their sin Ps 85:2 3680
thou hast *c* him with shame Ps 89:45 5844
the waters *c* their enemies Ps 106:11 3680
and *c* the company of Abiram Ps 106:17 3680
thou hast *c* me in my mother's Ps 139:13 5526
thou hast *c* my head in the day of Ps 140:7 5526
nettles had *c* the face thereof, Prov 24:31 3680
a potsherd *c* with silver dross Prov 26:23 6823
Whose hatred is *c* by deceit Prov 26:26 3680
his name shall be *c* with darkness Eccl 6:4 3680
with twain he *c* his face Is 6:2 3680
and with twain he *c* his feet Is 6:2 3680
your rulers, the seers hath he *c* Is 29:10 3680
c himself with sackcloth, and went Is 37:1 3680
of the priests *c* with sackcloth Is 37:2 3680
I have *c* thee in the shadow of Is 51:16 3680
he hath *c* me with the robe of Is 61:10 3271
and confounded, and *c* their heads Jer 14:3 2645
were ashamed, they *c* their heads Jer 14:4 2645
she is *c* with the multitude of Jer 51:42 3680
shame hath *c* our faces Jer 51:51 3680
How hath the Lord *c* the daughter Lam 2:1 5743
stones, he hath *c* me with ashes Lam 3:16 3728
Thou hast *c* with anger, and Lam 3:43 5526
Thou hast *c* thyself with a cloud, Lam 3:44 5526
to another, and two *c* their bodies Eze 1:11 3680
which *c* on this side, and every Eze 1:23 3680
which *c* on that side, their Eze 1:23 3680
over thee, and *c* thy nakedness Eze 16:8 3680
fine linen, and I *c* thee with silk Eze 16:10 3680
hath *c* the naked with a garment Eze 18:7 3680
hath *c* the naked with a garment, Eze 18:16 3680
a rock, that it should not be *c* Eze 24:8 3680
of Elishah was that which *c* thee Eze 27:7 4374
I *c* the deep for him, and I Eze 31:15 3680
them, and the skin *c* them above Eze 37:8 7159
windows, and the windows were *c* Eze 41:16 3680
c him with sackcloth, and sat in Jonah 3:6 3680
beast be *c* with sackcloth, and cry Jonah 3:8 3680
His glory *c* the heavens, and the Hab 3:3 3680
the ship was *c* with the waves Mt 8:24 *2572*
for there is nothing *c*, that Mt 10:26 *2572*
For there is nothing *c*, that Lk 12:2 *4780*
are forgiven, and whose sins are *c* Rom 4:7 *1943*
or prophesying, having his head *c* 1Cor 11:4 *2596*
For if the woman be not *c* 1Cor 11:6 *2619*
be shorn or shaven, let her be *c* 1Cor 11:6 *2619*

COVEREDST {2}

Thou *c* it with the deep as with a Ps 104:6 3680
thy broidered garments, and *c* them Eze 16:18

COVEREST {2}

vesture, wherewith thou *c* thyself Deut 22:12 3680
Who *c* thyself with light as with Ps 104:2 5844

COVERETH {27}

all the fat that *c* the inwards Ex 29:13 3680
and the fat that *c* the inwards Ex 29:22 3680
the fat that *c* the inwards Lev 3:3 3680
and the fat that *c* the inwards Lev 3:9 3680
the fat that *c* the inwards Lev 3:14 3680
the fat that *c* the inwards Lev 4:8 3680
and the fat that *c* the inwards Lev 7:3 3680
that which *c* the inwards, and the Lev 9:19 4374
which *c* the face of the earth Num 22:11 3680
Surely he *c* his feet in his Judg 3:24 5526
he *c* the faces of the judges Job 9:24 3680
Because he *c* his face with his Job 15:27 3680
it, and *c* the bottom of the sea Job 36:30 3680
With clouds he *c* the light Job 36:32 3680
violence *c* them as a garment Ps 73:6 5848
him as the garment which *c* him Ps 109:19 5844
Who *c* the heaven with clouds, who Ps 147:8 3680
but violence *c* the mouth of the Prov 10:6 3680
but violence *c* the mouth of the Prov 10:11 3680
but love *c* all sins Prov 10:12 3680
but a prudent man *c* shame Prov 12:16 3680
He that *c* a transgression seeketh Prov 17:9 3680
He that *c* his sins shall not Prov 28:13 3680
our shame, and our confusion *c* us Jer 3:25 3680
art the anointed cherub that *c* Eze 28:14 5526
for one *c* violence with his Mal 2:16 3680
c it with a vessel, or putteth it Lk 8:16 *2572*

COVERING {48}

and Noah removed the *c* of the ark Gen 8:13 4372
he is to thee a *c* of the eyes Gen 20:16 3682
For that is his *c* only, it is his Ex 22:27 3682
c the mercy seat with their wings Ex 25:20 5526
to be a *c* upon the tabernacle Ex 26:7 168
thou shalt make a *c* for the tent Ex 26:14 4372
a *c* above of badgers' skins Ex 26:14 4372
tabernacle, his tent, and his *c* Ex 35:11 4372
mercy seat, and the vail of the *c* Ex 35:12 4539
he made a *c* for the tent of rams' Ex 36:19 4372
a *c* of badgers' skins above that Ex 36:19 4372
the *c* of rams' skins dyed red, and Ex 39:34 4372
the *c* of badgers' skins Ex 39:34 4372
and the vail of the *c* Ex 39:34 4539
put the *c* of the tent above upon Ex 40:19 4372
and set up the vail of the *c* Ex 40:21 4539
he shall put a *c* upon his upper Lev 13:45 5844
the *c* thereof, and the hanging for Num 3:25 4372
they shall take down the *c* vail Num 4:5 4539
thereon the *c* of badgers' skins Num 4:6 3681
same with a *c* of badgers' skins Num 4:8 4372
within a *c* of badgers' skins Num 4:10 4372
cover it with a *c* of badgers' Num 4:11 4372
them with a *c* of badgers' skins Num 4:12 4372
upon it a *c* of badgers' skins Num 4:14 3681
made an end of *c* the sanctuary Num 4:15 3680
of the congregation, his *c* Num 4:25 4372
the *c* of the badgers' skins that Num 4:25 4372
broad plates for a *c* of the altar Num 16:38 6826
broad plates for a *c* of the altar Num 16:39 6826
which hath no *c* bound upon it Num 19:15 6781
spread a *c* over the well's mouth, 2Sa 17:19 4539
Thick clouds are a *c* to him Job 22:14 5643
that they have no *c* in the cold Job 24:7 3682
him, and destruction hath no *c* Job 26:6 3682
clothing, or any poor without *c* Job 31:19 3682
He spread a cloud for a *c* Ps 105:39 4539
the *c* of it of purple, the midst Song 3:10 4817
And he discovered the *c* of Judah Is 22:8 4539
of the *c* cast over all people Is 25:7 3875
the *c* narrower than that he can Is 28:20 4541
and that cover with a *c*, but not Is 30:1 4541
Ye shall defile also the *c* of thy Is 30:22 6826
and I make sackcloth their *c* Is 50:3 3682
every precious stone was thy *c* Eze 28:13 4540
O *c* cherub, from the midst of the Eze 28:16 5526
c the altar of the LORD with Mal 2:13 3680
for her hair is given her for a *c* 1Cor 11:15 *4018*

COVERINGS {2}

decked my bed with *c* of tapestry Prov 7:16 4765
She maketh herself *c* of tapestry Prov 31:22 4765

COVERS {3}

c thereof, and bowls thereof, to Ex 25:29 7184
his *c* to cover withal, of pure Ex 37:16 7184
the bowls, and *c* to cover withal Num 4:7 7184

COVERT {9}

came down by the *c* of the hill 1Sa 25:20 5643
the *c* for the sabbath that they 2Kin 16:18 4329
abide in the *c* to lie in wait Job 38:40 5521
in the *c* of the reed, and fens Job 40:21 5643
will trust in the *c* of thy wings Ps 61:4 5643
for a *c* from storm and from rain Is 4:6 4563
be thou a *c* to them from the face Is 16:4 5643
the wind, and a *c* from the tempest Is 32:2 5643
He hath forsaken his *c*, as the Jer 25:38 5520

COVET {8}

Thou shalt not *c* thy neighbour's Ex 20:17 2530
thou shalt not *c* thy neighbour's Ex 20:17 2530
wife, neither shalt thou *c* thy Deut 5:21 183
they *c* fields, and take them by Mic 2:2 2530
law had said, Thou shalt not *c* Rom 7:7 *1937*
false witness, Thou shalt not *c* Rom 13:9 *1937*
But *c* earnestly the best gifts 1Cor 12:31 *2206*
c to prophesy, and forbid not to 1Cor 14:39 *2206*

COVETED {3}

shekels weight, then I *c* them Josh 7:21 2530
I have *c* no man's silver, or gold Acts 20:33 *1937*
which while some *c* after, they 1Ti 6:10 *3713*

COVETETH {2}

He *c* greedily all the day long Prov 21:26 183
Woe to him that *c* an evil Hab 2:9 1214

COVETOUS {9}

heart's desire, and blesseth the *c* Ps 10:3 1214
And the Pharisees also, who were *c* Lk 16:14 *5366*
of this world, or with the *c* 1Cor 5:10 *4123*
a brother be a fornicator, or *c* 1Cor 5:11 *4123*
Nor thieves, nor *c*, nor drunkards 1Cor 6:10 *4123*
nor unclean person, nor *c* man Eph 5:5 *4123*
but patient, not a brawler, not *c* 1Ti 3:3 *866*
be lovers of their own selves, *c* 2Ti 3:2 *5366*
have exercised with *c* practices 2Pet 2:14 *4124*

COVETOUSNESS {19}

fear God, men of truth, hating *c* Ex 18:21 1215
unto thy testimonies, and not to *c* Ps 119:36 1215
but he that hateth *c* shall Prov 28:16 1215
the iniquity of his *c* was I wroth Is 57:17 1215
of them every one is given to *c* Jer 6:13 1215
unto the greatest is given to *c* Jer 8:10 1215
thine heart are not but for thy *c* Jer 22:17 1215
is come, and the measure of thy *c* Jer 51:13 1215
their heart goeth after their *c* Eze 33:31 1215
coveteth an evil *c* to his house Hab 2:9 1215
Thefts, *c*, wickedness, deceit, Mk 7:22 *4124*
them, Take heed, and beware of *c* Lk 12:15 *4124*
fornication, wickedness, *c* Rom 1:29 *4124*
matter of bounty, and not as of *c* 2Cor 9:5 *4124*
and all uncleanness, or *c* Eph 5:3 *4124*

evil concupiscence, and c ... Col 3:5 4124
as ye know, nor a cloke of c ... 1Th 2:5 4124
your conversation be without c ... Heb 13:5 866
through c shall they with feigned ... 2Pet 2:3 4124

COVOCATION {1}
month ye shall have an holy c ... Num 29:12

COW {6}
And whether it be c or ewe ... Lev 22:28 7794
But the firstling of a c, or the ... Num 18:17 7794
their c calveth, and casteth not ... Job 21:10 6510
a man shall nourish a young c ... Is 7:21 5697
And the c and the bear shall feed ... Is 11:7 6510
every c at that which is before ... Amos 4:3

COW'S {1}
I have given thee c dung for ... Eze 4:15 1241

COZ *(coz)* {1} *A descendant of Caleb.*
C begat Anub, and Zobebah, and the ... 1Chr 4:8 6976

COZBI *(coz'-bi)* {2} *A Midianite woman.*
woman that was slain was C ... Num 25:15 3579
of Peor, and in the matter of C ... Num 25:18 3579

COZEBA See CHOZEBA.

CRACKLING {1}
For as the c of thorns under a ... Eccl 7:6 6963

CRACKNELS {1}
take with thee ten loaves, and c ... 1Kin 14:3 5350

CRAFT {6}
cause c to prosper in his hand ... Dan 8:25 4820
how they might take him by c ... Mk 14:1 1388
And because he was of the same c ... Acts 18:3 3673
that by this c we have our wealth ... Acts 19:25 2039
our c is in danger to be set at ... Acts 19:27 3313
craftsman, of whatsoever c he be ... Rev 18:22 5078

CRAFTINESS {5}
He taketh the wise in their own c ... Job 5:13 6193
But he perceived their c, and said ... Lk 20:23 3834
He taketh the wise in their own c ... 1Cor 3:19 3834
of dishonesty, not walking in c ... 2Cor 4:2 3834
the sleight of men, and cunning c ... Eph 4:14 3834

CRAFTSMAN {2}
the work of the hands of the c ... Deut 27:15 2976
and no c, of whatsoever craft he ... Rev 18:22 5079

CRAFTSMEN {7}
thousand captives, and all the c ... 2Kin 24:14 2796
might, even seven thousand, and c ... 2Kin 24:16 2796
for they were c ... 1Chr 4:14 2796
Lod, and Ono, the valley of c ... Neh 11:35 2796
all of it the work of the c ... Hos 13:2 2796
brought no small gain unto the c ... Acts 19:24 5079
the c which are with him, have a ... Acts 19:38 5079

CRAFTY {4}
the devices of the c, so that ... Job 5:12 6175
thou choosest the tongue of the c ... Job 15:5 6175
They have taken c counsel against ... Ps 83:3 6191
nevertheless, being c, I caught ... 2Cor 12:16 3835

CRAG {1}
upon the c of the rock, and the ... Job 39:28 8127

CRANE {2}
Like a c or a swallow, so did I ... Is 38:14 5483
and the turtle and the c and the ... Jer 8:7 5483

CRASHING {1}
and a great c from the hills ... Zeph 1:10 7667

CRAVED {1}
Pilate, and c the body of Jesus ... Mk 15:43 154

CRAVETH {1}
for his mouth c it of him ... Prov 16:26 404

CREATE {8}
C in me a clean heart, O God ... Ps 51:10 1254
the LORD will c upon every ... Is 4:5 1254
I form the light, and c darkness ... Is 45:7 1254
I make peace, and c evil ... Is 45:7 1254
I c the fruit of the lips ... Is 57:19 1254
I c new heavens and a new earth ... Is 65:17 1254
for ever in that which I c ... Is 65:18 1254
I c Jerusalem a rejoicing, and her ... Is 65:18 1254

CREATED {45}
In the beginning God c the heaven ... Gen 1:1 1254
God c great whales, and every ... Gen 1:21 1254
So God c man in his own image ... Gen 1:27 1254
in the image of God c he him ... Gen 1:27 1254
male and female c he them ... Gen 1:27 1254
from all his work which God c ... Gen 2:3 1254
and of the earth when they were c ... Gen 2:4 1254
In the day that God c man ... Gen 5:1 1254
Male and female c he them ... Gen 5:2 1254
Adam, in the day when they were c ... Gen 5:2 1254
have c from the face of the earth ... Gen 6:7 1254
day that God c man upon the earth ... Deut 4:32 1254
and the south thou hast c them ... Ps 89:12 1254
shall be c shall praise the LORD ... Ps 102:18 1254
forth thy spirit, they are c ... Ps 104:30 1254
for he commanded, and they were c ... Ps 148:5 1254
and behold who hath c these things ... Is 40:26 1254
the Holy One of Israel hath c it ... Is 41:20 1254
he that c the heavens, and ... Is 42:5 1254
thus saith the LORD that c thee ... Is 43:1 1254
for I have c him for my glory, I ... Is 43:7 1254
I the LORD have c it ... Is 45:8 1254
made the earth, and c man upon it ... Is 45:12 1254
saith the LORD that c the heavens ... Is 45:18 1254
he c it not in vain, he formed it ... Is 45:18 1254
They are c now, and not from the ... Is 48:7 1254
I have c the smith that bloweth ... Is 54:16 1254
I have c the waster to destroy ... Is 54:16 1254
for the LORD hath c a new thing ... Jer 31:22 1254
in the place where thou wast c ... Eze 21:30 1254
thee in the day that thou wast c ... Eze 28:13 1254
from the day that thou wast c ... Eze 28:15 1254
hath not one God c us ... Mal 2:10 1254
which God c unto this time ... Mk 13:19 2936
was the man c for the woman ... 1Cor 11:9 2936
c in Christ Jesus unto good works ... Eph 2:10 2936
who c all things by Jesus Christ ... Eph 3:9 2936
after God is c in righteousness ... Eph 4:24 2936
For by him were all things c ... Col 1:16 2936
all things were c by him, and for ... Col 1:16 2936
after the image of him that c him ... Col 3:10 2936
which God hath c to be received ... 1Ti 4:3 2936
for thou hast c all things ... Rev 4:11 2936
thy pleasure they are and were c ... Rev 4:11 2936
who c heaven, and the things that ... Rev 10:6 2936

CREATETH {1}
c the wind, and declareth unto man ... Amos 4:13 1254

CREATION {6}
of the c God made them male ... Mk 10:6 2937
the c which God created unto this ... Mk 13:19 2937
things of him from the c of the ... Rom 1:20 2937
we know that the whole c groaneth ... Rom 8:22 2937
were from the beginning of the c ... 2Pet 3:4 2937
the beginning of the c of God ... Rev 3:14 2937

CREATOR {5}
Remember now thy C in the days of ... Eccl 12:1 1254
the C of the ends of the earth, ... Is 40:28 1254
the c of Israel, your King ... Is 43:15 1254
the creature more than the C ... Rom 1:25 2936
well doing, as unto a faithful C ... 1Pet 4:19 2939

CREATURE {29}
the moving c that hath life ... Gen 1:20 8318
and every living c that moveth ... Gen 1:21 5315
forth the living c after his kind ... Gen 1:24 5315
Adam called every living c ... Gen 2:19 5315
every living c that is with you ... Gen 9:10 5315
every living c that is with you, ... Gen 9:12 5315
and every living c of all flesh ... Gen 9:15 5315
every living c of all flesh that ... Gen 9:16 5315
of every living c that moveth in ... Lev 11:46 5315
of every c that creepeth upon the ... Lev 11:46 5315
of the living c was in the wheels ... Eze 1:20 2416
of the living c was in the wheels ... Eze 1:21 2416
living c was as the colour of the ... Eze 1:22 2416
This is the living c that I saw ... Eze 10:15 2416
of the living c was in them ... Eze 10:17 2416
This is the living c that I saw ... Eze 10:20 2416
and preach the gospel to every c ... Mk 16:15 2937
served the c more than the ... Rom 1:25 2937
c waiteth for the manifestation ... Rom 8:19 2937
For the c was made subject to ... Rom 8:20 2937
Because the c itself also shall ... Rom 8:21 2937
nor depth, nor any other c ... Rom 8:39 2937
man be in Christ, he is a new c ... 2Cor 5:17 2937
nor uncircumcision, but a new c ... Gal 6:15 2937
God, the firstborn of every c ... Col 1:15 2937
to every c which is under heaven ... Col 1:23 2937
For every c of God is good, and ... 1Ti 4:4 2938
Neither is there any c that is ... Heb 4:13 2937
every c which is in heaven, and on ... Rev 5:13 2938

CREATURES {12}
houses shall be full of doleful c ... Is 13:21 255
the likeness of four living c ... Eze 1:5 2416
for the likeness of the living c ... Eze 1:13 2416
up and down among the living c ... Eze 1:13 2416
And the living c ran and returned ... Eze 1:14 2416
Now as I beheld the living c ... Eze 1:15 2416
upon the earth by the living c ... Eze 1:15 2416
And when the living c went ... Eze 1:19 2416
when the living c were lifted up ... Eze 1:19 2416
living c that touched one another ... Eze 3:13 2416
be a kind of firstfruits of his c ... Jas 1:18 2938
of the c which were in the sea ... Rev 8:9 2938

CREDITOR {3}
Every c that lendeth ought ... Deut 15:2 1167,4874,3027
the c is come to take unto him my ... 2Kin 4:1 5383
There was a certain c which had ... Lk 7:41 1157

CREDITORS {1}
or which of my c is it to whom I ... Is 50:1 5383

CREEK {1}
a certain c with a shore, into ... Acts 27:39 2859

CREEP {7}
All fowls that c, going upon all ... Lev 11:20 8318
things that c upon the earth ... Lev 11:29 8317
unclean to you among all that c ... Lev 11:31 8318
things that c upon the earth ... Lev 11:42 8317
beasts of the forest do c forth ... Ps 104:20 7430
things that c upon the earth ... Eze 38:20 7430
sort are they which c into houses ... 2Ti 3:6 1744,1519

CREEPETH {14}
every thing that c upon the earth ... Gen 1:25 7431
thing that c upon the earth ... Gen 1:26 7430
every thing that c upon the earth ... Gen 1:30 7430
every thing that c upon the earth ... Gen 7:8 7430
every creeping thing that c upon ... Gen 7:14 7430
thing that c upon the earth ... Gen 7:21 8317
thing that c upon the earth ... Gen 8:17 7430
whatsoever c upon the earth, ... Gen 8:19 7430
every creeping thing that c upon ... Lev 11:41 8317
with any creeping thing that c ... Lev 11:43 8317
thing that c upon the earth ... Lev 11:44 7430
creature that c upon the earth ... Lev 11:46 8317
living thing that c on the ground ... Lev 20:25 7430
of any thing that c on the ground ... Deut 4:18 7430

CREEPING {29}
c thing, and beast of the earth ... Gen 1:24 7431
over every c thing that creepeth ... Gen 1:26 7431
the c thing, and the fowls of the ... Gen 6:7 7431
of every c thing of the earth ... Gen 6:20 7431
every c thing that creepeth upon ... Gen 7:14 7431
of every c thing that creepeth ... Gen 7:21 8318
the c things, and the fowl of the ... Gen 7:23 7431
of every c thing that creepeth ... Gen 8:17 7431
Every beast, every c thing ... Gen 8:19 7431
the carcase of unclean c things ... Lev 5:2 8318
may ye eat of every flying c ... Lev 11:21 8318
But all other flying c things ... Lev 11:23 8318
the c things that creep upon the ... Lev 11:29 8318
every c thing that creepeth upon ... Lev 11:41 8318
hath more feet among all c things ... Lev 11:42 8318
with any c thing that creepeth ... Lev 11:43 8318
of c thing that creepeth upon the ... Lev 11:44 8318
Or whosoever toucheth any c thing ... Lev 22:5 8318
every c thing that flieth is ... Deut 14:19 8318
of c things, and of fishes ... 1Kin 4:33 7431
wherein are things c innumerable ... Ps 104:25 7431
c things, and flying fowl ... Ps 148:10 7431
and behold every form of c things ... Eze 8:10 7431
all c things that creep upon the ... Eze 38:20 7431
with the c things of the ground ... Hos 2:18 7431
of the sea, as the c things ... Hab 1:14 7431
c things, and fowls of the air ... Acts 10:12 2062
c things, and fowls of the air ... Acts 11:6 2062
and fourfooted beasts, and c things ... Rom 1:23 2062

CREPT {1}
are certain men c in unawares ... Jude 4 3921

CRESCENS *(cres'-sens)* {1} *A companion of Paul.*
C to Galatia, Titus unto Dalmatia ... 2Ti 4:10 2913

CRETE *(creet)* {5} See CRETES. *An island south of Greece.*
suffering us, we sailed under C ... Acts 27:7 2914
which is an haven of C, and lieth ... Acts 27:12 2914
thence, they sailed close by C ... Acts 27:13 2914
me, and not have loosed from C ... Acts 27:21 2914
For this cause left I thee in C ... Titus 1:5 2914

CRETES *(creets)* {1} See CRETIANS. *Inhabitants of Crete.*
C and Arabians, we do hear them ... Acts 2:11 2912

CRETIANS *(cre'-shuns)* {2} See CRETES. *Same as Cretes.*
The C are alway liars, evil ... Titus 1:12 2912
bishop of the church of the C ... Titus s 2912

CREW {5}
And immediately the cock c ... Mt 26:74 5455
and the cock c ... Mk 14:68 5455
And the second time the cock c ... Mk 14:72 5455
while he yet spake, the cock c ... Lk 22:60 5455
and immediately the cock c ... Jn 18:27 5455

CRIB {3}
to serve thee, or abide by thy c ... Job 39:9 18
Where no oxen are, the c is clean ... Prov 14:4 18
owner, and the ass his master's c ... Is 1:3 18

CRIED {201}
he c with a great and exceeding ... Gen 27:34 6817
with me, and I c with a loud voice ... Gen 39:14 7121
that I lifted up my voice and c ... Gen 39:15 7121
as I lifted up my voice and c ... Gen 39:18 7121
they c before him, Bow the knee ... Gen 41:43 7121
the people c to Pharaoh for bread ... Gen 41:55 6817
and he c, Cause every man to go ... Gen 45:1 7121
reason of the bondage, and they c ... Ex 2:23 2199
c unto Pharaoh, saying, Wherefore ... Ex 5:15 6817
Moses c unto the LORD because of ... Ex 8:12 6817
of Israel c out unto the LORD ... Ex 14:10 6817
And he c unto the LORD ... Ex 15:25 6817
Moses c unto the LORD, saying, ... Ex 17:4 6817
And the people c unto Moses ... Num 11:2 6817
Moses c unto the LORD, saying, ... Num 12:13 6817
lifted up their voice, and c ... Num 14:1 5414
when we c unto the LORD, he heard ... Num 20:16 6817
the damsel, because she c not ... Deut 22:24 6817
field, and the betrothed damsel c ... Deut 22:27 6817
when we c unto the LORD God of ... Deut 26:7 6817
when they c unto the LORD, he put ... Josh 24:7 6817
of Israel c unto the LORD ... Judg 3:9 2199
of Israel c unto the LORD ... Judg 3:15 2199
of Israel c unto the LORD ... Judg 4:3 6817
c through the lattice, Why is his ... Judg 5:28 2980
of Israel c unto the LORD ... Judg 6:6 2199
when the children of Israel c ... Judg 6:7 2199
and they c, The sword of the LORD, ... Judg 7:20 7121
and all the host ran, and c ... Judg 7:21 7321
and lifted up his voice, and c ... Judg 9:7 7121
of Israel c unto the LORD ... Judg 10:10 2199
ye c to me, and I delivered you ... Judg 10:12 6817
they c unto the children of Dan ... Judg 18:23 7121
and told it, all the city c out ... 1Sa 4:13 2199
Ekron, that the Ekronites c out ... 1Sa 5:10 2199
Samuel c unto the LORD for Israel ... 1Sa 7:9 2199
your fathers c unto the LORD, ... 1Sa 12:8 2199
they c unto the LORD, and said, We ... 1Sa 12:10 2199
he c unto the LORD all night ... 1Sa 15:11 2199
c unto the armies of Israel, and ... 1Sa 17:8 7121
Jonathan c after the lad, and said ... 1Sa 20:37 7121
Jonathan c after the lad, Make ... 1Sa 20:38 7121

c after Saul, saying, My lord the	1Sa 24:8	7121
David c to the people, and to	1Sa 26:14	7121
Samuel, she c with a loud voice	1Sa 28:12	2199
And the watchman c, and told the	2Sa 18:25	7121
the king c with a loud voice, O	2Sa 19:4	2199
Then c a wise woman out of the	2Sa 20:16	7121
upon the LORD, and c to my God	2Sa 22:7	7121
he c against the altar in the	1Kin 13:2	7121
which had c against the altar in	1Kin 13:4	7121
he c unto the man of God that	1Kin 13:21	7121
For the saying which he c by the	1Kin 13:32	7121
he c unto the LORD, and said, O	1Kin 17:20	7121
c unto the LORD, and said, O LORD	1Kin 17:21	7121
they c aloud, and cut themselves	1Kin 18:28	7121
passed by, he c unto the king	1Kin 20:39	6817
and Jehoshaphat c out	1Kin 22:32	2199
And Elisha saw it, and he c	2Kin 2:12	6817
Now there c a certain woman of	2Kin 4:1	6817
of the pottage, that they c out	2Kin 4:40	6817
and he c, and said, Alas, master	2Kin 6:5	6817
there c a woman unto him, saying,	2Kin 6:26	6817
c to the king for her house and	2Kin 8:5	6817
Athaliah rent her clothes, and c	2Kin 11:14	7121
c with a loud voice in the Jews'	2Kin 18:28	7121
the prophet c unto the LORD	2Kin 20:11	7121
for they c to God in the battle,	1Chr 5:20	2199
they c unto the LORD, and the	2Chr 13:14	6817
Asa c unto the LORD his God, and	2Chr 14:11	7121
but Jehoshaphat c out, and the	2Chr 18:31	2199
Then they c with a loud voice in	2Chr 32:18	7121
of Amoz, prayed and c to heaven	2Chr 32:20	2199
c with a loud voice unto the LORD	Neh 9:4	2199
trouble, when they c unto thee	Neh 9:27	6817
c unto thee, thou heardest them	Neh 9:28	2199
c with a loud and a bitter cry	Est 4:1	2199
I delivered the poor that c	Job 29:12	7768
(they c after them as after a	Job 30:5	7321
up, and I c in the congregation	Job 30:28	7768
I c unto the LORD with my voice,	Ps 3:4	7121
upon the LORD, and c unto my God	Ps 18:6	7768
They c, but there was none to	Ps 18:41	7768
They c unto thee, and were	Ps 22:5	2199
but when he c unto him, he heard	Ps 22:24	7768
I c unto thee, and thou hast	Ps 30:2	7768
I c to thee, O LORD	Ps 30:8	7121
supplications when I c unto thee	Ps 31:22	7768
This poor man c, and the LORD	Ps 34:6	7121
I c unto him with my mouth, and he	Ps 66:17	7121
I c unto God with my voice, even	Ps 77:1	6817
God of my salvation, I have c day	Ps 88:1	6817
But unto thee have I c, O LORD	Ps 88:13	7768
Then they c unto the LORD in	Ps 107:6	6817
Then they c unto the LORD in	Ps 107:13	2199
I c with my whole heart	Ps 119:145	7121
I c unto thee	Ps 119:146	7121
the dawning of the morning, and c	Ps 119:147	7768
In my distress I c unto the LORD	Ps 120:1	7121
of the depths have I c unto thee	Ps 130:1	7121
In the day when I c thou	Ps 138:3	7121
I c unto the LORD with my voice	Ps 142:1	2199
I c unto thee, O LORD	Ps 142:5	2199
one c unto another, and said, Holy	Is 6:3	7121
moved at the voice of him that c	Is 6:4	7121
And he c, A lion	Is 21:8	7121
have I c concerning this, Their	Is 30:7	7121
c with a loud voice in the Jews'	Is 36:13	7121
Destruction upon destruction is c	Jer 4:20	7121
I c out, I c violence and	Jer 20:8	2199
c out, I c violence and spoil	Jer 20:8	7121
Their heart c unto the Lord, O	Lam 2:18	6817
They c unto them, Depart ye	Lam 4:15	7121
He c also in mine ears with a	Eze 9:1	7121
that I fell upon my face, and c	Eze 9:8	2199
it was c unto them in my hearing,	Eze 10:13	7121
c with a loud voice, and said, Ah	Eze 11:13	2199
Then an herald c aloud, To you it	Dan 3:4	7123
He c aloud, and said thus, Hew	Dan 4:14	7123
The king c aloud to bring in the	Dan 5:7	7123
he c with a lamentable voice unto	Dan 6:20	2200
they have not c unto me with	Hos 7:14	2199
c every man unto his god, and cast	Jonah 1:5	2199
Wherefore they c unto the LORD	Jonah 1:14	7121
I c by reason of mine affliction	Jonah 2:2	7121
out of the belly of hell c I	Jonah 2:2	7768
the city a day's journey, and he c	Jonah 3:4	7121
whom the former prophets have c	Zec 1:4	7121
Then c he upon me, and spake unto	Zec 6:8	2199
hath c by the former prophets	Zec 7:7	7121
it is come to pass, that as he c	Zec 7:13	7121
so they c, and I would not hear,	Zec 7:13	7121
And, behold, they c out, saying,	Mt 8:29	*2896*
and they c out for fear	Mt 14:26	*2896*
and beginning to sink, he c	Mt 14:30	*2896*
c unto him, saying, Have mercy on	Mt 15:22	*2905*
c out, saying, Have mercy on us,	Mt 20:30	*2896*
but they c the more, saying, Have	Mt 20:31	*2896*
went before, and that followed, c	Mt 21:9	*2896*
But they c out the more, saying,	Mt 27:23	*2896*
hour Jesus c with a loud voice	Mt 27:46	*310*
when he had c again with a loud	Mt 27:50	*2896*
an unclean spirit; and he c out	Mk 1:23	*349*
c with a loud voice, he came out	Mk 1:26	*2896*
him, fell down before him, and c	Mk 3:11	*2896*
c with a loud voice, and said,	Mk 5:7	*2896*
it had been a spirit, and c out	Mk 6:49	*349*
the father of the child c out	Mk 9:24	*2896*
And the spirit c, and rent him sore	Mk 9:26	*2896*
but he c the more a great deal,	Mk 10:48	*2896*
before, and they that followed, c	Mk 11:9	*2896*
they c out again, Crucify him	Mk 15:13	*2896*
they c out the more exceedingly,	Mk 15:14	*2896*
hour Jesus c with a loud voice	Mk 15:34	*994*
Jesus c with a loud voice, and	Mk 15:37	*863*
against him, saw that he so c out	Mk 15:39	*2896*
and c out with a loud voice,	Lk 4:33	*349*
he had said these things, he c	Lk 8:8	*5455*
he c out, and fell down before him	Lk 8:28	*349*
a man of the company c out	Lk 9:38	*310*
And he c and said, Father Abraham,	Lk 16:24	*5455*
And he c, saying, Jesus, thou son	Lk 18:38	*994*
but he c so much the more, Thou	Lk 18:39	*2896*
they c out all at once, saying,	Lk 23:18	*349*
But they c, saying, Crucify him,	Lk 23:21	*2019*
when Jesus had c with a loud	Lk 23:46	*5455*
John bare witness of him, and c	Jn 1:15	*2896*
Then c Jesus in the temple as he	Jn 7:28	*2896*
of the feast, Jesus stood and c	Jn 7:37	*2896*
he c with a loud voice, Lazarus,	Jn 11:43	*2905*
and went forth to meet him, and c	Jn 12:13	*2896*
Jesus c and said, He that	Jn 12:44	*2896*
Then c they all again, saying,	Jn 18:40	*2905*
and officers saw him, they c out	Jn 19:6	*2905*
but the Jews c out, saying, If	Jn 19:12	*2896*
But they c out, Away with him,	Jn 19:15	*2905*
Then they c out with a loud voice	Acts 7:57	*2896*
c with a loud voice, Lord, lay	Acts 7:60	*2896*
same followed Paul and us, and c	Acts 16:17	*2896*
But Paul c with a loud voice,	Acts 16:28	*5455*
c out, saying, Great is Diana of	Acts 19:28	*2896*
Some therefore c one thing	Acts 19:32	*2896*
the space of two hours c out	Acts 19:34	*2896*
some c one thing, some another,	Acts 21:34	*994*
And as they c out, and cast off	Acts 22:23	*2905*
wherefore they c so against him	Acts 22:24	*2019*
he c out in the council, Men and	Acts 23:6	*2896*
that I c standing among them,	Acts 24:21	*2896*
they c with a loud voice, saying,	Rev 6:10	*2896*
he c with a loud voice to the	Rev 7:2	*2896*
c with a loud voice, saying,	Rev 7:10	*2896*
c with a loud voice, as when a	Rev 10:3	*2896*
and when he had c, seven thunders	Rev 10:3	*2896*
And she being with child c	Rev 12:2	*2896*
c with a loud cry to him that had	Rev 14:18	*5455*
he c mightily with a strong voice	Rev 18:2	*2896*
c when they saw the smoke of her	Rev 18:18	*2896*
cast dust on their heads, and c	Rev 18:19	*2896*
he c with a loud voice, saying to	Rev 19:17	*2896*

CRIES {1}

the c of them which have reaped	Jas 5:4	*995*

CRIEST {5}

Moses, Wherefore c thou unto me	Ex 14:15	6817
Who art thou that c to the king	1Sa 26:14	7121
if thou c after knowledge, and	Prov 2:3	7121
When thou c, let thy companies	Is 57:13	2199
Why c thou for thine affliction	Jer 30:15	2199

CRIETH {17}

blood c unto me from the ground	Gen 4:10	6817
come to pass, when he c unto me	Ex 22:27	6817
and the soul of the wounded c out	Job 24:12	7768
shall deliver the needy when he c	Ps 72:12	7768
my flesh c out for the living God	Ps 84:2	7442
Wisdom c without	Prov 1:20	7442
She c in the chief place of	Prov 1:21	7121
She c at the gates, at the entry	Prov 8:3	7442
she c upon the highest places of	Prov 9:3	7121
is in pain, and c out in her pangs	Is 26:17	2199
of him that c in the wilderness	Is 40:3	7121
it c out against me	Jer 12:8	5414,6963
The LORD's voice c unto the city	Mic 6:9	7121
for she c after us	Mt 15:23	*2896*
taketh him, and he suddenly c out	Lk 9:39	*2896*
Esaias also c concerning Israel,	Rom 9:27	*2896*
is of you kept back by fraud, c	Jas 5:4	*2896*

CRIME {2}

For this is an heinous c	Job 31:11	2154
concerning the c laid against him	Acts 25:16	*1462*

CRIMES {2}

for the land is full of bloody c	Eze 7:23	4941
to signify the c laid against him	Acts 25:27	*156*

CRIMSON {5}

and in iron, and in purple, and c	2Chr 2:7	3758
blue, and in fine linen, and in c	2Chr 2:14	3758
the vail of blue, and purple, and c	2Chr 3:14	3758
though they be red like c	Is 1:18	8438
thou clothest thyself with c	Jer 4:30	8144

CRIPPLE {1}

being a c from his mother's womb,	Acts 14:8	*5560*

CRISPING {1}

and the wimples, and the c pins,	Is 3:22	2754

CRISPUS *(cris'-pus)* {2} *A convert of Paul.*

And C, the chief ruler of the	Acts 18:8	*2921*
I baptized none of you, but C	1Cor 1:14	*2921*

CROOKBACKT {1}

Or c, or a dwarf, or that hath a	Lev 21:20	1384

CROOKED {14}

are a perverse and c generation	Deut 32:5	6618
hand hath formed the c serpent	Job 26:13	1281
as turn aside unto their c ways	Ps 125:5	6128
Whose ways are c, and they froward	Prov 2:15	6141
That which is c cannot be made	Eccl 1:15	5791
straight, which he hath made c	Eccl 7:13	5791
even leviathan that c serpent	Is 27:1	6129
the c shall be made straight, and	Is 40:4	6121
before them, and c things straight	Is 42:16	4625
make the c places straight	Is 45:2	1921
they have made them c paths	Is 59:8	6140
stone, he hath made my paths c	Lam 3:9	5753
the c shall be made straight, and	Lk 3:5	*4646*
rebuke, in the midst of a c	Phil 2:15	*4646*

CROP {2}

away his c with his feathers	Lev 1:16	4760
I will c off from the top of his	Eze 17:22	6998

CROPPED {1}

He c off the top of his young	Eze 17:4	6998

CROSS {28}

And he that taketh not his c	Mt 10:38	*4716*
deny himself, and take up his c	Mt 16:24	*4716*
him they compelled to bear his c	Mt 27:32	*4716*
Son of God, come down from the c	Mt 27:40	*4716*
let him now come down from the c	Mt 27:42	*4716*
deny himself, and take up his c	Mk 8:34	*4716*
and come, take up the c, and follow	Mk 10:21	*4716*
Alexander and Rufus, to bear his c	Mk 15:21	*4716*
thyself, and come down from the c	Mk 15:30	*4716*
of Israel descend now from the c	Mk 15:32	*4716*
himself, and take up his c daily	Lk 9:23	*4716*
And whosoever doth not bear his c	Lk 14:27	*4716*
and on him they laid the c	Lk 23:26	*4716*
he bearing his c went forth into	Jn 19:17	*4716*
wrote a title, and put it on the c	Jn 19:19	*4716*
by the c of Jesus his mother	Jn 19:25	*4716*
upon the c on the sabbath day	Jn 19:31	*4716*
lest the c of Christ should be	1Cor 1:17	*4716*
of the c is to them that perish	1Cor 1:18	*4716*
is the offence of the c ceased	Gal 5:11	*4716*
persecution for the c of Christ	Gal 6:12	*4716*
save in the c of our Lord Jesus	Gal 6:14	*4716*
unto God in one body by the c	Eph 2:16	*4716*
death, even the death of the c	Phil 2:8	*4716*
the enemies of the c of Christ	Phil 3:18	*4716*
peace through the blood of his c	Col 1:20	*4716*
of the way, nailing it to his c	Col 2:14	*4716*
was set before him endured the c	Heb 12:2	*4716*

CROSSWAY {1}

thou have stood in the c, to cut	Obad 14	6563

CROUCH {1}

c to him for a piece of silver and	1Sa 2:36	7812

CROUCHETH {1}

He c, and humbleth himself, that	Ps 10:10	1794

CROW {7}

this night, before the cock c	Mt 26:34	*5455*
said unto him, Before the cock c	Mt 26:75	*5455*
night, before the cock c twice	Mk 14:30	*5455*
unto him, Before the cock c twice	Mk 14:72	*5455*
the cock shall not c this day	Lk 22:34	*5455*
said unto him, Before the cock c	Lk 22:61	*5455*
unto thee, The cock shall not c	Jn 13:38	*5455*

CROWN {66}

on the c of the head of him that	Gen 49:26	6936
upon it a c of gold round about	Ex 25:11	2213
make thereto a c of gold round	Ex 25:24	2213
thou shalt make a golden c to the	Ex 25:25	2213
put the holy c upon the mitre	Ex 29:6	5145
unto it a c of gold round about	Ex 30:3	2213
thou make to it under the c of it	Ex 30:4	2213
made a c of gold to it round	Ex 37:2	2213
made thereunto a c of gold round	Ex 37:11	2213
made a c of gold for the border	Ex 37:12	2213
unto it a c of gold round about	Ex 37:26	2213
gold for it under the c thereof	Ex 37:27	2213
plate of the holy c of pure gold	Ex 39:30	5145
put the golden plate, the holy c	Lev 8:9	5145
for the c of the anointing oil of	Lev 21:12	5145
the arm with the c of the head	Deut 33:20	6936
I took the c that was upon his	2Sa 1:10	5145
their king's c from off his head	2Sa 12:30	5850
to the c of his head there was no	2Sa 14:25	6936
put the c upon him, and gave him	2Kin 11:12	5145
David took the c of their king	1Chr 20:2	5850
king's son, and put upon him the c	2Chr 23:11	5145
before the king with the c royal	Est 1:11	3804
he set the royal c upon her head	Est 2:17	3804
the c royal which is set upon his	Est 6:8	3804
white, and with a great c of gold	Est 8:15	5850
the sole of his foot unto his c	Job 2:7	6936
and taken the c from my head	Job 19:9	5850
shoulder, and bind it as a c to me	Job 31:36	5850
thou settest a c of pure gold on	Ps 21:3	5850
thou hast profaned his c by	Ps 89:39	5145
upon himself shall his c flourish	Ps 132:18	5145
a c of glory shall she deliver to	Prov 4:9	5850
woman is a c to her husband	Prov 12:4	5850
The c of the wise is their riches	Prov 14:24	5850
The hoary head is a c of glory	Prov 16:31	5850
children are the c of old men	Prov 17:6	5850
doth the c endure to every	Prov 27:24	5145
c wherewith his mother crowned	Song 3:11	5850
c of the head of the daughters of	Is 3:17	6936
Woe to the c of pride, to the	Is 28:1	5850
The c of pride, the drunkards of	Is 28:3	5850
LORD of hosts be for a c of glory	Is 28:5	5850
Thou shalt also be a c of glory	Is 62:3	5850
have broken the c of thy head	Jer 2:16	6936
down, even the c of your glory	Jer 13:18	5850
Moab, and the c of the head of the	Jer 48:45	6936
The c is fallen from our head	Lam 5:16	5850
a beautiful c upon thine head	Eze 16:12	5850

the diadem, and take off the *c* ... Eze 21:26 5850
shall be as the stones of a *c* ... Zec 9:16 5145
they had platted a *c* of thorns ... Mt 27:29 *4735*
purple, and platted a *c* of thorns ... Mk 15:17 *4735*
soldiers platted a *c* of thorns ... Jn 19:2 *4735*
forth, wearing the *c* of thorns ... Jn 19:5 *4735*
do it to obtain a corruptible *c* ... 1Cor 9:25 *4735*
and longed for, my joy and *c* ... Phil 4:1 *4735*
hope, or joy, or *c* of rejoicing ... 1Th 2:19 *4735*
up for me a *c* of righteousness ... 2Ti 4:8 *4735*
he shall receive the *c* of life ... Jas 1:12 *4735*
ye shall receive a *c* of glory ... 1Pet 5:4 *4735*
and I will give thee a *c* of life ... Rev 2:10 *4735*
thou hast, that no man take thy *c* ... Rev 3:11 *4735*
and a *c* was given unto him ... Rev 6:2 *4735*
upon her head a *c* of twelve stars ... Rev 12:1 *4735*
having on his head a golden *c* ... Rev 14:14 *4735*

CROWNED {6}
hast *c* him with glory and honour ... Ps 8:5 5849
the prudent are *c* with knowledge ... Prov 14:18 3803
the crown wherewith his mother *c* ... Song 3:11 5849
Thy *c* are as the locusts, and thy ... Nah 3:17 4502
for masteries, yet is he not *c* ... 2Ti 2:5 *4737*
of death, *c* with glory and honour ... Heb 2:9 *4737*

CROWNEDST {1}
thou *c* him with glory and honour, ... Heb 2:7 *4737*

CROWNEST {1}
Thou *c* the year with thy goodness ... Ps 65:11 5849

CROWNETH {1}
who *c* thee with lovingkindness and ... Ps 103:4 5849

CROWNING {1}
the *c* city, whose merchants are ... Is 23:8 5849

CROWNS {9}
beautiful *c* upon their heads ... Eze 23:42 5850
take silver and gold, and make *c* ... Zec 6:11 5850
the *c* shall be to Helem, and to ... Zec 6:14 5850
they had on their heads *c* of gold ... Rev 4:4 *4735*
cast their *c* before the throne, ... Rev 4:10 *4735*
heads were as it were *c* like gold ... Rev 9:7 *4735*
horns, and seven *c* upon his heads ... Rev 12:3 *1238*
horns, and upon his horns ten *c* ... Rev 13:1 *1238*
fire, and on his head were many *c* ... Rev 19:12 *1238*

CRUCIFIED {37}
Son of man is betrayed to be *c* ... Mt 26:2 *4717*
all say unto him, Let him be *c* ... Mt 27:22 *4717*
the more, saying, Let him be *c* ... Mt 27:23 *4717*
Jesus, he delivered him to be *c* ... Mt 27:26 *4717*
And they *c* him, and parted his ... Mt 27:35 *4717*
were there two thieves *c* with him ... Mt 27:38 *4717*
also, which were *c* with him ... Mt 27:44 *4957*
that ye seek Jesus, which was *c* ... Mt 28:5 *4717*
when he had scourged him, to be *c* ... Mk 15:15 *4717*
And when they had *c* him, they ... Mk 15:24 *4717*
was the third hour, and they *c* him ... Mk 15:25 *4717*
they that were *c* with him reviled ... Mk 15:32 *4957*
Jesus of Nazareth, which was *c* ... Mk 16:6 *4717*
requiring that he might be *c* ... Lk 23:23 *4717*
called Calvary, there they *c* him ... Lk 23:33 *4717*
the hands of sinful men, and be *c* ... Lk 24:7 *4717*
condemned to death, and have *c* him ... Lk 24:20 *4717*
him therefore unto them to be *c* ... Jn 19:16 *4717*
Where they *c* him, and two others ... Jn 19:18 *4717*
Jesus was *c* was nigh to the city ... Jn 19:20 *4717*
soldiers, when they had *c* Jesus ... Jn 19:23 *4717*
of the other which was *c* with him ... Jn 19:32 *4957*
where he was *c* there was a garden ... Jn 19:41 *4717*
taken, and by wicked hands have *c* ... Acts 2:23 *4362*
that same Jesus, whom ye have *c* ... Acts 2:36 *4717*
Christ of Nazareth, whom ye *c* ... Acts 4:10 *4717*
that our old man is *c* with him ... Rom 6:6 *4957*
was Paul *c* for you? ... 1Cor 1:13 *4717*
But we preach Christ *c*, unto the ... 1Cor 1:23 *4717*
you, save Jesus Christ, and him *c* ... 1Cor 2:2 *4717*
not have *c* the Lord of glory ... 1Cor 2:8 *4717*
though he was *c* through weakness ... 2Cor 13:4 *4717*
I am *c* with Christ ... Gal 2:20 *4957*
evidently set forth, *c* among you ... Gal 3:1 *4717*
they that are Christ's have *c* the ... Gal 5:24 *4717*
by whom the world is *c* unto me ... Gal 6:14 *4717*
Egypt, where also our Lord was *c* ... Rev 11:8 *4717*

CRUCIFY {16}
mock, and to scourge, and to *c* him ... Mt 20:19 *4717*
some of them ye shall kill and *c* ... Mt 23:34 *4717*
on him, and led him away to *c* him ... Mt 27:31 *4717*
And they cried out again, *C* him ... Mk 15:13 *4717*
out the more exceedingly, *C* him ... Mk 15:14 *4717*
on him, and led him out to *c* him ... Mk 15:20 *4717*
And with him they *c* two thieves ... Mk 15:27 *4717*
cried, saying, *C* him, *c* him ... Lk 23:21 *4717*
out, saying, *C* him, *c* him ... Jn 19:6 *4717*
unto them, Take ye him, and *c* him ... Jn 19:6 *4717*
not that I have power to *c* thee ... Jn 19:10 *4717*
with him, away with him, *c* him ... Jn 19:15 *4717*
unto them, Shall I *c* your King ... Jn 19:15 *4717*
seeing they *c* to themselves the ... Heb 6:6 *388*

CRUEL {19}
and their wrath, for it was *c* ... Gen 49:7 7185
of spirit, and for *c* bondage ... Ex 6:9 7185
dragons, and the *c* venom of asps ... Deut 32:33 393
Thou art become *c* to me ... Job 30:21 393
and they hate me with *c* hatred ... Ps 25:19 2555
hand of the unrighteous and *c* man ... Ps 71:4 2556
others, and thy years unto the *c* ... Prov 5:9 394
but he that is *c* troubleth his ... Prov 11:17 394
mercies of the wicked are *c* ... Prov 12:10 394
therefore a *c* messenger shall be ... Prov 17:11 394
Wrath is *c*, and anger is ... Prov 27:4 395
jealousy is *c* as the grave ... Song 8:6
c both with wrath and fierce anger ... Is 13:9 394
over into the hand of a *c* lord ... Is 19:4 7186
they are *c*, and have no mercy ... Jer 6:23 394
with the chastisement of a *c* one ... Jer 30:14 394
they are *c*, and will not shew ... Jer 50:42 394
daughter of my people is become *c* ... Lam 4:3 393
And others had trial of *c* mockings ... Heb 11:36

CRUELLY {1}
father, because he *c* oppressed ... Eze 18:18 6233

CRUELTY {5}
instruments of *c* are in their ... Gen 49:5 2555
That the *c* done to the threescore ... Judg 9:24 2555
me, and such as breathe out *c* ... Ps 27:12 2555
are full of the habitations of *c* ... Ps 74:20 2555
with *c* have ye ruled them ... Eze 34:4 6531

CRUMBS {3}
yet the dogs eat of the *c* which ... Mt 15:27 *5589*
the table eat of the children's *c* ... Mk 7:28 *5589*
desiring to be fed with the *c* ... Lk 16:21 *5589*

CRUSE {9}
the *c* of water, and let us go ... 1Sa 26:11 6835
the *c* of water from Saul's ... 1Sa 26:12 6835
the *c* of water that was at his ... 1Sa 26:16 6835
a *c* of honey, and go to him ... 1Kin 14:3 1228
a barrel, and a little oil in a *c* ... 1Kin 17:12 6835
neither shall the *c* of oil fail ... 1Kin 17:14 6835
neither did the *c* of oil fail ... 1Kin 17:16 6835
and a *c* of water at his head ... 1Kin 19:6 6835
And he said, Bring me a new *c* ... 2Kin 2:20 6746

CRUSH {4}
that the foot may *c* them, or that ... Job 39:15 2115
against me to *c* my young men ... Lam 1:15 7665
To *c* under his feet all the ... Lam 3:34 1792
which *c* the needy, which say to ... Amos 4:1 7533

CRUSHED {7}
LORD that which is bruised, or *c* ... Lev 22:24 3807
c Balaam's foot against the wall ... Num 22:25 3905
be only oppressed and *c* alway ... Deut 28:33 7533
which are *c* before the moth ... Job 4:19 1792
they are *c* in the gate, neither ... Job 5:4 1792
that which is *c* breaketh out into ... Is 59:5 2116
hath devoured me, he hath *c* me ... Jer 51:34 2000

CRY {181}
LORD said, Because the *c* of Sodom ... Gen 18:20 2201
according to the *c* of it, which ... Gen 18:21 6818
because the *c* of them is waxen ... Gen 19:13 6818
a great and exceeding bitter *c* ... Gen 27:34 6818
their *c* came up unto God by ... Ex 2:23 7775
have heard their *c* by reason of ... Ex 3:7 6818
the *c* of the children of Israel ... Ex 3:9 6818
therefore they *c*, saying, Let us ... Ex 5:8 6817
And there shall be a great *c* ... Ex 11:6 6818
and there was a great *c* in Egypt ... Ex 12:30 6818
they *c* at all unto me ... Ex 22:23 6817
I will surely hear their *c* ... Ex 22:23 6818
of them that *c* for being overcome ... Ex 32:18 6030
upon his upper lip, and shall *c* ... Lev 13:45 7121
about them fled at the *c* of them ... Num 16:34 6963
he *c* unto the LORD against thee, ... Deut 15:9 7121
lest he *c* against thee unto the ... Deut 24:15 7121
c unto the gods which ye have ... Judg 10:14 2199
the *c* of the city went up to ... 1Sa 5:12 7775
Cease not to *c* unto the LORD our ... 1Sa 7:8 2199
ye shall *c* out in that day ... 1Sa 8:18 2199
because their *c* is come unto me ... 1Sa 9:16 6818
I yet to *c* any more unto the king ... 2Sa 19:28 2199
my *c* did enter into his ears ... 2Sa 22:7 7775
my God, to hearken unto the *c* ... 1Kin 8:28 7440
mocked them, and said, *C* aloud ... 1Kin 18:27 7121
she went forth to *c* unto the king ... 2Kin 8:3 6817
my God, to hearken unto the *c* ... 2Chr 6:19 7440
trumpets to *c* alarm against you ... 2Chr 13:12 7321
c unto thee in our affliction, ... 2Chr 20:9 2199
there was a great *c* of the people ... Neh 5:1 6818
very angry when I heard their *c* ... Neh 5:6 2201
heardest their *c* by the Red sea ... Neh 9:9 2201
cried with a loud and a bitter *c* ... Est 4:1 2201
of the fastings and their *c* ... Est 9:31 2201
blood, and let my *c* have no place ... Job 16:18 2201
I *c* out of wrong, but I am not ... Job 19:7 6817
I *c* aloud, but there is no ... Job 19:7 7768
Will God hear his *c* when trouble ... Job 27:9 6818
I *c* unto thee, and thou dost not ... Job 30:20 7768
though they *c* in his destruction ... Job 30:24 7769
If my land *c* against me, or that ... Job 31:38 2199
So that they cause the *c* of the ... Job 34:28 6818
he heareth the *c* of the afflicted ... Job 34:28 6818
they make the oppressed to *c* ... Job 35:9 2199
they *c* out by reason of the arm ... Job 35:9 7768
There they *c*, but none giveth ... Job 35:12 6817
they *c* not when he bindeth them ... Job 36:13 7768
when his young ones *c* unto God ... Job 38:41 7768
Hearken unto the voice of my *c* ... Ps 5:2 7773
not the *c* of the humble ... Ps 9:12 6818
right, O LORD, attend unto my *c* ... Ps 17:1 7440
my *c* came before him, even into ... Ps 18:6 7775
I *c* in the daytime, but thou ... Ps 22:2 7121
O LORD, when I *c* with my voice ... Ps 27:7 7121
Unto thee will I *c*, O LORD my ... Ps 28:1 7121
when I *c* unto thee, when I lift ... Ps 28:2 7768
and his ears are open unto their *c* ... Ps 34:15 7775
The righteous *c*, and the LORD ... Ps 34:17 6817
O LORD, and give ear unto my *c* ... Ps 39:12 7775
inclined unto me, and heard my *c* ... Ps 40:1 7775
at noon, will I pray, and *c* aloud ... Ps 55:17 1993
When I *c* unto thee, then shall ... Ps 56:9 7121
I will *c* unto God most high ... Ps 57:2 7121
Hear my *c*, O God ... Ps 61:1 7440
of the earth will I *c* unto thee ... Ps 61:2 7121
for I *c* unto thee daily ... Ps 86:3 7121
incline thine ear unto my *c* ... Ps 88:2 7440
He shall *c* unto me, Thou art my ... Ps 89:26 7121
LORD, and let my *c* come unto thee ... Ps 102:1 7775
affliction, when he heard their *c* ... Ps 106:44 7440
Then they *c* unto the LORD in ... Ps 107:19 2199
Then they *c* unto the LORD in ... Ps 107:28 6817
Let my *c* come near before thee, O ... Ps 119:169 7440
Lord, I *c* unto thee ... Ps 141:1 7121
unto my voice, when I *c* unto thee ... Ps 141:1 7121
Attend unto my *c* ... Ps 142:6 7440
he also will hear their *c* ... Ps 145:19 7775
and to the young ravens which *c* ... Ps 147:9 7121
Doth not wisdom *c* ... Prov 8:1 7121
his ears at the *c* of the poor ... Prov 21:13 2201
he also shall *c* himself ... Prov 21:13 7121
heard in quiet more than the *c* of ... Eccl 9:17 2201
for righteousness, but behold a *c* ... Is 5:7 6818
child shall have knowledge to *c* ... Is 8:4 7121
C out and shout, thou inhabitant ... Is 12:6 6670
shall *c* in their desolate houses ... Is 13:22 6030
c, O city ... Is 14:31 2199
And Heshbon shall *c*, and Elealeh ... Is 15:4 2199
soldiers of Moab shall *c* out ... Is 15:4 7321
My heart shall *c* out for Moab ... Is 15:5 2199
shall raise up a *c* of destruction ... Is 15:5 2201
For the *c* is gone round about the ... Is 15:8 2201
for they shall *c* unto the LORD ... Is 19:20 6817
they shall *c* aloud from the sea ... Is 24:14 6670
c ye out, and *c* ... Is 29:9 8173
unto thee at the voice of thy *c* ... Is 30:19 2201
valiant ones shall *c* without ... Is 33:7 6817
the satyr shall *c* to his fellow ... Is 34:14 7121
c unto her, that her warfare is ... Is 40:2 7121
The voice said, *C* ... Is 40:6 7121
And he said, What shall I *c* ... Is 40:6 7121
He shall not *c*, nor lift up, nor ... Is 42:2 6817
he shall *c*, yea, roar ... Is 42:13 7321
now will I *c* like a travailing ... Is 42:14 6463
whose *c* is in the ships ... Is 43:14 7440
yea, one shall *c* unto him ... Is 46:7 6817
c aloud, thou that didst not ... Is 54:1 6670
C aloud, spare not, lift up thy ... Is 58:1 7121
thou shalt *c*, and he shall say, ... Is 58:9 7768
but ye shall *c* for sorrow of ... Is 65:14 6817
c in the ears of Jerusalem, ... Jer 2:2 7121
thou not from this time *c* unto me ... Jer 3:4 7121
c, gather together, and say, ... Jer 4:5 7121
neither lift up *c* nor prayer for ... Jer 7:16 7440
Behold the voice of the *c* of the ... Jer 8:19 7775
and though they shall *c* unto me ... Jer 11:11 2199
c unto the gods unto whom they ... Jer 11:12 2199
neither lift up a *c* or prayer for ... Jer 11:14 7440
they *c* unto me for their trouble ... Jer 11:14 7121
the *c* of Jerusalem is gone up ... Jer 14:2 6682
fast, I will not hear their *c* ... Jer 14:12 7440
Let a *c* be heard from their ... Jer 18:22 2201
let him hear the *c* in the morning ... Jer 20:16 2201
Go up to Lebanon, and *c* ... Jer 22:20 6817
in Bashan, and *c* from the passages ... Jer 22:20 6817
Howl, ye shepherds, and *c* ... Jer 25:34 2199
A voice of the *c* of the shepherds ... Jer 25:36 6818
upon the mount Ephraim shall *c* ... Jer 31:6 7121
thy *c* hath filled the land ... Jer 46:12 6682
They did *c* there, Pharaoh king of ... Jer 46:17 7121
then the men shall *c*, and all the ... Jer 47:2 2199
ones have caused a *c* to be heard ... Jer 48:4 2201
have heard a *c* of destruction ... Jer 48:5 6818
howl and *c*; tell ye it in Arnon ... Jer 48:20 2199
I will *c* out for all Moab ... Jer 48:31 2199
From the *c* of Heshbon even unto ... Jer 48:34 2201
c, ye daughters of Rabbah, gird ... Jer 49:3 6817
at the *c* the noise thereof was ... Jer 49:21 6818
and they shall *c* unto them ... Jer 49:29 7121
the *c* is heard among the nations ... Jer 50:46 2201
A sound of a *c* cometh from ... Jer 51:54 2201
Arise, *c* out in the night ... Lam 2:19 7442
Also when I *c* and shout, he ... Lam 3:8 2199
ear at my breathing, at my *c* ... Lam 3:56 7775
though they *c* in mine ears with a ... Eze 8:18 7121
that *c* for all the abominations ... Eze 9:4 602
C and howl, son of man ... Eze 21:12 2199
Forbear to *c*, make no mourning ... Eze 24:17 602
of thy fall, when the wounded *c* ... Eze 26:15 602
the sound of the *c* of thy pilots ... Eze 27:28 2201
shall *c* bitterly, and shall cast ... Eze 27:30 2199
c aloud at Beth-aven, after thee, ... Hos 5:8 7321
Israel shall *c* unto me, My God, ... Hos 8:2 2199
your God, and *c* unto the LORD, ... Joel 1:14 2199
O LORD, to thee will I *c* ... Joel 1:19 7121
of the field *c* also unto thee ... Joel 1:20 6165
a young lion *c* out of his den ... Amos 3:4 5414,6963
that great city, and *c* against it ... Jonah 1:2 7121
sackcloth, and *c* mightily unto God ... Jonah 3:8 7121
Then shall they *c* unto the LORD ... Mic 3:4 2199
that bite with their teeth, and *c* ... Mic 3:5 7121
Now why dost thou *c* out aloud ... Mic 4:9 7321
Stand, stand, shall they *c* ... Nah 2:8
O LORD, how long shall I *c* ... Hab 1:2 7768
even *c* out unto thee of violence, ... Hab 1:2 2199
the stone shall *c* out of the wall ... Hab 2:11 2199

noise of a *c* from the fish gate ... Zeph 1:10 6818
mighty man shall *c* there bitterly ... Zeph 1:14 6873
C thou, saying, Thus saith the ... Zec 1:14 7121
C yet, saying, Thus saith the ... Zec 1:17 7121
He shall not strive, nor *c* ... Mt 12:19 *2905*
And at midnight there was a *c* made ... Mt 25:6 *2906*
of Nazareth, he began to *c* out ... Mk 10:47 *2896*
avenge his own elect, which *c* day ... Lk 18:7 *994*
stones would immediately *c* out ... Lk 19:40 *2896*
And there arose a great *c* ... Acts 23:9 *2906*
Spirit of adoption, whereby we *c* ... Rom 8:15 *2896*
break forth and *c*, thou that ... Gal 4:27 *994*
cried with a loud *c* to him that ... Rev 14:18 *2906*

CRYING {31}
when Eli heard the noise of the *c* ... 1Sa 4:14 6818
hand on her head, and went on *c* ... 2Sa 13:19 2201
regardeth he the *c* of the driver ... Job 39:7 8663
I am weary of my *c* ... Ps 69:3 7121
let not thy soul spare for his *c* ... Prov 19:18 4191
horseleach hath two daughters, *c* ... Prov 30:15
walls, and of *c* to the mountains ... Is 22:5 7771
There is a *c* for wine in the ... Is 24:11 6682
heard in her, nor the voice of *c* ... Is 65:19 2201
A voice of *c* shall be from ... Jer 48:3 6818
thereof with shoutings, *c* ... Zec 4:7
with weeping, and with *c* out ... Mal 2:13 603
The voice of one *c* in the ... Mt 3:3 *994*
two blind men followed him, *c* ... Mt 9:27 *2896*
the children *c* in the temple, and ... Mt 21:15 *2896*
The voice of one *c* in the ... Mk 1:3 *994*
the mountains, and in the tombs, *c* ... Mk 5:5 *2896*
the multitude *c* aloud began to ... Mk 15:8 *310*
The voice of one *c* in the ... Lk 3:4 *994*
c out, and saying, Thou art Christ ... Lk 4:41 *2896*
voice of one *c* in the wilderness ... Jn 1:23 *994*
c with loud voice, came out of ... Acts 8:7 *994*
ran in among the people, *c* out, ... Acts 14:14 *2896*
unto the rulers of the city, *c* ... Acts 17:6 *994*
C out, Men of Israel, help ... Acts 21:28 *2896*
of the people followed after, *c* ... Acts 21:36 *2896*
c that he ought not to live any ... Acts 25:24 *1916*
of his Son into your hearts, *c* ... Gal 4:6 *2896*
and supplications with strong *c* ... Heb 5:7 *2906*
c with a loud voice to him that ... Rev 14:15 *2896*
more death, neither sorrow, nor *c* ... Rev 21:4 *2906*

CRYSTAL {5}
The gold and the *c* cannot equal it ... Job 28:17 2137
as the colour of the terrible *c* ... Eze 1:22 7140
was a sea of glass like unto *c* ... Rev 4:6 *2930*
like a jasper stone, clear as *c* ... Rev 21:11 *2929*
of water of life, clear as *c* ... Rev 22:1 *2930*

CUBIT {47}
in a *c* shalt thou finish it above ... Gen 6:16 520
be the length thereof, and a *c* ... Ex 25:10 520
half the breadth thereof, and a *c* ... Ex 25:10 520
be the length thereof, and a *c* ... Ex 25:17 520
c the breadth thereof, and a *c* ... Ex 25:23 520
a *c* on the one side, and a *c* ... Ex 26:13 520
be the length of a board, and a *c* ... Ex 26:16 520
A *c* shall be the length thereof, ... Ex 30:2 520
and a *c* the breadth thereof ... Ex 30:2 520
and the breadth of a board one *c* ... Ex 36:21 520
half was the length of it, and a *c* ... Ex 37:1 520
a half the breadth of it, and a *c* ... Ex 37:1 520
was the length thereof, and one *c* ... Ex 37:6 520
c the breadth thereof, and a *c* ... Ex 37:10 520
a *c*, and the breadth of it a *c* ... Ex 37:25 520
of it, after the *c* of a man ... Deut 3:11 520
had two edges, of a *c* length ... Judg 3:16 1574
knops compassing it, ten in a *c* ... 1Kin 7:24 520
the chapiter and above was a *c* ... 1Kin 7:31 520
after the work of the base, a *c* ... 1Kin 7:31 520
a wheel was a *c* and half a *c* ... 1Kin 7:32 520
a round compass of half a *c* high ... 1Kin 7:35 520
ten in a *c*, compassing the sea ... 2Chr 4:3 520
reed of six cubits long by the *c* ... Eze 40:5 520
chambers was one *c* on this side ... Eze 40:12 520
the space was one *c* on that side ... Eze 40:12 520
a *c* and an half long, and a *c* ... Eze 40:42 520
and an half broad, and one *c* high ... Eze 40:42 520
breadth inward, a way of one *c* ... Eze 42:4 520
The *c* is a *c* and an hand ... Eze 43:13 520
The *c* is a *c* and an hand ... Eze 43:13 520
be a *c*, and the breadth a *c* ... Eze 43:13 520
two cubits, and the breadth one *c* ... Eze 43:14 520
four cubits, and the breadth one *c* ... Eze 43:14 520
border about it shall be half a *c* ... Eze 43:17 520
bottom thereof shall be a *c* about ... Eze 43:17 520
can add one *c* unto his stature ... Mt 6:27 *4083*
can add to his stature one *c* ... Lk 12:25 *4083*

CUBITS {215}
the ark shall be three hundred *c* ... Gen 6:15 520
c, the breadth of it fifty *c* ... Gen 6:15 520
and the height of it thirty *c* ... Gen 6:15 520
Fifteen *c* upward did the waters ... Gen 7:20 520
two *c* and a half shall be the ... Ex 25:10 520
two *c* and a half shall be the ... Ex 25:17 520
two *c* shall be the length thereof ... Ex 25:23 520
shall be eight and twenty *c* ... Ex 26:2 520
the breadth of one curtain four *c* ... Ex 26:2 520
of one curtain shall be thirty *c* ... Ex 26:8 520
the breadth of one curtain four *c* ... Ex 26:8 520
Ten *c* shall be the length of a ... Ex 26:16 520
five *c* long, and five *c* broad ... Ex 27:1 520
height thereof shall be three *c* ... Ex 27:1 520
of an hundred *c* long for one side ... Ex 27:9 520
be hangings of an hundred *c* long ... Ex 27:11
side shall be hangings of fifty *c* ... Ex 27:12 520
side eastward shall be fifty *c* ... Ex 27:13 520
of the gate shall be fifteen *c* ... Ex 27:14 520
side shall be hangings fifteen *c* ... Ex 27:15
shall be an hanging of twenty *c* ... Ex 27:16 520
the court shall be an hundred *c* ... Ex 27:18 520
the height five *c* of fine twined ... Ex 27:18 520
two *c* shall be the height thereof ... Ex 30:2 520
one curtain was twenty and eight *c* ... Ex 36:9 520
the breadth of one curtain four *c* ... Ex 36:9 520
of one curtain was thirty *c* ... Ex 36:15 520
four *c* was the breadth of one ... Ex 36:15 520
The length of a board was ten *c* ... Ex 36:21 520
two *c* and a half was the length of ... Ex 37:1 520
two *c* and a half was the length ... Ex 37:6 520
two *c* was the length thereof, and ... Ex 37:10 520
two *c* was the height of it ... Ex 37:25 520
five *c* was the length thereof, and ... Ex 38:1 520
five *c* the breadth thereof ... Ex 38:1 520
three *c* the height thereof ... Ex 38:1 520
fine twined linen, an hundred *c* ... Ex 38:9 520
the hangings were an hundred *c* ... Ex 38:11 520
side were hangings of fifty *c* ... Ex 38:12 520
the east side eastward fifty *c* ... Ex 38:13 520
side of the gate were fifteen *c* ... Ex 38:14 520
hand, were hangings of fifteen *c* ... Ex 38:15 520
twenty *c* was the length, and the ... Ex 38:18 520
height in the breadth was five *c* ... Ex 38:18 520
as it were two *c* high upon the ... Num 11:31 520
outward a thousand *c* round about ... Num 35:4 520
on the east side two thousand *c* ... Num 35:5 520
on the south side two thousand *c* ... Num 35:5 520
on the west side two thousand *c* ... Num 35:5 520
on the north side two thousand *c* ... Num 35:5 520
nine *c* was the length thereof, and ... Deut 3:11 520
four *c* the breadth of it, after ... Deut 3:11 520
about two thousand *c* by measure ... Josh 3:4 520
of Gath, whose height was six *c* ... 1Sa 17:4 520
length thereof was threescore *c* ... 1Kin 6:2 520
and the breadth thereof twenty *c* ... 1Kin 6:2
and the height thereof thirty *c* ... 1Kin 6:2 520
twenty *c* was the length thereof, ... 1Kin 6:3 520
ten *c* was the breadth thereof ... 1Kin 6:3 520
chamber was five *c* broad ... 1Kin 6:6 520
and the middle was six *c* broad ... 1Kin 6:6 520
and the third was seven *c* broad ... 1Kin 6:6 520
all the house, five *c* high ... 1Kin 6:10 520
he built twenty *c* on the sides of ... 1Kin 6:16 520
before it, was forty *c* long ... 1Kin 6:17 520
forepart was twenty *c* in length ... 1Kin 6:20 520
twenty *c* in breadth ... 1Kin 6:20 520
twenty *c* in the height thereof ... 1Kin 6:20 520
of olive tree, each ten *c* high ... 1Kin 6:23 520
five *c* was the one wing of the ... 1Kin 6:24 520
five *c* the other wing of the ... 1Kin 6:24 520
part of the other were ten *c* ... 1Kin 6:24 520
And the other cherub was ten *c* ... 1Kin 6:25 520
of the one cherub was ten *c* ... 1Kin 6:26 520
length thereof was an hundred *c* ... 1Kin 7:2 520
and the breadth thereof fifty *c* ... 1Kin 7:2 520
and the height thereof thirty *c* ... 1Kin 7:2 520
the length thereof was fifty *c* ... 1Kin 7:6 520
and the breadth thereof thirty *c* ... 1Kin 7:6 520
ten *c*, and stones of eight *c* ... 1Kin 7:10 520
brass, of eighteen *c* high apiece ... 1Kin 7:15 520
a line of twelve *c* did compass ... 1Kin 7:15 520
of the one chapiter was five *c* ... 1Kin 7:16 520
of the other chapiter was five *c* ... 1Kin 7:16 520
of lily work in the porch, four *c* ... 1Kin 7:19 520
ten *c* from the one brim to the ... 1Kin 7:23 520
about, and his height was five *c* ... 1Kin 7:23 520
a line of thirty *c* did compass it ... 1Kin 7:23 520
four *c* was the length of one base ... 1Kin 7:27 520
four *c* the breadth thereof, and ... 1Kin 7:27 520
and three *c* the height of it ... 1Kin 7:27 520
and every laver was four *c* ... 1Kin 7:38 520
the corner gate, four hundred *c* ... 2Kin 14:13 520
of the one pillar was eighteen *c* ... 2Kin 25:17 520
height of the chapiter three *c* ... 2Kin 25:17 520
man of great stature, five *c* high ... 1Chr 11:23 520
The length by *c* after the first ... 2Chr 3:3 520
first measure was threescore *c* ... 2Chr 3:3 520
c, and the breadth twenty *c* ... 2Chr 3:3 520
breadth of the house, twenty *c* ... 2Chr 3:4 520
breadth of the house, twenty *c* ... 2Chr 3:8 520
and the breadth thereof twenty *c* ... 2Chr 3:8 520
the cherubims were twenty *c* long ... 2Chr 3:11 520
wing of the one cherub was five *c* ... 2Chr 3:11 520
other wing was likewise five *c* ... 2Chr 3:11 520
of the other cherub was five *c* ... 2Chr 3:12 520
and the other wing was five *c* also ... 2Chr 3:12 520
spread themselves forth twenty *c* ... 2Chr 3:13 520
pillars of thirty and five *c* high ... 2Chr 3:15 520
top of each of them was five *c* ... 2Chr 3:15 520
twenty *c* the length thereof, and ... 2Chr 4:1 520
twenty *c* the breadth thereof, and ... 2Chr 4:1 520
and ten *c* the height thereof ... 2Chr 4:1 520
sea of ten *c* from brim to brim ... 2Chr 4:2 520
five *c* the height thereof ... 2Chr 4:2 520
a line of thirty *c* did compass it ... 2Chr 4:2 520
a brasen scaffold, of five *c* long ... 2Chr 6:13 520
five *c* broad, and three *c* ... 2Chr 6:13 520
the corner gate, four hundred *c* ... 2Chr 25:23 520
the height thereof threescore *c* ... Ezr 6:3 521
the breadth thereof threescore *c* ... Ezr 6:3 521
a thousand *c* on the wall unto the ... Neh 3:13 520
a gallows be made of fifty *c* high ... Est 5:14 520
also, the gallows fifty *c* high ... Est 7:9 520
of one pillar was eighteen *c* ... Jer 52:21 520
fillet of twelve *c* did compass it ... Jer 52:21 520
height of one chapiter was five *c* ... Jer 52:22 520
reed of six *c* long by the cubit ... Eze 40:5 520
the little chambers were five *c* ... Eze 40:7 520
he the porch of the gate, eight *c* ... Eze 40:9 520
and the posts thereof, two *c* ... Eze 40:9 520
of the entry of the gate, ten *c* ... Eze 40:11 520
length of the gate, thirteen *c* ... Eze 40:11 520
chambers were six *c* on this side ... Eze 40:12 520
and six *c* on that side ... Eze 40:12 520
the breadth was five and twenty *c* ... Eze 40:13 520
made also posts of threescore *c* ... Eze 40:14 520
of the inner gate were fifty *c* ... Eze 40:15 520
without, an hundred *c* eastward ... Eze 40:19 520
the length thereof was fifty *c* ... Eze 40:21 520
and the breadth five and twenty *c* ... Eze 40:21 520
from gate to gate an hundred *c* ... Eze 40:23 520
the length was fifty *c* ... Eze 40:25 520
and the breadth five and twenty *c* ... Eze 40:25 520
toward the south an hundred *c* ... Eze 40:27 520
it was fifty *c* long ... Eze 40:29 520
and five and twenty *c* broad ... Eze 40:29 520
about were five and twenty *c* long ... Eze 40:30 520
and five *c* broad ... Eze 40:30 520
it was fifty *c* long ... Eze 40:33 520
and five and twenty *c* broad ... Eze 40:33 520
the length was fifty *c*, and the ... Eze 40:36 520
and the breadth five and twenty *c* ... Eze 40:36 520
the court, an hundred *c* long ... Eze 40:47 520
and an hundred *c* broad ... Eze 40:47 520
five *c* on this side ... Eze 40:48 520
and five *c* on that side ... Eze 40:48 520
the gate was three *c* on this side ... Eze 40:48 520
and three *c* on that side ... Eze 40:48 520
length of the porch was twenty *c* ... Eze 40:49 520
and the breadth eleven *c* ... Eze 40:49 520
six *c* broad on the one side, and ... Eze 41:1 520
six *c* broad on the other side, ... Eze 41:1 520
the breadth of the door was ten *c* ... Eze 41:2 520
door were five *c* on the one side ... Eze 41:2 520
and five *c* on the other side ... Eze 41:2 520
the length thereof, forty *c* ... Eze 41:2 520
and the breadth, twenty *c* ... Eze 41:2 520
the post of the door, two *c* ... Eze 41:3 520
and the door, six *c* ... Eze 41:3 520
the breadth of the door, seven *c* ... Eze 41:3 520
the length thereof, twenty *c* ... Eze 41:4 520
and the breadth, twenty *c*, before ... Eze 41:4 520
the wall of the house, six *c* ... Eze 41:5 520
of every side chamber, four *c* ... Eze 41:5 520
were a full reed of six great *c* ... Eze 41:8 520
side chamber without, was five *c* ... Eze 41:9 520
was the wideness of twenty *c* ... Eze 41:10 520
was left was five *c* round about ... Eze 41:11 520
the west was seventy *c* broad ... Eze 41:12 520
was five *c* thick round about ... Eze 41:12 520
and the length thereof ninety *c* ... Eze 41:12 520
the house, an hundred *c* long ... Eze 41:13 520
walls thereof, an hundred *c* long ... Eze 41:13 520
toward the east, an hundred *c* ... Eze 41:14 520
on the other side, an hundred *c* ... Eze 41:15 520
altar of wood was three *c* high ... Eze 41:22 520
and the length thereof two *c* ... Eze 41:22 520
an hundred *c* was the north door ... Eze 42:2 520
and the breadth was fifty *c* ... Eze 42:2 520
Over against the twenty *c* which ... Eze 42:3
a walk of ten *c* breadth inward ... Eze 42:4 520
the length thereof was fifty *c* ... Eze 42:7 520
in the utter court was fifty *c* ... Eze 42:8 520
the temple were an hundred *c* ... Eze 42:8 520
measures of the altar after the *c* ... Eze 43:13 520
the lower settle shall be two *c* ... Eze 43:14 520
greater settle shall be four *c* ... Eze 43:14 520
So the altar shall be four *c* ... Eze 43:15 520
the altar shall be twelve *c* long ... Eze 43:16
settle shall be fourteen *c* long ... Eze 43:17
fifty *c* round about for the ... Eze 45:2 520
courts joined of forty *c* long ... Eze 46:22
he measured a thousand *c* ... Eze 47:3 520
whose height was threescore *c* ... Dan 3:1 521
and the breadth thereof six *c* ... Dan 3:1 521
the length thereof is twenty *c* ... Zec 5:2 520
and the breadth thereof ten *c* ... Zec 5:2 520
but as it were two hundred *c* ... Jn 21:8 *4088*
an hundred and forty and four *c* ... Rev 21:17 *4088*

CUCKOW {2}
owl, and the night hawk, and the *c* ... Lev 11:16 7828
owl, and the night hawk, and the *c* ... Deut 14:15 7828

CUCUMBERS {2}
the *c*, and the melons, and the ... Num 11:5 7180
as a lodge in a garden of *c* ... Is 1:8 4750

CUD {11}
is clovenfooted, and cheweth the *c* ... Lev 11:3 1625
not eat of them that chew the *c* ... Lev 11:4 1625
camel, because he cheweth the *c* ... Lev 11:4 1625
coney, because he cheweth the *c* ... Lev 11:5 1625
hare, because he cheweth the *c* ... Lev 11:6 1625
yet he cheweth not the *c* ... Lev 11:7 1625
clovenfooted, nor cheweth the *c* ... Lev 11:26 1625
cheweth the *c* among the beasts, ... Deut 14:6 1625
not eat of them that chew the *c* ... Deut 14:7 1625
for they chew the *c*, but divide ... Deut 14:7 1625
the hoof, yet cheweth not the *c* ... Deut 14:8 1625

CUMBERED {1}
But Martha was *c* about much ... Lk 10:40 *4049*

CUMBERETH {1}
why *c* it the ground ... Lk 13:7 *2673*

CUMBRANCE {1}
can I myself alone bear your *c* ... Deut 1:12 2960

CUMI *(coo'-mi)* {1}
hand, and said unto her, Talitha *c* ... Mk 5:41 *2891*

CUMMIN {4}
the fitches, and scatter the *c* ... Is 28:25 3646
wheel turned about upon the *c* ... Is 28:27 3646
with a staff, and the *c* with a rod ... Is 28:27 3646
pay tithe of mint and anise and *c* ... Mt 23:23 *2951*

CUN See CHUN.

CUNNING {33}
and Esau was a *c* hunter, a man of ... Gen 25:27 3045
with cherubims of *c* work shalt ... Ex 26:1 2803
and fine twined linen of *c* work ... Ex 26:31 2803
and fine twined linen, with *c* work ... Ex 28:6 2803
of judgment with *c* work ... Ex 28:15 2803
To devise *c* works, to work in ... Ex 31:4 4284
to make any manner of *c* work ... Ex 35:33 4284
of the *c* workman, and of the ... Ex 35:35 2803
and of those that devise *c* work ... Ex 35:35 4284
cherubims of *c* work made he them ... Ex 36:8 2803
cherubims made he it of *c* work ... Ex 36:35 2803
a *c* workman, and an embroiderer in ... Ex 38:23 2803
and in the fine linen, with *c* work ... Ex 39:3 2803
he made the breastplate of *c* work ... Ex 39:8 2803
who is a *c* player on an harp ... 1Sa 16:16 3045
that is *c* in playing, and a mighty ... 1Sa 16:18 3045
c to work all works in brass ... 1Kin 7:14 1847
all manner of *c* men for every ... 1Chr 22:15 2450
of the LORD, even all that were *c* ... 1Chr 25:7 995
therefore a man *c* to work in gold ... 2Chr 2:7 2450
can skill to grave with the *c* men ... 2Chr 2:7 2450
And now I have sent a *c* man ... 2Chr 2:13 2450
be put to him, with thy *c* men ... 2Chr 2:14 2450
with the *c* men of my lord David ... 2Chr 2:14 2450
engines, invented by *c* men ... 2Chr 26:15 2803
let my right hand forget her *c* ... Ps 137:5
work of the hands of a *c* workman ... Song 7:1 542
the *c* artificer, and the eloquent ... Is 3:3 2450
he seeketh unto him a *c* workman ... Is 40:20 2450
and send for *c* women, that they ... Jer 9:17 2450
they are all the work of *c* men ... Jer 10:9 2450
c in knowledge, and understanding ... Dan 1:4 3045
c craftiness, whereby they lie in ... Eph 4:14

CUNNINGLY {1}
not followed *c* devised fables ... 2Pet 1:16

CUP {68}
Pharaoh's *c* was in my hand ... Gen 40:11 3563
and pressed them into Pharaoh's *c* ... Gen 40:11 3563
I gave the *c* into Pharaoh's hand ... Gen 40:11 3563
deliver Pharaoh's *c* into his hand ... Gen 40:13 3563
he gave the *c* into Pharaoh's hand ... Gen 40:21 3563
And put my *c*, the silver *c* ... Gen 44:2 1375
the *c* was found in Benjamin's ... Gen 44:12 1375
he also with whom the *c* is found ... Gen 44:16 1375
man in whose hand the *c* is found ... Gen 44:17 1375
own meat, and drank of his own *c* ... 2Sa 12:3 3563
was wrought like the brim of a *c* ... 1Kin 7:26 3563
like the work of the brim of a *c* ... 2Chr 4:5 3563
shall be the portion of their *c* ... Ps 11:6 3563
of mine inheritance and of my *c* ... Ps 16:5 3563
my *c* runneth over ... Ps 23:5 3563
waters of a full *c* are wrung out ... Ps 73:10
the hand of the LORD there is a *c* ... Ps 75:8 3563
I will take the *c* of salvation ... Ps 116:13 3563
it giveth his colour in the *c* ... Prov 23:31 3599
of the LORD the *c* of his fury ... Is 51:17 3563
the dregs of the *c* of trembling ... Is 51:17 3563
of thine hand the *c* of trembling ... Is 51:22 3563
the dregs of the *c* of my fury ... Is 51:22 3563
the *c* of consolation to drink for ... Jer 16:7 3563
Take the wine *c* of this fury at ... Jer 25:15 3563
Then took I the *c* at the LORD's ... Jer 25:17 3563
take the *c* at thine hand to drink ... Jer 25:28 3563
of the *c* have assuredly drunken ... Jer 49:12 3563
a golden *c* in the LORD's hand ... Jer 51:7 3563
the *c* also shall pass through ... Lam 4:21 3563
will I give her *c* into thine hand ... Eze 23:31 3563
drink of thy sister's *c* deep ... Eze 23:32 3563
with the *c* of astonishment and ... Eze 23:33 3563
with the *c* of thy sister Samaria ... Eze 23:33 3563
the *c* of the LORD's right hand ... Hab 2:16 3563
I will make Jerusalem a *c* of ... Zec 12:2 5592
c of cold water only in the name ... Mt 10:42 *4221*
of the *c* that I shall drink of ... Mt 20:22 *4221*
Ye shall drink indeed of my *c* ... Mt 20:23 *4221*
make clean the outside of the *c* ... Mt 23:25 *4221*
first that which is within the *c* ... Mt 23:26 *4221*
And he took the *c*, and gave thanks, ... Mt 26:27 *4221*
possible, let this *c* pass from me ... Mt 26:39 *4221*
if this *c* may not pass away from ... Mt 26:42 *4221*
a *c* of water to drink in my name ... Mk 9:41 *4221*
ye drink of the *c* that I drink of ... Mk 10:38 *4221*
drink of the *c* that I drink of ... Mk 10:39 *4221*
And he took the *c*, and when he had ... Mk 14:23 *4221*
take away this *c* from me ... Mk 14:36 *4221*
make clean the outside of the *c* ... Lk 11:39 *4221*
And he took the *c*, and gave thanks, ... Lk 22:17 *4221*
Likewise also the *c* after supper ... Lk 22:20 *4221*
This *c* is the new testament in my ... Lk 22:20 *4221*
be willing, remove this *c* from me ... Lk 22:42 *4221*
the *c* which my Father hath given ... Jn 18:11 *4221*
The *c* of blessing which we bless, ... 1Cor 10:16 *4221*
Ye cannot drink the *c* of the Lord ... 1Cor 10:21 *4221*
and the *c* of devils ... 1Cor 10:21 *4221*
same manner also he took the *c* ... 1Cor 11:25 *4221*
This *c* is the new testament in my ... 1Cor 11:25 *4221*
eat this bread, and drink this *c* ... 1Cor 11:26 *4221*
drink this *c* of the Lord, ... 1Cor 11:27 *4221*
of that bread, and drink of that *c* ... 1Cor 11:28 *4221*
into the *c* of his indignation ... Rev 14:10 *4221*
to give unto her the *c* of the ... Rev 16:19 *4221*
having a golden *c* in her hand ... Rev 17:4 *4221*
in the *c* which she hath filled ... Rev 18:6 *4221*

CUPBEARER {1}
For I was the king's *c* ... Neh 1:11 4945

CUPBEARERS {2}
and their apparel, and his *c* ... 1Kin 10:5 4945
his *c* also, and their apparel ... 2Chr 9:4 4945

CUPS {6}
and the bowls, and the *c* ... 1Chr 28:17 7184
quantity, from the vessels of *c* ... Is 22:24 101
pots full of wine, and *c*, and I ... Jer 35:5 3563
and the spoons, and the *c* ... Jer 52:19 4518
to hold, as the washing of *c* ... Mk 7:4 *4221*
men, as the washing of pots and *c* ... Mk 7:8 *4221*

CURDLED {1}
out as milk, and *c* me like cheese ... Job 10:10 7087

CURE {4}
health and *c*, and I will *c* them ... Jer 33:6 7495
heal you, nor *c* you of your wound ... Hos 5:13 1455
and they could not *c* him ... Mt 17:16 *2323*
over all devils, and to *c* diseases ... Lk 9:1 *2323*

CURED {4}
for thou shalt not be *c* ... Jer 46:11 8585
the child was *c* from that very ... Mt 17:18 *2323*
in that same hour he *c* many of ... Lk 7:21 *2323*
said unto him that was *c*, It is ... Jn 5:10 *2323*

CURES {1}
I do *c* to day and to morrow, and ... Lk 13:32 *2392*

CURIOUS {10}
the *c* girdle of the ephod, which ... Ex 28:8
above the *c* girdle of the ephod ... Ex 28:27
above the *c* girdle of the ephod ... Ex 28:28
gird him with the *c* girdle of the ... Ex 29:5
And to devise *c* works, to work in ... Ex 35:32 4284
the *c* girdle of his ephod, that ... Ex 39:5
above the *c* girdle of the ephod ... Ex 39:20
above the *c* girdle of the ephod ... Ex 39:21
with the *c* girdle of the ephod ... Lev 8:7
used *c* arts brought their books ... Acts 19:19 *4021*

CURIOUSLY {1}
c wrought in the lowest parts of ... Ps 139:15 7551

CURRENT {1}
c money with the merchant ... Gen 23:16 5674

CURSE {101}
I will not again *c* the ground any ... Gen 8:21 7043
thee, and *c* him that curseth thee ... Gen 12:3 779
and I shall bring a *c* upon me ... Gen 27:12 7045
said unto him, Upon me be thy *c* ... Gen 27:13 7045
nor *c* the ruler of thy people ... Ex 22:28 779
Thou shalt not *c* the deaf ... Lev 19:14 7043
bitter water that causeth the *c* ... Num 5:18 779
bitter water that causeth the *c* ... Num 5:19 779
the woman, The LORD make thee a *c* ... Num 5:21 423
the *c* shall go into thy bowels ... Num 5:22 779
bitter water that causeth the *c* ... Num 5:24 779
the *c* shall enter into her ... Num 5:24 779
the *c* shall enter into her ... Num 5:27 779
shall be a *c* among her people ... Num 5:27 423
I pray thee, *c* me this people ... Num 22:6 779
come now, *c* me them ... Num 22:11 6895
thou shalt not *c* the people ... Num 22:12 779
I pray thee, *c* me this people ... Num 22:17 6895
c me Jacob, and come, defy Israel ... Num 23:7 779
How shall I *c*, whom God hath not ... Num 23:8 5344
I took thee to *c* mine enemies ... Num 23:11 6895
and *c* me them from thence ... Num 23:13 6895
Neither *c* them at all, nor bless ... Num 23:25 6895
thou mayest *c* me them from thence ... Num 23:27 6895
I called thee to *c* mine enemies ... Num 24:10 6895
you this day a blessing and a *c* ... Deut 11:26 7045
And a *c*, if ye will not obey the ... Deut 11:28 7045
Gerizim, and the *c* upon mount Ebal ... Deut 11:29 7045
Pethor of Mesopotamia, to *c* thee ... Deut 23:4 7043
the *c* into a blessing unto thee ... Deut 23:5 7045
shall stand upon mount Ebal to *c* ... Deut 27:13 7045
he heareth the words of this *c* ... Deut 29:19 423
upon thee, the blessing and the *c* ... Deut 30:1 7045
and make the camp of Israel a *c* ... Josh 6:18 2764
Balaam the son of Beor to *c* you ... Josh 24:9 7043
C ye Meroz, said the angel of the ... Judg 5:23 779
c ye bitterly the inhabitants ... Judg 5:23 779
upon them came the *c* of Jotham ... Judg 9:57 7045
this dead dog *c* my lord the king ... 2Sa 16:9 7043
so let him *c*, because the LORD ... 2Sa 16:10 7043
LORD hath said unto him, *C* David ... 2Sa 16:10 7043
let him alone, and let him *c* ... 2Sa 16:11 7043
c in the day when I went to ... 1Kin 2:8 7045
should become a desolation and a *c* ... 2Kin 22:19 7045
their nobles, and entered into a *c* ... Neh 10:29 423
them, that he should *c* them ... Neh 13:2 7043
God turned the *c* into a blessing ... Neh 13:2 7045
he will *c* thee to thy face ... Job 1:11 1288
he will *c* thee to thy face ... Job 2:5 1288
c God, and die ... Job 2:9 1288
Let them *c* it ... Job 3:8 5344
that *c* the day, who are ready ... Job 3:8 779
to sin by wishing a *c* to his soul ... Job 31:30 423
their mouth, but they *c* inwardly ... Ps 62:4 7043
Let them *c*, but bless thou ... Ps 109:28 7043
The *c* of the LORD is in the house ... Prov 3:33 3994
corn, the people shall *c* him ... Prov 11:26 5344
him shall the people *c*, nations ... Prov 24:24 5344
so the *c* causeless shall not come ... Prov 26:2 7045
it shall be counted a *c* to him ... Prov 27:14 7045
his eyes shall have many a *c* ... Prov 28:27 3994
unto his master, lest he *c* thee ... Prov 30:10 7043
lest thou hear thy servant *c* thee ... Eccl 7:21 7043
C not the king, no not in thy ... Eccl 10:20 7043
c not the rich in thy bedchamber ... Eccl 10:20 7043
c their king and their God, and ... Is 8:21 7043
hath the *c* devoured the earth ... Is 24:6 423
and upon the people of my *c* ... Is 34:5 2764
and have given Jacob to the *c* ... Is 43:28 2764
your name for a *c* unto my chosen ... Is 65:15 7621
yet every one of them doth *c* me ... Jer 15:10 7043
and a proverb, a taunt and a *c* ... Jer 24:9 7045
astonishment, an hissing, and a *c* ... Jer 25:18 7045
will make this city a *c* to all ... Jer 26:6 7045
kingdoms of the earth, to be a *c* ... Jer 29:18 423
of them shall be taken up a *c* by ... Jer 29:22 7045
and an astonishment, and a *c* ... Jer 42:18 7045
off, and that ye might be a *c* ... Jer 44:8 7045
and an astonishment, and a *c* ... Jer 44:12 7045
and an astonishment, and a *c* ... Jer 44:22 7045
a reproach, a waste, and a *c* ... Jer 49:13 7045
sorrow of heart, thy *c* unto them ... Lam 3:65 8381
therefore the *c* is poured upon us ... Dan 9:11 423
This is the *c* that goeth forth ... Zec 5:3 423
as ye were a *c* among the heathen ... Zec 8:13 7045
I will even send a *c* upon you ... Mal 2:2 3994
and I will *c* your blessings ... Mal 2:2 779
Ye are cursed with a *c* ... Mal 3:9 3994
come and smite the earth with a *c* ... Mal 4:6 2764
enemies, bless them that *c* you ... Mt 5:44 *2672*
Then began he to *c* and to swear, ... Mt 26:74 *2653*
But he began to *c* and to swear, ... Mk 14:71 *332*
Bless them that *c* you, and pray ... Lk 6:28 *2672*
and bound themselves under a *c* ... Acts 23:12 *332*
bound ourselves under a great *c* ... Acts 23:14 *332*
bless, and *c* not ... Rom 12:14 *2672*
works of the law are under the *c* ... Gal 3:10 *2671*
redeemed us from the *c* of the law ... Gal 3:13 *2671*
being made a *c* for us ... Gal 3:13 *2671*
and therewith *c* we men, which are ... Jas 3:9 *2672*
And there shall be no more *c* ... Rev 22:3 *2652*

CURSED {72}
thou art *c* above all cattle, and ... Gen 3:14 779
c is the ground for thy sake ... Gen 3:17 779
now art thou *c* from the earth, ... Gen 4:11 779
the ground which the LORD hath *c* ... Gen 5:29 779
And he said, *C* be Canaan ... Gen 9:25 779
c be every one that curseth thee, ... Gen 27:29 779
C be their anger, for it was ... Gen 49:7 779
he hath *c* his father or his ... Lev 20:9 7043
the name of the LORD, and *c* ... Lev 24:11 7043
him that hath *c* without the camp ... Lev 24:14 7043
him that had *c* out of the camp ... Lev 24:23 7043
and he whom thou cursest is *c* ... Num 22:6 779
I curse, whom God hath not *c* ... Num 23:8 6895
c is he that curseth thee ... Num 24:9 779
lest thou be a *c* thing like it ... Deut 7:26 2764
for it is a *c* thing ... Deut 7:26 2764
of the *c* thing to thine hand ... Deut 13:17 2764
C be the man that maketh any ... Deut 27:15 779
C be he that setteth light by his ... Deut 27:16 779
C be he that removeth his ... Deut 27:17 779
C be he that maketh the blind to ... Deut 27:18 779
C be he that perverteth the ... Deut 27:19 779
C be he that lieth with his ... Deut 27:20 779
C be he that lieth with any ... Deut 27:21 779
C be he that lieth with his ... Deut 27:22 779
C be he that lieth with his ... Deut 27:23 779
C be he that smiteth his ... Deut 27:24 779
C be he that taketh reward to ... Deut 27:25 779
C be he that confirmeth not all ... Deut 27:26 779
C shalt thou be in the city, and ... Deut 28:16 779
c shalt thou be in the field ... Deut 28:16 779
C shall be thy basket and thy ... Deut 28:17 779
C shall be the fruit of thy body, ... Deut 28:18 779
C shalt thou be when thou comest ... Deut 28:19 779
c shalt thou be when thou goest ... Deut 28:19 779
C be the man before the LORD, ... Josh 6:26 779
Now therefore ye are *c*, and there ... Josh 9:23 779
did eat and drink, and *c* Abimelech ... Judg 9:27 7043
C be he that giveth a wife to ... Judg 21:18 779
C be the man that eateth any food ... 1Sa 14:24 779
C be the man that eateth any food ... 1Sa 14:28 779
the Philistine *c* David by his ... 1Sa 17:43 7043
c be they before the LORD ... 1Sa 26:19 779
came forth, and *c* still as he came ... 2Sa 16:5 7043
And thus said Shimei when he *c* ... 2Sa 16:7 7043
c as he went, and threw stones at ... 2Sa 16:13 7043
because he *c* the LORD's anointed ... 2Sa 19:21 7043
which *c* me with a grievous curse ... 1Kin 2:8 7043
c them in the name of the LORD ... 2Kin 2:24 7043
and said, Go, see now this *c* woman ... 2Kin 9:34 779
c them, and smote certain of them, ... Neh 13:25 7043
sinned, and *c* God in their hearts ... Job 1:5 1288
Job his mouth, and *c* his day ... Job 3:1 7043
but suddenly I *c* his habitation ... Job 5:3 5344

their portion is c in the earth ... Job 24:18 7043
they that be c of him shall be ... Ps 37:22 7043
hast rebuked the proud that are c ... Ps 119:21 779
thyself likewise hast c others ... Eccl 7:22 7043
C be the man that obeyeth not the ... Jer 11:3 779
C be the man that trusteth in man ... Jer 17:5 779
C be the day wherein I was born ... Jer 20:14 779
C be the man who brought tidings ... Jer 20:15 779
C be he that doeth the work of ... Jer 48:10 779
c be he that keepeth back his ... Jer 48:10 779
But c be the deceiver, which hath ... Mal 1:14 779
I have c them already, because ye ... Mal 2:2 779
Ye are c with a curse ... Mal 3:9 779
left hand, Depart from me, ye c ... Mt 25:41 *2672*
who knoweth not the law are c ... Jn 7:49 *1944*
C is every one that continueth ... Gal 3:10 *1944*
C is every one that hangeth on a ... Gal 3:13 *1944*
with covetous practices; c children ... 2Pet 2:14 *2671*

CURSEDST {2}
from thee, about which thou c ... Judg 17:2 422
which thou c is withered away ... Mk 11:21 *2672*

CURSES {8}
shall write these c in a book ... Num 5:23 423
that all these c shall come upon ... Deut 28:15 7045
Moreover all these c shall come ... Deut 28:45 7045
all the c that are written in ... Deut 29:20 423
according to all the c of the ... Deut 29:21 423
to bring upon it all the c that ... Deut 29:27 7045
all these c upon thine enemies ... Deut 30:7 423
even all the c that are written ... 2Chr 34:24 423

CURSEST {1}
and he whom thou c is cursed ... Num 22:6 779

CURSETH {10}
thee, and curse him that c thee ... Gen 12:3 7043
cursed be every one that c thee ... Gen 27:29 779
he that c his father, or his ... Ex 21:17 7043
For every one that c his father ... Lev 20:9 7043
Whosoever c his God shall bear ... Lev 24:15 7043
thee, and cursed is he that c thee ... Num 24:9 779
Whoso c his father or his mother, ... Prov 20:20 7043
a generation that c their father ... Prov 30:11 7043
He that c father or mother, let ... Mt 15:4 *2551*
Whoso c father or mother, let him ... Mk 7:10 *2551*

CURSING {12}
the woman with an oath of c ... Num 5:21 423
The LORD shall send upon thee c ... Deut 28:20 3994
you life and death, blessing and c ... Deut 30:19 7045
me good for his c this day ... 2Sa 16:12 7045
His mouth is full of c and deceit ... Ps 10:7 423
and for c and lying which they ... Ps 59:12 423
As he loved c, so let it come ... Ps 109:17 7045
with c like as with his garment ... Ps 109:18 7045
he heareth c, and bewrayeth it not ... Prov 29:24 423
Whose mouth is full of c and ... Rom 3:14 *685*
is rejected, and is nigh unto c ... Heb 6:8 *2671*
mouth proceedeth blessing and c ... Jas 3:10 *2671*

CURSINGS {1}
of the law, the blessings and c ... Josh 8:34 7045

CURTAIN {26}
length of one c shall be eight ... Ex 26:2 3407
the breadth of one c four cubits ... Ex 26:2 3407
one c from the selvedge in the ... Ex 26:4 3407
the uttermost edge of another c ... Ex 26:4 3407
shalt thou make in the one c ... Ex 26:5 3407
thou make in the edge of the c ... Ex 26:5 3407
The length of one c shall be ... Ex 26:8 3407
the breadth of one c four cubits ... Ex 26:8 3407
shalt double the sixth c in the ... Ex 26:9 3407
loops on the edge of the one c ... Ex 26:10 3407
the c which coupleth the second ... Ex 26:10 3407
the half c that remaineth, shall ... Ex 26:12 3407
The length of one c was twenty ... Ex 36:9 3407
the breadth of one c four cubits ... Ex 36:9 3407
of one c from the selvedge in the ... Ex 36:11 3407
the uttermost side of another c ... Ex 36:11 3407
Fifty loops made he in one c ... Ex 36:12 3407
made he in the edge of the c ... Ex 36:12 3407
the loops held one c to another ... Ex 36:12
length of one c was thirty cubits ... Ex 36:15 3407
cubits was the breadth of one c ... Ex 36:15 3407
edge of the c in the coupling ... Ex 36:17 3407
the c which coupleth the second ... Ex 36:17 3407
the c for the door of the court, ... Num 3:26 4539
out the heavens like a c ... Ps 104:2 3407
stretcheth out the heavens as a c ... Is 40:22 1852

CURTAINS {31}
with ten c of fine twined linen ... Ex 26:1 3407
every one of the c shall have one ... Ex 26:2 3407
The five c shall be coupled ... Ex 26:3 3407
other five c shall be coupled one ... Ex 26:3 3407
couple the c together with the ... Ex 26:6 3407
thou shalt make c of goats' hair ... Ex 26:7 3407
eleven c shalt thou make ... Ex 26:7 3407
the eleven c shall be all of one ... Ex 26:8 3407
shalt couple five c by themselves ... Ex 26:9 3407
six c by themselves, and shalt ... Ex 26:9 3407
remaineth of the c of the tent ... Ex 26:12 3407
the length of the c of the tent ... Ex 26:13 3407
made ten c of fine twined linen ... Ex 36:8 3407
the c were all of one size ... Ex 36:9 3407
the five c one unto another ... Ex 36:10 3407
the other five c he coupled one ... Ex 36:10 3407
coupled the c one unto another ... Ex 36:13 3407
he made c of goats' hair for the ... Ex 36:14 3407
eleven c he made them ... Ex 36:14 3407
the eleven c were of one size ... Ex 36:15 3407
he coupled five c by themselves ... Ex 36:16 3407
and six c by themselves ... Ex 36:16 3407
bear the c of the tabernacle ... Num 4:25 3407
the ark of God dwelleth within c ... 2Sa 7:2 3407
of the LORD remaineth under c ... 1Chr 17:1 3407
of Kedar, as the c of Solomon ... Song 1:5 3407
forth the c of thine habitations ... Is 54:2 3407
spoiled, and my c in a moment ... Jer 4:20 3407
tent any more, and to set up my c ... Jer 10:20 3407
shall take to themselves their c ... Jer 49:29 3407
the c of the land of Midian did ... Hab 3:7 3407

CUSH *(cush)* {8} See ETHIOPIA.
1. A son of Ham.
C, and Mizraim, and Phut, and ... Gen 10:6 3568
the sons of C; Seba, and Havilah ... Gen 10:7 3568
And C begat Nimrod ... Gen 10:8 3568
C, and Mizraim, Put, and Canaan ... 1Chr 1:8 3568
the sons of C; Seba, and Havilah ... 1Chr 1:9 3568
And C begat Nimrod ... 1Chr 1:10 3568
2. A Benjaminite.
the words of C the Benjamite ... Ps 7:t 3568
3. Land of descendants of Cush.
Egypt, and from Pathros, and from C ... Is 11:11 3568

CUSHAN *(cu'-shan)* {1} See CHUSHAN-RISHATHAIM.
Same as Chushan-rishathaim.
saw the tents of C in affliction ... Hab 3:7 3572

CUSHI *(cu'-shi)* {10}
1. Messenger of David.
Then said Joab to C, Go tell the ... 2Sa 18:21 3569
C bowed himself unto Joab, and ran ... 2Sa 18:21 3569
me, I pray thee, also run after C ... 2Sa 18:22 3569
way of the plain, and overran C ... 2Sa 18:23 3569
And, behold, C came ... 2Sa 18:31 3569
C said, Tidings, my lord the king ... 2Sa 18:31 3569
And the king said unto C, Is the ... 2Sa 18:32 3569
C answered, The enemies of my ... 2Sa 18:32 3569
2. Ancestor of Jehudi.
son of Shelemiah, the son of C ... Jer 36:14 3569
3. Father of Zephaniah.
came unto Zephaniah the son of C ... Zeph 1:1 3569

CUSTODY {5}
And under the c and charge of the ... Num 3:36 6486
unto the c of Hege the king's ... Est 2:3 3027
to the c of Hegai, that Esther ... Est 2:8 3027
to the c of Hegai, keeper of the ... Est 2:8 3027
to the c of Shaashgaz, the king's ... Est 2:14 3027

CUSTOM {20}
for the c of women is upon me ... Gen 31:35 1870
And it was a c in Israel, ... Judg 11:39 2706
the priest's c with the people ... 1Sa 2:13 4941
by number, according to the c ... Ezr 3:4 4941
they not pay toll, tribute, and c ... Ezr 4:13 1983
and toll, tribute, and c, was paid ... Ezr 4:20 1983
to impose toll, tribute, or c ... Ezr 7:24 1983
sealed according to the law and c ... Jer 32:11 2706
sitting at the receipt of c ... Mt 9:9 *5058*
of the earth take c or tribute ... Mt 17:25 *5056*
sitting at the receipt of c ... Mk 2:14 *5058*
According to the c of the ... Lk 1:9 *1485*
do for him after the c of the law ... Lk 2:27 *1480*
after the c of the feast ... Lk 2:42 *1485*
and, as his c was, he went into ... Lk 4:16 *3588,1486*
Levi, sitting at the receipt of c ... Lk 5:27 *5058*
But ye have a c, that I should ... Jn 18:39 *4914*
c to whom c; fear to whom fear ... Rom 13:7 *5056*
be contentious, we have no such c ... 1Cor 11:16 *4914*

CUSTOMS {7}
not any one of these abominable c ... Lev 18:30 2708
For the c of the people are vain ... Jer 10:3 2708
shall change the c which Moses ... Acts 6:14 *1485*
And teach c, which are not lawful ... Acts 16:21 *1485*
neither to walk after the c ... Acts 21:21 *1485*
I know thee to be expert in all c ... Acts 26:3 *1485*
or c of our fathers, yet was I ... Acts 28:17 *1485*

CUT {320}
neither shall all flesh be c off ... Gen 9:11 3772
that soul shall be c off from his ... Gen 17:14 3772
c off the foreskin of her son, and ... Ex 4:25 3772
thou shalt be c off from the ... Ex 9:15 3582
soul shall be c off from Israel ... Ex 12:15 3772
even that soul shall be c off ... Ex 12:19 3772
and I will c them off ... Ex 23:23 3582
thou shalt c the ram in pieces, ... Ex 29:17 5408
shall even be c off from his ... Ex 30:33 3772
shall even be c off from his ... Ex 30:38 3772
that soul shall be c off from ... Ex 31:14 3772
images, and c down their groves ... Ex 34:13 3772
c it into wires, to work it in ... Ex 39:3 7112
offering, and c it into his pieces ... Lev 1:6 5408
he shall c it into his pieces, ... Lev 1:12 5408
shall be c off from his people ... Lev 7:20 3772
shall be c off from his people ... Lev 7:21 3772
it shall be c off from his people ... Lev 7:25 3772
shall be c off from his people ... Lev 7:27 3772
And he c the ram into pieces ... Lev 8:20 5408
that man shall be c off from ... Lev 17:4 3772
even that man shall be c off from ... Lev 17:9 3772
will c him off from among his ... Lev 17:10 3772
eateth it shall be c off ... Lev 17:14 3772
be c off from among their people ... Lev 18:29 3772
that soul shall be c off from ... Lev 19:8 3772
will c him off from among his ... Lev 20:3 3772
will c him off, and all that go a ... Lev 20:5 3772
will c him off from among his ... Lev 20:6 3772
they shall be c off in the sight ... Lev 20:17 3772
both of them shall be c off from ... Lev 20:18 3772
that soul shall be c off from my ... Lev 22:3 3772
or crushed, or broken, or c ... Lev 22:24 3772
he shall be c off from among his ... Lev 23:29 3772
c down your images, and cast your ... Lev 26:30 3772
C ye not off the tribe of the ... Num 4:18 3772
be c off from among his people ... Num 9:13 3772
c down from thence a branch with ... Num 13:23 3772
of Israel c down from thence ... Num 13:24 3772
that soul shall be c off from ... Num 15:30 3772
that soul shall utterly be c off ... Num 15:31 3772
soul shall be c off from Israel ... Num 19:13 3772
that soul shall be c off from ... Num 19:20 3772
c down their groves, and burn ... Deut 7:5 1438
c off the nations from before ... Deut 12:29 3772
ye shall not c yourselves ... Deut 14:1 1413
thy God hath c off the nations ... Deut 19:1 3772
with the axe to c down the tree ... Deut 19:5 3772
thou shalt not c them down (for ... Deut 20:19 3772
thou shalt destroy and c them down ... Deut 20:20 3772
or hath his privy member c off ... Deut 23:1 3772
Then thou shalt c off her hand ... Deut 25:12 7112
c off from the waters that come ... Josh 3:13 3772
salt sea, failed, and were c off ... Josh 3:16 3772
were c off before the ark of the ... Josh 4:7 3772
the waters of Jordan were c off ... Josh 4:7 3772
c off our name from the earth ... Josh 7:9 3772
c off the Anakims from the ... Josh 11:21 3772
c down for thyself there in the ... Josh 17:15 1254
a wood, and thou shalt c it down ... Josh 17:18 1254
all the nations that I have c off ... Josh 23:4 3772
c off his thumbs and his great ... Judg 1:6 7112
thumbs and their great toes c off ... Judg 1:7 7112
c down the grove that is by it ... Judg 6:25 3772
the grove which thou shalt c down ... Judg 6:26 3772
the grove was c down that was by ... Judg 6:28 3772
because he hath c down the grove ... Judg 6:30 3772
c down a bough from the trees, and ... Judg 9:48 3772
all the people likewise c down ... Judg 9:49 3772
c her in pieces, and sent her ... Judg 20:6 5408
There is one tribe c off from ... Judg 21:6 1438
not c off from among his brethren ... Ruth 4:10 3772
that I will c off thine arm, and ... 1Sa 2:31 1438
whom I shall not c off from mine ... 1Sa 2:33 3772
were c off upon the threshold ... 1Sa 5:4 3772
him, and c off his head therewith ... 1Sa 17:51 3772
But also thou shalt not c off thy ... 1Sa 20:15 3772
not when the LORD hath c off the ... 1Sa 20:15 3772
c off the skirt of Saul's robe ... 1Sa 24:4 3772
because he had c off Saul's skirt ... 1Sa 24:5 3772
for in that I c off the skirt of ... 1Sa 24:11 3772
that thou wilt not c off my seed ... 1Sa 24:21 3772
how he hath c off those that have ... 1Sa 28:9 3772
they c off his head, and stripped ... 1Sa 31:9 3772
c off their hands and their feet, ... 2Sa 4:12 7112
have c off all thine enemies out ... 2Sa 7:9 3772
c off their garments in the ... 2Sa 10:4 3772
they c off the head of Sheba the ... 2Sa 20:22 3772
Then will I c off Israel out of ... 1Kin 9:7 3772
until he had c off every male in ... 1Kin 11:16 3772
of Jeroboam, even to c it off ... 1Kin 13:34 3582
will c off from Jeroboam him that ... 1Kin 14:10 3772
who shall c off the house of ... 1Kin 14:14 3772
when Jezebel c off the prophets ... 1Kin 18:4 3772
c it in pieces, and lay it on wood ... 1Kin 18:23 5408
c themselves after their manner ... 1Kin 18:28 1413
c the bullock in pieces, and laid ... 1Kin 18:33 5408
will c off from Ahab him that ... 1Kin 21:21 3772
came to Jordan, they c down wood ... 2Kin 6:4 1504
he c down a stick, and cast it in ... 2Kin 6:6 7094
I will c off from Ahab him that ... 2Kin 9:8 3772
the LORD began to c Israel short ... 2Kin 10:32 7096
king Ahaz c off the borders of ... 2Kin 16:17 7112
c down the groves, and brake in ... 2Kin 18:4 3772
At that time did Hezekiah c off ... 2Kin 18:16 7112
will c down the tall cedar trees ... 2Kin 19:23 3772
c down the groves, and filled ... 2Kin 23:14 3772
c in pieces all the vessels of ... 2Kin 24:13 7112
have c off all thine enemies from ... 1Chr 17:8 3772
c off their garments in the midst ... 1Chr 19:4 3772
c them with saws, and with harrows ... 1Chr 20:3 7787
can skill to c timber in Lebanon ... 2Chr 2:8 3772
the hewers that c timber ... 2Chr 2:10 3772
we will c wood out of Lebanon, as ... 2Chr 2:16 3772
the images, and c down the groves ... 2Chr 14:3 1438
Asa c down her idol, and stamped ... 2Chr 15:16 3772
to c off the house of Ahab ... 2Chr 22:7 3772
for he was c off from the house ... 2Chr 26:21 1504
c in pieces the vessels of the ... 2Chr 28:24 7112
c down the groves, and threw down ... 2Chr 31:1 1438
which c off all the mighty men of ... 2Chr 32:21 3582
on high above them, he c down ... 2Chr 34:4 1438
c down all the idols throughout ... 2Chr 34:7 1438
or where were the righteous c off ... Job 4:7 3582
let loose his hand, and c me off ... Job 6:9 1214
not c down, it withereth before ... Job 8:12 6998
Whose hope shall be c off ... Job 8:14 6990
If he c off, and shut up, or ... Job 11:10 2498
forth like a flower, and is c down ... Job 14:2 5243
hope of a tree, if it be c down ... Job 14:7 3772
above shall his branch be c off ... Job 18:16 5243
his months is c off in the midst ... Job 21:21 2686
Which were c down out of time, ... Job 22:16 7059
our substance is not c down ... Job 22:20 3582
Because I was not c off before ... Job 23:17 6780
c off as the tops of the ears of ... Job 24:24 5243
Who c up mallows by the bushes, ... Job 30:4 6998

when people are c off in their ... Job 36:20 5927
The LORD shall c off all ... Ps 12:3 3772
I am c off from before thine eyes ... Ps 31:22 1629
to c off the remembrance of them ... Ps 34:16 3772
soon be c down like the grass ... Ps 37:2 5243
For evildoers shall be c off ... Ps 37:9 3772
be cursed of him shall be c off ... Ps 37:22 3772
seed of the wicked shall be c off ... Ps 37:28 3772
when the wicked are c off ... Ps 37:34 3772
end of the wicked shall be c off ... Ps 37:38 3772
c them off in thy truth ... Ps 54:5 6789
let them be as c in pieces ... Ps 58:7 4135
of the wicked also will I c off ... Ps 75:10 1438
He shall c off the spirit of ... Ps 76:12 1219
is burned with fire, it is c down ... Ps 80:16 3683
let us c them off from being a ... Ps 83:4 3582
they are c off from thy hand ... Ps 88:5 1504
thy terrors have c me off ... Ps 88:16 6789
in the evening it is c down ... Ps 90:6 4135
for it is soon c off, and we fly ... Ps 90:10 1504
shall c them off in their own ... Ps 94:23 6789
the LORD our God shall c them off ... Ps 94:23 6789
his neighbour, him will I c off ... Ps 101:5 6789
that I may c off all wicked doers ... Ps 101:8 3772
c the bars of iron in sunder ... Ps 107:16 1438
Let his posterity be c off ... Ps 109:13 3772
that he may c off the memory of ... Ps 109:15 3772
he hath c asunder the cords of ... Ps 129:4 7112
of thy mercy c off mine enemies, ... Ps 143:12 6789
shall be c off from the earth ... Prov 2:22 3772
the froward tongue shall be c out ... Prov 10:31 3772
expectation shall not be c off ... Prov 23:18 3772
expectation shall not be c off ... Prov 24:14 3772
the sycomores are c down, but we ... Is 9:10 1438
LORD will c off from Israel head ... Is 9:14 3772
and c off nations not a few ... Is 10:7 3772
he shall c down the thickets of ... Is 10:34 5362
of Judah shall be c off ... Is 11:13 3772
how art thou c down to the ground ... Is 14:12 1438
c off from Babylon the name, and ... Is 14:22 3772
be baldness, and every beard c off ... Is 15:2 1438
he shall both c off the sprigs ... Is 18:5 3772
take away and c down the branches ... Is 18:5 8456
be removed, and be c down, and fall ... Is 22:25 1438
that was upon it shall be c off ... Is 22:25 3772
that watch for iniquity are c off ... Is 29:20 3772
as thorns c up shall they be ... Is 33:12 3683
I will c down the tall cedars ... Is 37:24 3772
I have c off like a weaver my ... Is 38:12 7088
he will c me off with pining ... Is 38:12 1214
c in sunder the bars of iron ... Is 45:2 1438
for thee, that I c thee not off ... Is 48:9 3772
c off nor destroyed from before ... Is 48:19 3772
Art thou not it that hath c Rahab ... Is 51:9 2672
for he was c off out of the land ... Is 53:8 1504
sign that shall not be c off ... Is 55:13 3772
name, that shall not be c off ... Is 56:5 3772
as if he c off a dog's neck ... Is 66:3
is c off from their mouth ... Jer 7:28 3772
C off thine hair, O Jerusalem, and ... Jer 7:29 1494
to c off the children from ... Jer 9:21 3772
let us c him off from the land of ... Jer 11:19 3772
nor c themselves, nor make ... Jer 16:6 1413
they shall c down thy choice ... Jer 22:7 3772
are c down because of the fierce ... Jer 25:37 1826
when they c the calf in twain, and ... Jer 34:18 3772
he c it with the penknife, and ... Jer 36:23 7167
having c themselves, with ... Jer 41:5 1413
to c off from you man and woman, ... Jer 44:7 3772
that ye might c yourselves off, ... Jer 44:8 3772
for evil, and to c off all Judah ... Jer 44:11 3772
They shall c down her forest, ... Jer 46:23 3772
to c off from Tyrus and Zidon ... Jer 47:4 3772
Ashkelon is c off with the ... Jer 47:5 1820
how long wilt thou c thyself ... Jer 47:5 1413
let us c it off from being a ... Jer 48:2 3772
Also thou shalt be c down ... Jer 48:2 1826
The horn of Moab is c off ... Jer 48:25 1438
of war shall be c off in that day ... Jer 49:26 1826
C off the sower from Babylon, and ... Jer 50:16 3772
of the whole earth c in asunder ... Jer 50:23 1438
of war shall be c off in that day ... Jer 50:30 1826
be not c off in her iniquity ... Jer 51:6 1826
to c it off, that none shall ... Jer 51:62 3772
He hath c off in his fierce anger ... Lam 2:3 1438
They have c off my life in the ... Lam 3:53 6789
then I said, I am c off ... Lam 3:54 1504
and your images may be c down ... Eze 6:6 1438
I will c him off from the midst ... Eze 14:8 3772
will c off man and beast from it ... Eze 14:13 3772
so that I c off man and beast from ... Eze 14:17 3772
to c off from it man and beast ... Eze 14:19 3772
to c off from it man and beast ... Eze 14:21 3772
wast born thy navel was not c ... Eze 16:4 3772
c off the fruit thereof, that it ... Eze 17:9 7082
forts, to c off many persons ... Eze 17:17 3772
and will c off from thee the ... Eze 21:3 3772
Seeing then that I will c off ... Eze 21:4 3772
I will c thee off from the people ... Eze 25:7 3772
will c off man and beast from it ... Eze 25:13 3772
I will c off the Cherethims, and ... Eze 25:16 3772
c off man and beast out of thee ... Eze 29:8 3772
I will c off the multitude of No ... Eze 30:15 3772
have c him off, and have left him ... Eze 31:12 3772
c off from it him that passeth ... Eze 35:7 3772
we are c off for our parts ... Eze 37:11 1504
neither c down any out of the ... Eze 39:10 2404
thereof, ye shall be c in pieces ... Dan 2:5 5648
a stone was c out without hands ... Dan 2:34 1505
was c out of the mountain without ... Dan 2:45 1505
shall be c in pieces, and their ... Dan 3:29 5648
c off his branches, shake off his ... Dan 4:14 7113
two weeks shall Messiah be c off ... Dan 9:26 3772
idols, that they may be c off ... Hos 8:4 3772
her king is c off as the foam ... Hos 10:7 1820
king of Israel utterly be c off ... Hos 10:15 1820
for it is c off from your mouth ... Joel 1:5 3772
the drink offering is c off from ... Joel 1:9 3772
Is not the meat c off before our ... Joel 1:16 3772
c off the inhabitant from the ... Amos 1:5 3772
I will c off the inhabitant from ... Amos 1:8 3772
I will c off the judge from the ... Amos 2:3 3772
horns of the altar shall be c off ... Amos 3:14 1438
c them in the head, all of them ... Amos 9:1 1214
by night, (how art thou c off ... Obad 5 1820
of Esau may be c off by slaughter ... Obad 9 3772
and thou shalt be c off for ever ... Obad 10 3772
to c off those of his that did ... Obad 14 3772
all thine enemies shall be c off ... Mic 5:9 3772
that I will c off thy horses out ... Mic 5:10 3772
I will c off the cities of thy ... Mic 5:11 3772
I will c off witchcrafts out of ... Mic 5:12 3772
graven images also will I c off ... Mic 5:13 3772
yet thus shall they be c down ... Nah 1:12 1494
will I c off the graven image ... Nah 1:14 3772
he is utterly c off ... Nah 1:15 3772
I will c off thy prey from the ... Nah 2:13 3772
the sword shall c thee off ... Nah 3:15 3772
shall be c off from the fold ... Hab 3:17 1504
I will c off man from off the ... Zeph 1:3 3772
I will c off the remnant of Baal ... Zeph 1:4 3772
the merchant people are c down ... Zeph 1:11 1820
they that bear silver are c off ... Zeph 1:11 3772
I have c off the nations ... Zeph 3:6 3772
dwelling should not be c off ... Zeph 3:7 3772
one that stealeth shall be c off ... Zec 5:3 5352
one that sweareth shall be c off ... Zec 5:3 5352
I will c off the pride of the ... Zec 9:6 3772
I will c off the chariot from ... Zec 9:10 3772
and the battle bow shall be c off ... Zec 9:10 3772
also I c off in one month ... Zec 11:8 3582
is to be c off, let it be c off ... Zec 11:9 3582
c it asunder, that I might break ... Zec 11:10 1438
Then I c asunder mine other staff ... Zec 11:14 1438
not visit those that be c off ... Zec 11:16 3582
with it shall be c in pieces ... Zec 12:3 8295
that I will c off the names of ... Zec 13:2 3772
two parts therein shall be c off ... Zec 13:8 3772
shall not be c off from the city ... Zec 14:2 3772
The LORD will c off the man that ... Mal 2:12 3772
c it off, and cast it from thee ... Mt 5:30 1581
c them off, and cast them from ... Mt 18:8 1581
others c down branches from the ... Mt 21:8 2875
shall c him asunder, and appoint ... Mt 24:51 1371
if thy hand offend thee, c it off ... Mk 9:43 609
if thy foot offend thee, c it off ... Mk 9:45 609
others c down branches off the ... Mk 11:8 2875
the high priest, and c off his ear ... Mk 14:47 581
will c him in sunder, and will ... Lk 12:46 1371
c it down ... Lk 13:7 1581
after that thou shalt c it down ... Lk 13:9 1581
priest, and c off his right ear ... Lk 22:50 851
servant, and c off his right ear ... Jn 18:10 609
his kinsman whose ear Peter c off ... Jn 18:26 609
they were c to the heart, and took ... Acts 5:33 1282
they were c to the heart, and they ... Acts 7:54 1282
Then the soldiers c off the ropes ... Acts 27:32 609
c it short in righteousness ... Rom 9:28 4932
thou also shalt be c off ... Rom 11:22 1581
For if thou wert c out of the ... Rom 11:24 1581
that I may c off occasion from ... 2Cor 11:12 1581
were even c off which trouble you ... Gal 5:12 609

CUTH *(cuth)* {1} See CUTHAH. *A Babylonian city.*
the men of C made Nergal, and the ... 2Kin 17:30 3575

CUTHAH *(cu'-thah)* {1} See CUTH. *Same as Cuth.*
men from Babylon, and from C ... 2Kin 17:24 3575

CUTTEST {1}
When thou c down thine harvest in ... Deut 24:19 7114

CUTTETH {6}
He c out rivers among the rocks ... Job 28:10 1234
the bow, and c the spear in sunder ... Ps 46:9 7112
the grave's mouth, as when one c ... Ps 141:7 6398
the hand of a fool c off the feet ... Prov 26:6 7096
for one c a tree out of the ... Jer 10:3 3772
chambers, and c him out windows ... Jer 22:14 7167

CUTTING {5}
in c of stones, to set them, and ... Ex 31:5 2799
in the c of stones, to set them, ... Ex 35:33 2799
I said in the c off of my days, I ... Is 38:10 1824
to thy house by c off many people ... Hab 2:10 7096
crying, and c himself with stones ... Mk 5:5 2629

CUTTINGS {3}
Ye shall not make any c in your ... Lev 19:28 8296
nor make any c in their flesh ... Lev 21:5 8296
upon all the hands shall be c ... Jer 48:37 1417

CUZA See CHUZA.

CYMBAL {1}
sounding brass, or a tinkling c ... 1Cor 13:1 2950

CYMBALS {16}
timbrels, and on cornets, and on c ... 2Sa 6:5 6767
and with timbrels, and with c ... 1Chr 13:8 4700
musick, psalteries and harps and c ... 1Chr 15:16 4700
to sound with c of brass ... 1Chr 15:19 4700
and with trumpets, and with c ... 1Chr 15:28 4700
but Asaph made a sound with c ... 1Chr 16:5 4700
c for those that should make a ... 1Chr 16:42 4700
harps, with psalteries, and with c ... 1Chr 25:1 4700
in the house of the LORD, with c ... 1Chr 25:6 4700
arrayed in white linen, having c ... 2Chr 5:12 4700
voice with the trumpets and c ... 2Chr 5:13 4700
in the house of the LORD with c ... 2Chr 29:25 4700
Levites the sons of Asaph with c ... Ezr 3:10 4700
and with singing, with c, ... Neh 12:27 4700
Praise him upon the loud c ... Ps 150:5 6767
him upon the high sounding c ... Ps 150:5 6767

CYPRESS {1}
him down cedars, and taketh the c ... Is 44:14 8645

CYPRUS *(si'-prus)* {8} *An island off the Syrian coast.*
a Levite, and of the country of C ... Acts 4:36 2954
travelled as far as Phenice, and C ... Acts 11:19 2954
And some of them were men of C ... Acts 11:20 2954
and from thence they sailed to C ... Acts 13:4 2954
took Mark, and sailed unto C ... Acts 15:39 2954
Now when we had discovered C ... Acts 21:3 2954
brought with them one Mnason of C ... Acts 21:16 2954
from thence, we sailed under C ... Acts 27:4 2954

CYRENE *(si-re'-ne)* {4} See CYRENIAN. *A Libyan city.*
came out, they found a man of C ... Mt 27:32 2957
and in the parts of Libya about C ... Acts 2:10 2957
of them were men of Cyprus and C ... Acts 11:20 2957
was called Niger, and Lucius of C ... Acts 13:1 2957

CYRENIAN *(si-re'-ne-an)* {2} See CYRENIANS. *A native of Cyrene.*
And they compel one Simon a C ... Mk 15:21 2956
laid hold upon one Simon, a C ... Lk 23:26 2956

CYRENIANS *(si-re'-ne-ans)* {1}
synagogue of the Libertines, and C ... Acts 6:9 2956

CYRENIUS *(si-re'-ne-us)* {1} *A Roman governor of Syria.*
made when C was governor of Syria ... Lk 2:2 2958

CYRUS *(si'-rus)* {23} *Founder of the Persian Empire.*
first year of C king of Persia ... 2Chr 36:22 3566
up the spirit of C king of Persia ... 2Chr 36:22 3566
Thus saith C king of Persia, All ... 2Chr 36:23 3566
first year of C king of Persia ... Ezr 1:1 3566
up the spirit of C king of Persia ... Ezr 1:1 3566
Thus saith C king of Persia, The ... Ezr 1:2 3566
Also C the king brought forth the ... Ezr 1:7 3566
Even those did C king of Persia ... Ezr 1:8 3566
that they had of C king of Persia ... Ezr 3:7 3566
as king C the king of Persia hath ... Ezr 4:3 3566
all the days of C king of Persia ... Ezr 4:5 3566
But in the first year of C the ... Ezr 5:13 3567
C made a decree to build this ... Ezr 5:13 3567
those did C the king take out of ... Ezr 5:14 3567
that a decree was made of C the ... Ezr 5:17 3567
In the first year of C the king ... Ezr 6:3 3567
the same C the king made a decree ... Ezr 6:3 3567
according to the commandment of C ... Ezr 6:14 3567
That saith of C, He is my ... Is 44:28 3566
the LORD to his anointed, to C ... Is 45:1 3566
unto the first year of king C ... Dan 1:21 3566
and in the reign of C the Persian ... Dan 6:28 3567
In the third year of C king of ... Dan 10:1 3566

D

DABAREH *(dab'-a-reh)* {1} See DABERATH. *A Levitical city in Issachar.*
her suburbs, D with her suburbs, ... Josh 21:28 1705

DABBASHETH *(dab'-ba-sheth)* {1} *A border city of Issachar.*
sea, and Maralah, and reached to D ... Josh 19:11 1708

DABBESHETH See DABBASHETH.

DABERATH *(dab'-e-rath)* {2} See DABAREH. *Same as Dabareh.*
and then goeth out to D, and goeth ... Josh 19:12 1705
her suburbs, D with her suburbs, ... 1Chr 6:72 1705

DAGGER {3}
made him a d which had two edges ... Judg 3:16 2719
took the d from his right thigh, ... Judg 3:21 2719
not draw the d out of his belly ... Judg 3:22 2719

DAGON {12} See BETH-DAGON, DAGON'S. *A Philistine god.*
great sacrifice unto D their god ... Judg 16:23 1712
house of D, and set it by D ... 1Sa 5:2 1712
D was fallen upon his face to the ... 1Sa 5:3 1712
And they took D, and set him in his ... 1Sa 5:3 1712
D was fallen upon his face to the ... 1Sa 5:4 1712
and the head of D and both the ... 1Sa 5:4 1712

the stump of *D* was left to him 1Sa 5:4 1712
neither the priests of *D*, nor any 1Sa 5:5 1712
of *D* in Ashdod unto this day 1Sa 5:5 1712
sore upon us, and upon *D* our god 1Sa 5:7 1712
his head in the temple of *D* 1Chr 10:10 1712

DAGON'S {1}
nor any that come into *D* house 1Sa 5:5 1712

DAILY {63}
your *d* tasks, as when there was Ex 5:13 3117
from your bricks of your *d* task Ex 5:19 3117
be twice as much as they gather *d* Ex 16:5 3117
the *d* meat offering, and the Num 4:16 8548
this manner ye shall offer *d* Num 28:24 3117
the *d* burnt offering, and his meat Num 29:6 8548
she pressed him *d* with her words Judg 16:16 3117
a *d* rate for every day, all the 2Kin 25:30 3117
his *d* portion for their service 2Chr 31:16 3117
offered the *d* burnt offerings by Ezr 3:4 3117
prepared for me *d* was one ox Neh 5:18 3117,259
pass, when they spake *d* unto him Est 3:4 3117
soul, having sorrow in my heart *d* Ps 13:2 3119
they say *d* unto me, Where Ps 42:10 3605,3117
he fighting *d* oppresseth me Ps 56:1 3605,3117
enemies would *d* swallow me up Ps 56:2 3605,3117
that I may *d* perform my vows Ps 61:8 3117
who *d* loadeth us with benefits, Ps 68:19 3117
and *d* shall he be praised Ps 72:15 3605,3117
foolish man reproacheth thee *d* Ps 74:22 3605,3117
for I cry unto thee *d* Ps 86:3 3605,3117
LORD, I have called *d* upon thee Ps 88:9 3605,3117
round about me *d* like water Ps 88:17 3605,3117
I was *d* his delight, rejoicing Prov 8:30 3117
watching *d* at my gates, waiting Prov 8:34 3117
Yet they seek me *d*, and delight to Is 58:2 3117
d rising up early and sending them Jer 7:25 3117
I am in derision *d*, every one Jer 20:7 3605,3117
unto me, and a derision, *d* Jer 20:8 3605,3117
that they should give him *d* a Jer 37:21 3117
and Noph shall have distresses *d* Eze 30:16 3119
without blemish *d* the seven days Eze 45:23 3117
of the goats *d* for a sin offering Eze 45:23 3117
Thou shalt *d* prepare a burnt Eze 46:13 3117
the king appointed them a *d* Dan 1:5 3117
by him the *d* sacrifice was taken Dan 8:11 8548
the *d* sacrifice by reason of Dan 8:12 8548
vision concerning the *d* sacrifice Dan 8:13 8548
shall take away the *d* sacrifice Dan 11:31 8548
And from the time that the *d* Dan 12:11 8548
he *d* increaseth lies and Hos 12:1 3605,3117
Give us this day our *d* bread Mt 6:11 1967
I sat *d* with you teaching in the Mt 26:55 2596,2250
I was *d* with you in the temple Mk 14:49 2596,2250
himself, and take up his cross *d* Lk 9:23 2596,2250
Give us day by day our *d* bread Lk 11:3 1967
he taught *d* in the temple Lk 19:47 2596,2250
When I was *d* with you in the Lk 22:53 2596,2250
continuing *d* with one accord in Acts 2:46 2596,2250
church *d* such as should be saved Acts 2:47 2596,2250
whom they laid *d* at the gate of Acts 3:2 2596,2250
d in the temple, and in every Acts 5:42 3956,2250
neglected in the *d* ministration Acts 6:1 2522
faith, and increased in number *d* Acts 16:5 2596,2250
and searched the scriptures *d* Acts 17:11 2596,2250
in the market *d* with them Acts 17:17 2596,3956,2250
disputing *d* in the school of one Acts 19:9 2596,2250
in Christ Jesus our Lord, I die *d* 1Cor 15:31 2596,2250
that which cometh upon me *d* 2Cor 11:28 2596,2250
But exhort one another *d*, Heb 3:13 2596,1538,2250
Who needeth not *d*, as those high Heb 7:27 2596,2250
priest standeth *d* ministering Heb 10:11 2596,2250
be naked, and destitute of *d* food Jas 2:15 2184

DAINTIES {3}
be fat, and he shall yield royal *d* Gen 49:20 4574
and let me not eat of their *d* Ps 141:4 4516
Be not desirous of his *d* Prov 23:3 4303

DAINTY {3}
bread, and his soul *d* meat Job 33:20 8378
neither desire thou his *d* meats Prov 23:6 4303
thee, and all things which were *d* Rev 18:14 3045

DALAIAH *(dal-a-i'-ah)* {1} See DELAIAH. *A descendant of Judah.*
and Akkub, and Johanan, and *D* 1Chr 3:24 1806

DALE {2}
of Shaveh, which is the king's *d* Gen 14:17 6010
pillar, which is in the king's *d* 2Sa 18:18 6010

DALMANUTHA *(dal-ma-nu'-thah)* {1} *A village in Galilee.*
and came into the parts of *D* Mk 8:10 1148

DALMATIA *(dal-ma'-she-ah)* {1} *A Roman province west of Macedonia.*
Crescens to Galatia, Titus unto *D* 2Ti 4:10 1149

DALPHON *(dal'-fon)* {1} *A son of Haman.*
And Parshandatha, and *D*, Est 9:7 1813

DAM {5}
seven days it shall be with his *d* Ex 22:30 517
shall be seven days under the *d* Lev 22:27 517
the *d* sitting upon the young, or Deut 22:6 517
not take the *d* with the young Deut 22:6 517
shalt in any wise let the *d* go Deut 22:7 517

DAMAGE {6}
why should *d* grow to the hurt of Ezr 4:22 2257
not countervail the king's *d* Est 7:4 5143
off the feet, and drinketh *d* Prov 26:6 2555
and the king should have no *d* Dan 6:2 5142
will be with hurt and much *d* Acts 27:10 2209
might receive *d* by us in nothing 2Cor 7:9 2210

DAMARIS *(dam'-a-ris)* {1} *An Athenian convert of Paul.*
Areopagite, and a woman named *D* Acts 17:34 1152

DAMASCENES *(dam-as-senes')* {1} *Inhabitants of Damascus.*
the city of the *D* with a garrison 2Cor 11:32 1159

DAMASCUS *(da-mas'-cus)* {60} See DAMASCENES, SYRIA-DAMASCUS. *A city in Syria.*
which is on the left hand of *D* Gen 14:15 1834
of my house is this Eliezer of *D* Gen 15:2 1834
when the Syrians of *D* came to 2Sa 8:5 1834
David put garrisons in Syria of *D* 2Sa 8:6 1834
and they went to *D*, and dwelt 1Kin 11:24 1834
and dwelt therein, and reigned in *D* 1Kin 11:24 1834
king of Syria, that dwelt at *D* 1Kin 15:18 1834
on thy way to the wilderness of *D* 1Kin 19:15 1834
shalt make streets for thee in *D* 1Kin 20:34 1834
not Abana and Pharpar, rivers of *D* 2Kin 5:12 1834
And Elisha came to *D* 2Kin 8:7 1834
even of every good thing of *D* 2Kin 8:9 1834
he warred, and how he recovered *D* 2Kin 14:28 1834
king of Assyria went up against *D* 2Kin 16:9 1834
king Ahaz went to *D* to meet 2Kin 16:10 1834
and saw an altar that was at *D* 2Kin 16:10 1834
that king Ahaz had sent from *D* 2Kin 16:11 1834
it against king Ahaz came from *D* 2Kin 16:11 1834
And when the king was come from *D* 2Kin 16:12 1834
when the Syrians of *D* came to 1Chr 18:5 1834
king of Syria, that dwelt at *D* 2Chr 16:2 1834
spoil of them unto the king of *D* 2Chr 24:23 1834
captives, and brought them to *D* 2Chr 28:5 1834
he sacrificed unto the gods of *D* 2Chr 28:23 1834
of Lebanon which looketh toward *D* Song 7:4 1834
For the head of Syria is *D* Is 7:8 1834
and the head of *D* is Rezin Is 7:8 1834
and my mother, the riches of *D* Is 8:4 1834
is not Samaria as *D* Is 10:9 1834
The burden of *D* Is 17:1 1834
D is taken away from being a city Is 17:1 1834
Ephraim, and the kingdom from *D* Is 17:3 1834
Concerning *D*. Hamath is confounded Jer 49:23 1834
D is waxed feeble, and turneth Jer 49:24 1834
kindle a fire in the wall of *D* Jer 49:27 1834
D was thy merchant in the Eze 27:18 1834
which is between the border of *D* Eze 47:16 1834
be Hazar-enan, the border of *D* Eze 47:17 1834
measure from Hauran, and from *D* Eze 47:18 1834
the border of *D* northward Eze 48:1 1834
For three transgressions of *D* Amos 1:3 1834
I will break also the bar of *D* Amos 1:5 1834
of a bed, and in *D* in a couch Amos 3:12 1833
you to go into captivity beyond *D* Amos 5:27 1834
D shall be the rest thereof Zec 9:1 1834
letters to *D* to the synagogues Acts 9:2 1154
as he journeyed, he came near *D* Acts 9:3 1154
the hand, and brought him into *D* Acts 9:8 1154
there was a certain disciple at *D* Acts 9:10 1154
the disciples which were at *D* Acts 9:19 1154
the Jews which dwelt at *D* Acts 9:22 1154
boldly at *D* in the name of Jesus Acts 9:27 1154
unto the brethren, and went to *D* Acts 22:5 1154
was come nigh unto *D* about noon Acts 22:6 1154
said unto me, Arise, and go into *D* Acts 22:10 1154
that were with me, I came into *D* Acts 22:11 1154
as I went to *D* with authority Acts 26:12 1154
But shewed first unto them of *D* Acts 26:20 1154
In *D* the governor under Aretas 2Cor 11:32 1154
Arabia, and returned again unto *D* Gal 1:17 1154

DAMNABLE {1}
privily shall bring in *d* heresies 2Pet 2:1 684

DAMNATION {11}
ye shall receive the greater *d* Mt 23:14 2917
how can ye escape the *d* of hell Mt 23:33 2920
but is in danger of eternal *d* Mk 3:29 2920
these shall receive greater *d* Mk 12:40 2917
the same shall receive greater *d* Lk 20:47 2917
evil, unto the resurrection of *d* Jn 5:29 2920
whose *d* is just Rom 3:8 2917
shall receive to themselves *d* Rom 13:2 2917
drinketh *d* to himself, not 1Cor 11:29 2917
Having *d*, because they have cast 1Ti 5:12 2917
not, and their *d* slumbereth not 2Pet 2:3 684

DAMNED {3}
he that believeth not shall be *d* Mk 16:16 2632
he that doubteth is *d* if he eat Rom 14:23 2632
That they all might be *d* who 2Th 2:12 2919

DAMSEL {40}
that the *d* to whom I shall say, Gen 24:14 5291
the *d* was very fair to look upon, Gen 24:16 5291
And the *d* ran, and told them of her Gen 24:28 5291
Let the *d* abide with us a few Gen 24:55 5291
And they said, We will call the *d* Gen 24:57 5291
of Jacob, and he loved the *d* Gen 34:3 5291
and spake kindly unto the *d* Gen 34:3 5291
saying, Get me this *d* to wife Gen 34:4 3207
but give me the *d* to wife Gen 34:12 5291
Then shall the father of the *d* Deut 22:15 5291
them unto the father of the *d* Deut 22:19 5291
virginity be not found for the *d* Deut 22:20 5291
the *d* to the door of her father's Deut 22:21 5291
If a *d* that is a virgin be Deut 22:23 5291
the *d*, because she cried not, Deut 22:24 5291
find a betrothed *d* in the field Deut 22:25 5291
But unto the *d* thou shalt do Deut 22:26 5291
there is in the *d* no sin worthy Deut 22:26 5291
field, and the betrothed *d* cried Deut 22:27 5291
If a man find a *d* that is a Deut 22:28 5291
to every man a *d* or two Judg 5:30 7356
when the father of the *d* saw him Judg 19:3 5291
over the reapers, Whose *d* is this Ruth 2:5 5291
It is the Moabitish *d* that came Ruth 2:6 5291
So they sought for a fair *d* 1Kin 1:3 5291
the *d* was very fair, and cherished 1Kin 1:4 5291
in a charger, and given to the *d* Mt 14:11 2877
a *d* came unto him, saying, Thou Mt 26:69 3814
the *d* is not dead, but sleepeth Mk 5:39 3813
the father and the mother of the *d* Mk 5:40 3813
entereth in where the *d* was lying Mk 5:40 3813
And he took the *d* by the hand Mk 5:41 3813
which is, being interpreted, *D* Mk 5:41 2877
And straightway the *d* arose Mk 5:42 2877
him, the king said unto the *d* Mk 6:22 2877
in a charger, and gave it to the *d* Mk 6:28 2877
the *d* gave it to her mother Mk 6:28 2877
Then saith the *d* that kept the Jn 18:17 3814
a *d* came to hearken, named Rhoda Acts 12:13 3814
a certain *d* possessed with a Acts 16:16 3814

DAMSEL'S {8}
d virginity unto the elders of Deut 22:15 5291
the *d* father shall say unto the Deut 22:16 5291
with her shall give unto the *d* Deut 22:29 5291
the *d* father, retained him Judg 19:4 5291
the *d* father said unto his son in Judg 19:5 5291
for the *d* father had said unto Judg 19:6 5291
the *d* father said, Comfort thine Judg 19:8 5291
the *d* father, said unto him, Judg 19:9 5291

DAMSELS {3}
And Rebekah arose, and her *d* Gen 24:61 5291
with five *d* of hers that went 1Sa 25:42 5291
among them were the *d* playing Ps 68:25 5959

DAN *(dan)* {71} See DANITES, DAN-JAAN, LAISH, MAHANEH-DAN.
1. A son of Jacob.
therefore called she his name *D* Gen 30:6 1835
D, and Naphtali Gen 35:25 1835
And the sons of *D* Gen 46:23 1835
D shall judge his people, as one Gen 49:16 1835
D shall be a serpent by the way, Gen 49:17 1835
D, and Naphtali, Gad, and Asher Ex 1:4 1835
therein, and called Leshem, *D* Josh 19:47 1835
after the name of *D* their father Josh 19:47 1835
after the name of *D* their father Judg 18:29 1835
D, Joseph, and Benjamin, Naphtali, 1Chr 2:2 1835
D also and Javan going to and fro Eze 27:19 1835
2. A city and tribal territory in northern Canaan.
eighteen, and pursued them unto *D* Gen 14:14 1835
all the land of Gilead, unto *D* Deut 34:1 1835
called the name of the city *D* Judg 18:29 1835
from *D* even to Beer-sheba, with Judg 20:1 1835
all Israel from *D* even to 1Sa 3:20 1835
from *D* even to Beer-sheba 2Sa 3:10 1835
from *D* even to Beer-sheba, as the 2Sa 17:11 1835
from *D* even to Beer-sheba, and 2Sa 24:2 1835
from *D* even to Beer-sheba seventy 2Sa 24:15 1835
from *D* even to Beer-sheba, all 1Kin 4:25 1835
Beth-el, and the other put he in *D* 1Kin 12:29 1835
before the one, even unto *D* 1Kin 12:30 1835
of Israel, and smote Ijon, and *D* 1Kin 15:20 1835
in Beth-el, and that were in *D* 2Kin 10:29 1835
Israel from Beer-sheba even to *D* 1Chr 21:2 1835
and they smote Ijon, and *D*, and 2Chr 16:4 1835
Israel, from Beer-sheba even to *D* 2Chr 30:5 1835
For a voice declareth from *D* Jer 4:15 1835
of his horses was heard from *D* Jer 8:16 1835
a portion for *D* Eze 48:1 1835
And by the border of *D*, from the Eze 48:2 1835
gate of Benjamin, one gate of *D* Eze 48:32 1835
of Samaria, and say, Thy god, O *D* Amos 8:14 1835
3. Tribe descended from Dan 1.
of Ahisamach, of the tribe of *D* Ex 31:6 1835
of Ahisamach, of the tribe of *D* Ex 35:34 1835
of Ahisamach, of the tribe of *D* Ex 38:23 1835
of Dibri, of the tribe of *D* Lev 24:11 1835
Of *D*; Ahiezer the son Num 1:12 1835
Of the children of *D*, by their Num 1:38 1835
of them, even of the tribe of *D* Num 1:39 1835
The standard of the camp of *D* Num 2:25 1835
of *D* shall be Ahiezer the son of Num 2:25 1835
of *D* were an hundred thousand Num 2:31 1835
prince of the children of *D* Num 7:66 1835
of the children of *D* set forward Num 10:25 1835
Of the tribe of *D*, Ammiel the son Num 13:12 1835
sons of *D* after their families Num 26:42 1835
of *D* after their families Num 26:42 1835
of the tribe of the children of *D* Num 34:22 1835
Gad, and Asher, and Zebulun, *D* Deut 27:13 1835
Dan he said, *D* is a lion's whelp Deut 33:22 1835
of *D* according to their families Josh 19:40 1835
of *D* went out too little for them Josh 19:47 1835
therefore the children of *D* went Josh 19:47 1835
of *D* according to their families Josh 19:48 1835
Ephraim, and out of the tribe of *D* Josh 21:5 1835
And out of the tribe of *D*, Eltekeh Josh 21:23 1835
children of *D* into the mountain Judg 1:34 1835
why did *D* remain in ships Judg 5:17 1835
in the camp of *D* between Zorah Judg 13:25 1835
the children of *D* sent of their Judg 18:2 1835
which were of the children of *D* Judg 18:16 1835
and overtook the children of *D* Judg 18:22 1835
they cried unto the children of *D* Judg 18:23 1835
the children of *D* said unto him Judg 18:25 1835

the children of *D* went their way ... Judg 18:26 1835
the children of *D* set up the ... Judg 18:30 1835
were priests to the tribe of *D* ... Judg 18:30 1835
Of *D*, Azareel the son of Jeroham ... 1Chr 27:22 1835
of a woman of the daughters of *D* ... 2Chr 2:14 1835

DANCE {8}
of Shiloh come out to *d* in dances ... Judg 21:21 2342
like a flock, and their children *d* ... Job 21:11 7540
Let them praise his name in the *d* ... Ps 149:3 4234
Praise him with the timbrel and *d* ... Ps 150:4 4234
a time to mourn, and a time to *d* ... Eccl 3:4 7540
there, and satyrs shall *d* there ... Is 13:21 7540
shall the virgin rejoice in the *d* ... Jer 31:13 4234
our *d* is turned into mourning ... Lam 5:15 4234

DANCED {6}
to their number, of them that *d* ... Judg 21:23 2342
David *d* before the LORD with all ... 2Sa 6:14 3769
piped unto you, and ye have not *d* ... Mt 11:17 *3738*
of Herodias *d* before them ... Mt 14:6 *3738*
the said Herodias came in, and *d* ... Mk 6:22 *3738*
piped unto you, and ye have not *d* ... Lk 7:32 *3738*

DANCES {6}
after her with timbrels and with *d* ... Ex 15:20 4246
meet him with timbrels and with *d* ... Judg 11:34 4246
of Shiloh come out to dance in *d* ... Judg 21:21 4246
sing one to another of him in *d* ... 1Sa 21:11 4246
they sang one to another in *d* ... 1Sa 29:5 4246
shalt go forth in the *d* of them ... Jer 31:4

DANCING {7}
that he saw the calf, and the *d* ... Ex 32:19 4246
cities of Israel, singing and *d* ... 1Sa 18:6 4246
earth, eating and drinking, and *d* ... 1Sa 30:16 2287
leaping and *d* before the LORD ... 2Sa 6:16 3769
out at a window saw king David *d* ... 1Chr 15:29 7540
turned for me my mourning into *d* ... Ps 30:11 4234
the house, he heard musick and *d* ... Lk 15:25 *5525*

DANDLED {1}
her sides, and be *d* upon her knees ... Is 66:12 8173

DANGER {7}
shall be in *d* of the judgment ... Mt 5:21 *1777*
shall be in *d* of the judgment ... Mt 5:22 *1777*
shall be in *d* of the council ... Mt 5:22 *1777*
shall be in *d* of hell fire ... Mt 5:22 *1777*
but is in *d* of eternal damnation ... Mk 3:29 *1777*
craft is in *d* to be set at nought ... Acts 19:27 *2793*
For we are in *d* to be called in ... Acts 19:40 *2793*

DANGEROUS {1}
spent, and when sailing was now *d* ... Acts 27:9 *2000*

DANIEL {81} See BELTESHAZZAR.
1. A son of David.
the second *D*, of Abigail the ... 1Chr 3:1 1840
2. An Israelite who renewed the covenant.
of the sons of Ithamar; *D* ... Ezr 8:2 1840
D, Ginnethon, Baruch, ... Neh 10:6 1840
3. A major prophet.
Though these three men, Noah, *D* ... Eze 14:14 1840
Though Noah, *D*, and Job, were in ... Eze 14:20 1840
Behold, thou art wiser than *D* ... Eze 28:3 1840
were of the children of Judah, *D* ... Dan 1:6 1840
for he gave unto *D* the name of ... Dan 1:7 1840
But *D* purposed in his heart that ... Dan 1:8 1840
Now God had brought *D* into favour ... Dan 1:9 1840
prince of the eunuchs said unto *D* ... Dan 1:10 1840
Then said *D* to Melzar, whom the ... Dan 1:11 1840
of the eunuchs had set over *D* ... Dan 1:11 1840
D had understanding in all ... Dan 1:17 1840
them all was found none like *D* ... Dan 1:19 1840
D continued even unto the first ... Dan 1:21 1840
and they sought *D* and his fellows ... Dan 2:13 1841
Then *D* answered with counsel and ... Dan 2:14 1841
Arioch made the thing known to *D* ... Dan 2:15 1841
Then *D* went in, and desired of the ... Dan 2:16 1841
Then *D* went to his house, and made ... Dan 2:17 1841
that *D* and his fellows should not ... Dan 2:18 1841
revealed unto *D* in a night vision ... Dan 2:19 1841
Then *D* blessed the God of heaven ... Dan 2:19 1841
D answered and said, Blessed be ... Dan 2:20 1841
Therefore *D* went in unto Arioch, ... Dan 2:24 1841
Then Arioch brought in *D* before ... Dan 2:25 1841
The king answered and said to *D* ... Dan 2:26 1841
D answered in the presence of the ... Dan 2:27 1841
upon his face, and worshipped *D* ... Dan 2:46 1841
The king answered unto *D*, and said ... Dan 2:47 1841
Then the king made *D* a great man ... Dan 2:48 1841
Then *D* requested of the king, and ... Dan 2:49 1841
but *D* sat in the gate of the king ... Dan 2:49 1841
But at the last *D* came in before ... Dan 4:8 1841
Then *D*, whose name was ... Dan 4:19 1841
doubts, were found in the same *D* ... Dan 5:12 1841
now let *D* be called, and he will ... Dan 5:12 1841
Then was *D* brought in before the ... Dan 5:13 1841
said unto Daniel, Art thou that *D* ... Dan 5:13 1841
Then *D* answered and said before ... Dan 5:17 1841
and they clothed *D* with scarlet ... Dan 5:29 1841
of whom *D* was first ... Dan 6:2 1841
Then this *D* was preferred above ... Dan 6:3 1841
against *D* concerning the kingdom ... Dan 6:4 1841
find any occasion against this *D* ... Dan 6:5 1841
Now when *D* knew that the writing ... Dan 6:10 1841
found *D* praying and making ... Dan 6:11 1841
and said before the king, That *D* ... Dan 6:13 1841
set his heart on *D* to deliver him ... Dan 6:14 1841
king commanded, and they brought *D* ... Dan 6:16 1841
Now the king spake and said unto *D* ... Dan 6:16 1841
might not be changed concerning *D* ... Dan 6:17 1841
with a lamentable voice unto *D* ... Dan 6:20 1841
king spake and said to Daniel, O *D* ... Dan 6:20 1841
Then said *D* unto the king, O king ... Dan 6:21 1841
should take *D* up out of the den ... Dan 6:23 1841
So *D* was taken up out of the den, ... Dan 6:23 1841
those men which had accused *D* ... Dan 6:24 1841
and fear before the God of *D* ... Dan 6:26 1841
who hath delivered *D* from the ... Dan 6:27 1841
So this *D* prospered in the reign ... Dan 6:28 1841
king of Babylon *D* had a dream ... Dan 7:1 1841
D spake and said, I saw in my ... Dan 7:2 1841
I *D* was grieved in my spirit in ... Dan 7:15 1841
As for me *D*, my cogitations much ... Dan 7:28 1841
appeared unto me, even unto me *D* ... Dan 8:1 1840
it came to pass, when I, even I *D* ... Dan 8:15 1840
I *D* fainted, and was sick certain ... Dan 8:27 1840
the first year of his reign I *D* ... Dan 9:2 1840
and talked with me, and said, O *D* ... Dan 9:22 1840
a thing was revealed unto *D* ... Dan 10:1 1840
In those days I *D* was mourning ... Dan 10:2 1840
And I *D* alone saw the vision ... Dan 10:7 1840
And he said unto me, O *D*, a man ... Dan 10:11 1840
Then said he unto me, Fear not, *D* ... Dan 10:12 1840
But thou, O *D*, shut up the words, ... Dan 12:4 1840
Then I *D* looked, and, behold, ... Dan 12:5 1840
And he said, Go thy way, *D* ... Dan 12:9 1840
spoken of by *D* the prophet ... Mt 24:15 *1158*
spoken of by *D* the prophet ... Mk 13:14 *1158*

DANITES *(dan'-ites)* {4} *Descendants of Dan 1.*
of Zorah, of the family of the *D* ... Judg 13:2 1839
D sought them an inheritance to ... Judg 18:1 1839
thence of the family of the *D* ... Judg 18:11 1839
of the *D* expert in war twenty and ... 1Chr 12:35 1839

DAN-JAAN *(dan-ja'-an)* {1} *A place between Gilead and Zidon.*
and they came to *D*, and about to ... 2Sa 24:6 1842

DANNAH *(dan'-nah)* {1} *A city in Judah.*
And *D*, and Kirjath-sannah, which is ... Josh 15:49 1837

DARA *(da'-rah)* {1} See DARDA. *A son of Zerah.*
Ethan, and Heman, and Calcol, and *D* ... 1Chr 2:6 1873

DARDA *(dar'-dah)* {1} See DARA. *A wise man.*
and Heman, and Chalcol, and *D* ... 1Kin 4:31 1862

DARE {5}
is so fierce that *d* stir him up ... Job 41:10
good man some would even *d* to die ... Rom 5:7 *5111*
For I will not *d* to speak of any ... Rom 15:18 *5111*
D any of you, having a matter ... 1Cor 6:1 *5111*
For we *d* not make ourselves of ... 2Cor 10:12 *5111*

DARIUS *(da-ri'-us)* {25}
1. Darius Hystaspes, king of Persia.
the reign of *D* king of Persia ... Ezr 4:5 1867
of the reign of *D* king of Persia ... Ezr 4:24 1868
cease, till the matter came to *D* ... Ezr 5:5 1868
the river, sent unto *D* the king ... Ezr 5:6 1868
Unto *D* the king, all peace ... Ezr 5:7 1868
Then *D* the king made a decree, and ... Ezr 6:1 1868
I *D* have made a decree ... Ezr 6:12 1868
to that which *D* the king had sent ... Ezr 6:13 1868
to the commandment of Cyrus, and *D* ... Ezr 6:14 1868
year of the reign of *D* the king ... Ezr 6:15 1868
In the second year of *D* the king ... Hag 1:1 1867
in the second year of *D* the king ... Hag 1:15 1867
month, in the second year of *D* ... Hag 2:10 1867
month, in the second year of *D* ... Zec 1:1 1867
Sebat, in the second year of *D* ... Zec 1:7 1867
pass in the fourth year of king *D* ... Zec 7:1 1867
2. Darius Nothus, king of Persia.
to the reign of *D* the Persian ... Neh 12:22 1867
3. Cyaxares, king of Media.
D the Median took the kingdom, ... Dan 5:31 1868
It pleased *D* to set over the ... Dan 6:1 1868
and said thus unto him, King *D* ... Dan 6:6 1868
Wherefore king *D* signed the ... Dan 6:9 1868
Then king *D* wrote unto all people ... Dan 6:25 1868
prospered in the reign of *D* ... Dan 6:28 1868
year of *D* the son of Ahasuerus ... Dan 9:1 1867
I in the first year of *D* the Mede ... Dan 11:1 1867

DARK {43}
the sun went down, and it was *d* ... Gen 15:17 5939
if the plague be somewhat *d* ... Lev 13:6 3544
than the skin, but be somewhat *d* ... Lev 13:21 3544
the other skin, but be somewhat *d* ... Lev 13:26 3544
in the skin, but it be somewhat *d* ... Lev 13:28 3544
the plague be somewhat *d* after ... Lev 13:56 3544
apparently, and not in *d* speeches ... Num 12:8 2420
of the gate, when it was *d* ... Josh 2:5 2822
d waters, and thick clouds of the ... 2Sa 22:12 2841
began to be *d* before the sabbath ... Neh 13:19 6751
of the twilight thereof be *d* ... Job 3:9 2821
They grope in the *d* without light ... Job 12:25 2822
shall be *d* in his tabernacle ... Job 18:6 2821
can he judge through the *d* cloud ... Job 22:13 6205
In the *d* they dig through houses, ... Job 24:16 2822
round about him were *d* waters ... Ps 18:11 2824
Let their way be *d* and slippery ... Ps 35:6 2822
I will open my *d* saying upon the ... Ps 49:4 2420
for the *d* places of the earth are ... Ps 74:20 4285
I will utter *d* sayings of old ... Ps 78:2 2420
thy wonders be known in the *d* ... Ps 88:12 2822
He sent darkness, and made it *d* ... Ps 105:28 2821
of the wise, and their *d* sayings ... Prov 1:6 2420
evening, in the black and *d* night ... Prov 7:9 653
LORD, and their works are in the *d* ... Is 29:15 4285
in a *d* place of the earth ... Is 45:19 2822
feet stumble upon the *d* mountains ... Jer 13:16 5399
He hath set me in *d* places ... Lam 3:6 4285
the house of Israel do in the *d* ... Eze 8:12 2822
and make the stars thereof *d* ... Eze 32:7 6937
of heaven will I make *d* over thee ... Eze 32:8 6937
scattered in the cloudy and *d* day ... Eze 34:12 6205
and understanding *d* sentences ... Dan 8:23 2420
the sun and the moon shall be *d* ... Joel 2:10 6937
and maketh the day *d* with night ... Amos 5:8 2821
even very *d*, and no brightness in ... Amos 5:20 651
and it shall be *d* unto you ... Mic 3:6 2821
and the day shall be *d* over them ... Mic 3:6 6937
light shall not be clear, nor *d* ... Zec 14:6 7087
full of light, having no part *d* ... Lk 11:36 *4652*
And it was now *d*, and Jesus was not ... Jn 6:17 *4653*
early, when it was yet *d*, unto ... Jn 20:1 *4653*
a light that shineth in a *d* place ... 2Pet 1:19 *850*

DARKEN {1}
I will *d* the earth in the clear ... Amos 8:9 2821

DARKENED {19}
earth, so that the land was *d* ... Ex 10:15 2821
Let their eyes be *d*, that they ... Ps 69:23 2821
the moon, or the stars, be not *d* ... Eccl 12:2 2821
that look out of the windows be *d* ... Eccl 12:3 2821
the light is *d* in the heavens ... Is 5:30 2821
the LORD of hosts is the land *d* ... Is 9:19 6272
the sun shall be *d* in his going ... Is 13:10 2821
all joy is *d*, the mirth of the ... Is 24:11 6150
also the day shall be *d*, when I ... Eze 30:18 2821
The sun and the moon shall be *d* ... Joel 3:15 6937
his right eye shall be utterly *d* ... Zec 11:17 3543
of those days shall the sun be *d* ... Mt 24:29 *4654*
tribulation, the sun shall be *d* ... Mk 13:24 *4654*
And the sun was *d*, and the veil of ... Lk 23:45 *4654*
and their foolish heart was *d* ... Rom 1:21 *4654*
Let their eyes be *d*, that they ... Rom 11:10 *4654*
Having the understanding *d* ... Eph 4:18 *4654*
as the third part of them was *d* ... Rev 8:12 *4654*
the air were *d* by reason of the ... Rev 9:2 *4654*

DARKENETH {1}
Who is this that *d* counsel by ... Job 38:2 2821

DARKISH {1}
skin of their flesh be *d* white ... Lev 13:39 3544

DARKLY {1}
For now we see through a glass, *d* ... 1Cor 13:12 *1722,135*

DARKNESS {162}
d was upon the face of the deep ... Gen 1:2 2822
God divided the light from the *d* ... Gen 1:4 2822
Day, and the *d* he called Night ... Gen 1:5 2822
and to divide the light from the *d* ... Gen 1:18 2822
horror of great *d* fell upon him ... Gen 15:12 2825
that there may be *d* over the land ... Ex 10:21 2822
Egypt, even *d* which may be felt ... Ex 10:21 2822
there was a thick *d* in all the ... Ex 10:22 2822
d to them, but it gave light by ... Ex 14:20 2822
unto the thick *d* where God was ... Ex 20:21 6205
with *d*, clouds, and thick *d* ... Deut 4:11 6205
of the cloud, and of the thick *d* ... Deut 5:22 6205
voice out of the midst of the *d* ... Deut 5:23 2822
as the blind gropeth in *d* ... Deut 28:29 653
he put *d* between you and the ... Josh 24:7 3990
the wicked shall be silent in *d* ... 1Sa 2:9 2822
and *d* was under his feet ... 2Sa 22:10 6205
he made *d* pavilions round about ... 2Sa 22:12 2822
and the LORD will lighten my *d* ... 2Sa 22:29 2822
he would dwell in the thick *d* ... 1Kin 8:12 6205
he would dwell in the thick *d* ... 2Chr 6:1 6205
Let that day be *d* ... Job 3:4 2822
Let *d* and the shadow of death ... Job 3:5 2822
that night, let *d* seize upon it ... Job 3:6 652
They meet with *d* in the daytime ... Job 5:14 2822
not return, even to the land of *d* ... Job 10:21 2822
A land of *d*, as *d* itself ... Job 10:22 5890
order, and where the light is as *d* ... Job 10:22 652
discovereth deep things out of *d* ... Job 12:22 2822
not that he shall return out of *d* ... Job 15:22 2822
the day of *d* is ready at his hand ... Job 15:23 2822
He shall not depart out of *d* ... Job 15:30 2822
the light is short because of *d* ... Job 17:12 2822
I have made my bed in the *d* ... Job 17:13 2822
shall be driven from light into *d* ... Job 18:18 2822
and he hath set *d* in my paths ... Job 19:8 2822
All *d* shall be hid in his secret ... Job 20:26 2822
Or *d*, that thou canst not see ... Job 22:11 2822
I was not cut off before the *d* ... Job 23:17 2822
he covered the *d* from my face ... Job 23:17 652
He setteth an end to *d*, and ... Job 28:3 2822
the stones of *d*, and the shadow of ... Job 28:3 652
by his light I walked through *d* ... Job 29:3 2822
I waited for light, there came *d* ... Job 30:26 652
There is no *d*, nor shadow of ... Job 34:22 2822
order our speech by reason of *d* ... Job 37:19 2822
thick *d* a swaddlingband for it, ... Job 38:9 6205
and as for *d*, where is the place ... Job 38:19 2822
and *d* was under his feet ... Ps 18:9 6205
He made *d* his secret place ... Ps 18:11 2822
LORD my God will enlighten my *d* ... Ps 18:28 2822
they walk on in *d* ... Ps 82:5 2825
laid me in the lowest pit, in *d* ... Ps 88:6 4285
me, and mine acquaintance into *d* ... Ps 88:18 4285
the pestilence that walketh in *d* ... Ps 91:6 652
Clouds and *d* are round about him ... Ps 97:2 6205
Thou makest *d*, and it is night ... Ps 104:20 2822
He sent *d*, and made it dark ... Ps 105:28 2822
Such as sit in *d* and in the shadow ... Ps 107:10 2822
He brought them out of *d* and the ... Ps 107:14 2822
there ariseth light in the *d* ... Ps 112:4 2822

D

Surely the *d* shall cover me ... Ps 139:11 2822
the *d* hideth not from thee ... Ps 139:12 2822
the *d* and the light are both alike ... Ps 139:12 2825
he hath made me to dwell in *d* ... Ps 143:3 4285
to walk in the ways of *d* ... Prov 2:13 2822
The way of the wicked is as *d* ... Prov 4:19 653
shall be put out in obscure *d* ... Prov 20:20 2822
as far as light excelleth *d* ... Eccl 2:13 2822
but the fool walketh in *d* ... Eccl 2:14 2822
All his days also he eateth in *d* ... Eccl 5:17 2822
in with vanity, and departeth in *d* ... Eccl 6:4 2822
his name shall be covered with *d* ... Eccl 6:4 2822
let him remember the days of *d* ... Eccl 11:8 2822
that put *d* for light, and light ... Is 5:20 2822
for light, and light for *d* ... Is 5:20 2822
one look unto the land, behold *d* ... Is 5:30 2822
and behold trouble and *d*, dimness ... Is 8:22 2825
and they shall be driven to *d* ... Is 8:22 653
in *d* have seen a great light ... Is 9:2 2822
see out of obscurity, and out of *d* ... Is 29:18 2822
them that sit in *d* out of the ... Is 42:7 2822
I will make *d* light before them ... Is 42:16 4285
will give thee the treasures of *d* ... Is 45:3 2822
I form the light, and create *d* ... Is 45:7 2822
thou silent, and get thee into *d* ... Is 47:5 2822
to them that are in *d*, Shew ... Is 49:9 2822
of his servant, that walketh in *d* ... Is 50:10 2825
and thy *d* be as the noonday ... Is 58:10 653
for brightness, but we walk in *d* ... Is 59:9 653
the *d* shall cover the earth, and ... Is 60:2 2822
the earth, and gross *d* the people ... Is 60:2 6205
a land of *d* ... Jer 2:31 3991
LORD your God, before he cause *d* ... Jer 13:16 2821
of death, and make it gross *d* ... Jer 13:16 6205
them as slippery ways in the *d* ... Jer 23:12 653
hath led me, and brought me into *d* ... Lam 3:2 2822
set *d* upon thy land, saith the ... Eze 32:8 2822
he knoweth what is in the *d* ... Dan 2:22 2816
A day of *d* and of gloominess, a ... Joel 2:2 2822
a day of clouds and of thick *d* ... Joel 2:2 6205
The sun shall be turned into *d* ... Joel 2:31 2822
that maketh the morning *d* ... Amos 4:13 5890
the day of the LORD is *d*, and not ... Amos 5:18 2822
not the day of the LORD be *d* ... Amos 5:20 2822
when I sit in *d*, the LORD shall ... Mic 7:8 2822
d shall pursue his enemies ... Nah 1:8 2822
and desolation, a day of *d* ... Zeph 1:15 2822
a day of clouds and thick *d* ... Zeph 1:15 6205
which sat in *d* saw great light ... Mt 4:16 4655
thy whole body shall be full of *d* ... Mt 6:23 4652
be *d*, how great is that *d* ... Mt 6:23 4655
shall be cast out into outer *d* ... Mt 8:12 4655
What I tell you in *d*, that speak ... Mt 10:27 4653
away, and cast him into outer *d* ... Mt 22:13 4655
unprofitable servant into outer *d* ... Mt 25:30 4655
was *d* over all the land unto the ... Mt 27:45 4655
there was *d* over the whole land ... Mk 15:33 4655
give light to them that sit in *d* ... Lk 1:79 4655
evil, thy body also is full of *d* ... Lk 11:34 4652
light which is in thee be not *d* ... Lk 11:35 4655
in *d* shall be heard in the light ... Lk 12:3 4653
is your hour, and the power of *d* ... Lk 22:53 4655
there was a *d* over all the earth ... Lk 23:44 4655
And the light shineth in *d* ... Jn 1:5 4653
the *d* comprehended it not ... Jn 1:5 4653
men loved *d* rather than light ... Jn 3:19 4655
followeth me shall not walk in *d* ... Jn 8:12 4653
the light, lest *d* come upon you ... Jn 12:35 4653
for he that walketh in *d* knoweth ... Jn 12:35 4653
on me should not abide in *d* ... Jn 12:46 4653
The sun shall be turned into *d* ... Acts 2:20 4655
there fell on him a mist and a *d* ... Acts 13:11 4655
and to turn them from *d* to light ... Acts 26:18 4655
a light of them which are in *d* ... Rom 2:19 4655
therefore cast off the works of *d* ... Rom 13:12 4655
to light the hidden things of *d* ... 1Cor 4:5 4655
the light to shine out of *d* ... 2Cor 4:6 4655
what communion hath light with *d* ... 2Cor 6:14 4655
For ye were sometimes *d*, but now ... Eph 5:8 4655
with the unfruitful works of *d* ... Eph 5:11 4655
the rulers of the *d* of this world ... Eph 6:12 4655
delivered us from the power of *d* ... Col 1:13 4655
But ye, brethren, are not in *d* ... 1Th 5:4 4655
we are not of the night, nor of *d* ... 1Th 5:5 4655
fire, nor unto blackness, and *d* ... Heb 12:18 4655
of *d* into his marvellous light ... 1Pet 2:9 4655
delivered them into chains of *d* ... 2Pet 2:4 2217
to whom the mist of *d* is reserved ... 2Pet 2:17 4655
light, and in him is no *d* at all ... 1Jn 1:5 4653
fellowship with him, and walk in *d* ... 1Jn 1:6 4655
because the *d* is past, and the ... 1Jn 2:8 4653
brother, is in *d* even until now ... 1Jn 2:9 4653
is in *d*, and walketh in *d* ... 1Jn 2:11 4653
because that *d* hath blinded his ... 1Jn 2:11 4653
in everlasting chains under *d* ... Jude 6 2217
the blackness of *d* for ever ... Jude 13 4655
and his kingdom was full of *d* ... Rev 16:10 4656

DARKON *(dar'-kon)* {2} *A family of exiles.*
of Jaalah, the children of *D* ... Ezr 2:56 1874
of Jaala, the children of *D* ... Neh 7:58 1874

DARLING {2}
my *d* from the power of the dog ... Ps 22:20 3173
destructions, my *d* from the lions ... Ps 35:17 3173

DART {3}
the spear, the *d*, nor the ... Job 41:26 4551
Till a *d* strike through his liver ... Prov 7:23 2671
or thrust through with a *d* ... Heb 12:20 1002

DARTS {4}
And he took three *d* in his hand ... 2Sa 18:14 7626
in the city of David, and made *d* ... 2Chr 32:5 7973
D are counted as stubble ... Job 41:29 8455
all the fiery *d* of the wicked ... Eph 6:16 956

DASH {7}
wilt *d* their children, and rip up ... 2Kin 8:12 7376
thou shalt *d* them in pieces like ... Ps 2:9 5310
lest thou *d* thy foot against a ... Ps 91:12 5062
Their bows also shall *d* the young ... Is 13:18 7376
I will *d* them one against another ... Jer 13:14 5310
lest at any time thou *d* thy foot ... Mt 4:6 4350
lest at any time thou *d* thy foot ... Lk 4:11 4350

DASHED {5}
hath *d* in pieces the enemy ... Ex 15:6 7492
be *d* to pieces before their eyes ... Is 13:16 7376
the mother was *d* in pieces upon ... Hos 10:14 7376
infants shall be *d* in pieces ... Hos 13:16 7376
her young children also were *d* in ... Nah 3:10 7376

DASHETH {2}
d thy little ones against the ... Ps 137:9 5310
He that *d* in pieces is come up ... Nah 2:1 6327

DATHAN *(da'-than)* {10} *A conspirator against Moses.*
of Kohath, the son of Levi, and *D* ... Num 16:1 1885
And Moses sent to call *D* and Abiram ... Num 16:12 1885
about the tabernacle of Korah, *D* ... Num 16:24 1885
And Moses rose up and went unto *D* ... Num 16:25 1885
from the tabernacle of Korah, *D* ... Num 16:27 1885
D and Abiram came out, and stood ... Num 16:27 1885
Nemuel, and *D*, and Abiram ... Num 26:9 1885
This is that *D* and Abiram, which ... Num 26:9 1885
And what he did unto *D* and Abiram, ... Deut 11:6 1885
earth opened and swallowed up *D* ... Ps 106:17 1885

DAUB {1}
Say unto them which *d* it with ... Eze 13:11 2902

DAUBED {7}
d it with slime and with pitch, and ... Ex 2:3 2560
others *d* it with untempered ... Eze 13:10 2902
daubing wherewith ye have *d* it ... Eze 13:12 2902
ye have *d* with untempered morter ... Eze 13:14 2902
upon them that have *d* it with ... Eze 13:15 2902
no more, neither they that *d* it ... Eze 13:15 2902
her prophets have *d* them with ... Eze 22:28 2902

DAUBING {1}
Where is the *d* wherewith ye have ... Eze 13:12 2915

DAUGHTER {324}
the *d* of Haran, the father of ... Gen 11:29 1323
son's son, and Sarai his *d* in law ... Gen 11:31 3618
she is the *d* of my father, but ... Gen 20:12 1323
but not the *d* of my mother ... Gen 20:12 1323
And said, Whose *d* art thou ... Gen 24:23 1323
I am the *d* of Bethuel the son of ... Gen 24:24 1323
her, and said, Whose *d* art thou ... Gen 24:47 1323
The *d* of Bethuel, Nahor's son, ... Gen 24:47 1323
master's brother's *d* unto his son ... Gen 24:48 1323
the *d* of Bethuel the Syrian of ... Gen 25:20 1323
Judith the *d* of Beeri the Hittite ... Gen 26:34 1323
Bashemath the *d* of Elon the ... Gen 26:34 1323
the *d* of Ishmael Abraham's son ... Gen 28:9 1323
Rachel his *d* cometh with the ... Gen 29:6 1323
when Jacob saw Rachel the *d* of ... Gen 29:10 1323
years for Rachel thy younger *d* ... Gen 29:18 1323
evening, that he took Leah his *d* ... Gen 29:23 1323
Laban gave unto his *d* Leah Zilpah ... Gen 29:24 1323
him Rachel his *d* to wife also ... Gen 29:28 1323
Laban gave to Rachel his *d* Bilhah ... Gen 29:29 1323
And afterwards she bare a *d* ... Gen 30:21 1323
And Dinah the *d* of Leah, which she ... Gen 34:1 1323
clave unto Dinah the *d* of Jacob ... Gen 34:3 1323
that he had defiled Dinah his *d* ... Gen 34:5 1323
in Israel in lying with Jacob's *d* ... Gen 34:7 1323
my son Shechem longeth for your *d* ... Gen 34:8 1323
then will we take our *d*, and we ... Gen 34:17 1323
he had delight in Jacob's *d* ... Gen 34:19 1323
Adah the *d* of Elon the Hittite, ... Gen 36:2 1323
Aholibamah the *d* of Anah the ... Gen 36:2 1323
Anah the *d* of Zibeon the Hivite ... Gen 36:2 1323
And Bashemath Ishmael's *d*, sister ... Gen 36:3 1323
d of Anah the *d* of Zibeon ... Gen 36:14 1323
came of Aholibamah the *d* of Anah ... Gen 36:18 1323
and Aholibamah the *d* of Anah ... Gen 36:25 1323
the *d* of Matred, the *d* of ... Gen 36:39 1323
Judah saw there a *d* of a certain ... Gen 38:2 1323
said Judah to Tamar his *d* in law ... Gen 38:11 3618
in process of time the *d* of Shuah ... Gen 38:12 1323
not that she was his *d* in law ... Gen 38:16 3618
Tamar thy *d* in law hath played ... Gen 38:24 3618
the *d* of Poti-pherah priest of On ... Gen 41:45 1323
came, which Asenath the *d* of ... Gen 41:50 1323
in Padan-aram, with his *d* Dinah ... Gen 46:15 1323
whom Laban gave to Leah his *d* ... Gen 46:18 1323
Ephraim, which Asenath the *d* of ... Gen 46:20 1323
Laban gave unto Rachel his *d* ... Gen 46:25 1323
but if it be a *d*, then she shall ... Ex 1:16 1323
every *d* ye shall save alive ... Ex 1:22 1323
Levi, and took to wife a *d* of Levi ... Ex 2:1 1323
the *d* of Pharaoh came down to ... Ex 2:5 1323
said his sister to Pharaoh's *d* ... Ex 2:7 1323
Pharaoh's *d* said to her, Go ... Ex 2:8 1323
Pharaoh's *d* said unto her, Take ... Ex 2:9 1323
she brought him unto Pharaoh's *d* ... Ex 2:10 1323
and he gave Moses Zipporah his *d* ... Ex 2:21 1323
d of Amminadab, sister of Naashon ... Ex 6:23 1323
thou, nor thy son, nor thy *d* ... Ex 20:10 1323
if a man sell his *d* to be a ... Ex 21:7 1323
gored a son, or have gored a *d* ... Ex 21:31 1323
fulfilled, for a son, or for a *d* ... Lev 12:6 1323
the *d* of thy father, or *d* ... Lev 18:9 1323
d, or of thy daughter's *d* ... Lev 18:10 1323
of thy father's wife's *d*, ... Lev 18:11 1323
the nakedness of thy *d* in law ... Lev 18:15 3618
the nakedness of a woman and her *d* ... Lev 18:17 1323
son's *d*, or her daughter's *d* ... Lev 18:17 1323
Do not prostitute thy *d*, to cause ... Lev 19:29 1323
And if a man lie with his *d* in law ... Lev 20:12 3618
father's *d*, or his mother's *d* ... Lev 20:17 1323
and for his son, and for his *d* ... Lev 21:2 1323
the *d* of any priest, if she ... Lev 21:9 1323
If the priest's *d* also be married ... Lev 22:12 1323
But if the priest's *d* be a widow ... Lev 22:13 1323
the *d* of Dibri, of the tribe of ... Lev 24:11 1323
was slain was Cozbi, the *d* of Zur ... Num 25:15 1323
the *d* of a prince of Midian, ... Num 25:18 1323
the name of the *d* of Asher was ... Num 26:46 1323
the *d* of Levi, whom her mother ... Num 26:59 1323
inheritance to pass unto his *d* ... Num 27:8 1323
And if he have no *d*, then ye shall ... Num 27:9 1323
wife, between the father and his *d* ... Num 30:16 1323
And every *d*, that possesseth an ... Num 36:8 1323
thou, nor thy son, nor thy *d* ... Deut 5:14 1323
thy *d* thou shalt not give unto ... Deut 7:3 1323
nor his *d* shalt thou take unto ... Deut 7:3 1323
thou, and thy son, and thy *d* ... Deut 12:18 1323
thy mother, or thy son, or thy *d* ... Deut 13:6 1323
God, thou, and thy son, and thy *d* ... Deut 16:11 1323
feast, thou, and thy son, and thy *d* ... Deut 16:14 1323
or his *d* to pass through the fire ... Deut 18:10 1323
I gave my *d* unto this man to wife ... Deut 22:16 1323
saying, I found not thy *d* a maid ... Deut 22:17 1323
the *d* of his father, or the ... Deut 27:22 1323
father, or the *d* of his mother ... Deut 27:22 1323
toward her son, and toward her *d* ... Deut 28:56 1323
will I give Achsah my *d* to wife ... Josh 15:16 1323
he gave him Achsah his *d* to wife ... Josh 15:17 1323
will I give Achsah my *d* to wife ... Judg 1:12 1323
he gave him Achsah his *d* to wife ... Judg 1:13 1323
his *d* came out to meet him with ... Judg 11:34 1323
her he had neither son nor *d* ... Judg 11:34 1323
his clothes, and said, Alas, my *d* ... Judg 11:35 1323
went yearly to lament the *d* of ... Judg 11:40 1323
Behold, here is my *d* a maiden ... Judg 19:24 1323
give his *d* unto Benjamin to wife ... Judg 21:1 1323
her *d* in law, with her, which ... Ruth 1:22 3618
And she said unto her, Go, my *d* ... Ruth 2:2 1323
unto Ruth, Hearest thou not, my *d* ... Ruth 2:8 1323
And Naomi said unto her *d* in law ... Ruth 2:20 3618
d in law, It is good, my *d* ... Ruth 2:22 1323
mother in law said unto her, My *d* ... Ruth 3:1 1323
Blessed be thou of the LORD, my *d* ... Ruth 3:10 1323
And now, my *d*, fear not ... Ruth 3:11 1323
law, she said, Who art thou, my *d* ... Ruth 3:16 1323
Then said she, Sit still, my *d* ... Ruth 3:18 1323
for thy *d* in law, which loveth ... Ruth 4:15 3618
thine handmaid for a *d* of Belial ... 1Sa 1:16 1323
his *d* in law, Phinehas' wife, was ... 1Sa 4:19 3618
was Ahinoam, the *d* of Ahimaaz ... 1Sa 14:50 1323
riches, and will give him his *d* ... 1Sa 17:25 1323
to David, Behold my elder *d* Merab ... 1Sa 18:17 1323
at the time when Merab Saul's *d* ... 1Sa 18:19 1323
And Michal Saul's *d* loved David ... 1Sa 18:20 1323
gave him Michal his *d* to wife ... 1Sa 18:27 1323
and that Michal Saul's *d* loved him ... 1Sa 18:28 1323
But Saul had given Michal his *d* ... 1Sa 25:44 1323
the *d* of Talmai king of Geshur ... 2Sa 3:3 1323
name was Rizpah, the *d* of Aiah ... 2Sa 3:7 1323
thou first bring Michal Saul's *d* ... 2Sa 3:13 1323
Michal Saul's *d* looked through a ... 2Sa 6:16 1323
Michal the *d* of Saul came out to ... 2Sa 6:20 1323
Therefore Michal the *d* of Saul ... 2Sa 6:23 1323
the *d* of Eliam, the wife of Uriah ... 2Sa 11:3 1323
his bosom, and was unto him as a *d* ... 2Sa 12:3 1323
were born three sons, and one *d* ... 2Sa 14:27 1323
in to Abigail the *d* of Nahash ... 2Sa 17:25 1323
two sons of Rizpah the *d* of Aiah ... 2Sa 21:8 1323
five sons of Michal the *d* of Saul ... 2Sa 21:8 1323
Rizpah the *d* of Aiah took ... 2Sa 21:10 1323
David what Rizpah the *d* of Aiah ... 2Sa 21:11 1323
of Egypt, and took Pharaoh's *d* ... 1Kin 3:1 1323
Taphath the *d* of Solomon to wife ... 1Kin 4:11 1323
Basmath the *d* of Solomon to wife ... 1Kin 4:15 1323
also an house for Pharaoh's *d* ... 1Kin 7:8 1323
given it for a present unto his *d* ... 1Kin 9:16 1323
But Pharaoh's *d* came up out of ... 1Kin 9:24 1323
together with the *d* of Pharaoh ... 1Kin 11:1 1323
was Maachah, the *d* of Abishalom ... 1Kin 15:2 1323
was Maachah, the *d* of Abishalom ... 1Kin 15:10 1323
the *d* of Ethbaal king of the ... 1Kin 16:31 1323
name was Azubah the *d* of Shilhi ... 1Kin 22:42 1323
for the *d* of Ahab was his wife ... 2Kin 8:18 1323
the *d* of Omri king of Israel ... 2Kin 8:26 1323
for she is a king's *d* ... 2Kin 9:34 1323
the *d* of king Joram, sister of ... 2Kin 11:2 1323
Give thy *d* to my son to wife ... 2Kin 14:9 1323
name was Jerusha, the *d* of Zadok ... 2Kin 15:33 1323
also was Abi, the *d* of Zachariah ... 2Kin 18:2 1323
The virgin the *d* of Zion hath ... 2Kin 19:21 1323
the *d* of Jerusalem hath shaken ... 2Kin 19:21 1323
the *d* of Haruz of Jotbah ... 2Kin 21:19 1323
the *d* of Adaiah of Boscath ... 2Kin 22:1 1323
his *d* to pass through the fire to ... 2Kin 23:10 1323
the *d* of Jeremiah of Libnah ... 2Kin 23:31 1323
the *d* of Pedaiah of Rumah ... 2Kin 23:36 1323
the *d* of Elnathan of Jerusalem ... 2Kin 24:8 1323

the *d* of Jeremiah of Libnah ... 2Kin 24:18 1323
the *d* of Matred, the *d* of ... 1Chr 1:50 1323
of the *d* of Shua the Canaanitess ... 1Chr 2:3 1323
Tamar his *d* in law bare him ... 1Chr 2:4 3618
d of Machir the father of Gilead ... 1Chr 2:21 1323
Sheshan gave his *d* to Jarha his ... 1Chr 2:35 1323
and the *d* of Caleb was Achsa ... 1Chr 2:49 1323
the *d* of Talmai king of Geshur ... 1Chr 3:2 1323
of Bath-shua the *d* of Ammiel ... 1Chr 3:5 1323
sons of Bithiah the *d* of Pharaoh ... 1Chr 4:18 1323
his *d* was Sherah, who built ... 1Chr 7:24 1323
that Michal the *d* of Saul looking ... 1Chr 15:29 1323
Solomon brought up the *d* of ... 2Chr 8:11 1323
Rehoboam took him Mahalath the *d* ... 2Chr 11:18 1121
Abihail the *d* of Eliab the son of ... 2Chr 11:18 1323
he took Maachah the *d* of Absalom ... 2Chr 11:20 1323
Rehoboam loved Maachah the *d* of ... 2Chr 11:21 1323
Michaiah the *d* of Uriel of Gibeah ... 2Chr 13:2 1323
name was Azubah the *d* of Shilhi ... 2Chr 20:31 1323
for he had the *d* of Ahab to wife ... 2Chr 21:6 1323
also was Athaliah the *d* of Omri ... 2Chr 22:2 1323
the *d* of the king, took Joash the ... 2Chr 22:11
the *d* of king Jehoram, the wife ... 2Chr 22:11 1323
Give thy *d* to my son to wife ... 2Chr 25:18 1323
also was Jerushah, the *d* of Zadok ... 2Chr 27:1 1323
was Abijah, the *d* of Zechariah ... 2Chr 29:1 1323
the *d* of Meshullam the son of ... Neh 6:18 1323
that is, Esther, his uncle's *d* ... Est 2:7 1323
were dead, took for his own *d* ... Est 2:7 1323
the *d* of Abihail the uncle of ... Est 2:15 1323
who had taken her for his *d* ... Est 2:15 1323
the *d* of Abihail, and Mordecai the ... Est 9:29 1323
in the gates of the *d* of Zion ... Ps 9:14 1323
Hearken, O *d*, and consider, and ... Ps 45:10 1323
the *d* of Tyre shall be there with ... Ps 45:12 1323
The king's *d* is all glorious ... Ps 45:13 1323
O *d* of Babylon, who art to be ... Ps 137:8 1323
thy feet with shoes, O prince's *d* ... Song 7:1 1323
the *d* of Zion is left as a ... Is 1:8 1323
Lift up thy voice, O *d* of Gallim ... Is 10:30 1323
the mount of the *d* of Zion ... Is 10:32 1004
unto the mount of the *d* of Zion ... Is 16:1 1323
spoiling of the *d* of my people ... Is 22:4 1323
land as a river, O *d* of Tarshish ... Is 23:10 1323
thou oppressed virgin, *d* of Zidon ... Is 23:12 1323
the *d* of Zion, hath despised thee ... Is 37:22 1323
the *d* of Jerusalem hath shaken ... Is 37:22 1323
O virgin *d* of Babylon, sit on the ... Is 47:1 1323
no throne, O *d* of the Chaldeans ... Is 47:1 1323
darkness, O *d* of the Chaldeans ... Is 47:5 1323
of thy neck, O captive *d* of Zion ... Is 52:2 1323
world, Say ye to the *d* of Zion ... Is 62:11 1323
toward the *d* of my people ... Jer 4:11 1323
child, the voice of the *d* of Zion ... Jer 4:31 1323
I have likened the *d* of Zion to a ... Jer 6:2 1323
of the *d* of my people slightly ... Jer 6:14
for war against thee, O *d* of Zion ... Jer 6:23 1323
O *d* of my people, gird thee with ... Jer 6:26 1323
of the *d* of my people slightly ... Jer 8:11 1323
the voice of the cry of the *d* of ... Jer 8:19 1323
For the hurt of the *d* of my ... Jer 8:21 1323
of the *d* of my people recovered ... Jer 8:22 1323
the slain of the *d* of my people ... Jer 9:1 1323
shall I do for the *d* of my people ... Jer 9:7 1323
for the virgin *d* of my people is ... Jer 14:17 1323
go about, O thou backsliding *d* ... Jer 31:22 1323
balm, O virgin, the *d* of Egypt ... Jer 46:11 1323
O thou *d* dwelling in Egypt, ... Jer 46:19 1323
The *d* of Egypt shall be ... Jer 46:24 1323
Thou *d* that dost inhabit Dibon, ... Jer 48:18 1323
flowing valley, O backsliding *d* ... Jer 49:4 1323
against thee, O *d* of Babylon ... Jer 50:42 1323
The *d* of Babylon is like a ... Jer 51:33 1323
the *d* of Jeremiah of Libnah ... Jer 52:1 1323
from the *d* of Zion all her beauty ... Lam 1:6 1323
the *d* of Judah, as in a winepress ... Lam 1:15 1323
the *d* of Zion with a cloud in his ... Lam 2:1 1323
strong holds of the *d* of Judah ... Lam 2:2 1323
the tabernacle of the *d* of Zion ... Lam 2:4 1323
in the *d* of Judah mourning ... Lam 2:5 1323
destroy the wall of the *d* of Zion ... Lam 2:8 1323
The elders of the *d* of Zion sit ... Lam 2:10 1323
destruction of the *d* of my people ... Lam 2:11 1323
I liken to thee, O *d* of Jerusalem ... Lam 2:13 1323
comfort thee, O virgin *d* of Zion ... Lam 2:13 1323
their head at the *d* of Jerusalem ... Lam 2:15 1323
the Lord, O wall of the *d* of Zion ... Lam 2:18 1323
destruction of the *d* of my people ... Lam 3:48 1323
the *d* of my people is become ... Lam 4:3 1323
of the iniquity of the *d* of my ... Lam 4:6 1323
destruction of the *d* of my people ... Lam 4:10 1323
O *d* of Edom, that dwellest in the ... Lam 4:21 1323
is accomplished, O *d* of Zion ... Lam 4:22 1323
visit thine iniquity, O *d* of Edom ... Lam 4:22 1323
shall deliver neither son nor *d* ... Eze 14:20 1323
As is the mother, so is her *d* ... Eze 16:44 1323
Thou art thy mother's *d*, that ... Eze 16:45 1323
hath lewdly defiled his *d* in law ... Eze 22:11 3618
his sister, his father's *d* ... Eze 22:11 1323
for mother, or for son, or for *d* ... Eze 44:25 1323
for the king's *d* of the south ... Dan 11:6 1323
he shall give him the *d* of women ... Dan 11:17 1323
and took Gomer the *d* of Diblaim ... Hos 1:3 1323
she conceived again, and bare a *d* ... Hos 1:6 1323
of the sin to the *d* of Zion ... Mic 1:13 1323
the strong hold of the *d* of Zion ... Mic 4:8 1323
shall come to the *d* of Jerusalem ... Mic 4:8 1323
O *d* of Zion, like a woman in ... Mic 4:10 1323
Arise and thresh, O *d* of Zion ... Mic 4:13 1323
thyself in troops, O *d* of troops ... Mic 5:1 1323
the *d* riseth up against her ... Mic 7:6 1323
the *d* in law against her mother ... Mic 7:6 3618
even the *d* of my dispersed, shall ... Zeph 3:10 1323
Sing, O *d* of Zion ... Zeph 3:14 1323
all the heart, O *d* of Jerusalem ... Zeph 3:14 1323
dwellest with the *d* of Babylon ... Zec 2:7 1323
Sing and rejoice, O *d* of Zion ... Zec 2:10 1323
Rejoice greatly, O *d* of Zion ... Zec 9:9 1323
shout, O *d* of Jerusalem ... Zec 9:9 1323
married the *d* of a strange god ... Mal 2:11 1323
saying, My *d* is even now dead ... Mt 9:18 *2364*
and when he saw her, he said, *D* ... Mt 9:22 *2364*
the *d* against her mother, and the ... Mt 10:35 *2364*
the *d* in law against her mother ... Mt 10:35 *3565*
he that loveth son or *d* more than ... Mt 10:37 *2364*
the *d* of Herodias danced before ... Mt 14:6 *2364*
my *d* is grievously vexed with a ... Mt 15:22 *2364*
her *d* was made whole from that ... Mt 15:28 *2364*
Tell ye the *d* of Sion, Behold, ... Mt 21:5 *2364*
My little *d* lieth at the point of ... Mk 5:23 *2365*
And he said unto her, *D*, thy faith ... Mk 5:34 *2364*
certain which said, Thy *d* is dead ... Mk 5:35 *2364*
when the *d* of the said Herodias ... Mk 6:22 *2364*
whose young *d* had an unclean ... Mk 7:25 *2365*
cast forth the devil out of her *d* ... Mk 7:26 *2364*
the devil is gone out of thy *d* ... Mk 7:29 *2364*
out, and her *d* laid upon the bed ... Mk 7:30 *2364*
the *d* of Phanuel, of the tribe of ... Lk 2:36 *2364*
For he had one only *d*, about ... Lk 8:42 *2364*
And he said unto her, *D*, be of ... Lk 8:48 *2364*
saying to him, Thy *d* is dead ... Lk 8:49 *2364*
the mother against the *d* ... Lk 12:53 *2364*
and the *d* against the mother ... Lk 12:53 *2364*
in law against her *d* in law ... Lk 12:53 *3565*
the *d* in law against her mother ... Lk 12:53 *3565*
being a *d* of Abraham, whom Satan ... Lk 13:16 *2364*
Fear not, *d* of Sion ... Jn 12:15 *2364*
Pharaoh's *d* took him up, and ... Acts 7:21 *2364*
be called the son of Pharaoh's *d* ... Heb 11:24 *2364*

DAUGHTER'S {3}
daughter, or of thy *d* daughter ... Lev 18:10 1323
or her *d* daughter, to uncover her ... Lev 18:17 1323
are the tokens of my *d* virginity ... Deut 22:17 1323

DAUGHTERS {256}
and he begat sons and *d* ... Gen 5:4 1121
seven years, and begat sons and *d* ... Gen 5:7 1121
fifteen years, and begat sons and *d* ... Gen 5:10 1121
forty years, and begat sons and *d* ... Gen 5:13 1121
thirty years, and begat sons and *d* ... Gen 5:16 1121
hundred years, and begat sons and *d* ... Gen 5:19 1121
hundred years, and begat sons and *d* ... Gen 5:22 1121
and two years, and begat sons and *d* ... Gen 5:26 1121
and five years, and begat sons and *d* ... Gen 5:30 1121
earth, and *d* were born unto them, ... Gen 6:1 1121
the *d* of men that they were fair ... Gen 6:2 1121
of God came in unto the *d* of men ... Gen 6:4 1121
hundred years, and begat sons and *d* ... Gen 11:11 1121
three years, and begat sons and *d* ... Gen 11:13 1121
three years, and begat sons and *d* ... Gen 11:15 1121
thirty years, and begat sons and *d* ... Gen 11:17 1121
and nine years, and begat sons and *d* ... Gen 11:19 1121
seven years, and begat sons and *d* ... Gen 11:21 1121
hundred years, and begat sons and *d* ... Gen 11:23 1121
years, and begat sons and *d* ... Gen 11:25 1121
I have two *d* which have not known ... Gen 19:8 1121
son in law, and thy sons, and thy *d* ... Gen 19:12 1121
sons in law, which married his *d* ... Gen 19:14 1121
take thy wife, and thy two *d* ... Gen 19:15 1121
and upon the hand of his two *d* ... Gen 19:16 1121
mountain, and his two *d* with him ... Gen 19:30 1121
dwelt in a cave, he and his two *d* ... Gen 19:30 1121
Thus were both the *d* of Lot with ... Gen 19:36 1121
my son of the *d* of the Canaanites ... Gen 24:3 1121
the *d* of the men of the city come ... Gen 24:13 1121
my son of the *d* of the Canaanites ... Gen 24:37 1121
my life because of the *d* of Heth ... Gen 27:46 1121
take a wife of the *d* of Heth ... Gen 27:46 1121
which are of the *d* of the land ... Gen 27:46 1121
take a wife of the *d* of Canaan ... Gen 28:1 1121
d of Laban thy mother's brother ... Gen 28:2 1121
take a wife of the *d* of Canaan ... Gen 28:6 1121
Esau seeing that the *d* of Canaan ... Gen 28:8 1121
And Laban had two *d* ... Gen 29:16 1121
for the *d* will call me blessed ... Gen 30:13 1121
to me, and carried away my *d* ... Gen 31:26 1121
me to kiss my sons and my *d* ... Gen 31:28 1121
take by force thy *d* from me ... Gen 31:31 1121
thee fourteen years for thy two *d* ... Gen 31:41 1121
These *d* are my *d*, and ... Gen 31:43 1121
Jacob, These *d* are my *d* ... Gen 31:43 1121
can I do this day unto these my *d* ... Gen 31:43 1121
If thou shalt afflict my *d* ... Gen 31:50 1121
take other wives beside my *d* ... Gen 31:50 1121
up, and kissed his sons and his *d* ... Gen 31:55 1121
went out to see the *d* of the land ... Gen 34:1 1121
with us, and give your *d* unto us ... Gen 34:9 1121
unto us, and take our *d* unto you ... Gen 34:9 1121
Then will we give our *d* unto you ... Gen 34:16 1121
and we will take your *d* to us ... Gen 34:16 1121
us take their *d* to us for wives ... Gen 34:21 1121
and let us give them our *d* ... Gen 34:21 1121
took his wives of the *d* of Canaan ... Gen 36:2 1121
his wives, and his sons, and his *d* ... Gen 36:6 1121
all his *d* rose up to comfort him ... Gen 37:35 1121
his *d*, and his sons' *d* ... Gen 46:7 1121
his *d* were thirty and three ... Gen 46:15 1121
the priest of Midian had seven *d* ... Ex 2:16 1121
And he said unto his *d*, And where ... Ex 2:20 1121
upon your sons, and upon your *d* ... Ex 3:22 1121
one of the *d* of Putiel to wife ... Ex 6:25 1121
old, with our sons and with our *d* ... Ex 10:9 1121
and she have born him sons or *d* ... Ex 21:4 1121
with her after the manner of *d* ... Ex 21:9 1121
wives, of your sons, and of your *d* ... Ex 32:2 1121
take of their *d* unto thy sons ... Ex 34:16 1121
their *d* go a whoring after their ... Ex 34:16 1121
and thy sons, and thy *d* with thee ... Lev 10:14 1121
the flesh of your *d* shall ye eat ... Lev 26:29 1121
to thy *d* with thee, by a statute ... Num 18:11 1121
thy *d* with thee, by a statute for ... Num 18:19 1121
his sons that escaped, and his *d* ... Num 21:29 1121
whoredom with the *d* of Moab ... Num 25:1 1121
son of Hepher had no sons, but *d* ... Num 26:33 1121
the names of the *d* of Zelophehad ... Num 26:33 1121
Then came the *d* of Zelophehad ... Num 27:1 1121
and these are the names of his *d* ... Num 27:1 1121
The *d* of Zelophehad speak right ... Num 27:7 1121
Zelophehad our brother unto his *d* ... Num 36:2 1121
concerning the *d* of Zelophehad ... Num 36:6 1121
so did the *d* of Zelophehad ... Num 36:10 1121
the *d* of Zelophehad, were married ... Num 36:11 1121
God, ye, and your sons, and your *d* ... Deut 12:12 1121
their *d* they have burnt in the ... Deut 12:31 1121
be no whore of the *d* of Israel ... Deut 23:17 1121
thy *d* shall be given unto another ... Deut 28:32 1121
Thou shalt beget sons and *d* ... Deut 28:41 1121
the flesh of thy sons and of thy *d* ... Deut 28:53 1121
of his sons, and of his *d* ... Deut 32:19 1121
of gold, and his sons, and his *d* ... Josh 7:24 1121
of Manasseh, had no sons, but *d* ... Josh 17:3 1121
and these are the names of his *d* ... Josh 17:3 1121
Because the *d* of Manasseh had an ... Josh 17:6 1121
they took their *d* to be their ... Judg 3:6 1121
gave their *d* to their sons, and ... Judg 3:6 1121
That the *d* of Israel went yearly ... Judg 11:40 1121
he had thirty sons, and thirty *d* ... Judg 12:9 1121
took in thirty *d* from abroad for ... Judg 12:9 1121
of the *d* of the Philistines ... Judg 14:1 1121
of the *d* of the Philistines ... Judg 14:2 1121
woman among the *d* of thy brethren ... Judg 14:3 1121
not give them of our *d* to wives ... Judg 21:7 1121
may not give them wives of our *d* ... Judg 21:18 1121
if the *d* of Shiloh come out to ... Judg 21:21 1121
man his wife of the *d* of Shiloh ... Judg 21:21 1121
Then she arose with her *d* in law ... Ruth 1:6 3618
her two *d* in law with her ... Ruth 1:7 3618
Naomi said unto her two *d* in law ... Ruth 1:8 3618
And Naomi said, Turn again, my *d* ... Ruth 1:11 1121
Turn again, my *d*, go your way ... Ruth 1:12 1121
nay, my *d* ... Ruth 1:13 1121
wife, and to all her sons and her *d* ... 1Sa 1:4 1121
and bare three sons and two *d* ... 1Sa 2:21 1121
he will take your *d* to be ... 1Sa 8:13 1121
the names of his two *d* were these ... 1Sa 14:49 1121
wives, and their sons, and their *d* ... 1Sa 30:3 1121
man for his sons and for his *d* ... 1Sa 30:6 1121
nor great, neither sons nor *d* ... 1Sa 30:19 1121
lest the *d* of the Philistines ... 2Sa 1:20 1121
lest the *d* of the uncircumcised ... 2Sa 1:20 1121
Ye *d* of Israel, weep over Saul, ... 2Sa 1:24 1121
were yet sons and *d* born to David ... 2Sa 5:13 1121
d that were virgins apparelled ... 2Sa 13:18 1121
the lives of thy sons and of thy *d* ... 2Sa 19:5 1121
their *d* to pass through the fire, ... 2Kin 17:17 1121
Now Sheshan had no sons, but *d* ... 1Chr 2:34 1121
Shimei had sixteen sons and six *d* ... 1Chr 4:27 1121
and Zelophehad had *d* ... 1Chr 7:15 1121
and David begat more sons and *d* ... 1Chr 14:3 1121
died, and had no sons, but *d* ... 1Chr 23:22 1121
to Heman fourteen sons and three *d* ... 1Chr 25:5 1121
son of a woman of the *d* of Dan ... 2Chr 2:14 1121
and eight sons, and threescore *d* ... 2Chr 11:21 1121
twenty and two sons, and sixteen *d* ... 2Chr 13:21 1121
and he begat sons and *d* ... 2Chr 24:3 1121
thousand, women, sons, and *d* ... 2Chr 28:8 1121
the sword, and our sons and our *d* ... 2Chr 29:9 1121
wives, and their sons, and their *d* ... 2Chr 31:18 1121
which took a wife of the *d* of ... Ezr 2:61 1121
taken of their *d* for themselves ... Ezr 9:2 1121
give not your *d* unto their sons ... Ezr 9:12 1121
take their *d* unto your sons ... Ezr 9:12 1121
part of Jerusalem, he and his *d* ... Neh 3:12 1121
brethren, your sons, and your *d* ... Neh 4:14 1121
that said, We, our sons, and our *d* ... Neh 5:2 1121
our *d* to be servants ... Neh 5:5 1121
some of our *d* are brought unto ... Neh 5:5 1121
which took one of the *d* of ... Neh 7:63 1121
wives, their sons, and their *d* ... Neh 10:28 1121
that we would not give our *d* unto ... Neh 10:30 1121
nor take their *d* for our sons ... Neh 10:30 1121
not give your *d* unto their sons ... Neh 13:25 1121
nor take their *d* unto your sons ... Neh 13:25 1121
unto him seven sons and three *d* ... Job 1:2 1121
his *d* were eating and drinking ... Job 1:13 1121
thy *d* were eating and drinking ... Job 1:18 1121
He had also seven sons and three *d* ... Job 42:13 1121
found so fair as the *d* of Job ... Job 42:15 1121
Kings' *d* were among thy ... Ps 45:9 1121
let the *d* of Judah be glad, ... Ps 48:11 1121
the *d* of Judah rejoiced because ... Ps 97:8 1121
sons and their *d* unto devils, ... Ps 106:37 1121
blood of their sons and of their *d* ... Ps 106:38 1121
that our *d* may be as corner ... Ps 144:12 1121

The horseleach hath two *d* ... Prov 30:15 1121
Many *d* have done virtuously, but ... Prov 31:29 1121
all the *d* of musick shall be ... Eccl 12:4 1121
O ye *d* of Jerusalem, as the tents ... Song 1:5 1121
thorns, so is my love among the *d* ... Song 2:2 1121
O ye *d* of Jerusalem, by the roes, ... Song 2:7 1121
O ye *d* of Jerusalem, by the roes, ... Song 3:5 1121
with love, for the *d* of Jerusalem ... Song 3:10 1121
O ye *d* of Zion, and behold king ... Song 3:11 1121
O *d* of Jerusalem, if ye find my ... Song 5:8 1121
is my friend, O *d* of Jerusalem ... Song 5:16 1121
The *d* saw her, and blessed her ... Song 6:9 1121
O *d* of Jerusalem, that ye stir ... Song 8:4 1121
Because the *d* of Zion are haughty ... Is 3:16 1121
of the head of the *d* of Zion ... Is 3:17 1121
away the filth of the *d* of Zion ... Is 4:4 1121
so the *d* of Moab shall be at the ... Is 16:2 1121
hear my voice, ye careless *d* ... Is 32:9 1121
my *d* from the ends of the earth ... Is 43:6 1121
thy *d* shall be carried upon their ... Is 49:22 1121
name better than of sons and of *d* ... Is 56:5 1121
thy *d* shall be nursed at thy side ... Is 60:4 1121
herds, their sons and their *d* ... Jer 3:24 1121
thy sons and thy *d* should eat ... Jer 5:17 1121
their sons and their *d* in the fire ... Jer 7:31 1121
mouth, and teach your *d* wailing ... Jer 9:20 1121
their *d* shall die by famine ... Jer 11:22 1121
nor their sons, nor their *d* ... Jer 14:16 1121
thou have sons or *d* in this place ... Jer 16:2 1121
concerning the *d* that are born in ... Jer 16:3 1121
sons and the flesh of their *d* ... Jer 19:9 1121
Take ye wives, and beget sons and *d* ... Jer 29:6 1121
give your *d* to husbands ... Jer 29:6 1121
that they may bear sons and *d* ... Jer 29:6 1121
their *d* to pass through the fire ... Jer 32:35 1121
our wives, our sons, nor our *d* ... Jer 35:8 1121
were in Mizpah, even the king's *d* ... Jer 41:10 1121
and children, and the king's *d* ... Jer 43:6 1121
taken captives, and thy *d* captives ... Jer 48:46 1121
her *d* shall be burned with fire ... Jer 49:2 1121
ye *d* of Rabbah, gird you with ... Jer 49:3 1121
because of all the *d* of my city ... Lam 3:51 1121
face against the *d* of thy people ... Eze 13:17 1121
shall deliver neither sons nor *d* ... Eze 14:16 1121
shall deliver neither sons nor *d* ... Eze 14:18 1121
be brought forth, both sons and *d* ... Eze 14:22 1121
thou hast taken thy sons and thy *d* ... Eze 16:20 1121
the *d* of the Philistines, which ... Eze 16:27 1121
her *d* that dwell at thy left hand ... Eze 16:46 1121
thy right hand, is Sodom and her *d* ... Eze 16:46 1121
hath not done, she nor her *d* ... Eze 16:48 1121
as thou hast done, thou and thy *d* ... Eze 16:48 1121
idleness was in her and in her *d* ... Eze 16:49 1121
the captivity of Sodom and her *d* ... Eze 16:53 1121
the captivity of Samaria and her *d* ... Eze 16:53 1121
When thy sisters, Sodom and her *d* ... Eze 16:55 1121
her *d* shall return to their ... Eze 16:55 1121
thy *d* shall return to your former ... Eze 16:55 1121
of thy reproach of the *d* of Syria ... Eze 16:57 1121
the *d* of the Philistines, which ... Eze 16:57 1121
I will give them unto thee for *d* ... Eze 16:61 1121
two women, the *d* of one mother ... Eze 23:2 1121
were mine, and they bare sons and *d* ... Eze 23:4 1121
they took her sons and her *d* ... Eze 23:10 1121
they shall take thy sons and thy *d* ... Eze 23:25 1121
shall slay their sons and their *d* ... Eze 23:47 1121
your *d* whom ye have left shall ... Eze 24:21 1121
minds, their sons and their *d* ... Eze 24:25 1121
her *d* which are in the field ... Eze 26:6 1121
with the sword thy *d* in the field ... Eze 26:8 1121
her *d* shall go into captivity ... Eze 30:18 1121
the *d* of the nations shall lament ... Eze 32:16 1121
the *d* of the famous nations, unto ... Eze 32:18 1121
therefore your *d* shall commit ... Hos 4:13 1121
I will not punish your *d* when ... Hos 4:14 1121
your *d* shall prophesy, your old ... Joel 2:28 1121
your *d* into the hand of the ... Joel 3:8 1121
thy *d* shall fall by the sword, and ... Amos 7:17 1121
and his wife was of the *d* of Aaron ... Lk 1:5 *2364*
D of Jerusalem, weep not for me, ... Lk 23:28 *2364*
your *d* shall prophesy, and your ... Acts 2:17 *2364*
And the same man had four *d* ... Acts 21:9 *2364*
you, and ye shall be my sons and *d* ... 2Cor 6:18 *2364*
whose *d* ye are, as long as ye do ... 1Pet 3:6 *5043*

DAVID {1085} See DAVID'S. *Second king of Israel.*
father of Jesse, the father of *D* ... Ruth 4:17 1732
begat Jesse, and Jesse begat *D* ... Ruth 4:22 1732
came upon *D* from that day forward ... 1Sa 16:13 1732
Jesse, and said, Send me *D* thy son ... 1Sa 16:19 1732
sent them by *D* his son unto Saul ... 1Sa 16:20 1732
D came to Saul, and stood before ... 1Sa 16:21 1732
Saul sent to Jesse, saying, Let *D* ... 1Sa 16:22 1732
that *D* took an harp, and played ... 1Sa 16:23 1732
Now *D* was the son of that ... 1Sa 17:12 1732
And *D* was the youngest ... 1Sa 17:14 1732
But *D* went and returned from Saul ... 1Sa 17:15 1732
And Jesse said unto *D* his son ... 1Sa 17:17 1732
D rose up early in the morning, ... 1Sa 17:20 1732
D left his carriage in the hand ... 1Sa 17:22 1732
and *D* heard them ... 1Sa 17:23 1732
D spake to the men that stood by ... 1Sa 17:26 1732
anger was kindled against *D* ... 1Sa 17:28 1732
D said, What have I now done ... 1Sa 17:29 1732
words were heard which *D* spake ... 1Sa 17:31 1732
D said to Saul, Let no man's ... 1Sa 17:32 1732
And Saul said to *D*, Thou art not ... 1Sa 17:33 1732
D said unto Saul, Thy servant ... 1Sa 17:34 1732
D said moreover, The LORD that ... 1Sa 17:37 1732
And Saul said unto *D*, Go, and the ... 1Sa 17:37 1732
Saul armed *D* with his armour, and ... 1Sa 17:38 1732
D girded his sword upon his ... 1Sa 17:39 1732
D said unto Saul, I cannot go ... 1Sa 17:39 1732
And *D* put them off him ... 1Sa 17:39 1732
came on and drew near unto *D* ... 1Sa 17:41 1732
Philistine looked about, and saw *D* ... 1Sa 17:42 1732
And the Philistine said unto *D* ... 1Sa 17:43 1732
Philistine cursed *D* by his gods ... 1Sa 17:43 1732
And the Philistine said to *D* ... 1Sa 17:44 1732
Then said *D* to the Philistine, ... 1Sa 17:45 1732
and came and drew nigh to meet *D* ... 1Sa 17:48 1732
that *D* hasted, and ran toward the ... 1Sa 17:48 1732
D put his hand in his bag, and ... 1Sa 17:49 1732
So *D* prevailed over the ... 1Sa 17:50 1732
was no sword in the hand of *D* ... 1Sa 17:50 1732
Therefore *D* ran, and stood upon ... 1Sa 17:51 1732
D took the head of the Philistine ... 1Sa 17:54 1732
when Saul saw *D* go forth against ... 1Sa 17:55 1732
as *D* returned from the slaughter ... 1Sa 17:57 1732
D answered, I am the son of thy ... 1Sa 17:58 1732
was knit with the soul of *D* ... 1Sa 18:1 1732
D made a covenant, because he ... 1Sa 18:3 1732
was upon him, and gave it to *D* ... 1Sa 18:4 1732
D went out whithersoever Saul ... 1Sa 18:5 1732
when *D* was returned from the ... 1Sa 18:6 1732
thousands, and *D* his ten thousands ... 1Sa 18:7 1732
ascribed unto *D* ten thousands ... 1Sa 18:8 1732
Saul eyed *D* from that day and ... 1Sa 18:9 1732
D played with his hand, as at ... 1Sa 18:10 1732
I will smite *D* even to the wall ... 1Sa 18:11 1732
D avoided out of his presence ... 1Sa 18:11 1732
And Saul was afraid of *D*, because ... 1Sa 18:12 1732
D behaved himself wisely in all ... 1Sa 18:14 1732
But all Israel and Judah loved *D* ... 1Sa 18:16 1732
And Saul said to *D*, Behold my ... 1Sa 18:17 1732
D said unto Saul, Who am I ... 1Sa 18:18 1732
should have been given to *D* ... 1Sa 18:19 1732
And Michal Saul's daughter loved *D* ... 1Sa 18:20 1732
Wherefore Saul said to *D*, Thou ... 1Sa 18:21 1732
saying, Commune with *D* secretly ... 1Sa 18:22 1732
those words in the ears of *D* ... 1Sa 18:23 1732
D said, Seemeth it to you a light ... 1Sa 18:23 1732
saying, On this manner spake *D* ... 1Sa 18:24 1732
Saul said, Thus shall ye say to *D* ... 1Sa 18:25 1732
to make *D* fall by the hand of the ... 1Sa 18:25 1732
his servants told *D* these words ... 1Sa 18:26 1732
it pleased *D* well to be the ... 1Sa 18:26 1732
Wherefore *D* arose and went, he and ... 1Sa 18:27 1732
D brought their foreskins, and ... 1Sa 18:27 1732
and knew that the LORD was with *D* ... 1Sa 18:28 1732
Saul was yet the more afraid of *D* ... 1Sa 18:29 1732
that *D* behaved himself more ... 1Sa 18:30 1732
servants, that they should kill *D* ... 1Sa 19:1 1732
Saul's son delighted much in *D* ... 1Sa 19:2 1732
and Jonathan told *D*, saying, Saul ... 1Sa 19:2 1732
good of *D* unto Saul his father ... 1Sa 19:4 1732
against his servant, against *D* ... 1Sa 19:4 1732
to slay *D* without a cause ... 1Sa 19:5 1732
And Jonathan called *D* ... 1Sa 19:7 1732
And Jonathan brought *D* to Saul ... 1Sa 19:7 1732
D went out, and fought with the ... 1Sa 19:8 1732
and *D* played with his hand ... 1Sa 19:9 1732
Saul sought to smite *D* even to ... 1Sa 19:10 1732
D fled, and escaped that night ... 1Sa 19:10 1732
So Michal let *D* down through a ... 1Sa 19:12 1732
Saul sent messengers to take *D* ... 1Sa 19:14 1732
the messengers again to see *D* ... 1Sa 19:15 1732
So *D* fled, and escaped, and came to ... 1Sa 19:18 1732
Behold, *D* is at Naioth in Ramah ... 1Sa 19:19 1732
And Saul sent messengers to take *D* ... 1Sa 19:20 1732
and said, Where are Samuel and *D* ... 1Sa 19:22 1732
D fled from Naioth in Ramah, and ... 1Sa 20:1 1732
D sware moreover, and said, Thy ... 1Sa 20:3 1732
Then said Jonathan unto *D* ... 1Sa 20:4 1732
D said unto Jonathan, Behold, to ... 1Sa 20:5 1732
D earnestly asked leave of me ... 1Sa 20:6 1732
Then said *D* to Jonathan, Who ... 1Sa 20:10 1732
And Jonathan said unto *D*, Come, and ... 1Sa 20:11 1732
And Jonathan said unto *D*, O LORD ... 1Sa 20:12 1732
behold, if there be good toward *D* ... 1Sa 20:12 1732
hath cut off the enemies of *D* ... 1Sa 20:15 1732
a covenant with the house of *D* ... 1Sa 20:16 1732
Jonathan caused *D* to swear again ... 1Sa 20:17 1732
Then Jonathan said to *D*, To ... 1Sa 20:18 1732
So *D* hid himself in the field ... 1Sa 20:24 1732
D earnestly asked leave of me to ... 1Sa 20:28 1732
of his father to slay *D* ... 1Sa 20:33 1732
for he was grieved for *D*, because ... 1Sa 20:34 1732
at the time appointed with *D* ... 1Sa 20:35 1732
Jonathan and *D* knew the matter ... 1Sa 20:39 1732
D arose out of a place toward the ... 1Sa 20:41 1732
with another, until *D* exceeded ... 1Sa 20:41 1732
And Jonathan said to *D*, Go in ... 1Sa 20:42 1732
Then came *D* to Nob to Ahimelech ... 1Sa 21:1 1732
was afraid at the meeting of *D* ... 1Sa 21:1 1732
D said unto Ahimelech the priest, ... 1Sa 21:2 1732
And the priest answered *D*, and said ... 1Sa 21:4 1732
D answered the priest, and said ... 1Sa 21:5 1732
D said unto Ahimelech, And is ... 1Sa 21:8 1732
D said, There is none like that ... 1Sa 21:9 1732
D arose, and fled that day for ... 1Sa 21:10 1732
Is not this *D* the king of the ... 1Sa 21:11 1732
thousands, and *D* his ten thousands ... 1Sa 21:11 1732
D laid up these words in his ... 1Sa 21:12 1732
D therefore departed thence, and ... 1Sa 22:1 1732
D went thence to Mizpeh of Moab ... 1Sa 22:3 1732
the while that *D* was in the hold ... 1Sa 22:4 1732
And the prophet Gad said unto *D* ... 1Sa 22:5 1732
Then *D* departed, and came into the ... 1Sa 22:5 1732
Saul heard that *D* was discovered ... 1Sa 22:6 1732
among all thy servants as *D* ... 1Sa 22:14 1732
because their hand also is with *D* ... 1Sa 22:17 1732
escaped, and fled after *D* ... 1Sa 22:20 1732
Abiathar shewed *D* that Saul had ... 1Sa 22:21 1732
D said unto Abiathar, I knew it ... 1Sa 22:22 1732
Then they told *D*, saying, Behold, ... 1Sa 23:1 1732
Therefore *D* enquired of the LORD, ... 1Sa 23:2 1732
And the LORD said unto *D*, Go, and ... 1Sa 23:2 1732
Then *D* enquired of the LORD yet ... 1Sa 23:4 1732
So *D* and his men went to Keilah, ... 1Sa 23:5 1732
So *D* saved the inhabitants of ... 1Sa 23:5 1732
of Ahimelech fled to *D* to Keilah ... 1Sa 23:6 1732
Saul that *D* was come to Keilah ... 1Sa 23:7 1732
go down to Keilah, to besiege *D* ... 1Sa 23:8 1732
D knew that Saul secretly ... 1Sa 23:9 1732
Then said *D*, O LORD God of Israel ... 1Sa 23:10 1732
Then said *D*, Will the men of ... 1Sa 23:12 1732
Then *D* and his men, which were ... 1Sa 23:13 1732
it was told Saul that *D* was ... 1Sa 23:13 1732
D abode in the wilderness in ... 1Sa 23:14 1732
D saw that Saul was come out to ... 1Sa 23:15 1732
D was in the wilderness of Ziph ... 1Sa 23:15 1732
went to *D* into the wood, and ... 1Sa 23:16 1732
D abode in the wood, and Jonathan ... 1Sa 23:18 1732
Doth not *D* hide himself with us ... 1Sa 23:19 1732
but *D* and his men were in the ... 1Sa 23:24 1732
And they told *D* ... 1Sa 23:25 1732
he pursued after *D* in the ... 1Sa 23:25 1732
this side of the mountain, and *D* ... 1Sa 23:26 1732
D made haste to get away for fear ... 1Sa 23:26 1732
for Saul and his men compassed *D* ... 1Sa 23:26 1732
returned from pursuing after *D* ... 1Sa 23:28 1732
D went up from thence, and dwelt ... 1Sa 23:29 1732
D is in the wilderness of En-gedi ... 1Sa 24:1 1732
of all Israel, and went to seek *D* ... 1Sa 24:2 1732
and *D* and his men remained in the ... 1Sa 24:3 1732
the men of *D* said unto him, ... 1Sa 24:4 1732
Then *D* arose, and cut off the ... 1Sa 24:4 1732
So *D* stayed his servants with ... 1Sa 24:7 1732
D also arose afterward, and went ... 1Sa 24:8 1732
D stooped with his face to the ... 1Sa 24:8 1732
D said to Saul, Wherefore hearest ... 1Sa 24:9 1732
Behold, *D* seeketh thy hurt ... 1Sa 24:9 1732
when *D* had made an end of ... 1Sa 24:16 1732
said, Is this thy voice, my son *D* ... 1Sa 24:16 1732
And he said to *D*, Thou art more ... 1Sa 24:17 1732
And *D* sware unto Saul ... 1Sa 24:22 1732
but *D* and his men gat them up unto ... 1Sa 24:22 1732
D arose, and went down to the ... 1Sa 25:1 1732
D heard in the wilderness that ... 1Sa 25:4 1732
D sent out ten young men, and ... 1Sa 25:5 1732
D said unto the young men, Get ... 1Sa 25:5 1732
thy servants, and to thy son *D* ... 1Sa 25:8 1732
all those words in the name of *D* ... 1Sa 25:9 1732
servants, and said, Who is *D* ... 1Sa 25:10 1732
D said unto his men, Gird ye on ... 1Sa 25:13 1732
D also girded on his sword ... 1Sa 25:13 1732
there went up after *D* about four ... 1Sa 25:13 1732
D sent messengers out of the ... 1Sa 25:14 1732
covert of the hill, and, behold, *D* ... 1Sa 25:20 1732
Now *D* had said, Surely in vain ... 1Sa 25:21 1732
also do God unto the enemies of *D* ... 1Sa 25:22 1732
And when Abigail saw *D*, she hasted ... 1Sa 25:23 1732
ass, and fell before *D* on her face ... 1Sa 25:23 1732
D said to Abigail, Blessed be the ... 1Sa 25:32 1732
So *D* received of her hand that ... 1Sa 25:35 1732
when *D* heard that Nabal was dead, ... 1Sa 25:39 1732
D sent and communed with Abigail, ... 1Sa 25:39 1732
when the servants of *D* were come ... 1Sa 25:40 1732
D sent us unto thee, to take thee ... 1Sa 25:40 1732
went after the messengers of *D* ... 1Sa 25:42 1732
D also took Ahinoam of Jezreel ... 1Sa 25:43 1732
Doth not *D* hide himself in the ... 1Sa 26:1 1732
to seek *D* in the wilderness of ... 1Sa 26:2 1732
But *D* abode in the wilderness, and ... 1Sa 26:3 1732
D therefore sent out spies, and ... 1Sa 26:4 1732
D arose, and came to the place ... 1Sa 26:5 1732
D beheld the place where Saul lay ... 1Sa 26:5 1732
Then answered *D* and said to ... 1Sa 26:6 1732
So *D* and Abishai came to the ... 1Sa 26:7 1732
Then said Abishai to *D*, God hath ... 1Sa 26:8 1732
D said to Abishai, Destroy him ... 1Sa 26:9 1732
D said furthermore, As the LORD ... 1Sa 26:10 1732
So *D* took the spear and the cruse ... 1Sa 26:12 1732
Then *D* went over to the other ... 1Sa 26:13 1732
D cried to the people, and to ... 1Sa 26:14 1732
D said to Abner, Art not thou a ... 1Sa 26:15 1732
said, Is this thy voice, my son *D* ... 1Sa 26:17 1732
D said, It is my voice, my lord, ... 1Sa 26:17 1732
return, my son *D* ... 1Sa 26:21 1732
D answered and said, Behold the ... 1Sa 26:22 1732
D, Blessed be thou, my son *D* ... 1Sa 26:25 1732
So *D* went on his way, and Saul ... 1Sa 26:25 1732
D said in his heart, I shall now ... 1Sa 27:1 1732
D arose, and he passed over with ... 1Sa 27:2 1732
D dwelt with Achish at Gath, he ... 1Sa 27:3 1732
even *D* with his two wives, ... 1Sa 27:3 1732
told Saul that *D* was fled to Gath ... 1Sa 27:4 1732
D said unto Achish, If I have now ... 1Sa 27:5 1732
the time that *D* dwelt in the ... 1Sa 27:7 1732
And *D* and his men went up, and ... 1Sa 27:8 1732
D smote the land, and left neither ... 1Sa 27:9 1732
D said, Against the south of ... 1Sa 27:10 1732
D saved neither man nor woman ... 1Sa 27:11 1732

tell on us, saying, So did *D*	1Sa 27:11	1732
And Achish believed *D*, saying, He	1Sa 27:12	1732
And Achish said unto *D*, Know thou	1Sa 28:1	1732
D said to Achish, Surely thou	1Sa 28:2	1732
And Achish said to *D*, Therefore	1Sa 28:2	1732
it to thy neighbour, even to *D*	1Sa 28:17	1732
but *D* and his men passed on in the	1Sa 29:2	1732
of the Philistines, Is not this *D*	1Sa 29:3	1732
Is not this *D*, of whom they sang	1Sa 29:5	1732
thousands, and *D* his ten thousands	1Sa 29:5	1732
Then Achish called *D*, and said	1Sa 29:6	1732
D said unto Achish, But what have	1Sa 29:8	1732
And Achish answered and said to *D*	1Sa 29:9	1732
So *D* and his men rose up early to	1Sa 29:11	1732
And it came to pass, when *D*	1Sa 30:1	1732
So *D* and his men came to the city,	1Sa 30:3	1732
Then *D* and the people that were	1Sa 30:4	1732
And *D* was greatly distressed	1Sa 30:6	1732
but *D* encouraged himself in the	1Sa 30:6	1732
D said to Abiathar the priest,	1Sa 30:7	1732
brought thither the ephod to *D*	1Sa 30:7	1732
D enquired at the LORD, saying,	1Sa 30:8	1732
So *D* went, he and the six hundred	1Sa 30:9	1732
But *D* pursued, he and four hundred	1Sa 30:10	1732
in the field, and brought him to *D*	1Sa 30:11	1732
And *D* said unto him, To whom	1Sa 30:13	1732
D said to him, Canst thou bring	1Sa 30:15	1732
D smote them from the twilight	1Sa 30:17	1732
And *D* recovered all that the	1Sa 30:18	1732
and *D* rescued his two wives	1Sa 30:18	1732
D recovered all	1Sa 30:19	1732
D took all the flocks and the	1Sa 30:20	1732
D came to the two hundred men,	1Sa 30:21	1732
that they could not follow *D*	1Sa 30:21	1732
and they went forth to meet *D*	1Sa 30:21	1732
when *D* came near to the people,	1Sa 30:21	1732
Belial, of those that went with *D*	1Sa 30:22	1732
Then said *D*, Ye shall not do so,	1Sa 30:23	1732
when *D* came to Ziklag, he sent of	1Sa 30:26	1732
to all the places where *D* himself	1Sa 30:31	1732
when *D* was returned from the	2Sa 1:1	1732
D had abode two days in Ziklag	2Sa 1:1	1732
and so it was, when he came to *D*	2Sa 1:2	1732
D said unto him, From whence	2Sa 1:3	1732
D said unto him, How went the	2Sa 1:4	1732
D said unto the young man that	2Sa 1:5	1732
Then *D* took hold on his clothes,	2Sa 1:11	1732
D said unto the young man that	2Sa 1:13	1732
D said unto him, How wast thou	2Sa 1:14	1732
D called one of the young men, and	2Sa 1:15	1732
D said unto him, Thy blood be	2Sa 1:16	1732
D lamented with this lamentation	2Sa 1:17	1732
that *D* enquired of the LORD,	2Sa 2:1	1732
D said, Whither shall I go up	2Sa 2:1	1732
So *D* went up thither, and his two	2Sa 2:2	1732
that were with him did *D* bring up	2Sa 2:3	1732
there they anointed *D* king over	2Sa 2:4	1732
And they told *D*, saying, That the	2Sa 2:4	1732
D sent messengers unto the men of	2Sa 2:5	1732
But the house of Judah followed *D*	2Sa 2:10	1732
the time that *D* was king in	2Sa 2:11	1732
of Zeruiah, and the servants of *D*	2Sa 2:13	1732
and twelve of the servants of *D*	2Sa 2:15	1732
Israel, before the servants of *D*	2Sa 2:17	1732
But the servants of *D* had smitten	2Sa 2:31	1732
house of Saul and the house of *D*	2Sa 3:1	1732
but *D* waxed stronger and stronger,	2Sa 3:1	1732
unto *D* were sons born in Hebron	2Sa 3:2	1732
These were born to *D* in Hebron	2Sa 3:5	1732
house of Saul and the house of *D*	2Sa 3:6	1732
delivered thee into the hand of *D*	2Sa 3:8	1732
as the LORD hath sworn to *D*	2Sa 3:9	1732
up the throne of *D* over Israel	2Sa 3:10	1732
messengers to *D* on his behalf	2Sa 3:12	1732
D sent messengers to Ish-bosheth	2Sa 3:14	1732
Ye sought for *D* in times past to	2Sa 3:17	1732
for the LORD hath spoken of *D*	2Sa 3:18	1732
By the hand of my servant *D* I	2Sa 3:18	1732
also to speak in the ears of *D* in	2Sa 3:19	1732
So Abner came to *D* to Hebron	2Sa 3:20	1732
D made Abner and the men that were	2Sa 3:20	1732
And Abner said unto *D*, I will	2Sa 3:21	1732
And *D* sent Abner away	2Sa 3:21	1732
And, behold, the servants of *D*	2Sa 3:22	1732
Abner was not with *D* in Hebron	2Sa 3:22	1732
And when Joab was come out from *D*	2Sa 3:26	1732
but *D* knew it not	2Sa 3:26	1732
And afterward when *D* heard it	2Sa 3:28	1732
D said to Joab, and to all the	2Sa 3:31	1732
king *D* himself followed the bier	2Sa 3:31	1732
D to eat meat while it was yet	2Sa 3:35	1732
D sware, saying, So do God to me,	2Sa 3:35	1732
of Ish-bosheth unto *D* to Hebron	2Sa 4:8	1732
D answered Rechab and Baanah his	2Sa 4:9	1732
D commanded his young men, and	2Sa 4:12	1732
tribes of Israel to *D* unto Hebron	2Sa 5:1	1732
king *D* made a league with them in	2Sa 5:3	1732
they anointed *D* king over Israel	2Sa 5:3	1732
D was thirty years old when he	2Sa 5:4	1732
which spake unto *D*, saying,	2Sa 5:6	1732
thinking, *D* cannot come in	2Sa 5:6	1732
Nevertheless *D* took the strong	2Sa 5:7	1732
the same is the city of *D*	2Sa 5:7	1732
D said on that day, Whosoever	2Sa 5:8	1732
So *D* dwelt in the fort	2Sa 5:9	1732
and called it the city of *D*	2Sa 5:9	1732
D built round about from Millo and	2Sa 5:9	1732
D went on, and grew great, and the	2Sa 5:10	1732
king of Tyre sent messengers to *D*	2Sa 5:11	1732
and they built *D* an house	2Sa 5:11	1732
D perceived that the LORD had	2Sa 5:12	1732
D took him more concubines and	2Sa 5:13	1732
yet sons and daughters born to *D*	2Sa 5:13	1732
had anointed *D* king over Israel	2Sa 5:17	1732
the Philistines came up to seek *D*	2Sa 5:17	1732
D heard of it, and went down to	2Sa 5:17	1732
D enquired of the LORD, saying,	2Sa 5:19	1732
And the LORD said unto *D*, Go up	2Sa 5:19	1732
D came to Baal-perazim	2Sa 5:20	1732
D smote them there, and said, The	2Sa 5:20	1732
they left their images, and *D*	2Sa 5:21	1732
when *D* enquired of the LORD, he	2Sa 5:23	1732
D did so, as the LORD had	2Sa 5:25	1732
D gathered together all the	2Sa 6:1	1732
D arose, and went with all the	2Sa 6:2	1732
And *D* and all the house of Israel	2Sa 6:5	1732
D was displeased, because the	2Sa 6:8	1732
D was afraid of the LORD that day	2Sa 6:9	1732
So *D* would not remove the ark of	2Sa 6:10	1732
LORD unto him into the city of *D*	2Sa 6:10	1732
but *D* carried it aside into the	2Sa 6:10	1732
And it was told king *D*, saying,	2Sa 6:12	1732
So *D* went and brought up the ark	2Sa 6:12	1732
into the city of *D* with gladness	2Sa 6:12	1732
D danced before the LORD with all	2Sa 6:14	1732
D was girded with a linen ephod	2Sa 6:14	1732
So *D* and all the house of Israel	2Sa 6:15	1732
the LORD came into the city of *D*	2Sa 6:16	1732
a window, and saw king *D* leaping	2Sa 6:16	1732
that *D* had pitched for it	2Sa 6:17	
D offered burnt offerings and	2Sa 6:17	1732
as soon as *D* had made an end of	2Sa 6:18	1732
Then *D* returned to bless his	2Sa 6:20	1732
of Saul came out to meet *D*	2Sa 6:20	1732
D said unto Michal, It was before	2Sa 6:21	1732
Go and tell my servant *D*, Thus	2Sa 7:5	1732
shalt thou say unto my servant *D*	2Sa 7:8	1732
so did Nathan speak unto *D*	2Sa 7:17	1732
Then went king *D* in, and sat	2Sa 7:18	1732
what can *D* say more unto thee	2Sa 7:20	1732
D be established before thee	2Sa 7:26	1732
that *D* smote the Philistines, and	2Sa 8:1	1732
D took Metheg-ammah out of the	2Sa 8:1	1732
D smote also Hadadezer, the son	2Sa 8:3	1732
D took from him a thousand	2Sa 8:4	1732
D houghed all the chariot horses,	2Sa 8:4	1732
D slew of the Syrians two and	2Sa 8:5	1732
Then *D* put garrisons in Syria of	2Sa 8:6	1732
the Syrians became servants to *D*	2Sa 8:6	1732
And the LORD preserved *D*	2Sa 8:6	1732
D took the shields of gold that	2Sa 8:7	1732
king *D* took exceeding much brass	2Sa 8:8	1732
D had smitten all the host of	2Sa 8:9	1732
sent Joram his son unto king *D*	2Sa 8:10	1732
Which also king *D* did dedicate	2Sa 8:11	1732
D gat him a name when he returned	2Sa 8:13	1732
And the LORD preserved *D*	2Sa 8:14	1732
D reigned over all Israel	2Sa 8:15	1732
D executed judgment and justice	2Sa 8:15	1732
D said, Is there yet any that is	2Sa 9:1	1732
when they had called him unto *D*	2Sa 9:2	1732
Then king *D* sent, and fetched him	2Sa 9:5	1732
the son of Saul, was come unto *D*	2Sa 9:6	1732
And *D* said, Mephibosheth	2Sa 9:6	1732
D said unto him, Fear not	2Sa 9:7	1732
Then said *D*, I will shew kindness	2Sa 10:2	1732
D sent to comfort him by the hand	2Sa 10:2	1732
Thinkest thou that *D* doth honour	2Sa 10:3	1732
hath not *D* rather sent his	2Sa 10:3	1732
When they told it unto *D*, he sent	2Sa 10:5	1732
saw that they stank before *D*	2Sa 10:6	1732
when *D* heard of it, he sent Joab,	2Sa 10:7	1732
And when it was told *D*, he	2Sa 10:17	1732
set themselves in array against *D*	2Sa 10:17	1732
D slew the men of seven hundred	2Sa 10:18	1732
that *D* sent Joab, and his servants	2Sa 11:1	1732
But *D* tarried still at Jerusalem	2Sa 11:1	1732
that *D* arose from off his bed, and	2Sa 11:2	1732
D sent and enquired after the	2Sa 11:3	1732
D sent messengers, and took her	2Sa 11:4	1732
conceived, and sent and told *D*	2Sa 11:5	1732
D sent to Joab, saying, Send me	2Sa 11:6	1732
And Joab sent Uriah to *D*	2Sa 11:6	1732
D demanded of him how Joab did,	2Sa 11:7	1732
D said to Uriah, Go down to thy	2Sa 11:8	1732
And when they had told *D*, saying,	2Sa 11:10	1732
D said unto Uriah, Camest thou	2Sa 11:10	1732
And Uriah said unto *D*, The ark, and	2Sa 11:11	1732
D said to Uriah, Tarry here to	2Sa 11:12	1732
when *D* had called him, he did eat	2Sa 11:13	1732
that *D* wrote a letter to Joab, and	2Sa 11:14	1732
the people of the servants of *D*	2Sa 11:17	1732
told *D* all the things concerning	2Sa 11:18	1732
shewed *D* all that Joab had sent	2Sa 11:22	1732
And the messenger said unto *D*	2Sa 11:23	1732
Then *D* said unto the messenger,	2Sa 11:25	1732
D sent and fetched her to his	2Sa 11:27	1732
But the thing that *D* had done	2Sa 11:27	1732
And the LORD sent Nathan unto *D*	2Sa 12:1	1732
And Nathan said to *D*, Thou art the	2Sa 12:7	1732
D said unto Nathan, I have sinned	2Sa 12:13	1732
And Nathan said unto *D*, The LORD	2Sa 12:13	1732
that Uriah's wife bare unto *D*	2Sa 12:15	1732
D therefore besought God for the	2Sa 12:16	1732
D fasted, and went in, and lay all	2Sa 12:16	1732
the servants of *D* feared to tell	2Sa 12:18	1732
But when *D* saw that his servants	2Sa 12:19	1732
D perceived that the child was	2Sa 12:19	1732
therefore *D* said unto his	2Sa 12:19	1732
Then *D* arose from the earth, and	2Sa 12:20	1732
D comforted Bath-sheba his wife,	2Sa 12:24	1732
And Joab sent messengers to *D*	2Sa 12:27	1732
D gathered all the people	2Sa 12:29	1732
So *D* and all the people returned	2Sa 12:31	1732
the son of *D* had a fair sister	2Sa 13:1	1732
and Amnon the son of *D* loved her	2Sa 13:1	1732
Then *D* sent home to Tamar, saying	2Sa 13:7	1732
But when king *D* heard of all	2Sa 13:21	1732
the way, that tidings came to *D*	2Sa 13:30	1732
D mourned for his son every day	2Sa 13:37	
the soul of king *D* longed to go	2Sa 13:39	1732
And there came a messenger to *D*	2Sa 15:13	1732
D said unto all his servants that	2Sa 15:14	1732
D said to Ittai, Go and pass over	2Sa 15:22	1732
D went up by the ascent of mount	2Sa 15:30	1732
And one told *D*, saying, Ahithophel	2Sa 15:31	1732
D said, O LORD, I pray thee, turn	2Sa 15:31	1732
that when *D* was come to the top	2Sa 15:32	1732
Unto whom *D* said, If thou passest	2Sa 15:33	1732
when *D* was a little past the top	2Sa 16:1	1732
when king *D* came to Bahurim,	2Sa 16:5	1732
And he cast stones at *D*, and at all	2Sa 16:6	1732
and at all the servants of king *D*	2Sa 16:6	1732
LORD hath said unto him, Curse *D*	2Sa 16:10	1732
D said to Abishai, and to all his	2Sa 16:11	1732
And as *D* and his men went by the	2Sa 16:13	1732
counsel of Ahithophel both with *D*	2Sa 16:23	1732
and pursue after *D* this night	2Sa 17:1	1732
therefore send quickly, and tell *D*	2Sa 17:16	1732
and they went and told king *D*	2Sa 17:17	1732
told king *D*, and said unto *D*	2Sa 17:21	1732
Then *D* arose, and all the people	2Sa 17:22	1732
Then *D* came to Mahanaim	2Sa 17:24	1732
when *D* was come to Mahanaim, that	2Sa 17:27	1732
sheep, and cheese of kine, for *D*	2Sa 17:29	1732
D numbered the people that were	2Sa 18:1	1732
D sent forth a third part of the	2Sa 18:2	1732
slain before the servants of *D*	2Sa 18:7	1732
And Absalom met the servants of *D*	2Sa 18:9	1732
D sat between the two gates	2Sa 18:24	1732
king *D* sent to Zadok and to	2Sa 19:11	1732
the men of Judah to meet king *D*	2Sa 19:16	1732
D said, What have I to do with	2Sa 19:22	1732
have also more right in *D* than ye	2Sa 19:43	1732
and said, We have no part in *D*	2Sa 20:1	1732
of Israel went up from after *D*	2Sa 20:2	1732
D came to his house at Jerusalem	2Sa 20:3	1732
D said to Abishai, Now shall	2Sa 20:6	1732
Joab, and he that is for *D*	2Sa 20:11	1732
against the king, even against *D*	2Sa 20:21	1732
Jairite was a chief ruler about *D*	2Sa 20:26	1732
in the days of *D* three years	2Sa 21:1	1732
and *D* enquired of the LORD	2Sa 21:1	1732
Wherefore *D* said unto the	2Sa 21:3	1732
that was between them, between *D*	2Sa 21:7	1732
it was told *D* what Rizpah the	2Sa 21:11	1732
D went and took the bones of Saul	2Sa 21:12	1732
D went down, and his servants with	2Sa 21:15	1732
and *D* waxed faint	2Sa 21:15	1732
sword, thought to have slain *D*	2Sa 21:16	1732
Then the men of *D* sware unto him	2Sa 21:17	1732
Shimeah the brother of *D* slew him	2Sa 21:21	1732
in Gath, and fell by the hand of *D*	2Sa 21:22	1732
D spake unto the LORD the words	2Sa 22:1	1732
mercy to his anointed, unto *D*	2Sa 22:51	1732
Now these be the last words of *D*	2Sa 23:1	1732
D the son of Jesse said, and the	2Sa 23:1	1732
of the mighty men whom *D* had	2Sa 23:8	1732
of the three mighty men with *D*	2Sa 23:9	1732
came to *D* in the harvest time	2Sa 23:13	1732
D was then in an hold, and the	2Sa 23:14	1732
D longed, and said, Oh that one	2Sa 23:15	1732
and took it, and brought it to *D*	2Sa 23:16	1732
And *D* set him over his guard	2Sa 23:23	1732
he moved *D* against them to say,	2Sa 24:1	1732
D said unto the LORD, I have	2Sa 24:10	1732
For when *D* was up in the morning,	2Sa 24:11	1732
Go and say unto *D*, Thus saith the	2Sa 24:12	1732
So Gad came to *D*, and told him, and	2Sa 24:13	1732
D said unto Gad, I am in a great	2Sa 24:14	1732
D spake unto the LORD when he saw	2Sa 24:17	1732
And Gad came that day to *D*	2Sa 24:18	1732
And *D*, according to the saying of	2Sa 24:19	1732
D said, To buy the threshingfloor	2Sa 24:21	1732
And Araunah said unto *D*, Let my	2Sa 24:22	1732
So *D* bought the threshingfloor and	2Sa 24:24	1732
D built there an altar unto the	2Sa 24:25	1732
Now king *D* was old and stricken in	1Kin 1:1	1732
mighty men which belonged to *D*	1Kin 1:8	1732
D our lord knoweth it not	1Kin 1:11	1732
Go and get thee in unto king *D*	1Kin 1:13	1732
Then king *D* answered and said,	1Kin 1:28	1732
Let my lord king *D* live for ever	1Kin 1:31	1732
And king *D* said, Call me Zadok the	1Kin 1:32	1732
than the throne of my lord king *D*	1Kin 1:37	1732
Verily our lord king *D* hath made	1Kin 1:43	1732
came to bless our lord king *D*	1Kin 1:47	1732
Now the days of *D* drew nigh that	1Kin 2:1	1732
So *D* slept with his fathers	1Kin 2:10	1732
and was buried in the city of *D*	1Kin 2:10	1732
the days that *D* reigned over	1Kin 2:11	1732
upon the throne of *D* his father	1Kin 2:12	1732
me on the throne of *D* my father	1Kin 2:24	1732
the Lord GOD before *D* my father	1Kin 2:26	1732

my father *D* not knowing thereof, 1Kin 2:32 1732
but upon *D*, and upon his seed, and 1Kin 2:33 1732
that thou didst to *D* my father 1Kin 2:44 1732
and the throne of *D* shall be 1Kin 2:45 1732
and brought her into the city of *D* 1Kin 3:1 1732
in the statutes of *D* his father 1Kin 3:3 1732
servant *D* my father great mercy 1Kin 3:6 1732
king instead of *D* my father 1Kin 3:7 1732
as thy father *D* did walk 1Kin 3:14 1732
for Hiram was ever a lover of *D* 1Kin 5:1 1732
Thou knowest how that *D* my father 1Kin 5:3 1732
the LORD spake unto *D* my father 1Kin 5:5 1732
which hath given unto *D* a wise 1Kin 5:7 1732
which I spake unto *D* thy father 1Kin 6:12 1732
which *D* his father had dedicated 1Kin 7:51 1732
of the LORD out of the city of *D* 1Kin 8:1 1732
with his mouth unto *D* my father 1Kin 8:15 1732
but I chose *D* to be over my 1Kin 8:16 1732
it was in the heart of *D* my 1Kin 8:17 1732
And the LORD said unto *D* my father 1Kin 8:18 1732
up in the room of *D* my father 1Kin 8:20 1732
D my father that thou promisedst 1Kin 8:24 1732
keep with thy servant *D* my father 1Kin 8:25 1732
unto thy servant *D* my father 1Kin 8:26 1732
LORD had done for *D* his servant 1Kin 8:66 1732
as *D* thy father walked, in 1Kin 9:4 1732
as I promised to *D* thy father 1Kin 9:5 1732
came up out of the city of *D* unto 1Kin 9:24 1732
as was the heart of *D* his father 1Kin 11:4 1732
the LORD, as did *D* his father 1Kin 11:6 1732
not do it for *D* thy father's sake 1Kin 11:12 1732
thy son for *D* my servant's sake 1Kin 11:13 1732
when *D* was in Edom, and Joab the 1Kin 11:15 1732
that *D* slept with his fathers 1Kin 11:21 1732
when *D* slew them of Zobah 1Kin 11:24 1732
of the city of *D* his father 1Kin 11:27 1732
my judgments, as did *D* his father 1Kin 11:33 1732
his life for *D* my servant's sake 1Kin 11:34
that *D* my servant may have a 1Kin 11:36 1732
commandments, as *D* my servant did 1Kin 11:38 1732
a sure house, as I built for *D* 1Kin 11:38 1732
for this afflict the seed of *D* 1Kin 11:39 1732
in the city of *D* his father 1Kin 11:43 1732
saying, What portion have we in *D* 1Kin 12:16 1732
now see to thine own house, *D* 1Kin 12:16 1732
the house of *D* unto this day 1Kin 12:19 1732
none that followed the house of *D* 1Kin 12:20 1732
kingdom return to the house of *D* 1Kin 12:26 1732
shall be born unto the house of *D* 1Kin 13:2 1732
kingdom away from the house of *D* 1Kin 14:8 1732
hast not been as my servant *D* 1Kin 14:8 1732
with his fathers in the city of *D* 1Kin 14:31 1732
God, as the heart of *D* his father 1Kin 15:3 1732
Because *D* did that which was 1Kin 15:5 1732
they buried him in the city of *D* 1Kin 15:8 1732
of the LORD, as did *D* his father 1Kin 15:11 1732
in the city of *D* his father 1Kin 15:24 1732
in the city of *D* his father 1Kin 22:50 1732
Judah for *D* his servant's sake 2Kin 8:19 1732
with his fathers in the city of *D* 2Kin 8:24 1732
with his fathers in the city of *D* 2Kin 9:28 1732
with his fathers in the city of *D* 2Kin 12:21 1732
LORD, yet not like *D* his father 2Kin 14:3 1732
with his fathers in the city of *D* 2Kin 14:20 1732
with his fathers in the city of *D* 2Kin 15:7 1732
in the city of *D* his father 2Kin 15:38 1732
LORD his God, like *D* his father 2Kin 16:2 1732
with his fathers in the city of *D* 2Kin 16:20 1732
rent Israel from the house of *D* 2Kin 17:21 1732
to all that *D* his father did 2Kin 18:3 1732
the LORD, the God of *D* thy father 2Kin 20:5 1732
of which the LORD said to *D* 2Kin 21:7 1732
in all the way of *D* his father 2Kin 22:2 1732
Ozem the sixth, *D* the seventh 1Chr 2:15 1732
Now these were the sons of *D* 1Chr 3:1 1732
These were all the sons of *D* 1Chr 3:9 1732
their cities unto the reign of *D* 1Chr 4:31 1732
these are they whom *D* set over 1Chr 6:31 1732
number was in the days of *D* two 1Chr 7:2 1732
in their villages, whom *D* 1Chr 9:22 1732
kingdom unto *D* the son of Jesse 1Chr 10:14 1732
themselves to *D* unto Hebron 1Chr 11:1 1732
D made a covenant with them in 1Chr 11:3 1732
they anointed *D* king over Israel, 1Chr 11:3 1732
And *D* and all Israel went to 1Chr 11:4 1732
inhabitants of Jebus said to *D* 1Chr 11:5 1732
Nevertheless *D* took the castle of 1Chr 11:5 1732
of Zion, which is the city of *D* 1Chr 11:5 1732
D said, Whosoever smiteth the 1Chr 11:6 1732
And *D* dwelt in the castle 1Chr 11:7 1732
they called it the city of *D* 1Chr 11:7 1732
So *D* waxed greater and greater 1Chr 11:9 1732
of the mighty men whom *D* had 1Chr 11:10 1732
of the mighty men whom *D* had 1Chr 11:11
He was with *D* at Pas-dammim, and 1Chr 11:13 1732
went down to the rock to *D* 1Chr 11:15 1732
D was then in the hold, and the 1Chr 11:16 1732
D longed, and said, Oh that one 1Chr 11:17 1732
and took it, and brought it to *D* 1Chr 11:18 1732
but *D* would not drink of it, but 1Chr 11:18 1732
and *D* set him over his guard 1Chr 11:25 1732
are they that came to *D* to Ziklag 1Chr 12:1 1732
D into the hold to the wilderness 1Chr 12:8 1732
and Judah to the hold unto *D* 1Chr 12:16 1732
D went out to meet them, and 1Chr 12:17 1732
and he said, Thine are we, *D* 1Chr 12:18 1732
Then *D* received them, and made 1Chr 12:18 1732
there fell some of Manasseh to *D* 1Chr 12:19 1732
they helped *D* against the band of 1Chr 12:21 1732
day there came to *D* to help him 1Chr 12:22 1732
came to *D* to Hebron, to turn the 1Chr 12:23 1732
by name, to come and make *D* king 1Chr 12:31 1732
to make *D* king over all Israel 1Chr 12:38 1732
were of one heart to make *D* king 1Chr 12:38 1732
there they were with *D* three days 1Chr 12:39 1732
D consulted with the captains of 1Chr 13:1 1732
D said unto all the congregation 1Chr 13:2 1732
So *D* gathered all Israel together 1Chr 13:5 1732
D went up, and all Israel, to 1Chr 13:6 1732
And *D* and all Israel played before 1Chr 13:8 1732
D was displeased, because the 1Chr 13:11 1732
D was afraid of God that day, 1Chr 13:12 1732
So *D* brought not the ark home to 1Chr 13:13 1732
home to himself to the city of *D* 1Chr 13:13 1732
king of Tyre sent messengers to *D* 1Chr 14:1 1732
D perceived that the LORD had 1Chr 14:2 1732
D took more wives at Jerusalem 1Chr 14:3 1732
D begat more sons and daughters 1Chr 14:3 1732
that *D* was anointed king over all 1Chr 14:8 1732
the Philistines went up to seek *D* 1Chr 14:8 1732
D heard of it, and went out 1Chr 14:8 1732
D enquired of God, saying, Shall 1Chr 14:10 1732
and *D* smote them there 1Chr 14:11 1732
Then *D* said, God hath broken in 1Chr 14:11 1732
D gave a commandment, and they 1Chr 14:12 1732
Therefore *D* enquired again of God 1Chr 14:14 1732
D therefore did as God commanded 1Chr 14:16 1732
the fame of *D* went out into all 1Chr 14:17 1732
D made him houses in the city of 1Chr 15:1
made him houses in the city of *D* 1Chr 15:1 1732
Then *D* said, None ought to carry 1Chr 15:2 1732
D gathered all Israel together to 1Chr 15:3 1732
D assembled the children of Aaron 1Chr 15:4 1732
D called for Zadok and Abiathar 1Chr 15:11 1732
D spake to the chief of the 1Chr 15:16 1732
So *D*, and the elders of Israel, and 1Chr 15:25 1732
D was clothed with a robe of fine 1Chr 15:27 1732
D also had upon him an ephod of 1Chr 15:27 1732
of the LORD came to the city of *D* 1Chr 15:29 1732
at a window saw king *D* dancing 1Chr 15:29 1732
tent that *D* had pitched for it 1Chr 16:1 1732
when *D* had made an end of 1Chr 16:2 1732
Then on that day *D* delivered 1Chr 16:7 1732
D returned to bless his house 1Chr 16:43 1732
as *D* sat in his house 1Chr 17:1 1732
that *D* said to Nathan the prophet 1Chr 17:1 1732
Then Nathan said unto *D*, Do all 1Chr 17:2 1732
tell *D* my servant, Thus saith the 1Chr 17:4 1732
shalt thou say unto my servant *D* 1Chr 17:7 1732
so did Nathan speak unto *D* 1Chr 17:15 1732
D the king came and sat before the 1Chr 17:16 1732
What can *D* speak more to thee for 1Chr 17:18 1732
let the house of *D* thy servant be 1Chr 17:24 1732
that *D* smote the Philistines, and 1Chr 18:1 1732
D smote Hadarezer king of Zobah 1Chr 18:3 1732
D took from him a thousand 1Chr 18:4 1732
D also houghed all the chariot 1Chr 18:4 1732
D slew of the Syrians two and 1Chr 18:5 1732
Then *D* put garrisons in 1Chr 18:6 1732
preserved *D* whithersoever he went 1Chr 18:6 1732
D took the shields of gold that 1Chr 18:7 1732
brought *D* very much brass, 1Chr 18:8 1732
how *D* had smitten all the host of 1Chr 18:9 1732
He sent Hadoram his son to king *D* 1Chr 18:10 1732
Them also king *D* dedicated unto 1Chr 18:11 1732
preserved *D* whithersoever he went 1Chr 18:13 1732
So *D* reigned over all Israel, and 1Chr 18:14 1732
the sons of *D* were chief about 1Chr 18:17 1732
D said, I will shew kindness unto 1Chr 19:2 1732
D sent messengers to comfort him 1Chr 19:2 1732
So the servants of *D* came into 1Chr 19:2 1732
Thinkest thou that *D* doth honour 1Chr 19:3 1732
told *D* how the men were served 1Chr 19:5 1732
had made themselves odious to *D* 1Chr 19:6 1732
when *D* heard of it, he sent Joab, 1Chr 19:8 1732
And it was told *D* 1Chr 19:17 1732
So when *D* had put the battle in 1Chr 19:17 1732
D slew of the Syrians seven 1Chr 19:18 1732
Israel, they made peace with *D* 1Chr 19:19 1732
But *D* tarried at Jerusalem 1Chr 20:1 1732
D took the crown of their king 1Chr 20:2 1732
Even so dealt *D* with all the 1Chr 20:3 1732
And *D* and all the people returned 1Chr 20:3 1732
and they fell by the hand of *D* 1Chr 20:8 1732
provoked *D* to number Israel 1Chr 21:1 1732
D said to Joab and to the rulers 1Chr 21:2 1732
the number of the people unto *D* 1Chr 21:5 1732
D said unto God, I have sinned 1Chr 21:8 1732
Go and tell *D*, saying, Thus saith 1Chr 21:10 1732
So Gad came to *D*, and said unto 1Chr 21:11 1732
D said unto Gad, I am in a great 1Chr 21:13 1732
D lifted up his eyes, and saw the 1Chr 21:16 1732
Then *D* and the elders of Israel, 1Chr 21:16 1732
D said unto God, Is it not I that 1Chr 21:17 1732
LORD commanded Gad to say to *D* 1Chr 21:18 1732
that *D* should go up, and set up an 1Chr 21:18 1732
D went up at the saying of Gad, 1Chr 21:19 1732
as *D* came to Ornan 1Chr 21:21 1732
Ornan looked and saw *D* 1Chr 21:21 1732
bowed himself to *D* with his face 1Chr 21:21 1732
Then *D* said to Ornan, Grant me 1Chr 21:22 1732
And Ornan said unto *D*, Take it to 1Chr 21:23 1732
king *D* said to Ornan, Nay 1Chr 21:24 1732
So *D* gave to Ornan for the place 1Chr 21:25 1732
D built there an altar unto the 1Chr 21:26 1732
At that time when *D* saw that the 1Chr 21:28 1732
But *D* could not go before it to 1Chr 21:30 1732
Then *D* said, This is the house of 1Chr 22:1 1732
D commanded to gather together 1Chr 22:2 1732
D prepared iron in abundance for 1Chr 22:3 1732
Tyre brought much cedar wood to *D* 1Chr 22:4 1732
D said, Solomon my son is young 1Chr 22:5 1732
So *D* prepared abundantly before 1Chr 22:5 1732
D said to Solomon, My son, as for 1Chr 22:7 1732
D also commanded all the princes 1Chr 22:17 1732
So when *D* was old and full of days 1Chr 23:1 1732
instruments which I made, said *D* 1Chr 23:5 1732
D divided them into courses among 1Chr 23:6 1732
For *D* said, The LORD God of 1Chr 23:25 1732
For by the last words of *D* the 1Chr 23:27 1732
D distributed them, both Zadok of 1Chr 24:3 1732
in the presence of *D* the king 1Chr 24:31 1732
Moreover *D* and the captains of the 1Chr 25:1 1732
which *D* the king, and the chief 1Chr 26:26 1732
reign of *D* they were sought for 1Chr 26:31 1732
whom king *D* made rulers over the 1Chr 26:32 1732
Elihu, one of the brethren of *D* 1Chr 27:18 1732
But *D* took not the number of them 1Chr 27:23 1732
of the Chronicles of king *D* 1Chr 27:24 1732
D assembled all the princes of 1Chr 28:1 1732
Then *D* the king stood up upon his 1Chr 28:2 1732
Then *D* gave to Solomon his son 1Chr 28:11 1732
All this, said *D*, the LORD made 1Chr 28:19
D said to Solomon his son, Be 1Chr 28:20 1732
Furthermore *D* the king said unto 1Chr 29:1 1732
D the king also rejoiced with 1Chr 29:9 1732
Wherefore *D* blessed the LORD 1Chr 29:10 1732
D said, Blessed be thou, LORD God 1Chr 29:10 1732
D said to all the congregation, 1Chr 29:20 1732
the son of *D* king the second time 1Chr 29:22 1732
as king instead of *D* his father 1Chr 29:23 1732
all the sons likewise of king *D* 1Chr 29:24 1732
Thus *D* the son of Jesse reigned 1Chr 29:26 1732
Now the acts of *D* the king 1Chr 29:29 1732
And Solomon the son of *D* was 2Chr 1:1 1732
But the ark of God had *D* brought 2Chr 1:4 1732
to the place which *D* had prepared 2Chr 1:4 1732
great mercy unto *D* my father 2Chr 1:8 1732
let thy promise unto *D* my father 2Chr 1:9 1732
thou didst deal with *D* my father 2Chr 2:3 1732
whom *D* my father did provide 2Chr 2:7 1732
who hath given to *D* the king a 2Chr 2:12 1732
men of my lord *D* thy father 2Chr 2:14 1732
D his father had numbered them 2Chr 2:17 1732
LORD appeared unto *D* his father 2Chr 3:1 1732
in the place that *D* had prepared 2Chr 3:1 1732
that *D* his father had dedicated 2Chr 5:1 1732
of the LORD out of the city of *D* 2Chr 5:2 1732
with his mouth to my father *D* 2Chr 6:4 1732
have chosen *D* to be over my 2Chr 6:6 1732
Now it was in the heart of *D* my 2Chr 6:7 1732
But the LORD said to *D* my father 2Chr 6:8 1732
up in the room of *D* my father 2Chr 6:10 1732
hast kept with thy servant *D* my 2Chr 6:15 1732
keep with thy servant *D* my father 2Chr 6:16 1732
hast spoken unto thy servant *D* 2Chr 6:17 1732
the mercies of *D* thy servant 2Chr 6:42 1732
which *D* the king had made to 2Chr 7:6 1732
when *D* praised by their ministry 2Chr 7:6 1732
that the LORD had shewed unto *D* 2Chr 7:10 1732
as *D* thy father walked, and do 2Chr 7:17 1732
have covenanted with *D* thy father 2Chr 7:18 1732
of *D* unto the house that he had 2Chr 8:11 1732
in the house of *D* king of Israel 2Chr 8:11 1732
to the order of *D* his father 2Chr 8:14 1732
for so had *D* the man of God 2Chr 8:14 1732
in the city of *D* his father 2Chr 9:31 1732
saying, What portion have we in *D* 2Chr 10:16 1732
your tents, O Israel, and now, *D* 2Chr 10:16 1732
the house of *D* unto this day 2Chr 10:19 1732
years they walked in the way of *D* 2Chr 11:17 1732
of Jerimoth the son of *D* to wife 2Chr 11:18 1732
and was buried in the city of *D* 2Chr 12:16 1732
kingdom over Israel to *D* for ever 2Chr 13:5 1732
servant of Solomon the son of *D* 2Chr 13:6 1732
LORD in the hand of the sons of *D* 2Chr 13:8 1732
they buried him in the city of *D* 2Chr 14:1 1732
made for himself in the city of *D* 2Chr 16:14 1732
in the first ways of his father *D* 2Chr 17:3 1732
with his fathers in the city of *D* 2Chr 21:1 1732
would not destroy the house of *D* 2Chr 21:7 1732
covenant that he had made with *D* 2Chr 21:7 1732
the LORD God of *D* thy father 2Chr 21:12 1732
they buried him in the city of *D* 2Chr 21:20 1732
LORD hath said of the sons of *D* 2Chr 23:3 1732
whom *D* had distributed in the 2Chr 23:18 1732
singing, as it was ordained by *D* 2Chr 23:18 1732
in the city of *D* among the kings 2Chr 24:16 1732
they buried him in the city of *D* 2Chr 24:25 1732
they buried him in the city of *D* 2Chr 27:9 1732
of the LORD, like *D* his father 2Chr 28:1 1732
to all that *D* his father had done 2Chr 29:2 1732
according to the commandment of *D* 2Chr 29:25 1732
stood with the instruments of *D* 2Chr 29:26 1732
ordained by *D* king of Israel 2Chr 29:27 1732
unto the LORD with the words of *D* 2Chr 29:30 1732
of *D* king of Israel there was not 2Chr 30:26 1732
repaired Millo in the city of *D* 2Chr 32:5 1732
to the west side of the city of *D* 2Chr 32:30 1732
the sepulchres of the sons of *D* 2Chr 32:33 1732
God, of which God had said to *D* 2Chr 33:7 1732
a wall without the city of *D* 2Chr 33:14 1732
in the ways of *D* his father 2Chr 34:2 1732
after the God of *D* his father 2Chr 34:3 1732

son of *D* king of Israel did build ... 2Chr 35:3 1732
the writing of *D* king of Israel ... 2Chr 35:4 1732
according to the commandment of *D* ... 2Chr 35:15 1732
the ordinance of *D* king of Israel ... Ezr 3:10 1732
of the sons of *D* ... Ezr 8:2 1732
Also of the Nethinims, whom *D* ... Ezr 8:20 1732
that go down from the city of *D* ... Neh 3:15 1732
over against the sepulchres of *D* ... Neh 3:16 1732
commandment of *D* the man of God ... Neh 12:24 1732
instruments of *D* the man of God ... Neh 12:36 1732
up by the stairs of the city of *D* ... Neh 12:37 1732
of the wall, above the house of *D* ... Neh 12:37 1732
according to the commandment of *D* ... Neh 12:45 1732
For in the days of *D* and Asaph of ... Neh 12:46 1732
A Psalm of *D*, when he fled from ... Ps 3:*t* 1732
on Neginoth, A Psalm of *D* ... Ps 4:*t* 1732
upon Nehiloth, A Psalm of *D* ... Ps 5:*t* 1732
upon Sheminith, A Psalm of *D* ... Ps 6:*t* 1732
Shiggaion of *D*, which he sang ... Ps 7:*t* 1732
upon Gittith, A Psalm of *D* ... Ps 8:*t* 1732
upon Muth-labben, A Psalm of *D* ... Ps 9:*t* 1732
the chief Musician, A Psalm of *D* ... Ps 11:*t* 1732
upon Sheminith, A Psalm of *D* ... Ps 12:*t* 1732
the chief Musician, A Psalm of *D* ... Ps 13:*t* 1732
the chief Musician, A Psalm of *D* ... Ps 14:*t* 1732
A Psalm of *D* ... Ps 15:*t* 1732
Michtam of *D* ... Ps 16:*t* 1732
A Prayer of *D* ... Ps 17:*t* 1732
the chief Musician, A Psalm of *D* ... Ps 18:*t* 1732
mercy to his anointed, to *D* ... Ps 18:50 1732
the chief Musician, A Psalm of *D* ... Ps 19:*t* 1732
the chief Musician, A Psalm of *D* ... Ps 20:*t* 1732
the chief Musician, A Psalm of *D* ... Ps 21:*t* 1732
Aijeleth Shahar, A Psalm of *D* ... Ps 22:*t* 1732
A Psalm of *D* ... Ps 23:*t* 1732
A Psalm of *D* ... Ps 24:*t* 1732
A Psalm of *D* ... Ps 25:*t* 1732
A Psalm of *D* ... Ps 26:*t* 1732
A Psalm of *D* ... Ps 27:*t* 1732
A Psalm of *D* ... Ps 28:*t* 1732
A Psalm of *D* ... Ps 29:*t* 1732
the dedication of the house of *D* ... Ps 30:*t* 1732
the chief Musician, A Psalm of *D* ... Ps 31:*t* 1732
A Psalm of *D*, A Maschil ... Ps 32:*t* 1732
A Psalm of *D*, when he changed his ... Ps 34:*t* 1732
A Psalm of *D* ... Ps 35:*t* 1732
the chief Musician, A Psalm of *D* ... Ps 36:*t* 1732
A Psalm of *D* ... Ps 37:*t* 1732
A Psalm of *D*, to bring to ... Ps 38:*t* 1732
even to Jeduthun, A Psalm of *D* ... Ps 39:*t* 1732
the chief Musician, A Psalm of *D* ... Ps 40:*t* 1732
the chief Musician, A Psalm of *D* ... Ps 41:*t* 1732
the chief Musician, A Psalm of *D* ... Ps 51:*t* 1732
Musician, Maschil, A Psalm of *D* ... Ps 52:*t* 1732
D is come to the house of ... Ps 52:*t* 1732
Mahalath, Maschil, A Psalm of *D* ... Ps 53:*t* 1732
Neginoth, Maschil, A Psalm of *D* ... Ps 54:*t* 1732
Doth not *D* hide himself with us ... Ps 54:*t* 1732
Neginoth, Maschil, A Psalm of *D* ... Ps 55:*t* 1732
a Michtam of *D*, when the ... Ps 56:*t* 1732
Altaschith, Michtam of *D* ... Ps 57:*t* 1732
Altaschith, Michtam of *D* ... Ps 58:*t* 1732
Altaschith, Michtam of *D* ... Ps 59:*t* 1732
upon Shushan-eduth, Michtam of *D* ... Ps 60:*t* 1732
upon Neginah, A Psalm of *D* ... Ps 61:*t* 1732
to Jeduthun, A Psalm of *D* ... Ps 62:*t* 1732
A Psalm of *D*, when he was in the ... Ps 63:*t* 1732
the chief Musician, A Psalm of *D* ... Ps 64:*t* 1732
Musician, A Psalm and Song of *D* ... Ps 65:*t* 1732
Musician, A Psalm or Song of *D* ... Ps 68:*t* 1732
upon Shoshannim, A Psalm of *D* ... Ps 69:*t* 1732
the chief Musician, A Psalm of *D* ... Ps 70:*t* 1732
The prayers of *D* the son of Jesse ... Ps 72:20 1732
He chose *D* also his servant, and ... Ps 78:70 1732
A Prayer of *D* ... Ps 86:*t* 1732
I have sworn unto *D* my servant ... Ps 89:3 1732
I have found *D* my servant ... Ps 89:20 1732
that I will not lie unto *D* ... Ps 89:35 1732
thou swarest unto *D* in thy truth ... Ps 89:49 1732
A Psalm of *D* ... Ps 101:*t* 1732
A Psalm of *D* ... Ps 103:*t* 1732
A Song or Psalm of *D* ... Ps 108:*t* 1732
the chief Musician, A Psalm of *D* ... Ps 109:*t* 1732
A Psalm of *D* ... Ps 110:*t* 1732
A Song of degrees of *D* ... Ps 122:*t* 1732
the thrones of the house of *D* ... Ps 122:5 1732
A Song of degrees of *D* ... Ps 124:*t* 1732
A Song of degrees of *D* ... Ps 131:*t* 1732
Lord, remember *D*, and all his ... Ps 132:1 1732
LORD hath sworn in truth unto *D* ... Ps 132:11 1732
will I make the horn of *D* to bud ... Ps 132:17 1732
A Song of degrees of *D* ... Ps 133:*t* 1732
A Psalm of *D* ... Ps 138:*t* 1732
the chief Musician, A Psalm of *D* ... Ps 139:*t* 1732
the chief Musician, A Psalm of *D* ... Ps 140:*t* 1732
A Psalm of *D* ... Ps 141:*t* 1732
Maschil of *D* ... Ps 142:*t* 1732
A Psalm of *D* ... Ps 143:*t* 1732
A Psalm of *D* ... Ps 144:*t* 1732
who delivereth *D* his servant from ... Ps 144:10 1732
Proverbs of Solomon the son of *D* ... Prov 1:1 1732
of the Preacher, the son of *D* ... Eccl 1:1 1732
tower of *D* builded for an armoury ... Song 4:4 1732
And it was told the house of *D* ... Is 7:2 1732
said, Hear ye now, O house of *D* ... Is 7:13 1732
be no end, upon the throne of *D* ... Is 9:7 1732
in truth in the tabernacle of *D* ... Is 16:5 1732
the breaches of the city of *D* ... Is 22:9 1732
the key of the house of *D* will I ... Is 22:22 1732
to Ariel, the city where *D* dwelt ... Is 29:1 1732
the LORD, the God of *D* thy father ... Is 38:5 1732
you, even the sure mercies of *D* ... Is 55:3 1732
sitting upon the throne of *D* ... Jer 17:25 1732
O house of *D*, thus saith the LORD ... Jer 21:12 1732
that sittest upon the throne of *D* ... Jer 22:2 1732
sitting upon the throne of *D* ... Jer 22:4 1732
sitting upon the throne of *D* ... Jer 22:30 1732
raise unto *D* a righteous Branch ... Jer 23:5 1732
that sitteth upon the throne of *D* ... Jer 29:16 1732
D their king, whom I will raise ... Jer 30:9 1732
righteousness to grow up unto *D* ... Jer 33:15 1732
D shall never want a man to sit ... Jer 33:17 1732
be broken with *D* my servant ... Jer 33:21 1732
multiply the seed of *D* my servant ... Jer 33:22 1732
D my servant, so that I will not ... Jer 33:26 1732
none to sit upon the throne of *D* ... Jer 36:30 1732
feed them, even my servant *D* ... Eze 34:23 1732
my servant *D* a prince among them ... Eze 34:24 1732
D my servant shall be king over ... Eze 37:24 1732
my servant *D* shall be their ... Eze 37:25 1732
LORD their God, and *D* their king ... Hos 3:5 1732
instruments of musick, like *D* ... Amos 6:5 1732
tabernacle of *D* that is fallen ... Amos 9:11 1732
that the glory of the house of *D* ... Zec 12:7 1732
them at that day shall be as *D* ... Zec 12:8 1732
the house of *D* shall be as God ... Zec 12:8 1732
I will pour upon the house of *D* ... Zec 12:10 1732
family of the house of *D* apart ... Zec 12:12 1732
fountain opened to the house of *D* ... Zec 13:1 1732
of Jesus Christ, the son of *D* ... Mt 1:1 *1138*
And Jesse begat *D* the king ... Mt 1:6 *1138*
D the king begat Solomon of her ... Mt 1:6 *1138*
to *D* are fourteen generations ... Mt 1:17 *1138*
from *D* until the carrying away ... Mt 1:17 *1138*
saying, Joseph, thou son of *D* ... Mt 1:20 *1138*
crying, and saying, Thou son of *D* ... Mt 9:27 *1138*
them, Have ye not read what *D* did ... Mt 12:3 *1138*
and said, Is not this the son of *D* ... Mt 12:23 *1138*
on me, O Lord, thou son of *D* ... Mt 15:22 *1138*
on us, O Lord, thou son of *D* ... Mt 20:30 *1138*
on us, O Lord, thou son of *D* ... Mt 20:31 *1138*
saying, Hosanna to the son of *D* ... Mt 21:9 *1138*
saying, Hosanna to the son of *D* ... Mt 21:15 *1138*
They say unto him, The son of *D* ... Mt 22:42 *1138*
How then doth *D* in spirit call ... Mt 22:43 *1138*
If *D* then call him Lord ... Mt 22:45 *1138*
Have ye never read what *D* did ... Mk 2:25 *1138*
out, and say, Jesus, thou son of *D* ... Mk 10:47 *1138*
more a great deal, Thou son of *D* ... Mk 10:48 *1138*
be the kingdom of our father *D* ... Mk 11:10 *1138*
that Christ is the son of *D* ... Mk 12:35 *1138*
For *D* himself said by the Holy ... Mk 12:36 *1138*
D therefore himself calleth him ... Mk 12:37 *1138*
was Joseph, of the house of *D* ... Lk 1:27 *1138*
him the throne of his father *D* ... Lk 1:32 *1138*
us in the house of his servant *D* ... Lk 1:69 *1138*
into Judaea, unto the city of *D* ... Lk 2:4 *1138*
was of the house and lineage of *D* ... Lk 2:4 *1138*
day in the city of *D* a Saviour ... Lk 2:11 *1138*
of Nathan, which was the son of *D* ... Lk 3:31 *1138*
read so much as this, what *D* did ... Lk 6:3 *1138*
saying, Jesus, thou son of *D* ... Lk 18:38 *1138*
so much the more, Thou son of *D* ... Lk 18:39 *1138*
D himself saith in the book of ... Lk 20:42 *1138*
D therefore calleth him Lord, how ... Lk 20:44 *1138*
Christ cometh of the seed of *D* ... Jn 7:42 *1138*
town of Bethlehem, where *D* was ... Jn 7:42 *1138*
D spake before concerning Judas ... Acts 1:16 *1138*
For *D* speaketh concerning him, I ... Acts 2:25 *1138*
speak unto you of the patriarch *D* ... Acts 2:29 *1138*
For *D* is not ascended into the ... Acts 2:34 *1138*
mouth of thy servant *D* hast said ... Acts 4:25 *1138*
our fathers, unto the days of *D* ... Acts 7:45 *1138*
up unto them *D* to be their king ... Acts 13:22 *1138*
I have found *D* the son of Jesse ... Acts 13:22 *1138*
give you the sure mercies of *D* ... Acts 13:34 *1138*
For *D*, after he had served his ... Acts 13:36 *1138*
build again the tabernacle of *D* ... Acts 15:16 *1138*
seed of *D* according to the flesh ... Rom 1:3 *1138*
Even as *D* also describeth the ... Rom 4:6 *1138*
D saith, Let their table be made ... Rom 11:9 *1138*
of *D* was raised from the dead ... 2Ti 2:8 *1138*
a certain day, saying in *D* ... Heb 4:7 *1138*
of *D* also, and Samuel, and of the ... Heb 11:32 *1138*
true, he that hath the key of *D* ... Rev 3:7 *1138*
the tribe of Juda, the Root of *D* ... Rev 5:5 *1138*
am the root and the offspring of *D* ... Rev 22:16 *1138*

DAVID'S {54}
Saul became *D* enemy continually ... 1Sa 18:29 1732
also sent messengers unto *D* house ... 1Sa 19:11 1732
Michal *D* wife told him, saying ... 1Sa 19:11 1732
it at the hand of *D* enemies ... 1Sa 20:16 1732
Saul's side, and *D* place was empty ... 1Sa 20:25 1732
the month, that *D* place was empty ... 1Sa 20:27 1732
D men said unto him, Behold, we ... 1Sa 23:3 1732
that *D* heart smote him, because ... 1Sa 24:5 1732
when *D* young men came, they spake ... 1Sa 25:9 1732
And Nabal answered *D* servants ... 1Sa 25:10 1732
So *D* young men turned their way ... 1Sa 25:12 1732
D wife, to Phalti the son of ... 1Sa 25:44 1732
And Saul knew *D* voice, and said, Is ... 1Sa 26:17 1732
D two wives were taken captives ... 1Sa 30:5 1732
cattle, and said, This is *D* spoil ... 1Sa 30:20 1732
there lacked of *D* servants ... 2Sa 2:30 1732
sixth, Ithream, by Eglah *D* wife ... 2Sa 3:5 1732
blind, that are hated of *D* soul ... 2Sa 5:8 1732
so the Moabites became *D* servants ... 2Sa 8:2 1732
they of Edom became *D* servants ... 2Sa 8:14 1732
and *D* sons were chief rulers ... 2Sa 8:18 1732
D servants came into the land of ... 2Sa 10:2 1732
Wherefore Hanun took *D* servants ... 2Sa 10:4 1732
D anger was greatly kindled ... 2Sa 12:5 1732
and it was set on *D* head ... 2Sa 12:30 1732
the son of Shimeah *D* brother ... 2Sa 13:3 1732
the son of Shimeah *D* brother ... 2Sa 13:32 1732
D counsellor, from his city, even ... 2Sa 15:12 1732
So Hushai *D* friend came into the ... 2Sa 15:37 1732
D friend, was come unto Absalom ... 2Sa 16:16 1732
all *D* men with him, over Jordan ... 2Sa 19:41 1732
D heart smote him after that he ... 2Sa 24:10 1732
the prophet Gad, *D* seer, saying ... 2Sa 24:11 1732
Solomon to ride upon king *D* mule ... 1Kin 1:38 1732
one tribe for my servant *D* sake ... 1Kin 11:32 1732
Nevertheless for *D* sake did the ... 1Kin 15:4 1732
did the priest give king *D* spears ... 2Kin 11:10 1732
sake, and for my servant *D* sake ... 2Kin 19:34 1732
sake, and for my servant *D* sake ... 2Kin 20:6 1732
and the Moabites became *D* servants ... 1Chr 18:2 1732
and the Syrians became *D* servants ... 1Chr 18:6 1732
the Edomites became *D* servants ... 1Chr 18:13 1732
Wherefore Hanun took *D* servants ... 1Chr 19:4 1732
and it was set upon *D* head ... 1Chr 20:2 1732
son of Shimea *D* brother slew him ... 1Chr 20:7 1732
spake unto Gad, *D* seer, saying ... 1Chr 21:9 1732
of the substance which was king *D* ... 1Chr 27:31 1732
Also Jonathan *D* uncle was a ... 1Chr 27:32 1732
and shields, that had been king *D* ... 2Chr 23:9 1732
For thy servant *D* sake turn not ... Ps 132:10 1732
D Psalm of praise ... Ps 145:*t* 1732
sake, and for my servant *D* sake ... Is 37:35 1732
the kings that sit upon *D* throne ... Jer 13:13 1732
How say they that Christ is *D* son ... Lk 20:41 *1138*

DAWN {2}
as it began to *d* toward the first ... Mt 28:1 *2020*
in a dark place, until the day *d* ... 2Pet 1:19 *1306*

DAWNING {5}
rose early about the *d* of the day ... Josh 6:15 5927
the woman in the *d* of the day ... Judg 19:26 6437
let it see the *d* of the day ... Job 3:9 6079
to and fro unto the *d* of the day ... Job 7:4 5399
I prevented the *d* of the morning ... Ps 119:147 5399

DAY {1747}
And God called the light *D* ... Gen 1:5 3117
and the morning were the first *d* ... Gen 1:5 3117
and the morning were the second *d* ... Gen 1:8 3117
and the morning were the third *d* ... Gen 1:13 3117
to divide the *d* from the night ... Gen 1:14 3117
the greater light to rule the *d* ... Gen 1:16 3117
And to rule over the *d* and over the ... Gen 1:18 3117
and the morning were the fourth *d* ... Gen 1:19 3117
and the morning were the fifth *d* ... Gen 1:23 3117
and the morning were the sixth *d* ... Gen 1:31 3117
on the seventh *d* God ended his ... Gen 2:2 3117
he rested on the seventh *d* from ... Gen 2:2 3117
And God blessed the seventh *d* ... Gen 2:3 3117
in the *d* that the LORD God made ... Gen 2:4 3117
for in the *d* that thou eatest ... Gen 2:17 3117
know that in the *d* ye eat thereof ... Gen 3:5 3117
the garden in the cool of the *d* ... Gen 3:8 3117
this *d* from the face of the earth ... Gen 4:14 3117
In the *d* that God created man, in ... Gen 5:1 3117
in the *d* when they were created ... Gen 5:2 3117
the seventeenth *d* of the month ... Gen 7:11 3117
the same *d* were all the fountains ... Gen 7:11 3117
In the selfsame *d* entered Noah ... Gen 7:13 3117
on the seventeenth *d* of the month ... Gen 8:4 3117
on the first *d* of the month ... Gen 8:5 3117
the first *d* of the month, the ... Gen 8:13 3117
twentieth *d* of the month, was the ... Gen 8:14 3117
heat, and summer and winter, and *d* ... Gen 8:22 3117
In the same *d* the LORD made a ... Gen 15:18 3117
their foreskin in the selfsame *d* ... Gen 17:23 3117
In the selfsame *d* was Abraham ... Gen 17:26 3117
tent door in the heat of the *d* ... Gen 18:1 3117
of the Moabites unto this *d* ... Gen 19:37 3117
the children of Ammon unto this *d* ... Gen 19:38 3117
the same *d* that Isaac was weaned ... Gen 21:8 3117
yet heard I of it, but to *d* ... Gen 21:26 3117
Then on the third *d* Abraham ... Gen 22:4 3117
as it is said to this *d*, In the ... Gen 22:14 3117
thee, send me good speed this *d* ... Gen 24:12 3117
I came this *d* unto the well, and ... Gen 24:42 3117
Sell me this *d* thy birthright ... Gen 25:31 3117
And Jacob said, Swear to me this *d* ... Gen 25:33 3117
And it came to pass the same *d* ... Gen 26:32 3117
city is Beer-sheba unto this *d* ... Gen 26:33 3117
old, I know not the *d* of my death ... Gen 27:2 3117
also of you both in one *d* ... Gen 27:45 3117
And he said, Lo, it is yet high *d* ... Gen 29:7 3117
pass through all thy flock to *d* ... Gen 30:32 3117
he removed that *d* the he goats ... Gen 30:35 3117
the third *d* that Jacob was fled ... Gen 31:22 3117
require it, whether stolen by *d* ... Gen 31:39 3117
in the *d* the drought consumed me ... Gen 31:40 3117
what can I do this *d* unto these ... Gen 31:43 3117
witness between me and thee this *d* ... Gen 31:48 3117
him until the breaking of the *d* ... Gen 32:24 7837
Let me go, for the *d* breaketh ... Gen 32:26 7837
hollow of the thigh, unto this *d* ... Gen 32:32 3117
men should overdrive them one *d* ... Gen 33:13 3117
that *d* on his way unto Seir ... Gen 33:16 3117
And it came to pass on the third *d* ... Gen 34:25 3117

me in the *d* of my distress	Gen 35:3	3117
of Rachel's grave unto this *d*	Gen 35:20	3117
as she spake to Joseph *d* by *d*	Gen 39:10	3117
Wherefore look ye so sadly to *d*	Gen 40:7	3117
And it came to pass the third *d*	Gen 40:20	3117
I do remember my faults this *d*	Gen 41:9	3117
is this *d* with our father	Gen 42:13	3117
Joseph said unto them the third *d*	Gen 42:18	3117
the youngest is this *d* with our	Gen 42:32	3117
Behold, I have bought you this *d*	Gen 47:23	3117
the land of Egypt unto this *d*	Gen 47:26	3117
me all my life long unto this *d*	Gen 48:15	3117
And he blessed them that *d*	Gen 48:20	3117
to bring to pass, as it is this *d*	Gen 50:20	3117
And when he went out the second *d*	Ex 2:13	3117
it that ye are come so soon to *d*	Ex 2:18	3117
Pharaoh commanded the same *d* the	Ex 5:6	3117
brick both yesterday and to *d*	Ex 5:14	3117
it came to pass on the *d* when the	Ex 6:28	3117
in that *d* the land of Goshen	Ex 8:22	3117
since the *d* that they were upon	Ex 10:6	3117
were upon the earth unto this *d*	Ex 10:6	3117
wind upon the land all that *d*	Ex 10:13	3117
for in that *d* thou seest my face	Ex 10:28	3117
In the tenth *d* of this month they	Ex 12:3	
fourteenth *d* of the same month	Ex 12:6	3117
this *d* shall be unto you for a	Ex 12:14	3117
even the first *d* ye shall put	Ex 12:15	3117
the first *d* until the seventh *d*	Ex 12:15	3117
in the first *d* there shall be an	Ex 12:16	3117
in the seventh *d* there shall be	Ex 12:16	3117
for in this selfsame *d* have I	Ex 12:17	3117
this *d* in your generations by an	Ex 12:17	3117
on the fourteenth *d* of the month	Ex 12:18	3117
twentieth *d* of the month at even	Ex 12:18	3117
the selfsame *d* it came to pass	Ex 12:41	3117
And it came to pass the selfsame *d*	Ex 12:51	3117
unto the people, Remember this *d*	Ex 13:3	3117
This *d* came ye out in the month	Ex 13:4	3117
in the seventh *d* shall be a feast	Ex 13:6	3117
thou shalt shew thy son in that *d*	Ex 13:8	3117
them by *d* in a pillar of a cloud	Ex 13:21	3119
to go by *d* and night	Ex 13:21	3119
away the pillar of the cloud by *d*	Ex 13:22	3119
which he will shew to you to *d*	Ex 14:13	3117
Egyptians whom ye have seen to *d*	Ex 14:13	3117
that *d* out of the hand of the	Ex 14:30	3117
on the fifteenth *d* of the second	Ex 16:1	3117
and gather a certain rate every *d*	Ex 16:4	3117
that on the sixth *d* they shall	Ex 16:5	3117
that on the sixth *d* they gathered	Ex 16:22	3117
bake that which ye will bake to *d*	Ex 16:23	
And Moses said, Eat that to *d*	Ex 16:25	3117
for to *d* is a sabbath unto the	Ex 16:25	3117
to *d* ye shall not find it in the	Ex 16:25	3117
but on the seventh *d*, which is	Ex 16:26	3117
on the seventh *d* for to gather	Ex 16:27	3117
the sixth *d* the bread of two days	Ex 16:29	3117
out of his place on the seventh *d*	Ex 16:29	3117
people rested on the seventh *d*	Ex 16:30	3117
the same *d* came they into the	Ex 19:1	3117
the people, and sanctify them to *d*	Ex 19:10	3117
And be ready against the third *d*	Ex 19:11	3117
for the third *d* the LORD will	Ex 19:11	3117
Be ready against the third *d*	Ex 19:15	3117
on the third *d* in the morning	Ex 19:16	3117
Remember the sabbath *d*, to keep	Ex 20:8	3117
But the seventh *d* is the sabbath	Ex 20:10	3117
them is, and rested the seventh *d*	Ex 20:11	3117
the LORD blessed the sabbath *d*	Ex 20:11	3117
if he continue a *d* or two	Ex 21:21	3117
on the eighth *d* thou shalt give	Ex 22:30	3117
on the seventh *d* thou shalt rest	Ex 23:12	3117
the seventh *d* he called unto	Ex 24:16	3117
thou shalt offer every *d* a	Ex 29:36	3117
first year *d* by *d* continually	Ex 29:38	3117
doeth any work in the sabbath *d*	Ex 31:15	3117
and on the seventh *d* he rested	Ex 31:17	3117
that *d* about three thousand men	Ex 32:28	3117
yourselves to *d* to the LORD	Ex 32:29	
bestow upon you a blessing this *d*	Ex 32:29	3117
nevertheless in the *d* when I	Ex 32:34	3117
that which I command thee this *d*	Ex 34:11	3117
on the seventh *d* thou shalt rest	Ex 34:21	3117
but on the seventh *d* there shall	Ex 35:2	3117
there shall be to you an holy *d*	Ex 35:2	
habitations upon the sabbath *d*	Ex 35:3	3117
On the first *d* of the first month	Ex 40:2	3117
year, on the first *d* of the month	Ex 40:17	
till the *d* that it was taken up	Ex 40:37	3117
LORD was upon the tabernacle by *d*	Ex 40:38	3119
in the *d* of his trespass offering	Lev 6:5	3119
LORD in the *d* when he is anointed	Lev 6:20	3119
the same *d* that it is offered	Lev 7:15	3119
it shall be eaten the same *d* that	Lev 7:16	3119
third *d* shall be burnt with fire	Lev 7:17	3119
be eaten at all on the third *d*	Lev 7:18	3119
in the *d* when he presented them	Lev 7:35	3119
in the *d* that he anointed them,	Lev 7:36	3119
in the *d* that he commanded the	Lev 7:38	3119
As he hath done this *d*, so the	Lev 8:34	3117
tabernacle of the congregation *d*	Lev 8:35	3119
it came to pass on the eighth *d*	Lev 9:1	3117
for to *d* the LORD will appear	Lev 9:4	3117
this *d* have they offered their	Lev 10:19	3117
I had eaten the sin offering to *d*	Lev 10:19	3117
in the eighth *d* the flesh of his	Lev 12:3	3117
shall look on him the seventh *d*	Lev 13:5	3117
look on him again the seventh *d*	Lev 13:6	3117
shall look upon him the seventh *d*	Lev 13:27	3117
in the seventh *d* the priest shall	Lev 13:32	3117
in the seventh *d* the priest shall	Lev 13:34	3117
on the plague on the seventh *d*	Lev 13:51	3117
leper in the *d* of his cleansing	Lev 14:2	3117
But it shall be on the seventh *d*	Lev 14:9	3117
on the eighth *d* he shall take two	Lev 14:10	3117
d for his cleansing unto the	Lev 14:23	3117
shall come again the seventh *d*	Lev 14:39	3117
on the eighth *d* he shall take to	Lev 15:14	3117
on the eighth *d* she shall take	Lev 15:29	3117
on the tenth *d* of the month	Lev 16:29	
For on that *d* shall the priest	Lev 16:30	3117
be eaten the same *d* ye offer it	Lev 19:6	3117
if ought remain until the third *d*	Lev 19:6	3117
it be eaten at all on the third *d*	Lev 19:7	3117
and from the eighth *d* and	Lev 22:27	3117
it and her young both in one *d*	Lev 22:28	3117
On the same *d* it shall be eaten	Lev 22:30	3117
but the seventh *d* is the sabbath	Lev 23:3	3117
In the fourteenth *d* of the first	Lev 23:5	
on the fifteenth *d* of the same	Lev 23:6	3117
In the first *d* ye shall have an	Lev 23:7	3117
in the seventh *d* is an holy	Lev 23:8	3117
ye shall offer that *d* when ye	Lev 23:12	3117
until the selfsame *d* that ye have	Lev 23:14	3117
from the *d* that ye brought the	Lev 23:15	3117
shall proclaim on the selfsame *d*	Lev 23:21	3117
in the first *d* of the month	Lev 23:24	
Also on the tenth *d* of this	Lev 23:27	
there shall be a *d* of atonement	Lev 23:27	3117
shall do no work in that same *d*	Lev 23:28	3117
for it is a *d* of atonement, to	Lev 23:28	3117
not be afflicted in that same *d*	Lev 23:29	3117
doeth any work in that same *d*	Lev 23:30	3117
in the ninth *d* of the month at	Lev 23:32	
The fifteenth *d* of this seventh	Lev 23:34	3117
On the first *d* shall be an holy	Lev 23:35	3117
on the eighth *d* shall be an holy	Lev 23:36	3117
offerings, every thing upon his *d*	Lev 23:37	3117
fifteenth *d* of the seventh month	Lev 23:39	3117
on the first *d* shall be a sabbath	Lev 23:39	3117
on the eighth *d* shall be a	Lev 23:39	3117
d the boughs of goodly trees	Lev 23:40	3117
the tenth *d* of the seventh month	Lev 25:9	
in the *d* of atonement shall ye	Lev 25:9	3117
give thine estimation in that *d*	Lev 27:23	3117
on the first *d* of the second	Num 1:1	
the first *d* of the second month	Num 1:18	
Moses in the *d* that the LORD	Num 3:1	3117
for on the *d* that I smote all the	Num 3:13	3117
head in the *d* of his cleansing	Num 6:9	3117
on the seventh *d* shall he shave	Num 6:9	3117
on the eighth *d* he shall bring	Num 6:10	3117
shall hallow his head that same *d*	Num 6:11	3117
it came to pass on the *d* that	Num 7:1	3117
in the *d* that it was anointed	Num 7:10	3117
offering, each prince on his *d*	Num 7:11	3117
first *d* was Nahshon the son of	Num 7:12	3117
On the second *d* Nethaneel the son	Num 7:18	3117
On the third *d* Eliab the son of	Num 7:24	3117
On the fourth *d* Elizur the son of	Num 7:30	3117
On the fifth *d* Shelumiel the son	Num 7:36	3117
On the sixth *d* Eliasaph the son	Num 7:42	3117
On the seventh *d* Elishama the son	Num 7:48	3117
On the eighth *d* offered Gamaliel	Num 7:54	3117
On the ninth *d* Abidan the son of	Num 7:60	3117
On the tenth *d* Ahiezer the son of	Num 7:66	3117
On the eleventh *d* Pagiel the son	Num 7:72	3117
On the twelfth *d* Ahira the son of	Num 7:78	3117
in the *d* when it was anointed, by	Num 7:84	3117
on the *d* that I smote every	Num 8:17	3117
In the fourteenth *d* of this month	Num 9:3	3117
d of the first month at even in	Num 9:5	3117
not keep the passover on that *d*	Num 9:6	3117
Moses and before Aaron on that *d*	Num 9:6	3117
The fourteenth *d* of the second	Num 9:11	3117
on the *d* that the tabernacle was	Num 9:15	3117
the cloud covered it by *d*	Num 9:16	
whether it was by *d* or by night	Num 9:21	3119
Also in the *d* of your gladness,	Num 10:10	3117
twentieth *d* of the second month	Num 10:11	
of the LORD was upon them by *d*	Num 10:34	3119
Ye shall not eat one *d*, nor two	Num 11:19	3117
And the people stood up all that *d*	Num 11:32	3117
all that night, and all the next *d*	Num 11:32	3117
each *d* for a year, shall ye bear	Num 14:34	3117
Moses, from the *d* that the LORD	Num 15:23	3117
sticks upon the sabbath *d*	Num 15:32	3117
himself with it on the third *d*	Num 19:12	3117
on the seventh *d* he shall be	Num 19:12	3117
he purify not himself the third *d*	Num 19:12	3117
then the seventh *d* he shall not	Num 19:12	3117
third *d*, and on the seventh *d*	Num 19:19	3117
on the seventh *d* he shall purify	Num 19:19	3117
since I was thine unto this *d*	Num 22:30	3117
which was slain in the *d* of the	Num 25:18	3117
first year without spot *d* by *d*	Num 28:3	3117
on the sabbath *d* two lambs of the	Num 28:9	3117
in the fourteenth *d* of the first	Num 28:16	3117
in the fifteenth *d* of this month	Num 28:17	3117
In the first *d* shall be an holy	Num 28:18	3117
on the seventh *d* ye shall have an	Num 28:25	3117
Also in the *d* of the firstfruits,	Num 28:26	3117
on the first *d* of the month	Num 29:1	
it is a *d* of blowing the trumpets	Num 29:1	3117
ye shall have on the tenth *d* of	Num 29:7	
on the fifteenth *d* of the seventh	Num 29:12	3117
on the second *d* ye shall offer	Num 29:17	3117
on the third *d* eleven bullocks,	Num 29:20	3117
And on the fourth *d* ten bullocks	Num 29:23	3117
on the fifth *d* nine bullocks, two	Num 29:26	3117
on the sixth *d* eight bullocks,	Num 29:29	3117
on the seventh *d* seven bullocks	Num 29:32	3117
On the eighth *d* ye shall have a	Num 29:35	3117
her in the *d* that he heareth	Num 30:5	3117
at her in the *d* that he heard it	Num 30:7	3117
her on the *d* that he heard it	Num 30:8	3117
them void on the *d* he heard them	Num 30:12	3117
his peace at her from *d* to *d*	Num 30:14	3117
her in the *d* that he heard them	Num 30:14	3117
third *d*, and on the seventh *d*	Num 31:19	3117
your clothes on the seventh *d*	Num 31:24	3117
on the fifteenth *d* of the first	Num 33:3	3117
in the first *d* of the fifth month	Num 33:38	
on the first *d* of the month	Deut 1:3	
ye are this *d* as the stars of	Deut 1:10	3117
ye should go, and in a cloud by *d*	Deut 1:33	3119
which in that *d* had no knowledge	Deut 1:39	3117
Ar, the coast of Moab, this *d*	Deut 2:18	3117
in their stead even unto this *d*	Deut 2:22	3117
This *d* will I begin to put the	Deut 2:25	3117
thy hand, as appeareth this *d*	Deut 2:30	3117
Bashan-havoth-jair, unto this *d*	Deut 3:14	3117
are alive every one of you this *d*	Deut 4:4	3117
which I set before you this *d*	Deut 4:8	3117
Specially the *d* that thou	Deut 4:10	3117
no manner of similitude on the *d*	Deut 4:15	3117
of inheritance, as ye are this *d*	Deut 4:20	3117
to witness against you this *d*	Deut 4:26	3117
since the *d* that God created man	Deut 4:32	3117
an inheritance, as it is this *d*	Deut 4:38	3117
Know therefore this *d*, and	Deut 4:39	3117
which I command thee this *d*	Deut 4:40	3117
which I speak in your ears this *d*	Deut 5:1	3117
are all of us here alive this *d*	Deut 5:3	3117
Keep the sabbath *d* to sanctify it	Deut 5:12	3117
But the seventh *d* is the sabbath	Deut 5:14	3117
thee to keep the sabbath *d*	Deut 5:15	3117
we have seen this *d* that God doth	Deut 5:24	3117
which I command thee this *d*	Deut 6:6	3117
us alive, as it is at this *d*	Deut 6:24	3117
which I command thee this *d*	Deut 7:11	3117
this *d* shall ye observe to do	Deut 8:1	3117
which I command thee this *d*	Deut 8:11	3117
unto thy fathers, as it is this *d*	Deut 8:18	3117
I testify against you this *d* that	Deut 8:19	3117
art to pass over Jordan this *d*	Deut 9:1	3117
Understand therefore this *d*	Deut 9:3	3117
from the *d* that thou didst depart	Deut 9:7	3117
the fire in the *d* of the assembly	Deut 9:10	3117
LORD from the *d* that I knew you	Deut 9:24	3117
the fire in the *d* of the assembly	Deut 10:4	3117
to bless in his name, unto this *d*	Deut 10:8	3117
command thee this *d* for thy good	Deut 10:13	3117
above all people, as it is this *d*	Deut 10:15	3117
And know ye this *d*	Deut 11:2	3117
hath destroyed them unto this *d*	Deut 11:4	3117
which I command you this *d*	Deut 11:8	3117
which I command you this *d*	Deut 11:13	3117
set before you this *d* a blessing	Deut 11:26	3117
God, which I command you this *d*	Deut 11:27	3117
way which I command you this *d*	Deut 11:28	3117
which I set before you this *d*	Deut 11:32	3117
the things that we do here this *d*	Deut 12:8	3117
which I command thee this *d*	Deut 13:18	3117
which I command thee this *d*	Deut 15:5	3117
I command thee this thing to *d*	Deut 15:15	3117
d when thou camest forth out of	Deut 16:3	3117
sacrificedst the first *d* at even	Deut 16:4	3117
on the seventh *d* shall be a	Deut 16:8	3117
in Horeb in the *d* of the assembly	Deut 18:16	3117
them, which I command thee this *d*	Deut 19:9	3117
ye approach this *d* unto battle	Deut 20:3	3117
shalt in any wise bury him that *d*	Deut 21:23	3117
At his *d* thou shalt give him his	Deut 24:15	3117
I profess this *d* unto the LORD	Deut 26:3	3117
This *d* the LORD thy God hath	Deut 26:16	3117
the LORD this *d* to be thy God	Deut 26:17	3117
this *d* to be his peculiar people	Deut 26:18	3117
which I command you this *d*	Deut 27:1	3117
it shall be on the *d* when ye	Deut 27:2	3117
which I command you this *d*	Deut 27:4	3117
this *d* thou art become the people	Deut 27:9	3117
which I command thee this *d*	Deut 27:10	3117
charged the people the same *d*	Deut 27:11	3117
which I command thee this *d*	Deut 28:1	3117
God, which I command thee this *d*	Deut 28:13	3117
words which I command thee this *d*	Deut 28:14	3117
which I command thee this *d*	Deut 28:15	3117
longing for them all the *d* long	Deut 28:32	3117
and thou shalt fear *d* and night, and	Deut 28:66	3119
see, and ears to hear, unto this *d*	Deut 29:4	3117
Ye stand this *d* all of you before	Deut 29:10	3117
thy God maketh with thee this *d*	Deut 29:12	3117
to *d* for a people unto himself	Deut 29:13	3117
us this *d* before the LORD our God	Deut 29:15	3117
that is not here with us this *d*	Deut 29:15	3117
away this *d* from the LORD our God	Deut 29:18	3117
another land, as it is this *d*	Deut 29:28	3117
to all that I command thee this *d*	Deut 30:2	3117
which I command thee this *d*	Deut 30:8	3117
which I command thee this *d*	Deut 30:11	3117
have set before thee this *d* life	Deut 30:15	3117
this *d* to love the LORD thy God	Deut 30:16	3117

I denounce unto you this *d*	Deut 30:18	3117
to record this *d* against you	Deut 30:19	3117
and twenty years old this *d*	Deut 31:2	3117
be kindled against them in that *d*	Deut 31:17	3117
so that they will say in that *d*	Deut 31:17	3117
surely hide my face in that *d* for	Deut 31:18	3117
wrote this song the same *d*	Deut 31:22	3117
I am yet alive with you this *d*	Deut 31:27	3117
for the *d* of their calamity is at	Deut 32:35	3117
which I testify among you this *d*	Deut 32:46	3117
spake unto Moses that selfsame *d*	Deut 32:48	3117
shall cover him all the *d* long	Deut 33:12	3117
of his sepulchre unto this *d*	Deut 34:6	3117
but thou shalt meditate therein *d*	Josh 1:8	3119
This *d* will I begin to magnify	Josh 3:7	3117
and they are there unto this *d*	Josh 4:9	3117
On that *d* the LORD magnified	Josh 4:14	3117
on the tenth *d* of the first month	Josh 4:19	
This *d* have I rolled away the	Josh 5:9	3117
is called Gilgal unto this *d*	Josh 5:9	3117
d of the month at even in the	Josh 5:10	3117
and parched corn in the selfsame *d*	Josh 5:11	3117
the seventh *d* ye shall compass	Josh 6:4	3117
until the *d* I bid you shout	Josh 6:10	3117
the second *d* they compassed the	Josh 6:14	3117
it came to pass on the seventh *d*	Josh 6:15	3117
early about the dawning of the *d*	Josh 6:15	7837
only on that *d* they compassed the	Josh 6:15	3117
in Israel even unto this *d*	Josh 6:25	3117
LORD shall trouble thee this *d*	Josh 7:25	3117
great heap of stones unto this *d*	Josh 7:26	3117
The valley of Achor, unto this *d*	Josh 7:26	3117
it was, that all that fell that *d*	Josh 8:25	3117
even a desolation unto this *d*	Josh 8:28	3117
that remaineth unto this *d*	Josh 8:29	3117
out of our houses on the *d* we	Josh 9:12	3117
unto their cities on the third *d*	Josh 9:17	3117
made them that *d* hewers of wood	Josh 9:27	3117
of the LORD, even unto this *d*	Josh 9:27	3117
d when the LORD delivered up the	Josh 10:12	3117
not to go down about a whole *d*	Josh 10:13	3117
there was no *d* like that before	Josh 10:14	3117
which remain until this very *d*	Josh 10:27	3117
that *d* Joshua took Makkedah, and	Josh 10:28	3117
which took it on the second *d*	Josh 10:32	3117
And they took it on that *d*	Josh 10:35	3117
he utterly destroyed that *d*	Josh 10:35	3117
among the Israelites until this *d*	Josh 13:13	3117
And Moses sware on that *d*, saying,	Josh 14:9	3117
and now, lo, I am this *d* fourscore	Josh 14:10	3117
As yet I am as strong this *d* as I	Josh 14:11	3117
I was in the *d* that Moses sent me	Josh 14:11	3117
whereof the LORD spake in that *d*	Josh 14:12	3117
for thou heardest in that *d* how	Josh 14:12	3117
the Kenezite unto this *d*, because	Josh 14:14	3117
of Judah at Jerusalem unto this *d*	Josh 15:63	3117
among the Ephraimites unto this *d*	Josh 16:10	3117
these many days unto this *d*	Josh 22:3	3117
Israel, to turn away this *d* from	Josh 22:16	3117
rebel this *d* against the LORD	Josh 22:16	3117
we are not cleansed until this *d*	Josh 22:17	3117
this *d* from following the LORD	Josh 22:18	3117
ye rebel to *d* against the LORD	Josh 22:18	3117
the LORD, (save us not this *d*	Josh 22:22	3117
turn this *d* from following the	Josh 22:29	3117
This *d* we perceive that the LORD	Josh 22:31	3117
God, as ye have done unto this *d*	Josh 23:8	3117
to stand before you unto this *d*	Josh 23:9	3117
this *d* I am going the way of all	Josh 23:14	3117
choose you this *d* whom ye will	Josh 24:15	3117
a covenant with the people that *d*	Josh 24:25	3117
Benjamin in Jerusalem unto this *d*	Judg 1:21	3117
is the name thereof unto this *d*	Judg 1:26	3117
that *d* under the hand of Israel	Judg 3:30	3117
for this is the *d* in which the	Judg 4:14	3117
So God subdued on that *d* Jabin	Judg 4:23	3117
the son of Abinoam on that *d*	Judg 5:1	3117
unto this *d* it is yet in Ophrah	Judg 6:24	3117
that he could not do it by *d*	Judg 6:27	3119
Therefore on that *d* he called him	Judg 6:32	3117
against my father's house this *d*	Judg 9:18	3117
and with his house this *d*, then	Judg 9:19	3117
against the city all that *d*	Judg 9:45	3117
called Havoth-jair unto this *d*	Judg 10:4	3117
us only, we pray thee, this *d*	Judg 10:15	3117
LORD the Judge be judge this *d*	Judg 11:27	3117
are ye come up unto me this *d*	Judg 12:3	3117
the womb to the *d* of his death	Judg 13:7	3117
me, that came unto me the other *d*	Judg 13:10	3117
it came to pass on the seventh *d*	Judg 14:15	3117
it came to pass on the seventh *d*	Judg 14:17	3117
d before the sun went down	Judg 14:18	3117
which is in Lehi unto this *d*	Judg 15:19	3117
In the morning, when it is *d*	Judg 16:2	1242
for unto that *d* all their	Judg 18:1	3117
place Mahaneh-dan unto this *d*	Judg 18:12	3117
d of the captivity of the land	Judg 18:30	3117
it came to pass on the fourth *d*	Judg 19:5	3117
morning on the fifth *d* to depart	Judg 19:8	3117
now the *d* draweth toward evening,	Judg 19:9	3117
the *d* groweth to an end, lodge	Judg 19:9	3117
by Jebus, the *d* was far spent	Judg 19:11	3117
when the *d* began to spring, they	Judg 19:25	7837
the woman in the dawning of the *d*	Judg 19:26	1242
the *d* that the children of Israel	Judg 19:30	3117
of the land of Egypt unto this *d*	Judg 19:30	3117
of the Israelites that *d* twenty	Judg 20:21	3117
themselves in array the first *d*	Judg 20:22	3117
children of Benjamin the second *d*	Judg 20:24	3117
them out of Gibeah the second *d*	Judg 20:25	3117
LORD, and fasted that *d* until even	Judg 20:26	3117
of Benjamin on the third *d*	Judg 20:30	3117
of the Benjamites that *d* twenty	Judg 20:35	3117
that *d* of Benjamin were twenty	Judg 20:46	3117
that there should be to *d* one	Judg 21:3	3117
tribe cut off from Israel this *d*	Judg 21:6	3117
her, Where hast thou gleaned to *d*	Ruth 2:19	3117
with whom I wrought to *d* is Boaz	Ruth 2:19	3117
he have finished the thing this *d*	Ruth 3:18	3117
What *d* thou buyest the field of	Ruth 4:5	3117
people, Ye are witnesses this *d*	Ruth 4:9	3117
ye are witnesses this *d*	Ruth 4:10	3117
thee this *d* without a kinsman	Ruth 4:14	3117
in one *d* they shall die both of	1Sa 2:34	3117
In that *d* I will perform against	1Sa 3:12	3117
us to *d* before the Philistines	1Sa 4:3	3117
the same *d* with his clothes rent	1Sa 4:12	3117
I fled to *d* out of the army	1Sa 4:16	3117
of Dagon in Ashdod unto this *d*	1Sa 5:5	3117
the same *d* unto the LORD	1Sa 6:15	3117
they returned to Ekron the same *d*	1Sa 6:16	3117
this *d* in the field of Joshua	1Sa 6:18	3117
the LORD, and fasted on that *d*	1Sa 7:6	3117
on that *d* upon the Philistines	1Sa 7:10	3117
d that I brought them up out of	1Sa 8:8	3117
up out of Egypt even unto this *d*	1Sa 8:8	3117
ye shall cry out in that *d*	1Sa 8:18	3117
LORD will not hear you in that *d*	1Sa 8:18	3117
now, for he came to *d* to the city	1Sa 9:12	3117
the people to *d* in the high place	1Sa 9:12	3117
in his ear a *d* before Saul came	1Sa 9:15	3117
for ye shall eat with me to *d*	1Sa 9:19	3117
Saul did eat with Samuel that *d*	1Sa 9:24	3117
to pass about the spring of the *d*	1Sa 9:26	7837
thou art departed from me to *d*	1Sa 10:2	3117
those signs came to pass that *d*	1Sa 10:9	3117
ye have this *d* rejected your God,	1Sa 10:19	3117
Ammonites until the heat of the *d*	1Sa 11:11	3117
not a man be put to death this *d*	1Sa 11:13	3117
for to *d* the LORD hath wrought	1Sa 11:13	3117
you from my childhood unto this *d*	1Sa 12:2	3117
and his anointed is witness this *d*	1Sa 12:5	3117
Is it not wheat harvest to *d*	1Sa 12:17	3117
LORD sent thunder and rain that *d*	1Sa 12:18	3117
came to pass in the *d* of battle	1Sa 13:22	3117
Now it came to pass upon a *d*	1Sa 14:1	3117
So the LORD saved Israel that *d*	1Sa 14:23	3117
of Israel were distressed that *d*	1Sa 14:24	3117
man that eateth any food this *d*	1Sa 14:28	3117
d of the spoil of their enemies	1Sa 14:30	3117
that *d* from Michmash to Aijalon	1Sa 14:31	3117
roll a great stone unto me this *d*	1Sa 14:33	3117
But he answered him not that *d*	1Sa 14:37	3117
wherein this sin hath been this *d*	1Sa 14:38	3117
he hath wrought with God this *d*	1Sa 14:45	3117
of Israel from thee this *d*	1Sa 15:28	3117
see Saul until the *d* of his death	1Sa 15:35	3117
upon David from that *d* forward	1Sa 16:13	3117
defy the armies of Israel this *d*	1Sa 17:10	3117
This *d* will the LORD deliver thee	1Sa 17:46	3117
this *d* unto the fowls of the air	1Sa 17:46	3117
And Saul took him that *d*, and would	1Sa 18:2	3117
And Saul eyed David from that *d*	1Sa 18:9	3117
Thou shalt this *d* be my son in	1Sa 18:21	3117
and lay down naked all that *d*	1Sa 19:24	3117
field unto the third *d* at even	1Sa 20:5	
morrow any time, or the third *d*	1Sa 20:12	
Saul spake not any thing that *d*	1Sa 20:26	3117
was the second *d* of the month	1Sa 20:27	
meat, neither yesterday, nor to *d*	1Sa 20:27	3117
no meat the second *d* of the month	1Sa 20:34	3117
sanctified this *d* in the vessel	1Sa 21:5	3117
in the *d* when it was taken away	1Sa 21:6	3117
servants of Saul was there that *d*	1Sa 21:7	3117
fled that *d* for fear of Saul, and	1Sa 21:10	3117
me, to lie in wait, as at this *d*	1Sa 22:8	3117
me, to lie in wait, as at this *d*	1Sa 22:13	3117
and slew on that *d* fourscore	1Sa 22:18	3117
unto Abiathar, I knew it that *d*	1Sa 22:22	3117
And Saul sought him every *d*	1Sa 23:14	3117
Behold the *d* of which the LORD	1Sa 24:4	3117
this *d* thine eyes have seen how	1Sa 24:10	3117
to *d* into mine hand in the cave	1Sa 24:10	3117
thou hast shewed this *d* how that	1Sa 24:18	3117
thou hast done unto me this *d*	1Sa 24:19	3117
for we come in a good *d*	1Sa 25:8	3117
a wall unto us both by night and *d*	1Sa 25:16	3119
which sent thee this *d* to meet me	1Sa 25:32	3117
which hast kept me this *d* from	1Sa 25:33	3117
enemy into thine hand this *d*	1Sa 26:8	3117
or his *d* shall come to die	1Sa 26:10	3117
they have driven me out this *d*	1Sa 26:19	3117
was precious in thine eyes this *d*	1Sa 26:21	3117
delivered thee into my hand to *d*	1Sa 26:23	3117
much set by this *d* in mine eyes	1Sa 26:24	3117
perish one *d* by the hand of Saul	1Sa 27:1	3117
Achish gave him Ziklag that *d*	1Sa 27:6	3117
the kings of Judah unto this *d*	1Sa 27:6	3117
Whither have ye made a road to *d*	1Sa 27:10	3117
done this thing unto thee this *d*	1Sa 28:18	3117
he had eaten no bread all the *d*	1Sa 28:20	3117
since he fell unto me unto this *d*	1Sa 29:3	3117
found evil in thee since the *d* of	1Sa 29:6	3117
of thy coming unto me unto this *d*	1Sa 29:6	3117
I have been with thee unto this *d*	1Sa 29:8	3117
come to Ziklag on the third *d*	1Sa 30:1	3117
unto the evening of the next *d*	1Sa 30:17	4283
And it was so from that *d* forward	1Sa 30:25	3117
ordinance for Israel unto this *d*	1Sa 30:25	3117
all his men, that same *d* together	1Sa 31:6	3117
came even to pass on the third *d*	2Sa 1:2	3117
was a very sore battle that *d*	2Sa 2:17	3117
they came to Hebron at break of *d*	2Sa 2:32	215
this *d* unto the house of Saul thy	2Sa 3:8	3117
that thou chargest me to *d* with a	2Sa 3:8	3117
to eat meat while it was yet *d*	2Sa 3:35	3117
all Israel understood that *d* that	2Sa 3:37	3117
great man fallen this *d* in Israel	2Sa 3:38	3117
And I am this *d* weak, though	2Sa 3:39	3117
sojourners there until this *d*	2Sa 4:3	3117
came about the heat of the *d* to	2Sa 4:5	3117
my lord the king this *d* of Saul	2Sa 4:8	3117
And David said on that *d*,	2Sa 5:8	3117
the place Perez-uzzah to this *d*	2Sa 6:8	3117
was afraid of the LORD that *d*	2Sa 6:9	3117
to *d* in the eyes of the handmaids	2Sa 6:20	3117
no child unto the *d* of her death	2Sa 6:23	3117
out of Egypt, even to this *d*	2Sa 7:6	3117
to Uriah, Tarry here to *d* also	2Sa 11:12	3117
Uriah abode in Jerusalem that *d*	2Sa 11:12	3117
it came to pass on the seventh *d*	2Sa 12:18	3117
king's son, lean from *d* to *d*	2Sa 13:4	1242
king's son, lean from *d* to *d*	2Sa 13:4	1242
hath been determined from the *d*	2Sa 13:32	3117
David mourned for his son every *d*	2Sa 13:37	3117
should I this *d* make thee go up	2Sa 15:20	3117
me good for his cursing this *d*	2Sa 16:12	3117
that *d* of twenty thousand men	2Sa 18:7	3117
that *d* than the sword devoured	2Sa 18:8	3117
and it is called unto this *d*	2Sa 18:18	3117
shalt not bear tidings this *d*	2Sa 18:20	3117
thou shalt bear tidings another *d*	2Sa 18:20	3117
but this *d* thou shalt bear no	2Sa 18:20	3117
this *d* of all them that rose up	2Sa 18:31	3117
the victory that *d* was turned	2Sa 19:2	3117
d how the king was grieved for	2Sa 19:2	3117
by stealth that *d* into the city	2Sa 19:3	3117
said Thou hast shamed this *d* the	2Sa 19:5	3117
which this *d* have saved thy life,	2Sa 19:5	3117
For thou hast declared this *d*	2Sa 19:6	3117
for this *d* I perceive, that if	2Sa 19:6	3117
lived, and all we had died this *d*	2Sa 19:6	3117
d that my lord the king went out	2Sa 19:19	3117
I am come the first this *d* of all	2Sa 19:20	3117
Zeruiah, that ye should this *d* be	2Sa 19:22	3117
be put to death this *d* in Israel	2Sa 19:22	3117
that I am this *d* king over Israel	2Sa 19:22	3117
from the *d* the king departed	2Sa 19:24	3117
the *d* he came again in peace	2Sa 19:24	3117
I am this *d* fourscore years old	2Sa 19:35	3117
shut up unto the *d* of their death	2Sa 20:3	3117
of the air to rest on them by *d*	2Sa 21:10	3119
in the *d* that the LORD had	2Sa 22:1	3117
me in the *d* of my calamity	2Sa 22:19	3117
wrought a great victory that *d*	2Sa 23:10	3117
And Gad came that *d* to David	2Sa 24:18	3117
For he is gone down this *d*	1Kin 1:25	3117
so will I certainly do this *d*	1Kin 1:30	3117
one to sit on my throne this *d*	1Kin 1:48	3117
me to *d* that he will not slay his	1Kin 1:51	3117
in the *d* when I went to Mahanaim	1Kin 2:8	3117
shall be put to death this *d*	1Kin 2:24	3117
that on the *d* thou goest out, and	1Kin 2:37	3117
on the *d* thou goest out, and	1Kin 2:42	3117
on his throne, as it is this *d*	1Kin 3:6	3117
it came to pass the third *d* after	1Kin 3:18	3117
one *d* was thirty measures of fine	1Kin 4:22	3117
said, Blessed be the LORD this *d*	1Kin 5:7	3117
and there they are unto this *d*	1Kin 8:8	3117
Since the *d* that I brought forth	1Kin 8:16	3117
with thine hand, as it is this *d*	1Kin 8:24	3117
servant prayeth before thee to *d*	1Kin 8:28	3117
open toward this house night and *d*	1Kin 8:29	3117
be nigh unto the LORD our God *d*	1Kin 8:59	3119
his commandments, as at this *d*	1Kin 8:61	3117
The same *d* did the king hallow	1Kin 8:64	3117
On the eighth *d* he sent the	1Kin 8:66	3117
the land of Cabul unto this *d*	1Kin 9:13	3117
of bondservice unto this *d*	1Kin 9:21	3117
trees, nor were seen unto this *d*	1Kin 10:12	3117
a servant unto this people this *d*	1Kin 12:7	3117
came to Rehoboam the third *d*	1Kin 12:12	3117
Come to me again the third *d*	1Kin 12:12	3117
the house of David unto this *d*	1Kin 12:19	3117
on the fifteenth *d* of the month	1Kin 12:32	3117
fifteenth *d* of the eighth month	1Kin 12:33	3117
And he gave a sign the same *d*	1Kin 13:3	3117
of God had done that *d* in Beth-el	1Kin 13:11	3117
off the house of Jeroboam that *d*	1Kin 14:14	3117
over Israel that *d* in the camp	1Kin 16:16	3117
until the *d* that the LORD sendeth	1Kin 17:14	3117
surely shew myself unto him to *d*	1Kin 18:15	3117
let it be known this *d* that thou	1Kin 18:36	3117
deliver it into thine hand this *d*	1Kin 20:13	3117
that in the seventh *d* the battle	1Kin 20:29	3117
hundred thousand footmen in one *d*	1Kin 20:29	3117
at the word of the LORD to *d*	1Kin 22:5	3117
Behold, thou shalt see in that *d*	1Kin 22:25	3117
And the battle increased that *d*	1Kin 22:35	3117
thy master from thy head to *d*	2Kin 2:3	3117
thy master from thy head to *d*	2Kin 2:5	3117
waters were healed unto this *d*	2Kin 2:22	3117
And it fell on a *d*, that Elisha	2Kin 4:8	3117
And it fell on a *d*, that he came	2Kin 4:11	3117

child was grown, it fell on a *d*	2Kin 4:18	3117
wilt thou go to him to *d*	2Kin 4:23	3117
thy son, that we may eat him to *d*	2Kin 6:28	3117
and I said unto her on the next *d*	2Kin 6:29	3117
Shaphat shall stand on him this *d*	2Kin 6:31	3117
this *d* is a *d* of good tidings,	2Kin 7:9	3117
this *d* is a *d* of good tidings,	2Kin 7:9	3117
the *d* that she left the land	2Kin 8:6	3117
the hand of Judah unto this *d*	2Kin 8:22	3117
it a draught house unto this *d*	2Kin 10:27	3117
name of it Joktheel unto this *d*	2Kin 14:7	3117
a leper unto the *d* of his death	2Kin 15:5	3117
Elath, and dwelt there unto this *d*	2Kin 16:6	3117
own land to Assyria unto this *d*	2Kin 17:23	3117
Unto this *d* they do after the	2Kin 17:34	3117
fathers, so do they unto this *d*	2Kin 17:41	3117
This *d* is a *d* of trouble	2Kin 19:3	3117
on the third *d* thou shalt go up	2Kin 20:5	3117
the house of the LORD the third *d*	2Kin 20:8	3117
have laid up in store unto this *d*	2Kin 20:17	3117
since the *d* their fathers came	2Kin 21:15	3117
out of Egypt, even unto this *d*	2Kin 21:15	3117
in the tenth *d* of the month	2Kin 25:1	3117
on the ninth *d* of the fourth	2Kin 25:3	
on the seventh *d* of the month	2Kin 25:8	
twentieth *d* of the month, that	2Kin 25:27	
king, a daily rate for every *d*	2Kin 25:30	3117
them utterly unto this *d*, and	1Chr 4:41	3117
and dwelt there unto this *d*	1Chr 4:43	3117
to the river Gozan, unto this *d*	1Chr 5:26	3117
they were employed in that work *d*	1Chr 9:33	3119
slew a lion in a pit in a snowy *d*	1Chr 11:22	3117
For at that time *d* by *d* there	1Chr 12:22	3117
is called Perez-uzza to this *d*	1Chr 13:11	3117
And David was afraid of God that *d*	1Chr 13:12	3117
Then on that *d* David delivered	1Chr 16:7	3117
shew forth from *d* to *d* his	1Chr 16:23	3117
forth from *d* to *d* his salvation	1Chr 16:23	3117
d that I brought up Israel unto	1Chr 17:5	3117
I brought up Israel unto this *d*	1Chr 17:5	3117
four a *d*, southward four a *d*	1Chr 26:17	3117
and my judgments, as at this *d*	1Chr 28:7	3117
his service this *d* unto the LORD	1Chr 29:5	3117
LORD, on the morrow after that *d*	1Chr 29:21	3117
on that *d* with great gladness	1Chr 29:22	3117
the second *d* of the second month	2Chr 3:2	
And there it is unto this *d*	2Chr 5:9	3117
Since the *d* that I brought forth	2Chr 6:5	3117
with thine hand, as it is this *d*	2Chr 6:15	3117
may be open upon this house *d*	2Chr 6:20	3119
in the eighth *d* they made a	2Chr 7:9	3117
twentieth *d* of the seventh month	2Chr 7:10	3117
make to pay tribute until this *d*	2Chr 8:8	3117
Even after a certain rate every *d*	2Chr 8:13	3117
as the duty of every *d* required	2Chr 8:14	3117
Solomon was prepared unto the *d*	2Chr 8:16	3117
came to Rehoboam on the third *d*	2Chr 10:12	3117
Come again to me on the third *d*	2Chr 10:12	3117
the house of David unto this *d*	2Chr 10:19	3117
at the word of the LORD to *d*	2Chr 18:4	3117
thou shalt see on that *d* when	2Chr 18:24	3117
And the battle increased that *d*	2Chr 18:34	3117
on the fourth *d* they assembled	2Chr 20:26	3117
valley of Berachah, unto this *d*	2Chr 20:26	3117
the hand of Judah unto this *d*	2Chr 21:10	3117
reason of the sickness *d* by *d*	2Chr 21:15	3117
Thus they did *d* by *d*, and	2Chr 24:11	3117
a leper unto the *d* of his death	2Chr 26:21	3117
and twenty thousand in one *d*	2Chr 28:6	3117
Now they began on the first *d* of	2Chr 29:17	
on the eighth *d* of the month came	2Chr 29:17	
in the sixteenth *d* of the first	2Chr 29:17	
fourteenth *d* of the second month	2Chr 30:15	
priests praised the LORD *d* by *d*	2Chr 30:21	3117
fourteenth *d* of the first month	2Chr 35:1	
the LORD was prepared the same *d*	2Chr 35:16	3117
I come not against thee this *d*	2Chr 35:21	3117
in their lamentations to this *d*	2Chr 35:25	3117
as the duty of every *d* required	Ezr 3:4	3117
From the first *d* of the seventh	Ezr 3:6	3117
given them *d* by *d* without fail	Ezr 6:9	3118
on the third *d* of the month Adar	Ezr 6:15	3118
fourteenth *d* of the first month	Ezr 6:19	
For upon the first *d* of the first	Ezr 7:9	
on the first *d* of the fifth month	Ezr 7:9	
the twelfth *d* of the first month	Ezr 8:31	
on the fourth *d* was the silver	Ezr 8:33	3117
in a great trespass unto this *d*	Ezr 9:7	3117
of face, as it is this *d*	Ezr 9:7	3117
yet escaped, as it is this *d*	Ezr 9:15	3117
on the twentieth *d* of the month	Ezr 10:9	
is this a work of one *d* or two	Ezr 10:13	3117
sat down in the first *d* of the	Ezr 10:16	3117
by the first *d* of the first month	Ezr 10:17	3117
which I pray before thee now, *d*	Neh 1:6	3119
I pray thee, thy servant this *d*	Neh 1:11	3117
will they make an end in a *d*	Neh 4:2	3117
and set a watch against them *d*	Neh 4:9	3119
a guard to us, and labour on the *d*	Neh 4:22	3117
I pray you, to them, even this *d*	Neh 5:11	3117
fifth *d* of the month Elul, in	Neh 6:15	
upon the first *d* of the seventh	Neh 8:2	3117
This *d* is holy unto the LORD your	Neh 8:9	3117
for this *d* is holy unto our Lord	Neh 8:10	3117
your peace, for the *d* is holy	Neh 8:11	3117
on the second *d* were gathered	Neh 8:13	3117
d had not the children of Israel	Neh 8:17	3117
Also *d* by *d*, from the first *d*	Neh 8:18	3117
the first *d* unto the last *d*	Neh 8:18	3117
on the eighth *d* was a solemn	Neh 8:18	3117
fourth *d* of this month the	Neh 9:1	3117
God one fourth part of the *d*	Neh 9:3	3117
get thee a name, as it is this *d*	Neh 9:10	3117
them in the *d* by a cloudy pillar	Neh 9:12	3119
cloud departed not from them by *d*	Neh 9:19	3119
the kings of Assyria unto this *d*	Neh 9:32	3117
Behold, we are servants this *d*	Neh 9:36	3117
victuals on the sabbath *d* to sell	Neh 10:31	3117
on the sabbath, or on the holy *d*	Neh 10:31	3117
for the singers, due for every *d*	Neh 11:23	3117
Also that *d* they offered great	Neh 12:43	3117
the porters, every *d* his portion	Neh 12:47	3117
On that *d* they read in the book	Neh 13:1	3117
into Jerusalem on the sabbath *d*	Neh 13:15	3117
the *d* wherein they sold victuals	Neh 13:15	3117
ye do, and profane the sabbath *d*	Neh 13:17	3117
be brought in on the sabbath *d*	Neh 13:19	3117
gates, to sanctify the sabbath *d*	Neh 13:22	3117
On the seventh *d*, when the heart	Est 1:10	3117
Media say this *d* unto all the	Est 1:18	3117
Mordecai walked every *d* before	Est 2:11	3117
lot, before Haman from *d* to *d*	Est 3:7	3117
lot, before Haman from *d* to *d*	Est 3:7	3117
thirteenth *d* of the first month	Est 3:12	3117
children and women, in one *d*	Est 3:13	3117
thirteenth *d* of the twelfth month	Est 3:13	3117
should be ready against that *d*	Est 3:14	3117
nor drink three days, night or *d*	Est 4:16	3117
it came to pass on the third *d*	Est 5:1	3117
Haman come this *d* unto the	Est 5:4	3117
went Haman forth that *d* joyful	Est 5:9	3117
second *d* at the banquet of wine	Est 7:2	3117
On that *d* did the king Ahasuerus	Est 8:1	3117
the three and twentieth *d* thereof	Est 8:9	
Upon one *d* in all the provinces	Est 8:12	3117
upon the thirteenth *d* of the	Est 8:12	
should be ready against that *d* to	Est 8:13	3117
and gladness, a feast and a good *d*	Est 8:17	3117
on the thirteenth *d* of the same	Est 9:1	3117
in the *d* that the enemies of the	Est 9:1	3117
On that *d* the number of those	Est 9:11	3117
d also of the month Adar, and slew	Est 9:15	3117
thirteenth *d* of the month Adar	Est 9:17	3117
on the fourteenth *d* of the same	Est 9:17	
made it a *d* of feasting and	Est 9:17	3117
on the thirteenth *d* thereof	Est 9:18	
on the fifteenth *d* of the same	Est 9:18	
made it a *d* of feasting and	Est 9:18	3117
made the fourteenth *d* of the	Est 9:19	3117
of the month Adar a *d* of gladness	Est 9:19	
gladness and feasting, and a good *d*	Est 9:19	3117
fourteenth *d* of the month Adar	Est 9:21	
and the fifteenth *d* of the same	Est 9:21	3117
and from mourning into a good *d*	Est 9:22	3117
in their houses, every one his *d*	Job 1:4	3117
Now there was a *d* when the sons	Job 1:6	3117
there was a *d* when his sons and	Job 1:13	3117
Again there was a *d* when the sons	Job 2:1	3117
Job his mouth, and cursed his *d*	Job 3:1	3117
Let the *d* perish wherein I was	Job 3:3	3117
Let that *d* be darkness	Job 3:4	3117
the blackness of the *d* terrify it	Job 3:5	3117
them curse it that curse the *d*	Job 3:8	3117
let it see the dawning of the *d*	Job 3:9	7837
and fro unto the dawning of the *d*	Job 7:4	5399
accomplish, as an hireling, his *d*	Job 14:6	3117
he knoweth that the *d* of darkness	Job 15:23	3117
They change the night into *d*	Job 17:12	3117
him shall be astonied at his *d*	Job 18:20	3117
at the latter *d* upon the earth	Job 19:25	
flow away in the *d* of his wrath	Job 20:28	3117
reserved to the *d* of destruction	Job 21:30	3117
brought forth to the *d* of wrath	Job 21:30	3117
Even to *d* is my complaint bitter	Job 23:2	3117
waters with bounds, until the *d*	Job 26:10	216
trouble, against the *d* of battle	Job 38:23	3117
and in his law doth he meditate *d*	Ps 1:2	3119
this *d* have I begotten thee	Ps 2:7	3117
is angry with the wicked every *d*	Ps 7:11	3117
the *d* that the LORD delivered him	Ps 18:*t*	3117
me in the *d* of my calamity	Ps 18:18	3117
D unto *d* uttereth speech, and	Ps 19:2	3117
D unto *d* uttereth speech, and	Ps 19:2	3117
hear thee in the *d* of trouble	Ps 20:1	3117
on thee do I wait all the *d*	Ps 25:5	3117
through my roaring all the *d* long	Ps 32:3	3117
For *d* and night thy hand was heavy	Ps 32:4	3119
and of thy praise all the *d* long	Ps 35:28	3117
for he seeth that his *d* is coming	Ps 37:13	3117
I go mourning all the *d* long	Ps 38:6	3117
and imagine deceits all the *d* long	Ps 38:12	3117
My tears have been my meat *d*	Ps 42:3	3119
In God we boast all the *d* long	Ps 44:8	3117
sake are we killed all the *d* long	Ps 44:22	3117
call upon me in the *d* of trouble	Ps 50:15	3117
D and night they go about it upon	Ps 55:10	3119
Every *d* they wrest my words	Ps 56:5	3117
and refuge in the *d* of my trouble	Ps 59:16	3117
and with thy honour all the *d*	Ps 71:8	3117
and thy salvation all the *d*	Ps 71:15	3117
thy righteousness all the *d* long	Ps 71:24	3117
For all the *d* long have I been	Ps 73:14	3117
The *d* is thine, the night also is	Ps 74:16	3117
In the *d* of my trouble I sought	Ps 77:2	3117
turned back in the *d* of battle	Ps 78:9	3117
nor the *d* when he delivered them	Ps 78:42	3117
appointed, on our solemn feast *d*	Ps 81:3	3117
For a *d* in thy courts is better	Ps 84:10	3117
In the *d* of my trouble I will	Ps 86:7	3117
of my salvation, I have cried *d*	Ps 88:1	3117
name shall they rejoice all the *d*	Ps 89:16	3117
for the arrow that flieth by *d*	Ps 91:5	3119
A Psalm or Song for the sabbath *d*	Ps 92:*t*	3117
To *d* if ye will hear his voice,	Ps 95:7	3117
as in the *d* of temptation in the	Ps 95:8	3117
forth his salvation from *d* to *d*	Ps 96:2	3117
me in the *d* when I am in trouble	Ps 102:2	3117
in the *d* when I call answer me	Ps 102:2	3117
enemies reproach me all the *d*	Ps 102:8	3117
be willing in the *d* of thy power	Ps 110:3	3117
kings in the *d* of his wrath	Ps 110:5	3117
This is the *d* which the LORD hath	Ps 118:24	3117
They continue this *d* according to	Ps 119:91	3117
it is my meditation all the *d*	Ps 119:97	3117
Seven times a *d* do I praise thee	Ps 119:164	3117
The sun shall not smite thee by *d*	Ps 121:6	3119
The sun to rule by *d*	Ps 136:8	3117
of Edom in the *d* of Jerusalem	Ps 137:7	3117
In the *d* when I cried thou	Ps 138:3	3117
but the night shineth as the *d*	Ps 139:12	3117
my head in the *d* of battle	Ps 140:7	3117
Every *d* will I bless thee	Ps 145:2	3117
in that very *d* his thoughts	Ps 146:4	3117
more and more unto the perfect *d*	Prov 4:18	3117
not spare in the *d* of vengeance	Prov 6:34	3117
this *d* have I payed my vows	Prov 7:14	3117
will come home at the *d* appointed	Prov 7:20	3117
profit not in the *d* of wrath	Prov 11:4	3117
even the wicked for the *d* of evil	Prov 16:4	3117
coveteth greedily all the *d* long	Prov 21:26	3117
prepared against the *d* of battle	Prov 21:31	3117
I have made known to thee this *d*	Prov 22:19	3117
fear of the LORD all the *d* long	Prov 23:17	3117
thou faint in the *d* of adversity	Prov 24:10	3117
not what a *d* may bring forth	Prov 27:1	3117
house in the *d* of thy calamity	Prov 27:10	3117
dropping in a very rainy *d*	Prov 27:15	3117
the *d* of death than the *d* of	Eccl 7:1	3117
death than the *d* of one's birth	Eccl 7:1	3117
In the *d* of prosperity be joyful,	Eccl 7:14	3117
but in the *d* of adversity	Eccl 7:14	3117
hath he power in the *d* of death	Eccl 8:8	3117
d nor night seeth sleep with his	Eccl 8:16	3117
In the *d* when the keepers of the	Eccl 12:3	3117
Until the *d* break, and the shadows	Song 2:17	3117
him in the *d* of his espousals	Song 3:11	3117
in the *d* of the gladness of his	Song 3:11	3117
Until the *d* break, and the shadows	Song 4:6	3117
we do for our sister in the *d*	Song 8:8	3117
alone shall be exalted in that *d*	Is 2:11	3117
For the *d* of the LORD of hosts	Is 2:12	3117
alone shall be exalted in that *d*	Is 2:17	3117
In that *d* a man shall cast his	Is 2:20	3117
In that *d* shall he swear, saying,	Is 3:7	3117
In that *d* the Lord will take away	Is 3:18	3117
in that *d* seven women shall take	Is 4:1	3117
In that *d* shall the branch of the	Is 4:2	3117
assemblies, a cloud and smoke by *d*	Is 4:5	3119
in that *d* they shall roar against	Is 5:30	3117
from the *d* that Ephraim departed	Is 7:17	3117
it shall come to pass in that *d*	Is 7:18	3117
In the same *d* shall the Lord	Is 7:20	3117
it shall come to pass in that *d*	Is 7:21	3117
it shall come to pass in that *d*	Is 7:23	3117
oppressor, as in the *d* of Midian	Is 9:4	3117
and tail, branch and rush, in one *d*	Is 9:14	3117
will ye do in the *d* of visitation	Is 10:3	3117
his thorns and his briers in one *d*	Is 10:17	3117
it shall come to pass in that *d*	Is 10:20	3117
it shall come to pass in that *d*	Is 10:27	3117
yet shall he remain at Nob that *d*	Is 10:32	3117
in that *d* there shall be a root	Is 11:10	3117
it shall come to pass in that *d*	Is 11:11	3117
d that he came up out of the land	Is 11:16	3117
in that *d* thou shalt say, O LORD,	Is 12:1	3117
in that *d* shall ye say, Praise	Is 12:4	3117
for the *d* of the LORD is at hand	Is 13:6	3117
the *d* of the LORD cometh, cruel	Is 13:9	3117
in the *d* of his fierce anger	Is 13:13	3117
it shall come to pass in the *d*	Is 14:3	3117
in that *d* it shall come to pass,	Is 17:4	3117
At that *d* shall a man look to his	Is 17:7	3117
In that *d* shall his strong cities	Is 17:9	3117
In the *d* shalt thou make thy	Is 17:11	3117
shall be a heap in the *d* of grief	Is 17:11	3117
In that *d* shall Egypt be like	Is 19:16	3117
In that *d* shall five cities in	Is 19:18	3117
In that *d* shall there be an altar	Is 19:19	3117
shall know the LORD in that *d*	Is 19:21	3117
In that *d* shall there be a	Is 19:23	3117
In that *d* shall Israel be the	Is 19:24	3117
of this isle shall say in that *d*	Is 20:6	3117
For it is a *d* of trouble, and of	Is 22:5	3117
thou didst look in that *d* to the	Is 22:8	3117
in that *d* did the Lord GOD of	Is 22:12	3117
it shall come to pass in that *d*	Is 22:20	3117
In that *d*, saith the LORD of	Is 22:25	3117
it shall come to pass in that *d*	Is 23:15	3117
it shall come to pass in that *d*	Is 24:21	3117
And it shall be said in that *d*	Is 25:9	3117
In that *d* shall this song be sung	Is 26:1	3117
In that *d* the LORD with his sore	Is 27:1	3117
In that *d* sing ye unto her, A	Is 27:2	3117
it, I will keep it night and *d*	Is 27:3	3117

Context	Reference	Number
wind in the *d* of the east wind	Is 27:8	3117
it shall come to pass in that *d*	Is 27:12	3117
it shall come to pass in that *d*	Is 27:13	3117
In that *d* shall the LORD of hosts	Is 28:5	3117
morning shall it pass over, by *d*	Is 28:19	3117
the plowman plow all *d* to sow	Is 28:24	3117
in that *d* shall the deaf hear the	Is 29:18	3117
in that *d* shall thy cattle feed	Is 30:23	3117
in the *d* of the great slaughter	Is 30:25	3117
in the *d* that the LORD bindeth up	Is 30:26	3117
For in that *d* every man shall	Is 31:7	3117
For it is the *d* of the LORD's	Is 34:8	3117
shall not be quenched night nor *d*	Is 34:10	3119
This *d* is a *d* of trouble, and of	Is 37:3	3117
This *d* is a *d* of trouble	Is 37:3	3117
from *d* even to night wilt thou	Is 38:12	3117
from *d* even to night wilt thou	Is 38:13	3117
shall praise thee, as I do this *d*	Is 38:19	3117
laid up in store until this *d*	Is 39:6	3117
Yea, before the *d* was I am he	Is 43:13	3117
come to thee in a moment in one *d*	Is 47:9	3117
even before the *d* when thou	Is 48:7	3117
in a *d* of salvation have I helped	Is 49:8	3117
d because of the fury of the	Is 51:13	3117
continually every *d* is blasphemed	Is 52:5	3117
they shall know in that *d* that I	Is 52:6	3117
and to morrow shall be as this *d*	Is 56:12	3117
in the *d* of your fast ye find	Is 58:3	3117
ye shall not fast as ye do this *d*	Is 58:4	3117
a *d* for a man to afflict his soul	Is 58:5	3117
and an acceptable *d* to the LORD	Is 58:5	3117
doing thy pleasure on my holy *d*	Is 58:13	3117
shall not be shut *d* nor night	Is 60:11	3119
shall be no more thy light by *d*	Is 60:19	3117
the *d* of vengeance of our God	Is 61:2	3117
hold their peace *d* nor night	Is 62:6	3117
For the *d* of vengeance is in mine	Is 63:4	3117
the *d* unto a rebellious people	Is 65:2	3117
a fire that burneth all the *d*	Is 65:5	3117
be made to bring forth in one *d*	Is 66:8	3117
I have this *d* set thee over the	Jer 1:10	3117
made thee this *d* a defenced city	Jer 1:18	3117
from our youth even unto this *d*	Jer 3:25	3117
it shall come to pass at that *d*	Jer 4:9	3117
for the *d* goeth away, for the	Jer 6:4	3117
nor commanded them in the *d* that	Jer 7:22	3117
Since the *d* that your fathers	Jer 7:25	3117
d I have even sent unto you all	Jer 7:25	3117
of tears, that I might weep *d*	Jer 9:1	3119
d that I brought them forth out	Jer 11:4	3117
milk and honey, as it is this *d*	Jer 11:5	3117
unto your fathers in the *d* that I	Jer 11:7	3117
land of Egypt, even unto this *d*	Jer 11:7	3117
them for the *d* of slaughter	Jer 12:3	3117
run down with tears night and *d*	Jer 14:17	3119
is gone down while it was yet *d*	Jer 15:9	3119
there shall ye serve other gods *d*	Jer 16:13	3119
my refuge in the *d* of affliction	Jer 16:19	3117
have I desired the woeful *d*	Jer 17:16	3117
thou art my hope in the *d* of evil	Jer 17:17	3117
bring upon them the *d* of evil	Jer 17:18	3117
bear no burden on the sabbath *d*	Jer 17:21	3117
of your houses on the sabbath *d*	Jer 17:22	3117
work, but hallow ye the sabbath *d*	Jer 17:22	3117
of this city on the sabbath *d*	Jer 17:24	3117
but hallow the sabbath *d*	Jer 17:24	3117
unto me to hallow the sabbath *d*	Jer 17:27	3117
of Jerusalem on the sabbath *d*	Jer 17:27	3117
in the *d* of their calamity	Jer 18:17	3117
Cursed be the *d* wherein I was	Jer 20:14	3117
let not the *d* wherein my mother	Jer 20:14	3117
king of Judah, even unto this *d*	Jer 25:3	3117
as it is this *d*	Jer 25:18	3117
of the LORD shall be at that *d*	Jer 25:33	3117
be until the *d* that I visit them	Jer 27:22	3117
for that *d* is great, so that none	Jer 30:7	3117
it shall come to pass in that *d*	Jer 30:8	3117
For there shall be a *d*, that the	Jer 31:6	3117
made with their fathers in the *d*	Jer 31:32	3117
giveth the sun for a light by *d*	Jer 31:35	3119
land of Egypt, even unto this *d*	Jer 32:20	3119
made thee a name, as at this *d*	Jer 32:20	3119
of my fury from the *d* that they	Jer 32:31	3119
they built it even unto this *d*	Jer 32:31	3119
ye can break my covenant of the *d*	Jer 33:20	3117
and that there should not be *d*	Jer 33:20	3119
If my covenant be not with *d*	Jer 33:25	3119
with your fathers in the *d* that I	Jer 34:13	3117
for unto this *d* they drink none,	Jer 35:14	3117
from the *d* I spake unto thee,	Jer 36:2	3117
days of Josiah, even into this *d*	Jer 36:2	3117
LORD's house upon the fasting *d*	Jer 36:6	3117
be cast out in the *d* to the heat	Jer 36:30	3117
the *d* that Jerusalem was taken	Jer 38:28	3117
the ninth *d* of the month, the	Jer 39:2	3117
in that *d* before thee	Jer 39:16	3117
But I will deliver thee in that *d*	Jer 39:17	3117
I loose thee this *d* from the	Jer 40:4	3117
it came to pass the second *d*	Jer 41:4	3117
that I have admonished you this *d*	Jer 42:19	3117
now I have this *d* declared it to	Jer 42:21	3117
this *d* they are a desolation, and	Jer 44:2	3117
wasted and desolate, as at this *d*	Jer 44:6	3117
are not humbled even unto this *d*	Jer 44:10	3117
an inhabitant, as at this *d*	Jer 44:22	3117
happened unto you, as at this *d*	Jer 44:23	3117
For this is the *d* of the Lord GOD	Jer 46:10	3117
a *d* of vengeance, that he may	Jer 46:10	3117
because the *d* of their calamity	Jer 46:21	3117
Because of the *d* that cometh to	Jer 47:4	3117
that *d* shall be as the heart of a	Jer 48:41	3117
at that *d* shall the heart of the	Jer 49:22	3117
of war shall be cut off in that *d*	Jer 49:26	3117
for their *d* is come, the time of	Jer 50:27	3117
of war shall be cut off in that *d*	Jer 50:30	3117
for thy *d* is come, the time that	Jer 50:31	3117
for in the *d* of trouble they	Jer 51:2	3117
in the tenth *d* of the month	Jer 52:4	
in the ninth *d* of the month	Jer 52:6	
in prison till the *d* of his death	Jer 52:11	3117
in the tenth *d* of the month	Jer 52:12	
twentieth *d* of the month, that	Jer 52:31	
every *d* a portion until the *d*	Jer 52:34	3117
me in the *d* of his fierce anger	Lam 1:12	3117
me desolate and faint all the *d*	Lam 1:13	3117
thou wilt bring the *d* that thou	Lam 1:21	3117
footstool in the *d* of his anger	Lam 2:1	3117
as in the *d* of a solemn feast	Lam 2:7	3117
this is the *d* that we looked for	Lam 2:16	3117
let tears run down like a river *d*	Lam 2:18	3119
them in the *d* of thine anger	Lam 2:21	3117
a solemn *d* my terrors round about	Lam 2:22	3117
so that in the *d* of the LORD's	Lam 2:22	3117
his hand against me all the *d*	Lam 3:3	3117
and their song all the *d*	Lam 3:14	3117
in the *d* that I called upon thee	Lam 3:57	3117
their device against me all the *d*	Lam 3:62	3117
in the fifth *d* of the month	Eze 1:1	
In the fifth *d* of the month	Eze 1:2	
is in the cloud in the *d* of rain	Eze 1:28	3117
against me, even unto this very *d*	Eze 2:3	3117
appointed thee each *d* for a year	Eze 4:6	3117
be by weight, twenty shekels a *d*	Eze 4:10	3117
the *d* of trouble is near, and not	Eze 7:7	3117
Behold the *d*, behold, it is come	Eze 7:10	3117
time is come, the *d* draweth near	Eze 7:12	3117
in the *d* of the wrath of the LORD	Eze 7:19	3117
in the fifth *d* of the month	Eze 8:1	
remove by *d* in their sight	Eze 12:3	3119
thy stuff by *d* in their sight	Eze 12:4	3119
I brought forth my stuff by *d*	Eze 12:7	3119
the battle in the *d* of the LORD	Eze 13:5	3117
in the *d* thou wast born thy navel	Eze 16:4	3117
in the *d* that thou wast born	Eze 16:5	3117
thy mouth in the *d* of thy pride	Eze 16:56	3117
the tenth *d* of the month, that	Eze 20:1	
In the *d* when I chose Israel, and	Eze 20:5	3117
In the *d* that I lifted up mine	Eze 20:6	3117
is called Bamah unto this *d*	Eze 20:29	3117
all your idols, even unto this *d*	Eze 20:31	3117
whose *d* is come, when iniquity	Eze 21:25	3117
whose *d* is come, when their	Eze 21:29	3117
upon in the *d* of indignation	Eze 22:24	3117
my sanctuary in the same *d*	Eze 23:38	3117
then they came the same *d* into my	Eze 23:39	3117
in the tenth *d* of the month	Eze 24:1	
man, write thee the name of the *d*	Eze 24:2	3117
of the *d*, even of this same *d*	Eze 24:2	3117
against Jerusalem this same *d*	Eze 24:2	3117
shall it not be in the *d* when I	Eze 24:25	3117
in that *d* shall come unto thee	Eze 24:26	3117
In that *d* shall thy mouth be	Eze 24:27	3117
year, in the first *d* of the month	Eze 26:1	
tremble in the *d* of thy fall	Eze 26:18	3117
of the seas in the *d* of thy ruin	Eze 27:27	3117
in the *d* that thou wast created	Eze 28:13	3117
from the *d* that thou wast created	Eze 28:15	3117
in the twelfth *d* of the month	Eze 29:1	
in the first *d* of the month	Eze 29:17	
In that *d* will I cause the horn	Eze 29:21	3117
Howl ye, Woe worth the *d*	Eze 30:2	3117
even the *d* of the LORD is near, a	Eze 30:3	3117
of the LORD is near, a cloudy *d*	Eze 30:3	3117
In that *d* shall messengers go	Eze 30:9	3117
upon them, as in the *d* of Egypt	Eze 30:9	3117
also the *d* shall be darkened	Eze 30:18	3117
in the seventh *d* of the month	Eze 30:20	
in the first *d* of the month	Eze 31:1	
In the *d* when he went down to the	Eze 31:15	3117
in the first *d* of the month	Eze 32:1	
own life, in the *d* of thy fall	Eze 32:10	3117
in the fifteenth *d* of the month	Eze 32:17	
him in the *d* of his transgression	Eze 33:12	3117
in the *d* that he turneth from his	Eze 33:12	3117
in the *d* that he sinneth	Eze 33:12	3117
in the fifth *d* of the month	Eze 33:21	
seeketh out his flock in the *d*	Eze 34:12	3117
scattered in the cloudy and dark *d*	Eze 34:12	3117
In the *d* that I shall have	Eze 36:33	3117
In that *d* when my people of	Eze 38:14	3117
Surely in that *d* there shall be a	Eze 38:19	3117
this is the *d* whereof I have	Eze 39:8	3117
it shall come to pass in that *d*	Eze 39:11	3117
the *d* that I shall be glorified	Eze 39:13	3117
am the LORD their God from that *d*	Eze 39:22	3117
year, in the tenth *d* of the month	Eze 40:1	
in the selfsame *d* the hand of the	Eze 40:1	3117
in the *d* when they shall make it	Eze 43:18	3117
on the second *d* thou shalt offer	Eze 43:22	3117
every *d* a goat for a sin offering	Eze 43:25	3117
shall be, that upon the eighth *d*	Eze 43:27	3117
in the *d* that he goeth into the	Eze 44:27	3117
in the first *d* of the month	Eze 45:18	
so thou shalt do the seventh *d* of	Eze 45:20	
in the fourteenth *d* of the month	Eze 45:21	3117
upon that *d* shall the prince	Eze 45:22	3117
in the fifteenth *d* of the month	Eze 45:25	3117
in the *d* of the new moon it shall	Eze 46:1	3117
d shall be six lambs without	Eze 46:4	3117
in the *d* of the new moon it shall	Eze 46:6	3117
as he did on the sabbath *d*	Eze 46:12	3117
of the city from that *d* shall be	Eze 48:35	3117
upon his knees three times a *d*	Dan 6:10	3118
his petition three times a *d*	Dan 6:13	3118
confusion of faces, as at this *d*	Dan 9:7	3117
gotten thee renown, as at this *d*	Dan 9:15	3117
twentieth *d* of the first month,	Dan 10:4	3117
for from the first *d* that thou	Dan 10:12	3117
it shall come to pass at that *d*	Hos 1:5	3117
great shall be the *d* of Jezreel	Hos 1:11	3117
her as in the *d* that she was born	Hos 2:3	3117
as in the *d* when she came up out	Hos 2:15	3117
And it shall be at that *d*, saith	Hos 2:16	3117
in that *d* will I make a covenant	Hos 2:18	3117
it shall come to pass in that *d*	Hos 2:21	3117
shalt thou fall in the *d*, and the	Hos 4:5	3117
be desolate in the *d* of rebuke	Hos 5:9	3117
in the third *d* he will raise us	Hos 6:2	3117
In the *d* of our king the princes	Hos 7:5	3117
What will ye do in the solemn *d*	Hos 9:5	3117
in the *d* of the feast of the LORD	Hos 9:5	3117
Beth-arbel in the *d* of battle	Hos 10:14	3117
Alas for the *d*	Joel 1:15	3117
for the *d* of the LORD is at hand,	Joel 1:15	3117
for the *d* of the LORD cometh, for	Joel 2:1	3117
A *d* of darkness and of gloominess,	Joel 2:2	3117
a *d* of clouds and of thick	Joel 2:2	3117
for the *d* of the LORD is great and	Joel 2:11	3117
the terrible *d* of the LORD come	Joel 2:31	3117
for the *d* of the LORD is near in	Joel 3:14	3117
it shall come to pass in that *d*	Joel 3:18	3117
with shouting in the *d* of battle	Amos 1:14	3117
tempest in the *d* of the whirlwind	Amos 1:14	3117
shall flee away naked in that *d*	Amos 2:16	3117
That in the *d* that I shall visit	Amos 3:14	3117
maketh the *d* dark with night	Amos 5:8	3117
you that desire the *d* of the LORD	Amos 5:18	3117
the *d* of the LORD is darkness, and	Amos 5:18	3117
Shall not the *d* of the LORD be	Amos 5:20	3117
Ye that put far away the evil *d*	Amos 6:3	3117
shall be howlings in that *d*	Amos 8:3	3117
it shall come to pass in that *d*	Amos 8:9	3117
darken the earth in the clear *d*	Amos 8:9	3117
and the end thereof as a bitter *d*	Amos 8:10	3117
In that *d* shall the fair virgins	Amos 8:13	3117
In that *d* will I raise up the	Amos 9:11	3117
Shall I not in that *d*, saith the	Obad 8	3117
In the *d* that thou stoodest on	Obad 11	3117
in the *d* that the strangers	Obad 11	3117
not have looked on the *d* of thy	Obad 12	3117
the *d* that he became a stranger	Obad 12	3117
in the *d* of their destruction	Obad 12	3117
proudly in the *d* of distress	Obad 12	3117
people in the *d* of their calamity	Obad 13	3117
in the *d* of their calamity	Obad 13	3117
in the *d* of their calamity	Obad 13	3117
did remain in the *d* of distress	Obad 14	3117
For the *d* of the LORD is near	Obad 15	3117
when the morning rose the next *d*	Jonah 4:7	4283
In that *d* shall one take up a	Mic 2:4	3117
the *d* shall be dark over them	Mic 3:6	3117
In that *d*, saith the LORD, will I	Mic 4:6	3117
it shall come to pass in that *d*	Mic 5:10	3117
the *d* of thy watchmen and thy	Mic 7:4	3117
In the *d* that thy walls are to be	Mic 7:11	3117
in that *d* shall the decree be far	Mic 7:11	3117
In that *d* also he shall come even	Mic 7:12	3117
a strong hold in the *d* of trouble	Nah 1:7	3117
in the *d* of his preparation	Nah 2:3	3117
camp in the hedges in the cold *d*	Nah 3:17	3117
I might rest in the *d* of trouble	Hab 3:16	3117
for the *d* of the LORD is at hand	Zeph 1:7	3117
in the *d* of the LORD's sacrifice	Zeph 1:8	3117
In the same *d* also will I punish	Zeph 1:9	3117
it shall come to pass in that *d*	Zeph 1:10	3117
The great *d* of the LORD is near,	Zeph 1:14	3117
the voice of the *d* of the LORD	Zeph 1:14	3117
That *d* is a *d* of wrath, a *d*	Zeph 1:15	3117
a *d* of trouble and distress, a *d*	Zeph 1:15	3117
a *d* of wasteness and desolation, a	Zeph 1:15	3117
a *d* of darkness and gloominess, a	Zeph 1:15	3117
a *d* of clouds and thick darkness,	Zeph 1:15	3117
A *d* of the trumpet and alarm	Zeph 1:16	3117
them in the *d* of the LORD's wrath	Zeph 1:18	3117
before the *d* pass as the chaff,	Zeph 2:2	3117
before the *d* of the LORD's anger	Zeph 2:2	3117
hid in the *d* of the LORD's anger	Zeph 2:3	3117
until the *d* that I rise up to the	Zeph 3:8	3117
In that *d* shalt thou not be	Zeph 3:11	3117
In that *d* it shall be said to	Zeph 3:16	3117
in the first *d* of the month	Hag 1:1	3117
twentieth *d* of the sixth month,	Hag 1:15	3117
twentieth *d* of the month, came	Hag 2:1	
twentieth *d* of the ninth month,	Hag 2:10	
I pray you, consider from this *d*	Hag 2:15	3117
Consider now from this *d* and	Hag 2:18	3117
twentieth *d* of the ninth month,	Hag 2:18	3117
even from the *d* that the	Hag 2:18	3117
from this *d* will I bless you	Hag 2:19	3117
twentieth *d* of the month, saying,	Hag 2:20	
In that *d*, saith the LORD of	Hag 2:23	3117
twentieth *d* of the eleventh month	Zec 1:7	3117
be joined to the LORD in that *d*	Zec 2:11	3117
iniquity of that land in one *d*	Zec 3:9	3117

In that *d*, saith the LORD of ... Zec 3:10 3117
despised the *d* of small things ... Zec 4:10 3117
Babylon, and come thou the same *d* ... Zec 6:10 3117
the fourth *d* of the ninth month ... Zec 7:1
which were in the *d* that the ... Zec 8:9 3117
even to *d* do I declare that I ... Zec 9:12 3117
that *d* as the flock of his people ... Zec 9:16 3117
And it was broken in that *d* ... Zec 11:11 3117
in that *d* will I make Jerusalem a ... Zec 12:3 3117
In that *d*, saith the LORD, I will ... Zec 12:4 3117
In that *d* will I make the ... Zec 12:6 3117
In that *d* shall the LORD defend ... Zec 12:8 3117
them at that *d* shall be as David ... Zec 12:8 3117
it shall come to pass in that *d* ... Zec 12:9 3117
In that *d* shall there be a great ... Zec 12:11 3117
In that *d* there shall be a ... Zec 13:1 3117
it shall come to pass in that *d* ... Zec 13:2 3117
it shall come to pass in that *d* ... Zec 13:4 3117
the *d* of the LORD cometh, and thy ... Zec 14:1 3117
when he fought in the *d* of battle ... Zec 14:3 3117
that *d* upon the mount of Olives ... Zec 14:4 3117
it shall come to pass in that *d* ... Zec 14:6 3117
But it shall be one *d* which shall ... Zec 14:7 3117
shall be known to the LORD, not *d* ... Zec 14:7 3117
And it shall be in that *d*, that ... Zec 14:8 3117
in that *d* shall there be one LORD ... Zec 14:9 3117
it shall come to pass in that *d* ... Zec 14:13 3117
In that *d* shall there be upon the ... Zec 14:20 3117
in that *d* there shall be no more ... Zec 14:21 3117
who may abide the *d* of his coming ... Mal 3:2 3117
in that *d* when I make up my ... Mal 3:17 3117
the *d* cometh, that shall burn as ... Mal 4:1 3117
the *d* that cometh shall burn them ... Mal 4:1 3117
in the *d* that I shall do this ... Mal 4:3 3117
great and dreadful *d* of the LORD ... Mal 4:5 3117
Give us this *d* our daily bread ... Mt 6:11 *4594*
grass of the field, which to *d* is ... Mt 6:30 *4594*
unto the *d* is the evil thereof ... Mt 6:34 *2250*
Many will say to me in that *d* ... Mt 7:22 *2250*
and Gomorrha in the *d* of judgment ... Mt 10:15 *2250*
and Sidon at the *d* of judgment ... Mt 11:22 *2250*
would have remained until this *d* ... Mt 11:23 *4594*
of Sodom in the *d* of judgment ... Mt 11:24 *2250*
on the sabbath *d* through the corn ... Mt 12:1
lawful to do upon the sabbath *d* ... Mt 12:2
man is Lord even of the sabbath *d* ... Mt 12:8
fall into a pit on the sabbath *d* ... Mt 12:11
thereof in the *d* of judgment ... Mt 12:36 *2250*
The same *d* went Jesus out of the ... Mt 13:1 *2250*
It will be foul weather to *d* ... Mt 16:3 *4594*
and be raised again the third *d* ... Mt 16:21 *2250*
the third *d* he shall be raised ... Mt 17:23 *2250*
the labourers for a penny a *d* ... Mt 20:2 *2250*
Why stand ye here all the *d* idle ... Mt 20:6 *2250*
borne the burden and heat of the *d* ... Mt 20:12 *2250*
the third *d* he shall rise again ... Mt 20:19 *2250*
go work to *d* in my vineyard ... Mt 21:28 *4594*
The same *d* came to him the ... Mt 22:23 *2250*
that *d* forth ask him any more ... Mt 22:46 *2250*
winter, neither on the sabbath *d* ... Mt 24:20
But of that *d* and hour knoweth no ... Mt 24:36 *2250*
until the *d* that Noe entered into ... Mt 24:38 *2250*
a *d* when he looketh not for him ... Mt 24:50 *2250*
for ye know neither the *d* nor the ... Mt 25:13 *2250*
But they said, Not on the feast *d* ... Mt 26:5
Now the first *d* of the feast of ... Mt 26:17
until that *d* when I drink it new ... Mt 26:29 *2250*
The field of blood, unto this *d* ... Mt 27:8 *4594*
this *d* in a dream because of him ... Mt 27:19 *4594*
Now the next *d*, that followed the ... Mt 27:62 *1887*
that followed the *d* of the ... Mt 27:62
be made sure until the third *d* ... Mt 27:64 *2250*
toward the first *d* of the week ... Mt 28:1
among the Jews until this *d* ... Mt 28:15 *4595*
straightway on the sabbath *d* he ... Mk 1:21
rising up a great while before *d* ... Mk 1:35 *1773*
the corn fields on the sabbath *d* ... Mk 2:23
d that which is not lawful ... Mk 2:24
would heal him on the sabbath *d* ... Mk 3:2
should sleep, and rise night and *d* ... Mk 4:27 *2250*
And the same *d*, when the even was ... Mk 4:35 *2250*
And always, night and *d*, he was in ... Mk 5:5 *2250*
And when the sabbath *d* was come ... Mk 6:2
and Gomorrha in the *d* of judgment ... Mk 6:11 *2250*
And when a convenient *d* was come ... Mk 6:21 *2250*
when the *d* was now far spent, his ... Mk 6:35 *5610*
killed, he shall rise the third *d* ... Mk 9:31 *2250*
the third *d* he shall rise again ... Mk 10:34 *2250*
But of that *d* and that hour ... Mk 13:32 *2250*
But they said, Not on the feast *d* ... Mk 14:2
the first *d* of unleavened bread, ... Mk 14:12 *2250*
until that *d* that I drink it new ... Mk 14:25 *2250*
I say unto thee, That this *d* ... Mk 14:30 *4594*
the *d* before the sabbath, ... Mk 15:42
morning the first *d* of the week ... Mk 16:2
early the first *d* of the week ... Mk 16:9
until the *d* that these things ... Lk 1:20 *2250*
that on the eighth *d* they came to ... Lk 1:59 *2250*
the *d* of his shewing unto Israel ... Lk 1:80 *2250*
For unto you is born this *d* in ... Lk 2:11 *4594*
fastings and prayers night and *d* ... Lk 2:37 *2250*
the synagogue on the sabbath *d* ... Lk 4:16 *2250*
them, This *d* is this scripture ... Lk 4:21 *4594*
And when it was *d*, he departed and ... Lk 4:42 *2250*
And it came to pass on a certain *d* ... Lk 5:17 *2250*
We have seen strange things to *d* ... Lk 5:26 *4594*
he would heal on the sabbath *d* ... Lk 6:7
And when it was *d*, he called unto ... Lk 6:13 *2250*

Rejoice ye in that *d*, and leap for ... Lk 6:23 *2250*
And it came to pass the *d* after ... Lk 7:11 *2250*
it came to pass on a certain *d* ... Lk 8:22 *2250*
when the *d* began to wear away, ... Lk 9:12 *2250*
slain, and be raised the third *d* ... Lk 9:22 *2250*
came to pass, that on the next *d* ... Lk 9:37 *2250*
tolerable in that *d* for Sodom ... Lk 10:12 *2250*
us *d* by *d* our daily bread ... Lk 11:3 *3588,2596,2250*
us *d* by *d* our daily bread ... Lk 11:3 *3588,2596,2250*
which is to *d* in the field, and to ... Lk 12:28 *4594*
a *d* when he looketh not for him ... Lk 12:46 *2250*
Jesus had healed on the sabbath *d* ... Lk 13:14
healed, and not on the sabbath *d* ... Lk 13:14 *2250*
from this bond on the sabbath *d* ... Lk 13:16 *2250*
The same *d* there came certain of ... Lk 13:31 *2250*
out devils, and I do cures to *d* ... Lk 13:32 *4594*
the third *d* I shall be perfected ... Lk 13:32
Nevertheless I must walk to *d* ... Lk 13:33 *4594*
and to morrow, and the *d* following ... Lk 13:33
to eat bread on the sabbath *d* ... Lk 14:1
lawful to heal on the sabbath *d* ... Lk 14:3
pull him out on the sabbath *d* ... Lk 14:5 *2250*
and fared sumptuously every *d* ... Lk 16:19 *2250*
against thee seven times in a *d* ... Lk 17:4 *2250*
seven times in a *d* turn again to ... Lk 17:4 *2250*
also the Son of man be in his *d* ... Lk 17:24 *2250*
until the *d* that Noe entered into ... Lk 17:27 *2250*
But the same *d* that Lot went out ... Lk 17:29 *2250*
Even thus shall it be in the *d* ... Lk 17:30 *2250*
In that *d*, he which shall be upon ... Lk 17:31 *2250*
avenge his own elect, which cry *d* ... Lk 18:7 *2250*
the third *d* he shall rise again ... Lk 18:33 *2250*
for to *d* I must abide at thy ... Lk 19:5 *4594*
This *d* is salvation come to this ... Lk 19:9 *4594*
even thou, at least in this thy *d* ... Lk 19:42 *2250*
so that *d* come upon you unawares ... Lk 21:34 *2250*
in the *d* time he was teaching in ... Lk 21:37 *2250*
Then came the *d* of unleavened ... Lk 22:7 *2250*
the cock shall not crow this *d* ... Lk 22:34 *4594*
And as soon as it was *d*, the ... Lk 22:66 *2250*
And the same *d* Pilate and Herod ... Lk 23:12 *2250*
To *d* shalt thou be with me in ... Lk 23:43 *4594*
that *d* was the preparation, and ... Lk 23:54 *2250*
rested the sabbath *d* according to ... Lk 23:56
Now upon the first *d* of the week ... Lk 24:1
and the third *d* rise again ... Lk 24:7 *2250*
same *d* to a village called Emmaus ... Lk 24:13 *2250*
to *d* is the third *d* since these ... Lk 24:21 *4594*
to *d* is the third *d* since these ... Lk 24:21 *2250*
evening, and the *d* is far spent ... Lk 24:29 *2250*
to rise from the dead the third *d* ... Lk 24:46 *2250*
The next *d* John seeth Jesus ... Jn 1:29 *1887*
Again the next *d* after John stood ... Jn 1:35 *1887*
dwelt, and abode with him that *d* ... Jn 1:39 *2250*
The *d* following Jesus would go ... Jn 1:43 *1887*
the third *d* there was a marriage ... Jn 2:1 *2250*
at the passover, in the feast *d* ... Jn 2:23
on the same *d* was the sabbath ... Jn 5:9 *2250*
was cured, It is the sabbath *d* ... Jn 5:10
these things on the sabbath *d* ... Jn 5:16
The *d* following, when the people ... Jn 6:22 *1887*
raise it up again at the last *d* ... Jn 6:39 *2250*
I will raise him up at the last *d* ... Jn 6:40 *2250*
I will raise him up at the last *d* ... Jn 6:44 *2250*
I will raise him up at the last *d* ... Jn 6:54 *2250*
on the sabbath *d* circumcise a man ... Jn 7:22
sabbath *d* receive circumcision ... Jn 7:23
every whit whole on the sabbath *d* ... Jn 7:23
In the last *d*, that great *d* of ... Jn 7:37 *2250*
Abraham rejoiced to see my *d* ... Jn 8:56 *2250*
him that sent me, while it is *d* ... Jn 9:4 *2250*
it was the sabbath *d* when Jesus ... Jn 9:14
he keepeth not the sabbath *d* ... Jn 9:16
there not twelve hours in the *d* ... Jn 11:9 *2250*
If any man walk in the *d*, he ... Jn 11:9 *2250*
in the resurrection at the last *d* ... Jn 11:24 *2250*
Then from that *d* forth they took ... Jn 11:53 *2250*
against the *d* of my burying hath ... Jn 12:7 *2250*
On the next *d* much people that ... Jn 12:12 *1887*
shall judge him in the last *d* ... Jn 12:48 *2250*
At that *d* ye shall know that I am ... Jn 14:20 *2250*
in that *d* ye shall ask me nothing ... Jn 16:23 *2250*
At that *d* ye shall ask in my name ... Jn 16:26 *2250*
upon the cross on the sabbath *d* ... Jn 19:31
that sabbath *d* was an high *d* ... Jn 19:31 *2250*
of the Jews' preparation *d* ... Jn 19:42
The first *d* of the week cometh ... Jn 20:1
Then the same *d* at evening ... Jn 20:19 *2250*
being the first *d* of the week ... Jn 20:19 *2250*
Until the *d* in which he was taken ... Acts 1:2 *2250*
unto that same *d* that he was ... Acts 1:22 *2250*
when the *d* of Pentecost was fully ... Acts 2:1 *2250*
it is but the third hour of the *d* ... Acts 2:15 *2250*
notable *d* of the Lord come ... Acts 2:20 *2250*
sepulchre is with us unto this *d* ... Acts 2:29 *2250*
the same *d* there were added unto ... Acts 2:41 *2250*
put them in hold unto the next *d* ... Acts 4:3 *839*
If we this *d* be examined of the ... Acts 4:9 *4594*
and circumcised him the eighth *d* ... Acts 7:8 *2250*
the next *d* he shewed himself unto ... Acts 7:26 *2250*
And they watched the gates *d* ... Acts 9:24 *2250*
about the ninth hour of the *d* an ... Acts 10:3 *2250*
Him God raised up the third *d* ... Acts 10:40 *2250*
Now as soon as it was *d*, there ... Acts 12:18 *2250*
And upon a set *d* Herod, arrayed in ... Acts 12:21 *2250*
the synagogue on the sabbath *d* ... Acts 13:14 *2250*
which are read every sabbath *d* ... Acts 13:27
this *d* have I begotten thee ... Acts 13:33 *4594*

the next sabbath *d* came almost ... Acts 13:44
the next *d* he departed with ... Acts 14:20 *1887*
in the synagogues every sabbath *d* ... Acts 15:21
and the next *d* to Neapolis ... Acts 16:11
And when it was *d*, the magistrates ... Acts 16:35 *2250*
Because he hath appointed a *d* ... Acts 17:31 *2250*
And upon the first *d* of the week ... Acts 20:7
long while, even till break of *d* ... Acts 20:11 *827*
came the next *d* over against ... Acts 20:15
the next *d* we arrived at Samos, ... Acts 20:15
the next *d* we came to Miletus ... Acts 20:15
at Jerusalem the *d* of Pentecost ... Acts 20:16 *2250*
from the first *d* that I came into ... Acts 20:18 *2250*
I take you to record this *d* ... Acts 20:26 *4594*
every one night and *d* with tears ... Acts 20:31 *2250*
the *d* following unto Rhodes, and ... Acts 21:1
and abode with them one *d* ... Acts 21:7 *2250*
the next *d* we that were of Paul's ... Acts 21:8
the *d* following Paul went in with ... Acts 21:18
the next *d* purifying himself with ... Acts 21:26 *2250*
toward God, as ye all are this *d* ... Acts 22:3 *4594*
before God until this *d* ... Acts 23:1 *2250*
And when it was *d*, certain of the ... Acts 23:12 *2250*
called in question by you this *d* ... Acts 24:21 *4594*
the next *d* sitting on the ... Acts 25:6 *1887*
d before thee touching all the ... Acts 26:2 *4594*
tribes, instantly serving God *d* ... Acts 26:7 *2250*
of God, I continue unto this *d* ... Acts 26:22 *2250*
but also all that hear me this *d* ... Acts 26:29 *4594*
the next *d* we touched at Sidon ... Acts 27:3
the next *d* they lightened the ... Acts 27:18
the third *d* we cast out with our ... Acts 27:19
of the stern, and wished for the *d* ... Acts 27:29 *2250*
while the *d* was coming on, Paul ... Acts 27:33 *2250*
meat, saying, This *d* ... Acts 27:33 *4594*
fourteenth *d* that ye have tarried ... Acts 27:33 *2250*
And when it was *d*, they knew not ... Acts 27:39 *2250*
after one *d* the south wind blew, ... Acts 28:13 *2250*
and we came the next *d* to Puteoli ... Acts 28:13 *2250*
when they had appointed him a *d* ... Acts 28:23 *2250*
wrath against the *d* of wrath ... Rom 2:5 *2250*
In the *d* when God shall judge the ... Rom 2:16 *2250*
sake we are killed all the *d* long ... Rom 8:36 *2250*
All *d* long I have stretched forth ... Rom 10:21 *2250*
should not hear;) unto this *d* ... Rom 11:8 *4594,2250*
is far spent, the *d* is at hand ... Rom 13:12 *2250*
Let us walk honestly, as in the *d* ... Rom 13:13 *2250*
man esteemeth one *d* above another ... Rom 14:5 *2250*
another esteemeth every *d* alike ... Rom 14:5 *2250*
He that regardeth the *d*, ... Rom 14:6 *2250*
and he that regardeth not the *d* ... Rom 14:6 *2250*
in the *d* of our Lord Jesus Christ ... 1Cor 1:8 *2250*
for the *d* shall declare it, ... 1Cor 3:13 *2250*
of all things unto this *d* ... 1Cor 4:13 *737*
saved in the *d* of the Lord Jesus ... 1Cor 5:5 *2250*
committed, and fell in one *d* three ... 1Cor 10:8 *2250*
d according to the scriptures ... 1Cor 15:4 *2250*
Upon the first *d* of the week let ... 1Cor 16:2
ours in the *d* of the Lord Jesus ... 2Cor 1:14 *2250*
for until this *d* remaineth the ... 2Cor 3:14 *4594*
But even unto this *d*, when Moses ... 2Cor 3:15 *4594*
inward man is renewed *d* by *d* ... 2Cor 4:16 *2250*
in the *d* of salvation have I ... 2Cor 6:2 *2250*
now is the *d* of salvation ... 2Cor 6:2 *2250*
a *d* I have been in the deep ... 2Cor 11:25 *3574*
sealed unto the *d* of redemption ... Eph 4:30 *2250*
able to withstand in the evil *d* ... Eph 6:13 *2250*
gospel from the first *d* until now ... Phil 1:5 *2250*
it until the *d* of Jesus Christ ... Phil 1:6 *2250*
offence till the *d* of Christ ... Phil 1:10 *2250*
I may rejoice in the *d* of Christ ... Phil 2:16 *2250*
Circumcised the eighth *d*, of the ... Phil 3:5 *2250*
since the *d* ye heard of it, and ... Col 1:6 *2250*
since the *d* we heard it, do not ... Col 1:9 *2250*
for labouring night and *d*, because ... 1Th 2:9 *2250*
d praying exceedingly that we ... 1Th 3:10 *2250*
know perfectly that the *d* of the ... 1Th 5:2 *2250*
that that *d* should overtake you ... 1Th 5:4 *2250*
light, and the children of the *d* ... 1Th 5:5 *2250*
But let us, who are of the *d* ... 1Th 5:8 *2250*
among you was believed) in that *d* ... 2Th 1:10 *2250*
as that the *d* of Christ is at ... 2Th 2:2 *2250*
for that *d* shall not come, except ... 2Th 2:3
with labour and travail night and *d* ... 2Th 3:8 *2250*
and prayers night and *d* ... 1Ti 5:5 *2250*
of thee in my prayers night and *d* ... 2Ti 1:3 *2250*
committed unto him against that *d* ... 2Ti 1:12 *2250*
find mercy of the Lord in that *d* ... 2Ti 1:18 *2250*
judge, shall give me at that *d* ... 2Ti 4:8 *2250*
this *d* have I begotten thee ... Heb 1:5 *4594*
To *d* if ye will hear his voice, ... Heb 3:7 *4594*
in the *d* of temptation in the ... Heb 3:8 *2250*
daily, while it is called To *d* ... Heb 3:13 *4594*
To *d* if ye will hear his voice, ... Heb 3:15 *4594*
of the seventh *d* on this wise ... Heb 4:4
the seventh *d* from all his works ... Heb 4:4 *2250*
Again, he limiteth a certain *d* ... Heb 4:7 *2250*
saying in David, To *d* ... Heb 4:7 *4594*
To *d* if ye will hear his voice, ... Heb 4:7 *4594*
have spoken of another *d* ... Heb 4:8 *2250*
to *d* have I begotten thee ... Heb 5:5 *4594*
in the *d* when I took them by the ... Heb 8:9 *2250*
more, as ye see the *d* approaching ... Heb 10:25 *2250*
the same yesterday, and to *d* ... Heb 13:8 *4594*
To *d* or to morrow we will go into ... Jas 4:13 *4594*
hearts, as in a *d* of slaughter ... Jas 5:5 *2250*
God in the *d* of visitation ... 1Pet 2:12 *2250*
in a dark place, until the *d* dawn ... 2Pet 1:19 *2250*

the *d* star arise in your hearts ... 2Pet 1:19 5459
from *d* to *d* with their unlawful ... 2Pet 2:8 2250
to *d* with their unlawful deeds ... 2Pet 2:8 2250
the *d* of judgment to be punished ... 2Pet 2:9 2250
fire against the *d* of judgment ... 2Pet 3:7 2250
that one *d* is with the Lord as a ... 2Pet 3:8 2250
and a thousand years as one *d* ... 2Pet 3:8 2250
But the *d* of the Lord will come ... 2Pet 3:10 2250
unto the coming of the *d* of God ... 2Pet 3:12 2250
boldness in the *d* of judgment ... 1Jn 4:17 2250
unto the judgment of the great *d* ... Jude 6 2250
was in the Spirit on the Lord's *d* ... Rev 1:10 2250
and they rest not *d* and night, ... Rev 4:8 2250
For the great *d* of his wrath is ... Rev 6:17 2250
the throne of God, and serve him *d* ... Rev 7:15 2250
the *d* shone not for a third part ... Rev 8:12 2250
were prepared for an hour, and a *d* ... Rev 9:15 2250
accused them before our God *d* ... Rev 12:10 2250
and they have no rest *d* nor night ... Rev 14:11 2250
of that great *d* of God Almighty ... Rev 16:14 2250
shall her plagues come in one *d* ... Rev 18:8 2250
are, and shall be tormented *d* ... Rev 20:10 2250
it shall not be shut at all by *d* ... Rev 21:25 2250

DAY'S See APPENDIX.

DAYS See APPENDIX.

DAYS' See APPENDIX.

DAYSMAN {1}
Neither is there any *d* betwixt us ... Job 9:33 3198

DAYSPRING {2}
caused the *d* to know his place ... Job 38:12 7837
whereby the *d* from on high hath ... Lk 1:78 395

DAYTIME {9}
by *d* in a pillar of a cloud, and ... Num 14:14 3119
They meet with darkness in the *d* ... Job 5:14 3119
marked for themselves in the *d* ... Job 24:16 3119
O my God, I cry in the *d*, but ... Ps 22:2 3119
his lovingkindness in the *d* ... Ps 42:8 3119
In the *d* also he led them with a ... Ps 78:14 3119
a shadow in the *d* from the heat ... Is 4:6 3119
upon the watchtower in the *d* ... Is 21:8 3119
it pleasure to riot in the *d* ... 2Pet 2:13

DEACON {2}
let them use the office of a *d* ... 1Ti 3:10 1247
a *d* well purchase to themselves a ... 1Ti 3:13 1247

DEACONS {3}
Philippi, with the bishops and *d* ... Phil 1:1 1249
Likewise must the *d* be grave ... 1Ti 3:8 1249
Let the *d* be the husbands of one ... 1Ti 3:12 1249

DEAD {367}
him, Behold, thou art but a *d* man ... Gen 20:3 4191
stood up from before his *d* ... Gen 23:3 4191
I may bury my *d* out of my sight ... Gen 23:4 4191
of our sepulchres bury thy *d* ... Gen 23:6 4191
but that thou mayest bury thy *d* ... Gen 23:6 4191
should bury my *d* out of my sight ... Gen 23:8 4191
bury thy *d* ... Gen 23:11 4191
of me, and I will bury my *d* there ... Gen 23:13 4191
bury therefore thy *d* ... Gen 23:15 4191
for his brother is *d*, and he is ... Gen 42:38 4191
and his brother is *d*, and he alone ... Gen 44:20 4191
saw that their father was *d* ... Gen 50:15 4191
for all the men are *d* which ... Ex 4:19 4191
of the cattle of the Israelites *d* ... Ex 9:7 4191
a house where there was not one *d* ... Ex 12:30 4191
for they said, We be all *d* men ... Ex 12:33 4191
Egyptians *d* upon the sea shore ... Ex 14:30 4191
and the *d* beast shall be his ... Ex 21:34 4191
the *d* ox also they shall divide ... Ex 21:35 4191
and the *d* shall be his own ... Ex 21:36 4191
doth touch them, when they be *d* ... Lev 11:31 4194
any of them, when they are *d* ... Lev 11:32 4194
cuttings in your flesh for the *d* ... Lev 19:28 5315
for the *d* among his people ... Lev 21:1 5315
shall he go in to any *d* body ... Lev 21:11 4191
thing that is unclean by the *d* ... Lev 22:4 5315
and whosoever is defiled by the *d* ... Num 5:2 5315
LORD he shall come at no *d* body ... Num 6:6 4191
him, for that he sinned by the *d* ... Num 6:11 5315
defiled by the *d* body of a man ... Num 9:6 5315
defiled by the *d* body of a man ... Num 9:7 5315
be unclean by reason of a *d* body ... Num 9:10 5315
Let her not be as one *d*, of whom ... Num 12:12 4191
And he stood between the *d* ... Num 16:48 4191
He that toucheth the *d* body of ... Num 19:11 4191
Whosoever toucheth the *d* body of ... Num 19:13 4191
d body of any man that is *d* ... Num 19:13 4191
in the open fields, or a *d* body ... Num 19:16 4191
a bone, or one slain, or one *d* ... Num 19:18 4191
congregation saw that Aaron was *d* ... Num 20:29 1478
and *d* from among the people, ... Deut 2:16 4191
between your eyes for the *d* ... Deut 14:1 4191
flesh, nor touch their *d* carcase ... Deut 14:8 5038
the wife of the *d* shall not marry ... Deut 25:5 4191
name of his brother which is *d* ... Deut 25:6 4191
nor given ought thereof for the *d* ... Deut 26:14 4191
Moses my servant is *d* ... Josh 1:2 4191
to pass, when the judge was *d* ... Judg 2:19 4191
was fallen down *d* on the earth ... Judg 3:25 4191
of the LORD, when Ehud was *d* ... Judg 4:1 4191
her tent, behold, Sisera lay *d* ... Judg 4:22 4191
he bowed, there he fell down *d* ... Judg 5:27 7703
to pass, as soon as Gideon was *d* ... Judg 8:33 4191
Israel saw that Abimelech was *d* ... Judg 9:55 4191
So the *d* which he slew at his ... Judg 16:30 4191
have they forced, that she is *d* ... Judg 20:5 4191
you, as ye have dealt with the *d* ... Ruth 1:8 4191
to the living and to the *d* ... Ruth 2:20 4191
the Moabitess, the wife of the *d* ... Ruth 4:5 4191
of the *d* upon his inheritance ... Ruth 4:5 4191
of the *d* upon his inheritance ... Ruth 4:10 4191
that the name of the *d* be not cut ... Ruth 4:10 4191
also, Hophni and Phinehas, are *d* ... 1Sa 4:17 4191
in law and her husband were *d* ... 1Sa 4:19 4191
saw their champion was *d*, they ... 1Sa 17:51 4191
after a *d* dog, after a flea ... 1Sa 24:14 4191
when David heard that Nabal was *d* ... 1Sa 25:39 4191
Now Samuel was *d*, and all Israel ... 1Sa 28:3 4191
armourbearer saw that Saul was *d* ... 1Sa 31:5 4191
and that Saul and his sons were *d* ... 1Sa 31:7 4191
the people also are fallen and *d* ... 2Sa 1:4 4191
and Jonathan his son are *d* also ... 2Sa 1:4 4191
Saul and Jonathan his son be *d* ... 2Sa 1:5 4191
for your master Saul is *d* ... 2Sa 2:7 4191
heard that Abner was *d* in Hebron ... 2Sa 4:1 4191
me, saying, Behold, Saul is *d* ... 2Sa 4:10 4191
look upon such a *d* dog as I am ... 2Sa 9:8 4191
Uriah the Hittite is *d* also ... 2Sa 11:21 4191
some of the king's servants be *d* ... 2Sa 11:24 4191
Uriah the Hittite is *d* also ... 2Sa 11:24 4191
that Uriah her husband was *d* ... 2Sa 11:26 4191
to tell him that the child was *d* ... 2Sa 12:18 4191
we tell him that the child is *d* ... 2Sa 12:18 4191
perceived that the child was *d* ... 2Sa 12:19 4191
unto his servants, Is the child *d* ... 2Sa 12:19 4191
And they said, He is *d* ... 2Sa 12:19 4191
but when the child was *d*, thou ... 2Sa 12:21 4191
But now he is *d*, wherefore should ... 2Sa 12:23 4191
for Amnon only is *d* ... 2Sa 13:32 4191
that all the king's sons are *d* ... 2Sa 13:33 4191
for Amnon only is *d* ... 2Sa 13:33 4191
concerning Amnon, seeing he was *d* ... 2Sa 13:39 4191
had a long time mourned for the *d* ... 2Sa 14:2 4191
widow woman, and mine husband is *d* ... 2Sa 14:5 4191
Why should this *d* dog curse my ... 2Sa 16:9 4191
because the king's son is *d* ... 2Sa 18:20 4191
anointed over us, is *d* in battle ... 2Sa 19:10 4191
but *d* men before my lord the king ... 2Sa 19:28 4194
laid her *d* child in my bosom ... 1Kin 3:20 4191
my child suck, behold, it was *d* ... 1Kin 3:21 4191
is my son, and the *d* is thy son ... 1Kin 3:22 4191
but the *d* is thy son, and the ... 1Kin 3:22 4191
that liveth, and thy son is the *d* ... 1Kin 3:23 4191
but thy son is the *d*, and my son ... 1Kin 3:23 4191
the captain of the host was *d* ... 1Kin 11:21 4191
to his sons, saying, When I am *d* ... 1Kin 13:31 4191
saying, Naboth is stoned, and is *d* ... 1Kin 21:14 4191
that Naboth was stoned, and was *d* ... 1Kin 21:15 4191
for Naboth is not alive, but *d* ... 1Kin 21:15 4191
when Ahab heard that Naboth was *d* ... 1Kin 21:16 4191
it came to pass, when Ahab was *d* ... 2Kin 3:5 4191
Thy servant my husband is *d* ... 2Kin 4:1 4191
house, behold, the child was *d* ... 2Kin 4:32 4191
he had restored a *d* body to life ... 2Kin 8:5 4191
of Ahaziah saw that her son was *d* ... 2Kin 11:1 4191
behold, they were all *d* corpses ... 2Kin 19:35 4191
him in a chariot *d* from Megiddo ... 2Kin 23:30 4191
And when Bela was *d*, Jobab the son ... 1Chr 1:44 4191
And when Jobab was *d*, Husham of ... 1Chr 1:45 4191
And when Husham was *d*, Hadad the ... 1Chr 1:46 4191
And when Hadad was *d*, Samlah of ... 1Chr 1:47 4191
And when Samlah was *d*, Shaul of ... 1Chr 1:48 4191
And when Shaul was *d*, Baal-hanan ... 1Chr 1:49 4191
And when Baal-hanan was *d*, Hadad ... 1Chr 1:50 4191
And when Azubah was *d*, Caleb took ... 1Chr 2:19 4191
Hezron was *d* in Caleb-ephratah ... 1Chr 2:24 4194
armourbearer saw that Saul was *d* ... 1Chr 10:5 4191
and that Saul and his sons were *d* ... 1Chr 10:7 4191
they were *d* bodies fallen to the ... 2Chr 20:24 6297
both riches with the *d* bodies ... 2Chr 20:25 6297
of Ahaziah saw that her son was *d* ... 2Chr 22:10 4191
when her father and mother were *d* ... Est 2:7 4194
upon the young men, and they are *d* ... Job 1:19 4191
D things are formed from under ... Job 26:5 7496
forgotten as a *d* man out of mind ... Ps 31:12 4191
and horse are cast into a *d* sleep ... Ps 76:6
The *d* bodies of thy servants have ... Ps 79:2 5038
Free among the *d*, like the slain ... Ps 88:5 4191
Wilt thou shew wonders to the *d* ... Ps 88:10 4191
shall the *d* arise and praise thee ... Ps 88:10 7496
and ate the sacrifices of the *d* ... Ps 106:28 4191
fill the places with the *d* bodies ... Ps 110:6 1472
The *d* praise not the LORD, ... Ps 115:17 4191
as those that have been long *d* ... Ps 143:3 4191
death, and her paths unto the *d* ... Prov 2:18 7496
knoweth not that the *d* are there ... Prov 9:18 7496
in the congregation of the *d* ... Prov 21:16 7496
Wherefore I praised the *d* which ... Eccl 4:2 4191
the *d* which are already *d* more ... Eccl 4:2 4191
and after that they go to the *d* ... Eccl 9:3 4191
dog is better than a *d* lion ... Eccl 9:4 4191
but the *d* know not any thing, ... Eccl 9:5 4191
D flies cause the ointment of the ... Eccl 10:1 4194
for the living to the *d* ... Is 8:19 4191
it stirreth up the *d* for thee ... Is 14:9 7496
with the sword, nor *d* in battle ... Is 22:2 4191
They are *d*, they shall not live ... Is 26:14 4191
Thy *d* men shall live, together ... Is 26:19 4191
together with my *d* body shall ... Is 26:19 5038
and the earth shall cast out the *d* ... Is 26:19 7496
behold, they were all *d* corpses ... Is 37:36 4191
are in desolate places as *d* men ... Is 59:10 4191
to comfort them for the *d* ... Jer 16:7 4191
Weep ye not for the *d*, neither ... Jer 22:10 4191
cast his *d* body into the graves ... Jer 26:23 5038
the whole valley of the *d* bodies ... Jer 31:40 6297
them with the *d* bodies of men ... Jer 33:5 6297
their *d* bodies shall be for meat ... Jer 34:20 5038
his *d* body shall be cast out in ... Jer 36:30 5038
cast all the *d* bodies of the men ... Jer 41:9 6297
places, as they that be *d* of old ... Lam 3:6 4191
I will lay the *d* carcases of the ... Eze 6:5
cry, make no mourning for the *d* ... Eze 24:17 4191
they shall come at no *d* person to ... Eze 44:25 4191
of any thing that is *d* of itself ... Eze 44:31 5038
there shall be many *d* bodies in ... Amos 8:3 6297
by a *d* body touch any of these ... Hag 2:13
But when Herod was *d*, behold, an ... Mt 2:19 5053
for they are *d* which sought the ... Mt 2:20 2348
and let the *d* bury their *d* ... Mt 8:22 3498
saying, My daughter is even now *d* ... Mt 9:18 5053
for the maid is not *d*, but ... Mt 9:24 599
cleanse the lepers, raise the *d* ... Mt 10:8 3498
the *d* are raised up, and the poor ... Mt 11:5 3498
he is risen from the *d* ... Mt 14:2 3498
of man be risen again from the *d* ... Mt 17:9 3498
the resurrection of the *d* ... Mt 22:31 3498
God is not the God of the *d* ... Mt 22:32 3498
are within full of *d* men's bones ... Mt 23:27 3498
people, He is risen from the *d* ... Mt 27:64 3498
did shake, and became as *d* men ... Mt 28:4 3498
that he is risen from the *d* ... Mt 28:7 3498
which said, Thy daughter is *d* ... Mk 5:35 599
the damsel is not *d*, but sleepeth ... Mk 5:39 599
the Baptist was risen from the *d* ... Mk 6:14 3498
he is risen from the *d* ... Mk 6:16 3498
Son of man were risen from the *d* ... Mk 9:9 3498
the rising from the *d* should mean ... Mk 9:10 3498
and he was as one *d* ... Mk 9:26 3498
insomuch that many said, He is *d* ... Mk 9:26 599
when they shall rise from the *d* ... Mk 12:25 3498
And as touching the *d*, that they ... Mk 12:26 3498
He is not the God of the *d* ... Mk 12:27 3498
marvelled if he were already *d* ... Mk 15:44 2348
whether he had been any while *d* ... Mk 15:44 599
there was a *d* man carried out, ... Lk 7:12 2348
And he that was *d* sat up, and began ... Lk 7:15 3498
the *d* are raised, to the poor the ... Lk 7:22 3498
saying to him, Thy daughter is *d* ... Lk 8:49 2348
she is not *d*, but sleepeth ... Lk 8:52 599
to scorn, knowing that she was *d* ... Lk 8:53 599
that John was risen from the *d* ... Lk 9:7 3498
Let the *d* bury their *d* ... Lk 9:60 3498
and departed, leaving him half *d* ... Lk 10:30 2258
For this my son was *d*, and is ... Lk 15:24 3498
for this thy brother was *d* ... Lk 15:32 3498
if one went unto them from the *d* ... Lk 16:30 3498
though one rose from the *d* ... Lk 16:31 3498
and the resurrection from the *d* ... Lk 20:35 3498
Now that the *d* are raised ... Lk 20:37 3498
For he is not a God of the *d* ... Lk 20:38 3498
seek ye the living among the *d* ... Lk 24:5 3498
to rise from the *d* the third day ... Lk 24:46 3498
therefore he was risen from the *d* ... Jn 2:22 3498
as the Father raiseth up the *d* ... Jn 5:21 3498
when the *d* shall hear the voice ... Jn 5:25 3498
manna in the wilderness, and are *d* ... Jn 6:49 599
fathers did eat manna, and are *d* ... Jn 6:58 599
Abraham is *d*, and the prophets ... Jn 8:52 599
our father Abraham, which is *d* ... Jn 8:53 599
and the prophets are *d* ... Jn 8:53 599
unto them plainly, Lazarus is *d* ... Jn 11:14 599
believeth in me, though he were *d* ... Jn 11:25 599
the sister of him that was *d* ... Jn 11:39 2348
for he hath been *d* four days ... Jn 11:39
the place where the *d* was laid ... Jn 11:41 2348
And he that was *d* came forth ... Jn 11:44 2348
Lazarus was which had been *d* ... Jn 12:1 2348
d, whom he raised from the *d* ... Jn 12:1 3498
whom he had raised from the *d* ... Jn 12:9 3498
grave, and raised him from the *d* ... Jn 12:17 3498
and saw that he was *d* already ... Jn 19:33 2348
he must rise again from the *d* ... Jn 20:9 3498
that he was risen from the *d* ... Jn 21:14 3498
David, that he is both *d* and ... Acts 2:29 5053
whom God hath raised from the *d* ... Acts 3:15 3498
Jesus the resurrection from the *d* ... Acts 4:2 3498
whom God raised from the *d* ... Acts 4:10 3498
young men came in, and found her *d* ... Acts 5:10 3498
thence, when his father was *d* ... Acts 7:4 599
with him after he rose from the *d* ... Acts 10:41 3498
God to be the Judge of quick and *d* ... Acts 10:42 3498
But God raised him from the *d* ... Acts 13:30 3498
that he raised him up from the *d* ... Acts 13:34 3498
the city, supposing he had been *d* ... Acts 14:19 2348
and risen again from the *d* ... Acts 17:3 3498
he hath raised him from the *d* ... Acts 17:31 3498
of the resurrection of the *d* ... Acts 17:32 3498
the third loft, and was taken up *d* ... Acts 20:9 3498
resurrection of the *d* I am called ... Acts 23:6 3498
shall be a resurrection of the *d* ... Acts 24:15 3498
the resurrection of the *d* I am ... Acts 24:21 3498
and of one Jesus, which was *d* ... Acts 25:19 2348
you, that God should raise the *d* ... Acts 26:8 3498
first that should rise from the *d* ... Acts 26:23 3498
or fallen down *d* suddenly ... Acts 28:6 3498
by the resurrection from the *d* ... Rom 1:4 3498
even God, who quickeneth the *d* ... Rom 4:17 3498
considered not his own body now *d* ... Rom 4:19 3499
up Jesus our Lord from the *d* ... Rom 4:24 3498
the offence of one many be *d* ... Rom 5:15 599
How shall we, that are *d* to sin ... Rom 6:2 599

D

the *d* by the glory of the Father ... Rom 6:4 *3498*
For he that is *d* is freed from ... Rom 6:7 *599*
Now if we be *d* with Christ ... Rom 6:8 *599*
raised from the *d* dieth no more ... Rom 6:9 *3498*
to be *d* indeed unto sin, but ... Rom 6:11 *3498*
those that are alive from the *d* ... Rom 6:13 *3498*
but if the husband be *d*, she is ... Rom 7:2 *599*
but if her husband be *d*, she is ... Rom 7:3 *599*
ye also are become *d* to the law ... Rom 7:4 *2289*
to him who is raised from the *d* ... Rom 7:4 *3498*
that being *d* wherein we were held ... Rom 7:6 *599*
For without the law sin was *d* ... Rom 7:8 *3498*
the body is *d* because of sin ... Rom 8:10 *3498*
up Jesus from the *d* dwell in you ... Rom 8:11 *3498*
d shall also quicken your mortal ... Rom 8:11 *3498*
bring up Christ again from the *d* ... Rom 10:7 *3498*
God hath raised him from the *d* ... Rom 10:9 *3498*
of them be, but life from the *d* ... Rom 11:15 *3498*
he might be Lord both of the *d* ... Rom 14:9 *3498*
but if her husband be *d*, she is ... 1Cor 7:39 *2837*
preached that he rose from the *d* ... 1Cor 15:12 *3498*
there is no resurrection of the *d* ... 1Cor 15:12 *3498*
there be no resurrection of the *d* ... 1Cor 15:13 *3498*
up, if so be that the *d* rise not ... 1Cor 15:15 *3498*
For if the *d* rise not, then is ... 1Cor 15:16 *3498*
now is Christ risen from the *d* ... 1Cor 15:20 *3498*
also the resurrection of the *d* ... 1Cor 15:21 *3498*
do which are baptized for the *d* ... 1Cor 15:29 *3498*
if the *d* rise not at all ... 1Cor 15:29 *3498*
are they then baptized for the *d* ... 1Cor 15:29 *3498*
it me, if the *d* rise not ... 1Cor 15:32 *3498*
will say, How are the *d* raised up ... 1Cor 15:35 *3498*
also is the resurrection of the *d* ... 1Cor 15:42 *3498*
sound, and the *d* shall be raised ... 1Cor 15:52 *3498*
but in God which raiseth the *d* ... 2Cor 1:9 *3498*
one died for all, then were all *d* ... 2Cor 5:14 *599*
Father, who raised him from the *d* ... Gal 1:1 *3498*
I through the law am *d* to the law ... Gal 2:19 *599*
the law, then Christ is *d* in vain ... Gal 2:21 *599*
when he raised him from the *d* ... Eph 1:20 *3498*
who were *d* in trespasses and sins ... Eph 2:1 *3498*
Even when we were *d* in sins ... Eph 2:5 *3498*
sleepest, and arise from the *d* ... Eph 5:14 *3498*
unto the resurrection of the *d* ... Phil 3:11 *3498*
the firstborn from the *d* ... Col 1:18 *3498*
who hath raised him from the *d* ... Col 2:12 *3498*
being *d* in your sins and the ... Col 2:13 *3498*
Wherefore if ye be *d* with Christ ... Col 2:20 *599*
For ye are *d*, and your life is hid ... Col 3:3 *599*
heaven, whom he raised from the *d* ... 1Th 1:10 *3498*
the *d* in Christ shall rise first ... 1Th 4:16 *3498*
in pleasure is *d* while she liveth ... 1Ti 5:6 *2348*
from the *d* according to my gospel ... 2Ti 2:8 *3498*
For if we be *d* with him, we shall ... 2Ti 2:11 *4880*
the *d* at his appearing and his ... 2Ti 4:1 *3498*
of repentance from *d* works ... Heb 6:1 *3498*
and of resurrection of the *d* ... Heb 6:2 *3498*
purge your conscience from *d* ... Heb 9:14 *3498*
is of force after men are *d* ... Heb 9:17 *3498*
and by it he being *d* yet speaketh ... Heb 11:4 *599*
even of one, and him as good as *d* ... Heb 11:12 *3499*
to raise him up, even from the *d* ... Heb 11:19 *3498*
their *d* raised to life again ... Heb 11:35 *3498*
again from the *d* our Lord Jesus ... Heb 13:20 *3498*
faith, if it hath not works, is *d* ... Jas 2:17 *3498*
that faith without works is *d* ... Jas 2:20 *3498*
the body without the spirit is *d* ... Jas 2:26 *3498*
so faith without works is *d* also ... Jas 2:26 *3498*
of Jesus Christ from the *d* ... 1Pet 1:3 *3498*
that raised him up from the *d* ... 1Pet 1:21 *3498*
being *d* to sins, should live unto ... 1Pet 2:24 *581*
ready to judge the quick and the *d* ... 1Pet 4:5 *3498*
preached also to them that are *d* ... 1Pet 4:6 *3498*
withereth, without fruit, twice *d* ... Jude 12 *599*
and the first begotten of the *d* ... Rev 1:5 *3498*
saw him, I fell at his feet as *d* ... Rev 1:17 *3498*
I am he that liveth, and was *d* ... Rev 1:18 *3498*
first and the last, which was *d* ... Rev 2:8 *3498*
a name that thou livest, and art *d* ... Rev 3:1 *3498*
their *d* bodies shall lie in the ... Rev 11:8 *4430*
see their *d* bodies three days ... Rev 11:9 *4430*
shall not suffer their *d* bodies ... Rev 11:9 *4430*
is come, and the time of the *d* ... Rev 11:18 *3498*
Blessed are the *d* which die in ... Rev 14:13 *3498*
it became as the blood of a *d* man ... Rev 16:3 *3498*
But the rest of the *d* lived not ... Rev 20:5 *3498*
And I saw the *d*, small and great, ... Rev 20:12 *3498*
the *d* were judged out of those ... Rev 20:12 *3498*
gave up the *d* which were in it ... Rev 20:13 *3498*
up the *d* which were in them ... Rev 20:13 *3498*

DEADLY {7}
for there was a *d* destruction ... 1Sa 5:11 4194
oppress me, from my *d* enemies ... Ps 17:9 5315
the groanings of a *d* wounded man ... Eze 30:24
and if they drink any *d* thing ... Mk 16:18 *2286*
an unruly evil, full of *d* poison ... Jas 3:8 *2287*
and his *d* wound was healed ... Rev 13:3 *2288*
beast, whose *d* wound was healed ... Rev 13:12 *2288*

DEADNESS {1}
neither yet the *d* of Sarah's womb ... Rom 4:19 *3500*

DEAF {15}
or who maketh the dumb, or *d* ... Ex 4:11 2795
Thou shalt not curse the *d* ... Lev 19:14 2795
But I, as a *d* man, heard not ... Ps 38:13 2795
they are like the *d* adder that ... Ps 58:4 2795
in that day shall the *d* hear the ... Is 29:18 2795
the ears of the *d* shall be ... Is 35:5 2795
Hear, ye *d* ... Is 42:18 2795
or *d*, as my messenger that I sent ... Is 42:19 2795
eyes, and the *d* that have ears ... Is 43:8 2795
mouth, their ears shall be *d* ... Mic 7:16 2790
the *d* hear, the dead are raised, ... Mt 11:5 *2974*
bring unto him one that was *d* ... Mk 7:32 *2974*
he maketh both the *d* to hear ... Mk 7:37 *2974*
d spirit, I charge thee, come out ... Mk 9:25 *2974*
the *d* hear, the dead are raised, ... Lk 7:22 *2974*

DEAL {60}
now will we *d* worse with thee, ... Gen 19:9
thou wilt not *d* falsely with me ... Gen 21:23
And now if ye will *d* kindly ... Gen 24:49 6213
and I will *d* well with thee ... Gen 32:9
Should he *d* with our sister as ... Gen 34:31 6213
d kindly and truly with me ... Gen 47:29 6213
let us *d* wisely with them ... Ex 1:10
but let not Pharaoh *d* deceitfully ... Ex 8:29
he shall *d* with her after the ... Ex 21:9 6213
thou shalt *d* with thy vineyard ... Ex 23:11 6213
tenth *d* of flour mingled with the ... Ex 29:40
one tenth *d* of fine flour mingled ... Lev 14:21
not steal, neither *d* falsely ... Lev 19:11
if thou *d* thus with me, kill me, ... Num 11:15 6213
tenth *d* of flour mingled with the ... Num 15:4
a several tenth *d* of flour ... Num 28:13
A several tenth *d* shalt thou ... Num 28:21
A several tenth *d* unto one lamb ... Num 28:29
one tenth *d* for one lamb, ... Num 29:4
A several tenth *d* for one lamb ... Num 29:10
a several tenth *d* to each lamb of ... Num 29:15
But thus shall ye *d* with them ... Deut 7:5 6213
the land, that we will *d* kindly ... Josh 2:14 6213
the LORD *d* kindly with you, as ye ... Ruth 1:8 6213
Therefore thou shalt *d* kindly ... 1Sa 20:8 6213
D gently for my sake with the ... 2Sa 18:5
As thou didst *d* with David my ... 2Chr 2:3 6213
dwell therein, even so *d* with me ... 2Chr 2:3
D courageously, and the LORD shall ... 2Chr 19:11 6213
lest I *d* with you after your ... Job 42:8 6213
unto the fools, *D* not foolishly ... Ps 75:4
to *d* subtilly with his servants ... Ps 105:25
D bountifully with thy servant, ... Ps 119:17 1580
D with thy servant according unto ... Ps 119:124 6213
for thou shalt *d* bountifully with ... Ps 142:7 1580
but they that *d* truly are his ... Prov 12:22 6213
of uprightness will he *d* unjustly ... Is 26:10
make an end to *d* treacherously ... Is 33:1
they shall *d* treacherously with ... Is 33:1
wouldest *d* very treacherously ... Is 48:8
my servant shall *d* prudently ... Is 52:13
Is it not to *d* thy bread to the ... Is 58:7 6536
happy that *d* very treacherously ... Jer 12:1
d thus with them in the time of ... Jer 18:23 6213
if so be that the LORD will *d* ... Jer 21:2 6213
Therefore will I also *d* in fury ... Eze 8:18 6213
I will even *d* with thee as thou ... Eze 16:59 6213
kept my judgments, to *d* truly ... Eze 18:9 6213
the days that I shall *d* with thee ... Eze 22:14 6213
they shall *d* furiously with thee ... Eze 23:25 6213
they shall *d* with thee hatefully, ... Eze 23:29 6213
he shall surely *d* with him ... Eze 31:11 6213
thou seest, *d* with thy servants ... Dan 1:13 6213
shall *d* against them, and shall ... Dan 11:7 6213
upon them that *d* treacherously ... Hab 1:13
why do we *d* treacherously every ... Mal 2:10
let none *d* treacherously against ... Mal 2:15
that ye *d* not treacherously ... Mal 2:16
more a great *d* they published it ... Mk 7:36 *4054*
but he cried the more a great *d* ... Mk 10:48

DEALER {1}
the treacherous *d* dealeth ... Is 21:2

DEALERS {2}
the treacherous *d* have dealt ... Is 24:16
the treacherous *d* have dealt very ... Is 24:16

DEALEST {2}
Wherefore *d* thou thus with thy ... Ex 5:15 6213
d treacherously, and they dealt ... Is 33:1

DEALETH {10}
thus *d* Micah with me, and hath ... Judg 18:4 6213
told me that he *d* very subtilly ... 1Sa 23:22
poor that *d* with a slack hand ... Prov 10:4 6213
prudent man *d* with knowledge ... Prov 13:16 6213
He that is soon angry *d* foolishly ... Prov 14:17 6213
is his name, who *d* in proud wrath ... Prov 21:24 6213
dealer *d* treacherously, and the ... Is 21:2
the priest every one *d* falsely ... Jer 6:13 6213
the priest every one *d* falsely ... Jer 8:10 6213
God *d* with you as with sons ... Heb 12:7 *4374*

DEALING {1}
his violent *d* shall come down ... Ps 7:16

DEALINGS {2}
of your evil *d* by all this people ... 1Sa 2:23 1697
have no *d* with the Samaritans ... Jn 4:9 *4798*

DEALS {19}
three tenth *d* of fine flour for a ... Lev 14:10
thereof shall be two tenth *d* of ... Lev 23:13
two wave loaves of two tenth *d* ... Lev 23:17
two tenth *d* shall be in one cake ... Lev 24:5
for a meat offering two tenth *d* ... Num 15:6
d of flour mingled with half an ... Num 15:9
two tenth *d* of flour for a meat ... Num 28:9
three tenth *d* of flour for a meat ... Num 28:12
two tenth *d* of flour for a meat ... Num 28:12
three tenth *d* shall ye offer for ... Num 28:20
bullock, and two tenth *d* for a ram ... Num 28:20
three tenth *d* unto one bullock, ... Num 28:28
two tenth *d* unto one ram, ... Num 28:28
three tenth *d* for a bullock ... Num 29:3
and two tenth *d* for a ram ... Num 29:3
three tenth *d* to a bullock ... Num 29:9
and two tenth *d* to one ram, ... Num 29:9
three tenth *d* unto every bullock ... Num 29:14
two tenth *d* to each ram of the ... Num 29:14

DEALT {57}
when Sarai *d* hardly with her, she ... Gen 16:6
because God hath *d* graciously ... Gen 33:11
Wherefore *d* ye so ill with me, as ... Gen 43:6
Therefore God *d* well with the ... Ex 1:20
hast thou *d* thus with us, to ... Ex 14:11 6213
they *d* proudly he was above them ... Ex 18:11
seeing he hath *d* deceitfully with ... Ex 21:8
if ye have *d* well with Jerubbaal ... Judg 9:16 6213
If ye then have *d* truly and ... Judg 9:19 6213
and the men of Shechem *d* ... Judg 9:23
as ye have *d* with the dead, and ... Ruth 1:8 6213
hath *d* very bitterly with me ... Ruth 1:20
how that thou hast *d* well with me ... 1Sa 24:18 6213
shall have *d* well with my lord ... 1Sa 25:31
he *d* among all the people, even ... 2Sa 6:19 2505
for they *d* faithfully ... 2Kin 12:15 6213
d with familiar spirits and ... 2Kin 21:6 6213
hand, because they *d* faithfully ... 2Kin 22:7 6213
he *d* to every one of Israel, both ... 1Chr 16:3 2505
Even so *d* David with all the ... 1Chr 20:3 6213
done amiss, and have *d* wickedly ... 2Chr 6:37
he *d* wisely, and dispersed of all ... 2Chr 11:23
d with a familiar spirit, and with ... 2Chr 33:6 6213
We have *d* very corruptly against ... Neh 1:7
that they *d* proudly against them ... Neh 9:10
But they and our fathers *d* proudly ... Neh 9:16
yet they *d* proudly, and hearkened ... Neh 9:29
My brethren have *d* deceitfully as ... Job 6:15
because he hath *d* bountifully ... Ps 13:6 1580
neither have we *d* falsely in thy ... Ps 44:17
d unfaithfully like their fathers ... Ps 78:57
He hath not *d* with us after our ... Ps 103:10 6213
for the LORD hath *d* bountifully ... Ps 116:7 1580
Thou hast *d* well with thy servant ... Ps 119:65 6213
for they *d* perversely with me ... Ps 119:78
He hath not *d* so with any nation ... Ps 147:20 6213
dealers have *d* treacherously ... Is 24:16
dealers have *d* very treacherously ... Is 24:16
they *d* not treacherously with ... Is 33:1
so have ye *d* treacherously with ... Jer 3:20
the house of Judah have *d* very ... Jer 5:11
even they have *d* treacherously ... Jer 12:6
all her friends have *d* ... Lam 1:2
in the midst of thee have they *d* ... Eze 22:7 6213
Because that Edom hath *d* against ... Eze 25:12 6213
the Philistines have *d* by revenge ... Eze 25:15 6213
They have *d* treacherously against ... Hos 5:7
there have they *d* treacherously ... Hos 6:7
that hath *d* wondrously with you ... Joel 2:26 6213
our doings, so hath he *d* with us ... Zec 1:6 6213
Judah hath *d* treacherously, and an ... Mal 2:11
whom thou hast *d* treacherously ... Mal 2:14
Thus hath the Lord *d* with me in ... Lk 1:25 *4160*
Son, why hast thou thus *d* with us ... Lk 2:48 *4160*
The same *d* subtilly with our ... Acts 7:19 *2686*
of the Jews have *d* with me ... Acts 25:24 *1793*
according as God hath *d* to every ... Rom 12:3 *3307*

DEAR {7}
Is Ephraim my *d* son ... Jer 31:20 3357
who was *d* unto him, was sick, and ... Lk 7:2 *1784*
count I my life *d* unto myself ... Acts 20:24 *5093*
followers of God, as *d* children ... Eph 5:1 *27*
of Epaphras our *d* fellowservant ... Col 1:7 *27*
us into the kingdom of his *d* Son ... Col 1:13 *26*
souls, because ye were *d* unto us ... 1Th 2:8 *27*

DEARLY {10}
I have given the *d* beloved of my ... Jer 12:7
D beloved, avenge not yourselves, ... Rom 12:19
my *d* beloved, flee from idolatry ... 1Cor 10:14
these promises *d* beloved, let us ... 2Cor 7:1
d beloved, for your edifying ... 2Cor 12:19
Therefore, my brethren *d* beloved ... Phil 4:1
fast in the Lord, my *d* beloved ... Phil 4:1
To Timothy, my *d* beloved son ... 2Ti 1:2
unto Philemon our *d* beloved ... Philem 1
D beloved, I beseech you as ... 1Pet 2:11

DEARTH {8}
seven years of *d* began to come ... Gen 41:54 7458
and the *d* was in all lands ... Gen 41:54 7458
and there was a *d* in the land ... 2Kin 4:38 7458
If there be *d* in the land ... 2Chr 6:28 7458
might buy corn, because of the *d* ... Neh 5:3 7458
came to Jeremiah concerning the *d* ... Jer 14:1 1226
Now there came a *d* over all the ... Acts 7:11 *3042*
great *d* throughout all the world ... Acts 11:28 *3042*

DEATH {376}
Let me not see the *d* of the child ... Gen 21:16 4194
comforted after his mother's *d* ... Gen 24:67
to pass after the *d* of Abraham ... Gen 25:11 4194
his wife shall surely be put to *d* ... Gen 26:11 4191
them after the *d* of Abraham ... Gen 26:18 4194
old, I know not the day of my *d* ... Gen 27:2 4194
thee before the LORD before my *d* ... Gen 27:7 4194
he may bless thee before his *d* ... Gen 27:10 4194
may take away from me this *d* only ... Ex 10:17 4194
mount shall be surely put to *d* ... Ex 19:12 4191

Context	Reference	Number
he die, shall be surely put to *d*	Ex 21:12	4191
mother, shall be surely put to *d*	Ex 21:15	4191
hand, he shall surely be put to *d*	Ex 21:16	4191
mother, shall surely be put to *d*	Ex 21:17	4191
his owner also shall be put to *d*	Ex 21:29	4191
a beast shall surely be put to *d*	Ex 22:19	4191
it shall surely be put to *d*	Ex 31:14	4191
day, he shall surely be put to *d*	Ex 31:15	4191
work therein shall be put to *d*	Ex 35:2	4191
the *d* of the two sons of Aaron	Lev 16:1	4194
they shall not be put to *d*	Lev 19:20	4191
he shall surely be put to *d*	Lev 20:2	4191
mother shall be surely put to *d*	Lev 20:9	4191
shall surely be put to *d*	Lev 20:10	4191
of them shall surely be put to *d*	Lev 20:11	4191
of them shall surely be put to *d*	Lev 20:12	4191
they shall surely be put to *d*	Lev 20:13	4191
he shall surely be put to *d*	Lev 20:15	4191
they shall surely be put to *d*	Lev 20:16	4191
wizard, shall surely be put to *d*	Lev 20:27	4191
LORD, he shall surely be put to *d*	Lev 24:16	4191
of the LORD, shall be put to *d*	Lev 24:16	4191
any man shall surely be put to *d*	Lev 24:17	4191
a man, he shall be put to *d*	Lev 24:21	4191
but shall surely be put to *d*	Lev 27:29	4191
cometh nigh shall be put to *d*	Num 1:51	4191
cometh nigh shall be put to *d*	Num 3:10	4191
cometh nigh shall be put to *d*	Num 3:38	4191
The man shall be surely put to *d*	Num 15:35	4191
men die the common *d* of all men	Num 16:29	4194
cometh nigh shall be put to *d*	Num 18:7	4191
Let me die the *d* of the righteous	Num 23:10	4194
murderer shall surely be put to *d*	Num 35:16	4191
murderer shall surely be put to *d*	Num 35:17	4191
murderer shall surely be put to *d*	Num 35:18	4191
him shall surely be put to *d*	Num 35:21	4191
it unto the *d* of the high priest	Num 35:25	4194
until the *d* of the high priest	Num 35:28	4194
but after the *d* of the high	Num 35:28	4194
to *d* by the mouth of witnesses	Num 35:30	7523
a murderer, which is guilty of *d*	Num 35:31	4191
but he shall be surely put to *d*	Num 35:31	4191
until the *d* of the priest	Num 35:32	4194
of dreams, shall be put to *d*	Deut 13:5	4191
be first upon him to put him to *d*	Deut 13:9	4191
is worthy of *d* be put to *d*	Deut 17:6	4191
witness he shall not be put to *d*	Deut 17:6	4191
be first upon him to put him to *d*	Deut 17:7	4191
whereas he was not worthy of *d*	Deut 19:6	4194
have committed a sin worthy of *d*	Deut 21:22	4194
and he be to be put to *d*	Deut 21:22	4191
in the damsel no sin worthy of *d*	Deut 22:26	4194
not be put to *d* for the children	Deut 24:16	4191
be put to *d* for the fathers	Deut 24:16	4191
shall be put to *d* for his own sin	Deut 24:16	4191
thee this day life and good, and *d*	Deut 30:15	4194
I have set before you life and *d*	Deut 30:19	4194
and how much more after my *d*	Deut 31:27	4194
my *d* ye will utterly corrupt	Deut 31:29	4194
children of Israel before his *d*	Deut 33:1	4194
Now after the *d* of Moses the	Josh 1:1	4194
him, he shall be put to *d*	Josh 1:18	4191
have, and deliver our lives from *d*	Josh 2:13	4194
until the *d* of the high priest	Josh 20:6	4194
Now after the *d* of Joshua it came	Judg 1:1	4194
jeoparded their lives unto the *d*	Judg 5:18	4191
let him be put to *d* whilst it is	Judg 6:31	4191
from the womb to the day of his *d*	Judg 13:7	4194
so that his soul was vexed unto *d*	Judg 16:16	4191
d were more than they which he	Judg 16:30	4194
Gibeah, that we may put them to *d*	Judg 20:13	4191
He shall surely be put to *d*	Judg 21:5	4191
also, if ought but *d* part thee	Ruth 1:17	4194
law since the *d* of thine husband	Ruth 2:11	4194
about the time of her *d* the women	1Sa 4:20	4191
men, that we may put them to *d*	1Sa 11:12	4191
not a man be put to *d* this day	1Sa 11:13	4191
the bitterness of *d* is past	1Sa 15:32	4194
see Saul until the day of his *d*	1Sa 15:35	4194
is but a step between me and *d*	1Sa 20:3	4194
I have occasioned the *d* of all	1Sa 22:22	
came to pass after the *d* of Saul	2Sa 1:1	4194
in their *d* they were not divided	2Sa 1:23	4194
no child unto the day of her *d*	2Sa 6:23	4194
two lines measured he to put to *d*	2Sa 8:2	4191
shall be, whether in *d* or life	2Sa 15:21	4194
not Shimei be put to *d* for this	2Sa 19:21	4191
be put to *d* this day in Israel	2Sa 19:22	4191
shut up unto the day of their *d*	2Sa 20:3	4191
were put to *d* in the days of	2Sa 21:9	4191
When the waves of *d* compassed me	2Sa 22:5	4194
the snares of *d* prevented me	2Sa 22:6	4194
not put thee to *d* with the sword	1Kin 2:8	4191
shall be put to *d* this day	1Kin 2:24	4191
for thou art worthy of *d*	1Kin 2:26	4194
not at this time put thee to *d*	1Kin 2:26	4191
in Egypt until the *d* of Solomon	1Kin 11:40	4194
Israel after the *d* of Ahab	2Kin 1:1	4194
thence any more *d* or barren land	2Kin 2:21	4194
man of God, there is *d* in the pot	2Kin 4:40	4194
not be put to *d* for the children	2Kin 14:6	4191
be put to *d* for the fathers	2Kin 14:6	4191
shall be put to *d* for his own sin	2Kin 14:6	4191
king of Judah lived after the *d*	2Kin 14:17	4194
was a leper unto the day of his *d*	2Kin 15:5	4194
days was Hezekiah sick unto *d*	2Kin 20:1	4191
prepared abundantly before his *d*	1Chr 22:5	4194
God of Israel should be put to *d*	2Chr 15:13	4191
after the *d* of his father to his	2Chr 22:4	4194
the house, he shall be put to *d*	2Chr 23:7	4191
Now after the *d* of Jehoiada came	2Chr 24:17	4194
d of Joash son of Jehoahaz king	2Chr 25:25	4194
was a leper unto the day of his *d*	2Chr 26:21	4194
days Hezekiah was sick to the *d*	2Chr 32:24	4191
Jerusalem did him honour at his *d*	2Chr 32:33	4194
upon him, whether it be unto *d*	Ezr 7:26	4193
is one law of his to put him to *d*	Est 4:11	4191
and the shadow of *d* stain it	Job 3:5	6757
Which long for *d*, but it cometh	Job 3:21	4194
he shall redeem thee from *d*	Job 5:20	4194
and *d* rather than my life	Job 7:15	4194
of darkness and the shadow of *d*	Job 10:21	6757
and of the shadow of *d*, without	Job 10:22	6757
out to light the shadow of *d*	Job 12:22	6757
on my eyelids is the shadow of *d*	Job 16:16	6757
even the firstborn of *d* shall	Job 18:13	4194
to them even as the shadow of *d*	Job 24:17	6757
in the terrors of the shadow of *d*	Job 24:17	6757
of him shall be buried in *d*	Job 27:15	4194
of darkness, and the shadow of *d*	Job 28:3	6757
d say, We have heard the fame	Job 28:22	4194
know that thou wilt bring me to *d*	Job 30:23	4194
is no darkness, nor shadow of *d*	Job 34:22	6757
Have the gates of *d* been opened	Job 38:17	4194
seen the doors of the shadow of *d*	Job 38:17	6757
For in *d* there is no remembrance	Ps 6:5	4194
for him the instruments of *d*	Ps 7:13	4194
liftest me up from the gates of *d*	Ps 9:13	4194
eyes, lest I sleep the sleep of *d*	Ps 13:3	4194
The sorrows of *d* compassed me	Ps 18:4	4194
the snares of *d* prevented me	Ps 18:5	4194
brought me into the dust of *d*	Ps 22:15	4194
the valley of the shadow of *d*	Ps 23:4	6757
To deliver their soul from *d*	Ps 33:19	4194
covered us with the shadow of *d*	Ps 44:19	6757
he will be our guide even unto *d*	Ps 48:14	4192
d shall feed on them	Ps 49:14	4194
the terrors of *d* are fallen upon	Ps 55:4	4194
Let *d* seize upon them, and let	Ps 55:15	4194
hast delivered my soul from *d*	Ps 56:13	4194
the Lord belong the issues from *d*	Ps 68:20	4194
For there are no bands in their *d*	Ps 73:4	4194
he spared not their soul from *d*	Ps 78:50	4194
that liveth, and shall not see *d*	Ps 89:48	4194
those that are appointed to *d*	Ps 102:20	8546
in darkness and in the shadow of *d*	Ps 107:10	6757
of darkness and the shadow of *d*	Ps 107:14	6757
draw near unto the gates of *d*	Ps 107:18	4194
The sorrows of *d* compassed me	Ps 116:3	4194
hast delivered my soul from *d*	Ps 116:8	4194
the LORD is the *d* of his saints	Ps 116:15	4194
he hath not given me over unto *d*	Ps 118:18	4194
For her house inclineth unto *d*	Prov 2:18	4194
Her feet go down to *d*	Prov 5:5	4194
going down to the chambers of *d*	Prov 7:27	4194
all they that hate me love *d*	Prov 8:36	4194
righteousness delivereth from *d*	Prov 10:2	4194
righteousness delivereth from *d*	Prov 11:4	4194
evil pursueth it to his own *d*	Prov 11:19	4194
the pathway thereof there is no *d*	Prov 12:28	4194
to depart from the snares of *d*	Prov 13:14	4194
the end thereof are the ways of *d*	Prov 14:12	4194
to depart from the snares of *d*	Prov 14:27	4194
the righteous hath hope in his *d*	Prov 14:32	4194
of a king is as messengers of *d*	Prov 16:14	4194
the end thereof are the ways of *d*	Prov 16:25	4194
D and life are in the power of the	Prov 18:21	4194
to and fro of them that seek *d*	Prov 21:6	4194
them that are drawn unto *d*	Prov 24:11	4194
casteth firebrands, arrows, and *d*	Prov 26:18	4194
the day of *d* than the day of	Eccl 7:1	4194
find more bitter than *d* the woman	Eccl 7:26	4194
hath he power in the day of *d*	Eccl 8:8	4194
for love is strong as *d*	Song 8:6	4194
in the land of the shadow of *d*	Is 9:2	6757
He will swallow up *d* in victory	Is 25:8	4194
We have made a covenant with *d*	Is 28:15	4194
your covenant with *d* shall be	Is 28:18	4194
days was Hezekiah sick unto *d*	Is 38:1	4191
thee, *d* can not celebrate thee	Is 38:18	4194
wicked, and with the rich in his *d*	Is 53:9	4194
hath poured out his soul unto *d*	Is 53:12	4194
of drought, and of the shadow of *d*	Jer 2:6	6757
d shall be chosen rather than	Jer 8:3	4194
For *d* is come up into our windows	Jer 9:21	4194
he turn it into the shadow of *d*	Jer 13:16	6757
Such as are for *d*, to *d*	Jer 15:2	4194
Such as are for *d*, to *d*	Jer 15:2	4194
and let their men be put to *d*	Jer 18:21	4194
the way of life, and the way of *d*	Jer 21:8	4194
certain, that if ye put me to *d*	Jer 26:15	4191
and all Judah put him at all to *d*	Jer 26:19	4191
the king sought to put him to *d*	Jer 26:21	4191
of the people to put him to *d*	Jer 26:24	4191
thee, let this man be put to *d*	Jer 38:4	4191
wilt thou not surely put me to *d*	Jer 38:15	4191
soul, I will not put thee to *d*	Jer 38:16	4191
us, and we will not put thee to *d*	Jer 38:25	4191
that they might put us to *d*	Jer 43:3	4191
such as are for *d* to *d*	Jer 43:11	4194
in prison till the day of his *d*	Jer 52:11	4194
put them to *d* in Riblah in the	Jer 52:27	4191
a portion until the day of his *d*	Jer 52:34	4194
bereaveth, at home there is as *d*	Lam 1:20	4194
in the *d* of him that dieth	Eze 18:32	4194
for they are all delivered unto *d*	Eze 31:14	4194
pleasure in the *d* of the wicked	Eze 33:11	4194
I will redeem them from *d*	Hos 13:14	4194
O *d*, I will be thy plagues	Hos 13:14	4194
the shadow of *d* into the morning	Amos 5:8	6757
do well to be angry, even unto *d*	Jonah 4:9	4194
his desire as hell, and is as *d*	Hab 2:5	4194
And was there until the *d* of Herod	Mt 2:15	*5054*
shadow of *d* light is sprung up	Mt 4:16	*2288*
shall deliver up the brother to *d*	Mt 10:21	*2288*
and cause them to be put to *d*	Mt 10:21	*2289*
when he would have put him to *d*	Mt 14:5	*615*
or mother, let him die the *d*	Mt 15:4	*2288*
here, which shall not taste of *d*	Mt 16:28	*2288*
and they shall condemn him to *d*	Mt 20:18	*2288*
exceeding sorrowful, even unto *d*	Mt 26:38	*2288*
against Jesus, to put him to *d*	Mt 26:59	*2289*
and said, He is guilty of *d*	Mt 26:66	*2288*
against Jesus to put him to *d*	Mt 27:1	*2289*
daughter lieth at the point of *d*	Mk 5:23	*2079*
or mother, let him die the *d*	Mk 7:10	*2288*
here, which shall not taste of *d*	Mk 9:1	*2288*
and they shall condemn him to *d*	Mk 10:33	*2288*
shall betray the brother to *d*	Mk 13:12	*2288*
shall cause them to be put to *d*	Mk 13:12	*2289*
him by craft, and put him to *d*	Mk 14:1	*615*
is exceeding sorrowful unto *d*	Mk 14:34	*2288*
against Jesus to put him to *d*	Mk 14:55	*2289*
condemned him to be guilty of *d*	Mk 14:64	*2288*
in darkness and in the shadow of *d*	Lk 1:79	*2288*
Ghost, that he should not see *d*	Lk 2:26	*2288*
here, which shall not taste of *d*	Lk 9:27	*2288*
scourge him, and put him to *d*	Lk 18:33	*615*
shall they cause to be put to *d*	Lk 21:16	*2289*
thee, both into prison, and to *d*	Lk 22:33	*2288*
worthy of *d* is done unto him	Lk 23:15	*2288*
I have found no cause of *d* in him	Lk 23:22	*2288*
led with him to be put to *d*	Lk 23:32	*337*
him to be condemned to *d*, and have	Lk 24:20	*2288*
for he was at the point of *d*	Jn 4:47	*599*
but is passed from *d* unto life	Jn 5:24	*2288*
my saying, he shall never see *d*	Jn 8:51	*2288*
saying, he shall never taste of *d*	Jn 8:52	*2288*
said, This sickness is not unto *d*	Jn 11:4	*2288*
Howbeit Jesus spake of his *d*	Jn 11:13	*2288*
together for to put him to *d*	Jn 11:53	*615*
they might put Lazarus also to *d*	Jn 12:10	*615*
signifying what *d* he should die	Jn 12:33	*2288*
lawful for us to put any man to *d*	Jn 18:31	*615*
signifying what *d* he should die	Jn 18:32	*2288*
signifying by what *d* he should	Jn 21:19	*2288*
up, having loosed the pains of *d*	Acts 2:24	*2288*
And Saul was consenting unto his *d*	Acts 8:1	*336*
that they should be put to *d*	Acts 12:19	*520*
they found no cause of *d* in him	Acts 13:28	*2288*
I persecuted this way unto the *d*	Acts 22:4	*2288*
by, and consenting unto his *d*	Acts 22:20	*336*
charge worthy of *d* or of bonds	Acts 23:29	*336*
committed any thing worthy of *d*	Acts 25:11	*336*
had committed nothing worthy of *d*	Acts 25:25	*336*
and when they were put to *d*	Acts 26:10	*337*
nothing worthy of *d* or of bonds	Acts 26:31	*2288*
there was no cause of *d* in me	Acts 28:18	*2288*
such things are worthy of *d*	Rom 1:32	*2288*
to God by the *d* of his Son	Rom 5:10	*2288*
into the world, and *d* by sin	Rom 5:12	*2288*
so *d* passed upon all men, for	Rom 5:12	*2288*
Nevertheless *d* reigned from Adam	Rom 5:14	*2288*
man's offence *d* reigned by one	Rom 5:17	*2288*
That as sin hath reigned unto *d*	Rom 5:21	*2288*
Christ were baptized into his *d*	Rom 6:3	*2288*
buried with him by baptism into *d*	Rom 6:4	*2288*
together in the likeness of his *d*	Rom 6:5	*2288*
d hath no more dominion over him	Rom 6:9	*2288*
whether of sin unto *d*, or of	Rom 6:16	*2288*
for the end of those things is *d*	Rom 6:21	*2288*
For the wages of sin is *d*	Rom 6:23	*2288*
to bring forth fruit unto *d*	Rom 7:5	*2288*
to life, I found to be unto *d*	Rom 7:10	*2288*
that which is good made *d* unto me	Rom 7:13	*2288*
working *d* in me by that which is	Rom 7:13	*2288*
me from the body of this *d*	Rom 7:24	*2288*
me free from the law of sin and *d*	Rom 8:2	*2288*
For to be carnally minded is *d*	Rom 8:6	*2288*
I am persuaded, that neither *d*	Rom 8:38	*2288*
or the world, or life, or *d*	1Cor 3:22	*2288*
last, as it were appointed to *d*	1Cor 4:9	*1935*
do shew the Lord's *d* till he come	1Cor 11:26	*2288*
For since by man came *d*, by man	1Cor 15:21	*2288*
that shall be destroyed is *d*	1Cor 15:26	*2288*
D is swallowed up in victory	1Cor 15:54	*2288*
O *d*, where is thy sting	1Cor 15:55	*2288*
The sting of *d* is sin	1Cor 15:56	*2288*
the sentence of *d* in ourselves	2Cor 1:9	*2288*
delivered us from so great a *d*	2Cor 1:10	*2288*
we are the savour of *d* unto *d*	2Cor 2:16	*2288*
we are the savour of *d* unto *d*	2Cor 2:16	*2288*
But if the ministration of *d*	2Cor 3:7	*2288*
delivered unto *d* for Jesus' sake	2Cor 4:11	*2288*
So then *d* worketh in us, but life	2Cor 4:12	*2288*
the sorrow of the world worketh *d*	2Cor 7:10	*2288*
whether it be by life, or by *d*	Phil 1:20	*2288*
and became obedient unto *d*	Phil 2:8	*2288*
even the *d* of the cross	Phil 2:8	*2288*
indeed he was sick nigh unto *d*	Phil 2:27	*2288*
work of Christ he was nigh unto *d*	Phil 2:30	*2288*
being made conformable unto his *d*	Phil 3:10	*2288*
the body of his flesh through *d*	Col 1:22	*2288*
Christ, who hath abolished *d*	2Ti 1:10	*2288*

D

the angels for the suffering of *d* ... Heb 2:9 *2288*
God should taste *d* for every man ... Heb 2:9 *2288*
that through *d* he might destroy ... Heb 2:14 *2288*
him that had the power of *d* ... Heb 2:14 *2288*
them who through fear of *d* were ... Heb 2:15 *2288*
that was able to save him from *d* ... Heb 5:7 *2288*
to continue by reason of *d* ... Heb 7:23 *2288*
new testament, that by means of *d* ... Heb 9:15 *2288*
be the *d* of the testator ... Heb 9:16 *2288*
that he should not see *d* ... Heb 11:5 *2288*
it is finished, bringeth forth *d* ... Jas 1:15 *2288*
his way shall save a soul from *d* ... Jas 5:20 *2288*
God, being put to *d* in the flesh ... 1Pet 3:18 *2289*
we have passed from *d* unto life ... 1Jn 3:14 *2288*
not his brother abideth in *d* ... 1Jn 3:14 *2288*
sin a sin which is not unto *d* ... 1Jn 5:16 *2288*
life for them that sin not unto *d* ... 1Jn 5:16 *2288*
There is a sin unto *d* ... 1Jn 5:16 *2288*
and there is a sin not unto *d* ... 1Jn 5:17 *2288*
and have the keys of hell and of *d* ... Rev 1:18 *2288*
be thou faithful unto *d*, and I ... Rev 2:10 *2288*
shall not be hurt of the second *d* ... Rev 2:11 *2288*
I will kill her children with *d* ... Rev 2:23 *2288*
and his name that sat on him was *D* ... Rev 6:8 *2288*
sword, and with hunger, and with *d* ... Rev 6:8 *2288*
And in those days shall men seek *d* ... Rev 9:6 *2288*
to die, and *d* shall flee from them ... Rev 9:6 *2288*
loved not their lives unto the *d* ... Rev 12:11 *2288*
his heads as it were wounded to *d* ... Rev 13:3 *2288*
her plagues come in one day, *d* ... Rev 18:8 *2288*
such the second *d* hath no power ... Rev 20:6 *2288*
and *d* and hell delivered up the ... Rev 20:13 *2288*
And *d* and hell were cast into the ... Rev 20:14 *2288*
This is the second *d* ... Rev 20:14 *2288*
and there shall be no more *d* ... Rev 21:4 *2288*
which is the second *d* ... Rev 21:8 *2288*

DEATHS {4}
They shall die of grievous *d* ... Jer 16:4 4463
thou shalt die the *d* of them that ... Eze 28:8 4463
Thou shalt die the *d* of the ... Eze 28:10 4194
prisons more frequent, in *d* oft ... 2Cor 11:23 *2288*

DEBASE {1}
didst *d* thyself even unto hell ... Is 57:9 8213

DEBATE {4}
D thy cause with thy neighbour ... Prov 25:9 7378
forth, thou wilt *d* with it ... Is 27:8 7378
Behold, ye fast for strife and *d* ... Is 58:4 4683
full of envy, murder, *d*, deceit, ... Rom 1:29 *2054*

DEBATES {1}
lest there be *d*, envyings, wraths ... 2Cor 12:20 *2054*

DEBIR *(de'-bur)* {14} See KIRJATH-SANNAH, KIRJATH-SEPHER.
1. An Amorite king.
unto *D* king of Eglon, saying, ... Josh 10:3 1688
2. A city in Judah.
and all Israel with him, to *D* ... Josh 10:38 1688
done to Hebron, so he did to *D* ... Josh 10:39 1688
mountains, from Hebron, from *D* ... Josh 11:21 1688
The king of *D*, one ... Josh 12:13 1688
toward *D* from the valley of Achor ... Josh 15:7 1688
up thence to the inhabitants of *D* ... Josh 15:15 1688
and the name of *D* before was ... Josh 15:15 1688
and Kirjath-sannah, which is *D* ... Josh 15:49 1688
suburbs, and *D* with her suburbs ... Josh 21:15 1688
went against the inhabitants of *D* ... Judg 1:11 1688
and the name of *D* before was ... Judg 1:11 1688
her suburbs, *D* with her suburbs, ... 1Chr 6:58 1688
3. The boundary of Gad.
Mahanaim unto the border of *D* ... Josh 13:26 1688

DEBORAH *(deb'-o-rah)* {10}
1. Rebekah's nurse.
But *D* Rebekah's nurse died, and ... Gen 35:8 1683
2. A judge of Israel.
And *D*, a prophetess, the wife of ... Judg 4:4 1683
the palm tree of *D* between Ramah ... Judg 4:5 1683
D arose, and went with Barak to ... Judg 4:9 1683
and *D* went up with him ... Judg 4:10 1683
And *D* said unto Barak, Up ... Judg 4:14 1683
Then sang *D* and Barak the son of ... Judg 5:1 1683
in Israel, until that I *D* arose ... Judg 5:7 1683
Awake, awake, *D* ... Judg 5:12 1683
princes of Issachar were with *D* ... Judg 5:15 1683

DEBT {7}
and every one that was in *d* ... 1Sa 22:2 5378
Go, sell the oil, and pay thy *d* ... 2Kin 4:7 5386
year, and the exaction of every *d* ... Neh 10:31 3027
loosed him, and forgave him the *d* ... Mt 18:27 *1156*
prison, till he should pay the *d* ... Mt 18:30 *3784*
I forgave thee all that *d* ... Mt 18:32 *3782*
not reckoned of grace, but of *d* ... Rom 4:4 *3783*

DEBTOR {4}
hath restored to the *d* his pledge ... Eze 18:7 2326
the gold of the temple, he is a *d* ... Mt 23:16 *3784*
I am *d* both to the Greeks, and to ... Rom 1:14 *3781*
that he is a *d* to do the whole ... Gal 5:3 *3781*

DEBTORS {5}
us our debts, as we forgive our *d* ... Mt 6:12 *3781*
certain creditor which had two *d* ... Lk 7:41 *5533*
one of his lord's *d* unto him ... Lk 16:5 *5533*
Therefore, brethren, we are *d* ... Rom 8:12 *3781*
and their *d* they are ... Rom 15:27 *3781*

DEBTS {2}
of them that are sureties for *d* ... Prov 22:26 4859
And forgive us our *d*, as we ... Mt 6:12 *3783*

DECAPOLIS *(de-cap'-o-lis)* {3} *A district east of the Jordan River.*
of people from Galilee, and from *D* ... Mt 4:25 *1179*
began to publish in *D* how great ... Mk 5:20 *1179*
the midst of the coasts of *D* ... Mk 7:31 *1179*

DECAY {1}
poor, and fallen in *d* with thee ... Lev 25:35 4131

DECAYED {2}
of the bearers of burdens is *d* ... Neh 4:10 3782
raise up the *d* places thereof ... Is 44:26 2723

DECAYETH {3}
fail from the sea, and the flood *d* ... Job 14:11 2717
much slothfulness the building *d* ... Eccl 10:18 4355
Now that which *d* and waxeth old is ... Heb 8:13 *3822*

DECEASE {2}
spake of his *d* which he should ... Lk 9:31 *1841*
that ye may be able after my *d* to ... 2Pet 1:15 *1841*

DECEASED {2}
they are *d*, they shall not rise ... Is 26:14 7496
when he had married a wife, *d* ... Mt 22:25 *5053*

DECEIT {34}
and their belly prepareth *d* ... Job 15:35 4820
wickedness, nor my tongue utter *d* ... Job 27:4 7423
or if my foot hath hasted to *d* ... Job 31:5 4820
His mouth is full of cursing and *d* ... Ps 10:7 4820
of his mouth are iniquity and *d* ... Ps 36:3 4820
to evil, and thy tongue frameth *d* ... Ps 50:19 4820
d and guile depart not from her ... Ps 55:11 8496
He shall redeem their soul from *d* ... Ps 72:14 8496
He that worketh *d* shall not dwell ... Ps 101:7 7423
for their *d* is falsehood ... Ps 119:118 8649
the counsels of the wicked are *d* ... Prov 12:5 4820
but a false witness *d* ... Prov 12:17 4820
D is in the heart of them that ... Prov 12:20 4820
but the folly of fools is *d* ... Prov 14:8 4820
Bread of *d* is sweet to a man ... Prov 20:17 8267
lips, and layeth up *d* within him ... Prov 26:24 4820
Whose hatred is covered by *d* ... Prov 26:26 4860
neither was any *d* in his mouth ... Is 53:9 4820
so are their houses full of *d* ... Jer 5:27 4820
they hold fast *d*, they refuse to ... Jer 8:5 8649
habitation is in the midst of *d* ... Jer 9:6 4820
through *d* they refuse to know me, ... Jer 9:6 4820
it speaketh *d* ... Jer 9:8 4820
nought, and the *d* of their heart ... Jer 14:14 8649
of the *d* of their own heart ... Jer 23:26 8649
and the house of Israel with *d* ... Hos 11:12 4820
the balances of *d* are in his hand ... Hos 12:7 4820
and falsifying the balances by *d* ... Amos 8:5 4820
houses with violence and *d* ... Zeph 1:9 4820
covetousness, wickedness, *d* ... Mk 7:22 *1388*
full of envy, murder, debate, *d* ... Rom 1:29 *1388*
their tongues they have used *d* ... Rom 3:13 *1387*
you through philosophy and vain *d* ... Col 2:8 *539*
For our exhortation was not of *d* ... 1Th 2:3 *4106*

DECEITFUL {21}
will abhor the bloody and *d* man ... Ps 5:6 4820
but they devise *d* matters against ... Ps 35:20 4820
O deliver me from the *d* and unjust ... Ps 43:1 4820
devouring words, O thou *d* tongue ... Ps 52:4 4820
d men shall not live out half ... Ps 55:23 4820
were turned aside like a *d* bow ... Ps 78:57 7423
the mouth of the *d* are opened ... Ps 109:2 4820
lying lips, and from a *d* tongue ... Ps 120:2 7423
The wicked worketh a *d* work ... Prov 11:18 8267
but a *d* witness speaketh lies ... Prov 14:25 4820
for they are *d* meat ... Prov 23:3 3577
but the kisses of an enemy are *d* ... Prov 27:6 6280
poor and the *d* man meet together ... Prov 29:13 8501
Favour is *d*, and beauty is vain ... Prov 31:30 8267
The heart is *d* above all things, ... Jer 17:9 6121
they are like a *d* bow ... Hos 7:16 7423
and with the bag of *d* weights ... Mic 6:11 4820
their tongue is *d* in their mouth ... Mic 6:12 7423
neither shall a *d* tongue be found ... Zeph 3:13 8649
apostles, *d* workers, transforming ... 2Cor 11:13 *1386*
corrupt according to the *d* lusts ... Eph 4:22 *539*

DECEITFULLY {11}
Shechem and Hamor his father *d* ... Gen 34:13 4820
but let not Pharaoh deal *d* any ... Ex 8:29 2048
seeing he hath dealt *d* with her ... Ex 21:8 898
the thing which he hath *d* gotten ... Lev 6:4 6231
brethren have dealt *d* as a brook ... Job 6:15 898
and talk *d* for him ... Job 13:7 7423
his soul unto vanity, nor sworn *d* ... Ps 24:4 4820
like a sharp rasor, working *d* ... Ps 52:2 7423
that doeth the work of the LORD *d* ... Jer 48:10 7423
made with him he shall work *d* ... Dan 11:23 4820
nor handling the word of God *d* ... 2Cor 4:2 *1389*

DECEITFULNESS {3}
the *d* of riches, choke the word ... Mt 13:22 *539*
the *d* of riches, and the lusts of ... Mk 4:19 *539*
be hardened through the *d* of sin ... Heb 3:13 *539*

DECEITS {2}
imagine *d* all the day long ... Ps 38:12 4820
unto us smooth things, prophesy *d* ... Is 30:10 4123

DECEIVABLENESS {1}
with all *d* of unrighteousness in ... 2Th 2:10 *539*

DECEIVE {27}
of Ner, that he came to *d* thee ... 2Sa 3:25 6601
did I not say, Do not *d* me ... 2Kin 4:28 7952
the king, Let not Hezekiah *d* you ... 2Kin 18:29 5377
God in whom thou trustest *d* thee ... 2Kin 19:10 5377
therefore let not Hezekiah *d* you ... 2Chr 32:15 5377
and *d* not with thy lips ... Prov 24:28 6601
the king, Let not Hezekiah *d* you ... Is 36:14 5377
d thee, saying, Jerusalem shall ... Is 37:10 5377
they will *d* every one his ... Jer 9:5 2048
d you, neither hearken to your ... Jer 29:8 5377
D not yourselves, saying, The ... Jer 37:9 5377
they wear a rough garment to *d* ... Zec 13:4 3884
them, Take heed that no man *d* you ... Mt 24:4 *4105*
and shall *d* many ... Mt 24:5 *4105*
shall rise, and shall *d* many ... Mt 24:11 *4105*
they shall *d* the very elect ... Mt 24:24 *4105*
say, Take heed lest any man *d* you ... Mk 13:5 *4105*
and shall *d* many ... Mk 13:6 *4105*
fair speeches *d* the hearts of the ... Rom 16:18 *1818*
Let no man *d* himself ... 1Cor 3:18 *1818*
whereby they lie in wait to *d* ... Eph 4:14 *4106*
Let no man *d* you with vain words ... Eph 5:6 *538*
Let no man *d* you by any means ... 2Th 2:3 *1818*
we *d* ourselves, and the truth is ... 1Jn 1:8 *4105*
Little children, let no man *d* you ... 1Jn 3:7 *4105*
that he should *d* the nations no ... Rev 20:3 *4105*
shall go out to *d* the nations ... Rev 20:8 *4105*

DECEIVED {35}
And your father hath *d* me, and ... Gen 31:7 2048
violence, or hath *d* his neighbour ... Lev 6:2 6231
that your heart be not *d* ... Deut 11:16 6601
Michal, Why hast thou *d* me so ... 1Sa 19:17 7411
Saul, saying, Why hast thou *d* me ... 1Sa 28:12 7411
My lord, O king, my servant *d* me ... 2Sa 19:26 7411
the *d* and the deceiver are his ... Job 12:16 7683
not him that is *d* trust in vanity ... Job 15:31 8582
mine heart have been *d* by a woman ... Job 31:9 6601
whosoever is *d* thereby is not ... Prov 20:1 7686
fools, the princes of Noph are *d* ... Is 19:13 5377
a *d* heart hath turned him aside, ... Is 44:20 2048
thou hast greatly *d* this people ... Jer 4:10 5377
O LORD, thou hast *d* me, and I was ... Jer 20:7 6601
thou hast *d* me, and I was *d* ... Jer 20:7 6601
Thy terribleness hath *d* thee ... Jer 49:16 5377
for my lovers, but they *d* me ... Lam 1:19 7411
if the prophet be *d* when he hath ... Eze 14:9 6601
I the LORD have *d* that prophet ... Eze 14:9 6601
pride of thine heart hath *d* thee ... Obad 3 5377
at peace with thee have *d* thee ... Obad 7 5377
said, Take heed that ye be not *d* ... Lk 21:8 *4105*
them the Pharisees, Are ye also *d* ... Jn 7:47 *4105*
d me, and by it slew me ... Rom 7:11 *1818*
Be not *d*: neither fornicators ... 1Cor 6:9 *4105*
Be not *d*: evil communications ... 1Cor 15:33 *4105*
Be not *d*; God is not ... Gal 6:7 *4105*
And Adam was not *d*, but the woman ... 1Ti 2:14 *538*
but the woman being *d* was in the ... 1Ti 2:14 *538*
and worse, deceiving, and being *d* ... 2Ti 3:13 *4105*
sometimes foolish, disobedient, *d* ... Titus 3:3 *4105*
thy sorceries were all nations *d* ... Rev 18:23 *4105*
with which he *d* them that had ... Rev 19:20 *4105*
the devil that *d* them was cast ... Rev 20:10 *4105*

DECEIVER {5}
me, and I shall seem to him as a *d* ... Gen 27:12 8591
the deceived and the *d* are his ... Job 12:16 7686
But cursed be the *d*, which hath ... Mal 1:14 5230
Sir, we remember that that *d* said ... Mt 27:63 *4108*
This is a *d* and an antichrist ... 2Jn 7 *4108*

DECEIVERS {3}
as *d*, and yet true ... 2Cor 6:8 *4108*
many unruly and vain talkers and *d* ... Titus 1:10 *5423*
For many *d* are entered into the ... 2Jn 7 *4108*

DECEIVETH {6}
is the man that *d* his neighbour ... Prov 26:19 7411
but he *d* the people ... Jn 7:12 *4105*
when he is nothing, he *d* himself ... Gal 6:3 *5422*
but *d* his own heart, this man's ... Jas 1:26 *538*
and Satan, which *d* the whole world ... Rev 12:9 *4105*
d them that dwell on the earth by ... Rev 13:14 *4105*

DECEIVING {2}
shall wax worse and worse, *d* ... 2Ti 3:13 *4105*
hearers only, *d* your own selves ... Jas 1:22 *3884*

DECEIVINGS {1}
own *d* while they feast with you ... 2Pet 2:13 *539*

DECENTLY {1}
Let all things be done *d* and in ... 1Cor 14:40 *2156*

DECIDED {1}
thyself hast *d* it ... 1Kin 20:40 2782

DECISION {2}
multitudes in the valley of *d* ... Joel 3:14 2742
LORD is near in the valley of *d* ... Joel 3:14 2742

DECK {2}
D thyself now with majesty and ... Job 40:10 5710
They *d* it with silver and with ... Jer 10:4 3302

DECKED {6}
I have *d* my bed with coverings of ... Prov 7:16 7234
I *d* thee also with ornaments, and ... Eze 16:11 5710
Thus wast thou *d* with gold ... Eze 16:13 5710
she *d* herself with her earrings ... Hos 2:13 5710
d with gold and precious stones and ... Rev 17:4 *5558*
d with gold, and precious stones, ... Rev 18:16 *5558*

DECKEDST {2}
d thy high places with divers ... Eze 16:16 6213
d thyself with ornaments, ... Eze 23:40 5710

DECKEST {1}
though thou *d* thee with ornaments ... Jer 4:30 5710

DECKETH {1}
as a bridegroom *d* himself with ... Is 61:10 3547

D

DECLARATION {4}
the *d* of the greatness of ... Est 10:2 6575
my speech, and my *d* with your ears ... Job 13:17 262
d of those things which are most ... Lk 1:1 *1335*
Lord, and *d* of your ready mind ... 2Cor 8:19

DECLARE {95}
was none that could *d* it to me ... Gen 41:24 5046
Moab, began Moses to *d* this law ... Deut 1:5 874
shall *d* his cause in the ears of ... Josh 20:4 1696
if ye can certainly *d* it me ... Judg 14:12 5046
But if ye cannot *d* it me, then ... Judg 14:13 5046
that he may *d* unto us the riddle, ... Judg 14:15 5046
the words of the prophets *d* good ... 1Kin 22:13
D his glory among the heathen ... 1Chr 16:24 5608
d good to the king with one ... 2Chr 18:12
to *d* it unto her, and to charge ... Est 4:8 5046
of the sea shall *d* unto thee ... Job 12:8 5608
that which I have seen I will *d* ... Job 15:17 5608
Who shall *d* his way to his face ... Job 21:31 5046
Then did he see it, and *d* it ... Job 28:27 5608
I would *d* unto him the number of ... Job 31:37 5046
d, if thou hast understanding ... Job 38:4 5046
d if thou knowest it all ... Job 38:18 5046
demand of thee, and *d* thou unto me ... Job 40:7 3045
demand of thee, and *d* thou unto me ... Job 42:4 3045
I will *d* the decree ... Ps 2:7 5608
d among the people his doings ... Ps 9:11 5046
The heavens *d* the glory of God ... Ps 19:1 5608
I will *d* thy name unto my ... Ps 22:22 5608
shall *d* his righteousness unto a ... Ps 22:31 5046
shall it *d* thy truth ... Ps 30:9 5046
For I will *d* mine iniquity ... Ps 38:18 5046
if I would *d* and speak of them, ... Ps 40:5 5046
heavens shall *d* his righteousness ... Ps 50:6 5046
hast thou to do to *d* my statutes ... Ps 50:16 5608
fear, and shall *d* the work of God ... Ps 64:9 5046
I will *d* what he hath done for my ... Ps 66:16 5608
that I may *d* all thy works ... Ps 73:28 5608
name is near thy wondrous works *d* ... Ps 75:1 5608
But I will *d* for ever ... Ps 75:9 5046
arise and *d* them to their children ... Ps 78:6 5608
D his glory among the heathen, ... Ps 96:3 5608
The heavens *d* his righteousness, ... Ps 97:6 5046
To *d* the name of the LORD in Zion ... Ps 102:21 5608
d his works with rejoicing ... Ps 107:22 5608
live, and *d* the works of the LORD ... Ps 118:17 5608
and shall *d* thy mighty acts ... Ps 145:4 5046
and I will *d* thy greatness ... Ps 145:6 5608
in my heart even to *d* all this ... Eccl 9:1 952
they *d* their sin as Sodom, they ... Is 3:9 5046
d his doings among the people, ... Is 12:4 3045
watchman, let him *d* what he seeth ... Is 21:6 5046
or *d* us things for to come ... Is 41:22 8085
to pass, and new things do I *d* ... Is 42:9 5046
d his praise in the islands ... Is 42:12 5046
who among them can *d* this ... Is 43:9 5046
d thou, that thou mayest be ... Is 43:26 5608
as I, shall call, and shall *d* it ... Is 44:7 5046
I *d* things that are right ... Is 45:19 5046
and will not ye *d* it ... Is 48:6 5046
with a voice of singing *d* ye ... Is 48:20 5046
who shall *d* his generation ... Is 53:8 7878
I will *d* thy righteousness, and ... Is 57:12 5046
they shall *d* my glory among the ... Is 66:19 5046
D ye in Judah, and publish in ... Jer 4:5 5046
D this in the house of Jacob, and ... Jer 5:20 5046
hath spoken, that he may *d* it ... Jer 9:12 5046
d it in the isles afar off, and ... Jer 31:10 5046
If I *d* it unto thee, wilt thou ... Jer 38:15 5046
D unto us now what thou hast said ... Jer 38:25 5046
answer you, I will *d* it unto you ... Jer 42:4 5046
so *d* unto us, and we will do it ... Jer 42:20 5046
D ye in Egypt, and publish in ... Jer 46:14 5046
D ye among the nations, and ... Jer 50:2 5046
to *d* in Zion the vengeance of the ... Jer 50:28 5046
let us *d* in Zion the work of the ... Jer 51:10 5608
that they may *d* all their ... Eze 12:16 5608
d unto them their abominations ... Eze 23:36 5046
d all that thou seest to the ... Eze 40:4 5046
d the interpretation thereof, ... Dan 4:18 560
D ye it not at Gath, weep ye not ... Mic 1:10 5046
to *d* unto Jacob his transgression ... Mic 3:8 5046
even to day do I *d* that I will ... Zec 9:12 5046
D unto us the parable of the ... Mt 13:36 *5419*
unto him, *D* unto us this parable ... Mt 15:15 *5419*
unto them thy name, and will *d* it ... Jn 17:26 *1107*
who shall *d* his generation ... Acts 8:33 *1334*
we *d* unto you glad tidings, how ... Acts 13:32 *2097*
though a man *d* it unto you ... Acts 13:41 *1555*
worship, him *d* I unto you ... Acts 17:23 *2605*
For I have not shunned to *d* unto ... Acts 20:27 *312*
to *d* his righteousness for the ... Rom 3:25 *1732*
To *d*, I say, at this time his ... Rom 3:26 *1732*
for the day shall *d* it, because ... 1Cor 3:13 *1213*
Now in this that I *d* unto you I ... 1Cor 11:17 *3853*
I *d* unto you the gospel which I ... 1Cor 15:1 *1107*
state shall Tychicus *d* unto you ... Col 4:7 *1107*
I will *d* thy name unto my ... Heb 2:12 *518*
things *d* plainly that they seek a ... Heb 11:14 *1718*
heard *d* we unto you, that ye also ... 1Jn 1:3 *518*
d unto you, that God is light, and ... 1Jn 1:5 *312*

DECLARED {41}
that my name may be *d* throughout ... Ex 9:16 5608
Moses *d* unto the children of ... Lev 23:44 1696
they *d* their pedigrees after ... Num 1:18
because it was not *d* what should ... Num 15:34 6567
he *d* unto you his covenant, which ... Deut 4:13 5046
For thou hast *d* this day, that ... 2Sa 19:6 5046
the words that were *d* unto them ... Neh 8:12 3045
plentifully *d* the thing as it is ... Job 26:3 3045
I have *d* thy faithfulness and thy ... Ps 40:10 559
hitherto have I *d* thy wondrous ... Ps 71:17 5046
thou hast *d* thy strength among ... Ps 77:14 3045
lovingkindness be *d* in the grave ... Ps 88:11 5608
With my lips have I *d* all the ... Ps 119:13 5608
I have *d* my ways, and thou ... Ps 119:26 5608
A grievous vision is *d* unto me ... Is 21:2 5046
God of Israel, have I *d* unto you ... Is 21:10 5046
Who hath *d* from the beginning, ... Is 41:26 5046
I have *d*, and have saved, and I ... Is 43:12 5046
thee from that time, and have *d* it ... Is 44:8 5046
who hath *d* this from ancient time ... Is 45:21 8085
I have *d* the former things from ... Is 48:3 5046
from the beginning *d* it to thee ... Is 48:5 5046
among them hath *d* these things ... Is 48:14 5046
Then Michaiah *d* unto them all the ... Jer 36:13 5046
now I have this day *d* it to you ... Jer 42:21 5046
she *d* unto him before all the ... Lk 8:47 *518*
of the Father, he hath *d* him ... Jn 1:18 *1834*
I have *d* unto them thy name, and ... Jn 17:26 *1107*
d unto them how he had seen the ... Acts 9:27 *1334*
when he had *d* all these things ... Acts 10:8 *1834*
d unto them how the Lord had ... Acts 12:17 *1334*
they *d* all things that God had ... Acts 15:4 *312*
Simeon hath *d* how God at the ... Acts 15:14 *1834*
he *d* particularly what things God ... Acts 21:19 *1834*
Festus *d* Paul's cause unto the ... Acts 25:14 *394*
d to be the Son of God with power ... Rom 1:4 *3724*
thee, and that my name might be *d* ... Rom 9:17 *1229*
For it hath been *d* unto me of you ... 1Cor 1:11 *1213*
d to be the epistle of Christ ... 2Cor 3:3 *5319*
Who also *d* unto us your love in ... Col 1:8 *1213*
as he hath *d* to his servants the ... Rev 10:7 *2097*

DECLARETH {4}
yea, there is none that *d* ... Is 41:26 5046
For a voice *d* from Dan, and ... Jer 4:15 5046
and their staff *d* unto them ... Hos 4:12 5046
d unto man what is his thought, ... Amos 4:13 5046

DECLARING {4}
D the end from the beginning, and ... Is 46:10 5046
d the conversion of the Gentiles ... Acts 15:3 *1555*
d what miracles and wonders God ... Acts 15:12 *1834*
d unto you the testimony of God ... 1Cor 2:1 *2605*

DECLINE {5}
to *d* after many to wrest judgment ... Ex 23:2 5186
thou shalt not *d* from the ... Deut 17:11 5493
yet do I not *d* from thy ... Ps 119:157 5186
neither *d* from the words of my ... Prov 4:5 5186
Let not thine heart *d* to her ways ... Prov 7:25 7847

DECLINED {4}
d neither to the right hand, nor ... 2Chr 34:2 5493
his way have I kept, and not *d* ... Job 23:11 5186
have our steps *d* from thy way ... Ps 44:18 5186
yet have I not *d* from thy law ... Ps 119:51 5186

DECLINETH {2}
My days are like a shadow that *d* ... Ps 102:11 5186
am gone like the shadow when it *d* ... Ps 109:23 5186

DECREASE {2}
suffereth not their cattle to *d* ... Ps 107:38 4591
He must increase, but I must *d* ... Jn 3:30 *1642*

DECREASED {1}
the waters *d* continually until ... Gen 8:5 2637

DECREE {49}
So they established a *d* to make ... 2Chr 30:5 1697
a *d* to build this house of God ... Ezr 5:13 2942
that a *d* was made of Cyrus the ... Ezr 5:17 2942
Then Darius the king made a *d* ... Ezr 6:1 2942
d concerning the house of God at ... Ezr 6:3 2942
Moreover I make a *d* what ye shall ... Ezr 6:8 2942
Also I have made a *d*, that ... Ezr 6:11 2942
I Darius have made a *d* ... Ezr 6:12 2942
I make a *d*, that all they of the ... Ezr 7:13 2942
do make a *d* to all the treasurers ... Ezr 7:21 2942
when the king's *d* which he shall ... Est 1:20 6599
his *d* was heard, and when many ... Est 2:8 1881
the *d* was given in Shushan the ... Est 3:15 1881
his *d* came, there was great ... Est 4:3 1881
d that was given at Shushan to ... Est 4:8 1881
the *d* was given at Shushan the ... Est 8:14 1881
his *d* came, the Jews had joy and ... Est 8:17 1881
his *d* drew near to be put in ... Est 9:1 1881
also according unto this day's *d* ... Est 9:13 1881
the *d* was given at Shushan ... Est 9:14 1881
the *d* of Esther confirmed these ... Est 9:32 3982
Thou shalt also *d* a thing ... Job 22:28 1504
When he made a *d* for the rain ... Job 28:26 2706
I will declare the *d* ... Ps 2:7 2706
he hath made a *d* which shall not ... Ps 148:6 2706
kings reign, and princes *d* justice ... Prov 8:15 2710
When he gave to the sea his *d* ... Prov 8:29 2706
Woe unto them that *d* unrighteous ... Is 10:1 2710
bound of the sea by a perpetual *d* ... Jer 5:22 2706
dream, there is but one *d* for you ... Dan 2:9 1882
the *d* went forth that the wise ... Dan 2:13 1882
Why is the *d* so hasty from the ... Dan 2:15 1882
Thou, O king, hast made a *d* ... Dan 3:10 2942
Therefore I make a *d*, That every ... Dan 3:29 2942
Therefore made I a *d* to bring in ... Dan 4:6 2942
is by the *d* of the watchers ... Dan 4:17 1510
this is the *d* of the most High, ... Dan 4:24 1510
statute, and to make a firm *d* ... Dan 6:7 633
Now, O king, establish the *d* ... Dan 6:8 633
signed the writing and the *d* ... Dan 6:9 633
the king concerning the king's *d* ... Dan 6:12 633
Hast thou not signed a *d*, that ... Dan 6:12 633
nor the *d* that thou hast signed, ... Dan 6:13 633
That no *d* nor statute which the ... Dan 6:15 633
I make a *d*, That in every ... Dan 6:26 2942
Nineveh by the *d* of the king ... Jonah 3:7 2940
day shall the *d* be far removed ... Mic 7:11 2706
Before the *d* bring forth, before ... Zeph 2:2 2706
went out a *d* from Caesar Augustus ... Lk 2:1 *1378*

DECREED {5}
done, and what was *d* against her ... Est 2:1 1504
as they had *d* for themselves and ... Est 9:31 6965
And brake up for it my *d* place ... Job 38:10 2706
the consumption *d* shall overflow ... Is 10:22 2782
hath so *d* in his heart that he ... 1Cor 7:37 *2919*

DECREES {3}
them that decree unrighteous *d* ... Is 10:1 2711
delivered them the *d* for to keep ... Acts 16:4 *1378*
do contrary to the *d* of Caesar ... Acts 17:7 *1378*

DEDAN *(de'-dan)* {11} See DEDANIM.
1. A grandson of Cush.
sons of Raamah; Sheba, and *D* ... Gen 10:7 1719
sons of Raamah; Sheba, and *D* ... 1Chr 1:9 1719
2. A son of Jokshan.
And Jokshan begat Sheba, and *D* ... Gen 25:3 1719
the sons of *D* were Asshurim, and ... Gen 25:3 1719
sons of Jokshan; Sheba, and *D* ... 1Chr 1:32 1719
3. A district between Sela and the Salt Sea.
D, and Tema, and Buz, and all that ... Jer 25:23 1719
dwell deep, O inhabitants of *D* ... Jer 49:8 1719
they of *D* shall fall by the sword ... Eze 25:13 1719
The men of *D* were thy merchants ... Eze 27:15 1719
D was thy merchant in precious ... Eze 27:20 1719
Sheba, and *D*, and the merchants of ... Eze 38:13 1719

DEDANIM *(ded'-a-nim)* {1} See DODANIM. *Descendants of Raamah.*
O ye travelling companies of *D* ... Is 21:13 1720

DEDANITES See DEDANIM.

DEDICATE {4}
the battle, and another man *d* it ... Deut 20:5 2596
king David did *d* unto the LORD ... 2Sa 8:11 6942
d to maintain the house of the ... 1Chr 26:27 6942
to *d* it to him, and to burn before ... 2Chr 2:4 6942

DEDICATED {24}
a new house, and hath not *d* it ... Deut 20:5 2596
I had wholly *d* the silver unto ... Judg 17:3 6942
gold that he had *d* of all nations ... 2Sa 8:11 6942
which David his father had *d* ... 1Kin 7:51 6944
of Israel *d* the house of the LORD ... 1Kin 8:63 2596
the things which his father had *d* ... 1Kin 15:15 6944
and the things which himself had *d* ... 1Kin 15:15 6944
All the money of the *d* things ... 2Kin 12:4 6944
fathers, kings of Judah, had *d* ... 2Kin 12:18 6942
also king David *d* unto the LORD ... 1Chr 18:11 6942
the treasures of the *d* things ... 1Chr 26:20 6944
all the treasures of the *d* things ... 1Chr 26:26 6944
the captains of the host, had *d* ... 1Chr 26:26 6942
and Joab the son of Zeruiah, had *d* ... 1Chr 26:28 6942
and whosoever had *d* any thing ... 1Chr 26:28 6942
of the treasuries of the *d* things ... 1Chr 28:12 6944
that David his father had *d* ... 2Chr 5:1 6944
all the people *d* the house of God ... 2Chr 7:5 2596
the things that his father had *d* ... 2Chr 15:18 6944
and that he himself had *d* ... 2Chr 15:18 6944
also all the *d* things of the ... 2Chr 24:7 6944
tithes and the *d* things faithfully ... 2Chr 31:12 6944
every *d* thing in Israel shall be ... Eze 44:29 2764
testament was *d* without blood ... Heb 9:18 *1457*

DEDICATING {2}
the princes offered for *d* of the ... Num 7:10 2598
his day, for the *d* of the altar ... Num 7:11 2598

DEDICATION {11}
This was the *d* of the altar ... Num 7:84 2598
This was the *d* of the altar ... Num 7:88 2598
for they kept the *d* of the altar ... 2Chr 7:9 2598
kept the *d* of this house of God ... Ezr 6:16 2597
offered at the *d* of this house of ... Ezr 6:17 2597
at the *d* of the wall of Jerusalem ... Neh 12:27 2598
to keep the *d* with gladness, both ... Neh 12:27 2598
Song at the *d* of the house of ... Ps 30:t 2598
to come to the *d* of the image ... Dan 3:2 2597
unto the *d* of the image that ... Dan 3:3 2597
at Jerusalem the feast of the *d* ... Jn 10:22 *1456*

DEED {19}
What *d* is this that ye have done ... Gen 44:15 4639
in very *d* for this cause have I ... Ex 9:16 199
There was no such *d* done nor seen ... Judg 19:30
For in very *d*, as the LORD God of ... 1Sa 25:34 199
that Saul was come in very *d* ... 1Sa 26:4 3559
because by this *d* thou hast given ... 2Sa 12:14 1697
But will God in very *d* dwell with ... 2Chr 6:18
For this *d* of the queen shall ... Est 1:17 1697
have heard of the *d* of the queen ... Est 1:18 1697
to the counsel and *d* of them ... Lk 23:51 *4334*
which was a prophet mighty in *d* ... Lk 24:19 *2041*
good *d* done to the impotent man ... Acts 4:9 *2108*
Gentiles obedient, by word and *d* ... Rom 15:18 *2041*
that he that hath done this *d* ... 1Cor 5:2 *2041*
him that hath so done this *d* ... 1Cor 5:3
be also in *d* when we are present ... 2Cor 10:11 *2041*
And whatsoever ye do in word or *d* ... Col 3:17 *2041*
man shall be blessed in his *d* ... Jas 1:25 *4162*
but in *d* and in truth ... 1Jn 3:18 *2041*

DEEDS {33}
thou hast done *d* unto me that ... Gen 20:9 4639
make known his *d* among the people ... 1Chr 16:8 5949
And his *d*, first and last, behold, ... 2Chr 35:27 1697
is come upon us for our evil *d* ... Ezr 9:13 4639
reported his good *d* before me ... Neh 6:19
wipe not out my good *d* that I ... Neh 13:14
Give them according to their *d* ... Ps 28:4 6467
make known his *d* among the people ... Ps 105:1 5949
According to their *d*, accordingly ... Is 59:18 1578
they overpass the *d* of the wicked ... Jer 5:28 1697
them according to their *d* ... Jer 25:14 6467
ye allow the *d* of your fathers ... Lk 11:48 *2041*
receive the due reward of our *d* ... Lk 23:41 *3739,4238*
light, because their *d* were evil ... Jn 3:19 *2041*
lest his *d* should be reproved ... Jn 3:20 *2041*
that his *d* may be made manifest, ... Jn 3:21 *2041*
Ye do the *d* of your father ... Jn 8:41 *2041*
and was mighty in words and in *d* ... Acts 7:22 *2041*
and confessed, and shewed their *d* ... Acts 19:18 *4234*
that very worthy *d* are done unto ... Acts 24:2 *2735*
to every man according to his *d* ... Rom 2:6 *2041*
Therefore by the *d* of the law ... Rom 3:20 *2041*
by faith without the *d* of the law ... Rom 3:28 *2041*
do mortify the *d* of the body ... Rom 8:13 *4234*
in signs, and wonders, and mighty *d* ... 2Cor 12:12 *1411*
put off the old man with his *d* ... Col 3:9 *4234*
day to day with their unlawful *d* ... 2Pet 2:8 *2041*
speed is partaker of his evil *d* ... 2Jn 11 *2041*
remember his *d* which he doeth ... 3Jn 10 *2041*
ungodly *d* which they have ungodly ... Jude 15 *2041*
hatest the *d* of the Nicolaitanes ... Rev 2:6 *2041*
except they repent of their *d* ... Rev 2:22 *2041*
sores, and repented not of their *d* ... Rev 16:11 *2041*

DEEMED {1}
about midnight the shipmen *d* that ... Acts 27:27 *5282*

DEEP {67}
was upon the face of the *d* ... Gen 1:2 8415
the LORD God caused a *d* sleep to ... Gen 2:21 8639
of the great *d* broken up, and the ... Gen 7:11 8415
The fountains also of the *d* ... Gen 8:2 8415
a *d* sleep fell upon Abram ... Gen 15:12 8639
of the *d* that lieth under ... Gen 49:25 8415
for the *d* that coucheth beneath, ... Deut 33:13 8415
because a *d* sleep from the LORD ... 1Sa 26:12 8639
when *d* sleep falleth on men, ... Job 4:13 8639
He discovereth *d* things out of ... Job 12:22 6013
when *d* sleep falleth upon men, in ... Job 33:15 8639
and the face of the *d* is frozen ... Job 38:30 8415
He maketh the *d* to boil like a ... Job 41:31 4688
one would think the *d* to be hoary ... Job 41:32 8415
thy judgments are a great *d* ... Ps 36:6 8415
D calleth unto *d* at the noise ... Ps 42:7 8415
D calleth unto *d* at the noise ... Ps 42:7 8415
one of them, and the heart, is *d* ... Ps 64:6 6013
I sink in *d* mire, where there is ... Ps 69:2 4688
I am come into *d* waters, where ... Ps 69:2 4615
hate me, and out of the *d* waters ... Ps 69:14 4615
neither let the *d* swallow me up ... Ps 69:15 4688
and didst cause it to take *d* root ... Ps 80:9 8328
and thy thoughts are very *d* ... Ps 92:5 6009
are the *d* places of the earth ... Ps 95:4 4278
it with the *d* as with a garment ... Ps 104:6 8415
the LORD, and his wonders in the *d* ... Ps 107:24 4688
in the seas, and all *d* places ... Ps 135:6 8415
into *d* pits, that they rise not ... Ps 140:10 4113
the fountains of the *d* ... Prov 8:28 8415
of a man's mouth are as *d* waters ... Prov 18:4 6013
casteth into a *d* sleep ... Prov 19:15 8639
the heart of man is like *d* water ... Prov 20:5 6013
mouth of strange women is a *d* pit ... Prov 22:14 6013
For a whore is a *d* ditch ... Prov 23:27 6013
which is far off, and exceeding *d* ... Eccl 7:24 6013
upon you the spirit of *d* sleep ... Is 29:10 8639
Woe unto them that seek *d* to hide ... Is 29:15 6009
he hath made it *d* and large ... Is 30:33 6009
That saith to the *d*, Be dry, and I ... Is 44:27 6683
sea, the waters of the great *d* ... Is 51:10 8415
That led them through the *d* ... Is 63:13 8415
Flee ye, turn back, dwell *d* ... Jer 49:8 6009
Flee, get you far off, dwell *d* ... Jer 49:30 6009
shalt drink of thy sister's cup *d* ... Eze 23:32 6013
I shall bring up the *d* upon thee ... Eze 26:19 8415
the *d* set him up on high with her ... Eze 31:4 8415
I covered the *d* for him, and I ... Eze 31:15 8415
Then will I make their waters *d* ... Eze 32:14 8257
and to have drunk of the *d* waters ... Eze 34:18 4950
He revealeth the *d* and secret ... Dan 2:22 5994
I was in a *d* sleep on my face ... Dan 8:18 7290
then was I in a *d* sleep on my ... Dan 10:9 7290
fire, and it devoured the great *d* ... Amos 7:4 8415
For thou hadst cast me into the *d* ... Jonah 2:3 4688
the *d* uttered his voice, and ... Hab 3:10 8415
unto Simon, Launch out into the *d* ... Lk 5:4 *899*
built an house, and digged *d* ... Lk 6:48 *2532,900*
command them to go out into the *d* ... Lk 8:31 *12*
to draw with, and the well is *d* ... Jn 4:11 *901*
being fallen into a *d* sleep ... Acts 20:9 *901*
Or, Who shall descend into the *d* ... Rom 10:7 *12*
things, yea, the *d* things of God ... 1Cor 2:10 *899*
their *d* poverty abounded unto the ... 2Cor 8:2 *899*
and a day I have been in the *d* ... 2Cor 11:25 *1037*

DEEPER {9}
the plague in sight be *d* than the ... Lev 13:3 6013
in sight be not *d* than the skin ... Lev 13:4 6013
and it be in sight *d* than the skin ... Lev 13:25 6013
if it be in sight *d* than the skin ... Lev 13:30 6013
be not in sight *d* than the skin ... Lev 13:31 6013
be not in sight *d* than the skin ... Lev 13:32 6013
nor be in sight *d* than the skin ... Lev 13:34 6013
d than hell; what canst thou know? ... Job 11:8 6013
a people of a *d* speech than thou ... Is 33:19 6012

DEEPLY {3}
of Israel have *d* revolted ... Is 31:6 6009
They have *d* corrupted themselves, ... Hos 9:9 6009
he sighed *d* in his spirit, and ... Mk 8:12 *389*

DEEPNESS {1}
because they had no *d* of earth ... Mt 13:5 *899*

DEEPS {4}
thou threwest into the *d*, as a ... Neh 9:11 4688
lowest pit, in darkness, in the *d* ... Ps 88:6 4688
the earth, ye dragons, and all *d* ... Ps 148:7 8415
all the *d* of the river shall dry ... Zec 10:11 4688

DEER {1}
and the roebuck, and the fallow *d* ... Deut 14:5 3180

DEFAMED {1}
Being *d*, we intreat ... 1Cor 4:13 *987*

DEFAMING {1}
For I heard the *d* of many ... Jer 20:10 1681

DEFEAT {2}
then mayest thou for me *d* the ... 2Sa 15:34 6565
For the LORD had appointed to *d* ... 2Sa 17:14 6565

DEFENCE {22}
their *d* is departed from them, and ... Num 14:9 6738
and built cities for *d* in Judah ... 2Chr 11:5 4692
Yea, the Almighty shall be thy *d* ... Job 22:25 1220
My *d* is of God, which saveth the ... Ps 7:10 4043
for an house of *d* to save me ... Ps 31:2 4686
for God is my *d* ... Ps 59:9 4869
for thou hast been my *d* and refuge ... Ps 59:16 4869
for God is my *d*, and the God of my ... Ps 59:17 4869
he is my *d* ... Ps 62:2 4869
he is my *d* ... Ps 62:6 4869
For the LORD is our *d* ... Ps 89:18 4043
But the LORD is my *d* ... Ps 94:22 4869
For wisdom is a *d* ... Eccl 7:12 6738
and money is a *d* ... Eccl 7:12 6738
upon all the glory shall be a *d* ... Is 4:5 2646
the brooks of *d* shall be emptied ... Is 19:6 4692
his place of *d* shall be the ... Is 33:16 4869
and the *d* shall be prepared ... Nah 2:5 5526
have made his *d* unto the people ... Acts 19:33 *626*
hear ye my *d* which I make now ... Acts 22:1 *627*
as both in my bonds, and in the *d* ... Phil 1:7 *627*
I am set for the *d* of the gospel ... Phil 1:17 *627*

DEFENCED {9}
of a *d* city a ruin ... Is 25:2 1219
Yet the *d* city shall be desolate, ... Is 27:10 1219
against all the *d* cities of Judah ... Is 36:1 1219
waste *d* cities into ruinous heaps ... Is 37:26 1219
have made thee this day a *d* city ... Jer 1:18 4013
and let us go into the *d* cities ... Jer 4:5 4013
and let us enter into the *d* cities ... Jer 8:14 4013
for these *d* cities remained of ... Jer 34:7 4013
and to Judah in Jerusalem the *d* ... Eze 21:20 1219

DEFEND {11}
to *d* Israel Tola the son of Puah ... Judg 10:1 3467
For I will *d* this city, to save ... 2Kin 19:34 1598
I will *d* this city for mine own ... 2Kin 20:6 1598
name of the God of Jacob *d* thee ... Ps 20:1 7682
d me from them that rise up ... Ps 59:1 7682
D the poor and fatherless ... Ps 82:3 8199
the LORD of hosts *d* Jerusalem ... Is 31:5 1598
For I will *d* this city to save it ... Is 37:35 1598
and I will *d* this city ... Is 38:6 1598
The LORD of hosts shall *d* them ... Zec 9:15 1598
In that day shall the LORD *d* the ... Zec 12:8 1598

DEFENDED {2}
d it, and slew the Philistines ... 2Sa 23:12 5337
he *d* him, and avenged him that was ... Acts 7:24 *292*

DEFENDEST {1}
for joy, because thou *d* them ... Ps 5:11 5526

DEFENDING {1}
d also he will deliver it ... Is 31:5 1598

DEFER {3}
a vow unto God, *d* not to pay it ... Eccl 5:4 309
name's sake will I *d* mine anger ... Is 48:9 748
d not, for thine own sake, O my ... Dan 9:19 309

DEFERRED {3}
the young man *d* not to do the ... Gen 34:19 309
Hope *d* maketh the heart sick, but ... Prov 13:12 4900
he *d* them, and said, When Lysias ... Acts 24:22 *306*

DEFERRETH {1}
discretion of a man *d* his anger ... Prov 19:11 748

DEFIED {6}
I defy, whom the LORD hath not *d* ... Num 23:8 2194
seeing he hath *d* the armies of ... 1Sa 17:36 2778
of Israel, whom thou hast *d* ... 1Sa 17:45 2778
And when he *d* Israel, Jonathan the ... 2Sa 21:21 2778
when they *d* the Philistines that ... 2Sa 23:9 2778
But when he *d* Israel, Jonathan ... 1Chr 20:7 2778

DEFILE {39}
neither shall ye *d* yourselves ... Lev 11:44 2930
when they *d* my tabernacle that is ... Lev 15:31 2930
wife, to *d* thyself with her ... Lev 18:20 2930
any beast to *d* thyself therewith ... Lev 18:23 2930
D not ye yourselves in any of ... Lev 18:24 2930
not you out also, when ye *d* it ... Lev 18:28 2930
that ye *d* not yourselves therein ... Lev 18:30 2930
to *d* my sanctuary, and to profane ... Lev 20:3 2930
But he shall not *d* himself ... Lev 21:4 2930
nor *d* himself for his father, or ... Lev 21:11 2930
not eat to *d* himself therewith ... Lev 22:8 2930
that they *d* not their camps, in ... Num 5:3 2930
D not therefore the land which ye ... Num 35:34 2930
children of Ammon, did the king *d* ... 2Kin 23:13 2930
how shall I *d* them? ... Song 5:3 2936
Ye shall *d* also the covering of ... Is 30:22 2930
is called by my name, to *d* it ... Jer 32:34 2930
shall enter into it, and *d* it ... Eze 7:22 2490
D the house, and fill the courts ... Eze 9:7 2930
d not yourselves with the idols ... Eze 20:7 2930
nor *d* yourselves with their idols ... Eze 20:18 2930
against herself to *d* herself ... Eze 22:3 2930
they shall *d* thy brightness ... Eze 28:7 2490
ye *d* every one his neighbour's ... Eze 33:26 2930
Neither shall they *d* themselves ... Eze 37:23 2930
the house of Israel no more *d* ... Eze 43:7 2930
at no dead person to *d* themselves ... Eze 44:25 2930
no husband, they may *d* themselves ... Eze 44:25 2930
in his heart that he would not *d* ... Dan 1:8 1351
that he might not *d* himself ... Dan 1:8 1351
and they *d* the man ... Mt 15:18 *2840*
are the things which *d* a man ... Mt 15:20 *2840*
that entering into him can *d* him ... Mk 7:15 *2840*
those are they that *d* the man ... Mk 7:15 *2840*
into the man, it cannot *d* him ... Mk 7:18 *2840*
come from within, and *d* the man ... Mk 7:23 *2840*
If any man *d* the temple of God, ... 1Cor 3:17 *5351*
for them that *d* themselves with ... 1Ti 1:10 *733*
these filthy dreamers *d* the flesh ... Jude 8 *3392*

DEFILED {71}
her, and lay with her, and *d* her ... Gen 34:2 6031
that he had *d* Dinah his daughter ... Gen 34:5 2930
because he had *d* Dinah their ... Gen 34:13 2930
because they had *d* their sister ... Gen 34:27 2930
be that a man shall be *d* withal ... Lev 5:3 2930
them, that ye should be *d* thereby ... Lev 11:43 2933
shall be in him he shall be *d* ... Lev 13:46 2930
goeth from him, and is *d* therewith ... Lev 15:32 2930
are *d* which I cast out before you ... Lev 18:24 2930
And the land is *d* ... Lev 18:25 2930
were before you, and the land is *d* ... Lev 18:27 2930
after wizards, to be *d* by them ... Lev 19:31 2930
There shall none be *d* for the ... Lev 21:1 2930
for her may he be *d* ... Lev 21:3 2930
and whosoever is *d* by the dead ... Num 5:2 2931
and be kept close, and she be *d* ... Num 5:13 2930
jealous of his wife, and she be *d* ... Num 5:14 2930
of his wife, and she be not *d* ... Num 5:14 2930
of thy husband, and if thou be *d* ... Num 5:20 2930
come to pass, that, if she be *d* ... Num 5:27 2930
And if the woman be not *d*, but be ... Num 5:28 2930
instead of her husband, and is *d* ... Num 5:29 2930
he hath *d* the head of his ... Num 6:9 2930
because his separation was *d* ... Num 6:12 2930
who were *d* by the dead body of a ... Num 9:6 2931
We are *d* by the dead body of a ... Num 9:7 2931
because he hath *d* the sanctuary ... Num 19:20 2930
that thy land be not *d*, which ... Deut 21:23 2930
the fruit of thy vineyard, be *d* ... Deut 22:9 6942
be his wife, after that she is *d* ... Deut 24:4 2930
d the high places where the ... 2Kin 23:8 2930
he *d* Topheth, which is in the ... 2Kin 23:10 2930
forasmuch as he *d* his father's ... 1Chr 5:1 2490
they have *d* the priesthood ... Neh 13:29 1351
my skin, and *d* my horn in the dust ... Job 16:15 5953
they have *d* by casting down the ... Ps 74:7 2490
thy holy temple have they *d* ... Ps 79:1 2930
Thus were they *d* with their own ... Ps 106:39 2930
The earth also is *d* under the ... Is 24:5 2610
For your hands are *d* with blood ... Is 59:3 1351
ye *d* my land, and made mine ... Jer 2:7 2930
her whoredom, that she *d* the land ... Jer 3:9 2610
because they have *d* my land ... Jer 16:18 2490
shall be *d* as the place of Tophet ... Jer 19:13 2931
their *d* bread among the Gentiles ... Eze 4:13 2931
because thou hast *d* my sanctuary ... Eze 5:11 2930
and their holy places shall be *d* ... Eze 7:24 2490
neither hath *d* his neighbour's ... Eze 18:6 2930
and *d* his neighbour's wife, ... Eze 18:11 2930
hath not *d* his neighbour's wife, ... Eze 18:15 2930
doings, wherein ye have been *d* ... Eze 20:43 2930
hast *d* thyself in thine idols ... Eze 22:4 2930
hath lewdly *d* his daughter in law ... Eze 22:11 2930
all their idols she *d* herself ... Eze 23:7 2930
Then I saw that she was *d* ... Eze 23:13 2930
they *d* her with their whoredom, ... Eze 23:17 2930
they have *d* my sanctuary in the ... Eze 23:38 2930
Thou hast *d* thy sanctuaries by ... Eze 28:18 2490
they *d* it by their own way and by ... Eze 36:17 2930
they have even *d* my holy name by ... Eze 43:8 2930
whoredom, and Israel is *d* ... Hos 5:3 2930
whoredom of Ephraim, Israel is *d* ... Hos 6:10 2930
thee, that say, Let her be *d* ... Mic 4:11 2610
of his disciples eat bread with *d* ... Mk 7:2 *2839*
hall, lest they should be *d* ... Jn 18:28 *3392*
their conscience being weak is *d* ... 1Cor 8:7 *3435*
but unto them that are *d* and ... Titus 1:15 *3392*
their mind and conscience is *d* ... Titus 1:15 *3392*
trouble you, and thereby many be *d* ... Heb 12:15 *3392*
which have not *d* their garments ... Rev 3:4 *3435*
they which were not *d* with women ... Rev 14:4 *3435*

DEFILEDST {1}
then *d* thou it ... Gen 49:4 2490

DEFILETH {9}
every one that *d* it shall surely ... Ex 31:14 2490
d the tabernacle of the LORD ... Num 19:13 2930
for blood it *d* the land ... Num 35:33 2610
goeth into the mouth *d* a man ... Mt 15:11 *2840*
out of the mouth, this *d* a man ... Mt 15:11 *2840*
with unwashen hands *d* not a man ... Mt 15:20 *2840*
out of the man, that *d* the man ... Mk 7:20 *2840*
that it *d* the whole body, and ... Jas 3:6 *4695*
enter into it any thing that *d* ... Rev 21:27 *2840*

DEFRAUD {5}
Thou shalt not *d* thy neighbour ... Lev 19:13 6231
D not, Honour thy father and ... Mk 10:19 *650*
Nay, ye do wrong, and *d*, and that ... 1Cor 6:8 *650*
D ye not one the other, except it ... 1Cor 7:5 *650*
d his brother in any matter ... 1Th 4:6 *4122*

DEFRAUDED {4}
or whom have I *d*? ... 1Sa 12:3 6231
And they said, Thou hast not *d* us ... 1Sa 12:4 6231
rather suffer yourselves to be *d* ... 1Cor 6:7 *650*
no man, we have *d* no man ... 2Cor 7:2 *4122*

DEFY {5}
curse me Jacob, and come, *d* Israel ... Num 23:7 2194
or how shall I *d*, whom the LORD ... Num 23:8 2194
I *d* the armies of Israel this day ... 1Sa 17:10 2778
surely to *d* Israel is he come up ... 1Sa 17:25 2778
that he should *d* the armies of ... 1Sa 17:26 2778

DEGENERATE {1}
then art thou turned into the *d* ... Jer 2:21 5494

DEGREE {7}
their brethren of the second *d* ... 1Chr 15:18
to the estate of a man of high *d* ... 1Chr 17:17
Surely men of low *d* are vanity ... Ps 62:9
and men of high *d* are a lie ... Ps 62:9
seats, and exalted them of low *d* ... Lk 1:52 *5011*
purchase to themselves a good *d* ... 1Ti 3:13 *898*
Let the brother of low *d* rejoice ... Jas 1:9 *5011*

DEGREES {24}
shall the shadow go forward ten *d* ... 2Kin 20:9 4609
or go back ten *d* ... 2Kin 20:9 4609
for the shadow to go down ten *d* ... 2Kin 20:10 4609
the shadow return backward ten *d* ... 2Kin 20:10 4609
brought the shadow ten *d* backward ... 2Kin 20:11 4609
A Song of *d* ... Ps 120:*t* 4609
A Song of *d* ... Ps 121:*t* 4609
A Song of *d* of David ... Ps 122:*t* 4609
A Song of *d* ... Ps 123:*t* 4609
A Song of *d* of David ... Ps 124:*t* 4609
A Song of *d* ... Ps 125:*t* 4609
A Song of *d* ... Ps 126:*t* 4609
A Song of *d* for Solomon ... Ps 127:*t* 4609
A Song of *d* ... Ps 128:*t* 4609
A Song of *d* ... Ps 129:*t* 4609
A Song of *d* ... Ps 130:*t* 4609
A Song of *d* of David ... Ps 131:*t* 4609
A Song of *d* ... Ps 132:*t* 4609
A Song of *d* of David ... Ps 133:*t* 4609
A Song of *d* ... Ps 134:*t* 4609
bring again the shadow of the *d* ... Is 38:8 4609
sun dial of Ahaz, ten *d* backward ... Is 38:8 4609
So the sun returned ten *d* ... Is 38:8 4609
by which *d* it was gone down ... Is 38:8 4609

DEHAVITES *(de-ha'-vites)* {1} *Foreign settlers in Samaria.*
the Susanchites, the *D*, and the ... Ezr 4:9 1723

DEKAR *(de'-kar)* {1} *Father of an officer of Solomon.*
The son of *D*, in Makaz, and in ... 1Kin 4:9 1857

DELAIAH *(del-a-i'-ah)* {6} See DALAIAH.
1. A priest of David.
The three and twentieth to *D* ... 1Chr 24:18 1806
2. A family with a lost genealogy.
The children of *D*, the children ... Ezr 2:60 1806
The children of *D*, the children ... Neh 7:62 1806
3. An opponent of Nehemiah.
son of *D* the son of Mehetabeel ... Neh 6:10 1806
4. A prince of Judah.
D the son of Shemaiah, and ... Jer 36:12 1806
Nevertheless Elnathan and *D* ... Jer 36:25 1806

DELAY {3}
Thou shalt not *d* to offer the ... Ex 22:29 309
he would not *d* to come to them ... Acts 9:38 *3635*
without any *d* on the morrow I sat ... Acts 25:17 *311*

DELAYED {2}
d to come down out of the mount ... Ex 32:1 954
d not to keep thy commandments ... Ps 119:60 4102

DELAYETH {2}
his heart, My lord *d* his coming ... Mt 24:48 *5549*
his heart, My lord *d* his coming ... Lk 12:45 *5549*

DELECTABLE {1}
their *d* things shall not profit ... Is 44:9 2530

DELICACIES {1}
through the abundance of her *d* ... Rev 18:3 *4764*

DELICATE {5}
is tender among you, and very *d* ... Deut 28:54 6028
d woman among you, which would ... Deut 28:56 6028
no more be called tender and *d* ... Is 47:1 6028
of Zion to a comely and *d* woman ... Jer 6:2 6026
and poll thee for thy *d* children ... Mic 1:16 8588

DELICATELY {4}
And Agag came unto him *d* ... 1Sa 15:32 4574
He that *d* bringeth up his servant ... Prov 29:21 6445
They that did feed *d* are desolate ... Lam 4:5 4574
gorgeously apparelled, and live *d* ... Lk 7:25 *5172*

DELICATENESS {1}
of her foot upon the ground for *d* ... Deut 28:56 6026

DELICATES {1}
hath filled his belly with my *d* ... Jer 51:34 5730

DELICIOUSLY {2}
glorified herself, and lived *d* ... Rev 18:7 *4763*
lived *d* with her, shall bewail ... Rev 18:9 *4763*

DELIGHT {51}
because he had *d* in Jacob's ... Gen 34:19 2654
If the LORD *d* in us, then he will ... Num 14:8 2654
Only the LORD had a *d* in thy ... Deut 10:15 2836
be, if thou have no *d* in her ... Deut 21:14 2654
as great *d* in burnt offerings ... 1Sa 15:22 2656
Behold, the king hath *d* in thee ... 1Sa 18:22 2654
he thus say, I have no *d* in thee ... 2Sa 15:26 2654
my lord the king *d* in this thing ... 2Sa 24:3 2654
To whom would the king *d* to do ... Est 6:6 2654
thou have thy *d* in the Almighty ... Job 22:26 6026
Will he *d* himself in the Almighty ... Job 27:10 6026
that he should *d* himself with God ... Job 34:9 7521
But his *d* is in the law of the ... Ps 1:2 2656
excellent, in whom is all my *d* ... Ps 16:3 2656
D thyself also in the LORD ... Ps 37:4 6026
shall *d* themselves in the ... Ps 37:11 6026
I *d* to do thy will, O my God ... Ps 40:8 2654
they *d* in lies ... Ps 62:4 7521
thou the people that *d* in war ... Ps 68:30 2654
within me thy comforts *d* my soul ... Ps 94:19 8173
I will *d* myself in thy statutes ... Ps 119:16 8173
Thy testimonies also are my *d* ... Ps 119:24 8191
for therein do I *d* ... Ps 119:35 2654
And I will *d* myself in thy ... Ps 119:47 8173
but I *d* in thy law ... Ps 119:70 8173
for thy law is my *d* ... Ps 119:77 8191
and thy law is my *d* ... Ps 119:174 8191
the scorners *d* in their scorning, ... Prov 1:22 2531
d in the frowardness of the ... Prov 2:14 1523
and I was daily his *d*, rejoicing ... Prov 8:30 8191
but a just weight is his *d* ... Prov 11:1 7522
upright in their way are his *d* ... Prov 11:20 7522
they that deal truly are his *d* ... Prov 12:22 7522
prayer of the upright is his *d* ... Prov 15:8 7522
Righteous lips are the *d* of kings ... Prov 16:13 7522
A fool hath no *d* in understanding ... Prov 18:2 2654
D is not seemly for a fool ... Prov 19:10 8588
them that rebuke him shall be *d* ... Prov 24:25 5276
he shall give *d* unto thy soul ... Prov 29:17 4574
under his shadow with great *d* ... Song 2:3 2530
I *d* not in the blood of bullocks ... Is 1:11 2654
for gold, they shall not *d* in it ... Is 13:17 2654
let your soul *d* itself in fatness ... Is 55:2 6026
d to know my ways, as a nation ... Is 58:2 2654
they take *d* in approaching to God ... Is 58:2 2654
and call the sabbath a *d*, the holy ... Is 58:13 6027
Then shalt thou *d* thyself in the ... Is 58:14 6026
they have no *d* in it ... Jer 6:10 2654
for in these things I *d*, saith ... Jer 9:24 2654
of the covenant, whom ye *d* in ... Mal 3:1 2655
For I *d* in the law of God after ... Rom 7:22 *4913*

DELIGHTED {12}
Saul's son *d* much in David ... 1Sa 19:2 2654
delivered me, because he *d* in me ... 2Sa 22:20 2654
which *d* in thee, to set thee on ... 1Kin 10:9 2654
which *d* in thee to set thee on ... 2Chr 9:8 2654
d themselves in thy great ... Neh 9:25 5727
no more, except the king *d* in her ... Est 2:14 2654
delivered me, because he *d* in me ... Ps 18:19 2654
deliver him, seeing he *d* in him ... Ps 22:8 2654
as he *d* not in blessing, so let ... Ps 109:17 2654
did choose that wherein I *d* not ... Is 65:12 2654
and chose that in which I *d* not ... Is 66:4 2654
be *d* with the abundance of her ... Is 66:11 6026

DELIGHTEST {1}
thou *d* not in burnt offering ... Ps 51:16 7521

DELIGHTETH {14}
the man whom the king *d* to honour ... Est 6:6 2654
the man whom the king *d* to honour ... Est 6:7 2654
withal whom the king *d* to honour ... Est 6:9 2654
the man whom the king *d* to honour ... Est 6:9 2654
the man whom the king *d* to honour ... Est 6:11 2654
and he *d* in his way ... Ps 37:23 2654
the LORD, that *d* greatly in his ... Ps 112:1 2654
He *d* not in the strength of the ... Ps 147:10 2654
as a father the son in whom he *d* ... Prov 3:12 7521
mine elect, in whom my soul *d* ... Is 42:1 7521
for the LORD *d* in thee, and thy ... Is 62:4 2654
ways, and their soul *d* in their ... Is 66:3 2654
for ever, because he *d* in mercy ... Mic 7:18 2654
of the LORD, and he *d* in them ... Mal 2:17 2654

DELIGHTS {6}
you in scarlet, with other *d* ... 2Sa 1:24 5730
Unless thy law had been my *d* ... Ps 119:92 8191
yet thy commandments are my *d* ... Ps 119:143 8191
my *d* were with the sons of men ... Prov 8:31 8191
the *d* of the sons of men, as ... Eccl 2:8 8588
pleasant art thou, O love, for *d* ... Song 7:6 8588

DELIGHTSOME {1}
for ye shall be a *d* land, saith ... Mal 3:12 2656

DELILAH *(de-li'-lah)* {6} *Woman who betrayed Samson.*
valley of Sorek, whose name was *D* ... Judg 16:4 1807
D said to Samson, Tell me, I pray ... Judg 16:6 1807
D said unto Samson, Behold, thou ... Judg 16:10 1807
D therefore took new ropes, and ... Judg 16:12 1807
D said unto Samson, Hitherto thou ... Judg 16:13 1807
when *D* saw that he had told her ... Judg 16:18 1807

DELIVER {296}
D me, I pray thee, from the hand ... Gen 32:11 5337
to *d* him to his father again ... Gen 37:22 7725
thou shalt *d* Pharaoh's cup into ... Gen 40:13 5414
so will I *d* you your brother, and ... Gen 42:34 5414
d him into my hand, and I will ... Gen 42:37 5414
I am come down to *d* them out of ... Ex 3:8 5337
yet shall ye *d* the tale of bricks ... Ex 5:18 5414
but God *d* him into his hand ... Ex 21:13 579
If a man shall *d* unto his ... Ex 22:7 5414
If a man *d* unto his neighbour an ... Ex 22:10 5414
thou shalt *d* it unto him by that ... Ex 22:26 7725
for I will *d* the inhabitants of ... Ex 23:31 5414
they shall *d* you your bread again ... Lev 26:26 7725
If thou wilt indeed *d* this people ... Num 21:2 5414
the congregation shall *d* the ... Num 35:25 5337
to *d* us into the hand of the ... Deut 1:27 5414
that he might *d* him into thy hand ... Deut 2:30 5414
for I will *d* him, and all his ... Deut 3:2 5414
thy God shall *d* them before thee ... Deut 7:2 5414
the LORD thy God shall *d* thee ... Deut 7:16 5414
thy God shall *d* them unto thee ... Deut 7:23 5414
he shall *d* their kings into thine ... Deut 7:24 5414
d him into the hand of the ... Deut 19:12 5414
to *d* thee, and to give up thine ... Deut 23:14 5337
Thou shalt not *d* unto his master ... Deut 23:15 5462
In any case thou shalt *d* him the ... Deut 24:13 7725
d her husband out of the hand of ... Deut 25:11 5337
any that can *d* out of my hand ... Deut 32:39 5337
have, and *d* our lives from death ... Josh 2:13 5337
to *d* us into the hand of the ... Josh 7:7 5414
your God will *d* it into your hand ... Josh 8:7 5414
morrow about this time will I *d* ... Josh 11:6 5414
then they shall not *d* the slayer ... Josh 20:5 5462
I will *d* him into thine hand ... Judg 4:7 5414
d the Midianites into thine hand ... Judg 7:7 5414
Israel, Did not I *d* you from the ... Judg 10:11
wherefore I will *d* you no more ... Judg 10:13 3467
let them *d* you in the time of ... Judg 10:14 3467
d us only, we pray thee, this day ... Judg 10:15 5337
the LORD *d* them before me, shall ... Judg 11:9 5414
If thou shalt without fail *d* the ... Judg 11:30 5414
he shall begin to *d* Israel out of ... Judg 13:5 3467
that we may *d* thee into the hand ... Judg 15:12 5414
fast, and *d* thee into their hand ... Judg 15:13 5414
Now therefore *d* us the men ... Judg 20:13 5414
I will *d* them into thine hand ... Judg 20:28 5414
who shall *d* us out of the hand of ... 1Sa 4:8 5337
he will *d* you out of the hand of ... 1Sa 7:3 5337
Israel *d* out of the hands of the ... 1Sa 7:14 5337
but now *d* us out of the hand of ... 1Sa 12:10 5337
things, which cannot profit nor *d* ... 1Sa 12:21 5337
wilt thou *d* them into the hand of ... 1Sa 14:37 5414
he will *d* me out of the hand of ... 1Sa 17:37 5337
the LORD *d* thee into mine hand ... 1Sa 17:46 5462
for I will *d* the Philistines into ... 1Sa 23:4 5414
of Keilah *d* me up into his hand ... 1Sa 23:11 5462
Will the men of Keilah *d* me ... 1Sa 23:12 5462
LORD said, They will *d* thee up ... 1Sa 23:12 5462
our part shall be to *d* him into ... 1Sa 23:20 5462
I will *d* thine enemy into thine ... 1Sa 24:4 5414
cause, and *d* me out of thine hand ... 1Sa 24:15 8199
LORD, and let him *d* me out of all ... 1Sa 26:24 5337
Moreover the LORD will also *d* ... 1Sa 28:19 5414
the LORD also shall *d* the host of ... 1Sa 28:19 5414
nor *d* me into the hands of my ... 1Sa 30:15 5462
D me my wife Michal, which I ... 2Sa 3:14 5414
wilt thou *d* them into mine hand ... 2Sa 5:19 5414
for I will doubtless *d* the ... 2Sa 5:19 5414
D him that smote his brother, ... 2Sa 14:7 5414
to *d* his handmaid out of the hand ... 2Sa 14:16 5337
d him only, and I will depart from ... 2Sa 20:21 5414
d them to the enemy, so that they ... 1Kin 8:46 5414
that thou wouldest *d* thy servant ... 1Kin 18:9 5414
Thou shalt *d* me thy silver, and ... 1Kin 20:5 5414
I will *d* it into thine hand this ... 1Kin 20:13 5414
therefore will I *d* all this great ... 1Kin 20:28 5414
for the Lord shall *d* it into the ... 1Kin 22:6 5414
for the LORD shall *d* it into the ... 1Kin 22:12 5414
for the LORD shall *d* it into the ... 1Kin 22:15 5414
to *d* them into the hand of Moab ... 2Kin 3:10 5414
to *d* them into the hand of Moab ... 2Kin 3:13 5414
he will *d* the Moabites also into ... 2Kin 3:18 5414
but *d* it for the breaches of the ... 2Kin 12:7 5414
he shall *d* you out of the hand of ... 2Kin 17:39 5337
I will *d* thee two thousand horses ... 2Kin 18:23 5414
be able to *d* you out of his hand ... 2Kin 18:29 5337
saying, The LORD will surely *d* us ... 2Kin 18:30 5337
you, saying, The LORD will *d* us ... 2Kin 18:32 5337
that the LORD should *d* Jerusalem ... 2Kin 18:35 5337
and I will *d* thee and this city out ... 2Kin 20:6 5337
d them into the hand of their ... 2Kin 21:14 5414
let them *d* it into the hand of ... 2Kin 22:5 5414
wilt thou *d* them into mine hand ... 1Chr 14:10 5414
for I will *d* them into thine hand ... 1Chr 14:10 5414
d us from the heathen, that we ... 1Chr 16:35 5337
d them over before their enemies, ... 2Chr 6:36 5414
for God will *d* it into the king's ... 2Chr 18:5 5414
for the LORD shall *d* it into the ... 2Chr 18:11 5414
which could not *d* their own ... 2Chr 25:15 5337
that he might *d* them into the ... 2Chr 25:20 5414
d the captives again, which ye ... 2Chr 28:11 7725
The LORD our God shall *d* us out ... 2Chr 32:11 5337
to *d* their lands out of mine hand ... 2Chr 32:13 5337
that could *d* his people out of ... 2Chr 32:14 5337
be able to *d* you out of mine hand ... 2Chr 32:14 5337
to *d* his people out of mine hand ... 2Chr 32:15 5337
your God *d* you out of mine hand ... 2Chr 32:15 5337

D

d his people out of mine hand 2Chr 32:17 5337
those *d* thou before the God of Ezr 7:19 8000
many times didst thou *d* them Neh 9:28 5337
neither is there any to *d* them Job 5:4 5337
He shall *d* thee in six troubles Job 5:19 5337
D me from the enemy's hand Job 6:23 4422
none that can *d* out of thine hand Job 10:7 5337
He shall *d* the island of the Job 22:30 4422
D him from going down to the pit Job 33:24 6308
He will *d* his soul from going Job 33:28 6299
then a great ransom cannot *d* thee Job 36:18 5186
Return, O LORD, *d* my soul Ps 6:4 2502
them that persecute me, and *d* me Ps 7:1 5337
pieces, while there is none to *d* Ps 7:2 5337
d my soul from the wicked, which Ps 17:13 6403
trusted, and thou didst *d* them Ps 22:4 6403
on the LORD that he would *d* him Ps 22:8 6403
let him *d* him, seeing he Ps 22:8 5337
D my soul from the sword Ps 22:20 5337
O keep my soul, and *d* me Ps 25:20 5337
D me not over unto the will of Ps 27:12 5414
d me in thy righteousness Ps 31:1 6403
d me speedily Ps 31:2 5337
d me from the hand of mine Ps 31:15 5337
neither shall he *d* any by his Ps 33:17 4422
To *d* their soul from death, and to Ps 33:19 5337
LORD shall help them, and *d* them Ps 37:40 6403
he shall *d* them from the wicked, Ps 37:40 6403
D me from all my transgressions Ps 39:8 5337
Be pleased, O LORD, to *d* me Ps 40:13 5337
the LORD will *d* him in time of Ps 41:1 4422
thou wilt not *d* him unto the will Ps 41:2 5414
O *d* me from the deceitful and Ps 43:1 6403
I will *d* thee, and thou shalt Ps 50:15 2502
in pieces, and there be none to *d* Ps 50:22 5337
D me from bloodguiltiness, O God, Ps 51:14 5337
wilt not thou *d* my feet from Ps 56:13 5337
D me from mine enemies, O my God Ps 59:1 5337
D me from the workers of iniquity Ps 59:2 5337
D me out of the mire, and let me Ps 69:14 5337
d me because of mine enemies Ps 69:18 6299
Make haste, O God, to *d* me Ps 70:1 5337
D me in thy righteousness, and Ps 71:2 5337
D me, O my God, out of the hand Ps 71:4 6403
for there is none to *d* him Ps 71:11 5337
For he shall *d* the needy when he Ps 72:12 5337
O *d* not the soul of thy Ps 74:19 5414
d us, and purge away our sins, for Ps 79:9 5337
D the poor and needy Ps 82:4 6403
shall he *d* his soul from the hand Ps 89:48 4422
Surely he shall *d* thee from the Ps 91:3 5337
upon me, therefore will I *d* him Ps 91:14 6403
I will *d* him, and honour him Ps 91:15 2502
Many times did he *d* them Ps 106:43 5337
thy mercy is good, *d* thou me Ps 109:21 5337
O LORD, I beseech thee, *d* my soul Ps 116:4 4422
D me from the oppression of man Ps 119:134 6299
Consider mine affliction, and *d* me Ps 119:153 2502
Plead my cause, and *d* me Ps 119:154 1350
d me according to thy word Ps 119:170 5337
D my soul, O LORD, from lying Ps 120:2 5337
D me, O LORD, from the evil man Ps 140:1 2502
d me from my persecutors Ps 142:6 5337
D me, O LORD, from mine enemies Ps 143:9 5337
d me out of great waters, from Ps 144:7 5337
d me from the hand of strange Ps 144:11 5337
To *d* thee from the way of the Prov 2:12 5337
To *d* thee from the strange woman, Prov 2:16 5337
of glory shall she *d* to thee Prov 4:9 4042
d thyself, when thou art come Prov 6:3 5337
D thyself as a roe from the hand Prov 6:5 5337
of the upright shall *d* them Prov 11:6 5337
mouth of the upright shall *d* them Prov 12:6 5337
for if thou *d* him, yet thou must Prov 19:19 5337
shalt *d* his soul from hell Prov 23:14 5337
If thou forbear to *d* them that Prov 24:11 5337
neither shall wickedness *d* those Eccl 8:8 4422
it away safe, and none shall *d* it Is 5:29 5337
a great one, and he shall *d* them Is 19:20 5337
which men *d* to one that is Is 29:11 5414
defending also he will *d* it Is 31:5 5337
for he shall not be able to *d* you Is 36:14 5337
saying, The LORD will surely *d* us Is 36:15 5337
you, saying, The LORD will *d* us Is 36:18 5337
that the LORD should *d* Jerusalem Is 36:20 5337
And I will *d* thee and this city out Is 38:6 5337
is none that can *d* out of my hand Is 43:13 5337
prayeth unto it, and saith, *D* me Is 44:17 5337
aside, that he cannot *d* his soul Is 44:20 5337
they could not *d* the burden Is 46:2 4422
even I will carry, and will *d* you Is 46:4 4422
they shall not *d* themselves from Is 47:14 5337
or have I no power to *d* Is 50:2 5337
criest, let thy companies *d* thee Is 57:13 5337
for I am with thee to *d* thee Jer 1:8 5337
thee, saith the LORD, to *d* thee Jer 1:19 5337
I *d* to the sword before their Jer 15:9 5414
to *d* thee, saith the LORD Jer 15:20 5337
I will *d* thee out of the hand of Jer 15:21 5337
Therefore *d* up their children to Jer 18:21 5414
Moreover I will *d* all the Jer 20:5 5414
I will *d* Zedekiah king of Judah, Jer 21:7 5414
d him that is spoiled out of the Jer 21:12 5337
d the spoiled out of the hand of Jer 22:3 5337
I will *d* them to be removed into Jer 24:9 5414
will *d* them to be removed to all Jer 29:18 5414
I will *d* them into the hand of Jer 29:21 5414
lest they *d* me into their hand, Jer 38:19 5414
said, They shall not *d* thee Jer 38:20 5414
But I will *d* thee in that day, Jer 39:17 5337
For I will surely *d* thee, and thou Jer 39:18 4422
you, and to *d* you from his hand Jer 42:11 5337
for to *d* us into the hand of the Jer 43:3 5414
d such as are for death to death Jer 43:11
I will *d* them into the hand of Jer 46:26 5414
Babylon, and *d* every man his soul Jer 51:6 4422
d ye every man his soul from the Jer 51:45 4422
that doth *d* us out of their hand Lam 5:8 6561
d them in the day of the wrath of Eze 7:19 5337
d you into the hands of strangers Eze 11:9 5414
d my people out of your hand, and Eze 13:21 5337
for I will *d* my people out of Eze 13:23 5337
they should *d* but their own souls Eze 14:14 5337
they shall *d* neither sons nor Eze 14:16 5337
they shall *d* neither sons nor Eze 14:18 5337
they shall *d* neither son nor Eze 14:20 5337
they shall but *d* their own souls Eze 14:20 5337
d thee into the hand of brutish Eze 21:31 5414
I will *d* thee into the hand of Eze 23:28 5414
therefore I will *d* thee to the Eze 25:4 5414
will *d* thee for a spoil to the Eze 25:7 5414
taketh warning shall *d* his soul Eze 33:5 4422
shall not *d* him in the day of his Eze 33:12 5337
for I will *d* my flock from their Eze 34:10 5337
will *d* them out of all places Eze 34:12 5337
that shall *d* you out of my hands Dan 3:15 7804
to *d* us from the burning fiery Dan 3:17 7804
he will *d* us out of thine hand, O Dan 3:17 7804
God that can *d* after this sort Dan 3:29 5338
set his heart on Daniel to *d* him Dan 6:14 7804
going down of the sun to *d* him Dan 6:14 5338
continually, he will *d* thee Dan 6:16 7804
able to *d* thee from the lions Dan 6:20 7804
any that could *d* out of his hand Dan 8:4 5337
could *d* the ram out of his hand Dan 8:7 5337
none shall *d* her out of mine hand Hos 2:10 5337
how shall I *d* thee, Israel Hos 11:8 4042
captivity, to *d* them up to Edom Amos 1:6 5462
shall the mighty *d* himself Amos 2:14 4422
swift of foot shall not *d* himself Amos 2:15 4422
that rideth the horse *d* himself Amos 2:15 4422
therefore will I *d* up the city Amos 6:8 5462
his head, to *d* him from his grief Jonah 4:6 5337
thus shall he *d* us from the Mic 5:6 5337
teareth in pieces, and none can *d* Mic 5:8 5337
shalt take hold, but shalt not *d* Mic 6:14 6403
d them in the day of the LORD's Zeph 1:18 5337
D thyself, O Zion, that dwellest Zec 2:7 4422
I will *d* the men every one into Zec 11:6 4672
of their hand I will not *d* them Zec 11:6 5337
the adversary *d* thee to the judge Mt 5:25 *3860*
the judge *d* thee to the officer, Mt 5:25 *3860*
temptation, but *d* us from evil Mt 6:13 *4506*
for they will *d* you up to the Mt 10:17 *3860*
But when they *d* you up, take no Mt 10:19 *3860*
the brother shall *d* up the Mt 10:21 *3860*
shall *d* him to the Gentiles to Mt 20:19 *3860*
Then shall they *d* you up to be Mt 24:9 *3860*
give me, and I will *d* him unto you Mt 26:15 *3860*
let him *d* him now, if he will Mt 27:43 *4506*
shall *d* him to the Gentiles Mk 10:33 *3860*
for they shall *d* you up to Mk 13:9 *3860*
d you up, take no thought Mk 13:11 *3860*
but *d* us from evil Lk 11:4 *4506*
the judge *d* thee to the officer, Lk 12:58 *3860*
they might *d* him unto the power Lk 20:20 *3860*
that God by his hand would *d* them Acts 7:25 *1325*
and am come down to *d* them Acts 7:34 *1807*
shall *d* him into the hands of the Acts 21:11 *3860*
no man may *d* me unto them Acts 25:11 *5483*
of the Romans to *d* any man to die Acts 25:16 *5483*
who shall *d* me from the body of Rom 7:24 *4506*
To *d* such a one unto Satan for 1Cor 5:5 *3860*
from so great a death, and doth *d* 2Cor 1:10 *4506*
we trust that he will yet *d* us 2Cor 1:10 *4506*
that he might *d* us from this Gal 1:4 *1807*
the Lord shall *d* me from every 2Ti 4:18 *4506*
d them who through fear of death Heb 2:15 *525*
The Lord knoweth how to *d* the 2Pet 2:9 *4506*

DELIVERANCE {16}

to save your lives by a great *d* Gen 45:7 6413
Thou hast given this great *d* into Judg 15:18 8668
the LORD had given *d* unto Syria 2Kin 5:1 8668
said, The arrow of the LORD's *d* 2Kin 13:17 8668
and the arrow of *d* from Syria 2Kin 13:17 8668
the LORD saved them by a great *d* 1Chr 11:14 8668
but I will grant them some *d* 2Chr 12:7 6413
and hast given us such *d* as this Ezr 9:13 6413
d arise to the Jews from another Est 4:14 2020
Great *d* giveth he to his king Ps 18:50 3444
compass me about with songs of *d* Ps 32:7 6405
not wrought any *d* in the earth Is 26:18 3444
Zion and in Jerusalem shall be *d* Joel 2:32 6413
But upon mount Zion shall be *d* Obad 17 6413
to preach *d* to the captives, and Lk 4:18 *859*
were tortured, not accepting *d* Heb 11:35 *629*

DELIVERANCES {1}

command *d* for Jacob Ps 44:4 3444

DELIVERED {291}

into your hand are they *d* Gen 9:2 5414
which hath *d* thine enemies into Gen 14:20 4042
her days to be *d* were fulfilled Gen 25:24 3205
he *d* them into the hand of his Gen 32:16 5414
he *d* him out of their hands Gen 37:21 5337
are *d* ere the midwives come in Ex 1:19 3205
An Egyptian *d* us out of the hand Ex 2:19 5337
hast thou *d* thy people at all Ex 5:23 5337
the Egyptians, and *d* our houses Ex 12:27 5337
d me from the sword of Pharaoh Ex 18:4 5337
the way, and how the LORD *d* them Ex 18:8 5337
whom he had *d* out of the hand of Ex 18:9 5337
who hath *d* you out of the hand of Ex 18:10 5337
who hath *d* the people from under Ex 18:10 5337
in that which was *d* him to keep Lev 6:2 6487
or that which was *d* him to keep Lev 6:4 6487
ye shall be *d* into the hand of Lev 26:25 5414
of Israel, and *d* up the Canaanites Num 21:3 5414
for I have *d* him into thy hand, Num 21:34 5414
So there were *d* out of the Num 31:5 4560
the LORD our God *d* him before us Deut 2:33 5414
the LORD our God *d* all unto us Deut 2:36 5414
So the LORD our God *d* into our Deut 3:3 5414
of stone, and *d* them unto me Deut 5:22 5414
the LORD *d* unto me two tables of Deut 9:10 5414
God hath *d* it into thine hands Deut 20:13 5414
God hath *d* them into thine hands Deut 21:10 5414
d it unto the priests the sons of Deut 31:9 5414
Truly the LORD hath *d* into our Josh 2:24 5414
d them out of the hand of the Josh 9:26 5337
for I have *d* them into thine hand Josh 10:8 5414
LORD *d* up the Amorites before the Josh 10:12 5414
God hath *d* them into your hand Josh 10:19 5414
And the LORD *d* it also, and the Josh 10:30 5414
the LORD *d* Lachish into the hand Josh 10:32 5414
the LORD *d* them into the hand of Josh 11:8 5414
the LORD *d* all their enemies into Josh 21:44 5414
now ye have *d* the children of Josh 22:31 5337
so I *d* you out of his hand Josh 24:10 5337
and I *d* them into your hand Josh 24:11 5414
I have *d* the land into his hand Judg 1:2 5414
the LORD *d* the Canaanites and the Judg 1:4 5414
he *d* them into the hands of Judg 2:14 5414
which *d* them out of the hand of Judg 2:16 3467
d them out of the hand of their Judg 2:18 3467
neither *d* he them into the hand Judg 2:23 5414
who *d* them, even Othniel the son Judg 3:9 3467
the LORD *d* Chushan-rishathaim Judg 3:10 5414
for the LORD hath *d* your enemies Judg 3:28 5414
and he also *d* Israel Judg 3:31 3467
hath *d* Sisera into thine hand Judg 4:14 5414
They that are *d* from the noise of Judg 5:11
the LORD *d* them into the hand of Judg 6:1 5414
I *d* you out of the hand of the Judg 6:9 5337
d us into the hands of the Judg 6:13 5414
for I have *d* it into thine hand Judg 7:9 5414
into his hand hath God *d* Midian Judg 7:14 5414
for the LORD hath *d* into your Judg 7:15 5414
God hath *d* into your hands the Judg 8:3 5414
when the LORD hath *d* Zebah Judg 8:7 5414
for thou hast *d* us from the hand Judg 8:22 3467
who had *d* them out of the hands Judg 8:34 5337
d you out of the hand of Midian Judg 9:17 5337
I *d* you out of their hand Judg 10:12 3467
And the LORD God of Israel *d* Sihon Judg 11:21 5414
the LORD *d* them into his hands Judg 11:32 5414
ye *d* me not out of their hands Judg 12:2 3467
And when I saw that ye *d* me not Judg 12:3 3467
the LORD *d* them into my hand Judg 12:3 5414
the LORD *d* them into the hand of Judg 13:1 5414
Our god hath *d* Samson our enemy Judg 16:23 5414
Our god hath *d* into our hands our Judg 16:24 5414
was with child, near to be *d* 1Sa 4:19 3205
d you out of the hand of the 1Sa 10:18 5337
d you out of the hand of your 1Sa 12:11 5337
for the LORD hath *d* them into our 1Sa 14:10 5414
for the LORD hath *d* them into the 1Sa 14:12 5414
d Israel out of the hands of them 1Sa 14:48 5337
him, and *d* it out of his mouth 1Sa 17:35 5337
The LORD that *d* me out of the paw 1Sa 17:37 5337
God hath *d* him into mine hand 1Sa 23:7 5234
but God *d* him not into his hand 1Sa 23:14 5414
d thee to day into mine hand in 1Sa 24:10 5414
the LORD had *d* me into thine hand 1Sa 24:18 5462
God hath *d* thine enemy into thine 1Sa 26:8 5462
for the LORD *d* thee into my hand 1Sa 26:23 5414
d the company that came against 1Sa 30:23 5414
have not *d* thee into the hand of 2Sa 3:8 4672
the rest of the people he *d* into 2Sa 10:10 5414
I *d* thee out of the hand of Saul 2Sa 12:7 5337
the LORD hath *d* the kingdom into 2Sa 16:8 5414
which hath *d* up the men that 2Sa 18:28 5462
he *d* us out of the hand of the 2Sa 19:9 4422
men of his sons be *d* unto us 2Sa 21:6 5414
he *d* them into the hands of the 2Sa 21:9 5414
in the day that the LORD had *d* 2Sa 22:1 5337
He *d* me from my strong enemy, and 2Sa 22:18 5337
he *d* me, because he delighted in 2Sa 22:20 2502
Thou also hast *d* me from the 2Sa 22:44 6403
thou hast *d* me from the violent 2Sa 22:49 5337
I was *d* of a child with her in 1Kin 3:17 3205
the third day after that I was *d* 1Kin 3:18 3205
that this woman was *d* also 1Kin 3:18 3205
the LORD hath *d* him unto the lion 1Kin 13:26 5414
d them into the hand of his 1Kin 15:18 5414
house, and *d* him unto his mother 1Kin 17:23 5414
into whose hand they *d* the money 2Kin 12:15 5414
he *d* them into the hand of Hazael 2Kin 13:3 5414
d them into the hand of spoilers, 2Kin 17:20 5414
this city shall not be *d* into the 2Kin 18:30 5414
any of the gods of the nations *d* 2Kin 18:33 5337
have they *d* Samaria out of mine 2Kin 18:34 5337
that have *d* their country out of 2Kin 18:35 5337
Jerusalem shall not be *d* into the 2Kin 19:10 5414

and shalt thou be *d* 2Kin 19:11 5337
d them which my fathers have 2Kin 19:12 5337
money that was *d* into their hand 2Kin 22:7 5414
have *d* it into the hand of them 2Kin 22:9 5414
the priest hath *d* me a book 2Kin 22:10 5414
Hagarites were *d* into their hand 1Chr 5:20 5414
d it, and slew the Philistines 1Chr 11:14 5337
Then on that day David *d* first 1Chr 16:7 5414
the rest of the people he *d* unto 1Chr 19:11 5414
God *d* them into their hand 2Chr 13:16 5414
he *d* them into thine hand 2Chr 16:8 5414
they shall be *d* into your hand 2Chr 18:14 5414
d to the captains of hundreds 2Chr 23:9 5414
the LORD *d* a very great host into 2Chr 24:24 5414
Wherefore the LORD his God *d* him 2Chr 28:5 5414
he was also *d* into the hand of 2Chr 28:5 5414
he hath *d* them into your hand, and 2Chr 28:9 5414
he hath *d* them to trouble, to 2Chr 29:8 5414
d their people out of mine hand 2Chr 32:17 5337
they *d* the money that was brought 2Chr 34:9 5414
Hilkiah *d* the book to Shaphan 2Chr 34:15 5414
have *d* it into the hand of the 2Chr 34:17 5414
Babylon, and they were *d* unto one Ezr 5:14 3052
he *d* us from the hand of the Ezr 8:31 5337
they *d* the king's commissions Ezr 8:36 5414
been *d* into the hand of the kings Ezr 9:7 5414
horse be *d* to the hand of one of Est 6:9 5414
God hath *d* me to the ungodly, and Job 16:11 5462
it is *d* by the pureness of thine Job 22:30 4422
so should I be *d* for ever from my Job 23:7 6403
Because I *d* the poor that cried, Job 29:12 4422
I have *d* him that without cause Ps 7:4 2502
d him from the hand of all his Ps 18:*t* 5337
He *d* me from my strong enemy, and Ps 18:17 5337
he *d* me, because he delighted in Ps 18:19 2502
Thou hast *d* me from the strivings Ps 18:43 6403
thou hast *d* me from the violent Ps 18:48 5337
They cried unto thee, and were *d* Ps 22:5 4422
man is not *d* by much strength Ps 33:16 5337
me, and *d* me from all my fears Ps 34:4 5337
For he hath *d* me out of all Ps 54:7 5337
He hath *d* my soul in peace from Ps 55:18 6299
For thou hast *d* my soul from Ps 56:13 5337
That thy beloved may be *d* Ps 60:5 2502
let me be *d* from them that hate Ps 69:14 5337
day when he *d* them from the enemy Ps 78:42 6299
d his strength into captivity, and Ps 78:61 5414
his hands were *d* from the pots Ps 81:6 5674
calledst in trouble, and I *d* thee Ps 81:7 2502
thou hast *d* my soul from the Ps 86:13 5337
he *d* them out of their distresses Ps 107:6 5337
d them from their destructions Ps 107:20 4422
That thy beloved may be *d* Ps 108:6 2502
For thou hast *d* my soul from Ps 116:8 2502
The righteous is *d* out of trouble Prov 11:8 2502
knowledge shall the just be *d* Prov 11:9 2502
seed of the righteous shall be *d* Prov 11:21 4422
walketh wisely, he shall be *d* Prov 28:26 4422
and he by his wisdom *d* the city Eccl 9:15 4422
to be *d* from the king of Assyria Is 20:6 5337
the book is *d* to him that is not Is 29:12 5414
he hath *d* them to the slaughter Is 34:2 5414
this city shall not be *d* into the Is 36:15 5414
any of the gods of the nations *d* Is 36:18 5337
have they *d* Samaria out of my Is 36:19 5337
that have *d* their land out of my Is 36:20 5337
and shalt thou be *d* Is 37:11 5337
d them which my fathers have Is 37:12 5337
thou hast in love to my soul *d* it Is 38:17
mighty, or the lawful captive *d* Is 49:24 4422
prey of the terrible shall be *d* Is 49:25 4422
came, she was *d* of a man child Is 66:7 4422
and say, We are *d* to do all these Jer 7:10 5337
for he hath *d* the soul of the Jer 20:13 5337
but shall surely be *d* into the Jer 32:4 5414
Now when I had *d* the evidence of Jer 32:16 5414
It shall be *d* into the hand of Jer 32:36 5414
be taken, and *d* into his hand Jer 34:3 5414
thou shalt be *d* into the hand of Jer 37:17 5414
she shall be *d* into the hand of Jer 46:24 5414
the Lord hath *d* me into their Lam 1:14 5414
but thou hast *d* thy soul Eze 3:19 5337
also thou hast *d* thy soul Eze 3:21 5337
they only shall be *d*, but the Eze 14:16 5337
they only shall be *d* themselves Eze 14:18 5337
d them to cause them to pass Eze 16:21 5414
d thee unto the will of them that Eze 16:27 5414
he break the covenant, and be *d* Eze 17:15 4422
Wherefore I have *d* her into the Eze 23:9 5414
I have therefore *d* him into the Eze 31:11 5414
for they are all *d* unto death Eze 31:14 5414
she is *d* to the sword Eze 32:20 5414
but thou hast *d* thy soul Eze 33:9 5337
d them out of the hand of those Eze 34:27 5337
d his servants that trusted in Dan 3:28 7804
who hath *d* Daniel from the power Dan 6:27 7804
that time thy people shall be *d* Dan 12:1 4422
the name of the LORD shall be *d* Joel 2:32 4422
because they *d* up the whole Amos 1:6 5462
escapeth of them shall not be *d* Amos 9:1 4422
neither shouldest thou have *d* up Obad 14 5462
there shalt thou be *d* Mic 4:10 5337
that he may be *d* from the power Hab 2:9 5337
they that tempt God are even *d* Mal 3:15 4422
All things are *d* unto me of my Mt 11:27 *3860*
d him to the tormentors, till he Mt 18:34 *3860*
and *d* unto them his goods Mt 25:14 *3860*
d him to Pontius Pilate the Mt 27:2 *3860*
knew that for envy they had *d* him Mt 27:18 *3860*
Jesus, he *d* him to be crucified Mt 27:26 *3860*
Pilate commanded the body to be *d* Mt 27:58 *591*
your tradition, which ye have *d* Mk 7:13 *3860*
The Son of man is *d* into the Mk 9:31 *3860*
shall be *d* unto the chief priests Mk 10:33 *3860*
him away, and *d* him to Pilate Mk 15:1 *3860*
chief priests had *d* him for envy Mk 15:10 *3860*
d Jesus, when he had scourged him Mk 15:15 *3860*
Even as they *d* them unto us Lk 1:2 *3860*
time came that she should be *d* Lk 1:57 *5088*
being *d* out of the hand of our Lk 1:74 *4506*
accomplished that she should be *d* Lk 2:6 *5088*
for that is *d* unto me Lk 4:6 *3860*
there was *d* unto him the book of Lk 4:17 *1929*
And he *d* him to his mother Lk 7:15 *1325*
d him again to his father Lk 9:42 *591*
shall be *d* into the hands of men Lk 9:44 *3860*
All things are *d* to me of my Lk 10:22 *3860*
that thou mayest be *d* from him Lk 12:58 *525*
For he shall be *d* unto the Lk 18:32 *3860*
d them ten pounds, and said unto Lk 19:13 *1325*
but he *d* Jesus to their will Lk 23:25 *3860*
The Son of man must be *d* into the Lk 24:7 *3860*
our rulers *d* him to be condemned Lk 24:20 *3860*
as soon as she is *d* of the child Jn 16:21 *1080*
would not have *d* him up unto thee Jn 18:30 *3860*
chief priests have *d* thee unto me Jn 18:35 *3860*
I should not be *d* to the Jews Jn 18:36 *3860*
therefore he that *d* me unto thee Jn 19:11 *3860*
Then *d* he him therefore unto them Jn 19:16 *3860*
being *d* by the determinate Acts 2:23 *1560*
whom ye *d* up, and denied him in Acts 3:13 *3860*
the customs which Moses *d* us Acts 6:14 *3860*
d him out of all his afflictions, Acts 7:10 *1807*
d him to four quaternions of Acts 12:4 *3860*
hath *d* me out of the hand of Acts 12:11 *1807*
together, they *d* the epistle Acts 15:30 *1929*
they *d* them the decrees for to Acts 16:4 *3860*
d the epistle to the governor, Acts 23:33 *325*
sail into Italy, they *d* Paul Acts 27:1 *3860*
the centurion *d* the prisoners to Acts 28:16 *3860*
yet was I *d* prisoner from Acts 28:17 *3860*
Who was *d* for our offences, and Rom 4:25 *3860*
form of doctrine which was *d* you Rom 6:17 *3860*
But now we are *d* from the law Rom 7:6 *2673*
creature itself also shall be *d* Rom 8:21 *1659*
but *d* him up for us all, how Rom 8:32 *3860*
That I may be *d* from them that do Rom 15:31 *4506*
ordinances, as I *d* them to you 1Cor 11:2 *3860*
Lord that which also I *d* unto you 1Cor 11:23 *3860*
For I *d* unto you first of all 1Cor 15:3 *3860*
when he shall have *d* up the 1Cor 15:24 *3860*
Who *d* us from so great a death, 2Cor 1:10 *4506*
d unto death for Jesus' sake 2Cor 4:11 *3860*
Who hath *d* us from the power of Col 1:13 *4506*
which *d* us from the wrath to come 1Th 1:10 *4506*
And that we may be *d* from 2Th 3:2 *4506*
whom I have *d* unto Satan, that 1Ti 1:20 *3860*
but out of them all the Lord *d* me 2Ti 3:11 *4506*
I was *d* out of the mouth of the 2Ti 4:17 *4506*
was *d* of a child when she was Heb 11:11 *5088*
d them into chains of darkness, 2Pet 2:4 *3860*
d just Lot, vexed with the filthy 2Pet 2:7 *4506*
the holy commandment *d* unto them 2Pet 2:21 *3860*
which was once *d* unto the saints Jude 3 *3860*
in birth, and pained to be *d* Rev 12:2 *5088*
the woman which was ready to be *d* Rev 12:4 *5088*
hell *d* up the dead which were in Rev 20:13 *1325*

DELIVEREDST {3}
Therefore thou *d* them into the Neh 9:27 5414
thou *d* unto me five talents Mt 25:20 *3860*
thou *d* unto me two talents Mt 25:22 *3860*

DELIVERER {10}
the LORD raised up a *d* to the Judg 3:9 3467
LORD, the LORD raised them up a *d* Judg 3:15 3467
And there was no *d*, because it was Judg 18:28 5337
my rock, and my fortress, and my *d* 2Sa 22:2 6403
my rock, and my fortress, and my *d* Ps 18:2 6403
thou art my help and my *d* Ps 40:17 6403
thou art my help and my *d* Ps 70:5 6403
my high tower, and my *d* Ps 144:2 6403
a *d* by the hand of the angel Acts 7:35 *3086*
shall come out of Sion the *D* Rom 11:26 *4506*

DELIVEREST {2}
which *d* the poor from him that is Ps 35:10 5337
that which thou *d* will I give up Mic 6:14 6403

DELIVERETH {13}
He *d* the poor in his affliction, Job 36:15 2502
He *d* me from mine enemies Ps 18:48 6403
them that fear him, and *d* them Ps 34:7 2502
d them out of all their troubles Ps 34:17 5337
but the LORD *d* him out of them Ps 34:19 5337
he *d* them out of the hand of the Ps 97:10 5337
who *d* David his servant from the Ps 144:10 6475
but righteousness *d* from death Prov 10:2 5337
but righteousness *d* from death Prov 11:4 5337
A true witness *d* souls Prov 14:25 5337
d girdles unto the merchant Prov 31:24 5414
they are for a prey, and none *d* Is 42:22 5337
He *d* and rescueth, and he worketh Dan 6:27 7804

DELIVERING {3}
d you up to the synagogues, and Lk 21:12 *3860*
d into prisons both men and women Acts 22:4 *3860*
D thee from the people, and from Acts 26:17 *1807*

DELIVERY {1}
draweth near the time of her *d* Is 26:17 3205

DELUSION {1}
God shall send them strong *d* 2Th 2:11 *4106*

DELUSIONS {1}
I also will choose their *d* Is 66:4 8586

DEMAND {4}
for I will *d* of thee, and answer Job 38:3 7592
I will *d* of thee, and declare thou Job 40:7 7592
I will *d* of thee, and declare thou Job 42:4 7592
the *d* by the word of the holy Dan 4:17 7595

DEMANDED {7}
set over them, were beaten, and *d* Ex 5:14 559
David *d* of him how Joab did, and 2Sa 11:7 7592
king hath *d* cannot the wise men Dan 2:27 7593
he *d* of them where Christ should Mt 2:4 *4441*
And the soldiers likewise *d* of him Lk 3:14 *1905*
when he was *d* of the Pharisees, Lk 17:20 *1905*
d who he was, and what he had done Acts 21:33 *4441*

DEMAS *(de'-mas)* {3} *A companion of Paul.*
Luke, the beloved physician, and *D* Col 4:14 *1214*
For *D* hath forsaken me, having 2Ti 4:10 *1214*
Marcus, Aristarchus, *D*, Lucas, my Philem 24 *1214*

DEMETRIUS *(de-me'-tre-us)* {3}
1. An opponent of Paul.
For a certain man named *D* Acts 19:24 *1216*
Wherefore if *D*, and the craftsmen Acts 19:38 *1216*
2. Disciple commended by John.
D hath good report of all men, and 3Jn 12 *1216*

DEMONSTRATION {1}
but in *d* of the Spirit and of 1Cor 2:4 *585*

DEN {19}
wait secretly as a lion in his *d* Ps 10:9 5520
put his hand on the cockatrice' *d* Is 11:8 3975
become a *d* of robbers in your Jer 7:11 4631
heaps, and a *d* of dragons Jer 9:11 4583
Judah desolate, and a *d* of dragons Jer 10:22 4583
shall be cast into the *d* of lions Dan 6:7 1358
shall be cast into the *d* of lions Dan 6:12 1358
and cast him into the *d* of lions Dan 6:16 1358
and laid upon the mouth of the *d* Dan 6:17 1358
went in haste unto the *d* of lions Dan 6:19 1358
And when he came to the *d*, he Dan 6:20 1358
take Daniel up out of the *d* Dan 6:23 1358
Daniel was taken up out of the *d* Dan 6:23 1358
cast them into the *d* of lions Dan 6:24 1358
they came at the bottom of the *d* Dan 6:24 1358
a young lion cry out of his *d* Amos 3:4 4585
ye have made it a *d* of thieves Mt 21:13 *4693*
ye have made it a *d* of thieves Mk 11:17 *4693*
ye have made it a *d* of thieves Lk 19:46 *4693*

DENIED {19}
Then Sarah *d*, saying, I laughed Gen 18:15 3584
and I *d* him not 1Kin 20:7 4513
for I should have *d* the God that Job 31:28 3584
But he *d* before them all, saying, Mt 26:70 *720*
again he *d* with an oath, I do not Mt 26:72 *720*
But he *d*, saying, I know not, Mk 14:68 *720*
And he *d* it again Mk 14:70 *720*
When all *d*, Peter and they that Lk 8:45 *720*
be *d* before the angels of God Lk 12:9 *533*
he *d* him, saying, Woman, I know Lk 22:57 *720*
And he confessed, and *d* not Jn 1:20 *720*
crow, till thou hast *d* me thrice Jn 13:38 *533*
He *d* it, and said, I am not Jn 18:25 *720*
Peter then *d* again Jn 18:27 *720*
d him in the presence of Pilate, Acts 3:13 *720*
But ye *d* the Holy One and the Just Acts 3:14 *720*
he hath *d* the faith, and is worse 1Ti 5:8 *720*
my name, and hast not *d* my faith Rev 2:13 *720*
my word, and hast not *d* my name Rev 3:8 *720*

DENIETH {4}
But he that *d* me before men shall Lk 12:9 *720*
that *d* that Jesus is the Christ 1Jn 2:22 *720*
that *d* the Father and the Son 1Jn 2:22 *720*
Whosoever *d* the Son, the same 1Jn 2:23 *720*

DENOUNCE {1}
I *d* unto you this day, that ye Deut 30:18 5046

DENS {9}
of Israel made them the *d* which Judg 6:2 4492
Then the beasts go into *d* Job 37:8 695
When they couch in their *d* Job 38:40 4585
and lay them down in their *d* Ps 104:22 4585
and Hermon, from the lions' *d* Song 4:8 4585
and towers shall be for *d* for ever Is 32:14 4631
with prey, and his *d* with ravin Nah 2:12 4585
deserts, and in mountains, and in *d* Heb 11:38 *4693*
free man, hid themselves in the *d* Rev 6:15 *4693*

DENY {24}
unto you, lest ye *d* your God Josh 24:27 3584
one petition of thee, *d* me not 1Kin 2:16 7725
his place, then it shall *d* him Job 8:18 3584
d me them not before I die Prov 30:7 4513
d thee, and say, Who is the LORD Prov 30:9 3584
whosoever shall *d* me before men Mt 10:33 *720*
him will I also *d* before my Mt 10:33 *720*
come after me, let him *d* himself Mt 16:24 *533*
cock crow, thou shalt *d* me thrice Mt 26:34 *533*
with thee, yet will I not *d* thee Mt 26:35 *533*
cock crow, thou shalt *d* me thrice Mt 26:75 *533*
come after me, let him *d* himself Mk 8:34 *533*
twice, thou shalt *d* me thrice Mk 14:30 *533*
I will not *d* thee in any wise Mk 14:31 *533*
twice, thou shalt *d* me thrice Mk 14:72 *533*

D

come after me, let him *d* himself ... Lk 9:23 *533*
which *d* that there is any ... Lk 20:27 *483*
thrice *d* that thou knowest me ... Lk 22:34 *533*
cock crow, thou shalt *d* me thrice ... Lk 22:61 *533*
and we cannot *d* it ... Acts 4:16 *720*
if we *d* him, he also will *d* us ... 2Ti 2:12 *720*
he cannot *d* himself ... 2Ti 2:13 *720*
but in works they *d* him, being ... Titus 1:16 *720*

DENYING {4}
but *d* the power thereof ... 2Ti 3:5 *720*
d ungodliness and worldly lusts, ... Titus 2:12 *720*
even *d* the Lord that bought them, ... 2Pet 2:1 *720*
d the only Lord God, and our Lord ... Jude 4 *720*

DEPART {129}
or if thou *d* to the right hand, ... Gen 13:9
sceptre shall not *d* from Judah ... Gen 49:10 5493
And the frogs shall *d* from thee ... Ex 8:11 5493
of flies may *d* from Pharaoh ... Ex 8:29 5493
And Moses let his father in law *d* ... Ex 18:27 7971
so that her fruit *d* from her ... Ex 21:22 3318
And the LORD said unto Moses, *D* ... Ex 33:1 3212
And then shall he *d* from thee ... Lev 25:41 3318
but I will *d* to mine own land, and ... Num 10:30 3212
unto the congregation, saying, *D* ... Num 16:26 5493
lest they *d* from thy heart all ... Deut 4:9 5493
didst *d* out of the land of Egypt ... Deut 9:7 3318
law shall not *d* out of thy mouth ... Josh 1:8 4185
So Joshua let the people *d* ... Josh 24:28 7971
D not hence, I pray thee, until I ... Judg 6:18 4185
d early from mount Gilead ... Judg 7:3 6852
the morning, that he rose up to *d* ... Judg 19:5 3212
And when the man rose up to *d* ... Judg 19:7 3212
the morning on the fifth day to *d* ... Judg 19:8 3212
And when the man rose up to *d* ... Judg 19:9 3212
Saul said unto the Kenites, Go, *d* ... 1Sa 15:6 5493
d, and get thee into the land of ... 1Sa 22:5 3212
in the morning, and have light, *d* ... 1Sa 29:10 3212
rose up early to *d* in the morning ... 1Sa 29:11 3212
they may lead them away, and *d* ... 1Sa 30:22 3212
mercy shall not *d* away from him ... 2Sa 7:15 5493
and to morrow I will let thee *d* ... 2Sa 11:12 7971
shall never *d* from thine house ... 2Sa 12:10 5493
make speed to *d*, lest he overtake ... 2Sa 15:14 3212
only, and I will *d* from the city ... 2Sa 20:21 3212
statutes, I did not *d* from them ... 2Sa 22:23 5493
Hadad said to Pharaoh, Let me *d* ... 1Kin 11:21 7971
D yet for three days, then come ... 1Kin 12:5 3212
of the LORD, and returned to *d* ... 1Kin 12:24 3212
of Israel, that he may *d* from me ... 1Kin 15:19 5927
of Israel, that he may *d* from me ... 2Chr 16:3 5927
and God moved them to *d* from him ... 2Chr 18:31
they might not *d* from their ... 2Chr 35:15 5493
How long wilt thou not *d* from me ... Job 7:19 8159
He shall not *d* out of darkness ... Job 15:30 5493
The increase of his house shall *d* ... Job 20:28 1540
they say unto God, *D* from us ... Job 21:14 5493
Which said unto God, *D* from us ... Job 22:17 5493
to *d* from evil is understanding ... Job 28:28 5493
D from me, all ye workers of ... Ps 6:8 5493
D from evil, and do good ... Ps 34:14 5493
D from evil, and do good ... Ps 37:27 5493
guile *d* not from her streets ... Ps 55:11 4185
A froward heart shall *d* from me ... Ps 101:4 5493
D from me, ye evildoers ... Ps 119:115 5493
d from me therefore, ye bloody ... Ps 139:19 5493
fear the LORD, and *d* from evil ... Prov 3:7 5493
let not them *d* from thine eyes ... Prov 3:21 3868
Let them not *d* from thine eyes ... Prov 4:21 3868
d not from the words of my mouth ... Prov 5:7 5493
to *d* from the snares of death ... Prov 13:14 5493
to fools to *d* from evil ... Prov 13:19 5493
to *d* from the snares of death ... Prov 14:27 5493
that he may *d* from hell beneath ... Prov 15:24 5493
fear of the LORD men *d* from evil ... Prov 16:6 5493
of the upright is to *d* from evil ... Prov 16:17 5493
evil shall not *d* from his house ... Prov 17:13 4185
he is old, he will not *d* from it ... Prov 22:6 5493
not his foolishness *d* from him ... Prov 27:22 5493
The envy also of Ephraim shall *d* ... Is 11:13 5493
shall his yoke *d* from off them ... Is 14:25 5493
his burden *d* from off their ... Is 14:25 5493
D ye, *d* ye, go ye out from ... Is 52:11 5493
d ye, go ye out from thence, ... Is 52:11 5493
For the mountains shall *d* ... Is 54:10 4185
my kindness shall not *d* from thee ... Is 54:10 4185
shall not *d* out of thy mouth, nor ... Is 59:21 4185
lest my soul *d* from thee ... Jer 6:8 3363
they that *d* from me shall be ... Jer 17:13 3249
those ordinances *d* from before me ... Jer 31:36 4185
that they shall not *d* from me ... Jer 32:40 5493
Chaldeans shall surely *d* from us ... Jer 37:9 1980
for they shall not *d* ... Jer 37:9 1980
they shall remove, they shall *d* ... Jer 50:3 1980
They cried unto them, *D* ye ... Lam 4:15 5493
d, *d*, touch not ... Lam 4:15 5493
d, *d*, touch not ... Lam 4:15 5493
and my jealousy shall *d* from thee ... Eze 16:42 5493
also to them when I *d* from them ... Hos 9:12 5493
Arise ye, and *d* ... Mic 2:10 3212
the sceptre of Egypt shall *d* away ... Zec 10:11 5493
d from me, ye that work iniquity ... Mt 7:23 *672*
to *d* unto the other side ... Mt 8:18 *565*
he would *d* out of their coasts ... Mt 8:34 *3327*
when ye *d* out of that house or ... Mt 10:14 *1831*
said unto them, They need not *d* ... Mt 14:16 *565*
D from me, ye cursed, into ... Mt 25:41 *4198*
pray him to *d* out of their coasts ... Mk 5:17 *565*
abide till ye *d* from that place ... Mk 6:10 *1831*
nor hear you, when ye *d* thence ... Mk 6:11 *1607*
thou thy servant *d* in peace ... Lk 2:29 *630*
that he should not *d* from them ... Lk 4:42 *4198*
Jesus' knees, saying, *D* from me ... Lk 5:8 *1831*
about besought him to *d* from them ... Lk 8:37 *565*
into, there abide, and thence *d* ... Lk 9:4 *1831*
thee, thou shalt not *d* thence ... Lk 12:59 *1831*
d from me, all ye workers of ... Lk 13:27 *868*
him, Get thee out, and *d* hence ... Lk 13:31 *4198*
are in the midst of it *d* out ... Lk 21:21 *1633*
D hence, and go into Judaea, that ... Jn 7:3 *3327*
d out of this world unto the ... Jn 13:1 *3327*
but if I *d*, I will send him unto ... Jn 16:7 *4198*
they should not *d* from Jerusalem ... Acts 1:4 *5562*
now therefore *d*, and go in peace ... Acts 16:36 *1831*
desired them to *d* out of the city ... Acts 16:39 *1831*
commanded all Jews to *d* from Rome ... Acts 18:2 *5562*
them, ready to *d* on the morrow ... Acts 20:7 *1826*
And he said unto me, *D* ... Acts 22:21 *4198*
captain then let the young man *d* ... Acts 23:22 *630*
himself would *d* shortly thither ... Acts 25:4 *1607*
part advised to *d* thence also ... Acts 27:12 *321*
not the wife *d* from her husband ... 1Cor 7:10 *5562*
But and if she *d*, let her remain ... 1Cor 7:11 *5562*
But if the unbelieving *d*, let him ... 1Cor 7:15 *5562*
the unbelieving *d*, let him *d* ... 1Cor 7:15 *5562*
thrice, that it might *d* from me ... 2Cor 12:8 *868*
betwixt two, having a desire to *d* ... Phil 1:23 *360*
times some shall *d* from the faith ... 1Ti 4:1 *868*
name of Christ *d* from iniquity ... 2Ti 2:19 *868*
D in peace, be ye warmed and ... Jas 2:16 *5217*

DEPARTED {217}
So Abram *d*, as the LORD had ... Gen 12:4 3212
years old when he *d* out of Haran ... Gen 12:4 3318
in Sodom, and his goods, and *d* ... Gen 14:12 3212
and she *d*, and wandered in the ... Gen 21:14 3212
of the camels of his master, and *d* ... Gen 24:10 3212
Isaac *d* thence, and pitched his ... Gen 26:17 3212
away, and they *d* from him in peace ... Gen 26:31 3212
my sleep *d* from mine eyes ... Gen 31:40 5074
and Laban *d*, and returned unto his ... Gen 31:55 3212
And the man said, They are *d* hence ... Gen 37:17 5265
asses with the corn, and *d* thence ... Gen 42:26 3212
sent his brethren away, and they *d* ... Gen 45:24 3212
For they were *d* from Rephidim ... Ex 19:2 5265
d not out of the tabernacle ... Ex 33:11 4185
of the children of Israel *d* from ... Ex 35:20 3318
if the plague be *d* from them ... Lev 13:58 5493
they *d* from the mount of the LORD ... Num 10:33 5265
kindled against them; and he *d* ... Num 12:9 3212
And the cloud *d* from off the ... Num 12:10 5493
their defence is *d* from them ... Num 14:9 5493
and Moses, *d* not out of the camp ... Num 14:44 4185
the elders of Midian *d* with the ... Num 22:7 3212
they *d* from Rameses in the first ... Num 33:3 5265
they *d* from Succoth, and pitched ... Num 33:6 5265
they *d* from before Pi-hahiroth, ... Num 33:8 5265
they *d* from Dophkah, and encamped ... Num 33:13 5265
they *d* from Rephidim, and pitched ... Num 33:15 5265
they *d* from Kibroth-hattaavah, and ... Num 33:17 5265
they *d* from Hazeroth, and pitched ... Num 33:18 5265
they *d* from Rithmah, and pitched ... Num 33:19 5265
they *d* from Rimmon-parez, and ... Num 33:20 5265
they *d* from Tahath, and pitched at ... Num 33:27 5265
they *d* from Hashmonah, and ... Num 33:30 5265
they *d* from Moseroth, and pitched ... Num 33:31 5265
they *d* from Ebronah, and encamped ... Num 33:35 5265
they *d* from mount Hor, and pitched ... Num 33:41 5265
they *d* from Zalmonah, and pitched ... Num 33:42 5265
they *d* from Punon, and pitched in ... Num 33:43 5265
they *d* from Oboth, and pitched in ... Num 33:44 5265
they *d* from Iim, and pitched in ... Num 33:45 5265
they *d* from the mountains of ... Num 33:48 5265
when we *d* from Horeb, we went ... Deut 1:19 5265
when she is *d* out of his house, ... Deut 24:2 3318
And she sent them away, and they *d* ... Josh 2:21 3212
d from the children of Israel out ... Josh 22:9 3212
of the LORD *d* out of his sight ... Judg 6:21 1980
they *d* every man unto his place ... Judg 9:55 3212
not that the LORD was *d* from him ... Judg 16:20 5493
the man *d* out of the city from ... Judg 17:8 3212
Then the five men *d*, and came to ... Judg 18:7 3212
So they turned and *d*, and put the ... Judg 18:21 3212
that night, but he rose up and *d* ... Judg 19:10 3212
of Israel *d* thence at that time ... Judg 21:24 1980
The glory is *d* from Israel ... 1Sa 4:21 1540
said, The glory is *d* from Israel ... 1Sa 4:22 1540
not let the people go, and they *d* ... 1Sa 6:6 3212
When thou art *d* from me to day, ... 1Sa 10:2 3212
So the Kenites *d* from among the ... 1Sa 15:6 5493
Spirit of the LORD *d* from Saul ... 1Sa 16:14 5493
and the evil spirit *d* from him ... 1Sa 16:23 5493
was with him, and was *d* from Saul ... 1Sa 18:12 5493
And he arose and *d* ... 1Sa 20:42 3212
David therefore *d* thence, and ... 1Sa 22:1 3212
Then David *d*, and came into the ... 1Sa 22:5 3212
arose and *d* out of Keilah, and went ... 1Sa 23:13 3318
God is *d* from me, and answereth me ... 1Sa 28:15 5493
seeing the LORD is *d* from thee ... 1Sa 28:16 5493
So all the people *d* every one to ... 2Sa 6:19 3212
Uriah *d* out of the king's house, ... 2Sa 11:8 3318
And Nathan *d* unto his house ... 2Sa 12:15 3212
came to pass, after they were *d* ... 2Sa 17:21 3212
from the day the king *d* until the ... 2Sa 19:24 3212
have not wickedly *d* from my God ... 2Sa 22:22
And the people *d* ... 1Kin 12:5 3212
So Israel *d* unto their tents ... 1Kin 12:16 3212
And Jeroboam's wife arose, and *d* ... 1Kin 14:17 3212
So he *d* thence, and found Elisha ... 1Kin 19:19 3212
And the messengers *d*, and brought ... 1Kin 20:9 3212
as soon as thou art *d* from me ... 1Kin 20:36 1980
And as soon as he was *d* from him ... 1Kin 20:36 3212
So the prophet *d*, and waited for ... 1Kin 20:38 3212
And Elijah *d* ... 2Kin 1:4 3212
he *d* not therefrom ... 2Kin 3:3 5493
they *d* from him, and returned to ... 2Kin 3:27 5265
And he *d*, and took with him ten ... 2Kin 5:5 3212
So he *d* from him a little way ... 2Kin 5:19 3212
and he let the men go, and they *d* ... 2Kin 5:24 3212
So he *d* from Elisha, and came to ... 2Kin 8:14 3212
And he arose and *d*, and came to ... 2Kin 10:12 935
And when he was *d* thence, he ... 2Kin 10:15 3212
Jehu *d* not from after them, to ... 2Kin 10:29 5493
for he *d* not from the sins of ... 2Kin 10:31 5493
he *d* not therefrom ... 2Kin 13:2 5493
Nevertheless they *d* not from the ... 2Kin 13:6 5493
he *d* not from all the sins of ... 2Kin 13:11 5493
he *d* not from all the sins of ... 2Kin 14:24 5493
he *d* not from the sins of ... 2Kin 15:9 5493
he *d* not all his days from the ... 2Kin 15:18 5493
he *d* not from the sins of ... 2Kin 15:24 5493
he *d* not from the sins of ... 2Kin 15:28 5493
they *d* not from them ... 2Kin 17:22 5493
d not from following him, but ... 2Kin 18:6 5493
heard that he was *d* from Lachish ... 2Kin 19:8 5265
So Sennacherib king of Assyria *d* ... 2Kin 19:36 5265
all the people *d* every man to his ... 1Chr 16:43 3212
Wherefore Joab *d*, and went ... 1Chr 21:4 3318
they *d* not from the commandment ... 2Chr 8:15 5493
And the people *d* ... 2Chr 10:5 3212
d not from it, doing that which ... 2Chr 20:32 5493
years, and *d* without being desired ... 2Chr 21:20 3212
And when they were *d* from him ... 2Chr 24:25 3212
all his days they *d* not from ... 2Chr 34:33 5493
Then we *d* from the river of Ahava ... Ezr 8:31 5265
the cloud *d* not from them by day ... Neh 9:19 5493
have not wickedly *d* from my God ... Ps 18:21
who drove him away, and he *d* ... Ps 34:*t* 3212
Egypt was glad when they *d* ... Ps 105:38 3318
I have not *d* from thy judgments ... Ps 119:102 5493
the day that Ephraim *d* from Judah ... Is 7:17 5493
heard that he was *d* from Lachish ... Is 37:8 5265
So Sennacherib king of Assyria *d* ... Is 37:37 5265
Mine age is *d*, and is removed from ... Is 38:12 5265
the smiths, were *d* from Jerusalem ... Jer 29:2 3318
of them, they *d* from Jerusalem ... Jer 37:5 5927
d to go over to the Ammonites ... Jer 41:10 3212
And they *d*, and dwelt in the ... Jer 41:17 3212
of Zion all her beauty is *d* ... Lam 1:6 3318
heart, which hath *d* from me ... Eze 6:9 5493
Then the glory of the LORD *d* from ... Eze 10:18 3318
The kingdom is *d* from thee ... Dan 4:31 5709
thereof, because it is *d* from it ... Hos 10:5 1540
But ye are *d* out of the way ... Mal 2:8 5493
they had heard the king, they *d* ... Mt 2:9 *4198*
they *d* into their own country ... Mt 2:12 *402*
And when they were *d*, behold, the ... Mt 2:13 *402*
mother by night, and *d* into Egypt ... Mt 2:14 *402*
into prison, he *d* into Galilee ... Mt 4:12 *402*
And he arose, and *d* to his house ... Mt 9:7 *565*
And when Jesus *d* thence, two blind ... Mt 9:27 *3855*
But they, when they were *d* ... Mt 9:31 *1831*
he *d* thence to teach and to preach ... Mt 11:1 *3327*
And as they *d*, Jesus began to say ... Mt 11:7 *4198*
And when he was *d* thence, he went ... Mt 12:9 *3327*
these parables, he *d* thence ... Mt 13:53 *3332*
he *d* thence by ship into a desert ... Mt 14:13 *402*
d into the coasts of Tyre and ... Mt 15:21 *402*
Jesus *d* from thence, and came nigh ... Mt 15:29 *3327*
And he left them, and *d* ... Mt 16:4 *565*
and he *d* out of him ... Mt 17:18 *1831*
he *d* from Galilee, and came into ... Mt 19:1 *3332*
his hands on them, and *d* thence ... Mt 19:15 *4198*
as they *d* from Jericho, a great ... Mt 20:29 *1607*
went out, and *d* from the temple ... Mt 24:1 *4198*
of silver in the temple, and *d* ... Mt 27:5 *402*
the door of the sepulchre, and *d* ... Mt 27:60 *565*
they *d* quickly from the sepulchre ... Mt 28:8 *1831*
d into a solitary place, and there ... Mk 1:35 *565*
the leprosy *d* from him, and he was ... Mk 1:42 *565*
And he *d*, and began to publish in ... Mk 5:20 *565*
they *d* into a desert place by ... Mk 6:32 *565*
he *d* into a mountain to pray ... Mk 6:46 *565*
ship again *d* to the other side ... Mk 8:13 *565*
they *d* thence, and passed through ... Mk 9:30 *1831*
he *d* to his own house ... Lk 1:23 *565*
And the angel *d* from her ... Lk 1:38 *565*
which *d* not from the temple, but ... Lk 2:37 *868*
he *d* from him for a season ... Lk 4:13 *868*
And when it was day, he *d* and went ... Lk 4:42 *1831*
the leprosy *d* from him ... Lk 5:13 *565*
d to his own house, glorifying ... Lk 5:25 *565*
the messengers of John were *d* ... Lk 7:24 *565*
out of whom the devils were *d* ... Lk 8:35 *1831*
d besought him that he might be ... Lk 8:38 *1831*
And they *d*, and went through the ... Lk 9:6 *1831*
as they *d* from him, Peter said ... Lk 9:33 *1316*
his raiment, and wounded him, and *d* ... Lk 10:30 *565*
And on the morrow when he *d* ... Lk 10:35 *1831*
clothes laid by themselves, and *d* ... Lk 24:12 *565*
Judaea, and *d* again into Galilee ... Jn 4:3 *565*
Now after two days he *d* thence ... Jn 4:43 *565*
The man *d*, and told the Jews that ... Jn 5:15 *565*

he *d* again into a mountain ... Jn 6:15 *402*
These things spake Jesus, and *d* ... Jn 12:36 *565*
they *d* from the presence of the ... Acts 5:41 *4198*
which spake unto Cornelius was *d* ... Acts 10:7 *565*
Then *d* Barnabas to Tarsus, for to ... Acts 11:25 *1831*
and forthwith the angel *d* from him ... Acts 12:10 *868*
And he *d*, and went into another ... Acts 12:17 *1831*
the Holy Ghost, *d* unto Seleucia ... Acts 13:4 *2718*
But when they *d* from Perga ... Acts 13:14 *1330*
the next day he *d* with Barnabas ... Acts 14:20 *1831*
who *d* from them from Pamphylia, ... Acts 15:38 *868*
that they *d* in asunder one from ... Acts 15:39 *673*
And Paul chose Silas, and *d* ... Acts 15:40 *1831*
they comforted them, and *d* ... Acts 16:40 *1831*
to him with all speed, they *d* ... Acts 17:15 *1826*
So Paul *d* from among them ... Acts 17:33 *1831*
these things Paul *d* from Athens ... Acts 18:1 *5562*
he *d* thence, and entered into a ... Acts 18:7 *1831*
had spent some time there, he *d* ... Acts 18:23 *1831*
he *d* from them, and separated the ... Acts 19:9 *868*
and the diseases *d* from them ... Acts 19:12 *525*
d for to go into Macedonia ... Acts 20:1 *1831*
even till break of day, so he *d* ... Acts 20:11 *1831*
had accomplished those days, we *d* ... Acts 21:5 *1831*
we that were of Paul's company *d* ... Acts 21:8 *1831*
Then straightway they *d* from him ... Acts 22:29 *868*
and when we *d*, they laded us with ... Acts 28:10 *321*
after three months we *d* in a ship ... Acts 28:11 *321*
not among themselves, they *d* ... Acts 28:25 *630*
had said these words, the Jews *d* ... Acts 28:29 *565*
when I *d* from Macedonia, no ... Phil 4:15 *1831*
world, and is *d* unto Thessalonica ... 2Ti 4:10 *4198*
he therefore *d* for a season ... Philem 15 *5563*
the heaven *d* as a scroll when it ... Rev 6:14 *673*
soul lusted after are *d* from thee ... Rev 18:14 *565*
dainty and goodly are *d* from thee ... Rev 18:14 *565*

DEPARTETH {8}
wind carrieth him away, and he *d* ... Job 27:21 3212
wise man feareth, and *d* from evil ... Prov 14:16 5493
d in darkness, and his name shall ... Eccl 6:4 3212
he that *d* from evil maketh ... Is 59:15 5493
treacherously *d* from her husband ... Jer 3:20
whose heart *d* from the LORD ... Jer 17:5 5493
the prey *d* not ... Nah 3:1 4185
and bruising him hardly *d* from him ... Lk 9:39 *672*

DEPARTING {12}
to pass, as her soul was in *d* ... Gen 35:18 3318
their *d* out of the land of Egypt ... Ex 16:1 3318
d away from our God, speaking ... Is 59:13 5253
even by *d* from thy precepts and ... Dan 9:5 5493
transgressed thy law, even by *d* ... Dan 9:11 5493
great whoredom, *d* from the LORD ... Hos 1:2
And the people saw them *d*, and many ... Mk 6:33 *5217*
d from the coasts of Tyre and ... Mk 7:31 *1831*
John *d* from them returned to ... Acts 13:13 *672*
that after my *d* shall grievous ... Acts 20:29 *867*
in *d* from the living God ... Heb 3:12 *868*
made mention of the *d* of the ... Heb 11:22 *1841*

DEPARTURE {2}
sea shall be troubled at thy *d* ... Eze 26:18 3318
and the time of my *d* is at hand ... 2Ti 4:6 *359*

DEPOSED {1}
he was *d* from his kingly throne, ... Dan 5:20 5182

DEPRIVED {3}
why should I be *d* also of you ... Gen 27:45 7921
Because God hath *d* her of wisdom ... Job 39:17 5382
I am *d* of the residue of my years ... Is 38:10 6485

DEPTH {12}
The *d* saith, It is not in me ... Job 28:14 8415
walked in the search of the *d* ... Job 38:16 8415
he layeth up the *d* in storehouses ... Ps 33:7 8415
a compass upon the face of the *d* ... Prov 8:27 8415
for height, and the earth for *d* ... Prov 25:3 6012
ask it either in the *d*, or in the ... Is 7:11 6009
the *d* closed me round about, the ... Jonah 2:5 8415
were drowned in the *d* of the sea ... Mt 18:6 *3989*
up, because it had no *d* of earth ... Mk 4:5 *899*
Nor height, nor *d*, nor any other ... Rom 8:39 *899*
O the *d* of the riches both of the ... Rom 11:33 *899*
is the breadth, and length, and *d* ... Eph 3:18 *899*

DEPTHS {17}
The *d* have covered them ... Ex 15:5 8415
the *d* were congealed in the heart ... Ex 15:8 8415
d that spring out of valleys and ... Deut 8:7 8415
again from the *d* of the sea ... Ps 68:22 4688
up again from the *d* of the earth ... Ps 71:20 8415
the *d* also were troubled ... Ps 77:16 8415
them drink as out of the great *d* ... Ps 78:15 8415
so he led them through the *d* ... Ps 106:9 8415
they go down again to the *d* ... Ps 107:26 8415
Out of the *d* have I cried unto ... Ps 130:1 4615
his knowledge the *d* are broken up ... Prov 3:20 8415
When there were no *d*, I was ... Prov 8:24 8415
her guests are in the *d* of hell ... Prov 9:18 6010
that hath made the *d* of the sea a ... Is 51:10 4615
be broken by the seas in the *d* of ... Eze 27:34 4615
their sins into the *d* of the sea ... Mic 7:19 4688
have not known the *d* of Satan ... Rev 2:24 *899*

DEPUTED {1}
but there is no man *d* of the king ... 2Sa 15:3

DEPUTIES {3}
and to the lieutenants, and the *d* ... Est 8:9 6346
and the lieutenants, and the *d* ... Est 9:3 6346
the law is open, and there are *d* ... Acts 19:38 *446*

DEPUTY {5}
a *d* was king ... 1Kin 22:47 5324
was with the *d* of the country ... Acts 13:7 *446*
to turn away the *d* from the faith ... Acts 13:8 *446*
Then the *d*, when he saw what was ... Acts 13:12 *446*
when Gallio was the *d* of Achaia ... Acts 18:12 *446*

DERBE *(der'-by)* {4} *A south Galatian town.*
of it, and fled unto Lystra and *D* ... Acts 14:6 *1191*
he departed with Barnabas to *D* ... Acts 14:20 *1191*
Then came he to *D* and Lystra ... Acts 16:1 *1191*
and Gaius of *D*, and Timotheus ... Acts 20:4 *1191*

DERIDE {1}
they shall *d* every strong hold ... Hab 1:10 7832

DERIDED {2}
and they *d* him ... Lk 16:14 *1592*
the rulers also with them *d* him ... Lk 23:35 *1592*

DERISION {15}
are younger than I have me in *d* ... Job 30:1 7832
the Lord shall have them in *d* ... Ps 2:4 3932
a *d* to them that are round about ... Ps 44:13 7047
shalt have all the heathen in *d* ... Ps 59:8 3932
d to them that are round about us ... Ps 79:4 7047
proud have had me greatly in *d* ... Ps 119:51 3887
I am in *d* daily, every one ... Jer 20:7 7814
made a reproach unto me, and a *d* ... Jer 20:8 7047
vomit, and he also shall be in *d* ... Jer 48:26 7814
For was not Israel a *d* unto thee ... Jer 48:27 7814
so shall Moab be a *d* and a ... Jer 48:39 7814
I was a *d* to all my people ... Lam 3:14 7814
be laughed to scorn and had in *d* ... Eze 23:32 3932
d to the residue of the heathen ... Eze 36:4 3932
this shall be their *d* in the land ... Hos 7:16 3932

DESCEND {10}
and the border shall *d*, and shall ... Num 34:11 3381
or he shall *d* into battle ... 1Sa 26:10 3381
his glory shall not *d* after him ... Ps 49:17 3381
that rejoiceth, shall *d* into it ... Is 5:14 3381
with them that *d* into the pit ... Eze 26:20 3381
with them that *d* into the pit ... Eze 31:16 3381
of Israel *d* now from the cross ... Mk 15:32 *2597*
saw a vision, A certain vessel *d* ... Acts 11:5 *2597*
Who shall *d* into the deep ... Rom 10:7 *2597*
shall *d* from heaven with a shout ... 1Th 4:16 *2597*

DESCENDED {19}
the LORD *d* upon it in fire ... Ex 19:18 3381
tabernacle, the cloudy pillar *d* ... Ex 33:9 3381
the LORD *d* in the cloud, and stood ... Ex 34:5 3381
the brook that *d* out of the mount ... Deut 9:21 3381
d from the mountain, and passed ... Josh 2:23 3381
the coast *d* unto the river Kanah, ... Josh 17:9 3381
the border *d* to Ataroth-adar, ... Josh 18:13 3381
d to the valley of Hinnom, to the ... Josh 18:16 3381
on the south, and *d* to En-rogel, ... Josh 18:16 3381
d to the stone of Bohan the son ... Josh 18:17 3381
as the dew that *d* upon the ... Ps 133:3 3381
ascended up into heaven, or *d* ... Prov 30:4 3381
And the rain *d*, and the floods came ... Mt 7:25 *2597*
And the rain *d*, and the floods came ... Mt 7:27 *2597*
angel of the Lord *d* from heaven ... Mt 28:2 *2597*
the Holy Ghost *d* in a bodily ... Lk 3:22 *2597*
the high priest *d* with the elders ... Acts 24:1 *2597*
what is it but that he also *d* ... Eph 4:9 *2597*
He that *d* is the same also that ... Eph 4:10 *2597*

DESCENDETH {1}
This wisdom *d* not from above, but ... Jas 3:15 *2718*

DESCENDING {8}
of God ascending and *d* on it ... Gen 28:12 3381
the Spirit of God *d* like a dove ... Mt 3:16 *2597*
the Spirit like a dove *d* upon him ... Mk 1:10 *2597*
I saw the Spirit *d* from heaven ... Jn 1:32 *2597*
whom thou shalt see the Spirit *d* ... Jn 1:33 *2597*
and *d* upon the Son of man ... Jn 1:51 *2597*
and a certain vessel *d* unto him ... Acts 10:11 *2597*
d out of heaven from God, ... Rev 21:10 *2597*

DESCENT {3}
even now at the *d* of the mount of ... Lk 19:37 *2600*
father, without mother, without *d* ... Heb 7:3 *35*
But he whose *d* is not counted ... Heb 7:6 *1075*

DESCRIBE {4}
d it according to the inheritance ... Josh 18:4 3789
Ye shall therefore *d* the land ... Josh 18:6 3789
them that went to *d* the land ... Josh 18:8 3789
d it, and come again to me, that I ... Josh 18:8 3789

DESCRIBED {2}
d it by cities into seven parts ... Josh 18:9 3789
he *d* unto him the princes of ... Judg 8:14 3789

DESCRIBETH {2}
Even as David also *d* the ... Rom 4:6 *3004*
For Moses *d* the righteousness ... Rom 10:5 *1125*

DESCRIPTION {1}
bring the *d* hither to me, that I ... Josh 18:6

DESCRY {1}
house of Joseph sent to *d* Beth-el ... Judg 1:23 8446

DESERT {42}
flock to the backside of the *d* ... Ex 3:1 4057
three days' journey into the *d* ... Ex 5:3 4057
and were come to the *d* of Sinai ... Ex 19:2 4057
from the *d* unto the river ... Ex 23:31 4057
into the *d* of Zin in the first ... Num 20:1 4057
my commandment in the *d* of Zin ... Num 27:14 4057
they removed from the *d* of Sinai ... Num 33:16 4057
He found him in a *d* land, and in ... Deut 32:10 4057
Also he built towers in the *d* ... 2Chr 26:10 4057
Behold, as wild asses in the *d* ... Job 24:5 4057
render to them their *d* ... Ps 28:4 1576
and grieve him in the *d* ... Ps 78:40 3452
I am like an owl of the *d* ... Ps 102:6 2723
and tempted God in the *d* ... Ps 106:14 3452
beasts of the *d* shall lie there ... Is 13:21 6728
The burden of the *d* of the sea ... Is 21:1 4057
so it cometh from the *d*, from a ... Is 21:1 4057
The wild beasts of the *d* shall ... Is 34:14 6728
the *d* shall rejoice, and blossom ... Is 35:1 6160
break out, and streams in the *d* ... Is 35:6 6160
make straight in the *d* a highway ... Is 40:3 6160
I will set in the *d* the fir tree ... Is 41:19 6160
wilderness, and rivers in the *d* ... Is 43:19 3452
wilderness, and rivers in the *d* ... Is 43:20 3452
her *d* like the garden of the LORD ... Is 51:3 6160
shall be like the heath in the *d* ... Jer 17:6 6160
people that dwell in the *d* ... Jer 25:24 4057
a wilderness, a dry land, and a *d* ... Jer 50:12 6160
the wild beasts of the *d* with the ... Jer 50:39 6728
country, and go down into the *d* ... Eze 47:8 6160
by ship into a *d* place apart ... Mt 14:13 *2048*
to him, saying, This is a *d* place ... Mt 14:15 *2048*
unto you, Behold, he is in the *d* ... Mt 24:26 *2048*
city, but was without in *d* places ... Mk 1:45 *2048*
yourselves apart into a *d* place ... Mk 6:31 *2048*
they departed into a *d* place by ... Mk 6:32 *2048*
him, and said, This is a *d* place ... Mk 6:35 *2048*
departed and went into a *d* place ... Lk 4:42 *2048*
a *d* place belonging to the city ... Lk 9:10 *2048*
for we are here in a *d* place ... Lk 9:12 *2048*
fathers did eat manna in the *d* ... Jn 6:31 *2048*
Jerusalem unto Gaza, which is *d* ... Acts 8:26 *2048*

DESERTS {6}
when he led them through the *d* ... Is 48:21 2723
wilderness, through a land of *d* ... Jer 2:6 6160
to their *d* will I judge them ... Eze 7:27 4941
are like the foxes in the *d* ... Eze 13:4 2723
was in the *d* till the day of his ... Lk 1:80 *2048*
they wandered in *d*, and in ... Heb 11:38 *2047*

DESERVE {1}
us less than our iniquities *d* ... Ezr 9:13

DESERVETH {1}
thee less than thine iniquity *d* ... Job 11:6

DESERVING {1}
according to the *d* of his hands ... Judg 9:16 1576

DESIRABLE {3}
rulers, all of them *d* young men ... Eze 23:6 2531
horses, all of them *d* young men ... Eze 23:12 2531
all of them *d* young men, captains ... Eze 23:23 2531

DESIRE {111}
thy *d* shall be to thy husband, and ... Gen 3:16 8669
And unto thee shall be his *d* ... Gen 4:7 8669
for that ye did *d* ... Ex 10:11 1245
neither shall any man *d* thy land ... Ex 34:24 2530
Neither shalt thou *d* thy ... Deut 5:21 2530
thou shalt not *d* the silver or ... Deut 7:25 2530
come with all the *d* of his mind ... Deut 18:6 183
hast a *d* unto her, that thou ... Deut 21:11 2836
I would *d* a request of you, that ... Judg 8:24 7592
And on whom is all the *d* of Israel ... 1Sa 9:20 2532
the *d* of thy soul to come down ... 1Sa 23:20 183
is all my salvation, and all my *d* ... 2Sa 23:5 2656
I *d* one small petition of thee ... 1Kin 2:20 7592
I will do all thy *d* concerning ... 1Kin 5:8 2656
and thou shalt accomplish my *d* ... 1Kin 5:9 2656
fir trees according to all his *d* ... 1Kin 5:10 2656
all Solomon's *d* which he was ... 1Kin 9:1 2837
with gold, according to all his *d* ... 1Kin 9:11 2656
unto the queen of Sheba all her *d* ... 1Kin 10:13 2656
said, Did I *d* a son of my lord ... 2Kin 4:28 7592
to the queen of Sheba all her *d* ... 2Chr 9:12 2656
and sought him with their whole *d* ... 2Chr 15:15 7522
servants, who *d* to fear thy name ... Neh 1:11 2655
and I *d* to reason with God ... Job 13:3 2654
thou wilt have a *d* to the work of ... Job 14:15 3700
for we *d* not the knowledge of thy ... Job 21:14 2654
withheld the poor from their *d* ... Job 31:16 2656
behold, my *d* is, that the ... Job 31:35 8420
speak, for I *d* to justify thee ... Job 33:32 2654
My *d* is that Job may be tried ... Job 34:36 15
D not the night, when people are ... Job 36:20 7602
wicked boasteth of his heart's *d* ... Ps 10:3 8378
hast heard the *d* of the humble ... Ps 10:17 8378
Thou hast given him his heart's *d* ... Ps 21:2 8378
Lord, all my *d* is before thee ... Ps 38:9 8378
and offering thou didst not *d* ... Ps 40:6 2654
the king greatly *d* thy beauty ... Ps 45:11 183
hath seen his *d* upon mine enemies ... Ps 54:7
let me see my *d* upon mine enemies ... Ps 59:10
put to confusion, that *d* my hurt ... Ps 70:2 2655
upon earth that I *d* beside thee ... Ps 73:25 2654
for he gave them their own *d* ... Ps 78:29 8378
shall see my *d* on mine enemies ... Ps 92:11
mine ears shall hear my *d* of the ... Ps 92:11
he see his *d* upon his enemies ... Ps 112:8
the *d* of the wicked shall perish ... Ps 112:10 8378
I see my *d* upon them that hate me ... Ps 118:7
satisfiest the *d* of every living ... Ps 145:16 7522
He will fulfil the *d* of them that ... Ps 145:19 7522
all the things thou canst *d* are ... Prov 3:15 2656
but the *d* of the righteous shall ... Prov 10:24 8378
The *d* of the righteous is only ... Prov 11:23 8378
heart sick, but when the *d* cometh ... Prov 13:12 8378
The *d* accomplished is sweet to ... Prov 13:19 8378
Through *d* a man, having separated ... Prov 18:1 8378

D

The *d* of a man is his kindness — Prov 19:22 — 8378
The *d* of the slothful killeth him — Prov 21:25 — 8378
neither *d* thou his dainty meats — Prov 23:6 — 183
neither *d* to be with them — Prov 24:1 — 183
eyes than the wandering of the *d* — Eccl 6:9 — 5315
be a burden, and *d* shall fail — Eccl 12:5 — 35
beloved's, and his *d* is toward me — Song 7:10 — 8669
the *d* of our soul is to thy name, — Is 26:8 — 8378
is no beauty that we should *d* him — Is 53:2 — 2530
land whereunto they *d* to return — Jer 22:27 — 5375,5315
in the place whither ye *d* to go — Jer 42:22 — 2654
have a *d* to return to dwell there — Jer 44:14 — 5375,5315
I take away from thee the *d* of — Eze 24:16 — 4261
the *d* of your eyes, and that which — Eze 24:21 — 4261
the *d* of their eyes, and that — Eze 24:25 — 4261
That they would *d* mercies of the — Dan 2:18 — 1156
nor the *d* of women, nor regard — Dan 11:37 — 2532
It is in my *d* that I should — Hos 10:10 — 183
Woe unto you that *d* the day of — Amos 5:18 — 183
he uttereth his mischievous *d* — Mic 7:3 — 5315
home, who enlargeth his *d* as hell — Hab 2:5 — 5315
the *d* of all nations shall come — Hag 2:7 — 2532
If any man *d* to be first, the — Mk 9:35 — *2309*
do for us whatsoever we shall *d* — Mk 10:35 — *154*
unto you, What things soever ye *d* — Mk 11:24 — *154*
d him to do as he had ever done — Mk 15:8 — *154*
when ye shall *d* to see one of the — Lk 17:22 — *1937*
which *d* to walk in long robes, and — Lk 20:46 — *2309*
With *d* I have desired to eat this — Lk 22:15 — *1939*
The Jews have agreed to *d* thee — Acts 23:20 — *2065*
But we *d* to hear of thee what — Acts 28:22 — *515*
Brethren, my heart's *d* and prayer — Rom 10:1 — *2107*
having a great *d* these many years — Rom 15:23 — *1974*
d spiritual gifts, but rather — 1Cor 14:1 — *2206*
when he told us your earnest *d* — 2Cor 7:7 — *1972*
what fear, yea, what vehement *d* — 2Cor 7:11 — *1972*
from them which *d* occasion — 2Cor 11:12 — *2309*
For though I would *d* to glory — 2Cor 12:6 — *2309*
whereunto ye *d* again to be in — Gal 4:9 — *2309*
I *d* to be present with you now, — Gal 4:20 — *2309*
ye that *d* to be under the law, do — Gal 4:21 — *2309*
As many as *d* to make a fair shew — Gal 6:12 — *2309*
but *d* to have you circumcised, — Gal 6:13 — *2309*
Wherefore I *d* that ye faint not — Eph 3:13 — *154*
having a *d* to depart, and to be — Phil 1:23 — *1939*
Not because I *d* a gift — Phil 4:17 — *1934*
but I *d* fruit that may abound to — Phil 4:17 — *1934*
to *d* that ye might be filled with — Col 1:9 — *154*
to see your face with great *d* — 1Th 2:17 — *1939*
If a man *d* the office of a bishop — 1Ti 3:1 — *3713*
we *d* that every one of you do — Heb 6:11 — *1937*
But now they *d* a better country, — Heb 11:16 — *3713*
d to have, and cannot obtain — Jas 4:2 — *2206*
things the angels *d* to look into — 1Pet 1:12 — *1937*
d the sincere milk of the word, — 1Pet 2:2 — *1971*
shall *d* to die, and death shall — Rev 9:6 — *1937*

DESIRED {50}
a tree to be *d* to make one wise, — Gen 3:6 — 2530
ye have chosen, and whom ye have *d* — 1Sa 12:13 — 7592
that which Solomon *d* to build in — 1Kin 9:19 — 2836
all that Solomon *d* to build in — 2Chr 8:6 — 2836
And he *d* many wives — 2Chr 11:23 — 7592
and departed without being *d* — 2Chr 21:20 — 2532
whatsoever she *d* was given her to — Est 2:13 — 559
shall not save of that which he *d* — Job 20:20 — 2530
More to be *d* are they than gold, — Ps 19:10 — 2530
One thing have I *d* of the LORD — Ps 27:4 — 7592
bringeth them unto their *d* haven — Ps 107:30 — 2656
he hath *d* it for his habitation — Ps 132:13 — 183
for I have *d* it — Ps 132:14 — 183
all the things that may be *d* are — Prov 8:11 — 2656
There is treasure to be *d* — Prov 21:20 — 2530
mine eyes *d* I kept not from them — Eccl 2:10 — 7592
of the oaks which ye have *d* — Is 1:29 — 2530
soul have I *d* thee in the night — Is 26:9 — 183
neither have I *d* the woeful day — Jer 17:16 — 183
d of the king that he would give — Dan 2:16 — 1156
unto me now what we *d* of thee — Dan 2:23 — 1156
For I *d* mercy, and not sacrifice — Hos 6:6 — 2654
my soul *d* the firstripe fruit — Mic 7:1 — 183
gather together, O nation not *d* — Zeph 2:1 — 3700
righteous men have *d* to see those — Mt 13:17 — *1939*
tempting *d* him that he would shew — Mt 16:1 — *1905*
one prisoner, whomsoever they *d* — Mk 15:6 — *154*
one of the Pharisees *d* him that — Lk 7:36 — *2065*
And he *d* to see him — Lk 9:9 — *2212*
kings have *d* to see those things — Lk 10:24 — *2309*
With desire I have *d* to eat this — Lk 22:15 — *1937*
Satan hath *d* to have you, that he — Lk 22:31 — *1809*
cast into prison, whom they had *d* — Lk 23:25 — *154*
d him, saying, Sir, we would see — Jn 12:21 — *2065*
d a murderer to be granted unto — Acts 3:14 — *154*
d to find a tabernacle for the — Acts 7:46 — *154*
he *d* Philip that he would come up — Acts 8:31 — *3870*
d of him letters to Damascus to — Acts 9:2 — *154*
chamberlain their friend, *d* peace — Acts 12:20 — *154*
d to hear the word of God — Acts 13:7 — *1934*
And afterward they *d* a king — Acts 13:21 — *154*
yet *d* they Pilate that he should — Acts 13:28 — *154*
d them to depart out of the city — Acts 16:39 — *2065*
When they *d* him to tarry longer — Acts 18:20 — *2065*
d favour against him, that he — Acts 25:3 — *154*
were *d* to tarry with them seven — Acts 28:14 — *3870*
I greatly *d* him to come unto you — 1Cor 16:12 — *3870*
Insomuch that we *d* Titus, that as — 2Cor 8:6 — *3870*
I *d* Titus, and with him I sent a — 2Cor 12:18 — *3870*
the petitions that we *d* of him — 1Jn 5:15 — *154*

DESIREDST {2}
According to all that thou *d* of — Deut 18:16 — 7592
all that debt, because thou *d* me — Mt 18:32 — *3870*

DESIRES {3}
give thee the *d* of thine heart — Ps 37:4 — 4862
not, O LORD, the *d* of the wicked — Ps 140:8 — 3970
fulfilling the *d* of the flesh — Eph 2:3 — *2307*

DESIREST {2}
thou *d* truth in the inward parts — Ps 51:6 — 2654
For thou *d* not sacrifice — Ps 51:16 — 2654

DESIRETH {17}
or for whatsoever thy soul *d* — Deut 14:26 — 7592
then take as much as thy soul *d* — 1Sa 2:16 — 8378
The king *d* not any dowry, but an — 1Sa 18:25 — 2656
unto David, Whatsoever thy soul *d* — 1Sa 20:4 — 559
reign over all that thine heart *d* — 2Sa 3:21 — 8378
according to all that thy soul *d* — 1Kin 11:37 — 8378
a servant earnestly *d* the shadow — Job 7:2 — 7602
And what his soul *d*, even that he — Job 23:13 — 183
What man is he that *d* life — Ps 34:12 — 2655
the hill which God *d* to dwell in — Ps 68:16 — 2530
The wicked *d* the net of evil men — Prov 12:12 — 2530
The soul of the sluggard *d* — Prov 13:4 — 183
The soul of the wicked *d* evil — Prov 21:10 — 183
for his soul of all that he *d* — Eccl 6:2 — 183
drunk old wine straightway *d* new — Lk 5:39 — *2309*
and *d* conditions of peace — Lk 14:32 — *2065*
of a bishop, he *d* a good work — 1Ti 3:1 — *1937*

DESIRING {12}
without, *d* to speak with him — Mt 12:46 — *2212*
without, *d* to speak with thee — Mt 12:47 — *2212*
him, and *d* a certain thing of him — Mt 20:20 — *154*
stand without, *d* to see thee — Lk 8:20 — *2309*
d to be fed with the crumbs which — Lk 16:21 — *1937*
d him that he would not delay to — Acts 9:38 — *3870*
d him that he would not adventure — Acts 19:31 — *3870*
d to have judgment against him — Acts 25:15 — *154*
earnestly *d* to be clothed upon — 2Cor 5:2 — *1971*
d greatly to see us, as we also — 1Th 3:6 — *1971*
D to be teachers of the law — 1Ti 1:7 — *2309*
Greatly *d* to see thee, being — 2Ti 1:4 — *1971*

DESIROUS {6}
Be not *d* of his dainties — Prov 23:3 — 183
for he was *d* to see him of a long — Lk 23:8 — *2309*
knew that they were *d* to ask him — Jn 16:19 — *2309*
a garrison, *d* to apprehend me — 2Cor 11:32 — *2309*
Let us not be *d* of vain glory — Gal 5:26 — *2755*
So being affectionately *d* of you — 1Th 2:8 — *2442*

DESOLATE {148}
not die, that the land be not *d* — Gen 47:19 — 3456
lest the land become *d*, and the — Ex 23:29 — 8077
and your high ways shall be *d* — Lev 26:22 — 8074
and your land shall be *d*, and your — Lev 26:33 — 8077
sabbaths, as long as it lieth *d* — Lev 26:34 — 8074
long as it lieth *d* it shall rest — Lev 26:35 — 8074
while she lieth *d* without them — Lev 26:43 — 8074
So Tamar remained *d* in her — 2Sa 13:20 — 8076
as she lay *d* she kept sabbath — 2Chr 36:21 — 8074
earth, which built *d* places for — Job 3:14 — 2723
And he dwelleth in *d* cities — Job 15:28 — 3582
of hypocrites shall be *d*, and fire — Job 15:34 — 1565
thou hast made *d* all my company — Job 16:7 — 8074
the wilderness in former time *d* — Job 30:3 — 7722
To satisfy the *d* and waste ground — Job 38:27 — 7722
for I am *d* and afflicted — Ps 25:16 — 3173
hate the righteous shall be *d* — Ps 34:21 — 816
them that trust in him shall be *d* — Ps 34:22 — 816
Let them be *d* for a reward of — Ps 40:15 — 8074
Let their habitation be *d* — Ps 69:25 — 8074
bread also out of their *d* places — Ps 109:10 — 2723
my heart within me is *d* — Ps 143:4 — 8074
Your country is *d*, your cities — Is 1:7 — 8077
it in your presence, and it is *d* — Is 1:7 — 8077
she being *d* shall sit upon the — Is 3:26 — 5352
Of a truth many houses shall be *d* — Is 5:9 — 8047
man, and the land be utterly *d* — Is 6:11 — 8077
rest all of them in the *d* valleys — Is 7:19 — 1327
fierce anger, to lay the land *d* — Is 13:9 — 8047
shall cry in their *d* houses — Is 13:22 — 490
the waters of Nimrim shall be *d* — Is 15:6 — 4923
and they that dwell therein are *d* — Is 24:6 — 816
Yet the defenced city shall be *d* — Is 27:10 — 910
cause to inherit the *d* heritages — Is 49:8 — 8076
thy *d* places, and the land of thy — Is 49:19 — 8074
I have lost my children, and am *d* — Is 49:21 — 1565
of the *d* than the children of the — Is 54:1 — 8074
make the *d* cities to be inhabited — Is 54:3 — 8077
we are in *d* places as dead men — Is 59:10 — 820
thy land any more be termed *D* — Is 62:4 — 8077
be horribly afraid, be ye very *d* — Jer 2:12 — 2717
from his place to make thy land *d* — Jer 4:7 — 8047
said, The whole land shall be *d* — Jer 4:27 — 8077
lest I make thee *d*, a land not — Jer 6:8 — 8077
for the land shall be *d* — Jer 7:34 — 2723
I will make the cities of Judah *d* — Jer 9:11 — 8077
to make the cities of Judah *d* — Jer 10:22 — 8077
and have made his habitation *d* — Jer 10:25 — 8074
pleasant portion a *d* wilderness — Jer 12:10 — 8077
They have made it *d* — Jer 12:11 — 8074
being *d* it mourneth unto me — Jer 12:11 — 8077
the whole land is made *d*, because — Jer 12:11 — 8074
To make their land *d*, and a — Jer 18:16 — 8047
And I will make this city *d* — Jer 19:8 — 8047
for their land is *d* because of — Jer 25:38 — 8047
this city shall be *d* without an — Jer 26:9 — 2717
It is *d* without man or beast — Jer 32:43 — 8077
ye say shall be *d* without man — Jer 33:10 — 2717
streets of Jerusalem, that are *d* — Jer 33:10 — 8074
which is *d* without man and without — Jer 33:12 — 2717
and they are wasted and *d*, as at — Jer 44:6 — 8077
waste and *d* without an inhabitant — Jer 46:19 — 3341
for the cities thereof shall be *d* — Jer 48:9 — 8047
waters also of Nimrim shall be *d* — Jer 48:34 — 4923
and it shall be a *d* heap, and her — Jer 49:2 — 8077
their habitations *d* with them — Jer 49:20 — 8074
her, which shall make her land *d* — Jer 50:3 — 8047
but it shall be wholly *d* — Jer 50:13 — 8077
make their habitation *d* with them — Jer 50:45 — 8074
but thou shalt be *d* for ever — Jer 51:26 — 8077
but that it shall be *d* for ever — Jer 51:62 — 8077
all her gates are *d* — Lam 1:4 — 8076
he hath made me *d* and faint all — Lam 1:13 — 8076
my children are *d*, because the — Lam 1:16 — 8076
he hath made me *d* — Lam 3:11 — 8076
delicately are *d* in the streets — Lam 4:5 — 8074
the mountain of Zion, which is *d* — Lam 5:18 — 8074
And your altars shall be *d* — Eze 6:4 — 8074
and the high places shall be *d* — Eze 6:6 — 3456
may be laid waste and made *d* — Eze 6:6 — 816
upon them, and make the land *d* — Eze 6:14 — 8077
more *d* than the wilderness toward — Eze 6:14 — 8047
that her land may be *d* from all — Eze 12:19 — 3456
waste, and the land shall be *d* — Eze 12:20 — 8077
and they spoil it, so that it be *d* — Eze 14:15 — 8077
but the land shall be *d* — Eze 14:16 — 8077
And I will make the land *d* — Eze 15:8 — 8077
And he knew their *d* palaces — Eze 19:7 — 490
and the land was *d*, and the fulness — Eze 19:7 — 3456
womb, that I might make them *d* — Eze 20:26 — 8074
the land of Israel, when it was *d* — Eze 25:3 — 8074
and I will make it *d* from Teman — Eze 25:13 — 2723
When I shall make thee a *d* city — Eze 26:19 — 2717
of the earth, in places *d* of old — Eze 26:20 — 2723
And the land of Egypt shall be *d* — Eze 29:9 — 8077
land of Egypt utterly waste and *d* — Eze 29:10 — 8077
d in the midst of the countries — Eze 29:12 — 8077
midst of the countries that are *d* — Eze 29:12 — 8074
laid waste shall be *d* forty years — Eze 29:12 — 8077
they shall be *d* in the midst of — Eze 30:7 — 8074
midst of the countries that are *d* — Eze 30:7 — 8074
And I will make Pathros *d*, and will — Eze 30:14 — 8074
I shall make the land of Egypt *d* — Eze 32:15 — 8077
For I will lay the land most *d* — Eze 33:28 — 8077
mountains of Israel shall be *d* — Eze 33:28 — 8074
land most *d* because of all their — Eze 33:29 — 8077
thee, and I will make thee most *d* — Eze 35:3 — 8077
cities waste, and thou shalt be *d* — Eze 35:4 — 8077
will I make mount Seir most *d* — Eze 35:7 — 8077
Israel, saying, They are laid *d* — Eze 35:12 — 8074
rejoiceth, I will make thee *d* — Eze 35:14 — 8077
house of Israel, because it was *d* — Eze 35:15 — 8074
thou shalt be *d*, O mount Seir, and — Eze 35:15 — 8077
Because they have made you *d* — Eze 36:3 — 8074
to the valleys, to the *d* wastes — Eze 36:4 — 8076
the *d* land shall be tilled, — Eze 36:34 — 8074
whereas it lay *d* in the sight of — Eze 36:34 — 8077
This land that was *d* is become — Eze 36:35 — 8074
and the waste and *d* and ruined — Eze 36:35 — 8074
places, and plant that that was *d* — Eze 36:36 — 8074
to turn thine hand upon the *d* — Eze 38:12 — 2723
upon thy sanctuary that is *d* — Dan 9:17 — 8074
abominations he shall make it *d* — Dan 9:27 — 8074
shall be poured upon the *d* — Dan 9:27 — 8076
the abomination that maketh *d* — Dan 11:31 — 8074
abomination that maketh *d* set up — Dan 12:11 — 8074
Ephraim shall be *d* in the day of — Hos 5:9 — 8047
Samaria shall become *d* — Hos 13:16 — 816
clods, the garners are laid *d* — Joel 1:17 — 8074
the flocks of sheep are made *d* — Joel 1:18 — 816
and behind them a *d* wilderness — Joel 2:3 — 8077
drive him into a land barren and *d* — Joel 2:20 — 8077
and Edom shall be a *d* wilderness — Joel 3:19 — 8077
high places of Isaac shall be *d* — Amos 7:9 — 8074
the idols thereof will I lay *d* — Mic 1:7 — 8077
in making thee *d* because of thy — Mic 6:13 — 8074
the land shall be *d* because of — Mic 7:13 — 8077
their towers are *d* — Zeph 3:6 — 8074
Thus the land was *d* after them — Zec 7:14 — 8074
for they laid the pleasant land *d* — Zec 7:14 — 8047
will return and build the *d* places — Mal 1:4 — 2723
your house is left unto you *d* — Mt 23:38 — *2048*
your house is left unto you *d* — Lk 13:35 — *2048*
Psalms, Let his habitation be *d* — Acts 1:20 — *2048*
for the *d* hath many more children — Gal 4:27 — *2048*
she that is a widow indeed, and *d* — 1Ti 5:5 — *3443*
the whore, and shall make her *d* — Rev 17:16 — *2049*
for in one hour is she made *d* — Rev 18:19 — *2049*

DESOLATION {46}
and bring your sanctuaries unto *d* — Lev 26:31 — 8074
And I will bring the land into *d* — Lev 26:32 — 8074
for ever, even a *d* unto this day — Josh 8:28 — 8077
that they should become a *d* — 2Kin 22:19 — 8047
who therefore gave them up to *d* — 2Chr 30:7 — 8047
in the *d* they rolled themselves — Job 30:14 — 7722
How are they brought into *d* — Ps 73:19 — 8047
When your fear cometh as *d* — Prov 1:27 — 7584
neither of the *d* of the wicked — Prov 3:25 — 7722
in the *d* which shall come from — Is 10:3 — 7722
and there shall be *d* — Is 17:9 — 8077
In the city is left *d*, and the — Is 24:12 — 8047
d shall come upon thee suddenly, — Is 47:11 — 7722
d, and destruction, and the famine, — Is 51:19 — 7701
is a wilderness, Jerusalem a *d* — Is 64:10 — 8077

that this house shall become a *d* ... Jer 22:5 2723
And this whole land shall be a *d* ... Jer 25:11 2723
princes thereof, to make them a *d* ... Jer 25:18 2723
Judah a *d* without an inhabitant ... Jer 34:22 8077
and, behold, this day they are a *d* ... Jer 44:2 2723
therefore is your land a *d* ... Jer 44:22 2723
that Bozrah shall become a *d* ... Jer 49:13 8047
Also Edom shall be a *d* ... Jer 49:17 8047
for dragons, and a *d* for ever ... Jer 49:33 8077
become a *d* among the nations ... Jer 50:23 8047
Babylon a *d* without an inhabitant ... Jer 51:29 8047
Her cities are a *d*, a dry land, ... Jer 51:43 8047
and a snare is come upon us, *d* ... Lam 3:47 7612
prince shall be clothed with *d* ... Eze 7:27 8077
with the cup of astonishment and *d* ... Eze 23:33 8077
and the transgression of *d* ... Dan 8:13 8074
he daily increaseth lies and *d* ... Hos 12:1 7701
Egypt shall be a *d*, and Edom shall ... Joel 3:19 8077
that I should make thee a *d* ... Mic 6:16 8047
a booty, and their houses a *d* ... Zeph 1:13 8047
distress, a day of wasteness and *d* ... Zeph 1:15 4875
be forsaken, and Ashkelon a *d* ... Zeph 2:4 8077
and saltpits, and a perpetual *d* ... Zeph 2:9 8077
and will make Nineveh a *d*, and dry ... Zeph 2:13 8077
d shall be in the thresholds ... Zeph 2:14 2721
how is she become a *d*, a place ... Zeph 2:15 8047
against itself is brought to *d* ... Mt 12:25 *2049*
shall see the abomination of *d* ... Mt 24:15 *2050*
ye shall see the abomination of *d* ... Mk 13:14 *2050*
against itself is brought to *d* ... Lk 11:17 *2049*
know that the *d* thereof is nigh ... Lk 21:20 *2050*

DESOLATIONS {11}
God, and to repair the *d* thereof ... Ezr 9:9 2723
what *d* he hath made in the earth ... Ps 46:8 8047
up thy feet unto the perpetual *d* ... Ps 74:3 4876
they shall raise up the former *d* ... Is 61:4 8074
the *d* of many generations ... Is 61:4 8074
and an hissing, and perpetual *d* ... Jer 25:9 2723
and will make it perpetual *d* ... Jer 25:12 8077
I will make thee perpetual *d* ... Eze 35:9 8077
years in the *d* of Jerusalem ... Dan 9:2 2723
open thine eyes, and behold our *d* ... Dan 9:18 8074
end of the war *d* are determined ... Dan 9:26 8074

DESPAIR {3}
and Saul shall *d* of me, to seek me ... 1Sa 27:1 2976
d of all the labour which I took ... Eccl 2:20 2976
we are perplexed, but not in *d* ... 2Cor 4:8 *1820*

DESPAIRED {1}
insomuch that we *d* even of life ... 2Cor 1:8 *1820*

DESPERATE {2}
and the speeches of one that is *d* ... Job 6:26 2976
the day of grief and of *d* sorrow ... Is 17:11 605

DESPERATELY {1}
above all things, and *d* wicked ... Jer 17:9 605

DESPISE {37}
And if ye shall *d* my statutes ... Lev 26:15 3988
they that *d* me shall be lightly ... 1Sa 2:30 959
why then did ye *d* us, that our ... 2Sa 19:43 7043
so that they shall *d* their ... Est 1:17 959
therefore *d* not thou the ... Job 5:17 3988
I would *d* my life ... Job 9:21 3988
that thou shouldest *d* the work of ... Job 10:3 3988
If I did *d* the cause of my ... Job 31:13 3988
heart, O God, thou wilt not *d* ... Ps 51:17 959
awakest, thou shalt *d* their image ... Ps 73:20 959
destitute, and not *d* their prayer ... Ps 102:17 959
but fools *d* wisdom and instruction ... Prov 1:7 936
d not the chastening of the LORD ... Prov 3:11 3988
Men do not *d* a thief, if he steal ... Prov 6:30 936
for he will *d* the wisdom of thy ... Prov 23:9 936
d not thy mother when she is old ... Prov 23:22 936
of Israel, Because ye *d* this word ... Is 30:12 3988
thy lovers will *d* thee, they will ... Jer 4:30 3988
say still unto them that *d* me ... Jer 23:17 5006
all that honoured her *d* her ... Lam 1:8 2107
which *d* thee round about ... Eze 16:57 7590
that *d* them round about them ... Eze 28:26 7590
I *d* your feast days, and I will ... Amos 5:21 3988
you, O priests, that *d* my name ... Mal 1:6 959
hold to the one, and *d* the other ... Mt 6:24 *2706*
Take heed that ye *d* not one of ... Mt 18:10 *2706*
hold to the one, and *d* the other ... Lk 16:13 *2706*
that eateth *d* him that eateth not ... Rom 14:3 *1848*
or *d* ye the church of God, and ... 1Cor 11:22 *2706*
Let no man therefore *d* him ... 1Cor 16:11 *1848*
D not prophesyings ... 1Th 5:20 *1848*
Let no man *d* thy youth ... 1Ti 4:12 *2706*
masters, let them not *d* them ... 1Ti 6:2 *2706*
Let no man *d* thee ... Titus 2:15 *4065*
d not thou the chastening of the ... Heb 12:5 *3643*
of uncleanness, and *d* government ... 2Pet 2:10 *2706*
d dominion, and speak evil of ... Jude 8 *114*

DESPISED {60}
her mistress was *d* in her eyes ... Gen 16:4 7043
conceived, I was *d* in her eyes ... Gen 16:5 7043
thus Esau *d* his birthright ... Gen 25:34 959
even because they *d* my judgments ... Lev 26:43 3988
because that ye have *d* the LORD ... Num 11:20 3988
know the land which ye have *d* ... Num 14:31 3988
Because he hath *d* the word of the ... Num 15:31 959
this the people that thou hast *d* ... Judg 9:38 3988
And they *d* him, and brought him no ... 1Sa 10:27 959
and she *d* him in her heart ... 2Sa 6:16 959
Wherefore hast thou *d* the ... 2Sa 12:9 959
because thou hast *d* me, and hast ... 2Sa 12:10 959
the daughter of Zion hath *d* thee ... 2Kin 19:21 959
and she *d* him in her heart ... 1Chr 15:29 959
d his words, and misused his ... 2Chr 36:16 959
d us, and said, What is this thing ... Neh 2:19 959
for we are *d* ... Neh 4:4 939
d in the thought of him that is ... Job 12:5 937
Yea, young children *d* me ... Job 19:18 3988
of men, and *d* of the people ... Ps 22:6 959
For he hath not *d* nor abhorred ... Ps 22:24 959
to shame, because God hath *d* them ... Ps 53:5 3988
they *d* the pleasant land, they ... Ps 106:24 3988
I am small and *d* ... Ps 119:141 959
they *d* all my reproof ... Prov 1:30 5006
and my heart *d* reproof ... Prov 5:12 5006
is of a perverse heart shall be *d* ... Prov 12:8 937
He that is *d*, and hath a servant, ... Prov 12:9 7034
the poor man's wisdom is *d* ... Eccl 9:16 959
yea, I should not be *d* ... Song 8:1 937
d the word of the Holy One of ... Is 5:24 5006
he hath *d* the cities, he ... Is 33:8 3988
the daughter of Zion, hath *d* thee ... Is 37:22 959
He is *d* and rejected of men ... Is 53:3 959
he was *d*, and we esteemed him not ... Is 53:3 959
all they that *d* thee shall bow ... Is 60:14 5006
this man Coniah a *d* broken idol ... Jer 22:28 959
thus they have *d* my people ... Jer 33:24 5006
among the heathen, and *d* among men ... Jer 49:15 959
hath *d* in the indignation of his ... Lam 2:6 5006
which hast *d* the oath in breaking ... Eze 16:59 959
made him king, whose oath he *d* ... Eze 17:16 959
Seeing he *d* the oath by breaking ... Eze 17:18 959
surely mine oath that he hath *d* ... Eze 17:19 959
they *d* my judgments, which if a ... Eze 20:13 3988
Because they *d* my judgments ... Eze 20:16 3988
but had *d* my statutes, and had ... Eze 20:24 3988
Thou hast *d* mine holy things, and ... Eze 22:8 959
are round about them, that *d* them ... Eze 28:24 7590
because they have *d* the law of ... Amos 2:4 3988
thou art greatly *d* ... Obad 2 959
For who hath *d* the day of small ... Zec 4:10 937
say, Wherein have we *d* thy name ... Mal 1:6 959
they were righteous, and *d* others ... Lk 18:9 *1848*
goddess Diana should be *d* ... Acts 19:27 *1519,3762,3049*
the world, and things which are *d* ... 1Cor 1:28 *1848*
ye are honourable, but we are *d* ... 1Cor 4:10 *820*
which was in my flesh ye *d* not ... Gal 4:14 *1848*
He that *d* Moses' law died without ... Heb 10:28 *114*
But ye have *d* the poor ... Jas 2:6 *818*

DESPISERS {2}
Behold, ye *d*, and wonder, and ... Acts 13:41 *2707*
d of those that are good, ... 2Ti 3:3 *865*

DESPISEST {1}
Or *d* thou the riches of his ... Rom 2:4 *2706*

DESPISETH {19}
God is mighty, and *d* not any ... Job 36:5 3988
the poor, and *d* not his prisoners ... Ps 69:33 959
is void of wisdom *d* his neighbour ... Prov 11:12 936
Whoso *d* the word shall be ... Prov 13:13 936
is perverse in his ways *d* him ... Prov 14:2 959
He that *d* his neighbour sinneth ... Prov 14:21 936
A fool *d* his father's instruction ... Prov 15:5 5006
but a foolish man *d* his mother ... Prov 15:20 959
instruction *d* his own soul ... Prov 15:32 3988
but he that *d* his ways shall die ... Prov 19:16 959
d to obey his mother, the ravens ... Prov 30:17 936
he that *d* the gain of oppressions ... Is 33:15 3988
his Holy One, to him whom man *d* ... Is 49:7 960
he that *d* you *d* me ... Lk 10:16 *114*
d me *d* him that sent me ... Lk 10:16 *114*
He therefore that *d*, *d* not man ... 1Th 4:8 *114*

DESPISING {1}
d the shame, and is set down at ... Heb 12:2 *2706*

DESPITE {2}
thy *d* against the land of Israel ... Eze 25:6 7589
hath done *d* unto the Spirit of ... Heb 10:29 *1796*

DESPITEFUL {3}
taken vengeance with a *d* heart ... Eze 25:15 7589
with *d* minds, to cast it out for ... Eze 36:5 7589
Backbiters, haters of God, *d* ... Rom 1:30 *5197*

DESPITEFULLY {3}
and pray for them which *d* use you ... Mt 5:44 *1908*
and pray for them which *d* use you ... Lk 6:28 *1908*
with their rulers, to use them *d* ... Acts 14:5 *5195*

DESTITUTE {8}
who hath not left *d* my master of ... Gen 24:27 5800
will regard the prayer of the *d* ... Ps 102:17 6199
leave not my soul *d* ... Ps 141:8 6168
is joy to him that is *d* of wisdom ... Prov 15:21 2638
the country shall be *d* of that ... Eze 32:15 8047
d of the truth, supposing that ... 1Ti 6:5 *650*
being *d*, afflicted, tormented ... Heb 11:37 *5302*
be naked, and *d* of daily food, ... Jas 2:15 *3007*

DESTROY {261}
I will *d* man whom I have created ... Gen 6:7 4229
I will *d* them with the earth ... Gen 6:13 7843
to *d* all flesh, wherein is the ... Gen 6:17 7843
that I have made will I *d* from ... Gen 7:4 4229
more be a flood to *d* the earth ... Gen 9:11 7843
become a flood to *d* all flesh ... Gen 9:15 7843
Wilt thou also *d* the righteous ... Gen 18:23 5595
wilt thou also *d* and not spare the ... Gen 18:24 5595
wilt thou *d* all the city for lack ... Gen 18:28 7843
forty and five, I will not *d* it ... Gen 18:28 7843
I will not *d* it for twenty's sake ... Gen 18:31 7843
I will not *d* it for ten's sake ... Gen 18:32 7843
For we will *d* this place, because ... Gen 19:13 7843
and the LORD hath sent us to *d* it ... Gen 19:13 7843
for the LORD will *d* this city ... Gen 19:14 7843
to *d* the frogs from thee and thy ... Ex 8:9 3772
shall not be upon you to *d* you ... Ex 12:13 4889
my sword, my hand shall *d* them ... Ex 15:9 3423
will *d* all the people to whom ... Ex 23:27 2000
But ye shall *d* their altars ... Ex 34:13 5422
the same soul will I *d* from among ... Lev 23:30 6
d your cattle, and make you few in ... Lev 26:22 3772
I will *d* your high places, and cut ... Lev 26:30 8045
to *d* them utterly, and to break my ... Lev 26:44 3615
I will utterly *d* their cities ... Num 21:2 2763
d all the children of Sheth ... Num 24:17 6979
shall *d* him that remaineth of the ... Num 24:19 6
ye shall *d* all this people ... Num 32:15 7843
d all their pictures, and *d* ... Num 33:52 6
the hand of the Amorites, to *d* us ... Deut 1:27 8045
to *d* them from among the host, ... Deut 2:15 2000
not forsake thee, neither *d* thee ... Deut 4:31 7843
d thee from off the face of the ... Deut 6:15 8045
smite them, and utterly *d* them ... Deut 7:2 2763
against you, and *d* thee suddenly ... Deut 7:4 8045
ye shall *d* their altars, and break ... Deut 7:5 5422
hate him to their face, to *d* them ... Deut 7:10 6
shall *d* them with a mighty ... Deut 7:23 2000
thou shalt *d* their name from ... Deut 7:24 6
a consuming fire he shall *d* them ... Deut 9:3 8045
d them quickly, as the LORD hath ... Deut 9:3 6
Let me alone, that I may *d* them ... Deut 9:14 8045
was wroth against you to *d* you ... Deut 9:19 8045
the LORD had said he would *d* you ... Deut 9:25 8045
d not thy people and thine ... Deut 9:26 7843
and the LORD would not *d* thee ... Deut 10:10 7843
Ye shall utterly *d* all the places ... Deut 12:2 6
d the names of them out of that ... Deut 12:3 6
But thou shalt utterly *d* them ... Deut 20:17 2763
thou shalt not *d* the trees ... Deut 20:19 7843
not trees for meat, thou shalt *d* ... Deut 20:20 7843
will rejoice over you to *d* you ... Deut 28:63 6
he will *d* these nations from ... Deut 31:3 8045
shall *d* both the young man and the ... Deut 32:25 7921
and shall say, *D* them ... Deut 33:27 8045
the hand of the Amorites, to *d* us ... Josh 7:7 6
except ye *d* the accursed from ... Josh 7:12 8045
to *d* all the inhabitants of the ... Josh 9:24 8045
that he might *d* them utterly ... Josh 11:20 2763
favour, but that he might *d* them ... Josh 11:20 8045
to *d* the land wherein the ... Josh 22:33 7843
entered into the land to *d* it ... Judg 6:5 7843
do, Ye shall utterly *d* every male ... Judg 21:11 2763
utterly *d* all that they have, and ... 1Sa 15:3 2763
lest I *d* you with them ... 1Sa 15:6 622
good, and would not utterly *d* them ... 1Sa 15:9 2763
utterly *d* the sinners the ... 1Sa 15:18 2763
to *d* the city for my sake ... 1Sa 23:10 7843
that thou wilt not *d* my name out ... 1Sa 24:21 8045
David said to Abishai, *D* him not ... 1Sa 26:9 7843
people in to *d* the king thy lord ... 1Sa 26:15 7843
hand to *d* the LORD's anointed ... 2Sa 1:14 7843
and we will *d* the heir also ... 2Sa 14:7 8045
revengers of blood to *d* any more ... 2Sa 14:11 7843
lest they *d* my son ... 2Sa 14:11 8045
hand of the man that would *d* me ... 2Sa 14:16 8045
thou seekest to *d* a city and a ... 2Sa 20:19 4191
me, that I should swallow up or *d* ... 2Sa 20:20 7843
that I might *d* them that hate me ... 2Sa 22:41 6789
his hand upon Jerusalem to *d* it ... 2Sa 24:16 7843
also were not able utterly to *d* ... 1Kin 9:21 2763
to *d* it from off the face of the ... 1Kin 13:34 8045
Thus did Zimri *d* all the house of ... 1Kin 16:12 8045
Yet the LORD would not *d* Judah ... 2Kin 8:19 7843
might *d* the worshippers of Baal ... 2Kin 10:19 6
and Jacob, and would not *d* them ... 2Kin 13:23 7843
LORD against this place to *d* it ... 2Kin 18:25 7843
Go up against this land, and *d* it ... 2Kin 18:25 7843
sent them against Judah to *d* it ... 2Kin 24:2 6
an angel unto Jerusalem to *d* it ... 1Chr 21:15 7843
therefore I will not *d* them ... 2Chr 12:7 7843
he would not *d* him altogether ... 2Chr 12:12 7843
Seir, utterly to slay and *d* them ... 2Chr 20:23 8045
every one helped to *d* another ... 2Chr 20:23 4889
would not *d* the house of David ... 2Chr 21:7 7843
God hath determined to *d* thee ... 2Chr 25:16 7843
is with me, that he *d* thee not ... 2Chr 35:21 7843
name to dwell there *d* all kings ... Ezr 6:12 4049
to *d* this house of God which is ... Ezr 6:12 2255
to *d* all the Jews that were ... Est 3:6 8045
all the king's provinces, to *d* ... Est 3:13 8045
for the Jews, to *d* them ... Est 4:7 6
was given at Shushan to *d* them ... Est 4:8 8045
which he wrote to *d* the Jews ... Est 8:5 6
and to stand for their life, to *d* ... Est 8:11 8045
against the Jews to *d* them ... Est 9:24 6
to consume them, and to *d* them ... Est 9:24 6
him, to *d* him without cause ... Job 2:3 1104
that it would please God to *d* me ... Job 6:9 1792
If he *d* him from his place, then ... Job 8:18 1104
yet thou dost *d* me ... Job 10:8 1104
after my skin worms *d* this body ... Job 19:26 5362
Thou shalt *d* them that speak ... Ps 5:6 6
D thou them, O God ... Ps 5:10 816
that I might *d* them that hate me ... Ps 18:40 6789
fruit shalt thou *d* from the earth ... Ps 21:10 6
of his hands, he shall *d* them ... Ps 28:5 2040
that seek after my soul to *d* it ... Ps 40:14 5595
shall likewise *d* thee for ever ... Ps 52:5 5422
D, O Lord, and divide their ... Ps 55:9 1104

D

those that seek my soul, to *d* it	Ps 63:9	7722
they that would *d* me, being mine	Ps 69:4	6789
hearts, Let us *d* them together	Ps 74:8	3238
I will early *d* all the wicked of	Ps 101:8	6789
he said that he would *d* them	Ps 106:23	8045
his wrath, lest he should *d* them	Ps 106:23	7843
They did not *d* the nations	Ps 106:34	8045
name of the LORD will I *d* them	Ps 118:10	4135
name of the LORD I will *d* them	Ps 118:11	4135
name of the LORD I will *d* them	Ps 118:12	4135
wicked have waited for me to *d* me	Ps 119:95	6
d all them that afflict my soul	Ps 143:12	6
shoot out thine arrows, and *d* them	Ps 144:6	1949
but all the wicked will he *d*	Ps 145:20	8045
prosperity of fools shall *d* them	Prov 1:32	6
of transgressors shall *d* them	Prov 11:3	7703
The LORD will *d* the house of the	Prov 15:25	5255
of the wicked shall *d* them	Prov 21:7	1641
d the work of thine hands	Eccl 5:6	2254
why shouldest thou *d* thyself	Eccl 7:16	8074
to err, and *d* the way of thy paths	Is 3:12	1104
but it is in his heart to *d*	Is 10:7	8045
nor *d* in all my holy mountain	Is 11:9	7843
the LORD shall utterly *d* the	Is 11:15	2763
indignation, to *d* the whole land	Is 13:5	2254
he shall *d* the sinners thereof	Is 13:9	8045
I will *d* the counsel thereof	Is 19:3	1104
to *d* the strong holds thereof	Is 23:11	8045
he will *d* in this mountain the	Is 25:7	1104
to *d* the poor with lying words	Is 32:7	2254
LORD against this land to *d* it	Is 36:10	7843
Go up against this land, and *d* it	Is 36:10	7843
I will *d* and devour at once	Is 42:14	5395
as if he were ready to *d*	Is 51:13	7843
and I have created the waster to *d*	Is 54:16	2254
cluster, and one saith, *D* it not	Is 65:8	7843
sakes, that I may not *d* them all	Is 65:8	7843
nor *d* in all my holy mountain	Is 65:25	7843
out, and to pull down, and to *d*	Jer 1:10	6
Go ye up upon her walls, and *d*	Jer 5:10	7843
by night, and let us *d* her palaces	Jer 6:5	7843
Let us *d* the tree with the fruit	Jer 11:19	7843
d that nation, saith the LORD	Jer 12:17	6
spare, nor have mercy, but *d* them	Jer 13:14	7843
of the earth, to devour and *d*	Jer 15:3	7843
my hand against thee, and *d* thee	Jer 15:6	7843
I will *d* my people, since they	Jer 15:7	6
d them with double destruction	Jer 17:18	7665
up, and to pull down, and to *d* it	Jer 18:7	6
Woe be unto the pastors that *d*	Jer 23:1	6
about, and will utterly *d* them	Jer 25:9	2763
down, and to throw down, and to *d*	Jer 31:28	6
d this land, and shall cause to	Jer 36:29	7843
I will *d* the city and the	Jer 46:8	6
he shall *d* thy strong holds	Jer 48:18	7843
they will *d* till they have enough	Jer 49:9	7843
will *d* from thence the king and	Jer 49:38	6
utterly *d* after them, saith the	Jer 50:21	2763
her up as heaps, and *d* her utterly	Jer 50:26	2763
d ye utterly all her host	Jer 51:3	2763
is against Babylon, to *d* it	Jer 51:11	7843
and with thee will I *d* kingdoms	Jer 51:20	7843
The LORD hath purposed to *d* the	Lam 2:8	7843
d them in anger from under the	Lam 3:66	8045
and which I will send to *d* you	Eze 5:16	7843
I will *d* your high places	Eze 6:3	6
wilt thou *d* all the residue of	Eze 9:8	7843
will *d* him from the midst of my	Eze 14:9	8045
of brutish men, and skilful to *d*	Eze 21:31	4889
to *d* souls, to get dishonest gain	Eze 22:27	6
the land, that I should not *d* it	Eze 22:30	7843
I will *d* thee	Eze 25:7	8045
to *d* it for the old hatred	Eze 25:15	4889
d the remnant of the sea coast	Eze 25:16	9
they shall *d* the walls of Tyrus,	Eze 26:4	7843
walls, and *d* thy pleasant houses	Eze 26:12	5422
and I will *d* thee, O covering	Eze 28:16	6
shall be brought to *d* the land	Eze 30:11	7843
I will also *d* the idols, and I	Eze 30:13	6
I will *d* also all the beasts	Eze 32:13	6
but I will *d* the fat and the	Eze 34:16	8045
I saw when I came to *d* the city	Eze 43:3	7843
commanded to *d* all the wise men	Dan 2:12	7
to *d* the wise men of Babylon	Dan 2:24	7
D not the wise men of Babylon	Dan 2:24	7
Hew the tree down, and *d* it	Dan 4:23	2255
consume and to *d* it unto the end	Dan 7:26	7
he shall *d* wonderfully, and shall	Dan 8:24	7843
shall *d* the mighty and the holy	Dan 8:24	7843
heart, and by peace shall *d* many	Dan 8:25	7843
that shall come shall *d* the city	Dan 9:26	7843
portion of his meat shall *d* him	Dan 11:26	7665
go forth with great fury to *d*	Dan 11:44	8045
I will *d* her vines and her fig	Hos 2:12	8074
the night, and I will *d* thy mother	Hos 4:5	1820
I will not return to *d* Ephraim	Hos 11:9	7843
I will *d* it from off the face of	Amos 9:8	8045
not utterly *d* the house of Jacob	Amos 9:8	8045
even *d* the wise men out of Edom,	Obad 8	6
it is polluted, it shall *d* you	Mic 2:10	2254
of thee, and I will *d* thy chariots	Mic 5:10	6
so will I *d* thy cities	Mic 5:14	8045
Philistines, I will even *d* thee	Zeph 2:5	6
against the north, and *d* Assyria	Zeph 2:13	6
I will *d* the strength of the	Hag 2:22	8045
that I will seek to *d* all the	Zec 12:9	8045
he shall not *d* the fruits of your	Mal 3:11	7843
seek the young child to *d* him	Mt 2:13	*622*
not that I am come to *d* the law	Mt 5:17	*2647*
I am not come to *d*, but to fulfil	Mt 5:17	*2647*
him which is able to *d* both soul	Mt 10:28	*622*
against him, how they might *d* him	Mt 12:14	*622*
will miserably *d* those wicked men	Mt 21:41	*622*
I am able to *d* the temple of God,	Mt 26:61	*2647*
should ask Barabbas, and *d* Jesus	Mt 27:20	*622*
art thou come to *d* us	Mk 1:24	*622*
against him, how they might *d* him	Mk 3:6	*622*
and into the waters, to *d* him	Mk 9:22	*622*
and sought how they might *d* him	Mk 11:18	*622*
d the husbandmen, and will give	Mk 12:9	*622*
I will *d* this temple that is made	Mk 14:58	*2647*
art thou come to *d* us	Lk 4:34	*622*
to save life, or to *d* it	Lk 6:9	*622*
man is not come to *d* men's lives	Lk 9:56	*622*
of the people sought to *d* him	Lk 19:47	*622*
d these husbandmen, and shall give	Lk 20:16	*622*
D this temple, and in three days I	Jn 2:19	*3089*
for to steal, and to kill, and to *d*	Jn 10:10	*622*
of Nazareth shall *d* this place	Acts 6:14	*2647*
D not him with thy meat, for whom	Rom 14:15	*622*
For meat *d* not the work of God	Rom 14:20	*2647*
I will *d* the wisdom of the wise,	1Cor 1:19	*622*
temple of God, him shall God *d*	1Cor 3:17	*5351*
but God shall *d* both it and them	1Cor 6:13	*2673*
shall *d* with the brightness of	2Th 2:8	*2673*
that through death he might *d* him	Heb 2:14	*2673*
who is able to save and to *d*	Jas 4:12	*622*
that he might *d* the works of the	1Jn 3:8	*3089*
d them which *d* the earth	Rev 11:18	*1311*

DESTROYED {167}

every living substance was *d*	Gen 7:23	4229
they were *d* from the earth	Gen 7:23	4229
where, before the LORD *d* Sodom	Gen 13:10	7843
when God *d* the cities of the	Gen 19:29	7843
and I shall be *d*, I and my house	Gen 34:30	8045
thou not yet that Egypt is *d*	Ex 10:7	6
LORD only, he shall be utterly *d*	Ex 22:20	2763
and they utterly *d* them and their	Num 21:3	2763
d you in Seir, even unto Hormah	Deut 1:44	3807
when they had *d* them from before	Deut 2:12	8045
but the LORD *d* them before them	Deut 2:21	8045
when he *d* the Horims from before	Deut 2:22	8045
d them, and dwelt in their stead	Deut 2:23	8045
that time, and utterly *d* the men	Deut 2:34	2763
And we utterly *d* them, as we did	Deut 3:6	2763
God hath *d* them from among you	Deut 4:3	8045
upon it, but shall utterly be *d*	Deut 4:26	8045
hide themselves from thee, be *d*	Deut 7:20	6
destruction, until they be *d*	Deut 7:23	8045
thee, until thou have *d* them	Deut 7:24	8045
was angry with you to have *d* you	Deut 9:8	8045
angry with Aaron to have *d* him	Deut 9:20	8045
how the LORD hath *d* them unto	Deut 11:4	6
that they be *d* from before thee	Deut 12:30	8045
unto for to do, until thou be *d*	Deut 28:20	8045
down upon thee, until thou be *d*	Deut 28:24	8045
and overtake thee, till thou be *d*	Deut 28:45	8045
thy neck, until he have *d* thee	Deut 28:48	8045
of thy land, until thou be *d*	Deut 28:51	8045
thy sheep, until he have *d* thee	Deut 28:51	6
bring upon thee, until thou be *d*	Deut 28:61	8045
unto the land of them, whom he *d*	Deut 31:4	8045
Sihon and Og, whom ye utterly *d*	Josh 2:10	2763
they utterly *d* all that was in	Josh 6:21	2763
until he had utterly *d* all the	Josh 8:26	2763
had taken Ai, and had utterly *d* it	Josh 10:1	2763
and the king thereof he utterly *d*	Josh 10:28	2763
therein he utterly *d* that day	Josh 10:35	2763
but *d* it utterly, and all the	Josh 10:37	2763
utterly *d* all the souls that were	Josh 10:39	2763
but utterly *d* all that breathed,	Josh 10:40	2763
the sword, and he utterly *d* them	Josh 11:12	2763
the sword, until they had *d* them	Josh 11:14	8045
Joshua *d* them utterly with their	Josh 11:21	2763
until he have *d* you from off this	Josh 23:15	8045
and I *d* them from before you	Josh 24:8	8045
Zephath, and utterly *d* it	Judg 1:17	2763
until they had *d* Jabin king of	Judg 4:24	3772
d the increase of the earth, till	Judg 6:4	7843
d down to the ground of the	Judg 20:21	7843
d down to the ground of the	Judg 20:25	7843
the children of Israel *d* of the	Judg 20:35	7843
they *d* in the midst of them	Judg 20:42	7843
the women are *d* out of Benjamin	Judg 21:16	8045
a tribe be not *d* out of Israel	Judg 21:17	4229
he *d* them, and smote them with	1Sa 5:6	8074
utterly *d* all the people with the	1Sa 15:8	2763
and refuse, that they *d* utterly	1Sa 15:9	2763
and the rest we have utterly *d*	1Sa 15:15	2763
have utterly *d* the Amalekites	1Sa 15:20	2763
which should have been utterly *d*	1Sa 15:21	2764
they *d* the children of Ammon, and	2Sa 11:1	7843
be *d* from remaining in any of the	2Sa 21:5	8045
pursued mine enemies, and *d* them	2Sa 22:38	8045
to the angel that *d* the people	2Sa 24:16	7843
Asa *d* her idol, and burnt it by	1Kin 15:13	3772
that breathed, until he had *d* him	1Kin 15:29	8045
in Samaria, till he had *d* him	2Kin 10:17	8045
Thus Jehu *d* Baal out of Israel	2Kin 10:28	8045
she arose and *d* all the seed royal	2Kin 11:1	6
for the king of Syria had *d* them	2Kin 13:7	6
them which my fathers have *d*	2Kin 19:12	843
of Assyria have *d* the nations	2Kin 19:17	2717
therefore they have *d* them	2Kin 19:18	6
which Hezekiah his father had *d*	2Kin 21:3	6
d before the children of Israel	2Kin 21:9	8045
d them utterly unto this day, and	1Chr 4:41	2763
the land, whom God *d* before them	1Chr 5:25	8045
And Joab smote Rabbah, and *d* it	1Chr 20:1	2040
months to be *d* before thy foes	1Chr 21:12	5595
evil, and said to the angel that *d*	1Chr 21:15	7843
for they were *d* before the LORD,	2Chr 14:13	7665
And nation was *d* of nation	2Chr 15:6	3807
turned from them, and *d* them not	2Chr 20:10	8045
d all the seed royal of the house	2Chr 22:10	1696
d all the princes of the people	2Chr 24:23	7843
until they had utterly *d* them all	2Chr 31:1	3615
nations that my fathers utterly *d*	2Chr 32:14	2763
whom the LORD had *d* before the	2Chr 33:9	8045
which the kings of Judah had *d*	2Chr 34:11	7843
d all the goodly vessels thereof	2Chr 36:19	7843
for which cause was this city *d*	Ezr 4:15	2718
who *d* this house, and carried the	Ezr 5:12	5642
it be written that they may be *d*	Est 3:9	6
and thy father's house shall be *d*	Est 4:14	6
are sold, I and my people, to be *d*	Est 7:4	8045
Jews slew and *d* five hundred men	Est 9:6	6
d five hundred men in Shushan the	Est 9:12	6
They are *d* from morning to	Job 4:20	3807
He hath *d* me on every side, and I	Job 19:10	5422
in the night, so that they are *d*	Job 34:25	1792
thou hast *d* the wicked, thou hast	Ps 9:5	6
and thou hast *d* cities	Ps 9:6	5428
If the foundations be *d*, what can	Ps 11:3	2040
transgressors shall be *d* together	Ps 37:38	8045
thou hast *d* all them that go a	Ps 73:27	6789
their iniquity, and *d* them not	Ps 78:38	7843
and frogs, which *d* them	Ps 78:45	7843
He *d* their vines with hail, and	Ps 78:47	2026
is that they shall be *d* for ever	Ps 92:7	8045
of Babylon, who art to be *d*	Ps 137:8	7703
despiseth the word shall be *d*	Prov 13:13	2254
a companion of fools shall be *d*	Prov 13:20	7321
is that is *d* for want of judgment	Prov 13:23	5595
his neck, shall suddenly be *d*	Prov 29:1	7665
they that are led of them are *d*	Is 9:16	1104
the yoke shall be *d* because of	Is 10:27	2254
and *d* the cities thereof	Is 14:17	2040
because thou hast *d* thy land	Is 14:20	7843
d them, and made all their memory	Is 26:14	8045
he hath utterly *d* them, he hath	Is 34:2	2763
them which my fathers have *d*	Is 37:12	7843
therefore they have *d* them	Is 37:19	6
been cut off nor *d* from before me	Is 48:19	8045
Many pastors have *d* my vineyard	Jer 12:10	7843
for all thy lovers are *d*	Jer 22:20	7665
Moab is *d*	Jer 48:4	7665
perish, and the plain shall be *d*	Jer 48:8	8045
Moab shall be *d* from being a	Jer 48:42	8045
Babylon is suddenly fallen and *d*	Jer 51:8	7665
d out of her the great voice	Jer 51:55	6
he hath *d* his strong holds, and	Lam 2:5	7843
he hath *d* his places of the	Lam 2:6	7843
he hath *d* and broken her bars	Lam 2:9	6
and say to thee, How art thou *d*	Eze 26:17	6
like the *d* in the midst of the	Eze 27:32	1822
when all her helpers shall be *d*	Eze 30:8	7665
the multitude thereof shall be *d*	Eze 32:12	8045
a kingdom, which shall never be *d*	Dan 2:44	2255
kingdom that which shall not be *d*	Dan 6:26	2255
beast was slain, and his body *d*	Dan 7:11	7
kingdom that which shall not be *d*	Dan 7:14	2255
but within few days he shall be *d*	Dan 11:20	7665
My people are *d* for lack of	Hos 4:6	1820
the sin of Israel, shall be *d*	Hos 10:8	8045
O Israel, thou hast *d* thyself	Hos 13:9	7843
Yet *d* I the Amorite before them,	Amos 2:9	8045
yet I *d* his fruit from above, and	Amos 2:9	8045
their cities are *d*, so that there	Zeph 3:6	6658
d those murderers, and burned up	Mt 22:7	*622*
and the flood came, and *d* them all	Lk 17:27	*622*
from heaven, and *d* them all	Lk 17:29	*622*
shall be *d* from among the people	Acts 3:23	*1842*
Is not this he that *d* them which	Acts 9:21	*4199*
when he had *d* seven nations in	Acts 13:19	*2507*
and her magnificence should be *d*	Acts 19:27	*2507*
that the body of sin might be *d*	Rom 6:6	*2673*
tempted, and were *d* of serpents	1Cor 10:9	*622*
and were *d* of the destroyer	1Cor 10:10	*622*
enemy that shall be *d* is death	1Cor 15:26	*2673*
cast down, but not *d*	2Cor 4:9	*622*
the faith which once he *d*	Gal 1:23	*4199*
build again the things which I *d*	Gal 2:18	*2647*
lest he that *d* the firstborn	Heb 11:28	*3645*
beasts, made to be taken and *d*	2Pet 2:12	*5356*
afterward *d* them that believed	Jude 5	*622*
third part of the ships were *d*	Rev 8:9	*1311*

DESTROYER {7}

will not suffer the *d* to come in	Ex 12:23	7843
the *d* of our country, which slew	Judg 16:24	2717
in prosperity the *d* shall come	Job 15:21	7703
kept me from the paths of the *d*	Ps 17:4	6530
the same is the companion of a *d*	Prov 28:24	7843
the *d* of the Gentiles is on his	Jer 4:7	7843
and were destroyed of the *d*	1Cor 10:10	*3644*

DESTROYERS {4}

the grave, and his life to the *d*	Job 33:22	4191
thy *d* and they that made thee	Is 49:17	2040
And I will prepare *d* against thee	Jer 22:7	7843
O ye *d* of mine heritage, because	Jer 50:11	8154

DESTROYEST {4}
and thou *d* the hope of man ... Job 14:19 6
the LORD, which *d* all the earth ... Jer 51:25 7843
Thou that *d* the temple, and ... Mt 27:40 *2647*
thou that *d* the temple, and ... Mk 15:29 *2647*

DESTROYETH {8}
which the LORD *d* before your face ... Deut 8:20 6
He *d* the perfect and the wicked ... Job 9:22 3615
increaseth the nations, and *d* them ... Job 12:23 6
he that doeth it *d* his own soul ... Prov 6:32 7843
with his mouth *d* his neighbour ... Prov 11:9 7843
thy ways to that which *d* kings ... Prov 31:3 4229
and a gift *d* the heart ... Eccl 7:7 6
but one sinner *d* much good ... Eccl 9:18 6

DESTROYING {14}
of Heshbon, utterly *d* the men ... Deut 3:6 2763
d it utterly, and all that is ... Deut 13:15 2763
edge of the sword, utterly *d* them ... Josh 11:11 2763
to all lands, by *d* them utterly ... 2Kin 19:11 2763
land, and the angel of the LORD *d* ... 1Chr 21:12 7843
and as he was *d*, the LORD beheld, ... 1Chr 21:15 7843
a *d* storm, as a flood of mighty ... Is 28:2 6986
to all lands by *d* them utterly ... Is 37:11 2763
your prophets, like a *d* lion ... Jer 2:30 7843
that rise up against me, a *d* wind ... Jer 51:1 7843
O *d* mountain, saith the LORD, ... Jer 51:25 4889
not withdrawn his hand from *d* ... Lam 2:8 1104
man with his *d* weapon in his hand ... Eze 9:1 4892
mine eye spared them from *d* them ... Eze 20:17 7843

DESTRUCTION {94}
destroy them with a mighty *d* ... Deut 7:23 4103
burning heat, and with bitter *d* ... Deut 32:24 6986
the city with a very great *d* ... 1Sa 5:9 4103
for there was a deadly *d* ... 1Sa 5:11 4103
a man whom I appointed to utter *d* ... 1Kin 20:42 2764
the death of his father to his *d* ... 2Chr 22:4 4889
the *d* of Ahaziah was of God by ... 2Chr 22:7 8395
his heart was lifted up to his *d* ... 2Chr 26:16 7843
endure to see the *d* of my kindred ... Est 8:6 13
of the sword, and slaughter, and *d* ... Est 9:5 12
be afraid of *d* when it cometh ... Job 5:21 7701
At *d* and famine thou shalt laugh ... Job 5:22 7701
d shall be ready at his side ... Job 18:12 343
how oft cometh their *d* upon them ... Job 21:17 343
His eyes shall see his *d*, and he ... Job 21:20 3589
is reserved to the day of *d* ... Job 21:30 343
before him, and *d* hath no covering ... Job 26:6 11
D and death say, We have heard the ... Job 28:22 11
up against me the ways of their *d* ... Job 30:12 343
grave, though they cry in his *d* ... Job 30:24 6365
Is not *d* to the wicked ... Job 31:3 343
it is a fire that consumeth to *d* ... Job 31:12 11
For *d* from God was a terror to me ... Job 31:23 343
at the *d* of him that hated me ... Job 31:29 6365
Let *d* come upon him at unawares ... Ps 35:8 7722
into that very *d* let him fall ... Ps 35:8 7722
bring them down into the pit of *d* ... Ps 55:23 7845
thou castedst them down into *d* ... Ps 73:18 4876
or thy faithfulness in *d* ... Ps 88:11 11
Thou turnest man to *d* ... Ps 90:3 1793
nor for the *d* that wasteth at ... Ps 91:6 6986
Who redeemeth thy life from *d* ... Ps 103:4 7845
your *d* cometh as a whirlwind ... Prov 1:27 343
mouth of the foolish is near *d* ... Prov 10:14 4288
the *d* of the poor is their ... Prov 10:15 4288
but *d* shall be to the workers of ... Prov 10:29 4288
wide his lips shall have *d* ... Prov 13:3 4288
of people is the *d* of the prince ... Prov 14:28 4288
Hell and *d* are before the LORD ... Prov 15:11 11
Pride goeth before *d*, and an ... Prov 16:18 7667
that exalteth his gate seeketh *d* ... Prov 17:19 7667
A fool's mouth is his *d*, and his ... Prov 18:7 4288
Before *d* the heart of man is ... Prov 18:12 7667
but *d* shall be to the workers of ... Prov 21:15 4288
For their heart studieth *d* ... Prov 24:2 7701
Hell and *d* are never full ... Prov 27:20 10
of all such as are appointed to *d* ... Prov 31:8 2475
the *d* of the transgressors and of ... Is 1:28 7667
cease, and mine anger in their *d* ... Is 10:25 8399
come as a *d* from the Almighty ... Is 13:6 7701
will sweep it with the besom of *d* ... Is 14:23 8045
they shall raise up a cry of *d* ... Is 15:5 7667
shall be called, The city of *d* ... Is 19:18 2041
and the gate is smitten with *d* ... Is 24:12 7591
places, and the land of thy *d* ... Is 49:19 2035
desolation, and *d*, and the famine, ... Is 51:19 7667
wasting and *d* are in their paths ... Is 59:7 7667
wasting nor *d* within thy borders ... Is 60:18 7667
evil from the north, and a great *d* ... Jer 4:6 7667
D upon *d* is cried ... Jer 4:20 7667
out of the north, and great *d* ... Jer 6:1 7667
and destroy them with double *d* ... Jer 17:18 7670
a very fair heifer, but *d* cometh ... Jer 46:20 7171
Horonaim, spoiling and great *d* ... Jer 48:3 7667
the enemies have heard a cry of *d* ... Jer 48:5 7667
is in the land, and of great *d* ... Jer 50:22 7667
great *d* from the land of the ... Jer 51:54 7667
for the *d* of the daughter of my ... Lam 2:11 7667
is come upon us, desolation and *d* ... Lam 3:47 7667
d of the daughter of my people ... Lam 3:48 7667
they were their meat in the *d* of ... Lam 4:10 7667
which shall be for their *d* ... Eze 5:16 4889
D cometh; and they shall seek ... Eze 7:25 7089
bring thy *d* among the nations ... Eze 32:9 7667
fled from me: *d* unto them ... Hos 7:13 7701
lo, they are gone because of *d* ... Hos 9:6 7701
O grave, I will be thy *d* ... Hos 13:14 6987
as a *d* from the Almighty shall it ... Joel 1:15 7701
of Judah in the day of their *d* ... Obad 12 6
destroy you, even with a sore *d* ... Mic 2:10 2256
and there shall be no more utter *d* ... Zec 14:11 2764
is the way, that leadeth to *d* ... Mt 7:13 *684*
D and misery are in their ways ... Rom 3:16 *4938*
the vessels of wrath fitted to *d* ... Rom 9:22 *684*
unto Satan for the *d* of the flesh ... 1Cor 5:5 *3639*
edification, and not for your *d* ... 2Cor 10:8 *2506*
me to edification, and not to *d* ... 2Cor 13:10 *2506*
Whose end is *d*, whose God is ... Phil 3:19 *684*
then sudden *d* cometh upon them, ... 1Th 5:3 *3639*
be punished with everlasting *d* ... 2Th 1:9 *3639*
lusts, which drown men in *d* ... 1Ti 6:9 *3639*
and bring upon themselves swift *d* ... 2Pet 2:1 *684*
scriptures, unto their own *d* ... 2Pet 3:16 *684*

DESTRUCTIONS {3}
d are come to a perpetual end ... Ps 9:6 2723
rescue my soul from their *d* ... Ps 35:17 7722
and delivered them from their *d* ... Ps 107:20 7825

DETAIN {2}
LORD, I pray thee, let us *d* thee ... Judg 13:15 6113
unto Manoah, Though thou *d* me ... Judg 13:16 6113

DETAINED {1}
there that day, *d* before the LORD ... 1Sa 21:7 6113

DETERMINATE {1}
being delivered by the *d* counsel ... Acts 2:23 *3724*

DETERMINATION {1}
for my *d* is to gather the nations ... Zeph 3:8 4941

DETERMINE {1}
and he shall pay as the judges *d* ... Ex 21:22

DETERMINED {30}
be sure that evil is *d* by him ... 1Sa 20:7 3615
d by my father to come upon thee ... 1Sa 20:9 3615
Jonathan knew that it was *d* of ... 1Sa 20:33 3615
for evil is *d* against our master, ... 1Sa 25:17 3615
of Absalom this hath been *d* from ... 2Sa 13:32 7760
Solomon *d* to build an house for ... 2Chr 2:1 559
that God hath *d* to destroy thee ... 2Chr 25:16 3289
evil *d* against him by the king ... Est 7:7 3615
Seeing his days are *d*, the number ... Job 14:5 2782
shall make a consumption, even *d* ... Is 10:23 2782
hosts, which he hath *d* against it ... Is 19:17 3289
even *d* upon the whole earth ... Is 28:22 2782
weeks are *d* upon thy people ... Dan 9:24 2852
end of the war desolations are *d* ... Dan 9:26 2782
that *d* shall be poured upon the ... Dan 9:27 2782
for that that is *d* shall be done ... Dan 11:36 2782
the Son of man goeth, as it was *d* ... Lk 22:22 *3724*
when he was *d* to let him go ... Acts 3:13 *2919*
thy counsel *d* before to be done ... Acts 4:28 *4309*
d to send relief unto the ... Acts 11:29 *3724*
they *d* that Paul and Barnabas, and ... Acts 15:2 *5021*
Barnabas *d* to take with them John ... Acts 15:37 *1011*
hath *d* the times before appointed ... Acts 17:26 *3724*
it shall be *d* in a lawful ... Acts 19:39 *1956*
For Paul had *d* to sail by Ephesus ... Acts 20:16 *2919*
to Augustus, I have *d* to send him ... Acts 25:25 *2919*
when it was *d* that we should sail ... Acts 27:1 *2919*
For I *d* not to know any thing ... 1Cor 2:2 *2919*
But I *d* this with myself, that I ... 2Cor 2:1 *2919*
for I have *d* there to winter ... Titus 3:12 *2919*

DETEST {1}
but thou shalt utterly *d* it ... Deut 7:26 8262

DETESTABLE {6}
with the carcases of their *d* ... Jer 16:18 8251
sanctuary with all thy *d* things ... Eze 5:11 8251
of their *d* things therein ... Eze 7:20 8251
away all the *d* things thereof ... Eze 11:18 8251
after the heart of their *d* things ... Eze 11:21 8251
idols, nor with their *d* things ... Eze 37:23 8251

DEUEL *(de-oo'-el)* {4} See REUEL. *Father of Eliasaph.*
Eliasaph the son of *D* ... Num 1:14 1845
sixth day Eliasaph the son of *D* ... Num 7:42 1845
offering of Eliasaph the son of *D* ... Num 7:47 1845
of Gad was Eliasaph the son of *D* ... Num 10:20 1845

DEVICE {10}
to find out every *d* which shall ... 2Chr 2:14 4284
his *d* that he had devised against ... Est 8:3 4284
by letters that his wicked *d* ... Est 9:25 4284
they imagined a mischievous *d* ... Ps 21:11
further not his wicked *d* ... Ps 140:8
for there is no work, nor *d* ... Eccl 9:10 2808
you, and devise a *d* against you ... Jer 18:11 4284
for his *d* is against Babylon, to ... Jer 51:11 4209
their *d* against me all the day ... Lam 3:62 1902
stone, graven by art and man's *d* ... Acts 17:29 *1761*

DEVICES {16}
disappointeth the *d* of the crafty ... Job 5:12 4284
the *d* which ye wrongfully imagine ... Job 21:27 4209
in the *d* that they have imagined ... Ps 10:2 4209
he maketh the *d* of the people of ... Ps 33:10 4284
man who bringeth wicked *d* to pass ... Ps 37:7 4209
and be filled with their own *d* ... Prov 1:31 4156
a man of wicked *d* will he condemn ... Prov 12:2 4209
and a man of wicked *d* is hated ... Prov 14:17 4209
There are many *d* in a man's heart ... Prov 19:21 4284
he deviseth wicked *d* to destroy ... Is 32:7 2154
they had devised *d* against me ... Jer 11:19 4284
but we will walk after our own *d* ... Jer 18:12 4284
let us devise *d* against Jeremiah ... Jer 18:18 4284
he shall forecast his *d* against ... Dan 11:24 4284
they shall forecast *d* against him ... Dan 11:25 4284
for we are not ignorant of his *d* ... 2Cor 2:11 *3540*

DEVIL {61}
wilderness to be tempted of the *d* ... Mt 4:1 *1228*
Then the *d* taketh him up into the ... Mt 4:5 *1228*
the *d* taketh him up into an ... Mt 4:8 *1228*
Then the *d* leaveth him, and, ... Mt 4:11 *1228*
him a dumb man possessed with a *d* ... Mt 9:32 *1139*
when the *d* was cast out, the dumb ... Mt 9:33 *1140*
and they say, He hath a *d* ... Mt 11:18 *1140*
unto him one possessed with a *d* ... Mt 12:22 *1139*
enemy that sowed them is the *d* ... Mt 13:39 *1228*
is grievously vexed with a *d* ... Mt 15:22 *1139*
And Jesus rebuked the *d* ... Mt 17:18 *1140*
fire, prepared for the *d* and his ... Mt 25:41 *1228*
him that was possessed with the *d* ... Mk 5:15 *1139*
him that was possessed with the *d* ... Mk 5:16 *1139*
the *d* prayed him that he might be ... Mk 5:18 *1139*
forth the *d* out of her daughter ... Mk 7:26 *1140*
the *d* is gone out of thy daughter ... Mk 7:29 *1140*
house, she found the *d* gone out ... Mk 7:30 *1140*
Being forty days tempted of the *d* ... Lk 4:2 *1228*
the *d* said unto him, If thou be ... Lk 4:3 *1228*
And the *d*, taking him up into an ... Lk 4:5 *1228*
the *d* said unto him, All this ... Lk 4:6 *1228*
when the *d* had ended all the ... Lk 4:13 *1228*
had a spirit of an unclean *d* ... Lk 4:33 *1140*
when the *d* had thrown him in the ... Lk 4:35 *1140*
and ye say, He hath a *d* ... Lk 7:33 *1140*
then cometh the *d*, and taketh away ... Lk 8:12 *1228*
was driven of the *d* into the ... Lk 8:29 *1142*
the *d* threw him down, and tare him ... Lk 9:42 *1140*
And he was casting out a *d* ... Lk 11:14 *1140*
when the *d* was gone out, the dumb ... Lk 11:14 *1140*
you twelve, and one of you is a *d* ... Jn 6:70 *1228*
answered and said, Thou hast a *d* ... Jn 7:20 *1140*
Ye are of your father the *d* ... Jn 8:44 *1228*
thou art a Samaritan, and hast a *d* ... Jn 8:48 *1140*
Jesus answered, I have not a *d* ... Jn 8:49 *1140*
Now we know that thou hast a *d* ... Jn 8:52 *1140*
And many of them said, He hath a *d* ... Jn 10:20 *1140*
the words of him that hath a *d* ... Jn 10:21 *1139*
Can a *d* open the eyes of the ... Jn 10:21 *1140*
the *d* having now put into the ... Jn 13:2 *1228*
all that were oppressed of the *d* ... Acts 10:38 *1228*
all mischief, thou child of the *d* ... Acts 13:10 *1228*
Neither give place to the *d* ... Eph 4:27 *1228*
stand against the wiles of the *d* ... Eph 6:11 *1228*
into the condemnation of the *d* ... 1Ti 3:6 *1228*
reproach and the snare of the *d* ... 1Ti 3:7 *1228*
out of the snare of the *d* ... 2Ti 2:26 *1228*
power of death, that is, the *d* ... Heb 2:14 *1228*
Resist the *d*, and he will flee ... Jas 4:7 *1228*
because your adversary the *d* ... 1Pet 5:8 *1228*
that committeth sin is of the *d* ... 1Jn 3:8 *1228*
for the *d* sinneth from the ... 1Jn 3:8 *1228*
might destroy the works of the *d* ... 1Jn 3:8 *1228*
and the children of the *d* ... 1Jn 3:10 *1228*
when contending with the *d* he ... Jude 9 *1228*
the *d* shall cast some of you into ... Rev 2:10 *1228*
that old serpent, called the *D* ... Rev 12:9 *1228*
for the *d* is come down unto you, ... Rev 12:12 *1228*
that old serpent, which is the *D* ... Rev 20:2 *1228*
the *d* that deceived them was cast ... Rev 20:10 *1228*

DEVILISH {1}
above, but is earthly, sensual, *d* ... Jas 3:15 *1141*

DEVILS {55}
offer their sacrifices unto *d* ... Lev 17:7 8163
They sacrificed unto *d*, not to ... Deut 32:17 7700
for the high places, and for the *d* ... 2Chr 11:15 8163
sons and their daughters unto *d* ... Ps 106:37 7700
those which were possessed with *d* ... Mt 4:24 *1139*
and in thy name have cast out *d* ... Mt 7:22 *1140*
many that were possessed with *d* ... Mt 8:16 *1139*
met him two possessed with *d* ... Mt 8:28 *1139*
So the *d* besought him, saying, If ... Mt 8:31 *1142*
to the possessed of the *d* ... Mt 8:33 *1139*
He casteth out *d* through the ... Mt 9:34 *1140*
through the prince of the *d* ... Mt 9:34 *1140*
raise the dead, cast out *d* ... Mt 10:8 *1140*
This fellow doth not cast out *d* ... Mt 12:24 *1140*
by Beelzebub the prince of the *d* ... Mt 12:24 *1140*
And if I by Beelzebub cast out *d* ... Mt 12:27 *1140*
But if I cast out *d* by the Spirit ... Mt 12:28 *1140*
them that were possessed with *d* ... Mk 1:32 *1139*
diseases, and cast out many *d* ... Mk 1:34 *1140*
and suffered not the *d* to speak ... Mk 1:34 *1140*
all Galilee, and cast out *d* ... Mk 1:39 *1140*
heal sicknesses, and to cast out *d* ... Mk 3:15 *1140*
of the *d* casteth he out *d* ... Mk 3:22 *1140*
all the *d* besought him, saying, ... Mk 5:12 *1142*
And they cast out many *d*, and ... Mk 6:13 *1140*
saw one casting out *d* in thy name ... Mk 9:38 *1140*
out of whom he had cast seven *d* ... Mk 16:9 *1140*
In my name shall they cast out *d* ... Mk 16:17 *1140*
d also came out of many, crying ... Lk 4:41 *1140*
out of whom went seven *d* ... Lk 8:2 *1140*
man, which had *d* long time ... Lk 8:27 *1140*
because many *d* were entered into ... Lk 8:30 *1140*
Then went the *d* out of the man, ... Lk 8:33 *1140*
out of whom the *d* were departed ... Lk 8:35 *1140*
was possessed of the *d* was healed ... Lk 8:36 *1139*
Now the man out of whom the *d* ... Lk 8:38 *1140*
power and authority over all *d* ... Lk 9:1 *1140*
saw one casting out *d* in thy name ... Lk 9:49 *1140*
even the *d* are subject unto us ... Lk 10:17 *1140*
said, He casteth out *d* through ... Lk 11:15 *1140*
Beelzebub the chief of the *d* ... Lk 11:15 *1140*
I cast out *d* through Beelzebub ... Lk 11:18 *1140*

And if I by Beelzebub cast out *d* ... Lk 11:19 *1140*
with the finger of God cast out *d* ... Lk 11:20 *1140*
that fox, Behold, I cast out *d* ... Lk 13:32 *1140*
sacrifice, they sacrifice to *d* ... 1Cor 10:20 *1140*
ye should have fellowship with *d* ... 1Cor 10:20 *1140*
cup of the Lord, and the cup of *d* ... 1Cor 10:21 *1140*
table, and of the table of *d* ... 1Cor 10:21 *1140*
spirits, and doctrines of *d* ... 1Ti 4:1 *1140*
the *d* also believe, and tremble ... Jas 2:19 *1140*
that they should not worship *d* ... Rev 9:20 *1140*
For they are the spirits of *d* ... Rev 16:14 *1142*
and is become the habitation of *d* ... Rev 18:2 *1142*

DEVISE {16}
To *d* cunning works, to work in ... Ex 31:4 2803
to *d* curious works, to work in ... Ex 35:32 2803
and of those that *d* cunning work ... Ex 35:35 2803
yet doth he *d* means, that his ... 2Sa 14:14 2803
to confusion that *d* my hurt ... Ps 35:4 2803
but they *d* deceitful matters ... Ps 35:20 2803
against me do they *d* my hurt ... Ps 41:7 2803
D not evil against thy neighbour, ... Prov 3:29 2790
Do they not err that *d* evil ... Prov 14:22 2790
shall be to them that *d* good ... Prov 14:22 2790
his eyes to *d* froward things ... Prov 16:30 2803
you, and *d* a device against you ... Jer 18:11 2803
let us *d* devices against Jeremiah ... Jer 18:18 2803
these are the men that *d* mischief ... Eze 11:2 2803
Woe to them that *d* iniquity ... Mic 2:1 2803
this family do I *d* an evil ... Mic 2:3 2803

DEVISED {12}
that *d* against us that we should ... 2Sa 21:5 1819
which he had *d* of his own heart ... 1Kin 12:33 908
that he had *d* against the Jews ... Est 8:3 2803
d by Haman the son of Hammedatha ... Est 8:5 4284
had *d* against the Jews to destroy ... Est 9:24 2803
which he *d* against the Jews, ... Est 9:25 2803
they *d* to take away my life ... Ps 31:13 2161
they had *d* devices against me ... Jer 11:19 2803
they have *d* evil against it ... Jer 48:2 2803
for the LORD hath both *d* and done ... Jer 51:12 2161
hath done that which he had *d* ... Lam 2:17 2161
not followed cunningly *d* fables ... 2Pet 1:16 *4679*

DEVISETH {8}
He *d* mischief upon his bed ... Ps 36:4 2803
Thy tongue *d* mischiefs ... Ps 52:2 2803
he *d* mischief continually ... Prov 6:14 2790
An heart that *d* wicked ... Prov 6:18 2790
A man's heart *d* his way ... Prov 16:9 2803
He that *d* to do evil shall be ... Prov 24:8 2803
he *d* wicked devices to destroy ... Is 32:7 3289
But the liberal *d* liberal things ... Is 32:8 3289

DEVOTE {1}
that a man shall *d* unto the LORD ... Lev 27:28 2763

DEVOTED {7}
holy unto the LORD, as a field *d* ... Lev 27:21 2764
Notwithstanding no *d* thing ... Lev 27:28 2764
every *d* thing is most holy unto ... Lev 27:28 2764
None *d*, which shall be ... Lev 27:29 2764
which shall be *d* of men ... Lev 27:29 2763
Every thing *d* in Israel shall be ... Num 18:14 2764
thy servant, who is *d* to thy fear ... Ps 119:38

DEVOTIONS {1}
as I passed by, and beheld your *d* ... Acts 17:23 *4574*

DEVOUR {71}
the morning he shall *d* the prey ... Gen 49:27 398
blood, and my sword shall *d* flesh ... Deut 32:42 398
and *d* the cedars of Lebanon ... Judg 9:15 398
d the men of Shechem, and the ... Judg 9:20 398
house of Millo, and *d* Abimelech ... Judg 9:20 398
said, Shall the sword *d* for ever ... 2Sa 2:26 398
command the locusts to *d* the land ... 2Chr 7:13 398
It shall *d* the strength of his ... Job 18:13 398
of death shall *d* his strength ... Job 18:13 398
wrath, and the fire shall *d* them ... Ps 21:9 398
a fire shall *d* before him ... Ps 50:3 398
wild beast of the field doth *d* it ... Ps 80:13 7462
to *d* the poor from off the earth, ... Prov 30:14 398
strangers *d* it in your presence, ... Is 1:7 398
they shall *d* Israel with open ... Is 9:12 398
it shall *d* the briers and thorns, ... Is 9:18 398
d his thorns and his briers in one ... Is 10:17 398
of thine enemies shall *d* them ... Is 26:11 398
not of a mean man, shall *d* him ... Is 31:8 398
your breath, as fire, shall *d* you ... Is 33:11 398
I will destroy and *d* at once ... Is 42:14 7602
ye beasts of the field, come to *d* ... Is 56:9 398
all that *d* him shall offend ... Jer 2:3 398
people wood, and it shall *d* them ... Jer 5:14 398
beasts of the field, come to *d* ... Jer 12:9 402
d from the one end of the land ... Jer 12:12 398
and the beasts of the earth, to *d* ... Jer 15:3 398
it shall *d* the palaces of ... Jer 17:27 398
it shall *d* all things round about ... Jer 21:14 398
that *d* thee shall be devoured ... Jer 30:16 398
and the sword shall *d*, and it shall ... Jer 46:10 398
sword shall *d* round about thee ... Jer 46:14 398
shall *d* the corner of Moab, and ... Jer 48:45 398
it shall *d* all round about him ... Jer 50:32 398
famine and pestilence shall *d* him ... Eze 7:15 398
and another fire shall *d* them ... Eze 15:7 398
it shall *d* every green tree in ... Eze 20:47 398
them through the fire, to *d* them ... Eze 23:37 402
midst of thee, it shall *d* thee ... Eze 28:18 398
the beast of the land *d* them ... Eze 34:28 398
thou shalt *d* men no more, neither ... Eze 36:14 398
thus unto it, Arise, *d* much flesh ... Dan 7:5 399
shall *d* the whole earth, and shall ... Dan 7:23 399
now shall a month *d* them with ... Hos 5:7 398
it shall *d* the palaces thereof ... Hos 8:14 398
d them, because of their own ... Hos 11:6 398
there will I *d* them like a lion ... Hos 13:8 398
which shall *d* the palaces of ... Amos 1:4 398
which shall *d* the palaces thereof ... Amos 1:7 398
which shall *d* the palaces thereof ... Amos 1:10 398
which shall *d* the palaces of ... Amos 1:12 398
it shall *d* the palaces thereof, ... Amos 1:14 398
it shall *d* the palaces of Kirioth ... Amos 2:2 398
it shall *d* the palaces of ... Amos 2:5 398
d it, and there be none to quench ... Amos 5:6 398
shall kindle in them, and *d* them ... Obad 18 398
the sword shall *d* thy young lions ... Nah 2:13 398
the fire shall *d* thy bars ... Nah 3:13 398
There shall the fire *d* thee ... Nah 3:15 398
was as to *d* the poor secretly ... Hab 3:14 398
and they shall *d*, and subdue with ... Zec 9:15 398
that the fire may *d* thy cedars ... Zec 11:1 398
they shall *d* all the people round ... Zec 12:6 398
for ye *d* widows' houses, and for a ... Mt 23:14 *2719*
Which *d* widows' houses, and for a ... Mk 12:40 *2719*
Which *d* widows' houses, and for a ... Lk 20:47 *2719*
you into bondage, if a man *d* you ... 2Cor 11:20 *2719*
d one another, take heed that ye ... Gal 5:15 *2719*
which shall *d* the adversaries ... Heb 10:27 *2068*
about, seeking whom he may *d* ... 1Pet 5:8 *2666*
for to *d* her child as soon as it ... Rev 12:4 *2719*

DEVOURED {53}
hath quite *d* also our money ... Gen 31:15 398
say, Some evil beast hath *d* him ... Gen 37:20 398
an evil beast hath *d* him ... Gen 37:33 398
seven thin ears *d* the seven rank ... Gen 41:7 1104
the thin ears *d* the seven good ... Gen 41:24 1104
d them, and they died before the ... Lev 10:2 398
what time the fire *d* two hundred ... Num 26:10 398
from them, and they shall be *d* ... Deut 31:17 398
d with burning heat, and with ... Deut 32:24 3898
the wood *d* more people that day ... 2Sa 18:8 398
people that day than the sword *d* ... 2Sa 18:8 398
and fire out of his mouth *d* ... 2Sa 22:9 398
and fire out of his mouth *d* ... Ps 18:8 398
of flies among them, which *d* them ... Ps 78:45 398
For they have *d* Jacob, and laid ... Ps 79:7 398
d the fruit of their ground ... Ps 105:35 398
ye shall be *d* with the sword ... Is 1:20 398
hath the curse *d* the earth ... Is 24:6 398
own sword hath *d* your prophets ... Jer 2:30 398
For shame hath *d* the labour of ... Jer 3:24 398
have *d* the land, and all that is ... Jer 8:16 398
d him, and consumed him, and have ... Jer 10:25 398
they that devour thee shall be *d* ... Jer 30:16 398
All that found them have *d* them ... Jer 50:7 398
the king of Assyria hath *d* him ... Jer 50:17 398
the king of Babylon hath *d* me ... Jer 51:34 398
it hath *d* the foundations thereof ... Lam 4:11 398
any work, when the fire hath *d* it ... Eze 15:5 398
thou sacrificed unto them to be *d* ... Eze 16:20 398
to catch the prey; it *d* men ... Eze 19:3 398
to catch the prey, and *d* men ... Eze 19:6 398
branches, which hath *d* her fruit ... Eze 19:14 398
they have *d* souls ... Eze 22:25 398
residue shall be *d* by the fire ... Eze 23:25 398
will I give to the beasts to be *d* ... Eze 33:27 398
the beasts of the field to be *d* ... Eze 39:4 402
it *d* and brake in pieces, and ... Dan 7:7 399
which *d*, brake in pieces, and ... Dan 7:19 399
an oven, and have *d* their judges ... Hos 7:7 398
Strangers have *d* his strength ... Hos 7:9 398
for the fire hath *d* the pastures ... Joel 1:19 398
the fire hath *d* the pastures of ... Joel 1:20 398
increased, the palmerworm *d* them ... Amos 4:9 398
it *d* the great deep, and did eat ... Amos 7:4 398
they shall be *d* as stubble fully ... Nah 1:10 398
be *d* by the fire of his jealousy ... Zeph 1:18 398
for all the earth shall be *d* with ... Zeph 3:8 398
and she shall be *d* with fire ... Zec 9:4 398
and the fowls came and *d* them up ... Mt 13:4 *2719*
fowls of the air came and *d* it up ... Mk 4:4 *2719*
and the fowls of the air *d* it ... Lk 8:5 *2719*
which hath *d* thy living with ... Lk 15:30 *2719*
from God out of heaven, and *d* them ... Rev 20:9 *2719*

DEVOURER {1}
will rebuke the *d* for your sakes ... Mal 3:11 398

DEVOUREST {1}
say unto you, Thou land *d* up men ... Eze 36:13 398

DEVOURETH {10}
for the sword *d* one as well as ... 2Sa 11:25 398
mouth of the wicked *d* iniquity ... Prov 19:28 1104
the man who *d* that which is holy ... Prov 20:25 3216
as the fire *d* the stubble ... Is 5:24 398
flaming fire, which *d* round about ... Lam 2:3 398
the fire *d* both the ends of it, ... Eze 15:4 398
A fire *d* before them ... Joel 2:3 398
flame of fire that *d* the stubble ... Joel 2:5 398
thy tongue when the wicked *d* the ... Hab 1:13 1104
their mouth, and *d* their enemies ... Rev 11:5 *2719*

DEVOURING {6}
the glory of the LORD was like *d* ... Ex 24:17 398
Thou lovest all *d* words, O thou ... Ps 52:4 1105
tempest, and the flame of *d* fire ... Is 29:6 398
and his tongue as a *d* fire ... Is 30:27 398
and with the flame of a *d* fire ... Is 30:30 398
us shall dwell with the *d* fire ... Is 33:14 398

DEVOUT {9}
and the same man was just and *d* ... Lk 2:25 *2126*
d men, out of every nation under ... Acts 2:5 *2126*
d men carried Stephen to his ... Acts 8:2 *2126*
A *d* man, and one that feared God ... Acts 10:2 *2152*
a *d* soldier of them that waited ... Acts 10:7 *2152*
But the Jews stirred up the *d* ... Acts 13:50 *4576*
of the *d* Greeks a great multitude ... Acts 17:4 *4576*
the Jews, and with the *d* persons ... Acts 17:17 *4576*
a *d* man according to the law, ... Acts 22:12 *2152*

DEW {37}
God give thee of the *d* of heaven ... Gen 27:28 2919
of the *d* of heaven from above ... Gen 27:39 2919
in the morning the *d* lay round ... Ex 16:13 2919
when the *d* that lay was gone up, ... Ex 16:14 2919
when the *d* fell upon the camp in ... Num 11:9 2919
my speech shall distil as the *d* ... Deut 32:2 2919
things of heaven, for the *d* ... Deut 33:13 2919
his heavens shall drop down *d* ... Deut 33:28 2919
if the *d* be on the fleece only, ... Judg 6:37 2919
wringed the *d* out of the fleece, ... Judg 6:38 2919
all the ground let there be *d* ... Judg 6:39 2919
there was *d* on all the ground ... Judg 6:40 2919
of Gilboa, let there be no *d* ... 2Sa 1:21 2919
as the *d* falleth on the ground ... 2Sa 17:12 2919
there shall not be *d* nor rain ... 1Kin 17:1 2919
the *d* lay all night upon my ... Job 29:19 2919
who hath begotten the drops of *d* ... Job 38:28 2919
thou hast the *d* of thy youth ... Ps 110:3 2919
As the *d* of Hermon, and as the *d* ... Ps 133:3 2919
up, and the clouds drop down the *d* ... Prov 3:20 2919
his favour is as *d* upon the grass ... Prov 19:12 2919
for my head is filled with *d* ... Song 5:2 2919
like a cloud of *d* in the heat of ... Is 18:4 2919
for thy *d* is as the *d* of herbs, ... Is 26:19 2919
it be wet with the *d* of heaven ... Dan 4:15 2920
it be wet with the *d* of heaven ... Dan 4:23 2920
wet thee with the *d* of heaven ... Dan 4:25 2920
body was wet with the *d* of heaven ... Dan 4:33 2920
body was wet with the *d* of heaven ... Dan 5:21 2920
as the early *d* it goeth away ... Hos 6:4 2919
as the early *d* that passeth away, ... Hos 13:3 2919
I will be as the *d* unto Israel ... Hos 14:5 2919
many people as a *d* from the LORD ... Mic 5:7 2919
heaven over you is stayed from *d* ... Hag 1:10 2919
and the heavens shall give their *d* ... Zec 8:12 2919

DIADEM {4}
my judgment was as a robe and a *d* ... Job 29:14 6797
for a *d* of beauty, unto the ... Is 28:5 6843
a royal *d* in the hand of thy God ... Is 62:3 6797
Remove the *d*, and take off the ... Eze 21:26 4701

DIAL {2}
it had gone down in the *d* of Ahaz ... 2Kin 20:11 4609
is gone down in the sun *d* of Ahaz ... Is 38:8 4609

DIAMOND {4}
be an emerald, a sapphire, and a *d* ... Ex 28:18 3095
an emerald, a sapphire, and a *d* ... Ex 39:11 3095
of iron, and with the point of a *d* ... Jer 17:1 8068
the sardius, topaz, and the *d* ... Eze 28:13 3095

DIANA *(di-an'-ah)* {5} *A Greek goddess.*
which made silver shrines for *D* ... Acts 19:24 *735*
goddess *D* should be despised ... Acts 19:27 *735*
Great is *D* of the Ephesians ... Acts 19:28 *735*
Great is *D* of the Ephesians ... Acts 19:34 *735*
worshipper of the great goddess *D* ... Acts 19:35 *735*

DIBLAH See DIBLATH.

DIBLAIM *(dib'-la-im)* {1} *Father of Gomer.*
and took Gomer the daughter of *D* ... Hos 1:3 1691

DIBLATH *(dib'-lath)* {1} *A place in northern Canaan.*
than the wilderness toward *D* ... Eze 6:14 1689

DIBON *(di'-bon)* {9} See DIBON-GAD, DIMON.
1. A Moabite city.
Heshbon is perished even unto *D* ... Num 21:30 1769
Ataroth, and *D*, and Jazer, and ... Num 32:3 1769
And the children of Gad built *D* ... Num 32:34 1769
and all the plain of Medeba unto *D* ... Josh 13:9 1769
D, and Bamoth-baal, and ... Josh 13:17 1769
Thou daughter that dost inhabit *D* ... Jer 48:18 1769
upon *D*, and upon Nebo, and upon ... Jer 48:22 1769
He is gone up to Bajith, and to *D* ... Is 15:2 1769
2. A town in Judah.
in the villages thereof, and at *D* ... Neh 11:25 1769

DIBON-GAD *(di'-bon-gad')* {2} *An encampment during the Exodus.*
from Iim, and pitched in *D* ... Num 33:45 1769
And they removed from *D*, and ... Num 33:46 1769

DIBRI *(dib'-ri)* {1} *Father of Shelomith.*
was Shelomith, the daughter of *D* ... Lev 24:11 1704

DID {1011}
d eat, and gave also unto her ... Gen 3:6
and he *d* eat ... Gen 3:6
gave me of the tree, and I *d* eat ... Gen 3:12
serpent beguiled me, and I *d* eat ... Gen 3:13
to his wife *d* the LORD God make ... Gen 3:21
Thus *d* Noah ... Gen 6:22 6213
that God commanded him, so *d* he ... Gen 6:22 6213
Noah *d* according unto all that ... Gen 7:5 6213
upward *d* the waters prevail ... Gen 7:20
because the LORD *d* there confound ... Gen 11:9
from thence *d* the LORD scatter ... Gen 11:9
under the tree, and they *d* eat ... Gen 18:8
Wherefore *d* Sarah laugh, saying, ... Gen 18:13
d bake unleavened bread, and they ... Gen 19:3
unleavened bread, and they *d* eat ... Gen 19:3

Context	Reference	Number
the LORD *d* unto Sarah as he had	Gen 21:1	6213
that God *d* tempt Abraham, and said	Gen 22:1	
eight Milcah *d* bear to Nahor	Gen 22:23	
And they *d* eat and drink, he and the	Gen 24:54	
because he *d* eat of his venison	Gen 25:28	
he *d* eat and drink, and rose up, and	Gen 25:34	
the herdmen of Gerar *d* strive	Gen 26:20	
made them a feast, and they *d* eat	Gen 26:30	
it near to him, and he *d* eat	Gen 27:25	
d not I serve with thee for	Gen 29:25	
And Jacob *d* so, and fulfilled her	Gen 29:28	6213
Jacob *d* separate the lambs, and	Gen 30:40	
the stronger cattle *d* conceive	Gen 30:41	
they *d* eat there upon the heap	Gen 31:46	
they *d* eat bread, and tarried all	Gen 31:54	
they *d* not pursue after the sons	Gen 35:5	
the thing which he *d* displeased	Gen 38:10	6213
he die also, as his brethren *d*	Gen 38:11	
that he *d* to prosper in his hand	Gen 39:3	6213
save the bread which he *d* eat	Gen 39:6	
this manner *d* thy servant to me	Gen 39:19	6213
and whatsoever they *d* there	Gen 39:22	6213
was with him, and that which he *d*	Gen 39:23	6213
the birds *d* eat them out of the	Gen 40:17	
Yet *d* not the chief butler	Gen 40:23	
leanfleshed kine *d* eat up the	Gen 41:4	
to his dream he *d* interpret	Gen 41:12	
the ill favoured kine *d* eat up	Gen 41:20	
And they *d* so	Gen 42:20	6213
and thus *d* he unto them	Gen 42:25	6213
The man *d* solemnly protest unto	Gen 43:3	
And the man *d* as Joseph bade	Gen 43:17	6213
for his bowels *d* yearn upon his	Gen 43:30	
which *d* eat with him, by	Gen 43:32	
he *d* according to the word that	Gen 44:2	6213
for God *d* send me before you to	Gen 45:5	
And the children of Israel *d* so	Gen 45:21	6213
d eat their portion which Pharaoh	Gen 47:22	
fathers Abraham and Isaac *d* walk	Gen 48:15	
his sons *d* unto him according as	Gen 50:12	6213
all the evil which we *d* unto him	Gen 50:15	1580
Thy father *d* command before he	Gen 50:16	
for they *d* unto thee evil	Gen 50:17	1580
Therefore they *d* set over them	Ex 1:11	
d not as the king of Egypt	Ex 1:17	6213
he said to him that *d* the wrong	Ex 2:13	
d the signs in the sight of the	Ex 4:30	6213
which they *d* make heretofore, ye	Ex 5:8	
of the children of Israel *d* see	Ex 5:19	
concerning the which I *d* swear to	Ex 6:8	
Aaron *d* as the LORD commanded	Ex 7:6	6213
LORD commanded them, so *d* they	Ex 7:6	6213
they *d* so as the LORD had	Ex 7:10	6213
they also *d* in like manner with	Ex 7:11	6213
And Moses and Aaron *d* so, as the	Ex 7:20	6213
the magicians of Egypt *d* so with	Ex 7:22	6213
neither *d* he hearken unto them	Ex 7:22	6213
neither *d* he set his heart to	Ex 7:23	
the magicians *d* so with their	Ex 8:7	6213
the LORD *d* according to the word	Ex 8:13	6213
And they *d* so	Ex 8:17	6213
the magicians *d* so with their	Ex 8:18	6213
And the LORD *d* so	Ex 8:24	6213
the LORD *d* according to the word	Ex 8:31	6213
the LORD *d* that thing on the	Ex 9:6	6213
he *d* not let the people go	Ex 9:7	
for that ye *d* desire	Ex 10:11	
they *d* eat every herb of the land	Ex 10:15	
Aaron *d* all these wonders before	Ex 11:10	6213
d as the LORD had commanded Moses	Ex 12:28	6213
Moses and Aaron, so *d* they	Ex 12:28	6213
And the children of Israel *d*	Ex 12:35	6213
Thus *d* all the children of Israel	Ex 12:50	6213
Moses and Aaron, so *d* they	Ex 12:50	6213
that the LORD *d* bring the	Ex 12:51	
d unto me when I came forth out	Ex 13:8	6213
And they *d* so	Ex 14:4	6213
word that we *d* tell thee in Egypt	Ex 14:12	
the LORD *d* upon the Egyptians	Ex 14:31	6313
when we *d* eat bread to the full	Ex 16:3	
And the children of Israel *d* so	Ex 16:17	6213
when they *d* mete it with an omer,	Ex 16:18	
it *d* not stink, neither was there	Ex 16:24	
of Israel *d* eat manna forty years	Ex 16:35	
they *d* eat manna, until they came	Ex 16:35	
the people *d* chide with Moses	Ex 17:2	
Moses *d* so in the sight of the	Ex 17:6	6213
So Joshua *d* as Moses had said to	Ex 17:10	6213
d obeisance, and kissed him	Ex 18:7	
saw all that he *d* to the people	Ex 18:14	6213
in law, and *d* all that he had said	Ex 18:24	6213
seen what I *d* unto the Egyptians	Ex 19:4	6213
they saw God, and *d* eat and drink	Ex 24:11	
For mischief *d* he bring them out,	Ex 32:12	
What *d* this people unto thee,	Ex 32:21	6213
the children of Levi *d* according	Ex 32:28	6213
no man *d* put on him his ornaments	Ex 33:4	
he *d* neither eat bread, nor drink	Ex 34:28	
Every one that *d* offer an	Ex 35:24	
hearted *d* spin with their hands	Ex 35:25	
thus *d* he make for all the boards	Ex 36:22	
thus he *d* to both of them in both	Ex 36:29	6213
they *d* beat the gold into thin	Ex 39:3	
they *d* bind the breastplate by	Ex 39:21	
and the children of Israel *d*	Ex 39:32	6213
LORD commanded Moses, so *d* they	Ex 39:32	6213
Moses *d* look upon all the work,	Ex 39:43	
Thus *d* Moses: according to all	Ex 40:16	6213
the LORD commanded him, so *d* he	Ex 40:16	6213
he *d* with the bullock for a sin	Lev 4:20	6213
Moses *d* as the LORD commanded him	Lev 8:4	6213
d he put the golden plate, the	Lev 8:9	
his sons *d* all things which the	Lev 8:36	6213
he *d* wash the inwards and the legs	Lev 9:14	
they *d* according to the word of	Lev 10:7	6213
do with that blood as he *d* with	Lev 16:15	6213
he *d* as the LORD commanded Moses	Lev 16:34	6213
the children of Israel *d* as the	Lev 24:23	6213
because it *d* not rest in your	Lev 26:35	
possession of the land *d* belong	Lev 27:24	
And the children of Israel *d*	Num 1:54	6213
LORD commanded Moses, so *d* they	Num 1:54	6213
And the children of Israel *d*	Num 2:34	6213
Aaron *d* number according to the	Num 4:37	
Aaron *d* number according to the	Num 4:41	
And the children of Israel *d* so	Num 5:4	6213
so *d* the children of Israel	Num 5:4	6213
Zuar, prince of Issachar, *d* offer	Num 7:18	
the children of Zebulun, *d* offer	Num 7:24	
the children of Reuben, *d* offer	Num 7:30	
the children of Simeon, *d* offer	Num 7:36	
And Aaron *d* so; he lighted	Num 8:3	6213
d to the Levites according unto	Num 8:20	6213
so *d* the children of Israel unto	Num 8:20	6213
the Levites, so *d* they unto them	Num 8:22	6213
so *d* the children of Israel	Num 9:5	6213
the other *d* set up the tabernacle	Num 10:21	
which we *d* eat in Egypt freely	Num 11:5	
they prophesied, and *d* not cease	Num 11:25	
which I *d* in Egypt and in the	Num 14:22	6213
Even those men that *d* bring up	Num 14:37	
And Moses *d* so: as the LORD	Num 17:11	6213
the LORD commanded him, so *d* he	Num 17:11	6213
Moses *d* as the LORD commanded	Num 20:27	6213
What he *d* in the Red sea, and in	Num 21:14	2052
D I not earnestly send unto thee	Num 22:37	6213
Balak *d* as Balaam had spoken	Num 23:2	6213
Balak *d* as Balaam had said, and	Num 23:30	6213
and the people *d* eat, and bowed	Num 25:2	
Moses *d* as the LORD commanded him	Num 27:22	6213
Eleazar the priest *d* as the LORD	Num 31:31	6213
Thus *d* your fathers, when I sent	Num 32:8	6213
so *d* the daughters of Zelophehad	Num 36:10	6213
according to all that he *d* for	Deut 1:30	6213
Yet in this thing ye *d* not	Deut 1:32	369
as Israel *d* unto the land of his	Deut 2:12	6213
As he *d* to the children of Esau,	Deut 2:22	6213
which dwell in Ar, *d* unto me	Deut 2:29	6213
as we *d* unto Sihon king of	Deut 3:6	6213
the LORD *d* because of Baal-peor	Deut 4:3	6213
But ye that *d* cleave unto the	Deut 4:4	
D ever people hear the voice of	Deut 4:33	
d for you in Egypt before your	Deut 4:34	6213
for the mountain *d* burn with fire	Deut 5:23	
The LORD *d* not set his love upon	Deut 7:7	6213
the LORD thy God *d* unto Pharaoh	Deut 7:18	6213
neither *d* thy fathers know	Deut 8:3	
neither *d* thy foot swell, these	Deut 8:4	
I neither *d* eat bread nor drink	Deut 9:9	
I *d* neither eat bread, nor drink	Deut 9:18	
which he *d* in the midst of Egypt	Deut 11:3	6213
what he *d* unto the army of Egypt,	Deut 11:4	6213
what he *d* unto you in the	Deut 11:5	6213
what he *d* unto Dathan and Abiram,	Deut 11:6	6213
great acts of the LORD which he *d*	Deut 11:7	6213
How *d* these nations serve their	Deut 12:30	
thy God *d* unto Miriam by the way	Deut 24:9	6213
Amalek *d* unto thee by the way	Deut 25:17	6213
Ye have seen all that the LORD *d*	Deut 29:2	6213
do unto them as he *d* to Sihon	Deut 31:4	6213
So the LORD alone *d* lead him	Deut 32:12	
Which *d* eat the fat of their	Deut 32:38	
neither *d* he acknowledge his	Deut 33:9	
d as the LORD commanded Moses	Deut 34:9	6213
what ye *d* unto the two kings of	Josh 2:10	6213
these things, our hearts *d* melt	Josh 2:11	
neither *d* there remain any more	Josh 2:11	
Israel *d* so as Joshua commanded	Josh 4:8	6213
all his banks, as they *d* before	Josh 4:18	8032
Jordan, *d* Joshua pitch in Gilgal	Josh 4:20	
LORD your God *d* to the Red sea	Josh 4:23	6213
the cause why Joshua *d* circumcise	Josh 5:4	
they *d* eat of the old corn of the	Josh 5:11	
but they *d* eat of the fruit of	Josh 5:12	
d worship, and said unto him, What	Josh 5:14	
And Joshua *d* so	Josh 5:15	6213
so they *d* six days	Josh 6:14	6213
They *d* work wilily, and went and	Josh 9:4	6213
of him, and all that he *d* in Egypt	Josh 9:9	6213
all that he *d* to the two kings of	Josh 9:10	6213
so *d* he unto them, and delivered	Josh 9:26	6213
And they *d* so, and brought forth	Josh 10:23	6213
he *d* to the king of Makkedah as	Josh 10:28	6213
as he *d* unto the king of Jericho	Josh 10:28	6213
but *d* unto the king thereof as he	Josh 10:30	6213
as he *d* unto the king of Jericho	Josh 10:30	6213
so he *d* to Debir, and to the king	Josh 10:39	6213
their land *d* Joshua take at one	Josh 10:42	
Joshua *d* unto them as the LORD	Josh 11:9	6213
d Joshua take, and smote them with	Josh 11:12	
that *d* Joshua burn	Josh 11:13	
so *d* Moses command Joshua, and so	Josh 11:15	6213
command Joshua, and so *d* Joshua	Josh 11:15	6213
Them *d* Moses the servant of the	Josh 12:6	
for these *d* Moses smite, and cast	Josh 13:12	
d the children of Israel slay	Josh 13:22	
d distribute for inheritance in	Josh 13:32	
so the children of Israel *d*	Josh 14:5	6213
but *d* not utterly drive them out	Josh 17:13	
D not Achan the son of Zerah	Josh 22:20	3808
d not intend to go up against	Josh 22:33	
to that which I *d* among them	Josh 24:5	6213
a land for which ye *d* not labour	Josh 24:13	
which *d* those great signs in our	Josh 24:17	6213
the children of Benjamin *d* not	Judg 1:21	
Neither *d* Manasseh drive out the	Judg 1:27	
d not utterly drive them out	Judg 1:28	
Neither *d* Ephraim drive out the	Judg 1:29	
Neither *d* Zebulun drive out the	Judg 1:30	
Neither *d* Asher drive out the	Judg 1:31	
for they *d* not drive them out	Judg 1:32	
Neither *d* Naphtali drive out the	Judg 1:33	
of the LORD, that he *d* for Israel	Judg 2:7	6213
the children of Israel *d* evil in	Judg 2:11	6213
but they *d* not so	Judg 2:17	6213
as their fathers *d* keep it	Judg 2:22	
the children of Israel *d* evil in	Judg 3:7	6213
the children of Israel *d* evil	Judg 3:12	6213
he *d* gird it under his raiment	Judg 3:16	
the children of Israel again *d*	Judg 4:1	6213
why *d* Dan remain in ships	Judg 5:17	
the children of Israel *d* evil in	Judg 6:1	6213
D not the LORD bring us up from	Judg 6:13	6213
And he *d* so	Judg 6:20	6213
d as the LORD had said unto him	Judg 6:27	6213
it by day, that he *d* it by night	Judg 6:27	6213
And God *d* so that night	Judg 6:40	6213
they *d* chide with him sharply	Judg 8:1	
with whom ye *d* upbraid me	Judg 8:15	
d cast therein every man the	Judg 8:25	
d eat and drink, and cursed	Judg 9:27	
which he *d* unto his father, in	Judg 9:56	6213
d God render upon their heads	Judg 9:57	
the children of Israel *d* evil	Judg 10:6	6213
D not I deliver you from the	Judg 10:11	3808
and the Maonites, *d* oppress you	Judg 10:12	
D not ye hate me, and expel me out	Judg 11:7	
d he ever strive against Israel,	Judg 11:25	
or *d* he ever fight against them,	Judg 11:25	
why therefore *d* ye not recover	Judg 11:26	
who *d* with her according to his	Judg 11:39	6213
the children of Israel *d* evil	Judg 13:1	6213
and the angel *d* wonderously	Judg 13:19	6213
LORD *d* no more appear to Manoah	Judg 13:21	
and gave them, and they *d* eat	Judg 14:9	
said unto them, As they *d* unto me	Judg 15:11	6213
he *d* grind in the prison house	Judg 16:21	1961
but every man *d* that which was	Judg 17:6	6213
so they *d* eat and drink, and lodged	Judg 19:4	
d eat and drink both of them	Judg 19:6	
and they *d* eat both of them	Judg 19:8	
their feet, and *d* eat and drink	Judg 19:21	
for ye *d* not give unto them at	Judg 21:22	
And the children of Benjamin *d* so	Judg 21:23	6213
every man *d* that which was right	Judg 21:25	6213
her parched corn, and she *d* eat	Ruth 2:14	
blessed be he that *d* take	Ruth 2:19	
d according to all that her	Ruth 3:6	6213
which two *d* build the house of	Ruth 4:11	
as he *d* so year by year, when she	1Sa 1:7	6213
therefore she wept, and *d* not eat	1Sa 1:7	6213
d eat, and her countenance was no	1Sa 1:18	
the child *d* minister unto the	1Sa 2:11	1961
So they *d* in Shiloh unto all the	1Sa 2:14	6213
that his sons *d* unto all Israel	1Sa 2:22	6213
D I plainly appear unto the house	1Sa 2:27	
d I choose him out of all the	1Sa 2:28	
d I give unto the house of thy	1Sa 2:28	
Now Samuel *d* not yet know the	1Sa 3:7	
d let none of his words fall to	1Sa 3:19	
not, neither *d* she regard it	1Sa 4:20	
d they not let the people go, and	1Sa 6:6	
And the men *d* so	1Sa 6:10	6213
of Israel *d* put away Baalim	1Sa 7:4	
the coasts thereof *d* Israel	1Sa 7:14	
So Saul *d* eat with Samuel that	1Sa 9:24	
of the LORD, which he *d* to you	1Sa 12:7	6213
then the people *d* hide	1Sa 13:6	
the people *d* eat them with the	1Sa 14:32	
I *d* but taste a little honey with	1Sa 14:43	
that which Amalek *d* to Israel	1Sa 15:2	6213
Samuel *d* that which the LORD	1Sa 16:4	6213
For he *d* put his life in his hand	1Sa 19:5	
d eat no meat the second day of	1Sa 20:34	
d they not sing one to another of	1Sa 21:11	3808
D I then begin to enquire of God	1Sa 22:15	
he fled, and *d* not shew it to me	1Sa 22:17	
five persons that *d* wear a linen	1Sa 22:18	
that Nabal *d* shear his sheep	1Sa 25:4	
So *d* David, and so will be his	1Sa 27:11	6213
d bake unleavened bread thereof	1Sa 28:24	
and they *d* eat	1Sa 28:25	
and gave him bread, and he *d* eat	1Sa 30:11	
fell to the earth, and *d* obeisance	2Sa 1:2	
were with him *d* David bring up	2Sa 2:3	
the king *d* pleased all the people	2Sa 3:36	6213
And David *d* so, as the LORD had	2Sa 5:25	6213
so *d* Nathan speak unto David	2Sa 7:17	
Which also king David *d* dedicate	2Sa 8:11	
fell on his face, and *d* reverence	2Sa 9:6	
for he *d* eat continually at the	2Sa 9:13	
how Joab *d*, and how the people *d*	2Sa 11:7	7965
he *d* eat and drink before him	2Sa 11:13	
unto the city when ye *d* fight	2Sa 11:20	

d not a woman cast a piece of a 2Sa 11:21
it *d* eat of his own meat, and 2Sa 12:3
fourfold, because he *d* this thing 2Sa 12:6 6213
neither *d* he eat bread with them 2Sa 12:17
set bread before him, and he *d* eat 2Sa 12:20
thus *d* he unto all the cities of 2Sa 12:31 6213
in his sight, and *d* bake the cakes 2Sa 13:8
the servants of Absalom *d* unto 2Sa 13:29 6213
d obeisance, and said, Help, O 2Sa 14:4
on this manner *d* Absalom to all 2Sa 15:6 6213
thus *d* Ahithophel counsel Absalom 2Sa 17:15
d perversely the day that my lord 2Sa 19:19
that *d* eat at thine own table 2Sa 19:28
why then *d* ye despise us, that 2Sa 19:43
do us more harm than *d* Absalom 2Sa 20:6
of Saul, whom the LORD *d* choose 2Sa 21:6
he *d* hear my voice out of his 2Sa 22:7
my cry *d* enter into his ears 2Sa 22:7
he rode upon a cherub, and *d* fly 2Sa 22:11
I *d* not depart from them 2Sa 22:23
so that my feet *d* not slip 2Sa 22:37
Then *d* I beat them as small as 2Sa 22:43
I *d* stamp them as the mire of the 2Sa 22:43
street, and *d* spread them abroad 2Sa 22:43
These things *d* these three mighty 2Sa 23:17 6213
These things *d* Benaiah the son of 2Sa 23:22 6213
All these things *d* Araunah 2Sa 24:23
d obeisance unto the king 1Kin 1:16
d reverence to the king, and said, 1Kin 1:31
Joab the son of Zeruiah *d* to me 1Kin 2:5 6213
what he *d* to the two captains of 1Kin 2:5 6213
Zadok the priest *d* the king put 1Kin 2:35
D I not make thee to swear by the 1Kin 2:42
a thousand burnt offerings *d* 1Kin 3:4
as thy father David *d* walk 1Kin 3:14
it was not my son, which I *d* bear 1Kin 3:21
and Hiram's builders *d* hew them 1Kin 5:18
a line of twelve cubits *d* compass 1Kin 7:15
so *d* he for the other chapiter 1Kin 7:18 6213
cubits *d* compass it round about 1Kin 7:23
of Jordan *d* the king cast them 1Kin 7:46
d he put among the treasures of 1Kin 7:51
even those *d* the priests and the 1Kin 8:4
The same day *d* the king hallow 1Kin 8:64
upon those *d* Solomon levy a 1Kin 9:21
Israel *d* Solomon make no bondmen 1Kin 9:22
then *d* he build Millo 1Kin 9:24
three times in a year *d* Solomon 1Kin 9:25
d they bring them out by their 1Kin 10:29
Solomon *d* evil in the sight of 1Kin 11:6 6213
the LORD, as *d* David his father 1Kin 11:6
Then *d* Solomon build an high 1Kin 11:7
likewise *d* he for all his strange 1Kin 11:8 6213
(For six months *d* Joab remain 1Kin 11:16
beside the mischief that Hadad *d* 1Kin 11:25
judgments, as *d* David his father 1Kin 11:33
as David my servant *d* 1Kin 11:38 6213
acts of Solomon, and all that he *d* 1Kin 11:41 6213
thy father *d* put upon us lighter 1Kin 12:9
now whereas my father *d* lade you 1Kin 12:11
So *d* he in Beth-el, sacrificing 1Kin 12:32 6213
d eat bread in his house, and 1Kin 13:19
the which the LORD *d* say to thee 1Kin 13:22
And Jeroboam's wife *d* so, and arose 1Kin 14:4 6213
the sins of Jeroboam, who *d* sin 1Kin 14:16
the city which the LORD *d* choose 1Kin 14:21
Judah *d* evil in the sight of the 1Kin 14:22 6213
they *d* according to all the 1Kin 14:24 6213
of Rehoboam, and all that he *d* 1Kin 14:29 6213
d the LORD his God give him a 1Kin 15:4
Because David *d* that which was 1Kin 15:5 6213
acts of Abijam, and all that he *d* 1Kin 15:7 6213
Asa *d* that which was right in the 1Kin 15:11 6213
the LORD, as *d* David his father 1Kin 15:11
all his might, and all that he *d* 1Kin 15:23 6213
he *d* evil in the sight of the 1Kin 15:26 6213
king of Judah *d* Baasha slay him 1Kin 15:28
acts of Nadab, and all that he *d* 1Kin 15:31 6213
he *d* evil in the sight of the 1Kin 15:34 6213
the acts of Baasha, and what he *d* 1Kin 16:5 6213
he *d* in the sight of the LORD 1Kin 16:7 6213
Thus *d* Zimri destroy all the 1Kin 16:12
acts of Elah, and all that he *d* 1Kin 16:14 6213
Judah *d* Zimri reign seven days in 1Kin 16:15
and in his sin which he *d* 1Kin 16:19 6213
d worse than all that were before 1Kin 16:25
of the acts of Omri which he *d* 1Kin 16:27 6213
Ahab the son of Omri *d* evil in 1Kin 16:30 6213
Ahab *d* more to provoke the LORD 1Kin 16:33 6213
In his days *d* Hiel the Beth-elite 1Kin 16:34
d according unto the word of the 1Kin 17:5 6213
d according to the saying of 1Kin 17:15 6213
he, and her house, *d* eat many days 1Kin 17:15 6213
neither *d* the cruse of oil fail 1Kin 17:16
d when Jezebel slew the prophets 1Kin 18:13 6213
they *d* it the second time 1Kin 18:34
And they *d* it the third time 1Kin 18:34
he *d* eat and drink, and laid him 1Kin 19:6
d eat and drink, and went in the 1Kin 19:8
unto the people, and they *d* eat 1Kin 19:21
unto their voice, and *d* so 1Kin 20:25 6213
Now the men *d* diligently observe 1Kin 20:33
from him, and *d* hastily catch it 1Kin 20:33
d as Jezebel had sent unto them 1Kin 21:11 6213
Naboth *d* blaspheme God and the 1Kin 21:13
which *d* sell himself to work 1Kin 21:25
he *d* very abominably in following 1Kin 21:26
to all things as *d* the Amorites 1Kin 21:26 6213

D I not tell thee that he would 1Kin 22:18
acts of Ahab, and all that he *d* 1Kin 22:39 6213
he *d* evil in the sight of the 1Kin 22:52 6213
of the acts of Ahaziah which he *d* 2Kin 1:18 6213
D I not say unto you, Go not 2Kin 2:18
that thy servant *d* fear the LORD 2Kin 4:1 1961
D I desire a son of my lord 2Kin 4:28
d I not say, Do not deceive me 2Kin 4:28
set it before them, and they *d* eat 2Kin 4:44
and the iron *d* swim 2Kin 6:6
So we boiled my son, and *d* eat him 2Kin 6:29
d eat and drink, and carried thence 2Kin 7:8
d after the saying of the man of 2Kin 8:2 6213
of Israel, as *d* the house of Ahab 2Kin 8:18 6213
he *d* evil in the sight of the 2Kin 8:18 6213
acts of Joram, and all that he *d* 2Kin 8:23 6213
the son of Ahab king of Israel *d* 2Kin 8:25
d evil in the sight of the LORD, 2Kin 8:27 6213
as *d* the house of Ahab 2Kin 8:27
they *d* so at the going up to Gur, 2Kin 9:27
he *d* eat and drink, and said, Go, 2Kin 9:34
But Jehu *d* it in subtilty, to the 2Kin 10:19 6213
acts of Jehu, and all that he *d* 2Kin 10:34 6213
Athaliah *d* reign over the land 2Kin 11:3
d according to all things that 2Kin 11:9 6213
d the priest give king David's 2Kin 11:10
Jehoash *d* that which was right in 2Kin 12:2 6213
the hands of them that *d* the work 2Kin 12:11 6213
acts of Joash, and all that he *d* 2Kin 12:19 6213
he *d* that which was evil in the 2Kin 13:2 6213
Neither *d* he leave of the people 2Kin 13:7
of Jehoahaz, and all that he *d* 2Kin 13:8 6213
he *d* that which was evil in the 2Kin 13:11 6213
acts of Joash, and all that he *d* 2Kin 13:12 6213
Three times *d* Joash beat him, and 2Kin 13:25
he *d* that which was right in the 2Kin 14:3 6213
he *d* according to all things as 2Kin 14:3 6213
all things as Joash his father *d* 2Kin 14:3 6213
as yet the people *d* sacrifice 2Kin 14:4
of the acts of Jehoash which he *d* 2Kin 14:15 6213
he *d* that which was evil in the 2Kin 14:24 6213
of Jeroboam, and all that he *d* 2Kin 14:28 6213
he *d* that which was right in the 2Kin 15:3 6213
acts of Azariah, and all that he *d* 2Kin 15:6 6213
d Zachariah the son of Jeroboam 2Kin 15:8
he *d* that which was evil in the 2Kin 15:9 6213
he *d* that which was evil in the 2Kin 15:18 6213
acts of Menahem, and all that he *d* 2Kin 15:21 6213
he *d* that which was evil in the 2Kin 15:24 6213
of Pekahiah, and all that he *d* 2Kin 15:26 6213
he *d* that which was evil in the 2Kin 15:28 6213
acts of Pekah, and all that he *d* 2Kin 15:31 6213
he *d* that which was right in the 2Kin 15:34 6213
he *d* according to all that his 2Kin 15:34 6213
acts of Jotham, and all that he *d* 2Kin 15:36 6213
d not that which was right in the 2Kin 16:2 6213
Thus *d* Urijah the priest, 2Kin 16:16 6213
of the acts of Ahaz which he *d* 2Kin 16:19 6213
he *d* that which was evil in the 2Kin 17:2 6213
the children of Israel *d* secretly 2Kin 17:9
as *d* the heathen whom the LORD 2Kin 17:11
that *d* not believe in the LORD 2Kin 17:14
the sins of Jeroboam which he *d* 2Kin 17:22 6213
Howbeit they *d* not hearken 2Kin 17:40
but they *d* after their former 2Kin 17:40 6213
as *d* their fathers, so do they 2Kin 17:41 6213
he *d* that which was right in the 2Kin 18:3 6213
to all that David his father *d* 2Kin 18:3 6213
of Israel *d* burn incense to it 2Kin 18:4
the king of Assyria *d* carry away 2Kin 18:11
year of king Hezekiah *d* 2Kin 18:13
At that time *d* Hezekiah cut off 2Kin 18:16
he *d* that which was evil in the 2Kin 21:2 6213
a grove, as *d* Ahab king of Israel 2Kin 21:3 6213
than *d* the nations whom the LORD 2Kin 21:9
above all that the Amorites *d* 2Kin 21:11 6213
of Manasseh, and all that he *d* 2Kin 21:17 6213
he *d* that which was evil in the 2Kin 21:20 6213
LORD, as his father Manasseh *d* 2Kin 21:20 6213
of the acts of Amon which he *d* 2Kin 21:25 6213
he *d* that which was right in the 2Kin 22:2 6213
but they *d* eat of the unleavened 2Kin 23:9
d the king beat down, and brake 2Kin 23:12 6213
of Ammon, *d* the king defile 2Kin 23:13
d to them according to all the 2Kin 23:19 6213
d Josiah put away, that he might 2Kin 23:24
acts of Josiah, and all that he *d* 2Kin 23:28 6213
he *d* that which was evil in the 2Kin 23:32 6213
he *d* that which was evil in the 2Kin 23:37 6213
according to all that he *d* 2Kin 24:3 6213
of Jehoiakim, and all that he *d* 2Kin 24:5 6213
he *d* that which was evil in the 2Kin 24:9 6213
and his servants *d* besiege it 2Kin 24:11
he *d* that which was evil in the 2Kin 24:19 6213
d Nebuzar-adan the captain of the 2Kin 25:11
d the Chaldees break in pieces, 2Kin 25:13
d lift up the head of Jehoiachin 2Kin 25:27
he *d* eat bread continually before 2Kin 25:29
neither *d* all their family 1Chr 4:27
Samuel the seer *d* ordain in their 1Chr 9:22
These things *d* these three 1Chr 11:19 6213
These things *d* Benaiah the son of 1Chr 11:24 6213
David therefore *d* as God 1Chr 14:16 6213
For because ye *d* it not at the 1Chr 15:13 3808
d blow with the trumpets before 1Chr 15:24
so *d* Nathan speak unto David 1Chr 17:15
that *d* the work for the service 1Chr 23:24 6213
of the spoils won in battles *d* 1Chr 26:27

over them that *d* the work of the 1Chr 27:26 6213
d eat and drink before the LORD on 1Chr 29:22
In that night *d* God appear unto 2Chr 1:7
whom David my father *d* provide 2Chr 2:7
cubits *d* compass it round about 2Chr 4:2
which *d* compass it round about 2Chr 4:3
d Huram his father make to king 2Chr 4:16
of Jordan *d* the king cast them 2Chr 4:17
these *d* the priests and the 2Chr 5:5
d not then wait by course 2Chr 5:11 369
them *d* Solomon make to pay 2Chr 8:8
d Solomon make no servants for 2Chr 8:9
that thy father *d* put upon us 2Chr 10:9
he *d* evil, because he prepared 2Chr 12:14 6213
Neither *d* Jeroboam recover 2Chr 13:20
Asa *d* that which was good and 2Chr 14:2 6213
d turn unto the LORD God of 2Chr 15:4
for God *d* vex them with all 2Chr 15:6
I *d* see all Israel scattered upon 2Chr 18:16
D I not tell thee that he would 2Chr 18:17
Moreover in Jerusalem *d* 2Chr 19:8
after this *d* Jehoshaphat king of 2Chr 20:35
of Israel, who *d* very wickedly 2Chr 20:35 6213
like as *d* the house of Ahab 2Chr 21:6 6213
The same time also *d* Libnah 2Chr 21:10
Wherefore he *d* evil in the sight 2Chr 22:4 6213
all Judah *d* according to all 2Chr 23:8 6213
Joash *d* that which was right in 2Chr 24:2 6213
LORD *d* they bestow upon Baalim 2Chr 24:7
Thus they *d* day by day, and 2Chr 24:11 6213
Jehoiada gave it to such as *d* the 2Chr 24:12 6213
he *d* that which was right in the 2Chr 25:2 6213
but *d* as it is written in the law 2Chr 25:4
d the children of Judah carry 2Chr 25:12
d turn away from following the 2Chr 25:27
he *d* that which was right in the 2Chr 26:4 6213
to all that his father Amaziah *d* 2Chr 26:4 6213
d Isaiah the prophet, the son of 2Chr 26:22
he *d* that which was right in the 2Chr 27:2 6213
to all that his father Uzziah *d* 2Chr 27:2 6213
the people *d* yet corruptly 2Chr 27:2
So much *d* the children of Ammon 2Chr 27:5
but he *d* not that which was right 2Chr 28:1 6213
At that time *d* king Ahaz send 2Chr 28:16
in the time of his distress *d* he 2Chr 28:22
he *d* that which was right in the 2Chr 29:2 6213
which king Ahaz in his reign *d* 2Chr 29:19
brethren the Levites *d* help them 2Chr 29:34
yet *d* they eat the passover 2Chr 30:18
they *d* eat throughout the feast 2Chr 30:22
d give to the congregation a 2Chr 30:24
thus *d* Hezekiah throughout all 2Chr 31:20 6213
he *d* it with all his heart, and 2Chr 31:21 6213
and they *d* help him 2Chr 32:3
After this *d* Sennacherib king of 2Chr 32:9
d him honour at his death 2Chr 32:33 6213
But *d* that which was evil in the 2Chr 33:2 6213
Nevertheless the people *d* 2Chr 33:17
But he *d* that which was evil in 2Chr 33:22 6213
LORD, as *d* Manasseh his father 2Chr 33:22 6213
he *d* that which was right in the 2Chr 34:2 6213
so *d* he in the cities of Manasseh 2Chr 34:6
the men *d* the work faithfully 2Chr 34:12 6213
d according to the covenant of 2Chr 34:32 6213
of David king of Israel *d* build 2Chr 35:3
And so *d* they with the oxen 2Chr 35:12
neither *d* all the kings of Israel 2Chr 35:18 6213
he *d* that which was evil in the 2Chr 36:5 6213
and his abominations which he *d* 2Chr 36:8 6213
he *d* that which was evil in the 2Chr 36:9 6213
he *d* that which was evil in the 2Chr 36:12 6213
Even those *d* Cyrus king of Persia Ezr 1:8
All these *d* Sheshbazzar bring up Ezr 1:11
those *d* Cyrus the king take out Ezr 5:14
king had sent, so they *d* speedily Ezr 6:13 5648
the LORD God of Israel, *d* eat, Ezr 6:21
he *d* eat no bread, nor drink Ezr 10:6
children of the captivity *d* so Ezr 10:16 6213
not whither I went, or what I *d* Neh 2:16 6213
nor to the rest that *d* the work Neh 2:16 6213
But the fish gate *d* the sons of Neh 3:3
the people *d* according to this Neh 5:13 6213
but so *d* not I, because of the Neh 5:15 6213
so they *d* eat, and were filled, and Neh 9:25
they *d* evil again before thee Neh 9:28 6213
their brethren that *d* the work of Neh 11:12 6213
evil that Eliashib *d* for Tobiah Neh 13:7 6213
that *d* the work, were fled every Neh 13:10 6213
D not your fathers thus, and *d* Neh 13:18 6213
D not Solomon king of Israel sin Neh 13:26 3808
nevertheless even him *d* Neh 13:26
none *d* compel Est 1:8
the king *d* according to the word Est 1:21 6213
and he *d* so Est 2:4 6213
house, to know how Esther *d* Est 2:11 7965
for Esther *d* the commandment of Est 2:20 6213
After these things *d* king Est 3:1
bowed not, nor *d* him reverence Est 3:2
nor *d* him reverence, then was Est 3:5
d according to all that Esther Est 4:17 6213
Esther the queen *d* let no man Est 5:12
On that day *d* the king Ahasuerus Est 8:1
d what they would unto those that Est 9:5 6213
Thus *d* Job continually Job 1:5 6213
In all this *d* not Job sin with Job 2:10
why *d* I not give up the ghost Job 3:11
Why *d* the knees prevent me Job 3:12
D I say, Bring unto me Job 6:22

Then *d* he see it, and declare it ... Job 28:27
D not I weep for him that was in ... Job 30:25
If I *d* despise the cause of my ... Job 31:13
D not he that made me in the womb ... Job 31:15
d not one fashion us in the womb ... Job 31:15
The stranger *d* not lodge in the ... Job 31:32
D I fear a great multitude ... Job 31:34
or *d* the contempt of families ... Job 31:34
d according as the LORD commanded ... Job 42:9 6213
d eat bread with him in his house ... Job 42:11
there were any that *d* understand ... Ps 14:2
he rode upon a cherub, and *d* fly ... Ps 18:10
he *d* fly upon the wings of the ... Ps 18:10
I *d* not put away his statutes ... Ps 18:22
under me, that my feet *d* not slip ... Ps 18:36
neither *d* I turn again till they ... Ps 18:37
Then *d* I beat them small as the ... Ps 18:42
I *d* cast them out as the dirt in ... Ps 18:42
they that *d* see me without fled ... Ps 31:11
False witnesses *d* rise up ... Ps 35:11
they *d* tear me, and ceased not ... Ps 35:15
which *d* eat of my bread, hath ... Ps 41:9
neither *d* their own arm save them ... Ps 44:3
upon thy right hand *d* stand the ... Ps 45:9
in sin *d* my mother conceive me ... Ps 51:5
d understand, that *d* seek God ... Ps 53:2
that *d* magnify himself against me ... Ps 55:12
there *d* we rejoice in him ... Ps 66:6
Kings of armies *d* flee apace ... Ps 68:12
Marvellous things *d* he in the ... Ps 78:12 6213
Man *d* eat angels' food ... Ps 78:25
So they *d* eat, and were well ... Ps 78:29
their days *d* he consume in vanity ... Ps 78:33
Nevertheless they *d* flatter him ... Ps 78:36
d not stir up all his wrath ... Ps 78:38
How oft *d* they provoke him in the ... Ps 78:40
from heaven *d* the LORD behold the ... Ps 102:19
d eat up all the herbs in their ... Ps 105:35
They *d* not destroy the nations, ... Ps 106:34
Many times *d* he deliver them ... Ps 106:43
Princes also *d* sit and speak ... Ps 119:23
but thy servant *d* meditate in thy ... Ps 119:23
that *d* he in heaven, and in earth, ... Ps 135:6 6213
Thine eyes *d* see my substance, ... Ps 139:16
the LORD *d* I make my supplication ... Ps 142:1
d not choose the fear of the LORD ... Prov 1:29
and the hills *d* tremble, and their ... Is 5:25
his feet, and with twain he *d* fly ... Is 6:2
afterward *d* more grievously ... Is 9:1
whose graven images *d* excel them ... Is 10:10 4480
Isaiah the son of Amoz *d* see ... Is 13:1
to tremble, that *d* shake kingdoms ... Is 14:16
And he *d* so, walking naked and ... Is 20:2 6213
in that day *d* the Lord GOD of ... Is 22:12
or a swallow, so *d* I chatter ... Is 38:14
I *d* mourn as a dove ... Is 38:14
d not the LORD, he against whom ... Is 42:24 3808
I *d* them suddenly, and they came ... Is 48:3 6213
yet we *d* esteem him stricken, ... Is 53:4
as a nation that *d* righteousness ... Is 58:2 6213
when I called, ye *d* not answer ... Is 65:12
when I spake, ye *d* not hear ... Is 65:12
but *d* evil before mine eyes, and ... Is 65:12 6213
d choose that wherein I delighted ... Is 65:12
when I called, none *d* answer ... Is 66:4
when I spake, they *d* not hear ... Is 66:4
but they *d* evil before mine eyes, ... Is 66:4 6213
see what I *d* to it for the ... Jer 7:12 6213
they *d* worse than their fathers ... Jer 7:26
but they *d* them not ... Jer 11:8 6213
the wild asses *d* stand in the ... Jer 14:6
their eyes *d* fail, because there ... Jer 14:6
for that which he *d* in Jerusalem ... Jer 15:4 6213
words were found, and I *d* eat them ... Jer 15:16
d not thy father eat and drink, and ... Jer 22:15
D Hezekiah king of Judah and all ... Jer 26:19
d he not fear the LORD, and ... Jer 26:19
because I *d* bear the reproach of ... Jer 31:19
Baruch the son of Neriah *d* ... Jer 36:8 6213
d hearken unto the words of the ... Jer 37:2
And Jeremiah *d* so ... Jer 38:12 6213
there they *d* eat bread together ... Jer 41:1 6213
d we make her cakes to worship ... Jer 44:19
d not the LORD remember them, and ... Jer 44:21
because the LORD *d* drive them ... Jer 46:15
They *d* cry there, Pharaoh king of ... Jer 46:17
they *d* not stand, because the day ... Jer 46:21
he *d* that which was evil in the ... Jer 52:2 6213
of twelve cubits *d* compass it ... Jer 52:21
he *d* continually eat bread before ... Jer 52:33
of the enemy, and none *d* help her ... Lam 1:7
her, and *d* mock at her sabbaths ... Lam 1:7
They that *d* feed delicately are ... Lam 4:5
Then *d* I eat it ... Eze 3:3
the place where they *d* offer ... Eze 6:13
Then *d* the cherubims lift up ... Eze 11:22
I *d* so as I was commanded ... Eze 12:7 6213
neither *d* she strengthen the hand ... Eze 16:49
this vine *d* bend her roots toward ... Eze 17:7
d that which is not good among ... Eze 18:18 6213
they *d* not every man cast away ... Eze 20:8
neither *d* they forsake the idols ... Eze 20:8
neither *d* I make an end of them ... Eze 20:17
I *d* in the morning as I was ... Eze 24:18 6213
The ships of Tarshish *d* sing of ... Eze 27:25
under his branches *d* all the ... Eze 31:6
none *d* search or seek after them ... Eze 34:6
neither *d* my shepherds search for ... Eze 34:8

as they *d* cleanse it with the ... Eze 43:22
as he *d* on the sabbath day ... Eze 46:12 6213
than all the children which *d* eat ... Dan 1:15
D not we cast three men bound ... Dan 3:24
but they *d* not make known unto me ... Dan 4:7
d eat grass as oxen, and his body ... Dan 4:33
before his God, as he *d* aforetime ... Dan 6:10 5648
and the Ancient of days *d* sit ... Dan 7:9
but he *d* according to his will, ... Dan 8:4 6213
rose up, and *d* the king's business ... Dan 8:27 6213
neither *d* I anoint myself at all, ... Dan 10:3
For she *d* not know that I gave ... Hos 2:8
because they *d* not hearken unto ... Hos 9:17
of iniquity *d* not overtake them ... Hos 10:9
I *d* know thee in the wilderness, ... Hos 13:5
because he *d* pursue his brother ... Amos 1:11
d cast off all pity ... Amos 1:11
his anger *d* tear perpetually, and ... Amos 1:11
As if a man *d* flee from a lion, ... Amos 5:19
great deep, and *d* eat up a part ... Amos 7:4
off those of his that *d* escape ... Obad 14 6412
d remain in the day of distress ... Obad 11 0000
and he *d* it not ... Jonah 3:10 6213
to pass, when the sun *d* arise ... Jonah 4:8
The lion *d* tear in pieces enough ... Nah 2:12
which Habakkuk the prophet *d* see ... Hab 1:1
the perpetual hills *d* bow ... Hab 3:6
of the land of Midian *d* tremble ... Hab 3:7
brought it home, I *d* blow upon it ... Hag 1:9
the people *d* fear before the LORD ... Hag 1:12
d work in the house of the LORD ... Hag 1:14 6213
but they *d* not hear, nor hearken ... Zec 1:4
d they not take hold of your ... Zec 1:6
so that no man *d* lift up his head ... Zec 1:21
d ye at all fast unto me, even to ... Zec 7:5
And when ye *d* eat, and when ye *d* ... Zec 7:6
d not ye eat for yourselves, and ... Zec 7:6
Tyrus *d* build herself a strong ... Zec 9:3
d turn many away from iniquity ... Mal 2:6
And *d* not he make one ... Mal 2:15
d as the angel of the Lord had ... Mt 1:24 *4160*
when he heard that Archelaus *d* ... Mt 2:22
him, and so *d* his disciples ... Mt 9:19
Have ye not read what David *d* ... Mt 12:3 *4160*
d eat the shewbread, which was ... Mt 12:4
he *d* not many mighty works there ... Mt 13:58 *4160*
they *d* all eat, and were filled ... Mt 14:20
well *d* Esaias prophesy of you, ... Mt 15:7
they *d* all eat, and were filled ... Mt 15:37
they that *d* eat were four ... Mt 15:38
his face *d* shine as the sun, and ... Mt 17:2
Why *d* Moses then command to give ... Mt 19:7
and ninth hour, and *d* likewise ... Mt 20:5 *4160*
d as Jesus commanded them, ... Mt 21:6 *4160*
the wonderful things that he *d* ... Mt 21:15 *4160*
Why *d* ye not then believe him ... Mt 21:25
Whether of them twain *d* the will ... Mt 21:31 *4160*
they *d* unto them likewise ... Mt 21:36 *4160*
D ye never read in the scriptures ... Mt 21:42
and *d* not minister unto thee ... Mt 25:44
Inasmuch as ye *d* it not to one of ... Mt 25:45 *4160*
least of these, ye *d* it not to me ... Mt 25:45 *4160*
my body, she *d* it for my burial ... Mt 26:12 *4160*
the disciples *d* as Jesus had ... Mt 26:19 *4160*
And as they *d* eat, he said, Verily ... Mt 26:21
Then *d* they spit in his face, and ... Mt 26:67
of the children of Israel *d* value ... Mt 27:9
upon my vesture *d* they cast lots ... Mt 27:35
and the earth *d* quake, and the ... Mt 27:51
fear of him the keepers *d* shake ... Mt 28:4
d run to bring his disciples word ... Mt 28:8
money, and *d* as they were taught ... Mt 28:15 *4160*
John *d* baptize in the wilderness, ... Mk 1:4 *1096*
he *d* eat locusts and wild honey ... Mk 1:6
And at even, when the sun *d* set ... Mk 1:32
Have ye never read what David *d* ... Mk 2:25 *4160*
d eat the shewbread, which is not ... Mk 2:26
had heard what great things he *d* ... Mk 3:8 *4160*
d yield fruit that sprang up and ... Mk 4:8
and all men *d* marvel ... Mk 5:20
he *d* many things, and heard him ... Mk 6:20 *4160*
they *d* all eat, and were filled ... Mk 6:42
they that *d* eat of the loaves ... Mk 6:44
they *d* set them before the people ... Mk 8:6
So they *d* eat, and were filled ... Mk 8:8
them, What *d* Moses command you ... Mk 10:3
Why then *d* ye not believe him ... Mk 11:31
For all they *d* cast in of their ... Mk 12:44
but she of her want *d* cast in all ... Mk 12:44
d eat, Jesus said, Verily I say ... Mk 14:18
And as they *d* eat, Jesus took ... Mk 14:22
But neither so *d* their witness ... Mk 14:59 *2258*
the servants *d* strike him with ... Mk 14:65
d spit upon him, and bowing their ... Mk 15:19
And in those days he *d* eat nothing ... Lk 4:2
d eat, rubbing them in their ... Lk 6:1
so much as this, what David *d* ... Lk 6:3 *4160*
d take and eat the shewbread, and ... Lk 6:4
And he *d* so ... Lk 6:10 *4160*
for in the like manner *d* their ... Lk 6:23 *4160*
for so *d* their fathers to the ... Lk 6:26 *4160*
the stream *d* beat vehemently ... Lk 6:49
d wipe them with the hairs of her ... Lk 7:38
And they *d* so, and made them all ... Lk 9:15 *4160*
And they *d* eat, and were all filled ... Lk 9:17
one at all things which Jesus *d* ... Lk 9:43 *4160*
they *d* not receive him, because ... Lk 9:53
and consume them, even as Elias *d* ... Lk 9:54 *4160*

d not he that made that which is ... Lk 11:40
neither *d* according to his will, ... Lk 12:47 *4160*
d commit things worthy of stripes ... Lk 12:48
the husks that the swine *d* eat ... Lk 15:16
thank that servant because he *d* ... Lk 17:9 *4160*
They *d* eat, they drank, they ... Lk 17:27
they *d* eat, they drank, they ... Lk 17:28
down, and reaping that I *d* not sow ... Lk 19:22
D not our heart burn within us, ... Lk 24:32
he took it, and *d* eat before them ... Lk 24:43
d write, Jesus of Nazareth, the ... Jn 1:45
d Jesus in Cana of Galilee ... Jn 2:11 *4160*
they saw the miracles which he *d* ... Jn 2:23 *4160*
But Jesus *d* not commit himself ... Jn 2:24
told me all things that ever I *d* ... Jn 4:29 *4160*
He told me all that ever I *d* ... Jn 4:39 *4160*
he *d* at Jerusalem at the feast ... Jn 4:45 *4160*
the second miracle that Jesus *d* ... Jn 4:54 *4160*
therefore *d* the Jews persecute ... Jn 5:16
he *d* on them that were diseased ... Jn 6:2 *4160*
had seen the miracle that Jesus *d* ... Jn 6:14 *4160*
the place where they *d* eat bread ... Jn 6:23
but because ye *d* eat of the ... Jn 6:26
Our fathers *d* eat manna in the ... Jn 6:31
Your fathers *d* eat manna in the ... Jn 6:49
not as your fathers *d* eat manna ... Jn 6:58
For neither *d* his brethren ... Jn 7:5
D not Moses give you the law, and ... Jn 7:19
this *d* not Abraham ... Jn 8:40 *4160*
him, saying, Master, who *d* sin ... Jn 9:2
But the Jews *d* not believe ... Jn 9:18
that if any man *d* confess that he ... Jn 9:22
to him again, What *d* he to thee ... Jn 9:26 *4160*
you already, and ye *d* not hear ... Jn 9:27
but the sheep *d* not hear them ... Jn 10:8
him, and said, John *d* no miracle ... Jn 10:41 *4160*
had seen the things which Jesus *d* ... Jn 11:45 *4160*
and *d* hide himself from them ... Jn 12:36
Pharisees they *d* not confess him ... Jn 12:42
the works which none other man *d* ... Jn 15:24 *4160*
Jesus, and so *d* another disciple ... Jn 18:15
D not I see thee in the garden ... Jn 18:26
or *d* others tell it thee of me ... Jn 18:34
for my vesture they *d* cast lots ... Jn 19:24
things therefore the soldiers *d* ... Jn 19:24 *4160*
the other disciple *d* outrun Peter ... Jn 20:4
many other signs truly *d* Jesus in ... Jn 20:30 *4160*
d cast himself into the sea ... Jn 21:7
many other things which Jesus *d* ... Jn 21:25 *4160*
which God *d* by him in the midst ... Acts 2:22 *4160*
Therefore *d* my heart rejoice, and ... Acts 2:26
his flesh *d* see corruption ... Acts 2:31
many other words *d* he testify ... Acts 2:40
d eat their meat with gladness and ... Acts 2:46
that through ignorance ye *d* it ... Acts 3:17 *4238*
as *d* also your rulers ... Acts 3:17
Why *d* the heathen rage, and the ... Acts 4:25
D not we straitly command you ... Acts 5:28
d great wonders and miracles among ... Acts 6:8 *4160*
But he that *d* his neighbour wrong ... Acts 7:27 *91*
the same *d* God send to be a ruler ... Acts 7:35
as your fathers *d*, so do ye ... Acts 7:51
and seeing the miracles which he *d* ... Acts 8:6 *4160*
sight, and neither *d* eat nor drink ... Acts 9:9
works and almsdeeds which she *d* ... Acts 9:36 *4160*
of all things which he *d* both in ... Acts 10:39 *4160*
of God, even to us, who *d* eat ... Acts 10:41
the like gift as he *d* unto us ... Acts 11:17
Which also they *d*, and sent it to ... Acts 11:30 *4160*
And so he *d* ... Acts 12:8 *4160*
witness, in that he *d* good ... Acts 14:17 *15*
Holy Ghost, even as he *d* unto us ... Acts 15:8
at the first *d* visit the Gentiles ... Acts 15:14
And this *d* she many days ... Acts 16:18 *4160*
chief of the priests, which *d* so ... Acts 19:14 *4160*
virgins, which *d* prophesy ... Acts 21:9
Which thing I also *d* in Jerusalem ... Acts 26:10 *4160*
many of the saints *d* I shut up in ... Acts 26:10 *4160*
and Moses *d* say should come ... Acts 26:22
for even their women *d* change the ... Rom 1:26
even as they *d* not like to retain ... Rom 1:28
For what if some *d* not believe ... Rom 3:3
grace *d* much more abound ... Rom 5:20
d work in our members to bring ... Rom 7:5
For whom he *d* foreknow ... Rom 8:29
he also *d* predestinate to be ... Rom 8:29
Moreover whom he *d* predestinate ... Rom 8:30
But I say, *D* not Israel know ... Rom 10:19
and I would to God ye *d* reign ... 1Cor 4:8
d all eat the same spiritual meat ... 1Cor 10:3
d all drink the same spiritual ... 1Cor 10:4
which *d* put all things under him ... 1Cor 15:27
thus minded, *d* I use lightness ... 2Cor 1:17
For to this end also *d* I write ... 2Cor 2:9
as though God *d* beseech you by us ... 2Cor 5:20
do not repent, though I *d* repent ... 2Cor 7:8
I *d* it not for his cause that had ... 2Cor 7:12
And this they *d*, not as we hoped, ... 2Cor 8:5
But be it so, I *d* not burden you ... 2Cor 12:16
D I make a gain of you by any of ... 2Cor 12:17
D Titus make a gain of you ... 2Cor 12:18
he *d* eat with the Gentiles ... Gal 2:12
ye *d* service unto them which by ... Gal 4:8
Ye *d* run well ... Gal 5:7
who *d* hinder you that ye should ... Gal 5:7
that ye *d* communicate with my ... Phil 4:14
Neither *d* we eat any man's bread ... 2Th 3:8
because I *d* it ignorantly in ... 1Ti 1:13 *4160*

the coppersmith *d* me much evil 2Ti 4:14 *1731*
when they had heard, *d* provoke Heb 3:16
word preached *d* not profit them Heb 4:2
God *d* rest the seventh day from Heb 4:4
his own works, as God *d* from his Heb 4:10
bringing in of a better hope *d* Heb 7:19
for this he *d* once, when he Heb 7:27 *4160*
him that *d* the service perfect Heb 9:9 *3000*
which was in them *d* signify 1Pet 1:11
but unto us they *d* minister the 1Pet 1:12
Who *d* no sin, neither was guile 1Pet 2:22 *4160*
and *d* cast them to the earth Rev 12:4
the wound by a sword, and *d* live Rev 13:14
which *d* corrupt the earth with Rev 19:2
for the glory of God *d* lighten it Rev 21:23

DIDDEST {1}
as thou *d* the Egyptian yesterday Acts 7:28 *387*

DIDST {122}
why *d* thou not tell me that she Gen 12:18
but thou *d* laugh Gen 18:15
I know that thou *d* this in the Gen 20:6 6213
neither *d* thou tell me, neither Gen 21:26
Wherefore *d* thou flee away Gen 31:27
d not tell me, that I might have Gen 31:27
of my hand *d* thou require it, Gen 31:39
Thou *d* blow with thy wind, the Ex 15:10
as thou *d* anoint their father, Ex 40:15
thou shalt do to him as thou *d* Num 21:34 6213
thou shalt do unto him as thou *d* Deut 3:2 6213
from the day that thou *d* depart Deut 9:7
thou *d* drink the pure blood of Deut 32:14
whom thou *d* prove at Massah, and Deut 33:8
with whom thou *d* strive at the Deut 33:8
which thou *d* let us down by Josh 2:18
her king as thou *d* unto Jericho Josh 8:2 6213
d not call us to go with thee Judg 12:1 6213
thou *d* send come again unto us Judg 13:8 6213
for thou *d* call me 1Sa 3:6
for thou *d* call me 1Sa 3:8
Wherefore then *d* thou not obey 1Sa 15:19
but *d* fly upon the spoil, and 1Sa 15:19
d evil in the sight of the LORD 1Sa 15:19 6213
thou sawest it, and *d* rejoice 1Sa 19:5
come to the place where thou *d* 1Sa 20:19
men of my lord, whom thou *d* send 1Sa 25:25
why then *d* thou not go down unto 2Sa 11:10
For thou *d* it secretly 2Sa 12:12 6213
thou *d* fast and weep for the child 2Sa 12:21
the child was dead, thou *d* rise 2Sa 12:21
the other that thou *d* unto me 2Sa 13:16 6213
why *d* thou not smite him there to 2Sa 18:11
yet *d* thou set thy servant among 2Sa 19:28
D not thou, my lord, O king, 1Kin 1:13
that thou *d* to David my father 1Kin 2:44 6213
thou *d* well that it was in thine 1Kin 8:18
For thou *d* separate them from 1Kin 8:53 6213
All that thou *d* send for to thy 1Kin 20:9
Thou *d* blaspheme God and the king 1Kin 21:10
For thy people Israel *d* thou make 1Chr 17:22
As thou *d* deal with David my 2Chr 2:3
d send him cedars to build him an 2Chr 2:3
thou *d* well in that it was in 2Chr 6:8
because thou *d* rely on the LORD, 2Chr 16:8
who *d* drive out the inhabitants 2Chr 20:7
thou *d* humble thyself before God, 2Chr 34:27
d rend thy clothes, and weep 2Chr 34:27
who *d* choose Abram, and broughtest Neh 9:7
d see the affliction of our Neh 9:9
So *d* thou get thee a name, as it Neh 9:10
thou *d* divide the sea before them Neh 9:11
wonders that thou *d* among them Neh 9:17 6213
forty years *d* thou sustain them Neh 9:21
d divide them into corners Neh 9:22
many times *d* thou deliver them Neh 9:28
Yet many years *d* thou forbear Neh 9:30
thou *d* not utterly consume them Neh 9:31 6213
wherewith thou *d* testify against Neh 9:34
trusted, and thou *d* deliver them Ps 22:4
thou *d* make me hope when I was Ps 22:9
thou *d* hide thy face, and I was Ps 30:7
because thou *d* it Ps 39:9 6213
and offering thou *d* not desire Ps 40:6
what work thou *d* in their days Ps 44:1 6466
How thou *d* drive out the heathen Ps 44:2
how thou *d* afflict the people, and Ps 44:2
which *d* not go out with our Ps 60:10
when thou *d* march through the Ps 68:7
d send a plentiful rain Ps 68:9
whereby thou *d* confirm thine Ps 68:9
Surely thou *d* set them in Ps 73:18
Thou *d* divide the sea by thy Ps 74:13
Thou *d* cleave the fountain and the Ps 74:15
Thou *d* cause judgment to be heard Ps 76:8
d cause it to take deep root, and Ps 80:9
which *d* weaken the nations Is 14:12
thou *d* look in that day to the Is 22:8
thou *d* shew them no mercy Is 47:6
so that thou *d* not lay these Is 47:7
neither *d* remember the latter end Is 47:7
things, and thou *d* not know them Is 48:6
O barren, thou that *d* not bear Is 54:1
thou that *d* not travail with Is 54:1
d increase thy perfumes, and *d* Is 57:9
d debase thyself even unto hell Is 57:9
so *d* thou lead thy people, to Is 63:14
When thou *d* terrible things which Is 64:3 6213
which thou *d* swear to their Jer 32:22
How *d* thou write all these words Jer 36:17
Thou *d* say, Woe is me now Jer 45:3
whom thou *d* command that they Lam 1:10
thou *d* eat fine flour, and honey, Eze 16:13
thou *d* prosper into a kingdom Eze 16:13
But thou *d* trust in thine own Eze 16:15
And of thy garments thou *d* take Eze 16:16
d commit whoredom with them, Eze 16:17
which thou *d* give unto them Eze 16:36
for whom thou *d* wash thyself Eze 23:40
thou *d* enrich the kings of the Eze 27:33
thou *d* break, and rend all their Eze 29:7
As thou *d* rejoice at the Eze 35:15
from the first day that thou *d* Dan 10:12
because thou *d* trust in thy way, Hos 10:13
that thou *d* ride upon thine Hab 3:8
Thou *d* cleave the earth with Hab 3:9
Thou *d* march through the land in Hab 3:12
thou *d* thresh the heathen in Hab 3:12
Thou *d* strike through with his Hab 3:14
Thou *d* walk through the sea with Hab 3:15
d not thou sow good seed in thy Mt 13:27
faith, wherefore *d* thou doubt Mt 14:31
d not thou agree with me for a Mt 20:13
head with oil thou *d* not anoint Lk 7:46
and reapest that thou *d* not sow Lk 19:21
have believed that thou *d* send me Jn 17:8
uncircumcised, and *d* eat with them Acts 11:3
hast thou that thou *d* not receive 1Cor 4:7
now if thou *d* receive it, why 1Cor 4:7
d set him over the works of thy Heb 2:7
unto me, Wherefore *d* thou marvel Rev 17:7

DIDYMUS *(did'-i-mus)* {3} See THOMAS. *Another name for Thomas the apostle.*
said Thomas, which is called *D* Jn 11:16 *1324*
one of the twelve, called *D* Jn 20:24 *1324*
Simon Peter, and Thomas called *D* Jn 21:2 *1324*

DIE {321}
thereof thou shalt surely *d* Gen 2:17 4191
shall ye touch it, lest ye *d* Gen 3:3 4191
the woman, Ye shall not surely *d* Gen 3:4 4191
that is in the earth shall *d* Gen 6:17 1478
lest some evil take me, and I *d* Gen 19:19 4191
thou that thou shalt surely *d* Gen 20:7 4191
Behold, I am at the point to *d* Gen 25:32 4191
Because I said, Lest I *d* for her Gen 26:9 4191
my soul may bless thee before I *d* Gen 27:4 4191
Give me children, or else I *d* Gen 30:1 4191
one day, all the flock will *d* Gen 33:13 4191
said, Lest peradventure he *d* also Gen 38:11 4191
that we may live, and not *d* Gen 42:2 4191
be verified, and ye shall not *d* Gen 42:20 4191
that we may live, and not *d* Gen 43:8 4191
it be found, both let him *d* Gen 44:9 4191
his father, his father would *d* Gen 44:22 4191
is not with us, that he will *d* Gen 44:31 4191
I will go and see him before I *d* Gen 45:28 4191
said unto Joseph, Now let me *d* Gen 46:30 4191
why should we *d* in thy presence Gen 47:15 4191
shall we *d* before thine eyes Gen 47:19 4191
seed, that we may live, and not *d* Gen 47:19 4191
time drew nigh that Israel must *d* Gen 47:29 4191
said unto Joseph, Behold, I *d* Gen 48:21 4191
made me swear, saying, Lo, I *d* Gen 50:5 4191
said unto his brethren, I *d* Gen 50:24 4191
fish that is in the river shall *d* Ex 7:18 4191
there shall nothing *d* of all that Ex 9:4 4191
down upon them, and they shall *d* Ex 9:19 4191
thou seest my face thou shalt *d* Ex 10:28 4191
in the land of Egypt shall *d* Ex 11:5 4191
us away to *d* in the wilderness Ex 14:11 4191
we should *d* in the wilderness Ex 14:12 4191
not God speak with us, lest we *d* Ex 20:19 4191
that smiteth a man, so that he *d* Ex 21:12 4191
from mine altar, that he may *d* Ex 21:14 4191
he *d* not, but keepeth his bed Ex 21:18 4191
a rod, and he *d* under his hand Ex 21:20 4191
a man or a woman, that they *d* Ex 21:28 4191
ox hurt another's, that he *d* Ex 21:35 4191
up, and be smitten that he *d* Ex 22:2 4191
and it *d*, or be hurt, or driven Ex 22:10 4191
neighbour, and it be hurt, or *d* Ex 22:14 4191
when he cometh out, that he *d* not Ex 28:35 4191
that they bear not iniquity, and *d* Ex 28:43 4191
wash with water, that they *d* not Ex 30:20 4191
and their feet, that they *d* not Ex 30:21 4191
charge of the LORD, that ye *d* not Lev 8:35 4191
lest ye *d*, and lest wrath come Lev 10:6 4191
of the congregation, lest ye *d* Lev 10:7 4191
of the congregation, lest ye *d* Lev 10:9 4191
any beast, of which ye may eat, *d* Lev 11:39 4191
that they *d* not in their Lev 15:31 4191
that he *d* not Lev 16:2 4191
upon the testimony, that he *d* not Lev 16:13 4191
they shall *d* childless Lev 20:20 4191
d therefore, if they profane it Lev 22:9 4191
touch any holy thing, lest they *d* Num 4:15 4191
that they may live, and not *d* Num 4:19 4191
things are covered, lest they *d* Num 4:20 4191
or for his sister, when they *d* Num 6:7 4194
if any man *d* very suddenly by him Num 6:9 4191
consumed, and there they shall *d* Num 14:35 4191
If these men *d* the common death Num 16:29 4191
from me, that they *d* not Num 17:10 4191
unto Moses, saying, Behold, we *d* Num 17:12 1478
tabernacle of the LORD shall *d* Num 17:13 4191
that neither they, nor ye also, *d* Num 18:3 4191
lest they bear sin, and *d* Num 18:22 4191
the children of Israel, lest ye *d* Num 18:32 4191
we and our cattle should *d* there Num 20:4 4191
unto his people, and shall *d* there Num 20:26 4191
of Egypt to *d* in the wilderness Num 21:5 4191
Let me *d* the death of the Num 23:10 4191
shall surely *d* in the wilderness Num 26:65 4191
of Israel, saying, If a man *d* Num 27:8 4191
that the manslayer *d* not, until Num 35:12 4191
instrument of iron, so that he *d* Num 35:16 4191
wherewith he may *d*, and he *d* Num 35:17 4191
wherewith he may *d*, and he *d* Num 35:18 4191
him by laying of wait, that he *d* Num 35:20 4191
him with his hand, that he *d* Num 35:21 4191
any stone, wherewith a man may *d* Num 35:23 4191
and cast it upon him, that he *d* Num 35:23 4191
any person to cause him to *d* Num 35:30 4191
But I must *d* in this land, I must Deut 4:22 4191
Now therefore why should we *d* Deut 5:25 4191
our God any more, then we shall *d* Deut 5:25 4191
stone him with stones, that he *d* Deut 13:10 4191
them with stones, till they *d* Deut 17:5 4191
the judge, even that man shall *d* Deut 17:12 4191
great fire any more, that I *d* not Deut 18:16 4191
gods, even that prophet shall *d* Deut 18:20 4191
upon his neighbour, that he *d* Deut 19:5 4191
and smite him mortally that he *d* Deut 19:11 4191
avenger of blood, that he may *d* Deut 19:12 4191
lest he *d* in the battle, and Deut 20:5 4191
lest he *d* in the battle, and Deut 20:6 4191
lest he *d* in the battle, and Deut 20:7 4191
stone him with stones, that he *d* Deut 21:21 4191
stone her with stones that she *d* Deut 22:21 4191
then they shall both of them *d* Deut 22:22 4191
them with stones that they *d* Deut 22:24 4191
only that lay with her shall *d* Deut 22:25 4191
or if the latter husband *d* Deut 24:3 4191
then that thief shall *d* Deut 24:7 4191
dwell together, and one of them *d* Deut 25:5 4191
days approach that thou must *d* Deut 31:14 4191
d in the mount whither thou goest Deut 32:50 4191
Let Reuben live, and not *d* Deut 33:6 4191
not *d* by the hand of the avenger Josh 20:9 4191
thou shalt not *d* Judg 6:23 4191
Bring out thy son, that he may *d* Judg 6:30 4191
unto his wife, We shall surely *d* Judg 13:22 4191
and now shall I *d* for thirst Judg 15:18 4191
Let me *d* with the Philistines Judg 16:30 4191
Where thou diest, will I *d* Ruth 1:17 4191
d in the flower of their age 1Sa 2:33 4191
one day they shall *d* both of them 1Sa 2:34 4191
the LORD thy God, that we *d* not 1Sa 12:19 4191
my son, he shall surely *d* 1Sa 14:39 4191
in mine hand, and, lo, I must *d* 1Sa 14:43 4191
for thou shalt surely *d*, Jonathan 1Sa 14:44 4191
said unto Saul, Shall Jonathan *d* 1Sa 14:45 4191
thou shalt not *d* 1Sa 20:2 4191
of the LORD, that I *d* not 1Sa 20:14 4191
unto me, for he shall surely *d* 1Sa 20:31 4191
king said, Thou shalt surely *d* 1Sa 22:16 4191
or his day shall come to *d* 1Sa 26:10 4191
LORD liveth, ye are worthy to *d* 1Sa 26:16 4194
for my life, to cause me to *d* 1Sa 28:9 4191
him, that he may be smitten, and *d* 2Sa 11:15 4191
done this thing shall surely *d* 2Sa 12:5 4194
thou shalt not *d* 2Sa 12:13 4191
is born unto thee shall surely *d* 2Sa 12:14 4191
For we must needs *d*, and are as 2Sa 14:14 4191
neither if half of us *d*, will 2Sa 18:3 4191
unto Shimei, Thou shalt not *d* 2Sa 19:23 4191
that I may *d* in mine own city, and 2Sa 19:37 4191
shall be found in him, he shall *d* 1Kin 1:52 4191
David drew nigh that he should *d* 1Kin 2:1 4191
but I will *d* here 1Kin 2:30 4191
certain that thou shalt surely *d* 1Kin 2:37 4191
whither, that thou shalt surely *d* 1Kin 2:42 4191
into the city, the child shall *d* 1Kin 14:12 4191
my son, that we may eat it, and *d* 1Kin 17:12 4191
for himself that he might *d* 1Kin 19:4 4191
out, and stone him, that he may *d* 1Kin 21:10 4191
art gone up, but shalt surely *d* 2Kin 1:4 4191
art gone up, but shalt surely *d* 2Kin 1:6 4191
art gone up, but shalt surely *d* 2Kin 1:16 4191
Why sit we here until we *d* 2Kin 7:3 4191
in the city, and we shall *d* there 2Kin 7:4 4191
if we sit still here, we *d* also 2Kin 7:4 4191
if they kill us, we shall but *d* 2Kin 7:4 4191
shewed me that he shall surely *d* 2Kin 8:10 4191
honey, that ye may live, and not *d* 2Kin 18:32 4191
for thou shalt *d*, and not live 2Kin 20:1 4191
shall not *d* for the children 2Chr 25:4 4191
the children *d* for the fathers 2Chr 25:4 4191
every man shall *d* for his own sin 2Chr 25:4 4191
over yourselves to *d* by famine 2Chr 32:11 4191
curse God, and *d* Job 2:9 4191
they *d*, even without wisdom Job 4:21 4191
and wisdom shall *d* with you Job 12:2 4191
the stock thereof *d* in the ground Job 14:8 4191
If a man *d*, shall he live again Job 14:14 4191
till I *d* I will not remove mine Job 27:5 1478
I shall *d* in my nest, and I shall Job 29:18 1478
In a moment shall they *d*, and the Job 34:20 4191
they shall *d* without knowledge Job 36:12 1478
They *d* in youth, and their life is Job 36:14 4191
speak evil of me, When shall he *d* Ps 41:5 4191
For he seeth that wise men *d* Ps 49:10 4191
those that are appointed to *d* Ps 79:11 8546
But ye shall *d* like men, and fall Ps 82:7 4191

ready to *d* from my youth up ... Ps 88:15 1478
takest away their breath, they *d* ... Ps 104:29 1478
I shall not *d*, but live, and ... Ps 118:17 4191
He shall *d* without instruction ... Prov 5:23 4191
but fools *d* for want of wisdom ... Prov 10:21 4191
and he that hateth reproof shall *d* ... Prov 15:10 4191
that despiseth his ways shall *d* ... Prov 19:16 4191
him with the rod, he shall not *d* ... Prov 23:13 4191
deny me them not before I *d* ... Prov 30:7 4191
A time to be born, and a time to *d* ... Eccl 3:2 4191
shouldest thou *d* before thy time ... Eccl 7:17 4191
the living know that they shall *d* ... Eccl 9:5 4191
for to morrow we shall *d* ... Is 22:13 4191
not be purged from you till ye *d* ... Is 22:14 4191
there shalt thou *d*, and there the ... Is 22:18 4191
for thou shalt *d*, and not live ... Is 38:1 4191
therein shall *d* in like manner ... Is 51:6 4191
be afraid of a man that shall *d* ... Is 51:12 4191
that he should not *d* in the pit ... Is 51:14 4191
for the child shall *d* an hundred ... Is 65:20 4191
for their worm shall not *d* ... Is 66:24 4191
that thou *d* not by our hand ... Jer 11:21 4191
young men shall *d* by the sword ... Jer 11:22 4191
their daughters shall *d* by famine ... Jer 11:22 4191
They shall *d* of grievous deaths ... Jer 16:4 4191
and the small shall *d* in this land ... Jer 16:6 4191
to Babylon, and there thou shalt *d* ... Jer 20:6 4191
they shall *d* of a great ... Jer 21:6 4191
in this city shall *d* by the sword ... Jer 21:9 4191
But he shall *d* in the place ... Jer 22:12 4191
and there shall ye *d* ... Jer 22:26 4191
him, saying, Thou shalt surely *d* ... Jer 26:8 4191
saying, This man is worthy to *d* ... Jer 26:11 4194
This man is not worthy to *d* ... Jer 26:16 4194
Why will ye *d*, thou and thy people ... Jer 27:13 4191
this year thou shalt *d*, because ... Jer 28:16 4191
But every one shall *d* for his own ... Jer 31:30 4191
Thou shalt not *d* by the sword ... Jer 34:4 4191
But thou shalt *d* in peace ... Jer 34:5 4191
the scribe, lest I *d* there ... Jer 37:20 4191
in this city shall *d* by the sword ... Jer 38:2 4191
he is like to *d* for hunger in the ... Jer 38:9 4191
out of the dungeon, before he *d* ... Jer 38:10 4191
these words, and thou shalt not *d* ... Jer 38:24 4191
to Jonathan's house, to *d* there ... Jer 38:26 4191
and there ye shall *d* ... Jer 42:16 4191
they shall *d* by the sword, by the ... Jer 42:17 4191
that ye shall *d* by the sword ... Jer 42:22 4191
they shall *d*, from the least even ... Jer 44:12 4191
the wicked, Thou shalt surely *d* ... Eze 3:18 4191
man shall *d* in his iniquity ... Eze 3:18 4191
he shall *d* in his iniquity ... Eze 3:19 4191
before him, he shall *d* ... Eze 3:20 4191
he shall *d* in his sin, and his ... Eze 3:20 4191
thee shall *d* with the pestilence ... Eze 5:12 4191
far off shall *d* of the pestilence ... Eze 6:12 4191
is besieged shall *d* by the famine ... Eze 6:12 4191
the field shall *d* with the sword ... Eze 7:15 4191
see it, though he shall *d* there ... Eze 12:13 4191
slay the souls that should not *d* ... Eze 13:19 4191
the midst of Babylon he shall *d* ... Eze 17:16 4191
the soul that sinneth, it shall *d* ... Eze 18:4 4191
he shall surely *d* ... Eze 18:13 4191
he shall not *d* for the iniquity ... Eze 18:17 4191
even he shall *d* in his iniquity ... Eze 18:18 4191
The soul that sinneth, it shall *d* ... Eze 18:20 4191
shall surely live, he shall not *d* ... Eze 18:21 4191
at all that the wicked should *d* ... Eze 18:23 4194
hath sinned, in them shall he *d* ... Eze 18:24 4191
that he hath done shall he *d* ... Eze 18:26 4191
shall surely live, he shall not *d* ... Eze 18:28 4191
for why will ye *d*, O house of ... Eze 18:31 4191
thou shalt *d* the deaths of them ... Eze 28:8 4191
Thou shalt *d* the deaths of the ... Eze 28:10 4191
O wicked man, thou shalt surely *d* ... Eze 33:8 4191
man shall *d* in his iniquity ... Eze 33:8 4191
he shall *d* in his iniquity ... Eze 33:9 4191
for why will ye *d*, O house of ... Eze 33:11 4191
hath committed, he shall *d* for it ... Eze 33:13 4191
the wicked, Thou shalt surely *d* ... Eze 33:14 4191
shall surely live, he shall not *d* ... Eze 33:15 4191
iniquity, he shall even *d* thereby ... Eze 33:18 4191
caves shall *d* of the pestilence ... Eze 33:27 4191
Moab shall *d* with tumult, with ... Amos 2:2 4191
in one house, that they shall *d* ... Amos 6:9 4191
Jeroboam shall *d* by the sword ... Amos 7:11 4191
thou shalt *d* in a polluted land ... Amos 7:17 4191
of my people shall *d* by the sword ... Amos 9:10 4191
better for me to *d* than to live ... Jonah 4:3 4194
and wished in himself to *d* ... Jonah 4:8 4191
better for me to *d* than to live ... Jonah 4:8 4194
we shall not *d* ... Hab 1:12 4191
that that dieth, let it *d* ... Zec 11:9 4191
therein shall be cut off and *d* ... Zec 13:8 1478
or mother, let him *d* the death ... Mt 15:4 5053
Master, Moses said, If a man *d* ... Mt 22:24 599
him, Though I should *d* with thee ... Mt 26:35 599
or mother, let him *d* the death ... Mk 7:10 5053
unto us, If a man's brother *d* ... Mk 12:19 599
If I should *d* with thee, I will ... Mk 14:31 4880
unto him, was sick, and ready to *d* ... Lk 7:2 5053
unto us, If any man's brother *d* ... Lk 20:28 599
he *d* without children, that his ... Lk 20:28 599
Neither can they *d* any more ... Lk 20:36 599
Sir, come down ere my child *d* ... Jn 4:49 599
a man may eat thereof, and not *d* ... Jn 6:50 599
seek me, and shall *d* in your sins ... Jn 8:21 599
you, that ye shall *d* in your sins ... Jn 8:24 599
I am he, ye shall *d* in your sins ... Jn 8:24 599
also go, that we may *d* with him ... Jn 11:16 599
and believeth in me shall never *d* ... Jn 11:26 599
one man should *d* for the people ... Jn 11:50 599
Jesus should *d* for that nation ... Jn 11:51 599
wheat fall into the ground and *d* ... Jn 12:24 599
but if it *d*, it bringeth forth ... Jn 12:24 599
signifying what death he should *d* ... Jn 12:33 599
one man should *d* for the people ... Jn 18:14 622
signifying what death he should *d* ... Jn 18:32 599
law, and by our law he ought to *d* ... Jn 19:7 599
that that disciple should not *d* ... Jn 21:23 599
said not unto him, He shall not *d* ... Jn 21:23 599
but also to *d* at Jerusalem for ... Acts 21:13 599
of death, I refuse not to *d* ... Acts 25:11 599
Romans to deliver any man to *d* ... Acts 25:16 684
for a righteous man will one *d* ... Rom 5:7 599
man some would even dare to *d* ... Rom 5:7 599
live after the flesh, ye shall *d* ... Rom 8:13 599
we *d*, we *d* unto the Lord ... Rom 14:8 599
whether we live therefore, or *d* ... Rom 14:8 599
for it were better for me to *d* ... 1Cor 9:15 599
For as in Adam all *d*, even so in ... 1Cor 15:22 599
Christ Jesus our Lord, I *d* daily ... 1Cor 15:31 599
for to morrow we *d* ... 1Cor 15:32 599
is not quickened, except it *d* ... 1Cor 15:36 599
that ye are in our hearts to *d* ... 2Cor 7:3 4880
live is Christ, and to *d* is gain ... Phil 1:21 599
here men that *d* receive tithes ... Heb 7:8 599
is appointed unto men once to *d* ... Heb 9:27 599
which remain, that are ready to *d* ... Rev 3:2 599
and shall desire to *d*, and death ... Rev 9:6 599
Blessed are the dead which *d* in ... Rev 14:13 599

DIED {201}

and thirty years: and he *d* ... Gen 5:5 4191
and twelve years: and he *d* ... Gen 5:8 4191
and five years: and he *d* ... Gen 5:11 4191
and ten years: and he *d* ... Gen 5:14 4191
and five years: and he *d* ... Gen 5:17 4191
and two years: and he *d*. ... Gen 5:20 4191
and nine years: and he *d*. ... Gen 5:27 4191
and seven years: and he *d* ... Gen 5:31 4191
all flesh *d* that moved upon the ... Gen 7:21 1478
all that was in the dry land, *d* ... Gen 7:22 4191
and fifty years: and he *d* ... Gen 9:29 4191
Haran *d* before his father Terah ... Gen 11:28 4191
and Terah *d* in Haran ... Gen 11:32 4191
And Sarah *d* in Kirjath-arba ... Gen 23:2 4191
d in a good old age, an old man ... Gen 25:8 4191
and he gave up the ghost and *d* ... Gen 25:17 4191
he *d* in the presence of all his ... Gen 25:18 5307
But Deborah Rebekah's nurse *d* ... Gen 35:8 4191
(for she *d*) that she called his ... Gen 35:18 4191
And Rachel *d*, and was buried in the ... Gen 35:19 4191
And Isaac gave up the ghost, and *d* ... Gen 35:29 4191
And Bela *d*, and Jobab the son of ... Gen 36:33 4191
And Jobab *d*, and Husham of the land ... Gen 36:34 4191
And Husham *d*, and Hadad the son of ... Gen 36:35 4191
Hadad *d*, and Samlah of Masrekah ... Gen 36:36 4191
And Samlah *d*, and Saul of Rehoboth ... Gen 36:37 4191
And Saul *d*, and Baal-hanan the son ... Gen 36:38 4191
And Baal-hanan the son of Achbor *d* ... Gen 36:39 4191
daughter of Shuah Judah's wife *d* ... Gen 38:12 4191
Onan *d* in the land of Canaan ... Gen 46:12 4191
Rachel *d* by me in the land of ... Gen 48:7 4191
father did command before he *d* ... Gen 50:16 4194
So Joseph *d*, being an hundred and ... Gen 50:26 4191
And Joseph *d*, and all his brethren, ... Ex 1:6 4191
of time, that the king of Egypt *d* ... Ex 2:23 4191
the fish that was in the river *d* ... Ex 7:21 4191
the frogs *d* out of the houses, ... Ex 8:13 4191
and all the cattle of Egypt *d* ... Ex 9:6 4191
the children of Israel *d* not one ... Ex 9:6 4191
Would to God we had *d* by the hand ... Ex 16:3 4191
them, and they *d* before the LORD ... Lev 10:2 4191
offered before the LORD, and *d* ... Lev 16:1 4191
eateth that which *d* of itself ... Lev 17:15 5038
Abihu *d* before the LORD, when ... Num 3:4 4191
we had *d* in the land of Egypt ... Num 14:2 4191
God we had *d* in this wilderness ... Num 14:2 4191
d by the plague before the LORD ... Num 14:37 4191
stoned him with stones, and he *d* ... Num 15:36 4191
Now they that *d* in the plague ... Num 16:49 4191
beside them that *d* about the ... Num 16:49 4191
and Miriam *d* there, and was buried ... Num 20:1 4191
Would God that we had *d* when our ... Num 20:3 1478
our brethren *d* before the LORD ... Num 20:3 1478
Aaron *d* there in the top of the ... Num 20:28 4191
and much people of Israel *d* ... Num 21:6 4191
those that *d* in the plague were ... Num 25:9 4191
with Korah, when that company *d* ... Num 26:10 4194
the children of Korah *d* not ... Num 26:11 4191
Onan *d* in the land of Canaan ... Num 26:19 4191
And Nadab and Abihu *d*, when they ... Num 26:61 4191
Our father *d* in the wilderness, ... Num 27:3 4191
but *d* in his own sin, and had no ... Num 27:3 4191
d there, in the fortieth year ... Num 33:38 4191
years old when he *d* in mount Hor ... Num 33:39 4194
there Aaron *d*, and there he was ... Deut 10:6 4191
Aaron thy brother *d* in mount Hor ... Deut 32:50 4191
LORD *d* there in the land of Moab ... Deut 34:5 4191
and twenty years old when he *d* ... Deut 34:7 4194
d in the wilderness by the way, ... Josh 5:4 4191
upon them unto Azekah, and they *d* ... Josh 10:11 4191
they were more which *d* with ... Josh 10:11 4191
Nun, the servant of the LORD, *d* ... Josh 24:29 4191
And Eleazar the son of Aaron *d* ... Josh 24:33 4191
him to Jerusalem, and there he *d* ... Judg 1:7 4191
Nun, the servant of the LORD, *d* ... Judg 2:8 4191
which Joshua left when he *d* ... Judg 2:21 4191
And Othniel the son of Kenaz *d* ... Judg 3:11 4191
asleep and weary. So he *d* ... Judg 4:21 4191
son of Joash *d* in a good old age ... Judg 8:32 4191
of the tower of Shechem *d* also ... Judg 9:49 4191
man thrust him through, and he *d* ... Judg 9:54 4191
twenty and three years, and *d* ... Judg 10:2 4191
And Jair *d*, and was buried in Camon ... Judg 10:5 4191
Then *d* Jephthah the Gileadite, and ... Judg 12:7 4191
Then *d* Ibzan, and was buried at ... Judg 12:10 4191
And Elon the Zebulonite *d*, and was ... Judg 12:12 4191
son of Hillel the Pirathonite *d* ... Judg 12:15 4191
And Elimelech Naomi's husband *d* ... Ruth 1:3 4191
Chilion *d* also both of them ... Ruth 1:5 4191
gate, and his neck brake, and he *d* ... 1Sa 4:18 4191
the men that *d* not were smitten ... 1Sa 5:12 4191
rescued Jonathan, that he *d* not ... 1Sa 14:45 4191
And Samuel *d*; and all the Israelites ... 1Sa 25:1 4191
that his heart *d* within him ... 1Sa 25:37 4191
the LORD smote Nabal, that he *d* ... 1Sa 25:38 4191
upon his sword, and *d* with him ... 1Sa 31:5 4191
So Saul *d*, and his three sons, and ... 1Sa 31:6 4191
And he smote him that he *d* ... 2Sa 1:15 4191
there, and *d* in the same place ... 2Sa 2:23 4191
Asahel fell down and *d* stood still ... 2Sa 2:23 4191
three hundred and threescore men *d* ... 2Sa 2:31 4191
under the fifth rib, that he *d* ... 2Sa 3:27 4191
and said, *D* Abner as a fool dieth ... 2Sa 3:33 4191
there he *d* by the ark of God ... 2Sa 6:7 4191
king of the children of Ammon *d* ... 2Sa 10:1 4191
of their host, who *d* there ... 2Sa 10:18 4191
and Uriah the Hittite *d* also ... 2Sa 11:17 4191
the wall, that he *d* in Thebez ... 2Sa 11:21 4191
the seventh day, that the child *d* ... 2Sa 12:18 4191
in order, and hanged himself, and *d* ... 2Sa 17:23 4191
would God I had *d* for thee ... 2Sa 18:33 4191
lived, and all we had *d* this day ... 2Sa 19:6 4191
him not again; and he *d* ... 2Sa 20:10 4191
there *d* of the people from Dan ... 2Sa 24:15 4191
and he fell upon him that he *d* ... 1Kin 2:25 4191
out, and fell upon him, that he *d* ... 1Kin 2:46 4191
this woman's child *d* in the night ... 1Kin 3:19 4191
stoned him with stones, that he *d* ... 1Kin 12:18 4191
of the door, the child *d* ... 1Kin 14:17 4191
house over him with fire, and *d* ... 1Kin 16:18 4191
so Tibni *d*, and Omri reigned ... 1Kin 16:22 4191
stoned him with stones, that he *d* ... 1Kin 21:13 4191
against the Syrians, and *d* at even ... 1Kin 22:35 4191
So the king *d*, and was brought to ... 1Kin 22:37 4191
So he *d* according to the word of ... 2Kin 1:17 4191
on her knees till noon, and then *d* ... 2Kin 4:20 4191
upon him in the gate, and he *d* ... 2Kin 7:17 4191
upon him in the gate, and he *d* ... 2Kin 7:20 4191
it on his face, so that he *d* ... 2Kin 8:15 4191
And he fled to Megiddo, and *d* there ... 2Kin 9:27 4191
his servants, smote him, and he *d* ... 2Kin 12:21 4191
sick of his sickness whereof he *d* ... 2Kin 13:14 4191
And Elisha *d*, and they buried him ... 2Kin 13:20 4191
So Hazael king of Syria *d* ... 2Kin 13:24 4191
and he came to Egypt, and *d* there ... 2Kin 23:34 4191
him, and smote Gedaliah, that he *d* ... 2Kin 25:25 4191
Hadad *d* also. And the dukes ... 1Chr 1:51 4191
but Seled *d* without children ... 1Chr 2:30 4191
Jether *d* without children ... 1Chr 2:32 4191
fell likewise on the sword, and *d* ... 1Chr 10:5 4191
So Saul *d*, and his three sons ... 1Chr 10:6 4191
and all his house *d* together ... 1Chr 10:6 4191
So Saul *d* for his transgression ... 1Chr 10:13 4191
and there he *d* before God ... 1Chr 13:10 4191
king of the children of Ammon *d* ... 1Chr 19:1 4191
And Eleazar *d*, and had no sons, but ... 1Chr 23:22 4191
Abihu *d* before their father, and ... 1Chr 24:2 4191
he *d* in a good old age, full of ... 1Chr 29:28 4191
stoned him with stones, that he *d* ... 2Chr 10:18 4191
and the LORD struck him, and he *d* ... 2Chr 13:20 4191
d in the one and fortieth year of ... 2Chr 16:13 4191
time of the sun going down he *d* ... 2Chr 18:34 4191
so he *d* of sore diseases ... 2Chr 21:19 4191
and was full of days when he *d* ... 2Chr 24:15 4191
thirty years old was he when he *d* ... 2Chr 24:15 4194
And when he *d*, he said, The LORD ... 2Chr 24:22 4191
and slew him on his bed, and he *d* ... 2Chr 24:25 4191
brought him to Jerusalem, and he *d* ... 2Chr 35:24 4191
Why *d* I not from the womb ... Job 3:11 4191
So Job *d*, being old and full of ... Job 42:17 4191
d I saw also the Lord sitting ... Is 6:1 4194
that king Ahaz *d* was this burden ... Is 14:28 4194
So Hananiah the prophet *d* the ... Jer 28:17 4191
Pelatiah the son of Benaiah *d* ... Eze 11:13 4191
and at even my wife *d* ... Eze 24:18 4191
when he offended in Baal, he *d* ... Hos 13:1 4191
And last of all the woman *d* also ... Mt 22:27 599
And the second took her, and *d* ... Mk 12:21 599
last of all the woman *d* also ... Mk 12:22 599
came to pass, that the beggar *d* ... Lk 16:22 599
the rich man also *d*, and was ... Lk 16:22 599
a wife, and *d* without children ... Lk 20:29 599
her to wife, and he *d* childless ... Lk 20:30 599
and they left no children, and *d* ... Lk 20:31 599
Last of all the woman *d* also ... Lk 20:32 599
been here, my brother had not *d* ... Jn 11:21 599
been here, my brother had not *d* ... Jn 11:32 599
even this man should not have *d* ... Jn 11:37 599
Jacob went down into Egypt, and *d* ... Acts 7:15 5053
days, that she was sick, and *d* ... Acts 9:37 599
due time Christ *d* for the ungodly ... Rom 5:6 599

were yet sinners, Christ *d* for us ... Rom 5:8 *599*
that he *d*, he *d* unto sin once ... Rom 6:10 *599*
came, sin revived, and I *d* ... Rom 7:9 *599*
It is Christ that *d*, yea rather, ... Rom 8:34 *599*
For to this end Christ both *d* ... Rom 14:9 *599*
with thy meat, for whom Christ *d* ... Rom 14:15 *599*
brother perish, for whom Christ *d* ... 1Cor 8:11 *599*
how that Christ *d* for our sins ... 1Cor 15:3 *599*
thus judge, that if one *d* for all ... 2Cor 5:14 *599*
And that he *d* for all, that they ... 2Cor 5:15 *599*
but unto him which *d* for them ... 2Cor 5:15 *599*
For if we believe that Jesus *d* ... 1Th 4:14 *599*
Who *d* for us, that, whether we ... 1Th 5:10 *599*
law *d* without mercy under two or ... Heb 10:28 *599*
These all *d* in faith, not having ... Heb 11:13 *599*
By faith Joseph, when he *d* ... Heb 11:22 *5053*
were in the sea, and had life, *d* ... Rev 8:9 *599*
many men *d* of the waters, because ... Rev 8:11 *599*
and every living soul *d* in the sea ... Rev 16:3 *599*

DIEST {1}
Where thou *d*, will I die, and ... Ruth 1:17 4191

DIET {2}
And for his *d*, there was a ... Jer 52:34 737
there was a continual *d* given him ... Jer 52:34 737

DIETH {30}
fat of the beast that *d* of itself ... Lev 7:24 5038
That which *d* of itself, or is ... Lev 22:8 5038
the law, when a man *d* in a tent ... Num 19:14 4191
eat of any thing that *d* of itself ... Deut 14:21 5038
and said, Died Abner as a fool *d* ... 2Sa 3:33 4194
Him that *d* of Jeroboam in the ... 1Kin 14:11 4191
him that *d* in the field shall the ... 1Kin 14:11 4191
Him that *d* of Baasha in the city ... 1Kin 16:4 4191
him that *d* of his in the fields ... 1Kin 16:4 4191
Him that *d* of Ahab in the city ... 1Kin 21:24 4191
him that *d* in the field shall the ... 1Kin 21:24 4191
But man *d*, and wasteth away ... Job 14:10 4191
One *d* in his full strength, being ... Job 21:23 4191
another *d* in the bitterness of ... Job 21:25 4191
For when he *d* he shall carry ... Ps 49:17 4194
When a wicked man *d*, his ... Prov 11:7 4194
And how *d* the wise man ... Eccl 2:16 4191
as the one *d*, so *d* the other ... Eccl 3:19 4194
is no water, and *d* for thirst ... Is 50:2 4191
he that eateth of their eggs *d* ... Is 59:5 4191
eaten of that which *d* of itself ... Eze 4:14 5038
committeth iniquity, and *d* in them ... Eze 18:26 4191
in the death of him that *d* ... Eze 18:32 4191
that that *d*, let it die ... Zec 11:9 4191
Where their worm *d* not, and the ... Mk 9:44 *5053*
Where their worm *d* not, and the ... Mk 9:46 *5053*
Where their worm *d* not, and the ... Mk 9:48 *5053*
raised from the dead *d* no more ... Rom 6:9 *599*
himself, and no man *d* to himself ... Rom 14:7 *599*

DIFFER {1}
who maketh thee to *d* from another ... 1Cor 4:7 *1252*

DIFFERENCE {12}
put a *d* between the Egyptians ... Ex 11:7 6395
And that ye may put *d* between holy ... Lev 10:10 914
To make a *d* between the unclean ... Lev 11:47 914
put *d* between clean beasts ... Lev 20:25 914
have put no *d* between the holy ... Eze 22:26
they shewed *d* between the unclean ... Eze 22:26
my people the *d* between the holy ... Eze 44:23
put no *d* between us and them, ... Acts 15:9 *1252*
for there is no *d* ... Rom 3:22 *1293*
For there is no *d* between the Jew ... Rom 10:12 *1293*
There is *d* also between a wife and ... 1Cor 7:34 *3307*
some have compassion, making a *d* ... Jude 22 *1252*

DIFFERENCES {1}
there are *d* of administrations, ... 1Cor 12:5 *1243*

DIFFERETH {2}
for one star *d* from another star ... 1Cor 15:41 *1308*
d nothing from a servant, though ... Gal 4:1 *1308*

DIFFERING {1}
Having then gifts *d* according to ... Rom 12:6 *1313*

DIG {13}
a pit, or if a man shall *d* a pit ... Ex 21:33 3738
whose hills thou mayest *d* brass ... Deut 8:9 2672
abroad, thou shalt *d* therewith ... Deut 23:13 2658
d for it more than for hid ... Job 3:21 2658
ye *d* a pit for your friend ... Job 6:27 3738
yea, thou shalt *d* about thee ... Job 11:18 2658
In the dark they *d* through houses ... Job 24:16 2864
me, Son of man, *d* now in the wall ... Eze 8:8 2864
D thou through the wall in their ... Eze 12:5 2864
they shall *d* through the wall to ... Eze 12:12 2864
Though they *d* into hell, thence ... Amos 9:2 2864
also, till I shall *d* about it ... Lk 13:8 *4626*
I cannot *d* ... Lk 16:3 *4626*

DIGGED {37}
unto me, that I have *d* this well ... Gen 21:30 2658
had *d* in the days of Abraham his ... Gen 26:15 2658
Isaac *d* again the wells of water, ... Gen 26:18 2658
which they had *d* in the days of ... Gen 26:18 2658
Isaac's servants *d* in the valley ... Gen 26:19 2658
they *d* another well, and strove ... Gen 26:21 2658
from thence, and *d* another well ... Gen 26:22 2658
there Isaac's servants *d* a well ... Gen 26:25 3738
the well which they had *d* ... Gen 26:32 2658
their selfwill they *d* down a wall ... Gen 49:6 6131
in my grave which I have *d* for me ... Gen 50:5 3738
all the Egyptians *d* round about ... Ex 7:24 2658
The princes *d* the well ... Num 21:18 2658
the nobles of the people *d* it ... Num 21:18 3738
thou filledst not, and wells *d* ... Deut 6:11 2672
I have *d* and drunk strange waters, ... 2Kin 19:24 5365
in the desert, and *d* many wells ... 2Chr 26:10 2672
houses full of all goods, wells *d* ... Neh 9:25 2672
d it, and is fallen into the ditch ... Ps 7:15 2658
cause they have *d* for my soul ... Ps 35:7 2658
they have *d* a pit before me, into ... Ps 57:6 3738
until the pit be *d* for the wicked ... Ps 94:13 3738
The proud have *d* pits for me ... Ps 119:85 3738
it shall not be pruned, nor *d* ... Is 5:6 5737
that shall be *d* with the mattock ... Is 7:25 5737
I have *d*, and drunk water ... Is 37:25 5365
hole of the pit whence ye are *d* ... Is 51:1 5365
Then I went to Euphrates, and *d* ... Jer 13:7 2658
for they have *d* a pit for my soul ... Jer 18:20 3738
for they have *d* a pit to take me, ... Jer 18:22 3738
when I had *d* in the wall, behold ... Eze 8:8 2864
in the even I *d* through the wall ... Eze 12:7 2864
d a winepress in it, and built a ... Mt 21:33 *3736*
d in the earth, and hid his lord's ... Mt 25:18 *3736*
d a place for the winefat, and ... Mk 12:1 *3736*
d deep, and laid the foundation on ... Lk 6:48 *4626*
prophets, and *d* down thine altars ... Rom 11:3 *2679*

DIGGEDST {1}
and wells digged, which thou *d* not ... Deut 6:11 2672

DIGGETH {3}
An ungodly man *d* up evil ... Prov 16:27 3738
Whoso *d* a pit shall fall therein ... Prov 26:27 3738
He that *d* a pit shall fall into ... Eccl 10:8 2658

DIGNITIES {2}
are not afraid to speak evil of *d* ... 2Pet 2:10 *1891*
dominion, and speak evil of *d* ... Jude 8 *1891*

DIGNITY {4}
my strength, the excellency of *d* ... Gen 49:3 7613
d hath been done to Mordecai for ... Est 6:3 1420
Folly is set in great *d*, and the ... Eccl 10:6 4791
and their *d* shall proceed of ... Hab 1:7 7613

DIKLAH *(dik'-lah)* {2} *A son of Joktan.*
And Hadoram, and Uzal, and *D* ... Gen 10:27 1853
Hadoram also, and Uzal, and *D* ... 1Chr 1:21 1853

DILEAN *(dil'-e-an)* {1} *A city in Judah.*
And *D*, and Mizpeh, and Joktheel, ... Josh 15:38 1810

DILIGENCE {10}
Keep thy heart with all *d* ... Prov 4:23 4929
give *d* that thou mayest be ... Lk 12:58 *2039*
he that ruleth, with *d* ... Rom 12:8 *4710*
and knowledge, and in all *d* ... 2Cor 8:7 *4710*
Do thy *d* to come shortly unto me ... 2Ti 4:9 *4704*
Do thy *d* to come before winter ... 2Ti 4:21 *4704*
one of you do shew the same *d* to ... Heb 6:11 *4710*
And beside this, giving all *d* ... 2Pet 1:5 *4710*
give *d* to make your calling and ... 2Pet 1:10 *4710*
when I gave all *d* to write unto ... Jude 3 *4710*

DILIGENT {15}
judges shall make *d* inquisition ... Deut 19:18 3190
But take *d* heed to do the ... Josh 22:5 3966
they accomplish a *d* search ... Ps 64:6
and my spirit made *d* search ... Ps 77:6
but the hand of the *d* maketh rich ... Prov 10:4 2742
The hand of the *d* shall bear rule ... Prov 12:24 2742
substance of a *d* man is precious ... Prov 12:27 2742
soul of the *d* shall be made fat ... Prov 13:4 2742
The thoughts of the *d* tend only ... Prov 21:5 2742
thou a man *d* in his business ... Prov 22:29 4106
Be thou *d* to know the state of ... Prov 27:23
proved *d* in many things ... 2Cor 8:22 *4705*
but now much more *d* ... 2Cor 8:22 *4707*
be *d* to come unto me to Nicopolis ... Titus 3:12 *4704*
be *d* that ye may be found of him ... 2Pet 3:14 *4704*

DILIGENTLY {37}
If thou wilt *d* hearken to the ... Ex 15:26
Moses *d* sought the goat of the ... Lev 10:16
to thyself, and keep thy soul *d* ... Deut 4:9 3966
teach them *d* unto thy children ... Deut 6:7 8150
Ye shall *d* keep the commandments ... Deut 6:17
if ye shall hearken *d* unto my ... Deut 11:13
For if ye shall *d* keep all these ... Deut 11:22
enquire, and make search, and ask *d* ... Deut 13:14 3190
hast heard of it, and enquired *d* ... Deut 17:4 3190
of leprosy, that thou observe *d* ... Deut 24:8 3966
if thou shalt hearken *d* unto the ... Deut 28:1
Now the men did *d* observe whether ... 1Kin 20:33 5172
let it be *d* done for the house of ... Ezr 7:23 149
Hear *d* my speech, and my ... Job 13:17
Hear *d* my speech, and let this be ... Job 21:2
thou shalt *d* consider his place, ... Ps 37:10 995
us to keep thy precepts *d* ... Ps 119:4 3966
d to seek thy face, and I have ... Prov 7:15 7836
He that *d* seeketh good procureth ... Prov 11:27 7836
consider *d* what is before thee ... Prov 23:1
he hearkened *d* with much heed ... Is 21:7 7182
hearken *d* unto me, and eat ye that ... Is 55:2
and send unto Kedar, and consider *d* ... Jer 2:10 3966
if they will *d* learn the ways of ... Jer 12:16
if ye *d* hearken unto me, saith ... Jer 17:24
if ye will *d* obey the voice of ... Zec 6:15
enquired of them *d* what time the ... Mt 2:7
search *d* for the young child ... Mt 2:8 *199*
he had *d* enquired of the wise men ... Mt 2:16
house, and seek *d* till she find it ... Lk 15:8 *1960*
taught *d* the things of the Lord, ... Acts 18:25 *199*
if she have *d* followed every good ... 1Ti 5:10
in Rome, he sought me out very *d* ... 2Ti 1:17 *4706*
and Apollos on their journey *d* ... Titus 3:13 *4709*
rewarder of them that *d* seek him ... Heb 11:6 *1567*
Looking *d* lest any man fail of ... Heb 12:15
have enquired and searched *d* ... 1Pet 1:10

DIM {9}
Isaac was old, and his eyes were *d* ... Gen 27:1 3543
the eyes of Israel were *d* for age ... Gen 48:10 3513
his eye was not *d*, nor his ... Deut 34:7 3543
place, and his eyes began to wax *d* ... 1Sa 3:2 3544
and his eyes were *d*, that he could ... 1Sa 4:15 6965
Mine eye also is *d* by reason of ... Job 17:7 3543
of them that see shall not be *d* ... Is 32:3 8159
How is the gold become *d* ... Lam 4:1 6004
for these things our eyes are *d* ... Lam 5:17 2821

DIMINISH {8}
ye shall not *d* ought thereof ... Ex 5:8 1639
duty of marriage, shall he not *d* ... Ex 21:10 1639
thou shalt *d* the price of it ... Lev 25:16 4591
neither shall ye *d* ought from it ... Deut 4:2 1639
not add thereto, nor *d* from it ... Deut 12:32 1639
d not a word ... Jer 26:2 1639
therefore will I also *d* thee ... Eze 5:11 1639
for I will *d* them, that they ... Eze 29:15 4591

DIMINISHED {5}
not ought of your work shall be *d* ... Ex 5:11 1639
gotten by vanity shall be *d* ... Prov 13:11 4591
the children of Kedar, shall be *d* ... Is 21:17 4591
may be increased there, and not *d* ... Jer 29:6 4591
have *d* thine ordinary food, and ... Eze 16:27 1639

DIMINISHING {1}
the *d* of them the riches of the ... Rom 11:12 *2275*

DIMNAH *(dim'-nah)* {1} *A Levitical city in Zebulun.*
D with her suburbs, Nahalal with ... Josh 21:35 1829

DIMNESS {2}
trouble and darkness, *d* of anguish ... Is 8:22 4588
Nevertheless the *d* shall not be ... Is 9:1 4155

DIMON *(di'-mon)* {2} See DIBON, DIMONAH. *A Moabite city.*
For the waters of *D* shall be full ... Is 15:9 1775
for I will bring more upon *D* ... Is 15:9 1775

DIMONAH *(di-mo'-nah)* {1} See DIMON. *A city in Judah.*
And Kinah, and *D*, and Adadah, ... Josh 15:22 1776

DINAH {7} See DINAH'S. *A daughter of Jacob.*
a daughter, and called her name *D* ... Gen 30:21 1783
D the daughter of Leah, which she ... Gen 34:1 1783
his soul clave unto *D* the ... Gen 34:3 1783
he had defiled *D* his daughter ... Gen 34:5 1783
he had defiled *D* their sister ... Gen 34:13 1783
took *D* out of Shechem's house, and ... Gen 34:26 1783
Padan-aram, with his daughter *D* ... Gen 46:15 1783

DINAH'S {1}
D brethren, took each man his ... Gen 34:25 1783

DINAITES *(di'-na-ites)* {1} *Foreign settlers in Samaria.*
the *D*, the Apharsathchites, the ... Ezr 4:9 1784

DINE {3}
these men shall *d* with me at noon ... Gen 43:16 398
besought him to *d* with him ... Lk 11:37 *709*
Jesus saith unto them, Come and *d* ... Jn 21:12 *709*

DINED {1}
So when they had *d*, Jesus saith ... Jn 21:15 *709*

DINHABAH *(din'-ha-bah)* {2} *Capital of Edom.*
and the name of his city was *D* ... Gen 36:32 1838
and the name of his city was *D* ... 1Chr 1:43 1838

DINNER {4}
Better is a *d* of herbs where love ... Prov 15:17 737
Behold, I have prepared my *d* ... Mt 22:4 *712*
he had not first washed before *d* ... Lk 11:38 *712*
When thou makest a *d* or a supper ... Lk 14:12 *712*

DIONYSIUS *(di-on-ish'-yus)* {1} *An Athenian convert of Paul.*
the which was *D* the Areopagite ... Acts 17:34 *1354*

DIOTREPHES *(di-ot'-re-feez)* {1} *A believer condemned by John.*
but *D*, who loveth to have the ... 3Jn 9 *1361*

DIP {10}
d it in the blood that is in the ... Ex 12:22 2881
the priest shall *d* his finger in ... Lev 4:6 2881
the priest shall *d* his finger in ... Lev 4:17 2881
and the hyssop, and shall *d* them ... Lev 14:6 2881
the priest shall *d* his right ... Lev 14:16 2881
d them in the blood of the slain ... Lev 14:51 2881
d it in the water, and sprinkle it ... Num 19:18 2881
let him *d* his foot in oil ... Deut 33:24 2881
d thy morsel in the vinegar ... Ruth 2:14 2881
that he may *d* the tip of his ... Lk 16:24 *911*

DIPPED {10}
goats, and *d* the coat in the blood ... Gen 37:31 2881
he *d* his finger in the blood, and ... Lev 9:9 2881
were *d* in the brim of the water ... Josh 3:15 2881
d it in an honeycomb, and put his ... 1Sa 14:27 2881
d himself seven times in Jordan, ... 2Kin 5:14 2881
d it in water, and spread it on ... 2Kin 8:15 2881
That thy foot may be *d* in the ... Ps 68:23 4272
give a sop, when I have *d* it ... Jn 13:26 *911*
And when he had *d* the sop, he gave ... Jn 13:26 *1686*
clothed with a vesture *d* in blood ... Rev 19:13 *911*

DIPPETH {2}
He that *d* his hand with me in the ... Mt 26:23 *1686*
that *d* with me in the dish ... Mk 14:20 *1686*

DIRECT {10}
to *d* his face unto Goshen........ Gen 46:28 3384
will I *d* my prayer unto thee........ Ps 5:3 6186
him, and he shall *d* thy paths........ Prov 3:6 3474
of the perfect shall *d* his way........ Prov 11:5 3474
but wisdom is profitable to *d*........ Eccl 10:10 3787
and I will *d* all his ways........ Is 45:13 3474
I will *d* their work in truth, and........ Is 61:8 5414
man that walketh to *d* his steps........ Jer 10:23 3559
Jesus Christ, *d* our way unto you........ 1Th 3:11 *2720*
the Lord *d* your hearts into the........ 2Th 3:5 *2720*

DIRECTED {3}
Now he hath not *d* his words........ Job 32:14 6186
O that my ways were *d* to keep thy........ Ps 119:5 3559
Who hath *d* the Spirit of the LORD........ Is 40:13 8505

DIRECTETH {3}
He *d* it under the whole heaven,........ Job 37:3 3474
but the LORD *d* his steps........ Prov 16:9 3559
as for the upright, he *d* his way........ Prov 21:29 3559

DIRECTION {1}
by the *d* of the lawgiver, with........ Num 21:18

DIRECTLY {2}
sprinkle of her blood *d* before........ Num 19:4 413,5227
even the way *d* before the wall........ Eze 42:12 1903

DIRT {3}
and the *d* came out........ Judg 3:22 6574
them out as the *d* in the streets........ Ps 18:42 2916
whose waters cast up mire and *d*........ Is 57:20 2916

DISALLOW {1}
But if her father *d* her in the........ Num 30:5 5106

DISALLOWED {5}
her, because her father *d* her........ Num 30:5 5106
But if her husband *d* her on the........ Num 30:8 5106
his peace at her, and *d* her not........ Num 30:11 5106
d indeed of men, but chosen of........ 1Pet 2:4 *593*
the stone which the builders *d*........ 1Pet 2:7 *593*

DISANNUL {3}
Wilt thou also *d* my judgment........ Job 40:8 6565
hath purposed, and who shall *d* it........ Is 14:27 6565
and thirty years after, cannot *d*........ Gal 3:17 *208*

DISANNULLED {1}
covenant with death shall be *d*........ Is 28:18 3722

DISANNULLETH {1}
yet if it be confirmed, no man *d*........ Gal 3:15 *114*

DISANNULLING {1}
For there is verily a *d* of the........ Heb 7:18 *115*

DISAPPOINT {1}
O LORD, *d* him, cast him down........ Ps 17:13 6923

DISAPPOINTED {1}
Without counsel purposes are *d*........ Prov 15:22 6565

DISAPPOINTETH {1}
He *d* the devices of the crafty,........ Job 5:12 6565

DISCERN {17}
before our brethren *d* thou what........ Gen 31:32 5234
and she said, *D*, I pray thee,........ Gen 38:25 5234
so is my lord the king to *d* good........ 2Sa 14:17 8085
can I *d* between good and evil........ 2Sa 19:35 3045
that I may *d* between good and bad........ 1Kin 3:9 995
understanding to *d* judgment........ 1Kin 3:11 8085
So that the people could not *d*........ Ezr 3:13 5234
but I could not *d* the form........ Job 4:16 5234
cannot my taste *d* perverse things........ Job 6:30 995
cause them to *d* between the........ Eze 44:23 3045
cannot *d* between their right hand........ Jonah 4:11 3045
d between the righteous and the........ Mal 3:18 7200
ye can *d* the face of the sky........ Mt 16:3 *1252*
but can ye not *d* the signs of the........ Mt 16:3
ye can *d* the face of the sky and........ Lk 12:56 *1381*
is it that ye do not *d* this time........ Lk 12:56
senses exercised to *d* both good........ Heb 5:14 *1253*

DISCERNED {4}
he *d* him not, because his hands........ Gen 27:23 5234
the king of Israel *d* him that he........ 1Kin 20:41 5234
I *d* among the youths, a young man........ Prov 7:7 995
because they are spiritually *d*........ 1Cor 2:14 *350*

DISCERNER {1}
is a *d* of the thoughts and intents........ Heb 4:12 *2924*

DISCERNETH {1}
and a wise man's heart *d* both time........ Eccl 8:5 3045

DISCERNING {2}
to himself, not *d* the Lord's body........ 1Cor 11:29 *1252*
to another *d* of spirits........ 1Cor 12:10 *1253*

DISCHARGE {1}
and there is no *d* in that war........ Eccl 8:8 4917

DISCHARGED {1}
and will cause them to be *d* there........ 1Kin 5:9 5310

DISCIPLE {29}
The *d* is not above his master,........ Mt 10:24 *3101*
It is enough for the *d* that he be........ Mt 10:25 *3101*
water only in the name of a *d*........ Mt 10:42 *3101*
who also himself was Jesus' *d*........ Mt 27:57 *3100*
The *d* is not above his master........ Lk 6:40 *3101*
own life also, he cannot be my *d*........ Lk 14:26 *3101*
and come after me, cannot be my *d*........ Lk 14:27 *3101*
that he hath, he cannot be my *d*........ Lk 14:33 *3101*
him, and said, Thou art his *d*........ Jn 9:28 *3101*
Jesus, and so did another *d*........ Jn 18:15 *3101*
that *d* was known unto the high........ Jn 18:15 *3101*
Then went out that other *d*........ Jn 18:16 *3101*
the *d* standing by, whom he loved,........ Jn 19:26 *3101*
Then saith he to the *d*, Behold........ Jn 19:27 *3101*
from that hour that *d* took her........ Jn 19:27 *3101*
being a *d* of Jesus, but secretly........ Jn 19:38 *3101*
to Simon Peter, and to the other *d*........ Jn 20:2 *3101*
went forth, and that other *d*........ Jn 20:3 *3101*
the other *d* did outrun Peter, and........ Jn 20:4 *3101*
Then went in also that other *d*........ Jn 20:8 *3101*
Therefore that *d* whom Jesus loved........ Jn 21:7 *3101*
seeth the *d* whom Jesus loved........ Jn 21:20 *3101*
that that *d* should not die........ Jn 21:23 *3101*
This is the *d* which testifieth of........ Jn 21:24 *3101*
there was a certain *d* at Damascus........ Acts 9:10 *3101*
and believed not that he was a *d*........ Acts 9:26 *3101*
Joppa a certain *d* named Tabitha........ Acts 9:36 *3102*
and, behold, a certain *d* was there........ Acts 16:1 *3101*
one Mnason of Cyprus, an old *d*........ Acts 21:16 *3101*

DISCIPLES {243}
seal the law among my *d*........ Is 8:16 3928
he was set, his *d* came unto him........ Mt 5:1 *3101*
And another of his *d* said unto him........ Mt 8:21 *3101*
into a ship, his *d* followed him........ Mt 8:23 *3101*
his *d* came to him, and awoke him,........ Mt 8:25 *3101*
and sat down with him and his *d*........ Mt 9:10 *3101*
saw it, they said unto his *d*........ Mt 9:11 *3101*
Then came to him the *d* of John........ Mt 9:14 *3101*
fast oft, but thy *d* fast not........ Mt 9:14 *3101*
and followed him, and so did his *d*........ Mt 9:19 *3101*
Then saith he unto his *d*, The........ Mt 9:37 *3101*
had called unto him his twelve *d*........ Mt 10:1 *3101*
an end of commanding his twelve *d*........ Mt 11:1 *3101*
of Christ, he sent two of his *d*........ Mt 11:2 *3101*
his *d* were an hungred, and began........ Mt 12:1 *3101*
thy *d* do that which is not lawful........ Mt 12:2 *3101*
forth his hand toward his *d*........ Mt 12:49 *3101*
the *d* came, and said unto him, Why........ Mt 13:10 *3101*
his *d* came unto him, saying,........ Mt 13:36 *3101*
his *d* came, and took up the body,........ Mt 14:12 *3101*
his *d* came to him, saying, This........ Mt 14:15 *3101*
and gave the loaves to his *d*........ Mt 14:19 *3101*
and the *d* to the multitude........ Mt 14:19 *3101*
his *d* to get into a ship, and to........ Mt 14:22 *3101*
when the *d* saw him walking on the........ Mt 14:26 *3101*
Why do thy *d* transgress the........ Mt 15:2 *3101*
Then came his *d*, and said unto him........ Mt 15:12 *3101*
his *d* came and besought him,........ Mt 15:23 *3101*
Then Jesus called his *d* unto him........ Mt 15:32 *3101*
his *d* say unto him, Whence should........ Mt 15:33 *3101*
and brake them, and gave to his *d*........ Mt 15:36 *3101*
and the *d* to the multitude........ Mt 15:36 *3101*
when his *d* were come to the other........ Mt 16:5 *3101*
Caesarea Philippi, he asked his *d*........ Mt 16:13 *3101*
Then charged he his *d* that they........ Mt 16:20 *3101*
began Jesus to shew unto his *d*........ Mt 16:21 *3101*
Then said Jesus unto his *d*........ Mt 16:24 *3101*
And when the *d* heard it, they fell........ Mt 17:6 *3101*
his *d* asked him, saying, Why then........ Mt 17:10 *3101*
Then the *d* understood that he........ Mt 17:13 *3101*
And I brought him to thy *d*........ Mt 17:16 *3101*
Then came the *d* to Jesus apart,........ Mt 17:19 *3101*
same time came the *d* unto Jesus........ Mt 18:1 *3101*
His *d* say unto him, If the case........ Mt 19:10 *3101*
and the *d* rebuked them........ Mt 19:13 *3101*
Then said Jesus unto his *d*........ Mt 19:23 *3101*
When his *d* heard it, they were........ Mt 19:25 *3101*
the twelve *d* apart in the way........ Mt 20:17 *3101*
of Olives, then sent Jesus two *d*........ Mt 21:1 *3101*
the *d* went, and did as Jesus........ Mt 21:6 *3101*
And when the *d* saw it, they........ Mt 21:20 *3101*
him their *d* with the Herodians........ Mt 22:16 *3101*
to the multitude, and to his *d*........ Mt 23:1 *3101*
his *d* came to him for to shew him........ Mt 24:1 *3101*
the *d* came unto him privately,........ Mt 24:3 *3101*
these sayings, he said unto his *d*........ Mt 26:1 *3101*
But when his *d* saw it, they had........ Mt 26:8 *3101*
bread the *d* came to Jesus........ Mt 26:17 *3101*
passover at thy house with my *d*........ Mt 26:18 *3101*
the *d* did as Jesus had appointed........ Mt 26:19 *3101*
and brake it, and gave it to the *d*........ Mt 26:26 *3101*
Likewise also said all the *d*........ Mt 26:35 *3101*
Gethsemane, and saith unto the *d*........ Mt 26:36 *3101*
And he cometh unto the *d*, and........ Mt 26:40 *3101*
Then cometh he to his *d*, and saith........ Mt 26:45 *3101*
Then all the *d* forsook him........ Mt 26:56 *3101*
lest his *d* come by night, and........ Mt 27:64 *3101*
tell his *d* that he is risen from........ Mt 28:7 *3101*
and did run to bring his *d* word........ Mt 28:8 *3101*
And as they went to tell his *d*........ Mt 28:9 *3101*
His *d* came by night, and stole him........ Mt 28:13 *3101*
Then the eleven *d* went away into........ Mt 28:16 *3101*
also together with Jesus and his *d*........ Mk 2:15 *3101*
and sinners, they said unto his *d*........ Mk 2:16 *3101*
the *d* of John and of the Pharisees........ Mk 2:18 *3101*
unto him, Why do the *d* of John........ Mk 2:18 *3101*
fast, but thy *d* fast not........ Mk 2:18 *3101*
his *d* began, as they went, to........ Mk 2:23 *3101*
himself with his *d* to the sea........ Mk 3:7 *3101*
And he spake to his *d*, that a........ Mk 3:9 *3101*
he expounded all things to his *d*........ Mk 4:34 *3101*
his *d* said unto him, Thou seest........ Mk 5:31 *3101*
and his *d* follow him........ Mk 6:1 *3101*
when his *d* heard of it, they came........ Mk 6:29 *3101*
his *d* came unto him, and said,........ Mk 6:35 *3101*
gave them to his *d* to set before........ Mk 6:41 *3101*
his *d* to get into the ship........ Mk 6:45 *3101*
of his *d* eat bread with defiled........ Mk 7:2 *3101*
Why walk not thy *d* according to........ Mk 7:5 *3101*
his *d* asked him concerning the........ Mk 7:17 *3101*
eat, Jesus called his *d* unto him........ Mk 8:1 *3101*
his *d* answered him, From whence........ Mk 8:4 *3101*
gave to his *d* to set before them........ Mk 8:6 *3101*
he entered into a ship with his *d*........ Mk 8:10 *3101*
Now the *d* had forgotten to take........ Mk 8:14
And Jesus went out, and his *d*........ Mk 8:27 *3101*
and by the way he asked his *d*........ Mk 8:27 *3101*
turned about and looked on his *d*........ Mk 8:33 *3101*
people unto him with his *d* also........ Mk 8:34 *3101*
And when he came to his *d*, he saw........ Mk 9:14 *3101*
I spake to thy *d* that they should........ Mk 9:18 *3101*
his *d* asked him privately, Why........ Mk 9:28 *3101*
For he taught his *d*, and said unto........ Mk 9:31 *3101*
in the house his *d* asked him........ Mk 10:10 *3101*
his *d* rebuked those that brought........ Mk 10:13 *3101*
round about, and saith unto his *d*........ Mk 10:23 *3101*
the *d* were astonished at his........ Mk 10:24 *3101*
he went out of Jericho with his *d*........ Mk 10:46 *3101*
he sendeth forth two of his *d*........ Mk 11:1 *3101*
And his *d* heard it........ Mk 11:14 *3101*
And he called unto him his *d*........ Mk 12:43 *3101*
one of his *d* saith unto him,........ Mk 13:1 *3101*
his *d* said unto him, Where wilt........ Mk 14:12 *3101*
And he sendeth forth two of his *d*........ Mk 14:13 *3101*
shall eat the passover with my *d*........ Mk 14:14 *3101*
his *d* went forth, and came into........ Mk 14:16 *3101*
and he saith to his *d*, Sit ye here........ Mk 14:32 *3101*
But go your way, tell his *d*........ Mk 16:7 *3101*
Pharisees murmured against his *d*........ Lk 5:30 *3101*
Why do the *d* of John fast often,........ Lk 5:33 *3101*
likewise the *d* of the Pharisees........ Lk 5:33
his *d* plucked the ears of corn,........ Lk 6:1 *3101*
was day, he called unto him his *d*........ Lk 6:13 *3101*
plain, and the company of his *d*........ Lk 6:17 *3101*
And he lifted up his eyes on his *d*........ Lk 6:20 *3101*
many of his *d* went with him, and........ Lk 7:11 *3101*
the *d* of John shewed him of all........ Lk 7:18 *3101*
two of his *d* sent them to Jesus........ Lk 7:19 *3101*
his *d* asked him, saying, What........ Lk 8:9 *3101*
he went into a ship with his *d*........ Lk 8:22 *3101*
he called his twelve *d* together........ Lk 9:1 *3101*
And he said to his *d*, Make them........ Lk 9:14 *3101*
gave to the *d* to set before the........ Lk 9:16 *3101*
praying, his *d* were with him........ Lk 9:18 *3101*
I besought thy *d* to cast him out........ Lk 9:40 *3101*
Jesus did, he said unto his *d*........ Lk 9:43 *3101*
And when his *d* James and John saw........ Lk 9:54 *3101*
And he turned him unto his *d*........ Lk 10:23 *3101*
one of his *d* said unto him, Lord,........ Lk 11:1 *3101*
pray, as John also taught his *d*........ Lk 11:1 *3101*
to say unto his *d* first of all........ Lk 12:1 *3101*
And he said unto his *d*, Therefore........ Lk 12:22 *3101*
And he said also unto his *d*........ Lk 16:1 *3101*
Then said he unto the *d*, It is........ Lk 17:1 *3101*
And he said unto the *d*, The days........ Lk 17:22 *3101*
but when his *d* saw it, they........ Lk 18:15 *3101*
of Olives, he sent two of his *d*........ Lk 19:29 *3101*
of the *d* began to rejoice........ Lk 19:37 *3101*
unto him, Master, rebuke thy *d*........ Lk 19:39 *3101*
all the people he said unto his *d*........ Lk 20:45 *3101*
shall eat the passover with my *d*........ Lk 22:11 *3101*
and his *d* also followed him........ Lk 22:39 *3101*
from prayer, and was come to his *d*........ Lk 22:45 *3101*
after John stood, and two of his *d*........ Jn 1:35 *3101*
the two *d* heard him speak, and........ Jn 1:37 *3101*
both Jesus was called, and his *d*........ Jn 2:2 *3101*
and his *d* believed on him........ Jn 2:11 *3101*
mother, and his brethren, and his *d*........ Jn 2:12 *3101*
his *d* remembered that it was........ Jn 2:17 *3101*
his *d* remembered that he had said........ Jn 2:22 *3101*
his *d* into the land of Judaea........ Jn 3:22 *3101*
question between some of John's *d*........ Jn 3:25 *3101*
made and baptized more *d* than John........ Jn 4:1 *3101*
himself baptized not, but his *d*........ Jn 4:2 *3101*
(For his *d* were gone away unto........ Jn 4:8 *3101*
And upon this came his *d*, and........ Jn 4:27 *3101*
the mean while his *d* prayed him........ Jn 4:31 *3101*
said the *d* one to another........ Jn 4:33 *3101*
and there he sat with his *d*........ Jn 6:3 *3101*
One of his *d*, Andrew, Simon........ Jn 6:8 *3101*
thanks, he distributed to the *d*........ Jn 6:11 *3101*
the *d* to them that were set down........ Jn 6:11 *3101*
were filled, he said unto his *d*........ Jn 6:12 *3101*
his *d* went down unto the sea,........ Jn 6:16 *3101*
one whereinto his *d* were entered........ Jn 6:22 *3101*
went not with his *d* into the boat........ Jn 6:22 *3101*
but that his *d* were gone away........ Jn 6:22 *3101*
was not there, neither his *d*........ Jn 6:24 *3101*
Many therefore of his *d*, when........ Jn 6:60 *3101*
himself that his *d* murmured at it........ Jn 6:61 *3101*
that time many of his *d* went back........ Jn 6:66 *3101*
that thy *d* also may see the works........ Jn 7:3 *3101*
my word, then are ye my *d* indeed........ Jn 8:31 *3101*
his *d* asked him, saying, Master,........ Jn 9:2 *3101*
will ye also be his *d*........ Jn 9:27 *3101*
but we are Moses' *d*........ Jn 9:28 *3101*
Then after that saith he to his *d*........ Jn 11:7 *3101*
His *d* say unto him, Master, the........ Jn 11:8 *3101*
Then said his *d*, Lord, if he........ Jn 11:12 *3101*
and there continued with his *d*........ Jn 11:54 *3101*
Then saith one of his *d*, Judas........ Jn 12:4 *3101*
understood not his *d* at the first........ Jn 12:16 *3101*
Then the *d* looked one on another,........ Jn 13:22 *3101*
on Jesus' bosom one of his *d*........ Jn 13:23 *3101*
all men know that ye are my *d*........ Jn 13:35 *3101*
so shall ye be my *d*........ Jn 15:8 *3101*
some of his *d* among themselves........ Jn 16:17 *3101*
His *d* said unto him, Lo, now........ Jn 16:29 *3101*
with his *d* over the brook Cedron........ Jn 18:1 *3101*

D

the which he entered, and his *d* ... Jn 18:1 *3101*
resorted thither with his *d* ... Jn 18:2 *3101*
not thou also one of this man's *d* ... Jn 18:17 *3101*
priest then asked Jesus of his *d* ... Jn 18:19 *3101*
Art not thou also one of his *d* ... Jn 18:25 *3101*
Then the *d* went away again unto ... Jn 20:10 *3101*
told the *d* that she had seen the ... Jn 20:18 *3101*
the doors were shut where the *d* ... Jn 20:19 *3101*
Then were the *d* glad, when they ... Jn 20:20 *3101*
The other *d* therefore said unto ... Jn 20:25 *3101*
days again his *d* were within ... Jn 20:26 *3101*
Jesus in the presence of his *d* ... Jn 20:30 *3101*
to the *d* at the sea of Tiberias ... Jn 21:1 *3101*
of Zebedee, and two other of his *d* ... Jn 21:2 *3101*
but the *d* knew not that it was ... Jn 21:4 *3101*
the other *d* came in a little ship ... Jn 21:8 *3101*
none of the *d* durst ask him, Who ... Jn 21:12 *3101*
Jesus shewed himself to his *d* ... Jn 21:14 *3101*
stood up in the midst of the *d* ... Acts 1:15 *3101*
number of the *d* was multiplied ... Acts 6:1 *3101*
the multitude of the *d* unto them ... Acts 6:2 *3101*
the number of the *d* multiplied in ... Acts 6:7 *3101*
against the *d* of the Lord ... Acts 9:1 *3101*
with the *d* which were at Damascus ... Acts 9:19 *3101*
Then the *d* took him by night, and ... Acts 9:25 *3101*
assayed to join himself to the *d* ... Acts 9:26 *3101*
the *d* had heard that Peter was ... Acts 9:38 *3101*
the *d* were called Christians ... Acts 11:26 *3101*
Then the *d*, every man according ... Acts 11:29 *3101*
the *d* were filled with joy, and ... Acts 13:52 *3101*
as the *d* stood round about him, ... Acts 14:20 *3101*
Confirming the souls of the *d* ... Acts 14:22 *3101*
they abode long time with the *d* ... Acts 14:28 *3101*
put a yoke upon the neck of the *d* ... Acts 15:10 *3101*
in order, strengthening all the *d* ... Acts 18:23 *3101*
exhorting the *d* to receive him ... Acts 18:27 *3101*
and finding certain *d*, ... Acts 19:1 *3101*
from them, and separated the *d* ... Acts 19:9 *3101*
people, the *d* suffered him not ... Acts 19:30 *3101*
Paul called unto him the *d* ... Acts 20:1 *3101*
when the *d* came together to break ... Acts 20:7 *3101*
things, to draw away *d* after them ... Acts 20:30 *3101*
And finding *d*, we tarried there ... Acts 21:4 *3101*
also certain of the *d* of Caesarea ... Acts 21:16 *3101*

DISCIPLES' {1}
and began to wash the *d* feet ... Jn 13:5 *3101*

DISCIPLINE {1}
He openeth also their ear to *d* ... Job 36:10 4148

DISCLOSE {1}
the earth also shall *d* her blood ... Is 26:21 1540

DISCOMFITED {9}
And Joshua *d* Amalek and his people ... Ex 17:13 2522
them, and *d* them, even unto Hormah ... Num 14:45 3807
the LORD *d* them before Israel, and ... Josh 10:10 1949
And the LORD *d* Sisera, and all his ... Judg 4:15 2000
and Zalmunna, and *d* all the host ... Judg 8:12 2729
upon the Philistines, and *d* them ... 1Sa 7:10 1949
lightning, and *d* them ... 2Sa 22:15 2000
he shot out lightnings, and *d* them ... Ps 18:14 1949
and his young men shall be *d* ... Is 31:8 4522

DISCOMFITURE {1}
and there was a very great *d* ... 1Sa 14:20 4103

DISCONTENTED {1}
in debt, and every one that was *d* ... 1Sa 22:2 4751,5315

DISCONTINUE {1}
shalt *d* from thine heritage that ... Jer 17:4 8058

DISCORD {2}
he soweth *d* ... Prov 6:14 4066
he that soweth *d* among brethren ... Prov 6:19 4090

DISCOURAGE {1}
wherefore *d* ye the heart of the ... Num 32:7 5106

DISCOURAGED {6}
was much *d* because of the way ... Num 21:4 7114
they *d* the heart of the children ... Num 32:9 5106
fear not, neither be *d* ... Deut 1:21 2865
our brethren have *d* our heart ... Deut 1:28 4549
He shall not fail nor be *d* ... Is 42:4 7533
children to anger, lest they be *d* ... Col 3:21 *120*

DISCOVER {12}
wife, nor *d* his father's skirt ... Deut 22:30 1540
we will *d* ourselves unto them ... 1Sa 14:8 1540
Who can *d* the face of his garment ... Job 41:13 1540
but that his heart may *d* itself ... Prov 18:2 1540
d not a secret to another ... Prov 25:9 1540
the LORD will *d* their secret ... Is 3:17 6168
Therefore will I *d* thy skirts ... Jer 13:26 2834
he will *d* thy sins ... Lam 4:22 1540
will *d* thy nakedness unto them, ... Eze 16:37 1540
now will I *d* her lewdness in the ... Hos 2:10 1540
I will *d* the foundations thereof ... Mic 1:6 1540
I will *d* thy skirts upon thy face ... Nah 3:5 1540

DISCOVERED {22}
thy nakedness be not *d* thereon ... Ex 20:26 1540
he hath *d* her fountain, and she ... Lev 20:18 6168
both of them *d* themselves unto ... 1Sa 14:11 1540
When Saul heard that David was *d* ... 1Sa 22:6 3045
foundations of the world were *d* ... 2Sa 22:16 1540
of the world were *d* at thy rebuke ... Ps 18:15 1540
he *d* the covering of Judah, and ... Is 22:8 1540
for thou hast *d* thyself to ... Is 57:8 1540
thine iniquity are thy skirts *d* ... Jer 13:22 1540
they have not *d* thine iniquity, ... Lam 2:14 1540
the foundation thereof shall be *d* ... Eze 13:14 1540
thy nakedness *d* through thy ... Eze 16:36 1540
Before thy wickedness was *d* ... Eze 16:57 1540
in that your transgressions are *d* ... Eze 21:24 1540
In thee have they *d* their ... Eze 22:10 1540
These *d* her nakedness ... Eze 23:10 1540
So she *d* her whoredoms, and ... Eze 23:18 1540
her whoredoms, and *d* her nakedness ... Eze 23:18 1540
of thy whoredoms shall be *d* ... Eze 23:29 1540
the iniquity of Ephraim was *d* ... Hos 7:1 1540
Now when we had *d* Cyprus, we left ... Acts 21:3 *398*
but they *d* a certain creek with a ... Acts 27:39 *2657*

DISCOVERETH {2}
He *d* deep things out of darkness, ... Job 12:22 1540
hinds to calve, and *d* the forests ... Ps 29:9 2834

DISCOVERING {1}
by *d* the foundation unto the neck ... Hab 3:13 6168

DISCREET {3}
let Pharaoh look out a man *d* ... Gen 41:33 995
thee all this, there is none so *d* ... Gen 41:39 995
To be *d*, chaste, keepers at home, ... Titus 2:5 *4998*

DISCREETLY {1}
when Jesus saw that he answered *d* ... Mk 12:34 *3562*

DISCRETION {9}
he will guide his affairs with *d* ... Ps 112:5 4941
to the young man knowledge and *d* ... Prov 1:4 4209
D shall preserve thee, ... Prov 2:11 4209
keep sound wisdom and *d* ... Prov 3:21 4209
That thou mayest regard *d* ... Prov 5:2 4209
a fair woman which is without *d* ... Prov 11:22 2940
The *d* of a man deferreth his ... Prov 19:11 7922
his God doth instruct him to *d* ... Is 28:26 4941
out the heavens by his *d* ... Jer 10:12 8394

DISDAINED {2}
about, and saw David, he *d* him ... 1Sa 17:42 959
whose fathers I would have *d* to ... Job 30:1 3988

DISEASE {15}
whether I shall recover of this *d* ... 2Kin 1:2 2483
saying, Shall I recover of this *d* ... 2Kin 8:8 2483
saying, Shall I recover of this *d* ... 2Kin 8:9 2483
until his *d* was exceeding great ... 2Chr 16:12 2483
yet in his *d* he sought not to the ... 2Chr 16:12 2483
great sickness by *d* of thy bowels ... 2Chr 21:15 4245
in his bowels with an incurable *d* ... 2Chr 21:18 2483
of my *d* is my garment changed ... Job 30:18
are filled with a loathsome *d* ... Ps 38:7
An evil *d*, say they, cleaveth ... Ps 41:8 1697
is vanity, and it is an evil *d* ... Eccl 6:2 2483
all manner of *d* among the people ... Mt 4:23 *3119*
and every *d* among the people ... Mt 9:35 *3119*
of sickness and all manner of *d* ... Mt 10:1 *3119*
made whole of whatsoever *d* he had ... Jn 5:4 *3553*

DISEASED {8}
his old age he was *d* in his feet ... 1Kin 15:23 2470
of his reign was *d* in his feet ... 2Chr 16:12 2470
The *d* have ye not strengthened, ... Eze 34:4 2456
pushed all the *d* with your horns, ... Eze 34:21 2456
which was *d* with an issue of ... Mt 9:20
brought unto him all that were *d* ... Mt 14:35 *2560,2192*
brought unto him all that were *d* ... Mk 1:32 *2560,2192*
which he did on them that were *d* ... Jn 6:2 *770*

DISEASES {13}
put none of these *d* upon thee ... Ex 15:26 4245
put none of the evil *d* of Egypt ... Deut 7:15 4064
upon thee all the *d* of Egypt ... Deut 28:60 4064
so he died of sore *d* ... 2Chr 21:19 8463
(for they left him in great *d* ... 2Chr 24:25 4251
who healeth all thy *d* ... Ps 103:3 8463
that were taken with divers *d* ... Mt 4:24 *3554*
many that were sick of divers *d* ... Mk 1:34 *3554*
divers *d* brought them unto him ... Lk 4:40 *3554*
him, and to be healed of their *d* ... Lk 6:17 *3554*
over all devils, and to cure *d* ... Lk 9:1 *3554*
the *d* departed from them, and the ... Acts 19:12 *3554*
which had *d* in the island, came, ... Acts 28:9 *769*

DISFIGURE {1}
for they *d* their faces, that they ... Mt 6:16 *853*

DISGRACE {1}
do not *d* the throne of thy glory ... Jer 14:21 5034

DISGUISE {3}
d thyself, that thou be not known ... 1Kin 14:2 8138
unto Jehoshaphat, I will *d* myself ... 1Kin 22:30 2664
unto Jehoshaphat, I will *d* myself ... 2Chr 18:29 2664

DISGUISED {5}
Saul *d* himself, and put on other ... 1Sa 28:8 2664
d himself with ashes upon his ... 1Kin 20:38 2664
And the king of Israel *d* himself ... 1Kin 22:30 2664
So the king of Israel *d* himself ... 2Chr 18:29 2664
but *d* himself, that he might ... 2Chr 35:22 2664

DISGUISETH {1}
and *d* his face ... Job 24:15 5643

DISH {4}
forth butter in a lordly *d* ... Judg 5:25 5602
Jerusalem as a man wipeth a *d* ... 2Kin 21:13 6747
dippeth his hand with me in the *d* ... Mt 26:23 *5165*
that dippeth with me in the *d* ... Mk 14:20 *5165*

DISHAN *(di'-shan)* {5} See DISHON. *A son of Seir.*
And Dishon, and Ezer, and *D* ... Gen 36:21 1789
The children of *D* are these ... Gen 36:28 1789
Duke Dishon, duke Ezer, duke *D* ... Gen 36:30 1789
Anah, and Dishon, and Ezar, and *D* ... 1Chr 1:38 1789
The sons of *D* ... 1Chr 1:42 1789

DISHES {3}
And thou shalt make the *d* thereof ... Ex 25:29 7086
which were upon the table, his *d* ... Ex 37:16 7086
of blue, and put thereon the *d* ... Num 4:7 7086

DISHON *(di'-shon)* {7} See DISHAN.
1. A son of Seir.
And *D*, and Ezer, and Dishan ... Gen 36:21 1788
And these are the children of *D* ... Gen 36:26 1788
Duke *D*, duke Ezer, duke Dishan ... Gen 36:30 1788
Shobal, and Zibeon, and Anah, and *D* ... 1Chr 1:38 1788
2. A son of Anah.
D, and Aholibamah the daughter of ... Gen 36:25 1788
The sons of Anah; *D* ... 1Chr 1:41 1788
And the sons of *D* ... 1Chr 1:41 1788

DISHONEST {2}
thy *d* gain which thou hast made ... Eze 22:13 1215
to destroy souls, to get *d* gain ... Eze 22:27 1215

DISHONESTY {1}
renounced the hidden things of *d* ... 2Cor 4:2 *152*

DISHONOUR {11}
meet for us to see the king's *d* ... Ezr 4:14 6173
d that magnify themselves against ... Ps 35:26 3639
and my shame, and my *d* ... Ps 69:19 3639
reproach and *d* that seek my hurt ... Ps 71:13 3639
A wound and *d* shall he get ... Prov 6:33 7036
I honour my Father, and ye do *d* me ... Jn 8:49 *818*
to *d* their own bodies between ... Rom 1:24 *818*
unto honour, and another unto *d* ... Rom 9:21 *819*
It is sown in *d* ... 1Cor 15:43 *819*
By honour and *d*, by evil report and ... 2Cor 6:8 *819*
and some to honour, and some to *d* ... 2Ti 2:20 *819*

DISHONOUREST {1}
breaking the law *d* thou God ... Rom 2:23 *818*

DISHONOURETH {3}
For the son *d* the father, the ... Mic 7:6 5034
his head covered, *d* his head ... 1Cor 11:4 *2617*
her head uncovered *d* her head ... 1Cor 11:5 *2617*

DISINHERIT {1}
d them, and will make of thee a ... Num 14:12 3423

DISMAYED {31}
fear not, neither be *d* ... Deut 31:8 2865
be not afraid, neither be thou *d* ... Josh 1:9 2865
Fear not, neither be thou *d* ... Josh 8:1 2865
unto them, Fear not, nor be *d* ... Josh 10:25 2865
of the Philistine, they were *d* ... 1Sa 17:11 2865
were of small power, they were *d* ... 2Kin 19:26 2865
dread not, nor be *d* ... 1Chr 22:13 2865
fear not, nor be *d* ... 1Chr 28:20 2865
Be not afraid nor *d* by reason of ... 2Chr 20:15 2865
fear not, nor be *d* ... 2Chr 20:17 2865
be not afraid nor *d* for the king ... 2Chr 32:7 2865
I was *d* at the seeing of it ... Is 21:3 926
were of small power, they were *d* ... Is 37:27 2865
be not *d* ... Is 41:10 8159
or do evil, that we may be *d* ... Is 41:23 8159
be not *d* at their faces, lest I ... Jer 1:17 2865
wise men are ashamed, they are *d* ... Jer 8:9 2865
be not *d* at the signs of heaven ... Jer 10:2 2865
for the heathen are *d* at them ... Jer 10:2 2865
be *d*, but let not me be *d* ... Jer 17:18 2865
they shall fear no more, nor be *d* ... Jer 23:4 2865
neither be *d*, O Israel ... Jer 30:10 2865
Wherefore have I seen them *d* ... Jer 46:5 2844
O my servant Jacob, and be not *d* ... Jer 46:27 2865
Misgab is confounded and *d* ... Jer 48:1 2865
Elam to be *d* before their enemies ... Jer 49:37 2865
and they shall be *d* ... Jer 50:36 2865
nor be *d* at their looks, though ... Eze 2:6 2865
neither be *d* at their looks, ... Eze 3:9 2865
mighty men, O Teman, shall be *d* ... Obad 9 2865

DISMAYING {1}
a *d* to all them about him ... Jer 48:39 4288

DISMISSED {3}
the priest *d* not the courses ... 2Chr 23:8 6362
So when they were *d*, they came to ... Acts 15:30 *630*
thus spoken, he *d* the assembly ... Acts 19:41 *630*

DISOBEDIENCE {6}
For as by one man's *d* many were ... Rom 5:19 *3876*
in a readiness to revenge all *d* ... 2Cor 10:6 *3876*
now worketh in the children of *d* ... Eph 2:2 *543*
of God upon the children of *d* ... Eph 5:6 *543*
God cometh on the children of *d* ... Col 3:6 *543*
d received a just recompence of ... Heb 2:2 *3876*

DISOBEDIENT {13}
who was *d* unto the word of the ... 1Kin 13:26 4784
Nevertheless they were *d*, and ... Neh 9:26 4784
the *d* to the wisdom of the just ... Lk 1:17 *545*
I was not *d* unto the heavenly ... Acts 26:19 *545*
of evil things, *d* to parents, ... Rom 1:30 *545*
stretched forth my hands unto a *d* ... Rom 10:21 *544*
man, but for the lawless and *d* ... 1Ti 1:9 *506*
d to parents, unthankful, unholy, ... 2Ti 3:2 *545*
deny him, being abominable, and *d* ... Titus 1:16 *545*
also were sometimes foolish, *d* ... Titus 3:3 *545*
but unto them which be *d*, the ... 1Pet 2:7 *544*
stumble at the word, being *d* ... 1Pet 2:8 *544*
Which sometime were *d*, when once ... 1Pet 3:20 *544*

DISOBEYED {1}
thou hast *d* the mouth of the LORD ... 1Kin 13:21 4784

DISORDERLY {3}
from every brother that walketh *d* ... 2Th 3:6 *814*
behaved not ourselves *d* among you ... 2Th 3:7 *812*
are some which walk among you *d* ... 2Th 3:11 *814*

DISPATCH {1}
and *d* them with their swords .... Eze 23:47 1254

DISPENSATION {4}
a *d* of the gospel is committed 1Cor 9:17 *3622*
That in the *d* of the fulness of................ Eph 1:10 *3622*
If ye have heard of the *d* of the .... Eph 3:2 *3622*
according to the *d* of God which............. Col 1:25 *3622*

DISPERSE {8}
D yourselves among the people, and....... 1Sa 14:34 6327
The lips of the wise *d* knowledge........... Prov 15:7 2219
and *d* them in the countries .... Eze 12:15 2219
d them through the countries.................. Eze 20:23 2219
d thee in the countries, and will .... Eze 22:15 2219
will *d* them through the countries........... Eze 29:12 2219
will *d* them through the countries........... Eze 30:23 2219
d them among the countries .... Eze 30:26 2219

DISPERSED {10}
d of all his children throughout 2Chr 11:23 6555
d among the people in all the.................. Est 3:8 6504
He hath *d*, he hath given to the................ Ps 112:9 6340
Let thy fountains be *d* abroad.................. Prov 5:16 6327
gather together the *d* of Judah................ Is 11:12 5310
they were *d* through the countries .... Eze 36:19 2219
even the daughter of my *d*....................... Zeph 3:10 6327
go unto the *d* among the Gentiles .... Jn 7:35 *1290*
as many as obeyed him, were *d*................ Acts 5:37 *1287*
it is written, He hath *d* abroad 2Cor 9:9 *4650*

DISPERSIONS {1}
of your *d* are accomplished .... Jer 25:34 8600

DISPLAYED {1}
that it may be *d* because of the .... Ps 60:4 5127

DISPLEASE {5}
Let it not *d* my lord that I....................... Gen 31:35 2734
now therefore, if it *d* thee............... Num 22:34 7489,5869
that thou *d* not the lords of the 1Sa 29:7 6213,7451,5869
Joab, Let not this thing *d* thee 2Sa 11:25 7489,5869
it *d* him, and he turn away his .... Prov 24:18 7489,5869

DISPLEASED {25}
thing which he did *d* the LORD....... Gen 38:10 7489,5869
the head of Ephraim, it *d* him......... Gen 48:17 7489,5869
people complained, it *d* the LORD .. Num 11:1 7451,241
Moses also was *d* .... Num 11:10
the thing *d* Samuel, when they 1Sa 8:6 7489,5869
very wroth, and the saying *d* him.... 1Sa 18:8 7489,5869
And David was *d*, because the LORD...... 2Sa 6:8 2734
that David had done *d* the LORD.... 2Sa 11:27 7489,5869
his father had not *d* him at any 1Kin 1:6 6087
went to his house heavy and *d* 1Kin 20:43 2198
d because of the word which................... 1Kin 21:4 2198
And David was *d*, because the LORD...... 1Chr 13:11 2734
God was *d* with this thing.............. 1Chr 21:7 3415,5869
scattered us, thou hast been *d*............... Ps 60:1 599
it *d* him that there was no.............. Is 59:15 7489,5869
was sore *d* with himself, and set .... Dan 6:14 888
it *d* Jonah exceedingly, and he......... Jonah 4:1 7489,5869
Was the LORD *d* against the rivers .... Hab 3:8 2734
been sore *d* with your fathers................. Zec 1:2 7107
I am very sore *d* with the heathen.......... Zec 1:15 7107
for I was but a little *d*, and they .... Zec 1:15 7107
they were sore *d*,... Mt 21:15 *23*
when Jesus saw it, he was much *d* .... Mk 10:14 *23*
began to be much *d* with James .... Mk 10:41 *23*
Herod was highly *d* with them of............ Acts 12:20 *2371*

DISPLEASURE {5}
was afraid of the anger and hot *d*........... Deut 9:19 2534
Philistines, though I do them a *d*............ Judg 15:3 7451
wrath, and vex them in his sore *d*........... Ps 2:5 2740
neither chasten me in thy hot *d* .... Ps 6:1 2534
neither chasten me in thy hot *d* .... Ps 38:1 2534

DISPOSED {4}
Or who hath *d* the whole world .... Job 34:13 7760
Dost thou know when God *d* them .... Job 37:15 7760
when he was *d* to pass into Achaia .... Acts 18:27 *1014*
you to a feast, and ye be *d* to go 1Cor 10:27 *2309*

DISPOSING {1}
but the whole *d* thereof is of the............. Prov 16:33 4941

DISPOSITION {1}
the law by the *d* of angels .... Acts 7:53 *1296*

DISPOSSESS {2}
ye shall *d* the inhabitants of the .... Num 33:53 3423
how can I *d* them.. Deut 7:17 3423

DISPOSSESSED {2}
d the Amorite which was in it.................. Num 32:39 3423
d the Amorites from before his .... Judg 11:23 3423

DISPUTATION {1}
d with them, they determined that .... Acts 15:2 *4803*

DISPUTATIONS {1}
receive ye, but not to doubtful *d*............ Rom 14:1 *1253*

DISPUTE {1}
the righteous might *d* with him .... Job 23:7 3198

DISPUTED {5}
What was it that ye *d* among .... Mk 9:33 *1260*
way they had *d* among themselves.......... Mk 9:34 *1256*
Jesus, and *d* against the Grecians .... Acts 9:29 *4802*
Therefore *d* he in the synagogue .... Acts 17:17 *1256*
he *d* about the body of Moses.................. Jude 9 *1256*

DISPUTER {1}
where is the *d* of this world 1Cor 1:20 *4804*

DISPUTING {5}
and of Asia, *d* with Stephen.................... Acts 6:9 *4802*
And when there had been much *d* .... Acts 15:7 *4803*
for the space of three months, *d*............ Acts 19:8 *1256*
d daily in the school of one .... Acts 19:9 *1256*
me in the temple *d* with any man .... Acts 24:12 *1256*

DISPUTINGS {2}
things without murmurings and *d* .... Phil 2:14 *1261*
Perverse *d* of men of corrupt................... 1Ti 6:5 *3859*

DISQUIET {1}
d the inhabitants of Babylon.................. Jer 50:34 7264

DISQUIETED {6}
said to Saul, Why hast thou *d* me 1Sa 28:15 7264
surely they are *d* in vain......................... Ps 39:6 1993
and why art thou *d* in me........................ Ps 42:5 1993
and why art thou *d* within me................ Ps 42:11 1993
and why art thou *d* within me................ Ps 43:5 1993
For three things the earth is *d*.............. Prov 30:21 7264

DISQUIETNESS {1}
by reason of the *d* of my heart .... Ps 38:8 5100

DISSEMBLED {3}
d also, and they have put it even .... Josh 7:11 3584
For ye *d* in your hearts, when ye............. Jer 42:20 8582
the other Jews *d* likewise with .... Gal 2:13 *4942*

DISSEMBLERS {1}
neither will I go in with *d* .... Ps 26:4 5956

DISSEMBLETH {1}
He that hateth *d* with his lips .... Prov 26:24 5234

DISSENSION {3}
Paul and Barnabas had no small *d*.......... Acts 15:2 *4714*
there arose a *d* between the.................... Acts 23:7 *4714*
And when there arose a great *d* .... Acts 23:10 *4714*

DISSIMULATION {2}
Let love be without *d*.............................. Rom 12:9 *505*
was carried away with their *d*................ Gal 2:13 *5272*

DISSOLVE {1}
make interpretations, and *d* doubts .... Dan 5:16 8271

DISSOLVED {8}
all the inhabitants thereof are *d* .... Ps 75:3 4127
thou, whole Palestina, art *d* .... Is 14:31 4127
broken down, the earth is clean *d*............ Is 24:19 6565
all the host of heaven shall be *d*............. Is 34:4 4743
opened, and the palace shall be *d* .... Nah 2:6 4127
house of this tabernacle were *d*.............. 2Cor 5:1 *2647*
that all these things shall be *d*................ 2Pet 3:11 *3089*
heavens being on fire shall be *d*.............. 2Pet 3:12 *3089*

DISSOLVEST {1}
ride upon it, and *d* my substance........... Job 30:22 4127

DISSOLVING {1}
d of doubts, were found in the .... Dan 5:12 8271

DISTAFF {1}
spindle, and her hands hold the *d*........... Prov 31:19 6418

DISTANT {1}
equally *d* one from another .... Ex 36:22 7947

DISTIL {2}
my speech shall *d* as the dew .... Deut 32:2 5140
do drop and *d* upon man abundantly....... Job 36:28 7491

DISTINCTION {1}
they give a *d* in the sounds..................... 1Cor 14:7 *1293*

DISTINCTLY {1}
in the book in the law of God *d* .... Neh 8:8 6567

DISTRACTED {1}
while I suffer thy terrors I am *d*............. Ps 88:15 6323

DISTRACTION {1}
attend upon the Lord without *d*.............. 1Cor 7:35 *563*

DISTRESS {33}
answered me in the day of my *d*.............. Gen 35:3 6869
therefore is this *d* come upon us .... Gen 42:21 6869
D not the Moabites, neither .... Deut 2:9 6696
d them not, nor meddle with them.......... Deut 2:19 6696
thine enemies shall *d* thee .... Deut 28:53 6693
shall *d* thee in all thy gates .... Deut 28:55 6693
enemy shall *d* thee in thy gates .... Deut 28:57 6693
come unto me now when ye are in *d*......... Judg 11:7 6887
And every one that was in *d*.................... 1Sa 22:2 4689
In my *d* I called upon the LORD,.............. 2Sa 22:7 6862
redeemed my soul out of all *d* 1Kin 1:29 6869
in the time of his *d* did he...................... 2Chr 28:22 6887
Ye see the *d* that we are in, how............. Neh 2:17 7451
pleasure, and we are in great *d*.............. Neh 9:37 6869
hast enlarged me when I was in *d*........... Ps 4:1 6862
In my *d* I called upon the LORD,............... Ps 18:6 6862
I called upon the LORD in *d* .... Ps 118:5 4712
In my *d* I cried unto the LORD, and......... Ps 120:1 6869
when *d* and anguish cometh upon you.... Prov 1:27 6869
a strength to the needy in his *d*.............. Is 25:4 6862
Yet I will *d* Ariel, and there .... Is 29:2 6693
and her munition, and that *d* her........... Is 29:7 6693
land at this once, and will *d* them .... Jer 10:18 6887
for I am in *d* .... Lam 1:20 6887
spoken proudly in the day of *d*............... Obad 12 6869
that did remain in the day of *d*.............. Obad 14 6869
of wrath, a day of trouble and *d* .... Zeph 1:15 4691
And I will bring *d* upon men.................. Zeph 1:17 6887
shall be great *d* in the land .... Lk 21:23 *318*
and upon the earth of *d* of nations.......... Lk 21:25 *4928*
shall tribulation, or *d*, or......................... Rom 8:35 *4730*
this is good for the present *d*................. 1Cor 7:26 *318*
our affliction and *d* by your faith 1Th 3:7 *318*

DISTRESSED {11}
Jacob was greatly afraid and *d* .... Gen 32:7 3334
Moab was *d* because of the .... Num 22:3 6973
and they were greatly *d*......................... Judg 2:15 3334
so that Israel was sore *d*......................... Judg 10:9 3334
a strait, (for the people were *d*............... 1Sa 13:6 5065
the men of Israel were *d* that day 1Sa 14:24 5065
And Saul answered, I am sore *d*............. 1Sa 28:15 6887
And David was greatly *d*........................ 1Sa 30:6 3334
I am *d* for thee, my brother 2Sa 1:26 6887
d him, but strengthened him not............ 2Chr 28:20 6696
troubled on every side, yet not *d*............ 2Cor 4:8 *4729*

DISTRESSES {8}
O bring thou me out of my *d*................... Ps 25:17 4691
he delivered them out of their *d*............. Ps 107:6 4691
and he saved them out of their *d* .... Ps 107:13 4691
and he saveth them out of their *d* .... Ps 107:19 4691
he bringeth them out of their *d*.............. Ps 107:28 4691
and Noph shall have *d* daily................... Eze 30:16 6862
afflictions, in necessities, in *d* 2Cor 6:4 *4730*
in *d* for Christ's sake 2Cor 12:10 *4730*

DISTRIBUTE {5}
d for inheritance in the plains................ Josh 13:32 5157
to *d* the oblations of the LORD,................ 2Chr 31:14 5414
was to *d* unto their brethren .... Neh 13:13 2505
d unto the poor, and thou shalt.............. Lk 18:22 *1239*
be rich in good works, ready to *d*........... 1Ti 6:18 *2130*

DISTRIBUTED {6}
d for inheritance to them .... Josh 14:1 5157
And David *d* them, both Zadok of.......... 1Chr 24:3 2505
whom David had *d* in the house of 2Chr 23:18 2505
he *d* to the disciples, and the .... Jn 6:11 *1239*
But as God hath *d* to every man 1Cor 7:17 *3307*
the rule which God hath *d* to us 2Cor 10:13 *3307*

DISTRIBUTETH {1}
God *d* sorrows in his anger .... Job 21:17 2505

DISTRIBUTING {1}
D to the necessity of saints .... Rom 12:13 *2841*

DISTRIBUTION {2}
d was made unto every man.................... Acts 4:35 *1239*
and for your liberal *d* unto them............ 2Cor 9:13 *2842*

DITCH {6}
Yet shalt thou plunge me in the *d*........... Job 9:31 7845
fallen into the *d* which he made.............. Ps 7:15 7845
For a whore is a deep *d* .... Prov 23:27 7745
Ye made also a *d* between the two .... Is 22:11 4724
blind, both shall fall into the *d* .... Mt 15:14 *999*
they not both fall into the *d*.................... Lk 6:39 *999*

DITCHES {1}
LORD, Make this valley full of *d*............. 2Kin 3:16 1356

DIVERS {37}
not sow thy vineyard with *d* seeds.......... Deut 22:9 3610
not wear a garment of *d* sorts .... Deut 22:11 8162
not have in thy bag *d* weights .... Deut 25:13
have in thine house *d* measures............... Deut 25:14
to Sisera a prey of *d* colours .... Judg 5:30 6648
a prey of *d* colours of needlework........... Judg 5:30 6648
of *d* colours of needlework on .... Judg 5:30 6648
a garment of *d* colours upon her............ 2Sa 13:18 6446
rent her garment of *d* colours 2Sa 13:19 6446
of *d* colours, and all manner of.............. 1Chr 29:2 7553
d kinds of spices prepared by the........... 2Chr 16:14
d also of the princes of Israel................ 2Chr 21:4
Nevertheless *d* of Asher and.................... 2Chr 30:11 582
He sent *d* sorts of flies among .... Ps 78:45
there came *d* sorts of flies, and .... Ps 105:31
D weights, and *d* measures,..................... Prov 20:10
D weights are an abomination unto........ Prov 20:23
words there are also *d* vanities............... Eccl 5:7
thy high places with *d* colours .... Eze 16:16 2921
of feathers, which had *d* colours .... Eze 17:3 7553
that were taken with *d* diseases .... Mt 4:24 *4164*
and earthquakes, in *d* places.................. Mt 24:7
many that were sick of *d* diseases.......... Mk 1:34 *4164*
for *d* of them came from far.................... Mk 8:3 *5100*
shall be earthquakes in *d* places .... Mk 13:8
d diseases brought them unto him.......... Lk 4:40 *4164*
earthquakes shall be in *d* places .... Lk 21:11
But when *d* were hardened, and .... Acts 19:9 *5100*
to another *d* kinds of tongues 1Cor 12:10
with sins, led away with *d* lusts 2Ti 3:6 *4164*
deceived, serving *d* lusts .... Titus 3:3 *4164*
in *d* manners spake in time past .... Heb 1:1 *4187*
with *d* miracles, and gifts of the .... Heb 2:4 *4164*
d washings, and carnal ordinances,......... Heb 9:10 *1313*
Be not carried about with *d*..................... Heb 13:9 *4164*
when ye fall into *d* temptations .... Jas 1:2 *4164*

DIVERSE {8}
thy cattle gender with a *d* kind............... Lev 19:19 3610
vessels being *d* one from another .... Est 1:7 8138
their laws are *d* from all people .... Est 3:8 8138
from the sea, *d* one from another............ Dan 7:3 8133
it was *d* from all the beasts that .... Dan 7:7 8133
which was *d* from all the others,............. Dan 7:19 8133
which shall be *d* from all .... Dan 7:23 8133
he shall be *d* from the first, and............. Dan 7:24 8133

DIVERSITIES {3}
Now there are *d* of gifts, but the............. 1Cor 12:4 *1243*
there are *d* of operations, but it 1Cor 12:6 *1243*
helps, governments, *d* of tongues 1Cor 12:28 *1085*

DIVIDE {49}
let it *d* the waters from the .... Gen 1:6 914
to *d* the day from the night..................... Gen 1:14 914
to *d* the light from the darkness.............. Gen 1:18 914
I will *d* them in Jacob, and..................... Gen 49:7 2505
and at night he shall *d* the spoil .... Gen 49:27 2505
thine hand over the sea, and *d* it............ Ex 14:16 1234
will overtake, I will *d* the spoil .... Ex 15:9 2505
the live ox, and *d* the money of it .... Ex 21:35 2673
and the dead ox also they shall *d*........... Ex 21:35 2673

D

the vail shall *d* unto you between Ex 26:33 914
but shall not *d* it asunder Lev 1:17 914
neck, but shall not *d* it asunder Lev 5:8 2505
cud, or of them that *d* the hoof Lev 11:4 6536
the swine, though he *d* the hoof Lev 11:7 6536
d the prey into two parts Num 31:27 2673
ye shall *d* the land by lot for an Num 33:54 5157
which shall *d* the land unto you Num 34:17 5157
to *d* the land by inheritance Num 34:18 5157
to *d* the inheritance unto the Num 34:29
or of them that *d* the cloven hoof Deut 14:7 6536
chew the cud, but *d* not the hoof Deut 14:7 6536
d the coasts of thy land, which Deut 19:3
d for an inheritance the land Josh 1:6
only *d* thou it by lot unto the Josh 13:6 5307
Now therefore *d* this land for an Josh 13:7 2505
they shall *d* it into seven parts Josh 18:5 2505
d the spoil of your enemies with Josh 22:8 2505
said, Thou and Ziba *d* the land 2Sa 19:29 2505
D the living child in two, and 1Kin 3:25 1504
neither mine nor thine, but *d* it 1Kin 3:26 1504
thou didst *d* the sea before them, Neh 9:11 1234
didst *d* them into corners Neh 9:22 2505
the innocent shall *d* the silver Job 27:17 2505
O Lord, and *d* their tongues Ps 55:9 6385
I will *d* Shechem, and mete out the Ps 60:6 2505
Thou didst *d* the sea by thy Ps 74:13 6565
I will *d* Shechem, and mete out the Ps 108:7 2505
than to *d* the spoil with the Prov 16:19 2505
men rejoice when they *d* the spoil Is 9:3 2505
Therefore will I *d* him a portion Is 53:12 5312
he shall *d* the spoil with the Is 53:12 5312
balances to weigh, and *d* the hair Eze 5:1 2505
when ye shall *d* by lot the land Eze 45:1 5307
So shall ye *d* this land unto you Eze 47:21 2505
that ye shall *d* it by lot for an Eze 47:22 5307
shall *d* by lot unto the tribes of Eze 48:29 5307
shall *d* the land for gain Dan 11:39 2505
that he *d* the inheritance with me Lk 12:13 *3307*
this, and *d* it among yourselves Lk 22:17 *1266*

DIVIDED {69}
God *d* the light from the darkness Gen 1:4 914
d the waters which were under the Gen 1:7 914
of the Gentiles *d* in their lands Gen 10:5 6504
for in his days was the earth *d* Gen 10:25 6385
by these were the nations *d* in Gen 10:32 5504
he *d* himself against them, he and Gen 14:15 2505
d them in the midst, and laid each Gen 15:10 1334
but the birds *d* he not Gen 15:10 1334
he *d* the people that was with him Gen 32:7 2673
he *d* the children unto Leah, and Gen 33:1 2673
dry land, and the waters were *d* Ex 14:21 1234
Unto these the land shall be *d* Num 26:53 2505
the land shall be *d* by lot Num 26:55 2505
thereof be *d* between many Num 26:56 2505
which Moses *d* from the men that Num 31:42 2673
hath *d* unto all nations under the Deut 4:19 2505
When the Most High *d* to the Deut 32:8
of Israel did, and they *d* the land Josh 14:5 2505
there Joshua *d* the land unto the Josh 18:10 2505
d for an inheritance by lot in Josh 19:51
I have *d* unto you by lot these Josh 23:4 5307
have they not *d* the prey Judg 5:30 2505
he *d* the three hundred men into Judg 7:16 2673
d them into three companies, and Judg 9:43 2673
d her, together with her bones, Judg 19:29 5408
and in their death they were not *d* 2Sa 1:23 6504
people of Israel *d* into two parts 1Kin 16:21 2505
So they *d* the land between them 1Kin 18:6 2505
the waters, and they were *d* hither 2Kin 2:8 2673
in his days the earth was *d* 1Chr 1:19 6385
David *d* them into courses among 1Chr 23:6 2505
and thus were they *d* 1Chr 24:4 2505
Thus were they *d* by lot, one sort 1Chr 24:5 2505
d them speedily among all the 2Chr 35:13 7323
Who hath *d* a watercourse for the Job 38:25 6385
that tarried at home *d* the spoil Ps 68:12 2505
He *d* the sea, and caused them to Ps 78:13 1234
d them an inheritance by line, and Ps 78:55 5307
To him which *d* the Red sea into Ps 136:13 1504
is the prey of a great spoil *d* Is 33:23 2505
his hand hath *d* it unto them by Is 34:17 2505
that *d* the sea, whose waves Is 51:15 7280
The anger of the LORD hath *d* them Lam 4:16 2505
neither shall they be *d* into two Eze 37:22 2673
of iron, the kingdom shall be *d* Dan 2:41 6386
Thy kingdom is *d*, and given to the Dan 5:28 6537
shall be *d* toward the four winds Dan 11:4 2673
Their heart is *d* Hos 10:2 2505
and thy land shall be *d* by line Amos 7:17 2505
turning away he hath *d* our fields Mic 2:4 2505
thy spoil shall be *d* in the midst Zec 14:1 2505
Every kingdom *d* against itself is Mt 12:25 *3307*
every city or house *d* against Mt 12:25 *3307*
Satan, he is *d* against himself Mt 12:26 *3307*
if a kingdom be *d* against itself Mk 3:24 *3307*
if a house be *d* against itself, Mk 3:25 *3307*
rise up against himself, and be *d* Mk 3:26 *3307*
the two fishes *d* he among them Mk 6:41 *3307*
Every kingdom *d* against itself is Lk 11:17 *1266*
a house *d* against a house falleth Lk 11:17
Satan also be *d* against himself Lk 11:18 *1266*
shall be five in one house *d* Lk 12:52 *1266*
father shall be *d* against the son Lk 12:53 *1266*
he *d* unto them his living Lk 15:12 *1244*
he *d* their land to them by lot Acts 13:19 *2624*
the multitude of the city was *d* Acts 14:4 *4977*
and the multitude was *d* Acts 23:7 *4977*
Is Christ *d*? 1Cor 1:13 *3307*
great city was *d* into three parts Rev 16:19 *1096*

DIVIDER {1}
made me a judge or a *d* over you Lk 12:14 *3312*

DIVIDETH {10}
the cud, but *d* not the hoof Lev 11:4 6536
the cud, but *d* not the hoof Lev 11:5 6536
the cud, but *d* not the hoof Lev 11:6 6536
of every beast which *d* the hoof Lev 11:26 6536
the swine, because it *d* the hoof Deut 14:8 6536
He *d* the sea with his power, and Job 26:12 7280
of the LORD *d* the flames of fire Ps 29:7 2672
which *d* the sea when the waves Jer 31:35 7280
as a shepherd *d* his sheep from Mt 25:32 *873*
he trusted, and *d* his spoils Lk 11:22 *1239*

DIVIDING {7}
of *d* the land for inheritance by Josh 19:49
they made an end of *d* the country Josh 19:51 2505
d the water before them, to make Is 63:12 1234
a time and times and the *d* of time Dan 7:25 6387
d to every man severally as he 1Cor 12:11 *1244*
rightly *d* the word of truth 2Ti 2:15 *3718*
even to the *d* asunder of soul Heb 4:12 *3311*

DIVINATION {12}
the rewards of *d* in their hand Num 22:7 7081
is there any *d* against Israel Num 23:23 7081
through the fire, or that useth *d* Deut 18:10 7081
pass through the fire, and used *d* 2Kin 17:17 7081
unto you a false vision and *d* Jer 14:14 7081
d within the house of Israel Eze 12:24 4738
They have seen vanity and lying *d* Eze 13:6 7081
and have ye not spoken a lying *d* Eze 13:7 4738
head of the two ways, to use *d* Eze 21:21 7081
hand was the *d* for Jerusalem Eze 21:22 7081
them as a false *d* in their sight Eze 21:23 7080
with a spirit of *d* met us Acts 16:16 *4436*

DIVINATIONS {1}
see no more vanity, nor divine *d* Eze 13:23 7081

DIVINE {11}
such a man as I can certainly *d* Gen 44:15 5172
d unto me by the familiar spirit, 1Sa 28:8 7080
A *d* sentence is in the lips of Prov 16:10 7081
that see vanity, and that *d* lies Eze 13:9 7080
no more vanity, nor *d* divinations Eze 13:23 7181
whiles they *d* a lie unto thee, to Eze 21:29 7080
unto you, that ye shall not *d* Mic 3:6 7080
the prophets thereof *d* for money Mic 3:11 7080
had also ordinances of *d* service Heb 9:1 *2999*
According as his *d* power hath 2Pet 1:3 *2304*
be partakers of the *d* nature 2Pet 1:4 *2304*

DIVINERS {7}
observers of times, and unto *d* Deut 18:14 7080
called for the priests and the *d* 1Sa 6:2 7080
of the liars, and maketh *d* mad Is 44:25 7080
to your prophets, nor to your *d* Jer 27:9 7080
Let not your prophets and your *d* Jer 29:8 7080
be ashamed, and the *d* confounded Mic 3:7 7080
the *d* have seen a lie, and have Zec 10:2 7080

DIVINETH {1}
drinketh, and whereby indeed he *d* Gen 44:5 5172

DIVINING {1}
d lies unto them, saying, Thus Eze 22:28 7080

DIVISION {6}
I will put a *d* between my people Ex 8:23 6304
after the *d* of the families of 2Chr 35:5 2515
you, Nay; but rather *d* Lk 12:51 *1267*
So there was a *d* among the people Jn 7:43 *4978*
And there was a *d* among them Jn 9:16 *4978*
There was a *d* therefore again Jn 10:19 *4978*

DIVISIONS {17}
to their *d* by their tribes Josh 11:23 4256
a possession according to their *d* Josh 12:7 4256
of Israel according to their *d* Josh 18:10 4256
For the *d* of Reuben there were Judg 5:15 6391
For the *d* of Reuben there were Judg 5:16 6391
Now these are the *d* of the sons 1Chr 24:1 4256
Concerning the *d* of the porters 1Chr 26:1 4256
these were the *d* of the porters 1Chr 26:12 4256
These are the *d* of the porters 1Chr 26:19 4256
d of the families of the fathers 2Chr 35:5 6391
might give according to the *d* of 2Chr 35:12 4653
they set the priests in their *d* Ezr 6:18 6392
And of the Levites were *d* in Judah Neh 11:36 4256
brethren, mark them which cause *d* Rom 16:17 *1370*
and that there be no *d* among you 1Cor 1:10 *4978*
you envying, and strife, and *d* 1Cor 3:3 *1370*
I hear that there be *d* among you 1Cor 11:18 *4978*

DIVORCE {1}
away, and given her a bill of *d* Jer 3:8 3748

DIVORCED {4}
or a *d* woman, or profane, or an Lev 21:14 1644
daughter be a widow, or *d* Lev 22:13 1644
of a widow, and of her that is *d* Num 30:9 1644
her that is *d* committeth adultery Mt 5:32 *630*

DIVORCEMENT {6}
let him write her a bill of *d* Deut 24:1 3748
her, and write her a bill of *d* Deut 24:3 3748
is the bill of your mother's *d* Is 50:1 3748
let him give her a writing of *d* Mt 5:31 *647*
command to give a writing of *d* Mt 19:7 *647*
suffered to write a bill of *d* Mk 10:4 *647*

DIZAHAB *(diz'-a-hab)* {1} *A place in the Sinai wilderness.*
and Laban, and Hazeroth, and *D* Deut 1:1 1774

DO {1373}
d bring a flood of waters upon Gen 6:17
I *d* set my bow in the cloud, and Gen 9:13
and this they begin to *d* Gen 11:6 6213
which they have imagined to *d* Gen 11:6 6213
d to her as it pleaseth thee Gen 16:6 6213
And they said, So *d*, as thou hast Gen 18:5 6213
from Abraham that thing which I *d* Gen 18:17 6213
LORD, to *d* justice and judgment Gen 18:19 6213
from thee to *d* after this manner Gen 18:25 6213
Judge of all the earth *d* right Gen 18:25 6213
I will not *d* it for forty's sake Gen 18:29 6213
And he said, I will not *d* it Gen 18:30 6213
you, brethren, *d* not so wickedly Gen 19:7
d ye to them as is good in your Gen 19:8 6213
only unto these men *d* nothing Gen 19:8 6213
for I cannot *d* any thing till Gen 19:22 6213
unto thee, thou shalt *d* unto me Gen 21:23 6213
neither *d* thou any thing unto him Gen 22:12 6213
if now thou *d* prosper my way Gen 24:42 3426
shall this birthright *d* to me Gen 25:32
That thou wilt *d* us no hurt Gen 26:29 6213
what shall I *d* now unto thee, my Gen 27:37 6213
what good shall my life *d* me Gen 27:46
if thou wilt *d* this thing for me, Gen 30:31 6213
God hath said unto thee, *d* Gen 31:16 6213
power of my hand to *d* you hurt Gen 31:29 6213
what can I *d* this day unto these Gen 31:43 6213
saidst, I will surely *d* thee good Gen 32:12 3190
We cannot *d* this thing, to give Gen 34:14 6213
man deferred not to *d* the thing Gen 34:19 6213
D not thy brethren feed the flock Gen 37:13
how then can I *d* this great Gen 39:9 6213
into the house to *d* his business Gen 39:11 6213
D not interpretations belong to Gen 40:8 3808
I *d* remember my faults this day Gen 41:9
Pharaoh what he is about to *d* Gen 41:25 6213
What God is about to *d* he sheweth Gen 41:28 6213
Let Pharaoh *d* this, and let him Gen 41:34 6213
what he saith to you, *d* Gen 41:55 6213
Why *d* ye look one upon another Gen 42:1
unto them the third day, This *d* Gen 42:18 6213
D not sin against the child Gen 42:22
If it must be so now, *d* this Gen 43:11 6213
should *d* according to this thing Gen 44:7 6213
God forbid that I should *d* so Gen 44:17 6213
Say unto thy brethren, This *d* ye Gen 45:17 6213
Now thou art commanded, this *d* ye Gen 45:19 6213
I will *d* as thou hast said Gen 47:30 6213
When ye *d* the office of a midwife Ex 1:16
I will *d* in the midst thereof Ex 3:20 6213
and will teach you what ye shall *d* Ex 4:15 6213
wherewith thou shalt *d* signs Ex 4:17 6213
see that thou *d* all those wonders Ex 4:21 6213
said unto them, Wherefore *d* ye Ex 5:4
us go and *d* sacrifice to the LORD Ex 5:17
thou see what I will *d* to Pharaoh Ex 6:1 6213
that they may *d* sacrifice unto Ex 8:8
said, It is not meet so to *d* Ex 8:26 6213
shall *d* this thing in the land Ex 9:5 6213
wilt *d* that which is right in his Ex 15:26 6213
wherefore *d* ye tempt the LORD Ex 17:2
What shall I *d* unto this people Ex 17:4 6213
I *d* make them know the statutes Ex 18:16
and the work that they must *d* Ex 18:20 6213
If thou shalt *d* this thing Ex 18:23 6213
the LORD hath spoken we will *d* Ex 19:8 6213
thou labour, and *d* all thy work Ex 20:9 6213
in it thou shalt not *d* any work Ex 20:10 6213
not go out as the menservants *d* Ex 21:7 3318
if he *d* not these three unto her, Ex 21:11 6213
shalt thou *d* with thine oxen Ex 22:30 6213
not follow a multitude to *d* evil Ex 23:2
Six days thou shalt *d* thy work Ex 23:12 6213
his voice, and *d* all that I speak Ex 23:22 6213
them, nor *d* after their works Ex 23:24 6213
the LORD hath said will we *d* Ex 24:3 6213
that the LORD hath said will we *d* Ex 24:7 6213
if any man have any matters to *d* Ex 24:14 1167
shalt *d* unto them to hallow them Ex 29:1 6213
And thus shalt thou *d* unto Aaron Ex 29:35 6213
shalt *d* thereto according to the Ex 29:41 6213
have commanded thee shall they *d* Ex 31:11 6213
he thought to *d* unto his people Ex 32:14 6213
noise of them that sing *d* I hear Ex 32:18
I may know what to *d* unto thee Ex 33:5 6213
I will *d* this thing also that Ex 33:17 6213
all thy people I will *d* marvels Ex 34:10 6213
thing that I will *d* with thee Ex 34:10 6213
d sacrifice unto their gods, and Ex 34:15
commanded, that ye should *d* them Ex 35:1 6213
to *d* service in the holy place, Ex 35:19
even of them that *d* any work Ex 35:35 6213
up to come unto the work to *d* it Ex 36:2 6213
to *d* service in the holy place, Ex 39:1
The cloths of service to *d* Ex 39:41
shall *d* against any of them Lev 4:2 6213
If the priest that is anointed *d* Lev 4:3
he shall *d* with the bullock as he Lev 4:20 6213
offering, so shall he *d* with this Lev 4:20 6213
if he *d* not utter it, then he Lev 5:1
his lips to *d* evil, or to *d* good Lev 5:4 7489,3190
so the LORD hath commanded to *d* Lev 8:34 6213
LORD commanded that ye should *d* Lev 9:6 6213

D not drink wine nor strong drink Lev 10:9
d with that blood as he did with Lev 16:15 6213
so shall he *d* for the tabernacle Lev 16:16 6213
d no work at all, whether it be Lev 16:29 6213
wherein ye dwelt, shall ye not *d* Lev 18:3 6213
I bring you, shall ye not *d* Lev 18:3 6213
Ye shall *d* my judgments, and keep Lev 18:4 6213
which if a man *d*, he shall live Lev 18:5 6213
therefore I *d* visit the iniquity Lev 18:25
Ye shall *d* no unrighteousness in Lev 19:15 6213
D not prostitute thy daughter, to Lev 19:29
Ye shall *d* no unrighteousness in Lev 19:35 6213
and all my judgments, and *d* them Lev 19:37 6213
if the people of the land *d* any Lev 20:4
shall keep my statutes, and *d* them Lev 20:8 6213
and all my judgments, and *d* them Lev 20:22 6213
bread of their God, they *d* offer Lev 21:6
for I the LORD *d* sanctify him Lev 21:15
for I the LORD *d* sanctify them Lev 21:23
I the LORD *d* sanctify them Lev 22:9
for I the LORD *d* sanctify them Lev 22:16
keep my commandments, and *d* them Lev 22:31 6213
ye shall *d* no work therein Lev 23:3 6213
ye shall *d* no servile work Lev 23:7 6213
ye shall *d* no servile work Lev 23:8 6213
ye shall *d* no servile work Lev 23:21 6213
Ye shall *d* no servile work Lev 23:25 6213
ye shall *d* no work in that same Lev 23:28 6213
Ye shall *d* no manner of work Lev 23:31 6213
ye shall *d* no servile work Lev 23:35 6213
ye shall *d* no servile work Lev 23:36 6213
Wherefore ye shall *d* my statutes Lev 25:18 6213
and keep my judgments, and *d* them Lev 25:18 6213
that *d* sojourn among you, of them Lev 25:45
keep my commandments, and *d* them Lev 26:3 6213
will not *d* all these commandments Lev 26:14 6213
ye will not *d* all my commandments Lev 26:15 6213
I also will *d* this unto you Lev 26:16 6213
of which they *d* not offer a Lev 27:11
those that *d* pitch next unto him Num 2:5
to *d* the service of the Num 3:7 5647
Israel, to *d* the service of the Num 3:8 5647
to *d* the work in the tabernacle Num 4:3 6213
But thus *d* unto them, that they Num 4:19 6213
to *d* the work in the tabernacle Num 4:23 5647
to *d* the work of the tabernacle Num 4:30 5647
all that might *d* service in the Num 4:37 5647
of all that might *d* service in Num 4:41 5647
every one that came to *d* the Num 4:47 5647
to *d* a trespass against the LORD, Num 5:6 6213
so he must *d* after the law of his Num 6:21 6213
that they may be to *d* the service Num 7:5 5647
And thus shalt thou *d* unto them Num 8:7 6213
d the service of the tabernacle Num 8:15 5647
to *d* the service of the children Num 8:19 5647
that went the Levites in to *d* Num 8:22 5647
the charge, and shall *d* no service Num 8:26 5647
Thus shalt thou *d* unto the Num 8:26 6213
the manner thereof, so shall he *d* Num 9:14 6213
with us, and we will *d* thee good Num 10:29 3190
goodness the LORD shall *d* unto us Num 10:32 3190
the same will we *d* unto thee Num 10:32 3190
Medad *d* prophesy in the camp Num 11:27
in mine ears, so will I *d* to you Num 14:28 6213
I will surely *d* it unto all this Num 14:35 6213
Wherefore now *d* ye transgress the Num 14:41
so shall ye *d* to every one Num 15:12 6213
are born of the country shall *d* Num 15:13 6213
as ye *d*, so he shall *d* Num 15:14 6213
as ye *d* the heave offering of the Num 15:20
of the LORD, and *d* them Num 15:39 6213
d all my commandments, and be holy Num 15:40 6213
This *d*; Take you censers Num 16:6 6213
d the service of the tabernacle Num 16:9 5647
hath sent me to *d* all these works Num 16:28 6213
the LORD, to *d* the service of the Num 18:6 5647
But the Levites shall *d* the Num 18:23 5647
thou shalt *d* to him as thou didst Num 21:34 6213
I will *d* whatsoever thou sayest Num 22:17 6213
LORD my God, to *d* less or more Num 22:18 6213
say unto thee, that shalt thou *d* Num 22:20 6213
was I ever wont to *d* so unto thee Num 22:30 6213
he said, and shall he not *d* it Num 23:19 6213
the LORD speaketh, that I must *d* Num 23:26 6213
to *d* either good or bad of mine Num 24:13 6213
d to thy people in the latter Num 24:14 6213
and Israel shall *d* valiantly Num 24:18 6213
ye shall *d* no manner of servile Num 28:18 6213
ye shall *d* no servile work Num 28:25 6213
ye shall *d* no servile work Num 28:26 6213
ye shall *d* no servile work Num 29:1 6213
ye shall not *d* any work therein Num 29:7 6213
ye shall *d* no servile work, and ye Num 29:12 6213
ye shall *d* no servile work Num 29:35 6213
These things ye shall *d* unto the Num 29:39 6213
he shall *d* according to all that Num 30:2 6213
d ye abide without the camp seven Num 31:19 6213
them, If ye will *d* this thing Num 32:20 6213
But if ye will not *d* so, behold, Num 32:23 6213
d that which hath proceeded out Num 32:24 6213
Thy servants will *d* as my lord Num 32:25 6213
unto thy servants, so will we *d* Num 32:31 6213
to pass, that I shall *d* unto you Num 33:56 6213
as I thought to *d* unto them Num 33:56 6213
hast spoken is good for us to *d* Deut 1:14 6213
all the things which ye should *d* Deut 1:18 6213
you, and chased you, as bees *d* Deut 1:44 6213
thou shalt *d* unto him as thou Deut 3:2 6213
so shall the LORD *d* unto all the Deut 3:21 6213
that can *d* according to thy works Deut 3:24 6213
which I teach you, for to *d* them Deut 4:1 6213
that ye should *d* so in the land Deut 4:5 6213
Keep therefore and *d* them Deut 4:6 6213
that ye might *d* them in the land Deut 4:14 6213
shall *d* evil in the sight of the Deut 4:25 6213
learn them, and keep, and *d* them Deut 5:1 6213
shalt labour, and *d* all thy work Deut 5:13 6213
in it thou shalt not *d* any work Deut 5:14 6213
and we will hear it, and *d* it Deut 5:27 6213
that they may *d* them in the land Deut 5:31 6213
Ye shall observe to *d* therefore Deut 5:32 6213
that ye might *d* them in the land Deut 6:1 6213
O Israel, and observe to *d* it Deut 6:3 6213
thou shalt *d* that which is right Deut 6:18 6213
us to *d* all these statutes Deut 6:24 6213
if we observe to *d* all these Deut 6:25 6213
command thee this day, to *d* them Deut 7:11 6213
d them, that the LORD thy God Deut 7:12 6213
so shall the LORD thy God *d* unto Deut 7:19 6213
this day shall ye observe to *d* Deut 8:1 6213
to *d* thee good at thy latter end Deut 8:16 3190
if thou *d* at all forget the LORD Deut 8:19
to *d* them, to love the LORD your Deut 11:22 6213
observe to *d* all the statutes Deut 11:32 6213
ye shall observe to *d* in the land Deut 12:1 6213
Ye shall not *d* so unto the LORD Deut 12:4 6213
Ye shall not *d* after all the Deut 12:8 6213
things that we *d* here this day Deut 12:8 6213
there thou shalt *d* all that I Deut 12:14 6213
when thou shalt *d* that which is Deut 12:25 6213
even so will I *d* likewise Deut 12:30 6213
Thou shalt not *d* so unto the LORD Deut 12:31 6213
I command you, observe to *d* it Deut 12:32 6213
fear, and shall *d* no more any such Deut 13:11 6213
to *d* that which is right in the Deut 13:18 6213
to observe to *d* all these Deut 15:5 6213
maidservant thou shalt *d* likewise Deut 15:17 6213
thou shalt *d* no work with the Deut 15:19
thou shalt *d* no work therein Deut 16:8 6213
shalt observe and *d* these statutes Deut 16:12 6213
thou shalt *d* according to the Deut 17:10 6213
thou shalt observe to *d* according Deut 17:10 6213
shall tell thee, thou shalt *d* Deut 17:11 6213
man that will *d* presumptuously Deut 17:12 6213
fear, and *d* no more presumptuously Deut 17:13
law and these statutes, to *d* them Deut 17:19 6213
as all his brethren the Levites *d* Deut 18:7
thou shalt not learn to *d* after Deut 18:9 6213
For all that *d* these things are Deut 18:12 6213
hath not suffered thee so to *d* Deut 18:14
all these commandments to *d* them Deut 19:9 6213
Then shall ye *d* unto him, as he Deut 19:19 6213
d not tremble, neither be ye Deut 20:3
Thus shalt thou *d* unto all the Deut 20:15 6213
That they teach you not to *d* Deut 20:18 6213
when thou shalt *d* that which is Deut 21:9 6213
manner shalt thou *d* with his ass Deut 22:3 6213
so shalt thou *d* with his raiment Deut 22:3 6213
hast found, shalt thou *d* likewise Deut 22:3 6213
for all that *d* so are abomination Deut 22:5 6213
the damsel thou shalt *d* nothing Deut 22:26 6213
d according to all that the Deut 24:8 6213
them, so ye shall observe to *d* Deut 24:8 6213
I command thee to *d* this thing Deut 24:18 6213
I command thee to *d* this thing Deut 24:22 6213
For all that *d* such things Deut 25:16 6213
all that *d* unrighteously, are an Deut 25:16 6213
thee to *d* these statutes and Deut 26:16 6213
d them with all thine heart, and Deut 26:16 6213
d his commandments and his Deut 27:10 6213
the words of this law to *d* them Deut 27:26 6213
to *d* all his commandments which I Deut 28:1 6213
this day, to observe and to *d* them Deut 28:13 6213
thy God, to observe to *d* all his Deut 28:15 6213
settest thine hand unto for to *d* Deut 28:20 6213
If thou wilt not observe to *d* all Deut 28:58 6213
rejoiced over you to *d* you good Deut 28:63 3190
d them, that ye may prosper in Deut 29:9 6213
ye may prosper in all that ye *d* Deut 29:9 6213
you only *d* I make this covenant Deut 29:14
that we may *d* all the words of Deut 29:29 6213
he will *d* thee good, and multiply Deut 30:5 3190
d all his commandments which I Deut 30:8 6213
us, that we may hear it, and *d* it Deut 30:12 6213
us, that we may hear it, and *d* it Deut 30:13 6213
thy heart, that thou mayest *d* it Deut 30:14 6213
the LORD shall *d* unto them as he Deut 31:4 6213
that ye may *d* unto them according Deut 31:5 6213
observe to *d* all the words of Deut 31:12 6213
because ye will *d* evil in the Deut 31:29 6213
D ye thus requite the LORD, O Deut 32:6
your children to observe to *d* Deut 32:46 6213
which the LORD sent him to *d* in Deut 34:11 6213
the land which I *d* give to them Josh 1:2
to *d* according to all the law Josh 1:7 6213
to *d* according to all that is Josh 1:8 6213
that thou commandest us we will *d* Josh 1:16 6213
the country *d* faint because of us Josh 2:24
the LORD will *d* wonders among you Josh 3:5 6213
Thus shalt thou *d* six days Josh 6:3 6213
what wilt thou *d* unto thy great Josh 7:9 6213
And thou shalt *d* to Ai and her king Josh 8:2 6213
of the LORD shall ye *d* Josh 8:8 6213
This we will *d* to them Josh 9:20 6213
and right unto thee to *d* unto us Josh 9:25 6213
right unto thee to *d* unto us, *d* Josh 9:25 6213
for thus shall the LORD *d* to all Josh 10:25 6213
heed to *d* the commandment Josh 22:5 6213
What have ye to *d* with the LORD Josh 22:24
that we might *d* the service of Josh 22:27 5647
to *d* all that is written in the Josh 23:6 6213
Else if ye *d* in any wise go back, Josh 23:12
which ye planted not *d* ye eat Josh 24:13
d you hurt, and consume you, after Josh 24:20 7489
that he could not *d* it by day Judg 6:27 6213
them, Look on me, and *d* likewise Judg 7:17 6213
be that, as I *d*, so shall ye *d* Judg 7:17 6213
and what was I able to *d* in Judg 8:3 6213
then mayest thou *d* to them as Judg 9:33 6213
with him, What ye have seen me *d* Judg 9:48 6213
make haste, and *d* as I have done Judg 9:48 6213
d thou unto us whatsoever seemeth Judg 10:15 6213
if we *d* not so according to thy Judg 11:10 6213
What hast thou to *d* with me Judg 11:12
d to me according to that which Judg 11:36 6213
teach us what we shall *d* unto the Judg 13:8 6213
child, and how shall we *d* unto him Judg 13:12 4640
come to pass we may *d* thee honour Judg 13:17
for so used the young men to *d* Judg 14:10 6213
though I *d* them a displeasure Judg 15:3 6213
to *d* to him as he hath done to us Judg 15:10 6213
I that the LORD will *d* me good Judg 17:13 3190
D ye know that there is in these Judg 18:14
consider what ye have to *d* Judg 18:14 6213
the priest unto them, What *d* ye Judg 18:18 6213
I pray you, *d* not so wickedly Judg 19:23 7489
into mine house, *d* not this folly Judg 19:23 6213
d with them what seemeth good Judg 19:24 6213
but unto this man *d* not so vile a Judg 19:24 6213
thing which we will *d* to Gibeah Judg 20:9 6213
for the people, that they may *d* Judg 20:10 6213
How shall we *d* for wives for them Judg 21:7 6213
this is the thing that ye shall *d* Judg 21:11 6213
How shall we *d* for wives for them Judg 21:16 6213
the LORD *d* so to me, and more also Ruth 1:17 6213
be on the field that they *d* reap Ruth 2:9
will tell thee what thou shalt *d* Ruth 3:4 6213
that thou sayest unto me I will *d* Ruth 3:5 6213
I will *d* to thee all that thou Ruth 3:11 6213
let him *d* the kinsman's part Ruth 3:13
but if he will not *d* the part of Ruth 3:13
then will I *d* the part of a Ruth 3:13
d thou worthily in Ephratah, and Ruth 4:11 6213
her, *D* what seemeth thee good 1Sa 1:23 6213
unto them, Why *d* ye such things 1Sa 2:23 6213
that shall *d* according to that 1Sa 2:35 6213
I will *d* a thing in Israel, at 1Sa 3:11 6213
God *d* so to thee, and more also, 1Sa 3:17 6213
let him *d* what seemeth him good 1Sa 3:18 6213
What shall we *d* with the ark of 1Sa 5:8 6213
What shall we *d* to the ark of the 1Sa 6:2 6213
Wherefore then *d* ye harden your 1Sa 6:6
If ye *d* return unto the LORD with 1Sa 7:3
gods, so *d* they also unto thee 1Sa 8:8 6213
saying, What shall I *d* for my son 1Sa 10:2 6213
that thou *d* as occasion serve 1Sa 10:7 6213
and shew thee what thou shalt *d* 1Sa 10:8 6213
ye shall *d* with us all that 1Sa 11:10 6213
the LORD will *d* before your eyes 1Sa 12:16 6213
But if ye shall still *d* wickedly 1Sa 12:25 7489
D all that is in thine heart 1Sa 14:7 6213
D whatsoever seemeth good unto 1Sa 14:36 6213
D what seemeth good unto thee 1Sa 14:40 6213
And Saul answered, God *d* so 1Sa 14:44 6213
will shew thee what thou shalt *d* 1Sa 16:3 6213
my father will *d* nothing either 1Sa 20:2 6213
I will even *d* it for thee 1Sa 20:4 6213
The LORD *d* so and much more to 1Sa 20:13 6213
please my father to *d* thee evil 1Sa 20:13
d not I know that thou hast 1Sa 20:30
I know what God will *d* for me 1Sa 22:3 6213
that thou mayest *d* to him as it 1Sa 24:4 6213
d this thing unto my master 1Sa 24:6 6213
know and consider what thou wilt *d* 1Sa 25:17 6213
more also *d* God unto the enemies 1Sa 25:22 6213
for I will no more *d* thee harm 1Sa 26:21 7489
thou shalt both *d* great things 1Sa 26:25 6213
shalt know what thy servant can *d* 1Sa 28:2 6213
make known unto me what I shall *d* 1Sa 28:15 6213
What *d* these Hebrews here 1Sa 29:3
said David, Ye shall not *d* so 1Sa 30:23 6213
which against Judah *d* shew 2Sa 3:8 6213
So *d* God to Abner, and more also, 2Sa 3:9 6213
to David, even so I *d* to him 2Sa 3:9 6213
Now then *d* it 2Sa 3:18 6213
So *d* God to me, and more also, if 2Sa 3:35 6213
d all that is in thine heart 2Sa 7:3 6213
to *d* for you great things and 2Sa 7:23 6213
for ever, and *d* as thou hast said 2Sa 7:25 6213
servant, so shall thy servant *d* 2Sa 9:11 6213
the LORD *d* that which seemeth him 2Sa 10:12 6213
liveth, I will not *d* this thing 2Sa 11:11 6213
the LORD, to *d* evil in his sight 2Sa 12:9 6213
but I will *d* this thing before 2Sa 12:12 6213
for him to *d* any thing to her 2Sa 13:2 6213
Nay, my brother, *d* not force me 2Sa 13:12 6213
d not thou this folly 2Sa 13:12 6213
unto me, and I would *d* him justice 2Sa 15:4 6663
nigh to him to *d* him obeisance 2Sa 15:5 7812
thy servants are ready to *d* 2Sa 15:15
let him *d* to me as seemeth good 2Sa 15:26 6213
said, What have I to *d* with you 2Sa 16:10
more now may this Benjamite *d* it 2Sa 16:11
counsel among you what we shall *d* 2Sa 16:20 6213

Context	Reference	Number
shall we *d* after his saying	2Sa 17:6	6213
What seemeth you best I will *d*	2Sa 18:4	6213
rise against thee to *d* thee hurt	2Sa 18:32	
God *d* so to me, and more also, if	2Sa 19:13	6213
to *d* what he thought good	2Sa 19:18	6213
neither *d* thou remember that	2Sa 19:19	
said, What have I to *d* with you	2Sa 19:22	
for *d* not I know that I am this	2Sa 19:22	
d therefore what is good in thine	2Sa 19:27	6213
d to him what shall seem good	2Sa 19:37	6213
I will *d* to him that which shall	2Sa 19:38	6213
of me, that will I *d* for thee	2Sa 19:38	6213
d us more harm than did Absalom	2Sa 20:6	3415
And he answered, I *d* hear	2Sa 20:17	
What shall I *d* for you	2Sa 21:3	6213
shall say, that will I *d* for you	2Sa 21:4	6213
me, O LORD, that I should *d* this	2Sa 23:17	6213
that I may *d* it unto thee	2Sa 24:12	6213
so will I certainly *d* this day	1Kin 1:30	6213
D therefore according to thy	1Kin 2:6	6213
what thou oughtest to *d* unto him	1Kin 2:9	6213
God *d* so to me, and more also, if	1Kin 2:23	6213
D as he hath said, and fall upon	1Kin 2:31	6213
hath said, so will thy servant *d*	1Kin 2:38	6213
of God was in him, to *d* judgment	1Kin 3:28	6213
and I will *d* all thy desire	1Kin 5:8	6213
Then hear thou in heaven, and *d*	1Kin 8:32	6213
dwelling place, and forgive, and *d*	1Kin 8:39	6213
d according to all that the	1Kin 8:43	6213
fear thee, as *d* thy people Israel	1Kin 8:43	
desire which he was pleased to *d*	1Kin 9:1	6213
to *d* according to all that I have	1Kin 9:4	6213
king, to *d* judgment and justice	1Kin 10:9	6213
in thy days I will not *d* it for	1Kin 11:12	6213
to *d* that which is right in mine	1Kin 11:33	6213
d that is right in my sight, to	1Kin 11:38	6213
How *d* ye advise that I may answer	1Kin 12:6	
If this people go up to *d*	1Kin 12:27	6213
to *d* that only which was right in	1Kin 14:8	6213
go and *d* as thou hast said	1Kin 17:13	6213
What have I to *d* with thee	1Kin 17:18	
And he said, *D* it the second time	1Kin 18:34	8138
And he said, *D* it the third time	1Kin 18:34	8027
saying, So let the gods *d* to me	1Kin 19:2	6213
thy servant at the first I will *d*	1Kin 20:9	6213
but this thing I may not *d*	1Kin 20:9	6213
The gods *d* so unto me, and more	1Kin 20:10	6213
d this thing, Take the kings away	1Kin 20:24	6213
go forth, and *d* so	1Kin 22:22	6213
Ask what I shall *d* for thee	2Kin 2:9	6213
What have I to *d* with thee	2Kin 3:13	
unto her, What shall I *d* for thee	2Kin 4:2	6213
d not lie unto thine handmaid	2Kin 4:16	
did I not say, *D* not deceive me	2Kin 4:28	
had bid thee *d* some great thing	2Kin 5:13	
how shall we *d*?	2Kin 6:15	6213
If the LORD *d* not help thee,	2Kin 6:27	
Then he said, God *d* so and more	2Kin 6:31	6213
one to another, We *d* not well	2Kin 7:9	6213
d unto the children of Israel	2Kin 8:12	6213
that he should *d* this great thing	2Kin 8:13	6213
What hast thou to *d* with peace	2Kin 9:18	
What hast thou to *d* with peace	2Kin 9:19	
will *d* all that thou shalt bid us	2Kin 10:5	6213
d thou that which is good in	2Kin 10:5	6213
a great sacrifice to *d* to Baal	2Kin 10:19	
This is the thing that ye shall *d*	2Kin 11:5	6213
them, Ye shall not *d* this thing	2Kin 17:12	6213
that they should not *d* like them	2Kin 17:15	6213
sold themselves to *d* evil in the	2Kin 17:17	6213
Unto this day they *d* after the	2Kin 17:34	6213
neither *d* they after their	2Kin 17:34	6213
and to him shall ye *d* sacrifice	2Kin 17:36	
shall observe to *d* for evermore	2Kin 17:37	6213
fathers, so *d* they unto this day	2Kin 17:41	6213
would not hear them, nor *d* them	2Kin 18:12	6213
of the LORD of hosts shall *d* this	2Kin 19:31	6213
that the LORD will *d* the thing	2Kin 20:9	6213
to *d* according to all that I have	2Kin 21:8	6213
Manasseh seduced them to *d* more	2Kin 21:9	6213
the hand of them that *d* the work	2Kin 22:9	6213
to *d* according unto all that	2Kin 22:13	6213
it me, that I should *d* this thing	1Chr 11:19	6213
to know what Israel ought to *d*	1Chr 12:32	6213
said that they would *d* so	1Chr 13:4	6213
suffered no man to *d* them wrong	1Chr 16:21	6231
and *d* my prophets no harm	1Chr 16:22	7489
to *d* according to all that is	1Chr 16:40	
D all that is in thine heart	1Chr 17:2	6213
for ever, and *d* as thou hast said	1Chr 17:23	6213
let the LORD *d* that which is good	1Chr 19:13	6213
d away the iniquity of thy	1Chr 21:8	5674
that I may *d* it unto thee	1Chr 21:10	6213
let my lord the king *d* that which	1Chr 21:23	6213
be constant to *d* my commandments	1Chr 28:7	6213
be strong, and *d* it	1Chr 28:10	6213
and of good courage, and *d* it	1Chr 28:20	6213
to *d* all these things, and to	1Chr 29:19	6213
Then hear thou from heaven, and *d*	2Chr 6:23	6213
d according to all that the	2Chr 6:33	6213
d according to all that I have	2Chr 7:17	6213
them, to *d* judgment and justice	2Chr 9:8	6213
to *d* the law and the commandment	2Chr 14:4	6213
go out, and *d* even so	2Chr 18:21	6213
the judges, Take heed what ye *d*	2Chr 19:6	6213
take heed and *d* it	2Chr 19:7	6213
Thus shall ye *d* in the fear of	2Chr 19:9	6213
this *d*, and ye shall not trespass	2Chr 19:10	6213
neither know we what to *d*	2Chr 20:12	6213
was his counsellor to *d* wickedly	2Chr 22:3	7561
This is the thing that ye shall *d*	2Chr 23:4	6213
d it, be strong for the battle	2Chr 25:8	6213
But what shall we *d* for the	2Chr 25:9	6213
to *d* the commandment of the king	2Chr 30:12	6213
Whereon *d* ye trust, that ye abide	2Chr 32:10	
d all that I have commanded them	2Chr 33:8	6213
to *d* worse than the heathen, whom	2Chr 33:9	6213
to thy servants, they *d* it	2Chr 34:16	6213
to *d* after all that is written in	2Chr 34:21	6213
that they may *d* according to the	2Chr 35:6	6213
What have I to *d* with thee	2Chr 35:21	
for we seek your God, as ye *d*	Ezr 4:2	
we *d* sacrifice unto him since the	Ezr 4:2	
Ye have nothing to *d* with us to	Ezr 4:3	
now that ye fail not to *d* this	Ezr 4:22	5648
I make a decree what ye shall *d*	Ezr 6:8	5648
the law of the LORD, and to *d* it	Ezr 7:10	6213
to *d* with the rest of the silver	Ezr 7:18	5648
that *d* after the will of your God	Ezr 7:18	5648
d make a decree to all the	Ezr 7:21	
will not *d* the law of thy God	Ezr 7:26	5648
be of good courage, and *d* it	Ezr 10:4	6213
should *d* according to this word	Ezr 10:5	6213
your fathers, and *d* his pleasure	Ezr 10:11	6213
As thou hast said, so must we *d*	Ezr 10:12	6213
keep my commandments, and *d* them	Neh 1:9	6213
put in my heart to *d* at Jerusalem	Neh 2:12	6213
What is this thing that ye *d*	Neh 2:19	6213
and said, What *d* these feeble Jews	Neh 4:2	6213
I said, It is not good that ye *d*	Neh 5:9	6213
so will we *d* as thou sayest	Neh 5:12	6213
that they should *d* according to	Neh 5:12	6213
But they thought to *d* me mischief	Neh 6:2	6213
d so, and sin, and that they might	Neh 6:13	6213
that they might *d* with them as	Neh 9:24	6213
thy judgments, (which if a man *d*	Neh 9:29	6213
d all the commandments of the	Neh 10:29	6213
What evil thing is this that ye *d*	Neh 13:17	6213
if ye *d* so again, I will lay	Neh 13:21	8138
unto you to *d* all this great evil	Neh 13:27	6213
that they should *d* according to	Est 1:8	6213
What shall we *d* unto the queen	Est 1:15	6213
to *d* with them as it seemeth good	Est 3:11	6213
d know, that whosoever, whether	Est 4:11	
that he may *d* as Esther hath said	Est 5:5	6213
I will *d* to morrow as the king	Est 5:8	6213
to *d* honour more than to myself	Est 6:6	6213
d even so to Mordecai the Jew,	Est 6:10	6213
presume in his heart to *d* so	Est 7:5	6213
Jews which are in Shushan to *d* to	Est 9:13	6213
undertook to *d* as they had begun	Est 9:23	6213
the terrors of God *d* set	Job 6:4	
D ye imagine to reprove words, and	Job 6:26	
what shall I *d* unto thee, O thou	Job 7:20	6466
proud helpers *d* stoop under him	Job 9:13	
say unto God, *D* not condemn me	Job 10:2	
what canst thou *d*?	Job 11:8	6466
ye know, the same *d* I know also	Job 13:2	
mocketh another, *d* ye so mock him	Job 13:9	
if ye *d* secretly accept persons	Job 13:10	
Wherefore *d* I take my flesh in my	Job 13:14	
Only *d* not two things unto me	Job 13:20	6213
wherewith he can *d* no good	Job 15:3	5953
and what *d* thy eyes wink at,	Job 15:12	
I also could speak as ye *d*	Job 16:4	
you all, *d* ye return, and come now	Job 17:10	
Why *d* ye persecute me as God, and	Job 19:22	
Therefore *d* my thoughts cause me	Job 20:2	
Wherefore *d* the wicked live,	Job 21:7	
d ye not know their tokens,	Job 21:29	
what can the Almighty *d* for them	Job 22:17	6466
d they that know him not see his	Job 24:1	
What then shall I *d* when God	Job 31:14	6213
neither *d* the aged understand	Job 32:9	
God, that he should *d* wickedness	Job 34:10	
surely God will not *d* wickedly	Job 34:12	7561
done iniquity, I will *d* no more	Job 34:32	6466
Which the clouds *d* drop and distil	Job 36:28	
that they may *d* whatsoever he	Job 37:12	6467
Men *d* therefore fear him	Job 37:24	6213
thou mark when the hinds *d* calve	Job 39:1	
remember the battle, *d* no more	Job 41:8	3254
that thou canst *d* every thing	Job 42:2	3201
Why *d* the heathen rage, and the	Ps 2:1	
my God, in thee *d* I put my trust	Ps 7:1	
what can the righteous *d*	Ps 11:3	6466
with a double heart *d* they speak	Ps 12:2	
for in thee *d* I put my trust	Ps 16:1	
thee, O LORD, *d* I lift up my soul	Ps 25:1	
on thee *d* I wait all the day	Ps 25:5	
IN thee, O LORD, *d* I put my trust	Ps 31:1	6213
The young lions *d* lack, and suffer	Ps 34:10	6213
Depart from evil, and *d* good	Ps 34:14	6213
LORD is against them that *d* evil	Ps 34:16	6213
left off to be wise, and to *d* good	Ps 36:3	3190
Trust in the LORD, and *d* good	Ps 37:3	6213
not thyself in any wise to *d* evil	Ps 37:8	7489
Depart from evil, and *d* good	Ps 37:27	6213
For in thee, O LORD, *d* I hope	Ps 38:15	
I delight to *d* thy will, O my God	Ps 40:8	6213
against me *d* they devise my hurt	Ps 41:7	
What hast thou to *d* to declare my	Ps 50:16	
D good in thy good pleasure unto	Ps 51:18	3190
not fear what flesh can *d* unto me	Ps 56:4	6213
be afraid what man can *d* unto me	Ps 56:11	6213
D ye indeed speak righteousness,	Ps 58:1	
d ye judge uprightly, O ye sons	Ps 58:1	
Through God we shall *d* valiantly	Ps 60:12	6213
suddenly *d* they shoot at him, and	Ps 64:4	
In thee, O LORD, *d* I put my trust	Ps 71:1	
d we give thanks, unto thee *d* we	Ps 75:1	6213
which pass by the way *d* pluck her	Ps 80:12	6213
d justice to the afflicted and	Ps 82:3	6663
D unto them as unto the	Ps 83:9	6213
thee, O Lord, *d* I lift up my soul	Ps 86:4	
how I *d* bear in my bosom the	Ps 89:50	
workers of iniquity *d* flourish	Ps 92:7	
people that *d* err in their heart	Ps 95:10	
his commandments to *d* them	Ps 103:18	6213
that *d* his commandments,	Ps 103:20	6213
of his, that *d* his pleasure	Ps 103:21	6213
of the forest *d* creep forth	Ps 104:20	
suffered no man to *d* them wrong	Ps 105:14	6231
and *d* my prophets no harm	Ps 105:15	
that *d* business in great waters	Ps 107:23	6213
Through God we shall *d* valiantly	Ps 108:13	6213
But *d* thou for me, O GOD the Lord	Ps 109:21	6213
all they that *d* his commandments	Ps 111:10	6213
what can man *d* unto me	Ps 118:6	6213
They also *d* no iniquity	Ps 119:3	6466
which *d* err from thy commandments	Ps 119:21	
for therein *d* I delight	Ps 119:35	
yet *d* I not forget thy statutes	Ps 119:83	
yet *d* I not forget thy law	Ps 119:109	
but thy law *d* I love	Ps 119:113	
as thou usest to *d* unto those	Ps 119:132	4941
yet *d* not I forget thy precepts	Ps 119:141	
for I *d* not forget thy law	Ps 119:153	
yet *d* I not decline from thy	Ps 119:157	
but thy law *d* I love	Ps 119:163	
Seven times a day *d* I praise thee	Ps 119:164	
for I *d* not forget thy	Ps 119:176	
D good, O LORD, unto those that	Ps 125:4	
Neither *d* they which go by say,	Ps 129:8	
wait, and in his word *d* I hope	Ps 130:5	
neither *d* I exercise myself in	Ps 131:1	
If I *d* not remember thee, let my	Ps 137:6	
D not I hate them, O LORD, that	Ps 139:21	
for in thee *d* I trust	Ps 143:8	
Teach me to *d* thy will	Ps 143:10	6213
Who rejoice to *d* evil, and delight	Prov 2:14	6213
the power of thine hand to *d* it	Prov 3:27	6213
D this now, my son, and deliver	Prov 6:3	6213
Men *d* not despise a thief, if he	Prov 6:30	
and the froward mouth, *d* I hate	Prov 8:13	
as sport to a fool to *d* mischief	Prov 10:23	6213
D they not err that devise evil	Prov 14:22	
much less *d* lying lips a prince	Prov 17:7	
brethren of the poor *d* hate him	Prov 19:7	
how much more *d* his friends go	Prov 19:7	
him, yet thou must *d* it again	Prov 19:19	3254
so *d* stripes the inward parts of	Prov 20:30	
To *d* justice and judgment is more	Prov 21:3	6213
because they refuse to *d* judgment	Prov 21:7	6213
is joy to the just to *d* judgment	Prov 21:15	6213
He that deviseth to *d* evil shall	Prov 24:8	7489
I will *d* so to him as he hath	Prov 24:29	6213
not what to *d* in the end thereof	Prov 25:8	6213
When righteous men *d* rejoice	Prov 28:12	
She will *d* him good and not evil	Prov 31:12	1580
which they should *d* under the	Eccl 2:3	6213
labour that I had laboured to *d*	Eccl 2:11	6213
for what can the man *d* that	Eccl 2:12	
rejoice, and to *d* good in his life	Eccl 3:12	6213
saith he, For whom *d* I labour	Eccl 4:8	
consider not that they *d* evil	Eccl 5:1	6213
d not all go to one place	Eccl 6:6	
is fully set in them to *d* evil	Eccl 8:11	6213
Though a sinner *d* evil an hundred	Eccl 8:12	6213
to *d*, *d* it with thy might	Eccl 9:10	6213
he *d* not whet the edge, then must	Eccl 10:10	
nor how the bones *d* grow in the	Eccl 11:5	
therefore *d* the virgins love thee	Song 1:3	
what shall we *d* for our sister in	Song 8:8	6213
cease to *d* evil	Is 1:16	7489
Learn to *d* well	Is 1:17	3190
you what I will *d* to my vineyard	Is 5:5	6213
neither *d* they seek the LORD of	Is 9:13	
what will ye *d* in the day of	Is 10:3	6213
so *d* to Jerusalem and her idols	Is 10:11	6213
that they *d* not rise, nor possess	Is 14:21	
or tail, branch or rush, may *d*	Is 19:15	6213
shall *d* sacrifice and oblation	Is 19:21	5647
neither *d* I nourish up young men,	Is 23:4	
people of the earth *d* languish	Is 24:4	
all the merryhearted *d* sigh	Is 24:7	
foundations of the earth *d* shake	Is 24:18	
I the LORD *d* keep it	Is 27:3	
of Gibeon, that he may *d* his work	Is 28:21	6213
and with their lips *d* honour me	Is 29:13	
I will proceed to *d* a marvellous	Is 29:14	6381
of the LORD of hosts shall *d* this	Is 37:32	6213
that the LORD will *d* this thing	Is 38:7	6213
praise thee, as I *d* this day	Is 38:19	
d good, or *d* evil, that we may	Is 41:23	3190,7489
pass, and new things *d* I declare	Is 42:9	
These things will I *d* unto them	Is 42:16	6213
Behold, I will *d* a new thing	Is 43:19	6213
I the LORD *d* all these things	Is 45:7	6213
and I will *d* all my pleasure	Is 46:10	6213
purposed it, I will also *d* it	Is 46:11	6213
for mine own sake, will I *d* it	Is 48:11	6213
he will *d* his pleasure on Babylon	Is 48:14	6213
Wherefore *d* ye spend money for	Is 55:2	

Keep ye judgment, and *d* justice ... Is 56:1 6213
Against whom *d* ye sport ... Is 57:4
shall not fast as ye *d* this day ... Is 58:4
and we all *d* fade as a leaf ... Is 64:6
so will I *d* for my servants' ... Is 65:8 6213
after things that *d* not profit ... Jer 2:8
thou to *d* in the way of Egypt ... Jer 2:18 1870
or what hast thou to *d* in the way ... Jer 2:18 1870
they are wise to *d* evil ... Jer 4:22 7489
but to *d* good they have no ... Jer 4:22 3190
art spoiled, what wilt thou *d* ... Jer 4:30 6213
of the needy *d* they not judge ... Jer 5:28
what will ye *d* in the end thereof ... Jer 5:31 6213
We are delivered to *d* all these ... Jer 7:10 6213
will I *d* unto this house, which ... Jer 7:14 6213
they *d* in the cities of Judah ... Jer 7:17 6213
D they provoke me to anger ... Jer 7:19
d they not provoke themselves to ... Jer 7:19
How *d* ye say, We are wise, and the ... Jer 8:8
Why *d* we sit still ... Jer 8:14
for how shall I *d* for the ... Jer 9:7 6213
for they cannot *d* evil, neither ... Jer 10:5 7489
also is it in them to *d* good ... Jer 10:5 3190
d them, according to all which I ... Jer 11:4 6213
words of this covenant, and *d* them ... Jer 11:6 6213
which I commanded them to *d* ... Jer 11:8 6213
my beloved to *d* in mine house ... Jer 11:15
then how wilt thou *d* in the ... Jer 12:5 6213
D we not certainly know that ... Jer 13:12
then may ye also *d* good ... Jer 13:23 3190
that are accustomed to *d* evil ... Jer 13:23 7489
d thou it for thy name's sake ... Jer 14:7 6213
D not abhor us, for thy name's ... Jer 14:21
d not disgrace the throne of thy ... Jer 14:21
neither *d* ye any work, but hallow ... Jer 17:22 6213
sabbath day, to *d* no work therein ... Jer 17:24 6213
cannot I *d* with you as this ... Jer 18:6 6213
that I thought to *d* unto them ... Jer 18:8 6213
If it *d* evil in my sight, that it ... Jer 18:10 6213
and we will every one *d* the ... Jer 18:12 6213
Thus will I *d* unto this place, ... Jer 19:12 6213
d no wrong, *d* no violence to the ... Jer 22:3 3238,2554
For if ye *d* this thing indeed, ... Jer 22:4 6213
d judgment and justice, and then it ... Jer 22:15 6213
and for violence, to *d* it ... Jer 22:17 6213
D not I fill heaven and earth ... Jer 23:24
d tell them, and cause my people ... Jer 23:32 6213
and I will *d* you no hurt ... Jer 25:6
which I purpose to *d* unto them ... Jer 26:3 6213
d with me as seemeth good and meet ... Jer 26:14 6213
the LORD *d* so ... Jer 28:6 6213
good that I will *d* for my people ... Jer 29:32 6213
wherefore *d* I see every man with ... Jer 30:6
I *d* earnestly remember him still ... Jer 31:20
that thou commandedst them to *d* ... Jer 32:23 6213
they should *d* this abomination ... Jer 32:35 6213
away from them, to *d* them good ... Jer 32:40 2895
rejoice over them to *d* them good ... Jer 32:41 2895
all the good that I *d* unto them ... Jer 33:9 6213
to *d* sacrifice continually ... Jer 33:18 6213
which I purpose to *d* unto them ... Jer 36:3 6213
that can *d* any thing against you ... Jer 38:5 3201
well to him, and *d* him no harm ... Jer 39:12 6213
but *d* unto him even as he shall ... Jer 39:12 6213
Thou shalt not *d* this thing ... Jer 40:16 6213
many, as thine eyes *d* behold us ... Jer 42:2
walk, and the thing that we may *d* ... Jer 42:3 6213
if we *d* not even according to all ... Jer 42:5 6213
declare unto us, and we will *d* it ... Jer 42:20 6213
d not this abominable thing that ... Jer 44:4 6213
But we will certainly *d* ... Jer 44:17 6213
as she hath done, *d* unto her ... Jer 50:15 6213
d according to all that I have ... Jer 50:21 6213
that she hath done, *d* unto her ... Jer 50:29 6213
that I will *d* judgment upon the ... Jer 51:47 6485
that I will *d* judgment upon her ... Jer 51:52 6485
when her waves *d* roar like great ... Jer 51:55
The ways of Zion *d* mourn, because ... Lam 1:4
d unto them, as thou hast done ... Lam 1:22 5953
Mine eyes *d* fail with tears, my ... Lam 2:11
I *d* send thee unto them ... Eze 2:4
I will *d* in thee that which I ... Eze 5:9 6213
I will not *d* any more the like ... Eze 5:9 6213
I would *d* this evil unto them ... Eze 6:10 6213
I will *d* unto them after their ... Eze 7:27 6213
of man, seest thou what they *d* ... Eze 8:6 6213
abominations that they *d* here ... Eze 8:9 6213
the house of Israel *d* in the dark ... Eze 8:12 6213
greater abominations that they *d* ... Eze 8:13 6213
keep mine ordinances, and *d* them ... Eze 11:20 6213
be taken thereof to *d* any work ... Eze 15:3 6213
to *d* any of these unto thee, to ... Eze 16:5 6213
d that which is lawful and right, ... Eze 18:5 6213
d that which is lawful and right, ... Eze 18:21 6213
my judgments, which if a man *d* ... Eze 20:11 6213
my judgments, which if a man *d* ... Eze 20:13 6213
and keep my judgments, and *d* them ... Eze 20:19 6213
to *d* them, which if a man *d* ... Eze 20:21 6213
your doings your sins *d* appear ... Eze 21:24
LORD have spoken it, and will *d* it ... Eze 22:14 6213
I will *d* these things unto thee, ... Eze 23:30 6213
not to *d* after your lewdness ... Eze 23:48 6213
come to pass, and I will *d* it ... Eze 24:14 6213
ye shall *d* as I have done ... Eze 24:22 6213
all that he hath done shall ye *d* ... Eze 24:24 6213
Because that Moab and Seir *d* say ... Eze 25:8
they shall *d* in Edom according to ... Eze 25:14 6213
if he *d* not turn from his way, he ... Eze 33:9
d that which is lawful and right ... Eze 33:14 6213
d that which is lawful and right, ... Eze 33:19 6213
words, but they will not *d* them ... Eze 33:31 6213
thy words, but they *d* them not ... Eze 33:32 6213
of Israel that *d* feed themselves ... Eze 34:2
I will even *d* according to thine ... Eze 35:11 6213
desolate, so will I *d* unto thee ... Eze 35:15 6213
will *d* better unto you than at ... Eze 36:11 2895
I *d* not this for your sakes, O ... Eze 36:22 6213
keep my judgments, and *d* them ... Eze 36:27 6213
Not for your sakes *d* I this ... Eze 36:32 6213
have spoken it, and I will *d* it ... Eze 36:36 6213
house of Israel, to *d* it for them ... Eze 36:37 6213
and observe my statutes, and *d* them ... Eze 37:24 6213
that I the LORD *d* sanctify Israel ... Eze 37:28
that I *d* sacrifice for you ... Eze 39:17
the ordinances thereof, and *d* them ... Eze 43:11 6213
to *d* the office of a priest unto ... Eze 44:13 3547
so thou shalt *d* the seventh day ... Eze 45:20 6213
shall he *d* the like in the feast ... Eze 45:25 6213
d not ye serve my gods, nor ... Dan 3:14
known that the heavens *d* rule ... Dan 4:26
for we *d* not present our ... Dan 9:18
O Lord, hearken and *d* ... Dan 9:19 6213
and *d* according to his will ... Dan 11:3 6213
shall *d* according to his own will ... Dan 11:16 6213
thus shall he *d* ... Dan 11:17 6213
he shall *d* that which his fathers ... Dan 11:24 6213
hearts shall be to *d* mischief ... Dan 11:27
and he shall *d* exploits, and return ... Dan 11:28 6213
so shall he *d* ... Dan 11:30 6213
such as *d* wickedly against the ... Dan 11:32 7561
but the people that *d* know their ... Dan 11:32
shall be strong, and *d* exploits ... Dan 11:32 6213
the king shall *d* according to his ... Dan 11:36 6213
Thus shall he *d* in the most ... Dan 11:39 6213
but the wicked shall *d* wickedly ... Dan 12:10 7561
her rulers with shame *d* love ... Hos 4:18
Ephraim, what shall I *d* unto thee ... Hos 6:4 6213
O Judah, what shall I *d* unto thee ... Hos 6:4 6213
they *d* not return to the LORD ... Hos 7:10
yet *d* they imagine mischief ... Hos 7:15
What will ye *d* in the solemn day, ... Hos 9:5 6213
what then should a king *d* to us ... Hos 10:3 6213
So shall Beth-el *d* unto you ... Hos 10:15 6213
they *d* make a covenant with the ... Hos 12:1
What have I to *d* any more with ... Hos 14:8
How *d* the beasts groan ... Joel 1:18
for the LORD will *d* great things ... Joel 2:21 6213
of the wilderness *d* spring ... Joel 2:22
the vine *d* yield their strength ... Joel 2:22 6213
Yea, and what have ye to *d* with me ... Joel 3:4
the Lord GOD will *d* nothing ... Amos 3:7 6213
For they know not to *d* right ... Amos 3:10 6213
Therefore thus will I *d* unto thee ... Amos 4:12 6213
because I will *d* this unto thee ... Amos 4:12 6213
him, What shall we *d* unto thee ... Jonah 1:11 6213
said that he would *d* unto them ... Jonah 3:10 6213
I *d* well to be angry, even unto ... Jonah 4:9 3190
this family *d* I devise an evil ... Mic 2:3
d not my words *d* good to him ... Mic 2:7 3190
in the spirit and falsehood *d* lie ... Mic 2:11
require of thee, but to *d* justly ... Mic 6:8 6213
That they may *d* evil with both ... Mic 7:3
What *d* ye imagine against the ... Nah 1:9
heart, The LORD will not *d* good ... Zeph 1:12 3190
neither will he *d* evil ... Zeph 1:12 7487
he will not *d* iniquity ... Zeph 3:5 6213
of Israel shall not *d* iniquity ... Zeph 3:13 6213
and how *d* ye see it now ... Hag 2:3
and with his skirt *d* touch bread ... Hag 2:12
prophets, *d* they live for ever ... Zec 1:5
of hosts thought to *d* unto us ... Zec 1:6 6213
Then said I, What come these to *d* ... Zec 1:21 6213
Whither *d* these bear the ephah ... Zec 5:10
days to *d* good unto Jerusalem ... Zec 8:15 3190
are the things that ye shall *d* ... Zec 8:16 6213
even to day *d* I declare that I ... Zec 9:12
d not magnify themselves against ... Zec 12:7
neither *d* ye kindle fire on mine ... Mal 1:10
because ye *d* not lay it to heart ... Mal 2:2
why *d* we deal treacherously every ... Mal 2:10
yea, and all that *d* wickedly ... Mal 4:1 6213
in the day that I shall *d* this ... Mal 4:3 6213
Blessed are they which *d* hunger ... Mt 5:6
Neither *d* men light a candle, and ... Mt 5:15
but whosoever shall *d* and teach ... Mt 5:19 *4160*
d good to them that hate you, and ... Mt 5:44 *4160*
d not even the publicans the same ... Mt 5:46 *4160*
what *d* ye more than others ... Mt 5:47 *4160*
d not even the publicans so ... Mt 5:47 *4160*
Take heed that ye *d* not your alms ... Mt 6:1 *4160*
d not sound a trumpet before thee ... Mt 6:2
hypocrites *d* in the synagogues ... Mt 6:2 *4160*
repetitions, as the heathen *d* ... Mt 6:7
where thieves *d* not break through ... Mt 6:20
neither *d* they reap, nor gather ... Mt 6:26
toil not, neither *d* they spin ... Mt 6:28
these things *d* the Gentiles seek ... Mt 6:32
ye would that men should *d* to you ... Mt 7:12 *4160*
d ye even so to them ... Mt 7:12 *4160*
D men gather grapes of thorns, or ... Mt 7:16
servant, *D* this, and he doeth it ... Mt 8:9 *4160*
What have we to *d* with thee ... Mt 8:29 *4160*
of John, saying, Why *d* we ... Mt 9:14
Neither *d* men put new wine into ... Mt 9:17
ye that I am able to *d* this ... Mt 9:28 *4160*
come, or *d* we look for another ... Mt 11:3
those things which ye *d* hear ... Mt 11:4
thy disciples *d* that which is not ... Mt 12:2 *4160*
lawful to *d* upon the sabbath day ... Mt 12:2 *4160*
to *d* well on the sabbath days ... Mt 12:12 *4160*
by whom *d* your children cast them ... Mt 12:27
For whosoever shall *d* the will of ... Mt 12:50 *4160*
neither *d* they understand ... Mt 13:13
offend, and them which *d* iniquity ... Mt 13:41 *4160*
therefore mighty works *d* shew ... Mt 14:2
Why *d* thy disciples transgress ... Mt 15:2
Why *d* ye also transgress the ... Mt 15:3
But in vain they *d* worship me ... Mt 15:9 *4160*
D not ye yet understand, that ... Mt 15:17
D ye not yet understand, neither ... Mt 16:9
How is it that ye *d* not ... Mt 16:11
Whom *d* men say that I the Son of ... Mt 16:13
of whom *d* the kings of the earth ... Mt 17:25
That in heaven their angels *d* ... Mt 18:10
heavenly Father *d* also unto you ... Mt 18:35 *4160*
Master, what good thing shall I *d* ... Mt 19:16 *4160*
said, Thou shalt *d* no murder ... Mt 19:18
said, Friend, I *d* thee no wrong ... Mt 20:13 *91*
me to *d* what I will with mine own ... Mt 20:15 *4160*
will ye that I shall *d* unto you ... Mt 20:32 *4160*
ye shall not only *d* this which is ... Mt 21:21 *4160*
what authority I *d* these things ... Mt 21:24 *4160*
what authority I *d* these things ... Mt 21:27 *4160*
what will he *d* unto those ... Mt 21:40 *4160*
Ye *d* err, not knowing the ... Mt 22:29
you observe, that observe and *d* ... Mt 23:3 *4160*
but *d* not ye after their works ... Mt 23:3 *4160*
for they say, and *d* not ... Mt 23:3 *4160*
they *d* for to be seen of men ... Mt 23:5 *4160*
an oath, I *d* not know the man ... Mt 26:72
nothing to *d* with that just man ... Mt 27:19
What shall I *d* then with Jesus ... Mt 27:22 *4160*
what have we to *d* with thee ... Mk 1:24
spirits, and they *d* obey him ... Mk 1:27
Why *d* the disciples of John and of ... Mk 2:18
why *d* they on the sabbath day ... Mk 2:24 *4160*
Is it lawful to *d* good on the ... Mk 3:4 *15*
on the sabbath days, or to *d* evil ... Mk 3:4 *2554*
whosoever shall *d* the will of God ... Mk 3:35 *4160*
said, What have I to *d* with thee ... Mk 5:7
he could there *d* no mighty work ... Mk 6:5 *4160*
therefore mighty works *d* shew ... Mk 6:14
Howbeit in vain *d* they worship me ... Mk 7:7
many other such like things ye *d* ... Mk 7:8 *4160*
ye suffer him no more to *d* ought ... Mk 7:12 *4160*
and many such like things *d* ye ... Mk 7:13 *4160*
D ye not perceive, that ... Mk 7:18
and *d* ye not remember ... Mk 8:18
is it that ye *d* not understand ... Mk 8:21
them, Whom *d* men say that I am ... Mk 8:27
but if thou canst *d* any thing ... Mk 9:22 *1410*
shall *d* a miracle in my name ... Mk 9:39 *4160*
what shall I *d* that I may inherit ... Mk 10:17 *4160*
D not commit adultery, *D* not ... Mk 10:19
D not kill, *D* not steal ... Mk 10:19
D not bear false witness, Defraud ... Mk 10:19
d for us whatsoever we shall ... Mk 10:35 *4160*
would ye that I should *d* for you ... Mk 10:36 *4160*
thou that I should *d* unto thee ... Mk 10:51 *4160*
man say unto you, Why *d* ye this ... Mk 11:3 *4160*
there said unto them, What *d* ye ... Mk 11:5 *4160*
But if ye *d* not forgive, neither ... Mk 11:26
this authority to *d* these things ... Mk 11:28 *4160*
what authority I *d* these things ... Mk 11:29 *4160*
Neither *d* I tell you by what ... Mk 11:33 *4160*
what authority I *d* these things ... Mk 11:33 *4160*
the lord of the vineyard *d* ... Mk 12:9 *4160*
D ye not therefore err, because ... Mk 12:24
ye therefore *d* greatly err ... Mk 12:27
speak, neither *d* ye premeditate ... Mk 13:11
ye will ye may *d* them good ... Mk 14:7 *4160*
aloud began to desire him to *d* as ... Mk 15:8
d unto him whom ye call the King ... Mk 15:12 *4160*
to *d* for him after the custom of ... Lk 2:27 *4160*
him, saying, What shall we *d* then ... Lk 3:10 *4160*
hath meat, let him *d* likewise ... Lk 3:11 *4160*
unto him, Master, what shall we *d* ... Lk 3:12 *4160*
him, saying, And what shall we *d* ... Lk 3:14 *4160*
D violence to no man, neither ... Lk 3:14 *1286*
d also here in thy country ... Lk 4:23 *4160*
what have we to *d* with thee ... Lk 4:34
Why *d* ye eat and drink with ... Lk 5:30
Why *d* the disciples of John fast ... Lk 5:33
Why *d* ye that which is not lawful ... Lk 6:2 *4160*
lawful to *d* on the sabbath days ... Lk 6:2 *4160*
on the sabbath days to *d* good ... Lk 6:9 *15*
or to *d* evil? ... Lk 6:9 *2554*
what they might *d* to Jesus ... Lk 6:11 *4160*
d good to them which hate you, ... Lk 6:27 *4160*
ye would that men should *d* to you ... Lk 6:31 *4160*
d ye also to them likewise ... Lk 6:31 *4160*
if ye *d* good to them which ... Lk 6:33 *15*
good to them which *d* good to you ... Lk 6:33 *15*
for sinners also *d* even the same ... Lk 6:33 *4160*
d good, and lend, hoping for ... Lk 6:35 *15*
of thorns men *d* not gather figs ... Lk 6:44
d not the things which I say ... Lk 6:46 *4160*
worthy for whom he should *d* this ... Lk 7:4 *3930*
servant, *D* this, and he doeth it ... Lk 7:8 *4160*
hear the word of God, and *d* it ... Lk 8:21 *4160*
said, What have I to *d* with thee ... Lk 8:28
we *d* wipe off against you ... Lk 10:11
what shall I *d* to inherit eternal ... Lk 10:25 *4160*
this *d*, and thou shalt live ... Lk 10:28 *4160*

unto him, Go, and *d* thou likewise	Lk 10:37	*4160*
by whom *d* your sons cast them out	Lk 11:19	
Now *d* ye Pharisees make clean the	Lk 11:39	
that have no more that they can *d*	Lk 12:4	*4160*
himself, saying, What shall I *d*	Lk 12:17	*4160*
And he said, This will I *d*	Lk 12:18	*4160*
to *d* that thing which is least	Lk 12:26	*1410*
For all these things *d* the	Lk 12:30	
that ye *d* not discern this time	Lk 12:56	
I *d* cures to day and to morrow, and	Lk 13:32	*2005*
these many years *d* I serve thee	Lk 15:29	
within himself, What shall I *d*	Lk 16:3	*4160*
I am resolved what to *d*, that,	Lk 16:4	*4160*
done that which was our duty to *d*	Lk 17:10	*4160*
what shall I *d* to inherit eternal	Lk 18:18	*4160*
D not commit adultery	Lk 18:20	
D not kill, *D* not steal	Lk 18:20	
D not steal, *D* not bear false	Lk 18:20	
thou that I shall *d* unto thee	Lk 18:41	*4160*
man ask you, Why *d* ye loose him	Lk 19:31	
could not find what they might *d*	Lk 19:48	*4160*
what authority I *d* these things	Lk 20:8	*4160*
of the vineyard, What shall I *d*	Lk 20:13	*4160*
lord of the vineyard *d* unto them	Lk 20:15	*4160*
this *d* in remembrance of me	Lk 22:19	*4160*
it was that should *d* this thing	Lk 22:23	*4238*
For if they *d* these things in a	Lk 23:31	*4160*
for they know not what they *d*	Lk 23:34	*4160*
why *d* thoughts arise in your	Lk 24:38	
Woman, what have I to *d* with thee	Jn 2:4	
he saith unto you, *d* it	Jn 2:5	*4160*
for no man can *d* these miracles	Jn 3:2	*4160*
thee, We speak that we *d* know	Jn 3:11	
My meat is to *d* the will of him	Jn 4:34	*4160*
The Son can *d* nothing of himself,	Jn 5:19	*4160*
but what he seeth the Father *d*	Jn 5:19	*4160*
I can of mine own self *d* nothing	Jn 5:30	*4160*
finish, the same works that I *d*	Jn 5:36	*4160*
D not think that I will accuse	Jn 5:45	
he himself knew what he would *d*	Jn 6:6	*4160*
they unto him, What shall we *d*	Jn 6:28	*4160*
not to *d* mine own will, but the	Jn 6:38	*4160*
If thou *d* these things, shew	Jn 7:4	*4160*
If any man will *d* his will	Jn 7:17	*4160*
D the rulers know indeed that	Jn 7:26	
will he *d* more miracles than	Jn 7:31	*4160*
her, Neither *d* I condemn thee	Jn 8:11	
that I *d* nothing of myself	Jn 8:28	*4160*
for I *d* always those things that	Jn 8:29	*4160*
ye *d* that which ye have seen with	Jn 8:38	*4160*
ye would *d* the works of Abraham	Jn 8:39	*4160*
Ye *d* the deeds of your father	Jn 8:41	*4160*
Why *d* ye not understand my speech	Jn 8:43	
lusts of your father ye will *d*	Jn 8:44	*4160*
truth, why *d* ye not believe me	Jn 8:46	
my Father, and ye *d* dishonour me	Jn 8:49	
mine eyes, and I washed, and *d* see	Jn 9:15	
that is a sinner *d* such miracles	Jn 9:16	*4160*
not of God, he could *d* nothing	Jn 9:33	*4160*
the works that I *d* in my Father's	Jn 10:25	*4160*
of those works *d* ye stone me	Jn 10:32	
If I *d* not the works of my Father	Jn 10:37	*4160*
But if I *d*, though ye believe not	Jn 10:38	*4160*
if he sleep, he shall *d* well	Jn 11:12	*4982*
a council, and said, What *d* we	Jn 11:47	*4160*
What I *d* thou knowest not now	Jn 13:7	*4160*
that ye should *d* as I have done	Jn 13:15	*4160*
things, happy are ye if ye *d* them	Jn 13:17	*4160*
him, That thou doest, *d* quickly	Jn 13:27	*4160*
works that I *d* shall he *d* also	Jn 14:12	*4160*
works than these shall he *d*	Jn 14:12	*4160*
ask in my name, that will I *d*	Jn 14:13	*4160*
any thing in my name, I will *d* it	Jn 14:14	*4160*
gave me commandment, even so I *d*	Jn 14:31	*4160*
for without me ye can *d* nothing	Jn 15:5	*4160*
if ye *d* whatsoever I command you	Jn 15:14	*4160*
d unto you for my name's sake	Jn 15:21	*4160*
these things will they *d* unto you	Jn 16:3	*4160*
D ye enquire among yourselves of	Jn 16:19	
answered them, *D* ye now believe	Jn 16:31	
work which thou gavest me to *d*	Jn 17:4	*4160*
Lord, and what shall this man *d*	Jn 21:21	
of all that Jesus began both to *d*	Acts 1:1	*4160*
we *d* hear them speak in our	Acts 2:11	
Men and brethren, what shall we *d*	Acts 2:37	*4160*
What shall we *d* to these men	Acts 4:16	*4160*
For to *d* whatsoever thy hand and	Acts 4:28	*4160*
intend to *d* as touching these men	Acts 5:35	*4238*
why *d* ye wrong one to another	Acts 7:26	*91*
ye *d* always resist the Holy Ghost	Acts 7:51	
as your fathers did, so *d* ye	Acts 7:51	
Lord, what wilt thou have me to *d*	Acts 9:6	*4160*
be told thee what thou must *d*	Acts 9:6	*4160*
tell thee what thou oughtest to *d*	Acts 10:6	*4160*
Sirs, why *d* ye these things	Acts 14:15	*4160*
keep yourselves, ye shall *d* well	Acts 15:29	*4238*
of the Lord, and see how they *d*	Acts 15:36	*2192*
d exceedingly trouble our city,	Acts 16:20	
voice, saying, *D* thyself no harm	Acts 16:28	*4238*
Sirs, what must I *d* to be saved	Acts 16:30	*4160*
now *d* they thrust us out privily	Acts 16:37	
these all *d* contrary to the	Acts 17:7	*4160*
be quiet, and to *d* nothing rashly	Acts 19:36	*4160*
D therefore this that we say to	Acts 21:23	*4160*
And I said, What shall I *d*	Acts 22:10	*4160*
which are appointed for thee to *d*	Acts 22:10	*4160*
But *d* not thou yield unto them	Acts 23:21	
I *d* the more cheerfully answer	Acts 24:10	
herein *d* I exercise myself, to	Acts 24:16	
willing to *d* the Jews a pleasure,	Acts 25:9	*2698*
that I ought to *d* many things	Acts 26:9	*4238*
d works meet for repentance	Acts 26:20	*4238*
to *d* those things which are not	Rom 1:28	*4160*
of death, not only *d* the same	Rom 1:32	*4160*
have pleasure in them that *d* them	Rom 1:32	*4238*
judgest them which *d* such things	Rom 2:3	*4238*
d not obey the truth, but obey	Rom 2:8	*544*
d by nature the things contained	Rom 2:14	*4160*
that we say,) Let us *d* evil	Rom 3:8	*4160*
D we then make void the law	Rom 3:31	
For that which I *d* I allow not	Rom 7:15	*2716*
for what I would, that *d* I not	Rom 7:15	*4238*
but what I hate, that *d* I	Rom 7:15	*4160*
If then I *d* that which I would	Rom 7:16	*4160*
then it is no more I that *d* it	Rom 7:17	*2716*
For the good that I would I *d* not	Rom 7:19	*4160*
evil which I would not, that I *d*	Rom 7:19	*4238*
Now if I *d* that I would not	Rom 7:20	*4160*
it is no more I that *d* it	Rom 7:20	*2716*
a law, that, when I would *d* good	Rom 7:21	*4160*
For what the law could not *d*	Rom 8:3	*102*
d mind the things of the flesh	Rom 8:5	
but if ye through the Spirit *d*	Rom 8:13	
then *d* we with patience wait for	Rom 8:25	
let him *d* it with simplicity	Rom 12:8	
Rejoice with them that *d* rejoice	Rom 12:15	
d that which is good, and thou	Rom 13:3	*4160*
But if thou *d* that which is evil,	Rom 13:4	*4160*
them that *d* not believe in Judaea	Rom 15:31	*544*
For what have I to *d* to judge	1Cor 5:12	
d not ye judge them that are	1Cor 5:12	
D ye not know that the saints	1Cor 6:2	
Why *d* ye not rather take wrong	1Cor 6:7	
why *d* ye not rather suffer	1Cor 6:7	
ye *d* wrong, and defraud, and that	1Cor 6:8	
let him *d* what he will, he	1Cor 7:36	*4160*
to them that *d* examine me is this	1Cor 9:3	
D ye not know that they which	1Cor 9:13	
For if I *d* this thing willingly,	1Cor 9:17	*4238*
this I *d* for the gospel's sake,	1Cor 9:23	*4160*
Now they *d* it to obtain a	1Cor 9:25	
D we provoke the Lord to jealousy	1Cor 10:22	
eat, or drink, or whatsoever ye *d*	1Cor 10:31	*4160*
d all to the glory of God	1Cor 10:31	*4160*
this *d* in remembrance of me	1Cor 11:24	*4160*
this *d* ye, as oft as ye drink it,	1Cor 11:25	*4160*
ye *d* shew the Lord's death till	1Cor 11:26	
d all speak with tongues	1Cor 12:30	
d all interpret?	1Cor 12:30	
Else what shall they *d* which are	1Cor 15:29	*4160*
and with what body *d* they come	1Cor 15:35	
churches of Galatia, even so *d* ye	1Cor 16:1	*4160*
for I *d* pass through Macedonia	1Cor 16:5	
the work of the Lord, as I also *d*	1Cor 16:10	
d I purpose according to the	2Cor 1:17	
D we begin again to commend	2Cor 3:1	
are in this tabernacle *d* groan	2Cor 5:4	
I *d* not repent, though I did	2Cor 7:8	
we *d* you to wit of the grace of	2Cor 8:1	*1107*
have begun before, not only to *d*	2Cor 8:10	*4160*
Whether any *d* enquire of Titus,	2Cor 8:23	
we *d* not war after the flesh	2Cor 10:3	
D ye look on things after the	2Cor 10:7	
wages of them, to *d* you service	2Cor 11:8	
But what I *d*, that I will *d*,	2Cor 11:12	*4160*
But what I *d*, that I will *d*	2Cor 11:12	*4160*
but we *d* all things, dearly	2Cor 12:19	
I pray to God that ye *d* no evil	2Cor 13:7	*4160*
but that ye should *d* that which	2Cor 13:7	*4160*
For we can *d* nothing against the	2Cor 13:8	*1410*
For *d* I now persuade men, or God	Gal 1:10	
or *d* I seek to please men	Gal 1:10	
which I also was forward to *d*	Gal 2:10	*4160*
not as *d* the Jews, why compellest	Gal 2:14	
Gentiles to live as *d* the Jews	Gal 2:14	
I *d* not frustrate the grace of	Gal 2:21	
in the book of the law to *d* them	Gal 3:10	*4160*
the law, *d* ye not hear the law	Gal 4:21	
he is a debtor to *d* the whole law	Gal 5:3	*4160*
why *d* I yet suffer persecution	Gal 5:11	
so that ye cannot *d* the things	Gal 5:17	*4160*
that they which *d* such things	Gal 5:21	*4238*
let us *d* good unto all men,	Gal 6:10	*2038*
Now unto him that is able to *d*	Eph 3:20	*4160*
d the same things unto them,	Eph 6:9	*4160*
may know my affairs, and how I *d*	Eph 6:21	*4238*
and I therein *d* rejoice, yea, and	Phil 1:18	
to *d* of his good pleasure	Phil 2:13	*1754*
D all things without murmurings	Phil 2:14	*4160*
For the same cause also *d* ye joy	Phil 2:18	
d count them but dung, that I may	Phil 3:8	
but this one thing I *d*,	Phil 3:13	
and heard, and seen in me, *d*	Phil 4:9	*4238*
I can *d* all things through Christ	Phil 4:13	*2480*
d not cease to pray for you, and	Col 1:9	
Christ forgave you, so also *d* ye	Col 3:13	
whatsoever ye *d* in word or deed,	Col 3:17	*4160*
d all in the name of the Lord	Col 3:17	*4160*
And whatsoever ye *d*	Col 3:23	*4160*
d it heartily, as to the Lord, and	Col 3:23	*2038*
all men, even as we *d* toward you	1Th 3:12	
indeed ye *d* it toward all the	1Th 4:10	*4160*
to *d* your own business, and to	1Th 4:11	*4238*
let us not sleep, as *d* others	1Th 5:6	
one another, even as also ye *d*	1Th 5:11	*4160*
calleth you, who also will *d* it	1Th 5:24	*4160*
Lord touching you, that ye both *d*	2Th 3:4	*4160*
will *d* the things which we	2Th 3:4	*4160*
which is in faith: so *d*	1Ti 1:4	
but rather *d* them service,	1Ti 6:2	*1398*
That they *d* good, that they be	1Ti 6:18	*14*
that they *d* gender strifes	2Ti 2:23	
so *d* these also resist the truth	2Ti 3:8	
d the work of an evangelist, make	2Ti 4:5	*4160*
D thy diligence to come shortly	2Ti 4:9	*4704*
D thy diligence to come before	2Ti 4:21	*4704*
thy mind would I *d* nothing	Philem 14	*4160*
albeit I *d* not say to thee how	Philem 19	*4160*
thou wilt also *d* more than I say	Philem 21	*4160*
They *d* alway err in their heart	Heb 3:10	
have believed *d* enter into rest	Heb 4:3	
of him with whom we have to *d*	Heb 4:13	*3056*
And this will we *d*, if God permit	Heb 6:3	*4160*
to the saints, and *d* minister	Heb 6:10	
d shew the same diligence to the	Heb 6:11	
of me,) to *d* thy will, O God	Heb 10:7	*4160*
said he, Lo, I come to *d* thy will	Heb 10:9	*4160*
not made of things which *d* appear	Heb 11:3	
assaying to *d* were drowned	Heb 11:29	*2983*
not fear what man shall *d* unto me	Heb 13:6	*4160*
But to *d* good and to communicate	Heb 13:16	*2140*
that they may *d* it with joy	Heb 13:17	*4160*
beseech you the rather to *d* this	Heb 13:19	*4160*
in every good work to *d* his will	Heb 13:21	*4160*
D not err, my beloved brethren	Jas 1:16	
D not rich men oppress you, and	Jas 2:6	
D not they blaspheme that worthy	Jas 2:7	
neighbour as thyself, ye *d* well	Jas 2:8	4160
D not commit adultery, said also,	Jas 2:11	
adultery, said also, *D* not kill	Jas 2:11	
So speak ye, and so *d*, as they	Jas 2:12	*4160*
D ye think that the scripture	Jas 4:5	
we shall live, and *d* this, or that	Jas 4:15	*4160*
to him that knoweth to *d* good	Jas 4:17	*4160*
if any of you *d* err from the	Jas 5:19	
Who by him *d* believe in God, that	1Pet 1:21	
the praise of them that *d* well	1Pet 2:14	*17*
but if, when ye *d* well, and suffer	1Pet 2:20	*15*
ye are, as long as ye *d* well	1Pet 3:6	*15*
Let him eschew evil, and *d* good	1Pet 3:11	*4160*
Lord is against them that *d* evil	1Pet 3:12	*4160*
let him *d* it as of the ability	1Pet 4:11	
for if ye *d* these things, ye	2Pet 1:10	*4160*
whereunto ye *d* well that ye take	2Pet 1:19	*4160*
wrest, as they *d* also the other	2Pet 3:16	
we lie, and *d* not the truth	1Jn 1:6	*4160*
hereby we *d* know that we know him	1Jn 2:3	
d those things that are pleasing	1Jn 3:22	*4160*
d testify that the Father sent	1Jn 4:14	
I *d* not say that he shall pray	1Jn 5:16	
a godly sort, thou shalt *d* well	3Jn 6	*4160.*
and repent, and *d* the first works	Rev 2:5	*4160*
are Jews, and are not, but *d* lie	Rev 3:9	
of thy nakedness *d* not appear	Rev 3:18	
heads, and with them they *d* hurt	Rev 9:19	
to *d* in the sight of the beast	Rev 13:14	*4160*
and their works *d* follow them	Rev 14:13	
said unto me, See thou *d* it not	Rev 19:10	*3361*
of the earth *d* bring their glory	Rev 21:24	
he unto me, See thou *d* it not	Rev 22:9	*3361*
are they that *d* his commandments	Rev 22:14	*4160*

DOCTOR {1}

a *d* of the law, had in reputation	Acts 5:34	*3547*

DOCTORS {2}

sitting in the midst of the *d*	Lk 2:46	*1320*
d of the law sitting by, which	Lk 5:17	*3547*

DOCTRINE {51}

My *d* shall drop as the rain, my	Deut 32:2	3948
My *d* is pure, and I am clean in	Job 11:4	3948
For I give you good *d*, forsake ye	Prov 4:2	3948
shall he make to understand *d*	Is 28:9	8052
they that murmured shall learn *d*	Is 29:24	3948
the stock is a *d* of vanities	Jer 10:8	4148
people were astonished at his *d*	Mt 7:28	*1322*
but of the *d* of the Pharisees and	Mt 16:12	*1322*
they were astonished at his *d*	Mt 22:33	*1322*
And they were astonished at his *d*	Mk 1:22	*1322*
what new *d* is this	Mk 1:27	*1322*
and said unto them in his *d*	Mk 4:2	*1322*
people was astonished at his *d*	Mk 11:18	*1322*
And he said unto them in his *d*	Mk 12:38	*1322*
And they were astonished at his *d*	Lk 4:32	*1322*
My *d* is not mine, but his that	Jn 7:16	*1322*
his will, he shall know of the *d*	Jn 7:17	*1322*
of his disciples, and of his *d*	Jn 18:19	*1322*
stedfastly in the apostles' *d*	Acts 2:42	*1322*
have filled Jerusalem with your *d*	Acts 5:28	*1322*
astonished at the *d* of the Lord	Acts 13:12	*1322*
May we know what this new *d*	Acts 17:19	*1322*
form of *d* which was delivered you	Rom 6:17	*1322*
to the *d* which ye have learned	Rom 16:17	*1322*
or by prophesying, or by *d*	1Cor 14:6	*1322*
one of you hath a psalm, hath a *d*	1Cor 14:26	*1322*
about with every wind of *d*	Eph 4:14	*1319*
some that they teach no other *d*	1Ti 1:3	
thing that is contrary to sound *d*	1Ti 1:10	*1319*
the words of faith and of good *d*	1Ti 4:6	*1319*
to reading, to exhortation, to *d*	1Ti 4:13	*1319*
heed unto thyself, and unto the *d*	1Ti 4:16	*1319*
they who labour in the word and *d*	1Ti 5:17	*1319*
of God and his *d* be not blasphemed	1Ti 6:1	*1319*
to the *d* which is according to	1Ti 6:3	*1319*
But thou hast fully known my *d*	2Ti 3:10	*1319*

of God, and is profitable for *d* 2Ti 3:16 1319
with all longsuffering and *d* 2Ti 4:2 1322
when they will not endure sound *d* 2Ti 4:3 1319
be able by sound *d* both to exhort .... Titus 1:9 1319
the things which become sound *d* .... Titus 2:1 1319
in *d* shewing uncorruptness, ... Titus 2:7 1319
that they may adorn the *d* of God .... Titus 2:10 1319
the principles of the *d* of Christ .... Heb 6:1 3056
Of the *d* of baptisms, and of .... Heb 6:2 1322
and abideth not in the *d* of Christ 2Jn 9 1322
that abideth in the *d* of Christ 2Jn 9 1322
any unto you, and bring not this *d* 2Jn 10 1322
them that hold the *d* of Balaam .... Rev 2:14 1322
hold the *d* of the Nicolaitanes .... Rev 2:15 1322
as many as have not this *d* .... Rev 2:24 1322

DOCTRINES {5}
teaching for *d* the commandments .... Mt 15:9 1319
teaching for *d* the commandments .... Mk 7:7 1319
the commandments and *d* of men .... Col 2:22 1319
seducing spirits, and *d* of devils 1Ti 4:1 1319
about with divers and strange *d* .... Heb 13:9 1322

DODAI *(do'-dahee)* {1} See DODO. *A captain in David's army.*
the second month was *D* an Ahohite 1Chr 27:4 1739

DODANIM *(do'-da-nim)* {2} See RODANIM. *Descendants of Javan.*
and Tarshish, Kittim, and *D* .... Gen 10:4 1721
and Tarshish, Kittim, and *D* 1Chr 1:7 1721

DODAVAH *(do'-da-vah)* {1} *Father of Eliezer.*
Then Eliezer the son of *D* of 2Chr 20:37 1735

DODAVAHU See DODAVAH.

DODO *(do'-do)* {5} See DODAI.
1. Grandfather of Tola.
the son of Puah, the son of *D* .... Judg 10:1 1734
2. Father of Eleazar.
Eleazar the son of *D* the Ahohite 2Sa 23:9 1734
him was Eleazar the son of *D* 1Chr 11:12 1734
3. Father of Elhanan.
the son of *D* of Beth-lehem 2Sa 23:24 1734
the son of *D* of Beth-lehem 1Chr 11:26 1734

DOEG *(do'-eg)* {6} *Chief herdsman of King Saul.*
and his name was *D*, an Edomite, ... 1Sa 21:7 1673
Then answered *D* the Edomite 1Sa 22:9 1673
And the king said to *D*, Turn thou, ... 1Sa 22:18 1673
D the Edomite turned, and he fell 1Sa 22:18 1673
when *D* the Edomite was there, ... 1Sa 22:22 1673
when *D* the Edomite came and told .... Ps 52:*t* 1673

DOER {8}
did there, he was the *d* of it .... Gen 39:22 6218
the *d* of evil according to his 2Sa 3:39 6218
plentifully rewardeth the proud *d* .... Ps 31:23 6218
A wicked *d* giveth heed to false .... Prov 17:4
I suffer trouble, as an evil *d* 2Ti 2:9 2557
a hearer of the word, and not a *d* .... Jas 1:23 4163
but a *d* of the work, this man .... Jas 1:25 4163
law, thou art not a *d* of the law .... Jas 4:11 4163

DOERS {6}
the hand of the *d* of the work 2Kin 22:5 6213
let them give it to the *d* of the 2Kin 22:5 6213
neither will he help the evil *d* .... Job 8:20
d from the city of the LORD .... Ps 101:8 6466
but the *d* of the law shall be .... Rom 2:13 4163
But be ye *d* of the word, and not .... Jas 1:22 4163

DOEST {45}
If thou *d* well, shalt thou not be .... Gen 4:7 3190
if thou *d* not well, sin lieth at .... Gen 4:7 3190
is with thee in all that thou *d* .... Gen 21:22 6213
thing that thou *d* to the people .... Ex 18:14 6213
The thing that thou *d* is not good .... Ex 18:17 6213
when thou *d* that which is good and .... Deut 12:28 6213
work of thine hand which thou *d* .... Deut 14:29 6213
bless thee in all that thou *d* .... Deut 15:18 6213
but thou *d* me wrong to war .... Judg 11:27 6213
in, and to know all that thou *d* 2Sa 3:25 6213
mayest prosper in all that thou *d* 1Kin 2:3 6213
him, What *d* thou here, Elijah 1Kin 19:9
and said, What *d* thou here, Elijah 1Kin 19:13
and mark, and see what thou *d* 1Kin 20:22 6213
will say unto him, What *d* thou .... Job 9:12 6213
sinnest, what *d* thou against him .... Job 35:6 6466
multiplied, what *d* thou unto him .... Job 35:6 6213
when thou *d* well to thyself .... Ps 49:18 3190
Thou art the God that *d* wonders .... Ps 77:14 6213
art great, and *d* wondrous things .... Ps 86:10 6213
Thou art good, and *d* good .... Ps 119:68
who may say unto him, What *d* thou .... Eccl 8:4 6213
when thou *d* evil, then thou .... Jer 11:15
shall go aside to ask how thou *d* .... Jer 15:5 7965
said unto thee, What *d* thou .... Eze 12:9 6213
seeing thou *d* all these things, ... Eze 16:30 6213
things are to us, that thou *d* so .... Eze 24:19 6213
or say unto him, What *d* thou .... Dan 4:35 5648
the LORD, *D* thou well to be angry .... Jonah 4:4 3190
D thou well to be angry for the .... Jonah 4:9 3190
Therefore when thou *d* thine alms .... Mt 6:2 4160
But when thou *d* alms, let not thy .... Mt 6:3 4160
authority *d* thou these things .... Mt 21:23 4160
authority *d* thou these things .... Mk 11:28 4160
authority *d* thou these things .... Lk 20:2 4160
seeing that thou *d* these things .... Jn 2:18 4160
can do these miracles that thou *d* .... Jn 3:2 4160
may see the works that thou *d* .... Jn 7:3 4160
said Jesus unto him, That thou *d* .... Jn 13:27 4160
saying, Take heed what thou *d* .... Acts 22:26 4160

that judgest *d* the same things .... Rom 2:1 4238
d the same, that thou shalt .... Rom 2:3 4160
there is one God; thou *d* well .... Jas 2:19 4160
thou *d* faithfully whatsoever thou 3Jn 5 4160
whatsoever thou *d* to the brethren 3Jn 5 4160

DOETH {96}
seen all that Laban *d* unto thee .... Gen 31:12 6213
for whosoever *d* any work therein, ... Ex 31:14 6213
whosoever *d* any work in the .... Ex 31:15 6213
whosoever *d* work therein shall be .... Ex 35:2 6213
while he *d* somewhat against any .... Lev 4:27 6213
in any of all these that a man *d* .... Lev 6:3 6213
that *d* any work in that same day .... Lev 23:30 6213
But the soul that *d* ought .... Num 15:30 6213
who shall live when God *d* this .... Num 24:23 7760
Which *d* great things and .... Job 5:9 6213
Which *d* great things past finding .... Job 9:10 6213
his soul desireth, even that he *d* .... Job 23:13 6213
and *d* not good to the widow .... Job 24:21 3190
great things *d* he, which we .... Job 37:5 6213
and whatsoever he *d* shall prosper .... Ps 1:3 6213
works, there is none that *d* good .... Ps 14:1 6213
there is none that *d* good .... Ps 14:3 6213
nor *d* evil to his neighbour, nor .... Ps 15:3 6213
He that *d* these things shall .... Ps 15:5 6213
there is none that *d* good .... Ps 53:1 6213
there is none that *d* good .... Ps 53:3 6213
who only *d* wondrous things .... Ps 72:18 6213
he that *d* righteousness at all .... Ps 106:3 6213
hand of the LORD *d* valiantly .... Ps 118:15 6213
hand of the LORD *d* valiantly .... Ps 118:16 6213
To him who alone *d* great wonders .... Ps 136:4 6213
he that *d* it destroyeth his own .... Prov 6:32 6213
The merciful man *d* good to his .... Prov 11:17 1580
the heart of the foolish *d* not so .... Prov 15:7
a fool *d* it to his sorrow .... Prov 17:21
A merry heart *d* good like a .... Prov 17:22 3190
A man that *d* violence to the .... Prov 28:17 6231
and of mirth, What *d* it .... Eccl 2:2 6213
I know that, whatsoever God *d* .... Eccl 3:14 6213
and God *d* it, that men should fear .... Eccl 3:14 6213
just man upon earth, that *d* good .... Eccl 7:20 6213
for he *d* whatsoever pleaseth him .... Eccl 8:3 6213
bind them on thee, as a bride *d* .... Is 49:18
Blessed is the man that *d* this .... Is 56:2 6213
Wherefore *d* the LORD our God all .... Jer 5:19 6213
Cursed be he that *d* the work of .... Jer 48:10 6213
he escape that *d* such things .... Eze 17:15 6213
that *d* the like to any one of .... Eze 18:10 6213
that *d* not any of those duties, ... Eze 18:11 6213
considereth, and *d* not such like, ... Eze 18:14 6213
and *d* according to all the .... Eze 18:24 6213
that the wicked man *d*, shall he .... Eze 18:24 6213
d that which is lawful and right, ... Eze 18:27 6213
he *d* according to his will in the .... Dan 4:35 5648
in all his works which he *d* .... Dan 9:14 6213
name, saith the LORD that *d* this .... Amos 9:12 6213
will cut off the man that *d* this .... Mal 2:12 6213
Every one that *d* evil is good in .... Mal 2:17 6213
hand know what thy right hand *d* .... Mt 6:3 4160
but he that *d* the will of my .... Mt 7:21 4160
d them, I will liken him unto a .... Mt 7:24 4160
d them not, shall be likened unto .... Mt 7:26 4160
my servant, Do this, and he *d* it .... Mt 8:9 4160
d them, I will shew you to whom .... Lk 6:47 4160
d not, is like a man that without .... Lk 6:49 4160
my servant, Do this, and he *d* it .... Lk 7:8 4238
For every one that *d* evil hateth .... Jn 3:20 4160
But he that *d* truth cometh to the .... Jn 3:21 4160
for what things soever he *d* .... Jn 5:19 4160
these also *d* the Son likewise .... Jn 5:19 4160
him all things that himself *d* .... Jn 5:20 4160
no man that *d* any thing in secret .... Jn 7:4 4160
it hear him, and know what he *d* .... Jn 7:51 4160
d his will, him he heareth .... Jn 9:31 4160
for this man *d* many miracles .... Jn 11:47 4160
dwelleth in me, he *d* the works .... Jn 14:10 4160
knoweth not what his lord *d* .... Jn 15:15 4160
will think that he *d* God service .... Jn 16:2 4374
the Lord, who *d* all these things .... Acts 15:17 4160
This man *d* nothing worthy of .... Acts 26:31 4238
every soul of man that *d* evil .... Rom 2:9 2716
there is none that *d* good .... Rom 3:12 4160
That the man which *d* those things .... Rom 10:5 4160
wrath upon him that *d* evil .... Rom 13:4 4238
that a man *d* is without the body 1Cor 6:18 4160
he will keep his virgin, *d* well 1Cor 7:37 4160
giveth her in marriage *d* well 1Cor 7:38 4160
her not in marriage *d* better 1Cor 7:38 4160
d he it by the works of the law, ... Gal 3:5
The man that *d* them shall live in .... Gal 3:12 4160
whatsoever good thing any man *d* .... Eph 6:8 4160
But he that *d* wrong shall receive .... Col 3:25 91
d it not, to him it is sin .... Jas 4:17 4160
but he that *d* the will of God 1Jn 2:17 4160
ye know that every one that *d* 1Jn 2:29 4160
he that *d* righteousness is 1Jn 3:7 4160
whosoever *d* not righteousness is 1Jn 3:10 4160
remember his deeds which he *d* 3Jn 10 4160
He that *d* good is of God 3Jn 11 15
but he that *d* evil hath not seen 3Jn 11 2554
he *d* great wonders, so that he .... Rev 13:13 4160

DOG {15}
shall not a *d* move his tongue .... Ex 11:7 3611
of a whore, or the price of a *d* .... Deut 23:18 3611
as a *d* lappeth, him shalt thou .... Judg 7:5 3611
said unto David, Am I a *d* 1Sa 17:43 3611
after a dead *d*, after a flea 1Sa 24:14 3611
look upon such a dead *d* as I am 2Sa 9:8 3611
Why should this dead *d* curse my 2Sa 16:9 3611
But what, is thy servant a *d* 2Kin 8:13 3611
darling from the power of the *d* .... Ps 22:20 3611
they make a noise like a *d* .... Ps 59:6 3611
and let them make a noise like a *d* .... Ps 59:14 3611
As a *d* returneth to his vomit, so .... Prov 26:11 3611
one that taketh a *d* by the ears .... Prov 26:17 3611
for a living *d* is better than a .... Eccl 9:4 3611
The *d* is turned to his own vomit 2Pet 2:22 2965

DOG'S {2}
and said, Am I a *d* head, which 2Sa 3:8 3611
a lamb, as if he cut off a *d* neck .... Is 66:3 3611

DOGS {24}
ye shall cast it to the *d* .... Ex 22:31 3611
in the city shall the *d* eat 1Kin 14:11 3611
in the city shall the *d* eat 1Kin 16:4 3611
In the place where *d* licked the 1Kin 21:19 3611
of Naboth shall *d* lick thy blood 1Kin 21:19 3611
The *d* shall eat Jezebel by the 1Kin 21:23 3611
Ahab in the city the *d* shall eat 1Kin 21:24 3611
the *d* licked up his blood 1Kin 22:38 3611
the *d* shall eat Jezebel in the 2Kin 9:10 3611
shall *d* eat the flesh of Jezebel 2Kin 9:36 3611
have set with the *d* of my flock .... Job 30:1 3611
For *d* have compassed me .... Ps 22:16 3611
the tongue of thy *d* in the same .... Ps 68:23 3611
all ignorant, they are all dumb *d* .... Is 56:10 3611
they are greedy *d* which can never .... Is 56:11 3611
the *d* to tear, and the fowls of .... Jer 15:3 3611
not that which is holy unto the *d* .... Mt 7:6 2965
bread, and to cast it to *d* .... Mt 15:26 2952
yet the *d* eat of the crumbs which .... Mt 15:27 2952
bread, and to cast it unto the *d* .... Mk 7:27 2952
yet the *d* under the table eat of .... Mk 7:28 2952
moreover the *d* came and licked his .... Lk 16:21 2965
Beware of *d*, beware of evil .... Phil 3:2 2965
For without are *d*, and sorcerers, ... Rev 22:15 2965

DOING {40}
hast now done foolishly in so *d* .... Gen 31:28 6213
ye have done evil in so *d* .... Gen 44:5 6213
fearful in praises, *d* wonders .... Ex 15:11 6213
without *d* any thing else, go .... Num 20:19
in *d* wickedly in the sight of the .... Deut 9:18 6213
So Hiram made an end of *d* all the 1Kin 7:40 6213
d evil in the sight of the LORD 1Kin 16:19 6213
d that which was right in the 1Kin 22:43 6213
in *d* that which was evil in the 2Kin 21:16 6213
Arise therefore, and be *d*, and the 1Chr 22:16 6213
d that which was right in the 2Chr 20:32 6213
d according to their abominations .... Ezr 9:1
I am *d* a great work, so that I .... Neh 6:3 6213
in so *d* my maker would soon take .... Job 32:22
shall wisely consider of his *d* .... Ps 64:9 4640
he is terrible in his *d* toward .... Ps 66:5 5949
This is the LORD'S *d* .... Ps 118:23 854
keepeth his hand from *d* any evil .... Is 56:2 6213
from *d* thy pleasure on my holy .... Is 58:13 6213
not *d* thine own ways, nor finding .... Is 58:13 6213
this is the Lord's *d*, and it is .... Mt 21:42 1096
when he cometh shall find so *d* .... Mt 24:46 4160
This was the Lord's *d*, and it is .... Mk 12:11 1096
when he cometh shall find so *d* .... Lk 12:43 4160
who went about *d* good, and healing .... Acts 10:38 2109
they have found any evil *d* in me .... Acts 24:20 92
in well *d* seek for glory and .... Rom 2:7 2041
for in so *d* thou shalt heap coals .... Rom 12:20 4160
Now therefore perform the *d* of it 2Cor 8:11 4160
And let us not be weary in well *d* .... Gal 6:9 4160
d the will of God from the heart .... Eph 6:6 4160
With good will *d* service, as to .... Eph 6:7 1398
brethren, be not weary in well *d* 2Th 3:13 2569
for in *d* this thou shalt both 1Ti 4:16 4160
another, *d* nothing by partiality 1Ti 5:21 4160
that with well *d* ye may put to 1Pet 2:15 15
be so, that ye suffer for well *d* 1Pet 3:17 15
for well *d*, than for evil *d* 1Pet 3:17 2554
of their souls to him in well *d* 1Pet 4:19 16

DOINGS {51}
After the *d* of the land of Egypt, ... Lev 18:3 4640
after the *d* of the land of Canaan .... Lev 18:3 4640
of the wickedness of thy *d* .... Deut 28:20 4611
they ceased not from their own *d* .... Judg 2:19 4611
man was churlish and evil in his *d* 1Sa 25:3 4611
and not after the *d* of Israel 2Chr 17:4 4640
declare among the people his *d* .... Ps 9:11 5949
of all thy work, and talk of thy *d* .... Ps 77:12 5949
Even a child is known by his *d* .... Prov 20:11 4611
of your *d* from before mine eyes .... Is 1:16 4611
their *d* are against the LORD, to .... Is 3:8 4611
shall eat the fruit of their *d* .... Is 3:10 4611
declare his *d* among the people, ... Is 12:4 5949
it because of the evil of your *d* .... Jer 4:4 4611
thy *d* have procured these things .... Jer 4:18 4611
Israel, Amend your ways and your *d* .... Jer 7:3 4611
amend your ways and your *d* .... Jer 7:5 4611
then thou shewedst me their *d* .... Jer 11:18 4611
according to the fruit of his *d* .... Jer 17:10 4611
and make your ways and your *d* good .... Jer 18:11 4611
it, because of the evil of your *d* .... Jer 21:12 4611
according to the fruit of your *d* .... Jer 21:14 4611
visit upon you the evil of your *d* .... Jer 23:2 4611
way, and from the evil of their *d* .... Jer 23:22 4611
way, and from the evil of your *d* .... Jer 25:5 4611
because of the evil of their *d* .... Jer 26:3 4611

now amend your ways and your *d*	Jer 26:13	4611
according to the fruit of his *d*	Jer 32:19	4611
his evil way, and amend your *d*	Jer 35:15	4611
because of the evil of your *d*	Jer 44:22	4611
ye shall see their way and their *d*	Eze 14:22	5949
when ye see their ways and their *d*	Eze 14:23	5949
remember your ways, and all your *d*	Eze 20:43	5949
nor according to your corrupt *d*	Eze 20:44	5949
in all your *d* your sins do appear	Eze 21:24	5949
thy ways, and according to thy *d*	Eze 24:14	5949
it by their own way and by their *d*	Eze 36:17	5949
to their *d* I judged them	Eze 36:19	5949
your *d* that were not good, and	Eze 36:31	4611
ways, and reward them their *d*	Hos 4:9	4611
their *d* to turn unto their God	Hos 5:4	4611
now their own *d* have beset them	Hos 7:2	4611
for the wickedness of their *d* I	Hos 9:15	4611
according to his *d* will he	Hos 12:2	4611
are these his *d*	Mic 2:7	4611
behaved themselves ill in their *d*	Mic 3:4	4611
therein, for the fruit of their *d*	Mic 7:13	4611
early, and corrupted all their *d*	Zeph 3:7	5949
thou not be ashamed for all thy *d*	Zeph 3:11	5949
evil ways, and from your evil *d*	Zec 1:4	4611
our ways, and according to our *d*	Zec 1:6	4611

DOLEFUL {2}

shall be full of *d* creatures	Is 13:21	255
and lament with a *d* lamentation	Mic 2:4	5093

DOMINION {62}

let them have *d* over the fish of	Gen 1:26	7287
have *d* over the fish of the sea,	Gen 1:28	7287
pass when thou shalt have the *d*	Gen 27:40	7300
shalt thou indeed have *d* over us	Gen 37:8	4910
shall come he that shall have *d*	Num 24:19	7287
have *d* over the nobles among the	Judg 5:13	7287
made me have *d* over the mighty	Judg 5:13	7287
the Philistines had *d* over Israel	Judg 14:4	4910
For he had *d* over all the region	1Kin 4:24	7287
and in all the land of his *d*	1Kin 9:19	4475
in his house, nor in all his *d*	2Kin 20:13	4475
and Saraph, who had the *d* in Moab	1Chr 4:22	1166
his *d* by the river Euphrates	1Chr 18:3	3027
throughout all the land of his *d*	2Chr 8:6	4475
from under the *d* of Judah	2Chr 21:8	3027
so that they had the *d* over them	Neh 9:28	7287
also they have *d* over our bodies,	Neh 9:37	4910
D and fear are with him	Job 25:2	4910
canst thou set the *d* thereof in	Job 38:33	4896
Thou madest him to have *d* over	Ps 8:6	4910
let them not have *d* over me	Ps 19:13	4910
the upright shall have *d* over	Ps 49:14	7287
He shall have *d* also from sea to	Ps 72:8	7287
his works in all places of his *d*	Ps 103:22	4475
his sanctuary, and Israel his *d*	Ps 114:2	4475
not any iniquity have *d* over me	Ps 119:133	7980
thy *d* endureth throughout all	Ps 145:13	4475
besides thee have had *d* over us	Is 26:13	1196
in his house, nor in all his *d*	Is 39:2	4475
kingdoms of the earth of his *d*	Jer 34:1	4475
thereof, and all the land of his *d*	Jer 51:28	4475
his *d* is from generation to	Dan 4:3	7985
thy *d* to the end of the earth	Dan 4:22	7985
whose *d* is an everlasting *d*	Dan 4:34	7985
That in every *d* of my kingdom men	Dan 6:26	7985
his *d* shall be even unto the end	Dan 6:26	7985
and *d* was given to it	Dan 7:6	7985
they had their *d* taken away	Dan 7:12	7985
And there was given him *d*, and	Dan 7:14	7985
his *d* is an everlasting *d*,	Dan 7:14	7985
and they shall take away his *d*	Dan 7:26	7985
And the kingdom and *d*, and the	Dan 7:27	7985
up, that shall rule with great *d*	Dan 11:3	4474
according to his *d* which he ruled	Dan 11:4	4915
be strong above him, and have *d*	Dan 11:5	4910
his *d* shall be a great *d*	Dan 11:5	4474
shall it come, even the first *d*	Mic 4:8	4475
his *d* shall be from sea even to	Zec 9:10	4915
the Gentiles exercise *d* over them	Mt 20:25	*2634*
death hath no more *d* over him	Rom 6:9	*2961*
For sin shall not have *d* over you	Rom 6:14	*2961*
how that the law hath *d* over a	Rom 7:1	*2961*
that we have *d* over your faith	2Cor 1:24	*2961*
and power, and might, and *d*	Eph 1:21	*2963*
be praise and *d* for ever and ever	1Pet 4:11	*2904*
be glory and *d* for ever and ever	1Pet 5:11	*2904*
defile the flesh, despise *d*	Jude 8	*2963*
Saviour, be glory and majesty, *d*	Jude 25	*2904*
be glory and *d* for ever and ever	Rev 1:6	*2904*

DOMINIONS {2}

all *d* shall serve and obey him	Dan 7:27	7985
whether they be thrones, or *d*	Col 1:16	*2963*

DONE {564}

What is this that thou hast *d*	Gen 3:13	6213
serpent, Because thou hast *d* this	Gen 3:14	6213
And he said, What hast thou *d*	Gen 4:10	6213
every thing living, as I have *d*	Gen 8:21	6213
his younger son had *d* unto him	Gen 9:24	6213
is this that thou hast *d* unto me	Gen 12:18	6213
now, and see whether they have *d*	Gen 18:21	6213
of my hands have I *d* this	Gen 20:5	6213
him, What hast thou *d* unto us	Gen 20:9	6213
thou hast *d* deeds unto me that	Gen 20:9	6213
unto me that ought not to be *d*	Gen 20:9	6213
thou, that thou hast *d* this thing	Gen 20:10	6213
kindness that I have *d* unto thee	Gen 21:23	6213
I wot not who hath *d* this thing	Gen 21:26	6213
because thou hast *d* this thing	Gen 22:16	6213
to pass, before he had *d* speaking	Gen 24:15	3615
when she had *d* giving him drink,	Gen 24:19	3615
also, until they have *d* drinking	Gen 24:19	3615
as the camels had *d* drinking	Gen 24:22	3615
before I had *d* speaking in mine	Gen 24:45	3615
Isaac all things that he had *d*	Gen 24:66	6213
What is this thou hast *d* unto us	Gen 26:10	6213
as we have *d* unto thee nothing	Gen 26:29	6213
I have *d* according as thou badest	Gen 27:19	6213
that which thou hast *d* to him	Gen 27:45	6213
until I have *d* that which I have	Gen 28:15	6213
What is this thou hast *d* unto me	Gen 29:25	6213
must not be so *d* in our country	Gen 29:26	6213
my service which I have *d* thee	Gen 30:26	5647
said to Jacob, What hast thou *d*	Gen 31:26	6213
thou hast now *d* foolishly in so	Gen 31:28	5528
which thing ought not to be *d*	Gen 34:7	6213
here also have I *d* nothing that	Gen 40:15	6213
is this that God hath *d* unto us	Gen 42:28	6213
ye have *d* evil in so doing	Gen 44:5	7489
What deed is this that ye have *d*	Gen 44:15	6213
them, Why have ye *d* this thing	Ex 1:18	6213
to wit what would be *d* to him	Ex 2:4	6213
that which is *d* to you in Egypt	Ex 3:16	6213
he hath *d* evil to this people	Ex 5:23	7489
signs which I have *d* among them	Ex 10:2	7760
manner of work shall be *d* in them	Ex 12:16	6213
eat, that only may be *d* of you	Ex 12:16	6213
This is *d* because of that which	Ex 13:8	
and they said, Why have we *d* this	Ex 14:5	6213
of all that God had *d* for Moses	Ex 18:1	6213
that the LORD had *d* unto Pharaoh	Ex 18:8	6213
which the LORD had *d* to Israel	Ex 18:9	6213
judgment shall it be *d* unto him	Ex 21:31	6213
Six days may work be *d*	Ex 31:15	6213
have not been *d* in all the earth	Ex 34:10	1254
till Moses had *d* speaking with	Ex 34:33	3615
Six days shall work be *d*, but on	Ex 35:2	6213
they had *d* it as the LORD had	Ex 39:43	6213
commanded, even so had they *d* it	Ex 39:43	6213
things which ought not to be *d*	Lev 4:2	6213
they have *d* somewhat against any	Lev 4:13	6213
things which should not be *d*	Lev 4:13	6213
d somewhat through ignorance	Lev 4:22	6213
things which should not be *d*	Lev 4:22	6213
things which ought not to be *d*	Lev 4:27	6213
that he hath *d* in the holy thing	Lev 5:16	2398
which are forbidden to be *d* by	Lev 5:17	6213
he hath *d* in trespassing therein	Lev 6:7	6213
which the LORD commanded to be *d*	Lev 8:5	6213
As he hath *d* this day, so the	Lev 8:34	6213
it be, wherein any work is *d*	Lev 11:32	6213
have the men of the land *d*	Lev 18:27	6213
LORD for his sin which he hath *d*	Lev 19:22	2398
he hath *d* shall be forgiven him	Lev 19:22	2398
Six days shall work be *d*	Lev 23:3	6213
as he hath *d*, so shall it be *d*	Lev 24:19	6213
so shall it be *d* to him again	Lev 24:20	5414
their sin which they have *d*	Num 5:7	6213
have *d* trespass against her	Num 5:27	4603
us, wherein we have *d* foolishly	Num 12:11	2973
shall it be *d* for one bullock	Num 15:11	6213
declared what should be *d* to him	Num 15:34	6213
for I have not *d* them of mine own	Num 16:28	
that Israel had *d* to the Amorites	Num 22:2	6213
Balaam, What have I *d* unto thee	Num 22:28	6213
Balaam, What hast thou *d* unto me	Num 23:11	6213
the name of our father be *d* away	Num 27:4	1639
that had *d* evil in the sight of	Num 32:13	6213
God hath *d* unto these two kings	Deut 3:21	6213
that hath *d* for thee these great	Deut 10:21	6213
have they *d* unto their gods	Deut 12:31	6213
to have *d* unto his brother	Deut 19:19	6213
which they have *d* unto their gods	Deut 20:18	6213
So shall it be *d* unto that man	Deut 25:9	6213
have *d* according to all that thou	Deut 26:14	6213
the LORD *d* thus unto this land	Deut 29:24	6213
and the LORD hath not *d* all this	Deut 32:27	6466
when they had *d* circumcising all	Josh 5:8	8552
and tell me now what thou hast *d*	Josh 7:19	6213
Israel, and thus and thus have I *d*	Josh 7:20	6213
what Joshua had *d* unto Jericho	Josh 9:3	6213
of you, and have *d* this thing	Josh 9:24	6213
as he had *d* to Jericho and her	Josh 10:1	6213
and her king, so he had *d* to Ai	Josh 10:1	6213
to all that he had *d* to Libnah	Josh 10:32	6213
to all that he had *d* to Lachish	Josh 10:35	6213
to all that he had *d* to Eglon	Josh 10:37	6213
as he had *d* to Hebron, so he did	Josh 10:39	6213
as he had *d* also to Libnah, and to	Josh 10:39	6213
if we have not rather *d* it for	Josh 22:24	6213
d unto all these nations because	Josh 23:3	6213
as ye have *d* unto this day	Josh 23:8	6213
have seen what I have *d* in Egypt	Josh 24:7	6213
after that he hath *d* you good	Josh 24:20	3190
LORD, that he had *d* for Israel	Josh 24:31	6213
as I have *d*, so God hath requited	Judg 1:7	6213
why have ye *d* this	Judg 2:2	6213
works which he had *d* for Israel	Judg 2:10	6213
because they had *d* evil in the	Judg 3:12	6213
to another, Who hath *d* this thing	Judg 6:29	6213
son of Joash hath *d* this thing	Judg 6:29	6213
What have I *d* now in comparison	Judg 8:2	6213
Now therefore, if ye have *d* truly	Judg 9:16	6213
have *d* unto him according to the	Judg 9:16	6213
That the cruelty *d* to the	Judg 9:24	
do, make haste, and do as I have *d*	Judg 9:48	
Let this thing be *d* for me	Judg 11:37	6213
or his mother what he had *d*	Judg 14:6	6213
Philistines said, Who hath *d* this	Judg 15:6	6213
unto them, Though ye have *d* this	Judg 15:7	6213
to do to him as he hath *d* to us	Judg 15:10	6213
is this that thou hast *d* unto us	Judg 15:11	6213
unto me, so have I *d* unto them	Judg 15:11	6213
There was no such deed *d* nor seen	Judg 19:30	1961
is this that is *d* among you	Judg 20:12	1961
all that thou hast *d* unto thy	Ruth 2:11	6213
man, until he shall have *d* eating	Ruth 3:3	3615
her all that the man had *d* to her	Ruth 3:16	6213
And he said, What is there *d*	1Sa 4:16	1697
then he hath *d* us this great evil	1Sa 6:9	6213
d since the day that I brought	1Sa 8:8	6213
so shall it be *d* unto his oxen	1Sa 11:7	6213
which ye have *d* in the sight of	1Sa 12:17	6213
ye have *d* all this wickedness	1Sa 12:20	6213
great things he hath *d* for you	1Sa 12:24	1430
And Samuel said, What hast thou *d*	1Sa 13:11	6213
to Saul, Thou hast *d* foolishly	1Sa 13:13	5528
Tell me what thou hast *d*	1Sa 14:43	6213
What shall be *d* to the man that	1Sa 17:26	6213
So shall it be *d* to the man that	1Sa 17:27	6213
And David said, What have I now *d*	1Sa 17:29	6213
him all that Saul had *d* to him	1Sa 19:18	6213
before Jonathan, What have I *d*	1Sa 20:1	6213
what hath he *d*?	1Sa 20:32	6213
his father had *d* him shame	1Sa 20:34	3637
that thou hast *d* unto me this day	1Sa 24:19	6213
when the LORD shall have *d* to my	1Sa 25:30	6213
is not good that thou hast *d*	1Sa 26:16	6213
for what have I *d*	1Sa 26:18	6213
thou knowest what Saul hath *d*	1Sa 28:9	6213
And the LORD hath *d* to him	1Sa 28:17	6213
therefore hath the LORD *d* this	1Sa 28:18	6213
unto Achish, But what have I *d*	1Sa 29:8	6213
the Philistines had *d* to Saul	1Sa 31:11	6213
because ye have *d* this thing	2Sa 2:6	6213
king, and said, What hast thou *d*	2Sa 3:24	6213
hast thou *d* all these great	2Sa 7:21	6213
David had *d* displeased the LORD	2Sa 11:27	6213
the man that hath *d* this thing	2Sa 12:5	6213
thing is this that thou hast *d*	2Sa 12:21	6213
thing ought to be *d* in Israel	2Sa 13:12	6213
thy servant Joab *d* this thing	2Sa 14:20	6213
Behold now, I have *d* this thing	2Sa 14:21	6213
had *d* passing out of the city	2Sa 15:24	8552
say, Wherefore hast thou *d* so	2Sa 16:10	6213
the concubine of Saul, had *d*	2Sa 21:11	6213
who had *d* many acts, he slew two	2Sa 23:20	6213
sinned greatly in that I have *d*	2Sa 24:10	6213
for I have *d* very foolishly	2Sa 24:10	5528
have sinned, and I have *d* wickedly	2Sa 24:17	5753
but these sheep, what have they *d*	2Sa 24:17	6213
in saying, Why hast thou *d* so	1Kin 1:6	6213
Is this thing *d* by my lord the	1Kin 1:27	
I have *d* according to thy words	1Kin 3:12	6213
have *d* perversely, we have	1Kin 8:47	5753
LORD had *d* for David his servant	1Kin 8:66	6213
Why hath the LORD *d* thus unto	1Kin 9:8	6213
Forasmuch as this is *d* of thee	1Kin 11:11	1961
of God had *d* that day in Beth-el	1Kin 13:11	6213
But hast *d* evil above all that	1Kin 14:9	6213
all that their fathers had *d*	1Kin 14:22	6213
father, which he had *d* before him	1Kin 15:3	6213
that I have *d* all these things at	1Kin 18:36	6213
Jezebel all that Elijah had *d*	1Kin 19:1	6213
for what have I *d* to thee	1Kin 19:20	6213
to all that his father had *d*	1Kin 22:53	6213
what is to be *d* for thee	2Kin 4:13	6213
What then is to be *d* for her	2Kin 4:14	6213
wouldest thou not have *d* it	2Kin 5:13	6213
you what the Syrians have *d* to us	2Kin 7:12	6213
great things that Elisha hath *d*	2Kin 8:4	6213
for the LORD hath *d* that which he	2Kin 10:10	6213
Because thou hast *d* well in	2Kin 10:30	2895
hast *d* unto the house of Ahab	2Kin 10:30	6213
all that his father Amaziah had *d*	2Kin 15:3	6213
of the LORD, as his fathers had *d*	2Kin 15:9	6213
all that his father Uzziah had *d*	2Kin 15:34	6213
Assyria, as he had *d* year by year	2Kin 17:4	
of Assyria have *d* to all lands	2Kin 19:11	6213
heard long ago how I have *d* it	2Kin 19:25	6213
have *d* that which is good in thy	2Kin 20:3	6213
Judah hath *d* these abominations	2Kin 21:11	6213
hath *d* wickedly above all that	2Kin 21:11	6213
Because they have *d* that which	2Kin 21:15	6213
these things that thou hast *d*	2Kin 23:17	6213
the acts that he had *d* in Beth-el	2Kin 23:19	6213
to all that his fathers had *d*	2Kin 23:32	6213
to all that his fathers had *d*	2Kin 23:37	6213
to all that his father had *d*	2Kin 24:9	6213
to all that Jehoiakim had *d*	2Kin 24:19	6213
the Philistines had *d* to Saul	1Chr 10:11	6213
of Kabzeel, who had *d* many acts	1Chr 11:22	
marvellous works that he hath *d*	1Chr 16:12	6213
hast thou *d* all this greatness,	1Chr 17:19	6213
because I have *d* this thing	1Chr 21:8	6213
for I have *d* very foolishly	1Chr 21:8	5528
that have sinned and *d* evil indeed	1Chr 21:17	7489
for these sheep, what have they *d*	1Chr 21:17	6213
We have sinned, we have *d* amiss	2Chr 6:37	5753
Why hath the LORD *d* thus unto	2Chr 7:21	6213
for this thing is *d* of me	2Chr 11:4	1961
Herein thou hast *d* foolishly	2Chr 16:9	5528
because he had *d* good in Israel	2Chr 24:16	6213
Jehoiada his father had *d* to him	2Chr 24:22	6213

thee, because thou hast *d* this 2Chr 25:16 6213
all that David his father had *d* 2Chr 29:2 6213
d that which was evil in the eyes 2Chr 29:6 6213
for the thing was *d* suddenly 2Chr 29:36 1961
for they had not *d* it of a long 2Chr 30:5 6213
my fathers have *d* unto all the 2Chr 32:13 6213
to the benefit *d* unto him 2Chr 32:25
the wonder that was *d* in the land 2Chr 32:31 1961
let it be *d* with speed Ezr 6:12 5648
require of you, it be *d* speedily, Ezr 7:21 5648
let it be diligently *d* for the Ezr 7:23 5648
Now when these things were *d* Ezr 9:1 3615
let it be *d* according to the law Ezr 10:3 6213
all that I have *d* for this people Neh 5:19 6213
no such things *d* as thou sayest Neh 6:8 1961
from the work, that it be not *d* Neh 6:9 6213
not the children of Israel *d* so Neh 8:17 6213
for thou hast *d* right Neh 9:33 6213
but we have *d* wickedly Neh 9:33 7561
I have *d* for the house of my God Neh 13:14 6213
hath not *d* wrong to the king only Est 1:16 5753
Vashti, and what she had *d* Est 2:1 6213
Mordecai perceived all that was *d* Est 4:1 6213
dignity hath been *d* to Mordecai Est 6:3 6213
him, There is nothing *d* for him Est 6:3 6213
What shall be *d* unto the man whom Est 6:6 6213
Thus shall it be *d* to the man Est 6:9 6213
Thus shall it be *d* unto the man Est 6:11 6213
what have they *d* in the rest of Est 9:12 6213
and it shall be *d* Est 9:12 6213
the king commanded it so to be *d* Est 9:14 6213
shall repay him what he hath *d* Job 21:31 6213
whether it be *d* against a nation, Job 34:29
if I have *d* iniquity, I will do Job 34:32 6466
O LORD my God, if I have *d* this Ps 7:3 6213
they have *d* abominable works, Ps 14:1 8581
be born, that he hath *d* this Ps 22:31 6213
and all his works are *d* in truth Ps 33:4
For he spake, and it was *d* Ps 33:9 1961
wonderful works which thou hast *d* Ps 40:5 6213
These things hast thou *d*, and I Ps 50:21 6213
and *d* this evil in thy sight Ps 51:4 6213
for ever, because thou hast *d* it Ps 52:9 6213
have *d* abominable iniquity Ps 53:1 8581
what he hath *d* for my soul Ps 66:16 6213
high, who hast *d* great things Ps 71:19 6213
hath *d* wickedly in the sanctuary Ps 74:3 7489
wonderful works that he hath *d* Ps 78:4 6213
for he hath *d* marvellous things Ps 98:1 6213
marvellous works that he hath *d* Ps 105:5 6213
iniquity, we have *d* wickedly Ps 106:6 6213
which had *d* great things in Egypt Ps 106:21 6213
that thou, LORD, hast *d* it Ps 109:27 6213
are *d* in truth and uprightness Ps 111:8 6213
he hath *d* whatsoever he hath Ps 115:3 6213
I have *d* judgment and justice Ps 119:121 6213
salvation, and *d* thy commandments Ps 119:166 6213
or what shall be *d* unto thee Ps 120:3 3254
The LORD hath *d* great things for Ps 126:2 6213
The LORD hath *d* great things for Ps 126:3 6213
if he have *d* thee no harm Prov 3:30 1580
not, except they have *d* mischief Prov 4:16 7489
do so to him as he hath *d* to me Prov 24:29 6213
and saith, I have *d* no wickedness Prov 30:20 466
If thou hast *d* foolishly in Prov 30:32 5034
Many daughters have *d* virtuously Prov 31:29 6466
is *d* is that which shall be *d* Eccl 1:9 6466
things that are *d* under heaven Eccl 1:13 6466
works that are *d* under the sun Eccl 1:14 6466
that which hath been already *d* Eccl 2:12 6466
that are *d* under the sun Eccl 4:1 6466
evil work that is *d* under the sun Eccl 4:3 6466
work that is *d* under the sun Eccl 8:9 6466
in the city where they had so *d* Eccl 8:10 6466
vanity which is *d* upon the earth Eccl 8:14 6466
business that is *d* upon the earth Eccl 8:16 6466
the work that is *d* under the sun Eccl 8:17 6466
things that are *d* under the sun Eccl 9:3 6466
any thing that is *d* under the sun Eccl 9:6 6466
have been *d* more to my vineyard Is 5:4 6466
that I have not *d* in it Is 5:4 6466
as I have *d* unto Samaria and her Is 10:11 6466
strength of my hand I have *d* it Is 10:13 6466
for he hath *d* excellent things Is 12:5 6466
grapes when the vintage is *d* Is 24:13 3615
for thou hast *d* wonderful things Is 25:1 6213
that are far off, what I have *d* Is 33:13 6213
what the kings of Assyria have *d* Is 37:11 6213
heard long ago, how I have *d* it Is 37:26 6213
have *d* that which is good in thy Is 38:3 6213
unto me, and himself hath *d* it Is 38:15 6213
d it, calling the generations Is 41:4 6213
the hand of the LORD hath *d* this Is 41:20 6213
for the LORD hath *d* it Is 44:23 6213
the things that are not yet *d* Is 46:10 6213
say, Mine idol hath *d* them Is 48:5 6213
because he had *d* no violence Is 53:9 6213
the valley, know what thou hast *d* Jer 2:23 6213
d evil things as thou couldest Jer 3:5 6213
which backsliding Israel hath *d* Jer 3:6 6213
after she had *d* all these things Jer 3:7 6213
neither shall that be *d* any more Jer 3:16 6213
thus shall it be *d* unto them Jer 5:13 6213
because ye have *d* all these works Jer 7:13 6213
fathers, as I have *d* to Shiloh Jer 7:14 6213
of Judah have *d* evil in my sight Jer 7:30 6213
wickedness, saying, What have I *d* Jer 8:6 6213
which they have *d* against Jer 11:17 6213

ye have *d* worse than your fathers Jer 16:12 6213
hath *d* a very horrible thing Jer 18:13 6213
Wherefore hath the LORD *d* thus Jer 22:8 6213
I have *d* these things unto thee Jer 30:15 6213
not return, until he have *d* it Jer 30:24 6213
Israel for all that they have *d* Jer 31:37 6213
they have *d* nothing of all that Jer 32:23 6213
d evil before me from their youth Jer 32:30 6213
which they have *d* to provoke me Jer 32:32 6213
had *d* right in my sight, in Jer 34:15 6213
d according to all that Jonadab Jer 35:10 6213
d according unto all that he hath Jer 35:18 6213
these men have *d* evil in all that Jer 38:9 7489
have *d* to Jeremiah the prophet Jer 38:9 6213
d according as he hath said Jer 40:3 6213
the son of Nethaniah had *d* Jer 41:11 6213
the evil that I have *d* unto you Jer 42:10 6213
offerings unto her, as we have *d* Jer 44:17 6213
that escapeth, and say, What is *d* Jer 48:19 1961
as she hath *d*, do unto her Jer 50:15 6213
according to all that she hath *d* Jer 50:29 6213
d that which he spake against the Jer 51:12 6213
they have *d* in Zion in your sight Jer 51:24 6213
The violence *d* to me and to my Jer 51:35 6213
to all that Jehoiakim had *d* Jer 52:2 6213
my sorrow, which is *d* unto me Lam 1:12 5953
they are glad that thou hast *d* it Lam 1:21 6213
as thou hast *d* unto me for all my Lam 1:22 5953
The LORD hath *d* that which he had Lam 2:17 6213
consider to whom thou hast *d* this Lam 2:20 5953
he hath *d* shall not be remembered Eze 3:20 6213
neither have *d* according to the Eze 5:7 6213
in thee that which I have not *d* Eze 5:9 6213
that be *d* in the midst thereof Eze 9:4 6213
I have *d* as thou hast commanded Eze 9:11 6213
but have *d* after the manners of Eze 11:12 6213
d, so shall it be *d* unto them Eze 12:11 6213
which I have spoken shall be *d* Eze 12:28 6213
d without cause all that I have Eze 14:23 6213
cause all that I have *d* in it Eze 14:23 6213
nor *d* after their abominations Eze 16:47 6213
GOD, Sodom thy sister hath not *d* Eze 16:48 6213
nor her daughters, as thou hast *d* Eze 16:48 6213
abominations which thou hast *d* Eze 16:51 6213
in all that thou hast *d*, in that Eze 16:54 6213
deal with thee as thou hast *d* Eze 16:59 6213
thee for all that thou hast *d* Eze 16:63 6213
hath *d* all these things, he shall Eze 17:18 6213
the LORD have spoken and have *d* it Eze 17:24 6213
he hath *d* all these abominations Eze 18:13 6213
his father's sins which he hath *d* Eze 18:14 6213
When the son hath *d* that which is Eze 18:19 6213
all my statutes, and hath *d* them Eze 18:19 6213
that he hath *d* he shall live Eze 18:22 6213
he hath *d* shall not be mentioned Eze 18:24 6213
that he hath *d* shall he die Eze 18:26 6213
Moreover this they have *d* unto me Eze 23:38 6213
thus have they *d* in the midst of Eze 23:39 6213
And ye shall do as I have *d* Eze 24:22 6213
to all that he hath *d* shall ye do Eze 24:24 6213
he hath *d* that which is lawful and Eze 33:16 6213
Behold, it is come, and it is *d* Eze 39:8 1961
transgressions have I *d* unto them Eze 39:24 6213
ashamed of all that they have *d* Eze 43:11 6213
for all that shall be *d* therein Eze 44:14 6213
thee, O king, have I *d* no hurt Dan 6:22 5648
have *d* wickedly, and have rebelled Dan 9:5 7561
as hath been *d* upon Jerusalem Dan 9:12 6213
have sinned, we have *d* wickedly Dan 9:15 7561
that which his fathers have not *d* Dan 11:24 6213
that is determined shall be *d* Dan 11:36 6213
conceived them hath *d* shamefully Hos 2:5 3001
because he hath *d* great things Joel 2:20 6213
a city, and the LORD hath not *d* it Amos 3:6 6213
d, it shall be *d* unto thee Obad 15 6213
unto him, Why hast thou *d* this Jonah 1:10 6213
hast *d* as it pleased thee Jonah 1:14 6213
people, what have I *d* unto thee Mic 6:3 6213
they have *d* violence to the law Zeph 3:4 2554
as I have *d* these so many years Zec 7:3 6213
And this have ye *d* again, covering Mal 2:13 6213
Now all this was *d*, that it might Mt 1:22 *1096*
Thy will be *d* in earth, as it is Mt 6:10 *1096*
in thy name *d* many wonderful Mt 7:22 *4160*
believed, so be it *d* unto thee Mt 8:13 *1096*
most of his mighty works were *d* Mt 11:20 *1096*
d in you, had been *d* in Tyre Mt 11:21 *1096*
d in thee, had been *d* in Sodom Mt 11:23 *1096*
unto them, An enemy hath *d* this Mt 13:28 *4160*
but have *d* unto him whatsoever Mt 17:12 *4160*
it shall be *d* for them of my Mt 18:19 *1096*
his fellowservants saw what was *d* Mt 18:31 *1096*
unto their lord all that was *d* Mt 18:31 *1096*
All this was *d*, that it might be Mt 21:4 *1096*
this which is *d* to the fig tree Mt 21:21
into the sea; it shall be *d* Mt 21:21 *1096*
these ought ye to have *d*, and not Mt 23:23 *4160*
His lord said unto him, Well *d* Mt 25:21 *2095*
His lord said unto him, Well *d* Mt 25:23 *2095*
Inasmuch as ye have *d* it unto one Mt 25:40 *4160*
my brethren, ye have *d* it unto me Mt 25:40 *4160*
also this, that this woman hath *d* Mt 26:13 *4160*
except I drink it, thy will be *d* Mt 26:42 *1096*
But all this was *d*, that the Mt 26:56 *1096*
said, Why, what evil hath he *d* Mt 27:23 *4160*
and those things that were *d* Mt 27:54 *1096*
all the things that were *d* Mt 28:11 *1096*
these things are *d* in parables Mk 4:11 *1096*

out to see what it was that was *d* Mk 5:14 *1096*
things the Lord hath *d* for thee Mk 5:19 *4160*
great things Jesus had *d* for him Mk 5:20 *4160*
to see her that had *d* this thing Mk 5:32 *4160*
knowing what was *d* in her Mk 5:33 *1096*
all things, both what they had *d* Mk 6:30 *4160*
He hath *d* all things well Mk 7:37 *4160*
they have *d* unto him whatsoever Mk 9:13 *4160*
pass, till all these things be *d* Mk 13:30 *1096*
She hath *d* what she could Mk 14:8 *4160*
this also that she hath *d* shall Mk 14:9 *4160*
to do as he had ever *d* unto them Mk 15:8 *4160*
them, Why, what evil hath he *d* Mk 15:14 *4160*
mighty hath *d* to me great things Lk 1:49 *4160*
all the evils which Herod had *d* Lk 3:19 *4160*
we have heard *d* in Capernaum Lk 4:23 *1096*
And when they had this *d*, they Lk 5:6 *4160*
they that fed them saw what was *d* Lk 8:34 *1096*
they went out to see what was *d* Lk 8:35 *1096*
great things God hath *d* unto thee Lk 8:39 *4160*
great things Jesus had *d* unto him Lk 8:39 *4160*
should tell no man what was *d* Lk 8:56 *1096*
heard of all that was *d* by him Lk 9:7 *1096*
told him all that they had *d* Lk 9:10 *4160*
mighty works had been *d* in Tyre Lk 10:13 *1096*
Sidon, which have been *d* in you Lk 10:13 *1096*
Thy will be *d*, as in heaven, so Lk 11:2 *1096*
these ought ye to have *d*, and not Lk 11:42 *4160*
things that were *d* by him Lk 13:17 *1096*
it is *d* as thou hast commanded Lk 14:22 *1096*
steward, because he had *d* wisely Lk 16:8 *4160*
when ye shall have *d* all those Lk 17:10 *4160*
we have *d* that which was our duty Lk 17:10 *4160*
not my will, but thine, be *d* Lk 22:42 *1096*
have seen some miracle *d* by him Lk 23:8 *1096*
worthy of death is *d* unto him Lk 23:15 *4238*
time, Why, what evil hath he *d* Lk 23:22 *4160*
tree, what shall be *d* in the dry Lk 23:31 *1096*
but this man hath *d* nothing amiss Lk 23:41 *4238*
when the centurion saw what was *d* Lk 23:47 *1096*
beholding the things which were *d* Lk 23:48 *1096*
day since these things were *d* Lk 24:21 *1096*
what things were *d* in the way Lk 24:35
These things were *d* in Bethabara Jn 1:28 *1096*
because he had *d* these things on Jn 5:16 *4160*
they that have *d* good, unto the Jn 5:29 *4160*
and they that have *d* evil, unto Jn 5:29 *4238*
I have *d* one work, and ye all Jn 7:21 *4160*
than these which this man hath *d* Jn 7:31 *4160*
told them what things Jesus had *d* Jn 11:46 *4160*
that they had *d* these things unto Jn 12:16 *4160*
heard that he had *d* this miracle Jn 12:18 *4160*
But though he had *d* so many Jn 12:37 *4160*
Know ye what I have *d* to you Jn 13:12 *4160*
ye should do as I have *d* to you Jn 13:15 *4160*
will, and it shall be *d* unto you Jn 15:7 *1096*
If I had not *d* among them the Jn 15:24 *4160*
what hast thou *d*? Jn 18:35 *4160*
For these things were *d*, that the Jn 19:36 *1096*
signs were *d* by the apostles Acts 2:43 *1096*
or by what name, have ye *d* this Acts 4:7 *4160*
good deed *d* to the impotent man Acts 4:9
a notable miracle hath been *d* by Acts 4:16 *1096*
God for that which was *d* Acts 4:21 *1096*
counsel determined before to be *d* Acts 4:28 *1096*
wonders may be *d* by the name of Acts 4:30 *1096*
his wife, not knowing what was *d* Acts 5:7 *1096*
miracles and signs which were *d* Acts 8:13 *1096*
how much evil he hath *d* to thy Acts 9:13 *4160*
This was *d* thrice Acts 10:16 *1096*
thou hast well *d* that thou art Acts 10:33 *4160*
And this was *d* three times Acts 11:10 *1096*
was true which was *d* by the angel Acts 12:9 *1096*
deputy, when he saw what was *d* Acts 13:12 *1096*
wonders to be *d* by their hands Acts 14:3 *1096*
the people saw what Paul had *d* Acts 14:11 *4160*
would have *d* sacrifice with the Acts 14:13 *2309*
that they had not *d* sacrifice Acts 14:18
all that God had *d* with them Acts 14:27 *4160*
things that God had *d* with them Acts 15:4 *4160*
saying, The will of the Lord be *d* Acts 21:14 *1096*
who he was, and what he had *d* Acts 21:33 *4160*
are *d* unto this nation by thy Acts 24:2 *1096*
to the Jews have I *d* no wrong Acts 25:10 *91*
this thing was not *d* in a corner Acts 26:26 *4238*
So when this was *d*, others also, Acts 28:9 *1096*
neither having *d* any good or evil Rom 9:11 *4238*
that he that hath *d* this deed 1Cor 5:2 *4160*
him that hath so *d* this deed 1Cor 5:3 *2716*
that it should be so *d* unto me 1Cor 9:15 *1096*
which is in part shall be *d* away 1Cor 13:10 *2673*
Let all things be *d* unto edifying 1Cor 14:26 *1096*
Let all things be *d* decently 1Cor 14:40 *1096*
all your things be *d* with charity 1Cor 16:14 *1096*
which glory was to be *d* away 2Cor 3:7 *2673*
that which is *d* away was glorious 2Cor 3:11 *2673*
which vail is *d* away in Christ 2Cor 3:14 *2673*
receive the things *d* in his body 2Cor 5:10
according to that he hath *d* 2Cor 5:10 *4238*
his cause that had *d* the wrong 2Cor 7:12 *91*
which are *d* of them in secret Eph 5:12 *1096*
in the evil day, and having *d* all Eph 6:13 *2716*
Let nothing be *d* through strife Phil 2:3
Notwithstanding ye have well *d* Phil 4:14 *4160*
for the wrong which he hath *d* Col 3:25 *91*
you all things which are *d* here Col 4:9
of righteousness which we have *d* Titus 3:5 *4160*
hath *d* despite unto the Spirit of Heb 10:29 *1796*

D

after ye have *d* the will of God, Heb 10:36 *4160*
from the throne, saying, It is *d* Rev 16:17 *1096*
And he said unto me, It is *d* Rev 21:6 *1096*
things which must shortly be *d* Rev 22:6 *1096*

DOOR {189}
not well, sin lieth at the *d* Gen 4:7 6607
the *d* of the ark shalt thou set Gen 6:16 6607
he sat in the tent *d* in the heat Gen 18:1 6607
ran to meet them from the tent *d* Gen 18:2 6607
And Sarah heard it in the tent *d* Gen 18:10 6607
Lot went out at the *d* unto them Gen 19:6 6607
and shut the *d* after him Gen 19:6 1817
Lot, and came near to break the *d* Gen 19:9 1817
house to them, and shut to the *d* Gen 19:10 1817
the *d* of the house with blindness Gen 19:11 6607
wearied themselves to find the *d* Gen 19:11 6607
with him at the *d* of the house Gen 43:19 6607
on the upper *d* post of the houses Ex 12:7 4947
d of his house until the morning Ex 12:22 6607
the LORD will pass over the *d* Ex 12:23 6607
he shall also bring him to the *d* Ex 21:6 1817
or unto the *d* post Ex 21:6 4201
an hanging for the *d* of the tent Ex 26:36 6607
the *d* of the tabernacle of the Ex 29:4 6607
by the *d* of the tabernacle of the Ex 29:11 6607
by the *d* of the tabernacle of the Ex 29:32 6607
your generations at the *d* of the Ex 29:42 6607
and stood every man at his tent *d* Ex 33:8 6607
stood at the *d* of the tabernacle, Ex 33:9 6607
pillar stand at the tabernacle *d* Ex 33:10 6607
every man in his tent *d* Ex 33:10 6607
the hanging for the *d* at the Ex 35:15 6607
hanging for the *d* of the court Ex 35:17 8179
for the tabernacle *d* of blue Ex 36:37 6607
which assembled at the *d* of the Ex 38:8 6607
to the *d* of the tabernacle of the Ex 38:30 6607
the hanging for the tabernacle *d* Ex 39:38 6607
of the *d* to the tabernacle Ex 40:5 6607
d of the tabernacle of the tent Ex 40:6 6607
his sons unto the *d* of the Ex 40:12 6607
at the *d* of the tabernacle Ex 40:28 6607
d of the tabernacle of the tent Ex 40:29 6607
at the *d* of the tabernacle of the Lev 1:3 6607
by the *d* of the tabernacle of the Lev 1:5 6607
and kill it at the *d* of the Lev 3:2 6607
the *d* of the tabernacle of the Lev 4:4 6607
which is at the *d* of the Lev 4:7 6607
which is at the *d* of the Lev 4:18 6607
the *d* of the tabernacle of the Lev 8:3 6607
the *d* of the tabernacle of the Lev 8:4 6607
Boil the flesh at the *d* of the Lev 8:31 6607
of the *d* of the tabernacle of the Lev 8:33 6607
at the *d* of the tabernacle of the Lev 8:35 6607
the *d* of the tabernacle of the Lev 10:7 6607
unto the *d* of the tabernacle of Lev 12:6 6607
at the *d* of the tabernacle of the Lev 14:11 6607
unto the *d* of the tabernacle of Lev 14:23 6607
the house to the *d* of the house Lev 14:38 6607
the *d* of the tabernacle of the Lev 15:14 6607
to the *d* of the tabernacle of the Lev 15:29 6607
at the *d* of the tabernacle of the Lev 16:7 6607
the *d* of the tabernacle of the Lev 17:4 6607
unto the *d* of the tabernacle of Lev 17:5 6607
at the *d* of the tabernacle of the Lev 17:6 6607
the *d* of the tabernacle of the Lev 17:9 6607
unto the *d* of the tabernacle of Lev 19:21 6607
the hanging for the *d* of the Num 3:25 6607
curtain for the *d* of the court Num 3:26 6607
the hanging for the *d* of the Num 4:25 6607
the hanging for the *d* of the gate Num 4:26 6607
to the *d* of the tabernacle of the Num 6:10 6607
the *d* of the tabernacle of the Num 6:13 6607
at the *d* of the tabernacle of the Num 6:18 6607
at the *d* of the tabernacle of the Num 10:3 6607
every man in the *d* of his tent Num 11:10 6607
stood in the *d* of the tabernacle, Num 12:5 6607
stood in the *d* of the tabernacle Num 16:18 6607
against them unto the *d* of the Num 16:19 6607
stood in the *d* of their tents, and Num 16:27 6607
the *d* of the tabernacle of the Num 16:50 6607
the *d* of the tabernacle of the Num 20:6 6607
the *d* of the tabernacle of the Num 25:6 6607
by the *d* of the tabernacle of the Num 27:2 6607
upon the *d* posts of thine house Deut 11:20 4201
it through his ear unto the *d* Deut 15:17 1817
to the *d* of her father's house Deut 22:21 6607
over the *d* of the tabernacle Deut 31:15 6607
at the *d* of the tabernacle of the Josh 19:51 6607
her, Stand in the *d* of the tent Judg 4:20 6607
went hard unto the *d* of the tower Judg 9:52 6607
round about, and beat at the *d* Judg 19:22 1817
fell down at the *d* of the man's Judg 19:26 6607
fallen down at the *d* of the house Judg 19:27 6607
at the *d* of the tabernacle of the 1Sa 2:22 6607
But Uriah slept at the *d* of the 2Sa 11:9 6607
from me, and bolt the *d* after her 2Sa 13:17 1817
out, and bolted the *d* after her 2Sa 13:18 1817
The *d* for the middle chamber was 1Kin 6:8 6907
So also made he for the *d* of the 1Kin 6:33 6907
leaves of the one *d* were folding 1Kin 6:34 1817
of the other *d* were folding 1Kin 6:34 1817
her feet, as she came in at the *d* 1Kin 14:6 6607
came to the threshold of the *d* 1Kin 14:17 1004
which kept the *d* of the king's 1Kin 14:27 6607
thou shalt shut the *d* upon thee 2Kin 4:4 1817
from him, and shut the *d* upon her 2Kin 4:5 1817
called her, she stood in the *d* 2Kin 4:15 6607
of God, and shut the *d* upon him 2Kin 4:21
shut the *d* upon them twain, and 2Kin 4:33 1817
stood at the *d* of the house of 2Kin 5:9 6607
d, and hold him fast at the *d* 2Kin 6:32 1817
Then open the *d*, and flee, and 2Kin 9:3 1817
And he opened the *d*, and fled 2Kin 9:10 1817
the priests that kept the *d* put 2Kin 12:9 5592
which the keepers of the *d* have 2Kin 22:4 5592
order, and the keepers of the *d* 2Kin 23:4 5592
and the three keepers of the *d* 2Kin 25:18 5592
of the *d* of the tabernacle of the 1Chr 9:21 6607
d of the house of Eliashib the Neh 3:20 6607
from the *d* of the house of Neh 3:21 6607
Teresh, of those which kept the *d* Est 2:21 5592
the keepers of the *d*, who sought Est 6:2 5592
laid wait at my neighbour's *d* Job 31:9 6607
silence, and went not out of the *d* Job 31:34 6607
Keep the *d* of my lips Ps 141:3 1817
come not nigh the *d* of her house Prov 5:8 6607
she sitteth at the *d* of her house Prov 9:14 6607
As the *d* turneth upon his hinges, Prov 26:14 1817
in his hand by the hole of the *d* Song 5:4 6607
and if she be a *d*, we will inclose Song 8:9 1817
the posts of the *d* moved at the Is 6:4 5592
of Shallum, the keeper of the *d* Jer 35:4 5592
and the three keepers of the *d* Jer 52:24 5592
to the *d* of the inner gate, that Eze 8:3 6607
brought me to the *d* of the court Eze 8:7 6607
digged in the wall, behold a *d* Eze 8:8 6607
Then he brought me to the *d* of Eze 8:14 6607
at the *d* of the temple of the Eze 8:16 6607
every one stood at the *d* of the Eze 10:19 6607
behold at the *d* of the gate five Eze 11:1 6607
and twenty cubits, *d* against *d* Eze 40:13 6607
breadth of the *d* was ten cubits Eze 41:2 6607
the sides of the *d* were five Eze 41:2 6607
and measured the post of the *d* Eze 41:3 6607
and the *d*, six cubits Eze 41:3 6607
and the breadth of the *d*, seven Eze 41:3 6607
one *d* toward the north, and Eze 41:11 6607
another *d* toward the south Eze 41:11 6607
The *d* posts, and the narrow Eze 41:16 5592
three stories, over against the *d* Eze 41:16 5592
To that above the *d*, even unto Eze 41:17 6607
unto above the *d* were cherubims Eze 41:20 6607
two leaves for the one *d* Eze 41:24 1817
and two leaves for the other *d* Eze 41:24 1817
an hundred cubits was the north *d* Eze 42:2 6607
was a *d* in the head of the way Eze 42:12 6607
the land shall worship at the *d* Eze 46:3 6607
me again unto the *d* of the house Eze 47:1 6607
valley of Achor for a *d* of hope Hos 2:15 6607
said, Smite the lintel of the *d* Amos 9:1
and when thou hast shut thy *d* Mt 6:6 *2374*
and the *d* was shut Mt 25:10 *2374*
stone to the *d* of the sepulchre Mt 27:60 *2374*
rolled back the stone from the *d* Mt 28:2 *2374*
was gathered together at the *d* Mk 1:33 *2374*
no, not so much as about the *d* Mk 2:2 *2374*
found the colt tied by the *d* Mk 11:4 *2374*
stone unto the *d* of the sepulchre Mk 15:46 *2374*
stone from the *d* of the sepulchre Mk 16:3 *2374*
the *d* is now shut, and my children Lk 11:7 *2374*
risen up, and hath shut to the *d* Lk 13:25 *2374*
without, and to knock at the *d* Lk 13:25 *2374*
not by the *d* into the sheepfold Jn 10:1 *2374*
d is the shepherd of the sheep Jn 10:2 *2374*
unto you, I am the *d* of the sheep Jn 10:7 *2374*
I am the *d* Jn 10:9 *2374*
But Peter stood at the *d* without Jn 18:16 *2374*
and spake unto her that kept the *d* Jn 18:16 *2377*
damsel that kept the *d* unto Peter Jn 18:17 *2377*
buried thy husband are at the *d* Acts 5:9 *2374*
before the *d* kept the prison Acts 12:6 *2374*
knocked at the *d* of the gate Acts 12:13
and when they had opened the *d* Acts 12:16
how he had opened the *d* of faith Acts 14:27 *2374*
For a great *d* and effectual is 1Cor 16:9 *2374*
a *d* was opened unto me of the 2Cor 2:12 *2374*
open unto us a *d* of utterance Col 4:3 *2374*
the judge standeth before the *d* Jas 5:9 *2374*
I have set before thee an open *d* Rev 3:8 *2374*
Behold, I stand at the *d*, and Rev 3:20 *2374*
man hear my voice, and open the *d* Rev 3:20 *2374*
behold, a *d* was opened in heaven Rev 4:1 *2374*

DOORKEEPER {1}
I had rather be a *d* in the house Ps 84:10 5605

DOORKEEPERS {2}
and Elkanah were *d* for the ark 1Chr 15:23 7778
and Jehiah were *d* for the ark 1Chr 15:24 7778

DOORS {71}
d of thy house into the street Josh 2:19 1817
shut the *d* of the parlour upon Judg 3:23 1817
the *d* of the parlour were locked, Judg 3:24 1817
opened not the *d* of the parlour Judg 3:25 1817
of the *d* of my house to meet me Judg 11:31 1817
took the *d* of the gate of the Judg 16:3 1817
opened the *d* of the house, and Judg 19:27 1817
opened the *d* of the house of the 1Sa 3:15 1817
and scrabbled on the *d* of the gate 1Sa 21:13 1817
oracle he made *d* of olive tree 1Kin 6:31 1817
The two *d* also were of olive tree 1Kin 6:32 1817
the two *d* were of fir tree 1Kin 6:34 1817
And all the *d* and posts were square 1Kin 7:5 6607
both for the *d* of the inner house 1Kin 7:50 1817
for the *d* of the house, to wit, 1Kin 7:50 1817
the *d* of the temple of the LORD 2Kin 18:16 1817
the nails for the *d* of the gates 1Chr 22:3 1817
and the *d* thereof, with gold 2Chr 3:7 1817
great court, and *d* for the court 2Chr 4:9 1817
overlaid the *d* of them with brass 2Chr 4:9 1817
the inner *d* thereof for the most 2Chr 4:22 1817
the *d* of the house of the temple, 2Chr 4:22 1817
shall be porters of the *d* 2Chr 23:4 5592
shut up the *d* of the house of the 2Chr 28:24 1817
opened the *d* of the house of the 2Chr 29:3 1817
have shut up the *d* of the porch 2Chr 29:7 1817
the *d* had gathered of the hand of 2Chr 34:9 5592
it, and set up the *d* of it Neh 3:1 1817
thereof, and set up the *d* thereof Neh 3:3 1817
thereof, and set up the *d* thereof Neh 3:6 1817
built it, and set up the *d* thereof Neh 3:13 1817
build it, and set up the *d* thereof Neh 3:14 1817
it, and set up the *d* thereof Neh 3:15 1817
not set up the *d* upon the gates Neh 6:1 1817
let us shut the *d* of the temple Neh 6:10 1817
was built, and I had set up the *d* Neh 7:1 1817
stand by, let them shut the *d* Neh 7:3 1817
not up the *d* of my mother's womb Job 3:10 1817
but I opened my *d* to the Job 31:32 1817
Or who shut up the sea with *d* Job 38:8 1817
decreed place, and set bars and *d* Job 38:10 1817
or hast thou seen the *d* of the Job 38:17 8179
Who can open the *d* of his face Job 41:14 1817
be ye lifted up, ye everlasting *d* Ps 24:7 6607
lift them up, ye everlasting *d* Ps 24:9 6607
above, and opened the *d* of heaven Ps 78:23 1817
city, at the coming in at the *d* Prov 8:3 6607
waiting at the posts of my *d* Prov 8:34 6607
the *d* shall be shut in the Eccl 12:4 1817
and shut thy *d* about thee Is 26:20 1817
Behind the *d* also and the posts Is 57:8 1817
in the *d* of the houses, and speak Eze 33:30 6607
the *d* of the side chambers were Eze 41:11 6607
temple and the sanctuary had two *d* Eze 41:23 1817
the *d* had two leaves apiece, two Eze 41:24 1817
on the *d* of the temple, cherubims Eze 41:25 1817
and their *d* toward the north Eze 42:4 6607
fashions, and according to their *d* Eze 42:11 6607
according to the *d* of the Eze 42:12 6607
keep the *d* of thy mouth from her Mic 7:5 6607
Open thy *d*, O Lebanon, that the Zec 11:1 1817
that would shut the *d* for nought Mal 1:10 1817
that it is near, even at the *d* Mt 24:33 *2374*
that it is nigh, even at the *d* Mk 13:29 *2374*
when the *d* were shut where the Jn 20:19 *2374*
the *d* being shut, and stood in the Jn 20:26 *2374*
Lord by night opened the prison *d* Acts 5:19 *2374*
standing without before the *d* Acts 5:23 *2374*
immediately all the *d* were opened Acts 16:26 *2374*
and seeing the prison *d* open Acts 16:27 *2374*
and forthwith the *d* were shut Acts 21:30 *2374*

DOPHKAH *(dof'-kah)* {2} *An encampment during the Exodus.*
of Sin, and encamped in *D* Num 33:12 1850
And they departed from *D*, and Num 33:13 1850

DOR *(dor)* {7} See EN-DOR. *A Canaanite city.*
in the borders of *D* on the west Josh 11:2 1756
The king of *D* in the coast of *D* Josh 12:23 1756
towns, and the inhabitants of *D* Josh 17:11 1756
towns, nor the inhabitants of *D* Judg 1:27 1756
Abinadab, in all the region of *D* 1Kin 4:11 1756
towns, Megiddo and her towns, *D* 1Chr 7:29 1756

DORCAS *(dor'-cas)* {2} See TABITHA. *Disciple raised from the dead by Peter.*
by interpretation is called *D* Acts 9:36 *1393*
coats and garments which *D* made Acts 9:39 *1393*

DOST {56}
it that thou *d* ask after my name Gen 32:29
when thou *d* overtake them, say Gen 44:4
d thou go to possess their land Deut 9:5
When thou *d* lend thy brother any Deut 24:10
the man to whom thou *d* lend shall Deut 24:11
Thou *d* but hate me, and lovest me Judg 14:16
after whom *d* thou pursue 1Sa 24:14
Wherefore then *d* thou ask of me 1Sa 28:16
why *d* thou ask Abishag the 1Kin 2:22
D thou now govern the kingdom of 1Kin 21:7
Now on whom *d* thou trust, that 2Kin 18:20
sin, when thou *d* afflict them 2Chr 6:26
For what *d* thou make request Neh 2:4
D thou still retain thine Job 2:9
And why *d* thou not pardon my Job 7:21
yet thou *d* destroy me Job 10:8
d thou open thine eyes upon such Job 14:3
d thou not watch over my sin Job 14:16
d thou restrain wisdom to thyself Job 15:8
unto thee, and thou *d* not hear me Job 30:20
Why *d* thou strive against him Job 33:13
D thou know when God disposed Job 37:15
D thou know the balancings of the Job 37:16
When thou with rebukes *d* correct Ps 39:11
why *d* thou cast me off Ps 43:2
d not increase thy wealth by Ps 44:12
thou *d* establish equity, thou Ps 99:4
honour, when thou *d* embrace her Prov 4:8
for thou *d* not enquire wisely Eccl 7:10
beloved, that thou *d* so charge us Song 5:9
d weigh the path of the just Is 26:7
now on whom *d* thou trust, that Is 36:5
Wherefore *d* thou prophesy, and say Jer 32:3
D thou certainly know that Baalis Jer 40:14
daughter that *d* inhabit Dibon Jer 48:18

Wherefore *d* thou forget us for .... Lam 5:20
thou *d* dwell among scorpions .... Eze 2:6
Whom *d* thou pass in beauty .... Eze 32:19
if thou *d* not speak to warn the .... Eze 33:8
Now why *d* thou cry out aloud .... Mic 4:9
Why *d* thou shew me iniquity, and .... Hab 1:3
d thou not care that my sister .... Lk 10:40
D not thou fear God, seeing thou .... Lk 23:40
what *d* thou work? .... Jn 6:30
born in sins, and *d* thou teach us .... Jn 9:34
D thou believe on the Son of God .... Jn 9:35
How long *d* thou make us to doubt .... Jn 10:24
him, Lord, *d* thou wash my feet .... Jn 13:6
should not steal, *d* thou steal .... Rom 2:21
adultery, *d* thou commit adultery .... Rom 2:22
idols, *d* thou commit sacrilege .... Rom 2:22
circumcision *d* transgress the law .... Rom 2:27
But why *d* thou judge thy brother .... Rom 14:10
or why *d* thou set at nought thy .... Rom 14:10
why *d* thou glory, as if thou 1Cor 4:7
d thou not judge and avenge our .... Rev 6:10

DOTE {1}
and they shall *d*: a sword is .... Jer 50:36 2973

DOTED {6}
she *d* on her lovers, on the .... Eze 23:5 5689
and with all on whom she *d* .... Eze 23:7 5689
of the Assyrians, upon whom she *d* .... Eze 23:9 5689
She *d* upon the Assyrians her .... Eze 23:12 5689
eyes, she *d* upon them, and sent .... Eze 23:16 5689
For she *d* upon their paramours, ... Eze 23:20 5689

DOTH {207}
For God *d* know that in the day ye .... Gen 3:5
d comfort himself, purposing to .... Gen 27:42
d my father yet live .... Gen 45:3
d put a difference between the .... Ex 11:7
I am the LORD that *d* sanctify you .... Ex 31:13
why *d* thy wrath wax hot against .... Ex 32:11
whosoever *d* touch them, when they .... Lev 11:31
d fall, it shall be unclean .... Lev 11:32
of the fruits *d* he sell unto thee .... Lev 25:16
when the LORD *d* make thy thigh to .... Num 5:21
the man whom the LORD *d* choose .... Num 16:7
the LORD *d* command concerning the .... Num 36:6
the LORD our God *d* give unto us .... Deut 1:20
which the LORD our God *d* give us .... Deut 1:25
as a man *d* bear his son, in all .... Deut 1:31
this day that God *d* talk with man .... Deut 5:24
that man *d* not live by bread only .... Deut 8:3
the mouth of the LORD *d* man live .... Deut 8:3
of these nations the LORD *d* drive .... Deut 9:4
these nations the LORD thy God *d* .... Deut 9:5
what *d* the LORD thy God require .... Deut 10:12
He *d* execute the judgment of the .... Deut 10:18
for a gift *d* blind the eyes of .... Deut 16:19
abominations the LORD thy God *d* .... Deut 18:12
which the LORD thy God *d* give .... Deut 20:16
God, he it is that *d* go with thee .... Deut 31:6
he it is that *d* go before thee .... Deut 31:8
Whosoever he be that *d* rebel .... Josh 1:18
when he that *d* flee unto one of .... Josh 20:4
it shall be, when any man *d* come .... Judg 4:20
d know that thou art a virtuous .... Ruth 3:11
because he *d* bless the sacrifice 1Sa 9:13
D not David hide himself with us 1Sa 23:19
D not David hide himself in the 1Sa 26:1
Wherefore *d* my lord thus pursue 1Sa 26:18
as when one *d* hunt a partridge in 1Sa 26:20
that David *d* honour thy father 2Sa 10:3
for the king *d* speak this thing 2Sa 14:13
in that the king *d* not fetch home 2Sa 14:13
neither *d* God respect any person 2Sa 14:14
yet *d* he devise means, that his 2Sa 14:14
the king *d* sit in the gate 2Sa 19:8
For thy servant *d* know that I 2Sa 19:20
but why *d* my lord the king 2Sa 24:3
of that which *d* cost me nothing 2Sa 24:24
the son of Haggith *d* reign 1Kin 1:11
why then *d* Adonijah reign 1Kin 1:13
for he *d* not prophesy good 1Kin 22:8
spirit of Elijah *d* rest on Elisha 2Kin 2:15
that this man *d* send unto me to 2Kin 5:7
that David *d* honour thy father 1Chr 19:3
why then *d* my lord require this 1Chr 21:3
as *d* thy people Israel, and may 2Chr 6:33
D not Hezekiah persuade you to 2Chr 32:11
D Job fear God for nought .... Job 1:9
D not their excellency which is .... Job 4:21
neither *d* trouble spring out of .... Job 5:6
D the wild ass bray when he hath .... Job 6:5
but what *d* your arguing reprove .... Job 6:25
D God pervert judgment .... Job 8:3
or *d* the Almighty pervert justice .... Job 8:3
D not the ear try words .... Job 12:11
Why *d* thine heart carry thee away .... Job 15:12
my reins asunder, and *d* not spare .... Job 16:13
d not mine eye continue in their .... Job 17:2
And thou sayest, How *d* God know .... Job 22:13
On the left hand, where he *d* work .... Job 23:9
so *d* the grave those which have .... Job 24:19
upon whom *d* not his light arise .... Job 25:3
D not he see my ways, and count .... Job 31:4
Therefore *d* Job open his mouth in .... Job 35:16
he *d* establish them for ever, and .... Job 36:7
D the hawk fly by thy wisdom, and .... Job 39:26
D the eagle mount up at thy .... Job 39:27
By his neesings a light *d* shine .... Job 41:18
in his law *d* he meditate day and .... Ps 1:2
in his pride *d* persecute the poor .... Ps 10:2
in the secret places *d* he murder .... Ps 10:8
he *d* catch the poor, when he .... Ps 10:9
Wherefore *d* the wicked contemn .... Ps 10:13
his countenance *d* behold the .... Ps 11:7
in his temple *d* every one speak .... Ps 29:9
because mine enemy *d* not triumph .... Ps 41:11
D not David hide himself with us .... Ps 54:*t*
for who, say they, *d* hear .... Ps 59:7
he *d* send out his voice, and that .... Ps 68:33
And they say, How *d* God know .... Ps 73:11
why *d* thine anger smoke against .... Ps 74:1
d his promise fail for evermore .... Ps 77:8
boar out of the wood *d* waste it .... Ps 80:13
beast of the field *d* devour it .... Ps 80:13
neither *d* a fool understand this .... Ps 92:6
therefore *d* my soul keep them .... Ps 119:129
wait for the LORD, my soul *d* wait .... Ps 130:5
The LORD *d* build up Jerusalem .... Ps 147:2
These six things *d* the LORD hate .... Prov 6:16
D not wisdom cry? .... Prov 8:1
a stranger *d* not intermeddle with .... Prov 14:10
he that *d* keep his soul shall be .... Prov 22:5
d not he that pondereth the heart .... Prov 24:12
thy soul, *d* not he know it .... Prov 24:12
so *d* an angry countenance a .... Prov 25:23
so *d* the slothful upon his bed .... Prov 26:14
so *d* the sweetness of a man's .... Prov 27:9
d the crown endure to every .... Prov 27:24
but the righteous *d* sing and .... Prov 29:6
and *d* not bless their mother .... Prov 30:11
her husband *d* safely trust in her .... Prov 31:11
so *d* a little folly him that is .... Eccl 10:1
and his right hand *d* embrace me .... Song 2:6
but Israel *d* not know .... Is 1:3
my people *d* not consider .... Is 1:3
neither *d* the cause of the widow .... Is 1:23
d take away from Jerusalem and .... Is 3:1
d witness against them .... Is 3:9
neither *d* his heart think so .... Is 10:7
D the plowman plow all day to sow .... Is 28:24
d he open and break the clods of .... Is 28:24
d he not cast abroad the fitches, ... Is 28:25
For his God *d* instruct him to .... Is 28:26
him to discretion, and *d* teach him .... Is 28:26
stream of brimstone, *d* kindle it .... Is 30:33
the villages that Kedar *d* inhabit .... Is 42:11
an ash, and the rain *d* nourish it .... Is 44:14
day that I am he that *d* speak .... Is 52:6
neither *d* justice overtake us .... Is 59:9
glory for that which *d* not profit .... Jer 2:11
for to thee *d* it appertain .... Jer 10:7
Wherefore *d* the way of the wicked .... Jer 12:1
the LORD *d* not accept them .... Jer 14:10
yet every one of them *d* curse me .... Jer 15:10
that none *d* return from his .... Jer 23:14
see whether a man *d* travail with .... Jer 30:6
him, as a shepherd *d* his flock .... Jer 31:10
why then *d* their king inherit Gad .... Jer 49:1
neither *d* any son of man pass .... Jer 51:43
How *d* the city sit solitary, that .... Lam 1:1
For he *d* not afflict willingly .... Lam 3:33
Wherefore *d* a living man complain .... Lam 3:39
there is none that *d* deliver us .... Lam 5:8
When a righteous man *d* turn from .... Eze 3:20
he *d* not sin, he shall surely .... Eze 3:21
d not the son bear the iniquity .... Eze 18:19
of me, *D* he not speak parables .... Eze 20:49
that *d* not understand shall fall .... Hos 4:14
of Israel *d* testify to his face .... Hos 5:5
what *d* the LORD require of thee, ... Mic 6:8
judgment *d* never go forth .... Hab 1:4
for the wicked *d* compass about .... Hab 1:4
every morning *d* he bring his .... Zeph 3:5
rust *d* corrupt, and where thieves .... Mt 6:19
neither moth nor rust *d* corrupt .... Mt 6:20
This fellow *d* not cast out devils .... Mt 12:24
D not your master pay tribute .... Mt 17:24
d he not leave the ninety and nine .... Mt 18:12
is put away *d* commit adultery .... Mt 19:9
How then *d* David in spirit call .... Mt 22:43
not what hour your Lord *d* come .... Mt 24:42
he is at hand that *d* betray me .... Mt 26:46
Why *d* this man thus speak .... Mk 2:7
the new wine *d* burst the bottles .... Mk 2:22
Why *d* this generation seek after .... Mk 8:12
My soul *d* magnify the Lord, ... Lk 1:46
neither *d* a corrupt tree bring .... Lk 6:43
of a candle *d* give thee light .... Lk 11:36
d not each one of you on the .... Lk 13:15
as a hen *d* gather her brood under .... Lk 13:34
whosoever *d* not bear his cross, ... Lk 14:27
d not leave the ninety and nine in .... Lk 15:4
d not light a candle, and sweep .... Lk 15:8
D he thank that servant because .... Lk 17:9
that is chief, as he that *d* serve .... Lk 22:26
beginning *d* set forth good wine .... Jn 2:10
said unto them, *D* this offend you .... Jn 6:61
D our law judge any man, before .... Jn 7:51
how then *d* he now see .... Jn 9:19
Therefore *d* my Father love me, ... Jn 10:17
even by him *d* this man stand here .... Acts 4:10
what *d* hinder me to be baptized .... Acts 8:36
the high priest *d* bear me witness .... Acts 22:5
much learning *d* make thee mad .... Acts 26:24
man seeth, why *d* he yet hope for .... Rom 8:24
unto me, Why *d* he yet find fault .... Rom 9:19
to the Lord he *d* not regard it .... Rom 14:6
D God take care for oxen 1Cor 9:9
D not even nature itself teach 1Cor 11:14
D not behave itself unseemly, ... 1Cor 13:5
neither *d* corruption inherit 1Cor 15:50
so great a death, and *d* deliver 2Cor 1:10
much more *d* the ministration of 2Cor 3:9
for whatsoever *d* make manifest is .... Eph 5:13
as it *d* also in you, since the .... Col 1:6
as a father *d* his children, ... 1Th 2:11
of iniquity *d* already work 2Th 2:7
their word will eat as *d* a canker 2Ti 2:17
all shall wax old as *d* a garment .... Heb 1:11
the sin which *d* so easily beset .... Heb 12:1
What *d* it profit, my brethren, ... Jas 2:14
to the body; what *d* it profit? .... Jas 2:16
D a fountain send forth at the .... Jas 3:11
and he *d* not resist you .... Jas 5:6
d also now save us (not the 1Pet 3:21
and so *d* Marcus my son 1Pet 5:13
it *d* not yet appear what we shall 1Jn 3:2
is born of God *d* not commit sin 1Jn 3:9
neither *d* he himself receive the 3Jn 10
and in righteousness he *d* judge .... Rev 19:11

DOTHAN *(do'-than)* {3} *A city in Manasseh.*
I heard them say, Let us go to *D* .... Gen 37:17 1886
his brethren, and found them in *D* .... Gen 37:17 1886
him, saying, Behold, he is in *D* 2Kin 6:13 1886

DOTING {1}
but *d* about questions and strifes 1Ti 6:4 *3552*

DOUBLE {26}
take *d* money in your hand .... Gen 43:12 4932
they took *d* money in their hand, ... Gen 43:15 4932
he shall restore *d* .... Ex 22:4 8147
the thief be found, let him pay *d* .... Ex 22:7 8147
he shall pay *d* unto his neighbour .... Ex 22:9 8147
shalt *d* the sixth curtain in the .... Ex 26:9 3717
they made the breastplate *d* .... Ex 39:9 3717
worth a *d* hired servant to thee .... Deut 15:18 4932
by giving him a *d* portion of all .... Deut 21:17 8147
let a *d* portion of thy spirit be 2Kin 2:9 8147
they were not of *d* heart 1Chr 12:33
that they are *d* to that which is .... Job 11:6 3718
can come to him with his *d* bridle .... Job 41:13 3718
with a *d* heart do they speak .... Ps 12:2
LORD's hand *d* for all her sins .... Is 40:2 3718
For your shame ye shall have *d* .... Is 61:7 4932
land they shall possess the *d* .... Is 61:7 4932
their iniquity and their sin *d* .... Jer 16:18 4932
destroy them with *d* destruction .... Jer 17:18 4932
that I will render *d* unto thee .... Zec 9:12 4932
be counted worthy of *d* honour 1Ti 5:17 *1362*
A *d* minded man is unstable in all .... Jas 1:8 *1374*
purify your hearts, ye *d* minded .... Jas 4:8 *1374*
d unto her *d* according to .... Rev 18:6 *3588,1362*
she hath filled fill to her *d* .... Rev 18:6 *1362*

DOUBLED {4}
dream was *d* unto Pharaoh twice .... Gen 41:32 8138
Foursquare it shall be being *d* .... Ex 28:16 3717
span the breadth thereof, being *d* .... Ex 39:9 3717
let the sword be *d* the third time .... Eze 21:14 3717

DOUBLETONGUED {1}
must the deacons be grave, not *d* 1Ti 3:8 *1351*

DOUBT {13}
is without *d* rent in pieces .... Gen 37:33
life shall hang in *d* before thee .... Deut 28:66
No *d* but ye are the people, and .... Job 12:2 551
faith, wherefore didst thou *d* .... Mt 14:31 *1365*
d not, ye shall not only do this .... Mt 21:21 *1252*
shall not *d* in his heart, but .... Mk 11:23 *1252*
no *d* the kingdom of God is come .... Lk 11:20 *686*
How long dost thou make us to *d* .... Jn 10:24 *142,5590*
were all amazed, and were in *d* .... Acts 2:12 *1280*
No *d* this man is a murderer, whom .... Acts 28:4 *3843*
For our sakes, no *d*, this is 1Cor 9:10 *1063*
for I stand in *d* of you .... Gal 4:20 *639*
they would no *d* have continued 1Jn 2:19

DOUBTED {4}
but some *d* .... Mt 28:17 *1365*
they *d* of them whereunto this .... Acts 5:24 *1280*
Now while Peter *d* in himself what .... Acts 10:17 *1280*
because I *d* of such manner of .... Acts 25:20 *639*

DOUBTETH {1}
he that *d* is damned if he eat, ... Rom 14:23 *1252*

DOUBTFUL {2}
drink, neither be ye of *d* mind .... Lk 12:29 *3349*
but not to *d* disputations .... Rom 14:1 *1261*

DOUBTING {4}
on another, *d* of whom he spake .... Jn 13:22 *639*
down, and go with them, *d* nothing .... Acts 10:20 *1252*
bade me go with them, nothing *d* .... Acts 11:12 *1252*
up holy hands, without wrath and *d* 1Ti 2:8 *1261*

DOUBTLESS {7}
D ye shall not come into the land .... Num 14:30 518
for I will *d* deliver the 2Sa 5:19
shall *d* come again with rejoicing .... Ps 126:6
D thou art our father, though .... Is 63:16 3588
unto others, yet *d* I am to you 1Cor 9:2 *1065*
not expedient for me *d* to glory 2Cor 12:1 *1211*
Yea *d*, and I count all things but .... Phil 3:8 *3304*

DOUBTS {2}
sentences, and dissolving of *d* .... Dan 5:12 7001
interpretations, and dissolve *d* .... Dan 5:16 7001

D

DOUGH {8}
the people took their *d* before it ... Ex 12:34 1217
baked unleavened cakes of the *d* ... Ex 12:39 1217
of your *d* for an heave offering ... Num 15:20 6182
Of the first of your *d* ye shall ... Num 15:21 6182
bring the firstfruits of our *d* ... Neh 10:37 6182
fire, and the women knead their *d* ... Jer 7:18 1217
the priest the first of your *d* ... Eze 44:30 6182
after he hath kneaded the *d* ... Hos 7:4 1217

DOVE {18}
Also he sent forth a *d* from him ... Gen 8:8 3123
But the *d* found no rest for the ... Gen 8:9 3123
sent forth the *d* out of the ark ... Gen 8:10 3123
the *d* came in to him in the ... Gen 8:11 3123
and sent forth the *d* ... Gen 8:12 3123
Oh that I had wings like a *d* ... Ps 55:6 3123
wings of a *d* covered with silver ... Ps 68:13 3123
O my *d*, that art in the clefts of ... Song 2:14 3123
to me, my sister, my love, my *d* ... Song 5:2 3123
My *d*, my undefiled is but one ... Song 6:9 3123
I did mourn as a *d* ... Is 38:14 3123
be like the *d* that maketh her ... Jer 48:28 3123
is like a silly *d* without heart ... Hos 7:11 3123
as a *d* out of the land of Assyria ... Hos 11:11 3123
Spirit of God descending like a *d* ... Mt 3:16 *4058*
the Spirit like a *d* descending ... Mk 1:10 *4058*
a bodily shape like a *d* upon him ... Lk 3:22 *4058*
descending from heaven like a *d* ... Jn 1:32 *4058*

DOVE'S {1}
the fourth part of a cab of *d* ... 2Kin 6:25 1686

DOVES {10}
eyes of *d* by the rivers of waters ... Song 5:12 3123
like bears, and mourn sore like *d* ... Is 59:11 3123
as the *d* to their windows ... Is 60:8 3123
mountains like *d* of the valleys ... Eze 7:16 3123
lead her as with the voice of *d* ... Nah 2:7 3123
as serpents, and harmless as *d* ... Mt 10:16 *4058*
and the seats of them that sold *d* ... Mt 21:12 *4058*
and the seats of them that sold *d* ... Mk 11:15 *4058*
that sold oxen and sheep and *d* ... Jn 2:14 *4058*
And said unto them that sold *d* ... Jn 2:16 *4058*

DOVES' {2}
thou art fair; thou hast *d* eyes ... Song 1:15 3123
thou hast *d* eyes within thy locks ... Song 4:1 3123

DOWN See APPENDIX.

DOWNSITTING {1}
Thou knowest my *d* and mine ... Ps 139:2 3427

DOWNWARD {5}
Judah shall yet again take root *d* ... 2Kin 19:30 4295
beast that goeth *d* to the earth ... Eccl 3:21 4295
of Judah shall again take root *d* ... Is 37:31 4295
appearance of his loins even *d* ... Eze 1:27 4295
appearance of his loins even *d* ... Eze 8:2 4295

DOWRY {4}
God hath endued me with a good *d* ... Gen 30:20 2065
Ask me never so much *d* and gift ... Gen 34:12 4119
according to the *d* of virgins ... Ex 22:17 4119
The king desireth not any *d* ... 1Sa 18:25 4119

DRAG {2}
net, and gather them in their *d* ... Hab 1:15 4365
net, and burn incense unto their *d* ... Hab 1:16 4365

DRAGGING {1}
cubits,) *d* the net with fishes ... Jn 21:8 *4951*

DRAGON {19}
valley, even before the *d* well ... Neh 2:13 8577
the *d* shalt thou trample under ... Ps 91:13 8577
he shall slay the *d* that is in ... Is 27:1 8577
hath cut Rahab, and wounded the *d* ... Is 51:9 8577
he hath swallowed me up like a *d* ... Jer 51:34 8577
the great *d* that lieth in the ... Eze 29:3 8577
and behold a great red *d*, having ... Rev 12:3 *1404*
the *d* stood before the woman ... Rev 12:4 *1404*
his angels fought against the *d* ... Rev 12:7 *1404*
the *d* fought and his angels ... Rev 12:7 *1404*
the great *d* was cast out, that ... Rev 12:9 *1404*
when the *d* saw that he was cast ... Rev 12:13 *1404*
which the *d* cast out of his mouth ... Rev 12:16 *1404*
the *d* was wroth with the woman ... Rev 12:17 *1404*
the *d* gave him his power, and his ... Rev 13:2 *1404*
they worshipped the *d* which gave ... Rev 13:4 *1404*
like a lamb, and he spake as a *d* ... Rev 13:11 *1404*
come out of the mouth of the *d* ... Rev 16:13 *1404*
And he laid hold on the *d*, that ... Rev 20:2 *1404*

DRAGONS {16}
Their wine is the poison of *d* ... Deut 32:33 8577
I am a brother to *d*, and a ... Job 30:29 8577
sore broken us in the place of *d* ... Ps 44:19 8577
the heads of the *d* in the waters ... Ps 74:13 8577
the LORD from the earth, ye *d* ... Ps 148:7 8577
d in their pleasant palaces ... Is 13:22 8577
and it shall be an habitation of *d* ... Is 34:13 8577
in the habitation of *d*, where ... Is 35:7 8577
the field shall honour me, the *d* ... Is 43:20 8577
Jerusalem heaps, and a den of *d* ... Jer 9:11 8577
of Judah desolate, and a den of *d* ... Jer 10:22 8577
they snuffed up the wind like *d* ... Jer 14:6 8577
Hazor shall be a dwelling for *d* ... Jer 49:33 8577
heaps, a dwelling place for *d* ... Jer 51:37 8577
I will make a wailing like the *d* ... Mic 1:8 8577
waste for the *d* of the wilderness ... Mal 1:3 8568

DRAMS {6}
talents and ten thousand *d* ... 1Chr 29:7 150
and one thousand *d* of gold ... Ezr 2:69 1871
basons of gold, of a thousand *d* ... Ezr 8:27 150
the treasure a thousand *d* of gold ... Neh 7:70 1871
work twenty thousand *d* of gold ... Neh 7:71 1871
was twenty thousand *d* of gold ... Neh 7:72 1871

DRANK {19}
he *d* of the wine, and was drunken ... Gen 9:21 8354
so I *d*, and she made the camels ... Gen 24:46 8354
and he brought him wine, and he *d* ... Gen 27:25 8354
And they *d*, and were merry with him ... Gen 43:34 8354
abundantly, and the congregation *d* ... Num 20:11 8354
d the wine of their drink ... Deut 32:38 8354
d of his own cup, and lay in his ... 2Sa 12:3 8354
bread in his house, and *d* water ... 1Kin 13:19 8354
and he *d* of the brook ... 1Kin 17:6
meat, and of the wine which he *d* ... Dan 1:5 4960
nor with the wine which he *d* ... Dan 1:8 4960
d wine before the thousand ... Dan 5:1 8355
and his concubines, *d* in them ... Dan 5:3 8355
They *d* wine, and praised the gods ... Dan 5:4 8355
and they all *d* of it ... Mk 14:23 *4095*
They did eat, they *d*, they ... Lk 17:27 *4095*
they did eat, they *d*, they bought ... Lk 17:28 *4095*
d thereof himself, and his ... Jn 4:12 *4095*
for they *d* of that spiritual Rock ... 1Cor 10:4 *4095*

DRAUGHT {5}
made it a *d* house unto this day ... 2Kin 10:27 4280
belly, and is cast out into the *d* ... Mt 15:17 *856*
belly, and goeth out into the *d* ... Mk 7:19 *856*
and let down your nets for a *d* ... Lk 5:4 *61*
at the *d* of the fishes which they ... Lk 5:9 *61*

DRAVE {13}
wheels, that they *d* them heavily ... Ex 14:25 5090
they *d* not out the Canaanites ... Josh 16:10 3423
which *d* them out from before you ... Josh 24:12 1644
the LORD *d* out from before us all ... Josh 24:18 1644
he *d* out the inhabitants of the ... Judg 1:19 3423
d them out from before you, and ... Judg 6:9 1644
which they *d* before those other ... 1Sa 30:20 5090
sons of Abinadab, *d* the new cart ... 2Sa 6:3 5090
Syria, and *d* the Jews from Elath ... 2Kin 16:6 5394
Jeroboam *d* Israel from following ... 2Kin 17:21 5071
and Uzza and Ahio *d* the cart ... 1Chr 13:7 5090
whom God *d* out before the face of ... Acts 7:45 *1856*
he *d* them from the judgment seat ... Acts 18:16 *556*

DRAW {76}
time that women go out to *d* water ... Gen 24:11 7579
of the city come out to *d* water ... Gen 24:13 7579
I will *d* water for thy camels ... Gen 24:19 7579
again unto the well to *d* water ... Gen 24:20 7579
virgin cometh forth to *d* water ... Gen 24:43 7579
I will also *d* for thy camels ... Gen 24:44 7579
And he said, *D* not nigh hither ... Ex 3:5
them, *D* out and take you a lamb ... Ex 12:21 4900
I will *d* my sword, my hand shall ... Ex 15:9 7324
will *d* out a sword after you ... Lev 26:33 7324
so that he could not *d* the dagger ... Judg 3:22 8025
d toward mount Tabor, and take ... Judg 4:6 4900
I will *d* unto thee to the river ... Judg 4:7 4900
D thy sword, and slay me, that men ... Judg 9:54 8025
let us *d* near to one of these ... Judg 19:13
d them from the city unto the ... Judg 20:32 5423
maidens going out to *d* water ... 1Sa 9:11 7579
Let us *d* near hither unto God ... 1Sa 14:36
D ye near hither, all the chief ... 1Sa 14:38
D thy sword, and thrust me through ... 1Sa 31:4 8025
we will *d* it into the river ... 2Sa 17:13 5498
D thy sword, and thrust me through ... 1Chr 10:4 8025
and every man shall *d* after him ... Job 21:33 4900
he trusteth that he can *d* up ... Job 40:23 1518
Canst thou *d* out leviathan with ... Job 41:1 4900
D me not away with the wicked, and ... Ps 28:3 4900
D out also the spear, and stop the ... Ps 35:3 7324
D nigh unto my soul, and redeem it ... Ps 69:18
is good for me to *d* near to God ... Ps 73:28
wilt thou *d* out thine anger to ... Ps 85:5 4900
they *d* near unto the gates of ... Ps 107:18
They *d* nigh that follow after ... Ps 119:150
of understanding will *d* it out ... Prov 20:5 1802
come not, nor the years *d* nigh ... Eccl 12:1
D me, we will run after thee ... Song 1:4 4900
Woe unto them that *d* iniquity ... Is 5:18 4900
of the Holy One of Israel *d* nigh ... Is 5:19
ye *d* water out of the wells of ... Is 12:3 7579
people *d* near me with their mouth ... Is 29:13
d near together, ye that are ... Is 45:20
But *d* near hither, ye sons of the ... Is 57:3
a wide mouth, and *d* out the tongue ... Is 57:4 748
if thou *d* out thy soul to the ... Is 58:10 6329
that *d* the bow, to Tubal, and ... Is 66:19 4900
and I will cause him to *d* near ... Jer 30:21
and shield, and *d* near to battle ... Jer 46:3
of the flock shall *d* them out ... Jer 49:20 5498
of the flock shall *d* them out ... Jer 50:45 5498
the sea monsters *d* out the breast ... Lam 4:3 2502
I will *d* out a sword after them ... Eze 5:2 7324
I will *d* out a sword after them ... Eze 5:12 7324
charge over the city to *d* near ... Eze 9:1
I will *d* out the sword after them ... Eze 12:14 7324
will *d* forth my sword out of his ... Eze 21:3 3318
hast caused thy days to *d* near ... Eze 22:4
they shall *d* their swords against ... Eze 28:7 7324
they shall *d* their swords against ... Eze 30:11 7324
d her and all her multitudes ... Eze 32:20 4900
let all the men of war *d* near ... Joel 3:9
D thee waters for the siege ... Nah 3:14 7579
to *d* out fifty vessels out of the ... Hag 2:16 2834
D out now, and bear unto the ... Jn 2:8 *501*
a woman of Samaria to *d* water ... Jn 4:7 *501*
Sir, thou hast nothing to *d* with ... Jn 4:11 *502*
not, neither come hither to *d* ... Jn 4:15 *501*
Father which hath sent me *d* him ... Jn 6:44 *1670*
the earth, will *d* all men unto me ... Jn 12:32 *1670*
now they were not able to *d* it ... Jn 21:6 *1670*
to *d* away disciples after them ... Acts 20:30 *645*
by the which we *d* nigh unto God ... Heb 7:19
Let us *d* near with a true heart ... Heb 10:22 *4334*
but if any man *d* back, my soul ... Heb 10:38 *5288*
of them who *d* back unto perdition ... Heb 10:39 *5289*
d you before the judgment seats ... Jas 2:6 *1670*
D nigh to God, and he will *d* ... Jas 4:8

DRAWER {1}
thy wood unto the *d* of thy water ... Deut 29:11 7579

DRAWERS {3}
wood and *d* of water unto all the ... Josh 9:21 7579
d of water for the house of my ... Josh 9:23 7579
d of water for the congregation ... Josh 9:27 7579

DRAWETH {12}
the wife of the one *d* near for to ... Deut 25:11
now the day *d* toward evening, I ... Judg 19:9 7503
He *d* also the mighty with his ... Job 24:22 4900
his soul *d* near unto the grave ... Job 33:22
when he *d* him into his net ... Ps 10:9 4900
my life *d* nigh unto the grave ... Ps 88:3
that *d* near the time of her ... Is 26:17
The time is come, the day *d* near ... Eze 7:12
This people *d* nigh unto me with ... Mt 15:8
and the time *d* near ... Lk 21:8
for your redemption *d* nigh ... Lk 21:28
for the coming of the Lord *d* nigh ... Jas 5:8

DRAWING {2}
archers in the places of *d* water ... Judg 5:11 4857
the sea, and *d* nigh unto the ship ... Jn 6:19 *1096*

DRAWN {28}
way, and his sword *d* in his hand ... Num 22:23 8025
way, and his sword *d* in his hand ... Num 22:31 8025
and which hath not *d* in the yoke ... Deut 21:3 4900
not hear, but shalt be *d* away ... Deut 30:17 5080
him with his sword *d* in his hand ... Josh 5:13 8025
till we have *d* them from the city ... Josh 8:6 5423
were *d* away from the city ... Josh 8:16 5423
the border was *d* from the top of ... Josh 15:9 8388
and the border was *d* to Baalah ... Josh 15:9 8388
and the border was *d* to Shicron ... Josh 15:11 8388
And the border was *d* thence ... Josh 18:14 8388
was *d* from the north, and went ... Josh 18:17 8388
were *d* away from the city ... Judg 20:31 5423
that which the young men have *d* ... Ruth 2:9 7579
having a *d* sword in his hand ... 1Chr 21:16 8025
It is *d*, and cometh out of the ... Job 20:25 8025
The wicked have *d* out the sword ... Ps 37:14 6605
than oil, yet were they *d* swords ... Ps 55:21 6609
them that are *d* unto death ... Prov 24:11 3947
from the swords, from the *d* sword ... Is 21:15 5203
the milk, and *d* from the breasts ... Is 28:9 6267
with the burial of an ass, *d* ... Jer 22:19 5498
with lovingkindness have I *d* thee ... Jer 31:3 4900
he hath *d* back his right hand ... Lam 2:3 7725
have *d* forth my sword out of his ... Eze 21:5 3318
thou, The sword, the sword is *d* ... Eze 21:28 6605
all were *d* up again into heaven ... Acts 11:10 *385*
when he is *d* away of his own lust ... Jas 1:14 *1828*

DREAD {9}
the *d* of you shall be upon every ... Gen 9:2 2844
Fear and *d* shall fall upon them ... Ex 15:16 6343
D not, neither be afraid of them ... Deut 1:29 6206
will I begin to put the *d* of thee ... Deut 2:25 6343
the *d* of you upon all the land ... Deut 11:25 4172
d not, nor be dismayed ... 1Chr 22:13 3372
and his *d* fall upon you ... Job 13:11 6343
let not thy *d* make me afraid ... Job 13:21 367
your fear, and let him be your *d* ... Is 8:13 6206

DREADFUL {9}
and said, How *d* is this place ... Gen 28:17 3372
A *d* sound is in his ears ... Job 15:21 6343
were so high that they were *d* ... Eze 1:18 3374
and behold a fourth beast, *d* ... Dan 7:7 1763
from all the others, exceeding *d* ... Dan 7:19 1763
d God, keeping the covenant and ... Dan 9:4 3372
They are terrible and *d* ... Hab 1:7 3372
my name is *d* among the heathen ... Mal 1:14 3372
of the great and *d* day of the LORD ... Mal 4:5 3372

DREAM {74}
came to Abimelech in a *d* by night ... Gen 20:3 2472
And God said unto him in a *d* ... Gen 20:6 2472
up mine eyes, and saw in a *d* ... Gen 31:10 2472
angel of God spake unto me in a *d* ... Gen 31:11 2472
Laban the Syrian in a *d* by night ... Gen 31:24 2472
And Joseph dreamed a *d*, and he told ... Gen 37:5 2472
this *d* which I have dreamed ... Gen 37:6 2472
And he dreamed yet another *d* ... Gen 37:9 2472
Behold, I have dreamed a *d* more ... Gen 37:9 2472
What is this *d* that thou hast ... Gen 37:10 2472
And they dreamed a *d* both of them ... Gen 40:5 2472
each man his *d* in one night ... Gen 40:5 2472
to the interpretation of his *d* ... Gen 40:5 2472
unto him, We have dreamed a *d* ... Gen 40:8 2472
chief butler told his *d* to Joseph ... Gen 40:9 2472
and said to him, In my *d* ... Gen 40:9 2472
unto Joseph, I also was in my *d* ... Gen 40:16 2472
awoke, and, behold, it was a *d* ... Gen 41:7 2472
and Pharaoh told them his *d* ... Gen 41:8 2472
And we dreamed a *d* in one night ... Gen 41:11 2472

to the interpretation of his *d* ... Gen 41:11 2472
to his *d* he did interpret ... Gen 41:12 2472
unto Joseph, I have dreamed a *d* ... Gen 41:15 2472
understand a *d* to interpret it ... Gen 41:15 2472
Pharaoh said unto Joseph, In my *d* ... Gen 41:17 2472
And I saw in my *d*, and, behold, ... Gen 41:22 2472
Pharaoh, The *d* of Pharaoh is one ... Gen 41:25 2472
are seven years: the *d* is one ... Gen 41:26 2472
for that the *d* was doubled unto ... Gen 41:32 2472
and will speak unto him in a *d* ... Num 12:6 2472
man that told a *d* unto his fellow ... Judg 7:13 2472
and said, Behold, I dreamed a *d* ... Judg 7:13 2472
Gideon heard the telling of the *d* ... Judg 7:15 2472
to Solomon in a *d* by night ... 1Kin 3:5 2472
and, behold, it was a *d* ... 1Kin 3:15 2472
He shall fly away as a *d*, and ... Job 20:8 2472
In a *d*, in a vision of the night, ... Job 33:15 2472
As a *d* when one awaketh ... Ps 73:20 2472
of Zion, we were like them that *d* ... Ps 126:1 2472
For a *d* cometh through the ... Eccl 5:3 2472
shall be as a *d* of a night vision ... Is 29:7 2472
hath a *d*, let him tell a *d* ... Jer 23:28 2472
unto them, I have dreamed a *d* ... Dan 2:3 2472
spirit was troubled to know the *d* ... Dan 2:3 2472
tell thy servants the *d*, and we ... Dan 2:4 2493
will not make known unto me the *d* ... Dan 2:5 2493
But if ye shew the *d*, and the ... Dan 2:6 2493
therefore shew me the *d*, and the ... Dan 2:6 2493
the king tell his servants the *d* ... Dan 2:7 2493
will not make known unto me the *d* ... Dan 2:9 2493
therefore tell me the *d*, and I ... Dan 2:9 2493
unto me the *d* which I have seen ... Dan 2:26 2493
Thy *d*, and the visions of thy head ... Dan 2:28 2493
This is the *d*; and we will ... Dan 2:36 2493
and the *d* is certain, and the ... Dan 2:45 2493
I saw a *d* which made me afraid, ... Dan 4:5 2493
me the interpretation of the *d* ... Dan 4:6 2493
and I told the *d* before them ... Dan 4:7 2493
and before him I told the *d* ... Dan 4:8 2493
visions of my *d* that I have seen ... Dan 4:9 2493
This *d* I king Nebuchadnezzar have ... Dan 4:18 2493
said, Belteshazzar, let not the *d* ... Dan 4:19 2493
the *d* be to them that hate thee, ... Dan 4:19 2493
king of Babylon Daniel had a *d* ... Dan 7:1 2493
then he wrote the *d*, and told the ... Dan 7:1 2493
your old men shall *d* dreams ... Joel 2:28 2492
the Lord appeared unto him in a *d* ... Mt 1:20 *3677*
being warned of God in a *d* that ... Mt 2:12 *3677*
Lord appeareth to Joseph in a *d* ... Mt 2:13 *3677*
in a *d* to Joseph in Egypt ... Mt 2:19 *3677*
being warned of God in a *d* ... Mt 2:22 *3677*
this day in a *d* because of him ... Mt 27:19 *3677*
and your old men shall *d* dreams ... Acts 2:17 *1798*

DREAMED {20}
And he *d*, and behold a ladder set ... Gen 28:12 2492
Joseph *d* a dream, and he told it ... Gen 37:5 2492
you, this dream which I have *d* ... Gen 37:6 2492
he *d* yet another dream, and told ... Gen 37:9 2492
Behold, I have *d* a dream more ... Gen 37:9 2492
is this dream that thou hast *d* ... Gen 37:10 2492
they *d* a dream both of them, each ... Gen 40:5 2492
said unto him, We have *d* a dream ... Gen 40:8 2492
of two full years, that Pharaoh *d* ... Gen 41:1 2492
And he slept and *d* the second time ... Gen 41:5 2492
we *d* a dream in one night, I and ... Gen 41:11 2492
we *d* each man according to the ... Gen 41:11 2492
I have *d* a dream, and there is ... Gen 41:15 2492
the dreams which he *d* of them ... Gen 42:9 2492
I *d* a dream, and, lo, a cake of ... Judg 7:13 2492
saying, I have *d*, I have *d* ... Jer 23:25 2492
dreams which ye cause to be *d* ... Jer 29:8 2492
Nebuchadnezzar *d* dreams, ... Dan 2:1 2492
I have *d* a dream, and my spirit ... Dan 2:3 2492

DREAMER {4}
to another, Behold, this *d* cometh ... Gen 37:19 1167,2472
or a *d* of dreams, and giveth thee ... Deut 13:1 2492
that prophet, or that *d* of dreams ... Deut 13:3 2492
or that *d* of dreams, shall be put ... Deut 13:5 2492

DREAMERS {2}
to your diviners, nor to your *d* ... Jer 27:9 2492
these filthy *d* defile the flesh ... Jude 8 *1797*

DREAMETH {2}
even be as when an hungry man *d* ... Is 29:8 2492
or as when a thirsty man *d* ... Is 29:8 2492

DREAMS {21}
hated him yet the more for his *d* ... Gen 37:8 2472
see what will become of his *d* ... Gen 37:20 2472
and he interpreted to us our *d* ... Gen 41:12 2472
Joseph remembered the *d* which he ... Gen 42:9 2472
you a prophet, or a dreamer of *d* ... Deut 13:1 2472
prophet, or that dreamer of *d* ... Deut 13:3 2472
prophet, or that dreamer of *d* ... Deut 13:5 2472
answered him not, neither by *d* ... 1Sa 28:6 2472
neither by prophets, nor by *d* ... 1Sa 28:15 2472
Then thou scarest me with *d* ... Job 7:14 2472
For in the multitude of *d* ... Eccl 5:7 2472
to forget my name by their *d* ... Jer 23:27 2472
them that prophesy false *d* ... Jer 23:32 2472
neither hearken to your *d* which ... Jer 29:8 2472
understanding in all visions and *d* ... Dan 1:17 2472
Nebuchadnezzar dreamed *d* ... Dan 2:1 2472
for to shew the king his *d* ... Dan 2:2 2472
understanding, interpreting of *d* ... Dan 5:12 2493
your old men shall dream *d* ... Joel 2:28 2472
seen a lie, and have told false *d* ... Zec 10:2 2472
and your old men shall dream *d* ... Acts 2:17 *1797*

DREGS {3}
but the *d* thereof, all the wicked ... Ps 75:8 8105
thou hast drunken the *d* of the ... Is 51:17 6907
even the *d* of the cup of my fury ... Is 51:22 6907

DRESS {9}
into the garden of Eden to *d* it ... Gen 2:15 5647
and he hasted to *d* it ... Gen 18:7 6213
d them, but shalt neither drink ... Deut 28:39 5647
to *d* for the wayfaring man that ... 2Sa 12:4 6213
d the meat in my sight, that I ... 2Sa 13:5 6213
Amnon's house, and *d* him meat ... 2Sa 13:7 6213
d it for me and my son, that we ... 1Kin 17:12 6213
I will *d* the other bullock, and ... 1Kin 18:23 6213
for yourselves, and *d* it first ... 1Kin 18:25 6213

DRESSED {7}
milk, and the calf which he had *d* ... Gen 18:8 6213
all that is *d* in the fryingpan, ... Lev 7:9 6213
of wine, and five sheep ready *d* ... 1Sa 25:18 6213
d it for the man that was come to ... 2Sa 12:4 6213
king, and had neither *d* his feet ... 2Sa 19:24 6213
was given them, and they *d* it ... 1Kin 18:26 6213
meet for them by whom it is *d* ... Heb 6:7 *1090*

DRESSER {1}
he unto the *d* of his vineyard ... Lk 13:7 *289*

DRESSERS {1}
vine *d* in the mountains, and in ... 2Chr 26:10 3755

DRESSETH {1}
when he *d* the lamps, he shall ... Ex 30:7 3190

DREW {85}
And Abraham *d* near, and said, Wilt ... Gen 18:23
water, and *d* for all his camels ... Gen 24:20 8025
down unto the well, and *d* water ... Gen 24:45 7579
and they *d* and lifted up Joseph out ... Gen 37:28 4900
as he *d* back his hand, that, ... Gen 38:29 7725
the time *d* nigh that Israel must ... Gen 47:29
Because I *d* him out of the water ... Ex 2:10 4871
d water, and filled the troughs to ... Ex 2:16 1802
also *d* water enough for us, and ... Ex 2:19 1802
And when Pharaoh *d* nigh, the ... Ex 14:10
Moses *d* near unto the thick ... Ex 20:21
and all the congregation *d* near ... Lev 9:5
d nigh, and came before the city, ... Josh 8:11
For Joshua *d* not his hand back, ... Josh 8:26 7725
twenty thousand men that *d* sword ... Judg 8:10 8025
But the youth *d* not his sword ... Judg 8:20 8025
thousand footmen that *d* sword ... Judg 20:2 8025
and six thousand men that *d* sword ... Judg 20:15 8025
hundred thousand men that *d* sword ... Judg 20:17 8025
all these *d* the sword ... Judg 20:25 8025
all these *d* the sword ... Judg 20:35 8025
liers in wait *d* themselves along ... Judg 20:37 4900
thousand men that *d* the sword ... Judg 20:46 8025
So he *d* off his shoe ... Ruth 4:8 8025
d water, and poured it out before ... 1Sa 7:6 7579
the Philistines *d* near to battle ... 1Sa 7:10
Then Saul *d* near to Samuel in the ... 1Sa 9:18
And the Philistine *d* near morning ... 1Sa 17:16
he *d* near to the Philistine ... 1Sa 17:40
came on and *d* near unto David ... 1Sa 17:41
d nigh to meet David, that David ... 1Sa 17:48
d it out of the sheath thereof, ... 1Sa 17:51 8025
And Joab *d* nigh, and the people ... 2Sa 10:13
And he came apace, and *d* near ... 2Sa 18:25
he *d* me out of many waters ... 2Sa 22:17 4871
d water out of the well of ... 2Sa 23:16 7579
valiant men that *d* the sword ... 2Sa 24:9 8025
Now the days of David *d* nigh that ... 1Kin 2:1
they *d* out the staves, that the ... 1Kin 8:8 748
a certain man *d* a bow at a ... 1Kin 22:34 4900
seven hundred men that *d* swords ... 2Kin 3:26 8025
Jehu *d* a bow with his full ... 2Kin 9:24
d water out of the well of ... 1Chr 11:18 7579
d nigh before the Syrians unto ... 1Chr 19:14
d forth the Syrians that were ... 1Chr 19:16 3318
hundred thousand men that *d* sword ... 1Chr 21:5 8025
and ten thousand men that *d* sword ... 1Chr 21:5 8025
they *d* out the staves of the ark, ... 2Chr 5:9 748
d bows, two hundred and fourscore ... 2Chr 14:8 1869
a certain man *d* a bow at a ... 2Chr 18:33 4900
So Esther *d* near, and touched the ... Est 5:2
his decree *d* near to be put in ... Est 9:1
he *d* me out of many waters ... Ps 18:16 4871
were afraid, *d* near, and came ... Is 41:5
So they *d* up Jeremiah with cords, ... Jer 38:13 4900
I *d* them with cords of a man, ... Hos 11:4 4900
she *d* not near to her God ... Zeph 3:2
they *d* to shore, and sat down, and ... Mt 13:48 *307*
when they *d* nigh unto Jerusalem, ... Mt 21:1
when the time of the fruit *d* near ... Mt 21:34
d his sword, and struck a servant ... Mt 26:51 *645*
of Gennesaret, and *d* to the shore ... Mk 6:53 *4358*
of them that stood by *d* a sword ... Mk 14:47 *4685*
Then *d* near unto him all the ... Lk 15:1
d nigh to the house, he heard ... Lk 15:25
feast of unleavened bread *d* nigh ... Lk 22:1
d near unto Jesus to kiss him ... Lk 22:47
preparation, and the sabbath *d* on ... Lk 23:54 *2020*
and reasoned, Jesus himself *d* near ... Lk 24:15
they *d* nigh unto the village, ... Lk 24:28
servants which *d* the water knew ... Jn 2:9 *501*
Simon Peter having a sword *d* it ... Jn 18:10 *1670*
d the net to land full of great ... Jn 21:11 *1670*
d away much people after him ... Acts 5:37 *868*
the time of the promise *d* nigh ... Acts 7:17
as he *d* near to behold it, the ... Acts 7:31 *4334*
d nigh unto the city, Peter went ... Acts 10:9
d him out of the city, supposing ... Acts 14:19 *4951*
d them into the marketplace unto ... Acts 16:19 *1670*
he *d* out his sword, and would have ... Acts 16:27 *4685*
they *d* Jason and certain brethren ... Acts 17:6 *4951*
they *d* Alexander out of the ... Acts 19:33 *4264*
Paul, and *d* him out of the temple ... Acts 21:30 *1670*
that they *d* near to some country ... Acts 27:27 *4317*
his tail *d* the third part of the ... Rev 12:4 *4951*

DREWEST {1}
Thou *d* near in the day that I ... Lam 3:57

DRIED {39}
were *d* up from off the earth ... Gen 8:7 3001
the waters were *d* up from off the ... Gen 8:13 2717
day of the month, was the earth *d* ... Gen 8:14 3001
green ears of corn *d* by the fire ... Lev 2:14 7033
nor eat moist grapes, or *d* ... Num 6:3 3002
But now our soul is *d* away ... Num 11:6 3001
For we have heard how the LORD *d* ... Josh 2:10 3001
For the LORD your God *d* up the ... Josh 4:23 3001
which he *d* up from before us, ... Josh 4:23 3001
heard that the LORD had *d* up the ... Josh 5:1 3001
green withs that were never *d* ... Judg 16:7 2717
green withs which had not been *d* ... Judg 16:8 2717
d up, so that he could not pull ... 1Kin 13:4 3001
a while, that the brook *d* up ... 1Kin 17:7 3001
I *d* up all the rivers of besieged ... 2Kin 19:24 2717
His roots shall be *d* up beneath ... Job 18:16 3001
they are *d* up, they are gone away ... Job 28:4 1809
My strength is *d* up like a ... Ps 22:15 3001
my throat is *d* ... Ps 69:3 2787
the Red sea also, and it was *d* up ... Ps 106:9 2717
their multitude *d* up with thirst ... Is 5:13 6704
the river shall be wasted and *d* up ... Is 19:5 3001
defence shall be emptied and *d* up ... Is 19:6 2717
have I *d* up all the rivers of the ... Is 37:25 2717
thou not it which hath *d* the sea ... Is 51:10 2717
places of the wilderness are *d* up ... Jer 23:10 3001
and they shall be *d* up ... Jer 50:38 3001
have *d* up the green tree, and have ... Eze 17:24 3001
and the east wind *d* up her fruit ... Eze 19:12 3001
behold, they say, Our bones are *d* ... Eze 37:11 3001
is smitten, their root is *d* up ... Hos 9:16 3001
and his fountain shall be *d* up ... Hos 13:15 2717
the new wine is *d* up, the oil ... Joel 1:10 3001
The vine is *d* up, and the fig tree ... Joel 1:12 3001
for the rivers of waters are *d* up ... Joel 1:20 3001
his arm shall be clean *d* up ... Zec 11:17 3001
fountain of her blood was *d* up ... Mk 5:29 *3583*
the fig tree *d* up from the roots ... Mk 11:20 *3583*
and the water thereof was *d* up ... Rev 16:12 *3583*

DRIEDST {1}
thou *d* up mighty rivers ... Ps 74:15 3001

DRIETH {3}
and the flood decayeth and *d* up ... Job 14:11 3001
but a broken spirit *d* the bones ... Prov 17:22 3001
it dry, and *d* up all the rivers ... Nah 1:4 3001

DRINK {377}
let us make our father *d* wine ... Gen 19:32 8248
their father *d* wine that night ... Gen 19:33 8248
let us make him *d* wine this night ... Gen 19:34 8248
father *d* wine that night also ... Gen 19:35 8248
with water, and gave the lad *d* ... Gen 21:19 8248
I pray thee, that I may *d* ... Gen 24:14 8354
and she shall say, *D* ... Gen 24:14 8354
and I will give thy camels *d* also ... Gen 24:14 8248
d a little water of thy pitcher ... Gen 24:17 1572
And she said, *D*, my lord ... Gen 24:18 8354
upon her hand, and gave him *d* ... Gen 24:18 8248
And when she had done giving him *d* ... Gen 24:19 8248
little water of thy pitcher to *d* ... Gen 24:43 8248
And she say to me, Both *d* thou ... Gen 24:44 8354
and I said unto her, Let me *d* ... Gen 24:45 8248
from her shoulder, and said, *D* ... Gen 24:46 8354
and I will give thy camels *d* also ... Gen 24:46 8248
and she made the camels *d* also ... Gen 24:46 8354
And they did eat and *d*, he and the ... Gen 24:54 8354
and he did eat and *d*, and rose up, ... Gen 25:34 8354
a feast, and they did eat and *d* ... Gen 26:30 8354
troughs when the flocks came to *d* ... Gen 30:38 8354
conceive when they came to *d* ... Gen 30:38 8354
he poured a *d* offering thereon, ... Gen 35:14 5262
to *d* of the water of the river ... Ex 7:18 8354
the Egyptians could not *d* of the ... Ex 7:21 8354
about the river for water to *d* ... Ex 7:24 8354
for they could not *d* of the water ... Ex 7:24 8354
they could not *d* of the waters of ... Ex 15:23 8354
Moses, saying, What shall we *d* ... Ex 15:24 8354
was no water for the people to *d* ... Ex 17:1 8354
said, Give us water that we may *d* ... Ex 17:2 8354
out of it, that the people may *d* ... Ex 17:6 8354
they saw God, and did eat and *d* ... Ex 24:11 8354
an hin of wine for a *d* offering ... Ex 29:40 5262
to the *d* offering thereof ... Ex 29:41 5262
shall ye pour *d* offering thereon ... Ex 30:9 5262
people sat down to eat and to *d* ... Ex 32:6 8354
the children of Israel *d* of it ... Ex 32:20 8248
neither eat bread, nor *d* water ... Ex 34:28 8354
Do not *d* wine nor strong *d*, ... Lev 10:9 8354
Do not *d* wine nor strong *d* ... Lev 10:9 7941
all *d* that may be drunk in every ... Lev 11:34 4945
the *d* offering thereof shall be ... Lev 23:13 5262
their *d* offerings, even an ... Lev 23:18 5262
d offerings, every thing upon his ... Lev 23:37 5262
he shall cause the woman to *d* the ... Num 5:24 8248
cause the woman to *d* the water ... Num 5:26 8248
he hath made her to *d* the water ... Num 5:27 8248

himself from wine and strong *d* Num 6:3 7941
shall *d* no vinegar of wine, or Num 6:3 8354
of wine, or vinegar of strong *d* Num 6:3 7941
neither shall he *d* any liquor of Num 6:3 8354
offering, and their *d* offerings Num 6:15 5262
meat offering, and his *d* offering Num 6:17 5262
that the Nazarite may *d* wine Num 6:20 8354
a *d* offering shalt thou prepare Num 15:5 5262
for a *d* offering thou shalt offer Num 15:7 5262
thou shalt bring for a *d* offering Num 15:10 5262
his *d* offering, according to the Num 15:24 5262
neither is there any water to *d* Num 20:5 8354
congregation and their beasts *d* Num 20:8 8248
neither will we *d* of the water of Num 20:17 8354
my cattle *d* of thy water, then I Num 20:19 8354
we will not *d* of the waters of Num 21:22 8354
prey, and *d* the blood of the slain Num 23:24 8354
the *d* offering thereof shall be Num 28:7 5262
unto the LORD for a *d* offering Num 28:7 5262
as the *d* offering thereof, thou Num 28:8 5262
oil, and the *d* offering thereof Num 28:9 5262
burnt offering, and his *d* offering Num 28:10 5262
their *d* offerings shall be half Num 28:14 5262
burnt offering, and his *d* offering Num 28:15 5262
burnt offering, and his *d* offering Num 28:24 5262
blemish) and their *d* offerings Num 28:31 5262
their *d* offerings, according unto Num 29:6 5262
of it, and their *d* offerings Num 29:11 5262
meat offering, and his *d* offering Num 29:16 5262
their *d* offerings for the Num 29:18 5262
thereof, and their *d* offerings Num 29:19 5262
their *d* offerings for the Num 29:21 5262
meat offering, and his *d* offering Num 29:22 5262
their *d* offerings for the Num 29:24 5262
meat offering, and his *d* offering Num 29:25 5262
their *d* offerings for the Num 29:27 5262
meat offering, and his *d* offering Num 29:28 5262
their *d* offerings for the Num 29:30 5262
meat offering, and his *d* offering Num 29:31 5262
their *d* offerings for the Num 29:33 5262
meat offering, and his *d* offering Num 29:34 5262
their *d* offerings for the bullock Num 29:37 5262
meat offering, and his *d* offering Num 29:38 5262
for your *d* offerings, and for your Num 29:39 5262
was no water for the people to *d* Num 33:14 8354
of them for money, that ye may *d* Deut 2:6 8354
me water for money, that I may *d* Deut 2:28 8354
neither did eat bread nor *d* water Deut 9:9 8354
nor *d* water, because of all your Deut 9:18 8354
or for wine, or for strong *d* Deut 14:26 7941
but shalt neither *d* of the wine Deut 28:39 8354
have ye drunk wine or strong *d* Deut 29:6 7941
thou didst *d* the pure blood of Deut 32:14 8354
the wine of their *d* offerings Deut 32:38 5257
I pray thee, a little water to *d* Judg 4:19 8248
a bottle of milk, and gave him *d* Judg 4:19 8248
boweth down upon his knees to *d* Judg 7:5 8354
down upon their knees to *d* water Judg 7:6 8354
of their god, and did eat and *d* Judg 9:27 8354
d not wine nor strong *d* Judg 13:4 8354
and *d* not wine nor strong *d* Judg 13:4 7941
now *d* no wine nor strong Judg 13:7 7941
no wine nor strong *d* Judg 13:7 8354
neither let her *d* wine or strong Judg 13:14 8354
let her *d* wine or strong *d* Judg 13:14 7941
so they did eat and *d*, and lodged Judg 19:4 8354
eat and *d* both of them together Judg 19:6 8354
their feet, and did eat and *d* Judg 19:21 8354
d of that which the young men Ruth 2:9 8354
drunken neither wine nor strong *d* 1Sa 1:15 7941
and they made him *d* water 1Sa 30:11 8248
into mine house, to eat and to *d* 2Sa 11:11 8354
him, he did eat and *d* before him 2Sa 11:13 8354
be faint in the wilderness may *d* 2Sa 16:2 8354
taste what I eat or what I *d* 2Sa 19:35 8354
Oh that one would give me *d* of 2Sa 23:15 8248
he would not *d* thereof, but 2Sa 23:16 8354
therefore he would not *d* it 2Sa 23:17 8354
d before him, and say, God save 1Kin 1:25 8354
bread nor *d* water in this place 1Kin 13:8 8354
nor *d* water, nor turn again by 1Kin 13:9 8354
neither will I eat bread nor *d* 1Kin 13:16 8354
eat no bread nor *d* water there 1Kin 13:17 8354
that he may eat bread and *d* water 1Kin 13:18 8354
thee, Eat no bread, and *d* no water 1Kin 13:22 8354
that thou shalt *d* of the brook 1Kin 17:4 8354
water in a vessel, that I may *d* 1Kin 17:10 8354
unto Ahab, Get thee up, eat and *d* 1Kin 18:41 8354
So Ahab went up to eat and to *d* 1Kin 18:42 8354
And he did eat and *d*, and laid him 1Kin 19:6 8354
And he arose, and did eat and *d* 1Kin 19:8 8354
filled with water, that ye may *d* 2Kin 3:17 8354
them, that they may eat and *d* 2Kin 6:22 8354
into one tent, and did eat and *d* 2Kin 7:8 8354
he was come in, he did eat and *d* 2Kin 9:34 8354
and poured his *d* offering 2Kin 16:13 5262
offering, and their *d* offerings 2Kin 16:15 5262
d their own piss with you 2Kin 18:27 8354
d ye every one the waters of his 2Kin 18:31 8354
Oh that one would give me *d* of 1Chr 11:17 8248
but David would not *d* of it 1Chr 11:18 8354
shall I *d* the blood of these men 1Chr 11:19 8354
Therefore he would not *d* it 1Chr 11:19 8354
lambs, with their *d* offerings 1Chr 29:21 5262
d before the LORD on that day 1Chr 29:22 8353
them, and gave them to eat and to *d* 2Chr 28:15 8248
the *d* offerings for every burnt 2Chr 29:35 5262
and meat, and *d*, and oil, unto them Ezr 3:7 4960
their *d* offerings, and offer them Ezr 7:17 5261
he did eat no bread, nor *d* water Ezr 10:6 8354
d the sweet, and send portions Neh 8:10 8354
went their way to eat, and to *d* Neh 8:12 8354
they gave them *d* in vessels of Est 1:7 8248
the king and Haman sat down to *d* Est 3:15 8354
and neither eat nor *d* three days Est 4:16 8354
sisters to eat and to *d* with them Job 1:4 8354
he shall *d* of the wrath of the Job 21:20 8354
not given water to the weary to *d* Job 22:7 8248
their *d* offerings of blood will I Ps 16:4 5262
thou shalt make them *d* of the Ps 36:8 8248
of bulls, or *d* the blood of goats Ps 50:13 8354
thou hast made us to *d* the wine Ps 60:3 8248
thirst they gave me vinegar to *d* Ps 69:21 8248
shall wring them out, and *d* them Ps 75:8 8354
gave them *d* as out of the great Ps 78:15 8248
floods, that they could not *d* Ps 78:44 8354
them tears to *d* in great measure Ps 80:5 8248
mingled my *d* with weeping, Ps 102:9 8249
They give *d* to every beast of the Ps 104:11 8248
He shall *d* of the brook in the Ps 110:7 8354
and *d* the wine of violence Prov 4:17 8354
D waters out of thine own cistern Prov 5:15 8354
d of the wine which I have Prov 9:5 8354
is a mocker, strong *d* is raging Prov 20:1 7941
Eat and *d*, saith he to thee Prov 23:7 8354
be thirsty, give him water to *d* Prov 25:21 8248
it is not for kings to *d* wine Prov 31:4 8354
nor for princes strong *d* Prov 31:4 7941
Lest they *d*, and forget the law, Prov 31:5 8354
Give strong *d* unto him that is Prov 31:6 7941
Let him *d*, and forget his poverty, Prov 31:7 8354
man, than that he should eat and *d* Eccl 2:24 8354
that every man should eat and *d* Eccl 3:13 8354
and comely for one to eat and to *d* Eccl 5:18 8354
the sun, than to eat, and to *d* Eccl 8:15 8354
d thy wine with a merry heart Eccl 9:7 8354
d, yea, *d* abundantly, O Song 5:1 8354
yea, *d* abundantly, O beloved Song 5:1 7937
I would cause thee to *d* of spiced Song 8:2 8248
that they may follow strong *d* Is 5:11 7941
them that are mighty to *d* wine Is 5:22 8354
of strength to mingle strong *d* Is 5:22 7941
watch in the watchtower, eat, *d* Is 21:5 8354
let us eat and *d* Is 22:13 8354
They shall not *d* wine with a song Is 24:9 8354
strong *d* shall be bitter to them Is 24:9 7941
shall be bitter to them that *d* it Is 24:9 8354
through strong *d* are out of the Is 28:7 7941
have erred through strong *d* Is 28:7 7941
out of the way through strong *d* Is 28:7 7941
stagger, but not with strong *d* Is 29:9 7941
he will cause the *d* of the Is 32:6 4945
d their own piss with you Is 36:12 8354
d ye every one the waters of his Is 36:16 8354
to give *d* to my people, my chosen Is 43:20 8248
thou shalt no more *d* it again Is 51:22 8354
will fill ourselves with strong *d* Is 56:12 7941
hast thou poured a *d* offering Is 57:6 5262
the stranger shall not *d* thy wine Is 62:8 8354
have brought it together shall *d* Is 62:9 8354
that furnish the *d* offering unto Is 65:11 4469
behold, my servants shall *d* Is 65:13 8354
Egypt, to *d* the waters of Sihor Jer 2:18 8354
to *d* the waters of the river Jer 2:18 8354
to pour out *d* offerings unto Jer 7:18 5262
and given us water of gall to *d* Jer 8:14 8248
and give them water of gall to *d* Jer 9:15 8248
d for their father or for their Jer 16:7 8248
to sit with them to eat and to *d* Jer 16:8 8354
have poured out *d* offerings unto Jer 19:13 5262
did not thy father eat and *d* Jer 22:15 8354
make them *d* the water of gall Jer 23:15 8248
to whom I send thee, to *d* it Jer 25:15 8248
And they shall *d*, and be moved, and Jer 25:16 8354
and made all the nations to *d* Jer 25:17 8248
of Sheshach shall *d* after them Jer 25:26 8354
D ye, and be drunken, and spue, and Jer 25:27 8354
take the cup at thine hand to *d* Jer 25:28 8354
Ye shall certainly *d* Jer 25:28 8354
poured out *d* offerings unto other Jer 32:29 5262
chambers, and give them wine to *d* Jer 35:2 8248
and I said unto them, *D* ye wine Jer 35:5 8354
But they said, We will *d* no wine Jer 35:6 8354
us, saying, Ye shall *d* no wine Jer 35:6 8354
to *d* no wine all our days, we, Jer 35:8 8354
commanded his sons not to *d* wine Jer 35:14 8354
for unto this day they *d* none Jer 35:14 8354
to pour out *d* offerings unto her, Jer 44:17 5262
to pour out *d* offerings unto her, Jer 44:18 5262
poured out *d* offerings unto her, Jer 44:19 5262
pour out *d* offerings unto her, Jer 44:19 5262
to pour out *d* offerings unto her Jer 44:25 5262
to *d* of the cup have assuredly Jer 49:12 8354
but thou shalt surely *d* of it Jer 49:12 8354
Thou shalt *d* also water by Eze 4:11 8354
from time to time shalt thou *d* Eze 4:11 8354
they shall *d* water by measure, and Eze 4:16 8354
d thy water with trembling and Eze 12:18 8354
d their water with astonishment, Eze 12:19 8354
out there their *d* offerings Eze 20:28 5262
Thou shalt *d* of thy sister's cup Eze 23:32 8354
Thou shalt even *d* it and suck it Eze 23:34 8354
fruit, and they shall *d* thy milk Eze 25:4 8354
in their height, all that *d* water Eze 31:14 8354
best of Lebanon, all that *d* water Eze 31:16 8354
they *d* that which ye have fouled Eze 34:19 8354
that ye may eat flesh, and *d* blood Eze 39:17 8354
d the blood of the princes of the Eze 39:18 8354
d blood till ye be drunken, of my Eze 39:19 8354
Neither shall any priest *d* wine Eze 44:21 8354
d offerings, in the feasts, and in Eze 45:17 5262
appointed your meat and your *d* Dan 1:10 4960
us pulse to eat, and water to *d* Dan 1:12 8354
and the wine that they should *d* Dan 1:16 4960
his concubines, might *d* therein Dan 5:2 8355
wool and my flax, mine oil and my *d* Hos 2:5 8250
Their *d* is sour Hos 4:18 5435
the *d* offering is cut off from Joel 1:9 5262
the *d* offering is withholden from Joel 1:13 5262
a *d* offering unto the LORD your Joel 2:14 5262
girl for wine, that they might *d* Joel 3:3 8354
they *d* the wine of the condemned Amos 2:8 8354
ye gave the Nazarites wine to *d* Amos 2:12 8248
their masters, Bring, and let us *d* Amos 4:1 8354
unto one city, to *d* water Amos 4:8 8354
but ye shall not *d* wine of them Amos 5:11 8354
That *d* wine in bowls, and anoint Amos 6:6 8354
vineyards, and *d* the wine thereof Amos 9:14 8354
d continually, yea, they shall *d* Obad 16 8354
let them not feed, nor *d* water Jonah 3:7 8354
unto thee of wine and of strong *d* Mic 2:11 7941
sweet wine, but shalt not *d* wine Mic 6:15 8354
him that giveth his neighbour *d* Hab 2:15 8248
d thou also, and let thy foreskin Hab 2:16 8354
but not *d* the wine thereof Zeph 1:13 8354
ye *d*, but ye are not filled with Hag 1:6 8354
but ye are not filled with *d* Hag 1:6 7937
when ye did eat, and when ye did *d* Zec 7:6 8354
yourselves, and *d* for yourselves Zec 7:6 8354
and they shall *d*, and make a noise Zec 9:15 8354
ye shall eat, or what ye shall *d* Mt 6:25 *4095*
or, What shall we *d* Mt 6:31 *4095*
whosoever shall give to *d* unto Mt 10:42 *4222*
d of the cup that I shall *d* Mt 20:22 *4095*
Ye shall *d* indeed of my cup, and Mt 20:23 *4095*
and to eat and *d* with the drunken Mt 24:49 *4095*
I was thirsty, and ye gave me *d* Mt 25:35 *4222*
or thirsty, and gave thee *d* Mt 25:37 *4222*
I was thirsty, and ye gave me no *d* Mt 25:42 *4222*
to them, saying, *D* ye all of it Mt 26:27 *4095*
I will not *d* henceforth of this Mt 26:29 *4095*
until that day when I *d* it new Mt 26:29 *4095*
pass away from me, except I *d* it Mt 26:42 *4095*
vinegar to *d* mingled with gall Mt 27:34 *4095*
tasted thereof, he would not *d* Mt 27:34 *4095*
it on a reed, and gave him to *d* Mt 27:48 *4222*
a cup of water to *d* in my name Mk 9:41 *4222*
can ye *d* of the cup that I *d* Mk 10:38 *4095*
d of the cup that I *d* of Mk 10:39 *4095*
I will *d* no more of the fruit of Mk 14:25 *4095*
until that day that I *d* it new in Mk 14:25 *4095*
they gave him to *d* wine mingled Mk 15:23 *4095*
it on a reed, and gave him to *d* Mk 15:36 *4222*
if they *d* any deadly thing, it Mk 16:18 *4095*
shall *d* neither wine nor strong Lk 1:15 *4095*
neither wine nor strong *d* Lk 1:15 *4608*
d with publicans and sinners Lk 5:30 *4095*
but thine eat and *d* Lk 5:33 *4095*
take thine ease, eat, *d*, and be Lk 12:19 *4095*
ye shall eat, or what ye shall *d* Lk 12:29 *4095*
and maidens, and to eat and *d* Lk 12:45 *4095*
and afterward thou shalt eat and *d* Lk 17:8 *4095*
I will not *d* of the fruit of the Lk 22:18 *4095*
d at my table in my kingdom, and Lk 22:30 *4095*
saith unto her, Give me to *d* Jn 4:7 *4095*
thou, being a Jew, askest *d* of me Jn 4:9 *4095*
that saith to thee, Give me to *d* Jn 4:10 *4095*
d his blood, ye have no life in Jn 6:53 *4095*
indeed, and my blood is *d* indeed Jn 6:55 *4213*
let him come unto me, and *d* Jn 7:37 *4095*
hath given me, shall I not *d* it Jn 18:11 *4095*
sight, and neither did eat nor *d* Acts 9:9 *4095*
d with him after he rose from the Acts 10:41 *4844*
nor *d* till they had killed Paul Acts 23:12 *4095*
nor *d* till they have killed him Acts 23:21 *4095*
if he thirst, give him *d* Rom 12:20 *4222*
kingdom of God is not meat and *d* Rom 14:17 *4213*
to eat flesh, nor to *d* wine Rom 14:21 *4095*
Have we not power to eat and to *d* 1Cor 9:4 *4095*
all *d* the same spiritual *d* 1Cor 10:4 *4095*
all *d* the same spiritual *d* 1Cor 10:4 *4188*
The people sat down to eat and *d* 1Cor 10:7 *4095*
Ye cannot *d* the cup of the Lord, 1Cor 10:21 *4095*
Whether therefore ye eat, or *d* 1Cor 10:31 *4095*
ye not houses to eat and to *d* in 1Cor 11:22 *4095*
this do ye, as oft as ye *d* it 1Cor 11:25 *4095*
d this cup, ye do shew the Lord's 1Cor 11:26 *4095*
bread, and *d* this cup of the Lord, 1Cor 11:27 *4095*
of that bread, and *d* of that cup 1Cor 11:28 *4095*
all made to *d* into one Spirit 1Cor 12:13 *4222*
let us eat and *d* 1Cor 15:32 *4095*
judge you in meat, or in *d* Col 2:16 *4213*
D no longer water, but use a 1Ti 5:23 *5202*
because she made all nations *d* of Rev 14:8 *4222*
The same shall *d* of the wine of Rev 14:10 *4095*
thou hast given them blood to *d* Rev 16:6 *4095*

DRINKERS {1}

all ye *d* of wine, because of the Joel 1:5 8354

DRINKETH {17}

Is not this it in which my lord *d* Gen 44:5 8354
d water of the rain of heaven Deut 11:11 8354
the poison whereof *d* up my spirit Job 6:4 8354
which *d* iniquity like water Job 15:16 8354

who *d* up scorning like water ... Job 34:7 8354
he *d* up a river, and hasteth not ... Job 40:23 6231
cutteth off the feet, and *d* damage ... Prov 26:6 8354
man dreameth, and, behold, he *d* ... Is 29:8 8354
he *d* no water, and is faint ... Is 44:12 8354
d with publicans and sinners ... Mk 2:16 *4095*
Whosoever *d* of this water shall ... Jn 4:13 *4095*
But whosoever *d* of the water that ... Jn 4:14 *4095*
d my blood, hath eternal life ... Jn 6:54 *4095*
d my blood, dwelleth in me, and I ... Jn 6:56 *4095*
d unworthily, eateth and *d* ... 1Cor 11:29 *4095*
For the earth which *d* in the rain ... Heb 6:7 *4095*

DRINKING {21}
also, until they have done *d* ... Gen 24:19 8354
to pass, as the camels had done *d* ... Gen 24:22 8354
he shall have done eating and *d* ... Ruth 3:3 8354
upon all the earth, eating and *d* ... 1Sa 30:16 8354
the sea in multitude, eating and *d* ... 1Kin 4:20 8354
all king Solomon's *d* vessels were ... 1Kin 10:21 4945
d himself drunk in the house of ... 1Kin 16:9 8354
heard this message, as he was *d* ... 1Kin 20:12 8354
But Ben-hadad was *d* himself drunk ... 1Kin 20:16 8354
David three days, eating and *d* ... 1Chr 12:39 8354
all the *d* vessels of king Solomon ... 2Chr 9:20 4945
the *d* was according to the law ... Est 1:8 8360
d wine in their eldest brother's ... Job 1:13 8354
d wine in their eldest brother's ... Job 1:18 8354
sheep, eating flesh, and *d* wine ... Is 22:13 8354
John came neither eating nor *d* ... Mt 11:18 *4095*
The Son of man came eating and *d* ... Mt 11:19 *4095*
the flood they were eating and *d* ... Mt 24:38 *4095*
neither eating bread nor *d* wine ... Lk 7:33 *4095*
Son of man is come eating and *d* ... Lk 7:34 *4095*
d such things as they give ... Lk 10:7 *4095*

DRINKS {1}
Which stood only in meats and *d* ... Heb 9:10 *4188*

DRIVE {57}
shall he *d* them out of his land ... Ex 6:1 1644
which shall *d* out the Hivite, the ... Ex 23:28 1644
I will not *d* them out from before ... Ex 23:29 1644
little I will *d* them out from ... Ex 23:30 1644
thou shalt *d* them out before thee ... Ex 23:31 1644
I will *d* out the Canaanite, the ... Ex 33:2 1644
I *d* out before thee the Amorite, ... Ex 34:11 1644
that I may *d* them out of the land ... Num 22:6 1644
to overcome them, and *d* them out ... Num 22:11 1644
Then ye shall *d* out all the ... Num 33:52 3423
But if ye will not *d* out the ... Num 33:55 3423
To *d* out nations from before thee ... Deut 4:38 3423
so shalt thou *d* them out, and ... Deut 9:3 3423
doth *d* them out from before thee ... Deut 9:4 3423
doth *d* them out from before thee ... Deut 9:5 3423
Then will the LORD *d* out all ... Deut 11:23 3423
the LORD thy God doth *d* them out ... Deut 18:12 3423
fail *d* out from before you the ... Josh 3:10 3423
them will I *d* out from before the ... Josh 13:6 3423
I shall be able to *d* them out ... Josh 14:12 3423
of Judah could not *d* them out ... Josh 15:63 3423
d out the inhabitants of those ... Josh 17:12 3423
but did not utterly *d* them out ... Josh 17:13 3423
for thou shalt *d* out the ... Josh 17:18 3423
d them from out of your sight ... Josh 23:5 3423
d out any of these nations from ... Josh 23:13 3423
but could not *d* out the ... Judg 1:19 3423
did not *d* out the Jebusites that ... Judg 1:21 3423
Neither did Manasseh *d* out the ... Judg 1:27 3423
and did not utterly *d* them out ... Judg 1:28 3423
Neither did Ephraim *d* out the ... Judg 1:29 3423
Neither did Zebulun *d* out the ... Judg 1:30 3423
Neither did Asher *d* out the ... Judg 1:31 3423
for they did not *d* them out ... Judg 1:32 3423
Neither did Naphtali *d* out the ... Judg 1:33 3423
I will not *d* them out from before ... Judg 2:3 1644
I also will not henceforth *d* out ... Judg 2:21 3423
God shall *d* out from before us ... Judg 11:24 3423
an ass, and said to her servant, *D* ... 2Kin 4:24 5090
who didst *d* out the inhabitants ... 2Chr 20:7 3423
side, and shall *d* him to his feet ... Job 18:11 6327
They *d* away the ass of the ... Job 24:3 5090
How thou didst *d* out the heathen ... Ps 44:2 3423
is driven away, so *d* them away ... Ps 68:2 5086
shall *d* it far from him ... Prov 22:15
I will *d* thee from thy station, ... Is 22:19 1920
all places whither I shall *d* them ... Jer 24:9 5080
and that I should *d* you out ... Jer 27:10 5080
that I might *d* you out, and that ... Jer 27:15 5080
not, because the LORD did *d* them ... Jer 46:15 1920
Gentiles, whither I will *d* them ... Eze 4:13 5080
That they shall *d* thee from men ... Dan 4:25 2957
they shall *d* thee from men, and ... Dan 4:32 2957
I will *d* them out of mine house ... Hos 9:15 1644
will *d* him into a land barren and ... Joel 2:20 5080
they shall *d* out Ashdod at the ... Zeph 2:4 1644
up into the wind, we let her *d* ... Acts 27:15 *1929*

DRIVEN {49}
thou hast *d* me out this day from ... Gen 4:14 1644
they were *d* out from Pharaoh's ... Ex 10:11 1644
or *d* away, no man seeing it ... Ex 22:10 7617
until he hath *d* out his enemies ... Num 32:21 3423
shouldest be *d* to worship them, ... Deut 4:19 5080
the LORD thy God hath *d* thee ... Deut 30:1 5080
If any of thine be *d* out unto the ... Deut 30:4 5080
For the LORD hath *d* out from ... Josh 23:9 3423
for they have *d* me out this day ... 1Sa 26:19 1644
is wisdom *d* quite from me ... Job 6:13 5080
Wilt thou break a leaf *d* to ... Job 13:25 5086
He shall be *d* from light into ... Job 18:18 1920
They were *d* forth from among men, ... Job 30:5 1644
let them be *d* backward and put to ... Ps 40:14 5472
As smoke is *d* away, so drive them ... Ps 68:2 5086
Jordan was *d* back ... Ps 114:3 5437
Jordan, that thou wast *d* back ... Ps 114:5 5437
The wicked is *d* away in his ... Prov 14:32 1760
and they shall be *d* to darkness ... Is 8:22 5080
wither, be *d* away, and be no more ... Is 19:7 5086
sword, and as *d* stubble to his bow ... Is 41:2 5086
the places whither I have *d* them ... Jer 8:3 5080
the lands whither he had *d* them ... Jer 16:15 5080
d them away, and have not visited ... Jer 23:2 5080
countries whither I have *d* them ... Jer 23:3 5080
countries whither I had *d* them ... Jer 23:8 5080
they shall be *d* on, and fall ... Jer 23:12 1760
the places whither I have *d* you ... Jer 29:14 5080
the nations whither I have *d* them ... Jer 29:18 5080
whither I have *d* them in mine ... Jer 32:37 5080
of all places whither they were *d* ... Jer 40:12 5080
nations, whither they had been *d* ... Jer 43:5 5080
the nations whither I have *d* thee ... Jer 46:28 5080
ye shall be *d* out every man right ... Jer 49:5 5080
the lions have *d* him away ... Jer 50:17 5080
I have *d* him out for his ... Eze 31:11 1644
again that which was *d* away ... Eze 34:4 5080
bring again that which was *d* away ... Eze 34:16 5080
he was *d* from men, and did eat ... Dan 4:33 2957
he was *d* from the sons of men ... Dan 5:21 2957
whither thou hast *d* them, because ... Dan 9:7 5080
as the chaff that is *d* with the ... Hos 13:3 5590
I will gather her that is *d* out ... Mic 4:6 5080
and gather her that was *d* out ... Zeph 3:19 5080
was *d* of the devil into the ... Lk 8:29 *1643*
strake sail, and so were *d* ... Acts 27:17 *5342*
night was come, as we were *d* up ... Acts 27:27 *1308*
a wave of the sea *d* with the wind ... Jas 1:6 *416*
are *d* of fierce winds, yet are ... Jas 3:4 *1643*

DRIVER {2}
he said unto the *d* of his chariot ... 1Kin 22:34 7395
regardeth he the crying of the *d* ... Job 39:7 5065

DRIVETH {4}
for he *d* furiously ... 2Kin 9:20 5090
the chaff which the wind *d* away ... Ps 1:4 5086
The north wind *d* away rain ... Prov 25:23 2342
immediately the spirit *d* him into ... Mk 1:12 *1544*

DRIVING {6}
without *d* them out hastily ... Judg 2:23 3423
the *d* is like the *d* of Jehu ... 2Kin 9:20 4491
the *d* is like the *d* of Jehu ... 2Kin 9:20 4491
by *d* out nations from before thy ... 1Chr 17:21 1644

DROMEDARIES {3}
d brought they unto the place ... 1Kin 4:28 7409
on mules, camels, and young *d* ... Est 8:10 7424
thee, the *d* of Midian and Ephah ... Is 60:6 1070

DROMEDARY {1}
thou art a swift *d* traversing her ... Jer 2:23 1072

DROP {15}
My doctrine shall *d* as the rain ... Deut 32:2 6201
also his heavens shall *d* down dew ... Deut 33:28 6201
Which the clouds do *d* and distil ... Job 36:28 5140
and thy paths *d* fatness ... Ps 65:11 7491
They *d* upon the pastures of the ... Ps 65:12 7491
the clouds *d* down the dew ... Prov 3:20 7491
a strange woman *d* as an honeycomb ... Prov 5:3 5197
O my spouse, *d* as the honeycomb ... Song 4:11 5197
nations are as a *d* of a bucket ... Is 40:15 4752
D down, ye heavens, from above, ... Is 45:8 7491
d thy word toward the south, and ... Eze 20:46 5197
d thy word toward the holy places ... Eze 21:2 5197
mountains shall *d* down new wine ... Joel 3:18 5197
d not thy word against the house ... Amos 7:16 5197
the mountains shall *d* sweet wine ... Amos 9:13 5197

DROPPED {7}
earth trembled, and the heavens *d* ... Judg 5:4 5197
the clouds also *d* water ... Judg 5:4 5197
the wood, behold, the honey *d* ... 1Sa 14:26 1982
of harvest until water *d* upon ... 2Sa 21:10 5413
and my speech *d* upon them ... Job 29:22 5197
the heavens also *d* at the ... Ps 68:8 5197
my hands *d* with myrrh, and my ... Song 5:5 5197

DROPPETH {1}
of the hands the house *d* through ... Eccl 10:18 1811

DROPPING {3}
of a wife are a continual *d* ... Prov 19:13 1812
A continual *d* in a very rainy day ... Prov 27:15 1812
lilies, *d* sweet smelling myrrh ... Song 5:13 5197

DROPS {4}
he maketh small the *d* of water ... Job 36:27 5197
or who hath begotten the *d* of dew ... Job 38:28 96
my locks with the *d* of the night ... Song 5:2 7447
d of blood falling down to the ... Lk 22:44 *2361*

DROPSY {1}
man before him which had the *d* ... Lk 14:2 *5203*

DROSS {8}
the wicked of the earth like *d* ... Ps 119:119 5509
Take away the *d* from the silver, ... Prov 25:4 5509
a potsherd covered with silver *d* ... Prov 26:23 5509
Thy silver is become *d*, thy wine ... Is 1:22 5509
thee, and purely purge away thy *d* ... Is 1:25 5509
house of Israel is to me become *d* ... Eze 22:18 5509
they are even the *d* of silver ... Eze 22:18 5509
Because ye are all become *d* ... Eze 22:19 5509

DROUGHT {10}
in the day the *d* consumed me ... Gen 31:40 2721
serpents, and scorpions, and *d* ... Deut 8:15 6774
D and heat consume the snow waters ... Job 24:19 6723
is turned into the *d* of summer ... Ps 32:4 2725
and satisfy thy soul in *d* ... Is 58:11 6710
and of pits, through a land of *d* ... Jer 2:6 6723
not be careful in the year of *d* ... Jer 17:8 1226
A *d* is upon her waters ... Jer 50:38 2721
in the land of great *d* ... Hos 13:5 8514
And I called for a *d* upon the land ... Hag 1:11 2721

DROVE {13}
So he *d* out the man ... Gen 3:24 1644
the carcases, Abram *d* them away ... Gen 15:11 5380
servants, every *d* by themselves ... Gen 32:16 5739
me, and put a space betwixt *d* ... Gen 32:16 5739
and put a space betwixt *d* and *d* ... Gen 32:16 5739
thou by all this *d* which I met ... Gen 33:8 4264
the shepherds came and *d* them away ... Ex 2:17 1644
d out the Amorites that were ... Num 21:32 3423
Caleb *d* thence the three sons of ... Josh 15:14 3423
who *d* away the inhabitants of ... 1Chr 8:13 1272
who *d* him away, and he departed ... Ps 34:*t* 1644
beheld, and *d* asunder the nations ... Hab 3:6 5425
he *d* them all out of the temple, ... Jn 2:15 *1544*

DROVES {1}
third, and all that followed the *d* ... Gen 32:19 5739

DROWN {2}
love, neither can the floods *d* it ... Song 8:7 7857
which *d* men in destruction and ... 1Ti 6:9 *1036*

DROWNED {5}
also are *d* in the Red sea ... Ex 15:4 2823
and it shall be cast out and *d* ... Amos 8:8 8248
and shall be *d*, as by the flood of ... Amos 9:5 8248
that he were *d* in the depth of ... Mt 18:6 *2670*
Egyptians assaying to do were *d* ... Heb 11:29 *2666*

DROWSINESS {1}
d shall clothe a man with rags ... Prov 23:21 5124

DRUNK {29}
all drink that may be *d* in every ... Lev 11:34 8354
neither have ye *d* wine or strong ... Deut 29:6 8354
make mine arrows *d* with blood ... Deut 32:42 7937
and when he had *d*, his spirit came ... Judg 15:19 8354
And when Boaz had eaten and *d* ... Ruth 3:7 8354
in Shiloh, and after they had *d* ... 1Sa 1:9 8354
nor *d* any water, three days and ... 1Sa 30:12 8354
and he made him *d* ... 2Sa 11:13 7937
d water in the place, of the ... 1Kin 13:22 8354
eaten bread, and after he had *d* ... 1Kin 13:23 8354
drinking himself *d* in the house ... 1Kin 16:9 7910
himself *d* in the pavilions ... 1Kin 20:16 7910
and when they had eaten and *d* ... 2Kin 6:23 8354
d strange waters, and with the ... 2Kin 19:24 8354
I have *d* my wine with my milk ... Song 5:1 8354
I have digged, and *d* water ... Is 37:25 8354
which hast *d* at the hand of the ... Is 51:17 8354
make them *d* in my fury, and I will ... Is 63:6 7937
and made *d* with their blood ... Jer 46:10 7301
And I will make *d* her princes ... Jer 51:57 7937
to have *d* of the deep waters, but ... Eze 34:18 8354
concubines, have *d* wine in them ... Dan 5:23 8355
For as ye have *d* upon my holy ... Obad 16 8354
No man also having *d* old wine ... Lk 5:39 *4095*
d in thy presence, and thou hast ... Lk 13:26 *4095*
and when men have well *d*, then ... Jn 2:10 *3184*
be not *d* with wine, wherein is ... Eph 5:18 *3182*
been made *d* with the wine of her ... Rev 17:2 *3182*
For all nations have *d* of the ... Rev 18:3

DRUNKARD {5}
he is a glutton, and a *d* ... Deut 21:20 5435
For the *d* and the glutton shall ... Prov 23:21 5435
goeth up into the hand of a *d* ... Prov 26:9 7910
shall reel to and fro like a *d* ... Is 24:20 7910
an idolater, or a railer, or a *d* ... 1Cor 5:11 *3183*

DRUNKARDS {6}
and I was the song of the *d* ... Ps 69:12 8354,7941
to the *d* of Ephraim, whose ... Is 28:1 7910
the *d* of Ephraim, shall be ... Is 28:3 7910
Awake, ye *d*, and weep ... Joel 1:5 7910
and while they are drunken as *d* ... Nah 1:10 5435
Nor thieves, nor covetous, nor *d* ... 1Cor 6:10 *3183*

DRUNKEN {34}
And he drank of the wine, and was *d* ... Gen 9:21 7943
Eli thought she had been *d* ... 1Sa 1:13 7910
unto her, How long wilt thou be *d* ... 1Sa 1:14 7937
I have *d* neither wine nor strong ... 1Sa 1:15 7937
within him for he was very *d* ... 1Sa 25:36 7910
them to stagger like a *d* man ... Job 12:25 7910
and fro, and stagger like a *d* man ... Ps 107:27 7910
as a *d* man staggereth in his ... Is 19:14 7910
they are *d*, but not with wine ... Is 29:9 7937
they shall be *d* with their own ... Is 49:26 7937
thou hast *d* the dregs of the cup ... Is 51:17 8354
now this, thou afflicted, and *d* ... Is 51:21 7937
I am like a *d* man, and like a man ... Jer 23:9 7910
Drink ye, and be *d*, and spue, and ... Jer 25:27 7937
Make ye him *d*: for he magnified ... Jer 48:26 7937
drink of the cup have assuredly *d* ... Jer 49:12 7937
hand, that made all the earth *d* ... Jer 51:7 7937
the nations have *d* of her wine ... Jer 51:7 8354
feasts, and I will make them *d* ... Jer 51:39 7937
he hath made me *d* with wormwood ... Lam 3:15 7301
thou shalt be *d*, and shalt make ... Lam 4:21 7937
We have *d* our water for money ... Lam 5:4 8354
full, and drink blood till ye be *d* ... Eze 39:19 7943

D

and while they are *d* as drunkards Nah 1:10 5435
Thou also shalt be *d* Nah 3:11 7937
to him, and makest him *d* also Hab 2:15 7937
and to eat and drink with the *d* Mt 24:49 *3184*
and to eat and drink, and to be *d* Lk 12:45 *3182*
serve me, till I have eaten and *d* Lk 17:8 *4095*
For these are not *d*, as ye Acts 2:15 *3184*
and one is hungry, and another is *d* 1Cor 11:21 *3184*
be *d* are *d* in the night 1Th 5:7 *3184*
I saw the woman *d* with the blood Rev 17:6 *3184*

DRUNKENNESS {7}
of mine heart, to add *d* to thirst Deut 29:19 7302
for strength, and not for *d* Eccl 10:17 8358
inhabitants of Jerusalem, with *d* Jer 13:13 7943
Thou shalt be filled with *d* Eze 23:33 7943
overcharged with surfeiting, and *d* Lk 21:34 *3178*
not in rioting and *d*, not in Rom 13:13 *3178*
Envyings, murders, *d*, revellings, Gal 5:21 *3178*

DRUSILLA *(dru-sil'-lah)* {1} *Wife of Felix.*
when Felix came with his wife *D* Acts 24:24 *1409*

DRY {71}
place, and let the *d* land appear Gen 1:9 3004
And God called the *d* land Earth Gen 1:10 3004
of all that was in the *d* land Gen 7:22 2724
the face of the ground was *d* Gen 8:13 2720
river, and pour it upon the *d* land Ex 4:9 3004
become blood upon the *d* land Ex 4:9 3006
children of Israel shall go on *d* Ex 14:16 3004
night, and made the sea *d* land Ex 14:21 2724
of the sea upon the *d* ground Ex 14:22 3004
d land in the midst of the sea Ex 14:29 3004
on *d* land in the midst of the sea Ex 15:19 3004
offering, mingled with oil, and *d* Lev 7:10 2720
it is a *d* scall, even a leprosy Lev 13:30 5424
of the LORD stood firm on *d* Josh 3:17 2724
passed over on *d* ground, until Josh 3:17 2724
were lifted up unto the *d* land Josh 4:18 2724
came over this Jordan on *d* land Josh 4:22 3004
bread of their provision was *d* Josh 9:5 3004
but now, behold, it is *d*, and it Josh 9:12 3001
it be *d* upon all the earth beside Judg 6:37 2721
let it now be *d* only upon the Judg 6:39 2721
for it was *d* upon the fleece only Judg 6:40 2721
they two went over on *d* ground 2Kin 2:8 2724
midst of the sea on the *d* land Neh 9:11 3004
the waters, and they *d* up Job 12:15 3001
and wilt thou pursue the *d* stubble Job 13:25 3002
the flame shall *d* up his branches Job 15:30 3001
my flesh longeth for thee in a *d* Ps 63:1 6723
He turned the sea into *d* land Ps 66:6 3004
the rebellious dwell in a *d* land Ps 68:6 6707
and his hands formed the *d* land Ps 95:5 3006
they ran in the *d* places like a Ps 105:41 6723
and the watersprings into *d* ground Ps 107:33 6774
d ground into watersprings Ps 107:35 6723
Better is a *d* morsel, and Prov 17:1 2720
as the heat in a *d* place Is 25:5 6724
as rivers of water in a *d* place Is 32:2 6724
the *d* land springs of water Is 41:18 6723
and hills, and *d* up all their herbs Is 42:15 3001
islands, and I will *d* up the pools Is 42:15 3001
and floods upon the *d* ground Is 44:3 3004
That saith to the deep, Be *d* Is 44:27 2717
and I will *d* up thy rivers Is 44:27 3001
at my rebuke I *d* up the sea Is 50:2 2717
and as a root out of a *d* ground Is 53:2 6723
eunuch say, Behold, I am a *d* tree Is 56:3 3002
A *d* wind of the high places in Jer 4:11 6703
wilderness, a *d* land, and a desert Jer 50:12 6723
I will *d* up her sea Jer 51:36 2717
and make her springs *d* Jer 51:36 3001
a *d* land, and a wilderness, a land Jer 51:43 6723
have made the *d* tree to flourish Eze 17:24 3002
planted in the wilderness, in a *d* Eze 19:13 6723
tree in thee, and every *d* tree Eze 20:47 3002
And I will make the rivers *d* Eze 30:12 2724
and, lo, they were very *d* Eze 37:2 3002
O ye *d* bones, hear the word of Eze 37:4 3002
and set her like a *d* land Hos 2:3 6723
a miscarrying womb and *d* breasts Hos 9:14 6784
and his spring shall become *d* Hos 13:15 954
hath made the sea and the *d* land Jonah 1:9 3004
vomited out Jonah upon the *d* land Jonah 2:10 3004
rebuketh the sea, and maketh it *d* Nah 1:4 3001
be devoured as stubble fully *d* Nah 1:10 3002
and *d* like a wilderness Zeph 2:13 6723
earth, and the sea, and the *d* land Hag 2:6 2724
the deeps of the river shall *d* up Zec 10:11 3001
man, he walketh through *d* places Mt 12:43 *504*
man, he walketh through *d* places Lk 11:24 *504*
tree, what shall be done in the *d* Lk 23:31 *3584*
through the Red sea as by *d* land Heb 11:29 *3584*

DRYSHOD {1}
streams, and make men go over *d* Is 11:15 5275

DUE {31}
it is thy *d*, and thy sons' *d* Lev 10:13 2706
they be thy *d*, and thy sons' *d* Lev 10:14 2706
I will give you rain in *d* season Lev 26:4
offer unto me in their *d* season Num 28:2
rain of your land in his *d* season Deut 11:14
be the priest's *d* from the people Deut 18:3 4941
their foot shall slide in *d* time Deut 32:35
sought him not after the *d* order 1Chr 15:13
LORD the glory *d* unto his name 1Chr 16:29
for the singers, *d* for every day Neh 11:23 1697
LORD the glory *d* unto his name Ps 29:2
LORD the glory *d* unto his name Ps 96:8
give them their meat in *d* season Ps 104:27
them their meat in *d* season Ps 145:15
good from them to whom it is *d* Prov 3:27 1167
and a word spoken in *d* season Prov 15:23
and thy princes eat in *d* season Eccl 10:17
pay all that was *d* unto him Mt 18:34 *3784*
to give them meat in *d* season Mt 24:45
their portion of meat in *d* season Lk 12:42
for we receive the *d* reward of Lk 23:41 *514*
in *d* time Christ died for the Rom 5:6
tribute to whom tribute is *d* Rom 13:7
unto the wife *d* benevolence 1Cor 7:3 *3784*
as of one born out of *d* time 1Cor 15:8
for in *d* season we shall reap, if Gal 6:9 *2398*
all, to be testified in *d* time 1Ti 2:6 *2398*
But hath in *d* times manifested Titus 1:3 *2398*
that he may exalt you in *d* time 1Pet 5:6

DUES {1}
Render therefore to all their *d* Rom 13:7 *3782*

DUKE {46}
firstborn son of Esau; *d* Teman Gen 36:15 441
d Omar, *d* Zepho, *d* Kenaz, Gen 36:15 441
D Korah, *d* Gatam, and *d* Gen 36:16 441
D Korah, *d* Gatam, and *d* Amalek Gen 36:16 441
d Nahath, *d* Zerah Gen 36:17 441
d Shammah, *d* Gen 36:17 441
d Jeush, *d* Jaalam, *d* Korah Gen 36:18 441
came of the Horites; *d* Lotan Gen 36:29 441
d Shobal, *d* Zibeon, *d* Anah, Gen 36:29 441
D Dishon, *d* Ezer, *d* Dishan Gen 36:30 441
by their names; *d* Timnah Gen 36:40 441
d Alvah, *d* Jetheth Gen 36:40 441
D Aholibamah, *d* Elah, *d* Pinon Gen 36:41 441
D Kenaz, *d* Teman, *d* Mibzar, Gen 36:42 441
D Magdiel, *d* Iram Gen 36:43 441
of Edom were; *d* Timnah 1Chr 1:51 441
d Aliah, *d* Jetheth 1Chr 1:51 441
D Aholibamah, *d* Elah, *d* Pinon 1Chr 1:52 441
D Kenaz, *d* Teman, *d* Mibzar, 1Chr 1:53 441
D Magdiel, *d* Iram 1Chr 1:54 441

DUKES {15}
These were *d* of the sons of Esau Gen 36:15 441
these are the *d* that came of Gen 36:16 441
these are the *d* that came of Gen 36:17 441
these were the *d* that came of Gen 36:18 441
who is Edom, and these are their *d* Gen 36:19 441
these are the *d* of the Horites, Gen 36:21 441
These are the *d* that came of the Gen 36:29 441
these are the *d* that came of Hori Gen 36:30 441
among their *d* in the land of Seir Gen 36:30 441
names of the *d* that came of Esau Gen 36:40 441
these be the *d* of Edom, according Gen 36:43 441
Then the *d* of Edom shall be Ex 15:15 441
and Reba, which were *d* of Sihon Josh 13:21 5257
And the *d* of Edom were 1Chr 1:51 441
These are the *d* of Edom 1Chr 1:54

DULCIMER {3}
flute, harp, sackbut, psaltery, *d* Dan 3:5 5481
harp, sackbut, psaltery, and *d* Dan 3:10 5481
harp, sackbut, psaltery, and *d* Dan 3:15 5481

DULL {3}
and their ears are *d* of hearing Mt 13:15 *917*
and their ears are *d* of hearing Acts 28:27 *917*
seeing ye are *d* of hearing Heb 5:11 *3576*

DUMAH *(doo'-mah)* {4}
1. Son of Ishmael.
And Mishma, and *D*, and Massa, Gen 25:14 1746
Mishma, and *D*, Massa, Hadad, and 1Chr 1:30 1746
2. A city in Judah.
Arab, and *D*, and Eshean, Josh 15:52 1746
3. An undetermined city.
The burden of *D*. He calleth to Is 21:11 1746

DUMB {29}
or who maketh the *d*, or deaf, or Ex 4:11 483
I was as a *d* man that openeth not Ps 38:13 483
I was *d* with silence, I held my Ps 39:2 481
I was *d*, I opened not my mouth Ps 39:9 481
Open thy mouth for the *d* in the Prov 31:8 483
hart, and the tongue of the *d* sing Is 35:6 483
a sheep before her shearers is *d* Is 53:7 481
all ignorant, they are all *d* dogs Is 56:10 483
thy mouth, that thou shalt be *d* Eze 3:26 481
thou shalt speak, and be no more *d* Eze 24:27 481
was opened, and I was no more *d* Eze 33:22 481
toward the ground, and I became *d* Dan 10:15 481
trusteth therein, to make *d* idols Hab 2:18 483
to the *d* stone, Arise, it shall Hab 2:19 1748
they brought to him a *d* man Mt 9:32 *2974*
devil was cast out, the *d* spake Mt 9:33 *2974*
with a devil, blind, and *d* Mt 12:22 *2974*
the blind and *d* both spake and saw Mt 12:22 *2974*
those that were lame, blind, *d* Mt 15:30 *2974*
when they saw the *d* to speak Mt 15:31 *2974*
deaf to hear, and the *d* to speak Mk 7:37 *216*
my son, which hath a *d* spirit Mk 9:17 *216*
spirit, saying unto him, Thou *d* Mk 9:25 *216*
And, behold, thou shalt be *d* Lk 1:20 *4623*
casting out a devil, and it was *d* Lk 11:14 *2974*
devil was gone out, the *d* spake Lk 11:14 *2974*
like a lamb *d* before his shearer, Acts 8:32 *880*
carried away unto these *d* idols 1Cor 12:2 *880*
the *d* ass speaking with man's 2Pet 2:16 *880*

DUNG {30}
bullock, and his skin, and his *d* Ex 29:14 6569
legs, and his inwards, and his *d* Lev 4:11 6569
and his hide, his flesh, and his *d* Lev 8:17 6569
skins, and their flesh, and their *d* Lev 16:27 6569
flesh, and her blood, with her *d* Num 19:5 6569
Jeroboam, as a man taketh away *d* 1Kin 14:10 1557
d for five pieces of silver 2Kin 6:25 2755
d upon the face of the field in 2Kin 9:37 1828
that they may eat their own *d* 2Kin 18:27 2716,(6675)
the dragon well, and to the *d* port Neh 2:13 830
on the wall unto the *d* gate Neh 3:13 830
But the *d* gate repaired Malchiah Neh 3:14 830
upon the wall toward the *d* gate Neh 12:31 830
perish for ever like his own *d* Job 20:7 1561
they became as *d* for the earth Ps 83:10 1828
that they may eat their own *d* Is 36:12 2716,(6675)
they shall be for *d* upon the face Jer 8:2 1828
fall as *d* upon the open field Jer 9:22 1828
but they shall be as *d* upon the Jer 16:4 1828
they shall be *d* upon the ground Jer 25:33 1828
it with *d* that cometh out of man Eze 4:12 1561
given thee cow's *d* for man's *d* Eze 4:15 6832
given thee cow's *d* for man's *d* Eze 4:15 1561
as dust, and their flesh as the *d* Zeph 1:17 1561
spread *d* upon your faces Mal 2:3 6569
even the *d* of your solemn feasts Mal 2:3 6569
I shall dig about it, and *d* it Lk 13:8 *906,2874*
things, and do count them but *d* Phil 3:8 *4657*

DUNGEON {13}
they should put me into the *d* Gen 40:15 953
brought him hastily out of the *d* Gen 41:14 953
of the captive that was in the *d* Ex 12:29 953
Jeremiah was entered into the *d* Jer 37:16 953
cast him into the *d* of Malchiah Jer 38:6 953
in the *d* there was no water, but Jer 38:6 953
they had put Jeremiah in the *d* Jer 38:7 953
whom they have cast into the *d* Jer 38:9 953
Jeremiah the prophet out of the *d* Jer 38:10 953
by cords into the *d* to Jeremiah Jer 38:11 953
and took him up out of the *d* Jer 38:13 953
have cut off my life in the *d* Lam 3:53 953
name, O LORD, out of the low *d* Lam 3:55 953

DUNGHILL {7}
lifteth up the beggar from the *d* 1Sa 2:8 830
his house be made a *d* for this Ezr 6:11 5122
and lifteth the needy out of the *d* Ps 113:7 830
straw is trodden down for the *d* Is 25:10 4087
and your houses shall be made a *d* Dan 2:5 5122
and their houses shall be made a *d* Dan 3:29 5122
for the land, nor yet for the *d* Lk 14:35 *2874*

DUNGHILLS {1}
brought up in scarlet embrace *d* Lam 4:5 830

DURA *(doo'-rah)* {1} *A plain in Babylonia.*
he set it up in the plain of *D* Dan 3:1 1757

DURABLE {2}
d riches and righteousness Prov 8:18 6276
sufficiently, and for *d* clothing Is 23:18 6266

DURETH {1}
in himself, but *d* for a while Mt 13:21 *2076*

DURST {9}
that *d* presume in his heart to do Est 7:5
d not shew you mine opinion Job 32:6 3372
neither *d* any man from that day Mt 22:46 *5111*
no man after that *d* ask him any Mk 12:34 *5111*
after that they *d* not ask him any Lk 20:40 *5111*
none of the disciples *d* ask him Jn 21:12 *5111*
of the rest *d* no man join himself Acts 5:13 *5111*
Moses trembled, and *d* not behold Acts 7:32 *5111*
d not bring against him a railing Jude 9 *5111*

DUST {108}
formed man of the *d* of the ground Gen 2:7 6083
d shalt thou eat all the days of Gen 3:14 6083
for *d* thou art, and unto *d* Gen 3:19 6083
thy seed as the *d* of the earth Gen 13:16 6083
man can number the *d* of the earth Gen 13:16 6083
unto the Lord, which am but *d* Gen 18:27 6083
shall be as the *d* of the earth Gen 28:14 6083
smite the *d* of the land, that it Ex 8:16 6083
smote the *d* of the earth, and it Ex 8:17 6083
all the *d* of the land became lice Ex 8:17 6083
it shall become small *d* in all Ex 9:9 80
they shall pour out the *d* that Lev 14:41 6083
blood thereof, and cover it with *d* Lev 17:13 6083
of the *d* that is in the floor of Num 5:17 6083
Who can count the *d* of Jacob Num 23:10 6083
even until it was as small as *d* Deut 9:21 6083
I cast the *d* thereof into the Deut 9:21 6083
the rain of thy land powder and *d* Deut 28:24 6083
the poison of serpents of the *d* Deut 32:24 6083
Israel, and put *d* upon their heads Josh 7:6 6083
raiseth up the poor out of the *d* 1Sa 2:8 6083
and threw stones at him, and cast *d* 2Sa 16:13 6083
as small as the *d* of the earth 2Sa 22:43 6083
as I exalted thee out of the *d* 1Kin 16:2 6083
the wood, and the stones, and the *d* 1Kin 18:38 6083
if the *d* of Samaria shall suffice 1Kin 20:10 6083
made them like the *d* by threshing 2Kin 13:7 6083
cast the *d* of them into the brook 2Kin 23:12 6083
the *d* of the earth in multitude 2Chr 1:9 6083
made *d* of them, and strowed it 2Chr 34:4 1854
sprinkled *d* upon their heads Job 2:12 6083
whose foundation is in the *d* Job 4:19 6083
cometh not forth of the *d* Job 5:6 6083
clothed with worms and clods of *d* Job 7:5 6083

for now shall I sleep in the *d* Job 7:21 6083
wilt thou bring me into *d* again Job 10:9 6083
grow out of the *d* of the earth Job 14:19 6083
skin, and defiled my horn in the *d* Job 16:15 6083
our rest together is in the *d* Job 17:16 6083
shall lie down with him in the *d* Job 20:11 6083
shall lie down alike in the *d* Job 21:26 6083
Then shalt thou lay up gold as *d* Job 22:24 6083
Though he heap up silver as the *d* Job 27:16 6083
and it hath *d* of gold Job 28:6 6083
the mire, and I am become like *d* Job 30:19 6083
and man shall turn again unto *d* Job 34:15 6083
When the *d* groweth into hardness Job 38:38 6083
earth, and warmeth them in the *d* Job 39:14 6083
Hide them in the *d* together Job 40:13 6083
I abhor myself, and repent in *d* Job 42:6 6083
and lay mine honour in the *d* Ps 7:5 6083
small as the *d* before the wind Ps 18:42 6083
brought me into the *d* of death Ps 22:15 6083
to the *d* shall bow before him Ps 22:29 6083
shall the *d* praise thee Ps 30:9 6083
our soul is bowed down to the *d* Ps 44:25 6083
and his enemies shall lick the *d* Ps 72:9 6083
rained flesh also upon them as *d* Ps 78:27 6083
stones, and favour the *d* thereof Ps 102:14 6083
he remembereth that we are *d* Ps 103:14 6083
they die, and return to their *d* Ps 104:29 6083
raiseth up the poor out of the *d* Ps 113:7 6083
My soul cleaveth unto the *d* Ps 119:25 6083
part of the *d* of the world Prov 8:26 6083
the *d*, and all turn to *d* again Eccl 3:20 6083
Then shall the *d* return to the Eccl 12:7 6083
the rock, and hide thee in the *d* Is 2:10 6083
and their blossom shall go up as *d* Is 5:24 80
to the ground, even to the *d* Is 25:12 6083
he bringeth it even to the *d* Is 26:5 6083
Awake and sing, ye that dwell in *d* Is 26:19 6083
speech shall be low out of the *d* Is 29:4 6083
speech shall whisper out of the *d* Is 29:4 6083
strangers shall be like small *d* Is 29:5 80
their *d* made fat with fatness Is 34:7 6083
the *d* thereof into brimstone, and Is 34:9 6083
comprehended the *d* of the earth Is 40:12 6083
as the small *d* of the balance Is 40:15 7834
gave them as the *d* to his sword Is 41:2 6083
Come down, and sit in the *d* Is 47:1 6083
and lick up the *d* of thy feet Is 49:23 6083
Shake thyself from the *d* Is 52:2 6083
d shall be the serpent's meat Is 65:25 6083
have cast up *d* upon their heads Lam 2:10 6083
He putteth his mouth in the *d* Lam 3:29 6083
the ground, to cover it with *d* Eze 24:7 6083
I will also scrape her *d* from her Eze 26:4 6083
horses their *d* shall cover thee Eze 26:10 80
thy *d* in the midst of the water Eze 26:12 6083
shall cast up *d* upon their heads, Eze 27:30 6083
in the *d* of the earth shall awake Dan 12:2 6083
That pant after the *d* of the Amos 2:7 6083
of Aphrah roll thyself in the *d* Mic 1:10 6083
shall lick the *d* like a serpent Mic 7:17 6083
the clouds are the *d* of his feet Nah 1:3 80
thy nobles shall dwell in the *d* Nah 3:18
for they shall heap *d*, and take it Hab 1:10 6083
blood shall be poured out as *d* Zeph 1:17 6083
and heaped up silver as the *d* Zec 9:3 6083
shake off the *d* of your feet Mt 10:14 *2868*
shake off the *d* under your feet Mk 6:11 *5522*
shake off the very *d* from your Lk 9:5 *2868*
Even the very *d* of your city Lk 10:11 *2868*
But they shook off the *d* of their Acts 13:51 *2868*
clothes, and threw *d* into the air, Acts 22:23 *2868*
they cast *d* on their heads, and Rev 18:19 *5522*

DUTIES {1}
And that doeth not any of those *d* Eze 18:11

DUTY {8}
her *d* of marriage, shall he not Ex 21:10
perform the *d* of an husband's Deut 25:5
the *d* of my husband's brother Deut 25:7
as the *d* of every day required 2Chr 8:14 1697
as the *d* of every day required Ezr 3:4 1697
for this is the whole *d* of man Eccl 12:13
done that which was our *d* to do Lk 17:10 *3784*
their *d* is also to minister unto Rom 15:27 *3784*

DWARF {1}
Or crookbackt, or a *d*, or that Lev 21:20 1851

DWELL {338}
the father of such as *d* in tents Gen 4:20 3427
he shall *d* in the tents of Shem Gen 9:27 7931
them, that they might *d* together Gen 13:6 3427
so that they could not *d* together Gen 13:6 3427
he shall *d* in the presence of all Gen 16:12 7931
for he feared to *d* in Zoar Gen 19:30 3427
d where it pleaseth thee Gen 20:15 3427
of the Canaanites, among whom I *d* Gen 24:3 3427
the Canaanites, in whose land I *d* Gen 24:37 3427
d in the land which I shall tell Gen 26:2 7931
now will my husband *d* with me Gen 30:20 2082
And ye shall *d* with us Gen 34:10 3427
d and trade ye therein, and get you Gen 34:10 3427
we will *d* with you, and we will Gen 34:16 3427
therefore let them *d* in the land Gen 34:21 3427
consent unto us for to *d* with us Gen 34:22 3427
unto them, and they will *d* with us Gen 34:23 3427
go up to Beth-el, and *d* there Gen 35:1 3427
than that they might *d* together Gen 36:7 3427
thou shalt *d* in the land of Gen 45:10 3427
that ye may *d* in the land of Gen 46:34 3427
let thy servants *d* in the land of Gen 47:4 3427
make thy father and brethren to *d* Gen 47:6 3427
in the land of Goshen let them *d* Gen 47:6 3427
Zebulun shall *d* at the haven of Gen 49:13 7931
was content to *d* with the man Ex 2:21 3427
of Goshen, in which my people *d* Ex 8:22 5975
thou hast made for thee to *d* in Ex 15:17 3427
They shall not *d* in thy land Ex 23:33 3427
that I may *d* among them Ex 25:8 7931
I will *d* among the children of Ex 29:45 7931
of Egypt, that I may *d* among them Ex 29:46 7931
he shall *d* alone Lev 13:46 3427
whither I bring you to *d* therein Lev 20:22 3427
Ye shall *d* in booths seven days Lev 23:42 3427
Israelites born shall *d* in booths Lev 23:42 3427
children of Israel to *d* in booths Lev 23:43 3427
ye shall *d* in the land in safety Lev 25:18 3427
your fill, and *d* therein in safety Lev 25:19 3427
full, and *d* in your land safely Lev 26:5 3427
your enemies which *d* therein Lev 26:32 3427
camps, in the midst whereof I *d* Num 5:3 7931
what the land is that they *d* in Num 13:19 3427
cities they be that they *d* in Num 13:19 3427
be strong that *d* in the land Num 13:28 3427
The Amalekites *d* in the land of Num 13:29 3427
the Amorites, *d* in the mountains Num 13:29 3427
and the Canaanites *d* by the sea Num 13:29 3427
I sware to make you *d* therein Num 14:30 7931
lo, the people shall *d* alone Num 23:9 7931
our little ones shall *d* in the Num 32:17 3427
of the land, and *d* therein Num 33:53 3427
vex you in the land wherein ye *d* Num 33:55 3427
their possession cities to *d* in Num 35:2 3427
cities shall they have to *d* in Num 35:3 3427
come again to *d* in the land Num 35:32 3427
ye shall inhabit, wherein I *d* Num 35:34 7931
for I the LORD *d* among the Num 35:34 7931
children of Esau, which *d* in Seir Deut 2:4 3427
children of Esau which *d* in Seir Deut 2:29 3427
and the Moabites which *d* in Ar Deut 2:29 3427
which *d* in the champaign over Deut 11:30 3427
ye shall possess it, and *d* therein Deut 11:31 3427
d in the land which the LORD your Deut 12:10 3427
about, so that ye *d* in safety Deut 12:10 3427
to cause his name to *d* there Deut 12:11 7931
God hath given thee to *d* there Deut 13:12 3427
shalt *d* therein, and shalt say, I Deut 17:14 3427
He shall *d* with thee, even among Deut 23:16 3427
If brethren *d* together, and one of Deut 25:5 3427
and thou shalt not *d* therein Deut 28:30 3427
that thou mayest *d* in the land Deut 30:20 3427
the LORD shall *d* in safety by him Deut 33:12 7931
he shall *d* between his shoulders Deut 33:12 7931
then shall *d* in safety alone Deut 33:28 7931
Peradventure ye *d* among us Josh 9:7 3427
when ye *d* among us Josh 9:22 3427
d in the mountains are gathered Josh 10:6 3427
the Maachathites *d* among the Josh 13:13 3427
in the land, save cities to *d* in Josh 14:4 3427
but the Jebusites *d* with the Josh 15:63 3427
but the Canaanites *d* among the Josh 16:10 3427
Canaanites would *d* in that land Josh 17:12 3427
all the Canaanites that *d* in the Josh 17:16 3427
a place, that he may *d* among them Josh 20:4 3427
he shall *d* in that city, until he Josh 20:6 3427
Moses to give us cities to *d* in Josh 21:2 3427
ye built not, and ye *d* in them Josh 24:13 3427
the Amorites, in whose land ye *d* Josh 24:15 3427
but the Jebusites *d* with the Judg 1:21 3427
Canaanites would *d* in that land Judg 1:27 3427
But the Amorites would *d* in mount Judg 1:35 3427
the Amorites, in whose land ye *d* Judg 6:10 3427
that they should not *d* in Shechem Judg 9:41 3427
D with me, and be unto me a father Judg 17:10 3427
was content to *d* with the man Judg 17:11 3427
them an inheritance to *d* in Judg 18:1 3427
made them *d* in this place 1Sa 12:8 3427
the country, that I may *d* there 1Sa 27:5 3427
for why should thy servant *d* in 1Sa 27:5 3427
I *d* in an house of cedar, but the 2Sa 7:2 3427
build me an house for me to *d* in 2Sa 7:5 3427
that they may *d* in a place of 2Sa 7:10 7931
d there, and go not forth thence 1Kin 2:36 3427
this woman *d* in one house 1Kin 3:17 3427
I will *d* among the children of 1Kin 6:13 7931
he would *d* in the thick darkness 1Kin 8:12 7931
built thee an house to *d* in 1Kin 8:13 2073
will God indeed *d* on the earth 1Kin 8:27 3427
belongeth to Zidon, and *d* there 1Kin 17:9 3427
I *d* among mine own people 2Kin 4:13 3427
the place where we *d* with thee is 2Kin 6:1 3427
us a place there, where we may *d* 2Kin 6:2 3427
d there, and let him teach them 2Kin 17:27 3427
d in the land, and serve the king 2Kin 25:24 3427
I *d* in an house of cedars, but 1Chr 17:1 3427
not build me an house to *d* in 1Chr 17:4 3427
they shall *d* in their place, and 1Chr 17:9 7931
that they may *d* in Jerusalem for 1Chr 23:25 7931
build him an house to *d* therein 2Chr 2:3 3427
he would *d* in the thick darkness 2Chr 6:1 7931
very deed *d* with men on the earth 2Chr 6:18 3427
the children of Israel to *d* there 2Chr 8:2 3427
My wife shall not *d* in the house 2Chr 8:11 3427
brethren that *d* in their cities 2Chr 19:10 3427
companions that *d* in Samaria Ezr 4:17 3488
name to *d* there destroy all kings Ezr 6:12 7932
d in booths in the feast of the Neh 8:14 3427
to bring one of ten to *d* in Neh 11:1 3427
nine parts to *d* in other cities Neh 11:1 3427
themselves to *d* at Jerusalem Neh 11:2 3427
let a cloud *d* upon it Job 3:5 7931
in them that *d* in houses of clay Job 4:19 7931
wickedness *d* in thy tabernacles Job 11:14 7931
It shall *d* in his tabernacle, Job 18:15 7931
They that *d* in mine house, and my Job 19:15 1481
To *d* in the cliffs of the valleys Job 30:6 7931
LORD, only makest me *d* in safety Ps 4:8 3427
neither shall evil *d* with thee Ps 5:4 1481
who shall *d* in thy holy hill Ps 15:1 7931
I will *d* in the house of the LORD Ps 23:6 3427
the world, and they that *d* therein Ps 24:1 3427
His soul shall *d* at ease Ps 25:13 3885
that I may *d* in the house of the Ps 27:4 3427
so shalt thou *d* in the land Ps 37:3 7931
and *d* for evermore Ps 37:27 7931
the land, and *d* therein for ever Ps 37:29 7931
that he may *d* in thy courts Ps 65:4 7931
They also that *d* in the uttermost Ps 65:8 3427
the rebellious *d* in a dry land Ps 68:6 7931
hill which God desireth to *d* in Ps 68:16 3427
the LORD will *d* in it for ever Ps 68:16 7931
the LORD God might *d* among them Ps 68:18 7931
let none *d* in their tents Ps 69:25 3427
that they may *d* there, and have it Ps 69:35 3427
love his name shall *d* therein Ps 69:36 7931
They that *d* in the wilderness Ps 72:9
of Israel to *d* in their tents Ps 78:55 7931
are they that *d* in thy house Ps 84:4 3427
than to *d* in the tents of Ps 84:10 1752
that glory may *d* in our land Ps 85:9 7931
the world, and they that *d* therein Ps 98:7 3427
the land, that they may *d* with me Ps 101:6 3427
shall not *d* within my house Ps 101:7 3427
they found no city to *d* in Ps 107:4 4186
wickedness of them that *d* therein Ps 107:34 3427
there he maketh the hungry to *d* Ps 107:36 3427
that I *d* in the tents of Kedar Ps 120:5 7931
here will I *d*; for I have Ps 132:14 3427
brethren to *d* together in unity Ps 133:1 3427
d in the uttermost parts of the Ps 139:9 7931
upright shall *d* in thy presence Ps 140:13 3427
he hath made me to *d* in darkness Ps 143:3 3427
hearkeneth unto me shall *d* safely Prov 1:33 7931
the upright shall *d* in the land Prov 2:21 7931
I wisdom *d* with prudence, and find Prov 8:12 7931
It is better to *d* in a corner of Prov 21:9 3427
It is better to *d* in the Prov 21:19 3427
It is better to *d* in the corner Prov 25:24 3427
I *d* in the midst of a people of Is 6:5 3427
they that *d* in the land of the Is 9:2 3427
wolf also shall *d* with the lamb Is 11:6 1481
and owls shall *d* there, and satyrs Is 13:21 7931
Let mine outcasts *d* with thee Is 16:4 1481
for them that *d* in the wilderness Is 23:13
for them that *d* before the LORD Is 23:18 3427
they that *d* therein are desolate Is 24:6 3427
bringeth down them that *d* on high Is 26:5 3427
Awake and sing, ye that *d* in dust Is 26:19 7931
shall *d* in Zion at Jerusalem Is 30:19 3427
shall *d* in the wilderness Is 32:16 7931
my people shall *d* in a peaceable Is 32:18 3427
Who among us shall *d* with the Is 33:14 1481
who among us shall *d* with Is 33:14 1481
He shall *d* on high Is 33:16 7931
the people that *d* therein shall Is 33:24 3427
also and the raven shall *d* in it Is 34:11 7931
generation shall they *d* therein Is 34:17 7931
them out as a tent to *d* in Is 40:22 3427
give place to me that I may *d* Is 49:20 3427
they that *d* therein shall die in Is 51:6 3427
I *d* in the high and holy place, Is 57:15 7931
The restorer of paths to *d* in Is 58:12 3427
it, and my servants shall *d* there Is 65:9 7931
forsaken, and not a man *d* therein Jer 4:29 3427
will cause you to *d* in this place Jer 7:3 7931
I cause you to *d* in this place Jer 7:7 7931
the city, and those that *d* therein Jer 8:16 3427
of them that *d* in a far country Jer 8:19
corners, that *d* in the wilderness Jer 9:26 3427
wickedness of them that *d* therein Jer 12:4 3427
all that *d* in thine house shall Jer 20:6 3427
saved, and Israel shall *d* safely Jer 23:6 7931
they shall *d* in their own land Jer 23:8 3427
them that *d* in the land of Egypt Jer 24:8 3427
d in the land that the LORD hath Jer 25:5 3427
people that *d* in the desert Jer 25:24 7931
they shall till it, and *d* therein Jer 27:11 3427
Build ye houses, and *d* in them Jer 29:5 3427
build ye houses, and *d* in them Jer 29:28 3427
have a man to *d* among this people Jer 29:32 3427
there shall *d* in Judah itself, and Jer 31:24 3427
and I will cause them to *d* safely Jer 32:37 3427
and Jerusalem shall *d* safely Jer 33:16 7931
all your days ye shall *d* in tents Jer 35:7 3427
to build houses for us to *d* in Jer 35:9 3427
so we *d* at Jerusalem Jer 35:11 3427
ye shall *d* in the land which I Jer 35:15 3427
d with him among the people Jer 40:5 3427
d in the land, and serve the king Jer 40:9 3427
I will *d* at Mizpah to serve the Jer 40:10 3427
d in your cities that ye have Jer 40:10 3427
We will not *d* in this land, Jer 42:13 3427
and there will we *d* Jer 42:14 3427
to *d* in the land of Judah Jer 43:4 3427
to *d* in the land of Judah Jer 43:5 1481

Jews which *d* in the land of Egypt .... Jer 44:1 3427
which *d* at Migdol, and at .... Jer 44:1 3427
of Egypt, whither ye be gone to *d* .... Jer 44:8 1481
them that *d* in the land of Egypt .... Jer 44:13 3427
a desire to return to *d* there .... Jer 44:14 3427
all Judah that *d* in the land of .... Jer 44:26 3427
the city, and them that *d* therein .... Jer 47:2 3427
without any to *d* therein .... Jer 48:9 3427
O ye that *d* in Moab, leave the .... Jer 48:28 3427
d in the rock, and be like the .... Jer 48:28 7931
his people *d* in his cities .... Jer 49:1 3427
d deep, O inhabitants of Dedan .... Jer 49:8 3427
shall a son of man *d* in it .... Jer 49:18 1481
d deep, O ye inhabitants of Hazor .... Jer 49:30 3427
gates nor bars, which *d* alone .... Jer 49:31 7931
there, nor any son of man *d* in it .... Jer 49:33 1481
desolate, and none shall *d* therein .... Jer 50:3 3427
of the islands shall *d* there .... Jer 50:39 3427
and the owls shall *d* therein .... Jer 50:39 3427
shall any son of man *d* therein .... Jer 50:40 1481
against them that *d* in the midst .... Jer 51:1 3427
thou dost *d* among scorpions .... Eze 2:6 3427
of all them that *d* therein .... Eze 12:19 3427
daughters that *d* at thy left hand .... Eze 16:46 3427
under it shall *d* all fowl of .... Eze 17:23 7931
the branches thereof shall they *d* .... Eze 17:23 7931
then shall they *d* in their land .... Eze 28:25 3427
they shall *d* safely therein, and .... Eze 28:26 3427
they shall *d* with confidence, ... Eze 28:26 3427
smite all them that *d* therein .... Eze 32:15 3427
they shall *d* safely in the .... Eze 34:25 3427
but they shall *d* safely, and none .... Eze 34:28 3427
ye shall *d* in the land that I .... Eze 36:28 3427
also cause you to *d* in the cities .... Eze 36:33 3427
they shall *d* in the land that I .... Eze 37:25 3427
and they shall *d* therein, even .... Eze 37:25 3427
they shall *d* safely all of them .... Eze 38:8 3427
that *d* safely, all of them .... Eze 38:11 3427
that *d* in the midst of the land .... Eze 38:12 3427
among them that *d* carelessly in .... Eze 39:6 3427
they that *d* in the cities of .... Eze 39:9 3427
where I will *d* in the midst of .... Eze 43:7 7931
I will *d* in the midst of them for .... Eze 43:9 7931
wheresoever the children of men *d* .... Dan 2:38 1753
that *d* in all the earth .... Dan 4:1 1753
that *d* in all the earth .... Dan 6:25 1753
They shall not *d* in the LORD's .... Hos 9:3 3427
yet make thee to *d* in tabernacles .... Hos 12:9 3427
They that *d* under his shadow .... Hos 14:7 3427
But Judah shall *d* for ever .... Joel 3:20 3427
of Israel be taken out that *d* in .... Amos 3:12 3427
stone, but ye shall not *d* in them .... Amos 5:11 3427
all that *d* therein shall mourn .... Amos 9:5
thou shalt *d* in the field, and .... Mic 4:10 7931
because of them that *d* therein .... Mic 7:13 3427
which *d* solitarily in the wood, ... Mic 7:14 7931
the world, and all that *d* therein .... Nah 1:5 3427
thy nobles shall *d* in the dust .... Nah 3:18 7931
city, and of all that *d* therein .... Hab 2:8 3427
city, and of all that *d* therein .... Hab 2:17 3427
of all them that *d* in the land .... Zeph 1:18 3427
to *d* in your cieled houses, and .... Hag 1:4 3427
I will *d* in the midst of thee, ... Zec 2:10 7931
I will *d* in the midst of thee, and .... Zec 2:11 7931
will *d* in the midst of Jerusalem .... Zec 8:3 7931
old women *d* in the streets of .... Zec 8:4 3427
they shall *d* in the midst of .... Zec 8:8 7931
And a bastard shall *d* in Ashdod .... Zec 9:6 3427
And men shall *d* in it, and there .... Zec 14:11 3427
and they enter in and *d* there .... Mt 12:45 *2730*
and they enter in, and *d* there .... Lk 11:26 *2730*
d on the face of the whole earth .... Lk 21:35 *2521*
desolate, and let no man *d* therein .... Acts 1:20 *2730*
all ye that *d* at Jerusalem, be .... Acts 2:14 *2730*
to all them that *d* in Jerusalem .... Acts 4:16 *2730*
into this land, wherein ye now *d* .... Acts 7:4 *2730*
For they that *d* at Jerusalem .... Acts 13:27 *2730*
to *d* on all the face of the earth .... Acts 17:26 *2730*
but Paul was suffered to *d* by .... Acts 28:16 *3306*
that the Spirit of God *d* in you .... Rom 8:9 *3611*
up Jesus from the dead *d* in you .... Rom 8:11 *3611*
and she be pleased to *d* with him 1Cor 7:12 *3611*
and if he be pleased to *d* with her 1Cor 7:13 *3611*
I will *d* in them, and walk in them 2Cor 6:16 *1774*
That Christ may *d* in your hearts .... Eph 3:17 *2730*
that in him should all fulness *d* .... Col 1:19 *2730*
Let the word of Christ *d* in you .... Col 3:16 *1774*
d with them according to 1Pet 3:7 *4924*
Hereby know we that we *d* in him 1Jn 4:13 *3306*
to try them that *d* upon the earth .... Rev 3:10 *2730*
blood on them that *d* on the earth .... Rev 6:10 *2730*
on the throne shall *d* among them .... Rev 7:15 *4637*
they that *d* upon the earth shall .... Rev 11:10 *2730*
ye heavens, and ye that *d* in them .... Rev 12:12 *4637*
and them that *d* in heaven .... Rev 13:6 *4637*
all that *d* upon the earth shall .... Rev 13:8 *2730*
them which *d* therein to worship .... Rev 13:12 *2730*
deceiveth them that *d* on the .... Rev 13:14 *2730*
to them that *d* on the earth .... Rev 13:14 *2730*
unto them that *d* on the earth .... Rev 14:6 *2730*
they that *d* on the earth shall .... Rev 17:8 *2730*
he will *d* with them, and they .... Rev 21:3 *4637*

DWELLED {6}

the Perizzite *d* then in the land .... Gen 13:7 3427
Abram *d* in the land of Canaan, and .... Gen 13:12 3427
Lot *d* in the cities of the plain, ... Gen 13:12 3427
d between Kadesh and Shur, and .... Gen 20:1 3427
they *d* there about ten years .... Ruth 1:4 3427
on every side, and ye *d* safe 1Sa 12:11 3427

DWELLERS {3}

d on the earth, see ye, when he .... Is 18:3 7931
known unto all the *d* at Jerusalem .... Acts 1:19 *2730*
the *d* in Mesopotamia, and in .... Acts 2:9 *2730*

DWELLEST {19}

them, and *d* in their land .... Deut 12:29 3427
d in their cities, and in their .... Deut 19:1 3427
and possessest it, and *d* therein .... Deut 26:1 3427
which *d* between the cherubims 2Kin 19:15 3427
thou that *d* between the cherubims .... Ps 80:1 3427
O thou that *d* in the heavens .... Ps 123:1 3427
Thou that *d* in the gardens, the .... Song 8:13 3427
hosts, O my people that *d* in Zion .... Is 10:24 3427
that *d* between the cherubims, ... Is 37:16 3427
that *d* carelessly, that sayest in .... Is 47:8 3427
O thou that *d* in the clefts of .... Jer 49:16 7931
O thou that *d* upon many waters, ... Jer 51:13 7931
of Edom, that *d* in the land of Uz .... Lam 4:21 3427
thee, O thou that *d* in the land .... Eze 7:7 3427
of man, thou *d* in the midst of a .... Eze 12:2 3427
thou that *d* in the clefts of the .... Obad 3 7931
that *d* with the daughter of .... Zec 2:7 3427
Master,) where *d* thou .... Jn 1:38 *3306*
I know thy works, and where thou *d* .... Rev 2:13 *2730*

DWELLETH {58}

But the stranger that *d* with you .... Lev 19:34 1481
if thy brother that *d* by thee be .... Lev 25:39
brother that *d* by him wax poor .... Lev 25:47
and the people that *d* therein .... Num 13:18 3427
he *d* as a lion, and teareth the .... Deut 33:20 7931
she *d* in Israel even unto this .... Josh 6:25 3427
wherein the LORD's tabernacle *d* .... Josh 22:19 7931
which *d* between the cherubims 1Sa 4:4 3427
while he *d* in the country of the 1Sa 27:11 3427
that *d* between the cherubims 2Sa 6:2 3427
the ark of God *d* within curtains 2Sa 7:2 3427
that *d* between the cherubims, ... 1Chr 13:6 3427
he *d* in desolate cities, and in .... Job 15:28 7931
Where is the way where light *d* .... Job 38:19 7931
She *d* and abideth on the rock, ... Job 39:28 7931
to the LORD, which *d* in Zion .... Ps 9:11 3427
and the place where thine honour *d* .... Ps 26:8 4908
He that *d* in the secret place of .... Ps 91:1 3427
the LORD our God, who *d* on high, ... Ps 113:5 3427
out of Zion, which *d* at Jerusalem .... Ps 135:21 7931
seeing he *d* securely by thee .... Prov 3:29 3427
of hosts, which *d* in mount Zion .... Is 8:18 7931
for he *d* on high .... Is 33:5 7931
the people that *d* in this city .... Jer 29:16 3427
desolation, and no man *d* therein, ... Jer 44:2 3427
that *d* without care, saith the .... Jer 49:31 3427
a land wherein no man *d*, neither .... Jer 51:43 3427
she *d* among the heathen, she .... Lam 1:3 3427
that *d* at thy right hand, is .... Eze 16:46 3427
the king *d* that made him king .... Eze 17:16
when my people of Israel *d* safely .... Eze 38:14 3427
darkness, and the light *d* with him .... Dan 2:22 8271
every one that *d* therein shall .... Hos 4:3 3427
for the LORD *d* in Zion .... Joel 3:21 7931
and every one mourn that *d* therein .... Amos 8:8 3427
by it, and by him that *d* therein .... Mt 23:21 *2730*
my blood, *d* in me, and I in him .... Jn 6:56 *3306*
but the Father that *d* in me .... Jn 14:10 *3306*
for he *d* with you, and shall be in .... Jn 14:17 *3306*
Howbeit the most High *d* not in .... Acts 7:48 *2730*
d not in temples made with hands .... Acts 17:24 *2730*
that do it, but sin that *d* in me .... Rom 7:17 *3611*
is, in my flesh,) *d* no good thing .... Rom 7:18 *3611*
that do it, but sin that *d* in me .... Rom 7:20 *3611*
by his Spirit that *d* in you .... Rom 8:11 *1774*
that the Spirit of God *d* in you 1Cor 3:16 *3611*
For in him *d* all the fulness of .... Col 2:9 *2730*
by the Holy Ghost which *d* in us 2Ti 1:14 *1774*
The spirit that *d* in us lusteth .... Jas 4:5 *2730*
earth, wherein *d* righteousness 2Pet 3:13 *2730*
how *d* the love of God in him 1Jn 3:17 *3306*
keepeth his commandments *d* in him 1Jn 3:24 *3306*
God *d* in us, and his love is 1Jn 4:12 *3306*
God *d* in him, and he in God 1Jn 4:15 *3306*
he that *d* in love *d* in God 1Jn 4:16 *3306*
the truth's sake, which *d* in us 2Jn 2 *3306*
slain among you, where Satan *d* .... Rev 2:13 *2730*

DWELLING {53}

their *d* was from Mesha, as thou .... Gen 10:30 4186
Jacob was a plain man, *d* in tents .... Gen 25:27 3427
thy *d* shall be the fatness of the .... Gen 27:39 4186
if a man sell a *d* house in a .... Lev 25:29 4186
that goeth down to the *d* of Ar .... Num 21:15 3427
dukes of Sihon, *d* in the country .... Josh 13:21 3427
hear thou in heaven thy *d* place 1Kin 8:30 3427
hear thou in heaven thy *d* place 1Kin 8:39 3427
Hear thou in heaven thy *d* place 1Kin 8:43 3427
in heaven thy *d* place, and 1Kin 8:49 3427
were in his city, *d* with Naboth 1Kin 21:8 3427
at the beginning of their *d* there 2Kin 17:25 3427
they ministered before the *d* 1Chr 6:32 4908
Now these are their *d* places 1Chr 6:54 4186
and a place for thy *d* for ever 2Chr 6:2 3427
hear thou from thy *d* place 2Chr 6:21 3427
hear thou from heaven thy *d* place 2Chr 6:30 3427
heavens, even from thy *d* place 2Chr 6:33 3427
heavens, even from thy *d* place 2Chr 6:39 3427
came up to his holy *d* place 2Chr 30:27 4583
on his people, and on his *d* place 2Chr 36:15 4583
the *d* place of the wicked shall .... Job 8:22 168
where are the *d* places of the .... Job 21:28 4908
their *d* places to all generations .... Ps 49:11 4908
consume in the grave from their *d* .... Ps 49:14 2073
and pluck thee out of thy *d* place .... Ps 52:5 168
defiled by casting down the *d* .... Ps 74:7 4908
and his *d* place in Zion .... Ps 76:2 4585
Jacob, and laid waste his *d* place .... Ps 79:7 5116
thou hast been our *d* place in all .... Ps 90:1 4583
shall any plague come nigh thy *d* .... Ps 91:10 168
and oil in the *d* of the wise .... Prov 21:20 5116
against the *d* of the righteous .... Prov 24:15 5116
upon every *d* place of mount Zion .... Is 4:5 4349
I will consider in my *d* place .... Is 18:4 4349
O thou daughter *d* in Egypt .... Jer 46:19 3427
And Hazor shall be a *d* for dragons .... Jer 49:33 4583
a *d* place for dragons, an .... Jer 51:37 3427
all of them *d* without walls, and .... Eze 38:11 3427
profane place for the city, for *d* .... Eze 48:15 4186
whose *d* is not with flesh .... Dan 2:11 4070
thy *d* shall be with the beasts of .... Dan 4:25 4070
thy *d* shall be with the beasts of .... Dan 4:32 4070
his *d* was with the wild asses .... Dan 5:21 4070
I am the LORD your God *d* in Zion .... Joel 3:17 7931
Where is the *d* of the lions .... Nah 2:11 4583
so their *d* should not be cut off, ... Zeph 3:7 4583
Who had his *d* among the tombs .... Mk 5:3 *2731*
there were *d* at Jerusalem Jews, ... Acts 2:5 *2730*
Jews and Greeks also *d* at Ephesus .... Acts 19:17 *2730*
d in the light which no man can 1Ti 6:16 *3611*
d in tabernacles with Isaac and .... Heb 11:9 *2730*
that righteous man *d* among them 2Pet 2:8 *1460*

DWELLINGPLACE {2}

parable, and said, Strong is thy *d* .... Num 24:21 4186
and have no certain *d* place 1Cor 4:11 *790*

DWELLINGPLACES {5}

tents, and have mercy on his *d* .... Jer 30:18 4908
they have burned her *d* .... Jer 51:30 4908
In all your *d* the cities shall be .... Eze 6:6 4186
will save them out of all their *d* .... Eze 37:23 4186
to possess the *d* that are not .... Hab 1:6 4908

DWELLINGS {17}

of Israel had light in their *d* .... Ex 10:23 4186
generations throughout all your *d* .... Lev 3:17 4186
or of beast, in any of your *d* .... Lev 7:26 4186
sabbath of the LORD in all your *d* .... Lev 23:3 4186
your generations in all your *d* .... Lev 23:14 4186
d throughout your generations .... Lev 23:21 4186
your generations in all your *d* .... Lev 23:31 4186
your generations in all your *d* .... Num 35:29 4186
nor any remaining in his *d* .... Job 18:19 4033
such are the *d* of the wicked .... Job 18:21 4908
and the barren land his *d* .... Job 39:6 4908
for wickedness is in their *d* .... Ps 55:15 4033
Zion more than all the *d* of Jacob .... Ps 87:2 4908
habitation, and in sure *d*, and in .... Is 32:18 4908
because our *d* have cast us out .... Jer 9:19 4908
in thee, and make their *d* in thee .... Eze 25:4 4908
And the sea coast shall be *d* .... Zeph 2:6 5116

DWELT {226}

d in the land of Nod, on the east .... Gen 4:16 3427
and they *d* there .... Gen 11:2 3427
they came unto Haran, and *d* there .... Gen 11:31 3427
d in the plain of Mamre, which is .... Gen 13:18 3427
Amorites, that *d* in Hazezon-tamar .... Gen 14:7 3427
who *d* in Sodom, and his goods, and .... Gen 14:12 3427
for he *d* in the plain of Mamre .... Gen 14:13 7931
after Abram had *d* ten years in .... Gen 16:3 3427
the cities in the which Lot *d* .... Gen 19:29 3427
d in the mountain, and his two .... Gen 19:30 3427
he *d* in a cave, he and his two .... Gen 19:30 3427
d in the wilderness, and became an .... Gen 21:20 3427
he *d* in the wilderness of Paran .... Gen 21:21 3427
and Abraham *d* at Beer-sheba .... Gen 22:19 3427
Ephron *d* among the children of .... Gen 23:10 3427
for he *d* in the south country .... Gen 24:62 3427
Isaac *d* by the well Lahai-roi .... Gen 25:11 3427
they *d* from Havilah unto Shur, ... Gen 25:18 7931
And Isaac *d* in Gerar .... Gen 26:6 3427
the valley of Gerar, and *d* there .... Gen 26:17 3427
when Israel *d* in that land, that .... Gen 35:22 7931
Thus *d* Esau in mount Seir .... Gen 36:8 3427
Jacob *d* in the land wherein his .... Gen 37:1 3427
went and *d* in her father's house .... Gen 38:11 3427
Israel *d* in the land of Egypt, in .... Gen 47:27 3427
Joseph *d* in Egypt, he, and his .... Gen 50:22 3427
and *d* in the land of Midian .... Ex 2:15 3427
who *d* in Egypt, was four hundred .... Ex 12:40 3427
the land of Egypt, wherein ye *d* .... Lev 18:3 3427
your sabbaths, when ye *d* upon it .... Lev 26:35 3427
and the Canaanites *d* in the valley .... Num 14:25 3427
Canaanites which *d* in that hill .... Num 14:45 3427
we have *d* in Egypt a long time .... Num 20:15 3427
which *d* in the south, heard tell .... Num 21:1 3427
Israel *d* in all the cities of the .... Num 21:25 3427
Thus Israel *d* in the land of the .... Num 21:31 3427
the Amorites, which *d* at Heshbon .... Num 21:34 3427
all their cities wherein they *d* .... Num 31:10 4186
and he *d* therein .... Num 32:40 3427
which *d* in the south in the land .... Num 33:40 3427
which *d* in Heshbon, and Og the .... Deut 1:4 3427
which *d* at Astaroth in Edrei .... Deut 1:4 3427
Ye have *d* long enough in this .... Deut 1:6 3427
which *d* in that mountain, came .... Deut 1:44 3427
which *d* in Seir, through the way .... Deut 2:8 3427
The Emims *d* therein in times past .... Deut 2:10 3427

The Horims also *d* in Seir ... Deut 2:12 3427
before them, and *d* in their stead ... Deut 2:12 3427
giants *d* therein in old time ... Deut 2:20 3427
them, and *d* in their stead ... Deut 2:21 3427
of Esau, which *d* in Seir, when he ... Deut 2:22 3427
d in their stead even unto this ... Deut 2:22 3427
And the Avims which *d* in Hazerim ... Deut 2:23 3427
them, and *d* in their stead ... Deut 2:23 3427
the Amorites, which *d* at Heshbon ... Deut 3:2 3427
who *d* at Heshbon, whom Moses and ... Deut 4:46 3427
built goodly houses, and *d* therein ... Deut 8:12 3427
we have *d* in the land of Egypt ... Deut 29:16 3427
will of him that *d* in the bush ... Deut 33:16 7931
town wall, and she *d* upon the wall ... Josh 2:15 3427
d on the other side Jordan ... Josh 7:7 3427
and that they *d* among them ... Josh 9:16 3427
who *d* in Heshbon, and ruled from ... Josh 12:2 3427
that *d* at Ashtaroth and at Edrei, ... Josh 12:4 3427
the Canaanites that *d* in Gezer ... Josh 16:10 3427
d therein, and called Leshem, Dan, ... Josh 19:47 3427
he built the city, and *d* therein ... Josh 19:50 3427
they possessed it, and *d* therein ... Josh 21:43 3427
the children of Reuben and Gad *d* ... Josh 22:33 3427
Your fathers *d* on the other side ... Josh 24:2 3427
ye *d* in the wilderness a long ... Josh 24:7 3427
which *d* on the other side Jordan ... Josh 24:8 3427
the Amorites which *d* in the land ... Josh 24:18 3427
that *d* in the mountain, and in the ... Judg 1:9 3427
the Canaanites that *d* in Hebron ... Judg 1:10 3427
they went and *d* among the people ... Judg 1:16 3427
the Canaanites that *d* in Gezer ... Judg 1:29 3427
but the Canaanites *d* in Gezer ... Judg 1:29 3427
but the Canaanites *d* among them ... Judg 1:30 3427
But the Asherites *d* among the ... Judg 1:32 3427
but he *d* among the Canaanites, ... Judg 1:33 3427
Hivites that *d* in mount Lebanon ... Judg 3:3 3427
of Israel *d* among the Canaanites ... Judg 3:5 3427
which *d* in Harosheth of the ... Judg 4:2 3427
she *d* under the palm tree of ... Judg 4:5 3427
d in tents on the east of Nobah ... Judg 8:11 7931
Joash went and *d* in his own house ... Judg 8:29 3427
d there, for fear of Abimelech ... Judg 9:21 3427
And Abimelech *d* at Arumah ... Judg 9:41 3427
he *d* in Shamir in mount Ephraim ... Judg 10:1 3427
brethren, and *d* in the land of Tob ... Judg 11:3 3427
While Israel *d* in Heshbon ... Judg 11:26 3427
d in the top of the rock Etam ... Judg 15:8 3427
were therein, how they *d* careless ... Judg 18:7 3427
they built a city, and *d* therein ... Judg 18:28 3427
repaired the cities, and *d* in them ... Judg 21:23 3427
and *d* with her mother in law ... Ruth 2:23 3427
he and Samuel went and *d* in Naioth ... 1Sa 19:18 3427
they *d* with him all the while ... 1Sa 22:4 3427
d in strong holds at En-gedi ... 1Sa 23:29 3427
David *d* with Achish at Gath, he ... 1Sa 27:3 3427
the time that David *d* in the ... 1Sa 27:7 3427
the Philistines came and *d* in them ... 1Sa 31:7 3427
they *d* in the cities of Hebron ... 2Sa 2:3 3427
So David *d* in the fort, and called ... 2Sa 5:9 3427
Whereas I have not *d* in any house ... 2Sa 7:6 3427
all that *d* in the house of Ziba ... 2Sa 9:12 4186
So Mephibosheth *d* in Jerusalem ... 2Sa 9:13 3427
So Absalom *d* two full years in ... 2Sa 14:28 3427
Shimei *d* in Jerusalem many days ... 1Kin 2:38 3427
And Judah and Israel *d* safely ... 1Kin 4:25 3427
his house where he *d* had another ... 1Kin 7:8 3427
the Canaanites that *d* in the city ... 1Kin 9:16 3427
d therein, and reigned in Damascus ... 1Kin 11:24 3427
Solomon, and Jeroboam *d* in Egypt ... 1Kin 12:2 3427
which *d* in the cities of Judah ... 1Kin 12:17 3427
in mount Ephraim, and *d* therein ... 1Kin 12:25 3427
Now there *d* an old prophet in ... 1Kin 13:11 3427
the city where the old prophet *d* ... 1Kin 13:25 3427
that *d* at Damascus, saying, ... 1Kin 15:18 3427
building of Ramah, and *d* in Tirzah ... 1Kin 15:21 3427
d by the brook Cherith, that is ... 1Kin 17:5 3427
of Israel *d* in their tents ... 2Kin 13:5 3427
death, and *d* in a several house ... 2Kin 15:5 3427
Elath, and *d* there unto this day ... 2Kin 16:6 3427
and *d* in the cities thereof ... 2Kin 17:24 3427
d in Beth-el, and taught them how ... 2Kin 17:28 3427
in their cities wherein they *d* ... 2Kin 17:29 3427
went and returned, and *d* at Nineveh ... 2Kin 19:36 3427
(now she *d* in Jerusalem in the ... 2Kin 22:14 3427
of the scribes which *d* at Jabez ... 1Chr 2:55 3427
those that *d* among plants and ... 1Chr 4:23 3427
there they *d* with the king for ... 1Chr 4:23 3427
they *d* at Beer-sheba, and Moladah, ... 1Chr 4:28 3427
they of Ham had *d* there of old ... 1Chr 4:40 3427
this day, and *d* in their rooms ... 1Chr 4:41 3427
escaped, and *d* there unto this day ... 1Chr 4:43 3427
who *d* in Aroer, even unto Nebo and ... 1Chr 5:8 3427
they *d* in their tents throughout ... 1Chr 5:10 3427
of Gad *d* over against them ... 1Chr 5:11 3427
they *d* in Gilead in Bashan, and in ... 1Chr 5:16 3427
they *d* in their steads until the ... 1Chr 5:22 3427
tribe of Manasseh *d* in the land ... 1Chr 5:23 3427
In these *d* the children of Joseph ... 1Chr 7:29 3427
These *d* in Jerusalem ... 1Chr 8:28 3427
at Gibeon *d* the father of Gibeon ... 1Chr 8:29 3427
these also *d* with their brethren ... 1Chr 8:32 3427
d in their possessions in their ... 1Chr 9:2
in Jerusalem *d* of the children of ... 1Chr 9:3 3427
that *d* in the villages of the ... 1Chr 9:16 3427
these *d* at Jerusalem ... 1Chr 9:34 3427
in Gibeon *d* the father of Gibeon, ... 1Chr 9:35 3427
they also *d* with their brethren ... 1Chr 9:38 3427
the Philistines came and *d* in them ... 1Chr 10:7 3427
And David *d* in the castle ... 1Chr 11:7 3427
For I have not *d* in an house ... 1Chr 17:5 3427
that *d* in the cities of Judah ... 2Chr 10:17 3427
Rehoboam *d* in Jerusalem, and built ... 2Chr 11:5 3427
that *d* at Damascus, saying, ... 2Chr 16:2 3427
Jehoshaphat *d* at Jerusalem ... 2Chr 19:4 3427
they *d* therein, and have built ... 2Chr 20:8 3427
the Arabians that *d* in Gur-baal ... 2Chr 26:7 3427
d in a several house, being a ... 2Chr 26:21 3427
and they *d* there ... 2Chr 28:18 3427
that *d* in Judah, rejoiced ... 2Chr 30:25 3427
that *d* in Jerusalem to give the ... 2Chr 31:4 3427
that *d* in the cities of Judah, ... 2Chr 31:6 3427
(now she *d* in Jerusalem in the ... 2Chr 34:22 3427
d in their cities, and all Israel ... Ezr 2:70 3427
Moreover the Nethinims *d* in Ophel ... Neh 3:26 3427
the Jews which *d* by them came ... Neh 4:12 3427
and all Israel, *d* in their cities ... Neh 7:73 3427
of the people *d* at Jerusalem ... Neh 11:1 3427
the province that *d* in Jerusalem ... Neh 11:3 3427
but in the cities of Judah *d* ... Neh 11:3 3427
at Jerusalem *d* certain of the ... Neh 11:4 3427
All the sons of Perez that *d* at ... Neh 11:6 3427
But the Nethinims *d* in Ophel ... Neh 11:21 3427
of Judah *d* at Kirjath-arba ... Neh 11:25 3427
they *d* from Beer-sheba unto the ... Neh 11:30 2583
Benjamin from Geba *d* at Michmash ... Neh 11:31
There *d* men of Tyre also therein, ... Neh 13:16 3427
that *d* in the unwalled towns, ... Est 9:19 3427
and the honourable man *d* in it ... Job 22:8 3427
d as a king in the army, as one ... Job 29:25 7931
Thy congregation hath *d* therein ... Ps 68:10 3427
mount Zion, wherein thou hast *d* ... Ps 74:2 7931
my soul had almost *d* in silence ... Ps 94:17 7931
My soul hath long *d* with him that ... Ps 120:6 7931
neither shall it be *d* in from ... Is 13:20 7931
to Ariel, the city where David *d* ... Is 29:1 2583
went and returned, and *d* at Nineveh ... Is 37:37 3427
passed through, and where no man *d* ... Jer 2:6 3427
But we have *d* in tents, and have ... Jer 35:10 3427
so he *d* among the people ... Jer 39:14 3427
d with him among the people that ... Jer 40:6 3427
d in the habitation of Chimham, ... Jer 41:17 3427
that *d* in the land of Egypt ... Jer 44:15 3427
neither shall it be *d* in from ... Jer 50:39 7931
that *d* by the river of Chebar, and ... Eze 3:15 3427
under his shadow *d* all great ... Eze 31:6 3427
that *d* under his shadow in the ... Eze 31:17 3427
of Israel *d* in their own land ... Eze 36:17 3427
wherein your fathers have *d* ... Eze 37:25 3427
when they *d* safely in their land, ... Eze 39:26 3427
heaven *d* in the boughs thereof ... Dan 4:12 1753
which the beasts of the field *d* ... Dan 4:21 1753
rejoicing city that *d* carelessly ... Zeph 2:15 3427
d in a city called Nazareth ... Mt 2:23 *2730*
d in Capernaum, which is upon the ... Mt 4:13 *2730*
on all that *d* round about them ... Lk 1:65 *4039*
above all men that *d* in Jerusalem ... Lk 13:4 *2730*
d among us, (and we beheld his ... Jn 1:14 *4637*
They came and saw where he *d* ... Jn 1:39 *3306*
before he *d* in Charran, ... Acts 7:2 *2730*
the Chaldaeans, and *d* in Charran ... Acts 7:4 *2730*
the Jews which *d* at Damascus ... Acts 9:22 *2730*
to the saints which *d* at Lydda ... Acts 9:32 *2730*
And all that *d* at Lydda and Saron ... Acts 9:35 *2730*
the brethren which *d* in Judaea ... Acts 11:29 *2730*
d as strangers in the land of ... Acts 13:17 *3940*
so that all they which *d* in Asia ... Acts 19:10 *2730*
of all the Jews which *d* there ... Acts 22:12 *2730*
Paul *d* two whole years in his own ... Acts 28:30 *3306*
which *d* first in thy grandmother ... 2Ti 1:5 *1774*
them that *d* on the earth ... Rev 11:10 *2730*

DYED {7}
And rams' skins *d* red, and badgers' ... Ex 25:5
for the tent of rams' skins *d* red ... Ex 26:14
And rams' skins *d* red, and badgers' ... Ex 35:7
for the tent of rams' skins *d* red ... Ex 36:19
the covering of rams' skins *d* red ... Ex 39:34
with *d* garments from Bozrah ... Is 63:1 2556
exceeding in *d* attire upon their ... Eze 23:15 2871

DYING {6}
shall we be consumed with *d* ... Num 17:13 1478
took a wife, and *d* left no seed ... Mk 12:20 *599*
years of age, and she lay a *d* ... Lk 8:42 *599*
the body the *d* of the Lord Jesus ... 2Cor 4:10 *3500*
as *d*, and, behold, we live ... 2Cor 6:9 *599*
By faith Jacob, when he was a *d* ... Heb 11:21 *599*

E

EACH See APPENDIX.

EAGLE {23}
the *e*, and the ossifrage, and the ... Lev 11:13 5404
and the pelican, and the gier *e* ... Lev 11:18 7360
the *e*, and the ossifrage, and the ... Deut 14:12 5404
And the pelican, and the gier *e* ... Deut 14:17 7360
earth, as swift as the *e* flieth ... Deut 28:49 5404
As an *e* stirreth up her nest, ... Deut 32:11 5404
as the *e* that hasteth to the prey ... Job 9:26 5404
Doth the *e* mount up at thy ... Job 39:27 5404
fly away as an *e* toward heaven ... Prov 23:5 5404
The way of an *e* in the air ... Prov 30:19 5404
Behold, he shall fly as an *e* ... Jer 48:40 5404
make thy nest as high as the *e* ... Jer 49:16 5404
he shall come up and fly as the *e* ... Jer 49:22 5404
four also had the face of an *e* ... Eze 1:10 5404
and the fourth the face of an *e* ... Eze 10:14 5404
A great *e* with great wings, ... Eze 17:3 5404
another great *e* with great wings ... Eze 17:7 5404
He shall come as an *e* against the ... Hos 8:1 5404
thou exalt thyself as the *e* ... Obad 4 5404
enlarge thy baldness as the *e* ... Mic 1:16 5404
fly as the *e* that hasteth to eat ... Hab 1:8 5404
fourth beast was like a flying *e* ... Rev 4:7 *105*
were given two wings of a great *e* ... Rev 12:14 *105*

EAGLE'S {2}
thy youth is renewed like the *e* ... Ps 103:5 5404
was like a lion, and had *e* wings ... Dan 7:4 5403

EAGLES {7}
they were swifter than *e*, they ... 2Sa 1:23 5404
out, and the young *e* shall eat it ... Prov 30:17 5404
shall mount up with wings as *e* ... Is 40:31 5404
his horses are swifter than *e* ... Jer 4:13 5404
swifter than the *e* of the heaven ... Lam 4:19 5404
there will the *e* be gathered ... Mt 24:28 *105*
thither will the *e* be gathered ... Lk 17:37 *105*

EAGLES' {2}
and how I bare you on *e* wings ... Ex 19:4 5404
hairs were grown like *e* feathers ... Dan 4:33 5403

EAR {120}
for the barley was in the *e* ... Ex 9:31 24
wilt give *e* to his commandments, ... Ex 15:26 238
bore his *e* through with an aul ... Ex 21:6 241
the tip of the right *e* of Aaron ... Ex 29:20 241
tip of the right *e* of his sons ... Ex 29:20 241
upon the tip of Aaron's right *e* ... Lev 8:23 241
upon the tip of their right *e* ... Lev 8:24 241
it upon the tip of the right *e* of ... Lev 14:14 241
e of him that is to be cleansed ... Lev 14:17 241
it upon the tip of the right *e* of ... Lev 14:25 241
e of him that is to be cleansed ... Lev 14:28 241
your voice, nor give *e* unto you ... Deut 1:45 238
it through his *e* unto the door ... Deut 15:17 241
Give *e*, O ye heavens, and I will ... Deut 32:1 238
give *e*, O ye princes ... Judg 5:3 238
and will set them to *e* his ground ... 1Sa 8:12 2790
in his *e* a day before Saul came ... 1Sa 9:15 241
LORD, bow down thine *e*, and hear ... 2Kin 19:16 241
but they would not give *e* ... 2Chr 24:19 238
Let thine *e* now be attentive, and ... Neh 1:6 241
let now thine *e* be attentive to ... Neh 1:11 241
yet would they not give *e* ... Neh 9:30 238
mine *e* received a little thereof ... Job 4:12 241
Doth not the *e* try words ... Job 12:11 241
mine *e* hath heard and understood ... Job 13:1 241
When the *e* heard me, then it ... Job 29:11 241
Unto me men gave *e*, and waited, and ... Job 29:21 8085
I gave *e* to your reasons, whilst ... Job 32:11 238
give *e* unto me, ye that have ... Job 34:2 238
For the *e* trieth words, as the ... Job 34:3 241
also their *e* to discipline ... Job 36:10 241
of thee by the hearing of the *e* ... Job 42:5 241
Give *e* to my words, O LORD ... Ps 5:1 238
thou wilt cause thine *e* to hear ... Ps 10:17 241
give *e* unto my prayer, that goeth ... Ps 17:1 238
incline thine *e* unto me, and hear ... Ps 17:6 241
Bow down thine *e* to me ... Ps 31:2 241
O LORD, and give *e* unto my cry ... Ps 39:12 238
and consider, and incline thine *e* ... Ps 45:10 241
give *e*, all ye inhabitants of the ... Ps 49:1 238
will incline mine *e* to a parable ... Ps 49:4 241
give *e* to the words of my mouth ... Ps 54:2 238
Give *e* to my prayer, O God ... Ps 55:1 238
deaf adder that stoppeth her *e* ... Ps 58:4 241
incline thine *e* unto me, and save ... Ps 71:2 241
and he gave *e* unto me ... Ps 77:1 238
Give *e*, O my people, to my law ... Ps 78:1 238
Give *e*, O Shepherd of Israel, ... Ps 80:1 238
give *e*, O God of Jacob ... Ps 84:8 238
Bow down thine *e*, O LORD, hear me ... Ps 86:1 241
Give *e*, O LORD, unto my prayer ... Ps 86:6 238
incline thine *e* unto my cry ... Ps 88:2 241
He that planted the *e*, shall he ... Ps 94:9 241
incline thine *e* unto me ... Ps 102:2 241
he hath inclined his *e* unto me ... Ps 116:2 241
give *e* unto my voice, when I cry ... Ps 141:1 238
give *e* to my supplications ... Ps 143:1 238
thou incline thine *e* unto wisdom ... Prov 2:2 241
incline thine *e* unto my sayings ... Prov 4:20 241
bow thine *e* to my understanding ... Prov 5:1 241
nor inclined mine *e* to them that ... Prov 5:13 241
The *e* that heareth the reproof of ... Prov 15:31 241
a liar giveth *e* to a naughty ... Prov 17:4 238
the *e* of the wise seeketh ... Prov 18:15 241

The hearing *e*, and the seeing eye, ... Prov 20:12 241
Bow down thine *e*, and hear the ... Prov 22:17 241
wise reprover upon an obedient *e* ... Prov 25:12 241
away his *e* from hearing the law ... Prov 28:9 241
nor the *e* filled with hearing ... Eccl 1:8 241
Hear, O heavens, and give *e* ... Is 1:2 238
give *e* unto the law of our God, ... Is 1:10 238
and give *e*, all ye of far ... Is 8:9 238
Give ye *e*, and hear my voice ... Is 28:23 238
the young asses that *e* the ground ... Is 30:24 5647
give *e* unto my speech ... Is 32:9 238
Incline thine *e*, O LORD, and hear ... Is 37:17 241
Who among you will give *e* to this ... Is 42:23 238
time that thine *e* was not opened ... Is 48:8 241
he wakeneth mine *e* to hear as the ... Is 50:4 241
The Lord GOD hath opened mine *e* ... Is 50:5 241
give *e* unto me, O my nation ... Is 51:4 238
Incline your *e*, and come unto me ... Is 55:3 241
neither his *e* heavy, that it ... Is 59:1 241
not heard, nor perceived by the *e* ... Is 64:4 238
their *e* is uncircumcised, and they ... Jer 6:10 241
not, nor inclined their *e* ... Jer 7:24 241
not unto me, nor inclined their *e* ... Jer 7:26 241
let your *e* receive the word of ... Jer 9:20 241
obeyed not, nor inclined their *e* ... Jer 11:8 241
Hear ye, and give *e* ... Jer 13:15 238
not, neither inclined their *e* ... Jer 17:23 241
nor inclined your *e* to hear ... Jer 25:4 241
unto me, neither inclined their *e* ... Jer 34:14 241
but ye have not inclined your *e* ... Jer 35:15 241
nor inclined their *e* to turn from ... Jer 44:5 241
hide not thine *e* at my breathing, ... Lam 3:56 241
O my God, incline thine *e* ... Dan 9:18 241
and give ye *e*, O house of the king ... Hos 5:1 238
Hear this, ye old men, and give *e* ... Joel 1:2 238
lion two legs, or a piece of an *e* ... Amos 3:12 241
and what ye hear in the *e*, that ... Mt 10:27 *3775*
high priest's, and smote off his *e* ... Mt 26:51 *5621*
first the blade, then the *e* ... Mk 4:28 *4719*
after that the full corn in the *e* ... Mk 4:28 *4719*
the high priest, and cut off his *e* ... Mk 14:47 *5621*
which ye have spoken in the *e* in ... Lk 12:3 *3775*
priest, and cut off his right *e* ... Lk 22:50 *3775*
And he touched his *e*, and healed ... Lk 22:51 *5621*
servant, and cut off his right *e* ... Jn 18:10 *5621*
his kinsman whose *e* Peter cut off ... Jn 18:26 *5621*
nor *e* heard, neither have entered ... 1Cor 2:9 *3775*
if the *e* shall say, Because I am ... 1Cor 12:16 *3775*
He that hath an *e*, let him hear ... Rev 2:7 *3775*
He that hath an *e*, let him hear ... Rev 2:11 *3775*
He that hath an *e*, let him hear ... Rev 2:17 *3775*
He that hath an *e*, let him hear ... Rev 2:29 *3775*
He that hath an *e*, let him hear ... Rev 3:6 *3775*
He that hath an *e*, let him hear ... Rev 3:13 *3775*
He that hath an *e*, let him hear ... Rev 3:22 *3775*
If any man have an *e*, let him ... Rev 13:9 *3775*

EARED {1}
which is neither *e* nor sown ... Deut 21:4 5647

EARING {2}
shall neither be *e* nor harvest ... Gen 45:6 2758
in *e* time and in harvest thou ... Ex 34:21 2758

EARLY {87}
your feet, and ye shall rise up *e* ... Gen 19:2 7925
Abraham gat up *e* in the morning ... Gen 19:27 7925
Abimelech rose *e* in the morning ... Gen 20:8 7925
Abraham rose up *e* in the morning ... Gen 21:14 7925
Abraham rose up *e* in the morning ... Gen 22:3 7925
Jacob rose up *e* in the morning, ... Gen 28:18 7925
e in the morning Laban rose up, ... Gen 31:55 7925
Rise up *e* in the morning, and ... Ex 8:20 7925
Rise up *e* in the morning, and ... Ex 9:13 7925
rose up *e* in the morning, and ... Ex 24:4 7925
they rose up *e* on the morrow, and ... Ex 32:6 7925
Moses rose up *e* in the morning, ... Ex 34:4 7925
they rose up *e* in the morning, and ... Num 14:40 7925
Joshua rose *e* in the morning ... Josh 3:1 7925
Joshua rose *e* in the morning, and ... Josh 6:12 7925
that they rose *e* about the ... Josh 6:15 7925
Joshua rose up *e* in the morning ... Josh 7:16 7925
Joshua rose up *e* in the morning ... Josh 8:10 7925
it, that they hasted and rose up *e* ... Josh 8:14 7925
the city arose *e* in the morning ... Judg 6:28 7925
for he rose up *e* on the morrow ... Judg 6:38 7925
that were with him, rose up *e* ... Judg 7:1 7925
depart *e* from mount Gilead ... Judg 7:3 6852
the sun is up, thou shalt rise *e* ... Judg 9:33 7925
when they arose *e* in the morning ... Judg 19:5 7925
he arose *e* in the morning on the ... Judg 19:8 7925
to morrow get you *e* on your way ... Judg 19:9 7925
morrow, that the people rose *e* ... Judg 21:4 7925
And they rose up in the morning *e* ... 1Sa 1:19 7925
of Ashdod arose *e* on the morrow ... 1Sa 5:3 7925
when they arose *e* on the morrow ... 1Sa 5:4 7925
And they arose *e* ... 1Sa 9:26 7925
when Samuel rose *e* to meet Saul ... 1Sa 15:12 7925
David rose up *e* in the morning, ... 1Sa 17:20 7925
Wherefore now rise up *e* in the ... 1Sa 29:10 7925
soon as ye be up *e* in the morning ... 1Sa 29:10 7925
his men rose up *e* to depart in ... 1Sa 29:11 7925
And Absalom rose up *e*, and stood ... 2Sa 15:2 7925
they rose up *e* in the morning, and ... 2Kin 3:22 7925
of the man of God was risen *e* ... 2Kin 6:15 7925
when they arose *e* in the morning ... 2Kin 19:35 7925
they rose *e* in the morning, and ... 2Chr 20:20 7925
Then Hezekiah the king rose *e* ... 2Chr 29:20 7925
rose up *e* in the morning, and ... Job 1:5 7925
shall help her, and that right *e* ... Ps 46:5 1242
I myself will awake *e* ... Ps 57:8 7837
e will I seek thee ... Ps 63:1 7836
returned and enquired *e* after God ... Ps 78:34 7836
O satisfy us *e* with thy mercy ... Ps 90:14 1242
I will *e* destroy all the wicked ... Ps 101:8 1242
I myself will awake *e* ... Ps 108:2 7837
It is vain for you to rise up *e* ... Ps 127:2 7925
they shall seek me *e*, but they ... Prov 1:28 7836
that seek me *e* shall find me ... Prov 8:17 7836
rising *e* in the morning, it shall ... Prov 27:14 7925
Let us get up *e* to the vineyards ... Song 7:12 7925
that rise up *e* in the morning ... Is 5:11 7925
within me will I seek thee *e* ... Is 26:9 7836
when they arose *e* in the morning ... Is 37:36 7925
and I spake unto you, rising up *e* ... Jer 7:13 7925
the prophets, daily rising up *e* ... Jer 7:25 7925
even unto this day, rising *e* ... Jer 11:7 7925
I have spoken unto you, rising *e* ... Jer 25:3 7925
servants the prophets, rising *e* ... Jer 25:4 7925
I sent unto you, both rising up *e* ... Jer 26:5 7925
the prophets, rising up *e* ... Jer 29:19 7925
though I taught them, rising up *e* ... Jer 32:33 7925
I have spoken unto you, rising *e* ... Jer 35:14 7925
the prophets, rising up *e* ... Jer 35:15 7925
servants the prophets, rising *e* ... Jer 44:4 7925
king arose very *e* in the morning ... Dan 6:19 8238
affliction they will seek me *e* ... Hos 5:15 7836
as the *e* dew it goeth away ... Hos 6:4 7925
as the *e* dew that passeth away, ... Hos 13:3 7925
but they rose *e*, and corrupted all ... Zeph 3:7 7925
which went out *e* in the morning ... Mt 20:1 *260,4404*
very *e* in the morning the first ... Mk 16:2 *4404*
Now when Jesus was risen *e* the ... Mk 16:9 *4404*
all the people came *e* in the ... Lk 21:38 *3719*
very *e* in the morning, they came ... Lk 24:1 *3722*
which were *e* at the sepulchre ... Lk 24:22 *3721*
e in the morning he came again ... Jn 8:2 *3722*
of judgment: and it was *e* ... Jn 18:28 *4405*
the week cometh Mary Magdalene *e* ... Jn 20:1 *4404*
into the temple *e* in the morning ... Acts 5:21 *3722*
for it, until he receive the *e* ... Jas 5:7 *4406*

EARNEST {8}
For the *e* expectation of the ... Rom 8:19 *603*
given the *e* of the Spirit in our ... 2Cor 1:22 *728*
given unto us the *e* of the Spirit ... 2Cor 5:5 *728*
when he told us your *e* desire ... 2Cor 7:7 *1972*
which put the same *e* care into ... 2Cor 8:16 *4710*
Which is the *e* of our inheritance ... Eph 1:14 *728*
According to my *e* expectation ... Phil 1:20 *603*
we ought to give the more *e* heed ... Heb 2:1 *4056*

EARNESTLY {16}
Did I not *e* send unto thee to ... Num 22:37
David *e* asked leave of me that he ... 1Sa 20:6
David *e* asked leave of me to go ... 1Sa 20:28
Zabbai *e* repaired the other piece ... Neh 3:20 2734
As a servant *e* desireth the ... Job 7:2
For I *e* protested unto your ... Jer 11:7
I do *e* remember him still ... Jer 31:20
may do evil with both hands *e* ... Mic 7:3 3190
in an agony he prayed more *e* ... Lk 22:44 *1617*
e looked upon him, and said, This ... Lk 22:56 *816*
or why look ye so *e* on us ... Acts 3:12 *816*
e beholding the council, said, ... Acts 23:1 *816*
But covet *e* the best gifts ... 1Cor 12:31 *2206*
e desiring to be clothed upon ... 2Cor 5:2 *1971*
he prayed *e* that it might not ... Jas 5:17 *4335*
exhort you that ye should *e* ... Jude 3 *1864*

EARNETH {2}
he that *e* wages *e* wages to ... Hag 1:6 7936

EARRING {5}
golden *e* of half a shekel weight ... Gen 24:22 5141
came to pass, when he saw the *e* ... Gen 24:30 5141
I put the *e* upon her face, and the ... Gen 24:47 5141
money, and every one an *e* of gold ... Job 42:11 5141
As an *e* of gold, and an ornament ... Prov 25:12 5141

EARRINGS {12}
all their *e* which were in their ... Gen 35:4 5141
unto them, Break off the golden *e* ... Ex 32:2 5141
golden *e* which were in their ears ... Ex 32:3 5141
and brought bracelets, and *e* ... Ex 35:22 5141
chains, and bracelets, rings, *e* ... Num 31:50 5694
me every man the *e* of his prey ... Judg 8:24 5141
(For they had golden *e*, because ... Judg 8:24 5141
every man the *e* of his prey ... Judg 8:25 5141
golden *e* that he requested was a ... Judg 8:26 5141
and the tablets, and the *e* ... Is 3:20 3908
e in thine ears, and a beautiful ... Eze 16:12 5694
and she decked herself with her *e* ... Hos 2:13 5141

EARS {151}
told all these things in their *e* ... Gen 20:8 241
earrings which were in their *e* ... Gen 35:4 241
seven *e* of corn came up upon one ... Gen 41:5 7641
And, behold, seven thin *e* and ... Gen 41:6 7641
the seven thin *e* devoured the ... Gen 41:7 7641
devoured the seven rank and full *e* ... Gen 41:7 7641
seven *e* came up in one stalk, ... Gen 41:22 7641
And, behold, seven *e*, withered, ... Gen 41:23 7641
e devoured the seven good *e* ... Gen 41:24 7641
the seven good *e* are seven years ... Gen 41:26 7641
the seven empty *e* blasted with ... Gen 41:27 7641
thee, speak a word in my lord's *e* ... Gen 44:18 241
in the *e* of Pharaoh, saying, ... Gen 50:4 241
mayest tell in the *e* of thy son ... Ex 10:2 241
Speak now in the *e* of the people ... Ex 11:2 241
and rehearse it in the *e* of Joshua ... Ex 17:14 241
which are in the *e* of your wives ... Ex 32:2 241
earrings which were in their *e* ... Ex 32:3 241
of thy firstfruits green *e* of ... Lev 2:14 24
even corn beaten out of full *e* ... Lev 2:14 3759
nor parched corn, nor green *e* ... Lev 23:14 3759
ye have wept in the *e* of the LORD ... Num 11:18 241
LORD, as ye have spoken in mine *e* ... Num 14:28 241
which I speak in your *e* this day ... Deut 5:1 241
pluck the *e* with thine hand ... Deut 23:25 4425
see, and *e* to hear, unto this day ... Deut 29:4 241
may speak these words in their *e* ... Deut 31:28 241
Moses spake in the *e* of all the ... Deut 31:30 241
this song in the *e* of the people ... Deut 32:44 241
the *e* of the elders of that city ... Josh 20:4 241
proclaim in the *e* of the people ... Judg 7:3 241
in the *e* of all the men of ... Judg 9:2 241
brethren spake of him in the *e* of ... Judg 9:3 241
and spakest of also in mine *e* ... Judg 17:2 241
glean *e* of corn after him in ... Ruth 2:2 7641
at which both the *e* of every one ... 1Sa 3:11 241
them in the *e* of the LORD ... 1Sa 8:21 241
tidings in the *e* of the people ... 1Sa 11:4 241
bleating of the sheep in mine *e* ... 1Sa 15:14 241
those words in the *e* of David ... 1Sa 18:23 241
also spake in the *e* of Benjamin ... 2Sa 3:19 241
the *e* of David in Hebron all that ... 2Sa 3:19 241
all that we have heard with our *e* ... 2Sa 7:22 241
and my cry did enter into his *e* ... 2Sa 22:7 241
full *e* of corn in the husk ... 2Kin 4:42 3759
e of the people that are on the ... 2Kin 18:26 241
thy tumult is come up into mine *e* ... 2Kin 19:28 241
of it, both his *e* shall tingle ... 2Kin 21:12 241
he read in their *e* all the words ... 2Kin 23:2 241
all that we have heard with our *e* ... 1Chr 17:20 241
let thine *e* be attent unto the ... 2Chr 6:40 241
mine *e* attent unto the prayer ... 2Chr 7:15 241
he read in their *e* all the words ... 2Chr 34:30 241
the *e* of all the people were ... Neh 8:3 241
and my declaration with your *e* ... Job 13:17 241
A dreadful sound is in his *e* ... Job 15:21 241
off as the tops of the *e* of corn ... Job 24:24 7641
heard the fame thereof with our *e* ... Job 28:22 241
Then he openeth the *e* of men ... Job 33:16 241
and openeth their *e* in oppression ... Job 36:15 241
came before him, even into his *e* ... Ps 18:6 241
his *e* are open unto their cry ... Ps 34:15 241
mine *e* hast thou opened ... Ps 40:6 241
We have heard with our *e*, O God, ... Ps 44:1 241
incline your *e* to the words of my ... Ps 78:1 241
mine *e* shall hear my desire of ... Ps 92:11 241
They have *e*, but they hear not ... Ps 115:6 241
let thine *e* be attentive to the ... Ps 130:2 241
They have *e*, but they hear not ... Ps 135:17 241
Whoso stoppeth his *e* at the cry ... Prov 21:13 241
Speak not in the *e* of a fool ... Prov 23:9 241
thine *e* to the words of knowledge ... Prov 23:12 241
one that taketh a dog by the *e* ... Prov 26:17 241
In mine *e* said the LORD of hosts, ... Is 5:9 241
people fat, and make their *e* heavy ... Is 6:10 241
their eyes, and hear with their *e* ... Is 6:10 241
after the hearing of his *e* ... Is 11:3 241
reapeth the *e* with his arm ... Is 17:5 7641
e in the valley of Rephaim ... Is 17:5 7641
in mine *e* by the LORD of hosts ... Is 22:14 241
thine *e* shall hear a word behind ... Is 30:21 241
the *e* of them that hear shall ... Is 32:3 241
that stoppeth his *e* from hearing ... Is 33:15 241
the *e* of the deaf shall be ... Is 35:5 241
in the *e* of the people that are ... Is 36:11 241
tumult, is come up into mine *e* ... Is 37:29 241
opening the *e*, but he heareth not ... Is 42:20 241
eyes, and the deaf that have *e* ... Is 43:8 241
other, shall say again in thine *e* ... Is 49:20 241
cry in the *e* of Jerusalem, saying ... Jer 2:2 241
which have *e*, and hear not ... Jer 5:21 241
heareth, his *e* shall tingle ... Jer 19:3 241
as ye have heard with your *e* ... Jer 26:11 241
speak all these words in your *e* ... Jer 26:15 241
this word that I speak in thine *e* ... Jer 28:7 241
in the *e* of all the people ... Jer 28:7 241
in the *e* of Jeremiah the prophet ... Jer 29:29 241
the *e* of the people in the LORD's ... Jer 36:6 241
thou shalt read them in the *e* of ... Jer 36:6 241
in the *e* of all the people ... Jer 36:10 241
the book in the *e* of the people ... Jer 36:13 241
hast read in the *e* of the people ... Jer 36:14 241
Sit down now, and read it in our *e* ... Jer 36:15 241
So Baruch read it in their *e* ... Jer 36:15 241
the words in the *e* of the king ... Jer 36:20 241
read it in the *e* of the king ... Jer 36:21 241
in the *e* of all the princes which ... Jer 36:21 241
thine heart, and hear with thine *e* ... Eze 3:10 241
cry in mine *e* with a loud voice ... Eze 8:18 241
also in mine *e* with a loud voice ... Eze 9:1 241
they have *e* to hear, and hear not ... Eze 12:2 241
forehead, and earrings in thine *e* ... Eze 16:12 241
take away thy nose and thine *e* ... Eze 23:25 241
thee to hear it with thine *e* ... Eze 24:26 241
thine eyes, and hear with thine *e* ... Eze 40:4 241
hear with thine *e* all that I say ... Eze 44:5 241
mouth, their *e* shall be deaf ... Mic 7:16 241
the shoulder, and stopped their *e* ... Zec 7:11 241
He that hath *e* to hear, let him ... Mt 11:15 *3775*
and began to pluck the *e* of corn ... Mt 12:1 *4719*
Who hath *e* to hear, let him hear ... Mt 13:9 *3775*
their *e* are dull of hearing, and ... Mt 13:15 *3775*
their eyes, and hear with their *e* ... Mt 13:15 *3775*
and your *e*, for they hear ... Mt 13:16 *3775*
Who hath *e* to hear, let him hear ... Mt 13:43 *3775*

if this come to the governor's *e*	Mt 28:14	*191*
they went, to pluck the *e* of corn	Mk 2:23	*4719*
unto them, He that hath *e* to hear	Mk 4:9	*3775*
If any man have *e* to hear	Mk 4:23	*3775*
If any man have *e* to hear	Mk 7:16	*3775*
and put his fingers into his *e*	Mk 7:33	*3775*
And straightway his *e* were opened	Mk 7:35	*189*
and having *e*, hear ye not	Mk 8:18	*3775*
thy salutation sounded in mine *e*	Lk 1:44	*3775*
scripture fulfilled in your *e*	Lk 4:21	*3775*
disciples plucked the *e* of corn	Lk 6:1	*4719*
he cried, He that hath *e* to hear	Lk 8:8	*3775*
sayings sink down into your *e*	Lk 9:44	*3775*
He that hath *e* to hear, let him	Lk 14:35	*3775*
and uncircumcised in heart and *e*	Acts 7:51	*3775*
a loud voice, and stopped their *e*	Acts 7:57	*3775*
the *e* of the church which was in	Acts 11:22	*3775*
certain strange things to our *e*	Acts 17:20	*189*
their *e* are dull of hearing, and	Acts 28:27	*3775*
their eyes, and hear with their *e*	Acts 28:27	*3775*
e that they should not hear	Rom 11:8	*3775*
teachers, having itching *e*	2Ti 4:3	*189*
turn away their *e* from the truth	2Ti 4:4	*189*
into the *e* of the Lord of Sabaoth	Jas 5:4	*3775*
his *e* are open unto their prayers	1Pet 3:12	*3775*

EARTH {987}

God created the heaven and the *e*	Gen 1:1	776
the *e* was without form, and void	Gen 1:2	776
And God called the dry land *E*	Gen 1:10	776
Let the *e* bring forth grass, the	Gen 1:11	776
seed is in itself, upon the *e*	Gen 1:11	776
the *e* brought forth grass, and	Gen 1:12	776
heaven to give light upon the *e*	Gen 1:15	776
heaven to give light upon the *e*	Gen 1:17	776
fowl that may fly above the *e* in	Gen 1:20	776
and let fowl multiply in the *e*	Gen 1:22	776
Let the *e* bring forth the living	Gen 1:24	776
beast of the *e* after his kind	Gen 1:24	776
the beast of the *e* after his kind	Gen 1:25	776
upon the *e* after his kind	Gen 1:25	127
the cattle, and over all the *e*	Gen 1:26	776
thing that creepeth upon the *e*	Gen 1:26	776
and multiply, and replenish the *e*	Gen 1:28	776
thing that moveth upon the *e*	Gen 1:28	776
is upon the face of all the *e*	Gen 1:29	776
And to every beast of the *e*	Gen 1:30	776
thing that creepeth upon the *e*	Gen 1:30	776
the *e* were finished, and all the	Gen 2:1	776
of the *e* when they were created	Gen 2:4	776
day that the LORD God made the *e*	Gen 2:4	776
the field before it was in the *e*	Gen 2:5	776
not caused it to rain upon the *e*	Gen 2:5	776
there went up a mist from the *e*	Gen 2:6	776
And now art thou cursed from the *e*	Gen 4:11	127
a vagabond shalt thou be in the *e*	Gen 4:12	776
this day from the face of the *e*	Gen 4:14	127
a fugitive and a vagabond in the *e*	Gen 4:14	776
to multiply on the face of the *e*	Gen 6:1	127
giants in the *e* in those days	Gen 6:4	776
of man was great in the *e*	Gen 6:5	776
that he had made man on the *e*	Gen 6:6	776
created from the face of the *e*	Gen 6:7	127
The *e* also was corrupt before God	Gen 6:11	776
the *e* was filled with violence	Gen 6:11	776
And God looked upon the *e*, and	Gen 6:12	776
had corrupted his way upon the *e*	Gen 6:12	776
for the *e* is filled with violence	Gen 6:13	776
I will destroy them with the *e*	Gen 6:13	776
a flood of waters upon the *e*	Gen 6:17	776
thing that is in the *e* shall die	Gen 6:17	776
thing of the *e* after his kind	Gen 6:20	127
alive upon the face of all the *e*	Gen 7:3	776
it to rain upon the *e* forty days	Gen 7:4	776
from off the face of the *e*	Gen 7:4	127
flood of waters was upon the *e*	Gen 7:6	776
thing that creepeth upon the *e*	Gen 7:8	127
of the flood were upon the *e*	Gen 7:10	776
rain was upon the *e* forty days	Gen 7:12	776
upon the *e* after his kind	Gen 7:14	776
flood was forty days upon the *e*	Gen 7:17	776
and it was lift up above the *e*	Gen 7:17	776
were increased greatly upon the *e*	Gen 7:18	776
prevailed exceedingly upon the *e*	Gen 7:19	776
flesh died that moved upon the *e*	Gen 7:21	776
thing that creepeth upon the *e*	Gen 7:21	776
and they were destroyed from the *e*	Gen 7:23	776
prevailed upon the *e* an hundred	Gen 7:24	776
made a wind to pass over the *e*	Gen 8:1	776
from off the *e* continually	Gen 8:3	776
were dried up from off the *e*	Gen 8:7	776
were on the face of the whole *e*	Gen 8:9	776
waters were abated from off the *e*	Gen 8:11	776
were dried up from off the *e*	Gen 8:13	776
day of the month, was the *e* dried	Gen 8:14	776
thing that creepeth upon the *e*	Gen 8:17	776
may breed abundantly in the *e*	Gen 8:17	776
fruitful, and multiply upon the *e*	Gen 8:17	776
and whatsoever creepeth upon the *e*	Gen 8:19	776
While the *e* remaineth, seedtime	Gen 8:22	776
and multiply, and replenish the *e*	Gen 9:1	776
be upon every beast of the *e*	Gen 9:2	776
upon all that moveth upon the *e*	Gen 9:2	127
bring forth abundantly in the *e*	Gen 9:7	776
of every beast of the *e* with you	Gen 9:10	776
the ark, to every beast of the *e*	Gen 9:10	776
more be a flood to destroy the *e*	Gen 9:11	776
of a covenant between me and the *e*	Gen 9:13	776
when I bring a cloud over the *e*	Gen 9:14	776
of all flesh that is upon the *e*	Gen 9:16	776
and all flesh that is upon the *e*	Gen 9:17	776
them was the whole *e* overspread	Gen 9:19	776
began to be a mighty one in the *e*	Gen 10:8	776
for in his days was the *e* divided	Gen 10:25	776
divided in the *e* after the flood	Gen 10:32	776
the whole *e* was of one language,	Gen 11:1	776
upon the face of the whole *e*	Gen 11:4	776
thence upon the face of all the *e*	Gen 11:8	776
the language of all the *e*	Gen 11:9	776
abroad upon the face of all the *e*	Gen 11:9	776
all families of the *e* be blessed	Gen 12:3	127
thy seed as the dust of the *e*	Gen 13:16	776
man can number the dust of the *e*	Gen 13:16	776
God, possessor of heaven and *e*	Gen 14:19	776
God, the possessor of heaven and *e*	Gen 14:22	776
all the nations of the *e* shall be	Gen 18:18	776
the Judge of all the *e* do right	Gen 18:25	776
the *e* when Lot entered into Zoar	Gen 19:23	776
there is not a man in the *e* to	Gen 19:31	776
us after the manner of all the *e*	Gen 19:31	776
the nations of the *e* be blessed	Gen 22:18	776
of heaven, and the God of the *e*	Gen 24:3	776
the LORD, bowing himself to the *e*	Gen 24:52	776
the nations of the *e* be blessed	Gen 26:4	776
them, and filled them with *e*	Gen 26:15	6083
heaven, and the fatness of the *e*	Gen 27:28	776
shall be the fatness of the *e*	Gen 27:39	776
behold a ladder set up on the *e*	Gen 28:12	776
shall be as the dust of the *e*	Gen 28:14	776
the families of the *e* be blessed	Gen 28:14	127
down ourselves to thee to the *e*	Gen 37:10	776
the *e* brought forth by handfuls	Gen 41:47	776
was over all the face of the *e*	Gen 41:56	776
him with their faces to the *e*	Gen 42:6	776
bowed themselves to him to the *e*	Gen 43:26	776
preserve you a posterity in the *e*	Gen 45:7	776
himself with his face to the *e*	Gen 48:12	776
a multitude in the midst of the *e*	Gen 48:16	776
rod, and smote the dust of the *e*	Ex 8:17	776
am the LORD in the midst of the *e*	Ex 8:22	776
is none like me in all the *e*	Ex 9:14	776
thou shalt be cut off from the *e*	Ex 9:15	776
be declared throughout all the *e*	Ex 9:16	776
know how that the *e* is the LORD's	Ex 9:29	776
rain was not poured upon the *e*	Ex 9:33	776
shall cover the face of the *e*	Ex 10:5	776
one cannot be able to see the *e*	Ex 10:5	776
were upon the *e* unto this day	Ex 10:6	127
covered the face of the whole *e*	Ex 10:15	776
right hand, the *e* swallowed them	Ex 15:12	776
for all the *e* is mine	Ex 19:5	776
or that is in the *e* beneath	Ex 20:4	776
that is in the water under the *e*	Ex 20:4	776
days the LORD made heaven and *e*	Ex 20:11	776
An altar of *e* thou shalt make	Ex 20:24	127
days the LORD made heaven and *e*	Ex 31:17	776
them from the face of the *e*	Ex 32:12	127
that are upon the face of the *e*	Ex 33:16	127
and bowed his head toward the *e*	Ex 34:8	776
have not been done in all the *e*	Ex 34:10	776
all the beasts that are on the *e*	Lev 11:2	776
feet, to leap withal upon the *e*	Lev 11:21	776
things that creep upon the *e*	Lev 11:29	776
the *e* shall be an abomination	Lev 11:41	776
things that creep upon the *e*	Lev 11:42	776
thing that creepeth upon the *e*	Lev 11:44	776
creature that creepeth upon the *e*	Lev 11:46	776
And the vessel of *e*, that he	Lev 15:12	2789
as iron, and your *e* as brass	Lev 26:19	776
high upon the face of the *e*	Num 11:31	776
which were upon the face of the *e*	Num 12:3	127
all the *e* shall be filled with	Num 14:21	776
the *e* open her mouth, and swallow	Num 16:30	127
the *e* opened her mouth, and	Num 16:32	776
pit, and the *e* closed upon them	Num 16:33	776
Lest the *e* swallow us up also	Num 16:34	776
they cover the face of the *e*	Num 22:5	776
which covereth the face of the *e*	Num 22:11	776
the *e* opened her mouth, and	Num 26:10	776
God is there in heaven or in *e*	Deut 3:24	776
that they shall live upon the *e*	Deut 4:10	127
of any beast that is on the *e*	Deut 4:17	776
is in the waters beneath the *e*	Deut 4:18	776
e to witness against you this day	Deut 4:26	776
that God created man upon the *e*	Deut 4:32	776
upon *e* he shewed thee his great	Deut 4:36	776
above, and upon the *e* beneath	Deut 4:39	776
prolong thy days upon the *e*	Deut 4:40	127
or that is in the *e* beneath	Deut 5:8	776
is in the waters beneath the *e*	Deut 5:8	776
thee from off the face of the *e*	Deut 6:15	127
that are upon the face of the *e*	Deut 7:6	127
the *e* also, with all that therein	Deut 10:14	776
how the *e* opened her mouth, and	Deut 11:6	776
as the days of heaven upon the *e*	Deut 11:21	776
the days that ye live upon the *e*	Deut 12:1	127
shall pour it upon the *e* as water	Deut 12:16	776
as long as thou livest upon the *e*	Deut 12:19	127
shalt pour it upon the *e* as water	Deut 12:24	776
from the one end of the *e* even	Deut 13:7	776
even unto the other end of the *e*	Deut 13:7	776
the nations that are upon the *e*	Deut 14:2	127
first of all the fruit of the *e*	Deut 26:2	127
high above all nations of the *e*	Deut 28:1	776
all people of the *e* shall see	Deut 28:10	776
the *e* that is under thee shall be	Deut 28:23	776
into all the kingdoms of the *e*	Deut 28:25	776
air, and unto the beasts of the *e*	Deut 28:26	776
from far, from the end of the *e*	Deut 28:49	776
end of the *e* even unto the other	Deut 28:64	776
e to record this day against you,	Deut 30:19	776
and *e* to record against them	Deut 31:28	776
and hear, O *e*, the words of my	Deut 32:1	776
ride on the high places of the *e*	Deut 32:13	776
consume the *e* with her increase	Deut 32:22	776
for the precious things of the *e*	Deut 33:16	776
together to the ends of the *e*	Deut 33:17	776
in heaven above, and in *e* beneath	Josh 2:11	776
e passeth over before you into	Josh 3:11	776
the LORD, the Lord of all the *e*	Josh 3:13	776
That all the people of the *e*	Josh 4:24	776
Joshua fell on his face to the *e*	Josh 5:14	776
fell to the *e* upon his face	Josh 7:6	776
and cut off our name from the *e*	Josh 7:9	776
they are hid in the *e* in the	Josh 7:21	776
I am going the way of all the *e*	Josh 23:14	776
was fallen down dead on the *e*	Judg 3:25	776
the *e* trembled, and the heavens	Judg 5:4	776
destroyed the increase of the *e*	Judg 6:4	776
it be dry upon all the *e* beside	Judg 6:37	776
of any thing that is in the *e*	Judg 18:10	776
pillars of the *e* are the LORD's	1Sa 2:8	776
shall judge the ends of the *e*	1Sa 2:10	776
shout, so that the *e* rang again	1Sa 4:5	776
rent, and with *e* upon his head	1Sa 4:12	127
the *e* before the ark of the LORD	1Sa 5:3	776
also trembled, and the *e* quaked	1Sa 14:15	776
and to the wild beasts of the *e*	1Sa 17:46	776
that all the *e* may know that	1Sa 17:46	776
and he fell upon his face to the *e*	1Sa 17:49	776
every one from the face of the *e*	1Sa 20:15	127
stooped with his face to the *e*	1Sa 24:8	776
herself on her face to the *e*	1Sa 25:41	776
the spear even to the *e* at once	1Sa 26:8	776
the *e* before the face of the LORD	1Sa 26:20	776
I saw gods ascending out of the *e*	1Sa 28:13	776
straightway all along on the *e*	1Sa 28:20	776
So he arose from the *e*, and sat	1Sa 28:23	776
were spread abroad upon all the *e*	1Sa 30:16	776
clothes rent, and *e* upon his head	2Sa 1:2	127
to David, that he fell to the *e*	2Sa 1:2	776
hand, and take you away from the *e*	2Sa 4:11	776
the great men that are in the *e*	2Sa 7:9	776
in the *e* is like thy people	2Sa 7:23	776
in, and lay all night upon the *e*	2Sa 12:16	776
him, to raise him up from the *e*	2Sa 12:17	776
Then David arose from the *e*	2Sa 12:20	776
his garments, and lay on the *e*	2Sa 13:31	776
name nor remainder upon the *e*	2Sa 14:7	127
one hair of thy son fall to the *e*	2Sa 14:11	776
know all things that are in the *e*	2Sa 14:20	776
his coat rent, and *e* upon his head	2Sa 15:32	127
up between the heaven and the *e*	2Sa 18:9	776
he fell down to the *e* upon his	2Sa 18:28	776
Then the *e* shook and trembled	2Sa 22:8	776
as small as the dust of the *e*	2Sa 22:43	776
grass springing out of the *e* by	2Sa 23:4	776
bowed with her face to the *e*	1Kin 1:31	776
so that the *e* rent with the sound	1Kin 1:40	776
not an hair of him fall to the *e*	1Kin 1:52	776
I go the way of all the *e*	1Kin 2:2	776
Solomon, from all kings of the *e*	1Kin 4:34	776
or on *e* beneath, who keepest	1Kin 8:23	776
will God indeed dwell on the *e*	1Kin 8:27	776
people of the *e* may know thy name	1Kin 8:43	776
among all the people of the *e*	1Kin 8:53	776
That all the people of the *e* may	1Kin 8:60	776
all the kings of the *e* for riches	1Kin 10:23	776
all the *e* sought to Solomon, to	1Kin 10:24	776
it from off the face of the *e*	1Kin 13:34	127
the LORD sendeth rain upon the *e*	1Kin 17:14	127
and I will send rain upon the *e*	1Kin 18:1	127
he cast himself down upon the *e*	1Kin 18:42	776
that there is no God in all the *e*	2Kin 5:15	776
servant two mules' burden of *e*	2Kin 5:17	127
that there shall fall unto the *e*	2Kin 10:10	776
of all the kingdoms of the *e*	2Kin 19:15	776
thou hast made heaven and *e*	2Kin 19:15	776
that all the kingdoms of the *e*	2Kin 19:19	776
he began to be mighty upon the *e*	1Chr 1:10	776
in his days the *e* was divided	1Chr 1:19	776
his judgments are in all the *e*	1Chr 16:14	776
Sing unto the LORD, all the *e*	1Chr 16:23	776
Fear before him, all the *e*	1Chr 16:30	776
be glad, and let the *e* rejoice	1Chr 16:31	776
because he cometh to judge the *e*	1Chr 16:33	776
the great men that are in the *e*	1Chr 17:8	776
what one nation in the *e* is like	1Chr 17:21	776
of the LORD stand between the *e*	1Chr 21:16	776
much blood upon the *e* in my sight	1Chr 22:8	776
the heaven and in the *e* is thine	1Chr 29:11	776
our days on the *e* are as a shadow	1Chr 29:15	776
the dust of the *e* in multitude	2Chr 1:9	776
of Israel, that made heaven and *e*	2Chr 2:12	776
thee in the heaven, nor in the *e*	2Chr 6:14	776
very deed dwell with men on the *e*	2Chr 6:18	776
people of the *e* may know thy name	2Chr 6:33	776
all the kings of the *e* in riches	2Chr 9:22	776
all the kings of the *e* sought the	2Chr 9:23	776
to and fro throughout the whole *e*	2Chr 16:9	776
were dead bodies fallen to the *e*	2Chr 20:24	776
the gods of the people of the *e*	2Chr 32:19	776
All the kingdoms of the *e* hath	2Chr 36:23	776
me all the kingdoms of the *e*	Ezr 1:2	776

Context	Reference	No.
of the God of heaven and *e*	Ezr 5:11	772
with sackclothes, and *e* upon them	Neh 9:1	127
with all their host, the *e*	Neh 9:6	776
From going to and fro in the *e*	Job 1:7	776
there is none like him in the *e*	Job 1:8	776
From going to and fro in the *e*	Job 2:2	776
there is none like him in the *e*	Job 2:3	776
kings and counsellors of the *e*	Job 3:14	776
Who giveth rain upon the *e*	Job 5:10	776
be afraid of the beasts of the *e*	Job 5:22	776
offspring as the grass of the *e*	Job 5:25	776
an appointed time to man upon *e*	Job 7:1	776
our days upon *e* are a shadow	Job 8:9	776
out of the *e* shall others grow	Job 8:19	6083
shaketh the *e* out of her place	Job 9:6	776
The *e* is given into the hand of	Job 9:24	776
thereof is longer than the *e*	Job 11:9	776
Or speak to the *e*, and it shall	Job 12:8	776
them out, and they overturn the *e*	Job 12:15	776
the chief of the people of the *e*	Job 12:24	776
the root thereof wax old in the *e*	Job 14:8	776
grow out of the dust of the *e*	Job 14:19	776
Unto whom alone the *e* was given	Job 15:19	776
the perfection thereof upon the *e*	Job 15:29	776
O *e*, cover not thou my blood, and	Job 16:18	776
shall the *e* be forsaken for thee	Job 18:4	776
shall perish from the *e*, and he	Job 18:17	776
at the latter day upon the *e*	Job 19:25	6083
old, since man was placed upon *e*	Job 20:4	776
the *e* shall rise up against him	Job 20:27	776
for the mighty man, he had the *e*	Job 22:8	776
the poor of the *e* hide themselves	Job 24:4	776
their portion is cursed in the *e*	Job 24:18	776
hangeth the *e* upon nothing	Job 26:7	776
Iron is taken out of the *e*	Job 28:2	6083
As for the *e*, out of it cometh	Job 28:5	776
he looketh to the ends of the *e*	Job 28:24	776
of the valleys, in caves of the *e*	Job 30:6	6083
they were viler than the *e*	Job 30:8	776
given him a charge over the *e*	Job 34:13	776
us more than the beasts of the *e*	Job 35:11	776
lightning unto the ends of the *e*	Job 37:3	776
to the snow, Be thou on the *e*	Job 37:6	776
the face of the world in the *e*	Job 37:12	776
quieteth the *e* by the south wind	Job 37:17	776
I laid the foundations of the *e*	Job 38:4	776
take hold of the ends of the *e*	Job 38:13	776
perceived the breadth of the *e*	Job 38:18	776
the east wind upon the *e*	Job 38:24	776
To cause it to rain on the *e*	Job 38:26	776
set the dominion thereof in the *e*	Job 38:33	776
Which leaveth her eggs in the *e*	Job 39:14	776
Upon *e* there is not his like, who	Job 41:33	6083
The kings of the *e* set themselves	Ps 2:2	776
parts of the *e* for thy possession	Ps 2:8	776
be instructed, ye judges of the *e*	Ps 2:10	776
him tread down my life upon the *e*	Ps 7:5	776
is thy name in all the *e*	Ps 8:1	776
is thy name in all the *e*	Ps 8:9	776
man of the *e* may no more oppress	Ps 10:18	776
as silver tried in a furnace of *e*	Ps 12:6	776
to the saints that are in the *e*	Ps 16:3	776
their eyes bowing down to the *e*	Ps 17:11	776
Then the *e* shook and trembled	Ps 18:7	776
is gone out through all the *e*	Ps 19:4	776
shalt thou destroy from the *e*	Ps 21:10	776
they that be fat upon *e* shall eat	Ps 22:29	776
The *e* is the LORD's, and the	Ps 24:1	776
and his seed shall inherit the *e*	Ps 25:13	776
the *e* is full of the goodness of	Ps 33:5	776
Let all the *e* fear the LORD	Ps 33:8	776
upon all the inhabitants of the *e*	Ps 33:14	776
remembrance of them from the *e*	Ps 34:16	776
LORD, they shall inherit the *e*	Ps 37:9	776
But the meek shall inherit the *e*	Ps 37:11	776
of him shall inherit the *e*	Ps 37:22	776
and he shall be blessed upon the *e*	Ps 41:2	776
our belly cleaveth unto the *e*	Ps 44:25	776
mayest make princes in all the *e*	Ps 45:16	776
we fear, though the *e* be removed	Ps 46:2	776
uttered his voice, the *e* melted	Ps 46:6	776
desolations he hath made in the *e*	Ps 46:8	776
to cease unto the end of the *e*	Ps 46:9	776
I will be exalted in the *e*	Ps 46:10	776
he is a great King over all the *e*	Ps 47:2	776
For God is the King of all the *e*	Ps 47:7	776
shields of the *e* belong unto God	Ps 47:9	776
situation, the joy of the whole *e*	Ps 48:2	776
thy praise unto the ends of the *e*	Ps 48:10	776
called the *e* from the rising of	Ps 50:1	776
heavens from above, and to the *e*	Ps 50:4	776
let thy glory be above all the *e*	Ps 57:5	776
let thy glory be above all the *e*	Ps 57:11	776
violence of your hands in the *e*	Ps 58:2	776
he is a God that judgeth in the *e*	Ps 58:11	776
in Jacob unto the ends of the *e*	Ps 59:13	776
Thou hast made the *e* to tremble	Ps 60:2	776
From the end of the *e* will I cry	Ps 61:2	776
go into the lower parts of the *e*	Ps 63:9	776
of all the ends of the *e*, and of	Ps 65:5	776
Thou visitest the *e*, and waterest	Ps 65:9	776
All the *e* shall worship thee, and	Ps 66:4	776
That thy way may be known upon *e*	Ps 67:2	776
and govern the nations upon *e*	Ps 67:4	776
Then shall the *e* yield her	Ps 67:6	776
the ends of the *e* shall fear him	Ps 67:7	776
The *e* shook, the heavens also	Ps 68:8	776
unto God, ye kingdoms of the *e*	Ps 68:32	776
e praise him, the seas, and every	Ps 69:34	776
up again from the depths of the *e*	Ps 71:20	776
as showers that water the *e*	Ps 72:6	776
the river unto the ends of the *e*	Ps 72:8	776
be an handful of corn in the *e*	Ps 72:16	776
flourish like grass of the *e*	Ps 72:16	776
let the whole *e* be filled with	Ps 72:19	776
tongue walketh through the *e*	Ps 73:9	776
there is none upon *e* that I	Ps 73:25	776
salvation in the midst of the *e*	Ps 74:12	776
hast set all the borders of the *e*	Ps 74:17	776
for the dark places of the *e* are	Ps 74:20	776
The *e* and all the inhabitants	Ps 75:3	776
of the *e* shall wring them out	Ps 75:8	776
the *e* feared, and was still,	Ps 76:8	776
to save all the meek of the *e*	Ps 76:9	776
is terrible to the kings of the *e*	Ps 76:12	776
the *e* trembled and shook	Ps 77:18	776
palaces, like the *e* which he hath	Ps 78:69	776
saints unto the beasts of the *e*	Ps 79:2	776
of the *e* are out of course	Ps 82:5	776
Arise, O God, judge the *e*	Ps 82:8	776
they became as dung for the *e*	Ps 83:10	127
art the most high over all the *e*	Ps 83:18	776
Truth shall spring out of the *e*	Ps 85:11	776
are thine, the *e* also is thine	Ps 89:11	776
higher than the kings of the *e*	Ps 89:27	776
or ever thou hadst formed the *e*	Ps 90:2	776
up thyself, thou judge of the *e*	Ps 94:2	776
hand are the deep places of the *e*	Ps 95:4	776
sing unto the LORD, all the *e*	Ps 96:1	776
fear before him, all the *e*	Ps 96:9	776
rejoice, and let the *e* be glad	Ps 96:11	776
for he cometh to judge the *e*	Ps 96:13	776
let the *e* rejoice	Ps 97:1	776
the *e* saw, and trembled	Ps 97:4	776
of the LORD of the whole *e*	Ps 97:5	776
LORD, art high above all the *e*	Ps 97:9	776
all the ends of the *e* have seen	Ps 98:3	776
noise unto the LORD, all the *e*	Ps 98:4	776
for he cometh to judge the *e*	Ps 98:9	776
let the *e* be moved	Ps 99:1	776
all the kings of the *e* thy glory	Ps 102:15	776
heaven did the LORD behold the *e*	Ps 102:19	776
thou laid the foundation of the *e*	Ps 102:25	776
as the heaven is high above the *e*	Ps 103:11	776
Who laid the foundations of the *e*	Ps 104:5	776
turn not again to cover the *e*	Ps 104:9	776
the *e* is satisfied with the fruit	Ps 104:13	776
may bring forth food out of the *e*	Ps 104:14	776
the *e* is full of thy riches	Ps 104:24	776
thou renewest the face of the *e*	Ps 104:30	127
He looketh on the *e*, and it	Ps 104:32	776
sinners be consumed out of the *e*	Ps 104:35	776
his judgments are in all the *e*	Ps 105:7	776
The *e* opened and swallowed up	Ps 106:17	776
and thy glory above all the *e*	Ps 108:5	776
off the memory of them from the *e*	Ps 109:15	776
His seed shall be mighty upon *e*	Ps 112:2	776
that are in heaven, and in the *e*	Ps 113:6	776
Tremble, thou *e*, at the presence	Ps 114:7	776
the LORD which made heaven and *e*	Ps 115:15	776
but the *e* hath he given to the	Ps 115:16	776
I am a stranger in the *e*	Ps 119:19	776
The *e*, O LORD, is full of thy	Ps 119:64	776
had almost consumed me upon *e*	Ps 119:87	776
thou hast established the *e*	Ps 119:90	776
the wicked of the *e* like dross	Ps 119:119	776
the LORD, which made heaven and *e*	Ps 121:2	776
of the LORD, who made heaven and *e*	Ps 124:8	776
and *e* bless thee out of Zion	Ps 134:3	776
that did he in heaven, and in *e*	Ps 135:6	776
to ascend from the ends of the *e*	Ps 135:7	776
out the *e* above the waters	Ps 136:6	776
kings of the *e* shall praise thee	Ps 138:4	776
in the lowest parts of the *e*	Ps 139:15	776
speaker be established in the *e*	Ps 140:11	776
and cleaveth wood upon the *e*	Ps 141:7	776
forth, he returneth to his *e*	Ps 146:4	127
Which made heaven, and *e*, the sea,	Ps 146:6	776
who prepareth rain for the *e*	Ps 147:8	776
forth his commandment upon *e*	Ps 147:15	776
Praise the LORD from the *e*	Ps 148:7	776
Kings of the *e*, and all people	Ps 148:11	776
princes, and all judges of the *e*	Ps 148:11	776
his glory is above the *e* and	Ps 148:13	776
shall be cut off from the *e*	Prov 2:22	776
LORD by wisdom hath founded the *e*	Prov 3:19	776
even all the judges of the *e*	Prov 8:16	776
the beginning, or ever the *e* was	Prov 8:23	776
as yet he had not made the *e*	Prov 8:26	776
the foundations of the *e*	Prov 8:29	776
in the habitable part of his *e*	Prov 8:31	776
wicked shall not inhabit the *e*	Prov 10:30	776
shall be recompensed in the *e*	Prov 11:31	776
a fool are in the ends of the *e*	Prov 17:24	776
the *e* for depth, and the heart of	Prov 25:3	776
established all the ends of the *e*	Prov 30:4	776
to devour the poor from off the *e*	Prov 30:14	776
the *e* that is not filled with	Prov 30:16	776
three things the *e* is disquieted	Prov 30:21	776
which are little upon the *e*	Prov 30:24	776
but the *e* abideth for ever	Eccl 1:4	776
that goeth downward to the *e*	Eccl 3:21	776
God is in heaven, and thou upon *e*	Eccl 5:2	776
the profit of the *e* is for all	Eccl 5:9	776
there is not a just man upon *e*	Eccl 7:20	776
a vanity which is done upon the *e*	Eccl 8:14	776
business that is done upon the *e*	Eccl 8:16	776
walking as servants upon the *e*	Eccl 10:7	776
not what evil shall be upon the *e*	Eccl 11:2	776
they empty themselves upon the *e*	Eccl 11:3	776
dust return to the *e* as it was	Eccl 12:7	776
The flowers appear on the *e*	Song 2:12	776
Hear, O heavens, and give ear, O *e*	Is 1:2	776
rocks, and into the caves of the *e*	Is 2:19	6083
ariseth to shake terribly the *e*	Is 2:19	776
ariseth to shake terribly the *e*	Is 2:21	776
the fruit of the *e* shall be	Is 4:2	776
alone in the midst of the *e*	Is 5:8	776
unto them from the end of the *e*	Is 5:26	776
the whole *e* is full of his glory	Is 6:3	776
And they shall look unto the *e*	Is 8:22	776
left, have I gathered all the *e*	Is 10:14	776
with equity for the meek of the *e*	Is 11:4	776
he shall smite the *e* with the rod	Is 11:4	776
for the *e* shall be full of the	Is 11:9	776
from the four corners of the *e*	Is 11:12	776
this is known in all the *e*	Is 12:5	776
the *e* shall remove out of her	Is 13:13	776
The whole *e* is at rest, and is	Is 14:7	776
even all the chief ones of the *e*	Is 14:9	776
man that made the *e* to tremble	Is 14:16	776
that is purposed upon the whole *e*	Is 14:26	776
the world, and dwellers on the *e*	Is 18:3	776
and to the beasts of the *e*	Is 18:6	776
all the beasts of the *e* shall	Is 18:6	776
are the honourable of the *e*	Is 23:8	776
all the honourable of the *e*	Is 23:9	776
the world upon the face of the *e*	Is 23:17	127
the LORD maketh the *e* empty	Is 24:1	776
The *e* mourneth and fadeth away,	Is 24:4	776
people of the *e* do languish	Is 24:4	776
The *e* also is defiled under the	Is 24:5	776
hath the curse devoured the *e*	Is 24:6	776
inhabitants of the *e* are burned	Is 24:6	776
part of the *e* have we heard songs	Is 24:16	776
upon thee, O inhabitant of the *e*	Is 24:17	776
the foundations of the *e* do shake	Is 24:18	776
The *e* is utterly broken down	Is 24:19	776
the *e* is clean dissolved, the	Is 24:19	776
the *e* is moved exceedingly	Is 24:19	776
The *e* shall reel to and fro like a	Is 24:20	776
the kings of the *e* upon the *e*	Is 24:21	127
he take away from off all the *e*	Is 25:8	776
when thy judgments are in the *e*	Is 26:9	776
it far unto all the ends of the *e*	Is 26:15	776
wrought any deliverance in the *e*	Is 26:18	776
the *e* shall cast out the dead	Is 26:19	776
of the *e* for their iniquity	Is 26:21	776
the *e* also shall disclose her	Is 26:21	776
cast down to the *e* with the hand	Is 28:2	776
even determined upon the whole *e*	Is 28:22	776
and bread of the increase of the *e*	Is 30:23	127
The *e* mourneth and languisheth	Is 33:9	776
let the *e* hear, and all that is	Is 34:1	776
of all the kingdoms of the *e*	Is 37:16	776
thou hast made heaven and *e*	Is 37:16	776
that all the kingdoms of the *e*	Is 37:20	776
the dust of the *e* in a measure	Is 40:12	776
from the foundations of the *e*	Is 40:21	776
sitteth upon the circle of the *e*	Is 40:22	776
the judges of the *e* as vanity	Is 40:23	776
shall not take root in the *e*	Is 40:24	776
the Creator of the ends of the *e*	Is 40:28	776
the ends of the *e* were afraid	Is 41:5	776
have taken from the ends of the *e*	Is 41:9	776
he have set judgment in the *e*	Is 42:4	776
he that spread forth the *e*	Is 42:5	776
his praise from the end of the *e*	Is 42:10	776
daughters from the ends of the *e*	Is 43:6	776
shout, ye lower parts of the *e*	Is 44:23	776
spreadeth abroad the *e* by myself	Is 44:24	776
let the *e* open, and let them bring	Is 45:8	776
with the potsherds of the *e*	Is 45:9	127
I have made the *e*, and created man	Is 45:12	776
God himself that formed the *e*	Is 45:18	776
secret, in a dark place of the *e*	Is 45:19	776
ye saved, all the ends of the *e*	Is 45:22	776
hath laid the foundation of the *e*	Is 48:13	776
utter it even to the end of the *e*	Is 48:20	776
salvation unto the end of the *e*	Is 49:6	776
of the people, to establish the *e*	Is 49:8	776
and be joyful, O *e*	Is 49:13	776
thee with their face toward the *e*	Is 49:23	776
and look upon the *e* beneath	Is 51:6	776
the *e* shall wax old like a	Is 51:6	776
and laid the foundations of the *e*	Is 51:13	776
and lay the foundations of the *e*	Is 51:16	776
all the ends of the *e* shall see	Is 52:10	776
of the whole *e* shall he be called	Is 54:5	776
Noah should no more go over the *e*	Is 54:9	776
the heavens are higher than the *e*	Is 55:9	776
not thither, but watereth the *e*	Is 55:10	776
upon the high places of the *e*	Is 58:14	776
the darkness shall cover the *e*	Is 60:2	776
For as the *e* bringeth forth her	Is 61:11	776
make Jerusalem a praise in the *e*	Is 62:7	776
down their strength to the *e*	Is 63:6	776
e shall bless himself in the God	Is 65:16	776
he that sweareth in the *e* shall	Is 65:16	776
I create new heavens and a new *e*	Is 65:17	776
throne, and the *e* is my footstool	Is 66:1	776
Shall the *e* be made to bring	Is 66:8	776
as the new heavens and the new *e*	Is 66:22	776
I beheld the *e*, and, lo, it was	Jer 4:23	776

Context	Reference	Number
For this shall the *e* mourn	Jer 4:28	776
Hear, O *e*:	Jer 6:19	776
be raised from the sides of the *e*	Jer 6:22	776
and for the beasts of the *e*	Jer 7:33	776
for dung upon the face of the *e*	Jer 8:2	127
valiant for the truth upon the *e*	Jer 9:3	776
and righteousness, in the *e*	Jer 9:24	776
at his wrath the *e* shall tremble	Jer 10:10	776
not made the heavens and the *e*	Jer 10:11	778
even they shall perish from the *e*	Jer 10:11	772
He hath made the *e* by his power	Jer 10:12	776
to ascend from the ends of the *e*	Jer 10:13	776
for there was no rain in the *e*	Jer 14:4	776
heaven, and the beasts of the *e*	Jer 15:3	776
into all kingdoms of the *e*	Jer 15:4	776
man of contention to the whole *e*	Jer 15:10	776
be as dung upon the face of the *e*	Jer 16:4	127
and for the beasts of the *e*	Jer 16:4	776
unto thee from the ends of the *e*	Jer 16:19	776
from me shall be written in the *e*	Jer 17:13	776
and for the beasts of the *e*	Jer 19:7	776
O *e*, *e*, *e*, hear the word	Jer 22:29	776
judgment and justice in the *e*	Jer 23:5	776
Do not I fill heaven and *e*	Jer 23:24	776
kingdoms of the *e* for their hurt	Jer 24:9	776
which are upon the face of the *e*	Jer 25:26	127
upon all the inhabitants of the *e*	Jer 25:29	776
all the inhabitants of the *e*	Jer 25:30	776
come even to the ends of the *e*	Jer 25:31	776
up from the coasts of the *e*	Jer 25:32	776
day from one end of the *e*	Jer 25:33	776
even unto the other end of the *e*	Jer 25:33	776
curse to all the nations of the *e*	Jer 26:6	776
I have made the *e*, the man and the	Jer 27:5	776
thee from off the face of the *e*	Jer 28:16	127
to all the kingdoms of the *e*	Jer 29:18	776
them from the coasts of the *e*	Jer 31:8	776
hath created a new thing in the *e*	Jer 31:22	776
of the *e* searched out beneath	Jer 31:37	776
the *e* by thy great power and	Jer 32:17	776
before all the nations of the *e*	Jer 33:9	776
the ordinances of heaven and *e*	Jer 33:25	776
kingdoms of the *e* of his dominion	Jer 34:1	776
into all the kingdoms of the *e*	Jer 34:17	776
heaven, and to the beasts of the *e*	Jer 34:20	776
among all the nations of the *e*	Jer 44:8	776
I will go up, and will cover the *e*	Jer 46:8	776
The *e* is moved at the noise of	Jer 49:21	776
of the whole *e* cut in asunder	Jer 50:23	776
up from the coasts of the *e*	Jer 50:41	776
taking of Babylon the *e* is moved	Jer 50:46	776
hand, that made all the *e* drunken	Jer 51:7	776
He hath made the *e* by his power	Jer 51:15	776
to ascend from the ends of the *e*	Jer 51:16	776
LORD, which destroyest all the *e*	Jer 51:25	776
praise of the whole *e* surprised	Jer 51:41	776
Then the heaven and the *e*, and all	Jer 51:48	776
shall fall the slain of all the *e*	Jer 51:49	776
unto the *e* the beauty of Israel	Lam 2:1	776
my liver is poured upon the *e*	Lam 2:11	776
of beauty, The joy of the whole *e*	Lam 2:15	776
feet all the prisoners of the *e*	Lam 3:34	776
The kings of the *e*, and all the	Lam 4:12	776
the *e* by the living creatures	Eze 1:15	776
were lifted up from the *e*	Eze 1:19	776
those were lifted up from the *e*	Eze 1:21	776
the wicked of the *e* for a spoil	Eze 7:21	776
spirit lifted me up between the *e*	Eze 8:3	776
the LORD hath forsaken the *e*	Eze 8:12	776
say, The LORD hath forsaken the *e*	Eze 9:9	776
wings to mount up from the *e*	Eze 10:16	776
mounted up from the *e* in my sight	Eze 10:19	776
thee in the low parts of the *e*	Eze 26:20	776
the *e* with the multitude of thy	Eze 27:33	776
bring thee to ashes upon the *e* in	Eze 28:18	776
all the people of the *e* are gone	Eze 31:12	776
to the nether parts of the *e*	Eze 31:14	776
in the nether parts of the *e*	Eze 31:16	776
unto the nether parts of the *e*	Eze 31:18	776
beasts of the whole *e* with thee	Eze 32:4	776
unto the nether parts of the *e*	Eze 32:18	776
into the nether parts of the *e*	Eze 32:24	776
upon all the face of the *e*	Eze 34:6	776
the *e* shall yield her increase,	Eze 34:27	776
When the whole *e* rejoiceth	Eze 35:14	776
things that creep upon the *e*	Eze 38:20	127
that are upon the face of the *e*	Eze 38:20	127
remain upon the face of the *e*	Eze 39:14	776
the blood of the princes of the *e*	Eze 39:18	776
the *e* shined with his glory	Eze 43:2	776
There is not a man upon the *e*	Dan 2:10	3007
mountain, and filled the whole *e*	Dan 2:35	772
shall bear rule over all the *e*	Dan 2:39	772
that dwell in all the *e*	Dan 4:1	772
a tree in the midst of the *e*	Dan 4:10	772
thereof to the end of all the *e*	Dan 4:11	772
the stump of his roots in the *e*	Dan 4:15	772
the beasts in the grass of the *e*	Dan 4:15	772
and the sight thereof to all the *e*	Dan 4:20	772
thy dominion to the end of the *e*	Dan 4:22	772
of the roots thereof in the *e*	Dan 4:23	772
of the *e* are reputed as nothing	Dan 4:35	772
and among the inhabitants of the *e*	Dan 4:35	772
that dwell in all the *e*	Dan 6:25	772
and wonders in heaven and in *e*	Dan 6:27	772
and it was lifted up from the *e*	Dan 7:4	772
which shall arise out of the *e*	Dan 7:17	772
be the fourth kingdom upon *e*	Dan 7:23	772
and shall devour the whole *e*	Dan 7:23	772
west on the face of the whole *e*	Dan 8:5	776
in the dust of the *e* shall awake	Dan 12:2	127
sword and the battle out of the *e*	Hos 2:18	776
heavens, and they shall hear the *e*	Hos 2:21	776
the *e* shall hear the corn, and the	Hos 2:22	776
I will sow her unto me in the *e*	Hos 2:23	776
latter and former rain unto the *e*	Hos 6:3	776
The *e* shall quake before them	Joel 2:10	776
in the heavens and in the *e*	Joel 2:30	776
the heavens and the *e* shall shake	Joel 3:16	776
of the *e* on the head of the poor	Amos 2:7	776
of all the families of the *e*	Amos 3:2	127
a bird fall in a snare upon the *e*	Amos 3:5	776
one take up a snare from the *e*	Amos 3:5	127
upon the high places of the *e*	Amos 4:13	776
leave off righteousness in the *e*	Amos 5:7	776
them out upon the face of the *e*	Amos 5:8	776
darken the *e* in the clear day	Amos 8:9	776
hath founded his troop in the *e*	Amos 9:6	776
them out upon the face of the *e*	Amos 9:6	776
it from off the face of the *e*	Amos 9:8	127
the least grain fall upon the *e*	Amos 9:9	776
the *e* with her bars was about me	Jonah 2:6	776
hearken, O *e*, and all that therein	Mic 1:2	776
upon the high places of the *e*	Mic 1:3	776
unto the Lord of the whole *e*	Mic 4:13	776
be great unto the ends of the *e*	Mic 5:4	776
and ye strong foundations of the *e*	Mic 6:2	776
good man is perished out of the *e*	Mic 7:2	776
their holes like worms of the *e*	Mic 7:17	776
the *e* is burned at his presence,	Nah 1:5	776
will cut off thy prey from the *e*	Nah 2:13	776
For the *e* shall be filled with	Hab 2:14	776
let all the *e* keep silence before	Hab 2:20	776
the *e* was full of his praise	Hab 3:3	776
He stood, and measured the *e*	Hab 3:6	776
didst cleave the *e* with rivers	Hab 3:9	776
ye the LORD, all ye meek of the *e*	Zeph 2:3	776
will famish all the gods of the *e*	Zeph 2:11	776
for all the *e* shall be devoured	Zeph 3:8	776
praise among all people of the *e*	Zeph 3:20	776
the *e* is stayed from her fruit	Hag 1:10	776
will shake the heavens, and the *e*	Hag 2:6	776
I will shake the heavens and the *e*	Hag 2:21	776
to walk to and fro through the *e*	Zec 1:10	776
walked to and fro through the *e*	Zec 1:11	776
all the *e* sitteth still, and is at	Zec 1:11	776
run to and fro through the whole *e*	Zec 4:10	776
stand by the Lord of the whole *e*	Zec 4:14	776
over the face of the whole *e*	Zec 5:3	776
resemblance through all the *e*	Zec 5:6	776
lifted up the ephah between the *e*	Zec 5:9	776
before the Lord of all the *e*	Zec 6:5	776
walk to and fro through the *e*	Zec 6:7	776
walk to and fro through the *e*	Zec 6:7	776
walked to and fro through the *e*	Zec 6:7	776
river even to the ends of the *e*	Zec 9:10	776
and layeth the foundation of the *e*	Zec 12:1	776
though all the people of the *e* be	Zec 12:3	776
LORD shall be king over all the *e*	Zec 14:9	776
e unto Jerusalem to worship the	Zec 14:17	776
come and smite the *e* with a curse	Mal 4:6	776
for they shall inherit the *e*	Mt 5:5	*1093*
Ye are the salt of the *e*	Mt 5:13	*1093*
e pass, one jot or one tittle	Mt 5:18	*1093*
Nor by the *e*; for it is	Mt 5:35	*1093*
Thy will be done in *e*, as it is	Mt 6:10	*1093*
for yourselves treasures upon *e*	Mt 6:19	*1093*
hath power on *e* to forgive sins	Mt 9:6	*1093*
that I am come to send peace on *e*	Mt 10:34	*1093*
O Father, Lord of heaven and *e*	Mt 11:25	*1093*
nights in the heart of the *e*	Mt 12:40	*1093*
e to hear the wisdom of Solomon	Mt 12:42	*1093*
places, where they had not much *e*	Mt 13:5	*1093*
because they had no deepness of *e*	Mt 13:5	*1093*
on *e* shall be bound in heaven	Mt 16:19	*1093*
on *e* shall be loosed in heaven	Mt 16:19	*1093*
of the *e* take custom or tribute	Mt 17:25	*1093*
on *e* shall be bound in heaven	Mt 18:18	*1093*
on *e* shall be loosed in heaven	Mt 18:18	*1093*
if two of you shall agree on *e* as	Mt 18:19	*1093*
no man your father upon the *e*	Mt 23:9	*1093*
righteous blood shed upon the *e*	Mt 23:35	*1093*
all the tribes of the *e* mourn	Mt 24:30	*1093*
e shall pass away, but my words	Mt 24:35	*1093*
one went and digged in the *e*	Mt 25:18	*1093*
went and hid thy talent in the *e*	Mt 25:25	*1093*
the *e* did quake, and the rocks	Mt 27:51	*1093*
given unto me in heaven and in *e*	Mt 28:18	*1093*
hath power on *e* to forgive sins	Mk 2:10	*1093*
ground, where it had not much *e*	Mk 4:5	*1093*
up, because it had no depth of *e*	Mk 4:5	*1093*
For the *e* bringeth forth fruit of	Mk 4:28	*1093*
which, when it is sown in the *e*	Mk 4:31	*1093*
all the seeds that be in the *e*	Mk 4:31	*1093*
as no fuller on *e* can white them	Mk 9:3	*1093*
from the uttermost part of the *e*	Mk 13:27	*1093*
Heaven and *e* shall pass away	Mk 13:31	*1093*
on *e* peace, good will toward men	Lk 2:14	*1093*
hath power upon *e* to forgive sins	Lk 5:24	*1093*
built an house upon the *e*	Lk 6:49	*1093*
O Father, Lord of heaven and *e*	Lk 10:21	*1093*
be done, as in heaven, so in *e*	Lk 11:2	*1093*
from the utmost parts of the *e* to	Lk 11:31	*1093*
I am come to send fire on the *e*	Lk 12:49	*1093*
that I am come to give peace on *e*	Lk 12:51	*1093*
the face of the sky and of the *e*	Lk 12:56	*1093*
e to pass, than one tittle of the	Lk 16:17	*1093*
shall he find faith on the *e*	Lk 18:8	*1093*
upon the *e* distress of nations,	Lk 21:25	*1093*
things which are coming on the *e*	Lk 21:26	*3625*
Heaven and *e* shall pass away	Lk 21:33	*1093*
dwell on the face of the whole *e*	Lk 21:35	*1093*
all the *e* until the ninth hour	Lk 23:44	*1093*
bowed down their faces to the *e*	Lk 24:5	*1093*
he that is of the *e* is earthly	Jn 3:31	*1093*
is earthly, and speaketh of the *e*	Jn 3:31	*1093*
I, if I be lifted up from the *e*	Jn 12:32	*1093*
I have glorified thee on the *e*	Jn 17:4	*1093*
unto the uttermost part of the *e*	Acts 1:8	*1093*
above, and signs in the *e* beneath	Acts 2:19	*1093*
the kindreds of the *e* be blessed	Acts 3:25	*1093*
God, which hast made heaven, and *e*	Acts 4:24	*1093*
The kings of the *e* stood up	Acts 4:26	*1093*
my throne, and *e* is my footstool	Acts 7:49	*1093*
for his life is taken from the *e*	Acts 8:33	*1093*
And he fell to the *e*, and heard a	Acts 9:4	*1093*
And Saul arose from the *e*	Acts 9:8	*1093*
corners, and let down to the *e*	Acts 10:11	*1093*
of fourfooted beasts of the *e*	Acts 10:12	*1093*
and saw fourfooted beasts of the *e*	Acts 11:6	*1093*
salvation unto the ends of the *e*	Acts 13:47	*1093*
God, which made heaven, and *e*	Acts 14:15	*1093*
that he is Lord of heaven and *e*	Acts 17:24	*1093*
to dwell on all the face of the *e*	Acts 17:26	*1093*
with such a fellow from the *e*	Acts 22:22	*1093*
when we were all fallen to the *e*	Acts 26:14	*1093*
be declared throughout all the *e*	Rom 9:17	*1093*
will the Lord make upon the *e*	Rom 9:28	*1093*
their sound went into all the *e*	Rom 10:18	*1093*
gods, whether in heaven or in *e*	1Cor 8:5	*1093*
For the *e* is the Lord's, and the	1Cor 10:26	*1093*
for the *e* is the Lord's, and the	1Cor 10:28	*1093*
The first man is of the *e*	1Cor 15:47	*1093*
are in heaven, and which are on *e*	Eph 1:10	*1093*
family in heaven and *e* is named,	Eph 3:15	*1093*
into the lower parts of the *e*	Eph 4:9	*1093*
and thou mayest live long on the *e*	Eph 6:3	*1093*
things in heaven, and things in *e*	Phil 2:10	*1919*
and things under the *e*	Phil 2:10	*2709*
are in heaven, and that are in *e*	Col 1:16	*1093*
say, whether they be things in *e*	Col 1:20	*1093*
above, not on things on the *e*	Col 3:2	*1093*
your members which are upon the *e*	Col 3:5	*1093*
silver, but also of wood and of *e*	2Ti 2:20	*3749*
hast laid the foundation of the *e*	Heb 1:10	*1093*
For the *e* which drinketh in the	Heb 6:7	*1093*
For if he were on *e*, he should	Heb 8:4	*1093*
strangers and pilgrims on the *e*	Heb 11:13	*1093*
and in dens and caves of the *e*	Heb 11:38	*1093*
who refused him that spake on *e*	Heb 12:25	*1093*
Whose voice then shook the *e*	Heb 12:26	*1093*
once more I shake not the *e* only	Heb 12:26	*1093*
have lived in pleasure on the *e*	Jas 5:5	*1093*
for the precious fruit of the *e*	Jas 5:7	*1093*
by heaven, neither by the *e*	Jas 5:12	*1093*
it rained not on the *e* by the	Jas 5:17	*1093*
the *e* brought forth her fruit	Jas 5:18	*1093*
the *e* standing out of the water	2Pet 3:5	*1093*
But the heavens and the *e*, which	2Pet 3:7	*1093*
the *e* also and the works that are	2Pet 3:10	*1093*
look for new heavens and a new *e*	2Pet 3:13	*1093*
are three that bear witness in *e*	1Jn 5:8	*1093*
the prince of the kings of the *e*	Rev 1:5	*1093*
all kindreds of the *e* shall wail	Rev 1:7	*1093*
to try them that dwell upon the *e*	Rev 3:10	*1093*
nor in *e*, neither under the *e*	Rev 5:3	*1093*
of God sent forth into all the *e*	Rev 5:6	*1093*
and we shall reign on the *e*	Rev 5:10	*1093*
and on the *e*, and under the *e*	Rev 5:13	*1093*
thereon to take peace from the *e*	Rev 6:4	*1093*
over the fourth part of the *e*	Rev 6:8	*1093*
and with the beasts of the *e*	Rev 6:8	*1093*
blood on them that dwell on the *e*	Rev 6:10	*1093*
stars of heaven fell unto the *e*	Rev 6:13	*1093*
And the kings of the *e*, and the	Rev 6:15	*1093*
on the four corners of the *e*	Rev 7:1	*1093*
holding the four winds of the *e*	Rev 7:1	*1093*
the wind should not blow on the *e*	Rev 7:1	*1093*
whom it was given to hurt the *e*	Rev 7:2	*1093*
Saying, Hurt not the *e*, neither	Rev 7:3	*1093*
the altar, and cast it into the *e*	Rev 8:5	*1093*
and they were cast upon the *e*	Rev 8:7	*1093*
to the inhabiters of the *e* by	Rev 8:13	*1093*
star fall from heaven unto the *e*	Rev 9:1	*1093*
of the smoke locusts upon the *e*	Rev 9:3	*1093*
the scorpions of the *e* have power	Rev 9:3	*1093*
not hurt the grass of the *e*	Rev 9:4	*1093*
sea, and his left foot on the *e*	Rev 10:2	*1093*
upon the *e* lifted up his hand to	Rev 10:5	*1093*
things that therein are, and the *e*	Rev 10:6	*1093*
upon the sea and upon the *e*	Rev 10:8	*1093*
standing before the God of the *e*	Rev 11:4	*1093*
to smite the *e* with all plagues,	Rev 11:6	*1093*
the *e* shall rejoice over them	Rev 11:10	*1093*
them that dwell on the *e*	Rev 11:10	*1093*
destroy them which destroy the *e*	Rev 11:18	*1093*
heaven, and did cast them to the *e*	Rev 12:4	*1093*
he was cast out into the *e*	Rev 12:9	*1093*
Woe to the inhabiters of the *e*	Rev 12:12	*1093*
saw that he was cast unto the *e*	Rev 12:13	*1093*
the *e* helped the woman	Rev 12:16	*1093*
the *e* opened her mouth, and	Rev 12:16	*1093*
upon the *e* shall worship him	Rev 13:8	*1093*
beast coming up out of the *e*	Rev 13:11	*1093*

before him, and causeth the *e* ... Rev 13:12 *1093*
on the *e* in the sight of men ... Rev 13:13 *1093*
them that dwell on the *e* by the ... Rev 13:14 *1093*
to them that dwell on the *e* ... Rev 13:14 *1093*
which were redeemed from the *e* ... Rev 14:3 *1093*
unto them that dwell on the *e* ... Rev 14:6 *1093*
him that made heaven, and *e* ... Rev 14:7 *1093*
for the harvest of the *e* is ripe ... Rev 14:15 *1093*
thrust in his sickle on the *e* ... Rev 14:16 *1093*
and the *e* was reaped ... Rev 14:16 *1093*
the clusters of the vine of the *e* ... Rev 14:18 *1093*
thrust in his sickle into the *e* ... Rev 14:19 *1093*
and gathered the vine of the *e* ... Rev 14:19 *1093*
of the wrath of God upon the *e* ... Rev 16:1 *1093*
and poured out his vial upon the *e* ... Rev 16:2 *1093*
go forth unto the kings of the *e* ... Rev 16:14 *1093*
was not since men were upon the *e* ... Rev 16:18 *1093*
the *e* have committed fornication ... Rev 17:2 *1093*
the inhabitants of the *e* have ... Rev 17:2 *1093*
AND ABOMINATIONS OF THE *E* ... Rev 17:5 *1093*
that dwell on the *e* shall wonder ... Rev 17:8 *1093*
reigneth over the kings of the *e* ... Rev 17:18 *1093*
the *e* was lightened with his ... Rev 18:1 *1093*
the kings of the *e* have committed ... Rev 18:3 *1093*
the merchants of the *e* are waxed ... Rev 18:3 *1093*
And the kings of the *e*, who have ... Rev 18:9 *1093*
the merchants of the *e* shall weep ... Rev 18:11 *1093*
were the great men of the *e* ... Rev 18:23 *1093*
of all that were slain upon the *e* ... Rev 18:24 *1093*
the *e* with her fornication ... Rev 19:2 *1093*
the beast, and the kings of the *e* ... Rev 19:19 *1093*
are in the four quarters of the *e* ... Rev 20:8 *1093*
went up on the breadth of the *e* ... Rev 20:9 *1093*
sat on it, from whose face the *e* ... Rev 20:11 *1093*
And I saw a new heaven and a new *e* ... Rev 21:1 *1093*
the first *e* were passed away ... Rev 21:1 *1093*
the kings of the *e* do bring their ... Rev 21:24 *1093*

EARTHEN {10}
But the *e* vessel wherein it is ... Lev 6:28 2789
every *e* vessel, whereinto any of ... Lev 11:33 2789
in an *e* vessel over running water ... Lev 14:5 2789
in an *e* vessel over running water ... Lev 14:50 2789
take holy water in an *e* vessel ... Num 5:17 2789
e vessels, and wheat, and barley, ... 2Sa 17:28 3335
Go and get a potter's *e* bottle ... Jer 19:1 2789
and put them in an *e* vessel ... Jer 32:14 2789
are they esteemed as *e* pitchers ... Lam 4:2 2789
have this treasure in *e* vessels ... 2Cor 4:7 *3749*

EARTHLY {5}
If I have told you *e* things ... Jn 3:12 *1919*
he that is of the earth is *e* ... Jn 3:31 *1537,3588,1093*
For we know that if our *e* house ... 2Cor 5:1 *1919*
in their shame, who mind *e* things ... Phil 3:19 *1919*
not from above, but is *e*, sensual ... Jas 3:15 *1919*

EARTHQUAKE {16}
and after the wind an *e* ... 1Kin 19:11 7494
but the LORD was not in the *e* ... 1Kin 19:11 7494
And after the *e* a fire ... 1Kin 19:12 7494
of hosts with thunder, and with *e* ... Is 29:6 7494
of Israel, two years before the *e* ... Amos 1:1 7494
e in the days of Uzziah king of ... Zec 14:5 7494
him, watching Jesus, saw the *e* ... Mt 27:54 *4578*
And, behold, there was a great *e* ... Mt 28:2 *4578*
And suddenly there was a great *e* ... Acts 16:26 *4578*
seal, and, lo, there was a great *e* ... Rev 6:12 *4578*
and lightnings, and an *e* ... Rev 8:5 *4578*
the same hour was there a great *e* ... Rev 11:13 *4578*
in the *e* were slain of men seven ... Rev 11:13 *4578*
voices, and thunderings, and an *e* ... Rev 11:19 *4578*
and there was a great *e*, such as ... Rev 16:18 *4578*
upon the earth, so mighty an *e* ... Rev 16:18 *4578*

EARTHQUAKES {3}
be famines, and pestilences, and *e* ... Mt 24:7 *4578*
there shall be *e* in divers places ... Mk 13:8 *4578*
great *e* shall be in divers places ... Lk 21:11 *4578*

EARTHY {4}
The first man is of the earth, *e* ... 1Cor 15:47 *5517*
As is the *e*, such are they also ... 1Cor 15:48 *5517*
such are they also that are *e* ... 1Cor 15:48 *5517*
we have borne the image of the *e* ... 1Cor 15:49 *5517*

EASE {20}
when thou wilt *e* thyself abroad ... Deut 23:13 3427
nations shalt thou find no *e* ... Deut 28:65 7280
trode them down with *e* over ... Judg 20:43 4496
now therefore *e* thou somewhat the ... 2Chr 10:4 7043
E somewhat the yoke that thy ... 2Chr 10:9 7043
me, my couch shall *e* my complaint ... Job 7:13 5375
the thought of him that is at *e* ... Job 12:5 7600
I was at *e*, but he hath broken me ... Job 16:12 7961
full strength, being wholly at *e* ... Job 21:23 7946
His soul shall dwell at *e* ... Ps 25:13 2896
scorning of those that are at *e* ... Ps 123:4 7600
I will *e* me of mine adversaries, ... Is 1:24 5162
Rise up, ye women that are at *e* ... Is 32:9 7600
Tremble, ye women that are at *e* ... Is 32:11 7600
return, and be in rest and at *e* ... Jer 46:27 7599
hath been at *e* from his youth ... Jer 48:11 7599
multitude being at *e* was with her ... Eze 23:42 7961
Woe to them that are at *e* in Zion ... Amos 6:1 7600
with the heathen that are at *e* ... Zec 1:15 7600
take thine *e*, eat, drink, and be ... Lk 12:19 *373*

EASED {2}
and though I forbear, what am I *e* ... Job 16:6 1980
I mean not that other men be *e* ... 2Cor 8:13 *425*

EASIER {8}
so shall it be *e* for thyself ... Ex 18:22 7043
For whether is *e*, to say, Thy ... Mt 9:5 *2123*
It is *e* for a camel to go through ... Mt 19:24 *2123*
Whether is it *e* to say to the ... Mk 2:9 *2123*
It is *e* for a camel to go through ... Mk 10:25 *2123*
Whether is *e*, to say, Thy sins be ... Lk 5:23 *2123*
it is *e* for heaven and earth to ... Lk 16:17 *2123*
For it is *e* for a camel to go ... Lk 18:25 *2123*

EASILY {2}
is not *e* provoked, thinketh no ... 1Cor 13:5
the sin which doth so *e* beset us ... Heb 12:1

EAST {157}
goeth toward the *e* of Assyria ... Gen 2:14 6926
he placed at the *e* of the garden ... Gen 3:24 6924
the land of Nod, on the *e* of Eden ... Gen 4:16 6926
unto Sephar a mount of the *e* ... Gen 10:30 6924
as they journeyed from the *e* ... Gen 11:2 6924
a mountain on the *e* of Beth-el ... Gen 12:8 6924
on the west, and Hai on the *e* ... Gen 12:8 6924
and Lot journeyed *e* ... Gen 13:11 6924
eastward, unto the *e* country ... Gen 25:6 6924
abroad to the west, and to the *e* ... Gen 28:14 6924
the land of the people of the *e* ... Gen 29:1 6924
blasted with the *e* wind sprung up ... Gen 41:6 6921
thin, and blasted with the *e* wind ... Gen 41:23 6921
empty ears blasted with the *e* ... Gen 41:27 6921
the LORD brought an *e* wind upon ... Ex 10:13 6921
the *e* wind brought the locusts ... Ex 10:13 6921
by a strong *e* wind all that night ... Ex 14:21 6921
e side eastward shall be fifty ... Ex 27:13 6924
for the *e* side eastward fifty ... Ex 38:13 6924
it beside the altar on the *e* part ... Lev 1:16 6924
on the *e* side toward the rising ... Num 2:3 6924
the tabernacle toward the *e* ... Num 3:38 6924
on the *e* parts shall go forward ... Num 10:5 6924
out of the mountains of the *e* ... Num 23:7 6924
ye shall point out your *e* border ... Num 34:10 6924
to Riblah, on the *e* side of Ain ... Num 34:11 6924
on the *e* side two thousand cubits ... Num 35:5 6924
in the *e* border of Jericho ... Josh 4:19 4217
on the *e* side of Beth-el, and ... Josh 7:2 6924
And to the Canaanite on the *e* ... Josh 11:3 4217
Hermon, and all the plain on the *e* ... Josh 12:1 4217
to the sea of Chinneroth on the *e* ... Josh 12:3 4217
plain, even the salt sea on the *e* ... Josh 12:3 4217
the *e* border was the salt sea, ... Josh 15:5 6924
the water of Jericho on the *e* ... Josh 16:1 4217
on the *e* side was Ataroth-addar ... Josh 16:5 4217
passed by it on the *e* to Janohah ... Josh 16:6 4217
north, and in Issachar on the *e* ... Josh 17:10 4217
beyond Jordan on the *e*, which ... Josh 18:7 4217
the border of it on the *e* side ... Josh 18:20 6924
along on the *e* to Gittah-hepher ... Josh 19:13 6924
and the children of the *e* ... Judg 6:3 6924
the children of the *e* were ... Judg 6:33 6924
all the children of the *e* lay ... Judg 7:12 6924
hosts of the children of the *e* ... Judg 8:10 6924
dwelt in tents on the *e* of Nobah ... Judg 8:11 6924
came by the *e* side of the land of ... Judg 11:18 4217,8121
on the *e* side of the highway that ... Judg 21:19 4217,8121
all the children of the *e* country ... 1Kin 4:30 6924
and three looking toward the *e* ... 1Kin 7:25 4217
even unto the *e* side of the ... 1Chr 4:39 4217
all the *e* land of Gilead ... 1Chr 5:10 4217
on the *e* side of Jordan, were ... 1Chr 6:78 4217
were the porters, toward the *e* ... 1Chr 9:24 4217
of the valleys, both toward the *e* ... 1Chr 12:15 4217
and three looking toward the *e* ... 2Chr 4:4 4217
on the right side of the *e* end ... 2Chr 4:10 6924
stood at the *e* end of the altar, ... 2Chr 5:12 4217
them together into the *e* street ... 2Chr 29:4 4217
Levite, the porter toward the *e* ... 2Chr 31:14 4217
the water gate toward the *e* ... Neh 3:26 4217
the keeper of the *e* gate ... Neh 3:29 4217
greatest of all the men of the *e* ... Job 1:3 6924
and fill his belly with the *e* wind ... Job 15:2 6921
The *e* wind carrieth him away, and ... Job 27:21 6921
the *e* wind upon the earth ... Job 38:24 6921
ships of Tarshish with an *e* wind ... Ps 48:7 6921
cometh neither from the *e* ... Ps 75:6 4161
He caused an *e* wind to blow in ... Ps 78:26 6921
As far as the *e* is from the west, ... Ps 103:12 4217
them out of the lands, from the *e* ... Ps 107:3 4217
they be replenished from the *e* ... Is 2:6 6924
spoil them of the *e* together ... Is 11:14 6924
wind in the day of the *e* wind ... Is 27:8 6921
up the righteous man from the *e* ... Is 41:2 4217
I will bring thy seed from the *e* ... Is 43:5 4217
a ravenous bird from the *e* ... Is 46:11 4217
with an *e* wind before the enemy ... Jer 18:17 6921
is by the entry of the *e* gate ... Jer 19:2 2777
of the horse gate toward the *e* ... Jer 31:40 4217
Kedar, and spoil the men of the *e* ... Jer 49:28 6924
LORD, and their faces toward the *e* ... Eze 8:16 6924
worshipped the sun toward the *e* ... Eze 8:16 6924
of the *e* gate of the LORD's house ... Eze 10:19 6931
brought me unto the *e* gate of the ... Eze 11:1 6931
is on the *e* side of the city ... Eze 11:23 6924
when the *e* wind toucheth it ... Eze 17:10 6921
the *e* wind dried up her fruit ... Eze 19:12 6921
the men of the *e* for a possession ... Eze 25:4 6924
men of the *e* with the Ammonites ... Eze 25:10 6924
the *e* wind hath broken thee in ... Eze 27:26 6921
passengers on the *e* of the sea ... Eze 39:11 6926
gate which looketh toward the *e* ... Eze 40:6 6921
gate that looketh toward the *e* ... Eze 40:22 6921
toward the north, and toward the *e* ... Eze 40:23 6921
into the inner court toward the *e* ... Eze 40:32 6921
one at the side of the *e* gate ... Eze 40:44 6921
the separate place toward the *e* ... Eze 41:14 6921
was the entry on the *e* side ... Eze 42:9 6921
wall of the court toward the *e* ... Eze 42:10 6921
before the wall toward the *e* ... Eze 42:12 6921
whose prospect is toward the *e* ... Eze 42:15 6921
He measured the *e* side with the ... Eze 42:16 6921
gate that looketh toward the *e* ... Eze 43:1 6921
Israel came from the way of the *e* ... Eze 43:2 6921
whose prospect is toward the *e* ... Eze 43:4 6921
stairs shall look toward the *e* ... Eze 43:17 6921
which looketh toward the *e* ... Eze 44:1 6921
and from the *e* side eastward ... Eze 45:7 6924
the west border unto the *e* border ... Eze 45:7 6921
e shall be shut the six working ... Eze 46:1 6921
gate that looketh toward the *e* ... Eze 46:12 6921
of the house stood toward the *e* ... Eze 47:1 6921
issue out toward the *e* country ... Eze 47:8 6930
the *e* side ye shall measure from ... Eze 47:18 6921
from the border unto the *e* sea ... Eze 47:18 6931
And this is the *e* side ... Eze 47:18 6921
for these are his sides *e* ... Eze 48:1 6921
from the *e* side unto the west ... Eze 48:2 6921
from the *e* side even unto the ... Eze 48:3 6921
from the *e* side unto the west ... Eze 48:4 6921
from the *e* side unto the west ... Eze 48:5 6921
from the *e* side even unto the ... Eze 48:6 6921
from the *e* side unto the west ... Eze 48:7 6921
from the *e* side unto the west ... Eze 48:8 6921
from the *e* side unto the west ... Eze 48:8 6921
toward the *e* ten thousand in ... Eze 48:10 6921
on the *e* side four thousand and ... Eze 48:16 6921
toward the *e* two hundred and fifty ... Eze 48:17 6921
the oblation toward the *e* border ... Eze 48:21 6921
from the *e* side unto the west ... Eze 48:23 6921
from the *e* side unto the west ... Eze 48:24 6921
from the *e* side unto the west ... Eze 48:25 6921
from the *e* side unto the west ... Eze 48:26 6921
from the *e* side unto the west ... Eze 48:27 6921
at the *e* side four thousand and ... Eze 48:32 6921
toward the south, and toward the *e* ... Dan 8:9 4217
But tidings out of the *e* and out ... Dan 11:44 4217
and followeth after the *e* wind ... Hos 12:1 6921
an *e* wind shall come, the wind of ... Hos 13:15 6921
with his face toward the *e* sea ... Joel 2:20 6931
and from the north even to the *e* ... Amos 8:12 4217
sat on the *e* side of the city, and ... Jonah 4:5 6924
God prepared a vehement *e* wind ... Jonah 4:8 6921
faces shall sup up as the *e* wind ... Hab 1:9 6921
save my people from the *e* country ... Zec 8:7 4217
is before Jerusalem on the *e* ... Zec 14:4 6924
in the midst thereof toward the *e* ... Zec 14:4 4217
wise men from the *e* to Jerusalem ... Mt 2:1 *395*
we have seen his star in the *e* ... Mt 2:2 *395*
the star, which they saw in the *e* ... Mt 2:9 *395*
That many shall come from the *e* ... Mt 8:11 *395*
the lightning cometh out of the *e* ... Mt 24:27 *395*
And they shall come from the *e* ... Lk 13:29 *395*
angel ascending from the *e* ... Rev 7:2 *395*
kings of the *e* might be prepared ... Rev 16:12 *395*
On the *e* three gates ... Rev 21:13 *395*

EASTER {1} *Passover.*
intending after *E* to bring him ... Acts 12:4 *3957*

EASTWARD {40}
God planted a garden *e* in Eden ... Gen 2:8 6924
art northward, and southward, and *e* ... Gen 13:14 6924
his son, while he yet lived, *e* ... Gen 25:6 6924
east side *e* shall be fifty cubits ... Ex 27:13 4217
for the east side *e* fifty cubits ... Ex 38:13 4217
his finger upon the mercy seat *e* ... Lev 16:14 6924
tabernacle of the congregation *e* ... Num 3:38 4217
to us on this side Jordan *e* ... Num 32:19 4217
outmost coast of the salt sea *e* ... Num 34:3 6924
side of the sea of Chinnereth *e* ... Num 34:11 6924
this side Jordan near Jericho *e* ... Num 34:15 6924
salt sea, under Ashdoth-pisgah *e* ... Deut 3:17 4217
and northward, and southward, and *e* ... Deut 3:27 4217
the plain on this side Jordan *e* ... Deut 4:49 4217
and unto the valley of Mizpeh *e* ... Josh 11:8 4217
Moses gave them, beyond Jordan *e* ... Josh 13:8 4217
on the other side Jordan *e* ... Josh 13:27 4217
other side Jordan, by Jericho, *e* ... Josh 13:32 4217
went about *e* unto Taanath-shiloh ... Josh 16:6 4217
turned from Sarid *e* toward the ... Josh 19:12 6924
other side Jordan by Jericho *e* ... Josh 20:8 4217
in Michmash, *e* from Beth-aven ... 1Sa 13:5 6926
house *e* over against the south ... 1Kin 7:39 6924
Get thee hence, and turn thee *e* ... 1Kin 17:3 6924
From Jordan *e*, all the land of ... 2Kin 10:33 4217,8121
And he said, Open the window *e* ... 2Kin 13:17 6924
e he inhabited unto the entering ... 1Chr 5:9 4217
e Naaran, and westward Gezer, with ... 1Chr 7:28 4217
waited in the king's gate *e* ... 1Chr 9:18 4217
the lot *e* fell to Shelemiah ... 1Chr 26:14 4217
E were six Levites, northward ... 1Chr 26:17 4217
David, even unto the water gate *e* ... Neh 12:37 4217
the LORD's house, which looketh *e* ... Eze 11:1 6921
gate *e* were three on this side ... Eze 40:10 1870,6921
without, an hundred cubits *e* ... Eze 40:19 6921
westward, and from the east side *e* ... Eze 45:7 6921
the threshold of the house *e* ... Eze 47:1 6921
gate by the way that looketh *e* ... Eze 47:2 6921
the line in his hand went forth *e* ... Eze 47:3 6921
portion shall be ten thousand *e* ... Eze 48:18 6921

EASY {4}
but knowledge is *e* unto him that ... Prov 14:6 7043
For my yoke is *e*, and my burden is ... Mt 11:30 *5543*
tongue words *e* to be understood ... 1Cor 14:9 *2154*
e to be intreated, full of mercy ... Jas 3:17 *2138*

EAT {655}
the garden thou mayest freely *e* ... Gen 2:16 398
and evil, thou shalt not *e* of it ... Gen 2:17 398
Ye shall not *e* of every tree of ... Gen 3:1 398
We may *e* of the fruit of the ... Gen 3:2 398
hath said, Ye shall not *e* of it ... Gen 3:3 398
know that in the day ye *e* thereof ... Gen 3:5 398
of the fruit thereof, and did *e* ... Gen 3:6 398
and he did *e* ... Gen 3:6 398
thee that thou shouldest not *e* ... Gen 3:11 398
gave me of the tree, and I did *e* ... Gen 3:12 398
serpent beguiled me, and I did *e* ... Gen 3:13 398
dust shalt thou *e* all the days of ... Gen 3:14 398
saying, Thou shalt not *e* of it ... Gen 3:17 398
in sorrow shalt thou *e* of it all ... Gen 3:17 398
thou shalt *e* the herb of the ... Gen 3:18 398
of thy face shalt thou *e* bread ... Gen 3:19 398
also of the tree of life, and *e* ... Gen 3:22 398
the blood thereof, shall ye not *e* ... Gen 9:4 398
under the tree, and they did *e* ... Gen 18:8 398
unleavened bread, and they did *e* ... Gen 19:3 398
was set meat before him to *e* ... Gen 24:33 398
but he said, I will not *e* ... Gen 24:33 398
And they did *e* and drink, he and the ... Gen 24:54 398
because he did *e* of his venison ... Gen 25:28 6310
and he did *e* and drink, and rose up, ... Gen 25:34 398
made them a feast, and they did *e* ... Gen 26:30 398
and bring it to me, that I may *e* ... Gen 27:4 398
me savoury meat, that I may *e* ... Gen 27:7 398
it to thy father, that he may *e* ... Gen 27:10 398
e of my venison, that thy soul ... Gen 27:19 398
I will *e* of my son's venison, ... Gen 27:25 398
it near to him, and he did *e* ... Gen 27:25 398
e of his son's venison, that thy ... Gen 27:31 398
I go, and will give me bread to *e* ... Gen 28:20 398
they did *e* there upon the heap ... Gen 31:46 398
and called his brethren to *e* bread ... Gen 31:54 398
and they did *e* bread, and tarried ... Gen 31:54 398
the children of Israel *e* not of ... Gen 32:32 398
And they sat down to *e* bread ... Gen 37:25 398
save the bread which he did *e* ... Gen 39:6 398
the birds did *e* them out of the ... Gen 40:17 398
the birds shall *e* thy flesh from ... Gen 40:19 398
leanfleshed kine did *e* up the ... Gen 41:4 398
the ill favoured kine did *e* up ... Gen 41:20 398
that they should *e* bread there ... Gen 43:25 398
Egyptians, which did *e* with him ... Gen 43:32 398
not *e* bread with the Hebrews ... Gen 43:32 398
ye shall *e* the fat of the land ... Gen 45:18 398
did *e* their portion which Pharaoh ... Gen 47:22 398
call him, that he may *e* bread ... Ex 2:20 398
they shall *e* the residue of that ... Ex 10:5 398
shall *e* every tree which groweth ... Ex 10:5 398
e every herb of the land, even ... Ex 10:12 398
they did *e* every herb of the land ... Ex 10:15 398
houses, wherein they shall *e* it ... Ex 12:7 398
they shall *e* the flesh in that ... Ex 12:8 398
with bitter herbs they shall *e* it ... Ex 12:8 398
E not of it raw, nor sodden at ... Ex 12:9 398
And thus shall ye *e* it ... Ex 12:11 398
and ye shall *e* it in haste ... Ex 12:11 398
days shall ye *e* unleavened bread ... Ex 12:15 398
save that which every man must *e* ... Ex 12:16 398
ye shall *e* unleavened bread, ... Ex 12:18 398
Ye shall *e* nothing leavened ... Ex 12:20 398
shall ye *e* unleavened bread ... Ex 12:20 398
There shall no stranger *e* thereof ... Ex 12:43 398
him, then shall he *e* thereof ... Ex 12:44 398
hired servant shall not *e* thereof ... Ex 12:45 398
person shall *e* thereof ... Ex 12:48 398
thou shalt *e* unleavened bread ... Ex 13:6 398
when we did *e* bread to the full ... Ex 16:3 398
you in the evening flesh to *e* ... Ex 16:8 398
saying, At even ye shall *e* flesh ... Ex 16:12 398
the LORD hath given you to *e* ... Ex 16:15 402
And Moses said, *E* that to day ... Ex 16:25 398
of Israel did *e* manna forty years ... Ex 16:35 398
they did *e* manna, until they came ... Ex 16:35 398
to *e* bread with Moses' father in ... Ex 18:12 398
neither shall ye *e* any flesh that ... Ex 22:31 398
that the poor of thy people may *e* ... Ex 23:11 398
the beasts of the field shall *e* ... Ex 23:11 398
(thou shalt *e* unleavened bread ... Ex 23:15 398
also they saw God, and did *e* ... Ex 24:11 398
his sons shall *e* the flesh of the ... Ex 29:32 398
they shall *e* those things ... Ex 29:33 398
a stranger shall not *e* thereof ... Ex 29:33 398
and the people sat down to *e* ... Ex 32:6 398
thee, and thou *e* of his sacrifice ... Ex 34:15 398
thou shalt *e* unleavened bread ... Ex 34:18 398
he did neither *e* bread, nor drink ... Ex 34:28 398
that ye *e* neither fat nor blood ... Lev 3:17 398
thereof shall Aaron and his sons *e* ... Lev 6:16 398
the congregation they shall *e* it ... Lev 6:16 398
children of Aaron shall *e* of it ... Lev 6:18 398
offereth it for sin shall *e* it ... Lev 6:26 398
among the priests shall *e* thereof ... Lev 6:29 398
among the priests shall *e* thereof ... Lev 7:6 398
all that be clean shall *e* thereof ... Lev 7:19 398
e of the flesh of the sacrifice ... Lev 7:21 398
Ye shall *e* no manner of fat, of ... Lev 7:23 398
but ye shall in no wise *e* of it ... Lev 7:24 398
Moreover ye shall *e* no manner of ... Lev 7:26 398
there *e* it with the bread that is ... Lev 8:31 398
Aaron and his sons shall *e* it ... Lev 8:31 398
e it without leaven beside the ... Lev 10:12 398
ye shall *e* it in the holy place, ... Lev 10:13 398
shall ye *e* in a clean place ... Lev 10:14 398
e among all the beasts that are ... Lev 11:2 398
among the beasts, that shall ye *e* ... Lev 11:3 398
not *e* of them that chew the cud ... Lev 11:4 398
Of their flesh shall ye not *e* ... Lev 11:8 398
These shall ye *e* of all that are ... Lev 11:9 398
and in the rivers, them shall ye *e* ... Lev 11:9 398
ye shall not *e* of their flesh, ... Lev 11:11 398
Yet these may ye *e* of every ... Lev 11:21 398
Even these of them ye may *e* ... Lev 11:22 398
if any beast, of which ye may *e* ... Lev 11:39 402
the earth, them ye shall not *e* ... Lev 11:42 398
No soul of you shall *e* blood ... Lev 17:12 398
that sojourneth among you *e* blood ... Lev 17:12 398
Ye shall *e* the blood of no manner ... Lev 17:14 398
shall ye *e* of the fruit thereof ... Lev 19:25 398
Ye shall not *e* any thing with the ... Lev 19:26 398
He shall *e* the bread of his God, ... Lev 21:22 398
he shall not *e* of the holy things ... Lev 22:4 398
shall not *e* of the holy things, ... Lev 22:6 398
shall afterward *e* of the holy ... Lev 22:7 398
he shall not *e* to defile himself ... Lev 22:8 398
no stranger *e* of the holy thing ... Lev 22:10 398
shall not *e* of the holy thing ... Lev 22:10 398
with his money, he shall *e* of it ... Lev 22:11 398
they shall *e* of his meat ... Lev 22:11 398
she may not *e* of an offering of ... Lev 22:12 398
she shall *e* of her father's meat ... Lev 22:13 398
there shall no stranger *e* thereof ... Lev 22:13 398
if a man *e* of the holy thing ... Lev 22:14 398
when they *e* their holy things ... Lev 22:16 398
days ye must *e* unleavened bread ... Lev 23:6 398
ye shall *e* neither bread, nor ... Lev 23:14 398
they shall *e* it in the holy place ... Lev 24:9 398
ye shall *e* the increase thereof ... Lev 25:12 398
ye shall *e* your fill, and dwell ... Lev 25:19 398
What shall we *e* the seventh year ... Lev 25:20 398
e yet of old fruit until the ... Lev 25:22 398
in ye shall *e* of the old store ... Lev 25:22 398
ye shall *e* your bread to the full ... Lev 26:5 398
ye shall *e* old store, and bring ... Lev 26:10 398
vain, for your enemies shall *e* it ... Lev 26:16 398
and ye shall *e*, and not be ... Lev 26:26 398
ye shall *e* the flesh of your sons ... Lev 26:29 398
of your daughters shall ye *e* ... Lev 26:29 398
of your enemies shall *e* you up ... Lev 26:38 398
nor *e* moist grapes, or dried ... Num 6:3 398
he *e* nothing that is made of the ... Num 6:4 398
e it with unleavened bread and ... Num 9:11 398
Who shall give us flesh to *e* ... Num 11:4 398
which we did *e* in Egypt freely ... Num 11:5 398
Give us flesh, that we may *e* ... Num 11:13 398
to morrow, and ye shall *e* flesh ... Num 11:18 398
Who shall give us flesh to *e* ... Num 11:18 398
give you flesh, and ye shall *e* ... Num 11:18 398
Ye shall not *e* one day, nor two ... Num 11:19 398
that they may *e* a whole month ... Num 11:21 398
when ye *e* of the bread of the ... Num 15:19 398
most holy place shalt thou *e* it ... Num 18:10 398
every male shall *e* it ... Num 18:10 398
clean in thy house shall *e* of it ... Num 18:11 398
in thine house shall *e* of it ... Num 18:13 398
ye shall *e* it in every place, ye ... Num 18:31 398
lie down until he *e* of the prey ... Num 23:24 398
he shall *e* up the nations his ... Num 24:8 398
and the people did *e*, and bowed ... Num 25:2 398
of them for money, that ye may *e* ... Deut 2:6 398
me meat for money, that I may *e* ... Deut 2:28 398
neither see, nor hear, nor *e* ... Deut 4:28 398
shalt *e* bread without scarceness ... Deut 8:9 398
I neither did *e* bread nor drink ... Deut 9:9 398
I did neither *e* bread, nor drink ... Deut 9:18 398
thy cattle, that thou mayest *e* ... Deut 11:15 398
there ye shall *e* before the LORD ... Deut 12:7 398
e flesh in all thy gates, ... Deut 12:15 398
and the clean may *e* thereof ... Deut 12:15 398
Only ye shall not *e* the blood ... Deut 12:16 398
Thou mayest not *e* within thy ... Deut 12:17 398
But thou must *e* them before the ... Deut 12:18 398
and thou shalt say, I will *e* flesh ... Deut 12:20 398
thy soul longeth to *e* flesh ... Deut 12:20 398
thou mayest *e* flesh, whatsoever ... Deut 12:20 398
thou shalt *e* in thy gates ... Deut 12:21 398
is eaten, so thou shalt *e* them ... Deut 12:22 398
the clean shall *e* of them alike ... Deut 12:22 398
be sure that thou *e* not the blood ... Deut 12:23 398
thou mayest not *e* the life with ... Deut 12:23 398
Thou shalt not *e* it ... Deut 12:24 398
Thou shalt not *e* it ... Deut 12:25 398
God, and thou shalt *e* the flesh ... Deut 12:27 398
Thou shalt not *e* any abominable ... Deut 14:3 398
are the beasts which ye shall *e* ... Deut 14:4 398
among the beasts, that ye shall *e* ... Deut 14:6 398
not *e* of them that chew the cud ... Deut 14:7 398
ye shall not *e* of their flesh, ... Deut 14:8 398
These ye shall *e* of all that are ... Deut 14:9 398
have fins and scales shall ye *e* ... Deut 14:9 398
not fins and scales ye may not *e* ... Deut 14:10 398
Of all clean birds ye shall *e* ... Deut 14:11 398
are they of which ye shall not *e* ... Deut 14:12 398
But of all clean fowls ye may *e* ... Deut 14:20 398
Ye shall not *e* of any thing that ... Deut 14:21 398
is in thy gates, that he may *e* it ... Deut 14:21 398
thou shalt *e* before the LORD thy ... Deut 14:23 398
thou shalt *e* there before the ... Deut 14:26 398
thy gates, shall come, and shall *e* ... Deut 14:29 398
Thou shalt *e* it before the LORD ... Deut 15:20 398
Thou shalt *e* it within thy gates ... Deut 15:22 398
the clean person shall *e* it alike ... Deut 15:22 398
shalt not *e* the blood thereof ... Deut 15:23 398
Thou shalt *e* no leavened bread ... Deut 16:3 398
seven days shalt thou *e* ... Deut 16:3 398
e it in the place which the LORD ... Deut 16:7 398
thou shalt *e* unleavened bread ... Deut 16:8 398
they shall *e* the offerings of the ... Deut 18:1 398
shall have like portions to *e* ... Deut 18:8 398
battle, and another man *e* of it ... Deut 20:6 2490
thou shalt *e* the spoil of thine ... Deut 20:14 398
for thou mayest *e* of them ... Deut 20:19 398
then thou mayest *e* grapes thy ... Deut 23:24 398
that they may *e* within thy gates, ... Deut 26:12 398
peace offerings, and shalt *e* there ... Deut 27:7 398
eyes, and thou shalt not *e* thereof ... Deut 28:31 398
which thou knowest not *e* up ... Deut 28:33 398
for the worms shall *e* them ... Deut 28:39 398
he shall *e* the fruit of thy ... Deut 28:51 398
thou shalt *e* the fruit of thine ... Deut 28:53 398
of his children whom he shall *e* ... Deut 28:55 398
for she shall *e* them for want of ... Deut 28:57 398
that he might *e* the increase of ... Deut 32:13 398
Which did *e* the fat of their ... Deut 32:38 398
they did *e* of the old corn of the ... Josh 5:11 398
but they did *e* of the fruit of ... Josh 5:12 398
which ye planted not do ye *e* ... Josh 24:13 398
the house of their god, and did *e* ... Judg 9:27 398
drink, and *e* not any unclean thing ... Judg 13:4 398
neither *e* any unclean thing ... Judg 13:7 398
She may not *e* of any thing that ... Judg 13:14 398
drink, nor *e* any unclean thing ... Judg 13:14 398
I will not *e* of thy bread ... Judg 13:16 398
and gave them, and they did *e* ... Judg 14:9 398
so they did *e* and drink, and lodged ... Judg 19:4 398
And they sat down, and did *e* ... Judg 19:6 398
and they did *e* both of them ... Judg 19:8 398
they washed their feet, and did *e* ... Judg 19:21 398
e of the bread, and dip thy morsel ... Ruth 2:14 398
her parched corn, and she did *e* ... Ruth 2:14 398
therefore she wept, and did not *e* ... 1Sa 1:7 398
the woman went her way, and did *e* ... 1Sa 1:18 398
that I may *e* a piece of bread ... 1Sa 2:36 398
he go up to the high place to *e* ... 1Sa 9:13 398
people will not *e* until he come ... 1Sa 9:13 398
afterwards they *e* that be bidden ... 1Sa 9:13 398
for ye shall *e* with me to day, and ... 1Sa 9:19 398
set it before thee, and *e* ... 1Sa 9:24 398
So Saul did *e* with Samuel that ... 1Sa 9:24 398
the people did *e* them with the ... 1Sa 14:32 398
in that they *e* with the blood ... 1Sa 14:33 398
sheep, and slay them here, and *e* ... 1Sa 14:34 398
the king sat him down to *e* meat ... 1Sa 20:24 398
did *e* no meat the second day of ... 1Sa 20:34 398
and *e*, that thou mayest have ... 1Sa 28:22 398
he refused, and said, I will not *e* ... 1Sa 28:23 398
and they did *e* ... 1Sa 28:25 398
and gave him bread, and he did *e* ... 1Sa 30:11 398
to *e* meat while it was yet day ... 2Sa 3:35 1262
thou shalt *e* bread at my table ... 2Sa 9:7 398
master's son may have food to *e* ... 2Sa 9:10 398
thy master's son shall *e* bread ... 2Sa 9:10 398
he shall *e* at my table, as one of ... 2Sa 9:11 398
for he did *e* continually at the ... 2Sa 9:13 398
I then go into mine house, to *e* ... 2Sa 11:11 398
David had called him, he did *e* ... 2Sa 11:13 398
it did *e* of his own meat, and ... 2Sa 12:3 398
neither did he *e* bread with them ... 2Sa 12:17 1262
set bread before him, and he did *e* ... 2Sa 12:20 398
dead, thou didst rise and *e* bread ... 2Sa 12:21 398
I may see it, and *e* it at her hand ... 2Sa 13:5 398
sight, that I may *e* at her hand ... 2Sa 13:6 1262
but he refused to *e* ... 2Sa 13:9 398
that I may *e* of thine hand ... 2Sa 13:10 1262
had brought them unto him to *e* ... 2Sa 13:11 398
fruit for the young men to *e* ... 2Sa 16:2 398
people that were with him, to *e* ... 2Sa 17:29 398
that did *e* at thine own table ... 2Sa 19:28 398
taste what I *e* or what I drink ... 2Sa 19:35 398
and, behold, they *e* and drink ... 1Kin 1:25 398
be of those that *e* at thy table ... 1Kin 2:7 398
neither will I *e* bread nor drink ... 1Kin 13:8 398
E no bread, nor drink water, nor ... 1Kin 13:9 398
Come home with me, and *e* bread ... 1Kin 13:15 398
neither will I *e* bread nor drink ... 1Kin 13:16 398
Thou shalt *e* no bread nor drink ... 1Kin 13:17 398
thine house, that he may *e* bread ... 1Kin 13:18 398
did *e* bread in his house, and ... 1Kin 13:19 398
E no bread, and drink no water ... 1Kin 13:22 398
in the city shall the dogs *e* ... 1Kin 14:11 398
shall the fowls of the air *e* ... 1Kin 14:11 398
in the city shall the dogs *e* ... 1Kin 16:4 398
shall the fowls of the air *e* ... 1Kin 16:4 398
me and my son, that we may *e* it ... 1Kin 17:12 398
he, and her house, did *e* many days ... 1Kin 17:15 398
which *e* at Jezebel's table ... 1Kin 18:19 398
said unto Ahab, Get thee up, *e* ... 1Kin 18:41 398
So Ahab went up to *e* and to drink ... 1Kin 18:42 398
him, and said unto him, Arise and *e* ... 1Kin 19:5 398
And he did *e* and drink, and laid him ... 1Kin 19:6 398
touched him, and said, Arise and *e* ... 1Kin 19:7 398
And he arose, and did *e* and drink, ... 1Kin 19:8 398
unto the people, and they did *e* ... 1Kin 19:21 398
his face, and would *e* no bread ... 1Kin 21:4 398

e bread, and let thine heart be 1Kin 21:7 398
The dogs shall *e* Jezebel by the 1Kin 21:23 398
Ahab in the city the dogs shall *e* 1Kin 21:24 398
shall the fowls of the air *e* 1Kin 21:24 398
and she constrained him to *e* bread 2Kin 4:8 398
he turned in thither to *e* bread 2Kin 4:8 398
they poured out for the men to *e* 2Kin 4:40 398
And they could not *e* thereof 2Kin 4:40 398
for the people, that they may *e* 2Kin 4:41 398
unto the people, that they may *e* 2Kin 4:42 398
Give the people, that they may *e* 2Kin 4:43 398
thus saith the LORD, They shall *e* 2Kin 4:43 398
set it before them, and they did *e* 2Kin 4:44 398
before them, that they may *e* 2Kin 6:22 398
thy son, that we may *e* him to day 2Kin 6:28 398
we will *e* my son to morrow 2Kin 6:28 398
So we boiled my son, and did *e* him 2Kin 6:29 398
Give thy son, that we may *e* him 2Kin 6:29 398
eyes, but shalt not *e* thereof 2Kin 7:2 398
they went into one tent, and did *e* 2Kin 7:8 398
eyes, but shalt not *e* thereof 2Kin 7:19 398
the dogs shall *e* Jezebel in the 2Kin 9:10 398
And when he was come in, he did *e* 2Kin 9:34 398
shall dogs *e* the flesh of Jezebel 2Kin 9:36 398
that they may *e* their own dung, 2Kin 18:27 398
then *e* ye every man of his own 2Kin 18:31 398
Ye shall *e* this year such things 2Kin 19:29 398
and *e* the fruits thereof 2Kin 19:29 398
but they did *e* of the unleavened 2Kin 23:9 398
he did *e* bread continually before 2Kin 25:29 398
And did *e* and drink before the LORD 1Chr 29:22 398
and shod them, and gave them to *e* 2Chr 28:15 398
yet did they *e* the passover 2Chr 30:18 398
they did *e* throughout the feast 2Chr 30:22 398
the LORD, we have had enough to *e* 2Chr 31:10 398
that they should not *e* of the Ezr 2:63 398
the LORD God of Israel, did *e* Ezr 6:21 398
e the good of the land, and leave Ezr 9:12 398
he did *e* no bread, nor drink Ezr 10:6 398
up corn for them, that we may *e* Neh 5:2 398
that they should not *e* of the Neh 7:65 398
e the fat, and drink the sweet, and Neh 8:10 398
the people went their way to *e* Neh 8:12 398
so they did *e*, and were filled, and Neh 9:25 398
fathers to *e* the fruit thereof Neh 9:36 398
neither *e* nor drink three days, Est 4:16 398
for their three sisters to *e* Job 1:4 398
For my sighing cometh before I *e* Job 3:24 3899
Then let me sow, and let another *e* Job 31:8 398
did *e* bread with him in his house Job 42:11 398
e up my people as they *e* bread Ps 14:4 398
The meek shall *e* and be satisfied Ps 22:26 398
that be fat upon earth shall *e* Ps 22:29 398
came upon me to *e* up my flesh Ps 27:2 398
which did *e* of my bread, hath Ps 41:9 398
Will I *e* the flesh of bulls, or Ps 50:13 398
e up my people as they *e* bread Ps 53:4 398
rained down manna upon them to *e* Ps 78:24 398
Man did *e* angels' food Ps 78:25 398
So they did *e*, and were well Ps 78:29 398
so that I forget to *e* my bread Ps 102:4 398
did *e* up all the herbs in their Ps 105:35 398
to *e* the bread of sorrows Ps 127:2 398
For thou shalt *e* the labour of Ps 128:2 398
let me not *e* of their dainties Ps 141:4 3898
Therefore shall they *e* of the Prov 1:31 398
For they *e* the bread of Prov 4:17 3898
e of my bread, and drink of the Prov 9:5 3898
A man shall *e* good by the fruit Prov 13:2 398
transgressors shall *e* violence Prov 13:2 398
love it shall *e* the fruit thereof Prov 18:21 398
thou sittest to *e* with a ruler Prov 23:1 3898
E thou not the bread of him that Prov 23:6 3898
E and drink, saith he to thee Prov 23:7 398
e thou honey, because it is good Prov 24:13 398
e so much as is sufficient for Prov 25:16 398
be hungry, give him bread to *e* Prov 25:21 398
It is not good to *e* much honey Prov 25:27 398
tree shall *e* the fruit thereof Prov 27:18 398
and the young eagles shall *e* it Prov 30:17 398
for a man, than that he should *e* Eccl 2:24 398
For who can *e*, or who else can Eccl 2:25 398
And also that every man should *e* Eccl 3:13 398
they are increased that *e* them Eccl 5:11 398
whether he *e* little or much Eccl 5:12 398
it is good and comely for one to *e* Eccl 5:18 398
hath given him power to *e* thereof Eccl 5:19 398
giveth him not power to *e* thereof Eccl 6:2 398
thing under the sun, than to *e* Eccl 8:15 398
e thy bread with joy, and drink Eccl 9:7 398
thy princes *e* in the morning Eccl 10:16 398
thy princes *e* in due season, for Eccl 10:17 398
garden, and *e* his pleasant fruits Song 4:16 398
e, O friends Song 5:1 398
ye shall *e* the good of the land Is 1:19 398
for they shall *e* the fruit of Is 3:10 398
We will *e* our own bread, and wear Is 4:1 398
of the fat ones shall strangers *e* Is 5:17 398
Butter and honey shall he *e* Is 7:15 398
shall give, he shall *e* butter Is 7:22 398
honey shall every one *e* that is Is 7:22 398
he shall *e* on the left hand, and Is 9:20 398
they shall *e* every man the flesh Is 9:20 398
the lion shall *e* straw like the Is 11:7 398
table, watch in the watchtower, *e* Is 21:5 398
let us *e* and drink Is 22:13 398
to *e* sufficiently, and for durable Is 23:18 398
ground shall *e* clean provender Is 30:24 398
that they may *e* their own dung, Is 36:12 398
e ye every one of his vine, and Is 36:16 398
Ye shall *e* this year such as Is 37:30 398
vineyards, and *e* the fruit thereof Is 37:30 398
the moth shall *e* them up Is 50:9 398
For the moth shall *e* them up like Is 51:8 398
the worm shall *e* them like wool Is 51:8 398
come ye, buy, and *e* Is 55:1 398
e ye that which is good, and let Is 55:2 398
ye shall *e* the riches of the Is 61:6 398
that have gathered it shall *e* it Is 62:9 398
which *e* swine's flesh, and broth Is 65:4 398
GOD, Behold, my servants shall *e* Is 65:13 398
vineyards, and *e* the fruit of them Is 65:21 398
shall not plant, and another *e* Is 65:22 398
the lion shall *e* straw like the Is 65:25 398
to *e* the fruit thereof and the Jer 2:7 398
they shall *e* up thine harvest, and Jer 5:17 398
sons and thy daughters should *e* Jer 5:17 398
they shall *e* up thy flocks and Jer 5:17 398
they shall *e* up thy vines and thy Jer 5:17 398
unto your sacrifices, and *e* flesh Jer 7:21 398
words were found, and I did *e* them Jer 15:16 398
feasting, to sit with them to *e* Jer 16:8 398
I will cause them to *e* the flesh Jer 19:9 398
they shall *e* every one the flesh Jer 19:9 398
did not thy father *e* and drink, and Jer 22:15 398
The wind shall *e* up all thy Jer 22:22 7462
gardens, and *e* the fruit of them Jer 29:5 398
gardens, and *e* the fruit of them Jer 29:28 398
shall *e* them as common things Jer 31:5
there they did *e* bread together Jer 41:1 398
he did continually *e* bread before Jer 52:33 398
Shall the women *e* their fruit Lam 2:20 398
thy mouth, and *e* that I give thee Eze 2:8 398
Son of man, *e* that thou findest Eze 3:1 398
e this roll, and go speak unto the Eze 3:1 398
and he caused me to *e* that roll Eze 3:2 398
Son of man, cause thy belly to *e* Eze 3:3 398
Then did I *e* it Eze 3:3 398
ninety days shalt thou *e* thereof Eze 4:9 398
thou shalt *e* shall be by weight Eze 4:10 398
from time to time shalt thou *e* it Eze 4:10 398
thou shalt *e* it as barley cakes, Eze 4:12 398
shall the children of Israel *e* Eze 4:13 398
they shall *e* bread by weight, and Eze 4:16 398
Therefore the fathers shall *e* the Eze 5:10 398
and the sons shall *e* their fathers Eze 5:10 398
e thy bread with quaking, and Eze 12:18 398
They shall *e* their bread with Eze 12:19 398
thou didst *e* fine flour, and honey Eze 16:13 398
in thee they *e* upon the mountains Eze 22:9 398
lips, and *e* not the bread of men Eze 24:17 398
your lips, nor *e* the bread of men Eze 24:22 398
they shall *e* thy fruit, and they Eze 25:4 398
Ye *e* with the blood, and lift up Eze 33:25 398
Ye *e* the fat, and ye clothe you Eze 34:3 398
they *e* that which ye have trodden Eze 34:19 7462
of Israel, that ye may *e* flesh Eze 39:17 398
Ye shall *e* the flesh of the Eze 39:18 398
ye shall *e* fat till ye be full, Eze 39:19 398
LORD shall *e* the most holy things Eze 42:13 398
in it to *e* bread before the LORD Eze 44:3 398
They shall *e* the meat offering, Eze 44:29 398
The priests shall not *e* of any Eze 44:31 398
and let them give us pulse to *e* Dan 1:12 398
of the children that *e* of the Dan 1:13 398
e the portion of the king's meat Dan 1:15 398
make thee to *e* grass as oxen Dan 4:25 2939
make thee to *e* grass as oxen Dan 4:32 2939
did *e* grass as oxen, and his body Dan 4:33 399
beasts of the field shall *e* them Hos 2:12 398
They *e* up the sin of my people, Hos 4:8 398
For they shall *e*, and not have Hos 4:10 398
of mine offerings, and *e* it Hos 8:13 398
they shall *e* unclean things in Hos 9:3 398
all that *e* thereof shall be Hos 9:4 398
ye shall *e* in plenty, and be Joel 2:26 398
e the lambs out of the flock, and Amos 6:4 398
great deep, and did *e* up a part Amos 7:4 398
land of Judah, and there *e* bread Amos 7:12 398
gardens, and *e* the fruit of them Amos 9:14 398
they that *e* thy bread have laid a Obad 7
Who also *e* the flesh of my people Mic 3:3 398
Thou shalt *e*, but not be Mic 6:14 398
there is no cluster to *e* Mic 7:1 398
it shall *e* thee up like the Nah 3:15 398
as the eagle that hasteth to *e* Hab 1:8 398
ye *e*, but ye have not enough Hag 1:6 398
And when ye did *e*, and when ye did Zec 7:6 398
did not ye *e* for yourselves, and Zec 7:6 398
let the rest *e* every one the Zec 11:9 398
but he shall *e* the flesh of the Zec 11:16 398
for your life, what ye shall *e* Mt 6:25 *5315*
thought, saying, What shall we *e* Mt 6:31 *5315*
pluck the ears of corn, and to *e* Mt 12:1 *2068*
did *e* the shewbread, which was Mt 12:4 *5315*
which was not lawful for him to *e* Mt 12:4 *5315*
give ye them to *e* Mt 14:16 *5315*
And they did all *e*, and were filled Mt 14:20 *5315*
not their hands when they *e* bread Mt 15:2 *2068*
but to *e* with unwashen hands Mt 15:20 *5315*
yet the dogs *e* of the crumbs Mt 15:27 *2068*
three days, and have nothing to *e* Mt 15:32 *5315*
And they did all *e*, and were filled Mt 15:37 *5315*
they that did *e* were four Mt 15:38 *2068*
smite his fellowservants, and to *e* Mt 24:49 *2068*
for thee to *e* the passover Mt 26:17 *5315*
And as they did *e*, he said, Verily Mt 26:21 *2068*
the disciples, and said, Take, *e* Mt 26:26 *5315*
he did *e* locusts and wild honey Mk 1:6 *2068*
saw him *e* with publicans and Mk 2:16 *2068*
did *e* the shewbread, which is not Mk 2:26 *5315*
lawful to *e* but for the priests Mk 2:26 *5315*
they could not so much as *e* bread Mk 3:20 *5315*
should be given her to *e* Mk 5:43 *5315*
had no leisure so much as to *e* Mk 6:31 *5315*
for they have nothing to *e* Mk 6:36 *5315*
said unto them, Give ye them to *e* Mk 6:37 *5315*
of bread, and give them to *e* Mk 6:37 *5315*
And they did all *e*, and were filled Mk 6:42 *5315*
they that did *e* of the loaves Mk 6:44 *5315*
disciples *e* bread with defiled Mk 7:2 *2068*
e not, holding the tradition of Mk 7:3 *2068*
except they wash, they *e* not Mk 7:4 *2068*
but *e* bread with unwashen hands Mk 7:5 *2068*
table *e* of the children's crumbs Mk 7:28 *2068*
great, and having nothing to *e* Mk 8:1 *5315*
three days, and have nothing to *e* Mk 8:2 *5315*
So they did *e*, and were filled Mk 8:8 *5315*
No man *e* fruit of thee hereafter Mk 11:14 *5315*
that thou mayest *e* the passover Mk 14:12 *5315*
where I shall *e* the passover with Mk 14:14 *5315*
And as they sat and did *e*, Jesus Mk 14:18 *2068*
And as they did *e*, Jesus took Mk 14:22 *2068*
and gave to them, and said, Take, *e* Mk 14:22 *5315*
And in those days he did *e* nothing Lk 4:2 *5315*
disciples, saying, Why do ye *e* Lk 5:30 *2068*
but thine *e* and drink Lk 5:33 *2068*
the ears of corn, and did *e* Lk 6:1 *2068*
e the shewbread, and gave also to Lk 6:4 *5315*
to *e* but for the priests alone Lk 6:4 *5315*
him that he would *e* with him Lk 7:36 *5315*
said unto them, Give ye them to *e* Lk 9:13 *5315*
And they did *e*, and were all filled Lk 9:17 *5315*
e such things as are set before Lk 10:8 *2068*
take thine ease, *e*, drink, and be Lk 12:19 *5315*
for your life, what ye shall *e* Lk 12:22 *5315*
And seek not ye what ye shall *e* Lk 12:29 *5315*
menservants and maidens, and to *e* Lk 12:45 *2068*
to *e* bread on the sabbath day Lk 14:1 *5315*
Blessed is he that shall *e* bread Lk 14:15 *5315*
the husks that the swine did *e* Lk 15:16 *2068*
and let us *e*, and be merry Lk 15:23 *5315*
and afterward thou shalt *e* Lk 17:8 *5315*
They did *e*, they drank, they Lk 17:27 *2068*
they did *e*, they drank, they Lk 17:28 *2068*
us the passover, that we may *e* Lk 22:8 *5315*
where I shall *e* the passover with Lk 22:11 *5315*
With desire I have desired to *e* Lk 22:15 *5315*
I will not any more *e* thereof Lk 22:16 *5315*
That ye may *e* and drink at my Lk 22:30 *2068*
he took it, and did *e* before them Lk 24:43 *5315*
prayed him, saying, Master, *e* Jn 4:31 *5315*
I have meat to *e* that ye know not Jn 4:32 *5315*
any man brought him ought to *e* Jn 4:33 *5315*
we buy bread, that these may *e* Jn 6:5 *5315*
the place where they did *e* bread Jn 6:23 *5315*
because ye did *e* of the loaves Jn 6:26 *5315*
Our fathers did *e* manna in the Jn 6:31 *5315*
gave them bread from heaven to *e* Jn 6:31 *5315*
Your fathers did *e* manna in the Jn 6:49 *5315*
heaven, that a man may *e* thereof Jn 6:50 *5315*
if any man *e* of this bread, he Jn 6:51 *5315*
this man give us his flesh to *e* Jn 6:52 *5315*
Except ye *e* the flesh of the Son Jn 6:53 *5315*
not as your fathers did *e* manna Jn 6:58 *5315*
that they might *e* the passover Jn 18:28 *5315*
did *e* their meat with gladness and Acts 2:46 *3335*
sight, and neither did *e* nor drink Acts 9:9 *5315*
Rise, Peter; kill, and *e* Acts 10:13 *5315*
of God, even to us, who did *e* Acts 10:41 *4906*
and didst *e* with them Acts 11:3 *4906*
Arise, Peter; slay and *e* Acts 11:7 *5315*
e nor drink till they had killed Acts 23:12 *5315*
that we will *e* nothing until we Acts 23:14 *1089*
that they will neither *e* nor Acts 23:21 *5315*
he had broken it, he began to *e* Acts 27:35 *2068*
that he may *e* all things Rom 14:2 *5315*
It is good neither to *e* flesh Rom 14:21 *5315*
that doubteth is damned if he *e* Rom 14:23 *5315*
with such an one, no not to *e* 1Cor 5:11 *4906*
of the idol unto this hour *e* it 1Cor 8:7 *2068*
for neither, if we *e*, are we the 1Cor 8:8 *5315*
neither, if we *e* not, are we the 1Cor 8:8 *5315*
e those things which are offered 1Cor 8:10 *2068*
I will *e* no flesh while the world 1Cor 8:13 *5315*
Have we not power to *e* and to 1Cor 9:4 *5315*
did all *e* the same spiritual meat 1Cor 10:3 *5315*
written, The people sat down to *e* 1Cor 10:7 *5315*
are not they which *e* of the 1Cor 10:18 *2068*
is sold in the shambles, that *e* 1Cor 10:25 *2068*
whatsoever is set before you, *e* 1Cor 10:27 *2068*
e not for his sake that shewed it 1Cor 10:28 *2068*
Whether therefore ye *e*, or drink, 1Cor 10:31 *2068*
this is not to *e* the Lord's 1Cor 11:20 *5315*
have ye not houses to *e* and to 1Cor 11:22 *2068*
he brake it, and said, Take, *e* 1Cor 11:24 *5315*
For as often as ye *e* this bread 1Cor 11:26 *2068*
whosoever shall *e* this bread 1Cor 11:27 *2068*
so let him *e* of that bread, and 1Cor 11:28 *2068*
when ye come together to *e* 1Cor 11:33 *5315*
any man hunger, let him *e* at home 1Cor 11:34 *2068*
let us *e* and drink 1Cor 15:32 *5315*
he did *e* with the Gentiles Gal 2:12 *4906*
Neither did we *e* any man's bread 2Th 3:8 *5315*

not work, neither should he *e* ... 2Th 3:10 *2068*
they work, and *e* their own bread ... 2Th 3:12 *2068*
their word will *e* as doth a ... 2Ti 2:17 *3542,2192*
to *e* which serve the tabernacle ... Heb 13:10 *5315*
shall *e* your flesh as it were ... Jas 5:3 *5315*
I give to *e* of the tree of life ... Rev 2:7 *5315*
to *e* things sacrificed unto idols ... Rev 2:14 *5315*
I give to *e* of the hidden manna ... Rev 2:17 *5315*
to *e* things sacrificed unto idols ... Rev 2:20 *5315*
said unto me, Take it, and *e* it up ... Rev 10:9 *2719*
shall *e* her flesh, and burn her ... Rev 17:16 *5315*
That ye may *e* the flesh of kings, ... Rev 19:18 *5315*

EATEN {105}
Hast thou *e* of the tree, whereof ... Gen 3:11 398
hast *e* of the tree, of which I ... Gen 3:17 398
unto thee of all food that is *e* ... Gen 6:21 398
that which the young men have *e* ... Gen 14:24 398
I have *e* of all before thou ... Gen 27:33 398
rams of thy flock have I not *e* ... Gen 31:38 398
And when they had *e* them up.. Gen 41:21 935,413,7130
known that they had *e* them..... Gen 41:21 935,413,7130
when they had *e* up the corn which ... Gen 43:2 398
In one house shall it be *e* ... Ex 12:46 398
shall no leavened bread be *e* ... Ex 13:3 398
bread shall be *e* seven days ... Ex 13:7 398
and his flesh shall not be *e* ... Ex 21:28 398
cause a field or vineyard to be *e* ... Ex 22:5 1197
it shall not be *e*, because it is ... Ex 29:34 398
shall it be *e* in the holy place ... Lev 6:16 398
it shall not be *e* ... Lev 6:23 398
in the holy place shall it be *e* ... Lev 6:26 398
in the holy place, shall be *e* ... Lev 6:30 398
it shall be *e* in the holy place ... Lev 7:6 398
for thanksgiving shall be *e* the ... Lev 7:15 398
it shall be *e* the same day that ... Lev 7:16 398
the remainder of it shall be *e* ... Lev 7:16 398
be *e* at all on the third day ... Lev 7:18 398
any unclean thing shall not be *e* ... Lev 7:19 398
Wherefore have ye not *e* the sin ... Lev 10:17 398
have *e* it in the holy place ... Lev 10:18 398
if I had *e* the sin offering to ... Lev 10:19 398
they shall not be *e*, they are an ... Lev 11:13 398
Of all meat which may be *e* ... Lev 11:34 398
it shall not be *e* ... Lev 11:41 398
between the beast that may be *e* ... Lev 11:47 398
and the beast that may not be *e* ... Lev 11:47 398
any beast or fowl that may be *e* ... Lev 17:13 398
It shall be *e* the same day ye ... Lev 19:6 398
if it be *e* at all on the third ... Lev 19:7 398
it shall not be *e* of ... Lev 19:23 398
On the same day it shall be *e* up ... Lev 22:30 398
days shall unleavened bread be *e* ... Num 28:17 398
when thou shalt have *e* and be full ... Deut 6:11 398
When thou hast *e* and art full, ... Deut 8:10 398
Lest when thou hast *e* and art full ... Deut 8:12 398
as the roebuck and the hart is *e* ... Deut 12:22 398
they shall not be *e* ... Deut 14:19 398
vineyard, and hath not yet *e* of it ... Deut 20:6 2490
I have not *e* thereof in my ... Deut 26:14 398
Ye have not *e* bread, neither have ... Deut 29:6 398
and they shall have *e* and filled ... Deut 31:20 398
had *e* of the old corn of the land ... Josh 5:12 398
And when Boaz had *e* and drunk, and.... Ruth 3:7 398
up after they had *e* in Shiloh ... 1Sa 1:9 398
if haply the people had *e* freely ... 1Sa 14:30 398
for he had *e* no bread all the day ... 1Sa 28:20 398
and when he had *e*, his spirit came ... 1Sa 30:12 398
for he had *e* no bread, nor drunk ... 1Sa 30:12 398
have we *e* at all of the king's ... 2Sa 19:42 398
hast *e* bread and drunk water in ... 1Kin 13:22 398
to pass, after he had *e* bread ... 1Kin 13:23 398
the lion had not *e* the carcase ... 1Kin 13:28 398
and when they had *e* and drunk, he ... 2Kin 6:23 398
my brethren have not *e* the bread ... Neh 5:14 398
is unsavoury be *e* without salt ... Job 6:6 398
as a garment that is moth *e* ... Job 13:28 398
Or have *e* my morsel myself alone, ... Job 31:17 398
the fatherless hath not *e* thereof ... Job 31:17 398
If I have *e* the fruits thereof ... Job 31:39 398
zeal of thine house hath *e* me up ... Ps 69:9 398
For I have *e* ashes like bread, and ... Ps 102:9 398
bread *e* in secret is pleasant ... Prov 9:17 398
thou hast *e* shalt thou vomit up ... Prov 23:8 398
I have *e* my honeycomb with my ... Song 5:1 398
for ye have *e* up the vineyard ... Is 3:14 398
thereof, and it shall be *e* up ... Is 5:5 398
and it shall return, and shall be *e* ... Is 6:13 1197
I have roasted flesh, and *e* it ... Is 44:19 398
for they have *e* up Jacob, and ... Jer 10:25 398
figs, which could not be *e* ... Jer 24:2 398
evil, very evil, that cannot be *e* ... Jer 24:3 398
the evil figs, which cannot be *e* ... Jer 24:8 398
like vile figs, that cannot be *e* ... Jer 29:17 398
The fathers have *e* a sour grape ... Jer 31:29 398
up even till now have I not *e* of ... Eze 4:14 398
The fathers have *e* sour grapes ... Eze 18:2 398
hath not *e* upon the mountains, ... Eze 18:6 398
duties, but even hath *e* upon the ... Eze 18:11 398
That hath not *e* upon the ... Eze 18:15 398
you to have *e* up the good pasture ... Eze 34:18 7462
unleavened bread shall be *e* ... Eze 45:21 398
ye have *e* the fruit of lies ... Hos 10:13 398
hath left hath the locust *e* ... Joel 1:4 398
hath left hath the cankerworm *e* ... Joel 1:4 398
hath left hath the caterpiller *e* ... Joel 1:4 398
the years that the locust hath *e* ... Joel 2:25 398
they that had *e* were about five ... Mt 14:21 *2068*
they that had *e* were about four ... Mk 8:9 *5315*
shall ye begin to say, We have *e* ... Lk 13:26 *5315*
and serve me, till I have *e* ... Lk 17:8 *5315*
zeal of thine house hath *e* me up ... Jn 2:17 *2719*
and above unto them that had *e* ... Jn 6:13 *977*
very hungry, and would have *e* ... Acts 10:10 *1089*
for I have never *e* any thing that ... Acts 10:14 *5315*
he was *e* of worms, and gave up the ... Acts 12:23 *4662*
again, and had broken bread, and *e* ... Acts 20:11 *1089*
And when they had *e* enough ... Acts 27:38 *2880*
and as soon as I had *e* it, my ... Rev 10:10 *5315*

EATER {3}
Out of the *e* came forth meat, and ... Judg 14:14 398
to the sower, and bread to the *e* ... Is 55:10 398
even fall into the mouth of the *e* ... Nah 3:12 398

EATERS {1}
among riotous *e* of flesh ... Prov 23:20 2151

EATEST {3}
for in the day that thou *e* ... Gen 2:17 398
and why *e* thou not ... 1Sa 1:8 398
so sad, that thou *e* no bread ... 1Kin 21:5 398

EATETH {56}
for whosoever *e* leavened bread ... Ex 12:15 398
for whosoever *e* that which is ... Ex 12:19 398
the soul that *e* of it shall bear ... Lev 7:18 398
But the soul that *e* of the flesh ... Lev 7:20 398
For whosoever *e* the fat of the ... Lev 7:25 398
even the soul that *e* it shall be ... Lev 7:25 398
it be that *e* any manner of blood ... Lev 7:27 398
he that *e* of the carcase of it ... Lev 11:40 398
he that *e* in the house shall wash ... Lev 14:47 398
that *e* any manner of blood ... Lev 17:10 398
against that soul that *e* blood ... Lev 17:10 398
whosoever *e* it shall be cut off ... Lev 17:14 398
every soul that *e* that which died ... Lev 17:15 398
Therefore every one that *e* it ... Lev 19:8 398
it, is a land that *e* up the ... Num 13:32 398
man that *e* any food until evening ... 1Sa 14:24 398
the man that *e* any food this day ... 1Sa 14:28 398
Whose harvest the hungry *e* up ... Job 5:5 398
soul, and never *e* with pleasure ... Job 21:25 398
he *e* grass as an ox ... Job 40:15 398
similitude of an ox that *e* grass ... Ps 106:20 398
The righteous *e* to the satisfying ... Prov 13:25 398
she *e*, and wipeth her mouth, and ... Prov 30:20 398
e not the bread of idleness ... Prov 31:27 398
together, and *e* his own flesh ... Eccl 4:5 398
his days also he *e* in darkness ... Eccl 5:17 398
eat thereof, but a stranger *e* it ... Eccl 6:2 398
it is yet in his hand he *e* it up ... Is 28:4 1104
man dreameth, and, behold, he *e* ... Is 29:8 398
with part thereof he *e* flesh ... Is 44:16 398
he that *e* of their eggs dieth, and ... Is 59:5 398
every man that *e* the sour grape ... Jer 31:30 398
Why *e* your Master with publicans ... Mt 9:11 *2068*
disciples, How is it that he *e* ... Mk 2:16 *2068*
One of you which *e* with me shall ... Mk 14:18 *2068*
receiveth sinners, and *e* with them ... Lk 15:2 *4906*
Whoso *e* my flesh, and drinketh my ... Jn 6:54 *5176*
He that *e* my flesh, and drinketh ... Jn 6:56 *5176*
so he that *e* me, even he shall ... Jn 6:57 *5176*
he that *e* of this bread shall ... Jn 6:58 *5176*
He that *e* bread with me hath ... Jn 13:18 *5176*
another, who is weak, *e* herbs ... Rom 14:2 *2068*
e despise him that *e* not ... Rom 14:3 *2068*
which *e* not judge him that *e* ... Rom 14:3 *2068*
He that *e*, *e* to the Lord, ... Rom 14:6 *2068*
e not, to the Lord he *e* not ... Rom 14:6 *2068*
for that man who *e* with offence ... Rom 14:20 *2068*
because he *e* not of faith ... Rom 14:23 *2068*
e not of the fruit thereof ... 1Cor 9:7 *2068*
e not of the milk of the flock ... 1Cor 9:7 *2068*
e and drinketh unworthily, *e* ... 1Cor 11:29 *2068*

EATING {27}
every man according to his *e* ... Ex 12:4 400
it every man according to his *e* ... Ex 16:16 400
every man according to his *e* ... Ex 16:18 400
every man according to his *e* ... Ex 16:21 400
in his hands, and went on *e* ... Judg 14:9 398
man, until he shall have done *e* ... Ruth 3:3 398
the LORD in *e* with the blood ... 1Sa 14:34 398
abroad upon all the earth, *e* ... 1Sa 30:16 398
it as they had made an end of *e* ... 1Kin 1:41 398
is by the sea in multitude, *e* ... 1Kin 4:20 398
as they were *e* of the pottage, ... 2Kin 4:40 398
were with David three days, *e* ... 1Chr 12:39 398
his sons and his daughters were *e* ... Job 1:13 398
Thy sons and thy daughters were *e* ... Job 1:18 398
rain it upon him while he is *e* ... Job 20:23 3894
e flesh, and drinking wine ... Is 22:13 398
midst, *e* swine's flesh, and the ... Is 66:17 398
an end of *e* the grass of the land ... Amos 7:2 398
John came neither *e* nor drinking ... Mt 11:18 *2068*
The Son of man came *e* and drinking ... Mt 11:19 *2068*
were before the flood they were *e* ... Mt 24:38 *5176*
And as they were *e*, Jesus took ... Mt 26:26 *2068*
neither *e* bread nor drinking wine ... Lk 7:33 *2068*
The Son of man is come *e* and ... Lk 7:34 *2068*
And in the same house remain, *e* ... Lk 10:7 *2068*
the *e* of those things that are ... 1Cor 8:4 *1035*
For in *e* every one taketh before ... 1Cor 11:21 *5315*

EBAL *(e'-bal)* {8} *Son of Shobal.*
Alvan, and Manahath, and *E*, Shepho, ... Gen 36:23 5858
and the curse upon mount *E* ... Deut 11:29 5858
command you this day, in mount *E* ... Deut 27:4 5858
shall stand upon mount *E* to curse ... Deut 27:13 5858
the LORD God of Israel in mount *E* ... Josh 8:30 5858
half of them over against mount *E* ... Josh 8:33 5858
And *E*, and Abimael, and Sheba, ... 1Chr 1:22 5858
Alian, and Manahath, and *E*, Shephi, ... 1Chr 1:40 5858

EBED *(e'-bed)* {6} See EBED-MELECH.
1. Father of Gaal.
Gaal the son of *E* came with his ... Judg 9:26 5651
And Gaal the son of *E* said ... Judg 9:28 5651
the words of Gaal the son of *E* ... Judg 9:30 5651
saying, Behold, Gaal the son of *E* ... Judg 9:31 5651
And Gaal the son of *E* went out ... Judg 9:35 5651
2. A family of exiles.
E the son of Jonathan, and with ... Ezr 8:6 5651

EBED-MELECH *(e'-bed-me'-lek)* {6} *An Ethiopian eunuch.*
Now when *E* the Ethiopian, one of ... Jer 38:7 5663
E went forth out of the king's ... Jer 38:8 5663
king commanded *E* the Ethiopian ... Jer 38:10 5663
So *E* took the men with him, and ... Jer 38:11 5663
E the Ethiopian said unto ... Jer 38:12 5663
speak to *E* the Ethiopian, saying, ... Jer 39:16 5663

EBEN-EZER {3} *A Philistine city.*
to battle, and pitched beside *E* ... 1Sa 4:1 72
and brought it from *E* unto Ashdod ... 1Sa 5:1 72
Shen, and called the name of it *E* ... 1Sa 7:12 72

EBER *(e'-bur)* {13} See HEBER.
1. A great-grandson of Shem.
father of all the children of *E* ... Gen 10:21 5677
and Salah begat *E* ... Gen 10:24 5677
unto *E* were born two sons ... Gen 10:25 5677
lived thirty years, and begat *E* ... Gen 11:14 5677
after he begat *E* four hundred ... Gen 11:15 5677
E lived four and thirty years, and ... Gen 11:16 5677
E lived after he begat Peleg four ... Gen 11:17 5677
begat Shelah, and Shelah begat *E* ... 1Chr 1:18 5677
unto *E* were born two sons ... 1Chr 1:19 5677
E, Peleg, Reu, ... 1Chr 1:25 5677
2. Descendants of Eber 1.
Asshur, and shall afflict *E* ... Num 24:24 5677
3. Son of Elpaal.
E, and Misham, and Shamed, who ... 1Chr 8:12 5677
4. A priest of the Amok family.
Kallai; of Amok, *E* ... Neh 12:20 5677

EBEZ See ABEZ.

EBIASAPH *(e-bi'-a-saf)* {3} See ABIASAPH. *A great-grandson of Korah.*
E his son, and Assir his son, ... 1Chr 6:23 43
the son of Assir, the son of *E* ... 1Chr 6:37 43
the son of Kore, the son of *E* ... 1Chr 9:19 43

EBONY {1}
for a present horns of ivory and *e* ... Eze 27:15 1894

EBRONAH *(eb-ro'-nah)* {2} *An encampment during the Exodus.*
from Jotbathah, and encamped at *E* ... Num 33:34 5684
And they departed from *E*, and ... Num 33:35 5684

ECBATANA See ACHMETHA.

ED *(ed)* {1} *Name of an altar.*
of Gad called the altar *E* ... Josh 22:34

EDAR *(e'-dar)* {1} See EDER. *A name of a watchtower.*
his tent beyond the tower of *E* ... Gen 35:21 5740

EDEN *(e'-dun)* {20}
1. Original land of Adam and Eve.
planted a garden eastward in *E* ... Gen 2:8 5731
went out of *E* to water the garden ... Gen 2:10 5731
into the garden of *E* to dress it ... Gen 2:15 5731
him forth from the garden of *E* ... Gen 3:23 5731
east of the garden of *E* Cherubim ... Gen 3:24 5731
the land of Nod, on the east of *E* ... Gen 4:16 5731
will make her wilderness like *E* ... Is 51:3 5731
hast been in *E* the garden of God ... Eze 28:13 5731
so that all the trees of *E* ... Eze 31:9 5731
and all the trees of *E*, the choice ... Eze 31:16 5731
in greatness among the trees of *E* ... Eze 31:18 5731
of *E* unto the nether parts of the ... Eze 31:18 5731
is become like the garden of *E* ... Eze 36:35 5731
is as the garden of *E* before them ... Joel 2:3 5731
2. An undetermined place.
the children of *E* which were in ... 2Kin 19:12 5731
the children of *E* which were in ... Is 37:12 5731
Haran, and Canneh, and *E*, the ... Eze 27:23 5731
the sceptre from the house of *E* ... Amos 1:5 5731
3. Son of Joah.
of Zimmah, and *E* the son of Joah ... 2Chr 29:12 5731
4. A Levite during Hezekiah's time.
And next him were *E*, and Miniamin, ... 2Chr 31:15 5731

EDER *(e'-dur)* {3} See EDAR. *A city in southern Judah.*
Edom southward were Kabzeel, and *E* ... Josh 15:21 5740
2. A grandson of Merari.
Mahli, and *E*, and Jeremoth, three ... 1Chr 23:23 5740
Mahli, and *E*, and Jerimoth ... 1Chr 24:30 5740

EDGE {56}
his son with the *e* of the sword ... Gen 34:26 6310
in the *e* of the wilderness ... Ex 13:20 7097
people with the *e* of the sword ... Ex 17:13 5310
the *e* of the one curtain from the ... Ex 26:4 8193
uttermost *e* of another curtain ... Ex 26:4 8193
loops shalt thou make in the *e* of ... Ex 26:5 7097
the *e* of the one curtain that is ... Ex 26:10 8193
fifty loops in the *e* of the ... Ex 26:10 8193
on the *e* of one curtain from the ... Ex 36:11 8193
fifty loops made he in the *e* of ... Ex 36:12 7097
e of the curtain in the coupling ... Ex 36:17 7097

fifty loops made he upon the *e* of ... Ex 36:17 7097
smote him with the *e* of the sword ... Num 21:24 6310
Etham, which is in the *e* of the ... Num 33:6 7097
in the *e* of the land of Edom ... Num 33:37 7097
that city with the *e* of the sword ... Deut 13:15 6310
thereof, with the *e* of the sword ... Deut 13:15 6310
thereof with the *e* of the sword ... Deut 20:13 6310
and ass, with the *e* of the sword ... Josh 6:21 6310
all fallen on the *e* of the sword ... Josh 8:24 6310
smote it with the *e* of the sword ... Josh 8:24 6310
smote it with the *e* of the sword ... Josh 10:28 6310
smote it with the *e* of the sword ... Josh 10:30 6310
smote it with the *e* of the sword ... Josh 10:32 6310
smote it with the *e* of the sword ... Josh 10:35 6310
smote it with the *e* of the sword ... Josh 10:37 6310
them with the *e* of the sword ... Josh 10:39 6310
therein with the *e* of the sword ... Josh 11:11 6310
them with the *e* of the sword ... Josh 11:12 6310
smote with the *e* of the sword ... Josh 11:14 6310
even unto the *e* of the sea of ... Josh 13:27 7097
smote it with the *e* of the sword ... Josh 19:47 6310
it with the *e* of the sword ... Judg 1:8 6310
the city with the *e* of the sword ... Judg 1:25 6310
with the *e* of the sword before ... Judg 4:15 6310
fell upon the *e* of the sword ... Judg 4:16 6310
them with the *e* of the sword ... Judg 18:27 6310
the city with the *e* of the sword ... Judg 20:37 6310
them with the *e* of the sword ... Judg 20:48 6310
with the *e* of the sword, with the ... Judg 21:10 6310
people with the *e* of the sword ... 1Sa 15:8 6310
smote he with the *e* of the sword ... 1Sa 22:19 6310
and sheep, with the *e* of the sword ... 1Sa 22:19 6310
the city with the *e* of the sword ... 2Sa 15:14 6310
them with the *e* of the sword ... 2Kin 10:25 6310
servants with the *e* of the sword ... Job 1:15 6310
servants with the *e* of the sword ... Job 1:17 6310
also turned the *e* of his sword ... Ps 89:43 6697
be blunt, and he do not whet the *e* ... Eccl 10:10 6440
them with the *e* of the sword ... Jer 21:7 6310
the children's teeth are set on *e* ... Jer 31:29 6949
his teeth shall be set on *e* ... Jer 31:30 6949
the children's teeth are set on *e* ... Eze 18:2 6949
the border thereof by the *e* ... Eze 43:13
shall fall by the *e* of the sword ... Lk 21:24 *4750*
escaped the *e* of the sword, out ... Heb 11:34 *4750*

EDGES {4}
joined at the two *e* thereof ... Ex 28:7 7098
by the two *e* was it coupled ... Ex 39:4 7099
made him a dagger which had two *e* ... Judg 3:16 6366
hath the sharp sword with two *e* ... Rev 2:12 *1366*

EDIFICATION {4}
his neighbour for his good to *e* ... Rom 15:2 *3619*
speaketh unto men to *e*, and ... 1Cor 14:3 *3619*
the Lord hath given us for *e* ... 2Cor 10:8 *3619*
which the Lord hath given me to *e* ... 2Cor 13:10 *3619*

EDIFIED {2}
and Galilee and Samaria, and were *e* ... Acts 9:31 *3618*
well, but the other is not *e* ... 1Cor 14:17 *3618*

EDIFIETH {3}
puffeth up, but charity *e* ... 1Cor 8:1 *3618*
in an unknown tongue *e* himself ... 1Cor 14:4 *3618*
he that prophesieth *e* the church ... 1Cor 14:4 *3618*

EDIFY {3}
wherewith one may *e* another ... Rom 14:19 *3619*
for me, but all things *e* not ... 1Cor 10:23 *3618*
e one another, even as also ye do ... 1Th 5:11 *3618*

EDIFYING {8}
that the church may receive *e* ... 1Cor 14:5 *3619*
may excel to the *e* of the church ... 1Cor 14:12 *3619*
Let all things be done unto *e* ... 1Cor 14:26 *3619*
dearly beloved, for your *e* ... 2Cor 12:19 *3619*
for the *e* of the body of Christ ... Eph 4:12 *3619*
body unto the *e* of itself in love ... Eph 4:16 *3619*
which is good to the use of *e* ... Eph 4:29 *3619*
than godly *e* which is in faith ... 1Ti 1:4 *3618*

EDOM *(e'-dum)* {87} See EDOMITES, ESAU, IDUMEA, OBED-EDOM.
1. Another name for Esau.
children of Seir in the land of *E* ... Gen 36:21 123
that reigned in the land of *E* ... Gen 36:31 123
Bela the son of Beor reigned in *E* ... Gen 36:32 123
these be the dukes of *E*, ... Gen 36:43 123
the dukes of *E* shall be amazed ... Ex 15:15 123
from Kadesh unto the king of *E* ... Num 20:14 123
E said unto him, Thou shalt not ... Num 20:18 123
E came out against him with much ... Num 20:20 123
Thus *E* refused to give Israel ... Num 20:21 123
by the coast of the land of *E* ... Num 20:23 123
Red sea, to compass the land of *E* ... Num 21:4 123
E shall be a possession, Seir ... Num 24:18 123
Hor, in the edge of the land of *E* ... Num 33:37 123
of Zin along by the coast of *E* ... Num 34:3 123
even to the border of *E* the ... Josh 15:1 123
coast of *E* southward were Kabzeel ... Josh 15:21 123
marchedst out of the field of *E* ... Judg 5:4 123
messengers unto the king of *E* ... Judg 11:17 123
but the king of *E* would not ... Judg 11:17 123
and compassed the land of *E* ... Judg 11:18 123
children of Ammon, and against *E* ... 1Sa 14:47 123
And he put garrisons in *E* ... 2Sa 8:14 123
throughout all *E* put he garrisons ... 2Sa 8:14 123
all they of *E* became David's ... 2Sa 8:14 123
of the Red sea, in the land of *E* ... 1Kin 9:26 123
he was of the king's seed in *E* ... 1Kin 11:14 123
came to pass, when David was in *E* ... 1Kin 11:15 123
he had smitten every male in *E* ... 1Kin 11:15 123
he had cut off every male in *E* ... 1Kin 11:16 123
There was then no king in *E* ... 1Kin 22:47 123
way through the wilderness of *E* ... 2Kin 3:8 123
king of Judah, and the king of *E* ... 2Kin 3:9 123
the king of *E* went down to him ... 2Kin 3:12 123
there came water by the way of *E* ... 2Kin 3:20 123
through even unto the king of *E* ... 2Kin 3:26 123
In his days *E* revolted from under ... 2Kin 8:20 123
Yet *E* revolted from under the ... 2Kin 8:22 123
He slew of *E* in the valley of ... 2Kin 14:7 123
Thou hast indeed smitten *E* ... 2Kin 14:10 123
that reigned in the land of *E* ... 1Chr 1:43 123
And the dukes of *E* were ... 1Chr 1:51 123
These are the dukes of *E* ... 1Chr 1:54 123
from *E*, and from Moab, and from the ... 1Chr 18:11 123
And he put garrisons in *E* ... 1Chr 18:13 123
at the sea side in the land of *E* ... 2Chr 8:17 123
they sought after the gods of *E* ... 2Chr 25:20 123
smote of *E* in the valley of salt ... Ps 60:*t* 123
over *E* will I cast out my shoe ... Ps 60:8 123
who will lead me into *E* ... Ps 60:9 123
The tabernacles of *E*, and the ... Ps 83:6 123
over *E* will I cast out my shoe ... Ps 108:9 123
who will lead me into *E* ... Ps 108:10 123
the children of *E* in the day of ... Ps 137:7 123
they shall lay their hand upon *E* ... Is 11:14 123
Who is this that cometh from *E* ... Is 63:1 123
Egypt, and Judah, and *E*, and the ... Jer 9:26 123
E, and Moab, and the children of ... Jer 25:21 123
And send them to the king of *E* ... Jer 27:3 123
and among the Ammonites, and in *E* ... Jer 40:11 123
Concerning *E*, thus saith the LORD ... Jer 49:7 123
Also *E* shall be a desolation ... Jer 49:17 123
that he hath taken against *E* ... Jer 49:20 123
E be as the heart of a woman in ... Jer 49:22 123
and be glad, O daughter of *E* ... Lam 4:21 123
thine iniquity, O daughter of *E* ... Lam 4:22 123
Because that *E* hath dealt against ... Eze 25:12 123
also stretch out mine hand upon *E* ... Eze 25:13 123
I will lay my vengeance upon *E* by ... Eze 25:14 123
they shall do in *E* according to ... Eze 25:14 123
There is *E*, her kings, and all her ... Eze 32:29 123
escape out of his hand, even *E* ... Dan 11:41 123
E shall be a desolate wilderness, ... Joel 3:19 123
to deliver them up to *E* ... Amos 1:6 123
up the whole captivity to *E* ... Amos 1:9 123
For three transgressions of *E* ... Amos 1:11 123
bones of the king of *E* into lime ... Amos 2:1 123
they may possess the remnant of *E* ... Amos 9:12 123
saith the Lord GOD concerning *E* ... Obad 1 123
destroy the wise men out of *E* ... Obad 8 123
Whereas *E* saith, We are ... Mal 1:4 123
2. Descendants of Esau.
therefore was his name called *E* ... Gen 25:30 123
land of Seir, the country of *E* ... Gen 32:3 123
the generations of Esau, who is *E* ... Gen 36:1 123
Esau is *E* ... Gen 36:8 123
came of Eliphaz in the land of *E* ... Gen 36:16 123
came of Reuel in the land of *E* ... Gen 36:17 123
are the sons of Esau, who is *E* ... Gen 36:19 123

EDOMITE *(e'-dum-ite)* {7} See EDOMITES. *A descendant of Esau.*
Thou shalt not abhor an *E* ... Deut 23:7 130
and his name was Doeg, an *E* ... 1Sa 21:7 130
Then answered Doeg the *E*, which ... 1Sa 22:9 130
And Doeg the *E* turned, and he fell ... 1Sa 22:18 130
day, when Doeg the *E* was there ... 1Sa 22:22
unto Solomon, Hadad the *E* ... 1Kin 11:14 130
of David, when Doeg the *E* came ... Ps 52:*t* 130

EDOMITES *(e'-dum-ites)* {13}
the father of the *E* in mount Seir ... Gen 36:9 130
he is Esau the father of the *E* ... Gen 36:43 130
of the Moabites, Ammonites, *E* ... 1Kin 11:1 130
certain *E* of his father's ... 1Kin 11:17
smote the *E* which compassed him ... 2Kin 8:21 130
the son Zeruiah slew of the *E* in ... 1Chr 18:12 130
all the *E* became David's servants ... 1Chr 18:13 130
In his days the *E* revolted from ... 2Chr 21:8 130
smote the *E* which compassed him ... 2Chr 21:9 130
So the *E* revolted from under the ... 2Chr 21:10 130
come from the slaughter of the *E* ... 2Chr 25:14 130
Lo, thou hast smitten the *E* ... 2Chr 25:19 130
For again the *E* had come and ... 2Chr 28:17 130

EDREI *(ed'-re-i)* {8}
1. A city in Bashan.
his people, to the battle at *E* ... Num 21:33 154
which dwelt at Astaroth in *E* ... Deut 1:4 154
and all his people, to battle at *E* ... Deut 3:1 154
and all Bashan, unto Salchah and *E* ... Deut 3:10 154
that dwelt at Ashtaroth and at *E* ... Josh 12:4 154
reigned in Ashtaroth and in *E* ... Josh 13:12 154
half Gilead, and Ashtaroth, and *E* ... Josh 13:31 154
2. A city in Naphtali.
And Kedesh, and *E*, and En-hazor, ... Josh 19:37 154

EFFECT {14}
she bound her soul, of none *e* ... Num 30:8 6565
and they spake to her to that *e* ... 2Chr 34:22
devices of the people of none *e* ... Ps 33:10 5106
the *e* of righteousness quietness ... Is 32:17 5656
his lies shall not so *e* it ... Jer 48:30 6213
at hand, and the *e* of every vision ... Eze 12:23 1697
God of none *e* by your tradition ... Mt 15:6 *208*
of none *e* through your tradition ... Mk 7:13 *208*
make the faith of God without *e* ... Rom 3:3 *2673*
and the promise made of none *e* ... Rom 4:14 *2673*
the word of God hath taken none *e* ... Rom 9:6 *1601*
Christ should be made of none *e* ... 1Cor 1:17 *2758*
should make the promise of none *e* ... Gal 3:17 *2673*
Christ is become of no *e* unto you ... Gal 5:4 *2673*

EFFECTED {1}
his own house, he prosperously *e* ... 2Chr 7:11 6743

EFFECTUAL {6}
e is opened unto me, and there are ... 1Cor 16:9 *1756*
which is *e* in the enduring of the ... 2Cor 1:6 *1754*
me by the *e* working of his power ... Eph 3:7 *1753*
according to the *e* working in the ... Eph 4:16 *1753*
of thy faith may become *e* by the ... Philem 6 *1756*
The *e* fervent prayer of a ... Jas 5:16 *1754*

EFFECTUALLY {2}
(For he that wrought *e* in Peter ... Gal 2:8 *1754*
which *e* worketh also in you that ... 1Th 2:13 *1754*

EFFEMINATE {1}
idolaters, nor adulterers, nor *e* ... 1Cor 6:9 *3120*

EGG {2}
any taste in the white of an *e* ... Job 6:6 2495
Or if he shall ask an *e*, will he ... Lk 11:12 *5609*

EGGS {7}
whether they be young ones, or *e* ... Deut 22:6 1000
upon the young, or upon the *e* ... Deut 22:6 1000
Which leaveth her *e* in the earth ... Job 39:14 1000
as one gathereth *e* that are left ... Is 10:14 1000
They hatch cockatrice' *e*, and ... Is 59:5 1000
he that eateth of their *e* dieth ... Is 59:5 1000
As the partridge sitteth on *e* ... Jer 17:11

EGLAH *(eg'-lah)* {2} See MICHAL. *A wife of David.*
sixth, Ithream, by *E* David's wife ... 2Sa 3:5 5698
the sixth, Ithream by *E* his wife ... 1Chr 3:3 5698

EGLAIM *(eg'-la-im)* {1} See EN-EGLAIM. *A Moabite city.*
the howling thereof unto *E* ... Is 15:8 97

EGLON *(eg'-lon)* {13}
1. An Amorite city.
Lachish, and unto Debir king of *E* ... Josh 10:3 5700
king of Lachish, the king of *E* ... Josh 10:5 5700
king of Lachish, and the king of *E* ... Josh 10:23 5700
from Lachish Joshua passed unto *E* ... Josh 10:34 5700
And Joshua went up from *E*, and all ... Josh 10:36 5700
to all that he had done to *E* ... Josh 10:37 5700
The king of *E*, one ... Josh 12:12 5700
Lachish, and Bozkath, and *E* ... Josh 15:39 5700
2. A Moabite king.
the LORD strengthened *E* the king ... Judg 3:12 5700
the children of Israel served *E* ... Judg 3:14 5700
a present unto *E* the king of Moab ... Judg 3:15 5700
the present unto *E* king of Moab ... Judg 3:17 5700
and *E* was a very fat man ... Judg 3:17 5700

EGYPT *(e'-jipt)* {611} See EGYPTIAN, MIZRAIM. *Kingdom in northeast Africa.*
went down into *E* to sojourn there ... Gen 12:10 4714
he was come near to enter into *E* ... Gen 12:11 4714
that, when Abram was come into *E* ... Gen 12:14 4714
And Abram went up out of *E* ... Gen 13:1 4714
of the LORD, like the land of *E* ... Gen 13:10 4714
from the river of *E* unto the ... Gen 15:18 4714
him a wife out of the land of *E* ... Gen 21:21 4714
unto Shur, that is before *E* ... Gen 25:18 4714
him, and said, Go not down into *E* ... Gen 26:2 4714
going to carry it down to *E* ... Gen 37:25 4714
and they brought Joseph into *E* ... Gen 37:28 4714
sold him into *E* unto Potiphar ... Gen 37:36 4714
And Joseph was brought down to *E* ... Gen 39:1 4714
that the butler of the king of *E* ... Gen 40:1 4714
offended their lord the king of *E* ... Gen 40:1 4714
and the baker of the king of *E* ... Gen 40:5 4714
called for all the magicians of *E* ... Gen 41:8 4714
in all the land of *E* for badness ... Gen 41:19 4714
throughout all the land of *E* ... Gen 41:29 4714
be forgotten in the land of *E* ... Gen 41:30 4714
and set him over the land of *E* ... Gen 41:33 4714
of *E* in the seven plenteous years ... Gen 41:34 4714
which shall be in the land of *E* ... Gen 41:36 4714
set thee over all the land of *E* ... Gen 41:41 4714
him ruler over all the land of *E* ... Gen 41:43 4714
hand or foot in all the land of *E* ... Gen 41:44 4714
went out over all the land of *E* ... Gen 41:45 4714
he stood before Pharaoh king of *E* ... Gen 41:46 4714
went throughout all the land of *E* ... Gen 41:46 4714
which were in the land of *E* ... Gen 41:48 4714
that was in the land of *E* ... Gen 41:53 4714
all the land of *E* there was bread ... Gen 41:54 4714
all the land of *E* was famished ... Gen 41:55 4714
waxed sore in the land of *E* ... Gen 41:56 4714
all countries came into *E* to ... Gen 41:57 4714
saw that there was corn in *E* ... Gen 42:1 4714
heard that there is corn in *E* ... Gen 42:2 4714
went down to buy corn in *E* ... Gen 42:3 4714
which they had brought out of *E* ... Gen 43:2 4714
and rose up, and went down to *E* ... Gen 43:15 4714
your brother, whom ye sold into *E* ... Gen 45:4 4714
throughout all the land of *E* ... Gen 45:8 4714
God hath made me lord of all *E* ... Gen 45:9 4714
my father of all my glory in *E* ... Gen 45:13 4714
you the good of the land of *E* ... Gen 45:18 4714
land of *E* for your little ones ... Gen 45:19 4714
of all the land of *E* is yours ... Gen 45:20 4714
laden with the good things of *E* ... Gen 45:23 4714
And they went up out of *E*, and came ... Gen 45:25 4714
governor over all the land of *E* ... Gen 45:26 4714
fear not to go down into *E* ... Gen 46:3 4714

I will go down with thee into *E* .... Gen 46:4 4714
land of Canaan, and came into *E* .... Gen 46:6 4714
seed brought he with him into *E* .... Gen 46:7 4714
of Israel, which came into *E* .... Gen 46:8 4714
the land of *E* were born Manasseh .... Gen 46:20 4714
souls that came with Jacob into *E* .... Gen 46:26 4714
Joseph, which were born him in *E* .... Gen 46:27 4714
house of Jacob, which came into *E* .... Gen 46:27 4714
The land of *E* is before thee .... Gen 47:6 4714
a possession in the land of *E* .... Gen 47:11 4714
very sore, so that the land of *E* .... Gen 47:13 4714
that was found in the land of *E* .... Gen 47:14 4714
money failed in the land of *E* .... Gen 47:15 4714
all the land of *E* for Pharaoh .... Gen 47:20 4714
E even to the other end thereof .... Gen 47:21 4714
over the land of *E* unto this day .... Gen 47:26 4714
And Israel dwelt in the land of *E* .... Gen 47:27 4714
in the land of *E* seventeen years .... Gen 47:28 4714
bury me not, I pray thee, in *E* .... Gen 47:29 4714
and thou shalt carry me out of *E* .... Gen 47:30 4714
of *E* before I came unto thee into .... Gen 48:5 4714
before I came unto thee into *E* .... Gen 48:5 4714
all the elders of the land of *E* .... Gen 50:7 4714
And Joseph returned into *E* .... Gen 50:14 4714
And Joseph dwelt in *E*, he, and his .... Gen 50:22 4714
and he was put in a coffin in *E* .... Gen 50:26 4714
of Israel, which came into *E* .... Ex 1:1 4714
for Joseph was in *E* already .... Ex 1:5 4714
there arose up a new king over *E* .... Ex 1:8 4714
the king of *E* spake to the Hebrew .... Ex 1:15 4714
as the king of *E* commanded them .... Ex 1:17 4714
the king of *E* called for the .... Ex 1:18 4714
of time, that the king of *E* died .... Ex 2:23 4714
of my people which are in *E* .... Ex 3:7 4714
the children of Israel out of *E* .... Ex 3:10 4714
the children of Israel out of *E* .... Ex 3:11 4714
brought forth the people out of *E* .... Ex 3:12 4714
that which is done to you in *E* .... Ex 3:16 4714
E unto the land of the Canaanites .... Ex 3:17 4714
of Israel, unto the king of *E* .... Ex 3:18 4714
the king of *E* will not let you go .... Ex 3:19 4714
smite *E* with all my wonders which .... Ex 3:20 4714
unto my brethren which are in *E* .... Ex 4:18 4714
in Midian, Go, return into *E* .... Ex 4:19 4714
and he returned to the land of *E* .... Ex 4:20 4714
When thou goest to return into *E* .... Ex 4:21 4714
the king of *E* said unto them .... Ex 5:4 4714
throughout all the land of *E* to .... Ex 5:12 4714
in, speak unto Pharaoh king of *E* .... Ex 6:11 4714
Israel, and unto Pharaoh king of *E* .... Ex 6:13 4714
of Israel out of the land of *E* .... Ex 6:13 4714
of *E* according to their armies .... Ex 6:26 4714
which spake to Pharaoh king of *E* .... Ex 6:27 4714
out the children of Israel from *E* .... Ex 6:27 4714
spake unto Moses in the land of *E* .... Ex 6:28 4714
of *E* all that I say unto thee .... Ex 6:29 4714
and my wonders in the land of *E* .... Ex 7:3 4714
that I may lay my hand upon *E* .... Ex 7:4 4714
the land of *E* by great judgments .... Ex 7:4 4714
I stretch forth mine hand upon *E* .... Ex 7:5 4714
now the magicians of *E*, they also .... Ex 7:11 4714
thine hand upon the waters of *E* .... Ex 7:19 4714
throughout all the land of *E* .... Ex 7:19 4714
throughout all the land of *E* .... Ex 7:21 4714
the magicians of *E* did so with .... Ex 7:22 4714
to come up upon the land of *E* .... Ex 8:5 4714
out his hand over the waters of *E* .... Ex 8:6 4714
came up, and covered the land of *E* .... Ex 8:6 4714
up frogs upon the land of *E* .... Ex 8:7 4714
lice throughout all the land of *E* .... Ex 8:16 4714
lice throughout all the land of *E* .... Ex 8:17 4714
houses, and into all the land of *E* .... Ex 8:24 4714
of Israel and the cattle of *E* .... Ex 9:4 4714
and all the cattle of *E* died .... Ex 9:6 4714
small dust in all the land of *E* .... Ex 9:9 4714
throughout all the land of *E* .... Ex 9:9 4714
such as hath not been in *E* since .... Ex 9:18 4714
may be hail in all the land of *E* .... Ex 9:22 4714
field, throughout the land of *E* .... Ex 9:22 4714
rained hail upon the land of *E* .... Ex 9:23 4714
of *E* since it became a nation .... Ex 9:24 4714
of *E* all that was in the field .... Ex 9:25 4714
what things I have wrought in *E* .... Ex 10:2 4714
thou not yet that *E* is destroyed .... Ex 10:7 4714
the land of *E* for the locusts .... Ex 10:12 4714
may come up upon the land of *E* .... Ex 10:12 4714
forth his rod over the land of *E* .... Ex 10:13 4714
went up over all the land of *E* .... Ex 10:14 4714
and rested in all the coasts of *E* .... Ex 10:14 4714
field, through all the land of *E* .... Ex 10:15 4714
one locust in all the coasts of *E* .... Ex 10:19 4714
be darkness over the land of *E* .... Ex 10:21 4714
in all the land of *E* three days .... Ex 10:22 4714
more upon Pharaoh, and upon *E* .... Ex 11:1 4714
was very great in the land of *E* .... Ex 11:3 4714
will I go out into the midst of *E* .... Ex 11:4 4714
in the land of *E* shall die .... Ex 11:5 4714
cry throughout all the land of *E* .... Ex 11:6 4714
be multiplied in the land of *E* .... Ex 11:9 4714
Moses and Aaron in the land of *E* .... Ex 12:1 4714
through the land of *E* this night .... Ex 12:12 4714
the firstborn in the land of *E* .... Ex 12:12 4714
gods of *E* I will execute judgment .... Ex 12:12 4714
you, when I smite the land of *E* .... Ex 12:13 4714
your armies out of the land of *E* .... Ex 12:17 4714
of the children of Israel in *E* .... Ex 12:27 4714
the firstborn in the land of *E* .... Ex 12:29 4714
and there was a great cry in *E* .... Ex 12:30 4714
which they brought forth out of *E* .... Ex 12:39 4714
because they were thrust out of *E* .... Ex 12:39 4714
of Israel, who dwelt in *E* .... Ex 12:40 4714
LORD went out from the land of *E* .... Ex 12:41 4714
them out from the land of *E* .... Ex 12:42 4714
of the land of *E* by their armies .... Ex 12:51 4714
day, in which ye came out from *E* .... Ex 13:3 4714
me when I came forth out of *E* .... Ex 13:8 4714
the LORD brought thee out of *E* .... Ex 13:9 4714
the LORD brought us out from *E* .... Ex 13:14 4714
the firstborn in the land of *E* .... Ex 13:15 4714
LORD brought us forth out of *E* .... Ex 13:16 4714
they see war, and they return to *E* .... Ex 13:17 4714
up harnessed out of the land of *E* .... Ex 13:18 4714
king of *E* that the people fled .... Ex 14:5 4714
and all the chariots of *E* .... Ex 14:7 4714
the heart of Pharaoh king of *E* .... Ex 14:8 4714
Because there were no graves in *E* .... Ex 14:11 4714
us, to carry us forth out of *E* .... Ex 14:11 4714
word that we did tell thee in *E* .... Ex 14:12 4714
departing out of the land of *E* .... Ex 16:1 4714
hand of the LORD in the land of *E* .... Ex 16:3 4714
you out from the land of *E* .... Ex 16:6 4714
you forth from the land of *E* .... Ex 16:32 4714
thou hast brought us up out of *E* .... Ex 17:3 4714
LORD had brought Israel out of *E* .... Ex 18:1 4714
gone forth out of the land of *E* .... Ex 19:1 4714
brought thee out of the land of *E* .... Ex 20:2 4714
were strangers in the land of *E* .... Ex 22:21 4714
were strangers in the land of *E* .... Ex 23:9 4714
for in it thou camest out from *E* .... Ex 23:15 4714
them forth out of the land of *E* .... Ex 29:46 4714
us up out of the land of *E* .... Ex 32:1 4714
thee up out of the land of *E* .... Ex 32:4 4714
broughtest out of the land of *E* .... Ex 32:7 4714
thee up out of the land of *E* .... Ex 32:8 4714
of the land of *E* with great power .... Ex 32:11 4714
us up out of the land of *E* .... Ex 32:23 4714
brought up out of the land of *E* .... Ex 33:1 4714
month Abib thou camest out from *E* .... Ex 34:18 4714
you up out of the land of *E* .... Lev 11:45 4714
After the doings of the land of *E* .... Lev 18:3 4714
were strangers in the land of *E* .... Lev 19:34 4714
brought you out of the land of *E* .... Lev 19:36 4714
brought you out of the land of *E* .... Lev 22:33 4714
brought them out of the land of *E* .... Lev 23:43 4714
you forth out of the land of *E* .... Lev 25:38 4714
forth out of the land of *E* .... Lev 25:42 4714
forth out of the land of *E* .... Lev 25:55 4714
you forth out of the land of *E* .... Lev 26:13 4714
forth out of the land of *E* in the .... Lev 26:45 4714
were come out of the land of *E* .... Num 1:1 4714
of *E* I hallowed unto me all the .... Num 3:13 4714
of *E* I sanctified them for myself .... Num 8:17 4714
were come out of the land of *E* .... Num 9:1 4714
which we did eat in *E* freely .... Num 11:5 4714
for it was well with us in *E* .... Num 11:18 4714
Why came we forth out of *E* .... Num 11:20 4714
seven years before Zoan in *E* .... Num 13:22 4714
that we had died in the land of *E* .... Num 14:2 4714
better for us to return into *E* .... Num 14:3 4714
captain, and let us return into *E* .... Num 14:4 4714
people, from *E* even until now .... Num 14:19 4714
and my miracles, which I did in *E* .... Num 14:22 4714
brought you out of the land of *E* .... Num 15:41 4714
ye made us to come up out of *E* .... Num 20:5 4714
How our fathers went down into *E* .... Num 20:15 4714
and we have dwelt in *E* a long time .... Num 20:15 4714
and hath brought us forth out of *E* .... Num 20:16 4714
out of *E* to die in the wilderness .... Num 21:5 4714
there is a people come out from *E* .... Num 22:5 4714
there is a people come out of *E* .... Num 22:11 4714
God brought them out of *E* .... Num 23:22 4714
God brought him forth out of *E* .... Num 24:8 4714
went forth out of the land of *E* .... Num 26:4 4714
whom her mother bare to Levi in *E* .... Num 26:59 4714
of the men that came up out of *E* .... Num 32:11 4714
of *E* with their armies under the .... Num 33:1 4714
were come out of the land of *E* .... Num 33:38 4714
from Azmon unto the river of *E* .... Num 34:5 4714
us forth out of the land of *E* .... Deut 1:27 4714
did for you in *E* before your eyes .... Deut 1:30 4714
the iron furnace, even out of *E* .... Deut 4:20 4714
did for you in *E* before your eyes .... Deut 4:34 4714
with his mighty power out of *E* .... Deut 4:37 4714
after they came forth out of *E* .... Deut 4:45 4714
they were come forth out of *E* .... Deut 4:46 4714
brought thee out of the land of *E* .... Deut 5:6 4714
wast a servant in the land of *E* .... Deut 5:15 4714
thee forth out of the land of *E* .... Deut 6:12 4714
We were Pharaoh's bondmen in *E* .... Deut 6:21 4714
us out of *E* with a mighty hand .... Deut 6:21 4714
and wonders, great and sore, upon *E* .... Deut 6:22 4714
the hand of Pharaoh king of *E* .... Deut 7:8 4714
none of the evil diseases of *E* .... Deut 7:15 4714
did unto Pharaoh, and unto all *E* .... Deut 7:18 4714
thee forth out of the land of *E* .... Deut 8:14 4714
didst depart out of the land of *E* .... Deut 9:7 4714
of *E* have corrupted themselves .... Deut 9:12 4714
forth out of *E* with a mighty hand .... Deut 9:26 4714
were strangers in the land of *E* .... Deut 10:19 4714
went down into *E* with threescore .... Deut 10:22 4714
which he did in the midst of *E* .... Deut 11:3 4714
unto Pharaoh the king of *E* .... Deut 11:3 4714
And what he did unto the army of *E* .... Deut 11:4 4714
it, is not as the land of *E* .... Deut 11:10 4714
brought you out of the land of *E* .... Deut 13:5 4714
brought thee out of the land of *E* .... Deut 13:10 4714
wast a bondman in the land of *E* .... Deut 15:15 4714
thee forth out of *E* by night .... Deut 16:1 4714
out of the land of *E* in haste .... Deut 16:3 4714
of *E* all the days of thy life .... Deut 16:3 4714
that thou camest forth out of *E* .... Deut 16:6 4714
that thou wast a bondman in *E* .... Deut 16:12 4714
cause the people to return to *E* .... Deut 17:16 4714
thee up out of the land of *E* .... Deut 20:1 4714
way, when ye came forth out of *E* .... Deut 23:4 4714
that ye were come forth out of *E* .... Deut 24:9 4714
that thou wast a bondman in *E* .... Deut 24:18 4714
wast a bondman in the land of *E* .... Deut 24:22 4714
when ye were come forth out of *E* .... Deut 25:17 4714
my father, and he went down into *E* .... Deut 26:5 4714
forth out of *E* with a mighty hand .... Deut 26:8 4714
smite thee with the botch of *E* .... Deut 28:27 4714
upon thee all the diseases of *E* .... Deut 28:60 4714
thee into *E* again with ships .... Deut 28:68 4714
in the land of *E* unto Pharaoh .... Deut 29:2 4714
we have dwelt in the land of *E* .... Deut 29:16 4714
them forth out of the land of *E* .... Deut 29:25 4714
to do in the land of *E* to Pharaoh .... Deut 34:11 4714
for you, when ye came out of *E* .... Josh 2:10 4714
All the people that came out of *E* .... Josh 5:4 4714
the way, after they came out of *E* .... Josh 5:4 4714
way as they came forth out of *E* .... Josh 5:5 4714
men of war, which came out of *E* .... Josh 5:6 4714
the reproach of *E* from off you .... Josh 5:9 4714
of him, and all that he did in *E* .... Josh 9:9 4714
From Sihor, which is before *E* .... Josh 13:3 4714
and went out unto the river of *E* .... Josh 15:4 4714
her villages, unto the river of *E* .... Josh 15:47 4714
and his children went down into *E* .... Josh 24:4 4714
also and Aaron, and I plagued *E* .... Josh 24:5 4714
I brought your fathers out of *E* .... Josh 24:6 4714
have seen what I have done in *E* .... Josh 24:7 4714
other side of the flood, and in *E* .... Josh 24:14 4714
our fathers out of the land of *E* .... Josh 24:17 4714
of Israel brought up out of *E* .... Josh 24:32 4714
I made you to go up out of *E* .... Judg 2:1 4714
brought them out of the land of *E* .... Judg 2:12 4714
Israel, I brought you up from *E* .... Judg 6:8 4714
not the LORD bring us up from *E* .... Judg 6:13 4714
land, when they came up out of *E* .... Judg 11:13 4714
But when Israel came up from *E* .... Judg 11:16 4714
of the land of *E* unto this day .... Judg 19:30 4714
when they were in *E* in Pharaoh's 1Sa 2:27 4714
up out of *E* even unto this day 1Sa 8:8 4714
I brought up Israel out of *E* 1Sa 10:18 4714
fathers up out of the land of *E* 1Sa 12:6 4714
When Jacob was come into *E* 1Sa 12:8 4714
forth your fathers out of *E* 1Sa 12:8 4714
the way, when he came up from *E* 1Sa 15:2 4714
when they came up out of *E* 1Sa 15:6 4714
to Shur, that is over against *E* 1Sa 15:7 4714
to Shur, even unto the land of *E* 1Sa 27:8 4714
And he said, I am a young man of *E* 1Sa 30:13 4713
the children of Israel out of *E* 2Sa 7:6 4714
thou redeemedst to thee from *E* 2Sa 7:23 4714
affinity with Pharaoh king of *E* 1Kin 3:1 4714
and unto the border of *E* 1Kin 4:21 4714
country, and all the wisdom of *E* 1Kin 4:30 4714
were come out of the land of *E* 1Kin 6:1 4714
they came out of the land of *E* 1Kin 8:9 4714
forth my people Israel out of *E* 1Kin 8:16 4714
brought them out of the land of *E* 1Kin 8:21 4714
thou broughtest forth out of *E* 1Kin 8:51 4714
broughtest our fathers out of *E* 1Kin 8:53 4714
in of Hamath unto the river of *E* 1Kin 8:65 4714
fathers out of the land of *E* 1Kin 9:9 4714
For Pharaoh king of *E* had gone up 1Kin 9:16 4714
had horses brought out of *E* 1Kin 10:28 4714
went out of *E* for six hundred 1Kin 10:29 4714
servants with him, to go into *E* 1Kin 11:17 4714
to *E*, unto Pharaoh king of *E* 1Kin 11:18 4714
when Hadad heard in *E* that David 1Kin 11:21 4714
And Jeroboam arose, and fled into *E* 1Kin 11:40 4714
unto Shishak king of *E* 1Kin 11:40 4714
was in *E* until the death of 1Kin 11:40 4714
son of Nebat, who was yet in *E* 1Kin 12:2 4714
Solomon, and Jeroboam dwelt in *E* 1Kin 12:2 4714
thee up out of the land of *E* 1Kin 12:28 4714
that Shishak king of *E* came up 1Kin 14:25 4714
sent messengers to So king of *E* 2Kin 17:4 4714
them up out of the land of *E* 2Kin 17:7 4714
the hand of Pharaoh king of *E* 2Kin 17:7 4714
of the land of *E* with great power 2Kin 17:36 4714
of this bruised reed, even upon *E* 2Kin 18:21 4714
so is Pharaoh king of *E* unto all 2Kin 18:21 4714
put thy trust on *E* for chariots 2Kin 18:24 4714
their fathers came forth out of *E* 2Kin 21:15 4714
of *E* went up against the king of 2Kin 23:29 4714
and he came to *E*, and died there 2Kin 23:34 4714
the king of *E* came not again any 2Kin 24:7 4714
had taken from the river of *E* 2Kin 24:7 4714
that pertained to the king of *E* 2Kin 24:7 4714
the armies, arose, and came to *E* 2Kin 25:26 4714
from Shihor of *E* even unto the 1Chr 13:5 4714
whom thou hast redeemed out of *E* 1Chr 17:21 4714
had horses brought out of *E* 2Chr 1:16 4714
brought forth out of *E* a chariot 2Chr 1:17 4714
Israel, when they came out of *E* 2Chr 5:10 4714
my people out of the land of *E* I 2Chr 6:5 4714
in of Hamath unto the river of *E* 2Chr 7:8 4714
them forth out of the land of *E* 2Chr 7:22 4714
and to the border of *E* 2Chr 9:26 4714
unto Solomon horses out of *E* 2Chr 9:28 4714
the son of Nebat, who was in *E* 2Chr 10:2 4714

that Jeroboam returned out of *E* 2Chr 10:2 4714
of *E* came up against Jerusalem 2Chr 12:2 4714
that came with him out of *E* 2Chr 12:3 4714
So Shishak king of *E* came up 2Chr 12:9 4714
they came out of the land of *E* 2Chr 20:10 4714
even to the entering in of *E* 2Chr 26:8 4714
Necho king of *E* came up to fight 2Chr 35:20 4714
the king of *E* put him down at 2Chr 36:3 4714
the king of *E* made Eliakim his 2Chr 36:4 4714
his brother, and carried him to *E* 2Chr 36:4 4714
affliction of our fathers in *E* Neh 9:9 4714
God that brought thee up out of *E* Neh 9:18 4714
Princes shall come out of *E* Ps 68:31 4714
their fathers, in the land of *E* Ps 78:12 4714
How he had wrought his signs in *E* Ps 78:43 4714
And smote all the firstborn in *E* Ps 78:51 4714
Thou hast brought a vine out of *E* Ps 80:8 4714
he went out through the land of *E* Ps 81:5 4714
brought thee out of the land of *E* Ps 81:10 4714
Israel also came into *E* Ps 105:23 4714
E was glad when they departed Ps 105:38 4714
understood not thy wonders in *E* Ps 106:7 4714
which had done great things in *E* Ps 106:21 4714
When Israel went out of *E* Ps 114:1 4714
Who smote the firstborn of *E* Ps 135:8 4714
into the midst of thee, O *E* Ps 135:9 4714
To him that smote *E* in their Ps 136:10 4714
works, with fine linen of *E* Prov 7:16 4714
uttermost part of the rivers of *E* Is 7:18 4714
thee, after the manner of *E* Is 10:24 4714
lift it up after the manner of *E* Is 10:26 4714
be left, from Assyria, and from *E* Is 11:11 4714
he came up out of the land of *E* Is 11:16 4714
The burden of *E* Is 19:1 4714
swift cloud, and shall come into *E* Is 19:1 4714
the idols of *E* shall be moved at Is 19:1 4714
the heart of *E* shall melt in the Is 19:1 4714
the spirit of *E* shall fail in the Is 19:3 4714
of hosts hath purposed upon *E* Is 19:12 4714
they have also seduced *E*, even Is 19:13 4714
they have caused *E* to err in Is 19:14 4714
shall there be any work for *E* Is 19:15 4714
In that day shall *E* be like unto Is 19:16 4714
of Judah shall be a terror unto *E* Is 19:17 4714
five cities in the land of *E* Is 19:18 4714
in the midst of the land of *E* Is 19:19 4714
LORD of hosts in the land of *E* Is 19:20 4714
And the LORD shall be known to *E* Is 19:21 4714
And the LORD shall smite *E* Is 19:22 4714
be a highway out of *E* to Assyria Is 19:23 4714
and the Assyrian shall come into *E* Is 19:23 4714
shall Israel be the third with *E* Is 19:24 4714
saying, Blessed be *E* my people Is 19:25 4714
years for a sign and wonder upon *E* Is 20:3 4714
uncovered, to the shame of *E* Is 20:4 4714
expectation, and of *E* their glory Is 20:5 4714
As at the report concerning *E* Is 23:5 4714
of the river unto the stream of *E* Is 27:12 4714
and the outcasts in the land of *E* Is 27:13 4714
That walk to go down into *E* Is 30:2 4714
and to trust in the shadow of *E* Is 30:2 4714
in the shadow of *E* your confusion Is 30:3 4714
them that go down to *E* for help Is 31:1 4714
staff of this broken reed, on *E* Is 36:6 4714
so is Pharaoh king of *E* to all Is 36:6 4714
put thy trust on *E* for chariots Is 36:9 4714
I gave *E* for thy ransom, Ethiopia Is 43:3 4714
saith the LORD, The labour of *E* Is 45:14 4714
aforetime into *E* to sojourn there Is 52:4 4714
us up out of the land of *E* Jer 2:6 4714
hast thou to do in the way of *E* Jer 2:18 4714
thou also shalt be ashamed of *E* Jer 2:36 4714
brought them out of the land of *E* Jer 7:22 4714
came forth out of the land of *E* Jer 7:25 4714
E, and Judah, and Edom, and the Jer 9:26 4714
them forth out of the land of *E* Jer 11:4 4714
them up out of the land of *E* Jer 11:7 4714
of Israel out of the land of *E* Jer 16:14 4714
of Israel out of the land of *E* Jer 23:7 4714
them that dwell in the land of *E* Jer 24:8 4714
Pharaoh king of *E*, and his Jer 25:19 4714
afraid, and fled, and went into *E* Jer 26:21 4714
the king sent men into *E*, namely Jer 26:22 4714
and certain men with him into *E* Jer 26:22 4714
fetched forth Urijah out of *E* Jer 26:23 4714
bring them out of the land of *E* Jer 31:32 4714
signs and wonders in the land of *E* Jer 32:20 4714
out of the land of *E* with signs Jer 32:21 4714
them forth out of the land of *E* Jer 34:13 4714
army was come forth out of *E* Jer 37:5 4714
shall return to *E* into their own Jer 37:7 4714
Bethlehem, to go to enter into *E* Jer 41:17 4714
but we will go into the land of *E* Jer 42:14 4714
set your faces to enter into *E* Jer 42:15 4714
you there in the land of *E* Jer 42:16 4714
follow close after you there in *E* Jer 42:16 4714
to go into *E* to sojourn there Jer 42:17 4714
you, when ye shall enter into *E* Jer 42:18 4714
Go ye not into *E* Jer 42:19 4714
Go not into *E* to sojourn there Jer 43:2 4714
So they came into the land of *E* Jer 43:7 4714
he shall smite the land of *E* Jer 43:11 4714
in the houses of the gods of *E* Jer 43:12 4714
array himself with the land of *E* Jer 43:12 4714
that is in the land of *E* Jer 43:13 4714
Jews which dwell in the land of *E* Jer 44:1 4714
unto other gods in the land of *E* Jer 44:8 4714
the land of *E* to sojourn there Jer 44:12 4714
and fall in the land of *E* Jer 44:12 4714
them that dwell in the land of *E* Jer 44:13 4714
the land of *E* to sojourn there Jer 44:14 4714
that dwelt in the land of *E* Jer 44:15 4714
Judah that are in the land of *E* Jer 44:24 4714
Judah that dwell in the land of *E* Jer 44:26 4714
man of Judah in all the land of *E* Jer 44:26 4714
Judah that are in the land of *E* Jer 44:27 4714
land of *E* into the land of Judah Jer 44:28 4714
the land of *E* to sojourn there Jer 44:28 4714
give Pharaoh-hophra king of *E* Jer 44:30 4714
Against *E*, against the army of Jer 46:2 4714
army of Pharaoh-necho king of *E* Jer 46:2 4714
E riseth up like a flood, and his Jer 46:8 4714
balm, O virgin, the daughter of *E* Jer 46:11 4714
come and smite the land of *E* Jer 46:13 4714
Declare ye in *E*, and publish in Jer 46:14 4714
Pharaoh king of *E* is but a noise Jer 46:17 4714
O thou daughter dwelling in *E* Jer 46:19 4714
E is like a very fair heifer, but Jer 46:20 4714
The daughter of *E* shall be Jer 46:24 4714
multitude of No, and Pharaoh, and *E* Jer 46:25 4714
in sending his ambassadors into *E* Eze 17:15 4714
with chains unto the land of *E* Eze 19:4 4714
known unto them in the land of *E* Eze 20:5 4714
E into a land that I had espied Eze 20:6 4714
yourselves with the idols of *E* Eze 20:7 4714
did they forsake the idols of *E* Eze 20:8 4714
in the midst of the land of *E* Eze 20:8 4714
them forth out of the land of *E* Eze 20:9 4714
to go forth out of the land of *E* Eze 20:10 4714
the wilderness of the land of *E* Eze 20:36 4714
And they committed whoredoms in *E* Eze 23:3 4714
she her whoredoms brought from *E* Eze 23:8 4714
the harlot in the land of *E* Eze 23:19 4714
brought from the land of *E* Eze 23:27 4714
them, nor remember *E* any more Eze 23:27 4714
E was that which thou spreadest Eze 27:7 4714
face against Pharaoh king of *E* Eze 29:2 4714
against him, and against all *E* Eze 29:2 4714
against thee, Pharaoh king of *E* Eze 29:3 4714
all the inhabitants of *E* shall Eze 29:6 4714
the land of *E* shall be desolate Eze 29:9 4714
make the land of *E* utterly waste Eze 29:10 4714
I will make the land of *E* Eze 29:12 4714
bring again the captivity of *E* Eze 29:14 4714
I will give the land of *E* unto Eze 29:19 4714
of *E* for his labour wherewith he Eze 29:20 4714
And the sword shall come upon *E* Eze 30:4 4714
when the slain shall fall in *E* Eze 30:4 4714
also that uphold *E* shall fall Eze 30:6 4714
LORD, when I have set a fire in *E* Eze 30:8 4714
upon them, as in the day of *E* Eze 30:9 4714
of *E* to cease by the hand of Eze 30:10 4714
shall draw their swords against *E* Eze 30:11 4714
no more a prince of the land of *E* Eze 30:13 4714
will put a fear in the land of *E* Eze 30:13 4714
fury upon Sin, the strength of *E* Eze 30:15 4714
And I will set fire in *E* Eze 30:16 4714
shall break there the yokes of *E* Eze 30:18 4714
will I execute judgments in *E* Eze 30:19 4714
the arm of Pharaoh king of *E* Eze 30:21 4714
I am against Pharaoh king of *E* Eze 30:22 4714
stretch it out upon the land of *E* Eze 30:25 4714
man, speak unto Pharaoh king of *E* Eze 31:2 4714
lamentation for Pharaoh king of *E* Eze 32:2 4714
and they shall spoil the pomp of *E* Eze 32:12 4714
shall make the land of *E* desolate Eze 32:15 4714
shall lament for her, even for *E* Eze 32:16 4714
man, wail for the multitude of *E* Eze 32:18 4714
the land of *E* with a mighty hand Dan 9:15 4714
carry captives into *E* their gods Dan 11:8 4714
the land of *E* shall not escape Dan 11:42 4714
over all the precious things of *E* Dan 11:43 4714
she came up out of the land of *E* Hos 2:15 4714
they call to *E*, they go to Hos 7:11 4714
their derision in the land of *E* Hos 7:16 4714
they shall return to *E* Hos 8:13 4714
but Ephraim shall return to *E* Hos 9:3 4714
E shall gather them up, Memphis Hos 9:6 4714
him, and called my son out of *E* Hos 11:1 4714
not return into the land of *E* Hos 11:5 4714
shall tremble as a bird out of *E* Hos 11:11 4714
and oil is carried into *E* Hos 12:1 4714
LORD thy God from the land of *E* Hos 12:9 4714
the LORD brought Israel out of *E* Hos 12:13 4714
LORD thy God from the land of *E* Hos 13:4 4714
E shall be a desolation, and Edom Joel 3:19 4714
brought you up from the land of *E* Amos 2:10 4714
I brought up from the land of *E* Amos 3:1 4714
in the palaces in the land of *E* Amos 3:9 4714
pestilence after the manner of *E* Amos 4:10 4714
and drowned, as by the flood of *E* Amos 8:8 4714
be drowned, as by the flood of *E* Amos 9:5 4714
up Israel out of the land of *E* Amos 9:7 4714
thee up out of the land of *E* Mic 6:4 4714
thy coming out of the land of *E* Mic 7:15 4714
E were her strength, and it was Nah 3:9 4714
with you when ye came out of *E* Hag 2:5 4714
again also out of the land of *E* Zec 10:10 4714
the sceptre of *E* shall depart Zec 10:11 4714
And if the family of *E* go not up Zec 14:18 4714
This shall be the punishment of *E* Zec 14:19 4714
and his mother, and flee into *E* Mt 2:13 *125*
by night, and departed into *E* Mt 2:14 *125*
Out of *E* have I called my son Mt 2:15 *125*
in a dream to Joseph in *E* Mt 2:19 *125*
Phrygia, and Pamphylia, in *E* Acts 2:10 *125*
with envy, sold Joseph into *E* Acts 7:9 *125*
in the sight of Pharaoh king of *E* Acts 7:10 *125*
and he made him governor over *E* Acts 7:10 *125*
a dearth over all the land of *E* Acts 7:11 *125*
heard that there was corn in *E* Acts 7:12 *125*
So Jacob went down into *E* Acts 7:15 *125*
people grew and multiplied in *E* Acts 7:17 *125*
of my people which is in *E* Acts 7:34 *125*
now come, I will send thee into *E* Acts 7:34 *125*
wonders and signs in the land of *E* Acts 7:36 *125*
hearts turned back again into *E* Acts 7:39 *125*
brought us out of the land of *E* Acts 7:40 *125*
as strangers in the land of *E* Acts 13:17 *125*
all that came out of *E* by Moses Heb 3:16 *125*
to lead them out of the land of *E* Heb 8:9 *125*
riches than the treasures in *E* Heb 11:26 *125*
By faith he forsook *E*, not Heb 11:27 *125*
the people out of the land of *E* Jude 5 *125*
spiritually is called Sodom and *E* Rev 11:8 *125*

EGYPTIAN *(e-jip'-shun)* {23} See EGYPTIAN'S, EGYPTIANS.

1. An inhabitant of Egypt.

and she had an handmaid, an *E* Gen 16:1 4713
wife took Hagar her maid the *E* Gen 16:3 4713
Sarah saw the son of Hagar the *E* Gen 21:9 4713
Abraham's son, whom Hagar the *E* Gen 25:12 4713
captain of the guard, an *E* Gen 39:1 4713
in the house of his master the *E* Gen 39:2 4713
women are not as the *E* women Ex 1:19 4713
he spied an *E* smiting an Hebrew, Ex 2:11 4713
there was no man, he slew the *E* Ex 2:12 4713
kill me, as thou killedst the *E* Ex 2:14 4713
An *E* delivered us out of the hand Ex 2:19 4713
woman, whose father was an *E* Lev 24:10 4713
thou shalt not abhor an *E* Deut 23:7 4713
And they found an *E* in the field 1Sa 30:11 4713
And he slew an *E*, a goodly man 2Sa 23:21 4713
the *E* had a spear in his hand 2Sa 23:21 4713
And Sheshan had a servant, an *E* 1Chr 2:34 4713
And he slew an *E*, a man of great 1Chr 11:23 4713
the *E* into Assyria, and the Is 19:23 4714
was oppressed, and smote the *E* Acts 7:24 *124*
as thou diddest the *E* yesterday Acts 7:28 *124*
Art not thou that *E*, which before Acts 21:38 *124*

2. The Red Sea.

destroy the tongue of the *E* sea Is 11:15 4714

EGYPTIAN'S *(e-jip'-shuns)* {4}

the *E* house for Joseph's sake Gen 39:5 4713
the spear out of the *E* hand 2Sa 23:21 4713
in the *E* hand was a spear like a 1Chr 11:23 4713
the spear out of the *E* hand 1Chr 11:23 4713

EGYPTIANS *(e-jip'-shuns)* {98}

when the *E* shall see thee, that Gen 12:12 4713
the *E* beheld the woman that she Gen 12:14 4713
and Pharaoh said unto all the *E* Gen 41:55 4714
storehouses, and sold unto the *E* Gen 41:56 4714
them by themselves, and for the *E* Gen 43:32 4713
because the *E* might not eat bread Gen 43:32 4713
that is an abomination unto the *E* Gen 43:32 4714
and the *E* and the house of Pharaoh Gen 45:2 4714
is an abomination unto the *E* Gen 46:34 4714
all the *E* came unto Joseph, and Gen 47:15 4714
for the *E* sold every man his Gen 47:20 4714
the *E* mourned for him threescore Gen 50:3 4714
is a grievous mourning to the *E* Gen 50:11 4714
the *E* made the children of Israel Ex 1:13 4714
them out of the hand of the *E* Ex 3:8 4714
wherewith the *E* oppress them Ex 3:9 4714
favour in the sight of the *E* Ex 3:21 4714
and ye shall spoil the *E* Ex 3:22 4714
whom the *E* keep in bondage Ex 6:5 4714
from under the burdens of the *E* Ex 6:6 4714
from under the burdens of the *E* Ex 6:7 4714
the *E* shall know that I am the Ex 7:5 4714
the *E* shall lothe to drink of the Ex 7:18 4714
the *E* could not drink of the Ex 7:21 4714
all the *E* digged round about the Ex 7:24 4714
the houses of the *E* shall be full Ex 8:21 4714
of the *E* to the LORD our God Ex 8:26 4714
of the *E* before their eyes Ex 8:26 4714
the magicians, and upon all the *E* Ex 9:11 4714
and the houses of all the *E* Ex 10:6 4714
favour in the sight of the *E* Ex 11:3 4714
put a difference between the *E* Ex 11:7 4714
will pass through to smite the *E* Ex 12:23 4714
in Egypt, when he smote the *E* Ex 12:27 4714
and all his servants, and all the *E* Ex 12:30 4714
the *E* were urgent upon the people Ex 12:33 4714
of the *E* jewels of silver Ex 12:35 4714
favour in the sight of the *E* Ex 12:36 4714
And they spoiled the *E* Ex 12:36 4714
that the *E* may know that I am the Ex 14:4 4714
But the *E* pursued after them, all Ex 14:9 4714
behold, the *E* marched after them Ex 14:10 4714
us alone, that we may serve the *E* Ex 14:12 4714
been better for us to serve the *E* Ex 14:12 4714
for the *E* whom ye have seen to Ex 14:13 4714
I will harden the hearts of the *E* Ex 14:17 4714
the *E* shall know that I am the Ex 14:18 4714
it came between the camp of the *E* Ex 14:20 4714
the *E* pursued, and went in after Ex 14:23 4714
the *E* through the pillar of fire Ex 14:24 4714
and troubled the host of the *E* Ex 14:24 4714
so that the *E* said, Let us flee Ex 14:25 4714
fighteth for them against the *E* Ex 14:25 4714
waters may come again upon the *E* Ex 14:26 4714
and the *E* fled against it Ex 14:27 4714

the LORD overthrew the *E* in the ... Ex 14:27 4714
that day out of the hand of the *E* ... Ex 14:30 4714
Israel saw the *E* dead upon the ... Ex 14:30 4714
which the LORD did upon the *E* ... Ex 14:31 4714
which I have brought upon the *E* ... Ex 15:26 4714
to the *E* for Israel's sake, and ... Ex 18:8 4714
out of the hand of the *E* ... Ex 18:9 4714
you out of the hand of the *E* ... Ex 18:10 4714
from under the hand of the *E* ... Ex 18:10 4714
have seen what I did unto the *E* ... Ex 19:4 4714
Wherefore should the *E* speak ... Ex 32:12 4714
Then the *E* shall hear it, (for ... Num 14:13 4714
the *E* vexed us, and our fathers ... Num 20:15 4714
hand in the sight of all the *E* ... Num 33:3 4714
For the *E* buried all their ... Num 33:4 4714
the *E* evil entreated us, and ... Deut 26:6 4713
the *E* pursued after your fathers ... Josh 24:6 4714
put darkness between you and the *E* ... Josh 24:7 4713
you out of the hand of the *E* ... Judg 6:9 4714
Did not I deliver you from the *E* ... Judg 10:11 4714
the *E* with all the plagues in the ... 1Sa 4:8 4714
ye harden your hearts, as the *E* ... 1Sa 6:6 4714
you out of the hand of the *E* ... 1Sa 10:18 4714
Hittites, and the kings of the *E* ... 2Kin 7:6 4714
Ammonites, the Moabites, the *E* ... Ezr 9:1 4713
set the *E* against the *E* ... Is 19:2 4714
the *E* will I give over into the ... Is 19:4 4714
the *E* shall know the LORD in that ... Is 19:21 4714
the *E* shall serve with the ... Is 19:23 4714
Assyria lead away the *E* prisoners ... Is 20:4 4714
For the *E* shall help in vain, and ... Is 30:7 4714
Now the *E* are men, and not God ... Is 31:3 4714
of the *E* shall he burn with fire ... Jer 43:13 4714
We have given the hand to the *E* ... Lam 5:6 4714
with the *E* thy neighbours ... Eze 16:26 4714
the *E* for the paps of thy youth ... Eze 23:21 4714
scatter the *E* among the nations ... Eze 29:12 4714
E from the people whither they ... Eze 29:13 4714
scatter the *E* among the nations ... Eze 30:23 4714
scatter the *E* among the nations ... Eze 30:26 4714
in all the wisdom of the *E* ... Acts 7:22 *124*
which the *E* assaying to do were ... Heb 11:29 *124*

EHI *(e'-hi)* {1} See AHARAH. *A son of Benjamin.*
and Ashbel, Gera, and Naaman, *E* ... Gen 46:21 278

EHUD *(e'-hud)* {10}
1. A son of Gera.
E the son of Gera, a Benjamite, a ... Judg 3:15 261
But *E* made him a dagger which had ... Judg 3:16 261
And *E* came unto him ... Judg 3:20 261
E said, I have a message from God ... Judg 3:20 261
E put forth his left hand, and ... Judg 3:21 261
Then *E* went forth through the ... Judg 3:23 261
E escaped while they tarried, and ... Judg 3:26 261
of the LORD, when *E* was dead ... Judg 4:1 261
2. A great-grandson of Benjamin.
Jeush, and Benjamin, and *E*, and ... 1Chr 7:10 261
And these are the sons of *E* ... 1Chr 8:6 261

EIGHT {80}
Seth were *e* hundred years ... Gen 5:4 8083
after he begat Enos *e* hundred ... Gen 5:7 8083
after he begat Cainan *e* hundred ... Gen 5:10 8083
he begat Mahalaleel *e* hundred ... Gen 5:13 8083
after he begat Jared *e* hundred ... Gen 5:16 8083
Mahalaleel were *e* hundred ninety ... Gen 5:17 8083
he begat Enoch *e* hundred years ... Gen 5:19 8083
he that is *e* days old shall be ... Gen 17:12 8083
his son Isaac being *e* days old ... Gen 21:4 8083
these *e* Milcah did bear to Nahor, ... Gen 22:23 8083
length of one curtain shall be *e* ... Ex 26:2 8083
And they shall be *e* boards ... Ex 25:25 8083
e cubits, and the breadth of one ... Ex 36:9 8083
And there were *e* boards ... Ex 36:30 8083
e thousand and an hundred, ... Num 2:24 8083
were *e* thousand and six hundred, ... Num 3:28 8083
were *e* thousand and five hundred ... Num 4:48 8083
e oxen he gave unto the sons of ... Num 7:8 8083
And on the sixth day *e* bullocks ... Num 29:29 8083
shall be forty and *e* cities ... Num 35:7 8083
Zered, was thirty and *e* years ... Deut 2:14 8083
e cities with their suburbs ... Josh 21:41 8083
served Chushan-rishathaim *e* years ... Judg 3:8 8083
and he judged Israel *e* years ... Judg 12:14 8083
Now Eli was ninety and *e* years old ... 1Sa 4:15 8083
and he had *e* sons ... 1Sa 17:12 8083
up his spear against *e* hundred ... 2Sa 23:8 8083
there were in Israel *e* hundred ... 2Sa 24:9 8083
ten cubits, and stones of *e* cubits ... 1Kin 7:10 8083
he reigned *e* years in Jerusalem ... 2Kin 8:17 8083
in Samaria was twenty and *e* years ... 2Kin 10:36 8083
Josiah was *e* years old when he ... 2Kin 22:1 8083
e hundred, ready armed to the war ... 1Chr 12:24 8083
e hundred, mighty men of valour, ... 1Chr 12:30 8083
e thousand and six hundred ... 1Chr 12:35 8083
their brethren, threescore and *e* ... 1Chr 16:38 8083
by man, was thirty and *e* thousand ... 1Chr 23:3 8083
e among the sons of Ithamar ... 1Chr 24:4 8083
was two hundred fourscore and *e* ... 1Chr 25:7 8083
e sons, and threescore daughters ... 2Chr 11:21 8083
in array against him with *e* ... 2Chr 13:3 8083
he reigned *e* years in Jerusalem ... 2Chr 21:5 8083
he reigned in Jerusalem *e* years ... 2Chr 21:20 8083
the house of the LORD in *e* days ... 2Chr 29:17 8083
Josiah was *e* years old when he ... 2Chr 34:1 8083
Jehoiachin was *e* years old when ... 2Chr 36:9 8083
and Joab, two thousand *e* hundred ... Ezr 2:6 8083
of Ater of Hezekiah, ninety and *e* ... Ezr 2:16 8083
Anathoth, an hundred twenty and *e* ... Ezr 2:23 8083
of Asaph, an hundred twenty and *e* ... Ezr 2:41 8083
and with him twenty and *e* males ... Ezr 8:11 8083
thousand and *e* hundred and eighteen ... Neh 7:11 8083
of Zattu, *e* hundred forty and five ... Neh 7:13 8083
of Binnui, six hundred forty and *e* ... Neh 7:15 8083
of Bebai, six hundred twenty and *e* ... Neh 7:16 8083
of Ater of Hezekiah, ninety and *e* ... Neh 7:21 8083
Hashum, three hundred twenty and *e* ... Neh 7:22 8083
an hundred fourscore and *e* ... Neh 7:26 8083
Anathoth, an hundred twenty and *e* ... Neh 7:27 8083
of Asaph, an hundred forty and *e* ... Neh 7:44 8083
of Shobai, an hundred thirty and *e* ... Neh 7:45 8083
threescore and *e* valiant men ... Neh 11:6 8083
Sallai, nine hundred twenty and *e* ... Neh 11:8 8083
the house were *e* hundred twenty ... Neh 11:12 8083
of valour, an hundred twenty and *e* ... Neh 11:14 8083
a portion to seven, and also to *e* ... Eccl 11:2 8083
escaped from Johanan with *e* men ... Jer 41:15 8083
from Jerusalem *e* hundred thirty ... Jer 52:29 8083
the porch of the gate, *e* cubits ... Eze 40:9 8083
and the going up to it had *e* steps ... Eze 40:31 8083
and the going up to it had *e* steps ... Eze 40:34 8083
and the going up to it had *e* steps ... Eze 40:37 8083
e tables, whereupon they slew ... Eze 40:41 8083
shepherds, and *e* principal men ... Mic 5:5 8083
when *e* days were accomplished for ... Lk 2:21 *3638*
an *e* days after these sayings ... Lk 9:28 *3638*
an infirmity thirty and *e* years ... Jn 5:5 *3638*
after *e* days again his disciples ... Jn 20:26 *3638*
which had kept his bed *e* years ... Acts 9:33 *3638*
e souls were saved by water ... 1Pet 3:20 *3638*

EIGHTEEN {22}
house, three hundred and *e* ... Gen 14:14 8083,6240
Eglon the king of Moab *e* years ... Judg 3:14 8083,6240
e years, all the children of ... Judg 10:8 8083,6240
of Israel again *e* thousand men ... Judg 20:25 8083,6240
fell of Benjamin *e* thousand men ... Judg 20:44 8083,6240
of salt, being *e* thousand men ... 2Sa 8:13 8083,6240
of brass, of *e* cubits high apiece ... 1Kin 7:15 8083,6240
Jehoiachin was *e* years old when ... 2Kin 24:8 8083,6240
of the one pillar was *e* cubits ... 2Kin 25:17 8083,6240
tribe of Manasseh *e* thousand ... 1Chr 12:31 8083,6240
in the valley of salt *e* thousand ... 1Chr 18:12 8083,6240
sons and brethren, strong men, *e* ... 1Chr 26:9 8083,6240
of brass *e* thousand talents, and ... 1Chr 29:7 7239,8083
(for he took *e* wives, and ... 2Chr 11:21 8083,6240
with him two hundred and *e* males. Ezr 8:9 8083,6240
with his sons and his brethren, *e* ... Ezr 8:18 8083,6240
thousand and eight hundred and *e*.. Neh 7:11 8083,6240
height of one pillar was *e* cubits ... Jer 52:21 8083,6240
round about *e* thousand measures... Eze 48:35 8083,6240
those *e*, upon whom the tower.. Lk 13:4 *1176,2532,3638*
a spirit of infirmity *e* years ... Lk 13:11 *1176,2532,3638*
hath bound, lo, these *e* years ... Lk 13:16 *1176,2532,3638*

EIGHTEENTH {11}
Now in the *e* year of king ... 1Kin 15:1 8083,6240
over Israel in Samaria the *e* year ... 2Kin 3:1 8083,6240
pass in the *e* year of king Josiah ... 2Kin 22:3 8083,6240
But in the *e* year of king Josiah ... 2Kin 23:23 8083,6240
to Hezir, the *e* to Aphses, ... 1Chr 24:15 8083,6240
The *e* to Hanani, he, his sons ... 1Chr 25:25 8083,6240
Now in the *e* year of king ... 2Chr 13:1 8083,6240
Now in the *e* year of his reign, ... 2Chr 34:8 8083,6240
In the *e* year of the reign of ... 2Chr 35:19 8083,6240
of Judah, which was the *e* year of ... Jer 32:1 8083,6240
In the *e* year of Nebuchadrezzar ... Jer 52:29 8083,6240

EIGHTH {39}
on the *e* day thou shalt give it ... Ex 22:30 8066
And it came to pass on the *e* day ... Lev 9:1 8066
in the *e* day the flesh of his ... Lev 12:3 8066
on the *e* day he shall take two he ... Lev 14:10 8066
he shall bring them on the *e* day ... Lev 14:23 8066
on the *e* day he shall take to him ... Lev 15:14 8066
on the *e* day she shall take unto ... Lev 15:29 8066
and from the *e* day and thenceforth ... Lev 22:27 8066
on the *e* day shall be an holy ... Lev 23:36 8066
on the *e* day shall be a sabbath ... Lev 23:39 8066
And ye shall sow the *e* year ... Lev 25:22 8066
on the *e* day he shall bring two ... Num 6:10 8066
On the *e* day offered Gamaliel the ... Num 7:54 8066
On the *e* day ye shall have a ... Num 29:35 8066
month Bul, which is the *e* month ... 1Kin 6:38 8066
On the *e* day he sent the people ... 1Kin 8:66 8066
ordained a feast in the *e* month ... 1Kin 12:32 8066
the fifteenth day of the *e* month ... 1Kin 12:33 8066
e year of Asa king of Judah began ... 1Kin 16:29 8083
e year of Azariah king of Judah ... 2Kin 15:8 8083
him in the *e* year of his reign ... 2Kin 24:12 8083
Johanan the *e*, Elzabad the ninth, ... 1Chr 12:12 8066
to Hakkoz, the *e* to Abijah, ... 1Chr 24:10 8066
The *e* to Jeshaiah, he, his sons, ... 1Chr 25:15 8066
the seventh, Peulthai the *e* ... 1Chr 26:5 8066
e captain for the *e* month ... 1Chr 27:11 8066
in the *e* day they made a solemn ... 2Chr 7:9 8066
on the *e* day of the month came ... 2Chr 29:17 8066
For in the *e* year of his reign, ... 2Chr 34:3 8083
on the *e* day was a solemn ... Neh 8:18 8066
it shall be, that upon the *e* day ... Eze 43:27 8066
In the *e* month, in the second ... Zec 1:1 8066
that on the *e* day they came to ... Lk 1:59 *3590*
and circumcised him the *e* day ... Acts 7:8 *3590*
Circumcised the *e* day, of the ... Phil 3:5 *3637*
but saved Noah the *e* person ... 2Pet 2:5 *3590*
was, and is not, even he is the *e* ... Rev 17:11 *3590*
the *e*, beryl ... Rev 21:20 *3590*

EIGHTIETH {1}
e year after the children of ... 1Kin 6:1 8084

EIGHTY {3}
And Methuselah lived an hundred *e* ... Gen 5:25 8084
he begat Lamech seven hundred *e* ... Gen 5:26 8084
And Lamech lived an hundred *e* ... Gen 5:28 8084

EITHER See APPENDIX.

EKER *(e'-ker)* {1} *Descendant of Judah.*
were, Maaz, and Jamin, and *E* ... 1Chr 2:27 6134

EKRON *(ec'-ron)* {22} See EKRONITES. *A Philistine city.*
unto the borders of *E* northward ... Josh 13:3 6138
out unto the side of *E* northward ... Josh 15:11 6138
E, with her towns and her villages ... Josh 15:45 6138
From *E* even unto the sea, all ... Josh 15:46 6138
And Elon, and Thimnathah, and *E* ... Josh 19:43 6138
and *E* with the coast thereof ... Judg 1:18 6138
they sent the ark of God to *E* ... 1Sa 5:10 6138
pass, as the ark of God came to *E* ... 1Sa 5:10 6138
they returned to *E* the same day ... 1Sa 6:16 6138
one, for Gath one, for *E* one ... 1Sa 6:17 6138
to Israel, from *E* even unto Gath ... 1Sa 7:14 6138
the valley, and to the gates of *E* ... 1Sa 17:52 6138
even unto Gath, and unto *E* ... 1Sa 17:52 6138
of Baal-zebub the god of *E* ... 2Kin 1:2 6138
of Baal-zebub the god of *E* ... 2Kin 1:3 6138
of Baal-zebub the god of *E* ... 2Kin 1:6 6138
of Baal-zebub the god of *E* ... 2Kin 1:16 6138
and Ashkelon, and Azzah, and *E* ... Jer 25:20 6138
I will turn mine hand against *E* ... Amos 1:8 6138
noonday, and *E* shall be rooted up ... Zeph 2:4 6138
it, and be very sorrowful, and *E* ... Zec 9:5 6138
in Judah, and *E* as a Jebusite ... Zec 9:7 6138

EKRONITES *(ek'-ron-ites)* {2} *Inhabitants of Ekron.*
the Gittites, and the *E* ... Josh 13:3 6139
that the *E* cried out, saying, ... 1Sa 5:10 6139

ELADAH *(el'-a-dah)* {1} *A descendant of Ephraim.*
E his son, and Tahath his son, ... 1Chr 7:20 497

ELAH *(e'-lah)* {17}
1. An Edomite prince.
Duke Aholibamah, duke *E*, duke ... Gen 36:41 425
Duke Aholibamah, duke *E*, duke ... 1Chr 1:52 425
2. A valley in Judah.
and pitched by the valley of *E* ... 1Sa 17:2 425
Israel, were in the valley of *E* ... 1Sa 17:19 425
thou slewest in the valley of *E* ... 1Sa 21:9 425
3. Father of Shimei.
Shimei the son of *E*, in Benjamin ... 1Kin 4:18 425
4. Son of King Baasha of Israel.
E his son reigned in his stead ... 1Kin 16:6 425
E the son of Baasha to reign over ... 1Kin 16:8 425
Baasha, and the sins of *E* his son ... 1Kin 16:13 425
Now the rest of the acts of *E* ... 1Kin 16:14 425
5. Father of King Hoshea of Israel.
Hoshea the son of *E* made a ... 2Kin 15:30 425
Judah began Hoshea the son of *E* ... 2Kin 17:1 425
of Hoshea son of *E* king of Israel ... 2Kin 18:1 425
of Hoshea son of *E* king of Israel ... 2Kin 18:9 425
6. A son of Caleb.
of Jephunneh; Iru, *E* ... 1Chr 4:15 425
and the sons of *E*, even Kenaz ... 1Chr 4:15 425
7. A Benjamite.
E the son of Uzzi, the son of ... 1Chr 9:8 425

ELAM *(e'-lam)* {28} See ELAMITES, PERSIA.
1. A son of Shem.
E, and Asshur, and Arphaxad, and Lud . Gen 10:22 5867
E, and Asshur, and Arphaxad, and Lud . 1Chr 1:17 5867
2. Land of the Elamites.
Ellasar, Chedorlaomer king of *E* ... Gen 14:1 5867
With Chedorlaomer the king of *E* ... Gen 14:9 5867
Pathros, and from Cush, and from *E* ... Is 11:11 5867
Go up, O *E*: ... Is 21:2 5867
E bare the quiver with chariots ... Is 22:6 5867
of Zimri, and all the kings of *E* ... Jer 25:25 5867
E in the beginning of the reign ... Jer 49:34 5867
Behold, I will break the bow of *E* ... Jer 49:35 5867
upon *E* will I bring the four ... Jer 49:36 5867
the outcasts of *E* shall not come ... Jer 49:36 5867
For I will cause *E* to be dismayed ... Jer 49:37 5867
And I will set my throne in *E* ... Jer 49:38 5867
bring again the captivity of *E* ... Jer 49:39 5867
There is *E* and all her multitude ... Eze 32:24 5867
which is in the province of *E* ... Dan 8:2 5867
3. Son of Shashak.
And Hananiah, and *E*, and Antothijah, .. 1Chr 8:24 5867
4. A son of Meshelemiah.
E the fifth, Jehohanan the sixth, ... 1Chr 26:3 5867
5. A family of exiles with Zerubbabel.
The children of *E*, a thousand two ... Ezr 2:7 5867
The children of *E*, a thousand two ... Neh 7:12 5867
6. A family of exiles with Zerubbabel.
The children of the other *E* ... Ezr 2:31 5867
The children of the other *E* ... Neh 7:34 5867
7. A family of exiles with Ezra.
And of the sons of *E* ... Ezr 8:7 5867
8. An ancestor of Shechaniah.
of Jehiel, one of the sons of *E* ... Ezr 10:2 5867
And of the sons of *E* ... Ezr 10:26 5867
9. A chief who renewed the covenant.
Parosh, Pahath-moab, *E*, Zatthu, ... Neh 10:14 5867
10. A priest who purified the wall.
and Jehohanan, and Malchijah, and *E* ... Neh 12:42 5867

ELAMITES *(e'-lam-ites)* {2} See PERSIANS. *Foreign settlers in Samaria.*
the Dehavites, and the *E*, ... Ezr 4:9 5962
Parthians, and Medes, and *E* ... Acts 2:9 *1639*

ELASAH *(el'-a-sah)* {2} See ELEASAH.
1. Married a foreign wife.
Ishmael, Nethaneel, Jozabad, and *E* Ezr 10:22 501
2. An ambassador of Hezekiah.
By the hand of *E* the son of Jer 29:3 501

ELATH *(e'-lath)* {5} See ELOTH. *An Elamite port.*
the way of the plain from *E* Deut 2:8 359
He built *E*, and restored it to 2Kin 14:22 359
of Syria recovered *E* to Syria 2Kin 16:6 359
and drave the Jews from *E* 2Kin 16:6 359
and the Syrians came to *E*, and 2Kin 16:6 359

EL-BERITH See BERITH.

EL-BETH-EL {1} *Another name for Bethel.*
an altar, and called the place *E* Gen 35:7 416

ELDAAH *(el'-da-ah)* {2} *A son of Midian.*
Epher, and Hanoch, and Abidah, and *E* Gen 25:4 420
Epher, and Henoch, and Abida, and *E* 1Chr 1:33 420

ELDAD *(el'-dad)* {2} *An elder and prophet with Moses.*
camp, the name of the one was *E* Num 11:26 419
man, and told Moses, and said, *E* Num 11:27 419

ELDER {20}
the brother of Japheth the *e* Gen 10:21 1419
the *e* shall serve the younger Gen 25:23 7227
these words of Esau her *e* son Gen 27:42 1419
the name of the *e* was Leah Gen 29:16 1419
Behold my *e* daughter Merab, her 1Sa 18:17 1419
for he is mine *e* brother 1Kin 2:22 1419
aged men, much *e* than thy father Job 15:10
because they were *e* than he Job 32:4 2205,3117
thine *e* sister is Samaria, she and Eze 16:46 1419
receive thy sisters, thine *e* Eze 16:61 1419
names of them were Aholah the *e* Eze 23:4 1419
Now his *e* son was in the field Lk 15:25 *4245*
The *e* shall serve the younger Rom 9:12 *3187*
Rebuke not an *e*, but intreat him 1Ti 5:1 *4245*
The *e* women as mothers 1Ti 5:2 *4245*
Against an *e* receive not an 1Ti 5:19 *4245*
you I exhort, who am also an *e* 1Pet 5:1 *4850*
submit yourselves unto the *e* 1Pet 5:5 *4245*
The *e* unto the elect lady and her 2Jn 1 *4245*
The *e* unto the wellbeloved Gaius, 3Jn 1 *4245*

ELDERS {179}
of Pharaoh, the *e* of his house Gen 50:7 2205
all the *e* of the land of Egypt, Gen 50:7 2205
gather the *e* of Israel together, Ex 3:16 2205
the *e* of Israel, unto the king of Ex 3:18 2205
the *e* of the children of Israel Ex 4:29 2205
called for all the *e* of Israel Ex 12:21 2205
take with thee of the *e* of Israel Ex 17:5 2205
in the sight of the *e* of Israel Ex 17:6 2205
all the *e* of Israel, to eat bread Ex 18:12 2205
and called for the *e* of the people Ex 19:7 2205
and seventy of the *e* of Israel Ex 24:1 2205
and seventy of the *e* of Israel Ex 24:9 2205
And he said unto the *e*, Tarry ye Ex 24:14 2205
the *e* of the congregation shall Lev 4:15 2205
and his sons, and the *e* of Israel Lev 9:1 2205
me seventy men of the *e* of Israel Num 11:16 2205
knowest to be the *e* of the people Num 11:16 2205
men of the *e* of the people Num 11:24 2205
and gave it unto the seventy *e* Num 11:25 2205
the camp, he and the *e* of Israel Num 11:30 2205
the *e* of Israel followed him Num 16:25 2205
And Moab said unto the *e* of Midian Num 22:4 2205
e of Moab and the *e* of Midian Num 22:7 2205
heads of your tribes, and your *e* Deut 5:23 2205
Then the *e* of his city shall send Deut 19:12 2205
Then thy *e* and thy judges shall Deut 21:2 2205
even the *e* of that city shall Deut 21:3 2205
the *e* of that city shall bring Deut 21:4 2205
all the *e* of that city, that are Deut 21:6 2205
him out unto the *e* of his city Deut 21:19 2205
shall say unto the *e* of his city Deut 21:20 2205
the *e* of the city in the gate Deut 22:15 2205
father shall say unto the *e* Deut 22:16 2205
cloth before the *e* of the city Deut 22:17 2205
the *e* of that city shall take Deut 22:18 2205
wife go up to the gate unto the *e* Deut 25:7 2205
Then the *e* of his city shall call Deut 25:8 2205
unto him in the presence of the *e* Deut 25:9 2205
Moses with the *e* of Israel Deut 27:1 2205
captains of your tribes, your *e* Deut 29:10 2205
LORD, and unto all the *e* of Israel Deut 31:9 2205
unto me all the *e* of your tribes Deut 31:28 2205
thy *e*, and they will tell thee Deut 32:7 2205
the *e* of Israel, and put dust upon Josh 7:6 2205
the *e* of Israel, before the Josh 8:10 2205
And all Israel, and their *e* Josh 8:33 2205
Wherefore our *e* and all the Josh 9:11 2205
in the ears of the *e* of that city Josh 20:4 2205
for all Israel, and for their *e* Josh 23:2 2205
and called for the *e* of Israel Josh 24:1 2205
all the days of the *e* that Josh 24:31 2205
all the days of the *e* that Judg 2:7 2205
the *e* thereof, even threescore and Judg 8:14 2205
And he took the *e* of the city Judg 8:16 2205
the *e* of Gilead went to fetch Judg 11:5 2205
said unto the *e* of Gilead Judg 11:7 2205
the *e* of Gilead said unto Judg 11:8 2205
said unto the *e* of Gilead Judg 11:9 2205
the *e* of Gilead said unto Judg 11:10 2205
went with the *e* of Gilead Judg 11:11 2205
Then the *e* of the congregation Judg 21:16 2205
took ten men of the *e* of the city Ruth 4:2 2205
before the *e* of my people Ruth 4:4 2205
And Boaz said unto the *e*, and unto Ruth 4:9 2205
that were in the gate, and the *e* Ruth 4:11 2205
the *e* of Israel said, Wherefore 1Sa 4:3 2205
Then all the *e* of Israel gathered 1Sa 8:4 2205
the *e* of Jabesh said unto him, 1Sa 11:3 2205
before the *e* of my people, and 1Sa 15:30 2205
the *e* of the town trembled at his 1Sa 16:4 2205
of the spoil unto the *e* of Judah 1Sa 30:26 2205
with the *e* of Israel, saying, Ye 2Sa 3:17 2205
So all the *e* of Israel came to 2Sa 5:3 2205
the *e* of his house arose, and went 2Sa 12:17 2205
well, and all the *e* of Israel 2Sa 17:4 2205
Absalom and the *e* of Israel 2Sa 17:15 2205
saying, Speak unto the *e* of Judah 2Sa 19:11 2205
Solomon assembled the *e* of Israel 1Kin 8:1 2205
all the *e* of Israel came, and the 1Kin 8:3 2205
called all the *e* of the land 1Kin 20:7 2205
And all the *e* and all the people 1Kin 20:8 2205
and sent the letters unto the *e* 1Kin 21:8 2205
the men of his city, even the *e* 1Kin 21:11 2205
his house, and the *e* sat with him 2Kin 6:32 2205
came to him, he said to the *e* 2Kin 6:32 2205
the rulers of Jezreel, to the *e* 2Kin 10:1 2205
the *e* also, and the bringers up of 2Kin 10:5 2205
the *e* of the priests, covered 2Kin 19:2 2205
unto him all the *e* of Judah 2Kin 23:1 2205
Therefore came all the *e* of 1Chr 11:3 2205
the *e* of Israel, and the captains 1Chr 15:25 2205
the *e* of Israel, who were clothed 1Chr 21:16 2205
Solomon assembled the *e* of Israel 2Chr 5:2 2205
And all the *e* of Israel came 2Chr 5:4 2205
together all the *e* of Judah 2Chr 34:29 2205
God was upon the *e* of the Jews Ezr 5:5 7868
Then asked we those *e*, and said Ezr 5:9 7868
the *e* of the Jews build this Ezr 6:7 7868
e of these Jews for the building Ezr 6:8 7868
the *e* of the Jews builded, and Ezr 6:14 7868
counsel of the princes and the *e* Ezr 10:8 2205
and with them the *e* of every city Ezr 10:14 2205
him in the assembly of the *e* Ps 107:32 2205
sitteth among the *e* of the land Prov 31:23 2205
the *e* of the priests covered with Is 37:2 2205
up certain of the *e* of the land Jer 26:17 2205
of the *e* which were carried away Jer 29:1 2205
mine *e* gave up the ghost in the Lam 1:19 2205
The *e* of the daughter of Zion sit Lam 2:10 2205
priests, they favoured not the *e* Lam 4:16 2205
the faces of *e* were not honoured Lam 5:12 2205
The *e* have ceased from the gate, Lam 5:14 2205
the *e* of Judah sat before me, Eze 8:1 2205
of the *e* of Israel unto me Eze 14:1 2205
that certain of the *e* of Israel Eze 20:1 2205
man, speak unto the *e* of Israel Eze 20:3 2205
a solemn assembly, gather the *e* Joel 1:14 2205
the congregation, assemble the *e* Joel 2:16 2205
transgress the tradition of the *e* Mt 15:2 *4245*
and suffer many things of the *e* Mt 16:21 *4245*
the *e* of the people came unto him Mt 21:23 *4245*
the *e* of the people, unto the Mt 26:3 *4245*
chief priests and *e* of the people Mt 26:47 *4245*
scribes and the *e* were assembled Mt 26:57 *4245*
Now the chief priests, and *e* Mt 26:59 *4245*
e of the people took counsel Mt 27:1 *4245*
silver to the chief priests and *e* Mt 27:3 *4245*
accused of the chief priests and *e* Mt 27:12 *4245*
e persuaded the multitude that Mt 27:20 *4245*
him, with the scribes and *e* Mt 27:41 *4245*
they were assembled with the *e* Mt 28:12 *4245*
holding the tradition of the *e* Mk 7:3 *4245*
to the tradition of the *e* Mk 7:5 *4245*
things, and be rejected of the *e* Mk 8:31 *4245*
priests, and the scribes, and the *e* Mk 11:27 *4245*
priest and the scribes and the *e* Mk 14:43 *4245*
all the chief priests and the *e* Mk 14:53 *4245*
held a consultation with the *e* Mk 15:1 *4245*
sent unto him the *e* of the Jews Lk 7:3 *4245*
things, and be rejected of the *e* Lk 9:22 *4245*
scribes came upon him with the *e* Lk 20:1 *4245*
captains of the temple, and the *e* Lk 22:52 *4245*
the *e* of the people and the chief Lk 22:66 *4244*
morrow, that their rulers, and *e* Acts 4:5 *4245*
of the people, and *e* of Israel, Acts 4:8 *4245*
priests and *e* had said unto them Acts 4:23 *4245*
stirred up the people, and the *e* Acts 6:12 *4245*
sent it to the *e* by the hands of Acts 11:30 *4245*
ordained them *e* in every church Acts 14:23 *4245*
apostles and *e* about this question Acts 15:2 *4245*
church, and of the apostles and *e* Acts 15:4 *4245*
e came together for to consider Acts 15:6 *4245*
Then pleased it the apostles and *e* Acts 15:22 *4245*
The apostles and *e* and brethren Acts 15:23 *4245*
e which were at Jerusalem Acts 16:4 *4245*
called the *e* of the church Acts 20:17 *4245*
and all the *e* were present Acts 21:18 *4245*
and all the estate of the *e* Acts 22:5 *4244*
came to the chief priests and *e* Acts 23:14 *4245*
high priest descended with the *e* Acts 24:1 *4245*
the *e* of the Jews informed me, Acts 25:15 *4245*
Let the *e* that rule well be 1Ti 5:17 *4245*
ordain *e* in every city, as I had Titus 1:5 *4245*
For by it the *e* obtained a good Heb 11:2 *4245*
him call for the *e* of the church Jas 5:14 *4245*
The *e* which are among you I 1Pet 5:1 *4245*
twenty *e* sitting, clothed in Rev 4:4 *4245*
twenty *e* fall down before him Rev 4:10 *4245*
one of the *e* saith unto me, Weep Rev 5:5 *4245*
beasts, and in the midst of the *e* Rev 5:6 *4245*
twenty *e* fell down before the Rev 5:8 *4245*
the throne and the beasts and the *e* Rev 5:11 *4245*
twenty *e* fell down and worshipped Rev 5:14 *4245*
about the throne, and about the *e* Rev 7:11 *4245*
And one of the *e* answered, saying Rev 7:13 *4245*
And the four and twenty *e*, which Rev 11:16 *4245*
before the four beasts, and the *e* Rev 14:3 *4245*
And the four and twenty *e* and the Rev 19:4 *4245*

ELDEST {14}
unto his *e* servant of his house Gen 24:2 2205
not see, he called Esau his *e* son Gen 27:1 1419
goodly raiment of her *e* son Esau Gen 27:15 1419
And he searched, and began at the *e* Gen 44:12 1419
of Reuben, Israel's *e* son Num 1:20 1060
Reuben, the *e* son of Israel Num 26:5 1060
the three *e* sons of Jesse went and 1Sa 17:13 1419
the three *e* followed Saul 1Sa 17:14 1419
Eliab his *e* brother heard when he 1Sa 17:28 1419
Then he took his *e* son that 2Kin 3:27 1060
to the camp had slain all the *e* 2Chr 22:1 7223
wine in their *e* brother's house Job 1:13 1060
wine in their *e* brother's house Job 1:18 1060
one by one, beginning at the *e* Jn 8:9 *4245*

ELEAD *(e'-le-ad)* {1} *A descendant of Ephraim.*
Shuthelah his son, and Ezer, and *E* 1Chr 7:21 496

ELEADAH See ELADAH.

ELEALEH *(el-e-a'-leh)* {5} *An Amorite village.*
and Nimrah, and Heshbon, and *E* Num 32:3 500
of Reuben built Heshbon, and *E* Num 32:37 500
And Heshbon shall cry, and *E* Is 15:4 500
with my tears, O Heshbon, and *E* Is 16:9 500
the cry of Heshbon even unto *E* Jer 48:34 500

ELEASAH *(el-e'-a-sah)* {4} See ELASAH.
1. A son of Helez.
begat Helez, and Helez begat *E* 1Chr 2:39 501
E begat Sisamai, and Sisamai begat 1Chr 2:40 501
2. A descendant of King Saul.
his son, *E* his son, Azel his son 1Chr 8:37 501
his son, *E* his son, Azel his son 1Chr 9:43 501

ELEAZAR *(el-e-a'-zar)* {74}
1. A son of Aaron.
she bare him Nadab, and Abihu, *E* Ex 6:23 499
E Aaron's son took him one of the Ex 6:25 499
even Aaron, Nadab and Abihu, *E* Ex 28:1 499
Moses said unto Aaron, and unto *E* Lev 10:6 499
Moses spake unto Aaron, and unto *E* Lev 10:12 499
and he was angry with *E* and Ithamar Lev 10:16 499
Nadab the firstborn, and Abihu, *E* Num 3:2 499
and *E* and Ithamar ministered in the Num 3:4 499
E the son of Aaron the priest Num 3:32 499
to the office of *E* the son of Num 4:16 499
Speak unto *E* the son of Aaron the Num 16:37 499
E the priest took the brasen Num 16:39 499
shall give her unto *E* the priest Num 19:3 499
E the priest shall take of her Num 19:4 499
E his son, and bring them up unto Num 20:25 499
and put them upon *E* his son Num 20:26 499
and put them upon *E* his son Num 20:28 499
E came down from the mount Num 20:28 499
And when Phinehas, the son of *E* Num 25:7 499
Phinehas, the son of *E*, the son Num 25:11 499
unto *E* the son of Aaron the Num 26:1 499
E the priest spake with them in Num 26:3 499
Aaron was born Nadab, and Abihu, *E* Num 26:60 499
E the priest, who numbered the Num 26:63 499
before *E* the priest, and before Num 27:2 499
And set him before *E* the priest Num 27:19 499
shall stand before *E* the priest Num 27:21 499
and set him before *E* the priest Num 27:22 499
Phinehas the son of *E* the priest Num 31:6 499
E the priest, and unto the Num 31:12 499
E the priest, and all the princes Num 31:13 499
E the priest said unto the men of Num 31:21 499
E the priest, and the chief Num 31:26 499
and give it unto *E* the priest Num 31:29 499
E the priest did as the LORD Num 31:31 499
unto *E* the priest, as the LORD Num 31:41 499
E the priest took the gold of Num 31:51 499
E the priest took the gold of the Num 31:54 499
to *E* the priest, and unto the Num 32:2 499
them Moses commanded *E* the priest Num 32:28 499
E the priest, and Joshua the son Num 34:17 499
E his son ministered in the Deut 10:6 499
which *E* the priest, and Joshua the Josh 14:1 499
came near before *E* the priest Josh 17:4 499
which *E* the priest, and Joshua the Josh 19:51 499
of the Levites unto *E* the priest Josh 21:1 499
Phinehas the son of *E* the priest Josh 22:13 499
Phinehas the son of *E* the priest Josh 22:31 499
Phinehas the son of *E* the priest Josh 22:32 499
And *E* the son of Aaron died Josh 24:33 499
And Phinehas, the son of *E* Judg 20:28 499
Nadab, and Abihu, *E*, and Ithamar 1Chr 6:3 499
E begat Phinehas, Phinehas begat 1Chr 6:4 499
E his son, Phinehas his son, 1Chr 6:50 499
Phinehas the son of *E* was the 1Chr 9:20 499
Nadab, and Abihu, *E*, and Ithamar 1Chr 24:1 499
therefore *E* and Ithamar executed 1Chr 24:2 499
them, both Zadok of the sons of *E* 1Chr 24:3 499
of *E* than of the sons of Ithamar 1Chr 24:4 499
Among the sons of *E* there were 1Chr 24:4 499
of God, were of the sons of *E* 1Chr 24:5 499
household being taken for *E* 1Chr 24:6 499
the son of Phinehas, the son of *E* Ezr 7:5 499
2. Son of Abinadab.
sanctified *E* his son to keep the 1Sa 7:1 499

3. A son of Dodo.
after him was *E* the son of Dodo............2Sa 23:9 499
after him was *E* the son of Dodo,............1Chr 11:12 499
4. Son of Mahli.
The sons of Mahli; *E*, and Kish..............1Chr 23:21 499
E died, and had no sons, but..................1Chr 23:22 499
Of Mahli came *E*, who had no sons.........1Chr 24:28 499
5. Son of Phinehas.
with him was *E* the son of.......................Ezr 8:33 499
6. Married a foreign wife.
and Malchiah, and Miamin, and *E*..........Ezr 10:25
7. A priest in Nehemiah's time.
And Maaseiah, and Shemaiah, and *E*.....Neh 12:42 499
8. Son of Eliud; ancestor of Jesus.
And Eliud begat *E*.......................................Mt 1:15 *1648*
and *E* begat Matthan...................................Mt 1:15 *1648*

ELECT {17}
mine *e*, in whom my soul.........................Is 42:1 972
servant's sake, and Israel mine *e*............Is 45:4 972
mine *e* shall inherit it, and my................Is 65:9 972
mine *e* shall long enjoy the work ....Is 65:22 972
they shall deceive the very *e*..................Mt 24:24 *1588*
his *e* from the four winds........................Mt 24:31 *1588*
if it were possible, even the *e*.................Mk 13:22 *1588*
his *e* from the four winds........................Mk 13:27 *1588*
And shall not God avenge his own *e*.......Lk 18:7 *1588*
thing to the charge of God's *e*................Rom 8:33 *1588*
Put on therefore, as the *e* of God............Col 3:12 *1588*
the *e* angels, that thou observe................1Ti 5:21 *1588*
according to the faith of God's *e*............Titus 1:1 *1588*
E according to the foreknowledge...........1Pet 1:2 *1588*
in Sion a chief corner stone, *e*.................1Pet 2:6 *1588*
The elder unto the *e* lady 2Jn 1 *1588*
of thy *e* sister greet thee..........................2Jn 13 *1588*

ELECTED {1}
e together with you, saluteth you...........1Pet 5:13 *4899*

ELECTION {6}
of God according to *e* might stand..........Rom 9:11 *1589*
according to the *e* of grace......................Rom 11:5 *1589*
but the *e* hath obtained it, and ....Rom 11:7 *1589*
but as touching the *e*, they are...............Rom 11:28 *1589*
brethren beloved, your *e* of God..............1Th 1:4 *1589*
to make your calling and *e* sure..............2Pet 1:10 *1589*

ELECT'S {3}
but for the *e* sake those days...................Mt 24:22 *1588*
but for the *e* sake, whom he hath.............Mk 13:20 *1588*
endure all things for the *e* sakes 2Ti 2:10 *1588*

EL-ELOHE-ISRAEL *(el-el-o'-he-iz'-rah-el)* {1} *An altar of Jacob near Shechem.*
there an altar, and called it *E*..................Gen 33:20 415

ELEMENTS {4}
bondage under the *e* of the world ....Gal 4:3 *4747*
again to the weak and beggarly *e* ....Gal 4:9 *4747*
the *e* shall melt with fervent 2Pet 3:10 *4747*
the *e* shall melt with fervent 2Pet 3:12 *4747*

ELEPH *(e'-lef)* {1} *A town in Benjamin.*
And Zelah, *E*, and Jebusi, which is.........Josh 18:28 507

ELEVEN {24}
his *e* sons, and passed over the........Gen 32:22 259,6240
the *e* stars made obeisance to me.....Gen 37:9 259,6240
e curtains shalt thou make ....Ex 26:7 6249,6240
the *e* curtains shall be all of.............Ex 26:8 6249,6240
e curtains he made them ....Ex 36:14 6249,6240
the *e* curtains were of one size ....Ex 36:15 6249,6240
And on the third day *e* bullocks.........Num 29:20 6249,6240
(There are *e* days' journey from.......Deut 1:2 259,6240
e cities with their villages ....Josh 15:51 259,6240
of us *e* hundred pieces of silver........Judg 16:5 505,3967
The *e* hundred shekels of silver.........Judg 17:2 505,3967
when he had restored the *e* ....Judg 17:3 505,3967
he reigned *e* years in Jerusalem.........2Kin 23:36 259,6240
he reigned *e* years in Jerusalem.........2Kin 24:18 259,6240
he reigned *e* years in Jerusalem.........2Chr 36:5 259,6240
reigned *e* years in Jerusalem 2Chr 36:11 259,6240
he reigned *e* years in Jerusalem.........Jer 52:1 259,6240
cubits, and the breadth *e* cubits.......Eze 40:49 6249,6240
Then the *e* disciples went away...............Mt 28:16 *1733*
unto the *e* as they sat at meat ....Mk 16:14 *1733*
told all these things unto the *e*................Lk 24:9 *1733*
found the *e* gathered together, and ....Lk 24:33 *1733*
was numbered with the *e* apostles ....Acts 1:26 *1733*
But Peter, standing up with the *e*.............Acts 2:14 *1733*

ELEVENTH {20}
On the *e* day Pagiel the son of.........Num 7:72 6249,6240
the fortieth year, in the *e* month.......Deut 1:3 6249,6240
And in the *e* year, in the month.........1Kin 6:38 259,6240
in the *e* year of Joram the son of.......2Kin 9:29 259,6240
unto the *e* year of king Zedekiah 2Kin 25:2 6249,6240
the tenth, Machbanai the *e*.................1Chr 12:13 6249,6240
The *e* to Eliashib, the twelfth to........1Chr 24:12 6249,6240
The *e* to Azareel, he, his sons, ...1Chr 25:18 6249,6240
The *e* captain for the *e* 1Chr 27:14 6249,6240
unto the end of the *e* year of ....Jer 1:3 6249,6240
in the *e* year of Zedekiah, in the ....Jer 39:2 6249,6240
unto the *e* year of king Zedekiah ....Jer 52:5 6249,6240
And it came to pass in the *e* year.....Eze 26:1 6249,6240
And it came to pass in the *e* year.....Eze 30:20 259,6240
And it came to pass in the *e* year.....Eze 31:1 259,6240
and twentieth day of the *e* month....Zec 1:7 6249,6240
about the *e* hour he went out, and..........Mt 20:6 *1734*
that were hired about the *e* hour ....Mt 20:9 *1734*
the *e*, a jacinth..Rev 21:20 *1734*

ELHANAN *(el-ha'-nan)* {4}
1. Son of Jair.
where *E* the son of Jaare-oregim,...........2Sa 21:19 445
E the son of Jair slew Lahmi the 1Chr 20:5 445
2. Son of Dodo.
E the son of Dodo of Beth-lehem,...........2Sa 23:24 445
E the son of Dodo of Beth-lehem,...........1Chr 11:26 445

ELI *(e'-li)* {33} See ELI'S, ELOI.
1. A High Priest of Israel.
And the two sons of *E*, Hophni and.........1Sa 1:3 5941
Now *E* the priest sat upon a seat 1Sa 1:9 5941
the LORD, that *E* marked her mouth 1Sa 1:12 5941
therefore *E* thought she had been 1Sa 1:13 5941
E said unto her, How long wilt 1Sa 1:14 5941
Then *E* answered and said, Go in 1Sa 1:17 5941
and brought the child to *E* 1Sa 1:25 5941
unto the LORD before *E* the priest..........1Sa 2:11 5941
Now the sons of *E* were sons of...............1Sa 2:12 5941
E blessed Elkanah and his wife, and 1Sa 2:20 5941
Now *E* was very old, and heard all 1Sa 2:22 5941
And there came a man of God unto *E*.....1Sa 2:27 5941
ministered unto the LORD before *E*........1Sa 3:1 5941
when *E* was laid down in his place..........1Sa 3:2 5941
And he ran unto *E*, and said, Here..........1Sa 3:5 5941
And Samuel arose and went to *E*.............1Sa 3:6 5941
And he arose and went to *E*, and said 1Sa 3:8 5941
E perceived that the LORD had.................1Sa 3:8 5941
Therefore *E* said unto Samuel, Go, ...1Sa 3:9 5941
E all things which I have spoken 1Sa 3:12 5941
I have sworn unto the house of *E*............1Sa 3:14 5941
feared to shew *E* the vision 1Sa 3:15 5941
Then *E* called Samuel, and said,..............1Sa 3:16 5941
and the two sons of *E*, Hophni and..........1Sa 4:4 5941
and the two sons of *E*, Hophni and..........1Sa 4:11 5941
E sat upon a seat by the wayside 1Sa 4:13 5941
when *E* heard the noise of the..................1Sa 4:14 5941
man came in hastily, and told *E*..............1Sa 4:14 5941
Now *E* was ninety and eight years............1Sa 4:15 5941
And the man said unto *E*, I am he 1Sa 4:16 5941
the son of Phinehas, the son of *E*.............1Sa 14:3 5941
the house of *E* in Shiloh 1Kin 2:27 5941
2. An Aramaic term for God.
with a loud voice, saying, Eli, *E*..............Mt 27:46 *2241*

ELIAB *(e-li'-ab)* {20} See ELIAB'S, ELIEL.
1. Son of Helon.
E the son of Helon..Num 1:9 446
E the son of Helon shall be ....Num 2:7 446
the third day *E* the son of Helon,..............Num 7:24 446
offering of *E* the son of Helon...................Num 7:29 446
of Zebulun was *E* the son of Helon..........Num 10:16 446
2. Father of Dathan.
Dathan and Abiram, the sons of *E*...........Num 16:1 446
Dathan and Abiram, the sons of *E*...........Num 16:12 446
the sons of Pallu; *E*.....................................Num 26:8 446
And the sons of *E*...Num 26:9 446
Dathan and Abiram, the sons of *E*...........Deut 11:6 446
3. A son of Jesse.
were come, that he looked on *E* 1Sa 16:6 446
the battle were *E* the first born...............1Sa 17:13 446
E his eldest brother heard when 1Sa 17:28 446
And Jesse begat his firstborn *E*...............1Chr 2:13 446
daughter of *E* the son of Jesse...................2Chr 11:18 446
4. A Levite ancestor of Samuel.
E his son, Jeroham his son, ...1Chr 6:27 446
5. A leader in David's army.
Obadiah the second, *E* the third, ...1Chr 12:9 446
6. A Levite in David's time.
and Jehiel, and Unni, *E*, and......................1Chr 15:18 446
and Jehiel, and Unni, and *E*.......................1Chr 15:20 446
and Jehiel, and Mattithiah, and *E*.............1Chr 16:5 446

ELIAB'S *(e'-le-abs)* {1}
E anger was kindled against David 1Sa 17:28 446

ELIADA *(e'-li'-a-dah)* {3} See ELIADAH.
1. A son of David.
And Elishama, and *E*, and Eliphalet.......2Sa 5:16 450
And Elishama, and *E*, and Eliphelet,......1Chr 3:8 450
E a mighty man of valour, and with 2Chr 17:17 450

ELIADAH *(e-li'-a-dah)* {1} See ELIADA. *An opponent of King Saul.*
adversary, Rezon the son of *E* 1Kin 11:23 450

ELIAH *(e-li'-ah)* {2} See ELIJAH. *A son of Jeroham.*
And Jaresiah, and *E*, and Zichri, the 1Chr 8:27 452
and Abdi, and Jeremoth, and *E*.................Ezr 10:26 452

ELIAHBA *(e-li'-ah-bah)* {2} *A "mighty man" of David.*
E the Shaalbonite, of the sons of 2Sa 23:32 455
Baharumite, *E* the Shaalbonite,...............1Chr 11:33 455

ELIAKIM *(e-li'-a-kim)* {15} See JEHOIAKIM.
1. A son of Hilkiah.
out to them *E* the son of Hilkiah 2Kin 18:18 471
Then said *E* the son of Hilkiah,.................2Kin 18:26 471
Then came *E* the son of Hilkiah,...............2Kin 18:37 471
And he sent *E*, which was over the 2Kin 19:2 471
my servant *E* the son of Hilkiah................Is 22:20 471
Then came forth unto him *E* ....Is 36:3 471
Then said *E* and Shebna and Joah ....Is 36:11 471
Then came *E*, the son of Hilkiah,...............Is 36:22 471
And he sent *E*, who was over the..............Is 37:2 471
2. Original name of Jehoiakim.
Pharaoh-nechoh made *E* the son of 2Kin 23:34 471
the king of Egypt made *E* his....................2Chr 36:4 471
3. A priest who dedicated the wall.
E, Maaseiah, Miniamin, Michaiah,...........Neh 12:41 471

4. Son of Abiud; ancestor of Jesus.
and Abiud begat *E* ....Mt 1:13 *1662*
and *E* begat Azor..Mt 1:13 *1662*
of Jonan, which was the son of *E*............Lk 3:30 *1662*

ELIAM *(e'-le-am)* {2}
1. Father of Bathsheba.
Bath-sheba, the daughter of *E* 2Sa 11:3 463
2. A "mighty man" of David.
E the son of Ahithophel the 2Sa 23:34 463

ELIAS *(e-li'-as)* {30} See ELIJAH. *Greek form of Elijah.*
if ye will receive it, this is *E*...................Mt 11:14 *2243*
some, *E*; and others, Jeremias ....Mt 16:14 *2243*
them Moses and *E* talking with him ....Mt 17:3 *2243*
and one for Moses, and one for *E*............Mt 17:4 *2243*
scribes that *E* must first come................Mt 17:10 *2243*
E truly shall first come, and.....................Mt 17:11 *2243*
That *E* is come already, and they.............Mt 17:12 *2243*
said, This man calleth for *E* ....Mt 27:47 *2243*
let us see whether *E* will come to............Mt 27:49 *2243*
Others said, That it is *E* ....Mk 6:15 *2243*
but some say, *E*..Mk 8:28 *2243*
appeared unto them *E* with Moses...........Mk 9:4 *2243*
and one for Moses, and one for *E*............Mk 9:5 *2243*
scribes that *E* must first come................Mk 9:11 *2243*
E verily cometh first, and.........................Mk 9:12 *2243*
That *E* is indeed come, and they..............Mk 9:13 *2243*
it said, Behold, he calleth *E* ....Mk 15:35 *2243*
let us see whether *E* will come to............Mk 15:36 *2243*
him in the spirit and power of *E*..............Lk 1:17 *2243*
were in Israel in the days of *E* ....Lk 4:25 *2243*
But unto none of them was *E* sent...........Lk 4:26 *2243*
And of some, that *E* had appeared...........Lk 9:8 *2243*
but some say *E*...Lk 9:19 *2243*
two men, which were Moses and *E* ....Lk 9:30 *2243*
and one for Moses, and one for *E*.............Lk 9:33 *2243*
and consume them, even as *E* did ....Lk 9:54 *2243*
Art thou *E*?...Jn 1:21 *2243*
if thou be not that Christ, nor *E* ....Jn 1:25 *2243*
not what the scripture saith of *E* ....Rom 11:2 *2243*
E was a man subject to like ....Jas 5:17 *2243*

ELIASAPH *(e-li'-a-saf)* {6}
1. A chief of Gad.
E the son of Deuel.......................................Num 1:14 460
Gad shall be *E* the son of Reuel................Num 2:14 460
the sixth day *E* the son of Deuel..............Num 7:42 460
offering of *E* the son of Deuel...................Num 7:47 460
of Gad was *E* the son of Deuel.................Num 10:20 460
2. A Gershonite leader.
shall be *E* the son of Lael..........................Num 3:24 460

ELIASHIB *(e-li'-a-shib)* {17}
1. A descendant of Judah.
of Elioenai were, Hodaiah, and *E* 1Chr 3:24 475
2. A priest in David's time.
The eleventh to *E*, the twelfth to.............1Chr 24:12 475
3. Son of Joiakim.
chamber of Johanan the son of *E*..............Ezr 10:6 475
Joiakim, Joiakim also begat *E*...................Neh 12:10 475
and *E* begat Joiada ....Neh 12:10 475
The Levites in the days of *E*......................Neh 12:22 475
the days of Johanan the son of *E* ....Neh 12:23 475
4. Married a foreign wife.
Of the singers also; *E*...................................Ezr 10:24 475
5. Son of Zotta.
Elioenai, *E*, Mattaniah, and ....Ezr 10:27 475
6. Son of Bani.
Vaniah, Meremoth, *E*,...................................Ezr 10:36 475
7. High Priest during Nehemiah's time.
Then *E* the high priest rose up.................Neh 3:1 475
of the house of *E* the high priest...............Neh 3:20 475
from the door of the house of *E* ....Neh 3:21 475
even to the end of the house of *E*..............Neh 3:21 475
this, *E* the priest, having the......................Neh 13:4 475
of the evil that *E* did for Tobiah ....Neh 13:7 475
the son of *E* the high priest, was...............Neh 13:28 475

ELIATHAH *(e-li'-a-thah)* {2} *A son of Heman.*
and Jerimoth, Hananiah, Hanani, *E*.........1Chr 25:4 448
The twentieth to *E*, he, his sons, ...1Chr 25:27 448

ELIDAD *(e-li'-dad)* {1} *Son of Chislon.*
of Benjamin, *E* the son of Chislon.............Num 34:21 449

ELIEHOENAI See ELIHOENAI.

ELIEL *(e'-le-el)* {10} See ELIAH.
1. Head of the house of Manasseh.
even Epher, and Ishi, and *E* 1Chr 5:24 447
2. Son of Jeroham.
the son of Jeroham, the son of *E* 1Chr 6:34 447
3. A son of Shimhi.
And Elienai, and Zilthai, and *E*.................1Chr 8:20 447
4. A son of Shashak.
And Ishpan, and Heber, and *E* 1Chr 8:22 447
5. A captain in David's army.
E the Mahavite, and Jeribai, and 1Chr 11:46 447
6. A "mighty man" of David.
E, and Obed, and Jasiel the.........................1Chr 11:47 447
7. A Gadite ally of David.
Attai the sixth, *E* the seventh,...................1Chr 12:11 447
8. A chief of Judah.
E the chief, and his brethren.......................1Chr 15:9 447
9. A chief Levite.
Asaiah, and Joel, Shemaiah, and *E*..........1Chr 15:11 447
10. A Levite in Hezekiah's time.
and Jerimoth, and Jozabad, and *E* 2Chr 31:13 447

ELIENAI *(e-li-e'-nahee)* {1} *A son of Shimhi.*
And *E*, and Zilthai, and Eliel,.....................1Chr 8:20 462

ELIEZER {15}
of my house is this *E* of Damascus.......... Gen 15:2 461
And the name of the other was *E*........... Ex 18:4 461
Zemira, and Joash, and *E*, and.............. 1Chr 7:8 461
and Zechariah, and Benaiah, and *E*........ 1Chr 15:24 461
sons of Moses were, Gershom, and *E*....... 1Chr 23:15 461
And the sons of *E* were, Rehabiah......... 1Chr 23:17 461
And *E* had none other sons..................... 1Chr 23:17 461
And his brethren by *E*............................ 1Chr 26:25 461
was *E* the son of Zichri........................... 1Chr 27:16 461
Then *E* the son of Dodavah of................... 2Chr 20:37 461
Then sent I for *E*, for Ariel, for............... Ezr 8:16 461
Maaseiah, and *E*, and Jarib, and.............. Ezr 10:18 461
Kelita,) Pethahiah, Judah, and *E*............ Ezr 10:23 461
E, Ishijah, Malchiah, Shemaiah,.............. Ezr 10:31 461
of Jose, which was the son of *E*............... Lk 3:29 *1663*

ELIHOENAI *(e-li-ho-e'-nahee)* {1} See ELIOENAI. *A family of exiles.*
E the son of Zerahiah, and with .... Ezr 8:4 454

ELIHOREPH *(e-li-ho'-ref)* {1} *A scribe of Solomon.*
E and Ahiah, the sons of Shisha,............. 1Kin 4:3 456

ELIHU *(e-li'-hew)* {11}
1. Great-grandfather of Samuel.
the son of Jeroham, the son of *E*............ 1Sa 1:1 453
2. A soldier of David.
and Michael, and Jozabad, and *E*........... 1Chr 12:20 453
3. A Tabernacle servant.
whose brethren were strong men, *E*........ 1Chr 26:7 453
4. Brother of David.
Of Judah, *E*, one of the brethren............. 1Chr 27:18 453
5. A friend of Job.
Then was kindled the wrath of *E*............ Job 32:2 453
Now *E* had waited till Job had................ Job 32:4 453
When *E* saw that there was no................ Job 32:5 453
E the son of Barachel the Buzite............. Job 32:6 453
Furthermore *E* answered and said,.......... Job 34:1 453
E spake moreover, and said,.................... Job 35:1 453
E also proceeded, and said,.................... Job 36:1 453

ELIJAH *(e-li'-jah)* {69} See ELIAH, ELIAS.
1. The prophet.
E the Tishbite, who was of the............... 1Kin 17:1 452
E said unto her, Fear not....................... 1Kin 17:13 452
did according to the saying of *E*............ 1Kin 17:15 452
of the LORD, which he spake by *E*.......... 1Kin 17:16 452
And she said unto *E*, What have I.......... 1Kin 17:18 452
And the LORD heard the voice of *E*......... 1Kin 17:22 452
E took the child, and brought him......... 1Kin 17:23 452
E said, See, thy son liveth..................... 1Kin 17:23 452
And the woman said to *E*, Now by.......... 1Kin 17:24 452
LORD came to *E* in the third year........... 1Kin 18:1 452
E went to shew himself unto Ahab......... 1Kin 18:2 452
was in the way, behold, *E* met him......... 1Kin 18:7 452
and said, Art thou that my lord *E*........... 1Kin 18:7 452
tell thy lord, Behold, *E* is here.............. 1Kin 18:8 452
tell thy lord, Behold, *E* is here.............. 1Kin 18:11 452
tell thy lord, Behold, *E* is here.............. 1Kin 18:14 452
E said, As the LORD of hosts.................. 1Kin 18:15 452
and Ahab went to meet *E*......................... 1Kin 18:16 452
it came to pass, when Ahab saw *E*.......... 1Kin 18:17 452
E came unto all the people, and............. 1Kin 18:21 452
Then said *E* unto the people, I,............... 1Kin 18:22 452
E said unto the prophets of Baal,........... 1Kin 18:25 452
that *E* mocked them, and said, Cry......... 1Kin 18:27 452
E said unto all the people, Come............ 1Kin 18:30 452
E took twelve stones, according............. 1Kin 18:31 452
that *E* the prophet came near, and.......... 1Kin 18:36 452
E said unto them, Take the.................... 1Kin 18:40 452
E brought them down to the brook.......... 1Kin 18:40 452
E said unto Ahab, Get thee up,.............. 1Kin 18:41 452
E went up to the top of Carmel.............. 1Kin 18:42 452
And the hand of the LORD was on *E*......... 1Kin 18:46 452
told Jezebel all that *E* had done............. 1Kin 19:1 452
Jezebel sent a messenger unto *E*............ 1Kin 19:2 452
unto him, What doest thou here, *E*......... 1Kin 19:9 452
when *E* heard it, that he wrapped........... 1Kin 19:13 452
and said, What doest thou here, *E*......... 1Kin 19:13 452
E passed by him, and cast his............... 1Kin 19:19 452
he left the oxen, and ran after *E*........... 1Kin 19:20 452
Then he arose, and went after *E*............ 1Kin 19:21 452
the LORD came to *E* the Tishbite............. 1Kin 21:17 452
And Ahab said to *E*, Hast thou............... 1Kin 21:20 452
the LORD came to *E* the Tishbite............. 1Kin 21:28 452
the LORD said to *E* the Tishbite............. 2Kin 1:3 452
And *E* departed.. 2Kin 1:4 452
And he said, It is *E* the Tishbite............. 2Kin 1:8 452
E answered and said to the captain........ 2Kin 1:10 452
E answered and said unto them, If.......... 2Kin 1:12 452
and fell on his knees before *E*................ 2Kin 1:13 452
the angel of the LORD said unto *E*.......... 2Kin 1:15 452
of the LORD which *E* had spoken............ 2Kin 1:17 452
up *E* into heaven by a whirlwind............. 2Kin 2:1 452
that *E* went with Elisha from.................. 2Kin 2:1 452
E said unto Elisha, Tarry here, I............ 2Kin 2:2 452
E said unto him, Elisha, tarry................ 2Kin 2:4 452
E said unto him, Tarry, I pray............... 2Kin 2:6 452
E took his mantle, and wrapped it.......... 2Kin 2:8 452
that *E* said unto Elisha, Ask what........... 2Kin 2:9 452
E went up by a whirlwind into................ 2Kin 2:11 452
mantle of *E* that fell from him............... 2Kin 2:13 452
mantle of *E* that fell from him............... 2Kin 2:14 452
said, Where is the LORD God of *E*........... 2Kin 2:14 452
The spirit of *E* doth rest on.................... 2Kin 2:15 452
poured water on the hands of *E*.............. 2Kin 3:11 452
by his servant *E* the Tishbite................... 2Kin 9:36 452
which he spake by his servant *E*............ 2Kin 10:10 452
of the LORD, which he spake to *E*.......... 2Kin 10:17 452
writing to him from *E* the prophet.......... 2Chr 21:12 452
I will send you *E* the prophet.................. Mal 4:5 452
2. Married a foreign wife.
Maaseiah, and *E*, and Shemaiah, and....... Ezr 10:21 452

ELIKA *(e-li'-kah)* {1} *A guard of David.*
the Harodite, *E* the Harodite,.................. 2Sa 23:25 470

ELIM *(e'-lim)* {6} See BEER-ELIM. *An encampment during the Exodus.*
And they came to *E*, where were............. Ex 15:27 362
And they took their journey from *E*........ Ex 16:1 362
of Sin, which is between *E*..................... Ex 16:1 362
from Marah, and came unto *E*................. Num 33:9 362
in *E* were twelve fountains of.................. Num 33:9 362
And they removed from *E*, and.............. Num 33:10 362

ELIMELECH *(e-lim'-e-lek)* {4} See ELIMELECH'S. *Husband of Naomi.*
And the name of the man was *E*............. Ruth 1:2 458
And *E* Naomi's husband died................... Ruth 1:3 458
man of wealth, of the family of *E*........... Ruth 2:1 458
Boaz, who was of the kindred of *E*......... Ruth 2:3 458

ELIMELECH'S {2}
of land, which was our brother *E*........... Ruth 4:3 458
that I have bought all that was *E*........... Ruth 4:9 458

ELIOENAI *(e-li-o-e'-nahee)* {8} See ELIHOENAI.
1. A son of Neariah.
E, and Hezekiah, and Azrikam, three...... 1Chr 3:23 454
And the sons of *E* were, Hodaiah,........... 1Chr 3:24 454
2. A Simeonite prince.
And *E*, and Jaakobah, and....................... 1Chr 4:36 454
3. A son of Becher.
and Joash, and Eliezer, and *E*................ 1Chr 7:8 454
4. A Temple servant.
the sixth, *E* the seventh......................... 1Chr 26:3 454
5. Married a foreign wife.
E, Maaseiah, Ishmael, Nethaneel,............ Ezr 10:22 454
6. A son of Zattu.
E, Eliashib, Mattaniah, and.................... Ezr 10:27 454
7. A priest during Nehemiah's time.
Maaseiah, Miniamin, Michaiah, *E*............ Neh 12:41 454

ELIPHAL *(el'-i-fal)* {1} *A captain in David's army.*
the Hararite, *E* the son of Ur,................. 1Chr 11:35 465

ELIPHALET *(e-lif'-a-let)* {2} See ELIPHELET, ELPALET. *A son of David.*
And Elishama, and Eliada, and *E*........... 2Sa 5:16 467
And Elishama, and Beeliada, and *E*....... 1Chr 14:7 467

ELIPHAZ *(el'-if-az)* {15}
1. A son of Esau.
And Adah bare to Esau *E*....................... Gen 36:4 464
E the son of Adah the wife of................. Gen 36:10 464
And the sons of *E* were Teman................ Gen 36:11 464
was concubine to *E* Esau's son.............. Gen 36:12 464
and she bare to *E* Amalek...................... Gen 36:12 464
the sons of *E* the firstborn son.............. Gen 36:15 464
came of *E* in the land of Edom.............. Gen 36:16 464
E, Reuel, and Jeush, and Jaalam, and..... 1Chr 1:35 464
The sons of *E*; Teman, and...................... 1Chr 1:36 464
2. A friend of Job.
E the Temanite, and Bildad the............... Job 2:11 464
Then *E* the Temanite answered and........ Job 4:1 464
Then answered *E* the Temanite............... Job 15:1 464
Then *E* the Temanite answered and........ Job 22:1 464
the LORD said to *E* the Temanite............ Job 42:7 464
So *E* the Temanite and Bildad the.......... Job 42:9 464

ELIPHELEH *(e-lif'-e-leh)* {2} *A Levite singer.*
and Maaseiah, and Mattithiah, and *E*...... 1Chr 15:18 466
And Mattithiah, and *E*, and Mikneiah,... 1Chr 15:21 466

ELIPHELEHU See ELIPHELEH.

ELIPHELET *(e-lif'-e-let)* {6} See ELIPHALET.
1. A "mighty man" of David.
E the son of Ahasbai, the son of............. 2Sa 23:34 467
2. A son of David.
Ibhar also, and Elishama, and *E*............ 1Chr 3:6 467
3. Same as Eliphat.
And Elishama, and Eliada, and *E*........... 1Chr 3:8 467
4. A descendant of King Saul.
Jehush the second, and *E* the third......... 1Chr 8:39 467
5. A family of exiles.
whose names are these, *E*........................ Ezr 8:13 467
6. A son of Hashum.
Mattenai, Mattathah, Zabad, *E*............... Ezr 10:33 467

ELI'S *(e'-lize)* {1} *Refers to Eli 1.*
that the iniquity of *E* house.................... 1Sa 3:14 5941

ELISABETH *(e-liz'-a-beth)* {8} See ELISABETH'S. *Mother of John the Baptist.*
of Aaron, and her name was *E*............... Lk 1:5 *1665*
child, because that *E* was barren............ Lk 1:7 *1665*
thy wife *E* shall bear thee a son,............ Lk 1:13 *1665*
those days his wife *E* conceived............ Lk 1:24 *1665*
And, behold, thy cousin *E*, she............... Lk 1:36 *1665*
house of Zacharias, and saluted *E*.......... Lk 1:40 *1665*
when *E* heard the salutation of............... Lk 1:41 *1665*
E was filled with the Holy Ghost............ Lk 1:41 *1665*

ELISABETH'S *(e-liz'-a-beths)* {1}
Now *E* full time came that she............... Lk 1:57 *1665*

ELISEUS *(el-i-se'-us)* {1} See ELISHA. *Greek form of Elisha.*
in the time of *E* the prophet................... Lk 4:27 *1666*

ELISHA *(e-li'-shah)* {58} See ELISEUS. *A prophet.*
and *E* the son of Shaphat of.................... 1Kin 19:16 477
the sword of Jehu shall *E* slay................. 1Kin 19:17 477
found *E* the son of Shaphat, who............ 1Kin 19:19 477
Elijah went with *E* from Gilgal................ 2Kin 2:1 477
And Elijah said unto *E*, Tarry here......... 2Kin 2:2 477
E said unto him, As the LORD................. 2Kin 2:2 477
were at Beth-el came forth to *E*.............. 2Kin 2:3 477
And Elijah said unto him, *E*.................... 2Kin 2:4 477
that were at Jericho came to *E*............... 2Kin 2:5 477
over, that Elijah said unto *E*................... 2Kin 2:9 477
E said, I pray thee, let a double............. 2Kin 2:9 477
E saw it, and he cried, My father,........... 2Kin 2:12 477
and thither: and *E* went over.................. 2Kin 2:14 477
spirit of Elijah doth rest on *E*................ 2Kin 2:15 477
the men of the city said unto *E*.............. 2Kin 2:19 477
to the saying of *E* which he spake.......... 2Kin 2:22 477
Here is *E* the son of Shaphat,................. 2Kin 3:11 477
E said unto the king of Israel,................ 2Kin 3:13 477
E said, As the LORD of hosts.................. 2Kin 3:14 477
the sons of the prophets unto *E*............. 2Kin 4:1 477
E said unto her, What shall I do............. 2Kin 4:2 477
that *E* passed to Shunem, where............. 2Kin 4:8 477
season that *E* had said unto her............. 2Kin 4:17 477
when *E* was come into the house,........... 2Kin 4:32 477
And *E* came again to Gilgal.................... 2Kin 4:38 477
when *E* the man of God had heard.......... 2Kin 5:8 477
at the door of the house of *E*................. 2Kin 5:9 477
E sent a messenger unto him,................. 2Kin 5:10 477
the servant of *E* the man of God........... 2Kin 5:20 477
E said unto him, Whence comest............ 2Kin 5:25 477
sons of the prophets said unto *E*............ 2Kin 6:1 477
but *E*, the prophet that is in................... 2Kin 6:12 477
E prayed, and said, LORD, I pray............ 2Kin 6:17 477
and chariots of fire round about *E*.......... 2Kin 6:17 477
E prayed unto the LORD, and said,......... 2Kin 6:18 477
according to the word of *E*.................... 2Kin 6:18 477
E said unto them, This is not the............ 2Kin 6:19 477
come into Samaria, that *E* said.............. 2Kin 6:20 477
And the king of Israel said unto *E*.......... 2Kin 6:21 477
if the head of *E* the son of..................... 2Kin 6:31 477
But *E* sat in his house, and the.............. 2Kin 6:32 477
Then *E* said, Hear ye the word of........... 2Kin 7:1 477
Then spake *E* unto the woman,............... 2Kin 8:1 477
the great things that *E* hath done.......... 2Kin 8:4 477
her son, whom *E* restored to life............ 2Kin 8:5 477
And *E* came to Damascus........................ 2Kin 8:7 477
E said unto him, Go, say unto him.......... 2Kin 8:10 477
E answered, The LORD hath shewed......... 2Kin 8:13 477
So he departed from *E*, and came to........ 2Kin 8:14 477
said to him, What said *E* to thee............ 2Kin 8:14 477
E the prophet called one of the.............. 2Kin 9:1 477
Now *E* was fallen sick of his.................. 2Kin 13:14 477
E said unto him, Take bow and.............. 2Kin 13:15 477
E put his hands upon the king's............. 2Kin 13:16 477
Then *E* said, Shoot................................ 2Kin 13:17 477
E died, and they buried him.................. 2Kin 13:20 477
the man into the sepulchre of *E*............. 2Kin 13:21 477
down, and touched the bones of *E*.......... 2Kin 13:21 477

ELISHAH *(e-li'-shah)* {3} *A son of Javan.*
E, and Tarshish, Kittim, and.................... Gen 10:4 473
E, and Tarshish, Kittim, and.................... 1Chr 1:7 473
purple from the isles of *E* was................ Eze 27:7 473

ELISHAMA *(e-lish'-a-mah)* {17} See ELISHUA.
1. Grandfather of Joshua.
E the son of Ammihud........................... Num 1:10 476
shall be *E* the son of Ammihud............... Num 2:18 476
seventh day *E* the son of Ammihud.......... Num 7:48 476
offering of *E* the son of Ammihud............ Num 7:53 476
over his host was *E* the son of................. Num 10:22 476
son, Ammihud his son, *E* his son,........... 1Chr 7:26 476
2. A son of David.
And *E*, and Eliada, and Eliphalet............ 2Sa 5:16 476
Ibhar also, and *E*, and Eliphelet,............ 1Chr 3:6 476
And *E*, and Eliada, and Eliphelet,.......... 1Chr 3:8 476
And *E*, and Beeliada, and Eliphalet........ 1Chr 14:7 476
3. A descendant of Judah.
the son of Nethaniah the son of *E*........... Jer 41:1 476
4. Son of Jekamiah.
Jekamiah, and Jekamiah begat *E*............ 1Chr 2:41 476
5. Same as Elishua.
son of Nethaniah, the son of *E*................ 2Kin 25:25 476
6. A priest who taught the law.
and with them *E* and Jehoram,................ 2Chr 17:8 476
7. A scribe of Jehoiakim.
even *E* the scribe, and Delaiah the.......... Jer 36:12 476
in the chamber of *E* the scribe............... Jer 36:20 476
he took it out of *E* the scribe's.............. Jer 36:21 476

ELISHAPHAT *(e-lish'-a-fat)* {1} *Assisted in making Joash king.*
E the son of Zichri, into........................ 2Chr 23:1 478

ELISHEBA *(e-lish'-e-bah)* {1} *Daughter of Amminadab.*
And Aaron took him *E*, daughter of....... Ex 6:23 472

ELISHUA *(e-lish'-oo-ah)* {2} See ELISHAMA. *A son of David.*
Ibhar also, and *E*, and Nepheg, and........ 2Sa 5:15 474
And Ibhar, and *E*, and Elpalet,............... 1Chr 14:5 474

ELIUD *(e-li'-ud)* {2} *Son of Achim; ancestor of Jesus.*
and Achim begat *E*................................ Mt 1:14 *1664*
And *E* begat Eleazar............................... Mt 1:15 *1664*

ELIZABETH See ELISABETH.

ELIZAPHAN *(e-liz'-a-fan)* {4} See ELZAPHAN.
1. Son of Uzziel.
shall be *E* the son of Uzziel.................... Num 3:30 469
Of the sons of *E*.................................... 1Chr 15:8 469
2. Son of Parnach.
of Zebulun, *E* the son of Parnach........... Num 34:25 469
3. A family of Levites.
And of the sons of *E*.............................. 2Chr 29:13 469

ELIZUR *(e-li'-zur)* {5} *Son of Shedeur.*
E the son of Shedeur Num 1:5 468
shall be *E* the son of Shedeur Num 2:10 468
On the fourth day *E* the son of Num 7:30 468
offering of *E* the son of Shedeur Num 7:35 468
over his host was *E* the son of Num 10:18 468

ELKANAH *(el-ka'-nah)* {20}
1. A grandson of Korah.
Assir, and *E*, and Abiasaph Ex 6:24 511
E his son, and Ebiasaph his son, 1Chr 6:23 511
2. Father of Samuel.
mount Ephraim, and his name was *E* 1Sa 1:1 511
when the time was that *E* offered 1Sa 1:4 511
Then said *E* her husband to her, 1Sa 1:8 511
and *E* knew Hannah his wife 1Sa 1:19 511
And the man *E*, and all his house, 1Sa 1:21 511
E her husband said unto her, Do 1Sa 1:23 511
E went to Ramah to his house 1Sa 2:11 511
And Eli blessed *E* and his wife, and 1Sa 2:20 511
son, Jeroham his son, *E* his son 1Chr 6:27 511
The son of *E*, the son of Jeroham, 1Chr 6:34 511
3. A Levite.
the sons of *E*; Amasai, and 1Chr 6:25 511
The son of *E*, the son of Joel, 1Chr 6:36 511
4. A descendant of Kohath.
the sons of *E* 1Chr 6:26 511
The son of Zuph, the son of *E* 1Chr 6:35 511
5. Father of Asa.
the son of Asa, the son of *E* 1Chr 9:16 511
6. A soldier in David's army.
E, and Jesiah, and Azareel, and 1Chr 12:6 511
7. A Levite doorkeeper.
E were doorkeepers for the ark 1Chr 15:23 511
8. An officer of King Ahaz.
E that was next to the king 2Chr 28:7 511

ELKOSH See ELKOSHITE.

ELKOSHITE {1}
book of the vision of Nahum the *E* Nah 1:1 512

ELLASAR *(el'-la-sar)* {2} *A Babylonian city.*
king of Shinar, Arioch king of *E* Gen 14:1 495
of Shinar, and Arioch king of *E* Gen 14:9 495

ELMODAM *(el-mo'-dam)* {1} *Son of Er.*
of Cosam, which was the son of *E* Lk 3:28 *1678*

ELMS {1}
hills, under oaks and poplars and *e* Hos 4:13 424

ELNAAM *(el-na'-am)* {1} *Father of two of David's "mighty men."*
and Joshaviah, the sons of *E* 1Chr 11:46 493

ELNATHAN *(el-na'-than)* {7}
1. Father of Nehushta.
the daughter of *E* of Jerusalem 2Kin 24:8 494
E the son of Achbor, and certain Jer 26:22 494
E the son of Achbor, and Gemariah Jer 36:12 494
Nevertheless *E* and Delaiah and Jer 36:25 494
2. Name of three Levites during Ezra's time.
for Ariel, for Shemaiah, and for *E* Ezr 8:16 494
and for Jarib, and for *E* Ezr 8:16 494
also for Joiarib, and for *E* Ezr 8:16 494

ELOI *(e-lo'-ee)* {2} See ELI. *Same as Eli 2.*
a loud voice, saying, *E*, *E* Mk 15:34 *1682*

ELON *(e'-lon)* {7} See ELONITES.
1. Esau's father-in-law.
the daughter of *E* the Hittite Gen 26:34 356
the daughter of *E* the Hittite Gen 36:2 356
2. A son of Zebulun.
Sered, and *E*, and Jahleel Gen 46:14 356
of *E*, the family of the Elonites Num 26:26 356
3. A Danite town.
And *E*, and Thimnathah, and Ekron, Josh 19:43 356
4. A judge of Israel.
And after him *E*, a Zebulonite, Judg 12:11 356
E the Zebulonite died, and was Judg 12:12 356

ELON-BETH-HANAN *(e'-lon-beth-ha'-nan)* {1} *A Danite town.*
Shaalbim, and Beth-shemesh, and *E* 1Kin 4:9 358

ELONITES *(e'-lon-ites)* {1} *Descendants of Elon 2.*
of Elon, the family of the *E* Num 26:26 440

ELOQUENT {3}
the LORD, O my Lord, I am not *e* Ex 4:10 376,1697
artificer, and the *e* orator Is 3:3 995
an *e* man, and mighty in the Acts 18:24 *3052*

ELOTH *(e'-loth)* {3} See ELATH. *Same as Elath.*
in Ezion-geber, which is beside *E* 1Kin 9:26 359
Solomon to Ezion-geber, and to *E* 2Chr 8:17 359
He built *E*, and restored it to 2Chr 26:2 359

ELPAAL *(el-pa'-al)* {3} *A son of Shaharaim.*
of Hushim he begat Abitub, and *E* 1Chr 8:11 508
The sons of *E*; Eber, and Misham 1Chr 8:12 508
Jezliah, and Jobab, the sons of *E* 1Chr 8:18 508

ELPALET *(el-pa'-let)* {1} See ELIPHALET. *A son of David.*
And Ibhar, and Elishua, and *E* 1Chr 14:5 467

EL-PARAN *(el-pa'-ran)* {1} *A place in southern Canaan.*
in their mount Seir, unto *E* Gen 14:6 364

ELPELET See ELPALET.

ELSE See APPENDIX.

ELTEKE See ELTEKEH.

ELTEKEH *(el'-te-keh)* {2} *A Danite city.*
And *E*, and Gibbethon, and Baalath, Josh 19:44 514
E with her suburbs, Gibbethon Josh 21:23 514

ELTEKON *(el'-te-kon)* {1} *A city in Judah.*
And Maarath, and Beth-anoth, and *E* Josh 15:59 515

ELTOLAD *(el-to'-lad)* {2} *A city in Judah.*
And *E*, and Chesil, and Hormah, Josh 15:30 513
And *E*, and Bethul, and Hormah, Josh 19:4 513

ELUL *(e'-lul)* {1} *Sixth month of the Hebrew year.*
and fifth day of the month *E* Neh 6:15 435

ELUZAI *(e-loo'-zahee)* {1} *A soldier in David's army.*
E, and Jerimoth, and Bealiah, and 1Chr 12:5 498

ELYMAS *(el'-i-mas)* {1} See BAR-JESUS. *A sorcerer.*
But *E* the sorcerer (for so is his Acts 13:8 *1681*

ELZABAD *(el'-za-bad)* {2}
1. A soldier in David's army.
Johanan the eighth, *E* the ninth, 1Chr 12:12 443
2. Son of Shemaiah.
Othni, and Rephael, and Obed, *E* 1Chr 26:7 443

ELZAPHAN *(el'-za-fan)* {2} See ELIZAPHAN. *A son of Uzziel.*
Mishael, and *E*, and Zithri Ex 6:22 469
And Moses called Mishael and *E* Lev 10:4 469

EMBALM {1}
the physicians to *e* his father Gen 50:2 2590

EMBALMED {3}
and the physicians *e* Israel Gen 50:2 2590
the days of those which are *e* Gen 50:3 2590
and they *e* him, and he was put in a Gen 50:26 2590

EMBOLDENED {1}
of him which is weak be *e* to eat 1Cor 8:10 *3618*

EMBOLDENETH {1}
or what *e* thee that thou Job 16:3 4834

EMBRACE {8}
time of life, thou shalt *e* a son 2Kin 4:16 2263
e the rock for want of a shelter Job 24:8 2263
to honour, when thou dost *e* her Prov 4:8 2263
e the bosom of a stranger Prov 5:20 2263
a time to *e*, and a time to refrain Eccl 3:5 2263
head, and his right hand doth *e* me Song 2:6 2263
and his right hand should *e* me Song 8:3 2263
brought up in scarlet *e* dunghills Lam 4:5 2263

EMBRACED {5}
e him, and kissed him, and brought Gen 29:13 2263
e him, and fell on his neck, and Gen 33:4 2263
and he kissed them, and *e* them Gen 48:10 2263
e them, and departed for to go Acts 20:1 *782*
e them, and confessed that they Heb 11:13 *782*

EMBRACING {2}
and a time to refrain from *e* Eccl 3:5 2263
him, and *e* him said, Trouble not Acts 20:10 *4843*

EMBROIDER {1}
thou shalt *e* the coat of fine Ex 28:39 7660

EMBROIDERER {2}
the cunning workman, and of the *e* Ex 35:35 7551
an *e* in blue, and in purple, and in Ex 38:23 7551

EMEK KEZIZ See KEZIZ.

EMERALD {5}
And the second row shall be an *e* Ex 28:18 5306
And the second row, an *e*, a Ex 39:11 5306
the jasper, the sapphire, the *e* Eze 28:13 5306
throne, in sight like unto an *e* Rev 4:3 *4664*
a chalcedony; the fourth, an *e* Rev 21:19 *4665*

EMERALDS {1}
they occupied in thy fairs with *e* Eze 27:16 5306

EMERODS {8}
the botch of Egypt, and with the *e* Deut 28:27 6076
them, and smote them with *e* 1Sa 5:6 6076
they had *e* in their secret parts 1Sa 5:9 6076
died not were smitten with the *e* 1Sa 5:12 6076
They answered, Five golden *e* 1Sa 6:4 6076
ye shall make images of your *e* 1Sa 6:5 6076
of gold and the images of their *e* 1Sa 6:11 2914
these are the golden *e* which the 1Sa 6:17 2914

EMIM See EMIMS.

EMIMS *(e'-mims)* {3} *A race of giants.*
the *E* in Shaveh Kiriathaim, Gen 14:5 368
The *E* dwelt therein in times past Deut 2:10 368
but the Moabites call them *E* Deut 2:11 368

EMINENT {4}
also built unto thee an *e* place Eze 16:24 1354
In that thou buildest thine *e* Eze 16:31 1354
shall throw down thine *e* place Eze 16:39 1354
it upon an high mountain and *e* Eze 17:22 8524

EMITES See EMIMS.

EMMANUEL *(em-man'-uel)* {1} See IMMANUEL. *A Messianic name.*
and they shall call his name *E* Mt 1:23 *1694*

EMMAUS *(em'-ma-us)* {1} *A village near Jerusalem.*
same day to a village called *E* Lk 24:13 *1695*

EMMOR *(em'-mor)* {1} See HAMOR. *Father of Sychem.*
sons of *E* the father of Sychem Acts 7:16 *1697*

EMPIRE {1}
be published throughout all his *e* Est 1:20 4438

EMPLOY {1}
life) to *e* them in the siege Deut 20:19 935,6440

EMPLOYED {2}
for they were *e* in that work day 1Chr 9:33 5921
Tikvah were *e* about this matter Ezr 10:15 5975

EMPLOYMENT {1}
sever out men of continual *e* Eze 39:14

EMPTIED {8}
e her pitcher into the trough, and Gen 24:20 6168
to pass as they *e* their sacks Gen 42:35 7324
e the chest, and took it, and 2Chr 24:11 6168
even thus be he shaken out, and *e* Neh 5:13 7386
the brooks of defence shall be *e* Is 19:6 1809
The land shall be utterly *e* Is 24:3 1238
hath not been *e* from vessel to Jer 48:11 7324
for the emptiers have *e* them out Nah 2:2 1238

EMPTIERS {1}
for the *e* have emptied them out, Nah 2:2 1238

EMPTINESS {1}
of confusion, and the stones of *e* Is 34:11 922

EMPTY {38}
thou hadst sent me away now *e* Gen 31:42 7387
and the pit was *e*, there was no Gen 37:24 7386
the seven *e* ears blasted with the Gen 41:27 7386
when ye go, ye shall not go *e* Ex 3:21 7387
and none shall appear before me *e* Ex 23:15 7387
And none shall appear before me *e* Ex 34:20 7387
command that they *e* the house Lev 14:36 6437
thou shalt not let him go away *e* Deut 15:13 7387
not appear before the LORD *e* Deut 16:16 7387
with *e* pitchers, and lamps within Judg 7:16 7385
LORD hath brought me home again *e* Ruth 1:21 7387
Go not *e* unto thy mother in law Ruth 3:17 7387
the God of Israel, send it not *e* 1Sa 6:3 7387
because thy seat will be *e* 1Sa 20:18 6485
side, and David's place was *e* 1Sa 20:25 6485
month, that David's place was *e* 1Sa 20:27 6485
the sword of Saul returned not *e* 2Sa 1:22 7387
thy neighbours, even *e* vessels 2Kin 4:3 7385
Thou hast sent widows away *e* Job 22:9 7387
out the north over the *e* place Job 26:7 8414
they *e* themselves upon the earth Eccl 11:3 7324
the LORD maketh the earth *e* Is 24:1 1238
but he awaketh, and his soul is *e* Is 29:8 7385
to make *e* the soul of the hungry, Is 32:6 7324
returned with their vessels *e* Jer 14:3 7387
shall *e* his vessels, and break Jer 48:12 7324
fan her, and shall *e* her land Jer 51:2 1238
me, he hath made me an *e* vessel Jer 51:34 7385
Then set it *e* upon the coals Eze 24:11 7385
Israel is an *e* vine, he bringeth Hos 10:1 1238
She is *e*, and void, and waste Nah 2:10 950
Shall they therefore *e* their net Hab 1:17 7324
pipes *e* the golden oil out of Zec 4:12 7324
when he is come, he findeth it *e* Mt 12:44 *4980*
and beat him, and sent him away *e* Mk 12:3 *2756*
and the rich he hath sent *e* away Lk 1:53 *2756*
beat him, and sent him away *e* Lk 20:10 *2756*
shamefully, and sent him away *e* Lk 20:11 *2756*

EMULATION {1}
to *e* them which are my flesh Rom 11:14 *3863*

EMULATIONS {1}
witchcraft, hatred, variance, *e* Gal 5:20 *2205*

ENABLED {1}
Jesus our Lord, who hath *e* me 1Ti 1:12 *1743*

ENAM *(e'-nam)* {1} *A city in Judah.*
and En-gannim, Tappuah, and *E* Josh 15:34 5879

ENAN *(e'-nan)* {5} See HAZAR-ENAN. *Father of Ahira.*
Ahira the son of *E* Num 1:15 5881
shall be Ahira the son of *E* Num 2:29 5881
twelfth day Ahira the son of *E* Num 7:78 5881
offering of Ahira the son of *E* Num 7:83 5881
Naphtali was Ahira the son of *E* Num 10:27 5881

ENCAMP {11}
e before Pi-hahiroth, between Ex 14:2 2583
before it shall ye *e* by the sea Ex 14:2 2583
it, and shall *e* round about the Num 1:50 2583
as they *e*, so shall they set Num 2:17 2583
those that *e* by him shall be the Num 2:27 2583
But those that *e* before the Num 3:38 2583
how we are to *e* in the wilderness Num 10:31 2583
e against the city, and take it 2Sa 12:28 2583
e round about my tabernacle Job 19:12 2583
an host should *e* against me Ps 27:3 2583
I will *e* about mine house because Zec 9:8 2583

ENCAMPED {33}
e in Etham, in the edge of the Ex 13:20 2583
they *e* there by the waters Ex 15:27 2583
where he *e* at the mount of God Ex 18:5 2583
from Elim, and *e* by the Red sea Num 33:10 2583
e in the wilderness of Sin Num 33:11 2583
of Sin, and *e* in Dophkah Num 33:12 2583
from Dophkah, and *e* in Alush Num 33:13 2583
e at Rephidim, where was no water Num 33:14 2583
and *e* at Hazeroth Num 33:17 2583
mount Shapher, and *e* in Haradah Num 33:24 2583
from Makheloth, and *e* at Tahath Num 33:26 2583
from Hashmonah, and *e* at Moseroth Num 33:30 2583
Bene-jaakan, and *e* at Hor-hagidgad Num 33:32 2583
from Jotbathah, and *e* at Ebronah Num 33:34 2583
from Ebronah, and *e* at Ezion-gaber Num 33:35 2583
and *e* in Almon-diblathaim Num 33:46 2583
e in Gilgal, in the east border Josh 4:19 2583
children of Israel *e* in Gilgal Josh 5:10 2583
e before Gibeon, and made war Josh 10:5 2583
e against it, and fought against Josh 10:31 2583
they *e* against it, and fought Josh 10:34 2583
they *e* against them, and destroyed Judg 6:4 2583
e against Thebez, and took it Judg 9:50 2583
gathered together, and *e* in Gilead Judg 10:17 2583
together, and *e* in Mizpeh Judg 10:17 2583

the morning, and *e* against Gibeah ... Judg 20:19 2583
up, and *e* against Jabesh-gilead ... 1Sa 11:1 2583
but the Philistines *e* in Michmash ... 1Sa 13:16 2583
my lord, are *e* in the open fields ... 2Sa 11:11 2583
the people were *e* against ... 1Kin 16:15 2583
the people that were *e* heard say ... 1Kin 16:16 2583
e in the valley of Rephaim ... 1Chr 11:15 2583
e against the fenced cities, and ... 2Chr 32:1 2583

ENCAMPETH {2}
The angel of the LORD *e* round ... Ps 34:7 2583
bones of him that *e* against thee ... Ps 53:5 2583

ENCAMPING {1}
and overtook them *e* by the sea ... Ex 14:9 2583

ENCHANTER {1}
or an observer of times, or an *e* ... Deut 18:10 5172

ENCHANTERS {1}
to your dreamers, nor to your *e* ... Jer 27:9 6049

ENCHANTMENT {3}
neither shall ye use *e*, nor ... Lev 19:26 5172
there is no *e* against Jacob ... Num 23:23 5172
the serpent will bite without *e* ... Eccl 10:11 3908

ENCHANTMENTS {10}
did in like manner with their *e* ... Ex 7:11 3858
of Egypt did so with their *e* ... Ex 7:22 3909
the magicians did so with their *e* ... Ex 8:7 3909
with their *e* to bring forth lice ... Ex 8:18 3909
as at other times, to seek for *e* ... Num 24:1 5172
the fire, and used divination and *e* ... 2Kin 17:17 5172
and observed times, and used *e* ... 2Kin 21:6 5172
also he observed times, and used *e* ... 2Chr 33:6 5172
the great abundance of thine *e* ... Is 47:9 2267
Stand now with thine *e*, and with ... Is 47:12 2267

ENCOUNTERED {1}
and of the Stoicks, *e* him ... Acts 17:18 *4820*

ENCOURAGE {4}
e him: for he shall cause ... Deut 1:38 2388
and *e* him, and strengthen him ... Deut 3:28 2388
overthrow it: and *e* thou him ... 2Sa 11:25 2388
They *e* themselves in an evil ... Ps 64:5 2388

ENCOURAGED {5}
the men of Israel *e* themselves ... Judg 20:22 2388
but David *e* himself in the LORD ... 1Sa 30:6 2388
that they might be *e* in the law ... 2Chr 31:4 2388
e them to the service of the ... 2Chr 35:2 2388
So the carpenter *e* the goldsmith ... Is 41:7 2388

END {307}
The *e* of all flesh is come before ... Gen 6:13 7093
after the *e* of the hundred and ... Gen 8:3 7097
to pass at the *e* of forty days ... Gen 8:6 7093
which is in the *e* of his field ... Gen 23:9 7097
had made an *e* of blessing Jacob ... Gen 27:30 3615
pass at the *e* of two full years ... Gen 41:1 7093
e of the borders of Egypt even to ... Gen 47:21 7097
Egypt even to the other *e* thereof ... Gen 47:21 7097
made an *e* of commanding his sons ... Gen 49:33 3615
to the *e* thou mayest know that I ... Ex 8:22 4616
pass at the *e* of the four hundred ... Ex 12:41 7093
which is in the *e* of the year ... Ex 23:16 3318
And make one cherub on the one *e* ... Ex 25:19 7098
the other cherub on the other *e* ... Ex 25:19 7098
boards shall reach from *e* to *e* ... Ex 26:28 7097
Moses, when he had made an *e* of ... Ex 31:18 3615
of ingathering at the year's *e* ... Ex 34:22 8622
from the one *e* to the other ... Ex 36:33 7097
One cherub on the *e* on this side ... Ex 37:8 7098
on the other *e* on that side ... Ex 37:8 7098
of your consecration be at an *e* ... Lev 8:33 4390
when he hath made an *e* of ... Lev 16:20 3615
To the *e* that the children of ... Lev 17:5 4616
his sons have made an *e* of ... Num 4:15 3615
as he had made an *e* of speaking ... Num 16:31 3615
and let my last *e* be like his ... Num 23:10
but his latter *e* shall be that he ... Num 24:20
to do thee good at thy latter *e* ... Deut 8:16
to pass at the *e* of forty days ... Deut 9:11 7093
year even unto the *e* of the year ... Deut 11:12 319
from the one *e* of the earth even ... Deut 13:7 7097
unto the other *e* of the earth ... Deut 13:7 7097
At the *e* of three years thou ... Deut 14:28 7097
At the *e* of every seven years ... Deut 15:1 7093
to the *e* that he should multiply ... Deut 17:16 4616
to the *e* that he may prolong his ... Deut 17:20 4616
an *e* of speaking unto the people ... Deut 20:9 3615
When thou hast made an *e* of ... Deut 26:12 3615
from the *e* of the earth, as swift ... Deut 28:49 7097
from the one *e* of the earth even ... Deut 28:64 7097
At the *e* of every seven years, in ... Deut 31:10 7093
when Moses had made an *e* of ... Deut 31:24 3615
I will see what their *e* shall be ... Deut 32:20 319
would consider their latter *e* ... Deut 32:29
Moses made an *e* of speaking all ... Deut 32:45 3615
when Israel had made an *e* of ... Josh 8:24 3615
it came to pass at the *e* of three ... Josh 9:16 7097
an *e* of slaying them with a very ... Josh 10:20 3615
sea, even unto the *e* of Jordan ... Josh 15:5 7097
which is at the *e* of the valley ... Josh 15:8 7097
was from the *e* of Kirjath-jearim ... Josh 18:15 7097
the *e* of the mountain that lieth ... Josh 18:16 7097
salt sea at the south *e* of Jordan ... Josh 18:19 7097
When they had made an *e* of ... Josh 19:49 3615
So they made an *e* of dividing the ... Josh 19:51 3615
when he had made an *e* to offer ... Judg 3:18 3615
e of the staff that was in his ... Judg 6:21 7097
to pass at the *e* of two months ... Judg 11:39 7093
when he had made an *e* of speaking ... Judg 15:17 3615
behold, the day groweth to an *e* ... Judg 19:9 2583
unto the *e* of barley harvest ... Ruth 2:23 3615
down at the *e* of the heap of corn ... Ruth 3:7 7097
latter *e* than at the beginning ... Ruth 3:10
I begin, I will also make an *e* ... 1Sa 3:12 3615
going down to the *e* of the city ... 1Sa 9:27 7097
he had made an *e* of prophesying ... 1Sa 10:13 3615
e of offering the burnt offering ... 1Sa 13:10 3615
wherefore he put forth the *e* of ... 1Sa 14:27 7097
the *e* of the rod that was in mine ... 1Sa 14:43 7097
when he had made an *e* of speaking ... 1Sa 18:1 3615
when David had made an *e* of ... 1Sa 24:16 3615
e of the spear smote him under ... 2Sa 2:23
be bitterness in the latter *e* ... 2Sa 2:26
an *e* of offering burnt offerings ... 2Sa 6:18 3615
When thou hast made an *e* of ... 2Sa 11:19 3615
as he had made an *e* of speaking ... 2Sa 13:36 3615
every year's *e* that he polled it ... 2Sa 14:26 7093
Jerusalem at the *e* of nine months ... 2Sa 24:8 7097
as they had made an *e* of eating ... 1Kin 1:41 3615
to pass at the *e* of three years ... 1Kin 2:39 7093
until he had made an *e* of ... 1Kin 3:1 3615
So Hiram made an *e* of doing all ... 1Kin 7:40 3615
an *e* of praying all this prayer ... 1Kin 8:54 3615
to pass at the *e* of twenty years ... 1Kin 9:10 7097
to pass at the seven years' *e* ... 2Kin 8:3 7097
was full from one *e* to another ... 2Kin 10:21 6310
as soon as he had made an *e* of ... 2Kin 10:25 3615
at the *e* of three years they took ... 2Kin 18:10 7097
Jerusalem from one *e* to another ... 2Kin 21:16 6310
when David had made an *e* of ... 1Chr 16:2 3615
on the right side of the east *e* ... 2Chr 4:10
stood at the east *e* of the altar ... 2Chr 5:12
Solomon had made an *e* of praying ... 2Chr 7:1 3615
to pass at the *e* of twenty years ... 2Chr 8:1 7093
find them at the *e* of the brook ... 2Chr 20:16 5490
when they had made an *e* of the ... 2Chr 20:23 3615
after the *e* of two years, his ... 2Chr 21:19 7093
chest, until they had made an *e* ... 2Chr 24:10 3615
came to pass at the *e* of the year ... 2Chr 24:23 8622
of the first month they made an *e* ... 2Chr 29:17 3615
they had made an *e* of offering ... 2Chr 29:29 3615
from one *e* to another with their ... Ezr 9:11 6310
they made an *e* with all the men ... Ezr 10:17 3615
to the *e* of the house of Eliashib ... Neh 3:21 8503
will they make an *e* in a day ... Neh 4:2 3615
and what is mine *e*, that I should ... Job 6:11 7093
yet thy latter *e* should greatly ... Job 8:7
Shall vain words have an *e* ... Job 16:3 7093
it be ere ye make an *e* of words ... Job 18:2 7078
the day and night come to an *e* ... Job 26:10 8503
He setteth an *e* to darkness ... Job 28:3 7093
that Job may be tried unto the *e* ... Job 34:36 5331
e of Job more than his beginning ... Job 42:12
of the wicked come to an *e* ... Ps 7:9 1584
are come to a perpetual *e* ... Ps 9:6 8552
their words to the *e* of the world ... Ps 19:4 7097
forth is from the *e* of the heaven ... Ps 19:6 7097
To the *e* that my glory may sing ... Ps 30:12 4616
for the *e* of that man is peace ... Ps 37:37 319
the *e* of the wicked shall be cut ... Ps 37:38 319
LORD, make me to know mine *e* ... Ps 39:4 7093
to cease unto the *e* of the earth ... Ps 46:9 7097
From the *e* of the earth will I ... Ps 61:2 7097
then understood I their *e* ... Ps 73:17 319
and thy years shall have no *e* ... Ps 102:27 8552
man, and are at their wit's *e* ... Ps 107:27 1104
and I shall keep it unto the *e* ... Ps 119:33 6118
I have seen an *e* of all ... Ps 119:96 7093
statutes alway, even unto the *e* ... Ps 119:112 6118
But her *e* is bitter as wormwood ... Prov 5:4 319
but the *e* thereof are the ways of ... Prov 14:12 319
the *e* of that mirth is heaviness ... Prov 14:13 319
but the *e* thereof are the ways of ... Prov 16:25 319
mayest be wise in thy latter *e* ... Prov 19:20
but the *e* thereof shall not be ... Prov 20:21 319
For surely there is an *e* ... Prov 23:18 319
not what to do in the *e* thereof ... Prov 25:8 319
from the beginning to the *e* ... Eccl 3:11 5490
yet is there no *e* of all his ... Eccl 4:8 7093
There is no *e* of all the people ... Eccl 4:16 7093
for that is the *e* of all men ... Eccl 7:2 5490
Better is the *e* of a thing than ... Eccl 7:8 319
to the *e* that man should find ... Eccl 7:14 1700
the *e* of his talk is mischievous ... Eccl 10:13 319
making many books there is no *e* ... Eccl 12:12 7093
is there any *e* of their treasures ... Is 2:7 7097
is there any *e* of their chariots ... Is 2:7 7097
unto them from the *e* of the earth ... Is 5:26 7097
at the *e* of the conduit of the ... Is 7:3 7097
and peace there shall be no *e* ... Is 9:7 7093
from the *e* of heaven, even the ... Is 13:5 7093
for the extortioner is at an *e* ... Is 16:4 657
after the *e* of seventy years ... Is 23:15 7093
pass after the *e* of seventy years ... Is 23:17 7093
make an *e* to deal treacherously ... Is 33:1 5239
night wilt thou make an *e* of me ... Is 38:12 7999
night wilt thou make an *e* of me ... Is 38:13 7999
and know the latter *e* of them ... Is 41:22
praise from the *e* of the earth ... Is 42:10 7097
confounded world without *e* ... Is 45:17 5704,5769,5703
Declaring the *e* from the ... Is 46:10 319
didst remember the latter *e* of it ... Is 47:7
it even to the *e* of the earth ... Is 48:20 7097
salvation unto the *e* of the earth ... Is 49:6 7097
unto the *e* of the world, Say ye ... Is 62:11 7097
unto the *e* of the eleventh year ... Jer 1:3 8537
will he keep it to the *e* ... Jer 3:5 5331
yet will I not make a full *e* ... Jer 4:27 3615
but make not a full *e* ... Jer 5:10 3615
I will not make a full *e* with you ... Jer 5:18 3615
will ye do in the *e* thereof ... Jer 5:31 319
said, He shall not see our last *e* ... Jer 12:4
e of the land even to the other ... Jer 12:12 7097
even to the other *e* of the land ... Jer 12:12 7097
days, and at his *e* shall be a fool ... Jer 17:11 319
one *e* of the earth even unto the ... Jer 25:33 7097
unto the other *e* of the earth ... Jer 25:33 7097
when Jeremiah had made an *e* of ... Jer 26:8 3615
evil, to give you an expected *e* ... Jer 29:11 319
though I make a full *e* of all ... Jer 30:11 3615
will I not make a full *e* of thee ... Jer 30:11 3615
And there is hope in thine *e* ... Jer 31:17 319
At the *e* of seven years let ye go ... Jer 34:14 7093
that when Jeremiah had made an *e* ... Jer 43:1 3615
until there be an *e* of them ... Jer 44:27 3615
for I will make a full *e* of all ... Jer 46:28 3615
I will not make a full *e* of thee ... Jer 46:28 3615
thine *e* is come, and the measure ... Jer 51:13 7093
that his city is taken at one *e* ... Jer 51:31 7097
made an *e* of reading this book ... Jer 51:63 3615
she remembereth not her last *e* ... Lam 1:9
our *e* is near, our days are ... Lam 4:18 7093
for our *e* is come ... Lam 4:18 7093
to pass at the *e* of seven days ... Eze 3:16 7097
An *e*, the *e* is come upon the ... Eze 7:2 7093
Now is the *e* come upon thee, and I ... Eze 7:3 7093
An *e* is come, the *e* is come ... Eze 7:6 7093
wilt thou make a full *e* of the ... Eze 11:13 3615
neither did I make an *e* of them ... Eze 20:17 3615
to the *e* that they might know ... Eze 20:26 4616
when iniquity shall have an *e* ... Eze 21:25 7093
their iniquity shall have an *e* ... Eze 21:29 7093
At the *e* of forty years will I ... Eze 29:13 7093
To the *e* that none of all the ... Eze 31:14 4616
time that their iniquity had an *e* ... Eze 35:5 7093
after the *e* of seven months shall ... Eze 39:14 7097
the separate place at the *e* ... Eze 41:12 6285
Now when he had made an *e* of ... Eze 42:15 3615
hast made an *e* of cleansing it ... Eze 43:23 3615
From the north *e* to the coast of ... Eze 48:1 7097
that at the *e* thereof they might ... Dan 1:5 7117
at the *e* of ten days their ... Dan 1:15 7117
Now at the *e* of the days that the ... Dan 1:18 7117
thereof to the *e* of all the earth ... Dan 4:11 5491
dominion to the *e* of the earth ... Dan 4:22 5491
At the *e* of twelve months he ... Dan 4:29 7118
And at the *e* of the days I ... Dan 4:34 7118
dominion shall be even unto the *e* ... Dan 6:26 5491
and to destroy it unto the *e* ... Dan 7:26 5491
Hitherto is the *e* of the matter ... Dan 7:28 5491
time of the *e* shall be the vision ... Dan 8:17 7093
in the last *e* of the indignation ... Dan 8:19
the time appointed the *e* shall be ... Dan 8:19 7093
and to make an *e* of sins, and to ... Dan 9:24 2856
the *e* thereof shall be with a ... Dan 9:26 7093
unto the *e* of the war desolations ... Dan 9:26 7093
in the *e* of years they shall join ... Dan 11:6 7093
for yet the *e* shall be at the ... Dan 11:27 7093
white, even to the time of the *e* ... Dan 11:35 7093
at the time of the *e* shall the ... Dan 11:40 7093
yet he shall come to his *e* ... Dan 11:45 7093
book, even to the time of the *e* ... Dan 12:4 7093
it be to the *e* of these wonders ... Dan 12:6 7093
shall be the *e* of these things ... Dan 12:8 319
and sealed till the time of the *e* ... Dan 12:9 7093
But go thou thy way till the *e* be ... Dan 12:13 7093
in thy lot at the *e* of the days ... Dan 12:13 7093
the great houses shall have an *e* ... Amos 3:15 5486
to what *e* is it for you ... Amos 5:18
that when they had made an *e* of ... Amos 7:2 3615
The *e* is come upon my people of ... Amos 8:2 7093
the *e* thereof as a bitter day ... Amos 8:10 319
to the *e* that every one of the ... Obad 9 4616
an utter *e* of the place thereof ... Nah 1:8 3615
he will make an utter *e* ... Nah 1:9 3615
for there is none *e* of the store ... Nah 2:9 7097
there is none *e* of their corpses ... Nah 3:3 7097
but at the *e* it shall speak, and ... Hab 2:3 7093
endureth to the *e* shall be saved ... Mt 10:22 *5056*
when Jesus had made an *e* of ... Mt 11:1 *5055*
the harvest is the *e* of the world ... Mt 13:39 *4930*
it be in the *e* of this world ... Mt 13:40 *4930*
shall it be at the *e* of the world ... Mt 13:49 *4930*
coming, and of the *e* of the world ... Mt 24:3 *4930*
to pass, but the *e* is not yet ... Mt 24:6 *5056*
he that shall endure unto the *e* ... Mt 24:13 *5056*
and then shall the *e* come ... Mt 24:14 *5056*
from one *e* of heaven to the other ... Mt 24:31 *206*
with the servants, to see the *e* ... Mt 26:58 *5056*
In the *e* of the sabbath, as it ... Mt 28:1 *3796*
even unto the *e* of the world ... Mt 28:20 *4930*
he cannot stand, but hath an *e* ... Mk 3:26 *5056*
but the *e* shall not be yet ... Mk 13:7 *5056*
he that shall endure unto the *e* ... Mk 13:13 *5056*
his kingdom there shall be no *e* ... Lk 1:33 *5056*
a parable unto them to this *e* ... Lk 18:1
but the *e* is not by and by ... Lk 21:9 *5056*
things concerning me have an *e* ... Lk 22:37 *5056*
world, he loved them unto the *e* ... Jn 13:1 *5056*
To this *e* was I born, and for this ... Jn 18:37
to the *e* they might not live ... Acts 7:19 *1519*
to the *e* ye may be established ... Rom 1:11 *1519*
to the *e* the promise might be ... Rom 4:16 *1519*
for the *e* of those things is ... Rom 6:21 *5056*

and the e everlasting life ... Rom 6:22 5056
For Christ is the e of the law ... Rom 10:4 5056
For to this e Christ both died ... Rom 14:9
shall also confirm you unto the e ... 1Cor 1:8 5056
Then cometh the e, when he shall ... 1Cor 15:24 5056
shall acknowledge even to the e ... 2Cor 1:13 5056
For to this e also did I write ... 2Cor 2:9
the e of that which is abolished ... 2Cor 3:13 5056
whose e shall be according to ... 2Cor 11:15 5056
all ages, world without e ... Eph 3:21 165,3588,165
Whose e is destruction, whose God ... Phil 3:19 5056
To the e he may stablish your ... 1Th 3:13 1519
Now the e of the commandment is ... 1Ti 1:5 5056
of the hope firm unto the e ... Heb 3:6 5056
confidence stedfast unto the e ... Heb 3:14 5056
whose e is to be burned ... Heb 6:8 5056
full assurance of hope unto the e ... Heb 6:11 5056
is to them an e of all strife ... Heb 6:16 4009
beginning of days, nor e of life ... Heb 7:3 5056
but now once in the e of the ... Heb 9:26 4930
considering the e of their ... Heb 13:7 1545
and have seen the e of the Lord ... Jas 5:11 5056
Receiving the e of your faith ... 1Pet 1:9 5056
hope to the e for the grace that ... 1Pet 1:13 5049
But the e of all things is at ... 1Pet 4:7 5056
what shall the e be of them that ... 1Pet 4:17 5056
the latter e is worse with them ... 2Pet 2:20 2078
and keepeth my works unto the e ... Rev 2:26 5056
and Omega, the beginning and the e ... Rev 21:6 5056
and Omega, the beginning and the e ... Rev 22:13 5056

ENDAMAGE {1}
so thou shalt e the revenue of ... Ezr 4:13 5142

ENDANGER {1}
ye make me e my head to the king ... Dan 1:10 2325

ENDANGERED {1}
cleaveth wood shall be e thereby ... Eccl 10:9 5533

ENDEAVOUR {1}
Moreover I will e that ye may be ... 2Pet 1:15 4704

ENDEAVOURED {2}
immediately we e to go into ... Acts 16:10 2212
e the more abundantly to see your ... 1Th 2:17 4704

ENDEAVOURING {1}
E to keep the unity of the Spirit ... Eph 4:3 4704

ENDEAVOURS {1}
to the wickedness of their e ... Ps 28:4 4611

ENDED {21}
on the seventh day God e his work ... Gen 2:2 3615
was in the land of Egypt, were e ... Gen 41:53 3615
When that year was e, they came ... Gen 47:18 8552
of this song, until they were e ... Deut 31:30 8552
and mourning for Moses were e ... Deut 34:8 8552
until they have e all my harvest ... Ruth 2:21 3615
and so they e the matter ... 2Sa 20:18 8552
So was e all the work that king ... 1Kin 7:51 7999
help them, till the work was e ... 2Chr 29:34 3615
The words of Job are e ... Job 31:40 8552
of David the son of Jesse are e ... Ps 72:20 3615
days of thy mourning shall be e ... Is 60:20 7999
harvest is past, the summer is e ... Jer 8:20 3615
till thou hast e the days of thy ... Eze 4:8 3615
when Jesus had e these sayings ... Mt 7:28 4931
and when they were e, he afterward ... Lk 4:2 4931
devil had e all the temptation ... Lk 4:13 4931
Now when he had e all his sayings ... Lk 7:1 4137
And supper being e, the devil ... Jn 13:2 1096
After these things were e ... Acts 19:21 4137
when the seven days were almost e ... Acts 21:27 4931

ENDETH {1}
the noise of them that rejoice e ... Is 24:8 2308

ENDING {1}
and Omega, the beginning and the e ... Rev 1:8 5056

ENDLESS {2}
e genealogies, which minister ... 1Ti 1:4 562
but after the power of an e life ... Heb 7:16 179

EN-DOR *(en'-dor)* {3} *A village near Mt. Tabor.*
towns, and the inhabitants of E ... Josh 17:11 5874
that hath a familiar spirit at E ... 1Sa 28:7 5874
Which perished at E: they became ... Ps 83:10 5874

ENDOW {1}
he shall surely e her to be his ... Ex 22:16 4117

ENDS {51}
in the two e of the mercy seat ... Ex 25:18 7098
cherubims on the two e thereof ... Ex 25:19 7098
two chains of pure gold at the e ... Ex 28:14 4020
e of wreathen work of pure gold ... Ex 28:22 1383
on the two e of the breastplate ... Ex 28:23 7098
are on the e of the breastplate ... Ex 28:24 7098
the other two e of the two ... Ex 28:25 7098
two e of the breastplate in the ... Ex 28:26 7098
on the two e of the mercy seat ... Ex 37:7 7098
cherubims on the two e thereof ... Ex 37:8 7099
the four e of the grate of brass ... Ex 38:5 7099
the breastplate chains at the e ... Ex 39:15 1383
in the two e of the breastplate ... Ex 39:16 7098
rings on the e of the breastplate ... Ex 39:17 7098
the two e of the two wreathen ... Ex 39:18 7098
on the two e of the breastplate ... Ex 39:19 7098
together to the e of the earth ... Deut 33:17 657
shall judge the e of the earth ... 1Sa 2:10 657
that the e of the staves were ... 1Kin 8:8 7218
that the e of the staves were ... 2Chr 5:9 7218
he looketh to the e of the earth ... Job 28:24 7098
lightning unto the e of the earth ... Job 37:3 3671
take hold of the e of the earth ... Job 38:13 3671
and his circuit unto the e of it ... Ps 19:6 7098
All the e of the world shall ... Ps 22:27 657
praise unto the e of the earth ... Ps 48:10 7099
in Jacob unto the e of the earth ... Ps 59:13 657
of all the e of the earth ... Ps 65:5 7099
all the e of the earth shall fear ... Ps 67:7 657
the river unto the e of the earth ... Ps 72:8 657
all the e of the earth have seen ... Ps 98:3 657
to ascend from the e of the earth ... Ps 135:7 7097
a fool are in the e of the earth ... Prov 17:24 7097
all the e of the earth ... Prov 30:4 657
far unto all the e of the earth ... Is 26:15 7097
the Creator of the e of the earth ... Is 40:28 7098
the e of the earth were afraid ... Is 41:5 7098
taken from the e of the earth ... Is 41:9 7098
daughters from the e of the earth ... Is 43:6 7097
ye saved, all the e of the earth ... Is 45:22 657
all the e of the earth shall see ... Is 52:10 657
to ascend from the e of the earth ... Jer 10:13 7097
unto thee from the e of the earth ... Jer 16:19 657
come even to the e of the earth ... Jer 25:31 7097
to ascend from the e of the earth ... Jer 51:16 7097
fire devoureth both the e of it ... Eze 15:4 7098
be great unto the e of the earth ... Mic 5:4 657
river even to the e of the earth ... Zec 9:10 657
salvation unto the e of the earth ... Acts 13:47 2078
words unto the e of the world ... Rom 10:18 4009
upon whom the e of the world are ... 1Cor 10:11 5056

ENDUED {5}
God hath e me with a good dowry ... Gen 30:20 2064
e with prudence and understanding ... 2Chr 2:12 3045
e with understanding, of Huram my ... 2Chr 2:13 3045
until ye be e with power from on ... Lk 24:49 1746
e with knowledge among you ... Jas 3:13 1990

ENDURE {29}
me and the children be able to e ... Gen 33:14 7272
so, then thou shalt be able to e ... Ex 18:23 5975
For how can I e to see the evil ... Est 8:6 3201
or how can I e to see the ... Est 8:6 3201
hold it fast, but it shall not e ... Job 8:15 6965
of his highness I could not e ... Job 31:23
But the LORD shall e for ever ... Ps 9:7 3427
weeping may e for a night ... Ps 30:5 3885
thee as long as the sun and moon e ... Ps 72:5 6440
His name shall e for ever ... Ps 72:17 1961
also will I make to e for ever ... Ps 89:29
His seed shall e for ever ... Ps 89:36 1961
thou, O LORD, shalt e for ever ... Ps 102:12 3427
shall perish, but thou shalt e ... Ps 102:26 5975
of the LORD shall e for ever ... Ps 104:31 1961
doth the crown e to every ... Prov 27:24
Can thine heart e, or can thine ... Eze 22:14 5975
But he that shall e unto the end ... Mt 24:13 5278
and so e but for a time ... Mk 4:17 2076
but he that shall e unto the end ... Mk 13:13 5278
and tribulations that ye e ... 2Th 1:4 430
Thou therefore e hardness ... 2Ti 2:3 2553
Therefore I e all things for the ... 2Ti 2:10 5278
they will not e sound doctrine ... 2Ti 4:3 430
e afflictions, do the work of an ... 2Ti 4:5 2553
If ye e chastening, God dealeth ... Heb 12:7 5278
(For they could not e that which ... Heb 12:20 5342
we count them happy which e ... Jas 5:11 5278
for conscience toward God e grief ... 1Pet 2:19 5297

ENDURED {8}
their time should have e for ever ... Ps 81:15 1961
e with much longsuffering the ... Rom 9:22 5342
what persecutions I e ... 2Ti 3:11 5297
And so, after he had patiently e ... Heb 6:15 3114
ye e a great fight of afflictions ... Heb 10:32 5278
for he e, as seeing him who is ... Heb 11:27 2594
was set before him e the cross ... Heb 12:2 5278
For consider him that e such ... Heb 12:3 5278

ENDURETH {59}
for his mercy e for ever ... 1Chr 16:34
because his mercy e for ever ... 1Chr 16:41
for his mercy e for ever ... 2Chr 5:13
for his mercy e for ever ... 2Chr 7:3
because his mercy e for ever ... 2Chr 7:6
for his mercy e for ever ... 2Chr 20:21
for his mercy e for ever toward ... Ezr 3:11
For his anger e but a moment ... Ps 30:5
the goodness of God e continually ... Ps 52:1
of peace so long as the moon e ... Ps 72:7 1097
his truth e to all generations ... Ps 100:5
for his mercy e for ever ... Ps 106:1
for his mercy e for ever ... Ps 107:1
and his righteousness e for ever ... Ps 111:3 5975
his praise e for ever ... Ps 111:10 5975
and his righteousness e for ever ... Ps 112:3 5975
his righteousness e for ever ... Ps 112:9 5975
the truth of the LORD e for ever ... Ps 117:2
because his mercy e for ever ... Ps 118:1
say, that his mercy e for ever ... Ps 118:2
say, that his mercy e for ever ... Ps 118:3
say, that his mercy e for ever ... Ps 118:4
for his mercy e for ever ... Ps 118:29
righteous judgments e for ever ... Ps 119:160
Thy name, O LORD, e for ever ... Ps 135:13
for his mercy e for ever ... Ps 136:1
for his mercy e for ever ... Ps 136:2
for his mercy e for ever ... Ps 136:3
for his mercy e for ever ... Ps 136:4
for his mercy e for ever ... Ps 136:5
for his mercy e for ever ... Ps 136:6
for his mercy e for ever ... Ps 136:7
for his mercy e for ever ... Ps 136:8
for his mercy e for ever ... Ps 136:9
for his mercy e for ever ... Ps 136:10
for his mercy e for ever ... Ps 136:11
for his mercy e for ever ... Ps 136:12
for his mercy e for ever ... Ps 136:13
for his mercy e for ever ... Ps 136:14
for his mercy e for ever ... Ps 136:15
for his mercy e for ever ... Ps 136:16
for his mercy e for ever ... Ps 136:17
for his mercy e for ever ... Ps 136:18
for his mercy e for ever ... Ps 136:19
for his mercy e for ever ... Ps 136:20
for his mercy e for ever ... Ps 136:21
for his mercy e for ever ... Ps 136:22
for his mercy e for ever ... Ps 136:23
for his mercy e for ever ... Ps 136:24
for his mercy e for ever ... Ps 136:25
for his mercy e for ever ... Ps 136:26
thy mercy, O LORD, e for ever ... Ps 138:8
thy dominion e throughout all ... Ps 145:13
for his mercy e for ever ... Jer 33:11
but he that e to the end shall be ... Mt 10:22 5278
which e unto everlasting life ... Jn 6:27 3306
hopeth all things, e all things ... 1Cor 13:7 5278
is the man that e temptation ... Jas 1:12 5278
the word of the Lord e for ever ... 1Pet 1:25 3306

ENDURING {3}
of the LORD is clean, e for ever ... Ps 19:9 5975
which is effectual in the e of ... 2Cor 1:6 5281
heaven a better and an e substance ... Heb 10:34 3306

EN-EGLAIM *(en-eg'-la-im)* {1} *A place near the Salt Sea.*
upon it from En-gedi even unto E ... Eze 47:10 5882

ENEMIES {267}
delivered thine e into thy hand ... Gen 14:20 6862
shall possess the gate of his e ... Gen 22:17 341
shall be in the neck of thine e ... Gen 49:8 341
war, they join also unto our e ... Ex 1:10 8130
I will be an enemy unto thine e ... Ex 23:22 341
I will make all thine e turn ... Ex 23:27 341
unto their shame among their e ... Ex 32:25 6965
And ye shall chase your e, and they ... Lev 26:7 341
your e shall fall before you by ... Lev 26:8 341
in vain, for your e shall eat it ... Lev 26:16 341
ye shall be slain before your e ... Lev 26:17 341
your e which dwell therein shall ... Lev 26:32 341
hearts in the lands of their e ... Lev 26:36 341
no power to stand before your e ... Lev 26:37 341
land of your e shall eat you up ... Lev 26:38 341
them into the land of their e ... Lev 26:41 341
they be in the land of their e ... Lev 26:44 341
and ye shall be saved from your e ... Num 10:9 341
LORD, and let thine e be scattered ... Num 10:35 341
ye be not smitten before your e ... Num 14:42 341
I took thee to curse mine e ... Num 23:11 341
he shall eat up the nations his e ... Num 24:8 6862
I called thee to curse mine e ... Num 24:10 341
shall be a possession for his e ... Num 24:18 341
driven out his e from before him ... Num 32:21 341
lest ye be smitten before your e ... Deut 1:42 341
out all thine e from before thee ... Deut 6:19 341
rest from all your e round about ... Deut 12:10 341
out to battle against thine e ... Deut 20:1 341
day unto battle against your e ... Deut 20:3 341
to fight for you against your e ... Deut 20:4 341
shalt eat the spoil of thine e ... Deut 20:14 341
forth to war against thine e ... Deut 21:10 341
host goeth forth against thine e ... Deut 23:9 341
and to give up thine e before thee ... Deut 23:14 341
rest from all thine e round about ... Deut 25:19 341
The LORD shall cause thine e that ... Deut 28:7 341
thee to be smitten before thine e ... Deut 28:25 341
sheep shall be given unto thine e ... Deut 28:31 341
shalt thou serve thine e which ... Deut 28:48 341
wherewith thine e shall distress ... Deut 28:53 341
wherewith thine e shall distress ... Deut 28:55 341
be sold unto your e for bondmen ... Deut 28:68 341
put all these curses upon thine e ... Deut 30:7 341
even our e themselves being ... Deut 32:31 341
I will render vengeance to mine e ... Deut 32:41 6862
be thou an help to him from his e ... Deut 33:7 6862
thine e shall be found liars unto ... Deut 33:29 341
their backs before their e ... Josh 7:8 341
could not stand before their e ... Josh 7:12 341
turned their backs before their e ... Josh 7:12 341
canst not stand before thine e ... Josh 7:13 341
avenged themselves upon their e ... Josh 10:13 341
ye not, but pursue after your e ... Josh 10:19 341
all your e against whom ye fight ... Josh 10:25 341
a man of all their e before them ... Josh 21:44 341
all their e into their hand ... Josh 21:44 341
of your e with your brethren ... Josh 22:8 341
from all their e round about ... Josh 23:1 341
the hands of their e round about ... Judg 2:14 341
any longer stand before their e ... Judg 2:14 341
their e all the days of the judge ... Judg 2:18 341
e the Moabites into your hand ... Judg 3:28 341
So let all thine e perish ... Judg 5:31 341
of all their e on every side ... Judg 8:34 341
vengeance for thee of thine e ... Judg 11:36 341
my mouth is enlarged over mine e ... 1Sa 2:1 341
save us out of the hand of our e ... 1Sa 4:3 341
us out of the hand of our e ... 1Sa 12:10 341
the hand of your e on every side ... 1Sa 12:11 341
that I may be avenged on mine e ... 1Sa 14:24 341

spoil of their *e* which they found ... 1Sa 14:30 341
against all his *e* on every side ... 1Sa 14:47 341
to be avenged of the king's *e* ... 1Sa 18:25 341
the *e* of David every one from the ... 1Sa 20:15 341
it at the hand of David's *e* ... 1Sa 20:16 341
also do God unto the *e* of David ... 1Sa 25:22 341
thine own hand, now let thine *e* ... 1Sa 25:26 341
and the souls of thine *e*, them ... 1Sa 25:29 341
against the *e* of my lord the king ... 1Sa 29:8 341
of the spoil of the *e* of the LORD ... 1Sa 30:26 341
and out of the hand of all their *e* ... 2Sa 3:18 341
forth upon mine *e* before me ... 2Sa 5:20 341
rest round about from all his *e* ... 2Sa 7:1 341
off all thine *e* out of thy sight ... 2Sa 7:9 341
thee to rest from all thine *e* ... 2Sa 7:11 341
to the *e* of the LORD to blaspheme ... 2Sa 12:14 341
LORD hath avenged him of his *e* ... 2Sa 18:19 341
The *e* of my lord the king, and all ... 2Sa 18:32 341
In that thou lovest thine *e* ... 2Sa 19:6 8130
saved us out of the hand of our *e* ... 2Sa 19:9 341
him out of the hand of all his *e* ... 2Sa 22:1 341
so shall I be saved from mine *e* ... 2Sa 22:4 341
I have pursued mine *e*, and ... 2Sa 22:38 341
also given me the necks of mine *e* ... 2Sa 22:41 341
bringeth me forth from mine *e* ... 2Sa 22:49 341
flee three months before thine *e* ... 2Sa 24:13 6862
hast asked the life of thine *e* ... 1Kin 3:11 341
soul, in the land of their *e* ... 1Kin 8:48 341
you out of the hand of all your *e* ... 2Kin 17:39 341
them into the hand of their *e* ... 2Kin 21:14 341
a prey and a spoil to all their *e* ... 2Kin 21:14 341
ye be come to betray me to mine *e* ... 1Chr 12:17 6862
God hath broken in upon mine *e* by ... 1Chr 14:11 341
off all thine *e* from before thee ... 1Chr 17:8 341
I will subdue all thine *e* ... 1Chr 17:10 341
sword of thine *e* overtaketh thee ... 1Chr 21:12 341
rest from all his *e* round about ... 1Chr 22:9 341
honour, nor the life of thine *e* ... 2Chr 1:11 8130
if their *e* besiege them in the ... 2Chr 6:28 341
go out to war against their *e* by ... 2Chr 6:34 341
deliver them over before their *e* ... 2Chr 6:36 341
made them to rejoice over their *e* ... 2Chr 20:27 341
fought against the *e* of Israel ... 2Chr 20:29 341
them into the hand of their *e* ... 2Chr 25:20
when our *e* heard that it was ... Neh 4:15 341
the reproach of the heathen our *e* ... Neh 5:9 341
the Arabian, and the rest of our *e* ... Neh 6:1 341
that when all our *e* heard thereof ... Neh 6:16 341
them into the hand of their *e* ... Neh 9:27 6862
them out of the hand of their *e* ... Neh 9:27 6862
thou them in the hand of their *e* ... Neh 9:28 341
to avenge themselves on their *e* ... Est 8:13 341
in the day that the *e* of the Jews ... Est 9:1 341
e with the stroke of the sword ... Est 9:5 341
lives, and had rest from their *e* ... Est 9:16 341
the Jews rested from their *e* ... Est 9:22 341
me unto him as one of his *e* ... Job 19:11 6862
all mine *e* upon the cheek bone ... Ps 3:7 341
righteousness because of mine *e* ... Ps 5:8 8324
waxeth old because of all mine *e* ... Ps 6:7 6887
Let all mine *e* be ashamed ... Ps 6:10 341
because of the rage of mine *e* ... Ps 7:6 6887
strength because of thine *e* ... Ps 8:2 6887
When mine *e* are turned back, they ... Ps 9:3 341
as for all his *e*, he puffeth at ... Ps 10:5 6887
that oppress me, from my deadly *e* ... Ps 17:9 341
him from the hand of all his *e* ... Ps 18:*t* 341
so shall I be saved from mine *e* ... Ps 18:3 341
I have pursued mine *e*, and ... Ps 18:37 341
also given me the necks of mine *e* ... Ps 18:40 341
He delivereth me from mine *e* ... Ps 18:48 341
hand shall find out all thine *e* ... Ps 21:8 341
me in the presence of mine *e* ... Ps 23:5 6887
let not mine *e* triumph over me ... Ps 25:2 341
Consider mine *e*; for they are ... Ps 25:19 341
When the wicked, even mine *e* ... Ps 27:2 6862
up above mine *e* round about me ... Ps 27:6 341
a plain path, because of mine *e* ... Ps 27:11 8324
not over unto the will of mine *e* ... Ps 27:12 6862
I was a reproach among all mine *e* ... Ps 31:11 6887
me from the hand of mine *e* ... Ps 31:15 341
mine *e* wrongfully rejoice over me ... Ps 35:19 341
the *e* of the LORD shall be as the ... Ps 37:20 341
But mine *e* are lively, and they ... Ps 38:19 341
him unto the will of his *e* ... Ps 41:2 341
Mine *e* speak evil of me, When ... Ps 41:5 341
in my bones, mine *e* reproach me ... Ps 42:10 6887
thee will we push down our *e* ... Ps 44:5 6862
But thou hast saved us from our *e* ... Ps 44:7 6862
in the heart of the king's *e* ... Ps 45:5 341
He shall reward evil unto mine *e* ... Ps 54:5 8324
hath seen his desire upon mine *e* ... Ps 54:7 341
Mine *e* would daily swallow me up ... Ps 56:2 8324
thee, then shall mine *e* turn back ... Ps 56:9 341
Deliver me from mine *e*, O my God ... Ps 59:1 341
let me see my desire upon mine *e* ... Ps 59:10 8324
it is that shall tread down our *e* ... Ps 60:12 6862
of thy power shall thine *e* submit ... Ps 66:3 341
God arise, let his *e* be scattered ... Ps 68:1 341
God shall wound the head of his *e* ... Ps 68:21 341
be dipped in the blood of thine *e* ... Ps 68:23 341
me, being mine *e* wrongfully ... Ps 69:4 341
deliver me because of mine *e* ... Ps 69:18 341
For mine *e* speak against me ... Ps 71:10 341
his *e* shall lick the dust ... Ps 72:9 341
Thine *e* roar in the midst of thy ... Ps 74:4 6887
Forget not the voice of thine *e* ... Ps 74:23 6887
but the sea overwhelmed their *e* ... Ps 78:53 341
he smote his *e* in the hinder ... Ps 78:66 6862
our *e* laugh among themselves ... Ps 80:6 341
should soon have subdued their *e* ... Ps 81:14 341
For, lo, thine *e* make a tumult ... Ps 83:2 341
thine *e* with thy strong arm ... Ps 89:10 341
hast made all his *e* to rejoice ... Ps 89:42 341
Wherewith thine *e* have reproached ... Ps 89:51 341
For, lo, thine *e*, O LORD, for, lo ... Ps 92:9 341
for, lo, thine *e* shall perish ... Ps 92:9 341
shall see my desire on mine *e* ... Ps 92:11 7790
and burneth up his *e* round about ... Ps 97:3 6862
Mine *e* reproach me all the day ... Ps 102:8 341
made them stronger than their *e* ... Ps 105:24 6862
And the waters covered their *e* ... Ps 106:11 6862
Their *e* also oppressed them, and ... Ps 106:42 341
it is that shall tread down our *e* ... Ps 108:13 6862
I make thine *e* thy footstool ... Ps 110:1 341
rule thou in the midst of thine *e* ... Ps 110:2 341
he see his desire upon his *e* ... Ps 112:8 6862
hast made me wiser than mine *e* ... Ps 119:98 341
because mine *e* have forgotten thy ... Ps 119:139 6862
Many are my persecutors and mine *e* ... Ps 119:157 6862
speak with the *e* in the gate ... Ps 127:5 341
His *e* will I clothe with shame ... Ps 132:18 341
And hath redeemed us from our *e* ... Ps 136:24 6862
hand against the wrath of mine *e* ... Ps 138:7 341
thine *e* take thy name in vain ... Ps 139:20 6145
I count them mine *e* ... Ps 139:22 341
Deliver me, O LORD, from mine *e* ... Ps 143:9 341
And of thy mercy cut off mine *e* ... Ps 143:12 341
he maketh even his *e* to be at ... Prov 16:7 341
and avenge me of mine *e* ... Is 1:24 341
him, and join his *e* together ... Is 9:11 341
fire of thine *e* shall devour them ... Is 26:11 6862
he shall prevail against his *e* ... Is 42:13 341
adversaries, recompence to his *e* ... Is 59:18 341
thy corn to be meat for thine *e* ... Is 62:8 341
rendereth recompence to his *e* ... Is 66:6 341
and his indignation toward his *e* ... Is 66:14 341
of my soul into the hand of her *e* ... Jer 12:7 341
to the sword before their *e* ... Jer 15:9 341
make thee to pass with thine *e* ... Jer 15:14 341
e in the land which thou knowest ... Jer 17:4 341
fall by the sword before their *e* ... Jer 19:7 341
and straitness, wherewith their *e* ... Jer 19:9 341
fall by the sword of their *e* ... Jer 20:4 341
I give into the hand of their *e* ... Jer 20:5 341
and into the hand of their *e* ... Jer 21:7 341
them into the hand of their *e* ... Jer 34:20 341
I give into the hand of their *e* ... Jer 34:21 341
of Egypt into the hand of his *e* ... Jer 44:30 341
the going down of Horonaim the *e* ... Jer 48:5 6862
to be dismayed before their *e* ... Jer 49:37 341
with her, they are become her *e* ... Lam 1:2 341
are the chief, her *e* prosper ... Lam 1:5 341
all mine *e* have heard of my ... Lam 1:21 341
All thine *e* have opened their ... Lam 2:16 341
All our *e* have opened their ... Lam 3:46 341
Mine *e* chased me sore, like a ... Lam 3:52 341
them into the hand of their *e* ... Eze 39:23 6862
interpretation thereof to thine *e* ... Dan 4:19 6146
go into captivity before their *e* ... Amos 9:4 341
thee from the hand of thine *e* ... Mic 4:10 341
all thine *e* shall be cut off ... Mic 5:9 341
a man's *e* are the men of his own ... Mic 7:6 341
and he reserveth wrath for his *e* ... Nah 1:2 341
and darkness shall pursue his *e* ... Nah 1:8 341
be set wide open unto thine *e* ... Nah 3:13 341
which tread down their *e* in the ... Zec 10:5
But I say unto you, Love your *e* ... Mt 5:44 *2190*
till I make thine *e* thy footstool ... Mt 22:44 *2190*
till I make thine *e* thy footstool ... Mk 12:36 *2190*
we should be saved from our *e* ... Lk 1:71 *2190*
out of the hand of our *e* might ... Lk 1:74 *2190*
unto you which hear, Love your *e* ... Lk 6:27 *2190*
But love ye your *e*, and do good ... Lk 6:35 *2190*
But those mine *e*, which would not ... Lk 19:27 *2190*
that thine *e* shall cast a trench ... Lk 19:43 *2190*
Till I make thine *e* thy footstool ... Lk 20:43 *2190*
For if, when we were *e*, we were ... Rom 5:10 *2190*
they are *e* for your sakes ... Rom 11:28 *2190*
he hath put all *e* under his feet ... 1Cor 15:25 *2190*
that they are the *e* of the cross ... Phil 3:18 *2190*
e in your mind by wicked works ... Col 1:21 *2190*
I make thine *e* thy footstool ... Heb 1:13 *2190*
till his *e* be made his footstool ... Heb 10:13 *2190*
their mouth, and devoureth their *e* ... Rev 11:5 *2190*
and their *e* beheld them ... Rev 11:12 *2190*

ENEMIES' {3}

desolate, and ye be in your *e* land ... Lev 26:34 341
in their iniquity in your *e* lands ... Lev 26:39 341
them out of their *e* lands ... Eze 39:27 341

ENEMY {107}

LORD, hath dashed in pieces the *e* ... Ex 15:6 341
The *e* said, I will pursue, I will ... Ex 15:9 341
then I will be an *e* unto thine ... Ex 23:22 340
delivered into the hand of the *e* ... Lev 26:25 341
against the *e* that oppresseth you ... Num 10:9 341
that he die, and was not his *e* ... Num 35:23 341
wherewith thine *e* shall distress ... Deut 28:57 341
that I feared the wrath of the *e* ... Deut 32:27 341
beginning of revenges upon the *e* ... Deut 32:42 341
thrust out the *e* from before thee ... Deut 33:27 341
Samson our *e* into our hand ... Judg 16:23 341
delivered into our hands our *e* ... Judg 16:24 341
shalt see an *e* in my habitation ... 1Sa 2:32 6862
Saul became David's *e* continually ... 1Sa 18:29 341
me so, and sent away mine *e* ... 1Sa 19:17 341
deliver thine *e* into thine hand ... 1Sa 24:4 341
For if a man find his *e*, will he ... 1Sa 24:19 341
thine *e* into thine hand this day ... 1Sa 26:8 341
from thee, and is become thine *e* ... 1Sa 28:16 6145
the son of Saul thine *e*, which ... 2Sa 4:8 341
He delivered me from my strong *e* ... 2Sa 22:18 341
be smitten down before the *e* ... 1Kin 8:33 341
if their *e* besiege them in the ... 1Kin 8:37 341
go out to battle against their *e* ... 1Kin 8:44 341
them, and deliver them to the *e* ... 1Kin 8:46 341
captives unto the land of the *e* ... 1Kin 8:46 341
Hast thou found me, O mine *e* ... 1Kin 21:20 341
be put to the worse before the *e* ... 2Chr 6:24 341
shall make thee fall before the *e* ... 2Chr 25:8 341
to help the king against the *e* ... 2Chr 26:13 341
help us against the *e* in the way ... Ezr 8:22 341
us from the hand of the *e* ... Ezr 8:31 341
the Agagite, the Jews' *e* ... Est 3:10 6887
tongue, although the *e* could not ... Est 7:4 6862
and *e* is this wicked Haman ... Est 7:6 341
the Jews' *e* unto Esther the queen ... Est 8:1 6887
the *e* of the Jews, slew they ... Est 9:10 6887
the *e* of all the Jews, had ... Est 9:24 6887
face, and holdest me for thine *e* ... Job 13:24 341
mine *e* sharpeneth his eyes upon ... Job 16:9 6862
Let mine *e* be as the wicked, and ... Job 27:7 341
me, he counteth me for his *e* ... Job 33:10 341
him that without cause is mine *e* ... Ps 7:4 6887
Let the *e* persecute my soul, and ... Ps 7:5 341
that thou mightest still the *e* ... Ps 8:2 341
O thou *e*, destructions are come ... Ps 9:6 341
shall mine *e* be exalted over me ... Ps 13:2 341
Lest mine *e* say, I have prevailed ... Ps 13:4 341
He delivered me from my strong *e* ... Ps 18:17 341
shut me up into the hand of the *e* ... Ps 31:8 341
because mine *e* doth not triumph ... Ps 41:11 341
of the oppression of the *e* ... Ps 42:9 341
of the oppression of the *e* ... Ps 43:2 341
makest us to turn back from the *e* ... Ps 44:10 6862
by reason of the *e* and avenger ... Ps 44:16 341
Because of the voice of the *e* ... Ps 55:3 341
For it was not an *e* that ... Ps 55:12 341
me, and a strong tower from the *e* ... Ps 61:3 341
my life from fear of the *e* ... Ps 64:1 341
even all that the *e* hath done ... Ps 74:3 341
shall the *e* blaspheme thy name ... Ps 74:10 341
that the *e* hath reproached, O ... Ps 74:18 341
when he delivered them from the *e* ... Ps 78:42 6862
The *e* shall not exact upon him ... Ps 89:22 341
them from the hand of the *e* ... Ps 106:10 341
redeemed from the hand of the *e* ... Ps 107:2 6862
For the *e* hath persecuted my soul ... Ps 143:3 341
Rejoice not when thine *e* falleth ... Prov 24:17 341
If thine *e* be hungry, give him ... Prov 25:21 8130
the kisses of an *e* are deceitful ... Prov 27:6 8130
When the *e* shall come in like a ... Is 59:19 6862
he was turned to be their *e* ... Is 63:10 341
for the sword of the *e* and fear is ... Jer 6:25 341
verily I will cause the *e* to ... Jer 15:11 341
as with an east wind before the *e* ... Jer 18:17 341
thee with the wound of an *e* ... Jer 30:14 341
come again from the land of the *e* ... Jer 31:16 341
king of Babylon, his *e*, and that ... Jer 44:30 341
gone into captivity before the *e* ... Lam 1:5 6862
fell into the hand of the *e* ... Lam 1:7 6862
for the *e* hath magnified himself ... Lam 1:9 341
desolate, because the *e* prevailed ... Lam 1:16 341
his right hand from before the *e* ... Lam 2:3 341
He hath bent his bow like an *e* ... Lam 2:4 341
The Lord was as an *e* ... Lam 2:5 341
of the *e* the walls of her palaces ... Lam 2:7 341
thine *e* to rejoice over thee ... Lam 2:17 341
brought up hath mine *e* consumed ... Lam 2:22 341
the *e* should have entered into ... Lam 4:12 341
Because the *e* hath said against ... Eze 36:2 341
the *e* shall pursue him ... Hos 8:3 341
my people is risen up as an *e* ... Mic 2:8 341
Rejoice not against me, O mine *e* ... Mic 7:8 341
she that is mine *e* shall see it ... Mic 7:10 341
seek strength because of the *e* ... Nah 3:11 341
he hath cast out thine *e* ... Zeph 3:15 341
thy neighbour, and hate thine *e* ... Mt 5:43 *2190*
his *e* came and sowed tares among ... Mt 13:25 *2190*
unto them, An *e* hath done this ... Mt 13:28 *2190*
The *e* that sowed them is the ... Mt 13:39 *2190*
and over all the power of the *e* ... Lk 10:19 *2190*
thou *e* of all righteousness, wilt ... Acts 13:10 *2190*
Therefore if thine *e* hunger ... Rom 12:20 *2190*
The last *e* that shall be ... 1Cor 15:26 *2190*
Am I therefore become your *e* ... Gal 4:16 *2190*
Yet count him not as an *e* ... 2Th 3:15 *2190*
of the world is the *e* of God ... Jas 4:4 *2190*

ENEMY'S {3}

If thou meet thine *e* ox or his ... Ex 23:4 341
Or, Deliver me from the *e* hand ... Job 6:23 6862
and his glory into the *e* hand ... Ps 78:61 6862

ENFLAMING {1}

E yourselves with idols under ... Is 57:5 2552

ENGAGED {1}

for who is this that *e* his heart ... Jer 30:21 6148

EN-GANNIM *(en-gan'-nim)* {3}

1. A city in Judah.

and *E*, Tappuah, and Enam ... Josh 15:34 5873

2. A city in Issachar.
And Remeth, and *E*, and En-haddah, ... Josh 19:21 5873
her suburbs, *E* with her suburbs .... Josh 21:29 5873

EN-GEDI *(en-ghe'-di)* {6} See HAZAZON-TAMAR. *A town on the Salt Sea.*
and the city of Salt, and *E* .... Josh 15:62 5872
and dwelt in strong holds at *E* 1Sa 23:29 5872
David is in the wilderness of *E* 1Sa 24:1 5872
be in Hazazon-tamar, which is *E* 2Chr 20:2 5872
of camphire in the vineyards of *E* .... Song 1:14 5872
it from *E* even unto En-eglaim .... Eze 47:10 5872

ENGINES {2}
And he made in Jerusalem *e* 2Chr 26:15 2810
he shall set *e* of war against thy.............. Eze 26:9 4239

ENGRAFTED {1}
receive with meekness the *e* word .... Jas 1:21 *1721*

ENGRAVE {2}
shalt thou *e* the two stones with .... Ex 28:11 6605
I will *e* the graving thereof, ... Zec 3:9 6605

ENGRAVEN {1}
e in stones, was glorious, so 2Cor 3:7 *1795*

ENGRAVER {3}
With the work of an *e* in stone .... Ex 28:11 2796
work all manner of work, of the *e* .... Ex 35:35 2796
of the tribe of Dan, an *e* .... Ex 38:23 2796

ENGRAVINGS {5}
like the *e* of a signet, shalt .... Ex 28:11 6603
names, like the *e* of a signet .... Ex 28:21 6603
like the *e* of a signet, HOLINESS .... Ex 28:36 6603
like the *e* of a signet, every one .... Ex 39:14 6603
like to the *e* of a signet .... Ex 39:30 6603

EN-HADDAH *(en-had'-dah)* {1} *A city in Issachar.*
And Remeth, and En-gannim, and *E* ...... Josh 19:21 5876

EN-HAKKORE *(en-hak'-ko-re)* {1} *A spring.*
he called the name thereof *E* .... Judg 15:19 5875

EN-HAZOR *(en-ha'-zor)* {1} *A city in Naphtali.*
And Kedesh, and Edrei, and *E* .... Josh 19:37 5877

ENJOIN {1}
e thee that which is convenient .... Philem 8 *2004*

ENJOINED {3}
and Esther the queen had *e* them .... Est 9:31 6965
Who hath *e* him his way .... Job 36:23 6485
which God hath *e* unto you .... Heb 9:20 *1781*

ENJOY {14}
shall the land *e* her sabbaths .... Lev 26:34 7521
the land rest, and *e* her sabbaths .... Lev 26:34 7521
shall *e* her sabbaths, while she .... Lev 26:43 7521
e every man the inheritance of .... Num 36:8 3423
but thou shalt not *e* them .... Deut 28:41 1961
e it, which Moses the LORD's .... Josh 1:15 3423
with mirth, therefore *e* pleasure .... Eccl 2:1 7200
his soul *e* good in his labour .... Eccl 2:24 7200
e the good of all his labour, it .... Eccl 3:13 7200
to *e* the good of all his labour .... Eccl 5:18 7200
mine elect shall long *e* the work .... Is 65:22 1086
that by thee we *e* great quietness .... Acts 24:2 *5177*
giveth us richly all things to *e* 1Ti 6:17 *619*
than to *e* the pleasures of sin .... Heb 11:25 *2192,619*

ENJOYED {1}
until the land had *e* her sabbaths 2Chr 36:21 7521

ENLARGE {10}
God shall *e* Japheth, and he shall .... Gen 9:27 6601
before thee, and *e* thy borders .... Ex 34:24 7337
LORD thy God shall *e* thy border .... Deut 12:20 7337
if the LORD thy God *e* thy coast .... Deut 19:8 7337
e my coast, and that thine hand 1Chr 4:10 7235
when thou shalt *e* my heart .... Ps 119:32 7337
E the place of thy tent, and let .... Is 54:2 7337
that they might *e* their border .... Amos 1:13 7337
e thy baldness as the eagle .... Mic 1:16 7337
e the borders of their garments, ... Mt 23:5 *3170*

ENLARGED {11}
my mouth is *e* over mine enemies 1Sa 2:1 7337
Thou hast *e* my steps under me 2Sa 22:37 7337
thou hast *e* me when I was in .... Ps 4:1 7337
Thou hast *e* my steps under me, ... Ps 18:36 7337
The troubles of my heart are *e* .... Ps 25:17 7337
Therefore hell hath *e* herself .... Is 5:14 7337
thou hast *e* thy bed, and made thee .... Is 57:8 7337
thine heart shall fear, and be *e* .... Is 60:5 7337
is open unto you, our heart is *e* 2Cor 6:11 *4115*
unto my children,) be ye also *e* 2Cor 6:13 *4115*
that we shall be *e* by you 2Cor 10:15 *3170*

ENLARGEMENT {1}
at this time, then shall there *e* .... Est 4:14 7305

ENLARGETH {3}
he said, Blessed be he that *e* Gad .... Deut 33:20 7337
he *e* the nations, and straiteneth .... Job 12:23 7849
who *e* his desire as hell, and is .... Hab 2:5 7337

ENLARGING {1}
And there was an *e*, and a winding .... Eze 41:7 7337

ENLIGHTEN {1}
LORD my God will *e* my darkness .... Ps 18:28 5050

ENLIGHTENED {6}
and his eyes were *e* 1Sa 14:27 215
you, how mine eyes have been *e* 1Sa 14:29 215
to be *e* with the light of the .... Job 33:30 215
His lightnings *e* the world .... Ps 97:4 215
of your understanding being *e* .... Eph 1:18 *5461*
for those who were once *e* .... Heb 6:4 *5461*

ENLIGHTENING {1}
of the LORD is pure, *e* the eyes .... Ps 19:8 215

EN-MISHPAT *Another name for Kadesh.*
And they returned, and came to *E* .... Gen 14:7 5880

ENMITY {8}
I will put *e* between thee and the .... Gen 3:15 342
Or in *e* smite him with his hand, ... Num 35:21 342
he thrust him suddenly without *e* .... Num 35:22
they were at *e* between themselves .... Lk 23:12 *2189*
the carnal mind is *e* against God .... Rom 8:7 *2189*
abolished in his flesh the *e* .... Eph 2:15 *2189*
cross, having slain the *e* thereby .... Eph 2:16 *2189*
of the world is *e* with God .... Jas 4:4 *2189*

ENOCH *(e'-nok)* {12} See HENOCH.
1. A son of Cain.
and she conceived, and bare *E* .... Gen 4:17 2585
And unto *E* was born Irad .... Gen 4:18 2585
2. A city built by Cain.
after the name of his son, *E* .... Gen 4:17 2585
3. A son of Jared.
sixty and two years, and he begat *E* .... Gen 5:18 2585
he begat *E* eight hundred years .... Gen 5:19 2585
E lived sixty and five years, and .... Gen 5:21 2585
E walked with God after he begat .... Gen 5:22 2585
all the days of *E* were three .... Gen 5:23 2585
And *E* walked with God .... Gen 5:24 2585
Mathusala, which was the son of *E* .... Lk 3:37 *1802*
By faith *E* was translated that he .... Heb 11:5 *1802*
E also, the seventh from Adam, ... Jude 14 *1802*

ENOS *(e'-nos)* {7} See ENOSH. *Son of Seth.*
and he called his name *E* .... Gen 4:26 583
hundred and five years, and begat *E* .... Gen 5:6 583
after he begat *E* eight hundred .... Gen 5:7 583
E lived ninety years, and begat .... Gen 5:9 583
E lived after he begat Cainan .... Gen 5:10 583
all the days of *E* were nine .... Gen 5:11 583
Which was the son of *E*, which was .... Lk 3:38 *1800*

ENOSH *(e'-nosh)* {1} See ENOS. *Same as Enos.*
Adam, Sheth, *E*, ... 1Chr 1:1 583

ENOUGH See APPENDIX.

ENQUIRE {52}
the damsel, and *e* at her mouth .... Gen 24:57 7592
And she went to *e* of the LORD .... Gen 25:22 1875
people come unto me to *e* of God .... Ex 18:15 1875
that thou *e* not after their gods, ... Deut 12:30 1875
Then shalt thou *e*, and make search .... Deut 13:14 1875
that shall be in those days, and *e* .... Deut 17:9 1875
e of thee, and say, Is there any .... Judg 4:20 7592
when a man went to *e* of God 1Sa 9:9 1875
E thou whose son the stripling is 1Sa 17:56 7592
I then begin to *e* of God for him 1Sa 22:15 7592
that I may go to her, and *e* of her 1Sa 28:7 1875
said unto the king of Israel, *E* 1Kin 22:5 1875
besides, that we might *e* of him 1Kin 22:7 1875
by whom we may *e* of the LORD 1Kin 22:8 1875
e of Baal-zebub the god of Ekron 2Kin 1:2 1875
that ye go to *e* of Baal-zebub the 2Kin 1:3 1875
that thou sendest to *e* of 2Kin 1:6 1875
e of Baal-zebub the god of Ekron 2Kin 1:16 1875
no God in Israel to *e* of his word 2Kin 1:16 1875
that we may *e* of the LORD by him 2Kin 3:11 1875
e of the LORD by him, saying, ... 2Kin 8:8 1875
altar shall be for me to *e* by 2Kin 16:15 1239
e of the LORD for me, and for the 2Kin 22:13 1875
which sent you to *e* of the LORD 2Kin 22:18 1875
had a familiar spirit, to *e* of it 1Chr 10:13 1875
to *e* of his welfare, and to 1Chr 18:10 7592
not go before it to *e* of God 1Chr 21:30 1875
said unto the king of Israel, *E* 2Chr 18:4 1875
besides, that we might *e* of him 2Chr 18:6 1875
man, by whom we may *e* of the LORD 2Chr 18:7 1875
who sent unto him to *e* of the 2Chr 32:31 1875
e of the LORD for me, and for them 2Chr 34:21 1875
who sent you to *e* of the LORD 2Chr 34:26 1875
to *e* concerning Judah and .... Ezr 7:14 1240
For *e*, I pray thee, of the former .... Job 8:8 7592
the LORD, and to *e* in his temple .... Ps 27:4 1239
for thou dost not *e* wisely .... Eccl 7:10 7592
also the night: if ye will *e* .... Is 21:12 1158
e ye: return, come .... Is 21:12 1158
E, I pray thee, of the LORD for .... Jer 21:2 1875
that sent you unto me to *e* of me .... Jer 37:7 1875
prophet to *e* of him concerning me .... Eze 14:7 1875
of Israel came to *e* of the LORD .... Eze 20:1 1875
Are ye come to *e* of me .... Eze 20:3 1875
enter, *e* who in it is worthy .... Mt 10:11 *1833*
they began to *e* among themselves, ... Lk 22:23 *4802*
Do ye *e* among yourselves of that .... Jn 16:19 *2212*
e in the house of Judas for one .... Acts 9:11 *2212*
But if ye *e* any thing concerning .... Acts 19:39 *1934*
as though ye would *e* something .... Acts 23:15 *1231*
as though they would *e* somewhat .... Acts 23:20 *4441*
Whether any do *e* of Titus 2Cor 8:23

ENQUIRED {34}
e diligently, and, behold, it be .... Deut 17:4 1875
And when they *e* and asked, they .... Judg 6:29 1875
the men of Succoth, and *e* of him .... Judg 8:14 7592
children of Israel *e* of the LORD .... Judg 20:27 7592
Therefore they *e* of the LORD 1Sa 10:22 7592
he *e* of the LORD for him, and gave 1Sa 22:10 7592
hast *e* of God for him, that he 1Sa 22:13 7592
Therefore David *e* of the LORD 1Sa 23:2 7592
Then David *e* of the LORD yet 1Sa 23:4 7592
when Saul *e* of the LORD, the LORD 1Sa 28:6 7592
David *e* at the LORD, saying, ... 1Sa 30:8 7592
that David *e* of the LORD, saying, ... 2Sa 2:1 7592
David *e* of the LORD, saying, ... 2Sa 5:19 7592
when David *e* of the LORD, he said 2Sa 5:23 7592
David sent and *e* after the woman 2Sa 11:3 1875
was as if a man had *e* at the 2Sa 16:23 7592
and David *e* of the LORD 2Sa 21:1 1245
And *e* not of the LORD 1Chr 10:14 1875
for we *e* not at it in the days of 1Chr 13:3 1875
David *e* of God, saying, Shall I 1Chr 14:10 7592
Therefore David *e* again of God 1Chr 14:14 7592
returned and *e* early after God .... Ps 78:34 7836
should I be *e* of at all by them .... Eze 14:3 1875
GOD, I will not be *e* of by you .... Eze 20:3 1875
and shall I be *e* of by you .... Eze 20:31 1875
GOD, I will not be *e* of by you .... Eze 20:31
I will yet for this be *e* of by .... Eze 36:37 1875
that the king *e* of them, he .... Dan 1:20 1245
sought the LORD, nor *e* for him .... Zeph 1:6 1875
e of them diligently what time .... Mt 2:7 *198*
had diligently *e* of the wise men .... Mt 2:16 *198*
Then *e* he of them the hour when .... Jn 4:52 *4441*
or our brethren be *e* of, they are 2Cor 8:23
salvation the prophets have *e* 1Pet 1:10 *1567*

ENQUIREST {1}
That thou *e* after mine iniquity, ... Job 10:6 1245

ENQUIRY {2}
is holy, and after vows to make *e* .... Prov 20:25 1239
had made *e* for Simon's house .... Acts 10:17 *1331*

ENRICH {2}
the king will *e* him with great 1Sa 17:25 6238
thou didst *e* the kings of the .... Eze 27:33 6238

ENRICHED {2}
in every thing ye are *e* by him 1Cor 1:5 *4148*
Being *e* in every thing to all 2Cor 9:11 *4148*

ENRICHEST {1}
thou greatly *e* it with the river .... Ps 65:9 6238

EN-RIMMON *(en-rim'-mon)* {1} See AIN, RIMMON. *A city in Judah.*
And at *E*, and at Zareah, and at .... Neh 11:29 5884

EN-ROGEL *(en-ro'-ghel)* {4} *A fountain near Jerusalem.*
the goings out thereof were at *E* .... Josh 15:7 5883
on the south, and descended to *E* .... Josh 18:16 5883
Jonathan and Ahimaaz stayed by *E* 2Sa 17:17 5883
stone of Zoheleth, which is by *E* 1Kin 1:9 5883

ENSAMPLE {3}
walk so as ye have us for an *e* .... Phil 3:17 *5179*
an *e* unto you to follow us 2Th 3:9
making them an *e* unto those that 2Pet 2:6 *5262*

ENSAMPLES {3}
things happened unto them for *e* 1Cor 10:11 *5179*
So that we were *e* to all that 1Th 1:7 *5179*
but being *e* to the flock 1Pet 5:3 *5179*

EN-SHEMESH *(en-she'-mesh)* {2} *A spring.*
passed toward the waters of *E* .... Josh 15:7 5885
the north, and went forth to *E* .... Josh 18:17 5885

ENSIGN {8}
with the *e* of their father's .... Num 2:2 226
he will lift up an *e* to the .... Is 5:26 5251
stand for an *e* of the people .... Is 11:10 5251
shall set up an *e* for the nations .... Is 11:12 5251
lifteth up an *e* on the mountains .... Is 18:3 5251
a mountain, and as an *e* on an hill .... Is 30:17 5251
princes shall be afraid of the *e* .... Is 31:9 5251
lifted up as an *e* upon his land .... Zec 9:16 5264

ENSIGNS {1}
they set up their *e* for signs .... Ps 74:4 226

ENSNARED {1}
reign not, lest the people be *e* .... Job 34:30 4170

ENSUE {1}
let him seek peace, and *e* it 1Pet 3:11 *1377*

ENTANGLE {1}
how they might *e* him in his talk .... Mt 22:15 *3802*

ENTANGLED {3}
They are *e* in the land, the .... Ex 14:3 943
be not *e* again with the yoke of .... Gal 5:1 *1758*
Christ, they are again *e* therein 2Pet 2:20 *1707*

ENTANGLETH {1}
No man that warreth *e* himself 2Ti 2:4 *1707*

EN-TAPPUAH *(en-tap'-poo-ah)* {1} *A town in Manasseh.*
hand unto the inhabitants of *E* .... Josh 17:7 5887

ENTER {149}
he was come near to *e* into Egypt .... Gen 12:11 935
able to *e* into the tent of the .... Ex 40:35 935
all that *e* into the host, to do .... Num 4:3 935
all that *e* in to perform the .... Num 4:23 935
the curse shall *e* into her .... Num 5:24 935
the curse shall *e* into her .... Num 5:27 935
for he shall not *e* into the land .... Num 20:24 935
shall not *e* into the congregation .... Deut 23:1 935
A bastard shall not *e* into the .... Deut 23:2 935
e into the congregation of the .... Deut 23:2 935
e into the congregation of the .... Deut 23:3 935
e into the congregation of the .... Deut 23:3 935
e into the congregation of the .... Deut 23:8 935
That thou shouldest *e* into .... Deut 29:12 5674
them not to *e* into their cities .... Josh 10:19 935
go, and to *e* to possess the land .... Judg 18:9 935
my cry did *e* into his ears 2Sa 22:7
and when thy feet *e* into the city 1Kin 14:12 935
myself, and *e* into the battle 1Kin 22:30 935
We will *e* into the city, then the 2Kin 7:4 935

E

A third part of you that *e* in on ... 2Kin 11:5 935
I will *e* into the lodgings of his ... 2Kin 19:23 935
the priests could not *e* into the ... 2Chr 7:2 935
unclean in any thing should *e* in ... 2Chr 23:19 935
e into his sanctuary, which he ... 2Chr 30:8 935
for the house that I shall *e* into ... Neh 2:8 935
for none might *e* into the king's ... Est 4:2 935
will he *e* with thee into judgment ... Job 22:4 935
that he should *e* into judgment ... Job 34:23 1980
Their sword shall *e* into their ... Ps 37:15 935
they shall *e* into the king's ... Ps 45:15 935
they should not *e* into my rest ... Ps 95:11 935
E into his gates with ... Ps 100:4 935
into which the righteous shall *e* ... Ps 118:20 935
e not into judgment with thy ... Ps 143:2 935
E not into the path of the wicked ... Prov 4:14 935
A fool's lips *e* into contention, ... Prov 18:6 935
e not into the fields of the ... Prov 23:10 935
E into the rock, and hide thee in ... Is 2:10 935
The LORD will *e* into judgment ... Is 3:14 935
which keepeth the truth may *e* in ... Is 26:2 935
e thou into thy chambers, and shut ... Is 26:20 935
I will *e* into the height of his ... Is 37:24 935
He shall *e* into peace ... Is 57:2 935
in the street, and equity cannot *e* ... Is 59:14 935
that *e* in at these gates to ... Jer 7:2 935
let us *e* into the defenced cities ... Jer 8:14 935
if I *e* into the city, then behold ... Jer 14:18 935
E not into the house of mourning, ... Jer 16:5 935
that *e* in by these gates ... Jer 17:20 935
Then shall there *e* into the gates ... Jer 17:25 935
or who shall *e* into our ... Jer 21:13 935
thy people that *e* in by these ... Jer 22:2 935
then shall there *e* in by the ... Jer 22:4 935
Bethlehem, to go to *e* into Egypt, ... Jer 41:17 935
set your faces to *e* into Egypt ... Jer 42:15 935
you, when ye shall *e* into Egypt ... Jer 42:18 935
not *e* into thy congregation ... Lam 1:10 935
of his quiver to *e* into my reins ... Lam 3:13 935
for the robbers shall *e* into it ... Eze 7:22 935
neither shall they *e* into the ... Eze 13:9 935
they shall not *e* into the land of ... Eze 20:38 935
when he shall *e* into thy gates, ... Eze 26:10 935
as men *e* into a city wherein is ... Eze 26:10 935
I will cause breath to *e* into you ... Eze 37:5 935
When the priests *e* therein ... Eze 42:14 935
and no man shall *e* in by it ... Eze 44:2 935
he shall *e* by the way of the ... Eze 44:3 935
shall *e* into my sanctuary, of any ... Eze 44:9 935
They shall *e* into my sanctuary, ... Eze 44:16 935
that when they *e* in at the gates ... Eze 44:17 935
when they *e* into the inner court ... Eze 44:21 935
the prince shall *e* by the way of ... Eze 46:2 935
And when the prince shall *e* ... Eze 46:8 935
shall *e* into the fortress of the ... Dan 11:7 935
He shall also set his face to *e* ... Dan 11:17 935
He shall *e* peaceably even upon ... Dan 11:24 935
he shall *e* into the countries, and ... Dan 11:40 935
He shall *e* also into the glorious ... Dan 11:41 935
I will not *e* into the city ... Hos 11:9 935
they shall *e* in at the windows ... Joel 2:9 935
nor *e* into Gilgal, and pass not to ... Amos 5:5 935
Jonah began to *e* into the city a ... Jonah 3:4 935
it shall *e* into the house of the ... Zec 5:4 935
ye shall in no case *e* into the ... Mt 5:20 *1525*
e into thy closet, and when thou ... Mt 6:6 *1525*
E ye in at the strait gate ... Mt 7:13 *1525*
shall *e* into the kingdom of ... Mt 7:21 *1525*
city of the Samaritans *e* ye not ... Mt 10:5 *1525*
city or town ye shall *e*, enquire ... Mt 10:11 *1525*
Or else how can one *e* into a ... Mt 12:29 *1525*
wicked than himself, and they *e* in ... Mt 12:45 *1525*
ye shall not *e* into the kingdom ... Mt 18:3 *1525*
to *e* into life halt or maimed ... Mt 18:8 *1525*
thee to *e* into life with one cyc ... Mt 18:9 *1525*
but if thou wilt *e* into life ... Mt 19:17 *1525*
e into the kingdom of heaven ... Mt 19:23 *1525*
than for a rich man to *e* into the ... Mt 19:24 *1525*
e thou into the joy of thy lord ... Mt 25:21 *1525*
e thou into the joy of thy lord ... Mt 25:23 *1525*
that ye *e* not into temptation ... Mt 26:41 *1525*
no more openly *e* into the city ... Mk 1:45 *1525*
No man can *e* into a strong man's ... Mk 3:27 *1525*
swine, that we may *e* into them ... Mk 5:12 *1525*
place soever ye *e* into a house ... Mk 6:10 *1525*
out of him, and *e* no more into him ... Mk 9:25 *1525*
for thee to *e* into life maimed ... Mk 9:43 *1525*
for thee to *e* halt into life ... Mk 9:45 *1525*
it is better for thee to *e* into ... Mk 9:47 *1525*
child, he shall not *e* therein ... Mk 10:15 *1525*
riches *e* into the kingdom of God ... Mk 10:23 *1525*
to *e* into the kingdom of God ... Mk 10:24 *1525*
than for a rich man to *e* into the ... Mk 10:25 *1525*
into the house, neither *e* therein ... Mk 13:15 *1525*
lest ye *e* into temptation ... Mk 14:38 *1525*
thou shouldest *e* under my roof ... Lk 7:6 *1525*
that they which *e* in may see the ... Lk 8:16 *1531*
would suffer them to *e* into them ... Lk 8:32 *1525*
And whatsoever house ye *e* into ... Lk 9:4 *1525*
And into whatsoever house ye *e* ... Lk 10:5 *1525*
And into whatsoever city ye *e* ... Lk 10:8 *1525*
But into whatsoever city ye *e* ... Lk 10:10 *1525*
and they *e* in, and dwell there ... Lk 11:26 *1525*
Strive to *e* in at the strait gate ... Lk 13:24 *1525*
I say unto you, will seek to *e* in ... Lk 13:24 *1525*
child shall in no wise *e* therein ... Lk 18:17 *1525*
riches *e* into the kingdom of God ... Lk 18:24 *1525*
than for a rich man to *e* into the ... Lk 18:25 *1525*
are in the countries *e* thereinto ... Lk 21:21 *1525*
them, Pray that ye *e* not into ... Lk 22:40 *1525*
lest ye *e* into temptation ... Lk 22:46 *1525*
things, and to *e* into his glory ... Lk 24:26 *1525*
can he *e* the second time into his ... Jn 3:4 *1525*
he cannot *e* into the kingdom of ... Jn 3:5 *1525*
by me if any man *e* in, he shall ... Jn 10:9 *1525*
e into the kingdom of God ... Acts 14:22 *1525*
grievous wolves *e* in among you ... Acts 20:29 *1525*
They shall not *e* into my rest ... Heb 3:11 *1525*
they should not *e* into his rest ... Heb 3:18 *1525*
not *e* in because of unbelief ... Heb 3:19 *1525*
have believed do *e* into rest ... Heb 4:3 *1525*
if they shall *e* into my rest ... Heb 4:3 *1525*
If they shall *e* into my rest ... Heb 4:5 *1525*
that some must *e* therein, and they ... Heb 4:6 *1525*
therefore to *e* into that rest ... Heb 4:11 *1525*
boldness to *e* into the holiest by ... Heb 10:19 *1529*
man was able to *e* into the temple ... Rev 15:8 *1525*
there shall in no wise *e* into it ... Rev 21:27 *1525*
may *e* in through the gates into ... Rev 22:14 *1525*

ENTERED {107}
In the selfsame day *e* Noah ... Gen 7:13 935
in unto him, and *e* into his house ... Gen 19:3 935
the earth when Lot *e* into Zoar ... Gen 19:23 935
tent, and *e* into Rachel's tent ... Gen 31:33 935
he *e* into his chamber, and wept ... Gen 43:30 935
as Moses *e* into the tabernacle, ... Ex 33:9 935
which are *e* into thine house ... Josh 2:3 935
they *e* into the city, and took it, ... Josh 8:19 935
of them *e* into fenced cities ... Josh 10:20 935
they *e* into the land to destroy ... Judg 6:5 935
they *e* into an hold of the house ... Judg 9:46 935
Abishai, and *e* into the city ... 2Sa 10:14 935
e into another tent, and carried ... 2Kin 7:8 935
as Jehu *e* in at the gate, she ... 2Kin 9:31 935
his brother, and *e* into the city ... 1Chr 19:15 935
when the king *e* into the house of ... 2Chr 12:11 935
they *e* into a covenant to seek ... 2Chr 15:12 935
howbeit he *e* not into the temple ... 2Chr 27:2 935
e into Judah, and encamped against ... 2Chr 32:1 935
e by the gate of the valley, and ... Neh 2:15 935
e into a curse, and into an oath, ... Neh 10:29 935
Hast thou *e* into the springs of ... Job 38:16 935
Hast thou *e* into the treasures of ... Job 38:22 935
but when ye *e*, ye defiled my land ... Jer 2:7 935
is *e* into our palaces, to cut off ... Jer 9:21 935
which had *e* into the covenant, ... Jer 34:10 935
Jeremiah was *e* into the dungeon ... Jer 37:16 935
the heathen *e* into her sanctuary ... Lam 1:10 935
the enemy should have *e* into the ... Lam 4:12 935
the spirit *e* into me when he ... Eze 2:2 935
Then the spirit *e* into me ... Eze 3:24 935
e into a covenant with thee, ... Eze 16:8 935
when they *e* unto the heathen, ... Eze 36:20 935
they *e* into the wall which was of ... Eze 41:6 935
hath *e* in by it, therefore it ... Eze 44:2 935
foreigners *e* into his gates, and ... Obad 11 935
Thou shouldest not have *e* into ... Obad 13 935
rottenness *e* into my bones, and I ... Hab 3:16 935
when Jesus was *e* into Capernaum ... Mt 8:5 *1525*
And when he was *e* into a ship ... Mt 8:23 *1684*
he *e* into a ship, and passed over, ... Mt 9:1 *1684*
How he *e* into the house of God, ... Mt 12:4 *1525*
the day that Noe *e* into the ark ... Mt 24:38 *1525*
day he *e* into the synagogue ... Mk 1:21 *1525*
they *e* into the house of Simon and ... Mk 1:29 *2064*
again he *e* into Capernaum after ... Mk 2:1 *1525*
he *e* again into the synagogue ... Mk 3:1 *1525*
so that he *e* into a ship, and sat ... Mk 4:1 *1684*
went out, and *e* into the swine ... Mk 5:13 *1525*
And whithersoever he *e*, into ... Mk 6:56 *1531*
when he was *e* into the house from ... Mk 7:17 *1525*
e into an house, and would have no ... Mk 7:24 *1525*
straightway he *e* into a ship with ... Mk 8:10 *1684*
and as soon as ye be *e* into it ... Mk 11:2 *1531*
Jesus *e* into Jerusalem, and into ... Mk 11:11 *1525*
e into the house of Zacharias, and ... Lk 1:40 *1525*
and *e* into Simon's house ... Lk 4:38 *1525*
he *e* into one of the ships, which ... Lk 5:3 *1684*
that he *e* into the synagogue and ... Lk 6:6 *1525*
the people, he *e* into Capernaum ... Lk 7:1 *1525*
I *e* into thine house, thou gavest ... Lk 7:44 *1525*
many devils were *e* into him ... Lk 8:30 *1525*
of the man, and *e* into the swine ... Lk 8:33 *1525*
feared as they *e* into the cloud ... Lk 9:34 *1525*
went, and *e* into a village of the ... Lk 9:52 *1525*
that he *e* into a certain village ... Lk 10:38 *1525*
ye *e* not in yourselves, and them ... Lk 11:52 *1525*
as he *e* into a certain village, ... Lk 17:12 *1525*
the day that Noe *e* into the ark ... Lk 17:27 *1525*
And Jesus *e* and passed through ... Lk 19:1 *1525*
Then *e* Satan into Judas surnamed ... Lk 22:3 *1525*
when ye are *e* into the city, ... Lk 22:10 *1525*
And they *e* in, and found not the ... Lk 24:3 *1525*
ye are *e* into their labours ... Jn 4:38 *1525*
e into a ship, and went over the ... Jn 6:17 *1684*
whereinto his disciples were *e* ... Jn 6:22 *1684*
And after the sop Satan *e* into him ... Jn 13:27 *1525*
was a garden, into the which he *e* ... Jn 18:1 *1525*
Then Pilate *e* into the judgment ... Jn 18:33 *1525*
e into a ship immediately ... Jn 21:3 *305*
of them that *e* into the temple ... Acts 3:2 *1531*
e with them into the temple, ... Acts 3:8 *1525*
they *e* into the temple early in ... Acts 5:21 *1525*
went his way, and *e* into the house ... Acts 9:17 *1525*
morrow after they *e* into Caesarea ... Acts 10:24 *1525*
hath at any time *e* into my mouth ... Acts 11:8 *1525*
we *e* into the man's house ... Acts 11:12 *1525*
e into the house of Lydia ... Acts 16:40 *1525*
e into a certain man's house, ... Acts 18:7 *2064*
but he himself *e* into the ... Acts 18:19 *1525*
would have *e* in unto the people ... Acts 19:30 *1525*
we *e* into the house of Philip the ... Acts 21:8 *1525*
with them *e* into the temple ... Acts 21:26 *1524*
e into the castle, and told Paul ... Acts 23:16 *1525*
was *e* into the place of hearing, ... Acts 25:23 *1525*
to whom Paul *e* in, and prayed, and ... Acts 28:8 *1525*
by one man sin *e* into the world ... Rom 5:12 *1525*
Moreover the law *e*, that the ... Rom 5:20 *3922*
neither have *e* into the heart of ... 1Cor 2:9 *305*
e not in because of unbelief ... Heb 4:6 *1525*
For he that is *e* into his rest ... Heb 4:10 *1525*
the forerunner is for us *e* ... Heb 6:20 *1525*
but by his own blood he *e* in once ... Heb 9:12 *1525*
For Christ is not *e* into the holy ... Heb 9:24 *1525*
e into the ears of the Lord of ... Jas 5:4 *1525*
deceivers are *e* into the world ... 2Jn 7 *1525*
of life from God *e* into them ... Rev 11:11 *1525*

ENTERETH {20}
every one that *e* into the service ... Num 4:30 935
every one that *e* into the service ... Num 4:35 935
every one that *e* into the service ... Num 4:39 935
every one that *e* into the service ... Num 4:43 935
even unto every one that *e* into ... 2Chr 31:16 935
When wisdom *e* into thine heart, ... Prov 2:10 935
A reproof *e* more into a wise man ... Prov 17:10 5181
which *e* into their privy chambers ... Eze 21:14
the east, as one *e* into them ... Eze 42:12 935
he that *e* in by the way of the ... Eze 46:9 935
he that *e* by the way of the south ... Eze 46:9 935
that whatsoever *e* in at the mouth ... Mt 15:17 *1531*
e in where the damsel was lying ... Mk 5:40 *1531*
thing from without *e* into the man ... Mk 7:18 *1531*
Because it *e* not into his heart, ... Mk 7:19 *1531*
him into the house where he *e* in ... Lk 22:10 *1531*
He that *e* not by the door into ... Jn 10:1 *1535*
But he that *e* in by the door is ... Jn 10:2 *1535*
which *e* into that within the veil ... Heb 6:19 *1535*
as the high priest *e* into the ... Heb 9:25 *1535*

ENTERING {46}
at the *e* in of the tabernacle ... Ex 35:15 6607
cast it at the *e* of the gate of ... Josh 8:29 6607
Hermon unto the *e* into Hamath ... Josh 13:5 935
at the *e* of the gate of the city ... Josh 20:4 6607
unto the *e* in of Hamath ... Judg 3:3 935
stood in the *e* of the gate of the ... Judg 9:35 6607
even unto the *e* of the gate ... Judg 9:40 6607
stood in the *e* of the gate of the ... Judg 9:44 6607
Dan, stood by the *e* of the gate ... Judg 18:16 6607
the priest stood in the *e* of the ... Judg 18:17 6607
by *e* into a town that hath gates ... 1Sa 23:7 935
in array at the *e* in of the gate ... 2Sa 10:8 6607
them even unto the *e* of the gate ... 2Sa 11:23 6607
for the *e* of the oracle he made ... 1Kin 6:31 6607
from the *e* in of Hamath unto the ... 1Kin 8:65 935
stood in the *e* in of the cave ... 1Kin 19:13 6607
men at the *e* in of the gate ... 2Kin 7:3 6607
at the *e* in of the gate until the ... 2Kin 10:8 6607
the coast of Israel from the *e* of ... 2Kin 14:25 935
e in of the gate of Joshua the ... 2Kin 23:8 6607
at the *e* in of the house of the ... 2Kin 23:11 935
e in of the wilderness from the ... 1Chr 5:9 935
Egypt even unto the *e* of Hemath ... 1Chr 13:5 935
from the *e* in of Hamath unto the ... 2Chr 7:8 935
the *e* in of the gate of Samaria ... 2Chr 18:9 6607
part of you *e* on the sabbath ... 2Chr 23:4 935
stood at his pillar at the *e* in ... 2Chr 23:13 3996
when she was come to the *e* of the ... 2Chr 23:15 3996
abroad even to the *e* in of Egypt ... 2Chr 26:8 935
cvcn to thc *c* in at the fish gate ... 2Chr 33:14 935
that there is no house, no *e* in ... Is 23:1 935
the *e* of the gates of Jerusalem ... Jer 1:15 6607
even *e* in at the gates of ... Jer 17:27 935
mark well the *e* in of the house, ... Eze 44:5 3996
e in of Hemath unto the river of ... Amos 6:14 935
ye them that are *e* to go in ... Mt 23:13 *1525*
and the lusts of other things *e* in ... Mk 4:19 *1531*
that *e* into him can defile him ... Mk 7:15 *1531*
e into the ship again departed to ... Mk 8:13 *1684*
e into the sepulchre, they saw a ... Mk 16:5 *1525*
them that were *e* in ye hindered ... Lk 11:52 *1525*
in the which at your *e* ye shall ... Lk 19:30 *1531*
e into every house, and haling men ... Acts 8:3 *1531*
e into a ship of Adramyttium, we ... Acts 27:2 *1910*
manner of *e* in we had unto you ... 1Th 1:9 *1529*
being left us of *e* into his rest ... Heb 4:1 *1525*

ENTERPRISE {1}
hands cannot perform their *e* ... Job 5:12 8454

ENTERTAIN {1}
Be not forgetful to *e* strangers ... Heb 13:2 *5381*

ENTERTAINED {1}
some have *e* angels unawares ... Heb 13:2 *3579*

ENTICE {8}
if a man *e* a maid that is not ... Ex 22:16 6601
e thee secretly, saying, Let us ... Deut 13:6 5496
E thy husband, that he may ... Judg 14:15 6601
E him, and see wherein his great ... Judg 16:5 6601
Who shall *e* Ahab king of Israel, ... 2Chr 18:19 6601
the LORD, and said, I will *e* him ... 2Chr 18:20 6601
the LORD said, Thou shalt *e* him ... 2Chr 18:21 6601
My son, if sinners *e* thee ... Prov 1:10 6601

ENTICED {3}
And my heart hath been secretly e........ Job 31:27 6601
saying, Peradventure he will be e.......... Jer 20:10 6601
drawn away of his own lust, and e.......... Jas 1:14 1185

ENTICETH {1}
A violent man e his neighbour .... Prov 16:29 6601

ENTICING {2}
not with e words of man's wisdom.......... 1Cor 2:4 3981
should beguile you with e words............ Col 2:4 4086

ENTIRE {1}
work, that ye may be perfect and e......... Jas 1:4 3648

ENTRANCE {11}
your border unto the e of Hamath .... Num 34:8 935
the e into the city, and we will............. Judg 1:24 3996
shewed them the e into the city .... Judg 1:25 3996
before Ahab to the e of Jezreel.............. 1Kin 18:46 935
in the e of the gate of Samaria............... 1Kin 22:10 6607
And they went to the e of Gedor............. 1Chr 4:39 3996
that kept the e of the king's 2Chr 12:10 6607
The e of thy words giveth light .... Ps 119:130 6608
the face of the gate of the e................... Eze 40:15 2978
know our e in unto you, that it 1Th 2:1 1529
For so an e shall be ministered............... 2Pet 1:11 1529

ENTRANCES {1}
land of Nimrod in the e thereof .... Mic 5:6 6607

ENTREAT {2}
I will cause the enemy to e thee .... Jer 15:11 6293
e them evil four hundred years .... Acts 7:6 2559

ENTREATED {9}
he e Abram well for her sake .... Gen 12:16
hast thou so evil e this people................ Ex 5:22
And the Egyptians evil e us .... Deut 26:6
e them spitefully, and slew them........... Mt 22:6 5195
shall be mocked, and spitefully e........... Lk 18:32 5195
e him shamefully, and sent him.............. Lk 20:11 818
evil e our fathers, so that they .... Acts 7:19 2559
And Julius courteously e Paul .... Acts 27:3 5530
before, and were shamefully e............... 1Th 2:2 5195

ENTREATETH {1}
He evil e the barren that beareth............ Job 24:21

ENTRIES {1}
the e thereof were by the posts............... Eze 40:38 6607

ENTRY {15}
house, and the king's e without.............. 2Kin 16:18 3996
the LORD, were keepers of the e 1Chr 9:19 3996
the e of the house, the inner................. 2Chr 4:22 6607
at the e of the city, at the .... Prov 8:3 6310
which is by the e of the east.................. Jer 19:2 6607
sat down in the e of the new gate .... Jer 26:10 6607
at the e of the new gate of the .... Jer 36:10 6607
e that is in the house of the................... Jer 38:14 3996
which is at the e of Pharaoh's .... Jer 43:9 6607
this image of jealousy in the e............... Eze 8:5 872
art situate at the e of the sea................ Eze 27:3 3996
the breadth of the e of the gate.............. Eze 40:11 6607
up to the e of the north gate .... Eze 40:40 6607
was the e on the east side...................... Eze 42:9 3996
After he brought me through the e .... Eze 46:19 3996

ENVIED {6}
and the Philistines e him....................... Gen 26:14 7065
no children, Rachel e her sister.............. Gen 30:1 7065
And his brethren e him .... Gen 37:11 7065
They e Moses also in the camp, and....... Ps 106:16 7065
this a man is e of his neighbour .... Eccl 4:4 7068
were in the garden of God, e him........... Eze 31:9 7065

ENVIES {1}
all guile, and hypocrisies, and e............ 1Pet 2:1 5355

ENVIEST {1}
said unto him, E thou for my sake .... Num 11:29 7065

ENVIETH {1}
charity e not 1Cor 13:4 2206

ENVIOUS {4}
neither be thou e against the................ Ps 37:1 7065
For I was e at the foolish, when .... Ps 73:3 7065
Be not thou e against evil men.............. Prov 24:1 7065
neither be thou e at the wicked............. Prov 24:19 7065

ENVIRON {1}
shall e us round, and cut off our .... Josh 7:9 5437

ENVY {20}
man, and e slayeth the silly one .... Job 5:2 7068
E thou not the oppressor, and .... Prov 3:31 7065
but e the rottenness of the bones .... Prov 14:30 7068
Let not thine heart e sinners .... Prov 23:17 7065
but who is able to stand before e .... Prov 27:4 7068
love, and their hatred, and their e.......... Eccl 9:6 7068
The e also of Ephraim shall .... Is 11:13 7068
Ephraim shall not e Judah .... Is 11:13 7065
ashamed for their e at the people........... Is 26:11 7068
according to thine e which thou............ Eze 35:11 7068
For he knew that for e they had............ Mt 27:18 5355
priests had delivered him for e.............. Mk 15:10 5355
And the patriarchs, moved with e.......... Acts 7:9 2206
they were filled with e, and.................. Acts 13:45 2205
which believed not, moved with e.......... Acts 17:5 2206
full of e, murder, debate, deceit .... Rom 1:29 5355
indeed preach Christ even of e............... Phil 1:15 5355
of words, whereof cometh e.................... 1Ti 6:4 5355
pleasures, living in malice and e .... Titus 3:3 5355
that dwelleth in us lusteth to e .... Jas 4:5 5355

ENVYING {5}
and wantonness, not in strife and e .... Rom 13:13 2205
for whereas there is among you e.......... 1Cor 3:3 2205
one another, e one another .... Gal 5:26 5354
But if ye have bitter e and strife .... Jas 3:14 2205
For where e and strife is, there.............. Jas 3:16 2205

ENVYINGS {2}
lest there be debates, e, wraths, ... 2Cor 12:20 2205
E, murders, drunkenness, ... Gal 5:21 5355

EPAENETUS *(ep-en'-e-tus)* {1} *A Christian acquaintance of Paul.*
Salute my wellbeloved E, who is............ Rom 16:5 1866

EPAPHRAS *(ep'-a-fras)* {3} *A Christian acquaintance of Paul.*
As ye also learned of E our dear .... Col 1:7 1889
E, who is one of you, a servant .... Col 4:12 1889
There salute thee E, my......................... Philem 23 1889

EPAPHRODITUS *(e-paf-ro-di'-tus)* {3} *A fellow-worker with Paul.*
it necessary to send to you E.................. Phil 2:25 1891
having received of E the things.............. Phil 4:18 1891
to the Philippians from Rome by E......... Phil s 1891

EPENETUS See EPAENETUS.

EPHAH *(e'-fah)* {39}
1. A son of Midian; grandson of Abraham.
E, and Epher, and Hanoch, and Abidah.. Gen 25:4 5891
E, and Epher, and Henoch, and Abida,... 1Chr 1:33 5891
the dromedaries of Midian and E .... Is 60:6 5891
2. A concubine of Caleb.
And E, Caleb's concubine, bare............... 1Chr 2:46 5891
3. A son of Jahdai.
Jotham, and Gesham, and Pelet, and E... 1Chr 2:47 5891
4. A grain measure.
an omer is the tenth part of an e............ Ex 16:36 374
of an e of fine flour for a sin................. Lev 5:11 374
the tenth part of an e of fine.................. Lev 6:20 374
balances, just weights, a just e.............. Lev 19:36 374
tenth part of an e of barley meal .... Num 5:15 374
a tenth part of an e of flour for.............. Num 28:5 374
unleavened cakes of an e of flour........... Judg 6:19 374
and it was about an e of barley............... Ruth 2:17 374
one e of flour, and a bottle of................. 1Sa 1:24 374
an e of this parched corn........................ 1Sa 17:17 374
seed of an homer shall yield an e............ Is 5:10 374
have just balances, and a just e.............. Eze 45:10 374
The e and the bath shall be of one.......... Eze 45:11 374
the e the tenth part of an homer.............. Eze 45:11 374
part of an e of an homer of wheat........... Eze 45:13 374
of an e of an homer of barley.................. Eze 45:13 374
offering of an e for a bullock.................. Eze 45:24 374
an e for a ram, and an hin of oil .... Eze 45:24 374
a ram, and an hin of oil for an e .... Eze 45:24 374
offering shall be an e for a ram.............. Eze 46:5 374
to give, and an hin of oil to an e .... Eze 46:5 374
an e for a bullock, and .... Eze 46:7 374
an e for a ram, and for the lambs........... Eze 46:7 374
unto, and an hin of oil to an e................. Eze 46:7 374
shall be an e to a bullock .... Eze 46:11 374
an e to a ram, and to the lambs as.......... Eze 46:11 374
to give, and an hin of oil to an e .... Eze 46:11 374
morning, the sixth part of an e .... Eze 46:14 374
forth wheat, making the e small .... Amos 8:5 374
This is an e that goeth forth................... Zec 5:6 374
sitteth in the midst of the e.................... Zec 5:7 374
cast it into the midst of the e .... Zec 5:8 374
lifted up the e between the earth .... Zec 5:9 374
me, Whither do these bear the e............. Zec 5:10 374

EPHAI *(e'-fahee)* {1} *Family who remained in Jerusalem during captivity.*
the sons of E the Netophathite,............... Jer 40:8 5778

EPHER *(e'-fur)* {4}
1. A son of Midian; grandson of Abraham.
and E, and Hanoch, and Abidah .... Gen 25:4 6081
Ephah, and E, and Henoch, and Abida,.. 1Chr 1:33 6081
2. A descendant of Judah.
Ezra were, Jether, and Mered, and E....... 1Chr 4:17 6081
3. A chief of Manasseh.
house of their fathers, even E 1Chr 5:24 6081

EPHES-DAMMIM {1} *A city in Judah.*
between Shochoh and Azekah, in E........ 1Sa 17:1 658

EPHESIAN *(e-fe'-zheun)* {1} See EPHESIANS. *A resident of Ephesus.*
him in the city Trophimus an E .... Acts 21:29 2180

EPHESIANS *(e-fe'-zheuns)* {5}
saying, Great is Diana of the E............... Acts 19:28 2180
out, Great is Diana of the E.................... Acts 19:34 2180
E is a worshipper of the great................ Acts 19:35 2180
from Rome unto the E by Tychicus .... Eph s 2180
bishop of the church of the E.................. 2Ti s 2180

EPHESUS *(ef'-e-sus)* {17} See EPHESIAN. *Capital of Roman province of Asia.*
And he came to E, and left them .... Acts 18:19 2181
And he sailed from E.............................. Acts 18:21 2181
in the scriptures, came to E................... Acts 18:24 2181
the upper coasts came to E.................... Acts 19:1 2181
Jews and Greeks also dwelling at E........ Acts 19:17 2181
see and hear, that not alone at E............ Acts 19:26 2181
the people, he said, Ye men of E............ Acts 19:35 2181
Paul had determined to sail by E.......... Acts 20:16 2181
And from Miletus he sent to E............... Acts 20:17 2181
I have fought with beasts at E 1Cor 15:32 2181
I will tarry at E until Pentecost 1Cor 16:8 2181
God, to the saints which are at E........... Eph 1:1 2181
besought thee to abide still at E 1Ti 1:3 2181
things he ministered unto me at E......... 2Ti 1:18 2181
And Tychicus have I sent to E 2Ti 4:12 2181
unto E, and unto Smyrna, and unto........ Rev 1:11 2181
angel of the church of E write................ Rev 2:1 2181

EPHLAL *(ef'-lal)* {4} *A descendant of Pharez.*
And Zabad begat E, and E begat............ 1Chr 2:37 654
begat E, and E begat Obed,.................... 1Chr 2:37 654

EPHOD *(e'-fod)* {52}
1. Father of Hanniel.
of Manasseh, Hanniel the son of E.......... Num 34:23 641
2. A priestly garment.
and stones to be set in the e .... Ex 25:7 646
a breastplate, and an e, and a robe .... Ex 28:4 646
And they shall make the e of gold .... Ex 28:6 646
And the curious girdle of the e .... Ex 28:8 642
upon the shoulders of the e for .... Ex 28:12 646
work of the e thou shalt make it............. Ex 28:15 646
shoulderpieces of the e before it .... Ex 28:25 646
is in the side of the e inward.................. Ex 28:26 646
the two sides of the e underneath .... Ex 28:27 646
above the curious girdle of the e............. Ex 28:27 646
of the e with a lace of blue..................... Ex 28:28 646
above the curious girdle of the e............. Ex 28:28 646
be not loosed from the e .... Ex 28:28 646
the robe of the e all of blue.................... Ex 28:31 646
the coat, and the robe of the e .... Ex 29:5 646
and the e, and the breastplate................. Ex 29:5 646
with the curious girdle of the e............... Ex 29:5 646
and stones to be set for the e.................. Ex 35:9 646
and stones to be set, for the e................. Ex 35:27 646
And he made the e of gold, blue, ... Ex 39:2 646
And the curious girdle of his e............... Ex 39:5 642
them on the shoulders of the e................ Ex 39:7 646
work, like the work of the e .... Ex 39:8 646
on the shoulderpieces of the e................. Ex 39:18 646
was on the side of the e inward.............. Ex 39:19 646
the two sides of the e underneath .... Ex 39:20 646
above the curious girdle of the e............. Ex 39:20 646
of the e with a lace of blue..................... Ex 39:21 646
above the curious girdle of the e............. Ex 39:21 646
might not be loosed from the e .... Ex 39:21 646
the robe of the e of woven work.............. Ex 39:22 646
put the e upon him, and he girded.......... Lev 8:7 646
with the curious girdle of the e.............. Lev 8:7 646
And Gideon made an e thereof .... Judg 8:27 646
an house of gods, and made an e .... Judg 17:5 646
there is in these houses an e.................. Judg 18:14 646
took the graven image, and the e .... Judg 18:17 646
fetched the carved image, the e.............. Judg 18:18 646
heart was glad, and he took the e .... Judg 18:20 646
a child, girded with a linen e 1Sa 2:18 646
incense, to wear an e before me 1Sa 2:28 646
priest in Shiloh, wearing an e 1Sa 14:3 646
wrapped in a cloth behind the e 1Sa 21:9 646
persons that did wear a linen e.............. 1Sa 22:18 646
came down with an e in his hand 1Sa 23:6 646
the priest, Bring hither the e.................. 1Sa 23:9 646
pray thee, bring me hither the e............. 1Sa 30:7 646
brought thither the e to David 1Sa 30:7 646
David was girded with a linen e 2Sa 6:14 646
also had upon him an e of linen.............. 1Chr 15:27 646
without an image, and without an e .... Hos 3:4 646

EPHPHATHA {1}
he sighed, and saith unto him, E............ Mk 7:34 2188

EPHRAIM *(e'-fra-im)* {172} See EPHRAIMITE, EPHRAIM'S, EPHRAIN.
1. A son of Joseph.
name of the second called he E.............. Gen 41:52 669
of Egypt were born Manasseh and E ...... Gen 46:20 669
him his two sons, Manasseh and E .... Gen 48:1 669
And now thy two sons, E and................. Gen 48:5 669
E in his right hand toward...................... Gen 48:13 669
his right hand upon the head of E.......... Gen 48:17 669
bless, saying, God make thee as E.......... Gen 48:20 669
and he set E before Manasseh .... Gen 48:20 669
their families were Manasseh and E ...... Num 26:28 669
And the sons of E 1Chr 7:20 669
E their father mourned many days, ... 1Chr 7:22 669
2. One of the twelve tribes comprising Israel.
children of Joseph: of E......................... Num 1:10 669
namely, of the children of E .... Num 1:32 669
of them, even of the tribe of E .... Num 1:33 669
of E according to their armies................ Num 2:18 669
the captain of the sons of E .... Num 2:18 669
of E were an hundred thousand.............. Num 2:24 669
prince of the children of E .... Num 7:48 669
E set forward according to their .... Num 10:22 669
Of the tribe of E, Oshea the son.............. Num 13:8 669
sons of E after their families.................. Num 26:35 669
of E according to those that were .... Num 26:37 669
of the tribe of the children of E .... Num 34:24 669
they are the ten thousands of E.............. Deut 33:17 669
And all Naphtali, and the land of E .... Deut 34:2 669
were two tribes, Manasseh and E........... Josh 14:4 669
children of Joseph, Manasseh and E .... Josh 16:4 669
the border of the children of E............... Josh 16:5 669
children of E by their families .... Josh 16:8 669
cities for the children of E were.............. Josh 16:9 669
belonged to the children of E .... Josh 17:8 669
these cities of E are among the .... Josh 17:9 669
the house of Joseph, even to E .... Josh 17:17 669
of the families of the tribe of E.............. Josh 21:5 669
their lot out of the tribe of E .... Josh 21:20 669
Neither did E drive out the .... Judg 1:29 669
Out of E was there a root of them........... Judg 5:14 669
Then all the men of E gathered.............. Judg 7:24 669
the men of E said unto him, Why........... Judg 8:1 669
of E better than the vintage of............... Judg 8:2 669

E

and against the house of *E* ... Judg 10:9 669
the men of *E* gathered themselves ... Judg 12:1 669
men of Gilead, and fought with *E* ... Judg 12:4 669
and the men of Gilead smote *E* ... Judg 12:4 669
of *E* among the Ephraimites ... Judg 12:4 669
in Pirathon in the land of *E* ... Judg 12:15 669
and over Jezreel, and over *E* ... 2Sa 2:9 669
coasts out of the tribe of *E* ... 1Chr 6:66 669
Benjamin, and of the children of *E* ... 1Chr 9:3 669
the children of *E* twenty thousand ... 1Chr 12:30 669
Pelonite, of the children of *E* ... 1Chr 27:10 669
Pirathonite, of the children of *E* ... 1Chr 27:14 669
Of the children of *E*, Hoshea the ... 1Chr 27:20 669
the strangers with them out of *E* ... 2Chr 15:9 669
of Judah, and in the cities of *E* ... 2Chr 17:2 669
wit, with all the children of *E* ... 2Chr 25:7 669
that was come to him out of *E* ... 2Chr 25:10 669
And Zichri, a mighty man of *E* ... 2Chr 28:7 669
of the heads of the children of *E* ... 2Chr 28:12 669
Judah, and wrote letters also to *E* ... 2Chr 30:1 669
to city through the country of *E* ... 2Chr 30:10 669
of the people, even many of *E* ... 2Chr 30:18 669
in *E* also and Manasseh, until they ... 2Chr 31:1 669
in the cities of Manasseh, and *E* ... 2Chr 34:6 669
of the hand of Manasseh and *E* ... 2Chr 34:9 669
E also is the strength of mine ... Ps 60:7 669
The children of *E*, being armed, ... Ps 78:9 669
and chose not the tribe of *E* ... Ps 78:67 669
Before *E* and Benjamin and Manasseh ... Ps 80:2 669
E also is the strength of mine ... Ps 108:8 669
Syria is confederate with *E* ... Is 7:2 669
Because Syria, *E*, and the son of ... Is 7:5 669
and five years shall *E* be broken ... Is 7:8 669
And the head of *E* is Samaria ... Is 7:9 669
from the day that *E* departed from ... Is 7:17 669
all the people shall know, even *E* ... Is 9:9 669
Manasseh, *E* ... Is 9:21 669
and *E*, Manasseh ... Is 9:21 669
The envy also of *E* shall depart ... Is 11:13 669
E shall not envy Judah ... Is 11:13 669
and Judah shall not vex *E* ... Is 11:13 669
fortress also shall cease from *E* ... Is 17:3 669
of pride, to the drunkards of *E* ... Is 28:1 669
of pride, the drunkards of *E* ... Is 28:3 669
even the whole seed of *E* ... Jer 7:15 669
to Israel, and *E* is my firstborn ... Jer 31:9 669
I have surely heard *E* bemoaning ... Jer 31:18 669
Is *E* my dear son ... Jer 31:20 669
it, For Joseph, the stick of *E* ... Eze 37:16 669
Joseph, which is in the hand of *E* ... Eze 37:19 669
the west side, a portion for *E* ... Eze 48:5 669
And by the border of *E*, from the ... Eze 48:6 669
E is joined to idols ... Hos 4:17 669
I know *E*, and Israel is not hid ... Hos 5:3 669
for now, O *E*, thou committest ... Hos 5:3 669
and *E* fall in their iniquity ... Hos 5:5 669
E shall be desolate in the day of ... Hos 5:9 669
E is oppressed and broken in ... Hos 5:11 669
will I be unto *E* as a moth ... Hos 5:12 669
When *E* saw his sickness, and Judah ... Hos 5:13 669
then went *E* to the Assyrian, and ... Hos 5:13 669
For I will be unto *E* as a lion ... Hos 5:14 669
O *E*, what shall I do unto thee ... Hos 6:4 669
there is the whoredom of *E* ... Hos 6:10 669
the iniquity of *E* was discovered ... Hos 7:1 669
E, he hath mixed himself among ... Hos 7:8 669
E is a cake not turned ... Hos 7:8 669
E also is like a silly dove ... Hos 7:11 669
E hath hired lovers ... Hos 8:9 669
Because *E* hath made many altars ... Hos 8:11 669
but *E* shall return to Egypt, and ... Hos 9:3 669
The watchman of *E* was with my God ... Hos 9:8 669
As for *E*, their glory shall fly ... Hos 9:11 669
E, as I saw Tyrus, is planted in ... Hos 9:13 669
but *E* shall bring forth his ... Hos 9:13 669
E is smitten, their root is dried ... Hos 9:16 669
E shall receive shame, and Israel ... Hos 10:6 669
E is as an heifer that is taught, ... Hos 10:11 669
I will make *E* to ride ... Hos 10:11 669
I taught *E* also to go, taking ... Hos 11:3 669
How shall I give thee up, *E* ... Hos 11:8 669
I will not return to destroy *E* ... Hos 11:9 669
E compasseth me about with lies, ... Hos 11:12 669
E feedeth on wind, and followeth ... Hos 12:1 669
E said, Yet I am become rich, I ... Hos 12:8 669
E provoked him to anger most ... Hos 12:14 669
When *E* spake trembling, he ... Hos 13:1 669
The iniquity of *E* is bound up ... Hos 13:12 669
E shall say, What have I to do ... Hos 14:8 669
shall possess the fields of *E* ... Obad 19 669
I will cut off the chariot from *E* ... Zec 9:10 669
for me, filled the bow with *E* ... Zec 9:13 669
they of *E* shall be like a mighty ... Zec 10:7 669

3. Mountains in Samaria.

if mount *E* be too narrow for thee ... Josh 17:15 669
even Timnath-serah in mount *E* ... Josh 19:50 669
Naphtali, and Shechem in mount *E* ... Josh 20:7 669
with her suburbs in mount *E* ... Josh 21:21 669
which is in mount *E*, on the ... Josh 24:30 669
which was given him in mount *E* ... Josh 24:33 669
Timnath-heres, in the mount of *E* ... Judg 2:9 669
a trumpet in the mountain of *E* ... Judg 3:27 669
Ramah and Beth-el in mount *E* ... Judg 4:5 669
messengers throughout all mount *E* ... Judg 7:24 669
and he dwelt in Shamir in mount *E* ... Judg 10:1 669
And there was a man of mount *E* ... Judg 17:1 669
he came to mount *E* to the house ... Judg 17:8 669
who when they came to mount *E* ... Judg 18:2 669
they passed thence unto mount *E* ... Judg 18:13 669
sojourning on the side of mount *E* ... Judg 19:1 669
even, which was also of mount *E* ... Judg 19:16 669
toward the side of mount *E* ... Judg 19:18 669
of Ramathaim-zophim, of mount *E* ... 1Sa 1:1 669
And he passed through mount *E* ... 1Sa 9:4 669
had hid themselves in mount *E* ... 1Sa 14:22 669
but a man of mount *E*, Sheba the ... 2Sa 20:21 669
The son of Hur, in mount *E* ... 1Kin 4:8 669
Jeroboam built Shechem in mount *E* ... 1Kin 12:25 669
E two young men of the sons of ... 2Kin 5:22 669
in mount *E* with her suburbs ... 1Chr 6:67 669
Zemaraim, which is in mount *E* ... 2Chr 13:4 669
which he had taken from mount *E* ... 2Chr 15:8 669
people from Beer-sheba to mount *E* ... 2Chr 19:4 669
affliction from mount *E* ... Jer 4:15 669
upon the mount *E* shall cry ... Jer 31:6 669
shall be satisfied upon mount *E* ... Jer 50:19 669

4. A town near Absalom's farm.

in Baal-hazor, which is beside *E* ... 2Sa 13:23 669

5. Battle site between David's and Absalom's armies.

the battle was in the wood of *E* ... 2Sa 18:6 669

6. A northern gate at Jerusalem.

gate of *E* unto the corner gate ... 2Kin 14:13 669
the gate of *E* to the corner gate ... 2Chr 25:23 669
and in the street of the gate of *E* ... Neh 8:16 669
And from above the gate of *E* ... Neh 12:39 669

7. A city near Jerusalem.

wilderness, into a city called *E* ... Jn 11:54 *2187*

EPHRAIMITE *(e'-fra-im-ite)* {1} See EPHRAIMITES. *A descendant of Ephraim.*

said unto him, Art thou an *E* ... Judg 12:5 673

EPHRAIMITES *(e'-fra-im-ites)* {5}

dwell among the *E* unto this day ... Josh 16:10 669
fugitives of Ephraim among the *E* ... Judg 12:4 669
passages of Jordan before the *E* ... Judg 12:5 669
that when those *E* which were ... Judg 12:5 669
fell at that time of the *E* forty ... Judg 12:6 669

EPHRAIM'S *(e'-fra-ims)* {4}

1. Refers to Ephraim 1.

hand, and laid it upon *E* head ... Gen 48:14 669
to remove it from *E* head unto ... Gen 48:17 669
Joseph saw *E* children of the ... Gen 50:23 669

2. Refers to Ephraim 2.

Southward it was *E*, and northward ... Josh 17:10 669

EPHRAIN *(e'-fra-in)* {1} See EPHRAIM, EPHRON. *A city in Benjamin.*

and *E* with the towns thereof ... 2Chr 13:19 6085

EPHRATAH *(ef-rat-ah)* {5} See BETHLEHEM, CALEB-EPHRATAH, EPHRATH, EPHRATHITE.

1. Another name for Bethlehem-judah.

and do thou worthily in *E*, and be ... Ruth 4:11 672
Lo, we heard of it at *E* ... Ps 132:6 672
But thou, Beth-lehem *E*, though ... Mic 5:2 672

2. A wife of Caleb.

son of Hur, the firstborn of *E* ... 1Chr 2:50 672
sons of Hur, the firstborn of *E* ... 1Chr 4:4 672

EPHRATH *(e'-frath)* {5} See EPHRATAH.

1. A city in Judah.

was but a little way to come to *E* ... Gen 35:16 672
and was buried in the way to *E* ... Gen 35:19 672
but a little way to come unto *E* ... Gen 48:7 672
buried her there in the way of *E* ... Gen 48:7 672

2. Same as Ephratah 2.

was dead, Caleb took unto him *E* ... 1Chr 2:19 672

EPHRATHAH See EPHRATAH.

EPHRATHITE *(ef-rath-ite)* {3} See EPHRATHITES. *An inhabitant of Bethlehem-judah.*

of Tohu, the son of Zuph, an *E* ... 1Sa 1:1 673
son of that *E* of Beth-lehem-judah ... 1Sa 17:12 673
an *E* of Zereda, Solomon's servant ... 1Kin 11:26 673

EPHRATHITES *(ef-rath-ites)* {1}

and Chilion, *E* of Beth-lehem-judah ... Ruth 1:2 673

EPHRON *(e'-fron)* {13} See EPHRAIM, EPHRAIN.

1. Son of Zohar.

for me to *E* the son of Zohar ... Gen 23:8 6085
E dwelt among the children of ... Gen 23:10 6085
E the Hittite answered Abraham in ... Gen 23:10 6085
he spake unto *E* in the audience ... Gen 23:13 6085
E answered Abraham, saying unto ... Gen 23:14 6085
And Abraham hearkened unto *E* ... Gen 23:16 6085
Abraham weighed to *E* the silver ... Gen 23:16 6085
And the field of *E*, which was in ... Gen 23:17 6085
in the field of *E* the son of ... Gen 25:9 6085
is in the field of *E* the Hittite ... Gen 49:29 6085
bought with the field of *E* the ... Gen 49:30 6085
a buryingplace of *E* the Hittite ... Gen 50:13 6085

2. A mountain between Judah and Benjamin.

went out to the cities of mount *E* ... Josh 15:9 6085

EPICUREANS *(ep-i-cu-re'-ans)* {1} *Followers of the philosopher Epicurus.*

certain philosophers of the *E* ... Acts 17:18 *1946*

EPISTLE {19}

together, they delivered the *e* ... Acts 15:30 *1992*
delivered the *e* to the governor, ... Acts 23:33 *1992*
I Tertius, who wrote this *e* ... Rom 16:22 *1992*
I wrote unto you in an *e* not to ... 1Cor 5:9 *1992*
The first *e* to the Corinthians ... 1Cor *s*
Ye are our *e* written in our ... 2Cor 3:2 *1992*
the *e* of Christ ministered by us ... 2Cor 3:3 *1992*
the same *e* hath made you sorry ... 2Cor 7:8 *1992*
The second *e* to the Corinthians ... 2Cor *s*
when this *e* is read among you, ... Col 4:16 *1992*
likewise read the *e* from Laodicea ... Col 4:16
this *e* be read unto all the holy ... 1Th 5:27 *1992*
The first *e* unto the ... 1Th *s*
taught, whether by word, or our *e* ... 2Th 2:15 *1992*
man obey not our word by this *e* ... 2Th 3:14 *1992*
which is the token in every *e* ... 2Th 3:17 *1992*
The second *e* to the Thessalonians ... 2Th *s*
The second *e* unto Timotheus, ... 2Ti *s*
This second *e*, beloved, I now ... 2Pet 3:1 *1992*

EPISTLES {2}

e of commendation to you, or ... 2Cor 3:1 *1992*
As also in all his *e*, speaking in ... 2Pet 3:16 *1992*

EQUAL {21}

gold and the crystal cannot *e* it ... Job 28:17 6186
topaz of Ethiopia shall not *e* it ... Job 28:19 6186
eyes behold the things that are *e* ... Ps 17:2 4339
But it was thou, a man mine *e* ... Ps 55:13 6187
The legs of the lame are not *e* ... Prov 26:7 1809
will ye liken me, or shall I be *e* ... Is 40:25 7737
will ye liken me, and make me *e* ... Is 46:5 7737
what shall I *e* to thee, that I ... Lam 2:13 7737
say, The way of the Lord is not *e* ... Eze 18:25 8505
Is not my way *e* ... Eze 18:25 8505
The way of the Lord is not *e* ... Eze 18:29 8505
of Israel, are not my ways *e* ... Eze 18:29 8505
say, The way of the Lord is not *e* ... Eze 33:17 8505
as for them, their way is not *e* ... Eze 33:17 8505
say, The way of the Lord is not *e* ... Eze 33:20 8505
and thou hast made them *e* unto us ... Mt 20:12 *2470*
for they are *e* unto the angels ... Lk 20:36 *2465*
Father, making himself *e* with God ... Jn 5:18 *2470*
it not robbery to be *e* with God ... Phil 2:6 *2470*
servants that which is just and *e* ... Col 4:1 *2471*
breadth and the height of it are *e* ... Rev 21:16 *2470*

EQUALITY {2}

But by an *e*, that now at this ... 2Cor 8:14 *2471*
that there may be *e* ... 2Cor 8:14 *2471*

EQUALLY {1}

e distant one from another ... Ex 36:22 7947

EQUALS {1}

many my *e* in mine own nation ... Gal 1:14 *4915*

EQUITY {10}

the world, and the people with *e* ... Ps 98:9 4339
thou dost establish *e*, thou ... Ps 99:4 4339
justice, and judgment, and *e* ... Prov 1:3 4339
righteousness, and judgment, and *e* ... Prov 2:9 4339
good, nor to strike princes for *e* ... Prov 17:26 3476
wisdom, and in knowledge, and in *e* ... Eccl 2:21 3788
reprove with *e* for the meek of ... Is 11:4 4334
in the street, and *e* cannot enter ... Is 59:14 5229
abhor judgment, and pervert all *e* ... Mic 3:9 3477
he walked with me in peace and *e* ... Mal 2:6 4334

ER *(ur)* {11}

1. A son of Judah.

and he called his name *E* ... Gen 38:3 6147
took a wife for *E* his firstborn ... Gen 38:6 6147
And *E*, Judah's firstborn, was ... Gen 38:7 6147
E, and Onan, and Shelah, and Pharez, ... Gen 46:12 6147
but *E* and Onan died in the land of ... Gen 46:12 6147
The sons of Judah were *E* and Onan ... Num 26:19 6147
and *E* and Onan died in the land of ... Num 26:19 6147
E, and Onan, and Shelah ... 1Chr 2:3 6147
And *E*, the firstborn of Judah, was ... 1Chr 2:3 6147

2. A son of Shelah.

E the father of Lecah, and Laadah ... 1Chr 4:21 6147

3. Father of Elmodan; ancestor of Jesus.

Elmodam, which was the son of *E* ... Lk 3:28 *2262*

ERAN *(e'-ran)* {1} See ERANITES. *A son of Shath-elah.*

of *E*, the family of the Eranites ... Num 26:36 6197

ERANITES *(e'-ran-ites)* {1} *Descendants of Eran.*

of Eran, the family of the *E* ... Num 26:36 6198

ERASTUS *(e-ras'-tus)* {3}

1. A fellow-worker with Paul.

unto him, Timotheus and *E* ... Acts 19:22 *2037*
E abode at Corinth ... 2Ti 4:20 *2037*

2. A Corinthian city official.

E the chamberlain of the city ... Rom 16:23 *2037*

ERE {10}

are delivered *e* the midwives come ... Ex 1:19 2962
e it was chewed, the wrath of the ... Num 11:33 2962
long will it be *e* they believe me ... Num 14:11 3808
e the lamp of God went out in the ... 1Sa 3:3 2962
e thou bid the people return from ... 2Sa 2:26 3808
but *e* the messenger came to him, ... 2Kin 6:32 2962
How long will it be *e* ye make an ... Job 18:2
long will it be *e* thou be quiet ... Jer 47:6 3808
how long will it be *e* they attain ... Hos 8:5 3808
Sir, come down *e* my child die ... Jn 4:49 *4250*

ERECH *(e'-rek)* {1} See ARCHEVITES. *A city in Shinar.*

of his kingdom was Babel, and *E* ... Gen 10:10 751

ERECTED {1}

he *e* there an altar, and called it ... Gen 33:20 5324

ERI *(e'-ri)* {2} See ERITES. *A son of Gad.*

and Haggi, Shuni, and Ezbon, *E* ... Gen 46:16 6179
of *E*, the family of the Erites ... Num 26:16 6179

ERITES *(e'-rites)* {1} *Descendants of Eri.*

of Eri, the family of the *E* ... Num 26:16 6180

ERR {24}

the inhabitants of Jerusalem to *e* ... 2Chr 33:9 8582
a people that do *e* in their heart ... Ps 95:10 8582
which do *e* from thy commandments ... Ps 119:21 7686
all them that *e* from thy statutes ... Ps 119:118 7686
Do they not *e* that devise evil ... Prov 14:22 8582
to *e* from the words of knowledge ... Prov 19:27 7686

which lead thee cause thee to *e* ... Is 3:12 8582
of this people cause them to *e* ... Is 9:16 8582
Egypt to *e* in every work thereof ... Is 19:14 8582
they *e* in vision, they stumble in ... Is 28:7 7686
of the people, causing them to *e* ... Is 30:28 8582
though fools, shall not *e* therein ... Is 35:8 8582
thou made us to *e* from thy ways ... Is 63:17 8582
and caused my people Israel to *e* ... Jer 23:13 8582
my people to *e* by their lies ... Jer 23:32 8582
whoredoms hath caused them to *e* ... Hos 4:12 8582
and their lies caused them to *e* ... Amos 2:4 8582
prophets that make my people *e* ... Mic 3:5 8582
and said unto them, Ye do *e* ... Mt 22:29 *4105*
unto them, Do ye not therefore *e* ... Mk 12:24 *4105*
ye therefore do greatly *e* ... Mk 12:27 *4105*
They do alway *e* in their heart ... Heb 3:10 *4105*
Do not *e*, my beloved brethren ... Jas 1:16 *4105*
if any of you do *e* from the truth ... Jas 5:19 *4105*

ERRAND {3}
not eat, until I have told mine *e* ... Gen 24:33 1697
said, I have a secret *e* unto thee ... Judg 3:19 1697
and he said, I have an *e* to thee ... 2Kin 9:5 1697

ERRED {12}
his ignorance wherein he *e* ... Lev 5:18 7683
And if ye have *e*, and not observed ... Num 15:22 7683
the fool, and have *e* exceedingly ... 1Sa 26:21 7683
me to understand wherein I have *e* ... Job 6:24 7683
And be it indeed that I have *e* ... Job 19:4 7683
yet I *e* not from thy precepts ... Ps 119:110 8582
But they also have *e* through wine ... Is 28:7 7686
the prophet have *e* through strong ... Is 28:7 7686
They also that *e* in spirit shall ... Is 29:24 8582
they have *e* from the faith, and ... 1Ti 6:10 *635*
have *e* concerning the faith ... 1Ti 6:21 *795*
Who concerning the truth have *e* ... 2Ti 2:18 *795*

ERRETH {2}
but he that refuseth reproof *e* ... Prov 10:17 8582
of the month for every one that *e* ... Eze 45:20 7686

ERROR {13}
and God smote him there for his *e* ... 2Sa 6:7 7944
mine *e* remaineth with myself ... Job 19:4 4879
the angel, that it was an *e* ... Eccl 5:6 7684
as an *e* which proceedeth from the ... Eccl 10:5 7684
to utter *e* against the LORD, to ... Is 32:6 8432
there any *e* or fault found in him ... Dan 6:4 7960
so the last *e* shall be worse than ... Mt 27:64 *4106*
of their *e* which was meet ... Rom 1:27 *4106*
e of his way shall save a soul ... Jas 5:20 *4106*
escaped from them who live in *e* ... 2Pet 2:18 *4106*
led away with the *e* of the wicked ... 2Pet 3:17 *4106*
of truth, and the spirit of *e* ... 1Jn 4:6 *4106*
after the *e* of Balaam for reward ... Jude 11 *4106*

ERRORS {4}
Who can understand his *e* ... Ps 19:12 7691
They are vanity, and the work of *e* ... Jer 10:15 8595
They are vanity, the work of *e* ... Jer 51:18 8595
and for the *e* of the people ... Heb 9:7 *51*

ESAIAS *(e-sah'-yas)* {21} See ISAIAH. *Greek form of Isaiah.*
was spoken of by the prophet *E* ... Mt 3:3 *2268*
which was spoken by *E* the prophet ... Mt 4:14 *2268*
which was spoken by *E* the prophet ... Mt 8:17 *2268*
which was spoken by *E* the prophet ... Mt 12:17 *2268*
is fulfilled the prophecy of *E* ... Mt 13:14 *2268*
well did *E* prophesy of you ... Mt 15:7 *2268*
Well hath *E* prophesied of you ... Mk 7:6 *2268*
of the words of *E* the prophet ... Lk 3:4 *2268*
him the book of the prophet *E* ... Lk 4:17 *2268*
the Lord, as said the prophet *E* ... Jn 1:23 *2268*
That the saying of *E* the prophet ... Jn 12:38 *2268*
because that *E* said again ... Jn 12:39 *2268*
These things said *E*, when he saw ... Jn 12:41 *2268*
in his chariot read *E* the prophet ... Acts 8:28 *2268*
and heard him read the prophet *E* ... Acts 8:30 *2268*
by *E* the prophet unto our fathers ... Acts 28:25 *2268*
E also crieth concerning Israel ... Rom 9:27 *2268*
as *E* said before, Except the Lord ... Rom 9:29 *2268*
For *E* saith, Lord, who hath ... Rom 10:16 *2268*
But *E* is very bold, and saith, I ... Rom 10:20 *2268*
E saith, There shall be a root of ... Rom 15:12 *2268*

ESAR-HADDON *(e'-zar-had'-dun)* {3} *An Assyrian king.*
E his son reigned in his stead ... 2Kin 19:37 631
since the days of *E* king of Assur ... Ezr 4:2 634
E his son reigned in his stead ... Is 37:38 634

ESAU *(e'-saw)* {88}
1. A son of Isaac.
and they called his name *E* ... Gen 25:25 6215
E was a cunning hunter, a man of ... Gen 25:27 6215
And Isaac loved *E*, because he did ... Gen 25:28 6215
E came from the field, and he was ... Gen 25:29 6215
E said to Jacob, Feed me, I pray ... Gen 25:30 6215
E said, Behold, I am at the point ... Gen 25:32 6215
Then Jacob gave *E* bread and ... Gen 25:34 6215
thus *E* despised his birthright ... Gen 25:34 6215
E was forty years old when he ... Gen 26:34 6215
he called *E* his eldest son, and ... Gen 27:1 6215
when Isaac spake to *E* his son ... Gen 27:5 6215
E went to the field to hunt for ... Gen 27:5 6215
father speak unto *E* thy brother ... Gen 27:6 6215
E my brother is a hairy man, and I ... Gen 27:11 6215
raiment of her eldest son *E* ... Gen 27:15 6215
his father, I am *E* thy firstborn ... Gen 27:19 6215
thou be my very son *E* or not ... Gen 27:21 6215
but the hands are the hands of *E* ... Gen 27:22 6215
he said, Art thou my very son *E* ... Gen 27:24 6215
that *E* his brother came in from ... Gen 27:30 6215
I am thy son, thy firstborn *E* ... Gen 27:32 6215
when *E* heard the words of his ... Gen 27:34 6215
And Isaac answered and said unto *E* ... Gen 27:37 6215
E said unto his father, Hast thou ... Gen 27:38 6215
E lifted up his voice, and wept ... Gen 27:38 6215
E hated Jacob because of the ... Gen 27:41 6215
E said in his heart, The days of ... Gen 27:41 6215
these words of *E* her elder son ... Gen 27:42 6215
unto him, Behold, thy brother *E* ... Gen 27:42 6215
When *E* saw that Isaac had blessed ... Gen 28:6 6215
E seeing that the daughters of ... Gen 28:8 6215
Then went *E* unto Ishmael, and took ... Gen 28:9 6215
to *E* his brother unto the land of ... Gen 32:3 6215
shall ye speak unto my lord *E* ... Gen 32:4 6215
saying, We came to thy brother *E* ... Gen 32:6 6215
If *E* come to the one company, and ... Gen 32:8 6215
of my brother, from the hand of *E* ... Gen 32:11 6215
hand a present for *E* his brother ... Gen 32:13 6215
When *E* my brother meeteth thee ... Gen 32:17 6215
is a present sent unto my lord *E* ... Gen 32:18 6215
this manner shall ye speak unto *E* ... Gen 32:19 6215
E came, and with him four hundred ... Gen 33:1 6215
E ran to meet him, and embraced ... Gen 33:4 6215
E said, I have enough, my brother ... Gen 33:9 6215
E said, Let me now leave with ... Gen 33:15 6215
So *E* returned that day on his way ... Gen 33:16 6215
from the face of *E* thy brother ... Gen 35:1 6215
and his sons *E* and Jacob buried him ... Gen 35:29 6215
these are the generations of *E* ... Gen 36:1 6215
E took his wives of the daughters ... Gen 36:2 6215
And Adah bare to *E* Eliphaz ... Gen 36:4 6215
these are the sons of *E*, which ... Gen 36:5 6215
E took his wives, and his sons, and ... Gen 36:6 6215
E in mount Seir: *E* is Edom ... Gen 36:8 6215
these are the generations of *E* ... Gen 36:9 6215
the son of Adah the wife of *E* ... Gen 36:10 6215
son of Bashemath the wife of *E* ... Gen 36:10 6215
and she bare to *E* Jeush, and Jaalam ... Gen 36:14 6215
These were dukes of the sons of *E* ... Gen 36:15 6215
of Eliphaz the firstborn son of *E* ... Gen 36:15 6215
These are the sons of *E*, who is ... Gen 36:19 6215
names of the dukes that came of *E* ... Gen 36:40 6215
he is *E* the father of the ... Gen 36:43 6215
And I gave unto Isaac Jacob and *E* ... Josh 24:4 6215
and I gave unto *E* mount Seir ... Josh 24:4 6215
sons of Isaac; *E* and Israel ... 1Chr 1:34 6215
Was not *E* Jacob's brother ... Mal 1:2 6215
And I hated *E*, and laid his ... Mal 1:3 6215
or profane person, as *E*, who for ... Heb 12:16 *2269*
2. Descendants of Esau.
your brethren the children of *E* ... Deut 2:4 6215
Seir unto *E* for a possession ... Deut 2:5 6215
our brethren the children of *E* ... Deut 2:8 6215
the children of *E* succeeded them ... Deut 2:12 6215
As he did to the children of *E* ... Deut 2:22 6215
children of *E* which dwell in Seir ... Deut 2:29 6215
The sons of *E* ... 1Chr 1:35 6215
bring the calamity of *E* upon him ... Jer 49:8 6215
But I have made *E* bare, I have ... Jer 49:10 6215
are the things of *E* searched out ... Obad 6 6215
and the house of *E* for stubble ... Obad 18 6215
any remaining of the house of *E* ... Obad 18 6215
have I loved, but *E* have I hated ... Rom 9:13 *2269*
E concerning things to come ... Heb 11:20 *2269*
3. A mountain.
out of the mount of *E* ... Obad 8 6215
of *E* may be cut off by slaughter ... Obad 9 6215
shall possess the mount of *E* ... Obad 19 6215
Zion to judge the mount of *E* ... Obad 21 6215

ESAU'S *(e'-saws)* {12} *Refers to Esau 1.*
and his hand took hold on *E* heel ... Gen 25:26 6215
hairy, as his brother *E* hands ... Gen 27:23 6215
of Rebekah, Jacob's and *E* mother ... Gen 28:5 6215
These are the names of *E* sons ... Gen 36:10 6215
was concubine to Eliphaz *E* son ... Gen 36:12 6215
were the sons of Adah *E* wife ... Gen 36:12 6215
were the sons of Bashemath *E* wife ... Gen 36:13 6215
the daughter of Zibeon, *E* wife ... Gen 36:14 6215
these are the sons of Reuel *E* son ... Gen 36:17 6215
are the sons of Bashemath *E* wife ... Gen 36:17 6215
are the sons of Aholibamah *E* wife ... Gen 36:18 6215
the daughter of Anah, *E* wife ... Gen 36:18 6215

ESCAPE {59}
that he said, *E* for thy life ... Gen 19:17 4422
e to the mountain, lest thou be ... Gen 19:17 4422
I cannot *e* to the mountain, lest ... Gen 19:19 4422
let me *e* thither, (is it not a ... Gen 19:20 4422
Haste thee, *e* thither ... Gen 19:22 4422
company which is left shall *e* ... Gen 32:8 6413
they let none of them remain or *e* ... Josh 8:22 6412
speedily *e* into the land of the ... 1Sa 27:1 4422
so shall I *e* out of his hand ... 1Sa 27:1 4422
we shall not else *e* from Absalom ... 2Sa 15:14 6413
he get him fenced cities, and *e* us ... 2Sa 20:6 5337
let not one of them *e* ... 1Kin 18:40 4422
then let none go forth nor *e* out ... 2Kin 9:15 6412
I have brought into your hands *e* ... 2Kin 10:24 4422
they that *e* out of mount Zion ... 2Kin 19:31 6413
God, to leave us a remnant to *e* ... Ezr 9:8 6413
thou shalt *e* in the king's house ... Est 4:13 4422
shall fail, and they shall not *e* ... Job 11:20 4498,6
I would hasten my *e* from the ... Ps 55:8 4655
Shall they *e* by iniquity ... Ps 56:7 6405
righteousness, and cause me to *e* ... Ps 71:2 6403
own nets, whilst that I withal *e* ... Ps 141:10 5674
he that speaketh lies shall not *e* ... Prov 19:5 4422
pleaseth God shall *e* from her ... Eccl 7:26 4422
and how shall we *e* ... Is 20:6 4422
they that *e* out of mount Zion ... Is 37:32 6413
I will send those that *e* of them ... Is 66:19 6412
which they shall not be able to *e* ... Jer 11:11 3318
the principal of the flock to *e* ... Jer 25:35 6413
not *e* out of the hand of the ... Jer 32:4 4422
thou shalt not *e* out of his hand ... Jer 34:3 4422
thou shalt not *e* out of their ... Jer 38:18 4422
thou shalt not *e* out of their ... Jer 38:23 4422
none of them shall remain or *e* ... Jer 42:17 6412
shall *e* or remain, that they ... Jer 44:14 6412
shall return but such as shall *e* ... Jer 44:14 6412
Yet a small number that *e* the ... Jer 44:28 6412
flee away, nor the mighty man *e* ... Jer 46:6 4422
every city, and no city shall *e* ... Jer 48:8 4422
e out of the land of Babylon, to ... Jer 50:28 6412
let none thereof *e* ... Jer 50:29 6413
e the sword among the nations ... Eze 6:8 6412
they that *e* of you shall remember ... Eze 6:9 6412
But they that *e* of them shall ... Eze 7:16 6403
shall *e*, and shall be on the ... Eze 7:16 6412
shall he *e* that doeth such things ... Eze 17:15 4422
all these things, he shall not *e* ... Eze 17:18 4422
but these shall *e* out of his hand ... Dan 11:41 4422
and the land of Egypt shall not *e* ... Dan 11:42 6413
yea, and nothing shall *e* them ... Joel 2:3 6413
cut off those of his that did *e* ... Obad 14 6412
how can ye *e* the damnation of ... Mt 23:33 *5343,575*
to *e* all these things that shall ... Lk 21:36 *1628*
any of them should swim out, and *e* ... Acts 27:42 *1309*
that thou shalt *e* the judgment of ... Rom 2:3 *1628*
temptation also make a way to *e* ... 1Cor 10:13 *1545*
and they shall not *e* ... 1Th 5:3 *1628*
How shall we *e*, if we neglect so ... Heb 2:3 *1628*
earth, much more shall not we *e* ... Heb 12:25 *5343*

ESCAPED {58}
And there came one that had *e* ... Gen 14:13 6412
the residue of that which is *e* ... Ex 10:5 6413
he hath given his sons that *e* ... Num 21:29 6412
is *e* from his master unto thee ... Deut 23:15 5337
Ehud *e* while they tarried, and ... Judg 3:26 4422
the quarries, and *e* unto Seirath ... Judg 3:26 4422
and there *e* not a man ... Judg 3:29 4422
Ephraimites which were *e* said ... Judg 12:5 6412
for them that be *e* of Benjamin ... Judg 21:17 6413
but the people *e* ... 1Sa 14:41 3318
and David fled, and *e* that night ... 1Sa 19:10 4422
and he went, and fled, and *e* ... 1Sa 19:12 4422
away mine enemy, that he is *e* ... 1Sa 19:17 4422
So David fled, and *e*, and came to ... 1Sa 19:18 4422
thence, and *e* to the cave Adullam ... 1Sa 22:1 4422
son of Ahitub, named Abiathar, *e* ... 1Sa 22:20 4422
Saul that David was *e* from Keilah ... 1Sa 23:13 4422
there *e* not a man of them, save ... 1Sa 30:17 4422
Out of the camp of Israel am I *e* ... 2Sa 1:3 4422
and Rechab and Baanah his brother *e* ... 2Sa 4:6 4422
Ben-hadad the king of Syria *e* on ... 1Kin 20:20 4422
the remnant that is *e* of the ... 2Kin 19:30 6413
they *e* into the land of Armenia ... 2Kin 19:37 4422
of the Amalekites that were *e* ... 1Chr 4:43 6413
king of Syria *e* out of thine hand ... 2Chr 16:7 4422
fallen to the earth, and none *e* ... 2Chr 20:24 6413
that are *e* out of the hand of the ... 2Chr 30:6 6413
them that had *e* from the sword ... 2Chr 36:20 7611
for we remain yet *e*, as it is ... Ezr 9:15 6413
concerning the Jews that had *e* ... Neh 1:2 6413
I only am *e* alone to tell thee ... Job 1:15 4422
I only am *e* alone to tell thee ... Job 1:16 4422
I only am *e* alone to tell thee ... Job 1:17 4422
I only am *e* alone to tell thee ... Job 1:19 4422
I am *e* with the skin of my teeth ... Job 19:20 4422
Our soul is *e* as a bird out of ... Ps 124:7 4422
the snare is broken, and we are *e* ... Ps 124:7 4422
for them that are *e* of Israel ... Is 4:2 6413
such as are *e* of the house of ... Is 10:20 6413
the remnant that is *e* of the ... Is 37:31 6413
they *e* into the land of Armenia ... Is 37:38 4422
ye that are *e* of the nations ... Is 45:20 6412
e from Johanan with eight men ... Jer 41:15 4422
Ye that have *e* the sword, go away ... Jer 51:50 6412
LORD's anger none *e* nor remained ... Lam 2:22
mouth be opened to him which is *e* ... Eze 24:27 6412
that one that had *e* out of ... Eze 33:21 6412
evening, afore he that was *e* came ... Eze 33:22 6412
but he *e* out of their hand ... Jn 10:39 *1831*
that they *e* all safe to land ... Acts 27:44 *1295*
And when they were *e*, then they ... Acts 28:1 *1295*
whom, though he hath *e* the sea ... Acts 28:4 *1295*
down by the wall, and *e* his hands ... 2Cor 11:33 *1628*
e the edge of the sword, out of ... Heb 11:34 *5343*
For if they *e* not who refused him ... Heb 12:25 *5343*
having *e* the corruption that is ... 2Pet 1:4 *668*
those that were clean *e* from them ... 2Pet 2:18 *668*
For if after they have *e* the ... 2Pet 2:20 *668*

ESCAPETH {6}
that him that *e* the sword of ... 1Kin 19:17 4422
him that *e* from the sword of Jehu ... 1Kin 19:17 4422
lions upon him that *e* of Moab ... Is 15:9 6413
him that fleeth, and her that *e* ... Jer 48:19 4422
That he that *e* in that day shall ... Eze 24:26 6412
he that *e* of them shall not be ... Amos 9:1 6412

ESCAPING {1}
there should be no remnant nor *e* ... Ezr 9:14 6413

ESCHEW {1}
Let him *e* evil, and do good ... 1Pet 3:11 *1578*

ESCHEWED {1}
and one that feared God, and *e* evil ... Job 1:1 5493

ESCHEWETH {2}
one that feareth God, and *e* evil ... Job 1:8 5493
one that feareth God, and *e* evil ... Job 2:3 5493

ESEK *(e'-sek)* {1} *A well in the valley of Geran.*
he called the name of the well *E* ... Gen 26:20 6320

ESHAN See ESHEAN.

ESH-BAAL *(esh'-ba-al)* {2} See ISH-BOSHETH. *A son of King Saul.*
Malchi-shua, and Abinadab, and *E* ... 1Chr 8:33 792
Malchi-shua, and Abinadab, and *E* ... 1Chr 9:39 792

ESHBAN {2} A son of Dishon.
Hemdan, and *E*, and Ithran, and ... Gen 36:26 790
and *E*, and Ithran, and Cheran ... 1Chr 1:41 790

ESHCOL *(esh'-col)* {6}
1. Brother of Mamre and Aner.
Mamre the Amorite, brother of *E* ... Gen 14:13 812
men which went with me, Aner, *E* ... Gen 14:24 812
2. A valley or brook in Hebron.
And they came unto the brook of *E* ... Num 13:23 812
The place was called the brook *E* ... Num 13:24 812
they went up unto the valley of *E* ... Num 32:9 812
and came unto the valley of *E* ... Deut 1:24 812

ESHEAN *(esh'-e-an)* {1} *A city in Judea.*
Arab, and Dumah, and *E*, ... Josh 15:52 824

ESHEK *(e'-shek)* {1} *A descendant of King Saul.*
the sons of *E* his brother were, ... 1Chr 8:39 6232

ESHKALONITES *(esh'-ka-lon-ites)* {1} *Inhabitants of Ashkelon.*
and the Ashdothites, the *E* ... Josh 13:3 832

ESHTAOL *(esh'-ta-ol)* {7} See ESHTAULITES. *A town in Judah.*
And in the valley, *E*, and Zoreah, ... Josh 15:33 847
their inheritance was Zorah, and *E* ... Josh 19:41 847
camp of Dan between Zorah and *E* ... Judg 13:25 847
E in the buryingplace of Manoah ... Judg 16:31 847
of valour, from Zorah, and from *E* ... Judg 18:2 847
unto their brethren to Zorah and *E* ... Judg 18:8 847
Danites, out of Zorah and out of *E* ... Judg 18:11 847

ESHTAOLITES See ESHTAULITES.

ESHTAULITES *(esh'-ta-u-lites)* {1} *Inhabitants of Eshtaol.*
came the Zareathites, and the *E* ... 1Chr 2:53 848

ESHTEMOA *(esh-te-mo'-ah)* {5} See ESHTEMOH.
1. A Levitical town in Judah.
suburbs, and *E* with her suburbs, ... Josh 21:14 851
and to them which were in *E* ... 1Sa 30:28 851
with her suburbs, and Jattir, and *E* ... 1Chr 6:57 851
2. A descendant of Ezra.
and Ishbah the father of *E* ... 1Chr 4:17 851
the Garmite, and *E* the Maachathite ... 1Chr 4:19 851

ESHTEMOH *(esh'-te-moh)* {1} See ESHTEMOA. *Same as Eshtemoa 1.*
And Anab, and *E*, and Anim, ... Josh 15:50 851

ESHTON *(esh'-ton)* {2} *Grandson of Chelub.*
Mehir, which was the father of *E* ... 1Chr 4:11 850
E begat Beth-rapha, and Paseah, and ... 1Chr 4:12 850

ESLI *(es'-li)* {1} *Father of Naum; ancestor of Jesus.*
of Naum, which was the son of *E* ... Lk 3:25 *2069*

ESPECIALLY {5}
but *e* among my neighbours, and a ... Ps 31:11 3966
E because I know thee to be ... Acts 26:3 *3122*
e unto them who are of the ... Gal 6:10 *3122*
e they who labour in the word and ... 1Ti 5:17 *3122*
the books, but *e* the parchments ... 2Ti 4:13 *3122*

ESPIED {2}
in the inn, he *e* his money ... Gen 42:27 7200
into a land that I had *e* for them ... Eze 20:6 8446

ESPOUSALS {2}
crowned him in the day of his *e* ... Song 3:11 2861
of thy youth, the love of thine *e* ... Jer 2:2 3623

ESPOUSED {5}
which I *e* to me for an hundred ... 2Sa 3:14 781
his mother Mary was *e* to Joseph ... Mt 1:18 *3423*
To a virgin *e* to a man whose name ... Lk 1:27 *3423*
To be taxed with Mary his *e* wife ... Lk 2:5 *3423*
for I have *e* you to one husband, ... 2Cor 11:2 *718*

ESPY {2}
Kadesh-barnea to *e* out the land ... Josh 14:7 7270
of Aroer, stand by the way, and *e* ... Jer 48:19 6822

ESROM *(es'-rom)* {3} See HEZRON. *Son of Phares; ancestor of Jesus.*
and Phares begat *E* ... Mt 1:3 *2074*
and *E* begat Aram ... Mt 1:3 *2074*
of Aram, which was the son of *E* ... Lk 3:33 *2074*

ESTABLISH {44}
with thee will I *e* my covenant ... Gen 6:18 6965
I *e* my covenant with you, and with ... Gen 9:9 6965
I will *e* my covenant with you ... Gen 9:11 6965
I will *e* my covenant between me ... Gen 17:7 6965
I will *e* my covenant with him for ... Gen 17:19 6965
my covenant will I *e* with Isaac ... Gen 17:21 6965
you, and *e* my covenant with you ... Lev 26:9 6965
the soul, her husband may *e* it ... Num 30:13 6965
that he may *e* his covenant which ... Deut 8:18 6965
The LORD shall *e* thee an holy ... Deut 28:9 6965
That he may *e* thee to day for a ... Deut 29:13 6965
only the LORD *e* his word ... 1Sa 1:23 6965
bowels, and I will *e* his kingdom ... 2Sa 7:12 3559
e it for ever, and do as thou hast ... 2Sa 7:25 6965
Then I will *e* the throne of thy ... 1Kin 9:5 6965
son after him, and to *e* Jerusalem ... 1Kin 15:4 5975
and I will *e* his kingdom ... 1Chr 17:11 3559
I will *e* the throne of his ... 1Chr 22:10 3559
Moreover I will *e* his kingdom for ... 1Chr 28:7 3559
to *e* them for ever, therefore ... 2Chr 9:8 5975
he doth *e* them for ever, and they ... Job 36:7 3427
but *e* the just: for the righteous ... Ps 7:9 3559
God will *e* it for ever ... Ps 48:8 3559
the highest himself shall *e* her ... Ps 87:5 3559
shalt thou *e* in the very heavens ... Ps 89:2 3559
Thy seed will I *e* for ever ... Ps 89:4 3559
e thou the work of our hands upon ... Ps 90:17 3559
the work of our hands *e* thou it ... Ps 90:17 3559
thou dost *e* equity, thou ... Ps 99:4 3559
but he will *e* the border of the ... Prov 15:25 5324
to *e* it with judgment and with ... Is 9:7 5582
to *e* the earth, to cause to ... Is 49:8 6965
And give him no rest, till he *e* ... Is 62:7 3559
the LORD that formed it, to *e* it ... Jer 33:2 3559
I will *e* unto thee an everlasting ... Eze 16:60 6965
I will *e* my covenant with thee ... Eze 16:62 6965
together to *e* a royal statute ... Dan 6:7 6966
e the decree, and sign the writing ... Dan 6:8 6966
exalt themselves to *e* the vision ... Dan 11:14 5975
good, and *e* judgment in the gate ... Amos 5:15 3322
yea, we *e* the law ... Rom 3:31 *2476*
going about to *e* their own ... Rom 10:3 *2476*
to *e* you, and to comfort you ... 1Th 3:2 *4741*
first, that he may *e* the second ... Heb 10:9 *2476*

ESTABLISHED {74}
which I have *e* between me ... Gen 9:17 6965
is because the thing is *e* by God ... Gen 41:32 3559
I have also *e* my covenant with ... Ex 6:4 6965
O Lord, which thy hands have *e* ... Ex 15:17 3559
e for ever to him that bought it ... Lev 25:30 6965
witnesses, shall the matter be *e* ... Deut 19:15 6965
Hath he not made thee, and *e* thee ... Deut 32:6 3559
was *e* to be a prophet of the LORD ... 1Sa 3:20 539
e thy kingdom upon Israel for ... 1Sa 13:13 3559
the ground, thou shalt not be *e* ... 1Sa 20:31 3559
Israel shall be *e* in thine hand ... 1Sa 24:20 6965
LORD had *e* him king over Israel ... 2Sa 5:12 3559
shall be *e* for ever before thee ... 2Sa 7:16 539
thy throne shall be *e* for ever ... 2Sa 7:16 3559
servant David be *e* before thee ... 2Sa 7:26 3559
and his kingdom was *e* greatly ... 1Kin 2:12 3559
the LORD liveth, which hath *e* me ... 1Kin 2:24 3559
be *e* before the LORD for ever ... 1Kin 2:45 3559
the kingdom was *e* in the hand of ... 1Kin 2:46 3559
throne shall be *e* for evermore ... 1Chr 17:14 3559
his house be *e* for ever, and do as ... 1Chr 17:23 539
Let it even be *e*, that thy name ... 1Chr 17:24 539
thy servant be *e* before thee ... 1Chr 17:24 3559
promise unto David my father be *e* ... 2Chr 1:9 539
when Rehoboam had *e* the kingdom ... 2Chr 12:1 3559
LORD your God, so shall ye be *e* ... 2Chr 20:20 539
when the kingdom was *e* to him ... 2Chr 25:3 2388
So they *e* a decree to make ... 2Chr 30:5 5975
Their seed is *e* in their sight ... Job 21:8 3559
thing, and it shall be *e* unto thee ... Job 22:28 6965
the seas, and *e* it upon the floods ... Ps 24:2 3559
feet upon a rock, and *e* my goings ... Ps 40:2 3559
For he *e* a testimony in Jacob, and ... Ps 78:5 6965
earth which he hath *e* for ever ... Ps 78:69 3245
With whom my hand shall be *e* ... Ps 89:21 3559
It shall be *e* for ever as the ... Ps 89:37 3559
Thy throne is *e* of old ... Ps 93:2 3559
the world also shall be *e* that it ... Ps 96:10 3559
their seed shall be *e* before thee ... Ps 102:28 3559
His heart is *e*, he shall not be ... Ps 112:8 5564
thou hast *e* the earth, and it ... Ps 119:90 3559
an evil speaker be *e* in the earth ... Ps 140:11 3559
hath he *e* the heavens ... Prov 3:19 3559
feet, and let all thy ways be *e* ... Prov 4:26 3559
When he *e* the clouds above ... Prov 8:28 553
man shall not be *e* by wickedness ... Prov 12:3 3559
lip of truth shall be *e* for ever ... Prov 12:19 3559
of counsellors they are *e* ... Prov 15:22 6965
LORD, and thy thoughts shall be *e* ... Prov 16:3 3559
the throne is *e* by righteousness ... Prov 16:12 3559
Every purpose is *e* by counsel ... Prov 20:18 3559
and by understanding it is *e* ... Prov 24:3 3559
shall be *e* in righteousness ... Prov 25:5 3559
his throne shall be *e* for ever ... Prov 29:14 3559
who hath *e* all the ends of the ... Prov 30:4 6965
be *e* in the top of the mountains ... Is 2:2 3559
believe, surely ye shall not be *e* ... Is 7:9 539
And in mercy shall the throne be *e* ... Is 16:5 3559
he hath *e* it, he created it not ... Is 45:18 3559
In righteousness shalt thou be *e* ... Is 54:14 3559
he hath *e* the world by his wisdom ... Jer 10:12 3559
congregation shall be *e* before me ... Jer 30:20 3559
he hath *e* the world by his wisdom ... Jer 51:15 3559
I was *e* in my kingdom, and ... Dan 4:36 8627
be *e* in the top of the mountains ... Mic 4:1 3559
thou hast *e* them for correction ... Hab 1:12 3245
and it shall be *e*, and set there ... Zec 5:11 3559
witnesses every word may be *e* ... Mt 18:16 *2476*
were the churches *e* in the faith ... Acts 16:5 *4732*
gift, to the end ye may be *e* ... Rom 1:11 *4741*
witnesses shall every word be *e* ... 2Cor 13:1 *2476*
which was *e* upon better promises ... Heb 8:6 *3549*
that the heart be *e* with grace ... Heb 13:9 *950*
be *e* in the present truth ... 2Pet 1:12 *4741*

ESTABLISHETH {3}
then he *e* all her vows, or all ... Num 30:14 6965
The king by judgment *e* the land ... Prov 29:4 5975
which the king *e* may be changed ... Dan 6:15 6966

ESTABLISHMENT {1}
the *e* thereof, Sennacherib king ... 2Chr 32:1 571

ESTATE {17}
to the *e* of a man of high degree ... 1Chr 17:17 8448
e unto another that is better ... Est 1:19
Who remembered us in our low *e* ... Ps 136:23
saying, Lo, I am come to great *e* ... Eccl 1:16
the *e* of the sons of men, that ... Eccl 3:18 1700
shall return to their former *e* ... Eze 16:55
shall return to their former *e* ... Eze 16:55 3653
shall return to your former *e* ... Eze 16:55
roots shall one stand up in his *e* ... Dan 11:7 3653
Then shall stand up in his *e* a ... Dan 11:20 3653
in his *e* shall stand up a vile ... Dan 11:21 3653
But in his *e* shall he honour the ... Dan 11:38 3653
the low *e* of his handmaiden ... Lk 1:48
and all the *e* of the elders ... Acts 22:5
but condescend to men of low *e* ... Rom 12:16
that he might know your *e* ... Col 4:8 *3588,4012*
which kept not their first *e* ... Jude 6

ESTATES {2}
will settle you after your old *e* ... Eze 36:11
captains, and chief *e* of Galilee ... Mk 6:21

ESTEEM {5}
Will he *e* thy riches ... Job 36:19 6186
Therefore I *e* all thy precepts ... Ps 119:128
yet we did *e* him stricken, ... Is 53:4 2803
e other better than themselves ... Phil 2:3 *2233*
to *e* them very highly in love for ... 1Th 5:13 *2233*

ESTEEMED {11}
lightly *e* the Rock of his ... Deut 32:15 5034
despise me shall be lightly *e* ... 1Sa 2:30 7043
I am a poor man, and lightly *e* ... 1Sa 18:23 7043
I have *e* the words of his mouth ... Job 23:12 6845
lips is *e* a man of understanding ... Prov 17:28
shall be *e* as the potter's clay ... Is 29:16 2803
field shall be *e* as a forest ... Is 29:17 2803
he was despised, and we *e* him not ... Is 53:3
how are they *e* as earthen ... Lam 4:2 2803
for that which is highly *e* among ... Lk 16:15
who are least *e* in the church ... 1Cor 6:4 *1848*

ESTEEMETH {4}
He *e* iron as straw, and brass as ... Job 41:27 2803
One man *e* one day above another ... Rom 14:5 *2919*
another *e* every day alike ... Rom 14:5 *2919*
but to him that *e* any thing to be ... Rom 14:14 *3049*

ESTEEMING {1}
E the reproach of Christ greater ... Heb 11:26 *2233*

ESTHER *(est'-thur)* {53} See ESTHER'S, HADASSAH. *A Jewish queen.*
brought up Hadassah, that is, *E* ... Est 2:7 635
that *E* was brought also unto the ... Est 2:8 635
E had not shewed her people nor ... Est 2:10 635
women's house, to know how *E* did ... Est 2:11 635
Now when the turn of *E*, the ... Est 2:15 635
E obtained favour in the sight of ... Est 2:15 635
So *E* was taken unto king ... Est 2:16 635
the king loved *E* above all the ... Est 2:17 635
E had not yet shewed her kindred ... Est 2:20 635
for *E* did the commandment of ... Est 2:20 635
who told it unto *E* the queen ... Est 2:22 635
E certified the king thereof in ... Est 2:22 635
Then called *E* for Hatach, one of ... Est 4:5 635
destroy them, to shew it unto *E* ... Est 4:8 635
told *E* the words of Mordecai ... Est 4:9 635
Again *E* spake unto Hatach, and ... Est 4:10 635
Mordecai commanded to answer *E* ... Est 4:13 635
Then *E* bade them return Mordecai ... Est 4:15 635
to all that *E* had commanded him ... Est 4:17 635
that *E* put on her royal apparel, ... Est 5:1 635
when the king saw *E* the queen ... Est 5:2 635
the king held out to *E* the golden ... Est 5:2 635
So *E* drew near, and touched the ... Est 5:2 635
unto her, What wilt thou, queen *E* ... Est 5:3 635
E answered, If it seem good unto ... Est 5:4 635
that he may do as *E* hath said ... Est 5:5 635
the banquet that *E* had prepared ... Est 5:5 635
the king said unto *E* at the ... Est 5:6 635
Then answered *E*, and said, My ... Est 5:7 635
E the queen did let no man come ... Est 5:12 635
the banquet that *E* had prepared ... Est 6:14 635
came to banquet with *E* the queen ... Est 7:1 635
unto *E* on the second day at the ... Est 7:2 635
What is thy petition, queen *E* ... Est 7:2 635
Then *E* the queen answered and said ... Est 7:3 635
answered and said unto *E* the queen ... Est 7:5 635
E said, The adversary and enemy is ... Est 7:6 635
for his life to *E* the queen ... Est 7:7 635
fallen upon the bed whereon *E* was ... Est 7:8 635
the Jews' enemy unto *E* the queen ... Est 8:1 635
for *E* had told what he was unto ... Est 8:1 635
E set Mordecai over the house of ... Est 8:2 635
E spake yet again before the king ... Est 8:3 635
out the golden sceptre toward *E* ... Est 8:4 635
So *E* arose, and stood before the ... Est 8:4 635
Ahasuerus said unto *E* the queen ... Est 8:7 635
I have given *E* the house of Haman ... Est 8:7 635
And the king said unto *E* the queen ... Est 9:12 635
Then said *E*, If it please the ... Est 9:13 635

But when *E* came before the king, ... Est 9:25
Then *E* the queen, the daughter of .... Est 9:29 635
E the queen had enjoined them, and .... Est 9:31 635
the decree of *E* confirmed these .... Est 9:32 635

ESTHER'S *(es'-thurs)* {3}
and his servants, even *E* feast .... Est 2:18 635
So *E* maids and her chamberlains .... Est 4:4 635
And they told to Mordecai *E* words .... Est 4:12 635

ESTIMATE {2}
LORD, then the priest shall *e* it .... Lev 27:14 6186
as the priest shall *e* it, so .... Lev 27:14 6186

ESTIMATION {23}
with thy *e* by shekels of silver, ... Lev 5:15 6187
out of the flock, with thy *e* .... Lev 5:18 6187
out of the flock, with thy *e* .... Lev 6:6 6187
shall be for the LORD by thy *e* .... Lev 27:2 6187
thy *e* shall be of the male from .... Lev 27:3 6187
even thy *e* shall be fifty shekels .... Lev 27:3 6187
then thy *e* shall be thirty .... Lev 27:4 6187
then thy *e* shall be of the male .... Lev 27:5 6187
then thy *e* shall be of the male .... Lev 27:6 6187
for the female thy *e* shall be .... Lev 27:6 6187
then thy *e* shall be fifteen .... Lev 27:7 6187
But if he be poorer than thy *e* .... Lev 27:8 6187
a fifth part thereof unto thy *e* .... Lev 27:13 6187
of the money of thy *e* unto it .... Lev 27:15 6187
then thy *e* shall be according to .... Lev 27:16 6187
according to thy *e* it shall stand .... Lev 27:17 6187
and it shall be abated from thy *e* .... Lev 27:18 6187
of the money of thy *e* unto it .... Lev 27:19 6187
unto him the worth of thy *e* .... Lev 27:23 6187
he shall give thine *e* in that day .... Lev 27:23 6187
redeem it according to thine *e* .... Lev 27:27 6187
shall be sold according to thy *e* .... Lev 27:27 6187
thou redeem, according to thine *e* .... Num 18:16 6187

ESTIMATIONS {1}
all thy *e* shall be according to .... Lev 27:25 6187

ESTRANGED {5}
acquaintance are verily *e* from me .... Job 19:13 2114
The wicked are *e* from the womb .... Ps 58:3 2114
They were not *e* from their lust .... Ps 78:30 2114
have *e* this place, and have burned .... Jer 19:4 5234
because they are all *e* from me .... Eze 14:5 2114

ETAM *(e'-tam)* {5}
1. An area in western Judah.
and dwelt in the top of the rock *E* .... Judg 15:8 5862
went to the top of the rock *E* .... Judg 15:11 5862
2. A descendant of Judah.
And these were of the father of *E* 1Chr 4:3 5862
3. A village in Simeon.
And their villages were, *E* 1Chr 4:32 5862
4. A town in Judah.
He built even Beth-lehem, and *E* 2Chr 11:6 5862

ETERNAL {47}
The *e* God is thy refuge, and .... Deut 33:27 6924
I will make thee an *e* excellency .... Is 60:15 5769
I do, that I may have *e* life .... Mt 19:16 *166*
but the righteous into life *e* .... Mt 25:46 *166*
but is in danger of *e* damnation .... Mk 3:29 *166*
I do that I may inherit *e* life .... Mk 10:17 *166*
and in the world to come *e* life .... Mk 10:30 *166*
what shall I do to inherit *e* life .... Lk 10:25 *166*
what shall I do to inherit *e* life .... Lk 18:18 *166*
not perish, but have *e* life .... Jn 3:15 *166*
and gathereth fruit unto life *e* .... Jn 4:36 *166*
in them ye think ye have *e* life .... Jn 5:39 *166*
and drinketh my blood, hath *e* life .... Jn 6:54 *166*
thou hast the words of *e* life .... Jn 6:68 *166*
And I give unto them *e* life .... Jn 10:28 *166*
world shall keep it unto life *e* .... Jn 12:25 *166*
that he should give *e* life to as .... Jn 17:2 *166*
And this is life *e*, that they .... Jn 17:3 *166*
were ordained to *e* life believed .... Acts 13:48 *166*
that are made, even his *e* power .... Rom 1:20 *126*
and honour and immortality, *e* life .... Rom 2:7 *166*
through righteousness unto *e* life .... Rom 5:21 *166*
but the gift of God is *e* life .... Rom 6:23 *166*
exceeding and *e* weight of glory 2Cor 4:17 *166*
things which are not seen are *e* 2Cor 4:18 *166*
made with hands, *e* in the heavens 2Cor 5:1 *166*
According to the *e* purpose which .... Eph 3:11 *165*
Now unto the King *e*, immortal, ... 1Ti 1:17 *165*
of faith, lay hold on *e* life 1Ti 6:12 *166*
that they may lay hold on *e* life 1Ti 6:19 *166*
is in Christ Jesus with *e* glory 2Ti 2:10 *166*
In hope of *e* life, which God, ... Titus 1:2 *166*
according to the hope of *e* life .... Titus 3:7 *166*
he became the author of *e* .... Heb 5:9 *166*
of the dead, and of *e* judgment .... Heb 6:2 *166*
having obtained *e* redemption for .... Heb 9:12 *166*
who through the *e* Spirit offered .... Heb 9:14 *166*
the promise of *e* inheritance .... Heb 9:15 *166*
unto his *e* glory by Christ Jesus 1Pet 5:10 *166*
and shew unto you that *e* life 1Jn 1:2 *166*
he hath promised us, even *e* life 1Jn 2:25 *166*
hath *e* life abiding in him 1Jn 3:15 *166*
that God hath given to us *e* life 1Jn 5:11 *166*
ye may know that ye have *e* life 1Jn 5:13 *166*
This is the true God, and *e* life 1Jn 5:20 *166*
suffering the vengeance of *e* fire .... Jude 7 *166*
our Lord Jesus Christ unto *e* life .... Jude 21 *166*

ETERNITY {1}
and lofty One that inhabiteth *e* .... Is 57:15 5703

ETHAM *(e'-tham)* {4} *An encampment during the Exodus.*
from Succoth, and encamped in *E* .... Ex 13:20 864
from Succoth, and pitched in *E* .... Num 33:6 864
And they removed from *E*, and turned .... Num 33:7 864
journey in the wilderness of *E* .... Num 33:8 864

ETHAN *(e'-than)* {8}
1. A wise man in Solomon's time.
than *E* the Ezrahite, and Heman, and 1Kin 4:31 387
Maschil of *E* the Ezrahite .... Ps 89:*t* 387
2. A son of Zerah.
Zimri, and *E*, and Heman, and Calcol, ... 1Chr 2:6 387
And the sons of *E* 1Chr 2:8 387
3. A descendant of Gershon.
The son of *E*, the son of Zimmah, ... 1Chr 6:42 387
4. A descendant of Merari.
E the son of Kishi, the son of 1Chr 6:44 387
brethren, *E* the son of Kushaiah 1Chr 15:17 387
the singers, Heman, Asaph, and *E* 1Chr 15:19 387

ETHANIM *(eth'-a-nim)* {1} *Seventh month of the Hebrew year.*
at the feast in the month *E* 1Kin 8:2 388

ETHBAAL *(eth'-ba-al)* {1} *Father of Jezebel.*
of *E* king of the Zidonians 1Kin 16:31 856

ETHER *(e'-ther)* {2} *A city in Judah.*
Libnah, and *E*, and Ashan, ... Josh 15:42 6281
Ain, Remmon, and *E*, and Ashan .... Josh 19:7 6281

ETHIOPIA *(e-the-o'-pe-ah)* {20} See CUSH, ETHIOPIAN.
1. The land south of Egypt.
compasseth the whole land of *E* .... Gen 2:13 3568
reigned from India even unto *E* .... Est 1:1 3568
which are from India unto *E* .... Est 8:9 3568
The topaz of *E* shall not equal it .... Job 28:19 3568
behold Philistia, and Tyre, with *E* .... Ps 87:4 3568
which is beyond the rivers of *E* .... Is 18:1 3568
Syene even unto the border of *E* .... Eze 29:10 3568
the rivers of *E* my suppliants .... Zeph 3:10 3568
and, behold, a man of *E*, an eunuch .... Acts 8:27 *128*
2. Inhabitants of Ethiopia.
heard say of Tirhakah king of *E* 2Kin 19:9 3568
E shall soon stretch out her .... Ps 68:31 3568
and wonder upon Egypt and upon *E* .... Is 20:3 3568
ashamed of *E* their expectation, ... Is 20:5 3568
say concerning Tirhakah king of *E* .... Is 37:9 3568
I gave Egypt for thy ransom, *E* .... Is 43:3 3568
of Egypt, and merchandise of *E* .... Is 45:14 3568
and great pain shall be in *E* .... Eze 30:4 3568
E, and Libya, and Lydia, and all the .... Eze 30:5 3568
Persia, *E*, and Libya with them .... Eze 38:5 3568
E and Egypt were her strength, and .... Nah 3:9 3568

ETHIOPIAN {8}
the *E* woman whom he had married .... Num 12:1 3569
for he had married an *E* woman .... Num 12:1 3569
the *E* with an host of a thousand 2Chr 14:9 3569
Can the *E* change his skin, or the .... Jer 13:23 3569
Now when Ebed-melech the *E* .... Jer 38:7 3569
king commanded Ebed-melech the *E* .... Jer 38:10 3569
Ebed-melech the *E* said unto .... Jer 38:12 3569
Go and speak to Ebed-melech the *E* .... Jer 39:16 3569

ETHIOPIANS {13} *Inhabitants of Ethiopia.*
the Lubim, the Sukkiims, and the *E* 2Chr 12:3 3569
the LORD smote the *E* before Asa 2Chr 14:12 3569
before Judah; and the *E* fled 2Chr 14:12 3569
the *E* were overthrown, that they 2Chr 14:13 3569
Were not the *E* and the Lubims a 2Chr 16:8 3569
Arabians, that were near the *E* 2Chr 21:16 3569
the *E* captives, young and old, ... Is 20:4 3569
the *E* and the Libyans, that handle .... Jer 46:9 3569
to make the careless *E* afraid .... Eze 30:9 3569
the *E* shall be at his steps .... Dan 11:43 3569
not as children of the *E* unto me .... Amos 9:7 3569
Ye *E* also, ye shall be slain by .... Zeph 2:12 3569
under Candace queen of the *E* .... Acts 8:27 *128*

ETH KAZIN See ITTAH-KAZIN.

ETHNAN *(eth'-nan)* {1} *Grandson of Ashur.*
were, Zereth, and Jezoar, and *E* 1Chr 4:7 869

ETHNI *(eth'-ni)* {1} See JEATERAI. *Ancestor of Asaph.*
The son of *E*, the son of Zerah, ... 1Chr 6:41 867

EUBULUS *(yu-bu'-lus)* {1} *A Christian acquaintance of Paul.*
E greeteth thee, and Pudens, and 2Ti 4:21 *2103*

EUNICE *(yu-ni'-see)* {1} *Mother of Timothy.*
grandmother Lois, and thy mother *E* 2Ti 1:5 *2131*

EUNUCH {7}
neither let the *e* say, Behold, I .... Is 56:3 5631
He took also out of the city an *e* .... Jer 52:25 5631
an *e* of great authority under .... Acts 8:27 *2135*
the *e* answered Philip, and said, I .... Acts 8:34 *2135*
the *e* said, See, here is water .... Acts 8:36 *2135*
the water, both Philip and the *e* .... Acts 8:38 *2135*
that the *e* saw him no more .... Acts 8:39 *2135*

EUNUCHS {21}
looked out to him two or three *e* 2Kin 9:32 5631
they shall be *e* in the palace of 2Kin 20:18 5631
they shalt be *e* in the palace of .... Is 39:7 5631
unto the *e* that keep my sabbaths .... Is 56:4 5631
the king, and the queen, and the *e* .... Jer 29:2 5631
the princes of Jerusalem, the *e* .... Jer 34:19 5631
one of the *e* which was in the .... Jer 38:7 5631
women, and the children, and the *e* .... Jer 41:16 5631
unto Ashpenaz the master of his *e* .... Dan 1:3 5631
the prince of the *e* gave names .... Dan 1:7 5631
of the *e* that he might not defile .... Dan 1:8 5631
love with the prince of the *e* .... Dan 1:9 5631
prince of the *e* said unto Daniel .... Dan 1:10 5631
of the *e* had set over Daniel .... Dan 1:11 5631
of the *e* brought them in before .... Dan 1:18 5631
For there are some *e*, which were .... Mt 19:12 *2135*
and there are some *e*, which were .... Mt 19:12 *2134*
e, which were made *e* of men .... Mt 19:12 *2134*
and there be *e*, which have made .... Mt 19:12 *2135*
which have made themselves *e* for .... Mt 19:12 *2134*

EUODIAS *(yu-o'-de-as)* {1} *A Christian at Philippi.*
I beseech *E*, and beseech Syntyche, ... Phil 4:2 *2136*

EUPHRATES *(yu-fra'-teze)* {21} *A river in Mesopotamia.*
And the fourth river is *E* .... Gen 2:14 6578
unto the great river, the river *E* .... Gen 15:18 6578
unto the great river, the river *E* .... Deut 1:7 6578
from the river, the river *E* .... Deut 11:24 6578
unto the great river, the river *E* .... Josh 1:4 6578
recover his border at the river *E* 2Sa 8:3 6578
king of Assyria to the river *E* 2Kin 23:29 6578
river of Egypt unto the river *E* 2Kin 24:7 6578
the wilderness from the river *E* 1Chr 5:9 6578
his dominion by the river *E* 1Chr 18:3 6578
to fight against Charchemish by *E* 2Chr 35:20 6578
upon thy loins, and arise, go to *E* .... Jer 13:4 6578
So I went, and hid it by *E* .... Jer 13:5 6578
LORD said unto me, Arise, go to *E* .... Jer 13:6 6578
Then I went to *E*, and digged, and .... Jer 13:7 6578
was by the river *E* in Carchemish .... Jer 46:2 6578
toward the north by the river *E* .... Jer 46:6 6578
the north country by the river *E* .... Jer 46:10 6578
and cast it into the midst of *E* .... Jer 51:63 6578
are bound in the great river *E* .... Rev 9:14 *2166*
his vial upon the great river *E* .... Rev 16:12 *2166*

EURAQUILO See EUROCLYDON.

EUROCLYDON *(yu-roc'-lid-on)* {1} *A Mediterranean wind.*
it a tempestuous wind, called *E* .... Acts 27:14 *2148*

EUTYCHUS *(yu'-tik-us)* {1} *Youth restored to life.*
a certain young man named *E* .... Acts 20:9 *2161*

EVANGELIST {2}
into the house of Philip the *e* .... Acts 21:8 *2099*
afflictions, do the work of an *e* 2Ti 4:5 *2099*

EVANGELISTS {1}
and some, *e*; and some, pastors .... Eph 4:11 *2099*

EVE *(eev)* {4} *Wife of Adam.*
And Adam called his wife's name *E* .... Gen 3:20 2332
And Adam knew *E* his wife .... Gen 4:1 2332
beguiled *E* through his subtilty 2Cor 11:3 *2096*
For Adam was first formed, then *E* 1Ti 2:13 *2096*

EVEN See APPENDIX.

EVENING {60}
And the *e* and the morning were the .... Gen 1:5 6153
And the *e* and the morning were the .... Gen 1:8 6153
And the *e* and the morning were the .... Gen 1:13 6153
And the *e* and the morning were the .... Gen 1:19 6153
And the *e* and the morning were the .... Gen 1:23 6153
And the *e* and the morning were the .... Gen 1:31 6153
the dove came in to him in the *e* .... Gen 8:11 6153
of water at the time of the *e* .... Gen 24:11 6153
And it came to pass in the *e* .... Gen 29:23 6153
came out of the field in the *e* .... Gen 30:16 6153
of Israel shall kill it in the *e* .... Ex 12:6 6153
give you in the *e* flesh to eat .... Ex 16:8 6153
Moses from the morning unto the *e* .... Ex 18:13 6153
from *e* to morning before the LORD .... Ex 27:21 6153
the *e* unto the morning before the .... Lev 24:3 6153
when *e* cometh on, he shall wash .... Deut 23:11 6153
upon the trees until the *e* .... Josh 10:26 6153
now the day draweth toward *e* .... Judg 19:9 6150
man that eateth any food until *e* 1Sa 14:24 6153
Philistine drew near morning and *e* 1Sa 17:16 6150
even unto the *e* of the next day 1Sa 30:17 6153
and bread and flesh in the *e* 1Kin 17:6 6153
the offering of the *e* sacrifice 1Kin 18:29
the offering of the *e* sacrifice 1Kin 18:36
the *e* meat offering, and the 2Kin 16:15 6153
offering continually morning and *e* 1Chr 16:40 6153
the burnt offerings morning and *e* 2Chr 2:4 6153
every *e* burnt sacrifices and sweet 2Chr 13:11 6153
lamps thereof, to burn every *e* 2Chr 13:11 6153
e burnt offerings, and the burnt 2Chr 31:3 6153
even burnt offerings morning and *e* .... Ezr 3:3 6153
astonied until the *e* sacrifice .... Ezr 9:4 6153
at the *e* sacrifice I arose up .... Ezr 9:5 6153
In the *e* she went, and on the .... Est 2:14 6153
are destroyed from morning to *e* .... Job 4:20 6153
E, and morning, and at noon, will I .... Ps 55:17 6153
They return at *e*: they make a .... Ps 59:6 6153
And at *e* let them return .... Ps 59:14 6153
of the morning and *e* to rejoice .... Ps 65:8 6153
in the *e* it is cut down, and .... Ps 90:6 6153
work and to his labour until the *e* .... Ps 104:23 6153
up of my hands as the *e* sacrifice .... Ps 141:2 6153
In the twilight, in the *e* .... Prov 7:9 6153
in the *e* withhold not thine hand .... Eccl 11:6 6153
of the *e* are stretched out .... Jer 6:4 6153
of the LORD was upon me in the *e* .... Eze 33:22 6153
shall not be shut until the *e* .... Eze 46:2 6153
And the vision of the *e* and the .... Dan 8:26 6153
about the time of the *e* oblation .... Dan 9:21 6153
are more fierce than the *e* wolves .... Hab 1:8 6153
shall they lie down in the *e* .... Zeph 2:7 6153
her judges are *e* wolves .... Zeph 3:3 6153

that at *e* time it shall be light ... Zec 14:7 6153
And when it was *e*, his disciples ... Mt 14:15 *3798*
and when the *e* was come, he was ... Mt 14:23 *3798*
and said unto them, When it is *e* ... Mt 16:2 *3798*
in the *e* he cometh with the ... Mk 14:17 *3798*
for it is toward *e*, and the day is ... Lk 24:29 *2073*
Then the same day at *e*, being the ... Jn 20:19 *3798*
the prophets, from morning till *e* ... Acts 28:23 *2073*

EVENINGS {1}
a wolf of the *e* shall spoil them, ... Jer 5:6 6160

EVENINGTIDE {2}
And it came to pass in an *e* ... 2Sa 11:2 6256,6153
And behold at *e* trouble ... Is 17:14 6256,6153

EVENT {3}
that one *e* happeneth to them all ... Eccl 2:14 4745
there is one *e* to the righteous, ... Eccl 9:2 4745
sun, that there is one *e* unto all ... Eccl 9:3 4745

EVENTIDE {5}
to meditate in the field at the *e* ... Gen 24:63 6256,6153
the ark of the LORD until the *e* ... Josh 7:6 6153
of Ai he hanged on a tree until *e* ... Josh 8:29 6256,6153
now the *e* was come, he went out ... Mk 11:11
for it was now *e* ... Acts 4:3 *2073*

EVER {500}
of life, and eat, and live for *e* ... Gen 3:22 5769
I give it, and to thy seed for *e* ... Gen 13:15 5769
then let me bear the blame for *e* ... Gen 43:9 3605,3117
bear the blame to my father for *e* ... Gen 44:32 3605,3117
this is my name for *e*, and this is ... Ex 3:15 5769
it a feast by an ordinance for *e* ... Ex 12:14 5769
generations by an ordinance for *e* ... Ex 12:17 5769
to thee and to thy sons for *e* ... Ex 12:24 5769
see them again no more for *e* ... Ex 14:13 5769
The LORD shall reign for *e* ... Ex 15:18 5769
LORD shall reign for *e* and *e* ... Ex 15:18 5703
with thee, and believe thee for *e* ... Ex 19:9 5769
and he shall serve him for *e* ... Ex 21:6 5769
it shall be a statute for *e* unto ... Ex 27:21 5769
shall be a statute for *e* unto him ... Ex 28:43 5769
his sons' by a statute for *e* from ... Ex 29:28 5769
shall be a statute for *e* to them ... Ex 30:21 5769
and the children of Israel for *e* ... Ex 31:17 5769
and they shall inherit it for *e* ... Ex 32:13 5769
The fire shall *e* be burning upon ... Lev 6:13 8548
It shall be a statute for *e* in ... Lev 6:18 5769
is a statute for *e* unto the LORD ... Lev 6:22 5769
for *e* from among the children of ... Lev 7:34 5769
by a statute for *e* throughout ... Lev 7:36 5769
it shall be a statute for *e* ... Lev 10:9 5769
with thee, by a statute for *e* ... Lev 10:15 5769
shall be a statute for *e* unto you ... Lev 16:29 5769
your souls, by a statute for *e* ... Lev 16:31 5769
for *e* unto them throughout their ... Lev 17:7 5769
it shall be a statute for *e* ... Lev 23:14 5769
for *e* in all your dwellings ... Lev 23:21 5769
it shall be a statute for *e* ... Lev 23:31 5769
statute for *e* in your generations ... Lev 23:41 5769
statute for *e* in your generations ... Lev 24:3 5769
The land shall not be sold for *e* ... Lev 25:23 6783
for *e* to him that bought it ... Lev 25:30 6783
they shall be your bondmen for *e* ... Lev 25:46 5769
for *e* throughout your generations ... Num 10:8 5769
an ordinance for *e* in your ... Num 15:15 5769
thy sons, by an ordinance for *e* ... Num 18:8 5769
with thee, by a statute for *e* ... Num 18:11 5769
with thee, by a statute for *e* ... Num 18:19 5769
for *e* before the LORD unto thee ... Num 18:19 5769
it shall be a statute for *e* ... Num 18:23 5769
among them, for a statute for *e* ... Num 19:10 5769
upon which thou hast ridden *e* ... Num 22:30 5750
was I *e* wont to do so unto thee ... Num 22:30
end shall be that he perish for *e* ... Num 24:20 5703
and he also shall perish for *e* ... Num 24:24 5703
Did *e* people hear the voice of ... Deut 4:33
LORD thy God giveth thee, for *e* ... Deut 4:40 3605,3117
and with their children for *e* ... Deut 5:29 5769
thy children after thee for *e* ... Deut 12:28 5769
and it shall be an heap for *e* ... Deut 13:16 5769
and he shall be thy servant for *e* ... Deut 15:17 5769
the LORD, him and his sons for *e* ... Deut 18:5 3605,3117
thy God, and to walk *e* in his ways ... Deut 19:9 3605,3117
congregation of the LORD for *e* ... Deut 23:3 5769
prosperity all thy days for *e* ... Deut 23:6 5769
a wonder, and upon thy seed for *e* ... Deut 28:46 5769
unto us and to our children for *e* ... Deut 29:29 5769
to heaven, and say, I live for *e* ... Deut 32:40 5769
unto the children of Israel for *e* ... Josh 4:7 5769
fear the LORD your God for *e* ... Josh 4:24 3605,3117
Ai, and made it an heap for *e* ... Josh 8:28 5769
and thy children's for *e*, because ... Josh 14:9 5769
did he *e* strive against Israel, ... Judg 11:25
or did he *e* fight against them, ... Judg 11:25
the LORD, and there abide for *e* ... 1Sa 1:22 5769
should walk before me for *e* ... 1Sa 2:30 5769
an old man in thine house for *e* ... 1Sa 2:32 3605,3117
walk before mine anointed for *e* ... 1Sa 2:35 3605,3117
for *e* for the iniquity which he ... 1Sa 3:13 5769
with sacrifice nor offering for *e* ... 1Sa 3:14 5769
thy kingdom upon Israel for *e* ... 1Sa 13:13 5769
thy kindness from my house for *e* ... 1Sa 20:15 5769
LORD be between thee and me for *e* ... 1Sa 20:23 5769
between my seed and thy seed for *e* ... 1Sa 20:42 5769
he shall be my servant for *e* ... 1Sa 27:12 5769
thee keeper of mine head for *e* ... 1Sa 28:2 3605,3117
Shall the sword devour for *e* ... 2Sa 2:26 5331
guiltless before the LORD for *e* ... 2Sa 3:28 5769
the throne of his kingdom for *e* ... 2Sa 7:13 5769
be established for *e* before thee ... 2Sa 7:16 5769
throne shall be established for *e* ... 2Sa 7:16 5769
to be a people unto thee for *e* ... 2Sa 7:24 5769
his house, establish it for *e* ... 2Sa 7:25 5769
let thy name be magnified for *e* ... 2Sa 7:26 5769
it may continue for *e* before thee ... 2Sa 7:29 5769
of thy servant be blessed for *e* ... 2Sa 7:29 5769
Let my lord king David live for *e* ... 1Kin 1:31 5769
upon the head of his seed for *e* ... 1Kin 2:33 5769
be peace for *e* from the LORD ... 1Kin 2:33 5769
established before the LORD for *e* ... 1Kin 2:45
for Hiram was *e* a lover of David ... 1Kin 5:1 3605,3117
place for thee to abide in for *e* ... 1Kin 8:13 5769
built, to put my name there for *e* ... 1Kin 9:3 5769
of thy kingdom upon Israel for *e* ... 1Kin 9:5 5769
the LORD loved Israel for *e* ... 1Kin 10:9 5769
the seed of David, but not for *e* ... 1Kin 11:39 3605,3117
they will be thy servants for *e* ... 1Kin 12:7 3605,3117
unto thee, and unto thy seed for *e* ... 2Kin 5:27 5769
Israel, will I put my name for *e* ... 2Kin 21:7 5769
and to minister unto him for *e* ... 1Chr 15:2 5769
for his mercy endureth for *e* ... 1Chr 16:34 5769
be the LORD God of Israel for *e* ... 1Chr 16:36 5769
LORD God of Israel for *e* and *e* ... 1Chr 16:36 5769
because his mercy endureth for *e* ... 1Chr 16:41 5769
I will stablish his throne for *e* ... 1Chr 17:12 5769
mine house and in my kingdom for *e* ... 1Chr 17:14 5769
thou make thine own people for *e* ... 1Chr 17:22 5769
his house be established for *e* ... 1Chr 17:23 5769
thy name may be magnified for *e* ... 1Chr 17:24 5769
that it may be before thee for *e* ... 1Chr 17:27 5769
and it shall be blessed for *e* ... 1Chr 17:27 5769
of his kingdom over Israel for *e* ... 1Chr 22:10 5769
holy things, he and his sons for *e* ... 1Chr 23:13 5769
and to bless in his name for *e* ... 1Chr 23:13 5769
they may dwell in Jerusalem for *e* ... 1Chr 23:25 5769
to be king over Israel for *e* ... 1Chr 28:4 5769
will establish his kingdom for *e* ... 1Chr 28:7 5769
for your children after you for *e* ... 1Chr 28:8 5769
him, he will cast thee off for *e* ... 1Chr 28:9 5703
Israel our father, for *e* and *e* ... 1Chr 29:10 5704,5769
fathers, keep this for *e* in the ... 1Chr 29:18 5769
is an ordinance for *e* to Israel ... 2Chr 2:4 5769
for his mercy endureth for *e* ... 2Chr 5:13 5769
and a place for thy dwelling for *e* ... 2Chr 6:2 5769
for his mercy endureth for *e* ... 2Chr 7:3 5769
because his mercy endureth for *e* ... 2Chr 7:6 5769
that my name may be there for *e* ... 2Chr 7:16 5769
Israel, to establish them for *e* ... 2Chr 9:8 5769
they will be thy servants for *e* ... 2Chr 10:7 3605,3117
over Israel to David for *e* ... 2Chr 13:5 5769
seed of Abraham thy friend for *e* ... 2Chr 20:7 5769
for his mercy endureth for *e* ... 2Chr 20:21 5769
light to him and to his sons for *e* ... 2Chr 21:7 3605,3117
which he hath sanctified for *e* ... 2Chr 30:8 5769
Jerusalem shall my name be for *e* ... 2Chr 33:4 5769
Israel, will I put my name for *e* ... 2Chr 33:7 5865
endureth for *e* toward Israel ... Ezr 3:11 5769
their peace or their wealth for *e* ... Ezr 9:12 5769
to your children for *e* ... Ezr 9:12 5769
the king, Let the king live for *e* ... Neh 2:3 5769
the LORD your God for *e* and *e* ... Neh 9:5 5769
the congregation of God for *e* ... Neh 13:1 5769
who *e* perished, being innocent ... Job 4:7
they perish for *e* without any ... Job 4:20 5331
Thou prevailest for *e* against him ... Job 14:20 5331
pen and lead in the rock for *e* ... Job 19:24 5703
perish for *e* like his own dung ... Job 20:7 5331
be delivered for *e* from my judge ... Job 23:7 5331
yea, he doth establish them for *e* ... Job 36:7 5331
thou take him for a servant for *e* ... Job 41:4 5769
let them *e* shout for joy, because ... Ps 5:11 5769
hast put out their name for *e* ... Ps 9:5 5769
put out their name for *e* and *e* ... Ps 9:5 5703
But the LORD shall endure for *e* ... Ps 9:7 5769
the poor shall not perish for *e* ... Ps 9:18 5703
The LORD is King for *e* and *e* ... Ps 10:16 5769
The LORD is King for *e* and *e* ... Ps 10:16 5703
them from this generation for *e* ... Ps 12:7 5769
forget me, O Lord? for *e*? ... Ps 13:1 5331
the LORD is clean, enduring for *e* ... Ps 19:9 5703
it him, even length of days for *e* ... Ps 21:4 5769
even length of days for *e* and *e* ... Ps 21:4 5703
hast made him most blessed for *e* ... Ps 21:6 5703
your heart shall live for *e* ... Ps 22:26 5703
in the house of the LORD for *e* ... Ps 23:6 753,3117
for they have been *e* of old ... Ps 25:6
Mine eyes are *e* toward the LORD ... Ps 25:15 8548
them also, and lift them up for *e* ... Ps 28:9 5769
yea, the LORD sitteth King for *e* ... Ps 29:10 5769
will give thanks unto thee for *e* ... Ps 30:12 5769
of the LORD standeth for *e* ... Ps 33:11 5769
their inheritance shall be for *e* ... Ps 37:18 5769
He is *e* merciful, and lendeth ... Ps 37:26 3605,3117
they are preserved for *e* ... Ps 37:28 5769
the land, and dwell therein for *e* ... Ps 37:29 5703
settest me before thy face for *e* ... Ps 41:12 5769
long, and praise thy name for *e* ... Ps 44:8 5769
arise, cast us not off for *e* ... Ps 44:23 5331
God hath blessed thee for *e* ... Ps 45:2 5769
Thy throne, O God, is for *e* ... Ps 45:6 5769
throne, O God, is for *e* and *e* ... Ps 45:6 5703
the people praise thee for *e* ... Ps 45:17 5769
people praise thee for *e* and *e* ... Ps 45:17 5703
God will establish it for *e* ... Ps 48:8 5769
For this God is our God for *e* ... Ps 48:14 5769
this God is our God for *e* and *e* ... Ps 48:14 5703
is precious, and it ceaseth for *e* ... Ps 49:8 5769
That he should still live for *e* ... Ps 49:9 5331
their houses shall continue for *e* ... Ps 49:11 5769
and my sin is *e* before me ... Ps 51:3 8548
shall likewise destroy thee for *e* ... Ps 52:5 5331
I trust in the mercy of God for *e* ... Ps 52:8 5769
in the mercy of God for *e* and *e* ... Ps 52:8 5703
I will praise thee for *e*, because ... Ps 52:9 5769
abide in thy tabernacle for *e* ... Ps 61:4 5769
He shall abide before God for *e* ... Ps 61:7 5769
I sing praise unto thy name for *e* ... Ps 61:8 5703
He ruleth by his power for *e* ... Ps 66:7 5769
the LORD will dwell in it for *e* ... Ps 68:16 5331
His name shall endure for *e* ... Ps 72:17 5769
be his glorious name for *e* ... Ps 72:19 5769
of my heart, and my portion for *e* ... Ps 73:26 5769
why hast thou cast us off for *e* ... Ps 74:1 5331
enemy blaspheme thy name for *e* ... Ps 74:10 5331
congregation of thy poor for *e* ... Ps 74:19 5331
But I will declare for *e* ... Ps 75:9 5769
Will the Lord cast off for *e* ... Ps 77:7 5769
Is his mercy clean gone for *e* ... Ps 77:8 5331
which he hath established for *e* ... Ps 78:69 5769
wilt thou be angry for *e* ... Ps 79:5 5331
will give thee thanks for *e* ... Ps 79:13 5769
time should have endured for *e* ... Ps 81:15 5769
be confounded and troubled for *e* ... Ps 83:17 5703
Wilt thou be angry with us for *e* ... Ps 85:5 5769
of the mercies of the LORD for *e* ... Ps 89:1 5769
Mercy shall be built up for *e* ... Ps 89:2 5769
Thy seed will I establish for *e* ... Ps 89:4 5769
also will I make to endure for *e* ... Ps 89:29 5703
His seed shall endure for *e* ... Ps 89:36 5769
be established for *e* as the moon ... Ps 89:37 5769
wilt thou hide thyself for *e* ... Ps 89:46 5331
or *e* thou hadst formed the earth ... Ps 90:2
they shall be destroyed for *e* ... Ps 92:7 5703
thine house, O LORD, for *e* ... Ps 93:5 753,3117
thou, O LORD, shalt endure for *e* ... Ps 102:12 5769
will he keep his anger for *e* ... Ps 103:9 5769
it should not be removed for *e* ... Ps 104:5 5769,5703
of the LORD shall endure for *e* ... Ps 104:31 5769
remembered his covenant for *e* ... Ps 105:8 5769
for his mercy endureth for *e* ... Ps 106:1 5769
for his mercy endureth for *e* ... Ps 107:1 5769
Thou art a priest for *e* after the ... Ps 110:4 5769
his righteousness endureth for *e* ... Ps 111:3 5703
he will *e* be mindful of his ... Ps 111:5 5769
They stand fast for *e* and *e*, and ... Ps 111:8 5703
They stand fast for *e* and *e* ... Ps 111:8 5769
hath commanded his covenant for *e* ... Ps 111:9 5769
his praise endureth for *e* ... Ps 111:10 5769
his righteousness endureth for *e* ... Ps 112:3 5703
he shall not be moved for *e* ... Ps 112:6 5769
his righteousness endureth for *e* ... Ps 112:9 5703
truth of the LORD endureth for *e* ... Ps 117:2 5769
because his mercy endureth for *e* ... Ps 118:1 5769
that his mercy endureth for *e* ... Ps 118:2 5769
that his mercy endureth for *e* ... Ps 118:3 5769
that his mercy endureth for *e* ... Ps 118:4 5769
for his mercy endureth for *e* ... Ps 118:29 5769
I keep thy law continually for *e* ... Ps 119:44 5769
thy law continually for *e* and *e* ... Ps 119:44 5703
For *e*, O LORD, thy word is ... Ps 119:89 5769
for they are *e* with me ... Ps 119:98 5769
have I taken as an heritage for *e* ... Ps 119:111 5769
that thou hast founded them for *e* ... Ps 119:152 5769
judgments endureth for *e* ... Ps 119:160 5769
be removed, but abideth for *e* ... Ps 125:1 5769
people from henceforth even for *e* ... Ps 125:2 5769
the LORD from henceforth and for *e* ... Ps 131:3 5769
This is my rest for *e* ... Ps 132:14 5703
Thy name, O LORD, endureth for *e* ... Ps 135:13 5769
for his mercy endureth for *e* ... Ps 136:1 5769
for his mercy endureth for *e* ... Ps 136:2 5769
for his mercy endureth for *e* ... Ps 136:3 5769
for his mercy endureth for *e* ... Ps 136:4 5769
for his mercy endureth for *e* ... Ps 136:5 5769
for his mercy endureth for *e* ... Ps 136:6 5769
for his mercy endureth for *e* ... Ps 136:7 5769
for his mercy endureth for *e* ... Ps 136:8 5769
for his mercy endureth for *e* ... Ps 136:9 5769
for his mercy endureth for *e* ... Ps 136:10 5769
for his mercy endureth for *e* ... Ps 136:11 5769
for his mercy endureth for *e* ... Ps 136:12 5769
for his mercy endureth for *e* ... Ps 136:13 5769
for his mercy endureth for *e* ... Ps 136:14 5769
for his mercy endureth for *e* ... Ps 136:15 5769
for his mercy endureth for *e* ... Ps 136:16 5769
for his mercy endureth for *e* ... Ps 136:17 5769
for his mercy endureth for *e* ... Ps 136:18 5769
for his mercy endureth for *e* ... Ps 136:19 5769
for his mercy endureth for *e* ... Ps 136:20 5769
for his mercy endureth for *e* ... Ps 136:21 5769
for his mercy endureth for *e* ... Ps 136:22 5769
for his mercy endureth for *e* ... Ps 136:23 5769
for his mercy endureth for *e* ... Ps 136:24 5769
for his mercy endureth for *e* ... Ps 136:25 5769
for his mercy endureth for *e* ... Ps 136:26 5769
thy mercy, O LORD, endureth for *e* ... Ps 138:8 5769
and I will bless thy name for *e* ... Ps 145:1 5769
will bless thy name for *e* and *e* ... Ps 145:1 5703
and I will praise thy name for *e* ... Ps 145:2 5769
praise thy name for *e* and *e* ... Ps 145:2 5703
flesh bless his holy name for *e* ... Ps 145:21 5769
bless his holy name for *e* and *e* ... Ps 145:21 5703
which keepeth truth for *e* ... Ps 146:6 5769
The LORD shall reign for *e* ... Ps 146:10 5769

hath also stablished them for e ... Ps 148:6 5703
stablished them for e and e ... Ps 148:6 5769
the beginning, or e the earth was ... Prov 8:23 6924
truth shall be established for e ... Prov 12:19 5703
For riches are not for e ... Prov 27:24 5769
throne shall be established for e ... Prov 29:14 5703
but the earth abideth for e ... Eccl 1:4 5769
wise more than of the fool for e ... Eccl 2:16 5769
God doeth, it shall be for e ... Eccl 3:14 5769
they any more a portion for e in ... Eccl 9:6 5769
Or e the silver cord be loosed, ... Eccl 12:6
Or e I was aware, my soul made me ... Song 6:12 3808
from henceforth even for e ... Is 9:7 5769
Trust ye in the LORD for e ... Is 26:4 5703
he will not e be threshing it ... Is 28:28 5331
may be for the time to come for e ... Is 30:8 5703
the time to come for e and e ... Is 30:8 5769
and towers shall be for dens for e ... Is 32:14 5769
quietness and assurance for e ... Is 32:17 5769
stakes thereof shall e be removed ... Is 33:20 5331
smoke thereof shall go up for e ... Is 34:10 5769
none shall pass through it for e ... Is 34:10 5331
pass through it for e and e ... Is 34:10 5769
they shall possess it for e ... Is 34:17 5769
word of our God shall stand for e ... Is 40:8 5769
saidst, I shall be a lady for e ... Is 47:7 5769
but my salvation shall be for e ... Is 51:6 5769
my righteousness shall be for e ... Is 51:8 5769
For I will not contend for e ... Is 57:16 5769
LORD, from henceforth and for e ... Is 59:21 5769
they shall inherit the land for e ... Is 60:21 5769
neither remember iniquity for e ... Is 64:9 5703
rejoice for e in that which I ... Is 65:18 5703
Will he reserve his anger for e ... Jer 3:5
and I will not keep anger for e ... Jer 3:12 5769
to your fathers, for e and e ... Jer 7:7 5769
anger, which shall burn for e ... Jer 17:4 5769
and this city shall remain for e ... Jer 17:25 5769
and to your fathers for e and e ... Jer 25:5 5769
being a nation before me for e ... Jer 31:36 3605,3117
nor thrown down any more for e ... Jer 31:40 5769
way, that they may fear me for e ... Jer 32:39 3605,3117
for his mercy endureth for e ... Jer 33:11 5769
neither ye, nor your sons for e ... Jer 35:6 5769
a man to stand before me for e ... Jer 35:19 3605,3117
dragons, and a desolation for e ... Jer 49:33 5769
shall be no more inhabited for e ... Jer 50:39 5331
but thou shalt be desolate for e ... Jer 51:26 5769
that it shall be desolate for e ... Jer 51:62 5769
the Lord will not cast off for e ... Lam 3:31 5769
Thou, O LORD, remainest for e ... Lam 5:19 5769
dost thou forget us for e ... Lam 5:20 5331
their children's children for e ... Eze 37:25 5769
David shall be their prince for e ... Eze 37:25 5769
of the children of Israel for e ... Eze 43:7 5769
dwell in the midst of them for e ... Eze 43:9 5769
in Syriack, O king, live for e ... Dan 2:4 5957
Blessed be the name of God for e ... Dan 2:20 5957
be the name of God for e and e ... Dan 2:20 5957
kingdoms, and it shall stand for e ... Dan 2:44 5957
O king, live for e ... Dan 3:9 5957
and honoured him that liveth for e ... Dan 4:34 5957
spake and said, O king, live for e ... Dan 5:10 5957
unto him, King Darius, live for e ... Dan 6:6 5757
unto the king, O king, live for e ... Dan 6:21 5957
all their bones in pieces or e ... Dan 6:24 3809
the living God, and stedfast for e ... Dan 6:26 5957
the kingdom for e, even for e ... Dan 7:18 5957
for e, even for e and e ... Dan 7:18 5957
righteousness as the stars for e ... Dan 12:3 5769
as the stars for e and e ... Dan 12:3 5703
for e that it shall be for a time ... Dan 12:7 5769
I will betroth thee unto me for e ... Hos 2:19 5769
there hath not been e the like ... Joel 2:2 5769
But Judah shall dwell for e ... Joel 3:20 5769
and he kept his wrath for e ... Amos 1:11 5331
and thou shalt be cut off for e ... Obad 10 5769
with her bars was about me for e ... Jonah 2:6 5769
have ye taken away my glory for e ... Mic 2:9 5769
name of the LORD our God for e ... Mic 4:5 5769
of the LORD our God for e and e ... Mic 4:5 5703
Zion from henceforth, even for e ... Mic 4:7 5769
he retaineth not his anger for e ... Mic 7:18 5703
the prophets, do they live for e ... Zec 1:5 5769
the LORD hath indignation for e ... Mal 1:4 5769
and the power, and the glory, for e ... Mt 6:13 165
grow on thee henceforward for e ... Mt 21:19 165
to this time, no, nor e shall be ... Mt 24:21 3364
eat fruit of thee hereafter for e ... Mk 11:14 165
to do as he had e done unto them ... Mk 15:8 104
over the house of Jacob for e ... Lk 1:33 165
to Abraham, and to his seed for e ... Lk 1:55 165
unto him, Son, thou art e with me ... Lk 15:31 3842
told me all things that e I did ... Jn 4:29 3745
He told me all that e I did ... Jn 4:39 3745
this bread, he shall live for e ... Jn 6:51 165
of this bread shall live for e ... Jn 6:58 165
abideth not in the house for e ... Jn 8:35 165
but the Son abideth e ... Jn 8:35 165
All that e came before me are ... Jn 10:8 3745
the law that Christ abideth for e ... Jn 12:34 165
that he may abide with you for e ... Jn 14:16 165
I e taught in the synagogue, and ... Jn 18:20 3842
or e he come near, are ready to ... Acts 23:15 4253
the Creator, who is blessed for e ... Rom 1:25 165
is over all, God blessed for e ... Rom 9:5 165
to whom be glory for e ... Rom 11:36 165
glory through Jesus Christ for e ... Rom 16:27 165
his righteousness remaineth for e ... 2Cor 9:9 165
To whom be glory for e and e ... Gal 1:5 165
For no man e yet hated his own ... Eph 5:29 4218
our Father be glory for e and e ... Phil 4:20 165
so shall we e be with the Lord ... 1Th 4:17 3842
but e follow that which is good, ... 1Th 5:15 3842
be honour and glory for e and e ... 1Ti 1:17 165
E learning, and never able to come ... 2Ti 3:7 3842
to whom be glory for e and e ... 2Ti 4:18 165
thou shouldest receive him for e ... Philem 15 166
throne, O God, is for e and e ... Heb 1:8 165
Thou art a priest for e after the ... Heb 5:6 165
made an high priest for e after ... Heb 6:20 165
Thou art a priest for e after the ... Heb 7:17 165
Thou art a priest for e after the ... Heb 7:21 165
this man, because he continueth e ... Heb 7:24 165
seeing he e liveth to make ... Heb 7:25 3842
one sacrifice for sins for e ... Heb 10:12 1336
for e them that are sanctified ... Heb 10:14 1336
yesterday, and to day, and for e ... Heb 13:8 165
to whom be glory for e and e ... Heb 13:21 165
which liveth and abideth for e ... 1Pet 1:23 165
word of the Lord endureth for e ... 1Pet 1:25 165
praise and dominion for e and e ... 1Pet 4:11 165
glory and dominion for e and e ... 1Pet 5:11 165
of darkness is reserved for e ... 2Pet 2:17 165
him be glory both now and for e ... 2Pet 3:18 2250,165
the will of God abideth for e ... 1Jn 2:17 165
in us, and shall be with us for e ... 2Jn 2 165
the blackness of darkness for e ... Jude 13 165
and power, both now and e ... Jude 25 3956,165
glory and dominion for e and e ... Rev 1:6 165
throne, who liveth for e and e ... Rev 4:9 165
him that liveth for e and e ... Rev 4:10 165
and unto the Lamb for e and e ... Rev 5:13 165
him that liveth for e and e ... Rev 5:14 165
be unto our God for e and e ... Rev 7:12 165
by him that liveth for e and e ... Rev 10:6 165
and he shall reign for e and e ... Rev 11:15 165
ascendeth up for e and e ... Rev 14:11 165
of God, who liveth for e and e ... Rev 15:7 165
her smoke rose up for e and e ... Rev 19:3 165
day and night for e and e ... Rev 20:10 165
and they shall reign for e and e ... Rev 22:5 165

EVERLASTING {97}
the e covenant between God ... Gen 9:16 5769
generations for an e covenant ... Gen 17:7 5769
of Canaan, for an e possession ... Gen 17:8 5769
in your flesh for an e covenant ... Gen 17:13 5769
with him for an e covenant ... Gen 17:19 5769
the name of the LORD, the e God ... Gen 21:33 5769
after thee for an e possession ... Gen 48:4 5769
the utmost bound of the e hills ... Gen 49:26 5769
an e priesthood throughout their ... Ex 40:15 5769
shall be an e statute unto you ... Lev 16:34 5769
of Israel by an e covenant ... Lev 24:8 5769
the covenant of an e priesthood ... Num 25:13 5769
and underneath are the e arms ... Deut 33:27 5769
hath made with me an e covenant ... 2Sa 23:5 5769
and to Israel for an e covenant ... 1Chr 16:17 5769
and be ye lifted up, ye e doors ... Ps 24:7 5769
even lift them up, ye e doors ... Ps 24:9 5769
Israel from e, and to e ... Ps 41:13 5769
world, even from e to e ... Ps 90:2 5769
thou art from e ... Ps 93:2 5769
his mercy is e ... Ps 100:5 5769
e to e upon them that ... Ps 103:17 5769
and to Israel for an e covenant ... Ps 105:10 5769
of Israel from e to e ... Ps 106:48 5769
shall be in e remembrance ... Ps 112:6 5769
is an e righteousness, and thy law ... Ps 119:142 5769
of thy testimonies is e ... Ps 119:144 5769
in me, and lead me in the way e ... Ps 139:24 5769
Thy kingdom is an e kingdom ... Ps 145:13 5769
I was set up from e, from the ... Prov 8:23 5769
the righteous is an e foundation ... Prov 10:25 5769
The e Father, The Prince of Peace ... Is 9:6 5703
ordinance, broken the e covenant ... Is 24:5 5769
in the LORD JEHOVAH is e strength ... Is 26:4 5769
us shall dwell with e burnings ... Is 33:14 5769
songs and e joy upon their heads ... Is 35:10 5769
thou not heard, that the e God ... Is 40:28 5769
in the LORD with an e salvation ... Is 45:17 5769
e joy shall be upon their head ... Is 51:11 5769
but with e kindness will I have ... Is 54:8 5769
I will make an e covenant with ... Is 55:3 5769
for an e sign that shall not be ... Is 55:13 5769
I will give them an e name ... Is 56:5 5769
shall be unto thee an e light ... Is 60:19 5769
the LORD shall be thine e light ... Is 60:20 5769
e joy shall be unto them ... Is 61:7 5769
I will make an e covenant with ... Is 61:8 5769
them, to make himself an e name ... Is 63:12 5769
thy name is from e ... Is 63:16 5769
is the living God, and an e king ... Jer 10:10 5769
their e confusion shall never be ... Jer 20:11 5769
I will bring an e reproach upon ... Jer 23:40 5769
I have loved thee with an e love ... Jer 31:3 5769
I will make an e covenant with ... Jer 32:40 5769
establish unto thee an e covenant ... Eze 16:60 5769
it shall be an e covenant with ... Eze 37:26 5769
his kingdom is an e kingdom ... Dan 4:3 5957
whose dominion is an e dominion ... Dan 4:34 5957
his dominion is an e dominion ... Dan 7:14 5957
whose kingdom is an e kingdom ... Dan 7:27 5957
to bring in e righteousness, and ... Dan 9:24 5769
earth shall awake, some to e life ... Dan 12:2 5769
and some to shame and e contempt ... Dan 12:2 5769
have been from of old, from e ... Mic 5:2 5769
Art thou not from e, O LORD my ... Hab 1:12 6924
the e mountains were scattered, ... Hab 3:6 5703
his ways are e ... Hab 3:6 5769
two feet to be cast into e fire ... Mt 18:8 166
and shall inherit e life ... Mt 19:29 166
from me, ye cursed, into e fire ... Mt 25:41 166
shall go away into e punishment ... Mt 25:46 166
receive you into e habitations ... Lk 16:9 166
and in the world to come life e ... Lk 18:30 166
not perish, but have e life ... Jn 3:16 166
believeth on the Son hath e life ... Jn 3:36 166
of water springing up into e life ... Jn 4:14 166
on him that sent me, hath e life ... Jn 5:24 166
meat which endureth unto e life ... Jn 6:27 166
believeth on him, may have e life ... Jn 6:40 166
that believeth on me hath e life ... Jn 6:47 166
that his commandment is life e ... Jn 12:50 166
yourselves unworthy of e life ... Acts 13:46 166
unto holiness, and the end e life ... Rom 6:22 166
to the commandment of the e God ... Rom 16:26 166
shall of the Spirit reap life e ... Gal 6:8 166
Who shall be punished with e ... 2Th 1:9 166
and hath given us e consolation ... 2Th 2:16 166
believe on him to life e ... 1Ti 1:16 166
to whom be honour and power e ... 1Ti 6:16 166
the blood of the e covenant ... Heb 13:20 166
into the e kingdom of our Lord ... 2Pet 1:11 166
he hath reserved in e chains ... Jude 6 126
having the e gospel to preach ... Rev 14:6 166

EVERMORE {26}
be only oppressed and spoiled e ... Deut 28:29 3605,3117
unto David, and to his seed for e ... 2Sa 22:51 5769
you, ye shall observe to do for e ... 2Kin 17:37 3605,3117
throne shall be established for e ... 1Chr 17:14 5769
hand there are pleasures for e ... Ps 16:11 5331
to David, and to his seed for e ... Ps 18:50 5769
and dwell for e ... Ps 37:27 5769
doth his promise fail for e ... Ps 77:8 1755
and I will glorify thy name for e ... Ps 86:12 5769
mercy will I keep for him for e ... Ps 89:28 5769
Blessed be the LORD for e ... Ps 89:52 5769
thou, LORD, art most high for e ... Ps 92:8 5769
seek his face e ... Ps 105:4 8548
unto all generations for e ... Ps 106:31 5769
from this time forth and for e ... Ps 113:2 5769
from this time forth and for e ... Ps 115:18 5769
this time forth, and even for e ... Ps 121:8 5769
also sit upon thy throne for e ... Ps 132:12 5703
the blessing, even life for e ... Ps 133:3 5769
in the midst of them for e ... Eze 37:26 5769
be in the midst of them for e ... Eze 37:28 5769
him, Lord, e give us this bread ... Jn 6:34 3842
Christ, which is blessed for e ... 2Cor 11:31 3588,165
Rejoice e ... 1Th 5:16 3842
the Son, who is consecrated for e ... Heb 7:28 3588,165
and, behold, I am alive for e ... Rev 1:18 3588,165

EVERY See APPENDIX.

EVI *(e'-vi)* {2} *A Midian prince.*
namely, E, and Rekem, and Zur, and ... Num 31:8 189
with the princes of Midian, E ... Josh 13:21 189

EVIDENCE {7}
And I subscribed the e, and sealed ... Jer 32:10 5612
So I took the e of the purchase, ... Jer 32:11 5612
I gave the e of the purchase unto ... Jer 32:12 5612
this e of the purchase, both ... Jer 32:14 5612
sealed, and this e which is open ... Jer 32:14 5612
Now when I had delivered the e of ... Jer 32:16 5612
for, the e of things not seen ... Heb 11:1 1650

EVIDENCES {2}
Take these e, this evidence of ... Jer 32:14 5612
fields for money, and subscribe e ... Jer 32:44 5612

EVIDENT {5}
for it is e unto you if I lie ... Job 6:28 5921,6440
law in the sight of God, it is e ... Gal 3:11 1212
to them an e token of perdition ... Phil 1:28 1732
For it is e that our Lord sprang ... Heb 7:14 4271
And it is yet far more e ... Heb 7:15 2612

EVIDENTLY {2}
He saw in a vision e about the ... Acts 10:3 5320
Christ hath been e set forth ... Gal 3:1 4270

EVIL {616}
tree of knowledge of good and e ... Gen 2:9 7451
of the knowledge of good and e ... Gen 2:17 7451
be as gods, knowing good and e ... Gen 3:5 7451
as one of us, to know good and e ... Gen 3:22 7451
his heart was only e continually ... Gen 6:5 7451
man's heart is e from his youth ... Gen 8:21 7451
the mountain, lest some e take me ... Gen 19:19 7451
unto his father their e report ... Gen 37:2 7451
Some e beast hath devoured him ... Gen 37:20 7451
an e beast hath devoured him ... Gen 37:33 7451
have ye rewarded e for good ... Gen 44:4 7451
ye have done e in so doing ... Gen 44:5 7489
lest peradventure I see the e ... Gen 44:34 7451
e have the days of the years of ... Gen 47:9 7451
which redeemed me from all e ... Gen 48:16 7451
all the e which we did unto him ... Gen 50:15 7451
for they did unto thee e ... Gen 50:17 7451
for you, ye thought e against me ... Gen 50:20 7451
did see that they were in e case ... Ex 5:19 7451
thou so e entreated this people ... Ex 5:22 7489
he hath done e to this people ... Ex 5:23 7489
for e is before you ... Ex 10:10 7451

not follow a multitude to do *e* .... Ex 23:2 7451
repent of this *e* against thy .... Ex 32:12 7451
the LORD repented of the *e* which .... Ex 32:14 7451
the people heard these *e* tidings .... Ex 33:4 7451
pronouncing with his lips to do *e* .... Lev 5:4 7489
I will rid *e* beasts out of the .... Lev 26:6 7451
they brought up an *e* report of .... Num 13:32 1681
I bear with this *e* congregation .... Num 14:27 7451
it unto all this *e* congregation .... Num 14:35 7451
up the *e* report upon the land .... Num 14:37 7451
to bring us in unto this *e* place .... Num 20:5 7451
that had done *e* in the sight of .... Num 32:13 7451
not one of these men of this *e* .... Deut 1:35 7451
no knowledge between good and *e* .... Deut 1:39 7451
shall do *e* in the sight of the .... Deut 4:25 7451
none of the *e* diseases of Egypt .... Deut 7:15 7451
So shalt thou put the *e* away from .... Deut 13:5 7451
thine eye be *e* against thy poor .... Deut 15:9 7489
put the *e* away from among you .... Deut 17:7 7451
shalt put away the *e* from Israel .... Deut 17:12 7451
put the *e* away from among you .... Deut 19:19 7451
no more any such *e* among you .... Deut 19:20 7451
so shalt thou put *e* away from .... Deut 21:21 7451
bring up an *e* name upon her, and .... Deut 22:14 7451
an *e* name upon a virgin of Israel .... Deut 22:19 7451
so shalt thou put *e* away from .... Deut 22:21 7451
shalt thou put away *e* from Israel .... Deut 22:22 7451
shalt put away *e* from among you .... Deut 22:24 7451
thou shalt put *e* away from among .... Deut 24:7 7451
And the Egyptians *e* entreated us .... Deut 26:6 7489
his eye shall be *e* toward his .... Deut 28:54 7489
her eye shall be *e* toward the .... Deut 28:56 7489
LORD shall separate him unto *e* .... Deut 29:21 7451
day life and good, and death and *e* .... Deut 30:15 7451
e will befall you in the latter .... Deut 31:29 7451
because ye will do *e* in the sight .... Deut 31:29 7451
LORD bring upon you all *e* things .... Josh 23:15 7451
if it seem *e* unto you to serve .... Josh 24:15 7489
did *e* in the sight of the LORD .... Judg 2:11 7451
the LORD was against them for *e* .... Judg 2:15 7451
did *e* in the sight of the LORD .... Judg 3:7 7451
the children of Israel did *e* .... Judg 3:12 7451
because they had done *e* in the .... Judg 3:12 7451
did *e* in the sight of the LORD .... Judg 4:1 7451
did *e* in the sight of the LORD .... Judg 6:1 7451
Then God sent an *e* spirit between .... Judg 9:23 7451
all the *e* of the men of Shechem .... Judg 9:57 7451
the children of Israel did *e* .... Judg 10:6 7451
the children of Israel did *e* .... Judg 13:1 7451
death, and put away *e* from Israel .... Judg 20:13 7451
knew not that *e* was near them .... Judg 20:34 7451
for they saw that *e* was come upon .... Judg 20:41 7451
for I hear of your *e* dealings by 1Sa 2:23 7451
then he hath done us this great *e* 1Sa 6:9 7451
added unto all our sins this *e* 1Sa 12:19 7451
didst *e* in the sight of the LORD 1Sa 15:19 7451
an *e* spirit from the LORD 1Sa 16:14 7451
an *e* spirit from God troubleth 1Sa 16:15 7451
when the *e* spirit from God is 1Sa 16:16 7451
when the *e* spirit from God was 1Sa 16:23 7451
the *e* spirit departed from him 1Sa 16:23 7451
that the *e* spirit from God came 1Sa 18:10 7451
the *e* spirit from the LORD was 1Sa 19:9 7451
then be sure that *e* is determined 1Sa 20:7 7451
for if I knew certainly that *e* 1Sa 20:9 7451
it please my father to do thee *e* 1Sa 20:13 7451
see that there is neither *e* nor 1Sa 24:11 7451
whereas I have rewarded thee *e* 1Sa 24:17 7451
was churlish and *e* in his doings 1Sa 25:3 7451
for *e* is determined against our 1Sa 25:17 7451
and he hath requited me *e* for good 1Sa 25:21 7451
and they that seek *e* to my lord 1Sa 25:26 7451
e hath not been found in thee all 1Sa 25:28 7451
and hath kept his servant from *e* 1Sa 25:39 7451
or what *e* is in mine hand 1Sa 26:18 7451
for I have not found *e* in thee 1Sa 29:6 7451
of *e* according to his wickedness 2Sa 3:39 7451
of the LORD, to do *e* in his sight 2Sa 12:9 7451
I will raise up *e* against thee 2Sa 12:11 7451
this *e* in sending me away is 2Sa 13:16 7451
bring *e* upon us, and smite the 2Sa 15:14 7451
LORD might bring *e* upon Absalom 2Sa 17:14 7451
e that befell thee from thy youth 2Sa 19:7 7451
can I discern between good and *e* 2Sa 19:35 7451
the LORD repented him of the *e* 2Sa 24:16 7451
neither adversary nor *e* occurrent 1Kin 5:4 7451
LORD brought upon them all this *e* 1Kin 9:9 7451
Solomon did *e* in the sight of the 1Kin 11:6 7451
returned not from his *e* way 1Kin 13:33 7451
But hast done *e* above all that 1Kin 14:9 7489
I will bring *e* upon the house of 1Kin 14:10 7451
Judah did *e* in the sight of the 1Kin 14:22 7451
he did *e* in the sight of the LORD 1Kin 15:26 7451
he did *e* in the sight of the LORD 1Kin 15:34 7451
even for all the *e* that he did in 1Kin 16:7 7451
doing *e* in the sight of the LORD 1Kin 16:19 7451
But Omri wrought *e* in the eyes of 1Kin 16:25 7451
Ahab the son of Omri did *e* in the 1Kin 16:30 7451
hast thou also brought *e* upon the 1Kin 17:20 7489
work *e* in the sight of the LORD 1Kin 21:20 7451
Behold, I will bring *e* upon thee 1Kin 21:21 7451
will not bring the *e* in his days 1Kin 21:29 7451
will I bring the *e* upon his house 1Kin 21:29 7451
good concerning me, but *e* 1Kin 22:8 7451
no good concerning me, but *e* 1Kin 22:18 7451
hath spoken *e* concerning thee 1Kin 22:23 7451
he did *e* in the sight of the LORD 1Kin 22:52 7451
he wrought *e* in the sight of the 2Kin 3:2 7451
Behold, this *e* is of the LORD 2Kin 6:33 7451
Because I know the *e* that thou 2Kin 8:12 7451
he did *e* in the sight of the LORD 2Kin 8:18 7451
did *e* in the sight of the LORD, ... 2Kin 8:27 7451
he did that which was *e* in the 2Kin 13:2 7451
he did that which was *e* in the 2Kin 13:11 7451
he did that which was *e* in the 2Kin 14:24 7451
he did that which was *e* in the 2Kin 15:9 7451
he did that which was *e* in the 2Kin 15:18 7451
he did that which was *e* in the 2Kin 15:24 7451
he did that which was *e* in the 2Kin 15:28 7451
he did that which was *e* in the 2Kin 17:2 7451
saying, Turn ye from your *e* ways 2Kin 17:13 7451
sold themselves to do *e* in the 2Kin 17:17 7451
he did that which was *e* in the 2Kin 21:2 7451
seduced them to do more *e* than 2Kin 21:9 7451
am bringing such *e* upon Jerusalem 2Kin 21:12 7451
done that which was *e* in my sight 2Kin 21:15 7451
in doing that which was *e* in the 2Kin 21:16 7451
he did that which was *e* in the 2Kin 21:20 7451
I will bring *e* upon this place, ... 2Kin 22:16 7451
eyes shall not see all the *e* 2Kin 22:20 7451
he did that which was *e* in the 2Kin 23:32 7451
he did that which was *e* in the 2Kin 23:37 7451
he did that which was *e* in the 2Kin 24:9 7451
he did that which was *e* in the 2Kin 24:19 7451
was *e* in the sight of the LORD 1Chr 2:3 7451
that thou wouldest keep me from *e* 1Chr 4:10 7451
because it went *e* with his house 1Chr 7:23 7451
and he repented him of the *e* 1Chr 21:15 7451
that have sinned and done *e* indeed 1Chr 21:17 7489
he brought all this *e* upon them 2Chr 7:22 7451
And he did *e*, because he prepared 2Chr 12:14 7451
good unto me, but always *e* 2Chr 18:7 7451
not prophesy good unto me, but *e* 2Chr 18:17 7451
LORD hath spoken *e* against thee 2Chr 18:22 7451
when *e* cometh upon us, as the 2Chr 20:9 7451
was *e* in the eyes of the LORD 2Chr 21:6 7451
Wherefore he did *e* in the sight 2Chr 22:4 7451
done that which was *e* in the eyes 2Chr 29:6 7451
But did that which was *e* in the 2Chr 33:2 7451
he wrought much *e* in the sight of 2Chr 33:6 7451
was *e* in the sight of the LORD 2Chr 33:22 7451
I will bring *e* upon this place, ... 2Chr 34:24 7451
the *e* that I will bring upon this 2Chr 34:28 7451
he did that which was *e* in the 2Chr 36:5 7451
he did that which was *e* in the 2Chr 36:9 7451
he did that which was *e* in the 2Chr 36:12 7451
is come upon us for our *e* deeds .... Ezr 9:13 7451
might have matter for an *e* report .... Neh 6:13 7451
they did *e* again before thee .... Neh 9:28 7451
understood of the *e* that Eliashib .... Neh 13:7 7451
What *e* thing is this that ye do, ... Neh 13:17 7451
our God bring all this *e* upon us .... Neh 13:18 7451
unto you to do all this great *e* .... Neh 13:27 7451
for he saw that there was *e* .... Est 7:7 7451
e that shall come unto my people .... Est 8:6 7451
that feared God, and eschewed *e* .... Job 1:1 7451
that feareth God, and escheweth *e* .... Job 1:8 7451
that feareth God, and escheweth *e* .... Job 2:3 7451
of God, and shall we not receive *e* .... Job 2:10 7451
all this *e* that was come upon him .... Job 2:11 7451
seven there shall no *e* touch thee .... Job 5:19 7451
neither will he help the *e* doers .... Job 8:20 7489
He *e* entreateth the barren that .... Job 24:21 7462
to depart from *e* is understanding .... Job 28:28 7451
for good, then *e* came unto me .... Job 30:26 7451
lifted up myself when *e* found him .... Job 31:29 7451
because of the pride of *e* men .... Job 35:12 7451
comforted him over all the *e* that .... Job 42:11 7451
neither shall *e* dwell with thee .... Ps 5:4 7451
If I have rewarded *e* unto him .... Ps 7:4 7451
arm of the wicked and the *e* man .... Ps 10:15 7451
nor doeth *e* to his neighbour, nor .... Ps 15:3 7451
For they intended *e* against thee .... Ps 21:11 7451
shadow of death, I will fear no *e* .... Ps 23:4 7451
Keep thy tongue from *e*, and thy .... Ps 34:13 7451
Depart from *e*, and do good .... Ps 34:14 7451
LORD is against them that do *e* .... Ps 34:16 7451
E shall slay the wicked .... Ps 34:21 7451
They rewarded me *e* for good to .... Ps 35:12 7451
he abhorreth not *e* .... Ps 36:4 7451
not thyself in any wise to do *e* .... Ps 37:8 7489
not be ashamed in the *e* time .... Ps 37:19 7451
Depart from *e*, and do good .... Ps 37:27 7451
They also that render *e* for good .... Ps 38:20 7451
and put to shame that wish me *e* .... Ps 40:14 7451
Mine enemies speak *e* of me .... Ps 41:5 7451
An *e* disease, say they, cleaveth .... Ps 41:8 1100
should I fear in the days of *e* .... Ps 49:5 7451
Thou givest thy mouth to *e* .... Ps 50:19 7451
and done this *e* in thy sight .... Ps 51:4 7451
Thou lovest *e* more than good .... Ps 52:3 7451
He shall reward *e* unto mine .... Ps 54:5 7451
thoughts are against me for *e* .... Ps 56:5 7451
themselves in an *e* matter .... Ps 64:5 7451
by sending *e* angels among them .... Ps 78:49 7451
the years wherein we have seen *e* .... Ps 90:15 7451
There shall no *e* befall thee .... Ps 91:10 7451
Ye that love the LORD, hate *e* .... Ps 97:10 7451
they have rewarded me *e* for good .... Ps 109:5 7451
them that speak *e* against my soul .... Ps 109:20 7451
shall not be afraid of *e* tidings .... Ps 112:7 7451
my feet from every *e* way, that I .... Ps 119:101 7451
shall preserve thee from all *e* .... Ps 121:7 7451
me, O LORD, from the *e* man .... Ps 140:1 7451
Let not an *e* speaker be .... Ps 140:11
e shall hunt the violent man to .... Ps 140:11 7451
not my heart to any *e* thing .... Ps 141:4 7451
For their feet run to *e*, and make .... Prov 1:16 7451
and shall be quiet from fear of *e* .... Prov 1:33 7451
thee from the way of the *e* man .... Prov 2:12 7451
Who rejoice to do *e*, and delight .... Prov 2:14 7451
fear the LORD, and depart from *e* .... Prov 3:7 7451
Devise not *e* against thy .... Prov 3:29 7451
and go not in the way of *e* men .... Prov 4:14 7451
remove thy foot from *e* .... Prov 4:27 7451
in all *e* in the midst of the .... Prov 5:14 7451
To keep thee from the *e* woman .... Prov 6:24 7451
The fear of the LORD is to hate *e* .... Prov 8:13 7451
pride, and arrogancy, and the *e* way .... Prov 8:13 7451
so he that pursueth *e* pursueth it .... Prov 11:19 7451
wicked desireth the net of *e* men .... Prov 12:12 7451
the heart of them that imagine *e* .... Prov 12:20 7451
There shall no *e* happen to the .... Prov 12:21 205
to fools to depart from *e* .... Prov 13:19 7451
E pursueth sinners .... Prov 13:21 7451
man feareth, and departeth from *e* .... Prov 14:16 7451
The *e* bow before the good .... Prov 14:19 7451
Do they not err that devise *e* .... Prov 14:22 7451
in every place, beholding the *e* .... Prov 15:3 7451
the days of the afflicted are *e* .... Prov 15:15 7451
the wicked poureth out *e* things .... Prov 15:28 7451
even the wicked for the day of *e* .... Prov 16:4 7451
of the LORD men depart from *e* .... Prov 16:6 7451
the upright is to depart from *e* .... Prov 16:17 7451
An ungodly man diggeth up *e* .... Prov 16:27 7451
his lips he bringeth *e* to pass .... Prov 16:30 7451
An *e* man seeketh only rebellion .... Prov 17:11 7451
Whoso rewardeth *e* for good .... Prov 17:13 7451
e shall not depart from his house .... Prov 17:13 7451
he shall not be visited with *e* .... Prov 19:23 7451
away all *e* with his eyes .... Prov 20:8 7451
Say not thou, I will recompense *e* .... Prov 20:22 7451
of a wound cleanseth away *e* .... Prov 20:30 7451
The soul of the wicked desireth *e* .... Prov 21:10 7451
A prudent man foreseeth the *e* .... Prov 22:3 7451
bread of him that hath an *e* eye .... Prov 23:6 7451
Be not thou envious against *e* men .... Prov 24:1 7451
He that deviseth to do *e* shall be .... Prov 24:8 7489
Fret not thyself because of *e* men .... Prov 24:19 7489
shall be no reward to the *e* man .... Prov 24:20 7451
A prudent man foreseeth the *e* .... Prov 27:12 7451
E men understand not judgment .... Prov 28:5 7451
to go astray in an *e* way, he .... Prov 28:10 7451
hasteth to be rich hath an *e* eye .... Prov 28:22 7451
of an *e* man there is a snare .... Prov 29:6 7451
or if thou hast thought *e* .... Prov 30:32
not *e* all the days of her life .... Prov 31:12 7451
This also is vanity and a great *e* .... Eccl 2:21 7451
who hath not seen the *e* work that .... Eccl 4:3 7451
they consider not that they do *e* .... Eccl 5:1 7451
There is a sore *e* which I have .... Eccl 5:13 7451
those riches perish by *e* travail .... Eccl 5:14 7451
And this also is a sore *e*, that in .... Eccl 5:16 7451
There is an *e* which I have seen .... Eccl 6:1 7451
is vanity, and it is an *e* disease .... Eccl 6:2 7451
stand not in an *e* thing .... Eccl 8:3 7451
commandment shall feel no *e* thing .... Eccl 8:5 7451
Because sentence against an *e* .... Eccl 8:11 7451
men is fully set in them to do *e* .... Eccl 8:11 7451
a sinner do *e* an hundred times .... Eccl 8:12 7451
This is an *e* among all things .... Eccl 9:3 7451
of the sons of men is full of *e* .... Eccl 9:3 7451
fishes that are taken in an *e* net .... Eccl 9:12 7451
sons of men snared in an *e* time .... Eccl 9:12 7451
There is an *e* which I have seen .... Eccl 10:5 7451
what *e* shall be upon the earth .... Eccl 11:2 7451
put away *e* from thy flesh .... Eccl 11:10 7451
while the *e* days come not, nor .... Eccl 12:1 7451
it be good, or whether it be *e* .... Eccl 12:14 7451
put away the *e* of your doings .... Is 1:16 7455
cease to do *e* .... Is 1:16 7489
have rewarded *e* unto themselves .... Is 3:9 7451
that call *e* good, and good *e* .... Is 5:20 7451
have taken *e* counsel against thee .... Is 7:5 7451
that he may know to refuse the *e* .... Is 7:15 7451
child shall know to refuse the *e* .... Is 7:16 7451
will punish the world for their *e* .... Is 13:11 7451
he also is wise, and will bring *e* .... Is 31:2 7451
also of the churl are *e* .... Is 32:7 7451
shutteth his eyes from seeing *e* .... Is 33:15 7451
yea, do good, or do *e*, that we .... Is 41:23 7489
I make peace, and create *e* .... Is 45:7 7451
Therefore shall *e* come upon thee .... Is 47:11 7451
keepeth his hand from doing any *e* .... Is 56:2 7451
is taken away from the *e* to come .... Is 57:1 7451
Their feet run to *e*, and they make .... Is 59:7 7451
from *e* maketh himself a prey .... Is 59:15 7451
but did *e* before mine eyes, and .... Is 65:12 7451
but they did *e* before mine eyes .... Is 66:4 7451
Out of the north an *e* shall break .... Jer 1:14 7451
e shall come upon them, saith the .... Jer 2:3 7451
and see that it is an *e* thing .... Jer 2:19 7451
done *e* things as thou couldest .... Jer 3:5 7451
the imagination of their *e* heart .... Jer 3:17 7451
because of the *e* of your doings .... Jer 4:4 7455
for I will bring *e* from the north .... Jer 4:6 7451
they are wise to do *e*, but to do .... Jer 4:22 7489
neither shall *e* come upon us .... Jer 5:12 7451
for *e* appeareth out of the north, ... Jer 6:1 7451
I will bring *e* upon this people, ... Jer 6:19 7451
the imagination of their *e* heart .... Jer 7:24 7451
of Judah have done *e* in my sight .... Jer 7:30 7451
them that remain of this *e* family .... Jer 8:3 7451
for they proceed from *e* to *e* .... Jer 9:3 7451

for they cannot do *e*, neither ... Jer 10:5 7489
the imagination of their *e* heart ... Jer 11:8 7451
Behold, I will bring *e* upon them ... Jer 11:11 7451
when thou doest *e*, then thou ... Jer 11:15 7451
hath pronounced *e* against thee ... Jer 11:17 7451
for the *e* of the house of Israel ... Jer 11:17 7451
for I will bring *e* upon the men ... Jer 11:23 7451
against all mine *e* neighbours ... Jer 12:14 7451
This *e* people, which refuse to ... Jer 13:10 7451
good, that are accustomed to do *e* ... Jer 13:23 7489
thee well in the time of *e* ... Jer 15:11 7451
all this great *e* against us ... Jer 16:10 7451
the imagination of his *e* heart ... Jer 16:12 7451
thou art my hope in the day of *e* ... Jer 17:17 7451
bring upon them the day of *e* ... Jer 17:18 7451
pronounced, turn from their *e* ... Jer 18:8 7451
I will repent of the *e* that I ... Jer 18:8 7451
If it do *e* in my sight, that it ... Jer 18:10 7451
I frame *e* against you, and devise ... Jer 18:11 7451
ye now every one from his *e* way ... Jer 18:11 7451
do the imagination of his *e* heart ... Jer 18:12 7451
Shall *e* be recompensed for good ... Jer 18:20 7451
I will bring *e* upon this place, ... Jer 19:3 7451
upon all her towns all the *e* that ... Jer 19:15 7451
my face against this city for *e* ... Jer 21:10 7451
because of the *e* of your doings ... Jer 21:12 7455
upon you the *e* of your doings ... Jer 23:2 7455
dried up, and their course is *e* ... Jer 23:10 7451
for I will bring *e* upon them ... Jer 23:12 7451
heart, No *e* shall come upon you ... Jer 23:17 7451
have turned them from their *e* way ... Jer 23:22 7451
from the *e* of their doings ... Jer 23:22 7455
and the *e*, very *e* ... Jer 24:3 7451
cannot be eaten, they are so *e* ... Jer 24:3 7455
And as the *e* figs, which cannot be ... Jer 24:8 7451
cannot be eaten, they are so *e* ... Jer 24:8 7455
now every one from his *e* way ... Jer 25:5 7451
from the *e* of your doings, and ... Jer 25:5 7455
I begin to bring *e* on the city ... Jer 25:29 7489
e shall go forth from nation to ... Jer 25:32 7451
and turn every man from his *e* way ... Jer 26:3 7451
that I may repent me of the *e* ... Jer 26:3 7451
because of the *e* of their doings ... Jer 26:3 7455
e that he hath pronounced against ... Jer 26:13 7451
the LORD repented him of the *e* ... Jer 26:19 7451
procure great *e* against our souls ... Jer 26:19 7451
great kingdoms, of war, and of *e* ... Jer 28:8 7451
thoughts of peace, and not of *e* ... Jer 29:11 7451
cannot be eaten, they are so *e* ... Jer 29:17 7455
all this *e* to come upon them ... Jer 32:23 7451
of Judah have only done *e* before ... Jer 32:30 7451
Because of all the *e* of the ... Jer 32:32 7451
all this great *e* upon this people ... Jer 32:42 7451
ye now every man from his *e* way ... Jer 35:15 7451
of Jerusalem all the *e* that I ... Jer 35:17 7451
of Judah will hear all the *e* ... Jer 36:3 7451
return every man from his *e* way ... Jer 36:3 7451
return every one from his *e* way ... Jer 36:7 7451
all the *e* that I have pronounced ... Jer 36:31 7451
these men have done *e* in all that ... Jer 38:9 7489
my words upon this city for *e* ... Jer 39:16 7451
pronounced this *e* upon this place ... Jer 40:2 7451
heard of all the *e* that Ishmael ... Jer 41:11 7451
it be good, or whether it be *e* ... Jer 42:6 7451
for I repent me of the *e* that I ... Jer 42:10 7451
the *e* that I will bring upon them ... Jer 42:17 7451
Ye have seen all the *e* that I ... Jer 44:2 7451
this great *e* against your souls ... Jer 44:7 7451
set my face against you for *e* ... Jer 44:11 7451
and were well, and saw no *e* ... Jer 44:17 7451
because of the *e* of your doings ... Jer 44:22 7455
therefore this *e* is happened unto ... Jer 44:23 7451
I will watch over them for *e* ... Jer 44:27 7451
surely stand against you for *e* ... Jer 44:29 7451
I will bring *e* upon all flesh, ... Jer 45:5 7451
they have devised *e* against it ... Jer 48:2 7451
for they have heard *e* tidings ... Jer 49:23 7451
and I will bring *e* upon them ... Jer 49:37 7451
of Chaldea all their *e* that they ... Jer 51:24 7451
wrote in a book all the *e* that ... Jer 51:60 7451
shall not rise from the *e* that I ... Jer 51:64 7451
he did that which was *e* in the ... Jer 52:2 7451
of the most High proceedeth not *e* ... Lam 3:38 7451
upon them the *e* arrows of famine ... Eze 5:16 7451
e beasts, and they shall bereave ... Eze 5:17 7451
that I would do this *e* unto them ... Eze 6:10 7451
Alas for all the *e* abominations ... Eze 6:11 7451
An *e*, an only *e*, behold, is ... Eze 7:5 7451
the *e* that I have brought upon ... Eze 14:22 7451
turn ye, turn ye from your *e* ways ... Eze 33:11 7451
will cause the *e* beasts to cease ... Eze 34:25 7451
shall ye remember your own *e* ways ... Eze 36:31 7451
and thou shalt think an *e* thought ... Eze 38:10 7451
us, by bringing upon us a great *e* ... Dan 9:12 7451
all this *e* is come upon us ... Dan 9:13 7451
hath the LORD watched upon the *e* ... Dan 9:14 7451
and repenteth him of the *e* ... Joel 2:13 7451
shall there be *e* in a city ... Amos 3:6 7451
for it is an *e* time ... Amos 5:13 7451
Seek good, and not *e*, that ye may ... Amos 5:14 7451
Hate the *e*, and love the good, and ... Amos 5:15 7451
Ye that put far away the *e* day ... Amos 6:3 7451
set mine eyes upon them for *e* ... Amos 9:4 7451
The *e* shall not overtake nor ... Amos 9:10 7451
for whose cause this *e* is upon us ... Jonah 1:7 7451
for whose cause this *e* is upon us ... Jonah 1:8 7451
turn every one from his *e* way ... Jonah 3:8 7451
that they turned from their *e* way ... Jonah 3:10 7451

and God repented of the *e*, that he ... Jonah 3:10 7451
and repentest thee of the *e* ... Jonah 4:2 7451
but *e* came down from the LORD ... Mic 1:12 7451
and work *e* upon their beds ... Mic 2:1 7451
this family do I devise an *e* ... Mic 2:3 7451
for this time is *e* ... Mic 2:3 7451
Who hate the good, and love the *e* ... Mic 3:2 7451
none *e* can come upon us ... Mic 3:11 7451
That they may do *e* with both ... Mic 7:3 7451
that imagineth *e* against the LORD ... Nah 1:11 7451
of purer eyes than to behold *e* ... Hab 1:13 7451
an *e* covetousness to his house ... Hab 2:9 7451
be delivered from the power of *e* ... Hab 2:9 7451
not do good, neither will he do *e* ... Zeph 1:12 7489
thou shalt not see *e* any more ... Zeph 3:15 7451
e ways, and from your *e* doings ... Zec 1:4 7451
let none of you imagine *e* against ... Zec 7:10 7451
let none of you imagine *e* in your ... Zec 8:17 7451
blind for sacrifice, is it not *e* ... Mal 1:8 7451
the lame and sick, is it not *e* ... Mal 1:8 7451
Every one that doeth *e* is good in ... Mal 2:17 7451
manner of *e* against you falsely ... Mt 5:11 *4190,4487*
is more than these cometh of *e* ... Mt 5:37 *4190*
unto you, That ye resist not *e* ... Mt 5:39 *4190*
maketh his sun to rise on the *e* ... Mt 5:45 *4190*
temptation, but deliver us from *e* ... Mt 6:13 *4190*
But if thine eye be *e*, thy whole ... Mt 6:23 *4190*
unto the day is the *e* thereof ... Mt 6:34 *2549*
If ye then, being *e*, know how to ... Mt 7:11 *4190*
tree bringeth forth *e* fruit ... Mt 7:17 *4190*
tree cannot bring forth *e* fruit ... Mt 7:18 *4190*
think ye *e* in your hearts ... Mt 9:4 *4190*
of vipers, how can ye, being *e* ... Mt 12:34 *4190*
an *e* man out of the *e* treasure ... Mt 12:35 *4190*
bringeth forth *e* things ... Mt 12:35 *4190*
answered and said unto them, An *e* ... Mt 12:39 *4190*
of the heart proceed *e* thoughts ... Mt 15:19 *4190*
Is thine eye *e*, because I am good ... Mt 20:15 *4190*
if that *e* servant shall say in ... Mt 24:48 *2556*
said, Why, what *e* hath he done ... Mt 27:23 *2556*
on the sabbath days, or to do *e* ... Mk 3:4 *2554*
proceed *e* thoughts, adulteries, ... Mk 7:21 *2556*
an *e* eye, blasphemy, pride, ... Mk 7:22 *4190*
All these *e* things come from ... Mk 7:23 *4190*
that can lightly speak *e* of me ... Mk 9:39 *2551*
them, Why, what *e* hath he done ... Mk 15:14 *2556*
days to do good, or to do *e* ... Lk 6:9 *2554*
you, and cast out your name as *e* ... Lk 6:22 *4190*
unto the unthankful and to the *e* ... Lk 6:35 *4190*
an *e* man out of the *e* treasure ... Lk 6:45 *4190*
bringeth forth that which is *e* ... Lk 6:45 *4190*
and plagues, and of *e* spirits ... Lk 7:21 *4190*
had been healed of *e* spirits ... Lk 8:2 *4190*
but deliver us from *e* ... Lk 11:4 *4190*
If ye then, being *e*, know how to ... Lk 11:13 *4190*
to say, This is an *e* generation ... Lk 11:29 *4190*
but when thine eye is *e*, thy body ... Lk 11:34 *4190*
and likewise Lazarus *e* things ... Lk 16:25 *2556*
time, Why, what *e* hath he done ... Lk 23:22 *2556*
light, because their deeds were *e* ... Jn 3:19 *4190*
one that doeth *e* hateth the light ... Jn 3:20 *5337*
and they that have done *e*, unto ... Jn 5:29 *5337*
it, that the works thereof are *e* ... Jn 7:7 *4190*
shouldest keep them from the *e* ... Jn 17:15 *4190*
answered him, If I have spoken *e* ... Jn 18:23 *2560*
bear witness of the *e* ... Jn 18:23 *2556*
entreat them *e* four hundred years ... Acts 7:6 *2559*
e entreated our fathers, so that ... Acts 7:19 *2559*
how much *e* he hath done to thy ... Acts 9:13 *2556*
made their minds *e* affected ... Acts 14:2 *2559*
but spake *e* of that way before ... Acts 19:9
the *e* spirits went out of them ... Acts 19:12 *4190*
to call over them which had *e* ... Acts 19:13 *4190*
the *e* spirit answered and said, ... Acts 19:15 *4190*
the man in whom the *e* spirit was ... Acts 19:16 *4190*
Thou shalt not speak *e* of the ... Acts 23:5 *2560*
saying, We find no *e* in this man ... Acts 23:9 *2556*
they have found any *e* doing in me ... Acts 24:20 *92*
boasters, inventors of *e* things ... Rom 1:30 *2556*
every soul of man that doeth *e* ... Rom 2:9 *2556*
affirm that we say,) Let us do *e* ... Rom 3:8 *2556*
but the *e* which I would not, that ... Rom 7:19 *2556*
do good, *e* is present with me ... Rom 7:21 *2556*
neither having done any good or *e* ... Rom 9:11 *2556*
Abhor that which is *e* ... Rom 12:9 *4190*
Recompense to no man *e* for *e* ... Rom 12:17 *2556*
Recompense to no man *e* for *e* ... Rom 12:17 *2556*
Be not overcome of *e* ... Rom 12:21 *2556*
but overcome *e* with good ... Rom 12:21 *2556*
to good works, but to the *e* ... Rom 13:3 *2556*
But if thou do that which is *e* ... Rom 13:4 *2556*
wrath upon him that doeth *e* ... Rom 13:4 *2556*
not then your good be *e* spoken of ... Rom 14:16
but it is *e* for that man who ... Rom 14:20 *2556*
is good, and simple concerning *e* ... Rom 16:19 *2556*
we should not lust after *e* things ... 1Cor 10:6 *2556*
why am I *e* spoken of for that for ... 1Cor 10:30 *987*
easily provoked, thinketh no *e* ... 1Cor 13:5 *2556*
e communications corrupt good ... 1Cor 15:33 *2556*
by *e* report and good report ... 2Cor 6:8 *1426*
Now I pray to God that ye do no *e* ... 2Cor 13:7 *2556*
us from this present *e* world ... Gal 1:4 *4190*
e speaking, be put away from you, ... Eph 4:31 *988*
the time, because the days are *e* ... Eph 5:16 *4190*
be able to withstand in the *e* day ... Eph 6:13 *4190*
of dogs, beware of *e* workers ... Phil 3:2 *2556*
e concupiscence, and covetousness, ... Col 3:5 *2556*
See that none render *e* for *e* ... 1Th 5:15 *2556*

Abstain from all appearance of *e* ... 1Th 5:22 *4190*
stablish you, and keep you from *e* ... 2Th 3:3 *4190*
strife, railings, *e* surmisings, ... 1Ti 6:4 *4190*
of money is the root of all *e* ... 1Ti 6:10 *2556*
I suffer trouble, as an *e* doer ... 2Ti 2:9 *2557*
But *e* men and seducers shall wax ... 2Ti 3:13 *4190*
the coppersmith did me much *e* ... 2Ti 4:14 *2556*
deliver me from every *e* work ... 2Ti 4:18 *4190*
liars, *e* beasts, slow bellies ... Titus 1:12 *2556*
having no *e* thing to say of you ... Titus 2:8 *5337*
To speak *e* of no man, to be no ... Titus 3:2 *987*
any of you an *e* heart of unbelief ... Heb 3:12 *4190*
to discern both good and *e* ... Heb 5:14 *2556*
sprinkled from an *e* conscience ... Heb 10:22 *4190*
for God cannot be tempted with *e* ... Jas 1:13 *2556*
are become judges of *e* thoughts ... Jas 2:4 *4190*
it is an unruly *e*, full of deadly ... Jas 3:8 *2556*
is confusion and every *e* work ... Jas 3:16 *5337*
Speak not *e* one of another, ... Jas 4:11 *2635*
He that speaketh *e* of his brother ... Jas 4:11 *2635*
speaketh *e* of the law, and judgeth ... Jas 4:11 *2635*
all such rejoicing is *e* ... Jas 4:16 *4190*
and envies, and all *e* speakings, ... 1Pet 2:1 *2636*
Not rendering *e* for *e*, or ... 1Pet 3:9 *2556*
Not rendering *e* for *e*, or ... 1Pet 3:9 *2556*
let him refrain his tongue from *e* ... 1Pet 3:10 *2556*
Let him eschew *e*, and do good ... 1Pet 3:11 *2556*
Lord is against them that do *e* ... 1Pet 3:12 *2556*
that, whereas they speak *e* of you ... 1Pet 3:16 *2635*
for well doing, than for *e* doing ... 1Pet 3:17 *2554*
excess of riot, speaking *e* of you ... 1Pet 4:4 *987*
on their part he is *e* spoken of ... 1Pet 4:14 *987*
way of truth shall be *e* spoken of ... 2Pet 2:2 *987*
afraid to speak *e* of dignities ... 2Pet 2:10 *987*
speak *e* of the things that they ... 2Pet 2:12 *987*
Because his own works were *e* ... 1Jn 3:12 *4190*
speed is partaker of his *e* deeds ... 2Jn 11 *4190*
follow not that which is *e* ... 3Jn 11 *2556*
he that doeth *e* hath not seen God ... 3Jn 11 *2554*
dominion, and speak *e* of dignities ... Jude 8 *987*
But these speak *e* of those things ... Jude 10 *987*
canst not bear them which are *e* ... Rev 2:2 *2556*

EVILDOER {2}
every one is an hypocrite and an *e* ... Is 9:17 7489
or as a thief, or as an *e* ... 1Pet 4:15 *2555*

EVILDOERS {13}
have hated the congregation of *e* ... Ps 26:5
Fret not thyself because of *e* ... Ps 37:1 7489
For *e* shall be cut off ... Ps 37:9 7489
will rise up for me against the *e* ... Ps 94:16 7489
Depart from me, ye *e* ... Ps 119:115 7489
laden with iniquity, a seed of *e* ... Is 1:4 7489
the seed of *e* shall never be ... Is 14:20 7489
arise against the house of the *e* ... Is 31:2 7489
of the poor from the hand of *e* ... Jer 20:13 7489
strengthen also the hands of *e* ... Jer 23:14 7489
they speak against you as *e* ... 1Pet 2:12 *2555*
by him for the punishment of *e* ... 1Pet 2:14 *2555*
they speak evil of you, as of *e* ... 1Pet 3:16 *2555*

EVILFAVOUREDNESS {1}
wherein is blemish, or any *e* ... Deut 17:1

EVIL-MERODACH *(e'-vil-mer'-o-dak)* {2} *Son of Nebuchadnezzar.*
that *E* king of Babylon in the ... 2Kin 25:27 192
that *E* king of Babylon in the ... Jer 52:31 192

EVILS {9}
they shall be devoured, and many *e* ... Deut 31:17 7451
day, Are not these *e* come upon us ... Deut 31:17 7451
e which they shall have wrought ... Deut 31:18 7451
shall come to pass, when many *e* ... Deut 31:21 7451
For innumerable *e* have compassed ... Ps 40:12 7451
my people have committed two *e* ... Jer 2:13 7451
e which they have committed in ... Eze 6:9 7451
all your *e* that ye have committed ... Eze 20:43 7451
for all the *e* which Herod had ... Lk 3:19 *4190*

EWE {7}
Abraham set seven *e* lambs of the ... Gen 21:28 3535
What mean these seven *e* lambs ... Gen 21:29 3535
For these seven *e* lambs shalt ... Gen 21:30 3535
one *e* lamb of the first year ... Lev 14:10 3535
And whether it be cow or *e* ... Lev 22:28 7716
one *e* lamb of the first year ... Num 6:14 3535
nothing, save one little *e* lamb ... 2Sa 12:3 3535

EWES {3}
thy *e* and thy she goats have not ... Gen 31:38 7353
and twenty he goats, two hundred *e* ... Gen 32:14 7353
From following the *e* great with ... Ps 78:71 5763

EXACT {8}
he shall not *e* it of his ... Deut 15:2 5065
foreigner thou mayest *e* it again ... Deut 15:3 5065
Ye *e* usury, every one of his ... Neh 5:7 5378
might *e* of them money and corn ... Neh 5:10 5383
and the oil, that ye *e* of them ... Neh 5:11 5383
The enemy shall not *e* upon him ... Ps 89:22 5378
pleasure, and *e* all your labours ... Is 58:3 5065
E no more than that which is ... Lk 3:13 *4238*

EXACTED {2}
Menahem *e* the money of Israel, ... 2Kin 15:20 3318
he *e* the silver and the gold of ... 2Kin 23:35 5065

EXACTETH {1}
God *e* of thee less than thine ... Job 11:6 5382

EXACTION {1}
year, and the *e* of every debt ... Neh 10:31 4855

E

EXACTIONS {1}
take away your *e* from my people Eze 45:9 1646
EXACTORS {1}
peace, and thine *e* righteousness Is 60:17 5065
EXALT {26}
my father's God, and I will *e* him Ex 15:2 7311
e the horn of his anointed 1Sa 2:10 7311
therefore shalt thou not *e* them Job 17:4 7311
let us *e* his name together Ps 34:3 7311
he shall *e* thee to inherit the Ps 37:34 7311
not the rebellious *e* themselves Ps 66:7 7311
But my horn shalt thou *e* like the Ps 92:10 7311
E ye the LORD our God, and worship Ps 99:5 7311
E the LORD our God, and worship at Ps 99:9 7311
Let them *e* him also in the Ps 107:32 7311
thou art my God, I will *e* thee Ps 118:28 7311
lest they *e* themselves Ps 140:8 7311
E her, and she shall promote thee Prov 4:8 5549
e the voice unto them, shake the Is 13:2 7311
I will *e* my throne above the Is 14:13 7311
I will *e* thee, I will praise thy Is 25:1 7311
e him that is low, and abase him Eze 21:26 1361
neither shall it *e* itself any Eze 29:15 5375
e themselves for their height Eze 31:14 1361
e themselves to establish the Dan 11:14 5375
and he shall *e* himself, and magnify Dan 11:36 7311
High, none at all would *e* him Hos 11:7 7311
Though thou *e* thyself as the Obad 4 1361
whosoever shall *e* himself shall Mt 23:12 *5312*
take of you, if a man *e* himself 2Cor 11:20 *1869*
that he may *e* you in due time 1Pet 5:6 *5312*
EXALTED {64}
Agag, and his kingdom shall be *e* Num 24:7 5375
LORD, mine horn is *e* in the LORD 1Sa 2:1 7311
that he had *e* his kingdom for his 2Sa 5:12 5375
e be the God of the rock of my 2Sa 22:47 7311
the son of Haggith *e* himself 1Kin 1:5 5375
Forasmuch as I *e* thee from among 1Kin 14:7 7311
Forasmuch as I *e* thee out of the 1Kin 16:2 7311
whom hast thou *e* thy voice 2Kin 19:22 7311
thou art *e* as head above all 1Chr 29:11 5375
which is *e* above all blessing and Neh 9:5 7311
which mourn may be *e* to safety Job 5:11 7682
They are *e* for a little while, Job 24:24 7426
them for ever, and they are *e* Job 36:7 1361
side, when the vilest men are *e* Ps 12:8 7311
shall mine enemy be *e* over me Ps 13:2 7311
let the God of my salvation be *e* Ps 18:46 7311
Be thou *e*, LORD, in thine own Ps 21:13 7311
I will be *e* among the heathen Ps 46:10 7311
I will be *e* in the earth Ps 46:10 7311
he is greatly *e* Ps 47:9 5927
Be thou *e*, O God, above the Ps 57:5 7311
Be thou *e*, O God, above the Ps 57:11 7311
horns of the righteous shall be *e* Ps 75:10 7311
thy righteousness shall they be *e* Ps 89:16 7311
in thy favour our horn shall be *e* Ps 89:17 7311
I have *e* one chosen out of the Ps 89:19 7311
and in my name shall his horn be *e* Ps 89:24 7311
thou art *e* far above all gods Ps 97:9 5927
Be thou *e*, O God, above the Ps 108:5 7311
his horn shall be *e* with honour Ps 112:9 7311
The right hand of the LORD is *e* Ps 118:16 7426
of the upright the city is *e* Prov 11:11 7311
shall be *e* above the hills Is 2:2 5375
LORD alone shall be *e* in that day Is 2:11 7682
LORD alone shall be *e* in that day Is 2:17 7682
of hosts shall be *e* in judgment Is 5:16 1361
make mention that his name is *e* Is 12:4 7682
you, and therefore will he be *e* Is 30:18 7311
The LORD is *e* Is 33:5 7682
now will I be *e* Is 33:10 7311
whom hast thou *e* thy voice Is 37:23 7311
Every valley shall be *e*, and every Is 40:4 5375
a way, and my highways shall be *e* Is 49:11 7311
deal prudently, he shall be *e* Is 52:13 7311
have *e* the low tree, have dried Eze 17:24 1361
her stature was *e* among the thick Eze 19:11 1361
Therefore his height was *e* above Eze 31:5 1361
trembling, he *e* himself in Israel Hos 13:1 5375
were filled, and their heart was *e* Hos 13:6 7311
it shall be *e* above the hills Mic 4:1 5375
which art *e* unto heaven, shalt be Mt 11:23 *5312*
shall humble himself shall be *e* Mt 23:12 *5312*
seats, and *e* them of low degree Lk 1:52 *5312*
Capernaum, which art *e* to heaven Lk 10:15 *5312*
that humbleth himself shall be *e* Lk 14:11 *5312*
that humbleth himself shall be *e* Lk 18:14 *5312*
being by the right hand of God *e* Acts 2:33 *5312*
Him hath God *e* with his right Acts 5:31 *5312*
e the people when they dwelt as Acts 13:17 *5312*
abasing myself that ye might be *e* 2Cor 11:7 *5312*
lest I should be *e* above measure 2Cor 12:7 *5229*
lest I should be *e* above measure 2Cor 12:7 *5229*
God also hath highly *e* him Phil 2:9 *5251*
degree rejoice in that he is *e* Jas 1:9 *5311*
EXALTEST {1}
As yet *e* thou thyself against my Ex 9:17 5549
EXALTETH {9}
Behold, God *e* by his power Job 36:22 7682
He also *e* the horn of his people, Ps 148:14 7311
that is hasty of spirit *e* folly Prov 14:29 7311
Righteousness *e* a nation Prov 14:34 7311
he that *e* his gate seeketh Prov 17:19 1361
For whosoever *e* himself shall be Lk 14:11 *5312*
for every one that *e* himself Lk 18:14 *5312*
every high thing that *e* itself 2Cor 10:5 *1869*
e himself above all that is 2Th 2:4 *5229*
EXAMINATION {1}
O king Agrippa, that, after *e* had Acts 25:26 *351*
EXAMINE {5}
the tenth month to *e* the matter Ezr 10:16 1875
E me, O LORD, and prove me Ps 26:2 974
to them that do *e* me is this 1Cor 9:3 *350*
But let a man *e* himself, and so 1Cor 11:28 *1381*
E yourselves, whether ye be in 2Cor 13:5 *3985*
EXAMINED {6}
having *e* him before you, have Lk 23:14 *350*
If we this day be *e* of the good Acts 4:9 *350*
he *e* the keepers, and commanded Acts 12:19 *350*
that he should be *e* by scourging Acts 22:24 *426*
from him which should have *e* him Acts 22:29 *426*
Who, when they had *e* me, would Acts 28:18 *350*
EXAMINING {1}
by *e* of whom thyself mayest take Acts 24:8 *350*
EXAMPLE {8}
willing to make her a publick *e* Mt 1:19 *3856*
For I have given you an *e* Jn 13:15 *5262*
but be thou an *e* of the believers 1Ti 4:12 *5179*
fall after the same *e* of unbelief Heb 4:11 *5262*
Who serve unto the *e* and shadow of Heb 8:5 *5262*
for an *e* of suffering affliction, Jas 5:10 *5262*
suffered for us, leaving us an *e* 1Pet 2:21 *5261*
flesh, are set forth for an *e* Jude 7 *1164*
EXAMPLES {1}
Now these things were our *e* 1Cor 10:6 *5179*
EXCEED {4}
stripes he may give him, and not *e* Deut 25:3 3254
lest, if he should *e*, and beat him Deut 25:3 3254
shall *e* the righteousness of the Mt 5:20 *4052*
of righteousness *e* in glory 2Cor 3:9 *4052*
EXCEEDED {3}
one with another, until David *e* 1Sa 20:41 1431
So king Solomon *e* all the kings 1Kin 10:23 1431
transgressions that they have *e* Job 36:9 1396
EXCEEDEST {1}
for thou *e* the fame that I heard 2Chr 9:6 3254
EXCEEDETH {1}
prosperity *e* the fame which I 1Kin 10:7 3254
EXCEEDING {59}
thy shield, and thy *e* great reward Gen 15:1 3966
And I will make thee *e* fruitful Gen 17:6 3966
e bitter cry, and said unto his Gen 27:34 3966
and multiplied, and waxed *e* mighty Ex 1:7 3966
the voice of the trumpet *e* loud Ex 19:16 3966
to search it, is an *e* good land Num 14:7 3966
Talk no more so *e* proudly 1Sa 2:3
king David took *e* much brass 2Sa 8:8 3966
The rich man had *e* many flocks 2Sa 12:2 3966
wisdom and understanding *e* much 1Kin 4:29 3966
because they were *e* many 1Kin 7:47 3966
he brought also *e* much spoil out 1Chr 20:2 3966
for the LORD must be *e* magnifical 1Chr 22:5 4605
spears, and made them *e* strong 2Chr 11:12 7235,3966
for there was *e* much spoil in 2Chr 14:14 7235
until his disease was *e* great 2Chr 16:12 4605
And Hezekiah had *e* much riches 2Chr 32:27 3966
thou hast made him *e* glad with Ps 21:6 2302
altar of God, unto God my *e* joy Ps 43:4 8057
but thy commandment is *e* broad Ps 119:96 3966
the earth, but they are *e* wise Prov 30:24
e deep, who can find it out Eccl 7:24
(he is *e* proud) his loftiness, and Jer 48:29 3966
of Israel and Judah is *e* great Eze 9:9 3966
and thou wast *e* beautiful, and thou Eze 16:13 3966
e in dyed attire upon their heads Eze 23:15 5628
upon their feet, an *e* great army Eze 37:10 3966
the fish of the great sea, *e* many Eze 47:10 3966
was urgent, and the furnace *e* hot Dan 3:22 2493
Then was the king *e* glad for him Dan 6:23 7689
e dreadful, whose teeth were of Dan 7:19 3493
little horn, which waxed *e* great Dan 8:9 3499
Now Nineveh was an *e* great city Jonah 3:3 430
So Jonah was *e* glad of the gourd Jonah 4:6 1419
they rejoiced with *e* great joy Mt 2:10 *4970*
was *e* wroth, and sent forth, and Mt 2:16 *3029*
him up into an *e* high mountain Mt 4:8 *3029*
Rejoice, and be *e* glad Mt 5:12
e fierce, so that no man might Mt 8:28 *3029*
And they were *e* sorry Mt 17:23 *4970*
And they were *e* sorrowful, and Mt 26:22 *4970*
unto them, My soul is *e* sorrowful Mt 26:38 *4036*
And the king was *e* sorry Mk 6:26 *4036*
became shining, *e* white as snow Mk 9:3 *3029*
My soul is *e* sorrowful unto death Mk 14:34 *4036*
Herod saw Jesus, he was *e* glad Lk 23:8 *3029*
was *e* fair, and nourished up in Acts 7:20 *3588,2316*
commandment might become *e* Rom 7:13 *2596,5236*
worketh for us a far more *e* 2Cor 4:17 *1519,5236*
comfort, I am *e* joyful in all our 2Cor 7:4 *5248*
you for the *e* grace of God in you 2Cor 9:14 *5235*
what is the *e* greatness of his Eph 1:19 *5235*
the *e* riches of his grace in his Eph 2:7 *5235*
do *e* abundantly above all that we Eph 3:20 *5228*
Lord was *e* abundant with faith 1Ti 1:14 *5250*
ye may be glad also with *e* joy 1Pet 4:13
Whereby are given unto us *e* great 2Pet 1:4
presence of his glory with *e* joy Jude 24
the plague thereof was *e* great Rev 16:21 *4970*
EXCEEDINGLY {39}
waters prevailed *e* upon the earth Gen 7:19 3966
and sinners before the LORD *e* Gen 13:13 3966
her, I will multiply thy seed *e* Gen 16:10 7235
and thee, and will multiply thee *e* Gen 17:2 3966
fruitful, and will multiply him *e* Gen 17:20 3966
And Isaac trembled very *e*, and said Gen 27:33 1419
And the man increased *e*, and had Gen 30:43 3966
therein, and grew, and multiplied *e* Gen 47:27 3966
played the fool, and have erred *e* 1Sa 26:21 7235,3966
Then Amnon hated her *e* 2Sa 13:15 1419,3966
But they were *e* afraid, and said, 2Kin 10:4 3966
e in the sight of all Israel 1Chr 29:25 4605
was with him, and magnified him *e* 2Chr 1:1 4605
And Jehoshaphat waxed great *e* 2Chr 17:12 4605
for he strengthened himself *e* 2Chr 26:8 4605
it grieved them *e* that there was Neh 2:10 1419
Then was the queen *e* grieved Est 4:4 3966
Which rejoice *e*, and are glad, Job 3:22 413,1524
yea, let them *e* rejoice Ps 68:3 8057
But lusted *e* in the wilderness, Ps 106:14
and I love them *e* Ps 119:167 3966
for we are *e* filled with contempt Ps 123:3 7227
Our soul is *e* filled with the Ps 123:4 7227
dissolved, the earth is moved *e* Is 24:19
dreadful and terrible, and strong *e* Dan 7:7 3493
Then were the men *e* afraid Jonah 1:10 1419
Then the men feared the LORD *e* Jonah 1:16 1419
But it displeased Jonah *e* Jonah 4:1 1419
heard it, they were *e* amazed Mt 19:25 *4970*
And they feared *e*, and said one to Mk 4:41 *5401,3173*
And they cried out the more *e* Mk 15:14 *4056*
Jews, do *e* trouble our city, Acts 16:20 *1613*
being *e* mad against them, I Acts 26:11 *4057*
we being *e* tossed with a tempest, Acts 27:18 *4971*
e the more joyed we for the joy 2Cor 7:13 *4056*
being more *e* zealous of the Gal 1:14 *4056*
praying *e* that we might see 1Th 3:10 *5228,1537,4053*
because that your faith groweth *e* 2Th 1:3
Moses said, I *e* fear and quake Heb 12:21 *1630*
EXCEL {5}
as water, thou shalt not *e* Gen 49:4 3498
with harps on the Sheminith to *e* 1Chr 15:21 5329
that *e* in strength, that do his Ps 103:20 1368
images did *e* them of Jerusalem Is 10:10
seek that ye may *e* to the 1Cor 14:12 *4052*
EXCELLED {1}
Solomon's wisdom *e* the wisdom of 1Kin 4:30 7227
EXCELLENCY {26}
e of dignity, and the *e* of power Gen 49:3 3499
in the greatness of thine *e* thou Ex 15:7 1347
thy help, and in his *e* on the sky Deut 33:26 1346
and who is the sword of thy *e* Deut 33:29 1346
Doth not their *e* which is in them Job 4:21 3499
Shall not his *e* make you afraid Job 13:11 7613
Though his *e* mount up to the Job 20:6 7863
with the voice of his *e* Job 37:4 1347
thyself now with majesty and *e* Job 40:10 1363
the *e* of Jacob whom he loved Ps 47:4 1347
to cast him down from his *e* Ps 62:4 7613
his *e* is over Israel, and his Ps 68:34 1346
but the *e* of knowledge is, that Eccl 7:12 3504
the beauty of the Chaldees' *e* Is 13:19 1347
the *e* of Carmel and Sharon, they Is 35:2 1926
of the LORD, and the *e* of our God Is 35:2 1926
I will make thee an eternal *e* Is 60:15 1347
the *e* of your strength, the Eze 24:21 1347
of hosts, I abhor the *e* of Jacob Amos 6:8 1347
LORD hath sworn by the *e* of Jacob Amos 8:7 1347
hath turned away the *e* of Jacob Nah 2:2 1347
of Jacob, as the *e* of Israel Nah 2:2 1347
came not with *e* of speech or of 1Cor 2:1 *5247*
that the *e* of the power may be of 2Cor 4:7 *5236*
the *e* of the knowledge of Christ Phil 3:8 *5242*
EXCELLENT {34}
honour of his *e* majesty many days Est 1:4 1420
he is *e* in power, and in judgment, Job 37:23 7689
how *e* is thy name in all the Ps 8:1 117
how *e* is thy name in all the Ps 8:9 117
are in the earth, and to the *e* Ps 16:3 117
How *e* is thy lovingkindness, O Ps 36:7 3368
e than the mountains of prey Ps 76:4 117
it shall be an *e* oil, which shall Ps 141:5 7218
for his name alone is *e* Ps 148:13 7682
him according to his *e* greatness Ps 150:2 7230
for I will speak of *e* things Prov 8:6 5057
is more *e* than his neighbour Prov 12:26 8446
E speech becometh not a fool Prov 17:7 3499
understanding is of an *e* spirit Prov 17:27 7119
to thee *e* things in counsels Prov 22:20 7991
is as Lebanon, *e* as the cedars Song 5:15 977
the fruit of the earth shall be *e* Is 4:2 1347
for he hath done *e* things Is 12:5 1348
in counsel, and *e* in working Is 28:29 1431
and thou art come to *e* ornaments Eze 16:7 5716
image, whose brightness was *e* Dan 2:31 3493
e majesty was added unto me Dan 4:36 3493
Forasmuch as an *e* spirit, and Dan 5:12 3493
e wisdom is found in thee Dan 5:14 3493
because an *e* spirit was in him Dan 6:3 3493
thee in order, most *e* Theophilus, Lk 1:3 *2903*
Claudius Lysias unto the most *e* Acts 23:26 *2903*
the things that are more *e* Rom 2:18 *1308*
yet shew I unto you a more *e* way 1Cor 12:31 *2596,5236*
ye may approve things that are *e* Phil 1:10 *1308*
obtained a more *e* name than they Heb 1:4 *1313*

he obtained a more *e* ministry ... Heb 8:6 *1313*
God a more *e* sacrifice than Cain ... Heb 11:4 *4119*
a voice to him from the *e* glory ... 2Pet 1:17 *3169*

EXCELLEST {1}
virtuously, but thou *e* them all ... Prov 31:29 5927

EXCELLETH {3}
Then I saw that wisdom *e* folly ... Eccl 2:13 3504
as far as light *e* darkness ... Eccl 2:13 3504
by reason of the glory that *e* ... 2Cor 3:10 *5235*

EXCEPT See APPENDIX.

EXCEPTED See APPENDIX.

EXCESS {4}
they are full of extortion and *e* ... Mt 23:25 *192*
not drunk with wine, wherein is *e* ... Eph 5:18 *810*
lusts, *e* of wine, revellings, ... 1Pet 4:3 *3632*
with them to the same *e* of riot ... 1Pet 4:4 *401*

EXCHANGE {6}
gave them bread in *e* for horses ... Gen 47:17
the *e* thereof shall be holy ... Lev 27:10 8545
the *e* of it shall not be for ... Job 28:17 8545
shall not sell of it, neither *e* ... Eze 48:14 4171
a man give in *e* for his soul ... Mt 16:26 *465*
a man give in *e* for his soul ... Mk 8:37 *465*

EXCHANGERS {1}
to have put my money to the *e* ... Mt 25:27 *5133*

EXCLUDE {1}
yea, they would *e* you, that ye ... Gal 4:17 *1576*

EXCLUDED {1}
is boasting then? It is *e* ... Rom 3:27 *1576*

EXCUSE {3}
with one consent began to make *e* ... Lk 14:18 *3868*
so that they are without *e* ... Rom 1:20 *379*
think ye that we *e* ourselves unto ... 2Cor 12:19 *626*

EXCUSED {2}
I pray thee have me *e* ... Lk 14:18 *3868*
I pray thee have me *e* ... Lk 14:19 *3868*

EXCUSING {1}
accusing or else *e* one another ... Rom 2:15 *626*

EXECRATION {2}
and ye shall be an *e*, and an ... Jer 42:18 423
and they shall be an *e*, and an ... Jer 44:12 423

EXECUTE {32}
gods of Egypt I will *e* judgment ... Ex 12:12 6213
the priest shall *e* upon her all ... Num 5:30 6213
that they may *e* the service of ... Num 8:11 5647
He doth *e* the judgment of the ... Deut 10:18 6213
e my judgments, and keep all my ... 1Kin 6:12 6213
when wilt thou *e* judgment on them ... Ps 119:84 6213
To *e* vengeance upon the heathen, ... Ps 149:7 6213
To *e* upon them the judgment ... Ps 149:9 6213
Take counsel, *e* judgment ... Is 16:3 6213
if ye throughly *e* judgment ... Jer 7:5 6213
E judgment in the morning, and ... Jer 21:12 1777
E ye judgment and righteousness, ... Jer 22:3 6213
shall *e* judgment and justice in ... Jer 23:5 6213
and he shall *e* judgment and ... Jer 33:15 6213
will *e* judgments in the midst of ... Eze 5:8 6213
I will *e* judgments in thee, and ... Eze 5:10 6213
when I shall *e* judgments in thee ... Eze 5:15 6213
will *e* judgments among you ... Eze 11:9 6213
e judgments upon thee in the ... Eze 16:41 6213
I will *e* judgments upon Moab ... Eze 25:11 6213
I will *e* great vengeance upon ... Eze 25:17 6213
Zoan, and will *e* judgments in No ... Eze 30:14 6213
Thus will I *e* judgments in Egypt ... Eze 30:19 6213
e judgment and justice, take away ... Eze 45:9 6213
I will not *e* the fierceness of ... Hos 11:9 6213
I will *e* vengeance in anger and ... Mic 5:15 6213
my cause, and *e* judgment for me ... Mic 7:9 6213
E true judgment, and shew mercy and ... Zec 7:9 8199
e the judgment of truth and peace ... Zec 8:16 8199
him authority to *e* judgment also ... Jn 5:27 *4160*
a revenger to *e* wrath upon him ... Rom 13:4
To *e* judgment upon all, and to ... Jude 15 *4160*

EXECUTED {20}
gods also the LORD *e* judgments ... Num 33:4 6213
he *e* the justice of the LORD, and ... Deut 33:21 6213
David *e* judgment and justice unto ... 2Sa 8:15 6213
(he it is that *e* the priest's ... 1Chr 6:10
e judgment and justice among all ... 1Chr 18:14 6213
Ithamar *e* the priest's office ... 1Chr 24:2
So they *e* judgment against Joash ... 2Chr 24:24 6213
let judgment be *e* speedily upon ... Ezr 7:26 5648
stood up Phinehas, and *e* judgment ... Ps 106:30
an evil work is not *e* speedily ... Eccl 8:11 6213
shall not return, until he have *e* ... Jer 23:20 6213
neither *e* my judgments, but have ... Eze 11:12 6213
hath *e* true judgment between man ... Eze 18:8 6213
hath *e* my judgments, hath walked ... Eze 18:17 6213
they had not *e* my judgments ... Eze 20:24 6213
for they had *e* judgment upon her ... Eze 23:10 6213
I shall have *e* judgments in her ... Eze 28:22 6213
when I have *e* judgments upon all ... Eze 28:26 6213
see my judgment that I have *e* ... Eze 39:21 6213
that while he *e* the priest's ... Lk 1:8 *2407*

EXECUTEDST {1}
nor *e* his fierce wrath upon ... 1Sa 28:18 6213

EXECUTEST {1}
thou *e* judgment and righteousness ... Ps 99:4 6213

EXECUTETH {6}
known by the judgment which he *e* ... Ps 9:16 6213
The LORD *e* righteousness and ... Ps 103:6 6213
Which *e* judgment for the ... Ps 146:7 6213
the man that *e* my counsel from a ... Is 46:11
if there be any that *e* judgment ... Jer 5:1 6213
for he is strong that *e* his word ... Joel 2:11 6213

EXECUTING {3}
in *e* that which is right in mine ... 2Kin 10:30 6213
e the priest's office unto the ... 2Chr 11:14
when Jehu was *e* judgment upon the ... 2Chr 22:8

EXECUTION {1}
decree drew near to be put in *e* ... Est 9:1 6213

EXECUTIONER {1}
And immediately the king sent an *e* ... Mk 6:27 *4688*

EXEMPTED {1}
throughout all Judah; none was *e* ... 1Kin 15:22 5355

EXERCISE {11}
neither do I *e* myself in great ... Ps 131:1 1980
the LORD which *e* lovingkindness ... Jer 9:24 6213
the Gentiles *e* dominion over them ... Mt 20:25 *2634*
are great *e* authority upon them ... Mt 20:25 *2715*
the Gentiles *e* lordship over them ... Mk 10:42 *2634*
their great ones *e* authority upon ... Mk 10:42 *2715*
the Gentiles *e* lordship over them ... Lk 22:25 *2961*
they that *e* authority upon them ... Lk 22:25 *1850*
And herein do I *e* myself, to have ... Acts 24:16 *778*
e thyself rather unto godliness ... 1Ti 4:7 *1128*
For bodily *e* profiteth little ... 1Ti 4:8 *1129*

EXERCISED {6}
the sons of man to be *e* therewith ... Eccl 1:13 6031
to the sons of men to be *e* in it ... Eccl 3:10 6031
e robbery, and have vexed the poor ... Eze 22:29
senses *e* to discern both good ... Heb 5:14 *1128*
unto them which are *e* thereby ... Heb 12:11 *1128*
an heart they have *e* with ... 2Pet 2:14 *1128*

EXERCISETH {1}
he *e* all the power of the first ... Rev 13:12 *4160*

EXHORT {16}
other words did he testify and *e* ... Acts 2:40 *3870*
now I *e* you to be of good cheer ... Acts 27:22 *3867*
it necessary to *e* the brethren ... 2Cor 9:5 *3870*
e you by the Lord Jesus, that as ... 1Th 4:1 *3870*
Now we *e* you, brethren, warn them ... 1Th 5:14 *3870*
e by our Lord Jesus Christ, that ... 2Th 3:12 *3870*
I *e* therefore, that, first of all ... 1Ti 2:1 *3870*
These things teach and *e* ... 1Ti 6:2 *3870*
e with all longsuffering and ... 2Ti 4:2 *3870*
able by sound doctrine both to *e* ... Titus 1:9 *3870*
men likewise *e* to be sober minded ... Titus 2:6 *3870*
E servants to be obedient unto ... Titus 2:9
These things speak, and *e*, and ... Titus 2:15 *3870*
But *e* one another daily, while it ... Heb 3:13 *3870*
elders which are among you I *e* ... 1Pet 5:1 *3870*
e you that ye should earnestly ... Jude 3 *3870*

EXHORTATION {10}
many other things in his *e* ... Lk 3:18 *3870*
have any word of *e* for the people ... Acts 13:15 *3874*
parts, and had given them much *e* ... Acts 20:2 *3870*
Or he that exhorteth, on *e* ... Rom 12:8 *3874*
unto men to edification, and *e* ... 1Cor 14:3 *3874*
For indeed he accepted the *e* ... 2Cor 8:17 *3874*
For our *e* was not of deceit, nor ... 1Th 2:3 *3874*
give attendance to reading, to *e* ... 1Ti 4:13 *3874*
ye have forgotten the *e* which ... Heb 12:5 *3874*
brethren, suffer the word of *e* ... Heb 13:22 *3874*

EXHORTED {3}
e them all, that with purpose of ... Acts 11:23 *3870*
e the brethren with many words, ... Acts 15:32 *3870*
As ye know how we *e* and comforted ... 1Th 2:11 *3870*

EXHORTETH {1}
Or he that *e*, on exhortation ... Rom 12:8 *3870*

EXHORTING {4}
e them to continue in the faith, ... Acts 14:22 *3870*
e the disciples to receive him ... Acts 18:27 *4389*
but *e* one another ... Heb 10:25 *3870*
I have written briefly, *e* ... 1Pet 5:12 *3870*

EXILE {2}
thou art a stranger, and also an *e* ... 2Sa 15:19 1540
The captive *e* hasteneth that he ... Is 51:14 6808

EXORCISTS {1}
certain of the vagabond Jews, *e* ... Acts 19:13 *1845*

EXPECTATION {14}
the *e* of the poor shall not ... Ps 9:18 8615
for my *e* is from him ... Ps 62:5 8615
but the *e* of the wicked shall ... Prov 10:28 8615
man dieth, his *e* shall perish ... Prov 11:7 8615
but the *e* of the wicked is wrath ... Prov 11:23 8615
thine *e* shall not be cut off ... Prov 23:18 8615
thy *e* shall not be cut off ... Prov 24:14 8615
and ashamed of Ethiopia their *e* ... Is 20:5 4007
that day, Behold, such is our *e* ... Is 20:6 4007
for her *e* shall be ashamed ... Zec 9:5 4007
And as the people were in *e* ... Lk 3:15 *4328*
from all the *e* of the people of ... Acts 12:11 *4329*
For the earnest *e* of the creature ... Rom 8:19 *603*
According to my earnest *e* ... Phil 1:20 *603*

EXPECTED {1}
not of evil, to give you an *e* end ... Jer 29:11 8615

EXPECTING {2}
e to receive something of them ... Acts 3:5 *4328*
From henceforth *e* till his ... Heb 10:13 *1551*

EXPEDIENT {7}
Nor consider that it is *e* for us ... Jn 11:50 *4851*
It is *e* for you that I go away ... Jn 16:7 *4851*
that it was *e* that one man should ... Jn 18:14 *4851*
unto me, but all things are not *e* ... 1Cor 6:12 *4851*
for me, but all things are not *e* ... 1Cor 10:23 *4851*
for this is *e* for you, who have ... 2Cor 8:10 *4851*
It is not *e* for me doubtless to ... 2Cor 12:1 *4851*

EXPEL {2}
he shall *e* them from before you, ... Josh 23:5 1920
e me out of my father's house ... Judg 11:7 1644

EXPELLED {4}
of Israel *e* not the Geshurites ... Josh 13:13 3423
he *e* thence the three sons of ... Judg 1:20 3423
his banished be not *e* from him ... 2Sa 14:14 5080
e them out of their coasts ... Acts 13:50 *1544*

EXPENCES {2}
let the *e* be given out of the ... Ezr 6:4 5313
forthwith *e* be given unto these ... Ezr 6:8 5313

EXPERIENCE {4}
for I have learned by *e* that the ... Gen 30:27 5172
my heart had great *e* of wisdom ... Eccl 1:16 7200
And patience, *e* ... Rom 5:4 *1382*
and *e*, hope ... Rom 5:4 *1382*

EXPERIMENT {1}
Whiles by the *e* of this ... 2Cor 9:13 *1382*

EXPERT {6}
e in war, with all instruments of ... 1Chr 12:33 6186
And of the Danites *e* in war twenty ... 1Chr 12:35 6186
battle, *e* in war, forty thousand ... 1Chr 12:36 6186
all hold swords, being *e* in war ... Song 3:8 3925
shall be as of a mighty *e* man ... Jer 50:9 7919
know thee to be *e* in all customs ... Acts 26:3 *1109*

EXPIRED {9}
and the days were not *e* ... 1Sa 18:26 4390
to pass, after the year was *e* ... 2Sa 11:1 8666
when thy days be *e* that thou must ... 1Chr 17:11 4390
pass, that after the year was *e* ... 1Chr 20:1 8666
And when the year was *e*, king ... 2Chr 36:10 8666
And when these days were *e* ... Est 1:5 4390
And when these days are *e*, it ... Eze 43:27 3615
And when forty years were *e* ... Acts 7:30 *4137*
And when the thousand years are *e* ... Rev 20:7 *5055*

EXPLOITS {2}
and he shall do *e*, and return to ... Dan 11:28
God shall be strong, and do *e* ... Dan 11:32

EXPOUND {1}
not in three days *e* the riddle ... Judg 14:14 5046

EXPOUNDED {6}
unto them which *e* the riddle ... Judg 14:19 5046
he *e* all things to his disciples ... Mk 4:34 *1956*
he *e* unto them in all the ... Lk 24:27 *1329*
e it by order unto them, saying, ... Acts 11:4 *1620*
e unto him the way of God more ... Acts 18:26 *1620*
to whom he *e* and testified the ... Acts 28:23 *1620*

EXPRESS {1}
the *e* image of his person, and ... Heb 1:3 *5481*

EXPRESSED {6}
men which are *e* by their names ... Num 1:17 5344
thousand, which were *e* by name ... 1Chr 12:31 5344
were chosen, who were *e* by name ... 1Chr 16:41 5344
men which were *e* by name rose up ... 2Chr 28:15 5344
city, the men that were *e* by name ... 2Chr 31:19 5344
all of them were *e* by name ... Ezr 8:20

EXPRESSLY {3}
If I *e* say unto the lad, Behold, ... 1Sa 20:21 559
came *e* unto Ezekiel the priest ... Eze 1:3
Now the Spirit speaketh *e* ... 1Ti 4:1 *4490*

EXTEND {2}
there be none to *e* mercy unto him ... Ps 109:12 4900
I will *e* peace to her like a ... Is 66:12 5186

EXTENDED {2}
hath *e* mercy unto me before the ... Ezr 7:28 5186
but hath *e* mercy unto us in the ... Ezr 9:9 5186

EXTENDETH {1}
my goodness *e* not to thee ... Ps 16:2

EXTINCT {2}
breath is corrupt, my days are *e* ... Job 17:1 2193
they are *e*, they are quenched as ... Is 43:17 1846

EXTOL {4}
I will *e* thee, O LORD ... Ps 30:1 7311
e him that rideth upon the ... Ps 68:4 5549
I will *e* thee, my God, O king ... Ps 145:1 7311
Now I Nebuchadnezzar praise and *e* ... Dan 4:37 7313

EXTOLLED {2}
mouth, and he was *e* with my tongue ... Ps 66:17 7318
he shall be exalted and *e* ... Is 52:13 5375

EXTORTION {2}
gained of thy neighbours by *e* ... Eze 22:12 6233
but within they are full of *e* ... Mt 23:25 *724*

EXTORTIONER {3}
Let the *e* catch all that he hath ... Ps 109:11 5383
for the *e* is at an end, the ... Is 16:4 4160
a railer, or a drunkard, or an *e* ... 1Cor 5:11 *727*

EXTORTIONERS {3}
that I am not as other men are, *e* ... Lk 18:11 *727*
world, or with the covetous, or *e* ... 1Cor 5:10 *727*
drunkards, nor revilers, nor *e* ... 1Cor 6:10 *727*

EXTREME {1}
and with an *e* burning, and with ... Deut 28:22 2746

EXTREMITY {1}
yet he knoweth it not in great *e* ... Job 35:15 6580

EYE {116}

E for *e*, tooth for tooth, hand	Ex 21:24	5869
a man smite the *e* of his servant	Ex 21:26	5869
or the *e* of his maid, that it	Ex 21:26	5869
or that hath a blemish in his *e*	Lev 21:20	5869
e for *e*, tooth for tooth	Lev 24:20	5869
thine *e* shall have no pity upon	Deut 7:16	5869
neither shall thine *e* pity him	Deut 13:8	5869
thine *e* be evil against thy poor	Deut 15:9	5869
Thine *e* shall not pity him, but	Deut 19:13	5869
And thine *e* shall not pity	Deut 19:21	5869
e for *e*, tooth for tooth, hand	Deut 19:21	5869
thine *e* shall not pity her	Deut 25:12	5869
his *e* shall be evil toward his	Deut 28:54	5869
her *e* shall be evil toward the	Deut 28:56	5869
he kept him as the apple of his *e*	Deut 32:10	5869
his *e* was not dim, nor his	Deut 34:7	5869
but mine *e* spared thee	1Sa 24:10	5869
to my cleanness in his *e* sight	2Sa 22:25	5869
But the *e* of their God was upon	Ezr 5:5	5870
mine *e* shall no more see good	Job 7:7	5869
The *e* of him that hath seen me	Job 7:8	5869
up the ghost, and no *e* had seen me	Job 10:18	5869
mine *e* hath seen all this, mine	Job 13:1	5869
but mine *e* poureth out tears unto	Job 16:20	5869
doth not mine *e* continue in their	Job 17:2	5869
Mine *e* also is dim by reason of	Job 17:7	5869
The *e* also which saw him shall	Job 20:9	5869
The *e* also of the adulterer	Job 24:15	5869
saying, No *e* shall see me	Job 24:15	5869
the vulture's *e* hath not seen	Job 28:7	5869
his *e* seeth every precious thing	Job 28:10	5869
and when the *e* saw me, it gave	Job 29:11	5869
but now mine *e* seeth thee	Job 42:5	5869
Mine *e* is consumed because of	Ps 6:7	5869
Keep me as the apple of the *e*	Ps 17:8	5869
mine *e* is consumed with grief,	Ps 31:9	5869
I will guide thee with mine *e*	Ps 32:8	5869
the *e* of the LORD is upon them	Ps 33:18	5869
e that hate me without a cause	Ps 35:19	5869
Aha, aha, our *e* hath seen it	Ps 35:21	5869
mine *e* hath seen his desire upon	Ps 54:7	5869
Mine *e* mourneth by reason of	Ps 88:9	5869
Mine *e* also shall see my desire	Ps 92:11	5869
he that formed the *e*, shall he	Ps 94:9	5869
and my law as the apple of thine *e*	Prov 7:2	5869
winketh with the *e* causeth sorrow	Prov 10:10	5869
The hearing ear, and the seeing *e*	Prov 20:12	5869
a bountiful *e* shall be blessed	Prov 22:9	5869
bread of him that hath an evil *e*	Prov 23:6	5869
hasteth to be rich hath an evil *e*	Prov 28:22	5869
The *e* that mocketh at his father,	Prov 30:17	5869
the *e* is not satisfied with	Eccl 1:8	5869
neither is his *e* satisfied with	Eccl 4:8	5869
their *e* shall not spare children	Is 13:18	5869
for they shall see *e* to *e*	Is 52:8	5869
the ear, neither hath the *e* seen	Is 64:4	5869
mine *e* shall weep sore, and run	Jer 13:17	5869
mine *e*, mine *e* runneth down	Lam 1:16	5869
to the *e* in the tabernacle of the	Lam 2:4	5869
not the apple of thine *e* cease	Lam 2:18	5869
Mine *e* runneth down with rivers	Lam 3:48	5869
Mine *e* trickleth down, and ceaseth	Lam 3:49	5869
Mine *e* affecteth mine heart	Lam 3:51	5869
neither shall mine *e* spare	Eze 5:11	5869
mine *e* shall not spare thee,	Eze 7:4	5869
mine *e* shall not spare, neither	Eze 7:9	5869
mine *e* shall not spare, neither	Eze 8:18	5869
let not your *e* spare, neither	Eze 9:5	5869
mine *e* shall not spare, neither	Eze 9:10	5869
None *e* pitied thee, to do any of	Eze 16:5	5869
Nevertheless mine *e* spared them	Eze 20:17	5869
and let our *e* look upon Zion	Mic 4:11	5869
you toucheth the apple of his *e*	Zec 2:8	5869
upon his arm, and upon his right *e*	Zec 11:17	5869
his right *e* shall be utterly	Zec 11:17	5869
And if thy right *e* offend thee	Mt 5:29	*3788*
hath been said, An *e* for an *e*	Mt 5:38	*3788*
The light of the body is the *e*	Mt 6:22	*3788*
if therefore thine *e* be single	Mt 6:22	*3788*
But if thine *e* be evil, thy whole	Mt 6:23	*3788*
mote that is in thy brother's *e*	Mt 7:3	*3788*
the beam that is in thine own *e*	Mt 7:3	*3788*
pull out the mote out of thine *e*	Mt 7:4	*3788*
behold, a beam is in thine own *e*	Mt 7:4	*3788*
out the beam out of thine own *e*	Mt 7:5	*3788*
the mote out of thy brother's *e*	Mt 7:5	*3788*
if thine *e* offend thee, pluck it	Mt 18:9	*3788*
to enter into life with one *e*	Mt 18:9	*3442*
to go through the *e* of a needle	Mt 19:24	*5169*
Is thine *e* evil, because I am	Mt 20:15	*3788*
deceit, lasciviousness, an evil *e*	Mk 7:22	*3788*
if thine *e* offend thee, pluck it	Mk 9:47	*3788*
the kingdom of God with one *e*	Mk 9:47	*3442*
to go through the *e* of a needle	Mk 10:25	*5168*
mote that is in thy brother's *e*	Lk 6:41	*3788*
the beam that is in thine own *e*	Lk 6:41	*3788*
out the mote that is in thine *e*	Lk 6:42	*3788*
the beam that is in thine own *e*	Lk 6:42	*3788*
first the beam out of thine own *e*	Lk 6:42	*3788*
mote that is in thy brother's *e*	Lk 6:42	*3788*
The light of the body is the *e*	Lk 11:34	*3788*
therefore when thine *e* is single	Lk 11:34	*3788*
but when thine *e* is evil, thy	Lk 11:34	
camel to go through a needle's *e*	Lk 18:25	*5168*
E hath not seen, nor ear heard,	1Cor 2:9	*3788*
shall say, Because I am not the *e*	1Cor 12:16	*3788*
If the whole body were an *e*	1Cor 12:17	*3788*
the *e* cannot say unto the hand, I	1Cor 12:21	*3788*
moment, in the twinkling of an *e*	1Cor 15:52	*3788*
every *e* shall see him, and they	Rev 1:7	*3788*

EYEBROWS {1}

his head and his beard and his *e*	Lev 14:9	1354,5869

EYED {2}

Leah was tender *e*	Gen 29:17	5869
Saul *e* David from that day and	1Sa 18:9	5770

EYELIDS {9}

on my *e* is the shadow of death	Job 16:16	6079
are like the *e* of the morning	Job 41:18	6079
his eyes behold, his *e* try	Ps 11:4	6079
mine eyes, or slumber to mine *e*	Ps 132:4	6079
let thine *e* look straight before	Prov 4:25	6079
eyes, nor slumber to thine *e*	Prov 6:4	6079
let her take thee with her *e*	Prov 6:25	6079
and their *e* are lifted up	Prov 30:13	6079
our *e* gush out with waters	Jer 9:18	6079

EYE'S {1}

let him go free for his *e* sake	Ex 21:26	5869

EYES {504}

then your *e* shall be opened, and	Gen 3:5	5869
and that it was pleasant to the *e*	Gen 3:6	5869
the *e* of them both were opened,	Gen 3:7	5869
found grace in the *e* of the LORD	Gen 6:8	5869
And Lot lifted up his *e*, and beheld	Gen 13:10	5869
from him, Lift up now thine *e*	Gen 13:14	5869
mistress was despised in her *e*	Gen 16:4	5869
I was despised in her *e*	Gen 16:5	5869
And he lift up his *e* and looked, and	Gen 18:2	5869
ye to them as is good in your *e*	Gen 19:8	5869
he is to thee a covering of the *e*	Gen 20:16	5869
And God opened her *e*, and she saw a	Gen 21:19	5869
third day Abraham lifted up his *e*	Gen 22:4	5869
And Abraham lifted up his *e*	Gen 22:13	5869
and he lifted up his *e*, and saw, and	Gen 24:63	5869
And Rebekah lifted up her *e*	Gen 24:64	5869
his *e* were dim, so that he could	Gen 27:1	5869
if I have found favour in thine *e*	Gen 30:27	5869
e of the cattle in the gutters	Gen 30:41	5869
that I lifted up mine *e*, and saw	Gen 31:10	5869
And he said, Lift up now thine *e*	Gen 31:12	5869
and my sleep departed from mine *e*	Gen 31:40	5869
And Jacob lifted up his *e*, and	Gen 33:1	5869
And he lifted up his *e*, and saw the	Gen 33:5	5869
Let me find grace in your *e*	Gen 34:11	5869
and they lifted up their *e*	Gen 37:25	5869
wife cast her *e* upon Joseph	Gen 39:7	5869
was good in the *e* of Pharaoh	Gen 41:37	5869
in the *e* of all his servants	Gen 41:37	5869
and bound him before their *e*	Gen 42:24	5869
And he lifted up his *e*, and saw his	Gen 43:29	5869
that I may set mine *e* upon him	Gen 44:21	5869
And, behold, your *e* see, and the	Gen 45:12	5869
the *e* of my brother Benjamin,	Gen 45:12	5869
shall put his hand upon thine *e*	Gen 46:4	5869
shall we die before thine *e*	Gen 47:19	5869
Now the *e* of Israel were dim for	Gen 48:10	5869
His *e* shall be red with wine, and	Gen 49:12	5869
now I have found grace in your *e*	Gen 50:4	5869
be abhorred in the *e* of Pharaoh	Ex 5:21	5869
in the *e* of his servants, to put	Ex 5:21	5869
of the Egyptians before their *e*	Ex 8:26	5869
and for a memorial between thine *e*	Ex 13:9	5869
and for frontlets between thine *e*	Ex 13:16	5869
of Israel lifted up their *e*	Ex 14:10	5869
the *e* of the children of Israel	Ex 24:17	5869
be hid from the *e* of the assembly	Lev 4:13	5869
ways hide their *e* from the man	Lev 20:4	5869
ague, that shall consume the *e*	Lev 26:16	5869
be hid from the *e* of her husband	Num 5:13	5869
thou mayest be to us instead of *e*	Num 10:31	5869
beside this manna, before our *e*	Num 11:6	5869
your own heart and your own *e*	Num 15:39	5869
thou put out the *e* of these men	Num 16:14	5869
ye unto the rock before their *e*	Num 20:8	5869
to sanctify me in the *e* of the	Num 20:12	5869
the LORD opened the *e* of Balaam	Num 22:31	5869
And Balaam lifted up his *e*	Num 24:2	5869
the man whose *e* are open hath	Num 24:3	5869
a trance, but having his *e* open	Num 24:4	5869
the man whose *e* are open hath	Num 24:15	5869
a trance, but having his *e* open	Num 24:16	5869
me at the water before their *e*	Num 27:14	5869
of them shall be pricks in your *e*	Num 33:55	5869
for you in Egypt before your *e*	Deut 1:30	5869
Thine *e* have seen all that the	Deut 3:21	5869
and lift up thine *e* westward	Deut 3:27	5869
and behold it with thine *e*	Deut 3:27	5869
Your *e* have seen what the LORD	Deut 4:3	5869
things which thine *e* have seen	Deut 4:9	5869
thou lift up thine *e* unto heaven	Deut 4:19	5869
for you in Egypt before your *e*	Deut 4:34	5869
be as frontlets between thine *e*	Deut 6:8	5869
all his household, before our *e*	Deut 6:22	5869
temptations which thine *e* saw	Deut 7:19	5869
and brake them before your *e*	Deut 9:17	5869
things, which thine *e* have seen	Deut 10:21	5869
But your *e* have seen all the	Deut 11:7	5869
the *e* of the LORD thy God are	Deut 11:12	5869
be as frontlets between your *e*	Deut 11:18	5869
whatsoever is right in his own *e*	Deut 12:8	5869
in the *e* of the LORD thy God	Deut 13:18	5869
between your *e* for the dead	Deut 14:1	5869
gift doth blind the *e* of the wise	Deut 16:19	5869
blood, neither have our *e* seen it	Deut 21:7	5869
that she find no favour in his *e*	Deut 24:1	5869
ox shall be slain before thine *e*	Deut 28:31	5869
thine *e* shall look, and fail with	Deut 28:32	5869
of thine *e* which thou shalt see	Deut 28:34	5869
trembling heart, and failing of *e*	Deut 28:65	5869
of thine *e* which thou shalt see	Deut 28:67	5869
your *e* in the land of Egypt unto	Deut 29:2	5869
which thine *e* have seen, the	Deut 29:3	5869
e to see, and ears to hear, unto	Deut 29:4	5869
thee to see it with thine *e*	Deut 34:4	5869
Jericho, that he lifted up his *e*	Josh 5:13	5869
your sides, and thorns in your *e*	Josh 23:13	5869
your *e* have seen what I have done	Josh 24:7	5869
took him, and put out his *e*	Judg 16:21	5869
of the Philistines for my two *e*	Judg 16:28	5869
that which was right in his own *e*	Judg 17:6	5869
And when he had lifted up his *e*	Judg 19:17	5869
that which was right in his own *e*	Judg 21:25	5869
Let thine *e* be on the field that	Ruth 2:9	5869
Why have I found grace in thine *e*	Ruth 2:10	5869
shall be to consume thine *e*	1Sa 2:33	5869
his *e* began to wax dim, that he	1Sa 3:2	5869
his *e* were dim, that he could not	1Sa 4:15	5869
and they lifted up their *e*	1Sa 6:13	5869
I may thrust out all your right *e*	1Sa 11:2	5869
bribe to blind mine *e* therewith	1Sa 12:3	5869
the LORD will do before your *e*	1Sa 12:16	5869
and his *e* were enlightened	1Sa 14:27	5869
how mine *e* have been enlightened,	1Sa 14:29	5869
I have found grace in thine *e*	1Sa 20:3	5869
if I have found favour in thine *e*	1Sa 20:29	5869
this day thine *e* have seen how	1Sa 24:10	5869
young men find favour in thine *e*	1Sa 25:8	5869
was precious in thine *e* this day	1Sa 26:21	5869
much set by this day in mine *e*	1Sa 26:24	5869
much set by in the *e* of the LORD	1Sa 26:24	5869
I have now found grace in thine *e*	1Sa 27:5	5869
to day in the *e* of the handmaids	2Sa 6:20	5869
take thy wives before thine *e*	2Sa 12:11	5869
kept the watch lifted up his *e*	2Sa 13:34	5869
find favour in the *e* of the LORD	2Sa 15:25	5869
unto the wall, and lifted up his *e*	2Sa 18:24	5869
therefore what is good in thine *e*	2Sa 19:27	5869
but thine *e* are upon the haughty,	2Sa 22:28	5869
that the *e* of my lord the king	2Sa 24:3	5869
the *e* of all Israel are upon thee	1Kin 1:20	5869
this day, mine *e* even seeing it	1Kin 1:48	5869
That thine *e* may be open toward	1Kin 8:29	5869
That thine *e* may be open unto the	1Kin 8:52	5869
and mine *e* and mine heart shall be	1Kin 9:3	5869
I came, and mine *e* had seen it	1Kin 10:7	5869
do that which is right in mine *e*	1Kin 11:33	5869
for his *e* were set by reason of	1Kin 14:4	5869
only which was right in mine *e*	1Kin 14:8	5869
was right in the *e* of the LORD	1Kin 15:5	5869
was right in the *e* of the LORD	1Kin 15:11	5869
wrought evil in the *e* of the LORD	1Kin 16:25	5869
whatsoever is pleasant in thine *e*	1Kin 20:6	5869
was right in the *e* of the LORD	1Kin 22:43	5869
his *e* upon his *e*, and his hands	2Kin 4:34	5869
times, and the child opened his *e*	2Kin 4:35	5869
LORD, I pray thee, open his *e*	2Kin 6:17	5869
opened the *e* of the young man	2Kin 6:17	5869
open the *e* of these men, that	2Kin 6:20	5869
And the LORD opened their *e*	2Kin 6:20	5869
thou shalt see it with thine *e*	2Kin 7:2	5869
thou shalt see it with thine *e*	2Kin 7:19	5869
that which is good in thine *e*	2Kin 10:5	5869
that which is right in mine *e*	2Kin 10:30	5869
open, LORD, thine *e*, and see	2Kin 19:16	5869
and lifted up thine *e* on high	2Kin 19:22	5869
thine *e* shall not see all the	2Kin 22:20	5869
the sons of Zedekiah before his *e*	2Kin 25:7	5869
and put out the *e* of Zedekiah	2Kin 25:7	5869
right in the *e* of all the people	1Chr 13:4	5869
this was a small thing in thine *e*	1Chr 17:17	5869
And David lifted up his *e*, and saw	1Chr 21:16	5869
do that which is good in his *e*	1Chr 21:23	5869
That thine *e* may be open upon	2Chr 6:20	5869
thine *e* be open, and let thine	2Chr 6:40	5869
Now mine *e* shall be open, and mine	2Chr 7:15	5869
and mine *e* and mine heart shall be	2Chr 7:16	5869
I came, and mine *e* had seen it	2Chr 9:6	5869
right in the *e* of the LORD his	2Chr 14:2	5869
For the *e* of the LORD run to and	2Chr 16:9	5869
but our *e* are upon thee	2Chr 20:12	5869
was evil in the *e* of the LORD	2Chr 21:6	5869
evil in the *e* of the LORD our God	2Chr 29:6	5869
to hissing, as ye see with your *e*	2Chr 29:8	5869
neither shall thine *e* see all the	2Chr 34:28	5869
house was laid before their *e*	Ezr 3:12	5870
that our God may lighten our *e*	Ezr 9:8	5869
now be attentive, and thine *e* open	Neh 1:6	5869
much cast down in their own *e*	Neh 6:16	5869
despise their husbands in their *e*	Est 1:17	5869
king, and I be pleasing in his *e*	Est 8:5	5869
they lifted up their *e* afar off	Job 2:12	5869
womb, nor hid sorrow from mine *e*	Job 3:10	5869
an image was before mine *e*	Job 4:16	5869
thine *e* are upon me, and I am not	Job 7:8	5869
Hast thou *e* of flesh	Job 10:4	5869
is pure, and I am clean in thine *e*	Job 11:4	5869
But the *e* of the wicked shall	Job 11:20	5869
open thine *e* upon such an one	Job 14:3	5869
and what do thy *e* wink at,	Job 15:12	5869
enemy sharpeneth his *e* upon me	Job 16:9	5869
even the *e* of his children shall	Job 17:5	5869
mine *e* shall behold, and not	Job 19:27	5869

and their offspring before their *e* ... Job 21:8 5869
His *e* shall see his destruction, ... Job 21:20 5869
yet his *e* are upon their ways ... Job 24:23 5869
he openeth his *e*, and he is not ... Job 27:19 5869
is hid from the *e* of all living ... Job 28:21 5869
I was *e* to the blind, and feet was ... Job 29:15 5869
I made a covenant with mine *e* ... Job 31:1 5869
and mine heart walked after mine *e* ... Job 31:7 5869
or have caused the *e* of the widow ... Job 31:16 5869
he was righteous in his own *e* ... Job 32:1 5869
For his *e* are upon the ways of ... Job 34:21 5869
not his *e* from the righteous ... Job 36:7 5869
prey, and her *e* behold afar off ... Job 39:29 5869
He taketh it with his *e* ... Job 40:24 5869
his *e* are like the eyelids of the ... Job 41:18 5869
his *e* are privily set against the ... Ps 10:8 5869
his *e* behold, his eyelids try, ... Ps 11:4 5869
lighten mine *e*, lest I sleep the ... Ps 13:3 5869
In whose *e* a vile person is ... Ps 15:4 5869
let thine *e* behold the things ... Ps 17:2 5869
they have set their *e* bowing down ... Ps 17:11 5869
LORD is pure, enlightening the *e* ... Ps 19:8 5869
Mine *e* are ever toward the LORD ... Ps 25:15 5869
lovingkindness is before mine *e* ... Ps 26:3 5869
I am cut off from before thine *e* ... Ps 31:22 5869
The *e* of the LORD are upon the ... Ps 34:15 5869
is no fear of God before his *e* ... Ps 36:1 5869
flattereth himself in his own *e* ... Ps 36:2 5869
as for the light of mine *e* ... Ps 38:10 5869
set them in order before thine *e* ... Ps 50:21 5869
his *e* behold the nations ... Ps 66:7 5869
mine *e* fail while I wait for my ... Ps 69:3 5869
Let their *e* be darkened, that ... Ps 69:23 5869
Their *e* stand out with fatness ... Ps 73:7 5869
Thou holdest mine *e* waking ... Ps 77:4 5869
Only with thine *e* shalt thou ... Ps 91:8 5869
set no wicked thing before mine *e* ... Ps 101:3 5869
Mine *e* shall be upon the faithful ... Ps 101:6 5869
e have they, but they see not ... Ps 115:5 5869
mine *e* from tears, and my feet ... Ps 116:8 5869
it is marvellous in our *e* ... Ps 118:23 5869
Open thou mine *e*, that I may ... Ps 119:18 5869
Turn away mine *e* from beholding ... Ps 119:37 5869
Mine *e* fail for thy word, saying, ... Ps 119:82 5869
Mine *e* fail for thy salvation, and ... Ps 119:123 5869
Rivers of waters run down mine *e* ... Ps 119:136 5869
Mine *e* prevent the night watches, ... Ps 119:148 5869
lift up mine *e* unto the hills ... Ps 121:1 5869
Unto thee lift I up mine *e* ... Ps 123:1 5869
as the *e* of servants look unto ... Ps 123:2 5869
as the *e* of a maiden unto the ... Ps 123:2 5869
so our *e* wait upon the LORD our ... Ps 123:2 5869
is not haughty, nor mine *e* lofty ... Ps 131:1 5869
I will not give sleep to mine *e* ... Ps 132:4 5869
e have they, but they see not ... Ps 135:16 5869
Thine *e* did see my substance, yet ... Ps 139:16 5869
But mine *e* are unto thee, O GOD ... Ps 141:8 5869
The *e* of all wait upon thee ... Ps 145:15 5869
LORD openeth the *e* of the blind ... Ps 146:8
Be not wise in thine own *e* ... Prov 3:7 5869
let not them depart from thine *e* ... Prov 3:21 5869
Let them not depart from thine *e* ... Prov 4:21 5869
Let thine *e* look right on, and let ... Prov 4:25 5869
man are before the *e* of the LORD ... Prov 5:21 5869
Give not sleep to thine *e* ... Prov 6:4 5869
He winketh with his *e*, he ... Prov 6:13 5869
the teeth, and as smoke to the *e* ... Prov 10:26 5869
of a fool is right in his own *e* ... Prov 12:15 5869
The *e* of the LORD are in every ... Prov 15:3 5869
The light of the *e* rejoiceth the ... Prov 15:30 5869
of a man are clean in his own *e* ... Prov 16:2 5869
He shutteth his *e* to devise ... Prov 16:30 5869
in the *e* of him that hath it ... Prov 17:8 5869
but the *e* of a fool are in the ... Prov 17:24 5869
away all evil with his *e* ... Prov 20:8 5869
open thine *e*, and thou shalt be ... Prov 20:13 5869
of a man is right in his own *e* ... Prov 21:2 5869
findeth no favour in his *e* ... Prov 21:10 5869
The *e* of the LORD preserve ... Prov 22:12 5869
Wilt thou set thine *e* upon that ... Prov 23:5 5869
let thine *e* observe my ways ... Prov 23:26 5869
who hath redness of *e* ... Prov 23:29 5869
Thine *e* shall behold strange ... Prov 23:33 5869
the prince whom thine *e* have seen ... Prov 25:7 5869
so the *e* of man are never ... Prov 27:20 5869
but he that hideth his *e* shall ... Prov 28:27 5869
the LORD lighteneth both their *e* ... Prov 29:13 5869
that are pure in their own *e* ... Prov 30:12 5869
O how lofty are their *e* ... Prov 30:13 5869
whatsoever mine *e* desired I kept ... Eccl 2:10 5869
The wise man's *e* are in his head ... Eccl 2:14 5869
beholding of them with their *e* ... Eccl 5:11 5869
the *e* than the wandering of the ... Eccl 6:9 5869
nor night seeth sleep with his *e* ... Eccl 8:16 5869
it is for the *e* to behold the sun ... Eccl 11:7 5869
heart, and in the sight of thine *e* ... Eccl 11:9 5869
thou hast doves' *e* ... Song 1:15 5869
hast doves' *e* within thy locks ... Song 4:1 5869
my heart with one of thine *e* ... Song 4:9 5869
His *e* are as the *e* of doves by ... Song 5:12 5869
Turn away thine *e* from me ... Song 6:5 5869
thine *e* like the fishpools in ... Song 7:4 5869
then was I in his *e* as one that ... Song 8:10 5869
I will hide mine *e* from you ... Is 1:15 5869
of your doings from before mine *e* ... Is 1:16 5869
to provoke the *e* of his glory ... Is 3:8 5869
stretched forth necks and wanton *e* ... Is 3:16 5869
the *e* of the lofty shall be ... Is 5:15 5869
them that are wise in their own *e* ... Is 5:21 5869
for mine *e* have seen the King, ... Is 6:5 5869
their ears heavy, and shut their *e* ... Is 6:10 5869
lest they see with their *e* ... Is 6:10 5869
judge after the sight of his *e* ... Is 11:3 5869
dashed to pieces before their *e* ... Is 13:16 5869
his *e* shall have respect to the ... Is 17:7 5869
deep sleep, and hath closed your *e* ... Is 29:10 5869
the *e* of the blind shall see out ... Is 29:18 5869
but thine *e* shall see thy ... Is 30:20 5869
the *e* of them that see shall not ... Is 32:3 5869
shutteth his *e* from seeing evil ... Is 33:15 5869
Thine *e* shall see the king in his ... Is 33:17 5869
thine *e* shall see Jerusalem a ... Is 33:20 5869
Then the *e* of the blind shall be ... Is 35:5 5869
open thine *e*, O LORD, and see ... Is 37:17 5869
and lifted up thine *e* on high ... Is 37:23 5869
mine *e* fail with looking upward ... Is 38:14 5869
Lift up your *e* on high, and behold ... Is 40:26 5869
To open the blind *e*, to bring out ... Is 42:7 5869
the blind people that have *e* ... Is 43:8 5869
for he hath shut their *e*, that ... Is 44:18 5869
be glorious in the *e* of the LORD ... Is 49:5 5869
Lift up thine *e* round about ... Is 49:18 5869
Lift up your *e* to the heavens, and ... Is 51:6 5869
arm in the *e* of all the nations ... Is 52:10 5869
and we grope as if we had no *e* ... Is 59:10 5869
Lift up thine *e* round about ... Is 60:4 5869
but did evil before mine *e* ... Is 65:12 5869
because they are hid from mine *e* ... Is 65:16 5869
but they did evil before mine *e* ... Is 66:4 5869
Lift up thine *e* unto the high ... Jer 3:2 5869
are not thine *e* upon the truth ... Jer 5:3 5869
which have *e*, and see not ... Jer 5:21 5869
become a den of robbers in your *e* ... Jer 7:11 5869
mine *e* a fountain of tears, that ... Jer 9:1 5869
that our *e* may run down with ... Jer 9:18 5869
Lift up your *e*, and behold them ... Jer 13:20 5869
their *e* did fail, because there ... Jer 14:6 5869
Let mine *e* run down with tears ... Jer 14:17 5869
cease out of this place in your *e* ... Jer 16:9 5869
For mine *e* are upon all their ... Jer 16:17 5869
is their iniquity hid from mine *e* ... Jer 16:17 5869
and thine *e* shall behold it ... Jer 20:4 5869
But thine *e* and thine heart are ... Jer 22:17 5869
set mine *e* upon them for good ... Jer 24:6 5869
he shall slay them before your *e* ... Jer 29:21 5869
weeping, and thine *e* from tears ... Jer 31:16 5869
his *e* shall behold his *e* ... Jer 32:4 5869
for thine *e* are open upon all the ... Jer 32:19 5869
thine *e* shall behold the *e* of ... Jer 34:3 5869
the *e* of the king of Babylon ... Jer 34:3 5869
Zedekiah in Riblah before his *e* ... Jer 39:6 5869
Moreover he put out Zedekiah's *e* ... Jer 39:7 5869
of many, as thine *e* do behold us ... Jer 42:2 5869
was evil in the *e* of the LORD ... Jer 52:2 5869
the sons of Zedekiah before his *e* ... Jer 52:10 5869
Then he put out the *e* of Zedekiah ... Jer 52:11 5869
Mine *e* do fail with tears, my ... Lam 2:11 5869
our *e* as yet failed for our vain ... Lam 4:17 5869
for these things our *e* are dim ... Lam 5:17 5869
full of *e* round about them four ... Eze 1:18 5869
departed from me, and with their *e* ... Eze 6:9 5869
lift up thine *e* now the way ... Eze 8:5 5869
So I lifted up mine *e* the way ... Eze 8:5 5869
were full of *e* round about ... Eze 10:12 5869
house, which have *e* to see ... Eze 12:2 5869
he see not the ground with his *e* ... Eze 12:12 5869
neither hath lifted up his *e* to ... Eze 18:6 5869
hath lifted up his *e* to the idols ... Eze 18:12 5869
neither hath lifted up his *e* to ... Eze 18:15 5869
man the abominations of his *e* ... Eze 20:7 5869
away the abominations of their *e* ... Eze 20:8 5869
their *e* were after their fathers' ... Eze 20:24 5869
bitterness sigh before their *e* ... Eze 21:6 5869
have hid their *e* from my sabbaths ... Eze 22:26 5869
soon as she saw them with her *e* ... Eze 23:16 5869
not lift up thine *e* unto them ... Eze 23:27 5869
wash thyself, paintedst thy *e* ... Eze 23:40 5869
desire of thine *e* with a stroke ... Eze 24:16 5869
strength, the desire of your *e* ... Eze 24:21 5869
glory, the desire of their *e* ... Eze 24:25 5869
lift up your *e* toward your idols, ... Eze 33:25 5869
sanctified in you before their *e* ... Eze 36:23 5869
be in thine hand before their *e* ... Eze 37:20 5869
in thee, O Gog, before their *e* ... Eze 38:16 5869
be known in the *e* of many nations ... Eze 38:23 5869
Son of man, behold with thine *e* ... Eze 40:4 5869
mark well, and behold with thine *e* ... Eze 44:5 5869
lifted up mine *e* unto heaven ... Dan 4:34 5870
in this horn were *e* like the *e* ... Dan 7:8 5870
horn were like the *e* of man ... Dan 7:8 5870
even of that horn that had *e* ... Dan 7:20 5870
Then I lifted up mine *e*, and saw, ... Dan 8:3 5869
had a notable horn between his *e* ... Dan 8:5 5869
between his *e* is the first king ... Dan 8:21 5869
open thine *e*, and behold our ... Dan 9:18 5869
Then I lifted up mine *e*, and ... Dan 10:5 5869
his *e* as lamps of fire, and his ... Dan 10:6 5869
shall be hid from mine *e* ... Hos 13:14 5869
not the meat cut off before our *e* ... Joel 1:16 5869
I will set mine *e* upon them for ... Amos 9:4 5869
the *e* of the Lord GOD are upon ... Amos 9:8 5869
mine *e* shall behold her ... Mic 7:10 5869
Thou art of purer *e* than to ... Hab 1:13 5869
back your captivity before your *e* ... Zeph 3:20 5869
is it not in your *e* in comparison ... Hag 2:3 5869
Then lifted I up mine *e*, and saw, ... Zec 1:18 5869
I lifted up mine *e* again, and ... Zec 2:1 5869
upon one stone shall be seven *e* ... Zec 3:9 5869
they are the *e* of the LORD ... Zec 4:10 5869
I turned, and lifted up mine *e* ... Zec 5:1 5869
said unto me, Lift up now thine *e* ... Zec 5:5 5869
Then lifted I up mine *e*, and ... Zec 5:9 5869
And I turned, and lifted up mine *e* ... Zec 6:1 5869
If it be marvellous in the *e* of ... Zec 8:6 5869
it also be marvellous in mine *e* ... Zec 8:6 5869
when the *e* of man, as of all the ... Zec 9:1 5869
for now have I seen with mine *e* ... Zec 9:8 5869
I will open mine *e* upon the house ... Zec 12:4 5869
their *e* shall consume away in ... Zec 14:12 5869
your *e* shall see, and ye shall say ... Mal 1:5 5869
Then touched he their *e*, saying, ... Mt 9:29 *3788*
And their *e* were opened ... Mt 9:30 *3788*
and their *e* they have closed ... Mt 13:15 *3788*
time they should see with their *e* ... Mt 13:15 *3788*
But blessed are your *e*, for they ... Mt 13:16 *3788*
when they had lifted up their *e* ... Mt 17:8 *3788*
rather than having two *e* to be ... Mt 18:9 *3788*
Lord, that our *e* may be opened ... Mt 20:33 *3788*
on them, and touched their *e* ... Mt 20:34
their *e* received sight, and they ... Mt 20:34 *3788*
and it is marvellous in our *e* ... Mt 21:42 *3788*
for their *e* were heavy ... Mt 26:43 *3788*
Having *e*, see ye not ... Mk 8:18 *3788*
and when he had spit on his *e* ... Mk 8:23 *3659*
he put his hands again upon his *e* ... Mk 8:25 *3788*
than having two *e* to be cast into ... Mk 9:47 *3788*
and it is marvellous in our *e* ... Mk 12:11 *3788*
again, (for their *e* were heavy ... Mk 14:40 *3788*
For mine *e* have seen thy ... Lk 2:30 *3788*
the *e* of all them that were in ... Lk 4:20 *3788*
lifted up his *e* on his disciples ... Lk 6:20 *3788*
Blessed are the *e* which see the ... Lk 10:23 *3788*
And in hell he lift up his *e* ... Lk 16:23 *3788*
up so much as his *e* unto heaven ... Lk 18:13 *3788*
but now they are hid from thine *e* ... Lk 19:42 *3788*
But their *e* were holden that they ... Lk 24:16 *3788*
their *e* were opened, and they knew ... Lk 24:31 *3788*
I say unto you, Lift up your *e* ... Jn 4:35 *3788*
When Jesus then lifted up his *e* ... Jn 6:5 *3788*
he anointed the *e* of the blind ... Jn 9:6 *3788*
unto him, How were thine *e* opened ... Jn 9:10 *3788*
made clay, and anointed mine *e* ... Jn 9:11 *3788*
made the clay, and opened his *e* ... Jn 9:14 *3788*
them, He put clay upon mine *e* ... Jn 9:15 *3788*
him, that he hath opened thine *e* ... Jn 9:17 *3788*
or who hath opened his *e*, we know ... Jn 9:21 *3788*
how opened he thine *e* ... Jn 9:26 *3788*
is, and yet he hath opened mine *e* ... Jn 9:30 *3788*
the *e* of one that was born blind ... Jn 9:32 *3788*
a devil open the *e* of the blind ... Jn 10:21 *3788*
which opened the *e* of the blind ... Jn 11:37 *3788*
And Jesus lifted up his *e*, and said ... Jn 11:41 *3788*
He hath blinded their *e*, and ... Jn 12:40 *3788*
they should not see with their *e* ... Jn 12:40 *3788*
and lifted up his *e* to heaven ... Jn 17:1 *3788*
fastening his *e* upon him with ... Acts 3:4
when his *e* were opened, he saw no ... Acts 9:8 *3788*
from his *e* as it had been scales ... Acts 9:18 *3788*
And she opened her *e* ... Acts 9:40 *3788*
which when I had fastened mine *e* ... Acts 11:6
the Holy Ghost, set his *e* on him ... Acts 13:9
To open their *e*, and to turn them ... Acts 26:18 *3788*
and their *e* have they closed ... Acts 28:27 *3788*
lest they should see with their *e* ... Acts 28:27 *3788*
is no fear of God before their *e* ... Rom 3:18 *3788*
e that they should not see, and ... Rom 11:8 *3788*
Let their *e* be darkened, that ... Rom 11:10 *3788*
before whose *e* Jesus Christ hath ... Gal 3:1 *3788*
would have plucked out your own *e* ... Gal 4:15 *3788*
The *e* of your understanding being ... Eph 1:18 *3788*
opened unto the *e* of him with ... Heb 4:13 *3788*
For the *e* of the Lord are over ... 1Pet 3:12 *3788*
Having *e* full of adultery, and ... 2Pet 2:14 *3788*
which we have seen with our *e* ... 1Jn 1:1 *3788*
that darkness hath blinded his *e* ... 1Jn 2:11 *3788*
the flesh, and the lust of the *e* ... 1Jn 2:16 *3788*
his *e* were as a flame of fire ... Rev 1:14 *3788*
who hath his *e* like unto a flame ... Rev 2:18 *3788*
anoint thine *e* with eyesalve, ... Rev 3:18 *3788*
were four beasts full of *e* before ... Rev 4:6 *3788*
and they were full of *e* within ... Rev 4:8 *3788*
having seven horns and seven *e* ... Rev 5:6 *3788*
wipe away all tears from their *e* ... Rev 7:17 *3788*
His *e* were as a flame of fire, and ... Rev 19:12 *3788*
wipe away all tears from their *e* ... Rev 21:4 *3788*

EYESALVE {1}
and anoint thine eyes with *e* ... Rev 3:18 *2854*

EYESERVICE {2}
Not with *e*, as menpleasers ... Eph 6:6 *3787*
not with *e*, as menpleasers ... Col 3:22 *3787*

EYESIGHT {1}
cleanness of my hands in his *e* ... Ps 18:24 5869

EYEWITNESSES {2}
which from the beginning were *e* ... Lk 1:2 *845*
but were *e* of his majesty ... 2Pet 1:16 *2030*

EZAR *(e'-zar)* {1} See EZER. *A son of Seir.*
Zibeon, and Anah, and Dishon, and *E* ... 1Chr 1:38 687

EZBAI *(ez'-bahee)* {1} *Father of Naarai.*
Carmelite, Naarai the son of *E* ... 1Chr 11:37 229

EZBON *(ez'-bon)* {2}
1. Son of Gad.
Ziphion, and Haggi, Shuni, and *E* ... Gen 46:16 675
2. Son of Bela.
E, and Uzzi, and Uzziel, and ... 1Chr 7:7 675

EZEKIAS *(ez-e-ki'-as)* {2} See HEZEKIAH. *Greek form of Hezekiah.*
and Achaz begat *E* ... Mt 1:9 *1478*
And *E* begat Manasses ... Mt 1:10 *1478*

EZEKIEL {2} *A priest and prophet.*
came expressly unto *E* the priest ... Eze 1:3 3168
Thus *E* is unto you a sign ... Eze 24:24 3168

EZEL {1} *A boundary stone.*
and shalt remain by the stone *E* ... 1Sa 20:19 237

EZEM {1} *A city in Judah.*
And at Bilhah, and at *E*, and at ... 1Chr 4:29 6107

EZER {9}
1. Son of Seir the Horite.
And Dishon, and *E*, and Dishan ... Gen 36:21 687
The children of *E* are these ... Gen 36:27 687
Duke Dishon, duke *E*, duke Dishan ... Gen 36:30 687
The sons of *E*; Bilhan ... 1Chr 1:42 687
2. A descendant of Judah.
Gedor, and *E* the father of Hushah ... 1Chr 4:4 5829
3. A son of Ephraim.
son, and Shuthelah his son, and *E* ... 1Chr 7:21 5827
4. A Gadite who fought for David.
E the first, Obadiah the second, ... 1Chr 12:9 5829
5. A Levite who repaired the Jerusalem wall.
him repaired *E* the son of Jeshua ... Neh 3:19 5829
6. A priest in the time of Nehemiah.
and Malchijah, and Elam, and *E* ... Neh 12:42 5829

EZION-GABER {4} *Same as Ezion-geber.*
from Ebronah, and encamped at *E* ... Num 33:35 6100
And they removed from *E*, and ... Num 33:36 6100
the plain from Elath, and from *E* ... Deut 2:8 6100
and they made the ships in *E* ... 2Chr 20:36 6100

EZION-GEBER *(e'-ze-on-ghe'-bur)* {3} See EZION-GABER. *An Israelite seaport.*
Solomon made a navy of ships in *E* ... 1Kin 9:26 6100
for the ships were broken at *E* ... 1Kin 22:48 6100
Then went Solomon to *E*, and to ... 2Chr 8:17 6100

EZNITE *(ez'-nite)* {1} *Descendant of Adino.*
the same was Adino the *E* ... 2Sa 23:8 6112

EZRA *(ez'-rah)* {26} See AZARIAH, EZRAHITE.
1. A descendant of Judah.
And the sons of *E* were, Jether, and ... 1Chr 4:17 5830
2. Priest who led exiles back to Jerusalem.
E the son of Seraiah, the son of ... Ezr 7:1 5830
This *E* went up from Babylon ... Ezr 7:6 5830
For *E* had prepared his heart to ... Ezr 7:10 5830
Artaxerxes gave unto *E* the priest ... Ezr 7:11 5830
unto *E* the priest, a scribe of ... Ezr 7:12 5830
that whatsoever *E* the priest ... Ezr 7:21 5830
And thou, *E*, after the wisdom of ... Ezr 7:25 5830
Now when *E* had prayed, and when he ... Ezr 10:1 5830
of Elam, answered and said unto *E* ... Ezr 10:2 5830
Then arose *E*, and made the chief ... Ezr 10:5 5830
Then *E* rose up from before the ... Ezr 10:6 5830
E the priest stood up, and said ... Ezr 10:10 5830
E the priest, with certain chief ... Ezr 10:16 5830
they spake unto *E* the scribe to ... Neh 8:1 5830
E the priest brought the law ... Neh 8:2 5830
E the scribe stood upon a pulpit ... Neh 8:4 5830
E opened the book in the sight of ... Neh 8:5 5830
E blessed the LORD, the great God ... Neh 8:6 5830
E the priest the scribe, and the ... Neh 8:9 5830
unto *E* the scribe, even to ... Neh 8:13 5830
Of *E*, Meshullam ... Neh 12:13 5830
of *E* the priest, the scribe ... Neh 12:26 5830
And Azariah, *E*, and Meshullam, ... Neh 12:33 5830
God, and *E* the scribe before them ... Neh 12:36 5830
3. A priest who returned from exile.
Seraiah, Jeremiah, *E*, ... Neh 12:1 5830

EZRAH See EZRA.

EZRAHITE *(ez'-rah-hite)* {3}
than Ethan the *E*, and Heman, and ... 1Kin 4:31 250
Leannoth, Maschil of Heman the *E* ... Ps 88:*t* 250
Maschil of Ethan the *E* ... Ps 89:*t* 250

EZRI *(ez'-ri)* {1} *A superindendent of David.*
ground was *E* the son of Chelub ... 1Chr 27:26 5836

F

FABLES {5}
Neither give heed to *f* and endless ... 1Ti 1:4 *3454*
refuse profane and old wives' *f* ... 1Ti 4:7 *3454*
truth, and shall be turned unto *f* ... 2Ti 4:4 *3454*
Not giving heed to Jewish *f* ... Titus 1:14 *3454*
not followed cunningly devised *f* ... 2Pet 1:16 *3454*

FACE {422}
was upon the *f* of the deep ... Gen 1:2 6440
moved upon the *f* of the waters ... Gen 1:2 6440
is upon the *f* of all the earth ... Gen 1:29 6440
watered the whole *f* of the ground ... Gen 2:6 6440
In the sweat of thy *f* shalt thou ... Gen 3:19 639
this day from the *f* of the earth ... Gen 4:14 6440
from thy *f* shall I be hid ... Gen 4:14 6440
to multiply on the *f* of the earth ... Gen 6:1 6440
created from the *f* of the earth ... Gen 6:7 6440
alive upon the *f* of all the earth ... Gen 7:3 6440
from off the *f* of the earth ... Gen 7:4 6440
ark went upon the *f* of the waters ... Gen 7:18 6440
was upon the *f* of the ground ... Gen 7:23 6440
from off the *f* of the ground ... Gen 8:8 6440
were on the *f* of the whole earth ... Gen 8:9 6440
the *f* of the ground was dry ... Gen 8:13 6440
upon the *f* of the whole earth ... Gen 11:4 6440
upon the *f* of all the earth ... Gen 11:8 6440
upon the *f* of all the earth ... Gen 11:9 6440
with her, she fled from her *f* ... Gen 16:6 6440
I flee from the *f* of my mistress ... Gen 16:8 6440
And Abram fell on his *f* ... Gen 17:3 6440
Then Abraham fell upon his *f* ... Gen 17:17 6440
with his *f* toward the ground ... Gen 19:1 639
great before the *f* of the LORD ... Gen 19:13 6440
and I put the earring upon her *f* ... Gen 24:47 639
come for my hire before thy *f* ... Gen 30:33 6440
set his *f* toward the mount Gilead ... Gen 31:21 6440
me, and afterward I will see his *f* ... Gen 32:20 6440
for I have seen God *f* to *f* ... Gen 32:30 6440
for therefore I have seen thy *f* ... Gen 33:10 6440
as though I had seen the *f* of God ... Gen 33:10 6440
from the *f* of Esau thy brother ... Gen 35:1 6440
he fled from the *f* of his brother ... Gen 35:7 6440
from the *f* of his brother Jacob ... Gen 36:6 6440
because she had covered her *f* ... Gen 38:15 6440
was over all the *f* of the earth ... Gen 41:56 6440
us, saying, Ye shall not see my *f* ... Gen 43:3 6440
unto us, Ye shall not see my *f* ... Gen 43:5 6440
And he washed his *f*, and went out, ... Gen 43:31 6440
you, ye shall see my *f* no more ... Gen 44:23 6440
for we may not see the man's *f* ... Gen 44:26 6440
to direct his *f* unto Goshen ... Gen 46:28 6440
me die, since I have seen thy *f* ... Gen 46:30 6440
I had not thought to see thy *f* ... Gen 48:11 6440
himself with his *f* to the earth ... Gen 48:12 639
Joseph fell upon his father's *f* ... Gen 50:1 6440
went and fell down before his *f* ... Gen 50:18 6440
Moses fled from the *f* of Pharaoh ... Ex 2:15 6440
And Moses hid his *f* ... Ex 3:6 6440
shall cover the *f* of the earth ... Ex 10:5 5869
covered the *f* of the whole earth ... Ex 10:15 5869
heed to thyself, see my *f* no more ... Ex 10:28 6440
thou seest my *f* thou shalt die ... Ex 10:28 6440
I will see thy *f* again no more ... Ex 10:29 6440
cloud went from before their *f* ... Ex 14:19 6440
Let us flee from the *f* of Israel ... Ex 14:25 6440
upon the *f* of the wilderness ... Ex 16:14 6440
them from the *f* of the earth ... Ex 32:12 6440
LORD spake unto Moses *f* to *f* ... Ex 33:11 6440
that are upon the *f* of the earth ... Ex 33:16 6440
he said, Thou canst not see my *f* ... Ex 33:20 6440
but my *f* shall not be seen ... Ex 33:23 6440
wist not that the skin of his *f* ... Ex 34:29 6440
behold, the skin of his *f* shone ... Ex 34:30 6440
with them, he put a vail on his *f* ... Ex 34:33 6440
of Israel saw the *f* of Moses ... Ex 34:35 6440
that the skin of Moses' *f* shone ... Ex 34:35 6440
put the vail upon his *f* again ... Ex 34:35 6440
the part of his head toward his *f* ... Lev 13:41 6440
I will even set my *f* against that ... Lev 17:10 6440
honour the *f* of the old man, and ... Lev 19:32 6440
I will set my *f* against that man, ... Lev 20:3 6440
I will set my *f* against that man ... Lev 20:5 6440
even set my *f* against that soul ... Lev 20:6 6440
And I will set my *f* against you ... Lev 26:17 6440
LORD make his *f* shine upon thee ... Num 6:25 6440
high upon the *f* of the earth ... Num 11:31 6440
were upon the *f* of the earth ... Num 12:3 6440
her father had but spit in her *f* ... Num 12:14 6440
that thou LORD art seen *f* to *f* ... Num 14:14 5869
heard it, he fell upon his *f* ... Num 16:4 6440
one shall slay her before his *f* ... Num 19:3 6440
they cover the *f* of the earth ... Num 22:5 5869
which covereth the *f* of the earth ... Num 22:11 5869
his head, and fell flat on his *f* ... Num 22:31 639
but he set his *f* toward the ... Num 24:1 6440
not be afraid of the *f* of man ... Deut 1:17 6440
LORD talked with you *f* to *f* in ... Deut 5:4 6440
thee from off the *f* of the earth ... Deut 6:15 6440
that are upon the *f* of the earth ... Deut 7:6 6440
them that hate him to their *f* ... Deut 7:10 6440
him, he will repay him to his *f* ... Deut 7:10 6440
the LORD destroyeth before your *f* ... Deut 8:20
bring them down before thy *f* ... Deut 9:3
and to be beaten before his *f* ... Deut 25:2
off his foot, and spit in his *f* ... Deut 25:9 6440
thee to be smitten before thy *f* ... Deut 28:7
taken away from before thy *f* ... Deut 28:31
shall give them up before your *f* ... Deut 31:5
and I will hide my *f* from them ... Deut 31:17 6440
I will surely hide my *f* in that ... Deut 31:18 6440
said, I will hide my *f* from them ... Deut 32:20 6440
whom the LORD knew *f* to *f* ... Deut 34:10 6440
Joshua fell on his *f* to the earth ... Josh 5:14 6440
his *f* before the ark of the LORD ... Josh 7:6 6440
liest thou thus upon thy *f* ... Josh 7:10 6440
an angel of the LORD *f* to *f* ... Judg 6:22 6440
Then she fell on her *f*, and bowed ... Ruth 2:10 6440
Dagon was fallen upon his *f* to ... 1Sa 5:3 6440
Dagon was fallen upon his *f* to ... 1Sa 5:4 6440
he fell upon his *f* to the earth ... 1Sa 17:49 6440
every one from the *f* of the earth ... 1Sa 20:15 6440
fell on his *f* to the ground, and ... 1Sa 20:41 639
stooped with his *f* to the earth ... 1Sa 24:8 639
and fell before David on her *f* ... 1Sa 25:23 6440
herself on her *f* to the earth ... 1Sa 25:41 639
earth before the *f* of the LORD ... 1Sa 26:20 6440
stooped with his *f* to the ground ... 1Sa 28:14 639
hold up my *f* to Joab thy brother ... 2Sa 2:22 6440
that is, Thou shalt not see my *f* ... 2Sa 3:13 6440
when thou comest to see my *f* ... 2Sa 3:13 6440
come unto David, he fell on his *f* ... 2Sa 9:6 6440
she fell on her *f* to the ground ... 2Sa 14:4 639
Joab fell to the ground on his *f* ... 2Sa 14:22 6440
house, and let him not see my *f* ... 2Sa 14:24 6440
house, and saw not the king's *f* ... 2Sa 14:24 6440
and saw not the king's *f* ... 2Sa 14:28 6440
therefore let me see the king's *f* ... 2Sa 14:32 6440
bowed himself on his *f* to the ... 2Sa 14:33 639
over the *f* of all the country ... 2Sa 18:8 6440
earth upon his *f* before the king ... 2Sa 18:28 639
But the king covered his *f* ... 2Sa 19:4 6440
the king on his *f* upon the ground ... 2Sa 24:20 639
the king with his *f* to the ground ... 1Kin 1:23 639
bowed with her *f* to the earth ... 1Kin 1:31 639
And the king turned his *f* about ... 1Kin 8:14 6440
Intreat now the *f* of the LORD thy ... 1Kin 13:6 6440
it from off the *f* of the earth ... 1Kin 13:34 6440
and he knew him, and fell on his *f* ... 1Kin 18:7 6440
put his *f* between his knees, ... 1Kin 18:42 6440
he wrapped his *f* in his mantle ... 1Kin 19:13 6440
himself with ashes upon his *f* ... 1Kin 20:38 5869
and took the ashes away from his *f* ... 1Kin 20:41 5869
his bed, and turned away his *f* ... 1Kin 21:4 6440
my staff upon the *f* of the child ... 2Kin 4:29 6440
the staff upon the *f* of the child ... 2Kin 4:31 6440
in water, and spread it on his *f* ... 2Kin 8:15 6440
and she painted her *f*, and tired ... 2Kin 9:30 5869
he lifted up his *f* to the window ... 2Kin 9:32 6440
shall be as dung upon the *f* of ... 2Kin 9:37 6440
Hazael set his *f* to go up to ... 2Kin 12:17 6440
down unto him, and wept over his *f* ... 2Kin 13:14 6440
let us look one another in the *f* ... 2Kin 14:8 6440
another in the *f* at Beth-shemesh ... 2Kin 14:11 6440
then wilt thou turn away the *f* of ... 2Kin 18:24 6440
Then he turned his *f* to the wall ... 2Kin 20:2 6440
strength, seek his *f* continually ... 1Chr 16:11 6440
to David with his *f* to the ground ... 1Chr 21:21 639
And the king turned his *f*, and ... 2Chr 6:3 6440
not away the *f* of thine anointed ... 2Chr 6:42 6440
themselves, and pray, and seek my *f* ... 2Chr 7:14 6440
his head with his *f* to the ground ... 2Chr 20:18 639
let us see one another in the *f* ... 2Chr 25:17 6440
and they saw one another in the *f* ... 2Chr 25:21 6440
will not turn away his *f* from you ... 2Chr 30:9 6440
with shame of *f* to his own land ... 2Chr 32:21 6440
would not turn his *f* from him ... 2Chr 35:22 6440
and blush to lift up my *f* to thee ... Ezr 9:6 6440
to a spoil, and to confusion of *f* ... Ezr 9:7 6440
and Media, which saw the king's *f* ... Est 1:14 6440
mouth, they covered Haman's *f* ... Est 7:8 6440
and he will curse thee to thy *f* ... Job 1:11 6440
and he will curse thee to thy *f* ... Job 2:5 6440
Then a spirit passed before my *f* ... Job 4:15 6440
thou lift up thy *f* without spot ... Job 11:15 6440
Wherefore hidest thou thy *f* ... Job 13:24 6440
covereth his *f* with his fatness ... Job 15:27 6440
up in me beareth witness to my *f* ... Job 16:8 6440
My *f* is foul with weeping, and on ... Job 16:16 6440
shall declare his way to his *f* ... Job 21:31 6440
and shalt lift up thy *f* unto God ... Job 22:26 6440
he covered the darkness from my *f* ... Job 23:17 6440
and disguiseth his *f* ... Job 24:15 6440
holdeth back the *f* of his throne ... Job 26:9 6440
me, and spare not to spit in my *f* ... Job 30:10 6440
and he shall see his *f* with joy ... Job 33:26 6440
and when he hideth his *f*, who then ... Job 34:29 6440
the *f* of the world in the earth ... Job 37:12 6440
the *f* of the deep is frozen ... Job 38:30 6440
can discover the *f* of his garment ... Job 41:13 6440
Who can open the doors of his *f* ... Job 41:14 6440
make thy way straight before my *f* ... Ps 5:8 6440
he hideth his *f* ... Ps 10:11 6440
long wilt thou hide thy *f* from me ... Ps 13:1 6440
behold thy *f* in righteousness ... Ps 17:15 6440
thy strings against the *f* of them ... Ps 21:12 6440
hath he hid his *f* from him ... Ps 22:24 6440
that seek him, that seek thy *f* ... Ps 24:6 6440
When thou saidst, Seek ye my *f* ... Ps 27:8 6440
my heart said unto thee, Thy *f* ... Ps 27:8 6440
Hide not thy *f* far from me ... Ps 27:9 6440
thou didst hide thy *f*, and I was ... Ps 30:7 6440
Make thy *f* to shine upon thy ... Ps 31:16 6440
The *f* of the LORD is against them ... Ps 34:16 6440
settest me before thy *f* for ever ... Ps 41:12 6440

the shame of my *f* hath covered me ... Ps 44:15 6440
Wherefore hidest thou thy *f* ... Ps 44:24 6440
Hide thy *f* from my sins, and blot ... Ps 51:9 6440
cause his *f* to shine upon us ... Ps 67:1 6440
shame hath covered my *f* ... Ps 69:7 6440
hide not thy *f* from thy servant ... Ps 69:17 6440
O God, and cause thy *f* to shine ... Ps 80:3 6440
of hosts, and cause thy *f* to shine ... Ps 80:7 6440
of hosts, cause thy *f* to shine ... Ps 80:19 6440
look upon the *f* of thine anointed ... Ps 84:9 6440
why hidest thou thy *f* from me ... Ps 88:14 6440
and truth shall go before thy *f* ... Ps 89:14 6440
beat down his foes before his *f* ... Ps 89:23 6440
Hide not thy *f* from me in the day ... Ps 102:2 6440
and oil to make his *f* to shine ... Ps 104:15 6440
Thou hidest thy *f*, they are ... Ps 104:29 6440
thou renewest the *f* of the earth ... Ps 104:30 6440
seek his *f* evermore ... Ps 105:4 6440
Make thy *f* to shine upon thy ... Ps 119:135 6440
not away the *f* of thine anointed ... Ps 132:10 6440
hide not thy *f* from me, lest I be ... Ps 143:7 6440
with an impudent *f* said unto him ... Prov 7:13 6440
thee, diligently to seek thy *f* ... Prov 7:15 6440
a compass upon the *f* of the depth ... Prov 8:27 6440
A wicked man hardeneth his *f* ... Prov 21:29 6440
nettles had covered the *f* thereof ... Prov 24:31 6440
As in water *f* answereth to *f*, ... Prov 27:19 6440
wisdom maketh his *f* to shine ... Eccl 8:1 6440
of his *f* shall be changed ... Eccl 8:1 6440
with twain he covered his *f* ... Is 6:2 6440
that hideth his *f* from the house ... Is 8:17 6440
nor fill the *f* of the world with ... Is 14:21 6440
to them from the *f* of the spoiler ... Is 16:4 6440
the world upon the *f* of the earth ... Is 23:17 6440
destroy in this mountain the *f* of ... Is 25:7 6440
fill the *f* of the world with ... Is 27:6 6440
he hath made plain the *f* thereof ... Is 28:25 6440
neither shall his *f* now wax pale ... Is 29:22 6440
then wilt thou turn away the *f* of ... Is 36:9 6440
turned his *f* toward the wall ... Is 38:2 6440
with their *f* toward the earth ... Is 49:23 639
I hid not my *f* from shame ... Is 50:6 6440
have I set my *f* like a flint ... Is 50:7 6440
I hid my *f* from thee for a moment ... Is 54:8 6440
your sins have hid his *f* from you ... Is 59:2 6440
for thou hast hid thy *f* from us ... Is 64:7 6440
me to anger continually to my *f* ... Is 65:3 6440
the *f* thereof is toward the north ... Jer 1:13 6440
back unto me, and not their *f* ... Jer 2:27 6440
thou rentest thy *f* with painting ... Jer 4:30 5869
for dung upon the *f* of the earth ... Jer 8:2 6440
I discover thy skirts upon thy *f* ... Jer 13:26 6440
as dung upon the *f* of the earth ... Jer 16:4 6440
they are not hid from my *f* ... Jer 16:17 6440
shew them the back, and not the *f* ... Jer 18:17 6440
For I have set my *f* against this ... Jer 21:10 6440
hand of them whose *f* thou fearest ... Jer 22:25 6440
which are upon the *f* of the earth ... Jer 25:26 6440
thee from off the *f* of the earth ... Jer 28:16 6440
should remove it from before my *f* ... Jer 32:31 6440
unto me the back, and not the *f* ... Jer 32:33 6440
I have hid my *f* from this city ... Jer 33:5 6440
I will set my *f* against you for ... Jer 44:11 6440
water before the *f* of the Lord ... Lam 2:19 6440
man before the *f* of the most High ... Lam 3:35 6440
they four had the *f* of a man ... Eze 1:10 6440
the *f* of a lion, on the right ... Eze 1:10 6440
they four had the *f* of an ox on ... Eze 1:10 6440
four also had the *f* of an eagle ... Eze 1:10 6440
when I saw it, I fell upon my *f* ... Eze 1:28 6440
I have made thy *f* strong against ... Eze 3:8 6440
and I fell on my *f* ... Eze 3:23 6440
set thy *f* against it, and it shall ... Eze 4:3 6440
Therefore thou shalt set thy *f* ... Eze 4:7 6440
set thy *f* toward the mountains of ... Eze 6:2 6440
My *f* will I turn also from them, ... Eze 7:22 6440
I was left, that I fell upon my *f*, ... Eze 9:8 6440
first *f* was the *f* of a cherub ... Eze 10:14 6440
second *f* was the *f* of a man ... Eze 10:14 6440
and the third the *f* of a lion ... Eze 10:14 6440
and the fourth the *f* of an eagle ... Eze 10:14 6440
Then fell I down upon my *f* ... Eze 11:13 6440
thou shalt cover thy *f*, that thou ... Eze 12:6 6440
he shall cover his *f*, that he see ... Eze 12:12 6440
set thy *f* against the daughters ... Eze 13:17 6440
of their iniquity before their *f* ... Eze 14:3 6440
of his iniquity before his *f* ... Eze 14:4 6440
of his iniquity before his *f* ... Eze 14:7 6440
I will set my *f* against that man, ... Eze 14:8 6440
And I will set my *f* against them ... Eze 15:7 6440
when I set my *f* against them ... Eze 15:7 6440
will I plead with you *f* to *f* ... Eze 20:35 6440
will I plead with you *f* to *f* ... Eze 20:35 6440
set thy *f* toward the south, and ... Eze 20:46 6440
set thy *f* toward Jerusalem, and ... Eze 21:2 6440
left, whithersoever thy *f* is set ... Eze 21:16 6440
set thy *f* against the Ammonites, ... Eze 25:2 6440
set thy *f* against Zidon, and ... Eze 28:21 6440
set thy *f* against Pharaoh king of ... Eze 29:2 6440
upon all the *f* of the earth ... Eze 34:6 6440
set thy *f* against mount Seir, and ... Eze 35:2 6440
set thy *f* against Gog, the land ... Eze 38:2 6440
my fury shall come up in my *f* ... Eze 38:18 639
that are upon the *f* of the earth ... Eze 38:20 6440
remain upon the *f* of the earth ... Eze 39:14 6440
therefore hid I my *f* from them ... Eze 39:23 6440
unto them, and hid my *f* from them ... Eze 39:24 6440
I hide my *f* any more from them ... Eze 39:29 6440
from the *f* of the gate of the ... Eze 40:15 6440
gate of the entrance unto the *f* ... Eze 40:15 6440
the breadth of the *f* of the house ... Eze 41:14 6440
So that the *f* of a man was toward ... Eze 41:19 6440
the *f* of a young lion toward the ... Eze 41:19 6440
and the *f* of the sanctuary ... Eze 41:21 6440
upon the *f* of the porch without ... Eze 41:25 6440
and I fell upon my *f* ... Eze 43:3 6440
and I fell upon my *f* ... Eze 44:4 6440
Nebuchadnezzar fell upon his *f* ... Dan 2:46 600
west on the *f* of the whole earth ... Dan 8:5 6440
I was afraid, and fell upon my *f* ... Dan 8:17 6440
sleep on my *f* toward the ground ... Dan 8:18 6440
I set my *f* unto the Lord God, to ... Dan 9:3 6440
to us belongeth confusion of *f* ... Dan 9:8 6440
cause thy *f* to shine upon thy ... Dan 9:17 6440
his *f* as the appearance of ... Dan 10:6 6440
was I in a deep sleep on my *f* ... Dan 10:9 6440
and my *f* toward the ground ... Dan 10:9 6440
I set my *f* toward the ground, and ... Dan 10:15 6440
He shall also set his *f* to enter ... Dan 11:17 6440
he turn his *f* unto the isles ... Dan 11:18 6440
Then he shall turn his *f* toward ... Dan 11:19 6440
of Israel doth testify to his *f* ... Hos 5:5 6440
their offence, and seek my *f* ... Hos 5:15 6440
they are before my *f* ... Hos 7:2 6440
of Israel testifieth to his *f* ... Hos 7:10 6440
Before their *f* the people shall ... Joel 2:6 6440
with his *f* toward the east sea, ... Joel 2:20 6440
them out upon the *f* of the earth ... Amos 5:8 6440
them out upon the *f* of the earth ... Amos 9:6 6440
it from off the *f* of the earth ... Amos 9:8 6440
he will even hide his *f* from them ... Mic 3:4 6440
in pieces is come up before thy *f* ... Nah 2:1 6440
discover thy skirts upon thy *f* ... Nah 3:5 6440
over the *f* of the whole earth ... Zec 5:3 6440
anoint thine head, and wash thy *f* ... Mt 6:17 *4383*
I send my messenger before thy *f* ... Mt 11:10 *4383*
ye can discern the *f* of the sky ... Mt 16:3 *4383*
his *f* did shine as the sun, and ... Mt 17:2 *4383*
heard it, they fell on their *f* ... Mt 17:6 *4383*
angels do always behold the *f* of ... Mt 18:10 *4383*
little farther, and fell on his *f* ... Mt 26:39 *4383*
Then did they spit in his *f* ... Mt 26:67 *4383*
I send my messenger before thy *f* ... Mk 1:2 *4383*
to spit on him, and to cover his *f* ... Mk 14:65 *4383*
for thou shalt go before the *f* of ... Lk 1:76 *4383*
before the *f* of all people ... Lk 2:31 *4383*
who seeing Jesus fell on his *f* ... Lk 5:12 *4383*
I send my messenger before thy *f* ... Lk 7:27 *4383*
set his *f* to go to Jerusalem ... Lk 9:51 *4383*
And sent messengers before his *f* ... Lk 9:52 *4383*
because his *f* was as though he ... Lk 9:53 *4383*
two before his *f* into every city ... Lk 10:1 *4383*
ye can discern the *f* of the sky ... Lk 12:56 *4383*
And fell down on his *f* at his feet ... Lk 17:16 *4383*
dwell on the *f* of the whole earth ... Lk 21:35 *4383*
him, they struck him on the *f* ... Lk 22:64 *4383*
his *f* was bound about with a ... Jn 11:44 *3799*
the Lord always before my *f* ... Acts 2:25 *1799*
saw his *f* as it had been the *f* ... Acts 6:15 *4383*
out before the *f* of our fathers ... Acts 7:45 *4383*
dwell on all the *f* of the earth ... Acts 17:26 *4383*
of God, shall see my *f* no more ... Acts 20:25 *4383*
they should see his *f* no more ... Acts 20:38 *4383*
have the accusers *f* to *f* ... Acts 25:16 *4383*
but then *f* to *f* ... 1Cor 13:12 *4383*
down on his *f* he will worship God ... 1Cor 14:25 *4383*
f of Moses for the glory of his ... 2Cor 3:7 *4383*
which put a vail over his *f* ... 2Cor 3:13 *4383*
with open *f* beholding as in a ... 2Cor 3:18 *4383*
of God in the *f* of Jesus Christ ... 2Cor 4:6 *4383*
if a man smite you on the *f* ... 2Cor 11:20 *4383*
was unknown by *f* unto the ... Gal 1:22 *4383*
Antioch, I withstood him to the *f* ... Gal 2:11 *4383*
have not seen my *f* in the flesh ... Col 2:1 *4383*
to see your *f* with great desire ... 1Th 2:17 *4383*
that we might see your *f*, and ... 1Th 3:10 *4383*
his natural *f* in a glass ... Jas 1:23 *4383*
but the *f* of the Lord is against ... 1Pet 3:12 *4383*
speak *f* to *f*, that our joy may ... 2Jn 12 *4750*
come unto you, and speak *f* to *f* ... 2Jn 12 *4750*
thee, and we shall speak *f* to *f* ... 3Jn 14 *4750*
thee, and we shall speak *f* to *f* ... 3Jn 14 *4750*
the third beast had a *f* as a man ... Rev 4:7 *4383*
hide us from the *f* of him that ... Rev 6:16 *4383*
his *f* was as it were the sun, and ... Rev 10:1 *4383*
from the *f* of the serpent ... Rev 12:14 *4383*
sat on it, from whose *f* the earth ... Rev 20:11 *4383*
And they shall see his *f* ... Rev 22:4 *4383*

FACES {73}

their *f* were backward, and they ... Gen 9:23 6440
men turned their *f* from thence ... Gen 18:22
set the *f* of the flocks toward ... Gen 30:40 6440
him with their *f* to the earth ... Gen 42:6 639
laid before their *f* all these ... Ex 19:7 6440
his fear may be before your *f* ... Ex 20:20 6440
their *f* shall look one to another ... Ex 25:20 6440
shall the *f* of the cherubims be ... Ex 25:20 6440
with their *f* one to another ... Ex 37:9 6440
were the *f* of the cherubims ... Ex 37:9 6440
they shouted, and fell on their *f* ... Lev 9:24 6440
Aaron fell on their *f* before all ... Num 14:5 6440
And they fell upon their *f* ... Num 16:22 6440
And they fell upon their *f* ... Num 16:45 6440
and they fell upon their *f* ... Num 20:6 6440
and fell on their *f* to the ground ... Judg 13:20 6440
And they turned their *f*, and said ... Judg 18:23 6440
day the *f* of all thy servants ... 2Sa 19:5 6440
that all Israel set their *f* on me ... 1Kin 2:15 6440
saw it, they fell on their *f* ... 1Kin 18:39 6440
f were like the *f* of lions ... 1Chr 12:8 6440
in sackcloth, fell upon their *f* ... 1Chr 21:16 6440
feet, and their *f* were inward ... 2Chr 3:13 6440
bowed themselves with their *f* to ... 2Chr 7:3 639
have turned away their *f* from the ... 2Chr 29:6 6440
LORD with their *f* to the ground ... Neh 8:6 639
he covereth the *f* of the judges ... Job 9:24 6440
and bind their *f* in secret ... Job 40:13 6440
and their *f* were not ashamed ... Ps 34:5 6440
Fill their *f* with shame ... Ps 83:16 6440
and grind the *f* of the poor ... Is 3:15 6440
their *f* shall be as flames ... Is 13:8 6440
wipe away tears from off all *f* ... Is 25:8 6440
we hid as it were our *f* from him ... Is 53:3 6440
Be not afraid of their *f* ... Jer 1:8 6440
be not dismayed at their *f* ... Jer 1:17 6440
made their *f* harder than a rock ... Jer 5:3 6440
to the confusion of their own *f* ... Jer 7:19 6440
all *f* are turned into paleness ... Jer 30:6 6440
set your *f* to enter into Egypt ... Jer 42:15 6440
f to go into Egypt to sojourn ... Jer 42:17 6440
that have set their *f* to go into ... Jer 44:12 6440
to Zion with their *f* thitherward ... Jer 50:5 6440
shame hath covered our *f* ... Jer 51:51 6440
the *f* of elders were not honoured ... Lam 5:12 6440
And every one had four *f*, and every ... Eze 1:6 6440
and they four had their *f* and their ... Eze 1:8 6440
As for the likeness of their *f* ... Eze 1:10 6440
Thus were their *f* ... Eze 1:11 6440
living creatures, with his four *f* ... Eze 1:15 6440
thy face strong against their *f* ... Eze 3:8 6440
and shame shall be upon all *f* ... Eze 7:18 6440
LORD, and their *f* toward the east ... Eze 8:16 6440
And every one had four *f* ... Eze 10:14 6440
Every one had four *f* apiece ... Eze 10:21 6440
the likeness of their *f* was the ... Eze 10:22 6440
f which I saw by the river of ... Eze 10:22 6440
turn away your *f* from all your ... Eze 14:6 6440
all *f* from the south to the north ... Eze 20:47 6440
and every cherub had two *f* ... Eze 41:18 6440
for why should he see your *f* ... Dan 1:10 6440
thee, but unto us confusion of *f* ... Dan 9:7 6440
all *f* shall gather blackness ... Joel 2:6 6440
and the *f* of them all gather ... Nah 2:10 6440
their *f* shall sup up as the east ... Hab 1:9 6440
seed, and spread dung upon your *f* ... Mal 2:3 6440
for they disfigure their *f* ... Mt 6:16 *4383*
bowed down their *f* to the earth ... Lk 24:5 *4383*
fell before the throne on their *f* ... Rev 7:11 *4383*
their *f* were as the *f* of men ... Rev 9:7 *4383*
on their seats, fell upon their *f* ... Rev 11:16 *4383*

FADE {6}

Strangers shall *f* away, and they ... 2Sa 22:46 5034
The strangers shall *f* away ... Ps 18:45 5034
and we all do *f* as a leaf ... Is 64:6 5034
the fig tree, and the leaf shall *f* ... Jer 8:13 5034
for meat, whose leaf shall not *f* ... Eze 47:12 5034
the rich man *f* away in his ways ... Jas 1:11 *3133*

FADETH {7}

shall be as an oak whose leaf *f* ... Is 1:30 5034
f away, the world languisheth and ... Is 24:4 5034
f away, the haughty people of the ... Is 24:4 5034
The grass withereth, the flower *f* ... Is 40:7 5034
The grass withereth, the flower *f* ... Is 40:8 5034
that *f* not away, reserved in ... 1Pet 1:4 *263*
a crown of glory that *f* not away ... 1Pet 5:4 *262*

FADING {2}

glorious beauty is a *f* flower ... Is 28:1 5034
fat valley, shall be a *f* flower ... Is 28:4 5034

FAIL {64}

you for your cattle, if money *f* ... Gen 47:16 656
f with longing for them all the ... Deut 28:32 3615
he will not *f* thee, nor forsake ... Deut 31:6 7503
be with thee, he will not *f* thee ... Deut 31:8 7503
I will not *f* thee, nor forsake ... Josh 1:5 7503
that he will without *f* drive out ... Josh 3:10
If thou shalt without *f* deliver ... Judg 11:30
Let them not *f* to burn the fat ... 1Sa 2:16
no man's heart *f* because of him ... 1Sa 17:32 5307
I should not *f* to sit with the ... 1Sa 20:5
them, and without *f* recover all ... 1Sa 30:8
let there not *f* from the house of ... 2Sa 3:29 3772
there shall not *f* thee (said he) ... 1Kin 2:4 3772
There shall not *f* thee a man in ... 1Kin 8:25 3772
There shall not *f* thee a man upon ... 1Kin 9:5 3772
neither shall the cruse of oil *f* ... 1Kin 17:14 2637
neither did the cruse of oil *f* ... 1Kin 17:16 2638
he will not *f* thee, nor forsake ... 1Chr 28:20 7503
There shall not *f* thee a man in ... 2Chr 6:16 3772
There shall not *f* thee a man to ... 2Chr 7:18 3772
heed now that ye *f* not to do this ... Ezr 4:22 7960
given them day by day without *f* ... Ezr 6:9 7960
let nothing *f* of all that thou ... Est 6:10 5307
unto them, so as it should not *f* ... Est 9:27 5674
should not *f* from among the Jews ... Est 9:28 5674
the eyes of the wicked shall *f* ... Job 11:20 3615
As the waters *f* from the sea ... Job 14:11 235
the eyes of his children shall *f* ... Job 17:5 3615
caused the eyes of the widow to *f* ... Job 31:16 3615
for the faithful *f* from among the ... Ps 12:1 6461
mine eyes *f* while I wait for my ... Ps 69:3 3615
doth his promise *f* for evermore ... Ps 77:8 1584

F

nor suffer my faithfulness to *f* ... Ps 89:33 8266
Mine eyes *f* for thy word, saying, ... Ps 119:82 3615
Mine eyes *f* for thy salvation, and ... Ps 119:123 3615
and the rod of his anger shall *f* ... Prov 22:8 3615
be a burden, and desire shall *f* ... Eccl 12:5 6565
shall *f* in the midst thereof ... Is 19:3 1238
the waters shall *f* from the sea ... Is 19:5 5405
and all the glory of Kedar shall *f* ... Is 21:16 3615
and they all shall *f* together ... Is 31:3 3615
the drink of the thirsty to *f* ... Is 32:6 2637
for the vintage shall *f*, the ... Is 32:10 3615
no one of these shall *f*, none ... Is 34:16 5737
mine eyes *f* with looking upward ... Is 38:14 1809
He shall not *f* nor be discouraged ... Is 42:4 3543
pit, nor that his bread should *f* ... Is 51:14 2637
for the spirit should *f* before me ... Is 57:16 5848
of water, whose waters *f* not ... Is 58:11 3576
their eyes did *f*, because there ... Jer 14:6 3615
me as a liar, and as waters that *f* ... Jer 15:18 3808,539
wine to *f* from the winepresses ... Jer 48:33 7673
Mine eyes do *f* with tears ... Lam 2:11 3615
because his compassions *f* not ... Lam 3:22 3615
and the new wine shall *f* in her ... Hos 9:2 3584
to make the poor of the land to *f* ... Amos 8:4 7673
the labour of the olive shall *f* ... Hab 3:17 3584
that, when ye *f*, they may receive ... Lk 16:9 *1587*
than one tittle of the law to *f* ... Lk 16:17 *4098*
for thee, that thy faith *f* not ... Lk 22:32 *1587*
there be prophecies, they shall *f* ... 1Cor 13:8 *2673*
same, and thy years shall not *f* ... Heb 1:12 *1587*
for the time would *f* me to tell ... Heb 11:32 *1952*
any man *f* of the grace of God ... Heb 12:15 *5302*

FAILED {12}
and their heart *f* them, and they ... Gen 42:28 3318
when money *f* in the land of Egypt ... Gen 47:15 8552
the plain, even the salt sea, *f* ... Josh 3:16 8552
There *f* not ought of any good ... Josh 21:45 5307
that not one thing hath *f* of all ... Josh 23:14 5307
and not one thing hath *f* thereof ... Josh 23:14 5307
there hath not *f* one word of all ... 1Kin 8:56 5307
My kinsfolk have *f*, and my ... Job 19:14 2308
refuge *f* me; no man cared ... Ps 142:4 6
my soul *f* when he spake ... Song 5:6 3318
their might hath *f* ... Jer 51:30 5405
our eyes as yet *f* for our vain ... Lam 4:17 3615

FAILETH {19}
for the money *f* ... Gen 47:15 656
Their bull gendereth, and *f* not ... Job 21:10 1602
my strength *f* because of mine ... Ps 31:10 3782
heart panteth, my strength *f* me ... Ps 38:10 5800
therefore my heart *f* me ... Ps 40:12 5800
forsake me not when my strength *f* ... Ps 71:9 3615
My flesh and my heart *f* ... Ps 73:26 3615
and my flesh *f* of fatness ... Ps 109:24 3584
my spirit *f* ... Ps 143:7 3615
by the way, his wisdom *f* him ... Eccl 10:3 2638
hay is withered away, the grass *f* ... Is 15:6 3615
strong in power; not one *f* ... Is 40:26 5737
and their tongue *f* for thirst ... Is 41:17 5405
he is hungry, and his strength *f* ... Is 44:12 369
Yea, truth *f* ... Is 59:15 5737
are prolonged, and every vision *f* ... Eze 12:22 6
his judgment to light, he *f* not ... Zeph 3:5 5737
in the heavens that *f* not ... Lk 12:33 *413*
Charity never *f* ... 1Cor 13:8 *1601*

FAILING {2}
f of eyes, and sorrow of mind ... Deut 28:65 3631
Men's hearts *f* them for fear, and ... Lk 21:26 *674*

FAIN {2}
he would *f* flee out of his hand ... Job 27:22 1272
he would *f* have filled his belly ... Lk 15:16 *1937*

FAINT {41}
came from the field, and he was *f* ... Gen 25:29 5889
red pottage; for I am *f* ... Gen 25:30 5889
let not your hearts *f*, fear not, ... Deut 20:3 7401
heart *f* as well as his heart ... Deut 20:8 4549
behind thee, when thou wast *f* ... Deut 25:18 5889
of the land *f* because of you ... Josh 2:9 4127
of the country do *f* because of us ... Josh 2:24 4127
hundred men that were with him, *f* ... Judg 8:4 5889
for they be *f*, and I am pursuing ... Judg 8:5 5889
And the people were *f* ... 1Sa 14:28 5774
and the people were very *f* ... 1Sa 14:31 5774
which were so *f* that they could ... 1Sa 30:10 6296
which were so *f* that they could ... 1Sa 30:21 6296
wine, that such as be *f* in the ... 2Sa 16:2 3287
and David waxed *f* ... 2Sa 21:15 5774
If thou *f* in the day of adversity ... Prov 24:10 7503
is sick, and the whole heart *f* ... Is 1:5 1742
Therefore shall all hands be *f* ... Is 13:7 7503
he awaketh, and, behold, he is *f* ... Is 29:8 5889
He giveth power to the *f* ... Is 40:29 3287
Even the youths shall *f* and be ... Is 40:30 3286
and they shall walk, and not *f* ... Is 40:31 3286
he drinketh no water, and is *f* ... Is 44:12 3286
sorrow, my heart is *f* in me ... Jer 8:18 1742
And lest your heart *f*, and ye fear ... Jer 51:46 7401
made me desolate and *f* all the day ... Lam 1:13 1738
sighs are many, and my heart is *f* ... Lam 1:22 1742
that *f* for hunger in the top of ... Lam 2:19 5848
For this our heart is *f* ... Lam 5:17 1739
feeble, and every spirit shall *f* ... Eze 21:7 3543
gates, that their heart may *f* ... Eze 21:15 4127
virgins and young men *f* for thirst ... Amos 8:13 5968
fasting, lest they *f* in the way ... Mt 15:32 *1590*
houses, they will *f* by the way ... Mk 8:3 *1590*
ought always to pray, and not to *f* ... Lk 18:1 *1573*
we have received mercy, we *f* not ... 2Cor 4:1 *1573*
For which cause we *f* not ... 2Cor 4:16 *1573*
season we shall reap, if we *f* not ... Gal 6:9 *1590*
Wherefore I desire that ye *f* not ... Eph 3:13 *1573*
ye be wearied and *f* in your minds ... Heb 12:3 *1590*
nor *f* when thou art rebuked of ... Heb 12:5 *1590*

FAINTED {12}
And Jacob's heart *f*, for he ... Gen 45:26 6313
all the land of Canaan *f* by ... Gen 47:13 3856
I had *f*, unless I had believed to ... Ps 27:13
and thirsty, their soul *f* in them ... Ps 107:5 5848
Thy sons have *f*, they lie at the ... Is 51:20 5968
I *f* in my sighing, and I find no ... Jer 45:3 3021
the trees of the field *f* for him ... Eze 31:15 5969
And I Daniel *f*, and was sick ... Dan 8:27 1961
When my soul *f* within me I ... Jonah 2:7 5848
upon the head of Jonah, that he *f* ... Jonah 4:8 5968
on them, because they *f*, and were ... Mt 9:36 *1590*
sake hast laboured, and hast not *f* ... Rev 2:3 *2577*

FAINTEST {1}
it is come upon thee, and thou *f* ... Job 4:5 3811

FAINTETH {4}
even *f* for the courts of the LORD ... Ps 84:2 3615
My soul *f* for thy salvation ... Ps 119:81 3615
be as when a standard-bearer *f* ... Is 10:18 4549
earth, *f* not, neither is weary ... Is 40:28 3286

FAINTHEARTED {3}
man is there that is fearful and *f* ... Deut 20:8 7390,3824
neither be *f* for the two tails of ... Is 7:4 3824,7401
they are *f* ... Jer 49:23 4127

FAINTNESS {1}
f into their hearts in the lands ... Lev 26:36 4816

FAIR {53}
daughters of men that they were *f* ... Gen 6:2 2896
thou art a *f* woman to look upon ... Gen 12:11 3303
the woman that she was very *f* ... Gen 12:14 3303
damsel was very *f* to look upon ... Gen 24:16 2896
because she was *f* to look upon ... Gen 26:7 2896
and ruddy, and of a *f* countenance ... 1Sa 17:42 3303
the son of David had a *f* sister ... 2Sa 13:1 3303
was a woman of a *f* countenance ... 2Sa 14:27 3303
So they sought for a *f* damsel ... 1Kin 1:3 3303
And the damsel was very *f*, and ... 1Kin 1:4 3303
for she was *f* to look on ... Est 1:11 2896
Let there be *f* young virgins ... Est 2:2 2896,4758
may gather together all the *f* ... Est 2:3 2897,4758
nor mother, and the maid was *f* ... Est 2:7 3303,8389
F weather cometh out of the north ... Job 37:22 2091
so *f* as the daughters of Job ... Job 42:15 3303
With her much *f* speech she caused ... Prov 7:21 3948
so is a *f* woman which is without ... Prov 11:22 3303
When he speaketh *f*, believe him ... Prov 26:25 2603
Behold, thou art *f*, my love ... Song 1:15 3302
behold, thou art *f* ... Song 1:15 3302
Behold, thou art *f*, my beloved, ... Song 1:16 3302
my love, my *f* one, and come away ... Song 2:10 3302
my love, my *f* one, and come away ... Song 2:13 3302
Behold, thou art *f*, my love ... Song 4:1 3302
behold, thou art *f* ... Song 4:1 3302
Thou art all *f*, my love ... Song 4:7 3302
How *f* is thy love, my sister, my ... Song 4:10 3302
f as the moon, clear as the sun, ... Song 6:10 3303
How *f* and how pleasant art thou, O ... Song 7:6 3302
be desolate, even great and *f* ... Is 5:9 2896
will lay thy stones with *f* colors ... Is 54:11 6320
in vain shalt thou make thyself *f* ... Jer 4:30 3302
thy name, A green olive tree, *f* ... Jer 11:16 3303
they speak *f* words unto thee ... Jer 12:6 2896
Egypt is like a very *f* heifer ... Jer 46:20 3304
taken thy *f* jewels of my gold ... Eze 16:17 8597
and shall take thy *f* jewels ... Eze 16:39 8597
and take away thy *f* jewels ... Eze 23:26 8597
cedar in Lebanon with *f* branches ... Eze 31:3 3303
Thus was he *f* in his greatness, ... Eze 31:7 3302
I have made him *f* by the ... Eze 31:9 3303
The leaves thereof were *f* ... Dan 4:12 8209
Whose leaves were *f*, and the fruit ... Dan 4:21 8209
but I passed over upon her *f* neck ... Hos 10:11 2898
In that day shall the *f* virgins ... Amos 8:13 3303
Let them set a *f* mitre upon his ... Zec 3:5 2889
So they set a *f* mitre upon his ... Zec 3:5 2889
ye say, It will be *f* weather ... Mt 16:2 *2105*
was born, and was exceeding *f* ... Acts 7:20 *791*
which is called The *f* havens ... Acts 27:8 *2568*
f speeches deceive the hearts of ... Rom 16:18 *2129*
to make a *f* shew in the flesh ... Gal 6:12 *2146*

FAIRER {3}
not her younger sister *f* than she ... Judg 15:2 2896
Thou art *f* than the children of ... Ps 45:2 3302
their countenances appeared *f* ... Dan 1:15 2896

FAIREST {3}
O thou *f* among women, go thy way ... Song 1:8 3303
beloved, O thou *f* among women ... Song 5:9 3303
gone, O thou *f* among women ... Song 6:1 3303

FAIRS {6}
and lead, they traded in thy *f* ... Eze 27:12 5801
traded in thy *f* with horses ... Eze 27:14 5801
occupied in thy *f* with emeralds ... Eze 27:16 5801
going to and fro occupied in thy *f* ... Eze 27:19 5801
they occupied in thy *f* with chief ... Eze 27:22 5801
Thy riches, and thy *f*, thy ... Eze 27:27 5801

FAITH {247}
children in whom is no *f* ... Deut 32:20 529
but the just shall live by his *f* ... Hab 2:4 530
more clothe you, O ye of little *f* ... Mt 6:30 *3640*
you, I have not found so great *f* ... Mt 8:10 *4102*
are ye fearful, O ye of little *f* ... Mt 8:26 *3640*
Jesus seeing their *f* said unto ... Mt 9:2 *4102*
thy *f* hath made thee whole ... Mt 9:22 *4102*
to your *f* be it unto you ... Mt 9:29 *4102*
said unto him, O thou of little *f* ... Mt 14:31 *3640*
unto her, O woman, great is thy *f* ... Mt 15:28 *4102*
said unto them, O ye of little *f* ... Mt 16:8 *3640*
If ye have *f* as a grain of ... Mt 17:20 *4102*
I say unto you, If ye have *f* ... Mt 21:21 *4102*
of the law, judgment, mercy, and *f* ... Mt 23:23 *4102*
When Jesus saw their *f*, he said ... Mk 2:5 *4102*
how is it that ye have no *f* ... Mk 4:40 *4102*
thy *f* hath made thee whole ... Mk 5:34 *4102*
thy *f* hath made thee whole ... Mk 10:52 *4102*
saith unto them, Have *f* in God ... Mk 11:22 *4102*
And when he saw their *f*, he said ... Lk 5:20 *4102*
you, I have not found so great *f* ... Lk 7:9 *4102*
the woman, Thy *f* hath saved thee ... Lk 7:50 *4102*
said unto them, Where is your *f* ... Lk 8:25 *4102*
thy *f* hath made thee whole ... Lk 8:48 *4102*
he clothe you, O ye of little *f* ... Lk 12:28 *3640*
unto the Lord, Increase our *f* ... Lk 17:5 *4102*
If ye had *f* as a grain of mustard ... Lk 17:6 *4102*
thy *f* hath made thee whole ... Lk 17:19 *4102*
shall he find *f* on the earth ... Lk 18:8 *4102*
thy *f* hath saved thee ... Lk 18:42 *4102*
for thee, that thy *f* fail not ... Lk 22:32 *4102*
his name through *f* in his name ... Acts 3:16 *4102*
the *f* which is by him hath given ... Acts 3:16 *4102*
chose Stephen, a man full of *f* ... Acts 6:5 *4102*
priests were obedient to the *f* ... Acts 6:7 *4102*
And Stephen, full of *f* and power, ... Acts 6:8 *4102*
and full of the Holy Ghost and of *f* ... Acts 11:24 *4102*
turn away the deputy from the *f* ... Acts 13:8 *4102*
that he had *f* to be healed ... Acts 14:9 *4102*
them to continue in the *f* ... Acts 14:22 *4102*
the door of *f* unto the Gentiles ... Acts 14:27 *4102*
them, purifying their hearts by *f* ... Acts 15:9 *4102*
the churches established in the *f* ... Acts 16:5 *4102*
f toward our Lord Jesus Christ ... Acts 20:21 *4102*
him concerning the *f* in Christ ... Acts 24:24 *4102*
are sanctified by *f* that is in me ... Acts 26:18 *4102*
to the *f* among all nations ... Rom 1:5 *4102*
you all, that your *f* is spoken of ... Rom 1:8 *4102*
you by the mutual *f* both of you ... Rom 1:12 *4102*
of God revealed from *f* to *f* ... Rom 1:17 *4102*
written, The just shall live by *f* ... Rom 1:17 *4102*
make the *f* of God without effect ... Rom 3:3 *4102*
of God which is by *f* of Jesus ... Rom 3:22 *4102*
through *f* in his blood, to ... Rom 3:25 *4102*
but by the law of *f* ... Rom 3:27 *4102*
that a man is justified by *f* ... Rom 3:28 *4102*
justify the circumcision by *f* ... Rom 3:30 *4102*
and uncircumcision through *f* ... Rom 3:30 *4102*
then make void the law through *f* ... Rom 3:31 *4102*
the ungodly, his *f* is counted for ... Rom 4:5 *4102*
for we say that *f* was reckoned to ... Rom 4:9 *4102*
of the *f* which he had yet being ... Rom 4:11 *4102*
of that *f* of our father Abraham ... Rom 4:12 *4102*
through the righteousness of *f* ... Rom 4:13 *4102*
f is made void, and the promise ... Rom 4:14 *4102*
Therefore it is of *f*, that it ... Rom 4:16 *4102*
also which is of the *f* of Abraham ... Rom 4:16 *4102*
And being not weak in *f*, he ... Rom 4:19 *4102*
but was strong in *f*, giving glory ... Rom 4:20 *4102*
Therefore being justified by *f* ... Rom 5:1 *4102*
by *f* into this grace wherein we ... Rom 5:2 *4102*
the righteousness which is of *f* ... Rom 9:30 *4102*
Because they sought it not by *f* ... Rom 9:32 *4102*
is of *f* speaketh on this wise ... Rom 10:6 *4102*
that is, the word of *f*, which we ... Rom 10:8 *4102*
So then *f* cometh by hearing, and ... Rom 10:17 *4102*
broken off, and thou standest by *f* ... Rom 11:20 *4102*
to every man the measure of *f* ... Rom 12:3 *4102*
according to the proportion of *f* ... Rom 12:6 *4102*
that is weak in the *f* receive ye ... Rom 14:1 *4102*
Hast thou *f*? ... Rom 14:22 *4102*
eat, because he eateth not of *f* ... Rom 14:23 *4102*
for whatsoever is not of *f* is sin ... Rom 14:23 *4102*
nations for the obedience of *f* ... Rom 16:26 *4102*
That your *f* should not stand in ... 1Cor 2:5 *4102*
To another *f* by the same Spirit ... 1Cor 12:9 *4102*
and though I have all *f*, so that I ... 1Cor 13:2 *4102*
And now abideth *f*, hope, charity, ... 1Cor 13:13 *4102*
vain, and your *f* is also vain ... 1Cor 15:14 *4102*
be not raised, your *f* is vain ... 1Cor 15:17 *4102*
Watch ye, stand fast in the *f* ... 1Cor 16:13 *4102*
that we have dominion over your *f* ... 2Cor 1:24 *4102*
for by *f* ye stand ... 2Cor 1:24 *4102*
We having the same spirit of *f* ... 2Cor 4:13 *4102*
(For we walk by *f*, not by sight ... 2Cor 5:7 *4102*
as ye abound in every thing, in *f* ... 2Cor 8:7 *4102*
when your *f* is increased, that we ... 2Cor 10:15 *4102*
whether ye be in the *f* ... 2Cor 13:5 *4102*
the *f* which once he destroyed ... Gal 1:23 *4102*
but by the *f* of Jesus Christ, ... Gal 2:16 *4102*
be justified by the *f* of Christ ... Gal 2:16 *4102*
I live by the *f* of the Son of God ... Gal 2:20 *4102*
the law, or by the hearing of *f* ... Gal 3:2 *4102*
the law, or by the hearing of *f* ... Gal 3:5 *4102*
that they which are of *f*, the ... Gal 3:7 *4102*
justify the heathen through *f* ... Gal 3:8 *4102*
So then they which be of *f* are ... Gal 3:9 *4102*

for, The just shall live by *f* Gal 3:11 *4102*
And the law is not of *f* Gal 3:12 *4102*
promise of the Spirit through *f* Gal 3:14 *4102*
that the promise by *f* of Jesus Gal 3:22 *4102*
But before *f* came, we were kept Gal 3:23 *4102*
shut up unto the *f* which should Gal 3:23 *4102*
that we might be justified by *f* Gal 3:24 *4102*
But after that *f* is come, we are Gal 3:25 *4102*
of God by *f* in Christ Jesus Gal 3:26 *4102*
the hope of righteousness by *f* Gal 5:5 *4102*
but *f* which worketh by love Gal 5:6 *4102*
gentleness, goodness, *f* Gal 5:22 *4102*
who are of the household of *f* Gal 6:10 *4102*
heard of your *f* in the Lord Jesus Eph 1:15 *4102*
by grace are ye saved through *f* Eph 2:8 *4102*
with confidence by the *f* of him Eph 3:12 *4102*
may dwell in your hearts by *f* Eph 3:17 *4102*
One Lord, one *f*, one baptism, Eph 4:5 *4102*
we all come in the unity of the *f* Eph 4:13 *4102*
Above all, taking the shield of *f* Eph 6:16 *4102*
to the brethren, and love with *f* Eph 6:23 *4102*
for your furtherance and joy of *f* Phil 1:25 *4102*
together for the *f* of the gospel Phil 1:27 *4102*
sacrifice and service of your *f* Phil 2:17 *4102*
which is through the *f* of Christ Phil 3:9 *4102*
which is of God by *f* Phil 3:9 *4102*
heard of your *f* in Christ Jesus Col 1:4 *4102*
If ye continue in the *f* grounded Col 1:23 *4102*
stedfastness of your *f* in Christ Col 2:5 *4102*
up in him, and stablished in the *f* Col 2:7 *4102*
the *f* of the operation of God Col 2:12 *4102*
without ceasing your work of *f* 1Th 1:3 *4102*
f to God-ward is spread abroad 1Th 1:8 *4102*
to comfort you concerning your *f* 1Th 3:2 *4102*
forbear, I sent to know your *f* 1Th 3:5 *4102*
brought us good tidings of your *f* 1Th 3:6 *4102*
affliction and distress by your *f* 1Th 3:7 *4102*
that which is lacking in your *f* 1Th 3:10 *4102*
putting on the breastplate of *f* 1Th 5:8 *4102*
because that your *f* groweth 2Th 1:3 *4102*
f in all your persecutions and 2Th 1:4 *4102*
and the work of *f* with power 2Th 1:11 *4102*
for all men have not *f* 2Th 3:2 *4102*
Unto Timothy, my own son in the *f* 1Ti 1:2 *4102*
than godly edifying which is in *f* 1Ti 1:4 *4102*
conscience, and of *f* unfeigned 1Ti 1:5 *4102*
was exceeding abundant with *f* 1Ti 1:14 *4102*
Holding *f*, and a good conscience 1Ti 1:19 *4102*
concerning *f* have made shipwreck 1Ti 1:19 *4102*
a teacher of the Gentiles in *f* 1Ti 2:7 *4102*
if they continue in *f* and charity 1Ti 2:15 *4102*
of the *f* in a pure conscience 1Ti 3:9 *4102*
great boldness in the *f* which is 1Ti 3:13 *4102*
some shall depart from the *f* 1Ti 4:1 *4102*
nourished up in the words of *f* 1Ti 4:6 *4102*
in charity, in spirit, in *f* 1Ti 4:12 *4102*
own house, he hath denied the *f* 1Ti 5:8 *4102*
they have cast off their first *f* 1Ti 5:12 *4102*
after, they have erred from the *f* 1Ti 6:10 *4102*
after righteousness, godliness, *f* 1Ti 6:11 *4102*
Fight the good fight of *f* 1Ti 6:12 *4102*
have erred concerning the *f* 1Ti 6:21 *4102*
the unfeigned *f* that is in thee 2Ti 1:5 *4102*
which thou hast heard of me, in *f* 2Ti 1:13 *4102*
and overthrow the *f* of some 2Ti 2:18 *4102*
but follow righteousness, *f* 2Ti 2:22 *4102*
minds, reprobate concerning the *f* 2Ti 3:8 *4102*
manner of life, purpose, *f* 2Ti 3:10 *4102*
f which is in Christ Jesus 2Ti 3:15 *4102*
my course, I have kept the *f* 2Ti 4:7 *4102*
according to the *f* of God's elect Titus 1:1 *4102*
mine own son after the common *f* Titus 1:4 *4102*
that they may be sound in the *f* Titus 1:13 *4102*
grave, temperate, sound in *f* Titus 2:2 *4102*
Greet them that love us in the *f* Titus 3:15 *4102*
Hearing of thy love and *f*, which Philem 5 *4102*
thy *f* may become effectual by the Philem 6 *4102*
not being mixed with *f* in them Heb 4:2 *4102*
dead works, and of *f* toward God, Heb 6:1 *4102*
followers of them who through *f* Heb 6:12 *4102*
true heart in full assurance of *f* Heb 10:22 *4102*
of our *f* without wavering Heb 10:23 *1680*
Now the just shall live by *f* Heb 10:38 *4102*
Now *f* is the substance of things Heb 11:1 *4102*
Through *f* we understand that the Heb 11:3 *4102*
By *f* Abel offered unto God a more Heb 11:4 *4102*
By *f* Enoch was translated that he Heb 11:5 *4102*
But without *f* it is impossible to Heb 11:6 *4102*
By *f* Noah, being warned of God of Heb 11:7 *4102*
the righteousness which is by *f* Heb 11:7 *4102*
By *f* Abraham, when he was called Heb 11:8 *4102*
By *f* he sojourned in the land of Heb 11:9 *4102*
Through *f* also Sara herself Heb 11:11 *4102*
These all died in *f*, not having Heb 11:13 *4102*
By *f* Abraham, when he was tried, Heb 11:17 *4102*
By *f* Isaac blessed Jacob and Esau Heb 11:20 *4102*
By *f* Jacob, when he was a dying, Heb 11:21 *4102*
By *f* Joseph, when he died, made Heb 11:22 *4102*
By *f* Moses, when he was born, was Heb 11:23 *4102*
By *f* Moses, when he was come to Heb 11:24 *4102*
By *f* he forsook Egypt, not Heb 11:27 *4102*
Through *f* he kept the passover, Heb 11:28 *4102*
By *f* they passed through the Red Heb 11:29 *4102*
By *f* the walls of Jericho fell Heb 11:30 *4102*
By *f* the harlot Rahab perished Heb 11:31 *4102*
Who through *f* subdued kingdoms, Heb 11:33 *4102*
obtained a good report through *f* Heb 11:39 *4102*
the author and finisher of our *f* Heb 12:2 *4102*
whose *f* follow, considering the Heb 13:7 *4102*
trying of your *f* worketh patience Jas 1:3 *4102*
But let him ask in *f*, nothing Jas 1:6 *4102*
have not the *f* of our Lord Jesus Jas 2:1 *4102*
the poor of this world rich in *f* Jas 2:5 *4102*
though a man say he hath *f* Jas 2:14 *4102*
can *f* save him? Jas 2:14 *4102*
Even so *f*, if it hath not works, Jas 2:17 *4102*
Yea, a man may say, Thou hast *f* Jas 2:18 *4102*
shew me thy *f* without thy works, Jas 2:18 *4102*
I will shew thee my *f* by my works Jas 2:18 *4102*
that *f* without works is dead Jas 2:20 *4102*
Seest thou how *f* wrought with his Jas 2:22 *4102*
and by works was *f* made perfect Jas 2:22 *4102*
is justified, and not by *f* only Jas 2:24 *4102*
so *f* without works is dead also Jas 2:26 *4102*
the prayer of *f* shall save the Jas 5:15 *4102*
f unto salvation ready to be 1Pet 1:5 *4102*
That the trial of your *f*, being 1Pet 1:7 *4102*
Receiving the end of your *f* 1Pet 1:9 *4102*
that your *f* and hope might be in 1Pet 1:21 *4102*
Whom resist stedfast in the *f* 1Pet 5:9 *4102*
precious *f* with us through the 2Pet 1:1 *4102*
diligence, add to your *f* virtue 2Pet 1:5 *4102*
overcometh the world, even our *f* 1Jn 5:4 *4102*
earnestly contend for the *f* which Jude 3 *4102*
up yourselves on your most holy *f* Jude 20 *4102*
my name, and hast not denied my *f* Rev 2:13 *4102*
and charity, and service, and *f* Rev 2:19 *4102*
patience and the *f* of the saints Rev 13:10 *4102*
of God, and the *f* of Jesus Rev 14:12 *4102*

FAITHFUL {82}
who is *f* in all mine house Num 12:7 539
thy God, he is God, the *f* God Deut 7:9 539
And I will raise me up a *f* priest 1Sa 2:35 539
who is so *f* among all thy 1Sa 22:14 539
that are peaceable and *f* in Israel 2Sa 20:19 539
for he was a *f* man, and feared God Neh 7:2 571
foundest his heart *f* before thee Neh 9:8 539
for they were counted *f*, and their Neh 13:13 539
for the *f* fail from among the Ps 12:1 539
for the LORD preserveth the *f* Ps 31:23 539
moon, and as a *f* witness in heaven Ps 89:37 539
shall be upon the *f* of the land Ps 101:6 539
All thy commandments are *f* Ps 119:86 530
commanded are righteous and very *f* Ps 119:138 530
but he that is of a *f* spirit Prov 11:13 539
but a *f* ambassador is health Prov 13:17 529
A *f* witness will not lie Prov 14:5 529
but a *f* man who can find Prov 20:6 529
so is a *f* messenger to them that Prov 25:13 539
F are the wounds of a friend Prov 27:6 539
A *f* man shall abound with Prov 28:20 530
How is the *f* city become an Is 1:21 539
city of righteousness, the *f* city Is 1:26 539
I took unto me *f* witnesses to Is 8:2 539
because of the LORD that is *f* Is 49:7 539
f witness between us, if we do Jer 42:5 539
forasmuch as he was *f*, neither Dan 6:4 540
with God, and is *f* with the saints Hos 11:12 539
Who then is a *f* and wise servant, Mt 24:45 *4103*
Well done, thou good and *f* servant Mt 25:21 *4103*
thou hast been *f* over a few Mt 25:21 *4103*
him, Well done, good and *f* servant Mt 25:23 *4103*
thou hast been *f* over a few Mt 25:23 *4103*
the Lord said, Who then is that *f* Lk 12:42 *4103*
He that is *f* in that which is Lk 16:10 *4103*
which is least is *f* also in much Lk 16:10 *4103*
been *f* in the unrighteous mammon Lk 16:11 *4103*
if ye have not been *f* in that Lk 16:12 *4103*
thou hast been *f* in a very little Lk 19:17 *4103*
judged me to be *f* to the Lord Acts 16:15 *4103*
God is *f*, by whom ye were called 1Cor 1:9 *4103*
stewards, that a man be found *f* 1Cor 4:2 *4103*
f in the Lord, who shall bring 1Cor 4:17 *4103*
mercy of the Lord to be *f* 1Cor 7:25 *4103*
but God is *f*, who will not suffer 1Cor 10:13 *4103*
faith are blessed with *f* Abraham Gal 3:9 *4103*
and to the *f* in Christ Jesus Eph 1:1 *4103*
f minister in the Lord, shall Eph 6:21 *4103*
f brethren in Christ which are at Col 1:2 *4103*
who is for you a *f* minister of Col 1:7 *4103*
a *f* minister and fellowservant in Col 4:7 *4103*
With Onesimus, a *f* and beloved Col 4:9 *4103*
F is he that calleth you, who 1Th 5:24 *4103*
But the Lord is *f*, who shall 2Th 3:3 *4103*
me, for that he counted me *f* 1Ti 1:12 *4103*
This is a *f* saying, and worthy of 1Ti 1:15 *4103*
sober, *f* in all things 1Ti 3:11 *4103*
This is a *f* saying and worthy of 1Ti 4:9 *4103*
them service, because they are *f* 1Ti 6:2 *4103*
the same commit thou to *f* men 2Ti 2:2 *4103*
It is a *f* saying 2Ti 2:11 *4103*
we believe not, yet he abideth *f* 2Ti 2:13 *4103*
having *f* children not accused of Titus 1:6 *4103*
Holding fast the *f* word as he Titus 1:9 *4103*
This is a *f* saying, and these Titus 3:8 *4103*
and *f* high priest in things Heb 2:17 *4103*
Who was *f* to him that appointed Heb 3:2 *4103*
also Moses was *f* in all his house Heb 3:2
verily was *f* in all his house Heb 3:5 *4103*
(for he is *f* that promised Heb 10:23 *4103*
she judged him *f* who had promised Heb 11:11 *4103*
well doing, as unto a *f* Creator 1Pet 4:19 *4103*
a *f* brother unto you, as I 1Pet 5:12 *4103*
If we confess our sins, he is *f* 1Jn 1:9 *4103*
Christ, who is the *f* witness Rev 1:5 *4103*
be thou *f* unto death, and I will Rev 2:10 *4103*
wherein Antipas was my *f* martyr Rev 2:13 *4103*
things saith the Amen, the *f* Rev 3:14 *4103*
him are called, and chosen, and *f* Rev 17:14 *4103*
he that sat upon him was called *F* Rev 19:11 *4103*
for these words are true and *f* Rev 21:5 *4103*
said unto me, These sayings are *f* Rev 22:6 *4103*

FAITHFULLY {8}
for they dealt *f* 2Kin 12:15 530
their hand, because they dealt *f* 2Kin 22:7 530
ye do in the fear of the LORD, *f* 2Chr 19:9 530
tithes and the dedicated things *f* 2Chr 31:12 530
And the men did the work *f* 2Chr 34:12 530
The king that *f* judgeth the poor, Prov 29:14 571
my word, let him speak my word *f* Jer 23:28 571
thou doest *f* whatsoever thou 3Jn 5 *4103*

FAITHFULNESS {19}
man his righteousness and his *f* 1Sa 26:23 530
For there is no *f* in their mouth Ps 5:9 3559
thy *f* reacheth unto the clouds Ps 36:5 530
I have declared thy *f* and thy Ps 40:10 530
or thy *f* in destruction Ps 88:11 530
known thy *f* to all generations Ps 89:1 530
thy *f* shalt thou establish in the Ps 89:2 530
thy *f* also in the congregation of Ps 89:5 530
or to thy *f* round about thee Ps 89:8 530
But my *f* and my mercy shall be Ps 89:24 530
from him, nor suffer my *f* to fail Ps 89:33 530
morning, and thy *f* every night, Ps 92:2 530
that thou in *f* hast afflicted me Ps 119:75 530
Thy *f* is unto all generations Ps 119:90 530
in thy *f* answer me, and in thy Ps 143:1 530
f the girdle of his reins Is 11:5 530
thy counsels of old are *f* Is 25:1 530
great is thy *f* Lam 3:23 530
even betroth thee unto me in *f* Hos 2:20 530

FAITHLESS {4}
Then Jesus answered and said, O *f* Mt 17:17 *571*
O *f* generation, how long shall I Mk 9:19 *571*
And Jesus answering said, O *f* Lk 9:41 *571*
and be not *f*, but believing Jn 20:27 *571*

FALL {252}
a deep sleep to *f* upon Adam Gen 2:21 5307
f upon us, and take us for bondmen Gen 43:18 5307
See that ye *f* not out by the way Gen 45:24 7264
that his rider shall *f* backward Gen 49:17 5307
lest he *f* upon us with pestilence Ex 5:3 6293
Fear and dread shall *f* upon them Ex 15:16 5307
it, and an ox or an ass *f* therein Ex 21:33 5307
them, when they are dead, doth *f* Lev 11:32 5307
if any part of their carcase *f* Lev 11:37 5307
part of their carcase *f* thereon Lev 11:38 5307
lest the land *f* to whoredom Lev 19:29
they shall *f* before you by the Lev 26:7 5307
your enemies shall *f* before you Lev 26:8 5307
they shall *f* when none pursueth Lev 26:36 5307
they shall *f* one upon another, as Lev 26:37 3782
let them *f* by the camp, as it Num 11:31 5203
to *f* by the sword, that our wives Num 14:3 5307
shall *f* in this wilderness Num 14:29 5307
they shall *f* in this wilderness Num 14:32 5307
you, and ye shall *f* by the sword Num 14:43 5307
f unto you for an inheritance Num 34:2 5307
ass or his ox *f* down by the way Deut 22:4 5307
house, if any man *f* from thence Deut 22:8 5307
of the city shall *f* down flat Josh 6:5 5307
said, Rise thou, and *f* upon us Judg 8:21 6293
that ye will not *f* upon me Judg 15:12 6293
thirst, and *f* into the hand of the Judg 15:18 5307
let *f* also some of the handfuls Ruth 2:16 7997
thou know how the matter will *f* Ruth 3:18 5307
none of his words *f* to the ground 1Sa 3:19 5307
hair of his head *f* to the ground 1Sa 14:45 5307
f by the hand of the Philistines 1Sa 18:25 5307
let his spittle *f* down upon his 1Sa 21:13 3381
not put forth their hand to *f* 1Sa 22:17 6293
Turn thou, and *f* upon the priests 1Sa 22:18 6293
let not my blood *f* to the earth 1Sa 26:20 5307
and said, Go near, and *f* upon him 2Sa 1:15 6293
hair of thy son *f* to the earth 2Sa 14:11 5307
let us *f* now into the hand of the 2Sa 24:14 5307
let me not *f* into the hand of man 2Sa 24:14 5307
not an hair of him *f* to the earth 1Kin 1:52 5307
Jehoiada, saying, Go, *f* upon him 1Kin 2:29 6293
said, and *f* upon him, and bury him 1Kin 2:31 6293
may go up and *f* at Ramoth-gilead 1Kin 22:20 5307
let us *f* unto the host of the 2Kin 7:4 5307
Know now that there shall *f* unto 2Kin 10:10 5307
thy hurt, that thou shouldest *f* 2Kin 14:10 5307
I will cause him to *f* by the 2Kin 19:7 5307
He will *f* to his master Saul to 1Chr 12:19 5307
let me *f* now into the hand of the 1Chr 21:13 5307
but let me not *f* into the hand of 1Chr 21:13 5307
may go up and *f* at Ramoth-gilead 2Chr 18:19 5307
until thy bowels *f* out by reason 2Chr 21:15 3318
make thee *f* before the enemy 2Chr 25:8 3782
thine hurt, that thou shouldest *f* 2Chr 25:19 5307
before whom thou hast begun to *f* Est 6:13 5307
but shalt surely *f* before him Est 6:13 5307
and his dread *f* upon you Job 13:11 5307
Then let mine arm *f* from my Job 31:22 5307
let them *f* by their own counsels Ps 5:10 5307
are turned back, they shall *f* Ps 9:3 3782
that the poor may *f* by his strong Ps 10:10 5307
that very destruction let him *f* Ps 35:8 5307
Though he *f*, he shall not be Ps 37:24 5307

whereby the people *f* under thee Ps 45:5 5307
They shall *f* by the sword Ps 63:10 5064
own tongue to *f* upon themselves Ps 64:8 3782
all kings shall *f* down before him Ps 72:11 7812
he let it *f* in the midst of their Ps 78:28 5307
f like one of the princes Ps 82:7 5307
A thousand shall *f* at thy side Ps 91:7 5307
thrust sore at me that I might *f* Ps 118:13 5307
Let burning coals *f* upon them Ps 140:10 4131
Let the wicked *f* into their own Ps 141:10 5307
The LORD upholdeth all that *f* Ps 145:14 5307
away, unless they cause some to *f* Prov 4:16 3782
but a prating fool shall *f* Prov 10:8 3832
but a prating fool shall *f* Prov 10:10 3832
but the wicked shall *f* by his own Prov 11:5 5307
Where no counsel is, the people *f* Prov 11:14 5307
trusteth in his riches shall *f* Prov 11:28 5307
and an haughty spirit before a *f* Prov 16:18 3783
of the LORD shall *f* therein Prov 22:14 5307
the wicked shall *f* into mischief Prov 24:16 3782
diggeth a pit shall *f* therein Prov 26:27 5307
he shall *f* himself into his own Prov 28:10 5307
his heart shall *f* into mischief Prov 28:14 5307
in his ways shall *f* at once Prov 28:18 5307
the righteous shall see their *f* Prov 29:16 4658
For if they *f*, the one will lift Eccl 4:10 5307
diggeth a pit shall *f* into it Eccl 10:8 5307
if the tree *f* toward the south Eccl 11:3 5307
Thy men shall *f* by the sword Is 3:25 5307
among them shall stumble, and *f* Is 8:15 5307
they shall *f* under the slain Is 10:4 5307
Lebanon shall *f* by a mighty one Is 10:34 5307
unto them shall *f* by the sword Is 13:15 5307
be removed, and be cut down, and *f* Is 22:25 5307
of the fear shall *f* into the pit Is 24:18 5307
and it shall *f*, and not rise again Is 24:20 5307
f backward, and be broken, and Is 28:13 3782
be to you as a breach ready to *f* Is 30:13 5307
slaughter, when the towers *f* Is 30:25 5307
both he that helpeth shall *f* Is 31:3 3782
and he that is holpen shall *f* down Is 31:3 5307
the Assyrian *f* with the sword Is 31:8 5307
and all their host shall *f* down Is 34:4 5034
I will cause him to *f* by the Is 37:7 5307
and the young men shall utterly *f* Is 40:30 3782
shall I *f* down to the stock of a Is 44:19 5456
they shall *f* down unto thee, they Is 45:14 7812
they *f* down, yea, they worship Is 46:6 5456
and mischief shall *f* upon thee Is 47:11 5307
against thee shall *f* for thy sake Is 54:15 5307
cause mine anger to *f* upon you Jer 3:12 5307
they shall *f* among them that *f* Jer 6:15 5307
sons together shall *f* upon them Jer 6:21 3782
Shall they *f*, and not arise Jer 8:4 5307
shall they *f* among them that *f* Jer 8:12 5307
f as dung upon the open field Jer 9:22 5307
caused him to *f* upon it suddenly Jer 15:8 5307
I will cause them to *f* by the Jer 19:7 5307
they shall *f* by the sword of Jer 20:4 5307
shall be driven on, and *f* therein Jer 23:12 5307
it shall *f* grievously upon the Jer 23:19 2342
ye, and be drunken, and spue, and *f* Jer 25:27 5307
ye shall *f* like a pleasant vessel Jer 25:34 5307
it shall *f* with pain upon the Jer 30:23 2342
I *f* not away to the Chaldeans Jer 37:14 5307
and thou shalt not *f* by the sword Jer 39:18 5307
and *f* in the land of Egypt Jer 44:12 5307
f toward the north by the river Jer 46:6 5307
He made many to *f*, yea, one fell Jer 46:16 3782
the fear shall *f* into the pit Jer 48:44 5307
is moved at the noise of their *f* Jer 49:21 5307
young men shall *f* in her streets Jer 49:26 5307
her young men *f* in the streets Jer 50:30 5307
the most proud shall stumble and *f* Jer 50:32 5307
Thus the slain shall *f* in the Jer 51:4 5307
yea, the wall of Babylon shall *f* Jer 51:44 5307
slain shall *f* in the midst of her Jer 51:47 5307
caused the slain of Israel to *f* Jer 51:49 5307
so at Babylon shall *f* the slain Jer 51:49 5307
he hath made my strength to *f* Lam 1:14 3782
a third part shall *f* by the sword Eze 5:12 5307
the slain shall *f* in the midst of Eze 6:7 5307
for they shall *f* by the sword Eze 6:11 5307
that is near shall *f* by the sword Eze 6:12 5307
Ye shall *f* by the sword Eze 11:10 5307
morter, that it shall *f* Eze 13:11 5307
ye, O great hailstones, shall *f* Eze 13:11 5307
be discovered, and it shall *f* Eze 13:14 5307
his bands shall *f* by the sword Eze 17:21 5307
thy remnant shall *f* by the sword Eze 23:25 5307
let no lot *f* upon it Eze 24:6 5307
ye have left shall *f* by the sword Eze 24:21 5307
of Dedan shall *f* by the sword Eze 25:13 5307
isles shake at the sound of thy *f* Eze 26:15 4658
isles tremble in the day of thy *f* Eze 26:18 4658
shall *f* into the midst of the Eze 27:27 5307
in the midst of thee shall *f* Eze 27:34 5307
thou shalt *f* upon the open fields Eze 29:5 5307
when the slain shall *f* in Egypt Eze 30:4 5307
shall *f* with them by the sword Eze 30:5 5307
also that uphold Egypt shall *f* Eze 30:6 5307
shall they *f* in it by the sword Eze 30:6 5307
of Pi-beseth shall *f* by the sword Eze 30:17 5307
the sword to *f* out of his hand Eze 30:22 5307
the arms of Pharaoh shall *f* down Eze 30:25 5307
to shake at the sound of his *f* Eze 31:16 4658
his own life, in the day of thy *f* Eze 32:10 4658
will I cause thy multitude to *f* Eze 32:12 4658
They shall *f* in the midst of them Eze 32:20 4658
he shall not *f* thereby in the day Eze 33:12 3782
the wastes shall *f* by the sword Eze 33:27 5307
shall they *f* that are slain with Eze 35:8 5307
cause thy nations to *f* any more Eze 36:15 3782
down, and the steep places shall *f* Eze 38:20 5307
every wall shall *f* to the ground Eze 38:20 5307
arrows to *f* out of thy right hand Eze 39:3 5307
Thou shalt *f* upon the mountains Eze 39:4 5307
Thou shalt *f* upon the open field Eze 39:5 5307
of Israel to *f* into iniquity Eze 44:12 4383
this land shall *f* unto you for Eze 47:14 5307
ye *f* down and worship the golden Dan 3:5 5308
all kinds of musick, shall *f* down Dan 3:10 5308
ye *f* down and worship the image Dan 3:15 5308
but they shall *f* Dan 11:14 3782
but he shall stumble and *f* Dan 11:19 5307
and many shall *f* down slain Dan 11:26 5307
yet they shall *f* by the sword Dan 11:33 3782
Now when they shall *f*, they shall Dan 11:34 3782
of them of understanding shall *f* Dan 11:35 3782
Therefore shalt thou *f* in the day Hos 4:5 3782
shall *f* with thee in the night Hos 4:5 3782
that doth not understand shall *f* Hos 4:14 3832
Ephraim *f* in their iniquity Hos 5:5 3782
Judah also shall *f* with them Hos 5:5 3782
their princes shall *f* by the Hos 7:16 5307
and to the hills, *F* on us Hos 10:8 5307
they shall *f* by the sword Hos 13:16 5307
the transgressors shall *f* therein Hos 14:9 3872
when they *f* upon the sword, they Joel 2:8 5307
Can a bird *f* in a snare upon the Amos 3:5 5307
be cut off, and *f* to the ground Amos 3:14 5307
daughters shall *f* by the sword Amos 7:17 5307
even they shall *f*, and never rise Amos 8:14 5307
the least grain *f* upon the earth Amos 9:9 5307
when I *f*, I shall arise Mic 7:8 5307
they shall even *f* into the mouth Nah 3:12 5307
I give thee, if thou wilt *f* down Mt 4:9 *4098*
and great was the *f* of it Mt 7:27 *4431*
one of them shall not *f* on the Mt 10:29 *4098*
if it *f* into a pit on the sabbath Mt 12:11 *1706*
both shall *f* into the ditch Mt 15:14 *4098*
which *f* from their masters' table Mt 15:27 *4098*
whosoever shall *f* on this stone Mt 21:44 *4098*
but on whomsoever it shall *f* Mt 21:44 *4098*
and the stars shall *f* from heaven Mt 24:29 *4098*
And the stars of heaven shall *f* Mk 13:25 *1601*
this child is set for the *f* Lk 2:34 *4431*
they not both *f* into the ditch Lk 6:39 *4098*
and in time of temptation *f* away Lk 8:13 *868*
Satan as lightning *f* from heaven Lk 10:18 *4098*
Whosoever shall *f* upon that stone Lk 20:18 *4098*
but on whomsoever it shall *f* Lk 20:18 *4098*
they shall *f* by the edge of the Lk 21:24 *4098*
to say to the mountains, *F* on us Lk 23:30 *4098*
a corn of wheat *f* into the ground Jn 12:24 *4098*
they should *f* into the quicksands Acts 27:17 *1601*
of the boat, and let her *f* off Acts 27:32 *1601*
f from the head of any of you Acts 27:34 *4098*
they stumbled that they should *f* Rom 11:11 *4098*
but rather through their *f* Rom 11:11 *3900*
Now if the *f* of them be the Rom 11:12 *3900*
or an occasion to *f* in his Rom 14:13 *4625*
he standeth take heed lest he *f* 1Cor 10:12 *4098*
he *f* into the condemnation of the 1Ti 3:6 *1706*
lest he *f* into reproach and the 1Ti 3:7
will be rich *f* into temptation 1Ti 6:9
lest any man *f* after the same Heb 4:11 *4098*
If they shall *f* away, to renew Heb 6:6 *3895*
It is a fearful thing to *f* into Heb 10:31 *1706*
when ye *f* into divers temptations Jas 1:2 *4045*
lest ye *f* into condemnation Jas 5:12 *4098*
do these things, ye shall never *f* 2Pet 1:10 *4417*
f from your own stedfastness 2Pet 3:17 *1601*
twenty elders *f* down before him Rev 4:10 *4098*
F on us, and hide us from the face Rev 6:16 *4098*
I saw a star *f* from heaven unto Rev 9:1 *4098*

FALLEN {80}
and why is thy countenance *f* Gen 4:6 5307
man whose hair is *f* off his head Lev 13:40 4803
he that hath his hair *f* off from Lev 13:41 4803
poor, and *f* in decay with thee Lev 25:35 4131,3027
is *f* to us on this side Jordan Num 32:19 935
and that your terror is *f* upon us Josh 2:9 5307
when they were all *f* on the edge Josh 8:24 5307
their lord was *f* down dead on the Judg 3:25 5307
f unto them among the tribes of Judg 18:1 5307
the woman his concubine was *f* Judg 19:27 5307
Dagon was *f* upon his face to the 1Sa 5:3 5307
Dagon was *f* upon his face to the 1Sa 5:4 5307
from the LORD was *f* upon them 1Sa 26:12 5307
his three sons *f* in mount Gilboa 1Sa 31:8 5307
and many of the people also are *f* 2Sa 1:4 5307
not live after that he was *f* 2Sa 1:10 5307
because they were *f* by the sword 2Sa 1:12 5307
how are the mighty *f* 2Sa 1:19 5307
How are the mighty *f* in the midst 2Sa 1:25 5307
How are the mighty *f*, and the 2Sa 1:27 5307
a great man *f* this day in Israel 2Sa 3:38 5307
yea, they are *f* under my feet 2Sa 22:39 5307
Now Elisha was *f* sick of his 2Kin 13:14
his sons *f* in mount Gilboa 1Chr 10:8 5307
were dead bodies *f* to the earth 2Chr 20:24 5307
our fathers have *f* by the sword 2Chr 29:9 5307
Haman was *f* upon the bed whereon Est 7:8 5307
The fire of God is *f* from heaven Job 1:16 5307
is *f* into the ditch which he made Ps 7:15 5307
The lines are *f* unto me in Ps 16:6 5307
they are *f* under my feet Ps 18:38 5307
They are brought down and *f* Ps 20:8 5307
are the workers of iniquity *f* Ps 36:12 5307
terrors of death are *f* upon me Ps 55:4 5307
whereof they are *f* themselves Ps 57:6 5307
reproached thee are *f* upon me Ps 69:9 5307
is ruined, and Judah is *f* Is 3:8 5307
The bricks are *f* down, but we Is 9:10 5307
How art thou *f* from heaven Is 14:12 5307
fruits and for thy harvest is *f* Is 16:9 5307
he answered and said, Babylon is *f* Is 21:9 5307
and said, Babylon is *f*, is *f* Is 21:9 5307
the inhabitants of the world *f* Is 26:18 5307
for truth is *f* in the street, and Is 59:14 3782
Jews that are *f* to the Chaldeans Jer 38:19 5307
and they are *f* both together Jer 46:12 5307
the spoiler is *f* upon thy summer Jer 48:32 5307
her foundations are *f*, her walls Jer 50:15 5307
Babylon is suddenly *f* and Jer 51:8 5307
my young men are *f* by the sword Lam 2:21 5307
The crown is *f* from our head Lam 5:16 5307
Lo, when the wall is *f*, shall it Eze 13:12 5307
the valleys his branches are *f* Eze 31:12 5307
all of them slain, *f* by the sword Eze 32:22 5307
f by the sword, which caused Eze 32:23 5307
f by the sword, which are gone Eze 32:24 5307
that are *f* of the uncircumcised Eze 32:27 5307
all their kings are *f* Hos 7:7 5307
for thou hast *f* by thine iniquity Hos 14:1 3782
The virgin of Israel is *f* Amos 5:2 5307
the tabernacle of David that is *f* Amos 9:11 5307
for the cedar is *f* Zec 11:2 5307
have an ass or an ox *f* into a pit Lk 14:5 *1706*
as yet he was *f* upon none of them Acts 8:16 *1968*
of David, which is *f* down Acts 15:16 *4098*
being *f* into a deep sleep Acts 20:9 *2702*
when we were all *f* to the earth Acts 26:14 *2667*
lest we should have *f* upon rocks Acts 27:29 *1601*
swollen, or *f* down dead suddenly Acts 28:6 *2667*
present, but some are *f* asleep 1Cor 15:6 *2837*
Then they also which are *f* asleep 1Cor 15:18 *2837*
ye are *f* from grace Gal 5:4 *1601*
which happened unto me have *f* out Phil 1:12 *2064*
therefore from whence thou art *f* Rev 2:5 *1601*
saying, Babylon is *f*, is *f* Rev 14:8 *4098*
five are *f*, and one is, and the Rev 17:10 *4098*
Babylon the great is *f*, is *f* Rev 18:2 *4098*

FALLEST {1}
Thou *f* away to the Chaldeans Jer 37:13 5307

FALLETH {28}
when there *f* out any war, they Ex 1:10 7122
vessel, whereinto any of them *f* Lev 11:33 5307
their carcase *f* shall be unclean Lev 11:35 5307
be in the place where his lot *f* Num 33:54 3918
or that *f* on the sword, or that 2Sa 3:29 5307
as a man *f* before wicked men, so 2Sa 3:34 5307
him as the dew *f* on the ground 2Sa 17:12 5307
night, when deep sleep *f* on men Job 4:13 5307
night, when deep sleep *f* upon men Job 33:15 5307
wicked messenger *f* into mischief Prov 13:17 5307
a perverse tongue *f* into mischief Prov 17:20 5307
For a just man *f* seven times Prov 24:16 5307
Rejoice not when thine enemy *f* Prov 24:17 5307
to him that is alone when he *f* Eccl 4:10 5307
when it *f* suddenly upon them Eccl 9:12 5307
in the place where the tree *f* Eccl 11:3 5307
as the leaf *f* off from the vine Is 34:4 5034
a graven image, and *f* down thereto Is 44:15 5456
he *f* down unto it, and worshippeth Is 44:17 5456
f to the Chaldeans that besiege Jer 21:9 5307
whoso *f* not down and worshippeth Dan 3:6 5308
whoso *f* not down and worshippeth, Dan 3:11 5308
for ofttimes he *f* into the fire Mt 17:15 *4098*
a house divided against a house *f* Lk 11:17 *4098*
the portion of goods that *f* to me Lk 15:12 *1911*
his own master he standeth or *f* Rom 14:4 *4098*
grass, and the flower thereof *f* Jas 1:11 *1601*
and the flower thereof *f* away 1Pet 1:24 *1601*

FALLING {15}
f into a trance, but having his Num 24:4 5307
f into a trance, but having his Num 24:16 5307
have upholden him that was *f* Job 4:4 3782
the mountain *f* cometh to nought Job 14:18 5307
not thou deliver my feet from *f* Ps 56:13 1762
from tears, and my feet from *f* Ps 116:8 1762
A righteous man *f* down before the Prov 25:26 4131
as a *f* fig from the fig tree Is 34:4 5034
f down before him, she declared Lk 8:47 *4363*
of blood *f* down to the ground Lk 22:44 *2597*
f headlong, he burst asunder in Acts 1:18 *4248,1096*
f into a place where two seas met Acts 27:41 *4045*
so *f* down on his face he will 1Cor 14:25 *4098*
except there come a *f* away first 2Th 2:3 *646*
that is able to keep you from *f* Jude 24 *679*

FALLOW {3}
the *f* deer, and the wild goat, and Deut 14:5 3180
Jerusalem, Break up your *f* ground Jer 4:3 5215
break up your *f* ground Hos 10:12 5215

FALLOWDEER {1}
beside harts, and roebucks, and *f* 1Kin 4:23 3180

FALSE {64}
Thou shalt not bear *f* witness Ex 20:16 8267
Thou shalt not raise a *f* report Ex 23:1 7723
Keep thee far from a *f* matter Ex 23:7 8267

Neither shalt thou bear *f* witness... Deut 5:20 7723
If a *f* witness rise up against... Deut 19:16 2555
if the witness be a *f* witness... Deut 19:18 8267
And they said, It is *f*... 2Kin 9:12 8267
For truly my words shall not be *f*... Job 36:4 8267
for *f* witnesses are risen up... Ps 27:12 8267
F witnesses did rise up... Ps 35:11 2555
therefore I hate every *f* way... Ps 119:104 8267
and I hate every *f* way... Ps 119:128 8267
be done unto thee, thou *f* tongue... Ps 120:3 7423
A *f* witness that speaketh lies,... Prov 6:19 8267
A *f* balance is abomination to the... Prov 11:1 4820
but a *f* witness deceit... Prov 12:17 8267
but a *f* witness will utter lies... Prov 14:5 8267
wicked doer giveth heed to *f* lips... Prov 17:4 205
A *f* witness shall not be... Prov 19:5 8267
A *f* witness shall not be... Prov 19:9 8267
and a *f* balance is not good... Prov 20:23 4820
A *f* witness shall perish... Prov 21:28 3577
of a *f* gift is like clouds... Prov 25:14 8267
A man that beareth *f* witness... Prov 25:18 8267
they prophesy unto you a *f* vision... Jer 14:14 8267
them that prophesy *f* dreams... Jer 23:32 8267
Then said Jeremiah, It is *f*... Jer 37:14 8267
but have seen for thee *f* burdens... Lam 2:14 7723
as a *f* divination in their sight... Eze 21:23 7723
and love no *f* oath... Zec 8:17 8267
seen a lie, and have told *f* dreams... Zec 10:2 7723
against *f* swearers, and against... Mal 3:5 8267
Beware of *f* prophets, which come... Mt 7:15 *5573*
thefts, *f* witness, blasphemies... Mt 15:19 *5577*
Thou shalt not bear *f* witness... Mt 19:18 *5576*
many *f* prophets shall rise, and... Mt 24:11 *5573*
For there shall arise *f* Christs... Mt 24:24
f prophets, and shall shew great... Mt 24:24 *5573*
sought *f* witness against Jesus,... Mt 26:59 *5580*
though many *f* witnesses came, yet... Mt 26:60 *5575*
At the last came two *f* witnesses... Mt 26:60 *5575*
not steal, Do not bear *f* witness... Mk 10:19 *5576*
For *f* Christs and *f* prophets... Mk 13:22 *5580*
For many bare *f* witness against... Mk 14:56 *5576*
bare *f* witness against him,... Mk 14:57 *5576*
their fathers to the *f* prophets... Lk 6:26 *5573*
not steal, Do not bear *f* witness... Lk 18:20 *5576*
from any man by *f* accusation... Lk 19:8 *4811*
set up *f* witnesses, which said,... Acts 6:13 *5571*
a *f* prophet, a Jew, whose name... Acts 13:6 *5578*
Thou shalt not bear *f* witness... Rom 13:9 *5576*
we are found *f* witnesses of God... 1Cor 15:15 *5575*
For such are *f* apostles,... 2Cor 11:13 *5570*
sea, in perils among *f* brethren... 2Cor 11:26 *5569*
that because of *f* brethren... Gal 2:4 *5569*
f accusers, incontinent, fierce,... 2Ti 3:3 *1228*
not *f* accusers, not given to much... Titus 2:3 *1228*
But there were *f* prophets also... 2Pet 2:1 *5578*
shall be *f* teachers among you... 2Pet 2:1 *5572*
because many *f* prophets are gone... 1Jn 4:1 *5578*
out of the mouth of the *f* prophet... Rev 16:13 *5578*
with him the *f* prophet that... Rev 19:20 *5578*
the *f* prophet are, and shall be... Rev 20:10 *5578*

FALSEHOOD {14}

wrought *f* against mine own life... 2Sa 18:13 8267
in your answers there remaineth *f*... Job 21:34 4604
mischief, and brought forth *f*... Ps 7:14 8267
for their deceit is *f*... Ps 119:118 8267
right hand is a right hand of *f*... Ps 144:8 8267
right hand is a right hand of *f*... Ps 144:11 8267
under *f* have we hid ourselves... Is 28:15 8267
of transgression, a seed of *f*... Is 57:4 8267
from the heart words of *f*... Is 59:13 8267
for his molten image is *f*... Jer 10:14 8267
forgotten me, and trusted in *f*... Jer 13:25 8267
for his molten image is *f*... Jer 51:17 8267
for they commit *f*; and the thief... Hos 7:1 8267
f do lie, saying, I will prophesy... Mic 2:11 8267

FALSELY {21}

that thou wilt not deal *f* with me... Gen 21:23 8266
concerning it, and sweareth *f*... Lev 6:3 5921,8267
that about which he hath sworn *f*... Lev 6:5 8267
shall not steal, neither deal *f*... Lev 19:11 3584
ye shall not swear by my name *f*... Lev 19:12 8267
hath testified *f* against his... Deut 19:18 8267
have we dealt *f* in thy covenant... Ps 44:17 8266
surely they swear *f*... Jer 5:2 8267
The prophets prophesy *f*, and the... Jer 5:31 8267
the priest every one dealeth *f*... Jer 6:13 8267
and commit adultery, and swear *f*... Jer 7:9 8267
the priest every one dealeth *f*... Jer 8:10 8267
For they prophesy *f* unto you in... Jer 29:9 8267
for thou speakest *f* of Ishmael... Jer 40:16 8267
unto Jeremiah, Thou speakest *f*... Jer 43:2 8267
swearing *f* in making a covenant... Hos 10:4 7723
of him that sweareth *f* by my name... Zec 5:4 8267
all manner of evil against you *f*... Mt 5:11 *5574*
to no man, neither accuse any *f*... Lk 3:14
of science *f* so called... 1Ti 6:20 *5581*
they may be ashamed that *f* accuse... 1Pet 3:16

FALSIFYING {1}

and *f* the balances by deceit... Amos 8:5 5791

FAME {24}

the *f* thereof was heard in... Gen 45:16 6963
heard the *f* of thee will speak... Num 14:15 8088
his *f* was noised throughout all... Josh 6:27 8089
for we have heard the *f* of him... Josh 9:9 8089
his *f* was in all nations round... 1Kin 4:31 8034
f of Solomon concerning the name... 1Kin 10:1 8088
exceedeth the *f* which I heard... 1Kin 10:7 8052
the *f* of David went out into all... 1Chr 14:17 8034
be exceeding magnifical, of *f*... 1Chr 22:5 8034
Sheba heard of the *f* of Solomon... 2Chr 9:1 8088
thou exceedest the *f* that I heard... 2Chr 9:6 8052
his *f* went out throughout all the... Est 9:4 8089
We have heard the *f* thereof with... Job 28:22 8088
off, that have not heard my *f*... Is 66:19 8088
We have heard the *f* thereof... Jer 6:24 8089
f in every land where they have... Zeph 3:19 8034
his *f* went throughout all Syria... Mt 4:24 *189*
the *f* hereof went abroad into all... Mt 9:26 *5345*
spread abroad his *f* in all that... Mt 9:31 *1310*
tetrarch heard of the *f* of Jesus... Mt 14:1 *189*
immediately his *f* spread abroad... Mk 1:28 *189*
there went out a *f* of him through... Lk 4:14 *5345*
the *f* of him went out into every... Lk 4:37 *2279*
more went there a *f* abroad of him... Lk 5:15 *3056*

FAMILIAR {18}

not them that have *f* spirits... Lev 19:31
after such as have *f* spirits... Lev 20:6
or woman that hath a *f* spirit... Lev 20:27
or a consulter with *f* spirits... Deut 18:11
put away those that had *f* spirits... 1Sa 28:3
me a woman that hath a *f* spirit... 1Sa 28:7
that hath a *f* spirit at En-dor... 1Sa 28:7
divine unto me by the *f* spirit... 1Sa 28:8
cut off those that have *f* spirits... 1Sa 28:9
and dealt with *f* spirits and... 2Kin 21:6
the workers with *f* spirits... 2Kin 23:24
of one that had a *f* spirit... 1Chr 10:13
and dealt with a *f* spirit... 2Chr 33:6
my *f* friends have forgotten me... Job 19:14 3045
Yea, mine own *f* friend, in whom I... Ps 41:9 7965
unto them that have *f* spirits... Is 8:19
and to them that have *f* spirits... Is 19:3
as of one that hath a *f* spirit... Is 29:4

FAMILIARS {1}

All my *f* watched for my halting,... Jer 20:10 7965

FAMILIES {175}

after his tongue, after their *f*... Gen 10:5 4940
afterward were the *f* of the... Gen 10:18 4940
the sons of Ham, after their *f*... Gen 10:20 4940
the sons of Shem, after their *f*... Gen 10:31 4940
These are the *f* of the sons of... Gen 10:32 4940
in thee shall all *f* of the earth... Gen 12:3 4940
all the *f* of the earth be blessed... Gen 28:14 4940
of Esau, according to their *f*... Gen 36:40 4940
with bread, according to their *f*... Gen 47:12 2945
these be the *f* of Reuben... Ex 6:14 4940
these are the *f* of Simeon... Ex 6:15 4940
and Shimi, according to their *f*... Ex 6:17 4940
these are the *f* of Levi according... Ex 6:19 4940
these are the *f* of the Korhites... Ex 6:24 4940
the Levites according to their *f*... Ex 6:25 4940
you a lamb according to your *f*... Ex 12:21 4940
of their *f* that are with you,... Lev 25:45 4940
children of Israel, after their *f*... Num 1:2 4940
their pedigrees after their *f*... Num 1:18 4940
their generations, after their *f*... Num 1:20 4940
their generations, after their *f*... Num 1:22 4940
their generations, after their *f*... Num 1:24 4940
their generations, after their *f*... Num 1:26 4940
their generations, after their *f*... Num 1:28 4940
their generations, after their *f*... Num 1:30 4940
their generations, after their *f*... Num 1:32 4940
their generations, after their *f*... Num 1:34 4940
their generations, after their *f*... Num 1:36 4940
their generations, after their *f*... Num 1:38 4940
their generations, after their *f*... Num 1:40 4940
their generations, after their *f*... Num 1:42 4940
forward, every one after their *f*... Num 2:34 4940
of their fathers, by their *f*... Num 3:15 4940
of the sons of Gershon by their *f*... Num 3:18 4940
And the sons of Kohath by their *f*... Num 3:19 4940
And the sons of Merari by their *f*... Num 3:20 4940
These are the *f* of the Levites... Num 3:20 4940
these are the *f* of the... Num 3:21 4940
The *f* of the Gershonites shall... Num 3:23 4940
these are the *f* of the Kohathites... Num 3:27 4940
The *f* of the sons of Kohath shall... Num 3:29 4940
the *f* of the Kohathites shall be... Num 3:30 4940
these are the *f* of Merari... Num 3:33 4940
the house of the father of the *f*... Num 3:35 4940
of the LORD, throughout their *f*... Num 3:39 4940
the sons of Levi, after their *f*... Num 4:2 4940
f of the Kohathites from among... Num 4:18 4940
of their fathers, by their *f*... Num 4:22 4940
of the *f* of the Gershonites... Num 4:24 4940
This is the service of the *f* of... Num 4:28 4940
shalt number them after their *f*... Num 4:29 4940
of the *f* of the sons of Merari... Num 4:33 4940
of the Kohathites after their *f*... Num 4:34 4940
were numbered of them by their *f*... Num 4:36 4940
of the *f* of the Kohathites... Num 4:37 4940
of Gershon, throughout their *f*... Num 4:38 4940
of them, throughout their *f*... Num 4:40 4940
of the *f* of the sons of Gershon... Num 4:41 4940
of the *f* of the sons of Merari... Num 4:42 4940
throughout their *f*, by the house... Num 4:42 4940
numbered of them after their *f*... Num 4:44 4940
of the *f* of the sons of Merari... Num 4:45 4940
of Israel numbered, after their *f*... Num 4:46 4940
people weep throughout their *f*... Num 11:10 4940
These are the *f* of the Reubenites... Num 26:7 4940
The sons of Simeon after their *f*... Num 26:12 4940
These are the *f* of the Simeonites... Num 26:14 4940
The children of Gad after their *f*... Num 26:15 4940
These are the *f* of the children... Num 26:18 4940
sons of Judah after their *f* were... Num 26:20 4940
These are the *f* of Judah... Num 26:22 4940
sons of Issachar after their *f*... Num 26:23 4940
These are the *f* of Issachar... Num 26:25 4940
the sons of Zebulun after their *f*... Num 26:26 4940
These are the *f* of the... Num 26:27 4940
after their *f* were Manasseh... Num 26:28 4940
These are the *f* of Manasseh... Num 26:34 4940
the sons of Ephraim after their *f*... Num 26:35 4940
These are the *f* of the sons of... Num 26:37 4940
the sons of Joseph after their *f*... Num 26:37 4940
sons of Benjamin after their *f*... Num 26:38 4940
sons of Benjamin after their *f*... Num 26:41 4940
are the sons of Dan after their *f*... Num 26:42 4940
These are the *f* of Dan after... Num 26:42 4940
the *f* of Dan after their *f*... Num 26:42 4940
All the *f* of the Shuhamites,... Num 26:43 4940
children of Asher after their *f*... Num 26:44 4940
These are the *f* of the sons of... Num 26:47 4940
sons of Naphtali after their *f*... Num 26:48 4940
These are the *f* of Naphtali... Num 26:50 4940
of Naphtali according to their *f*... Num 26:50 4940
of the Levites after their *f*... Num 26:57 4940
These are the *f* of the Levites... Num 26:58 4940
of the *f* of Manasseh the son of... Num 27:1 4940
for an inheritance among your *f*... Num 33:54 4940
the chief fathers of the *f* of the... Num 36:1 4940
of the *f* of the sons of Joseph,... Num 36:1 4940
they were married into the *f* of... Num 36:12 4940
come according to the *f* thereof... Josh 7:14 4940
inheritance according to their *f*... Josh 13:15 4940
children of Reuben after their *f*... Josh 13:23 4940
children of Gad according their *f*... Josh 13:24 4940
the children of Gad after their *f*... Josh 13:28 4940
children of Manasseh by their *f*... Josh 13:29 4940
the children of Machir by their *f*... Josh 13:31 4940
the children of Judah by their *f*... Josh 15:1 4940
round about according to their *f*... Josh 15:12 4940
of Judah according to their *f*... Josh 15:20 4940
according to their *f* was thus... Josh 16:5 4940
children of Ephraim by their *f*... Josh 16:8 4940
children of Manasseh by their *f*... Josh 17:2 4940
the son of Joseph by their *f*... Josh 17:2 4940
came up according to their *f*... Josh 18:11 4940
round about, according to their *f*... Josh 18:20 4940
according to their *f* were Jericho... Josh 18:21 4940
of Benjamin according to their *f*... Josh 18:28 4940
of Simeon according to their *f*... Josh 19:1 4940
of Simeon according to their *f*... Josh 19:8 4940
of Zebulun according to their *f*... Josh 19:10 4940
of Zebulun according to their *f*... Josh 19:16 4940
of Issachar according to their *f*... Josh 19:17 4940
of Issachar according to their *f*... Josh 19:23 4940
of Asher according to their *f*... Josh 19:24 4940
of Asher according to their *f*... Josh 19:31 4940
of Naphtali according to their *f*... Josh 19:32 4940
of Naphtali according to their *f*... Josh 19:39 4940
of Dan according to their *f*... Josh 19:40 4940
of Dan according to their *f*... Josh 19:48 4940
out for the *f* of the Kohathites... Josh 21:4 4940
of the *f* of the tribe of Ephraim... Josh 21:5 4940
of the *f* of the tribe of Issachar... Josh 21:6 4940
f had out of the tribe of Reuben... Josh 21:7 4940
being of the *f* of the Kohathites,... Josh 21:10 4940
the *f* of the children of Kohath,... Josh 21:20 4940
f of the children of Kohath that... Josh 21:26 4940
of the *f* of the Levites, out of... Josh 21:27 4940
Gershonites according to their *f*... Josh 21:33 4940
unto the *f* of the children of... Josh 21:34 4940
the children of Merari by their *f*... Josh 21:40 4940
remaining of the *f* of the Levites... Josh 21:40 4940
the *f* of the tribe of Benjamin... 1Sa 9:21 4940
Benjamin to come near by their *f*... 1Sa 10:21 4940
And the *f* of Kirjath-jearim... 1Chr 2:53 4940
the *f* of the scribes which dwelt... 1Chr 2:55 4940
These are the *f* of the Zorathites... 1Chr 4:2 4940
the *f* of Aharhel the son of Harum... 1Chr 4:8 4940
the *f* of the house of them that... 1Chr 4:21 4940
names were princes in their *f*... 1Chr 4:38 4940
And his brethren by their *f*... 1Chr 5:7 4940
these are the *f* of the Levites... 1Chr 6:19 4940
of the *f* of the Kohathites... 1Chr 6:54 4940
their *f* were thirteen cities... 1Chr 6:60 4940
of Gershom throughout their *f* out... 1Chr 6:62 4940
given by lot, throughout their *f*... 1Chr 6:63 4940
the residue of the *f* of the sons... 1Chr 6:66 4940
their brethren among all the *f* of... 1Chr 7:5 4940
to the divisions of the *f* of the... 2Chr 35:5 1004,1
division of the *f* of the Levites... 2Chr 35:5 1004,1
the divisions of the *f* of the people... 2Chr 35:12 1004
after their *f* with their swords... Neh 4:13 4940
did the contempt of *f* terrify me... Job 31:34 4940
God setteth the solitary in *f*... Ps 68:6 1004
maketh him *f* like a flock... Ps 107:41 4940
I will call all the *f* of the... Jer 1:15 4940
all the *f* of the house of Israel... Jer 2:4 4940
upon the *f* that call not on thy... Jer 10:25 4940
and take all the *f* of the north... Jer 25:9 4940
be the God of all the *f* of Israel... Jer 31:1 4940
The two *f* which the LORD hath... Jer 33:24 4940
as the *f* of the countries, to... Eze 20:32 4940
I known of all the *f* of the earth... Amos 3:2 4940
f through her witchcrafts... Nah 3:4 4940
All the *f* that remain, every... Zec 12:14 4940
will not come up of all the *f* of... Zec 14:17 4940

FAMILY {123}
- that man, and against his *f* ... Lev 20:5 4940
- shall return every man unto his *f* ... Lev 25:10 4940
- and shall return unto his own *f* ... Lev 25:41 4940
- to the stock of the stranger's *f* ... Lev 25:47 4940
- unto him of his *f* may redeem him ... Lev 25:49 4940
- Gershon was the *f* of the Libnites ... Num 3:21 4940
- and the *f* of the Shimites ... Num 3:21 4940
- Kohath was the *f* of the Amramites ... Num 3:27 4940
- the *f* of the Izeharites, and the ... Num 3:27 4940
- the *f* of the Hebronites, and the ... Num 3:27 4940
- and the *f* of the Uzzielites ... Num 3:27 4940
- Merari was the *f* of the Mahlites ... Num 3:33 4940
- and the *f* of the Mushites ... Num 3:33 4940
- cometh the *f* of the Hanochites ... Num 26:5 4940
- of Pallu, the *f* of the Palluites ... Num 26:5 4940
- Hezron, the *f* of the Hezronites ... Num 26:6 4940
- of Carmi, the *f* of the Carmites ... Num 26:6 4940
- Nemuel, the *f* of the Nemuelites ... Num 26:12 4940
- of Jamin, the *f* of the Jaminites ... Num 26:12 4940
- Jachin, the *f* of the Jachinites ... Num 26:12 4940
- Of Zerah, the *f* of the Zarhites ... Num 26:13 4940
- of Shaul, the *f* of the Shaulites ... Num 26:13 4940
- Zephon, the *f* of the Zephonites ... Num 26:15 4940
- of Haggi, the *f* of the Haggites ... Num 26:15 4940
- of Shuni, the *f* of the Shunites ... Num 26:15 4940
- Of Ozni, the *f* of the Oznites ... Num 26:16 4940
- of Eri, the *f* of the Erites ... Num 26:16 4940
- Of Arod, the *f* of the Arodites ... Num 26:17 4940
- of Areli, the *f* of the Arelites ... Num 26:17 4940
- Shelah, the *f* of the Shelanites ... Num 26:20 4940
- of Pharez, the *f* of the Pharzites ... Num 26:20 4940
- of Zerah, the *f* of the Zarhites ... Num 26:20 4940
- Hezron, the *f* of the Hezronites ... Num 26:21 4940
- of Hamul, the *f* of the Hamulites ... Num 26:21 4940
- of Tola, the *f* of the Tolaites ... Num 26:23 4940
- of Pua, the *f* of the Punites ... Num 26:23 4940
- Jashub, the *f* of the Jashubites ... Num 26:24 4940
- Shimron, the *f* of the Shimronites ... Num 26:24 4940
- of Sered, the *f* of the Sardites ... Num 26:26 4940
- of Elon, the *f* of the Elonites ... Num 26:26 4940
- Jahleel, the *f* of the Jahleelites ... Num 26:26 4940
- Machir, the *f* of the Machirites ... Num 26:29 4940
- come the *f* of the Gileadites ... Num 26:29 4940
- Jeezer, the *f* of the Jeezerites ... Num 26:30 4940
- of Helek, the *f* of the Helekites ... Num 26:30 4940
- Asriel, the *f* of the Asrielites ... Num 26:31 4940
- Shechem, the *f* of the Shechemites ... Num 26:31 4940
- Shemida, the *f* of the Shemidaites ... Num 26:32 4940
- Hepher, the *f* of the Hepherites ... Num 26:32 4940
- the *f* of the Shuthalhites ... Num 26:35 4940
- of Becher, the *f* of the Bachrites ... Num 26:35 4940
- of Tahan, the *f* of the Tahanites ... Num 26:35 4940
- of Eran, the *f* of the Eranites ... Num 26:36 4940
- of Bela, the *f* of the Belaites ... Num 26:38 4940
- Ashbel, the *f* of the Ashbelites ... Num 26:38 4940
- Ahiram, the *f* of the Ahiramites ... Num 26:38 4940
- Shupham, the *f* of the Shuphamites ... Num 26:39 4940
- Hupham, the *f* of the Huphamites ... Num 26:39 4940
- of Ard, the *f* of the Ardites ... Num 26:40 4940
- of Naaman, the *f* of the Naamites ... Num 26:40 4940
- Shuham, the *f* of the Shuhamites ... Num 26:42 4940
- of Jimna, the *f* of the Jimnites ... Num 26:44 4940
- of Jesui, the *f* of the Jesuites ... Num 26:44 4940
- of Beriah, the *f* of the Beriites ... Num 26:44 4940
- of Heber, the *f* of the Heberites ... Num 26:45 4940
- the *f* of the Malchielites ... Num 26:45 4940
- Jahzeel, the *f* of the Jahzeelites ... Num 26:48 4940
- of Guni, the *f* of the Gunites ... Num 26:48 4940
- Of Jezer, the *f* of the Jezerites ... Num 26:49 4940
- Shillem, the *f* of the Shillemites ... Num 26:49 4940
- Gershon, the *f* of the Gershonites ... Num 26:57 4940
- Kohath, the *f* of the Kohathites ... Num 26:57 4940
- of Merari, the *f* of the Merarites ... Num 26:57 4940
- the *f* of the Libnites ... Num 26:58 4940
- the *f* of the Hebronites ... Num 26:58 4940
- the *f* of the Mahlites ... Num 26:58 4940
- the *f* of the Mushites ... Num 26:58 4940
- Mushites, the *f* of the Korathites ... Num 26:58 4940
- be done away from among his *f* ... Num 27:4 4940
- that is next to him of his *f* ... Num 27:11 4940
- only to the *f* of the tribe of ... Num 36:6 4940
- the *f* of the tribe of her father ... Num 36:8 4940
- tribe of the *f* of their father ... Num 36:12 4940
- be among you man, or woman, or *f* ... Deut 29:18 4940
- the *f* which the LORD shall take ... Josh 7:14 4940
- And he brought the *f* of Judah ... Josh 7:17 4940
- he took the *f* of the Zarhites ... Josh 7:17 4940
- he brought the *f* of the Zarhites ... Josh 7:17 4940
- they let go the man and all his *f* ... Judg 1:25 4940
- my *f* is poor in Manasseh, and I am ... Judg 6:15 504
- with all the *f* of the house of ... Judg 9:1 4940
- of the *f* of the Danites, whose ... Judg 13:2 4940
- of the *f* of Judah, who was a ... Judg 17:7 4940
- *f* five men from their coasts ... Judg 18:2 4940
- thence of the *f* of the Danites ... Judg 18:11 4940
- unto a tribe and a *f* in Israel ... Judg 18:19 4940
- man to his tribe and to his *f* ... Judg 21:24 4940
- of wealth, of the *f* of Elimelech ... Ruth 2:1 4940
- my *f* the least of all the ... 1Sa 9:21 4940
- the *f* of Matri was taken, and Saul ... 1Sa 10:21 4940
- life, or my father's *f* in Israel ... 1Sa 18:18 4940
- sacrifice there for all the *f* ... 1Sa 20:6 4940
- for our *f* hath a sacrifice in the ... 1Sa 20:29 4940
- the whole *f* is risen against ... 2Sa 14:7 4940
- man of the *f* of the house of Saul ... 2Sa 16:5 4940
- neither did all their *f* multiply ... 1Chr 4:27 4940
- were left of the *f* of that tribe ... 1Chr 6:61 4940
- for the *f* of the remnant of the ... 1Chr 6:70 4940
- *f* of the half tribe of Manasseh ... 1Chr 6:71 4940
- ark of God remained with the *f* of ... 1Chr 13:14 1004
- every generation, every *f* ... Est 9:28 4940
- you one of a city, and two of a *f* ... Jer 3:14 4940
- them that remain of this evil *f* ... Jer 8:3 4940
- against the whole *f* which I ... Amos 3:1 4940
- against this *f* do I devise an ... Mic 2:3 4940
- land shall mourn, every *f* apart ... Zec 12:12 4940
- the *f* of the house of David apart ... Zec 12:12 4940
- the *f* of the house of Nathan ... Zec 12:12 4940
- The *f* of the house of Levi apart ... Zec 12:13 4940
- the *f* of Shimei apart, and their ... Zec 12:13 4940
- that remain, every *f* apart ... Zec 12:14 4940
- if the *f* of Egypt go not up, and ... Zec 14:18 4940
- Of whom the whole *f* in heaven ... Eph 3:15 *3965*

FAMINE {96}
- And there was a *f* in the land ... Gen 12:10 7458
- for the *f* was grievous in the ... Gen 12:10 7458
- And there was a *f* in the land ... Gen 26:1 7458
- beside the first *f* that was in ... Gen 26:1 7458
- wind shall be seven years of *f* ... Gen 41:27 7458
- arise after them seven years of *f* ... Gen 41:30 7458
- the *f* shall consume the land ... Gen 41:30 7458
- by reason of that *f* following ... Gen 41:31 7458
- land against the seven years of *f* ... Gen 41:36 7458
- the land perish not through the *f* ... Gen 41:36 7458
- sons before the years of *f* came ... Gen 41:50 7458
- the *f* was over all the face of ... Gen 41:56 7458
- the *f* waxed sore in the land of ... Gen 41:56 7458
- because that the *f* was so sore in ... Gen 41:57 7458
- for the *f* was in the land of ... Gen 42:5 7458
- corn for the *f* of your houses ... Gen 42:19 7459
- take food for the *f* of your ... Gen 42:33 7459
- the *f* was sore in the land ... Gen 43:1 7458
- years hath the *f* been in the land ... Gen 45:6 7458
- for yet there are five years of *f* ... Gen 45:11 7458
- for the *f* is sore in the land of ... Gen 47:4 7458
- for the *f* was very sore, so that ... Gen 47:13 7458
- Canaan fainted by reason of the *f* ... Gen 47:13 7458
- because the *f* prevailed over them ... Gen 47:20 7458
- that there was a *f* in the land ... Ruth 1:1 7458
- Then there was a *f* in the days of ... 2Sa 21:1 7458
- Shall seven years of *f* come unto ... 2Sa 24:13 7458
- If there be in the land *f* ... 1Kin 8:37 7458
- And there was a sore *f* in Samaria ... 1Kin 18:2 7458
- And there was a great *f* in Samaria ... 2Kin 6:25 7458
- then the *f* is in the city, and we ... 2Kin 7:4 7458
- for the LORD hath called for a *f* ... 2Kin 8:1 7458
- month the *f* prevailed in the city ... 2Kin 25:3 7458
- Either three years' *f* ... 1Chr 21:12 7458
- judgment, or pestilence, or *f* ... 2Chr 20:9 7458
- give over yourselves to die by *f* ... 2Chr 32:11 7458
- In *f* he shall redeem thee from ... Job 5:20 7458
- destruction and *f* thou shalt laugh ... Job 5:22 3720
- For want and *f* they were solitary ... Job 30:3 3720
- death, and to keep them alive in *f* ... Ps 33:19 7458
- in the days of *f* they shall be ... Ps 37:19 7459
- he called for a *f* upon the land ... Ps 105:16 7458
- and I will kill thy root with *f* ... Is 14:30 7458
- and destruction, and the *f* ... Is 51:19 7458
- neither shall we see sword nor *f* ... Jer 5:12 7458
- and their daughters shall die by *f* ... Jer 11:22 7458
- them by the sword, and by the *f* ... Jer 14:12 7458
- sword, neither shall ye have *f* ... Jer 14:13 7458
- *f* shall not be in this land ... Jer 14:15 7458
- *f* shall those prophets be ... Jer 14:15 7458
- of Jerusalem because of the *f* ... Jer 14:16 7458
- behold them that are sick with *f* ... Jer 14:18 7458
- as are for the *f*, to the *f* ... Jer 15:2 7458
- be consumed by the sword, and by *f* ... Jer 16:4 7458
- up their children to the *f* ... Jer 18:21 7458
- from the sword, and from the *f* ... Jer 21:7 7458
- die by the sword, and by the *f* ... Jer 21:9 7458
- And I will send the sword, the *f* ... Jer 24:10 7458
- with the sword, and with the *f* ... Jer 27:8 7458
- people, by the sword, by the *f* ... Jer 27:13 7458
- send upon them the sword, the *f* ... Jer 29:17 7458
- them with the sword, with the *f* ... Jer 29:18 7458
- because of the sword, and of the *f* ... Jer 32:24 7458
- Babylon by the sword, and by the *f* ... Jer 32:36 7458
- to the pestilence, and to the *f* ... Jer 34:17 7458
- shall die by the sword, by the *f* ... Jer 38:2 7458
- in the land of Egypt, and the *f* ... Jer 42:16 7458
- shall die by the sword, by the *f* ... Jer 42:17 7458
- shall die by the sword, by the *f* ... Jer 42:22 7458
- consumed by the sword and by the *f* ... Jer 44:12 7458
- by the sword and by the *f* ... Jer 44:12 7458
- Jerusalem, by the sword, by the *f* ... Jer 44:13 7458
- consumed by the sword and by the *f* ... Jer 44:18 7458
- consumed by the sword and by the *f* ... Jer 44:27 7458
- the *f* was sore in the city, so ... Jer 52:6 7458
- an oven because of the terrible *f* ... Lam 5:10 7458
- with *f* shall they be consumed in ... Eze 5:12 7458
- upon them the evil arrows of *f* ... Eze 5:16 7458
- and I will increase the *f* upon you ... Eze 5:16 7458
- So will I send upon you *f* ... Eze 5:17 7458
- shall fall by the sword, by the *f* ... Eze 6:11 7458
- and is besieged shall die by the *f* ... Eze 6:12 7458
- and the pestilence and the *f* within ... Eze 7:15 7458
- and he that is in the city, *f* ... Eze 7:15 7458
- them from the sword, from the *f* ... Eze 12:16 7458
- thereof, and will send *f* upon it ... Eze 14:13 7458
- Jerusalem, the sword, and the *f* ... Eze 14:21 7458
- increase it, and lay no *f* upon you ... Eze 36:29 7458
- reproach of *f* among the heathen ... Eze 36:30 7458
- that I will send a *f* in the land ... Amos 8:11 7458
- not a *f* of bread, nor a thirst ... Amos 8:11 7458
- when great *f* was throughout all ... Lk 4:25 *3042*
- arose a mighty *f* in that land ... Lk 15:14 *3042*
- or distress, or persecution, or *f* ... Rom 8:35 *3042*
- one day, death, and mourning, and *f* ... Rev 18:8 *3042*

FAMINES {3}
- and there shall be *f*, and ... Mt 24:7 *3042*
- places, and there shall be *f* ... Mk 13:8 *3042*
- shall be in divers places, and *f* ... Lk 21:11 *3042*

FAMISH {2}
- the soul of the righteous to *f* ... Prov 10:3 7456
- for he will *f* all the gods of the ... Zeph 2:11 7329

FAMISHED {2}
- when all the land of Egypt was *f* ... Gen 41:55 7456
- and their honourable men are *f* ... Is 5:13 7458

FAMOUS {10}
- *f* in the congregation, men of ... Num 16:2 7148
- which were *f* in the congregation, ... Num 26:9 7121
- Ephratah, and be *f* in Beth-lehem ... Ruth 4:11 8034
- that his name may be *f* in Israel ... Ruth 4:14 7121
- *f* men, and heads of the house of ... 1Chr 5:24 8034
- *f* throughout the house of their ... 1Chr 12:30 8034
- A man was *f* according as he had ... Ps 74:5 3045
- And slew *f* kings ... Ps 136:18 117
- and she became *f* among women ... Eze 23:10 8034
- and the daughters of the *f* nations ... Eze 32:18 117

FAN {8}
- with the shovel and with the *f* ... Is 30:24 4214
- Thou shalt *f* them, and the wind ... Is 41:16 2219
- daughter of my people, not to *f* ... Jer 4:11 2219
- I will *f* them with a *f* in the ... Jer 15:7 2219
- Babylon fanners, that shall *f* her ... Jer 51:2 2219
- Whose *f* is in his hand, and he ... Mt 3:12 *4425*
- Whose *f* is in his hand, and he ... Lk 3:17 *4425*

FANNERS {1}
- And will send unto Babylon *f* ... Jer 51:2 2114

FAR See APPENDIX.

FARE {3}
- and look how thy brethren *f* ... 1Sa 17:18 7965
- so he paid the *f* thereof, and went ... Jonah 1:3 7939
- shall do well. *F* ye well ... Acts 15:29 *4517*

FARED {1}
- linen, and *f* sumptuously every day ... Lk 16:19 *2165*

FAREWELL {4}
- but let me first go bid them *f* ... Lk 9:61 *657*
- But bade them *f*, saying, I must ... Acts 18:21 *657*
- what they had against him. *F* ... Acts 23:30 *4517*
- Finally, brethren, *f* ... 2Cor 13:11 *5463*

FARM {1}
- and went their ways, one to his *f* ... Mt 22:5 *68*

FARTHER {3} See APPENDIX.

FARTHING {3}
- thou hast paid the uttermost *f* ... Mt 5:26 *2835*
- Are not two sparrows sold for a *f* ... Mt 10:29 *787*
- in two mites, which make a *f* ... Mk 12:42 *2835*

FARTHINGS {1}
- not five sparrows sold for two *f* ... Lk 12:6 *787*

FASHION {13}
- this is the *f* which thou shalt ... Gen 6:15
- *f* thereof which was shewed thee ... Ex 26:30 4941
- the *f* of almonds in one branch ... Ex 37:19
- and according to all the *f* of it ... 1Kin 6:38 4941
- the priest the *f* of the altar ... 2Kin 16:10 1823
- did not one *f* us in the womb ... Job 31:15 3559
- the *f* thereof, and the goings out ... Eze 43:11 8498
- saying, We never saw it on this *f* ... Mk 2:12 *3778*
- the *f* of his countenance was ... Lk 9:29 *1491*
- to the *f* that he had seen ... Acts 7:44 *5179*
- for the *f* of this world passeth ... 1Cor 7:31 *4976*
- And being found in *f* as a man ... Phil 2:8 *4976*
- grace of the *f* of it perisheth ... Jas 1:11 *4383*

FASHIONED {7}
- *f* it with a graving tool, after ... Ex 32:4 3335
- *f* me together round about ... Job 10:8 6213
- Thy hands have made me and *f* me ... Ps 119:73 3559
- which in continuance were *f* ... Ps 139:16 3335
- unto him that *f* it long ago ... Is 22:11 3335
- thy breasts are *f*, and thine hair ... Eze 16:7 3559
- that it may be *f* like unto his ... Phil 3:21 *4832*

FASHIONETH {3}
- He *f* their hearts alike ... Ps 33:15 3335
- *f* it with hammers, and worketh it ... Is 44:12 3335
- the clay say to him that *f* it ... Is 45:9 3335

FASHIONING {1}
- not *f* yourselves according to the ... 1Pet 1:14 *4964*

FASHIONS {1}
- were both according to their *f* ... Eze 42:11 4941

FAST {86}
- For the LORD had *f* closed up all ... Gen 20:18
- for he was *f* asleep and weary ... Judg 4:21
- but we will bind thee *f*, and ... Judg 15:13
- If they bind me *f* with new ropes ... Judg 16:11
- but abide here *f* by my maidens ... Ruth 2:8
- Thou shalt keep *f* by my young men ... Ruth 2:21
- So she kept *f* by the maidens of ... Ruth 2:23
- thou didst *f* and weep for the ... 2Sa 12:21 6684
- he is dead, wherefore should I *f* ... 2Sa 12:23 6684
- the letters, saying, Proclaim a *f* ... 1Kin 21:9 6685
- They proclaimed a *f*, and set ... 1Kin 21:12 6685
- door, and hold him *f* at the door ... 2Kin 6:32
- proclaimed a *f* throughout all ... 2Chr 20:3 6685

walls, and this work goeth *f* on ... Ezr 5:8 629
Then I proclaimed a *f* there ... Ezr 8:21 6685
f ye for me, and neither eat nor ... Est 4:16 6684
and my maidens will *f* likewise ... Est 4:16 6684
still he holdeth *f* his integrity ... Job 2:3
he shall hold it *f*, but it shall ... Job 8:15
My righteousness I hold *f* ... Job 27:6
and the clods cleave *f* together ... Job 38:38
he commanded, and it stood *f* ... Ps 33:9
For thine arrows stick *f* in me ... Ps 38:2
say they, cleaveth *f* unto him ... Ps 41:8
strength setteth *f* the mountains ... Ps 65:6
covenant shall stand *f* with him ... Ps 89:28
They stand *f* for ever and ever, and ... Ps 111:8
Take *f* hold of instruction ... Prov 4:13
day of your *f* ye find pleasure ... Is 58:3 6685
ye *f* for strife and debate, and to ... Is 58:4 6684
ye shall not *f* as ye do this day, ... Is 58:4 6684
Is it such a *f* that I have chosen ... Is 58:5 6685
wilt thou call this a *f*, and an ... Is 58:5 6685
Is not this the *f* that I have ... Is 58:6 6685
they hold *f* deceit, they refuse ... Jer 8:5
When they *f*, I will not hear ... Jer 14:12 6684
that they proclaimed a *f* before ... Jer 36:9 6685
say ye, Stand *f*, and prepare thee ... Jer 46:14
come, and his affliction hasteth *f* ... Jer 48:16 3966
took them captives held them *f* ... Jer 50:33
Sanctify ye a *f*, call a solemn ... Joel 1:14 6685
the trumpet in Zion, sanctify a *f* ... Joel 2:15 6685
and he lay, and was *f* asleep ... Jonah 1:5
believed God, and proclaimed a *f* ... Jonah 3:5 6685
years, did ye at all *f* unto me ... Zec 7:5 6684
The *f* of the fourth month, and the ... Zec 8:19 6685
the *f* of the fifth ... Zec 8:19 6685
the *f* of the seventh ... Zec 8:19 6685
and the *f* of ... Zec 8:19 6685
Moreover when ye *f*, be not, as ... Mt 6:16 *3522*
they may appear unto men to *f* ... Mt 6:16 *3522*
thou appear not unto men to *f* ... Mt 6:18 *3522*
Why do we and the Pharisees *f* oft ... Mt 9:14 *3522*
f oft, but thy disciples *f* not ... Mt 9:14 *3522*
from them, and then shall they *f* ... Mt 9:15 *3522*
hold him *f* ... Mt 26:48
and of the Pharisees used to *f* ... Mk 2:18 *3522*
of John and of the Pharisees *f* ... Mk 2:18 *3522*
but thy disciples *f* not ... Mk 2:18 *3522*
children of the bridechamber *f* ... Mk 2:19 *3522*
with them, they cannot *f* ... Mk 2:19 *3522*
then shall they *f* in those days ... Mk 2:20 *3522*
do the disciples of John *f* often ... Lk 5:33 *3522*
children of the bridechamber *f* ... Lk 5:34 *3522*
then shall they *f* in those days ... Lk 5:35 *3522*
I *f* twice in the week, I give ... Lk 18:12 *3522*
made their feet *f* in the stocks ... Acts 16:24 *805*
because the *f* was now already ... Acts 27:9 *3521*
and the forepart stuck *f*, and ... Acts 27:41
stand *f* in the faith, quit you ... 1Cor 16:13
Stand *f* therefore in the liberty ... Gal 5:1
that ye stand *f* in one spirit ... Phil 1:27
so stand *f* in the Lord, my dearly ... Phil 4:1
live, if ye stand *f* in the Lord ... 1Th 3:8
hold *f* that which is good ... 1Th 5:21 *2722*
Therefore, brethren, stand *f* ... 2Th 2:15
Hold *f* the form of sound words, ... 2Ti 1:13
Holding *f* the faithful word as he ... Titus 1:9 *472*
if we hold *f* the confidence and ... Heb 3:6 *2722*
let us hold *f* our profession ... Heb 4:14
Let us hold *f* the profession of ... Heb 10:23 *2722*
and thou holdest *f* my name ... Rev 2:13
have already hold *f* till I come ... Rev 2:25
hast received and heard, and hold *f* ... Rev 3:3
hold that *f* which thou hast, that ... Rev 3:11

FASTED {15}

f that day until even, and offered ... Judg 20:26 6684
f on that day, and said there, We ... 1Sa 7:6 6684
a tree at Jabesh, and *f* seven days ... 1Sa 31:13 6684
f until even, for Saul, and for ... 2Sa 1:12 6684
and David *f*, and went in, and lay ... 2Sa 12:16 6684
the child was yet alive, I *f* ... 2Sa 12:22 6684
sackcloth upon his flesh, and *f* ... 1Kin 21:27 6684
oak in Jabesh, and *f* seven days ... 1Chr 10:12 6684
So we *f* and besought our God for ... Ezr 8:23 6684
and mourned certain days, and *f* ... Neh 1:4 6684
Wherefore have we *f*, say they, and ... Is 58:3 6684
to the priests, saying, When ye *f* ... Zec 7:5 6684
And when he had *f* forty days ... Mt 4:2 *3522*
they ministered to the Lord, and *f* ... Acts 13:2 *3522*
And when they had *f* and prayed, and ... Acts 13:3 *3522*

FASTEN {5}

f the wreathen chains to the ... Ex 28:14 5414
thou shalt *f* in the two ouches ... Ex 28:25 5414
to *f* it on high upon the mitre ... Ex 39:31 5414
I will *f* him as a nail in a sure ... Is 22:23 8628
they *f* it with nails and with ... Jer 10:4 2388

FASTENED {18}

chains they *f* in the two ouches ... Ex 39:18 5414
f his sockets, and set up the ... Ex 40:18 5414
temples, and *f* it into the ground ... Judg 4:21 6795
she *f* it with the pin, and said ... Judg 16:14 8628
they *f* his body to the wall of ... 1Sa 31:10 8628
f upon his loins in the sheath ... 2Sa 20:8 6775
be *f* in the walls of the house ... 1Kin 6:6 270
f his head in the temple of Dagon ... 1Chr 10:10 8628
which were *f* to the throne, and ... 2Chr 9:18 270
f with cords of fine linen and ... Est 1:6 270
are the foundations thereof *f* ... Job 38:6 2883
as nails *f* by the masters of ... Eccl 12:11 5193
shall the nail that is *f* in the ... Is 22:25 8628
he *f* it with nails, that it ... Is 41:7 2388
an hand broad, *f* round about ... Eze 40:43 3559
in the synagogue were *f* on him ... Lk 4:20 *816*
the which when I had *f* mine eyes ... Acts 11:6 *816*
out of the heat, and *f* on his hand ... Acts 28:3 *2510*

FASTENING {1}

f his eyes upon him with John, ... Acts 3:4 *816*

FASTEST {1}

But thou, when thou *f*, anoint ... Mt 6:17 *2522*

FASTING {17}

of Israel were assembled with *f* ... Neh 9:1 6685
mourning among the Jews, and *f* ... Est 4:3 6685
I humbled my soul with *f* ... Ps 35:13 6685
wept, and chastened my soul with *f* ... Ps 69:10 6685
My knees are weak through *f* ... Ps 109:24 6685
the LORD's house upon the *f* day ... Jer 36:6 6685
his palace, and passed the night *f* ... Dan 6:18 2908
prayer and supplications, with *f* ... Dan 9:3 6685
me with all your heart, and with *f* ... Joel 2:12 6685
and I will not send them away *f* ... Mt 15:32 *3523*
goeth not out but by prayer and *f* ... Mt 17:21 *3521*
them away *f* to their own houses ... Mk 8:3 *3523*
by nothing, but by prayer and *f* ... Mk 9:29 *3521*
days ago I was *f* until this hour ... Acts 10:30 *3522*
church, and had prayed with *f* ... Acts 14:23 *3521*
ye have tarried and continued *f* ... Acts 27:33 *777*
that ye may give yourselves to *f* ... 1Cor 7:5 *3521*

FASTINGS {4}

their seed, the matters of the *f* ... Est 9:31 6685
the temple, but served God with *f* ... Lk 2:37 *3521*
in labours, in watchings, in *f* ... 2Cor 6:5 *3521*
in *f* often, in cold and nakedness ... 2Cor 11:27 *3521*

FAT {130}

of his flock and of the *f* thereof ... Gen 4:4 2459
the seven well favoured and *f* kine ... Gen 41:4 1277
did eat up the first seven *f* kine ... Gen 41:20 1277
and ye shall eat the *f* of the land ... Gen 45:18 2459
Out of Asher his bread shall be *f* ... Gen 49:20 8082
neither shall the *f* of my ... Ex 23:18 2459
thou shalt take all the *f* that ... Ex 29:13 2459
the *f* that is upon them, and burn ... Ex 29:13 2459
thou shalt take of the ram the *f* ... Ex 29:22 2459
the *f* that covereth the inwards, ... Ex 29:22 2459
the *f* that is upon them, and the ... Ex 29:22 2459
lay the parts, the head, and the *f* ... Lev 1:8 6309
pieces, with his head and his *f* ... Lev 1:12 6309
the *f* that covereth the inwards, ... Lev 3:3 2459
all the *f* that is upon the ... Lev 3:3 2459
the *f* that is on them, which is ... Lev 3:4 2459
the *f* thereof, and the whole rump, ... Lev 3:9 2459
the *f* that covereth the inwards, ... Lev 3:9 2459
all the *f* that is upon the ... Lev 3:9 2459
the *f* that is upon them, which is ... Lev 3:10 2459
the *f* that covereth the inwards, ... Lev 3:14 2459
all the *f* that is upon the ... Lev 3:14 2459
the *f* that is upon them, which is ... Lev 3:15 2459
all the *f* is the LORD's ... Lev 3:16 2459
that ye eat neither *f* nor blood ... Lev 3:17 2459
the *f* of the bullock for the sin ... Lev 4:8 2459
the *f* that covereth the inwards, ... Lev 4:8 2459
all the *f* that is upon the ... Lev 4:8 2459
the *f* that is upon them, which is ... Lev 4:9 2459
he shall take all his *f* from him ... Lev 4:19 2459
burn all his *f* upon the altar ... Lev 4:26 2459
as the *f* of the sacrifice of ... Lev 4:26 2459
shall take away all the *f* thereof ... Lev 4:31 2459
as the *f* is taken away from off ... Lev 4:31 2459
shall take away all the *f* thereof ... Lev 4:35 2459
as the *f* of the lamb is taken ... Lev 4:35 2459
the *f* of the peace offerings ... Lev 6:12 2459
offer of it all the *f* thereof ... Lev 7:3 2459
the *f* that covereth the inwards, ... Lev 7:3 2459
the *f* that is on them, which is ... Lev 7:4 2459
Ye shall eat no manner of *f* ... Lev 7:23 2459
the *f* of the beast that dieth of ... Lev 7:24 2459
the *f* of that which is torn with ... Lev 7:24 2459
eateth the *f* of the beast ... Lev 7:25 2459
the *f* with the breast, it shall ... Lev 7:30 2459
shall burn the *f* upon the altar ... Lev 7:31 2459
of the peace offerings, and the *f* ... Lev 7:33 2459
he took all the *f* that was upon ... Lev 8:16 2459
and the two kidneys, and their *f* ... Lev 8:16 2459
the head, and the pieces, and the *f* ... Lev 8:20 6309
And he took the *f*, and the rump, and ... Lev 8:25 2459
all the *f* that was upon the ... Lev 8:25 2459
and the two kidneys, and their *f* ... Lev 8:25 2459
one wafer, and put them on the *f* ... Lev 8:26 2459
But the *f*, and the kidneys, and the ... Lev 9:10 2459
the *f* of the bullock and of the ... Lev 9:19 2459
they put the *f* upon the breasts, ... Lev 9:20 2459
he burnt the *f* upon the altar ... Lev 9:20 2459
altar the burnt offering and the *f* ... Lev 9:24 2459
offerings made by fire of the *f* ... Lev 10:15 2459
the *f* of the sin offering shall ... Lev 16:25 2459
burn the *f* for a sweet savour ... Lev 17:6 2459
land is, whether it be *f* or lean ... Num 13:20 8082
shalt burn their *f* for an ... Num 18:17 2459
and filled themselves, and waxen *f* ... Deut 31:20 1878
with *f* of lambs, and rams of the ... Deut 32:14 2459
with the *f* of kidneys of wheat ... Deut 32:14 2459
But Jeshurun waxed *f*, and kicked ... Deut 32:15 8080
thou art waxen *f*, thou art grown ... Deut 32:15 8080
Which did eat the *f* of their ... Deut 32:38 2459
and Eglon was a very *f* man ... Judg 3:17 1277
the *f* closed upon the blade, so ... Judg 3:22 2459
Also before they burnt the *f* ... 1Sa 2:15 2459
not fail to burn the *f* presently ... 1Sa 2:16 2459
to make yourselves *f* with the ... 1Sa 2:29 1254
and to hearken than the *f* of rams ... 1Sa 15:22 2459
the woman had a *f* calf in the ... 1Sa 28:24 4770
from the *f* of the mighty, the bow ... 2Sa 1:22 2459
f cattle by the stone of Zoheleth ... 1Kin 1:9 4806
f cattle and sheep in abundance, ... 1Kin 1:19 4806
f cattle and sheep in abundance, ... 1Kin 1:25 4806
Ten *f* oxen, and twenty oxen out of ... 1Kin 4:23 1277
the *f* of the peace offerings ... 1Kin 8:64 2459
the *f* of the peace offerings ... 1Kin 8:64 2459
And they found *f* pasture and good, ... 1Chr 4:40 8082
the *f* of the peace offerings, ... 2Chr 7:7 2459
and the meat offerings, and the *f* ... 2Chr 7:7 2459
with the *f* of the peace offerings ... 2Chr 29:35 2459
offerings and the *f* until night ... 2Chr 35:14 2459
unto them, Go your way, eat the *f* ... Neh 8:10 4924
a *f* land, and possessed houses ... Neh 9:25 8082
eat, and were filled, and became *f* ... Neh 9:25 8082
f land which thou gavest before ... Neh 9:35 8082
maketh collops of *f* on his flanks ... Job 15:27 6371
They are inclosed in their own *f* ... Ps 17:10 2459
All they that be *f* upon earth ... Ps 22:29 1879
LORD shall be as the *f* of lambs ... Ps 37:20 3368
they shall be *f* and flourishing ... Ps 92:14 1879
Their heart is as *f* as grease ... Ps 119:70 2954
The liberal soul shall be made *f* ... Prov 11:25 1878
of the diligent shall be made *f* ... Prov 13:4 1878
a good report maketh the bones *f* ... Prov 15:30 1878
trust in the LORD shall be made *f* ... Prov 28:25 1878
of rams, and the *f* of fed beasts ... Is 1:11 2459
the waste places of the *f* ones ... Is 5:17 4220
Make the heart of this people *f* ... Is 6:10 8082
send among his *f* ones leanness ... Is 10:16 4924
all people a feast of *f* things ... Is 25:6 8081
of *f* things full of marrow, of ... Is 25:6 8081
of the *f* valleys of them that are ... Is 28:1 8081
is on the head of the *f* valley ... Is 28:4 8081
of the earth, and it shall be *f* ... Is 30:23 1879
it is made *f* with fatness, and ... Is 34:6 1878
with the *f* of the kidneys of rams ... Is 34:6 2459
and their dust made *f* with fatness ... Is 34:7 1878
me with the *f* of thy sacrifices ... Is 43:24 2459
in drought, and make *f* thy bones ... Is 58:11 2502
They are waxen *f*, they shine ... Jer 5:28 8080
because ye are grown *f* as the ... Jer 50:11 6335
Ye eat the *f*, and ye clothe you ... Eze 34:3 2459
in a *f* pasture shall they feed ... Eze 34:14 8082
but I will destroy the *f* and the ... Eze 34:16 8082
will judge between the *f* cattle ... Eze 34:20 1277
ye shall eat *f* till ye be full, ... Eze 39:19 2459
when ye offer my bread, the *f* ... Eze 44:7 2459
before me to offer unto me the *f* ... Eze 44:15 2459
out of the *f* pastures of Israel ... Eze 45:15 4945
peace offerings of your *f* beasts ... Amos 5:22 4806
by them their portion is *f* ... Hab 1:16 8082
he shall eat the flesh of the *f* ... Zec 11:16 1277

FATFLESHED {2}

seven well favoured kine and *f* ... Gen 41:2 1277
up out of the river seven kine, *f* ... Gen 41:18 1277

FATHER {985}

Therefore shall a man leave his *f* ... Gen 2:24 1
he was the *f* of such as dwell in ... Gen 4:20 1
he was the *f* of all such as ... Gen 4:21 1
and Ham is the *f* of Canaan ... Gen 9:18 1
And Ham, the *f* of Canaan ... Gen 9:22 1
saw the nakedness of his *f* ... Gen 9:22 1
covered the nakedness of their *f* ... Gen 9:23 1
the *f* of all the children of Eber ... Gen 10:21 1
Haran died before his *f* Terah in ... Gen 11:28 1
the *f* of Milcah, and the *f* of ... Gen 11:29 1
thou shalt be a *f* of many nations ... Gen 17:4 1
for a *f* of many nations have I ... Gen 17:5 1
Our *f* is old, and there is not a ... Gen 19:31 1
let us make our *f* drink wine ... Gen 19:32 1
we may preserve seed of our *f* ... Gen 19:32 1
they made their *f* drink wine that ... Gen 19:33 1
went in, and lay with her *f* ... Gen 19:33 1
I lay yesternight with my *f* ... Gen 19:34 1
we may preserve seed of our *f* ... Gen 19:34 1
they made their *f* drink wine that ... Gen 19:35 1
of Lot with child by their *f* ... Gen 19:36 1
the same is the *f* of the Moabites ... Gen 19:37 1
the same is the *f* of the children ... Gen 19:38 1
she is the daughter of my *f* ... Gen 20:12 1
Abraham his *f*, and said, My *f* ... Gen 22:7 1
brother, and Kemuel the *f* of Aram ... Gen 22:21 1
which I sware unto Abraham thy *f* ... Gen 26:3 1
in the days of Abraham his *f* ... Gen 26:15 1
in the days of Abraham his *f* ... Gen 26:18 1
by which his *f* had called them ... Gen 26:18 1
I am the God of Abraham thy *f* ... Gen 26:24 1
I heard thy *f* speak unto Esau thy ... Gen 27:6 1
make them savoury meat for thy *f* ... Gen 27:9 1
And thou shalt bring it to thy *f* ... Gen 27:10 1
My *f* peradventure will feel me, ... Gen 27:12 1
savoury meat, such as his *f* loved ... Gen 27:14 1
unto his *f*, and said, My *f* ... Gen 27:18 1
And Jacob said unto his *f*, I am ... Gen 27:19 1
Jacob went near unto Isaac his *f* ... Gen 27:22 1
his *f* Isaac said unto him, Come ... Gen 27:26 1
from the presence of Isaac his *f* ... Gen 27:30 1
his *f*, and said unto his *f* ... Gen 27:31 1
unto his *f*, Let my *f* arise ... Gen 27:31 1
Isaac his *f* said unto him, Who ... Gen 27:32 1
Esau heard the words of his *f* ... Gen 27:34 1

Context	Reference	No.
bitter cry, and said unto his *f*	Gen 27:34	1
Bless me, even me also, O my *f*	Gen 27:34	1
And Esau said unto his *f*	Gen 27:38	1
Hast thou but one blessing, my *f*	Gen 27:38	1
bless me, even me also, O my *f*	Gen 27:38	1
And Isaac his *f* answered and said	Gen 27:39	1
wherewith his *f* blessed him	Gen 27:41	1
of mourning for my *f* are at hand	Gen 27:41	1
house of Bethuel thy mother's *f*	Gen 28:2	1
And that Jacob obeyed his *f*	Gen 28:7	1
of Canaan pleased not Isaac his *f*	Gen 28:8	1
am the LORD God of Abraham thy *f*	Gen 28:13	1
and she ran and told her *f*	Gen 29:12	1
the God of my *f* hath been with me	Gen 31:5	1
all my power I have served your *f*	Gen 31:6	1
your *f* hath deceived me, and	Gen 31:7	1
taken away the cattle of your *f*	Gen 31:9	1
which God hath taken from our *f*	Gen 31:16	1
Isaac his *f* in the land of Canaan	Gen 31:18	1
but the God of your *f* spake unto	Gen 31:29	1
And she said to her *f*, Let it not	Gen 31:35	1
Except the God of my *f*, the God	Gen 31:42	1
God of Nahor, the God of their *f*	Gen 31:53	1
sware by the fear of his *f* Isaac	Gen 31:53	1
Jacob said, O God of my *f* Abraham	Gen 32:9	1
and God of my *f* Isaac	Gen 32:9	1
children of Hamor, Shechem's *f*	Gen 33:19	1
And Shechem spake unto his *f* Hamor	Gen 34:4	1
Hamor the *f* of Shechem went out	Gen 34:6	1
And Shechem said unto her *f*	Gen 34:11	1
Hamor his *f* deceitfully, and said,	Gen 34:13	1
than all the house of his *f*	Gen 34:19	1
but his *f* called him Benjamin	Gen 35:18	1
came unto Isaac his *f* unto Mamre	Gen 35:27	1
f of the Edomites in mount Seir	Gen 36:9	1
he fed the asses of Zibeon his *f*	Gen 36:24	1
he is Esau the *f* of the Edomites	Gen 36:43	1
land wherein his *f* was a stranger	Gen 37:1	1
unto his *f* their evil report	Gen 37:2	1
f loved him more than all his	Gen 37:4	1
And he told it to his *f*, and to his	Gen 37:10	1
his *f* rebuked him, and said unto	Gen 37:10	1
but his *f* observed the saying	Gen 37:11	1
to deliver him to his *f* again	Gen 37:22	1
and they brought it to their *f*	Gen 37:32	1
Thus his *f* wept for him	Gen 37:35	1
Behold thy *f* in law goeth up to	Gen 38:13	2524
forth, she sent to her *f* in law	Gen 38:25	2524
youngest is this day with our *f*	Gen 42:13	1
their *f* unto the land of Canaan	Gen 42:29	1
be twelve brethren, sons of our *f*	Gen 42:32	1
with our *f* in the land of Canaan	Gen 42:32	1
their *f* saw the bundles of money,	Gen 42:35	1
Jacob their *f* said unto them, Me	Gen 42:36	1
And Reuben spake unto his *f*	Gen 42:37	1
their *f* said unto them, Go again,	Gen 43:2	1
saying, Is your *f* yet alive	Gen 43:7	1
And Judah said unto Israel his *f*	Gen 43:8	1
their *f* Israel said unto them, If	Gen 43:11	1
your God, and the God of your *f*	Gen 43:23	1
welfare, and said, Is your *f* well	Gen 43:27	1
Thy servant our *f* is in good	Gen 43:28	1
get you up in peace unto your *f*	Gen 44:17	1
his servants, saying, Have ye a *f*	Gen 44:19	1
we said unto my lord, We have a *f*	Gen 44:20	1
his mother, and his *f* loveth him	Gen 44:20	1
lord, The lad cannot leave his *f*	Gen 44:22	1
leave his *f*, his *f* would die	Gen 44:22	
we came up unto thy servant my *f*	Gen 44:24	1
our *f* said, Go again, and buy us a	Gen 44:25	1
And thy servant my *f* said unto us	Gen 44:27	1
when I come to thy servant my *f*	Gen 44:30	1
our *f* with sorrow to the grave	Gen 44:31	1
surety for the lad unto my *f*	Gen 44:32	1
bear the blame to my *f* for ever	Gen 44:32	1
For how shall I go up to my *f*	Gen 44:34	1
the evil that shall come on my *f*	Gen 44:34	1
doth my *f* yet live	Gen 45:3	1
and he hath made me a *f* to Pharaoh	Gen 45:8	1
Haste ye, and go up to my *f*	Gen 45:9	1
ye shall tell my *f* of all my	Gen 45:13	1
haste and bring down my *f* hither	Gen 45:13	
And take your *f* and your households	Gen 45:18	1
for your wives, and bring your *f*	Gen 45:19	1
to his *f* he sent after this	Gen 45:23	1
and meat for his *f* by the way	Gen 45:23	1
land of Canaan unto Jacob their *f*	Gen 45:25	1
spirit of Jacob their *f* revived	Gen 45:27	1
unto the God of his *f* Isaac	Gen 46:1	1
said, I am God, the God of thy *f*	Gen 46:3	1
of Israel carried Jacob their *f*	Gen 46:5	1
and went up to meet Israel his *f*	Gen 46:29	1
and told Pharaoh, and said, My *f*	Gen 47:1	1
spake unto Joseph, saying, Thy *f*	Gen 47:5	1
the best of the land make thy *f*	Gen 47:6	1
And Joseph brought in Jacob his *f*	Gen 47:7	1
And Joseph placed his *f* and his	Gen 47:11	1
And Joseph nourished his *f*	Gen 47:12	1
Joseph, Behold, thy *f* is sick	Gen 48:1	1
And Joseph said unto his *f*	Gen 48:9	1
when Joseph saw that his *f* laid	Gen 48:17	1
unto his *f*, Not so, my *f*	Gen 48:18	1
his *f* refused, and said, I know it	Gen 48:19	1
and hearken unto Israel your *f*	Gen 49:2	1
Even by the God of thy *f*, who	Gen 49:25	1
The blessings of thy *f* have	Gen 49:26	1
it that their *f* spake unto them	Gen 49:28	1
the physicians to embalm his *f*	Gen 50:2	1
My *f* made me swear, saying, Lo, I	Gen 50:5	1
go up, I pray thee, and bury my *f*	Gen 50:5	1
said, Go up, and bury thy *f*	Gen 50:6	1
And Joseph went up to bury his *f*	Gen 50:7	1
a mourning for his *f* seven days	Gen 50:10	1
went up with him to bury his *f*	Gen 50:14	1
after he had buried his *f*	Gen 50:14	1
saw that their *f* was dead	Gen 50:15	1
Thy *f* did command before he died,	Gen 50:16	1
the servants of the God of thy *f*	Gen 50:17	1
when they came to Reuel their *f*	Ex 2:18	1
the flock of Jethro his *f* in law	Ex 3:1	2859
he said, I am the God of thy *f*	Ex 3:6	1
returned to Jethro his *f* in law	Ex 4:18	2859
priest of Midian, Moses' *f* in law	Ex 18:1	2859
Then Jethro, Moses' *f* in law	Ex 18:2	2859
for the God of my *f*, said he, was	Ex 18:4	1
And Jethro, Moses' *f* in law	Ex 18:5	2859
I thy *f* in law Jethro am come	Ex 18:6	2859
went out to meet his *f* in law	Ex 18:7	2859
Moses told his *f* in law all that	Ex 18:8	2859
And Jethro, Moses' *f* in law	Ex 18:12	2859
with Moses' *f* in law before God	Ex 18:12	2859
when Moses' *f* in law saw all that	Ex 18:14	2859
And Moses said unto his *f* in law	Ex 18:15	2859
Moses' *f* in law said unto him,	Ex 18:17	2589
to the voice of his *f* in law	Ex 18:24	2859
And Moses let his *f* in law depart	Ex 18:27	2859
Honour thy *f* and thy mother	Ex 20:12	1
And he that smiteth his *f*, or his	Ex 21:15	1
And he that curseth his *f*, or his	Ex 21:17	1
If her *f* utterly refuse to give	Ex 22:17	1
as thou didst anoint their *f*	Ex 40:15	1
The nakedness of thy *f*, or the	Lev 18:7	1
thy sister, the daughter of thy *f*	Lev 18:9	1
daughter, begotten of thy *f*	Lev 18:11	1
every man his mother, and his *f*	Lev 19:3	1
f or his mother shall be surely	Lev 20:9	1
hath cursed his *f* or his mother	Lev 20:9	1
is, for his mother, and for his *f*	Lev 21:2	1
the whore, she profaneth her *f*	Lev 21:9	1
nor defile himself for his *f*	Lev 21:11	1
whose *f* was an Egyptian, went out	Lev 24:10	1121
in the sight of Aaron their *f*	Num 3:4	1
the *f* of the Gershonites shall be	Num 3:24	1
of the *f* of the families of the	Num 3:30	1
f of the families of Merari was	Num 3:35	1
make himself unclean for his *f*	Num 6:7	1
the Midianite, Moses' *f* in law	Num 10:29	2859
as a nursing *f* beareth the	Num 11:12	
If her *f* had but spit in her face	Num 12:14	1
tribe of Levi, the tribe of thy *f*	Num 18:2	1
Our *f* died in the wilderness, and	Num 27:3	1
Why should the name of our *f* be	Num 27:4	1
among the brethren of our *f*	Num 27:4	1
of their *f* to pass unto them	Num 27:7	1
if his *f* have no brethren, then	Num 27:11	1
her *f* hear her vow, and her bond	Num 30:4	1
her *f* shall hold his peace at her	Num 30:4	1
But if her *f* disallow her in the	Num 30:5	1
because her *f* disallowed her	Num 30:5	1
a man and his wife, between the *f*	Num 30:16	1
tribe of their *f* shall they marry	Num 36:6	1
the family of the tribe of her *f*	Num 36:8	1
tribe of the family of their *f*	Num 36:12	1
Honour thy *f* and thy mother, as	Deut 5:16	1
in thine house, and bewail her *f*	Deut 21:13	1
will not obey the voice of his *f*	Deut 21:18	1
Then shall his *f* and his mother	Deut 21:19	1
Then shall the *f* of the damsel	Deut 22:15	1
the damsel's *f* shall say unto the	Deut 22:16	1
them unto the *f* of the damsel	Deut 22:19	1
f fifty shekels of silver	Deut 22:29	1
A Syrian ready to perish was my *f*	Deut 26:5	1
light by his *f* or his mother	Deut 27:16	1
his sister, the daughter of his *f*	Deut 27:22	1
is not he thy *f* that hath bought	Deut 32:6	1
ask thy *f*, and he will shew thee	Deut 32:7	1
Who said unto his *f* and to his	Deut 33:9	1
And that ye will save alive my *f*	Josh 2:13	1
and thou shalt bring thy *f*	Josh 2:18	1
and brought out Rahab, and her *f*	Josh 6:23	1
the city of Arba the *f* of Anak	Josh 15:13	1
moved him to ask of her *f* a field	Josh 15:18	1
of Manasseh, the *f* of Gilead	Josh 17:1	1
among the brethren of their *f*	Josh 17:4	1
after the name of Dan their *f*	Josh 19:47	1
the city of Arba the *f* of Anak	Josh 21:11	1
the *f* of Abraham, and the *f*	Josh 24:2	1
I took your *f* Abraham from the	Josh 24:3	1
the *f* of Shechem for an hundred	Josh 24:32	1
moved him to ask of her *f* a field	Judg 1:14	1
of the Kenite, Moses' *f* in law	Judg 1:16	2859
of Hobab the *f* in law of Moses	Judg 4:11	2859
the altar of Baal that thy *f* hath	Judg 6:25	1
in the sepulchre of Joash his *f*	Judg 8:32	1
of the house of his mother's *f*	Judg 9:1	1
(For my *f* fought for you, and	Judg 9:17	1
the men of Hamor the *f* of Shechem	Judg 9:28	1
which he did unto his *f*, in	Judg 9:56	1
And she said unto him, My *f*	Judg 11:36	1
And she said unto her *f*, Let this	Judg 11:37	1
that she returned unto her *f*	Judg 11:39	1
And he came up, and told his *f*	Judg 14:2	1
Then his *f* and his mother said	Judg 14:3	1
And Samson said unto his *f*	Judg 14:3	1
But his *f* and his mother knew not	Judg 14:4	1
Then went Samson down, and his *f*	Judg 14:5	1
but he told not his *f* or his	Judg 14:6	1
went on eating, and came to his *f*	Judg 14:9	1
So his *f* went down unto the woman	Judg 14:10	1
not told it my *f* nor my mother	Judg 14:16	1
But her *f* would not suffer him to	Judg 15:1	1
her *f* said, I verily thought that	Judg 15:2	1
and burnt her and her *f* with fire	Judg 15:6	1
all the house of his *f* came down	Judg 16:31	1
the buryingplace of Manoah his *f*	Judg 16:31	1
Dwell with me, and be unto me a *f*	Judg 17:10	1
and go with us, and be to us a *f*	Judg 18:19	1
after the name of Dan their *f*	Judg 18:29	1
when the *f* of the damsel saw him,	Judg 19:3	1
his *f* in law, the damsel's *f*	Judg 19:4	2859
his *f* in law, the damsel's *f*	Judg 19:4	1
the damsel's *f* said unto his son	Judg 19:5	1
for the damsel's *f* had said unto	Judg 19:6	1
to depart, his *f* in law urged him	Judg 19:7	2859
and the damsel's *f* said, Comfort	Judg 19:8	1
his *f* in law, the damsel's *f*	Judg 19:9	2859
his *f* in law, the damsel's *f*	Judg 19:9	1
and how thou hast left thy *f*	Ruth 2:11	1
f of Jesse, the *f* of David	Ruth 4:17	1
not unto the voice of their *f*	1Sa 2:25	1
appear unto the house of thy *f*	1Sa 2:27	1
I give unto the house of thy *f*	1Sa 2:28	1
thy house, and the house of thy *f*	1Sa 2:30	1
was taken, and that her *f* in law	1Sa 4:19	2524
taken, and because of her *f* in law	1Sa 4:21	2524
asses of Kish Saul's *f* were lost	1Sa 9:3	1
lest my *f* leave caring for the	1Sa 9:5	1
thy *f* hath left the care of the	1Sa 10:2	1
and said, But who is their *f*	1Sa 10:12	1
But he told not his *f*	1Sa 14:1	1
his *f* charged the people with the	1Sa 14:27	1
Thy *f* straitly charged the people	1Sa 14:28	1
My *f* hath troubled the land	1Sa 14:29	1
And Kish was the *f* of Saul	1Sa 14:51	1
Ner the *f* of Abner was the son of	1Sa 14:51	1
Saul my *f* seeketh to kill thee	1Sa 19:2	1
stand beside my *f* in the field	1Sa 19:3	1
I will commune with my *f* of thee	1Sa 19:3	1
good of David unto Saul his *f*	1Sa 19:4	1
and what is my sin before thy *f*	1Sa 20:1	1
my *f* will do nothing either great	1Sa 20:2	1
why should my *f* hide this thing	1Sa 20:2	1
Thy *f* certainly knoweth that I	1Sa 20:3	1
If thy *f* at all miss me, then say	1Sa 20:6	1
shouldest thou bring me to thy *f*	1Sa 20:8	1
by my *f* to come upon thee	1Sa 20:9	1
or what if thy *f* answer thee	1Sa 20:10	1
when I have sounded my *f* about to	1Sa 20:12	1
if it please my *f* to do thee evil	1Sa 20:13	1
thee, as he hath been with my *f*	1Sa 20:13	1
And Jonathan answered Saul his *f*	1Sa 20:32	1
determined of his *f* to slay David	1Sa 20:33	1
because his *f* had done him shame	1Sa 20:34	1
unto the king of Moab, Let my *f*	1Sa 22:3	1
nor to all the house of my *f*	1Sa 22:15	1
of Saul my *f* shall not find thee	1Sa 23:17	1
and that also Saul my *f* knoweth	1Sa 23:17	1
Moreover, my *f*, see, yea, see the	1Sa 24:11	1
him in the sepulchre of his *f*	2Sa 2:32	1
day unto the house of Saul thy *f*	2Sa 3:8	1
LORD, which chose me before thy *f*	2Sa 6:21	1
I will be his *f*, and he shall be	2Sa 7:14	1
thee all the land of Saul thy *f*	2Sa 9:7	1
as his *f* shewed kindness unto me	2Sa 10:2	1
hand of his servants for his *f*	2Sa 10:2	1
thou that David doth honour thy *f*	2Sa 10:3	1
when thy *f* cometh to see thee,	2Sa 13:5	1
restore me the kingdom of my *f*	2Sa 16:3	1
that thou art abhorred of thy *f*	2Sa 16:21	1
said Hushai, thou knowest thy *f*	2Sa 17:8	1
thy *f* is a man of war, and will	2Sa 17:8	1
that thy *f* is a mighty man	2Sa 17:10	1
buried in the sepulchre of his *f*	2Sa 17:23	1
and be buried by the grave of my *f*	2Sa 19:37	1
in the sepulchre of Kish his *f*	2Sa 21:14	1
his *f* had not displeased him at	1Kin 1:6	1
upon the throne of David his *f*	1Kin 2:12	1
me on the throne of David my *f*	1Kin 2:24	1
of the Lord GOD before David my *f*	1Kin 2:26	1
in all wherein my *f* was afflicted	1Kin 2:26	1
me, and from the house of my *f*	1Kin 2:31	1
my *f* David not knowing thereof,	1Kin 2:32	1
to, that thou didst to David my *f*	1Kin 2:44	1
in the statutes of David his *f*	1Kin 3:3	1
servant David my *f* great mercy	1Kin 3:6	1
king instead of David my *f*	1Kin 3:7	1
as thy *f* David did walk, then I	1Kin 3:14	1
him king in the room of his *f*	1Kin 5:1	1
f could not build an house unto	1Kin 5:3	1
as the LORD spake unto David my *f*	1Kin 5:5	1
which I spake unto David thy *f*	1Kin 6:12	1
his *f* was a man of Tyre, a worker	1Kin 7:14	1
which David his *f* had dedicated	1Kin 7:51	1
with his mouth unto David my *f*	1Kin 8:15	1
f to build an house for the name	1Kin 8:17	1
And the LORD said unto David my *f*	1Kin 8:18	1
up in the room of David my *f*	1Kin 8:20	1
my *f* that thou promisedst him	1Kin 8:24	1
my *f* that thou promisedst him	1Kin 8:25	1
unto thy servant David my *f*	1Kin 8:26	1
before me, as David thy *f* walked	1Kin 9:4	1
as I promised to David thy *f*	1Kin 9:5	1
as was the heart of David his *f*	1Kin 11:4	1
the LORD, as did David his *f*	1Kin 11:6	1

of the city of David his *f* 1Kin 11:27 1
my judgments, as did David his *f* 1Kin 11:33 1
buried in the city of David his *f* 1Kin 11:43 1
Thy *f* made our yoke grievous 1Kin 12:4 1
the grievous service of thy *f* 1Kin 12:4 1
Solomon his *f* while he yet lived 1Kin 12:6 1
thy *f* did put upon us lighter 1Kin 12:9 1
Thy *f* made our yoke heavy, but 1Kin 12:10 1
now whereas my *f* did lade you 1Kin 12:11 1
my *f* hath chastised you with 1Kin 12:11 1
My *f* made your yoke heavy, and I 1Kin 12:14 1
my *f* also chastised you with 1Kin 12:14 1
them they told also to their *f* 1Kin 13:11 1
their *f* said unto them, What way 1Kin 13:12 1
walked in all the sins of his *f* 1Kin 15:3 1
God, as the heart of David his *f* 1Kin 15:3 1
of the LORD, as did David his *f* 1Kin 15:11 1
things which his *f* had dedicated 1Kin 15:15 1
and between my *f* and thy *f* 1Kin 15:19 1
in the city of David his *f* 1Kin 15:24 1
and walked in the way of his *f* 1Kin 15:26 1
Let me, I pray thee, kiss my *f* 1Kin 19:20 1
which my *f* took from thy *f* 1Kin 20:34 1
Damascus, as my *f* made in Samaria 1Kin 20:34 1
in all the ways of Asa his *f* 1Kin 22:43 1
remained in the days of his *f* Asa 1Kin 22:46 1
in the city of David his *f* 1Kin 22:50 1
and walked in the way of his *f* 1Kin 22:52 1
to all that his *f* had done 1Kin 22:53 1
it, and he cried, My *f*, my *f* 2Kin 2:12 1
but not like his *f*, and like his 2Kin 3:2 1
image of Baal that his *f* had made 2Kin 3:2 1
get thee to the prophets of thy *f* 2Kin 3:13 1
went out to his *f* to the reapers 2Kin 4:18 1
And he said unto his *f*, My head, 2Kin 4:19 1
and spake unto him, and said, My *f* 2Kin 5:13 1
Elisha, when he saw them, My *f* 2Kin 6:21 1
rode together after Ahab his *f* 2Kin 9:25 1
face, and said, O my *f*, my *f* 2Kin 13:14 1
the hand of Jehoahaz his *f* by war 2Kin 13:25 1
LORD, yet not like David his *f* 2Kin 14:3 1
to all things as Joash his *f* did 2Kin 14:3 1
which had slain the king his *f* 2Kin 14:5 1
him king instead of his *f* Amaziah 2Kin 14:21 1
all that his *f* Amaziah had done 2Kin 15:3 1
to all that his *f* Uzziah had done 2Kin 15:34 1
in the city of David his *f* 2Kin 15:38 1
LORD his God, like David his *f* 2Kin 16:2 1
to all that David his *f* did 2Kin 18:3 1
the LORD, the God of David thy *f* 2Kin 20:5 1
Hezekiah his *f* had destroyed 2Kin 21:3 1
the LORD, as his *f* Manasseh did 2Kin 21:20 1
all the way that his *f* walked in 2Kin 21:21 1
the idols that his *f* served 2Kin 21:21 1
in all the way of David his *f* 2Kin 22:2 1
king in the room of Josiah his *f* 2Kin 23:34 1
to all that his *f* had done 2Kin 24:9 1
the *f* of Amasa was Jether the 1Chr 2:17 1
of Machir the *f* of Gilead 1Chr 2:21 1
sons of Machir the *f* of Gilead 1Chr 2:23 1
bare him Ashur the *f* of Tekoa 1Chr 2:24 1
which was the *f* of Ziph 1Chr 2:42 1
sons of Mareshah the *f* of Hebron 1Chr 2:42 1
begat Raham, the *f* of Jorkoam 1Chr 2:44 1
and Maon was the *f* of Beth-zur 1Chr 2:45 1
also Shaaph the *f* of Madmannah 1Chr 2:49 1
Sheva the *f* of Machbenah, and the 1Chr 2:49 1
of Machbenah, and the *f* of Gibea 1Chr 2:49 1
Shobal the *f* of Kirjath-jearim, 1Chr 2:50 1
Salma the *f* of Beth-lehem 1Chr 2:51 1
Hareph the *f* of Beth-gader 1Chr 2:51 1
Shobal the *f* of Kirjath-jearim 1Chr 2:52 1
the *f* of the house of Rechab 1Chr 2:55 1
And these were of the *f* of Etam 1Chr 4:3 1
And Penuel the *f* of Gedor, and Ezer 1Chr 4:4 1
of Gedor, and Ezer the *f* of Hushah 1Chr 4:4 1
of Ephratah, the *f* of Beth-lehem 1Chr 4:4 1
Ashur the *f* of Tekoa had two 1Chr 4:5 1
Mehir, which was the *f* of Eshton 1Chr 4:11 1
and Tehinnah the *f* of Ir-nahash 1Chr 4:12 1
the *f* of the valley of Charashim 1Chr 4:14 1
and Ishbah the *f* of Eshtemoa 1Chr 4:17 1
bare Jered the *f* of Gedor 1Chr 4:18 1
and Heber the *f* of Socho 1Chr 4:18 1
and Jekuthiel the *f* of Zanoah 1Chr 4:18 1
the *f* of Keilah the Garmite, and 1Chr 4:19 1
Er the *f* of Lecah 1Chr 4:21 1
Laadah the *f* of Mareshah, and the 1Chr 4:21 1
bare Machir the *f* of Gilead 1Chr 7:14 1
Ephraim their *f* mourned many days 1Chr 7:22 1
who is the *f* of Birzavith 1Chr 7:31 1
at Gibeon dwelt the *f* of Gibeon 1Chr 8:29 25
brethren, of the house of his *f* 1Chr 9:19 1
in Gibeon dwelt the *f* of Gibeon 1Chr 9:35 25
I will be his *f*, and he shall be 1Chr 17:13 25
because his *f* shewed kindness to 1Chr 19:2 25
to comfort him concerning his *f* 1Chr 19:2 25
thou that David doth honour thy *f* 1Chr 19:3 25
be my son, and I will be his *f* 1Chr 22:10 25
and Abihu died before their *f* 1Chr 24:2 25
their manner, under Aaron their *f* 1Chr 24:19 25
the hands of their *f* Jeduthun 1Chr 25:3 25
f for song in the house of the 1Chr 25:6 25
throughout the house of their *f* 1Chr 26:6 25
yet his *f* made him the chief 1Chr 26:10 25
me before all the house of my *f* 1Chr 28:4 25
house of Judah, the house of my *f* 1Chr 28:4 25
among the sons of my *f* he liked 1Chr 28:4 25
to be my son, and I will be his *f* 1Chr 28:6 25
son, know thou the God of thy *f* 1Chr 28:9 25
be thou, LORD God of Israel our *f* 1Chr 29:10 25
as king instead of David his *f* 1Chr 29:23 25
great mercy unto David my *f* 2Chr 1:8 25
unto David my *f* be established 2Chr 1:9 25
thou didst deal with David my *f* 2Chr 2:3 25
whom David my *f* did provide 2Chr 2:7 25
his *f* was a man of Tyre, skilful 2Chr 2:14 25
men of my lord David thy *f* 2Chr 2:14 25
David his *f* had numbered them 2Chr 2:17 25
LORD appeared unto David his *f* 2Chr 3:1 25
did Huram his *f* make to king 2Chr 4:16 25
that David his *f* had dedicated 2Chr 5:1 25
with his mouth to my *f* David 2Chr 6:4 25
f to build an house for the name 2Chr 6:7 25
But the LORD said to David my *f* 2Chr 6:8 25
up in the room of David my *f* 2Chr 6:10 25
f that which thou hast promised 2Chr 6:15 25
f that which thou hast promised 2Chr 6:16 25
before me, as David thy *f* walked 2Chr 7:17 25
have covenanted with David thy *f* 2Chr 7:18 25
to the order of David his *f* 2Chr 8:14 25
buried in the city of David his *f* 2Chr 9:31 25
Thy *f* made our yoke grievous 2Chr 10:4 25
the grievous servitude of thy *f* 2Chr 10:4 25
Solomon his *f* while he yet lived 2Chr 10:6 25
yoke that thy *f* did put upon us 2Chr 10:9 25
Thy *f* made our yoke heavy, but 2Chr 10:10 25
For whereas my *f* put a heavy yoke 2Chr 10:11 25
my *f* chastised you with whips, 2Chr 10:11 25
My *f* made your yoke heavy, but I 2Chr 10:14 25
my *f* chastised you with whips, 2Chr 10:14 25
things that his *f* had dedicated 2Chr 15:18 25
was between my *f* and thy *f* 2Chr 16:3 25
which Asa his *f* had taken 2Chr 17:2 25
in the first ways of his *f* David 2Chr 17:3 25
sought to the LORD God of his *f* 2Chr 17:4 25
he walked in the way of Asa his *f* 2Chr 20:32 25
their *f* gave them great gifts of 2Chr 21:3 25
risen up to the kingdom of his *f* 2Chr 21:4 25
saith the LORD God of David thy *f* 2Chr 21:12 25
in the ways of Jehoshaphat thy *f* 2Chr 21:12 25
death of his *f* to his destruction 2Chr 22:4 25
Jehoiada his *f* had done to him 2Chr 24:22 25
that had killed the king his *f* 2Chr 25:3 25
king in the room of his *f* Amaziah 2Chr 26:1 25
to all that his *f* Amaziah did 2Chr 26:4 25
to all that his *f* Uzziah did 2Chr 27:2 25
of the LORD, like David his *f* 2Chr 28:1 25
to all that David his *f* had done 2Chr 29:2 25
Hezekiah his *f* had broken down 2Chr 33:3 1
the LORD, as did Manasseh his *f* 2Chr 33:22 1
which Manasseh his *f* had made 2Chr 33:22 1
as Manasseh his *f* had humbled 2Chr 33:23 1
walked in the ways of David his *f* 2Chr 34:2 1
seek after the God of David his *f* 2Chr 34:3 1
for she had neither *f* nor mother Est 2:7 1
whom Mordecai, when her *f* Est 2:7 1
aged men, much elder than thy *f* Job 15:10 1
said to corruption, Thou art my *f* Job 17:14 1
I was a *f* to the poor Job 29:16 1
brought up with me, as with a *f* Job 31:18 1
Hath the rain a *f* Job 38:28 1
their *f* gave them inheritance Job 42:15 1
When my *f* and my mother forsake me Ps 27:10 1
A *f* of the fatherless, and a judge Ps 68:5 1
shall cry unto me, Thou art my *f* Ps 89:26 1
Like as a *f* pitieth his children, Ps 103:13 1
hear the instruction of thy *f* Prov 1:8 1
even as a *f* the son in whom he Prov 3:12 1
children, the instruction of a *f* Prov 4:1 1
A wise son maketh a glad *f* Prov 10:1 1
A wise son maketh a glad *f* Prov 15:20 1
the *f* of a fool hath no joy Prov 17:21 1
A foolish son is a grief to his *f* Prov 17:25 1
son is the calamity of his *f* Prov 19:13 1
He that wasteth his *f*, and chaseth Prov 19:26 1
Whoso curseth his *f* or his mother Prov 20:20 1
unto thy *f* that begat thee Prov 23:22 1
The *f* of the righteous shall Prov 23:24 1
Thy *f* and thy mother shall be glad Prov 23:25 1
of riotous men shameth his *f* Prov 28:7 1
Whoso robbeth his *f* or his mother Prov 28:24 1
loveth wisdom rejoiceth his *f* Prov 29:3 1
a generation that curseth their *f* Prov 30:11 1
The eye that mocketh at his *f* Prov 30:17 1
his brother of the house of his *f* Is 3:6 1
shall have knowledge to cry, My *f* Is 8:4 1
The mighty God, The everlasting *F* Is 9:6 1
and he shall be a *f* to the Is 22:21 1
the LORD, the God of David thy *f* Is 38:5 1
the *f* to the children shall make Is 38:19 1
Thy first *f* hath sinned, and thy Is 43:27 1
unto him that saith unto his *f* Is 45:10 1
Look unto Abraham your *f*, and unto Is 51:2 1
with the heritage of Jacob thy *f* Is 58:14 1
Doubtless thou art our *f*, though Is 63:16 1
thou, O LORD, art our *f*, our Is 63:16 1
But now, O LORD, thou art our *f* Is 64:8 1
Saying to a stock, Thou art my *f* Jer 2:27 1
from this time cry unto me, My *f* Jer 3:4 1
I said, Thou shalt call me, My *f* Jer 3:19 1
brethren, and the house of thy *f* Jer 12:6 1
for their *f* or for their mother Jer 16:7 1
man who brought tidings to my *f* Jer 20:15 1
reigned instead of Josiah his *f* Jer 22:11 1
did not thy *f* eat and drink, and do Jer 22:15 1
for I am a *f* to Israel, and Jer 31:9 1
son of Rechab our *f* commanded us Jer 35:6 1
Jonadab the son of Rechab our *f* Jer 35:8 1
that Jonadab our *f* commanded us Jer 35:10 1
the commandment of their *f* Jer 35:16 1
the commandment of Jonadab your *f* Jer 35:18 1
thy *f* was an Amorite, and thy Eze 16:3 1
an Hittite, and your *f* an Amorite Eze 16:45 1
as the soul of the *f*, so also the Eze 18:4 1
not die for the iniquity of his *f* Eze 18:17 1
As for his *f*, because he cruelly Eze 18:18 1
son bear the iniquity of the *f* Eze 18:19 1
not bear the iniquity of the *f* Eze 18:20 1
neither shall the *f* bear the Eze 18:20 1
In thee have they set light by *f* Eze 22:7 1
but for *f*, or for mother, or for Eze 44:25 1
silver vessels which his *f* Dan 5:2 2
and in the days of thy *f* light Dan 5:11 2
the king Nebuchadnezzar thy *f* Dan 5:11 2
the king, I say, thy *f* Dan 5:11 2
whom the king my *f* brought out of Dan 5:13 2
Nebuchadnezzar thy *f* a kingdom Dan 5:18 2
his *f* will go in unto the same Amos 2:7 2
For the son dishonoureth the *f* Mic 7:6 2
shall yet prophesy, then his *f* Zec 13:3 2
and his *f* and his mother that begat Zec 13:3 2
A son honoureth his *f*, and a Mal 1:6 2
if then I be a *f*, where is mine Mal 1:6 2
Have we not all one *f* Mal 2:10 2
Judaea in the room of his *f* Herod Mt 2:22 *3962*
We have Abraham to our *f* Mt 3:9 *3962*
in a ship with Zebedee their *f* Mt 4:21 *3962*
left the ship and their *f*, and Mt 4:22 *3962*
glorify your *F* which is in heaven Mt 5:16 *3962*
of your *F* which is in heaven Mt 5:45 *3962*
even as your *F* which is in heaven Mt 5:48 *3962*
of your *F* which is in heaven Mt 6:1 *3962*
thy *F* which seeth in secret Mt 6:4 *3962*
pray to thy *F* which is in secret Mt 6:6 *3962*
thy *F* which seeth in secret shall Mt 6:6 *3962*
for your *F* knoweth what things ye Mt 6:8 *3962*
Our *F* which art in heaven, Mt 6:9 *3962*
your heavenly *F* will also forgive Mt 6:14 *3962*
neither will your *F* forgive your Mt 6:15 *3962*
but unto thy *F* which is in secret Mt 6:18 *3962*
and thy *F*, which seeth in secret, Mt 6:18 *3962*
yet your heavenly *F* feedeth them Mt 6:26 *3962*
for your heavenly *F* knoweth that Mt 6:32 *3962*
how much more shall your *F* which Mt 7:11 *3962*
will of my *F* which is in heaven Mt 7:21 *3962*
me first to go and bury my *f* Mt 8:21 *3962*
of your *F* which speaketh in you Mt 10:20 *3962*
to death, and the *f* the child Mt 10:21 *3962*
fall on the ground without your *F* Mt 10:29 *3962*
before my *F* which is in heaven Mt 10:32 *3962*
before my *F* which is in heaven Mt 10:33 *3962*
a man at variance against his *f* Mt 10:35 *3962*
He that loveth *f* or mother more Mt 10:37 *3962*
and said, I thank thee, O *F* Mt 11:25 *3962*
Even so, *F*: for so it seemed Mt 11:26 *3962*
are delivered unto me of my *F* Mt 11:27 *3962*
no man knoweth the Son, but the *F* Mt 11:27 *3962*
neither knoweth any man the *F* Mt 11:27 *3962*
will of my *F* which is in heaven Mt 12:50 *3962*
the sun in the kingdom of their *F* Mt 13:43 *3962*
commanded, saying, Honour thy *f* Mt 15:4 *3962*
and, He that curseth *f* or mother Mt 15:4 *3962*
shall say to his *f* or his mother Mt 15:5 *3962*
And honour not his *f* or his mother Mt 15:6 *3962*
my heavenly *F* hath not planted Mt 15:13 *3962*
but my *F* which is in heaven Mt 16:17 *3962*
glory of his *F* with his angels Mt 16:27 *3962*
face of my *F* which is in heaven Mt 18:10 *3962*
will of your *F* which is in heaven Mt 18:14 *3962*
them of my *F* which is in heaven Mt 18:19 *3962*
my heavenly *F* do also unto you Mt 18:35 *3962*
this cause shall a man leave *f* Mt 19:5 *3962*
Honour thy *f* and thy mother Mt 19:19 *3962*
or brethren, or sisters, or *f* Mt 19:29 *3962*
for whom it is prepared of my *F* Mt 20:23 *3962*
them twain did the will of his *f* Mt 21:31 *3962*
call no man your *f* upon the earth Mt 23:9 *3962*
for one is your *F*, which is in Mt 23:9 *3962*
angels of heaven, but my *F* only Mt 24:36 *3962*
hand, Come, ye blessed of my *F* Mt 25:34 *3962*
face, and prayed, saying, O my *F* Mt 26:39 *3962*
time, and prayed, saying, O my *F* Mt 26:42 *3962*
that I cannot now pray to my *F* Mt 26:53 *3962*
them in the name of the *F* Mt 28:19 *3962*
they left their *f* Zebedee in the Mk 1:20 *3962*
put them all out, he taketh the *f* Mk 5:40 *3962*
For Moses said, Honour thy *f* Mk 7:10 *3962*
and, Whoso curseth *f* or mother Mk 7:10 *3962*
man shall say to his *f* or mother Mk 7:11 *3962*
do ought for his *f* or his mother Mk 7:12 *3962*
of his *F* with the holy angels Mk 8:38 *3962*
And he asked his *f*, How long is it Mk 9:21 *3962*
straightway the *f* of the child Mk 9:24 *3962*
cause shall a man leave his *f* Mk 10:7 *3962*
Defraud not, Honour thy *f* Mk 10:19 *3962*
or brethren, or sisters, or *f* Mk 10:29 *3962*
be the kingdom of our *f* David Mk 11:10 *3962*
that your *F* also which is in Mk 11:25 *3962*
neither will your *F* which is in Mk 11:26 *3962*
to death, and the *f* the son Mk 13:12 *3962*
neither the Son, but the *F* Mk 13:32 *3962*
And he said, Abba, *F*, all things Mk 14:36 *3962*
the *f* of Alexander and Rufus, to Mk 15:21 *3962*

him the throne of his *f* David... Lk 1:32 3962
after the name of his *f*... Lk 1:59 3962
And they made signs to his *f*... Lk 1:62 3962
his *f* Zacharias was filled with... Lk 1:67 3962
which he sware to our *f* Abraham... Lk 1:73 3962
behold, thy *f* and I have sought... Lk 2:48 3962
We have Abraham to our *f*... Lk 3:8 3962
as your *F* also is merciful... Lk 6:36 3962
and James, and John, and the *f*... Lk 8:51 3962
and delivered him again to his *f*... Lk 9:42 3962
me first to go and bury my *f*... Lk 9:59 3962
and said, I thank thee, O *F*... Lk 10:21 3962
even so, *F*; for so it seemed... Lk 10:21 3962
are delivered to me of my *F*... Lk 10:22 3962
knoweth who the Son is, but the *F*... Lk 10:22 3962
and who the *F* is, but the Son, and... Lk 10:22 3962
Our *F* which art in heaven,... Lk 11:2 3962
bread of any of you that is a *f*... Lk 11:11 3962
F give the Holy Spirit to them... Lk 11:13 3962
your *F* knoweth that ye have need... Lk 12:30 3962
The *f* shall be divided against... Lk 12:53 3962
the son, and the son against the *f*... Lk 12:53 3962
man come to me, and hate not his *f*... Lk 14:26 3962
the younger of them said to his *f*... Lk 15:12 3962
of them said to his *f*, *F*... Lk 15:12 3962
I will arise and go to my *f*... Lk 15:18 3962
and will say unto him, *F*... Lk 15:18 3962
And he arose, and came to his *f*... Lk 15:20 3962
his *f* saw him, and had compassion,... Lk 15:20 3962
And the son said unto him, *F*... Lk 15:21 3962
But the *f* said to his servants,... Lk 15:22 3962
thy *f* hath killed the fatted calf... Lk 15:27 3962
therefore came his *f* out, and... Lk 15:28 3962
And he answering said to his *f*... Lk 15:29 3962
F Abraham, have mercy on me, and... Lk 16:24 3962
he said, I pray thee therefore, *f*... Lk 16:27 3962
And he said, Nay, *f* Abraham... Lk 16:30 3962
bear false witness, Honour thy *f*... Lk 18:20 3962
as my *F* hath appointed unto me... Lk 22:29 3962
Saying, *F*, if thou be willing,... Lk 22:42 3962
Then said Jesus, *F*, forgive them... Lk 23:34 3962
with a loud voice, he said, *F*... Lk 23:46 3962
send the promise of my *F* upon you... Lk 24:49 3962
as of the only begotten of the *F*... Jn 1:14 3962
which is in the bosom of the *F*... Jn 1:18 3962
The *F* loveth the Son, and hath... Jn 3:35 3962
Art thou greater than our *f* Jacob... Jn 4:12 3962
yet at Jerusalem, worship the *F*... Jn 4:21 3962
shall worship the *F* in spirit... Jn 4:23 3962
for the *F* seeketh such to worship... Jn 4:23 3962
So the *f* knew that it was at the... Jn 4:53 3962
My *F* worketh hitherto, and I work... Jn 5:17 3962
but said also that God was his *F*... Jn 5:18 3962
but what he seeth the *F* do... Jn 5:19 3962
For the *F* loveth the Son, and... Jn 5:20 3962
For as the *F* raiseth up the dead,... Jn 5:21 3962
For the *F* judgeth no man, but... Jn 5:22 3962
Son, even as they honour the *F*... Jn 5:23 3962
not the *F* which hath sent him... Jn 5:23 3962
For as the *F* hath life in himself... Jn 5:26 3962
will of the *F* which hath sent me... Jn 5:30 3962
the *F* hath given me to finish... Jn 5:36 3962
of me, that the *F* hath sent me... Jn 5:36 3962
the *F* himself, which hath sent me... Jn 5:37 3962
that I will accuse you to the *F*... Jn 5:45 3962
for him hath God the *F* sealed... Jn 6:27 3962
but my *F* giveth you the true... Jn 6:32 3962
All that the *F* giveth me shall... Jn 6:37 3962
Jesus, the son of Joseph, whose *f*... Jn 6:42 3962
except the *F* which hath sent me... Jn 6:44 3962
heard, and hath learned of the *F*... Jn 6:45 3962
Not that any man hath seen the *F*... Jn 6:46 3962
is of God, he hath seen the *F*... Jn 6:46 3962
As the living *F* hath sent me... Jn 6:57 3962
hath sent me, and I live by the *F*... Jn 6:57 3962
it were given unto him of my *F*... Jn 6:65 3962
but I and the *F* that sent me... Jn 8:16 3962
the *F* that sent me beareth... Jn 8:18 3962
they unto him, Where is thy *F*... Jn 8:19 3962
Ye neither know me, nor my *F*... Jn 8:19 3962
ye should have known my *F* also... Jn 8:19 3962
that he spake to them of the *F*... Jn 8:27 3962
but as my *F* hath taught me, I... Jn 8:28 3962
the *F* hath not left me alone... Jn 8:29 3962
that which I have seen with my *F*... Jn 8:38 3962
which ye have seen with your *f*... Jn 8:38 3962
said unto him, Abraham is our *f*... Jn 8:39 3962
Ye do the deeds of your *f*... Jn 8:41 3962
we have one *F*, even God... Jn 8:41 3962
unto them, If God were your *F*... Jn 8:42 3962
Ye are of your *f* the devil... Jn 8:44 3962
and the lusts of your *f* ye will do... Jn 8:44 3962
for he is a liar, and the *f* of it... Jn 8:44 3962
but I honour my *F*, and ye do... Jn 8:49 3962
thou greater than our *f* Abraham... Jn 8:53 3962
it is my *F* that honoureth me... Jn 8:54 3962
Your *f* Abraham rejoiced to see my... Jn 8:56 3962
As the *F* knoweth me, even so know... Jn 10:15 3962
knoweth me, even so know I the *F*... Jn 10:15 3962
Therefore doth my *F* love me... Jn 10:17 3962
have I received of my *F*... Jn 10:18 3962
My *F*, which gave them me, is... Jn 10:29 3962
I and my *F* are one... Jn 10:30 3962
works have I shewed you from my *F*... Jn 10:32 3962
whom the *F* hath sanctified, and... Jn 10:36 3962
If I do not the works of my *F*... Jn 10:37 3962
and believe, that the *F* is in me... Jn 10:38 3962
lifted up his eyes, and said, *F*... Jn 11:41 3962
serve me, him will my *F* honour... Jn 12:26 3962
F, save me from this hour... Jn 12:27 3962
F, glorify thy name... Jn 12:28 3962
but the *F* which sent me, he gave... Jn 12:49 3962
even as the *F* said unto me, so I... Jn 12:50 3962
out of this world unto the *F*... Jn 13:1 3962
Jesus knowing that the *F* had... Jn 13:3 3962
no man cometh unto the *F*, but by... Jn 14:6 3962
ye should have known my *F* also... Jn 14:7 3962
unto him, Lord, shew us the *F*... Jn 14:8 3962
that hath seen me hath seen the *F*... Jn 14:9 3962
sayest thou then, Shew us the *F*... Jn 14:9 3962
am in the *F*, and the *F* in me... Jn 14:10 3962
but the *F* that dwelleth in me, he... Jn 14:10 3962
am in the *F*, and the *F* in me... Jn 14:11 3962
because I go unto my *F*... Jn 14:12 3962
that the *F* may be glorified in... Jn 14:13 3962
And I will pray the *F*, and he shall... Jn 14:16 3962
ye shall know that I am in my *F*... Jn 14:20 3962
loveth me shall be loved of my *F*... Jn 14:21 3962
my *F* will love him, and we will... Jn 14:23 3962
whom the *F* will send in my name,... Jn 14:26 3962
because I said, I go unto the *F*... Jn 14:28 3962
for my *F* is greater than I... Jn 14:28 3962
world may know that I love the *F*... Jn 14:31 3962
as the *F* gave me commandment,... Jn 14:31 3962
vine, and my *F* is the husbandman... Jn 15:1 3962
Herein is my *F* glorified, that ye... Jn 15:8 3962
As the *F* hath loved me, so have I... Jn 15:9 3962
my *F* I have made known unto you... Jn 15:15 3962
ye shall ask of the *F* in my name... Jn 15:16 3962
that hateth me hateth my *F* also... Jn 15:23 3962
seen and hated both me and my *F*... Jn 15:24 3962
I will send unto you from the *F*... Jn 15:26 3962
which proceedeth from the *F*... Jn 15:26 3962
because they have not known the *F*... Jn 16:3 3962
because I go to my *F*, and ye see... Jn 16:10 3962
things that the *F* hath are mine... Jn 16:15 3962
see me, because I go to the *F*... Jn 16:16 3962
and, Because I go to the *F*... Jn 16:17 3962
ye shall ask the *F* in my name... Jn 16:23 3962
I shall shew you plainly of the *F*... Jn 16:25 3962
that I will pray the *F* for you... Jn 16:26 3962
For the *F* himself loveth you,... Jn 16:27 3962
I came forth from the *F*, and am... Jn 16:28 3962
I leave the world, and go to the *F*... Jn 16:28 3962
alone, because the *F* is with me... Jn 16:32 3962
up his eyes to heaven, and said, *F*... Jn 17:1 3962
And now, O *F*, glorify thou me with... Jn 17:5 3962
Holy *F*, keep through thine own... Jn 17:11 3962
as thou, *F*, art in me, and I in... Jn 17:21 3962
F, I will that they also, whom... Jn 17:24 3962
O righteous *F*, the world hath not... Jn 17:25 3962
the cup which my *F* hath given me... Jn 18:11 3962
for he was *f* in law to Caiaphas,... Jn 18:13 3995
for I am not yet ascended to my *F*... Jn 20:17 3962
ascend unto my *F*, and your *F*... Jn 20:17 3962
as my *F* hath sent me, even so... Jn 20:21 3962
but wait for the promise of the *F*... Acts 1:4 3962
which the *F* hath put in his own... Acts 1:7 3962
having received of the *F* the... Acts 2:33 3962
glory appeared unto our *f* Abraham... Acts 7:2 3962
from thence, when his *f* was dead... Acts 7:4 3962
called his *f* Jacob to him, and all... Acts 7:14 3962
the sons of Emmor the *f* of Sychem... Acts 7:16
but his *f* was a Greek... Acts 16:1 3962
knew all that his *f* was a Greek... Acts 16:3 3962
that the *f* of Publius lay sick of... Acts 28:8 3962
to you and peace from God our *F*... Rom 1:7 3962
we say then that Abraham our *f*... Rom 4:1 3962
that he might be the *f* of all... Rom 4:11 3962
the *f* of circumcision to them who... Rom 4:12 3962
of that faith of our *f* Abraham... Rom 4:12 3962
who is the *f* of us all,... Rom 4:16 3962
made thee a *f* of many nations... Rom 4:17 3962
become the *f* of many nations... Rom 4:18 3962
the dead by the glory of the *F*... Rom 6:4 3962
adoption, whereby we cry, Abba, *F*... Rom 8:15 3962
by one, even by our *f* Isaac... Rom 9:10 3962
even the *F* of our Lord Jesus... Rom 15:6 3962
you, and peace, from God our *F*... 1Cor 1:3 3962
to us there is but one God, the *F*... 1Cor 8:6 3962
up the kingdom to God, even the *F*... 1Cor 15:24 3962
be to you and peace from God our *F*... 2Cor 1:2 3962
even the *F* of our Lord Jesus... 2Cor 1:3 3962
the *F* of mercies, and the God of... 2Cor 1:3 3962
And will be a *F* unto you, and ye... 2Cor 6:18 3962
F of our Lord Jesus Christ, which... 2Cor 11:31 3962
but by Jesus Christ, and God the *F*... Gal 1:1 3962
be to you and peace from God the *F*... Gal 1:3 3962
to the will of God and our *F*... Gal 1:4 3962
until the time appointed of the *f*... Gal 4:2 3962
into your hearts, crying, Abba, *F*... Gal 4:6 3962
to you, and peace, from God our *F*... Eph 1:2 3962
F of our Lord Jesus Christ, who... Eph 1:3 3962
the *F* of glory, may give unto you... Eph 1:17 3962
access by one Spirit unto the *F*... Eph 2:18 3962
the *F* of our Lord Jesus Christ... Eph 3:14 3962
F of all, who is above all, and... Eph 4:6 3962
the *F* in the name of our Lord... Eph 5:20 3962
cause shall a man leave his *f*... Eph 5:31 3962
Honour thy *f* and mother... Eph 6:2 3962
love with faith, from God the *F*... Eph 6:23 3962
you, and peace, from God our *F*... Phil 1:2 3962
Lord, to the glory of God the *F*... Phil 2:11 3962
of him, that, as a son with the *f*... Phil 2:22 3962
our *F* be glory for ever and ever... Phil 4:20 3962
you, and peace, from God our *F*... Col 1:2 3962
the *F* of our Lord Jesus Christ,... Col 1:3 3962
Giving thanks unto the *F*, which... Col 1:12 3962
For it pleased the *F* that in him... Col 1:19
the mystery of God, and of the *F*... Col 2:2 3962
thanks to God and the *F* by him... Col 3:17 3962
which is in God the *F* and in the... 1Th 1:1 3962
you, and peace, from God our *F*... 1Th 1:1 3962
in the sight of God and our *F*... 1Th 1:3 3962
as a *f* doth his children,... 1Th 2:11 3962
Now God himself and our *F*, and our... 1Th 3:11 3962
holiness before God, even our *F*... 1Th 3:13 3962
of the Thessalonians in God our *F*... 2Th 1:1 3962
you, and peace, from God our *F*... 2Th 1:2 3962
himself, and God, even our *F*... 2Th 2:16 3962
mercy, and peace, from God our *F*... 1Ti 1:2 3962
an elder, but intreat him as a *f*... 1Ti 5:1 3962
mercy, and peace, from God the *F*... 2Ti 1:2 3962
mercy, and peace, from God the *F*... Titus 1:4 3962
to you, and peace, from God our *F*... Philem 3 3962
And again, I will be to him a *F*... Heb 1:5 3962
Without *f*, without mother,... Heb 7:3 540
he was yet in the loins of his *f*... Heb 7:10 3962
is he whom the *f* chasteneth not... Heb 12:7 3962
subjection unto the *F* of spirits... Heb 12:9 3962
cometh down from the *F* of lights... Jas 1:17 3962
the *F* is this, To visit the... Jas 1:27 3962
Abraham our *f* justified by works... Jas 2:21 3962
bless we God, even the *F*... Jas 3:9 3962
to the foreknowledge of God the *F*... 1Pet 1:2 3962
F of our Lord Jesus Christ, which... 1Pet 1:3 3962
And if ye call on the *F*, who... 1Pet 1:17 3962
he received from God the *F* honour... 2Pet 1:17 3962
life, which was with the *F*... 1Jn 1:2 3962
our fellowship is with the *F*... 1Jn 1:3 3962
we have an advocate with the *F*... 1Jn 2:1 3962
because ye have known the *F*... 1Jn 2:13 3962
the love of the *F* is not in him... 1Jn 2:15 3962
pride of life, is not of the *F*... 1Jn 2:16 3962
is antichrist, that denieth the *F*... 1Jn 2:22 3962
the Son, the same hath not the *F*... 1Jn 2:23 3962
the Son hath the *F* also... 1Jn 2:23
continue in the Son, and in the *F*... 1Jn 2:24 3962
love the *F* hath bestowed upon us... 1Jn 3:1 3962
do testify that the *F* sent the... 1Jn 4:14 3962
that bear record in heaven, the *F*... 1Jn 5:7 3962
mercy, and peace, from God the *F*... 2Jn 3 3962
Jesus Christ, the Son of the *F*... 2Jn 3 3962
received a commandment from the *F*... 2Jn 4 3962
of Christ, he hath both the *F*... 2Jn 9 3962
that are sanctified by God the *F*... Jude 1 3962
and priests unto God and his *F*... Rev 1:6 3962
even as I received of my *F*... Rev 2:27 3962
will confess his name before my *F*... Rev 3:5 3962
set down with my *F* in his throne... Rev 3:21 3962

FATHERLESS {43}

not afflict any widow, or *f* child... Ex 22:22 3490
be widows, and your children *f*... Ex 22:24 3490
execute the judgment of the *f*... Deut 10:18 3490
thee,) and the stranger, and the *f*... Deut 14:29 3490
gates, and the stranger, and the *f*... Deut 16:11 3490
Levite, the stranger, and the *f*... Deut 16:14 3490
of the stranger, nor of the *f*... Deut 24:17 3490
be for the stranger, for the *f*... Deut 24:19 3490
be for the stranger, for the *f*... Deut 24:20 3490
be for the stranger, for the *f*... Deut 24:21 3490
the Levite, the stranger, the *f*... Deut 26:12 3490
and unto the stranger, to the *f*... Deut 26:13 3490
the judgment of the stranger, *f*... Deut 27:19 3490
Yea, ye overwhelm the *f*, and ye... Job 6:27 3490
the arms of the *f* have been... Job 22:9 3490
They drive away the ass of the *f*... Job 24:3 3490
They pluck the *f* from the breast,... Job 24:9 3490
the poor that cried, and the *f*... Job 29:12 3490
the *f* hath not eaten thereof... Job 31:17 3490
lifted up my hand against the *f*... Job 31:21 3490
thou art the helper of the *f*... Ps 10:14 3490
To judge the *f* and the oppressed,... Ps 10:18 3490
A father of the *f*, and a judge of... Ps 68:5 3490
Defend the poor and *f*... Ps 82:3 3490
and the stranger, and murder the *f*... Ps 94:6 3490
Let his children be *f*, and his... Ps 109:9 3490
be any to favour his *f* children... Ps 109:12 3490
he relieveth the *f* and widow... Ps 146:9 3490
not into the fields of the *f*... Prov 23:10 3490
the oppressed, judge the *f*... Is 1:17 3490
they judge not the *f*, neither... Is 1:23 3490
shall have mercy on their *f*... Is 9:17 3490
prey, and that they may rob the *f*... Is 10:2 3490
not the cause, the cause of the *f*... Jer 5:28 3490
oppress not the stranger, the *f*... Jer 7:6 3490
violence to the stranger, the *f*... Jer 22:3 3490
Leave thy *f* children, I will... Jer 49:11 3490
We are orphans and *f*,... Lam 5:3 369,1
in thee have they vexed the *f*... Eze 22:7 3490
for in thee the *f* findeth mercy... Hos 14:3 3490
oppress not the widow, nor the *f*... Zec 7:10 3490
in his wages, the widow, and the *f*... Mal 3:5 3490
Father is this, To visit the *f*... Jas 1:27 3737

FATHER'S {147}

and they saw not their *f* nakedness... Gen 9:23 1
thy kindred, and from thy *f* house... Gen 12:1 1
me to wander from my *f* house... Gen 20:13 1
which took me from my *f* house... Gen 24:7 1
is there room in thy *f* house for... Gen 24:23 1
But thou shalt go unto my *f* house... Gen 24:38 1
of my kindred, and of my *f* house... Gen 24:40 1
For all the wells which his *f*... Gen 26:15 1

come again to my *f* house in peace......... Gen 28:21 1
Rachel came with her *f* sheep.................. Gen 29:9 1
Rachel that he was her *f* brother............. Gen 29:12 1
taken away all that was our *f*................. Gen 31:1 1
of that which was our *f* hath he.............. Gen 31:1 1
I see your *f* countenance, that it............ Gen 31:5 1
inheritance for us in our *f* house............ Gen 31:14 1
stolen the images that were her *f*............ Gen 31:19 1
sore longedst after thy *f* house.............. Gen 31:30 1
lay with Bilhah his *f* concubine.............. Gen 35:22 1
the sons of Zilpah, his *f* wives............... Gen 37:2 1
to feed their *f* flock in Shechem............. Gen 37:12 1
Remain a widow at thy *f* house................ Gen 38:11 1
went and dwelt in her *f* house................. Gen 38:11 1
all my toil, and all my *f* house............... Gen 41:51 1
his brethren, and unto his *f* house........... Gen 46:31 1
my *f* house, which were in the................. Gen 46:31 1
all his *f* household, with bread,.............. Gen 47:12 1
and he held up his *f* hand, to................. Gen 48:17 1
thou wentest up to thy *f* bed.................. Gen 49:4 1
thy *f* children shall bow down................. Gen 49:8 1
And Joseph fell upon his *f* face.............. Gen 50:1 1
and his brethren, and his *f* house............ Gen 50:8 1
in Egypt, he, and his *f* house................. Gen 50:22 1
troughs to water their *f* flock................ Ex 2:16 1
him Jochebed his *f* sister to wife............ Ex 6:20 1733
my *f* God, and I will exalt him................ Ex 15:2 1
priest's office in his *f* stead.................. Lev 16:32 1
The nakedness of thy *f* wife shalt............ Lev 18:8 1
it is thy *f* nakedness............................ Lev 18:8 1
of thy *f* wife's daughter,........................ Lev 18:11 1
the nakedness of thy *f* sister.................. Lev 18:12 1
she is thy *f* near kinswoman.................... Lev 18:12 1
the nakedness of thy *f* brother................ Lev 18:14 1
his *f* wife hath uncovered his.................. Lev 20:11 1
hath uncovered his *f* nakedness................ Lev 20:11 1
his *f* daughter, or his mother's................. Lev 20:17 1
sister, nor of thy *f* sister........................ Lev 20:19 1
and is returned unto her *f* house.............. Lev 22:13 1
she shall eat of her *f* meat...................... Lev 22:13 1
with the ensign of their *f* house.............. Num 2:2 1
thy *f* house with thee shall bear.............. Num 18:1 1
among their *f* brethren........................... Num 27:7 1
inheritance unto his *f* brethren................. Num 27:10 1
being in her *f* house in her youth............ Num 30:3 1
yet in her youth in her *f* house................. Num 30:16 1
unto their *f* brothers' sons...................... Num 36:11 1730
damsel to the door of her *f* house............. Deut 22:21 1
to play the whore in her *f* house............... Deut 22:21 1
A man shall not take his *f* wife................. Deut 22:30 1
nor discover his *f* skirt........................... Deut 22:30 1
be he that lieth with his *f* wife................. Deut 27:20 1
because he uncovereth his *f* skirt.............. Deut 27:20 1
shew kindness unto my *f* house................. Josh 2:12 1
all thy *f* household, home unto................. Josh 2:18 1
her *f* household, and all that she............... Josh 6:25 1
and I am the least in my *f* house.............. Judg 6:15 1
Take thy *f* young bullock, even.................. Judg 6:25 1
because he feared his *f* household............. Judg 6:27 1
went unto his *f* house at Ophrah............... Judg 9:5 1
up against my *f* house this day................. Judg 9:18 1
shalt not inherit in our *f* house................ Judg 11:2 1
me, and expel me out of my *f* house........... Judg 11:7 1
thee and thy *f* house with fire.................. Judg 14:15 1
and he went up to his *f* house.................. Judg 14:19 1
her *f* house to Beth-lehem-judah................ Judg 19:2 1
she brought him into her *f* house.............. Judg 19:3 1
arm, and the arm of thy *f* house............... 1Sa 2:31 1
on thee, and on all thy *f* house................ 1Sa 9:20 1
to feed his *f* sheep at Beth-lehem............. 1Sa 17:15 1
make his *f* house free in Israel................. 1Sa 17:25 1
Thy servant kept his *f* sheep..................... 1Sa 17:34 1
go no more home to his *f* house................ 1Sa 18:2 1
or my *f* family in Israel, that I................... 1Sa 18:18 1
all his *f* house heard it, they..................... 1Sa 22:1 1
son of Ahitub, and all his *f* house.............. 1Sa 22:11 1
thou, and all thy *f* house.......................... 1Sa 22:16 1
of all the persons of thy *f* house............... 1Sa 22:22 1
destroy my name out of my *f* house............ 1Sa 24:21 1
thou gone in unto my *f* concubine.............. 2Sa 3:7 1
of Joab, and on all his *f* house................. 2Sa 3:29 1
kindness for Jonathan thy *f* sake............... 2Sa 9:7 1
be on me, and on my *f* house.................... 2Sa 14:9 1
have been thy *f* servant hitherto............... 2Sa 15:34 1
I have served in thy *f* presence................ 2Sa 16:19 1
Go in unto thy *f* concubines...................... 2Sa 16:21 1
Absalom went in unto his *f*....................... 2Sa 16:22 1
For all of my *f* house were but.................. 2Sa 19:28 1
against me, and against my *f* house........... 2Sa 24:17 1
not do it for David thy *f* sake.................... 1Kin 11:12 1
of his *f* servants with him........................ 1Kin 11:17 1
shall be thicker than my *f* loins................. 1Kin 12:10 1
thy *f* house, in that ye have..................... 1Kin 18:18 1
sons, and set him on his *f* throne............... 2Kin 10:3 1
and made him king in his *f* stead............... 2Kin 23:30 1
his *f* brother king in his stead.................... 2Kin 24:17 1730
forasmuch as he defiled his *f* bed............... 1Chr 5:1 1
Shemuel, heads of their *f* house................. 1Chr 7:2 1
of Asher, heads of their *f* house................ 1Chr 7:40 1
of his *f* house twenty and two................... 1Chr 12:28 1
God, be on me, and on my *f* house.............. 1Chr 21:17 1
according to their *f* house........................ 1Chr 23:11 1
with understanding, of Huram my *f*............ 2Chr 2:13 1
shall be thicker than my *f* loins................. 2Chr 10:10 1
slain thy brethren of thy *f* house............... 2Chr 21:13 1
king in his *f* stead in Jerusalem................. 2Chr 36:1 1
they could not shew their *f* house.............. Ezr 2:59 1
both I and my *f* house have sinned............. Neh 1:6 1
they could not shew their *f* house.............. Neh 7:61 1
thy *f* house shall be destroyed.................. Est 4:14 1
thine own people, and thy *f* house............. Ps 45:10 1
For I was my *f* son, tender and.................. Prov 4:3 1
keep thy *f* commandment, and................... Prov 6:20 1
son heareth his *f* instruction.................... Prov 13:1 1
fool despiseth his *f* instruction................. Prov 15:5 1
thy *f* friend, forsake not............................ Prov 27:10 1
thy people, and upon thy *f* house............... Is 7:17 1
a glorious throne to his *f* house................. Is 22:23 1
him all the glory of his *f* house................. Is 22:24 1
but obey their *f* commandment.................. Jer 35:14 1
that seeth all his *f* sins which.................... Eze 18:14 1
his sister, his *f* daughter........................... Eze 22:11 1
it new with you in my *F* kingdom............... Mt 26:29 *3962*
I must be about my *F* business.................. Lk 2:49 *3962*
in his own glory, and in his *F*................... Lk 9:26 *3962*
for it is your *F* good pleasure to............... Lk 12:32 *3962*
of my *f* have bread enough......................... Lk 15:17 *3962*
wouldest send him to my *f* house............... Lk 16:27 *3962*
make not my *F* house an house of............... Jn 2:16 *3962*
I am come in my *F* name, and ye................. Jn 5:43 *3962*
this is the *F* will which hath...................... Jn 6:39 *3962*
the works that I do in my *F* name.............. Jn 10:25 *3962*
to pluck them out of my *F* hand................. Jn 10:29 *3962*
In my *F* house are many mansions............... Jn 14:2 *3962*
not mine, but the *F* which sent me............. Jn 14:24 *3962*
as I have kept my *F* commandments............ Jn 15:10 *3962*
up in his *f* house three months.................. Acts 7:20 *3962*
that one should have his *f* wife................. 1Cor 5:1 *3962*
having his *F* name written in..................... Rev 14:1 *3962*

FATHERS {540}

thou shalt go to thy *f* in peace.................. Gen 15:15 1
Return unto the land of thy *f*..................... Gen 31:3 1
until now, both we, and also our *f*............. Gen 46:34 1
shepherds, both we, and also our *f*............ Gen 47:3 1
of the years of the life of my *f*.................. Gen 47:9 1
But I will lie with my *f*, and thou................ Gen 47:30 1
God, before whom my *f* Abraham................ Gen 48:15 1
them, and the name of my *f* Abraham.......... Gen 48:16 1
you again unto the land of your *f*............... Gen 48:21 1
bury me with my *f* in the cave.................... Gen 49:29 1
The God of your *f* hath sent me.................. Ex 3:13 1
of Israel, The LORD God of your *f*............... Ex 3:15 1
unto them, The LORD God of your *f*.............. Ex 3:16 1
that the LORD God of their *f*....................... Ex 4:5 1
these are the heads of the *f* of.................. Ex 6:25 1
the Egyptians; which neither thy *f*............. Ex 10:6 1
nor thy fathers' *f* have seen....................... Ex 10:6 1
according to the house of their *f*............... Ex 12:3 1
he sware unto thy *f* to give thee................ Ex 13:5 1
as he sware unto thee and to thy *f*............. Ex 13:11 1
the *f* upon the children unto the................ Ex 20:5 1
of the *f* upon the children......................... Ex 34:7 1
of his *f* shall he return............................. Lev 25:41 1
f shall they pine away with them............... Lev 26:39 1
and the iniquity of their *f*......................... Lev 26:40 1
families, by the house of their *f*................. Num 1:2 1
one head of the house of his *f*................... Num 1:4 1
princes of the tribes of their *f*.................. Num 1:16 1
families, by the house of their *f*................. Num 1:18 1
families, by the house of their *f*................. Num 1:20 1
families, by the house of their *f*................. Num 1:22 1
families, by the house of their *f*................. Num 1:24 1
families, by the house of their *f*................. Num 1:26 1
families, by the house of their *f*................. Num 1:28 1
families, by the house of their *f*................. Num 1:30 1
families, by the house of their *f*................. Num 1:32 1
families, by the house of their *f*................. Num 1:34 1
families, by the house of their *f*................. Num 1:36 1
families, by the house of their *f*................. Num 1:38 1
families, by the house of their *f*................. Num 1:40 1
families, by the house of their *f*................. Num 1:42 1
one was for the house of his *f*................... Num 1:44 1
Israel, by the house of their *f*................... Num 1:45 1
after the tribe of their *f* were.................. Num 1:47 1
of Israel by the house of their *f*................ Num 2:32 1
according to the house of their *f*............... Num 2:34 1
Levi after the house of their *f*.................. Num 3:15 1
according to the house of their *f*............... Num 3:20 1
families, by the house of their *f*................. Num 4:2 1
throughout the houses of their *f*............... Num 4:22 1
families, by the house of their *f*................. Num 4:29 1
and after the house of their *f*................... Num 4:34 1
and by the house of their *f*....................... Num 4:38 1
families, by the house of their *f*................. Num 4:40 1
families, by the house of their *f*................. Num 4:42 1
and after the house of their *f*................... Num 4:46 1
heads of the house of their *f*..................... Num 7:2 1
which thou swarest unto their *f*................. Num 11:12 1
of their *f* shall ye send a man................... Num 13:2 1
the *f* upon the children unto the................ Num 14:18 1
land which I sware unto their *f*................. Num 14:23 1
according to the house of their *f*............... Num 17:2 1
the house of their *f* twelve rods................. Num 17:2 1
the head of the house of their *f*................. Num 17:3 1
How our *f* went down into Egypt,................ Num 20:15 1
the Egyptians vexed us, and our *f*.............. Num 20:15 1
of their *f* they shall inherit...................... Num 26:55 1
the chief *f* of the congregation.................. Num 31:26 1
Thus did your *f*, when I sent them.............. Num 32:8 1
the chief *f* of the tribes of the.................. Num 32:28 1
tribes of your *f* ye shall inherit................. Num 33:54 1
according to the house of their *f*............... Num 34:14 1
according to the house of their *f*............... Num 34:14 1
the chief *f* of the families of...................... Num 36:1 1
the chief *f* of the children of...................... Num 36:1 1
from the inheritance of our *f*..................... Num 36:3 1
inheritance of the tribe of our *f*................. Num 36:4 1
inheritance of the tribe of his *f*................. Num 36:7 1
man the inheritance of his *f*..................... Num 36:8 1
which the LORD sware unto your *f*............... Deut 1:8 1
(The LORD God of your *f* make you.............. Deut 1:11 1
God of thy *f* hath said unto thee................ Deut 1:21 1
which I sware to give unto your *f*.............. Deut 1:35 1
the LORD God of your *f* giveth you.............. Deut 4:1 1
of thy *f* which he sware unto them.............. Deut 4:31 1
And because he loved thy *f*....................... Deut 4:37 1
made not this covenant with our *f*.............. Deut 5:3 1
the *f* upon the children unto the................ Deut 5:9 1
God of thy *f* hath promised thee................ Deut 6:3 1
land which he sware unto thy *f*.................. Deut 6:10 1
which the LORD sware unto thy *f*................ Deut 6:18 1
land which he sware unto our *f*.................. Deut 6:23 1
which he had sworn unto your *f*.................. Deut 7:8 1
mercy which he sware unto thy *f*................ Deut 7:12 1
he sware unto thy *f* to give thee................ Deut 7:13 1
which the LORD sware unto your *f*.............. Deut 8:1 1
not, neither did thy *f* know....................... Deut 8:3 1
with manna, which thy *f* knew not.............. Deut 8:16 1
which he sware unto thy *f*......................... Deut 8:18 1
which the LORD sware unto thy *f*................ Deut 9:5 1
unto their *f* to give unto them................... Deut 10:11 1
a delight in thy *f* to love them.................. Deut 10:15 1
Thy *f* went down into Egypt with.............. Deut 10:22 1
unto your *f* to give unto them................... Deut 11:9 1
sware unto your *f* to give them................. Deut 11:21 1
thy *f* giveth thee to possess it.................. Deut 12:1 1
hast not known, thou, nor thy *f*................. Deut 13:6 1
thee, as he hath sworn unto thy *f*............. Deut 13:17 1
as he hath sworn unto thy *f*...................... Deut 19:8 1
he promised to give unto thy *f*.................. Deut 19:8 1
The *f* shall not be put to death................. Deut 24:16 1
be put to death for the *f*.......................... Deut 24:16 1
sware unto our *f* for to give us.................. Deut 26:3 1
cried unto the LORD God of our *f*................ Deut 26:7 1
us, as thou swarest unto our *f*.................. Deut 26:15 1
God of thy *f* hath promised thee............... Deut 27:3 1
sware unto thy *f* to give thee.................... Deut 28:11 1
neither thou nor thy *f* have known............ Deut 28:36 1
neither thou nor thy *f* have known............ Deut 28:64 1
and as he hath sworn unto thy *f*............... Deut 29:13 1
of the LORD God of their *f*........................ Deut 29:25 1
the land which thy *f* possessed.................. Deut 30:5 1
and multiply thee above thy *f*.................... Deut 30:5 1
good, as he rejoiced over thy *f*.................. Deut 30:9 1
which the LORD sware unto thy *f*................ Deut 30:20 1
sworn unto their *f* to give them................. Deut 31:7 1
thou shalt sleep with thy *f*........................ Deut 31:16 1
land which I sware unto their *f*................. Deut 31:20 1
newly up, whom your *f* feared not.............. Deut 32:17 1
I sware unto their *f* to give them.............. Josh 1:6 1
ask their *f* in time to come........................ Josh 4:6
shall ask their *f* in time to come............... Josh 4:21 1
their *f* that he would give us.................... Josh 5:6 1
the heads of the *f* of the tribes.................. Josh 14:1 1
LORD God of your *f* hath given you............. Josh 18:3 1
the heads of the *f* of the tribes.................. Josh 19:51 1
f of the Levites unto Eleazar the................ Josh 21:1 1
unto the heads of the *f* of the................... Josh 21:1 1
he sware to give unto their *f*.................... Josh 21:43 1
to all that he sware unto their *f*............... Josh 21:44 1
f among the thousands of Israel................ Josh 22:14 1
of the LORD, which our *f* made.................. Josh 22:28 1
Your *f* dwelt on the other side of............... Josh 24:2 1
And I brought your *f* out of Egypt............. Josh 24:6 1
after your *f* with chariots........................ Josh 24:6 1
put away the gods which your *f*................. Josh 24:14 1
whether the gods which your *f*.................. Josh 24:15 1
our *f* out of the land of Egypt,.................. Josh 24:17 1
land which I sware unto your *f*................. Judg 2:1 1
were gathered unto their *f*........................ Judg 2:10 1
forsook the LORD God of their *f*................. Judg 2:12 1
the way which their *f* walked in................. Judg 2:17 1
themselves more than their *f*..................... Judg 2:19 1
which I commanded their *f*........................ Judg 2:20 1
as their *f* did keep it, or not..................... Judg 2:22 1
their *f* by the hand of Moses..................... Judg 3:4 1
miracles which our *f* told us of.................. Judg 6:13 1
when their *f* or their brethren.................. Judg 21:22 1
that brought your *f* up out of the.............. 1Sa 12:6 1
which he did to you and to your *f*.............. 1Sa 12:7 1
your *f* cried unto the LORD, then.............. 1Sa 12:8 1
brought forth your *f* out of Egypt.............. 1Sa 12:8 1
you, as it was against your *f*..................... 1Sa 12:15 1
and thou shalt sleep with thy *f*................... 2Sa 7:12 1
the king shall sleep with his *f*.................... 1Kin 1:21 1
So David slept with his *f*........................... 1Kin 2:10 1
the chief of the *f* of the............................. 1Kin 8:1 1
LORD, which he made with our *f*................. 1Kin 8:21 1
which thou gavest unto their *f*.................. 1Kin 8:34 1
land which thou gavest unto our *f*.............. 1Kin 8:40 1
which thou gavest unto their *f*.................. 1Kin 8:48 1
broughtest our *f* out of Egypt.................... 1Kin 8:53 1
be with us, as he was with our *f*................ 1Kin 8:57 1
which he commanded our *f*........................ 1Kin 8:58 1
who brought forth their *f* out of................ 1Kin 9:9 1
Egypt that David slept with his *f*............... 1Kin 11:21 1
And Solomon slept with his *f*..................... 1Kin 11:43 1
come unto the sepulchre of thy *f*............... 1Kin 13:22 1
land, which he gave to their *f*................... 1Kin 14:15 1
and he slept with his *f*, and Nadab............ 1Kin 14:20 1
above all that their *f* had done................. 1Kin 14:22 1
And Rehoboam slept with his *f*.................. 1Kin 14:31 1
was buried with his *f* in the city................ 1Kin 14:31 1

And Abijam slept with his f	1Kin 15:8	1
all the idols that his f had made	1Kin 15:12	1
And Asa slept with his f	1Kin 15:24	1
was buried with his f in the city	1Kin 15:24	1
So Baasha slept with his f	1Kin 16:6	1
So Omri slept with his f, and was	1Kin 16:28	1
for I am not better than my f	1Kin 19:4	1
the inheritance of my f unto thee	1Kin 21:3	1
give thee the inheritance of my f	1Kin 21:4	1
So Ahab slept with his f	1Kin 22:40	1
And Jehoshaphat slept with his f	1Kin 22:50	1
was buried with his f in the city	1Kin 22:50	1
And Joram slept with his f	2Kin 8:24	1
was buried with his f in the city	2Kin 8:24	1
with his f in the city of David	2Kin 9:28	1
And Jehu slept with his f	2Kin 10:35	1
and Jehoram, and Ahaziah, his f	2Kin 12:18	1
with his f in the city of David	2Kin 12:21	1
And Jehoahaz slept with his f	2Kin 13:9	1
And Joash slept with his f	2Kin 13:13	1
The f shall not be put to death	2Kin 14:6	1
be put to death for the f	2Kin 14:6	1
And Jehoash slept with his f	2Kin 14:16	1
with his f in the city of David	2Kin 14:20	1
that the king slept with his f	2Kin 14:22	1
And Jeroboam slept with his f	2Kin 14:29	1
So Azariah slept with his f	2Kin 15:7	1
with his f in the city of David	2Kin 15:7	1
of the LORD, as his f had done	2Kin 15:9	1
And Menahem slept with his f	2Kin 15:22	1
And Jotham slept with his f	2Kin 15:38	1
was buried with his f in the city	2Kin 15:38	1
And Ahaz slept with his f, and was	2Kin 16:20	1
was buried with his f in the city	2Kin 16:20	1
the law which I commanded your f	2Kin 17:13	1
like to the neck of their f	2Kin 17:14	1
that he made with their f	2Kin 17:15	1
as did their f, so do they unto	2Kin 17:41	1
them which my f have destroyed	2Kin 19:12	1
that which thy f have laid up in	2Kin 20:17	1
And Hezekiah slept with his f	2Kin 20:21	1
of the land which I gave their f	2Kin 21:8	1
since the day their f came forth	2Kin 21:15	1
And Manasseh slept with his f	2Kin 21:18	1
he forsook the LORD God of his f	2Kin 21:22	1
because our f have not hearkened	2Kin 22:13	1
I will gather thee unto thy f	2Kin 22:20	1
to all that his f had done	2Kin 23:32	1
to all that his f had done	2Kin 23:37	1
So Jehoiakim slept with his f	2Kin 24:6	1
of their f increased greatly	1Chr 4:38	1
of the house of their f were	1Chr 5:13	1
chief of the house of their f	1Chr 5:15	1
the heads of the house of their f	1Chr 5:24	1
and heads of the house of their f	1Chr 5:24	1
against the God of their f	1Chr 5:25	1
the Levites according to their f	1Chr 6:19	1
after the house of their f	1Chr 7:4	1
heads of the house of their f	1Chr 7:7	1
heads of the house of their f	1Chr 7:9	1
Jediael, by the heads of their f	1Chr 7:11	1
the f of the inhabitants of Geba	1Chr 8:6	1
were his sons, heads of the f	1Chr 8:10	1
who were heads of the f of the	1Chr 8:13	1
These were heads of the f	1Chr 8:28	1
f in the house of their f	1Chr 9:9	1
f in the house of their f	1Chr 9:9	1
heads of the house of their f	1Chr 9:13	1
and their f, being over the host	1Chr 9:19	1
chief of the f of the Levites,	1Chr 9:33	1
These chief f of the Levites were	1Chr 9:34	1
the God of our f look thereon	1Chr 12:17	1
throughout the house of their f	1Chr 12:30	1
the chief of the f of the Levites	1Chr 15:12	1
thou must go to be with thy f	1Chr 17:11	1
were the chief of the f of Laadan	1Chr 23:9	1
Levi after the house of their f	1Chr 23:24	1
even the chief of the f, as they	1Chr 23:24	1
chief men of the house of their f	1Chr 24:4	1
according to the house of their f	1Chr 24:4	1
the chief of the f of the priests	1Chr 24:6	1
after the house of their f	1Chr 24:30	1
the chief of the f of the priests	1Chr 24:31	1
even the principal f over against	1Chr 24:31	1
according to the house of their f	1Chr 26:13	1
of the Gershonite Laadan, chief f	1Chr 26:21	1
David the king, and the chief f	1Chr 26:26	1
to the generations of his f	1Chr 26:31	1
thousand and seven hundred chief f	1Chr 26:32	1
their number, to wit, the chief f	1Chr 27:1	1
Then the chief of the f and	1Chr 29:6	1
and sojourners, as were all our f	1Chr 29:15	1
Isaac, and of Israel, our f	1Chr 29:18	1
blessed the LORD God of their f	1Chr 29:20	1
in all Israel, the chief of the f	2Chr 1:2	1
the chief of the f of the	2Chr 5:2	1
thou gavest to them and to their f	2Chr 6:25	1
land which thou gavest unto our f	2Chr 6:31	1
which thou gavest unto their f	2Chr 6:38	1
forsook the LORD God of their f	2Chr 7:22	1
And Solomon slept with his f	2Chr 9:31	1
unto the LORD God of their f	2Chr 11:16	1
And Rehoboam slept with his f	2Chr 12:16	1
against the LORD God of your f	2Chr 13:12	1
upon the LORD God of their f	2Chr 13:18	1
So Abijah slept with his f	2Chr 14:1	1
to seek the LORD God of their f	2Chr 14:4	1
of their f with all their heart	2Chr 15:12	1
And Asa slept with his f, and died	2Chr 16:13	1
according to the house of their f	2Chr 17:14	1
back unto the LORD God of their f	2Chr 19:4	1
of the chief of the f of Israel	2Chr 19:8	1
And said, O LORD God of our f	2Chr 20:6	1
hearts unto the God of their f	2Chr 20:33	1
Now Jehoshaphat slept with his f	2Chr 21:1	1
was buried with his f in the city	2Chr 21:1	1
forsaken the LORD God of his f	2Chr 21:10	1
him, like the burning of his f	2Chr 21:19	1
and the chief of the f of Israel	2Chr 23:2	1
house of the LORD God of their f	2Chr 24:18	1
forsaken the LORD God of their f	2Chr 24:24	1
The f shall not die for the	2Chr 25:4	1
shall the children die for the f	2Chr 25:4	1
to the houses of their f,	2Chr 25:5	1
buried him with his f in the city	2Chr 25:28	1
that the king slept with his f	2Chr 26:2	1
number of the chief of the f of	2Chr 26:12	1
So Uzziah slept with his f	2Chr 26:23	1
they buried him with his f in the	2Chr 26:23	1
And Jotham slept with his f	2Chr 27:9	1
forsaken the LORD God of their f	2Chr 28:6	1
of your f was wroth with Judah	2Chr 28:9	1
to anger the LORD God of his f	2Chr 28:25	1
And Ahaz slept with his f, and they	2Chr 28:27	1
house of the LORD God of your f	2Chr 29:5	1
For our f have trespassed, and	2Chr 29:6	1
our f have fallen by the sword,	2Chr 29:9	1
And be not ye like your f, and like	2Chr 30:7	1
against the LORD God of their f	2Chr 30:7	1
not stiffnecked, as your f were	2Chr 30:8	1
seek God, the LORD God of his f	2Chr 30:19	1
to the LORD God of their f	2Chr 30:22	1
priests by the house of their f	2Chr 31:17	1
my f have done unto all the	2Chr 32:13	1
that my f utterly destroyed	2Chr 32:14	1
hand, and out of the hand of my f	2Chr 32:15	1
And Hezekiah slept with his f	2Chr 32:33	1
which I have appointed for your f	2Chr 33:8	1
greatly before the God of his f	2Chr 33:12	1
So Manasseh slept with his f	2Chr 33:20	1
because our f have not kept the	2Chr 34:21	1
I will gather thee to thy f	2Chr 34:28	1
of God, the God of their f	2Chr 34:32	1
the LORD, the God of their f	2Chr 34:33	1
by the houses of your f, after	2Chr 35:4	1
of the families of the f of your	2Chr 35:5	1
in one of the sepulchres of his f	2Chr 35:24	1
the LORD God of their f sent to	2Chr 36:15	1
up the chief of the f of Judah	Ezr 1:5	1
And some of the chief of the f	Ezr 2:68	1
and Levites and chief of the f	Ezr 3:12	1
and to the chief of the f	Ezr 4:2	1
of the chief of the f of Israel	Ezr 4:3	1
the book of the records of thy f	Ezr 4:15	2
But after that our f had provoked	Ezr 5:12	2
Blessed be the LORD God of our f	Ezr 7:27	1
are now the chief of their f	Ezr 8:1	1
unto the LORD God of your f	Ezr 8:28	1
and chief of the f of Israel	Ezr 8:29	1
Since the days of our f have we	Ezr 9:7	1
unto the LORD God of your f	Ezr 10:11	1
with certain chief of the f	Ezr 10:16	1
after the house of their f	Ezr 10:16	1
chief of the f gave unto the work	Neh 7:70	1
some of the chief of the f gave	Neh 7:71	1
chief of the f of all the people	Neh 8:13	1
and the iniquities of their f	Neh 9:2	1
the affliction of our f in Egypt	Neh 9:9	1
our f dealt proudly, and hardened	Neh 9:16	1
thou hadst promised to their f	Neh 9:23	1
and on our prophets, and on our f	Neh 9:32	1
princes, our priests, nor our f	Neh 9:34	1
our f to eat the fruit thereof	Neh 9:36	1
God, after the houses of our f	Neh 10:34	1
And his brethren, chief of the f	Neh 11:13	1
were priests, the chief of the f	Neh 12:12	1
were recorded chief of the f	Neh 12:22	1
sons of Levi, the chief of the f	Neh 12:23	1
Did not your f thus, and did not	Neh 13:18	1
thyself to the search of their f	Job 8:8	1
wise men have told from their f	Job 15:18	1
whose f I would have disdained to	Job 30:1	1
Our f trusted in thee	Ps 22:4	1
and a sojourner, as all my f were	Ps 39:12	1
our f have told us, what work	Ps 44:1	1
Instead of thy f shall be thy	Ps 45:16	1
go to the generation of his f	Ps 49:19	1
and known, and our f have told us	Ps 78:3	1
Israel, which he commanded our f	Ps 78:5	1
And might not be as their f	Ps 78:8	1
did he in the sight of their f	Ps 78:12	1
dealt unfaithfully like their f	Ps 78:57	1
When your f tempted me, proved me	Ps 95:9	1
We have sinned with our f	Ps 106:6	1
Our f understood not thy wonders	Ps 106:7	1
Let the iniquity of his f be	Ps 109:14	1
the glory of children are their f	Prov 17:6	1
riches are the inheritance of f	Prov 19:14	1
landmark, which thy f have set	Prov 22:28	1
for the iniquity of their f	Is 14:21	1
them which my f have destroyed	Is 37:12	1
that which thy f have laid up in	Is 39:6	1
And kings shall be thy nursing f	Is 49:23	
where our f praised thee, is	Is 64:11	1
the iniquities of your f together	Is 65:7	1
iniquity have your f found in me	Jer 2:5	1
for an inheritance unto your f	Jer 3:18	1
labour of our f from our youth	Jer 3:24	1
the LORD our God, we and our f	Jer 3:25	1
before this people, and the f	Jer 6:21	1
in the land that I gave to your f	Jer 7:7	1
which I gave to you and to your f	Jer 7:14	1
the f kindle the fire, and the	Jer 7:18	1
For I spake not unto your f	Jer 7:22	1
Since the day that your f came	Jer 7:25	1
they did worse than their f	Jer 7:26	1
Baalim, which their f taught them	Jer 9:14	1
they nor their f have known	Jer 9:16	1
Which I commanded your f in the	Jer 11:4	1
which I have sworn unto your f	Jer 11:5	1
f in the day that I brought them	Jer 11:7	1
which I made with their f	Jer 11:10	1
one against another, even the f	Jer 13:14	1
and the iniquity of our f	Jer 14:20	1
concerning their f that begat	Jer 16:3	1
Because your f have forsaken me,	Jer 16:11	1
And ye have done worse than your f	Jer 16:12	1
know not, neither ye nor your f	Jer 16:13	1
land that I gave unto their f	Jer 16:15	1
Surely our f have inherited lies,	Jer 16:19	1
day, as I commanded your f	Jer 17:22	1
they nor their f have known	Jer 19:4	1
as their f have forgotten my name	Jer 23:27	1
city that I gave you and your f	Jer 23:39	1
I gave unto them and to their f	Jer 24:10	1
to your f for ever and ever	Jer 25:5	1
the land that I gave to their f	Jer 30:3	1
The f have eaten a sour grape, and	Jer 31:29	1
f in the day that I took them by	Jer 31:32	1
the iniquity of the f into the	Jer 32:18	1
swear to their f to give them	Jer 32:22	1
and with the burnings of thy f	Jer 34:5	1
I made a covenant with your f in	Jer 34:13	1
but your f hearkened not unto me,	Jer 34:14	1
I have given to you and to your f	Jer 35:15	1
not, neither they, ye, nor your f	Jer 44:3	1
the wickedness of your f, and the	Jer 44:9	1
I set before you and before your f	Jer 44:10	1
as we have done, we, and our f	Jer 44:17	1
of Jerusalem, ye, and your f	Jer 44:21	1
the f shall not look back to	Jer 47:3	1
the LORD, the hope of their f	Jer 50:7	1
Our f have sinned, and are not	Lam 5:7	1
their f have transgressed against	Eze 2:3	1
Therefore the f shall eat the	Eze 5:10	1
and the sons shall eat their f	Eze 5:10	1
The f have eaten sour grapes, and	Eze 18:2	1
know the abominations of their f	Eze 20:4	1
ye not in the statutes of your f	Eze 20:18	1
Yet in this your f have	Eze 20:27	1
after the manner of your f	Eze 20:30	1
Like as I pleaded with your f in	Eze 20:36	1
up mine hand to give it to your f	Eze 20:42	1
in the land that I gave to your f	Eze 36:28	1
wherein your f have dwelt	Eze 37:25	1
mine hand to give it unto your f	Eze 47:14	1
praise thee, O thou God of my f	Dan 2:23	2
our kings, our princes, and our f	Dan 9:6	1
to our princes, and to our f	Dan 9:8	1
and for the iniquities of our f	Dan 9:16	1
do that which his f have not done	Dan 11:24	1
have not done, nor his fathers' f	Dan 11:24	1
shall he regard the God of his f	Dan 11:37	1
a god whom his f knew not shall	Dan 11:38	1
I saw your f as the firstripe in	Hos 9:10	1
or even in the days of your f	Joel 1:2	1
the which their f have walked	Amos 2:4	1
unto our f from the days of old	Mic 7:20	1
been sore displeased with your f	Zec 1:2	1
Be ye not as your f, unto whom	Zec 1:4	1
Your f, where are they	Zec 1:5	1
did they not take hold of your f	Zec 1:6	1
when your f provoked me to wrath,	Zec 8:14	1
profaning the covenant of our f	Mal 2:10	1
your f ye are gone away from mine	Mal 3:7	1
heart of the f to the children	Mal 4:6	1
heart of the children to their f	Mal 4:6	1
we had been in the days of our f	Mt 23:30	*3962*
ye up then the measure of your f	Mt 23:32	*3962*
hearts of the f to the children	Lk 1:17	*3962*
As he spake to our f, to Abraham,	Lk 1:55	*3962*
the mercy promised to our f	Lk 1:72	*3962*
did their f unto the prophets	Lk 6:23	*3962*
for so did their f to the false	Lk 6:26	*3962*
prophets, and your f killed them	Lk 11:47	*3962*
that ye allow the deeds of your f	Lk 11:48	*3962*
Our f worshipped in this mountain	Jn 4:20	*3962*
Our f did eat manna in the desert	Jn 6:31	*3962*
Your f did eat manna in the	Jn 6:49	*3962*
not as your f did eat manna, and	Jn 6:58	*3962*
it is of Moses, but of the f	Jn 7:22	*3962*
and of Jacob, the God of our f	Acts 3:13	*3962*
For Moses truly said unto the f	Acts 3:22	*3962*
which God made with our f	Acts 3:25	*3962*
The God of our f raised up Jesus,	Acts 5:30	*3962*
And he said, Men, brethren, and f	Acts 7:2	*3962*
our f found no sustenance	Acts 7:11	*3962*
in Egypt, he sent out our f first	Acts 7:12	*3962*
into Egypt, and died, he, and our f	Acts 7:15	*3962*
kindred, and evil entreated our f	Acts 7:19	*3962*
Saying, I am the God of thy f	Acts 7:32	*3962*
in the mount Sina, and with our f	Acts 7:38	*3962*
To whom our f would not obey, but	Acts 7:39	*3962*
Our f had the tabernacle of	Acts 7:44	*3962*

Which also our *f* that came after ... Acts 7:45 *3962*
out before the face of our *f* ... Acts 7:45 *3962*
as your *f* did, so do ye ... Acts 7:51 *3962*
have not your *f* persecuted ... Acts 7:52 *3962*
this people of Israel chose our *f* ... Acts 13:17 *3962*
promise which was made unto the *f* ... Acts 13:32 *3962*
on sleep, and was laid unto his *f* ... Acts 13:36 *3962*
which neither our *f* nor we were ... Acts 15:10 *3962*
Men, brethren, and *f*, hear ye my ... Acts 22:1 *3962*
manner of the law of the *f* ... Acts 22:3 *3971*
The God of our *f* hath chosen thee ... Acts 22:14 *3962*
so worship I the God of my *f* ... Acts 24:14 *3971*
promise made of God unto our *f* ... Acts 26:6 *3962*
the people, or customs of our *f* ... Acts 28:17 *3971*
by Esaias the prophet unto our *f* ... Acts 28:25 *3962*
Whose are the *f*, and of whom as ... Rom 9:5 *3962*
the promises made unto the *f* ... Rom 15:8 *3962*
in Christ, yet have ye not many *f* ... 1Cor 4:15 *3962*
how that all our *f* were under the ... 1Cor 10:1 *3962*
zealous of the traditions of my *f* ... Gal 1:14 *3967*
And, ye *f*, provoke not your ... Eph 6:4 *3962*
F, provoke not your children to ... Col 3:21 *3962*
and profane, for murderers of *f* ... 1Ti 1:9 *3964*
past unto the *f* by the prophets ... Heb 1:1 *3962*
When your *f* tempted me, proved me ... Heb 3:9 *3962*
covenant that I made with their *f* ... Heb 8:9 *3962*
Furthermore we have had *f* of our ... Heb 12:9 *3962*
received by tradition from your *f* ... 1Pet 1:18 *3970*
for since the *f* fell asleep ... 2Pet 3:4 *3962*
I write unto you, *f*, because ye ... 1Jn 2:13 *3962*
I have written unto you, *f* ... 1Jn 2:14 *3962*

FATHERS' {11}
be the heads of their *f* houses ... Ex 6:14 1
nor thy *f* fathers have seen, ... Ex 10:6 1
one, according to their *f* houses ... Num 17:6 1
upward, throughout their *f* house ... Num 26:2 1
ye are risen up in your *f* stead ... Num 32:14 1
the place of my *f* sepulchres ... Neh 2:3 1
unto the city of my *f* sepulchres ... Neh 2:5 1
eyes were after their *f* idols ... Eze 20:24 1
they discovered their *f* nakedness ... Eze 22:10 1
have not done, nor his *f* fathers ... Dan 11:24 1
they are beloved for the *f* sakes ... Rom 11:28 *3962*

FATHOMS {2}
And sounded, and found it twenty *f* ... Acts 27:28 *3712*
again, and found it fifteen *f* ... Acts 27:28 *3712*

FATLING {1}
the young lion and the *f* together ... Is 11:6 4806

FATLINGS {5}
and of the oxen, and of the *f* ... 1Sa 15:9 4932
paces, he sacrificed oxen and *f* ... 2Sa 6:13 4806
unto thee burnt sacrifices of *f* ... Ps 66:15 4220
bullocks, all of them *f* of Bashan ... Eze 39:18 4806
my *f* are killed, and all things ... Mt 22:4 *4619*

FATNESS {17}
the *f* of the earth, and plenty of ... Gen 27:28 4924
shall be the *f* of the earth ... Gen 27:39 4924
thick, thou art covered with *f* ... Deut 32:15
unto them, Should I leave my *f* ... Judg 9:9 1880
he covereth his face with his *f* ... Job 15:27 2459
on thy table should be full of *f* ... Job 36:16 1880
satisfied with the *f* of thy house ... Ps 36:8 1880
be satisfied as with marrow and *f* ... Ps 63:5 1880
and thy paths drop *f* ... Ps 65:11 1880
Their eyes stand out with *f* ... Ps 73:7 2459
and my flesh faileth of *f* ... Ps 109:24 8081
the *f* of his flesh shall wax lean ... Is 17:4 4924
with blood, it is made fat with *f* ... Is 34:6 2459
and their dust made fat with *f* ... Is 34:7 2459
let your soul delight itself in *f* ... Is 55:2 1880
the soul of the priests with *f* ... Jer 31:14 1880
the root and *f* of the olive tree ... Rom 11:17 *4096*

FATS {2}
the *f* shall overflow with wine and ... Joel 2:24 3342
the press is full, the *f* overflow ... Joel 3:13 3342

FATTED {5}
and fallowdeer, and *f* fowl ... 1Kin 4:23 75
the midst of her like *f* bullocks ... Jer 46:21 4770
And bring hither the *f* calf ... Lk 15:23 *4618*
thy father hath killed the *f* calf ... Lk 15:27 *4618*
hast killed for him the *f* calf ... Lk 15:30 *4618*

FATTER {1}
f in flesh than all the children ... Dan 1:15 1277

FATTEST {2}
upon them, and slew the *f* of them ... Ps 78:31 4924
upon the *f* places of the province ... Dan 11:24 4924

FAULT {19}
but the *f* is in thine own people ... Ex 5:16 2398
his face, according to his *f* ... Deut 25:2 7564
I have found no *f* in him since he ... 1Sa 29:3 3972
with a *f* concerning this woman ... 2Sa 3:8 5771
prepare themselves without my *f* ... Ps 59:4 5771
could find none occasion nor *f* ... Dan 6:4 7844
there any error or *f* found in him ... Dan 6:4 7844
go and tell him his *f* between thee ... Mt 18:15 *1651*
unwashen, hands, they found *f* ... Mk 7:2 *3201*
people, I find no *f* in this man ... Lk 23:4 *158*
have found no *f* in this man ... Lk 23:14 *158*
them, I find in him no *f* at all ... Jn 18:38 *156*
may know that I find no *f* in him ... Jn 19:4 *156*
for I find no *f* in him ... Jn 19:6 *156*
unto me, Why doth he yet find *f* ... Rom 9:19 *3201*
there is utterly a *f* among you ... 1Cor 6:7 *2275*
if a man be overtaken in a *f* ... Gal 6:1 *3900*

For finding *f* with them, he saith ... Heb 8:8 *3201*
for they are without *f* before the ... Rev 14:5 *299*

FAULTLESS {2}
if that first covenant had been *f* ... Heb 8:7 *278*
to present you *f* before the ... Jude 24 *299*

FAULTS {4}
I do remember my *f* this day ... Gen 41:9 2399
cleanse thou me from secret *f* ... Ps 19:12
Confess your *f* one to another, and ... Jas 5:16 *3900*
when ye be buffeted for your *f* ... 1Pet 2:20 *264*

FAULTY {2}
this thing as one which is *f* ... 2Sa 14:13 818
now shall they be found *f* ... Hos 10:2 816

FAVOUR {70}
now I have found *f* in thy sight ... Gen 18:3 2580
if I have found *f* in thine eyes ... Gen 30:27 2580
gave him *f* in the sight of the ... Gen 39:21 2580
I will give this people *f* in the ... Ex 3:21 2580
the LORD gave the people *f* in the ... Ex 11:3 2580
the LORD gave the people *f* in the ... Ex 12:36 2580
have I not found *f* in thy sight ... Num 11:11 2580
if I have found *f* in thy sight ... Num 11:15 2580
that she find no *f* in his eyes ... Deut 24:1 2580
the old, nor shew *f* to the young ... Deut 28:50 2603
O Naphtali, satisfied with *f* ... Deut 33:23 7522
and that they might have no *f* ... Josh 11:20 8467
Let me find *f* in thy sight, my ... Ruth 2:13 2580
was in *f* both with the LORD, and ... 1Sa 2:26 2896
for he hath found *f* in my sight ... 1Sa 16:22 2580
if I have found *f* in thine eyes ... 1Sa 20:29 2580
young men find *f* in thine eyes ... 1Sa 25:8 2580
nevertheless the lords *f* thee not ... 1Sa 29:6 2896
if I shall find *f* in the eyes of ... 2Sa 15:25 2580
Hadad found great *f* in the sight ... 1Kin 11:19 2580
servant have found *f* in thy sight ... Neh 2:5 3190
Esther obtained *f* in the sight of ... Est 2:15 2580
f in his sight more than all the ... Est 2:17 2617
that she obtained *f* in his sight ... Est 5:2 2580
If I have found *f* in the sight of ... Est 5:8 2580
If I have found *f* in thy sight ... Est 7:3 2580
and if I have found *f* in his sight ... Est 8:5 2580
Thou hast granted me life and *f* ... Job 10:12 2617
with *f* wilt thou compass him as ... Ps 5:12 7522
in his *f* is life ... Ps 30:5 7522
by thy *f* thou hast made my ... Ps 30:7 7522
that *f* my righteous cause ... Ps 35:27 2655
because thou hadst a *f* unto them ... Ps 44:3 7520
the people shall intreat thy *f* ... Ps 45:12 6440
in thy *f* our horn shall be ... Ps 89:17 7522
for the time to *f* her, yea, the ... Ps 102:13 2603
her stones, and *f* the dust thereof ... Ps 102:14 2603
with the *f* that thou bearest unto ... Ps 106:4 7522
any to *f* his fatherless children ... Ps 109:12 2603
A good man sheweth *f*, and lendeth ... Ps 112:5 2603
I intreated thy *f* with my whole ... Ps 119:58 6440
So shalt thou find *f* and good ... Prov 3:4 2580
and shall obtain *f* of the LORD ... Prov 8:35 7522
seeketh good procureth *f* ... Prov 11:27 7522
good man obtaineth *f* of the LORD ... Prov 12:2 7522
Good understanding giveth *f* ... Prov 13:15 2580
among the righteous there is *f* ... Prov 14:9 7522
The king's *f* is toward a wise ... Prov 14:35 7522
his *f* is as a cloud of the latter ... Prov 16:15 7522
thing, and obtaineth *f* of the LORD ... Prov 18:22 7522
will intreat the *f* of the prince ... Prov 19:6 6440
but his *f* is as dew upon the ... Prov 19:12 7522
findeth no *f* in his eyes ... Prov 21:10 2603
loving *f* rather than silver and ... Prov 22:1 2580
f than he that flattereth with ... Prov 28:23 2580
Many seek the ruler's *f* ... Prov 29:26 6440
F is deceitful, and beauty is vain ... Prov 31:30 2580
nor yet *f* to men of skill ... Eccl 9:11 2580
I in his eyes as one that found *f* ... Song 8:10 7965
Let *f* be shewed to the wicked, ... Is 26:10 2603
formed them will shew them no *f* ... Is 27:11 2603
but in my *f* have I had mercy on ... Is 60:10 7522
where I will not shew you *f* ... Jer 16:13 2594
Now God had brought Daniel into *f* ... Dan 1:9 2617
for thou hast found *f* with God ... Lk 1:30 *5485*
stature, and in *f* with God and man ... Lk 2:52 *5485*
having *f* with all the people ... Acts 2:47 *5485*
his afflictions, and gave him *f* ... Acts 7:10 *5485*
Who found *f* before God, and ... Acts 7:46 *5485*
desired *f* against him, that he ... Acts 25:3 *5485*

FAVOURABLE {4}
Be *f* unto them for our sakes ... Judg 21:22 2603
God, and he will be *f* unto him ... Job 33:26 7520
and will he be *f* no more ... Ps 77:7 7520
thou hast been *f* unto thy land ... Ps 85:1 7520

FAVOURED {14}
Rachel was beautiful and well *f* ... Gen 29:17 4758
was a goodly person, and well *f* ... Gen 39:6 4758
of the river seven well *f* kine ... Gen 41:2 4758
them out of the river, ill *f* ... Gen 41:3 4758
And the ill *f* and leanfleshed kine ... Gen 41:4 4758
kine did eat up the seven well *f* ... Gen 41:4 4758
seven kine, fatfleshed and well *f* ... Gen 41:18 8389
up after them, poor and very ill *f* ... Gen 41:19 8389
the ill *f* kine did eat up the ... Gen 41:20
but they were still ill *f* ... Gen 41:21
ill *f* kine that came up after ... Gen 41:27
priests, they *f* not the elders ... Lam 4:16 2603
whom was no blemish, but well *f* ... Dan 1:4 4758
Hail, thou that art highly *f* ... Lk 1:28 *5487*

FAVOUREST {1}
By this I know that thou *f* me ... Ps 41:11 2654

FAVOURETH {1}
by him, and said, He that *f* Joab ... 2Sa 20:11 2654

FEAR {404}
the *f* of you and the dread of you ... Gen 9:2 4172
in a vision, saying, *F* not, Abram ... Gen 15:1 3372
Surely the *f* of God is not in ... Gen 20:11 3374
f not; for God hath heard ... Gen 21:17 3372
f not, for I am with thee, and ... Gen 26:24 3372
the *f* of Isaac, had been with me, ... Gen 31:42 6343
Jacob sware by the *f* of his ... Gen 31:53 6343
for I *f* him, lest he will come and ... Gen 32:11 3373
the midwife said unto her, *F* not ... Gen 35:17 3372
for I *f* God ... Gen 42:18 3373
he said, Peace be to you, *f* not ... Gen 43:23 3372
f not to go down into Egypt ... Gen 46:3 3372
And Joseph said unto them, *F* not ... Gen 50:19 3372
Now therefore *f* ye not ... Gen 50:21 3372
ye will not yet *f* the LORD God ... Ex 9:30 3372
F ye not, stand still, and see the ... Ex 14:13 3372
F and dread shall fall upon them ... Ex 15:16 367
people able men, such as *f* God ... Ex 18:21 3373
Moses said unto the people, *F* not ... Ex 20:20 3372
that his *f* may be before your ... Ex 20:20 3374
I will send my *f* before thee ... Ex 23:27 367
Ye shall *f* every man his mother, ... Lev 19:3 3372
the blind, but shalt *f* thy God ... Lev 19:14 3372
face of the old man, and *f* thy God ... Lev 19:32 3372
but thou shalt *f* thy God ... Lev 25:17 3372
but *f* thy God ... Lev 25:36 3372
but shalt *f* thy God ... Lev 25:43 3372
neither *f* ye the people of the ... Num 14:9 3372
LORD is with us: *f* them not ... Num 14:9 3372
LORD said unto Moses, *F* him not ... Num 21:34 3372
f not, neither be discouraged ... Deut 1:21 3372
the *f* of thee upon the nations ... Deut 2:25 3374
the LORD said unto me, *F* him not ... Deut 3:2 3372
Ye shall not *f* them ... Deut 3:22 3372
that they may learn to *f* me all ... Deut 4:10 3372
in them, that they would *f* me ... Deut 5:29 3372
thou mightest *f* the LORD thy God ... Deut 6:2 3372
Thou shalt *f* the LORD thy God, and ... Deut 6:13 3372
to *f* the LORD our God, for our ... Deut 6:24 3372
to walk in his ways, and to *f* him ... Deut 8:6 3372
but to *f* the LORD thy God, to ... Deut 10:12 3372
Thou shalt *f* the LORD thy God ... Deut 10:20 3372
your God shall lay the *f* of you ... Deut 11:25 6343
f him, and keep his commandments, ... Deut 13:4 3372
And all Israel shall hear, and *f* ... Deut 13:11 3372
to *f* the LORD thy God always ... Deut 14:23 3372
all the people shall hear, and *f* ... Deut 17:13 3372
may learn to *f* the LORD his God ... Deut 17:19 3372
which remain shall hear, and *f* ... Deut 19:20 3372
f not, and do not tremble, neither ... Deut 20:3 3372
and all Israel shall hear, and *f* ... Deut 21:21 3372
that thou mayest *f* this glorious ... Deut 28:58 3372
and thou shalt *f* day and night, and ... Deut 28:66 6342
for the *f* of thine heart ... Deut 28:67 6343
heart wherewith thou shalt *f* ... Deut 28:67 6342
f not, nor be afraid of them ... Deut 31:6 3372
f not, neither be dismayed ... Deut 31:8 3372
f the LORD your God, and observe ... Deut 31:12 3372
learn to *f* the LORD your God, as ... Deut 31:13 3372
that ye might *f* the LORD your God ... Josh 4:24 3372
F not, neither be thou dismayed ... Josh 8:1 3372
LORD said unto Joshua, *F* them not ... Josh 10:8 3372
F not, nor be dismayed, be strong ... Josh 10:25 3372
done it for *f* of this thing ... Josh 22:24 1674
Now therefore *f* the LORD, and ... Josh 24:14 3372
turn in to me; *f* not ... Judg 4:18 3372
f not the gods of the Amorites, ... Judg 6:10 3372
f not: thou shalt not die ... Judg 6:23 3372
But if thou *f* to go down, go thou ... Judg 7:10 3373
for *f* of Abimelech his brother ... Judg 9:21 6440
And now, my daughter, *f* not ... Ruth 3:11 3372
stood by her said unto her, *F* not ... 1Sa 4:20 3372
the *f* of the LORD fell on the ... 1Sa 11:7 6343
If ye will *f* the LORD, and serve ... 1Sa 12:14 3372
said unto the people, *F* not ... 1Sa 12:20 3372
Only *f* the LORD, and serve him in ... 1Sa 12:24 3372
and fled that day for *f* of Saul ... 1Sa 21:10 6440
Abide thou with me, *f* not ... 1Sa 22:23 3372
And he said unto him, *F* not ... 1Sa 23:17 3372
haste to get away for *f* of Saul ... 1Sa 23:26 6440
And David said unto him, *F* not ... 2Sa 9:7 3372
then kill him, *f* not ... 2Sa 13:28 3372
be just, ruling in the *f* of God ... 2Sa 23:3 3374
That they may *f* thee all the days ... 1Kin 8:40 3372
to *f* thee, as do thy people ... 1Kin 8:43 3372
And Elijah said unto her, *F* not ... 1Kin 17:13 3372
but I thy servant *f* the LORD from ... 1Kin 18:12 3372
that thy servant did *f* the LORD ... 2Kin 4:1 3373
And he answered, *F* not ... 2Kin 6:16 3372
them how they should *f* the LORD ... 2Kin 17:28 3372
they *f* not the LORD, neither do ... 2Kin 17:34 3373
saying, Ye shall not *f* other gods ... 2Kin 17:35 3372
stretched out arm, him shall ye *f* ... 2Kin 17:36 3372
and ye shall not *f* other gods ... 2Kin 17:37 3372
neither shall ye *f* other gods ... 2Kin 17:38 3372
But the LORD your God ye shall *f* ... 2Kin 17:39 3372
F not to be the servants of the ... 2Kin 25:24 3372
the LORD brought the *f* of him ... 1Chr 14:17 6343
F before him, all the earth ... 1Chr 16:30 2342
f not, nor be dismayed ... 1Chr 28:20 3372
That they may *f* thee, to walk in ... 2Chr 6:31 3372
f thee, as doth thy people Israel ... 2Chr 6:33 3372

for the *f* of the LORD came upon ... 2Chr 14:14 6343
the *f* of the LORD fell upon all ... 2Chr 17:10 6343
Wherefore now let the *f* of the ... 2Chr 19:7 6343
shall ye do in the *f* of the LORD ... 2Chr 19:9 3374
f not, nor be dismayed ... 2Chr 20:17 3372
the *f* of God was on all the ... 2Chr 20:29 6343
for *f* was upon them because of ... Ezr 3:3 367
who desire to *f* thy name ... Neh 1:11 3372
the *f* of our God because of the ... Neh 5:9 3374
not I, because of the *f* of God ... Neh 5:15 3374
that would have put me in *f* ... Neh 6:14 3372
sent letters to put me in *f* ... Neh 6:19 3372
for the *f* of the Jews fell upon ... Est 8:17 6343
for the *f* of them fell upon all ... Est 9:2 6343
because the *f* of Mordecai fell ... Est 9:3 6343
Doth Job *f* God for nought ... Job 1:9 3372
Is not this thy *f*, thy confidence ... Job 4:6 3374
F came upon me, and trembling, ... Job 4:14 6343
forsaketh the *f* of the Almighty ... Job 6:14 3374
me, and let not his *f* terrify me ... Job 9:34 367
Then would I speak, and not *f* him ... Job 9:35 3372
shalt be stedfast, and shalt not *f* ... Job 11:15 3372
Yea, thou castest off *f*, and ... Job 15:4 3374
Their houses are safe from *f* ... Job 21:9 6343
he reprove thee for *f* of thee ... Job 22:4 3374
thee, and sudden *f* troubleth thee ... Job 22:10 6343
Dominion and *f* are with him ... Job 25:2 6343
the *f* of the LORD, that is wisdom ... Job 28:28 3374
Did I *f* a great multitude, or did ... Job 31:34 6206
Men do therefore *f* him ... Job 37:24 3372
her labour is in vain without *f* ... Job 39:16 6343
He mocketh at *f*, and is not ... Job 39:22 6343
his like, who is made without *f* ... Job 41:33 2844
Serve the LORD with *f*, and rejoice ... Ps 2:11 3374
in thy *f* will I worship toward ... Ps 5:7 3374
Put them in *f*, O LORD ... Ps 9:20 4172
There were they in great *f* ... Ps 14:5 6342
he honoureth them that *f* the LORD ... Ps 15:4 3373
The *f* of the LORD is clean, ... Ps 19:9 3374
Ye that *f* the LORD, praise him ... Ps 22:23 3373
f him, all ye the seed of Israel ... Ps 22:23 1481
my vows before them that *f* him ... Ps 22:25 3373
shadow of death, I will *f* no evil ... Ps 23:4 3372
the LORD is with them that *f* him ... Ps 25:14 3373
whom shall I *f*? ... Ps 27:1 3372
against me, my heart shall not *f* ... Ps 27:3 3372
and a *f* to mine acquaintance ... Ps 31:11 6343
f was on every side ... Ps 31:13 4032
hast laid up for them that *f* thee ... Ps 31:19 3373
Let all the earth *f* the LORD ... Ps 33:8 3372
the LORD is upon them that *f* him ... Ps 33:18 3373
round about them that *f* him ... Ps 34:7 3373
O *f* the LORD, ye his saints ... Ps 34:9 3372
is no want to them that *f* him ... Ps 34:9 3373
will teach you the *f* of the LORD ... Ps 34:11 3374
that there is no *f* of God before ... Ps 36:1 6343
many shall see it, and *f*, and shall ... Ps 40:3 3372
Therefore will not we *f*, though ... Ps 46:2 3372
F took hold upon them there, and ... Ps 48:6 7461
Wherefore should I *f* in the days ... Ps 49:5 3372
righteous also shall see, and *f* ... Ps 52:6 3372
There were they in great *f* ... Ps 53:5 6343
in great *f*, where no *f* was ... Ps 53:5 6343
changes, therefore they *f* not God ... Ps 55:19 3372
I will not *f* what flesh can do ... Ps 56:4 3372
a banner to them that *f* thee ... Ps 60:4 3373
heritage of those that *f* thy name ... Ps 61:5 3373
my life from *f* of the enemy ... Ps 64:1 6343
do they shoot at him, and *f* not ... Ps 64:4 3372
And all men shall *f*, and shall ... Ps 64:9 3372
Come and hear, all ye that *f* God ... Ps 66:16 3373
the ends of the earth shall *f* him ... Ps 67:7 3372
They shall *f* thee as long as the ... Ps 72:5 3372
salvation is nigh them that *f* him ... Ps 85:9 3373
unite my heart to *f* thy name ... Ps 86:11 3372
even according to thy *f*, so is ... Ps 90:11 3374
f before him, all the earth ... Ps 96:9 2342
shall *f* the name of the LORD ... Ps 102:15 3372
his mercy toward them that *f* him ... Ps 103:11 3373
the LORD pitieth them that *f* him ... Ps 103:13 3373
everlasting upon them that *f* him ... Ps 103:17 3373
for the *f* of them fell upon them ... Ps 105:38 6343
given meat unto them that *f* him ... Ps 111:5 3373
The *f* of the LORD is the ... Ps 111:10 3374
Ye that *f* the LORD, trust in the ... Ps 115:11 3373
will bless them that *f* the LORD ... Ps 115:13 3373
Let them now that *f* the LORD say ... Ps 118:4 3373
I will not *f* ... Ps 118:6 3372
servant, who is devoted to thy *f* ... Ps 119:38 3374
Turn away my reproach which I *f* ... Ps 119:39 3025
companion of all them that *f* thee ... Ps 119:63 3372
They that *f* thee will be glad ... Ps 119:74 3373
Let those that *f* thee turn unto ... Ps 119:79 3373
My flesh trembleth for *f* of thee ... Ps 119:120 6343
ye that *f* the LORD, bless the ... Ps 135:20 3373
the desire of them that *f* him ... Ps 145:19 3373
pleasure in them that *f* him ... Ps 147:11 3373
The *f* of the LORD is the ... Prov 1:7 3374
I will mock when your *f* cometh ... Prov 1:26 6343
When your *f* cometh as desolation, ... Prov 1:27 6343
did not choose the *f* of the LORD ... Prov 1:29 3374
and shall be quiet from *f* of evil ... Prov 1:33 6343
thou understand the *f* of the LORD ... Prov 2:5 3374
f the LORD, and depart from evil ... Prov 3:7 3372
Be not afraid of sudden *f* ... Prov 3:25 6343
The *f* of the LORD is to hate evil ... Prov 8:13 3374
The *f* of the LORD is the ... Prov 9:10 3374
The *f* of the wicked, it shall ... Prov 10:24 4034
The *f* of the LORD prolongeth days ... Prov 10:27 3374
In the *f* of the LORD is strong ... Prov 14:26 3374
The *f* of the LORD is a fountain ... Prov 14:27 3374
Better is little with the *f* of ... Prov 15:16 3374
The *f* of the LORD is the ... Prov 15:33 3374
by the *f* of the LORD men depart ... Prov 16:6 3374
The *f* of the LORD tendeth to life ... Prov 19:23 3374
The *f* of a king is as the roaring ... Prov 20:2 367
the *f* of the LORD are riches, and ... Prov 22:4 3374
but be thou in the *f* of the LORD ... Prov 23:17 3374
f thou the LORD and the king ... Prov 24:21 3372
The *f* of man bringeth a snare ... Prov 29:25 2731
it, that men should *f* before him ... Eccl 3:14 3372
but *f* thou God ... Eccl 5:7 3372
be well with them that *f* God ... Eccl 8:12 3373
that *f* God, which *f* before him ... Eccl 8:12 3372
F God, and keep his commandments ... Eccl 12:13 3372
thigh because of *f* in the night ... Song 3:8 6343
for *f* of the LORD, and for the ... Is 2:10 6343
for *f* of the LORD, and for the ... Is 2:19 6343
for *f* of the LORD, and for the ... Is 2:21 6343
f not, neither be fainthearted ... Is 7:4 3372
not come thither the *f* of briers ... Is 7:25 3374
neither *f* ye their *f*, nor be ... Is 8:12 3372
neither *f* ye their *f*, nor be ... Is 8:12 4172
and let him be your *f*, and let him ... Is 8:13 4172
knowledge and of the *f* of the LORD ... Is 11:2 3374
in the *f* of the LORD ... Is 11:3 3374
from thy sorrow, and from thy *f* ... Is 14:3 7267
f because of the shaking of the ... Is 19:16 6342
hath he turned into *f* unto me ... Is 21:4 2731
F, and the pit, and the snare, are ... Is 24:17 6343
of the *f* shall fall into the pit ... Is 24:18 6343
the terrible nations shall *f* thee ... Is 25:3 3372
their *f* toward me is taught by ... Is 29:13 3374
shall *f* the God of Israel ... Is 29:23 6206
over to his strong hold for *f* ... Is 31:9 4032
the *f* of the LORD is his treasure ... Is 33:6 3374
a fearful heart, Be strong, *f* not ... Is 35:4 3372
F thou not; for I am ... Is 41:10 3372
hand, saying unto thee, *F* not ... Is 41:13 3372
F not, thou worm Jacob, and ye men ... Is 41:14 3372
that formed thee, O Israel, *F* not ... Is 43:1 3372
F not: for I am with thee ... Is 43:5 3372
F not, O Jacob, my servant ... Is 44:2 3372
F ye not, neither be afraid ... Is 44:8 6342
yet they shall *f*, and they shall ... Is 44:11 6342
f ye not the reproach of men, ... Is 51:7 3372
F not; for thou shalt not be ashamed ... Is 54:4 3372
for thou shalt not *f* ... Is 54:14 3372
So shall they *f* the name of the ... Is 59:19 3372
together, and thine heart shall *f* ... Is 60:5 6342
and hardened our heart from thy *f* ... Is 63:17 3374
that my *f* is not in thee, saith ... Jer 2:19 6345
F ye not me? saith the LORD ... Jer 5:22 3372
Let us now *f* the LORD our God, ... Jer 5:24 3372
the enemy and *f* is on every side ... Jer 6:25 4032
Who would not *f* thee, O King of ... Jer 10:7 3372
defaming of many, *f* on every side ... Jer 20:10 4032
and they shall *f* no more, nor be ... Jer 23:4 3372
did he not *f* the LORD, and ... Jer 26:19 3373
heard a voice of trembling, of *f* ... Jer 30:5 6343
Therefore *f* thou not, O my ... Jer 30:10 3372
way, that they may *f* me for ever ... Jer 32:39 3372
I will put my *f* in their hearts ... Jer 32:40 3374
and they shall *f* and tremble for ... Jer 33:9 6342
let us go to Jerusalem for *f* of ... Jer 35:11 6440
for *f* of the army of the Syrians ... Jer 35:11 6440
Jerusalem for *f* of Pharaoh's army ... Jer 37:11 6440
F not to serve the Chaldeans ... Jer 40:9 3372
for *f* of Baasha king of Israel ... Jer 41:9 6440
for *f* was round about, saith the ... Jer 46:5 4032
But *f* not thou, O my servant ... Jer 46:27 3372
F thou not, O Jacob my servant, ... Jer 46:28 3372
F, and the pit, and the snare, ... Jer 48:43 6343
the *f* shall fall into the pit ... Jer 48:44 6343
I will bring a *f* upon thee ... Jer 49:5 6343
to flee, and *f* hath seized on her ... Jer 49:24 7374
cry unto them, *F* is on every side ... Jer 49:29 4032
for *f* of the oppressing sword ... Jer 50:16 6440
ye *f* for the rumour that shall be ... Jer 51:46 3372
F and a snare is come upon us, ... Lam 3:47 6343
thou saidst, *F* not ... Lam 3:57 3372
f them not, neither be dismayed ... Eze 3:9 3372
I will put a *f* in the land of ... Eze 30:13 3374
I *f* my lord the king, who hath ... Dan 1:10 3373
f before the God of Daniel ... Dan 6:26 1763
said he unto me, *F* not, Daniel ... Dan 10:12 3372
O man greatly beloved, *f* not ... Dan 10:19 3372
shall *f* the LORD and his goodness ... Hos 3:5 6342
shall *f* because of the calves of ... Hos 10:5 1481
F not, O land ... Joel 2:21 3372
lion hath roared, who will not *f* ... Amos 3:8 3372
I *f* the LORD, the God of heaven, ... Jonah 1:9 3373
God, and shall *f* because of thee ... Mic 7:17 3372
I said, Surely thou wilt *f* me ... Zeph 3:7 3372
be said to Jerusalem, *F* thou not ... Zeph 3:16 3372
the people did *f* before the LORD ... Hag 1:12 3372
remaineth among you: *f* ye not ... Hag 2:5 3372
f not, but let your hands be ... Zec 8:13 3372
to the house of Judah: *f* ye not ... Zec 8:15 3372
Ashkelon shall see it, and *f* ... Zec 9:5 3372
if I be a master, where is my *f* ... Mal 1:6 4172
for the *f* wherewith he feared me ... Mal 2:5 4172
f not me, saith the LORD of hosts ... Mal 3:5 3372
But unto you that *f* my name shall ... Mal 4:2 3373
f not to take unto thee Mary thy ... Mt 1:20 5399
F them not therefore ... Mt 10:26 5399
f not them which kill the body, ... Mt 10:28 5399
but rather *f* him which is able to ... Mt 10:28 5399
F ye not therefore, ye are of ... Mt 10:31 5399
and they cried out for *f* ... Mt 14:26 5401
we *f* the people ... Mt 21:26 5399
for *f* of him the keepers did ... Mt 28:4 5401
and said unto the women, *F* not ye ... Mt 28:5 5399
quickly from the sepulchre with *f* ... Mt 28:8 5401
was troubled, and *f* fell upon him ... Lk 1:12 5401
said unto him, *F* not, Zacharias ... Lk 1:13 5399
angel said unto her, *F* not, Mary ... Lk 1:30 5399
that *f* him from generation to ... Lk 1:50 5399
f came on all that dwelt round ... Lk 1:65 5401
enemies might serve him without *f* ... Lk 1:74 870
the angel said unto them, *F* not ... Lk 2:10 5399
And Jesus said unto Simon, *F* not ... Lk 5:10 5399
God, and were filled with *f* ... Lk 5:26 5401
And there came a *f* on all ... Lk 7:16 5401
for they were taken with great *f* ... Lk 8:37 5401
he answered him, saying, *F* not ... Lk 8:50 5399
will forewarn you whom ye shall *f* ... Lk 12:5 5399
F him, which after he hath killed ... Lk 12:5 5399
yea, I say unto you, *F* him ... Lk 12:5 5399
F not therefore ... Lk 12:7 5399
F not, little flock ... Lk 12:32 5399
himself, Though I *f* not God ... Lk 18:4 5399
Men's hearts failing them for *f* ... Lk 21:26 5401
him, saying, Dost not thou *f* God ... Lk 23:40 5399
openly of him for *f* of the Jews ... Jn 7:13 5401
F not, daughter of Sion ... Jn 12:15 5399
but secretly for *f* of the Jews ... Jn 19:38 5401
were assembled for *f* of the Jews ... Jn 20:19 5401
And *f* came upon every soul ... Acts 2:43 5401
great *f* came on all them that ... Acts 5:5 5401
great *f* came upon all the church, ... Acts 5:11 5401
and walking in the *f* of the Lord ... Acts 9:31 5401
Men of Israel, and ye that *f* God ... Acts 13:16 5399
f fell on them all, and the name ... Acts 19:17 5401
Saying, *F* not, Paul ... Acts 27:24 5399
There is no *f* of God before their ... Rom 3:18 5401
the spirit of bondage again to *f* ... Rom 8:15 5401
Be not highminded, but *f* ... Rom 11:20 5399
to whom custom; *f* to whom ... Rom 13:7 5401
to whom *f*; honour to whom ... Rom 13:7 5401
was with you in weakness, and in *f* ... 1Cor 2:3 5401
that he may be with you without *f* ... 1Cor 16:10 820
holiness in the *f* of God ... 2Cor 7:1 5401
what indignation, yea, what *f* ... 2Cor 7:11 5401
obedience of you all, how with *f* ... 2Cor 7:15 5401
But I *f*, lest by any means, as ... 2Cor 11:3 5399
For I *f*, lest, when I come, I ... 2Cor 12:20 5399
one to another in the *f* of God ... Eph 5:21 5401
according to the flesh, with *f* ... Eph 6:5 5401
bold to speak the word without *f* ... Phil 1:14 870
out your own salvation with *f* ... Phil 2:12 5401,2192
all, that others also may *f* ... 1Ti 5:20 5401
hath not given us the spirit of *f* ... 2Ti 1:7 1167
through *f* of death were all their ... Heb 2:15 5401
Let us therefore *f*, lest, a ... Heb 4:1 5399
not seen as yet, moved with *f* ... Heb 11:7 2125
that Moses said, I exceedingly *f* ... Heb 12:21 1630,1510
with reverence and godly *f* ... Heb 12:28 2124
I will not *f* what man shall do ... Heb 13:6 5399
time of your sojourning here in *f* ... 1Pet 1:17 5401
F God. Honour the king ... 1Pet 2:17 5399
to your masters with all *f* ... 1Pet 2:18 5401
conversation coupled with *f* ... 1Pet 3:2 5401
that is in you with meekness and *f* ... 1Pet 3:15 5401
There is no *f* in love ... 1Jn 4:18 5401
but perfect love casteth out *f* ... 1Jn 4:18 5401
because *f* hath torment ... 1Jn 4:18 5401
you, feeding themselves without *f* ... Jude 12 870
And others save with *f*, pulling ... Jude 23 5401
upon me, saying unto me, *F* not ... Rev 1:17 5399
F none of those things which thou ... Rev 2:10 5399
great *f* fell upon them which saw ... Rev 11:11 5401
saints, and them that *f* thy name ... Rev 11:18 5399
F God, and give glory to him ... Rev 14:7 5399
Who shall not *f* thee, O Lord, and ... Rev 15:4 5399
afar off for the *f* of her torment ... Rev 18:10 5401
afar off for the *f* of her torment ... Rev 18:15 5401
ye his servants, and ye that *f* him ... Rev 19:5 5399

FEARED {74}

for he *f* to dwell in Zoar ... Gen 19:30 3372
for he *f* to say, She is my wife ... Gen 26:7 3372
But the midwives *f* God, and did ... Ex 1:17 3372
pass, because the midwives *f* God ... Ex 1:21 3372
And Moses *f*, and said, Surely this ... Ex 2:14 3372
He that *f* the word of the LORD ... Ex 9:20 3373
and the people *f* the LORD, and ... Ex 14:31 3372
and he *f* not God ... Deut 25:18 3373
newly up, whom your fathers *f* not ... Deut 32:17 8175
Were it not that I *f* the wrath of ... Deut 32:27 1481
and they *f* him, as they *f* ... Josh 4:14 3372
That they *f* greatly, because ... Josh 10:2 3372
because he *f* his father's ... Judg 6:27 3372
for he *f*, because he was yet a ... Judg 8:20 3372
Samuel *f* to shew Eli the vision ... 1Sa 3:15 3372
all the people greatly *f* the LORD ... 1Sa 12:18 3372
for the people *f* the oath ... 1Sa 14:26 3372
because I *f* the people, and obeyed ... 1Sa 15:24 3372
a word again, because he *f* him ... 2Sa 3:11 3372
So the Syrians *f* to help the ... 2Sa 10:19 3372
the servants of David *f* to tell ... 2Sa 12:18 3372
Adonijah *f* because of Solomon, and ... 1Kin 1:50 3372
and they *f* the king ... 1Kin 3:28 3372
(Now Obadiah *f* the LORD greatly ... 1Kin 18:3 3373

of Egypt, and had *f* other gods, ... 2Kin 17:7 3372
there, that they *f* not the LORD ... 2Kin 17:25 3372
So they *f* the LORD, and made unto ... 2Kin 17:32 3373
They *f* the LORD, and served their ... 2Kin 17:33 3373
So these nations *f* the LORD ... 2Kin 17:41 3373
he also is to be *f* above all gods ... 1Chr 16:25 3372
And Jehoshaphat *f*, and set himself ... 2Chr 20:3 3372
faithful man, and *f* God above many ... Neh 7:2 3372
and upright, and one that *f* God ... Job 1:1 3373
which I greatly *f* is come upon me ... Job 3:25 6342
Thou, even thou, art to be *f* ... Ps 76:7 3372
the earth *f*, and was still, ... Ps 76:8 3372
unto him that ought to be *f* ... Ps 76:11 4172
on safely, so that they *f* not ... Ps 78:53 6342
God is greatly to be *f* in the ... Ps 89:7 6206
he is to be *f* above all gods ... Ps 96:4 3372
with thee, that thou mayest be *f* ... Ps 130:4 3372
The isles saw it, and *f* ... Is 41:5 3372
hast *f* continually every day ... Is 51:13 6342
whom hast thou been afraid or *f* ... Is 57:11 3372
treacherous sister Judah *f* not ... Jer 3:8 3372
pass, that the sword, which ye *f* ... Jer 42:16 3373
this day, neither have they *f* ... Jer 44:10 3372
Ye have *f* the sword ... Eze 11:8 3372
trembled and *f* before him ... Dan 5:19 1763
because we *f* not the LORD ... Hos 10:3 3372
Then the men *f* the LORD ... Jonah 1:16 3372
for the fear wherewith he *f* me ... Mal 2:5 3372
Then they that *f* the LORD spake ... Mal 3:16 3372
him for them that *f* the LORD ... Mal 3:16 3372
he *f* the multitude, because they ... Mt 14:5 *5399*
they *f* the multitude, because ... Mt 21:46 *5399*
they *f* greatly, saying, Truly ... Mt 27:54 *5399*
they *f* exceedingly, and said one ... Mk 4:41 *5399,5401*
For Herod *f* John, knowing that he ... Mk 6:20 *5399*
for they *f* him, because all the ... Mk 11:18 *5399*
they *f* the people ... Mk 11:32 *5399*
lay hold on him, but *f* the people ... Mk 12:12 *5399*
they *f* as they entered into the ... Lk 9:34 *5399*
they *f* to ask him of that saying ... Lk 9:45 *5399*
which *f* not God, neither regarded ... Lk 18:2 *5399*
For I *f* thee, because thou art an ... Lk 19:21 *5399*
and they *f* the people ... Lk 20:19 *5399*
for they *f* the people ... Lk 22:2 *5399*
parents, because they *f* the Jews ... Jn 9:22 *5399*
for they *f* the people, lest they ... Acts 5:26 *5399*
one that *f* God with all his house ... Acts 10:2 *5399*
and they *f*, when they heard that ... Acts 16:38 *5399*
death, and was heard in that he *f* ... Heb 5:7 *2124*

FEAREST {3}
for now I know that thou *f* God ... Gen 22:12 3373
even of old, and thou *f* me not ... Is 57:11 3372
hand of them whose face thou *f* ... Jer 22:25 1481

FEARETH {20}
Behold, Adonijah *f* king Solomon ... 1Kin 1:51 3372
and an upright man, one that *f* God ... Job 1:8 3373
and an upright man, one that *f* God ... Job 2:3 3373
What man is he that *f* the LORD ... Ps 25:12 3373
is the man that *f* the LORD ... Ps 112:1 3372
is every one that *f* the Lord ... Ps 128:1 3373
man be blessed that *f* the LORD ... Ps 128:4 3373
but he that *f* the commandment ... Prov 13:13 3373
in his uprightness *f* the LORD ... Prov 14:2 3373
A wise man *f*, and departeth from ... Prov 14:16 3373
Happy is the man that *f* alway ... Prov 28:14 6342
but a woman that *f* the LORD ... Prov 31:30 3373
for he that *f* God shall come ... Eccl 7:18 3373
because he *f* not before God ... Eccl 8:13 3373
sweareth, as he that *f* an oath ... Eccl 9:2 3373
Who is among you that *f* the LORD ... Is 50:10 3373
a just man, and one that *f* God ... Acts 10:22 *5399*
But in every nation he that *f* him ... Acts 10:35 *5399*
and whosoever among you *f* God ... Acts 13:26 *5399*
He that *f* is not made perfect in ... 1Jn 4:18 *5399*

FEARFUL {11}
f in praises, doing wonders ... Ex 15:11 3372
say, What man is there that is *f* ... Deut 20:8 3373
and *f* name, THE LORD THY GOD ... Deut 28:58 3372
people, saying, Whosoever is *f* ... Judg 7:3 3373
Say to them that are of a *f* heart ... Is 35:4 4116
he saith unto them, Why are ye *f* ... Mt 8:26 *1169*
said unto them, Why are ye so *f* ... Mk 4:40 *1169*
f sights and great signs shall ... Lk 21:11 *5400*
But a certain *f* looking for of ... Heb 10:27 *5398*
It is a *f* thing to fall into the ... Heb 10:31 *5398*
But the *f*, and unbelieving, and the ... Rev 21:8 *1169*

FEARFULLY {1}
for I am *f* and wonderfully made ... Ps 139:14 3372

FEARFULNESS {3}
F and trembling are come upon me, ... Ps 55:5 3374
My heart panted, *f* affrighted me ... Is 21:4 6427
f hath surprised the hypocrites ... Is 33:14 7461

FEARING {8}
children cease from *f* the LORD ... Josh 22:25 3372
But the woman *f* and trembling, ... Mk 5:33 *5399*
f lest Paul should have been ... Acts 23:10 *2125*
f lest they should fall into the ... Acts 27:17 *5399*
Then *f* lest we should have fallen ... Acts 27:29 *5399*
himself, *f* them which were of the ... Gal 2:12 *5399*
but in singleness of heart, *f* God ... Col 3:22 *5399*
not *f* the wrath of the king ... Heb 11:27 *5399*

FEARS {4}
me, and delivered me from all my *f* ... Ps 34:4 4035
f shall be in the way, and the ... Eccl 12:5 2849
and will bring their *f* upon them ... Is 66:4 4035
were fightings, within were *f* ... 2Cor 7:5 *5401*

FEAST {123}
and he made them a *f*, and did bake ... Gen 19:3 4960
Abraham made a great *f* the same ... Gen 21:8 4960
And he made them a *f*, and they did ... Gen 26:30 4960
the men of the place, and made a *f* ... Gen 29:22 4960
that he made a *f* unto all his ... Gen 40:20 4960
that they may hold a *f* unto me in ... Ex 5:1 2287
we must hold a *f* unto the LORD ... Ex 10:9 2282
ye shall keep it a *f* to the LORD ... Ex 12:14 2282
ye shall keep it a *f* by an ... Ex 12:14 2287
observe the *f* of unleavened bread ... Ex 12:17
day shall be a *f* to the LORD ... Ex 13:6 2282
keep a *f* unto me in the year ... Ex 23:14 2287
keep the *f* of unleavened bread ... Ex 23:15 2282
the *f* of harvest, the firstfruits ... Ex 23:16 2282
the *f* of ingathering, which is in ... Ex 23:16 2282
To morrow is a *f* to the LORD ... Ex 32:5 2282
The *f* of unleavened bread shalt ... Ex 34:18 2282
thou shalt observe the *f* of weeks ... Ex 34:22 2282
the *f* of ingathering at the ... Ex 34:22 2282
shall the sacrifice of the *f* of ... Ex 34:25 2282
f of unleavened bread unto the ... Lev 23:6 2282
f of tabernacles for seven days ... Lev 23:34 2282
ye shall keep a *f* unto the LORD ... Lev 23:39 2282
ye shall keep it a *f* unto the ... Lev 23:41 2282
day of this month is the *f* ... Num 28:17 2282
ye shall keep a *f* unto the LORD ... Num 29:12 2282
thou shalt keep the *f* of weeks ... Deut 16:10 2282
Thou shalt observe the *f* of ... Deut 16:13 2282
And thou shalt rejoice in thy *f* ... Deut 16:14 2282
f unto the LORD thy God in the ... Deut 16:15 2287
in the *f* of unleavened bread, and ... Deut 16:16 2282
bread, and in the *f* of weeks ... Deut 16:16 2282
and in the *f* of tabernacles ... Deut 16:16 2282
release, in the *f* of tabernacles, ... Deut 31:10 2282
and Samson made there a *f* ... Judg 14:10 4960
me within the seven days of the *f* ... Judg 14:12 4960
seven days, while their *f* lasted ... Judg 14:17 4960
there is a *f* of the LORD in ... Judg 21:19 2282
he held a *f* in his house, like ... 1Sa 25:36 4960
his house, like the *f* of a king ... 1Sa 25:36 4960
and the men that were with him a *f* ... 2Sa 3:20 4960
made a *f* to all his servants ... 1Kin 3:15 4960
at the *f* in the month Ethanim ... 1Kin 8:2 2282
And at that time Solomon held a *f* ... 1Kin 8:65 2282
ordained a *f* in the eighth month ... 1Kin 12:32 2282
like unto the *f* that is in Judah, ... 1Kin 12:32 2282
ordained a *f* unto the children of ... 1Kin 12:33 2282
f which was in the seventh month ... 2Chr 5:3 2282
Solomon kept the *f* seven days ... 2Chr 7:8 2282
seven days, and the *f* seven days ... 2Chr 7:9 2282
even in the *f* of unleavened bread ... 2Chr 8:13 2282
bread, and in the *f* of weeks ... 2Chr 8:13 2282
and in the *f* of tabernacles ... 2Chr 8:13 2282
much people to keep the *f* of ... 2Chr 30:13 2282
present at Jerusalem kept the *f* ... 2Chr 30:21 2282
eat throughout the *f* seven days ... 2Chr 30:22 4150
the *f* of unleavened bread seven ... 2Chr 35:17 2282
kept also the *f* of tabernacles ... Ezr 3:4 2282
kept the *f* of unleavened bread ... Ezr 6:22 2282
in the *f* of the seventh month ... Neh 8:14 2282
And they kept the *f* seven days ... Neh 8:18 2282
he made a *f* unto all his princes ... Est 1:3 4960
the king made a *f* unto all the ... Est 1:5 4960
a *f* for the women in the royal ... Est 1:9 4960
a great *f* unto all his princes ... Est 2:18 4960
and his servants, even Esther's *f* ... Est 2:18 4960
the Jews had joy and gladness, a *f* ... Est 8:17 4960
appointed, on our solemn *f* day ... Ps 81:3 2282
a merry heart hath a continual *f* ... Prov 15:15 4960
A *f* is made for laughter, and wine ... Eccl 10:19 3899
unto all people a *f* of fat things ... Is 25:6 4960
a *f* of wines on the lees, of fat ... Is 25:6 4960
LORD, as in the day of a solemn *f* ... Lam 2:7 4150
the passover, a *f* of seven days ... Eze 45:21 2282
seven days of the *f* he shall ... Eze 45:23 2282
like in the *f* of the seven days ... Eze 45:25 2282
the king made a great *f* to a ... Dan 5:1 3900
her *f* days, her new moons, and her ... Hos 2:11 2282
in the day of the *f* of the LORD ... Hos 9:5 2282
as in the days of the solemn *f* ... Hos 12:9 4150
I hate, I despise your *f* days ... Amos 5:21 2282
to keep the *f* of tabernacles ... Zec 14:16 2282
up to keep the *f* of tabernacles ... Zec 14:18 2282
up to keep the *f* of tabernacles ... Zec 14:19 2282
two days is the *f* of the passover ... Mt 26:2
But they said, Not on the *f* day ... Mt 26:5 *1859*
of the *f* of unleavened bread the ... Mt 26:17
Now at that *f* the governor was ... Mt 27:15 *1859*
days was the *f* of the passover ... Mk 14:1
But they said, Not on the *f* day ... Mk 14:2 *1859*
Now at that *f* he released unto ... Mk 15:6 *1859*
year at the *f* of the passover ... Lk 2:41 *1859*
after the custom of the *f* ... Lk 2:42 *1859*
him a great *f* in his own house ... Lk 5:29 *1408*
But when thou makest a *f*, call ... Lk 14:13 *1408*
Now the *f* of unleavened bread ... Lk 22:1 *1859*
release one unto them at the *f* ... Lk 23:17 *1859*
bear unto the governor of the *f* ... Jn 2:8 *755*
When the ruler of the *f* had ... Jn 2:9 *755*
the governor of the *f* called the ... Jn 2:9 *755*
at the passover, in the *f* day ... Jn 2:23 *1859*
that he did at Jerusalem at the *f* ... Jn 4:45 *1859*
for they also went unto the *f* ... Jn 4:45 *1859*
this there was a *f* of the Jews ... Jn 5:1 *1859*
a *f* of the Jews, was nigh ... Jn 6:4 *1859*
Now the Jews' *f* of tabernacles ... Jn 7:2 *1859*
Go ye up unto this *f* ... Jn 7:8 *1859*
I go not up yet unto this *f* ... Jn 7:8 *1859*
then went he also up unto the *f* ... Jn 7:10 *1859*
Then the Jews sought him at the *f* ... Jn 7:11 *1859*
Now about the midst of the *f* ... Jn 7:14 *1859*
last day, that great day of the *f* ... Jn 7:37 *1859*
Jerusalem the *f* of the dedication ... Jn 10:22 *1456*
that he will not come to the *f* ... Jn 11:56 *1859*
people that were come to the *f* ... Jn 12:12 *1859*
that came up to worship at the *f* ... Jn 12:20 *1859*
Now before the *f* of the passover, ... Jn 13:1 *1859*
we have need of against the *f* ... Jn 13:29 *1859*
this *f* that cometh in Jerusalem ... Acts 18:21 *1859*
Therefore let us keep the *f* ... 1Cor 5:8 *1858*
that believe not bid you to a *f* ... 1Cor 10:27
deceivings while they *f* with you ... 2Pet 2:13 *4910*
of charity, when they *f* with you ... Jude 12 *4910*

FEASTED {1}
f in their houses, every one his ... Job 1:4 6213,4960

FEASTING {7}
they, and made it a day of *f* ... Est 9:17 4960
rested, and made it a day of *f* ... Est 9:18 4960
month Adar a day of gladness and *f* ... Est 9:19 4960
they should make them days of *f* ... Est 9:22 4960
days of their *f* were gone about ... Job 1:5 4960
than to go to the house of *f* ... Eccl 7:2 4960
not also go into the house of *f* ... Jer 16:8 4960

FEASTS {32}
Concerning the *f* of the LORD ... Lev 23:2 4150
convocations, even these are my *f* ... Lev 23:2 4150
These are the *f* of the LORD ... Lev 23:4 4150
These are the *f* of the LORD ... Lev 23:37 4150
of Israel the *f* of the LORD ... Lev 23:44 4150
offering, or in your solemn *f* ... Num 15:3 4150
do unto the LORD in your set *f* ... Num 29:39 4150
in the new moons, and on the set *f* ... 1Chr 23:31 4150
on the solemn *f* of the LORD our ... 2Chr 2:4 4150
the new moons, and on the solemn *f* ... 2Chr 8:13 4150
the new moons, and for the set *f* ... 2Chr 31:3 4150
of all the set *f* of the LORD that ... Ezr 3:5 4150
of the new moons, for the set *f* ... Neh 10:33 4150
With hypocritical mockers in *f* ... Ps 35:16 4580
your appointed *f* my soul hateth ... Is 1:14
and pipe, and wine, are in their *f* ... Is 5:12 4960
In their heat I will make their *f* ... Jer 51:39 4960
because none come to the solemn *f* ... Lam 1:4 4150
the LORD hath caused the solemn *f* ... Lam 2:6 4150
of Jerusalem in her solemn *f* ... Eze 36:38 4150
and drink offerings, in the *f* ... Eze 45:17 2282
before the LORD in the solemn *f* ... Eze 46:9 4150
And in the *f* and in the solemnities ... Eze 46:11 2282
her sabbaths, and all her solemn *f* ... Hos 2:11 4150
I will turn your *f* into mourning ... Amos 8:10 2282
O Judah, keep thy solemn *f* ... Nah 1:15 2282
joy and gladness, and cheerful *f* ... Zec 8:19 4150
even the dung of your solemn *f* ... Mal 2:3 2282
And love the uppermost rooms at *f* ... Mt 23:6 *1173*
and the uppermost rooms at *f* ... Mk 12:39 *1173*
and the chief rooms at *f* ... Lk 20:46 *1173*
are spots in your *f* of charity ... Jude 12

FEATHERED {2}
f fowls like as the sand of the ... Ps 78:27 3671
Speak unto every *f* fowl, and to ... Eze 39:17 3671

FEATHERS {7}
pluck away his crop with his *f* ... Lev 1:16 5133
or wings and *f* unto the ostrich ... Job 39:13 2624
silver, and her *f* with yellow gold ... Ps 68:13 84
He shall cover thee with his *f* ... Ps 91:4 84
wings, longwinged, full of *f* ... Eze 17:3 5133
eagle with great wings and many *f* ... Eze 17:7 5133
hairs were grown like eagles' *f* ... Dan 4:33

FED {31}
Jacob *f* the rest of Laban's ... Gen 30:36 7462
as he *f* the asses of Zibeon his ... Gen 36:24 7462
and they *f* in a meadow ... Gen 41:2 7462
and they *f* in a meadow ... Gen 41:18 7462
he *f* them with bread for all ... Gen 47:17 5095
the God which *f* me all my life ... Gen 48:15 7462
I have *f* you in the wilderness ... Ex 16:32 398
f thee with manna, which thou ... Deut 8:3 398
Who *f* thee in the wilderness with ... Deut 8:16 398
f them, but went not in unto them ... 2Sa 20:3 3557
f them with bread and water ... 1Kin 18:4 3557
f them with bread and water ... 1Kin 18:13 3557
over the herds that *f* in Sharon ... 1Chr 27:29 7462
land, and verily thou shalt be *f* ... Ps 37:3 7462
So he *f* them according to the ... Ps 78:72 7462
He should have *f* them also with ... Ps 81:16 398
of rams, and the fat of *f* beasts ... Is 1:11 4806
when I had *f* them to the full, ... Jer 5:7
They were as *f* horses in the ... Jer 5:8 2109
oil, and honey, wherewith I *f* thee ... Eze 16:19 398
the wool, ye kill them that are *f* ... Eze 34:3 1277
f themselves, and *f* not my flock ... Eze 34:8 7462
thereof, and all flesh was *f* of it ... Dan 4:12 2110
they *f* him with grass like oxen, ... Dan 5:21 2939
and I *f* the flock ... Zec 11:7 7462
saw we thee an hungred, and *f* thee ... Mt 25:37 *5142*
they that *f* the swine fled, and ... Mk 5:14 *1006*
When they that *f* them saw what ... Lk 8:34 *1006*
desiring to be *f* with the crumbs ... Lk 16:21 *5526*
I have *f* you with milk, and not ... 1Cor 3:2 *4222*

FEEBLE {20}
But when the cattle were *f* ... Gen 30:42 5848
even all that were *f* behind thee ... Deut 25:18 2826
hath many children is waxed *f* ... 1Sa 2:5 535
dead in Hebron, his hands were *f* ... 2Sa 4:1 7503
carried all the *f* of them upon ... 2Chr 28:15 3782
and said, What do these *f* Jews ... Neh 4:2 537
hast strengthened the *f* knees ... Job 4:4 3766
I am *f* and sore broken ... Ps 38:8 6313
there was not one *f* person among ... Ps 105:37 3782
The conies are but a *f* folk ... Prov 30:26 3808,6099
remnant shall be very small and *f* ... Is 16:14 3808,3524
hands, and confirm the *f* knees ... Is 35:3 3782
our hands wax *f* ... Jer 6:24 7503
Damascus is waxed *f*, and turneth ... Jer 49:24 7503
of them, and his hands waxed *f* ... Jer 50:43 7503
All hands shall be *f*, and all ... Eze 7:17 7503
melt, and all hands shall be *f* ... Eze 21:7 7503
he that is *f* among them at that ... Zec 12:8 3782
the body, which seem to be more *f* ... 1Cor 12:22 *772*
which hang down, and the *f* knees ... Heb 12:12 *3886*

FEEBLEMINDED {1}
that are unruly, comfort the *f* ... 1Th 5:14 *3642*

FEEBLENESS {1}
to their children for *f* of hands ... Jer 47:3 7510

FEEBLER {1}
so the *f* were Laban's, and the ... Gen 30:42 5848

FEED {81}
F me, I pray thee, with that same ... Gen 25:30 3938
ye the sheep, and go and *f* them ... Gen 29:7 7462
this thing for me, I will again *f* ... Gen 30:31 7462
his brethren went to *f* their ... Gen 37:12 7462
Do not thy brethren *f* the flock ... Gen 37:13 7462
where they *f* their flocks ... Gen 37:16 7462
their trade hath been to *f* cattle ... Gen 46:32
shall *f* in another man's field ... Ex 22:5 1197
nor herds *f* before that mount ... Ex 34:3 7462
Saul to *f* his father's sheep at ... 1Sa 17:15 7462
Thou shalt *f* my people Israel, and ... 2Sa 5:2 7462
I commanded to *f* my people Israel ... 2Sa 7:7 7462
me, and I will *f* thee with me in ... 2Sa 19:33 3557
the ravens to *f* thee there ... 1Kin 17:4 3557
f him with bread of affliction and ... 1Kin 22:27 398
Thou shalt *f* my people Israel, and ... 1Chr 11:2 7462
whom I commanded to *f* my people ... 1Chr 17:6 7462
f him with bread of affliction and ... 2Chr 18:26 398
take away flocks, and *f* thereof ... Job 24:2 7462
the worm shall *f* sweetly on him ... Job 24:20
f them also, and lift them up for ... Ps 28:9 7462
death shall *f* on them ... Ps 49:14 7462
brought him to *f* Jacob his people ... Ps 78:71 7462
The lips of the righteous *f* many ... Prov 10:21 7462
f me with food convenient for me ... Prov 30:8 2963
f thy kids beside the shepherds' ... Song 1:8 7462
twins, which *f* among the lilies ... Song 4:5 7462
to *f* in the gardens, and to gather ... Song 6:2 7462
the lambs *f* after their manner ... Is 5:17 7462
And the cow and the bear shall *f* ... Is 11:7 7462
the firstborn of the poor shall *f* ... Is 14:30 7462
there shall the calf *f*, and there ... Is 27:10 7462
thy cattle *f* in large pastures ... Is 30:23 7462
He shall *f* his flock like a ... Is 40:11 7462
They shall *f* in the ways, and ... Is 49:9 7462
I will *f* them that oppress thee ... Is 49:26 398
f thee with the heritage of Jacob ... Is 58:14 398
f your flocks, and the sons of the ... Is 61:5 7462
wolf and the lamb shall *f* together ... Is 65:25 7462
which shall *f* you with knowledge ... Jer 3:15 7462
they shall *f* every one in his ... Jer 6:3 7462
Behold, I will *f* them, even this ... Jer 9:15 398
the pastors that *f* my people ... Jer 23:2 7462
over them which shall *f* them ... Jer 23:4 7462
I will *f* them with wormwood, and ... Jer 23:15 398
he shall *f* on Carmel and Bashan, ... Jer 50:19 7462
They that did *f* delicately are ... Lam 4:5 398
of Israel that do *f* themselves ... Eze 34:2 7462
not the shepherds *f* the flocks ... Eze 34:2 7462
but ye *f* not the flock ... Eze 34:3 7462
shepherds *f* themselves any more ... Eze 34:10 7462
f them upon the mountains of ... Eze 34:13 7462
I will *f* them in a good pasture, ... Eze 34:14 7462
in a fat pasture shall they *f* ... Eze 34:14 7462
I will *f* my flock, and I will ... Eze 34:15 7462
I will *f* them with judgment ... Eze 34:16 7462
over them, and he shall *f* them ... Eze 34:23 7462
he shall *f* them, and he shall be ... Eze 34:23 7462
they that *f* of the portion of his ... Dan 11:26 398
now the LORD will *f* them as a ... Hos 4:16 7462
and the winepress shall not *f* them ... Hos 9:2 7462
let them not *f*, nor drink water ... Jonah 3:7 7462
f in the strength of the LORD, in ... Mic 5:4 7462
F thy people with thy rod, the ... Mic 7:14 7462
let them *f* in Bashan and Gilead, ... Mic 7:14 7462
they shall *f* thereupon ... Zeph 2:7 7462
for they shall *f* and lie down, and ... Zeph 3:13 7462
F the flock of the slaughter ... Zec 11:4 7462
I will *f* the flock of slaughter, ... Zec 11:7 7462
Then said I, I will not *f* you ... Zec 11:9 7462
nor *f* that that standeth still ... Zec 11:16 3557
him into his fields to *f* swine ... Lk 15:15 *1006*
He saith unto him, *F* my lambs ... Jn 21:15 *1006*
He saith unto him, *F* my sheep ... Jn 21:16 *4165*
Jesus saith unto him, *F* my sheep ... Jn 21:17 *1006*
to *f* the church of God, which he ... Acts 20:28 *4165*
if thine enemy hunger, *f* him ... Rom 12:20 *5595*
bestow all my goods to *f* the poor ... 1Cor 13:3 *5595*
F the flock of God which is among ... 1Pet 5:2 *4165*
midst of the throne shall *f* them ... Rev 7:17 *4165*
that they should *f* her there a ... Rev 12:6 *5142*

FEEDEST {2}
Thou *f* them with the bread of ... Ps 80:5 398
whom my soul loveth, where thou *f* ... Song 1:7 7462

FEEDETH {8}
mouth of fools *f* on foolishness ... Prov 15:14 7462
he *f* among the lilies ... Song 2:16 7462
he *f* among the lilies ... Song 6:3 7462
He *f* on ashes ... Is 44:20 7462
Ephraim *f* on wind, and followeth ... Hos 12:1 7462
yet your heavenly Father *f* them ... Mt 6:26 *5142*
and God *f* them ... Lk 12:24 *5142*
or who *f* a flock, and eateth not ... 1Cor 9:7 *4165*

FEEDING {9}
was *f* the flock with his brethren ... Gen 37:2 7462
and the asses *f* beside them ... Job 1:14 7462
them to cease from *f* the flock ... Eze 34:10 7462
the *f* place of the young lions, ... Nah 2:11 4829
from them an herd of many swine *f* ... Mt 8:30 *1006*
mountains a great herd of swine *f* ... Mk 5:11 *1006*
of many swine *f* on the mountain ... Lk 8:32 *1006*
a servant plowing or *f* cattle ... Lk 17:7 *4165*
f themselves without fear ... Jude 12 *4165*

FEEL {7}
My father peradventure will *f* me ... Gen 27:12 4959
I pray thee, that I may *f* thee ... Gen 27:21 4184
Suffer me that I may *f* the ... Judg 16:26 4184
Surely he shall not *f* quietness ... Job 20:20 3045
Before your pots can *f* the thorns ... Ps 58:9 995
commandment shall *f* no evil thing ... Eccl 8:5 3045
if haply they might *f* after him ... Acts 17:27 *5584*

FEELING {2}
Who being past *f* have given ... Eph 4:19 *524*
with the *f* of our infirmities ... Heb 4:15 *4834*

FEET {256}
you, be fetched, and wash your *f* ... Gen 18:4 7272
tarry all night, and wash your *f* ... Gen 19:2 7272
camels, and water to wash his *f* ... Gen 24:32 7272
the men's *f* that were with him ... Gen 24:32 7272
water, and they washed their *f* ... Gen 43:24 7272
nor a lawgiver from between his *f* ... Gen 49:10 7272
he gathered up his *f* into the bed ... Gen 49:33 7272
put off thy shoes from off thy *f* ... Ex 3:5 7272
of her son, and cast it at his *f* ... Ex 4:25 7272
girded, your shoes on your *f* ... Ex 12:11 7272
there was under his *f* as it were ... Ex 24:10 7272
that are on the four *f* thereof ... Ex 25:26 7272
their hands and their *f* thereat ... Ex 30:19 7272
shall wash their hands and their *f* ... Ex 30:21 7272
that were in the four *f* thereof ... Ex 37:13 7272
their hands and their *f* thereat ... Ex 40:31 7272
the great toes of their right *f* ... Lev 8:24 7272
which have legs above their *f* ... Lev 11:21 7272
things, which have four *f* ... Lev 11:23 7272
or whatsoever hath more *f* among ... Lev 11:42 7272
thing else, go through on my *f* ... Num 20:19 7272
only I will pass through on my *f* ... Deut 2:28 7272
your *f* shall tread shall be yours ... Deut 11:24 7272
cometh out from between her *f* ... Deut 28:57 7272
and they sat down at thy *f* ... Deut 33:3 7272
as soon as the soles of the *f* of ... Josh 3:13 7272
the *f* of the priests that bare ... Josh 3:15 7272
where the priests' *f* stood firm ... Josh 4:3 7272
in the place where the *f* of the ... Josh 4:9 7272
the soles of the priests' *f* were ... Josh 4:18 7272
old shoes and clouted upon their *f* ... Josh 9:5 7272
put your *f* upon the necks of ... Josh 10:24 7272
put their *f* upon the necks of ... Josh 10:24 7272
thy *f* have trodden shall be thine ... Josh 14:9 7272
his *f* in his summer chamber ... Judg 3:24 7272
up with ten thousand men at his *f* ... Judg 4:10 7272
chariot, and fled away on his *f* ... Judg 4:15 7272
f to the tent of Jael the wife of ... Judg 4:17 7272
At her *f* he bowed, he fell, he ... Judg 5:27 7272
at her *f* he bowed, he fell ... Judg 5:27 7272
and they washed their *f*, and did ... Judg 19:21 7272
shalt go in, and uncover his *f* ... Ruth 3:4 4772
came softly, and uncovered his *f* ... Ruth 3:7 4772
and, behold, a woman lay at his *f* ... Ruth 3:8 4772
she lay at his *f* until the ... Ruth 3:14 4772
He will keep the *f* of his saints ... 1Sa 2:9 7272
up upon his hands and upon his *f* ... 1Sa 14:13 7272
and Saul went in to cover his *f* ... 1Sa 24:3 7272
And fell at his *f*, and said, Upon ... 1Sa 25:24 7272
be a servant to wash the *f* of the ... 1Sa 25:41 7272
nor thy *f* put into fetters ... 2Sa 3:34 7272
had a son that was lame of his *f* ... 2Sa 4:4 7272
and cut off their hands and their *f* ... 2Sa 4:12 7272
yet a son, which is lame on his *f* ... 2Sa 9:3 7272
and was lame on both his *f* ... 2Sa 9:13 7272
down to thy house, and wash thy *f* ... 2Sa 11:8 7272
and had neither dressed his *f* ... 2Sa 19:24 7272
and darkness was under his *f* ... 2Sa 22:10 7272
He maketh my *f* like hinds' *f* ... 2Sa 22:34 7272
so that my *f* did not slip ... 2Sa 22:37 7166
yea, they are fallen under my *f* ... 2Sa 22:39 7272
in his shoes that were on his *f* ... 1Kin 2:5 7272
put them under the soles of his *f* ... 1Kin 5:3 7272
Ahijah heard the sound of her *f* ... 1Kin 14:6 7272
when thy *f* enter into the city, ... 1Kin 14:12 7272
old age he was diseased in his *f* ... 1Kin 15:23 7272
the hill, she caught him by the *f* ... 2Kin 4:27 7272
she went in, and fell at his *f* ... 2Kin 4:37 7272
of his master's *f* behind him ... 2Kin 6:32 7272
of her than the skull, and the *f* ... 2Kin 9:35 7272
he revived, and stood up on his *f* ... 2Kin 13:21 7272
with the sole of my *f* have I ... 2Kin 19:24 6471
Neither will I make the *f* of ... 2Kin 21:8 7272
the king stood up upon his *f* ... 1Chr 28:2 7272
and they stood on their *f*, and ... 2Chr 3:13 7272
his reign was diseased in his *f* ... 2Chr 16:12 7272
not old, and their *f* swelled not ... Neh 9:21 7272
the king, and fell down at his *f* ... Est 8:3 7272
f is as a lamp despised in the ... Job 12:5 7272
Thou puttest my *f* also in the ... Job 13:27 7272
a print upon the heels of my *f* ... Job 13:27 7272
is cast into a net by his own *f* ... Job 18:8 7272
side, and shall drive him to his *f* ... Job 18:11 7272
the blind, and *f* was I to the lame ... Job 29:15 7272
they push away my *f*, and they ... Job 30:12 7272
He putteth my *f* in the stocks ... Job 33:11 7272
hast put all things under his *f* ... Ps 8:6 7272
and darkness was under his *f* ... Ps 18:9 7272
He maketh my *f* like hinds' *f*, ... Ps 18:33 7272
under me, that my *f* did not slip ... Ps 18:36 7166
they are fallen under my *f* ... Ps 18:38 7272
they pierced my hands and my *f* ... Ps 22:16 7272
shall pluck my *f* out of the net ... Ps 25:15 7272
hast set my *f* in a large room ... Ps 31:8 7272
clay, and set my *f* upon a rock, and ... Ps 40:2 7272
us, and the nations under our *f* ... Ps 47:3 7272
thou deliver my *f* from falling ... Ps 56:13 7272
he shall wash his *f* in the blood ... Ps 58:10 6471
suffereth not our *f* to be moved ... Ps 66:9 7272
as for me, my *f* were almost gone ... Ps 73:2 7272
Lift up thy *f* unto the perpetual ... Ps 74:3 6471
dragon shalt thou trample under *f* ... Ps 91:13
Whose *f* they hurt with fetters ... Ps 105:18 7272
f have they, but they walk not ... Ps 115:7 7272
from tears, and my *f* from falling ... Ps 116:8 7272
turned my *f* unto thy testimonies ... Ps 119:59 7272
my *f* from every evil way, that I ... Ps 119:101 7272
Thy word is a lamp unto my *f* ... Ps 119:105 7272
Our *f* shall stand within thy ... Ps 122:2 7272
For their *f* run to evil, and make ... Prov 1:16 7272
Ponder the path of thy *f*, and let ... Prov 4:26 7272
Her *f* go down to death ... Prov 5:5 7272
his eyes, he speaketh with his *f* ... Prov 6:13 7272
f that be swift in running to ... Prov 6:18 7272
hot coals, and his *f* not be burned ... Prov 6:28 7272
her *f* abide not in her house ... Prov 7:11 7272
that hasteth with his *f* sinneth ... Prov 19:2 7272
hand of a fool cutteth off the *f* ... Prov 26:6 7272
spreadeth a net for his *f* ... Prov 29:5 6471
I have washed my *f* ... Song 5:3 7272
beautiful are thy *f* with shoes ... Song 7:1 6471
and making a tinkling with their *f* ... Is 3:16 7272
tinkling ornaments about their *f* ... Is 3:18
and with twain he covered his *f* ... Is 6:2 7272
the head, and the hair of the *f* ... Is 7:20 7272
as a carcase trodden under *f* ... Is 14:19
her own *f* shall carry her afar ... Is 23:7 7272
even the *f* of the poor, and the ... Is 26:6 7272
Ephraim, shall be trodden under *f* ... Is 28:3 7272
forth thither the *f* of the ox ... Is 32:20 7272
with the sole of my *f* have I ... Is 37:25 6471
that he had not gone with his *f* ... Is 41:3 7272
and lick up the dust of thy *f* ... Is 49:23 7272
the *f* of him that bringeth good ... Is 52:7 7272
Their *f* run to evil, and they make ... Is 59:7 7272
make the place of my *f* glorious ... Is 60:13 7272
down at the soles of thy *f* ... Is 60:14 7272
before your *f* stumble upon the ... Jer 13:16 7272
they have not refrained their *f* ... Jer 14:10 7272
take me, and hid snares for my *f* ... Jer 18:22 7272
thy *f* are sunk in the mire, and ... Jer 38:22 7272
he hath spread a net for my *f* ... Lam 1:13 7272
To crush under his *f* all the ... Lam 3:34 7272
And their *f* were straight *f* ... Eze 1:7 7272
the sole of their *f* was like the ... Eze 1:7 7272
me, Son of man, stand upon thy *f* ... Eze 2:1 7272
unto me, and set me upon my *f* ... Eze 2:2 7272
into me, and set me upon my *f* ... Eze 3:24 7272
hast opened thy *f* to every one ... Eze 16:25 7272
and put on thy shoes upon thy *f* ... Eze 24:17 7272
heads, and your shoes upon your *f* ... Eze 24:23 7272
hands, and stamped with the *f* ... Eze 25:6 7272
troubledst the waters with thy *f* ... Eze 32:2 7272
f the residue of your pastures ... Eze 34:18 7272
must foul the residue with your *f* ... Eze 34:18 7272
which ye have trodden with your *f* ... Eze 34:19 7272
which ye have fouled with your *f* ... Eze 34:19 7272
lived, and stood up upon their *f* ... Eze 37:10 7272
and the place of the soles of my *f* ... Eze 43:7 7272
his *f* part of iron and part of ... Dan 2:33 7271
upon his *f* that were of iron ... Dan 2:34 7271
And whereas thou sawest the *f* ... Dan 2:41 7271
toes of the *f* were part of iron ... Dan 2:42 7271
and made stand upon the *f* as a man ... Dan 7:4 7271
the residue with the *f* of it ... Dan 7:7 7271
and stamped the residue with his *f* ... Dan 7:19 7271
his *f* like in colour to polished ... Dan 10:6 4772
the clouds are the dust of his *f* ... Nah 1:3 7272
the *f* of him that bringeth good ... Nah 1:15 7272
burning coals went forth at his *f* ... Hab 3:5 7272
will make my *f* like hinds' *f* ... Hab 3:19 7272
his *f* shall stand in that day ... Zec 14:4 7272
while they stand upon their *f* ... Zec 14:12 7272
ashes under the soles of your *f* ... Mal 4:3 7272
they trample them under their *f* ... Mt 7:6 *4228*
shake off the dust of your *f* ... Mt 10:14 *4228*
and cast them down at Jesus' *f* ... Mt 15:30 *4228*

two f to be cast into everlasting ... Mt 18:8 4228
fellowservant fell down at his f ... Mt 18:29 4228
And they came and held him by the f ... Mt 28:9 4228
when he saw him, he fell at his f ... Mk 5:22 4228
f for a testimony against them ... Mk 6:11 4228
of him, and came and fell at his f ... Mk 7:25 4228
than having two f to be cast into ... Mk 9:45 4228
to guide our f into the way of ... Lk 1:79 4228
stood at his f behind him weeping ... Lk 7:38 4228
and began to wash his f with tears ... Lk 7:38 4228
of her head, and kissed his f ... Lk 7:38 4228
thou gavest me no water for my f ... Lk 7:44 4228
she hath washed my f with tears ... Lk 7:44 4228
in hath not ceased to kiss my f ... Lk 7:45 4228
hath anointed my f with ointment ... Lk 7:46 4228
sitting at the f of Jesus ... Lk 8:35 4228
and he fell down at Jesus' f ... Lk 8:41 4228
off the very dust from your f for ... Lk 9:5 4228
Mary, which also sat at Jesus' f ... Lk 10:39 4228
on his hand, and shoes on his f ... Lk 15:22 4228
And fell down on his face at his f ... Lk 17:16 4228
Behold my hands and my f, that it ... Lk 24:39 4228
he shewed them his hands and his f ... Lk 24:40 4228
wiped his f with her hair, whose ... Jn 11:2 4228
saw him, she fell down at his f ... Jn 11:32 4228
and anointed the f of Jesus ... Jn 12:3 4228
wiped his f with her hair ... Jn 12:3 4228
and began to wash the disciples' f ... Jn 13:5 4228
him, Lord, dost thou wash my f ... Jn 13:6 4228
him, Thou shalt never wash my f ... Jn 13:8 4228
unto him, Lord, not my f only ... Jn 13:9 4228
needeth not save to wash his f ... Jn 13:10 4228
So after he had washed their f ... Jn 13:12 4228
and Master, have washed your f ... Jn 13:14 4228
ought to wash one another's f ... Jn 13:14 4228
the head, and the other at the f ... Jn 20:12 4228
and immediately his f and ancle ... Acts 3:7 939
laid them down at the apostles' f ... Acts 4:35 4228
and laid it at the apostles' f ... Acts 4:37 4228
and laid it at the apostles' f ... Acts 5:2 4228
the f of them which have buried ... Acts 5:9 4228
she down straightway at his f ... Acts 5:10 4228
him, Put off thy shoes from thy f ... Acts 7:33 4228
their clothes at a young man's f ... Acts 7:58 4228
met him, and fell down at his f ... Acts 10:25 4228
whose shoes of his f I am not ... Acts 13:25 4228
the dust of their f against them ... Acts 13:51 4228
man at Lystra, impotent in his f ... Acts 14:8 4228
voice, Stand upright on thy f ... Acts 14:10 4228
made their f fast in the stocks ... Acts 16:24 4228
and bound his own hands and f ... Acts 21:11 4228
in this city at the f of Gamaliel ... Acts 22:3 4228
But rise, and stand upon thy f ... Acts 26:16 4228
Their f are swift to shed blood ... Rom 3:15 4228
How beautiful are the f of them ... Rom 10:15 4228
bruise Satan under your f shortly ... Rom 16:20 4228
nor again the head to the f ... 1Cor 12:21 4228
hath put all enemies under his f ... 1Cor 15:25 4228
hath put all things under his f ... 1Cor 15:27 4228
hath put all things under his f ... Eph 1:22 4228
your f shod with the preparation ... Eph 6:15 4228
if she have washed the saints' f ... 1Ti 5:10 4228
things in subjection under his f ... Heb 2:8 4228
And make straight paths for your f ... Heb 12:13 4228
his f like unto fine brass, as if ... Rev 1:15 4228
saw him, I fell at his f as dead ... Rev 1:17 4228
his f are like fine brass ... Rev 2:18 4228
to come and worship before thy f ... Rev 3:9 4228
sun, and his f as pillars of fire ... Rev 10:1 4228
them, and they stood upon their f ... Rev 11:11 4228
the sun, and the moon under her f ... Rev 12:1 4228
his f were as the f of a bear ... Rev 13:2 4228
I fell at his f to worship him ... Rev 19:10 4228
f of the angel which shewed me ... Rev 22:8 4228

FEIGN {3}
f thyself to be a mourner, and put ... 2Sa 14:2
that she shall f herself to be ... 1Kin 14:5 5234
which should f themselves just ... Lk 20:20 5271

FEIGNED {3}
f himself mad in their hands, and ... 1Sa 21:13
that goeth not out of f lips ... Ps 17:1 4820
covetousness shall they with f ... 2Pet 2:3 4112

FEIGNEDLY {1}
me with her whole heart, but f ... Jer 3:10 8267

FEIGNEST {2}
why f thou thyself to be another ... 1Kin 14:6 5234
but thou f them out of thine own ... Neh 6:8 908

FELIX *(fe'-lix)* {8} See FELIX'. *A Roman procurator of Judea.*
him safe unto F the governor ... Acts 23:24 5344
governor F sendeth greeting ... Acts 23:26 5344
and in all places, most noble F ... Acts 24:3 5344
when F heard these things, having ... Acts 24:22 5344
when F came with his wife ... Acts 24:24 5344
F trembled, and answered, Go thy ... Acts 24:25 5344
and F, willing to shew the Jews a ... Acts 24:27 5344
a certain man left in bonds by F ... Acts 25:14 5344

FELIX' *(fe'-lix)* {1}
Porcius Festus came into F room ... Acts 24:27 5344

FELL {243}
very wroth, and his countenance f ... Gen 4:5 5307
and Gomorrah fled, and f there ... Gen 14:10 5307
down, a deep sleep f upon Abram ... Gen 15:12 5307
of great darkness f upon him ... Gen 15:12 5307
And Abram f on his face ... Gen 17:3 5307
Then Abraham f upon his face, and ... Gen 17:17 5307
f on his neck, and kissed him ... Gen 33:4 5307
they f before him on the ground ... Gen 44:14 5307
he f upon his brother Benjamin's ... Gen 45:14 5307
he f on his neck, and wept on his ... Gen 46:29 5307
Joseph f upon his father's face, ... Gen 50:1 5307
went and f down before his face ... Gen 50:18 5307
there f of the people that day ... Ex 32:28 5307
they shouted, and f on their faces ... Lev 9:24 5307
goat upon which the LORD's lot f ... Lev 16:9 5927
on which the lot f to be the ... Lev 16:10 5927
that was among them f a lusting ... Num 11:4
when the dew f upon the camp in ... Num 11:9 3381
in the night, the manna f upon it ... Num 11:9 3381
Aaron f on their faces before all ... Num 14:5 5307
heard it, he f upon his face ... Num 16:4 5307
they f upon their faces, and said, ... Num 16:22 5307
And they f upon their faces ... Num 16:45 5307
and they f upon their faces ... Num 20:6 5307
the LORD, she f down under Balaam ... Num 22:27 7257
his head, and f flat on his face ... Num 22:31 7812
I f down before the LORD, as at ... Deut 9:18 5307
Thus I f down before the LORD ... Deut 9:25 5307
nights, as I f down at the first ... Deut 9:25 5307
Joshua f on his face to the earth ... Josh 5:14 5307
shout, that the wall f down flat ... Josh 6:20 5307
f to the earth upon his face ... Josh 7:6 5307
it was, that all that f that day ... Josh 8:25 5307
and they f upon them ... Josh 11:7 5307
Joseph f from Jordan by Jericho ... Josh 16:1 3318
there f ten portions to Manasseh, ... Josh 17:5 5307
wrath f on all the congregation ... Josh 22:20 1961
all the host of Sisera f upon the ... Judg 4:16 5307
At her feet he bowed, he f ... Judg 5:27 5307
at her feet he bowed, he f ... Judg 5:27 5307
he bowed, there he f down dead, ... Judg 5:27 5307
a tent, and smote it that it f ... Judg 7:13 5307
for there f an hundred and twenty ... Judg 8:10 5307
there f at that time of the ... Judg 12:6 5307
f on their faces to the ground ... Judg 13:20 5307
the house f upon the lords, and ... Judg 16:30 5307
f down at the door of the man's ... Judg 19:26 5307
there f of Benjamin eighteen ... Judg 20:44 5307
So that all which f that day of ... Judg 20:46 5307
Then she f on her face, and bowed ... Ruth 2:10 5307
for there f of Israel thirty ... 1Sa 4:10 5307
that he f from off the seat ... 1Sa 4:18 5307
fear of the LORD f on the people ... 1Sa 11:7 5307
and they f before Jonathan ... 1Sa 14:13 5307
he f upon his face to the earth ... 1Sa 17:49 5307
f down by the way to Shaaraim ... 1Sa 17:52 5307
f on his face to the ground, and ... 1Sa 20:41 5307
he f upon the priests, and slew on ... 1Sa 22:18 6298
f before David on her face, and ... 1Sa 25:23 5307
f at his feet, and said, Upon me, ... 1Sa 25:24 5307
Then Saul f straightway all along ... 1Sa 28:20 5307
since he f unto me unto this day ... 1Sa 29:3 5307
because three days agone I f sick ... 1Sa 30:13
f down slain in mount Gilboa ... 1Sa 31:1 5307
Saul took a sword, and f upon it ... 1Sa 31:4 5307
he f likewise upon his sword, and ... 1Sa 31:5 5307
that he f to the earth, and did ... 2Sa 1:2 5307
so they f down together ... 2Sa 2:16 5307
he f down there, and died in the ... 2Sa 2:23 5307
to the place where Asahel f down ... 2Sa 2:23 5307
she made haste to flee, that he f ... 2Sa 4:4 5307
David, he f on his face, and did ... 2Sa 9:6 5307
there f some of the people of the ... 2Sa 11:17 5307
that he f sick for his sister ... 2Sa 13:2
she f on her face to the ground, ... 2Sa 14:4 5307
Joab f to the ground on his face, ... 2Sa 14:22 5307
he f down to the earth upon his ... 2Sa 18:28 7812
of Gera f down before the king ... 2Sa 19:18 5307
and as he went forth it f out ... 2Sa 20:8 5307
they f all seven together, and ... 2Sa 21:9 5307
f by the hand of David, and by the ... 2Sa 21:22 5307
he f upon him that he died ... 1Kin 2:25 6293
who f upon two men more righteous ... 1Kin 2:32 6293
up, and f upon him, and slew him ... 1Kin 2:34 6293
out, and f upon him, that he died ... 1Kin 2:46 6293
Abijah the son of Jeroboam f sick ... 1Kin 14:1
the mistress of the house, f sick ... 1Kin 17:17
f on his face, and said, Art thou ... 1Kin 18:7 5307
Then the fire of the LORD f ... 1Kin 18:38 5307
saw it, they f on their faces ... 1Kin 18:39 5307
and there a wall f upon twenty ... 1Kin 20:30 5307
Ahaziah f down through a lattice ... 2Kin 1:2 5307
f on his knees before Elijah, and ... 2Kin 1:13 3766
mantle of Elijah that f from him ... 2Kin 2:13 5307
mantle of Elijah that f from him ... 2Kin 2:14 5307
shall f every good tree, and stop ... 2Kin 3:19 5307
it f on a day, that Elisha passed ... 2Kin 4:8 1961
it f on a day, that he came ... 2Kin 4:11 1961
it f on a day, that he went out ... 2Kin 4:18 1961
f at his feet, and bowed herself ... 2Kin 4:37 5307
the ax head f into the water ... 2Kin 6:5 5307
the man of God said, Where f it ... 2Kin 6:6 5307
And so it f out unto him ... 2Kin 7:20 1961
the fugitives that f away to the ... 2Kin 25:11 5307
Hagarites, who f by their hand ... 1Chr 5:10 5307
For there f down many slain, ... 1Chr 5:22 5307
f down slain in mount Gilboa ... 1Chr 10:1 5307
Saul took a sword, and f upon it ... 1Chr 10:4 5307
he f likewise on the sword, and ... 1Chr 10:5 5307
there f some of Manasseh to David ... 1Chr 12:19 5307
there f to him of Manasseh, Adnah ... 1Chr 12:20 5307
they f by the hand of David, and ... 1Chr 20:8 5307
there f of Israel seventy ... 1Chr 21:14 5307
in sackcloth, f upon their faces ... 1Chr 21:16 5307
the lot eastward f to Shelemiah ... 1Chr 26:14 5307
because there f wrath for it ... 1Chr 27:24 1961
so there f down slain of Israel ... 2Chr 13:17 5307
for they f to him out of Israel ... 2Chr 15:9 5307
the fear of the LORD f upon all ... 2Chr 17:10 1961
of Jerusalem f before the LORD ... 2Chr 20:18 5307
his bowels f out by reason of his ... 2Chr 21:19 3318
f upon the cities of Judah, from ... 2Chr 25:13 6584
I f upon my knees, and spread out ... Ezr 9:5 3766
f down at his feet, and besought ... Est 8:3 5307
the fear of the Jews f upon them ... Est 8:17 5307
fear of them f upon all people ... Est 9:2 5307
the fear of Mordecai f upon them ... Est 9:3 5307
And the Sabeans f upon them ... Job 1:15 5307
f upon the camels, and have ... Job 1:17 6584
it f upon the young men, and they ... Job 1:19 5307
f down upon the ground, and ... Job 1:20 5307
up my flesh, they stumbled and f ... Ps 27:2 5307
Their priests f by the sword ... Ps 78:64 5307
for the fear of them f upon them ... Ps 105:38 5307
they f down, and there was none to ... Ps 107:12 3782
in the city, and those that f away ... Jer 39:9 5307
that f to him, with the rest of ... Jer 39:9 5307
to fall, yea, one f upon another ... Jer 46:16 5307
in the city, and those that f away ... Jer 52:15 5307
that f to the king of Babylon, and ... Jer 52:15 5307
when her people f into the hand ... Lam 1:7 5307
the children f under the wood ... Lam 5:13 3782
I f upon my face, and I heard a ... Eze 1:28 5307
and I f on my face ... Eze 3:23 5307
of the Lord GOD f there upon me ... Eze 8:1 5307
that I f upon my face, and cried, ... Eze 9:8 5307
the Spirit of the LORD f upon me ... Eze 11:5 5307
Then f I down upon my face, and ... Eze 11:13 5307
so f they all by the sword ... Eze 39:23 5307
and I f upon my face ... Eze 43:3 5307
and I f upon my face ... Eze 44:4 5307
Nebuchadnezzar f upon his face ... Dan 2:46 5308
f down and worshipped the golden ... Dan 3:7 5308
f down bound into the midst of ... Dan 3:23 5308
there f a voice from heaven, ... Dan 4:31 5308
came up, and before whom three f ... Dan 7:20 5308
I was afraid, and f upon my face ... Dan 8:17 5307
but a great quaking f upon them ... Dan 10:7 5307
lots, and the lot f upon Jonah ... Jonah 1:7 5307
f down, and worshipped him ... Mt 2:11 4098
and it f not: for it was founded ... Mt 7:25 4098
and it f: and great was the fall ... Mt 7:27 4098
some seeds f by the way side, and ... Mt 13:4 4098
Some f upon stony places, where ... Mt 13:5 4098
And some f among thorns ... Mt 13:7 4098
But other f into good ground, and ... Mt 13:8 4098
they f on their face, and were ... Mt 17:6 4098
The servant therefore f down ... Mt 18:26 4098
fellowservant f down at his feet ... Mt 18:29 4098
f on his face, and prayed, saying, ... Mt 26:39 4098
f down before him, and cried, ... Mk 3:11 4363
some f by the way side, and the ... Mk 4:4 4098
some f on stony ground, where it ... Mk 4:5 4098
some f among thorns, and the ... Mk 4:7 4098
other f on good ground, and did ... Mk 4:8 4098
he saw him, he f at his feet, ... Mk 5:22 4098
f down before him, and told him ... Mk 5:33 4363
of him, and came and f at his feet ... Mk 7:25 4363
he f on the ground, and wallowed ... Mk 9:20 4098
f on the ground, and prayed that, ... Mk 14:35 4098
was troubled, and fear f upon him ... Lk 1:12 1968
he f down at Jesus' knees, saying ... Lk 5:8 4363
who seeing Jesus f on his face ... Lk 5:12 4098
vehemently, and immediately it f ... Lk 6:49 4098
he sowed, some f by the way side ... Lk 8:5 4098
And some f upon a rock ... Lk 8:6 4098
And some f among thorns ... Lk 8:7 4098
other f on good ground, and sprang ... Lk 8:8 4098
that which f among thorns are ... Lk 8:14 4098
But as they sailed he f asleep ... Lk 8:23
f down before him, and with a loud ... Lk 8:28 4363
he f down at Jesus' feet, and ... Lk 8:41 4098
f among thieves, which stripped ... Lk 10:30 4045
unto him that f among the thieves ... Lk 10:36 1706
upon whom the tower in Siloam f ... Lk 13:4 4098
f on his neck, and kissed him ... Lk 15:20 1968
which f from the rich man's table ... Lk 16:21 4098
f down on his face at his feet, ... Lk 17:16 4098
she f down at his feet, saying ... Jn 11:32 4098
went backward, and f to the ground ... Jn 18:6 4098
which Judas by transgression f ... Acts 1:25
and the lot f upon Matthias ... Acts 1:26 4098
hearing these words f down ... Acts 5:5 4098
Then f she down straightway at ... Acts 5:10 4098
he had said this, he f asleep ... Acts 7:60
he f to the earth, and heard a ... Acts 9:4 4098
immediately there f from his eyes ... Acts 9:18 634
made ready, he f into a trance, ... Acts 10:10 1968
f down at his feet, and worshipped ... Acts 10:25 4098
the Holy Ghost f on all them ... Acts 10:44 1968
speak, the Holy Ghost f on them ... Acts 11:15 1968
his chains f off from his hands ... Acts 12:7 1601
immediately there f on him a mist ... Acts 13:11 1968
f on sleep, and was laid unto his ... Acts 13:36
f down before Paul and Silas, ... Acts 16:29 4363
fear f on them all, and the name ... Acts 19:17 1968
image which f down from Jupiter ... Acts 19:35 1356
f down from the third loft, and ... Acts 20:9 4098
f on him, and embracing him said, ... Acts 20:10 1968
f on Paul's neck, and kissed him, ... Acts 20:37 1968
I f unto the ground, and heard a ... Acts 22:7 4098

on them which *f*, severity ... Rom 11:22 *4098*
them that reproached thee *f* on me ... Rom 15:3 *1968*
f in one day three and twenty ... 1Cor 10:8 *4098*
sinned, whose carcases *f* in the ... Heb 3:17 *4098*
faith the walls of Jericho *f* down ... Heb 11:30 *4098*
for since the fathers *f* asleep ... 2Pet 3:4
saw him, I *f* at his feet as dead ... Rev 1:17 *4098*
twenty elders *f* down before the ... Rev 5:8 *4098*
the four and twenty elders *f* down ... Rev 5:14 *4098*
stars of heaven *f* unto the earth ... Rev 6:13 *4098*
f before the throne on their ... Rev 7:11 *4098*
there *f* a great star from heaven, ... Rev 8:10 *4098*
it *f* upon the third part of the ... Rev 8:10 *4098*
great fear *f* upon them which saw ... Rev 11:11 *4098*
and the tenth part of the city *f* ... Rev 11:13 *4098*
f upon their faces, and worshipped ... Rev 11:16 *4098*
there *f* a noisome and grievous ... Rev 16:2 *1096*
and the cities of the nations *f* ... Rev 16:19 *4098*
there *f* upon men a great hail out ... Rev 16:21 *2597*
elders and the four beasts *f* down ... Rev 19:4 *4098*
I *f* at his feet to worship him ... Rev 19:10 *4098*
I *f* down to worship before the ... Rev 22:8 *4098*

FELLED {1}
of water, and *f* all the good trees ... 2Kin 3:25 5307

FELLER {1}
no *f* is come up against us ... Is 14:8 3772

FELLEST {1}
before wicked men, so *f* thou ... 2Sa 3:34 5307

FELLING {1}
But as one was *f* a beam, the ax ... 2Kin 6:5 5307

FELLOES {1}
and their naves, and their *f* ... 1Kin 7:33 2839

FELLOW {29}
This one *f* came in to sojourn, and ... Gen 19:9 7453
Wherefore smitest thou thy *f* ... Ex 2:13 7453
man that told a dream unto his *f* ... Judg 7:13 7453
his *f* answered and said, This is ... Judg 7:14 7453
every man's sword against his *f* ... Judg 7:22 7453
man's sword was against his *f* ... 1Sa 14:20 7453
this *f* to play the mad man in my ... 1Sa 21:15
shall this *f* come into my house ... 1Sa 21:15
this *f* hath in the wilderness ... 1Sa 25:21
said unto him, Make this *f* return ... 1Sa 29:4 376
every one his *f* by the head ... 2Sa 2:16 7453
Put this *f* in the prison, and feed ... 1Kin 22:27
wherefore came this mad *f* to thee ... 2Kin 9:11
Put this *f* in the prison, and feed ... 2Chr 18:26
fall, the one will lift up his *f* ... Eccl 4:10 2270
and the satyr shall cry to his *f* ... Is 34:14 7453
And they said every one to his *f* ... Jonah 1:7 7453
and against the man that is my *f* ... Zec 13:7 5997
This *f* doth not cast out devils, ... Mt 12:24
And said, This *f* said, I am able ... Mt 26:61
This *f* was also with Jesus of ... Mt 26:71
Of a truth this *f* also was with ... Lk 22:59
We found this *f* perverting the ... Lk 23:2
as for this *f*, we know not from ... Jn 9:29
This *f* persuadeth men to worship ... Acts 18:13
Away with such a *f* from the earth ... Acts 22:22
have found this man a pestilent *f* ... Acts 24:5
f soldier, but your messenger, and ... Phil 2:25
These only are my *f* workers unto ... Col 4:11

FELLOWCITIZENS {1}
but *f* with the saints, and of the ... Eph 2:19 *4847*

FELLOWDISCIPLES {1}
is called Didymus, unto his *f* ... Jn 11:16 *4827*

FELLOWHEIRS {1}
That the Gentiles should be *f* ... Eph 3:6 *4789*

FELLOWHELPER {1}
is my partner and *f* concerning you ... 2Cor 8:23 *4904*

FELLOWHELPERS {1}
that we might be *f* to the truth ... 3Jn 8 *4904*

FELLOWLABOURER {2}
our *f* in the gospel of Christ, to ... 1Th 3:2 *4904*
Philemon our dearly beloved, and *f* ... Philem 1 *4904*

FELLOWLABOURERS {2}
Clement also, and with other my *f* ... Phil 4:3 *4904*
Aristarchus, Demas, Lucas, my *f* ... Philem 24 *4904*

FELLOWPRISONER {2}
Aristarchus my *f* saluteth you ... Col 4:10 *4869*
Epaphras, my *f* in Christ Jesus ... Philem 23 *4869*

FELLOWPRISONERS {1}
and Junia, my kinsmen, and my *f* ... Rom 16:7 *4869*

FELLOW'S {1}
and thrust his sword in his *f* side ... 2Sa 2:16 7453

FELLOWS {13}
and bewail my virginity, I and my *f* ... Judg 11:37 7464
lest angry *f* run upon thee, and ... Judg 18:25 582
as one of the vain *f* shamelessly ... 2Sa 6:20
the oil of gladness above thy *f* ... Ps 45:7 2270
all his *f* shall be ashamed ... Is 44:11 2270
and the tribes of Israel his *f* ... Eze 37:19 2270
Daniel and his *f* to be slain ... Dan 2:13 2269
his *f* should not perish with the ... Dan 2:18 2269
look was more stout than his *f* ... Dan 7:20 2273
thy *f* that sit before thee ... Zec 3:8 7453
markets, and calling unto their *f* ... Mt 11:16 *2083*
certain lewd *f* of the baser sort ... Acts 17:5 *435*
the oil of gladness above thy *f* ... Heb 1:9 *3353*

FELLOWSERVANT {6}
his *f* fell down at his feet, and ... Mt 18:29 *4889*
also have had compassion on thy *f* ... Mt 18:33 *4889*
learned of Epaphras our dear *f* ... Col 1:7 *4889*
minister and *f* in the Lord ... Col 4:7 *4889*
I am thy *f*, and of thy brethren ... Rev 19:10 *4889*
for I am thy *f*, and of thy ... Rev 22:9 *4889*

FELLOWSERVANTS {4}
went out, and found one of his *f* ... Mt 18:28 *4889*
So when his *f* saw what was done, ... Mt 18:31 *4889*
And shall begin to smite his *f* ... Mt 24:49 *4889*
little season, until their *f* also ... Rev 6:11 *4889*

FELLOWSHIP {17}
delivered him to keep, or in *f* ... Lev 6:2 8667,3027
of iniquity have *f* with thee ... Ps 94:20 2266
in the apostles' doctrine and *f* ... Acts 2:42 *2842*
the *f* of his Son Jesus Christ our ... 1Cor 1:9 *2842*
that ye should have *f* with devils ... 1Cor 10:20 *2844*
for what *f* hath righteousness ... 2Cor 6:14 *3352*
take upon us the *f* of the ... 2Cor 8:4 *2842*
and Barnabas the right hands of *f* ... Gal 2:9 *2842*
see what is the *f* of the mystery ... Eph 3:9 *2842*
have no *f* with the unfruitful ... Eph 5:11 *4790*
For your *f* in the gospel from the ... Phil 1:5 *2842*
if any *f* of the Spirit, if any ... Phil 2:1 *2842*
the *f* of his sufferings, being ... Phil 3:10 *2842*
that ye also may have *f* with us ... 1Jn 1:3 *2842*
truly our *f* is with the Father, ... 1Jn 1:3 *2842*
If we say that we have *f* with him ... 1Jn 1:6 *2842*
we have *f* one with another, and ... 1Jn 1:7 *2842*

FELLOWSOLDIER {1}
Apphia, and Archippus our *f* ... Philem 2 *4961*

FELT {5}
he *f* him, and said, The voice is ... Gen 27:22 4959
even darkness which may be *f* ... Ex 10:21 4959
have beaten me, and I *f* it not ... Prov 23:35 3045
she *f* in her body that she was ... Mk 5:29 *1097*
beast into the fire, and *f* no harm ... Acts 28:5 *3958*

FEMALE {24}
male and *f* created he them ... Gen 1:27 5347
Male and *f* created he them ... Gen 5:2 5347
they shall be male and *f* ... Gen 6:19 5347
thee by sevens, the male and his *f* ... Gen 7:2 802
clean by two, the male and his *f* ... Gen 7:2 802
air by sevens, the male and the *f* ... Gen 7:3 5347
into the ark, the male and the *f* ... Gen 7:9 5347
f of all flesh, as God had ... Gen 7:16 5347
whether it be a male or *f* ... Lev 3:1 5347
male or *f*, he shall offer it ... Lev 3:6 5347
a *f* without blemish, for his sin ... Lev 4:28 5347
bring it a *f* without blemish ... Lev 4:32 5347
a *f* from the flock, a lamb or a ... Lev 5:6 5347
her that hath born a male or a *f* ... Lev 12:7 5347
And if it be a *f*, then thy ... Lev 27:4 5347
shekels, and for the *f* ten shekels ... Lev 27:5 5347
for the *f* thy estimation shall be ... Lev 27:6 5347
shekels, and for the *f* ten shekels ... Lev 27:7 5347
f shall ye put out, without the ... Num 5:3 5347
figure, the likeness of male or *f* ... Deut 4:16 5347
not be male or *f* barren among you ... Deut 7:14 5347
the beginning made them male and *f* ... Mt 19:4 *2338*
creation God made them male and *f* ... Mk 10:6 *2338*
free, there is neither male nor *f* ... Gal 3:28 *2338*

FENCE {1}
shall ye be, and as a tottering *f* ... Ps 62:3 1447

FENCED {38}
in the *f* cities because of the ... Num 32:17 4013
and Beth-haran, *f* cities ... Num 32:36 4013
cities were *f* with high walls ... Deut 3:5 1219
cities great and *f* up to heaven, ... Deut 9:1 1219
f walls come down, wherein thou ... Deut 28:52 1219
of them entered into *f* cities ... Josh 10:20 4013
that the cities were great and *f* ... Josh 14:12 1219
the *f* cities are Ziddim, Zer, and ... Josh 19:35 4013
the five lords, both of *f* cities ... 1Sa 6:18 4013
him, lest he get him *f* cities ... 2Sa 20:6 1211
touch them must be *f* with iron ... 2Sa 23:7 4390
And ye shall smite every *f* city ... 2Kin 3:19 4013
horses, a *f* city also, and armour ... 2Kin 10:2 4013
of the watchmen to the *f* city ... 2Kin 17:9 4013
of the watchmen to the *f* city ... 2Kin 18:8 4013
against all the *f* cities of Judah ... 2Kin 18:13 1219
waste *f* cities into ruinous heaps ... 2Kin 19:25 1219
f cities, with walls, gates, and ... 2Chr 8:5 4692
in Judah and in Benjamin *f* cities ... 2Chr 11:10 4694
and Benjamin, unto every *f* city ... 2Chr 11:23 4694
he took the *f* cities which ... 2Chr 12:4 4694
he built *f* cities in Judah ... 2Chr 14:6 4694
in all the *f* cities of Judah ... 2Chr 17:2 1219
the *f* cities throughout all Judah ... 2Chr 17:19 4013
all the *f* cities of Judah ... 2Chr 19:5 1219
things, with *f* cities in Judah ... 2Chr 21:3 4694
and encamped against the *f* cities ... 2Chr 32:1 1219
war in all the *f* cities of Judah ... 2Chr 33:14 1219
hast *f* me with bones and sinews ... Job 10:11 7753
He hath *f* up my way that I cannot ... Job 19:8 1443
high tower, and upon every *f* wall ... Is 2:15 1219
And he *f* it, and gathered out the ... Is 5:2 5823
shall impoverish thy *f* cities ... Jer 5:17 4013
unto this people a *f* brasen wall ... Jer 15:20 1219
and ruined cities are become *f* ... Eze 36:35 1219
mount, and take the most *f* cities ... Dan 11:15 4013
and Judah hath multiplied *f* cities ... Hos 8:14 1219
and alarm against the *f* cities ... Zeph 1:16 1219

FENS {1}
in the covert of the reed, and *f* ... Job 40:21 1207

FERRET {1}
And the *f*, and the chameleon, and ... Lev 11:30 604

FERRY {1}
there went over a *f* boat to carry ... 2Sa 19:18 5679

FERVENT {7}
being *f* in the spirit, he spake ... Acts 18:25 *2204*
f in spirit; serving the Lord ... Rom 12:11 *2204*
mourning, your *f* mind toward me ... 2Cor 7:7 *2205*
The effectual *f* prayer of a ... Jas 5:16
above all things have *f* charity ... 1Pet 4:8 *1618*
elements shall melt with *f* heat ... 2Pet 3:10
elements shall melt with *f* heat ... 2Pet 3:12

FERVENTLY {2}
always labouring *f* for you in ... Col 4:12
one another with a pure heart *f* ... 1Pet 1:22 *1619*

FESTUS *(fes'-tus)* {12} See FESTUS'. *A Roman procurator of Judea.*
Porcius *F* came into Felix' room ... Acts 24:27 *5347*
Now when *F* was come into the ... Acts 25:1 *5347*
But *F* answered, that Paul should ... Acts 25:4 *5347*
But *F*, willing to do the Jews a ... Acts 25:9 *5347*
Then *F*, when he had conferred ... Acts 25:12 *5347*
came unto Caesarea to salute *F* ... Acts 25:13 *5347*
F declared Paul's cause unto the ... Acts 25:14 *5347*
Then Agrippa said unto *F*, I would ... Acts 25:22 *5347*
F said, King Agrippa, and all men ... Acts 25:24 *5347*
F said with a loud voice, Paul, ... Acts 26:24 *5347*
said, I am not mad, most noble *F* ... Acts 26:25 *5347*
Then said Agrippa unto *F*, This ... Acts 26:32 *5347*

FESTUS' *(fes'-tus)* {1}
at *F* commandment Paul was brought ... Acts 25:23 *5347*

FETCH {31}
I will *f* a morsel of bread, and ... Gen 18:5 3947
f me from thence two good kids of ... Gen 27:9 3947
obey my voice, and go *f* me them ... Gen 27:13 3947
will send, and *f* thee from thence ... Gen 27:45 3947
let him *f* your brother, and ye ... Gen 42:16 3947
flags, she sent her maid to *f* it ... Ex 2:5 3947
must we *f* you water out of this ... Num 20:10 3318
the border shall *f* a compass from ... Num 34:5
f him thence, and deliver him into ... Deut 19:12 3947
go into his house to *f* his pledge ... Deut 24:10 5670
thou shalt not go again to *f* it ... Deut 24:19 3947
and from thence will he *f* thee ... Deut 30:4 3947
the elders of Gilead went to *f* ... Judg 11:5 3947
to *f* victual for the people, that ... Judg 20:10 3947
Let us *f* the ark of the covenant ... 1Sa 4:3 3947
come ye down, and *f* it up to you ... 1Sa 6:21 5927
said unto Jesse, Send and *f* him ... 1Sa 16:11 3947
f him unto me, for he shall ... 1Sa 20:31 3947
the young men come over and *f* it ... 1Sa 26:22 3947
but *f* a compass behind them, and ... 2Sa 5:23
not *f* home again his banished ... 2Sa 14:13 7725
To *f* about this form of speech ... 2Sa 14:20 5437
F me, I pray thee, a little water ... 1Kin 17:10 3947
And as she was going to *f* it ... 1Kin 17:11 3947
he is, that I may send and *f* him ... 2Kin 6:13 3947
F quickly Micaiah the son of Imla ... 2Chr 18:8
f olive branches, and pine ... Neh 8:15 935
I will *f* my knowledge from afar, ... Job 36:3 5375
Come ye, say they, I will *f* wine ... Is 56:12 3947
king sent Jehudi to *f* the roll ... Jer 36:21 3947
them come themselves and *f* us out ... Acts 16:37 *1806*

FETCHED {17}
a little water, I pray you, be *f* ... Gen 18:4 3947
And he went, and *f*, and brought them ... Gen 27:14 3947
to Adar, and *f* a compass to Karkaa ... Josh 15:3
f the carved image, the ephod, and ... Judg 18:18 3947
And they ran and *f* him thence ... 1Sa 10:23 3947
as though they would have *f* wheat ... 2Sa 4:6 3947
f him out of the house of Machir, ... 2Sa 9:5 3947
f her to his house, and she became ... 2Sa 11:27 622
f thence a wise woman, and said ... 2Sa 14:2 3947
sent and *f* Hiram out of Tyre ... 1Kin 7:13 3947
f from thence gold, four hundred ... 1Kin 9:28 3947
they *f* a compass of seven days' ... 2Kin 3:9
f the rulers over hundreds, with ... 2Kin 11:4 3947
And they *f* up, and brought forth ... 2Chr 1:17 5927
f them, and brought them again ... 2Chr 12:11 5375
they *f* forth Urijah out of Egypt, ... Jer 26:23 3318
And from thence we *f* a compass ... Acts 28:13

FETCHETH {1}
his hand *f* a stroke with the axe ... Deut 19:5 5080

FETCHT {1}
f a calf tender and good, and gave ... Gen 18:7 3947

FETTERS {11}
and bound him with *f* of brass ... Judg 16:21 5178
bound, nor thy feet put into *f* ... 2Sa 3:34 5178
and bound him with *f* of brass ... 2Kin 25:7 5178
the thorns, and bound him with *f* ... 2Chr 33:11 5178
of Babylon, and bound him in *f* ... 2Chr 36:6 5178
And if they be bound in *f*, and be ... Job 36:8 2131
Whose feet they hurt with *f* ... Ps 105:18 3525
and their nobles with *f* of iron ... Ps 149:8 3525
he had been often bound with *f* ... Mk 5:4 *3976*
by him, and the *f* broken in pieces ... Mk 5:4 *3976*
kept bound with chains and in *f* ... Lk 8:29 *3976*

FEVER {9}
with a consumption, and with a *f* ... Deut 28:22 6920
mother laid, and sick of a *f* ... Mt 8:14 *4445*
her hand, and the *f* left her ... Mt 8:15 *4446*
wife's mother lay sick of a *f* ... Mk 1:30 *4445*
and immediately the *f* left her ... Mk 1:31 *4446*
mother was taken with a great *f* ... Lk 4:38 *4446*
stood over her, and rebuked the *f* ... Lk 4:39 *4446*

the seventh hour the *f* left him ... Jn 4:52 *4446*
father of Publius lay sick of a *f* ... Acts 28:8 *4446*

FEW {69} See APPENDIX.

FEWER {1} See APPENDIX.

FEWEST {1}
for ye were the *f* of all people ... Deut 7:7 4592

FEWNESS {1}
according to the *f* of years thou ... Lev 25:16 4591

FIDELITY {1}
but shewing all good *f* ... Titus 2:10 *4102*

FIELD {293}
every plant of the *f* before it ... Gen 2:5 7704
herb of the *f* before it grew ... Gen 2:5 7704
God formed every beast of the *f* ... Gen 2:19 7704
air, and to every beast of the *f* ... Gen 2:20 7704
the *f* which the LORD God had made ... Gen 3:1 7704
and above every beast of the *f* ... Gen 3:14 7704
thou shalt eat the herb of the *f* ... Gen 3:18 7704
to pass, when they were in the *f* ... Gen 4:8 7704
which is in the end of his *f* ... Gen 23:9 7704
the *f* give I thee, and the cave ... Gen 23:11 7704
I will give thee money for the *f* ... Gen 23:13 7704
the *f* of Ephron, which was in ... Gen 23:17 7704
which was before Mamre, the *f* ... Gen 23:17 7704
all the trees that were in the *f* ... Gen 23:17 7704
the *f* of Machpelah before Mamre ... Gen 23:19 7704
And the *f*, and the cave that is ... Gen 23:20 7704
meditate in the *f* at the eventide ... Gen 24:63 7704
that walketh in the *f* to meet us ... Gen 24:65 7704
in the *f* of Ephron the son of ... Gen 25:9 7704
The *f* which Abraham purchased of ... Gen 25:10 7704
a cunning hunter, a man of the *f* ... Gen 25:27 7704
and Esau came from the *f*, and he ... Gen 25:29 7704
and thy bow, and go out to the *f* ... Gen 27:3 7704
Esau went to the *f* to hunt for ... Gen 27:5 7704
a *f* which the LORD hath blessed ... Gen 27:27 7704
looked, and behold a well in the *f* ... Gen 29:2 7704
and found mandrakes in the *f* ... Gen 30:14 7704
came out of the *f* in the evening ... Gen 30:16 7704
Leah to the *f* unto his flock ... Gen 31:4 7704
And he bought a parcel of a *f* ... Gen 33:19 7704
were with his cattle in the *f* ... Gen 34:5 7704
out of the *f* when they heard it ... Gen 34:7 7704
city, and that which was in the *f* ... Gen 34:28 7704
who smote Midian in the *f* of Moab ... Gen 36:35 7704
we were binding sheaves in the *f* ... Gen 37:7 7704
behold, he was wandering in the *f* ... Gen 37:15 7704
he had in the house, and in the *f* ... Gen 39:5 7704
the food of the *f*, which was ... Gen 41:48 7704
Egyptians sold every man his *f* ... Gen 47:20 7704
be your own, for seed of the *f* ... Gen 47:24 7704
is in the *f* of Ephron the Hittite ... Gen 49:29 7704
that is in the *f* of Machpelah ... Gen 49:30 7704
the *f* of Ephron the Hittite for a ... Gen 49:30 7704
The purchase of the *f* and of the ... Gen 49:32 7704
in the cave of the *f* of Machpelah ... Gen 50:13 7704
with the *f* for a possession of a ... Gen 50:13 7704
in all manner of service in the *f* ... Ex 1:14 7704
upon thy cattle which is in the *f* ... Ex 9:3 7704
and all that thou hast in the *f* ... Ex 9:19 7704
which shall be found in the *f* ... Ex 9:19 7704
servants and his cattle in the *f* ... Ex 9:21 7704
and upon every herb of the *f* ... Ex 9:22 7704
of Egypt all that was in the *f* ... Ex 9:25 7704
hail smote every herb of the *f* ... Ex 9:25 7704
and brake every tree of the *f* ... Ex 9:25 7704
groweth for you out of the *f* ... Ex 10:5 7704
trees, or in the herbs of the *f* ... Ex 10:15 7704
day ye shall not find it in the *f* ... Ex 16:25 7704
If a man shall cause a *f* or ... Ex 22:5 7704
and shall feed in another man's *f* ... Ex 22:5 7704
of the best of his own *f*, and of ... Ex 22:5 7704
or the standing corn, or the *f* ... Ex 22:6 7704
that is torn of beasts in the *f* ... Ex 22:31 7704
the beasts of the *f* shall eat ... Ex 23:11 7704
which thou hast sown in the *f* ... Ex 23:16 7704
in thy labours out of the *f* ... Ex 23:16 7704
the beast of the *f* multiply ... Ex 23:29 7704
living bird loose into the open *f* ... Lev 14:7 7704
which they offer in the open *f* ... Lev 17:5 7704
wholly reap the corners of thy *f* ... Lev 19:9 7704
not sow thy *f* with mingled seed ... Lev 19:19 7704
of thy *f* when thou reapest ... Lev 23:22 7704
Six years thou shalt sow thy *f* ... Lev 25:3 7704
thou shalt neither sow thy *f* ... Lev 25:4 7704
the increase thereof out of the *f* ... Lev 25:12 7704
But the *f* of the suburbs of their ... Lev 25:34 7704
the trees of the *f* shall yield ... Lev 26:4 7704
part of a *f* of his possession ... Lev 27:16 7704
If he sanctify his *f* from the ... Lev 27:17 7704
sanctify his *f* after the jubile ... Lev 27:18 7704
if he that sanctified the *f* will ... Lev 27:19 7704
And if he will not redeem the *f* ... Lev 27:20 7704
he have sold the *f* to another man ... Lev 27:20 7704
But the *f*, when it goeth out in ... Lev 27:21 7704
unto the LORD, as a *f* devoted ... Lev 27:21 7704
the LORD a *f* which he hath bought ... Lev 27:22 7704
f shall return unto him of whom ... Lev 27:24 7704
of the *f* of his possession, shall ... Lev 27:28 7704
ox licketh up the grass of the *f* ... Num 22:4 7704
of the way, and went into the *f* ... Num 22:23 7704
brought him into the *f* of Zophim ... Num 23:14 7704
thy neighbour's house, his *f* ... Deut 5:21 7704
of the *f* increase upon thee ... Deut 7:22 7704
that the *f* bringeth forth year by ... Deut 14:22 7704
f is man's life) to employ them ... Deut 20:19 7704
to possess it, lying in the *f* ... Deut 21:1 7704
find a betrothed damsel in the *f* ... Deut 22:25 7704
For he found her in the *f* ... Deut 22:27 7704
down thine harvest in thy *f* ... Deut 24:19 7704
and hast forgot a sheaf in the *f* ... Deut 24:19 7704
and blessed shalt thou be in the *f* ... Deut 28:3 7704
and cursed shalt thou be in the *f* ... Deut 28:16 7704
carry much seed out into the *f* ... Deut 28:38 7704
the inhabitants of Ai in the *f* ... Josh 8:24 7704
him to ask of her father a *f* ... Josh 15:18 7704
him to ask of her father a *f* ... Judg 1:14 7704
marchedst out of the *f* of Edom ... Judg 5:4 7704
death in the high places of the *f* ... Judg 5:18 7704
thee, and lie in wait in the *f* ... Judg 9:32 7704
the people went out into the *f* ... Judg 9:42 7704
companies, and laid wait in the *f* ... Judg 9:43 7704
the woman as she sat in the *f* ... Judg 13:9 7704
his work out of the *f* at even ... Judg 19:16 7704
and the other to Gibeah in the *f* ... Judg 20:31 7704
Naomi, Let me now go to the *f* ... Ruth 2:2 7704
gleaned in the *f* after the ... Ruth 2:3 7704
part of the *f* belonging unto Boaz ... Ruth 2:3 7704
Go not to glean in another *f* ... Ruth 2:8 7704
be on the *f* that they do reap ... Ruth 2:9 7704
she gleaned in the *f* until even ... Ruth 2:17 7704
they meet thee not in any other *f* ... Ruth 2:22 7704
buyest the *f* of the hand of Naomi ... Ruth 4:5 7704
in the *f* about four thousand men ... 1Sa 4:2 7704
cart came into the *f* of Joshua ... 1Sa 6:14 7704
unto this day in the *f* of Joshua ... 1Sa 6:18 7704
came after the herd out of the *f* ... 1Sa 11:5 7704
trembling in the host, in the *f* ... 1Sa 14:15 7704
air, and to the beasts of the *f* ... 1Sa 17:44 7704
my father in the *f* where thou art ... 1Sa 19:3 7704
the *f* unto the third day at even ... 1Sa 20:5 7704
Come, and let us go out into the *f* ... 1Sa 20:11 7704
went out both of them into the *f* ... 1Sa 20:11 7704
So David hid himself in the *f* ... 1Sa 20:24 7704
the *f* at the time appointed with ... 1Sa 20:35 7704
they found an Egyptian in the *f* ... 1Sa 30:11 7704
were by themselves in the *f* ... 2Sa 10:8 7704
and came out unto us into the *f* ... 2Sa 11:23 7704
they two strove together in the *f* ... 2Sa 14:6 7704
Joab's *f* is near mine, and he hath ... 2Sa 14:30 2513
servants set the *f* on fire ... 2Sa 14:30 2513
thy servants set my *f* on fire ... 2Sa 14:31 2513
robbed of her whelps in the *f* ... 2Sa 17:8 7704
out into the *f* against Israel ... 2Sa 18:6 7704
out of the highway into the *f* ... 2Sa 20:12 7704
nor the beasts of the *f* by night ... 2Sa 21:10 7704
and they two were alone in the *f* ... 1Kin 11:29 7704
him that dieth in the *f* shall the ... 1Kin 14:11 7704
him that dieth in the *f* shall the ... 1Kin 21:24 7704
out into the *f* to gather herbs ... 2Kin 4:39 7704
camp to hide themselves in the *f* ... 2Kin 7:12 7704
all the fruits of the *f* since the ... 2Kin 8:6 7704
of the *f* of Naboth the Jezreelite ... 2Kin 9:25 7704
the *f* in the portion of Jezreel ... 2Kin 9:37 7704
in the highway of the fuller's *f* ... 2Kin 18:17 7704
they were as the grass of the *f* ... 2Kin 19:26 7704
smote Midian in the *f* of Moab ... 1Chr 1:46 7704
come were by themselves in the *f* ... 1Chr 19:9 7704
f for tillage of the ground was ... 1Chr 27:26 7704
him with his fathers in the *f* of ... 2Chr 26:23 7704
and of all the increase of the *f* ... 2Chr 31:5 7704
were fled every one to his *f* ... Neh 13:10 7704
league with the stones of the *f* ... Job 5:23 7704
the beasts of the *f* shall be at ... Job 5:23 7704
reap every one his corn in the *f* ... Job 24:6 7704
all the beasts of the *f* play ... Job 40:20 7704
oxen, yea, and the beasts of the *f* ... Ps 8:7 7704
the wild beasts of the *f* are mine ... Ps 50:11 7704
land of Egypt, in the *f* of Zoan ... Ps 78:12 7704
and his wonders in the *f* of Zoan ... Ps 78:43 7704
beast of the *f* doth devour it ... Ps 80:13 7704
Let the *f* be joyful, and all that ... Ps 96:12 7704
as a flower of the *f*, so he ... Ps 103:15 7704
drink to every beast of the *f* ... Ps 104:11 7704
make it fit for thyself in the *f* ... Prov 24:27 7704
I went by the *f* of the slothful ... Prov 24:30 7704
the goats are the price of the *f* ... Prov 27:26 7704
She considereth a *f*, and buyeth it ... Prov 31:16 7704
king himself is served by the *f* ... Eccl 5:9 7704
roes, and by the hinds of the *f* ... Song 2:7 7704
roes, and by the hinds of the *f* ... Song 3:5 7704
let us go forth into the *f* ... Song 7:11 7704
to house, that lay *f* to *f* ... Is 5:8 7704
to house, that lay *f* to *f* ... Is 5:8 7704
in the highway of the fuller's *f* ... Is 7:3 7704
his forest, and of his fruitful *f* ... Is 10:18
and joy out of the plentiful *f* ... Is 16:10
shall be turned into a fruitful *f* ... Is 29:17
the fruitful *f* shall be esteemed ... Is 29:17
and the wilderness be a fruitful *f* ... Is 32:15
the fruitful *f* be counted for a ... Is 32:15
remain in the fruitful *f* ... Is 32:16
in the highway of the fuller's *f* ... Is 36:2 7704
they were as the grass of the *f* ... Is 37:27 7704
thereof is as the flower of the *f* ... Is 40:6 7704
beast of the *f* shall honour me ... Is 43:20 7704
all the trees of the *f* shall clap ... Is 55:12 7704
All ye beasts of the *f*, come to ... Is 56:9 7704
As keepers of a *f*, are they ... Jer 4:17 7704
Go not forth into the *f*, nor walk ... Jer 6:25 7704
beast, and upon the trees of the *f* ... Jer 7:20 7704
fall as dung upon the open *f* ... Jer 9:22 7704
and the herbs of every *f* wither ... Jer 12:4 7704
assemble all the beasts of the *f* ... Jer 12:9 7704
the hind also calved in the *f* ... Jer 14:5 7704
If I go forth into the *f*, then ... Jer 14:18 7704
O my mountain in the *f*, I will ... Jer 17:3 7704
cometh from the rock of the *f* ... Jer 18:14 7704
Zion shall be plowed like a *f* ... Jer 26:18 7704
the beasts of the *f* have I given ... Jer 27:6 7704
him the beasts of the *f* also ... Jer 28:14 7704
Buy thee my *f* that is in Anathoth ... Jer 32:7 7704
LORD, and said unto me, Buy my *f* ... Jer 32:8 7704
I bought the *f* of Hanameel my ... Jer 32:9 7704
GOD, Buy thee the *f* for money ... Jer 32:25 7704
neither have we vineyard, nor *f* ... Jer 35:9 7704
for we have treasures in the *f* ... Jer 41:8 7704
is taken from the plentiful *f* ... Jer 48:33
for want of the fruits of the *f* ... Lam 4:9 7704
he that is in the *f* shall die ... Eze 7:15 7704
thou wast cast out in the open *f* ... Eze 16:5 7704
to multiply as the bud of the *f* ... Eze 16:7 7704
and planted it in a fruitful *f* ... Eze 17:5 7704
all the trees of the *f* shall know ... Eze 17:24 7704
against the forest of the south *f* ... Eze 20:46 7704
the *f* shall be slain by the sword ... Eze 26:6 7704
the sword thy daughters in the *f* ... Eze 26:8 7704
for meat to the beasts of the *f* ... Eze 29:5 776
unto all the trees of the *f* ... Eze 31:4 7704
above all the trees of the *f* ... Eze 31:5 7704
of the *f* bring forth their young ... Eze 31:6 7704
all the beasts of the *f* shall be ... Eze 31:13 7704
trees of the *f* fainted for him ... Eze 31:15 7704
cast thee forth upon the open *f* ... Eze 32:4 7704
him that is in the open *f* will I ... Eze 33:27 7704
meat to all the beasts of the *f* ... Eze 34:5 7704
meat to every beast of the *f* ... Eze 34:8 7704
the tree of the *f* shall yield her ... Eze 34:27 7704
tree, and the increase of the *f* ... Eze 36:30 7704
heaven, and the beasts of the *f* ... Eze 38:20 7704
beasts of the *f* to be devoured ... Eze 39:4 7704
Thou shalt fall upon the open *f* ... Eze 39:5 7704
shall take no wood out of the *f* ... Eze 39:10 7704
fowl, and to every beast of the *f* ... Eze 39:17 7704
of men dwell, the beasts of the *f* ... Dan 2:38 1251
the beasts of the *f* had shadow ... Dan 4:12 1251
in the tender grass of the *f* ... Dan 4:15 1251
which the beasts of the *f* dwelt ... Dan 4:21 1251
in the tender grass of the *f* ... Dan 4:23 1251
be with the beasts of the *f* ... Dan 4:23 1251
shall be with the beasts of the *f* ... Dan 4:25 1251
shall be with the beasts of the *f* ... Dan 4:32 1251
beasts of the *f* shall eat them ... Hos 2:12 7704
for them with the beasts of the *f* ... Hos 2:18 7704
with the beasts of the *f* ... Hos 4:3 7704
hemlock in the furrows of the *f* ... Hos 10:4 7704
The *f* is wasted, the land ... Joel 1:10 7704
the harvest of the *f* is perished ... Joel 1:11 7704
tree, even all the trees of the *f* ... Joel 1:12 7704
burned all the trees of the *f* ... Joel 1:19 7704
The beasts of the *f* cry also unto ... Joel 1:20 7704
Be not afraid, ye beasts of the *f* ... Joel 2:22 7704
make Samaria as an heap of the *f* ... Mic 1:6 7704
for your sake be plowed as a *f* ... Mic 3:12 7704
and thou shalt dwell in the *f* ... Mic 4:10 7704
rain, to every one grass in the *f* ... Zec 10:1 7704
fruit before the time in the *f* ... Mal 3:11 7704
Consider the lilies of the *f* ... Mt 6:28 *68*
God so clothe the grass of the *f* ... Mt 6:30 *68*
which sowed good seed in his *f* ... Mt 13:24 *68*
not thou sow good seed in thy *f* ... Mt 13:27 *68*
a man took, and sowed in his *f* ... Mt 13:31 *68*
the parable of the tares of the *f* ... Mt 13:36 *68*
The *f* is the world ... Mt 13:38 *68*
is like unto treasure hid in a *f* ... Mt 13:44 *68*
that he hath, and buyeth that *f* ... Mt 13:44 *68*
f return back to take his clothes ... Mt 24:18 *68*
Then shall two be in the *f* ... Mt 24:40 *68*
bought with them the potter's *f* ... Mt 27:7 *68*
Wherefore that *f* was called ... Mt 27:8 *68*
The *f* of blood, unto this day ... Mt 27:8 *68*
And gave them for the potter's *f* ... Mt 27:10 *68*
let him that is in the *f* not turn ... Mk 13:16 *68*
shepherds abiding in the *f* ... Lk 2:8 *68*
grass, which is to day in the *f* ... Lk 12:28 *68*
Now his elder son was in the *f* ... Lk 15:25 *68*
and by, when he is come from the *f* ... Lk 17:7 *68*
and he that is in the *f*, let him ... Lk 17:31 *68*
Two men shall be in the *f* ... Lk 17:36 *68*
Now this man purchased a *f* with ... Acts 1:18 *5564*
insomuch as that *f* is called in ... Acts 1:19 *5564*
that is to say, The *f* of blood ... Acts 1:19 *5564*

FIELDS {59}
of the villages, and out of the *f* ... Ex 8:13 7704
out of the city into the open *f* ... Lev 14:53 7704
counted as the *f* of the country ... Lev 25:31 7704
is not of the *f* of his possession ... Lev 27:22 7704
or given us inheritance of *f* ... Num 16:14 7704
slain with a sword in the open *f* ... Num 19:16 7704
we will not pass through the *f* ... Num 20:17 7704
we will not turn into the *f* ... Num 21:22 7704
grass in thy *f* for thy cattle ... Deut 11:15 7704
might eat the increase of the *f* ... Deut 32:13 7704
of Sodom, and of the *f* of Gomorrah ... Deut 32:32 7709
But the *f* of the city, and the ... Josh 21:12 7704
And they went out into the *f* ... Judg 9:27 7704
all the people that were in the *f* ... Judg 9:44 7704
And he will take your *f*, and your ... 1Sa 8:14 7704
of Jesse give every one of you *f* ... 1Sa 22:7 7704
with them, when we were in the *f* ... 1Sa 25:15 7704
upon you, nor *f* of offerings ... 2Sa 1:21 7704

lord, are encamped in the open *f*.............2Sa 11:11 7704
to Anathoth, unto thine own *f*.................1Kin 2:26 7704
him that dieth of his in the *f*...................1Kin 16:4 7704
Jerusalem in the *f* of Kidron...................2Kin 23:4 7709
But the *f* of the city, and the 1Chr 6:56 7704
let the *f* rejoice, and all that is 1Chr 16:32 7704
and over the storehouses in the *f*.............1Chr 27:25 7704
which were in the *f* of the 2Chr 31:19 7704
And for the villages, with their *f*............Neh 11:25 7704
the *f* thereof, at Azekah, and in...............Neh 11:30 7704
Gilgal, and out of the *f* of Geba ....Neh 12:29 7704
f of the cities the portions of ....Neh 12:44 7704
and sendeth waters upon the *f*..................Job 5:10 2351
And sow the *f*, and plant vineyards,.........Ps 107:37 7704
we found it in the *f* of the wood..............Ps 132:6 7704
had not made the earth, nor the *f*............Prov 8:26 2351
not into the *f* of the fatherless.................Prov 23:10 7704
For the *f* of Heshbon languish, and ....Is 16:8 7709
for the teats, for the pleasant *f*...............Is 32:12 7704
turned unto others, with their *f*..............Jer 6:12 7704
their *f* to them that shall..........................Jer 8:10 7704
on the hills in the *f*...................................Jer 13:27 7704
all the *f* unto the brook of ....Jer 31:40 8309
Houses and *f* and vineyards shall be.......Jer 32:15 7704
f shall be bought in this land, ...Jer 32:43 7704
Men shall buy *f* for money.......................Jer 32:44 7704
vineyards and *f* at the same time ....Jer 39:10 3010
of the forces which were in the *f*.............Jer 40:7 7704
of the forces that were in the *f*................Jer 40:13 7704
thou shalt fall upon the open *f*.................Eze 29:5 7704
as heaps in the furrows of the *f*...............Hos 12:11 7704
shall possess the *f* of Ephraim.................Obad 19 7704
of Ephraim, and the *f* of Samaria ....Obad 19 7704
And they covet *f*, and take them by ....Mic 2:2 7704
away he hath divided our *f*......................Mic 2:4 7704
the *f* shall yield no meat...........................Hab 3:17 7709
the corn *f* on the sabbath day...................Mk 2:23
that he went through the corn *f*................Lk 6:1
sent him into his *f* to feed swine ....Lk 15:15 *68*
up your eyes, and look on the *f*...............Jn 4:35 *5561*
who have reaped down your *f*...................Jas 5:4 *5561*

FIERCE {41}
be their anger, for it was *f*........................Gen 49:7 5794
Turn from thy *f* wrath, and repent ....Ex 32:12 2740
that the *f* anger of the LORD may.............Num 25:4 2740
to augment yet the *f* anger of the ....Num 32:14 2740
A nation of *f* countenance ....Deut 28:50 5794
arose from the table in *f* anger 1Sa 20:34 2750
his *f* wrath upon Amalek,...........................1Sa 28:18 2740
for the *f* wrath of the LORD is 2Chr 28:11 2740
there is *f* wrath against Israel 2Chr 28:13 2740
that his *f* wrath may turn away..................2Chr 29:10 2740
until the *f* wrath of our God for...............Ezr 10:14 2740
lion, and the voice of the *f* lion ....Job 4:10 7826
Thou huntest me as a *f* lion.......................Job 10:16 7826
nor the *f* lion passed by it.........................Job 28:8 7826
None is so *f* that dare stir him ....Job 41:10 393
Thy *f* wrath goeth over me ....Ps 88:16
for the *f* anger of Rezin with ....Is 7:4 2750
f anger, to lay the land desolate ....Is 13:9 2740
and in the day of his *f* anger ....Is 13:13 2740
a *f* king shall rule over them, ...Is 19:4 5794
Thou shalt not see a *f* people....................Is 33:19 3267
for the *f* anger of the LORD is....................Jer 4:8 2740
of the LORD, and by his *f* anger................Jer 4:26 2740
of the *f* anger of the LORD ....Jer 12:13 2740
of the *f* anger of the LORD ....Jer 25:37 2740
and because of his *f* anger.........................Jer 25:38 2740
The *f* anger of the LORD shall not ....Jer 30:24 2740
evil upon them, even my *f* anger ....Jer 49:37 2740
soul from the *f* anger of the LORD ....Jer 51:45 2740
me in the day of his *f* anger.......................Lam 1:12 2740
He hath cut off in his *f* anger ....Lam 2:3 2750
he hath poured out his *f* anger...................Lam 4:11 2740
a king of *f* countenance, and ....Dan 8:23 5794
and turn away from his *f* anger.................Jonah 3:9 2740
are more *f* than the evening.......................Hab 1:8 2300
before the *f* anger of the LORD ....Zeph 2:2 2740
indignation, even all my *f* anger..............Zeph 3:8 2740
out of the tombs, exceeding *f*....................Mt 8:28 *5467*
And they were the more *f*, saying,............Lk 23:5 *2001*
false accusers, incontinent, *f*....................2Ti 3:3 *434*
great, and are driven of *f* winds ....Jas 3:4 *4642*

FIERCENESS {12}
may turn from the *f* of his anger ....Deut 13:17 2740
turned from the *f* of his anger ....Josh 7:26 2740
not from the *f* of his great wrath..............2Kin 23:26 2740
that the *f* of his wrath may turn................2Chr 30:8 2740
He swalloweth the ground with *f*..............Job 39:24 7494
cast upon them the *f* of his anger..............Ps 78:49 2740
thyself from the *f* of thine anger ....Ps 85:3 2740
because of the *f* of the oppressor..............Jer 25:38 2740
not execute the *f* of mine anger................Hos 11:9 2740
can abide in the *f* of his anger...................Nah 1:6 2740
of the wine of the *f* of his wrath ....Rev 16:19 *2372*
treadeth the winepress of the *f*.................Rev 19:15 *2372*

FIERCER {1}
f than the words of the men of 2Sa 19:43 7185

FIERY {20}
the LORD sent *f* serpents among ....Num 21:6 8314
unto Moses, Make thee a *f* serpent ....Num 21:8 8314
wherein were *f* serpents, and...................Deut 8:15 8314
right hand went a *f* law for them ....Deut 33:2 799
Thou shalt make them as a *f* oven.............Ps 21:9 784
fruit shall be a *f* flying serpent.................Is 14:29 8314
f flying serpent, they will carry..................Is 30:6 8314
the midst of a burning *f* furnace ....Dan 3:6 5135
the midst of a burning *f* furnace ....Dan 3:11 5135
the midst of a burning *f* furnace ....Dan 3:15 5135
us from the burning *f* furnace ....Dan 3:17 5135
them into the burning *f* furnace...............Dan 3:20 5135
midst of the burning *f* furnace ....Dan 3:21 5135
midst of the burning *f* furnace ....Dan 3:23 5135
mouth of the burning *f* furnace.................Dan 3:26 5135
his throne was like the *f* flame.................Dan 7:9 5135
A *f* stream issued and came forth..............Dan 7:10 5135
all the *f* darts of the wicked ....Eph 6:16 *4448*
f indignation, which shall devour ....Heb 10:27 *4442*
the *f* trial which is to try you 1Pet 4:12 *4451*

FIFTEEN {24}
f years, and begat sons and ....Gen 5:10 2568,6240
F cubits upward did the waters ....Gen 7:20 2568,6240
an hundred threescore and *f* years ....Gen 25:7 7657,2568
of the gate shall be *f* cubits ....Ex 27:14 2568,6240
side shall be hangings *f* cubits ....Ex 27:15 2568,6240
side of the gate were *f* cubits..................Ex 38:14 2568,6240
hand, were hangings of *f* cubits ....Ex 38:15 2568,6240
f shekels, after the shekel of....................Ex 38:25 7657,2568
thy estimation shall be *f* shekels ....Lev 27:7 2568,6240
six hundred and threescore and *f*..............Num 31:37 7657,2568
about *f* thousand men, all that ....Judg 8:10 2568,6240
Now Ziba had *f* sons and twenty 2Sa 9:10 2568,6240
his *f* sons and his twenty servants...........2Sa 19:17 2568,6240
on forty five pillars, *f* in a row 1Kin 7:3 2568,6240
Jehoahaz king of Israel *f* years 2Kin 14:17 2568,6240
I will add unto thy days *f* years................2Kin 20:6 2568,6240
Jehoahaz king of Israel *f* years 2Chr 25:25 2568,6240
I will add unto thy days *f* years................Is 38:5 2568,6240
f shekels, shall be your maneh..................Eze 45:12 6235,2568
her to me for *f* pieces of silver..................Hos 3:2 2568,6240
Jerusalem, about *f* furlongs off.................Jn 11:18 *1178*
kindred, threescore and *f* souls................Acts 7:14 *1440,4002*
again, and found it *f* fathoms....................Acts 27:28 *1178*
Peter, and abode with him *f* days..............Gal 1:18 *1178*

FIFTEENTH {18}
on the *f* day of the second month ....Ex 16:1 2568,6240
on the *f* day of the same month is ....Lev 23:6 2568,6240
The *f* day of this seventh month ....Lev 23:34 2568,6240
Also in the *f* day of the seventh................Lev 23:39 2568,6240
in the *f* day of this month is the ....Num 28:17 2568,6240
on the *f* day of the seventh month.............Num 29:12 2568,6240
on the *f* day of the first month ....Num 33:3 2568,6240
on the *f* day of the month, like 1Kin 12:32 2568,6240
the *f* day of the eighth month 1Kin 12:33 2568,6240
In the *f* year of Amaziah the son 2Kin 14:23 2568,6240
The *f* to Bilgah, the sixteenth to...............1Chr 24:14 2568,6240
The *f* to Jeremoth, he, his sons, ...1Chr 25:22 2568,6240
in the *f* year of the reign of Asa 2Chr 15:10 2568,6240
on the *f* day of the same they ....Est 9:18 2568,6240
the *f* day of the same, yearly,.....................Est 9:21 2568,6240
in the *f* day of the month, that ....Eze 32:17 2568,6240
in the *f* day of the month, shall ....Eze 45:25 2568,6240
Now in the *f* year of the reign of...............Lk 3:1 *4003*

FIFTH {61}
and the morning were the *f* day ....Gen 1:23 2549
and bare Jacob the *f* son............................Gen 30:17 2549
take up the *f* part of the land of................Gen 41:34 2567
give the *f* part unto Pharaoh ....Gen 47:24 2549
Pharaoh should have the *f* part ....Gen 47:26 2569
and shall add the *f* part thereto ....Lev 5:16 2549
shall add the *f* part more thereto ....Lev 6:5 2549
in the *f* year shall ye eat of the..................Lev 19:25 2549
put the *f* part thereof unto it......................Lev 22:14 2549
then he shall add a *f* part ....Lev 27:13 2549
then he shall add the *f* part of...................Lev 27:15 2549
then he shall add the *f* part of...................Lev 27:19 2549
shall add a *f* part of it thereto ....Lev 27:27 2549
add thereto the *f* part thereof....................Lev 27:31 2549
and add unto it the *f* part thereof ....Num 5:7 2549
On the *f* day Shelumiel the son of ....Num 7:36 2549
on the *f* day nine bullocks, two ....Num 29:26 2549
in the first day of the *f* month ....Num 33:38 2549
the *f* lot came out for the tribe...................Josh 19:24 2549
morning on the *f* day to depart ....Judg 19:8 2549
spear smote him under the *f* rib 2Sa 2:23 2570
and the *f*, Shephatiah the son of 2Sa 3:4 2549
smote him there under the *f* rib 2Sa 3:27 2570
and they smote him under the *f* rib.............2Sa 4:6 2570
smote him therewith in the *f* rib 2Sa 20:10 2570
posts were a *f* part of the wall.....................1Kin 6:31 2549
in the *f* year of king Rehoboam 1Kin 14:25 2549
in the *f* year of Joram the son of 2Kin 8:16 2568
And in the *f* month, on the seventh.............2Kin 25:8 2549
the fourth, Raddai the *f*,..............................1Chr 2:14 2549
The *f*, Shephatiah of Abital..........................1Chr 3:3 2549
Nohah the fourth, and Rapha the *f*...............1Chr 8:2 2549
the fourth, Jeremiah the *f*...........................1Chr 12:10 2549
The *f* to Malchijah, the sixth to....................1Chr 24:9 2549
The *f* to Nethaniah, he, his sons,.................1Chr 25:12 2549
Elam the *f*, Jehohanan the sixth,................1Chr 26:3 2549
the fourth, and Nethaneel the *f*..................1Chr 26:4 2549
The *f* captain for the *f* month 1Chr 27:8 2549
that in the *f* year of king 2Chr 12:2 2549
came to Jerusalem in the *f* month ....Ezr 7:8 2549
on the first day of the *f* month ....Ezr 7:9 2549
unto me in like manner the *f* time...............Neh 6:5 2549
f day of the month Elul, in fifty ....Neh 6:15 2568
Jerusalem captive in the *f* month ....Jer 1:3 2549
fourth year, and in the *f* month...................Jer 28:1 2549
it came to pass in the *f* year of ....Jer 36:9 2549
Now in the *f* month, in the tenth..................Jer 52:12 2549
in the *f* day of the month, as I.....................Eze 1:1 2568
In the *f* day of the month.............................Eze 1:2 2568
which was the *f* year of king ....Eze 1:2 2549
in the *f* day of the month, as I......................Eze 8:1 2568
the seventh year, in the *f* month.................Eze 20:1 2549
in the *f* day of the month, that ....Eze 33:21 2568
Should I weep in the *f* month......................Zec 7:3 2549
ye fasted and mourned in the *f* ....Zec 7:5 2549
month, and the fast of the *f*........................Zec 8:19 2549
And when he had opened the *f* seal ....Rev 6:9 *3991*
the *f* angel sounded, and I saw a ....Rev 9:1 *3991*
the *f* angel poured out his vial ....Rev 16:10 *3991*
The *f*, sardonyx; the sixth...........................Rev 21:20 *3991*

FIFTIES {8}
rulers of hundreds, rulers of *f* ....Ex 18:21 2572
rulers of hundreds, rulers of *f* ....Ex 18:25 2572
over hundreds, and captains over *f*.............Deut 1:15 2572
thousands, and captains over *f*...................1Sa 8:12 2572
the former *f* with their *f*...........................2Kin 1:14 2572
in ranks, by hundreds, and by *f*...................Mk 6:40 *4004*
them sit down by *f* in a company ....Lk 9:14 *4004*

FIFTIETH {4}
And ye shall hallow the *f* year....................Lev 25:10 2572
shall that *f* year be unto you ....Lev 25:11 2572
In the *f* year of Azariah king of..................2Kin 15:23 2572
f year of Azariah king of Judah 2Kin 15:27 2572

FIFTY {157}
the breadth of it *f* cubits ....Gen 6:15 2572
the earth an hundred and *f* days ....Gen 7:24 2572
f days the waters were abated....................Gen 8:3 2572
flood three hundred and *f* years ....Gen 9:28 2572
Noah were nine hundred and *f* years ....Gen 9:29 2572
Peradventure there be *f* righteous ....Gen 18:24 2572
the *f* righteous that are therein ....Gen 18:24 2572
If I find in Sodom *f* righteous ....Gen 18:26 2572
lack five of the *f* righteous..........................Gen 18:28 2572
F loops shalt thou make in the....................Ex 26:5 2572
f loops shalt thou make in the.....................Ex 26:5 2572
thou shalt make *f* taches of gold ....Ex 26:6 2572
thou shalt make *f* loops on the ....Ex 26:10 2572
f loops in the edge of the ....Ex 26:10 2572
thou shalt make *f* taches of brass...............Ex 26:11 2572
shall be hangings of *f* cubits ....Ex 27:12 2572
side eastward shall be *f* cubits ....Ex 27:13 2572
and the breadth *f* every where.....................Ex 27:18 2572
f shekels, and of sweet calamus...................Ex 30:23 2572
calamus two hundred and *f* shekels, ...Ex 30:23 2572
F loops made he in one curtain, ...Ex 36:12 2572
f loops made he in the edge of.....................Ex 36:12 2572
he made *f* taches of gold, and......................Ex 36:13 2572
And he made *f* loops upon the.....................Ex 36:17 2572
f loops made he upon the edge of................Ex 36:17 2572
he made *f* taches of brass to........................Ex 36:18 2572
side were hangings of *f* cubits.....................Ex 38:12 2572
the east side eastward *f* cubits ....Ex 38:13 2572
thousand and five hundred and *f* men ....Ex 38:26 2572
sabbath shall ye number *f* days..................Lev 23:16 2572
shall be *f* shekels of silver ....Lev 27:3 2572
be valued at *f* shekels of silver ....Lev 27:16 2572
of the tribe of Simeon, were *f*......................Num 1:23 2572
and five thousand six hundred and *f* ....Num 1:25 2572
of the tribe of Issachar, were *f*....................Num 1:29 2572
of the tribe of Zebulun, were *f*.....................Num 1:31 2572
of the tribe of Naphtali, were *f*....................Num 1:43 2572
thousand and five hundred and *f*................Num 1:46 2572
were numbered thereof, were *f*.....................Num 2:6 2572
were numbered thereof, were *f*.....................Num 2:8 2572
were numbered of them, were *f*....................Num 2:13 2572
five thousand and six hundred and *f* ....Num 2:15 2572
were an hundred thousand and *f*.................Num 2:16 2572
one thousand and four hundred and *f*...........Num 2:16 2572
were numbered of them, were *f*....................Num 2:30 2572
Dan were an hundred thousand and *f*...........Num 2:31 2572
thousand and five hundred and *f*................Num 2:32 2572
and upward even until *f* years old...............Num 4:3 2572
upward until *f* years old shalt ....Num 4:23 2572
upward even unto *f* years old ....Num 4:30 2572
and upward even unto *f* years old ....Num 4:35 2572
two thousand seven hundred and *f* ....Num 4:36 2572
and upward even unto *f* years old ....Num 4:39 2572
and upward even unto *f* years old ....Num 4:43 2572
and upward even unto *f* years old................Num 4:47 2572
from the age of *f* years they.......................Num 8:25 2572
f princes of the assembly, famous...............Num 16:2 2572
censer, two hundred and *f* censers..............Num 16:17 2572
f men that offered incense ....Num 16:35 2572
devoured two hundred and *f* men ....Num 26:10 2572
that were numbered of them, *f*....................Num 26:34 2572
who were *f* and three thousand and.............Num 26:47 2572
thou shalt take one portion of *f*..................Num 31:30 2572
half, Moses took one portion of *f* ....Num 31:47 2572
seven hundred and *f* shekels........................Num 31:52 2572
father *f* shekels of silver ....Deut 22:29 2572
wedge of gold of *f* shekels weight ....Josh 7:21 2572
he smote of the people *f* thousand..............1Sa 6:19 2572
and *f* men to run before him 2Sa 15:1 2572
the oxen for *f* shekels of silver 2Sa 24:24 2572
and *f* men to run before him 1Kin 1:5 2572
and the breadth thereof *f* cubits.................1Kin 7:2 2572
the length thereof was *f* cubits...................1Kin 7:6 2572
Solomon's work, five hundred and *f*.............1Kin 9:23 2572
and an horse for an hundred and *f*.............1Kin 10:29 2572
and hid them by *f* in a cave........................1Kin 18:4 2572
LORD's prophets by *f* in a cave....................1Kin 18:13 2572
of Baal four hundred and *f*..........................1Kin 18:22 2572
are four hundred and *f* men 1Kin 18:22 2572
him a captain of *f* with his *f*........................2Kin 1:9 2572
and said to the captain of *f* 2Kin 1:10 2572
heaven, and consume thee and thy *f* 2Kin 1:10 2572

heaven, and consumed him and his *f* 2Kin 1:10 2572
captain of *f* with his *f* 2Kin 1:11 2572
heaven, and consume thee and thy *f* 2Kin 1:12 2572
heaven, and consumed him and his *f* 2Kin 1:12 2572
of the third *f* with his *f* 2Kin 1:13 2572
And the third captain of *f* went up 2Kin 1:13 2572
the life of these *f* thy servants 2Kin 1:13 2572
f men of the sons of the prophets 2Kin 2:7 2572
be with thy servants *f* strong men 2Kin 2:16 2572
They sent therefore *f* men 2Kin 2:17 2572
people to Jehoahaz but *f* horsemen 2Kin 13:7 2572
two and *f* years in Jerusalem 2Kin 15:2 2572
of each man *f* shekels of silver, ... 2Kin 15:20 2572
with him *f* men of the Gileadites 2Kin 15:25 2572
he began to reign, and reigned *f* 2Kin 21:1 2572
of their camels *f* thousand 1Chr 5:21 2572
f thousand, and of asses two 1Chr 5:21 2572
and sons' sons, an hundred and *f* 1Chr 8:40 2572
generations, nine hundred and *f* 1Chr 9:9 2572
f thousand, which could keep rank 1Chr 12:33 2572
and an horse for an hundred and *f* 2Chr 1:17 2572
f thousand and three thousand and 2Chr 2:17 2572
the nails was *f* shekels of gold 2Chr 3:9 2572
officers, even two hundred and *f* 2Chr 8:10 2572
f talents of gold, and brought 2Chr 8:18 2572
began to reign, and he reigned *f* 2Chr 26:3 2572
began to reign, and he reigned *f* 2Chr 33:1 2572
of Elam, a thousand two hundred *f* ...... Ezr 2:7 2572
of Bigvai, two thousand *f* ...... Ezr 2:14 2572
children of Adin, four hundred *f* ...... Ezr 2:15 2572
The men of Netophah, *f* and six ...... Ezr 2:22 2572
The children of Nebo, *f* and two ...... Ezr 2:29 2572
children of Magbish, an hundred *f* ...... Ezr 2:30 2572
Elam, a thousand two hundred *f* ...... Ezr 2:31 2572
children of Immer, a thousand *f* ...... Ezr 2:37 2572
children of Nekoda, six hundred *f* ...... Ezr 2:60 2572
of the males an hundred and *f* ...... Ezr 8:3 2572
of Jonathan, and with him *f* males ...... Ezr 8:6 2572
f talents of silver, and silver ...... Ezr 8:26 2572
f of the Jews and rulers, beside ...... Neh 5:17 2572
fifth day of the month Elul, in *f* ...... Neh 6:15 2572
children of Arah, six hundred *f* ...... Neh 7:10 2572
of Elam, a thousand two hundred *f* ...... Neh 7:12 2572
children of Adin, six hundred *f* ...... Neh 7:20 2572
The men of the other Nebo, *f* ...... Neh 7:33 2572
Elam, a thousand two hundred *f* ...... Neh 7:34 2572
children of Immer, a thousand *f* ...... Neh 7:40 2572
f basons, five hundred and thirty ...... Neh 7:70 2572
gallows be made of *f* cubits high ...... Est 5:14 2572
also, the gallows *f* cubits high ...... Est 7:9 2572
The captain of *f*, and the ...... Is 3:3 2572
of the inner gate were *f* cubits ...... Eze 40:15 2572
the length thereof was *f* cubits ...... Eze 40:21 2572
the length was *f* cubits, and the ...... Eze 40:25 2572
it was *f* cubits long, and five and ...... Eze 40:29 2572
it was *f* cubits long, and five and ...... Eze 40:33 2572
the length was *f* cubits, and the ...... Eze 40:36 2572
door, and the breadth was *f* cubits ...... Eze 42:2 2572
the length thereof was *f* cubits ...... Eze 42:7 2572
in the utter court was *f* cubits ...... Eze 42:8 2572
f cubits round about for the ...... Eze 45:2 2572
toward the north two hundred and *f* ...... Eze 48:17 2572
toward the south two hundred and *f* ...... Eze 48:17 2572
toward the east two hundred and *f* ...... Eze 48:17 2572
toward the west two hundred and *f* ...... Eze 48:17 2572
out *f* vessels out of the press ...... Hag 2:16 2572
hundred pence, and the other *f* ...... Lk 7:41 *4004*
and sit down quickly, and write *f* ...... Lk 16:6 *4004*
him, Thou art not yet *f* years old ...... Jn 8:57 *4004*
of great fishes, an hundred and *f* ...... Jn 21:11 *4004*
f years, until Samuel the prophet ...... Acts 13:20 *4004*
found it *f* thousand pieces of ...... Acts 19:19 *4002,3461*

FIG {41}
they sewed *f* leaves together, and ...... Gen 3:7 8384
and *f* trees, and pomegranates ...... Deut 8:8 8384
And the trees said to the *f* tree ...... Judg 9:10 8384
But the *f* tree said unto them, ... Judg 9:11 8384
his vine and under his *f* tree 1Kin 4:25 8384
vine, and every one of his *f* tree 2Kin 18:31 8384
their vines also and their *f* trees ...... Ps 105:33 8384
Whoso keepeth the *f* tree shall ...... Prov 27:18 8384
The *f* tree putteth forth her ...... Song 2:13 8384
as a falling *f* from the *f* tree ...... Is 34:4 8384
vine, and every one of his *f* tree ...... Is 36:16 8384
eat up thy vines and thy *f* trees ...... Jer 5:17 8384
the vine, nor figs on the *f* tree ...... Jer 8:13 8384
her *f* trees, whereof she hath ...... Hos 2:12 8384
in the *f* tree at her first time ...... Hos 9:10 8384
vine waste, and barked my *f* tree ...... Joel 1:7 8384
up, and the *f* tree languisheth ...... Joel 1:12 8384
the *f* tree and the vine do yield ...... Joel 2:22 8384
your *f* trees and your olive trees ...... Amos 4:9 8384
his vine and under his *f* tree ...... Mic 4:4 8384
f trees with the firstripe figs ...... Nah 3:12 8384
Although the *f* tree shall not ...... Hab 3:17 8384
the *f* tree, and the pomegranate, ... Hag 2:19 8384
the vine and under the *f* tree ...... Zec 3:10 8384
when he saw a *f* tree in the way, ... Mt 21:19 *4808*
presently the *f* tree withered ...... Mt 21:19 *4808*
How soon is the *f* tree withered ...... Mt 21:20 *4808*
this which is done to the *f* tree ...... Mt 21:21 *4808*
Now learn a parable of the *f* tree ...... Mt 24:32 *4808*
seeing a *f* tree afar off having ...... Mk 11:13 *4808*
they saw the *f* tree dried up from ...... Mk 11:20 *4808*
the *f* tree which thou cursedst is ...... Mk 11:21 *4808*
Now learn a parable of the *f* tree ...... Mk 13:28 *4808*
A certain man had a *f* tree ...... Lk 13:6 *4808*
come seeking fruit on this *f* tree ...... Lk 13:7 *4808*
Behold the *f* tree, and all the ...... Lk 21:29 *4808*
when thou wast under the *f* tree ...... Jn 1:48 *4808*
thee, I saw thee under the *f* tree ...... Jn 1:50 *4808*
Can the *f* tree, my brethren, bear ...... Jas 3:12 *4808*
even as a *f* tree casteth her ...... Rev 6:13 *4808*

FIGHT {107}
f against us, and so get them up ...... Ex 1:10 3898
The LORD shall *f* for you, and ye ...... Ex 14:14 3898
out men, and go out, *f* with Amalek ...... Ex 17:9 3898
before you, he shall *f* for you ...... Deut 1:30 3898
the LORD, we will go up and *f* ...... Deut 1:41 3898
unto them, Go not up, neither *f* ...... Deut 1:42 3898
and all his people, to *f* at Jahaz ...... Deut 2:32 4421
LORD your God he shall *f* for you ...... Deut 3:22 3898
to *f* for you against your enemies ...... Deut 20:4 3898
nigh unto a city to *f* against it ...... Deut 20:10 3898
to *f* with Joshua and with Israel, ... Josh 9:2 3898
your enemies against whom ye *f* ...... Josh 10:25 3898
of Merom, to *f* against Israel ...... Josh 11:5 3898
Dan went up to *f* against Leshem ...... Josh 19:47 3898
first, to *f* against them ...... Judg 1:1 3898
that we may *f* against the ...... Judg 1:3 3898
down to *f* against the Canaanites ...... Judg 1:9 3898
wentest to *f* with the Midianites ...... Judg 8:1 3898
out, I pray now, and *f* with them ...... Judg 9:38 3898
Jordan to *f* also against Judah ...... Judg 10:9 3898
man is he that will begin to *f* ...... Judg 10:18 3898
that we may *f* with the children ...... Judg 11:6 3898
f against the children of Ammon, ... Judg 11:8 3898
If ye bring me home again to *f* ...... Judg 11:9 3898
come against me to *f* in my land ...... Judg 11:12 3898
or did he ever *f* against them ...... Judg 11:25 3898
of Ammon to *f* against them ...... Judg 11:32 3898
f against the children of Ammon ...... Judg 12:1 3898
unto me this day, to *f* against me ...... Judg 12:3 3898
array to *f* against them at Gibeah ...... Judg 20:20 4421
quit yourselves like men, and *f* 1Sa 4:9 3898
out before us, and *f* our battles 1Sa 8:20 3898
together to *f* with Israel 1Sa 13:5 3898
f against them until they be 1Sa 15:18 3898
If he be able to *f* with me 1Sa 17:9 3898
me a man, that we may *f* together 1Sa 17:10 3898
the host was going forth to the *f* 1Sa 17:20 4634
will go and *f* with this Philistine 1Sa 17:32 3898
this Philistine to *f* with him 1Sa 17:33 3898
for me, and *f* the LORD's battles 1Sa 18:17 3898
the Philistines *f* against Keilah 1Sa 23:1 3898
for warfare, to *f* with Israel 1Sa 28:1 3898
that I may not go *f* against the 1Sa 29:8 3898
nigh unto the city when ye did *f* 2Sa 11:20 3898
to *f* against the house of Israel, ... 1Kin 12:21 3898
nor *f* against your brethren the 1Kin 12:24 3898
but let us *f* against them in the 1Kin 20:23 3898
we will *f* against them in the 1Kin 20:25 3898
up to Aphek, to *f* against Israel 1Kin 20:26 4421
F neither with small nor great, ... 1Kin 22:31 3898
turned aside to *f* against him 1Kin 22:32 3898
were come up to *f* against them 2Kin 3:21 3898
f for your master's house 2Kin 10:3 3898
he is come out to *f* against thee 2Kin 19:9 3898
to *f* against Israel, that he 2Chr 11:1 3898
nor *f* against your brethren 2Chr 11:4 3898
f ye not against the LORD God of 2Chr 13:12 3898
F ye not with small or great, ... 2Chr 18:30 3898
they compassed about him to *f* 2Chr 18:31 3898
not need to *f* in this battle 2Chr 20:17 3898
purposed to *f* against Jerusalem 2Chr 32:2 4421
to help us, and to *f* our battles 2Chr 32:8 3898
up to *f* against Charchemish by 2Chr 35:20 3898
himself, that he might *f* with him 2Chr 35:22 3898
came to *f* in the valley of 2Chr 35:22 3898
to *f* against Jerusalem, and to ...... Neh 4:8 3898
f for your brethren, your sons, ... Neh 4:14 3898
our God shall *f* for us ...... Neh 4:20 3898
f against them that *f* against ...... Ps 35:1 3898
they be many that *f* against me ...... Ps 56:2 3898
hands to war, and my fingers to *f* ...... Ps 144:1 4421
they shall *f* every one against ...... Is 19:2 3898
the nations that *f* against Ariel ...... Is 29:7 6633
even all that *f* against her ...... Is 29:7 6633
that *f* against mount Zion ...... Is 29:8 6633
of shaking will he *f* with it ...... Is 30:32 3898
come down to *f* for mount Zion ...... Is 31:4 6633
they shall *f* against thee ...... Jer 1:19 3898
they shall *f* against thee, but ...... Jer 15:20 3898
wherewith ye *f* against the king ...... Jer 21:4 3898
I myself will *f* against you with ...... Jer 21:5 3898
though ye *f* with the Chaldeans, ... Jer 32:5 3898
that *f* against it, because of the ...... Jer 32:24 3898
that *f* against this city, shall ...... Jer 32:29 3898
They come to *f* with the Chaldeans ...... Jer 33:5 3898
and they shall *f* against it ...... Jer 34:22 3898
f against this city, and take it, ... Jer 37:8 3898
the Chaldeans that *f* against you ...... Jer 37:10 3898
went to *f* with Ishmael the son of ...... Jer 41:12 3898
men of Babylon have forborn to *f* ...... Jer 51:30 3898
now will I return to *f* with the ...... Dan 10:20 3898
f with him, even with the king of ...... Dan 11:11 3898
and they shall *f*, because the LORD ...... Zec 10:5 3898
f against those nations, as when ...... Zec 14:3 3898
Judah also shall *f* at Jerusalem ...... Zec 14:14 3898
world, then would my servants *f* ...... Jn 18:36 *75*
ye be found even to *f* against God ...... Acts 5:39 *2314*
to him, let us not *f* against God ...... Acts 23:9 *2313*
so *f* I, not as one that beateth 1Cor 9:26 *4438*
F the good *f* of faith 1Ti 6:12 *73*
I have fought a good *f*, I have 2Ti 4:7 *75*
endured a great *f* of afflictions ...... Heb 10:32 *119*
made strong, waxed valiant in *f* ...... Heb 11:34 *4171*
ye *f* and war, yet ye have not, ... Jas 4:2 *3164*
will *f* against them with the ...... Rev 2:16 *4170*

FIGHTETH {3}
for the LORD *f* for them against ...... Ex 14:25 3898
your God, he it is that *f* for you ...... Josh 23:10 3898
because my lord *f* the battles of 1Sa 25:28 3898

FIGHTING {3}
of Elah, *f* with the Philistines 1Sa 17:19 3898
Uzziah had an host of *f* men 2Chr 26:11 6213,4421
he *f* daily oppresseth me ...... Ps 56:1 3898

FIGHTINGS {2}
without were *f*, within were fears 2Cor 7:5 *3163*
whence come wars and *f* among you ...... Jas 4:1 *3163*

FIGS {25}
of the pomegranates, and of the *f* ...... Num 13:23 8384
it is no place of seed, or of *f* ...... Num 20:5 8384
and two hundred cakes of *f* 1Sa 25:18 1690
gave him a piece of a cake of *f* 1Sa 30:12 1690
And Isaiah said, Take a lump of *f* 2Kin 20:7 8384
oxen, and meat, meal, cakes of *f* 1Chr 12:40 1690
as also wine, grapes, and *f* ...... Neh 13:15 8384
tree putteth forth her green *f* ...... Song 2:13 6291
said, Let them take a lump of *f* ...... Is 38:21 8384
nor *f* on the fig tree, and the ...... Jer 8:13 8384
two baskets of *f* were set before ...... Jer 24:1 8384
One basket had very good *f* ...... Jer 24:2 8384
even like the *f* that are first ...... Jer 24:2 8384
other basket had very naughty *f* ...... Jer 24:2 8384
And I said, *F* ...... Jer 24:3 8384
the good *f*, very good ...... Jer 24:3 8384
Like these good *f*, so will I ...... Jer 24:5 8384
And as the evil *f*, which cannot be ...... Jer 24:8 8384
and will make them like vile *f* ...... Jer 29:17 8384
fig trees with the firstripe *f* ...... Nah 3:12 1061
of thorns, or *f* of thistles ...... Mt 7:16 *4810*
for the time of *f* was not yet ...... Mk 11:13 *4810*
For of thorns men do not gather *f* ...... Lk 6:44 *4810*
either a vine, *f*? ...... Jas 3:12 *4810*
a fig tree casteth her untimely *f* ...... Rev 6:13 *3653*

FIGURE {7}
image, the similitude of any *f* ...... Deut 4:16 5566
and maketh it after the *f* of a man ...... Is 44:13 8403
who is the *f* of him that was to ...... Rom 5:14 *5179*
I have in a *f* transferred to 1Cor 4:6 *3345*
Which was a *f* for the time then ...... Heb 9:9 *3850*
also he received him in a *f* ...... Heb 11:19 *3850*
The like *f* whereunto even baptism 1Pet 3:21 *499*

FIGURES {3}
about with carved *f* of cherubims 1Kin 6:29 4734
f which ye made to worship them ...... Acts 7:43 *5179*
which are the *f* of the true ...... Heb 9:24 *499*

FILE {1}
Yet they had a *f* for the mattocks 1Sa 13:21 6477,6310

FILL {49}
f the waters in the seas, and let ...... Gen 1:22 4390
to *f* their sacks with corn ...... Gen 42:25 4390
F the men's sacks with food, as ...... Gen 44:1 4390
And they shall *f* thy houses ...... Ex 10:6 4390
F an omer of it to be kept for ...... Ex 16:32 4393
her fruit, and ye shall eat your *f* ...... Lev 25:19 7648
thy *f* at thine own pleasure ...... Deut 23:24 7648
f thine horn with oil, and go, I 1Sa 16:1 4390
F four barrels with water, and 1Kin 18:33 4390
Till he *f* thy mouth with laughing ...... Job 8:21 4390
f his belly with the east wind ...... Job 15:2 4390
When he is about to *f* his belly ...... Job 20:23 4390
f my mouth with arguments ...... Job 23:4 4390
or *f* the appetite of the young ...... Job 38:39 4390
Canst thou *f* his skin with barbed ...... Job 41:7 4390
thy mouth wide, and I will *f* it ...... Ps 81:10 4390
F their faces with shame ...... Ps 83:16 4390
he shall *f* the places with the ...... Ps 110:6 4390
we shall *f* our houses with spoil ...... Prov 1:13 4390
let us take our *f* of love until ...... Prov 7:18 7301
and I will *f* their treasures ...... Prov 8:21 4390
out of his wings shall *f* the ...... Is 8:8 4393
nor *f* the face of the world with ...... Is 14:21 4390
f the face of the world with ...... Is 27:6 4390
we will *f* ourselves with strong ...... Is 56:12 5433
I will *f* all the inhabitants of ...... Jer 13:13 4390
Do not I *f* heaven and earth ...... Jer 23:24 4390
but it is to *f* them with the dead ...... Jer 33:5 4390
Surely I will *f* thee with men ...... Jer 51:14 4390
f thy bowels with this roll that ...... Eze 3:3 4390
souls, neither *f* their bowels ...... Eze 7:19 4390
f the courts with the slain ...... Eze 9:7 4390
f thine hand with coals of fire ...... Eze 10:2 4390
f it with the choice bones ...... Eze 24:4 4390
f the land with the slain ...... Eze 30:11 4390
I will *f* the beasts of the whole ...... Eze 32:4 7646
f the valleys with thy height ...... Eze 32:5 4390
I will *f* his mountains with his ...... Eze 35:8 4390
which *f* their masters' houses ...... Zeph 1:9 4390
I will *f* this house with glory, ... Hag 2:7 4390
for that which is put in to *f* it ...... Mt 9:16 *4138*
as to *f* so great a multitude ...... Mt 15:33 *5526*
F ye up then the measure of your ...... Mt 23:32 *4137*
F the waterpots with water ...... Jn 2:7 *1072*
God of hope *f* you with all joy ...... Rom 15:13 *4137*
that he might *f* all things ...... Eph 4:10 *4137*
f up that which is behind of the ...... Col 1:24 *466*

F

saved, to *f* up their sins alway ... 1Th 2:16 *878*
she hath filled *f* to her double ... Rev 18:6 *2767*

FILLED {159}
and the earth was *f* with violence ... Gen 6:11 4390
for the earth is *f* with violence ... Gen 6:13 4390
f the bottle with water, and gave ... Gen 21:19 4390
f her pitcher, and came up ... Gen 24:16 4390
them, and *f* them with earth ... Gen 26:15 4390
and the land was *f* with them ... Ex 1:7 4390
f the troughs to water their ... Ex 2:16 4390
morning ye shall be *f* with bread ... Ex 16:12 7646
whom I have *f* with the spirit of ... Ex 28:3 4390
I have *f* him with the spirit of ... Ex 31:3 4390
he hath *f* him with the spirit of ... Ex 35:31 4390
Them hath he *f* with wisdom of ... Ex 35:35 4390
of the LORD *f* the tabernacle ... Ex 40:34 4390
of the LORD *f* the tabernacle ... Ex 40:35 4390
all the earth shall be *f* with the ... Num 14:21 4390
may eat within thy gates, and be *f* ... Deut 26:12 7646
f themselves, and waxen fat ... Deut 31:20 7646
these bottles of wine, which we *f* ... Josh 9:13 4390
and he was *f* with wisdom, and ... 1Kin 7:14 4390
that the cloud *f* the house of the ... 1Kin 8:10 4390
LORD had *f* the house of the LORD ... 1Kin 8:11 4390
he *f* the trench also with water ... 1Kin 18:35 4390
but the Syrians *f* the country ... 1Kin 20:27 4390
that valley shall be *f* with water ... 2Kin 3:17 4390
and the country was *f* with water ... 2Kin 3:20 4390
cast every man his stone, and *f* it ... 2Kin 3:25 4390
till he had *f* Jerusalem from one ... 2Kin 21:16 4390
f their places with the bones of ... 2Kin 23:14 4390
for he *f* Jerusalem with innocent ... 2Kin 24:4 4390
then the house was *f* with a cloud ... 2Chr 5:13 4390
the LORD had *f* the house of God ... 2Chr 5:14 4390
the glory of the LORD *f* the house ... 2Chr 7:1 4390
the LORD had *f* the LORD's house ... 2Chr 7:2 4390
bed which was *f* with sweet odours ... 2Chr 16:14 4390
which have *f* it from one end to ... Ezr 9:11 4390
so they did eat, and were *f* ... Neh 9:25 7646
who *f* their houses with silver ... Job 3:15 4390
thou hast *f* me with wrinkles, ... Job 16:8 7059
Yet he *f* their houses with good ... Job 22:18 4390
For my loins are *f* with a ... Ps 38:7 4390
Let my mouth be *f* with thy praise ... Ps 71:8 4390
whole earth be *f* with his glory ... Ps 72:19 4390
So they did eat, and were well *f* ... Ps 78:29 7646
take deep root, and it *f* the land ... Ps 80:9 4390
thine hand, they are *f* with good ... Ps 104:28 7646
are exceedingly *f* with contempt ... Ps 123:3 7646
Our soul is exceedingly *f* with ... Ps 123:4 7646
was our mouth *f* with laughter ... Ps 126:2 4390
be *f* with their own devices ... Prov 1:31 7646
shall thy barns be *f* with plenty ... Prov 3:10 4390
strangers be *f* with thy wealth ... Prov 5:10 7646
wicked shall be *f* with mischief ... Prov 12:21 4390
shall be *f* with his own ways ... Prov 14:14 7646
of his lips shall he be *f* ... Prov 18:20 7646
his mouth shall be *f* with gravel ... Prov 20:17 4390
chambers be *f* with all precious ... Prov 24:4 4390
thee, lest thou be *f* therewith ... Prov 25:16 7646
earth that is not *f* with water ... Prov 30:16 7646
and a fool when he is *f* with meat ... Prov 30:22 7646
nor the ear *f* with hearing ... Eccl 1:8 4390
and his soul be not *f* with good ... Eccl 6:3 7646
and yet the appetite is not *f* ... Eccl 6:7 4390
for my head is *f* with dew ... Song 5:2 4390
up, and his train *f* the temple ... Is 6:1 4390
and the house was *f* with smoke ... Is 6:4 4390
are my loins *f* with pain ... Is 21:3 4390
he hath *f* Zion with judgment and ... Is 33:5 4390
sword of the LORD is *f* with blood ... Is 34:6 4390
neither hast thou *f* me with the ... Is 43:24 7301
old man that hath not *f* his days ... Is 65:20 4390
Every bottle shall be *f* with wine ... Jer 13:12 4390
every bottle shall be *f* with wine ... Jer 13:12 4390
for thou hast *f* me with ... Jer 15:17 4390
they have *f* mine inheritance with ... Jer 16:18 4390
have *f* this place with the blood ... Jer 19:4 4390
f it with them that were slain ... Jer 41:9 4390
shame, and thy cry hath *f* the land ... Jer 46:12 4390
though their land was *f* with sin ... Jer 51:5 4390
he hath *f* his belly with my ... Jer 51:34 4390
He hath *f* me with bitterness, he ... Lam 3:15 7646
he is *f* full with reproach ... Lam 3:30 7646
for they have *f* the land with ... Eze 8:17 4390
the cloud *f* the inner court ... Eze 10:3 4390
the house was *f* with the cloud, ... Eze 10:4 4390
ye have *f* the streets thereof ... Eze 11:6 4390
Thou shalt be *f* with drunkenness ... Eze 23:33 4390
of thy merchandise they have *f* ... Eze 28:16 4390
cities be *f* with flocks of men ... Eze 36:38 4390
Thus ye shall be *f* at my table ... Eze 39:20 7646
the glory of the LORD *f* the house ... Eze 43:5 4390
the LORD *f* the house of the LORD ... Eze 44:4 4390
mountain, and *f* the whole earth ... Dan 2:35 4391
to their pasture, so were they *f* ... Hos 13:6 7646
they were *f*, and their heart was ... Hos 13:6 7646
f his holes with prey, and his ... Nah 2:12 4390
For the earth shall be *f* with the ... Hab 2:14 4390
Thou art *f* with shame for glory ... Hab 2:16 7646
but ye are not *f* with drink ... Hag 1:6
f the bow with Ephraim, and raised ... Zec 9:13 4390
and they shall be *f* like bowls ... Zec 9:15 4390
for they shall be *f* ... Mt 5:6 *5526*
And they did all eat, and were *f* ... Mt 14:20 *5526*
And they did all eat, and were *f* ... Mt 15:37 *5526*
f it with vinegar, and put it on a ... Mt 27:48 *4130*
else the new piece that *f* it up ... Mk 2:21 *4138*
And they did all eat, and were *f* ... Mk 6:42 *5526*
her, Let the children first be *f* ... Mk 7:27 *5526*
So they did eat, and were *f* ... Mk 8:8 *5526*
f a spunge full of vinegar, and ... Mk 15:36 *1072*
he shall be *f* with the Holy Ghost ... Lk 1:15 *4130*
Elisabeth was *f* with the Holy ... Lk 1:41 *4130*
He hath *f* the hungry with good ... Lk 1:53 *1705*
was *f* with the Holy Ghost ... Lk 1:67 *4130*
strong in spirit, *f* with wisdom ... Lk 2:40 *4137*
Every valley shall be *f*, and every ... Lk 3:5 *4137*
these things, were *f* with wrath, ... Lk 4:28 *4130*
f both the ships, so that they ... Lk 5:7 *4130*
were *f* with fear, saying, We have ... Lk 5:26 *4130*
And they were *f* with madness ... Lk 6:11 *4130*
for ye shall be *f* ... Lk 6:21 *5526*
they were *f* with water, and were ... Lk 8:23 *4845*
And they did eat, and were all *f* ... Lk 9:17 *5526*
come in, that my house may be *f* ... Lk 14:23 *1072*
he would fain have *f* his belly ... Lk 15:16 *1072*
they *f* them up to the brim ... Jn 2:7 *1072*
When they were *f*, he said unto ... Jn 6:12 *1705*
f twelve baskets with the ... Jn 6:13 *1072*
did eat of the loaves, and were *f* ... Jn 6:26 *5526*
the house was *f* with the odour of ... Jn 12:3 *4137*
you, sorrow hath *f* your heart ... Jn 16:6 *4137*
they *f* a spunge with vinegar, and ... Jn 19:29 *4130*
it *f* all the house where they ... Acts 2:2 *4137*
they were all *f* with the Holy ... Acts 2:4 *4130*
they were *f* with wonder and ... Acts 3:10 *4130*
f with the Holy Ghost, said unto ... Acts 4:8 *4130*
they were all *f* with the Holy ... Acts 4:31 *4130*
why hath Satan *f* thine heart to ... Acts 5:3 *4137*
and were *f* with indignation, ... Acts 5:17 *4137*
ye have *f* Jerusalem with your ... Acts 5:28 *4137*
and be *f* with the Holy Ghost ... Acts 9:17 *4130*
f with the Holy Ghost, set his ... Acts 13:9 *4130*
multitudes, they were *f* with envy ... Acts 13:45 *4130*
And the disciples were *f* with joy ... Acts 13:52 *4137*
whole city was *f* with confusion ... Acts 19:29 *4130*
Being *f* with all unrighteousness, ... Rom 1:29 *4137*
f with all knowledge, able also ... Rom 15:14 *4137*
I be somewhat *f* with your company ... Rom 15:24 *1705*
I am *f* with comfort, I am ... 2Cor 7:4 *4137*
that ye might be *f* with all the ... Eph 3:19 *4137*
but be *f* with the Spirit ... Eph 5:18 *4137*
Being *f* with the fruits of ... Phil 1:11 *4137*
to desire that ye might be *f* with ... Col 1:9 *4137*
tears, that I may be *f* with joy ... 2Ti 1:4 *4137*
in peace, be ye warmed and *f* ... Jas 2:16 *5526*
f it with fire of the altar, and ... Rev 8:5 *1072*
for in them is *f* up the wrath of ... Rev 15:1 *5055*
the temple was *f* with smoke from ... Rev 15:8 *1072*
she hath *f* fill to her double ... Rev 18:6 *2767*
the fowls were *f* with their flesh ... Rev 19:21 *5526*

FILLEDST {2}
all good things, which thou *f* not ... Deut 6:11 4390
of the seas, thou *f* many people ... Eze 27:33 7646

FILLEST {1}
whose belly thou *f* with thy hid ... Ps 17:14 4390

FILLET {1}
a *f* of twelve cubits did compass ... Jer 52:21 2339

FILLETED {3}
the court shall be *f* with silver ... Ex 27:17 2836
of the court were *f* with silver ... Ex 38:17 2836
their chapiters, and *f* them ... Ex 38:28 2836

FILLETH {6}
breath, but *f* me with bitterness ... Job 9:18 7646
the rain also *f* the pools ... Ps 84:6 5844
f the hungry soul with goodness ... Ps 107:9 4390
the mower *f* not his hand ... Ps 129:7 4390
f thee with the finest of the ... Ps 147:14 7646
fulness of him that *f* all in all ... Eph 1:23 *4131*

FILLETS {8}
their *f* shall be of silver ... Ex 27:10 2838
the pillars and their *f* of silver ... Ex 27:11 2838
chapiters and their *f* with gold ... Ex 36:38 2838
pillars and their *f* were of silver ... Ex 38:10 2838
the pillars and their *f* of silver ... Ex 38:11 2838
the pillars and their *f* of silver ... Ex 38:12 2838
the pillars and their *f* of silver ... Ex 38:17 2838
chapiters and their *f* of silver ... Ex 38:19 2838

FILLING {1}
f our hearts with food and ... Acts 14:17 *1705*

FILTH {4}
the *f* of the daughters of Zion ... Is 4:4 6675
will cast abominable *f* upon thee ... Nah 3:6
we are made as the *f* of the world ... 1Cor 4:13 *4027*
away of the *f* of the flesh ... 1Pet 3:21 *4509*

FILTHINESS {16}
carry forth the *f* out of the holy ... 2Chr 29:5 5079
the *f* of the heathen of the land ... Ezr 6:21 2932
the *f* of the people of the lands ... Ezr 9:11 5079
and yet is not washed from their *f* ... Prov 30:12 6675
all tables are full of vomit and *f* ... Is 28:8 6675
Her *f* is in her skirts ... Lam 1:9 2932
Because thy *f* was poured out, and ... Eze 16:36 5178
and will consume thy *f* out of thee ... Eze 22:15 2932
that the *f* of it may be molten in ... Eze 24:11 2932
In thy *f* is lewdness ... Eze 24:13 2932
not be purged from thy *f* any more ... Eze 24:13 2932
from all your *f*, and from all your ... Eze 36:25 2932
ourselves from all *f* of the flesh ... 2Cor 7:1 *3436*
Neither *f*, nor foolish talking, ... Eph 5:4 *151*
Wherefore lay apart all *f* ... Jas 1:21 *4507*
and *f* of her fornication ... Rev 17:4 *168*

FILTHY {17}
f is man, which drinketh iniquity ... Job 15:16 444
they are all together become *f* ... Ps 14:3 444
they are altogether become *f* ... Ps 53:3 444
our righteousnesses are as *f* rags ... Is 64:6 5708
Woe to her that is *f* and polluted, ... Zeph 3:1 4754
was clothed with *f* garments ... Zec 3:3 6674
Take away the *f* garments from him ... Zec 3:4 6674
f communication out of your mouth ... Col 3:8 *148*
no striker, not greedy of *f* lucre ... 1Ti 3:3
much wine, not greedy of *f* lucre ... 1Ti 3:8
no striker, not given to *f* lucre ... Titus 1:7 *150*
ought not, for *f* lucre's sake ... Titus 1:11 *150*
not for *f* lucre, but of a ready ... 1Pet 5:2 *147*
vexed with the *f* conversation of ... 2Pet 2:7 *766*
Likewise also these *f* dreamers ... Jude 8
and he which is *f*, let him be ... Rev 22:11 *4510*
let him be *f* still ... Rev 22:11 *4510*

FINALLY {6}
F, brethren, farewell ... 2Cor 13:11 *3063*
F, my brethren, be strong in the ... Eph 6:10 *3063*
F, my brethren, rejoice in the ... Phil 3:1 *3063*
F, brethren, whatsoever things ... Phil 4:8 *3063*
F, brethren, pray for us, that ... 2Th 3:1 *3063*
F, be ye all of one mind, having ... 1Pet 3:8 *5056*

FIND {156}
If I *f* in Sodom fifty righteous ... Gen 18:26 4672
If I *f* there forty and five, I ... Gen 18:28 4672
not do it, if I *f* thirty there ... Gen 18:30 4672
wearied themselves to *f* the door ... Gen 19:11 4672
that I may *f* grace in thy sight ... Gen 32:5 4672
ye speak unto Esau, when ye *f* him ... Gen 32:19 4672
These are to *f* grace in the sight ... Gen 33:8 4672
let me *f* grace in the sight of my ... Gen 33:15 4672
Let me *f* grace in your eyes, and ... Gen 34:11 4672
to Judah, and said, I cannot *f* her ... Gen 38:22 4672
Can we *f* such a one as this is, a ... Gen 41:38 4672
let us *f* grace in the sight of my ... Gen 47:25 4672
get you straw where ye can *f* it ... Ex 5:11 4672
ye shall not *f* it in the field ... Ex 16:25 4672
that I may *f* grace in thy sight ... Ex 33:13 4672
be sure your sin will *f* you out ... Num 32:23 4672
the revenger of blood *f* him ... Num 35:27 4672
LORD thy God, thou shalt *f* him ... Deut 4:29 4672
a man *f* her in the city, and lie ... Deut 22:23 4672
But if a man *f* a betrothed damsel ... Deut 22:25 4672
If a man *f* a damsel that is a ... Deut 22:28 4672
that she *f* no favour in his eyes ... Deut 24:1 4672
nations shalt thou *f* no ease ... Deut 28:65
to them as thou shalt *f* occasion ... Judg 9:33 4672
f it out, then I will give you ... Judg 14:12 4672
sojourn where he could *f* a place ... Judg 17:8 4672
to sojourn where I may *f* a place ... Judg 17:9 4672
LORD grant you that ye may *f* rest ... Ruth 1:9 4672
in whose sight I shall *f* grace ... Ruth 2:2 4672
Let me *f* favour in thy sight, my ... Ruth 2:13 4672
handmaid *f* grace in thy sight ... 1Sa 1:18 4672
city, ye shall straightway *f* him ... 1Sa 9:13 4672
about this time ye shall *f* him ... 1Sa 9:13 4672
then thou shalt *f* two men by ... 1Sa 10:2 4672
lad, saying, Go, *f* out the arrows ... 1Sa 20:21 4672
f out now the arrows which I ... 1Sa 20:36 4672
Saul my father shall not *f* thee ... 1Sa 23:17 4672
For if a man *f* his enemy, will he ... 1Sa 24:19 4672
young men *f* favour in thine eyes ... 1Sa 25:8 4672
if I shall *f* favour in the eyes ... 2Sa 15:25 4672
that I may *f* grace in thy sight ... 2Sa 16:4 4672
had sought and could not *f* them ... 2Sa 17:20 4672
peradventure we may *f* grass to ... 1Kin 18:5 4672
and tell Ahab, and he cannot *f* thee ... 1Kin 18:12 4672
to *f* out every device which shall ... 2Chr 2:14 2803
ye shall *f* them at the end of the ... 2Chr 20:16 4672
your children shall *f* compassion ... 2Chr 30:9
of Assyria come, and *f* much water ... 2Chr 32:4 4672
so shalt thou *f* in the book of ... Ezr 4:15 7912
gold that thou canst *f* in all the ... Ezr 7:16 7912
glad, when they can *f* the grave ... Job 3:22 4672
Canst thou by searching *f* out God ... Job 11:7 4672
canst thou *f* out the Almighty ... Job 11:7 4672
for I cannot *f* one wise man among ... Job 17:10 4672
that I knew where I might *f* him ... Job 23:3 4672
cause every man to *f* according to ... Job 34:11 4672
the Almighty, we cannot *f* him out ... Job 37:23 4672
his wickedness till thou *f* none ... Ps 10:15 4672
hast tried me, and shalt *f* nothing ... Ps 17:3 4672
Thine hand shall *f* out all thine ... Ps 21:8 4672
thy right hand shall *f* out those ... Ps 21:8 4672
Until I *f* out a place for the ... Ps 132:5 4672
We shall *f* all precious substance ... Prov 1:13 4672
me early, but they shall not *f* me ... Prov 1:28 4672
LORD, and *f* the knowledge of God ... Prov 2:5 4672
So shalt thou *f* favour and good ... Prov 3:4 4672
are life unto those that *f* them ... Prov 4:22 4672
and right to them that *f* knowledge ... Prov 8:9 4672
and *f* out knowledge of witty ... Prov 8:12 4672
that seek me early shall *f* me ... Prov 8:17 4672
a matter wisely shall *f* good ... Prov 16:20 4672
understanding shall *f* good ... Prov 19:8 4672
but a faithful man who can *f* ... Prov 20:6 4672
shall *f* more favour than he that ... Prov 28:23 4672
Who can *f* a virtuous woman ... Prov 31:10 4672
so that no man can *f* out the work ... Eccl 3:11 4672
man should *f* nothing after him ... Eccl 7:14 4672
exceeding deep, who can *f* it out ... Eccl 7:24 4672
I *f* more bitter than death the ... Eccl 7:26 4672

one by one, to *f* out the account Eccl 7:27 4672
yet my soul seeketh, but I *f* not Eccl 7:28 4672
that a man cannot *f* out the work Eccl 8:17 4672
it out, yet he shall not *f* it Eccl 8:17 4672
yet shall he not be able to *f* it Eccl 8:17 4672
for thou shalt *f* it after many Eccl 11:1 4672
sought to *f* out acceptable words Eccl 12:10 4672
sought him, but I could not *f* him Song 5:6 4672
if ye *f* my beloved, that ye tell Song 5:8 4672
when I should *f* thee without Song 8:1 4672
f for herself a place of rest Is 34:14 4672
seek them, and shalt not *f* them Is 41:12 4672
day of your fast ye *f* pleasure Is 58:3 4672
in her month they shall *f* her Jer 2:24 4672
places thereof, if ye can *f* a man Jer 5:1 4672
ye shall *f* rest for your souls Jer 6:16 4672
them, that they may *f* it so Jer 10:18 4672
f me, when ye shall search for me Jer 29:13 4672
in my sighing, and I *f* no rest Jer 45:3 4672
like harts that *f* no pasture Lam 1:6 4672
her prophets also *f* no vision Lam 2:9 4672
princes sought to *f* occasion Dan 6:4 7912
but they could *f* none occasion Dan 6:4 7912
We shall not *f* any occasion Dan 6:5 7912
except we *f* it against him Dan 6:5 7912
that she shall not *f* her paths Hos 2:6 4672
seek them, but shall not *f* them Hos 2:7 4672
but they shall not *f* him Hos 5:6 4672
in all my labours they shall *f* Hos 12:8 4672
of the LORD, and shall not *f* it Amos 8:12 4672
seek, and ye shall *f* Mt 7:7 2147
life, and few there be that *f* it Mt 7:14 2147
his life for my sake shall *f* it Mt 10:39 2147
ye shall *f* rest unto your souls Mt 11:29 2147
his life for my sake shall *f* it Mt 16:25 2147
thou shalt *f* a piece of money Mt 17:27 2147
And if so be that he *f* it, verily Mt 18:13 2147
ye shall *f* an ass tied, and a colt Mt 21:2 2147
and as many as ye shall *f* Mt 22:9 2147
when he cometh shall *f* so doing Mt 24:46 2147
ye shall *f* a colt tied, whereon Mk 11:2 2147
he might *f* any thing thereon Mk 11:13 2147
coming suddenly he *f* you sleeping Mk 13:36 2147
Ye shall *f* the babe wrapped in Lk 2:12 2147
when they could not *f* by what way Lk 5:19 2147
that they might *f* an accusation Lk 6:7 2147
seek, and ye shall *f* Lk 11:9 2147
when he cometh shall *f* watching Lk 12:37 2147
f them so, blessed are those Lk 12:38 2147
when he cometh shall *f* so doing Lk 12:43 2147
fruit on this fig tree, and *f* none Lk 13:7 2147
that which is lost, until he *f* it Lk 15:4 2147
and seek diligently till she *f* it Lk 15:8 2147
shall he *f* faith on the earth Lk 18:8 2147
entering ye shall *f* a colt tied Lk 19:30 2147
could not *f* what they might do Lk 19:48 2147
people, I *f* no fault in this man Lk 23:4 2147
shall seek me, and shall not *f* me Jn 7:34 2147
he go, that we shall not *f* him Jn 7:35 2147
shall seek me, and shall not *f* me Jn 7:36 2147
shall go in and out, and *f* pasture Jn 10:9 2147
I *f* in him no fault at all Jn 18:38 2147
may know that I *f* no fault in him Jn 19:4 2147
for I *f* no fault in him Jn 19:6 2147
side of the ship, and ye shall *f* Jn 21:6 2147
desired to *f* a tabernacle for the Acts 7:46 2147
f him, though he be not far from Acts 17:27 2147
saying, We *f* no evil in this man Acts 23:9 2147
that which is good I *f* not Rom 7:18 2147
I *f* then a law, that, when I Rom 7:21 2147
unto me, Why doth he yet *f* fault Rom 9:19
f you unprepared, we (that we say 2Cor 9:4 2147
I shall not *f* you such as I would 2Cor 12:20 2147
f mercy of the Lord in that day 2Ti 1:18 2147
f grace to help in time of need Heb 4:16 2147
men seek death, and shall not *f* it Rev 9:6 2147
thou shalt *f* them no more at all Rev 18:14 2147

FINDEST {2}
With whomsoever thou *f* thy gods Gen 31:32 4672
me, Son of man, eat that thou *f* Eze 3:1 4672

FINDETH {27}
every one that *f* me shall slay me Gen 4:14 4672
he *f* occasions against me, he Job 33:10 4672
word, as one that *f* great spoil Ps 119:162 4672
Happy is the man that *f* wisdom Prov 3:13 4672
For whoso *f* me *f* life Prov 8:35 4672
seeketh wisdom, and *f* it not Prov 14:6 4672
hath a froward heart *f* no good Prov 17:20 4672
Whoso *f* a wife *f* a good Prov 18:22 4672
his neighbour *f* no favour in his Prov 21:10
righteousness and mercy *f* life Prov 21:21 4672
Whatsoever thy hand *f* to do Eccl 9:10 4672
among the heathen, she *f* no rest Lam 1:3 4672
in thee the fatherless *f* mercy Hos 14:3
and he that seeketh *f* Mt 7:8 2147
He that *f* his life shall lose it Mt 10:39 2147
places, seeking rest, and *f* none Mt 12:43 2147
is come, he *f* it empty, swept, and Mt 12:44 2147
f them asleep, and saith unto Mt 26:40 2147
f them sleeping, and saith unto Mk 14:37 2147
and he that seeketh *f* Lk 11:10 2147
he *f* it swept and garnished Lk 11:25 2147
He first *f* his own brother Simon, Jn 1:41 2147
f Philip, and saith unto him, Jn 1:43 2147
Philip *f* Nathanael, and saith unto Jn 1:45 2147
Afterward Jesus *f* him in the Jn 5:14 2147

FINDING {10}
lest any *f* him should kill him Gen 4:15 4672
doeth great things past *f* out Job 9:10 2714
nor *f* thine own pleasure, nor Is 58:13 4672
f none, he saith, I will return Lk 11:24 2147
f nothing how they might punish Acts 4:21 2147
and *f* certain disciples, Acts 19:1 2147
f a ship sailing over unto Acts 21:2 2147
f disciples, we tarried there Acts 21:4 429
judgments, and his ways past *f* out Rom 11:33 421
For *f* fault with them, he saith, Heb 8:8

FINE {113}
quickly three measures of *f* meal Gen 18:6
him in vestures of *f* linen Gen 41:42
and *f* linen, and goats' hair, Ex 25:4
ten curtains of *f* twined linen Ex 26:1
f twined linen of cunning work Ex 26:31
f twined linen, wrought with Ex 26:36
of *f* twined linen of an hundred Ex 27:9
f twined linen, wrought with Ex 27:16
five cubits of *f* twined linen Ex 27:18
and purple, and scarlet, and *f* linen Ex 28:5
f twined linen, with cunning work Ex 28:6
and scarlet, and *f* twined linen Ex 28:8
of *f* twined linen, shalt thou Ex 28:15
embroider the coat of *f* linen Ex 28:39
shalt make the mitre of *f* linen Ex 28:39
and *f* linen, and goats' hair, Ex 35:6
f linen, and goats' hair, and red Ex 35:23
and of scarlet, and of *f* linen Ex 35:25
in *f* linen, and of the weaver, Ex 35:35
ten curtains of *f* twined linen Ex 36:8
and scarlet, and *f* twined linen Ex 36:35
f twined linen, of needlework Ex 36:37
the court were of *f* twined linen Ex 38:9
about were of *f* twined linen Ex 38:16
and scarlet, and *f* twined linen Ex 38:18
purple, and in scarlet, and *f* linen Ex 38:23
and scarlet, and *f* twined linen Ex 39:2
in the scarlet, and in the *f* linen Ex 39:3
and scarlet, and *f* twined linen Ex 39:5
and scarlet, and *f* twined linen Ex 39:8
they made coats of *f* linen of Ex 39:27
And a mitre of *f* linen Ex 39:28
and goodly bonnets of *f* linen Ex 39:28
linen breeches of *f* twined linen Ex 39:28
a girdle of *f* twined linen, and Ex 39:29
his offering shall be of *f* flour Lev 2:1
cakes of *f* flour mingled with oil Lev 2:4
it shall be of *f* flour unleavened Lev 2:5
shall be made of *f* flour with oil Lev 2:7
of *f* flour for a sin offering Lev 5:11
of *f* flour for a meat offering Lev 6:20
with oil, of *f* flour, fried Lev 7:12
three tenth deals of *f* flour for Lev 14:10
one tenth deal of *f* flour mingled Lev 14:21
deals of *f* flour mingled with oil Lev 23:13
they shall be of *f* flour Lev 23:17
And thou shalt take *f* flour Lev 24:5
cakes of *f* flour mingled with oil Num 6:15
both of them were full of *f* flour Num 7:13
both of them full of *f* flour Num 7:19
both of them full of *f* flour Num 7:25
both of them full of *f* flour Num 7:31
both of them full of *f* flour Num 7:37
both of them full of *f* flour Num 7:43
both of them full of *f* flour Num 7:49
both of them full of *f* flour Num 7:55
both of them full of *f* flour Num 7:61
both of them full of *f* flour Num 7:67
both of them full of *f* flour Num 7:73
both of them full of *f* flour Num 7:79
even *f* flour mingled with oil, and Num 8:8
was thirty measures of *f* flour 1Kin 4:22
of *f* flour be sold for a shekel 2Kin 7:1
So a measure of *f* flour was sold 2Kin 7:16
a measure of *f* flour for a shekel 2Kin 7:18
of them that wrought *f* linen 1Chr 4:21
the *f* flour, and the wine, and the 1Chr 9:29
clothed with a robe of *f* linen 1Chr 15:27
for the *f* flour for meat offering 1Chr 23:29
in *f* linen, and in crimson 2Chr 2:14
which he overlaid with *f* gold 2Chr 3:5 2896
and he overlaid it with *f* gold 2Chr 3:8 2896
f linen, and wrought cherubims 2Chr 3:14
and two vessels of *f* copper Ezr 8:27 6668
fastened with cords of *f* linen Est 1:6
and with a garment of *f* linen Est 8:15
a place for gold where they *f* it Job 28:1 2212
shall not be for jewels of *f* gold Job 28:17
hope, or have said to the *f* gold Job 31:24
than gold, yea, than much *f* gold Ps 19:10
yea, above *f* gold Ps 119:127
and the gain thereof than *f* gold Prov 3:14
works, with *f* linen of Egypt Prov 7:16
than gold, yea, than *f* gold Prov 8:19
of gold, and an ornament of *f* gold Prov 25:12
She maketh *f* linen, and selleth it Prov 31:24
His head is as the most *f* gold Song 5:11
set upon sockets of *f* gold Song 5:15
the *f* linen, and the hoods, and the Is 3:23
a man more precious than *f* gold Is 13:12
Moreover they that work in *f* flax Is 19:9 8305
how is the most *f* gold changed Lam 4:1
of Zion, comparable to *f* gold Lam 4:2
I girded thee about with *f* linen Eze 16:10
and thy raiment was of *f* linen Eze 16:13
thou didst eat *f* flour, and honey, Eze 16:13
f flour, and oil, and honey, Eze 16:19
F linen with broidered work from Eze 27:7
f linen, and coral, and agate Eze 27:16
oil, to temper with the *f* flour Eze 46:14
This image's head was of *f* gold Dan 2:32 2869
were girded with *f* gold of Uphaz Dan 10:5
f gold as the mire of the streets Zec 9:3
And he bought *f* linen, and took him Mk 15:46
f linen, and fared sumptuously Lk 16:19
And his feet like unto *f* brass Rev 1:15
and his feet are like *f* brass Rev 2:18
f linen, and purple, and silk, and Rev 18:12
f flour, and wheat, and beasts, and Rev 18:13 4585
city, that was clothed in *f* linen Rev 18:16
she should be arrayed in *f* linen Rev 19:8
for the *f* linen is the Rev 19:8
white horses, clothed in *f* linen Rev 19:14

FINER {1}
come forth a vessel for the *f* Prov 25:4 6884

FINEST {2}
them also with the *f* of the wheat Ps 81:16 2459
thee with the *f* of the wheat Ps 147:14 2459

FINGER {26}
Pharaoh, This is the *f* of God Ex 8:19 676
the horns of the altar with thy *f* Ex 29:12 676
stone, written with the *f* of God Ex 31:18 676
shall dip his *f* in the blood Lev 4:6 676
dip his *f* in some of the blood Lev 4:17 676
of the sin offering with his *f* Lev 4:25 676
of the blood thereof with his *f* Lev 4:30 676
of the sin offering with his *f* Lev 4:34 676
the altar round about with his *f* Lev 8:15 676
and he dipped his *f* in the blood Lev 9:9 676
f in the oil that is in his left Lev 14:16 676
his *f* seven times before the LORD Lev 14:16 676
shall sprinkle with his right *f* Lev 14:27 676
sprinkle it with his *f* upon the Lev 16:14 676
the blood with his *f* seven times Lev 16:14 676
upon it with his *f* seven times Lev 16:19 676
take of her blood with his *f* Num 19:4 676
stone written with the *f* of God Deut 9:10 676
My little *f* shall be thicker than 1Kin 12:10
My little *f* shall be thicker than 2Chr 10:10
yoke, the putting forth of the *f* Is 58:9 676
But if I with the *f* of God cast Lk 11:20 1147
may dip the tip of his *f* in water Lk 16:24 1147
with his *f* wrote on the ground, Jn 8:6 1147
put my *f* into the print of the Jn 20:25 1147
he to Thomas, Reach hither thy *f* Jn 20:27 1147

FINGERS {15}
that had on every hand six *f* 2Sa 21:20 676
a man of great stature, whose *f* 1Chr 20:6 676
thy heavens, the work of thy *f* Ps 8:3 676
my hands to war, and my *f* to fight Ps 144:1 676
his feet, he teacheth with his *f* Prov 6:13 676
Bind them upon thy *f*, write them Prov 7:3 676
my *f* with sweet smelling myrrh, Song 5:5 676
that which their own *f* have made Is 2:8 676
that which his *f* have made Is 17:8 676
blood, and your *f* with iniquity Is 59:3 676
the thickness thereof was four *f* Jer 52:21 676
hour came forth *f* of a man's hand Dan 5:5 677
not move them with one of their *f* Mt 23:4 1147
put his *f* into his ears, and he Mk 7:33 1147
the burdens with one of your *f* Lk 11:46 1147

FINING {2}
The *f* pot is for silver, and the Prov 17:3 4715
As the *f* pot for silver, and the Prov 27:21 4715

FINISH {11}
in a cubit shalt thou *f* it above Gen 6:16 3615
to *f* the transgression, and to Dan 9:24 3607
his hands shall also *f* it Zec 4:9 1214
he have sufficient to *f* it Lk 14:28 535
and is not able to *f* it, all that Lk 14:29 1615
to build, and was not able to *f* Lk 14:30 1615
that sent me, and to *f* his work Jn 4:34 5048
the Father hath given me to *f* Jn 5:36 5048
so that I might *f* my course with Acts 20:24 5048
For he will *f* the work, and cut it Rom 9:28 4931
so he would also *f* in you the 2Cor 8:6 2005

FINISHED {42}
the heavens and the earth were *f* Gen 2:1 3615
of the tent of the congregation *f* Ex 39:32 3615
So Moses *f* the work Ex 40:33 3615
law in a book, until they were *f* Deut 31:24 8552
until every thing was *f* that the Josh 4:10 8552
until he have *f* the thing this Ruth 3:18 3615
So he built the house, and *f* it 1Kin 6:9 3615
Solomon built the house, and *f* it 1Kin 6:14 3615
until he had *f* all the house 1Kin 6:22 8552
was the house *f* throughout all 1Kin 6:38 3615
years, and he *f* all his house 1Kin 7:1 3615
so was the work of the pillars *f* 1Kin 7:22 8552
when Solomon had *f* the building 1Kin 9:1 3615
So he *f* the house 1Kin 9:25 7999
began to number, but he *f* not 1Chr 27:24 3615
until thou hast *f* all the work 1Chr 28:20 3615
Huram *f* the work that he was to 2Chr 4:11 3615
for the house of the LORD was *f* 2Chr 5:1 7999
Thus Solomon *f* the house of the 2Chr 7:11 3615
of the LORD, and until it was *f* 2Chr 8:16 3615
And when they had *f* it, they 2Chr 24:14 3615
until the burnt offering was *f* 2Chr 29:28 3615
Now when all this was *f*, all 2Chr 31:1 3615

F

f them in the seventh month ... 2Chr 31:7 3615
in building, and yet it is not *f* ... Ezr 5:16 8000
and *f* it, according to the ... Ezr 6:14 3635
this house was *f* on the third day ... Ezr 6:15 3319
So the wall was *f* in the twenty ... Neh 6:15 7999
numbered thy kingdom, and *f* it ... Dan 5:26 8000
all these things shall be *f* ... Dan 12:7 3615
when Jesus had *f* these parables ... Mt 13:53 *5055*
when Jesus had *f* these sayings ... Mt 19:1 *5055*
when Jesus had *f* all these ... Mt 26:1 *5055*
I have *f* the work which thou ... Jn 17:4 *5048*
the vinegar, he said, It is *f* ... Jn 19:30 *5055*
when we had *f* our course from ... Acts 21:7 *1274*
I have *f* my course, I have kept ... 2Ti 4:7 *5055*
although the works were *f* from ... Heb 4:3 *1096*
and sin, when it is *f*, bringeth ... Jas 1:15 *658*
the mystery of God should be *f* ... Rev 10:7 *5055*
they shall have *f* their testimony ... Rev 11:7 *5055*
until the thousand years were *f* ... Rev 20:5 *5055*

FINISHER {1}
the author and *f* of our faith ... Heb 12:2 *5047*

FINS {5}
whatsoever hath *f* and scales in ... Lev 11:9 5579
And all that have not *f* and scales ... Lev 11:10 5579
Whatsoever hath no *f* nor scales ... Lev 11:12 5579
all that have *f* and scales shall ... Deut 14:9 5579
And whatsoever hath not *f* and ... Deut 14:10 5579

FIR {21}
of instruments made of *f* wood ... 2Sa 6:5 1265
cedar, and concerning timber of *f* ... 1Kin 5:8 1265
f trees according to all his ... 1Kin 5:10 1265
of the house with planks of *f* ... 1Kin 6:15 1265
And the two doors were of *f* tree ... 1Kin 6:34 1265
f trees, and with gold, according ... 1Kin 9:11 1265
the choice *f* trees thereof ... 2Kin 19:23 1265
f trees, and algum trees, out of ... 2Chr 2:8 1265
house he cieled with *f* tree ... 2Chr 3:5 1265
the *f* trees are her house ... Ps 104:17 1265
are cedar, and our rafters of *f* ... Song 1:17 1266
the *f* trees rejoice at thee, and ... Is 14:8 1265
the choice *f* trees thereof ... Is 37:24 1265
will set in the desert the *f* tree ... Is 41:19 1265
thorn shall come up the *f* tree ... Is 55:13 1265
the *f* tree, the pine tree, and the ... Is 60:13 1265
ship boards of *f* trees of Senir ... Eze 27:5 1265
the *f* trees were not like his ... Eze 31:8 1265
I am like a green *f* tree ... Hos 14:8 1265
the *f* trees shall be terribly ... Nah 2:3 1265
Howl, *f* tree ... Zec 11:2 1265

FIRE {549}
f from the LORD out of heaven ... Gen 19:24 784
and he took the *f* in his hand ... Gen 22:6 784
And he said, Behold the *f* and the ... Gen 22:7 784
of *f* out of the midst of a bush ... Ex 3:2 784
behold, the bush burned with *f* ... Ex 3:2 784
the *f* ran along upon the ground ... Ex 9:23 784
f mingled with the hail, very ... Ex 9:24 784
flesh in that night, roast with *f* ... Ex 12:8 784
all with water, but roast with *f* ... Ex 12:9 784
the morning ye shall burn with *f* ... Ex 12:10 784
and by night in a pillar of *f* ... Ex 13:21 784
day, nor the pillar of *f* by night ... Ex 13:22 784
Egyptians through the pillar of *f* ... Ex 14:24 784
the LORD descended upon it in *f* ... Ex 19:18 784
If *f* break out, and catch in ... Ex 22:6 784
he that kindled the *f* shall ... Ex 22:6 1200
f on the top of the mount in the ... Ex 24:17 784
thou burn with *f* without the camp ... Ex 29:14 784
offering made by *f* unto the LORD ... Ex 29:18
offering made by *f* unto the LORD ... Ex 29:25
shalt burn the remainder with *f* ... Ex 29:34 784
offering made by *f* unto the LORD ... Ex 29:41
offering made by *f* unto the LORD ... Ex 30:20
had made, and burnt it in the *f* ... Ex 32:20 784
then I cast it into the *f* ... Ex 32:24 784
Ye shall kindle no *f* throughout ... Ex 35:3 784
f was on it by night, in the ... Ex 40:38 784
priest shall put *f* upon the altar ... Lev 1:7 784
lay the wood in order upon the *f* ... Lev 1:7 784
on the *f* which is upon the altar ... Lev 1:8 784
sacrifice, an offering made by *f* ... Lev 1:9
on the *f* which is upon the altar ... Lev 1:12 784
sacrifice, an offering made by *f* ... Lev 1:13
upon the wood that is upon the *f* ... Lev 1:17 784
sacrifice, an offering made by *f* ... Lev 1:17
to be an offering made by *f* ... Lev 2:2
offerings of the LORD made by *f* ... Lev 2:3
it is an offering made by *f* ... Lev 2:9
offerings of the LORD made by *f* ... Lev 2:10
offering of the LORD made by *f* ... Lev 2:11
green ears of corn dried by the *f* ... Lev 2:14 784
offering made by *f* unto the LORD ... Lev 2:16
offering made by *f* unto the LORD ... Lev 3:3
is upon the wood that is on the *f* ... Lev 3:5 784
it is an offering made by *f* ... Lev 3:5
offering made by *f* unto the LORD ... Lev 3:9
offering made by *f* unto the LORD ... Lev 3:11
offering made by *f* unto the LORD ... Lev 3:14
made by *f* for a sweet savour ... Lev 3:16
and burn him on the wood with *f* ... Lev 4:12 784
offerings made by *f* unto the LORD ... Lev 4:35
offerings made by *f* unto the LORD ... Lev 5:12
the *f* of the altar shall be ... Lev 6:9 784
take up the ashes which the *f* ... Lev 6:10 784
the *f* upon the altar shall be ... Lev 6:12 784
The *f* shall ever be burning upon ... Lev 6:13 784
portion of my offerings made by *f* ... Lev 6:17
offerings of the LORD made by *f* ... Lev 6:18
it shall be burnt in the *f* ... Lev 6:30 784
offering made by *f* unto the LORD ... Lev 7:5
third day shall be burnt with *f* ... Lev 7:17 784
it shall be burnt with *f* ... Lev 7:19 784
offering made by *f* unto the LORD ... Lev 7:25
offerings of the LORD made by *f* ... Lev 7:30
offerings of the LORD made by *f* ... Lev 7:35
he burnt with *f* without the camp ... Lev 8:17 784
offering made by *f* unto the LORD ... Lev 8:21
offering made by *f* unto the LORD ... Lev 8:28
of the bread shall ye burn with *f* ... Lev 8:32 784
he burnt with *f* without the camp ... Lev 9:11 784
there came a *f* out from before ... Lev 9:24 784
put *f* therein, and put incense ... Lev 10:1 784
offered strange *f* before the LORD ... Lev 10:1 784
And there went out *f* from the LORD ... Lev 10:2 784
offerings of the LORD made by *f* ... Lev 10:12
sacrifices of the LORD made by *f* ... Lev 10:13
offerings made by *f* of the fat ... Lev 10:15
it shall be burnt in the *f* ... Lev 13:52 784
thou shalt burn it in the *f* ... Lev 13:55 784
that wherein the plague is with *f* ... Lev 13:57 784
f from off the altar before the ... Lev 16:12 784
upon the *f* before the LORD ... Lev 16:13 784
shall burn in the *f* their skins ... Lev 16:27 784
seed pass through the *f* to Molech ... Lev 18:21
day, it shall be burnt in the *f* ... Lev 19:6 784
they shall be burnt with *f* ... Lev 20:14 784
offerings of the LORD made by *f* ... Lev 21:6
she shall be burnt with *f* ... Lev 21:9 784
offerings of the LORD made by *f* ... Lev 21:21
nor make an offering by *f* of them ... Lev 22:22
offering made by *f* unto the LORD ... Lev 22:27
by *f* unto the LORD seven days ... Lev 23:8 784
an offering made by *f* unto the ... Lev 23:13
even an offering made by *f* ... Lev 23:18
offering made by *f* unto the LORD ... Lev 23:25
offering made by *f* unto the LORD ... Lev 23:27 784
offering made by *f* unto the LORD ... Lev 23:36
offering made by *f* unto the LORD ... Lev 23:36
offering made by *f* unto the LORD ... Lev 23:37
offering made by *f* unto the LORD ... Lev 24:7
made by *f* by a perpetual statute ... Lev 24:9
offered strange *f* before the LORD ... Num 3:4 784
put it in the *f* which is under ... Num 6:18 784
as it were the appearance of *f* ... Num 9:15 784
and the appearance of *f* by night ... Num 9:16 784
the *f* of the LORD burnt among ... Num 11:1 784
unto the LORD, the *f* was quenched ... Num 11:2 784
because the *f* of the LORD burnt ... Num 11:3 784
and in a pillar of *f* by night ... Num 14:14 784
an offering by *f* unto the LORD ... Num 15:3
wine, for an offering made by *f* ... Num 15:10
in offering an offering made by *f* ... Num 15:13
will offer an offering made by *f* ... Num 15:14
sacrifice made by *f* unto the LORD ... Num 15:25
put *f* therein, and put incense in ... Num 16:7 784
put *f* in them, and laid incense ... Num 16:18 784
there came out a *f* from the LORD ... Num 16:35 784
and scatter thou the *f* yonder ... Num 16:37 784
put *f* therein from off the altar, ... Num 16:46 784
holy things, reserved from the *f* ... Num 18:9 784
fat for an offering made by *f* ... Num 18:17
For there is a *f* gone out of ... Num 21:28 784
what time the *f* devoured two ... Num 26:10 784
offered strange *f* before the LORD ... Num 26:61 784
bread for my sacrifices made by *f* ... Num 28:2
This is the offering made by *f* ... Num 28:3
sacrifice made by *f* unto the LORD ... Num 28:6
offer it, a sacrifice made by *f* ... Num 28:8
sacrifice made by *f* unto the LORD ... Num 28:13
f for a burnt offering unto the ... Num 28:19
meat of the sacrifice made by *f* ... Num 28:24
sacrifice made by *f* unto the LORD ... Num 29:6
offering, a sacrifice made by *f* ... Num 29:13
offering, a sacrifice made by *f* ... Num 29:36
all their goodly castles, with *f* ... Num 31:10 784
Every thing that may abide the *f* ... Num 31:23 784
ye shall make it go through the *f* ... Num 31:23 784
all that abideth not the *f* ye ... Num 31:23 784
in *f* by night, to shew you by ... Deut 1:33 784
with *f* unto the midst of heaven ... Deut 4:11 784
you out of the midst of the *f* ... Deut 4:12 784
Horeb out of the midst of the *f* ... Deut 4:15 784
the LORD thy God is a consuming *f* ... Deut 4:24 784
out of the midst of the *f* ... Deut 4:33 784
earth he shewed thee his great *f* ... Deut 4:36 784
words out of the midst of the *f* ... Deut 4:36 784
mount out of the midst of the *f* ... Deut 5:4 784
ye were afraid by reason of the *f* ... Deut 5:5 784
mount out of the midst of the *f* ... Deut 5:22 784
(for the mountain did burn with *f* ... Deut 5:23 784
voice out of the midst of the *f* ... Deut 5:24 784
for this great *f* will consume us ... Deut 5:25 784
out of the midst of the *f* ... Deut 5:26 784
burn their graven images with *f* ... Deut 7:5 784
their gods shall ye burn with *f* ... Deut 7:25 784
as a consuming *f* he shall destroy ... Deut 9:3 784
the *f* in the day of the assembly ... Deut 9:10 784
mount, and the mount burned with *f* ... Deut 9:15 784
ye had made, and burnt it with *f* ... Deut 9:21 784
the *f* in the day of the assembly ... Deut 10:4 784
and burn their groves with *f* ... Deut 12:3 784
have burnt in the *f* to their gods ... Deut 12:31 784
and shalt burn with *f* the city ... Deut 13:16 784
offerings of the LORD made by *f* ... Deut 18:1
daughter to pass through the *f* ... Deut 18:10 784
let me see this great *f* any more ... Deut 18:16 784
For a *f* is kindled in mine anger, ... Deut 32:22 784
set on *f* the foundations of the ... Deut 32:22 3857
And they burnt the city with *f* ... Josh 6:24 784
thing shall be burnt with *f* ... Josh 7:15 784
stones, and burned them with *f* ... Josh 7:25 784
that ye shall set the city on *f* ... Josh 8:8 784
and hasted and set the city on *f* ... Josh 8:19 784
and burn their chariots with *f* ... Josh 11:6 784
and burnt their chariots with *f* ... Josh 11:9 784
and he burnt Hazor with *f* ... Josh 11:11 784
made by *f* are their inheritance ... Josh 13:14
the sword, and set the city on *f* ... Judg 1:8 784
there rose up *f* out of the rock, ... Judg 6:21 784
let *f* come out of the bramble, and ... Judg 9:15 784
let *f* come out from Abimelech, and ... Judg 9:20 784
let *f* come out from the men of ... Judg 9:20 784
and set the hold on *f* upon them ... Judg 9:49 784
of the tower to burn it with *f* ... Judg 9:52 784
burn thine house upon thee with *f* ... Judg 12:1 784
thee and thy father's house with *f* ... Judg 14:15 784
when he had set the brands on *f* ... Judg 15:5 784
and burnt her and her father with *f* ... Judg 15:6 784
as flax that was burnt with *f* ... Judg 15:14 784
is broken when it toucheth the *f* ... Judg 16:9 784
sword, and burnt the city with *f* ... Judg 18:27 784
also they set on *f* all the cities ... Judg 20:48 784
by *f* of the children of Israel ... 1Sa 2:28
Ziklag, and burned it with *f* ... 1Sa 30:1 784
and, behold, it was burned with *f* ... 1Sa 30:3 784
and we burned Ziklag with *f* ... 1Sa 30:14 784
go and set it on *f* ... 2Sa 14:30 784
servants set the field on *f* ... 2Sa 14:30 784
thy servants set my field on *f* ... 2Sa 14:31 784
f out of his mouth devoured ... 2Sa 22:9 784
him were coals of *f* kindled ... 2Sa 22:13 784
burned with *f* in the same place ... 2Sa 23:7 784
taken Gezer, and burnt it with *f* ... 1Kin 9:16 784
the king's house over him with *f* ... 1Kin 16:18 784
lay it on wood, and put no *f* under ... 1Kin 18:23 784
lay it on wood, and put no *f* under ... 1Kin 18:23 784
and the God that answereth by *f* ... 1Kin 18:24 784
of your gods, but put no *f* under ... 1Kin 18:25 784
Then the *f* of the LORD fell, and ... 1Kin 18:38 784
And after the earthquake a *f* ... 1Kin 19:12 784
but the LORD was not in the *f* ... 1Kin 19:12 784
after the *f* a still small voice ... 1Kin 19:12 784
then let *f* come down from heaven, ... 2Kin 1:10 784
And there came down *f* from heaven ... 2Kin 1:10 784
let *f* come down from heaven, and ... 2Kin 1:12 784
the *f* of God came down from ... 2Kin 1:12 784
there came *f* down from heaven, and ... 2Kin 1:14 784
a chariot of *f*, and horses of *f* ... 2Kin 2:11 784
chariots of *f* round about Elisha ... 2Kin 6:17 784
strong holds wilt thou set on *f* ... 2Kin 8:12 784
his son to pass through the *f* ... 2Kin 16:3 784
daughters to pass through the *f* ... 2Kin 17:17 784
children in *f* to Adrammelech ... 2Kin 17:31 784
have cast their gods into the *f* ... 2Kin 19:18 784
made his son pass through the *f* ... 2Kin 21:6 784
to pass through the *f* to Molech ... 2Kin 23:10 784
the chariots of the sun with *f* ... 2Kin 23:11 784
great man's house burnt he with *f* ... 2Kin 25:9 784
and they were burned with *f* ... 1Chr 14:12 784
by *f* upon the altar of burnt ... 1Chr 21:26 784
the *f* came down from heaven, and ... 2Chr 7:1 784
of Israel saw how the *f* came down ... 2Chr 7:3 784
and burnt his children in the *f* ... 2Chr 28:3 784
the *f* in the valley of the son of ... 2Chr 33:6 784
with *f* according to the ordinance ... 2Chr 35:13 784
all the palaces thereof with *f* ... 2Chr 36:19 784
gates thereof are burned with *f* ... Neh 1:3 784
gates thereof are consumed with *f* ... Neh 2:3 784
thereof were consumed with *f* ... Neh 2:13 784
gates thereof are burned with *f* ... Neh 2:17 784
and in the night by a pillar of *f* ... Neh 9:12 784
neither the pillar of *f* by night ... Neh 9:19 784
The *f* of God is fallen from ... Job 1:16 784
f shall consume the tabernacles ... Job 15:34 784
spark of his *f* shall not shine ... Job 18:5 784
a *f* not blown shall consume him ... Job 20:26 784
remnant of them the *f* consumeth ... Job 22:20 784
it is turned up as it were *f* ... Job 28:5 784
For it is a *f* that consumeth to ... Job 31:12 784
lamps, and sparks of *f* leap out ... Job 41:19 784
wicked he shall rain snares, *f* ... Ps 11:6 784
f out of his mouth devoured ... Ps 18:8 784
passed, hail stones and coals of *f* ... Ps 18:12 784
hail stones and coals of *f* ... Ps 18:13 784
wrath, and the *f* shall devour them ... Ps 21:9 784
the LORD divideth the flames of *f* ... Ps 29:7 784
while I was musing the *f* burned ... Ps 39:3 784
he burneth the chariot in the *f* ... Ps 46:9 784
a *f* shall devour before him, and ... Ps 50:3 784
even among them that are set on *f* ... Ps 57:4 3857
we went through *f* and through ... Ps 66:12 784
as wax melteth before the *f* ... Ps 68:2 784
They have cast *f* into thy ... Ps 74:7 784
all the night with a light of *f* ... Ps 78:14 784
so a *f* was kindled against Jacob, ... Ps 78:21 784
The *f* consumed their young men ... Ps 78:63 784
shall thy jealousy burn like *f* ... Ps 79:5 784
It is burned with *f*, it is cut ... Ps 80:16 784
As the *f* burneth a wood, and as ... Ps 83:14 784
flame setteth the mountains on *f* ... Ps 83:14 3857
shall thy wrath burn like *f* ... Ps 89:46 784
A *f* goeth before him, and burneth ... Ps 97:3 784

his ministers a flaming f ... Ps 104:4 784
rain, and flaming f in their land ... Ps 105:32 784
f to give light in the night ... Ps 105:39 784
a f was kindled in their company ... Ps 106:18 784
are quenched as the f of thorns ... Ps 118:12 784
let them be cast into the f ... Ps 140:10 784
F, and hail; snow, and ... Ps 148:8 784
Can a man take f in his bosom ... Prov 6:27 784
his lips there is as a burning f ... Prov 16:27 784
heap coals of f upon his head ... Prov 25:22
no wood is, there the f goeth out ... Prov 26:20 784
to burning coals, and wood to f ... Prov 26:21 784
the f that saith not, It is ... Prov 30:16 784
the coals thereof are coals of f ... Song 8:6 784
your cities are burned with f ... Is 1:7 784
shining of a flaming f by night ... Is 4:5 784
Therefore as the f devoureth the ... Is 5:24 784
be with burning and fuel of f ... Is 9:5 784
For wickedness burneth as the f ... Is 9:18 784
shall be as the fuel of the f ... Is 9:19 784
a burning like the burning of a f ... Is 10:16 784
light of Israel shall be for a f ... Is 10:17 784
the f of thine enemies shall ... Is 26:11 784
the women come, and set them on f ... Is 27:11 215
and the flame of devouring f ... Is 29:6 784
a sherd to take f from the hearth ... Is 30:14 784
and his tongue as a devouring f ... Is 30:27 784
with the flame of a devouring f ... Is 30:30 784
the pile thereof is f and much ... Is 30:33 784
whose f is in Zion, and his ... Is 31:9 217
your breath, as f, shall devour ... Is 33:11 784
up shall they be burned in the f ... Is 33:12 784
shall dwell with the devouring f ... Is 33:14 784
have cast their gods into the f ... Is 37:19 784
it hath set him on f round about ... Is 42:25 3857
when thou walkest through the f ... Is 43:2 784
He burneth part thereof in the f ... Is 44:16 784
Aha, I am warm, I have seen the f ... Is 44:16 217
I have burned part of it in the f ... Is 44:19 784
the f shall burn them ... Is 47:14 784
warm at, nor f to sit before it ... Is 47:14 217
Behold, all ye that kindle a f ... Is 50:11 784
walk in the light of your f ... Is 50:11 784
that bloweth the coals in the f ... Is 54:16 784
As when the melting f burneth ... Is 64:2 784
the f causeth the waters to boil ... Is 64:2 784
praised thee, is burned up with f ... Is 64:11 784
a f that burneth all the day ... Is 65:5 784
behold, the LORD will come with f ... Is 66:15 784
and his rebuke with flames of f ... Is 66:15 784
For by f and by his sword will the ... Is 66:16 784
neither shall their f be quenched ... Is 66:24 784
lest my fury come forth like f ... Jer 4:4 784
will make my words in thy mouth f ... Jer 5:14 784
up a sign of f in Beth-haccerem ... Jer 6:1
the lead is consumed of the f ... Jer 6:29 784
wood, and the fathers kindle the f ... Jer 7:18 784
sons and their daughters in the f ... Jer 7:31 784
tumult he hath kindled f upon it ... Jer 11:16 784
for a f is kindled in mine anger ... Jer 15:14 784
ye have kindled a f in mine anger ... Jer 17:4 784
I kindle a f in the gates thereof ... Jer 17:27 784
to burn their sons with f for ... Jer 19:5 784
a burning f shut up in my bones ... Jer 20:9 784
and he shall burn it with f ... Jer 21:10 784
lest my fury go out like f ... Jer 21:12 784
I will kindle a f in the forest ... Jer 21:14 784
cedars, and cast them into the f ... Jer 22:7 784
Is not my word like as a f ... Jer 23:29 784
king of Babylon roasted in the f ... Jer 29:22 784
set f on this city, and burn it ... Jer 32:29 784
to pass through the f unto Molech ... Jer 32:35
and he shall burn it with f ... Jer 34:2 784
and take it, and burn it with f ... Jer 34:22 784
there was a f on the hearth ... Jer 36:22
cast it into the f that was on ... Jer 36:23 784
in the f that was on the hearth ... Jer 36:23 784
king of Judah had burned in the f ... Jer 36:32 784
and take it, and burn it with f ... Jer 37:8 784
tent, and burn this city with f ... Jer 37:10 784
city shall not be burned with f ... Jer 38:17 784
and they shall burn it with f ... Jer 38:18 784
this city to be burned with f ... Jer 38:23 784
the houses of the people, with f ... Jer 39:8 784
I will kindle a f in the houses ... Jer 43:12 784
Egyptians shall he burn with f ... Jer 43:13 784
but a f shall come forth out of ... Jer 48:45 784
daughters shall be burned with f ... Jer 49:2 784
I will kindle a f in the wall of ... Jer 49:27 784
I will kindle a f in his cities ... Jer 50:32 784
the reeds they have burned with f ... Jer 51:32 784
high gates shall be burned with f ... Jer 51:58 784
in vain, and the folk in the f ... Jer 51:58 784
the great men, burned he with f ... Jer 52:13 784
hath he sent f into my bones ... Lam 1:13 784
against Jacob like a flaming f ... Lam 2:3 784
he poured out his fury like f ... Lam 2:4 784
and hath kindled a f in Zion ... Lam 4:11 784
a f infolding itself, and a ... Eze 1:4 784
amber, out of the midst of the f ... Eze 1:4 784
was like burning coals of f ... Eze 1:13 784
living creatures; and the f was bright ... Eze 1:13 784
out of the f went forth lightning ... Eze 1:13 784
as the appearance of f round ... Eze 1:27 784
as it were the appearance of f ... Eze 1:27 784
Thou shalt burn with f a third ... Eze 5:2 217
cast them into the midst of the f ... Eze 5:4 784
and burn them in the f ... Eze 5:4 784
for thereof shall a f come forth ... Eze 5:4 784
a likeness as the appearance of f ... Eze 8:2 784
of his loins even downward, f ... Eze 8:2 784
of f from between the cherubims ... Eze 10:2 784
Take f from between the wheels, ... Eze 10:6 784
f that was between the cherubims ... Eze 10:7 784
it is cast into the f for fuel ... Eze 15:4 784
the f devoureth both the ends of ... Eze 15:4 784
when the f hath devoured it, and ... Eze 15:5 784
I have given to the f for fuel ... Eze 15:6 784
they shall go out from one f ... Eze 15:7 784
another f shall devour them ... Eze 15:7 784
to pass through the f for them ... Eze 16:21
shall burn thine houses with f ... Eze 16:41 784
the f consumed them ... Eze 19:12 784
f is gone out of a rod of her ... Eze 19:14 784
the f all that openeth the womb ... Eze 20:26
your sons to pass through the f ... Eze 20:31 784
Behold, I will kindle a f in thee ... Eze 20:47 784
against thee in the f of my wrath ... Eze 21:31 784
Thou shalt be for fuel to the f ... Eze 21:32 784
furnace, to blow the f upon it ... Eze 22:20 784
upon you in the f of my wrath ... Eze 22:21 784
them with the f of my wrath ... Eze 22:31 784
shall be devoured by the f ... Eze 23:25 784
to pass for them through the f ... Eze 23:37
and burn up their houses with f ... Eze 23:47 784
even make the pile for f great ... Eze 24:9
Heap on wood, kindle the f ... Eze 24:10 784
her scum shall be in the f ... Eze 24:12 784
in the midst of the stones of f ... Eze 28:14 784
from the midst of the stones of f ... Eze 28:16 784
forth a f from the midst of thee ... Eze 28:18 784
when I have set a f in Egypt ... Eze 30:8 784
desolate, and will set f in Zoan ... Eze 30:14 784
And I will set f in Egypt ... Eze 30:16 784
Surely in the f of my jealousy ... Eze 36:5 784
in the f of my wrath have I ... Eze 38:19 784
rain, and great hailstones, f ... Eze 38:22 784
And I will send a f on Magog ... Eze 39:6 784
shall go forth, and shall set on f ... Eze 39:9 784
burn them with f seven years ... Eze 39:9 784
shall burn the weapons with f ... Eze 39:10 784
the flame of the f slew those men ... Dan 3:22 5135
men bound into the midst of the f ... Dan 3:24 5135
walking in the midst of the f ... Dan 3:25 5135
came forth of the midst of the f ... Dan 3:26 5135
whose bodies the f had no power ... Dan 3:27 5135
nor the smell of f had passed on ... Dan 3:27 5135
flame, and his wheels as burning f ... Dan 7:9 5135
and his eyes as lamps of f ... Dan 10:6 784
morning it burneth as a flaming f ... Hos 7:6 784
I will send a f upon his cities ... Hos 8:14 784
for the f hath devoured the ... Joel 1:19 784
the f hath devoured the pastures ... Joel 1:20 784
A f devoureth before them ... Joel 2:3 784
of f that devoureth the stubble ... Joel 2:5 784
and in the earth, blood, and f ... Joel 2:30 784
But I will send a f into the ... Amos 1:4 784
But I will send a f on the wall ... Amos 1:7 784
But I will send a f on the wall ... Amos 1:10 784
But I will send a f upon Teman ... Amos 1:12 784
But I will kindle a f in the wall ... Amos 1:14 784
But I will send a f upon Moab ... Amos 2:2 784
But I will send a f upon Judah ... Amos 2:5 784
out like f in the house of Joseph ... Amos 5:6 784
Lord GOD called to contend by f ... Amos 7:4 784
the house of Jacob shall be a f ... Obad 18 784
be cleft, as wax before the f ... Mic 1:4 784
shall be burned with the f ... Mic 1:7 784
his fury is poured out like f ... Nah 1:6 784
the f shall devour thy bars ... Nah 3:13 784
There shall the f devour thee ... Nah 3:15 784
people shall labour in the very f ... Hab 2:13 784
devoured by the f of his jealousy ... Zeph 1:18 784
with the f of my jealousy ... Zeph 3:8 784
unto her a wall of f round about ... Zec 2:5 784
this a brand plucked out of the f ... Zec 3:2 784
and she shall be devoured with f ... Zec 9:4 784
that the f may devour thy cedars ... Zec 11:1 784
an hearth of f among the wood ... Zec 12:6 784
and like a torch of f in a sheaf ... Zec 12:6 784
the third part through the f ... Zec 13:9 784
neither do ye kindle f on mine ... Mal 1:10
for he is like a refiner's f ... Mal 3:2 784
is hewn down, and cast into the f ... Mt 3:10 4442
with the Holy Ghost, and with f ... Mt 3:11 4442
up the chaff with unquenchable f ... Mt 3:12 4442
shall be in danger of hell f ... Mt 5:22 4442
is hewn down, and cast into the f ... Mt 7:19 4442
are gathered and burned in the f ... Mt 13:40 4442
cast them into a furnace of f ... Mt 13:42 4442
cast them into the furnace of f ... Mt 13:50 4442
ofttimes he falleth into the f ... Mt 17:15 4442
to be cast into everlasting f ... Mt 18:8 4442
two eyes to be cast into hell f ... Mt 18:9 4442
me, ye cursed, into everlasting f ... Mt 25:41 4442
it hath cast him into the f ... Mk 9:22 4442
into the f that never shall be ... Mk 9:43 4442
not, and the f is not quenched ... Mk 9:44 4442
into the f that never shall be ... Mk 9:45 4442
not, and the f is not quenched ... Mk 9:46 4442
two eyes to be cast into hell f ... Mk 9:47 4442
not, and the f is not quenched ... Mk 9:48 4442
every one shall be salted with f ... Mk 9:49 4442
and warmed himself at the f ... Mk 14:54 5457
is hewn down, and cast into the f ... Lk 3:9 4442
you with the Holy Ghost and with f ... Lk 3:16 4442
he will burn with f unquenchable ... Lk 3:17 4442
f to come down from heaven ... Lk 9:54 4442
I am come to send f on the earth ... Lk 12:49 4442
Lot went out of Sodom it rained f ... Lk 17:29 4442
when they had kindled a f in the ... Lk 22:55 4442
beheld him as he sat by the f ... Lk 22:56 5457
them, and cast them into the f ... Jn 15:6 4442
there, who had made a f of coals ... Jn 18:18
they saw a f of coals there, and ... Jn 21:9
them cloven tongues like as of f ... Acts 2:3 4442
blood, and f, and vapour of smoke ... Acts 2:19 4442
Lord in a flame of f in a bush ... Acts 7:30 4442
for they kindled a f, and received ... Acts 28:2 4443
of sticks, and laid them on the f ... Acts 28:3 4443
he shook off the beast into the f ... Acts 28:5 4442
shalt heap coals of f on his head ... Rom 12:20 4442
because it shall be revealed by f ... 1Cor 3:13 4442
the f shall try every man's work ... 1Cor 3:13 4442
yet so as by f ... 1Cor 3:15 4442
In flaming f taking vengeance on ... 2Th 1:8 4442
and his ministers a flame of f ... Heb 1:7 4442
Quenched the violence of f ... Heb 11:34 4442
be touched, and that burned with f ... Heb 12:18 4442
For our God is a consuming f ... Heb 12:29 4442
a matter a little f kindleth ... Jas 3:5 4442
And the tongue is a f, a world of ... Jas 3:6 4442
setteth on f the course of nature ... Jas 3:6 5394
and it is set on f of hell ... Jas 3:6 5394
shall eat your flesh as it were f ... Jas 5:3 4442
though it be tried with f ... 1Pet 1:7 4442
reserved unto f against the day ... 2Pet 3:7 4442
being on f shall be dissolved ... 2Pet 3:12 4448
the vengeance of eternal f ... Jude 7 4442
fear, pulling them out of the f ... Jude 23 4442
and his eyes were as a flame of f ... Rev 1:14 4442
his eyes like unto a flame of f ... Rev 2:18 4442
to buy of me gold tried in the f ... Rev 3:18 4442
of f burning before the throne ... Rev 4:5 4442
and filled it with f of the altar ... Rev 8:5 4442
f mingled with blood, and they ... Rev 8:7 4442
with f was cast into the sea ... Rev 8:8 4442
on them, having breastplates of f ... Rev 9:17 4447
and out of their mouths issued f ... Rev 9:17 4442
part of men killed, by the f ... Rev 9:18 4442
sun, and his feet as pillars of f ... Rev 10:1 4442
f proceedeth out of their mouth, ... Rev 11:5 4442
so that he maketh f come down ... Rev 13:13 4442
and he shall be tormented with f ... Rev 14:10 4442
the altar, which had power over f ... Rev 14:18 4442
a sea of glass mingled with f ... Rev 15:2 4442
unto him to scorch men with f ... Rev 16:8 4442
eat her flesh, and burn her with f ... Rev 17:16 4442
shall be utterly burned with f ... Rev 18:8 4442
His eyes were as a flame of f ... Rev 19:12 4442
lake of f burning with brimstone ... Rev 19:20 4442
f came down from God out of ... Rev 20:9 4442
them was cast into the lake of f ... Rev 20:10 4442
hell were cast into the lake of f ... Rev 20:14 4442
life was cast into the lake of f ... Rev 20:15 4442
in the lake which burneth with f ... Rev 21:8 4442

FIREBRAND {2}
put a f in the midst between two ... Judg 15:4 3940
ye were as a f plucked out of the ... Amos 4:11 181

FIREBRANDS {3}
three hundred foxes, and took f ... Judg 15:4 3940
As a mad man who casteth f ... Prov 26:18 2131
the two tails of these smoking f ... Is 7:4 181

FIREPANS {4}
and his fleshhooks, and his f ... Ex 27:3 4289
and the fleshhooks, and the f ... Ex 38:3 4289
And the f, and the bowls, and such ... 2Kin 25:15 4289
And the basons, and the f, and the ... Jer 52:19 4289

FIRES {1}
glorify ye the LORD in the f ... Is 24:15 217

FIRKINS {1}
containing two or three f apiece ... Jn 2:6 3355

FIRM {7}
f on dry ground in the midst of ... Josh 3:17 3559
where the priests' feet stood f ... Josh 4:3 3559
they are f in themselves ... Job 41:23 3332
His heart is as f as a stone ... Job 41:24 3332
but their strength is f ... Ps 73:4 1277
statute, and to make a f decree ... Dan 6:7 8631
of the hope f unto the end ... Heb 3:6 949

FIRMAMENT {17}
Let there be a f in the midst of ... Gen 1:6 7549
And God made the f, and divided the ... Gen 1:7 7549
the f from the waters which were ... Gen 1:7 7549
the waters which were above the f ... Gen 1:7 7549
And God called the f Heaven ... Gen 1:8 7549
Let there be lights in the f of ... Gen 1:14 7549
the f of the heaven to give light ... Gen 1:15 7549
God set them in the f of the ... Gen 1:17 7549
the earth in the open f of heaven ... Gen 1:20 7549
the f sheweth his handywork ... Ps 19:1 7549
praise him in the f of his power ... Ps 150:1 7549
the likeness of the f upon the ... Eze 1:22 7549
under the f were their wings ... Eze 1:23 7549
the f that was over their heads ... Eze 1:25 7549
above the f that was over their ... Eze 1:26 7549
in the f that was above the head ... Eze 10:1 7549
shine as the brightness of the f ... Dan 12:3 7549

FIRST {441}
and the morning were the f day ... Gen 1:5 259
The name of the f is Pison ... Gen 2:11 259

on the *f* day of the month, were	Gen 8:5	259
and *f* year, in the *f* month	Gen 8:13	7223
the *f* day of the month, the	Gen 8:13	259
which he had made there at the *f*	Gen 13:4	7223
the *f* came out red, all over like	Gen 25:25	7223
beside the *f* famine that was in	Gen 26:1	7223
that city was called Luz at the *f*	Gen 28:19	7223
thread, saying, This came out *f*	Gen 38:28	7223
did eat up the *f* seven fat kine	Gen 41:20	7223
at the *f* time are we brought in	Gen 43:18	8462
down at the *f* time to buy food	Gen 43:20	8462
to the voice of the *f* sign	Ex 4:8	7223
it shall be the *f* month of the	Ex 12:2	7223
blemish, a male of the *f* year	Ex 12:5	1121
even the *f* day ye shall put away	Ex 12:15	7223
the *f* day until the seventh day	Ex 12:15	7223
in the *f* day there shall be an	Ex 12:16	7223
In the *f* month, on the fourteenth	Ex 12:18	7223
to offer the *f* of thy ripe fruits	Ex 22:29	4395
The *f* of the firstfruits of thy	Ex 23:19	7225
the *f* row shall be a sardius, a	Ex 28:17	
this shall be the *f* row	Ex 28:17	259
two lambs of the *f* year day by	Ex 29:38	1121
tables of stone like unto the *f*	Ex 34:1	7223
words that were in the *f* tables	Ex 34:1	7223
tables of stone like unto the *f*	Ex 34:4	7223
The *f* of the firstfruits of thy	Ex 34:26	7225
the *f* row was a sardius, a topaz,	Ex 39:10	
this was the *f* row	Ex 39:10	259
On the *f* day of the *f* month	Ex 40:2	7223
On the *f* day of the *f* month	Ex 40:2	259
it came to pass in the *f* month in	Ex 40:17	7223
on the *f* day of the month, that	Ex 40:17	259
him as he burned the *f* bullock	Lev 4:21	7223
which is for the sin offering *f*	Lev 5:8	7223
and a lamb, both of the *f* year	Lev 9:3	1121
and offered it for sin, as the *f*	Lev 9:15	7223
the *f* year for a burnt offering	Lev 12:6	1121
one ewe lamb of the *f* year	Lev 14:10	1323
the *f* month at even is the LORD's	Lev 23:5	7223
In the *f* day ye shall have an	Lev 23:7	7223
f year for a burnt offering unto	Lev 23:12	1121
without blemish of the *f* year	Lev 23:18	1121
two lambs of the *f* year for a	Lev 23:19	1121
the *f* fruits for a wave offering	Lev 23:20	
in the *f* day of the month, shall	Lev 23:24	259
On the *f* day shall be an holy	Lev 23:35	7223
on the *f* day shall be a sabbath,	Lev 23:39	7223
ye shall take you on the *f* day	Lev 23:40	7223
on the *f* day of the second month,	Num 1:1	259
on the *f* day of the second month	Num 1:18	259
These shall *f* set forth	Num 2:9	7223
shall bring a lamb of the *f* year	Num 6:12	1121
one he lamb of the *f* year without	Num 6:14	1121
one ewe lamb of the *f* year	Num 6:14	1323
the *f* day was Nahshon the son of	Num 7:12	7223
one ram, one lamb of the *f* year	Num 7:15	1121
goats, five lambs of the *f* year	Num 7:17	1121
one ram, one lamb of the *f* year	Num 7:21	1121
goats, five lambs of the *f* year	Num 7:23	1121
one ram, one lamb of the *f* year	Num 7:27	1121
goats, five lambs of the *f* year	Num 7:29	1121
one ram, one lamb of the *f* year	Num 7:33	1121
goats, five lambs of the *f* year	Num 7:35	1121
one ram, one lamb of the *f* year	Num 7:39	1121
goats, five lambs of the *f* year	Num 7:41	1121
one ram, one lamb of the *f* year	Num 7:45	1121
goats, five lambs of the *f* year	Num 7:47	1121
one ram, one lamb of the *f* year	Num 7:51	1121
goats, five lambs of the *f* year	Num 7:53	1121
one ram, one lamb of the *f* year	Num 7:57	1121
goats, five lambs of the *f* year	Num 7:59	1121
one ram, one lamb of the *f* year	Num 7:63	1121
goats, five lambs of the *f* year	Num 7:65	1121
one ram, one lamb of the *f* year	Num 7:69	1121
goats, five lambs of the *f* year	Num 7:71	1121
one ram, one lamb of the *f* year	Num 7:75	1121
goats, five lambs of the *f* year	Num 7:77	1121
one ram, one lamb of the *f* year	Num 7:81	1121
goats, five lambs of the *f* year	Num 7:83	1121
the lambs of the *f* year twelve	Num 7:87	1121
the lambs of the *f* year sixty	Num 7:88	1121
in the *f* month of the second year	Num 9:1	7223
on the fourteenth day of the *f*	Num 9:5	7223
they *f* took their journey	Num 10:13	7223
In the *f* place went the standard	Num 10:14	7223
the *f* of your dough for an heave	Num 15:20	7225
Of the *f* of your dough ye shall	Num 15:21	7225
of the *f* year for a sin offering	Num 15:27	1323
whatsoever is *f* ripe in the land,	Num 18:13	1061
the desert of Zin in the *f* month	Num 20:1	7223
Amalek was the *f* of the nations	Num 24:20	7225
two lambs of the *f* year without	Num 28:3	1121
lambs of the *f* year without spot	Num 28:9	1121
lambs of the *f* year without spot	Num 28:11	1121
f month is the passover of the	Num 28:16	7223
In the *f* day shall be an holy	Num 28:18	7223
ram, and seven lambs of the *f* year	Num 28:19	1121
ram, seven lambs of the *f* year	Num 28:27	1121
on the *f* day of the month, ye	Num 29:1	259
seven lambs of the *f* year without	Num 29:2	1121
ram, and seven lambs of the *f* year	Num 29:8	1121
and fourteen lambs of the *f* year	Num 29:13	1121
lambs of the *f* year without spot	Num 29:17	1121
of the *f* year without blemish	Num 29:20	1121
of the *f* year without blemish	Num 29:23	1121
lambs of the *f* year without spot	Num 29:26	1121
of the *f* year without blemish	Num 29:29	1121
of the *f* year without blemish	Num 29:32	1121
seven lambs of the *f* year without	Num 29:36	1121
from Rameses in the *f* month	Num 33:3	7223
the fifteenth day of the *f* month	Num 33:3	7223
in the *f* day of the fifth month	Num 33:38	259
on the *f* day of the month, that	Deut 1:3	259
down before the LORD, as at the *f*	Deut 9:18	7223
nights, as I fell down at the *f*	Deut 9:25	
tables of stone like unto the *f*	Deut 10:1	7223
the *f* tables which thou brakest	Deut 10:2	7223
tables of stone like unto the *f*	Deut 10:3	7223
according to the *f* writing	Deut 10:4	7223
mount, according to the *f* time	Deut 10:10	7223
the *f* rain and the latter rain,	Deut 11:14	3138
thine hand shall be *f* upon him to	Deut 13:9	7223
sacrificedst the *f* day at even	Deut 16:4	7223
be *f* upon him to put him to death	Deut 17:7	7223
the *f* of the fleece of thy sheep,	Deut 18:4	7225
That thou shalt take of the *f* of	Deut 26:2	7225
he provided the *f* part for	Deut 33:21	7225
on the tenth day of the *f* month	Josh 4:19	7223
come out against us, as at the *f*	Josh 8:5	7223
They flee before us, as at the *f*	Josh 8:6	7223
for theirs was the *f* lot	Josh 21:10	7223
for us against the Canaanites *f*	Judg 1:1	8462
of the city was Laish at the *f*	Judg 18:29	7223
Which of us shall go up *f* to the	Judg 20:18	8462
LORD said, Judah shall go up *f*	Judg 20:18	8462
put themselves in array the *f* day	Judg 20:22	7223
down before us, as at the *f*	Judg 20:32	7223
before us, as in the *f* battle	Judg 20:39	7223
that *f* slaughter, which Jonathan	1Sa 14:14	7223
the same was the *f* altar that he	1Sa 14:35	2490
the battle were Eliab the *f* born	1Sa 17:13	
except thou *f* bring Michal Saul's	2Sa 3:13	6440
of them be overthrown at the *f*	2Sa 17:9	8462
I am come the *f* this day of all	2Sa 19:20	7223
f had in bringing back our king	2Sa 19:43	7223
days of harvest, in the *f* days	2Sa 21:9	7223
he attained not unto the *f* three	2Sa 23:19	
he attained not to the *f* three	2Sa 23:23	
f year of Asa king of Judah began	1Kin 16:23	259
make me thereof a little cake *f*	1Kin 17:13	7223
for yourselves, and dress it *f*	1Kin 18:25	7223
to thy servant at the *f* I will do	1Kin 20:9	7223
of the provinces went out *f*	1Kin 20:17	7223
Now the *f* inhabitants that dwelt	1Chr 9:2	7223
the Jebusites *f* shall be chief	1Chr 11:6	7223
Joab the son of Zeruiah went *f* up	1Chr 11:6	7223
he attained not to the *f* three	1Chr 11:21	
but attained not to the *f* three	1Chr 11:25	
Ezer the *f*, Obadiah the second,	1Chr 12:9	7218
went over Jordan in the *f* month	1Chr 12:15	7223
because ye did it not at the *f*	1Chr 15:13	7223
on that day David delivered *f*	1Chr 16:7	7218
Jeriah the *f*, Amariah the second,	1Chr 23:19	7218
Micah the *f*, and Jesiah the second	1Chr 23:20	7218
Now the *f* lot came forth to	1Chr 24:7	7223
of Rehabiah, the *f* was Isshiah	1Chr 24:21	7218
Jeriah the *f*, Amariah the second,	1Chr 24:23	
Now the *f* lot came forth for	1Chr 25:9	7223
Over the *f* course for the *f*	1Chr 27:2	7223
of the host for the *f* month	1Chr 27:3	7223
Now the acts of David the king, *f*	1Chr 29:29	7223
f measure was threescore cubits	2Chr 3:3	7223
rest of the acts of Solomon, *f*	2Chr 9:29	7223
Now the acts of Rehoboam, *f*	2Chr 12:15	7223
And, behold, the acts of Asa, *f*	2Chr 16:11	7223
in the *f* ways of his father David	2Chr 17:3	7223
of the acts of Jehoshaphat, *f*	2Chr 20:34	7223
rest of the acts of Amaziah, *f*	2Chr 25:26	7223
the rest of the acts of Uzziah, *f*	2Chr 26:22	7223
of his acts and of all his ways, *f*	2Chr 28:26	7223
He in the *f* year of his reign, in	2Chr 29:3	7223
year of his reign, in the *f* month	2Chr 29:3	7223
Now they began on the *f* day of	2Chr 29:17	7223
day of the *f* month to sanctify	2Chr 29:17	7223
of the *f* month they made an end	2Chr 29:17	7223
the fourteenth day of the *f* month	2Chr 35:1	7223
And his deeds, *f* and last, behold,	2Chr 35:27	7223
Now in the *f* year of Cyrus king	2Chr 36:22	259
Now in the *f* year of Cyrus king	Ezr 1:1	259
From the *f* day of the seventh	Ezr 3:6	259
men, that had seen the *f* house	Ezr 3:12	7223
But in the *f* year of Cyrus the	Ezr 5:13	2298
In the *f* year of Cyrus the king	Ezr 6:3	2298
the fourteenth day of the *f* month	Ezr 6:19	7223
For upon the *f* day of the	Ezr 7:9	259
f month began he to go up from	Ezr 7:9	7223
on the *f* day of the fifth month	Ezr 7:9	259
on the twelfth day of the *f* month	Ezr 8:31	7223
sat down in the *f* day of the	Ezr 10:16	259
by the *f* day of the *f* month	Ezr 10:17	259
by the *f* day of the *f* month	Ezr 10:17	7223
of them which came up at the *f*	Neh 7:5	7223
upon the *f* day of the seventh	Neh 8:2	259
from the *f* day unto the last day,	Neh 8:18	7223
which sat the *f* in the kingdom	Est 1:14	7223
In the *f* month, that is, the	Est 3:7	7223
the thirteenth day of the *f* month	Est 3:12	7223
Art thou the *f* man that was born	Job 15:7	7223
And he called the name of the *f*	Job 42:14	7223
He that is *f* in his own cause	Prov 18:17	7223
restore thy judges as at the *f*	Is 1:26	7223
when at the *f* he lightly	Is 9:1	7223
I the LORD, the *f*, and with the	Is 41:4	7223
The *f* shall say to Zion, Behold,	Is 41:27	7223
Thy *f* father hath sinned, and thy	Is 43:27	7223
I am the *f*, and I am the last	Is 44:6	7223
I am the *f*, I also am the last	Is 48:12	7223
me, and the ships of Tarshish *f*	Is 60:9	7223
that bringeth forth her *f* child	Jer 4:31	1069
where I set my name at the *f*	Jer 7:12	7223
f I will recompense their	Jer 16:18	7223
like the figs that are *f* ripe	Jer 24:2	1073
of Judah, that was the *f* year of	Jer 25:1	7224
and will build them, as at the *f*	Jer 33:7	7223
of the land, as at the *f*, saith	Jer 33:11	7223
words that were in the *f* roll	Jer 36:28	7223
f the king of Assyria hath	Jer 50:17	7223
king of Babylon in the *f* year of	Jer 52:31	
the *f* face was the face of a	Eze 10:14	259
in the *f* day of the month, that	Eze 26:1	259
and twentieth year, in the *f* month	Eze 29:17	7223
in the *f* day of the month, the	Eze 29:17	259
the eleventh year, in the *f* month	Eze 30:20	7223
in the *f* day of the month, that	Eze 31:1	259
in the *f* day of the month, that	Eze 32:1	259
after the measure of the *f* gate	Eze 40:21	7223
the *f* of all the firstfruits of	Eze 44:30	7225
the priest the *f* of your dough	Eze 44:30	7225
In the *f* month, in the	Eze 45:18	7223
in the *f* day of the month, thou	Eze 45:18	259
In the *f* month, in the fourteenth	Eze 45:21	7223
of the *f* year without blemish	Eze 46:13	1121
unto the *f* year of king Cyrus	Dan 1:21	259
of whom Daniel was *f*	Dan 6:2	2298
In the *f* year of Belshazzar king	Dan 7:1	2298
The *f* was like a lion, and had	Dan 7:4	6933
whom there were three of the *f*	Dan 7:8	6933
and he shall be diverse from the *f*	Dan 7:24	6933
which appeared unto me at the *f*	Dan 8:1	8462
is between his eyes is the *f* king	Dan 8:21	7223
In the *f* year of Darius the son	Dan 9:1	259
In the *f* year of his reign I	Dan 9:2	259
and twentieth day of the *f* month	Dan 10:4	7223
for from the *f* day that thou	Dan 10:12	7223
Also I in the *f* year of Darius	Dan 11:1	259
will go and return to my *f* husband	Hos 2:7	7223
in the fig tree at her *f* time	Hos 9:10	7225
and the latter rain in the *f* month	Joel 2:23	7223
with the *f* that go captive	Amos 6:7	7218
it come, even the *f* dominion	Mic 4:8	7223
in the *f* day of the month, came	Hag 1:1	259
saw this house in her *f* glory	Hag 2:3	7223
In the *f* chariot were red horses	Zec 6:2	7223
shall save the tents of Judah *f*	Zec 12:7	7223
gate unto the place of the *f* gate	Zec 14:10	7223
f be reconciled to thy brother,	Mt 5:24	*4412*
But seek ye *f* the kingdom of God,	Mt 6:33	*4412*
f cast out the beam out of thine	Mt 7:5	*4412*
unto him, Lord, suffer me *f* to go	Mt 8:21	*4412*
The *f*, Simon, who is called Peter	Mt 10:2	*4413*
except he *f* bind the strong man	Mt 12:29	*4412*
of that man is worse than the *f*	Mt 12:45	*4413*
Gather ye together *f* the tares	Mt 13:30	*4412*
scribes that Elias must *f* come	Mt 17:10	*4412*
them, Elias truly shall *f* come	Mt 17:11	*4412*
take up the fish that *f* cometh up	Mt 17:27	*4413*
But many that are *f* shall be last	Mt 19:30	*4412*
and the last shall be *f*	Mt 19:30	*4413*
from the last unto the *f*	Mt 20:8	*4413*
But when the *f* came, they	Mt 20:10	*4413*
shall be *f*, and the *f* last	Mt 20:16	*4413*
and he came to the *f*, and said, Son	Mt 21:28	*4413*
They say unto him, The *f*	Mt 21:31	*4413*
other servants more than the *f*	Mt 21:36	*4413*
and the *f*, when he had married a	Mt 22:25	*4413*
This is the *f* and great	Mt 22:38	*4413*
cleanse *f* that which is within	Mt 23:26	*4412*
Now the *f* day of the feast of	Mt 26:17	*4413*
error shall be worse than the *f*	Mt 27:64	*4413*
dawn toward the *f* day of the week	Mt 28:1	*3391*
except he will *f* bind the strong	Mk 3:27	*4412*
f the blade, then the ear, after	Mk 4:28	*4412*
her, Let the children *f* be filled	Mk 7:27	*4412*
scribes that Elias must *f* come	Mk 9:11	*4412*
told them, Elias verily cometh *f*	Mk 9:12	*4412*
them, If any man desire to be *f*	Mk 9:35	*4413*
But many that are *f* shall be last	Mk 10:31	*4413*
and the last *f*	Mk 10:31	*4413*
the *f* took a wife, and dying left	Mk 12:20	*4413*
Which is the *f* commandment of all	Mk 12:28	*4413*
The *f* of all the commandments is,	Mk 12:29	*4413*
this is the *f* commandment	Mk 12:30	*4413*
the gospel must *f* be published	Mk 13:10	*4412*
the *f* day of unleavened bread,	Mk 14:12	*4413*
the morning the *f* day of the week	Mk 16:2	*3391*
risen early the *f* day of the week	Mk 16:9	*4413*
he appeared *f* to Mary Magdalene,	Mk 16:9	*4412*
of all things from the very *f*	Lk 1:3	*509*
this taxing was *f* made when	Lk 2:2	*4413*
on the second sabbath after the *f*	Lk 6:1	*1207*
cast out *f* the beam out of thine	Lk 6:42	*4412*
he said, Lord, suffer me *f* to go	Lk 9:59	*4412*
but let me *f* go bid them farewell	Lk 9:61	*4412*
f say, Peace be to this house	Lk 10:5	*4412*
of that man is worse than the *f*	Lk 11:26	*4413*
he had not *f* washed before dinner	Lk 11:38	*4412*
say unto his disciples *f* of all	Lk 12:1	*4412*
there are last which shall be *f*	Lk 13:30	*4413*
there are *f* which shall be last	Lk 13:30	*4413*
The *f* said unto him, I have	Lk 14:18	*4413*
build a tower, sitteth not down *f*	Lk 14:28	*4412*
another king, sitteth not down *f*	Lk 14:31	*4412*
unto him, and said unto the *f*	Lk 16:5	*4413*

But f must he suffer many things, ... Lk 17:25 4412
Then came the f, saying, Lord, ... Lk 19:16 4413
the f took a wife, and died ... Lk 20:29 4413
these things must f come to pass ... Lk 21:9 4412
Now upon the f day of the week, ... Lk 24:1 3391
He f findeth his own brother ... Jn 1:41 4413
whosoever then f after the ... Jn 5:4 4413
let him f cast a stone at her ... Jn 8:7 4413
place where John at f baptized ... Jn 10:40 4412
not his disciples at the f ... Jn 12:16 4412
And led him away to Annas f ... Jn 18:13 4412
and brake the legs of the f ... Jn 19:32 4413
which at the f came to Jesus by ... Jn 19:39 4412
The f day of the week cometh Mary ... Jn 20:1 3391
Peter, and came f to the sepulchre ... Jn 20:4 4413
which came f to the sepulchre, and ... Jn 20:8 4413
being the f day of the week, when ... Jn 20:19 3391
Unto you f God, having raised up ... Acts 3:26 4412
Egypt, he sent out our fathers f ... Acts 7:12 4412
called Christians f in Antioch ... Acts 11:26 4412
When they were past the f ... Acts 12:10 4413
When John had f preached before ... Acts 13:24
should f have been spoken to you ... Acts 13:46 4412
at the f did visit the Gentiles ... Acts 15:14 4412
upon the f day of the week, when ... Acts 20:7 3391
from the f day that I came into ... Acts 20:18 4413
which was at the f among mine own ... Acts 26:4 746
But shewed f unto them of ... Acts 26:20 4412
that he should be the f that ... Acts 26:23 4413
cast themselves f into the sea ... Acts 27:43 4413
F, I thank my God through Jesus ... Rom 1:8 4412
to the Jew f, and also to the ... Rom 1:16 4412
man that doeth evil, of the Jew f ... Rom 2:9 4412
that worketh good, to the Jew f ... Rom 2:10 4412
F Moses saith, I will provoke you ... Rom 10:19 4413
Or who hath f given to him, and it ... Rom 11:35 4272
if f I be somewhat filled with ... Rom 15:24 4412
For f of all, when ye come ... 1Cor 11:18 4412
f apostles, secondarily prophets, ... 1Cor 12:28 4412
by, let the f hold his peace ... 1Cor 14:30 4413
you f of all that which I also ... 1Cor 15:3 1722,4413
The f man Adam was made a living ... 1Cor 15:45 4413
that was not f which is spiritual ... 1Cor 15:46 4412
The f man is of the earth, earthy ... 1Cor 15:47 4413
Upon the f day of the week let ... 1Cor 16:2 3391
The f epistle to the Corinthians ... 1Cor s 4413
but f gave their own selves to ... 2Cor 8:5 4412
For if there be f a willing mind ... 2Cor 8:12 4295
the gospel unto you at the f ... Gal 4:13 4386
glory, who f trusted in Christ ... Eph 1:12 4276
f into the lower parts of the ... Eph 4:9 4412
which is the f commandment with ... Eph 6:2 4413
gospel from the f day until now ... Phil 1:5 4413
the dead in Christ shall rise f ... 1Th 4:16 4412
The f epistle unto the ... 1Th s 4413
there come a falling away f ... 2Th 2:3 4412
that in me f Jesus Christ might ... 1Ti 1:16 4413
f of all, supplications, prayers, ... 1Ti 2:1 4412
For Adam was f formed, then Eve ... 1Ti 2:13 4413
And let these also f be proved ... 1Ti 3:10 4412
let them learn f to shew piety at ... 1Ti 5:4 4412
they have cast off their f faith ... 1Ti 5:12 4413
The f to Timothy was written from ... 1Ti s 4413
which dwelt f in thy grandmother ... 2Ti 1:5 4412
must be f partaker of the fruits ... 2Ti 2:6 4413
At my f answer no man stood with ... 2Ti 4:16 4413
ordained the f bishop of the ... 2Ti s 4413
that is an heretick after the f ... Titus 3:10 3391
ordained the f bishop of the ... Titus s 4413
which at the f began to be spoken ... Heb 2:3 746
they to whom it was f preached ... Heb 4:6 4386
f principles of the oracles of ... Heb 5:12 746
f being by interpretation King of ... Heb 7:2 4412
f for his own sins, and then for ... Heb 7:27 4386
For if that f covenant had been ... Heb 8:7 4413
covenant, he hath made the f old ... Heb 8:13 4413
Then verily the f covenant had ... Heb 9:1 4413
the f, wherein was the ... Heb 9:2 4413
went always into the f tabernacle ... Heb 9:6 4413
while as the f tabernacle was yet ... Heb 9:8 4413
that were under the f testament ... Heb 9:15 4413
Whereupon neither the f testament ... Heb 9:18 4413
He taketh away the f, that he may ... Heb 10:9 4413
that is from above is f pure ... Jas 3:17 4412
if it f begin at us, what shall ... 1Pet 4:17 4412
Knowing this f, that no prophecy ... 2Pet 1:20 4412
Knowing this f, that there shall ... 2Pet 3:3 4412
love him, because he f loved us ... 1Jn 4:19 4413
which kept not their f estate ... Jude 6 746
the f begotten of the dead, and ... Rev 1:5 4416
I am Alpha and Omega, the f ... Rev 1:11 4413
I am the f and the last ... Rev 1:17 4413
because thou hast left thy f love ... Rev 2:4 4413
and repent, and do the f works ... Rev 2:5 4413
These things saith the f and the ... Rev 2:8 4413
and the last to be more than the f ... Rev 2:19 4413
the f voice which I heard was as ... Rev 4:1 4413
the f beast was like a lion, and ... Rev 4:7 4413
The f angel sounded, and there ... Rev 8:7 4413
power of the f beast before him ... Rev 13:12 4413
therein to worship the f beast ... Rev 13:12 4413
the f went, and poured out his ... Rev 16:2 4413
This is the f resurrection ... Rev 20:5 4413
hath part in the f resurrection ... Rev 20:6 4413
f heaven and the f earth ... Rev 21:1 4413
The f foundation was jasper ... Rev 21:19 4413
the beginning and the end, the f ... Rev 22:13 4413

FIRSTBEGOTTEN {1}

bringeth in the f into the world ... Heb 1:6 4416

FIRSTBORN {116}

And Canaan begat Sidon his f ... Gen 10:15 1060
the f said unto the younger, Our ... Gen 19:31 1067
the f went in, and lay with her ... Gen 19:33 1067
that the f said unto the younger, ... Gen 19:34 1067
the f bare a son, and called his ... Gen 19:37 1067
Huz his f, and Buz his brother, and ... Gen 22:21 1060
the f of Ishmael, Nebajoth ... Gen 25:13 1060
unto his father, I am Esau thy f ... Gen 27:19 1060
he said, I am thy son, thy f Esau ... Gen 27:32 1060
to give the younger before the f ... Gen 29:26 1067
Reuben, Jacob's f, and Simeon, and ... Gen 35:23 1060
sons of Eliphaz the f son of Esau ... Gen 36:15 1060
And Judah took a wife for Er his f ... Gen 38:6 1060
And Er, Judah's f, was wicked in ... Gen 38:7 1060
called the name of the f Manasseh ... Gen 41:51 1060
the f according to his birthright ... Gen 43:33 1060
Reuben, Jacob's f ... Gen 46:8 1060
for Manasseh was the f ... Gen 48:14 1060
for this is the f ... Gen 48:18 1060
Reuben, thou art my f, my might, ... Gen 49:3 1060
LORD, Israel is my son, even my f ... Ex 4:22 1060
I will slay thy son, even thy f ... Ex 4:23 1060
sons of Reuben the f of Israel ... Ex 6:14 1060
all the f in the land of Egypt ... Ex 11:5 1060
from the f of Pharaoh that ... Ex 11:5 1060
throne, even unto the f of the ... Ex 11:5 1060
and all the f of beasts ... Ex 11:5 1060
will smite all the f in the land ... Ex 12:12 1060
all the f in the land of Egypt ... Ex 12:29 1060
from the f of Pharaoh that sat on ... Ex 12:29 1060
f of the captive that was in the ... Ex 12:29 1060
and all the f of cattle ... Ex 12:29 1060
Sanctify unto me all the f ... Ex 13:2 1060
all the f of man among thy ... Ex 13:13 1060
all the f in the land of Egypt ... Ex 13:15 1060
land of Egypt, both the f of man ... Ex 13:15 1060
of man, and the f of beast ... Ex 13:15 1060
but all the f of my children I ... Ex 13:15 1060
the f of thy sons shalt thou give ... Ex 22:29 1060
All the f of thy sons thou shalt ... Ex 34:20 1060
Nadab the f, and Abihu, Eleazar, ... Num 3:2 1060
of Israel instead of all the f ... Num 3:12 1060
Because all the f are mine ... Num 3:13 1060
f in the land of Egypt I hallowed ... Num 3:13 1060
unto me all the f in Israel ... Num 3:13 1060
Number all the f of the males of ... Num 3:40 1060
f among the children of Israel ... Num 3:41 1060
all the f among the children of ... Num 3:42 1060
all the f males by the number of ... Num 3:43 1060
f among the children of Israel ... Num 3:45 1060
thirteen of the f of the children ... Num 3:46 1060
Of the f of the children of ... Num 3:50 1060
even instead of the f of all the ... Num 8:16 1060
For all the f of the children of ... Num 8:17 1060
every f in the land of Egypt I ... Num 8:17 1060
the f of the children of Israel ... Num 8:18 1060
nevertheless the f of man shalt ... Num 18:15 1060
the Egyptians buried all their f ... Num 33:4 1060
if the f son be hers that was ... Deut 21:15 1060
f before the son of the hated ... Deut 21:16 1069
which is indeed the f ... Deut 21:16 1060
the son of the hated for the f ... Deut 21:17 1060
the right of the f is his ... Deut 21:17 1062
that the f which she beareth ... Deut 25:6 1060
the foundation thereof in his f ... Josh 6:26 1060
for he was the f of Joseph ... Josh 17:1 1060
wit, for Machir the f of Manasseh ... Josh 17:1 1060
And he said unto Jether his f ... Judg 8:20 1060
Now the name of his f was Joel ... 1Sa 8:2 1060
the name of the f Merab, and the ... 1Sa 14:49 1067
his f was Amnon, of Ahinoam the ... 2Sa 3:2 1060
thereof in Abiram his f, and set ... 1Kin 16:34 1060
And Canaan begat Zidon his f ... 1Chr 1:13 1060
The f of Ishmael, Nebaioth ... 1Chr 1:29 1060
the f of Judah, was evil in the ... 1Chr 2:3 1060
And Jesse begat his f Eliab ... 1Chr 2:13 1060
of Jerahmeel the f of Hezron were ... 1Chr 2:25 1060
Ram the f, and Bunah ... 1Chr 2:25 1060
of Ram the f of Jerahmeel were ... 1Chr 2:27 1060
of Jerahmeel were, Mesha his f ... 1Chr 2:42 1060
the son of Hur, the f of Ephratah ... 1Chr 2:50 1060
the f Amnon, of Ahinoam the ... 1Chr 3:1 1060
the f Johanan, the second ... 1Chr 3:15 1060
the f of Ephratah, the father of ... 1Chr 4:4 1060
sons of Reuben the f of Israel ... 1Chr 5:1 1060
(for he was the f; ... 1Chr 5:1 1060
of Reuben the f of Israel were, ... 1Chr 5:3 1060
the f Vashni, and Abiah ... 1Chr 6:28 1060
Now Benjamin begat Bela his f ... 1Chr 8:1 1060
his f son Abdon, and Zur, and Kish, ... 1Chr 8:30 1060
his brother were, Ulam his f ... 1Chr 8:39 1060
Asaiah the f, and his sons ... 1Chr 9:5 1060
who was the f of Shallum the ... 1Chr 9:31 1060
his f son Abdon, then Zur, and ... 1Chr 9:36 1060
Meshelemiah were, Zechariah the f ... 1Chr 26:2 1060
of Obed-edom were, Shemaiah the f ... 1Chr 26:4 1060
(for though he was not the f ... 1Chr 26:10 1060
because he was the f ... 2Chr 21:3 1060
Also the f of our sons, and of our ... Neh 10:36 1060
even the f of death shall devour ... Job 18:13 1060
And smote all the f in Egypt ... Ps 78:51 1060
Also I will make him my f ... Ps 89:27 1060
also all the f in their land ... Ps 105:36 1060
Who smote the f of Egypt, both of ... Ps 135:8 1060
him that smote Egypt in their f ... Ps 136:10 1060
the f of the poor shall feed, and ... Is 14:30 1060
to Israel, and Ephraim is my f ... Jer 31:9 1060
shall I give my f for my ... Mic 6:7 1060
that is in bitterness for his f ... Zec 12:10 1060
she had brought forth her f son ... Mt 1:25 4416
And she brought forth her f son ... Lk 2:7 4416
be the f among many brethren ... Rom 8:29 4416
God, the f of every creature ... Col 1:15 4416
beginning, the f from the dead ... Col 1:18 4416
destroyed the f should touch them ... Heb 11:28 4416
assembly and church of the f ... Heb 12:23 4416

FIRSTFRUIT {2}

The f also of thy corn, of thy ... Deut 18:4 7225
For if the f be holy, the lump is ... Rom 11:16 536

FIRSTFRUITS {31}

the f of thy labours, which thou ... Ex 23:16 1061
The first of the f of thy land ... Ex 23:19 1061
of the f of wheat harvest, and the ... Ex 34:22 1061
The first of the f of thy land ... Ex 34:26 1061
As for the oblation of the f ... Lev 2:12 7225
offering of thy f unto the LORD ... Lev 2:14 1061
for the meat offering of thy f ... Lev 2:14 1061
ye shall bring a sheaf of the f ... Lev 23:10 7225
they are the f unto the LORD ... Lev 23:17 1061
the f of them which they shall ... Num 18:12 7225
Also in the day of the f, when ye ... Num 28:26 1061
I have brought the f of the land ... Deut 26:10 7225
the man of God bread of the f ... 2Kin 4:42 1061
in abundance the f of corn ... 2Chr 31:5 7225
to bring the f of our ground, and ... Neh 10:35 1061
the f of all fruit of all trees, ... Neh 10:35 1061
should bring the f of our dough ... Neh 10:37 7225
for the offerings, for the f ... Neh 12:44 7225
at times appointed, and for the f ... Neh 13:31 1061
with the f of all thine increase ... Prov 3:9 7225
LORD, and the f of his increase ... Jer 2:3 7225
the f of your oblations, with all ... Eze 20:40 7225
first of all the f of all things ... Eze 44:30 1061
nor alienate the f of the land ... Eze 48:14 7225
which have the f of the Spirit ... Rom 8:23 536
who is the f of Achaia unto ... Rom 16:5 536
become the f of them that slept ... 1Cor 15:20 536
Christ the f ... 1Cor 15:23 536
that it is the f of Achaia ... 1Cor 16:15 536
be a kind of f of his creatures ... Jas 1:18 536
among men, being the f unto God ... Rev 14:4 536

FIRSTLING {14}

every f that cometh of a beast ... Ex 13:12 6363
every f of an ass thou shalt ... Ex 13:13 6363
every f among thy cattle, whether ... Ex 34:19 6363
But the f of an ass thou shalt ... Ex 34:20 6363
Only the f of the beasts, which ... Lev 27:26 1060
which should be the LORD's f ... Lev 27:26 1069
the f of unclean beasts shalt ... Num 18:15 1060
f of a cow, or the f ... Num 18:17 1060
or the f of a goat, thou shalt ... Num 18:17 1060
All the f males that come of thy ... Deut 15:19 1060
no work with the f of thy bullock ... Deut 15:19 1060
nor shear the f of thy sheep ... Deut 15:19 1060
is like the f of his bullock ... Deut 33:17 1060

FIRSTLINGS {6}

brought of the f of his flock ... Gen 4:4 1062
all the f among the cattle of the ... Num 3:41 1060
the f of your herds and of your ... Deut 12:6 1062
or the f of thy herds or of thy ... Deut 12:17 1062
the f of thy herds and of thy ... Deut 14:23 1062
the f of our herds and of our ... Neh 10:36 1062

FIRSTRIPE {4}

time was the time of the f grapes ... Num 13:20 1061
I saw your fathers as the f in ... Hos 9:10 1063
my soul desired the f fruit ... Mic 7:1 1063
be like fig trees with the f figs ... Nah 3:12 1063

FISH {35}

dominion over the f of the sea ... Gen 1:26 1710
dominion over the f of the sea ... Gen 1:28 1710
the f that is in the river shall ... Ex 7:18 1710
the f that was in the river died ... Ex 7:21 1710
We remember the f, which we did ... Num 11:5 1710
or shall all the f of the sea be ... Num 11:22 1709
the likeness of any f that is in ... Deut 4:18 1710
to the entering in at the f gate ... 2Chr 33:14 1709
But the f gate did the sons of ... Neh 3:3 1709
the old gate, and above the f gate ... Neh 12:39 1709
also therein, which brought f ... Neh 13:16 1709
or his head with f spears ... Job 41:7 1709
the f of the sea, and whatsoever ... Ps 8:8 1709
into blood, and slew their f ... Ps 105:29 1710
that make sluices and ponds for f ... Is 19:10 5315
their f stinketh, because there ... Is 50:2 1710
the LORD, and they shall f them ... Jer 16:16 1770
I will cause the f of thy rivers ... Eze 29:4 1710
all the f of thy rivers shall ... Eze 29:4 1710
thee and all the f of thy rivers ... Eze 29:5 1710
be a very great multitude of f ... Eze 47:9 1710
their f shall be according to ... Eze 47:10 1710
as the f of the great sea, ... Eze 47:10 1710
a great f to swallow up Jonah ... Jonah 1:17 1709
in the belly of the f three days ... Jonah 1:17 1709
And the LORD spake unto the f ... Jonah 2:10 1709
noise of a cry from the f gate ... Zeph 1:10 1709
Or if he ask a f, will he give ... Mt 7:10 2486
take up the f that first cometh ... Mt 17:27 2486
or if he ask a f ... Lk 11:11 2486
will he for a f give him a ... Lk 11:11 2486
gave him a piece of a broiled f ... Lk 24:42 2486

F

and *f* laid thereon, and bread ... Jn 21:9 *3795*
Bring of the *f* which ye have now ... Jn 21:10 *3795*
and giveth them, and *f* likewise ... Jn 21:13 *3795*

FISHERMEN {1}
but the *f* were gone out of them, ... Lk 5:2 *231*

FISHER'S {1}
he girt his *f* coat unto him, (for ... Jn 21:7 *1903*

FISHERS {7}
The *f* also shall mourn, and all ... Is 19:8 1771
Behold, I will send for many *f* ... Jer 16:16 1728
that the *f* shall stand upon it ... Eze 47:10 1728
for they were *f* ... Mt 4:18 *231*
me, and I will make you *f* of men ... Mt 4:19 *231*
for they were *f* ... Mk 1:16 *231*
will make you to become *f* of men ... Mk 1:17 *231*

FISHES {27}
and upon all the *f* of the sea ... Gen 9:2 1709
and of creeping things, and of *f* ... 1Kin 4:33 1709
the *f* of the sea shall declare ... Job 12:8 1709
as the *f* that are taken in an ... Eccl 9:12 1709
So that the *f* of the sea, and the ... Eze 38:20 1709
the *f* of the sea also shall be ... Hos 4:3 1709
And makest men as the *f* of the sea ... Hab 1:14 1709
and the *f* of the sea, and the ... Zeph 1:3 1709
here but five loaves, and two *f* ... Mt 14:17 *2486*
the five loaves, and the two *f* ... Mt 14:19 *2486*
said, Seven, and a few little *f* ... Mt 15:34 *2485*
he took the seven loaves and the *f* ... Mt 15:36 *2486*
knew, they say, Five, and two *f* ... Mk 6:38 *2486*
the five loaves and the two *f* ... Mk 6:41 *2486*
the two *f* divided he among them ... Mk 6:41 *2486*
of the fragments, and of the *f* ... Mk 6:43 *2486*
And they had a few small *f* ... Mk 8:7 *2485*
inclosed a great multitude of *f* ... Lk 5:6 *2486*
of the *f* which they had taken ... Lk 5:9 *2486*
no more but five loaves and two *f* ... Lk 9:13 *2486*
took the five loaves and the two *f* ... Lk 9:16 *2486*
barley loaves, and two small *f* ... Jn 6:9 *3795*
likewise of the *f* as much as they ... Jn 6:11 *3795*
to draw it for the multitude of *f* ... Jn 21:6 *2486*
cubits,) dragging the net with *f* ... Jn 21:8 *2486*
the net to land full of great *f* ... Jn 21:11 *2486*
flesh of beasts, another of *f* ... 1Cor 15:39 *2486*

FISHHOOKS {1}
hooks, and your posterity with *f* ... Amos 4:2 5518,1729

FISHING {1}
Peter saith unto them, I go a *f* ... Jn 21:3 *232*

FISHPOOLS {1}
thine eyes like the *f* in Heshbon ... Song 7:4 1295

FISH'S {1}
LORD his God out of the *f* belly ... Jonah 2:1 1710

FIST {2}
with a stone, or with his *f* ... Ex 21:18 106
to smite with the *f* of wickedness ... Is 58:4 106

FISTS {1}
hath gathered the wind in his *f* ... Prov 30:4 2651

FIT {9}
of a *f* man into the wilderness ... Lev 16:21 6261
f to go out for war and battle ... 1Chr 7:11
men of war *f* for the battle, that ... 1Chr 12:8
Is it *f* to say to a king, Thou ... Job 34:18
make it *f* for thyself in the ... Prov 24:27 6257
is *f* for the kingdom of God ... Lk 9:62 *2111*
It is neither *f* for the land ... Lk 14:35 *2111*
for it is not *f* that he should ... Acts 22:22 *2520*
husbands, as it is *f* in the Lord ... Col 3:18 *433*

FITCHES {4}
doth he not cast abroad the *f* ... Is 28:25 7100
For the *f* are not threshed with a ... Is 28:27 7100
but the *f* are beaten out with a ... Is 28:27 7100
and lentiles, and millet, and *f* ... Eze 4:9 3698

FITLY {4}
A word *f* spoken is like apples of ... Prov 25:11 5921,655
washed with milk, and *f* set ... Song 5:12 5921,4402
In whom all the building *f* framed ... Eph 2:21 *4883*
the whole body *f* joined together ... Eph 4:16 *4883*

FITTED {3}
with gold *f* upon the carved work ... 1Kin 6:35 3474
shall withal be *f* in thy lips ... Prov 22:18 3559
vessels of wrath *f* to destruction ... Rom 9:22 *2675*

FITTETH {1}
he *f* it with planes, and he ... Is 44:13 6213

FIVE {350}
hundred and *f* years, and begat Enos ... Gen 5:6 2568
Enos were nine hundred and *f* years ... Gen 5:11 2568
sixty and *f* years, and begat Jared ... Gen 5:15 2568
eight hundred ninety and *f* years ... Gen 5:17 2568
f years, and begat Methuselah ... Gen 5:21 2568
three hundred sixty and *f* years ... Gen 5:23 2568
he begat Noah *f* hundred ninety ... Gen 5:30 2568
f years, and begat sons and ... Gen 5:30 2568
Noah was *f* hundred years old ... Gen 5:32 2568
he begat Arphaxad *f* hundred years ... Gen 11:11 2568
And Arphaxad lived *f* and thirty ... Gen 11:12 2568
Terah were two hundred and *f* years ... Gen 11:32 2568
f years old when he departed out ... Gen 12:4 2568
Ellasar; four kings with *f* ... Gen 14:9 2568
lack *f* of the fifty righteous ... Gen 18:28 2568
all the city for lack of *f* ... Gen 18:28 2568
said, If I find there forty and *f* ... Gen 18:28 2568
but Benjamin's mess was *f* times ... Gen 43:34 2568
and yet there are *f* years, in the ... Gen 45:6 2568
yet there are *f* years of famine ... Gen 45:11 2568
silver, and *f* changes of raiment ... Gen 45:22 2568
some of his brethren, even *f* men ... Gen 47:2 2568
he shall restore *f* oxen for an ox ... Ex 22:1 2568
The *f* curtains shall be coupled ... Ex 26:3 2568
other *f* curtains shall be coupled ... Ex 26:3 2568
thou shalt couple *f* curtains by ... Ex 26:9 2568
f for the boards of the one side ... Ex 26:26 2568
f bars for the boards of the ... Ex 26:27 2568
f bars for the boards of the side ... Ex 26:27 2568
hanging *f* pillars of shittim wood ... Ex 26:37 2568
thou shalt cast *f* sockets of ... Ex 26:37 2568
f cubits long, and *f* cubits ... Ex 27:1 2568
the height *f* cubits of fine ... Ex 27:18 2568
of pure myrrh *f* hundred shekels ... Ex 30:23 2568
of cassia *f* hundred shekels, ... Ex 30:24 2568
he coupled the *f* curtains one ... Ex 36:10 2568
the other *f* curtains he coupled ... Ex 36:10 2568
And he coupled *f* curtains by ... Ex 36:16 2568
f for the boards of the one side ... Ex 36:31 2568
f bars for the boards of the ... Ex 36:32 2568
f bars for the boards of the ... Ex 36:32 2568
the *f* pillars of it with their ... Ex 36:38 2568
but their *f* sockets were of brass ... Ex 36:38 2568
f cubits was the length thereof, ... Ex 38:1 2568
f cubits the breadth thereof ... Ex 38:1 2568
in the breadth was *f* cubits ... Ex 38:18 2568
and *f* hundred and fifty men ... Ex 38:26 2568
f shekels he made hooks for the ... Ex 38:28 2568
f of you shall chase an hundred, ... Lev 26:8 2568
if it be from *f* years old even ... Lev 27:5 2568
a month old even unto *f* years old ... Lev 27:6 2568
of the male *f* shekels of silver ... Lev 27:6 2568
and six thousand and *f* hundred ... Num 1:21 2568
f thousand six hundred and fifty ... Num 1:25 2568
were forty thousand and *f* hundred ... Num 1:33 2568
f thousand and four hundred ... Num 1:37 2568
and one thousand and *f* hundred ... Num 1:41 2568
thousand and *f* hundred and fifty ... Num 1:46 2568
and six thousand and *f* hundred ... Num 2:11 2568
f thousand and six hundred and ... Num 2:15 2568
were forty thousand and *f* hundred ... Num 2:19 2568
f thousand and four hundred ... Num 2:23 2568
and one thousand and *f* hundred ... Num 2:28 2568
thousand and *f* hundred and fifty ... Num 2:32 2568
were seven thousand and *f* hundred ... Num 3:22 2568
Thou shalt even take *f* shekels ... Num 3:47 2568
f shekels, after the shekel of ... Num 3:50 2568
and *f* hundred and fourscore ... Num 4:48 2568
f rams, *f* he goats, *f* lambs ... Num 7:17 2568
f rams, *f* he goats, *f* lambs ... Num 7:23 2568
f rams, *f* he goats, *f* lambs ... Num 7:29 2568
f rams, *f* he goats, *f* lambs ... Num 7:35 2568
f rams, *f* he goats, *f* lambs ... Num 7:41 2568
f rams, *f* he goats, *f* lambs ... Num 7:47 2568
f rams, *f* he goats, *f* lambs ... Num 7:53 2568
f rams, *f* he goats, *f* lambs ... Num 7:59 2568
f rams, *f* he goats, *f* lambs ... Num 7:65 2568
f rams, *f* he goats, *f* lambs ... Num 7:71 2568
f he goats, *f* lambs of the ... Num 7:71 2568
f rams, *f* he goats, *f* lambs ... Num 7:77 2568
f rams, *f* he goats, *f* lambs ... Num 7:83 2568
f years old and upward they shall ... Num 8:24 2568
nor *f* days, neither ten days, nor ... Num 11:19 2568
for the money of *f* shekels ... Num 18:16 2568
them, forty thousand and *f* hundred ... Num 26:18 2568
and sixteen thousand and *f* hundred ... Num 26:22 2568
threescore thousand and *f* hundred ... Num 26:27 2568
and two thousand and *f* hundred ... Num 26:37 2568
f thousand and six hundred ... Num 26:41 2568
f thousand and four hundred ... Num 26:50 2568
Hur, and Reba, *f* kings of Midian ... Num 31:8 2568
one soul of *f* hundred, both of ... Num 31:28 2568
thousand and *f* thousand sheep, ... Num 31:32 2568
thousand and *f* hundred sheep ... Num 31:36 2568
were thirty thousand and *f* hundred ... Num 31:39 2568
thousand and *f* hundred sheep, ... Num 31:43 2568
thousand asses and *f* hundred, ... Num 31:45 2568
And he took about *f* thousand men ... Josh 8:12 2568
Therefore the *f* kings of the ... Josh 10:5 2568
But these *f* kings fled, and hid ... Josh 10:16 2568
The *f* kings are found hid in a ... Josh 10:17 2568
bring out those *f* kings unto me ... Josh 10:22 2568
brought forth those *f* kings unto ... Josh 10:23 2568
them, and hanged them on *f* trees ... Josh 10:26 2568
f lords of the Philistines ... Josh 13:3 2568
f years, even since the LORD ... Josh 14:10 2568
this day fourscore and *f* years old ... Josh 14:10 2568
f lords of the Philistines, and ... Judg 3:3 2568
family *f* men from their coasts ... Judg 18:2 2568
Then the *f* men departed, and came ... Judg 18:7 2568
Then answered the *f* men that went ... Judg 18:14 2568
the *f* men that went to spy out ... Judg 18:17 2568
f thousand and an hundred men ... Judg 20:35 2568
in the highways *f* thousand men ... Judg 20:45 2568
f thousand men that drew the ... Judg 20:46 2568
F golden emerods, and *f* golden ... 1Sa 6:4 2568
f golden mice, according to the ... 1Sa 6:4 2568
And when the *f* lords of the ... 1Sa 6:16 2568
belonging to the *f* lords, both of ... 1Sa 6:18 2568
was *f* thousand shekels of brass ... 1Sa 17:5 2568
chose him *f* smooth stones out of ... 1Sa 17:40 2568
give me *f* loaves of bread in mine ... 1Sa 21:3 2568
f persons that did wear a linen ... 1Sa 22:18 2568
f sheep ready dressed, and ... 1Sa 25:18 2568
f measures of parched corn, and an ... 1Sa 25:18 2568
with *f* damsels of hers that went ... 1Sa 25:42 2568
He was *f* years old when the ... 2Sa 4:4 2568
the *f* sons of Michal the daughter ... 2Sa 21:8 2568
Judah were *f* hundred thousand men ... 2Sa 24:9 2568
and his songs were a thousand and *f* ... 1Kin 4:32 2568
chamber was *f* cubits broad ... 1Kin 6:6 2568
all the house, *f* cubits high ... 1Kin 6:10 2568
f cubits was the one wing of the ... 1Kin 6:24 2568
f cubits the other wing of the ... 1Kin 6:24 2568
that lay on forty *f* pillars ... 1Kin 7:3 2568
of the one chapiter was *f* cubits ... 1Kin 7:16 2568
the other chapiter was *f* cubits ... 1Kin 7:16 2568
about, and his height was *f* cubits ... 1Kin 7:23 2568
he put *f* bases on the right side ... 1Kin 7:39 2568
f on the left side of the house ... 1Kin 7:39 2568
f on the right side, and *f* on ... 1Kin 7:49 2568
f on the left, before the oracle, ... 1Kin 7:49 2568
f hundred and fifty, which bare ... 1Kin 9:23 2568
f years old when he began to ... 1Kin 22:42 2568
twenty and *f* years in Jerusalem ... 1Kin 22:42 2568
dung for *f* pieces of silver ... 2Kin 6:25 2568
f of the horses that remain, ... 2Kin 7:13 2568
have smitten *f* or six times ... 2Kin 13:19 2568
f years old when he began to ... 2Kin 14:2 2568
F and twenty years old was he when ... 2Kin 15:33 2568
f years old was he when he began ... 2Kin 18:2 2568
hundred fourscore and *f* thousand ... 2Kin 19:35 2568
fifty and *f* years in Jerusalem ... 2Kin 21:1 2568
f years old when he began to ... 2Kin 23:36 2568
f men of them that were in the ... 2Kin 25:19 2568
All the sons of Judah were *f* ... 1Chr 2:4 2568
f of them in all ... 1Chr 2:6 2568
and Hasadiah, Jushab-hesed, *f* ... 1Chr 3:20 2568
and Tochen, and Ashan, *f* cities ... 1Chr 4:32 2568
f hundred men, went to mount Seir ... 1Chr 4:42 2568
and Obadiah, and Joel, Ishiah, *f* ... 1Chr 7:3 2568
and Uzziel, and Jerimoth, and Iri, *f* ... 1Chr 7:7 2568
of great stature, *f* cubits high ... 1Chr 11:23 2568
of God of gold *f* thousand talents ... 1Chr 29:7 2568
of the one cherub was *f* cubits ... 2Chr 3:11 2568
other wing was likewise *f* cubits ... 2Chr 3:11 2568
of the other cherub was *f* cubits ... 2Chr 3:12 2568
the other wing was *f* cubits also ... 2Chr 3:12 2568
f cubits high, and the chapiter ... 2Chr 3:15 2568
top of each of them was *f* cubits ... 2Chr 3:15 2568
f cubits the height thereof ... 2Chr 4:2 2568
put *f* on the right hand, and ... 2Chr 4:6 2568
f on the left, to wash in them ... 2Chr 4:6 2568
f on the right hand, and *f* on ... 2Chr 4:7 2568
f on the right side, and *f* on ... 2Chr 4:8 2568
of *f* cubits long, and *f* cubits ... 2Chr 6:13 2568
f hundred thousand chosen men ... 2Chr 13:17 2568
there was no more war unto the *f* ... 2Chr 15:19 2568
f years old when he began to ... 2Chr 20:31 2568
twenty and *f* years in Jerusalem ... 2Chr 20:31 2568
f years old when he began to ... 2Chr 25:1 2568
f hundred, that made war with ... 2Chr 26:13 2568
f years old when he began to ... 2Chr 27:1 2568
He was *f* and twenty years old when ... 2Chr 27:8 2568
began to reign when he was *f* ... 2Chr 29:1 2568
fifty and *f* years in Jerusalem ... 2Chr 33:1 2568
offerings *f* thousand small cattle ... 2Chr 35:9 2568
small cattle, and *f* hundred oxen ... 2Chr 35:9 2568
f years old when he began to ... 2Chr 36:5 2568
gold and of silver were *f* thousand ... Ezr 1:11 2568
Arah, seven hundred seventy and *f* ... Ezr 2:5 2568
of Zattu, nine hundred forty and *f* ... Ezr 2:8 2568
children of Gibbar, ninety and *f* ... Ezr 2:20 2568
and Ono, seven hundred twenty and *f* ... Ezr 2:33 2568
Jericho, three hundred forty and *f* ... Ezr 2:34 2568
mules, two hundred forty and *f* ... Ezr 2:66 2568
camels, four hundred thirty and *f* ... Ezr 2:67 2568
f thousand pound of silver, and ... Ezr 2:69 2568
Zattu, eight hundred forty and *f* ... Neh 7:13 2568
of Adin, six hundred fifty and *f* ... Neh 7:20 2568
children of Gibeon, ninety and *f* ... Neh 7:25 2568
Jericho, three hundred forty and *f* ... Neh 7:36 2568
f singing men and singing women ... Neh 7:67 2568
mules, two hundred forty and *f* ... Neh 7:68 2568
camels, four hundred thirty and *f* ... Neh 7:69 2568
f hundred and thirty priests' ... Neh 7:70 2568
slew and destroyed *f* hundred men ... Est 9:6 2568
destroyed *f* hundred men in ... Est 9:12 2568
f thousand, but they laid not ... Est 9:16 2568
f hundred yoke of oxen, and *f* ... Job 1:3 2568
f hundred she asses, and a very ... Job 1:3 2568
f years shall Ephraim be broken, ... Is 7:8 2568
four or *f* in the outmost fruitful ... Is 17:6 2568
In that day shall *f* cities in the ... Is 19:18 2568
at the rebuke of *f* shall ye flee ... Is 30:17 2568
and fourscore and *f* thousand ... Is 37:36 2568
of one chapiter was *f* cubits ... Jer 52:22 2568
seven hundred forty and *f* persons ... Jer 52:30 2568
in the twelfth month, in the *f* ... Jer 52:31 2568
porch and the altar, were about *f* ... Eze 8:16 2568
behold at the door of the gate *f* ... Eze 11:1 2568
In the *f* and twentieth year of our ... Eze 40:1 2568
the little chambers were *f* cubits ... Eze 40:7 2568
the breadth was *f* and twenty ... Eze 40:13 2568
fifty cubits, and the breadth *f* ... Eze 40:21 2568
fifty cubits, and the breadth *f* ... Eze 40:25 2568
it was fifty cubits long, and *f* ... Eze 40:29 2568
And the arches round about were *f* ... Eze 40:30 2568
cubits long, and *f* cubits broad ... Eze 40:30 2568
it was fifty cubits long, and *f* ... Eze 40:33 2568
fifty cubits, and the breadth *f* ... Eze 40:36 2568
f cubits on this side ... Eze 40:48 2568
and *f* cubits on that side ... Eze 40:48 2568
were *f* cubits on the one side ... Eze 41:2 2568
f cubits on the other side ... Eze 41:2 2568
chamber without, was *f* cubits ... Eze 41:9 2568

was left was f cubits round about ... Eze 41:11 2568
was f cubits thick round about ... Eze 41:12 2568
f hundred reeds, with the ... Eze 42:16 2568
f hundred reeds, with the ... Eze 42:17 2568
f hundred reeds, with the ... Eze 42:18 2568
measured f hundred reeds with the ... Eze 42:19 2568
f hundred reeds long, and ... Eze 42:20 2568
f hundred broad, to make a ... Eze 42:20 2568
length shall be the length of f ... Eze 45:1 2568
the sanctuary f hundred in length ... Eze 45:2 2568
with f hundred in breadth, square ... Eze 45:2 2568
thou measure the length of f ... Eze 45:3 2568
And the f and twenty thousand of ... Eze 45:5 2568
city f thousand broad, and f ... Eze 45:6 2568
twenty shekels, f and twenty ... Eze 45:12 2568
which ye shall offer of f ... Eze 48:8 2568
offer unto the LORD shall be of f ... Eze 48:9 2568
toward the north f and twenty ... Eze 48:10 2568
in breadth, and toward the south f ... Eze 48:10 2568
priests the Levites shall have f ... Eze 48:13 2568
all the length shall be f ... Eze 48:13 2568
the f thousand, that are left in ... Eze 48:15 2568
in the breadth over against the f ... Eze 48:15 2568
f hundred, and the south side four ... Eze 48:16 2568
f hundred, and on the east side ... Eze 48:16 2568
f hundred, and the west side four ... Eze 48:16 2568
side four thousand and f hundred ... Eze 48:16 2568
be f and twenty thousand by f ... Eze 48:20 2568
of the city, over against the f ... Eze 48:21 2568
and westward over against the f ... Eze 48:21 2568
thousand and f hundred measures ... Eze 48:30 2568
side four thousand and f hundred ... Eze 48:32 2568
thousand and f hundred measures ... Eze 48:33 2568
f hundred, with their three gates ... Eze 48:34 2568
the thousand three hundred and f ... Dan 12:12 2568
him, We have here but f loaves ... Mt 14:17 4002
the grass, and took the f loaves ... Mt 14:19 4002
eaten were about f thousand men ... Mt 14:21 4000
neither remember the f loaves of ... Mt 16:9 4002
the f thousand, and how many baskets ... Mt 16:9 4000
f of them were wise, and f were ... Mt 25:2 4000
And unto one he gave f talents ... Mt 25:15 4000
had received the f talents went ... Mt 25:16 4000
and made them other f talents ... Mt 25:16 4000
that had received f talents came ... Mt 25:20 4000
came and brought other f talents ... Mt 25:20 4000
deliveredst unto me f talents ... Mt 25:20 4000
gained beside them f talents more ... Mt 25:20 4000
And when they knew, they say, F ... Mk 6:38 4000
And when he had taken the f loaves ... Mk 6:41 4000
loaves were about f thousand men ... Mk 6:44 4000
When I brake the f loaves among ... Mk 8:19 4002
f thousand, how many baskets ... Mk 8:19 4000
and hid herself f months, saying ... Lk 1:24 4002
the one owed f hundred pence, and ... Lk 7:41 4001
We have no more but f loaves ... Lk 9:13 4002
they were about f thousand men ... Lk 9:14 4000
Then he took the f loaves ... Lk 9:16 4002
Are not f sparrows sold for two ... Lk 12:6 4002
shall be f in one house divided ... Lk 12:52 4002
I have bought f yoke of oxen ... Lk 14:19 4002
For I have f brethren ... Lk 16:28 4002
thy pound hath gained f pounds ... Lk 19:18 4002
him, Be thou also over f cities ... Lk 19:19 4002
For thou hast had f husbands ... Jn 4:18 4002
tongue Bethesda, having f porches ... Jn 5:2 4002
which hath f barley loaves, and ... Jn 6:9 4002
down, in number about f thousand ... Jn 6:10 4000
fragments of the f barley loaves ... Jn 6:13 4002
So when they had rowed about f ... Jn 6:19 4002
of the men was about f thousand ... Acts 4:4 4002
came unto them to Troas in f days ... Acts 20:6 4002
after f days Ananias the high ... Acts 24:1 4002
f words with my understanding ... 1Cor 14:19 4002
he was seen of above f hundred ... 1Cor 15:6 4001
Of the Jews f times received I ... 2Cor 11:24 3999
they should be tormented f months ... Rev 9:5 4002
power was to hurt men f months ... Rev 9:10 4002
f are fallen, and one is, and the ... Rev 17:10 4002

FIXED {6}
My heart is f, O God, my heart is ... Ps 57:7 3559
is f, O God, my heart is f ... Ps 57:7 3559
O God, my heart is f ... Ps 108:1 3559
his heart is f, trusting in the ... Ps 112:7 3559
us and you there is a great gulf f ... Lk 16:26 4741

FLAG {1}
can the f grow without water ... Job 8:11 260

FLAGON {2}
piece of flesh, and a f of wine ... 2Sa 6:19 809
piece of flesh, and a f of wine ... 1Chr 16:3 809

FLAGONS {3}
Stay me with f, comfort me with ... Song 2:5 809
even to all the vessels of f ... Is 22:24 5035
to other gods, and love f of wine ... Hos 3:1 809

FLAGS {3}
she laid it in the f by the ... Ex 2:3 5488
when she saw the ark among the f ... Ex 2:5 5488
the reeds and f shall wither ... Is 19:6 5488

FLAKES {1}
The f of his flesh are joined ... Job 41:23 4651

FLAME {34}
a f of fire out of the midst of a ... Ex 3:2 3827
a f from the city of Sihon ... Num 21:28 3852
when the f went up toward heaven ... Judg 13:20 3851
ascended in the f of the altar ... Judg 13:20 3851
f with smoke rise up out of the ... Judg 20:38 4864
But when the f began to arise up ... Judg 20:40 4864
the f of the city ascended up to ... Judg 20:40 3632
the f shall dry up his branches ... Job 15:30 7957
a f goeth out of his mouth ... Job 41:21 3851
as the f setteth the mountains on ... Ps 83:14 3852
the f burned up the wicked ... Ps 106:18 3852
which hath a most vehement f ... Song 8:6 7957
the f consumeth the chaff, so ... Is 5:24 3852
a fire, and his Holy One for a f ... Is 10:17 3852
and the f of devouring fire ... Is 29:6 3851
with the f of a devouring fire ... Is 30:30 3851
shall the f kindle upon thee ... Is 43:2 3852
from the power of the f ... Is 47:14 3852
a f from the midst of Sihon, and ... Jer 48:45 3852
the flaming f shall not be ... Eze 20:47 7957
the f of the fire slew those men ... Dan 3:22 7631
his throne was like the fiery f ... Dan 7:9 7631
and given to the burning f ... Dan 7:11 785
shall fall by the sword, and by f ... Dan 11:33 3852
the f hath burned all the trees ... Joel 1:19 3852
and behind them a f burneth ... Joel 2:3 3852
like the noise of a f of fire ... Joel 2:5 3851
fire, and the house of Joseph a f ... Obad 18 3852
for I am tormented in this f ... Lk 16:24 5395
the Lord in a f of fire in a bush ... Acts 7:30 5395
and his ministers a f of fire ... Heb 1:7 5395
and his eyes were as a f of fire ... Rev 1:14 5395
his eyes like unto a f of fire ... Rev 2:18 5395
His eyes were as a f of fire ... Rev 19:12 5395

FLAMES {3}
the LORD divideth the f of fire ... Ps 29:7 3852
their faces shall be as f ... Is 13:8 3851
and his rebuke with f of fire ... Is 66:15 3851

FLAMING {9}
a f sword which turned every way ... Gen 3:24 3858
his ministers a f fire ... Ps 104:4 3857
for rain, and f fire in their land ... Ps 105:32 3852
the shining of a f fire by night ... Is 4:5 3852
against Jacob like a f fire ... Lam 2:3 3852
the f flame shall not be quenched ... Eze 20:47 3852
morning it burneth as a f fire ... Hos 7:6 3852
with f torches in the day of his ... Nah 2:3 784
In f fire taking vengeance on ... 2Th 1:8 5395

FLANKS {6}
is on them, which is by the f ... Lev 3:4 3689
is upon them, which is by the f ... Lev 3:10 3689
is upon them, which is by the f ... Lev 3:15 3689
is upon them, which is by the f ... Lev 4:9 3689
is on them, which is by the f ... Lev 7:4 3689
and maketh collops of fat on his f ... Job 15:27 3689

FLASH {1}
appearance of a f of lightning ... Eze 1:14 965

FLAT {4}
a lame, or he that hath a f nose ... Lev 21:18 2763
his head, and fell f on his face ... Num 22:31 639
of the city shall fall down f ... Josh 6:5 8478
shout, that the wall fell down f ... Josh 6:20 8478

FLATTER {2}
they f with their tongue ... Ps 5:9 2505
they did f him with their mouth ... Ps 78:36 6601

FLATTERETH {6}
For he f himself in his own eyes ... Ps 36:2 2505
stranger which f with her words ... Prov 2:16 2505
stranger which f with her words ... Prov 7:5 2505
not with him that f with his lips ... Prov 20:19 6601
than he that f with the tongue ... Prov 28:23 2505
A man that f his neighbour ... Prov 29:5 2505

FLATTERIES {3}
and obtain the kingdom by f ... Dan 11:21 2519
covenant shall he corrupt by f ... Dan 11:32 2514
many shall cleave to them with f ... Dan 11:34 2519

FLATTERING {8}
let me give f titles unto man ... Job 32:21 3665
For I know not to give f titles ... Job 32:22 3665
with f lips and with a double ... Ps 12:2 2513
The LORD shall cut off all f lips ... Ps 12:3 2513
with the f of her lips she forced ... Prov 7:21 2506
and a f mouth worketh ruin ... Prov 26:28 2509
f divination within the house of ... Eze 12:24 2509
at any time used we f words ... 1Th 2:5 2850

FLATTERY {2}
He that speaketh f to his friends ... Job 17:5 2506
from the f of the tongue of a ... Prov 6:24 2513

FLAX {11}
And the f and the barley was ... Ex 9:31 6594
in the ear, and the f was bolled ... Ex 9:31 6594
and hid them with the stalks of f ... Josh 2:6 6593
as f that was burnt with fire ... Judg 15:14 6593
She seeketh wool, and f, and ... Prov 31:13 6593
Moreover they that work in fine f ... Is 19:9 6593
the smoking f shall he not quench ... Is 42:3 6594
with a line of f in his hand ... Eze 40:3 6593
and my water, my wool and my f ... Hos 2:5 6593
my f given to cover her nakedness ... Hos 2:9 6593
smoking f shall he not quench ... Mt 12:20 3043

FLAY {3}
he shall f the burnt offering, and ... Lev 1:6 6584
so that they could not f all the ... 2Chr 29:34 6584
f their skin from off them ... Mic 3:3 6584

FLAYED {1}
hands, and the Levites f them ... 2Chr 35:11 6584

FLEA {2}
after a dead dog, after a f ... 1Sa 24:14 6550
of Israel is come out to seek a f ... 1Sa 26:20 6550

FLED {148}
the kings of Sodom and Gomorrah f ... Gen 14:10 5127
that remained f to the mountain ... Gen 14:10 5127
with her, she f from her face ... Gen 16:6 1272
in that he told him not that he f ... Gen 31:20 1272
So he f with all that he had ... Gen 31:21 1272
on the third day that Jacob was f ... Gen 31:22 1272
when he f from the face of his ... Gen 35:7 1272
his garment in her hand, and f ... Gen 39:12 5127
in her hand, and was f forth ... Gen 39:13 5127
he left his garment with me, and f ... Gen 39:15 5127
his garment with me, and f out ... Gen 39:18 5127
But Moses f from the face of ... Ex 2:15 1272
and Moses f from before it ... Ex 4:3 5127
king of Egypt that the people f ... Ex 14:5 1272
and the Egyptians f against it ... Ex 14:27 5127
about them f at the cry of them ... Num 16:34 5127
of his refuge, whither he was f ... Num 35:25 5127
of his refuge, whither he was f ... Num 35:26 5127
is f to the city of his refuge ... Num 35:32 5127
they f before the men of Ai ... Josh 7:4 5127
f by the way of the wilderness ... Josh 8:15 5127
and the people that f to the ... Josh 8:20 5127
as they f from before Israel, and ... Josh 10:11 5127
But these five kings f, and hid ... Josh 10:16 5127
unto the city from whence he f ... Josh 20:6 5127
But Adoni-bezek f ... Judg 1:6 5127
chariot, and f away on his feet ... Judg 4:15 5127
Howbeit Sisera f away on his feet ... Judg 4:17 5127
all the host ran, and cried, and f ... Judg 7:21 5127
the host f to Beth-shittah in ... Judg 7:22 5127
And when Zebah and Zalmunna f ... Judg 8:12 5127
And Jotham ran away, and f, and went ... Judg 9:21 1272
he f before him, and many were ... Judg 9:40 5127
thither f all the men and women ... Judg 9:51 5127
Then Jephthah f from his brethren ... Judg 11:3 1272
f toward the wilderness unto the ... Judg 20:45 5127
f to the wilderness unto the rock ... Judg 20:47 5127
they f every man into his tent ... 1Sa 4:10 5127
I f to day out of the army ... 1Sa 4:16 5127
and said, Israel is f before the ... 1Sa 4:17 5127
they heard that the Philistines f ... 1Sa 14:22 5127
f from him, and were sore afraid ... 1Sa 17:24 5127
their champion was dead, they f ... 1Sa 17:51 5127
and they f from him ... 1Sa 19:8 5127
and David f, and escaped that night ... 1Sa 19:10 5127
and he went, and f, and escaped ... 1Sa 19:12 1272
So David f, and escaped, and came ... 1Sa 19:18 1272
David f from Naioth in Ramah, and ... 1Sa 20:1 1272
f that day for fear of Saul, and ... 1Sa 21:10 1272
and because they knew when he f ... 1Sa 22:17 1272
escaped, and f after David ... 1Sa 22:20 1272
of Ahimelech f to David to Keilah ... 1Sa 23:6 1272
Saul that David was f to Gath ... 1Sa 27:4 1272
men, which rode upon camels, and f ... 1Sa 30:17 5127
the men of Israel f from before ... 1Sa 31:1 5127
saw that the men of Israel f ... 1Sa 31:7 5127
they forsook the cities, and f ... 1Sa 31:7 5127
the people are f from the battle ... 2Sa 1:4 5127
And the Beerothites f to Gittaim ... 2Sa 4:3 1272
and his nurse took him up, and f ... 2Sa 4:4 5127
and they f before him ... 2Sa 10:13 5127
Ammon saw that the Syrians were f ... 2Sa 10:14 5127
then f they also before Abishai ... 2Sa 10:14 5127
the Syrians f before Israel ... 2Sa 10:18 5127
gat him up upon his mule, and f ... 2Sa 13:29 5127
But Absalom f. And the young man ... 2Sa 13:34 1272
But Absalom f, and went to Talmai ... 2Sa 13:37 1272
So Absalom f, and went to Geshur ... 2Sa 13:38 1272
all Israel f every one to his ... 2Sa 18:17 5127
for Israel had f every man to his ... 2Sa 19:8 5127
now he is f out of the land for ... 2Sa 19:9 1272
the people f from the Philistines ... 2Sa 23:11 5127
for so they came to me when I f ... 1Kin 2:7 1272
Joab f unto the tabernacle of the ... 1Kin 2:28 5127
f unto the tabernacle of the LORD ... 1Kin 2:29 5127
That Hadad f, he and certain ... 1Kin 11:17 1272
which f from his lord Hadadezer ... 1Kin 11:23 1272
f into Egypt, unto Shishak king ... 1Kin 11:40 1272
(for he was f from the presence ... 1Kin 12:2 1272
and the Syrians f ... 1Kin 20:20 5127
But the rest f to Aphek, into the ... 1Kin 20:30 5127
And Ben-hadad f, and came into the ... 1Kin 20:30 5127
so that they f before them ... 2Kin 3:24 5127
f in the twilight, and left their ... 2Kin 7:7 5127
as it was, and f for their life ... 2Kin 7:7 5127
the people f into their tents ... 2Kin 8:21 5127
And he opened the door, and f ... 2Kin 9:10 5127
And Joram turned his hands, and f ... 2Kin 9:23 5127
he f by the way of the garden ... 2Kin 9:27 5127
he f to Megiddo, and died there ... 2Kin 9:27 5127
they f every man to their tents ... 2Kin 14:12 5127
and he f to Lachish ... 2Kin 14:19 5127
all the men of war f by night by ... 2Kin 25:4
the men of Israel f from before ... 1Chr 10:1 5127
in the valley saw that they f ... 1Chr 10:7 5127
they forsook their cities, and f ... 1Chr 10:7 5127
the people f from before the ... 1Chr 11:13 5127
and they f before him ... 1Chr 19:14 5127
Ammon saw that the Syrians were f ... 1Chr 19:15 5127
they likewise f before Abishai ... 1Chr 19:15 5127
But the Syrians f before Israel ... 1Chr 19:18 5127
whither he had f from the ... 2Chr 10:2 1272
children of Israel f before Judah ... 2Chr 13:16 5127

and the Ethiopians *f* 2Chr 14:12 5127
they *f* every man to his tent 2Chr 25:22 5127
and he *f* to Lachish 2Chr 25:27 5127
were *f* every one to his field Neh 13:10 1272
when he *f* from Absalom his son Ps 3:*t* 1272
that did see me without *f* from me Ps 31:11 5074
when he *f* from Saul in the cave Ps 57:*t* 1272
At thy rebuke they *f* Ps 104:7 5127
The sea saw it, and *f* Ps 114:3 5127
Gibeah of Saul is *f* Is 10:29 5127
with their bread him that *f* Is 21:14 5074
For they *f* from the swords, from Is 21:15 5074
All thy rulers are *f* together Is 22:3 5074
together, which have *f* from far Is 22:3 1272
noise of the tumult the people *f* Is 33:3 5074
the birds of the heavens were *f* Jer 4:25 5074
of the heavens and the beast are *f* Jer 9:10 5074
heard it, he was afraid, and *f* Jer 26:21 1272
all the men of war, then they *f* Jer 39:4 1272
are *f* apace, and look not back Jer 46:5 5127
back, and are *f* away together Jer 46:21 5127
They that *f* stood under the Jer 48:45 5127
up, and all the men of war *f* Jer 52:7 1272
when they *f* away and wandered, Lam 4:15 5132
so that they *f* to hide themselves Dan 10:7 1272
for they have *f* from me Hos 7:13 5074
Jacob *f* into the country of Syria Hos 12:12 1272
For the men knew that he *f* from Jonah 1:10 1272
Therefore I *f* before unto Jonah 4:2 1272
like as ye *f* from before the Zec 14:5 5127
And they that kept them *f*, and went Mt 8:33 5343
the disciples forsook him, and *f* Mt 26:56 5343
And they that fed the swine *f* Mk 5:14 5343
And they all forsook him, and *f* Mk 14:50 5343
linen cloth, and *f* from them naked Mk 14:52 5343
quickly, and *f* from the sepulchre Mk 16:8 5343
them saw what was done, they *f* Lk 8:34 5343
Then *f* Moses at this saying, and Acts 7:29 5343
f unto Lystra and Derbe, cities of Acts 14:6 2703
that the prisoners had been *f* Acts 16:27 1628
so that they *f* out of that house Acts 19:16 1628
who have *f* for refuge to lay hold Heb 6:18 2703
the woman *f* into the wilderness, Rev 12:6 5343
And every island *f* away, and the Rev 16:20 5343
the earth and the heaven *f* away Rev 20:11 5343

FLEDDEST {2}

thou *f* from the face of Esau thy Gen 35:1 1272
thee, O thou sea, that thou *f* Ps 114:5 5127

FLEE {105}

I *f* from the face of my mistress Gen 16:8 1272
now, this city is near to *f* unto Gen 19:20 5127
f thou to Laban my brother to Gen 27:43 1272
didst thou *f* away secretly Gen 31:27 1272
his cattle *f* into the houses Ex 9:20 5127
Let us *f* from the face of Israel Ex 14:25 5127
thee a place whither he shall *f* Ex 21:13 5127
ye shall *f* when none pursueth you Lev 26:17 5127
and they shall *f*, as fleeing from Lev 26:36 5127
them that hate thee *f* before thee Num 10:35 5127
Therefore now *f* thou to thy place Num 24:11 1272
manslayer, that he may *f* thither Num 35:6 5127
that the slayer may *f* thither Num 35:11 5127
any person unawares may *f* thither Num 35:15 5127
That the slayer might *f* thither Deut 4:42 5127
that every slayer may *f* thither Deut 19:3 5127
the slayer, which shall *f* thither Deut 19:4 5127
he shall *f* unto one of those Deut 19:5 5127
way, and *f* before thee seven ways Deut 28:7 5127
them, and *f* seven ways before them Deut 28:25 5127
first, that we will *f* before them Josh 8:5 5127
They *f* before us, as at the first Josh 8:6 5127
therefore we will *f* before them Josh 8:6 5127
power to *f* this way or that way Josh 8:20 5127
and unwittingly may *f* thither Josh 20:3 5127
when he that doth *f* unto one of Josh 20:4 5127
at unawares might *f* thither Josh 20:9 5127
children of Israel said, Let us *f* Judg 20:32 5127
to pass, as she made haste to *f* 2Sa 4:4 5127
at Jerusalem, Arise, and let us *f* 2Sa 15:14 1227
people that are with him shall *f* 2Sa 17:2 5127
for if we *f* away, they will not 2Sa 18:3 5127
steal away when they *f* in battle 2Sa 19:3 5127
or wilt thou *f* three months 2Sa 24:13 5127
to his chariot, to *f* to Jerusalem 1Kin 12:18 5127
Then open the door, and *f*, and 2Kin 9:3 5127
to his chariot, to *f* to Jerusalem 2Chr 10:18 5127
I said, Should such a man as I *f* Neh 6:11 1272
they *f* away, they see no good Job 9:25 1272
He shall *f* from the iron weapon, Job 20:24 1272
he would fain *f* out of his hand Job 27:22 1272
they *f* far from me, and spare not Job 30:10 7368
The arrow cannot make him *f* Job 41:28 1272
F as a bird to your mountain Ps 11:1 5110
all that see them shall *f* away Ps 64:8 5074
also that hate him *f* before him Ps 68:1 5127
Kings of armies did *f* apace Ps 68:12 5074
shall I *f* from thy presence Ps 139:7 1272
I *f* unto thee to hide me Ps 143:9 3680
The wicked *f* when no man pursueth Prov 28:1 5127
of any person shall *f* to the pit Prov 28:17 5127
day break, and the shadows *f* away Song 2:17 5127
day break, and the shadows *f* away Song 4:6 5127
to whom will ye *f* for help Is 10:3 5127
of Gebim gather themselves to *f* Is 10:31
f every one into his own land Is 13:14 5127
his fugitives shall *f* unto Zoar Is 15:5
them, and they shall *f* far off Is 17:13 5127
whither we *f* for help to be Is 20:6 5127
for we will *f* upon horses Is 30:16 5127
therefore shall ye *f* Is 30:16 5127
One thousand shall *f* at the Is 30:17
at the rebuke of five shall ye *f* Is 30:17 5127
but he shall *f* from the sword, and Is 31:8 5127
and sorrow and sighing shall *f* away Is 35:10 5127
f ye from the Chaldeans, with a Is 48:20 1272
sorrow and mourning shall *f* away Is 51:11 5127
The whole city shall *f* for the Jer 4:29 1272
gather yourselves to *f* out of the Jer 6:1 5756
shepherds shall have no way to *f* Jer 25:35 4498
Let not the swift *f* away, nor the Jer 46:6 5127
F, save your lives, and be like Jer 48:6 5127
wings unto Moab, that it may *f* Jer 48:9 5323
F ye, turn back, dwell deep, O Jer 49:8 5127
feeble, and turneth herself to *f* Jer 49:24 5127
F, get you far off, dwell deep, O Jer 49:30 5127
they shall *f* every one to his own Jer 50:16 5127
The voice of them that *f* and Jer 50:28 5127
F out of the midst of Babylon, and Jer 51:6 5127
shall *f* away naked in that day Amos 2:16 5127
As if a man did *f* from a lion Amos 5:19 5127
f thee away into the land of Amos 7:12 1272
fleeth of them shall not *f* away Amos 9:1 5127
But Jonah rose up to *f* unto Jonah 1:3 1272
yet they shall *f* away Nah 2:8 5127
look upon thee shall *f* from thee Nah 3:7 5074
when the sun ariseth they *f* away Nah 3:17 5074
f from the land of the north, Zec 2:6 5127
ye shall *f* to the valley of the Zec 14:5 5127
yea, ye shall *f*, like as ye fled Zec 14:5 5127
f into Egypt, and be thou there Mt 2:13 5343
you to *f* from the wrath to come Mt 3:7 5343
in this city, *f* ye into another Mt 10:23 5343
be in Judaea *f* to the mountains Mt 24:16 5343
be in Judaea *f* to the mountains Mk 13:14 5343
you to *f* from the wrath to come Lk 3:7 5343
are in Judaea *f* to the mountains Lk 21:21 5343
not follow, but will *f* from him Jn 10:5 5343
were about to *f* out of the ship Acts 27:30 5343
F fornication 1Cor 6:18 5343
dearly beloved, *f* from idolatry 1Cor 10:14 5343
O man of God, *f* these things 1Ti 6:11 5343
F also youthful lusts 2Ti 2:22 5343
the devil, and he will *f* from you Jas 4:7 5343
die, and death shall *f* from them Rev 9:6 5343

FLEECE {9}

the first of the *f* of thy sheep Deut 18:4 1488
I will put a *f* of wool in the Judg 6:37 1492
and if the dew be on the *f* only Judg 6:37 1492
morrow, and thrust the *f* together Judg 6:38 1492
and wringed the dew out of the *f* Judg 6:38 1492
thee, but this once with the *f* Judg 6:39 1492
let it now be dry only upon the *f* Judg 6:39 1492
for it was dry upon the *f* only Judg 6:40 1492
not warmed with the *f* of my sheep Job 31:20 1488

FLEEING {3}

shall flee, as *f* from a sword Lev 26:36 4499
that *f* unto one of these cities Deut 4:42 5127
f into the wilderness in former Job 30:3 6207

FLEETH {9}

f into one of these cities Deut 19:11 5127
he *f* also as a shadow, and Job 14:2 1272
that he who *f* from the noise of Is 24:18 5127
ask him that *f*, and her that Jer 48:19 5127
He that *f* from the fear shall Jer 48:44 5211
he that *f* of them shall not flee Amos 9:1 5127
cankerworm spoileth, and *f* away Nah 3:16 5775
and leaveth the sheep, and *f* Jn 10:12 5343
The hireling *f*, because he is an Jn 10:13 5343

FLESH {423}

closed up the *f* instead thereof Gen 2:21 1320
of my bones, and *f* of my *f* Gen 2:23 1320
and they shall be one *f* Gen 2:24 1320
with man, for that he also is *f* Gen 6:3 1320
for all *f* had corrupted his way Gen 6:12 1320
The end of all *f* is come before Gen 6:13 1320
upon the earth, to destroy all *f* Gen 6:17 1320
And of every living thing of all *f* Gen 6:19 1320
into the ark, two and two of all *f* Gen 7:15 1320
went in male and female of all *f* Gen 7:16 1320
all *f* died that moved upon the Gen 7:21 1320
thing that is with thee, of all *f* Gen 8:17 1320
But *f* with the life thereof, Gen 9:4 1320
neither shall all *f* be cut off Gen 9:11 1320
and every living creature of all *f* Gen 9:15 1320
become a flood to destroy all *f* Gen 9:15 1320
of all *f* that is upon the earth Gen 9:16 1320
all *f* that is upon the earth Gen 9:17 1320
circumcise the *f* of your foreskin Gen 17:11 1320
f for an everlasting covenant Gen 17:13 1320
whose *f* of his foreskin is not Gen 17:14 1320
circumcised the *f* of their Gen 17:23 1320
in the *f* of his foreskin Gen 17:24 1320
in the *f* of his foreskin Gen 17:25 1320
Surely thou art my bone and my *f* Gen 29:14 1320
for he is our brother and our *f* Gen 37:27 1320
shall eat thy *f* from off thee Gen 40:19 1320
was turned again as his other *f* Ex 4:7 1320
shall eat the *f* in that night Ex 12:8 1320
of the *f* abroad out of the house Ex 12:46 1320
Egypt, when we sat by the *f* pots Ex 16:3 1320
give you in the evening *f* to eat Ex 16:8 1320
saying, At even ye shall eat *f* Ex 16:12 1320
and his *f* shall not be eaten Ex 21:28 1320
neither shall ye eat any *f* that Ex 22:31 1320
But the *f* of the bullock, and his Ex 29:14 1320
seethe his *f* in the holy place Ex 29:31 1320
sons shall eat the *f* of the ram Ex 29:32 1320
And if ought of the *f* of the Ex 29:34 1320
Upon man's *f* shall it not be Ex 30:32 1320
skin of the bullock, and all his *f* Lev 4:11 1320
breeches shall he put upon his *f* Lev 6:10 1320
touch the *f* thereof shall be holy Lev 6:27 1320
the *f* of the sacrifice of his Lev 7:15 1320
But the remainder of the *f* of the Lev 7:17 1320
if any of the *f* of the sacrifice Lev 7:18 1320
the *f* that toucheth any unclean Lev 7:19 1320
and as for the *f*, all that be Lev 7:19 1320
the *f* of the sacrifice of peace Lev 7:20 1320
eat of the *f* of the sacrifice of Lev 7:21 1320
the bullock, and his hide, his *f* Lev 8:17 1320
Boil the *f* at the door of the Lev 8:31 1320
And that which remaineth of the *f* Lev 8:32 1320
And the *f* and the hide he burnt Lev 9:11 1320
Of their *f* shall ye not eat, and Lev 11:8 1320
ye shall not eat of their *f* Lev 11:11 1320
in the eighth day the *f* of his Lev 12:3 1320
in the skin of his *f* a rising Lev 13:2 1320
it be in the skin of his *f* like Lev 13:2 1320
the plague in the skin of the *f* Lev 13:3 1320
be deeper than the skin of his *f* Lev 13:3 1320
be white in the skin of his *f* Lev 13:4 1320
be quick raw *f* in the rising Lev 13:10 1320
old leprosy in the skin of his *f* Lev 13:11 1320
leprosy have covered all his *f* Lev 13:13 1320
But when raw *f* appeareth in him, Lev 13:14 1320
And the priest shall see the raw *f* Lev 13:15 1320
for the raw *f* is unclean Lev 13:15 1320
Or if the raw *f* turn again Lev 13:16 1320
The *f* also, in which, even in the Lev 13:18 1320
Or if there be any *f*, in the skin Lev 13:24 1320
the quick *f* that burneth have a Lev 13:24
the skin of their *f* bright spots Lev 13:38 1320
skin of their *f* be darkish white Lev 13:39 1320
appeareth in the skin of the *f* Lev 13:43 1320
also he shall wash his *f* in water Lev 14:9 1320
hath a running issue out of his *f* Lev 15:2 1320
whether his *f* run with his issue, Lev 15:3 1320
or his *f* be stopped from his Lev 15:3 1320
he that toucheth the *f* of him Lev 15:7 1320
bathe his *f* in running water, and Lev 15:13 1320
he shall wash all his *f* in water Lev 15:16 1320
and her issue in her *f* be blood Lev 15:19 1320
the linen breeches upon his *f* Lev 16:4 1320
shall he wash his *f* in water Lev 16:4 1320
he shall wash his *f* with water in Lev 16:24 1320
clothes, and bathe his *f* in water Lev 16:26 1320
the fire their skins, and their *f* Lev 16:27 1320
clothes, and bathe his *f* in water Lev 16:28 1320
the life of the *f* is in the blood Lev 17:11 1320
For it is the life of all *f* Lev 17:14 1320
eat the blood of no manner of *f* Lev 17:14 1320
for the life of all *f* is the Lev 17:14 1320
he wash them not, nor bathe his *f* Lev 17:16 1320
cuttings in your *f* for the dead Lev 19:28 1320
nor make any cuttings in their *f* Lev 21:5 1320
unless he wash his *f* with water Lev 22:6 1320
ye shall eat the *f* of your sons Lev 26:29 1320
the *f* of your daughters shall ye Lev 26:29 1320
and let them shave all their *f* Num 8:7 1320
said, Who shall give us *f* to eat Num 11:4 1320
Whence should I have *f* to give Num 11:13 1320
weep unto me, saying, Give us *f* Num 11:13 1320
to morrow, and ye shall eat *f* Num 11:18 1320
Who shall give us *f* to eat Num 11:18 1320
the LORD will give you *f*, and ye Num 11:18 1320
hast said, I will give them *f* Num 11:21 1320
while the *f* was yet between their Num 11:33 1320
of whom the *f* is half consumed Num 12:12 1320
the God of the spirits of all *f* Num 16:22 1320
that openeth the matrix in all *f* Num 18:15 1320
the *f* of them shall be thine, as Num 18:18 1320
her skin, and her *f*, and her blood, Num 19:5 1320
and he shall bathe his *f* in water Num 19:7 1320
in water, and bathe his *f* in water Num 19:8 1320
the God of the spirits of all *f* Num 27:16 1320
For who is there of all *f* Deut 5:26 1320
kill and eat *f* in all thy gates, Deut 12:15 1320
and thou shalt say, I will eat *f* Deut 12:20 1320
because thy soul longeth to eat *f* Deut 12:20 1320
thou mayest eat *f*, whatsoever thy Deut 12:20 1320
not eat the life with the *f* Deut 12:23 1320
offer thy burnt offerings, the *f* Deut 12:27 1320
thy God, and thou shalt eat the *f* Deut 12:27 1320
ye shall not eat of their *f* Deut 14:8 1320
shall there any thing of the *f* Deut 16:4 1320
the *f* of thy sons and of thy Deut 28:53 1320
f of his children whom he shall Deut 28:55 1320
blood, and my sword shall devour *f* Deut 32:42 1320
the *f* he put in a basket, and he Judg 6:19 1320
of God said unto him, Take the *f* Judg 6:20 1320
was in his hand, and touched the *f* Judg 6:21 1320
of the rock, and consumed the *f* Judg 6:21 1320
then I will tear your *f* with the Judg 8:7 1320
that I am your bone and your *f* Judg 9:2 1320
while the *f* was in seething, with 1Sa 2:13 1320
Give *f* to roast for the priest 1Sa 2:15 1320
he will not have sodden *f* of thee 1Sa 2:15 1320
I will give thy *f* unto the fowls 1Sa 17:44 1320
my *f* that I have killed for my 1Sa 25:11 2878
Behold, we are thy bone and thy *f* 2Sa 5:1 1320
of bread, and a good piece of *f* 2Sa 6:19 829

brethren, ye are my bones and my f ... 2Sa 19:12 1320
thou not of my bone, and of my f ... 2Sa 19:13 1320
f in the morning, and bread and ... 1Kin 17:6 1320
and bread and f in the evening ... 1Kin 17:6 1320
them, and boiled their f with the ... 1Kin 19:21 1320
and put sackcloth upon his f ... 1Kin 21:27 1320
the f of the child waxed warm ... 2Kin 4:34 1320
thy f shall come again to thee, ... 2Kin 5:10 1320
his f came again like unto the ... 2Kin 5:14 1320
like unto the f of a little child ... 2Kin 5:14 1320
had sackcloth within upon his f ... 2Kin 6:30 1320
shall dogs eat the f of Jezebel ... 2Kin 9:36 1320
Behold, we are thy bone and thy f ... 1Chr 11:1 1320
of bread, and a good piece of f ... 1Chr 16:3 829
With his is an arm of f ... 2Chr 32:8 1320
f is as the f of our brethren ... Neh 5:5 1320
now, and touch his bone and his f ... Job 2:5 1320
the hair of my f stood up ... Job 4:15 1320
or is my f of brass ... Job 6:12 1320
My f is clothed with worms and ... Job 7:5 1320
Hast thou eyes of f ... Job 10:4 1320
hast clothed me with skin and f ... Job 10:11 1320
do I take my f in my teeth ... Job 13:14 1320
But his f upon him shall have ... Job 14:22 1320
cleaveth to my skin and to my f ... Job 19:20 1320
and are not satisfied with my f ... Job 19:22 1320
yet in my f shall I see God ... Job 19:26 1320
and trembling taketh hold on my f ... Job 21:6 1320
said not, Oh that we had of his f ... Job 31:31 1320
His f is consumed away, that it ... Job 33:21 1320
His f shall be fresher than a ... Job 33:25 1320
All f shall perish together, and ... Job 34:15 1320
The flakes of his f are joined ... Job 41:23 1320
my f also shall rest in hope ... Ps 16:9 1320
foes, came upon me to eat up my f ... Ps 27:2 1320
in my f because of thine anger ... Ps 38:3 1320
and there is no soundness in my f ... Ps 38:7 1320
Will I eat the f of bulls ... Ps 50:13 1320
not fear what f can do unto me ... Ps 56:4 1320
my f longeth for thee in a dry and ... Ps 63:1 1320
unto thee shall all f come ... Ps 65:2 1320
My f and my heart faileth ... Ps 73:26 7607
can he provide f for his people ... Ps 78:20 7607
He rained f also upon them as ... Ps 78:27 7607
remembered that they were but f ... Ps 78:39 1320
the f of thy saints unto the ... Ps 79:2 1320
my f crieth out for the living ... Ps 84:2 1320
and my f faileth of fatness ... Ps 109:24 1320
My f trembleth for fear of thee ... Ps 119:120 1320
Who giveth food to all f ... Ps 136:25 1320
let all f bless his holy name for ... Ps 145:21 1320
them, and health to all their f ... Prov 4:22 1320
mourn at the last, when thy f ... Prov 5:11 1320
that is cruel troubleth his own f ... Prov 11:17 7607
sound heart is the life of the f ... Prov 14:30 1320
among riotous eaters of f ... Prov 23:20 1320
together, and eateth his own f ... Eccl 4:5 1320
thy mouth to cause thy f to sin ... Eccl 5:6 1320
and put away evil from thy f ... Eccl 11:10 1320
study is a weariness of the f ... Eccl 12:12 1320
every man the f of his own arm ... Is 9:20 1320
fatness of his f shall wax lean ... Is 17:4 1320
oxen, and killing sheep, eating f ... Is 22:13 1320
and their horses f, and not spirit ... Is 31:3 1320
all f shall see it together ... Is 40:5 1320
All f is grass, and all the ... Is 40:6 1320
with part thereof he eateth f ... Is 44:16 1320
I have roasted f, and eaten it ... Is 44:19 1320
oppress thee with their own f ... Is 49:26 1320
all f shall know that I the LORD ... Is 49:26 1320
hide not thyself from thine own f ... Is 58:7 1320
monuments, which eat swine's f ... Is 65:4 1320
will the LORD plead with all f ... Is 66:16 1320
in the midst, eating swine's f ... Is 66:17 1320
shall all f come to worship ... Is 66:23 1320
shall be an abhorring unto all f ... Is 66:24 1320
unto your sacrifices, and eat f ... Jer 7:21 1320
the holy f is passed from thee ... Jer 11:15 1320
no f shall have peace ... Jer 12:12 1320
maketh f his arm, and whose heart ... Jer 17:5 1320
them to eat the f of their sons ... Jer 19:9 1320
the f of their daughters, and they ... Jer 19:9 1320
the f of his friend in the siege ... Jer 19:9 1320
nations, he will plead with all f ... Jer 25:31 1320
I am the LORD, the God of all f ... Jer 32:27 1320
I will bring evil upon all f ... Jer 45:5 1320
to my f be upon Babylon, shall ... Jer 51:35 7607
My f and my skin hath he made old ... Lam 3:4 1320
there abominable f into my mouth ... Eze 4:14 1320
is the caldron, and we be the f ... Eze 11:3 1320
the midst of it, they are the f ... Eze 11:7 1320
ye be the f in the midst thereof ... Eze 11:11 1320
the stony heart out of their f ... Eze 11:19 1320
and will give them an heart of f ... Eze 11:19 1320
thy neighbours, great of f ... Eze 16:26 1320
all f shall see that I the LORD ... Eze 20:48 1320
all f from the south to the north ... Eze 21:4 1320
That all f may know that I the ... Eze 21:5 1320
whose f is as the f of asses, ... Eze 23:20 1320
kindle the fire, consume the f ... Eze 24:10 1320
I will lay thy f upon the ... Eze 32:5 1320
the stony heart out of your f ... Eze 36:26 1320
and I will give you an heart of f ... Eze 36:26 1320
you, and will bring up f upon you ... Eze 37:6 1320
the f came up upon them, and the ... Eze 37:8 1320
of Israel, that ye may eat f ... Eze 39:17 1320
Ye shall eat the f of the mighty ... Eze 39:18 1320
tables was the f of the offering ... Eze 40:43 1320
in heart, and uncircumcised in f ... Eze 44:7 1320
in heart, nor uncircumcised in f ... Eze 44:9 1320
fatter in f than all the children ... Dan 1:15 1320
whose dwelling is not with f ... Dan 2:11 1321
thereof, and all f was fed of it ... Dan 4:12 1321
unto it, Arise, devour much f ... Dan 7:5 1321
neither came f nor wine in my ... Dan 10:3 1320
They sacrifice f for the ... Hos 8:13 1320
pour out my spirit upon all f ... Joel 2:28 1320
their f from off their bones ... Mic 3:2 7607
Who also eat the f of my people ... Mic 3:3 7607
pot, and as f within the caldron ... Mic 3:3 1320
as dust, and their f as the dung ... Zeph 1:17 3894
If one bear holy f in the skirt ... Hag 2:12 1320
Be silent, O all f, before the ... Zec 2:13 1320
eat every one the f of another ... Zec 11:9 1320
but he shall eat the f of the fat ... Zec 11:16 1320
Their f shall consume away while ... Zec 14:12 1320
for f and blood hath not revealed ... Mt 16:17 4561
and they twain shall be one f ... Mt 19:5 4561
they are no more twain, but one f ... Mt 19:6 4561
there should no f be saved ... Mt 24:22 4561
is willing, but the f is weak ... Mt 26:41 4561
And they twain shall be one f ... Mk 10:8 4561
they are no more twain, but one f ... Mk 10:8 4561
those days, no f should be saved ... Mk 13:20 4561
truly is ready, but the f is weak ... Mk 14:38 4561
all f shall see the salvation of ... Lk 3:6 4561
for a spirit hath not f and bones, ... Lk 24:39 4561
blood, nor of the will of the f ... Jn 1:13 4561
And the Word was made f, and dwelt ... Jn 1:14 4561
which is born of the f is f ... Jn 3:6 4561
which is born of the f is f ... Jn 3:6 4561
bread that I will give is my f ... Jn 6:51 4561
can this man give us his f to eat ... Jn 6:52 4561
ye eat the f of the Son of man ... Jn 6:53 4561
Whoso eateth my f, and drinketh my ... Jn 6:54 4561
For my f is meat indeed, and my ... Jn 6:55 4561
He that eateth my f, and drinketh ... Jn 6:56 4561
the f profiteth nothing ... Jn 6:63 4561
Ye judge after the f ... Jn 8:15 4561
hast given him power over all f ... Jn 17:2 4561
pour out of my Spirit upon all f ... Acts 2:17 4561
moreover also my f shall rest in ... Acts 2:26 4561
of his loins, according to the f ... Acts 2:30 4561
neither his f did see corruption ... Acts 2:31 4561
seed of David according to the f ... Rom 1:3 4561
which is outward in the f ... Rom 2:28 4561
no f be justified in his sight ... Rom 3:20 4561
father, as pertaining to the f ... Rom 4:1 4561
of the infirmity of your f ... Rom 6:19 4561
For when we were in the f ... Rom 7:5 4561
know that in me (that is, in my f ... Rom 7:18 4561
but with the f the law of sin ... Rom 7:25 4561
Jesus, who walk not after the f ... Rom 8:1 4561
in that it was weak through the f ... Rom 8:3 4561
Son in the likeness of sinful f ... Rom 8:3 4561
for sin, condemned sin in the f ... Rom 8:3 4561
in us, who walk not after the f ... Rom 8:4 4561
f do mind the things of the f ... Rom 8:5 4561
are in the f cannot please God ... Rom 8:8 4561
But ye are not in the f, but in ... Rom 8:9 4561
to the f, to live after the f ... Rom 8:12 4561
For if ye live after the f ... Rom 8:13 4561
my kinsmen according to the f ... Rom 9:3 4561
as concerning the f Christ came ... Rom 9:5 4561
which are the children of the f ... Rom 9:8 4561
to emulation them which are my f ... Rom 11:14 4561
and make not provision for the f ... Rom 13:14 4561
It is good neither to eat f ... Rom 14:21 2907
not many wise men after the f ... 1Cor 1:26 4561
That no f should glory in his ... 1Cor 1:29 4561
for the destruction of the f ... 1Cor 5:5 4561
for two, saith he, shall be one f ... 1Cor 6:16 4561
such shall have trouble in the f ... 1Cor 7:28 4561
I will eat no f while the world ... 1Cor 8:13 2907
Behold Israel after the f ... 1Cor 10:18 4561
All f is not the same f ... 1Cor 15:39 4561
but there is one kind of f of men ... 1Cor 15:39 4561
another f of beasts, another of ... 1Cor 15:39 4561
Now this I say, brethren, that f ... 1Cor 15:50 4561
do I purpose according to the f ... 2Cor 1:17 4561
be made manifest in our mortal f ... 2Cor 4:11 4561
know we no man after the f ... 2Cor 5:16 4561
we have known Christ after the f ... 2Cor 5:16 4561
from all filthiness of the f ... 2Cor 7:1 4561
our f had no rest, but we were ... 2Cor 7:5 4561
if we walked according to the f ... 2Cor 10:2 4561
For though we walk in the f ... 2Cor 10:3 4561
we do not war after the f ... 2Cor 10:3 4561
that many glory after the f ... 2Cor 11:18 4561
was given to me a thorn in the f ... 2Cor 12:7 4561
I conferred not with f and blood ... Gal 1:16 4561
the law shall no f be justified ... Gal 2:16 4561
life which I now live in the f I ... Gal 2:20 4561
are ye now made perfect by the f ... Gal 3:3 4561
how through infirmity of the f I ... Gal 4:13 4561
which was in my f ye despised not ... Gal 4:14 4561
bondwoman was born after the f ... Gal 4:23 4561
f persecuted him that was born ... Gal 4:29 4561
liberty for an occasion to the f ... Gal 5:13 4561
not fulfil the lust of the f ... Gal 5:16 4561
For the f lusteth against the ... Gal 5:17 4561
and the Spirit against the f ... Gal 5:17 4561
the works of the f are manifest ... Gal 5:19 4561
the f with the affections ... Gal 5:24 4561
to his f shall of the f reap ... Gal 6:8 4561
to make a fair shew in the f ... Gal 6:12 4561
that they may glory in your f ... Gal 6:13 4561
times past in the lusts of our f ... Eph 2:3 4561
fulfilling the desires of the f ... Eph 2:3 4561
in time past Gentiles in the f ... Eph 2:11 4561
in the f made by hands ... Eph 2:11 4561
abolished in his f the enmity ... Eph 2:15 4561
no man ever yet hated his own f ... Eph 5:29 4561
are members of his body, of his f ... Eph 5:30 4561
wife, and they two shall be one f ... Eph 5:31 4561
your masters according to the f ... Eph 6:5 4561
For we wrestle not against f ... Eph 6:12 4561
But if I live in the f, this is ... Phil 1:22 4561
in the f is more needful for you ... Phil 1:24 4561
and have no confidence in the f ... Phil 3:3 4561
also have confidence in the f ... Phil 3:4 4561
whereof he might trust in the f ... Phil 3:4 4561
the body of his f through death ... Col 1:22 4561
in my f for his body's sake ... Col 1:24 4561
as have not seen my face in the f ... Col 2:1 4561
For though I be absent in the f ... Col 2:5 4561
f by the circumcision of Christ ... Col 2:11 4561
and the uncircumcision of your f ... Col 2:13 4561
honour to the satisfying of the f ... Col 2:23 4561
your masters according to the f ... Col 3:22 4561
God was manifest in the f ... 1Ti 3:16 4561
more unto thee, both in the f ... Philem 16 4561
the children are partakers of f ... Heb 2:14 4561
Who in the days of his f, when he ... Heb 5:7 4561
to the purifying of the f ... Heb 9:13 4561
the veil, that is to say, his f ... Heb 10:20 4561
of our f which corrected us ... Heb 12:9 4561
shall eat your f as it were fire ... Jas 5:3 4561
For all f is as grass, and all the ... 1Pet 1:24 4561
God, being put to death in the f ... 1Pet 3:18 4561
away of the filth of the f ... 1Pet 3:21 4561
hath suffered for us in the f ... 1Pet 4:1 4561
in the f hath ceased from sin ... 1Pet 4:1 4561
time in the f to the lusts of men ... 1Pet 4:2 4561
judged according to men in the f ... 1Pet 4:6 4561
them that walk after the f in the ... 2Pet 2:10 4561
allure through the lusts of the f ... 2Pet 2:18 4561
in the world, the lust of the f ... 1Jn 2:16 4561
Christ is come in the f is of God ... 1Jn 4:2 4561
is come in the f is not of God ... 1Jn 4:3 4561
Jesus Christ is come in the f ... 2Jn 7 4561
and going after strange f ... Jude 7 4561
filthy dreamers defile the f ... Jude 8 4561
even the garment spotted by the f ... Jude 23 4561
and naked, and shall eat her f ... Rev 17:16 4561
That ye may eat the f of kings ... Rev 19:18 4561
the f of captains, and the f ... Rev 19:18 4561
the f of mighty men ... Rev 19:18 4561
the f of horses, and of them that ... Rev 19:18 4561
the f of all men, both free and ... Rev 19:18 4561
fowls were filled with their f ... Rev 19:21 4561

FLESHHOOK {2}
with a f of three teeth in his ... 1Sa 2:13 4207
all that the f brought up the ... 1Sa 2:14 4207

FLESHHOOKS {5}
shovels, and his basons, and his f ... Ex 27:3 4207
shovels, and the basons, and the f ... Ex 38:3 4207
about it, even the censers, the f ... Num 4:14 4207
Also pure gold for the f, and the ... 1Chr 28:17 4207
also, and the shovels, and the f ... 2Chr 4:16 4207

FLESHLY {3}
sincerity, not with f wisdom ... 2Cor 1:12 4559
vainly puffed up by his f mind ... Col 2:18
and pilgrims, abstain from f lusts ... 1Pet 2:11 4559

FLESHY {1}
but in f tables of the heart ... 2Cor 3:3 4560

FLEW {2}
the people f upon the spoil, and ... 1Sa 14:32 6213
Then f one of the seraphims unto ... Is 6:6 5774

FLIES {10}
I will send swarms of f upon thee ... Ex 8:21
shall be full of swarms of f ... Ex 8:21
no swarms of f shall be there ... Ex 8:22
of f into the house of Pharaoh ... Ex 8:24
by reason of the swarm of f ... Ex 8:24
of f may depart from Pharaoh ... Ex 8:29
the swarms of f from Pharaoh ... Ex 8:31
sent divers sorts of f among them ... Ps 78:45 6157
and there came divers sorts of f ... Ps 105:31 6157
Dead f cause the ointment of the ... Eccl 10:1 2070

FLIETH {4}
any winged fowl that f in the air ... Deut 4:17 5774
thing that f is unclean unto you ... Deut 14:19 5775
earth, as swift as the eagle f ... Deut 28:49 1675
nor for the arrow that f by day ... Ps 91:5 5774

FLIGHT {8}
you shall put ten thousand to f ... Lev 26:8 7291
and two put ten thousand to f ... Deut 32:30 5127
they put to f all them of the ... 1Chr 12:15 1272
go out with haste, nor go by f ... Is 52:12 4499
Therefore the f shall perish from ... Amos 2:14 4498
that your f be not in the winter ... Mt 24:20 5437
pray ye that your f be not in the ... Mk 13:18 5437
turned to f the armies of the ... Heb 11:34

FLINT {5}
forth water out of the rock of f ... Deut 8:15 2496
the f into a fountain of waters ... Ps 114:8 2496
hoofs shall be counted like f ... Is 5:28 6864
have I set my face like a f ... Is 50:7 2496
than f have I made thy forehead ... Eze 3:9 6864

FLINTY {1}
rock, and oil out of the *f* rock ... Deut 32:13 2496

FLOATS {1}
I will convey them by sea in *f* ... 1Kin 5:9 1702

FLOCK {112}
of the firstlings of his *f* ... Gen 4:4 6629
ewe lambs of the *f* by themselves ... Gen 21:28 6629
Go now to the *f*, and fetch me from ... Gen 27:9 6629
watered the *f* of Laban his ... Gen 29:10 6629
I will again feed and keep thy *f* ... Gen 30:31 6629
pass through all thy *f* to day ... Gen 30:32 6629
all the brown in the *f* of Laban ... Gen 30:40 6629
and Leah to the field unto his *f* ... Gen 31:4 6629
the rams of thy *f* have I not ... Gen 31:38 6629
them one day, all the *f* will die ... Gen 33:13 6629
was feeding the *f* with his ... Gen 37:2 6629
feed their father's *f* in Shechem ... Gen 37:12 6629
brethren feed the *f* in Shechem ... Gen 37:13
I will send thee a kid from the *f* ... Gen 38:17 6629
troughs to water their father's *f* ... Ex 2:16 6629
helped them, and watered their *f* ... Ex 2:17 6629
enough for us, and watered the *f* ... Ex 2:19 6629
Now Moses kept the *f* of Jethro ... Ex 3:1 6629
he led the *f* to the backside of ... Ex 3:1 6629
even of the herd, and of the *f* ... Lev 1:2 6629
unto the LORD be of the *f* ... Lev 3:6 6629
hath sinned, a female from the *f* ... Lev 5:6 6629
ram without blemish out of the *f* ... Lev 5:18 6629
ram without blemish out of the *f* ... Lev 6:6 6629
tithe of the herd, or of the *f* ... Lev 27:32 6629
LORD, of the herd, or of the *f* ... Num 15:3 6629
of thy herds or of thy *f*, nor any ... Deut 12:17 6629
kill of thy herd and of thy *f* ... Deut 12:21 6629
him liberally out of thy *f* ... Deut 15:14 6629
of thy *f* thou shalt sanctify unto ... Deut 15:19 6629
unto the LORD thy God, of the *f* ... Deut 16:2 6629
bear, and took a lamb out of the *f* ... 1Sa 17:34 5739
and he spared to take of his own *f* ... 2Sa 12:4 6629
gave to the people, of the *f* ... 2Chr 35:7 6629
a ram of the *f* for their trespass ... Ezr 10:19 6629
forth their little ones like a *f* ... Job 21:11 6629
to have set with the dogs of my *f* ... Job 30:1 6629
like a *f* by the hand of Moses ... Ps 77:20 6629
them in the wilderness like a *f* ... Ps 78:52 5739
thou that leadest Joseph like a *f* ... Ps 80:1 6629
and maketh him families like a *f* ... Ps 107:41 6629
thou makest thy *f* to rest at noon ... Song 1:7
forth by the footsteps of the *f* ... Song 1:8 6629
thy hair is as a *f* of goats ... Song 4:1 5739
Thy teeth are like a *f* of sheep ... Song 4:2 5739
thy hair is as a *f* of goats that ... Song 6:5 5739
Thy teeth are as a *f* of sheep ... Song 6:6 5739
shall feed his *f* like a shepherd ... Is 40:11 5739
sea with the shepherd of his *f* ... Is 63:11 6629
because the LORD's *f* is carried ... Jer 13:17 5739
where is the *f* that was given ... Jer 13:20 5739
was given thee, thy beautiful *f* ... Jer 13:20 6629
Ye have scattered my *f*, and driven ... Jer 23:2 6629
f out of all countries whither I ... Jer 23:3 6629
the ashes, ye principal of the *f* ... Jer 25:34 6629
the principal of the *f* to escape ... Jer 25:35 6629
howling of the principal of the *f* ... Jer 25:36 6629
him, as a shepherd doth his *f* ... Jer 31:10 5739
oil, and for the young of the *f* ... Jer 31:12 6629
of the *f* shall draw them out ... Jer 49:20 6629
of the *f* shall draw them out ... Jer 50:45 6629
with thee the shepherd and his *f* ... Jer 51:23 5739
Take the choice of the *f*, and burn ... Eze 24:5 6629
but ye feed not the *f* ... Eze 34:3 6629
my *f* was scattered upon all the ... Eze 34:6 6629
surely because my *f* became a prey ... Eze 34:8 6629
my *f* became meat to every beast ... Eze 34:8 6629
did my shepherds search for my *f* ... Eze 34:8 6629
fed themselves, and fed not my *f* ... Eze 34:8 6629
I will require my *f* at their hand ... Eze 34:10 6629
them to cease from feeding the *f* ... Eze 34:10 6629
deliver my *f* from their mouth ... Eze 34:10 6629
As a shepherd seeketh out his *f* ... Eze 34:12 5739
I will feed my *f*, and I will cause ... Eze 34:15 6629
And as for you, O my *f*, thus saith ... Eze 34:17 6629
And as for my *f*, they eat that ... Eze 34:19 6629
Therefore will I save my *f* ... Eze 34:22 6629
And ye my *f*, the *f* of my ... Eze 34:31 6629
the *f* of my pasture, are men, and ... Eze 34:31 6629
increase them with men like a *f* ... Eze 36:37 6629
As the holy *f*, as the *f* of ... Eze 36:38 6629
ram out of the *f* without blemish ... Eze 43:23 6629
bullock, and a ram out of the *f* ... Eze 43:25 6629
And one lamb out of the *f*, out of ... Eze 45:15 6629
and eat the lambs out of the *f* ... Amos 6:4 6629
LORD took me as I followed the *f* ... Amos 7:15 6629
neither man nor beast, herd nor *f* ... Jonah 3:7 6629
as the *f* in the midst of their ... Mic 2:12 5739
And thou, O tower of the *f* ... Mic 4:8 5739
the *f* of thine heritage, which ... Mic 7:14 6629
the *f* shall be cut off from the ... Hab 3:17 6629
that day as the *f* of his people ... Zec 9:16 6629
they went their way as a *f* ... Zec 10:2 6629
visited his *f* the house of Judah ... Zec 10:3 5739
Feed the *f* of the slaughter ... Zec 11:4 6629
And I will feed the *f* of slaughter ... Zec 11:7 6629
even you, O poor of the *f* ... Zec 11:7 6629
and I fed the *f* ... Zec 11:7 6629
so the poor of the *f* that waited ... Zec 11:11 6629
idol shepherd that leaveth the *f* ... Zec 11:17 6629
which hath in his *f* a male ... Mal 1:14 5739
the sheep of the *f* shall be ... Mt 26:31 *4167*
watch over their *f* by night ... Lk 2:8 *4167*
Fear not, little *f* ... Lk 12:32 *4168*
unto yourselves, and to all the *f* ... Acts 20:28 *4168*
in among you, not sparing the *f* ... Acts 20:29 *4168*
or who feedeth a *f*, and eateth not ... 1Cor 9:7 *4167*
eateth not of the milk of the *f* ... 1Cor 9:7 *4167*
Feed the *f* of God which is among ... 1Pet 5:2 *4168*
but being ensamples to the *f* ... 1Pet 5:3 *4168*

FLOCKS {80}
which went with Abram, had *f* ... Gen 13:5 6629
and he hath given him *f*, and herds, ... Gen 24:35 6629
For he had possession of *f* ... Gen 26:14 6629
there were three *f* of sheep lying ... Gen 29:2 5739
of that well they watered the *f* ... Gen 29:2 5739
thither were all the *f* gathered ... Gen 29:3 5739
until all the *f* be gathered ... Gen 29:8 5739
Jacob fed the rest of Laban's *f* ... Gen 30:36 6629
f in the gutters in the watering ... Gen 30:38 6629
troughs when the *f* came to drink ... Gen 30:38 6629
the *f* conceived before the rods, ... Gen 30:39 6629
set the faces of the *f* toward the ... Gen 30:40 6629
and he put his own *f* by themselves ... Gen 30:40 5739
And I have oxen, and asses, *f* ... Gen 32:5 6629
that was with him, and the *f* ... Gen 32:7 6629
the children are tender, and the *f* ... Gen 33:13 6629
thy brethren, and well with the *f* ... Gen 37:14 6629
thee, where they feed their *f* ... Gen 37:16
thy children's children, and thy *f* ... Gen 45:10 6629
and they have brought their *f* ... Gen 46:32 6629
father and my brethren, and their *f* ... Gen 47:1 6629
have no pasture for their *f* ... Gen 47:4 6629
exchange for horses, and for the *f* ... Gen 47:17 6629
their little ones, and their *f* ... Gen 50:8 6629
and with our daughters, with our *f* ... Ex 10:9 6629
only let your *f* and your herds be ... Ex 10:24 6629
Also take your *f* and your herds, ... Ex 12:32 6629
and *f*, and herds, even very much ... Ex 12:38 6629
neither let the *f* nor herds feed ... Ex 34:3 6629
And if his offering be of the *f* ... Lev 1:10 6629
ram without blemish out of the *f* ... Lev 5:15 6629
Shall the *f* and the herds be slain ... Num 11:22 6629
all their cattle, and all their *f* ... Num 31:9 4735
beeves, of the asses, and of the *f* ... Num 31:30 6629
Our little ones, our wives, our *f* ... Num 32:26 4735
the *f* of thy sheep, in the land ... Deut 7:13 6251
thy *f* multiply, and thy silver and ... Deut 8:13 6629
of your herds and of your *f* ... Deut 12:6 6629
of thy herds and of thy *f* ... Deut 14:23 6629
thy kine, and the *f* of thy sheep ... Deut 28:4 6251
thy kine, and the *f* of thy sheep ... Deut 28:18 6251
or *f* of thy sheep, until he have ... Deut 28:51 6251
to hear the bleatings of the *f* ... Judg 5:16 5739
And David took all the *f* and the ... 1Sa 30:20 6629
The rich man had exceeding many *f* ... 2Sa 12:2 6629
them like two little *f* of kids ... 1Kin 20:27 2835
to seek pasture for their *f* ... 1Chr 4:39 6629
was pasture there for their *f* ... 1Chr 4:41 6629
over the *f* was Jaziz the Hagerite ... 1Chr 27:31 6629
and the Arabians brought him *f* ... 2Chr 17:11 6629
manner of beasts, and cotes for *f* ... 2Chr 32:28 5739
him cities, and possessions of *f* ... 2Chr 32:29 6629
of our herds and of our *f*, to ... Neh 10:36 6629
they violently take away *f* ... Job 24:2 5739
The pastures are clothed with *f* ... Ps 65:13 6629
their *f* to hot thunderbolts ... Ps 78:48 4735
to know the state of thy *f* ... Prov 27:23 6629
aside by the *f* of thy companions ... Song 1:7 5739
they shall be for *f*, which shall ... Is 17:2 5739
joy of wild asses, a pasture of *f* ... Is 32:14 5739
All the *f* of Kedar shall be ... Is 60:7 6629
shall stand and feed your *f* ... Is 61:5 6629
And Sharon shall be a fold of *f* ... Is 65:10 6629
their *f* and their herds, their ... Jer 3:24 6629
they shall eat up thy *f* and thine ... Jer 5:17 6629
with their *f* shall come unto her ... Jer 6:3 5739
all their *f* shall be scattered ... Jer 10:21 4830
and they that go forth with *f* ... Jer 31:24 5739
causing their *f* to lie down ... Jer 33:12 6629
shall the *f* pass again under the ... Jer 33:13 6629
their *f* shall they take away ... Jer 49:29 6629
be as the he goats before the *f* ... Jer 50:8 6629
Ammonites a couchingplace for *f* ... Eze 25:5 6629
not the shepherds feed the *f* ... Eze 34:2 6629
cities be filled with *f* of men ... Eze 36:38 6629
They shall go with their *f* ... Hos 5:6 6629
the *f* of sheep are made desolate ... Joel 1:18 5739
a young lion among the *f* of sheep ... Mic 5:8 5739
for shepherds, and folds for *f* ... Zeph 2:6 6629
f shall lie down in the midst of ... Zeph 2:14 5739

FLOOD {43}
do bring a *f* of waters upon the ... Gen 6:17 3999
f of waters was upon the earth ... Gen 7:6 3999
because of the waters of the *f* ... Gen 7:7 3999
of the *f* were upon the earth ... Gen 7:10 3999
the *f* was forty days upon the ... Gen 7:17 3999
off any more by the waters of a *f* ... Gen 9:11 3999
more be a *f* to destroy the earth ... Gen 9:11 3999
become a *f* to destroy all flesh ... Gen 9:15 3999
lived after the *f* three hundred ... Gen 9:28 3999
them were sons born after the *f* ... Gen 10:1 3999
divided in the earth after the *f* ... Gen 10:32 3999
Arphaxad two years after the *f* ... Gen 11:10 3999
other side of the *f* in old time ... Josh 24:2 5104
from the other side of the *f* ... Josh 24:3 5104
served on the other side of the *f* ... Josh 24:14 5104
were on the other side of the *f* ... Josh 24:15 5104
the *f* decayeth and drieth up ... Job 14:11 5104
foundation was overflown with a *f* ... Job 22:16 5104
The *f* breaketh out from the ... Job 28:4 5158
The LORD sitteth upon the *f* ... Ps 29:10 3999
they went through the *f* on foot ... Ps 66:6 5104
cleave the fountain and the *f* ... Ps 74:15 5158
carriest them away as with a *f* ... Ps 90:5 2229
storm, as a *f* of mighty waters ... Is 28:2 2230
the enemy shall come in like a *f* ... Is 59:19 5104
Who is this that cometh up as a *f* ... Jer 46:7 2975
Egypt riseth up like a *f*, and his ... Jer 46:8 2975
and shall be an overflowing *f* ... Jer 47:2 5158
the end thereof shall be with a *f* ... Dan 9:26 7858
with the arms of a *f* shall they ... Dan 11:22 7858
and it shall rise up wholly as a *f* ... Amos 8:8 2975
and drowned, as by the *f* of Egypt ... Amos 8:8 2975
it shall rise up wholly like a *f* ... Amos 9:5 2975
be drowned, as by the *f* of Egypt ... Amos 9:5 2975
But with an overrunning *f* he will ... Nah 1:8 7858
before the *f* they were eating ... Mt 24:38 *2627*
And knew not until the *f* came ... Mt 24:39 *2627*
and when the *f* arose, the stream ... Lk 6:48 *4182*
the *f* came, and destroyed them all ... Lk 17:27 *2627*
bringing in the *f* upon the world ... 2Pet 2:5 *2627*
water as a *f* after the woman ... Rev 12:15 *4215*
her to be carried away of the *f* ... Rev 12:15 *4216*
swallowed up the *f* which the ... Rev 12:16 *4215*

FLOODS {19}
the *f* stood upright as an heap, ... Ex 15:8 5140
the *f* of ungodly men made me ... 2Sa 22:5 5158
shall not see the rivers, the *f* ... Job 20:17 5104
He bindeth the *f* from overflowing ... Job 28:11 5104
the *f* of ungodly men made me ... Ps 18:4 5158
and established it upon the *f* ... Ps 24:2 5104
surely in the *f* of great waters ... Ps 32:6 7858
waters, where the *f* overflow me ... Ps 69:2 7641
and their *f*, that they could not ... Ps 78:44 5140
The *f* have lifted up, O LORD, the ... Ps 93:3 5104
the *f* have lifted up their voice ... Ps 93:3 5104
the *f* lift up their waves ... Ps 93:3 5104
Let the *f* clap their hands ... Ps 98:8 5104
love, neither can the *f* drown it ... Song 8:7 5104
thirsty, and *f* upon the dry ground ... Is 44:3 5140
and I restrained the *f* thereof ... Eze 31:15 5104
and the *f* compassed me about ... Jonah 2:3 5104
the *f* came, and the winds blew, and ... Mt 7:25 *4215*
the *f* came, and the winds blew, and ... Mt 7:27 *4215*

FLOOR {19}
saw the mourning in the *f* of Atad ... Gen 50:11 1637
of the dust that is in the *f* of ... Num 5:17 7172
out of thy flock, and out of thy *f* ... Deut 15:14 1637
put a fleece of wool in the *f* ... Judg 6:37 1637
thee, and get thee down to the *f* ... Ruth 3:3 1637
And she went down unto the *f* ... Ruth 3:6 1637
that a woman came into the *f* ... Ruth 3:14 1637
both the *f* of the house, and the ... 1Kin 6:15 7172
covered the *f* of the house with ... 1Kin 6:15 7172
sides of the house, both the *f* ... 1Kin 6:16 7172
the *f* of the house he overlaid ... 1Kin 6:30 7172
one side of the *f* to the other ... 1Kin 7:7 7172
to *f* the houses which the kings ... 2Chr 34:11 7136
my threshing, and the corn of my *f* ... Is 21:10 1637
The *f* and the winepress shall not ... Hos 9:2 1637
with the whirlwind out of the *f* ... Hos 13:3 1637
them as the sheaves into the *f* ... Mic 4:12 1637
and he will throughly purge his *f* ... Mt 3:12 *257*
and he will throughly purge his *f* ... Lk 3:17 *257*

FLOORS {1}
the *f* shall be full of wheat, and ... Joel 2:24 1637

FLOTES {1}
it to thee in *f* by sea to Joppa ... 2Chr 2:16 7513

FLOUR {58}
of wheaten *f* shalt thou make them ... Ex 29:2 5560
the one lamb a tenth deal of *f* ... Ex 29:40 5560
his offering shall be of fine *f* ... Lev 2:1 5560
his handful of the *f* thereof ... Lev 2:2 5560
cakes of fine *f* mingled with oil ... Lev 2:4 5560
it shall be of fine *f* unleavened ... Lev 2:5 5560
shall be made of fine *f* with oil ... Lev 2:7 5560
of fine *f* for a sin offering ... Lev 5:11 5560
of the *f* of the meat offering, and ... Lev 6:15 5560
f for a meat offering perpetual ... Lev 6:20 5560
cakes mingled with oil, of fine *f* ... Lev 7:12 5560
of fine *f* for a meat offering ... Lev 14:10 5560
one tenth deal of fine *f* mingled ... Lev 14:21 5560
deals of fine *f* mingled with oil ... Lev 23:13 5560
they shall be of fine *f* ... Lev 23:17 5560
And thou shalt take fine *f* ... Lev 24:5 5560
cakes of fine *f* mingled with oil, ... Num 6:15 5560
f mingled with oil for a meat ... Num 7:13 5560
both of them full of fine *f* ... Num 7:19 5560
both of them full of fine *f* ... Num 7:25 5560
both of them full of fine *f* ... Num 7:31 5560
both of them full of fine *f* ... Num 7:37 5560
both of them full of fine *f* ... Num 7:43 5560
both of them full of fine *f* ... Num 7:49 5560
both of them full of fine *f* ... Num 7:55 5560
both of them full of fine *f* ... Num 7:61 5560
both of them full of fine *f* ... Num 7:67 5560
both of them full of fine *f* ... Num 7:73 5560
both of them full of fine *f* ... Num 7:79 5560
even fine *f* mingled with oil, and ... Num 8:8 5560
offering of a tenth deal of *f* ... Num 15:4 5560
offering two tenth deals of *f* ... Num 15:6 5560
of three tenth deals of *f* mingled ... Num 15:9 5560
an ephah of *f* for a meat offering ... Num 28:5 5560
two tenth deals of *f* for a meat ... Num 28:9 5560

deals of f for a meat offering ... Num 28:12 5560
two tenth deals of f for a meat ... Num 28:12 5560
a several tenth deal of f mingled ... Num 28:13 5560
shall be of f mingled with oil ... Num 28:20 5560
offering of f mingled with oil ... Num 28:28 5560
shall be of f mingled with oil ... Num 29:3 5560
shall be of f mingled with oil ... Num 29:9 5560
shall be of f mingled with oil ... Num 29:14 5560
unleavened cakes of an ephah of f ... Judg 6:19 7058
three bullocks, and one ephah of f ... 1Sa 1:24 7058
hasted, and killed it, and took f ... 1Sa 28:24 7058
And she took f, and kneaded it, and ... 2Sa 13:8 1217
and wheat, and barley, and f ... 2Sa 17:28 7058
day was thirty measures of fine f ... 1Kin 4:22 5560
of fine f be sold for a shekel ... 2Kin 7:1 5560
So a measure of fine f was sold ... 2Kin 7:16 5560
a measure of fine f for a shekel ... 2Kin 7:18 5560
of the sanctuary, and the fine f ... 1Chr 9:29 5560
for the fine f for meat offering, ... 1Chr 23:29 5560
thou didst eat fine f, and honey, ... Eze 16:13 5560
also which I gave thee, fine f ... Eze 16:19 5560
of oil, to temper with the fine f ... Eze 46:14 5560
and wine, and oil, and fine f ... Rev 18:13 4585

FLOURISH {13}
In his days shall the righteous f ... Ps 72:7 6524
they of the city shall f like ... Ps 72:16 6692
all the workers of iniquity do f ... Ps 92:7 6692
shall f like the palm tree ... Ps 92:12 6524
shall f in the courts of our God ... Ps 92:13 6524
upon himself shall his crown f ... Ps 132:18 6692
the righteous shall f as a branch ... Prov 11:28 6524
tabernacle of the upright shall f ... Prov 14:11 6524
way, and the almond tree shall f ... Eccl 12:5 5006
let us see if the vine f, whether ... Song 7:12 6524
shalt thou make thy seed to f ... Is 17:11 6524
your bones shall f like an herb ... Is 66:14 6524
and have made the dry tree to f ... Eze 17:24 6524

FLOURISHED {2}
and to see whether the vine f ... Song 6:11 6524
last your care of me hath f again ... Phil 4:10 330

FLOURISHETH {2}
In the morning it f, and groweth ... Ps 90:6 6692
as a flower of the field, so he f ... Ps 103:15 6692

FLOURISHING {2}
they shall be fat and f ... Ps 92:14 7488
in mine house, and f in my palace ... Dan 4:4 7487

FLOW {13}
his goods shall f away in the day ... Job 20:28 5064
his wind to blow, and the waters f ... Ps 147:18 5140
that the spices thereof may f out ... Song 4:16 5140
and all nations shall f unto it ... Is 2:2 5102
he caused the waters to f out of ... Is 48:21 5140
f together, and thine heart shall ... Is 60:5 5102
might f down at thy presence ... Is 64:1 2151
shall f together to the goodness ... Jer 31:12 5102
the nations shall not f together ... Jer 51:44 5102
and the hills shall f with milk ... Joel 3:18 3212
of Judah shall f with waters ... Joel 3:18 3212
and people shall f unto it ... Mic 4:1 5102
shall f rivers of living water ... Jn 7:38 4482

FLOWED {3}
f over all his banks, as they did ... Josh 4:18 3212
the mountains f down at thy ... Is 64:3 2151
Waters f over mine head ... Lam 3:54 6687

FLOWER {20}
with a knop and a f in one branch ... Ex 25:33 6525
other branch, with a knop and a f ... Ex 25:33 6525
in one branch, a knop and a f ... Ex 37:19 6525
in another branch, a knop and a f ... Ex 37:19 6525
shall die in the f of their age ... 1Sa 2:33 582
He cometh forth like a f, and is ... Job 14:2 6731
shall cast off his f as the olive ... Job 15:33 5328
as a f of the field, so he ... Ps 103:15 6731
sour grape is ripening in the f ... Is 18:5 5328
glorious beauty is a fading f ... Is 28:1 6731
fat valley, shall be a fading f ... Is 28:4 6733
thereof is as the f of the field ... Is 40:6 6731
The grass withereth, the f fadeth ... Is 40:7 6731
The grass withereth, the f fadeth ... Is 40:8 6731
the f of Lebanon languisheth ... Nah 1:4 6525
if she pass the f of her age ... 1Cor 7:36 5230
because as the f of the grass he ... Jas 1:10 438
the f thereof falleth, and the ... Jas 1:11 438
glory of man as the f of grass ... 1Pet 1:24 438
the f thereof falleth away ... 1Pet 1:24 438

FLOWERS {17}
his bowls, his knops, and his f ... Ex 25:31 6525
with their knops and their f ... Ex 25:34 6525
his bowls, his knops, and his f ... Ex 37:17 6525
like almonds, his knops, and his f ... Ex 37:20 6525
her f be upon him, he shall be ... Lev 15:24 5079
And of her that is sick of her f ... Lev 15:33 5079
shaft thereof, unto the f thereof ... Num 8:4 6525
was carved with knops and open f ... 1Kin 6:18 6731
cherubims and palm trees and open f ... 1Kin 6:29 6731
cherubims and palm trees and open f ... 1Kin 6:32 6731
cherubims and palm trees and open f ... 1Kin 6:35 6731
brim of a cup, with f of lilies ... 1Kin 7:26 6525
before the oracle, with the f ... 1Kin 7:49 6525
brim of a cup, with f of lilies ... 2Chr 4:5 6525
And the f, and the lamps, and the ... 2Chr 4:21 6525
The f appear on the earth ... Song 2:12 5339
as a bed of spices, as sweet f ... Song 5:13 4026

FLOWETH {12}
it, a land that f with milk ... Lev 20:24 2100
us, and surely it f with milk ... Num 13:27 2100
a land which f with milk and honey ... Num 14:8 2100
up out of a land that f with milk ... Num 16:13 2100
us into a land that f with milk ... Num 16:14 2100
in the land that f with milk ... Deut 6:3 2100
seed, a land that f with milk ... Deut 11:9 2100
even a land that f with milk ... Deut 26:9 2100
fathers, a land that f with milk ... Deut 26:15 2100
thee, a land that f with milk ... Deut 27:3 2100
that f with milk and honey ... Deut 31:20 2100
give us, a land that f with milk ... Josh 5:6 2100

FLOWING {12}
a large, unto a land f with milk ... Ex 3:8 2100
unto a land f with milk and honey ... Ex 3:17 2100
a land f with milk and honey, that ... Ex 13:5 2100
Unto a land f with milk and honey ... Ex 33:3 2100
wellspring of wisdom as a f brook ... Prov 18:4 5042
of the Gentiles like a f stream ... Is 66:12 7857
to give them a land f with milk ... Jer 11:5 2100
or shall the cold f waters that ... Jer 18:14 5140
a land f with milk and honey ... Jer 32:22 2100
thy f valley, O backsliding ... Jer 49:4 2100
f with milk and honey, which is ... Eze 20:6 2100
f with milk and honey, which is ... Eze 20:15 2100

FLUTE {4}
hear the sound of the cornet, f ... Dan 3:5 4953
heard the sound of the cornet, f ... Dan 3:7 4953
hear the sound of the cornet, f ... Dan 3:10 4953
hear the sound of the cornet, f ... Dan 3:15 4953

FLUTTERETH {1}
f over her young, spreadeth ... Deut 32:11 7363

FLUX {1}
sick of a fever and of a bloody f ... Acts 28:8 1420

FLY {25}
fowl that may f above the earth ... Gen 1:20 5774
but didst f upon the spoil, and ... 1Sa 15:19 5860
he rode upon a cherub, and did f ... 2Sa 22:11 5774
trouble, as the sparks f upward ... Job 5:7 5774
He shall f away as a dream, and ... Job 20:8 5774
Doth the hawk f by thy wisdom ... Job 39:26 82
he rode upon a cherub, and did f ... Ps 18:10 5774
he did f upon the wings of the ... Ps 18:10 1675
for then would I f away, and be at ... Ps 55:6 5774
it is soon cut off, and we f away ... Ps 90:10 5774
they f away as an eagle toward ... Prov 23:5 5774
his feet, and with twain he did f ... Is 6:2 5774
the LORD shall hiss for the f ... Is 7:18 2070
But they shall f upon the ... Is 11:14 5774
Who are these that f as a cloud ... Is 60:8 5774
he shall f as an eagle, and shall ... Jer 48:40 1675
f as the eagle, and spread his ... Jer 49:22 1675
hunt the souls to make them f ... Eze 13:20 6524
souls that ye hunt to make them f ... Eze 13:20 6524
being caused to f swiftly ... Dan 9:21 3286
glory shall f away like a bird ... Hos 9:11 5774
they shall f as the eagle that ... Hab 1:8 5774
that she might f into the ... Rev 12:14 4072
I saw another angel f in the ... Rev 14:6 4072
that f in the midst of heaven ... Rev 19:17 4072

FLYING {11}
Yet these may ye eat of every f ... Lev 11:21 5775
But all other f creeping things, ... Lev 11:23 5775
creeping things, and f fowl ... Ps 148:10 3671
by wandering, as the swallow by f ... Prov 26:2 5774
fruit shall be a fiery f serpent ... Is 14:29 5774
fiery f serpent, they will carry ... Is 30:6 5774
As birds f, so will the LORD of ... Is 31:5 5774
and looked, and behold a f roll ... Zec 5:1 5774
And I answered, I see a f roll ... Zec 5:2 5774
fourth beast was like a f eagle ... Rev 4:7 4072
heard an angel f through the ... Rev 8:13 4072

FOAL {3}
Binding his f unto the vine, and ... Gen 49:11 5895
and upon a colt the f of an ass ... Zec 9:9 1121
an ass, and a colt the f of an ass ... Mt 21:5 5207

FOALS {1}
bulls, twenty she asses, and ten f ... Gen 32:15 5895

FOAM {1}
cut off as the f upon the water ... Hos 10:7 7110

FOAMETH {2}
and he f, and gnasheth with his ... Mk 9:18 875
and it teareth him that he f again ... Lk 9:39 876

FOAMING {2}
fell on the ground, and wallowed f ... Mk 9:20 875
of the sea, f out their own shame ... Jude 13 1890

FODDER {1}
or loweth the ox over his f ... Job 6:5 1098

FOES {7}
to be destroyed before thy f ... 1Chr 21:12 6862
and slew of their f seventy ... Est 9:16 8130
wicked, even mine enemies and my f ... Ps 27:2 341
hast not made my f to rejoice ... Ps 30:1 341
beat down his f before his face ... Ps 89:23 6862
a man's f shall be they of his ... Mt 10:36 2190
Until I make thy f thy footstool ... Acts 2:35 2190

FOLD {9}
the shepherds make their f there ... Is 13:20 7257
And Sharon shall be a f of flocks ... Is 65:10 5116
of Israel shall their f be ... Eze 34:14 5116
there shall they lie in a good f ... Eze 34:14 5116
the flock in the midst of their f ... Mic 2:12 1699
flock shall be cut off from the f ... Hab 3:17 4356
I have, which are not of this f ... Jn 10:16 833
and there shall be one f, and one ... Jn 10:16 4167
as a vesture shalt thou f them up ... Heb 1:12 1667

FOLDEN {1}
For while they be f together as ... Nah 1:10 5440

FOLDETH {1}
The fool f his hands together, and ... Eccl 4:5 2263

FOLDING {4}
two leaves of the one door were f ... 1Kin 6:34 1550
leaves of the other door were f ... 1Kin 6:34 1550
a little f of the hands to sleep ... Prov 6:10 2264
a little f of the hands to sleep ... Prov 24:33 2264

FOLDS {5}
little ones, and f for your sheep ... Num 32:24 1448
and f of sheep ... Num 32:36 1448
house, nor he goats out of thy f ... Ps 50:9 4356
will bring them again to their f ... Jer 23:3 5116
for shepherds, and f for flocks ... Zeph 2:6 1448

FOLK {5}
some of the f that are with me ... Gen 33:15 5971
The conies are but a feeble f ... Prov 30:26 5971
the f in the fire, and they shall ... Jer 51:58 3816
laid his hands upon a few sick f ... Mk 6:5
a great multitude of impotent f ... Jn 5:3

FOLKS {1}
unto Jerusalem, bringing sick f ... Acts 5:16

FOLLOW {86}
be willing to f me unto this land ... Gen 24:5 3212,310
will not be willing to f thee ... Gen 24:8 3212,310
the woman will not f me ... Gen 24:39 3212,310
his steward, Up, f after the men ... Gen 44:4 7291
and all the people that f thee ... Ex 11:8 7272
heart, that he shall f after them ... Ex 14:4 7291
Egyptians, and they shall f them ... Ex 14:17 310
from her, and yet no mischief f ... Ex 21:22 1961
And if any mischief f, then thou ... Ex 21:23 1961
Thou shalt not f a multitude to ... Ex 23:2 1961,310
is altogether just shalt thou f ... Deut 16:20 7291
of the LORD, if the thing f not ... Deut 18:22 1961
And he said unto them, F after me ... Judg 3:28 7291
bread unto the people that f me ... Judg 8:5 7272
hearts inclined to f Abimelech ... Judg 9:3 935,310
unto the young men that f my lord ... 1Sa 25:27 1980,7272
faint that they could not f David ... 1Sa 30:21 3212,310
among the people that f Absalom ... 2Sa 17:9 310
if the LORD be God, f him ... 1Kin 18:21 3212,310
but if Baal, then f him ... 1Kin 18:21 3212,310
my mother, and then I will f thee ... 1Kin 19:20 3212,310
for all the people that f me ... 1Kin 20:10 7272
f me, and I will bring you to the ... 2Kin 6:19 3212,310
mercy shall f me all the days of ... Ps 23:6 7291
because I f the thing that good ... Ps 38:20 7291
f her shall be brought unto thee ... Ps 45:14 310
the upright in heart shall f it ... Ps 94:15 310
draw nigh that f after mischief ... Ps 119:150 7291
that they may f strong drink ... Is 5:11 7291
ye that f after righteousness, ye ... Is 51:1 7291
from being a pastor to f thee ... Jer 17:16 310
shall f close after you there in ... Jer 42:16 1692
that f their own spirit, and have ... Eze 13:3 1980,310
she shall f after her lovers, but ... Hos 2:7 7291
if we f on to know the LORD ... Hos 6:3 7291
F me, and I will make you fishers ... Mt 4:19 1205,3694
I will f thee whithersoever thou ... Mt 8:19 190
But Jesus said unto him, F me ... Mt 8:22 190
and he saith unto him, F me ... Mt 9:9 190
and take up his cross, and f me ... Mt 16:24 190
and come and f me ... Mt 19:21 190
of custom, and said unto him, F me ... Mk 2:14 190
And he suffered no man to f him ... Mk 5:37 4870
and his disciples f him ... Mk 6:1 190
and take up his cross, and f me ... Mk 8:34 190
come, take up the cross, and f me ... Mk 10:21 190
bearing a pitcher of water: f him ... Mk 14:13 190
signs shall f them that believe ... Mk 16:17 3877
and he said unto him, F me ... Lk 5:27 190
take up his cross daily, and f me ... Lk 9:23 190
I will f thee whithersoever thou ... Lk 9:57 190
And he said unto another, F me ... Lk 9:59 190
also said, Lord, I will f thee ... Lk 9:61 190
go not after them, nor f them ... Lk 17:23 1377
in heaven: and come, f me ... Lk 18:22 190
f him into the house where he ... Lk 22:10 190
were about him saw what would f ... Lk 22:49 2071
Philip, and saith unto him, F me ... Jn 1:43 190
before them, and the sheep f him ... Jn 10:4 190
And a stranger will they not f ... Jn 10:5 190
and I know them, and they f me ... Jn 10:27 190
If any man serve me, let him f me ... Jn 12:26 190
I go, thou canst not f me now ... Jn 13:36 190
but thou shalt f me afterwards ... Jn 13:36 190
Lord, why cannot I f thee now ... Jn 13:37 190
this, he saith unto him, F me ... Jn 21:19 190
is that to thee? f thou me ... Jn 21:22 190
from Samuel and those that f after ... Acts 3:24 2517
thy garment about thee, and f me ... Acts 12:8 190
Let us therefore f after the ... Rom 14:19 1377
F after charity, and desire ... 1Cor 14:1 1377
but I f after, if that I may ... Phil 3:12 1377
but ever f that which is good, ... 1Th 5:15 1377
know how ye ought to f us ... 2Th 3:7 3401
an ensample unto you to f us ... 2Th 3:9 3401
and some men they f after ... 1Ti 5:24 1872
f after righteousness, godliness, ... 1Ti 6:11 1377

F

but f righteousness, faith, 2Ti 2:22 1377
F peace with all men, and holiness Heb 12:14 1377
whose faith f, considering the Heb 13:7 3401
and the glory that should f 1Pet 1:11 3326,5023
that ye should f his steps 1Pet 2:21 1872
many shall f their pernicious 2Pet 2:2 1811
f not that which is evil, but 3Jn 11 3401
These are they which f the Lamb Rev 14:4 190
and their works do f them Rev 14:13 190

FOLLOWED {108}
upon the camels, and f the man Gen 24:61 3212,310
all that f the droves, saying, On Gen 32:19 1980,310
hath f me fully, him will I bring Num 14:24 310
and the elders of Israel f him Num 16:25 3212,310
because they have not wholly f me Num 32:11 310
for they have wholly f the LORD Num 32:12 310
because he hath wholly f the LORD Deut 1:36 310
for all the men that f Baal-peor Deut 4:3 1980,310
the covenant of the LORD f them Josh 6:8 1980,310
but I wholly f the LORD my God Josh 14:8 310
hast wholly f the LORD my God Josh 14:9 310
wholly f the LORD God of Israel Josh 14:14 310
f other gods, of the gods of the Judg 2:12 3212,310
and light persons, which f him Judg 9:4 3212,310
f Abimelech, and put them to the Judg 9:49 3212,310
and all the people f him trembling 1Sa 13:7 310
even they also f hard after them 1Sa 14:22 1692
went and f Saul to the battle 1Sa 17:13 1980,310
and the three eldest f Saul 1Sa 17:14 1980,310
the Philistines f hard upon Saul 1Sa 31:2 1692
horsemen f hard after him 2Sa 1:6 1692
But the house of Judah f David 2Sa 2:10 1961,310
And king David himself f the bier 2Sa 3:31 1980,310
there f him a mess of meat from 2Sa 11:8 3318,310
saw that his counsel was not f 2Sa 17:23 6213
f Sheba the son of Bichri 2Sa 20:2 310
none that f the house of David 1Kin 12:20 310
who f me with all his heart, to 1Kin 14:8 1980,310
half of the people f Tibni the 1Kin 16:21 1961,310
and half f Omri 1Kin 16:21 310
But the people that f Omri 1Kin 16:22 310
that f Tibni the son of Ginath 1Kin 16:22 310
the LORD, and thou hast f Baalim 1Kin 18:18 3212,310
city, and the army which f them 1Kin 20:19 310
and for the cattle that f them 2Kin 3:9 7272
And he arose, and f her 2Kin 4:30 3112,310
So Gehazi f after Naaman 2Kin 5:21 7291
Jehu f after him, and said, Smite 2Kin 9:27 7291
f the sins of Jeroboam the son of 2Kin 13:2 3212,310
they f vanity, and became vain, 2Kin 17:15 3212,310
the Philistines f hard after Saul 1Chr 10:2 1692
the men of the guard which f me Neh 4:23 310
players on instruments f after Ps 68:25
whither the head looked they f it Eze 10:11 3212,310
the LORD took me as I f the flock Amos 7:15 310
left their nets, and f him Mt 4:20 190
ship and their father, and f him Mt 4:22 190
there f him great multitudes of Mt 4:25 190
mountain, great multitudes f him Mt 8:1 190
marvelled, and said to them that f Mt 8:10 190
into a ship, his disciples f him Mt 8:23 190
And he arose, and f him Mt 9:9 190
f him, and so did his disciples Mt 9:19 190
thence, two blind men f him Mt 9:27 190
and great multitudes f him Mt 12:15 190
they f him on foot out of the Mt 14:13 190
And great multitudes f him Mt 19:2 190
we have forsaken all, and f thee Mt 19:27 190
unto you, That ye which have f me Mt 19:28 190
Jericho, a great multitude f him Mt 20:29 190
received sight, and they f him Mt 20:34 190
that went before, and that f Mt 21:9 190
But Peter f him afar off unto the Mt 26:58 190
which f Jesus from Galilee, Mt 27:55 190
that f the day of the preparation Mt 27:62 2076,3326
they forsook their nets, and f him Mk 1:18 190
that were with him f after him Mk 1:36 2614
And he arose and f him Mk 2:14 190
there were many, and they f him Mk 2:15 190
multitude from Galilee f him Mk 3:7 190
and much people f him, and thronged Mk 5:24 190
we have left all, and have f thee Mk 10:28 190
and as they f, they were afraid Mk 10:32 190
his sight, and f Jesus in the way Mk 10:52 190
that went before, and they that f Mk 11:9 190
there f him a certain young man, Mk 14:51 190
Peter f him afar off, even into Mk 14:54 190
f him, and ministered unto him Mk 15:41 190
land, they forsook all, and f him Lk 5:11 190
And he left all, rose up, and f him Lk 5:28 190
said unto the people that f him Lk 7:9 190
people, when they knew it, f him Lk 9:11 190
Lo, we have left all, and f thee Lk 18:28 190
sight, and f him, glorifying God Lk 18:43 190
and his disciples also f him Lk 22:39 190
And Peter f afar off Lk 22:54 190
there f him a great company of Lk 23:27 190
the women that f him from Galilee Lk 23:49 4870
f after, and beheld the sepulchre, Lk 23:55 2628
heard him speak, and they f Jesus Jn 1:37 190
f him, was Andrew, Simon Peter's Jn 1:40 190
And a great multitude f him Jn 6:2 190
f her, saying, She goeth unto the Jn 11:31 190
And Simon Peter f Jesus, and so did Jn 18:15 190
And he went out, and f him Acts 12:9 190
and religious proselytes f Paul Acts 13:43 190
The same f Paul and us, and cried, Acts 16:17 2628
multitude of the people f after Acts 21:36 190
which f not after righteousness, Rom 9:30 1377
Israel, which f after the law of Rom 9:31 1377
that spiritual Rock that f them 1Cor 10:4 190
have diligently f every good work 1Ti 5:10 1872
For we have not f cunningly 2Pet 1:16 1811
him was Death, and Hell f with him Rev 6:8 190
angel sounded, and there f hail Rev 8:7 1096
there f another angel, saying, Rev 14:8 190
And the third angel f them Rev 14:9 190
in heaven f him upon white horses Rev 19:14 190

FOLLOWEDST {1}
inasmuch as thou f not young men Ruth 3:10 3212,310

FOLLOWERS {8}
I beseech you, be ye f of me 1Cor 4:16 3402
Be ye f of me, even as I also am 1Cor 11:1 3402
Be ye therefore f of God, as dear Eph 5:1 3402
be f together of me, and mark them Phil 3:17 4831
And ye became f of us, and of the 1Th 1:6 3402
became f of the churches of God 1Th 2:14 3402
but f of them who through faith Heb 6:12 3402
if ye be f of that which is good 1Pet 3:13 3402

FOLLOWETH {15}
him that f her kill with the 2Kin 11:15 935,310
and whoso f her, let him be slain 2Chr 23:14 935,310
My soul f hard after thee Ps 63:8 1692
but he that f vain persons is Prov 12:11 7291
him that f after righteousness Prov 15:9 7291
He that f after righteousness and Prov 21:21 7291
but he that f after vain persons Prov 28:19 7291
loveth gifts, and f after rewards Is 1:23 7291
whereas none f thee to commit Eze 16:34 310
on wind, and f after the east wind Hos 12:1 7291
f after me, is not worthy of me Mt 10:38 190
in thy name, and he f not us Mk 9:38 190
forbad him, because he f not us Mk 9:38 190
him, because he f not with us Lk 9:49 190
he that f me shall not walk in Jn 8:12 190

FOLLOWING {43}
land by reason of that famine f Gen 41:31 310,3651
will turn away thy son from f me Deut 7:4 310
that thou be not snared by f them Deut 12:30 310
away this day from f the LORD Josh 22:16 310
away this day from f the LORD Josh 22:18 310
an altar to turn from f the LORD Josh 22:23 310
and turn this day from f the LORD Josh 22:29 310
in f other gods to serve them, and Judg 2:19 3212,310
or to return from f after thee Ruth 1:16
you continue f the LORD your God 1Sa 12:14 310
turn not aside from f the LORD 1Sa 12:20 310
went up from f the Philistines 1Sa 14:46 310
for he is turned back from f me 1Sa 15:11 310
returned from f the Philistines 1Sa 24:1 310
hand nor to the left from f Abner 2Sa 2:19 310
not turn aside from f of him 2Sa 2:21 310
Asahel, Turn thee aside from f me 2Sa 2:22 310
return from f their brethren 2Sa 2:26 310
up every one from f his brother 2Sa 2:27 310
And Joab returned from f Abner 2Sa 2:30 310
from f the sheep, to be ruler 2Sa 7:8 310
they f Adonijah helped him 1Kin 1:7 310
if ye shall at all turn from f me 1Kin 9:6 310
he did very abominably in f idols 1Kin 21:26 3212,310
drave Israel from f the LORD 2Kin 17:21 310
LORD, and departed not from f him 2Kin 18:6 310
sheepcote, even from f the sheep 1Chr 17:7 310
f the LORD they made a conspiracy 2Chr 25:27 310
they departed not from f the LORD 2Chr 34:33 310
may tell it to the generation f Ps 48:13 314
From f the ewes great with young Ps 78:71 310
in the generation f let their Ps 109:13 312
confirming the word with signs f Mk 16:20 1872
day, and to morrow, and the day f Lk 13:33 2192
Then Jesus turned, and saw them f Jn 1:38 190
The day f Jesus would go forth Jn 1:43 1887
The day f, when the people which Jn 6:22 1887
Then cometh Simon Peter f him Jn 20:6 190
the disciple whom Jesus loved f Jn 21:20 190
the day f unto Rhodes, and from Acts 21:1 1836
the day f Paul went in with us Acts 21:18 1966
the night f the Lord stood by him Acts 23:11
f the way of Balaam the son of 2Pet 2:15 1811

FOLLY {37}
because he had wrought f in Gen 34:7 5039
she hath wrought f in Israel Deut 22:21 5039
he hath wrought f in Israel Josh 7:15 5039
into mine house, do not this f Judg 19:23 5039
committed lewdness and f in Israel Judg 20:6 5039
according to all the f that they Judg 20:10 5039
is his name, and f is with him 1Sa 25:25 5039
do not thou this f 2Sa 13:12 5039
and his angels he charged with f Job 4:18 8417
yet God layeth not f to them Job 24:12 8604
lest I deal with you after your f Job 42:8 5039
This their way is their f Ps 49:13 3689
but let them not turn again to f Ps 85:8 3690
of his f he shall go astray Prov 5:23 200
but a fool layeth open his f Prov 13:16 200
but the f of fools is deceit Prov 14:8 200
The simple inherit f Prov 14:18 200
but the foolishness of fools is f Prov 14:24 200
is hasty of spirit exalteth f Prov 14:29 200
F is joy to him that is destitute Prov 15:21 200
but the instruction of fools is f Prov 16:22 200
man, rather than a fool in his f Prov 17:12 200
before he heareth it, it is f Prov 18:13 200
not a fool according to his f Prov 26:4 200
Answer a fool according to his f Prov 26:5 200
so a fool returneth to his f Prov 26:11 200
wisdom, and to know madness and f Eccl 1:17 5531
and to lay hold on f, till I might Eccl 2:3 5531
behold wisdom, and madness, and f Eccl 2:12 5531
I saw that wisdom excelleth f Eccl 2:13 5531
and to know the wickedness of f Eccl 7:25 3689
so doth a little f him that is in Eccl 10:1 5531
F is set in great dignity, and the Eccl 10:6 5529
and every mouth speaketh f Is 9:17 5039
I have seen f in the prophets of Jer 23:13 8604
bear with me a little in my f 2Cor 11:1 877
for their f shall be manifest 2Ti 3:9 454

FOOD {55}
to the sight, and good for f Gen 2:9 3978
saw that the tree was good for f Gen 3:6 3978
unto thee of all f that is eaten Gen 6:21 3978
and it shall be for f for thee Gen 6:21 402
let them gather all the f of Gen 41:35 400
and let them keep f in the cities Gen 41:35 400
that f shall be for store to the Gen 41:36 400
up all the f of the seven years Gen 41:48 400
laid up the f in the cities Gen 41:48 400
the f of the field, which was Gen 41:48 400
From the land of Canaan to buy f Gen 42:7 400
but to buy f are thy servants Gen 42:10 400
take f for the famine of your Gen 42:33
them, Go again, buy us a little f Gen 43:2 400
us, we will go down and buy thee f Gen 43:4 400
down at the first time to buy f Gen 43:20 400
down in our hands to buy f Gen 43:22 400
Fill the men's sacks with f Gen 44:1 400
Go again, and buy us a little f Gen 44:25 400
seed of the field, and for your f Gen 47:24 400
for f for your little ones Gen 47:24 398
her f, her raiment, and her duty Ex 21:10 7607
it is the f of the offering made Lev 3:11 3899
it is the f of the offering made Lev 3:16 3899
planted all manner of trees for f Lev 19:23 3978
because it is his f Lev 22:7 3899
the stranger, in giving him f Deut 10:18 3899
that eateth any f until evening 1Sa 14:24 3899
none of the people tasted any f 1Sa 14:24 3899
man that eateth any f this day 1Sa 14:28 3899
master's son may have f to eat 2Sa 9:10 3899
in giving f for my household 1Kin 5:9 3899
of wheat for f to his household 1Kin 5:11 4361
mouth more than my necessary f Job 23:12
wilderness yieldeth f for them Job 24:5 3899
Who provideth for the raven his f Job 38:41 6718
the mountains bring him forth f Job 40:20 944
Man did eat angels' f Ps 78:25 3899
bring forth f out of the earth Ps 104:14 3899
Who giveth f to all flesh Ps 136:25 3899
which giveth f to the hungry Ps 146:7 3899
He giveth to the beast his f Ps 147:9 3899
gathereth her f in the harvest Prov 6:8 3978
Much f is in the tillage of the Prov 13:23 400
have goats' milk enough for thy f Prov 27:27 3899
for the f of thy household, and Prov 27:27 3899
sweeping rain which leaveth no f Prov 28:3 3899
feed me with f convenient for me Prov 30:8 3899
she bringeth her f from afar Prov 31:14 3899
have diminished thine ordinary f Eze 16:27
f unto them that serve the city Eze 48:18 3899
filling our hearts with f Acts 14:17 5160
both minister bread for your f 2Cor 9:10 1035
And having f and raiment let us be 1Ti 6:8 1304
be naked, and destitute of daily f Jas 2:15 5160

FOOL {66}
behold, I have played the f 1Sa 26:21 5528
and said, Died Abner as a f dieth 2Sa 3:33 5036
The f hath said in his heart, Ps 14:1 5036
that wise men die, likewise the f Ps 49:10 3684
The f hath said in his heart, Ps 53:1 5036
neither doth a f understand this Ps 92:6 3684
or as a f to the correction of Prov 7:22 191
but a prating f shall fall Prov 10:8 191
but a prating f shall fall Prov 10:10 191
that uttereth a slander, is a f Prov 10:18 3684
is as sport to a f to do mischief Prov 10:23 3684
the f shall be servant to the Prov 11:29 191
The way of a f is right in his Prov 12:15 191
but a f layeth open his folly Prov 13:16 3684
but the f rageth, and is confident Prov 14:16 3684
A f despiseth his father's Prov 15:5 191
Excellent speech becometh not a f Prov 17:7 5036
than an hundred stripes into a f Prov 17:10 3684
man, rather than a f in his folly Prov 17:12 3684
in the hand of a f to get wisdom Prov 17:16 3684
He that begetteth a f doeth it to Prov 17:21 3684
and the father of a f hath no joy Prov 17:21 5036
but the eyes of a f are in the Prov 17:24 3684
Even a f, when he holdeth his Prov 17:28 191
A f hath no delight in Prov 18:2 3684
perverse in his lips, and is a f Prov 19:1 3684
Delight is not seemly for a f Prov 19:10 3684
but every f will be meddling Prov 20:3 191
Speak not in the ears of a f Prov 23:9 3684
Wisdom is too high for a f Prov 24:7 191
so honour is not seemly for a f Prov 26:1 3684
Answer not a f according to his Prov 26:4 3684
Answer a f according to his folly Prov 26:5 3684
hand of a f cutteth off the feet Prov 26:6 3684
is he that giveth honour to a f Prov 26:8 3684
all things both rewardeth the f Prov 26:10 3684

so a *f* returneth to his folly ... Prov 26:11 3684
is more hope of a *f* than of him ... Prov 26:12 3684
Though thou shouldest bray a *f* in ... Prov 27:22 191
trusteth in his own heart is a *f* ... Prov 28:26 3684
A *f* uttereth all his mind ... Prov 29:11 3684
is more hope of a *f* than of him ... Prov 29:20 3684
a *f* when he is filled with meat ... Prov 30:22 5030
but the *f* walketh in darkness ... Eccl 2:14 3684
heart, As it happeneth to the *f* ... Eccl 2:15 3684
wise more than of the *f* for ever ... Eccl 2:16 3684
the wise man? as the *f* ... Eccl 2:16 3684
he shall be a wise man or a *f* ... Eccl 2:19 5530
The *f* foldeth his hands together, ... Eccl 4:5 3684
hath the wise more than the *f* ... Eccl 6:8 3684
pot, so is the laughter of the *f* ... Eccl 7:6 3684
when he that is a *f* walketh by ... Eccl 10:3 5530
saith to every one that he is a *f* ... Eccl 10:3 5530
but the lips of a *f* will swallow ... Eccl 10:12 3684
A *f* also is full of words ... Eccl 10:14 5536
days, and at his end shall be a *f* ... Jer 17:11 5036
the prophet is a *f*, the spiritual ... Hos 9:7 191
but whosoever shall say, Thou *f* ... Mt 5:22 *3474*
But God said unto him, Thou *f* ... Lk 12:20 *876*
in this world, let him become a *f* ... 1Cor 3:18 *3474*
Thou *f*, that which thou sowest is ... 1Cor 15:36 *876*
again, Let no man think me a *f* ... 2Cor 11:16 *876*
yet as a *f* receive me, that I may ... 2Cor 11:16 *876*
(I speak as a *f*) I am more ... 2Cor 11:23 *3912*
to glory, I shall not be a *f* ... 2Cor 12:6 *876*
I am become a *f* in glorying ... 2Cor 12:11 *876*

FOOLISH {52}
the LORD, O *f* people and unwise ... Deut 32:6 5036
them to anger with a *f* nation ... Deut 32:21 5036
as one of the *f* women speaketh ... Job 2:10 5039
For wrath killeth the *f* man ... Job 5:2 191
I have seen the *f* taking root ... Job 5:3 191
The *f* shall not stand in thy ... Ps 5:5 1984
make me not the reproach of the *f* ... Ps 39:8 5036
For I was envious at the *f* ... Ps 73:3 1984
So *f* was I, and ignorant ... Ps 73:22 1198
that the *f* people have blasphemed ... Ps 74:18 5036
remember how the *f* man ... Ps 74:22 5036
Forsake the *f*, and live ... Prov 9:6 6612
A *f* woman is clamorous ... Prov 9:13 3687
but a *f* son is the heaviness of ... Prov 10:1 3684
of the *f* is near destruction ... Prov 10:14 191
but the *f* plucketh it down with ... Prov 14:1 200
mouth of the *f* is a rod of pride ... Prov 14:3 191
Go from the presence of a *f* man ... Prov 14:7 3684
the heart of the *f* doeth not so ... Prov 15:7 3684
but a *f* man despiseth his mother ... Prov 15:20 3684
A *f* son is a grief to his father, ... Prov 17:25 3684
A *f* son is the calamity of his ... Prov 19:13 3684
but a *f* man spendeth it up ... Prov 21:20 3684
wise man contendeth with a *f* man ... Prov 29:9 191
f king, who will no more be ... Eccl 4:13 3684
much wicked, neither be thou *f* ... Eccl 7:17 5530
The labour of the *f* wearieth ... Eccl 10:15 3684
and maketh their knowledge *f* ... Is 44:25 5528
For my people is *f*, they have not ... Jer 4:22 191
these are poor; they are *f* ... Jer 5:4 2973
now this, O *f* people, and without ... Jer 5:21 5530
they are altogether brutish and *f* ... Jer 10:8 3688
seen vain and *f* things for thee ... Lam 2:14 8602
Woe unto the *f* prophets, that ... Eze 13:3 5036
the instruments of a *f* shepherd ... Zec 11:15 196
shall be likened unto a *f* man ... Mt 7:26 *3474*
of them were wise, and five were *f* ... Mt 25:2 *3474*
They that were *f* took their lamps ... Mt 25:3 *3474*
the *f* said unto the wise, Give us ... Mt 25:8 *3474*
their *f* heart was darkened ... Rom 1:21 *801*
An instructor of the *f*, a teacher ... Rom 2:20 *878*
by a *f* nation I will anger you ... Rom 10:19 *801*
hath not God made *f* the wisdom of ... 1Cor 1:20 *3471*
But God hath chosen the *f* things ... 1Cor 1:27 *3474*
O *f* Galatians, who hath bewitched ... Gal 3:1 *453*
Are ye so *f*? ... Gal 3:3 *453*
nor *f* talking, nor jesting, which ... Eph 5:4 *3473*
and a snare, and into many *f* ... 1Ti 6:9 *453*
But *f* and unlearned questions ... 2Ti 2:23 *3474*
ourselves also were sometimes *f* ... Titus 3:3 *453*
But avoid *f* questions, and ... Titus 3:9 *3474*
to silence the ignorance of *f* men ... 1Pet 2:15 *878*

FOOLISHLY {12}
thou hast now done *f* in so doing ... Gen 31:28 5528
upon us, wherein we have done *f* ... Num 12:11 2973
said to Saul, Thou hast done *f* ... 1Sa 13:13 5528
for I have done very *f* ... 2Sa 24:10 5528
for I have done very *f* ... 1Chr 21:8 5528
Herein thou hast done *f* ... 2Chr 16:9 5528
Job sinned not, nor charged God *f* ... Job 1:22 8604
I said unto the fools, Deal not *f* ... Ps 75:4 1984
He that is soon angry dealeth *f* ... Prov 14:17 200
If thou hast done *f* in lifting up ... Prov 30:32 5034
after the Lord, but as it were *f* ... 2Cor 11:17 *1722,877*
any is bold, (I speak *f*,) I am ... 2Cor 11:21 *1722,877*

FOOLISHNESS {20}
the counsel of Ahithophel into *f* ... 2Sa 15:31 5528
and are corrupt because of my *f* ... Ps 38:5 200
O God, thou knowest my *f* ... Ps 69:5 200
the heart of fools proclaimeth *f* ... Prov 12:23 200
but the *f* of fools is folly ... Prov 14:24 200
the mouth of fools poureth out *f* ... Prov 15:2 200
the mouth of fools feedeth on *f* ... Prov 15:14 200
The *f* of man perverteth his way ... Prov 19:3 200
F is bound in the heart of a ... Prov 22:15 200
The thought of *f* is sin ... Prov 24:9 200
will not his *f* depart from him ... Prov 27:22 200
wickedness of folly, even of *f* ... Eccl 7:25 5531
of the words of his mouth is *f* ... Eccl 10:13 5531
an evil eye, blasphemy, pride, *f* ... Mk 7:22 *877*
cross is to them that perish *f* ... 1Cor 1:18 *3472*
it pleased God by the *f* of ... 1Cor 1:21 *3472*
and unto the Greeks *f* ... 1Cor 1:23 *3472*
Because the *f* of God is wiser ... 1Cor 1:25 *3474*
for they are *f* unto him ... 1Cor 2:14 *3472*
of this world is *f* with God ... 1Cor 3:19 *3472*

FOOL'S {7}
A *f* wrath is presently known ... Prov 12:16 191
A *f* lips enter into contention, ... Prov 18:6 3684
A *f* mouth is his destruction, and ... Prov 18:7 3684
the ass, and a rod for the *f* back ... Prov 26:3 3684
but a *f* wrath is heavier than ... Prov 27:3 191
a *f* voice is known by multitude ... Eccl 5:3 3684
but a *f* heart at his left ... Eccl 10:2 3684

FOOLS {42}
be as one of the *f* in Israel ... 2Sa 13:13 5036
spoiled, and maketh the judges *f* ... Job 12:17 1984
They were children of *f*, yea, ... Job 30:8 5036
I said unto the *f*, Deal not ... Ps 75:4 1984
and ye *f*, when will ye be wise ... Ps 94:8 3684
F, because of their transgression ... Ps 107:17 191
but *f* despise wisdom and ... Prov 1:7 191
scorning, and *f* hate knowledge ... Prov 1:22 3684
the prosperity of *f* shall destroy ... Prov 1:32 3684
shame shall be the promotion of *f* ... Prov 3:35 3684
and, ye *f*, be ye of an ... Prov 8:5 3684
but *f* die for want of wisdom ... Prov 10:21 191
but the heart of *f* proclaimeth ... Prov 12:23 3684
to *f* to depart from evil ... Prov 13:19 3684
companion of *f* shall be destroyed ... Prov 13:20 3684
but the folly of *f* is deceit ... Prov 14:8 3684
F make a mock at sin ... Prov 14:9 191
but the foolishness of *f* is folly ... Prov 14:24 3684
in the midst of *f* is made known ... Prov 14:33 3684
but the mouth of *f* poureth out ... Prov 15:2 3684
but the mouth of *f* feedeth on ... Prov 15:14 3684
but the instruction of *f* is folly ... Prov 16:22 191
and stripes for the back of *f* ... Prov 19:29 3684
so is a parable in the mouth of *f* ... Prov 26:7 3684
so is a parable in the mouth of *f* ... Prov 26:9 3684
than to give the sacrifice of *f* ... Eccl 5:1 3684
for he hath no pleasure in *f* ... Eccl 5:4 3684
but the heart of *f* is in the ... Eccl 7:4 3684
for a man to hear the song of *f* ... Eccl 7:5 3684
anger resteth in the bosom of *f* ... Eccl 7:9 3684
cry of him that ruleth among *f* ... Eccl 9:17 3684
Surely the princes of Zoan are *f* ... Is 19:11 191
The princes of Zoan are become *f* ... Is 19:13 2973
the wayfaring men, though *f* ... Is 35:8 191
Ye *f* and blind ... Mt 23:17 *3474*
Ye *f* and blind ... Mt 23:19 *3474*
Ye *f*, did not he that made that ... Lk 11:40 *878*
Then he said unto them, O *f* ... Lk 24:25 *453*
to be wise, they became *f* ... Rom 1:22 *3471*
We are *f* for Christ's sake, but ... 1Cor 4:10 *3474*
For ye suffer *f* gladly, seeing ye ... 2Cor 11:19 *878*
ye walk circumspectly, not as *f* ... Eph 5:15 *781*

FOOT {94}
no rest for the sole of her *f* ... Gen 8:9 7272
or *f* in all the land of Egypt ... Gen 41:44 7272
thousand on *f* that were men ... Ex 12:37 7273
tooth, hand for hand, *f* for *f*, ... Ex 21:24 7272
the great toe of their right *f* ... Ex 29:20 7272
his *f* also of brass, to wash ... Ex 30:18 3653
vessels, and the laver and his *f* ... Ex 30:28 3653
furniture, and the laver and his *f* ... Ex 31:9 3653
his vessels, the laver and his *f* ... Ex 35:16 3653
the *f* of it of brass, of the ... Ex 38:8 3653
his vessels, the laver and his *f* ... Ex 39:39 3653
shalt anoint the laver and his *f* ... Ex 40:11 3653
vessels, both the laver and his *f* ... Lev 8:11 3653
upon the great toe of his right *f* ... Lev 8:23 7272
from his head even to his *f* ... Lev 13:12 7272
upon the great toe of his right *f* ... Lev 14:14 7272
upon the great toe of his right *f* ... Lev 14:17 7272
upon the great toe of his right *f* ... Lev 14:25 7272
upon the great toe of his right *f* ... Lev 14:28 7272
Balaam's *f* against the wall ... Num 22:25 7272
thee, neither did thy *f* swell ... Deut 8:4 7272
seed, and wateredst it with thy *f* ... Deut 11:10 7272
tooth, hand for hand, *f* for *f* ... Deut 19:21 7272
and loose his shoe from off his *f* ... Deut 25:9 7272
from the sole of thy *f* unto the ... Deut 28:35 7272
sole of her *f* upon the ground for ... Deut 28:56 7272
shall the sole of thy *f* have rest ... Deut 28:65 7272
shoe is not waxen old upon thy *f* ... Deut 29:5 7272
their *f* shall slide in due time ... Deut 32:35 7272
and let him dip his *f* in oil ... Deut 33:24 7272
sole of your *f* shall tread upon ... Josh 1:3 7272
Loose thy shoe from off thy *f* ... Josh 5:15 7272
he was sent on *f* into the valley ... Judg 5:15 7272
was as light of *f* as a wild roe ... 2Sa 2:18 7272
from the sole of his *f* even to ... 2Sa 14:25 7272
fingers, and on every *f* six toes ... 2Sa 21:20 7272
and he trode her under *f* ... 2Kin 9:33
on each hand, and six on each *f* ... 1Chr 20:6
will I any more remove the *f* of ... 2Chr 33:8 7272
the sole of his *f* unto his crown ... Job 2:7 7272
My *f* hath held his steps, his way ... Job 23:11 7272
the waters forgotten of the *f* ... Job 28:4 7272
or if my *f* hath hasted to deceit ... Job 31:5 7272
that the *f* may crush them ... Job 39:15 7272
they hid is their own *f* taken ... Ps 9:15 7272
My *f* standeth in an even place ... Ps 26:12 7272
Let not the *f* of pride come ... Ps 36:11 7272
when my *f* slippeth, they magnify ... Ps 38:16 7272
they went through the flood on *f* ... Ps 66:6 7272
That thy *f* may be dipped in the ... Ps 68:23 7272
thou dash thy *f* against a stone ... Ps 91:12 7272
When I said, My *f* slippeth ... Ps 94:18 7272
will not suffer thy *f* to be moved ... Ps 121:3 7272
refrain thy *f* from their path ... Prov 1:15 7272
and thy *f* shall not stumble ... Prov 3:23 7272
shall keep thy *f* from being taken ... Prov 3:26 7272
remove thy *f* from evil ... Prov 4:27 7272
Withdraw thy *f* from thy ... Prov 25:17 7272
broken tooth, and a *f* out of joint ... Prov 25:19 7272
Keep thy *f* when thou goest to the ... Eccl 5:1 7272
From the sole of the *f* even unto ... Is 1:6 7272
my mountains tread him under *f* ... Is 14:25 947
meted out and trodden under *f* ... Is 18:7 4001
and put off thy shoe from thy *f* ... Is 20:2 7272
The *f* shall tread it down, even ... Is 26:6 7272
the east, called him to his *f* ... Is 41:2 7272
turn away thy *f* from the sabbath ... Is 58:13 7272
Withhold thy *f* from being unshod, ... Jer 2:25 7272
have trodden my portion under *f* ... Jer 12:10 947
The Lord hath trodden under *f* all ... Lam 1:15 5541
was like the sole of a calf's *f* ... Eze 1:7 7272
thine hand, and stamp with thy *f* ... Eze 6:11 7272
No *f* of man shall pass through it ... Eze 29:11 7272
nor *f* of beast shall pass through ... Eze 29:11 7272
neither shall the *f* of man ... Eze 32:13 7272
and the host to be trodden under *f* ... Dan 8:13 4823
he that is swift of *f* shall not ... Amos 2:15 7272
thou dash thy *f* against a stone ... Mt 4:6 *4228*
and to be trodden under *f* of men ... Mt 5:13 *2662*
him on *f* out of the cities ... Mt 14:13 *3979*
if thy hand or thy *f* offend thee ... Mt 18:8 *4228*
the servants, Bind him hand and *f* ... Mt 22:13 *4228*
if thy *f* offend thee, cut it off ... Mk 9:45 *4228*
thou dash thy *f* against a stone ... Lk 4:11 *4228*
bound hand and *f* with graveclothes ... Jn 11:44 *4228*
not so much as to set his *f* on ... Acts 7:5 *4228*
If the *f* shall say, Because I am ... 1Cor 12:15 *4228*
trodden under *f* the Son of God ... Heb 10:29 *2662*
with a garment down to the *f* ... Rev 1:13 *4158*
he set his right *f* upon the sea ... Rev 10:2 *4228*
and his left *f* on the earth ... Rev 10:2
shall they tread under *f* forty ... Rev 11:2

FOOTBREADTH {1}
land, no, not so much as a *f* ... Deut 2:5

FOOTMEN {12}
I am, are six hundred thousand *f* ... Num 11:21 7273
thousand *f* that drew sword ... Judg 20:2 376,7273
fell of Israel thirty thousand *f* ... 1Sa 4:10 7273
in Telaim, two hundred thousand *f* ... 1Sa 15:4 7273
unto the *f* that stood about him ... 1Sa 22:17 7328
horsemen, and twenty thousand *f* ... 2Sa 8:4 376,7273
of Zoba, twenty thousand *f* ... 2Sa 10:6 7273
an hundred thousand *f* in one day ... 1Kin 20:29 7273
ten chariots, and ten thousand *f* ... 2Kin 13:7 7273
horsemen, and twenty thousand *f* ... 1Chr 18:4 376,7273
in chariots, and forty thousand *f* ... 1Chr 19:18 376,7273
If thou hast run with the *f* ... Jer 12:5 7273

FOOTSTEPS {4}
in thy paths, that my *f* slip not ... Ps 17:5 6471
waters, and thy *f* are not known ... Ps 77:19 6119
the *f* of thine anointed ... Ps 89:51 6119
way forth by the *f* of the flock ... Song 1:8 6119

FOOTSTOOL {16}
for the *f* of our God, and had made. 1Chr 28:2 1916,7272
with a *f* of gold, which were ... 2Chr 9:18 3534
our God, and worship at his *f* ... Ps 99:5 1916,7272
until I make thine enemies thy *f* ... Ps 110:1 1916,7272
we will worship at his *f* ... Ps 132:7 1916,7272
my throne, and the earth is my *f* ... Is 66:1 1916,7272
remembered not his *f* in the day ... Lam 2:1 1916,7272
for it is his *f* ... Mt 5:35 *5286,3588,4228*
till I make thine enemies thy *f*.. Mt 22:44 *5286,3588,4228*
till I make thine enemies thy *f*.. Mk 12:36 *5286,3588,4228*
Till I make thine enemies thy *f*. Lk 20:43 *5286,3588,4228*
Until I make thy foes thy *f* ... Acts 2:35 *5286,3588,4228*
my throne, and earth is my *f* ... Acts 7:49 *5286,3588,4228*
I make thine enemies thy *f* ... Heb 1:13 *5286,3588,4228*
till his enemies be made his *f* ... Heb 10:13 *5286,3588,4228*
there, or sit here under my *f* ... Jas 2:3 *5286*

FOR See APPENDIX.

FORASMUCH {43}
F as God hath shewed thee all ... Gen 41:39 310
f as thou knowest how we are ... Num 10:31 3588,5921,3651
f as he hath no part nor ... Deut 12:12 3588
f as the LORD hath said unto you, ... Deut 17:16
f as the LORD hath blessed me ... Josh 17:14 5704
f as the LORD hath taken ... Judg 11:36 310,834
f as we have sworn both of us in ... 1Sa 20:42
f as when the LORD had delivered .. 1Sa 24:18 854,834
f as my lord the king is come ... 2Sa 19:30 310,834
F as this is done of thee, and ... 1Kin 11:11 3282,834
F as thou hast disobeyed the ... 1Kin 13:21 3282,834
F as I exalted thee from among ... 1Kin 14:7 3282,834
F as I exalted thee out of the ... 1Kin 16:2 3282,834
F as thou hast sent messengers to ... 2Kin 1:16 3282,834
f as he defiled his father's bed, ... 1Chr 5:1
F as it was in thine heart to ... 2Chr 6:8
F as thou art sent of the king, .. Ezr 7:14 3606,6903,1768
F as this people refuseth the ... Is 8:6 3282,365
F as this people draw near me ... Is 29:13 3282,365
F as there is none like unto thee ... Jer 10:6

F

f as among all the wise men of ... Jer 10:7
f as iron breaketh in pieces ... Dan 2:40 3606,6903,1768
f as thou sawest the iron ... Dan 2:41 3606,6903,1768
F as thou sawest that the ... Dan 2:45 3606,6903,1768
f as all the wise men of my ... Dan 4:18 3606,6903,1768
F as an excellent spirit, and ... Dan 5:12 3606,6903,1768
f as he was faithful, neither ... Dan 6:4 3606,6903,1768
f as before him innocency was .. Dan 6:22 3606,6903,1768
F therefore as your treading is ... Amos 5:11 3282
But *f* as he had not to pay, his ... Mt 18:25
F as many have taken in hand to ... Lk 1:1 *1895*
f as Lydda was nigh to Joppa, and ... Acts 9:38 *5607*
F then as God gave them the like ... Acts 11:17 *1487*
F as we have heard, that certain ... Acts 15:24 *1894*
F then as we are the offspring of ... Acts 17:29
F as I know that thou hast been ... Acts 24:10
f as he is the image and glory of ... 1Cor 11:7
f as ye are zealous of spiritual ... 1Cor 14:12 *1893*
f as ye know that your labour is ... 1Cor 15:58
F as ye are manifestly declared ... 2Cor 3:3
F then as the children are ... Heb 2:14 *1893*
F as ye know that ye were not ... 1Pet 1:18
F then as Christ hath suffered ... 1Pet 4:1

FORBAD {5}
whatsoever the LORD our God *f* us ... Deut 2:37 6680
But John *f* him, saying, I have ... Mt 3:14 *1254*
we *f* him, because he followeth ... Mk 9:38 *2967*
we *f* him, because he followeth ... Lk 9:49 *2967*
f the madness of the prophet ... 2Pet 2:16 *2967*

FORBARE {3}
and he *f* to go forth ... 1Sa 23:13 2308
Then the prophet *f*, and said, I ... 2Chr 25:16 2308
So he *f*, and slew them not among ... Jer 41:8 2308

FORBEAR {22}
wouldest *f* to help him, thou ... Ex 23:5 2308
But if thou shalt *f* to vow ... Deut 23:22 2308
to battle, or shall I *f* ... 1Kin 22:6 2308
to battle, or shall we *f* ... 1Kin 22:15 2308
to battle, or shall I *f* ... 2Chr 18:5 2308
to battle, or shall I *f* ... 2Chr 18:14 2308
f; why shouldest thou be smitten ... 2Chr 25:16 2308
f thee from meddling with God, ... 2Chr 35:21 2308
Yet many years didst thou *f* them ... Neh 9:30 4900
and though I *f*, what am I eased ... Job 16:6 2308
If thou *f* to deliver them that ... Prov 24:11 2820
to come with me into Babylon, *f* ... Jer 40:4 2308
will hear, or whether they will *f* ... Eze 2:5 2308
will hear, or whether they will *f* ... Eze 2:7 2308
will hear, or whether they will *f* ... Eze 3:11 2308
and he that forbeareth, let him *f* ... Eze 3:27 2308
F to cry, make no mourning for ... Eze 24:17 1826
my price; and if not, *f* ... Zec 11:12 2308
have not we power to *f* working ... 1Cor 9:6 *3361*
but now I *f*, lest any man should ... 2Cor 12:6 *5339*
when we could no longer *f* ... 1Th 3:1 *4722*
cause, when I could no longer *f* ... 1Th 3:5 *4722*

FORBEARANCE {2}
the riches of his goodness and *f* ... Rom 2:4 *463*
are past, through the *f* of God ... Rom 3:25 *463*

FORBEARETH {2}
f to keep the passover, even the ... Num 9:13 2308
and he that *f*, let him forbear ... Eze 3:27 2310

FORBEARING {5}
By long *f* is a prince persuaded, ... Prov 25:15 639
my bones, and I was weary with *f* ... Jer 20:9 3557
f one another in love ... Eph 4:2 *430*
things unto them, *f* threatening ... Eph 6:9 *447*
F one another, and forgiving one ... Col 3:13 *430*

FORBID {37}
God *f* that thy servants should do ... Gen 44:7 2486
God *f* that I should do so ... Gen 44:17 2486
and said, My lord Moses, *f* them ... Num 11:28 3607
God *f* that we should rebel ... Josh 22:29 2486
God *f* that we should forsake the ... Josh 24:16 2486
God *f* that I should sin against ... 1Sa 12:23 2486
God *f*: as the LORD liveth ... 1Sa 14:45 2486
And he said unto him, God *f* ... 1Sa 20:2 2486
The LORD *f* that I should do this ... 1Sa 24:6 2486
The LORD *f* that I should stretch ... 1Sa 26:11 2486
said to Ahab, The LORD *f* it me ... 1Kin 21:3 2486
And said, My God *f* it me, that I ... 1Chr 11:19 2486
God *f* that I should justify you ... Job 27:5 2486
f them not, to come unto me ... Mt 19:14 *2967*
But Jesus said, *F* him not ... Mk 9:39 *2967*
to come unto me, and *f* them not ... Mk 10:14 *2967*
cloke *f* not to take thy coat also ... Lk 6:29 *2967*
And Jesus said unto him, *F* him not ... Lk 9:50 *2967*
to come unto me, and *f* them not ... Lk 18:16 *2967*
they heard it, they said, God *f* ... Lk 20:16 *3361,1096*
Can any man *f* water, that these ... Acts 10:47 *2967*
that he should *f* none of his ... Acts 24:23 *2967*
God *f*: yea, let God be true ... Rom 3:4 *3361,1096*
God *f*: for then how shall God ... Rom 3:6 *3361,1096*
God *f*: yea, we establish the law ... Rom 3:31 *3361,1096*
God *f*. How shall we ... Rom 6:2 *3361,1096*
but under grace? God *f* ... Rom 6:15 *3361,1096*
Is the law sin? God *f* ... Rom 7:7 *3361,1096*
good made death unto me? God *f* ... Rom 7:13 *3361,1096*
unrighteousness with God? God *f* ... Rom 9:14 *3361,1096*
God cast away his people? God *f* ... Rom 11:1 *3361,1096*
that they should fall? God *f* ... Rom 11:11 *3361,1096*
members of an harlot? God *f* ... 1Cor 6:15
f not to speak with tongues ... 1Cor 14:39 *2967*
the minister of sin? God *f* ... Gal 2:17 *3361,1096*
the promises of God? God *f* ... Gal 3:21 *3361,1096*
But God *f* that I should glory, ... Gal 6:14 *3361,1096*

FORBIDDEN {3}
any of these things which are *f* ... Lev 5:17 3808
the LORD thy God hath *f* thee ... Deut 4:23 6680
were *f* of the Holy Ghost to ... Acts 16:6 *2967*

FORBIDDETH {1}
f them that would, and casteth ... 3Jn 10 *2967*

FORBIDDING {4}
f to give tribute to Caesar, ... Lk 23:2 *2967*
with all confidence, no man *f* him ... Acts 28:31 *209*
F us to speak to the Gentiles ... 1Th 2:16 *2967*
F to marry, and commanding to ... 1Ti 4:3 *2967*

FORBORN {1}
men of Babylon have *f* to fight ... Jer 51:30 2308

FORCE {19}
take by *f* thy daughters from me ... Gen 31:31 1497
in the field, and the man *f* her ... Deut 22:25 2388
not dim, nor his natural *f* abated ... Deut 34:7 3893
and if not, I will take it by *f* ... 1Sa 2:16 2394
him, Nay, my brother, do not *f* me ... 2Sa 13:12 6031
Jews, and made them to cease by *f* ... Ezr 4:23 153
Will he *f* the queen also before ... Est 7:8 3533
By the great *f* of my disease is ... Job 30:18 3581
his *f* is in the navel of his ... Job 40:16 202
their blood by the *f* of the sword ... Jer 18:21 3027
is evil, and their *f* is not right ... Jer 23:10 1369
of Heshbon because of the *f* ... Jer 48:45 3581
but with *f* and with cruelty have ... Eze 34:4 2394
the *f* of the sword in the time of ... Eze 35:5 3027
strong shall not strengthen his *f* ... Amos 2:14 3581
and the violent take it by *f* ... Mt 11:12 *726*
they would come and take him by *f* ... Jn 6:15 *726*
to take him by *f* from among them, ... Acts 23:10 *726*
is of *f* after men are dead ... Heb 9:17 *949*

FORCED {7}
the Amorites *f* the children of ... Judg 1:34 3905
and my concubine have they *f* ... Judg 20:5 6031
I *f* myself therefore, and offered ... 1Sa 13:12 662
than she, *f* her, and lay with her ... 2Sa 13:14 6031
because he had *f* his sister Tamar ... 2Sa 13:22 6031
day that he *f* his sister Tamar ... 2Sa 13:32 6031
flattering of her lips she *f* him ... Prov 7:21 5080

FORCES {16}
he placed *f* in all the fenced ... 2Chr 17:2 2428
gold, nor all the *f* of strength ... Job 36:19 3981
the *f* of the Gentiles shall come ... Is 60:5 2428
unto thee the *f* of the Gentiles ... Is 60:11 2428
of the *f* which were in the fields ... Jer 40:7 2428
of the *f* that were in the fields ... Jer 40:13 2428
of the *f* that were with him ... Jer 41:11 2428
of the *f* that were with him ... Jer 41:13 2428
of the *f* that were with him ... Jer 41:16 2428
Then all the captains of the *f* ... Jer 42:1 2428
of the *f* which were with him ... Jer 42:8 2428
and all the captains of the *f* ... Jer 43:4 2428
and all the captains of the *f* ... Jer 43:5 2428
assemble a multitude of great *f* ... Dan 11:10 2428
shall he honour the God of *f* ... Dan 11:38 4581
carried away captive his *f* ... Obad 11 2428

FORCIBLE {1}
How *f* are right words ... Job 6:25 4834

FORCING {2}
thereof by *f* an ax against them ... Deut 20:19 5080
so the *f* of wrath bringeth forth ... Prov 30:33 4330

FORD {1}
sons, and passed over the *f* Jabbok ... Gen 32:22 4569

FORDS {3}
them the way to Jordan unto the *f* ... Josh 2:7 4569
took the *f* of Jordan toward Moab, ... Judg 3:28 4569
Moab shall be at the *f* of Arnon ... Is 16:2 4569

FORECAST {2}
he shall *f* his devices against ... Dan 11:24 2803
for they shall *f* devices against ... Dan 11:25 2803

FOREFATHERS {2}
back to the iniquities of their *f* ... Jer 11:10
from my *f* with pure conscience ... 2Ti 1:3 *4269*

FOREFRONT {10}
in the *f* of the tabernacle ... Ex 26:9 4136,6640
upon the *f* of the mitre it shall ... Ex 28:37 4136,6640
upon the mitre, even upon his *f* ... Lev 8:9 4136,6640
The *f* of the one was situate ... 1Sa 14:5 8127
Set ye Uriah in the *f* of the ... 2Sa 11:15 4136,6440
from the *f* of the house, from ... 2Kin 16:14 6440
and Jehoshaphat in the *f* of them ... 2Chr 20:27 7218
the *f* of the lower gate unto the ... Eze 40:19 6440
the *f* of the inner court without ... Eze 40:19 6440
for the *f* of the house stood ... Eze 47:1 6440

FOREHEAD {16}
And it shall be upon Aaron's *f* ... Ex 28:38 4696
and it shall be always upon his *f* ... Ex 28:38 4696
toward his face, he is *f* bald ... Lev 13:41 1371
be in the bald head, or bald *f* ... Lev 13:42 1372
in his bald head, or his bald *f* ... Lev 13:42 1372
his bald head, or in his bald *f* ... Lev 13:43 1372
and smote the Philistine in his *f* ... 1Sa 17:49 4696
that the stone sunk into his *f* ... 1Sa 17:49 4696
f before the priests in the house ... 2Chr 26:19 4696
behold, he was leprous in his *f* ... 2Chr 26:20 4696
and thou hadst a whore's *f* ... Jer 3:3 4696
thy *f* strong against their ... Eze 3:8 4696
than flint have I made thy *f* ... Eze 3:9 4696
And I put a jewel on thy *f* ... Eze 16:12 639
and receive his mark in his *f* ... Rev 14:9 *3359*
upon her *f* was a name written, ... Rev 17:5 *3359*

FOREHEADS {8}
forehead strong against their *f* ... Eze 3:8 4696
set a mark upon the *f* of the men ... Eze 9:4 4696
servants of our God in their *f* ... Rev 7:3 *3359*
not the seal of God in their *f* ... Rev 9:4 *3359*
their right hand, or in their *f* ... Rev 13:16 *3359*
Father's name written in their *f* ... Rev 14:1 *3359*
received his mark upon their *f* ... Rev 20:4 *3359*
and his name shall be in their *f* ... Rev 22:4 *3359*

FOREIGNER {2}
A *f* and an hired servant shall not ... Ex 12:45 8453
Of a *f* thou mayest exact it again ... Deut 15:3 5237

FOREIGNERS {2}
f entered into his gates, and cast ... Obad 11 5237
ye are no more strangers and *f* ... Eph 2:19 *3941*

FOREKNEW {1}
cast away his people which he *f* ... Rom 11:2 *4267*

FOREKNOW {1}
For whom he did *f*, he also did ... Rom 8:29 *4267*

FOREKNOWLEDGE {2}
f of God, ye have taken, and by ... Acts 2:23 *4268*
to the *f* of God the Father ... 1Pet 1:2 *4268*

FOREMOST See APPENDIX.

FOREORDAINED {1}
Who verily was *f* before the ... 1Pet 1:20 *4267*

FOREPART {5}
underneath, toward the *f* thereof ... Ex 28:27 6440
underneath, toward the *f* of it ... Ex 39:20 6440
the oracle in the *f* was twenty ... 1Kin 6:20 6440
court on the *f* of the chambers ... Eze 42:7 6440
the *f* stuck fast, and remained ... Acts 27:41 *4408*

FORERUNNER {1}
Whither the *f* is for us entered, ... Heb 6:20 *4274*

FORESAW {1}
I *f* the Lord always before my ... Acts 2:25 *4308*

FORESEEING {1}
f that God would justify the ... Gal 3:8 *4375*

FORESEETH {2}
A prudent man *f* the evil, and ... Prov 22:3 7200
A prudent man *f* the evil, and ... Prov 27:12 7200

FORESHIP {1}
have cast anchors out of the *f* ... Acts 27:30 *4408*

FORESKIN {9}
circumcise the flesh of your *f* ... Gen 17:11 6190
flesh of his *f* is not circumcised ... Gen 17:14 6190
of their *f* in the selfsame day ... Gen 17:23 6190
circumcised in the flesh of his *f* ... Gen 17:24 6190
circumcised in the flesh of his *f* ... Gen 17:25 6190
and cut off the *f* of her son ... Ex 4:25 6190
of his *f* shall be circumcised ... Lev 12:3 6190
therefore the *f* of your heart ... Deut 10:16 6190
also, and let thy *f* be uncovered ... Hab 2:16 6188

FORESKINS {5}
of Israel at the hill of the *f* ... Josh 5:3 6190
dowry, but an hundred *f* of the ... 1Sa 18:25 6190
and David brought their *f*, and they ... 1Sa 18:27 6190
an hundred *f* of the Philistines ... 2Sa 3:14 6190
and take away the *f* of your heart ... Jer 4:4 6190

FOREST {38}
and came into the *f* of Hareth ... 1Sa 22:5 3293
the house of the *f* of Lebanon ... 1Kin 7:2 3293
in the house of the *f* of Lebanon ... 1Kin 10:17 3293
f of Lebanon were of pure gold ... 1Kin 10:21 3293
and into the *f* of his Carmel ... 2Kin 19:23 3293
in the house of the *f* of Lebanon ... 2Chr 9:16 3293
f of Lebanon were of pure gold ... 2Chr 9:20 3293
Asaph the keeper of the king's *f* ... Neh 2:8 6508
For every beast of the *f* is mine ... Ps 50:10 3293
beasts of the *f* do creep forth ... Ps 104:20 3293
kindle in the thickets of the *f* ... Is 9:18 3293
shall consume the glory of his *f* ... Is 10:18 3293
the trees of his *f* shall be few ... Is 10:19 3293
the thickets of the *f* with iron ... Is 10:34 3293
In the *f* in Arabia shall ye lodge ... Is 21:13 3293
the armour of the house of the *f* ... Is 22:8 3293
field shall be esteemed as a *f* ... Is 29:17 3293
fruitful field be counted for a *f* ... Is 32:15 3293
shall hail, coming down on the *f* ... Is 32:19 3293
border, and the *f* of his Carmel ... Is 37:24 3293
himself among the trees of the *f* ... Is 44:14 3293
into singing, ye mountains, O *f* ... Is 44:23 3293
yea, all ye beasts in the *f* ... Is 56:9 3293
lion out of the *f* shall slay them ... Jer 5:6 3293
one cutteth a tree out of the *f* ... Jer 10:3 3293
is unto me as a lion in the *f* ... Jer 12:8 3293
kindle a fire in the *f* thereof ... Jer 21:14 3293
house as the high places of a *f* ... Jer 26:18 3293
They shall cut down her *f* ... Jer 46:23 3293
which is among the trees of the *f* ... Eze 15:2 3293
tree among the trees of the *f* ... Eze 15:6 3293
against the *f* of the south field ... Eze 20:46 3293
say to the *f* of the south, Hear ... Eze 20:47 3293
and I will make them a *f*, and the ... Hos 2:12 3293
Will a lion roar in the *f* ... Amos 3:4 3293
house as the high places of the *f* ... Mic 3:12 3293
a lion among the beasts of the *f* ... Mic 5:8 3293
for the *f* of the vintage is come ... Zec 11:2 3293

FORESTS {3}
in the *f* he built castles and ... 2Chr 27:4 2793
to calve, and discovereth the *f*. ... Ps 29:9 3295
neither cut down any out of the *f*. ... Eze 39:10 3293

FORETELL {1}
f you, as if I were present, the ... 2Cor 13:2 *4302*

FORETOLD {2}
behold, I have *f* you all things ... Mk 13:23 *4280*
have likewise *f* of these days ... Acts 3:24 *4293*

FOREWARN {1}
But I will *f* you whom ye shall ... Lk 12:5 *5263*

FOREWARNED {1}
all such, as we also have *f* you ... 1Th 4:6 *4277*

FORFEITED {1}
all his substance should be *f* ... Ezr 10:8 2763

FORGAT {8}
butler remember Joseph, but *f* him ... Gen 40:23 7911
f the LORD their God, and served ... Judg 3:7 7911
when they *f* the LORD their God, ... 1Sa 12:9 7911
f his works, and his wonders that ... Ps 78:11 7911
They soon *f* his works ... Ps 106:13 7911
They *f* God their saviour, which ... Ps 106:21 7911
I *f* prosperity ... Lam 3:17 5382
lovers, and *f* me, saith the LORD ... Hos 2:13 7911

FORGAVE {9}
f their iniquity, and destroyed ... Ps 78:38 3722
and loosed him, and *f* him the debt ... Mt 18:27 *863*
I *f* thee all that debt, because ... Mt 18:32 *863*
to pay, he frankly *f* them both ... Lk 7:42 *5483*
that he, to whom he *f* most ... Lk 7:43 *5483*
f any thing, to whom I *f* it ... 2Cor 2:10 *5483*
for your sakes *f* I it in the ... 2Cor 2:10
even as Christ *f* you, so also do ... Col 3:13 *5483*

FORGAVEST {2}
thou *f* the iniquity of my sin ... Ps 32:5 5375
thou wast a God that *f* them ... Ps 99:8 5375

FORGED {1}
The proud have *f* a lie against me ... Ps 119:69 2950

FORGERS {1}
But ye are *f* of lies, ye are all ... Job 13:4 2950

FORGET {55}
he *f* that which thou hast done to ... Gen 27:45 7911
he, hath made me *f* all my toil ... Gen 41:51 5382
lest thou *f* the things which ... Deut 4:9 7911
lest ye *f* the covenant of the ... Deut 4:23 7911
nor *f* the covenant of thy fathers ... Deut 4:31 7911
Then beware lest thou *f* the LORD ... Deut 6:12 7911
Beware that thou *f* not the LORD ... Deut 8:11 7911
thou *f* the LORD thy God, which ... Deut 8:14 7911
thou do at all *f* the LORD thy God ... Deut 8:19 7911
f not, how thou provokedst the ... Deut 9:7 7911
thou shalt not *f* it ... Deut 25:19 7911
not *f* thine handmaid, but wilt ... 1Sa 1:11 7911
have made with you ye shall not *f* ... 2Kin 17:38 7911
are the paths of all that *f* God ... Job 8:13 7911
I will *f* my complaint, I will ... Job 9:27 7911
Because thou shalt *f* thy misery ... Job 11:16 7911
The womb shall *f* him ... Job 24:20 7911
and all the nations that *f* God ... Ps 9:17 7913
f not the humble ... Ps 10:12 7911
How long wilt thou *f* me, O LORD ... Ps 13:1 7911
f also thine own people, and thy ... Ps 45:10 7911
Now consider this, ye that *f* God ... Ps 50:22 7911
Slay them not, lest my people *f* ... Ps 59:11 7911
f not the congregation of thy ... Ps 74:19 7911
F not the voice of thine enemies ... Ps 74:23 7911
not *f* the works of God, but keep ... Ps 78:7 7911
so that I *f* to eat my bread ... Ps 102:4 7911
soul, and *f* not all his benefits ... Ps 103:2 7911
I will not *f* thy word ... Ps 119:16 7911
yet do I not *f* thy statutes ... Ps 119:83 7911
I will never *f* thy precepts ... Ps 119:93 7911
yet do I not *f* thy law ... Ps 119:109 7911
yet do not I *f* thy precepts ... Ps 119:141 7911
for I do not *f* thy law ... Ps 119:153 7911
for I do not *f* thy commandments ... Ps 119:176 7911
If I *f* thee, O Jerusalem ... Ps 137:5 7911
let my right hand *f* her cunning ... Ps 137:5 7911
My son, *f* not my law ... Prov 3:1 7911
get understanding: *f* it not ... Prov 4:5 7911
f the law, and pervert the ... Prov 31:5 7911
f his poverty, and remember his ... Prov 31:7 7911
Can a woman *f* her sucking child, ... Is 49:15 7911
yea, they may *f*, yet will I not ... Is 49:15 7911
may *f*, yet will I not *f* thee ... Is 49:15 7911
for thou shalt *f* the shame of thy ... Is 54:4 7911
that *f* my holy mountain, that ... Is 65:11 7913
Can a maid *f* her ornaments, or a ... Jer 2:32 7911
think to cause my people to *f* my ... Jer 23:27 7911
I, even I, will utterly *f* you ... Jer 23:39 5382
Wherefore dost thou *f* us for ever ... Lam 5:20 7911
I will also *f* thy children ... Hos 4:6 7911
I will never *f* any of their works ... Amos 8:7 7911
is not unrighteous to *f* your work ... Heb 6:10 *1950*
do good and to communicate *f* not ... Heb 13:16 *1950*

FORGETFUL {2}
Be not *f* to entertain strangers ... Heb 13:2 *1950*
therein, he being not a *f* hearer ... Jas 1:25 *1953*

FORGETFULNESS {1}
righteousness in the land of *f* ... Ps 88:12 5388

FORGETTEST {2}
face, and *f* our affliction and our ... Ps 44:24 7911
f the LORD thy maker, that hath ... Is 51:13 7911

FORGETTETH {4}
f that the foot may crush them, ... Job 39:15 7911
he *f* not the cry of the humble ... Ps 9:12 7911
f the covenant of her God ... Prov 2:17 7913
straightway *f* what manner of man ... Jas 1:24 *1950*

FORGETTING {1}
f those things which are behind, ... Phil 3:13 *1950*

FORGIVE {56}
So shall ye say unto Joseph, *F* ... Gen 50:17 5375
f the trespass of the servants of ... Gen 50:17 5375
Now therefore *f*, I pray thee, my ... Ex 10:17 5375
Yet now, if thou wilt *f* their sin ... Ex 32:32 5375
and the LORD shall *f* her, because ... Num 30:5 5545
and the LORD shall *f* her ... Num 30:8 5545
and the LORD shall *f* her ... Num 30:12 5545
he will not *f* your transgressions ... Josh 24:19 5375
f the trespass of thine handmaid ... 1Sa 25:28 5375
and when thou hearest, *f* ... 1Kin 8:30 5545
f the sin of thy people Israel, ... 1Kin 8:34 5545
f the sin of thy servants, and of ... 1Kin 8:36 5545
heaven thy dwelling place, and *f* ... 1Kin 8:39 5545
f thy people that have sinned ... 1Kin 8:50 5545
and when thou hearest, *f* ... 2Chr 6:21 5545
f the sin of thy people Israel, ... 2Chr 6:25 5545
f the sin of thy servants, and of ... 2Chr 6:27 5545
heaven thy dwelling place, and *f* ... 2Chr 6:30 5545
f thy people which have sinned ... 2Chr 6:39 5545
will *f* their sin, and will heal ... 2Chr 7:14 5545
and *f* all my sins ... Ps 25:18 5375
Lord, art good, and ready to *f* ... Ps 86:5 5546
therefore *f* them not ... Is 2:9 5375
f not their iniquity, neither ... Jer 18:23 3722
for I will *f* their iniquity, and I ... Jer 31:34 5545
that I may *f* their iniquity and ... Jer 36:3 5545
O Lord, hear; O Lord, *f* ... Dan 9:19 5545
land, then I said, O Lord GOD, *f* ... Amos 7:2 5545
f us our debts, as we *f* our ... Mt 6:12 *863*
For if ye *f* men their trespasses, ... Mt 6:14 *863*
heavenly Father will also *f* you ... Mt 6:14 *863*
But if ye *f* not men their ... Mt 6:15 *863*
your Father *f* your trespasses ... Mt 6:15 *863*
man hath power on earth to *f* sins ... Mt 9:6 *863*
sin against me, and I *f* him ... Mt 18:21 *863*
If ye from your hearts *f* not ... Mt 18:35 *863*
who can *f* sins but God only ... Mk 2:7 *863*
man hath power on earth to *f* sins ... Mk 2:10 *863*
And when ye stand praying, *f* ... Mk 11:25 *863*
heaven may *f* you your trespasses ... Mk 11:25 *863*
But if ye do not *f*, neither will ... Mk 11:26 *863*
is in heaven *f* your trespasses ... Mk 11:26 *863*
Who can *f* sins, but God alone ... Lk 5:21 *863*
hath power upon earth to *f* sins ... Lk 5:24 *863*
f, and ye shall be forgiven ... Lk 6:37 *630*
And *f* us our sins ... Lk 11:4 *863*
for we also *f* every one that is ... Lk 11:4 *863*
and if he repent, *f* him ... Lk 17:3 *863*
thou shalt *f* him ... Lk 17:4 *863*
Then said Jesus, Father, *f* them ... Lk 23:34 *863*
ye ought rather to *f* him, and ... 2Cor 2:7 *5483*
ye *f* any thing, I *f* also ... 2Cor 2:10 *5483*
f me this wrong ... 2Cor 12:13 *5483*
just to *f* us our sins, and to ... 1Jn 1:9 *863*

FORGIVEN {42}
for them, and it shall be *f* them ... Lev 4:20 5545
his sin, and it shall be *f* him ... Lev 4:26 5545
for him, and it shall be *f* him ... Lev 4:31 5545
committed, and it shall be *f* him ... Lev 4:35 5545
hath sinned, and it shall be *f* him ... Lev 5:10 5545
of these, and it shall be *f* him ... Lev 5:13 5545
offering, and it shall be *f* him ... Lev 5:16 5545
wist it not, and it shall be *f* him ... Lev 5:18 5545
it shall be *f* him for any thing ... Lev 6:7 5545
which he hath done shall be *f* him ... Lev 19:22 5545
and as thou hast *f* this people ... Num 14:19 5375
of Israel, and it shall be *f* them ... Num 15:25 5545
And it shall be *f* all the ... Num 15:26 5545
and it shall be *f* him ... Num 15:28 5545
And the blood shall be *f* them ... Deut 21:8 3722
is he whose transgression is *f* ... Ps 32:1 5375
Thou hast *f* the iniquity of thy ... Ps 85:2 5375
therein shall be *f* their iniquity ... Is 33:24 5375
thy sins be *f* thee ... Mt 9:2 *863*
to say, Thy sins be *f* thee ... Mt 9:5 *863*
and blasphemy shall be *f* unto men ... Mt 12:31 *863*
Ghost shall not be *f* unto men ... Mt 12:31 *863*
the Son of man, it shall be *f* him ... Mt 12:32 *863*
Holy Ghost, it shall not be *f* him ... Mt 12:32 *863*
palsy, Son, thy sins be *f* thee ... Mk 2:5 *863*
of the palsy, Thy sins be *f* thee ... Mk 2:9 *863*
All sins shall be *f* unto the sons ... Mk 3:28 *863*
and their sins should be *f* them ... Mk 4:12 *863*
him, Man, thy sins are *f* thee ... Lk 5:20 *863*
to say, Thy sins be *f* thee ... Lk 5:23 *863*
forgive, and ye shall be *f* ... Lk 6:37 *630*
Her sins, which are many, are *f* ... Lk 7:47 *863*
but to whom little is *f*, the same ... Lk 7:47 *863*
he said unto her, Thy sins are *f* ... Lk 7:48 *863*
the Son of man, it shall be *f* him ... Lk 12:10 *863*
the Holy Ghost it shall not be *f* ... Lk 12:10 *863*
of thine heart may be *f* thee ... Acts 8:22 *863*
are they whose iniquities are *f* ... Rom 4:7 *863*
God for Christ's sake hath *f* you ... Eph 4:32 *5483*
having *f* you all trespasses ... Col 2:13 *5483*
sins, they shall be *f* him ... Jas 5:15 *863*
because your sins are *f* you for ... 1Jn 2:12 *863*

FORGIVENESS {7}
But there is *f* with thee, that ... Ps 130:4 5547
the Holy Ghost hath never *f* ... Mk 3:29 *859*
to Israel, and *f* of sins ... Acts 5:31 *859*
preached unto you the *f* of sins ... Acts 13:38 *859*
that they may receive *f* of sins ... Acts 26:18 *859*
the *f* of sins, according to the ... Eph 1:7 *859*
his blood, even the *f* of sins ... Col 1:14 *859*

FORGIVENESSES {1}
Lord our God belong mercies and *f* ... Dan 9:9 5547

FORGIVETH {2}
Who *f* all thine iniquities ... Ps 103:3 5545
Who is this that *f* sins also ... Lk 7:49 *863*

FORGIVING {4}
f iniquity and transgression and ... Ex 34:7 5375
f iniquity and transgression, and ... Num 14:18 5375
f one another, even as God for ... Eph 4:32 *5483*
f one another, if any man have a ... Col 3:13 *5483*

FORGOT {1}
hast *f* a sheaf in the field, thou ... Deut 24:19 7911

F

FORGOTTEN {46}
shall be *f* in the land of Egypt ... Gen 41:30 7911
neither have I *f* them ... Deut 26:13 7911
for it shall not be *f* out of the ... Deut 31:21 7911
hast *f* God that formed thee ... Deut 32:18 7911
and my familiar friends have *f* me ... Job 19:14 7911
even the waters *f* of the foot ... Job 28:4 7911
the needy shall not alway be *f* ... Ps 9:18 7911
said in his heart, God hath *f* ... Ps 10:11 7911
I am *f* as a dead man out of mind ... Ps 31:12 7911
God my rock, Why hast thou *f* me ... Ps 42:9 7911
yet have we not *f* thee, neither ... Ps 44:17 7911
If we have *f* the name of our God, ... Ps 44:20 7911
Hath God *f* to be gracious ... Ps 77:9 7911
but I have not *f* thy law ... Ps 119:61 7911
mine enemies have *f* thy words ... Ps 119:139 7911
the days to come shall all be *f* ... Eccl 2:16 7911
they were *f* in the city where ... Eccl 8:10 7911
for the memory of them is *f* ... Eccl 9:5 7911
Because thou hast *f* the God of ... Is 17:10 7911
Tyre shall be *f* seventy years ... Is 23:15 7911
thou harlot that hast been *f* ... Is 23:16 7911
Israel, thou shalt not be *f* of me ... Is 44:21 5382
forsaken me, and my Lord hath *f* me ... Is 49:14 7913
because the former troubles are *f* ... Is 65:16 7911
yet my people have *f* me days ... Jer 2:32 7911
they have *f* the LORD their God ... Jer 3:21 7911
because thou hast *f* me, and ... Jer 13:25 7911
Because my people hath *f* me ... Jer 18:15 7911
confusion shall never be *f* ... Jer 20:11 7911
fathers have *f* my name for Baal ... Jer 23:27 7911
shame, which shall not be *f* ... Jer 23:40 7911
All thy lovers have *f* thee ... Jer 30:14 7911
Have ye *f* the wickedness of your ... Jer 44:9 7911
covenant that shall not be *f* ... Jer 50:5 7911
they have *f* their restingplace ... Jer 50:6 7911
and sabbaths to be *f* in Zion ... Lam 2:6 7911
by extortion, and hast *f* me ... Eze 22:12 7911
Because thou hast *f* me, and cast ... Eze 23:35 7911
seeing thou hast *f* the law of thy ... Hos 4:6 7911
For Israel hath *f* his Maker ... Hos 8:14 7911
therefore have they *f* me ... Hos 13:6 7911
side, they had *f* to take bread ... Mt 16:5 *1950*
the disciples had *f* to take bread ... Mk 8:14 *1950*
not one of them is *f* before God ... Lk 12:6 *1950*
ye have *f* the exhortation which ... Heb 12:5 *1585*
hath *f* that he was purged from ... 2Pet 1:9 *3024,2983*

FORKS {1}
and for the coulters, and for the *f* ... 1Sa 13:21 7969,7053

FORM {24}
And the earth was without *f* ... Gen 1:2 8414
he said unto her, What *f* is he of ... 1Sa 28:14 8389
To fetch about this *f* of speech ... 2Sa 14:20 6440
of gold according to their *f* ... 2Chr 4:7 4941
I could not discern the *f* thereof ... Job 4:16 4758
I *f* the light, and create darkness ... Is 45:7 3335
his *f* more than the sons of men ... Is 52:14 8389
he hath no *f* nor comeliness ... Is 53:2 8389
earth, and, lo, it was without *f* ... Jer 4:23 8414
And he put forth the *f* of an hand ... Eze 8:3 8403
behold every *f* of creeping things ... Eze 8:10 8403
the *f* of a man's hand under their ... Eze 10:8 8403
shew them the *f* of the house ... Eze 43:11 6699
they may keep the whole *f* thereof ... Eze 43:11 6699
the *f* thereof was terrible ... Dan 2:31 7299
the *f* of his visage was changed ... Dan 3:19 6755
the *f* of the fourth is like the ... Dan 3:25 7299
in another *f* unto two of them ... Mk 16:12 *3444*
which hast the *f* of knowledge ... Rom 2:20 *3446*
f of doctrine which was delivered ... Rom 6:17 *5179*
Who, being in the *f* of God ... Phil 2:6 *3444*
took upon him the *f* of a servant ... Phil 2:7 *3444*
Hold fast the *f* of sound words, ... 2Ti 1:13 *5296*
Having a *f* of godliness, but ... 2Ti 3:5 *3446*

FORMED {34}
the LORD God *f* man of the dust of ... Gen 2:7 3335
he put the man whom he had *f* ... Gen 2:8 3335
God *f* every beast of the field ... Gen 2:19 3335
and hast forgotten God that *f* thee ... Deut 32:18 2342
of ancient times that I have *f* it ... 2Kin 19:25 3335
Dead things are *f* from under the ... Job 26:5 2342
his hand hath *f* the crooked ... Job 26:13 2342
I also am *f* out of the clay ... Job 33:6 7169
or ever thou hadst *f* the earth ... Ps 90:2 2342
he that *f* the eye, shall he not ... Ps 94:9 3335

and his hands *f* the dry land ... Ps 95:5 3335
The great God that *f* all things ... Prov 26:10 2342
he that *f* them will shew them no ... Is 27:11 3335
ancient times, that I have *f* it ... Is 37:26 3335
thee, O Jacob, and he that *f* thee ... Is 43:1 3335
him for my glory, I have *f* him ... Is 43:7 3335
before me there was no God *f* ... Is 43:10 3335
This people have I *f* for myself ... Is 43:21 3335
f thee from the womb, which will ... Is 44:2 3335
Who hath *f* a god, or molten a ... Is 44:10 3335
I have *f* thee ... Is 44:21 3335
he that *f* thee from the womb, I ... Is 44:24 3335
God himself that *f* the earth ... Is 45:18 3335
in vain, he *f* it to be inhabited ... Is 45:18 3335
saith the LORD that *f* me from the ... Is 49:5 3335
No weapon that is *f* against thee ... Is 54:17 3335
Before I *f* thee in the belly I ... Jer 1:5 3335
maker thereof, the LORD that *f* it ... Jer 33:2 3335
behold, he *f* grasshoppers in the ... Amos 7:1 3335
Shall the thing *f* say to him that ... Rom 9:20 *4110*
thing *f* say to him that *f* it ... Rom 9:20 *4110*
again until Christ be *f* in you ... Gal 4:19 *3445*
For Adam was first *f*, then Eve ... 1Ti 2:13 *4111*

FORMER {50}
after the *f* manner when thou wast ... Gen 40:13 7223
fought against the *f* king of Moab ... Num 21:26 7223
Her *f* husband, which sent her ... Deut 24:4 7223
in *f* time in Israel concerning ... Ruth 4:7 6440
him again after the *f* manner ... 1Sa 17:30 7223
the *f* fifties with their fifties ... 2Kin 1:14 7223
day they do after the *f* manners ... 2Kin 17:34 7223
but they did after their *f* manner ... 2Kin 17:40 7223
But the *f* governors that had been ... Neh 5:15 7223
I pray thee, of the *f* age ... Job 8:8 7223
the wilderness in *f* time desolate ... Job 30:3 570
not against us *f* iniquities ... Ps 79:8 7223
where are thy *f* lovingkindnesses, ... Ps 89:49 7223
is no remembrance of *f* things ... Eccl 1:11 7223
What is the cause that the *f* days ... Eccl 7:10 7223
let them shew the *f* things ... Is 41:22 7223
the *f* things are come to pass, and ... Is 42:9 7223
declare this, and shew us *f* things ... Is 43:9 7223
Remember ye not the *f* things ... Is 43:18 7223
Remember the *f* things of old ... Is 46:9 7223
I have declared the *f* things from ... Is 48:3 7223
shall raise up the *f* desolations ... Is 61:4 7223
their *f* work into their bosom ... Is 65:7 7223
because the *f* troubles are ... Is 65:16 7223
the *f* shall not be remembered, ... Is 65:17 7223
God, that giveth rain, both the *f* ... Jer 5:24 3138
for he is the *f* of all things ... Jer 10:16 3335
the *f* kings which were before ... Jer 34:5 7223
write in it all the *f* words that ... Jer 36:28 7223
for he is the *f* of all things ... Jer 51:19 3335
shall return to their *f* estate ... Eze 16:55 6927
shall return to their *f* estate ... Eze 16:55 6927
shall return to your *f* estate ... Eze 16:55 6927
a multitude greater than the *f* ... Dan 11:13 7223
but it shall not be as the *f* ... Dan 11:29 7223
latter and *f* rain unto the earth ... Hos 6:3 3138
given you the *f* rain moderately ... Joel 2:23 4175
the *f* rain, and the latter rain in ... Joel 2:23 4175
shall be greater than of the *f* ... Hag 2:9 7223
unto whom the *f* prophets have ... Zec 1:4 7223
LORD hath cried by the *f* prophets ... Zec 7:7 7223
in his spirit by the *f* prophets ... Zec 7:12 7223
of this people as in the *f* days ... Zec 8:11 7223
half of them toward the *f* sea ... Zec 14:8 6931
the days of old, and as in *f* years ... Mal 3:4 6931
The *f* treatise have I made, O ... Acts 1:1 *4413*
the *f* conversation the old man ... Eph 4:22 *4387*
call to remembrance the *f* days ... Heb 10:32 *4386*
to the *f* lusts in your ignorance ... 1Pet 1:14 *4386*
for the *f* things are passed away ... Rev 21:4 *4413*

FORMETH {2}
he that *f* the mountains, and ... Amos 4:13 3335
f the spirit of man within him ... Zec 12:1 3335

FORMS {2}
in thereof, and all the *f* thereof ... Eze 43:11 6699
thereof, and all the *f* thereof ... Eze 43:11 6699

FORNICATION {36}
of Jerusalem to commit *f*, and ... 2Chr 21:11 2181
shall commit *f* with all the ... Is 23:17 2181
f with the Egyptians thy ... Eze 16:26 2181
thy *f* in the land of Canaan unto ... Eze 16:29 8457
wife, saving for the cause of *f* ... Mt 5:32 *4202*
away his wife, except it be for *f* ... Mt 19:9 *4202*
they to him, We be not born of *f* ... Jn 8:41 *4202*
pollutions of idols, and from *f* ... Acts 15:20 *4202*
from things strangled, and from *f* ... Acts 15:29 *4202*
and from strangled, and from *f* ... Acts 21:25 *4202*
with all unrighteousness, *f* ... Rom 1:29 *4202*
that there is *f* among you ... 1Cor 5:1 *4202*
such *f* as is not so much as named ... 1Cor 5:1 *4202*
Now the body is not for *f* ... 1Cor 6:13 *4202*
Flee *f*. Every sin that ... 1Cor 6:18 *4202*
but he that committeth *f* sinneth ... 1Cor 6:18 *4203*
Nevertheless, to avoid *f*, let ... 1Cor 7:2 *4202*
Neither let us commit *f*, as some ... 1Cor 10:8 *4203*
repented of the uncleanness and *f* ... 2Cor 12:21 *4202*
Adultery, *f*, uncleanness, ... Gal 5:19 *4202*
But *f*, and all uncleanness, or ... Eph 5:3 *4202*
f, uncleanness, inordinate ... Col 3:5 *4202*
that ye should abstain from *f* ... 1Th 4:3 *4202*
giving themselves over to *f* ... Jude 7 *1608*
unto idols, and to commit *f* ... Rev 2:14 *4203*
to seduce my servants to commit *f* ... Rev 2:20 *4203*
gave her space to repent of her *f* ... Rev 2:21 *4202*
their sorceries, nor of their *f* ... Rev 9:21 *4202*
of the wine of the wrath of her *f* ... Rev 14:8 *4202*
of the earth have committed *f* ... Rev 17:2 *4203*
made drunk with the wine of her *f* ... Rev 17:2 *4202*
and filthiness of her *f* ... Rev 17:4 *4202*
of the wine of the wrath of her *f* ... Rev 18:3 *4202*
earth have committed *f* with her ... Rev 18:3 *4203*
the earth, who have committed *f* ... Rev 18:9 *4203*
did corrupt the earth with her *f* ... Rev 19:2 *4202*

FORNICATIONS {3}
pouredst out thy *f* on every one ... Eze 16:15 8457
thoughts, murders, adulteries, *f* ... Mt 15:19 *4202*
evil thoughts, adulteries, *f* ... Mk 7:21 *4202*

FORNICATOR {2}
that is called a brother be a *f* ... 1Cor 5:11 *4205*
Lest there be any *f*, or profane ... Heb 12:16 *4205*

FORNICATORS {3}
an epistle not to company with *f* ... 1Cor 5:9 *4205*
with the *f* of this world, or with ... 1Cor 5:10 *4205*
neither *f*, nor idolaters, nor ... 1Cor 6:9 *4205*

FORSAKE {58}
he will not *f* thee, neither ... Deut 4:31 7503
f not the Levite as long as thou ... Deut 12:19 5800
thou shalt not *f* him ... Deut 14:27 5800
he will not fail thee, nor *f* thee ... Deut 31:6 5800
not fail thee, neither *f* thee ... Deut 31:8 5800
go to be among them, and will *f* me ... Deut 31:16 5800
in that day, and I will *f* them ... Deut 31:17 5800
I will not fail thee, nor *f* thee ... Josh 1:5 5800
forbid that we should *f* the LORD ... Josh 24:16 5800
If ye *f* the LORD, and serve ... Josh 24:20 5800
Should I *f* my sweetness, and my ... Judg 9:11 2308
For the LORD will not *f* his ... 1Sa 12:22 5203
will not *f* my people Israel ... 1Kin 6:13 5800
let him not leave us, nor *f* us ... 1Kin 8:57 5203
I will *f* the remnant of mine ... 2Kin 21:14 5203
but if thou *f* him, he will cast ... 1Chr 28:9 5800
nor *f* thee, until thou hast ... 1Chr 28:20 5800
f my statutes and my commandments, ... 2Chr 7:19 5800
if ye *f* him, he will *f* you ... 2Chr 15:2 5800
is against all them that *f* him ... Ezr 8:22 5800
utterly consume them, nor *f* them ... Neh 9:31 5800
we will not *f* the house of our ... Neh 10:39 5800
f it not, but keep it still ... Job 20:13 5800
leave me not, neither *f* me ... Ps 27:9 5800
When my father and my mother *f* me ... Ps 27:10 5800
Cease from anger, and *f* wrath ... Ps 37:8 5800
F me not, O LORD ... Ps 38:21 5800
f me not when my strength faileth ... Ps 71:9 5800
and greyheaded, O God, *f* me not ... Ps 71:18 5800
If his children *f* my law, and walk ... Ps 89:30 5800
neither will he *f* his inheritance ... Ps 94:14 5800
O *f* me not utterly ... Ps 119:8 5800
of the wicked that *f* thy law ... Ps 119:53 5800
f not the works of thine own ... Ps 138:8 7503
f not the law of thy mother ... Prov 1:8 5203
Let not mercy and truth *f* thee ... Prov 3:3 5800
good doctrine, *f* ye not my law ... Prov 4:2 5800
F her not, and she shall preserve ... Prov 4:6 5800
f not the law of thy mother ... Prov 6:20 5203
F the foolish, and live ... Prov 9:6 5800
and thy father's friend, *f* not ... Prov 27:10 5800
They that *f* the law praise the ... Prov 28:4 5800
they that *f* the LORD shall be ... Is 1:28 5800
the God of Israel will not *f* them ... Is 41:17 5800
I do unto them, and not *f* them ... Is 42:16 5800
Let the wicked *f* his way, and the ... Is 55:7 5800
But ye are they that *f* the LORD ... Is 65:11 5800
all that *f* thee shall be ashamed, ... Jer 17:13 5800
I will even *f* you, saith the LORD ... Jer 23:33 5203
forget you, and I will *f* you ... Jer 23:39 5203
f her, and let us go every one ... Jer 51:9 5800
us for ever, and *f* us so long time ... Lam 5:20 5800
neither did they *f* the idols of ... Eze 20:8 5800
them that *f* the holy covenant ... Dan 11:30 5800
lying vanities *f* their own mercy ... Jonah 2:8 5800
are among the Gentiles to *f* Moses .. Acts 21:21 *646,575*
will never leave thee, nor *f* thee ... Heb 13:5 *1459*

FORSAKEN {76}
doings, whereby thou hast *f* me ... Deut 28:20 5800
Because they have *f* the covenant ... Deut 29:25 5800
but now the LORD hath *f* us ... Judg 6:13 5203
both because we have *f* our God ... Judg 10:10 5800
Yet ye have *f* me, and served other ... Judg 10:13 5800
day, wherewith they have *f* me ... 1Sa 8:8 5800
because we have *f* the LORD ... 1Sa 12:10 5800
Because that they have *f* me ... 1Kin 11:33 5800
house, in that ye have *f* the ... 1Kin 18:18 5800
of Israel have *f* thy covenant ... 1Kin 19:10 5800
of Israel have *f* thy covenant ... 1Kin 19:14 5800
Because they have *f* me, and have ... 2Kin 22:17 5800
Thus saith the LORD, Ye have *f* me ... 2Chr 12:5 5800
is our God, and we have not *f* him ... 2Chr 13:10 5800
but ye have *f* him ... 2Chr 13:11 5800
because he had *f* the LORD God of ... 2Chr 21:10 5800
because ye have *f* the LORD ... 2Chr 24:20 5800
he hath also *f* you ... 2Chr 24:20 5800
because they had *f* the LORD God ... 2Chr 24:24 5800
because they had *f* the LORD God ... 2Chr 28:6 5800
the LORD our God, and have *f* him ... 2Chr 29:6 5800
Because they have *f* me, and have ... 2Chr 34:25 5800
God hath not *f* us in our bondage ... Ezr 9:9 5800
for we have *f* thy commandments, ... Ezr 9:10 5800
said, Why is the house of God *f* ... Neh 13:11 5800
shall the earth be *f* for thee ... Job 18:4 5800
hath oppressed and hath *f* the poor ... Job 20:19 5800
hast not *f* them that seek thee ... Ps 9:10 5800
God, my God, why hast thou *f* me ... Ps 22:1 5800
have I not seen the righteous *f* ... Ps 37:25 5800
Saying, God hath *f* him ... Ps 71:11 5800
they have *f* the LORD, they have ... Is 1:4 5800
Therefore thou hast *f* thy people ... Is 2:6 5203
shall be *f* of both her kings ... Is 7:16 5800
The cities of Aroer are *f* ... Is 17:2 5800
his strong cities be as a *f* bough ... Is 17:9 5800
be desolate, and the habitation *f* ... Is 27:10 7971
Because the palaces shall be *f* ... Is 32:14 5203
But Zion said, The LORD hath *f* me ... Is 49:14 5800
hath called thee as a woman *f* ... Is 54:6 5800
For a small moment have I *f* thee ... Is 54:7 5800
Whereas thou hast been *f* and hated ... Is 60:15 5800
Thou shalt no more be termed *F* ... Is 62:4 5800
called, Sought out, A city not *f* ... Is 62:12 5800
their wickedness, who have *f* me ... Jer 1:16 5800
they have *f* me the fountain of ... Jer 2:13 5800
that thou hast *f* the LORD thy God ... Jer 2:17 5800
that thou hast *f* the LORD thy God ... Jer 2:19 5800
every city shall be *f*, and not a ... Jer 4:29 5800
thy children have *f* me, and sworn ... Jer 5:7 5800
answer them, Like as ye have *f* me ... Jer 5:19 5800
f the generation of his wrath ... Jer 7:29 5203
Because they have *f* my law which ... Jer 9:13 5800
because we have *f* the land ... Jer 9:19 5800
I have *f* mine house, I have left ... Jer 12:7 5800
Thou hast *f* me, saith the LORD, ... Jer 15:6 5203
Because your fathers have *f* me ... Jer 16:11 5800
worshipped them, and have *f* me ... Jer 16:11 5800
because they have *f* the LORD ... Jer 17:13 5800
that come from another place be *f* ... Jer 18:14 5428
Because they have *f* me, and have ... Jer 19:4 5800
Because they have *f* the covenant ... Jer 22:9 5800
He hath *f* his covert, as the lion ... Jer 25:38 5800
For Israel hath not been *f* ... Jer 51:5 488
the LORD hath *f* the earth ... Eze 8:12 5800
say, The LORD hath *f* the earth ... Eze 9:9 5800
and to the cities that are *f* ... Eze 36:4 5800
she is *f* upon her land ... Amos 5:2 5203
For Gaza shall be *f*, and Ashkelon ... Zeph 2:4 5800
unto him, Behold, we have *f* all ... Mt 19:27 *863*
And every one that hath *f* houses ... Mt 19:29 *863*
God, my God, why hast thou *f* me ... Mt 27:46 *1459*
God, my God, why hast thou *f* me ... Mk 15:34 *1459*
Persecuted, but not *f* ... 2Cor 4:9 *1459*
For Demas hath *f* me, having loved ... 2Ti 4:10 *1459*
Which have *f* the right way, and ... 2Pet 2:15 *2641*

FORSAKETH {6}
but he *f* the fear of the Almighty ... Job 6:14 5800
judgment, and *f* not his saints ... Ps 37:28 5800
Which *f* the guide of her youth, ... Prov 2:17 5800
grievous unto him that *f* the way ... Prov 15:10 5800
and *f* them shall have mercy ... Prov 28:13 5800
you that *f* not all that he hath ... Lk 14:33 *657*

FORSAKING {2}
there be a great *f* in the midst ... Is 6:12 5805
Not *f* the assembling of ourselves ... Heb 10:25 *1459*

FORSOMUCH {1}
f as he also is a son of Abraham ... Lk 19:9 *2530*

FORSOOK {24}
then he *f* God which made him, and ... Deut 32:15 5203
they *f* the LORD God of their ... Judg 2:12 5800
they *f* the LORD, and served Baal ... Judg 2:13 5800
f the LORD, and served not him ... Judg 10:6 5800
they *f* the cities, and fled ... 1Sa 31:7 5800
Because they *f* the LORD their God ... 1Kin 9:9 5800
But he *f* the counsel of the old ... 1Kin 12:8 5800
f the old men's counsel that they ... 1Kin 12:13 5800
he *f* the LORD God of his fathers, ... 2Kin 21:22 5800
then they *f* their cities, and fled ... 1Chr 10:7 5800
Because they *f* the LORD God of ... 2Chr 7:22 5800
But he *f* the counsel which the ... 2Chr 10:8 5800
king Rehoboam *f* the counsel of ... 2Chr 10:13 5800
he *f* the law of the LORD, and all ... 2Chr 12:1 5800
So that he *f* the tabernacle of ... Ps 78:60 5203
but I *f* not thy precepts ... Ps 119:87 5800
f not the ordinance of their God ... Is 58:2 5800
f it, because there was no grass ... Jer 14:5 5800
Then all the disciples *f* him ... Mt 26:56 *863*
And straightway they *f* their nets ... Mk 1:18 *863*
And they all *f* him, and fled ... Mk 14:50 *863*
their ships to land, they *f* all ... Lk 5:11 *863*
stood with me, but all men *f* me ... 2Ti 4:16 *1459*
By faith he *f* Egypt, not fearing ... Heb 11:27 *2641*

FORSOOKEST {2}
of great kindness, and *f* them not ... Neh 9:17 5800
f them not in the wilderness ... Neh 9:19 5800

FORSWEAR {1}
time, Thou shalt not *f* thyself ... Mt 5:33 *1964*

FORT {6}
So David dwelt in the *f*, and ... 2Sa 5:9 4686
the fortress of the high *f* of thy ... Is 25:12 4869
build a *f* against it, and cast a ... Eze 4:2 1785
to cast a mount, and to build a *f* ... Eze 21:22 1785
and he shall make a *f* against thee ... Eze 26:8 1785
face toward the *f* of his own land ... Dan 11:19 4581

FORTH See APPENDIX.

FORTHWITH {10}
f expences be given unto these ... Ezr 6:8 629
f they sprung up, because they ... Mt 13:5 *2112*
f he came to Jesus, and said, Hail ... Mt 26:49 *2112*

f, when they were come out of the .... Mk 1:29 *2112*
charged him, and *f* sent him away.......... Mk 1:43 *2112*
And *f* Jesus gave them leave .... Mk 5:13 *2112*
f came there out blood and water .... Jn 19:34 *2117*
and he received sight *f*, and arose, ... Acts 9:18 *3916*
f the angel departed from him.............. Acts 12:10 *2112*
and *f* the doors were shut .... Acts 21:30 *2112*

FORTIETH {4}
in the *f* year after the children .... Num 33:38 705
And it came to pass in the *f* year .... Deut 1:3 705
In the *f* year of the reign of 1Chr 26:31 705
in the one and *f* year of his reign 2Chr 16:13 705

FORTIFIED {4}
he *f* the strong holds, and put 2Chr 11:11 2388
turning of the wall, and *f* them 2Chr 26:9 2388
they *f* Jerusalem unto the broad.............. Neh 3:8 5800
Assyria, and from the *f* cities .... Mic 7:12 4692

FORTIFY {6}
they *f* the city against thee .... Judg 9:31 6696
will they *f* themselves .... Neh 4:2 5800
have ye broken down to *f* the wall .... Is 22:10 1219
though she should *f* the height of............ Jer 51:53 1219
strong, *f* thy power mightily .... Nah 2:1 553
for the siege, *f* thy strong holds.............. Nah 3:14 2388

FORTRESS {15}
The LORD is my rock, and my *f* 2Sa 22:2 4686
The LORD is my rock, and my *f* .... Ps 18:2 4686
For thou art my rock and my *f* .... Ps 31:3 4686
me, for thou art my rock and my *f* .... Ps 71:3 4686
the LORD, He is my refuge and my *f*....... Ps 91:2 4686
My goodness, and my *f* .... Ps 144:2 4686
The *f* also shall cease from .... Is 17:3 4013
the *f* of the high fort of thy..................... Is 25:12 4013
a *f* among my people, that thou............... Jer 6:27 4013
the land, O inhabitant of the *f* .... Jer 10:17 4693
O LORD, my strength, and my *f* .... Jer 16:19 4581
shall enter into the *f* of the..................... Dan 11:7 4581
and be stirred up, even to his *f*................ Dan 11:10 4581
spoiled shall come against the *f* .... Amos 5:9 4013
from the *f* even to the river, and............. Mic 7:12 4693

FORTRESSES {2}
and brambles in the *f* thereof.................. Is 34:13 4013
all thy *f* shall be spoiled, as..................... Hos 10:14 4013

FORTS {6}
they built *f* against it round 2Kin 25:1 1785
and I will raise *f* against thee.................. Is 29:3 4694
the *f* and towers shall be for dens .... Is 32:14 6076
built *f* against it round about.................. Jer 52:4 1785
casting up mounts, and building *f* .... Eze 17:17 1785
and they that be in the *f*........................... Eze 33:27 4679

FORTUNATUS *(for-chu-na'-tus)* {2} *A Christian acquaintance of Paul.*
of the coming of Stephanas and *F* 1Cor 16:17 *5415*
from Philippi by Stephanus, and *F*.......... 1Cor *s* *5415*

FORTY {158}
f years, and begat sons and .... Gen 5:13 705
it to rain upon the earth *f* days .... Gen 7:4 705
the earth *f* days and *f* nights.................... Gen 7:4 705
the earth *f* days and *f* nights.................... Gen 7:12 705
the flood was *f* days upon the .... Gen 7:17 705
came to pass at the end of *f* days .... Gen 8:6 705
And he said, If I find there *f* .... Gen 18:28 705
there shall be *f* found there .... Gen 18:29 705
Isaac was *f* years old when he .... Gen 25:20 705
Esau was *f* years old when he took .... Gen 26:34 705
f kine, and ten bulls, twenty she .... Gen 32:15 705
age of Jacob was an hundred *f*.................. Gen 47:28 705
f days were fulfilled for him..................... Gen 50:3 705
of Israel did eat manna *f* years................. Ex 16:35 705
the mount *f* days and *f* nights.................... Ex 24:18 705
thou shalt make *f* sockets of..................... Ex 26:19 705
their *f* sockets of silver .... Ex 26:21 705
the LORD *f* days and *f* nights .... Ex 34:28 705
f sockets of silver he made under .... Ex 36:24 705
their *f* sockets of silver .... Ex 36:26 705
of years shall be unto thee *f*..................... Lev 25:8 705
of the tribe of Reuben, were *f*................... Num 1:21 705
even of the tribe of Gad, were *f*................ Num 1:25 705
were *f* thousand and five hundred............. Num 1:33 705
of the tribe of Asher, were *f*..................... Num 1:41 705
were numbered thereof, were *f*................. Num 2:11 705
were numbered of them, were *f*................. Num 2:15 705
were *f* thousand and five hundred............. Num 2:19 705
were numbered of them, were *f* .... Num 2:28 705
of the land after *f* days .... Num 13:25 705
wander in the wilderness *f* years............... Num 14:33 705
ye searched the land, even *f* days .... Num 14:34 705
even *f* years, and ye shall know my.......... Num 14:34 705
that were numbered of them were *f*......... Num 26:7 705
f thousand and five hundred .... Num 26:18 705
that were numbered of them were *f*......... Num 26:41 705
that were numbered of them were *f*......... Num 26:50 705
wander in the wilderness *f* years............... Num 32:13 705
and to them ye shall add *f*........................ Num 35:6 705
give to the Levites shall be *f*.................... Num 35:7 705
these *f* years the LORD thy God .... Deut 2:7 705
these *f* years in the wilderness .... Deut 8:2 705
did thy foot swell, these *f* years............... Deut 8:4 705
then I abode in the mount *f* days .... Deut 9:9 705
f nights, I neither did eat bread .... Deut 9:9 705
came to pass at the end of *f* days .... Deut 9:11 705
f nights, that the LORD gave me .... Deut 9:11 705
the first, *f* days and *f* nights .... Deut 9:18 705
fell down before the LORD *f* days .... Deut 9:25 705
f nights, as I fell down at the .... Deut 9:25 705
time, *f* days and *f* nights .... Deut 10:10 705
F stripes he may give him, and not .... Deut 25:3 705
I have led you *f* years in the .... Deut 29:5 705
About *f* thousand prepared for war .... Josh 4:13 705
walked *f* years in the wilderness .... Josh 5:6 705
F years old was I when Moses the............. Josh 14:7 705
me alive, as he said, these *f* .... Josh 14:10 705
of the children of Israel were *f*................. Josh 21:41 705
And the land had rest *f* years.................... Judg 3:11 705
seen among *f* thousand in Israel............... Judg 5:8 705
And the land had rest *f* years.................... Judg 5:31 705
f years in the days of Gideon.................... Judg 8:28 705
at that time of the Ephraimites *f* .... Judg 12:6 705
And he had *f* sons and thirty.................... Judg 12:14 705
hand of the Philistines *f* years................... Judg 13:1 705
And he had judged Israel *f* years 1Sa 4:18 705
and presented himself *f* days.................... 1Sa 17:16 705
was *f* years old when he began to 2Sa 2:10 705
to reign, and he reigned *f* years............... 2Sa 5:4 705
f thousand horsemen, and smote.............. 2Sa 10:18 705
And it came to pass after *f* years.............. 2Sa 15:7 705
reigned over Israel were *f* years............... 1Kin 2:11 705
Solomon had *f* thousand stalls of............ 1Kin 4:26 705
before it, was *f* cubits long 1Kin 6:17 705
that lay on *f* five pillars,.......................... 1Kin 7:3 705
one laver contained *f* baths 1Kin 7:38 705
over all Israel was *f* years........................ 1Kin 11:42 705
Rehoboam was *f* and one years old 1Kin 14:21 705
And *f* and one years reigned he in............ 1Kin 15:10 705
the strength of that meat *f* days............... 1Kin 19:8 705
f nights unto Horeb the mount of............. 1Kin 19:8 705
bears out of the wood, and tare *f* 2Kin 2:24 705
f camels' burden, and came and............... 2Kin 8:9 705
shearing house, even two and *f* men 2Kin 10:14 705
f years reigned he in Jerusalem............... 2Kin 12:1 705
to reign in Samaria, and reigned *f* 2Kin 14:23 705
f thousand seven hundred and 1Chr 5:18 705
battle, expert in war, *f* thousand 1Chr 12:36 705
f thousand footmen, and killed 1Chr 19:18 705
reigned over Israel was *f* years 1Chr 29:27 705
Jerusalem over all Israel *f* years.............. 2Chr 9:30 705
f years old when he began to.................... 2Chr 12:13 705
F and two years old was Ahaziah 2Chr 22:2 705
he reigned *f* years in Jerusalem............... 2Chr 24:1 705
children of Zattu, nine hundred *f* .... Ezr 2:8 705
children of Bani, six hundred *f* .... Ezr 2:10 705
The children of Azmaveth, *f* .... Ezr 2:24 705
and Beeroth, seven hundred and *f*........... Ezr 2:25 705
of Jericho, three hundred *f* .... Ezr 2:34 705
Pashur, a thousand two hundred *f* .... Ezr 2:38 705
whole congregation together was *f*.. Ezr 2:64 702,7239
their mules, two hundred *f*........................ Ezr 2:66 705
beside *f* shekels of silver........................... Neh 5:15 705
of Zattu, eight hundred *f*.......................... Neh 7:13 705
children of Binnui, six hundred *f*.............. Neh 7:15 705
The men of Beth-azmaveth, *f*.................... Neh 7:28 705
and Beeroth, seven hundred *f*................... Neh 7:29 705
of Jericho, three hundred *f*....................... Neh 7:36 705
Pashur, a thousand two hundred *f* .... Neh 7:41 705
children of Asaph, an hundred *f* .... Neh 7:44 705
children of Nekoda, six hundred *f*............ Neh 7:62 705
whole congregation together was *f*.. Neh 7:66 702,7239
and they had two hundred *f*...................... Neh 7:67 705
their mules, two hundred *f*....................... Neh 7:68 705
f years didst thou sustain them .... Neh 9:21 705
of the fathers, two hundred *f* .... Neh 11:13 705
f years, and saw his sons, and his............. Job 42:16 705
F years long was I grieved with .... Ps 95:10 705
of the Jews seven hundred *f* .... Jer 52:30 705
of the house of Judah *f* days..................... Eze 4:6 705
shall it be inhabited *f* years...................... Eze 29:11 705
waste shall be desolate *f* years .... Eze 29:12 705
At the end of *f* years will I .... Eze 29:13 705
the length thereof, *f* cubits .... Eze 41:2 705
courts joined of *f* cubits long................... Eze 46:22 705
led you *f* years through the....................... Amos 2:10 705
in the wilderness *f* years........................... Amos 5:25 705
Yet *f* days, and Nineveh shall be .... Jonah 3:4 705
And when he had fasted *f* days .... Mt 4:2 *5062*
f nights, he was afterward an.................... Mt 4:2 *5062*
there in the wilderness *f* days................... Mk 1:13 *5062*
Being *f* days tempted of the devil.............. Lk 4:2 *5062*
Then said the Jews, *F* and six .... Jn 2:20 *5062*
proofs, being seen of them *f* days .... Acts 1:3 *5062*
For the man was above *f* years old............ Acts 4:22 *5062*
And when he was full *f* years old.............. Acts 7:23 *5063*
when *f* years were expired, there .... Acts 7:30 *5062*
sea, and in the wilderness *f* years............. Acts 7:36 *5062*
of *f* years in the wilderness .... Acts 7:42 *5062*
about the time of *f* years .... Acts 13:18 *5063*
Benjamin, by the space of *f* years............. Acts 13:21 *5062*
they were more than *f* which had............. Acts 23:13 *5062*
for him of them more than *f* men .... Acts 23:21 *5062*
received I *f* stripes save one..................... 2Cor 11:24 *5062*
me, and saw my works *f* years.................. Heb 3:9 *5062*
with whom was he grieved *f* years .... Heb 3:17 *5062*
there were sealed an hundred and *f* .... Rev 7:4 *5062*
shall they tread under foot *f*.................... Rev 11:2 *5062*
was given unto him to continue *f*............ Rev 13:5 *5062*
Sion, and with him an hundred *f*............. Rev 14:1 *5062*
that song but the hundred and *f* .... Rev 14:3 *5062*
the wall thereof, an hundred and *f*.......... Rev 21:17 *5062*

FORTY'S {1}
said, I will not do it for *f* sake................. Gen 18:29 705

FORUM {1}
came to meet us as far as Appii *f*............ Acts 28:15 *675*

FORWARD {47}
And the man waxed great, and went *f*.... Gen 26:13 1980
of Israel, that they go *f*............................ Ex 14:15 5265
And when the tabernacle setteth *f*.......... Num 1:51 5265
of the congregation shall set *f*.................. Num 2:17 5265
they encamp, so shall they set *f*............... Num 2:17 5265
they shall go *f* in the third rank .... Num 2:24 5265
their standards, and so they set *f*............. Num 2:34 5265
And when the camp setteth *f* .... Num 4:5 5265
as the camp is to set *f*............................... Num 4:15 5265
lie on the east parts shall go *f* .... Num 10:5 5265
and the sons of Merari set *f*..................... Num 10:17 5265
set *f* according to their armies.................. Num 10:18 5265
And the Kohathites set *f*, bearing .... Num 10:21 5265
set *f* according to their armies................... Num 10:22 5265
camp of the children of Dan set *f*............ Num 10:25 5265
to their armies, when they set *f*............... Num 10:28 5265
came to pass, when the ark set *f* .... Num 10:35 5265
And the children of Israel set *f*............... Num 21:10 5265
And the children of Israel set *f*............... Num 22:1 5265
them on yonder side Jordan, or *f*............. Num 32:19 1973
that was with him, rushed *f* .... Judg 9:44 6584
shalt thou go on *f* from thence 1Sa 10:3 1973
came upon David from that day *f* 1Sa 16:13 4605
eyed David from that day and *f* 1Sa 18:9 1973
And it was so from that day *f*.................. 1Sa 30:25 4605
but they went *f* smiting the 2Kin 3:24
to her servant, Drive, and go *f*................. 2Kin 4:24
shall the shadow go *f* ten degrees............ 2Kin 20:9
four thousand were to set *f* the 1Chr 23:4 5921
of the Kohathites, to set it *f* 2Chr 34:12
to set *f* the work of the house of.............. Ezr 3:8 5921
to set *f* the workmen in the house .... Ezr 3:9 5921
Behold, I go *f*, but he is not...................... Job 23:8 6924
they set *f* my calamity, they have .... Job 30:13 3276
heart, and went backward, and not *f* .... Jer 7:24 6440
they went every one straight *f*................. Eze 1:9 6440
And they went every one straight *f*......... Eze 1:12 6440
they went every one straight *f*................. Eze 10:22 6440
LORD their God from that day and *f*...... Eze 39:22 1973
that upon the eighth day, and so *f*.......... Eze 43:27 1973
they helped *f* the affliction .... Zec 1:15
he went *f* a little, and fell on .... Mk 14:35 *4281*
multitude, the Jews putting him *f*........... Acts 19:33 *4261*
do, but also to be *f* a year ago 2Cor 8:10 *2309*
but being more *f*, of his own 2Cor 8:17 *4707*
the same which I also was *f* to do .... Gal 2:10 *4704*
whom if thou bring *f* on their 3Jn 6 *4311*

FORWARDNESS {2}
by occasion of the *f* of others 2Cor 8:8 *4710*
For I know the *f* of your mind 2Cor 9:2 *4288*

FOUGHT {64}
f with Israel in Rephidim .... Ex 17:8 3898
had said to him, and *f* with Amalek......... Ex 17:10 3898
then he *f* against Israel, and took............. Num 21:1 3898
to Jahaz, and *f* against Israel .... Num 21:23 3898
who had *f* against the former king .... Num 21:26 3898
for the LORD *f* for Israel .... Josh 10:14 3898
unto Libnah, and *f* against Libnah .... Josh 10:29 3898
against it, and *f* against it .... Josh 10:31 3898
against it, and *f* against it .... Josh 10:34 3898
and they *f* against it .... Josh 10:36 3898
to Debir; and *f* against it .... Josh 10:38 3898
LORD God of Israel *f* for Israel............... Josh 10:42 3898
God is he that hath *f* for you.................. Josh 23:3 3898
and they *f* with you .... Josh 24:8 3898
the men of Jericho *f* against you .... Josh 24:11 3898
they *f* against him, and they slew .... Judg 1:5 3898
of Judah had *f* against Jerusalem............ Judg 1:8 3898
The kings came and *f*.............................. Judg 5:19 3898
then *f* the kings of Canaan in.................. Judg 5:19 3898
They *f* from heaven.................................. Judg 5:20 3898
in their courses *f* against Sisera .... Judg 5:20 3898
(For my father *f* for you, and.................. Judg 9:17 3898
of Shechem, and *f* with Abimelech .... Judg 9:39 3898
Abimelech *f* against the city all .... Judg 9:45 3898
f against it, and went hard unto.............. Judg 9:52 3898
in Jahaz, and *f* against Israel .... Judg 11:20 3898
men of Gilead, and *f* with Ephraim .... Judg 12:4 3898
And the Philistines *f*, and Israel............. 1Sa 4:10 3898
of Moab, and they *f* against them............ 1Sa 12:9 3898
f against all his enemies on 1Sa 14:47 3898
f with the Philistines, and slew 1Sa 19:8 3898
f with the Philistines, and 1Sa 23:5 3898
the Philistines *f* against Israel................. 1Sa 31:1 3898
no more, neither *f* they any more 2Sa 2:28 3898
him, because he had *f* against 2Sa 8:10 3898
against David, and *f* with him................. 2Sa 10:17 3898
the city went out, and *f* with Joab 2Sa 11:17 3898
Joab *f* against Rabbah of the.................... 2Sa 12:26 3898
I have *f* against Rabbah, and have 2Sa 12:27 3898
and *f* against it, and took it..................... 2Sa 12:29 3898
f against the Philistines 2Sa 21:15 3898
when he *f* against Hazael king of............ 2Kin 8:29 3898
when he *f* with Hazael king of 2Kin 9:15 3898
f against Gath, and took it 2Kin 12:17 3898
his might wherewith he *f* against............ 2Kin 13:12 3898
how he *f* with Amaziah king of.............. 2Kin 14:15 3898
the Philistines *f* against Israel................. 1Chr 10:1 3898
him, because he had *f* against 1Chr 18:10 3898
the Syrians, they *f* with him..................... 1Chr 19:17 3898
thousand men which *f* in chariots 1Chr 19:18
they had heard that the LORD *f*............... 2Chr 20:29 3898
when he *f* with Hazael king of 2Chr 22:6 3898
He *f* also with the king of the................. 2Chr 27:5 3898
f against me without a cause................... Ps 109:3 3898
f against Ashdod, and took it.................. Is 20:1 3898

F

their enemy, and he *f* against them .... Is 63:10 3898
f against Jerusalem, and against .... Jer 34:1 3898
army *f* against Jerusalem, and .... Jer 34:7 3898
as when he *f* in the day of battle .... Zec 14:3 3898
that have *f* against Jerusalem .... Zec 14:12 6633
I have *f* with beasts at Ephesus 1Cor 15:32 *2341*
I have *f* a good fight, I have 2Ti 4:7 *75*
his angels *f* against the dragon .... Rev 12:7 *4170*
and the dragon *f* and his angels, ... Rev 12:7 *4170*

FOUL {5}
My face is *f* with weeping, and on .... Job 16:16 2560
but ye must *f* the residue with .... Eze 34:18 7515
It will be *f* weather to day .... Mt 16:3 *5494*
together, he rebuked the *f* spirit .... Mk 9:25 *169*
and the hold of every *f* spirit .... Rev 18:2 *169*

FOULED {1}
which ye have *f* with your feet .... Eze 34:19 4833

FOULEDST {1}
with thy feet, and *f* their rivers .... Eze 32:2 7515

FOUND {403}
was not *f* an help meet for him .... Gen 2:20 4672
But Noah *f* grace in the eyes of .... Gen 6:8 4672
But the dove *f* no rest for the .... Gen 8:9 4672
that they *f* a plain in the land .... Gen 11:2 4672
the angel of the LORD *f* her by a .... Gen 16:7 4672
if now I have *f* favour in thy .... Gen 18:3 4672
there shall be forty *f* there .... Gen 18:29 4672
there shall thirty be *f* there .... Gen 18:30 4672
there shall be twenty *f* there .... Gen 18:31 4672
Peradventure ten shall be *f* there .... Gen 18:32 4672
thy servant hath *f* grace in thy .... Gen 19:19 4672
f there a well of springing water .... Gen 26:19 4672
and said unto him, We have *f* water .... Gen 26:32 4672
it that thou hast *f* it so quickly .... Gen 27:20 4672
f mandrakes in the field, and .... Gen 30:14 4672
if I have *f* favour in thine eyes, ... Gen 30:27 4672
but he *f* them not .... Gen 31:33 4672
all the tent, but *f* them not .... Gen 31:34 4672
he searched, but *f* not the images .... Gen 31:35 4672
what hast thou *f* of all thy .... Gen 31:37 4672
if now I have *f* grace in thy .... Gen 33:10 4672
this was that Anah that *f* the .... Gen 36:24 4672
And a certain man *f* him, and, ... Gen 37:15 4672
his brethren, and *f* them in Dothan .... Gen 37:17 4672
and said, This have we *f* .... Gen 37:32 4672
but he *f* her not .... Gen 38:20 4672
this kid, and thou hast not *f* her .... Gen 38:23 4672
Joseph *f* grace in his sight, and .... Gen 39:4 4672
which we *f* in our sacks' mouths, ... Gen 44:8 4672
of thy servants it be *f*, both let .... Gen 44:9 4672
he with whom it is *f* shall be my .... Gen 44:10 4672
the cup was *f* in Benjamin's sack .... Gen 44:12 4672
God hath *f* out the iniquity of .... Gen 44:16 4672
and he also with whom the cup is *f* .... Gen 44:16 4672
man in whose hand the cup is *f* .... Gen 44:17 4672
that was *f* in the land of Egypt .... Gen 47:14 4672
If now I have *f* grace in thy .... Gen 47:29 4672
If now I have *f* grace in your .... Gen 50:4 4672
which shall be *f* in the field .... Ex 9:19 4672
be no leaven *f* in your houses .... Ex 12:19 4672
in the wilderness, and *f* no water .... Ex 15:22 4672
day for to gather, and they *f* none .... Ex 16:27 4672
him, or if he be *f* in his hand .... Ex 21:16 4672
If a thief be *f* breaking up .... Ex 22:2 4672
be certainly *f* in his hand alive .... Ex 22:4 4672
if the thief be *f*, let him pay .... Ex 22:7 4672
If the thief be not *f*, then the .... Ex 22:8 4672
thou hast also *f* grace in my .... Ex 33:12 4672
if I have *f* grace in thy sight, ... Ex 33:13 4672
thy people have *f* grace in thy .... Ex 33:16 4672
for thou hast *f* grace in my sight .... Ex 33:17 4672
If now I have *f* grace in thy .... Ex 34:9 4672
every man, with whom was *f* blue .... Ex 35:23 4672
with whom was *f* shittim wood for .... Ex 35:24 4672
Or have *f* that which was lost, and .... Lev 6:3 4672
or the lost thing which he *f* .... Lev 6:4 4672
have I not *f* favour in thy sight .... Num 11:11 4672
if I have *f* favour in thy sight .... Num 11:15 4672
they *f* a man that gathered sticks .... Num 15:32 4672
they that *f* him gathering sticks .... Num 15:33 4672
if we have *f* grace in thy sight, ... Num 32:5 4672
If there be *f* among you, within .... Deut 17:2 4672
There shall not be *f* among you .... Deut 18:10 4672
that all the people that is *f* .... Deut 20:11 4672
If one be *f* slain in the land .... Deut 21:1 4672
he hath lost, and thou hast *f* .... Deut 22:3 4672
I came to her, I *f* her not a maid .... Deut 22:14 4672
I *f* not thy daughter a maid .... Deut 22:17 4672
virginity be not *f* for the damsel .... Deut 22:20 4672
If a man be *f* lying with a woman .... Deut 22:22 4672
For he *f* her in the field, and the .... Deut 22:27 4672
and lie with her, and they be *f* .... Deut 22:28 4672
his eyes, because he hath *f* some .... Deut 24:1 4672
If a man be *f* stealing any of his .... Deut 24:7 4672
He *f* him in a desert land, and in .... Deut 32:10 4672
shall be *f* liars unto thee .... Deut 33:29
all the way, but *f* them not .... Josh 2:22 4672
The five kings are *f* hid in a .... Josh 10:17 4672
they *f* Adoni-bezek in Bezek .... Judg 1:5 4672
If now I have *f* grace in thy .... Judg 6:17 4672
ye had not *f* out my riddle .... Judg 14:18 4672
he *f* a new jawbone of an ass, and .... Judg 15:15 4672
they *f* among the inhabitants of .... Judg 21:12 4672
Why have I *f* grace in thine eyes, ... Ruth 2:10 4672
of Shalisha, but they *f* them not 1Sa 9:4 4672
Benjamites, but they *f* them not 1Sa 9:4 4672
they *f* young maidens going out to 1Sa 9:11 4672
for they are *f* 1Sa 9:20 4672
which thou wentest to seek are *f* 1Sa 10:2 4672
us plainly that the asses were *f* 1Sa 10:16 4672
sought him, he could not be *f* 1Sa 10:21 4672
ye have not *f* ought in my hand 1Sa 12:5 4672
Now there was no smith *f* 1Sa 13:19 4672
spear *f* in the hand of any of the 1Sa 13:22 4672
with Jonathan his son was there *f* 1Sa 13:22 4672
of their enemies which they *f* 1Sa 14:30 4672
for he hath *f* favour in my sight 1Sa 16:22 4672
that I have *f* grace in thine eyes 1Sa 20:3 4672
if I have *f* favour in thine eyes, ... 1Sa 20:29 4672
evil hath not been *f* in thee all 1Sa 25:28 4672
If I have now *f* grace in thine 1Sa 27:5 4672
I have *f* no fault in him since he 1Sa 29:3 4672
for I have not *f* evil in thee 1Sa 29:6 4672
what hast thou *f* in thy servant 1Sa 29:8 4672
they *f* an Egyptian in the field, ... 1Sa 30:11 4672
strip the slain, that they *f* Saul 1Sa 31:8 4672
f in his heart to pray this 2Sa 7:27 4672
that I have *f* grace in thy sight 2Sa 14:22 4672
in some place where he shall be *f* 2Sa 17:12 4672
be not one small stone *f* there 2Sa 17:13
f Abishag a Shunammite, and 1Kin 1:3 4672
if wickedness shall be *f* in him 1Kin 1:52 4672
was the weight of the brass *f* out 1Kin 7:47 2713
Hadad *f* great favour in the sight 1Kin 11:19 4672
the Shilonite *f* him in the way 1Kin 11:29 4672
f him sitting under an oak 1Kin 13:14 4672
f his carcase cast in the way, and 1Kin 13:28 4672
because in him there is *f* some 1Kin 14:13 4672
and nation, that they *f* thee not 1Kin 18:10 4672
f Elisha the son of Shaphat, who 1Kin 19:19 4672
departed from him, a lion *f* him 1Kin 20:36 4672
Then he *f* another man, and said, ... 1Kin 20:37 4672
said to Elijah, Hast thou *f* me 1Kin 21:20 4672
And he answered, I have *f* thee 1Kin 21:20 4672
sought three days, but *f* him not 2Kin 2:17 4672
f a wild vine, and gathered 2Kin 4:39 4672
but they *f* no more of her than 2Kin 9:35 4672
wheresoever any breach shall be *f* 2Kin 12:5 4672
told the money that was *f* in the 2Kin 12:10 4672
all the gold that was *f* in the 2Kin 12:18 4672
were *f* in the house of the LORD 2Kin 14:14 4672
gold that was *f* in the house of 2Kin 16:8 4672
the king of Assyria *f* conspiracy 2Kin 17:4 4672
was *f* in the house of the LORD 2Kin 18:15 4672
f the king of Assyria warring 2Kin 19:8 4672
all that was *f* in his treasures 2Kin 20:13 4672
I have *f* the book of the law in 2Kin 22:8 4672
the money that was *f* in the house 2Kin 22:9 4672
the words of this book that is *f* 2Kin 22:13 4672
was *f* in the house of the LORD 2Kin 23:2 4672
priest *f* in the house of the LORD 2Kin 23:24 4672
which were *f* in the city, and the 2Kin 25:19 4672
the land that were *f* in the city 2Kin 25:19 4672
they *f* fat pasture and good, and 1Chr 4:40 4672
the habitations that were *f* there 1Chr 4:41 4672
strip the slain, that they *f* Saul 1Chr 10:8 4672
therefore thy servant hath *f* in 1Chr 17:25 4672
f it to weigh a talent of gold, ... 1Chr 20:2 4672
there were more chief men *f* of 1Chr 24:4 4672
there were *f* among them mighty 1Chr 26:31 4672
seek him, he will be *f* of thee 1Chr 28:9 4672
f gave them to the treasure of 1Chr 29:8 4672
they were *f* an hundred and fifty 2Chr 2:17 4672
of the brass could not be *f* out 2Chr 4:18 2713
ye seek him, he will be *f* of you 2Chr 15:2 4672
and sought him, he was *f* of them 2Chr 15:4 4672
and he was *f* of them 2Chr 15:15 4672
there are good things *f* in thee 2Chr 19:3 4672
they *f* among them in abundance 2Chr 20:25 4672
that was *f* in the king's house 2Chr 21:17 4672
f the princes of Judah, and the 2Chr 22:8 4672
f them three hundred thousand 2Chr 25:5 4672
were *f* in the house of God with 2Chr 25:24 4672
all the uncleanness that they *f* 2Chr 29:16 4672
Hilkiah the priest *f* a book of 2Chr 34:14 4672
I have *f* the book of the law in 2Chr 34:15 4672
was *f* in the house of the LORD 2Chr 34:17 4672
the words of the book that is *f* 2Chr 34:21 4672
was *f* in the house of the LORD 2Chr 34:30 4672
did, and that which was *f* in him 2Chr 36:8 4672
by genealogy, but they were not *f* .... Ezr 2:62 4672
it is *f* that this city of old .... Ezr 4:19 7912
there was *f* at Achmetha, in the .... Ezr 6:2 7912
f there none of the sons of Levi .... Ezr 8:15 4672
f that had taken strange wives .... Ezr 10:18 4672
have *f* favour in thy sight .... Neh 2:5
peace, and *f* nothing to answer .... Neh 5:8 4672
I *f* a register of the genealogy .... Neh 7:5 4672
the first, and *f* written therein, ... Neh 7:5 4672
by genealogy, but it was not *f* .... Neh 7:64 4672
they *f* written in the law which .... Neh 8:14 4672
and therein was *f* written, that .... Neh 13:1 4672
made of the matter, it was *f* out .... Est 2:23 4672
If I have *f* favour in the sight .... Est 5:8 4672
it was *f* written, that Mordecai .... Est 6:2 4672
If I have *f* favour in thy sight, ... Est 7:3 4672
if I have *f* favour in his sight, ... Est 8:5 4672
the root of the matter is *f* in me .... Job 19:28 4672
as a dream, and shall not be *f* .... Job 20:8 4672
But where shall wisdom be *f* .... Job 28:12 4672
neither is it *f* in the land of .... Job 28:13 4672
lifted up myself when evil *f* him .... Job 31:29 4672
because they had *f* no answer .... Job 32:3 4672
should say, We have *f* out wisdom .... Job 32:13 4672
I have *f* a ransom .... Job 33:24 4672
in all the land were no women *f* .... Job 42:15 4672
in a time when thou mayest be *f* .... Ps 32:6 4672
his iniquity be *f* to be hateful .... Ps 36:2 4672
sought him, but he could not be *f* .... Ps 37:36 4672
and for comforters, but I *f* none .... Ps 69:20 4672
men of might have *f* their hands .... Ps 76:5 4672
Yea, the sparrow hath *f* an house .... Ps 84:3 4672
I have *f* David my servant .... Ps 89:20 4672
they *f* no city to dwell in .... Ps 107:4 4672
I *f* trouble and sorrow .... Ps 116:3 4672
we *f* it in the fields of the wood .... Ps 132:6 4672
But if he be *f*, he shall restore .... Prov 6:31 4672
seek thy face, and I have *f* thee .... Prov 7:15 4672
hath understanding wisdom is *f* .... Prov 10:13 4672
glory, if it be *f* in the way of .... Prov 16:31 4672
when thou hast *f* it, then there .... Prov 24:14 4672
Hast thou *f* honey .... Prov 25:16 4672
reprove thee, and thou be *f* a liar .... Prov 30:6
curse thee, and thou be *f* guilty .... Prov 30:10
Behold, this have I *f*, saith the .... Eccl 7:27 4672
one man among a thousand have I *f* .... Eccl 7:28 4672
among all those have I not *f* .... Eccl 7:28 4672
Lo, this only have I *f*, that God .... Eccl 7:29 4672
Now there was *f* in it a poor wise .... Eccl 9:15 4672
I sought him, but I *f* him not .... Song 3:1 4672
I sought him, but I *f* him not .... Song 3:2 4672
that go about the city *f* me .... Song 3:3 4672
but I *f* him whom my soul loveth .... Song 3:4 4672
that went about the city *f* me .... Song 5:7 4672
in his eyes as one that *f* favour .... Song 8:10 4672
As my hand hath *f* the kingdoms of .... Is 10:10 4672
my hand hath *f* as a nest the .... Is 10:14 4672
Every one that is *f* shall be .... Is 13:15 4672
all that are *f* in thee are bound .... Is 22:3 4672
so that there shall not be *f* in .... Is 30:14 4672
thereon, it shall not be *f* there .... Is 35:9 4672
f the king of Assyria warring .... Is 37:8 4672
all that was *f* in his treasures .... Is 39:2 4672
and gladness shall be *f* therein .... Is 51:3 4672
ye the LORD while he may be *f* .... Is 55:6 4672
thou hast *f* the life of thine .... Is 57:10 4672
I am *f* of them that sought me not .... Is 65:1 4672
the new wine is *f* in the cluster .... Is 65:8 4672
have your fathers *f* in me .... Jer 2:5 4672
the thief is ashamed when he is *f* .... Jer 2:26 4672
Also in thy skirts is *f* the blood .... Jer 2:34 4672
I have not *f* it by secret search, ... Jer 2:34 4672
among my people are *f* wicked men .... Jer 5:26 4672
A conspiracy is *f* among the men .... Jer 11:9 4672
came to the pits, and *f* no water .... Jer 14:3 4672
Thy words were *f*, and I did eat .... Jer 15:16 4672
house have I *f* their wickedness .... Jer 23:11 4672
And I will be *f* of you, saith the .... Jer 29:14 4672
sword *f* grace in the wilderness .... Jer 31:2 4672
the Chaldeans that were *f* there .... Jer 41:3 4672
But ten men were *f* among them .... Jer 41:8 4672
f him by the great waters that .... Jer 41:12 4672
was he *f* among thieves .... Jer 48:27 4672
All that *f* them have devoured .... Jer 50:7 4672
of Judah, and they shall not be *f* .... Jer 50:20 4672
thou art *f*, and also caught, ... Jer 50:24 4672
person, which were *f* in the city .... Jer 52:25 4672
that were *f* in the midst of the .... Jer 52:25 4672
we have *f*, we have seen it .... Lam 2:16 4672
not destroy it: but I *f* none .... Eze 22:30 4672
yet shalt thou never be *f* again .... Eze 26:21 4672
till iniquity was *f* in thee .... Eze 28:15 4672
them all was *f* none like Daniel .... Dan 1:19 4672
he *f* them ten times better than .... Dan 1:20 4672
I have *f* a man of the captives of .... Dan 2:25 4672
that no place was *f* for them .... Dan 2:35 7912
wisdom of the gods, was *f* in him .... Dan 5:11 7912
were *f* in the same Daniel, whom .... Dan 5:12 7912
and excellent wisdom is *f* in thee .... Dan 5:14 7912
in the balances, and art *f* wanting .... Dan 5:27 7912
there any error or fault *f* in him .... Dan 6:4 7912
f Daniel praying and making .... Dan 6:11 7912
before him innocency was *f* in me .... Dan 6:22 7912
no manner of hurt was *f* upon him .... Dan 6:23 7912
stumble and fall, and not be *f* .... Dan 11:19 4672
shall be *f* written in the book .... Dan 12:1 4672
I *f* Israel like grapes in the .... Hos 9:10 4672
now shall they be *f* faulty .... Hos 10:2
he *f* him in Beth-el, and there he .... Hos 12:4 4672
I have *f* me out substance .... Hos 12:8 4672
From me is thy fruit *f* .... Hos 14:8 4672
he *f* a ship going to Tarshish .... Jonah 1:3 4672
of Israel were *f* in thee .... Mic 1:13 4672
tongue be *f* in their mouth .... Zeph 3:13
and place shall not be *f* for them .... Zec 10:10 4672
and iniquity was not *f* in his lips .... Mal 2:6 4672
she was *f* with child of the Holy .... Mt 1:18 *2147*
and when ye have *f* him, bring me .... Mt 2:8 *2147*
I have not *f* so great faith, no, ... Mt 8:10 *2147*
the which when a man hath *f* .... Mt 13:44 *2147*
when he had *f* one pearl of great .... Mt 13:46 *2147*
f one of his fellowservants, ... Mt 18:28 *2147*
f others standing idle, and saith .... Mt 20:6 *2147*
f nothing thereon, but leaves .... Mt 21:19 *2147*
together all as many as they *f* .... Mt 22:10 *2147*
And he came and *f* them asleep again .... Mt 26:43 *2147*
But *f* none: yea, though .... Mt 26:60 *2147*
witnesses came, yet *f* they none .... Mt 26:60
they *f* a man of Cyrene, Simon by .... Mt 27:32 *2147*
And when they had *f* him, they said .... Mk 1:37 *2147*
unwashen, hands, they *f* fault .... Mk 7:2
she *f* the devil gone out, and her .... Mk 7:30 *2147*

f the colt tied by the door ... Mk 11:4 2147
to it, he f nothing but leaves ... Mk 11:13 2147
f as he had said unto them ... Mk 14:16 2147
he f them asleep again, (for ... Mk 14:40 2147
and f none. ... Mk 14:55 2147
for thou hast f favour with God ... Lk 1:30 2147
f Mary, and Joseph, and the babe ... Lk 2:16 429
And when they f him not, they ... Lk 2:45 2147
days they f him in the temple ... Lk 2:46 2147
he f the place where it was ... Lk 4:17 2147
I have not f so great faith, no, ... Lk 7:9 2147
f the servant whole that had been ... Lk 7:10 2147
f the man, out of whom the devils ... Lk 8:35 2147
voice was past, Jesus was f alone ... Lk 9:36 2147
sought fruit thereon, and f none. ... Lk 13:6 2147
And when he hath f it, he layeth ... Lk 15:5 2147
for I have f my sheep which was ... Lk 15:6 2147
And when she hath f it, she ... Lk 15:9 2147
for I have f the piece which I ... Lk 15:9 2147
he was lost, and is f ... Lk 15:24 2147
and was lost, and is f ... Lk 15:32 2147
There are not f that returned to ... Lk 17:18 2147
f even so as he had said unto them ... Lk 19:32 2147
f as he had said unto them ... Lk 22:13 2147
he f them sleeping for sorrow, ... Lk 22:45 2147
We f this fellow perverting the ... Lk 23:2 2147
have f no fault in this man ... Lk 23:14 2147
I have f no cause of death in him ... Lk 23:22 2147
they f the stone rolled away from ... Lk 24:2 2147
f not the body of the Lord Jesus ... Lk 24:3 2147
when they f not his body, they ... Lk 24:23 2147
f it even so as the women had ... Lk 24:24 2147
f the eleven gathered together, ... Lk 24:33 2147
We have f the Messias, which is, ... Jn 1:41 2147
and saith unto him, We have f him ... Jn 1:45 2147
f in the temple those that sold ... Jn 2:14 2147
when they had f him on the other ... Jn 6:25 2147
and when he had f him, he said ... Jn 9:35 2147
he f that he had lain in the ... Jn 11:17 2147
Jesus, when he had f a young ass ... Jn 12:14 2147
f her dead, and, carrying her ... Acts 5:10 2147
f them not in the prison, they ... Acts 5:22 2147
The prison truly f we shut with ... Acts 5:23 2147
we had opened, we f no man within ... Acts 5:23 2147
lest haply ye be f even to fight ... Acts 5:39 2147
our fathers f no sustenance ... Acts 7:11 2147
Who f favour before God, and ... Acts 7:46 2147
But Philip was f at Azotus ... Acts 8:40 2147
that if he f any of this way, ... Acts 9:2 2147
there he f a certain man named ... Acts 9:33 2147
f many that were come together ... Acts 10:27 2147
And when he had f him, he brought ... Acts 11:26 2147
f him not, he examined the ... Acts 12:19 2147
they f a certain sorcerer, a ... Acts 13:6 2147
I have f David the son of Jesse, ... Acts 13:22 2147
though they f no cause of death ... Acts 13:28 2147
And when they f them not, they ... Acts 17:6 2147
devotions, I f an altar with this ... Acts 17:23 2147
f a certain Jew named Aquila, ... Acts 18:2 2147
f it fifty thousand pieces of ... Acts 19:19 2147
For we have f this man a ... Acts 24:5 2147
they neither f me in the temple ... Acts 24:12 2147
certain Jews from Asia f me ... Acts 24:18 2147
if they have f any evil doing in ... Acts 24:20 2147
But when I f that he had ... Acts 25:25 2638
there the centurion f a ship of ... Acts 27:6 2147
sounded, and f it twenty fathoms ... Acts 27:28 2147
again, and f it fifteen fathoms ... Acts 27:28 2147
Where we f brethren, and were ... Acts 28:14 2147
pertaining to the flesh, hath f ... Rom 4:1 2147
to life, I f to be unto death ... Rom 7:10 2147
I was f of them that sought me ... Rom 10:20 2147
that a man be f faithful ... 1Cor 4:2 2147
we are f false witnesses of God ... 1Cor 15:15 2147
because I f not Titus my brother ... 2Cor 2:13 2147
clothed we shall not be f naked ... 2Cor 5:3 2147
I made before Titus, is f a truth ... 2Cor 7:14 1096
glory, they may be f even as we ... 2Cor 11:12 2147
that I shall be f unto you such ... 2Cor 12:20 2147
we ourselves also are f sinners ... Gal 2:17 2147
being f in fashion as a man, he ... Phil 2:8 2147
be f in him, not having mine own ... Phil 3:9 2147
of a deacon, being f blameless ... 1Ti 3:10
me out very diligently, and f me ... 2Ti 1:17 2147
and was not f, because God had ... Heb 11:5 2147
for he f no place of repentance, ... Heb 12:17 2147
might be f unto praise and honour ... 1Pet 1:7 2147
neither was guile f in his mouth ... 1Pet 2:22 2147
that ye may be f of him in peace ... 2Pet 3:14 2147
I rejoiced greatly that I f of ... 2Jn 4 2147
and are not, and hast f them liars ... Rev 2:2 2147
for I have not f thy works ... Rev 3:2 2147
no man was f worthy to open ... Rev 5:4 2147
their place f any more in heaven ... Rev 12:8 2147
And in their mouth was f no guile ... Rev 14:5 2147
away, and the mountains were not f ... Rev 16:20 2147
shall be f no more at all ... Rev 18:21 2147
shall be f any more in thee ... Rev 18:22 2147
in her was f the blood of ... Rev 18:24 2147
there was f no place for them ... Rev 20:11 2147
whosoever was not f written in ... Rev 20:15 2147

FOUNDATION {54}
the f thereof even until now ... Ex 9:18 3245
he shall lay the f thereof in his ... Josh 6:26 3245
to lay the f of the house ... 1Kin 5:17 3245
In the fourth year was the f of ... 1Kin 6:37 3245
even from the f unto the coping, ... 1Kin 7:9 4527
the f was of costly stones, even ... 1Kin 7:10 3245
he laid the f thereof in Abiram ... 1Kin 16:34 3245
of the f of the house of the LORD ... 2Chr 8:16 4143
a third part at the gate of the f ... 2Chr 23:5 3247
began to lay the f of the heaps ... 2Chr 31:7 3245
But the f of the temple of the ... Ezr 3:6 3245
the f of the temple of the LORD ... Ezr 3:10 3245
because the f of the house of the ... Ezr 3:11 3245
when the f of this house was laid ... Ezr 3:12 3245
laid the f of the house of God ... Ezr 5:16 787
whose f is in the dust, which are ... Job 4:19 3247
whose f was overflown with a ... Job 22:16 3247
His f is in the holy mountains ... Ps 87:1 3248
hast thou laid the f of the earth ... Ps 102:25 3245
rase it, even to the f thereof ... Ps 137:7 3247
the righteous is an everlasting f ... Prov 10:25 3247
I lay in Zion for a f a stone ... Is 28:16 3248
a precious corner stone, a sure f ... Is 28:16 4143
the temple, Thy f shall be laid ... Is 44:28 3245
also hath laid the f of the earth ... Is 48:13 3245
so that the f thereof shall be ... Eze 13:14 3247
discovering the f unto the neck ... Hab 3:13 3247
even from the day that the f of ... Hag 2:18 3245
have laid the f of this house ... Zec 4:9 3248
the f of the house of the LORD of ... Zec 8:9 3248
layeth the f of the earth, and ... Zec 12:1 3248
secret from the f of the world ... Mt 13:35 2602
for you from the f of the world ... Mt 25:34 2602
deep, and laid the f on a rock ... Lk 6:48 2310
is like a man that without a f ... Lk 6:49 2310
was shed from the f of the world ... Lk 11:50 2602
haply, after he hath laid the f ... Lk 14:29 2310
me before the f of the world ... Jn 17:24 2602
should build upon another man's f ... Rom 15:20 2310
masterbuilder, I have laid the f ... 1Cor 3:10 2310
For other f can no man lay than ... 1Cor 3:11 2310
if any man build upon this f gold ... 1Cor 3:12 2310
in him before the f of the world ... Eph 1:4 2602
built upon the f of the apostles ... Eph 2:20 2310
a good f against the time to come ... 1Ti 6:19 2310
Nevertheless the f of God ... 2Ti 2:19 2310
hast laid the f of the earth ... Heb 1:10 2311
finished from the f of the world ... Heb 4:3 2602
not laying again the f of ... Heb 6:1 2310
suffered since the f of the world ... Heb 9:26 2602
before the f of the world ... 1Pet 1:20 2602
slain from the f of the world ... Rev 13:8 2602
of life from the f of the world ... Rev 17:8 2602
The first f was jasper ... Rev 21:19 2310

FOUNDATIONS {32}
and set on fire the f of the ... Deut 32:22 4146
the f of heaven moved and shook, ... 2Sa 22:8 4146
appeared, the f of the world were ... 2Sa 22:16 4146
walls thereof, and joined the f ... Ezr 4:12 787
let the f thereof be strongly ... Ezr 6:3 787
when I laid the f of the earth ... Job 38:4 3245
are the f thereof fastened ... Job 38:6 134
If the f be destroyed, what can ... Ps 11:3 8356
the f also of the hills moved and ... Ps 18:7 4146
seen, and the f of the world were ... Ps 18:15 4146
all the f of the earth are out of ... Ps 82:5 4146
Who laid the f of the earth ... Ps 104:5 4349
he appointed the f of the earth ... Prov 8:29 4146
for the f of Kir-hareseth shall ... Is 16:7 808
the f of the earth do shake ... Is 24:18 4146
from the f of the earth ... Is 40:21 4146
and laid the f of the earth ... Is 51:13 3245
lay the f of the earth, and say ... Is 51:16 3245
and lay thy f with sapphires ... Is 54:11 3245
up the f of many generations ... Is 58:12 4146
the f of the earth searched out ... Jer 31:37 4146
her f are fallen, her walls are ... Jer 50:15 803
for a corner, nor a stone for f ... Jer 51:26 4146
and it hath devoured the f thereof ... Lam 4:11 3247
her f shall be broken down ... Eze 30:4 3247
the f of the side chambers were a ... Eze 41:8 4328
and I will discover the f thereof ... Mic 1:6 3247
and ye strong f of the earth ... Mic 6:2 4146
so that the f of the prison were ... Acts 16:26 2310
he looked for a city which hath f ... Heb 11:10 2310
the wall of the city had twelve f ... Rev 21:14 2310
the f of the wall of the city ... Rev 21:19 2310

FOUNDED {10}
For he hath f it upon the seas, ... Ps 24:2 3245
fulness thereof, thou hast f them ... Ps 89:11 3245
place which thou hast f for them ... Ps 104:8 3245
that thou hast f them for ever ... Ps 119:152 3245
LORD by wisdom hath f the earth ... Prov 3:19 3245
That the LORD hath f Zion ... Is 14:32 3245
til the Assyrian f it for them ... Is 23:13 3245
hath f his troop in the earth ... Amos 9:6 3245
for it was f upon a rock ... Mt 7:25 2311
for it was f upon a rock ... Lk 6:48 2311

FOUNDER {5}
of silver, and gave them to the f ... Judg 17:4 6884
the f melteth in vain ... Jer 6:29 6884
workman, and of the hands of the f ... Jer 10:9 6884
every f is confounded by the ... Jer 10:14 6884
every f is confounded by the ... Jer 51:17 6884

FOUNDEST {1}
f his heart faithful before thee, ... Neh 9:8 4672

FOUNTAIN {33}
by a f of water in the wilderness ... Gen 16:7 5869
by the f in the way to Shur ... Gen 16:7 5869
Nevertheless a f or pit, wherein ... Lev 11:36 4599
he hath discovered her f, and she ... Lev 20:18 4726
hath uncovered the f of her blood ... Lev 20:18 4726
the f of Jacob shall be upon a ... Deut 33:28 5869
the f of the water of Nephtoah ... Josh 15:9 4599
by a f which is in Jezreel ... 1Sa 29:1 5869
I went on to the gate of the f ... Neh 2:14 5869
But the gate of the f repaired ... Neh 3:15 5869
And at the f gate, which was over ... Neh 12:37 5869
For with thee is the f of life ... Ps 36:9 4726
the Lord, from the f of Israel ... Ps 68:26 4726
Thou didst cleave the f and the ... Ps 74:15 4599
the flint into a f of waters ... Ps 114:8 4599
Let thy f be blessed ... Prov 5:18 4726
law of the wise is a f of life ... Prov 13:14 4726
fear of the LORD is a f of life ... Prov 14:27 4726
the wicked is as a troubled f ... Prov 25:26 4599
or the pitcher be broken at the f ... Eccl 12:6 4002
a spring shut up, a f sealed ... Song 4:12 4599
A f of gardens, a well of living ... Song 4:15 4599
me the f of living waters ... Jer 2:13 4726
As a f casteth out her waters, so ... Jer 6:7 953
waters, and mine eyes a f of tears ... Jer 9:1 4726
the LORD, the f of living waters ... Jer 17:13 4726
dry, and his f shall be dried up ... Hos 13:15 4599
a f shall come forth of the house ... Joel 3:18 4599
a f opened to the house of David ... Zec 13:1 4726
straightway the f of her blood ... Mk 5:29 4077
Doth a f send forth at the same ... Jas 3:11 4077
so can no f both yield salt water ... Jas 3:12 4077
the f of the water of life freely ... Rev 21:6 4077

FOUNTAINS {15}
the same day were all the f of ... Gen 7:11 4599
The f also of the deep and the ... Gen 8:2 4599
and in Elim were twelve f of water ... Num 33:9 5869
a land of brooks of water, of f ... Deut 8:7 5869
the land, unto all f of water ... 1Kin 18:5 4599
the f which were without the city ... 2Chr 32:3 5869
together, who stopped all the f ... 2Chr 32:4 4599
Let thy f be dispersed abroad, and ... Prov 5:16 4599
when there were no f abounding ... Prov 8:24 4599
he strengthened the f of the deep ... Prov 8:28 5869
f in the midst of the valleys ... Is 41:18 4599
lead them unto living f of waters ... Rev 7:17 4077
rivers, and upon the f of waters ... Rev 8:10 4077
and the sea, and the f of waters ... Rev 14:7 4077
upon the rivers and f of waters ... Rev 16:4 4077

FOUR {328}
parted, and became into f heads ... Gen 2:10 702
after he begat Salah f hundred ... Gen 11:13 702
after he begat Eber f hundred ... Gen 11:15 702
And Eber lived f and thirty years, ... Gen 11:16 702
after he begat Peleg f hundred ... Gen 11:17 702
f kings with five ... Gen 14:9 702
afflict them f hundred years ... Gen 15:13 702
the land is worth f hundred ... Gen 23:15 702
f hundred shekels of silver, ... Gen 23:16 702
thee, and f hundred men with him ... Gen 32:6 702
came, and with him f hundred men ... Gen 33:1 702
f parts shall be your own, for ... Gen 47:24 702
was f hundred and thirty years ... Ex 12:40 702
pass at the end of the f hundred ... Ex 12:41 702
for an ox, and f sheep for a sheep ... Ex 22:1 702
thou shalt cast f rings of gold ... Ex 25:12 702
put them in the f corners thereof ... Ex 25:12 702
shalt make for it f rings of gold ... Ex 25:26 702
put the rings in the f corners ... Ex 25:26 702
that are on the f feet thereof ... Ex 25:26 702
in the candlestick shall be f ... Ex 25:34 702
breadth of one curtain f cubits ... Ex 26:2 702
breadth of one curtain f cubits ... Ex 26:8 702
it upon f pillars of shittim wood ... Ex 26:32 702
upon the f sockets of silver ... Ex 26:32 702
of it upon the f corners thereof ... Ex 27:2 702
make f brasen rings in the f ... Ex 27:4 702
shall be f, and their sockets f ... Ex 27:16 702
of stones, even f rows of stones ... Ex 28:17 702
breadth of one curtain f cubits ... Ex 36:9 702
f cubits was the breadth of one ... Ex 36:15 702
he made thereunto f pillars of ... Ex 36:36 702
he cast for them f sockets of ... Ex 36:36 702
And he cast for it f rings of gold ... Ex 37:3 702
to be set by the f corners of it ... Ex 37:3 702
And he cast for it f rings of gold ... Ex 37:13 702
put the rings upon the f corners ... Ex 37:13 702
that were in the f feet thereof ... Ex 37:13 702
were f bowls made like almonds ... Ex 37:20 702
thereof on the f corners of it ... Ex 38:2 702
he cast f rings for the f ends ... Ex 38:5 702
And their pillars were f ... Ex 38:19 702
and their sockets of brass f ... Ex 38:19 702
two thousand and f hundred shekels ... Ex 38:29 702
they set in it f rows of stones ... Ex 39:10 702
that creep, going upon all f ... Lev 11:20 702
thing that goeth upon all f ... Lev 11:21 702
things, which have f feet ... Lev 11:23 702
manner of beasts that go on all f ... Lev 11:27 702
and whatsoever goeth upon all f ... Lev 11:42 702
and f thousand and f hundred ... Num 1:29 702
and seven thousand and f hundred ... Num 1:31 702
and five thousand and f hundred ... Num 1:37 702
and three thousand and f hundred ... Num 1:43 702
and f thousand and f hundred ... Num 2:6 702
and seven thousand and f hundred ... Num 2:8 702
f hundred, throughout their ... Num 2:9 702
f hundred and fifty, throughout ... Num 2:16 702
and five thousand and f hundred ... Num 2:23 702
and three thousand and f hundred ... Num 2:30 702
f oxen he gave unto the sons of ... Num 7:7 702

F

f wagons and eight oxen he gave ... Num 7:8 702
f hundred shekels, after the ... Num 7:85 702
f bullocks, the rams sixty, the ... Num 7:88 702
plague were twenty and *f* thousand ... Num 25:9 702
f thousand and three hundred ... Num 26:25 702
and *f* thousand and *f* hundred ... Num 26:43 702
and three thousand and *f* hundred ... Num 26:47 702
and five thousand and *f* hundred ... Num 26:50 702
f cubits the breadth of it, after ... Deut 3:11 702
the *f* quarters of thy vesture ... Deut 22:12 702
f cities and their villages ... Josh 19:7 702
Almon with her suburbs; *f* cities ... Josh 21:18 702
Beth-horon with her suburbs; *f* cities ... Josh 21:22 702
with her suburbs; *f* cities ... Josh 21:24 702
with her suburbs; *f* cities ... Josh 21:29 702
Rehob with her suburbs; *f* cities ... Josh 21:31 702
with her suburbs; *f* cities ... Josh 21:35 702
with her suburbs; *f* cities ... Josh 21:37 702
Jazer with her suburbs; *f* cities ... Josh 21:39 702
against Shechem in *f* companies ... Judg 9:34 702
the Gileadite *f* days in a year ... Judg 11:40 702
and was there *f* whole months ... Judg 19:2 702
f hundred thousand footmen that ... Judg 20:2 702
were numbered *f* hundred thousand ... Judg 20:17 702
abode in the rock Rimmon *f* months ... Judg 20:47 702
f hundred young virgins, that had ... Judg 21:12 702
in the field about *f* thousand men ... 1Sa 4:2 702
were with him about *f* hundred men ... 1Sa 22:2 702
after David about *f* hundred men ... 1Sa 25:13 702
was a full year and *f* months ... 1Sa 27:7 702
pursued, he and *f* hundred men ... 1Sa 30:10 702
save *f* hundred young men, which ... 1Sa 30:17 702
and on every foot six toes, *f* ... 2Sa 21:20 702
These *f* were born to the giant in ... 2Sa 21:22 702
it came to pass in the *f* hundred ... 1Kin 6:1 702
upon *f* rows of cedar pillars, ... 1Kin 7:2 702
lily work in the porch, *f* cubits ... 1Kin 7:19 702
f cubits was the length of one ... 1Kin 7:27 702
f cubits the breadth thereof, and ... 1Kin 7:27 702
And every base had *f* brasen wheels ... 1Kin 7:30 702
the *f* corners thereof had ... 1Kin 7:30 702
under the borders were *f* wheels ... 1Kin 7:32 702
there were *f* undersetters to the ... 1Kin 7:34 702
to the *f* corners of one base ... 1Kin 7:34 702
and every laver was *f* cubits ... 1Kin 7:38 702
f hundred pomegranates for the ... 1Kin 7:42 702
f hundred and twenty talents, and ... 1Kin 9:28 702
f hundred chariots, and twelve ... 1Kin 10:26 702
in Tirzah, twenty and *f* years ... 1Kin 15:33 702
and the prophets of Baal *f* hundred ... 1Kin 18:19 702
prophets of the groves *f* hundred ... 1Kin 18:19 702
but Baal's prophets are *f* hundred ... 1Kin 18:22 702
Fill *f* barrels with water, and ... 1Kin 18:33 702
about *f* hundred men, and said unto ... 1Kin 22:6 702
there were *f* leprous men at the ... 2Kin 7:3 702
the corner gate, *f* hundred cubits ... 2Kin 14:13 702
Shobab, and Nathan, and Solomon, *f* ... 1Chr 3:5 702
bow, and skilful in war, were *f* ... 1Chr 5:18 702
and Puah, Jashub, and Shimrom, *f* ... 1Chr 7:1 702
and two thousand and thirty and *f* ... 1Chr 7:7 702
In *f* quarters were the porters, ... 1Chr 9:24 702
the *f* chief porters, were in ... 1Chr 9:26 702
the children of Levi *f* thousand ... 1Chr 12:26 702
whose fingers and toes were *f* ... 1Chr 20:6 702
Judah was *f* hundred threescore and ... 1Chr 21:5 702
and his *f* sons with him hid ... 1Chr 21:20 702
f thousand were to set forward ... 1Chr 23:4 702
Moreover *f* thousand were porters ... 1Chr 23:5 702
f thousand praised the LORD with ... 1Chr 23:5 702
These *f* were the sons of Shimei ... 1Chr 23:10 702
Izhar, Hebron, and Uzziel, *f* ... 1Chr 23:12 702
and twentieth to Delaiah, the *f* ... 1Chr 24:18 702
The *f* and twentieth to ... 1Chr 25:31 702
f a day, southward *f* a day ... 1Chr 26:17 702
f at the causeway, and two at ... 1Chr 26:18 702
course were twenty and *f* thousand ... 1Chr 27:1 702
course were twenty and *f* thousand ... 1Chr 27:2 702
were twenty and *f* thousand ... 1Chr 27:4 702
course were twenty and *f* thousand ... 1Chr 27:5 702
course were twenty and *f* thousand ... 1Chr 27:7 702
course were twenty and *f* thousand ... 1Chr 27:8 702
course were twenty and *f* thousand ... 1Chr 27:9 702
course were twenty and *f* thousand ... 1Chr 27:10 702
course were twenty and *f* thousand ... 1Chr 27:11 702
course were twenty and *f* thousand ... 1Chr 27:12 702
course were twenty and *f* thousand ... 1Chr 27:13 702
course were twenty and *f* thousand ... 1Chr 27:14 702
course were twenty and *f* thousand ... 1Chr 27:15 702
f hundred chariots, and twelve ... 2Chr 1:14 702
f hundred pomegranates on the two ... 2Chr 4:13 702
Ophir, and took thence *f* hundred ... 2Chr 8:18 702
Solomon had *f* thousand stalls for ... 2Chr 9:25 702
even *f* hundred thousand chosen ... 2Chr 13:3 702
of prophets *f* hundred men ... 2Chr 18:5 702
the corner gate, *f* hundred cubits ... 2Chr 25:23 702
basons of a second sort *f* hundred ... Ezr 1:10 702
were five thousand and *f* hundred ... Ezr 1:11 702
a thousand two hundred fifty and *f* ... Ezr 2:7 702
of Adin, *f* hundred fifty and *f* ... Ezr 2:15 702
a thousand two hundred fifty and *f* ... Ezr 2:31 702
of Hodaviah, seventy and *f* ... Ezr 2:40 702
camels, *f* hundred thirty and five ... Ezr 2:67 702
two hundred rams, *f* hundred lambs ... Ezr 6:17 703
unto me *f* times after this sort ... Neh 6:4 702
a thousand two hundred fifty and *f* ... Neh 7:12 702
Bezai, three hundred twenty and *f* ... Neh 7:23 702
a thousand two hundred fifty and *f* ... Neh 7:34 702
children of Hodevah, seventy and *f* ... Neh 7:43 702
camels, *f* hundred thirty and five ... Neh 7:69 702
were *f* hundred threescore ... Neh 11:6 702
were two hundred fourscore and *f* ... Neh 11:18 702
smote the *f* corners of the house, ... Job 1:19 702
sons' sons, even *f* generations ... Job 42:16 702
f things say not, It is enough ... Prov 30:15 702
for me, yea, *f* which I know not ... Prov 30:18 702
for *f* which it cannot bear ... Prov 30:21 702
There be *f* things which are ... Prov 30:24 702
well, yea, *f* are comely in going ... Prov 30:29 702
from the *f* corners of the earth ... Is 11:12 702
f or five in the outmost fruitful ... Is 17:6 702
I will appoint over them *f* kinds ... Jer 15:3 702
Jehudi had read three or *f* leaves ... Jer 36:23 702
upon Elam will I bring the *f* ... Jer 49:36 702
from the *f* quarters of heaven ... Jer 49:36 702
thickness thereof was *f* fingers ... Jer 52:21 702
all the persons were *f* thousand ... Jer 52:30 702
likeness of *f* living creatures ... Eze 1:5 702
And every one had *f* faces ... Eze 1:6 702
and every one had *f* wings ... Eze 1:6 702
their wings on their *f* sides ... Eze 1:8 702
they *f* had their faces and their ... Eze 1:8 702
they *f* had the face of a man, and ... Eze 1:10 702
they *f* had the face of an ox on ... Eze 1:10 702
they *f* also had the face of an ... Eze 1:10 702
creatures, with his *f* faces ... Eze 1:15 702
and they *f* had one likeness ... Eze 1:16 702
they went upon their *f* sides ... Eze 1:17 702
full of eyes round about them *f* ... Eze 1:18 702
upon the *f* corners of the land ... Eze 7:2 702
behold the *f* wheels by the ... Eze 10:9 702
they *f* had one likeness, as if a ... Eze 10:10 702
they went upon their *f* sides ... Eze 10:11 702
even the wheels that they *f* had ... Eze 10:12 702
And every one had *f* faces ... Eze 10:14 702
Every one had *f* faces apiece ... Eze 10:21 702
and every one *f* wings ... Eze 10:21 702
How much more when I send my *f* ... Eze 14:21 702
Come from the *f* winds, O breath, ... Eze 37:9 702
F tables were on this side, and ... Eze 40:41 702
f tables on that side, by the ... Eze 40:41 702
the *f* tables were of hewn stone ... Eze 40:42 702
f cubits, round about the house ... Eze 41:5 702
He measured it by the *f* sides ... Eze 42:20 702
greater settle shall be *f* cubits ... Eze 43:14 702
So the altar shall be *f* cubits ... Eze 43:15 702
altar and upward shall be *f* horns ... Eze 43:15 702
square in the *f* squares thereof ... Eze 43:16 702
broad in the *f* squares thereof ... Eze 43:17 702
and put it on the *f* horns of it ... Eze 43:20 702
on the *f* corners of the settle, ... Eze 43:20 702
upon the *f* corners of the settle ... Eze 45:19 702
by the *f* corners of the court ... Eze 46:21 702
In the *f* corners of the court ... Eze 46:22 702
these *f* corners were of one ... Eze 46:22 702
about in them, round about them *f* ... Eze 46:23 702
the north side *f* thousand ... Eze 48:16 702
and the south side *f* thousand ... Eze 48:16 702
and on the east side *f* thousand ... Eze 48:16 702
and the west side *f* thousand ... Eze 48:16 702
f thousand and five hundred ... Eze 48:30 702
And at the east side *f* thousand ... Eze 48:32 702
And at the south side *f* thousand ... Eze 48:33 702
At the west side *f* thousand ... Eze 48:34 702
As for these *f* children, God gave ... Dan 1:17 702
I see *f* men loose, walking in the ... Dan 3:25 703
the *f* winds of the heaven strove ... Dan 7:2 703
f great beasts came up from the ... Dan 7:3 703
the back of it *f* wings of a fowl ... Dan 7:6 703
the beast had also *f* heads ... Dan 7:6 703
These great beasts, which are *f* ... Dan 7:17 703
are *f* kings, which shall arise ... Dan 7:17 703
for it came up *f* notable ones ... Dan 8:8 702
ones toward the *f* winds of heaven ... Dan 8:8 702
whereas *f* stood up for it ... Dan 8:22 702
f kingdoms shall stand up out of ... Dan 8:22 702
And in the *f* and twentieth day of ... Dan 10:4 702
toward the *f* winds of heaven ... Dan 11:4 702
of Damascus, and for *f*, I will not ... Amos 1:3 702
transgressions of Gaza, and for *f* ... Amos 1:6 702
transgressions of Tyrus, and for *f* ... Amos 1:9 702
transgressions of Edom, and for *f* ... Amos 1:11 702
the children of Ammon, and for *f* ... Amos 1:13 702
transgressions of Moab, and for *f* ... Amos 2:1 702
transgressions of Judah, and for *f* ... Amos 2:4 702
of Israel, and for *f*, I will not ... Amos 2:6 702
In the *f* and twentieth day of the ... Hag 1:15 702
In the *f* and twentieth day of the ... Hag 2:10 702
this day and upward, from the *f* ... Hag 2:18 702
LORD came unto Haggai in the *f* ... Hag 2:20 702
Upon the *f* and twentieth day of ... Zec 1:7 702
eyes, and saw, and behold *f* horns ... Zec 1:18 702
the LORD shewed me *f* carpenters ... Zec 1:20 702
as the *f* winds of the heaven ... Zec 2:6 702
there came *f* chariots out from ... Zec 6:1 702
These are the *f* spirits of the ... Zec 6:5 702
that did eat were *f* thousand men ... Mt 15:38 *5070*
seven loaves of the *f* thousand ... Mt 16:10 *5070*
his elect from the *f* winds ... Mt 24:31 *5064*
the palsy, which was borne of *f* ... Mk 2:3 *5064*
had eaten were about *f* thousand ... Mk 8:9 *5070*
when the seven among *f* thousand ... Mk 8:20 *5070*
his elect from the *f* winds ... Mk 13:27 *5064*
f years, which departed not from ... Lk 2:37 *5064*
not ye, There are yet *f* months ... Jn 4:35 *5072*
lain in the grave *f* days already ... Jn 11:17 *5064*
for he hath been dead *f* days ... Jn 11:39 *5066*
made *f* parts, to every soldier a ... Jn 19:23 *5064*
of men, about *f* hundred, joined ... Acts 5:36 *5064*
entreat them evil *f* hundred years ... Acts 7:6 *5064*
great sheet knit at the *f* corners ... Acts 10:11 *5064*
F days ago I was fasting until ... Acts 10:30 *5067*
let down from heaven by *f* corners ... Acts 11:5 *5064*
delivered him to *f* quaternions of ... Acts 12:4 *5064*
about the space of *f* hundred ... Acts 13:20 *5071*
And the same man had *f* daughters ... Acts 21:9 *5064*
We have *f* men which have a vow on ... Acts 21:23 *5064*
f thousand men that were ... Acts 21:38 *5070*
they cast *f* anchors out of the ... Acts 27:29 *5064*
the law, which was *f* hundred ... Gal 3:17 *5071*
And round about the throne were *f* ... Rev 4:4 *5064*
and upon the seats I saw *f* ... Rev 4:4 *5064*
were *f* beasts full of eyes before ... Rev 4:6 *5064*
the *f* beasts had each of them six ... Rev 4:8 *5064*
The *f* and twenty elders fall down ... Rev 4:10 *5064*
of the throne and of the *f* beasts ... Rev 5:6 *5064*
the *f* beasts and *f* and twenty ... Rev 5:8 *5064*
And the *f* beasts said, Amen ... Rev 5:14 *5064*
And the *f* and twenty elders fell ... Rev 5:14 *5064*
one of the *f* beasts saying, Come ... Rev 6:1 *5064*
in the midst of the *f* beasts say ... Rev 6:6 *5064*
after these things I saw *f* angels ... Rev 7:1 *5064*
on the *f* corners of the earth ... Rev 7:1 *5064*
holding the *f* winds of the earth, ... Rev 7:1 *5064*
with a loud voice to the *f* angels ... Rev 7:2 *5064*
f thousand of all the tribes of ... Rev 7:4 *5064*
the *f* beasts, and fell before the ... Rev 7:11 *5064*
I heard a voice from the *f* horns ... Rev 9:13 *5064*
Loose the *f* angels which are ... Rev 9:14 *5064*
the *f* angels were loosed, which ... Rev 9:15 *5064*
And the *f* and twenty elders, which ... Rev 11:16 *5064*
f thousand, having his Father's ... Rev 14:1 *5064*
throne, and before the *f* beasts ... Rev 14:3 *5064*
f thousand, which were redeemed ... Rev 14:3 *5064*
one of the *f* beasts gave unto the ... Rev 15:7 *5064*
And the *f* and twenty elders and the ... Rev 19:4 *5064*
the *f* beasts fell down and ... Rev 19:4 *5064*
in the *f* quarters of the earth ... Rev 20:8 *5064*
f cubits, according to the ... Rev 21:17 *5064*

FOURFOLD {2}

And he shall restore the lamb *f* ... 2Sa 12:6 706
false accusation, I restore him *f* ... Lk 19:8 *5073*

FOURFOOTED {3}

manner of *f* beasts of the earth ... Acts 10:12 *5074*
saw *f* beasts of the earth, and ... Acts 11:6 *5074*
f beasts, and creeping things ... Rom 1:23 *5074*

FOURSCORE {37}

And Abram was *f* and six years old, ... Gen 16:16 8084
Isaac were an hundred and *f* years ... Gen 35:28 8084
And Moses was *f* years old, and ... Ex 7:7 8084
f years old, and Aaron *f* ... Ex 7:7 8084
f thousand and six thousand and ... Num 2:9 8084
thousand and five hundred and *f* ... Num 4:48 8084
and now, lo, I am this day *f* ... Josh 14:10 8084
And the land had rest *f* years ... Judg 3:30 8084
priests, and slew on that day *f* ... 1Sa 22:18 8084
a very aged man, even *f* years old ... 2Sa 19:32 8084
I am this day *f* years old ... 2Sa 19:35 8084
and *f* thousand hewers in the ... 1Kin 5:15 8084
f thousand chosen men, which were ... 1Kin 12:21 8084
was sold for *f* pieces of silver ... 2Kin 6:25 8084
Jehu appointed *f* men without ... 2Kin 10:24 8084
of the Assyrians an hundred *f* ... 2Kin 19:35 8084
in all by their genealogies *f* ... 1Chr 7:5 8084
the chief, and his brethren *f* ... 1Chr 15:9 8084
were cunning, was two hundred *f* ... 1Chr 25:7 8084
f thousand to hew in the mountain ... 2Chr 2:2 8084
f thousand to be hewers in the ... 2Chr 2:18 8084
f thousand chosen men, which were ... 2Chr 11:1 8084
bows, two hundred and *f* thousand ... 2Chr 14:8 8084
him two hundred and *f* thousand ... 2Chr 17:15 8084
f thousand ready prepared for the ... 2Chr 17:18 8084
with him *f* priests of the LORD, ... 2Chr 26:17 8084
of Michael, and with him *f* males ... Ezr 8:8 8084
and Netophah, an hundred *f* ... Neh 7:26 8084
the holy city were two hundred *f* ... Neh 11:18 8084
days, even an hundred and *f* days ... Est 1:4 8084
of strength they be *f* years ... Ps 90:10 8084
f concubines, and virgins without ... Song 6:8 8084
of the Assyrians an hundred and *f* ... Is 37:36 8084
and from Samaria, even *f* men ... Jer 41:5 8084
And she was a widow of about *f* ... Lk 2:37 *3589*
him, Take thy bill, and write *f* ... Lk 16:7 *3589*

FOURSQUARE {10}

the altar shall be *f* ... Ex 27:1 7251
F it shall be being doubled ... Ex 28:16 7251
breadth thereof; *f* shall it be ... Ex 30:2 7251
of it a cubit; it was *f* ... Ex 37:25 7251
the breadth thereof; it was *f* ... Ex 38:1 7251
It was *f*; they made the ... Ex 39:9 7251
gravings with their borders, *f* ... 1Kin 7:31 7251
and an hundred cubits broad, *f* ... Eze 40:47 7251
shall offer the holy oblation *f* ... Eze 48:20 7243
And the city lieth *f*, and the ... Rev 21:16 *5068*

FOURTEEN {26}

I served thee *f* years for thy two ... Gen 31:41 702,6240
all the souls were *f* ... Gen 46:22 702,6240
f thousand and six hundred ... Num 1:27 702,7657
f thousand and six hundred ... Num 2:4 702,7657
in the plague were *f* thousand ... Num 16:49 702,7657
f lambs of the first year ... Num 29:13 702,6246
deal to each lamb of the *f* lambs ... Num 29:15 702,6246
f lambs of the first year without ... Num 29:17 702,6246

f lambs of the first year without ..... Num 29:20 702,6246
f lambs of the first year without .... Num 29:23
f lambs of the first year without .... Num 29:26
f lambs of the first year without .... Num 29:29
f lambs of the first year without .... Num 29:32
f cities with their villages...................... Josh 15:36
f cities with their villages...................... Josh 18:28
days and seven days, even *f* days............ 1Kin 8:65
And God gave to Heman *f* sons 1Chr 25:5
waxed mighty, and married *f* wives 2Chr 13:21
for he had *f* thousand sheep, and .... Job 42:12
the settle shall be *f* cubits long .... Eze 43:17
f broad in the four squares .... Eze 43:17
to David are *f* generations........................ Mt 1:17 *1180*
into Babylon are *f* generations .... Mt 1:17 *1180*
unto Christ are *f* generations................... Mt 1:17 *1180*
a man in Christ above *f* years ago.......... 2Cor 12:2 *1180*
Then *f* years after I went up.................... Gal 2:1 *1180*

FOURTEENTH {25}
in the *f* year came Chedorlaomer,.... Gen 14:5 702,6240
until the *f* day of the same month ... Ex 12:6 702,6240
on the *f* day of the month at even ... Ex 12:18 702,6240
In the *f* day of the first month......... Lev 23:5 702,6240
In the *f* day of this month, at......... Num 9:3 702,6240
they kept the passover on the *f*........ Num 9:5 702,6240
The *f* day of the second month at.... Num 9:11 702,6240
in the *f* day of the first month......... Num 28:16 702,6240
kept the passover on the *f* day of .... Josh 5:10 702,6240
Now in the *f* year of king 2Kin 18:13 702,6240
to Huppah, the *f* to Jeshebeab,........ 1Chr 24:13 702,6240
The *f* to Mattithiah, he, his sons....... 1Chr 25:21 702,6240
on the *f* day of the second month 2Chr 30:15 702,6240
on the *f* day of the first month 2Chr 35:1 702,6240
upon the *f* day of the first month .... Ezr 6:19 702,6240
the *f* day also of the month Adar..... Est 9:15 702,6240
on the *f* day of the same rested......... Est 9:17 702,6240
day thereof, and on the *f* thereof..... Est 9:18 702,6240
made the *f* day of the month Adar .. Est 9:19 702,6240
keep the *f* day of the month Adar ... Est 9:21 702,6240
in the *f* year of king Hezekiah......... Is 36:1 702,6240
in the *f* year after that the city........ Eze 40:1 702,6240
in the *f* day of the month, ye .... Eze 45:21 702,6240
But when the *f* night was come, as.......... Acts 27:27 *5065*
This day is the *f* day that ye.................. Acts 27:33 *5065*

FOURTH {86}
and the morning were the *f* day .... Gen 1:19 7243
And the *f* river is Euphrates.................... Gen 2:14 7243
But in the *f* generation they .... Gen 15:16 7243
f generation of them that hate me........... Ex 20:5 7256
the *f* row a beryl, and an onyx, and .... Ex 28:20 7243
f part of an hin of beaten oil.................. Ex 29:40 7253
the *f* part of an hin of wine for .... Ex 29:40 7243
the third and to the *f* generation............. Ex 34:7 7256
And the *f* row, a beryl, an onyx,............... Ex 39:13 7243
But in the *f* year all the fruit.................. Lev 19:24 7243
be of wine, the *f* part of a hin .... Lev 23:13 7243
On the *f* day Elizur the son of.................. Num 7:30 7243
unto the third and *f* generation............... Num 14:18 7256
with the *f* part of an hin of oil .... Num 15:4 7243
the *f* part of an hin of wine for .... Num 15:5 7243
number of the *f* part of Israel.................. Num 23:10 7255
mingled with the *f* part of an hin............ Num 28:5 7243
offering thereof shall be the *f*................ Num 28:7 7243
a *f* part of an hin unto a lamb.................. Num 28:14 7243
on the *f* day ten bullocks, two................ Num 29:23 7243
f generation of them that hate me........... Deut 5:9 7256
the *f* lot came out to Issachar,.............. Josh 19:17 7243
And it came to pass on the *f* day............. Judg 19:5 7243
I have here at hand the *f* part of 1Sa 9:8 7253
And the *f*, Adonijah the son of............... 2Sa 3:4 7243
in the *f* year of Solomon's reign 1Kin 6:1 7243
olive tree, a *f* part of the wall................. 1Kin 6:33 7243
In the *f* year was the foundation 1Kin 6:37 7243
to reign over Judah in the *f* year 1Kin 22:41 702
the *f* part of a cab of dove's.................... 2Kin 6:25 7255
thy children of the *f* generation............... 2Kin 10:30 7243
of Israel unto the *f* generation................. 2Kin 15:12 7243
in the *f* year of king Hezekiah.................. 2Kin 18:9 7243
on the ninth day of the *f* month 2Kin 25:3
Nethaneel the *f*, Raddai the fifth 1Chr 2:14 7243
the *f*, Adonijah the son of........................ 1Chr 3:2 7243
the third Zedekiah, the *f* Shallum........... 1Chr 3:15 7243
Nohah the *f*, and Rapha the fifth............ 1Chr 8:2 7243
Mishmannah the *f*, Jeremiah the 1Chr 12:10 7243
the third, and Jekameam the *f*................. 1Chr 23:19 7243
third to Harim, the *f* to Seorim, ... 1Chr 24:8 7243
the third, Jekameam the *f*........................ 1Chr 24:23 7243
The *f* to Izri, he, his sons, and 1Chr 25:11 7243
the third, Jathniel the *f* 1Chr 26:2 7243
Joah the third, and Sacar the *f*............... 1Chr 26:4 7243
the third, Zechariah the *f* 1Chr 26:11 7243
The *f* captain for the *f*.......................... 1Chr 27:7 7243
The *f* captain for the *f*.......................... 1Chr 27:7 7243
in the *f* year of his reign 2Chr 3:2 702
on the *f* day they assembled 2Chr 20:26 7243
Now on the *f* day was the silver .... Ezr 8:33 7243
f day of this month the children............... Neh 9:1 702
their God one *f* part of the day .... Neh 9:3 7243
another *f* part they confessed, and.......... Neh 9:3 7243
f year of Jehoiakim the son of................. Jer 25:1 7243
king of Judah, in the *f* year .... Jer 28:1 7243
it came to pass in the *f* year of............... Jer 36:1 7243
year of Zedekiah, in the *f* month............. Jer 39:2 7243
in the *f* year of Jehoiakim the................. Jer 45:1 7243
f year of Jehoiakim the son of................. Jer 46:2 7243
in the *f* year of his reign .... Jer 51:59 7243
And in the *f* month, in the ninth............. Jer 52:6 7243

thirtieth year, in the *f* month.................. Eze 1:1 7243
the *f* the face of an eagle .... Eze 10:14 7243
the *f* kingdom shall be strong as .... Dan 2:40 7244
the form of the *f* is like the Son .... Dan 3:25 7244
visions, and behold a *f* beast .... Dan 7:7 7244
know the truth of the *f* beast .... Dan 7:19 7244
The *f* beast shall be the *f*........................ Dan 7:23 7244
the *f* shall be far richer than .... Dan 11:2 7243
in the *f* chariot grisled and bay.............. Zec 6:3 7243
pass in the *f* year of king Darius............. Zec 7:1 702
in the *f* day of the ninth month .... Zec 7:1 702
The fast of the *f* month, and the............... Zec 8:19 7243
in the *f* watch of the night Jesus .... Mt 14:25 *5067*
about the *f* watch of the night he............. Mk 6:48 *5067*
the *f* beast was like a flying..................... Rev 4:7 *5067*
And when he had opened the *f* seal .... Rev 6:7 *5067*
the voice of the *f* beast say...................... Rev 6:7 *5067*
them over the *f* part of the earth.............. Rev 6:8 *5067*
the *f* angel sounded, and the third .... Rev 8:12 *5067*
the *f* angel poured out his vial .... Rev 16:8 *5067*
the *f*, an emerald.. Rev 21:19 *5067*

FOWL {31}
f that may fly above the earth in............. Gen 1:20 5775
every winged *f* after his kind .... Gen 1:21 5775
let *f* multiply in the earth........................ Gen 1:22 5775
over the *f* of the air, and over .... Gen 1:26 5775
over the *f* of the air, and over .... Gen 1:28 5775
to every *f* of the air, and to..................... Gen 1:30 5775
the field, and every *f* of the air............... Gen 2:19 5775
to the *f* of the air, and to every................ Gen 2:20 5775
every *f* after his kind, every.................... Gen 7:14 5775
moved upon the earth, both of *f*.............. Gen 7:21 5775
things, and the *f* of the heaven .... Gen 7:23 5775
thee, of all flesh, both of *f*..................... Gen 8:17 5775
every creeping thing, and every *f* .... Gen 8:19 5775
clean beast, and of every clean *f* .... Gen 8:20 5775
earth, and upon every *f* of the air........... Gen 9:2 5775
that is with you, of the *f*......................... Gen 9:10 5775
whether it be of *f* or of beast.................. Lev 7:26 5775
law of the beasts, and of the *f* .... Lev 11:46 5775
any beast or *f* that may be eaten .... Lev 17:13 5775
abominable by beast, or by *f*.................... Lev 20:25 5775
winged *f* that flieth in the air................. Deut 4:17 6833
and fallowdeer, and fatted *f*................... 1Kin 4:23 1257
he spake also of beasts, and of *f*............. 1Kin 4:33 5775
is a path which no *f* knoweth.................... Job 28:7 5861
The *f* of the air, and the fish of .... Ps 8:8 6833
creeping things, and flying *f*................... Ps 148:10 6833
both the *f* of the heavens and the............ Jer 9:10 5775
shall dwell all *f* of every wing .... Eze 17:23 6833
Speak unto every feathered *f* .... Eze 39:17 6833
or torn, whether it be *f* or beast.............. Eze 44:31 5775
the back of it four wings of a *f*................ Dan 7:6 5776

FOWLER {3}
thee from the snare of the *f*..................... Ps 91:3 3353
as a bird from the hand of the *f* .... Prov 6:5 3353
is a snare of a *f* in all his ways .... Hos 9:8 3353

FOWLERS {1}
a bird out of the snare of the *f* .... Ps 124:7 3369

FOWLS {55}
thing, and the *f* of the air .... Gen 6:7 5775
Of *f* after their kind, and of .... Gen 6:20 5775
Of *f* also of the air by sevens,................... Gen 7:3 5775
that are not clean, and of *f*...................... Gen 7:8 5775
when the *f* came down upon the .... Gen 15:11 5861
his offering to the LORD be of *f*................ Lev 1:14 5775
have in abomination among the *f*............ Lev 11:13 5775
All *f* that creep, going upon all .... Lev 11:20 5775
and unclean, and between unclean *f*....... Lev 20:25 5775
But of all clean *f* ye may eat.................... Deut 14:20 5775
be meat unto all *f* of the air .... Deut 28:26 5775
thy flesh unto the *f* of the air 1Sa 17:44 5775
this day unto the *f* of the air 1Sa 17:46 5775
field shall the *f* of the air eat 1Kin 14:11 5775
fields shall the *f* of the air eat................ 1Kin 16:4 5775
field shall the *f* of the air eat 1Kin 21:24 5775
also *f* were prepared for me, and............ Neh 5:18 6833
the *f* of the air, and they shall .... Job 12:7 5775
kept close from the *f* of the air.............. Job 28:21 5775
us wiser than the *f* of heaven .... Job 35:11 5775
I know all the *f* of the mountains........... Ps 50:11 5775
feathered *f* like as the sand of............... Ps 78:27 5775
be meat unto the *f* of the heaven............ Ps 79:2 5775
By them shall the *f* of the heaven............ Ps 104:12 5775
unto the *f* of the mountains..................... Is 18:6 5861
the *f* shall summer upon them, and......... Is 18:6 5861
be meat for the *f* of the heaven............... Jer 7:33 5775
the *f* of the heaven, and the.................... Jer 15:3 5775
shall be meat for the *f* of heaven .... Jer 16:4 5775
be meat for the *f* of the heaven............... Jer 19:7 5775
for meat unto the *f* of the heaven........... Jer 34:20 5775
field and to the *f* of the heaven .... Eze 29:5 5775
All the *f* of heaven made their................. Eze 31:6 5775
all the *f* of the heaven remain................. Eze 31:13 5775
will cause all the *f* of the........................ Eze 32:4 5775
the *f* of the heaven, and the .... Eze 38:20 5775
the *f* of the heaven hath he given .... Dan 2:38 5776
the *f* of the heaven dwelt in the.............. Dan 4:12 6853
it, and the *f* from his branches .... Dan 4:14 6853
the *f* of the heaven had their .... Dan 4:21 6853
with the *f* of heaven, and with the .... Hos 2:18 5775
field, and with the *f* of heaven .... Hos 4:3 5775
them down as the *f* of the heaven............ Hos 7:12 5775
will consume the *f* of the heaven............. Zeph 1:3 5775
Behold the *f* of the air .... Mt 6:26 *4071*
the *f* came and devoured them up .... Mt 13:4 *4071*

the *f* of the air came and devoured .... Mk 4:4 *4071*
so that the *f* of the air may..................... Mk 4:32 *4071*
the *f* of the air devoured it .... Lk 8:5 *4071*
more are ye better than the *f*................... Lk 12:24 *4071*
the *f* of the air lodged in the .... Lk 13:19 *4071*
creeping things, and *f* of the air............. Acts 10:12 *4071*
creeping things, and *f* of the air .... Acts 11:6 *4071*
saying to all the *f* that fly in................... Rev 19:17 *3732*
all the *f* were filled with their .... Rev 19:21 *3732*

FOX {2}
if a *f* go up, he shall even break .... Neh 4:3 7776
unto them, Go ye, and tell that *f*............. Lk 13:32 *258*

FOXES {10}
went and caught three hundred *f*........... Judg 15:4 7776
they shall be a portion for *f*................... Ps 63:10 7776
Take us the *f*, the little *f*, ... Song 2:15 7776
Take us the *f*, the little *f* .... Song 2:15 7776
is desolate, the *f* walk upon it .... Lam 5:18 7776
are like the *f* in the deserts.................... Eze 13:4 7776
The *f* have holes, and the birds of .... Mt 8:20 *258*
F have holes, and birds of the air............ Lk 9:58 *258*

FRAGMENTS {7}
they took up of the *f* that .... Mt 14:20 *2801*
up twelve baskets full of the *f*................ Mk 6:43 *2801*
many baskets full of *f* took ye up........... Mk 8:19 *2801*
many baskets full of *f* took ye up........... Mk 8:20 *2801*
there was taken up of *f* that................... Lk 9:17 *2801*
Gather up the *f* that remain .... Jn 6:12 *2801*
the *f* of the five barley loaves .... Jn 6:13 *2801*

FRAIL {1}
that I may know how *f* I am .... Ps 39:4 2310

FRAME {5}
for he could not *f* to pronounce.............. Judg 12:6 3559
For he knoweth our *f*............................... Ps 103:14 3336
I *f* evil against you, and devise a............ Jer 18:11 3335
by which was as the *f* of a city .... Eze 40:2 4011
They will not *f* their doings to................. Hos 5:4 5414

FRAMED {5}
or shall the thing *f* say of him .... Is 29:16 3336
thing *f* say of him that *f* it .... Is 29:16 3335
f together groweth unto an holy .... Eph 2:21 *4883*
worlds were *f* by the word of God............ Heb 11:3 *2675*

FRAMETH {2}
to evil, and thy tongue *f* deceit............... Ps 50:19 6775
which *f* mischief by a law......................... Ps 94:20 3335

FRANKINCENSE {17}
these sweet spices with pure *f*................. Ex 30:34 3828
oil upon it, and put *f* thereon .... Lev 2:1 3828
thereof, with all the *f* thereof .... Lev 2:2 3828
put oil upon it, and lay *f* thereon .... Lev 2:15 3828
thereof, with all the *f* thereof .... Lev 2:16 3828
shall he put any *f* thereon....................... Lev 5:11 3828
all the *f* which is upon the meat.............. Lev 6:15 3828
shalt put pure *f* upon each row .... Lev 24:7 3828
no oil upon it, nor put *f* thereon.............. Num 5:15 3828
and the wine, and the oil, and the *f* 1Chr 9:29 3828
laid the meat offerings, the *f*.................. Neh 13:5 3828
with the meat offering and the *f*.............. Neh 13:9 3828
smoke, perfumed with myrrh and *f*......... Song 3:6 3828
of myrrh, and to the hill of *f* .... Song 4:6 3828
and cinnamon, with all trees of *f* .... Song 4:14 3828
gold, and *f*, and myrrh.............................. Mt 2:11 *3030*
and odours, and ointments, and *f*........... Rev 18:13 *3030*

FRANKLY {1}
to pay, he *f* forgave them both .... Lk 7:42 *5435*

FRAUD {2}
is full of cursing and deceit and *f* .... Ps 10:7 8496
which is of you kept back by *f* .... Jas 5:4 *650*

FRAY {3}
and no man shall *f* them away .... Deut 28:26 2729
and none shall *f* them away..................... Jer 7:33 2729
but these are come to *f* them .... Zec 1:21 2729

FRECKLED {1}
it is a *f* spot that groweth in.................. Lev 13:39 933

FREE {60}
he shall go out *f* for nothing.................... Ex 21:2 2670
I will not go out *f*................................... Ex 21:5 2670
shall she go out *f* without money .... Ex 21:11 2600
let him go *f* for his eye's sake .... Ex 21:26 2670
he shall let him go *f* for his .... Ex 21:27 2670
him *f* offerings every morning .... Ex 36:3 5071
to death, because she was not *f*.............. Lev 19:20 2666
be thou *f* from this bitter water .... Num 5:19 5352
then she shall be *f*, and shall................... Num 5:28 5352
thou shalt let him go *f* from thee............ Deut 15:12 2670
thou sendest him out *f* from thee .... Deut 15:13 2670
thou sendest him away *f* from thee .... Deut 15:18 2670
but he shall be *f* at home one .... Deut 24:5 5355
his father's house *f* in Israel 1Sa 17:25 2670
remaining in the chambers were *f*........... 1Chr 9:33 6362
as many as were of a *f* heart.................... 2Chr 29:31 5081
the servant is *f* from his master.............. Job 3:19 2670
Who hath sent out the wild ass *f*............. Job 39:5 2670
and uphold me with thy *f* spirit .... Ps 51:12 5082
F among the dead, like the slain .... Ps 88:5 2670
of the people, and let him go *f* .... Ps 105:20 6605
and to let the oppressed go *f* .... Is 58:6 2670
an Hebrew or an Hebrewess, go *f*............ Jer 34:9 2670
every one his maidservant, go *f*.............. Jer 34:10 2670
handmaids, whom they had let go *f* .... Jer 34:11 2670
thou shalt let him go *f* from thee............ Jer 34:14 2670
and publish the *f* offerings .... Amos 4:5 5071
or his mother, he shall be *f*..................... Mt 15:6
unto him, Then are the children *f* .... Mt 17:26 *1658*

he shall be *f* ... Mk 7:11
and the truth shall make you *f* ... Jn 8:32 *1659*
sayest thou, Ye shall be made *f* ... Jn 8:33 *1658*
Son therefore shall make you *f* ... Jn 8:36 *1659*
ye shall be *f* indeed ... Jn 8:36 *1658*
And Paul said, But I was *f* born ... Acts 22:28
offence, so also is the *f* gift ... Rom 5:15 *5486*
but the *f* gift is of many ... Rom 5:16 *5486*
the *f* gift came upon all men unto ... Rom 5:18
Being then made *f* from sin ... Rom 6:18 *1659*
ye were *f* from righteousness ... Rom 6:20 *1658*
But now being made *f* from sin ... Rom 6:22 *1659*
be dead, she is *f* from that law ... Rom 7:3 *1658*
made me *f* from the law of sin ... Rom 8:2 *1659*
but if thou mayest be made *f* ... 1Cor 7:21 *1658*
also he that is called, being *f* ... 1Cor 7:22 *1658*
am I not *f*? ... 1Cor 9:1 *1658*
For though I be *f* from all men ... 1Cor 9:19 *1658*
Gentiles, whether we be bond or *f* ... 1Cor 12:13 *1658*
there is neither bond nor *f* ... Gal 3:28 *1658*
But Jerusalem which is above is *f* ... Gal 4:26 *1658*
heir with the son of the *f* woman ... Gal 4:30 *1658*
of the bondwoman, but of the *f* ... Gal 4:31 *1658*
wherewith Christ hath made us *f* ... Gal 5:1 *1659*
the Lord, whether he be bond or *f* ... Eph 6:8 *1658*
Barbarian, Scythian, bond nor *f* ... Col 3:11 *1658*
of the Lord may have *f* course ... 2Th 3:1
As *f*, and not using your liberty ... 1Pet 2:16 *1658*
and every bondman, and every *f* man ... Rev 6:15 *1658*
small and great, rich and poor, *f* ... Rev 13:16 *1658*
and the flesh of all men, both *f* ... Rev 19:18 *1658*

FREED {2}
of you be *f* from being bondmen ... Josh 9:23 3772
For he that is dead is *f* from sin ... Rom 6:7 *1344*

FREEDMEN See LIBERTINES.

FREEDOM {2}
at all redeemed, nor *f* given her ... Lev 19:20 2668
a great sum obtained I this *f* ... Acts 22:28 *4174*

FREELY {19}
of the garden thou mayest *f* eat ... Gen 2:16
fish, which we did eat in Egypt *f* ... Num 11:5 2600
f to day of the spoil of their ... 1Sa 14:30
offered *f* for the house of God to ... Ezr 2:68
his counsellors have *f* offered ... Ezr 7:15
I will *f* sacrifice unto thee ... Ps 54:6 5071
backsliding, I will love them *f* ... Hos 14:4 5071
f ye have received, *f* give ... Mt 10:8 *1432*
f ye have received, *f* give ... Mt 10:8 *1432*
let me *f* speak unto you of the ... Acts 2:29 *3326,3954*
before whom also I speak *f* ... Acts 26:26 *3955*
Being justified *f* by his grace ... Rom 3:24 *1432*
him also *f* give us all things ... Rom 8:32
that are *f* given to us of God ... 1Cor 2:12
to you the gospel of God *f* ... 2Cor 11:7 *1432*
fountain of the water of life *f* ... Rev 21:6 *1432*
let him take the water of life *f* ... Rev 22:17 *1432*

FREEMAN {1}
being a servant, is the Lord's *f* ... 1Cor 7:22 *558*

FREEWILL {17}
vows, and for all his *f* offerings ... Lev 22:18 5071
or a *f* offering in beeves or ... Lev 22:21 5071
thou offer for a *f* offering ... Lev 22:23 5071
and beside all your *f* offerings ... Lev 23:38 5071
or in a *f* offering, or in your ... Num 15:3 5071
your *f* offerings, for your burnt ... Num 29:39 5071
vows, and your *f* offerings, and the ... Deut 12:6 5071
nor thy *f* offerings, or heave ... Deut 12:17 5071
of a *f* offering of thine hand ... Deut 16:10 5071
even a *f* offering, according as ... Deut 23:23 5071
was over the *f* offerings of God, ... 2Chr 31:14 5071
beside the *f* offering for the ... Ezr 1:4 5071
a *f* offering unto the LORD ... Ezr 3:5 5071
their own *f* to go up to Jerusalem ... Ezr 7:13 5069
with the *f* offering of the people ... Ezr 7:16 5069
the gold are a *f* offering unto ... Ezr 8:28 5071
the *f* offerings of my mouth, O ... Ps 119:108 5071

FREEWOMAN {2}
by a bondmaid, the other by a *f* ... Gal 4:22 *1658*
but he of the *f* was by promise ... Gal 4:23 *1658*

FREQUENT {1}
above measure, in prisons more *f* ... 2Cor 11:23 *4056*

FRESH {4}
of it was as the taste of *f* oil ... Num 11:8 3955
My glory was *f* in me, and my bow ... Job 29:20 2319
I shall be anointed with *f* oil ... Ps 92:10 7488
both yield salt water and *f* ... Jas 3:12 *1099*

FRESHER {1}
flesh shall be *f* than a child's ... Job 33:25 7375

FRET {7}
it is *f* inward, whether it be ... Lev 13:55 6356
her sore, for to make her *f* ... 1Sa 1:6 7481
F not thyself because of ... Ps 37:1 2734
f not thyself because of him who ... Ps 37:7 2734
f not thyself in any wise to do ... Ps 37:8 2734
F not thyself because of evil men ... Prov 24:19 2734
hungry, they shall *f* themselves ... Is 8:21 7107

FRETTED {1}
but hast *f* me in all these things ... Eze 16:43 7264

FRETTETH {1}
his heart *f* against the LORD ... Prov 19:3 2196

FRETTING {3}
the plague is a *f* leprosy ... Lev 13:51 3992
for it is a *f* leprosy ... Lev 13:52 3992
it is a *f* leprosy in the house ... Lev 14:44 3992

FRIED {2}
with oil, of fine flour, *f* ... Lev 7:12 7246
the pan, and for that which is *f* ... 1Chr 23:29 7246

FRIEND {54}
his *f* Hirah the Adullamite ... Gen 38:12 7453
the hand of his *f* the Adullamite ... Gen 38:20 7453
as a man speaketh unto his *f* ... Ex 33:11 7453
the wife of thy bosom, or thy *f* ... Deut 13:6 7453
whom he had used as his *f* ... Judg 14:20 7462
But Amnon had a *f*, whose name was ... 2Sa 13:3 7453
So Hushai David's *f* came into the ... 2Sa 15:37 7463
Hushai the Archite, David's *f* ... 2Sa 16:16 7463
Is this thy kindness to thy *f* ... 2Sa 16:17 7453
why wentest thou not with thy *f* ... 2Sa 16:17 7453
officer, and the king's *f* ... 1Kin 4:5 7463
seed of Abraham thy *f* for ever ... 2Chr 20:7 157
pity should be shewed from his *f* ... Job 6:14 7453
and ye dig a pit for your *f* ... Job 6:27 7451
he had been my *f* or brother ... Ps 35:14 7453
Yea, mine own familiar *f*, in whom ... Ps 41:9
f hast thou put far from me, and ... Ps 88:18 7453
son, if thou be surety for thy *f* ... Prov 6:1 7453
art come into the hand of thy *f* ... Prov 6:3 7453
thyself, and make sure thy *f* ... Prov 6:3 7453
A *f* loveth at all times, and a ... Prov 17:17 7453
surety in the presence of his *f* ... Prov 17:18 7453
there is a *f* that sticketh closer ... Prov 18:24 157
every man is a *f* to him that ... Prov 19:6 7453
his lips the king shall be his *f* ... Prov 22:11 7453
Faithful are the wounds of a *f* ... Prov 27:6 157
of a man's *f* by hearty counsel ... Prov 27:9 7453
Thine own *f*, and thy father's ... Prov 27:10 7453
own *f*, and thy father's *f* ... Prov 27:10 7453
blesseth his *f* with a loud voice ... Prov 27:14 7453
the countenance of his *f* ... Prov 27:17 7453
is my beloved, and this is my *f* ... Song 5:16 7453
chosen, the seed of Abraham my *f* ... Is 41:8 157
neighbour and his *f* shall perish ... Jer 6:21 7453
the flesh of his *f* in the siege ... Jer 19:9 7453
love a woman beloved of her *f* ... Hos 3:1 7453
Trust ye not in a *f*, put ye not ... Mic 7:5 7453
a *f* of publicans and sinners ... Mt 11:19 *5384*
answered one of them, and said, *F* ... Mt 20:13 *2083*
And he saith unto him, *F*, how ... Mt 22:12 *2083*
And Jesus said unto him, *F* ... Mt 26:50 *2083*
a *f* of publicans and sinners ... Lk 7:34 *5384*
them, Which of you shall have a *f* ... Lk 11:5 *5384*
at midnight, and say unto him, *F* ... Lk 11:5 *5384*
For a *f* of mine in his journey is ... Lk 11:6 *5384*
and give him, because he is his *f* ... Lk 11:8 *5384*
cometh, he may say unto thee, *F* ... Lk 14:10 *5384*
but the *f* of the bridegroom, ... Jn 3:29 *5384*
unto them, Our *f* Lazarus sleepeth ... Jn 11:11 *5384*
man go, thou art not Caesar's *f* ... Jn 19:12 *5384*
the king's chamberlain their *f* ... Acts 12:20 *3982*
and he was called the *F* of God ... Jas 2:23 *5384*
a *f* of the world is the enemy of ... Jas 4:4 *5384*

FRIENDLY {3}
after her, to speak *f* unto her ... Judg 19:3 3820
hast spoken *f* unto thine handmaid ... Ruth 2:13 3820
hath friends must shew himself *f* ... Prov 18:24 7489

FRIENDS {49}
Gerar, and Ahuzzath one of his *f* ... Gen 26:26 4828
elders of Judah, even to his *f* ... 1Sa 30:26 7453
to his brethren, and to his *f* ... 2Sa 3:8 4828
thine enemies, and hatest thy *f* ... 2Sa 19:6 157
of his kinsfolks, nor of his *f* ... 1Kin 16:11 7453
home, he sent and called for his *f* ... Est 5:10 157
all his *f* unto him, Let a gallows ... Est 5:14 157
all his *f* every thing that had ... Est 6:13 157
Now when Job's three *f* heard of ... Job 2:11 7453
My *f* scorn me ... Job 16:20 7453
that speaketh flattery to his *f* ... Job 17:5 7453
my familiar *f* have forgotten me ... Job 19:14
All my inward *f* abhorred me ... Job 19:19 4962
me, have pity upon me, O ye my *f* ... Job 19:21 7453
his three *f* was his wrath kindled ... Job 32:3 7453
thee, and against thy two *f* ... Job 42:7 7453
of Job, when he prayed for his *f* ... Job 42:10 7453
my *f* stand aloof from my sore ... Ps 38:11 7453
but the rich hath many *f* ... Prov 14:20 157
and a whisperer separateth chief *f* ... Prov 16:28 441
a matter separateth very *f* ... Prov 17:9 441
A man that hath *f* must shew ... Prov 18:24 7453
Wealth maketh many *f* ... Prov 19:4 7453
more do his *f* go far from him ... Prov 19:7 4828
eat, O *f*; drink, yea ... Song 5:1 7453
to thyself, and to all thy *f* ... Jer 20:4 157
buried there, thou, and all thy *f* ... Jer 20:6 157
Thy *f* have set thee on, and have ... Jer 38:22 605,7965
all her *f* have dealt ... Lam 1:2 7453
was wounded in the house of my *f* ... Zec 13:6 157
when his *f* heard of it, they went ... Mk 3:21 *3588,3844*
saith unto him, Go home to thy *f* ... Mk 5:19 *4674*
the centurion sent *f* to him ... Lk 7:6 *5384*
And I say unto you my *f*, Be not ... Lk 12:4 *5384*
or a supper, call not thy *f* ... Lk 14:12 *5384*
home, he calleth together his *f* ... Lk 15:6 *5384*
hath found it, she calleth her *f* ... Lk 15:9 *5384*
that I might make merry with my *f* ... Lk 15:29 *5384*
to yourselves *f* of the mammon of ... Lk 16:9 *5384*
and brethren, and kinsfolks, and *f* ... Lk 21:16 *5384*
and Herod were made *f* together ... Lk 23:12 *5384*
a man lay down his life for his *f* ... Jn 15:13 *5384*
Ye are my *f*, if ye do whatsoever ... Jn 15:14 *5384*
but I have called you *f* ... Jn 15:15 *5384*
together his kinsmen and near *f* ... Acts 10:24 *5384*
chief of Asia, which were his *f* ... Acts 19:31 *5384*
go unto his *f* to refresh himself ... Acts 27:3 *5384*
Our *f* salute thee ... 3Jn 14 *5384*
Greet the *f* by name ... 3Jn 14 *5384*

FRIENDSHIP {2}
Make no *f* with an angry man ... Prov 22:24 7462
know ye not that the *f* of the ... Jas 4:4 *5373*

FRINGE {2}
that they put upon the *f* of the ... Num 15:38 6734
And it shall be unto you for a *f* ... Num 15:39 6734

FRINGES {2}
them *f* in the borders of their ... Num 15:38 6734
Thou shalt make thee *f* upon the ... Deut 22:12 1434

FRO See APPENDIX.

FROGS {14}
will smite all thy borders with *f* ... Ex 8:2 6854
shall bring forth *f* abundantly ... Ex 8:3 6854
the *f* shall come up both on thee, ... Ex 8:4 6854
cause *f* to come up upon the land ... Ex 8:5 6854
the *f* came up, and covered the ... Ex 8:6 6854
brought up *f* upon the land of ... Ex 8:7 6854
he may take away the *f* from me ... Ex 8:8 6854
to destroy the *f* from thee ... Ex 8:9 6854
the *f* shall depart from thee, and ... Ex 8:11 6854
f which he had brought against ... Ex 8:12 6854
the *f* died out of the houses, out ... Ex 8:13 6854
and *f*, which destroyed them ... Ps 78:45 6854
land brought forth *f* in abundance ... Ps 105:30 6854
f come out of the mouth of the ... Rev 16:13 *944*

FROM See APPENDIX.

FRONT See APPENDIX.

FRONTIERS {1}
his cities which are on his *f* ... Eze 25:9 7097

FRONTLETS {3}
hand, and for *f* between thine eyes ... Ex 13:16 2903
they shall be as *f* between thine ... Deut 6:8 2903
may be as *f* between your eyes ... Deut 11:18 2903

FROST {7}
consumed me, and the *f* by night ... Gen 31:40 7140
small as the hoar *f* on the ground ... Ex 16:14 3713
By the breath of God *f* is given ... Job 37:10 7140
and the hoary *f* of heaven, who ... Job 38:29 3713
and their sycomore trees with *f* ... Ps 78:47 2602
scattereth the hoar *f* like ashes ... Ps 147:16 3713
heat, and in the night to the *f* ... Jer 36:30 7140

FROWARD {21}
for they are a very *f* generation ... Deut 32:20 8419
with the *f* thou wilt shew thyself ... 2Sa 22:27 6141
the counsel of the *f* is carried ... Job 5:13 6617
thyself pure; and with the *f* ... Ps 18:26 6141
thou wilt shew thyself *f* ... Ps 18:26 6617
A *f* heart shall depart from me ... Ps 101:4 6141
the man that speaketh *f* things ... Prov 2:12 8419
crooked, and they *f* in their paths ... Prov 2:15 3868
For the *f* is abomination to the ... Prov 3:32 3868
Put away from thee a *f* mouth ... Prov 4:24 6143
man, walketh with a *f* mouth ... Prov 6:12 6143
there is nothing *f* or perverse in ... Prov 8:8 6617
way, and the *f* mouth, do I hate ... Prov 8:13 8419
but the *f* tongue shall be cut out ... Prov 10:31 8419
They that are of a *f* heart are ... Prov 11:20 6141
A *f* man soweth strife ... Prov 16:28 8419
his eyes to devise *f* things ... Prov 16:30 8419
He that hath a *f* heart findeth no ... Prov 17:20 6141
The way of man is *f* and strange ... Prov 21:8 2019
and snares are in the way of the *f* ... Prov 22:5 6141
good and gentle, but also to the *f* ... 1Pet 2:18 *4646*

FROWARDLY {1}
he went on *f* in the way of his ... Is 57:17 7726

FROWARDNESS {3}
and delight in the *f* of the wicked ... Prov 2:14 8419
F is in his heart, he deviseth ... Prov 6:14 8419
mouth of the wicked speaketh *f* ... Prov 10:32 8419

FROZEN {1}
and the face of the deep is *f* ... Job 38:30 3920

FRUIT {210}
the *f* tree yielding *f* after ... Gen 1:11 6529
his kind, and the tree yielding *f* ... Gen 1:12 6529
in the which is the *f* of a tree ... Gen 1:29 6529
We may eat of the *f* of the trees ... Gen 3:2 6529
But of the *f* of the tree which is ... Gen 3:3 6529
wise, she took of the *f* thereof ... Gen 3:6 6529
that Cain brought of the *f* of the ... Gen 4:3 6529
from thee the *f* of the womb ... Gen 30:2 6529
all the *f* of the trees which the ... Ex 10:15 6529
so that her *f* depart from her, and ... Ex 21:22 3206
then ye shall count the *f* thereof ... Lev 19:23 6529
But in the fourth year all the *f* ... Lev 19:24 6529
shall ye eat of the *f* thereof ... Lev 19:25 6529
gathered in the *f* of the land ... Lev 23:39 8393
and gather in the *f* thereof ... Lev 25:3 8393
And the land shall yield her *f* ... Lev 25:19 6529
bring forth *f* for three years ... Lev 25:21 8393
eat yet of old *f* until the ninth ... Lev 25:22 8393
of the field shall yield their *f* ... Lev 26:4 6529
or of the *f* of the tree, is the ... Lev 27:30 6529
and bring of the *f* of the land ... Num 13:20 6529
and shewed them the *f* of the land ... Num 13:26 6529

and this is the *f* of it ... Num 13:27 6529
they took of the *f* of the land in ... Deut 1:25 6529
will also bless the *f* of thy womb ... Deut 7:13 6529
the *f* of thy land, thy corn, and ... Deut 7:13 6529
and that the land yield not her *f* ... Deut 11:17 2981
lest the *f* of thy seed which thou ... Deut 22:9 4395
the *f* of thy vineyard, be defiled ... Deut 22:9 8393
first of all the *f* of the earth ... Deut 26:2 6529
shall be the *f* of thy body ... Deut 28:4 6529
the *f* of thy ground, and the *f* ... Deut 28:4 6529
the *f* of thy cattle, the increase ... Deut 28:4 6529
in the *f* of thy body, and in the ... Deut 28:11 6529
in the *f* of thy cattle, and in the ... Deut 28:11 6529
in the *f* of thy ground, in the ... Deut 28:11 6529
Cursed shall be the *f* of thy body ... Deut 28:18 6529
the *f* of thy land, the increase ... Deut 28:18 6529
The *f* of thy land, and all thy ... Deut 28:33 6529
for thine olive shall cast his *f* ... Deut 28:40
f of thy land shall the locust ... Deut 28:42 6529
he shall eat the *f* of thy cattle ... Deut 28:51 6529
the *f* of thy land, until thou be ... Deut 28:51 6529
shalt eat the *f* of thine own body ... Deut 28:53 6529
in the *f* of thy body ... Deut 30:9 6529
in the *f* of thy cattle ... Deut 30:9 6529
in the *f* of thy land, for good ... Deut 30:9 6529
but they did eat of the *f* of the ... Josh 5:12 8393
my sweetness, and my good *f* ... Judg 9:11 8270
summer *f* for the young men to eat ... 2Sa 16:2
root downward, and bear *f* upward ... 2Kin 19:30 6529
and *f* trees in abundance ... Neh 9:25 3978
our fathers to eat the *f* thereof ... Neh 9:36 6529
firstfruits of all *f* of all trees ... Neh 10:35 6529
the *f* of all manner of trees, of ... Neh 10:37 6529
forth his *f* in his season ... Ps 1:3 6529
Their *f* shalt thou destroy from ... Ps 21:10 6529
the *f* thereof shall shake like ... Ps 72:16 6529
still bring forth *f* in old age ... Ps 92:14 5107
satisfied with the *f* of thy works ... Ps 104:13 6529
devoured the *f* of their ground ... Ps 105:35 6529
the *f* of the womb is his reward ... Ps 127:3 6529
Of the *f* of thy body will I set ... Ps 132:11 6529
eat of the *f* of their own way ... Prov 1:31 6529
My *f* is better than gold, yea, ... Prov 8:19 6529
the *f* of the wicked to sin ... Prov 10:16 8393
The *f* of the righteous is a tree ... Prov 11:30 6529
root of the righteous yieldeth *f* ... Prov 12:12
with good by the *f* of his mouth ... Prov 12:14 6529
eat good by the *f* of his mouth ... Prov 13:2 6529
satisfied with the *f* of his mouth ... Prov 18:20 6529
love it shall eat the *f* thereof ... Prov 18:21 6529
fig tree shall eat the *f* thereof ... Prov 27:18 6529
with the *f* of her hands she ... Prov 31:16 6529
Give her of the *f* of her hands ... Prov 31:31 6529
his *f* was sweet to my taste ... Song 2:3 6529
every one for the *f* thereof was ... Song 8:11 6529
keep the *f* thereof two hundred ... Song 8:12 6529
shall eat the *f* of their doings ... Is 3:10 6529
the *f* of the earth shall be ... Is 4:2 6529
I will punish the *f* of the stout ... Is 10:12 6529
have no pity on the *f* of the womb ... Is 13:18 6529
his *f* shall be a fiery flying ... Is 14:29 6529
fill the face of the world with *f* ... Is 27:6 8570
this is all the *f* to take away ... Is 27:9 6529
as the hasty *f* before the summer ... Is 28:4 1061
vineyards, and eat the *f* thereof ... Is 37:30 6529
root downward, and bear *f* upward ... Is 37:31 6529
I create the *f* of the lips ... Is 57:19 5108
vineyards, and eat the *f* of them ... Is 65:21 6529
country, to eat the *f* thereof ... Jer 2:7 6529
even the *f* of their thoughts, ... Jer 6:19 6529
and upon the *f* of the ground ... Jer 7:20 6529
olive tree, fair, and of goodly *f* ... Jer 11:16 6529
the tree with the *f* thereof ... Jer 11:19 3899
grow, yea, they bring forth *f* ... Jer 12:2 6529
shall cease from yielding *f* ... Jer 17:8 6529
according to the *f* of his doings ... Jer 17:10 6529
according to the *f* of your doings ... Jer 21:14 6529
gardens, and eat the *f* of them ... Jer 29:5 6529
gardens, and eat the *f* of them ... Jer 29:28 6529
according to the *f* of his doings ... Jer 32:19 6529
Shall the women eat their *f* ... Lam 2:20 6529
branches, and that it might bear *f* ... Eze 17:8 6529
thereof, and cut off the *f* thereof ... Eze 17:9 6529
bring forth boughs, and bear *f* ... Eze 17:23 6529
and the east wind dried up her *f* ... Eze 19:12 6529
which hath devoured her *f* ... Eze 19:14 6529
they shall eat thy *f*, and they ... Eze 25:4 6529
of the field shall yield her *f* ... Eze 34:27 6529
yield your *f* to my people of ... Eze 36:8 6529
and they shall increase and bring *f* ... Eze 36:11 6509
I will multiply the *f* of the tree ... Eze 36:30 6529
neither shall the *f* thereof be ... Eze 47:12 6529
new *f* according to his months ... Eze 47:12 1061
the *f* thereof shall be for meat, ... Eze 47:12 6529
the *f* thereof much, and in it was ... Dan 4:12 4
off his leaves, and scatter his *f* ... Dan 4:14 4
the *f* thereof much, and in it was ... Dan 4:21 4
is dried up, they shall bear no *f* ... Hos 9:16 6529
even the beloved *f* of their womb ... Hos 9:16
he bringeth forth *f* unto himself ... Hos 10:1 6529
to the multitude of his *f* he hath ... Hos 10:1 6529
ye have eaten the *f* of lies ... Hos 10:13 6529
From me is thy *f* found ... Hos 14:8 6529
for the tree beareth her *f* ... Joel 2:22 6529
yet I destroyed his *f* from above ... Amos 2:9 6529
the *f* of righteousness into ... Amos 6:12 6529
and a gatherer of sycomore *f* ... Amos 7:14

and behold a basket of summer *f* ... Amos 8:1
And I said, A basket of summer *f* ... Amos 8:2
gardens, and eat the *f* of them ... Amos 9:14 6529
the *f* of my body for the sin of ... Mic 6:7 6529
my soul desired the firstripe *f* ... Mic 7:1
for the *f* of their doings ... Mic 7:13 6529
neither shall *f* be in the vines ... Hab 3:17 2981
and the earth is stayed from her *f* ... Hag 1:10 2981
the vine shall give her *f* ... Zec 8:12 6529
the *f* thereof, even his meat, is ... Mal 1:12 5108
shall your vine cast her *f* before ... Mal 3:11 7920
not forth good *f* is hewn down ... Mt 3:10 2590
good tree bringeth forth good *f* ... Mt 7:17 2590
tree bringeth forth evil *f* ... Mt 7:17 2590
tree cannot bring forth evil *f* ... Mt 7:18 2590
a corrupt tree bring forth good *f* ... Mt 7:18 2590
not forth good *f* is hewn down ... Mt 7:19 2590
make the tree good, and his *f* good ... Mt 12:33 2590
tree corrupt, and his *f* corrupt ... Mt 12:33 2590
for the tree is known by his *f* ... Mt 12:33 2590
good ground, and brought forth *f* ... Mt 13:8 2590
which also beareth *f*, and bringeth ... Mt 13:23 2592
was sprung up, and brought forth *f* ... Mt 13:26 2590
unto it, Let no *f* grow on thee ... Mt 21:19 2590
when the time of the *f* drew near ... Mt 21:34 2590
henceforth of this *f* of the vine ... Mt 26:29 1081
and choked it, and it yielded no *f* ... Mk 4:7 2590
did yield *f* that sprang up and ... Mk 4:8 2590
and receive it, and bring forth *f* ... Mk 4:20 2592
earth bringeth forth *f* of herself ... Mk 4:28 2592
But when the *f* is brought forth, ... Mk 4:29 2590
No man eat *f* of thee hereafter ... Mk 11:14 2590
of the *f* of the vineyard ... Mk 12:2 2590
no more of the *f* of the vine ... Mk 14:25 1081
and blessed is the *f* of thy womb ... Lk 1:42 2590
not forth good *f* is hewn down ... Lk 3:9 2590
tree bringeth not forth corrupt *f* ... Lk 6:43 2590
a corrupt tree bring forth good *f* ... Lk 6:43 2590
every tree is known by his own *f* ... Lk 6:44 2590
up, and bare *f* an hundredfold ... Lk 8:8 2590
life, and bring no *f* to perfection ... Lk 8:14 5052
bring forth *f* with patience ... Lk 8:15 2592
sought *f* thereon, and found none ... Lk 13:6 2590
I come seeking *f* on this fig tree ... Lk 13:7 2590
And if it bear *f*, well ... Lk 13:9 2590
give him of the *f* of the vineyard ... Lk 20:10 2590
not drink of the *f* of the vine ... Lk 22:18 1081
gathereth *f* unto life eternal ... Jn 4:36 2590
it die, it bringeth forth much *f* ... Jn 12:24 2590
that beareth not *f* he taketh away ... Jn 15:2 2590
and every branch that beareth *f* ... Jn 15:2 2590
that it may bring forth more *f* ... Jn 15:2 2590
branch cannot bear *f* of itself ... Jn 15:4 2590
the same bringeth forth much *f* ... Jn 15:5 2590
glorified, that ye bear much *f* ... Jn 15:8 2590
ye should go and bring forth *f* ... Jn 15:16 2590
that your *f* should remain ... Jn 15:16 2590
that of the *f* of his loins, ... Acts 2:30 2590
might have some *f* among you also ... Rom 1:13 2590
What *f* had ye then in those ... Rom 6:21 2590
ye have your *f* unto holiness, and ... Rom 6:22 2590
we should bring forth *f* unto God ... Rom 7:4 2592
to bring forth *f* unto death ... Rom 7:5 2592
and have sealed to them this *f* ... Rom 15:28 2590
and eateth not of the *f* thereof ... 1Cor 9:7 2590
But the *f* of the Spirit is love, ... Gal 5:22 2590
(For the *f* of the Spirit is in ... Eph 5:9 2590
this is the *f* of my labour ... Phil 1:22 2590
but I desire *f* that may abound to ... Phil 4:17 2590
and bringeth forth *f*, as it doth ... Col 1:6 2592
it yieldeth the peaceable *f* of ... Heb 12:11 2590
the *f* of our lips giving thanks ... Heb 13:15 2590
the *f* of righteousness is sown in ... Jas 3:18 2590
for the precious *f* of the earth ... Jas 5:7 2590
and the earth brought forth her *f* ... Jas 5:18 2590
trees whose *f* withereth, without ... Jude 12 5352
whose *f* withereth, without *f* ... Jude 12 175
and yielded her *f* every month ... Rev 22:2 2590

FRUITFUL {35}
And God blessed them, saying, Be *f* ... Gen 1:22 6509
them, and God said unto them, Be *f* ... Gen 1:28 6509
abundantly in the earth, and be *f* ... Gen 8:17 6509
his sons, and said unto them, Be *f* ... Gen 9:1 6509
And you, be ye *f*, and multiply ... Gen 9:7 6509
And I will make thee exceeding *f* ... Gen 17:6 6509
blessed him, and will make him *f* ... Gen 17:20 6509
us, and we shall be *f* in the land ... Gen 26:22 6509
bless thee, and make thee *f* ... Gen 28:3 6509
be *f* and multiply ... Gen 35:11 6509
be *f* in the land of my affliction ... Gen 41:52 6509
me, Behold, I will make thee *f* ... Gen 48:4 6509
Joseph is a *f* bough ... Gen 49:22 6509
even a *f* bough by a well ... Gen 49:22 6509
And the children of Israel were *f* ... Ex 1:7 6509
respect unto you, and make you *f* ... Lev 26:9 6509
A *f* land into barrenness, for the ... Ps 107:34 6529
Thy wife shall be as a *f* vine by ... Ps 128:3 6509
f trees, and all cedars ... Ps 148:9 6529
hath a vineyard in a very *f* hill ... Is 5:1 1121,8081
of his forest, and of his *f* field ... Is 10:18 3759
in the outmost *f* branches thereof ... Is 17:6 6509
shall be turned into a *f* field ... Is 29:17 3759
the *f* field shall be esteemed as ... Is 29:17 3759
pleasant fields, for the *f* vine ... Is 32:12 6509
and the wilderness be a *f* field ... Is 32:15 3759
the *f* field be counted for a ... Is 32:15 3759
remain in the *f* field ... Is 32:16 3759
the *f* place was a wilderness, and ... Jer 4:26 3759
and they shall be *f* and increase ... Jer 23:3 6509
land, and planted it in a *f* field ... Eze 17:5 2233
she was *f* and full of branches by ... Eze 19:10 6509
Though he be *f* among his brethren ... Hos 13:15 6500
f seasons, filling our hearts ... Acts 14:17 2593
being *f* in every good work, and ... Col 1:10 2592

FRUITS {43}
take of the best *f* in the land in ... Gen 43:11 2173
to offer the first of thy ripe *f* ... Ex 22:29 4395
and shalt gather in the *f* thereof ... Ex 23:10 8393
with the bread of the first *f* for ... Lev 23:20 1061
of the *f* he shall sell unto thee ... Lev 25:15 8393
of the *f* doth he sell unto thee ... Lev 25:16 8393
until her *f* come in ye shall eat ... Lev 25:22 8393
trees of the land yield their *f* ... Lev 26:20 6529
for the precious *f* brought forth ... Deut 33:14 8393
him, and thou shalt bring in the *f* ... 2Sa 9:10
and an hundred of summer *f* ... 2Sa 16:1
all the *f* of the field since the ... 2Kin 8:6 8393
vineyards, and eat the *f* thereof ... 2Kin 19:29 6529
If I have eaten the *f* thereof ... Job 31:39 3581
which may yield *f* of increase ... Ps 107:37 6529
trees in them of all kind of *f* ... Eccl 2:5 6529
of pomegranates, with pleasant *f* ... Song 4:13 6529
his garden, and eat his pleasant *f* ... Song 4:16 6529
nuts to see the *f* of the valley ... Song 6:11 3
are all manner of pleasant *f* ... Song 7:13
for the shouting for thy summer *f* ... Is 16:9
and Carmel shake off their *f* ... Is 33:9
ye, gather ye wine, and summer *f* ... Jer 40:10
wine and summer *f* very much ... Jer 40:12
is fallen upon thy summer *f* ... Jer 48:32
for want of the *f* of the field ... Lam 4:9 8570
they have gathered the summer *f* ... Mic 7:1
not destroy the *f* of your ground ... Mal 3:11 6529
therefore *f* meet for repentance ... Mt 3:8 2590
Ye shall know them by their *f* ... Mt 7:16 2590
by their *f* ye shall know them ... Mt 7:20 2590
they might receive the *f* of it ... Mt 21:34 2590
render him the *f* in their seasons ... Mt 21:41 2590
bringing forth the *f* thereof ... Mt 21:43 2590
therefore *f* worthy of repentance ... Lk 3:8 2590
have no room where to bestow my *f* ... Lk 12:17 2590
and there will I bestow all my *f* ... Lk 12:18 1081
sown, and increase the *f* of your ... 2Cor 9:10 1081
with the *f* of righteousness ... Phil 1:11 2590
must be first partaker of the *f* ... 2Ti 2:6 2590
full of mercy and good *f*, without ... Jas 3:17 2590
the *f* that thy soul lusted after ... Rev 18:14 3703
which bare twelve manner of *f* ... Rev 22:2 2590

FRUSTRATE {2}
to *f* their purpose, all the days ... Ezr 4:5 656
I do not *f* the grace of God ... Gal 2:21 114

FRUSTRATETH {1}
That *f* the tokens of the liars, ... Is 44:25 6565

FRYING {1}
meat offering baken in the *f* pan ... Lev 2:7 4802

FRYINGPAN {1}
and all that is dressed in the *f* ... Lev 7:9 4802

FUEL {5}
be with burning and *f* of fire ... Is 9:5 3980
shall be as the *f* of the fire ... Is 9:19 3980
it is cast into the fire for *f* ... Eze 15:4 402
I have given to the fire for *f* ... Eze 15:6 402
Thou shalt be for *f* to the fire ... Eze 21:32 402

FUGITIVE {2}
a *f* and a vagabond shalt thou be ... Gen 4:12 5128
and I shall be a *f* and a vagabond ... Gen 4:14 5128

FUGITIVES {4}
Ye Gileadites are *f* of Ephraim ... Judg 12:4 6412
the *f* that fell away to the king ... 2Kin 25:11 5307
his *f* shall flee unto Zoar, an ... Is 15:5 1280
all his *f* with all his bands ... Eze 17:21 4015

FULFIL {24}
F her week, and we will give thee ... Gen 29:27 4390
F your works, your daily tasks, ... Ex 5:13 3615
the number of thy days I will *f* ... Ex 23:26 4390
that he might *f* the word of the ... 1Kin 2:27 4390
takest heed to *f* the statutes ... 1Chr 22:13 6213
To *f* the word of the LORD by the ... 2Chr 36:21 4390
to *f* threescore and ten years ... 2Chr 36:21 4390
number the months that they *f* ... Job 39:2
own heart, and *f* all thy counsel ... Ps 20:4 4390
the LORD *f* all thy petitions ... Ps 20:5 4390
He will *f* the desire of them that ... Ps 145:19 6213
us to *f* all righteousness ... Mt 3:15 4137
am not come to destroy, but to *f* ... Mt 5:17 4137
heart, which shall *f* all my will ... Acts 13:22 4160
if it *f* the law, judge thee, who ... Rom 2:27 5055
the flesh, to *f* the lusts thereof ... Rom 13:14
ye shall not *f* the lust of the ... Gal 5:16 5055
and so *f* the law of Christ ... Gal 6:2 378
F ye my joy, that ye be ... Phil 2:2 4137
me for you, to *f* the word of God ... Col 1:25 4137
in the Lord, that thou *f* it ... Col 4:17 4137
f all the good pleasure of his ... 2Th 1:11 4137
If ye *f* the royal law according ... Jas 2:8 5055
put in their hearts to *f* his will ... Rev 17:17 4160

FULFILLED {82}
her days to be delivered were *f* ... Gen 25:24 4390
me my wife, for my days are *f* ... Gen 29:21 4390

And Jacob did so, and *f* her week ... Gen 29:28 4390
And forty days were *f* for him ... Gen 50:3 4390
for so are *f* the days of those ... Gen 50:3 4390
Wherefore have ye not *f* your task ... Ex 5:14 3615
And seven days were *f*, after that ... Ex 7:25 4390
the days of her purifying be *f* ... Lev 12:4 4390
the days of her purifying are *f* ... Lev 12:6 4390
until the days be *f*, in the which ... Num 6:5 4390
the days of his separation are *f* ... Num 6:13 4390
And when thy days be *f*, and thou ... 2Sa 7:12 4390
in that the king hath *f* the ... 2Sa 14:22 6213
and hath with his hand *f* it ... 1Kin 8:15 4390
hast *f* it with thine hand, as it ... 1Kin 8:24 4390
who hath with his hands *f* that ... 2Chr 6:4 4390
hast *f* it with thine hand, as it ... 2Chr 6:15 4390
the mouth of Jeremiah might be *f* ... Ezr 1:1 3615
But thou hast *f* the judgment of ... Job 36:17 4390
f with your hand, saying, We will ... Jer 44:25 4390
he hath *f* his word that he had ... Lam 2:17 1214
our end is near, our days are *f* ... Lam 4:18 4390
when the days of the siege are *f* ... Eze 5:2 4390
the thing *f* upon Nebuchadnezzar ... Dan 4:33 5487
till three whole weeks were *f* ... Dan 10:3 4390
that it might be *f* which was ... Mt 1:22 *4137*
that it might be *f* which was ... Mt 2:15 *4137*
Then was *f* that which was spoken ... Mt 2:17 *4137*
that it might be *f* which was ... Mt 2:23 *4137*
That it might be *f* which was ... Mt 4:14 *4137*
pass from the law, till all be *f* ... Mt 5:18 *1096*
That it might be *f* which was ... Mt 8:17 *4137*
That it might be *f* which was ... Mt 12:17 *4137*
in them is *f* the prophecy of ... Mt 13:14 *378*
That it might be *f* which was ... Mt 13:35 *4137*
that it might be *f* which was ... Mt 21:4 *4137*
pass, till all these things be *f* ... Mt 24:34 *1096*
then shall the scriptures be *f* ... Mt 26:54 *4137*
of the prophets might be *f* ... Mt 26:56 *4137*
Then was *f* that which was spoken ... Mt 27:9 *4137*
that it might be *f* which was ... Mt 27:35 *4137*
And saying, The time is *f*, and the ... Mk 1:15 *4137*
when all these things shall be *f* ... Mk 13:4 *4931*
but the scriptures must be *f* ... Mk 14:49 *4137*
And the scripture was *f*, which ... Mk 15:28 *4137*
which shall be *f* in their season ... Lk 1:20 *4137*
And when they had *f* the days ... Lk 2:43 *5048*
is this scripture *f* in your ears ... Lk 4:21 *4137*
things which are written may be *f* ... Lk 21:22 *4137*
the times of the Gentiles be *f* ... Lk 21:24 *4137*
not pass away, till all be *f* ... Lk 21:32 *1096*
until it be *f* in the kingdom of ... Lk 22:16 *4137*
you, that all things must be *f* ... Lk 24:44 *4137*
this my joy therefore is *f* ... Jn 3:29 *4137*
of Esaias the prophet might be *f* ... Jn 12:38 *4137*
but that the scripture may be *f* ... Jn 13:18 *4137*
that the word might be *f* that is ... Jn 15:25 *4137*
that the scripture might be *f* ... Jn 17:12 *4137*
might have my joy *f* in themselves ... Jn 17:13 *4137*
That the saying might be *f* ... Jn 18:9 *4137*
the saying of Jesus might be *f* ... Jn 18:32 *4137*
that the scripture might be *f* ... Jn 19:24 *4137*
that the scripture might be *f* ... Jn 19:28 *5048*
that the scripture should be *f* ... Jn 19:36 *4137*
scripture must needs have been *f* ... Acts 1:16 *4137*
should suffer, he hath so *f* ... Acts 3:18 *4137*
And after that many days were *f* ... Acts 9:23 *4137*
when they had *f* their ministry, ... Acts 12:25 *4137*
as John *f* his course, he said, ... Acts 13:25 *4137*
they have *f* them in condemning ... Acts 13:27 *4137*
when they had *f* all that was ... Acts 13:29 *5055*
God hath *f* the same unto us their ... Acts 13:33 *1603*
of God for the work which they *f* ... Acts 14:26 *4137*
of the law might be *f* in us ... Rom 8:4 *4137*
loveth another hath *f* the law ... Rom 13:8 *4137*
when your obedience is *f* ... 2Cor 10:6 *4137*
For all the law is *f* in one word ... Gal 5:14 *4137*
the scripture was *f* which saith ... Jas 2:23 *4137*
killed as they were, should be *f* ... Rev 6:11 *4137*
of the seven angels were *f* ... Rev 15:8 *5055*
until the words of God shall be *f* ... Rev 17:17 *5055*
the thousand years should be *f* ... Rev 20:3 *5055*

FULFILLING {3}
stormy wind *f* his word ... Ps 148:8 6213
love is the *f* of the law ... Rom 13:10 *4138*
f the desires of the flesh and of ... Eph 2:3 *4160*

FULL {260}
vale of Siddim was *f* of slimepits ... Gen 14:10
of the Amorites is not yet *f* ... Gen 15:16 8003
age, an old man, and *f* of years ... Gen 25:8 7649
people, being old and *f* of days ... Gen 35:29 7649
to pass at the end of two *f* years ... Gen 41:1 3117
devoured the seven rank and *f* ears ... Gen 41:7 4392
ears came up in one stalk, *f* ... Gen 41:22 4392
his sack, our money in *f* weight ... Gen 43:21
shall be *f* of swarms of flies ... Ex 8:21 4390
and when we did eat bread to the *f* ... Ex 16:3 7648
and in the morning bread to the *f* ... Ex 16:8 7646
put an omer *f* of manna therein, ... Ex 16:33 4393
for he should make *f* restitution ... Ex 22:3 7999
even corn beaten out of *f* ears ... Lev 2:14 3759
he shall take a censer *f* of ... Lev 16:12 4393
his hands *f* of sweet incense ... Lev 16:12 4393
the land become *f* of wickedness ... Lev 19:29 4390
within a *f* year may he redeem it ... Lev 25:29 3117
within the space of a *f* year ... Lev 25:30 8549
ye shall eat your bread to the *f* ... Lev 26:5 7648
both of them were *f* of fine flour ... Num 7:13 4392
ten shekels of gold, *f* of incense ... Num 7:14 4392
both of them *f* of fine flour ... Num 7:19 4392
gold of ten shekels, *f* of incense ... Num 7:20 4392
both of them *f* of fine flour ... Num 7:25 4392
of ten shekels, *f* of incense ... Num 7:26 4392
both of them *f* of fine flour ... Num 7:31 4392
of ten shekels, *f* of incense ... Num 7:32 4392
both of them *f* of fine flour ... Num 7:37 4392
of ten shekels, *f* of incense ... Num 7:38 4392
both of them *f* of fine flour ... Num 7:43 4392
of ten shekels, *f* of incense ... Num 7:44 4392
both of them *f* of fine flour ... Num 7:49 4392
of ten shekels, *f* of incense ... Num 7:50 4392
both of them *f* of fine flour ... Num 7:55 4392
of ten shekels, *f* of incense ... Num 7:56 4392
both of them *f* of fine flour ... Num 7:61 4392
of ten shekels, *f* of incense ... Num 7:62 4392
both of them *f* of fine flour ... Num 7:67 4392
of ten shekels, *f* of incense ... Num 7:68 4392
both of them *f* of fine flour ... Num 7:73 4392
of ten shekels, *f* of incense ... Num 7:74 4392
both of them *f* of fine flour ... Num 7:79 4392
of ten shekels, *f* of incense ... Num 7:80 4392
f of incense, weighing ten ... Num 7:86 4392
give me his house *f* of silver ... Num 22:18 4393
give me his house *f* of silver ... Num 24:13 4393
houses *f* of all good things, ... Deut 6:11 4392
thou shalt have eaten and be *f* ... Deut 6:11 7646
When thou hast eaten and art *f* ... Deut 8:10 7646
when thou hast eaten and art *f* ... Deut 8:12 7646
that thou mayest eat and be *f* ... Deut 11:15 7646
father and her mother a *f* month ... Deut 21:13 3117
f with the blessing of the LORD, ... Deut 33:23 4392
Nun was *f* of the spirit of wisdom ... Deut 34:9 4392
of the fleece, a bowl *f* of water ... Judg 6:38 4392
Now the house was *f* of men ... Judg 16:27 4390
I went out *f*, and the LORD hath ... Ruth 1:21 4390
a *f* reward be given thee of the ... Ruth 2:12 8003
They that were *f* have hired out ... 1Sa 2:5 7646
gave them in *f* tale to the king ... 1Sa 18:27 4390
of the Philistines was a *f* year ... 1Sa 27:7 3117
with one *f* line to keep alive ... 2Sa 8:2 4393
it came to pass after two *f* years ... 2Sa 13:23 3117
dwelt two *f* years in Jerusalem ... 2Sa 14:28 3117
a piece of ground *f* of lentiles ... 2Sa 23:11 4392
Make this valley *f* of ditches ... 2Kin 3:16
shalt set aside that which is *f* ... 2Kin 4:4 4392
to pass, when the vessels were *f* ... 2Kin 4:6 4390
thereof wild gourds his lap *f* ... 2Kin 4:39 4393
f ears of corn in the husk ... 2Kin 4:42
the mountain was *f* of horses ... 2Kin 6:17 4390
lo, all the way was *f* of garments ... 2Kin 7:15 4392
drew a bow with his *f* strength ... 2Kin 9:24 4390
the house of Baal was *f* from one ... 2Kin 10:21 4390
he reigned a *f* month in Samaria ... 2Kin 15:13 3117
a parcel of ground *f* of barley ... 1Chr 11:13 4392
shalt grant it me for the *f* price ... 1Chr 21:22 4392
verily buy it for the *f* price ... 1Chr 21:24 4392
f of days, he made Solomon his ... 1Chr 23:1 7646
f of days, riches, and honour ... 1Chr 29:28 7646
was *f* of days when he died ... 2Chr 24:15 7646
possessed houses *f* of all goods ... Neh 9:25 4392
then was Haman *f* of wrath ... Est 3:5 4390
he was *f* of indignation against ... Est 5:9 4390
come to thy grave in a *f* age ... Job 5:26 3624
I am *f* of tossings to and fro unto ... Job 7:4 7646
I am *f* of confusion ... Job 10:15 7646
should a man *f* of talk be ... Job 11:2
is of few days, and *f* of trouble ... Job 14:1 7646
His bones are *f* of the sin of his ... Job 20:11 4390
One dieth in his *f* strength ... Job 21:23 8537
His breasts are *f* of milk ... Job 21:24 4390
For I am *f* of matter ... Job 32:18 4390
thy table should be *f* of fatness ... Job 36:16 4390
Job died, being old and *f* of days ... Job 42:17 7646
His mouth is *f* of cursing ... Ps 10:7 4390
they are *f* of children, and leave ... Ps 17:14 7646
their right hand is *f* of bribes ... Ps 26:10 4390
voice of the LORD is *f* of majesty ... Ps 29:4
the earth is *f* of the goodness of ... Ps 33:5 4390
right hand is *f* of righteousness ... Ps 48:10 4390
river of God, which is *f* of water ... Ps 65:9 4390
and I am *f* of heaviness ... Ps 69:20
waters of a *f* cup are wrung out ... Ps 73:10 4392
dark places of the earth are *f* of ... Ps 74:20 4390
it is *f* of mixture ... Ps 75:8 4392
he sent them meat to the *f* ... Ps 78:25 7648
being *f* of compassion, forgave ... Ps 78:38
art a God *f* of compassion, and ... Ps 86:15
For my soul is *f* of troubles ... Ps 88:3 7654
trees of the LORD are *f* of sap ... Ps 104:16 7654
the earth is *f* of thy riches ... Ps 104:24 4390
is gracious and *f* of compassion ... Ps 111:4
f of compassion, and righteous ... Ps 112:4
earth, O LORD, is *f* of thy mercy ... Ps 119:64 4390
that hath his quiver *f* of them ... Ps 127:5 4390
That our garners may be *f* ... Ps 144:13 4392
is gracious, and *f* of compassion ... Ps 145:8
than an house *f* of sacrifices ... Prov 17:1 4392
The *f* soul loatheth an honeycomb ... Prov 27:7 7646
Hell and destruction are never *f* ... Prov 27:20 7646
Lest I be *f*, and deny thee, and say ... Prov 30:9 7646
yet the sea is not *f* ... Eccl 1:7 4392
All things are *f* of labour ... Eccl 1:8
both the hands *f* with travail ... Eccl 4:6 4393
of the sons of men is *f* of evil ... Eccl 9:3 4390
A fool also is *f* of words ... Eccl 10:14 7235
If the clouds be *f* of rain ... Eccl 11:3 4390
I am *f* of the burnt offerings of ... Is 1:11 7646
your hands are *f* of blood ... Is 1:15 4390
it was *f* of judgment ... Is 1:21 4392
Their land also is *f* of silver ... Is 2:7 4390
their land is also *f* of horses ... Is 2:7 4390
Their land also is *f* of idols ... Is 2:8 4390
the whole earth is *f* of his glory ... Is 6:3 4393
for the earth shall be *f* of the ... Is 11:9 4390
shall be *f* of doleful creatures ... Is 13:21 4390
of Dimon shall be *f* of blood ... Is 15:9 4390
Thou that art *f* of stirs, a ... Is 22:2 4392
valleys shall be *f* of chariots ... Is 22:7 4390
lees, of fat things *f* of marrow ... Is 25:6
For all tables are *f* of vomit ... Is 28:8 4390
his lips are *f* of indignation, and ... Is 30:27 4390
they are *f* of the fury of the ... Is 51:20 4392
Even a *f* wind from those places ... Jer 4:12 4392
yet will I not make a *f* end ... Jer 4:27
when I had fed them to the *f* ... Jer 5:7 7646
but make not a *f* end ... Jer 5:10
I will not make a *f* end with you ... Jer 5:18
As a cage is *f* of birds, so are ... Jer 5:27 4392
so are their houses *f* of deceit ... Jer 5:27 4392
Therefore I am *f* of the fury of ... Jer 6:11 4392
aged with him that is *f* of days ... Jer 6:11 4390
For the land is *f* of adulterers ... Jer 23:10 4390
Within two *f* years will I bring ... Jer 28:3 3117
within the space of two *f* years ... Jer 28:11 3117
though I make a *f* end of all ... Jer 30:11
will I not make a *f* end of thee ... Jer 30:11
of the Rechabites pots *f* of wine ... Jer 35:5 4392
for I will make a *f* end of all ... Jer 46:28
I will not make a *f* end of thee ... Jer 46:28
solitary, that was *f* of people ... Lam 1:1 7227
he is filled *f* with reproach ... Lam 3:30 7646
their rings were *f* of eyes round ... Eze 1:18 4392
for the land is *f* of bloody ... Eze 7:23 4390
and the city is *f* of violence ... Eze 7:23 4390
great, and the land is *f* of blood ... Eze 9:9 4390
the city *f* of perverseness ... Eze 9:9 4390
the court was *f* of the brightness ... Eze 10:4 4390
were *f* of eyes round about, even ... Eze 10:12 4392
wilt thou make a *f* end of the ... Eze 11:13
f of feathers, which had divers ... Eze 17:3 4392
f of branches by reason of many ... Eze 19:10
f of wisdom, and perfect in beauty ... Eze 28:12 4392
and the rivers shall be *f* of thee ... Eze 32:6 4390
of that whereof it was *f*, when I ... Eze 32:15 4393
the valley which was *f* of bones ... Eze 37:1 4392
And ye shall eat fat till ye be *f* ... Eze 39:19 7654
were a *f* reed of six great cubits ... Eze 41:8 4393
Then was Nebuchadnezzar *f* of fury ... Dan 3:19 4391
transgressors are come to the *f* ... Dan 8:23 8552
Daniel was mourning three *f* weeks ... Dan 10:2 3117
And the floors shall be *f* of wheat ... Joel 2:24 4390
for the press is *f*, the fats ... Joel 3:13 4390
is pressed that is *f* of sheaves ... Amos 2:13 4392
But truly I am *f* of power by the ... Mic 3:8 4390
men thereof are *f* of violence ... Mic 6:12 4390
it is all *f* of lies and robbery ... Nah 3:1 4392
and the earth was *f* of his praise ... Hab 3:3 4390
of the city shall be *f* of boys ... Zec 8:5 4390
whole body shall be *f* of light ... Mt 6:22 *5460*
whole body shall be *f* of darkness ... Mt 6:23
Which, when it was *f*, they drew ... Mt 13:48 *4137*
that remained twelve baskets *f* ... Mt 14:20 *4134*
that was left seven baskets *f* ... Mt 15:37 *4134*
within they are *f* of extortion ... Mt 23:25 *1073*
but are within *f* of dead men's ... Mt 23:27 *1073*
but within ye are *f* of hypocrisy ... Mt 23:28 *3324*
after that the *f* corn in the ear ... Mk 4:28 *4134*
the ship, so that it was now *f* ... Mk 4:37 *1072*
twelve baskets *f* of the fragments ... Mk 6:43 *4134*
F well ye reject the commandment ... Mk 7:9
how many baskets *f* of fragments ... Mk 8:19 *4134*
how many baskets *f* of fragments ... Mk 8:20 *4138*
and filled a spunge *f* of vinegar ... Mk 15:36
Now Elisabeth's *f* time came that ... Lk 1:57 *4130*
Jesus being *f* of the Holy Ghost ... Lk 4:1 *4134*
city, behold a man *f* of leprosy ... Lk 5:12 *4134*
Woe unto you that are *f* ... Lk 6:25 *1705*
thy whole body also is *f* of light ... Lk 11:34 *5460*
thy body also is *f* of darkness ... Lk 11:34
body therefore be *f* of light ... Lk 11:36 *5460*
the whole shall be *f* of light ... Lk 11:36 *5460*
your inward part is *f* of ravening ... Lk 11:39 *1073*
was laid at his gate, *f* of sores, ... Lk 16:20
the Father,) *f* of grace and truth ... Jn 1:14 *4134*
for my time is not yet *f* come ... Jn 7:8 *4137*
you, and that your joy might be *f* ... Jn 15:11 *4137*
receive, that your joy may be *f* ... Jn 16:24 *4137*
was set a vessel *f* of vinegar ... Jn 19:29 *3324*
the net to land *f* of great fishes ... Jn 21:11 *3324*
said, These men are *f* of new wine ... Acts 2:13 *3325*
thou shalt make me *f* of joy with ... Acts 2:28 *4137*
f of the Holy Ghost and wisdom, ... Acts 6:3 *4134*
a man *f* of faith and of the Holy ... Acts 6:5 *4134*
f of faith and power, did great ... Acts 6:8 *4134*
when he was *f* forty years old, it ... Acts 7:23 *4137*
being *f* of the Holy Ghost, looked ... Acts 7:55 *4134*
this woman was *f* of good works ... Acts 9:36 *4134*
f of the Holy Ghost and of faith ... Acts 11:24 *4134*
O *f* of all subtilty and all ... Acts 13:10 *4134*

sayings, they were *f* of wrath ... Acts 19:28 4134
f of envy, murder, debate, deceit ... Rom 1:29 3324
Whose mouth is *f* of cursing ... Rom 3:14 1073
that ye also are *f* of goodness ... Rom 15:14 3324
Now ye are *f*, now ye are rich, ye ... 1Cor 4:8 2880
was *f* of heaviness, because that ... Phil 2:26
I am instructed both to be *f* ... Phil 4:12 5526
I am *f*, having received of ... Phil 4:18 4137
love, and unto all riches of the *f* ... Col 2:2 4136
make *f* proof of thy ministry ... 2Ti 4:5 4135
to them that are of *f* age ... Heb 5:14 5046
f assurance of hope unto the end ... Heb 6:11 4136
heart in *f* assurance of faith ... Heb 10:22 4136
unruly evil, *f* of deadly poison ... Jas 3:8 3324
f of mercy and good fruits, ... Jas 3:17 3324
joy unspeakable and *f* of glory ... 1Pet 1:8
Having eyes *f* of adultery ... 2Pet 2:14 3324
unto you, that your joy may be *f* ... 1Jn 1:4 4137
but that we receive a *f* reward ... 2Jn 8 4134
to face, that our joy may be *f* ... 2Jn 12 4137
were four beasts *f* of eyes before ... Rev 4:6 1073
they were *f* of eyes within ... Rev 4:8 1073
and golden vials *f* of odours ... Rev 5:8 1073
vials *f* of the wrath of God ... Rev 15:7 1073
and his kingdom was *f* of darkness ... Rev 16:10
f of names of blasphemy, having ... Rev 17:3 1073
cup in her hand *f* of abominations ... Rev 17:4 1073
vials *f* of the seven last plagues ... Rev 21:9 1073

FULLER {1}
so as no *f* on earth can white ... Mk 9:3 1102

FULLER'S {3}
is in the highway of the *f* field ... 2Kin 18:17 3526
in the highway of the *f* field ... Is 7:3 3526
in the highway of the *f* field ... Is 36:2 3526

FULLERS' {1}
a refiner's fire, and like *f* sope ... Mal 3:2 3526

FULLY {13}
Moses had *f* set up the tabernacle ... Num 7:1 3615
with him, and hath followed me *f* ... Num 14:24 4392
It hath *f* been shewed me, all ... Ruth 2:11 5046
went not *f* after the LORD, as did ... 1Kin 11:6 4390
men is *f* set in them to do evil ... Eccl 8:11 4390
be devoured as stubble *f* dry ... Nah 1:10 4390
the day of Pentecost was *f* come ... Acts 2:1 4845
being *f* persuaded that, what he ... Rom 4:21 4135
Let every man be *f* persuaded in ... Rom 14:5 4135
I have *f* preached the gospel of ... Rom 15:19 4137
But thou hast *f* known my doctrine ... 2Ti 3:10 3877
me the preaching might be *f* known ... 2Ti 4:17 4135
for her grapes are *f* ripe ... Rev 14:18

FULNESS {25}
as the *f* of the winepress ... Num 18:27 4395
f thereof, and for the good will ... Deut 33:16 4393
the sea roar, and the *f* thereof ... 1Chr 16:32 4393
In the *f* of his sufficiency he ... Job 20:22 4390
in thy presence is *f* of joy ... Ps 16:11 7648
is the LORD's, and the *f* thereof ... Ps 24:1 4393
world is mine, and the *f* thereof ... Ps 50:12 4393
the *f* thereof, thou hast founded ... Ps 89:11 4393
the sea roar, and the *f* thereof ... Ps 96:11 4393
the sea roar, and the *f* thereof ... Ps 98:7 4393
f of bread, and abundance of ... Eze 16:49 7653
the *f* thereof, by the noise of ... Eze 19:7 4393
of his *f* have all we received, and ... Jn 1:16 4138
how much more their *f* ... Rom 11:12 4138
until the *f* of the Gentiles be ... Rom 11:25 4138
I shall come in the *f* of the ... Rom 15:29 4138
is the Lord's, and the *f* thereof ... 1Cor 10:26 4138
is the Lord's, and the *f* thereof ... 1Cor 10:28 4138
But when the *f* of the time was ... Gal 4:4 4138
of the *f* of times he might gather ... Eph 1:10 4138
the *f* of him that filleth all in ... Eph 1:23 4138
be filled with all the *f* of God ... Eph 3:19 4138
of the stature of the *f* of Christ ... Eph 4:13 4138
that in him should all *f* dwell ... Col 1:19 4138
all the *f* of the Godhead bodily ... Col 2:9 4138

FURBISH {1}
f the spears, and put on the ... Jer 46:4 4838

FURBISHED {5}
a sword is sharpened, and also *f* ... Eze 21:9 4803
it is *f* that it may glitter ... Eze 21:10 4803
And he hath given it to be *f* ... Eze 21:11 4803
sword is sharpened, and it is *f* ... Eze 21:11 4803
for the slaughter it is *f* ... Eze 21:28 4803

FURIOUS {6}
with a *f* man thou shalt not go ... Prov 22:24 2534
strife, and a *f* man aboundeth in ... Prov 29:22 2534
anger and in fury and in *f* rebukes ... Eze 5:15 2534
upon them with *f* rebukes ... Eze 25:17 2534
the king was angry and very *f* ... Dan 2:12 7108
the LORD revengeth, and is *f* ... Nah 1:2 1167,2534

FURIOUSLY {2}
for he driveth *f* ... 2Kin 9:20 7697
and they shall deal *f* with thee ... Eze 23:25 2534

FURLONGS {5}
from Jerusalem about threescore *f* ... Lk 24:13 4712
about five and twenty or thirty *f* ... Jn 6:19 4712
Jerusalem, about fifteen *f* off ... Jn 11:18 4712
of a thousand and six hundred *f* ... Rev 14:20 4712
with the reed, twelve thousand *f* ... Rev 21:16 4712

FURNACE {30}
it was dark, behold a smoking *f* ... Gen 15:17 8574
went up as the smoke of a *f* ... Gen 19:28 3536
to you handfuls of ashes of the *f* ... Ex 9:8 3536
And they took ashes of the *f* ... Ex 9:10 3536
ascended as the smoke of a *f* ... Ex 19:18 3536
you forth out of the iron *f* ... Deut 4:20 3564
from the midst of the *f* of iron ... 1Kin 8:51 3564
as silver tried in a *f* of earth ... Ps 12:6 5948
is for silver, and the *f* for gold ... Prov 17:3 3564
pot for silver, and the *f* for gold ... Prov 27:21 3564
is in Zion, and his *f* in Jerusalem ... Is 31:9 8574
thee in the *f* of affliction ... Is 48:10 3564
land of Egypt, from the iron *f* ... Jer 11:4 3564
and lead, in the midst of the *f* ... Eze 22:18 3564
and tin, into the midst of the *f* ... Eze 22:20 3564
is melted in the midst of the *f* ... Eze 22:22 3564
the midst of a burning fiery *f* ... Dan 3:6 861
the midst of a burning fiery *f* ... Dan 3:11 861
the midst of a burning fiery *f* ... Dan 3:15 861
us from the burning fiery *f* ... Dan 3:17 861
that they should heat the *f* one ... Dan 3:19 861
them into the burning fiery *f* ... Dan 3:20 861
the midst of the burning fiery *f* ... Dan 3:21 861
the *f* exceeding hot, the flame of ... Dan 3:22 861
the midst of the burning fiery *f* ... Dan 3:23 861
the mouth of the burning fiery *f* ... Dan 3:26 861
shall cast them into a *f* of fire ... Mt 13:42 2575
cast them into the *f* of fire ... Mt 13:50 2575
brass, as if they burned in a *f* ... Rev 1:15 2575
pit, as the smoke of a great *f* ... Rev 9:2 2575

FURNACES {2}
piece, and the tower of the *f* ... Neh 3:11 8574
of the *f* even unto the broad wall ... Neh 12:38 8574

FURNISH {4}
Thou shalt *f* him liberally out of ... Deut 15:14 6059
said, Can God *f* a table in the ... Ps 78:19 6186
that *f* the drink offering unto ... Is 65:11 4390
f thyself to go into captivity ... Jer 46:19 6213,3627

FURNISHED {6}
had *f* Solomon with cedar trees ... 1Kin 9:11 5375
she hath also *f* her table ... Prov 9:2 6186
and the wedding was *f* with guests ... Mt 22:10 4130
shew you a large upper room *f* ... Mk 14:15 4766
shew you a large upper room *f* ... Lk 22:12 4766
throughly *f* unto all good works ... 2Ti 3:17 1822

FURNITURE {8}
and put them in the camel's *f* ... Gen 31:34 3733
all the *f* of the tabernacle, ... Ex 31:7 3627
And the table and his *f*, and the ... Ex 31:8 3627
pure candlestick with all his *f* ... Ex 31:8 3627
of burnt offering with all his *f* ... Ex 31:9 3627
also for the light, and his *f* ... Ex 35:14 3627
Moses, the tent, and all his *f* ... Ex 39:33 3627
glory out of all the pleasant *f* ... Nah 2:9 3627

FURROW {1}
unicorn with his band in the *f* ... Job 39:10 8525

FURROWS {8}
or that the *f* likewise thereof ... Job 31:38 8525
thou settlest the *f* thereof ... Ps 65:10 1417
they made long their *f* ... Ps 129:3 4618
it by the *f* of her plantation ... Eze 17:7 6170
wither in the *f* where it grew ... Eze 17:10 6170
as hemlock in the *f* of the field ... Hos 10:4 8525
bind themselves in their two *f* ... Hos 10:10 5869
as heaps in the *f* of the fields ... Hos 12:11 8525

FURTHER See APPENDIX.

FURTHERANCE {2}
rather unto the *f* of the gospel ... Phil 1:12 4297
continue with you all for your *f* ... Phil 1:25 4297

FURTHERED {1}
they *f* the people, and the house ... Ezr 8:36 5375

FURTHERMORE See APPENDIX.

FURY {70}
until thy brother's *f* turn away ... Gen 27:44 2534
walk contrary unto you also in *f* ... Lev 26:28 2534
God shall cast the *f* of his wrath ... Job 20:23 2740
F is not in me ... Is 27:4 2534
his *f* upon all their armies ... Is 34:2 2534
upon him the *f* of his anger ... Is 42:25 2534
because of the *f* of the oppressor ... Is 51:13 2534
where is the *f* of the oppressor ... Is 51:13 2534
hand of the LORD the cup of his *f* ... Is 51:17 2534
are full of the *f* of the LORD ... Is 51:20 2534
even the dregs of the cup of my *f* ... Is 51:22 2534
f to his adversaries, recompence ... Is 59:18 2534
anger, and trample them in my *f* ... Is 63:3 2534
and my *f*, it upheld me ... Is 63:5 2534
anger, and make them drunk in my *f* ... Is 63:6 2534
to render his anger with *f* ... Is 66:15 2534
lest my *f* come forth like fire, ... Jer 4:4 2534
I am full of the *f* of the LORD ... Jer 6:11 2534
my *f* shall be poured out upon ... Jer 7:20 2534
Pour out thy *f* upon the heathen ... Jer 10:25 2534
arm, even in anger, and in *f* ... Jer 21:5 2534
lest my *f* go out like fire, and ... Jer 21:12 2534
of the LORD is gone forth in *f* ... Jer 23:19 2534
the wine cup of this *f* at my hand ... Jer 25:15 2534
of the LORD goeth forth with *f* ... Jer 30:23 2534
of my *f* from the day that they ... Jer 32:31 2534
them in mine anger, and in my *f* ... Jer 32:37 2534
slain in mine anger and in my *f* ... Jer 33:5 2534
anger and the *f* that the LORD hath ... Jer 36:7 2534
my *f* hath been poured forth upon ... Jer 42:18 2534
so shall my *f* be poured forth ... Jer 42:18 2534
Wherefore my *f* and mine anger was ... Jer 44:6 2534
he poured out his *f* like fire ... Lam 2:4 2534
The LORD hath accomplished his *f* ... Lam 4:11 2534
I will cause my *f* to rest upon ... Eze 5:13 2534
I have accomplished my *f* in them ... Eze 5:13 2534
in thee in anger and in *f* and in ... Eze 5:15 2534
will I accomplish my *f* upon them ... Eze 6:12 2534
I shortly pour out my *f* upon thee ... Eze 7:8 2534
Therefore will I also deal in *f* ... Eze 8:18 2534
out of thy *f* upon Jerusalem ... Eze 9:8 2534
it with a stormy wind in my *f* ... Eze 13:13 2534
hailstones in my *f* to consume it ... Eze 13:13 2534
pour out my *f* upon it in blood, ... Eze 14:19 2534
and I will give thee blood in *f* ... Eze 16:38 2534
So will I make my *f* toward thee ... Eze 16:42 2534
But she was plucked up in *f* ... Eze 19:12 2534
I will pour out my *f* upon them ... Eze 20:8 2534
I would pour out my *f* upon them ... Eze 20:13 2534
I would pour out my *f* upon them ... Eze 20:21 2534
with *f* poured out, will I rule ... Eze 20:33 2534
out arm, and with *f* poured out ... Eze 20:34 2534
and I will cause my *f* to rest ... Eze 21:17 2534
you in mine anger and in my *f* ... Eze 22:20 2534
have poured out my *f* upon you ... Eze 22:22 2534
That it might cause *f* to come up ... Eze 24:8 2534
caused my *f* to rest upon thee ... Eze 24:13 2534
mine anger and according to my *f* ... Eze 25:14 2534
And I will pour my *f* upon Sin ... Eze 30:15 2534
spoken in my jealousy and in my *f* ... Eze 36:6 2534
Wherefore I poured my *f* upon them ... Eze 36:18 2534
that my *f* shall come up in my ... Eze 38:18 2534
f commanded to bring Shadrach, ... Dan 3:13 2528
Then was Nebuchadnezzar full of *f* ... Dan 3:19 2528
unto him in the *f* of his power ... Dan 8:6 2534
thy *f* be turned away from thy ... Dan 9:16 2534
go forth with great *f* to destroy ... Dan 11:44 2534
f upon the heathen, such as they ... Mic 5:15 2534
his *f* is poured out like fire, and ... Nah 1:6 2534
was jealous for her with great *f* ... Zec 8:2 2534

G

GAAL *(ga'-al)* {9} *A son of Ebed.*
G the son of Ebed came with his ... Judg 9:26 1603
G the son of Ebed said, Who is ... Judg 9:28 1603
the words of *G* the son of Ebed ... Judg 9:30 1603
G the son of Ebed and his brethren ... Judg 9:31 1603
G the son of Ebed went out, and ... Judg 9:35 1603
when *G* saw the people, he said to ... Judg 9:36 1603
G spake again and said, See there ... Judg 9:37 1603
G went out before the men of ... Judg 9:39 1603
and Zebul thrust out *G* and his ... Judg 9:41 1603

GAASH *(ga'-ash)* {4} *A mountain near Mt. Ephraim.*
the north side of the hill of *G* ... Josh 24:30 1608
on the north side of the hill *G* ... Judg 2:9 1608
Hiddai of the brooks of *G* ... 2Sa 23:30 1608
Hurai of the brooks of *G*, Abiel ... 1Chr 11:32 1608

GABA *(ga'-bah)* {3} See GEBA. *A Levitical city in Benjamin.*
and Ophni, and *G* ... Josh 18:24 1387
The children of Ramah and *G* ... Ezr 2:26 1387
The men of Ramah and *G*, six ... Neh 7:30 1387

GABBAI *(gab'-bahee)* {1} *A family of exiles.*
And after him *G*, Sallai, nine ... Neh 11:8 1373

GABBATHA *(gab'-ba-thah)* {1} *Place where Pilate judged.*
Pavement, but in the Hebrew, *G* ... Jn 19:13 1042

GABRIEL *(ga'-bre-el)* {4} *An angel.*
of Ulai, which called, and said, *G* ... Dan 8:16 1403
in prayer, even the man *G* ... Dan 9:21 1403
answering said unto him, I am *G* ... Lk 1:19 1043
in the sixth month the angel *G* ... Lk 1:26 1043

GAD *(gad)* {74}
1. A son of Jacob.
and she called his name *G* ... Gen 30:11 1410
Leah's handmaid; *G*, and Asher ... Gen 35:26 1410
And the sons of *G* ... Gen 46:16 1410
G, a troop shall overcome him ... Gen 49:19 1410
Dan, and Naphtali, *G*, and Asher ... Ex 1:4 1410
the children of *G* dwelt over ... 1Chr 5:11 1410
2. The tribe descended from Gad 1.
Of *G*; Eliasaph the son ... Num 1:14 1410
Of the children of *G*, by their ... Num 1:24 1410
of them, even of the tribe of *G* ... Num 1:25 1410
Then the tribe of *G* ... Num 2:14 1410
the captain of the sons of *G* ... Num 2:14 1410
prince of the children of *G* ... Num 7:42 1410
G was Eliasaph the son of Deuel ... Num 10:20 1410

G

Of the tribe of G, Geuel the son ... Num 13:15 1410
The children of G after their ... Num 26:15 1410
of G according to those that were ... Num 26:18 1410
the children of G had a very ... Num 32:1 1410
The children of G and the children ... Num 32:2 1410
Moses said unto the children of G ... Num 32:6 1410
And the children of G and the ... Num 32:25 1410
unto them, If the children of G ... Num 32:29 1410
And the children of G and the ... Num 32:31 1410
them, even to the children of G ... Num 32:33 1410
And the children of G built Dibon ... Num 32:34 1410
the tribe of the children of G ... Num 34:14 1410
Reuben, G, and Asher, and Zebulun, ... Deut 27:13 1410
of G he said, Blessed be he that ... Deut 33:20 1410
Blessed be he that enlargeth G ... Deut 33:20 1410
of Reuben, and the children of G ... Josh 4:12 1410
inheritance unto the tribe of G ... Josh 13:24 1410
of G according their families ... Josh 13:24 1410
of G after their families ... Josh 13:28 1410
and G, and Reuben, and half the ... Josh 18:7 1410
in Gilead out of the tribe of G ... Josh 20:8 1410
Reuben, and out of the tribe of G ... Josh 21:7 1410
And out of the tribe of G, Ramoth ... Josh 21:38 1410
of Reuben and the children of G ... Josh 22:9 1410
of Reuben and the children of G ... Josh 22:10 1410
of Reuben and the children of G ... Josh 22:11 1410
Reuben, and to the children of G ... Josh 22:13 1410
Reuben, and to the children of G ... Josh 22:15 1410
of Reuben and the children of G ... Josh 22:21 1410
of Reuben and children of G ... Josh 22:25 1410
of Reuben and the children of G ... Josh 22:30 1410
Reuben, and to the children of G ... Josh 22:31 1410
Reuben, and from the children of G ... Josh 22:32 1410
the children of Reuben and G dwelt ... Josh 22:33 1410
the children of G called the ... Josh 22:34 1410
went over Jordan to the land of G ... 1Sa 13:7 1410
in the midst of the river of G ... 2Sa 24:5 1410
Joseph, and Benjamin, Naphtali, G ... 1Chr 2:2 1410
Reuben, and out of the tribe of G ... 1Chr 6:63 1410
And out of the tribe of G ... 1Chr 6:80 1410
These were of the sons of G ... 1Chr 12:14 1410
then doth their king inherit G ... Jer 49:1 1410
unto the west side, G a portion ... Eze 48:27 1410
And by the border of G, at the ... Eze 48:28 1410
one gate of G, one gate of Asher, ... Eze 48:34 1410
Of the tribe of G were sealed ... Rev 7:5 1045

3. A prophet who assisted David.
the prophet G said unto David, ... 1Sa 22:5 1410
the LORD came unto the prophet G ... 2Sa 24:11 1410
So G came to David, and told him, ... 2Sa 24:13 1410
And David said unto G, I am in a ... 2Sa 24:14 1410
G came that day to David, and said ... 2Sa 24:18 1410
according to the saying of G ... 2Sa 24:19 1410
And the LORD spake unto G, David's ... 1Chr 21:9 1410
So G came to David, and said unto ... 1Chr 21:11 1410
And David said unto G, I am in a ... 1Chr 21:13 1410
LORD commanded G to say to David ... 1Chr 21:18 1410
David went up at the saying of G ... 1Chr 21:19 1410
and in the book of G the seer ... 1Chr 29:29 1410
of G the king's seer, and Nathan ... 2Chr 29:25 1410

GADARENES *(gad-a-renes')* {3} *Inhabitants of Gadara.*
sea, into the country of the G ... Mk 5:1 1046
arrived at the country of the G ... Lk 8:26 1046
the G round about besought him to ... Lk 8:37 1046

GADDEST {1}
Why g thou about so much to ... Jer 2:36 235

GADDI *(gad'-di)* {1} *One of the twelve spies.*
of Manasseh, G the son of Susi ... Num 13:11 1426

GADDIEL *(gad'-de-el)* {1} *One of the twelve spies.*
of Zebulun, G the son of Sodi ... Num 13:10 1427

GADI *(ga'-di)* {2} *Father of Menahem.*
the son of G went up from Tirzah ... 2Kin 15:14 1424
the son of G to reign over Israel ... 2Kin 15:17 1424

GADITE *(gad'-ite)* {1} See GADITES. *A member of the tribe of Dan.*
of Nathan of Zobah, Bani the G ... 2Sa 23:36 1425

GADITES *(gad'-ites)* {14}
I unto the Reubenites and to the G ... Deut 3:12 1425
unto the G I gave from Gilead ... Deut 3:16 1425
and Ramoth in Gilead, of the G ... Deut 4:43 1425
unto the Reubenites, and to the G ... Deut 29:8 1425
And to the Reubenites, and to the G ... Josh 1:12 1425
unto the Reubenites, and the G ... Josh 12:6 1425
the G have received their ... Josh 13:8 1425
called the Reubenites, and the G ... Josh 22:1 1425
all the land of Gilead, the G ... 2Kin 10:33 1425
The sons of Reuben, and the G ... 1Chr 5:18 1425
even the Reubenites, and the G ... 1Chr 5:26 1425
And of the G there separated ... 1Chr 12:8 1425
of the Reubenites, and the G ... 1Chr 12:37 1425
rulers over the Reubenites, the G ... 1Chr 26:32 1425

GAHAM *(ga'-ham)* {1} *A son of Nahor.*
Reumah, she bare also Tebah, and G ... Gen 22:24 1514

GAHAR *(ga'-har)* {2} *A family of exiles.*
of Giddel, the children of G ... Ezr 2:47 1515
of Giddel, the children of G ... Neh 7:49 1515

GAHER See GAHAR.

GAIN {30}
they took no g of money ... Judg 5:19 1214
or is it g to him, that thou ... Job 22:3 1214
of every one that is greedy of g ... Prov 1:19 1214
the g thereof than fine gold ... Prov 3:14 8393
He that is greedy of g troubleth ... Prov 15:27 1214
unjust g increaseth his substance ... Prov 28:8 8636
despiseth the g of oppressions ... Is 33:15 1214
own way, every one for his g ... Is 56:11 1214
dishonest g which thou hast made ... Eze 22:13 1214
destroy souls, to get dishonest g ... Eze 22:27 1214
that ye would g the time, because ... Dan 2:8 2084
and shall divide the land for g ... Dan 11:39 4242
consecrate their g unto the LORD ... Mic 4:13 1214
if he shall g the whole world, and ... Mt 16:26 2770
if he shall g the whole world, and ... Mk 8:36 2770
if he g the whole world, and lose ... Lk 9:25 2770
her masters much g by soothsaying ... Acts 16:16 2039
brought no small g unto the ... Acts 19:24 2039
unto all, that I might g the more ... 1Cor 9:19 2770
as a Jew, that I might g the Jews ... 1Cor 9:20 2770
that I might g them that are ... 1Cor 9:20 2770
that I might g them that are ... 1Cor 9:21 2770
as weak, that I might g the weak ... 1Cor 9:22 2770
Did I make a g of you by any of ... 2Cor 12:17 4122
Did Titus make a g of you ... 2Cor 12:18 4122
to live is Christ, and to die is g ... Phil 1:21 2771
But what things were g to me ... Phil 3:7 2771
supposing that g is godliness ... 1Ti 6:5 4200
with contentment is great g ... 1Ti 6:6 4200
a year, and buy and sell, and get g ... Jas 4:13 2770

GAINED {10}
the hypocrite, though he hath g ... Job 27:8 1214
thou hast greedily g of thy ... Eze 22:12 1214
thee, thou hast g thy brother ... Mt 18:15 2770
received two, he also g other two ... Mt 25:17 2770
I have g beside them five talents ... Mt 25:20 2770
I have g two other talents beside ... Mt 25:22 2770
much every man had g by trading ... Lk 19:15 1281
Lord, thy pound hath g ten pounds ... Lk 19:16 4333
thy pound hath g five pounds ... Lk 19:18 4160
to have g this harm and loss ... Acts 27:21 2770

GAINS {1}
that the hope of their g was gone ... Acts 16:19 2039

GAINSAY {1}
shall not be able to g nor resist ... Lk 21:15 471

GAINSAYERS {1}
to exhort and to convince the g ... Titus 1:9 483

GAINSAYING {3}
came I unto you without g ... Acts 10:29 369
unto a disobedient and g people ... Rom 10:21 483
and perished in the g of Core ... Jude 11 485

GAIUS *(gah'-yus)* {5}
1. A native of Macedonia.
and having caught G and Aristarchus ... Acts 19:29 1050
2. A native of Derbe.
and G of Derbe, and Timotheus ... Acts 20:4 1050
3. A native of Corinth.
G mine host, and of the whole ... Rom 16:23 1050
none of you, but Crispus and G ... 1Cor 1:14 1050
4. Addressee of John's third epistle.
The elder unto the wellbeloved G ... 3Jn 1 1050

GALAL *(ga'-lal)* {3}
1. Son of Jeduthun.
And Bakbakkar, Heresh, and G ... 1Chr 9:15 1559
2. A Levite exile.
the son of Shemaiah, the son of G ... 1Chr 9:16 1559
the son of Shammua, the son of G ... Neh 11:17 1559

GALATIA *(ga-la'-she-ah)* {6} See GALATIANS. *A Roman province in Asia Minor.*
Phrygia and the region of G ... Acts 16:6 1054
and went over all the country of G ... Acts 18:23 1054
given order to the churches of G ... 1Cor 16:1 1053
with me, unto the churches of G ... Gal 1:2 1053
Crescens to G, Titus unto ... 2Ti 4:10 1053
scattered throughout Pontus, G ... 1Pet 1:1 1053

GALATIANS *(ga-la'-she-uns)* {2} *Inhabitants of Galatia.*
O foolish G, who hath bewitched ... Gal 3:1 1052
Unto the G written from Rome ... Gal s 1052

GALBANUM {1}
spices, stacte, and onycha, and g ... Ex 30:34 2464

GALEED *(ga'-le-ed)* {2} See JAGAR-SAHADUTHA. *A memorial mound of stones.*
but Jacob called it G ... Gen 31:47 1567
was the name of it called G ... Gen 31:48 1567

GALILAEAN *(gal-i-le'-un)* {3} See GALILAEANS. *An inhabitant of Galilee.*
for thou art a G, and thy speech ... Mk 14:70 1057
for he is a G ... Lk 22:59 1057
he asked whether the man were a G ... Lk 23:6 1057

GALILAEANS *(gal-i-le'-uns)* {5}
some that told him of the G ... Lk 13:1 1057
Suppose ye that these G were ... Lk 13:2 1057
were sinners above all the G ... Lk 13:2 1057
the G received him, having seen ... Jn 4:45 1057
are not all these which speak G ... Acts 2:7 1057

GALILEE *(gal'-i-lee)* {72} See GALILAEAN. *A district north of Samaria.*
Kedesh in G in mount Naphtali ... Josh 20:7 1551
Kedesh in G with her suburbs, to ... Josh 21:32 1551
twenty cities in the land of G ... 1Kin 9:11 1551
Kedesh, and Hazor, and Gilead, and G ... 2Kin 15:29 1551
Kedesh in G with her suburbs, and ... 1Chr 6:76 1551
Jordan, in G of the nations ... Is 9:1 1551
turned aside into the parts of G ... Mt 2:22 1056
Jesus from G to Jordan unto John ... Mt 3:13 1056
into prison, he departed into G ... Mt 4:12 1056
beyond Jordan, G of the Gentiles ... Mt 4:15 1056
And Jesus, walking by the sea of G ... Mt 4:18 1056
And Jesus went about all G ... Mt 4:23 1056
great multitudes of people from G ... Mt 4:25 1056
and came nigh unto the sea of G ... Mt 15:29 1056
And while they abode in G, Jesus ... Mt 17:22 1056
these sayings, he departed from G ... Mt 19:1 1056
the prophet of Nazareth of G ... Mt 21:11 1056
I will go before you into G ... Mt 26:32 1056
Thou also wast with Jesus of G ... Mt 26:69 1056
off, which followed Jesus from G ... Mt 27:55 1056
he goeth before you into G ... Mt 28:7 1056
my brethren that they go into G ... Mt 28:10 1056
eleven disciples went away into G ... Mt 28:16 1056
Jesus came from Nazareth of G ... Mk 1:9 1056
put in prison, Jesus came into G ... Mk 1:14 1056
Now as he walked by the sea of G ... Mk 1:16 1056
all the region round about G ... Mk 1:28 1056
their synagogues throughout all G ... Mk 1:39 1056
multitude from G followed him ... Mk 3:7 1056
captains, and chief estates of G ... Mk 6:21 1056
Sidon, he came unto the sea of G ... Mk 7:31 1056
thence, and passed through G ... Mk 9:30 1056
I will go before you into G ... Mk 14:28 1056
(Who also, when he was in G ... Mk 15:41 1056
that he goeth before you into G ... Mk 16:7 1056
sent from God unto a city of G ... Lk 1:26 1056
And Joseph also went up from G ... Lk 2:4 1056
of the Lord, they returned into G ... Lk 2:39 1056
and Herod being tetrarch of G ... Lk 3:1 1056
in the power of the Spirit into G ... Lk 4:14 1056
down to Capernaum, a city of G ... Lk 4:31 1056
preached in the synagogues of G ... Lk 4:44 1056
were come out of every town of G ... Lk 5:17 1056
which is over against G ... Lk 8:26 1056
through the midst of Samaria and G ... Lk 17:11 1056
beginning from G to this place ... Lk 23:5 1056
When Pilate heard of G, he asked ... Lk 23:6 1056
women that followed him from G ... Lk 23:49 1056
also, which came with him from G ... Lk 23:55 1056
unto you when he was yet in G ... Lk 24:6 1056
Jesus would go forth into G ... Jn 1:43 1056
there was a marriage in Cana of G ... Jn 2:1 1056
miracles did Jesus in Cana of G ... Jn 2:11 1056
Judaea, and departed again into G ... Jn 4:3 1056
departed thence, and went into G ... Jn 4:43 1056
Then when he was come into G ... Jn 4:45 1056
Jesus came again into Cana of G ... Jn 4:46 1056
was come out of Judaea into G ... Jn 4:47 1056
he was come out of Judaea into G ... Jn 4:54 1056
Jesus went over the sea of G ... Jn 6:1 1056
these things Jesus walked in G ... Jn 7:1 1056
unto them, he abode still in G ... Jn 7:9 1056
said, Shall Christ come out of G ... Jn 7:41 1056
said unto him, Art thou also of G ... Jn 7:52 1056
for out of G ariseth no prophet ... Jn 7:52 1056
which was of Bethsaida of G ... Jn 12:21 1056
and Nathanael of Cana in G ... Jn 21:2 1056
Which also said, Ye men of G ... Acts 1:11 1056
of G in the days of the taxing ... Acts 5:37 1056
rest throughout all Judaea and G ... Acts 9:31 1056
all Judaea, and began from G ... Acts 10:37 1056
up with him from G to Jerusalem ... Acts 13:31 1056

GALL {14}
among you a root that beareth g ... Deut 29:18 7219
their grapes are grapes of g ... Deut 32:32 7219
poureth out my g upon the ground ... Job 16:13 4845
it is the g of asps within him ... Job 20:14 4846
sword cometh out of his g ... Job 20:25 4846
They gave me also g for my meat ... Ps 69:21 7219
and given us water of g to drink ... Jer 8:14 7219
and give them water of g to drink ... Jer 9:15 7219
and make them drink the water of g ... Jer 23:15 7219
me, and compassed me with g ... Lam 3:5 7219
my misery, the wormwood and the g ... Lam 3:19 7219
ye have turned judgment into g ... Amos 6:12 7219
vinegar to drink mingled with g ... Mt 27:34 5521
thou art in the g of bitterness ... Acts 8:23 5521

GALLANT {1}
neither shall g ship pass thereby ... Is 33:21 117

GALLERIES {4}
the king is held in the g ... Song 7:5 7298
the g thereof on the one side and ... Eze 41:15 862
the g round about on their three ... Eze 41:16 862
for the g were higher than these, ... Eze 42:5 862

GALLERY {2}
was g against g in three ... Eze 42:3 862

GALLEY {1}
wherein shall go no g with oars ... Is 33:21 590

GALLIM *(gal'-lim)* {2} *A city in Benjamin.*
the son of Laish, which was of G ... 1Sa 25:44 1554
up thy voice, O daughter of G ... Is 10:30 1554

GALLIO *(gal'-le-o)* {3} *A Roman proconsul of Achaia.*
when G was the deputy of Achaia, ... Acts 18:12 1058
G said unto the Jews, If it were ... Acts 18:14 1058
G cared for none of those things ... Acts 18:17 1058

GALLOWS {8}
Let a g be made of fifty cubits ... Est 5:14 6086
and he caused the g to be made ... Est 5:14 6086
g that he had prepared for him ... Est 6:4 6086
the g fifty cubits high, which ... Est 7:9 6086
on the g that he had prepared for ... Est 7:10 6086
him they have hanged upon the g ... Est 8:7 6086
ten sons be hanged upon the g ... Est 9:13 6086
sons should be hanged on the g ... Est 9:25 6086

GAMAD See GAMMADIMS.

GAMALIEL *(gam-a'-le-el)* {7}
1. A chief of Manasseh.
G the son of Pedahzur ... Num 1:10 1583
shall be *G* the son of Pedahzur ... Num 2:20 1583
day offered *G* the son of Pedahzur ... Num 7:54 1583
offering of *G* the son of Pedahzur ... Num 7:59 1583
was *G* the son of Pedahzur ... Num 10:23 1583
2. A noted Rabbinic teacher.
the council, a Pharisee, named *G* ... Acts 5:34 *1059*
up in this city at the feet of *G* ... Acts 22:3 *1059*

GAMMAD See GAMMADIMS.

GAMMADIM See GAMMADIMS.

GAMMADIMS *(gam'-ma-dims)* {1} *Defenders of Tyre.*
and the *G* were in thy towers ... Eze 27:11 1575

GAMUL *(ga'-mul)* {1} See BETH-GAMUL. *A sanctuary servant in David's time.*
Jachin, the two and twentieth to *G* ... 1Chr 24:17 1577

GAP {1}
stand in the *g* before me for the ... Eze 22:30 6556

GAPED {2}
They have *g* upon me with their ... Job 16:10 6473
They *g* upon me with their mouths, ... Ps 22:13 6475

GAPS {1}
Ye have not gone up into the *g* ... Eze 13:5 6556

GARDEN {52}
God planted a *g* eastward in Eden ... Gen 2:8 1588
life also in the midst of the *g* ... Gen 2:9 1588
went out of Eden to water the *g* ... Gen 2:10 1588
put him into the *g* of Eden to ... Gen 2:15 1588
Of every tree of the *g* thou ... Gen 2:16 1588
not eat of every tree of the *g* ... Gen 3:1 1588
the fruit of the trees of the *g* ... Gen 3:2 1588
which is in the midst of the *g* ... Gen 3:3 1588
in the *g* in the cool of the day ... Gen 3:8 1588
God amongst the trees of the *g* ... Gen 3:8 1588
said, I heard thy voice in the *g* ... Gen 3:10 1588
sent him forth from the *g* of Eden ... Gen 3:23 1588
east of the *g* of Eden Cherubim ... Gen 3:24 1588
even as the *g* of the LORD ... Gen 13:10 1588
it with thy foot, as a *g* of herbs ... Deut 11:10 1588
I may have it for a *g* of herbs ... 1Kin 21:2 1588
he fled by the way of the *g* house ... 2Kin 9:27 1588
buried in the *g* of his own house ... 2Kin 21:18 1588
his own house, in the *g* of Uzza ... 2Kin 21:18 1588
in his sepulchre in the *g* of Uzza ... 2Kin 21:26 1588
walls, which is by the king's *g* ... 2Kin 25:4 1588
pool of Siloah by the king's *g* ... Neh 3:15 1588
in the court of the *g* of the ... Est 1:5 1594
his wrath went into the palace *g* ... Est 7:7 1594
g into the place of the banquet ... Est 7:8 1594
branch shooteth forth in his *g* ... Job 8:16 1593
A *g* inclosed is my sister, my ... Song 4:12 1588
blow upon my *g*, that the spices ... Song 4:16 1588
Let my beloved come into his *g* ... Song 4:16 1588
I am come into my *g*, my sister, ... Song 5:1 1588
beloved is gone down into his *g* ... Song 6:2 1588
I went down into the *g* of nuts to ... Song 6:11 1594
as a lodge in a *g* of cucumbers ... Is 1:8
as a *g* that hath no water ... Is 1:30 1593
her desert like the *g* of the LORD ... Is 51:3 1588
and thou shalt be like a watered *g* ... Is 58:11 1588
as the *g* causeth the things that ... Is 61:11 1593
soul shall be as a watered *g* ... Jer 31:12 1588
night, by the way of the king's *g* ... Jer 39:4 1588
walls, which was by the king's *g* ... Jer 52:7 1588
tabernacle, as if it were of a *g* ... Lam 2:6 1588
hast been in Eden the *g* of God ... Eze 28:13 1588
The cedars in the *g* of God could ... Eze 31:8 1588
nor any tree in the *g* of God was ... Eze 31:8 1588
Eden, that were in the *g* of God ... Eze 31:9 1588
is become like the *g* of Eden ... Eze 36:35 1588
the land is as the *g* of Eden ... Joel 2:3 1588
a man took, and cast into his *g* ... Lk 13:19 *2779*
the brook Cedron, where was a *g* ... Jn 18:1 *2779*
not I see thee in the *g* with him ... Jn 18:26 *2779*
he was crucified there was a *g* ... Jn 19:41 *2779*
in the *g* a new sepulchre, wherein ... Jn 19:41 *2779*

GARDENER {1}
She, supposing him to be the *g* ... Jn 20:15 *2780*

GARDENS {12}
as *g* by the river's side, as the ... Num 24:6 1593
I made me *g* and orchards, and I ... Eccl 2:5 1593
A fountain of *g*, a well of living ... Song 4:15 1588
beds of spices, to feed in the *g* ... Song 6:2 1588
Thou that dwellest in the *g* ... Song 8:13 1588
for the *g* that ye have chosen ... Is 1:29 1593
that sacrificeth in *g*, and burneth ... Is 65:3 1593
purify themselves in the *g* behind ... Is 66:17 1593
and plant *g*, and eat the fruit of ... Jer 29:5 1593
and plant *g*, and eat the fruit of ... Jer 29:28 1593
when your *g* and your vineyards and ... Amos 4:9 1593
they shall also make *g*, and eat ... Amos 9:14 1593

GAREB *(ga'-reb)* {3}
1. A "mighty man" of David.
Ira an Ithrite, *G* an Ithrite, ... 2Sa 23:38 1619
Ira the Ithrite, *G* the Ithrite, ... 1Chr 11:40 1619
2. A hill near Jerusalem.
over against it upon the hill *G* ... Jer 31:39 1619

GARLANDS {1}
g unto the gates, and would have ... Acts 14:13 *4725*

GARLICK {1}
leeks, and the onions, and the *g* ... Num 11:5 7762

GARMENT {86}
And Shem and Japheth took a *g* ... Gen 9:23 8071
out red, all over like an hairy *g* ... Gen 25:25 155
And she caught him by his *g* ... Gen 39:12 899
and he left his *g* in her hand ... Gen 39:12 899
he had left his *g* in her hand ... Gen 39:13 899
cried, that he left his *g* with me ... Gen 39:15 899
And she laid up his *g* by her ... Gen 39:16 899
cried, that he left his *g* with me ... Gen 39:18 899
priest shall put on his linen *g* ... Lev 6:10 4055
of the blood thereof upon any *g* ... Lev 6:27 899
The *g* also that the plague of ... Lev 13:47 899
a woollen *g*, or a linen *g* ... Lev 13:47 899
be greenish or reddish in the *g* ... Lev 13:49 899
if the plague be spread in the *g* ... Lev 13:51 899
He shall therefore burn that *g* ... Lev 13:52 899
the plague be not spread in the *g* ... Lev 13:53 899
he shall rend it out of the *g* ... Lev 13:56 899
And if it appear still in the *g* ... Lev 13:57 899
And the *g*, either warp, or woof, ... Lev 13:58 899
in a *g* of woollen or linen ... Lev 13:59 899
And for the leprosy of a *g* ... Lev 14:55 899
And every *g*, and every skin, ... Lev 15:17 899
neither shall a *g* mingled of ... Lev 19:19 899
shall a man put on a woman's *g* ... Deut 22:5 8071
not wear a *g* of divers sorts ... Deut 22:11 8162
the spoils a goodly Babylonish *g* ... Josh 7:21 155
of Zerah, and the silver, and the *g* ... Josh 7:24 155
And they spread a *g*, and did cast ... Judg 8:25 8071
she had a *g* of divers colours ... 2Sa 13:18 3801
rent her *g* of divers colours that ... 2Sa 13:19 3801
Joab's *g* that he had put on was ... 2Sa 20:8 4055
he had clad himself with a new *g* ... 1Kin 11:29 8008
caught the new *g* that was on him ... 1Kin 11:30 8008
hasted, and took every man his *g* ... 2Kin 9:13 899
I heard this thing, I rent my *g* ... Ezr 9:3 899
and having rent my *g* and my mantle, ... Ezr 9:5 899
with a *g* of fine linen and purple ... Est 8:15 8509
as a *g* that is moth eaten ... Job 13:28 899
of my disease is my *g* changed ... Job 30:18 3830
I made the cloud the *g* thereof ... Job 38:9 3830
and they stand as a *g* ... Job 38:14 3830
can discover the face of his *g* ... Job 41:13 3830
I made sackcloth also my *g* ... Ps 69:11 3830
violence covereth them as a *g* ... Ps 73:6 7897
of them shall wax old like a *g* ... Ps 102:26 899
thyself with light as with a *g* ... Ps 104:2 8008
it with the deep as with a *g* ... Ps 104:6 3830
with cursing like as with his *g* ... Ps 109:18 4055
him as the *g* which covereth him ... Ps 109:19 899
Take his *g* that is surety for a ... Prov 20:16 899
taketh away a *g* in cold weather ... Prov 25:20 899
Take his *g* that is surety for a ... Prov 27:13 899
who hath bound the waters in a *g* ... Prov 30:4 8071
lo, they all shall wax old as a *g* ... Is 50:9 899
the earth shall wax old like a *g* ... Is 51:6 899
moth shall eat them up like a *g* ... Is 51:8 899
the *g* of praise for the spirit of ... Is 61:3 4594
as a shepherd putteth on his *g* ... Jer 43:12 899
hath covered the naked with a *g* ... Eze 18:7 899
hath covered the naked with a *g* ... Eze 18:16 899
whose *g* was white as snow, and the ... Dan 7:9 3831
ye pull off the robe with the *g* ... Mic 2:8 8008
holy flesh in the skirt of his *g* ... Hag 2:12 899
they wear a rough *g* to deceive ... Zec 13:4 155
one covereth violence with his *g* ... Mal 2:16 3830
piece of new cloth unto an old *g* ... Mt 9:16 *2440*
to fill it up taketh from the *g* ... Mt 9:16 *2440*
him, and touched the hem of his *g* ... Mt 9:20 *2440*
herself, If I may but touch his *g* ... Mt 9:21 *2440*
might only touch the hem of his *g* ... Mt 14:36 *2440*
man which had not on a wedding *g* ... Mt 22:11 *1742*
in hither not having a wedding *g* ... Mt 22:12 *1742*
a piece of new cloth on an old *g* ... Mk 2:21 *2440*
press behind, and touched his *g* ... Mk 5:27 *2440*
it were but the border of his *g* ... Mk 6:56 *2440*
And he, casting away his *g* ... Mk 10:50 *2440*
back again for to take up his *g* ... Mk 13:16 *2440*
side, clothed in a long white *g* ... Mk 16:5 *4749*
a piece of a new *g* upon an old ... Lk 5:36 *2440*
and touched the border of his *g* ... Lk 8:44 *2440*
hath no sword, let him sell his *g* ... Lk 22:36 *2440*
Cast thy *g* about thee, and follow ... Acts 12:8 *2440*
all shall wax old as doth a *g* ... Heb 1:11 *2440*
hating even the *g* spotted by the ... Jude 23 *5509*
clothed with a *g* down to the foot ... Rev 1:13 *4158*

GARMENTS {103}
and be clean, and change your *g* ... Gen 35:2 8071
put her widow's *g* off from her ... Gen 38:14 899
put on the *g* of her widowhood ... Gen 38:19 899
he washed his *g* in wine, and his ... Gen 49:11 3830
thou shalt make holy *g* for Aaron ... Ex 28:2 899
make Aaron's *g* to consecrate him ... Ex 28:3 899
these are the *g* which they shall ... Ex 28:4 899
they shall make holy *g* for Aaron ... Ex 28:4 899
And thou shalt take the *g*, and put ... Ex 29:5 899
it upon Aaron, and upon his *g* ... Ex 29:21 899
upon the *g* of his sons with him ... Ex 29:21 899
and he shall be hallowed, and his *g* ... Ex 29:21 899
his sons, and his sons' *g* with him ... Ex 29:21 899
the holy *g* of Aaron shall be his ... Ex 29:29 899
the holy *g* for Aaron the priest, ... Ex 31:10 899
the *g* of his sons, to minister in ... Ex 31:10 899
the holy *g* for Aaron the priest, ... Ex 35:19 899
the *g* of his sons, to minister in ... Ex 35:19 899
his service, and for the holy *g* ... Ex 35:21 899
and made the holy *g* for Aaron ... Ex 39:1 899
the holy *g* for Aaron the priest, ... Ex 39:41 899
Aaron the priest, and his sons' *g* ... Ex 39:41 899
shalt put upon Aaron the holy *g* ... Ex 40:13 899
his *g*, and put on other *g* ... Lev 6:11 899
and his sons with him, and the *g* ... Lev 8:2 899
it upon Aaron, and upon his *g* ... Lev 8:30 899
and upon his sons' *g* with him ... Lev 8:30 899
and sanctified Aaron, and his *g* ... Lev 8:30 899
his sons, and his sons' *g* with him ... Lev 8:30 899
these are holy *g* ... Lev 16:4 899
and shall put off the linen *g* ... Lev 16:23 899
the holy place, and put on his *g* ... Lev 16:24 899
linen clothes, even the holy *g* ... Lev 16:32 899
is consecrated to put on the *g* ... Lev 21:10 899
g throughout their generations ... Num 15:38 899
And strip Aaron of his *g*, and put ... Num 20:26 899
And Moses stripped Aaron of his *g* ... Num 20:28 899
their feet, and old *g* upon them ... Josh 9:5 8008
and these our *g* and our shoes are ... Josh 9:13 8008
sheets and thirty change of *g* ... Judg 14:12 899
sheets and thirty change of *g* ... Judg 14:13 899
gave change of *g* unto them which ... Judg 14:19
and gave it to David, and his *g* ... 1Sa 18:4 4055
and cut off their *g* in the middle ... 2Sa 10:4 4063
the king arose, and tare his *g* ... 2Sa 13:31 899
silver, and vessels of gold, and *g* ... 1Kin 10:25 8008
of silver, and two changes of *g* ... 2Kin 5:22 899
two bags, with two changes of *g* ... 2Kin 5:23 899
to receive money, and to receive *g* ... 2Kin 5:26 899
and, lo, all the way was full of *g* ... 2Kin 7:15 899
And changed his prison *g* ... 2Kin 25:29 899
cut off their *g* in the midst hard ... 1Chr 19:4 4063
silver, and one hundred priests' *g* ... Ezr 2:69 3801
five hundred and thirty priests' *g* ... Neh 7:70 3801
and threescore and seven priests' *g* ... Neh 7:72 3801
How thy *g* are warm, when he ... Job 37:17 899
They part my *g* among them ... Ps 22:18 899
All thy *g* smell of myrrh, and ... Ps 45:8 899
went down to the skirts of his *g* ... Ps 133:2 4060
Let thy *g* be always white ... Eccl 9:8 899
the smell of thy *g* is like the ... Song 4:11 8008
noise, and *g* rolled in blood ... Is 9:5 8071
put on thy beautiful *g*, O ... Is 52:1 899
Their webs shall not become *g* ... Is 59:6 899
he put on the *g* of vengeance for ... Is 59:17 899
me with the *g* of salvation ... Is 61:10 899
Edom, with dyed *g* from Bozrah ... Is 63:1 899
thy *g* like him that treadeth in ... Is 63:2 899
shall be sprinkled upon my *g* ... Is 63:3 899
were not afraid, nor rent their *g* ... Jer 36:24 899
And changed his prison *g* ... Jer 52:33 899
that men could not touch their *g* ... Lam 4:14 3830
of thy *g* thou didst take, and ... Eze 16:16 899
And tookest thy broidered *g* ... Eze 16:18 899
and put off their broidered *g* ... Eze 26:16 899
lay their *g* wherein they minister ... Eze 42:14 899
and shall put on other *g*, and shall ... Eze 42:14 899
shall be clothed with linen *g* ... Eze 44:17 899
their *g* wherein they ministered ... Eze 44:19 899
and they shall put on other *g* ... Eze 44:19 899
sanctify the people with their *g* ... Eze 44:19 899
and their hats, and their other *g* ... Dan 3:21 3831
And rend your heart, and not your *g* ... Joel 2:13 899
Joshua was clothed with filthy *g* ... Zec 3:3 899
Take away the filthy *g* from him ... Zec 3:4 899
his head, and clothed him with *g* ... Zec 3:5 899
spread their *g* in the way ... Mt 21:8 *2440*
and enlarge the borders of their *g* ... Mt 23:5 *2440*
crucified him, and parted his *g* ... Mt 27:35 *2440*
They parted my *g* among them ... Mt 27:35 *2440*
to Jesus, and cast their *g* on him ... Mk 11:7 *2440*
And many spread their *g* in the way ... Mk 11:8 *2440*
crucified him, they parted his *g* ... Mk 15:24 *2440*
they cast their *g* upon the colt ... Lk 19:35 *2440*
men stood by them in shining *g* ... Lk 24:4 *2067*
from supper, and laid aside his *g* ... Jn 13:4 *2440*
their feet, and had taken his *g* ... Jn 13:12 *2440*
had crucified Jesus, took his *g* ... Jn 19:23 *2440*
g which Dorcas made, while she ... Acts 9:39 *2440*
and your *g* are motheaten ... Jas 5:2 *2440*
which have not defiled their *g* ... Rev 3:4 *2440*
that watcheth, and keepeth his *g* ... Rev 16:15 *2440*

GARMITE *(gar'-mite)* {1} *A descendant of Judah.*
Naham, the father of Keilah the *G* ... 1Chr 4:19 1636

GARNER {2}
and gather his wheat into the *g* ... Mt 3:12 *596*
will gather the wheat into his *g* ... Lk 3:17 *596*

GARNERS {2}
That our *g* may be full, affording ... Ps 144:13 4200
the *g* are laid desolate, the ... Joel 1:17 214

GARNISH {1}
g the sepulchres of the righteous ... Mt 23:29 *2885*

GARNISHED {5}
he *g* the house with precious ... 2Chr 3:6 6823
his spirit he hath *g* the heavens ... Job 26:13 8235
he findeth it empty, swept, and *g* ... Mt 12:44 *2885*
cometh, he findeth it swept and *g* ... Lk 11:25 *2885*
g with all manner of precious ... Rev 21:19 *2885*

GARRISON {13}
where is the *g* of the Philistines ... 1Sa 10:5 5333
Jonathan smote the *g* of the ... 1Sa 13:3 5333
smitten a *g* of the Philistines ... 1Sa 13:4 5333
the *g* of the Philistines went out ... 1Sa 13:23 4673
us go over to the Philistines' *g* ... 1Sa 14:1 4673
go over unto the Philistines' *g* ... 1Sa 14:4 4673
unto the *g* of these uncircumcised ... 1Sa 14:6 4673

G

unto the *g* of the Philistines 1Sa 14:11 4673
the men of the *g* answered 1Sa 14:12 4675
the *g*, and the spoilers, they also 1Sa 14:15 4673
the *g* of the Philistines was then 2Sa 23:14 4673
the Philistines' *g* was then at 1Chr 11:16 5333
city of the Damascenes with a *g* 2Cor 11:32 *5432*

GARRISONS {7}
Then David put *g* in Syria of 2Sa 8:6 5333
And he put *g* in Edom 2Sa 8:14 5333
throughout all Edom put he *g* 2Sa 8:14 5333
Then David put *g* in 1Chr 18:6
And he put *g* in Edom 1Chr 18:13 5333
set *g* in the land of Judah, and in 2Chr 17:2 5333
thy strong *g* shall go down to the Eze 26:11 4676

GASHMU *(gash'-mu)* {1} See GESHEM. *A Samaritan in Nehemiah's time.*
G saith it, that thou and the Jews Neh 6:6 1654

GAT {20}
Abraham *g* up early in the morning Gen 19:27
cloud, and *g* him up into the mount Ex 24:18 5927
Moses *g* him into the camp, he and Num 11:30 622
g them up into the top of the Num 14:40 5927
So they *g* up from the tabernacle Num 16:27 5927
Abimelech *g* him up to mount Judg 9:48 5927
g them up to the top of the tower Judg 9:51 5927
rose up, and *g* him unto his place Judg 19:28 3212
g him up from Gilgal unto Gibeah 1Sa 13:15 5927
his men *g* them up unto the hold 1Sa 24:22 5927
they *g* them away, and no man saw 1Sa 26:12 3212
g them away through the plain all 2Sa 4:7 3212
David *g* him a name when he 2Sa 8:13 6213
every man *g* him up upon his mule 2Sa 13:29 7392
g him home to his house, to his 2Sa 17:23 3212
the people *g* them by stealth that 2Sa 19:3 935
with clothes, but he *g* no heat 1Kin 1:1
the pains of hell *g* hold upon me Ps 116:3
I *g* me men singers and women Eccl 2:8 6213
We *g* our bread with the peril of Lam 5:9 935

GATAM *(ga'-tam)* {3} *A son of Eliphaz.*
were Teman, Omar, Zepho, and *G* Gen 36:11 1609
Duke Korah, duke *G*, and duke Gen 36:16 1609
Teman, and Omar, Zephi, and *G* 1Chr 1:36 1609

GATE {274}
and Lot sat in the *g* of Sodom Gen 19:1 8179
possess the *g* of his enemies Gen 22:17 8179
that went in at the *g* of his city Gen 23:10 8179
that went in at the *g* of his city Gen 23:18 8179
the *g* of those which hate them Gen 24:60 8179
God, and this is the *g* of heaven Gen 28:17 8179
son came unto the *g* of their city Gen 34:20 8179
went out of the *g* of his city Gen 34:24 8179
went out of the *g* of his city Gen 34:24 8179
of the *g* shall be fifteen cubits Ex 27:14
for the *g* of the court shall be Ex 27:16 8179
Moses stood in the *g* of the camp Ex 32:26 8179
out from *g* to *g* throughout the Ex 32:27 8179
side of the *g* were fifteen cubits Ex 38:14
for the other side of the court *g* Ex 38:15 8179
the hanging for *g* of the Ex 38:18 8179
and the sockets of the court *g* Ex 38:31 8179
and the hanging for the court *g* Ex 39:40 8179
up the hanging at the court *g* Ex 40:8 8179
set up the hanging of the court *g* Ex 40:33 8179
the door of the *g* of the court Num 4:26 8179
city, and unto the *g* of his place Deut 21:19 8179
the elders of the city in the *g* Deut 22:15 8179
both out unto the *g* of that city Deut 22:24 8179
go up to the *g* unto the elders Deut 25:7 8179
the time of shutting of the *g* Josh 2:5 8179
were gone out, they shut the *g* Josh 2:7 8179
before the *g* even unto Shebarim Josh 7:5 8179
the entering of the *g* of the city Josh 8:29 8179
the entering of the *g* of the city Josh 20:4 8179
the entering of the *g* of the city Judg 9:35 8179
even unto the entering of the *g* Judg 9:40 8179
the entering of the *g* of the city Judg 9:44 8179
all night in the *g* of the city Judg 16:2 8179
the doors of the *g* of the city Judg 16:3 8179
stood by the entering of the *g* Judg 18:16 8179
stood in the entering of the *g* Judg 18:17 8179
Then went Boaz up to the *g* Ruth 4:1 8179
and from the *g* of his place Ruth 4:10 8179
all the people that were in the *g* Ruth 4:11 8179
backward by the side of the *g* 1Sa 4:18 8179
Saul drew near to Samuel in the *g* 1Sa 9:18 8179
scrabbled on the doors of the *g* 1Sa 21:13 8179
the *g* to speak with him quietly 2Sa 3:27 8179
array at the entering in of the *g* 2Sa 10:8 8179
even unto the entering of the *g* 2Sa 11:23 8179
and stood beside the way of the *g* 2Sa 15:2 8179
And the king stood by the *g* side 2Sa 18:4 8179
the roof over the *g* unto the wall 2Sa 18:24 8179
went up to the chamber over the *g* 2Sa 18:33 8179
the king arose, and sat in the *g* 2Sa 19:8 8179
the king doth sit in the *g* 2Sa 19:8 8179
of Beth-lehem, which is by the *g* 2Sa 23:15 8179
of Beth-lehem, that was by the *g* 2Sa 23:16 8179
when he came to the *g* of the city 1Kin 17:10 6607
the entrance of the *g* of Samaria 1Kin 22:10 8179
for a shekel, in the *g* of Samaria 2Kin 7:1 8179
men at the entering in of the *g* 2Kin 7:3 8179
to have the charge of the *g* 2Kin 7:17 8179
people trode upon him in the *g* 2Kin 7:17 8179
this time in the *g* of Samaria 2Kin 7:18 8179
people trode upon him in the *g* 2Kin 7:20 8179
And as Jehu entered in at the *g* 2Kin 9:31 8179
in of the *g* until the morning 2Kin 10:8 8179
part shall be at the *g* of Sur 2Kin 11:6 8179
part at the *g* behind the guard 2Kin 11:6 8179
came by the way of the *g* of the 2Kin 11:19 8179
g of Ephraim unto the corner *g* 2Kin 14:13 8179
He built the higher *g* of the 2Kin 15:35 8179
g of Joshua the governor of the 2Kin 23:8 8179
left hand at the *g* of the city 2Kin 23:8 8179
way of the *g* between two walls 2Kin 25:4 8179
waited in the king's *g* eastward 1Chr 9:18 8179
of Beth-lehem, that is at the *g* 1Chr 11:17 8179
of Beth-lehem, that was by the *g* 1Chr 11:18 8179
in array before the *g* of the city 1Chr 19:9 6607
of their fathers, for every *g* 1Chr 26:13 8179
with the *g* Shallecheth, by the 1Chr 26:16 8179
also by their courses at every *g* 2Chr 8:14 8179
entering in of the *g* of Samaria 2Chr 18:9 8179
part at the *g* of the foundation 2Chr 23:5 8179
the horse *g* by the king's house 2Chr 23:15 8179
the high *g* into the king's house 2Chr 23:20 8179
set it without at the *g* of the 2Chr 24:8 8179
g of Ephraim to the corner *g* 2Chr 25:23 8179
corner *g*, and at the valley *g* 2Chr 26:9 8179
He built the high *g* of the house 2Chr 27:3 8179
the street of the *g* of the city 2Chr 32:6 8179
to the entering in at the fish *g* 2Chr 33:14 8179
and the porters waited at every *g* 2Chr 35:15 8179
by night by the *g* of the valley Neh 2:13 8179
went on to the *g* of the fountain Neh 2:14 8179
and entered by the *g* of the valley Neh 2:15 8179
and they builded the sheep *g* Neh 3:1 8179
But the fish *g* did the sons of Neh 3:3 8179
Moreover the old *g* repaired Neh 3:6 8179
The valley *g* repaired Hanun, and Neh 3:13 8179
on the wall unto the dung *g* Neh 3:13 8179
But the dung *g* repaired Malchiah Neh 3:14 8179
But the *g* of the fountain Neh 3:15 8179
the water *g* toward the east Neh 3:26 8179
the horse *g* repaired the priests Neh 3:28 8179
the keeper of the east *g* Neh 3:29 8179
over against the *g* Miphkad Neh 3:31 8179
sheep *g* repaired the goldsmiths Neh 3:32 8179
that was before the water *g* Neh 8:1 8179
that was before the water *g* from Neh 8:3 8179
and in the street of the water *g* Neh 8:16 8179
in the street of the *g* of Ephraim Neh 8:16 8179
upon the wall toward the dung *g* Neh 12:31 8179
And at the fountain *g*, which was Neh 12:37 8179
even unto the water *g* eastward Neh 12:37 8179
And from above the *g* of Ephraim Neh 12:39 8179
the old *g*, and above the fish *g* Neh 12:39 8179
of Meah, even unto the sheep *g* Neh 12:39 8179
they stood still in the prison *g* Neh 12:39 8179
then Mordecai sat in the king's *g* Est 2:19 8179
Mordecai sat in the king's *g* Est 2:21 8179
that were in the king's *g* Est 3:2 8179
which were in the king's *g* Est 3:3 8179
And came even before the king's *g* Est 4:2 8179
king's *g* clothed with sackcloth Est 4:2 8179
which was before the king's *g* Est 4:6 8179
over against the *g* of the house Est 5:1 6607
saw Mordecai in the king's *g* Est 5:9 8179
the Jew sitting at the king's *g* Est 5:13 8179
Jew, that sitteth at the king's *g* Est 6:10 8179
came again to the king's *g* Est 6:12 8179
and they are crushed in the *g* Job 5:4 8179
out to the *g* through the city Job 29:7 8179
when I saw my help in the *g* Job 31:21 8179
sit in the *g* speak against me Ps 69:12 8179
This *g* of the LORD, into which Ps 118:20 8179
speak with the enemies in the *g* Ps 127:5 8179
his *g* seeketh destruction Prov 17:19 6607
oppress the afflicted in the *g* Prov 22:22 8179
he openeth not his mouth in the *g* Prov 24:7 8179
Heshbon, by the *g* of Bath-rabbim Song 7:4 8179
Howl, O *g*; cry, O city Is 14:31 8179
set themselves in array at the *g* Is 22:7 8179
the *g* is smitten with destruction Is 24:12 8179
that turn the battle to the *g* Is 28:6 8179
for him that reproveth in the *g* Is 29:21 8179
Stand in the *g* of the LORD's Jer 7:2 8179
stand in the *g* of the children of Jer 17:19 8179
is by the entry of the east *g* Jer 19:2 8179
were in the high *g* of Benjamin Jer 20:2 8179
of the new *g* of the LORD's house Jer 26:10 8179
Hananeel unto the *g* of the corner Jer 31:38 8179
of the horse *g* toward the east Jer 31:40 8179
of the new *g* of the LORD's house Jer 36:10 8179
when he was in the *g* of Benjamin Jer 37:13 8179
then sitting in the *g* of Benjamin Jer 38:7 8179
came in, and sat in the middle *g* Jer 39:3 8179
by the *g* betwixt the two walls Jer 39:4 8179
of the *g* between the two walls Jer 52:7 8179
The elders have ceased from the *g* Lam 5:14 8179
to the door of the inner *g* Eze 8:3 8179
behold northward at the *g* of the Eze 8:5 8179
g of the LORD's house which was Eze 8:14 8179
came from the way of the higher *g* Eze 9:2 8179
of the east *g* of the LORD's house Eze 10:19 8179
the east *g* of the LORD's house Eze 11:1 8179
behold at the door of the *g* five Eze 11:1 8179
and he stood in the *g* Eze 40:3 8179
Then came he unto the *g* which Eze 40:6 8179
measured the threshold of the *g* Eze 40:6 8179
and the other threshold of the *g* Eze 40:6
the threshold of the *g* by the Eze 40:7 8179
of the *g* within was one reed Eze 40:7 8179
also the porch of the *g* within Eze 40:8 8179
measured he the porch of the *g* Eze 40:9 8179
and the porch of the *g* was inward Eze 40:9 8179
the little chambers of the *g* Eze 40:10 8179
the breadth of the entry of the *g* Eze 40:11 8179
and the length of the *g*, thirteen Eze 40:11 8179
He measured then the *g* from the Eze 40:13 8179
of the court round about the *g* Eze 40:14 8179
from the face of the *g* of the Eze 40:15 8179
of the inner *g* were fifty cubits Eze 40:15 8179
posts within the *g* round about Eze 40:16 8179
g unto the forefront of the inner Eze 40:19 8179
the *g* of the outward court that Eze 40:20 8179
after the measure of the first *g* Eze 40:21 8179
g that looketh toward the east Eze 40:22 8179
the *g* of the inner court was over Eze 40:23 8179
against the *g* toward the north Eze 40:23 8179
from *g* to *g* an hundred cubits Eze 40:23 8179
behold a *g* toward the south Eze 40:24 8179
there was a *g* in the inner court Eze 40:27 8179
he measured from *g* to *g* toward Eze 40:27 8179
to the inner court by the south *g* Eze 40:28 8179
he measured the south *g* according Eze 40:28 8179
he measured the *g* according to Eze 40:32 8179
And he brought me to the north *g* Eze 40:35 8179
in the porch of the *g* were two Eze 40:39 8179
up to the entry of the north *g* Eze 40:40 8179
which was at the porch of the *g* Eze 40:40 8179
that side, by the side of the *g* Eze 40:41 8179
without the inner *g* were the Eze 40:44 8179
was at the side of the north *g* Eze 40:44 8179
one at the side of the east *g* Eze 40:44 8179
the breadth of the *g* was three Eze 40:48 8179
g whose prospect is toward the Eze 42:15 8179
Afterward he brought me to the *g* Eze 43:1 8179
even the *g* that looketh toward Eze 43:1 8179
the house by the way of the *g* Eze 43:4 8179
g of the outward sanctuary which Eze 44:1 8179
This *g* shall be shut, it shall Eze 44:2 8179
by the way of the porch of that *g* Eze 44:3 8179
of the north *g* before the house Eze 44:4 8179
posts of the *g* of the inner court Eze 45:19 8179
The *g* of the inner court that Eze 46:1 8179
of the porch of that *g* without Eze 46:2 8179
shall stand by the post of the *g* Eze 46:2 8179
worship at the threshold of the *g* Eze 46:2 8179
but the *g* shall not be shut until Eze 46:2 8179
worship at the door of this *g* Eze 46:3 8179
by the way of the porch of that *g* Eze 46:8 8179
in by the way of the north *g* to Eze 46:9 8179
go out by the way of the south *g* Eze 46:9 8179
by the way of the south *g* shall Eze 46:9 8179
forth by the way of the north *g* Eze 46:9 8179
way of the *g* whereby he came in Eze 46:9 8179
one shall then open him the *g* Eze 46:12 8179
going forth one shall shut the *g* Eze 46:12 8179
which was at the side of the *g* Eze 46:19 8179
out of the way of the *g* northward Eze 47:2 8179
utter *g* by the way that looketh Eze 47:2 8179
one *g* of Reuben Eze 48:31 8179
one *g* of Judah, one *g* of Levi Eze 48:31 8179
one *g* of Joseph Eze 48:32 8179
g of Benjamin, one *g* of Dan Eze 48:32 8179
one *g* of Simeon Eze 48:33 8179
of Issachar, one *g* of Zebulun Eze 48:33 8179
one *g* of Gad Eze 48:34 8179
g of Asher, one *g* of Naphtali Eze 48:34 8179
Daniel sat in the *g* of the king Dan 2:49 8651
hate him that rebuketh in the *g* Amos 5:10 8179
poor in the *g* from their right Amos 5:12 8179
and establish judgment in the *g* Amos 5:15 8179
not have entered into the *g* of my Obad 13 8179
is come unto the *g* of my people Mic 1:9 8179
the LORD unto the *g* of Jerusalem Mic 1:12 8179
up, and have passed through the *g* Mic 2:13 8179
noise of a cry from the fish *g* Zeph 1:10 8179
from Benjamin's *g* unto the place Zec 14:10 8179
the first *g*, unto the corner *g* Zec 14:10 8179
Enter ye in at the strait *g* Mt 7:13 *4439*
for wide is the *g*, and broad is Mt 7:13 *4439*
Because strait is the *g*, and Mt 7:14 *4439*
he came nigh to the *g* of the city Lk 7:12 *4439*
to enter in at the strait *g* Lk 13:24 *4439*
Lazarus, which was laid at his *g* Lk 16:20 *4440*
whom they laid daily at the *g* of Acts 3:2 *2374*
at the Beautiful *g* of the temple Acts 3:10 *4439*
house, and stood before the *g* Acts 10:17 *4440*
they came unto the iron *g* that Acts 12:10 *4439*
knocked at the door of the *g* Acts 12:13 *4440*
she opened not the *g* for gladness Acts 12:14 *4440*
told how Peter stood before the *g* Acts 12:14 *4440*
own blood, suffered without the *g* Heb 13:12 *4439*
every several *g* was of one pearl Rev 21:21

GATES {144}
thy stranger that is within thy *g* Ex 20:10 8179
were fenced with high walls, *g* Deut 3:5 1817
thy stranger that is within thy *g* Deut 5:14 8179
posts of thy house, and on thy *g* Deut 6:9 8179
of thine house, and upon thy *g* Deut 11:20 8179
the Levite that is within your *g* Deut 12:12 8179
kill and eat flesh in all thy *g* Deut 12:15 8179
thy *g* the tithe of thy corn Deut 12:17 8179
the Levite that is within thy *g* Deut 12:18 8179
thee, and thou shalt eat in thy *g* Deut 12:21 8179
the stranger that is in thy *g* Deut 14:21 8179
the Levite that is within thy *g* Deut 14:27 8179
and shalt lay it up within thy *g* Deut 14:28 8179
the widow, which are within thy *g* Deut 14:29 8179

g in thy land which the LORD thy ... Deut 15:7 8179
Thou shalt eat it within thy *g* ... Deut 15:22 8179
the passover within any of thy *g* ... Deut 16:5 8179
the Levite that is within thy *g* ... Deut 16:11 8179
the widow, that are within thy *g* ... Deut 16:14 8179
shalt thou make thee in all thy *g* ... Deut 16:18 8179
within any of thy *g* which the ... Deut 17:2 8179
that wicked thing, unto thy *g* ... Deut 17:5 8179
of controversy within thy *g* ... Deut 17:8 8179
any of thy *g* out of all Israel ... Deut 18:6 8179
he shall choose in one of thy *g* ... Deut 23:16 8179
that are in thy land within thy *g* ... Deut 24:14 8179
that they may eat within thy *g* ... Deut 26:12 8179
shall besiege thee in all thy *g* ... Deut 28:52 8179
all thy *g* throughout all thy land ... Deut 28:52 8179
shall distress thee in all thy *g* ... Deut 28:55 8179
shall distress thee in thy *g* ... Deut 28:57 8179
thy stranger that is within thy *g* ... Deut 31:12 8179
son shall he set up the *g* of it ... Josh 6:26 1817
then was war in the *g* ... Judg 5:8 8179
of the LORD go down to the *g* ... Judg 5:11 8179
the valley, and to the *g* of Ekron ... 1Sa 17:52 8179
entering into a town that hath *g* ... 1Sa 23:7 1817
And David sat between the two *g* ... 2Sa 18:24 8179
set up the *g* thereof in his ... 1Kin 16:34 1817
down the high places of the *g* ... 2Kin 23:8 8179
service, keepers of the *g* of the ... 1Chr 9:19 5592
porters in the *g* were two hundred ... 1Chr 9:22 5592
of the *g* of the house of the LORD ... 1Chr 9:23 8179
the nails for the doors of the *g* ... 1Chr 22:3 8179
fenced cities, with walls, *g* ... 2Chr 8:5 1817
about them walls, and towers, *g* ... 2Chr 14:7 1817
at the *g* of the house of the LORD ... 2Chr 23:19 8179
to praise in the *g* of the tents ... 2Chr 31:2 8179
the *g* thereof are burned with ... Neh 1:3 8179
the *g* thereof are consumed with ... Neh 2:3 8179
g of the palace which appertained ... Neh 2:8 8179
the *g* thereof were consumed with ... Neh 2:13 8179
the *g* thereof are burned with ... Neh 2:17 8179
not set up the doors upon the *g* ... Neh 6:1 8179
Let not the *g* of Jerusalem be ... Neh 7:3 8179
and their brethren that kept the *g* ... Neh 11:19 8179
ward at the thresholds of the *g* ... Neh 12:25 8179
and purified the people, and the *g* ... Neh 12:30 8179
that when the *g* of Jerusalem ... Neh 13:19 8179
that the *g* should be shut ... Neh 13:19 1817
of my servants set I at the *g* ... Neh 13:19 8179
they should come and keep the *g* ... Neh 13:22 8179
Have the *g* of death been opened ... Job 38:17 8179
liftest me up from the *g* of death ... Ps 9:13 8179
in the *g* of the daughter of Zion ... Ps 9:14 8179
Lift up your heads, O ye *g* ... Ps 24:7 8179
Lift up your heads, O ye *g* ... Ps 24:9 8179
The LORD loveth the *g* of Zion ... Ps 87:2 8179
Enter into his *g* with ... Ps 100:4 8179
For he hath broken the *g* of brass ... Ps 107:16 1817
draw near unto the *g* of death ... Ps 107:18 8179
Open to me the *g* of righteousness ... Ps 118:19 8179
Our feet shall stand within thy *g* ... Ps 122:2 8179
strengthened the bars of thy *g* ... Ps 147:13 8179
in the openings of the *g* ... Prov 1:21 8179
She crieth at the *g*, at the entry ... Prov 8:3 8179
me, watching daily at my *g* ... Prov 8:34 1817
wicked at the *g* of the righteous ... Prov 14:19 8179
Her husband is known in the *g* ... Prov 31:23 8179
her own works praise her in the *g* ... Prov 31:31 8179
at our *g* are all manner of ... Song 7:13 6607
her *g* shall lament and mourn ... Is 3:26 6607
may go into the *g* of the nobles ... Is 13:2 6607
Open ye the *g*, that the righteous ... Is 26:2 8179
I shall go to the *g* of the grave ... Is 38:10 8179
open before him the two leaved *g* ... Is 45:1 1817
and the *g* shall not be shut ... Is 45:1 8179
break in pieces the *g* of brass ... Is 45:2 1817
thy *g* of carbuncles, and all thy ... Is 54:12 8179
Therefore thy *g* shall be open ... Is 60:11 8179
walls Salvation, and thy *g* Praise ... Is 60:18 8179
Go through, go through the *g* ... Is 62:10 8179
entering of the *g* of Jerusalem ... Jer 1:15 8179
in at these *g* to worship the LORD ... Jer 7:2 8179
and the *g* thereof languish ... Jer 14:2 8179
with a fan in the *g* of the land ... Jer 15:7 8179
in all the *g* of Jerusalem ... Jer 17:19 8179
that enter in by these *g* ... Jer 17:20 8179
bring it in by the *g* of Jerusalem ... Jer 17:21 8179
bring in no burden through the *g* ... Jer 17:24 8179
into the *g* of this city kings ... Jer 17:25 8179
even entering in at the *g* of ... Jer 17:27 8179
I kindle a fire in the *g* thereof ... Jer 17:27 8179
people that enter in by these *g* ... Jer 22:2 8179
the *g* of this house kings sitting ... Jer 22:4 8179
forth beyond the *g* of Jerusalem ... Jer 22:19 8179
which have neither *g* nor bars ... Jer 49:31 1817
her high *g* shall be burned with ... Jer 51:58 8179
all her *g* are desolate ... Lam 1:4 8179
Her *g* are sunk into the ground ... Lam 2:9 8179
entered into the *g* of Jerusalem ... Lam 4:12 8179
of the sword against all their *g* ... Eze 21:15 8179
battering rams against the *g* ... Eze 21:22 8179
that was the *g* of the people ... Eze 26:2 1817
when he shall enter into thy *g* ... Eze 26:10 8179
and having neither bars nor *g* ... Eze 38:11 1817
g over against the length of the ... Eze 40:18 8179
of the *g* was the lower pavement ... Eze 40:18 8179
were by the posts of the *g* ... Eze 40:38 8179
charge at the *g* of the house ... Eze 44:11 8179
in at the *g* of the inner court ... Eze 44:17 8179
in the *g* of the inner court ... Eze 44:17 8179
the *g* of the city shall be after ... Eze 48:31 8179
three *g* northward ... Eze 48:31 8179
five hundred: and three *g* ... Eze 48:32 8179
measures: and three *g* ... Eze 48:33 8179
five hundred, with their three *g* ... Eze 48:34 8179
and foreigners entered into his *g* ... Obad 11 8179
The *g* of the rivers shall be ... Nah 2:6 8179
the *g* of thy land shall be set ... Nah 3:13 8179
of truth and peace in your *g* ... Zec 8:16 8179
the *g* of hell shall not prevail ... Mt 16:18 *4439*
And they watched the *g* day ... Acts 9:24 *4439*
oxen and garlands unto the *g* ... Acts 14:13 *4440*
great and high, and had twelve *g* ... Rev 21:12 *4440*
at the *g* twelve angels, and names ... Rev 21:12 *4440*
On the east three *g* ... Rev 21:13 *4440*
on the north three *g* ... Rev 21:13 *4440*
on the south three *g* ... Rev 21:13 *4440*
and on the west three *g* ... Rev 21:13 *4440*
the *g* thereof, and the wall ... Rev 21:15 *4440*
the twelve *g* were twelve pearls ... Rev 21:21 *4440*
the *g* of it shall not be shut at ... Rev 21:25 *4440*
in through the *g* into the city ... Rev 22:14 *4440*

GATH *(gath)* {33} See GATH-HEPHER, GATH-RIMMON, GITTITE, MORESHETH-GATH. *A royal Philistine city.*

only in Gaza, in *G*, and in Ashdod, ... Josh 11:22 1661
of Israel be carried about unto *G* ... 1Sa 5:8 1661
one, for Askelon one, for *G* one ... 1Sa 6:17 1661
to Israel, from Ekron even unto *G* ... 1Sa 7:14 1661
Philistines, named Goliath, of *G* ... 1Sa 17:4 1661
the champion, the Philistine of *G* ... 1Sa 17:23 1661
the way to Shaaraim, even unto *G* ... 1Sa 17:52 1661
and went to Achish the king of *G* ... 1Sa 21:10 1661
afraid of Achish the king of *G* ... 1Sa 21:12 1661
the son of Maoch, king of *G* ... 1Sa 27:2 1661
And David dwelt with Achish at *G* ... 1Sa 27:3 1661
Saul that David was fled to *G* ... 1Sa 27:4 1661
alive, to bring tidings to *G* ... 1Sa 27:11 1661
Tell it not in *G*, publish it not ... 2Sa 1:20 1661
men which came after him from *G* ... 2Sa 15:18 1661
And there was yet a battle in *G* ... 2Sa 21:20 1661
four were born to the giant in *G* ... 2Sa 21:22 1661
Achish son of Maachah king of *G* ... 1Kin 2:39 1661
Behold, thy servants be in *G* ... 1Kin 2:39 1661
went to *G* to Achish to seek his ... 1Kin 2:40 1661
and brought his servants from *G* ... 1Kin 2:40 1661
had gone from Jerusalem to *G* ... 1Kin 2:41 1661
went up, and fought against *G* ... 2Kin 12:17 1661
whom the men of *G* that were born ... 1Chr 7:21 1661
drove away the inhabitants of *G* ... 1Chr 8:13 1661
and subdued them, and took *G* ... 1Chr 18:1 1661
And yet again there was war at *G* ... 1Chr 20:6 1661
were born unto the giant in *G* ... 1Chr 20:8 1661
And *G*, and Mareshah, and Ziph, ... 2Chr 11:8 1661
and brake down the wall of *G* ... 2Chr 26:6 1661
the Philistines took him in *G* ... Ps 56:t 1661
then go down to *G* of the ... Amos 6:2 1661
Declare ye it not at *G*, weep ye ... Mic 1:10 1661

GATHER {165}

eaten, and thou shalt *g* it to thee ... Gen 6:21 622
said unto his brethren, *G* stones ... Gen 31:46 3950
they shall *g* themselves together ... Gen 34:30 622
let them *g* all the food of those ... Gen 41:35 6908
G yourselves together, that I may ... Gen 49:1 622
G yourselves together, and hear, ... Gen 49:2 6908
g the elders of Israel together, ... Ex 3:16 622
them go and *g* straw for themselves ... Ex 5:7 7197
to *g* stubble instead of straw ... Ex 5:12 7197
g thy cattle, and all that thou ... Ex 9:19 5756
g a certain rate every day, that ... Ex 16:4 3950
be twice as much as they *g* daily ... Ex 16:5 3950
G of it every man according to ... Ex 16:16 3950
Six days ye shall *g* it ... Ex 16:26 3950
on the seventh day for to *g* ... Ex 16:27 3950
shalt *g* in the fruits thereof ... Ex 23:10 622
g thou all the congregation ... Lev 8:3 6950
field, neither shalt thou *g* the ... Lev 19:9 3950
neither shalt thou *g* every grape ... Lev 19:10 3950
neither shalt thou *g* any gleaning ... Lev 23:22 3950
and *g* in the fruit thereof ... Lev 25:3 622
neither *g* the grapes of thy vine ... Lev 25:5 1219
nor *g* the grapes in it of thy ... Lev 25:11 1219
not sow, nor *g* in our increase ... Lev 25:20 622
thou shalt *g* the whole assembly ... Num 8:9 6950
shall *g* themselves unto thee ... Num 10:4 3259
G unto me seventy men of the ... Num 11:16 622
a man that is clean shall *g* up ... Num 19:9 622
g thou the assembly together, ... Num 20:8 6950
G the people together, and I will ... Num 21:16 622
G me the people together, and I ... Deut 4:10 6950
that thou mayest *g* in thy corn ... Deut 11:14 622
thou shalt *g* all the spoil of it ... Deut 13:16 6908
shalt not *g* the grapes thereof ... Deut 28:30 2490
field, and shalt *g* but little in ... Deut 28:38 622
of the wine, nor *g* the grapes ... Deut 28:39 103
g thee from all the nations, ... Deut 30:3 6908
will the LORD thy God *g* thee ... Deut 30:4 6908
G the people together, men, and ... Deut 31:12 6950
G unto me all the elders of your ... Deut 31:28 6950
g after the reapers among the ... Ruth 2:7 622
G all Israel to Mizpeh, and I will ... 1Sa 7:5 6908
will *g* all Israel unto my lord ... 2Sa 3:21 6908
Now therefore *g* the rest of the ... 2Sa 12:28 622
g to me all Israel unto mount ... 1Kin 18:19 6908
out into the field to *g* herbs ... 2Kin 4:39 3950
I will *g* thee unto thy fathers, ... 2Kin 22:20 622
that they may *g* themselves unto ... 1Chr 13:2 6908
g us together, and deliver us from ... 1Chr 16:35 6908
David commanded to *g* together the ... 1Chr 22:2 3664
g of all Israel money to repair ... 2Chr 24:5 6908
I will *g* thee to thy fathers, and ... 2Chr 34:28 622
that they should *g* themselves ... Ezr 10:7 6908
yet will I *g* them from thence, and ... Neh 1:9 6908
heart to *g* together the nobles ... Neh 7:5 6908
to *g* into them out of the fields ... Neh 12:44 3664
that they may *g* together all the ... Est 2:3 6908
g together all the Jews that are ... Est 4:16 3664
city to *g* themselves together ... Est 8:11 6950
or *g* together, then who can ... Job 11:10 6950
they *g* the vintage of the wicked ... Job 24:6 3953
if he *g* unto himself his spirit ... Job 34:14 622
thy seed, and *g* it into thy barn ... Job 39:12 622
G not my soul with sinners, nor ... Ps 26:9 622
and knoweth not who shall *g* them ... Ps 39:6 622
G my saints together unto me ... Ps 50:5 622
They *g* themselves together, they ... Ps 56:6 1481
They *g* themselves together ... Ps 94:21 1413
they *g* themselves together, and ... Ps 104:22 622
That thou givest them they *g* ... Ps 104:28 3950
g us from among the heathen, to ... Ps 106:47 6908
he shall *g* it for him that will ... Prov 28:8 6908
sinner he giveth travail, to *g* ... Eccl 2:26 622
a time to *g* stones together ... Eccl 3:5 3664
in the gardens, and to *g* lilies ... Song 6:2 3950
of Gebim *g* themselves to flee ... Is 10:31 5756
g together the dispersed of Judah ... Is 11:12 6908
and hatch, and *g* under her shadow ... Is 34:15 1716
he shall *g* the lambs with his arm ... Is 40:11 6908
the east, and *g* thee from the west ... Is 43:5 6908
all these *g* themselves together, ... Is 49:18 6908
with great mercies will I *g* thee ... Is 54:7 6908
they shall surely *g* together ... Is 54:15 1481
whosoever shall *g* together ... Is 54:15 1481
Yet will I *g* others to him, ... Is 56:8 6908
all they *g* themselves together, ... Is 60:4 6908
g out the stones ... Is 62:10 5619
come, that I will *g* all nations ... Is 66:18 6908
g together, and say, Assemble ... Jer 4:5 4390
g yourselves to flee out of the ... Jer 6:1 5756
The children *g* wood, and the ... Jer 7:18 3950
harvestman, and none shall *g* them ... Jer 9:22 622
G up thy wares out of the land, O ... Jer 10:17 622
I will *g* the remnant of my flock ... Jer 23:3 6908
I will *g* you from all the nations ... Jer 29:14 6908
g them from the coasts of the ... Jer 31:8 6908
that scattered Israel will *g* him ... Jer 31:10 6908
Behold, I will *g* them out of all ... Jer 32:37 6908
g ye wine, and summer fruits, and ... Jer 40:10 622
and none shall *g* up him that ... Jer 49:5 6908
G ye together, and come against ... Jer 49:14 6908
bright the arrows; *g* the shields ... Jer 51:11 4390
I will even *g* you from the people ... Eze 11:17 6908
therefore I will *g* all thy lovers ... Eze 16:37 6908
I will even *g* them round about ... Eze 16:37 6908
will *g* you out of the countries ... Eze 20:34 6908
g you out of the countries ... Eze 20:41 6908
therefore I will *g* you into the ... Eze 22:19 6908
As they *g* silver, and brass, and ... Eze 22:20 6910
so will I *g* you in mine anger and ... Eze 22:20 6908
Yea, I will *g* you, and blow upon ... Eze 22:21 3664
G the pieces thereof into it, ... Eze 24:4 622
I *g* the Egyptians from the people ... Eze 29:13 6908
g them from the countries, and ... Eze 34:13 6908
g you out of all countries, and ... Eze 36:24 6908
will *g* them on every side, and ... Eze 37:21 6908
g yourselves on every side to my ... Eze 39:17 622
sent to *g* together the princes ... Dan 3:2 3673
the nations, now will I *g* them ... Hos 8:10 6908
Egypt shall *g* them up, Memphis ... Hos 9:6 6908
assembly, *g* the elders and all the ... Joel 1:14 622
all faces shall *g* blackness ... Joel 2:6 6908
G the people, sanctify the ... Joel 2:16 622
g the children, and those that ... Joel 2:16 622
I will also *g* all nations ... Joel 3:2 6908
g yourselves together round about ... Joel 3:11 6908
I will surely *g* the remnant of ... Mic 2:12 6908
I will *g* her that is driven out, ... Mic 4:6 6908
for he shall *g* them as the ... Mic 4:12 6908
Now *g* thyself in troops, O ... Mic 5:1 1413
the faces of them all *g* blackness ... Nah 2:10 6908
they shall *g* the captivity as the ... Hab 1:9 622
net, and *g* them in their drag ... Hab 1:15 622
G yourselves together, yea, ... Zeph 2:1 7197
g together, O nation not desired ... Zeph 2:1 7197
determination is to *g* the nations ... Zeph 3:8 622
I will *g* them that are sorrowful ... Zeph 3:18 622
g her that was driven out ... Zeph 3:19 6908
even in the time that I *g* you ... Zeph 3:20 6908
I will hiss for them, and *g* them ... Zec 10:8 6908
Egypt, and *g* them out of Assyria ... Zec 10:10 6908
For I will *g* all nations against ... Zec 14:2 622
g his wheat into the garner ... Mt 3:12 *4863*
do they reap, nor *g* into barns ... Mt 6:26 *4863*
Do men *g* grapes of thorns, or ... Mt 7:16 *4816*
thou then that we go and *g* them up ... Mt 13:28 *4816*
lest while ye *g* up the tares ... Mt 13:29 *4816*
G ye together first the tares, and ... Mt 13:30 *4816*
but *g* the wheat into my barn ... Mt 13:30 *4863*
they shall *g* out of his kingdom ... Mt 13:41 *4816*
they shall *g* together his elect ... Mt 24:31 *1996*
g where I have not strawed ... Mt 25:26 *4863*
shall *g* together his elect from ... Mk 13:27 *1996*
will *g* the wheat into his garner ... Lk 3:17 *4863*
For of thorns men do not *g* figs ... Lk 6:44 *4816*
of a bramble bush *g* they grapes ... Lk 6:44 *5166*
as a hen doth *g* her brood under ... Lk 13:34

G up the fragments that remain, Jn 6:12 4863
but that also he should g Jn 11:52 4863
men g them, and cast them into the Jn 15:6 4863
g together in one all things in Eph 1:10 346
g the clusters of the vine of the Rev 14:18 5166
to g them to the battle of that Rev 16:14 4863
g yourselves together unto the Rev 19:17 4863
to g them together to battle Rev 20:8 4863

GATHERED {267}

be g together unto one place Gen 1:9 6960
their substance that they had g Gen 12:5 7408
and was g to his people Gen 25:8 622
and was g unto his people Gen 25:17 622
And thither were all the flocks g Gen 29:3 622
the cattle should be g together Gen 29:7 622
all the flocks be g together Gen 29:8 622
Laban g together all the men of Gen 29:22 622
was g unto his people, being old Gen 35:29 622
he g up all the food of the seven Gen 41:48 6908
Joseph g corn as the sand of the Gen 41:49 6651
Joseph g up all the money that Gen 47:14 3950
I am to be g unto my people Gen 49:29 622
he g up his feet into the bed, and Gen 49:33 622
ghost, and was g unto his people Gen 49:33 622
g together all the elders of the Ex 4:29 622
they g them together upon heaps Ex 8:14 6651
the waters were g together Ex 15:8 6192
children of Israel did so, and g Ex 16:17 3950
he that g much had nothing over, Ex 16:18
he that g little had no lack Ex 16:18
they g every man according to his Ex 16:18 3950
they g it every morning, every Ex 16:21 3950
day they g twice as much bread Ex 16:22 3950
when thou hast g in thy labours Ex 23:16 622
the people g themselves together Ex 32:1 6950
all the sons of Levi g themselves Ex 32:26 622
Moses g all the congregation of Ex 35:1 6950
the assembly was g together unto Lev 8:4 6950
when ye have g in the fruit of Lev 23:39 622
when ye are g together within Lev 26:25 622
congregation is to be g together Num 10:7 6950
g it, and ground it in mills, or Num 11:8 3950
of the sea be g together for them Num 11:22 622
g the seventy men of the elders Num 11:24 622
next day, and they g the quails Num 11:32 622
that g least g ten homers Num 11:32 622
that are g together against me Num 14:35 3259
they found a man that g sticks Num 15:32 7197
they g themselves together Num 16:3 6950
all thy company are g together Num 16:11 3259
Korah g all the congregation Num 16:19 6950
congregation was g against Moses Num 16:42 6950
they g themselves together Num 20:2 6950
Aaron g the congregation together Num 20:10 6950
Aaron shall be g unto his people Num 20:24 622
Aaron shall be g unto his people, Num 20:26 622
but Sihon g all his people Num 21:23 622
g themselves together against the Num 27:3 3259
also shalt be g unto thy people Num 27:13 622
as Aaron thy brother was g Num 27:13 622
shalt thou be g unto thy people Num 31:2 622
that thou hast g in thy corn Deut 16:13 622
goest up, and be g unto thy people Deut 32:50 622
Hor, and was g unto his people Deut 32:50 622
tribes of Israel were g together Deut 33:5 622
That they g themselves together, Josh 9:2 6908
g themselves together, and went up Josh 10:5 622
are g together against us Josh 10:6 6908
of the children of Israel g Josh 22:12 6950
Joshua g all the tribes of Israel Josh 24:1 622
g their meat under my table Judg 1:7 3950
were g unto their fathers Judg 2:10 622
he g unto him the children of Judg 3:13 622
Sisera g together all his Judg 4:13 2199
of the east were g together Judg 6:33 622
and Abi-ezer was g after him Judg 6:34 2199
who also was g after him Judg 6:35 2199
the men of Israel g themselves Judg 7:23 6817
of Ephraim g themselves together Judg 7:24 6817
all the men of Shechem g together Judg 9:6 622
g their vineyards, and trode the Judg 9:27 1219
tower of Shechem were g together Judg 9:47 6908
children of Ammon were g together Judg 10:17 6817
there were g vain men to Jephthah Judg 11:3 3950
but Sihon g all his people Judg 11:20 622
the men of Ephraim g themselves Judg 12:1 6817
Then Jephthah g together all the Judg 12:4 6908
g them together for to offer a Judg 16:23 6908
to Micah's house were g together Judg 18:22 2199
was g together as one man Judg 20:1 6950
of Israel were g against the city Judg 20:11 622
But the children of Benjamin g Judg 20:14 622
and g all the lords of the 1Sa 5:8 622
g together all the lords of the 1Sa 5:11 622
they g together to Mizpeh, and 1Sa 7:6 6908
Israel were g together to Mizpeh 1Sa 7:7 6908
of Israel g themselves together 1Sa 8:4 6908
the Philistines g themselves 1Sa 13:5 622
that the Philistines g themselves 1Sa 13:11 622
he g an host, and smote the 1Sa 14:48 6213
Saul g the people together, and 1Sa 15:4 8085
Now the Philistines g together 1Sa 17:1 622
were g together at Shochoh, which 1Sa 17:1 622
the men of Israel were g together 1Sa 17:2 622
And Jonathan's lad g up the arrows 1Sa 20:38 3950
g themselves unto him 1Sa 22:2 6908
the Israelites were g together 1Sa 25:1 6908
that the Philistines g their 1Sa 28:1 6908
the Philistines g themselves 1Sa 28:4 6908
Saul g all Israel together, and 1Sa 28:4 6908
Now the Philistines g together 1Sa 29:1 6908
the children of Benjamin g 2Sa 2:25 6908
when he had g all the people 2Sa 2:30 6908
David g together all the chosen 2Sa 6:1 3254
they g themselves together 2Sa 10:15 622
he g all Israel together, and 2Sa 10:17 622
David g all the people together, 2Sa 12:29 622
which cannot be g up again 2Sa 14:14 622
Israel be generally g unto thee 2Sa 17:11 622
and they were g together, and went 2Sa 20:14 7035
they g the bones of them that 2Sa 21:13 622
were there g together to battle 2Sa 23:9 622
the Philistines were g together 2Sa 23:11 622
Solomon g together chariots and 1Kin 10:26 622
he g men unto him, and became 1Kin 11:24 6908
g the prophets together unto 1Kin 18:20 6908
of Syria g all his host together 1Kin 20:1 6908
of Israel g the prophets together 1Kin 22:6 6908
they g all that were able to put 2Kin 3:21 6817
g thereof wild gourds his lap 2Kin 4:39 3950
king of Syria g all his host 2Kin 6:24 6908
Jehu g all the people together, 2Kin 10:18 6908
of the door have g of the people 2Kin 22:4 622
Thy servants have g the money 2Kin 22:9 5413
thou shalt be g into thy grave in 2Kin 22:20 622
they g unto him all the elders of 2Kin 23:1 622
Then all Israel g themselves to 1Chr 11:1 6908
were g together to battle 1Chr 11:13 622
So David g all Israel together, 1Chr 13:5 6950
David g all Israel together to 1Chr 15:3 6950
And the children of Ammon g 1Chr 19:7 622
he g all Israel, and passed over 1Chr 19:17 622
he g together all the princes of 1Chr 23:2 622
Solomon g chariots and horsemen 2Chr 1:14 622
he g of the house of Judah and 2Chr 11:1 6950
that were g together to Jerusalem 2Chr 12:5 622
there are g unto him vain men, 2Chr 13:7 6908
he g all Judah and Benjamin, and 2Chr 15:9 6908
So they g themselves together at 2Chr 15:10 6908
g together of prophets four 2Chr 18:5 6908
Judah g themselves together, to 2Chr 20:4 6908
g the Levites out of all the 2Chr 23:2 6908
he g together the priests and the 2Chr 24:5 6908
by day, and g money in abundance 2Chr 24:11 622
Moreover Amaziah g Judah together 2Chr 25:5 6908
Ahaz g together the vessels of 2Chr 28:24 622
g them together into the east 2Chr 29:4 622
they g their brethren, and 2Chr 29:15 622
g the rulers of the city, and went 2Chr 29:20 622
people g themselves together to 2Chr 30:3 622
So there was g much people 2Chr 32:4 6908
g them together to him in the 2Chr 32:6 6908
had g of the hand of Manasseh 2Chr 34:9 622
they have g together the money 2Chr 34:17 5413
thou shalt be g to thy grave in 2Chr 34:28 622
g together all the elders of 2Chr 34:29 622
the people g themselves together Ezr 3:1 622
I g together out of Israel chief Ezr 7:28 6908
I g them together to the river Ezr 8:15 6908
Benjamin g themselves together Ezr 10:9 6908
all my servants were g thither Neh 5:16 6908
all the people g themselves Neh 8:1 622
on the second day were g together Neh 8:13 622
the singers g themselves together Neh 12:28 622
I g them together, and set them in Neh 13:11 6908
when many maidens were g together Est 2:8 6908
when the virgins were g together Est 2:19 6908
The Jews g themselves together in Est 9:2 6950
g themselves together on the Est 9:15 6950
provinces g themselves together Est 9:16 6950
they have g themselves together Job 16:10 4390
lie down, but he shall not be g Job 27:19 622
the nettles they were g together Job 30:7 5596
and g themselves together Ps 35:15 622
the abjects g themselves together Ps 35:15 622
of the people are g together Ps 47:9 622
the mighty are g against me Ps 59:3 1481
When the people are g together Ps 102:22 6908
g them out of the lands, from the Ps 107:3 6908
are they g together for war Ps 140:2 1481
and herbs of the mountains are g Prov 27:25 622
who hath g the wind in his fists Prov 30:4 622
I g me also silver and gold, and Eccl 2:8 3664
I have g my myrrh with my spice Song 5:1 717
g out the stones thereof, and Is 5:2
are left, have I g all the earth Is 10:14 622
kingdoms of nations g together Is 13:4 622
ye g together the waters of the Is 22:9 6908
And they shall be g together Is 24:22 622
as prisoners are g in the pit Is 24:22 626
and ye shall be g one by one Is 27:12 3950
your spoil shall be g like the Is 33:4 622
shall the vultures also be g Is 34:15 6908
and his spirit it hath g them Is 34:16 6908
Let all the nations be g together Is 43:9 6908
let them all be g together Is 44:11 6908
to him, Though Israel be not g Is 49:5 622
beside those that are g unto him Is 56:8 6908
shall be g together unto thee Is 60:7 6908
they that have g it shall eat it Is 62:9 622
the nations shall be g unto it Jer 3:17 6960
they shall not be g, nor be Jer 8:2 622
shall not be lamented, neither g Jer 25:33 622
all the people were g against Jer 26:9 6950
g wine and summer fruits very much Jer 40:12 622
that all the Jews which are g Jer 40:15 6908
When I shall have g the house of Eze 28:25 6908
not be brought together, nor g Eze 29:5 6908
is g out of many people, against Eze 38:8 6908
that are g out of the nations Eze 38:12 622
hast thou g thy company to take a Eze 38:13 6950
g them out of their enemies' Eze 39:27 6908
but I have g them unto their own Eze 39:28 3664
were g together unto the Dan 3:3 3673
being g together, saw these men, Dan 3:27 3673
children of Israel be g together Hos 1:11 6908
people shall be g against them Hos 10:10 622
for she g it of the hire of an Mic 1:7 6908
many nations are g against thee Mic 4:11 622
they have g the summer fruits Mic 7:1 622
earth be g together against it Zec 12:3 622
round about shall be g together Zec 14:14 622
when he had g all the chief Mt 2:4 4863
were g together unto him, so that Mt 13:2 4863
As therefore the tares are g Mt 13:40 4816
into the sea, and g of every kind Mt 13:47 4863
g the good into vessels, but cast Mt 13:48 4816
three are g together in my name Mt 18:20 4863
g together all as many as they Mt 22:10 4863
to silence, they were g together Mt 22:34 4863
the Pharisees were g together Mt 22:41 4863
I have g thy children together Mt 23:37 1996
will the eagles be g together Mt 24:28 4863
before him shall be g all nations Mt 25:32 4863
when they were g together Mt 27:17 4863
g unto him the whole band of Mt 27:27 4863
all the city was g together at Mk 1:33 1996
straightway many were g together Mk 2:2 4863
there was g unto him a great Mk 4:1 4863
side, much people g unto him Mk 5:21 4863
the apostles g themselves Mk 6:30 4863
when much people were g together Lk 8:4 4896
the people were g thick together Lk 11:29 1865
when there were g together an Lk 12:1 1996
I have g thy children together Lk 13:34 1996
the younger son g all together Lk 15:13 4863
will the eagles be g together Lk 17:37 4863
and found the eleven g together Lk 24:33 4867
Therefore they g them together Jn 6:13 4863
Then g the chief priests and the Jn 11:47 4863
were g together at Jerusalem Acts 4:6 4863
the rulers were g together Acts 4:26 4863
of Israel, were g together, Acts 4:27 4863
where many were g together Acts 12:12 4863
had g the church together, they Acts 14:27 4863
when they had g the multitude Acts 15:30 4863
g a company, and set all the city Acts 17:5 3792
where they were g together Acts 20:8 4863
when Paul had g a bundle of Acts 28:3 4962
Christ, when ye are g together 1Cor 5:4 4863
He that had g much had nothing 2Cor 8:15
he that had g little had no lack 2Cor 8:15
g the vine of the earth, and cast Rev 14:19 5166
he g them together into a place Rev 16:16 4863
g together to make war against Rev 19:19 4863

GATHERER {1}

herdman, and a g of sycomore fruit Amos 7:14 1103

GATHEREST {1}

When thou g the grapes of thy Deut 24:21 1219

GATHERETH {17}

he that g the ashes of the heifer Num 19:10 622
He g the waters of the sea Ps 33:7 3664
his heart g iniquity to itself Ps 41:6 6908
he g together the outcasts of Ps 147:2 3664
g her food in the harvest Prov 6:8 103
He that g in summer is a wise son Prov 10:5 103
but he that g by labour shall Prov 13:11 6908
as one g eggs that are left, have Is 10:14 622
as when the harvestman g the corn Is 17:5 622
it shall be as he that g ears in Is 17:5 3950
The Lord GOD which g the outcasts Is 56:8 6908
the mountains, and no man g them Nah 3:18 6908
but g unto him all nations, and Hab 2:5 622
he that g not with me scattereth Mt 12:30 4863
even as a hen g her chickens Mt 23:37 1996
he that g not with me scattereth Lk 11:23 4863
g fruit unto life eternal Jn 4:36 4863

GATHERING {11}

the g together of the waters Gen 1:10 4723
him shall the g of the people be Gen 49:10 3349
they that found him g sticks Num 15:33 7197
widow woman was there g of sticks 1Kin 17:10 7197
I am g two sticks, that I may go 1Kin 17:12 7197
were three days in g of the spoil 2Chr 20:25 962
shall fail, the g shall not come Is 32:10 625
like the g of the caterpiller Is 33:4 625
g where thou hast not strawed Mt 25:24 4863
assuredly g that the Lord had Acts 16:10 4822
by our g together unto him, 2Th 2:1 1997

GATHERINGS {1}

that there be no g when I come 1Cor 16:2 3048

GATH-HEPHER *(gath-he'-fer)* {1} See GITTAH-HEPHER. *A town in Zebulun.*

the prophet, which was of G 2Kin 14:25 1662

GATH-RIMMON *(gath-rim'-mon)* {4}

1. A Levitical town in Dan.

And Jehud, and Bene-berak, and G Josh 19:45 1667

2. *A Levitical town in Manasseh.*
her suburbs, *G* with her suburbs ... Josh 21:24 1667
suburbs, and *G* with her suburbs ... Josh 21:25 1667
suburbs, and *G* with her suburbs ... 1Chr 6:69 1667

GAVE {465}
Adam *g* names to all cattle, and to ... Gen 2:20 7121
g also unto her husband with her ... Gen 3:6 5414
she *g* me of the tree, and I did ... Gen 3:12 5414
And he *g* him tithes of all ... Gen 14:20 5414
g her to her husband Abram to be ... Gen 16:3 5414
and good, and *g* it unto a young man ... Gen 18:7 5414
g them unto Abraham, and restored ... Gen 20:14 5414
g it unto Hagar, putting it on ... Gen 21:14 5414
with water, and *g* the lad drink ... Gen 21:19
and oxen, and *g* them unto Abimelech ... Gen 21:27 5414
upon her hand, and *g* him drink ... Gen 24:18
g straw and provender for the ... Gen 24:32 5414
and raiment, and *g* them to Rebekah ... Gen 24:53 5414
he *g* also to her brother and to ... Gen 24:53 5414
Abraham *g* all that he had unto ... Gen 25:5 5414
Abraham had, Abraham *g* gifts ... Gen 25:6 5414
Then Abraham *g* up the ghost ... Gen 25:8
he *g* up the ghost and died ... Gen 25:17
Then Jacob *g* Esau bread and ... Gen 25:34 5414
she *g* the savoury meat and the ... Gen 27:17 5414
which God *g* unto Abraham ... Gen 28:4 5414
he blessed him he *g* him a charge ... Gen 28:6
Laban *g* unto his daughter Leah ... Gen 29:24 5414
he *g* him Rachel his daughter to ... Gen 29:28 5414
Laban *g* to Rachel his daughter ... Gen 29:29 5414
she *g* him Bilhah her handmaid to ... Gen 30:4 5414
her maid, and *g* her Jacob to wife ... Gen 30:9 5414
g them into the hand of his sons ... Gen 30:35 5414
they *g* unto Jacob all the strange ... Gen 35:4 5414
And the land which I *g* Abraham ... Gen 35:12 5414
Isaac *g* up the ghost, and died, and ... Gen 35:29
he *g* it her, and came in unto her, ... Gen 38:18 5414
because that I *g* her not to ... Gen 38:26 5414
g him favour in the sight of the ... Gen 39:21 5414
I *g* the cup into Pharaoh's hand ... Gen 40:11 5414
he *g* the cup into Pharaoh's hand ... Gen 40:21 5414
he *g* him to wife Asenath the ... Gen 41:45 5414
g them water, and they washed ... Gen 43:24 5414
he *g* their asses provender ... Gen 43:24 5414
Joseph *g* them wagons, according ... Gen 45:21 5414
g them provision for the way ... Gen 45:21 5414
To all of them he *g* each man ... Gen 45:22 5414
but to Benjamin he *g* three ... Gen 45:22 5414
whom Laban *g* to Leah his daughter ... Gen 46:18 5414
which Laban *g* unto Rachel his ... Gen 46:25 5414
g them a possession in the land ... Gen 47:11 5414
Joseph *g* them bread in exchange ... Gen 47:17 5414
portion which Pharaoh *g* them ... Gen 47:22 5414
he *g* Moses Zipporah his daughter ... Ex 2:21 5414
g them a charge unto the children ... Ex 6:13
the LORD *g* the people favour in ... Ex 11:3 5414
the LORD *g* the people favour in ... Ex 12:36 5414
but it *g* light by night to these ... Ex 14:20
he *g* unto Moses, when he had made ... Ex 31:18 5414
So they *g* it me ... Ex 32:24 5414
he *g* them in commandment all that ... Ex 34:32
Moses *g* commandment, and they ... Ex 36:6
Moses *g* the money of them that ... Num 3:51 5414
oxen, and *g* them unto the Levites ... Num 7:6 5414
four oxen he *g* unto the sons of ... Num 7:7 5414
eight oxen he *g* unto the sons of ... Num 7:8 5414
unto the sons of Kohath he *g* none ... Num 7:9 5414
g it unto the seventy elders ... Num 11:25 5414
their princes *g* him a rod apiece ... Num 17:6 5414
g him a charge, as the LORD ... Num 27:23
Moses *g* the tribute, which was ... Num 31:41 5414
g them unto the Levites, which ... Num 31:47 5414
Moses *g* unto them, even to the ... Num 32:33 5414
g other names unto the cities ... Num 32:38 7121
Moses *g* Gilead unto Machir the ... Num 32:40 5414
which the LORD *g* unto them ... Deut 2:12 5414
g I unto the Reubenites and to the ... Deut 3:12 5414
g I unto the half tribe of ... Deut 3:13 5414
And I *g* Gilead unto Machir ... Deut 3:15 5414
unto the Gadites I *g* from Gilead ... Deut 3:16 5414
that the LORD *g* me the two tables ... Deut 9:11 5414
and the LORD *g* them unto me ... Deut 10:4 5414
I *g* my daughter unto this man to ... Deut 22:16 5414
g it for an inheritance unto the ... Deut 29:8 5414
he *g* Joshua the son of Nun a ... Deut 31:23
Moses *g* you on this side Jordan ... Josh 1:14 5414
g you on this side Jordan toward ... Josh 1:15 5414
Joshua *g* it for an inheritance ... Josh 11:23 5414
g it for a possession unto the ... Josh 12:6 5414
which Joshua *g* unto the tribes of ... Josh 12:7 5414
inheritance, which Moses *g* them ... Josh 13:8 5414
the servant of the LORD *g* them ... Josh 13:8 5414
of Levi he *g* none inheritance ... Josh 13:14 5414
Moses *g* unto the tribe of the ... Josh 13:15 5414
Moses *g* inheritance unto the ... Josh 13:24 5414
Moses *g* inheritance unto the half ... Josh 13:29 5414
Levi Moses *g* not any inheritance ... Josh 13:33 5414
but unto the Levites he *g* none ... Josh 14:3 5414
therefore they *g* no part unto the ... Josh 14:4 5414
g unto Caleb the son of Jephunneh ... Josh 14:13 5414
he *g* a part among the children of ... Josh 15:13 5414
he *g* him Achsah his daughter to ... Josh 15:17 5414
he *g* her the upper springs, and ... Josh 15:19 5414
g them an inheritance among the ... Josh 17:4 5414
the servant of the LORD *g* them ... Josh 18:7 5414
the children of Israel *g* an ... Josh 19:49 5414
g him the city which he asked ... Josh 19:50 5414
the children of Israel *g* unto the ... Josh 21:3 5414
the children of Israel *g* by lot ... Josh 21:8 5414
they *g* out of the tribe of the ... Josh 21:9 5414
they *g* them the city of Arba the ... Josh 21:11 5414
g they to Caleb the son of ... Josh 21:12 5414
Thus they *g* to the children of ... Josh 21:13 5414
For they *g* them Shechem with her ... Josh 21:21 5414
they *g* Golan in Bashan with her ... Josh 21:27
the LORD *g* unto Israel all the ... Josh 21:43 5414
the LORD *g* them rest round about, ... Josh 21:44
g you on the other side Jordan ... Josh 22:4 5414
g Joshua among their brethren on ... Josh 22:7 5414
his seed, and *g* him Isaac ... Josh 24:3 5414
I *g* unto Isaac Jacob and Esau ... Josh 24:4 5414
I *g* unto Esau mount Seir, to ... Josh 24:4 5414
I *g* them into your hand, that ye ... Josh 24:8 5414
he *g* him Achsah his daughter to ... Judg 1:13 5414
Caleb *g* her the upper springs and ... Judg 1:15 5414
they *g* Hebron unto Caleb, as ... Judg 1:20 5414
g their daughters to their sons, ... Judg 3:6 5414
g him drink, and covered him ... Judg 4:19
He asked water, and she *g* him milk ... Judg 5:25 5414
before you, and *g* you their land ... Judg 6:9 5414
they *g* him threescore and ten ... Judg 9:4 5414
and *g* them, and they did eat ... Judg 14:9 5414
g change of garments unto them ... Judg 14:19 5414
therefore I *g* her to thy ... Judg 15:2 5414
g them to the founder, who made ... Judg 17:4 5414
g provender unto the asses ... Judg 19:21
for the men of Israel *g* place to ... Judg 20:36 5414
they *g* them wives which they had ... Judg 21:14 5414
g to her that she had reserved ... Ruth 2:18 5414
six measures of barley *g* he me ... Ruth 3:17 5414
shoe, and *g* it to his neighbour ... Ruth 4:7 5414
the LORD *g* her conception, and she ... Ruth 4:13 5414
women her neighbours *g* it a name ... Ruth 4:17 7121
he *g* to Peninnah his wife, and to ... 1Sa 1:4 5414
unto Hannah he *g* a worthy portion ... 1Sa 1:5 5414
g her son suck until she weaned ... 1Sa 1:23
Bring the portion which I *g* thee ... 1Sa 9:23 5414
Samuel, God *g* him another heart ... 1Sa 10:9
g it to David, and his garments, ... 1Sa 18:4 5414
they *g* them in full tale to the ... 1Sa 18:27
Saul *g* him Michal his daughter to ... 1Sa 18:27 5414
Jonathan *g* his artillery unto his ... 1Sa 20:40 5414
So the priest *g* him hallowed ... 1Sa 21:6 5414
g him victuals, and *g* him the ... 1Sa 22:10 5414
Then Achish *g* him Ziklag that day ... 1Sa 27:6 5414
g him bread, and he did eat ... 1Sa 30:11 5414
they *g* him a piece of a cake of ... 1Sa 30:12 5414
I *g* thee thy master's house, and ... 2Sa 12:8 5414
g thee the house of Israel and of ... 2Sa 12:8 5414
king *g* all the captains charge ... 2Sa 18:5
Joab *g* up the sum of the number ... 2Sa 24:9 5414
And God *g* Solomon wisdom and ... 1Kin 4:29 5414
So Hiram *g* Solomon cedar trees and ... 1Kin 5:10 5414
Solomon *g* Hiram twenty thousand ... 1Kin 5:11 5414
thus *g* Solomon to Hiram year by ... 1Kin 5:11 5414
the LORD *g* Solomon wisdom, as he ... 1Kin 5:12 5414
that then king Solomon *g* Hiram ... 1Kin 9:11 5414
she *g* the king an hundred and ... 1Kin 10:10 5414
queen of Sheba *g* to king Solomon ... 1Kin 10:10 5414
king Solomon *g* unto the queen of ... 1Kin 10:13 5414
Solomon *g* her of his royal bounty ... 1Kin 10:13 5414
which *g* him an house, and ... 1Kin 11:18 5414
him victuals, and *g* him land ... 1Kin 11:18 5414
so that he *g* him to wife the ... 1Kin 11:19 5414
old men's counsel that they *g* him ... 1Kin 12:13 3289
he *g* a sign the same day, saying, ... 1Kin 13:3 5414
the house of David, and *g* it thee ... 1Kin 14:8 5414
which he *g* to their fathers, and ... 1Kin 14:15 5414
g unto the people, and they did ... 1Kin 19:21 5414
And he *g* him his hand ... 2Kin 10:15 5414
upon him, and *g* him the testimony ... 2Kin 11:12
they *g* the money, being told, ... 2Kin 12:11 5414
But they *g* that to the workmen, ... 2Kin 12:14 5414
the LORD *g* Israel a saviour, so ... 2Kin 13:5 5414
Menahem *g* Pul a thousand talents ... 2Kin 15:19 5414
his servant, and *g* him presents ... 2Kin 17:3 7725
Hezekiah *g* him all the silver ... 2Kin 18:15 5414
g it to the king of Assyria ... 2Kin 18:16 5414
the land which I *g* their fathers ... 2Kin 21:8 5414
Hilkiah *g* the book to Shaphan, and ... 2Kin 22:8 5414
Jehoiakim *g* the silver and the ... 2Kin 23:35 5414
and they *g* judgment upon him ... 2Kin 25:6 1696
Sheshan *g* his daughter to Jarha ... 1Chr 2:35 5414
they *g* them Hebron in the land of ... 1Chr 6:55 5414
they *g* to Caleb the son of ... 1Chr 6:56 5414
Aaron they *g* the cities of Judah ... 1Chr 6:57 5414
the children of Israel *g* to the ... 1Chr 6:64 5414
they *g* by lot out of the tribe of ... 1Chr 6:65 5414
they *g* unto them, of the cities ... 1Chr 6:67 5414
they *g* also Gezer with her ... 1Chr 6:67
David *g* a commandment, and they ... 1Chr 14:12
Joab *g* the sum of the number of ... 1Chr 21:5 5414
So David *g* to Ornan for the place ... 1Chr 21:25 5414
God *g* to Heman fourteen sons and ... 1Chr 25:5 5414
Then David *g* to Solomon his son ... 1Chr 28:11 5414
He *g* of gold by weight for things ... 1Chr 28:14
by weight he *g* gold for the ... 1Chr 28:16
for the golden basons he *g* gold ... 1Chr 28:17
g for the service of the house of ... 1Chr 29:7 5414
g them to the treasure of the ... 1Chr 29:8 5414
she *g* the king an hundred and ... 2Chr 9:9 5414
the queen of Sheba *g* king Solomon ... 2Chr 9:9 5414
king Solomon *g* to the queen of ... 2Chr 9:12 5414
counsel which the old men *g* him ... 2Chr 10:8 3289
he *g* them victual in abundance ... 2Chr 11:23 5414
g the kingdom over Israel to ... 2Chr 13:5 5414
Then the men of Judah *g* a shout ... 2Chr 13:15
the LORD *g* them rest round about ... 2Chr 15:15
for his God *g* him rest round ... 2Chr 20:30
their father *g* them great gifts ... 2Chr 21:3 5414
but the kingdom *g* he to Jehoram ... 2Chr 21:3 5414
g him the testimony, and made him ... 2Chr 23:11
Jehoiada *g* it to such as did the ... 2Chr 24:12 5414
the Ammonites *g* gifts to Uzziah ... 2Chr 26:8 5414
the children of Ammon *g* him the ... 2Chr 27:5 5414
g them to eat and to drink, and ... 2Chr 28:15
g it unto the king of Assyria ... 2Chr 28:21 5414
who therefore *g* them up to ... 2Chr 30:7 5414
the princes *g* to the congregation ... 2Chr 30:24 7311
unto him, and he *g* him a sign ... 2Chr 32:24 5414
they *g* it to the workmen that ... 2Chr 34:10 5414
artificers and builders *g* they it ... 2Chr 34:11 5414
Josiah *g* to the people, of the ... 2Chr 35:7 7311
his princes *g* willingly unto the ... 2Chr 35:8 7311
g unto the priests for the ... 2Chr 35:8 5414
g unto the Levites for passover ... 2Chr 35:9 7311
he *g* them all into his hand ... 2Chr 36:17 5414
They *g* after their ability unto ... Ezr 2:69 5414
They *g* money also unto the masons ... Ezr 3:7 5414
he *g* them into the hand of ... Ezr 5:12 3052
Artaxerxes *g* unto Ezra the priest ... Ezr 7:11 5414
they *g* their hands that they ... Ezr 10:19 5414
the wine, and *g* it unto the king ... Neh 2:1 5414
g them the king's letters ... Neh 2:9 5414
That I *g* my brother Hanani, and ... Neh 7:2
of the fathers *g* unto the work ... Neh 7:70 5414
The Tirshatha *g* to the treasure a ... Neh 7:70 5414
g to the treasure of the work ... Neh 7:71 5414
g was twenty thousand drams of ... Neh 7:72 5414
g the sense, and caused them to ... Neh 8:8 7760
companies of them that *g* thanks ... Neh 12:31
g thanks went over against them ... Neh 12:38
that *g* thanks in the house of God ... Neh 12:40
g the portions of the singers and ... Neh 12:47 5414
they *g* them drink in vessels of ... Est 1:7
he speedily *g* her her things for ... Est 2:9 5414
g gifts, according to the state ... Est 2:18 5414
g it unto Haman the son of ... Est 3:10 5414
g him a commandment to Mordecai, ... Est 4:5
Also he *g* him the copy of the ... Est 4:8 5414
g him commandment unto Mordecai ... Est 4:10
from Haman, and *g* it unto Mordecai ... Est 8:2 5414
the LORD *g*, and the LORD hath ... Job 1:21 5414
my servant, and he *g* me no answer ... Job 19:16
eye saw me, it *g* witness to me ... Job 29:11
Unto me men *g* ear, and waited, and ... Job 29:21
I *g* ear to your reasons, whilst ... Job 32:11
also the LORD *g* Job twice as much ... Job 42:10 3254
every man also *g* him a piece of ... Job 42:11 5414
their father *g* them inheritance ... Job 42:15 5414
and the Highest *g* his voice ... Ps 18:13 5414
The Lord *g* the word ... Ps 68:11 5414
They *g* me also gall for my meat ... Ps 69:21 5414
in my thirst they *g* me vinegar to ... Ps 69:21
and he *g* ear unto me ... Ps 77:1
g them drink as out of the great ... Ps 78:15
for he *g* them their own desire ... Ps 78:29 935
He *g* also their increase unto the ... Ps 78:46 5414
He *g* up their cattle also to the ... Ps 78:48 5462
but *g* their life over to the ... Ps 78:50 5462
He *g* his people over also unto ... Ps 78:62 5462
So I *g* them up unto their own ... Ps 81:12 7971
and the ordinance that he *g* them ... Ps 99:7 5414
He *g* them hail for rain, and ... Ps 105:32 5414
g them the lands of the heathen ... Ps 105:44 5414
And he *g* them their request ... Ps 106:15 5414
he *g* them into the hand of the ... Ps 106:41 5414
g their land for an heritage, an ... Ps 135:12 5414
g their land for an heritage ... Ps 136:21 5414
When he *g* to the sea his decree, ... Prov 8:29 7760
I *g* my heart to seek and search ... Eccl 1:13 5414
I *g* my heart to know wisdom, and ... Eccl 1:17 5414
shall return unto God who *g* it ... Eccl 12:7 5414
he *g* good heed, and sought out, and ... Eccl 12:9
called him, but he *g* me no answer ... Song 5:6
g the nations before him, and made ... Is 41:2 5414
he *g* them as the dust to his ... Is 41:2 5414
Who *g* Jacob for a spoil, and ... Is 42:24 5414
I *g* Egypt for thy ransom, ... Is 43:3 5414
I *g* my back to the smiters, and my ... Is 50:6 5414
the land that I *g* to your fathers ... Jer 7:7 5414
unto the place which I *g* to you ... Jer 7:14 5414
land that I *g* unto their fathers ... Jer 16:15 5414
from thine heritage that I *g* thee ... Jer 17:4 5414
you, and the city that I *g* you ... Jer 23:39 5414
off the land that I *g* unto them ... Jer 24:10 5414
land that I *g* to their fathers ... Jer 30:3 5414
I *g* the evidence of the purchase ... Jer 32:12 5414
g it to Baruch the scribe, the ... Jer 36:32 5414
where he *g* judgment upon him ... Jer 39:5 1696
g them vineyards and fields at the ... Jer 39:10 5414
g charge concerning Jeremiah to ... Jer 39:11
of the guard *g* him victuals ... Jer 40:5 5414
as I *g* Zedekiah king of Judah ... Jer 44:30 5414
where he *g* judgment upon him ... Jer 52:9 1696
mine elders *g* up the ghost in the ... Lam 1:19
My meat also which I *g* thee ... Eze 16:19 5414
I *g* them my statutes, and shewed ... Eze 20:11 5414
Moreover also I *g* them my ... Eze 20:12 5414
Wherefore I *g* them also statutes ... Eze 20:25 5414
the land that I *g* to your fathers ... Eze 36:28 5414
g them into the hand of their ... Eze 39:23 5414
the Lord *g* Jehoiakim king of ... Dan 1:2 5414

the prince of the eunuchs *g* names ... Dan 1:7 7760
for he *g* unto Daniel the name of ... Dan 1:7 7760
and *g* them pulse ... Dan 1:16 5414
God *g* them knowledge and skill in ... Dan 1:17 5414
g him many great gifts, and made ... Dan 2:48 3052
O thou king, the most high God *g* ... Dan 5:18 3052
And for the majesty that he *g* him ... Dan 5:19 3052
g thanks before his God, as he ... Dan 6:10
did not know that I *g* her corn ... Hos 2:8 5414
I *g* thee a king in mine anger, and ... Hos 13:11 5414
But ye *g* the Nazarites wine to ... Amos 2:12
I *g* them to him for the fear ... Mal 2:5 5414
he *g* commandment to depart unto ... Mt 8:18 *2753*
he *g* them power against unclean ... Mt 10:1 *1325*
g the loaves to his disciples, and ... Mt 14:19 *1325*
g thanks, and brake them ... Mt 15:36 *1325*
g to his disciples, and the ... Mt 15:36 *1325*
who *g* thee this authority ... Mt 21:23 *1325*
unto one he *g* five talents, to ... Mt 25:15 *1325*
I was an hungred, and ye *g* me meat ... Mt 25:35 *1325*
I was thirsty, and ye *g* me drink ... Mt 25:35 *4222*
or thirsty, and *g* thee drink ... Mt 25:37 *4222*
an hungred, and ye *g* me no meat ... Mt 25:42 *1325*
was thirsty, and ye *g* me no drink ... Mt 25:42 *4222*
g it to the disciples, and said, ... Mt 26:26 *1325*
g thanks, and *g* it to them, ... Mt 26:27 *1325*
that betrayed him *g* them a sign ... Mt 26:48 *1325*
g them for the potter's field, as ... Mt 27:10 *1325*
They *g* him vinegar to drink ... Mt 27:34 *1325*
it on a reed, and *g* him to drink ... Mt 27:48 *4222*
they *g* large money unto the ... Mt 28:12 *1325*
g also to them which were with ... Mk 2:26 *1325*
And forthwith Jesus *g* them leave ... Mk 5:13 *2010*
g them power over unclean spirits ... Mk 6:7 *1325*
a charger, and *g* it to the damsel ... Mk 6:28 *1325*
the damsel *g* it to her mother ... Mk 6:28 *1325*
g them to his disciples to set ... Mk 6:41 *1325*
g thanks, and brake ... Mk 8:6 *1325*
g to his disciples to set before ... Mk 8:6 *1325*
who *g* thee this authority to do ... Mk 11:28 *1325*
g authority to his servants, and ... Mk 13:34 *1325*
g to them, and said, Take, eat ... Mk 14:22 *1325*
had given thanks, he *g* it to them ... Mk 14:23 *1325*
they *g* him to drink wine mingled ... Mk 15:23 *1325*
g him to drink, saying, Let alone ... Mk 15:36 *4222*
a loud voice, and *g* up the ghost ... Mk 15:37
g up the ghost, he said, Truly ... Mk 15:39
he *g* the body to Joseph ... Mk 15:45 *1433*
she coming in that instant *g* ... Lk 2:38 *437*
he *g* it again to the minister, and ... Lk 4:20 *591*
g also to them that were with him ... Lk 6:4 *1325*
many that were blind he *g* sight ... Lk 7:21 *5483*
g them power and authority over ... Lk 9:1 *1325*
g to the disciples to set before ... Lk 9:16 *1325*
g them to the host, and said unto ... Lk 10:35 *1325*
and no man *g* unto him ... Lk 15:16 *1325*
they saw it, *g* praise unto God ... Lk 18:43 *1325*
or who is he that *g* thee this ... Lk 20:2 *1325*
g thanks, and said, Take this, and ... Lk 22:17
g thanks, and brake it ... Lk 22:19
g unto them, saying, This is my ... Lk 22:19 *1325*
Pilate *g* sentence that it should ... Lk 23:24
and the paps which never *g* suck ... Lk 23:29
said thus, he *g* up the ghost ... Lk 23:46
it, and brake, and *g* to them ... Lk 24:30 *1929*
they *g* him a piece of a broiled ... Lk 24:42 *1929*
to them *g* he power to become the ... Jn 1:12 *1325*
that he *g* his only begotten Son, ... Jn 3:16 *1325*
that Jacob *g* to his son Joseph ... Jn 4:5 *1325*
which *g* us the well, and drank ... Jn 4:12 *1325*
He *g* them bread from heaven to ... Jn 6:31 *1325*
Moses *g* you not that bread from ... Jn 6:32 *1325*
Moses therefore *g* unto you ... Jn 7:22 *1325*
which *g* them me, is greater than ... Jn 10:29 *1325*
he *g* me a commandment, what I ... Jn 12:49 *1325*
he *g* it to Judas Iscariot, the ... Jn 13:26 *1325*
as the Father *g* me commandment, ... Jn 14:31 *1781*
which *g* counsel to the Jews, that ... Jn 18:14 *4823*
But Jesus *g* him no answer ... Jn 19:9 *1325*
bowed his head, and *g* up the ghost ... Jn 19:30 *3860*
and Pilate *g* him leave ... Jn 19:38 *2010*
And they *g* forth their lots ... Acts 1:26 *1325*
as the Spirit *g* them utterance ... Acts 2:4 *1325*
he *g* heed unto them, expecting to ... Acts 3:5 *1907*
with great power *g* the apostles ... Acts 4:33 *591*
fell down, and *g* up the ghost ... Acts 5:5
he *g* him none inheritance in it, ... Acts 7:5 *1325*
And he *g* him the covenant of ... Acts 7:8 *1325*
g him favour and wisdom in the ... Acts 7:10 *1325*
g them up to worship the host of ... Acts 7:42 *3860*
the people with one accord *g* heed ... Acts 8:6 *4337*
To whom they all *g* heed, from the ... Acts 8:10 *4337*
he *g* her his hand, and lifted her ... Acts 9:41 *1325*
which *g* much alms to the people, ... Acts 10:2 *4160*
Forasmuch then as God *g* them the ... Acts 11:17 *1325*
And the people *g* a shout, saying, ... Acts 12:22
because he *g* not God the glory ... Acts 12:23 *1325*
eaten of worms, and *g* up the ghost ... Acts 12:23
after that he *g* unto them judges ... Acts 13:20 *1325*
God *g* unto them Saul the son of ... Acts 13:21 *1325*
to whom also he *g* testimony ... Acts 13:22 *3140*
which *g* testimony unto the word ... Acts 14:3 *3140*
g us rain from heaven, and ... Acts 14:17 *1325*
g audience to Barnabas and Paul, ... Acts 15:12
to whom we *g* no such commandment ... Acts 15:24 *1291*
they *g* him audience unto this ... Acts 22:22
g commandment to his accusers ... Acts 23:30
I *g* my voice against them ... Acts 26:10 *2702*
g him liberty to go unto his ... Acts 27:3 *2010*
g thanks to God in presence of ... Acts 27:35
Wherefore God also *g* them up to ... Rom 1:24 *3860*
For this cause God *g* them up unto ... Rom 1:26 *3860*
God *g* them over to a reprobate ... Rom 1:28 *3860*
even as the Lord *g* to every man ... 1Cor 3:5 *1325*
but God *g* the increase ... 1Cor 3:6
but first *g* their own selves to ... 2Cor 8:5 *1325*
Who *g* himself for our sins, that ... Gal 1:4 *1325*
To whom we *g* place by subjection, ... Gal 2:5 *1502*
they *g* to me and Barnabas the ... Gal 2:9 *1325*
who loved me, and *g* himself for me ... Gal 2:20 *3860*
but God *g* it to Abraham by ... Gal 3:18 *5483*
g him to be the head over all ... Eph 1:22 *1325*
captive, and *g* gifts unto men ... Eph 4:8 *1325*
And he *g* some, apostles ... Eph 4:11 *1325*
the church, and *g* himself for it ... Eph 5:25 *3860*
we *g* you by the Lord Jesus ... 1Th 4:2 *1325*
Who *g* himself a ransom for all, ... 1Ti 2:6 *1325*
Who *g* himself for us, that he ... Titus 2:14 *1325*
Abraham *g* a tenth part of all ... Heb 7:2
Abraham *g* the tenth of the spoils ... Heb 7:4 *1325*
of which no man *g* attendance at ... Heb 7:13 *4337*
g commandment concerning his ... Heb 11:22
us, and we *g* them reverence ... Heb 12:9 *1788*
again, and the heaven *g* rain ... Jas 5:18 *1325*
up from the dead, and *g* him glory ... 1Pet 1:21 *1325*
another, as he *g* us commandment ... 1Jn 3:23 *1325*
the record that God *g* of his Son ... 1Jn 5:10 *3140*
when I *g* all diligence to write ... Jude 3 *4160*
Christ, which God *g* unto him ... Rev 1:1 *1325*
I *g* her space to repent of her ... Rev 2:21 *1325*
g glory to the God of heaven ... Rev 11:13 *1325*
the dragon *g* him his power, and ... Rev 13:2 *1325*
which *g* power unto the beast ... Rev 13:4 *1325*
one of the four beasts *g* unto the ... Rev 15:7 *1325*
the sea *g* up the dead which were ... Rev 20:13 *1325*

GAVEST {34}
woman whom thou *g* to be with me ... Gen 3:12 5414
which thou *g* unto their fathers ... 1Kin 8:34 5414
which thou *g* unto our fathers ... 1Kin 8:40 5414
which thou *g* unto their fathers, ... 1Kin 8:48 5414
the land which thou *g* to them ... 2Chr 6:25 5414
which thou *g* unto our fathers ... 2Chr 6:31 5414
which thou *g* unto their fathers, ... 2Chr 6:38 5414
g it to the seed of Abraham thy ... 2Chr 20:7 5414
g him the name of Abraham ... Neh 9:7 7760
g them right judgments, and true ... Neh 9:13 5414
g them bread from heaven for ... Neh 9:15 5414
Thou *g* also thy good spirit to ... Neh 9:20 5414
g them water for their thirst ... Neh 9:20 5414
Moreover thou *g* them kingdoms ... Neh 9:22 5414
g them into their hands, with ... Neh 9:24 5414
mercies thou *g* them saviours ... Neh 9:27 5414
therefore *g* thou them into the ... Neh 9:30 5414
great goodness that thou *g* them ... Neh 9:35 5414
fat land which thou *g* before them ... Neh 9:35 5414
for the land that thou *g* unto our ... Neh 9:36 5414
G thou the goodly wings unto the ... Job 39:13
thou *g* it him, even length of ... Ps 21:4 5414
g him to be meat to the people ... Ps 74:14 5414
thou *g* me no water for my feet ... Lk 7:44 *1325*
Thou *g* me no kiss ... Lk 7:45 *1325*
and yet thou never *g* me a kid ... Lk 15:29 *1325*
Wherefore then *g* not thou my ... Lk 19:23 *1325*
the work which thou *g* me to do ... Jn 17:4 *1325*
which thou *g* me out of the world ... Jn 17:6 *1325*
they were, and thou *g* them me ... Jn 17:6 *1325*
them the words which thou *g* me ... Jn 17:8 *1325*
those that thou *g* me I have kept ... Jn 17:12 *1325*
which thou *g* me I have given them ... Jn 17:22 *1325*
Of them which thou *g* me have I ... Jn 18:9 *1325*

GAY {1}
him that weareth the *g* clothing ... Jas 2:3 *2986*

GAZA *(ga'-zah)* {19} See AZZAH, GAZITES.
1. A royal Philistine city.
as thou comest to Gerar, unto *G* ... Gen 10:19 5804
from Kadesh-barnea even unto *G* ... Josh 10:41 5804
only in *G*, in Gath, and in Ashdod, ... Josh 11:22 5804
G with her towns and her villages, ... Josh 15:47 5804
Also Judah took *G* with the coast ... Judg 1:18 5804
Then went Samson to *G*, and saw ... Judg 16:1 5804
eyes, and brought him down to *G* ... Judg 16:21 5804
for Ashdod one, for *G* one ... 1Sa 6:17 5804
the Philistines, even unto *G* ... 2Kin 18:8 5804
before that Pharaoh smote *G* ... Jer 47:1 5804
Baldness is come upon *G* ... Jer 47:5 5804
For three transgressions of *G* ... Amos 1:6 5804
will send a fire on the wall of *G* ... Amos 1:7 5804
For *G* shall be forsaken, and ... Zeph 2:4 5804
G also shall see it, and be very ... Zec 9:5 5804
and the king shall perish from *G* ... Zec 9:5 5804
goeth down from Jerusalem unto *G* ... Acts 8:26 *1048*
2. A city in Ephraim.
the earth, till thou come unto *G* ... Judg 6:4 5804
also and the towns thereof, unto *G* ... 1Chr 7:28 5804

GAZATHITES *(ga'-zath-ites)* {1} See GAZITES. *Inhabitants of Gaza.*
the *G*, and the Ashdothites, the ... Josh 13:3 5841

GAZE {1}
break through unto the LORD to *g* ... Ex 19:21 7200

GAZER *(ga'-zur)* {2} See GEZER. *A Canaanite city.*
from Geba until thou come to *G* ... 2Sa 5:25 1507
Philistines from Gibeon even to *G* ... 1Chr 14:16 1507

GAZEZ *(ga'-zez)* {2} *A son of Caleb.*
bare Haran, and Moza, and *G* ... 1Chr 2:46 1495
and Haran begat *G* ... 1Chr 2:46 1495

GAZING {1}
why stand ye *g* up into heaven ... Acts 1:11 *1689*

GAZINGSTOCK {2}
vile, and will set thee as a *g* ... Nah 3:6 7210
were made a *g* both by reproaches ... Heb 10:33 *2301*

GAZITES *(ga'-zites)* {1} See GAZATHITES. *Inhabitants of Gaza.*
And it was told the *G*, saying, ... Judg 16:2 5841

GAZZAM *(gaz'-zam)* {2} *A family of exiles.*
of Nekoda, the children of *G* ... Ezr 2:48 1502
The children of *G*, the children ... Neh 7:51 1502

GEBA *(ghe'-bah)* {12} See GABA, GIBEAH, GIBEON. *A Levitical city in Benjamin.*
her suburbs, *G* with her suburbs, ... Josh 21:17 1387
of the Philistines that was in *G* ... 1Sa 13:3 1387
from *G* until thou come to Gazer ... 2Sa 5:25 1387
Asa built with them *G* of Benjamin ... 1Kin 15:22 1387
from *G* to Beer-sheba, and brake ... 2Kin 23:8 1387
G with her suburbs, and Alemeth ... 1Chr 6:60 1387
fathers of the inhabitants of *G* ... 1Chr 8:6 1387
and he built therewith *G* and Mizpah ... 2Chr 16:6 1387
Benjamin from *G* dwelt at Michmash ... Neh 11:31 1387
Gilgal, and out of the fields of *G* ... Neh 12:29 1387
have taken up their lodging at *G* ... Is 10:29 1387
G to Rimmon south of Jerusalem ... Zec 14:10 1387

GEBAL *(ghe'-bal)* {2} See GIBLITES.
1. An Edomite territory.
G, and Ammon, and Amalek ... Ps 83:7 1381
2. A Phoenician trade city.
The ancients of *G* and the wise men ... Eze 27:9 1381

GEBALITES See GIBLITES.

GEBER {2} See EZION-GEBER.
1. Father of an officer of Solomon.
The son of *G*, in Ramoth-gilead ... 1Kin 4:13 1398
2. The son of Uri.
G the son of Uri was in the ... 1Kin 4:19 1398

GEBIM *(ghe'-bim)* {1} *A city in Benjamin.*
the inhabitants of *G* gather ... Is 10:31 1374

GEDALIAH *(ghed-a-li'-ah)* {32}
1. Son of Ahikam.
them he made *G* the son of Ahikam ... 2Kin 25:22 1436
of Babylon had made *G* governor ... 2Kin 25:23 1436
there came to *G* to Mizpah ... 2Kin 25:23 1436
G sware to them, and to their men, ... 2Kin 25:24 1436
and ten men with him, and smote *G* ... 2Kin 25:25 1436
committed him unto *G* the son of ... Jer 39:14 1436
Go back also to *G* the son of ... Jer 40:5 1436
Then went Jeremiah unto *G* the son ... Jer 40:6 1436
the king of Babylon had made *G* ... Jer 40:7 1436
Then they came to *G* to Mizpah ... Jer 40:8 1436
G the son of Ahikam the son of ... Jer 40:9 1436
that he had set over them *G* the ... Jer 40:11 1436
came to the land of Judah, to *G* ... Jer 40:12 1436
the fields, came to *G* to Mizpah, ... Jer 40:13 1436
But *G* the son of Ahikam believed ... Jer 40:14 1436
spake to *G* in Mizpah secretly ... Jer 40:15 1436
But *G* the son of Ahikam said unto ... Jer 40:16 1436
came unto *G* the son of Ahikam to ... Jer 41:1 1436
smote *G* the son of Ahikam the son ... Jer 41:2 1436
that were with him, even with *G* ... Jer 41:3 1436
second day after he had slain *G* ... Jer 41:4 1436
Come to *G* the son of Ahikam ... Jer 41:6 1436
whom he had slain because of *G* ... Jer 41:9 1436
committed to *G* the son of Ahikam ... Jer 41:10 1436
he had slain *G* the son of Ahikam ... Jer 41:16 1436
had slain *G* the son of Ahikam ... Jer 41:18 1436
of the guard had left with *G* the ... Jer 43:6 1436
2. A son of Jeduthun.
G, and Zeri, and Jeshaiah, ... 1Chr 25:3 1436
the second to *G*, who with his ... 1Chr 25:9 1436
3. Priest who married a foreigner.
and Eliezer, and Jarib, and *G* ... Ezr 10:18 1436
4. Grandfather of Zephaniah.
the son of Cushi, the son of *G* ... Zeph 1:1 1436
5. A prince who had Jeremiah imprisoned.
G the son of Pashur, and Jucal the ... Jer 38:1 1436

GEDEON *(ghed'-e-on)* {1} See GIDEON. *Greek form of Gideon.*
time would fail me to tell of *G* ... Heb 11:32 *1066*

GEDER *(ghe'-dur)* {1} See BETH-GADER, GEDERITE, GEDOR. *A Canaanite city.*
the king of *G*, one ... Josh 12:13 1445

GEDERAH *(ghed'-e-rah)* {1} See GEDERATHITE. *A city in Judah.*
And Sharaim, and Adithaim, and *G* ... Josh 15:36 1449

GEDERATHITE *(ghed'-e-rath-ite)* {1} *An inhabitant of Gederah.*
and Johanan, and Josabad the *G* ... 1Chr 12:4 1452

GEDERITE *(ghed'-e-rite)* {1} *An inhabitant of Geder.*
low plains was Baal-hanan the *G* ... 1Chr 27:28 1451

GEDEROTH *(ghed'-e-roth)* {2} *A town in Judah.*
And *G*, Beth-dagon, and Naamah, and ... Josh 15:41 1450
Beth-shemesh, and Ajalon, and *G* ... 2Chr 28:18 1450

GEDEROTHAIM *(ghed-e-ro-tha'-im)* {1} *A town in Judah.*
and Adithaim, and Gederah, and *G* ... Josh 15:36 1453

GEDOR *(ghe'-dor)* {7} See GEDER.
1. A city in Judah.
Halhul, Beth-zur, and *G*, ... Josh 15:58 1446

2. Hometown of Jeroham.
the sons of Jeroham of *G* ... 1Chr 12:7 1446
3. Son of Jehiel.
And *G*, and Ahio, and Zacher ... 1Chr 8:31 1446
And *G*, and Ahio, and Zechariah, and ... 1Chr 9:37 1446
4. A descendant of Judah.
And Penuel the father of *G* ... 1Chr 4:4 1446
bare Jered the father of *G* ... 1Chr 4:18 1446
5. A place in Judah.
And they went to the entrance of *G* ... 1Chr 4:39 1446

GE-HARASHIM See CHARASHIM.

GEHAZI *(ghe-ha'-zi)* {12} *A servant of Elijah.*
he said to *G* his servant, Call ... 2Kin 4:12 1522
G answered, Verily she hath no ... 2Kin 4:14 1522
that he said to *G* his servant ... 2Kin 4:25 1522
but *G* came near to thrust her ... 2Kin 4:27 1522
Then he said to *G*, Gird up thy ... 2Kin 4:29 1522
G passed on before them, and laid ... 2Kin 4:31 1522
And he called *G*, and said, Call ... 2Kin 4:36 1522
But *G*, the servant of Elisha the ... 2Kin 5:20 1522
So *G* followed after Naaman ... 2Kin 5:21 1522
unto him, Whence comest thou, *G* ... 2Kin 5:25 1522
the king talked with *G* the ... 2Kin 8:4 1522
G said, My lord, O king, this is ... 2Kin 8:5 1522

GELILOTH *(ghel'-il-oth)* {1} *Place on boundary of Benjamin and Judah.*
and went forth toward *G*, which is ... Josh 18:17 1553

GEMALLI *(ghe-mal'-li)* {1} *One of the twelve spies.*
tribe of Dan, Ammiel the son of *G* ... Num 13:12 1582

GEMARIAH *(ghem-a-ri'-ah)* {5}
1. Son of Shaphan.
in the chamber of *G* the son of ... Jer 36:10 1587
When Michaiah the son of *G* ... Jer 36:11 1587
G the son of Shaphan, and Zedekiah ... Jer 36:12 1587
G had made intercession to the ... Jer 36:25 1587
2. Son of Hilkiah.
G the son of Hilkiah, (whom ... Jer 29:3 1587

GENDER {2}
thy cattle *g* with a diverse kind ... Lev 19:19 7250
knowing that they do *g* strifes ... 2Ti 2:23 *1080*

GENDERED {1}
frost of heaven, who hath *g* it ... Job 38:29 3205

GENDERETH {2}
Their bull *g*, and faileth not ... Job 21:10 5674
which *g* to bondage, which is Agar ... Gal 4:24 *1080*

GENEALOGIES {8}
All these were reckoned by *g* in ... 1Chr 5:17 3187
in all by their *g* fourscore ... 1Chr 7:5 3187
were reckoned by their *g* twenty ... 1Chr 7:7 3187
So all Israel were reckoned by *g* ... 1Chr 9:1 3187
and of Iddo the seer concerning *g* ... 2Chr 12:15 3187
reckoned by *g* among the Levites ... 2Chr 31:19 3187
give heed to fables and endless *g* ... 1Ti 1:4 *1076*
But avoid foolish questions, and *g* ... Titus 3:9 *1076*

GENEALOGY {15}
their habitations, and their *g* ... 1Chr 4:33 3188
the *g* is not to be reckoned after ... 1Chr 5:1 3188
when the *g* of their generations ... 1Chr 5:7 3188
of them, after their *g* by their ... 1Chr 7:9 3188
the number throughout the *g* of ... 1Chr 7:40 3188
by their *g* in their villages ... 1Chr 9:22 3188
Beside their *g* of males, from ... 2Chr 31:16 3188
Both to the *g* of the priests by ... 2Chr 31:17 3188
to the *g* of all their little ones ... 2Chr 31:18 3188
those that were reckoned by *g* ... Ezr 2:62 3188
this is the *g* of them that went ... Ezr 8:1 3188
by *g* of the males an hundred ... Ezr 8:3 3188
that they might be reckoned by *g* ... Neh 7:5 3188
I found a register of the *g* of ... Neh 7:5 3188
those that were reckoned by *g* ... Neh 7:64 3188

GENERAL {2}
the *g* of the king's army was Joab ... 1Chr 27:34 8269
To the *g* assembly and church of ... Heb 12:23 *3831*

GENERALLY {2}
Israel be *g* gathered unto thee ... 2Sa 17:11
There shall be lamentation *g* upon ... Jer 48:38 3605

GENERATION {106}
righteous before me in this *g* ... Gen 7:1 1755
But in the fourth *g* they shall ... Gen 15:16 1755
Ephraim's children of the third *g* ... Gen 50:23
all his brethren, and all that *g* ... Ex 1:6 1755
with Amalek from *g* to *g* ... Ex 17:16 1755
fourth *g* of them that hate me ... Ex 20:5
unto the third and to the fourth *g* ... Ex 34:7
unto the third and fourth *g* ... Num 14:18
forty years, until all the *g* ... Num 32:13 1755
of this evil *g* see that good land ... Deut 1:35 1755
until all the *g* of the men of war ... Deut 2:14 1755
fourth *g* of them that hate me, ... Deut 5:9
even to his tenth *g* shall he not ... Deut 23:2 1755
even to their tenth *g* shall they ... Deut 23:3 1755
of the LORD in their third *g* ... Deut 23:8 1755
So that the *g* to come of your ... Deut 29:22 1755
they are a perverse and crooked *g* ... Deut 32:5 1755
for they are a very froward *g* ... Deut 32:20 1755
also all that *g* were gathered ... Judg 2:10 1755
there arose another *g* after them ... Judg 2:10 1755
g shall sit on the throne of ... 2Kin 10:30
of Israel unto the fourth *g* ... 2Kin 15:12
and kept throughout every *g* ... Est 9:28 1755
them from this *g* for ever ... Ps 12:7 1755
God is in the *g* of the righteous ... Ps 14:5 1755
be accounted to the Lord for a *g* ... Ps 22:30 1755
This is the *g* of them that seek ... Ps 24:6 1755
ye may tell it to the *g* following ... Ps 48:13 1755
shall go to the *g* of his fathers ... Ps 49:19 1755
shewed thy strength unto this *g* ... Ps 71:18 1755
against the *g* of thy children ... Ps 73:15 1755
shewing to the *g* to come the ... Ps 78:4 1755
That the *g* to come might know ... Ps 78:6 1755
a stubborn and rebellious *g* ... Ps 78:8 1755
a *g* that set not their heart ... Ps 78:8 1755
long was I grieved with this *g* ... Ps 95:10 1755
be written for the *g* to come ... Ps 102:18 1755
in the *g* following let their name ... Ps 109:13 1755
the *g* of the upright shall be ... Ps 112:2 1755
One *g* shall praise thy works to ... Ps 145:4 1755
doth the crown endure to every *g* ... Prov 27:24 1755
There is a *g* that curseth their ... Prov 30:11 1755
There is a *g* that are pure in ... Prov 30:12 1755
There is a *g*, O how lofty are ... Prov 30:13 1755
There is a *g*, whose teeth are as ... Prov 30:14 1755
passeth away, and another *g* cometh ... Eccl 1:4 1755
be dwelt in from *g* to *g* ... Is 13:20 1755
from *g* to *g* it shall lie ... Is 34:10 1755
from *g* to *g* shall they ... Is 34:17 1755
my salvation from *g* to *g* ... Is 51:8 1755
and who shall declare his *g* ... Is 53:8 1755
O *g*, see ye the word of the LORD ... Jer 2:31 1755
and forsaken the *g* of his wrath ... Jer 7:29 1755
be dwelt in from *g* to *g* ... Jer 50:39 1755
thy throne from *g* to *g* ... Lam 5:19 1755
dominion is from *g* to *g* ... Dan 4:3 1859
kingdom is from *g* to *g* ... Dan 4:34 1859
and their children another *g* ... Joel 1:3 1755
and Jerusalem from *g* to *g* ... Joel 3:20 1755
The book of the *g* of Jesus Christ ... Mt 1:1 *1078*
O *g* of vipers, who hath warned ... Mt 3:7 *1081*
whereunto shall I liken this *g* ... Mt 11:16 *1074*
O *g* of vipers, how can ye, being ... Mt 12:34 *1081*
adulterous *g* seeketh after a sign ... Mt 12:39 *1074*
rise in judgment with this *g* ... Mt 12:41 *1074*
up in the judgment with this *g* ... Mt 12:42 *1074*
it be also unto this wicked *g* ... Mt 12:45 *1074*
adulterous *g* seeketh after a sign ... Mt 16:4 *1074*
said, O faithless and perverse *g* ... Mt 17:17 *1074*
ye *g* of vipers, how can ye escape ... Mt 23:33 *1081*
things shall come upon this *g* ... Mt 23:36 *1074*
This *g* shall not pass, till all ... Mt 24:34 *1074*
Why doth this *g* seek after a sign ... Mk 8:12 *1074*
no sign be given unto this *g* ... Mk 8:12 *1074*
in this adulterous and sinful *g* ... Mk 8:38 *1074*
him, and saith, O faithless *g* ... Mk 9:19 *1074*
that this *g* shall not pass, till ... Mk 13:30 *1074*
fear him from *g* to *g* ... Lk 1:50 *1074*
O *g* of vipers, who hath warned ... Lk 3:7 *1081*
shall I liken the men of this *g* ... Lk 7:31 *1074*
said, O faithless and perverse *g* ... Lk 9:41 *1074*
began to say, This is an evil *g* ... Lk 11:29 *1074*
also the Son of man be to this *g* ... Lk 11:30 *1074*
judgment with the men of this *g* ... Lk 11:31 *1074*
up in the judgment with this *g* ... Lk 11:32 *1074*
world, may be required of this *g* ... Lk 11:50 *1074*
It shall be required of this *g* ... Lk 11:51 *1074*
g wiser than the children of ... Lk 16:8 *1074*
things, and be rejected of this *g* ... Lk 17:25 *1074*
This *g* shall not pass away, till ... Lk 21:32 *1074*
yourselves from this untoward *g* ... Acts 2:40 *1074*
and who shall declare his *g* ... Acts 8:33 *1074*
his own *g* by the will of God ... Acts 13:36 *1074*
I was grieved with that *g* ... Heb 3:10 *1074*
But ye are a chosen *g*, a royal ... 1Pet 2:9 *1085*

GENERATIONS {118}
These are the *g* of the heavens and ... Gen 2:4 8435
This is the book of the *g* of Adam ... Gen 5:1 8435
These are the *g* of Noah ... Gen 6:9 8435
a just man and perfect in his *g* ... Gen 6:9 8435
that is with you, for perpetual *g* ... Gen 9:12 1755
Now these are the *g* of the sons ... Gen 10:1 8435
the sons of Noah, after their *g* ... Gen 10:32 8435
These are the *g* of Shem ... Gen 11:10 8435
Now these are the *g* of Terah ... Gen 11:27 8435
g for an everlasting covenant ... Gen 17:7 1755
and thy seed after thee in their *g* ... Gen 17:9 1755
you, every man child in your *g* ... Gen 17:12 1755
Now these are the *g* of Ishmael ... Gen 25:12 8435
their names, according to their *g* ... Gen 25:13 8435
And these are the *g* of Isaac ... Gen 25:19 8435
Now these are the *g* of Esau ... Gen 36:1 8435
these are the *g* of Esau the ... Gen 36:9 8435
These are the *g* of Jacob ... Gen 37:2 8435
and this is my memorial unto all *g* ... Ex 3:15 1755
sons of Levi according to their *g* ... Ex 6:16 8435
of Levi according to their *g* ... Ex 6:19 8435
to the LORD throughout your *g* ... Ex 12:14 1755
your *g* by an ordinance for ever ... Ex 12:17 1755
the children of Israel in their *g* ... Ex 12:42 1755
omer of it to be kept for your *g* ... Ex 16:32 1755
the LORD, to be kept for your *g* ... Ex 16:33 1755
g on the behalf of the children ... Ex 27:21 1755
g at the door of the tabernacle ... Ex 29:42 1755
before the LORD throughout your *g* ... Ex 30:8 1755
upon it throughout your *g* ... Ex 30:10 1755
and to his seed throughout their *g* ... Ex 30:21 1755
oil unto me throughout your *g* ... Ex 30:31 1755
me and you throughout your *g* ... Ex 31:13 1755
the sabbath throughout their *g* ... Ex 31:16 1755
priesthood throughout their *g* ... Ex 40:15 1755
g throughout all your dwellings ... Lev 3:17 1755
be a statute for ever in your *g* ... Lev 6:18 1755
for ever throughout their *g* ... Lev 7:36 1755
for ever throughout your *g* ... Lev 10:9 1755
ever unto them throughout their *g* ... Lev 17:7 1755
in their *g* that hath any blemish ... Lev 21:17 1755
be of all your seed among your *g* ... Lev 22:3 1755
your *g* in all your dwellings ... Lev 23:14 1755
your dwellings throughout your *g* ... Lev 23:21 1755
your *g* in all your dwellings ... Lev 23:31 1755
be a statute for ever in your *g* ... Lev 23:41 1755
That your *g* may know that I made ... Lev 23:43 1755
be a statute for ever in your *g* ... Lev 24:3 1755
that bought it throughout his *g* ... Lev 25:30 1755
Israel's eldest son, by their *g* ... Num 1:20 8435
children of Simeon, by their *g* ... Num 1:22 8435
the children of Gad, by their *g* ... Num 1:24 8435
the children of Judah, by their *g* ... Num 1:26 8435
children of Issachar, by their *g* ... Num 1:28 8435
children of Zebulun, by their *g* ... Num 1:30 8435
children of Ephraim, by their *g* ... Num 1:32 8435
children of Manasseh, by their *g* ... Num 1:34 8435
children of Benjamin, by their *g* ... Num 1:36 8435
the children of Dan, by their *g* ... Num 1:38 8435
the children of Asher, by their *g* ... Num 1:40 8435
of Naphtali, throughout their *g* ... Num 1:42 8435
These also are the *g* of Aaron ... Num 3:1 8435
for ever throughout your *g* ... Num 10:8 1755
whosoever be among you in your *g* ... Num 15:14 1755
an ordinance for ever in your *g* ... Num 15:15 1755
LORD an heave offering in your *g* ... Num 15:21 1755
and henceforward among your *g* ... Num 15:23 1755
their garments throughout their *g* ... Num 15:38 1755
for ever throughout your *g* ... Num 18:23 1755
your *g* in all your dwellings ... Num 35:29 1755
his commandments to a thousand *g* ... Deut 7:9 1755
old, consider the years of many *g* ... Deut 32:7 1755
our *g* after us, that we might do ... Josh 22:27 1755
to us or to our *g* in time to come ... Josh 22:28 1755
Only that the *g* of the children ... Judg 3:2 1755
Now these are the *g* of Pharez ... Ruth 4:18 8435
These are their *g* ... 1Chr 1:29 8435
genealogy of their *g* was reckoned ... 1Chr 5:7 8435
valiant men of might in their *g* ... 1Chr 7:2 8435
And with them, by their *g*, after ... 1Chr 7:4 8435
after their genealogy by their *g* ... 1Chr 7:9 8435
heads of the fathers, by their *g* ... 1Chr 8:28 8435
brethren, according to their *g* ... 1Chr 9:9 8435
were chief throughout their *g* ... 1Chr 9:34 8435
he commanded to a thousand *g* ... 1Chr 16:15 1755
according to the *g* of his fathers ... 1Chr 26:31 8435
and his sons' sons, even four *g* ... Job 42:16 1755
thoughts of his heart to all *g* ... Ps 33:11 1755
name to be remembered in all *g* ... Ps 45:17 1755
and their dwelling places to all *g* ... Ps 49:11 1755
and his years as many *g* ... Ps 61:6 1755
and moon endure, throughout all *g* ... Ps 72:5 1755
shew forth thy praise to all *g* ... Ps 79:13 1755
draw out thine anger to all *g* ... Ps 85:5 1755
known thy faithfulness to all *g* ... Ps 89:1 1755
and build up thy throne to all *g* ... Ps 89:4 1755
been our dwelling place in all *g* ... Ps 90:1 1755
and his truth endureth to all *g* ... Ps 100:5 1755
and thy remembrance unto all *g* ... Ps 102:12 1755
thy years are throughout all *g* ... Ps 102:24 1755
he commanded to a thousand *g* ... Ps 105:8 1755
unto all *g* for evermore ... Ps 106:31 1755
Thy faithfulness is unto all *g* ... Ps 119:90 1755
O LORD, throughout all *g* ... Ps 135:13 1755
endureth throughout all *g* ... Ps 145:13 1755
even thy God, O Zion, unto all *g* ... Ps 146:10 1755
calling the *g* from the beginning ... Is 41:4 1755
the ancient days, in the *g* of old ... Is 51:9 1755
up the foundations of many *g* ... Is 58:12 1755
excellency, a joy of many *g* ... Is 60:15 1755
cities, the desolations of many *g* ... Is 61:4 1755
it, even to the years of many *g* ... Joel 2:2 1755
So all the *g* from Abraham to ... Mt 1:17 *1074*
Abraham to David are fourteen *g* ... Mt 1:17 *1074*
away into Babylon are fourteen *g* ... Mt 1:17 *1074*
unto Christ are fourteen *g* ... Mt 1:17 *1074*
from henceforth all *g* shall call ... Lk 1:48 *1074*
hath been hid from ages and from *g* ... Col 1:26 *1074*

GENNESARET *(ghen-nes'-a-ret)* {3} See CHINNERETH. *Same as Galilee.*
they came into the land of *G* ... Mt 14:34 *1082*
they came into the land of *G* ... Mk 6:53 *1082*
of God, he stood by the lake of *G* ... Lk 5:1 *1082*

GENTILE *(jen'-tile)* {2} See GENTILES. *A non-Jew.*
the Jew first, and also of the *G* ... Rom 2:9 *1672*
the Jew first, and also to the *G* ... Rom 2:10 *1672*

GENTILES {130}
of the *G* divided in their lands ... Gen 10:5 1471
which dwelt in Harosheth of the *G* ... Judg 4:2 1471
from Harosheth of the *G* unto the ... Judg 4:13 1471
the host, unto Harosheth of the *G* ... Judg 4:16 1471
to it shall the *G* seek ... Is 11:10 1471
bring forth judgment to the *G* ... Is 42:1 1471
the people, for a light of the *G* ... Is 42:6 1471
give thee for a light to the *G* ... Is 49:6 1471
I will lift up mine hand to the *G* ... Is 49:22 1471
and thy seed shall inherit the *G* ... Is 54:3 1471
the *G* shall come to thy light, and ... Is 60:3 1471
the forces of the *G* shall come ... Is 60:5 1471
unto thee the forces of the *G* ... Is 60:11 1471
shalt also suck the milk of the *G* ... Is 60:16 1471
ye shall eat the riches of the *G* ... Is 61:6 1471
seed shall be known among the *G* ... Is 61:9 1471
the *G* shall see thy righteousness ... Is 62:2 1471
the glory of the *G* like a flowing ... Is 66:12 1471

G

declare my glory among the G Is 66:19 1471
destroyer of the G is on his way Jer 4:7 1471
of the G that can cause rain Jer 14:22 1471
the G shall come unto thee from Jer 16:19 1471
the prophet against the G Jer 46:1 1471
and her princes are among the G Lam 2:9 1471
their defiled bread among the G Eze 4:13 1471
the G as a vessel wherein is no Hos 8:8 1471
Proclaim ye this among the G Joel 3:9 1471
of Jacob shall be among the G in Mic 5:8 1471
to cast out the horns of the G Zec 1:21 1471
name shall be great among the G Mal 1:11 1471
beyond Jordan, Galilee of the G Mt 4:15 *1484*
all these things do the G seek Mt 6:32 *1484*
Go not into the way of the G Mt 10:5 *1484*
a testimony against them and the G Mt 10:18 *1484*
he shall shew judgment to the G Mt 12:18 *1484*
And in his name shall the G trust Mt 12:21 *1484*
deliver him to the G to mock Mt 20:19 *1484*
the G exercise dominion over them Mt 20:25 *1484*
and shall deliver him to the G Mk 10:33 *1484*
the G exercise lordship over them Mk 10:42 *1484*
A light to lighten the G, and the Lk 2:32 *1484*
he shall be delivered unto the G Lk 18:32 *1484*
shall be trodden down of the G Lk 21:24 *1484*
the times of the G be fulfilled Lk 21:24 *1484*
The kings of the G exercise Lk 22:25 *1484*
go unto the dispersed among the G Jn 7:35 *1672*
the G, and teach the G Jn 7:35 *1672*
and Pontius Pilate, with the G Acts 4:27 *1484*
into the possession of the G Acts 7:45 *1484*
me, to bear my name before the G Acts 9:15 *1484*
because that on the G also was Acts 10:45 *1484*
G had also received the word of Acts 11:1 *1484*
Then hath God also to the G Acts 11:18 *1484*
the G besought that these words Acts 13:42 *1484*
life, lo, we turn to the G Acts 13:46 *1484*
set thee to be a light of the G Acts 13:47 *1484*
when the G heard this, they were Acts 13:48 *1484*
unbelieving Jews stirred up the G Acts 14:2 *1484*
was an assault made both of the G Acts 14:5 *1484*
the door of faith unto the G Acts 14:27 *1484*
declaring the conversion of the G Acts 15:3 *1484*
that the G by my mouth should Acts 15:7 *1484*
had wrought among the G by them Acts 15:12 *1484*
God at the first did visit the G Acts 15:14 *1484*
seek after the Lord, and all the G Acts 15:17 *1484*
among the G are turned to God Acts 15:19 *1484*
which are of the G in Antioch Acts 15:23 *1484*
henceforth I will go unto the G Acts 18:6 *1484*
him into the hands of the G Acts 21:11 *1484*
among the G by his ministry Acts 21:19 *1484*
are among the G to forsake Moses Acts 21:21 *1484*
As touching the G which believe Acts 21:25 *1484*
send thee far hence unto the G Acts 22:21 *1484*
from the people, and from the G Acts 26:17 *1484*
of Judaea, and then to the G Acts 26:20 *1484*
unto the people, and to the G Acts 26:23 *1484*
of God is sent unto the G Acts 28:28 *1484*
you also, even as among other G Rom 1:13 *1484*
For when the G, which have not Rom 2:14 *1484*
among the G through you, as it is Rom 2:24 *1484*
have before proved both Jews and G Rom 3:9 *1672*
is he not also of the G Rom 3:29 *1484*
Yes, of the G also Rom 3:29 *1484*
the Jews only, but also of the G Rom 9:24 *1484*
That the G, which followed not Rom 9:30 *1484*
fall salvation is come unto the G Rom 11:11 *1484*
of them the riches of the G Rom 11:12 *1484*
For I speak to you G, inasmuch as Rom 11:13 *1484*
as I am the apostle of the G Rom 11:13 *1484*
the fulness of the G be come in Rom 11:25 *1484*
that the G might glorify God for Rom 15:9 *1484*
will confess to thee among the G Rom 15:9 *1484*
And again he saith, Rejoice, ye G Rom 15:10 *1484*
again, Praise the Lord, all ye G Rom 15:11 *1484*
shall rise to reign over the G Rom 15:12 *1484*
in him shall the G trust Rom 15:12 *1484*
minister of Jesus Christ to the G Rom 15:16 *1484*
up of the G might be acceptable Rom 15:16 *1484*
by me, to make the G obedient Rom 15:18 *1484*
For if the G have been made Rom 15:27 *1484*
also all the churches of the G Rom 16:4 *1484*
not so much as named among the G 1Cor 5:1 *1484*
the things which the G sacrifice 1Cor 10:20 *1484*
neither to the Jews, nor to the G 1Cor 10:32 *1672*
Ye know that ye were G, carried 1Cor 12:2 *1484*
one body, whether we be Jews or G 1Cor 12:13 *1672*
gospel which I preach among the G Gal 2:2 *1484*
was mighty in me toward the G Gal 2:8 *1484*
from James, he did eat with the G Gal 2:12 *1484*
Jew, livest after the manner of G Gal 2:14 *1483*
thou the G to live as do the Jews Gal 2:14 *1484*
nature, and not sinners of the G Gal 2:15 *1484*
on the G through Jesus Christ Gal 3:14 *1484*
being in time past G in the flesh Eph 2:11 *1484*
of Jesus Christ for you G Eph 3:1 *1484*
That the G should be fellowheirs, Eph 3:6 *1484*
the G the unsearchable riches of Eph 3:8 *1484*
walk not as other G walk, in the Eph 4:17 *1484*
glory of this mystery among the G Col 1:27 *1484*
to the G that they might be saved 1Th 2:16 *1484*
even as the G which know not God 1Th 4:5 *1484*
a teacher of the G in faith 1Ti 2:7 *1484*
of angels, preached unto the G 1Ti 3:16 *1484*
an apostle, and a teacher of the G 2Ti 1:11 *1484*
and that all the G might hear 2Ti 4:17 *1484*
conversation honest among the G 1Pet 2:12 *1484*
to have wrought the will of the G 1Pet 4:3 *1484*
forth, taking nothing of the G 3Jn 7 *1484*
for it is given unto the G Rev 11:2 *1484*

GENTLE {5}
But we were g among you, even as 1Th 2:7 *2261*
but be g unto all men, apt to 2Ti 2:24 *2261*
no man, to be no brawlers, but g Titus 3:2 *1933*
is first pure, then peaceable, g Jas 3:17 *1933*
not only to the good and g 1Pet 2:18 *1933*

GENTLENESS {4}
and thy g hath made me great 2Sa 22:36 6031
up, and thy g hath made me great Ps 18:35 6038
g of Christ, who in presence am 2Cor 10:1 *1932*
joy, peace, longsuffering, g Gal 5:22 *5544*

GENTLY {2}
Deal g for my sake with the young 2Sa 18:5 3814
shall g lead those that are with Is 40:11

GENUBATH *(ghen'-u-bath)* {2} *Son of Hadad.*
of Tahpenes bare him G his son 1Kin 11:20 1592
G was in Pharaoh's household 1Kin 11:20 1592

GERA *(ghe'-rah)* {9} *A son of Bela.*
Belah, and Becher, and Ashbel, G Gen 46:21 1617
up a deliverer, Ehud the son of G Judg 3:15 1617
name was Shimei, the son of G 2Sa 16:5 1617
And Shimei the son of G, a 2Sa 19:16 1617
Shimei the son of G fell down 2Sa 19:18 1617
with thee Shimei the son of G 1Kin 2:8 1617
sons of Bela were, Addar, and G 1Chr 8:3 1617
And G, and Shephuphan, and Huram 1Chr 8:5 1617
And Naaman, and Ahiah, and G 1Chr 8:7 1617

GERAHS {5}
(a shekel is twenty g Ex 30:13 1626
twenty g shall be the shekel Lev 27:25 1626
(the shekel is twenty g Num 3:47 1626
the sanctuary, which is twenty g Num 18:16 1626
And the shekel shall be twenty g Eze 45:12 1626

GERAR *(ghe'-rar)* {10} *A city in Gaza.*
from Sidon, as thou comest to G Gen 10:19 1642
Kadesh and Shur, and sojourned in G Gen 20:1 1642
and Abimelech king of G sent Gen 20:2 1642
king of the Philistines unto G Gen 26:1 1642
And Isaac dwelt in G Gen 26:6 1642
his tent in the valley of G Gen 26:17 1642
the herdmen of G did strive with Gen 26:20 1642
Then Abimelech went to him from G Gen 26:26 1642
were with him pursued them unto G 2Chr 14:13 1642
all the cities round about G 2Chr 14:14 1642

GERGESENES *(ghur'-ghes-enes')* {1} *Inhabitants of an area near Sea of Galilee.*
side into the country of the G Mt 8:28 *1086*

GERIZIM *(gher'-iz-im)* {4} *A mountain in central Palestine.*
put the blessing upon mount G Deut 11:29 1630
upon mount G to bless the people Deut 27:12 1630
half of them over against mount G Josh 8:33 1630
and stood in the top of mount G Judg 9:7 1630

GERSHOM *(ghur'-shom)* {14} See GERSHON.
1. Firstborn son of Moses.
a son, and he called his name G Ex 2:22 1648
which the name of the one was G Ex 18:3 1648
The sons of Moses were, G 1Chr 23:15 1648
Of the sons of G, Shebuel was the 1Chr 23:16 1648
And Shebuel the son of G, the son 1Chr 26:24 1648
2. A son of Levi.
G, Kohath, and Merari 1Chr 6:16 1648
be the names of the sons of G 1Chr 6:17 1648
Of G 1Chr 6:20 1648
The son of Jahath, the son of G 1Chr 6:43 1648
to the sons of G throughout their 1Chr 6:62 1648
Unto the sons of G were given out 1Chr 6:71 1648
Of the sons of G 1Chr 15:7 1648
3. A descendant of Phinehas.
of the sons of Phinehas; G Ezr 8:2 1648
4. Father of Jonathan.
and Jonathan, the son of G Judg 18:30 1648

GERSHON *(ghur'-shon)* {18} See GERSHOM, GERSHONITE. *A form of Gershom 2.*
G, Kohath, and Merari Gen 46:11 1647
G, and Kohath, and Merari Ex 6:16 1647
The sons of G Ex 6:17 1647
G, and Kohath, and Merari Num 3:17 1647
the sons of G by their families Num 3:18 1647
Of G was the family of the Num 3:21 1647
of G in the tabernacle of the Num 3:25 1647
also the sum of the sons of G Num 4:22 1647
of G in the tabernacle of the Num 4:28 1647
were numbered of the sons of G Num 4:38 1647
of the families of the sons of G Num 4:41
oxen he gave unto the sons of G Num 7:7 1647
and the sons of G and the sons of Num 10:17 1647
of G, the family of the Num 26:57 1647
the children of G had by lot out Josh 21:6 1647
And unto the children of G Josh 21:27 1647
G, Kohath, and Merari 1Chr 6:1 1647
among the sons of Levi, namely, G 1Chr 23:6 1647

GERSHONITE *(ghur'-shon-ite)* {3} See GERSHONITES. *Descendant of Gershom 2.*
the sons of the G Laadan, chief 1Chr 26:21 1649
fathers, even of Laadan the G 1Chr 26:21 1649
LORD, by the hand of Jehiel the G 1Chr 29:8 1649

GERSHONITES *(ghur'-shon-ites)* {9}
these are the families of the G Num 3:21 1649
The families of the G shall pitch Num 3:23 1649
G shall be Eliasaph the son of Num 3:24 1649
service of the families of the G Num 4:24 1649
the service of the sons of the G Num 4:27 1649
of Gershon, the family of the G Num 26:57 1649
All the cities of the G according Josh 21:33 1649
Of the G were, Laadan, and Shimei 1Chr 23:7 1649
and of the G 2Chr 29:12 1649

GERUTH See CHIMHAM.

GERUTH KIMHAM See CHIMHAM.

GESHAM *(ghe'-sham)* {1} *A son of Jahdai.*
Regem, and Jotham, and G, and Pelet, 1Chr 2:47 1529

GESHAN See GESHAM.

GESHEM *(ghe'-shem)* {3} See GASHMU. *An opponent of Nehemiah.*
G the Arabian, heard it, they Neh 2:19 1654
G the Arabian, and the rest of our Neh 6:1 1654
G sent unto me, saying, Come, let Neh 6:2 1654

GESHUR *(ghe'-shur)* {8} See GESHURITES. *A kingdom in Bashan.*
the daughter of Talmai king of G 2Sa 3:3 1650
the son of Ammihud, king of G 2Sa 13:37 1650
So Absalom fled, and went to G 2Sa 13:38 1650
So Joab arose and went to G 2Sa 14:23 1650
say, Wherefore am I come from G 2Sa 14:32 1650
a vow while I abode at G in Syria 2Sa 15:8 1650
And he took G, and Aram, with the 1Chr 2:23 1650
the daughter of Talmai king of G 1Chr 3:2 1650

GESHURI *(ghesh'-u-ri)* {2} See GESHURITES.
1. Inhabitants of Geshur.
of Argob unto the coasts of G Deut 3:14 1651
2. A people dwelling between Arabia and Philistia.
of the Philistines, and all G Josh 13:2 1651

GESHURITES *(ghesh'-u-rites)* {5}
1. Inhabitants of Geshur.
Bashan, unto the border of the G Josh 12:5 1651
And Gilead, and the border of the G Josh 13:11 1651
of Israel expelled not the G Josh 13:13 1651
but the G and the Maachathites Josh 13:13 1651
2. Same as Geshuri 2.
his men went up, and invaded the G 1Sa 27:8 1651

GET {118}
G thee out of thy country, and Gen 12:1 3212
said, Up, g you out of this place Gen 19:14 3318
g thee into the land of Moriah Gen 22:2 3212
g thee out from this land, and Gen 31:13 3318
saying, G me this damsel to wife Gen 34:4 3947
g you possessions therein Gen 34:10
g you down thither, and buy for us Gen 42:2 3381
g you up in peace unto your Gen 44:17 5927
g you unto the land of Canaan Gen 45:17 935
so g them up out of the land Ex 1:10 5927
g you unto your burdens Ex 5:4 3212
g you straw where ye can find it Ex 5:11 3947
G thee unto Pharaoh in the Ex 7:15 3212
G thee from me, take heed to Ex 10:28 3212
G thee out, and all the people Ex 11:8 3318
g you forth from among my people, Ex 12:31 3318
I will g me honour upon Pharaoh, Ex 14:17 3513
g thee down, and thou shalt come Ex 19:24 3381
said unto Moses, Go, g thee down Ex 32:7 3381
he be poor, and cannot g so much Lev 14:21 5381
pigeons, such as he is able to g Lev 14:22 5381
young pigeons, such as he can g Lev 14:30 5381
Even such as he is able to g Lev 14:31 5381
whose hand is not able to g that Lev 14:32 5381
beside that that his hand shall g Num 6:21 5381
G you up this way southward, and Num 13:17 5927
g you into the wilderness by the Num 14:25 5265
saying, G you up from about the Num 16:24 5927
G you up from among this Num 16:45 7426
of Balak, G you into your land Num 22:13 3212
thee, I will g me back again Num 22:34
G thee up into this mount Abarim, Num 27:12 5927
g you over the brook Zered Deut 2:13 5674
G thee up into the top of Pisgah, Deut 3:27 5927
G you into your tents again Deut 5:30 7725
giveth thee power to g wealth Deut 8:18 6213
g thee down quickly from hence Deut 9:12 3381
g thee up into the place which Deut 17:8 5927
shall g up above thee very high Deut 28:43 5927
G thee up into this mountain Deut 32:49 5927
G you to the mountain, lest the Josh 2:16 3212
LORD said unto Joshua, G thee up Josh 7:10 6965
then g thee up to the wood Josh 17:15 5927
g you unto your tents, and unto Josh 22:4 3212
g thee down unto the host Judg 7:9 3381
now therefore g her for me to Judg 14:2 3947
unto his father, G her for me Judg 14:3 3947
to morrow g you early on your way Judg 19:9
thee, and g thee down to the floor Ruth 3:3 3381
Now therefore g you up 1Sa 9:13 5927
g you down from among the 1Sa 15:6 3381
in thine eyes, let me g away 1Sa 20:29 4422
g thee into the land of Judah 1Sa 22:5 935
David made haste to g away for 1Sa 23:26 3212
G you up to Carmel, and go to 1Sa 25:5 5927
lest he g him fenced cities, and 2Sa 20:6 4672
that my lord the king may g heat 1Kin 1:2
g thee in unto king David, and say 1Kin 1:13 935
G thee to Anathoth, unto thine 1Kin 2:26 3212
speed to g him up to his chariot 1Kin 12:18 5927
and g thee to Shiloh 1Kin 14:2 1980
g thee to thine own house 1Kin 14:12 3212
G thee hence, and turn thee 1Kin 17:3 3212
g thee to Zarephath, which 1Kin 17:9 3212
Ahab, G thee up, eat and drink 1Kin 18:41 5927

g thee down, that the rain stop ... 1Kin 18:44 3381
g thee to the prophets of thy ... 2Kin 3:13 3212
them alive, and g into the city ... 2Kin 7:12 935
speed to g him up to his chariot ... 2Chr 10:18 5927
So didst thou g thee a name ... Neh 9:10 6213
thy precepts I g understanding ... Ps 119:104
G wisdom, g understanding ... Prov 4:5 7069
therefore g wisdom ... Prov 4:7 7069
all thy getting g understanding ... Prov 4:7 7069
A wound and dishonour shall he g ... Prov 6:33 4672
is it to g wisdom than gold ... Prov 16:16 7069
to g understanding rather to be ... Prov 16:16 7069
in the hand of a fool to g wisdom ... Prov 17:16 7069
ways, and g a snare to thy soul ... Prov 22:25 3947
A time to g, and a time to lose ... Eccl 3:6 1245
I will g me to the mountain of ... Song 4:6 3212
Let us g up early to the ... Song 7:12
g thee unto this treasurer, even ... Is 22:15 935
G you out of the way, turn aside ... Is 30:11
shalt say unto it, G thee hence ... Is 30:22 3318
g thee up into the high mountain ... Is 40:9 5927
g thee into darkness, O daughter ... Is 47:5 935
I will g me unto the great men, ... Jer 5:5 3212
g thee a linen girdle, and put it ... Jer 13:1 7069
g a potter's earthen bottle, and ... Jer 19:1 7069
g up, ye horsemen, and stand forth ... Jer 46:4 5927
Moab, that it may flee and g away ... Jer 48:9 3318
g you far off, dwell deep, O ye ... Jer 49:30 5110
g you up unto the wealthy nation, ... Jer 49:31 5927
me about, that I cannot g out ... Lam 3:7 3318
g thee unto the house of Israel, ... Eze 3:4 935
g thee to them of the captivity, ... Eze 3:11 935
said, G you far from the LORD ... Eze 11:15
souls, to g dishonest gain ... Eze 22:27 1214
let the beasts g away from under ... Dan 4:14 5111
come, g you down ... Joel 3:13 3381
I will g them praise and fame in ... Zeph 3:19 776
G you hence, walk to and fro ... Zec 6:7 3212
unto him, G thee hence, Satan ... Mt 4:10 5217
his disciples to g into a ship ... Mt 14:22 1684
Peter, G thee behind me, Satan ... Mt 16:23 5217
his disciples to g into the ship ... Mk 6:45 1684
saying, G thee behind me, Satan ... Mk 8:33 5217
unto him, G thee behind me, Satan ... Lk 4:8 5217
about, and lodge, and g victuals ... Lk 9:12 2147
G thee out, and depart hence ... Lk 13:31 1831
G thee out of thy country, and ... Acts 7:3 1831
g thee down, and go with them, ... Acts 10:20 2597
g thee quickly out of Jerusalem ... Acts 22:18 1831
first into the sea, and g to land ... Acts 27:43 1826
Lest Satan should g an advantage ... 2Cor 2:11 4122
a year, and buy and sell, and g gain ... Jas 4:13

GETHER (ghe'-ther) {2} A son of Aram.
Uz, and Hul, and G, and Mash ... Gen 10:23 1666
Aram, and Uz, and Hul, and G ... 1Chr 1:17 1666

GETHSEMANE (gheth-sem'-a-ne) {2} A garden near Jerusalem.
with them unto a place called G ... Mt 26:36 1068
came to a place which was named G ... Mk 14:32 1068

GETTETH {9}
Whosoever g up to the gutter, and ... 2Sa 5:8 5060
the man that g understanding ... Prov 3:13 6329
a scorner g to himself shame ... Prov 9:7 3947
a wicked man g himself a blot ... Prov 9:7
heareth reproof g understanding ... Prov 15:32 7069
heart of the prudent g knowledge ... Prov 18:15 7069
He that g wisdom loveth his own ... Prov 19:8 7069
so he that g riches, and not by ... Jer 17:11 6213
he that g up out of the pit shall ... Jer 48:44 5927

GETTING {3}
had gotten, the cattle of his g ... Gen 31:18 7075
with all thy g get understanding ... Prov 4:7 7069
The g of treasures by a lying ... Prov 21:6 6467

GEUEL (ghe-u'-el) {1} A son of Machri.
tribe of Gad, G the son of Machi ... Num 13:15 1345

GEZER (ghe'-zur) {13} See GAZER, GEZRITES. A Canaanite city.
Then Horam king of G came up to ... Josh 10:33 1507
the king of G, one ... Josh 12:12 1507
of Beth-horon the nether, and to G ... Josh 16:3 1507
the Canaanites that dwelt in G ... Josh 16:10 1507
and G with her suburbs, ... Josh 21:21 1507
the Canaanites that dwelt in G ... Judg 1:29 1507
Canaanites dwelt in G among them ... Judg 1:29 1507
and Hazor, and Megiddo, and G ... 1Kin 9:15 1507
of Egypt had gone up, and taken G ... 1Kin 9:16 1507
And Solomon built G, and Beth-horon ... 1Kin 9:17 1507
they gave also G with her suburbs ... 1Chr 6:67 1507
Naaran, and westward G ... 1Chr 7:28 1507
war at G with the Philistines ... 1Chr 20:4 1507

GEZRITES (ghez'-rites) {1} Inhabitants of Gezer.
invaded the Geshurites, and the G ... 1Sa 27:8 1511

GHOST {9}
Then Abraham gave up the g ... Gen 25:8 1478
and he gave up the g and died ... Gen 25:17 1478
And Isaac gave up the g, and died, ... Gen 35:29 1478
into the bed, and yielded up the g ... Gen 49:33 1478
why died I not give up the g when ... Job 3:11 1478
Oh that I had given up the g ... Job 10:18 1478
be as the giving up of the g ... Job 11:20 5315
my tongue, I shall give up the g ... Job 13:19 1478
yea, man giveth up the g, and ... Job 14:10 1478
she hath given up the g ... Jer 15:9 5315
elders gave up the g in the city ... Lam 1:19 1478
found with child of the Holy G ... Mt 1:18 4151
conceived in her is of the Holy G ... Mt 1:20 4151
shall baptize you with the Holy G ... Mt 3:11 4151
G shall not be forgiven unto men ... Mt 12:31 4151
speaketh against the Holy G ... Mt 12:32 4151
a loud voice, yielded up the g ... Mt 27:50 4151
and of the Son, and of the Holy G ... Mt 28:19 4151
shall baptize you with the Holy G ... Mk 1:8 4151
the Holy G hath never forgiveness ... Mk 3:29 4151
David himself said by the Holy G ... Mk 12:36 4151
not ye that speak, but the Holy G ... Mk 13:11 4151
a loud voice, and gave up the g ... Mk 15:37 1606
he so cried out, and gave up the g ... Mk 15:39 1606
shall be filled with the Holy G ... Lk 1:15 4151
The Holy G shall come upon thee, ... Lk 1:35 4151
was filled with the Holy G ... Lk 1:41 4151
was filled with the Holy G ... Lk 1:67 4151
and the Holy G was upon him ... Lk 2:25 4151
revealed unto him by the Holy G ... Lk 2:26 4151
shall baptize you with the Holy G ... Lk 3:16 4151
the Holy G descended in a bodily ... Lk 3:22 4151
the Holy G returned from Jordan ... Lk 4:1 4151
Holy G it shall not be forgiven ... Lk 12:10 4151
For the Holy G shall teach you in ... Lk 12:12 4151
said thus, he gave up the g ... Lk 23:46 1606
which baptizeth with the Holy G ... Jn 1:33 4151
for the Holy G was not yet given ... Jn 7:39 4151
Comforter, which is the Holy G ... Jn 14:26 4151
bowed his head, and gave up the g ... Jn 19:30 4151
unto them, Receive ye the Holy G ... Jn 20:22 4151
after that he through the Holy G ... Acts 1:2 4151
the Holy G not many days hence ... Acts 1:5 4151
that the Holy G is come upon you ... Acts 1:8 4151
which the Holy G by the mouth of ... Acts 1:16 4151
were all filled with the Holy G ... Acts 2:4 4151
Father the promise of the Holy G ... Acts 2:33 4151
receive the gift of the Holy G ... Acts 2:38 4151
Peter, filled with the Holy G ... Acts 4:8 4151
were all filled with the Holy G ... Acts 4:31 4151
thine heart to lie to the Holy G ... Acts 5:3 4151
words fell down, and gave up the g ... Acts 5:5 1634
at his feet, and yielded up the g ... Acts 5:10 1634
and so is also the Holy G, whom ... Acts 5:32 4151
honest report, full of the Holy G ... Acts 6:3 4151
full of faith and of the Holy G ... Acts 6:5 4151
ye do always resist the Holy G ... Acts 7:51 4151
But he, being full of the Holy G ... Acts 7:55 4151
they might receive the Holy G ... Acts 8:15 4151
them, and they received the Holy G ... Acts 8:17 4151
hands the Holy G was given ... Acts 8:18 4151
hands, he may receive the Holy G ... Acts 8:19 4151
and be filled with the Holy G ... Acts 9:17 4151
and in the comfort of the Holy G ... Acts 9:31 4151
Jesus of Nazareth with the Holy G ... Acts 10:38 4151
the Holy G fell on all them which ... Acts 10:44 4151
poured out the gift of the Holy G ... Acts 10:45 4151
received the Holy G as well as we ... Acts 10:47 4151
the Holy G fell on them, as on us ... Acts 11:15 4151
shall be baptized with the Holy G ... Acts 11:16 4151
a good man, and full of the Holy G ... Acts 11:24 4151
eaten of worms, and gave up the g ... Acts 12:23 1634
Lord, and fasted, the Holy G said ... Acts 13:2 4151
being sent forth by the Holy G ... Acts 13:4 4151
Paul,) filled with the Holy G ... Acts 13:9 4151
with joy, and with the Holy G ... Acts 13:52 4151
witness, giving them the Holy G ... Acts 15:8 4151
For it seemed good to the Holy G ... Acts 15:28 4151
Holy G to preach the word in Asia ... Acts 16:6 4151
the Holy G since ye believed ... Acts 19:2 4151
heard whether there be any Holy G ... Acts 19:2 4151
them, the Holy G came on them ... Acts 19:6 4151
Save that the Holy G witnesseth ... Acts 20:23 4151
Holy G hath made you overseers ... Acts 20:28 4151
and said, Thus saith the Holy G ... Acts 21:11 4151
Well spake the Holy G by Esaias ... Acts 28:25 4151
the Holy G which is given unto us ... Rom 5:5 4151
bearing me witness in the Holy G ... Rom 9:1 4151
and peace, and joy in the Holy G ... Rom 14:17 4151
through the power of the Holy G ... Rom 15:13 4151
being sanctified by the Holy G ... Rom 15:16 4151
but which the Holy G teacheth ... 1Cor 2:13 4151
of the Holy G which is in you ... 1Cor 6:19 4151
is the Lord, but by the Holy G ... 1Cor 12:3 4151
by kindness, by the Holy G ... 2Cor 6:6 4151
and the communion of the Holy G ... 2Cor 13:14 4151
also in power, and in the Holy G ... 1Th 1:5 4151
with joy of the Holy G ... 1Th 1:6 4151
the Holy G which dwelleth in us ... 2Ti 1:14 4151
and renewing of the Holy G ... Titus 3:5 4151
miracles, and gifts of the Holy G ... Heb 2:4 4151
Wherefore (as the Holy G saith ... Heb 3:7 4151
were made partakers of the Holy G ... Heb 6:4 4151
The Holy G this signifying, that ... Heb 9:8 4151
Whereof the Holy G also is a ... Heb 10:15 4151
the Holy G sent down from heaven ... 1Pet 1:12 4151
as they were moved by the Holy G ... 2Pet 1:21 4151
Father, the Word, and the Holy G ... 1Jn 5:7 4151
holy faith, praying in the Holy G ... Jude 20 4151

GIAH (ghi'-ah) {1} A place near the wilderness of Gibeon.
that lieth before G by the way of ... 2Sa 2:24 1520

GIANT {8}
which was of the sons of the g ... 2Sa 21:16 7497
which was of the sons of the g ... 2Sa 21:18 7497
and he also was born to the g ... 2Sa 21:20 7497
four were born to the g in Gath ... 2Sa 21:22 7497
that was of the children of the g ... 1Chr 20:4 7497
and he also was the son of the g ... 1Chr 20:6 7497
were born unto the g in Gath ... 1Chr 20:8 7497
he runneth upon me like a g ... Job 16:14 1368

GIANTS {13}
There were g in the earth in ... Gen 6:4 5303
And there we saw the g ... Num 13:33 5303
sons of Anak, which come of the g ... Num 13:33 1368
Which also were accounted g ... Deut 2:11 7497
also was accounted a land of g ... Deut 2:20 7497
g dwelt therein in old time ... Deut 2:20 7497
remained of the remnant of g ... Deut 3:11 7497
which was called the land of g ... Deut 3:13 7497
which was of the remnant of the g ... Josh 12:4 7497
remained of the remnant of the g ... Josh 13:12 7497
of the valley of the g northward ... Josh 15:8 7497
of the Perizzites and of the g ... Josh 17:15 7497
the valley of the g on the north ... Josh 18:16 7497

GIBALITES See GIBLITES.

GIBBAR (ghib'-bar) {1} See GIBEON. A family of exiles.
The children of G, ninety and five ... Ezr 2:20 1402

GIBBETHON (ghib'-be-thon) {6} A town in Dan.
And Eltekeh, and G, and Baalath, ... Josh 19:44 1405
her suburbs, G with her suburbs, ... Josh 21:23 1405
and Baasha smote him at G, which ... 1Kin 15:27 1405
and all Israel laid siege to G ... 1Kin 15:27 1405
people were encamped against G ... 1Kin 16:15 1405
And Omri went up from G, and all ... 1Kin 16:17 1405

GIBEA (ghib'-e-ah) {1} See GIBEAH. Son of Sheva.
of Machbenah, and the father of G ... 1Chr 2:49 1388

GIBEAH (ghib'-e-ah) {48} A city in Judah.
Cain, G, and Timnah ... Josh 15:57 1390
we will pass over to G ... Judg 19:12 1390
places to lodge all night, in G ... Judg 19:13 1390
upon them when they were by G ... Judg 19:14 1390
to go in and to lodge in G ... Judg 19:15 1390
and he sojourned in G ... Judg 19:16 1390
I came into G that belongeth to ... Judg 20:4 1390
the men of G rose against me, and ... Judg 20:5 1390
the thing which we will do to G ... Judg 20:9 1390
when they come to G of Benjamin ... Judg 20:10 1390
of Belial, which are in G ... Judg 20:13 1390
together out of the cities unto G ... Judg 20:14 1390
beside the inhabitants of G ... Judg 20:15 1390
morning, and encamped against G ... Judg 20:19 1390
array to fight against them at G ... Judg 20:20 1390
of Benjamin came forth out of G ... Judg 20:21 1390
them out of G the second day ... Judg 20:25 1390
set liers in wait round about G ... Judg 20:29 1390
put themselves in array against G ... Judg 20:30 1390
and the other to G in the field ... Judg 20:31 1390
even out of the meadows of G ... Judg 20:33 1390
there came against G ten thousand ... Judg 20:34 1390
wait which they had set beside G ... Judg 20:36 1390
in wait hasted, and rushed upon G ... Judg 20:37 1390
against G toward the sunrising ... Judg 20:43 1390
And Saul also went home to G ... 1Sa 10:26 1390
came the messengers to G of Saul ... 1Sa 11:4 1390
with Jonathan in G of Benjamin ... 1Sa 13:2 1390
up from Gilgal unto G of Benjamin ... 1Sa 13:15 1390
with them, abode in G of Benjamin ... 1Sa 13:16 1390
in the uttermost part of G under ... 1Sa 14:2 1390
other southward over against G ... 1Sa 14:5 1390
of Saul in G of Benjamin looked ... 1Sa 14:16 1390
went up to his house to G of Saul ... 1Sa 15:34 1390
(now Saul abode in G under a tree ... 1Sa 22:6 1390
came up the Ziphites to Saul to G ... 1Sa 23:19 1390
the Ziphites came unto Saul to G ... 1Sa 26:1 1390
house of Abinadab that was in G ... 2Sa 6:3 1390
house of Abinadab which was at G ... 2Sa 6:4 1390
up unto the LORD in G of Saul ... 2Sa 21:6 1390
of G of the children of Benjamin ... 2Sa 23:29 1390
Ithai the son of Ribai of G ... 1Chr 11:31 1390
the daughter of Uriel of G ... 2Chr 13:2 1390
G of Saul is fled ... Is 10:29 1390
Blow ye the cornet in G, and the ... Hos 5:8 1390
themselves, as in the days of G ... Hos 9:9 1390
hast sinned from the days of G ... Hos 10:9 1390
the battle in G against the ... Hos 10:9 1390

GIBEATH (ghib'-e-ath) {1} See GIBEAH, GIBEATHITE. Same as Gibeah.
and Jebusi, which is Jerusalem, G ... Josh 18:28 1394

GIBEATH-HAARALOTH See FORESKINS.

GIBEATHITE (ghib'-e-ath-ite) {1} An inhabitant of Gibeah.
Joash, the sons of Shemaah the G ... 1Chr 12:3 1395

GIBEON (ghib'-e-on) {35} See GEBA, GIBEAH, GIBEONITE.
1. A Hivite city.
when the inhabitants of G heard ... Josh 9:3 1391
Now their cities were G, and ... Josh 9:17 1391
how the inhabitants of G had made ... Josh 10:1 1391
because G was a great city, as ... Josh 10:2 1391
and help me, that we may smite G ... Josh 10:4 1391
their hosts, and encamped before G ... Josh 10:5 1391
the men of G sent unto Joshua to ... Josh 10:6 1391
them with a great slaughter at G ... Josh 10:10 1391
Sun, stand thou still upon G ... Josh 10:12 1391
country of Goshen, even unto G ... Josh 10:41 1391
the Hivites the inhabitants of G ... Josh 11:19 1391
2. A city in Benjamin.
G, and Ramah, and Beeroth, ... Josh 18:25 1391
G with her suburbs, Geba with her ... Josh 21:17 1391
Saul, went out from Mahanaim to G ... 2Sa 2:12 1391
and met together by the pool of G ... 2Sa 2:13 1391
Helkath-hazzurim, which is in G ... 2Sa 2:16 1391

by the way of the wilderness of G 2Sa 2:24 1391
brother Asahel at G in the battle 2Sa 3:30 1391
at the great stone which is in G 2Sa 20:8 1391
the king went to G to sacrifice 1Kin 3:4 1391
In G the LORD appeared to Solomon 1Kin 3:5 1391
as he had appeared unto him at G 1Kin 9:2 1391
at G dwelt the father of Gibeon 1Chr 8:29 1391
in G dwelt the father of Gibeon, 1Chr 9:35 1391
Philistines from G even to Gazer 1Chr 14:16 1391
in the high place that was at G 1Chr 16:39 1391
season in the high place at G 1Chr 21:29 1391
to the high place that was at G 2Chr 1:3 1391
place that was at G to Jerusalem 2Chr 1:13 1391
the Meronothite, the men of G Neh 3:7 1391
The children of G, ninety and five Neh 7:25 1391
be wroth as in the valley of G Is 28:21 1391
Azur the prophet, which was of G Jer 28:1 1391
by the great waters that are in G Jer 41:12 1391
whom he had brought again from G Jer 41:16 1391

GIBEONITE *(ghib'-e-on-ite)* {2} See GIBEONITES. *An inhabitant of Gibeon.*
And Ismaiah the G, a mighty man 1Chr 12:4 1393
unto them repaired Melatiah the G Neh 3:7 1393

GIBEONITES *(ghib'-e-on-ites)* {6}
house, because he slew the G 2Sa 21:1 1393
And the king called the G, and said 2Sa 21:2 1393
(now the G were not of the 2Sa 21:2 1393
Wherefore David said unto the G 2Sa 21:3 1393
the G said unto him, We will have 2Sa 21:4 1393
them into the hands of the G 2Sa 21:9 1393

GIBLITES *(ghib'-lites)* {1} *Inhabitants of Gebal.*
And the land of the G, and all Josh 13:5 1382

GIDDALTI *(ghid-dal'-ti)* {2} *A son of Heman.*
Hananiah, Hanani, Eliathah, G 1Chr 25:4 1437
The two and twentieth to G 1Chr 25:29 1437

GIDDEL *(ghid'-del)* {4}
1. A family of exiles.
The children of G, the children Ezr 2:47 1435
of Hanan, the children of G Neh 7:49 1435
2. Servants of Solomon.
of Darkon, the children of G Ezr 2:56 1435
of Darkon, the children of G Neh 7:58 1435

GIDEON *(ghid'-e-on)* {39} See GEDEON, JERUBBAAL. *A judge of Israel.*
his son G threshed wheat by the Judg 6:11 1439
G said unto him, Oh my Lord, if Judg 6:13 1439
G went in, and made ready a kid, Judg 6:19 1439
when G perceived that he was an Judg 6:22 1439
LORD, G said, Alas, O Lord GOD Judg 6:22 1439
Then G built an altar there unto Judg 6:24 1439
Then G took ten men of his Judg 6:27 1439
G the son of Joash hath done this Judg 6:29 1439
Spirit of the LORD came upon G Judg 6:34 1439
G said unto God, If thou wilt Judg 6:36 1439
G said unto God, Let not thine Judg 6:39 1439
Then Jerubbaal, who is G, and all Judg 7:1 1439
And the LORD said unto G, The Judg 7:2 1439
And the LORD said unto G, The Judg 7:4 1439
and the LORD said unto G, Every Judg 7:5 1439
And the LORD said unto G, By the Judg 7:7 1439
when G was come, behold, there Judg 7:13 1439
the sword of G the son of Joash Judg 7:14 1439
when G heard the telling of the Judg 7:15 1439
The sword of the LORD, and of G Judg 7:18 1439
So G, and the hundred men that Judg 7:19 1439
The sword of the LORD, and of G Judg 7:20 1439
G sent messengers throughout all Judg 7:24 1439
Zeeb to G on the other side Judg 7:25 1439
G came to Jordan, and passed over, Judg 8:4 1439
G said, Therefore when the LORD Judg 8:7 1439
G went up by the way of them that Judg 8:11 1439
G the son of Joash returned from Judg 8:13 1439
G arose, and slew Zebah and Judg 8:21 1439
the men of Israel said unto G Judg 8:22 1439
G said unto them, I will not rule Judg 8:23 1439
G said unto them, I would desire Judg 8:24 1439
G made an ephod thereof, and put Judg 8:27 1439
which thing became a snare unto G Judg 8:27 1439
forty years in the days of G Judg 8:28 1439
G had threescore and ten sons of Judg 8:30 1439
G the son of Joash died in a good Judg 8:32 1439
to pass, as soon as G was dead Judg 8:33 1439
the house of Jerubbaal, namely, G Judg 8:35 1439

GIDEONI *(ghid-e-o'-ni)* {5} *A Benjamite who counted the people.*
Abidan the son of G Num 1:11 1441
shall be Abidan the son of G Num 2:22 1441
the ninth day Abidan the son of G Num 7:60 1441
offering of Abidan the son of G Num 7:65 1441
Benjamin was Abidan the son of G Num 10:24 1441

GIDOM *(ghi'-dom)* {1} *A place near Bethel.*
and pursued hard after them unto G Judg 20:45 1440

GIER {2}
and the pelican, and the g eagle, Lev 11:18 7360
the g eagle, and the cormorant, Deut 14:17 7360

GIFT {59}
Ask me never so much dowry and g Gen 34:12 4976
And thou shalt take no g Ex 23:8 7810
for the g blindeth the wise, and Ex 23:8 7810
given the Levites as a g to Aaron Num 8:19
are given as a g for the LORD Num 18:6 4979
office unto you as a service of g Num 18:7 4979
the heave offering of their g Num 18:11 4976
respect persons, neither take a g Deut 16:19 7810
for a g doth blind the eyes of Deut 16:19 7810
or hath he given us any g 2Sa 19:42 5379
of Tyre shall be there with a g Ps 45:12 4503
A g is as a precious stone in the Prov 17:8 7810
A wicked man taketh a g out of Prov 17:23 7810
A man's g maketh room for him, and Prov 18:16 4976
A g in secret pacifieth anger Prov 21:14 4976
of a false g is like clouds Prov 25:14 4991
his labour, it is the g of God Eccl 3:13 4991
this is the g of God Eccl 5:19 4991
and a g destroyeth the heart Eccl 7:7 4979
give a g unto any of his sons Eze 46:16 4979
But if he give a g of his Eze 46:17 4979
if thou bring thy g to the altar Mt 5:23 1435
Leave there thy g before the Mt 5:24 1435
and then come and offer thy g Mt 5:24 1435
offer the g that Moses commanded, Mt 8:4 1435
father or his mother, It is a g Mt 15:5 1435
sweareth by the g that is upon it Mt 23:18 1435
for whether is greater, the g Mt 23:19 1435
the altar that sanctifieth the g Mt 23:19 1435
It is Corban, that is to say, a g Mk 7:11 1435
her, If thou knewest the g of God Jn 4:10 1431
receive the g of the Holy Ghost Acts 2:38 1431
thou hast thought that the g of Acts 8:20 1431
out the g of the Holy Ghost Acts 10:45 1431
them the like g as he did unto us Acts 11:17 1431
impart unto you some spiritual g Rom 1:11 5486
offence, so also is the free g Rom 5:15 5486
the g by grace, which is by one Rom 5:15 1431
by one that sinned, so is the g Rom 5:16 1434
but the free g is of many Rom 5:16 5486
of the g of righteousness shall Rom 5:17 1431
the free g came upon all men unto Rom 5:18
but the g of God is eternal life Rom 6:23 5486
So that ye come behind in no g 1Cor 1:7 5486
man hath his proper g of God 1Cor 7:7 5486
though I have the g of prophecy 1Cor 13:2
that for the g bestowed upon us 2Cor 1:11 5486
that we would receive the g 2Cor 8:4 5485
be unto God for his unspeakable g 2Cor 9:15 1431
it is the g of God Eph 2:8 1435
according to the g of the grace Eph 3:7 1431
to the measure of the g of Christ Eph 4:7 1431
Not because I desire a g Phil 4:17 1390
Neglect not the g that is in thee 1Ti 4:14 5486
that thou stir up the g of God 2Ti 1:6 5486
and have tasted of the heavenly g Heb 6:4 1431
good g and every perfect g Jas 1:17 1394
As every man hath received the g 1Pet 4:10 5486

GIFTS {53}
which Abraham had, Abraham gave g Gen 25:6 4979
shall hallow in all their holy g Ex 28:38 4979
of the LORD, and beside your g Lev 23:38 4979
Out of all your g ye shall offer Num 18:29 4979
David's servants, and brought g 2Sa 8:2 4503
servants to David, and brought g 2Sa 8:6 4503
David's servants, and brought g 1Chr 18:2 4503
David's servants, and brought g 1Chr 18:6 4503
of persons, nor taking of g 2Chr 19:7 7810
gave them great g of silver 2Chr 21:3 4979
And the Ammonites gave g to Uzziah 2Chr 26:8 4503
many brought g unto the LORD to 2Chr 32:23 4503
to the provinces, and gave g Est 2:18 4864
one to another, and g to the poor Est 9:22 4979
thou hast received g for men Ps 68:18 4979
of Sheba and Seba shall offer g Ps 72:10 814
though thou givest many g Prov 6:35 7810
but he that hateth g shall live Prov 15:27 4979
is a friend to him that giveth g Prov 19:6 4976
that receiveth g overthroweth it Prov 29:4 8641
every one loveth g, and followeth Is 1:23 7810
They give g to all whores Eze 16:33 5078
givest thy g to all thy lovers Eze 16:33 5083
And I polluted them in their own g Eze 20:26 4979
For when ye offer your g, when ye Eze 20:31 4979
my holy name no more with your g Eze 20:39 4979
have they taken g to shed blood Eze 22:12 7810
thereof, ye shall receive of me g Dan 2:6 4978
man, and gave him many great g Dan 2:48 4978
Let thy g be to thyself, and give Dan 5:17 4978
they presented unto him g Mt 2:11 1435
to give good g unto your children Mt 7:11 1435
to give good g unto your children Lk 11:13 1390
casting their g into the treasury Lk 21:1 1435
adorned with goodly stones and g Lk 21:5 334
For the g and calling of God are Rom 11:29 5486
Having then g differing according Rom 12:6 5486
Now concerning spiritual g 1Cor 12:1
Now there are diversities of g 1Cor 12:4 5486
to another the g of healing by 1Cor 12:9 5486
then g of healings, helps, 1Cor 12:28 5486
Have all the g of healing 1Cor 12:30 5486
But covet earnestly the best g 1Cor 12:31 5486
charity, and desire spiritual g 1Cor 14:1
as ye are zealous of spiritual g 1Cor 14:12
captive, and gave g unto men Eph 4:8 1390
g of the Holy Ghost, according to Heb 2:4 3311
to God, that he may offer both g Heb 5:1 1435
priest is ordained to offer g Heb 8:3 1435
that offer g according to the law Heb 8:4 1435
in which were offered both g Heb 9:9 1435
God testifying of his g Heb 11:4 1435
shall send g one to another Rev 11:10 1435

GIHON *(ghi'-hon)* {6}
1. A river in the Garden of Eden.
the name of the second river is G Gen 2:13 1521
2. A place near Jerusalem.
own mule, and bring him down to G 1Kin 1:33 1521
David's mule, and brought him to G 1Kin 1:38 1521
have anointed him king in G 1Kin 1:45 1521
the upper watercourse of G 2Chr 32:30 1521
of David, on the west side of G 2Chr 33:14 1521

GILALAI *(ghil'-a-lahee)* {1} *A priest who dedicated the wall.*
Shemaiah, and Azarael, Milalai, G Neh 12:36 1562

GILBOA *(ghil-bo'-ah)* {8}
1. A district in Manasseh.
together, and they pitched in G 1Sa 28:4 1533
Philistines had slain Saul in G 2Sa 21:12 1533
2. A mountain near the valley Jezreel.
and fell down slain in mount G 1Sa 31:1 1533
his three sons fallen in mount G 1Sa 31:8 1533
I happened by chance upon mount G 2Sa 1:6 1533
Ye mountains of G, let there be 2Sa 1:21 1533
and fell down slain in mount G 1Chr 10:1 1533
and his sons fallen in mount G 1Chr 10:8 1533

GILEAD *(ghil'-e-ad)* {100} See GILEADITE, GILEAD'S, JABESH-GILEAD, RAMOTH-GILEAD.
1. District east of the Jordan River.
of Ishmeelites came from G with Gen 37:25 1568
land of Jazer, and the land of G Num 32:1 1568
shall be there in the cities of G Num 32:26 1568
the land of G for a possession Num 32:29 1568
the son of Manasseh went to G Num 32:39 1568
Moses gave G unto Machir the son Num 32:40 1568
that is by the river, even unto G Deut 2:36 1568
the cities of the plain, and all G Deut 3:10 1568
And the rest of G, and all Bashan, Deut 3:13 1568
And I gave G unto Machir Deut 3:15 1568
unto the Gadites I gave from G Deut 3:16 1568
and Ramoth in G, of the Gadites Deut 4:43 1568
LORD shewed him all the land of G Deut 34:1 1568
of the river, and from half G Josh 12:2 1568
and the Maachathites, and half G Josh 12:5 1568
And G, and the border of the Josh 13:11 1568
was Jazer, and all the cities of G Josh 13:25 1568
And half G, and Ashtaroth, and Edrei Josh 13:31 1568
a man of war, therefore he had G Josh 17:1 1568
to Manasseh, beside the land of G Josh 17:5 1568
Manasseh's sons had the land of G Josh 17:6 1568
Ramoth in G out of the tribe of Josh 20:8 1568
Ramoth in G with her suburbs, to Josh 21:38 1568
to go unto the country of G Josh 22:9 1568
of Manasseh, into the land of G Josh 22:13 1568
of Manasseh, unto the land of G Josh 22:15 1568
of Gad, out of the land of G Josh 22:32 1568
G abode beyond Jordan Judg 5:17 1568
day, which are in the land of G Judg 10:4 1568
of the Amorites, which is in G Judg 10:8 1568
together, and encamped in G Judg 10:17 1568
princes of G said one to another, Judg 10:18 1568
over all the inhabitants of G Judg 10:18 1568
the elders of G went to fetch Judg 11:5 1568
said unto the elders of G Judg 11:7 1568
the elders of G said unto Judg 11:8 1568
over all the inhabitants of G Judg 11:8 1568
said unto the elders of G Judg 11:9 1568
the elders of G said unto Judg 11:10 1568
went with the elders of G Judg 11:11 1568
Jephthah, and he passed over G Judg 11:29 1568
and passed over Mizpeh of G Judg 11:29 1568
from Mizpeh of G he passed over Judg 11:29 1568
together all the men of G Judg 12:4 1568
the men of G smote Ephraim, Judg 12:4 1568
that the men of G said unto him Judg 12:5 1568
buried in one of the cities of G Judg 12:7 1568
to Beer-sheba, with the land of G Judg 20:1 1568
Jordan to the land of Gad and G 1Sa 13:7 1568
And made him king over G, and over 2Sa 2:9 1568
Absalom pitched in the land of G 2Sa 17:26 1568
Then they came to G, and to the 2Sa 24:6 1568
son of Manasseh, which are in G 1Kin 4:13 1568
of Uri was in the country of G 1Kin 4:19 1568
who was of the inhabitants of G 1Kin 17:1 1568
Know ye that Ramoth in G is ours 1Kin 22:3 1568
eastward, all the land of G 2Kin 10:33 1568
is by the river Arnon, even G 2Kin 10:33 1568
and Kedesh, and Hazor, and G 2Kin 15:29 1568
and twenty cities in the land of G 1Chr 2:22 1568
were multiplied in the land of G 1Chr 5:9 1568
throughout all the east land of G 1Chr 5:10 1568
And they dwelt in G in Bashan 1Chr 5:16 1568
Ramoth in G with her suburbs, and 1Chr 6:80 1568
men of valour at Jazer of G 1Chr 26:31 1568
the half tribe of Manasseh in G 1Chr 27:21 1568
G is mine, and Manasseh is mine Ps 60:7 1568
G is mine Ps 108:8 1568
flock of goats that appear from G Song 6:5 1568
Is there no balm in G Jer 8:22 1568
Thou art G unto me, and the head Jer 22:6 1568
Go up into G, and take balm, O Jer 46:11 1568
satisfied upon mount Ephraim and G Jer 50:19 1568
and from Damascus, and from G Eze 47:18 1568
G is a city of them that work Hos 6:8 1568
Is there iniquity in G Hos 12:11 1568
because they have threshed G with Amos 1:3 1568
the women with child of G Amos 1:13 1568
and Benjamin shall possess G Obad 19 1568
let them feed in Bashan and G Mic 7:14 1568
bring them into the land of G Zec 10:10 1568
2. A mountain range in Gilead 1.
set his face toward the mount G Gen 31:21 1568
they overtook him in the mount G Gen 31:23 1568

pitched in the mount of G ......Gen 31:25 1568
the river Arnon, and half mount G ......Deut 3:12 1568
and depart early from mount G ......Judg 7:3 1568
goats, that appear from mount G......Song 4:1 1568
3. Son of Machir.
and Machir begat G......Num 26:29 1568
of G come the family of the......Num 26:29 1568
These are the sons of G ......Num 26:30 1568
the son of Hepher, the son of G......Num 27:1 1568
the families of the children of G ......Num 36:1 1568
of Manasseh, the father of G......Josh 17:1 1568
the son of Hepher, the son of G......Josh 17:3 1568
of Machir the father of G 1Chr 2:21 1568
sons of Machir the father of G 1Chr 2:23 1568
bare Machir the father of G 1Chr 7:14 1568
These were the sons of G, the son 1Chr 7:17 1568
4. Father of Jephthah.
and G begat Jephthah ......Judg 11:1 1568
5. A chief of Gad.
the son of Jaroah, the son of G 1Chr 5:14 1568

GILEADITE *(ghil'-e-ad-ite)* {9} See GILEADITES. *A descendant of Gilead.*
And after him arose Jair, a G......Judg 10:3 1569
Now Jephthah the G was a mighty ......Judg 11:1 1569
the G four days in a year......Judg 11:40 1569
Then died Jephthah the G, and was......Judg 12:7 1569
and Barzillai the G of Rogelim 2Sa 17:27 1569
Barzillai the G came down from......2Sa 19:31 1569
unto the sons of Barzillai the G 1Kin 2:7 1569
the daughters of Barzillai the G ......Ezr 2:61 1569
of Barzillai the G to wife ......Neh 7:63 1569

GILEADITES *(ghil'-e-ad-ites)* {4}
Gilead come the family of the G ......Num 26:29 1569
Ye G are fugitives of Ephraim......Judg 12:4 1569
the G took the passages of Jordan ......Judg 12:5 1569
and with him fifty men of the G 2Kin 15:25 1569

GILEAD'S *(ghil'-e-ads)* {1} *Refers to Gilead 4.*
And G wife bare him sons......Judg 11:2 1568

GILGAL *(ghil'-gal)* {41}
1. A place near Jericho.
in the champaign over against G ......Deut 11:30 1537
the first month, and encamped in G ......Josh 4:19 1537
of Jordan, did Joshua pitch in G......Josh 4:20 1537
place is called G unto this day......Josh 5:9 1537
children of Israel encamped in G......Josh 5:10 1537
sent unto Joshua to the camp to G......Josh 10:6 1537
So Joshua ascended from G ......Josh 10:7 1537
and went up from G all night ......Josh 10:9 1537
with him, unto the camp to G......Josh 10:15 1537
with him, unto the camp to G......Josh 10:43 1537
of Judah came unto Joshua in G......Josh 14:6 1537
and so northward, looking toward G ......Josh 15:7 1537
the LORD came up from G to Bochim ......Judg 2:1 1537
from the quarries that were by G......Judg 3:19 1537
year in circuit to Beth-el, and G 1Sa 7:16
thou shalt go down before me to G......1Sa 10:8
people, Come, and let us go to G 1Sa 11:14 1537
And all the people went to G 1Sa 11:15 1537
Saul king before the LORD in G......1Sa 11:15 1537
called together after Saul to G......1Sa 13:4 1537
As for Saul, he was yet in G......1Sa 13:7 1537
but Samuel came not to G 1Sa 13:8 1537
will come down now upon me to G......1Sa 13:12 1537
gat him up from G unto Gibeah of 1Sa 13:15 1537
and passed on, and gone down to G 1Sa 15:12 1537
unto the LORD thy God in G 1Sa 15:21 1537
in pieces before the LORD in G......1Sa 15:33 1537
And Judah came to G, to go to meet......2Sa 19:15 1537
Then the king went on to G 2Sa 19:40 1537
Also from the house of G, and out ......Neh 12:29 1537
and come not ye unto G, neither go ......Hos 4:15 1537
All their wickedness is in G ......Hos 9:15 1537
they sacrifice bullocks in G......Hos 12:11 1537
at G multiply transgression......Amos 4:4 1537
not Beth-el, nor enter into G......Amos 5:5 1537
for G shall surely go into......Amos 5:5 1537
answered him from Shittim unto G ......Mic 6:5 1537
2. A city between Dor and Tirsa.
the king of the nations of G ......Josh 12:23 1537
3. A city north of Joppa.
went to Joshua unto the camp at G ......Josh 9:6 1537
4. A place south of Ebal and Gerizim.
Elijah went with Elisha from G......2Kin 2:1 1537
And Elisha came again to G 2Kin 4:38 1537

GILO See GILOH.

GILOH *(ghi'-loh)* {2} See GILONITE. *A town in Judah.*
And Goshen, and Holon, and G ......Josh 15:51 1542
from his city, even from G......2Sa 15:12 1542

GILONITE *(ghi'-lo-nite)* {2} *An inhabitant of Giloh.*
Absalom sent for Ahithophel the G 2Sa 15:12 1526
Eliam the son of Ahithophel the G 2Sa 23:34 1526

GIMZO *(ghim'-zo)* {1} *A city in Judah.*
G also and the villages thereof......2Chr 28:18 1579

GIN {3}
The g shall take him by the heel, ...Job 18:9 6341
the houses of Israel, for a g......Is 8:14 6341
the earth, where no g is for him......Amos 3:5 4170

GINATH *(ghi'-nath)* {2} *Father of Tibni.*
followed Tibni the son of G......1Kin 16:21 1527
that followed Tibni the son of G......1Kin 16:22 1527

GINNETHO *(ghin'-ne-tho)* {1} See GINNETHON. *A priest who renewed the covenant.*
Iddo, G, Abijah,......Neh 12:4 1599

GINNETHOI See GINNETHO.

GINNETHON *(ghin'-ne-thon)* {2} See GINNETHO. *Same as Ginnetho.*
Daniel, G, Baruch,......Neh 10:6 1599
of G, Meshullam ......Neh 12:16 1599

GINS {2}
they have set g for me ......Ps 140:5 4170
the g of the workers of iniquity ......Ps 141:9 4170

GIRD {27}
g him with the curious girdle of......Ex 29:5 640
thou shalt g them with girdles, ...Ex 29:9 2296
he did g it under his raiment ......Judg 3:16 2296
G ye on every man his sword 1Sa 25:13 2296
g you with sackcloth, and mourn......2Sa 3:31 2296
G up thy loins, and take my staff......2Kin 4:29 2296
G up thy loins, and take this box......2Kin 9:1 2296
G up now thy loins like a man ......Job 38:3 247
G up thy loins now like a man ......Job 40:7 247
G thy sword upon thy thigh, O......Ps 45:3 2296
g yourselves, and ye shall be ......Is 8:9 247
g yourselves, and ye shall be ......Is 8:9 247
shall g themselves with sackcloth ......Is 15:3 2296
g sackcloth upon your loins ......Is 32:11 2290
Thou therefore g up thy loins......Jer 1:17 2296
For this g you with sackcloth, ...Jer 4:8 2296
g thee with sackcloth, and wallow......Jer 6:26 2296
of Rabbah, g you with sackcloth ......Jer 49:3 2296
They shall also g themselves with......Eze 7:18 2296
g them with sackcloth, and they ......Eze 27:31 2296
they shall not g themselves with ......Eze 44:18 2296
G yourselves, and lament, ye......Joel 1:13 2296
unto you, that he shall g himself......Lk 12:37 *4024*
g thyself, and serve me, till I......Lk 17:8 *4024*
hands, and another shall g thee ......Jn 21:18 *2224*
G thyself, and bind on thy sandals ......Acts 12:8 *2224*
Wherefore g up the loins of your......1Pet 1:13 *328*

GIRDED {33}
with your loins g, your shoes on ......Ex 12:11 2296
g him with the girdle, and clothed......Lev 8:7 2296
he g him with the curious girdle ......Lev 8:7 2296
g them with girdles, and put......Lev 8:13 2296
shall be g with a linen girdle,......Lev 16:4 2296
when ye had g on every man his ......Deut 1:41 2296
that stumbled are g with strength 1Sa 2:4 247
a child, g with a linen ephod......1Sa 2:18 2296
David g his sword upon his armour 1Sa 17:39 2296
they g on every man his sword......1Sa 25:13 2296
David also g on his sword 1Sa 25:13 2296
David was g with a linen ephod......2Sa 6:14 2296
that he had put on was g unto him 2Sa 20:8 2296
he being g with a new sword,......2Sa 21:16 2296
For thou hast g me with strength......2Sa 22:40 247
he g up his loins, and ran before......1Kin 18:46 8151
So they g sackcloth on their......1Kin 20:32 2296
one had his sword g by his side......Neh 4:18 631
For thou hast g me with strength......Ps 18:39 247
sackcloth, and g me with gladness......Ps 30:11 247
being g with power......Ps 65:6 247
wherewith he hath g himself......Ps 93:1 247
wherewith he is g continually......Ps 109:19 2296
I g thee, though thou hast not......Is 45:5 247
they have g themselves with......Lam 2:10 2296
I g thee about with fine linen,......Eze 16:10 2280
G with girdles upon their loins, ...Eze 23:15 2289
whose loins were g with fine gold......Dan 10:5 2296
Lament like a virgin g with......Joel 1:8 2296
Let your loins be g about ......Lk 12:35 *4024*
and took a towel, and g himself ......Jn 13:4 *1241*
with the towel wherewith he was g......Jn 13:5 *1241*
breasts g with golden girdles ......Rev 15:6 *4024*

GIRDEDST {1}
thou g thyself, and walkedst ......Jn 21:18 *2224*

GIRDETH {4}
Let not him that g on his harness 1Kin 20:11 2296
g their loins with a girdle......Job 12:18 631
It is God that g me with strength......Ps 18:32 247
She g her loins with strength, and ......Prov 31:17 2296

GIRDING {2}
of a stomacher a g of sackcloth......Is 3:24 4228
baldness, and to g with sackcloth ......Is 22:12 2296

GIRDLE {38}
a broidered coat, a mitre, and a g ......Ex 28:4 73
the curious g of the ephod, which ......Ex 28:8 2805
above the curious g of the ephod ......Ex 28:27 2805
above the curious g of the ephod ......Ex 28:28 2805
shalt make the g of needlework ......Ex 28:39 73
with the curious g of the ephod ......Ex 29:5 2805
the curious g of his ephod, that ......Ex 39:5 2805
above the curious g of the ephod ......Ex 39:20 2805
above the curious g of the ephod ......Ex 39:21 2805
a g of fine twined linen, and blue ......Ex 39:29 73
coat, and girded him with the g......Lev 8:7 73
with the curious g of the ephod ......Lev 8:7 2805
and shall be girded with a linen g ......Lev 16:4 73
sword, and to his bow, and to his g......1Sa 18:4 2290
ten shekels of silver, and a g 2Sa 18:11 2290
upon it a g with a sword fastened......2Sa 20:8 2290
his g that was about his loins......1Kin 2:5 2290
girt with a g of leather about......2Kin 1:8 232
and girdeth their loins with a g ......Job 12:18 232
for a g wherewith he is girded ......Ps 109:19 4206
and instead of a g a rent ......Is 3:24 2290
neither shall the g of their......Is 5:27 232
shall be the g of his loins ......Is 11:5 232
faithfulness the g of his reins......Is 11:5 232
and strengthen him with thy g......Is 22:21 73
unto me, Go and get thee a linen g......Jer 13:1 232
So I got a g according to the......Jer 13:2 232
Take the g that thou hast got,......Jer 13:4 232
take the g from thence, which I ......Jer 13:6 232
took the g from the place where I......Jer 13:7 232
behold, the g was marred, it was ......Jer 13:7 232
them, shall even be as this g ......Jer 13:10 232
For as the g cleaveth to the ......Jer 13:11 232
a leathern g about his loins......Mt 3:4 *2223*
with a g of a skin about his......Mk 1:6 *2223*
come unto us, he took Paul's g......Acts 21:11 *2223*
bind the man that owneth this g......Acts 21:11 *2223*
about the paps with a golden g......Rev 1:13 *2223*

GIRDLES {6}
and thou shalt make for them g......Ex 28:40 73
And thou shalt gird them with g......Ex 29:9 73
upon them, and girded them with g......Lev 8:13 73
delivereth g unto the merchant ......Prov 31:24 2289
Girded with g upon their loins,......Eze 23:15 232
breasts girded with golden g ......Rev 15:6 *2223*

GIRGASHITE *(ghur'-gash-ite)* {1} See GIRGASHITES, GIRGASITE. *A Canaanite tribe.*
also, and the Amorite, and the G......1Chr 1:14 1622

GIRGASHITES *(ghur'-gash-ites)* {5}
and the Canaanites, and the G......Gen 15:21 1622
thee, the Hittites, and the G......Deut 7:1 1622
and the Perizzites, and the G ......Josh 3:10 1622
and the Hittites, and the G ......Josh 24:11 1622
and the Jebusites, and the G ......Neh 9:8 1622

GIRGASITE *(ghur'-ga-site)* {1} See GIRGASHITE. *Same as Girgashite.*
and the Amorite, and the G ......Gen 10:16 1622

GIRL {1}
sold a g for wine, that they ......Joel 3:3 3207

GIRLS {1}
g playing in the streets thereof......Zec 8:5 3207

GIRT {4}
g with a girdle of leather about 2Kin 1:8 247
he g his fisher's coat unto him, ...Jn 21:7 *1241*
your loins g about with truth......Eph 6:14 *4024*
g about the paps with a golden......Rev 1:13 *4024*

GIRZITES See GEZRITES.

GISHPA See GISPA.

GISPA *(ghis'-pah)* {1} *An overseer of the Nethinim.*
G were over the Nethinims......Neh 11:21 1658

GISPHA See GISPA.

GITTAH-HEPHER *(ghit'-tah-he'-fer)* {1} See GATH-HEPHER. *A town in Zebulun.*
passeth on along on the east to G ......Josh 19:13 1662

GITTAIM *(ghit-ta'-im)* {2}
1. A city of refuge.
And the Beerothites fled to G 2Sa 4:3 1664
2. A Benjamite city.
Hazor, Ramah, G,......Neh 11:33 1664

GITTITE *(ghit'-tite)* {8} See GITTITES, GITTITH. *An inhabitant of Gath.*
into the house of Obed-edom the G......2Sa 6:10 1663
of Obed-edom the G three months......2Sa 6:11 1663
Then said the king to Ittai the G 2Sa 15:19 1663
Ittai the G passed over, and all 2Sa 15:22 1663
under the hand of Ittai the G......2Sa 18:2 1663
slew the brother of Goliath the G......2Sa 21:19 1663
into the house of Obed-edom the G 1Chr 13:13 1663
the brother of Goliath the G 1Chr 20:5 1663

GITTITES {2}
the Eshkalonites, the G, and the......Josh 13:3 1663
all the Pelethites, and all the G......2Sa 15:18 1663

GITTITH *(ghit'-tith)* {3} *A musical instrument.*
To the chief Musician upon G ......Ps 8:t 1665
To the chief Musician upon G ......Ps 81:t 1665
To the chief Musician upon G ......Ps 84:t 1665

GIVE {882}
heaven to g light upon the earth......Gen 1:15
heaven to g light upon the earth......Gen 1:17
Unto thy seed will I g this land......Gen 12:7 5414
thou seest, to thee will I g it......Gen 13:15 5414
for I will g it unto thee......Gen 13:17 5414
G me the persons, and take the......Gen 14:21 5414
Lord GOD, what wilt thou g me......Gen 15:2 5414
to g thee this land to inherit it......Gen 15:7 5414
I will g unto thee, and to thy......Gen 17:8 5414
her, and g thee a son also of her......Gen 17:16 5414
g me a possession of a ......Gen 23:4 5414
That he may g me the cave of......Gen 23:9 5414
g it me for a possession of a......Gen 23:9 5414
the field g I thee, and the cave......Gen 23:11 5414
cave that is therein, I g it thee ......Gen 23:11 5414
the sons of my people g I it thee ......Gen 23:11 5414
saying, But if thou wilt g it......Gen 23:13
I will g thee money for the field......Gen 23:13 5414
Unto thy seed will I g this land......Gen 24:7 5414
I will g thy camels drink also......Gen 24:14
if they g not thee one, thou ......Gen 24:41 5414
G me, I pray thee, a little water......Gen 24:43
I will g thy camels drink also......Gen 24:46
I will g all these countries, and......Gen 26:3 5414
will g unto thy seed all these......Gen 26:4 5414
Therefore God g thee of the dew......Gen 27:28 5414
g thee the blessing of Abraham,......Gen 28:4 5414
thou liest, to thee will I g it......Gen 28:13 5414
will g me bread to eat, and ......Gen 28:20 5414
of all that thou shalt g me I ......Gen 28:22 5414

will surely *g* the tenth unto thee ... Gen 28:22
It is better that I *g* her to thee ... Gen 29:19 5414
I should *g* her to another man ... Gen 29:19 5414
G me my wife, for my days are ... Gen 29:21 3051
to *g* the younger before the ... Gen 29:26 5414
we will *g* thee this also for the ... Gen 29:27 5414
G me children, or else I die ... Gen 30:1 3051
G me, I pray thee, of thy son's ... Gen 30:14 5414
G me my wives and my children, for ... Gen 30:26 5414
me thy wages, and I will *g* it ... Gen 30:28 5414
And he said, What shall I *g* thee ... Gen 30:31 5414
Thou shalt not *g* me any thing ... Gen 30:31 5414
I pray you *g* her him to wife ... Gen 34:8 5414
g your daughters unto us, and take ... Gen 34:9 5414
ye shall say unto me I will *g* ... Gen 34:11 5414
I will *g* according as ye shall ... Gen 34:12 5414
but *g* me the damsel to wife ... Gen 34:12 5414
to *g* our sister to one that is ... Gen 34:14 5414
Then will we *g* our daughters unto ... Gen 34:16 5414
let us *g* them our daughters ... Gen 34:21 5414
and Isaac, to thee I will *g* it ... Gen 35:12 5414
seed after thee will I *g* the land ... Gen 35:12 5414
he should *g* seed to his brother ... Gen 38:9 5414
And she said, What wilt thou *g* me ... Gen 38:16 5414
Wilt thou *g* me a pledge, till ... Gen 38:17 5414
said, What pledge shall I *g* thee ... Gen 38:18 5414
God shall *g* Pharaoh an answer of ... Gen 41:16
to *g* them provision for the way ... Gen 42:25 5414
to *g* his ass provender in the inn ... Gen 42:27 5414
God Almighty *g* you mercy before ... Gen 43:14 5414
I will *g* you the good of the land ... Gen 45:18 5414
unto Joseph, and said, *G* us bread ... Gen 47:15 3051
And Joseph said, *G* your cattle ... Gen 47:16 3051
I will *g* you for your cattle, if ... Gen 47:16 5414
g us seed, that we may live, and ... Gen 47:19 5414
that ye shall *g* the fifth part ... Gen 47:24 5414
will *g* this land to thy seed ... Gen 48:4 5414
me, and I will *g* thee thy wages ... Ex 2:9 5414
I will *g* this people favour in ... Ex 3:21 5414
Ye shall no more *g* the people ... Ex 5:7 5414
Pharaoh, I will not *g* you straw ... Ex 5:10 5414
to *g* them the land of Canaan, the ... Ex 6:4 5414
I did swear to *g* it to Abraham ... Ex 6:8 5414
I will *g* it you for an heritage ... Ex 6:8 5414
Thou must *g* us also sacrifices and ... Ex 10:25 5414
land which the LORD will *g* you ... Ex 12:25 5414
sware unto thy fathers to *g* thee ... Ex 13:5 5414
thy fathers, and shall *g* it thee, ... Ex 13:11 5414
a pillar of fire, to *g* them light ... Ex 13:21
wilt *g* ear to his commandments, ... Ex 15:26
when the LORD shall *g* you in the ... Ex 16:8 5414
G us water that we may drink ... Ex 17:2 5414
I will *g* thee counsel, and God ... Ex 18:19
then thou shalt *g* life for life ... Ex 21:23 5414
then he shall *g* for the ransom of ... Ex 21:30 5414
he shall *g* unto their master ... Ex 21:32 5414
g money unto the owner of them ... Ex 21:34 7725
utterly refuse to *g* her unto him ... Ex 22:17 5414
of thy sons shalt thou *g* unto me ... Ex 22:29 5414
the eighth day thou shalt *g* it me ... Ex 22:30 5414
I will *g* thee tables of stone, and ... Ex 24:12 5414
testimony which I shall *g* thee ... Ex 25:16 5414
the testimony that I shall *g* thee ... Ex 25:21 5414
of all things which I will *g* thee ... Ex 25:22
that they may *g* light over ... Ex 25:37
then shall they *g* every man a ... Ex 30:12 5414
This they shall *g*, every one that ... Ex 30:13 5414
shall *g* an offering unto the LORD ... Ex 30:14 5414
The rich shall not *g* more ... Ex 30:15
the poor shall not *g* less than ... Ex 30:15
when they *g* an offering unto the ... Ex 30:15 5414
spoken of will I *g* unto your seed ... Ex 32:13 5414
saying, Unto thy seed will I *g* it ... Ex 33:1 5414
with thee, and I will *g* thee rest ... Ex 33:14
thereto, and *g* it unto the priest ... Lev 5:16 5414
and *g* it unto him to whom it ... Lev 6:5 5414
the right shoulder shall ye *g* ... Lev 7:32 5414
which I *g* to you for a possession ... Lev 14:34 5414
and *g* them unto the priest ... Lev 15:14 5414
I will *g* it unto you to possess ... Lev 20:24 5414
shall *g* it unto the priest with ... Lev 22:14 5414
into the land which I *g* unto you ... Lev 23:10 5414
which ye *g* unto the LORD ... Lev 23:38 5414
come into the land which I *g* you ... Lev 25:2 5414
Thou shalt not *g* him thy money ... Lev 25:37 5414
to *g* you the land of Canaan, and ... Lev 25:38 5414
he shall *g* again the price of his ... Lev 25:51 7725
unto his years shall he *g* him ... Lev 25:52 7725
Then I will *g* you rain in due ... Lev 26:4 5414
I will *g* peace in the land, and ye ... Lev 26:6 5414
he shall *g* thine estimation in ... Lev 27:23 5414
thou shalt *g* the Levites unto ... Num 3:9 5414
And thou shalt *g* the money ... Num 3:48 5414
g it unto him against whom he ... Num 5:7 5414
upon thee, and *g* thee peace ... Num 6:26 7760
thou shalt *g* them unto the ... Num 7:5 5414
the seven lamps shall *g* light ... Num 8:2
the LORD said, I will *g* it you ... Num 10:29 5414
Who shall *g* us flesh to eat ... Num 11:4
flesh to *g* unto all this people ... Num 11:13 5414
G us flesh, that we may eat ... Num 11:13 5414
Who shall *g* us flesh to eat ... Num 11:18
the LORD will *g* you flesh ... Num 11:18 5414
I will *g* them flesh, that they ... Num 11:21 5414
which I *g* unto the children of ... Num 13:2 5414
us into this land, and *g* it us ... Num 14:8 5414
habitations, which I *g* unto you, ... Num 15:2 5414
first of your dough ye shall *g* ... Num 15:21 5414
ye shall *g* thereof the LORD's ... Num 18:28 5414
ye shall *g* her unto Eleazar the ... Num 19:3 5414
it shall *g* forth his water, and ... Num 20:8 5414
so thou shalt *g* the congregation ... Num 20:8
Thus Edom refused to *g* Israel ... Num 20:21 5414
together, and I will *g* them water ... Num 21:16 5414
to *g* me leave to go with you ... Num 22:13 5414
If Balak would *g* me his house ... Num 22:18 5414
If Balak would *g* me his house ... Num 24:13 5414
I *g* unto him my covenant of peace ... Num 25:12 5414
To many thou shalt *g* the more ... Num 26:54
to few thou shalt *g* the less ... Num 26:54
G unto us therefore a possession ... Num 27:4 5414
thou shalt surely *g* them a ... Num 27:7 5414
then ye shall *g* his inheritance ... Num 27:9 5414
then ye shall *g* his inheritance ... Num 27:10 5414
then ye shall *g* his inheritance ... Num 27:11 5414
g him a charge in their sight ... Num 27:19
g it unto Eleazar the priest, for ... Num 31:29 5414
g them unto the Levites, which ... Num 31:30 5414
then ye shall *g* them the land of ... Num 32:29 5414
ye shall *g* the more inheritance ... Num 33:54
ye shall *g* the less inheritance ... Num 33:54
to *g* unto the nine tribes ... Num 34:13 5414
that they *g* unto the Levites of ... Num 35:2 5414
ye shall *g* also unto the Levites ... Num 35:2 5414
which ye shall *g* unto the Levites ... Num 35:4 5414
g unto the Levites there shall be ... Num 35:6 5414
g to the Levites shall be forty ... Num 35:7 5414
them shall ye *g* with their ... Num 35:7
the cities which ye shall *g* shall ... Num 35:8 5414
that have many ye shall *g* many ... Num 35:8
them that have few ye shall *g* few ... Num 35:8
every one shall *g* of his cities ... Num 35:8 5414
g six cities shall ye have for ... Num 35:13 5414
Ye shall *g* three cities on this ... Num 35:14 5414
shall ye *g* in the land of Canaan ... Num 35:14 5414
The LORD commanded my lord to *g* ... Num 36:2 5414
was commanded by the LORD to *g* ... Num 36:2 5414
to *g* unto them and to their seed ... Deut 1:8 5414
the LORD our God doth *g* unto us ... Deut 1:20 5414
which the LORD our God doth *g* us ... Deut 1:25 5414
which I sware to *g* unto your ... Deut 1:35 5414
to him will I *g* the land that he ... Deut 1:36 5414
thither, and unto them will I *g* it ... Deut 1:39 5414
to your voice, nor *g* ear unto you ... Deut 1:45
for I will not *g* you of their ... Deut 2:5 5414
for I will not *g* thee of their ... Deut 2:9 5414
for I will not *g* thee of the land ... Deut 2:19 5414
g me water for money, that I may ... Deut 2:28 5414
Behold, I have begun to *g* Sihon ... Deut 2:31 5414
to *g* thee their land for an ... Deut 4:38 5414
land which I *g* them to possess it ... Deut 5:31 5414
to *g* thee great and goodly cities, ... Deut 6:10 5414
to *g* us the land which he sware ... Deut 6:23 5414
thou shalt not *g* unto his son ... Deut 7:3 5414
sware unto thy fathers to *g* thee ... Deut 7:13 5414
unto their fathers to *g* unto them ... Deut 10:11 5414
unto your fathers to *g* unto them ... Deut 11:9 5414
That I will *g* you the rain of ... Deut 11:14 5414
sware unto your fathers to *g* them ... Deut 11:21 5414
thou shalt *g* it unto the stranger ... Deut 14:21 5414
Thou shalt surely *g* him, and thine ... Deut 15:10 5414
thee thou shalt *g* unto him ... Deut 15:14 5414
which thou shalt *g* unto the LORD ... Deut 16:10 5414
Every man shall *g* as he is able ... Deut 16:17
they shall *g* unto the priest the ... Deut 18:3 5414
of thy sheep, shalt thou *g* him ... Deut 18:4 5414
g thee all the land which he ... Deut 19:8 5414
he promised to *g* unto thy fathers ... Deut 19:8 5414
doth *g* thee for an inheritance ... Deut 20:16 5414
g occasions of speech against her ... Deut 22:14 7760
g them unto the father of the ... Deut 22:19 5414
g unto the damsel's father fifty ... Deut 22:29 5414
to *g* up thine enemies before thee ... Deut 23:14 5414
g it in her hand, and send her out ... Deut 24:1 5414
his day thou shalt *g* him his hire ... Deut 24:15 5414
Forty stripes he may *g* him ... Deut 25:3
unto our fathers for to *g* us ... Deut 26:3 5414
sware unto thy fathers to *g* thee ... Deut 28:11 5414
the heaven to *g* the rain unto thy ... Deut 28:12 5414
So that he will not *g* to any of ... Deut 28:55 5414
but the LORD shall *g* thee there a ... Deut 28:65 5414
to Isaac, and to Jacob, to *g* them ... Deut 30:20 5414
the LORD shall *g* them up before ... Deut 31:5 5414
unto their fathers to *g* them ... Deut 31:7 5414
that I may *g* him a charge ... Deut 31:14
G ear, O ye heavens, and I will ... Deut 32:1
which I *g* unto the children of ... Deut 32:49 5414
which I *g* the children of Israel ... Deut 32:52 5414
I will *g* it unto thy seed ... Deut 34:4 5414
the land which I do *g* to them ... Josh 1:2 5414
unto their fathers to *g* them ... Josh 1:6 5414
house, and *g* me a true token ... Josh 2:12 5414
their fathers that he would *g* us ... Josh 5:6 5414
Joshua said unto Achan, My son, *g* ... Josh 7:19 7760
for I will *g* it into thine hand ... Josh 8:18 5414
Moses to *g* you all the land ... Josh 9:24 5414
Now therefore *g* me this mountain, ... Josh 14:12 5414
to him will I *g* Achsah my ... Josh 15:16 5414
Who answered, *G* me a blessing ... Josh 15:19 5414
g me also springs of water ... Josh 15:19 5414
to *g* us an inheritance among our ... Josh 17:4 5414
G out from among you three men ... Josh 18:4 3051
g him a place, that he may dwell ... Josh 20:4 5414
Moses to *g* us cities to dwell in ... Josh 21:2 5414
he sware to *g* unto their fathers ... Josh 21:43 5414
to him will I *g* Achsah my ... Judg 1:12 5414
said unto him, *G* me a blessing ... Judg 1:15 3051
g me also springs of water ... Judg 1:15 5414
G me, I pray thee, a little water ... Judg 4:19
g ear, O ye princes ... Judg 5:3
thee are too many for me to *g* the ... Judg 7:2 5414
said unto the men of Succoth, *G* ... Judg 8:5 5414
that we should *g* bread unto thine ... Judg 8:6 5414
that we should *g* bread unto thy ... Judg 8:15 5414
that ye would *g* me every man the ... Judg 8:24 5414
We will willingly *g* them ... Judg 8:25 5414
then I will *g* you thirty sheets ... Judg 14:12 5414
then shall ye *g* me thirty sheets ... Judg 14:13 5414
we will *g* thee every one of us ... Judg 16:5 5414
I will *g* thee ten shekels of ... Judg 17:10 5414
g here your advice and counsel ... Judg 20:7 3051
There shall not any of us *g* his ... Judg 21:1 5414
by the LORD that we will not *g* ... Judg 21:7 5414
Howbeit we may not *g* them wives ... Judg 21:18 5414
for ye did not *g* unto them at ... Judg 21:22 5414
shall *g* thee of this young woman ... Ruth 4:12 5414
but wilt *g* unto thine handmaid a ... 1Sa 1:11 5414
then I will *g* him unto the LORD ... 1Sa 1:11 5414
he shall *g* strength unto his king ... 1Sa 2:10 5414
G flesh to roast for the priest ... 1Sa 2:15 5414
but thou shalt *g* it me now ... 1Sa 2:16 5414
The LORD *g* thee seed of this ... 1Sa 2:20 7760
did I *g* unto the house of thy ... 1Sa 2:28 5414
wealth which God shall *g* Israel ... 1Sa 2:32 3190
ye shall *g* glory unto the God of ... 1Sa 6:5 5414
said, *G* us a king to judge us ... 1Sa 8:6 5414
them, and *g* them to his servants ... 1Sa 8:14 5414
g to his officers, and to his ... 1Sa 8:15 5414
that will I *g* to the man of God, ... 1Sa 9:8 5414
g thee two loaves of bread ... 1Sa 10:4 5414
G us seven days' respite, that we ... 1Sa 11:3
God of Israel, *G* a perfect lot ... 1Sa 14:41 3051
g me a man, that we may fight ... 1Sa 17:10 5414
will *g* him his daughter, and make ... 1Sa 17:25 5414
I will *g* thy flesh unto the fowls ... 1Sa 17:44 5414
I will *g* the carcases of the host ... 1Sa 17:46 5414
he will *g* you into our hands ... 1Sa 17:47 5414
her will I *g* thee to wife ... 1Sa 18:17 5414
I will *g* him her, that she may be ... 1Sa 18:21 5414
g me five loaves of bread in mine ... 1Sa 21:3 5414
none like that; *g* it me ... 1Sa 21:9 5414
will the son of Jesse *g* every one ... 1Sa 22:7 5414
g, I pray thee, whatsoever cometh ... 1Sa 25:8 5414
g it unto men, whom I know not ... 1Sa 25:11 5414
let them *g* me a place in some ... 1Sa 27:5 5414
we will not *g* them ought of the ... 1Sa 30:22 5414
g them unto thy neighbour, and he ... 2Sa 12:11 5414
g me meat, and dress the meat in ... 2Sa 13:5 1262
I will *g* charge concerning thee ... 2Sa 14:8
G counsel among you what we shall ... 2Sa 16:20 3051
And the king said, I will *g* them ... 2Sa 21:6 5414
I will *g* thanks unto thee ... 2Sa 22:50
Oh that one would *g* me drink of ... 2Sa 23:15
as a king, *g* unto the king ... 2Sa 24:23 5414
g thee counsel, that thou mayest ... 1Kin 1:12
that he *g* me Abishag the ... 1Kin 2:17 5414
God said, Ask what I shall *g* thee ... 1Kin 3:5 5414
G therefore thy servant an ... 1Kin 3:9 5414
in the morning to *g* my child suck ... 1Kin 3:21
g half to the one, and half to the ... 1Kin 3:25 5414
g her the living child, and in no ... 1Kin 3:26 5414
G her the living child, and in no ... 1Kin 3:27 5414
unto thee will I *g* hire for thy ... 1Kin 5:6 5414
to *g* him according to his ... 1Kin 8:32 5414
g rain upon thy land, which thou ... 1Kin 8:36 5414
g to every man according to his ... 1Kin 8:39 5414
g them compassion before them who ... 1Kin 8:50 5414
thee, and will *g* it to thy servant ... 1Kin 11:11 5414
but will *g* one tribe to thy son ... 1Kin 11:13 5414
will *g* ten tribes to thee ... 1Kin 11:31 5414
will *g* it unto thee, even ten ... 1Kin 11:35 5414
unto his son will I *g* one tribe ... 1Kin 11:36 5414
David, and will *g* Israel unto thee ... 1Kin 11:38 5414
What counsel *g* ye that we may ... 1Kin 12:9
and I will *g* thee a reward ... 1Kin 13:7 5414
If thou wilt *g* me half thine ... 1Kin 13:8 5414
he shall *g* Israel up because of ... 1Kin 14:16 5414
his God *g* him a lamp in Jerusalem ... 1Kin 15:4 5414
And he said unto her, *G* me thy son ... 1Kin 17:19 5414
them therefore *g* us two bullocks ... 1Kin 18:23 5414
G me thy vineyard, that I may ... 1Kin 21:2 5414
I will *g* thee for it a better ... 1Kin 21:2 5414
I will *g* thee the worth of it in ... 1Kin 21:2 5414
that I should *g* the inheritance ... 1Kin 21:3 5414
I will not *g* thee the inheritance ... 1Kin 21:4 5414
G me thy vineyard for money ... 1Kin 21:6 5414
I will *g* thee another vineyard ... 1Kin 21:6 5414
I will not *g* thee my vineyard ... 1Kin 21:6 5414
I will *g* thee the vineyard of ... 1Kin 21:7 5414
he refused to *g* thee for money ... 1Kin 21:15 5414
G unto the people, that they may ... 2Kin 4:42 5414
G the people, that they may eat ... 2Kin 4:43 5414
g them, I pray thee, a talent of ... 2Kin 5:22 5414
G thy son, that we may eat him to ... 2Kin 6:28 5414
G thy son, that we may eat him ... 2Kin 6:29 5414
him to *g* him alway a light ... 2Kin 8:19 5414
If it be, *g* me thine hand ... 2Kin 10:15 5414
the priest *g* king David's spears ... 2Kin 11:10 5414
G thy daughter to my son to wife ... 2Kin 14:9 5414
to *g* to the king of Assyria ... 2Kin 15:20 5414
g pledges to my lord the king of ... 2Kin 18:23
let them *g* it to the doers of the ... 2Kin 22:5 5414
but he taxed the land to *g* the ... 2Kin 23:35 5414
to *g* it unto Pharaoh-nechoh ... 2Kin 23:35 5414

Oh that one would *g* me drink of ... 1Chr 11:17
G thanks unto the LORD, call upon ... 1Chr 16:8
Unto thee will I *g* the land of ... 1Chr 16:18 5414
G unto the LORD, ye kindreds of ... 1Chr 16:28 3051
g unto the LORD glory and strength ... 1Chr 16:28 3051
G unto the LORD the glory due ... 1Chr 16:29 3051
O *g* thanks unto the LORD ... 1Chr 16:34
that we may *g* thanks to thy holy ... 1Chr 16:35
to *g* thanks to the LORD, because ... 1Chr 16:41
I *g* thee the oxen also for burnt ... 1Chr 21:23 5414
meat offering; I *g* it all ... 1Chr 21:23 5414
I will *g* him rest from all his ... 1Chr 22:9
be Solomon, and I will *g* peace ... 1Chr 22:9 5414
Only the LORD *g* thee wisdom ... 1Chr 22:12 5414
g thee charge concerning Israel, ... 1Chr 22:12
to *g* thanks and to praise the LORD ... 1Chr 25:3
great, and to *g* strength unto all ... 1Chr 29:12
g unto Solomon my son a perfect ... 1Chr 29:19 5414
unto him, Ask what I shall *g* thee ... 2Chr 1:7 5414
G me now wisdom and knowledge, ... 2Chr 1:10 5414
I will *g* thee riches, and wealth, ... 2Chr 1:12 5414
I will *g* to thy servants, the ... 2Chr 2:10 5414
What counsel *g* ye me to return ... 2Chr 10:6
What advice *g* ye that we may ... 2Chr 10:9
he promised to *g* a light to him ... 2Chr 21:7 5414
but they would not *g* ear ... 2Chr 24:19
The LORD is able to *g* thee much ... 2Chr 25:9 5414
G thy daughter to my son to wife ... 2Chr 25:18 5414
was to *g* them one heart to do the ... 2Chr 30:12 5414
g to the congregation a thousand ... 2Chr 30:24 7311
to *g* thanks, and to praise in the ... 2Chr 31:2
to *g* the portion of the priests ... 2Chr 31:4 5414
to *g* to their brethren by courses ... 2Chr 31:15 5414
to *g* portions to all the males ... 2Chr 31:19 5414
to *g* over yourselves to die by ... 2Chr 32:11 5414
that they might *g* according to ... 2Chr 35:12 5414
G ye now commandment to cause ... Ezr 4:21 7761
to *g* us a nail in his holy place, ... Ezr 9:8 5414
g us a little reviving in our ... Ezr 9:8 5414
to *g* us a reviving, to set up the ... Ezr 9:9 5414
to *g* us a wall in Judah and in ... Ezr 9:9 5414
Now therefore *g* not your ... Ezr 9:12 5414
that he may *g* me timber to make ... Neh 2:8 5414
g them for a prey in the land of ... Neh 4:4 5414
to *g* the land of the Canaanites ... Neh 9:8 5414
and the Girgashites, to *g* it ... Neh 9:8 5414
to *g* them light in the way ... Neh 9:12
which thou hadst sworn to *g* them ... Neh 9:15 5414
yet would they not *g* ear ... Neh 9:30
that we would not *g* our daughters ... Neh 10:30 5414
to *g* thanks, according to the ... Neh 12:24
Ye shall not *g* your daughters ... Neh 13:25 5414
let the king *g* her royal estate ... Est 1:19 5414
all the wives shall *g* to their ... Est 1:20 5414
g the house of Haman the Jews' ... Est 8:1 5414
a man hath will he *g* for his life ... Job 2:4 5414
why did I not *g* up the ghost when ... Job 3:11 1478
G a reward for me of your ... Job 6:22
my tongue, I shall *g* up the ghost ... Job 13:19 1478
neither let me *g* flattering ... Job 32:21 1478
I know not to *g* flattering titles ... Job 32:22
g ear unto me, ye that have ... Job 34:2
I shall *g* thee the heathen for ... Ps 2:8 5415
G ear to my words, O LORD ... Ps 5:1
the grave who shall *g* thee thanks ... Ps 6:5
g ear unto my prayer, that goeth ... Ps 17:1
will I *g* thanks unto thee ... Ps 18:49
G them according to their deeds, ... Ps 28:4 5414
g them after the work of their ... Ps 28:4 5414
G unto the LORD, O ye mighty, ... Ps 29:1 3051
g unto the LORD glory and strength ... Ps 29:1 3051
G unto the LORD the glory due ... Ps 29:2 3051
The LORD will *g* strength unto his ... Ps 29:11 5414
g thanks at the remembrance of ... Ps 30:4
I will *g* thanks unto thee for ... Ps 30:12
I will *g* thee thanks in the great ... Ps 35:18
he shall *g* thee the desires of ... Ps 37:4 5414
O LORD, and *g* ear unto my cry ... Ps 39:12
g ear, all ye inhabitants of the ... Ps 49:1
nor *g* to God a ransom for him ... Ps 49:7 5414
else would I *g* it ... Ps 51:16 5414
g ear to the words of my mouth ... Ps 54:2
G ear to my prayer, O God ... Ps 55:1
I will sing and *g* praise ... Ps 57:7
G us help from trouble ... Ps 60:11 3051
G the king thy judgments, O God, ... Ps 72:1 5414
O God, do we *g* ... Ps 75:1
unto thee do we *g* thanks ... Ps 75:1
G ear, O my people, to my law ... Ps 78:1
can he *g* bread also ... Ps 78:20 5414
will *g* thee thanks for ever ... Ps 79:13
G ear, O Shepherd of Israel, thou ... Ps 80:1
g ear, O God of Jacob ... Ps 84:8
the LORD will *g* grace and glory ... Ps 84:11 5414
the LORD shall *g* that which is ... Ps 85:12 5414
G ear, O LORD, unto my prayer ... Ps 86:6
g thy strength unto thy servant, ... Ps 86:16 5414
For he shall *g* his angels charge ... Ps 91:11
thing to *g* thanks unto the LORD ... Ps 92:1
That thou mayest *g* him rest from ... Ps 94:13
G unto the LORD, O ye kindreds of ... Ps 96:7 3051
g unto the LORD glory and strength ... Ps 96:7 3051
G unto the LORD the glory due ... Ps 96:8 3051
g thanks at the remembrance of ... Ps 97:12
They *g* drink to every beast of ... Ps 104:11
that thou mayest *g* them their ... Ps 104:27 5414
O *g* thanks unto the LORD ... Ps 105:1
Unto thee will I *g* the land of ... Ps 105:11 5414
fire to *g* light in the night ... Ps 105:39
O *g* thanks unto the LORD ... Ps 106:1
to *g* thanks unto thy holy name, ... Ps 106:47
O *g* thanks unto the LORD, for he ... Ps 107:1
g praise, even with my glory ... Ps 108:1
G us help from trouble ... Ps 108:12 3051
but I *g* myself unto prayer ... Ps 109:4
that he may *g* them the heritage ... Ps 111:6 5441
us, but unto thy name *g* glory ... Ps 115:1
O *g* thanks unto the LORD ... Ps 118:1
O *g* thanks unto the LORD ... Ps 118:29
G me understanding, and I shall ... Ps 119:34
At midnight I will rise to *g* ... Ps 119:62
g me understanding, that I may ... Ps 119:73
g me understanding, that I may ... Ps 119:125
g me understanding, and I shall ... Ps 119:144
g me understanding according to ... Ps 119:169
to *g* thanks unto the name of the ... Ps 122:4
I will not *g* sleep to mine eyes, ... Ps 132:4 5414
O *G* thanks unto the LORD ... Ps 136:1
O *g* thanks unto the God of gods ... Ps 136:2
O *g* thanks to the Lord of lords ... Ps 136:3
O *g* thanks unto the God of heaven ... Ps 136:26
shall *g* thanks unto thy name ... Ps 140:13
g ear unto my voice, when I cry ... Ps 141:1
g ear to my supplications ... Ps 143:1
To *g* subtilty to the simple, to ... Prov 1:4 5414
come again, and to morrow I will *g* ... Prov 3:28 5414
For I *g* you good doctrine, ... Prov 4:2 5414
She shall *g* to thine head an ... Prov 4:9 5414
Lest thou *g* thine honour unto ... Prov 5:9 5414
G not sleep to thine eyes, nor ... Prov 6:4 5414
he shall *g* all the substance of ... Prov 6:31 5414
G instruction to a wise man, and ... Prov 9:9 5414
g me thine heart, and let thine ... Prov 23:26 5414
be hungry, *g* him bread to eat ... Prov 25:21
be thirsty, *g* him water to drink ... Prov 25:21
The rod and reproof *g* wisdom ... Prov 29:15 5414
thy son, and he shall *g* thee rest ... Prov 29:17
he shall *g* delight unto thy soul ... Prov 29:17 5414
g me neither poverty nor riches ... Prov 30:8 5414
two daughters, crying, *G*, *g* ... Prov 30:15 3051
two daughters, crying, *G*, *g* ... Prov 30:15 3051
G not thy strength unto women, ... Prov 31:3 5414
G strong drink unto him that is ... Prov 31:6 5414
G her of the fruit of her hands ... Prov 31:31 5414
mine heart to *g* myself unto wine ... Eccl 2:3 4900
that he may *g* to him that is good ... Eccl 2:26 5414
than to *g* the sacrifice of fools ... Eccl 5:1 5414
G a portion to seven, and also to ... Eccl 11:2 5414
the tender grape *g* a good smell ... Song 2:13 5414
there will I *g* thee my loves ... Song 7:12 5414
The mandrakes *g* a smell, and at ... Song 7:13 5414
if a man would *g* all the ... Song 8:7 5414
O heavens, and *g* ear, O earth ... Is 1:2
g ear unto the law of our God, ye ... Is 1:10
I will *g* children to be their ... Is 3:4 5414
Lord himself shall *g* you a sign ... Is 7:14 5414
of milk that they shall *g* ... Is 7:22 6213
g ear, all ye of far countries ... Is 8:9
of my wrath will I *g* him a charge ... Is 10:6
thereof shall not *g* their light ... Is 13:10
shall *g* thee rest from thy sorrow ... Is 14:3
the Egyptians will I *g* over into ... Is 19:4 5534
G ye ear, and hear my voice ... Is 28:23
though the Lord *g* you the bread ... Is 30:20 5414
Then shall he *g* the rain of thy ... Is 30:23 5414
g ear unto my speech ... Is 32:9
Now therefore *g* pledges, I pray ... Is 36:8
I will *g* thee two thousand horses ... Is 36:8 5414
I will *g* to Jerusalem one that ... Is 41:27 5414
g thee for a covenant of the ... Is 42:6 5414
my glory will I not *g* to another ... Is 42:8 5414
Let them *g* glory unto the LORD, ... Is 42:12 7760
Who among you will *g* ear to this ... Is 42:23
therefore will I *g* men for thee ... Is 43:4 5414
I will say to the north, *G* up ... Is 43:6 5414
because I *g* waters in the ... Is 43:20 5414
to *g* drink to my people, my ... Is 43:20
I will *g* thee the treasures of ... Is 45:3 5414
I will not *g* my glory unto ... Is 48:11 5414
I will also *g* thee for a light to ... Is 49:6 5414
g thee for a covenant of the ... Is 49:8 5414
g place to me that I may dwell ... Is 49:20 5066
g ear unto me, O my nation ... Is 51:4
that it may *g* seed to the sower, ... Is 55:10 5414
unto them will I *g* in mine house ... Is 56:5 5414
I will *g* them an everlasting name ... Is 56:5 5414
shall the moon *g* light unto thee ... Is 60:19
to *g* unto them beauty for ashes, ... Is 61:3 5414
g him no rest, till he establish, ... Is 62:7 5414
Surely I will no more *g* thy corn ... Is 62:8 5414
I will *g* you pastors according to ... Jer 3:15 5414
g thee a pleasant land, a goodly ... Jer 3:19 5414
now also will I *g* sentence ... Jer 4:12 1696
g out their voice against the ... Jer 4:16 5414
g warning, that they may hear ... Jer 6:10
Therefore will I *g* their wives ... Jer 8:10 5414
g them water of gall to drink ... Jer 9:15
to *g* them a land flowing with ... Jer 11:5 5414
Hear ye, and *g* ear ... Jer 13:15
G glory to the LORD your God, ... Jer 13:16 5414
but I will *g* you assured peace in ... Jer 14:13 5414
or can the heavens *g* showers ... Jer 14:22 5414
thy treasures will I *g* to the ... Jer 15:13 5414
neither shall men *g* them the cup ... Jer 16:7
I will *g* thy substance and all thy ... Jer 17:3 5414
even to *g* every man according to ... Jer 17:10 5414
let us not *g* heed to any of his ... Jer 18:18
G heed to me, O LORD, and hearken ... Jer 18:19
their carcases will I *g* to be ... Jer 19:7 5414
I will *g* all Judah into the hand ... Jer 20:4 5414
of the kings of Judah will I *g* ... Jer 20:5 5414
I will *g* thee into the hand of ... Jer 22:25 5414
I will *g* them an heart to know me ... Jer 24:7 5414
So will I *g* Zedekiah the king of ... Jer 24:8 5414
he shall *g* a shout, as they that ... Jer 25:30
he will *g* them that are wicked to ... Jer 25:31 5414
that they should not *g* him into ... Jer 26:24 5414
g your daughters to husbands, ... Jer 29:6 5414
of evil, to *g* you an expected end ... Jer 29:11 5414
upon thee will I *g* for a prey ... Jer 30:16 5414
I will *g* this city into the hand ... Jer 32:3 5414
to *g* every one according to his ... Jer 32:19 5414
swear to their fathers to *g* them ... Jer 32:22 5414
I will *g* this city into the hand ... Jer 32:28 5414
I will *g* them one heart, and one ... Jer 32:39 5414
I will *g* this city into the hand ... Jer 34:2 5414
I will *g* the men that have ... Jer 34:18 5414
I will even *g* them into the hand ... Jer 34:20 5414
his princes will I *g* into the ... Jer 34:21 5414
chambers, and *g* them wine to drink ... Jer 35:2
that they should *g* him daily a ... Jer 37:21 5414
if I *g* thee counsel, wilt thou ... Jer 38:15
neither will I *g* thee into the ... Jer 38:16 5414
I will *g* Pharaoh-hophra king of ... Jer 44:30 5414
but thy life will I *g* unto thee ... Jer 45:5 5414
G wings unto Moab, that it may ... Jer 48:9 5414
that he may *g* rest to the land, ... Jer 50:34
g thyself no rest ... Lam 2:18 5414
G them sorrow of heart, thy curse ... Lam 3:65 5414
they *g* suck to their young ones ... Lam 4:3
thy mouth, and eat that I *g* thee ... Eze 2:8 5414
with this roll that I *g* thee ... Eze 3:3 5414
mouth, and *g* them warning from me ... Eze 3:17
I will *g* it into the hands of the ... Eze 7:21 5414
g wicked counsel in this city ... Eze 11:2
I will *g* you the land of Israel ... Eze 11:17 5414
I will *g* them one heart, and I ... Eze 11:19 5414
will *g* them an heart of flesh ... Eze 11:19 5414
so will I *g* the inhabitants of ... Eze 15:6 5414
They *g* gifts to all whores ... Eze 16:33 5414
which thou didst *g* unto them ... Eze 16:36 5414
I will *g* thee blood in fury and ... Eze 16:38 5414
I will also *g* thee into their ... Eze 16:39 5414
thou also shalt *g* no hire any ... Eze 16:41 5414
I will *g* them unto thee for ... Eze 16:61 5414
that they might *g* him horses ... Eze 17:15 5414
up mine hand to *g* it to them ... Eze 20:28 5414
mine hand to *g* it to your fathers ... Eze 20:42 5414
to *g* it into the hand of the ... Eze 21:11 5414
and I will *g* it him ... Eze 21:27 5414
therefore will I *g* her cup into ... Eze 23:31 5414
will *g* them to be removed and ... Eze 23:46 5414
will *g* them in possession, that ... Eze 25:10 5414
I will *g* the land of Egypt unto ... Eze 29:19 5414
I will *g* thee the opening of the ... Eze 29:21 5414
and the moon shall not *g* her light ... Eze 32:7
g again that he had robbed, walk ... Eze 33:15 7999
is in the open field will I *g* to ... Eze 33:27 5414
A new heart also will I *g* you ... Eze 36:26 5414
I will *g* you an heart of flesh ... Eze 36:26 5414
I will *g* thee unto the ravenous ... Eze 39:4 5414
that I will *g* unto Gog a place ... Eze 39:11 5414
thou shalt *g* to the priests the ... Eze 43:19 5414
ye shall *g* them no possession in ... Eze 44:28 5414
ye shall also *g* unto the priest ... Eze 44:30 5414
they *g* to the house of Israel ... Eze 45:8 5414
ye shall *g* the sixth part of an ... Eze 45:13
the people of the land shall *g* ... Eze 45:16 1961,413
part to *g* burnt offerings ... Eze 45:17
lambs as he shall be able to *g* ... Eze 46:5 4991
to the lambs as he is able to *g* ... Eze 46:11 4991
If the prince *g* a gift unto any ... Eze 46:16 5414
But if he *g* a gift of his ... Eze 46:17 5414
but he shall *g* his sons ... Eze 46:18
hand to *g* it unto your fathers ... Eze 47:14 5414
there shall ye *g* him his ... Eze 47:23 5414
let them *g* us pulse to eat, and ... Dan 1:12 5414
the king that he would *g* him time ... Dan 2:16 5415
and *g* thy rewards to another ... Dan 5:17 3052
might *g* accounts unto them ... Dan 6:2 3052
to *g* both the sanctuary and the ... Dan 8:13 5414
am now come forth to *g* thee skill ... Dan 9:22
he shall *g* him the daughter of ... Dan 11:17 5414
to whom they shall not *g* the ... Dan 11:21 5414
that *g* me my bread and my water, ... Hos 2:5 5414
I will *g* her her vineyards from ... Hos 2:15 5414
rulers with shame do love, *G* ye ... Hos 4:18 3051
g ye ear, O house of the king ... Hos 5:1
G them, O LORD ... Hos 9:14 5414
what wilt thou *g* ... Hos 9:14 5414
g them a miscarrying womb and dry ... Hos 9:14 5414
How shall I *g* thee up, Ephraim ... Hos 11:8 5414
saidst, *G* me a king and princes ... Hos 13:10 5414
g ear, all ye inhabitants of the ... Joel 1:2
g not thine heritage to reproach, ... Joel 2:17 5414
Therefore shalt thou *g* presents ... Mic 1:14 5414
Therefore will he *g* them up ... Mic 5:3 5414
shall I *g* my firstborn for my ... Mic 6:7 5414
will I *g* up to the sword ... Mic 6:14 5414
and in this place will I *g* peace ... Hag 2:9 5414
I will *g* thee places to walk ... Zec 3:7 5414
the vine shall *g* her fruit ... Zec 8:12 5414
the ground shall *g* her increase ... Zec 8:12 5414
and the heavens shall *g* their dew ... Zec 8:12 5414

g them showers of rain, to every Zec 10:1 5414
If ye think good, *g* me my price Zec 11:12 3051
to *g* glory unto my name, saith Mal 2:2 5414
He shall *g* his angels charge Mt 4:6
All these things will I *g* thee Mt 4:9 1325
let him *g* her a writing of Mt 5:31 1325
G to him that asketh thee, and Mt 5:42 1325
G us this day our daily bread Mt 6:11 1325
G not that which is holy unto the Mt 7:6 1325
ask bread, will he *g* him a stone Mt 7:9 1929
a fish, will he *g* him a serpent Mt 7:10 1929
know how to *g* good gifts unto Mt 7:11 1325
g good things to them that ask Mt 7:11 1325
He said unto them, *G* place Mt 9:24 402
freely ye have received, freely *g* Mt 10:8 1325
whosoever shall *g* to drink unto Mt 10:42 4222
heavy laden, and I will *g* you rest Mt 11:28
they shall *g* account thereof in Mt 12:36 591
he promised with an oath to *g* her Mt 14:7 1325
G me here John Baptist's head in Mt 14:8 1325
g ye them to eat Mt 14:16 1325
I will *g* unto thee the keys of Mt 16:19 1325
or what shall a man *g* in exchange Mt 16:26 1325
g unto them for me and thee Mt 17:27 1325
to *g* a writing of divorcement Mt 19:7 1325
g to the poor, and thou shalt have Mt 19:21 1325
whatsoever is right I will *g* you Mt 20:4
g them their hire, beginning from Mt 20:8 591
I will *g* unto this last, even as Mt 20:14 1325
and on my left, is not mine to *g* Mt 20:23 1325
to *g* his life a ransom for many Mt 20:28 1325
Is it lawful to *g* tribute unto Mt 22:17 1325
to them that *g* suck in those days Mt 24:19
and the moon shall not *g* her light Mt 24:29 1325
to *g* them meat in due season Mt 24:45 1325
unto the wise, *G* us of your oil Mt 25:8 1325
g it unto him which hath ten Mt 25:28 1325
said unto them, What will ye *g* me Mt 26:15 1325
he shall presently *g* me more than Mt 26:53 3936
thou wilt, and I will *g* it thee Mk 6:22 1325
I will *g* it thee, unto the half Mk 6:23 1325
saying, I will that thou *g* me by Mk 6:25 1325
said unto them, *G* ye them to eat Mk 6:37 1325
of bread, and *g* them to eat Mk 6:37 1325
Or what shall a man *g* in exchange Mk 8:37 1325
For whosoever shall *g* you a cup Mk 9:41 4222
g to the poor, and thou shalt have Mk 10:21 1325
on my left hand is not mine to *g* Mk 10:40 1325
to *g* his life a ransom for many Mk 10:45 1325
will *g* the vineyard unto others Mk 12:9 1325
Is it lawful to *g* tribute to Mk 12:14 1325
Shall we *g*, or shall we not *g* Mk 12:15 1325
to them that *g* suck in those days Mk 13:17
and the moon shall not *g* her light Mk 13:24 1325
glad, and promised to *g* him money Mk 14:11 1325
the Lord God shall *g* unto him the Lk 1:32 1325
To *g* knowledge of salvation unto Lk 1:77 1325
To *g* light to them that sit in Lk 1:79 2014
him, All this power will I *g* thee Lk 4:6 1325
and to whomsoever I will I *g* it Lk 4:6 1325
He shall *g* his angels charge over Lk 4:10
G to every man that asketh of Lk 6:30 1325
G, and it shall be given unto you Lk 6:38 1325
shall men *g* into your bosom Lk 6:38 1325
and he commanded to *g* her meat Lk 8:55 1325
said unto them, *G* ye them to eat Lk 9:13 1325
and drinking such things as they *g* Lk 10:7 3844
I *g* unto you power to tread on Lk 10:19 1325
G us day by day our daily bread Lk 11:3 1325
I cannot rise and *g* thee Lk 11:7 1325
g him, because he is his friend, Lk 11:8 1325
g him as many as he needeth Lk 11:8 1325
a father, will he *g* him a stone Lk 11:11 1929
he for a fish *g* him a serpent Lk 11:11 1929
know how to *g* good gifts unto Lk 11:13 1325
g the Holy Spirit to them that Lk 11:13 1325
of a candle doth *g* thee light Lk 11:36 5461
But rather *g* alms of such things Lk 11:41 1325
pleasure to *g* you the kingdom Lk 12:32 1325
Sell that ye have, and *g* alms Lk 12:33 1325
to *g* them their portion of meat Lk 12:42 1325
I am come to *g* peace on earth Lk 12:51 1325
g diligence that thou mayest be Lk 12:58 1325
and say to thee, *G* this man place Lk 14:9 1325
g me the portion of goods that Lk 15:12 1325
g an account of thy stewardship Lk 16:2 591
who shall *g* you that which is Lk 16:12 1325
that returned to *g* glory to God Lk 17:18 1325
I *g* tithes of all that I possess Lk 18:12
half of my goods I *g* to the poor Lk 19:8 1325
g it to him that hath ten pounds Lk 19:24 1325
that they should *g* him of the Lk 20:10 1325
shall *g* the vineyard to others Lk 20:16 1325
for us to *g* tribute unto Caesar Lk 20:22 1325
For I will *g* you a mouth and Lk 21:15 1325
child, and to them that *g* suck Lk 21:23
and covenanted to *g* him money Lk 22:5 1325
forbidding to *g* tribute to Caesar Lk 23:2 1325
that we may *g* an answer to them Jn 1:22 1325
saith unto her, *G* me to drink Jn 4:7 1325
that saith to thee, *G* me to drink Jn 4:10 1325
I shall *g* him shall never thirst Jn 4:14 1325
but the water that I shall *g* him Jn 4:14 1325
g me this water, that I thirst Jn 4:15 1325
the Son of man shall *g* unto you Jn 6:27 1325
Lord, evermore *g* us this bread Jn 6:34 1325
bread that I will *g* is my flesh Jn 6:51 1325
which I will *g* for the life of Jn 6:51 1325
How can this man *g* us his flesh Jn 6:52 1325
Did not Moses *g* you the law Jn 7:19 1325
said unto him, *G* God the praise Jn 9:24 1325
I *g* unto them eternal life Jn 10:28 1325
ask of God, God will *g* it thee Jn 11:22 1325
He it is, to whom I shall *g* a sop Jn 13:26 1929
that he should *g* something to the Jn 13:29 1325
A new commandment I *g* unto you Jn 13:34 1325
he shall *g* you another Comforter, Jn 14:16 1325
with you, my peace I *g* unto you Jn 14:27 1325
as the world giveth, *g* I unto you Jn 14:27 1325
in my name, he may *g* it you Jn 15:16 1325
in my name, he will *g* it you Jn 16:23 1325
that he should *g* eternal life to Jn 17:2 1325
but such as I have *g* I thee Acts 3:6 1325
for to *g* repentance to Israel, and Acts 5:31 1325
But we will *g* ourselves Acts 6:4 4342
g it to him for a possession Acts 7:5 1325
the lively oracles to *g* unto us Acts 7:38 1325
G me also this power, that on Acts 8:19 1325
To him *g* all the prophets witness Acts 10:43
and ye that fear God, *g* audience Acts 13:16
I will *g* you the sure mercies of Acts 13:34 1325
g an account of this concourse Acts 19:40 591
to *g* you an inheritance among all Acts 20:32 1325
more blessed to *g* than to receive Acts 20:35 1325
him also freely *g* us all things Rom 8:32 5483
but rather *g* place unto wrath Rom 12:19 1325
if he thirst, *g* him drink Rom 12:20 4222
shall *g* account of himself to God Rom 14:12 1325
unto whom not only I *g* thanks Rom 16:4
that ye may *g* yourselves to 1Cor 7:5 4980
yet I *g* my judgment, as one that 1Cor 7:25 1325
of for that for which I *g* thanks 1Cor 10:30
G none offence, neither to the 1Cor 10:32 1096
Wherefore I *g* you to understand, 1Cor 12:3
though I *g* my body to be burned, 1Cor 13:3 3860
except they *g* a distinction in 1Cor 14:7 1325
the trumpet *g* an uncertain sound 1Cor 14:8 1325
to *g* the light of the knowledge 2Cor 4:6
but *g* you occasion to glory on 2Cor 5:12 1325
And herein I *g* my advice 2Cor 8:10 1325
in his heart, so let him *g* 2Cor 9:7
Cease not to *g* thanks for you, Eph 1:16
may *g* unto you the spirit of Eph 1:17 1325
Neither *g* place to the devil Eph 4:27 1325
may have to *g* to him that needeth Eph 4:28 3330
and Christ shall *g* thee light Eph 5:14
We *g* thanks to God and the Father Col 1:3
g unto your servants that which Col 4:1 3930
We *g* thanks to God always for you 1Th 1:2
In every thing *g* thanks 1Th 5:18
But we are bound to *g* thanks 2Th 2:13
g you peace always by all means 2Th 3:16 1325
Neither *g* heed to fables and 1Ti 1:4
g attendance to reading, to 1Ti 4:13
g thyself wholly to them 1Ti 4:15 2468
And these things *g* in charge 1Ti 5:7
g none occasion to the adversary 1Ti 5:14 1325
I *g* thee charge in the sight of 1Ti 6:13
The Lord *g* mercy unto the house 2Ti 1:16 1325
the Lord *g* thee understanding in 2Ti 2:7 1325
will *g* them repentance to the 2Ti 2:25 1325
judge, shall *g* me at that day 2Ti 4:8 591
Therefore we ought to *g* the more Heb 2:1
as they that must *g* account Heb 13:17 591
notwithstanding ye *g* them not Jas 2:16 1325
be ready always to *g* an answer to 1Pet 3:15
Who shall *g* account to him that 1Pet 4:5 591
g diligence to make your calling 2Pet 1:10
he shall *g* him life for them that 1Jn 5:16 1325
I *g* to eat of the tree of life Rev 2:7 1325
I will *g* thee a crown of life Rev 2:10 1325
I *g* to eat of the hidden manna Rev 2:17 1325
will *g* him a white stone, and in Rev 2:17 1325
I will *g* unto every one of you Rev 2:23 1325
to him will I *g* power over the Rev 2:26 1325
I will *g* him the morning star Rev 2:28 1325
And when those beasts *g* glory Rev 4:9 1325
unto him, *G* me the little book Rev 10:9 1325
I will *g* power unto my two Rev 11:3 1325
We *g* thee thanks, O Lord God Rev 11:17
that thou shouldest *g* reward unto Rev 11:18 1325
he had power to *g* life unto the Rev 13:15 1325
Fear God, and *g* glory to him Rev 14:7 1325
they repented not to *g* him glory Rev 16:9 1325
to *g* unto her the cup of the wine Rev 16:19 1325
shall *g* their power and strength Rev 17:13 1239
g their kingdom unto the beast, Rev 17:17 1325
so much torment and sorrow *g* her Rev 18:7 1325
and rejoice, and *g* honour to him Rev 19:7 1325
I will *g* unto him that is athirst Rev 21:6 1325
to *g* every man according as his Rev 22:12 591

GIVEN {498}

I have *g* you every herb bearing Gen 1:29 5414
I have *g* every green herb for Gen 1:30
herb have I *g* you all things Gen 9:3 5414
Behold, to me thou hast *g* no seed Gen 15:3 5414
Unto thy seed have I *g* this land Gen 15:18 5414
I have *g* my maid into thy bosom Gen 16:5 5414
I have *g* thy brother a thousand Gen 20:16 5414
Sarah should have *g* children suck Gen 21:7
he hath *g* him flocks, and herds, Gen 24:35 5414
him hath he *g* all that he hath Gen 24:36 5414
have I *g* to him for servants Gen 27:37 5414
hath therefore *g* me this son also Gen 29:33 5414
my voice, and hath *g* me a son Gen 30:6 5414
God hath *g* me my hire Gen 30:18 5414
because I have *g* my maiden to my Gen 30:18 5414
of your father, and *g* them to me Gen 31:9 5414
God hath graciously *g* thy servant Gen 33:5 2603
she was not *g* unto him to wife Gen 38:14 5414
hath *g* you treasure in your sacks Gen 43:23 5414
whom God hath *g* me in this place Gen 48:9 5414
Moreover I have *g* to thee one Gen 48:22 5414
is no straw *g* unto thy servants Ex 5:16 5414
for there shall no straw be *g* you Ex 5:18 5414
which the LORD hath *g* you to eat Ex 16:15 5414
the LORD hath *g* you the sabbath Ex 16:29 5414
If his master have *g* him a wife Ex 21:4 5414
I have *g* with him Aholiab, the Ex 31:6 5414
I have *g* it unto them for their Lev 6:17 5414
have *g* them unto Aaron the priest Lev 7:34 5414
g them of the children of Israel Lev 7:36 5414
which are *g* out of the sacrifices Lev 10:14 5414
God hath *g* it you to bear the Lev 10:17 5414
I have *g* it to you upon the altar Lev 17:11 5414
all redeemed, nor freedom *g* her Lev 19:20 5414
because he hath *g* of his seed Lev 20:3 5414
they are wholly *g* unto him out of Num 3:9 5414
For they are wholly *g* unto me Num 8:16 5414
I have *g* the Levites as a gift to Num 8:19 5414
or *g* us inheritance of fields and Num 16:14 5414
to you they are *g* as a gift for Num 18:6 5414
I have *g* your priest's office Num 18:7 5414
I also have *g* thee the charge of Num 18:8 5414
unto thee have I *g* them by reason Num 18:8 5414
I have *g* them unto thee, and to Num 18:11 5414
unto the LORD, them have I *g* thee Num 18:12 5414
unto the LORD, have I *g* thee Num 18:19 5414
I have *g* the children of Levi all Num 18:21 5414
I have *g* to the Levites to Num 18:24 5414
I have *g* you from them for your Num 18:26 5414
into the land which I have *g* them Num 20:12 5414
into the land which I have *g* unto Num 20:24 5414
he hath *g* his sons that escaped, Num 21:29 5414
be *g* according to those that were Num 26:54 5414
there was no inheritance *g* them Num 26:62 5414
see the land which I have *g* unto Num 27:12 5414
let this land be *g* unto thy Num 32:5 5414
land which the LORD hath *g* them Num 32:7 5414
land which the LORD had *g* them Num 32:9 5414
for I have *g* you the land to Num 33:53 5414
unto all that the LORD had *g* him Deut 1:3 6680
because I have *g* mount Seir unto Deut 2:5 5414
because I have *g* Ar unto the Deut 2:9 5414
because I have *g* it unto the Deut 2:19 5414
I have *g* into thine hand Sihon Deut 2:24 5414
The LORD your God hath *g* you this Deut 3:18 5414
in your cities which I have *g* you Deut 3:19 5414
Until the LORD have *g* rest unto Deut 3:20 5117
God hath *g* them beyond Jordan Deut 3:20 5414
possession, which I have *g* you Deut 3:20 5414
good land which he hath *g* thee Deut 8:10 5414
the land which I have *g* you Deut 9:23 5414
LORD thy God which he hath *g* thee Deut 12:15 5414
flock, which the LORD hath *g* thee Deut 12:21 5414
God hath *g* thee to dwell there Deut 13:12 5414
LORD thy God which he hath *g* thee Deut 16:17 5414
the LORD thy God hath *g* thee Deut 20:14 5414
he hath *g* occasions of speech Deut 22:17 7760
hath *g* thee rest from all thine Deut 25:19 5117
hath *g* us this land, even a land Deut 26:9 5414
which thou, O LORD, hast *g* me Deut 26:10 5414
the LORD thy God hath *g* unto thee Deut 26:11 5414
hast *g* it unto the Levite, the Deut 26:12 5414
also have *g* them unto the Levite, Deut 26:13 5414
nor *g* ought thereof for the dead Deut 26:14 5414
and the land which thou hast *g* us Deut 26:15 5414
shall be *g* unto thine enemies Deut 28:31 5414
shall be *g* unto another people Deut 28:32 5414
the LORD thy God hath *g* thee Deut 28:52 5414
the LORD thy God hath *g* thee Deut 28:53 5414
Yet the LORD hath not *g* you an Deut 29:4 5414
and whom he had not *g* unto them Deut 29:26 2505
upon, that have I *g* unto you Josh 1:3 5414
The LORD your God hath *g* you rest Josh 1:13 5117
and hath *g* you this land Josh 1:13 5414
LORD have *g* your brethren rest Josh 1:15 5117
brethren rest, as he hath *g* you Josh 1:15 5117
that the LORD hath *g* you the land Josh 2:9 5414
when the LORD hath *g* us the land Josh 2:14 5414
I have *g* into thine hand Jericho, Josh 6:2 5414
for the LORD hath *g* you the city Josh 6:16 5414
I have *g* into thy hand the king Josh 8:1 5414
For Moses had *g* the inheritance Josh 14:3 5414
for thou hast *g* me a south land Josh 15:19 5414
Why hast thou *g* me but one lot and Josh 17:14 5414
God of your fathers hath *g* you Josh 18:3 5414
hath *g* rest unto your brethren Josh 22:4 5117
Moses had *g* possession in Bashan Josh 22:7 5414
time after that the LORD had *g* Josh 23:1 5117
the LORD your God hath *g* you Josh 23:13 5414
the LORD your God hath *g* you Josh 23:15 5414
land which he hath *g* unto you Josh 23:16 5414
I have *g* you a land for which ye Josh 24:13 5414
which was *g* him in mount Ephraim Josh 24:33 5414
for thou hast *g* me a south land Judg 1:15 5414
wife was *g* to his companion Judg 14:20
wife, and *g* her to his companion Judg 15:6 5414
and said, Thou hast *g* this great Judg 15:18 5414
for God hath *g* it into your hands Judg 18:10 5414
a full reward be *g* thee of the Ruth 2:12
the LORD hath *g* me my petition 1Sa 1:27 5414
hath *g* it to a neighbour of thine 1Sa 15:28 5414

should have been *g* to David 1Sa 18:19 5414
that she was *g* unto Adriel the 1Sa 18:19 5414
in that thou hast *g* him bread 1Sa 22:13 5414
let it even be *g* unto the young 1Sa 25:27 5414
But Saul had *g* Michal his 1Sa 25:44 5414
g it to thy neighbour, even to 1Sa 28:17 5414
that which the LORD hath *g* us 1Sa 30:23 5414
g him a reward for his tidings 2Sa 4:10 5414
the LORD had *g* him rest round 2Sa 7:1 5117
I have *g* unto thy master's son 2Sa 9:9 5414
moreover have *g* unto thee such 2Sa 12:8 3254
g great occasion to the enemies 2Sa 12:14 5006
hath *g* is not good at this time 2Sa 17:7 3289
I would have *g* thee ten shekels 2Sa 18:11 5414
or hath he *g* us any gift 2Sa 19:42 5375
Thou hast also *g* me the shield of 2Sa 22:36 5414
Thou hast also *g* me the necks of 2Sa 22:41 5414
which hath *g* one to sit on my 1Kin 1:48 5414
Let Abishag the Shunammite be *g* 1Kin 2:21 5414
that thou hast *g* him a son to sit 1Kin 3:6 5414
I have *g* thee a wise and an 1Kin 3:12 5414
I have also *g* thee that which 1Kin 3:13 5414
God hath *g* me rest on every side 1Kin 5:4 5117
which hath *g* unto David a wise 1Kin 5:7 5414
which thou hast *g* to thy people 1Kin 8:36 5414
that hath *g* rest unto his people 1Kin 8:56 5414
of the land which I have *g* them 1Kin 9:7 5414
cities which Solomon had *g* him 1Kin 9:12 5414
are these which thou hast *g* me 1Kin 9:13 5414
g it for a present unto his 1Kin 9:16 5414
the old men, which they had *g* him 1Kin 12:8 3289
God had *g* by the word of the LORD 1Kin 13:5 5414
took the bullock which was *g* them 1Kin 18:26 5414
LORD had *g* deliverance unto Syria 2Kin 5:1 5414
be *g* to thy servant two mules' 2Kin 5:17 5414
the Syrians had *g* him at Ramah 2Kin 8:29 5221
which the Syrians had *g* him 2Kin 9:15 5221
kings of Judah had *g* to the sun 2Kin 23:11 5414
allowance *g* him of the king 2Kin 25:30 5414
his birthright was *g* unto the 1Chr 5:1 5414
were cities *g* out of the half 1Chr 6:61
the sons of Merari were *g* by lot 1Chr 6:63
g out of the family of the half 1Chr 6:71
g out of the tribe of Zebulun 1Chr 6:77
were *g* them out of the tribe of 1Chr 6:78
hath he not *g* you rest on every 1Chr 22:18 5117
for he hath *g* the inhabitants of 1Chr 22:18 5414
hath *g* rest unto his people 1Chr 23:25 5117
(for the LORD hath *g* me many sons 1Chr 28:5 5414
which I have *g* to the house of my 1Chr 29:3 5414
and of thine own have we *g* thee 1Chr 29:14 5414
who hath *g* to David the king a 2Chr 2:12 5414
which thou hast *g* unto thy people 2Chr 6:27 5414
of my land which I have *g* them 2Chr 7:20 5414
because the LORD had *g* him rest 2Chr 14:6 5117
he hath *g* us rest on every side 2Chr 14:7 5117
which thou hast *g* us to inherit 2Chr 20:11
wounds which were *g* him at Ramah 2Chr 22:6 5221
I have *g* to the army of Israel 2Chr 25:9 5414
for God had *g* him substance very 2Chr 32:29 5414
of the law of the LORD *g* by Moses 2Chr 34:14
the priest hath *g* me a book 2Chr 34:18 5414
hath the LORD God of heaven *g* me 2Chr 36:23 5414
hath *g* me all the kingdoms of the Ezr 1:2 5414
commandment shall be *g* from me Ezr 4:21 7761
let the expences be *g* out of the Ezr 6:4 3052
expences be *g* unto these men Ezr 6:8 3052
let it be *g* them day by day Ezr 6:9 3052
the LORD God of Israel had *g* Ezr 7:6 5414
The vessels also that are *g* thee Ezr 7:19 3052
hast *g* us such deliverance as Ezr 9:13 5414
let letters be *g* me to the Neh 2:7 5414
which was *g* by Moses the servant Neh 10:29 5414
commanded to be *g* to the Levites Neh 13:5
the Levites had not been *g* them Neh 13:10 5414
things for purification be *g* them Est 2:3 5414
which were meet to be *g* her Est 2:9 5414
whatsoever she desired was *g* her Est 2:13 5414
Haman, The silver is *g* to thee Est 3:11 5414
g in every province was published Est 3:14 5414
the decree was *g* in Shushan the Est 3:15 5414
was *g* at Shushan to destroy them Est 4:8 5414
it shall be even *g* thee to the Est 5:3 5414
let my life be *g* me at my Est 7:3 5414
I have *g* Esther the house of Est 8:7 5414
g in every province was published Est 8:13 5414
the decree was *g* at Shushan the Est 8:14 5414
and the decree was *g* at Shushan Est 9:14 5414
Wherefore is light *g* to him that Job 3:20 5414
Why is light *g* to a man whose way Job 3:23
The earth is *g* into the hand of Job 9:24 5414
Oh that I had *g* up the ghost Job 10:18 1478
Unto whom alone the earth was *g* Job 15:19 5414
Thou hast not *g* water to the Job 22:7 8248
Though it be *g* him to be in Job 24:23 5414
of the Almighty hath *g* me life Job 33:4 2421
Who hath *g* him a charge over the Job 34:13 6485
By the breath of God frost is *g* Job 37:10 5414
or who hath *g* understanding to Job 38:36 5414
Hath thou *g* the horse strength Job 39:19 5414
the LORD, who hath *g* me counsel Ps 16:7 3289
Thou hast also *g* me the shield of Ps 18:35 5414
Thou hast also *g* me the necks of Ps 18:40 5414
Thou hast *g* him his heart's Ps 21:2 5414
Thou hast *g* us like sheep Ps 44:11 5414
Thou hast *g* a banner to them that Ps 60:4 5414
thou hast *g* me the heritage of Ps 61:5 5414
thou hast *g* commandment to save Ps 71:3 6680

to him shall be *g* of the gold of Ps 72:15 5414
had *g* them of the corn of heaven Ps 78:24 5414
maidens were not *g* to marriage Ps 78:63 1984
of thy servants have they *g* to be Ps 79:2 5414
He hath *g* meat unto them that Ps 111:5 5414
dispersed, he hath *g* to the poor Ps 112:9 5414
but the earth hath he *g* to the Ps 115:16 5414
but he hath not *g* me over unto Ps 118:18 5414
What shall be *g* unto thee Ps 120:3 5414
who hath not *g* us as a prey to Ps 124:6 5414
that which he hath *g* will he pay Prov 19:17 1576
if thou be a man *g* to appetite Prov 23:2 1167
with them that are *g* to change Prov 24:21 8138
God *g* to the sons of man to be Eccl 1:13 5414
which God hath *g* to the sons of Eccl 3:10 5414
also to whom God hath *g* riches Eccl 5:19 5414
hath *g* him power to eat thereof, Eccl 5:19 7980
A man to whom God hath *g* riches Eccl 6:2 5414
deliver those that are *g* to it Eccl 8:8 1167
which he hath *g* thee under the Eccl 9:9 5414
which are *g* from one shepherd Eccl 12:11 5414
of his hands shall be *g* him Is 3:11 6213
the LORD hath *g* me are for signs Is 8:18 5414
child is born, unto us a son is *g* Is 9:6 5414
the LORD hath *g* a commandment Is 23:11 6680
bread shall be *g* him Is 33:16 5414
of Lebanon shall be *g* unto it Is 35:2 5414
Jerusalem shall not be *g* into the Is 37:10 5414
have *g* Jacob to the curse, and Is 43:28 5414
and *g* them into thine hand Is 47:6 5414
thou that art *g* to pleasures Is 47:8 5719
The Lord GOD hath *g* me the tongue Is 50:4 5414
I have *g* him for a witness to the Is 55:4 5414
away, and *g* her a bill of divorce Jer 3:8 5414
g for an inheritance unto your Jer 3:18
every one is *g* to covetousness Jer 6:13 1214
the greatest is *g* to covetousness Jer 8:10 1214
the things that I have *g* them Jer 8:13 5414
g us water of gall to drink Jer 8:14
the LORD hath *g* me knowledge of Jer 11:18
I have *g* the dearly beloved of my Jer 12:7 5414
is the flock that was *g* thee Jer 13:20 5414
she hath *g* up the ghost Jer 15:9 5301
it shall be *g* into the hand of Jer 21:10 5414
that the LORD hath *g* unto you Jer 25:5 5414
have *g* it unto whom it seemed Jer 27:5 5414
now have I *g* all these lands into Jer 27:6 5414
field have I *g* also to serve him Jer 27:6 5414
I have *g* him the beasts of the Jer 28:14 5414
hast *g* them this land, which thou Jer 32:22 5414
the city is *g* into the hand of Jer 32:24 5414
for the city is *g* into the hand Jer 32:25 5414
it is *g* into the hand of the Jer 32:43 5414
in the land which I have *g* to you Jer 35:15 5414
This city shall surely be *g* into Jer 38:3 5414
then shall this city be *g* into Jer 38:18 5414
thou shalt not be *g* into the hand Jer 39:17 5414
which had *g* him that answer Jer 44:20
seeing the LORD hath *g* it a Jer 47:7 6680
she hath *g* her hand Jer 50:15 5414
diet *g* him of the king of Babylon Jer 52:34 5414
they have *g* their pleasant things Lam 1:11 5414
he hath *g* up into the hand of the Lam 2:7 5462
We have *g* the hand to the Lam 5:6 5414
thou hast not *g* him warning Eze 3:20
I have *g* thee cow's dung for Eze 4:15 5414
us is this land *g* in possession Eze 11:15 5414
which I have *g* to the fire for Eze 15:6 5414
of my silver, which I had *g* thee Eze 16:17 5414
and no reward is *g* unto thee Eze 16:34 5414
he had *g* his hand, and hath done Eze 17:18 5414
hath *g* his bread to the hungry, Eze 18:7 5414
that hath not *g* forth upon usury Eze 18:8 5414
Hath *g* forth upon usury, and hath Eze 18:13 5414
but hath *g* his bread to the Eze 18:16 5414
into the land which I had *g* them Eze 20:15 5414
he hath *g* it to be furbished, Eze 21:11 5414
that I have *g* to my servant Jacob Eze 28:25 5414
I have *g* thee for meat to the Eze 29:5 5414
I have *g* him the land of Egypt Eze 29:20 5414
the land is *g* us for inheritance Eze 33:24 5414
they are *g* us to consume Eze 35:12 5414
I have *g* unto Jacob my servant Eze 37:25 5414
they shall be *g* to salt Eze 47:11 5414
hast *g* me wisdom and might Dan 2:23 3052
of heaven hath *g* thee a kingdom Dan 2:37 3052
heaven hath he *g* into thine hand Dan 2:38 3052
let a beast's heart be *g* unto him Dan 4:16 3052
g to the Medes and Persians Dan 5:28 3052
man, and a man's heart was *g* to it Dan 7:4 3052
and dominion was *g* to it Dan 7:6 3052
and *g* to the burning flame Dan 7:11 3052
there was *g* him dominion, and Dan 7:14 3052
judgment was *g* to the saints of Dan 7:22 3052
they shall be *g* into his hand Dan 7:25 3052
shall be *g* to the people of the Dan 7:27 3052
an host was *g* him against the Dan 8:12 5414
but she shall be *g* up, and they Dan 11:6 5414
shall be *g* into his hand Dan 11:11 5414
my flax *g* to cover her nakedness Hos 2:9
rewards that my lovers have *g* me Hos 2:12 5414
for he hath *g* you the former rain Joel 2:23 5414
have *g* a boy for an harlot, and Joel 3:3 5414
I also have *g* you cleanness of Amos 4:6 5414
of their land which I have *g* them Amos 9:15 5414
the LORD hath *g* a commandment Nah 1:14 6680
Ask, and it shall be *g* you Mt 7:7 *1325*
which had *g* such power unto men Mt 9:8 *1325*

for it shall be *g* you in that Mt 10:19 *1325*
and there shall no sign be *g* to it Mt 12:39 *1325*
Because it is *g* unto you to know Mt 13:11 *1325*
heaven, but to them it is not *g* Mt 13:11 *1325*
whosoever hath, to him shall be *g* Mt 13:12 *1325*
meat, he commanded it to be *g* her Mt 14:9 *1325*
in a charger, and *g* to the damsel Mt 14:11 *1325*
there shall no sign be *g* unto it Mt 16:4 *1325*
saying, save they to whom it is *g* Mt 19:11 *1325*
but it shall be *g* to them for Mt 20:23
g to a nation bringing forth the Mt 21:43 *1325*
nor are *g* in marriage, but are as Mt 22:30 *1547*
every one that hath shall be *g* Mt 25:29 *1325*
sold for much, and *g* to the poor Mt 26:9 *1325*
All power is *g* unto me in heaven Mt 28:18 *1325*
Unto you it is *g* to know the Mk 4:11 *1325*
you that hear shall more be *g* Mk 4:24 *4369*
he that hath, to him shall be *g* Mk 4:25 *1325*
something should be *g* her to eat Mk 5:43 *1325*
is this which is *g* unto him Mk 6:2 *1325*
no sign be *g* unto this generation Mk 8:12 *1325*
but it shall be *g* to them for Mk 10:40
marry, nor are *g* in marriage Mk 12:25
shall be *g* you in that hour Mk 13:11 *1325*
pence, and have been *g* to the poor Mk 14:5 *1325*
the cup, and when he had *g* thanks Mk 14:23 *2168*
betrayed him had *g* them a token Mk 14:44 *1325*
Give, and it shall be *g* unto you Lk 6:38 *1325*
Unto you it is *g* to know the Lk 8:10 *1325*
whosoever hath, to him shall be *g* Lk 8:18 *1325*
you, Ask, and it shall be *g* you Lk 11:9 *1325*
and there shall no sign be *g* it Lk 11:29 *1325*
For unto whomsoever much is *g* Lk 12:48 *1325*
they were *g* in marriage, until Lk 17:27
him, to whom he had *g* the money Lk 19:15 *1325*
every one which hath shall be *g* Lk 19:26 *1325*
world marry, and are *g* in marriage Lk 20:34
marry, nor are *g* in marriage Lk 20:35
is my body which is *g* for you Lk 22:19 *1325*
For the law was *g* by Moses Jn 1:17 *1325*
except it be *g* him from heaven Jn 3:27 *1325*
hath *g* all things into his hand Jn 3:35 *1325*
he would have *g* thee living water Jn 4:10 *1325*
so hath he *g* to the Son to have Jn 5:26 *1325*
hath *g* him authority to execute Jn 5:27 *1325*
the Father hath *g* me to finish Jn 5:36 *1325*
and when he had *g* thanks, he Jn 6:11 *2168*
after that the Lord had *g* thanks Jn 6:23 *2168*
hath *g* me I should lose nothing Jn 6:39 *1325*
except it were *g* unto him of my Jn 6:65 *1325*
for the Holy Ghost was not yet *g* Jn 7:39
the Pharisees had *g* a commandment Jn 11:57 *1325*
hundred pence, and *g* to the poor Jn 12:5 *1325*
had *g* all things into his hands Jn 13:3 *1325*
For I have *g* you an example, that Jn 13:15 *1325*
As thou hast *g* him power over all Jn 17:2 *1325*
to as many as thou hast *g* him Jn 17:2 *1325*
thou hast *g* me are of thee Jn 17:7 *1325*
For I have *g* unto them the words Jn 17:8 *1325*
but for them which thou hast *g* me Jn 17:9 *1325*
name those whom thou hast *g* me Jn 17:11 *1325*
I have *g* them thy word Jn 17:14 *1325*
thou gavest me I have *g* them Jn 17:22 *1325*
they also, whom thou hast *g* me Jn 17:24 *1325*
my glory, which thou hast *g* me Jn 17:24 *1325*
the cup which my Father hath *g* me Jn 18:11 *1325*
except it were *g* thee from above Jn 19:11 *1325*
he through the Holy Ghost had *g* Acts 1:2 *1781*
g him this perfect soundness in Acts 3:16 *1325*
name under heaven *g* among men Acts 4:12 *1325*
whom God hath *g* to them that obey Acts 5:32 *1325*
hands the Holy Ghost was *g* Acts 8:18 *1325*
saw the city wholly *g* to idolatry Acts 17:16
whereof he hath *g* assurance unto Acts 17:31 *3930*
had *g* them much exhortation, he Acts 20:2 *3870*
And when he had *g* him licence Acts 21:40 *2010*
should have been *g* him of Paul Acts 24:26 *1325*
God hath *g* thee all them that Acts 27:24 *5483*
the Holy Ghost which is *g* unto us Rom 5:5 *1325*
God hath *g* them the spirit of Rom 11:8 *1325*
Or who hath first *g* to him Rom 11:35 *4272*
say, through the grace *g* unto me Rom 12:3 *1325*
to the grace that is *g* to us Rom 12:6 *1325*
g to hospitality Rom 12:13 *1377*
the grace that is *g* to me of God Rom 15:15 *1325*
which is *g* you by Jesus Christ 1Cor 1:4 *1325*
that are freely *g* to us of God 1Cor 2:12 *5483*
grace of God which is *g* unto me 1Cor 3:10 *1325*
for her hair is *g* her for a 1Cor 11:15 *1325*
And when he had *g* thanks, he brake 1Cor 11:24 *2168*
g to every man to profit withal 1Cor 12:7 *1325*
For to one is *g* by the Spirit the 1Cor 12:8 *1325*
having *g* more abundant honour to 1Cor 12:24 *1325*
as I have *g* order to the churches 1Cor 16:1 *1299*
may be *g* by many on our behalf 2Cor 1:11 *2168*
g the earnest of the Spirit in 2Cor 1:22 *1325*
who also hath *g* unto us the 2Cor 5:5 *1325*
hath *g* to us the ministry of 2Cor 5:18 *1325*
he hath *g* to the poor 2Cor 9:9 *1325*
Lord hath *g* us for edification 2Cor 10:8 *1325*
there was *g* to me a thorn in the 2Cor 12:7 *1325*
the Lord hath *g* me to edification 2Cor 13:10 *1325*
the grace that was *g* unto me Gal 2:9 *1325*
if there had been a law *g* Gal 3:21 *1325*
which could have *g* life Gal 3:21 *2227*
might be *g* to them that believe Gal 3:22 *1325*
own eyes, and have *g* them to me Gal 4:15 *1325*
of God which is *g* me to you-ward Eph 3:2 *1325*

G

of God *g* unto me by the effectual ... Eph 3:7 *1325*
of all saints, is this grace *g* ... Eph 3:8 *1325*
But unto every one of us is *g* ... Eph 4:7 *1325*
have *g* themselves over unto ... Eph 4:19 *3860*
hath *g* himself for us an offering ... Eph 5:2 *3860*
that utterance may be *g* unto me ... Eph 6:19 *1325*
For unto you it is *g* in the ... Phil 1:29 *5483*
g him a name which is above every ... Phil 2:9 *5483*
of God which is *g* to me for you ... Col 1:25 *1325*
who hath also *g* unto us his holy ... 1Th 4:8 *1325*
hath *g* us everlasting consolation ... 2Th 2:16 *1325*
g to hospitality, apt to teach ... 1Ti 3:2
Not *g* to wine, no striker, not ... 1Ti 3:3 *3943*
not *g* to much wine, not greedy of ... 1Ti 3:8 *4337*
which was *g* thee by prophecy, ... 1Ti 4:14 *1325*
For God hath not *g* us the spirit ... 2Ti 1:7 *1325*
which was *g* us in Christ Jesus ... 2Ti 1:9 *1325*
All scripture is *g* by inspiration ... 2Ti 3:16
not soon angry, not *g* to wine ... Titus 1:7 *3943*
not *g* to filthy lucre ... Titus 1:7
not *g* to much wine, teachers of ... Titus 2:3 *1402*
prayers I shall be *g* unto you ... Philem 22 *5483*
the children which God hath *g* me ... Heb 2:13 *1325*
For if Jesus had *g* them rest ... Heb 4:8 *2664*
and it shall be *g* him ... Jas 1:5 *1325*
as his divine power hath *g* unto ... 2Pet 1:3 *1433*
Whereby are *g* unto us exceeding ... 2Pet 1:4 *1433*
also according to the wisdom *g* ... 2Pet 3:15 *1325*
by the Spirit which he hath *g* us ... 1Jn 3:24 *1325*
because he hath *g* us of his ... 1Jn 4:13 *1325*
that God hath *g* to us eternal ... 1Jn 5:11 *1325*
hath *g* us an understanding, that ... 1Jn 5:20 *1325*
and a crown was *g* unto him ... Rev 6:2 *1325*
power was *g* to him that sat ... Rev 6:4 *1325*
there was *g* unto him a great ... Rev 6:4 *1325*
power was *g* unto them over the ... Rev 6:8 *1325*
white robes were *g* unto every one ... Rev 6:11 *1325*
to whom it was *g* to hurt the ... Rev 7:2 *1325*
to them were *g* seven trumpets ... Rev 8:2 *1325*
there was *g* unto him much incense ... Rev 8:3 *1325*
to him was *g* the key of the ... Rev 9:1 *1325*
and unto them was *g* power, as the ... Rev 9:3 *1325*
to them it was *g* that they should ... Rev 9:5 *1325*
there was *g* me a reed like unto a ... Rev 11:1 *1325*
for it is *g* unto the Gentiles ... Rev 11:2 *1325*
to the woman were *g* two wings of ... Rev 12:14 *1325*
there was *g* unto him a mouth ... Rev 13:5 *1325*
power was *g* unto him to continue ... Rev 13:5 *1325*
it was *g* unto him to make war ... Rev 13:7 *1325*
power was *g* him over all kindreds ... Rev 13:7 *1325*
thou hast *g* them blood to drink ... Rev 16:6 *1325*
power was *g* unto him to scorch ... Rev 16:8 *1325*
them, and judgment was *g* unto them ... Rev 20:4 *1325*

GIVER {2}
so with the *g* of usury to him ... Is 24:2
for God loveth a cheerful *g* ... 2Cor 9:7 *1395*

GIVEST {12}
brother, and thou *g* him nought ... Deut 15:9 5414
be grieved when thou *g* unto him ... Deut 15:10 5414
be righteous, what *g* thou him ... Job 35:7 5414
Thou *g* thy mouth to evil, and thy ... Ps 50:19 7971
g them tears to drink in great ... Ps 80:5
That thou *g* them they gather ... Ps 104:28 5414
thou *g* them their meat in due ... Ps 145:15 5414
content, though thou *g* many gifts ... Prov 6:35
thou *g* him not warning, nor ... Eze 3:18
but thou *g* thy gifts to all thy ... Eze 16:33 5414
and in that thou *g* a reward ... Eze 16:34 5414
For thou verily *g* thanks well ... 1Cor 14:17

GIVETH {126}
he *g* goodly words ... Gen 49:21 5414
therefore he *g* you on the sixth ... Ex 16:29 5414
which the LORD thy God *g* thee ... Ex 20:12 5414
of every man that *g* it willingly ... Ex 25:2 5068
that *g* any of his seed unto ... Lev 20:2 5414
when he *g* of his seed unto Molech ... Lev 20:4 5414
all that any man *g* of such unto ... Lev 27:9 5414
whatsoever any man *g* the priest ... Num 5:10 5414
land which the LORD our God *g* us ... Deut 2:29 5414
LORD God of your fathers *g* you ... Deut 4:1 5414
which the LORD thy God *g* thee for ... Deut 4:21 5414
which the LORD thy God *g* thee ... Deut 4:40 5414
which the LORD thy God *g* thee ... Deut 5:16 5414
for it is he that *g* thee power to ... Deut 8:18 5414
that the LORD thy God *g* thee not ... Deut 9:6 5414
good land which the LORD *g* you ... Deut 11:17 5414
which the LORD your God *g* you ... Deut 11:31 5414
thy fathers *g* thee to possess it ... Deut 12:1 5414
which the LORD your God *g* you ... Deut 12:9 5414
LORD your God *g* you to inherit ... Deut 12:10
when he *g* you rest from all your ... Deut 12:10
g thee a sign or a wonder, ... Deut 13:1 5414
God *g* thee for an inheritance to ... Deut 15:4 5414
which the LORD thy God *g* thee ... Deut 15:7 5414
which the LORD thy God *g* thee ... Deut 16:5 5414
which the LORD thy God *g* thee ... Deut 16:18 5414
which the LORD thy God *g* thee ... Deut 16:20 5414
which the LORD thy God *g* thee ... Deut 17:2 5414
which the LORD thy God *g* thee ... Deut 17:14 5414
which the LORD thy God *g* thee ... Deut 18:9 5414
land the LORD thy God *g* thee ... Deut 19:1 5414
LORD thy God *g* thee to possess it ... Deut 19:2 5414
LORD thy God *g* thee to inherit ... Deut 19:3
which the LORD thy God *g* thee for ... Deut 19:10 5414
LORD thy God *g* thee to possess it ... Deut 19:14 5414
LORD thy God *g* thee to possess it ... Deut 21:1 5414
which the LORD thy God *g* thee for ... Deut 21:23 5414
g it in her hand, and sendeth her ... Deut 24:3 5414
which the LORD thy God *g* thee for ... Deut 24:4 5414
which the LORD thy God *g* thee ... Deut 25:15 5414
God *g* thee for an inheritance to ... Deut 25:19 5414
thy God *g* thee for an inheritance ... Deut 26:1 5414
land that the LORD thy God *g* thee ... Deut 26:2 5414
which the LORD thy God *g* thee ... Deut 27:2 5414
which the LORD thy God *g* thee ... Deut 27:3 5414
which the LORD thy God *g* thee ... Deut 28:8 5414
LORD your God *g* you to possess it ... Josh 1:11 5414
which the LORD your God *g* them ... Josh 1:15 5414
Chemosh thy god *g* thee to possess ... Judg 11:24
Cursed be he that *g* a wife to ... Judg 21:18 5414
Who *g* rain upon the earth, and ... Job 5:10 5414
man *g* up the ghost, and where is ... Job 14:10 1478
the Almighty *g* them understanding ... Job 32:8
for he *g* not account of any of ... Job 33:13 6030
When he *g* quietness, who then can ... Job 34:29 8252
maker, who *g* songs in the night ... Job 35:10 5414
There they cry, but none *g* answer ... Job 35:12
but *g* right to the poor ... Job 36:6 5414
he *g* meat in abundance ... Job 36:31 5414
deliverance *g* he to his king ... Ps 18:50
the righteous sheweth mercy, and *g* ... Ps 37:21 5414
of Israel is he that *g* strength ... Ps 68:35 5414
The entrance of thy words *g* light ... Ps 119:130
it *g* understanding unto the ... Ps 119:130
for so he *g* his beloved sleep ... Ps 127:2 5414
Who *g* food to all flesh ... Ps 136:25 5414
It is he that *g* salvation unto ... Ps 144:10 5414
which *g* food to the hungry ... Ps 146:7 5414
He *g* to the beast his food, and to ... Ps 147:9 5414
He *g* snow like wool ... Ps 147:16 5414
For the LORD *g* wisdom ... Prov 2:6 5414
but he *g* grace unto the lowly ... Prov 3:34 5414
Good understanding *g* favour ... Prov 13:15 5414
A wicked doer *g* heed to false ... Prov 17:4
a liar *g* ear to a naughty tongue ... Prov 17:4
is a friend to him that *g* gifts ... Prov 19:6
but the righteous *g* and spareth ... Prov 21:26 5414
for he *g* of his bread to the poor ... Prov 22:9 5414
he that *g* to the rich, shall ... Prov 22:16 5414
when it *g* his colour in the cup, ... Prov 23:31 5414
his lips that *g* a right answer ... Prov 24:26 7725
so is he that *g* honour to a fool ... Prov 26:8 5414
He that *g* unto the poor shall not ... Prov 28:27 5414
g meat to her household, and a ... Prov 31:15 5414
For God *g* to a man that is good ... Eccl 2:26 5414
but to the sinner he *g* travail ... Eccl 2:26 5414
days of his life, which God *g* him ... Eccl 5:18 5414
yet God *g* him not power to eat ... Eccl 6:2
that wisdom *g* life to them that ... Eccl 7:12
which God *g* him under the sun ... Eccl 8:15 5414
He *g* power to the faint ... Is 40:29 5414
he that *g* breath unto the people ... Is 42:5 5414
the LORD our God, that *g* rain ... Jer 5:24 5414
wages, and *g* him not for his work ... Jer 22:13 5414
which *g* the sun for a light by ... Jer 31:35 5414
He *g* his cheek to him that ... Lam 3:30 5414
he *g* wisdom unto the wise, and ... Dan 2:21 3052
g it to whomsoever he will, and ... Dan 4:17 5415
g it to whomsoever he will ... Dan 4:25 5415
g it to whomsoever he will ... Dan 4:32 5415
Woe unto him that *g* his neighbour ... Hab 2:15
it *g* light unto all that are in ... Mt 5:15 *2989*
for God *g* not the Spirit by ... Jn 3:34 *1325*
but my Father *g* you the true ... Jn 6:32 *1325*
heaven, and *g* life unto the world ... Jn 6:33 *1325*
the Father *g* me shall come to me ... Jn 6:37 *1325*
the good shepherd *g* his life for ... Jn 10:11 *5087*
not as the world *g*, give I unto ... Jn 14:27 *1325*
and *g* them, and fish likewise ... Jn 21:13 *1325*
seeing he *g* to all life, and ... Acts 17:25 *1325*
he that *g*, let him do it with ... Rom 12:8 *3330*
to the Lord, for he *g* God thanks ... Rom 14:6 *2168*
he eateth not, and *g* God thanks ... Rom 14:6 *2168*
but God that *g* the increase ... 1Cor 3:7 *837*
So then he that *g* her in marriage ... 1Cor 7:38 *1547*
but he that *g* her not in marriage ... 1Cor 7:38 *1547*
But God *g* it a body as it hath ... 1Cor 15:38 *1325*
which *g* us the victory through ... 1Cor 15:57 *1325*
killeth, but the spirit *g* life ... 2Cor 3:6 *2226*
who *g* us richly all things to ... 1Ti 6:17 *3930*
that *g* to all men liberally, and ... Jas 1:5 *1325*
But he *g* more grace ... Jas 4:6 *1325*
but *g* grace unto the humble ... Jas 4:6 *1325*
it as of the ability which God *g* ... 1Pet 4:11 *5524*
proud, and *g* grace to the humble ... 1Pet 5:5 *1325*
for the Lord God *g* them light ... Rev 22:5 *5461*

GIVING {29}
And when she had done *g* him drink ... Gen 24:19
in *g* him food and raiment ... Deut 10:18 5414
by *g* him a double portion of all ... Deut 21:17 5414
his people in *g* them bread ... Ruth 1:6 5414
in *g* food for my household ... 1Kin 5:9 5414
by *g* him according to his ... 2Chr 6:23 5414
and *g* thanks unto the LORD ... Ezr 3:11
shall be as the *g* up of the ghost ... Job 11:20 4646
g in marriage, until the day that ... Mt 24:38
face at his feet, *g* him thanks ... Lk 17:16
g out that himself was some great ... Acts 8:9 *3004*
g them the Holy Ghost, even as he ... Acts 15:8 *1325*
strong in faith, *g* glory to God ... Rom 4:20
the *g* of the law, and the service ... Rom 9:4 *3548*
even things without life *g* sound ... 1Cor 14:7 *1325*
say Amen at thy *g* of thanks ... 1Cor 14:16
G no offence in any thing, that ... 2Cor 6:3 *1325*
but rather *g* of thanks ... Eph 5:4
G thanks always for all things ... Eph 5:20
with me as concerning *g* and ... Phil 4:15 *1394*
G thanks unto the Father, which ... Col 1:12
g thanks to God and the Father by ... Col 3:17
g of thanks, be made for all men ... 1Ti 2:1
g heed to seducing spirits, and ... 1Ti 4:1
Not *g* heed to Jewish fables, and ... Titus 1:14
of our lips *g* thanks to his name ... Heb 13:15
g honour unto the wife, as unto ... 1Pet 3:7 *632*
g all diligence, add to your ... 2Pet 1:5 *3923*
g themselves over to fornication, ... Jude 7

GIZONITE *(ghi'-zo-nite)* {1} *A bodyguard of David.*
The sons of Hashem the *G*, ... 1Chr 11:34 1493

GLAD {89}
he will be *g* in his heart ... Ex 4:14 8056
And the priest's heart was *g* ... Judg 18:20 8190
and they were *g* ... 1Sa 11:9 8056
g of heart for all the goodness ... 1Kin 8:66 2896
Let the heavens be *g*, and let the ... 1Chr 16:31 8056
people away into their tents, *g* ... 2Chr 7:10 8056
that day joyful and with a *g* heart ... Est 5:9 2896
city of Shushan rejoiced and was *g* ... Est 8:15 8056
rejoice exceedingly, and are *g* ... Job 3:22 7797
The righteous see it, and are *g* ... Job 22:19 8056
I will be *g* and rejoice in thee ... Ps 9:2 8056
rejoice, and Israel shall be *g* ... Ps 14:7 8056
Therefore my heart is *g*, and my ... Ps 16:9 8056
exceeding *g* with thy countenance ... Ps 21:6 2302
I will be *g* and rejoice in thy ... Ps 31:7 1523
Be *g* in the LORD, and rejoice, ye ... Ps 32:11 8056
shall hear thereof, and be *g* ... Ps 34:2 8056
Let them shout for joy, and be *g* ... Ps 35:27 8056
seek thee rejoice and be *g* in thee ... Ps 40:16 8056
whereby they have made thee *g* ... Ps 45:8 8056
shall make *g* the city of God ... Ps 46:4 8056
let the daughters of Judah be *g* ... Ps 48:11 1528
rejoice, and Israel shall be *g* ... Ps 53:6 8056
righteous shall be *g* in the LORD ... Ps 64:10 8056
O let the nations be *g* and sing ... Ps 67:4 8056
But let the righteous be *g* ... Ps 68:3 8056
humble shall see this, and be *g* ... Ps 69:32 8056
seek thee rejoice and be *g* in thee ... Ps 70:4 8056
may rejoice and be *g* all our days ... Ps 90:14 8056
Make us *g* according to the days ... Ps 90:15 8056
hast made me *g* through thy work ... Ps 92:4 8056
rejoice, and let the earth be *g* ... Ps 96:11 1523
multitude of isles be *g* thereof ... Ps 97:1 8056
Zion heard, and was *g* ... Ps 97:8 8056
that maketh *g* the heart of man ... Ps 104:15 8056
I will be *g* in the LORD ... Ps 104:34 8056
Egypt was *g* when they departed ... Ps 105:38 8056
Then are they *g* because they be ... Ps 107:30 8056
we will rejoice and be *g* in it ... Ps 118:24 8056
thee will be *g* when they see me ... Ps 119:74 8056
I was *g* when they said unto me, ... Ps 122:1 8056
whereof we are *g* ... Ps 126:3 8056
A wise son maketh a *g* father ... Prov 10:1 8056
but a good word maketh it *g* ... Prov 12:25 8056
A wise son maketh a *g* father ... Prov 15:20 8056
he that is *g* at calamities shall ... Prov 17:5 8056
father and thy mother shall be *g* ... Prov 23:25 8056
heart be *g* when he stumbleth ... Prov 24:17 1523
son, be wise, and make my heart *g* ... Prov 27:11 8056
we will be *g* and rejoice in thee, ... Song 1:4 1528
have waited for him, we will be *g* ... Is 25:9 1528
place shall be *g* for them ... Is 35:1 7996
And Hezekiah was *g* of them ... Is 39:2 8056
But be ye *g* and rejoice for ever ... Is 65:18 7796
be *g* with her, all ye that love ... Is 66:10 1528
making him very *g* ... Jer 20:15 8056
were with him, then they were *g* ... Jer 41:13 8056
Because ye were *g*, because ye ... Jer 50:11 8056
they are *g* that thou hast done it ... Lam 1:21 7796
Rejoice and be *g*, O daughter of ... Lam 4:21 8056
was the king exceeding *g* for him ... Dan 6:23 2868
They make the king *g* with their ... Hos 7:3 8056
be *g* and rejoice ... Joel 2:21 1523
Be *g* then, ye children of Zion, ... Joel 2:23 1523
was exceeding *g* of the gourd ... Jonah 4:6 8056
therefore they rejoice and are *g* ... Hab 1:15 1523
be *g* and rejoice with all the ... Zeph 3:14 8056
children shall see it, and be *g* ... Zec 10:7 8056
Rejoice, and be exceeding *g* ... Mt 5:12 *21*
when they heard it, they were *g* ... Mk 14:11 *5463*
and to shew thee these *g* tidings ... Lk 1:19 *2097*
shewing the *g* tidings of the ... Lk 8:1 *2097*
we should make merry, and be *g* ... Lk 15:32 *5463*
And they were *g*, and covenanted to ... Lk 22:5 *5463*
saw Jesus, he was exceeding *g* ... Lk 23:8 *5463*
and he saw it, and was *g* ... Jn 8:56 *5463*
I am *g* for your sakes that I was ... Jn 11:15 *5463*
Then were the disciples *g* ... Jn 20:20 *5463*
heart rejoice, and my tongue was *g* ... Acts 2:26 *21*
had seen the grace of God, was *g* ... Acts 11:23 *5463*
And we declare unto you *g* tidings ... Acts 13:32 *2097*
Gentiles heard this, they were *g* ... Acts 13:48 *5463*
bring *g* tidings of good things ... Rom 10:15 *2097*
I am *g* therefore on your behalf ... Rom 16:19 *5463*
I am *g* of the coming of Stephanas ... 1Cor 16:17 *5463*
who is he then that maketh me *g* ... 2Cor 2:2 *2165*
For we are *g*, when we are weak, ... 2Cor 13:9 *5463*
ye may be *g* also with exceeding ... 1Pet 4:13 *5463*
Let us be *g* and rejoice, and give ... Rev 19:7 *5463*

GLADLY {8}
did many things, and heard him *g* .... Mk 6:20 2234
And the common people heard him *g* .... Mk 12:37 2234
the people *g* received him.......................... Lk 8:40
Then they that *g* received his .... Acts 2:41 780
the brethren received us *g* .... Acts 21:17 780
For ye suffer fools *g*, seeing ye 2Cor 11:19 2234
Most *g* therefore will I rather..................... 2Cor 12:9 2236
And I will very *g* spend and be 2Cor 12:15 2236

GLADNESS {47}
Also in the day of your *g*............................ Num 10:10 8057
and with *g* of heart, for the........................ Deut 28:47 2898
into the city of David with *g*........................ 2Sa 6:12 8057
strength and *g* are in his place.................. 1Chr 16:27 2304
the LORD on that day with great *g*......... 1Chr 29:22 8057
And they sang praises with *g*.................... 2Chr 29:30 8057
bread seven days with great *g*................... 2Chr 30:21 8057
they kept other seven days with *g*........... 2Chr 30:23 8057
And there was very great *g* .... Neh 8:17 8057
to keep the dedication with *g*.................... Neh 12:27 8057
The Jews had light, and *g*, and joy, ... Est 8:16 8057
came, the Jews had joy and *g* .... Est 8:17 8342
and made it a day of feasting and *g*........ Est 9:17 8057
and made it a day of feasting and *g*........ Est 9:18 8057
day of the month Adar a day of *g* .... Est 9:19 8057
Thou hast put *g* in my heart....................... Ps 4:7 8057
my sackcloth, and girded me with *g* .... Ps 30:11 8057
the oil of *g* above thy fellows .... Ps 45:7 8342
With *g* and rejoicing shall they be .... Ps 45:15 8057
Make me to hear joy and *g*......................... Ps 51:8 8057
g for the upright in heart........................... Ps 97:11 8057
Serve the LORD with *g*................................ Ps 100:2 8057
with joy, and his chosen with *g* .... Ps 105:43 7440
rejoice in the *g* of thy nation.................... Ps 106:5 8057
hope of the righteous shall be *g* .... Prov 10:28 8057
in the day of the *g* of his heart................. Song 3:11 8057
g is taken away, and joy out of................. Is 16:10 8057
And behold joy and *g*, slaying oxen, ... Is 22:13 8057
g of heart, as when one goeth................... Is 30:29 8057
they shall obtain joy and *g*......................... Is 35:10 8057
g shall be found therein,............................ Is 51:3 8057
they shall obtain *g* and joy......................... Is 51:11 8057
voice of mirth, and the voice of *g*............ Jer 7:34 8057
voice of mirth, and the voice of *g*............ Jer 16:9 8057
voice of mirth, and the voice of *g*............ Jer 25:10 8057
Sing with *g* for Jacob, and shout .... Jer 31:7 8057
voice of joy, and the voice of *g* .... Jer 33:11 8057
g is taken from the plentiful .... Jer 48:33 8057
g from the house of our God .... Joel 1:16 1524
be to the house of Judah joy and *g*........... Zec 8:19 8057
immediately receive it with *g*..................... Mk 4:16 5479
And thou shalt have joy and *g* .... Lk 1:14 20
house, did eat their meat with *g* .... Acts 2:46 20
she opened not the gate for *g*.................... Acts 12:14 5479
filling our hearts with food and *g*.............. Acts 14:17 2167
therefore in the Lord with all *g*................. Phil 2:29 5479
the oil of *g* above thy fellows .... Heb 1:9 20

GLASS {9}
strong, and as a molten looking *g*............ Job 37:18 7209
For now we see through a *g*...................... 1Cor 13:12 2072
as in a *g* the glory of the Lord.................. 2Cor 3:18 2734
beholding his natural face in a *g* .... Jas 1:23 2072
was a sea of *g* like unto crystal................. Rev 4:6 5193
were a sea of *g* mingled with fire............... Rev 15:2 5193
his name, stand on the sea of *g*................ Rev 15:2 5193
was pure gold, like unto clear *g* .... Rev 21:18 5194
gold, as it were transparent *g*.................. Rev 21:21 5194

GLASSES {1}
The *g*, and the fine linen, and the .... Is 3:23 1549

GLEAN {10}
And thou shalt not *g* thy vineyard .... Lev 19:10 5953
thou shalt not *g* it afterward.................... Deut 24:21 5953
g ears of corn after him in whose............ Ruth 2:2 3950
And she said, I pray you, let me *g*........... Ruth 2:7 3950
Go not to *g* in another field,...................... Ruth 2:8 3950
And when she was risen up to *g* .... Ruth 2:15 3950
Let her *g* even among the sheaves,........... Ruth 2:15 3950
leave them, that she may *g* them............... Ruth 2:16 3950
g unto the end of barley harvest .... Ruth 2:23 3950
They shall throughly *g* the .... Jer 6:9 5953

GLEANED {6}
they *g* of them in the highways.............. Judg 20:45 5953
g in the field after the reapers .... Ruth 2:3 3950
So she *g* in the field until even,............... Ruth 2:17 3950
even, and beat out that she had *g*........... Ruth 2:17 3950
mother in law saw what she had *g*........... Ruth 2:18 3950
her, Where hast thou *g* to day .... Ruth 2:19 3950

GLEANING {5}
thou gather any *g* of thy harvest .... Lev 23:22 3951
Is not the *g* of the grapes of .... Judg 8:2 5955
Yet *g* grapes shall be left in it,................ Is 17:6 5955
as the *g* grapes when the vintage............ Is 24:13 5955
they not leave some *g* grapes.................. Jer 49:9 5955

GLEANINGS {1}
thou gather the *g* of thy harvest............. Lev 19:9 3951

GLEDE {1}
And the *g*, and the kite, and the .... Deut 14:13 7201

GLISTERING {2}
g stones, and of divers colours, ... 1Chr 29:2 6320
and his raiment was white and *g* .... Lk 9:29 1823

GLITTER {1}
it is furbished that it may *g* .... Eze 21:10 1300

GLITTERING {6}
If I whet my *g* sword, and mine .... Deut 32:41 1300
the *g* sword cometh out of his................... Job 20:25 1300
the *g* spear and the shield .... Job 39:23 3851
to consume because of the *g*..................... Eze 21:28 1300
the bright sword and the *g* spear .... Nah 3:3 1300
and at the shining of thy *g* spear .... Hab 3:11 1300

GLOOMINESS {2}
A day of darkness and of *g*....................... Joel 2:2 653
a day of darkness and *g*, a day of............ Zeph 1:15 653

GLORIEST {1}
Wherefore *g* thou in the valleys,............... Jer 49:4 1984

GLORIETH {3}
But let him that *g* glory in this .... Jer 9:24 1984
as it is written, He that *g* 1Cor 1:31 2744
But he that *g*, let him glory in.................. 2Cor 10:17 2744

GLORIFIED {51}
before all the people I will be *g* .... Lev 10:3 3513
thou art *g*... Is 26:15 3513
Jacob, and *g* himself in Israel.................... Is 44:23 6286
O Israel, in whom I will be *g*..................... Is 49:3 6286
for he hath *g* thee .... Is 55:5 6286
of Israel, because he hath *g* thee.............. Is 60:9 6286
work of my hands, that I may be *g* .... Is 60:21 6286
of the LORD, that he might be *g* .... Is 61:3 6286
sake, said, Let the LORD be *g*................... Is 66:5 3513
I will be *g* in the midst of thee................. Eze 28:22 3513
renown the day that I shall be *g* .... Eze 39:13 3513
are all thy ways, hast thou not *g*.............. Dan 5:23 1922
pleasure in it, and I will be *g* .... Hag 1:8 3513
g God, which had given such power........ Mt 9:8 1392
and they *g* the God of Israel..................... Mt 15:31 1392
g God, saying, We never saw it on........... Mk 2:12 1392
their synagogues, being *g* of all............... Lk 4:15 1392
were all amazed, and they *g* God............ Lk 5:26 1392
and they *g* God, saying, That a .... Lk 7:16 1392
she was made straight, and *g* God .... Lk 13:13 1392
back, and with a loud voice *g* God.......... Lk 17:15 1392
he *g* God, saying, Certainly this.............. Lk 23:47 1392
because that Jesus was not yet *g*............ Jn 7:39 1392
the Son of God might be *g* thereby .... Jn 11:4 1392
but when Jesus was *g*, then .... Jn 12:16 1392
that the Son of man should be *g*.............. Jn 12:23 1392
heaven, saying, I have both *g* it............... Jn 12:28 1392
said, Now is the Son of man *g* .... Jn 13:31 1392
man *g*, and God is *g* in him.................... Jn 13:31 1392
If God be *g* in him, God shall................... Jn 13:32 1392
the Father may be *g* in the Son .... Jn 14:13 1392
Herein is my Father *g*, that ye.................. Jn 15:8 1392
I have *g* thee on the earth....................... Jn 17:4 1392
and I am *g* in them .... Jn 17:10 1392
our fathers, hath *g* his Son Jesus .... Acts 3:13 1392
for all men *g* God for that which .... Acts 4:21 1392
g God, saying, Then hath God also .... Acts 11:18 1392
glad, and *g* the word of the Lord .... Acts 13:48 1392
they *g* the Lord, and said unto him......... Acts 21:20 1392
they *g* him not as God, neither................ Rom 1:21 1392
that we may be also *g* together .... Rom 8:17 4888
whom he justified, them he also *g*.......... Rom 8:30 1392
And they *g* God in me .... Gal 1:24 1392
shall come to be *g* in his saints 2Th 1:10 1740
Lord Jesus Christ may be *g* in you 2Th 1:12 1740
may have free course, and be *g* 2Th 3:1 1392
So also Christ *g* not himself to................. Heb 5:5 1392
may be *g* through Jesus Christ 1Pet 4:11 1392
of, but on your part he is *g*....................... 1Pet 4:14 1392
How much she hath *g* herself.................. Rev 18:7 1392

GLORIFIETH {1}
Whoso offereth praise *g* me .... Ps 50:23 3513

GLORIFY {25}
all ye the seed of Jacob, *g* him................. Ps 22:23 3513
deliver thee, and thou shalt *g* me........... Ps 50:15 3513
and shall *g* thy name .... Ps 86:9 3513
I will *g* thy name for evermore .... Ps 86:12 3513
Wherefore *g* ye the LORD in the .... Is 24:15 3513
shall the strong people *g* thee .... Is 25:3 3513
I will *g* the house of my glory.................. Is 60:7 6286
I will also *g* them, and they shall............ Jer 30:19 3513
g your Father which is in heaven .... Mt 5:16 1392
Father, *g* thy name..................................... Jn 12:28 1392
glorified it, and will *g* it again................. Jn 12:28 1392
God shall also *g* him in himself .... Jn 13:32 1392
and shall straightway *g* him..................... Jn 13:32 1392
He shall *g* me.. Jn 16:14 1392
the hour is come; *g* thy Son...................... Jn 17:1 1392
that thy Son also may *g* thee.................... Jn 17:1 1392
g thou me with thine own self.................. Jn 17:5 1392
by what death he should *g* God .... Jn 21:19 1392
with one mind and one mouth *g* God...... Rom 15:6 1392
might *g* God for his mercy .... Rom 15:9 1392
therefore *g* God in your body, and.......... 1Cor 6:20 1392
they *g* God for your professed 2Cor 9:13 1392
g God in the day of visitation 1Pet 2:12 1392
but let him *g* God on this behalf.............. 1Pet 4:16 1392
fear thee, O Lord, and *g* thy name .... Rev 15:4 1392

GLORIFYING {3}
And the shepherds returned, *g*................. Lk 2:20 1392
departed to his own house, *g* God.......... Lk 5:25 1392
his sight, and followed him, *g* God .... Lk 18:43 1392

GLORIOUS {45}
O LORD, is become *g* in power................. Ex 15:6 142
g in holiness, fearful in praises .... Ex 15:11 142
that thou mayest fear this *g* .... Deut 28:58 3513
How *g* was the king of Israel.................... 2Sa 6:20 3513
thank thee, and praise thy *g* name.......... 1Chr 29:13 8597
and blessed be thy *g* name, which........... Neh 9:5 3519
the riches of his *g* kingdom .... Est 1:4 3519
king's daughter is all *g* within.................. Ps 45:13 3520
make his praise *g*....................................... Ps 66:2 3519
And blessed be his *g* name for ever......... Ps 72:19 3519
Thou art more *g* and excellent than......... Ps 76:4 215
G things are spoken of thee, O................. Ps 87:3 3513
His work is honourable and *g* .... Ps 111:3 1926
I will speak of the *g* honour of................. Ps 145:5 3519
the *g* majesty of his kingdom .... Ps 145:12 3519
of the LORD be beautiful and *g*............... Is 4:2 3519
and his rest shall be *g*............................... Is 11:10 3519
he shall be for a *g* throne to his .... Is 22:23 3519
whose *g* beauty is a fading flower........... Is 28:1 6643
the *g* beauty, which is on the.................... Is 28:4 6643
cause his *g* voice to be heard.................. Is 30:30 1935
But there the *g* LORD will be unto .... Is 33:21 117
yet shall I be *g* in the eyes of.................... Is 49:5 3513
will make the place of my feet *g*............. Is 60:13 3513
this that is *g* in his apparel, ... Is 63:1 1921
hand of Moses with his *g* arm.................. Is 63:12 8597
people, to make thyself a *g* name .... Is 63:14 8597
A *g* high throne from the.......................... Jer 17:12 3519
made very *g* in the midst of the .... Eze 27:25 3519
and he shall stand in the *g* land.............. Dan 11:16 6643
shall enter also into the *g* land................ Dan 11:41 6643
the seas in the *g* holy mountain .... Dan 11:45 6643
g things that were done by him............... Lk 13:17 1741
g liberty of the children of God .... Rom 8:21 1391
and engraven in stones, was *g*......... 2Cor 3:7 1722,1391
of the spirit be rather *g* 2Cor 3:8 1722,1391
g had no glory in this respect.................. 2Cor 3:10 1392
if that which is done away was *g* 2Cor 3:11 1223,1391
more that which remaineth is *g*....... 2Cor 3:11 1722,1391
light of the *g* gospel of Christ 2Cor 4:4 1391
present it to himself a *g* church............... Eph 5:27 1741
be fashioned like unto his *g* body .... Phil 3:21 1391
might, according to his *g* power.............. Col 1:11 1391
According to the *g* gospel of the 1Ti 1:11 1391
the *g* appearing of the great God .... Titus 2:13 1391

GLORIOUSLY {3}
the LORD, for he hath triumphed *g* .... Ex 15:1
the LORD, for he hath triumphed *g* .... Ex 15:21
and before his ancients *g*......................... Is 24:23 3519

GLORY {402}
hath he gotten all this *g* .... Gen 31:1 3519
my father of all my *g* in Egypt .... Gen 45:13 3519
said unto Pharaoh, *G* over me.................. Ex 8:9 6286
ye shall see the *g* of the LORD .... Ex 16:7 3519
the *g* of the LORD appeared in the .... Ex 16:10 3519
the *g* of the LORD abode upon................. Ex 24:16 3519
the sight of the *g* of the LORD .... Ex 24:17 3519
for Aaron thy brother for *g* .... Ex 28:2 3519
shalt thou make for them, for *g* .... Ex 28:40 3519
shall be sanctified by my *g*...................... Ex 29:43 3519
I beseech thee, shew me thy *g* .... Ex 33:18 3519
while my *g* passeth by, that I.................. Ex 33:22 3519
the *g* of the LORD filled the..................... Ex 40:34 3519
the *g* of the LORD filled the..................... Ex 40:35 3519
the *g* of the LORD shall appear................ Lev 9:6 3519
the *g* of the LORD appeared unto .... Lev 9:23 3519
the *g* of the LORD appeared in the .... Num 14:10 3519
be filled with the *g* of the LORD.............. Num 14:21 3519
those men which have seen my *g*............. Num 14:22 3519
the *g* of the LORD appeared unto .... Num 16:19 3519
the *g* of the LORD appeared...................... Num 16:42 3519
the *g* of the LORD appeared unto .... Num 20:6 3519
LORD our God hath shewed us his *g* ...... Deut 5:24 3519
His *g* is like the firstling of .... Deut 33:17 1926
g to the LORD God of Israel, and............. Josh 7:19 3519
make them inherit the throne of *g* 1Sa 2:8 3519
The *g* is departed from Israel 1Sa 4:21 3519
The *g* is departed from Israel 1Sa 4:22 3519
ye shall give *g* unto the God of................ 1Sa 6:5 3519
for the *g* of the LORD had filled 1Kin 8:11 3519
g of this, and tarry at home..................... 2Kin 14:10 3513
G ye in his holy name................................. 1Chr 16:10 1984
Declare his *g* among the heathen 1Chr 16:24 3519
G and honour are in his presence 1Chr 16:27 1935
the people, give unto the LORD *g*........... 1Chr 16:28 3519
the LORD the *g* due unto his name 1Chr 16:29 3519
thy holy name, and *g* in thy praise......... 1Chr 16:35 7623
of *g* throughout all countries................... 1Chr 22:5 8597
greatness, and the power, and the *g* 1Chr 29:11 8597
for the *g* of the LORD had filled 2Chr 5:14 3519
the *g* of the LORD filled the 2Chr 7:1 3519
because the *g* of the LORD had................ 2Chr 7:2 3519
the *g* of the LORD upon the house, ... 2Chr 7:3 3519
told them of the *g* of his riches .... Est 5:11 3519
He hath stripped me of my *g*.................... Job 19:9 3519
My *g* was fresh in me, and my bow......... Job 29:20 3519
the *g* of his nostrils is terrible................ Job 39:20 1935
and array thyself with *g* and beauty....... Job 40:10 1935
my *g*, and the lifter up of mine .... Ps 3:3 3519
long will ye turn my *g* into shame........... Ps 4:2 3519
who hast set thy *g* above the .... Ps 8:1 1935
and hast crowned him with *g*................... Ps 8:5 3519
heart is glad, and my *g* rejoiceth........... Ps 16:9 3519
The heavens declare the *g* of God .... Ps 19:1 3519
His *g* is great in thy salvation .... Ps 21:5 3519
the King of *g* shall come in .... Ps 24:7 3519
Who is this King of *g*................................ Ps 24:8 3519
the King of *g* shall come in .... Ps 24:9 3519
Who is this King of *g*................................ Ps 24:10 3519
of hosts, he is the King of *g*.................... Ps 24:10 3519
O ye mighty, give unto the LORD *g* .... Ps 29:1 3519
the LORD the *g* due unto his name .... Ps 29:2 3519

the God of *g* thundereth	Ps 29:3	3519
doth every one speak of his *g*	Ps 29:9	3519
To the end that my *g* may sing	Ps 30:12	3519
thigh, O most mighty, with thy *g*	Ps 45:3	1935
when the *g* of his house is	Ps 49:16	3519
his *g* shall not descend after him	Ps 49:17	3519
let thy *g* be above all the earth	Ps 57:5	3519
Awake up, my *g*	Ps 57:8	3519
let thy *g* be above all the earth	Ps 57:11	3519
In God is my salvation and my *g*	Ps 62:7	3519
To see thy power and thy *g*	Ps 63:2	3519
one that sweareth by him shall *g*	Ps 63:11	1984
all the upright in heart shall *g*	Ps 64:10	1984
whole earth be filled with his *g*	Ps 72:19	3519
and afterward receive me to *g*	Ps 73:24	3519
his *g* into the enemy's hand	Ps 78:61	8597
salvation, for the *g* of thy name	Ps 79:9	3519
the LORD will give grace and *g*	Ps 84:11	3519
that *g* may dwell in our land	Ps 85:9	3519
For thou art the *g* of their	Ps 89:17	8597
Thou hast made his *g* to cease	Ps 89:44	2892
thy *g* unto their children	Ps 90:16	1926
Declare his *g* among the heathen,	Ps 96:3	3519
the people, give unto the LORD *g*	Ps 96:7	3519
the LORD the *g* due unto his name	Ps 96:8	3519
and all the people see his *g*	Ps 97:6	3519
all the kings of the earth thy *g*	Ps 102:15	3519
up Zion, he shall appear in his *g*	Ps 102:16	3519
The *g* of the LORD shall endure	Ps 104:31	3519
G ye in his holy name	Ps 105:3	1984
nation, that I may *g* with thine	Ps 106:5	1984
Thus they changed their *g* into	Ps 106:20	3519
and give praise, even with my *g*	Ps 108:1	3519
thy *g* above all the earth	Ps 108:5	3519
and his *g* above the heavens	Ps 113:4	3519
unto us, but unto thy name give *g*	Ps 115:1	3519
for great is the *g* of the LORD	Ps 138:5	3519
speak of the *g* of thy kingdom	Ps 145:11	3519
his *g* is above the earth and	Ps 148:13	1935
Let the saints be joyful in *g*	Ps 149:5	3519
The wise shall inherit *g*	Prov 3:35	3519
a crown of *g* shall she deliver to	Prov 4:9	8597
The hoary head is a crown of *g*	Prov 16:31	8597
the *g* of children are their	Prov 17:6	8597
it is his *g* to pass over a	Prov 19:11	8597
The *g* of young men is their	Prov 20:29	8597
It is the *g* of God to conceal a	Prov 25:2	3519
search their own *g* is not *g*	Prov 25:27	3519
men do rejoice, there is great *g*	Prov 28:12	8597
LORD, and for the *g* of his majesty	Is 2:10	1926
for the *g* of his majesty, when he	Is 2:19	1926
for the *g* of his majesty, when he	Is 2:21	1926
to provoke the eyes of his *g*	Is 3:8	3519
for upon all the *g* shall be a	Is 4:5	3519
and their *g*, and their multitude,	Is 5:14	1926
the whole earth is full of his *g*	Is 6:3	3519
the king of Assyria, and all his *g*	Is 8:7	3519
and where will ye leave your *g*	Is 10:3	3519
and the *g* of his high looks	Is 10:12	8597
under his *g* he shall kindle a	Is 10:16	3519
shall consume the *g* of his forest	Is 10:18	3519
the *g* of kingdoms, the beauty of	Is 13:19	6643
even all of them, lie in *g*	Is 14:18	3519
the *g* of Moab shall be contemned,	Is 16:14	3519
they shall be as the *g* of the	Is 17:3	3519
that the *g* of Jacob shall be made	Is 17:4	3519
expectation, and of Egypt their *g*	Is 20:5	8597
all the *g* of Kedar shall fail	Is 21:16	3519
thy *g* shall be the shame of thy	Is 22:18	3519
all the *g* of his father's house	Is 22:24	3519
it, to stain the pride of all *g*	Is 23:9	6643
songs, even *g* to the righteous	Is 24:16	6643
LORD of hosts be for a crown of *g*	Is 28:5	6643
the *g* of Lebanon shall be given	Is 35:2	3519
they shall see the *g* of the LORD	Is 35:2	3519
the *g* of the LORD shall be	Is 40:5	3519
shalt *g* in the Holy One of Israel	Is 41:16	1984
my *g* will I not give to another,	Is 42:8	3519
Let them give *g* unto the LORD	Is 42:12	3519
for I have created him for my *g*	Is 43:7	3519
Israel be justified, and shall *g*	Is 45:25	1984
salvation in Zion for Israel my *g*	Is 46:13	8597
I will not give my *g* unto another	Is 48:11	3519
the *g* of the LORD shall be thy	Is 58:8	3519
his *g* from the rising of the sun	Is 59:19	3519
the *g* of the LORD is risen upon	Is 60:1	3519
his *g* shall be seen upon thee	Is 60:2	3519
I will glorify the house of my *g*	Is 60:7	8597
The *g* of Lebanon shall come unto	Is 60:13	3519
light, and thy God thy *g*	Is 60:19	8597
in their *g* shall ye boast	Is 61:6	3519
righteousness, and all kings thy *g*	Is 62:2	3519
of *g* in the hand of the LORD	Is 62:3	8597
of thy holiness and of thy *g*	Is 63:15	8597
with the abundance of her *g*	Is 66:11	3519
the *g* of the Gentiles like a	Is 66:12	3519
and they shall come, and see my *g*	Is 66:18	3519
my fame, neither have seen my *g*	Is 66:19	3519
declare my *g* among the Gentiles	Is 66:19	3519
my people have changed their *g*	Jer 2:11	3519
in him, and in him shall they *g*	Jer 4:2	1984
not the wise man *g* in his wisdom	Jer 9:23	1984
let the mighty man *g* in his might	Jer 9:23	1984
not the rich man *g* in his riches	Jer 9:23	1984
let him that glorieth *g* in this	Jer 9:24	1984
name, and for a praise, and for a *g*	Jer 13:11	8597
Give *g* to the LORD your God,	Jer 13:16	3519
down, even the crown of your *g*	Jer 13:18	8597
not disgrace the throne of thy *g*	Jer 14:21	3519
Ah lord! or, Ah his *g*!	Jer 22:18	1935
Dibon, come down from thy *g*	Jer 48:18	3519
the likeness of the *g* of the LORD	Eze 1:28	3519
Blessed be the *g* of the LORD from	Eze 3:12	3519
the *g* of the LORD stood there, as	Eze 3:23	3519
as the *g* which I saw by the river	Eze 3:23	3519
the *g* of the God of Israel was	Eze 8:4	3519
the *g* of the God of Israel was	Eze 9:3	3519
Then the *g* of the LORD went up	Eze 10:4	3519
of the brightness of the LORD's *g*	Eze 10:4	3519
Then the *g* of the LORD departed	Eze 10:18	3519
the *g* of the God of Israel was	Eze 10:19	3519
the *g* of the God of Israel was	Eze 11:22	3519
the *g* of the LORD went up from	Eze 11:23	3519
which is the *g* of all lands	Eze 20:6	6643
which is the *g* of all lands	Eze 20:15	6643
strength, the joy of their *g*	Eze 24:25	8597
frontiers, the *g* of the country,	Eze 25:9	6643
I shall set *g* in the land of the	Eze 26:20	6643
To whom art thou thus like in *g*	Eze 31:18	3519
I will set my *g* among the heathen	Eze 39:21	3519
the *g* of the God of Israel came	Eze 43:2	3519
and the earth shined with his *g*	Eze 43:2	3519
the *g* of the LORD came into the	Eze 43:4	3519
the *g* of the LORD filled the	Eze 43:5	3519
the *g* of the LORD filled the	Eze 44:4	3519
kingdom, power, and strength, and *g*	Dan 2:37	3367
for the *g* of my kingdom, mine	Dan 4:36	3367
father a kingdom and majesty, and *g*	Dan 5:18	3367
and they took his *g* from him	Dan 5:20	3367
was given him dominion, and *g*	Dan 7:14	3367
of taxes in the *g* of the kingdom	Dan 11:20	1925
acknowledge and increase with *g*	Dan 11:39	3519
will I change their *g* into shame	Hos 4:7	3519
their *g* shall fly away like a	Hos 9:11	3519
rejoiced on it, for the *g* thereof	Hos 10:5	3519
come unto Adullam the *g* of Israel	Mic 1:15	3519
have ye taken away my *g* for ever	Mic 2:9	1926
g out of all the pleasant	Nah 2:9	3519
knowledge of the *g* of the LORD	Hab 2:14	3519
Thou art filled with shame for *g*	Hab 2:16	3519
spewing shall be on thy *g*	Hab 2:16	3519
His *g* covered the heavens, and the	Hab 3:3	1935
saw this house in her first *g*	Hag 2:3	3519
and I will fill this house with *g*	Hag 2:7	3519
The *g* of this latter house shall	Hag 2:9	3519
will be the *g* in the midst of her	Zec 2:5	3519
After the *g* hath he sent me unto	Zec 2:8	3519
and he shall bear the *g*, and shall	Zec 6:13	1935
for their *g* is spoiled	Zec 11:3	155
that the *g* of the house of David	Zec 12:7	8597
the *g* of the inhabitants of	Zec 12:7	8597
to give *g* unto my name, saith the	Mal 2:2	3519
of the world, and the *g* of them	Mt 4:8	*1391*
that they may have *g* of men	Mt 6:2	*1392*
kingdom, and the power, and the *g*	Mt 6:13	*1391*
his *g* was not arrayed like one of	Mt 6:29	*1391*
Son of man shall come in the *g* of	Mt 16:27	*1391*
shall sit in the throne of his *g*	Mt 19:28	*1391*
of heaven with power and great *g*	Mt 24:30	*1391*
Son of man shall come in his *g*	Mt 25:31	*1391*
he sit upon the throne of his *g*	Mt 25:31	*1391*
when he cometh in the *g* of his	Mk 8:38	*1391*
other on thy left hand, in thy *g*	Mk 10:37	*1391*
the clouds with great power and *g*	Mk 13:26	*1391*
the *g* of the Lord shone round	Lk 2:9	*1391*
G to God in the highest, and on	Lk 2:14	*1391*
the *g* of thy people Israel	Lk 2:32	*1391*
I give thee, and the *g* of them	Lk 4:6	*1391*
when he shall come in his own *g*	Lk 9:26	*1391*
Who appeared in *g*, and spake of	Lk 9:31	*1391*
they were awake, they saw his *g*	Lk 9:32	*1391*
that Solomon in all his *g* was not	Lk 12:27	*1391*
that returned to give *g* to God	Lk 17:18	*1391*
in heaven, and *g* in the highest	Lk 19:38	*1391*
in a cloud with power and great *g*	Lk 21:27	*1391*
things, and to enter into his *g*	Lk 24:26	*1391*
among us, (and we beheld his *g*	Jn 1:14	*1391*
the *g* as of the only begotten of	Jn 1:14	*1391*
and manifested forth his *g*	Jn 2:11	*1391*
of himself seeketh his own *g*	Jn 7:18	*1391*
that seeketh his *g* that sent him	Jn 7:18	*1391*
And I seek not mine own *g*	Jn 8:50	*1391*
unto death, but for the *g* of God	Jn 11:4	*1391*
thou shouldest see the *g* of God	Jn 11:40	*1391*
said Esaias, when he saw his *g*	Jn 12:41	*1391*
g which I had with thee before	Jn 17:5	*1391*
the *g* which thou gavest me I have	Jn 17:22	*1391*
that they may behold my *g*	Jn 17:24	*1391*
The God of *g* appeared unto our	Acts 7:2	*1391*
into heaven, and saw the *g* of God	Acts 7:55	*1391*
because he gave not God the *g*	Acts 12:23	*1391*
not see for the *g* of that light	Acts 22:11	*1391*
And changed the *g* of the	Rom 1:23	*1391*
in well doing seek for *g* and	Rom 2:7	*1391*
But *g*, honour, and peace, to every	Rom 2:10	*1391*
through my lie unto his *g*	Rom 3:7	*1391*
and come short of the *g* of God	Rom 3:23	*1391*
by works, he hath whereof to *g*	Rom 4:2	*2745*
strong in faith, giving *g* to God	Rom 4:20	*1391*
rejoice in hope of the *g* of God	Rom 5:2	*1391*
but we *g* in tribulations also	Rom 5:3	*2744*
the dead by the *g* of the Father	Rom 6:4	*1391*
g which shall be revealed in us	Rom 8:18	*1391*
pertaineth the adoption, and the *g*	Rom 9:4	*1391*
of his *g* on the vessels of mercy	Rom 9:23	*1391*
he had afore prepared unto *g*	Rom 9:23	*1391*
to whom be *g* for ever	Rom 11:36	*1391*
also received us to the *g* of God	Rom 15:7	*1391*
g through Jesus Christ in those	Rom 15:17	*2746*
be *g* through Jesus Christ for	Rom 16:27	*1391*
no flesh should *g* in his presence	1Cor 1:29	*2744*
glorieth, let him *g* in the Lord	1Cor 1:31	*2744*
before the world unto our *g*	1Cor 2:7	*1391*
not have crucified the Lord of *g*	1Cor 2:8	*1391*
Therefore let no man *g* in men	1Cor 3:21	*2744*
didst receive it, why dost thou *g*	1Cor 4:7	*2744*
gospel, I have nothing to *g* of	1Cor 9:16	*2745*
ye do, do all to the *g* of God	1Cor 10:31	*1391*
as he is the image and *g* of God	1Cor 11:7	*1391*
but the woman is the *g* of the man	1Cor 11:7	*1391*
have long hair, it is a *g* to her	1Cor 11:15	*1391*
but the *g* of the celestial is one	1Cor 15:40	*1391*
the *g* of the terrestrial is	1Cor 15:40	*1391*
There is one *g* of the sun	1Cor 15:41	*1391*
another *g* of the moon	1Cor 15:41	*1391*
and another *g* of the stars	1Cor 15:41	*1391*
differeth from another star in *g*	1Cor 15:41	*1391*
it is raised in *g*	1Cor 15:43	*1391*
him Amen, unto the *g* of God by us	2Cor 1:20	*1391*
for the *g* of his countenance	2Cor 3:7	*1391*
which *g* was to be done away	2Cor 3:7	*1391*
ministration of condemnation be *g*	2Cor 3:9	*1391*
of righteousness exceed in *g*	2Cor 3:9	*1391*
glorious had no *g* in this respect	2Cor 3:10	*1392*
by reason of the *g* that excelleth	2Cor 3:10	*1391*
as in a glass the *g* of the Lord	2Cor 3:18	*1391*
the same image from *g* to *g*	2Cor 3:18	*1391*
the *g* of God in the face of Jesus	2Cor 4:6	*1391*
of many redound to the *g* of God	2Cor 4:15	*1391*
exceeding and eternal weight of *g*	2Cor 4:17	*1391*
you occasion to *g* on our behalf	2Cor 5:12	*2745*
answer them which *g* in appearance	2Cor 5:12	*2744*
by us to the *g* of the same Lord	2Cor 8:19	*1391*
the churches, and the *g* of Christ	2Cor 8:23	*1391*
glorieth, let him *g* in the Lord	2Cor 10:17	*2744*
that wherein they *g*, they may be	2Cor 11:12	*2744*
g after the flesh, I will *g* also	2Cor 11:18	*2744*
If I must needs *g*, I will *g*	2Cor 11:30	*2744*
expedient for me doubtless to *g*	2Cor 12:1	*2744*
Of such an one will I *g*	2Cor 12:5	*2744*
yet of myself I will not *g*	2Cor 12:5	*2744*
For though I would desire to *g*	2Cor 12:6	*2744*
will I rather *g* in my infirmities	2Cor 12:9	*2744*
To whom be *g* for ever and ever	Gal 1:5	*1391*
Let us not be desirous of vain *g*	Gal 5:26	*2755*
that they may *g* in your flesh	Gal 6:13	*2744*
But God forbid that I should *g*	Gal 6:14	*2744*
the praise of the *g* of his grace	Eph 1:6	*1391*
should be to the praise of his *g*	Eph 1:12	*1391*
unto the praise of his *g*	Eph 1:14	*1391*
Jesus Christ, the Father of *g*	Eph 1:17	*1391*
what the riches of the *g* of his	Eph 1:18	*1391*
for you, which is your *g*	Eph 3:13	*1391*
according to the riches of his *g*	Eph 3:16	*1391*
Unto him be *g* in the church by	Eph 3:21	*1391*
are by Jesus Christ, unto the *g*	Phil 1:11	*1391*
to the *g* of God the Father	Phil 2:11	*1391*
whose *g* is in their shame, who	Phil 3:19	*1391*
his riches in *g* by Christ Jesus	Phil 4:19	*1391*
God and our Father be *g* for ever	Phil 4:20	*1391*
the *g* of this mystery among the	Col 1:27	*1391*
is Christ in you, the hope of *g*	Col 1:27	*1391*
ye also appear with him in *g*	Col 3:4	*1391*
Nor of men sought we *g*, neither	1Th 2:6	*1391*
called you unto his kingdom and *g*	1Th 2:12	*1391*
For ye are our *g* and joy	1Th 2:20	*1391*
So that we ourselves *g* in you in	2Th 1:4	*2744*
Lord, and from the *g* of his power	2Th 1:9	*1391*
to the obtaining of the *g* of our	2Th 2:14	*1391*
be honour and *g* for ever and ever	1Ti 1:17	*1391*
in the world, received up into *g*	1Ti 3:16	*1391*
is in Christ Jesus with eternal *g*	2Ti 2:10	*1391*
to whom be *g* for ever and ever	2Ti 4:18	*1391*
Who being the brightness of his *g*	Heb 1:3	*1391*
thou crownedst him with *g*	Heb 2:7	*1391*
of death, crowned with *g* and	Heb 2:9	*1391*
in bringing many sons unto *g*	Heb 2:10	*1391*
worthy of more *g* than Moses	Heb 3:3	*1391*
of *g* shadowing the mercyseat	Heb 9:5	*1391*
to whom be *g* for ever and ever	Heb 13:21	*1391*
Lord Jesus Christ, the Lord of *g*	Jas 2:1	*1391*
g not, and lie not against the	Jas 3:14	*2620*
g at the appearing of Jesus	1Pet 1:7	*1391*
with joy unspeakable and full of *g*	1Pet 1:8	*1392*
and the *g* that should follow	1Pet 1:11	*1391*
up from the dead, and gave him *g*	1Pet 1:21	*1391*
all the *g* of man as the flower of	1Pet 1:24	*1391*
For what *g* is it, if, when ye be	1Pet 2:20	*2811*
when his *g* shall be revealed, ye	1Pet 4:13	*1391*
for the spirit of *g* and of God	1Pet 4:14	*1391*
of the *g* that shall be revealed	1Pet 5:1	*1391*
a crown of *g* that fadeth not away	1Pet 5:4	*1391*
his eternal *g* by Christ Jesus	1Pet 5:10	*1391*
To him be *g* and dominion for ever	1Pet 5:11	*1391*
of him that hath called us to *g*	2Pet 1:3	*1391*
from God the Father honour and *g*	2Pet 1:17	*1391*
voice to him from the excellent *g*	2Pet 1:17	*1391*
To him be *g* both now and for ever	2Pet 3:18	*1391*
of his *g* with exceeding joy	Jude 24	*1391*
only wise God our Saviour, be *g*	Jude 25	*1391*
to him be *g* and dominion for ever	Rev 1:6	*1391*
And when those beasts give *g*	Rev 4:9	*1391*
art worthy, O Lord, to receive *g*	Rev 4:11	*1391*
and strength, and honour, and *g*	Rev 5:12	*1391*

saying, Blessing, and honour, and *g* Rev 5:13 *1391*
Blessing, and *g*, and wisdom, and Rev 7:12 *1391*
gave *g* to the God of heaven Rev 11:13 *1391*
voice, Fear God, and give *g* to him Rev 14:7 *1391*
with smoke from the *g* of God Rev 15:8 *1391*
they repented not to give him *g* Rev 16:9 *1391*
earth was lightened with his *g* Rev 18:1 *1391*
Salvation, and *g*, and honour, and Rev 19:1 *1391*
Having the *g* of God Rev 21:11 *1391*
for the *g* of God did lighten it, Rev 21:23 *1391*
of the earth do bring their *g* Rev 21:24 *1391*
And they shall bring the *g* Rev 21:26 *1391*

GLORYING {4}
Your *g* is not good 1Cor 5:6 *2745*
any man should make my *g* void 1Cor 9:15 *2745*
toward you, great is my *g* of you 2Cor 7:4 *2746*
I am become a fool in *g* 2Cor 12:11 *2744*

GLUTTON {2}
he is a *g*, and a drunkard Deut 21:20 2151
the *g* shall come to poverty Prov 23:21 2151

GLUTTONOUS {2}
and they say, Behold a man *g* Mt 11:19 *5314*
and ye say, Behold a *g* man Lk 7:34 *5314*

GNASH {2}
he shall *g* with his teeth, and Ps 112:10 2786
they hiss and *g* the teeth Lam 2:16 2786

GNASHED {2}
they *g* upon me with their teeth Ps 35:16 2786
they *g* on him with their teeth Acts 7:54 *1031*

GNASHETH {3}
he *g* upon me with his teeth Job 16:9 2786
g upon him with his teeth Ps 37:12 2786
g with his teeth, and pineth away Mk 9:18 *5149*

GNASHING {7}
shall be weeping and *g* of teeth Mt 8:12 *1030*
shall be wailing and *g* of teeth Mt 13:42 *1030*
shall be wailing and *g* of teeth Mt 13:50 *1030*
shall be weeping and *g* of teeth Mt 22:13 *1030*
shall be weeping and *g* of teeth Mt 24:51 *1030*
shall be weeping and *g* of teeth Mt 25:30 *1030*
g of teeth, when ye shall see Lk 13:28 *1030*

GNAT {1}
blind guides, which strain at a *g* Mt 23:24 *2971*

GNAW {1}
they *g* not the bones till the Zeph 3:3 1633

GNAWED {1}
they *g* their tongues for pain, Rev 16:10 *3145*

GO {1497}
upon thy belly shalt thou *g* Gen 3:14 3212
G forth of the ark, thou, and thy Gen 8:16 3318
from all that *g* out of the ark, Gen 9:10 3318
G to, let us make brick, and burn Gen 11:3 3051
G to, let us build us a city and a Gen 11:4 3051
G to, let us *g* down, and there Gen 11:7 3051
G to, let us *g* down, and there Gen 11:7 3381
to *g* into the land of Canaan Gen 11:31 3212
they went forth to *g* into the Gen 12:5 3212
thy wife, take her, and *g* thy way Gen 12:19 3212
then I will *g* to the right Gen 13:9 3231
hand, then I will *g* to the left Gen 13:9 8041
seeing I *g* childless, and the Gen 15:2 1980
thou shalt *g* to thy fathers in Gen 15:15 935
I pray thee, *g* in unto my maid Gen 16:2 935
and whither wilt thou *g* Gen 16:8 3212
I will *g* down now, and see whether Gen 18:21 3381
rise up early, and *g* on your ways Gen 19:2 1980
g thou in, and lie with him, that Gen 19:34 935
and I and the lad will *g* yonder Gen 22:5 3212
But thou shalt *g* unto my country, Gen 24:4 3212
that women *g* out to draw water Gen 24:11 3318
But thou shalt *g* unto my father's Gen 24:38 3212
thou do prosper my way which I *g* Gen 24:42 1980
is before thee, take her, and *g* Gen 24:51 3212
after that she shall *g* Gen 24:55 3212
me away that I may *g* to my master Gen 24:56 3212
Wilt thou *g* with this man Gen 24:58 3212
And she said, I will *g* Gen 24:58 3212
and said, *G* not down into Egypt Gen 26:2 3381
said unto Isaac, *G* from us Gen 26:16 3212
g out to the field, and take me Gen 27:3 3318
G now to the flock, and fetch me Gen 27:9 3212
obey my voice, and *g* fetch me them Gen 27:13 3212
g to Padan-aram, to the house of Gen 28:2 3212
will keep me in this way that I *g* Gen 28:20 1980
water ye the sheep, and *g* and feed Gen 29:7 3212
that I may *g* in unto her Gen 29:21 935
my maid Bilhah, *g* in unto her Gen 30:3 935
that I may *g* unto mine own place, Gen 30:25 3212
I have served thee, and let me *g* Gen 30:26 3212
for to *g* to Isaac his father in Gen 31:18 935
And he said, Let me *g*, for the day Gen 32:26 7971
And he said, I will not let thee *g* Gen 32:26 7971
us *g*, and I will *g* before thee Gen 33:12 3212
g up to Beth-el, and dwell there Gen 35:1 5927
let us arise, and *g* up to Beth-el Gen 35:3 5927
And he said to him, *G*, I pray thee Gen 37:14 3212
them say, Let us *g* to Dothan Gen 37:17 3212
and I, whither shall I *g* Gen 37:30 935
For I will *g* down into the grave Gen 37:35 3381
G in unto thy brother's wife, and Gen 38:8 935
G to, I pray thee, let me come in Gen 38:16 3051
all the Egyptians, *G* unto Joseph Gen 41:55 3212
ye shall not *g* forth hence Gen 42:15 3318
g ye, carry corn for the famine Gen 42:19 3212

My son shall not *g* down with you Gen 42:38 3381
him by the way in the which ye *g* Gen 42:38 3212
G again, buy us a little food Gen 43:2 7725
brother with us, we will *g* down Gen 43:4 3381
not send him, we will not *g* down Gen 43:5 3381
with me, and we will arise and *g* Gen 43:8 3212
and arise, *g* again unto the man Gen 43:13 7725
G again, and buy us a little food Gen 44:25 7725
And we said, We cannot *g* down Gen 44:26 3381
be with us, then will we *g* down Gen 44:26 3381
let the lad *g* up with his Gen 44:33 5927
For how shall I *g* up to my father Gen 44:34 5927
Cause every man to *g* out from me Gen 45:1 3318
g up to my father, and say unto Gen 45:9 5927
lade your beasts, and *g*, get you Gen 45:17 3212
I will *g* and see him before I die Gen 45:28 3212
fear not to *g* down into Egypt Gen 46:3 3381
I will *g* down with thee into Gen 46:4 3381
his father's house, I will *g* up Gen 46:31 5927
Now therefore let me *g* up Gen 50:5 5927
G up, and bury thy father, Gen 50:6 5927
to Pharaoh's daughter, Shall I *g* Ex 2:7 3212
Pharaoh's daughter said to her, *G* Ex 2:8 3212
I, that I should *g* unto Pharaoh Ex 3:11 3212
G, and gather the elders of Israel Ex 3:16 3212
and now let us *g*, we beseech thee, Ex 3:18 3212
king of Egypt will not let you *g* Ex 3:19 1980
and after that he will let you *g* Ex 3:20 7971
when ye *g*, ye shall not *g* empty Ex 3:21 3212
Now therefore *g*, and I will be Ex 4:12 3212
law, and said unto him, Let me *g* Ex 4:18 3212
Jethro said to Moses, *G* in peace Ex 4:18 3212
LORD said unto Moses in Midian, *G* Ex 4:19 3212
he shall not let the people *g* Ex 4:21 7971
And I say unto thee, Let my son *g* Ex 4:23 7971
and if thou refuse to let him *g* Ex 4:23 7971
So he let him *g* Ex 4:26 7503
G into the wilderness to meet Ex 4:27 3212
God of Israel, Let my people *g* Ex 5:1 7971
obey his voice to let Israel *g* Ex 5:2 7971
LORD, neither will I let Israel *g* Ex 5:2 7971
let us *g*, we pray thee, three Ex 5:3 3212
let them *g* and gather straw for Ex 5:7 3212
they cry, saying, Let us *g* Ex 5:8 3212
G ye, get you straw where ye can Ex 5:11 3212
therefore ye say, Let us *g* Ex 5:17 3212
G therefore now, and work Ex 5:18 3212
a strong hand shall he let them *g* Ex 6:1 7971
G in, speak unto Pharaoh king of Ex 6:11 935
of Israel *g* out of his land Ex 6:11 7971
he refuseth to let the people *g* Ex 7:14 7971
thee, saying, Let my people *g* Ex 7:16 7971
G unto Pharaoh, and say unto him, Ex 8:1 935
saith the LORD, Let my people *g* Ex 8:1 7971
And if thou refuse to let them *g* Ex 8:2 7971
abundantly, which shall *g* up Ex 8:3 5927
and I will let the people *g* Ex 8:8 7971
saith the LORD, Let my people *g* Ex 8:20 7971
if thou wilt not let my people *g* Ex 8:21 7971
G ye, sacrifice to your God in Ex 8:25 3212
We will *g* three days' journey Ex 8:27 3212
And Pharaoh said, I will let you *g* Ex 8:28 7971
only ye shall not *g* very far away Ex 8:28 3212
I *g* out from thee, and I will Ex 8:29 3318
people *g* to sacrifice to the LORD Ex 8:29 7971
neither would he let the people *g* Ex 8:32 7971
G in unto Pharaoh, and tell him, Ex 9:1 935
of the Hebrews, Let my people *g* Ex 9:1 7971
For if thou refuse to let them *g* Ex 9:2 7971
and he did not let the people *g* Ex 9:7 7971
of the Hebrews, Let my people *g* Ex 9:13 7971
that thou wilt not let them *g* Ex 9:17 7971
and I will let you *g*, and ye shall Ex 9:28 7971
he let the children of Israel *g* Ex 9:35 7971
unto Moses, *G* in unto Pharaoh Ex 10:1 935
let my people *g*, that they may Ex 10:3 7971
if thou refuse to let my people *g* Ex 10:4 7971
let the men *g*, that they may Ex 10:7 7971
and he said unto them, *G*, serve Ex 10:8 3212
but who are they that shall *g* Ex 10:8 1980
We will *g* with our young and with Ex 10:9 3212
and with our herds will we *g* Ex 10:9 3212
so with you, as I will let you *g* Ex 10:10 7971
g now ye that are men, and serve Ex 10:11 3212
not let the children of Israel *g* Ex 10:20 7971
and said, *G* ye, serve the LORD Ex 10:24 3212
your little ones also *g* with you Ex 10:24 3212
Our cattle also shall *g* with us Ex 10:26 3212
heart, and he would not let them *g* Ex 10:27 7971
he will let you *g* hence Ex 11:1 7971
when he shall let you *g*, he shall Ex 11:1 7971
About midnight will I *g* out into Ex 11:4 3318
and after that I will *g* out Ex 11:8 3318
of Israel *g* out of his land Ex 11:10 7971
none of you shall *g* out at the Ex 12:22 3318
and *g*, serve the LORD, as ye have Ex 12:31 3212
Pharaoh would hardly let us *g* Ex 13:15 7971
when Pharaoh had let the people *g* Ex 13:17 7971
to *g* by day and night Ex 13:21 3212
have let Israel *g* from serving us Ex 14:5 7971
of Israel, that they *g* forward Ex 14:15 5265
the children of Israel shall *g* on Ex 14:16 935
the LORD caused the sea to *g* back Ex 14:21 3212
and the people shall *g* out Ex 16:4 3318
let no man *g* out of his place on Ex 16:29 3318
G on before the people, and take Ex 17:5 5674
river, take in thine hand, and *g* Ex 17:5 1980
men, and *g* out, fight with Amalek Ex 17:9 3318

also *g* to their place in peace Ex 18:23 935
G unto the people, and sanctify Ex 19:10 3212
that ye *g* not up into the mount, Ex 19:12 5927
G down, charge the people, lest Ex 19:21 3381
Neither shalt thou *g* up by steps Ex 20:26 5927
he shall *g* out free for nothing Ex 21:2 3318
he shall *g* out by himself Ex 21:3 3318
his wife shall *g* out with him Ex 21:3 3318
he shall *g* out by himself Ex 21:4 3318
I will not *g* out free Ex 21:5 3318
she shall not *g* out as the Ex 21:7 3318
then shall she *g* out free without Ex 21:11 3318
he shall let him *g* free for his Ex 21:26 7971
he shall let him *g* free for his Ex 21:27 7971
mine Angel shall *g* before thee Ex 23:23 3212
shall the people *g* up with him Ex 24:2 5927
When they *g* into the tabernacle Ex 30:20 935
us gods, which shall *g* before us Ex 32:1 3212
And the LORD said unto Moses, *G* Ex 32:7 3212
us gods, which shall *g* before us Ex 32:23 3212
g in and out from gate to gate Ex 32:27 5674
now I will *g* up unto the LORD Ex 32:30 5927
Therefore now *g*, lead the people Ex 32:34 3212
mine Angel shall *g* before thee Ex 32:34 3212
g up hence, thou and the people Ex 33:1 5927
for I will not *g* up in the midst Ex 33:3 5927
My presence shall *g* with thee Ex 33:14 3212
If thy presence *g* not with me Ex 33:15 1980
my Lord, I pray thee, *g* among us Ex 34:9 3212
they *g* a whoring after their gods Ex 34:15 2181
their daughters *g* a whoring after Ex 34:16 2181
make thy sons *g* a whoring after Ex 34:16 2181
when thou shalt *g* up to appear Ex 34:24 5927
it shall never *g* out Lev 6:13 3518
ye shall not *g* out of the door of Lev 8:33 3318
G unto the altar, and offer thy Lev 9:7 7126
ye shall not *g* out from the door Lev 10:7 3318
when ye *g* into the tabernacle of Lev 10:9 935
of beasts that *g* on all four Lev 11:27 1980
the priest shall *g* forth out of Lev 14:3 3318
before the priest *g* into it to Lev 14:36 935
shall *g* in to see the house Lev 14:36 935
Then the priest shall *g* out of Lev 14:38 3318
But he shall let *g* the living Lev 14:53 7971
seed of copulation *g* out from him Lev 15:16 3318
to let him *g* for a scapegoat into Lev 16:10 7971
he shall *g* out unto the altar Lev 16:18 3318
he shall let *g* the goat in the Lev 16:22 7971
he that let *g* the goat for the Lev 16:26 7971
Thou shalt not *g* up and down as a Lev 19:16 3212
all that *g* a whoring after him, Lev 20:5 2181
to *g* a whoring after them, I will Lev 20:6 2181
Neither shall he *g* in to any dead Lev 21:11 935
Neither shall he *g* out of the Lev 21:12 3318
he shall not *g* in unto the vail Lev 21:23 935
and in the jubile it shall *g* out Lev 25:28 3318
it shall not *g* out in the jubile Lev 25:30 3318
they shall *g* out in the jubile Lev 25:31 3318
shall *g* out in the year of jubile Lev 25:33 3318
then he shall *g* out in the year Lev 25:54 3318
the sword *g* through your land Lev 26:6 5674
your yoke, and made you *g* upright Lev 26:13 3212
all that are able to *g* forth to Num 1:3 3318
that were able to *g* forth to war Num 1:20 3318
that were able to *g* forth to war Num 1:22 3318
that were able to *g* forth to war Num 1:24 3318
that were able to *g* forth to war Num 1:26 3318
that were able to *g* forth to war Num 1:28 3318
that were able to *g* forth to war Num 1:30 3318
that were able to *g* forth to war Num 1:32 3318
that were able to *g* forth to war Num 1:34 3318
that were able to *g* forth to war Num 1:36 3318
that were able to *g* forth to war Num 1:38 3318
that were able to *g* forth to war Num 1:40 3318
that were able to *g* forth to war Num 1:42 3318
all that were able to *g* forth to Num 1:45 3318
they shall *g* forward in the third Num 2:24 5265
They shall *g* hindmost with their Num 2:31 5265
Aaron and his sons shall *g* in Num 4:19 935
But they shall not *g* in to see Num 4:20 935
them, If any man's wife *g* aside Num 5:12 7847
the curse shall *g* into thy bowels Num 5:22 935
g in to do the service of the Num 8:15 935
upward they shall *g* in to wait Num 8:24 935
on the east parts shall *g* forward Num 10:5 5265
if ye *g* to war in your land Num 10:9 935
And he said unto him, I will not *g* Num 10:30 3212
And it shall be, if thou *g* with us Num 10:32 3212
and *g* up into the mountain Num 13:17 5927
Let us *g* up at once, and possess Num 13:30 5927
We be not able to *g* up against Num 13:31 5927
will *g* up unto the place which Num 14:40 5927
G not up, for the LORD is not Num 14:42 5927
to *g* up unto the hill top Num 14:44 5927
after which ye use to *g* a whoring Num 15:39 2181
they *g* down quick into the pit Num 16:30 3381
g quickly unto the congregation, Num 16:46 3212
we will *g* by the king's high way, Num 20:17 3212
We will *g* by the high way Num 20:19 5927
thing else, *g* through on my feet Num 20:19 5674
he said, Thou shalt not *g* through Num 20:20 5674
but we will *g* along by the king's Num 21:22 3212
Thou shalt not *g* with them Num 22:12 3212
to give me leave to *g* with you Num 22:13 1980
I cannot *g* beyond the word of the Num 22:18 5674
thee, rise up, and *g* with them Num 22:20 3212
said unto Balaam, *G* with the men Num 22:35 3212
thy burnt offering, and I will *g* Num 23:3 3212

G

G again unto Balak, and say thus .... Num 23:16 7725
I cannot *g* beyond the commandment ..... Num 24:13 5674
now, behold, I *g* unto my people .... Num 24:14 1980
are able to *g* to war in Israel .... Num 26:2 3318
Which may *g* out before them, and .... Num 27:17 3318
which may *g* in before them, and .... Num 27:17 935
at his word shall they *g* out .... Num 27:21 3318
let them *g* against the Midianites .... Num 31:3 1961
shall make it *g* through the fire .... Num 31:23 5674
ye shall make *g* through the water .... Num 31:23 5674
Shall your brethren *g* to war .... Num 32:6 935
that they should not *g* into the .... Num 32:9 935
But we ourselves will *g* ready .... Num 32:17 2502
if ye will *g* armed before the .... Num 32:20 2502
will *g* all of you armed over .... Num 32:21 5674
shall *g* on to Hazar-addar, and .... Num 34:4 3318
the border shall *g* on to Ziphron .... Num 34:9 3318
the coast shall *g* down from .... Num 34:11 3381
the border shall *g* down to Jordan .... Num 34:12 3381
g to the mount of the Amorites, ... Deut 1:7 935
g in and possess the land which .... Deut 1:8 935
g up and possess it, as the LORD .... Deut 1:21 5927
again by what way we must *g* up .... Deut 1:22 5927
Notwithstanding ye would not *g* up .... Deut 1:26 5927
Whither shall we *g* up .... Deut 1:28 5927
shew you by what way ye should *g* .... Deut 1:33 3212
Thou also shalt not *g* in thither .... Deut 1:37 935
thee, he shall *g* in thither .... Deut 1:38 935
and evil, they shall *g* in thither .... Deut 1:39 935
against the LORD, we will *g* up .... Deut 1:41 5927
were ready to *g* up into the hill .... Deut 1:41 5927
them, *G* not up, neither fight .... Deut 1:42 5927
I will *g* along by the high way, I .... Deut 2:27 3212
I pray thee, let me *g* over .... Deut 3:25 5674
thou shalt not *g* over this Jordan .... Deut 3:27 5674
for he shall *g* over before this .... Deut 3:28 5674
g in and possess the land which .... Deut 4:1 935
land whither ye *g* to possess it .... Deut 4:5 935
whither ye *g* over to possess it .... Deut 4:14 5674
that I should not *g* over Jordan .... Deut 4:21 5674
that I should not *g* in unto that .... Deut 4:21 935
land, I must not *g* over Jordan .... Deut 4:22 5674
but ye shall *g* over, and possess .... Deut 4:22 5674
ye *g* over Jordan to possess it .... Deut 4:26 5674
Or hath God assayed to *g* and take .... Deut 4:34 935
that it may *g* well with thee, and .... Deut 4:40 3190
that it may *g* well with thee, in .... Deut 5:16 3190
G thou near, and hear all that the .... Deut 5:27 7126
G say to them, Get you into your .... Deut 5:30 3212
land whither ye *g* to possess it .... Deut 6:1 5674
Ye shall not *g* after other gods, ... Deut 6:14 3212
thee, and that thou mayest *g* in .... Deut 6:18 935
g in and possess the land which .... Deut 8:1 935
to *g* in to possess nations .... Deut 9:1 935
dost thou *g* to possess their land .... Deut 9:5 935
G up and possess the land which I .... Deut 9:23 5927
the people, that they may *g* in .... Deut 10:11 935
g in and possess the land .... Deut 11:8 935
whither ye *g* to possess it .... Deut 11:8 5674
whither ye *g* to possess it, is a .... Deut 11:11 935
to *g* after other gods, which ye .... Deut 11:28 3212
to *g* in to possess the land which .... Deut 11:31 935
But when ye *g* over Jordan .... Deut 12:10 5674
that it may *g* well with thee, and .... Deut 12:25 3190
g unto the place which the LORD .... Deut 12:26 935
that it may *g* well with thee, and .... Deut 12:28 3190
Let us *g* after other gods, which .... Deut 13:2 3212
thee secretly, saying, Let us *g* .... Deut 13:6 3212
of their city, saying, Let us *g* .... Deut 13:13 3212
shalt *g* unto the place which the .... Deut 14:25 1980
shalt let him *g* free from thee .... Deut 15:12 7971
shalt not let him *g* away empty .... Deut 15:13 7971
I will not *g* away from thee .... Deut 15:16 3318
the morning, and *g* unto thy tents .... Deut 16:7 1980
that it may *g* well with thee .... Deut 19:13 2895
but life shall *g* for life .... Deut 19:21
let him *g* and return to his house, ... Deut 20:5 3212
let him also *g* and return unto his .... Deut 20:6 3212
let him *g* and return unto his .... Deut 20:7 3212
let him *g* and return unto his .... Deut 20:8 3212
that thou shalt *g* in unto her .... Deut 21:13 935
shalt let her *g* whither she will .... Deut 21:14 7971
ox or his sheep *g* astray, and hide .... Deut 22:1 5080
shalt in any wise let the dam *g* .... Deut 22:7 7971
g in unto her, and hate her, ... Deut 22:13 935
then shall he *g* abroad out of the .... Deut 23:10 3318
whither thou shalt *g* forth abroad .... Deut 23:12 3318
out of his house, she may *g* .... Deut 24:2 1980
wife, he shall not *g* out to war .... Deut 24:5 3318
thou shalt not *g* into his house .... Deut 24:10 935
shall the sun *g* down upon it .... Deut 24:15 935
thou shalt not *g* again to fetch .... Deut 24:19 7725
thou shalt not *g* over the boughs .... Deut 24:20 6286
brother shall *g* in unto her .... Deut 25:5 935
then let his brother's wife *g* up .... Deut 25:7 5927
shalt *g* unto the place which the .... Deut 26:2 1980
thou shalt *g* unto the priest that .... Deut 26:3 935
that thou mayest *g* in unto the .... Deut 27:3 935
thou shalt not *g* aside from any .... Deut 28:14 5493
to *g* after other gods to serve .... Deut 28:14 3212
thou shalt *g* out one way against .... Deut 28:25 3318
for they shall *g* into captivity .... Deut 28:41 3212
day from the LORD our God, to *g* .... Deut 29:18 3212
Who shall *g* up for us to heaven, ... Deut 30:12 5927
Who shall *g* over the sea for us, ... Deut 30:13 5674
over Jordan to *g* to possess it .... Deut 30:18 935
I can no more *g* out and come in .... Deut 31:2 3318
Thou shalt not *g* over this Jordan .... Deut 31:2 5674

he will *g* over before thee, and he .... Deut 31:3 5674
he shall *g* over before thee, as .... Deut 31:3 5674
he it is that doth *g* with thee .... Deut 31:6 1980
for thou must *g* with this people .... Deut 31:7 935
he it is that doth *g* before thee .... Deut 31:8 1980
ye *g* over Jordan to possess it .... Deut 31:13 5674
g a whoring after the gods of the .... Deut 31:16 2181
whither they *g* to be among them, ... Deut 31:16 935
imagination which they *g* about .... Deut 31:21 6213
whither ye *g* over Jordan to .... Deut 32:47 5674
but thou shalt not *g* thither unto .... Deut 32:52 935
but thou shalt not *g* over thither .... Deut 34:4 5674
g over this Jordan, thou, and all .... Josh 1:2 5674
to *g* in to possess the land, ... Josh 1:11 935
thou sendest us, we will *g* .... Josh 1:16 3212
G view the land, even Jericho .... Josh 2:1 3212
and afterward may ye *g* your way .... Josh 2:16 3212
that whosoever shall *g* out of the .... Josh 2:19 3318
from your place, and *g* after it .... Josh 3:3 1980
know the way by which ye must *g* .... Josh 3:4 3212
g round about the city once .... Josh 6:3 5362
G into the harlot's house, and .... Josh 6:22 935
saying, *G* up and view the country .... Josh 7:2 5927
him, Let not all the people *g* up .... Josh 7:3 5927
two or three thousand men *g* up .... Josh 7:3 5927
with thee, and arise, *g* up to Ai .... Josh 8:1 5927
people of war, to *g* up against Ai .... Josh 8:3 5927
g not very far from the city, but .... Josh 8:4 7368
g to meet them, and say unto them, ... Josh 9:11 3212
day we came forth to *g* unto you .... Josh 9:12 3212
hasted not to *g* down about a .... Josh 10:13 935
now, for war, both to *g* out .... Josh 14:11 3318
ye slack to *g* to possess the land .... Josh 18:3 935
g through the land, and describe .... Josh 18:4 1980
to describe the land, saying, *G* .... Josh 18:8 3212
to *g* unto the country of Gilead, ... Josh 22:9 3212
to *g* up to war against them .... Josh 22:12 5927
did not intend to *g* up against .... Josh 22:33 5927
Else if ye do in any wise *g* back .... Josh 23:12 7725
g in unto them, and they to you .... Josh 23:12 935
Who shall *g* up for us against the .... Judg 1:1 5927
the LORD said, Judah shall *g* up .... Judg 1:2 5927
I likewise will *g* with thee into .... Judg 1:3 1980
but they let *g* the man and all his .... Judg 1:25 7971
I made you to *g* up out of Egypt, ... Judg 2:1 5927
when Joshua had let the people *g* .... Judg 2:6 7971
of Israel commanded, saying, *G* .... Judg 4:6 3212
unto her, If thou wilt *g* with me .... Judg 4:8 3212
then I will *g* .... Judg 4:8 1982
but if thou wilt not *g* with me .... Judg 4:8 3212
then I will not *g* .... Judg 4:8 3212
said, I will surely *g* with thee .... Judg 4:9 3212
of the LORD *g* down to the gates .... Judg 5:11 3381
G in this thy might, and thou .... Judg 6:14 3212
Now therefore *g* to, proclaim in .... Judg 7:3 4994
unto thee, This shall *g* with thee .... Judg 7:4 3212
the same shall *g* with thee .... Judg 7:4 3212
thee, This shall not *g* with thee .... Judg 7:4 3212
the same shall not *g* .... Judg 7:4 3212
people *g* every man unto his place .... Judg 7:7 3212
But if thou fear to *g* down .... Judg 7:10 3381
g thou with Phurah thy servant .... Judg 7:10 3381
to *g* down unto the host .... Judg 7:11 3381
g to be promoted over the trees .... Judg 9:9 1980
g to be promoted over the trees .... Judg 9:11 1980
g to be promoted over the trees .... Judg 9:13 1980
g out, I pray now, and fight with .... Judg 9:38 3318
G and cry unto the gods which ye .... Judg 10:14 3212
now, that thou mayest *g* with us .... Judg 11:8 1980
unto the LORD, and I cannot *g* back .... Judg 11:35 7725
alone two months, that I may *g* up .... Judg 11:37 3212
And he said, *G* .... Judg 11:38 3212
didst not call us to *g* with thee .... Judg 12:1 3212
were escaped said, Let me *g* over .... Judg 12:5 5674
I will *g* in to my wife into the .... Judg 15:1 935
would not suffer him to *g* in .... Judg 15:1 935
he let them *g* into the standing .... Judg 15:5 7971
then my strength will *g* from me .... Judg 16:17 5493
I will *g* out as at other times .... Judg 16:20 3318
I *g* to sojourn where I may find a .... Judg 17:9 1980
and they said unto them, *G* .... Judg 18:2 3212
which we *g* shall be prosperous .... Judg 18:5 1980
priest said unto them, *G* in peace .... Judg 18:6 3212
the LORD is your way wherein ye *g* .... Judg 18:6 3212
that we may *g* up against them .... Judg 18:9 5927
be not slothful to *g*, and to enter .... Judg 18:9 3212
When ye *g*, ye shall come unto a .... Judg 18:10 935
g with us, and be to us a father .... Judg 18:19 3212
of bread, and afterward *g* your way .... Judg 19:5 3212
your way, that thou mayest *g* home .... Judg 19:9 1980
turned aside thither, to *g* in .... Judg 19:15 935
began to spring, they let her *g* .... Judg 19:25 7971
house, and went out to *g* his way .... Judg 19:27 3212
will not any of us *g* to his tent .... Judg 20:8 3212
we will *g* up by lot against it .... Judg 20:9 3212
to *g* out to battle against the .... Judg 20:14 3318
Which of us shall *g* up first to .... Judg 20:18 5927
LORD said, Judah shall *g* up first .... Judg 20:18 3212
Shall I *g* up again to battle .... Judg 20:23 5066
the LORD said, *G* up against him .... Judg 20:23 5927
Shall I yet again *g* out to battle .... Judg 20:28 3318
And the LORD said, *G* up .... Judg 20:28 5927
and commanded them, saying, *G* .... Judg 21:10 3212
children of Benjamin, saying, *G* .... Judg 21:20 3212
g to the land of Benjamin .... Judg 21:21 1980
unto her two daughters in law, *G* .... Ruth 1:8 3212
why will ye *g* with me .... Ruth 1:11 3212
again, my daughters, *g* your way .... Ruth 1:12 3212

for whither thou goest, I will *g* .... Ruth 1:16 3212
stedfastly minded to *g* with her .... Ruth 1:18 3212
Let me now *g* to the field, and .... Ruth 2:2 3212
And she said unto her, *G*, my .... Ruth 2:2 3212
G not to glean in another field, ... Ruth 2:8 3212
neither *g* from hence, but abide .... Ruth 2:8 5674
do reap, and *g* thou after them .... Ruth 2:9 1980
g unto the vessels, and drink of .... Ruth 2:9 1980
that thou *g* out with his maidens, ... Ruth 2:22 3318
he shall lie, and thou shalt *g* in .... Ruth 3:4 935
G not empty unto thy mother in .... Ruth 3:17 935
Eli answered and said, *G* in peace 1Sa 1:17 3212
I will not *g* up until the child 1Sa 1:22
Therefore Eli said unto Samuel, *G* 1Sa 3:9 3212
let it *g* again to his own place, ... 1Sa 5:11 7725
did they not let the people *g* 1Sa 6:6 7971
and send it away, that it may *g* 1Sa 6:8 1980
and to whom shall he *g* up from us 1Sa 6:20 5927
g out before us, and fight our 1Sa 8:20 3318
G ye every man unto his city 1Sa 8:22 3212
thee, and arise, *g* seek the asses 1Sa 9:3 3212
now let us *g* thither 1Sa 9:6 3212
shew us our way that we should *g* 1Sa 9:6 1980
his servant, But, behold, if we *g* 1Sa 9:7 3212
Come, and let us *g* to the seer 1Sa 9:9 3212
come, let us *g* 1Sa 9:10 3212
before he *g* up to the high place 1Sa 9:13 5927
for to *g* up to the high place 1Sa 9:14 5927
g up before me unto the high 1Sa 9:19 5927
and to morrow I will let thee *g* 1Sa 9:19 7971
Then shalt thou *g* on forward from 1Sa 10:3 2498
thou shalt *g* down before me to 1Sa 10:8 3381
turned his back to *g* from Samuel 1Sa 10:9 3212
let us *g* to Gilgal, and renew the 1Sa 11:14 3212
should ye *g* after vain things 1Sa 12:21 3212
let us *g* over to the Philistines' 1Sa 14:1 5674
to *g* over unto the Philistines' 1Sa 14:4 5674
let us *g* over unto the garrison 1Sa 14:6 5674
place, and will not *g* up unto them 1Sa 14:9 5927
then we will *g* up 1Sa 14:10 5927
said, Let us *g* down after the 1Sa 14:36 3381
of God, Shall I *g* down after the 1Sa 14:37 3381
Now *g* and smite Amalek, and utterly 1Sa 15:3 3212
And Saul said unto the Kenites, *G* 1Sa 15:6 3212
thee on a journey, and said, *G* 1Sa 15:18 3212
as Samuel turned about to *g* away 1Sa 15:27 3212
fill thine horn with oil, and *g* 1Sa 16:1 3212
And Samuel said, How can I *g* 1Sa 16:2 3212
thy servant will *g* and fight with 1Sa 17:32 3212
Thou art not able to *g* against 1Sa 17:33 3212
And Saul said unto David, *G* 1Sa 17:37 3212
his armour, and he assayed to *g* 1Sa 17:39 3212
unto Saul, I cannot *g* with these 1Sa 17:39 3212
when Saul saw David *g* forth 1Sa 17:55 3318
would let him *g* no more home to 1Sa 18:2 7725
And I will *g* out and stand beside 1Sa 19:3 3318
Saul, He said unto me, Let me *g* 1Sa 19:17 7971
but let me *g*, that I may hide 1Sa 20:5 7971
let us *g* out into the field 1Sa 20:11 3318
away, that thou mayest *g* in peace 1Sa 20:13 1980
then thou shalt *g* down quickly 1Sa 20:19 3381
I will send a lad, saying, *G* 1Sa 20:21 3212
g thy way: for the LORD hath 1Sa 20:22 3212
leave of me to *g* to Beth-lehem 1Sa 20:28
And he said, Let me *g*, I pray thee 1Sa 20:29 7971
unto his lad, and said unto him, *G* 1Sa 20:40 3212
G in peace, forasmuch as we have 1Sa 20:42 3212
of the LORD, saying, Shall I *g* 1Sa 23:2 3212
And the LORD said unto David, *G* 1Sa 23:2 3212
and said, Arise, *g* down to Keilah 1Sa 23:4 3381
to *g* down to Keilah, to besiege 1Sa 23:8 3381
went whithersoever they could *g* 1Sa 23:13 1980
and he forbare to *g* forth 1Sa 23:13 3318
G, I pray you, prepare yet, and 1Sa 23:22 3212
certainty, and I will *g* with you 1Sa 23:23 1980
will he let him *g* well away 1Sa 24:19 7971
g to Nabal, and greet him in my 1Sa 25:5 935
unto her servants, *G* on before me 1Sa 25:19 5674
G up in peace to thine house 1Sa 25:35 5927
Who will *g* down with me to Saul 1Sa 26:6 3381
said, I will *g* down with thee 1Sa 26:6 3381
the cruse of water, and let us *g* 1Sa 26:11 3212
of the LORD, saying, *G*, serve 1Sa 26:19 3212
that thou shalt *g* out with me to 1Sa 28:1 3318
spirit, that I may *g* to her 1Sa 28:7 3212
that he may *g* again to his place 1Sa 29:4 7725
let him not *g* down with us to 1Sa 29:4 3381
g in peace, that thou displease 1Sa 29:7 3212
that I may not *g* fight against 1Sa 29:8 3212
He shall not *g* up with us to the 1Sa 29:9 5927
could not *g* over the brook Besor 1Sa 30:10 5674
and said, *G* near, and fall upon him 2Sa 1:15 5066
Shall I *g* up into any of the 2Sa 2:1 5927
And the LORD said unto him, *G* up 2Sa 2:1 5927
David said, Whither shall I *g* up 2Sa 2:1 5927
Then said Abner unto him, *G* 2Sa 3:16 3212
unto David, I will arise and *g* 2Sa 3:21 3212
Shall I *g* up to the Philistines 2Sa 5:19 5927
And the LORD said unto David, *G* up 2Sa 5:19 5927
he said, Thou shalt not *g* up 2Sa 5:23 5927
shall the LORD *g* out before thee 2Sa 5:24 3318
And Nathan said to the king, *G* 2Sa 7:3 3212
G and tell my servant David, Thus 2Sa 7:5 3212
time when kings *g* forth to battle 2Sa 11:1 3318
G down to thy house, and wash thy 2Sa 11:8 3381
thou not *g* down unto thine house 2Sa 11:10 3381
shall I then *g* into mine house, ... 2Sa 11:11 935
I shall *g* to him, but he shall 2Sa 12:23 1980

G now to thy brother Amnon's 2Sa 13:7 3212
shall I cause my shame to *g* 2Sa 13:13 3212
his servants *g* with thy servant 2Sa 13:24 3212
Nay, my son, let us not all now *g* 2Sa 13:25 3212
howbeit he would not *g*, but 2Sa 13:25 3212
let my brother Amnon *g* with us 2Sa 13:26 3212
him, Why should he *g* with thee 2Sa 13:26 3212
and all the king's sons *g* with him 2Sa 13:27 7971
longed to *g* forth unto Absalom 2Sa 13:39 3318
G to thine house, and I will give 2Sa 14:8 3212
g therefore, bring the young man 2Sa 14:21 3212
g and set it on fire 2Sa 14:30 3212
the king, I pray thee, let me *g* 2Sa 15:7 3212
king said unto him, *G* in peace 2Sa 15:9 3212
should I this day make thee *g* up 2Sa 15:20 3212
seeing I *g* whither I may, return 2Sa 15:20 1980
And David said to Ittai, *G* 2Sa 15:22 3212
let me *g* over, I pray thee, and 2Sa 16:9 5674
G in unto thy father's concubines 2Sa 16:21 935
that thou *g* to battle in thine 2Sa 17:11 1980
I will surely *g* forth with you 2Sa 18:2 3318
answered, Thou shalt not *g* forth 2Sa 18:3 3318
G tell the king what thou hast 2Sa 18:21 3212
g forth, and speak comfortably 2Sa 19:7 3318
if thou *g* not forth, there will 2Sa 19:7 3318
to *g* to meet the king, to conduct 2Sa 19:15 3212
g down to meet my lord the king 2Sa 19:20 3381
ride thereon, and *g* to the king 2Sa 19:26 3212
that I should *g* up with the king 2Sa 19:34 5927
Thy servant will *g* a little way 2Sa 19:36 5674
let him *g* over with my lord the 2Sa 19:37 5674
Chimham shall *g* over with me 2Sa 19:38 5674
for David, let him *g* after Joab 2Sa 20:11 3212
Thou shalt *g* no more out with us 2Sa 21:17 3318
David against them to say, *G* 2Sa 24:1 3212
G now through all the tribes of 2Sa 24:2 7751
G and say unto David, Thus saith 2Sa 24:12 1980
G up, rear an altar unto the LORD 2Sa 24:18 5927
G and get thee in unto king David, 1Kin 1:13 3212
said unto him, *G* to thine house 1Kin 1:53 3212
I *g* the way of all the earth 1Kin 2:2 1980
let not his hoar head *g* down to 1Kin 2:6 3381
the son of Jehoiada, saying, *G* 1Kin 2:29 3212
g not forth thence any whither 1Kin 2:36 3318
know not how to *g* out or come in 1Kin 3:7 3318
If thy people *g* out to battle 1Kin 8:44 3318
I have set before you, but *g* 1Kin 9:6 1980
Israel, Ye shall not *g* in to them 1Kin 11:2 935
he should not *g* after other gods 1Kin 11:10 3212
with him, to *g* into Egypt 1Kin 11:17 935
that I may *g* to mine own country 1Kin 11:21 3212
thou seekest to *g* to thine own 1Kin 11:22 3212
howbeit let me *g* in any wise 1Kin 11:22 7971
saith the LORD, Ye shall not *g* up 1Kin 12:24 5927
If this people *g* up to do 1Kin 12:27 5927
g again to Rehoboam king of Judah 1Kin 12:27 7725
much for you to *g* up to Jerusalem 1Kin 12:28 5927
I will not *g* in with thee, 1Kin 13:8 935
with thee, nor *g* in with thee 1Kin 13:16 935
nor turn again to *g* by the way 1Kin 13:17 3212
and a cruse of honey, and *g* to him 1Kin 14:3 935
G, tell Jeroboam, Thus saith the 1Kin 14:7 3212
g out or come in to Asa king of 1Kin 15:17 3318
two sticks, that I may *g* in 1Kin 17:12 935
g and do as thou hast said 1Kin 17:13 935
in the third year, saying, *G* 1Kin 18:1 3212
G into the land, unto all 1Kin 18:5 3212
g, tell thy lord, Behold, Elijah 1Kin 18:8 3212
And now thou sayest, *G*, tell thy 1Kin 18:11 3212
And now thou sayest, *G*, tell thy 1Kin 18:14 3212
G up now, look toward the sea 1Kin 18:43 5927
And he said, *G* again seven times 1Kin 18:43 7725
G up, say unto Ahab, Prepare thy 1Kin 18:44 5927
G forth, and stand upon the mount 1Kin 19:11 3318
And the LORD said unto him, *G* 1Kin 19:15 3212
And he said unto him, *G* back again 1Kin 19:20 3212
of Israel, and said unto him, *G* 1Kin 20:22 3212
g out to the king of Israel 1Kin 20:31 3318
Then he said, *G* ye, bring him 1Kin 20:33 935
Because thou hast let *g* out of 1Kin 20:42 7971
thy life shall *g* for his life 1Kin 20:42 1961
that Ahab rose up to *g* down to 1Kin 21:16 3381
g down to meet Ahab king of 1Kin 21:18 3381
Wilt thou *g* with me to battle to 1Kin 22:4 3212
Shall I *g* against Ramoth-gilead 1Kin 22:6 3212
And they said, *G* up 1Kin 22:6 5927
G up to Ramoth-gilead, and prosper 1Kin 22:12 5927
shall we *g* against Ramoth-gilead 1Kin 22:15 3212
And he answered him, *G*, and prosper 1Kin 22:15 5927
persuade Ahab, that he may *g* up 1Kin 22:20 5927
And he said, I will *g* forth 1Kin 22:22 3318
g forth, and do so 1Kin 22:22 3318
when thou shalt *g* into an inner 1Kin 22:25 935
Tharshish to *g* to Ophir for gold 1Kin 22:48 3212
Let my servants *g* with thy 1Kin 22:49 3212
messengers, and said unto them, *G* 2Kin 1:2 3212
g up to meet the messengers of 2Kin 1:3 5927
Israel, that ye *g* to enquire of 2Kin 1:3 1980
up to meet us, and said unto us, *G* 2Kin 1:6 3212
said unto Elijah, *G* down with him 2Kin 1:15 3381
let them *g*, we pray thee, and seek 2Kin 2:16 3212
Did I not say unto you, *G* not 2Kin 2:18 3212
unto him, *G* up, thou bald head 2Kin 2:23 5927
g up, thou bald head 2Kin 2:23 5927
wilt thou *g* with me against Moab 2Kin 3:7 3212
And he said, I will *g* up 2Kin 3:7 5927
he said, Which way shall we *g* up 2Kin 3:8 5927
Then he said, *G*, borrow thee 2Kin 4:3 3212

And he said, *G*, sell the oil, and 2Kin 4:7 3212
wilt thou *g* to him to day 2Kin 4:23 1980
her servant, Drive, and *g* forward 2Kin 4:24 3212
staff in thine hand, and *g* thy way 2Kin 4:29 3212
G to, *g*, and I will send a letter 2Kin 5:5 3212
the king of Syria said, *G* to, *g* 2Kin 5:5 935
a messenger unto him, saying, *G* 2Kin 5:10 1980
And he said unto him, *G* in peace 2Kin 5:19 3212
and he let the men *g*, and they 2Kin 5:24 7971
Let us *g*, we pray thee, unto 2Kin 6:2 3212
And he answered, *G* ye 2Kin 6:2 3212
pray thee, and *g* with thy servants 2Kin 6:3 3212
And he answered, I will *g* 2Kin 6:3 3212
And he said, *G* and spy where he is, 2Kin 6:13 3212
and drink, and *g* to their master 2Kin 6:22 3212
to *g* unto the camp of the Syrians 2Kin 7:5 935
now therefore come, that we may *g* 2Kin 7:9 935
host of the Syrians, saying, *G* 2Kin 7:14 3212
g thou and thine household, and 2Kin 8:1 3212
a present in thine hand, and *g* 2Kin 8:8 3212
And Elisha said unto him, *G* 2Kin 8:10 3212
thine hand, and *g* to Ramoth-gilead 2Kin 9:1 3212
g in, and make him arise up from 2Kin 9:2 935
then let none *g* forth nor escape 2Kin 9:15 3318
city to *g* to tell it in Jezreel 2Kin 9:15 3212
he did eat and drink, and said, *G* 2Kin 9:34 6485
we *g* down to salute the children 2Kin 10:13 3381
escape, he that letteth him *g* 2Kin 10:24
the captains, *G* in, and slay them 2Kin 10:25 935
you that *g* forth on the sabbath 2Kin 11:7 3318
that should *g* out on the sabbath 2Kin 11:9 3318
set his face to *g* up to Jerusalem 2Kin 12:17 5927
and let them *g* and dwell there, and 2Kin 17:27 3212
it will *g* into his hand, and 2Kin 18:21 935
G up against this land, and 2Kin 18:25 5927
Jerusalem shall *g* forth a remnant 2Kin 19:31 3318
on the third day thou shalt *g* up 2Kin 20:5 5927
that I shall *g* up into the house 2Kin 20:8 5927
shall the shadow *g* forward ten 2Kin 20:9 1980
degrees, or *g* back ten degrees 2Kin 20:9 7725
the shadow to *g* down ten degrees 2Kin 20:10 5186
G up to Hilkiah the high priest, 2Kin 22:4 5927
G ye, enquire of the LORD for me, 2Kin 22:13 3212
fit to *g* out for war and battle 1Chr 7:11 3318
saying, Shall I *g* up against the 1Chr 14:10 5927
And the LORD said unto him, *G* up 1Chr 14:10 5927
unto him, *G* not up after them 1Chr 14:14 5927
then thou shalt *g* out to battle 1Chr 14:15 3318
G and tell David my servant, Thus 1Chr 17:4 3212
must *g* to be with thy fathers 1Chr 17:11 3212
time that kings *g* out to battle 1Chr 20:1 3318
and to the rulers of the people, *G* 1Chr 21:2 3212
G and tell David, saying, Thus 1Chr 21:10 3212
to David, that David should *g* up 1Chr 21:18 5927
But David could not *g* before it 1Chr 21:30 3212
and knowledge, that I may *g* out 2Chr 1:10 3318
If thy people *g* out to war 2Chr 6:34 3318
I have set before you, and shall *g* 2Chr 7:19 1980
saith the LORD, Ye shall not *g* up 2Chr 11:4 5927
in thy name we *g* against this 2Chr 14:11 935
g out or come in to Asa king of 2Chr 16:1 3318
g, break thy league with Baasha 2Chr 16:3 3212
persuaded him to *g* up with him to 2Chr 18:2 5927
of Judah, Wilt thou *g* with me to 2Chr 18:3 3212
Shall we *g* to Ramoth-gilead to 2Chr 18:5 3212
And they said, *G* up 2Chr 18:5 5927
G up to Ramoth-gilead, and prosper 2Chr 18:11 5927
shall we *g* to Ramoth-gilead to 2Chr 18:14 3212
G ye up, and prosper, and they 2Chr 18:14 5927
king of Israel, that he may *g* up 2Chr 18:19 5927
And he said, I will *g* out, and be a 2Chr 18:21 3318
g out, and do even so 2Chr 18:21 3318
g into an inner chamber to hide 2Chr 18:24 935
myself, and will *g* to the battle 2Chr 18:29 935
To morrow *g* ye down against them 2Chr 20:16 3381
to morrow *g* out against them 2Chr 20:17 3318
to *g* again to Jerusalem with joy 2Chr 20:27 7725
to make ships to *g* to Tarshish 2Chr 20:36 3212
were not able to *g* to Tarshish 2Chr 20:37 3212
of Jerusalem to *g* a whoring 2Chr 21:13 2181
they shall *g* in, for they are 2Chr 23:6 935
that were to *g* out on the sabbath 2Chr 23:8 3318
G out unto the cities of Judah, 2Chr 24:5 3318
able to *g* forth to war, that 2Chr 25:5 3318
the army of Israel *g* with thee 2Chr 25:7 935
But if thou wilt *g*, do it, be 2Chr 25:8 935
out of Ephraim, to *g* home again 2Chr 25:10 3212
should not *g* with him to battle 2Chr 25:13 3212
g out of the sanctuary 2Chr 26:18 3318
yea, himself hasted also to *g* out 2Chr 26:20 3318
G, enquire of the LORD for me, and 2Chr 34:21 3212
God be with him, and let him *g* up 2Chr 36:23 5927
let him *g* up to Jerusalem, which Ezr 1:3 5927
to *g* up to build the house of the Ezr 1:5 5927
unto him, Take these vessels, *g* Ezr 5:15 236
began he to *g* up from Babylon Ezr 7:9 4609
g up to Jerusalem, *g* with thee Ezr 7:13 1946
Israel chief men to *g* up with me Ezr 7:28 5927
first month, to *g* unto Jerusalem Ezr 8:31 3212
unto which ye *g* to possess it Ezr 9:11 935
unto the stairs that *g* down from Neh 3:15 3381
which they build, if a fox *g* up Neh 4:3 5927
would *g* into the temple to save Neh 6:11 935
I will not *g* in Neh 6:11 935
G your way, eat the fat, and drink Neh 8:10 3212
G forth unto the mount, and fetch Neh 8:15 3318
in the way wherein they should *g* Neh 9:12 3212
them that they should *g* in to Neh 9:15 935

and the way wherein they should *g* Neh 9:19 3212
they should *g* in to possess it Neh 9:23 935
let there *g* a royal commandment Est 1:19 3318
come to *g* in to king Ahasuerus Est 2:12 935
to *g* with her out of the house of Est 2:13 935
was come to *g* in unto the king, Est 2:15 935
she should *g* in unto the king Est 4:8 935
G, gather together all the Jews Est 4:16 3212
so will I *g* in unto the king, Est 4:16 935
then *g* thou in merrily with the Est 5:14 935
which is in them *g* away Job 4:21 5265
they *g* to nothing, and perish Job 6:18 5927
Before I *g* whence I shall not Job 10:21 3212
such words *g* out of thy mouth Job 15:13 3318
of his mouth shall he *g* away Job 15:30 5493
then I shall *g* the way whence I Job 16:22 1980
They shall *g* down to the bars of Job 17:16 3381
it shall *g* ill with him that is Job 20:26 3415
in a moment *g* down to the grave Job 21:13 5181
not asked them that *g* by the way Job 21:29 5674
I *g* forward, but he is not there Job 23:8 1980
g they forth to their work Job 24:5 3318
They cause him to *g* naked without Job 24:10 1980
I hold fast, and will not let it *g* Job 27:6 7503
a prince would I *g* near unto him Job 31:37 7126
Then the beasts *g* into dens Job 37:8 935
send lightnings, that they may *g* Job 38:35 3212
they *g* forth, and return not unto Job 39:4 3318
Out of his mouth *g* burning lamps Job 41:19 1980
g to my servant Job, and offer up Job 42:8 3212
all they that *g* down to the dust Ps 22:29 3381
persons, neither will I *g* in with Ps 26:4 935
them that *g* down into the pit Ps 28:1 3381
I should not *g* down to the pit Ps 30:3 3381
blood, when I *g* down to the pit Ps 30:9 3381
in the way which thou shalt *g* Ps 32:8 3212
I *g* mourning all the day long Ps 38:6 1980
strength, before I *g* hence Ps 39:13 3212
why *g* I mourning because of the Ps 42:9 3212
Why *g* I mourning because of the Ps 43:2 1980
Then will I *g* unto the altar of Ps 43:4 935
about Zion, and *g* round about her Ps 48:12 5362
He shall *g* to the generation of Ps 49:19 935
night they *g* about it upon the Ps 55:10 5437
let them *g* down quick into hell Ps 55:15 3381
they *g* astray as soon as they be Ps 58:3 8582
a dog, and *g* round about the city Ps 59:6 5437
a dog, and *g* round about the city Ps 59:14 5437
which didst not *g* out with our Ps 60:10 3318
shall *g* into the lower parts of Ps 63:9 935
I will *g* into thy house with Ps 66:13 935
I will *g* in the strength of the Ps 71:16 935
them that *g* a whoring from thee Ps 73:27 2181
own people to *g* forth like sheep Ps 78:52 5265
So will not we *g* back from thee Ps 80:18 5472
They *g* from strength to strength, Ps 84:7 3212
Righteousness shall *g* before him Ps 85:13 1980
them that *g* down into the pit Ps 88:4 3381
truth shall *g* before thy face Ps 89:14 6923
They *g* up by the mountains Ps 104:8 5927
they *g* down by the valleys unto Ps 104:8 3381
There *g* the ships Ps 104:26 1980
of the people, and let him *g* free Ps 105:20
that they might *g* to a city of Ps 107:7 3212
They that *g* down to the sea in Ps 107:23 3381
they *g* down again to the depths Ps 107:26 3381
O God, *g* forth with our hosts Ps 108:11 3318
neither any that *g* down into Ps 115:17 3381
I will *g* into them, and I will Ps 118:19 935
Make me to *g* in the path of thy Ps 119:35 1869
Let us *g* into the house of the Ps 122:1 3212
Whither the tribes *g* up, the Ps 122:4 5927
Neither do they which *g* by say Ps 129:8 5674
of my house, nor *g* up into my bed Ps 132:3 5927
We will *g* into his tabernacles Ps 132:7 935
Whither shall I *g* from thy spirit Ps 139:7 3212
them that *g* down into the pit Ps 143:7 3381
as those that *g* down into the pit Prov 1:12 3381
None that *g* unto her return again Prov 2:19 935
Say not unto thy neighbour, *G* Prov 3:28 3212
let her not *g* Prov 4:13 7503
g not in the way of evil men Prov 4:14 833
Her feet *g* down to death Prov 5:5 3381
of his folly he shall *g* astray Prov 5:23 7686
g, humble thyself, and make sure Prov 6:3 3212
G to the ant, thou sluggard Prov 6:6 3212
Can one *g* upon hot coals, and his Prov 6:28 1980
g not astray in her paths Prov 7:25 8582
g in the way of understanding Prov 9:6 833
who *g* right on their ways Prov 9:15 3474
G from the presence of a foolish Prov 14:7 3212
neither will he *g* unto the wise Prov 15:12 3212
they *g* down into the innermost Prov 18:8 3381
do his friends *g* far from him Prov 19:7 7368
up a child in the way he should *g* Prov 22:6 6310
and contention shall *g* out Prov 22:10 3318
a furious man thou shalt not *g* Prov 22:24 935
they that *g* to seek mixed wine Prov 23:30 935
G not forth hastily to strive, Prov 25:8 3318
they *g* down into the innermost Prov 26:22 3381
neither *g* into thy brother's Prov 27:10 935
to *g* astray in an evil way Prov 28:10 7686
yet *g* they forth all of them by Prov 30:27 3318
be three things which *g* well Prov 30:29 6806
G to now, I will prove thee with Eccl 2:1 3212
All *g* unto one place Eccl 3:20 1980
shall he return to *g* as he came Eccl 5:15 3212
points as he came, so shall he *g* Eccl 5:16 3212

G

do not all *g* to one place	Eccl 6:6	1980
It is better to *g* to the house of	Eccl 7:2	3212
than to *g* to the house of	Eccl 7:2	3212
Be not hasty to *g* out of his	Eccl 8:3	3212
and after that they *g* to the dead	Eccl 9:3	
G thy way, eat thy bread with joy	Eccl 9:7	3212
knoweth not how to *g* to the city	Eccl 10:15	3212
the mourners *g* about the streets	Eccl 12:5	5437
g thy way forth by the footsteps	Song 1:8	3318
g about the city in the streets,	Song 3:2	5437
The watchmen that *g* about the	Song 3:3	5437
held him, and would not let him *g*	Song 3:4	7503
G forth, O ye daughters of Zion,	Song 3:11	3318
sheep which *g* up from the washing	Song 6:6	5927
I will *g* up to the palm tree, I	Song 7:8	5927
let us *g* forth into the field	Song 7:11	3318
And many people shall *g* and say,	Is 2:3	1980
let us *g* up to the mountain of	Is 2:3	5927
out of Zion shall *g* forth the law	Is 2:3	3318
they shall *g* into the holes of	Is 2:19	935
To *g* into the clefts of the rocks	Is 2:21	935
walking and mincing as they *g*	Is 3:16	3212
And now *g* to	Is 5:5	
their blossom shall *g* up as dust	Is 5:24	5927
I send, and who will *g* for us	Is 6:8	3212
And he said, *G*, and tell this	Is 6:9	3212
G forth now to meet Ahaz, thou,	Is 7:3	3318
Let us *g* up against Judah, and vex	Is 7:6	5927
waters of Shiloah that *g* softly	Is 8:6	1980
channels, and *g* over all his banks	Is 8:7	1980
g over, he shall reach even to	Is 8:8	5674
and make men *g* over dryshod	Is 11:15	1869
that they may *g* into the gates of	Is 13:2	935
that *g* down to the stones of the	Is 14:19	3381
with weeping shall they *g* it up	Is 15:5	5927
upon the waters, saying, *G*	Is 18:2	3212
Isaiah the son of Amoz, saying, *G*	Is 20:2	3212
G up, O Elam	Is 21:2	5927
hath the Lord said unto me, *G*	Is 21:6	3212
saith the Lord GOD of hosts, *G*	Is 22:15	3212
g about the city, thou harlot	Is 23:16	5437
I would *g* through them, I would	Is 27:4	6585
that they might *g*, and fall	Is 28:13	3212
That walk to *g* down into Egypt,	Is 30:2	3381
Now *g*, write it before them in a	Is 30:8	935
Woe to them that *g* down to Egypt	Is 31:1	3381
wherein shall *g* no galley with	Is 33:21	3212
smoke thereof shall *g* up for ever	Is 34:10	5927
ravenous beast shall *g* up thereon	Is 35:9	5927
it will *g* into his hand, and	Is 36:6	935
G up against this land, and	Is 36:10	5927
Jerusalem shall *g* forth a remnant	Is 37:32	3318
G, and say to Hezekiah, Thus saith	Is 38:5	1980
I shall *g* to the gates of the	Is 38:10	3212
I shall *g* softly all my years in	Is 38:15	1718
they that *g* down into the pit	Is 38:18	3381
g up to the house of the LORD	Is 38:22	5927
ye that *g* down to the sea, and all	Is 42:10	3381
The LORD shall *g* forth as a	Is 42:13	3318
I will *g* before thee, and make the	Is 45:2	3212
and he shall let *g* my captives	Is 45:13	7971
they shall *g* to confusion	Is 45:16	1980
by the way that thou shouldest *g*	Is 48:17	3212
G ye forth of Babylon, flee ye	Is 48:20	3318
say to the prisoners, *G* forth	Is 49:9	3318
thee waste shall *g* forth of thee	Is 49:17	3318
Bow down, that we may *g* over	Is 51:23	5674
g ye out from thence, touch no	Is 52:11	3318
g ye out of the midst of her	Is 52:11	3318
For ye shall not *g* out with haste	Is 52:12	3318
nor *g* by flight: for the LORD	Is 52:12	3212
for the LORD will *g* before you	Is 52:12	1980
should no more *g* over the earth	Is 54:9	5674
For ye shall *g* out with joy	Is 55:12	3318
and to let the oppressed *g* free	Is 58:6	7971
righteousness shall *g* before thee	Is 58:8	1980
Thy sun shall no more *g* down	Is 60:20	935
thereof *g* forth as brightness	Is 62:1	3318
G through, *g* through the gates	Is 62:10	5674
And they shall *g* forth, and look	Is 66:24	3318
for thou shalt *g* to all that I	Jer 1:7	3212
G and cry in the ears of Jerusalem	Jer 2:2	1980
strangers, and after them will I *g*	Jer 2:25	3212
thou shalt *g* forth from him, and	Jer 2:37	3318
she *g* from him, and become another	Jer 3:1	1980
G and proclaim these words toward	Jer 3:12	1980
let us *g* into the defenced cities	Jer 4:5	935
they shall *g* into thickets, and	Jer 4:29	935
G ye up upon her walls, and	Jer 5:10	5927
arise, and let us *g* up at noon	Jer 6:4	5927
let us *g* by night, and let us	Jer 6:5	5927
G not forth into the field, nor	Jer 6:25	3318
But *g* ye now unto my place which	Jer 7:12	3212
leave my people, and *g* from them	Jer 9:2	3212
be borne, because they cannot *g*	Jer 10:5	6805
and inhabitants of Jerusalem *g*	Jer 11:12	1980
Thus saith the LORD unto me, *G*	Jer 13:1	1980
g to Euphrates, and hide it there	Jer 13:4	3212
g to Euphrates, and take the	Jer 13:6	3212
If I *g* forth into the field, then	Jer 14:18	3318
the priest *g* about into a land	Jer 14:18	5503
of my sight, and let them *g* forth	Jer 15:1	3318
thee, Whither shall we *g* forth	Jer 15:2	3318
or who shall *g* aside to ask how	Jer 15:5	5493
neither *g* to lament nor bemoan	Jer 16:5	3212
Thou shalt not also *g* into the	Jer 16:8	935
G and stand in the gate of the	Jer 17:19	1980
in, and by the which they *g* out	Jer 17:19	3318
g down to the potter's house, and	Jer 18:2	3381
Now therefore *g* to, speak to the	Jer 18:11	4994
Thus saith the LORD, *G* and get a	Jer 19:1	1980
g forth unto the valley of the	Jer 19:2	3318
sight of the men that *g* with thee	Jer 19:10	1980
house shall *g* into captivity	Jer 20:6	3212
works, that he may *g* up from us	Jer 21:2	5927
lest my fury *g* out like fire, and	Jer 21:12	3318
G down to the house of the king	Jer 22:1	3381
G up to Lebanon, and cry	Jer 22:20	5927
thy lovers shall *g* into captivity	Jer 22:22	3212
g not after other gods to serve	Jer 25:6	3212
evil shall *g* forth from nation to	Jer 25:32	3318
and at Jerusalem, *g* not to Babylon	Jer 27:18	935
G and tell Hananiah, saying, Thus	Jer 28:13	1980
ye call upon me, and ye shall *g*	Jer 29:12	1980
of them, shall *g* into captivity	Jer 30:16	3212
shalt *g* forth in the dances of	Jer 31:4	3318
let us *g* up to Zion unto the LORD	Jer 31:6	5927
How long wilt thou *g* about	Jer 31:22	2559
they that *g* forth with flocks	Jer 31:24	5265
the measuring line shall yet *g*	Jer 31:39	3318
G and speak to Zedekiah king of	Jer 34:2	1980
mouth, and thou shalt *g* to Babylon	Jer 34:3	935
an Hebrew or an Hebrewess, *g* free	Jer 34:9	7971
g free, that none should serve	Jer 34:10	7971
then they obeyed, and let them *g*	Jer 34:10	7971
whom they had let *g* free	Jer 34:11	7971
the end of seven years let ye *g*	Jer 34:14	7971
shalt let him *g* free from thee	Jer 34:14	7971
G unto the house of the	Jer 35:2	1980
let us *g* to Jerusalem for fear of	Jer 35:11	935
G and tell the men of Judah and the	Jer 35:13	1980
g not after other gods to serve	Jer 35:15	3212
I cannot *g* into the house of the	Jer 36:5	935
Therefore *g* thou, and read in the	Jer 36:6	935
said the princes unto Baruch, *G*	Jer 36:19	3212
to *g* into the land of Benjamin	Jer 37:12	3212
g forth unto the king of	Jer 38:17	3318
But if thou wilt not *g* forth to	Jer 38:18	3318
But if thou refuse to *g* forth	Jer 38:21	3318
G and speak to Ebed-melech the	Jer 39:16	1980
guard had let him *g* from Ramah	Jer 40:1	7971
for thee to *g*, thither *g*	Jer 40:4	3212
G back also to Gedaliah the son	Jer 40:5	7725
or *g* wheresoever it seemeth	Jer 40:5	3212
seemeth convenient unto thee to *g*	Jer 40:5	3212
and a reward, and let him *g*	Jer 40:5	7971
Mizpah secretly, saying, Let me *g*	Jer 40:15	3212
departed to *g* over to the	Jer 41:10	5674
to *g* to enter into Egypt,	Jer 41:17	3212
but we will *g* into the land of	Jer 42:14	935
into Egypt, and *g* to sojourn there	Jer 42:15	935
to *g* into Egypt to sojourn there	Jer 42:17	935
G ye not into Egypt	Jer 42:19	935
the place whither ye desire to *g*	Jer 42:22	935
G not into Egypt to sojourn there	Jer 43:2	935
he shall *g* forth from thence in	Jer 43:12	3318
to *g* into the land of Egypt to	Jer 44:12	935
and he saith, I will *g* up, and will	Jer 46:8	5927
G up into Gilead, and take balm, O	Jer 46:11	5927
let us *g* again to our own people,	Jer 46:16	7725
thyself to *g* into captivity	Jer 46:19	
thereof shall *g* like a serpent	Jer 46:22	3212
continual weeping shall *g* up	Jer 48:5	5927
Chemosh shall *g* forth into	Jer 48:7	3318
their king shall *g* into captivity	Jer 49:3	3212
shall altogether *g* unpunished	Jer 49:12	5352
thou shalt not *g* unpunished	Jer 49:12	3212
g up to Kedar, and spoil the men	Jer 49:28	5927
they shall *g*, and seek the LORD	Jer 50:4	3212
have caused them to *g* astray	Jer 50:6	8582
g forth out of the land of the	Jer 50:8	3318
G up against the land of	Jer 50:21	5927
let them *g* down to the slaughter	Jer 50:27	3381
they refused to let them *g*	Jer 50:33	7971
let us *g* every one into his own	Jer 51:9	3212
g ye out of the midst of her, and	Jer 51:45	3318
sword, *g* away, stand not still	Jer 51:50	1980
that we cannot *g* in our streets	Lam 4:18	3212
whither the spirit was to *g*	Eze 1:12	3212
Whithersoever the spirit was to *g*	Eze 1:20	3212
thither was their spirit to *g*	Eze 1:20	3212
g speak unto the house of Israel	Eze 3:1	3212
And he said unto me, Son of man, *g*	Eze 3:4	3212
And *g*, get thee to them of the	Eze 3:11	3212
g forth into the plain, and I will	Eze 3:22	3318
spake with me, and said unto me, *G*	Eze 3:24	935
thou shalt not *g* out among them	Eze 3:25	3318
which *g* a whoring after their	Eze 6:9	2181
that I should *g* far off from my	Eze 8:6	7368
G in, and behold the wicked	Eze 8:9	935
G through the midst of the city,	Eze 9:4	5674
G ye after him through the city,	Eze 9:5	5674
with the slain: *g* ye forth	Eze 9:7	3318
G in between the wheels, even	Eze 10:2	935
thou shalt *g* forth at even in	Eze 12:4	3318
as they that *g* forth into	Eze 12:4	4161
shall remove and *g* into captivity	Eze 12:11	3212
in the twilight, and shall *g* forth	Eze 12:12	3318
arms, and will let the souls *g*	Eze 13:20	7971
may *g* no more astray from me	Eze 14:11	8582
and say, Sword, *g* through the land	Eze 14:17	5674
they shall *g* out from one fire,	Eze 15:7	3318
Wherefore I caused them to *g*	Eze 20:10	3318
is the high place whereunto ye *g*	Eze 20:29	935
G ye, serve ye every one his	Eze 20:39	3212
therefore shall my sword *g* forth	Eze 21:4	3318
G thee one way or other, either	Eze 21:16	258
as they *g* in unto a woman that	Eze 23:44	935
I will not *g* back, neither will I	Eze 24:14	6544
shall *g* down to the ground	Eze 26:11	3381
with them that *g* down to the pit,	Eze 26:20	3381
In that day shall messengers *g*	Eze 30:9	3318
cities shall *g* into captivity	Eze 30:17	3212
daughters shall *g* into captivity	Eze 30:18	3212
with them that *g* down to the pit	Eze 31:14	3381
with them that *g* down into the	Eze 32:18	3381
g down, and be thou laid with the	Eze 32:19	3381
with them that *g* down to the pit	Eze 32:24	3381
with them that *g* down to the pit	Eze 32:25	3381
with them that *g* down to the pit	Eze 32:29	3381
with them that *g* down to the pit	Eze 32:30	3381
I will *g* up to the land of	Eze 38:11	5927
I will *g* to them that are at rest	Eze 38:11	935
cities of Israel shall *g* forth	Eze 39:9	3318
were seven steps to *g* up to it	Eze 40:26	5930
then shall they not *g* out of the	Eze 42:14	3318
shall *g* out by the way of the	Eze 44:3	3318
when they *g* forth into the utter	Eze 44:19	3318
then he shall *g* forth	Eze 46:2	3318
he shall *g* in by the way of the	Eze 46:8	935
he shall *g* forth by the way	Eze 46:8	3318
g out by the way of the south	Eze 46:9	3318
g forth by the way of the north	Eze 46:9	3318
but shall *g* forth over against it	Eze 46:9	3318
the midst of them, when they *g* in	Eze 46:10	935
them, when they *g* in, shall *g* in	Eze 46:10	3318
when they *g* forth, shall *g* forth	Eze 46:10	3318
then he shall *g* forth	Eze 46:12	3318
g down into the desert	Eze 47:8	3381
and *g* into the sea	Eze 47:8	935
way of Hethlon, as men *g* to Zedad	Eze 47:15	935
therefore he shall *g* forth with	Dan 11:44	3318
And he said, *G* thy way, Daniel	Dan 12:9	3212
But *g* thou thy way till the end	Dan 12:13	3212
And the LORD said to Hosea, *G*	Hos 1:2	3212
I will *g* after my lovers, that	Hos 2:5	3212
then shall she say, I will *g*	Hos 2:7	3212
G yet, love a woman beloved of	Hos 3:1	3212
neither *g* ye up to Beth-aven, nor	Hos 4:15	5927
They shall *g* with their flocks and	Hos 5:6	3212
I, even I, will tear and *g* away	Hos 5:14	3212
I will *g* and return to my place,	Hos 5:15	3212
call to Egypt, they *g* to Assyria	Hos 7:11	1980
When they shall *g*, I will spread	Hos 7:12	3212
I taught Ephraim also to *g*	Hos 11:3	8637
let the bridegroom *g* forth of his	Joel 2:16	3318
shall *g* into captivity unto Kir	Amos 1:5	1540
their king shall *g* into captivity	Amos 1:15	1980
his father will *g* in unto the	Amos 2:7	3212
ye shall *g* out at the breaches,	Amos 4:3	3318
shall surely *g* into captivity	Amos 5:5	1540
Therefore will I cause you to *g*	Amos 5:27	1540
from thence *g* ye to Hamath the	Amos 6:2	3212
then *g* down to Gath of the	Amos 6:2	3381
Therefore now shall they *g*	Amos 6:7	1540
with the first that *g* captive	Amos 6:7	1540
said unto Amos, O thou seer, *g*	Amos 7:12	3212
and the LORD said unto me, *G*	Amos 7:15	3212
Israel shall surely *g* into	Amos 7:17	1540
cause the sun to *g* down at noon	Amos 8:9	935
though they *g* into captivity	Amos 9:4	3212
g to Nineveh, that great city, and	Jonah 1:2	3212
to *g* with them unto Tarshish from	Jonah 1:3	935
g unto Nineveh, that great city,	Jonah 3:2	3312
I will *g* stripped and naked	Mic 1:8	3212
neither shall ye *g* haughtily	Mic 2:3	3212
the sun shall *g* down over the	Mic 3:6	935
let us *g* up to the mountain of	Mic 4:2	5927
for the law shall *g* forth of Zion	Mic 4:2	3318
for now shalt thou *g* forth out of	Mic 4:10	3318
thou shalt *g* even to Babylon	Mic 4:10	935
if he *g* through, both treadeth	Mic 5:8	5674
g into clay, and tread the morter,	Nah 3:14	935
and judgment doth never *g* forth	Hab 1:4	3318
G up to the mountain, and bring	Hag 1:8	5927
which *g* forth from standing	Zec 6:5	3318
g forth into the north country	Zec 6:6	3318
the white *g* forth after them	Zec 6:6	3318
the grisled *g* forth toward the	Zec 6:6	3318
sought to *g* that they might walk	Zec 6:7	3212
these that *g* toward the north	Zec 6:8	3318
g into the house of Josiah the	Zec 6:10	935
of one city shall *g* to another	Zec 8:21	1980
Let us *g* speedily to pray before	Zec 8:21	3212
I will *g* also	Zec 8:21	3212
a Jew, saying, We will *g* with you	Zec 8:23	3212
his arrow shall *g* forth as the	Zec 9:14	3318
shall *g* with whirlwinds of the	Zec 9:14	1980
city shall *g* forth into captivity	Zec 14:2	3318
Then shall the LORD *g* forth	Zec 14:3	3318
waters shall *g* out from Jerusalem	Zec 14:8	3318
against Jerusalem shall even *g* up	Zec 14:16	5927
if the family of Egypt *g* not up	Zec 14:18	5927
and ye shall *g* forth, and grow up	Mal 4:2	3318
them to Bethlehem, and said, *G*	Mt 2:8	*4198*
g into the land of Israel	Mt 2:20	*4198*
Herod, he was afraid to *g* thither	Mt 2:22	*565*
before the altar, and *g* thy way	Mt 5:24	*5217*
shall compel thee to *g* a mile	Mt 5:41	
g with him twain	Mt 5:41	*5217*
many there be which *g* in thereat	Mt 7:13	*1525*
but *g* thy way, shew thyself to	Mt 8:4	*5217*
and I say to this man, *G*, and he	Mt 8:9	*4198*
unto the centurion, *G* thy way	Mt 8:13	*5217*

him, Lord, suffer me first to g ... Mt 8:21 565
suffer us to g away into the herd ... Mt 8:31 565
And he said unto them, G ... Mt 8:32 5217
up thy bed, and g unto thine house ... Mt 9:6 5217
But g ye and learn what that ... Mt 9:13 4198
G not into the way of the ... Mt 10:5 565
But g rather to the lost sheep of ... Mt 10:6 4198
And as ye g, preach, saying, The ... Mt 10:7 4198
and there abide till ye g thence ... Mt 10:11 1831
answered and said unto them, G ... Mt 11:4 4198
him, Wilt thou then that we g ... Mt 13:28 565
that they may g into the villages ... Mt 14:15 565
to g before him unto the other ... Mt 14:22 4254
on the water, to g to Jesus ... Mt 14:29 2064
how that he must g unto Jerusalem ... Mt 16:21 565
g thou to the sea, and cast an ... Mt 17:27 4198
shall trespass against thee, g ... Mt 18:15 5217
him, If thou wilt be perfect, g ... Mt 19:21 5217
to g through the eye of a needle ... Mt 19:24 1330
G ye also into the vineyard, and ... Mt 20:4 5217
G ye also into the vineyard ... Mt 20:7 5217
Take that thine is, and g thy way ... Mt 20:14 5217
Behold, we g up to Jerusalem ... Mt 20:18 305
G into the village over against ... Mt 21:2 4198
g work to day in my vineyard ... Mt 21:28 5217
And he answered and said, I g sir ... Mt 21:30 5217
the harlots g into the kingdom of ... Mt 21:31 4254
G ye therefore into the highways, ... Mt 22:9 4198
for ye neither g in yourselves ... Mt 23:13 1525
ye them that are entering to g in ... Mt 23:13 1525
g not forth ... Mt 24:26 1831
g ye out to meet him ... Mt 25:6 1831
but g ye rather to them that sell ... Mt 25:9 4198
And these shall g away into ... Mt 25:46 565
G into the city to such a man, and ... Mt 26:18 5217
I will g before you into Galilee ... Mt 26:32 4254
disciples, Sit ye here, while I g ... Mt 26:36 565
g your way, make it as sure as ye ... Mt 27:65 5217
g quickly, and tell his disciples ... Mt 28:7 4198
g tell my brethren ... Mt 28:10 565
that they g into Galilee ... Mt 28:10 5217
G ye therefore, and teach all ... Mt 28:19 4198
Let us g into the next towns, ... Mk 1:38 71
but g thy way, shew thyself to ... Mk 1:44 5217
g thy way into thine house ... Mk 2:11 5217
G home to thy friends, and tell ... Mk 5:19 5217
g in peace, and be whole of thy ... Mk 5:34 5217
that they may g into the country ... Mk 6:36 565
And they say unto him, Shall we g ... Mk 6:37 565
g and see ... Mk 6:38 5217
to g to the other side before ... Mk 6:45 4254
her, For this saying g thy way ... Mk 7:29 5217
Neither g into the town, nor tell ... Mk 8:26 1525
having two hands to g into hell ... Mk 9:43 565
g thy way, sell whatsoever thou ... Mk 10:21 5217
to g through the eye of a needle ... Mk 10:25 1525
Behold, we g up to Jerusalem ... Mk 10:33 305
And Jesus said unto him, G thy way ... Mk 10:52 5217
G your way into the village over ... Mk 11:2 5217
and they let them g ... Mk 11:6 863
which love to g in long clothing, ... Mk 12:38 4043
not g down into the house ... Mk 13:15 2597
him, Where wilt thou that we g ... Mk 14:12 565
G ye into the city, and there ... Mk 14:13 5217
And wheresoever he shall g in ... Mk 14:14 1525
I will g before you into Galilee ... Mk 14:28 4254
Rise up, let us g ... Mk 14:42 71
But g your way, tell his ... Mk 16:7 5217
G ye into all the world, and ... Mk 16:15 4198
he shall g before him in the ... Lk 1:17 4281
for thou shalt g before the face ... Lk 1:76 4313
Let us now g even unto Bethlehem, ... Lk 2:15 1330
but g, and shew thyself to the ... Lk 5:14 565
thy couch, and g into thine house ... Lk 5:24 4198
me soldiers, and I say unto one, G ... Lk 7:8 4198
G your way, and tell John what ... Lk 7:22 4198
faith hath saved thee; g in peace ... Lk 7:50 4198
g forth, and are choked with cares ... Lk 8:14 4198
Let us g over unto the other side ... Lk 8:22 1330
them to g out into the deep ... Lk 8:31 565
made thee whole; g in peace ... Lk 8:48 4198
house, he suffered no man to g in ... Lk 8:51 1525
when ye g out of that city, shake ... Lk 9:5 1831
that they may g into the towns and ... Lk 9:12 565
except we should g and buy meat ... Lk 9:13 4198
set his face to g to Jerusalem ... Lk 9:51 4198
as though he would g to Jerusalem ... Lk 9:53 4198
said, Lord, suffer me first to g ... Lk 9:59 565
but g thou and preach the kingdom ... Lk 9:60 565
but let me first g bid them ... Lk 9:61
G your ways: behold, I send ... Lk 10:3 4198
G not from house to house ... Lk 10:7 3327
g your ways out into the streets ... Lk 10:10 1831
Then said Jesus unto him, G ... Lk 10:37 4198
shall g unto him at midnight, and ... Lk 11:5 4198
G ye, and tell that fox, Behold, I ... Lk 13:32 4198
him, and healed him, and let him g ... Lk 14:4 630
But when thou art bidden, g ... Lk 14:10 4198
unto thee, Friend, g up higher ... Lk 14:10 4320
of ground, and I must needs g ... Lk 14:18 1831
of oxen, and I g to prove them ... Lk 14:19 4198
G out quickly into the streets and ... Lk 14:21 1831
G out into the highways and hedges ... Lk 14:23 1831
g after that which is lost, until ... Lk 15:4 4198
g to my father, and will say unto ... Lk 15:18 4198
he was angry, and would not g in ... Lk 15:28 1525
when he is come from the field, G ... Lk 17:7 3928
G shew yourselves unto the ... Lk 17:14 4198
said unto him, Arise, g thy way ... Lk 17:19 4198
g not after them, nor follow them ... Lk 17:23 565
camel to g through a needle's eye ... Lk 18:25 1525
we g up to Jerusalem, and all ... Lk 18:31 305
G ye into the village over ... Lk 19:30 5217
g ye not therefore after them ... Lk 21:8 4198
he sent Peter and John, saying, G ... Lk 22:8 4198
Lord, I am ready to g with thee ... Lk 22:33 4198
will not answer me, nor let me g ... Lk 22:68 630
chastise him, and let him g ... Lk 23:22 630
Jesus would g forth into Galilee ... Jn 1:43 1831
he must needs g through Samaria ... Jn 4:4 1330
Jesus saith unto her, G, call thy ... Jn 4:16 5217
Jesus saith unto him, G thy way ... Jn 4:50 4198
the twelve, Will ye also g away ... Jn 6:67 5217
him, Lord, to whom shall we g ... Jn 6:68 565
g into Judaea, that thy disciples ... Jn 7:3 5217
G ye up unto this feast ... Jn 7:8 305
I g not up yet unto this feast ... Jn 7:8 305
Why g ye about to kill me ... Jn 7:19 2212
then I g unto him that sent me ... Jn 7:33 5217
themselves, Whither will he g ... Jn 7:35 4198
will he g unto the dispersed ... Jn 7:35 4198
g, and sin no more ... Jn 8:11 4198
whence I came, and whither I g ... Jn 8:14 5217
whence I come, and whither I g ... Jn 8:14 5217
I g my way, and ye shall seek me, ... Jn 8:21 5217
whither I g, ye cannot come ... Jn 8:21 5217
because he saith, Whither I g ... Jn 8:22 5217
And said unto him, G, wash in the ... Jn 9:7 5217
G to the pool of Siloam, and wash ... Jn 9:11 5217
he shall be saved, and shall g in ... Jn 10:9 1525
Let us g into Judaea again ... Jn 11:7 71
but I g, that I may awake him out ... Jn 11:11 4198
nevertheless let us g unto him ... Jn 11:15 71
fellowdisciples, Let us also g ... Jn 11:16 71
them, Loose him, and let him g ... Jn 11:44 5217
I said unto the Jews, Whither I g ... Jn 13:33 5217
Jesus answered him, Whither I g ... Jn 13:36 5217
I g to prepare a place for you ... Jn 14:2 4198
And if I g and prepare a place for ... Jn 14:3 4198
And whither I g ye know, and the ... Jn 14:4 5217
because I g unto my Father ... Jn 14:12 4198
I g away, and come again unto you ... Jn 14:28 5217
I said, I g unto the Father ... Jn 14:28 4198
Arise, let us g hence ... Jn 14:31 71
and ordained you, that ye should g ... Jn 15:16 5217
But now I g my way to him that ... Jn 16:5 5217
expedient for you that I g away ... Jn 16:7 565
for if I g not away, the ... Jn 16:7 565
because I g to my Father, and ye ... Jn 16:10 5217
because I g to the Father ... Jn 16:16 5217
Because I g to the Father ... Jn 16:17 5217
the world, and g to the Father ... Jn 16:28 4198
ye seek me, let these g their way ... Jn 18:8 5217
saying, If thou let this man g ... Jn 19:12 630
but g to my brethren, and say unto ... Jn 20:17 4198
saith unto them, I g a fishing ... Jn 21:3 5217
say unto him, We also g with thee ... Jn 21:3 2064
as ye have seen him g into heaven ... Acts 1:11 4198
that he might g to his own place ... Acts 1:25 4198
John about to g into the temple ... Acts 3:3 1524
he was determined to let him g ... Acts 3:13 630
to g aside out of the council ... Acts 4:15 565
threatened them, they let them g ... Acts 4:21 630
And being let g, they went to ... Acts 4:23 630
G, stand and speak in the temple ... Acts 5:20 4198
the name of Jesus, and let them g ... Acts 5:40 630
Make us gods to g before us ... Acts 7:40 4313
g toward the south unto the way ... Acts 8:26 4198
G near, and join thyself to this ... Acts 8:29 4334
g into the city, and it shall be ... Acts 9:6 1525
g into the street which is called ... Acts 9:11 4198
the Lord said unto him, G thy way ... Acts 9:15 4198
g with them, doubting nothing ... Acts 10:20 4198
And the Spirit bade me g with them ... Acts 11:12 4905
that he should g as far as ... Acts 11:22 1330
G shew these things unto James, ... Acts 12:17
should g up to Jerusalem unto the ... Acts 15:2 305
they were let g in peace from the ... Acts 15:33 630
unto Barnabas, Let us g again ... Acts 15:36 1994
Paul have to g forth with him ... Acts 16:3 1831
they assayed to g into Bithynia ... Acts 16:7 4198
endeavoured to g into Macedonia ... Acts 16:10 1831
saying, Let those men g ... Acts 16:35 630
have sent to let you g ... Acts 16:36 630
therefore depart, and g in peace ... Acts 16:36 4198
and of the other, they let them g ... Acts 17:9 630
Paul to g as it were to the sea ... Acts 17:14 4198
I will g unto the Gentiles ... Acts 18:6 4198
to g to Jerusalem, saying, After ... Acts 19:21 4198
departed for to g into Macedonia ... Acts 20:1 4198
minding himself to g afoot ... Acts 20:13 3978
I g bound in the spirit unto ... Acts 20:22 4198
he should not g up to Jerusalem ... Acts 21:4 305
him not to g up to Jerusalem ... Acts 21:12 305
me, Arise, and g into Damascus ... Acts 22:10 4198
commanded the soldiers to g down ... Acts 23:10 2597
hundred soldiers to g to Caesarea ... Acts 23:23 4198
left the horsemen to g with him ... Acts 23:32 4198
answered, G thy way for this time ... Acts 24:25 4198
g down with me, and accuse this ... Acts 25:5 4782
Wilt thou g up to Jerusalem, and ... Acts 25:9 305
unto Caesar shalt thou g ... Acts 25:12 4198
whether he would g to Jerusalem ... Acts 25:20 4198
gave him liberty to g unto his ... Acts 27:3 4198
examined me, would have let me g ... Acts 28:18 630
G unto this people, and say, ... Acts 28:26 4198
But now I g unto Jerusalem to ... Rom 15:25 4198
must ye needs g out of the world ... 1Cor 5:10 1831
g to law before the unjust, and ... 1Cor 6:1
because ye g to law one with ... 1Cor 6:7
a feast, and ye be disposed to g ... 1Cor 10:27 4198
I g also, they shall g with me ... 1Cor 16:4 4198
on my journey whithersoever I g ... 1Cor 16:6 4198
that they would g before unto you ... 2Cor 9:5 4281
that we should g unto the heathen ... Gal 2:9
let not the sun g down upon your ... Eph 4:26 1931
I shall see how it will g with me ... Phil 2:23
That no man g beyond and defraud ... 1Th 4:6 5233
let us g on unto perfection ... Heb 6:1 5342
when he was called to g out into ... Heb 11:8 1831
Let us g forth therefore unto him ... Heb 13:13 1831
G to now, ye that say, To day or ... Jas 4:13 33
morrow we will g into such a city ... Jas 4:13 4198
G to now, ye rich men, weep and ... Jas 5:1 33
my God, and he shall g no more out ... Rev 3:12 1831
spake unto me again, and said, G ... Rev 10:8 5217
captivity shall g into captivity ... Rev 13:10 5217
G your ways, and pour out the ... Rev 16:1 5217
which g forth unto the kings of ... Rev 16:14 1607
pit, and g into perdition ... Rev 17:8 5217
shall g out to deceive the ... Rev 20:8 1831

GOAD {1}
six hundred men with an ox g ... Judg 3:31 4451

GOADS {2}
for the axes, and to sharpen the g ... 1Sa 13:21 1861
The words of the wise are as g ... Eccl 12:11 1861

GOAH See GOATH.

GOAT {35}
a she g of three years old, and a ... Gen 15:9 5795
And if his offering be a g ... Lev 3:12 5795
his hand upon the head of the g ... Lev 4:24 8163
fat, of ox, or of sheep, or of g ... Lev 7:23 5795
people's offering, and took the g ... Lev 9:15 8163
sought the g of the sin offering ... Lev 10:16 8163
Aaron shall bring the g upon ... Lev 16:9 8163
But the g, on which the lot fell ... Lev 16:10 8163
he kill the g of the sin offering ... Lev 16:15 8163
bullock, and of the blood of the g ... Lev 16:18 8163
altar, he shall bring the live g ... Lev 16:20 8163
hands upon the head of the live g ... Lev 16:21 8163
them upon the head of the g ... Lev 16:21 8163
the g shall bear upon him all ... Lev 16:22 8163
let go the g in the wilderness ... Lev 16:22 8163
he that let go the g for the ... Lev 16:26 8163
the g for the sin offering, whose ... Lev 16:27 8163
that killeth an ox, or lamb, or g ... Lev 17:3 5795
a bullock, or a sheep, or a g ... Lev 22:27 5795
then he shall bring a she g of ... Num 15:27 5795
a sheep, or the firstling of a g ... Num 18:17 5795
one g for a sin offering, to make ... Num 28:22 8163
And one g for a sin offering ... Num 29:22 8163
And one g for a sin offering ... Num 29:28 8163
And one g for a sin offering ... Num 29:31 8163
And one g for a sin offering ... Num 29:34 8163
And one g for a sin offering ... Num 29:38 8163
the ox, the sheep, and the g ... Deut 14:4 5795
and the fallow deer, and the wild g ... Deut 14:5 689
an he g also ... Prov 30:31 8495
every day a g for a sin offering ... Eze 43:25 8163
an he g came from the west on the ... Dan 8:5 5795
the g had a notable horn between ... Dan 8:5 6842
the he g waxed very great ... Dan 8:8 6842
the rough g is the king of Grecia ... Dan 8:21 6842

GOATH (go'-ath) {1} *A place near Jerusalem.*
and shall compass about to G ... Jer 31:39 1601

GOATS {87}
thence two good kids of the g ... Gen 27:9 5795
the kids of the g upon his hands ... Gen 27:16 5795
spotted and speckled among the g ... Gen 30:32 5795
speckled and spotted among the g ... Gen 30:33 5795
the he g that were ringstraked ... Gen 30:35 8495
all the she g that were speckled ... Gen 30:35 5795
thy she g have not cast their ... Gen 31:38 5795
Two hundred she g ... Gen 32:14 5795
and twenty he g ... Gen 32:14 8495
coat, and killed a kid of the g ... Gen 37:31 5795
out from the sheep, or from the g ... Ex 12:5 5795
namely, of the sheep, or of the g ... Lev 1:10 5795
his offering, a kid of the g ... Lev 4:23 5795
his offering, a kid of the g ... Lev 4:28 5795
flock, a lamb or a kid of the g ... Lev 5:6 5795
a kid of the g for a sin offering ... Lev 9:3 5795
kids of the g for a sin offering ... Lev 16:5 5795
And he shall take the two g ... Lev 16:7 8163
shall cast lots upon the two g ... Lev 16:8 8163
beeves, of the sheep, or of the g ... Lev 22:19 5795
kid of the g for a sin offering ... Lev 23:19 5795
One kid of the g for a sin ... Num 7:16 5795
two oxen, five rams, five he g ... Num 7:17 6260
One kid of the g for a sin ... Num 7:22 5795
two oxen, five rams, five he g ... Num 7:23 6260
One kid of the g for a sin ... Num 7:28 5795
two oxen, five rams, five he g ... Num 7:29 6260
One kid of the g for a sin ... Num 7:34 5795
two oxen, five rams, five he g ... Num 7:35 6260
One kid of the g for a sin ... Num 7:40 5795
two oxen, five rams, five he g ... Num 7:41 6260
One kid of the g for a sin ... Num 7:46 5795
two oxen, five rams, five he g ... Num 7:47 6260
One kid of the g for a sin ... Num 7:52 5795
two oxen, five rams, five he g ... Num 7:53 6260
One kid of the g for a sin ... Num 7:58 5795

two oxen, five rams, five he *g* ... Num 7:59 6260
One kid of the *g* for a sin ... Num 7:64 5795
two oxen, five rams, five he *g* ... Num 7:65 6260
One kid of the *g* for a sin ... Num 7:70 5795
two oxen, five rams, five he *g* ... Num 7:71 6260
One kid of the *g* for a sin ... Num 7:76 5795
two oxen, five rams, five he *g* ... Num 7:77 6260
One kid of the *g* for a sin ... Num 7:82 5795
two oxen, five rams, five he *g* ... Num 7:83 6260
the kids of the *g* for sin ... Num 7:87 5795
the rams sixty, the he *g* sixty ... Num 7:88 6260
one kid of the *g* for a sin ... Num 15:24 5795
one kid of the *g* for a sin ... Num 28:15 5795
And one kid of the *g*, to make an ... Num 28:30 5795
one kid of the *g* for a sin ... Num 29:5 5795
One kid of the *g* for a sin ... Num 29:11 5795
one kid of the *g* for a sin ... Num 29:16 5795
one kid of the *g* for a sin ... Num 29:19 5795
one kid of the *g* for a sin ... Num 29:25 5795
rams of the breed of Bashan, and *g* ... Deut 32:14 6260
men upon the rocks of the wild *g* ... 1Sa 24:2 3277
thousand sheep, and a thousand *g* ... 1Sa 25:2 5795
thousand and seven hundred he *g* ... 2Chr 17:11 8495
and seven lambs, and seven he *g* ... 2Chr 29:21 5795
they brought forth the he *g* for ... 2Chr 29:23 8163
for all Israel, twelve he *g* ... Ezr 6:17 5795
twelve he *g* for a sin offering ... Ezr 8:35 6842
wild *g* of the rock bring forth ... Job 39:1 3277
nor he *g* out of thy folds ... Ps 50:9 6260
of bulls, or drink the blood of *g* ... Ps 50:13 6260
I will offer bullocks with *g* ... Ps 66:15 6260
hills are a refuge for the wild *g* ... Ps 104:18 3277
the *g* are the price of the field ... Prov 27:26 6260
thy hair is as a flock of *g* ... Song 4:1 5795
of *g* that appear from Gilead ... Song 6:5 5795
bullocks, or of lambs, or of he *g* ... Is 1:11 6260
and with the blood of lambs and *g* ... Is 34:6 6260
be as the he *g* before the flocks ... Jer 50:8 6260
slaughter, like rams with he *g* ... Jer 51:40 6260
with thee in lambs, and rams, and *g* ... Eze 27:21 6260
between the rams and the he *g* ... Eze 34:17 6260
earth, of rams, of lambs, and of *g* ... Eze 39:18 6260
the *g* without blemish for a sin ... Eze 43:22 5795
a kid of the *g* daily for a sin ... Eze 45:23 5795
shepherds, and I punished the *g* ... Zec 10:3 6260
divideth his sheep from the *g* ... Mt 25:32 *2056*
right hand, but the *g* on the left ... Mt 25:33 *2055*
Neither by the blood of *g* ... Heb 9:12 *5131*
For if the blood of bulls and of *g* ... Heb 9:13 *5131*
took the blood of calves and of *g* ... Heb 9:19 *5131*
of *g* should take away sins ... Heb 10:4 *5131*

GOATS' {10}
and fine linen, and *g* hair, ... Ex 25:4 5795
thou shalt make curtains of *g* ... Ex 26:7 5795
and fine linen, and *g* hair, ... Ex 35:6 5795
g hair, and red skins of rams, and ... Ex 35:23 5795
them up in wisdom spun *g* hair ... Ex 35:26 5795
he made curtains of *g* hair for ... Ex 36:14 5795
of skins, and all work of *g* hair ... Num 31:20 5795
put a pillow of *g* hair for his ... 1Sa 19:13 5795
with a pillow of *g* hair for his ... 1Sa 19:16 5795
thou shalt have *g* milk enough for ... Prov 27:27 5795

GOATSKINS {1}
about in sheepskins and *g* ... Heb 11:37 *122,1192*

GOB (gob) {2} *A place where David battled the Philistines.*
battle with the Philistines at *G* ... 2Sa 21:18 1359
battle in *G* with the Philistines ... 2Sa 21:19 1359

GOBLET {1}
Thy navel is like a round *g* ... Song 7:2 101

GOD (god) {4456} See GODDESS, GODHEAD, GOD'S, GODS, GOD-WARD.
1. Creator and Ruler of the world, Israel, and the church.
In the beginning *G* created the ... Gen 1:1 430
the Spirit of *G* moved upon the ... Gen 1:2 430
G said, Let there be light ... Gen 1:3 430
G saw the light, that it was good ... Gen 1:4 430
G divided the light from the ... Gen 1:4 430
G called the light Day, and the ... Gen 1:5 430
G said, Let there be a firmament ... Gen 1:6 430
G made the firmament, and divided ... Gen 1:7 430
G called the firmament Heaven ... Gen 1:8 430
G said, Let the waters under the ... Gen 1:9 430
G called the dry land Earth ... Gen 1:10 430
and *G* saw that it was good ... Gen 1:10 430
G said, Let the earth bring forth ... Gen 1:11 430
and *G* saw that it was good ... Gen 1:12 430
G said, Let there be lights in ... Gen 1:14 430
And *G* made two great lights ... Gen 1:16 430
G set them in the firmament of ... Gen 1:17 430
and *G* saw that it was good ... Gen 1:18 430
G said, Let the waters bring ... Gen 1:20 430
G created great whales, and every ... Gen 1:21 430
and *G* saw that it was good ... Gen 1:21 430
G blessed them, saying, Be ... Gen 1:22 430
G said, Let the earth bring forth ... Gen 1:24 430
G made the beast of the earth ... Gen 1:25 430
and *G* saw that it was good ... Gen 1:25 430
G said, Let us make man in our ... Gen 1:26 430
So *G* created man in his own image ... Gen 1:27 430
in the image of *G* created he him ... Gen 1:27 430
G blessed them, and *G* said unto ... Gen 1:28 430
G said unto them, Be fruitful, and ... Gen 1:28 430
G said, Behold, I have given you ... Gen 1:29 430
G saw every thing that he had ... Gen 1:31 430
on the seventh day *G* ended his ... Gen 2:2 430
G blessed the seventh day, and ... Gen 2:3 430
from all his work which *G* created ... Gen 2:3 430
that the LORD *G* made the earth ... Gen 2:4 430
for the LORD *G* had not caused it ... Gen 2:5 430
the LORD *G* formed man of the dust ... Gen 2:7 430
the LORD *G* planted a garden ... Gen 2:8 430
LORD *G* to grow every tree that is ... Gen 2:9 430
the LORD *G* took the man, and put ... Gen 2:15 430
the LORD *G* commanded the man, ... Gen 2:16 430
And the LORD *G* said, It is not ... Gen 2:18 430
out of the ground the LORD *G* ... Gen 2:19 430
the LORD *G* caused a deep sleep to ... Gen 2:21 430
which the LORD *G* had taken from ... Gen 2:22 430
field which the LORD *G* had made ... Gen 3:1 430
unto the woman, Yea, hath *G* said ... Gen 3:1 430
G hath said, Ye shall not eat of ... Gen 3:3 430
For *G* doth know that in the day ... Gen 3:5 430
heard the voice of the LORD *G* ... Gen 3:8 430
from the presence of the LORD *G* ... Gen 3:8 430
the LORD *G* called unto Adam, and ... Gen 3:9 430
the LORD *G* said unto the woman, ... Gen 3:13 430
the LORD *G* said unto the serpent, ... Gen 3:14 430
the LORD *G* make coats of skins ... Gen 3:21 430
And the LORD *G* said, Behold, the ... Gen 3:22 430
Therefore the LORD *G* sent him ... Gen 3:23 430
For *G*, said she, hath appointed ... Gen 4:25 430
In the day that *G* created man ... Gen 5:1 430
in the likeness of *G* made he him ... Gen 5:1 430
Enoch walked with *G* after he ... Gen 5:22 430
And Enoch walked with *G* ... Gen 5:24 430
for *G* took him ... Gen 5:24 430
That the sons of *G* saw the ... Gen 6:2 430
when the sons of *G* came in unto ... Gen 6:4 430
G saw that the wickedness of man ... Gen 6:5 3068
and Noah walked with *G* ... Gen 6:9 430
earth also was corrupt before *G* ... Gen 6:11 430
G looked upon the earth, and, ... Gen 6:12 430
G said unto Noah, The end of all ... Gen 6:13 430
to all that *G* commanded him ... Gen 6:22 430
female, as *G* had commanded Noah ... Gen 7:9 430
all flesh, as *G* had commanded him ... Gen 7:16 430
G remembered Noah, and every ... Gen 8:1 430
G made a wind to pass over the ... Gen 8:1 430
G spake unto Noah, saying, ... Gen 8:15 430
G blessed Noah and his sons, and ... Gen 9:1 430
for in the image of *G* made he man ... Gen 9:6 430
G spake unto Noah, and to his sons ... Gen 9:8 430
G said, This is the token of the ... Gen 9:12 430
everlasting covenant between *G* ... Gen 9:16 430
G said unto Noah, This is the ... Gen 9:17 430
Blessed be the LORD *G* of Shem ... Gen 9:26 430
G shall enlarge Japheth, and he ... Gen 9:27 430
was the priest of the most high *G* ... Gen 14:18 410
be Abram of the most high *G* ... Gen 14:19 410
And blessed be the most high *G* ... Gen 14:20 410
unto the LORD, the most high *G* ... Gen 14:22 410
And Abram said, Lord *G*, what wilt ... Gen 15:2 3069
And he said, Lord *G*, whereby shall ... Gen 15:8 3069
spake unto her, Thou *G* seest me ... Gen 16:13 410
unto him, I am the Almighty *G* ... Gen 17:1 410
G talked with him, saying, ... Gen 17:3 430
to be a *G* unto thee, and to thy ... Gen 17:7 430
and I will be their *G* ... Gen 17:8 430
G said unto Abraham, Thou shalt ... Gen 17:9 430
G said unto Abraham, As for Sarai ... Gen 17:15 430
And Abraham said unto *G*, O that ... Gen 17:18 430
G said, Sarah thy wife shall bear ... Gen 17:19 430
him, and *G* went up from Abraham ... Gen 17:22 430
day, as *G* had said unto him ... Gen 17:23 430
when *G* destroyed the cities of ... Gen 19:29 430
that *G* remembered Abraham, and ... Gen 19:29 430
But *G* came to Abimelech in a ... Gen 20:3 430
G said unto him in a dream, Yea, ... Gen 20:6 430
Surely the fear of *G* is not in ... Gen 20:11 430
when *G* caused me to wander from ... Gen 20:13 430
So Abraham prayed unto *G* ... Gen 20:17 430
G healed Abimelech, and his wife, ... Gen 20:17 430
time of which *G* had spoken to him ... Gen 21:2 430
days old, as *G* had commanded him ... Gen 21:4 430
G hath made me to laugh, so that ... Gen 21:6 430
G said unto Abraham, Let it not ... Gen 21:12 430
G heard the voice of the lad ... Gen 21:17 430
the angel of *G* called to Hagar ... Gen 21:17 430
for *G* hath heard the voice of the ... Gen 21:17 430
G opened her eyes, and she saw a ... Gen 21:19 430
And *G* was with the lad ... Gen 21:20 430
G is with thee in all that thou ... Gen 21:22 430
G that thou wilt not deal falsely ... Gen 21:23 430
of the LORD, the everlasting *G* ... Gen 21:33 410
that *G* did tempt Abraham, and said ... Gen 22:1 430
the place of which *G* had told him ... Gen 22:3 430
G will provide himself a lamb for ... Gen 22:8 430
the place which *G* had told him of ... Gen 22:9 430
now I know that thou fearest *G* ... Gen 22:12 430
the *G* of heaven ... Gen 24:3 430
the *G* of the earth ... Gen 24:3 430
The LORD *G* of heaven, which took ... Gen 24:7 430
O LORD *G* of my master Abraham, I ... Gen 24:12 430
Blessed be the LORD *G* of my ... Gen 24:27 430
O LORD *G* of my master Abraham, if ... Gen 24:42 430
blessed the LORD *G* of my master ... Gen 24:48 430
that *G* blessed his son Isaac ... Gen 25:11 430
I am the *G* of Abraham thy father ... Gen 26:24 430
the LORD thy *G* brought it to me ... Gen 27:20 430
Therefore *G* give thee of the dew ... Gen 27:28 430
G Almighty bless thee, and make ... Gen 28:3 410
which *G* gave unto Abraham ... Gen 28:4 430
behold the angels of *G* ascending ... Gen 28:12 430
I am the LORD *G* of Abraham thy ... Gen 28:13 430
thy father, and the *G* of Isaac ... Gen 28:13 430
is none other but the house of *G* ... Gen 28:17 430
If *G* will be with me, and will ... Gen 28:20 430
then shall the LORD be my *G* ... Gen 28:21 430
G hath judged me, and hath also ... Gen 30:6 430
G hearkened unto Leah, and she ... Gen 30:17 430
G hath given me my hire, because ... Gen 30:18 430
G hath endued me with a good ... Gen 30:20 430
G remembered Rachel ... Gen 30:22 430
G hearkened to her, and opened her ... Gen 30:22 430
G hath taken away my reproach ... Gen 30:23 430
but the *G* of my father hath been ... Gen 31:5 430
but *G* suffered him not to hurt me ... Gen 31:7 430
Thus *G* hath taken away the cattle ... Gen 31:9 430
the angel of *G* spake unto me in a ... Gen 31:11 430
I am the *G* of Beth-el, where thou ... Gen 31:13 410
For all the riches which *G* hath ... Gen 31:16 430
whatsoever *G* hath said unto thee, ... Gen 31:16 430
G came to Laban the Syrian in a ... Gen 31:24 430
but the *G* of your father spake ... Gen 31:29 430
Except the *G* of my father ... Gen 31:42 430
the *G* of Abraham, and the fear of ... Gen 31:42 430
G hath seen mine affliction and ... Gen 31:42 430
G is witness betwixt me and thee ... Gen 31:50 430
The *G* of Abraham ... Gen 31:53 430
the *G* of Nahor ... Gen 31:53 430
the *G* of their father, judge ... Gen 31:53 430
way, and the angels of *G* met him ... Gen 32:1 430
O *G* of my father Abraham ... Gen 32:9 430
G of my father Isaac, the LORD ... Gen 32:9 430
a prince hast thou power with *G* ... Gen 32:28 430
for I have seen *G* face to face ... Gen 32:30 430
The children which *G* hath ... Gen 33:5 430
though I had seen the face of *G* ... Gen 33:10 430
because *G* hath dealt graciously ... Gen 33:11 430
G said unto Jacob, Arise, go up ... Gen 35:1 430
and make there an altar unto *G* ... Gen 35:1 410
I will make there an altar unto *G* ... Gen 35:3 410
the terror of *G* was upon the ... Gen 35:5 430
because there *G* appeared unto him ... Gen 35:7 430
G appeared unto Jacob again, when ... Gen 35:9 430
G said unto him, Thy name is ... Gen 35:10 430
And *G* said unto him ... Gen 35:11 430
I am *G* Almighty ... Gen 35:11 410
G went up from him in the place ... Gen 35:13 430
the place where *G* spake with him ... Gen 35:15 430
wickedness, and sin against *G* ... Gen 39:9 430
not interpretations belong to *G* ... Gen 40:8 430
G shall give Pharaoh an answer of ... Gen 41:16 430
G hath shewed Pharaoh what he is ... Gen 41:25 430
What *G* is about to do he sheweth ... Gen 41:28 430
the thing is established by *G* ... Gen 41:32 430
G will shortly bring it to pass ... Gen 41:32 430
a man in whom the Spirit of *G* is ... Gen 41:38 430
Forasmuch as *G* hath shewed thee ... Gen 41:39 430
For *G*, said he, hath made me ... Gen 41:51 430
For *G* hath caused me to be ... Gen 41:52 430
for I fear *G* ... Gen 42:18 430
is this that *G* hath done unto us ... Gen 42:28 430
G Almighty give you mercy before ... Gen 43:14 410
your *G*, and the *G* of your father ... Gen 43:23 430
G be gracious unto thee, my son ... Gen 43:29 430
G forbid that thy servants should ... Gen 44:7
G hath found out the iniquity of ... Gen 44:16 430
G forbid that I should do so ... Gen 44:17
for *G* did send me before you to ... Gen 45:5 430
G sent me before you to preserve ... Gen 45:7 430
you that sent me hither, but *G* ... Gen 45:8 430
G hath made me lord of all Egypt ... Gen 45:9 430
unto the *G* of his father Isaac ... Gen 46:1 430
G spake unto Israel in the ... Gen 46:2 430
I am *G*, the *G* of thy father ... Gen 46:3 430
G Almighty appeared unto me at ... Gen 48:3 410
whom *G* hath given me in this ... Gen 48:9 430
G hath shewed me also thy seed ... Gen 48:11 430
And he blessed Joseph, and said, *G* ... Gen 48:15 430
the *G* which fed me all my life ... Gen 48:15 430
G make thee as Ephraim and as ... Gen 48:20 430
but *G* shall be with you, and bring ... Gen 48:21 430
hands of the mighty *G* of Jacob ... Gen 49:24
Even by the *G* of thy father, who ... Gen 49:25 410
servants of the *G* of thy father ... Gen 50:17 430
for am I in the place of *G* ... Gen 50:19 430
but *G* meant it unto good, to ... Gen 50:20 430
G will surely visit you, and bring ... Gen 50:24 430
G will surely visit you, and ye ... Gen 50:25 430
But the midwives feared *G* ... Ex 1:17 430
Therefore *G* dealt well with the ... Ex 1:20 430
because the midwives feared *G* ... Ex 1:21 430
their cry came up unto *G* by ... Ex 2:23 430
G heard their groaning ... Ex 2:24 430
G remembered his covenant with ... Ex 2:24 430
G looked upon the children of ... Ex 2:25 430
and *G* had respect unto them ... Ex 2:25 430
and came to the mountain of *G* ... Ex 3:1 430
G called unto him out of the ... Ex 3:4 430
I am the *G* of thy father ... Ex 3:6 430
the *G* of Abraham ... Ex 3:6 430
G of Isaac, and the *G* of Jacob ... Ex 3:6 430
for he was afraid to look upon *G* ... Ex 3:6 430
And Moses said unto *G*, Who am I, ... Ex 3:11 430
ye shall serve *G* upon this ... Ex 3:12 430
And Moses said unto *G*, Behold, ... Ex 3:13 430
The *G* of your fathers hath sent ... Ex 3:13 430
G said unto Moses, I AM THAT I AM ... Ex 3:14 430
G said moreover unto Moses, Thus ... Ex 3:15 430

Context	Reference	Number
The LORD *G* of your fathers	Ex 3:15	430
the *G* of Abraham	Ex 3:15	430
the *G* of Isaac	Ex 3:15	430
the *G* of Jacob	Ex 3:15	430
The LORD *G* of your fathers	Ex 3:16	430
the *G* of Abraham, of Isaac, and of	Ex 3:16	430
The LORD *G* of the Hebrews hath	Ex 3:18	430
may sacrifice to the LORD our *G*	Ex 3:18	430
that the LORD *G* of their fathers	Ex 4:5	430
the *G* of Abraham	Ex 4:5	430
the *G* of Isaac	Ex 4:5	430
the *G* of Jacob	Ex 4:5	430
thou shalt be to him instead of *G*	Ex 4:16	430
took the rod of *G* in his hand	Ex 4:20	430
and met him in the mount of *G*	Ex 4:27	430
Thus saith the LORD *G* of Israel	Ex 5:1	430
The *G* of the Hebrews hath met	Ex 5:3	430
and sacrifice unto the LORD our *G*	Ex 5:3	430
Let us go and sacrifice to our *G*	Ex 5:8	430
G spake unto Moses, and said unto	Ex 6:2	430
Jacob, by the name of *G* Almighty	Ex 6:3	410
a people, and I will be to you a *G*	Ex 6:7	430
know that I am the LORD your *G*	Ex 6:7	430
The LORD *G* of the Hebrews hath	Ex 7:16	430
is none like unto the LORD our *G*	Ex 8:10	430
Pharaoh, This is the finger of *G*	Ex 8:19	430
sacrifice to your *G* in the land	Ex 8:25	430
the Egyptians to the LORD our *G*	Ex 8:26	430
and sacrifice to the LORD our *G*	Ex 8:27	430
the LORD your *G* in the wilderness	Ex 8:28	430
saith the LORD *G* of the Hebrews	Ex 9:1	430
saith the LORD *G* of the Hebrews	Ex 9:13	430
ye will not yet fear the LORD *G*	Ex 9:30	430
saith the LORD *G* of the Hebrews	Ex 10:3	430
they may serve the LORD their *G*	Ex 10:7	430
them, Go, serve the LORD your *G*	Ex 10:8	430
sinned against the LORD your *G*	Ex 10:16	430
once, and intreat the LORD your *G*	Ex 10:17	430
may sacrifice unto the LORD our *G*	Ex 10:25	430
we take to serve the LORD our *G*	Ex 10:26	430
that *G* led them not through the	Ex 13:17	430
for *G* said, Lest peradventure the	Ex 13:17	430
But *G* led the people about,	Ex 13:18	430
saying, *G* will surely visit you	Ex 13:19	430
And the angel of *G*, which went	Ex 14:19	430
he is my *G*, and I will prepare him	Ex 15:2	410
my father's *G*, and I will exalt	Ex 15:2	430
to the voice of the LORD thy *G*	Ex 15:26	430
Would to *G* we had died by the	Ex 16:3	
know that I am the LORD your *G*	Ex 16:12	430
with the rod of *G* in mine hand	Ex 17:9	430
heard of all that *G* had done for	Ex 18:1	430
for the *G* of my father, said he,	Ex 18:4	430
he encamped at the mount of *G*	Ex 18:5	430
offering and sacrifices for *G*	Ex 18:12	430
Moses' father in law before *G*	Ex 18:12	430
come unto me to enquire of *G*	Ex 18:15	430
make them know the statutes of *G*	Ex 18:16	430
counsel, and *G* shall be with thee	Ex 18:19	430
mayest bring the causes unto *G*	Ex 18:19	430
people able men, such as fear *G*	Ex 18:21	430
G command thee so, then thou	Ex 18:23	430
And Moses went up unto *G*, and the	Ex 19:3	430
out of the camp to meet with *G*	Ex 19:17	430
G answered him by a voice	Ex 19:19	430
G spake all these words, saying,	Ex 20:1	430
I am the LORD thy *G*, which have	Ex 20:2	430
I the LORD thy *G* am a jealous *G*	Ex 20:5	430
I the LORD thy *G* am a jealous *G*	Ex 20:5	410
name of the LORD thy *G* in vain	Ex 20:7	430
is the sabbath of the LORD thy *G*	Ex 20:10	430
which the LORD thy *G* giveth thee	Ex 20:12	430
but let not *G* speak with us, lest	Ex 20:19	430
for *G* is come to prove you, and	Ex 20:20	430
the thick darkness where *G* was	Ex 20:21	430
but *G* deliver him into his hand	Ex 21:13	430
shall appear before the Lord *G*	Ex 23:17	3068
into the house of the LORD thy *G*	Ex 23:19	430
And ye shall serve the LORD your *G*	Ex 23:25	430
And they saw the *G* of Israel	Ex 24:10	430
also they saw *G*, and did eat and	Ex 24:11	430
Moses went up into the mount of *G*	Ex 24:13	430
of Israel, and will be their *G*	Ex 29:45	430
know that I am the LORD their *G*	Ex 29:46	430
I am the LORD their *G*	Ex 29:46	430
filled him with the spirit of *G*	Ex 31:3	430
written with the finger of *G*	Ex 31:18	430
And Moses besought the LORD his *G*	Ex 32:11	430
And the tables were the work of *G*	Ex 32:16	430
the writing was the writing of *G*	Ex 32:16	430
Thus saith the LORD *G* of Israel	Ex 32:27	430
proclaimed, The LORD, The LORD *G*	Ex 34:6	410
name is Jealous, is a jealous *G*	Ex 34:14	410
children appear before the Lord *G*	Ex 34:23	3068
the *G* of Israel	Ex 34:23	430
the LORD thy *G* thrice in the year	Ex 34:24	430
unto the house of the LORD thy *G*	Ex 34:26	430
filled him with the spirit of *G*	Ex 35:31	430
thy *G* to be lacking from thy meat	Lev 2:13	430
commandments of the LORD his *G*	Lev 4:22	430
G hath given it you to bear the	Lev 10:17	
For I am the LORD your *G*	Lev 11:44	430
the land of Egypt, to be your *G*	Lev 11:45	430
unto them, I am the LORD your *G*	Lev 18:2	430
I am the LORD your *G*	Lev 18:4	430
thou profane the name of thy *G*	Lev 18:21	430
I am the LORD your *G*	Lev 18:30	430
for I the LORD your *G* am holy	Lev 19:2	430
I am the LORD your *G*	Lev 19:3	430
I am the LORD your *G*	Lev 19:4	430
I am the LORD your *G*	Lev 19:10	430
thou profane the name of thy *G*	Lev 19:12	430
the blind, but shalt fear thy *G*	Lev 19:14	430
I am the LORD your *G*	Lev 19:25	430
I am the LORD your *G*	Lev 19:31	430
of the old man, and fear thy *G*	Lev 19:32	430
I am the LORD your *G*	Lev 19:34	430
I am the LORD your *G*, which	Lev 19:36	430
for I am the LORD your *G*	Lev 20:7	430
I am the LORD your *G*, which have	Lev 20:24	430
They shall be holy unto their *G*	Lev 21:6	430
not profane the name of their *G*	Lev 21:6	430
by fire, and the bread of their *G*	Lev 21:6	430
for he is holy unto his *G*	Lev 21:7	430
he offereth the bread of thy *G*	Lev 21:8	430
profane the sanctuary of his *G*	Lev 21:12	430
oil of his *G* is upon him	Lev 21:12	430
to offer the bread of his *G*	Lev 21:17	430
nigh to offer the bread of his *G*	Lev 21:21	430
He shall eat the bread of his *G*	Lev 21:22	430
bread of your *G* of any of these	Lev 22:25	430
the land of Egypt, to be your *G*	Lev 22:33	430
brought an offering unto your *G*	Lev 23:14	430
I am the LORD your *G*	Lev 23:22	430
for you before the LORD your *G*	Lev 23:28	430
before the LORD your *G* seven days	Lev 23:40	430
I am the LORD your *G*	Lev 23:43	430
curseth his *G* shall bear his sin	Lev 24:15	430
for I am the LORD your *G*	Lev 24:22	430
but thou shalt fear thy *G*	Lev 25:17	430
for I am the LORD your *G*	Lev 25:17	430
but fear thy *G*	Lev 25:36	430
I am the LORD your *G*, which	Lev 25:38	430
land of Canaan, and to be your *G*	Lev 25:38	430
but shalt fear thy *G*	Lev 25:43	430
I am the LORD your *G*	Lev 25:55	430
for I am the LORD your *G*	Lev 26:1	430
walk among you, and will be your *G*	Lev 26:12	430
I am the LORD your *G*, which	Lev 26:13	430
for I am the LORD their *G*	Lev 26:44	430
heathen, that I might be their *G*	Lev 26:45	430
of his *G* is upon his head	Num 6:7	430
remembered before the LORD your *G*	Num 10:9	430
you for a memorial before your *G*	Num 10:10	430
I am the LORD your *G*	Num 10:10	430
would *G* that all the LORD's	Num 11:29	
LORD, saying, Heal her now, O *G*	Num 12:13	410
Would *G* that we had died in the	Num 14:2	
or would *G* we had died in this	Num 14:2	
and be holy unto your *G*	Num 15:40	430
I am the LORD your *G*, which	Num 15:41	430
the land of Egypt, to be your *G*	Num 15:41	430
I am the LORD your *G*	Num 15:41	430
that the *G* of Israel hath	Num 16:9	430
upon their faces, and said, O *G*	Num 16:22	410
the *G* of the spirits of all flesh	Num 16:22	430
Would *G* that we had died when our	Num 20:3	
And the people spake against *G*	Num 21:5	430
G came unto Balaam, and said, What	Num 22:9	430
And Balaam said unto *G*, Balak the	Num 22:10	430
G said unto Balaam, Thou shalt	Num 22:12	430
beyond the word of the LORD my *G*	Num 22:18	430
G came unto Balaam at night, and	Num 22:20	430
the word that *G* putteth in my	Num 22:38	430
And *G* met Balaam	Num 23:4	430
I curse, whom *G* hath not cursed	Num 23:8	410
G is not a man, that he should	Num 23:19	410
the LORD his *G* is with him	Num 23:21	430
G brought them out of Egypt	Num 23:22	410
and of Israel, What hath *G* wrought	Num 23:23	410
peradventure it will please *G*	Num 23:27	430
and the spirit of *G* came upon him	Num 24:2	430
said, which heard the words of *G*	Num 24:4	410
G brought him forth out of Egypt	Num 24:8	410
said, which heard the words of *G*	Num 24:16	410
who shall live when *G* doeth this	Num 24:23	410
because he was zealous for his *G*	Num 25:13	430
the *G* of the spirits of all flesh	Num 27:16	430
The LORD our *G* spake unto us in	Deut 1:6	430
The LORD your *G* hath multiplied	Deut 1:10	430
(The LORD *G* of your fathers make	Deut 1:11	430
as the LORD our *G* commanded us	Deut 1:19	430
the LORD our *G* doth give unto us	Deut 1:20	430
the LORD thy *G* hath set the land	Deut 1:21	430
as the LORD *G* of thy fathers hath	Deut 1:21	430
which the LORD our *G* doth give us	Deut 1:25	430
commandment of the LORD your *G*	Deut 1:26	430
The LORD your *G* which goeth	Deut 1:30	430
how that the LORD thy *G* bare thee	Deut 1:31	430
did not believe the LORD your *G*	Deut 1:32	430
that the LORD our *G* commanded us	Deut 1:41	430
For the LORD thy *G* hath blessed	Deut 2:7	430
LORD thy *G* hath been with thee	Deut 2:7	430
which the LORD our *G* giveth us	Deut 2:29	430
for the LORD thy *G* hardened his	Deut 2:30	430
the LORD our *G* delivered him	Deut 2:33	430
the LORD our *G* delivered all unto	Deut 2:36	430
the LORD our *G* forbad us	Deut 2:37	430
So the LORD our *G* delivered into	Deut 3:3	430
The LORD your *G* hath given you	Deut 3:18	430
the land which the LORD your *G*	Deut 3:20	430
seen all that the LORD your *G*	Deut 3:21	430
for the LORD your *G* he shall	Deut 3:22	430
O Lord *G*, thou hast begun to shew	Deut 3:24	3069
for what *G* is there in heaven or	Deut 3:24	410
LORD *G* of your fathers giveth you	Deut 4:1	430
LORD your *G* which I command you	Deut 4:2	430
the LORD thy *G* hath destroyed	Deut 4:3	430
did cleave unto the LORD your *G*	Deut 4:4	430
as the LORD my *G* commanded me	Deut 4:5	430
who hath *G* so nigh unto them	Deut 4:7	430
as the LORD our *G* is in all	Deut 4:7	430
before the LORD thy *G* in Horeb	Deut 4:10	430
which the LORD thy *G* hath divided	Deut 4:19	430
which the LORD thy *G* giveth thee	Deut 4:21	430
the covenant of the LORD your *G*	Deut 4:23	430
which the LORD thy *G* hath	Deut 4:23	430
For the LORD thy *G* is a consuming	Deut 4:24	430
consuming fire, even a jealous *G*	Deut 4:24	410
in the sight of the LORD thy *G*	Deut 4:25	430
thou shalt seek the LORD thy *G*	Deut 4:29	430
if thou turn to the LORD thy *G*	Deut 4:30	430
the LORD thy *G* is a merciful *G*	Deut 4:31	430
the LORD thy *G* is a merciful *G*	Deut 4:31	410
since the day that *G* created man	Deut 4:32	430
of *G* speaking out of the midst of	Deut 4:33	430
Or hath *G* assayed to go and take	Deut 4:34	430
to all that the LORD your *G* did	Deut 4:34	430
know that the LORD he is *G*	Deut 4:35	430
the LORD he is *G* in heaven above	Deut 4:39	430
which the LORD thy *G* giveth thee	Deut 4:40	430
The LORD our *G* made a covenant	Deut 5:2	430
I am the LORD thy *G*, which	Deut 5:6	430
I the LORD thy *G* am a jealous *G*	Deut 5:9	430
I the LORD thy *G* am a jealous *G*	Deut 5:9	410
name of the LORD thy *G* in vain	Deut 5:11	430
as the LORD thy *G* hath commanded	Deut 5:12	430
is the sabbath of the LORD thy *G*	Deut 5:14	430
that the LORD thy *G* brought thee	Deut 5:15	430
therefore the LORD thy *G*	Deut 5:15	430
as the LORD thy *G* hath commanded	Deut 5:16	430
which the LORD thy *G* giveth thee	Deut 5:16	430
the LORD our *G* hath shewed us his	Deut 5:24	430
day that *G* doth talk with man	Deut 5:24	430
voice of the LORD our *G* any more	Deut 5:25	430
G speaking out of the midst of	Deut 5:26	430
all that the LORD our *G* shall say	Deut 5:27	430
LORD our *G* shall speak unto thee	Deut 5:27	430
LORD your *G* hath commanded you	Deut 5:32	430
LORD your *G* hath commanded you	Deut 5:33	430
which the LORD your *G* commanded	Deut 6:1	430
thou mightest fear the LORD thy *G*	Deut 6:2	430
as the LORD *G* of thy fathers hath	Deut 6:3	430
The LORD our *G* is one LORD	Deut 6:4	430
LORD thy *G* with all thine heart	Deut 6:5	430
when the LORD thy *G* shall have	Deut 6:10	430
Thou shalt fear the LORD thy *G*	Deut 6:13	430
(For the LORD thy *G* is a jealous	Deut 6:15	430
G among you) lest the anger of	Deut 6:15	410
thy *G* be kindled against thee	Deut 6:15	430
shall not tempt the LORD your *G*	Deut 6:16	430
commandments of the LORD your *G*	Deut 6:17	430
the LORD our *G* hath commanded you	Deut 6:20	430
statutes, to fear the LORD our *G*	Deut 6:24	430
before the LORD our *G*, as he hath	Deut 6:25	430
When the LORD thy *G* shall bring	Deut 7:1	430
when the LORD thy *G* shall deliver	Deut 7:2	430
holy people unto the LORD thy *G*	Deut 7:6	430
the LORD thy *G* hath chosen thee	Deut 7:6	430
that the LORD thy *G*, he is *G*	Deut 7:9	430
the faithful *G*, which keepeth covenant	Deut 7:9	410
that the LORD thy *G* shall keep	Deut 7:12	430
the LORD thy *G* shall deliver thee	Deut 7:16	430
the LORD thy *G* did unto Pharaoh	Deut 7:18	430
the LORD thy *G* brought thee out	Deut 7:19	430
so shall the LORD thy *G* do unto	Deut 7:19	430
Moreover the LORD thy *G* will send	Deut 7:20	430
for the LORD thy *G* is among you	Deut 7:21	430
a mighty *G* and terrible	Deut 7:21	410
the LORD thy *G* will put out those	Deut 7:22	430
But the LORD thy *G* shall deliver	Deut 7:23	430
an abomination to the LORD thy *G*	Deut 7:25	430
G led thee these forty years in	Deut 8:2	430
so the LORD thy *G* chasteneth thee	Deut 8:5	430
commandments of the LORD thy *G*	Deut 8:6	430
For the LORD thy *G* bringeth thee	Deut 8:7	430
thou shalt bless the LORD thy *G*	Deut 8:10	430
thou forget not the LORD thy *G*	Deut 8:11	430
up, and thou forget the LORD thy *G*	Deut 8:14	430
shalt remember the LORD thy *G*	Deut 8:18	430
do at all forget the LORD thy *G*	Deut 8:19	430
unto the voice of the LORD your *G*	Deut 8:20	430
that the LORD thy *G* is he which	Deut 9:3	430
after that the LORD thy *G* hath	Deut 9:4	430
of these nations the LORD thy *G*	Deut 9:5	430
that the LORD thy *G* giveth thee	Deut 9:6	430
thy *G* to wrath in the wilderness	Deut 9:7	430
written with the finger of *G*	Deut 9:10	430
sinned against the LORD your *G*	Deut 9:16	430
commandment of the LORD your *G*	Deut 9:23	430
unto the LORD, and said, O Lord *G*	Deut 9:26	3069
as the LORD thy *G* promised him	Deut 10:9	430
the LORD thy *G* require of thee	Deut 10:12	430
but to fear the LORD thy *G*	Deut 10:12	430
the LORD thy *G* with all thy heart	Deut 10:12	430
of heavens is the LORD's thy *G*	Deut 10:14	430
the LORD your *G* is *G* of gods	Deut 10:17	430
gods, and Lord of lords, a great *G*	Deut 10:17	410
Thou shalt fear the LORD thy *G*	Deut 10:20	430
He is thy praise, and he is thy *G*	Deut 10:21	430
now the LORD thy *G* hath made thee	Deut 10:22	430
thou shalt love the LORD thy *G*	Deut 11:1	430
chastisement of the LORD your *G*	Deut 11:2	430
which the LORD thy *G* careth for	Deut 11:12	430

the LORD thy G are always upon it ... Deut 11:12 430
this day, to love the LORD your G ... Deut 11:13 430
do them, to love the LORD your G ... Deut 11:22 430
for the LORD your G shall lay the ... Deut 11:25 430
commandments of the LORD your G ... Deut 11:27 430
commandments of the LORD your G ... Deut 11:28 430
when the LORD thy G hath brought ... Deut 11:29 430
which the LORD your G giveth you ... Deut 11:31 430
which the LORD G of thy fathers ... Deut 12:1 430
not do so unto the LORD your G ... Deut 12:4 430
G shall choose out of all your ... Deut 12:5 430
shall eat before the LORD your G ... Deut 12:7 430
the LORD thy G hath blessed thee ... Deut 12:7 430
which the LORD your G giveth you ... Deut 12:9 430
LORD your G giveth you to inherit ... Deut 12:10 430
G shall choose to cause his name ... Deut 12:11 430
rejoice before the LORD your G ... Deut 12:12 430
thy G which he hath given thee ... Deut 12:15 430
eat them before the LORD thy G in ... Deut 12:18 430
which the LORD thy G shall choose ... Deut 12:18 430
rejoice before the LORD thy G in ... Deut 12:18 430
When the LORD thy G shall enlarge ... Deut 12:20 430
thy G hath chosen to put his name ... Deut 12:21 430
upon the altar of the LORD thy G ... Deut 12:27 430
upon the altar of the LORD thy G ... Deut 12:27 430
in the sight of the LORD thy G ... Deut 12:28 430
When the LORD thy G shall cut off ... Deut 12:29 430
not do so unto the LORD thy G ... Deut 12:31 430
for the LORD your G proveth you ... Deut 13:3 430
LORD your G with all your heart ... Deut 13:3 430
shall walk after the LORD your G ... Deut 13:4 430
you away from the LORD your G ... Deut 13:5 430
thy G commanded thee to walk in ... Deut 13:5 430
thee away from the LORD thy G ... Deut 13:10 430
which the LORD thy G hath given ... Deut 13:12 430
every whit, for the LORD thy G ... Deut 13:16 430
to the voice of the LORD thy G ... Deut 13:18 430
in the eyes of the LORD thy G ... Deut 13:18 430
the children of the LORD your G ... Deut 14:1 430
holy people unto the LORD thy G ... Deut 14:2 430
holy people unto the LORD thy G ... Deut 14:21 430
shalt eat before the LORD thy G ... Deut 14:23 430
to fear the LORD thy G always ... Deut 14:23 430
which the LORD thy G shall choose ... Deut 14:24 430
the LORD thy G hath blessed thee ... Deut 14:24 430
which the LORD thy G shall choose ... Deut 14:25 430
eat there before the LORD thy G ... Deut 14:26 430
that the LORD thy G may bless ... Deut 14:29 430
G giveth thee for an inheritance ... Deut 15:4 430
unto the voice of the LORD thy G ... Deut 15:5 430
For the LORD thy G blesseth thee ... Deut 15:6 430
which the LORD thy G giveth thee ... Deut 15:7 430
thy G shall bless thee in all thy ... Deut 15:10 430
G hath blessed thee thou shalt ... Deut 15:14 430
the LORD thy G redeemed thee ... Deut 15:15 430
the LORD thy G shall bless thee ... Deut 15:18 430
sanctify unto the LORD thy G ... Deut 15:19 430
eat it before the LORD thy G year ... Deut 15:20 430
sacrifice it unto the LORD thy G ... Deut 15:21 430
the passover unto the LORD thy G ... Deut 16:1 430
the month of Abib the LORD thy G ... Deut 16:1 430
the passover unto the LORD thy G ... Deut 16:2 430
which the LORD thy G giveth thee ... Deut 16:5 430
G shall choose to place his name ... Deut 16:6 430
which the LORD thy G shall choose ... Deut 16:7 430
solemn assembly to the LORD thy G ... Deut 16:8 430
of weeks unto the LORD thy G with ... Deut 16:10 430
shalt give unto the LORD thy G ... Deut 16:10
the LORD thy G hath blessed thee ... Deut 16:10 430
rejoice before the LORD thy G ... Deut 16:11 430
G hath chosen to place his name ... Deut 16:11 430
thy G in the place which the LORD ... Deut 16:15 430
because the LORD thy G shall ... Deut 16:15 430
appear before the LORD thy G in ... Deut 16:16 430
thy G which he hath given thee ... Deut 16:17 430
which the LORD thy G giveth thee ... Deut 16:18 430
which the LORD thy G giveth thee ... Deut 16:20 430
unto the altar of the LORD thy G ... Deut 16:21 430
which the LORD thy G hateth ... Deut 16:22 430
unto the LORD thy G any bullock ... Deut 17:1 430
abomination unto the LORD thy G ... Deut 17:1 430
which the LORD thy G giveth thee ... Deut 17:2 430
in the sight of the LORD thy G ... Deut 17:2 430
which the LORD thy G shall choose ... Deut 17:8 430
there before the LORD thy G ... Deut 17:12 430
which the LORD thy G giveth thee ... Deut 17:14 430
whom the LORD thy G shall choose ... Deut 17:15 430
may learn to fear the LORD his G ... Deut 17:19 430
For the LORD thy G hath chosen ... Deut 18:5 430
in the name of the LORD his G ... Deut 18:7 430
which the LORD thy G giveth thee ... Deut 18:9 430
G doth drive them out from before ... Deut 18:12 430
be perfect with the LORD thy G ... Deut 18:13 430
the LORD thy G hath not suffered ... Deut 18:14 430
The LORD thy G will raise up unto ... Deut 18:15 430
thy G in Horeb in the day of the ... Deut 18:16 430
again the voice of the LORD my G ... Deut 18:16 430
When the LORD thy G hath cut off ... Deut 19:1 430
land the LORD thy G giveth thee ... Deut 19:1 430
which the LORD thy G giveth thee ... Deut 19:2 430
which the LORD thy G giveth thee ... Deut 19:3 430
if the LORD thy G enlarge thy ... Deut 19:8 430
this day, to love the LORD thy G ... Deut 19:9 430
which the LORD thy G giveth thee ... Deut 19:10 430
thy G giveth thee to possess it ... Deut 19:14 430
for the LORD thy G is with thee ... Deut 20:1 430
For the LORD your G is he that ... Deut 20:4 430
And when the LORD thy G hath ... Deut 20:13 430

the LORD thy G hath given thee ... Deut 20:14 430
which the LORD thy G doth give ... Deut 20:16 430
as the LORD thy G hath commanded ... Deut 20:17 430
ye sin against the LORD your G ... Deut 20:18 430
thy G giveth thee to possess it ... Deut 21:1 430
for them the LORD thy G hath ... Deut 21:5 430
the LORD thy G hath delivered ... Deut 21:10 430
that is hanged is accursed of G ... Deut 21:23 430
which the LORD thy G giveth thee ... Deut 21:23 430
abomination unto the LORD thy G ... Deut 22:5 430
Nevertheless the LORD thy G would ... Deut 23:5 430
but the LORD thy G turned the ... Deut 23:5 430
because the LORD thy G loved thee ... Deut 23:5 430
For the LORD thy G walketh in the ... Deut 23:14 430
of the LORD thy G for any vow ... Deut 23:18 430
abomination unto the LORD thy G ... Deut 23:18 430
that the LORD thy G may bless ... Deut 23:20 430
vow a vow unto the LORD thy G ... Deut 23:21 430
for the LORD thy G will surely ... Deut 23:21 430
hast vowed unto the LORD thy G ... Deut 23:23 430
which the LORD thy G giveth thee ... Deut 24:4 430
thy G did unto Miriam by the way ... Deut 24:9 430
unto thee before the LORD thy G ... Deut 24:13 430
the LORD thy G redeemed thee ... Deut 24:18 430
that the LORD thy G may bless ... Deut 24:19 430
which the LORD thy G giveth thee ... Deut 25:15 430
abomination unto the LORD thy G ... Deut 25:16 430
and he feared not G ... Deut 25:18 430
when the LORD thy G hath given ... Deut 25:19 430
G giveth thee for an inheritance ... Deut 25:19 430
the land which the LORD thy G ... Deut 26:1 430
that the LORD thy G giveth thee ... Deut 26:2 430
the place which the LORD thy G ... Deut 26:2 430
this day unto the LORD thy G ... Deut 26:3 430
the altar of the LORD thy G ... Deut 26:4 430
and say before the LORD thy G ... Deut 26:5 430
unto the LORD G of our fathers ... Deut 26:7 430
set it before the LORD thy G ... Deut 26:10 430
and worship before the LORD thy G ... Deut 26:10 430
LORD thy G hath given unto thee ... Deut 26:11 430
shalt say before the LORD thy G ... Deut 26:13 430
to the voice of the LORD my G ... Deut 26:14 430
This day the LORD thy G hath ... Deut 26:16 430
the LORD this day to be thy G ... Deut 26:17 430
holy people unto the LORD thy G ... Deut 26:19 430
which the LORD thy G giveth thee ... Deut 27:2 430
which the LORD thy G giveth thee ... Deut 27:3 430
as the LORD G of thy fathers hath ... Deut 27:3 430
an altar unto the LORD thy G ... Deut 27:5 430
of the LORD thy G of whole stones ... Deut 27:6 430
thereon unto the LORD thy G ... Deut 27:6 430
and rejoice before the LORD thy G ... Deut 27:7 430
the people of the LORD thy G ... Deut 27:9 430
obey the voice of the LORD thy G ... Deut 27:10 430
unto the voice of the LORD thy G ... Deut 28:1 430
that the LORD thy G will set thee ... Deut 28:1 430
unto the voice of the LORD thy G ... Deut 28:2 430
which the LORD thy G giveth thee ... Deut 28:8 430
commandments of the LORD thy G ... Deut 28:9 430
commandments of the LORD thy G ... Deut 28:13 430
unto the voice of the LORD thy G ... Deut 28:15 430
unto the voice of the LORD thy G ... Deut 28:45 430
the LORD thy G with joyfulness ... Deut 28:47 430
the LORD thy G hath given thee ... Deut 28:52 430
the LORD thy G hath given thee ... Deut 28:53 430
and fearful name, THE LORD THY G ... Deut 28:58 430
obey the voice of the LORD thy G ... Deut 28:62 430
shalt say, Would G it were even ... Deut 28:67
say, Would G it were morning ... Deut 28:67
know that I am the LORD your G ... Deut 29:6 430
all of you before the LORD your G ... Deut 29:10 430
into covenant with the LORD thy G ... Deut 29:12 430
which the LORD thy G maketh with ... Deut 29:12 430
and that he may be unto thee a G ... Deut 29:13 430
us this day before the LORD our G ... Deut 29:15 430
away this day from the LORD our G ... Deut 29:18 430
of the LORD G of their fathers ... Deut 29:25 430
things belong unto the LORD our G ... Deut 29:29 430
the LORD thy G hath driven thee ... Deut 30:1 430
shalt return unto the LORD thy G ... Deut 30:2 430
That then the LORD thy G will ... Deut 30:3 430
LORD thy G hath scattered thee ... Deut 30:3 430
will the LORD thy G gather thee ... Deut 30:4 430
the LORD thy G will bring thee ... Deut 30:5 430
the LORD thy G will circumcise ... Deut 30:6 430
LORD thy G with all thine heart ... Deut 30:6 430
the LORD thy G will put all these ... Deut 30:7 430
the LORD thy G will make thee ... Deut 30:9 430
unto the voice of the LORD thy G ... Deut 30:10 430
LORD thy G with all thine heart ... Deut 30:10 430
this day to love the LORD thy G ... Deut 30:16 430
the LORD thy G shall bless thee ... Deut 30:16 430
thou mayest love the LORD thy G ... Deut 30:20 430
The LORD thy G, he will go over ... Deut 31:3 430
for the LORD thy G, he it is that ... Deut 31:6 430
thy G in the place which he shall ... Deut 31:11 430
learn, and fear the LORD your G ... Deut 31:12 430
and learn to fear the LORD your G ... Deut 31:13 430
because our G is not among us ... Deut 31:17 430
the covenant of the LORD your G ... Deut 31:26 430
ascribe ye greatness unto our G ... Deut 32:3 430
a G of truth and without iniquity, ... Deut 32:4 410
then he forsook G which made him ... Deut 32:15 433
sacrificed unto devils, not to G ... Deut 32:17 433
hast forgotten G that formed thee ... Deut 32:18 410
jealousy with that which is not G ... Deut 32:21 410
wherewith Moses the man of G ... Deut 33:1 430
none like unto the G of Jeshurun ... Deut 33:26 410

The eternal G is thy refuge, and ... Deut 33:27 430
for the LORD thy G is with thee ... Josh 1:9 430
which the LORD your G giveth you ... Josh 1:11 430
The LORD your G hath given you ... Josh 1:13 430
which the LORD your G giveth them ... Josh 1:15 430
only the LORD thy G be with thee ... Josh 1:17 430
for the LORD your G, he is G in ... Josh 2:11 430
the covenant of the LORD your G ... Josh 3:3 430
hear the words of the LORD your G ... Josh 3:9 430
that the living G is among you ... Josh 3:10 410
your G into the midst of Jordan ... Josh 4:5 430
For the LORD your G dried up the ... Josh 4:23 430
as the LORD your G did to the Red ... Josh 4:23 430
fear the LORD your G for ever ... Josh 4:24 430
And Joshua said, Alas, O Lord G ... Josh 7:7 3069
would to G we had been content, ... Josh 7:7
thus saith the LORD G of Israel ... Josh 7:13 430
glory to the LORD G of Israel ... Josh 7:19 430
against the LORD G of Israel ... Josh 7:20 430
for the LORD your G will deliver ... Josh 8:7 430
LORD G of Israel in mount Ebal ... Josh 8:30 430
of the name of the LORD thy G ... Josh 9:9 430
unto them by the LORD G of Israel ... Josh 9:18 430
unto them by the LORD G of Israel ... Josh 9:19 430
of water for the house of my G ... Josh 9:23 430
how that the LORD thy G commanded ... Josh 9:24 430
for the LORD your G hath ... Josh 10:19 430
as the LORD G of Israel commanded ... Josh 10:40 430
because the LORD G of Israel ... Josh 10:42 430
LORD G of Israel made by fire are ... Josh 13:14 430
the LORD G of Israel was their ... Josh 13:33 430
Moses the man of G concerning me ... Josh 14:6 430
I wholly followed the LORD my G ... Josh 14:8 430
wholly followed the LORD my G ... Josh 14:9 430
followed the LORD G of Israel ... Josh 14:14 430
which the LORD G of your fathers ... Josh 18:3 430
you here before the LORD our G ... Josh 18:6 430
commandment of the LORD your G ... Josh 22:3 430
now the LORD your G hath given ... Josh 22:4 430
you, to love the LORD your G ... Josh 22:5 430
committed against the G of Israel ... Josh 22:16 430
the altar of the LORD our G ... Josh 22:19 430
The LORD G of gods, the LORD G ... Josh 22:22 410
to do with the LORD G of Israel ... Josh 22:24 430
G forbid that we should rebel ... Josh 22:29
the altar of the LORD our G that ... Josh 22:29 430
the children of Israel blessed G ... Josh 22:33 430
between us that the LORD is G ... Josh 22:34 430
your G hath done unto all these ... Josh 23:3 430
for the LORD your G is he that ... Josh 23:3 430
And the LORD your G, he shall ... Josh 23:5 430
as the LORD your G hath promised ... Josh 23:5 430
But cleave unto the LORD your G ... Josh 23:8 430
for the LORD your G, he it is ... Josh 23:10 430
that ye love the LORD your G ... Josh 23:11 430
G will no more drive out any of ... Josh 23:13 430
the LORD your G hath given you ... Josh 23:13 430
LORD your G spake concerning you ... Josh 23:14 430
the LORD your G promised you ... Josh 23:15 430
the LORD your G hath given you ... Josh 23:15 430
the covenant of the LORD your G ... Josh 23:16 430
presented themselves before G ... Josh 24:1 430
Thus saith the LORD G of Israel ... Josh 24:2 430
G forbid that we should forsake ... Josh 24:16
For the LORD our G, he it is that ... Josh 24:17 430
for he is our G ... Josh 24:18 430
for he is an holy G ... Josh 24:19 430
he is a jealous G ... Josh 24:19 410
heart unto the LORD G of Israel ... Josh 24:23 430
The LORD our G will we serve, and ... Josh 24:24 430
words in the book of the law of G ... Josh 24:26 430
unto you, lest ye deny your G ... Josh 24:27 430
have done, so G hath requited me ... Judg 1:7 430
the LORD G of their fathers ... Judg 2:12 430
LORD, and forgat the LORD their G ... Judg 3:7 430
I have a message from G unto thee ... Judg 3:20 430
Hath not the LORD G of Israel ... Judg 4:6 430
So G subdued on that day Jabin ... Judg 4:23 430
praise to the LORD G of Israel ... Judg 5:3 430
from before the LORD G of Israel ... Judg 5:5 430
Thus saith the LORD G of Israel ... Judg 6:8 430
unto you, I am the LORD your G ... Judg 6:10 430
the angel of G said unto him, ... Judg 6:20 430
LORD, Gideon said, Alas, O Lord G ... Judg 6:22 3069
thy G upon the top of this rock ... Judg 6:26 430
And Gideon said unto G, If thou ... Judg 6:36 430
And Gideon said unto G, Let not ... Judg 6:39 430
And G did so that night ... Judg 6:40 430
his hand hath G delivered Midian ... Judg 7:14 430
G hath delivered into your hands ... Judg 8:3 430
remembered not the LORD their G ... Judg 8:34 430
that G may hearken unto you ... Judg 9:7 430
wherewith by me they honour G ... Judg 9:9 430
I leave my wine, which cheereth G ... Judg 9:13 430
Then G sent an evil spirit ... Judg 9:23 430
would to G this people were under ... Judg 9:29
Thus G rendered the wickedness of ... Judg 9:56 430
did G render upon their heads ... Judg 9:57 430
because we have forsaken our G ... Judg 10:10 430
the LORD G of Israel delivered ... Judg 11:21 430
So now the LORD G of Israel hath ... Judg 11:23 430
So whomsoever the LORD our G ... Judg 11:24 430
a Nazarite unto G from the womb ... Judg 13:5 430
A man of G came unto me, and his ... Judg 13:6 430
the countenance of an angel of G ... Judg 13:6 430
child shall be a Nazarite to G ... Judg 13:7 430
let the man of G which thou didst ... Judg 13:8 430
G hearkened to the voice of ... Judg 13:9 430

the angel of *G* came again unto Judg 13:9 430
die, because we have seen *G* Judg 13:22 430
But *G* clave an hollow place that Judg 15:19 430
unto *G* from my mother's womb Judg 16:17 430
unto the LORD, and said, O Lord *G* Judg 16:28 3069
I pray thee, only this once, O *G* Judg 16:28 430
Ask counsel, we pray thee, of *G* Judg 18:5 430
for *G* hath given it into your Judg 18:10 430
that the house of *G* was in Shiloh Judg 18:31 430
the assembly of the people of *G* Judg 20:2 430
and went up to the house of *G* Judg 20:18 1008
and asked counsel of *G* Judg 20:18 430
up, and came unto the house of *G* Judg 20:26 1008
of *G* was there in those days Judg 20:27 430
one goeth up to the house of *G* Judg 20:31 1008
the people came to the house of *G* Judg 21:2 1008
and abode there till even before *G* Judg 21:2 430
O LORD *G* of Israel, why is this Judg 21:3 430
thee of the LORD *G* of Israel Ruth 2:12 430
the *G* of Israel grant thee thy 1Sa 1:17 430
is there any rock like our *G* 1Sa 2:2 430
for the LORD is a *G* of knowledge 1Sa 2:3 410
And there came a man of *G* unto Eli 1Sa 2:27 430
the LORD *G* of Israel saith 1Sa 2:30 430
wealth which *G* shall give Israel 1Sa 2:32
ere the lamp of *G* went out in the 1Sa 3:3 430
the LORD, where the ark of *G* was 1Sa 3:3 430
G do so to thee, and more also, if 1Sa 3:17 430
with the ark of the covenant of *G* 1Sa 4:4 430
said, *G* is come into the camp 1Sa 4:7 430
And the ark of *G* was taken 1Sa 4:11 430
heart trembled for the ark of *G* 1Sa 4:13 430
dead, and the ark of *G* is taken 1Sa 4:17 430
he made mention of the ark of *G* 1Sa 4:18 430
that the ark of *G* was taken 1Sa 4:19 430
because the ark of *G* was taken 1Sa 4:21 430
for the ark of *G* is taken 1Sa 4:22 430
the Philistines took the ark of *G* 1Sa 5:1 430
the Philistines took the ark of *G* 1Sa 5:2 430
The ark of the *G* of Israel shall 1Sa 5:7 430
with the ark of the *G* of Israel 1Sa 5:8 430
Let the ark of the *G* of Israel be 1Sa 5:8 430
of the *G* of Israel about thither 1Sa 5:8 430
they sent the ark of *G* to Ekron 1Sa 5:10 430
as the ark of *G* came to Ekron 1Sa 5:10 430
the ark of the *G* of Israel to us 1Sa 5:10 430
away the ark of the *G* of Israel 1Sa 5:11 430
the hand of *G* was very heavy 1Sa 5:11 430
away the ark of the *G* of Israel 1Sa 6:3 430
give glory unto the *G* of Israel 1Sa 6:5 430
to stand before this holy LORD *G* 1Sa 6:20 430
to cry unto the LORD our *G* for us 1Sa 7:8 430
there is in this city a man of *G* 1Sa 9:6 430
present to bring to the man of *G* 1Sa 9:7 430
that will I give to the man of *G* 1Sa 9:8 430
when a man went to enquire of *G* 1Sa 9:9 430
the city where the man of *G* was 1Sa 9:10 430
I may shew thee the word of *G* 1Sa 9:27 430
men going up to *G* to Beth-el 1Sa 10:3 430
thou shalt come to the hill of *G* 1Sa 10:5 430
for *G* is with thee 1Sa 10:7 430
Samuel, *G* gave him another heart 1Sa 10:9 430
and the Spirit of *G* came upon him 1Sa 10:10 430
Thus saith the LORD *G* of Israel 1Sa 10:18 430
ye have this day rejected your *G* 1Sa 10:19 430
shouted, and said, *G* save the king 1Sa 10:24
men, whose hearts *G* had touched 1Sa 10:26 430
the Spirit of *G* came upon Saul 1Sa 11:6 430
when they forgat the LORD their *G* 1Sa 12:9 430
the LORD your *G* was your king 1Sa 12:12 430
following the LORD your *G* 1Sa 12:14 430
thy servants unto the LORD thy *G* 1Sa 12:19 430
G forbid that I should sin 1Sa 12:23
the commandment of the LORD thy *G* 1Sa 13:13 430
Ahiah, Bring hither the ark of *G* 1Sa 14:18 430
For the ark of *G* was at that time 1Sa 14:18 430
Let us draw near hither unto *G* 1Sa 14:36 430
And Saul asked counsel of *G* 1Sa 14:37 430
said unto the LORD *G* of Israel 1Sa 14:41 430
answered, *G* do so and more also 1Sa 14:44 430
G forbid: as the LORD liveth 1Sa 14:45
he hath wrought with *G* this day 1Sa 14:45 430
to sacrifice unto the LORD thy *G* 1Sa 15:15 430
unto the LORD thy *G* in Gilgal 1Sa 15:21 430
that I may worship the LORD thy *G* 1Sa 15:30 430
evil spirit from *G* troubleth thee 1Sa 16:15 430
evil spirit from *G* is upon thee 1Sa 16:16 430
evil spirit from *G* was upon Saul 1Sa 16:23 430
defy the armies of the living *G* 1Sa 17:26 430
defied the armies of the living *G* 1Sa 17:36 430
the *G* of the armies of Israel, 1Sa 17:45 430
know that there is a *G* in Israel 1Sa 17:46 430
evil spirit from *G* came upon Saul 1Sa 18:10 430
the Spirit of *G* was upon the 1Sa 19:20 430
the Spirit of *G* was upon him also 1Sa 19:23 430
And he said unto him, *G* forbid 1Sa 20:2
O LORD *G* of Israel, when I have 1Sa 20:12 430
till I know what *G* will do for me 1Sa 22:3 430
and hast enquired of *G* for him 1Sa 22:13 430
begin to enquire of *G* for him 1Sa 22:15 430
G hath delivered him into mine 1Sa 23:7 430
O LORD *G* of Israel, thy servant 1Sa 23:10 430
O LORD *G* of Israel, I beseech 1Sa 23:11 430
but *G* delivered him not into his 1Sa 23:14 430
and strengthened his hand in *G* 1Sa 23:16 430
more also do *G* unto the enemies 1Sa 25:22 430
of life with the LORD thy *G* 1Sa 25:29 430
Blessed be the LORD *G* of Israel 1Sa 25:32 430

as the LORD *G* of Israel liveth, 1Sa 25:34 430
G hath delivered thine enemy into 1Sa 26:8 430
G is departed from me, and 1Sa 28:15 430
in my sight, as an angel of *G* 1Sa 29:9 430
himself in the LORD his *G* 1Sa 30:6 430
And he said, Swear unto me by *G* 1Sa 30:15 430
As *G* liveth, unless thou hadst 2Sa 2:27 430
So do *G* to Abner, and more also, 2Sa 3:9 430
sware, saying, So do *G* to me 2Sa 3:35 430
the LORD *G* of hosts was with him 2Sa 5:10 430
bring up from thence the ark of *G* 2Sa 6:2 430
set the ark of *G* upon a new cart 2Sa 6:3 430
Gibeah, accompanying the ark of *G* 2Sa 6:4 430
forth his hand to the ark of *G* 2Sa 6:6 430
G smote him there for his error 2Sa 6:7 430
and there he died by the ark of *G* 2Sa 6:7 430
unto him, because of the ark of *G* 2Sa 6:12 430
brought up the ark of *G* from the 2Sa 6:12 430
but the ark of *G* dwelleth within 2Sa 7:2 430
and he said, Who am I, O Lord *G* 2Sa 7:18 3069
thing in thy sight, O Lord *G* 2Sa 7:19 3069
this the manner of man, O Lord *G* 2Sa 7:19 3069
for thou, Lord *G*, knowest thy 2Sa 7:20 3069
thou art great, O LORD *G* 2Sa 7:22 430
is there any *G* beside thee 2Sa 7:22 430
whom *G* went to redeem for a 2Sa 7:23 430
and thou, LORD, art become their *G* 2Sa 7:24 430
And now, O LORD *G*, the word that 2Sa 7:25 430
of hosts is the *G* over Israel 2Sa 7:26 430
G of Israel, hast revealed to thy 2Sa 7:27 430
And now, O Lord *G* 2Sa 7:28 3069
thou art that *G* 2Sa 7:28 430
for thou, O Lord *G*, hast spoken 2Sa 7:29 3069
shew the kindness of *G* unto him 2Sa 9:3 430
and for the cities of our *G* 2Sa 10:12 430
Thus saith the LORD *G* of Israel 2Sa 12:7 430
besought *G* for the child 2Sa 12:16 430
Who can tell whether *G* will be 2Sa 12:22 3068
the king remember the LORD thy *G* 2Sa 14:11 430
a thing against the people of *G* 2Sa 14:13 430
neither doth *G* respect any person 2Sa 14:14 430
out of the inheritance of *G* 2Sa 14:16 430
for as an angel of *G*, so is my 2Sa 14:17 430
the LORD thy *G* will be with thee 2Sa 14:17 430
to the wisdom of an angel of *G* 2Sa 14:20 430
the ark of the covenant of *G* 2Sa 15:24 430
and they set down the ark of *G* 2Sa 15:24 430
back the ark of *G* into the city 2Sa 15:25 430
the ark of *G* again to Jerusalem 2Sa 15:29 430
the mount, where he worshipped *G* 2Sa 15:32 430
G save the king, *G* save the 2Sa 16:16
had enquired at the oracle of *G* 2Sa 16:23 430
said, Blessed be the LORD thy *G* 2Sa 18:28 430
would *G* I had died for thee, O 2Sa 18:33
G do so to me, and more also, if 2Sa 19:13 430
lord the king is as an angel of *G* 2Sa 19:27 430
after that *G* was intreated for 2Sa 21:14 430
The *G* of my rock 2Sa 22:3 430
upon the LORD, and cried to my *G* 2Sa 22:7 430
not wickedly departed from my *G* 2Sa 22:22 430
by my *G* have I leaped over a wall 2Sa 22:30 430
As for *G*, his way is perfect 2Sa 22:31 410
For who is *G*, save the LORD 2Sa 22:32 410
and who is a rock, save our *G* 2Sa 22:32 430
G is my strength and power 2Sa 22:33 410
exalted be the *G* of the rock of 2Sa 22:47 430
It is *G* that avengeth me, and that 2Sa 22:48 410
the anointed of the *G* of Jacob 2Sa 23:1 430
The *G* of Israel said, the Rock of 2Sa 23:3 430
be just, ruling in the fear of *G* 2Sa 23:3 430
my house be not so with *G* 2Sa 23:5 410
Now the LORD thy *G* add unto the 2Sa 24:3 430
king, The LORD thy *G* accept thee 2Sa 24:23 430
my *G* of that which doth cost me 2Sa 24:24 430
LORD thy *G* unto thine handmaid 1Kin 1:17 430
him, and say, *G* save king Adonijah 1Kin 1:25
unto thee by the LORD *G* of Israel 1Kin 1:30 430
and say, *G* save king Solomon 1Kin 1:34
the LORD *G* of my lord the king 1Kin 1:36 430
people said, *G* save king Solomon 1Kin 1:39
G make the name of Solomon better 1Kin 1:47 430
Blessed be the LORD *G* of Israel 1Kin 1:48 430
keep the charge of the LORD thy *G* 1Kin 2:3 430
G do so to me, and more also, if 1Kin 2:23 430
the Lord *G* before David my father 1Kin 2:26 3069
G said, Ask what I shall give 1Kin 3:5 430
And now, O LORD my *G*, thou hast 1Kin 3:7 430
G said unto him, Because thou 1Kin 3:11 430
that the wisdom of *G* was in him 1Kin 3:28 430
And *G* gave Solomon wisdom and 1Kin 4:29 430
G for the wars which were about 1Kin 5:3 430
But now the LORD my *G* hath given 1Kin 5:4 430
unto the name of the LORD my *G* 1Kin 5:5 430
Blessed be the LORD *G* of Israel 1Kin 8:15 430
the name of the LORD *G* of Israel 1Kin 8:17 430
the name of the LORD *G* of Israel 1Kin 8:20 430
LORD *G* of Israel, there is no *G* 1Kin 8:23 430
LORD *G* of Israel, keep with thy 1Kin 8:25 430
O *G* of Israel, let thy word, I 1Kin 8:26 430
But will *G* indeed dwell on the 1Kin 8:27 430
to his supplication, O LORD my *G* 1Kin 8:28 430
fathers out of Egypt, O Lord *G* 1Kin 8:53 3069
The LORD our *G* be with us 1Kin 8:57 430
be nigh unto the LORD our *G* day 1Kin 8:59 430
earth may know that the LORD is *G* 1Kin 8:60 430
be perfect with the LORD our *G* 1Kin 8:61 430
of Egypt, before the LORD our *G* 1Kin 8:65 430
they forsook the LORD their *G* 1Kin 9:9 430

Blessed be the LORD thy *G* 1Kin 10:9 430
which *G* had put in his heart 1Kin 10:24 430
not perfect with the LORD his *G* 1Kin 11:4 430
turned from the LORD *G* of Israel 1Kin 11:9 430
And *G* stirred him up another 1Kin 11:23 430
the *G* of Israel, Behold, I will 1Kin 11:31 430
But the word of *G* came unto 1Kin 12:22 430
came unto Shemaiah the man of *G* 1Kin 12:22 430
there came a man of *G* out of 1Kin 13:1 430
heard the saying of the man of *G* 1Kin 13:4 430
of *G* had given by the word of the 1Kin 13:5 430
and said unto the man of *G* 1Kin 13:6 430
now the face of the LORD thy *G* 1Kin 13:6 430
the man of *G* besought the LORD, 1Kin 13:6 430
the king said unto the man of *G* 1Kin 13:7 430
the man of *G* said unto the king, 1Kin 13:8 430
of *G* had done that day in Beth-el 1Kin 13:11 430
seen what way the man of *G* went 1Kin 13:12 430
And went after the man of *G* 1Kin 13:14 430
Art thou the man of *G* that camest 1Kin 13:14 430
the man of *G* that came from Judah 1Kin 13:21 430
the LORD thy *G* commanded thee 1Kin 13:21 430
he said, It is the man of *G* 1Kin 13:26 430
up the carcase of the man of *G* 1Kin 13:29 430
wherein the man of *G* is buried 1Kin 13:31 430
Thus saith the LORD *G* of Israel 1Kin 14:7 430
LORD *G* of Israel in the house of 1Kin 14:13 430
not perfect with the LORD his *G* 1Kin 15:3 430
G give him a lamp in Jerusalem 1Kin 15:4 430
the LORD *G* of Israel to anger 1Kin 15:30 430
in provoking the LORD *G* of Israel 1Kin 16:13 430
to provoke the LORD *G* of Israel 1Kin 16:26 430
did more to provoke the LORD *G* of 1Kin 16:33 430
As the LORD *G* of Israel liveth, 1Kin 17:1 430
said, As the LORD thy *G* liveth 1Kin 17:12 430
thus saith the LORD *G* of Israel 1Kin 17:14 430
to do with thee, O thou man of *G* 1Kin 17:18 430
the LORD, and said, O LORD my *G* 1Kin 17:20 430
the LORD, and said, O LORD my *G* 1Kin 17:21 430
I know that thou art a man of *G* 1Kin 17:24 430
As the LORD thy *G* liveth, there 1Kin 18:10 430
if the LORD be *G*, follow him 1Kin 18:21 430
the *G* that answereth by fire, let 1Kin 18:24 430
answereth by fire, let him be *G* 1Kin 18:24 430
LORD *G* of Abraham, Isaac, and of 1Kin 18:36 430
day that thou art *G* in Israel 1Kin 18:36 430
may know that thou art the LORD *G* 1Kin 18:37 430
they said, The LORD, he is the *G* 1Kin 18:39 430
the LORD, he is the *G* 1Kin 18:39 430
nights unto Horeb the mount of *G* 1Kin 19:8 430
jealous for the LORD *G* of hosts 1Kin 19:10 430
jealous for the LORD *G* of hosts 1Kin 19:14 430
And there came a man of *G*, and 1Kin 20:28 430
The LORD is *G* of the hills 1Kin 20:28 430
but he is not *G* of the valleys, 1Kin 20:28 430
saying, Thou didst blaspheme *G* 1Kin 21:10 430
saying, Naboth did blaspheme *G* 1Kin 21:13 430
to anger the LORD *G* of Israel 1Kin 22:53 430
there is not a *G* in Israel 2Kin 1:3 430
there is not a *G* in Israel 2Kin 1:6 430
he spake unto him, Thou man of *G* 2Kin 1:9 430
of fifty, If I be a man of *G* 2Kin 1:10 430
and said unto him, O man of *G* 2Kin 1:11 430
unto them, If I be a man of *G* 2Kin 1:12 430
the fire of *G* came down from 2Kin 1:12 430
him, and said unto him, O man of *G* 2Kin 1:13 430
no *G* in Israel to enquire of his 2Kin 1:16 430
Where is the LORD *G* of Elijah 2Kin 2:14 430
she came and told the man of *G* 2Kin 4:7 430
that this is an holy man of *G* 2Kin 4:9 430
said, Nay, my lord, thou man of *G* 2Kin 4:16 430
him on the bed of the man of *G* 2Kin 4:21 430
that I may run to the man of *G* 2Kin 4:22 430
unto the man of *G* to mount Carmel 2Kin 4:25 430
when the man of *G* saw her afar 2Kin 4:25 430
came to the man of *G* to the hill 2Kin 4:27 430
And the man of *G* said, Let her 2Kin 4:27 430
out, and said, O thou man of *G* 2Kin 4:40 430
brought the man of *G* bread of the 2Kin 4:42 430
Would *G* my lord were with the 2Kin 5:3
rent his clothes, and said, Am I *G* 2Kin 5:7 430
when Elisha the man of *G* had 2Kin 5:8 430
on the name of the LORD his *G* 2Kin 5:11 430
to the saying of the man of *G* 2Kin 5:14 430
And he returned to the man of *G* 2Kin 5:15 430
there is no *G* in all the earth 2Kin 5:15 430
servant of Elisha the man of *G* 2Kin 5:20 430
And the man of *G* said, Where fell 2Kin 6:6 430
the man of *G* sent unto the king 2Kin 6:9 430
place which the man of *G* told him 2Kin 6:10 430
of the man of *G* was risen early 2Kin 6:15 430
G do so and more also to me, if 2Kin 6:31 430
king leaned answered the man of *G* 2Kin 7:2 430
he died, as the man of *G* had said 2Kin 7:17 430
man of *G* had spoken to the king 2Kin 7:18 430
that lord answered the man of *G* 2Kin 7:19 430
after the saying of the man of *G* 2Kin 8:2 430
the servant of the man of *G* 2Kin 8:4 430
The man of *G* is come hither 2Kin 8:7 430
hand, and go, meet the man of *G* 2Kin 8:8 430
and the man of *G* wept 2Kin 8:11 430
Thus saith the LORD *G* of Israel 2Kin 9:6 430
G of Israel with all his heart 2Kin 10:31 430
hands, and said, *G* save the king 2Kin 11:12
the man of *G* was wroth with him, 2Kin 13:19 430
the word of the LORD *G* of Israel 2Kin 14:25 430
in the sight of the LORD his *G* 2Kin 16:2 430
sinned against the LORD their *G* 2Kin 17:7 430

G

Context	Reference	Strong's
right against the LORD their G	2Kin 17:9	430
not believe in the LORD their G	2Kin 17:14	430
commandments of the LORD their G	2Kin 17:16	430
commandments of the LORD their G	2Kin 17:19	430
the manner of the G of the land	2Kin 17:26	430
the manner of the G of the land	2Kin 17:26	430
the manner of the G of the land	2Kin 17:27	430
But the LORD your G ye shall fear	2Kin 17:39	430
trusted in the LORD G of Israel	2Kin 18:5	430
not the voice of the LORD their G	2Kin 18:12	430
me, We trust in the LORD our G	2Kin 18:22	430
It may be the LORD thy G will	2Kin 19:4	430
sent to reproach the living G	2Kin 19:4	430
which the LORD thy G hath heard	2Kin 19:4	430
Let not thy G in whom thou	2Kin 19:10	430
O LORD G of Israel, which	2Kin 19:15	430
the cherubims, thou art the G	2Kin 19:15	430
sent him to reproach the living G	2Kin 19:16	430
Now therefore, O LORD our G	2Kin 19:19	430
may know that thou art the LORD G	2Kin 19:19	430
Thus saith the LORD G of Israel	2Kin 19:20	430
the G of David thy father, I have	2Kin 20:5	430
thus saith the LORD G of Israel	2Kin 21:12	430
forsook the LORD G of his fathers	2Kin 21:22	430
Thus saith the LORD G of Israel	2Kin 22:15	430
Thus saith the LORD G of Israel	2Kin 22:18	430
which the man of G proclaimed	2Kin 23:16	430
is the sepulchre of the man of G	2Kin 23:17	430
the passover unto the LORD your G	2Kin 23:21	430
Jabez called on the G of Israel	1Chr 4:10	430
G granted him that which he	1Chr 4:10	430
for they cried to G in the battle	1Chr 5:20	430
slain, because the war was of G	1Chr 5:22	430
against the G of their fathers	1Chr 5:25	430
whom G destroyed before them	1Chr 5:25	430
the G of Israel stirred up the	1Chr 5:26	430
the tabernacle of the house of G	1Chr 6:48	430
the servant of G had commanded	1Chr 6:49	430
the ruler of the house of G	1Chr 9:11	430
of the service of the house of G	1Chr 9:13	430
and treasuries of the house of G	1Chr 9:26	430
lodged round about the house of G	1Chr 9:27	430
the LORD thy G said unto thee,	1Chr 11:2	430
My G forbid it me, that I should	1Chr 11:19	430
the G of our fathers look thereon	1Chr 12:17	430
for thy G helpeth thee	1Chr 12:18	430
a great host, like the host of G	1Chr 12:22	430
and that it be of the LORD our G	1Chr 13:2	430
again the ark of our G to us	1Chr 13:3	430
the ark of G from Kirjath-jearim	1Chr 13:5	430
up thence the ark of G the LORD	1Chr 13:6	430
they carried the ark of G in a	1Chr 13:7	430
before G with all their might	1Chr 13:8	430
and there he died before G	1Chr 13:10	430
And David was afraid of G that day	1Chr 13:12	430
I bring the ark of G home to me	1Chr 13:12	430
the ark of G remained with the	1Chr 13:14	430
And David enquired of G, saying,	1Chr 14:10	430
G hath broken in upon mine	1Chr 14:11	430
David enquired again of G	1Chr 14:14	430
G said unto him, Go not up after	1Chr 14:14	430
for G is gone forth before thee	1Chr 14:15	430
therefore did as G commanded him	1Chr 14:16	430
prepared a place for the ark of G	1Chr 15:1	430
the ark of G but the Levites	1Chr 15:2	430
LORD chosen to carry the ark of G	1Chr 15:2	430
bring up the ark of the LORD G of	1Chr 15:12	430
the LORD our G made a breach upon	1Chr 15:13	430
the ark of the LORD G of Israel	1Chr 15:14	430
G upon their shoulders with the	1Chr 15:15	430
the trumpets before the ark of G	1Chr 15:24	430
when G helped the Levites that	1Chr 15:26	430
So they brought the ark of G	1Chr 16:1	430
and peace offerings before G	1Chr 16:1	430
and praise the LORD G of Israel	1Chr 16:4	430
the ark of the covenant of G	1Chr 16:6	430
He is the LORD our G	1Chr 16:14	430
O G of our salvation, and gather	1Chr 16:35	430
be the LORD G of Israel for ever	1Chr 16:36	430
and with musical instruments of G	1Chr 16:42	430
for G is with thee	1Chr 17:2	430
that the word of G came to Nathan	1Chr 17:3	430
LORD, and said, Who am I, O LORD G	1Chr 17:16	430
a small thing in thine eyes, O G	1Chr 17:17	430
of a man of high degree, O LORD G	1Chr 17:17	430
is there any G beside thee	1Chr 17:20	430
whom G went to redeem to be his	1Chr 17:21	430
and thou, LORD, becamest their G	1Chr 17:22	430
G of Israel, even a G to Israel	1Chr 17:24	430
For thou, O my G, hast told thy	1Chr 17:25	430
And now, LORD, thou art G, and hast	1Chr 17:26	430
and for the cities of our G	1Chr 19:13	430
G was displeased with this thing	1Chr 21:7	430
And David said unto G, I have	1Chr 21:8	430
G sent an angel unto Jerusalem to	1Chr 21:15	430
And David said unto G, Is it not I	1Chr 21:17	430
hand, I pray thee, O LORD my G	1Chr 21:17	430
not go before it to enquire of G	1Chr 21:30	430
This is the house of the LORD G	1Chr 22:1	430
stones to build the house of G	1Chr 22:2	430
an house for the LORD G of Israel	1Chr 22:6	430
unto the name of the LORD my G	1Chr 22:7	430
build the house of the LORD thy G	1Chr 22:11	430
keep the law of the LORD thy G	1Chr 22:12	430
Is not the LORD your G with you	1Chr 22:18	430
your soul to seek the LORD your G	1Chr 22:19	430
ye the sanctuary of the LORD G	1Chr 22:19	430
LORD, and the holy vessels of G	1Chr 22:19	430
Now concerning Moses the man of G	1Chr 23:14	430
The LORD G of Israel hath given	1Chr 23:25	430
of the service of the house of G	1Chr 23:28	430
and governors of the house of G	1Chr 24:5	430
as the LORD G of Israel had	1Chr 24:19	430
the king's seer in the words of G	1Chr 25:5	430
G gave to Heman fourteen sons and	1Chr 25:5	430
for the service of the house of G	1Chr 25:6	430
for G blessed him	1Chr 26:5	430
the treasures of the house of G	1Chr 26:20	430
for every matter pertaining to G	1Chr 26:32	430
and for the footstool of our G	1Chr 28:2	430
But G said unto me, Thou shalt	1Chr 28:3	430
Howbeit the LORD G of Israel	1Chr 28:4	430
LORD, and in the audience of our G	1Chr 28:8	430
commandments of the LORD your G	1Chr 28:8	430
know thou the G of thy father	1Chr 28:9	430
the treasuries of the house of G	1Chr 28:12	430
for the LORD G, even my G	1Chr 28:20	430
all the service of the house of G	1Chr 28:21	430
whom alone G hath chosen, is yet	1Chr 29:1	430
not for man, but for the LORD G	1Chr 29:1	430
my might for the house of my G	1Chr 29:2	430
my affection to the house of my G	1Chr 29:3	430
I have given to the house of my G	1Chr 29:3	430
G of gold five thousand talents	1Chr 29:7	430
LORD G of Israel our father, for	1Chr 29:10	430
Now therefore, our G, we thank	1Chr 29:13	430
O LORD our G, all this store that	1Chr 29:16	430
I know also, my G, that thou	1Chr 29:17	430
O LORD G of Abraham, Isaac, and of	1Chr 29:18	430
Now bless the LORD your G	1Chr 29:20	430
the LORD G of their fathers	1Chr 29:20	430
and the LORD his G was with him	2Chr 1:1	430
of the congregation of G, which	2Chr 1:3	430
But the ark of G had David	2Chr 1:4	430
In that night did G appear unto	2Chr 1:7	430
And Solomon said unto G, Thou hast	2Chr 1:8	430
Now, O LORD G, let thy promise	2Chr 1:9	430
G said to Solomon, Because this	2Chr 1:11	430
to the name of the LORD my G	2Chr 2:4	430
solemn feasts of the LORD our G	2Chr 2:4	430
for great is our G above all gods	2Chr 2:5	430
Blessed be the LORD G of Israel	2Chr 2:12	430
the building of the house of G	2Chr 3:3	430
king Solomon for the house of G	2Chr 4:11	430
that were for the house of G	2Chr 4:19	430
the treasures of the house of G	2Chr 5:1	430
LORD had filled the house of G	2Chr 5:14	430
Blessed be the LORD G of Israel	2Chr 6:4	430
the name of the LORD G of Israel	2Chr 6:7	430
the name of the LORD G of Israel	2Chr 6:10	430
O LORD G of Israel	2Chr 6:14	430
there is no G like thee in the	2Chr 6:14	430
O LORD G of Israel, keep with thy	2Chr 6:16	430
O LORD G of Israel, let thy word	2Chr 6:17	430
But will G in very deed dwell	2Chr 6:18	430
to his supplication, O LORD my G	2Chr 6:19	430
Now, my G, let, I beseech thee,	2Chr 6:40	430
Now therefore arise, O LORD G,	2Chr 6:41	430
let thy priests, O LORD G	2Chr 6:41	430
O LORD G, turn not away the face	2Chr 6:42	430
people dedicated the house of G	2Chr 7:5	430
the LORD G of their fathers	2Chr 7:22	430
had David the man of G commanded	2Chr 8:14	430
Blessed be the LORD thy G	2Chr 9:8	430
to be king for the LORD thy G	2Chr 9:8	430
because thy G loved Israel, to	2Chr 9:8	430
that G had put in his heart	2Chr 9:23	430
for the cause was of G, that the	2Chr 10:15	430
came to Shemaiah the man of G	2Chr 11:2	430
G of Israel came to Jerusalem	2Chr 11:16	430
unto the LORD G of their fathers	2Chr 11:16	430
ye not to know that the LORD G of	2Chr 13:5	430
But as for us, the LORD is our G	2Chr 13:10	430
keep the charge of the LORD our G	2Chr 13:11	430
G himself is with us for our	2Chr 13:12	430
the LORD G of your fathers	2Chr 13:12	430
that G smote Jeroboam and all	2Chr 13:15	430
G delivered them into their hand	2Chr 13:16	430
upon the LORD G of their fathers	2Chr 13:18	430
in the eyes of the LORD his G	2Chr 14:2	430
seek the LORD G of their fathers	2Chr 14:4	430
we have sought the LORD our G	2Chr 14:7	430
And Asa cried unto the LORD his G	2Chr 14:11	430
help us, O LORD our G	2Chr 14:11	430
O LORD, thou art our G	2Chr 14:11	430
the Spirit of G came upon Azariah	2Chr 15:1	430
hath been without the true G	2Chr 15:3	430
turn unto the LORD G of Israel	2Chr 15:4	430
for G did vex them with all	2Chr 15:6	430
that the LORD his G was with him	2Chr 15:9	430
a covenant to seek the LORD G of	2Chr 15:12	430
would not seek the LORD G of	2Chr 15:13	430
he brought into the house of G	2Chr 15:18	430
and not relied on the LORD thy G	2Chr 16:7	430
to the LORD G of his father	2Chr 17:4	430
for G will deliver it into the	2Chr 18:5	430
LORD liveth, even what my G saith	2Chr 18:13	430
G moved them to depart from him	2Chr 18:31	430
prepared thine heart to seek G	2Chr 19:3	430
unto the LORD G of their fathers	2Chr 19:4	430
no iniquity with the LORD our G	2Chr 19:7	430
O LORD G of our fathers	2Chr 20:6	430
art not thou G in heaven	2Chr 20:6	430
Art not thou our G, who didst	2Chr 20:7	430
O our G, wilt thou not judge them	2Chr 20:12	430
stood up to praise the LORD G of	2Chr 20:19	430
Believe in the LORD your G	2Chr 20:20	430
the fear of G was on all the	2Chr 20:29	430
for his G gave him rest round	2Chr 20:30	430
unto the G of their fathers	2Chr 20:33	430
the LORD G of his fathers	2Chr 21:10	430
the LORD G of David thy father	2Chr 21:12	430
was of G by coming to Joram	2Chr 22:7	430
hid in the house of G six years	2Chr 22:12	430
with the king in the house of G	2Chr 23:3	430
which were in the house of G	2Chr 23:9	430
him, and said, G save the king	2Chr 23:11	
house of your G from year to year	2Chr 24:5	430
had broken up the house of G	2Chr 24:7	430
of G laid upon Israel in the	2Chr 24:9	430
set the house of G in his state	2Chr 24:13	430
good in Israel, both toward G	2Chr 24:16	430
of the LORD G of their fathers	2Chr 24:18	430
the Spirit of G came upon	2Chr 24:20	430
and said unto them, Thus saith G	2Chr 24:20	430
the LORD G of their fathers	2Chr 24:24	430
the repairing of the house of G	2Chr 24:27	430
But there came a man of G to him	2Chr 25:7	430
G shall make thee fall before the	2Chr 25:8	430
for G hath power to help, and to	2Chr 25:8	430
And Amaziah said to the man of G	2Chr 25:9	430
And the man of G answered, The	2Chr 25:9	430
I know that G hath determined to	2Chr 25:16	430
for it came of G, that he might	2Chr 25:20	430
in the house of G with Obed-edom	2Chr 25:24	430
he sought G in the days of	2Chr 26:5	430
understanding in the visions of G	2Chr 26:5	430
the LORD, G made him to prosper	2Chr 26:5	430
And G helped him against the	2Chr 26:7	430
against the LORD his G, and went	2Chr 26:16	430
for thine honour from the LORD G	2Chr 26:18	430
his ways before the LORD his G	2Chr 27:6	430
Wherefore the LORD his G	2Chr 28:5	430
the LORD G of their fathers	2Chr 28:6	430
because the LORD G of your	2Chr 28:9	430
you, sins against the LORD your G	2Chr 28:10	430
the vessels of the house of G	2Chr 28:24	430
the vessels of the house of G	2Chr 28:24	430
anger the LORD G of his fathers	2Chr 28:25	430
of the LORD G of your fathers	2Chr 29:5	430
in the eyes of the LORD our G	2Chr 29:6	430
holy place unto the G of Israel	2Chr 29:7	430
with the LORD G of Israel	2Chr 29:10	430
that G had prepared the people	2Chr 29:36	430
unto the LORD G of Israel	2Chr 30:1	430
the LORD G of Israel at Jerusalem	2Chr 30:5	430
again unto the LORD G of Abraham	2Chr 30:6	430
the LORD G of their fathers	2Chr 30:7	430
and serve the LORD your G, that	2Chr 30:8	430
for the LORD your G is gracious	2Chr 30:9	430
Also in Judah the hand of G was	2Chr 30:12	430
to the law of Moses the man of G	2Chr 30:16	430
prepareth his heart to seek G	2Chr 30:19	430
the LORD G of his fathers, though	2Chr 30:19	430
to the LORD G of their fathers	2Chr 30:22	430
consecrated unto the LORD their G	2Chr 31:6	430
the ruler of the house of G	2Chr 31:13	430
over the freewill offerings of G	2Chr 31:14	430
and truth before the LORD his G	2Chr 31:20	430
in the service of the house of G	2Chr 31:21	430
the commandments, to seek his G	2Chr 31:21	430
us is the LORD our G to help us	2Chr 32:8	430
The LORD our G shall deliver us	2Chr 32:11	430
that your G should be able to	2Chr 32:14	430
how much less shall your G	2Chr 32:15	430
spake yet more against the LORD G	2Chr 32:16	430
to rail on the LORD G of Israel	2Chr 32:17	430
so shall not the G of Hezekiah	2Chr 32:17	430
spake against the G of Jerusalem	2Chr 32:19	430
for G had given him substance	2Chr 32:29	430
G left him, to try him, that he	2Chr 32:31	430
he had made, in the house of G	2Chr 33:7	430
of which G had said to David and	2Chr 33:7	430
he besought the LORD his G	2Chr 33:12	430
before the G of his fathers	2Chr 33:12	430
knew that the LORD he was G	2Chr 33:13	430
to serve the LORD G of Israel	2Chr 33:16	430
yet unto the LORD their G only	2Chr 33:17	430
and his prayer unto his G	2Chr 33:18	430
the name of the LORD G of Israel	2Chr 33:18	430
how G was intreated of him, and	2Chr 33:19	
after the G of David his father	2Chr 34:3	430
the house of the LORD his G	2Chr 34:8	430
was brought into the house of G	2Chr 34:9	430
Thus saith the LORD G of Israel	2Chr 34:23	430
Thus saith the LORD G of Israel	2Chr 34:26	430
didst humble thyself before G	2Chr 34:27	430
according to the covenant of G	2Chr 34:32	430
the G of their fathers	2Chr 34:32	430
even to serve the LORD their G	2Chr 34:33	430
the LORD, the G of their fathers	2Chr 34:33	430
serve now the LORD your G	2Chr 35:3	430
Jehiel, rulers of the house of G	2Chr 35:8	430
for G commanded me to make haste	2Chr 35:21	430
forbear thee from meddling with G	2Chr 35:21	430
of Necho from the mouth of G	2Chr 35:22	430
in the sight of the LORD his G	2Chr 36:5	430
in the sight of the LORD his G	2Chr 36:12	430
who had made him swear by G	2Chr 36:13	430
turning unto the LORD G of Israel	2Chr 36:13	430
the LORD G of their fathers sent	2Chr 36:15	430
they mocked the messengers of G	2Chr 36:16	430
all the vessels of the house of G	2Chr 36:18	430
And they burnt the house of G	2Chr 36:19	430

the LORD G of heaven given me 2Chr 36:23 430
The LORD his G be with him 2Chr 36:23 430
The LORD G of heaven hath given Ezr 1:2 430
his G be with him, and let him go Ezr 1:3 430
LORD G of Israel, (he is the G Ezr 1:3 430
house of G that is in Jerusalem Ezr 1:4 430
them whose spirit G had raised Ezr 1:5 430
of G to set it up in his place Ezr 2:68 430
the altar of the G of Israel Ezr 3:2 430
in the law of Moses the man of G Ezr 3:2 430
unto the house of G at Jerusalem Ezr 3:8 430
the workmen in the house of G Ezr 3:9 430
temple unto the LORD G of Israel Ezr 4:1 430
for we seek your G, as ye do Ezr 4:2 430
us to build an house unto our G Ezr 4:3 430
build unto the LORD G of Israel Ezr 4:3 430
house of G which is at Jerusalem Ezr 4:24 426
in the name of the G of Israel Ezr 5:1 426
house of G which is at Jerusalem Ezr 5:2 426
the prophets of G helping them Ezr 5:2 426
But the eye of their G was upon Ezr 5:5 426
to the house of the great G Ezr 5:8 426
the servants of the G of heaven Ezr 5:11 426
the G of heaven unto wrath Ezr 5:12 426
a decree to build this house of G Ezr 5:13 426
gold and silver of the house of G Ezr 5:14 426
let the house of G be builded in Ezr 5:15 426
house of G which is in Jerusalem Ezr 5:16 426
this house of G at Jerusalem Ezr 5:17 426
the house of G at Jerusalem Ezr 6:3 426
silver vessels of the house of G Ezr 6:5 426
and place them in the house of G Ezr 6:5 426
the work of this house of G alone Ezr 6:7 426
this house of G in his place Ezr 6:7 426
the building of this house of G Ezr 6:8 426
offerings of the G of heaven Ezr 6:9 426
savours unto the G of heaven Ezr 6:10 426
the G that hath caused his name Ezr 6:12 426
house of G which is at Jerusalem Ezr 6:12 426
commandment of the G of Israel Ezr 6:14 426
of this house of G with joy Ezr 6:16 426
house of G an hundred bullocks Ezr 6:17 426
courses, for the service of G Ezr 6:18 426
to seek the LORD G of Israel Ezr 6:21 430
the house of G, the G of Israel Ezr 6:22 430
which the LORD G of Israel had Ezr 7:6 430
hand of the LORD his G upon him Ezr 7:6 430
the good hand of his G upon him Ezr 7:9 430
of the law of the G of heaven Ezr 7:12 426
of thy G which is in thine hand Ezr 7:14 426
offered unto the G of Israel Ezr 7:15 426
of their G which is in Jerusalem Ezr 7:16 426
of your G which is in Jerusalem Ezr 7:17 426
that do after the will of your G Ezr 7:18 426
the service of the house of thy G Ezr 7:19 426
thou before the G of Jerusalem Ezr 7:19 426
be needful for the house of thy G Ezr 7:20 426
of the law of the G of heaven Ezr 7:21 426
is commanded by the G of heaven Ezr 7:23 426
for the house of the G of heaven Ezr 7:23 426
or ministers of this house of G Ezr 7:24 426
Ezra, after the wisdom of thy G Ezr 7:25 426
such as know the laws of thy G Ezr 7:25 426
will not do the law of thy G Ezr 7:26 426
be the LORD G of our fathers Ezr 7:27 430
hand of the LORD my G was upon me Ezr 7:28 430
ministers for the house of our G Ezr 8:17 430
by the good hand of our G upon us Ezr 8:18 430
afflict ourselves before our G Ezr 8:21 430
The hand of our G is upon all Ezr 8:22 430
fasted and besought our G for this Ezr 8:23 430
offering of the house of our G Ezr 8:25 430
unto the LORD G of your fathers Ezr 8:28 430
Jerusalem unto the house of our G Ezr 8:30 430
and the hand of our G was upon us Ezr 8:31 430
weighed in the house of our G by Ezr 8:33 430
offerings unto the G of Israel Ezr 8:35 430
the people, and the house of G Ezr 8:36 430
at the words of the G of Israel Ezr 9:4 430
out my hands unto the LORD my G Ezr 9:5 430
And said, O my G, I am ashamed and Ezr 9:6 430
to lift up my face to thee, my G Ezr 9:6 430
been shewed from the LORD our G Ezr 9:8 430
that our G may lighten our eyes Ezr 9:8 430
yet our G hath not forsaken us in Ezr 9:9 430
to set up the house of our G Ezr 9:9 430
And now, O our G, what shall we Ezr 9:10 430
seeing that thou our G hast Ezr 9:13 430
O LORD G of Israel, thou art Ezr 9:15 430
down before the house of G Ezr 10:1 430
We have trespassed against our G Ezr 10:2 430
our G to put away all the wives Ezr 10:3 430
at the commandment of our G Ezr 10:3 430
up from before the house of G Ezr 10:6 430
in the street of the house of G Ezr 10:9 430
unto the LORD G of your fathers Ezr 10:11 430
until the fierce wrath of our G Ezr 10:14 430
and prayed before the G of heaven Neh 1:4 430
O LORD G of heaven Neh 1:5 430
the great and terrible G Neh 1:5 410
So I prayed to the G of heaven Neh 2:4 430
to the good hand of my G upon me Neh 2:8 430
my G had put in my heart to do at Neh 2:12 430
of my G which was good upon me Neh 2:18 430
The G of heaven, he will prosper Neh 2:20 430
Hear, O our G Neh 4:4 430
we made our prayer unto our G Neh 4:9 430
G had brought their counsel to Neh 4:15 430
our G shall fight for us Neh 4:20 430
G because of the reproach of the Neh 5:9 430
So G shake out every man from his Neh 5:13 430
not I, because of the fear of G Neh 5:15 430
Think upon me, my G, for good, Neh 5:19 430
Now therefore, O G, strengthen my Neh 6:9
meet together in the house of G Neh 6:10 430
perceived that G had not sent him Neh 6:12 430
My G, think thou upon Tobiah and Neh 6:14 430
this work was wrought of our G Neh 6:16 430
man, and feared G above many Neh 7:2 430
my G put into mine heart to Neh 7:5 430
blessed the LORD, the great G Neh 8:6 430
book in the law of G distinctly Neh 8:8 430
day is holy unto the LORD your G Neh 8:9 430
in the courts of the house of G Neh 8:16 430
read in the book of the law of G Neh 8:18 430
G one fourth part of the day Neh 9:3 430
and worshipped the LORD their G Neh 9:3 430
loud voice unto the LORD their G Neh 9:4 430
and bless the LORD your G for ever Neh 9:5 430
Thou art the LORD the G, who Neh 9:7 430
but thou art a G ready to pardon, Neh 9:17 433
This is thy G that brought thee Neh 9:18 430
thou art a gracious and merciful G Neh 9:31 410
Now therefore, our G, the great, Neh 9:32 430
the mighty, and the terrible G Neh 9:32 410
of the lands unto the law of G Neh 10:28 430
given by Moses the servant of G Neh 10:29 430
the service of the house of our G Neh 10:32 430
the work of the house of our G Neh 10:33 430
bring it into the house of our G Neh 10:34 430
upon the altar of the LORD our G Neh 10:34 430
to bring to the house of our G Neh 10:36 430
minister in the house of our G Neh 10:36 430
chambers of the house of our G Neh 10:37 430
tithes unto the house of our G Neh 10:38 430
not forsake the house of our G Neh 10:39 430
was the ruler of the house of G Neh 11:11 430
business of the house of G Neh 11:16 430
the business of the house of G Neh 11:22 430
commandment of David the man of G Neh 12:24 430
instruments of David the man of G Neh 12:36 430
gave thanks in the house of G Neh 12:40 430
for G had made them rejoice with Neh 12:43 430
porters kept the ward of their G Neh 12:45 430
of praise and thanksgiving unto G Neh 12:46 430
the congregation of G for ever Neh 13:1 430
howbeit our G turned the curse Neh 13:2 430
the chamber of the house of our G Neh 13:4 430
in the courts of the house of G Neh 13:7 430
the vessels of the house of G Neh 13:9 430
Why is the house of G forsaken Neh 13:11 430
Remember me, O my G, concerning Neh 13:14 430
I have done for the house of my G Neh 13:14 430
did not our G bring all this evil Neh 13:18 430
Remember me, O my G, concerning Neh 13:22 430
hair, and made them swear by G Neh 13:25 430
him, who was beloved of his G Neh 13:26 430
G made him king over all Israel Neh 13:26 430
our G in marrying strange wives Neh 13:27 430
Remember them, O my G, because Neh 13:29 430
Remember me, O my G, for good Neh 13:31 430
and upright, and one that feared G Job 1:1 430
and cursed G in their hearts Job 1:5 430
of G came to present themselves Job 1:6 430
upright man, one that feareth G Job 1:8 430
said, Doth Job fear G for nought Job 1:9 430
The fire of G is fallen from Job 1:16 430
not, nor charged G foolishly Job 1:22 430
of G came to present themselves Job 2:1 430
upright man, one that feareth G Job 2:3 430
curse G, and die Job 2:9 430
we receive good at the hand of G Job 2:10 430
let not G regard it from above Job 3:4 433
is hid, and whom G hath hedged in Job 3:23 433
By the blast of G they perish Job 4:9 433
mortal man be more just than G Job 4:17 433
I would seek unto G Job 5:8 410
unto G would I commit my cause Job 5:8 430
is the man whom G correcteth Job 5:17 433
the terrors of G do set Job 6:4 433
that G would grant me the thing Job 6:8 433
it would please G to destroy me Job 6:9 433
Doth G pervert judgment Job 8:3 410
thou wouldest seek unto G betimes Job 8:5 410
the paths of all that forget G Job 8:13 410
G will not cast away a perfect Job 8:20 410
but how should man be just with G Job 9:2 410
If G will not withdraw his anger Job 9:13 433
I will say unto G, Do not condemn Job 10:2 433
But oh that G would speak Job 11:5 433
Know therefore that G exacteth of Job 11:6 433
thou by searching find out G Job 11:7 433
his neighbour, who calleth upon G Job 12:4 433
and they that provoke G are secure Job 12:6 410
into whose hand G bringeth Job 12:6 433
and I desire to reason with G Job 13:3 410
Will ye speak wickedly for G Job 13:7 410
will ye contend for G Job 13:8 410
and restrainest prayer before G Job 15:4 410
Hast thou heard the secret of G Job 15:8 433
consolations of G small with thee Job 15:11 410
thou turnest thy spirit against G Job 15:13 410
stretcheth out his hand against G Job 15:25 410
G hath delivered me to the Job 16:11 410
mine eye poureth out tears unto G Job 16:20 433
one might plead for a man with G Job 16:21 433
place of him that knoweth not G Job 18:21 410
Know now that G hath overthrown Job 19:6 433
for the hand of G hath touched me Job 19:21 433
Why do ye persecute me as G Job 19:22 410
yet in my flesh shall I see G Job 19:26 433
G shall cast them out of his Job 20:15 410
G shall cast the fury of his Job 20:23
portion of a wicked man from G Job 20:29 430
heritage appointed unto him by G Job 20:29 410
neither is the rod of G upon them Job 21:9 433
Therefore they say unto G Job 21:14 410
G distributeth sorrows in his Job 21:17
G layeth up his iniquity for his Job 21:19 433
Shall any teach G knowledge Job 21:22 410
Can a man be profitable unto G Job 22:2 410
Is not G in the height of heaven Job 22:12 433
And thou sayest, How doth G know Job 22:13 410
Which said unto G, Depart from us Job 22:17 410
and shalt lift up thy face unto G Job 22:26 433
For G maketh my heart soft, and Job 23:16 410
yet G layeth not folly to them Job 24:12 433
then can man be justified with G Job 25:4 410
As G liveth, who hath taken away Job 27:2 410
the spirit of G is in my nostrils Job 27:3 433
G forbid that I should justify Job 27:5
when G taketh away his soul Job 27:8 433
Will G hear his cry when trouble Job 27:9 401
will he always call upon G Job 27:10 433
I will teach you by the hand of G Job 27:11 410
portion of a wicked man with G Job 27:13 410
For G shall cast upon him, and not Job 27:22
G understandeth the way thereof, Job 28:23 430
in the days when G preserved me Job 29:2 433
when the secret of G was upon my Job 29:4 433
portion of G is there from above Job 31:2 433
that G may know mine integrity Job 31:6 433
then shall I do when G riseth up Job 31:14 410
from G was a terror to me Job 31:23 410
have denied the G that is above Job 31:28 410
justified himself rather than G Job 32:2 430
G thrusteth him down, not man Job 32:13 410
The spirit of G hath made me Job 33:4 410
that G is greater than man Job 33:12 433
For G speaketh once, yea twice, Job 33:14 410
He shall pray unto G, and he will Job 33:26 433
worketh G oftentimes with man Job 33:29 410
G hath taken away my judgment Job 34:5 410
he should delight himself with G Job 34:9 430
far be it from G, that he should Job 34:10 410
surely G will not do wickedly, Job 34:12 410
should enter into judgment with G Job 34:23 410
it is meet to be said unto G Job 34:31 410
multiplieth his words against G Job 34:37 410
none saith, Where is G my maker Job 35:10 433
Surely G will not hear vanity Job 35:13 410
G is mighty, and despiseth not any Job 36:5 410
Behold, G exalteth by his power Job 36:22 410
G is great, and we know him not, Job 36:26 410
G thundereth marvellously with Job 37:5 410
By the breath of G frost is given Job 37:10 410
consider the wondrous works of G Job 37:14 410
thou know when G disposed them Job 37:15 433
with G is terrible majesty Job 37:22 433
all the sons of G shouted for joy Job 38:7 430
when his young ones cry unto G Job 38:41 410
Because G hath deprived her of Job 39:17 433
he that reproveth G, let him Job 40:2 433
Hast thou an arm like G Job 40:9 410
He is the chief of the ways of G Job 40:19 410
There is no help for him in G Ps 3:2 430
save me, O my G Ps 3:7 430
I call, O G of my righteousness Ps 4:1 430
voice of my cry, my King, and my G Ps 5:2 430
For thou art not a G that hath Ps 5:4 410
Destroy thou them, O G Ps 5:10 430
O lord my G, in thee do I put my Ps 7:1 430
O LORD my G, if I have done this Ps 7:3 430
the righteous G trieth the hearts Ps 7:9 430
My defence is of G, which saveth Ps 7:10 430
G judgeth the righteous Ps 7:11 430
G is angry with the wicked every Ps 7:11 410
and all the nations that forget G Ps 9:17 430
will not seek after G Ps 10:4
G is not in all his thoughts Ps 10:4 430
in his heart, G hath forgotten Ps 10:11 410
O G, lift up thine hand Ps 10:12 410
doth the wicked contemn G Ps 10:13 430
Consider and hear me, O LORD my G Ps 13:3 430
said in his heart, There is no G Ps 14:1 430
that did understand, and seek G Ps 14:2 430
for G is in the generation of the Ps 14:5 430
Preserve me, O G Ps 16:1 410
thee, for thou wilt hear me, O G Ps 17:6 410
my G, my strength, in whom I will Ps 18:2 410
upon the LORD, and cried unto my G Ps 18:6 430
not wickedly departed from my G Ps 18:21 430
the LORD my G will enlighten my Ps 18:28 430
by my G have I leaped over a wall Ps 18:29 430
As for G, his way is perfect Ps 18:30 410
For who is G save the LORD Ps 18:31 433
or who is a rock save our G Ps 18:31 430
It is G that girdeth me with Ps 18:32 410
let the G of my salvation be Ps 18:46 430
It is G that avengeth me, and Ps 18:47 410
heavens declare the glory of G Ps 19:1 410
the name of the G of Jacob defend Ps 20:1 430
in the name of our G we will set Ps 20:5 430
the name of the LORD our G Ps 20:7 430

Context	Reference	Number
My *G*, my *G*, why hast thou	Ps 22:1	410
O my *G*, I cry in the daytime, but	Ps 22:2	430
thou art my *G* from my mother's	Ps 22:10	410
from the *G* of his salvation	Ps 24:5	430
O my *G*, I trust in thee	Ps 25:2	430
thou art the *G* of my salvation	Ps 25:5	430
Redeem Israel, O *G*, out of all	Ps 25:22	430
forsake me, O *G* of my salvation	Ps 27:9	430
the *G* of glory thundereth	Ps 29:3	410
O LORD my *G*, I cried unto thee,	Ps 30:2	430
O LORD my *G*, I will give thanks	Ps 30:12	430
redeemed me, O LORD *G* of truth	Ps 31:5	410
I said, Thou art my *G*	Ps 31:14	430
is the nation whose *G* is the LORD	Ps 33:12	430
even unto my cause, my *G*	Ps 35:23	430
Judge me, O LORD my *G*, according	Ps 35:24	430
is no fear of *G* before his eyes	Ps 36:1	430
is thy lovingkindness, O *G*	Ps 36:7	430
The law of his *G* is in his heart	Ps 37:31	430
thou wilt hear, O Lord my *G*	Ps 38:15	430
O my *G*, be not far from me	Ps 38:21	430
my mouth, even praise unto our *G*	Ps 40:3	430
Many, O LORD my *G*, are thy	Ps 40:5	430
I delight to do thy will, O my *G*	Ps 40:8	430
make no tarrying, O my *G*	Ps 40:17	430
Blessed be the LORD *G* of Israel	Ps 41:13	430
panteth my soul after thee, O *G*	Ps 42:1	430
My soul thirsteth for *G*	Ps 42:2	430
for the living *G*	Ps 42:2	410
shall I come and appear before *G*	Ps 42:2	430
say unto me, Where is thy *G*	Ps 42:3	430
went with them to the house of *G*	Ps 42:4	430
hope thou in *G*	Ps 42:5	430
O my *G*, my soul is cast down	Ps 42:6	430
my prayer unto the *G* of my life	Ps 42:8	410
I will say unto *G* my rock	Ps 42:9	410
say daily unto me, Where is thy *G*	Ps 42:10	430
hope thou in *G*	Ps 42:11	430
health of my countenance, and my *G*	Ps 42:11	430
Judge me, O *G*, and plead my cause	Ps 43:1	430
For thou art the *G* of my strength	Ps 43:2	430
will I go unto the altar of *G*	Ps 43:4	430
of *G*, unto *G* my exceeding joy	Ps 43:4	410
will I praise thee, O *G* my *G*	Ps 43:4	430
hope in *G*: for I shall yet praise	Ps 43:5	430
health of my countenance, and my *G*	Ps 43:5	430
We have heard with our ears, O *G*	Ps 44:1	430
Thou art my King, O *G*	Ps 44:4	430
In *G* we boast all the day long,	Ps 44:8	430
have forgotten the name of our *G*	Ps 44:20	430
Shall not *G* search this out	Ps 44:21	430
therefore *G* hath blessed thee for	Ps 45:2	430
Thy throne, O *G*, is for ever and	Ps 45:6	430
therefore *G*, thy *G*, hath	Ps 45:7	430
G is our refuge and strength, a	Ps 46:1	430
shall make glad the city of *G*	Ps 46:4	430
G is in the midst of her	Ps 46:5	430
G shall help her, and that right	Ps 46:5	430
the *G* of Jacob is our refuge	Ps 46:7	430
Be still, and know that I am *G*	Ps 46:10	430
the *G* of Jacob is our refuge	Ps 46:11	430
shout unto *G* with the voice of	Ps 47:1	430
G is gone up with a shout, the	Ps 47:5	430
Sing praises to *G*, sing praises	Ps 47:6	430
For *G* is the King of all the	Ps 47:7	430
G reigneth over the heathen	Ps 47:8	430
G sitteth upon the throne of his	Ps 47:8	430
the people of the *G* of Abraham	Ps 47:9	430
of the earth belong unto *G*	Ps 47:9	430
be praised in the city of our *G*	Ps 48:1	430
G is known in her palaces for a	Ps 48:3	430
of hosts, in the city of our *G*	Ps 48:8	430
G will establish it for ever	Ps 48:8	430
of thy lovingkindness, O *G*	Ps 48:9	430
According to thy name, O *G*	Ps 48:10	430
For this *G* is our *G* for ever	Ps 48:14	430
nor give to *G* a ransom for him	Ps 49:7	430
But *G* will redeem my soul from	Ps 49:15	430
The mighty *G*, even the LORD, hath	Ps 50:1	410
of beauty, *G* hath shined	Ps 50:2	430
Our *G* shall come, and shall not	Ps 50:3	430
for *G* is judge himself	Ps 50:6	430
I am *G*, even thy *G*	Ps 50:7	430
Offer unto *G* thanksgiving	Ps 50:14	430
But unto the wicked *G* saith	Ps 50:16	430
consider this, ye that forget *G*	Ps 50:22	433
will I shew the salvation of *G*	Ps 50:23	430
Have mercy upon me, O *G*,	Ps 51:1	430
Create in me a clean heart, O *G*	Ps 51:10	430
O *G*, thou *G* of my salvation	Ps 51:14	430
The sacrifices of *G* are a broken	Ps 51:17	430
a broken and a contrite heart, O *G*	Ps 51:17	430
the goodness of *G* endureth	Ps 52:1	410
G shall likewise destroy thee for	Ps 52:5	410
man that made not *G* his strength	Ps 52:7	430
olive tree in the house of *G*	Ps 52:8	430
trust in the mercy of *G* for ever	Ps 52:8	430
said in his heart, There is no *G*	Ps 53:1	430
G looked down from heaven upon	Ps 53:2	430
did understand, that did seek *G*	Ps 53:2	430
they have not called upon *G*	Ps 53:4	430
for *G* hath scattered the bones of	Ps 53:5	430
because *G* hath despised them	Ps 53:5	430
When *G* bringeth back the	Ps 53:6	430
Save me, O *G*, by thy name, and	Ps 54:1	430
Hear my prayer, O *G*	Ps 54:2	430
they have not set *G* before them	Ps 54:3	430
Behold, *G* is mine helper	Ps 54:4	430
Give ear to my prayer, O *G*	Ps 55:1	430
unto the house of *G* in company	Ps 55:14	430
As for me, I will call upon *G*	Ps 55:16	430
G shall hear, and afflict them,	Ps 55:19	410
therefore they fear not *G*	Ps 55:19	430
But thou, O *G*, shalt bring them	Ps 55:23	430
Be merciful unto me, O *G*	Ps 56:1	430
In *G* I will praise his word	Ps 56:4	430
in *G* I have put my trust	Ps 56:4	430
anger cast down the people, O *G*	Ps 56:7	430
for *G* is for me	Ps 56:9	430
In *G* will I praise his word	Ps 56:10	430
In *G* have I put my trust	Ps 56:11	430
Thy vows are upon me, O *G*	Ps 56:12	430
that I may walk before *G* in the	Ps 56:13	430
Be merciful unto me, O *G*, be	Ps 57:1	430
I will cry unto *G* most high	Ps 57:2	430
unto *G* that performeth all things	Ps 57:2	410
G shall send forth his mercy and	Ps 57:3	430
Be thou exalted, O *G*, above the	Ps 57:5	430
My heart is fixed, O *G*, my heart	Ps 57:7	430
Be thou exalted, O *G*, above the	Ps 57:11	430
Break their teeth, O *G*, in their	Ps 58:6	430
verily he is a *G* that judgeth in	Ps 58:11	430
me from mine enemies, O my *G*	Ps 59:1	430
O LORD *G* of hosts, the *G* of	Ps 59:5	430
for *G* is my defence	Ps 59:9	430
The *G* of my mercy shall prevent	Ps 59:10	430
G shall let me see my desire upon	Ps 59:10	430
let them know that *G* ruleth in	Ps 59:13	430
for *G* is my defence, and the *G*	Ps 59:17	430
O *G*, thou hast cast us off, thou	Ps 60:1	430
G hath spoken in his holiness	Ps 60:6	430
Wilt not thou, O *G*, which hadst	Ps 60:10	430
and thou, O *G*, which didst not go	Ps 60:10	430
Through *G* we shall do valiantly	Ps 60:12	430
Hear my cry, O *G*	Ps 61:1	430
For thou, O *G*, hast heard my vows	Ps 61:5	430
He shall abide before *G* for ever	Ps 61:7	430
Truly my soul waiteth upon *G*	Ps 62:1	430
My soul, wait thou only upon *G*	Ps 62:5	430
In *G* is my salvation and my glory	Ps 62:7	430
strength, and my refuge, is in *G*	Ps 62:7	430
G is a refuge for us	Ps 62:8	430
G hath spoken once	Ps 62:11	430
that power belongeth unto *G*	Ps 62:11	430
O *g*, thou art	Ps 63:1	430
thou art my *G*	Ps 63:1	410
But the king shall rejoice in *G*	Ps 63:11	430
Hear my voice, O *G*, in my prayer	Ps 64:1	430
But *G* shall shoot at them with an	Ps 64:7	430
and shall declare the work of *G*	Ps 64:9	430
waiteth for thee, O *G* in Sion	Ps 65:1	430
answer us, O *G* of our salvation	Ps 65:5	430
enrichest it with the river of *G*	Ps 65:9	430
Make a joyful noise unto *G*	Ps 66:1	430
Say unto *G*, How terrible art thou	Ps 66:3	430
Come and see the works of *G*	Ps 66:5	430
O bless our *G*, ye people, and make	Ps 66:8	430
For thou, O *G*, hast proved us	Ps 66:10	430
Come and hear, all ye that fear *G*	Ps 66:16	430
But verily *G* hath heard me	Ps 66:19	430
Blessed be *G*, which hath not	Ps 66:20	430
G be merciful unto us, and bless	Ps 67:1	430
Let the people praise thee, O *G*	Ps 67:3	430
Let the people praise thee, O *G*	Ps 67:5	430
and *G*, even our own *G*, shall	Ps 67:6	430
G shall bless us	Ps 67:7	430
Let *G* arise, let his enemies be	Ps 68:1	430
perish at the presence of *G*	Ps 68:2	430
let them rejoice before *G*	Ps 68:3	430
Sing unto *G*, sing praises to his	Ps 68:4	430
is *G* in his holy habitation	Ps 68:5	430
G setteth the solitary in	Ps 68:6	430
O *G*, when thou wentest forth	Ps 68:7	430
also dropped at the presence of *G*	Ps 68:8	430
presence of *G*, the *G* of Israel	Ps 68:8	430
Thou, O *G*, didst send a plentiful	Ps 68:9	430
thou, O *G*, hast prepared of thy	Ps 68:10	430
The hill of *G* is as the hill of	Ps 68:15	430
hill which *G* desireth to dwell in	Ps 68:16	430
The chariots of *G* are twenty	Ps 68:17	430
that the LORD *G* might dwell among	Ps 68:18	430
even the *G* of our salvation	Ps 68:19	410
is our *G* is the *G* of salvation	Ps 68:20	410
unto *G* the Lord belong the issues	Ps 68:20	3069
But *G* shall wound the head of his	Ps 68:21	430
They have seen thy goings, O *G*	Ps 68:24	430
even the goings of my *G*, my King,	Ps 68:24	410
Bless ye *G* in the congregations,	Ps 68:26	430
Thy *G* hath commanded thy strength	Ps 68:28	430
strengthen, O *G*, that which thou	Ps 68:28	430
soon stretch out her hands unto *G*	Ps 68:31	430
Sing unto *G*, ye kingdoms of the	Ps 68:32	430
Ascribe ye strength unto *G*	Ps 68:34	430
O *G*, thou art terrible out of thy	Ps 68:35	430
the *G* of Israel is he that giveth	Ps 68:35	410
Blessed be *G*	Ps 68:35	430
Save me, O *G*	Ps 69:1	430
eyes fail while I wait for my *G*	Ps 69:3	430
O *G*, thou knowest my foolishness	Ps 69:5	430
O Lord *G* of hosts, be ashamed for	Ps 69:6	3069
for my sake, O *G* of Israel	Ps 69:6	430
O *G*, in the multitude of thy	Ps 69:13	430
let thy salvation, O *G*, set me up	Ps 69:29	430
praise the name of *G* with a song	Ps 69:30	430
your heart shall live that seek *G*	Ps 69:32	430
For *G* will save Zion, and will	Ps 69:35	430
Make haste, O *G*, to deliver me	Ps 70:1	430
continually, Let *G* be magnified	Ps 70:4	430
make haste unto me, O *G*	Ps 70:5	430
Deliver me, O my *G*, out of the	Ps 71:4	430
For thou art my hope, O Lord *G*	Ps 71:5	3069
Saying, *G* hath forsaken him	Ps 71:11	430
O *G*, be not far from me	Ps 71:12	430
O my *G*, make haste for my help	Ps 71:12	430
go in the strength of the Lord *G*	Ps 71:16	3069
O *G*, thou hast taught me from my	Ps 71:17	430
when I am old and greyheaded, O *G*	Ps 71:18	430
Thy righteousness also, O *G*	Ps 71:19	430
O *G*, who is like unto thee	Ps 71:19	430
psaltery, even thy truth, O my *G*	Ps 71:22	430
Give the king thy judgments, O *G*	Ps 72:1	430
Blessed be the LORD *G*	Ps 72:18	430
the *G* of Israel, who only doeth	Ps 72:18	430
Truly *G* is good to Israel, even	Ps 73:1	430
And they say, How doth *G* know	Ps 73:11	4010
I went into the sanctuary of *G*	Ps 73:17	410
but *G* is the strength of my heart	Ps 73:26	430
is good for me to draw near to *G*	Ps 73:28	430
I have put my trust in the Lord *G*	Ps 73:28	3069
O *G*, why hast thou cast us off	Ps 74:1	430
the synagogues of *G* in the land	Ps 74:8	410
O *G*, how long shall the adversary	Ps 74:10	430
For *G* is my King of old, working	Ps 74:12	430
Arise, O *G*, plead thine own cause	Ps 74:22	430
Unto thee, O *G*, do we give thanks	Ps 75:1	430
But *G* is the judge	Ps 75:7	430
sing praises to the *G* of Jacob	Ps 75:9	430
In Judah is *G* known	Ps 76:1	430
O *G* of Jacob, both the chariot and	Ps 76:6	430
When *G* arose to judgment, to save	Ps 76:9	430
Vow, and pay unto the LORD your *G*	Ps 76:11	430
I cried unto *G* with my voice,	Ps 77:1	430
even unto *G* with my voice	Ps 77:1	430
I remembered *G*, and was troubled	Ps 77:3	430
Hath *G* forgotten to be gracious	Ps 77:9	410
Thy way, O *G*, is in the sanctuary	Ps 77:13	430
who is so great a *G*	Ps 77:13	410
as our *G*	Ps 77:13	430
Thou art the *G* that doest wonders	Ps 77:14	410
The waters saw thee, O *G*, the	Ps 77:16	430
they might set their hope in *G*	Ps 78:7	430
and not forget the works of *G*	Ps 78:7	410
spirit was not stedfast with *G*	Ps 78:8	410
They kept not the covenant of *G*	Ps 78:10	430
they tempted *G* in their heart by	Ps 78:18	410
Yea, they spake against *G*	Ps 78:19	430
Can *G* furnish a table in the	Ps 78:19	410
Because they believed not in *G*	Ps 78:22	430
The wrath of *G* came upon them, and	Ps 78:31	430
and enquired early after *G*	Ps 78:34	410
remembered that *G* was their rock	Ps 78:35	430
the high *G* their redeemer	Ps 78:35	410
they turned back and tempted *G*	Ps 78:41	410
and provoked the most high *G*	Ps 78:56	430
When *G* heard this, he was wroth,	Ps 78:59	430
O *g*, the heathen are come into	Ps 79:1	430
O *G* of our salvation, for the	Ps 79:9	430
the heathen say, Where is their *G*	Ps 79:10	430
Turn us again, O *G*, and cause thy	Ps 80:3	430
O LORD *G* of hosts, how long wilt	Ps 80:4	430
O *G* of hosts, and cause thy face	Ps 80:7	430
we beseech thee, O *G* of hosts	Ps 80:14	430
O LORD *G* of hosts, cause thy face	Ps 80:19	430
Sing aloud unto *G* our strength	Ps 81:1	430
joyful noise unto the *G* of Jacob	Ps 81:1	430
and a law of the *G* of Jacob	Ps 81:4	430
I am the LORD thy *G*, which	Ps 81:10	430
G standeth in the congregation of	Ps 82:1	430
Arise, O *G*, judge the earth	Ps 82:8	430
Keep not thou silence, O *G*	Ps 83:1	430
thy peace, and be not still, O *G*	Ps 83:1	410
the houses of *G* in possession	Ps 83:12	430
O my *G*, make them like a wheel	Ps 83:13	430
flesh crieth out for the living *G*	Ps 84:2	410
O LORD of hosts, my King, and my *G*	Ps 84:3	430
them in Zion appeareth before *G*	Ps 84:7	430
O LORD *G* of hosts, hear my prayer	Ps 84:8	430
give ear, O *G* of Jacob	Ps 84:8	430
O *G* our shield, and look upon the	Ps 84:9	430
a doorkeeper in the house of my *G*	Ps 84:10	430
For the LORD *G* is a sun and shield	Ps 84:11	430
O *G* of our salvation, and cause	Ps 85:4	430
I will hear what *G* the LORD will	Ps 85:8	410
O thou my *G*, save thy servant	Ps 86:2	430
thou art *G* alone	Ps 86:10	430
I will praise thee, O Lord my *G*	Ps 86:12	430
O *G*, the proud are risen against	Ps 86:14	430
art a *G* full of compassion, and	Ps 86:15	410
are spoken of thee, O city of *G*	Ps 87:3	430
O lord *G* of my salvation, I have	Ps 88:1	430
G is greatly to be feared in the	Ps 89:7	410
O LORD *G* of hosts, who is a	Ps 89:8	430
unto me, Thou art my father, my *G*	Ps 89:26	410
A Prayer of Moses, the man of *G*	Ps 90:*t*	430
to everlasting, thou art *G*	Ps 90:2	410
of the LORD our *G* be upon us	Ps 90:17	430
refuge and my fortress: my *G*	Ps 91:2	430
flourish in the courts of our *G*	Ps 92:13	430
O LORD *G*, to whom vengeance	Ps 94:1	410
O *G*, to whom vengeance belongeth,	Ps 94:1	410
neither shall the *G* of Jacob	Ps 94:7	430
my *G* is the rock of my refuge	Ps 94:22	430
the LORD our *G* shall cut them off	Ps 94:23	430
For the LORD is a great *G*	Ps 95:3	410

For he is our *G*	Ps 95:7	430
have seen the salvation of our *G*	Ps 98:3	430
Exalt ye the LORD our *G*, and	Ps 99:5	430
answeredst them, O LORD our *G*	Ps 99:8	430
thou wast a *G* that forgavest them	Ps 99:8	410
Exalt the LORD our *G*, and worship	Ps 99:9	430
for the LORD our *G* is holy	Ps 99:9	430
Know ye that the LORD he is *G*	Ps 100:3	430
I said, O my *G*, take me not away	Ps 102:24	410
O LORD my *G*, thou art very great	Ps 104:1	430
prey, and seek their meat from *G*	Ps 104:21	410
to my *G* while I have my being	Ps 104:33	430
He is the LORD our *G*	Ps 105:7	430
and tempted *G* in the desert	Ps 106:14	410
They forgat *G* their saviour,	Ps 106:21	410
Save us, O LORD our *G*, and gather	Ps 106:47	430
Blessed be the LORD *G* of Israel	Ps 106:48	430
rebelled against the words of *G*	Ps 107:11	410
O *G*, my heart is fixed	Ps 108:1	430
Be thou exalted, O *G*, above the	Ps 108:5	430
G hath spoken in his holiness	Ps 108:7	430
Wilt not thou, O *G*, who hast cast	Ps 108:11	430
and wilt not thou, O *G*, go forth	Ps 108:11	430
Through *G* we shall do valiantly	Ps 108:13	430
not thy peace, O *G* of my praise	Ps 109:1	430
O *G* the Lord, for thy name's sake	Ps 109:21	3069
Help me, O LORD my *G*	Ps 109:26	430
Who is like unto the LORD our *G*	Ps 113:5	430
at the presence of the *G* of Jacob	Ps 114:7	433
heathen say, Where is now their *G*	Ps 115:2	430
But our *G* is in the heavens	Ps 115:3	430
yea, our *G* is merciful	Ps 116:5	430
G is the LORD, which hath shewed	Ps 118:27	410
Thou art my *G*, and I will praise	Ps 118:28	410
thou art my *G*, I will exalt thee	Ps 118:28	430
keep the commandments of my *G*	Ps 119:115	430
LORD our *G* I will seek thy good	Ps 122:9	430
our eyes wait upon the LORD our *G*	Ps 123:2	430
vowed unto the mighty *G* of Jacob	Ps 132:2	
for the mighty *G* of Jacob	Ps 132:5	
the courts of the house of our *G*	Ps 135:2	430
O give thanks unto the *G* of gods	Ps 136:2	430
give thanks unto the *G* of heaven	Ps 136:26	410
are thy thoughts unto me, O *G*	Ps 139:17	410
thou wilt slay the wicked, O *G*	Ps 139:19	433
Search me, O *G*, and know my heart	Ps 139:23	410
said unto the LORD, Thou art my *G*	Ps 140:6	410
O *G* the Lord, the strength of my	Ps 140:7	
eyes are unto thee, O *G* the Lord	Ps 141:8	3069
for thou art my *G*	Ps 143:10	430
sing a new song unto thee, O *G*	Ps 144:9	430
that people, whose *G* is the LORD	Ps 144:15	430
I will extol thee, my *G*, O king	Ps 145:1	430
unto my *G* while I have any being	Ps 146:2	430
hath the *G* of Jacob for his help	Ps 146:5	410
whose hope is in the LORD his *G*	Ps 146:5	430
shall reign for ever, even thy *G*	Ps 146:10	430
good to sing praises unto our *G*	Ps 147:1	430
praise upon the harp unto our *G*	Ps 147:7	430
praise thy *G*, O Zion	Ps 147:12	430
praises of *G* be in their mouth	Ps 149:6	410
Praise *G* in his sanctuary	Ps 150:1	410
LORD, and find the knowledge of *G*	Prov 2:5	430
forgetteth the covenant of her *G*	Prov 2:17	430
understanding in the sight of *G*	Prov 3:4	430
but *G* overthroweth the wicked for	Prov 21:12	
the glory of *G* to conceal a thing	Prov 25:2	430
The great *G* that formed all	Prov 26:10	
Every word of *G* is pure	Prov 30:5	433
and take the name of my *G* in vain	Prov 30:9	430
this sore travail hath *G* given to	Eccl 1:13	430
that it was from the hand of *G*	Eccl 2:24	430
For *G* giveth to a man that is	Eccl 2:26	
give to him that is good before *G*	Eccl 2:26	430
which *G* hath given to the sons of	Eccl 3:10	430
G maketh from the beginning to	Eccl 3:11	430
his labour, it is the gift of *G*	Eccl 3:13	430
I know that, whatsoever *G* doeth	Eccl 3:14	430
G doeth it, that men should fear	Eccl 3:14	430
G requireth that which is past	Eccl 3:15	430
G shall judge the righteous and	Eccl 3:17	430
that *G* might manifest them, and	Eccl 3:18	430
when thou goest to the house of *G*	Eccl 5:1	430
hasty to utter any thing before *G*	Eccl 5:2	430
for *G* is in heaven, and thou upon	Eccl 5:2	430
When thou vowest a vow unto *G*	Eccl 5:4	430
wherefore should *G* be angry at	Eccl 5:6	430
but fear thou *G*	Eccl 5:7	430
of his life, which *G* giveth him	Eccl 5:18	430
also to whom *G* hath given riches	Eccl 5:19	430
this is the gift of *G*	Eccl 5:19	430
because *G* answereth him in the	Eccl 5:20	430
A man to whom *G* hath given riches	Eccl 6:2	430
yet *G* giveth him not power to eat	Eccl 6:2	430
Consider the work of *G*	Eccl 7:13	430
G also hath set the one over	Eccl 7:14	430
for he that feareth *G* shall come	Eccl 7:18	430
whoso pleaseth *G* shall escape	Eccl 7:26	430
that *G* hath made man upright	Eccl 7:29	430
that in regard of the oath of *G*	Eccl 8:2	430
be well with them that fear *G*	Eccl 8:12	430
because he feareth not before *G*	Eccl 8:13	430
which *G* giveth him under the sun	Eccl 8:15	430
Then I beheld all the work of *G*	Eccl 8:17	430
their works, are in the hand of *G*	Eccl 9:1	430
for *G* now accepteth thy works	Eccl 9:7	430
not the works of *G* who maketh all	Eccl 11:5	430
that for all these things *G* will	Eccl 11:9	430
shall return unto *G* who gave it	Eccl 12:7	430
Fear *G*, and keep his commandments	Eccl 12:13	430
For *G* shall bring every work into	Eccl 12:14	430
give ear unto the law of our *G*	Is 1:10	430
to the house of the *G* of Jacob	Is 2:3	430
saith the Lord *G* of hosts	Is 3:15	3069
and *G* that is holy shall be	Is 5:16	410
Thus saith the Lord *G*, It shall	Is 7:7	3069
Ask thee a sign of the LORD thy *G*	Is 7:11	430
men, but will ye weary my *G* also	Is 7:13	430
for *G* is with us	Is 8:10	410
not a people seek unto their *G*	Is 8:19	430
and curse their king and their *G*	Is 8:21	430
Counsellor, The mighty *G*	Is 9:6	410
of Jacob, unto the mighty *G*	Is 10:21	410
For the Lord *G* of hosts shall	Is 10:23	3069
thus saith the Lord *G* of hosts	Is 10:24	3069
Behold, *G* is my salvation	Is 12:2	410
be as when *G* overthrew Sodom	Is 13:19	430
my throne above the stars of *G*	Is 14:13	410
saith the LORD *G* of Israel	Is 17:6	430
forgotten the *G* of thy salvation	Is 17:10	430
but *G* shall rebuke them, and they	Is 17:13	
the *G* of Israel, have I declared	Is 21:10	430
for the LORD *G* of Israel hath	Is 21:17	430
Lord *G* of hosts in the valley of	Is 22:5	3069
Lord *G* of hosts call to weeping	Is 22:12	3069
ye die, saith the Lord *G* of hosts	Is 22:14	3069
Thus saith the Lord *G* of hosts	Is 22:15	3069
even the name of the LORD *G* of	Is 24:15	430
O lord, thou art my *G*	Is 25:1	430
the Lord *G* will wipe away tears	Is 25:8	3069
in that day, Lo, this is our *G*	Is 25:9	430
salvation will *G* appoint for	Is 26:1	
O LORD our *G*, other lords besides	Is 26:13	430
Therefore thus saith the Lord *G*	Is 28:16	3069
the Lord *G* of hosts a consumption	Is 28:22	3069
For his *G* doth instruct him to	Is 28:26	430
and shall fear the *G* of Israel	Is 29:23	430
For thus saith the Lord *G*	Is 30:15	3069
for the LORD is a *G* of judgment	Is 30:18	430
the Egyptians are men, and not *G*	Is 31:3	410
LORD, and the excellency of our *G*	Is 35:2	430
your *G* will come with vengeance,	Is 35:4	430
even *G* with a recompence	Is 35:4	430
to me, We trust in the LORD our *G*	Is 36:7	430
LORD thy *G* will hear the words of	Is 37:4	430
sent to reproach the living *G*	Is 37:4	430
which the LORD thy *G* hath heard	Is 37:4	430
of Judah, saying, Let not thy *G*	Is 37:10	430
G of Israel, that dwellest	Is 37:16	430
the cherubims, thou art the *G*	Is 37:16	430
sent to reproach the living *G*	Is 37:17	430
Now therefore, O LORD our *G*	Is 37:20	430
Thus saith the LORD *G* of Israel	Is 37:21	430
in the house of Nisroch his *g*	Is 37:38	430
the *G* of David thy father, I have	Is 38:5	430
ye my people, saith your *G*	Is 40:1	430
in the desert a highway for our *G*	Is 40:3	430
but the word of our *G* shall stand	Is 40:8	430
cities of Judah, Behold your *G*	Is 40:9	430
the Lord *G* will come with strong	Is 40:10	3069
To whom then will ye liken *G*	Is 40:18	410
judgment is passed over from my *G*	Is 40:27	430
not heard, that the everlasting *G*	Is 40:28	430
for I am thy *G*	Is 41:10	430
For I the LORD thy *G* will hold	Is 41:13	430
I the *G* of Israel will not	Is 41:17	430
Thus saith *G* the LORD, he that	Is 42:5	410
For I am the LORD thy *G*, the Holy	Is 43:3	430
before me there was no *G* formed	Is 43:10	410
saith the LORD, that I am *G*	Is 43:12	410
and beside me there is no *G*	Is 44:6	430
Is there a *G* beside me	Is 44:8	433
yea, there is no *G*	Is 44:8	6697
by thy name, am the *G* of Israel	Is 45:3	430
else, there is no *G* beside me	Is 45:5	430
thee, saying, Surely *G* is in thee	Is 45:14	410
there is none else, there is no *G*	Is 45:14	430
Verily thou art a *G* that hidest	Is 45:15	410
O *G* of Israel, the Saviour	Is 45:15	430
G himself that formed the earth	Is 45:18	430
there is no *G* else beside me	Is 45:21	430
a just *G* and a Saviour	Is 45:21	410
for I am *G*, and there is none else	Is 45:22	410
for I am *G*, and there is none else	Is 46:9	410
I am *G*, and there is none like me,	Is 46:9	430
make mention of the *G* of Israel	Is 48:1	430
themselves upon the *G* of Israel	Is 48:2	430
and now the Lord *G*, and his Spirit,	Is 48:16	3069
I am the LORD thy *G* which	Is 48:17	430
the LORD, and my work with my *G*	Is 49:4	430
my *G* shall be my strength	Is 49:5	430
Thus saith the Lord *G*, Behold, I	Is 49:22	3069
The Lord *G* hath given me the	Is 50:4	3069
The Lord *G* hath opened mine ear,	Is 50:5	3069
For the Lord *G* will help me	Is 50:7	3069
Behold, the Lord *G* will help me	Is 50:9	3609
of the LORD, and stay upon his *G*	Is 50:10	430
But I am the LORD thy *G*, that	Is 51:15	430
of the LORD, the rebuke of thy *G*	Is 51:20	430
thy *G* that pleadeth the cause of	Is 51:22	430
For thus saith the Lord *G*	Is 52:4	3069
saith unto Zion, Thy *G* reigneth	Is 52:7	430
shall see the salvation of our *G*	Is 52:10	430
the *G* of Israel will be your	Is 52:12	430
esteem him stricken, smitten of *G*	Is 53:4	430
The *G* of the whole earth shall he	Is 54:5	430
thou wast refused, saith thy *G*	Is 54:6	430
thee because of the LORD thy *G*	Is 55:5	430
and to our *G*, for he will	Is 55:7	430
The Lord *G* which gathereth the	Is 56:8	3069
There is no peace, saith my *G*	Is 57:21	430
not the ordinance of their *G*	Is 58:2	430
take delight in approaching to *G*	Is 58:2	430
separated between you and your *G*	Is 59:2	430
and departing away from our *G*	Is 59:13	430
unto the name of the LORD thy *G*	Is 60:9	430
light, and thy *G* thy glory	Is 60:19	430
Spirit of the Lord *G* is upon me	Is 61:1	3069
and the day of vengeance of our *G*	Is 61:2	430
call you the Ministers of our *G*	Is 61:6	430
my soul shall be joyful in my *G*	Is 61:10	430
so the Lord *G* will cause	Is 61:11	3069
royal diadem in the hand of thy *G*	Is 62:3	430
so shall thy *G* rejoice over thee	Is 62:5	430
neither hath the eye seen, O *G*	Is 64:4	430
Therefore thus saith the Lord *G*	Is 65:13	3069
for the Lord *G* shall slay thee,	Is 65:15	3069
bless himself in the *G* of truth	Is 65:16	430
shall swear by the *G* of truth	Is 65:16	430
saith thy *G*	Is 66:9	430
Then said I, Ah, Lord *G*	Jer 1:6	3069
thou hast forsaken the LORD thy *G*	Jer 2:17	430
thou hast forsaken the LORD thy *G*	Jer 2:19	430
thee, saith the Lord *G* of hosts	Jer 2:19	3069
before me, saith the Lord *G*	Jer 2:22	3069
against the LORD thy *G*, and hast	Jer 3:13	430
have forgotten the LORD their *G*	Jer 3:21	430
for thou art the LORD our *G*	Jer 3:22	430
truly in the LORD our *G* is the	Jer 3:23	430
sinned against the LORD our *G*	Jer 3:25	430
the voice of the LORD our *G*	Jer 3:25	430
Then said I, Ah, Lord *G*	Jer 4:10	3069
LORD, nor the judgment of their *G*	Jer 5:4	430
LORD, and the judgment of their *G*	Jer 5:5	430
thus saith the LORD *G* of hosts	Jer 5:14	430
our *G* all these things unto us	Jer 5:19	430
Let us now fear the LORD our *G*	Jer 5:24	430
the *G* of Israel, Amend your ways	Jer 7:3	430
Therefore thus saith the Lord *G*	Jer 7:20	3069
LORD of hosts, the *G* of Israel	Jer 7:21	430
my voice, and I will be your *G*	Jer 7:23	430
not the voice of the LORD their *G*	Jer 7:28	430
for the LORD our *G* hath put us to	Jer 8:14	430
LORD of hosts, the *G* of Israel	Jer 9:15	430
the true *G*, he is the living *G*	Jer 10:10	430
Thus saith the LORD *G* of Israel	Jer 11:3	430
be my people, and I will be your *G*	Jer 11:4	430
Thus saith the LORD *G* of Israel	Jer 13:12	430
Give glory to the LORD your *G*	Jer 13:16	430
Then said I, Ah, Lord *G*	Jer 14:13	3069
art not thou he, O LORD our *G*	Jer 14:22	430
by thy name, O LORD *G* of hosts	Jer 15:16	430
LORD of hosts, the *G* of Israel	Jer 16:9	430
committed against the LORD our *G*	Jer 16:10	430
LORD of hosts, the *G* of Israel	Jer 19:3	430
LORD of hosts, the *G* of Israel	Jer 19:15	430
Thus saith the LORD *G* of Israel	Jer 21:4	430
the covenant of the LORD their *G*	Jer 22:9	430
G of Israel against the pastors	Jer 23:2	430
Am I a *G* at hand, saith the LORD,	Jer 23:23	430
and not a *G* afar off	Jer 23:23	430
the words of the living *G*	Jer 23:36	430
of the LORD of hosts our *G*	Jer 23:36	430
saith the LORD, the *G* of Israel	Jer 24:5	430
my people, and I will be their *G*	Jer 24:7	430
the LORD *G* of Israel unto me	Jer 25:15	430
LORD of hosts, the *G* of Israel	Jer 25:27	430
obey the voice of the LORD your *G*	Jer 26:13	430
us in the name of the LORD our *G*	Jer 26:16	430
LORD of hosts, the *G* of Israel	Jer 27:4	430
the *G* of Israel, concerning the	Jer 27:21	430
the *G* of Israel, saying, I have	Jer 28:2	430
LORD of hosts, the *G* of Israel	Jer 28:14	430
the *G* of Israel, unto all that	Jer 29:4	430
LORD of hosts, the *G* of Israel	Jer 29:8	430
the *G* of Israel, of Ahab the son	Jer 29:21	430
the *G* of Israel, saying, Because	Jer 29:25	430
speaketh the LORD *G* of Israel	Jer 30:2	430
they shall serve the LORD their *G*	Jer 30:9	430
be my people, and I will be your *G*	Jer 30:22	430
will I be the *G* of all the	Jer 31:1	430
go up to Zion unto the LORD our *G*	Jer 31:6	430
for thou art the LORD my *G*	Jer 31:18	430
LORD of hosts, the *G* of Israel	Jer 31:23	430
and will be their *G*, and they shall	Jer 31:33	430
LORD of hosts, the *G* of Israel	Jer 32:14	430
LORD of hosts, the *G* of Israel	Jer 32:15	430
Ah Lord *G*!	Jer 32:17	3069
the Great, the Mighty *G*, the LORD	Jer 32:18	410
thou hast said unto me, O Lord *G*	Jer 32:25	3069
I am the LORD, the *G* of all flesh	Jer 32:27	430
the *G* of Israel, concerning this	Jer 32:36	430
my people, and I will be their *G*	Jer 32:38	430
the *G* of Israel, concerning the	Jer 33:4	430
saith the LORD, the *G* of Israel	Jer 34:2	430
saith the LORD, the *G* of Israel	Jer 34:13	430
the son of Igdaliah, a man of *G*	Jer 35:4	430
LORD of hosts, the *G* of Israel	Jer 35:13	430
G of hosts, the *G* of Israel	Jer 35:17	430
LORD of hosts, the *G* of Israel	Jer 35:18	430
LORD of hosts, the *G* of Israel	Jer 35:19	430
now unto the LORD our *G* for us	Jer 37:3	430
saith the LORD, the *G* of Israel	Jer 37:7	430
the *G* of hosts, the *G* of Israel	Jer 38:17	430

G

Context	Reference	Number
LORD of hosts, the *G* of Israel	Jer 39:16	430
The LORD thy *G* hath pronounced	Jer 40:2	430
pray for us unto the LORD thy *G*	Jer 42:2	430
That the LORD thy *G* may shew us	Jer 42:3	430
your *G* according to your words	Jer 42:4	430
LORD thy *G* shall send thee to us	Jer 42:5	430
obey the voice of the LORD our *G*	Jer 42:6	430
obey the voice of the LORD our *G*	Jer 42:6	430
the *G* of Israel, unto whom ye	Jer 42:9	430
obey the voice of the LORD your *G*	Jer 42:13	430
LORD of hosts, the *G* of Israel	Jer 42:15	430
LORD of hosts, the *G* of Israel	Jer 42:18	430
ye sent me unto the LORD your *G*	Jer 42:20	430
Pray for us unto the LORD our *G*	Jer 42:20	430
all that the LORD our *G* shall say	Jer 42:20	430
the voice of the LORD your *G*	Jer 42:21	430
all the words of the LORD their *G*	Jer 43:1	430
LORD their *G* had sent him to them	Jer 43:1	430
the LORD our *G* hath not sent thee	Jer 43:2	430
LORD of hosts, the *G* of Israel	Jer 43:10	430
LORD of hosts, the *G* of Israel	Jer 44:2	430
the *G* of hosts, the *G* of Israel	Jer 44:7	430
LORD of hosts, the *G* of Israel	Jer 44:11	430
of hosts, the *G* of Israel, saying	Jer 44:25	430
Egypt, saying, The Lord *G* liveth	Jer 44:26	3069
the *G* of Israel, unto thee, O	Jer 45:2	430
is the day of the Lord *G* of hosts	Jer 46:10	3069
for the Lord *G* of hosts hath a	Jer 46:10	3069
of hosts, the *G* of Israel, saith	Jer 46:25	430
LORD of hosts, the *G* of Israel	Jer 48:1	430
thee, saith the Lord *G* of hosts	Jer 49:5	3069
go, and seek the LORD their *G*	Jer 50:4	430
LORD of hosts, the *G* of Israel	Jer 50:18	430
G of hosts in the land of the	Jer 50:25	3069
the vengeance of the LORD our *G*	Jer 50:28	430
proud, saith the Lord *G* of hosts	Jer 50:31	3069
As *G* overthrew Sodom and Gomorrah	Jer 50:40	430
been forsaken, nor Judah of his *G*	Jer 51:5	430
Zion the work of the LORD our *G*	Jer 51:10	430
LORD of hosts, the *G* of Israel	Jer 51:33	430
for the LORD *G* of recompences	Jer 51:56	410
our hands unto *G* in the heavens	Lam 3:41	410
opened, and I saw visions of *G*	Eze 1:1	430
unto them, Thus saith the Lord *G*	Eze 2:4	3069
tell them, Thus saith the Lord *G*	Eze 3:11	3069
unto them, Thus saith the Lord *G*	Eze 3:27	3069
Then said I, Ah Lord *G*	Eze 4:14	3069
Thus saith the Lord *G*	Eze 5:5	3069
Therefore thus saith the Lord *G*	Eze 5:7	3069
Therefore thus saith the Lord *G*	Eze 5:8	3069
as I live, saith the Lord *G*	Eze 5:11	3069
hear the word of the Lord *G*	Eze 6:3	3069
saith the Lord *G* to the mountains	Eze 6:3	3069
Thus saith the Lord *G*	Eze 6:11	3069
thus saith the Lord *G* unto the	Eze 7:2	3069
Thus saith the Lord *G*	Eze 7:5	3069
of the Lord *G* fell there upon me	Eze 8:1	3069
in the visions of *G* to Jerusalem	Eze 8:3	430
the glory of the *G* of Israel was	Eze 8:4	430
the glory of the *G* of Israel was	Eze 9:3	430
and cried, and said, Ah Lord *G*	Eze 9:8	3069
the Almighty *G* when he speaketh	Eze 10:5	410
the glory of the *G* of Israel was	Eze 10:19	430
the *G* of Israel by the river of	Eze 10:20	430
Therefore thus saith the Lord *G*	Eze 11:7	3069
sword upon you, saith the Lord *G*	Eze 11:8	3069
a loud voice, and said, Ah Lord *G*	Eze 11:13	3069
say, Thus saith the Lord *G*	Eze 11:16	3069
say, Thus saith the Lord *G*	Eze 11:17	3069
my people, and I will be their *G*	Eze 11:20	430
their own heads, saith the Lord *G*	Eze 11:21	3069
the glory of the *G* of Israel was	Eze 11:22	430
by the Spirit of *G* into Chaldea	Eze 11:24	430
unto them, Thus saith the Lord *G*	Eze 12:10	3069
Thus saith the Lord *G* of the	Eze 12:19	3069
therefore, Thus saith the Lord *G*	Eze 12:23	3069
will perform it, saith the Lord *G*	Eze 12:25	3069
unto them, Thus saith the Lord *G*	Eze 12:28	3069
shall be done, saith the Lord *G*	Eze 12:28	3069
Thus saith the Lord *G*	Eze 13:3	3069
Therefore thus saith the Lord *G*	Eze 13:8	3069
am against you, saith the Lord *G*	Eze 13:8	3069
shall know that I am the Lord *G*	Eze 13:9	3069
Therefore thus saith the Lord *G*	Eze 13:13	3069
is no peace, saith the Lord *G*	Eze 13:16	3069
And say, Thus saith the Lord *G*	Eze 13:18	3069
Wherefore thus saith the Lord *G*	Eze 13:20	3069
unto them, Thus saith the Lord *G*	Eze 14:4	3069
of Israel, Thus saith the Lord *G*	Eze 14:6	3069
be my people, and I may be their *G*	Eze 14:11	430
saith the Lord *G*	Eze 14:11	3069
righteousness, saith the Lord *G*	Eze 14:14	3069
it, as I live, saith the Lord *G*	Eze 14:16	3069
it, as I live, saith the Lord *G*	Eze 14:18	3069
it, as I live, saith the Lord *G*	Eze 14:20	3069
For thus saith the Lord *G*	Eze 14:21	3069
have done in it, saith the Lord *G*	Eze 14:23	3069
Therefore thus saith the Lord *G*	Eze 15:6	3069
a trespass, saith the Lord *G*	Eze 15:8	3069
saith the Lord *G* unto Jerusalem	Eze 16:3	3069
with thee, saith the Lord *G*	Eze 16:8	3069
put upon thee, saith the Lord *G*	Eze 16:14	3069
and thus it was, saith the Lord *G*	Eze 16:19	3069
saith the Lord *G*	Eze 16:23	3069
is thine heart, saith the Lord *G*	Eze 16:30	3069
Thus saith the Lord *G*	Eze 16:36	3069
upon thine head, saith the Lord *G*	Eze 16:43	3069
As I live, saith the Lord *G*	Eze 16:48	3069
For thus saith the Lord *G*	Eze 16:59	3069
thou hast done, saith the Lord *G*	Eze 16:63	3069
And say, Thus saith the Lord *G*	Eze 17:3	3069
Say thou, Thus saith the Lord *G*	Eze 17:9	3069
As I live, saith the Lord *G*	Eze 17:16	3069
Therefore thus saith the Lord *G*	Eze 17:19	3069
Thus saith the Lord *G*	Eze 17:22	3069
As I live, saith the Lord *G*	Eze 18:3	3069
surely live, saith the Lord *G*	Eze 18:9	3069
saith the Lord *G*	Eze 18:23	3069
to his ways, saith the Lord *G*	Eze 18:30	3069
him that dieth, saith the Lord *G*	Eze 18:32	3069
unto them, Thus saith the Lord *G*	Eze 20:3	3069
As I live, saith the Lord *G*	Eze 20:3	3069
unto them, Thus saith the Lord *G*	Eze 20:5	3069
saying, I am the LORD your *G*	Eze 20:5	430
I am the LORD your *G*	Eze 20:7	430
I am the LORD your *G*	Eze 20:19	430
know that I am the LORD your *G*	Eze 20:20	430
unto them, Thus saith the Lord *G*	Eze 20:27	3069
of Israel, Thus saith the Lord *G*	Eze 20:30	3069
As I live, saith the Lord *G*	Eze 20:31	3069
As I live, saith the Lord *G*	Eze 20:33	3069
plead with you, saith the Lord *G*	Eze 20:36	3069
of Israel, thus saith the Lord *G*	Eze 20:39	3069
of Israel, saith the Lord *G*	Eze 20:40	3069
house of Israel, saith the Lord *G*	Eze 20:44	3069
Thus saith the Lord *G*	Eze 20:47	3069
Then said I, Ah Lord *G*	Eze 20:49	3069
brought to pass, saith the Lord *G*	Eze 21:7	3069
be no more, saith the Lord *G*	Eze 21:13	3069
Therefore thus saith the Lord *G*	Eze 21:24	3069
Thus saith the Lord *G*	Eze 21:26	3069
Thus saith the Lord *G* concerning	Eze 21:28	3069
say thou, Thus saith the Lord *G*	Eze 22:3	3069
forgotten me, saith the Lord *G*	Eze 22:12	3069
Therefore thus saith the Lord *G*	Eze 22:19	3069
saying, Thus saith the Lord *G*	Eze 22:28	3069
their heads, saith the Lord *G*	Eze 22:31	3069
O Aholibah, thus saith the Lord *G*	Eze 23:22	3069
For thus saith the Lord *G*	Eze 23:28	3069
Thus saith the Lord *G*	Eze 23:32	3069
have spoken it, saith the Lord *G*	Eze 23:34	3069
Therefore thus saith the Lord *G*	Eze 23:35	3069
For thus saith the Lord *G*	Eze 23:46	3069
shall know that I am the Lord *G*	Eze 23:49	3069
unto them, Thus saith the Lord *G*	Eze 24:3	3069
Wherefore thus saith the Lord *G*	Eze 24:6	3069
Therefore thus saith the Lord *G*	Eze 24:9	3069
they judge thee, saith the Lord *G*	Eze 24:14	3069
of Israel, Thus saith the Lord *G*	Eze 24:21	3069
shall know that I am the Lord *G*	Eze 24:24	3069
Hear the word of the Lord *G*	Eze 25:3	3069
Thus saith the Lord *G*	Eze 25:3	3069
For thus saith the Lord *G*	Eze 25:6	3069
Thus saith the Lord *G*	Eze 25:8	3069
Thus saith the Lord *G*	Eze 25:12	3069
Therefore thus saith the Lord *G*	Eze 25:13	3069
my vengeance, saith the Lord *G*	Eze 25:14	3069
Thus saith the Lord *G*	Eze 25:15	3069
Therefore thus saith the Lord *G*	Eze 25:16	3069
Therefore thus saith the Lord *G*	Eze 26:3	3069
have spoken it, saith the Lord *G*	Eze 26:5	3069
For thus saith the Lord *G*	Eze 26:7	3069
have spoken it, saith the Lord *G*	Eze 26:14	3069
Thus saith the Lord *G* to Tyrus	Eze 26:15	3069
For thus saith the Lord *G*	Eze 26:19	3069
be found again, saith the Lord *G*	Eze 26:21	3069
many isles, Thus saith the Lord *G*	Eze 27:3	3069
of Tyrus, Thus saith the Lord *G*	Eze 28:2	3069
up, and thou hast said, I am a *G*	Eze 28:2	410
I sit in the seat of *G*	Eze 28:2	430
yet thou art a man, and not *G*	Eze 28:2	410
set thine heart as the heart of *G*	Eze 28:2	430
Therefore thus saith the Lord *G*	Eze 28:6	3069
set thine heart as the heart of *G*	Eze 28:6	430
him that slayeth thee, I am *G*	Eze 28:9	430
but thou shalt be a man, and no *G*	Eze 28:9	410
have spoken it, saith the Lord *G*	Eze 28:10	3069
unto him, Thus saith the Lord *G*	Eze 28:12	3069
hast been in Eden the garden of *G*	Eze 28:13	430
wast upon the holy mountain of *G*	Eze 28:14	430
profane out of the mountain of *G*	Eze 28:16	430
And say, Thus saith the Lord *G*	Eze 28:22	3069
shall know that I am the Lord *G*	Eze 28:24	3069
Thus saith the Lord *G*	Eze 28:25	3069
know that I am the LORD their *G*	Eze 28:26	430
and say, Thus saith the Lord *G*	Eze 29:3	3069
Therefore thus saith the Lord *G*	Eze 29:8	3069
Yet thus saith the Lord *G*	Eze 29:13	3069
shall know that I am the Lord *G*	Eze 29:16	3069
Therefore thus saith the Lord *G*	Eze 29:19	3069
wrought for me, saith the Lord *G*	Eze 29:20	3069
and say, Thus saith the Lord *G*	Eze 30:2	3069
it by the sword, saith the Lord *G*	Eze 30:6	3069
Thus saith the Lord *G*	Eze 30:10	3069
Thus saith the Lord *G*	Eze 30:13	3069
Therefore thus saith the Lord *G*	Eze 30:22	3069
garden of *G* could not hide him	Eze 31:8	430
nor any tree in the garden of *G*	Eze 31:8	430
that were in the garden of *G*	Eze 31:9	430
Therefore thus saith the Lord *G*	Eze 31:10	3069
Thus saith the Lord *G*	Eze 31:15	430
his multitude, saith the Lord *G*	Eze 31:18	3069
Thus saith the Lord *G*	Eze 32:3	3069
upon thy land, saith the Lord *G*	Eze 32:8	3069
For thus saith the Lord *G*	Eze 32:11	3069
to run like oil, saith the Lord *G*	Eze 32:14	3069
her multitude, saith the Lord *G*	Eze 32:16	3069
by the sword, saith the Lord *G*	Eze 32:31	3069
his multitude, saith the Lord *G*	Eze 32:32	3069
them, As I live, saith the Lord *G*	Eze 33:11	3069
unto them, Thus saith the Lord *G*	Eze 33:25	3069
unto them, Thus saith the Lord *G*	Eze 33:27	3069
the Lord *G* unto the shepherds	Eze 34:2	3069
As I live saith the Lord *G*	Eze 34:8	3069
Thus saith the Lord *G*	Eze 34:10	3069
For thus saith the Lord *G*	Eze 34:11	3069
to lie down, saith the Lord *G*	Eze 34:15	3069
O my flock, thus saith the Lord *G*	Eze 34:17	3069
thus saith the Lord *G* unto them	Eze 34:20	3069
And I the LORD will be their *G*	Eze 34:24	430
I the LORD their *G* am with them	Eze 34:30	430
are my people, saith the Lord *G*	Eze 34:30	3069
pasture, are men, and I am your *G*	Eze 34:31	430
saith the Lord *G*	Eze 34:31	3069
unto it, Thus saith the Lord *G*	Eze 35:3	3069
as I live, saith the Lord *G*	Eze 35:6	3069
as I live, saith the Lord *G*	Eze 35:11	3069
Thus saith the Lord *G*	Eze 35:14	3069
Thus saith the Lord *G*	Eze 36:2	3069
and say, Thus saith the Lord *G*	Eze 36:3	3069
hear the word of the Lord *G*	Eze 36:4	3069
saith the Lord *G* to the mountains	Eze 36:4	3069
Therefore thus saith the Lord *G*	Eze 36:5	3069
valleys, Thus saith the Lord *G*	Eze 36:6	3069
Therefore thus saith the Lord *G*	Eze 36:7	3069
Thus saith the Lord *G*	Eze 36:13	3069
any more, saith the Lord *G*	Eze 36:14	3069
fall any more, saith the Lord *G*	Eze 36:15	3069
of Israel, Thus saith the Lord *G*	Eze 36:22	3069
I am the LORD, saith the Lord *G*	Eze 36:23	3069
be my people, and I will be your *G*	Eze 36:28	430
sakes do I this, saith the Lord *G*	Eze 36:32	3069
Thus saith the Lord *G*	Eze 36:33	3069
Thus saith the Lord *G*	Eze 36:37	3069
And I answered, O Lord *G*, thou	Eze 37:3	3069
saith the Lord *G* unto these bones	Eze 37:5	3069
the wind, Thus saith the Lord *G*	Eze 37:9	3069
unto them, Thus saith the Lord *G*	Eze 37:12	3069
unto them, Thus saith the Lord *G*	Eze 37:19	3069
unto them, Thus saith the Lord *G*	Eze 37:21	3069
my people, and I will be their *G*	Eze 37:23	430
yea, I will be their *G*, and they	Eze 37:27	430
And say, Thus saith the Lord *G*	Eze 38:3	3069
Thus saith the Lord *G*	Eze 38:10	3069
unto Gog, Thus saith the Lord *G*	Eze 38:14	3069
Thus saith the Lord *G*	Eze 38:17	3069
land of Israel, saith the Lord *G*	Eze 38:18	3069
my mountains, saith the Lord *G*	Eze 38:21	3069
and say, Thus saith the Lord *G*	Eze 39:1	3069
have spoken it, saith the Lord *G*	Eze 39:5	3069
and it is done, saith the Lord *G*	Eze 39:8	3069
robbed them, saith the Lord *G*	Eze 39:10	3069
be glorified, saith the Lord *G*	Eze 39:13	3069
son of man, thus saith the Lord *G*	Eze 39:17	3069
all men of war, saith the Lord *G*	Eze 39:20	3069
am the LORD their *G* from that day	Eze 39:22	430
Therefore thus saith the Lord *G*	Eze 39:25	3069
know that I am the LORD their *G*	Eze 39:28	430
house of Israel, saith the Lord *G*	Eze 39:29	3069
In the visions of *G* brought he me	Eze 40:2	430
the glory of the *G* of Israel came	Eze 43:2	430
Son of man, thus saith the Lord *G*	Eze 43:18	3069
unto me, saith the Lord *G*	Eze 43:19	3069
will accept you, saith the Lord *G*	Eze 43:27	3069
the *G* of Israel, hath entered in	Eze 44:2	430
of Israel, Thus saith the Lord *G*	Eze 44:6	3069
Thus saith the Lord *G*	Eze 44:9	3069
against them, saith the Lord *G*	Eze 44:12	3069
and the blood, saith the Lord *G*	Eze 44:15	3069
sin offering, saith the Lord *G*	Eze 44:27	3069
Thus saith the Lord *G*	Eze 45:9	3069
from my people, saith the Lord *G*	Eze 45:9	3069
for them, saith the Lord *G*	Eze 45:15	3069
Thus saith the Lord *G*	Eze 45:18	3069
Thus saith the Lord *G*	Eze 46:1	3069
Thus saith the Lord *G*	Eze 46:16	3069
Thus saith the Lord *G*	Eze 47:13	3069
his inheritance, saith the Lord *G*	Eze 47:23	3069
their portions, saith the Lord *G*	Eze 48:29	3069
of the vessels of the house of *G*	Dan 1:2	430
Now *G* had brought Daniel into	Dan 1:9	430
G gave them knowledge and skill in	Dan 1:17	430
the *G* of heaven concerning this	Dan 2:18	426
Daniel blessed the *G* of heaven	Dan 2:19	426
Blessed be the name of *G* for ever	Dan 2:20	426
O thou *G* of my fathers, who hast	Dan 2:23	426
But there is a *G* in heaven that	Dan 2:28	426
for the *G* of heaven hath given	Dan 2:37	426
the *G* of heaven set up a kingdom	Dan 2:44	426
the great *G* hath made known to	Dan 2:45	426
is, that your *G* is a *G* of gods	Dan 2:47	426
who is that *G* that shall deliver	Dan 3:15	426
our *G* whom we serve is able to	Dan 3:17	426
the fourth is like the Son of *G*	Dan 3:25	426
ye servants of the most high *G*	Dan 3:26	426
Blessed be the *G* of Shadrach	Dan 3:28	426
except their own *G*	Dan 3:28	426
amiss against the *G* of Shadrach	Dan 3:29	426
because there is no other *G* that	Dan 3:29	426
wonders that the high *G* hath	Dan 4:2	426
house of *G* which was at Jerusalem	Dan 5:3	426
O thou king, the most high *G* gave	Dan 5:18	426
G ruled in the kingdom of men	Dan 5:21	426
the *G* in whose hand thy breath is	Dan 5:23	426

G

G hath numbered thy kingdom, and	Dan 5:26	426
him concerning the law of his *G*	Dan 6:5	426
of any *G* or man for thirty days	Dan 6:7	426
and gave thanks before his *G*	Dan 6:10	426
making supplication before his *G*	Dan 6:11	426
any *G* or man within thirty days	Dan 6:12	426
Daniel, Thy *G* whom thou servest	Dan 6:16	426
of the living *G*, is thy *G*	Dan 6:20	426
My *G* hath sent his angel, and hath	Dan 6:22	426
him, because he believed in his *G*	Dan 6:23	426
and fear before the *G* of Daniel	Dan 6:26	426
for he is the living *G*, and	Dan 6:26	426
And I set my face unto the Lord *G*	Dan 9:3	430
And I prayed unto the LORD my *G*	Dan 9:4	430
O Lord, the great and dreadful *G*	Dan 9:4	410
To the Lord our *G* belong mercies	Dan 9:9	430
the voice of the LORD our *G*	Dan 9:10	430
the law of Moses the servant of *G*	Dan 9:11	430
our prayer before the LORD our *G*	Dan 9:13	430
for the LORD our *G* is righteous	Dan 9:14	430
And now, O Lord our *G*, that hast	Dan 9:15	430
Now therefore, O our *G*, hear the	Dan 9:17	430
O my *G*, incline thine ear, and	Dan 9:18	430
not, for thine own sake, O my *G*	Dan 9:19	430
G for the holy mountain of my *G*	Dan 9:20	430
to chasten thyself before thy *G*	Dan 10:12	430
do know their *G* shall be strong	Dan 11:32	430
things against the *G* of gods	Dan 11:36	410
he regard the *G* of his fathers	Dan 11:37	430
shall he honour the *G* of forces	Dan 11:38	433
G said unto him, Call her name	Hos 1:6	
save them by the LORD their *G*	Hos 1:7	430
Then said *G*, Call his name	Hos 1:9	
people, and I will not be your *G*	Hos 1:9	
Ye are the sons of the living *G*	Hos 1:10	410
and they shall say, Thou art my *G*	Hos 2:23	430
return, and seek the LORD their *G*	Hos 3:5	430
nor knowledge of *G* in the land	Hos 4:1	430
hast forgotten the law of thy *G*	Hos 4:6	430
gone a whoring from under their *G*	Hos 4:12	430
their doings to turn unto their *G*	Hos 5:4	430
the knowledge of *G* more than	Hos 6:6	430
do not return to the LORD their *G*	Hos 7:10	430
Israel shall cry unto me, My *G*	Hos 8:2	430
therefore it is not *G*	Hos 8:6	430
hast gone a whoring from thy *G*	Hos 9:1	430
watchman of Ephraim was with my *G*	Hos 9:8	430
and hatred in the house of his *G*	Hos 9:8	430
My *G* will cast them away, because	Hos 9:17	430
for I am *G*, and not man	Hos 11:9	410
but Judah yet ruleth with *G*	Hos 11:12	410
his strength he had power with *G*	Hos 12:3	430
Even the LORD *G* of hosts	Hos 12:5	430
Therefore turn thou to thy *G*	Hos 12:6	430
and wait on thy *G* continually	Hos 12:6	430
I that am the LORD thy *G* from the	Hos 12:9	430
Yet I am the LORD thy *G* from the	Hos 13:4	430
she hath rebelled against her *G*	Hos 13:16	430
return unto the LORD thy *G*	Hos 14:1	430
sackcloth, ye ministers of my *G*	Joel 1:13	430
from the house of your *G*	Joel 1:13	430
into the house of the LORD your *G*	Joel 1:14	430
gladness from the house of our *G*	Joel 1:16	430
and turn unto the LORD your *G*	Joel 2:13	430
offering unto the LORD your *G*	Joel 2:14	430
the people, Where is their *G*	Joel 2:17	430
and rejoice in the LORD your *G*	Joel 2:23	430
the name of the LORD your *G*	Joel 2:26	430
and that I am the LORD your *G*	Joel 2:27	430
the LORD your *G* dwelling in Zion	Joel 3:17	430
shall perish, saith the Lord *G*	Amos 1:8	3069
Surely the Lord *G* will do nothing	Amos 3:7	3069
the Lord *G* hath spoken, who can	Amos 3:8	3069
Therefore thus saith the Lord *G*	Amos 3:11	3069
house of Jacob, saith the Lord *G*	Amos 3:13	3069
the *G* of hosts,	Amos 3:13	430
The Lord *G* hath sworn by his	Amos 4:2	3069
of Israel, saith the Lord *G*	Amos 4:5	3069
as *G* overthrew Sodom and Gomorrah,	Amos 4:11	430
unto thee, prepare to meet thy *G*	Amos 4:12	430
The *G* of hosts, is his name	Amos 4:13	430
For thus saith the Lord *G*	Amos 5:3	3069
the *G* of hosts, shall be with you	Amos 5:14	430
it may be that the LORD *G* of	Amos 5:15	430
the *G* of hosts, the Lord, saith	Amos 5:16	430
whose name is The *G* of hosts	Amos 5:27	430
The Lord *G* hath sworn by himself,	Amos 6:8	3069
saith the LORD the *G* of hosts	Amos 6:8	430
saith the LORD the *G* of hosts	Amos 6:14	430
hath the Lord *G* shewed unto me	Amos 7:1	3069
the land, then I said, O Lord *G*	Amos 7:2	3069
hath the Lord *G* shewed unto me	Amos 7:4	3069
the Lord *G* called to contend by	Amos 7:4	3069
Then said I, O Lord *G*, cease, I	Amos 7:5	3069
shall not be, saith the Lord *G*	Amos 7:6	3069
hath the Lord *G* shewed unto me	Amos 8:1	3069
in that day, saith the Lord *G*	Amos 8:3	3069
in that day, saith the Lord *G*	Amos 8:9	3069
the days come, saith the Lord *G*	Amos 8:11	3069
the Lord *G* of hosts is he that	Amos 9:5	3069
the eyes of the Lord *G* are upon	Amos 9:8	3069
given them, saith the LORD thy *G*	Amos 9:15	430
saith the Lord *G* concerning Edom	Obad 1	3069
arise, call upon thy *G*	Jonah 1:6	430
if so be that *G* will think upon	Jonah 1:6	430
the *G* of heaven, which hath made	Jonah 1:9	430
his *G* out of the fish's belly	Jonah 2:1	430
life from corruption, O LORD my *G*	Jonah 2:6	430
the people of Nineveh believed *G*	Jonah 3:5	430
sackcloth, and cry mightily unto *G*	Jonah 3:8	430
Who can tell if *G* will turn	Jonah 3:9	430
G saw their works, that they	Jonah 3:10	430
G repented of the evil, that he	Jonah 3:10	430
I knew that thou art a gracious *G*	Jonah 4:2	410
the LORD *G* prepared a gourd, and	Jonah 4:6	430
But *G* prepared a worm when the	Jonah 4:7	430
that *G* prepared a vehement east	Jonah 4:8	430
G said to Jonah, Doest thou well	Jonah 4:9	430
let the Lord *G* be witness against	Mic 1:2	3069
for there is no answer of *G*	Mic 3:7	430
and to the house of the *G* of Jacob	Mic 4:2	430
name of the LORD our *G* for ever	Mic 4:5	430
of the name of the LORD his *G*	Mic 5:4	430
and bow myself before the high *G*	Mic 6:6	430
and to walk humbly with thy *G*	Mic 6:8	430
wait for the *G* of my salvation	Mic 7:7	430
my *G* will hear me	Mic 7:7	430
unto me, Where is the LORD thy *G*	Mic 7:10	430
shall be afraid of the LORD our *G*	Mic 7:17	430
Who is a *G* like unto thee, that	Mic 7:18	410
G is jealous, and the LORD	Nah 1:2	410
not from everlasting, O LORD my *G*	Hab 1:12	430
and, O mighty *G*, thou hast	Hab 1:12	6697
G came from Teman, and the Holy	Hab 3:3	433
will joy in the *G* of my salvation	Hab 3:18	430
The LORD *G* is my strength, and he	Hab 3:19	136
at the presence of the Lord *G*	Zeph 1:7	3069
the LORD their *G* shall visit them	Zeph 2:7	430
the *G* of Israel, Surely Moab	Zeph 2:9	430
she drew not near to her *G*	Zeph 3:2	430
The LORD thy *G* in the midst of	Zeph 3:17	430
the voice of the LORD their *G*	Hag 1:12	430
as the LORD their *G* had sent him	Hag 1:12	430
of the LORD of hosts, their *G*	Hag 1:14	430
obey the voice of the LORD your *G*	Zec 6:15	430
sent unto the house of *G* Sherezer	Zec 7:2	1008
my people, and I will be their *G*	Zec 8:8	430
we have heard that *G* is with you	Zec 8:23	430
even he, shall be for our *G*	Zec 9:7	430
the Lord *G* shall blow the trumpet	Zec 9:14	3069
the LORD their *G* shall save them	Zec 9:16	430
for I am the LORD their *G*	Zec 10:6	430
Thus saith the LORD my *G*	Zec 11:4	430
in the LORD of hosts their *G*	Zec 12:5	430
the house of David shall be as *G*	Zec 12:8	430
they shall say, The LORD is my *G*	Zec 13:9	430
and the LORD my *G* shall come	Zec 14:5	430
beseech *G* that he will be	Mal 1:9	410
hath not one *G* created us	Mal 2:10	410
the *G* of Israel, saith that he	Mal 2:16	430
or, Where is the *G* of judgment	Mal 2:17	430
Will a man rob *G*	Mal 3:8	430
have said, It is vain to serve *G*	Mal 3:14	430
they that tempt *G* are even	Mal 3:15	430
between him that serveth *G*	Mal 3:18	430
being interpreted is, *G* with us	Mt 1:23	*2316*
being warned of *G* in a dream that	Mt 2:12	
being warned of *G* in a dream	Mt 2:22	
that *G* is able of these stones to	Mt 3:9	*2316*
he saw the Spirit of *G* descending	Mt 3:16	*2316*
he said, If thou be the Son of *G*	Mt 4:3	*2316*
proceedeth out of the mouth of *G*	Mt 4:4	*2316*
unto him, If thou be the Son of *G*	Mt 4:6	*2316*
shalt not tempt the Lord thy *G*	Mt 4:7	*2316*
Thou shalt worship the Lord thy *G*	Mt 4:10	*2316*
for they shall see *G*	Mt 5:8	*2316*
shall be called the children of *G*	Mt 5:9	*2316*
Ye cannot serve *G* and mammon	Mt 6:24	*2316*
if *G* so clothe the grass of the	Mt 6:30	*2316*
seek ye first the kingdom of *G*	Mt 6:33	*2316*
with thee, Jesus, thou Son of *G*	Mt 8:29	*2316*
they marvelled, and glorified *G*	Mt 9:8	*2316*
he entered into the house of *G*	Mt 12:4	*2316*
out devils by the Spirit of *G*	Mt 12:28	*2316*
the kingdom of *G* is come unto you	Mt 12:28	*2316*
Of a truth thou art the Son of *G*	Mt 14:33	*2316*
of *G* by your tradition	Mt 15:3	*2316*
For *G* commanded, saying, Honour	Mt 15:4	*2316*
of *G* of none effect by your	Mt 15:6	*2316*
and they glorified the *G* of Israel	Mt 15:31	*2316*
Christ, the Son of the living *G*	Mt 16:16	*2316*
not the things that be of *G*	Mt 16:23	*2316*
What therefore *G* hath joined	Mt 19:6	*2316*
is none good but one, that is, *G*	Mt 19:17	*2316*
to enter into the kingdom of *G*	Mt 19:24	*2316*
but with *G* all things are	Mt 19:26	*2316*
Jesus went into the temple of *G*	Mt 21:12	*2316*
into the kingdom of *G* before you	Mt 21:31	*2316*
The kingdom of *G* shall be taken	Mt 21:43	*2316*
and teachest the way of *G* in truth	Mt 22:16	*2316*
unto *G* the things that are God's	Mt 22:21	*2316*
scriptures, nor the power of *G*	Mt 22:29	*2316*
are as the angels of *G* in heaven	Mt 22:30	*2316*
which was spoken unto you by *G*	Mt 22:31	*2316*
I am the *G* of Abraham	Mt 22:32	*2316*
G of Isaac, and the *G* of Jacob	Mt 22:32	*2316*
G is not the *G* of the dead	Mt 22:32	*2316*
the Lord thy *G* with all thy heart	Mt 22:37	*2316*
sweareth by the throne of *G*	Mt 23:22	*2316*
able to destroy the temple of *G*	Mt 26:61	*2316*
I adjure thee by the living *G*	Mt 26:63	*2316*
thou be the Christ, the Son of *G*	Mt 26:63	*2316*
If thou be the Son of *G*, come	Mt 27:40	*2316*
He trusted in *G*	Mt 27:43	*2316*
for he said, I am the Son of *G*	Mt 27:43	*2316*
that is to say, My *G*, my *G*	Mt 27:46	*2316*
Truly this was the Son of *G*	Mt 27:54	*2316*
of Jesus Christ, the Son of *G*	Mk 1:1	*2316*
the gospel of the kingdom of *G*	Mk 1:14	*2316*
and the kingdom of *G* is at hand	Mk 1:15	*2316*
who thou art, the Holy One of *G*	Mk 1:24	*2316*
who can forgive sins but *G* only	Mk 2:7	*2316*
were all amazed, and glorified *G*	Mk 2:12	*2316*
of *G* in the days of Abiathar the	Mk 2:26	*2316*
saying, Thou art the Son of *G*	Mk 3:11	*2316*
whosoever shall do the will of *G*	Mk 3:35	*2316*
the mystery of the kingdom of *G*	Mk 4:11	*2316*
he said, So is the kingdom of *G*	Mk 4:26	*2316*
shall we liken the kingdom of *G*	Mk 4:30	*2316*
thou Son of the most high *G*	Mk 5:7	*2316*
I adjure thee by *G*, that thou	Mk 5:7	*2316*
laying aside the commandment of *G*	Mk 7:8	*2316*
ye reject the commandment of *G*	Mk 7:9	*2316*
Making the word of *G* of none	Mk 7:13	*2316*
not the things that be of *G*	Mk 8:33	*2316*
the kingdom of *G* come with power	Mk 9:1	*2316*
the kingdom of *G* with one eye	Mk 9:47	*2316*
of the creation *G* made them male	Mk 10:6	*2316*
What therefore *G* hath joined	Mk 10:9	*2316*
for of such is the kingdom of *G*	Mk 10:14	*2316*
kingdom of *G* as a little child	Mk 10:15	*2316*
is none good but one, that is, *G*	Mk 10:18	*2316*
enter into the kingdom of *G*	Mk 10:23	*2316*
to enter into the kingdom of *G*	Mk 10:24	*2316*
to enter into the kingdom of *G*	Mk 10:25	*2316*
it is impossible, but not with *G*	Mk 10:27	*2316*
for with *G* all things are	Mk 10:27	*2316*
saith unto them, Have faith in *G*	Mk 11:22	*2316*
teachest the way of *G* in truth	Mk 12:14	*2316*
to *G* the things that are God's	Mk 12:17	*2316*
neither the power of *G*	Mk 12:24	*2316*
how in the bush *G* spake unto him	Mk 12:26	*2316*
I am the *G* of Abraham	Mk 12:26	*2316*
G of Isaac, and the *G* of Jacob	Mk 12:26	*2316*
He is not the *G* of the dead	Mk 12:27	*2316*
but the *G* of the living	Mk 12:27	*2316*
The Lord our *G* is one Lord	Mk 12:29	*2316*
the Lord thy *G* with all thy heart	Mk 12:30	*2316*
for there is one *G*	Mk 12:32	*2316*
art not far from the kingdom of *G*	Mk 12:34	*2316*
which *G* created unto this time	Mk 13:19	*2316*
drink it new in the kingdom of *G*	Mk 14:25	*2316*
being interpreted, My *G*, my *G*	Mk 15:34	*2316*
Truly this man was the Son of *G*	Mk 15:39	*2316*
also waited for the kingdom of *G*	Mk 15:43	*2316*
and sat on the right hand of *G*	Mk 16:19	*2316*
they were both righteous before *G*	Lk 1:6	*2316*
G in the order of his course	Lk 1:8	*2316*
shall he turn to the Lord their *G*	Lk 1:16	*2316*
that stand in the presence of *G*	Lk 1:19	*2316*
from *G* unto a city of Galilee	Lk 1:26	*2316*
for thou hast found favour with *G*	Lk 1:30	*2316*
the Lord *G* shall give unto him	Lk 1:32	*2316*
thee shall be called the Son of *G*	Lk 1:35	*2316*
For with *G* nothing shall be	Lk 1:37	*2316*
hath rejoiced in *G* my Saviour	Lk 1:47	*2316*
loosed, and he spake, and praised *G*	Lk 1:64	*2316*
Blessed be the Lord *G* of Israel	Lk 1:68	*2316*
Through the tender mercy of our *G*	Lk 1:78	*2316*
of the heavenly host praising *G*	Lk 2:13	*2316*
Glory to *G* in the highest, and on	Lk 2:14	*2316*
praising *G* for all the things	Lk 2:20	*2316*
him up in his arms, and blessed *G*	Lk 2:28	*2316*
but served *G* with fastings and	Lk 2:37	
and the grace of *G* was upon him	Lk 2:40	*2316*
and stature, and in favour with *G*	Lk 2:52	*2316*
the word of *G* came unto John the	Lk 3:2	*2316*
shall see the salvation of *G*	Lk 3:6	*2316*
That *G* is able of these stones to	Lk 3:8	*2316*
of Adam, which was the son of *G*	Lk 3:38	*2316*
unto him, If thou be the Son of *G*	Lk 4:3	*2316*
alone, but by every word of *G*	Lk 4:4	*2316*
Thou shalt worship the Lord thy *G*	Lk 4:8	*2316*
unto him, If thou be the Son of *G*	Lk 4:9	*2316*
shalt not tempt the Lord thy *G*	Lk 4:12	*2316*
the Holy One of *G*	Lk 4:34	*2316*
Thou art Christ the Son of *G*	Lk 4:41	*2316*
kingdom of *G* to other cities also	Lk 4:43	*2316*
upon him to hear the word of *G*	Lk 5:1	*2316*
Who can forgive sins, but *G* alone	Lk 5:21	*2316*
to his own house, glorifying *G*	Lk 5:25	*2316*
all amazed, and they glorified *G*	Lk 5:26	*2316*
How he went into the house of *G*	Lk 6:4	*2316*
all night in prayer to *G*	Lk 6:12	*2316*
for yours is the kingdom of *G*	Lk 6:20	*2316*
and they glorified *G*, saying, That	Lk 7:16	*2316*
That *G* hath visited his people	Lk 7:16	*2316*
kingdom of *G* is greater than he	Lk 7:28	*2316*
and the publicans, justified *G*	Lk 7:29	*2316*
counsel of *G* against themselves	Lk 7:30	*2316*
glad tidings of the kingdom of *G*	Lk 8:1	*2316*
the mysteries of the kingdom of *G*	Lk 8:10	*2316*
The seed is the word of *G*	Lk 8:11	*2316*
these which hear the word of *G*	Lk 8:21	*2316*
Jesus, thou Son of *G* most high	Lk 8:28	*2316*
things *G* hath done unto thee	Lk 8:39	*2316*
them to preach the kingdom of *G*	Lk 9:2	*2316*
unto them of the kingdom of *G*	Lk 9:11	*2316*
answering said, The Christ of *G*	Lk 9:20	*2316*
till they see the kingdom of *G*	Lk 9:27	*2316*
amazed at the mighty power of *G*	Lk 9:43	*2316*
thou and preach the kingdom of *G*	Lk 9:60	*2316*
back, is fit for the kingdom of *G*	Lk 9:62	*2316*
The kingdom of *G* is come nigh	Lk 10:9	*2316*

that the kingdom of G is come	Lk 10:11	2316
the Lord thy G with all thy heart	Lk 10:27	2316
the finger of G cast out devils	Lk 11:20	2316
the kingdom of G is come upon you	Lk 11:20	2316
are they that hear the word of G	Lk 11:28	2316
over judgment and the love of G	Lk 11:42	2316
also said the wisdom of G	Lk 11:49	2316
one of them is forgotten before G	Lk 12:6	2316
confess before the angels of G	Lk 12:8	2316
be denied before the angels of G	Lk 12:9	2316
But G said unto him, Thou fool,	Lk 12:20	2316
himself, and is not rich toward G	Lk 12:21	2316
and G feedeth them	Lk 12:24	2316
If then G so clothe the grass,	Lk 12:28	2316
rather seek ye the kingdom of G	Lk 12:31	2316
was made straight, and glorified G	Lk 13:13	2316
what is the kingdom of G like	Lk 13:18	2316
shall I liken the kingdom of G	Lk 13:20	2316
the prophets, in the kingdom of G	Lk 13:28	2316
sit down in the kingdom of G	Lk 13:29	2316
eat bread in the kingdom of G	Lk 14:15	2316
the presence of the angels of G	Lk 15:10	2316
Ye cannot serve G and mammon	Lk 16:13	2316
but G knoweth your hearts	Lk 16:15	2316
is abomination in the sight of G	Lk 16:15	2316
time the kingdom of G is preached	Lk 16:16	2316
and with a loud voice glorified G	Lk 17:15	2316
that returned to give glory to G	Lk 17:18	2316
when the kingdom of G should come	Lk 17:20	2316
The kingdom of G cometh not with	Lk 17:20	2316
the kingdom of G is within you	Lk 17:21	2316
city a judge, which feared not G	Lk 18:2	2316
himself, Though I fear not G	Lk 18:4	2316
shall not G avenge his own elect,	Lk 18:7	2316
and prayed thus with himself, G	Lk 18:11	2316
G be merciful to me a sinner	Lk 18:13	2316
for of such is the kingdom of G	Lk 18:16	2316
not receive the kingdom of G as a	Lk 18:17	2316
is good, save one, that is, G	Lk 18:19	2316
enter into the kingdom of G	Lk 18:24	2316
to enter into the kingdom of G	Lk 18:25	2316
with men are possible with G	Lk 18:27	2316
and followed him, glorifying G	Lk 18:43	2316
they saw it, gave praise unto G	Lk 18:43	2316
of G should immediately appear	Lk 19:11	2316
praise G with a loud voice for	Lk 19:37	2316
heard it, they said, G forbid	Lk 20:16	3361,1096
but teachest the way of G truly	Lk 20:21	2316
unto G the things which be God's	Lk 20:25	2316
and are the children of G, being	Lk 20:36	2316
calleth the Lord the G of Abraham	Lk 20:37	2316
G of Isaac, and the G of Jacob	Lk 20:37	2316
For he is not a G of the dead	Lk 20:38	2316
cast in unto the offerings of G	Lk 21:4	2316
the kingdom of G is nigh at hand	Lk 21:31	2316
be fulfilled in the kingdom of G	Lk 22:16	2316
until the kingdom of G shall come	Lk 22:18	2316
the right hand of the power of G	Lk 22:69	2316
all, Art thou then the Son of G	Lk 22:70	2316
if he be Christ, the chosen of G	Lk 23:35	2316
him, saying, Dost not thou fear G	Lk 23:40	2316
saw what was done, he glorified G	Lk 23:47	2316
waited for the kingdom of G	Lk 23:51	2316
mighty in deed and word before G	Lk 24:19	2316
temple, praising and blessing G	Lk 24:53	2316
was with G, and the Word was G	Jn 1:1	2316
same was in the beginning with G	Jn 1:2	2316
There was a man sent from G	Jn 1:6	2316
he power to become the sons of G	Jn 1:12	2316
nor of the will of man, but of G	Jn 1:13	2316
No man hath seen G at any time	Jn 1:18	2316
and saith, Behold the Lamb of G	Jn 1:29	2316
record that this is the Son of G	Jn 1:34	2316
he saith, Behold the Lamb of G	Jn 1:36	2316
him, Rabbi, thou art the Son of G	Jn 1:49	2316
and the angels of G ascending	Jn 1:51	2316
thou art a teacher come from G	Jn 3:2	2316
thou doest, except G be with him	Jn 3:2	2316
he cannot see the kingdom of G	Jn 3:3	2316
enter into the kingdom of G	Jn 3:5	2316
For G so loved the world, that he	Jn 3:16	2316
For G sent not his Son into the	Jn 3:17	2316
of the only begotten Son of G	Jn 3:18	2316
that they are wrought in G	Jn 3:21	2316
set to his seal that G is true	Jn 3:33	2316
For he whom G hath sent speaketh	Jn 3:34	2316
hath sent speaketh the words of G	Jn 3:34	2316
for G giveth not the Spirit by	Jn 3:34	2316
but the wrath of G abideth on him	Jn 3:36	2316
If thou knewest the gift of G	Jn 4:10	2316
G is a Spirit	Jn 4:24	2316
said also that G was his Father	Jn 5:18	2316
making himself equal with G	Jn 5:18	2316
hear the voice of the Son of G	Jn 5:25	2316
ye have not the love of G in you	Jn 5:42	2316
honour that cometh from G only	Jn 5:44	2316
for him hath G the Father sealed	Jn 6:27	2316
that we might work the works of G	Jn 6:28	2316
unto them, This is the work of G	Jn 6:29	2316
For the bread of G is he which	Jn 6:33	2316
And they shall be all taught of G	Jn 6:45	2316
the Father, save he which is of G	Jn 6:46	2316
Christ, the Son of the living G	Jn 6:69	2316
the doctrine, whether it be of G	Jn 7:17	2316
truth, which I have heard of G	Jn 8:40	2316
we have one Father, even G	Jn 8:41	2316
If G were your Father, ye would	Jn 8:42	2316
I proceeded forth and came from G	Jn 8:42	2316
He that is of G heareth God's	Jn 8:47	2316
them not, because ye are not of G	Jn 8:47	2316
of whom ye say, that he is your G	Jn 8:54	2316
but that the works of G should be	Jn 9:3	2316
Pharisees, This man is not of G	Jn 9:16	2316
said unto him, Give G the praise	Jn 9:24	2316
We know that G spake unto Moses	Jn 9:29	2316
Now we know that G heareth not	Jn 9:31	2316
if any man be a worshipper of G	Jn 9:31	2318
If this man were not of G	Jn 9:33	2316
Dost thou believe on the Son of G	Jn 9:35	2316
being a man, makest thyself G	Jn 10:33	2316
unto whom the word of G came	Jn 10:35	2316
because I said, I am the Son of G	Jn 10:36	2316
death, but for the glory of G	Jn 11:4	2316
that the Son of G might be	Jn 11:4	2316
ask of G, G will give it thee	Jn 11:22	2316
thou art the Christ, the Son of G	Jn 11:27	2316
thou shouldest see the glory of G	Jn 11:40	2316
of G that were scattered abroad	Jn 11:52	2316
of men more than the praise of G	Jn 12:43	2316
was come from G, and went to G	Jn 13:3	2316
and G is glorified in him	Jn 13:31	2316
If G be glorified in him	Jn 13:32	2316
G shall also glorify him in	Jn 13:32	2316
ye believe in G, believe also in	Jn 14:1	2316
think that he doeth G service	Jn 16:2	2316
believed that I came out from G	Jn 16:27	2316
that thou camest forth from G	Jn 16:30	2316
might know thee the only true G	Jn 17:3	2316
he made himself the Son of G	Jn 19:7	2316
and to my G, and your G	Jn 20:17	2316
and said unto him, My Lord and my G	Jn 20:28	2316
Jesus is the Christ, the Son of G	Jn 20:31	2316
by what death he should glorify G	Jn 21:19	2316
pertaining to the kingdom of G	Acts 1:3	2316
tongues the wonderful works of G	Acts 2:11	2316
to pass in the last days, saith G	Acts 2:17	2316
a man approved of G among you by	Acts 2:22	2316
which G did by him in the midst	Acts 2:22	2316
counsel and foreknowledge of G	Acts 2:23	2316
Whom G hath raised up, having	Acts 2:24	2316
knowing that G had sworn with an	Acts 2:30	2316
This Jesus hath G raised up	Acts 2:32	2316
by the right hand of G exalted	Acts 2:33	2316
that G hath made that same Jesus,	Acts 2:36	2316
many as the Lord our G shall call	Acts 2:39	2316
Praising G, and having favour with	Acts 2:47	2316
and leaping, and praising G	Acts 3:8	2316
saw him walking and praising G	Acts 3:9	2316
The G of Abraham, and of Isaac, and	Acts 3:13	2316
the G of our fathers, hath	Acts 3:13	2316
whom G hath raised from the dead	Acts 3:15	2316
which G before had shewed by the	Acts 3:18	2316
which G hath spoken by the mouth	Acts 3:21	2316
your G raise up unto you of your	Acts 3:22	2316
which G made with our fathers	Acts 3:25	2316
Unto you first G, having raised	Acts 3:26	2316
whom G raised from the dead, even	Acts 4:10	2316
it be right in the sight of G to	Acts 4:19	2316
hearken unto you more than unto G	Acts 4:19	2316
for all men glorified G for that	Acts 4:21	2316
their voice to G with one accord	Acts 4:24	2316
and said, Lord, thou art G	Acts 4:24	2316
spake the word of G with boldness	Acts 4:31	2316
not lied unto men, but unto G	Acts 5:4	2316
ought to obey G rather than men	Acts 5:29	2316
The G of our fathers raised up	Acts 5:30	2316
Him hath G exalted with his right	Acts 5:31	2316
whom G hath given to them that	Acts 5:32	2316
But if it be of G, ye cannot	Acts 5:39	2316
be found even to fight against G	Acts 5:39	2314
we should leave the word of G	Acts 6:2	2316
And the word of G increased	Acts 6:7	2316
words against Moses, and against G	Acts 6:11	2316
The G of glory appeared unto our	Acts 7:2	2316
G spake on this wise, That his	Acts 7:6	2316
in bondage will I judge, said G	Acts 7:7	2316
but G was with him,	Acts 7:9	2316
which G had sworn to Abraham, the	Acts 7:17	2316
G by his hand would deliver them	Acts 7:25	2316
I am the G of thy fathers	Acts 7:32	2316
the G of Abraham	Acts 7:32	2316
G of Isaac, and the G of Jacob	Acts 7:32	2316
the same did G send to be a ruler	Acts 7:35	2316
your G raise up unto you of your	Acts 7:37	2316
Then G turned, and gave them up to	Acts 7:42	2316
whom G drave out before the face	Acts 7:45	2316
Who found favour before G	Acts 7:46	2316
a tabernacle for the G of Jacob	Acts 7:46	2316
heaven, and saw the glory of G	Acts 7:55	2316
standing on the right hand of G	Acts 7:55	2316
standing on the right hand of G	Acts 7:56	2316
stoned Stephen, calling upon G	Acts 7:59	
This man is the great power of G	Acts 8:10	2316
concerning the kingdom of G	Acts 8:12	2316
had received the word of G	Acts 8:14	2316
of G may be purchased with money	Acts 8:20	2316
is not right in the sight of G	Acts 8:21	2316
of this thy wickedness, and pray G	Acts 8:22	2316
that Jesus Christ is the Son of G	Acts 8:37	2316
that he is the Son of G	Acts 9:20	2316
one that feared G with all his	Acts 10:2	2316
the people, and prayed to G alway	Acts 10:2	2316
an angel of G coming in to him	Acts 10:3	2316
come up for a memorial before G	Acts 10:4	2316
What G hath cleansed, that call	Acts 10:15	2316
a just man, and one that feareth G	Acts 10:22	2316
was warned from G by an holy	Acts 10:22	
but G hath shewed me that I	Acts 10:28	2316
in remembrance in the sight of G	Acts 10:31	2316
are we all here present before G	Acts 10:33	2316
that are commanded thee of G	Acts 10:33	2316
that G is no respecter of persons	Acts 10:34	2316
The word which G sent unto the	Acts 10:36	
How G anointed Jesus of Nazareth	Acts 10:38	2316
for G was with him	Acts 10:38	2316
Him G raised up the third day, and	Acts 10:40	2316
unto witnesses chosen before of G	Acts 10:41	2316
of G to be the Judge of quick	Acts 10:42	2316
speak with tongues, and magnify G	Acts 10:46	2316
had also received the word of G	Acts 11:1	2316
What G hath cleansed, that call	Acts 11:9	2316
Forasmuch then as G gave them the	Acts 11:17	2316
was I, that I could withstand G	Acts 11:17	2316
held their peace, and glorified G	Acts 11:18	2316
Then hath G also to the Gentiles	Acts 11:18	2316
came, and had seen the grace of G	Acts 11:23	2316
of the church unto G for him	Acts 12:5	2316
because he gave not G the glory	Acts 12:23	2316
But the word of G grew and	Acts 12:24	2316
they preached the word of G in	Acts 13:5	2316
and desired to hear the word of G	Acts 13:7	2316
Men of Israel, and ye that fear G	Acts 13:16	2316
The G of this people of Israel	Acts 13:17	2316
G gave unto them Saul the son of	Acts 13:21	2316
Of this man's seed hath G	Acts 13:23	2316
and whosoever among you feareth G	Acts 13:26	2316
But G raised him from the dead	Acts 13:30	2316
G hath fulfilled the same unto us	Acts 13:33	2316
own generation by the will of G	Acts 13:36	2316
whom G raised again, saw no	Acts 13:37	2316
to continue in the grace of G	Acts 13:43	2316
together to hear the word of G	Acts 13:44	2316
G should first have been spoken	Acts 13:46	2316
these vanities unto the living G	Acts 14:15	2316
enter into the kingdom of G	Acts 14:22	2316
of G for the work which they	Acts 14:26	2316
all that G had done with them	Acts 14:27	2316
things that G had done with them	Acts 15:4	2316
while ago G made choice among us	Acts 15:7	2316
And G, which knoweth the hearts,	Acts 15:8	2316
Now therefore why tempt ye G	Acts 15:10	2316
wonders G had wrought among the	Acts 15:12	2316
Simeon hath declared how G at the	Acts 15:14	2316
Known unto G are all his works	Acts 15:18	2316
the Gentiles are turned to G	Acts 15:19	2316
the brethren unto the grace of G	Acts 15:40	2316
of Thyatira, which worshipped G	Acts 16:14	2316
the servants of the most high G	Acts 16:17	2316
prayed, and sang praises unto G	Acts 16:25	2316
believing in G with all his house	Acts 16:34	2316
G was preached of Paul at Berea	Acts 17:13	2316
inscription, TO THE UNKNOWN G	Acts 17:23	2316
G that made the world and all	Acts 17:24	2316
then as we are the offspring of G	Acts 17:29	2316
of this ignorance G winked at	Acts 17:30	2316
Justus, one that worshipped G	Acts 18:7	2316
teaching the word of G among them	Acts 18:11	2316
to worship G contrary to the law	Acts 18:13	2316
return again unto you, if G will	Acts 18:21	2316
him the way of G more perfectly	Acts 18:26	2316
concerning the kingdom of G	Acts 19:8	2316
G wrought special miracles by the	Acts 19:11	2316
So mightily grew the word of G	Acts 19:20	2962
the Greeks, repentance toward G	Acts 20:21	2316
the gospel of the grace of G	Acts 20:24	2316
gone preaching the kingdom of G	Acts 20:25	2316
unto you all the counsel of G	Acts 20:27	2316
to feed the church of G, which	Acts 20:28	2316
now, brethren, I commend you to G	Acts 20:32	2316
particularly what things G had	Acts 21:19	2316
fathers, and was zealous toward G	Acts 22:3	2316
The G of our fathers hath chosen	Acts 22:14	2316
before G until this day	Acts 23:1	2316
G shall smite thee, thou whited	Acts 23:3	2316
him, let us not fight against G	Acts 23:9	2313
so worship I the G of my fathers	Acts 24:14	2316
And have hope toward G, which they	Acts 24:15	2316
void of offence toward G, and	Acts 24:16	2316
made of G unto our fathers	Acts 26:6	2316
tribes, instantly serving G day	Acts 26:7	
that G should raise the dead	Acts 26:8	2316
and from the power of Satan unto G	Acts 26:18	2316
they should repent and turn to G	Acts 26:20	2316
therefore obtained help of G	Acts 26:22	2316
And Paul said, I would to G	Acts 26:29	2316
by me this night the angel of G	Acts 27:23	2316
G hath given thee all them that	Acts 27:24	2316
for I believe G, that it shall be	Acts 27:25	2316
gave thanks to G in presence of	Acts 27:35	2316
whom when Paul saw, he thanked G	Acts 28:15	2316
and testified the kingdom of G	Acts 28:23	2316
that the salvation of G is sent	Acts 28:28	2316
Preaching the kingdom of G	Acts 28:31	2316
separated unto the gospel of G	Rom 1:1	2316
to be the Son of G with power	Rom 1:4	2316
all that be in Rome, beloved of G	Rom 1:7	2316
to you and peace from G our Father	Rom 1:7	2316
I thank my G through Jesus Christ	Rom 1:8	2316
For G is my witness, whom I serve	Rom 1:9	2316
by the will of G to come unto you	Rom 1:10	2316
for it is the power of G unto	Rom 1:16	2316
of G revealed from faith to faith	Rom 1:17	2316
For the wrath of G is revealed	Rom 1:18	2316
be known of G is manifest in them	Rom 1:19	2316

for G hath shewed it unto them	Rom 1:19	2316
Because that, when they knew G	Rom 1:21	2316
they glorified him not as G	Rom 1:21	2316
G into an image made like to	Rom 1:23	2316
Wherefore G also gave them up to	Rom 1:24	2316
changed the truth of G into a lie	Rom 1:25	2316
For this cause G gave them up	Rom 1:26	2316
to retain G in their knowledge	Rom 1:28	2316
G gave them over to a reprobate	Rom 1:28	2316
Backbiters, haters of G,	Rom 1:30	2319
Who knowing the judgment of G	Rom 1:32	2316
G is according to truth against	Rom 2:2	2316
shalt escape the judgment of G	Rom 2:3	2316
of G leadeth thee to repentance	Rom 2:4	2316
of the righteous judgment of G	Rom 2:5	2316
is no respect of persons with G	Rom 2:11	2316
of the law are just before G	Rom 2:13	2316
In the day when G shall judge the	Rom 2:16	2316
the law, and makest thy boast of G	Rom 2:17	2316
the law dishonourest thou G	Rom 2:23	2316
For the name of G is blasphemed	Rom 2:24	2316
praise is not of men, but of G	Rom 2:29	2316
were committed the oracles of G	Rom 3:2	2316
the faith of G without effect	Rom 3:3	2316
G forbid: yea,	Rom 3:4	3361,1096
let G be true, but every man a	Rom 3:4	2316
commend the righteousness of G	Rom 3:5	2316
Is G unrighteous who taketh	Rom 3:5	2316
G forbid: for then how	Rom 3:6	3361,1096
then how shall G judge the world	Rom 3:6	2316
For if the truth of G hath more	Rom 3:7	2316
is none that seeketh after G	Rom 3:11	2316
is no fear of G before their eyes	Rom 3:18	2316
world may become guilty before G	Rom 3:19	2316
But now the righteousness of G	Rom 3:21	2316
Even the righteousness of G which	Rom 3:22	2316
and come short of the glory of G	Rom 3:23	2316
Whom G hath set forth to be a	Rom 3:25	2316
through the forbearance of G	Rom 3:25	2316
Is he the G of the Jews only	Rom 3:29	2316
Seeing it is one G, which shall	Rom 3:30	2316
G forbid: yea, we establish	Rom 3:31	3361,1096
but not before G	Rom 4:2	2316
Abraham believed G, and it was	Rom 4:3	2316
of the man, unto whom G imputeth	Rom 4:6	2316
him whom he believed, even G	Rom 4:17	2316
the promise of G through unbelief	Rom 4:20	2316
in faith, giving glory to G	Rom 4:20	2316
we have peace with G through our	Rom 5:1	2316
rejoice in hope of the glory of G	Rom 5:2	2316
because the love of G is shed	Rom 5:5	2316
But G commendeth his love toward	Rom 5:8	2316
we were reconciled to G by the	Rom 5:10	2316
but we also joy in G through our	Rom 5:11	2316
be dead, much more the grace of G	Rom 5:15	2316
G forbid. How shall we	Rom 6:2	3361,1096
that he liveth, he liveth unto G	Rom 6:10	2316
but alive unto G through Jesus	Rom 6:11	2316
but yield yourselves unto G	Rom 6:13	2316
of righteousness unto G	Rom 6:13	2316
but under grace? G forbid	Rom 6:15	3361,1096
But G be thanked, that ye were	Rom 6:17	2316
from sin, and become servants to G	Rom 6:22	2316
but the gift of G is eternal life	Rom 6:23	2316
should bring forth fruit unto G	Rom 7:4	2316
Is the law sin? G forbid	Rom 7:7	3361,1096
made death unto me? G forbid	Rom 7:13	3361,1096
the law of G after the inward man	Rom 7:22	2316
I thank G through Jesus Christ	Rom 7:25	2316
mind I myself serve the law of G	Rom 7:25	2316
G sending his own Son in the	Rom 8:3	2316
carnal mind is enmity against G	Rom 8:7	2316
it is not subject to the law of G	Rom 8:7	2316
are in the flesh cannot please G	Rom 8:8	2316
that the Spirit of G dwell in you	Rom 8:9	2316
as are led by the Spirit of G	Rom 8:14	2316
they are the sons of G	Rom 8:14	2316
that we are the children of G	Rom 8:16	2316
heirs of G, and joint-heirs with	Rom 8:17	2316
manifestation of the sons of G	Rom 8:19	2316
liberty of the children of G	Rom 8:21	2316
saints according to the will of G	Rom 8:27	2316
for good to them that love G	Rom 8:28	2316
If G be for us, who can be	Rom 8:31	2316
It is G that justifieth	Rom 8:33	2316
is even at the right hand of G	Rom 8:34	2316
to separate us from the love of G	Rom 8:39	2316
of the law, and the service of G	Rom 9:4	2316
is over all, G blessed for ever	Rom 9:5	2316
word of G hath taken none effect	Rom 9:6	2316
these are not the children of G	Rom 9:8	2316
that the purpose of G according	Rom 9:11	2316
Is there unrighteousness with G?	Rom 9:14	2316
G forbid	Rom 9:14	3361,1096
but of G that sheweth mercy	Rom 9:16	2316
art thou that repliest against G	Rom 9:20	2316
What if G, willing to shew his	Rom 9:22	2316
the children of the living G	Rom 9:26	2316
prayer to G for Israel is, that	Rom 10:1	2316
record that they have a zeal of G	Rom 10:2	2316
unto the righteousness of G	Rom 10:3	2316
believe in thine heart that G	Rom 10:9	2316
and hearing by the word of G	Rom 10:17	2316
Hath G cast away his people	Rom 11:1	2316
cast away his people? G forbid	Rom 11:1	3361,1096
G hath not cast away his people	Rom 11:2	2316
intercession to G against Israel	Rom 11:2	2316
saith the answer of G unto him	Rom 11:4	2316
G hath given them the spirit of	Rom 11:8	2316
that they should fall? G forbid	Rom 11:11	3361,1096
For if G spared not the natural	Rom 11:21	2316
the goodness and severity of G	Rom 11:22	2316
for G is able to graff them in	Rom 11:23	2316
gifts and calling of G are without	Rom 11:29	2316
in times past have not believed G	Rom 11:30	2316
For G hath concluded them all in	Rom 11:32	2316
of the wisdom and knowledge of G	Rom 11:33	2316
brethren, by the mercies of G	Rom 12:1	2316
holy, acceptable unto G, which	Rom 12:1	2316
acceptable, and perfect, will of G	Rom 12:2	2316
according as G hath dealt to	Rom 12:3	2316
For there is no power but of G	Rom 13:1	2316
powers that be are ordained of G	Rom 13:1	2316
resisteth the ordinance of G	Rom 13:2	2316
minister of G to thee for good	Rom 13:4	2316
for he is the minister of G	Rom 13:4	2316
for G hath received him	Rom 14:3	2316
for G is able to make him stand	Rom 14:4	2316
the Lord, for he giveth G thanks	Rom 14:6	2316
he eateth not, and giveth G thanks	Rom 14:6	2316
every tongue shall confess to G	Rom 14:11	2316
give account of himself to G	Rom 14:12	2316
For the kingdom of G is not meat	Rom 14:17	2316
serveth Christ is acceptable to G	Rom 14:18	2316
meat destroy not the work of G	Rom 14:20	2316
have it to thyself before G	Rom 14:22	2316
Now the G of patience and	Rom 15:5	2316
one mind and one mouth glorify G	Rom 15:6	2316
received us to the glory of G	Rom 15:7	2316
circumcision for the truth of G	Rom 15:8	2316
might glorify G for his mercy	Rom 15:9	2316
Now the G of hope fill you with	Rom 15:13	2316
grace that is given to me of G	Rom 15:15	2316
ministering the gospel of G	Rom 15:16	2316
those things which pertain to G	Rom 15:17	2316
by the power of the Spirit of G	Rom 15:19	2316
me in your prayers to G for me	Rom 15:30	2316
you with joy by the will of G	Rom 15:32	2316
Now the G of peace be with you	Rom 15:33	2316
the G of peace shall bruise Satan	Rom 16:20	2316
commandment of the everlasting G	Rom 16:26	2316
To G only wise, be glory through	Rom 16:27	2316
Christ through the will of G,	1Cor 1:1	2316
Unto the church of G which is at	1Cor 1:2	2316
from G our Father, and from the	1Cor 1:3	2316
I thank my G always on your	1Cor 1:4	2316
for the grace of G which is given	1Cor 1:4	2316
G is faithful, by whom ye were	1Cor 1:9	2316
I thank G that I baptized none of	1Cor 1:14	2316
are saved it is the power of G	1Cor 1:18	2316
hath not G made foolish the	1Cor 1:20	2316
that in the wisdom of G	1Cor 1:21	2316
the world by wisdom knew not G	1Cor 1:21	2316
it pleased G by the foolishness	1Cor 1:21	2316
power of G, and the wisdom of G	1Cor 1:24	2316
of G is wiser than men	1Cor 1:25	2316
the weakness of G is stronger	1Cor 1:25	2316
But G hath chosen the foolish	1Cor 1:27	2316
G hath chosen the weak things of	1Cor 1:27	2316
hath G chosen, yea, and things	1Cor 1:28	2316
who of G is made unto us wisdom,	1Cor 1:30	2316
unto you the testimony of G	1Cor 2:1	2316
of men, but in the power of G	1Cor 2:5	2316
the wisdom of G in a mystery	1Cor 2:7	2316
which G ordained before the world	1Cor 2:7	2316
the things which G hath prepared	1Cor 2:9	2316
But G hath revealed them unto us	1Cor 2:10	2316
things, yea, the deep things of G	1Cor 2:10	2316
so the things of G knoweth no man	1Cor 2:11	2316
but the Spirit of G	1Cor 2:11	2316
but the spirit which is of G	1Cor 2:12	2316
that are freely given to us of G	1Cor 2:12	2316
not the things of the Spirit of G	1Cor 2:14	2316
but G gave the increase	1Cor 3:6	2316
but G that giveth the increase	1Cor 3:7	2316
we are labourers together with G	1Cor 3:9	2316
grace of G which is given unto me	1Cor 3:10	2316
not that ye are the temple of G	1Cor 3:16	2316
the Spirit of G dwelleth in you	1Cor 3:16	2316
If any man defile the temple of G	1Cor 3:17	2316
him shall G destroy	1Cor 3:17	2316
for the temple of G is holy	1Cor 3:17	2316
this world is foolishness with G	1Cor 3:19	2316
and stewards of the mysteries of G	1Cor 4:1	2316
shall every man have praise of G	1Cor 4:5	2316
I would to G ye did reign, that	1Cor 4:8	
For I think that G hath set forth	1Cor 4:9	2316
the kingdom of G is not in word	1Cor 4:20	2316
them that are without G judgeth	1Cor 5:13	2316
not inherit the kingdom of G	1Cor 6:9	2316
shall inherit the kingdom of G	1Cor 6:10	2316
Jesus, and by the Spirit of our G	1Cor 6:11	2316
but G shall destroy both it and	1Cor 6:13	2316
G hath both raised up the Lord,	1Cor 6:14	2316
members of an harlot? G forbid	1Cor 6:15	3361,1096
is in you, which ye have of G	1Cor 6:19	2316
therefore glorify G in your body	1Cor 6:20	2316
man hath his proper gift of G	1Cor 7:7	2316
but G hath called us to peace	1Cor 7:15	2316
But as G hath distributed to	1Cor 7:17	2316
keeping of the commandments of G	1Cor 7:19	2316
is called, therein abide with G	1Cor 7:24	2316
also that I have the Spirit of G	1Cor 7:40	2316
But if any man love G, the same	1Cor 8:3	2316
there is none other G but one	1Cor 8:4	2316
But to us there is but one G	1Cor 8:6	2316
But meat commendeth us not to G	1Cor 8:8	2316
Doth G take care for oxen	1Cor 9:9	2316
law, (being not without law to G	1Cor 9:21	2316
of them G was not well pleased	1Cor 10:5	2316
but G is faithful, who will not	1Cor 10:13	2316
sacrifice to devils, and not to G	1Cor 10:20	2316
ye do, do all to the glory of G	1Cor 10:31	2316
Gentiles, nor to the church of G	1Cor 10:32	2316
and the head of Christ is G	1Cor 11:3	2316
as he is the image and glory of G	1Cor 11:7	2316
but all things of G	1Cor 11:12	2316
a woman pray unto G uncovered	1Cor 11:13	2316
custom, neither the churches of G	1Cor 11:16	2316
or despise ye the church of G	1Cor 11:22	2316
of G calleth Jesus accursed	1Cor 12:3	2316
but it is the same G which	1Cor 12:6	2316
But now hath G set the members	1Cor 12:18	2316
but G hath tempered the body	1Cor 12:24	2316
G hath set some in the church,	1Cor 12:28	2316
speaketh not unto men, but unto G	1Cor 14:2	2316
I thank my G, I speak with	1Cor 14:18	2316
on his face he will worship G	1Cor 14:25	2316
report that G is in you of a	1Cor 14:25	2316
let him speak to himself, and to G	1Cor 14:28	2316
For G is not the author of	1Cor 14:33	2316
came the word of G out from you	1Cor 14:36	2316
I persecuted the church of G	1Cor 15:9	2316
by the grace of G I am what I am	1Cor 15:10	2316
but the grace of G which was with	1Cor 15:10	2316
we are found false witnesses of G	1Cor 15:15	2316
of G that he raised up Christ	1Cor 15:15	2316
delivered up the kingdom to G	1Cor 15:24	2316
him, that G may be all in all	1Cor 15:28	2316
some have not the knowledge of G	1Cor 15:34	2316
But G giveth it a body as it hath	1Cor 15:38	2316
cannot inherit the kingdom of G	1Cor 15:50	2316
But thanks be to G, which giveth	1Cor 15:57	2316
as G hath prospered him, that	1Cor 16:2	
of Jesus Christ by the will of G	2Cor 1:1	2316
unto the church of G which is at	2Cor 1:1	2316
to you and peace from G our Father	2Cor 1:2	2316
Blessed be G, even the Father of	2Cor 1:3	2316
mercies, and the G of all comfort	2Cor 1:3	2316
we ourselves are comforted of G	2Cor 1:4	2316
but in G which raiseth the dead	2Cor 1:9	2316
wisdom, but by the grace of G	2Cor 1:12	2316
But as G is true, our word toward	2Cor 1:18	2316
For the Son of G, Jesus Christ,	2Cor 1:19	2316
the promises of G in him are yea	2Cor 1:20	2316
Amen, unto the glory of G by us	2Cor 1:20	2316
Christ, and hath anointed us, is G	2Cor 1:21	2316
Moreover I call G for a record	2Cor 1:23	2316
Now thanks be unto G, which	2Cor 2:14	2316
For we are unto G a sweet savour	2Cor 2:15	2316
many, which corrupt the word of G	2Cor 2:17	2316
but as of sincerity, but as of G	2Cor 2:17	2316
in the sight of G speak we in	2Cor 2:17	2316
with the Spirit of the living G	2Cor 3:3	2316
but our sufficiency is of G	2Cor 3:5	2316
the word of G deceitfully	2Cor 4:2	2316
conscience in the sight of G	2Cor 4:2	2316
of Christ, who is the image of G	2Cor 4:4	2316
For G, who commanded the light to	2Cor 4:6	2316
of G in the face of Jesus Christ	2Cor 4:6	2316
of the power may be of G, and not	2Cor 4:7	2316
of many redound to the glory of G	2Cor 4:15	2316
we have a building of G, an	2Cor 5:1	2316
us for the selfsame thing is G	2Cor 5:5	2316
but we are made manifest unto G	2Cor 5:11	2316
be beside ourselves, it is to G	2Cor 5:13	2316
And all things are of G, who hath	2Cor 5:18	2316
that G was in Christ, reconciling	2Cor 5:19	2316
as though G did beseech you by us	2Cor 5:20	2316
stead, be ye reconciled to G	2Cor 5:20	2316
the righteousness of G in him	2Cor 5:21	2316
not the grace of G in vain	2Cor 6:1	2316
ourselves as the ministers of G	2Cor 6:4	2316
word of truth, by the power of G	2Cor 6:7	2316
hath the temple of G with idols	2Cor 6:16	2316
ye are the temple of the living G	2Cor 6:16	2316
as G hath said, I will dwell in	2Cor 6:16	2316
and I will be their G, and they	2Cor 6:16	2316
holiness in the fear of G	2Cor 7:1	2316
Nevertheless G, that comforteth	2Cor 7:6	2316
sight of G might appear unto you	2Cor 7:12	2316
of G bestowed on the churches of	2Cor 8:1	2316
Lord, and unto us by the will of G	2Cor 8:5	2316
But thanks be to G, which put the	2Cor 8:16	2316
for G loveth a cheerful giver	2Cor 9:7	2316
G is able to make all grace	2Cor 9:8	2316
through us thanksgiving to G	2Cor 9:11	2316
also by many thanksgivings unto G	2Cor 9:12	2316
G for your professed subjection	2Cor 9:13	2316
the exceeding grace of G in you	2Cor 9:14	2316
Thanks be unto G for his	2Cor 9:15	2316
but mighty through G to the	2Cor 10:4	2316
itself against the knowledge of G	2Cor 10:5	2316
which G hath distributed to us	2Cor 10:13	2316
Would to G ye could bear with me	2Cor 11:1	
to you the gospel of G freely	2Cor 11:7	2316
I love you not? G knoweth	2Cor 11:11	2316
The G and Father of our Lord Jesus	2Cor 11:31	2316
body, I cannot tell: G knoweth	2Cor 12:2	2316
I cannot tell: G knoweth	2Cor 12:3	2316
we speak before G in Christ	2Cor 12:19	2316
my G will humble me among you, and	2Cor 12:21	2316
yet he liveth by the power of G	2Cor 13:4	2316
him by the power of G toward you	2Cor 13:4	2316

Now I pray to *G* that ye do no ... 2Cor 13:7 *2316*
the *G* of love and peace shall be ... 2Cor 13:11 *2316*
Jesus Christ, and the love of *G* ... 2Cor 13:14 *2316*
G the Father, who raised him from ... Gal 1:1 *2316*
to you and peace from *G* the Father ... Gal 1:3 *2316*
world, according to the will of *G* ... Gal 1:4 *2316*
For do I now persuade men, or *G* ... Gal 1:10 *2316*
I persecuted the church of *G* ... Gal 1:13 *2316*
But when it pleased *G*, who ... Gal 1:15 *2316*
write unto you, behold, before *G* ... Gal 1:20 *2316*
And they glorified *G* in me ... Gal 1:24 *2316*
G accepteth no man's person ... Gal 2:6 *2316*
minister of sin? *G* forbid ... Gal 2:17 *3361,1096*
the law, that I might live unto *G* ... Gal 2:19 *2316*
live by the faith of the Son of *G* ... Gal 2:20 *2316*
I do not frustrate the grace of *G* ... Gal 2:21 *2316*
Even as Abraham believed *G* ... Gal 3:6 *2316*
foreseeing that *G* would justify ... Gal 3:8 *2316*
by the law in the sight of *G* ... Gal 3:11 *2316*
confirmed before of *G* in Christ ... Gal 3:17 *2316*
but *G* gave it to Abraham by ... Gal 3:18 *2316*
a mediator of one, but *G* is one ... Gal 3:20 *2316*
then against the promises of *G* ... Gal 3:21 *2316*
G forbid for if there had ... Gal 3:21 *3361,1096*
of *G* by faith in Christ Jesus ... Gal 3:26 *2316*
G sent forth his Son, made of a ... Gal 4:4 *2316*
G hath sent forth the Spirit of ... Gal 4:6 *2316*
then an heir of *G* through Christ ... Gal 4:7 *2316*
Howbeit then, when ye knew not *G* ... Gal 4:8 *2316*
now, after that ye have known *G* ... Gal 4:9 *2316*
or rather are known of *G* ... Gal 4:9 *2316*
but received me as an angel of *G* ... Gal 4:14 *2316*
not inherit the kingdom of *G* ... Gal 5:21 *2316*
G is not mocked ... Gal 6:7 *2316*
But *G* forbid that I should glory, ... Gal 6:14 *3361,1096*
and mercy, and upon the Israel of *G* ... Gal 6:16 *2316*
of Jesus Christ by the will of *G* ... Eph 1:1 *2316*
from *G* our Father, and from the ... Eph 1:2 *2316*
Blessed be the *G* and Father of our ... Eph 1:3 *2316*
That the *G* of our Lord Jesus ... Eph 1:17 *2316*
But *G*, who is rich in mercy, for ... Eph 2:4 *2316*
it is the gift of *G* ... Eph 2:8 *2316*
which *G* hath before ordained that ... Eph 2:10 *2316*
hope, and without *G* in the world ... Eph 2:12 *112*
unto *G* in one body by the cross ... Eph 2:16 *2316*
saints, and of the household of *G* ... Eph 2:19 *2316*
of *G* through the Spirit ... Eph 2:22 *2316*
dispensation of the grace of *G* ... Eph 3:2 *2316*
to the gift of the grace of *G* ... Eph 3:7 *2316*
of the world hath been hid in *G* ... Eph 3:9 *2316*
church the manifold wisdom of *G* ... Eph 3:10 *2316*
filled with all the fulness of *G* ... Eph 3:19 *2316*
One *G* and Father of all, who is ... Eph 4:6 *2316*
of the knowledge of the Son of *G* ... Eph 4:13 *2316*
alienated from the life of *G* ... Eph 4:18 *2316*
which after *G* is created in ... Eph 4:24 *2316*
grieve not the holy Spirit of *G* ... Eph 4:30 *2316*
even as *G* for Christ's sake hath ... Eph 4:32 *2316*
Be ye therefore followers of *G* ... Eph 5:1 *2316*
and a sacrifice to *G* for a ... Eph 5:2 *2316*
in the kingdom of Christ and of *G* ... Eph 5:5 *2316*
wrath of *G* upon the children of ... Eph 5:6 *2316*
always for all things unto *G* ... Eph 5:20 *2316*
one to another in the fear of *G* ... Eph 5:21 *2316*
the will of *G* from the heart ... Eph 6:6 *2316*
Put on the whole armour of *G* ... Eph 6:11 *2316*
unto you the whole armour of *G* ... Eph 6:13 *2316*
Spirit, which is the word of *G* ... Eph 6:17 *2316*
from *G* the Father and the Lord ... Eph 6:23 *2316*
from *G* our Father, and from the ... Phil 1:2 *2316*
I thank my *G* upon every ... Phil 1:3 *2316*
For *G* is my record, how greatly I ... Phil 1:8 *2316*
unto the glory and praise of *G* ... Phil 1:11 *2316*
to you of salvation, and that of *G* ... Phil 1:28 *2316*
Who, being in the form of *G* ... Phil 2:6 *2316*
it not robbery to be equal with *G* ... Phil 2:6 *2316*
Wherefore *G* also hath highly ... Phil 2:9 *2316*
to the glory of *G* the Father ... Phil 2:11 *2316*
For it is *G* which worketh in you ... Phil 2:13 *2316*
and harmless, the sons of *G* ... Phil 2:15 *2316*
but *G* had mercy on him ... Phil 2:27 *2316*
which worship *G* in the spirit ... Phil 3:3 *2316*
which is of *G* by faith ... Phil 3:9 *2316*
high calling of *G* in Christ Jesus ... Phil 3:14 *2316*
G shall reveal even this unto you ... Phil 3:15 *2316*
whose *G* is their belly, and whose ... Phil 3:19 *2316*
requests be made known unto *G* ... Phil 4:6 *2316*
And the peace of *G*, which passeth ... Phil 4:7 *2316*
the *G* of peace shall be with you ... Phil 4:9 *2316*
acceptable, wellpleasing to *G* ... Phil 4:18 *2316*
But my *G* shall supply all your ... Phil 4:19 *2316*
Now unto *G* and our Father be glory ... Phil 4:20 *2316*
of Jesus Christ by the will of *G* ... Col 1:1 *2316*
from *G* our Father and the Lord ... Col 1:2 *2316*
We give thanks to *G* and the Father ... Col 1:3 *2316*
and knew the grace of *G* in truth ... Col 1:6 *2316*
increasing in the knowledge of *G* ... Col 1:10 *2316*
is the image of the invisible *G* ... Col 1:15 *2316*
to the dispensation of *G* which is ... Col 1:25 *2316*
for you, to fulfil the word of *G* ... Col 1:25 *2316*
To whom *G* would make known what ... Col 1:27 *2316*
of the mystery of *G*, and of the ... Col 2:2 *2316*
the faith of the operation of *G* ... Col 2:12 *2316*
increaseth with the increase of *G* ... Col 2:19 *2316*
sitteth on the right hand of *G* ... Col 3:1 *2316*
your life is hid with Christ in *G* ... Col 3:3 *2316*
of *G* cometh on the children of ... Col 3:6 *2316*
on therefore, as the elect of *G* ... Col 3:12 *2316*
let the peace of *G* rule in your ... Col 3:15 *2316*
Lord Jesus, giving thanks to *G* ... Col 3:17 *2316*
in singleness of heart, fearing *G* ... Col 3:22 *2316*
that *G* would open unto us a door ... Col 4:3 *2316*
workers unto the kingdom of *G* ... Col 4:11 *2316*
and complete in all the will of *G* ... Col 4:12 *2316*
which is in *G* the Father and in ... 1Th 1:1 *2316*
from *G* our Father, and the Lord ... 1Th 1:1 *2316*
We give thanks to *G* always for ... 1Th 1:2 *2316*
Jesus Christ, in the sight of *G* ... 1Th 1:3 *2316*
beloved, your election of *G* ... 1Th 1:4 *2316*
how ye turned to *G* from idols to ... 1Th 1:9 *2316*
to serve the living and true *G* ... 1Th 1:9 *2316*
we were bold in our *G* to speak ... 1Th 2:2 *2316*
gospel of *G* with much contention ... 1Th 2:2 *2316*
But as we were allowed of *G* to be ... 1Th 2:4 *2316*
not as pleasing men, but *G* ... 1Th 2:4 *2316*
cloke of covetousness; *G* is witness ... 1Th 2:5 *2316*
you, not the gospel of *G* only ... 1Th 2:8 *2316*
preached unto you the gospel of *G* ... 1Th 2:9 *2316*
G also, how holily and justly and ... 1Th 2:10 *2316*
That ye would walk worthy of *G* ... 1Th 2:12 *2316*
also thank we *G* without ceasing ... 1Th 2:13 *2316*
word of *G* which ye heard of us ... 1Th 2:13 *2316*
as it is in truth, the word of *G* ... 1Th 2:13 *2316*
followers of the churches of *G* ... 1Th 2:14 *2316*
and they please not *G*, and are ... 1Th 2:15 *2316*
our brother, and minister of *G* ... 1Th 3:2 *2316*
can we render to *G* again for you ... 1Th 3:9 *2316*
joy for your sakes before our *G* ... 1Th 3:9 *2316*
Now *G* himself and our Father, and ... 1Th 3:11 *2316*
unblameable in holiness before *G* ... 1Th 3:13 *2316*
ye ought to walk and to please *G* ... 1Th 4:1 *2316*
For this is the will of *G* ... 1Th 4:3 *2316*
as the Gentiles which know not *G* ... 1Th 4:5 *2316*
For *G* hath not called us unto ... 1Th 4:7 *2316*
despiseth not man, but *G* ... 1Th 4:8 *2316*
taught of *G* to love one another ... 1Th 4:9 *2312*
in Jesus will *G* bring with him ... 1Th 4:14 *2316*
archangel, and with the trump of *G* ... 1Th 4:16 *2316*
For *G* hath not appointed us to ... 1Th 5:9 *2316*
for this is the will of *G* in ... 1Th 5:18 *2316*
the very *G* of peace sanctify you ... 1Th 5:23 *2316*
I pray *G* your whole spirit and ... 1Th 5:23
the Thessalonians in *G* our Father ... 2Th 1:1 *2316*
from *G* our Father and the Lord ... 2Th 1:2 *2316*
bound to thank *G* always for you ... 2Th 1:3 *2316*
churches of *G* for your patience ... 2Th 1:4 *2316*
of the righteous judgment of *G* ... 2Th 1:5 *2316*
worthy of the kingdom of *G* ... 2Th 1:5 *2316*
G to recompense tribulation to ... 2Th 1:6 *2316*
vengeance on them that know not *G* ... 2Th 1:8 *2316*
that our *G* would count you worthy ... 2Th 1:11 *2316*
according to the grace of our *G* ... 2Th 1:12 *2316*
above all that is called *G* ... 2Th 2:4 *2316*
as *G* sitteth in the temple of *G* ... 2Th 2:4 *2316*
shewing himself that he is *G* ... 2Th 2:4 *2316*
for this cause *G* shall send them ... 2Th 2:11 *2316*
to give thanks alway to *G* for you ... 2Th 2:13 *2316*
because *G* hath from the beginning ... 2Th 2:13 *2316*
Lord Jesus Christ himself, and *G* ... 2Th 2:16 *2316*
your hearts into the love of *G* ... 2Th 3:5 *2316*
the commandment of *G* our Saviour ... 1Ti 1:1 *2316*
from *G* our Father and Jesus Christ ... 1Ti 1:2 *2316*
glorious gospel of the blessed *G* ... 1Ti 1:11 *2316*
invisible, the only wise *G* ... 1Ti 1:17 *2316*
in the sight of *G* our Saviour ... 1Ti 2:3 *2316*
For there is one *G* ... 1Ti 2:5 *2316*
and one mediator between *G* ... 1Ti 2:5 *2316*
he take care of the church of *G* ... 1Ti 3:5 *2316*
behave thyself in the house of *G* ... 1Ti 3:15 *2316*
is the church of the living *G* ... 1Ti 3:15 *2316*
G was manifest in the flesh, ... 1Ti 3:16 *2316*
which *G* hath created to be ... 1Ti 4:3 *2316*
For every creature of *G* is good ... 1Ti 4:4 *2316*
it is sanctified by the word of *G* ... 1Ti 4:5 *2316*
because we trust in the living *G* ... 1Ti 4:10 *2316*
is good and acceptable before *G* ... 1Ti 5:4 *2316*
and desolate, trusteth in *G* ... 1Ti 5:5 *2316*
I charge thee before *G*, and the ... 1Ti 5:21 *2316*
of all honour, that the name of *G* ... 1Ti 6:1 *2316*
But thou, O man of *G*, flee these ... 1Ti 6:11 *2316*
thee charge in the sight of *G* ... 1Ti 6:13 *2316*
riches, but in the living *G* ... 1Ti 6:17 *2316*
of Jesus Christ by the will of *G* ... 2Ti 1:1 *2316*
from *G* the Father and Christ Jesus ... 2Ti 1:2 *2316*
I thank *G*, whom I serve from my ... 2Ti 1:3 *2316*
that thou stir up the gift of *G* ... 2Ti 1:6 *2316*
For *G* hath not given us the ... 2Ti 1:7 *2316*
according to the power of *G* ... 2Ti 1:8 *2316*
but the word of *G* is not bound ... 2Ti 2:9 *2316*
to shew thyself approved unto *G* ... 2Ti 2:15 *2316*
the foundation of *G* standeth sure ... 2Ti 2:19 *2316*
if *G* peradventure will give them ... 2Ti 2:25 *2316*
pleasures more than lovers of *G* ... 2Ti 3:4 *5377*
is given by inspiration of *G* ... 2Ti 3:16 *2315*
That the man of *G* may be perfect ... 2Ti 3:17 *2316*
I charge thee therefore before *G* ... 2Ti 4:1 *2316*
I pray *G* that it may not be laid ... 2Ti 4:16
Paul, a servant of *G*, and an ... Titus 1:1 *2316*
In hope of eternal life, which *G* ... Titus 1:2 *2316*
the commandment of *G* our Saviour ... Titus 1:3 *2316*
from *G* the Father and the Lord ... Titus 1:4 *2316*
be blameless, as the steward of *G* ... Titus 1:7 *2316*
They profess that they know *G* ... Titus 1:16 *2316*
that the word of *G* be not ... Titus 2:5 *2316*
of *G* our Saviour in all things ... Titus 2:10 *2316*
For the grace of *G* that bringeth ... Titus 2:11 *2316*
glorious appearing of the great *G* ... Titus 2:13 *2316*
love of *G* our Saviour toward man ... Titus 3:4 *2316*
they which have believed in *G* ... Titus 3:8 *2316*
from *G* our Father and the Lord ... Philem 3 *2316*
I thank my *G*, making mention of ... Philem 4 *2316*
G, who at sundry times and in ... Heb 1:1 *2316*
all the angels of *G* worship him ... Heb 1:6 *2316*
the Son he saith, Thy throne, O *G* ... Heb 1:8 *2316*
therefore *G*, even thy *G* ... Heb 1:9 *2316*
G also bearing them witness, both ... Heb 2:4 *2316*
that he by the grace of *G* should ... Heb 2:9 *2316*
children which *G* hath given me ... Heb 2:13 *2316*
priest in things pertaining to *G* ... Heb 2:17 *2316*
but he that built all things is *G* ... Heb 3:4 *2316*
in departing from the living *G* ... Heb 3:12 *2316*
G did rest the seventh day from ... Heb 4:4 *2316*
a rest to the people of *G* ... Heb 4:9 *2316*
his own works, as *G* did from his ... Heb 4:10 *2316*
For the word of *G* is quick ... Heb 4:12 *2316*
the heavens, Jesus the Son of *G* ... Heb 4:14 *2316*
for men in things pertaining to *G* ... Heb 5:1 *2316*
but he that is called of *G* ... Heb 5:4 *2316*
Called of *G* an high priest after ... Heb 5:10 *2316*
principles of the oracles of *G* ... Heb 5:12 *2316*
dead works, and of faith toward *G* ... Heb 6:1 *2316*
And this will we do, if *G* permit ... Heb 6:3 *2316*
And have tasted the good word of *G* ... Heb 6:5 *2316*
to themselves the Son of *G* afresh ... Heb 6:6 *2316*
receiveth blessing from *G* ... Heb 6:7 *2316*
For *G* is not unrighteous to ... Heb 6:10 *2316*
For when *G* made promise to ... Heb 6:13 *2316*
Wherein *G*, willing more ... Heb 6:17 *2316*
it was impossible for *G* to lie ... Heb 6:18 *2316*
Salem, priest of the most high *G* ... Heb 7:1 *2316*
but made like unto the Son of *G* ... Heb 7:3 *2316*
by the which we draw nigh unto *G* ... Heb 7:19 *2316*
uttermost that come unto *G* by him ... Heb 7:25 *2316*
as Moses was admonished of *G* when ... Heb 8:5 *5537*
and I will be to them a *G*, and they ... Heb 8:10 *2316*
accomplishing the service of *G* ... Heb 9:6
offered himself without spot to *G* ... Heb 9:14 *2316*
dead works to serve the living *G* ... Heb 9:14 *2316*
which *G* hath enjoined unto you ... Heb 9:20 *2316*
in the presence of *G* for us ... Heb 9:24 *2316*
of me,) to do thy will, O *G* ... Heb 10:7 *2316*
Lo, I come to do thy will, O *G* ... Heb 10:9 *2316*
sat down on the right hand of *G* ... Heb 10:12 *2316*
high priest over the house of *G* ... Heb 10:21 *2316*
trodden under foot the Son of *G* ... Heb 10:29 *2316*
into the hands of the living *G* ... Heb 10:31 *2316*
after ye have done the will of *G* ... Heb 10:36 *2316*
were framed by the word of *G* ... Heb 11:3 *2316*
By faith Abel offered unto *G* a ... Heb 11:4 *2316*
G testifying of his gifts ... Heb 11:4 *2316*
because *G* had translated him ... Heb 11:5 *2316*
this testimony, that he pleased *G* ... Heb 11:5 *2316*
for he that cometh to *G* must ... Heb 11:6 *2316*
being warned of *G* of things not ... Heb 11:7
whose builder and maker is *G* ... Heb 11:10 *2316*
wherefore *G* is not ashamed to be ... Heb 11:16 *2316*
not ashamed to be called their *G* ... Heb 11:16 *2316*
Accounting that *G* was able to ... Heb 11:19 *2316*
affliction with the people of *G* ... Heb 11:25 *2316*
G having provided some better ... Heb 11:40 *2316*
the right hand of the throne of *G* ... Heb 12:2 *2316*
G dealeth with you as with sons ... Heb 12:7 *2316*
any man fail of the grace of *G* ... Heb 12:15 *2316*
and unto the city of the living *G* ... Heb 12:22 *2316*
to *G* the Judge of all, and to the ... Heb 12:23 *2316*
whereby we may serve *G* acceptably ... Heb 12:28 *2316*
For our *G* is a consuming fire ... Heb 12:29 *2316*
and adulterers *G* will judge ... Heb 13:4 *2316*
spoken unto you the word of *G* ... Heb 13:7 *2316*
of praise to *G* continually ... Heb 13:15 *2316*
such sacrifices *G* is well pleased ... Heb 13:16 *2316*
Now the *G* of peace, that brought ... Heb 13:20 *2316*
James, a servant of *G* and of the ... Jas 1:1 *2316*
you lack wisdom, let him ask of *G* ... Jas 1:5 *2316*
he is tempted, I am tempted of *G* ... Jas 1:13 *2316*
for *G* cannot be tempted with evil ... Jas 1:13 *2316*
not the righteousness of *G* ... Jas 1:20 *2316*
religion and undefiled before *G* ... Jas 1:27 *2316*
Hath not *G* chosen the poor of ... Jas 2:5 *2316*
believest that there is one *G* ... Jas 2:19 *2316*
which saith, Abraham believed *G* ... Jas 2:23 *2316*
and he was called the Friend of *G* ... Jas 2:23 *2316*
Therewith bless we *G*, even the ... Jas 3:9 *2316*
made after the similitude of *G* ... Jas 3:9 *2316*
of the world is enmity with *G* ... Jas 4:4 *2316*
of the world is the enemy of *G* ... Jas 4:4 *2316*
G resisteth the proud, but giveth ... Jas 4:6 *2316*
Submit yourselves therefore to *G* ... Jas 4:7 *2316*
Draw nigh to *G*, and he will draw ... Jas 4:8 *2316*
the foreknowledge of *G* the Father ... 1Pet 1:2 *2316*
Blessed be the *G* and Father of our ... 1Pet 1:3 *2316*
of *G* through faith unto salvation ... 1Pet 1:5 *2316*
Who by him do believe in *G* ... 1Pet 1:21 *2316*
your faith and hope might be in *G* ... 1Pet 1:21 *2316*
incorruptible, by the word of *G* ... 1Pet 1:23 *2316*
indeed of men, but chosen of *G* ... 1Pet 2:4 *2316*
acceptable to *G* by Jesus Christ ... 1Pet 2:5 *2316*
but are now the people of *G* ... 1Pet 2:10 *2316*
behold, glorify *G* in the day of ... 1Pet 2:12 *2316*
For so is the will of *G*, that ... 1Pet 2:15 *2316*
but as the servants of *G* ... 1Pet 2:16 *2316*
Fear *G*. Honour the king. ... 1Pet 2:17 *2316*
conscience toward *G* endure grief ... 1Pet 2:19 *2316*
this is acceptable with *G* ... 1Pet 2:20 *2316*

in the sight of *G* of great price 1Pet 3:4 *2316*
holy women also, who trusted in *G* 1Pet 3:5 *2316*
the Lord *G* in your hearts 1Pet 3:15 *2316*
is better, if the will of *G* be so 1Pet 3:17 *2316*
that he might bring us to *G* 1Pet 3:18 *2316*
of *G* waited in the days of Noah 1Pet 3:20 *2316*
of a good conscience toward *G* 1Pet 3:21 *2316*
and is on the right hand of *G* 1Pet 3:22 *2316*
of men, but to the will of *G* 1Pet 4:2 *2316*
live according to *G* in the spirit 1Pet 4:6 *2316*
of the manifold grace of *G* 1Pet 4:10 *2316*
let him speak as the oracles of *G* 1Pet 4:11 *2316*
as of the ability which *G* giveth 1Pet 4:11 *2316*
that *G* in all things may be 1Pet 4:11 *2316*
of glory and of *G* resteth upon you 1Pet 4:14 *2316*
let him glorify *G* on this behalf 1Pet 4:16 *2316*
must begin at the house of *G* 1Pet 4:17 *2316*
that obey not the gospel of *G* 1Pet 4:17 *2316*
of *G* commit the keeping of their 1Pet 4:19 *2316*
Feed the flock of *G* which is 1Pet 5:2 *2316*
for *G* resisteth the proud, and 1Pet 5:5 *2316*
under the mighty hand of *G* 1Pet 5:6 *2316*
But the *G* of all grace, who hath 1Pet 5:10 *2316*
true grace of *G* wherein ye stand 1Pet 5:12 *2316*
us through the righteousness of *G* 2Pet 1:1 *2316*
you through the knowledge of *G* 2Pet 1:2 *2316*
received from *G* the Father honour 2Pet 1:17 *2316*
but holy men of *G* spake as they 2Pet 1:21 *2316*
For if *G* spared not the angels 2Pet 2:4 *2316*
that by the word of *G* the heavens 2Pet 3:5 *2316*
unto the coming of the day of *G* 2Pet 3:12 *2316*
that *G* is light, and in him is no 1Jn 1:5 *2316*
verily is the love of *G* perfected 1Jn 2:5 *2316*
the word of *G* abideth in you, and 1Jn 2:14 *2316*
the will of *G* abideth for ever 1Jn 2:17 *2316*
we should be called the sons of *G* 1Jn 3:1 *2316*
Beloved, now are we the sons of *G* 1Jn 3:2 *2316*
the Son of *G* was manifested 1Jn 3:8 *2316*
is born of *G* doth not commit sin 1Jn 3:9 *2316*
sin, because he is born of *G* 1Jn 3:9 *2316*
the children of *G* are manifest 1Jn 3:10 *2316*
not righteousness is not of *G* 1Jn 3:10 *2316*
Hereby perceive we the love of *G* 1Jn 3:16 *2316*
how dwelleth the love of *G* in him 1Jn 3:17 *2316*
G is greater than our heart, and 1Jn 3:20 *2316*
then have we confidence toward *G* 1Jn 3:21 *2316*
the spirits whether they are of *G* 1Jn 4:1 *2316*
Hereby know ye the Spirit of *G* 1Jn 4:2 *2316*
is come in the flesh is of *G* 1Jn 4:2 *2316*
is come in the flesh is not of *G* 1Jn 4:3 *2316*
Ye are of *G*, little children, and 1Jn 4:4 *2316*
We are of *G* 1Jn 4:6 *2316*
he that knoweth *G* heareth us 1Jn 4:6 *2316*
that is not of *G* heareth not us 1Jn 4:6 *2316*
for love is of *G* 1Jn 4:7 *2316*
is born of *G*, and knoweth *G* 1Jn 4:7 *2316*
He that loveth not knoweth not *G* 1Jn 4:8 *2316*
for *G* is love 1Jn 4:8 *2316*
the love of *G* toward us, because 1Jn 4:9 *2316*
because that *G* sent his only 1Jn 4:9 *2316*
is love, not that we loved *G* 1Jn 4:10 *2316*
if *G* so loved us, we ought also 1Jn 4:11 *2316*
No man hath seen *G* at any time 1Jn 4:12 *2316*
G dwelleth in us, and his love is 1Jn 4:12 *2316*
that Jesus is the Son of *G* 1Jn 4:15 *2316*
G dwelleth in him, and he in *G* 1Jn 4:15 *2316*
the love that *G* hath to us 1Jn 4:16 *2316*
G is love 1Jn 4:16 *2316*
love dwelleth in *G*, and *G* in him 1Jn 4:16 *2316*
If a man say, I love *G*, and hateth 1Jn 4:20 *2316*
how can he love *G* whom he hath 1Jn 4:20 *2316*
That he who loveth *G* love his 1Jn 4:21 *2316*
Jesus is the Christ is born of *G* 1Jn 5:1 *2316*
children of *G*, when we love *G* 1Jn 5:2 *2316*
For this is the love of *G* 1Jn 5:3 *2316*
is born of *G* overcometh the world 1Jn 5:4 *2316*
that Jesus is the Son of *G* 1Jn 5:5 *2316*
men, the witness of *G* is greater 1Jn 5:9 *2316*
for this is the witness of *G* 1Jn 5:9 *2316*
of *G* hath the witness in himself 1Jn 5:10 *2316*
not *G* hath made him a liar 1Jn 5:10 *2316*
the record that *G* gave of his Son 1Jn 5:10 *2316*
that *G* hath given to us eternal 1Jn 5:11 *2316*
not the Son of *G* hath not life 1Jn 5:12 *2316*
on the name of the Son of *G* 1Jn 5:13 *2316*
on the name of the Son of *G* 1Jn 5:13 *2316*
is born of *G* sinneth not 1Jn 5:18 *2316*
is begotten of *G* keepeth himself 1Jn 5:18 *2316*
And we know that we are of *G* 1Jn 5:19 *2316*
we know that the Son of *G* is come 1Jn 5:20 *2316*
This is the true *G*, and eternal 1Jn 5:20 *2316*
from *G* the Father, and from the 2Jn 3 *2316*
doctrine of Christ, hath not *G* 2Jn 9 *2316*
house, neither bid him *G* speed 2Jn 10
For he that biddeth him *G* speed 2Jn 11
He that doeth good is of *G* 3Jn 11 *2316*
that doeth evil hath not seen *G* 3Jn 11 *2316*
are sanctified by *G* the Father Jude 1 *2316*
of our *G* into lasciviousness Jude 4 *2316*
and denying the only Lord *G* Jude 4 *2316*
Keep yourselves in the love of *G* Jude 21 *2316*
To the only wise *G* our Saviour Jude 25 *2316*
which *G* gave unto him, to shew Rev 1:1 *2316*
Who bare record of the word of *G* Rev 1:2 *2316*
made us kings and priests unto *G* Rev 1:6 *2316*
called Patmos, for the word of *G* Rev 1:9 *2316*
in the midst of the paradise of *G* Rev 2:7 *2316*
These things saith the Son of *G* Rev 2:18 *2316*
that hath the seven Spirits of *G* Rev 3:1 *2316*
found thy works perfect before *G* Rev 3:2 *2316*
a pillar in the temple of my *G* Rev 3:12 *2316*
write upon him the name of my *G* Rev 3:12 *2316*
and the name of the city of my *G* Rev 3:12 *2316*
down out of heaven from my *G* Rev 3:12 *2316*
beginning of the creation of *G* Rev 3:14 *2316*
which are the seven Spirits of *G* Rev 4:5 *2316*
Lord *G* Almighty, which was, and is Rev 4:8 *2316*
G sent forth into all the earth Rev 5:6 *2316*
hast redeemed us to *G* by thy Rev 5:9 *2316*
And hast made us unto our *G* kings Rev 5:10 *2316*
that were slain for the word of *G* Rev 6:9 *2316*
having the seal of the living *G* Rev 7:2 *2316*
of our *G* in their foreheads Rev 7:3 *2316*
Salvation to our *G* which sitteth Rev 7:10 *2316*
on their faces, and worshipped *G* Rev 7:11 *2316*
and might, be unto our *G* for ever Rev 7:12 *2316*
are they before the throne of *G* Rev 7:15 *2316*
G shall wipe away all tears from Rev 7:17 *2316*
seven angels which stood before *G* Rev 8:2 *2316*
ascended up before *G* out of the Rev 8:4 *2316*
the seal of *G* in their foreheads Rev 9:4 *2316*
golden altar which is before *G* Rev 9:13 *2316*
the mystery of *G* should be Rev 10:7 *2316*
Rise, and measure the temple of *G* Rev 11:1 *2316*
before the *G* of the earth Rev 11:4 *2316*
of life from *G* entered into them Rev 11:11 *2316*
and gave glory to the *G* of heaven Rev 11:13 *2316*
which sat before *G* on their seats Rev 11:16 *2316*
upon their faces, and worshipped *G* Rev 11:16 *2316*
O Lord *G* Almighty, which art, and Rev 11:17 *2316*
the temple of *G* was opened in Rev 11:19 *2316*
and her child was caught up unto *G* Rev 12:5 *2316*
she hath a place prepared of *G* Rev 12:6 *2316*
strength, and the kingdom of our *G* Rev 12:10 *2316*
accused them before our *G* day Rev 12:10 *2316*
which keep the commandments of *G* Rev 12:17 *2316*
his mouth in blasphemy against *G* Rev 13:6 *2316*
men, being the firstfruits unto *G* Rev 14:4 *2316*
fault before the throne of *G* Rev 14:5 *2316*
Saying with a loud voice, Fear *G* Rev 14:7 *2316*
of the wine of the wrath of *G* Rev 14:10 *2316*
that keep the commandments of *G* Rev 14:12 *2316*
great winepress of the wrath of *G* Rev 14:19 *2316*
them is filled up the wrath of *G* Rev 15:1 *2316*
of glass, having the harps of *G* Rev 15:2 *2316*
song of Moses the servant of *G* Rev 15:3 *2316*
are thy works, Lord *G* Almighty Rev 15:3 *2316*
vials full of the wrath of *G* Rev 15:7 *2316*
with smoke from the glory of *G* Rev 15:8 *2316*
of the wrath of *G* upon the earth Rev 16:1 *2316*
Even so, Lord *G* Almighty, true and Rev 16:7 *2316*
heat, and blasphemed the name of *G* Rev 16:9 *2316*
blasphemed the *G* of heaven Rev 16:11 *2316*
of that great day of *G* Almighty Rev 16:14 *2316*
came in remembrance before *G* Rev 16:19 *2316*
men blasphemed *G* because of the Rev 16:21 *2316*
For *G* hath put in their hearts to Rev 17:17 *2316*
the words of *G* shall be fulfilled Rev 17:17 *2316*
G hath remembered her iniquities Rev 18:5 *2316*
is the Lord *G* who judgeth her Rev 18:8 *2316*
for *G* hath avenged you on her Rev 18:20 *2316*
and power, unto the Lord our *G* Rev 19:1 *2316*
worshipped *G* that sat on the Rev 19:4 *2316*
the throne, saying, Praise our *G* Rev 19:5 *2316*
for the Lord *G* omnipotent Rev 19:6 *2316*
These are the true sayings of *G* Rev 19:9 *2316*
worship *G* Rev 19:10 *2316*
his name is called The Word of *G* Rev 19:13 *2316*
fierceness and wrath of Almighty *G* Rev 19:15 *2316*
unto the supper of the great *G* Rev 19:17 *2316*
of Jesus, and for the word of *G* Rev 20:4 *2316*
but they shall be priests of *G* Rev 20:6 *2316*
came down from *G* out of heaven Rev 20:9 *2316*
small and great, stand before *G* Rev 20:12 *2316*
coming down from *G* out of heaven Rev 21:2 *2316*
the tabernacle of *G* is with men Rev 21:3 *2316*
G himself shall be with them Rev 21:3 *2316*
and be their *G* Rev 21:3 *2316*
G shall wipe away all tears from Rev 21:4 *2316*
and I will be his *G*, and he shall Rev 21:7 *2316*
descending out of heaven from *G* Rev 21:10 *2316*
Having the glory of *G* Rev 21:11 *2316*
for the Lord *G* Almighty and the Rev 21:22 *2316*
for the glory of *G* did lighten it Rev 21:23 *2316*
proceeding out of the throne of *G* Rev 22:1 *2316*
but the throne of *G* and of the Rev 22:3 *2316*
for the Lord *G* giveth them light Rev 22:5 *2316*
the Lord *G* of the holy prophets Rev 22:6 *2316*
worship *G* Rev 22:9 *2316*
G shall add unto him the plagues Rev 22:18 *2316*
G shall take away his part out of Rev 22:19 *2316*

2. Any deity other than God 1.

I have made thee a *g* to Pharaoh Ex 7:1 430
He that sacrificeth unto any *g* Ex 22:20 430
For thou shalt worship no other *g* Ex 34:14 410
there was no strange *g* with him Deut 32:12 410
am he, and there is no *g* with me Deut 32:39 430
if he be a *g*, let him plead for Judg 6:31 430
and made Baal-berith their *g* Judg 8:33 430
and went into the house of their *g* Judg 9:27 430
hold of the house of the *g* Berith Judg 9:46 410
thy *g* giveth thee to possess Judg 11:24 430
sacrifice unto Dagon their *g* Judg 16:23 430
Our *g* hath delivered Samson our Judg 16:23 430
saw him, they praised their *g* Judg 16:24 430
Our *g* hath delivered into our Judg 16:24 430
sore upon us, and upon Dagon our *g* 1Sa 5:7 430
Chemosh the *g* of the Moabites, and 1Kin 11:33 430
Milcom the *g* of the children of 1Kin 11:33 430
for he is a *g* 1Kin 18:27 430
the *g* of Ekron whether I shall 2Kin 1:2 430
of Baal-zebub the *g* of Ekron 2Kin 1:3 430
of Baal-zebub the *g* of Ekron 2Kin 1:6 430
of Baal-zebub the *g* of Ekron 2Kin 1:16 430
in the house of Nisroch his *g* 2Kin 19:37 430
for no *g* of any nation or kingdom 2Chr 32:15 433
was come into the house of his *g* 2Chr 32:21 430
that hasten after another *g* Ps 16:4
out our hands to a strange *g* Ps 44:20 410
shall no strange *g* be in thee Ps 81:9 410
shalt thou worship any strange *g* Ps 81:9 410
there was no strange *g* among you Is 43:12
Who hath formed a *g*, or molten a Is 44:10 410
yea, he maketh a *g*, and Is 44:15 410
the residue thereof he maketh a *g* Is 44:17 410
for thou art my *g* Is 44:17 410
pray unto a *g* that cannot save Is 45:20 410
and he maketh it a *g* Is 46:6 410
of Shinar to the house of his *g* Dan 1:2 430
into the treasure house of his *g* Dan 1:2 430
might not serve nor worship any *g* Dan 3:28 426
according to the name of my *g* Dan 4:8 426
and magnify himself above every *g* Dan 11:36 410
desire of women, nor regard any *g* Dan 11:37 433
a *g* whom his fathers knew not Dan 11:38 433
strong holds with a strange *g* Dan 11:39 433
and thou shalt know no *g* but me Hos 13:4 430
condemned in the house of their *g* Amos 2:8 430
your images, the star of your *g* Amos 5:26 430
the sin of Samaria, and say, Thy *g* Amos 8:14 430
and cried every man unto his *g* Jonah 1:5 430
every one in the name of his *g* Mic 4:5 430
this his power unto his *g* Hab 1:11 430
the daughter of a strange *g* Mal 2:11 410
and the star of your *g* Remphan Acts 7:43 *2316*
saying, It is the voice of a *g* Acts 12:22 *2316*
minds, and said that he was a *g* Acts 28:6 *2316*
In whom the *g* of this world hath 2Cor 4:4 *2316*

GODDESS {5}

Ashtoreth the *g* of the Zidonians 1Kin 11:5 430
Ashtoreth the *g* of the Zidonians 1Kin 11:33 430
great *g* Diana should be despised Acts 19:27 *2299*
a worshipper of the great *g* Diana Acts 19:35 *2299*
nor yet blasphemers of your *g* Acts 19:37 *2299*

GODHEAD {3} *That which is divine.*

that the G is like unto gold Acts 17:29 *2304*
made, even his eternal power and G Rom 1:20 *2305*
all the fulness of the G bodily Col 2:9 *2320*

GODLINESS {15}

quiet and peaceable life in all *g* 1Ti 2:2 *2150*
professing *g*) with good works 1Ti 2:10 *2317*
great is the mystery of *g* 1Ti 3:16 *2150*
and exercise thyself rather unto *g* 1Ti 4:7 *2150*
but *g* is profitable unto all 1Ti 4:8 *2150*
doctrine which is according to *g* 1Ti 6:3 *2150*
truth, supposing that gain is *g* 1Ti 6:5 *2150*
But *g* with contentment is great 1Ti 6:6 *2150*
and follow after righteousness, *g* 1Ti 6:11 *2150*
Having a form of *g*, but denying 2Ti 3:5 *2150*
of the truth which is after *g* Titus 1:1 *2150*
that pertain unto life and *g* 2Pet 1:3 *2150*
and to patience *g* 2Pet 1:6 *2150*
And to *g* brotherly kindness 2Pet 1:7 *2150*
be in all holy conversation and *g* 2Pet 3:11 *2150*

GODLY {15}

apart him that is *g* for himself Ps 4:3 2623
for the *g* man ceaseth Ps 12:1 2623
this shall every one that is *g* Ps 32:6 2623
That he might seek a *g* seed Mal 2:15 430
g sincerity, not with fleshly 2Cor 1:12 *2316*
were made sorry after a *g* manner 2Cor 7:9 *2596,2316*
For *g* sorrow worketh repentance 2Cor 7:10 *2596,2316*
that ye sorrowed after a *g* sort 2Cor 7:11 *2596,2316*
jealous over you with *g* jealousy 2Cor 11:2 *2316*
rather than *g* edifying which is 1Ti 1:4 *2316*
all that will live *g* in Christ 2Ti 3:12 *2153*
live soberly, righteously, and *g* Titus 2:12 *2153*
with reverence and *g* fear Heb 12:28
deliver the *g* out of temptations 2Pet 2:9 *2152*
on their journey after a *g* sort 3Jn 6 *516,2316*

GOD'S {26} *Refers to God 1.*

for a pillar, shall be *G* house Gen 28:22 430
and he said, Am I in *G* stead Gen 30:2 430
saw them, he said, This is *G* host Gen 32:2 430
G anger was kindled because he Num 22:22 430
for the judgment is *G* Deut 1:17 430
the battle is not yours, but *G* 2Chr 20:15 430
and into an oath, to walk in *G* law Neh 10:29 430
according to thy wish in *G* stead Job 33:6 410
My righteousness is more than *G* Job 35:2 410
I have yet to speak on *G* behalf Job 36:2 433
for it is *G* throne Mt 5:34 *2316*
and unto God the things that are *G* Mt 22:21 *2316*
and to God the things that are *G* Mk 12:17 *2316*
for the kingdom of *G* sake Lk 18:29 *2316*
and unto God the things which be *G* Lk 20:25 *2316*
He that is of God heareth *G* words Jn 8:47 *2316*
said, Revilest thou *G* high priest Acts 23:4 *2316*
thing to the charge of *G* elect Rom 8:33 *2316*
being ignorant of *G* righteousness Rom 10:3 *2316*
for they are *G* ministers, Rom 13:6 *2316*
ye are *G* husbandry, ye are *G* 1Cor 3:9 *2316*

and Christ is *G* ... 1Cor 3:23 *2316*
and in your spirit, which are *G* ... 1Cor 6:20 *2316*
according to the faith of *G* elect ... Titus 1:1 *2316*
as being lords over *G* heritage ... 1Pet 5:3 *2316*

GODS {246} *Refers to God 2.*
be opened, and ye shall be as *g* ... Gen 3:5 430
wherefore hast thou stolen my *g* ... Gen 31:30 430
whomsoever thou findest thy *g* ... Gen 31:32 430
the strange *g* that are among you ... Gen 35:2 430
g which were in their hand ... Gen 35:4 430
against all the *g* of Egypt I will ... Ex 12:12 430
unto thee, O LORD, among the *g* ... Ex 15:11 410
the LORD is greater than all *g* ... Ex 18:11 430
shalt have no other *g* before me ... Ex 20:3 430
not make with me *g* of silver ... Ex 20:23 430
shall ye make unto you *g* of gold ... Ex 20:23 430
Thou shalt not revile the *g* ... Ex 22:28 430
no mention of the name of other *g* ... Ex 23:13 430
shalt not bow down to their *g* ... Ex 23:24 430
with them, nor with their *g* ... Ex 23:32 430
for if thou serve their *g* ... Ex 23:33 430
and said unto him, Up, make us *g* ... Ex 32:1 430
and they said, These be thy *g* ... Ex 32:4 430
and said, These be thy *g*, O ... Ex 32:8 430
For they said unto me, Make us *g* ... Ex 32:23 430
sin, and have made them *g* of gold ... Ex 32:31 430
they go a whoring after their *g* ... Ex 34:15 430
and do sacrifice unto their *g* ... Ex 34:15 430
go a whoring after their *g* ... Ex 34:16 430
sons go a whoring after their *g* ... Ex 34:16 430
Thou shalt make thee no molten *g* ... Ex 34:17 430
nor make to yourselves molten *g* ... Lev 19:4 430
unto the sacrifices of their *g* ... Num 25:2 430
did eat, and bowed down to their *g* ... Num 25:2 430
upon their *g* also the LORD ... Num 33:4 430
And there ye shall serve *g* ... Deut 4:28 430
shalt have none other *g* before me ... Deut 5:7 430
Ye shall not go after other *g* ... Deut 6:14 430
of the *g* of the people which are ... Deut 6:14 430
me, that they may serve other *g* ... Deut 7:4 430
neither shalt thou serve their *g* ... Deut 7:16 430
their *g* shall ye burn with fire ... Deut 7:25 430
thy God, and walk after other *g* ... Deut 8:19 430
For the LORD your God is God of *g* ... Deut 10:17 430
ye turn aside, and serve other *g* ... Deut 11:16 430
you this day, to go after other *g* ... Deut 11:28 430
ye shall possess served their *g* ... Deut 12:2 430
down the graven images of their *g* ... Deut 12:3 430
thou enquire not after their *g* ... Deut 12:30 430
did these nations serve their *g* ... Deut 12:30 430
have they done unto their *g* ... Deut 12:31 430
have burnt in the fire to their *g* ... Deut 12:31 430
saying, Let us go after other *g* ... Deut 13:2 430
Let us go and serve other *g* ... Deut 13:6 430
of the *g* of the people which are ... Deut 13:7 430
Let us go and serve other *g* ... Deut 13:13 430
And hath gone and served other *g* ... Deut 17:3 430
speak in the name of other *g* ... Deut 18:20 430
which they have done unto their *g* ... Deut 20:18 430
to go after other *g* to serve them ... Deut 28:14 430
and there shalt thou serve other *g* ... Deut 28:36 430
and there thou shalt serve other *g* ... Deut 28:64 430
serve the *g* of these nations ... Deut 29:18 430
For they went and served other *g* ... Deut 29:26 430
g whom they knew not, and whom he ... Deut 29:26 430
be drawn away, and worship other *g* ... Deut 30:17 430
go a whoring after the *g* of the ... Deut 31:16 430
that they are turned unto other *g* ... Deut 31:18 430
then will they turn unto other *g* ... Deut 31:20 430
him to jealousy with strange *g* ... Deut 32:16
to *g* whom they knew not ... Deut 32:17 430
to new *g* that came newly up, whom ... Deut 32:17
he shall say, Where are their *g* ... Deut 32:37 430
God of *g*, the LORD God of *g* ... Josh 22:22 430
mention of the names of their *g* ... Josh 23:7 430
and have gone and served other *g* ... Josh 23:16 430
and they served other *g* ... Josh 24:2 430
put away the *g* which your fathers ... Josh 24:14 430
whether the *g* which your fathers ... Josh 24:15 430
or the *g* of the Amorites, in ... Josh 24:15 430
the LORD, to serve other *g* ... Josh 24:16 430
the LORD, and serve strange *g* ... Josh 24:20 430
the strange *g* which are among you ... Josh 24:23 430
their *g* shall be a snare unto you ... Judg 2:3 430
of Egypt, and followed other *g* ... Judg 2:12 430
of the *g* of the people that were ... Judg 2:12 430
they went a whoring after other *g* ... Judg 2:17 430
following other *g* to serve them ... Judg 2:19 430
to their sons, and served their *g* ... Judg 3:6 430
They chose new *g* ... Judg 5:8 430
fear not the *g* of the Amorites ... Judg 6:10 430
the *g* of Syria ... Judg 10:6 430
the *g* of Zidon ... Judg 10:6 430
the *g* of Moab ... Judg 10:6 430
the *g* of the children of Ammon ... Judg 10:6 430
the *g* of the Philistines, and ... Judg 10:6 430
forsaken me, and served other *g* ... Judg 10:13 430
cry unto the *g* which ye have ... Judg 10:14 430
the strange *g* from among them ... Judg 10:16 430
the man Micah had an house of *g* ... Judg 17:5 430
have taken away my *g* which I made ... Judg 18:24 430
unto her people, and unto her *g* ... Ruth 1:15 430
out of the hand of these mighty *G* ... 1Sa 4:8 430
these are the *G* that smote the ... 1Sa 4:8 430
from off you, and from off your *g* ... 1Sa 6:5 430
then put away the strange *g* ... 1Sa 7:3 430
forsaken me, and served other *g* ... 1Sa 8:8 430
Philistine cursed David by his *g* ... 1Sa 17:43 430
LORD, saying, Go, serve other *g* ... 1Sa 26:19 430
I saw *g* ascending out of the ... 1Sa 28:13 430
from the nations and their *g* ... 2Sa 7:23 430
you, but go and serve other *g* ... 1Kin 9:6 430
and have taken hold upon other *g* ... 1Kin 9:9 430
away your heart after their *g* ... 1Kin 11:2 430
away his heart after other *g* ... 1Kin 11:4 430
and sacrificed unto their *g* ... 1Kin 11:8 430
he should not go after other *g* ... 1Kin 11:10 430
behold thy *g*, O Israel, which ... 1Kin 12:28 430
hast gone and made thee other *g* ... 1Kin 14:9 430
And call ye on the name of your *g* ... 1Kin 18:24 430
and call on the name of your *g* ... 1Kin 18:25 430
saying, So let the *g* do to me ... 1Kin 19:2 430
The *g* do so unto me, and more also ... 1Kin 20:10 430
Their *g* are *g* of the hills ... 1Kin 20:23 430
Their *g* are *g* of the hills ... 1Kin 20:23 430
nor sacrifice unto other *g* ... 2Kin 5:17 430
of Egypt, and had feared other *g* ... 2Kin 17:7 430
every nation made *g* of their own ... 2Kin 17:29 430
Anammelech, the *g* of Sepharvaim ... 2Kin 17:31 430
the LORD, and served their own *g* ... 2Kin 17:33 430
saying, Ye shall not fear other *g* ... 2Kin 17:35 430
and ye shall not fear other *g* ... 2Kin 17:37 430
neither shall ye fear other *g* ... 2Kin 17:38 430
Hath any of the *g* of the nations ... 2Kin 18:33 430
Where are the *g* of Hamath ... 2Kin 18:34 430
where are the *g* of Sepharvaim ... 2Kin 18:34 430
among all the *g* of the countries ... 2Kin 18:35 430
Have the *g* of the nations ... 2Kin 19:12 430
have cast their *g* into the fire ... 2Kin 19:18 430
for they were no *g*, but the work ... 2Kin 19:18 430
have burned incense unto other *g* ... 2Kin 22:17 430
went a whoring after the *g* of the ... 1Chr 5:25 430
armour in the house of their *g* ... 1Chr 10:10 430
when they had left their *g* there ... 1Chr 14:12 430
also is to be feared above all *g* ... 1Chr 16:25 430
For all the *g* of the people are ... 1Chr 16:26 430
for great is our God above all *g* ... 2Chr 2:5 430
you, and shall go and serve other *g* ... 2Chr 7:19 430
of Egypt, and laid hold on other *g* ... 2Chr 7:22 430
which Jeroboam made you for *g* ... 2Chr 13:8 430
be a priest of them that are no *g* ... 2Chr 13:9 430
away the altars of the strange *g* ... 2Chr 14:3
that he brought the *g* of the ... 2Chr 25:14 430
Seir, and set them up to be his *g* ... 2Chr 25:14 430
sought after the *g* of the people ... 2Chr 25:15 430
they sought after the *g* of Edom ... 2Chr 25:20 430
sacrificed unto the *g* of Damascus ... 2Chr 28:23 430
Because the *g* of the kings of ... 2Chr 28:23 430
to burn incense unto other *g* ... 2Chr 28:25 430
were the *g* of the nations of ... 2Chr 32:13 430
the *g* of those nations that my ... 2Chr 32:14 430
As the *g* of the nations of other ... 2Chr 32:17 430
as against the *g* of the people of ... 2Chr 32:19 430
And he took away the strange *g* ... 2Chr 33:15 430
have burned incense unto other *g* ... 2Chr 34:25 430
put them in the house of his *g* ... Ezr 1:7 430
he judgeth among the *g* ... Ps 82:1 430
I have said, Ye are *g* ... Ps 82:6 430
Among the *g* there is none like ... Ps 86:8 430
God, and a great King above all *g* ... Ps 95:3 430
he is to be feared above all *g* ... Ps 96:4 430
For all the *g* of the nations are ... Ps 96:5 430
worship him, all ye *g* ... Ps 97:7 430
thou art exalted far above all *g* ... Ps 97:9 430
and that our Lord is above all *g* ... Ps 135:5 430
O give thanks unto the God of *g* ... Ps 136:2 430
before the *g* will I sing praise ... Ps 138:1 430
all the graven images of her *g* he ... Is 21:9 430
Hath any of the *g* of the nations ... Is 36:18 430
Where are the *g* of Hamath ... Is 36:19 430
where are the *g* of Sepharvaim ... Is 36:19 430
among all the *g* of these lands ... Is 36:20 430
Have the *g* of the nations ... Is 37:12 430
have cast their *g* into the fire ... Is 37:19 430
for they were no *g*, but the work ... Is 37:19 430
that we may know that ye are *g* ... Is 41:23 430
the molten images, Ye are our *g* ... Is 42:17 430
have burned incense unto other *g* ... Jer 1:16 430
their *g*, which are yet no *g* ... Jer 2:11 430
But where are thy *g* that thou ... Jer 2:28 430
number of thy cities are thy *g* ... Jer 2:28 430
and sworn by them that are no *g* ... Jer 5:7 430
and served strange *g* in your land ... Jer 5:19 430
walk after other *g* to your hurt ... Jer 7:6 430
after other *g* whom ye know not ... Jer 7:9 430
out drink offerings unto other *g* ... Jer 7:18 430
The *g* that have not made the ... Jer 10:11 426
went after other *g* to serve them ... Jer 11:10 430
cry unto the *g* unto whom they ... Jer 11:12 430
number of thy cities were thy *g* ... Jer 11:13 430
heart, and walk after other *g* ... Jer 13:10 430
and have walked after other *g* ... Jer 16:11 430
there shall ye serve other *g* day ... Jer 16:13 430
Shall a man make *g* unto himself ... Jer 16:20 430
and they are no *g* ... Jer 16:20 430
burned incense in it unto other *g* ... Jer 19:4 430
out drink offerings unto other *g* ... Jer 19:13 430
their God, and worshipped other *g* ... Jer 22:9 430
not after other *g* to serve them ... Jer 25:6 430
out drink offerings unto other *g* ... Jer 32:29 430
not after other *g* to serve them ... Jer 35:15 430
in the houses of the *g* of Egypt ... Jer 43:12 430
the houses of the *g* of the ... Jer 43:13 430
burn incense, and to serve other *g* ... Jer 44:3 430
to burn no incense unto other *g* ... Jer 44:5 430
unto other *g* in the land of Egypt ... Jer 44:8 430
had burned incense unto other *g* ... Jer 44:15 430
Pharaoh, and Egypt, with their *g* ... Jer 46:25 430
him that burneth incense to his *g* ... Jer 48:35 430
it before the king, except the *g* ... Dan 2:11 426
is, that your God is a God of *g* ... Dan 2:47 426
they serve not thy *g*, nor worship ... Dan 3:12 426
Abed-nego, do not ye serve my *g* ... Dan 3:14 426
that we will not serve thy *g* ... Dan 3:18 426
whom is the spirit of the holy *g* ... Dan 4:8 426
spirit of the holy *g* is in thee ... Dan 4:9 426
spirit of the holy *g* is in thee ... Dan 4:18 426
wine, and praised the *g* of gold ... Dan 5:4 426
whom is the spirit of the holy *g* ... Dan 5:11 426
wisdom, like the wisdom of the *g* ... Dan 5:11 426
the spirit of the *g* is in thee ... Dan 5:14 426
thou hast praised the *g* of silver ... Dan 5:23 426
carry captives into Egypt their *g* ... Dan 11:8 430
things against the God of *g* ... Dan 11:36 410
of Israel, who look to other *g* ... Hos 3:1 430
work of our hands, Ye are our *g* ... Hos 14:3 430
out of the house of thy *g* will I ... Nah 1:14 430
famish all the *g* of the earth ... Zeph 2:11 430
in your law, I said, Ye are *g* ... Jn 10:34 *2316*
If he called them *g*, unto whom ... Jn 10:35 *2316*
Make us *g* to go before us ... Acts 7:40 *2316*
The *g* are come down to us in the ... Acts 14:11 *2316*
to be a setter forth of strange *g* ... Acts 17:18 *1140*
people, saying that they be no *g* ... Acts 19:26 *2316*
though there be that are called *g* ... 1Cor 8:5 *2316*
or in earth, (as there be *g* many ... 1Cor 8:5 *2316*
them which by nature are no *g* ... Gal 4:8 *2316*

GOD-WARD {3}
Be thou for the people to *G* ... Ex 18:19 4136,430
trust have we through Christ to *G* .. 2Cor 3:4 *4314,2316*
your faith to *G* is spread abroad ... 1Th 1:8 *4314,2316*

GOEST {46}
as thou *g*, unto Sodom, and ... Gen 10:19 935
as thou *g* unto Sephar a mount of ... Gen 10:30 935
Egypt, as thou *g* toward Assyria ... Gen 25:18 935
thee in all places whither thou *g* ... Gen 28:15 3212
and whither *g* thou ... Gen 32:17 3212
When thou *g* to return into Egypt ... Ex 4:21 3212
is it not in that thou *g* with us ... Ex 33:16 3212
of the land whither thou *g* ... Ex 34:12 935
that thou *g* before them, by ... Num 14:14 1980
land whither thou *g* to possess it ... Deut 7:1 935
whither thou *g* in to possess it ... Deut 11:10 935
land whither thou *g* to possess it ... Deut 11:29 935
whither thou *g* to possess them ... Deut 12:29 935
When thou *g* out to battle against ... Deut 20:1 3318
When thou *g* forth to war against ... Deut 21:10 3318
land whither thou *g* to possess it ... Deut 23:20 935
shalt thou be when thou *g* out ... Deut 28:6 3318
shalt thou be when thou *g* out ... Deut 28:19 3318
whither thou *g* to possess it ... Deut 28:21 935
land whither thou *g* to possess it ... Deut 28:63 935
land whither thou *g* to possess it ... Deut 30:16 935
in the mount whither thou *g* up ... Deut 32:50 5927
prosper whithersoever thou *g* ... Josh 1:7 3212
is with thee whithersoever thou *g* ... Josh 1:9 3212
that thou *g* to take a wife of the ... Judg 14:3 1980
the old man said, Whither *g* thou ... Judg 19:17 3212
for whither thou *g*, I will go ... Ruth 1:16 3212
of the land, as thou *g* to Shur ... 1Sa 27:8 935
strength, when thou *g* on thy way ... 1Sa 28:22 3212
Wherefore *g* thou also with us ... 2Sa 15:19 3212
be, that on the day thou *g* out ... 1Kin 2:37 3318
a certain, on the day thou *g* out ... 1Kin 2:42 3318
g not forth with our armies ... Ps 44:9 3318
When thou *g*, thy steps shall not ... Prov 4:12 3212
When thou *g*, it shall lead thee ... Prov 6:22 1980
when thou *g* to the house of God ... Eccl 5:1 3212
in the grave, whither thou *g* ... Eccl 9:10 1980
prey in all places whither thou *g* ... Jer 45:5 3212
Then said I, Whither *g* thou ... Zec 2:2 1980
follow thee whithersoever thou *g* ... Mt 8:19 *565*
follow thee whithersoever thou *g* ... Lk 9:57 *565*
When thou *g* with thine adversary ... Lk 12:58 *5217*
and *g* thou thither again ... Jn 11:8 *5217*
unto him, Lord, whither *g* thou ... Jn 13:36 *5217*
Lord, we know not whither thou *g* ... Jn 14:5 *5217*
of you asketh me, Whither *g* thou ... Jn 16:5 *5217*

GOETH {135}
that is it which *g* toward the ... Gen 2:14 1980
with the present that *g* before me ... Gen 32:20 1980
as the cattle that *g* before me ... Gen 33:14
Behold thy father in law *g* up to ... Gen 38:13 5927
lo, he *g* out unto the water ... Ex 7:15 3318
unto him by that the sun *g* down ... Ex 22:26 935
when he *g* in unto the holy place ... Ex 28:29 935
when he *g* in before the LORD ... Ex 28:30 935
sound shall be heard when he *g* in ... Ex 28:35 935
thing that *g* upon all four ... Lev 11:21 1980
whatsoever *g* upon his paws, among ... Lev 11:27 1980
Whatsoever *g* upon the belly, and ... Lev 11:42 1980
whatsoever *g* upon all four, or ... Lev 11:42 1980
Moreover he that *g* into the house ... Lev 14:46 935
and of him whose seed *g* from him ... Lev 15:32 3318
of the congregation when he *g* in ... Lev 16:17 935
that *g* unto the holy things ... Lev 22:3 7126
or a man whose seed *g* from him ... Lev 22:4 3318
when it *g* out in the jubile ... Lev 27:21 3318
when a wife *g* aside to another ... Num 5:29 7847
that *g* down to the dwelling of Ar ... Num 21:15 5186
LORD your God which *g* before you ... Deut 1:30 1980
is he which *g* over before thee ... Deut 9:3 5674

by the way where the sun *g* down Deut 11:30 3996
As when a man *g* into the wood Deut 19:5 935
your God is he that *g* with you Deut 20:4 1980
When the host *g* forth against Deut 23:9 3318
pledge again when the sun *g* down Deut 24:13 935
the way that *g* up to Beth-horon Josh 10:10 4609
that *g* up to Seir, even unto Josh 11:17 5927
mount Halak, that *g* up to Seir Josh 12:7 5927
to the wilderness that *g* up from Josh 16:1 5927
g out from Beth-el to Luz, and Josh 16:2 3318
g down westward to the coast of Josh 16:3 3381
then *g* out to Daberath, and *g* Josh 19:12 3318
g out to Remmon-methoar to Neah Josh 19:13 3318
g out to Cabul on the left hand, Josh 19:27 3318
g out from thence to Hukkok, and Josh 19:34 3318
sun when he *g* forth in his might Judg 5:31 3318
of which one *g* up to the house of Judg 20:31 5927
that *g* up from Beth-el to Shechem Judg 21:19 5927
if it *g* up by the way of his own 1Sa 6:9 5927
law, and *g* at thy bidding, and is 1Sa 22:14 5493
part is that *g* down to the battle 1Sa 30:24 3381
that when my master *g* into the 2Kin 5:18 935
be ye with the king as he *g* out 2Kin 11:8 3318
of Millo, which *g* down to Silla 2Kin 12:20 3381
he cometh in, and when he *g* out 2Chr 23:7 3318
the walls, and this work *g* fast on Ezr 5:8 5648
so he that *g* down to the grave Job 7:9 3381
he *g* by me, and I see him not Job 9:11 5674
Which *g* in company with the Job 34:8 732
the sound that *g* out of his mouth Job 37:2 3318
he *g* on to meet the armed men Job 39:21 3318
Out of his nostrils *g* smoke Job 41:20 3318
a flame *g* out of his mouth Job 41:21 3318
that *g* not out of feigned lips Ps 17:1
when he *g* abroad, he telleth it Ps 41:6 3318
as *g* on still in his trespasses Ps 68:21 1980
Thy fierce wrath *g* over me Ps 88:16 5674
A fire *g* before him, and burneth Ps 97:3 3212
Man *g* forth unto his work and to Ps 104:23 3318
He that *g* forth and weepeth, Ps 126:6 3212
His breath *g* forth, he returneth Ps 146:4 3318
So he that *g* in to his Prov 6:29 935
He *g* after her straightway Prov 7:22 1980
as an ox *g* to the slaughter, or Prov 7:22 925
When it *g* well with the righteous Prov 11:10
Pride *g* before destruction, and an Prov 16:18
He that *g* about as a talebearer Prov 20:19 1980
As a thorn *g* up into the hand of Prov 26:9 5927
no wood is, there the fire *g* out Prov 26:20 3518
her candle *g* not out by night Prov 31:18 3518
also ariseth, and the sun *g* down Eccl 1:5 935
The wind *g* toward the south, and Eccl 1:6 1980
the spirit of man that *g* upward Eccl 3:21 5927
that *g* downward to the earth Eccl 3:21 3381
because man *g* to his long home, Eccl 12:5 1980
that *g* down sweetly, causing the Song 7:9 1980
From the time that it *g* forth it Is 28:19 5674
as when one *g* with a pipe to come Is 30:29 1980
be that *g* forth out of my mouth Is 55:11 3318
whosoever *g* therein shall not Is 59:8 1869
As a beast *g* down into the valley Is 63:14 3318
every one that *g* out thence shall Jer 5:6 3318
for the day *g* away, for the Jer 6:4 6437
but he that *g* out, and falleth to Jer 21:9 3318
but weep sore for him that *g* away Jer 22:10 1980
of the LORD *g* forth with fury Jer 30:23 3318
but he that *g* forth to the Jer 38:2 3318
g forth out of our own mouth Jer 44:17 3318
every one that *g* by it shall be Jer 49:17 5674
every one that *g* by Babylon shall Jer 50:13 5674
but none *g* to the battle Eze 7:14 1980
but their heart *g* after their Eze 33:31 1980
as one *g* up to the entry of the Eze 40:40 5927
as one *g* into them from the utter Eze 42:9 935
day that he *g* into the sanctuary Eze 44:27 935
as one *g* to Hamath, Hazar-enan, Eze 48:1 935
and as the early dew it *g* away Hos 6:4 1980
are as the light that *g* forth Hos 6:5 3318
This is the curse that *g* forth Zec 5:3 3318
and see what is this that *g* forth Zec 5:5 3318
This is an ephah that *g* forth Zec 5:6 3318
and I say to this man, Go, and he *g* Mt 8:9 *4198*
Then *g* he, and taketh with himself Mt 12:45 *4198*
he hideth, and for joy thereof *g* Mt 13:44 *5217*
Not that which *g* into the mouth Mt 15:11 *1525*
in at the mouth *g* into the belly Mt 15:17 *5562*
Howbeit this kind *g* not out but Mt 17:21 *1607*
g into the mountains, and seeketh Mt 18:12 *4198*
The Son of man *g* as it is written Mt 26:24 *5217*
he *g* before you into Galilee Mt 28:7 *4254*
he *g* up into a mountain, and Mk 3:13 *305*
g out into the draught, purging Mk 7:19 *1607*
The Son of man indeed *g*, as it is Mk 14:21 *5217*
he *g* straightway to him, and saith Mk 14:45 *4334*
Peter that he *g* before you into Mk 16:7 *4254*
and I say unto one, Go, and he *g* Lk 7:8 *4198*
Then *g* he, and taketh to him seven Lk 11:26 *4198*
And truly the Son of man *g* Lk 22:22 *4198*
whence it cometh, and whither it *g* Jn 3:8 *5217*
who *g* about to kill thee Jn 7:20 *2212*
he *g* before them, and the sheep Jn 10:4 *4198*
She *g* unto the grave to weep Jn 11:31 *5217*
darkness knoweth not whither he *g* Jn 12:35 *5217*
the south unto the way that *g* Acts 8:26 *3597*
But brother *g* to law with brother 1Cor 6:6
Who *g* a warfare any time at his 1Cor 9:7
g his way, and straightway Jas 1:24 *565*
and knoweth not whither he *g* 1Jn 2:11 *5217*
the Lamb whithersoever he *g* Rev 14:4 *5217*
of the seven, and *g* into perdition Rev 17:11 *5217*
out of his mouth *g* a sharp sword Rev 19:15 *1607*

GOG {11} See HAMON-GOG, MAGOG.
1. Son of Shemarah.
G his son, Shimei his son, 1Chr 5:4 1463
2. A prince of Scythia.
of man, set thy face against *G* Eze 38:2 1463
Behold, I am against thee, O *G* Eze 38:3 1463
of man, prophesy and say unto *G* Eze 38:14 1463
shall be sanctified in thee, O *G* Eze 38:16 1463
to pass at the same time when *G* Eze 38:18 1463
son of man, prophesy against *G* Eze 39:1 1463
Behold, I am against thee, O *G* Eze 39:1 1463
that I will give unto *G* a place Eze 39:11 1463
and there shall they bury *G* Eze 39:11 1463
the four quarters of the earth, *G* Rev 20:8 *1136*

GOIIM See NATIONS

GOING {92}
g on still toward the south Gen 12:9 1980
And when the sun was *g* down Gen 15:12 935
g to carry it down to Egypt Gen 37:25 1980
until the *g* down of the sun Ex 17:12 935
enemy's ox or his ass *g* astray Ex 23:4 8582
six branches *g* out of the sides Ex 37:18 3318
branches *g* out of the candlestick Ex 37:19 3318
to the six branches *g* out of it Ex 37:21 3318
g upon all four, shall be an Lev 11:20 1980
g over into the land which the Num 32:7 5674
the *g* forth thereof shall be from Num 34:4 8444
at the *g* down of the sun, at the Deut 16:6 935
Rejoice, Zebulun, in thy *g* out Deut 33:18 3318
sea toward the *g* down of the sun Josh 1:4 3996
after the ark, the priests *g* on Josh 6:9 1980
the city, *g* about it once Josh 6:11 5362
ark of the LORD, the priests *g* on Josh 6:13 1980
and smote them in the *g* down Josh 7:5 4174
were in the *g* down to Beth-horon, Josh 10:11 4174
the time of the *g* down of the sun Josh 10:27 935
is before the *g* up to Adummim Josh 15:7 4608
over against the *g* up of Adummim Josh 18:17 4608
this day I am *g* the way of all Josh 23:14 1980
was from the *g* up to Akrabbim Judg 1:36 4608
but I am now *g* to the house of Judg 19:18 1980
said unto her, Up, and let us be *g* Judg 19:28 3212
young maidens *g* out to draw water 1Sa 9:11 3318
as they were *g* down to the end of 1Sa 9:27 3381
three men *g* up to God to Beth-el 1Sa 10:3 5927
as the host was *g* forth to the 1Sa 17:20 3318
hast been upright, and thy *g* out 1Sa 29:6 3318
in *g* he turned not to the right 2Sa 2:19 3212
thee, and to know thy *g* out 2Sa 3:25 4161
a *g* in the tops of the mulberry 2Sa 5:24 6807
as she was *g* to fetch it, he 1Kin 17:11 3212
host about the *g* down of the sun 1Kin 22:36 935
as he was *g* up by the way, there 2Kin 2:23 5927
And they did so at the *g* up to Gur 2Kin 9:27 4608
I know thy abode, and thy *g* out 2Kin 19:27 3318
of *g* in the tops of the mulberry 1Chr 14:15 6807
by the causeway of the *g* up 1Chr 26:16 5927
returned from *g* against Jeroboam 2Chr 11:4 3212
time of the sun *g* down he died 2Chr 18:34 935
the *g* up to the armoury at the Neh 3:19 5927
to the *g* up of the corner Neh 3:31 5944
between the *g* up of the corner Neh 3:32 5944
at the *g* up of the wall, above Neh 12:37 4608
the LORD, and said, From *g* to Job 1:7 7751
the LORD, and said, From *g* to Job 2:2 7751
him from *g* down to the pit Job 33:24 3381
his soul from *g* into the pit Job 33:28 5674
His *g* forth is from the end of Ps 19:6 4161
the sun unto the *g* down thereof Ps 50:1 3996
the sun knoweth his *g* down Ps 104:19 3996
the *g* down of the same the LORD's Ps 113:3 3996
The LORD shall preserve thy *g* out Ps 121:8 3318
be no breaking in, nor *g* out Ps 144:14 3318
g down to the chambers of death Prov 7:27 3381
prudent man looketh well to his *g* Prov 14:15 838
well, yea, four are comely in *g* Prov 30:29 3212
shall be darkened in his *g* forth Is 13:10 3318
I know thy abode, and thy *g* out Is 37:28 3318
For in the *g* up of Luhith Jer 48:5 4608
for in the *g* down of Horonaim the Jer 48:5 4174
the children of Judah together, *g* Jer 50:4 1980
Dan also and Javan *g* to and fro Eze 27:19 235
the *g* up to it had eight steps Eze 40:31 4608
the *g* up to it had eight steps Eze 40:34 4608
the *g* up to it had eight steps Eze 40:37 4608
with every *g* forth of the Eze 44:5 4161
after his *g* forth one shall shut Eze 46:12 3318
he laboured till the *g* down of Dan 6:14 4606
that from the *g* forth of the Dan 9:25 4161
his *g* forth is prepared as the Hos 6:3 4161
and he found a ship *g* to Tarshish Jonah 1:3 935
g down of the same my name shall Mal 1:11 3996
g on from thence, he saw other Mt 4:21 *4260*
Jesus *g* up to Jerusalem took the Mt 20:17 *305*
Rise, let us be *g* Mt 26:46 *71*
Now when they were *g*, behold, Mt 28:11 *4108*
for there were many coming and *g* Mk 6:31 *5217*
were in the way *g* up to Jerusalem Mk 10:32 *305*
g to make war against another Lk 14:31 *4198*
And as he was now *g* down, his Jn 4:51 *2597*
g through the midst of them, and Jn 8:59 *1330*
coming in and *g* out at Jerusalem Acts 9:28 *1607*
These *g* before tarried for us at Acts 20:5 *4281*
g about to establish their own Rom 10:3 *2212*
beforehand, *g* before to judgment 1Ti 5:24 *4254*
g before for the weakness Heb 7:18 *4254*
For ye were as sheep *g* astray 1Pet 2:25 *4105*
g after strange flesh, are set Jude 7 *565*

GOINGS {26}
Moses wrote their *g* out according Num 33:2 4161
journeys according to their *g* out Num 33:2 4161
the *g* out of it shall be at the Num 34:5 8444
the *g* forth of the border shall Num 34:8 8444
the *g* out of it shall be at Num 34:9 8444
the *g* out of it shall be at the Num 34:12 8444
the *g* out of that coast were at Josh 15:4 8444
the *g* out thereof were at Josh 15:7 8444
the *g* out of the border were at Josh 15:11 8444
the *g* out thereof are at the sea Josh 16:3 8444
the *g* out thereof were at the sea Josh 16:8 8444
the *g* out thereof were at the Josh 18:12 8444
the *g* out thereof were at Josh 18:14 8444
of man, and he seeth all his *g* Job 34:21 6806
Hold up my *g* in thy paths, that Ps 17:5 838
upon a rock, and established my *g* Ps 40:2 838
They have seen thy *g*, O God Ps 68:24 1979
even the *g* of my God, my King, in Ps 68:24 1979
have purposed to overthrow my *g* Ps 140:4 6471
LORD, and he pondereth all his *g* Prov 5:21 4570
Man's *g* are of the LORD Prov 20:24 4703
there is no judgment in their *g* Is 59:8 4570
all their *g* out were both Eze 42:11 4161
the *g* out thereof, and the comings Eze 43:11 4161
these are the *g* out of the city Eze 48:30 8444
whose *g* forth have been from of Mic 5:2 4163

GOLAN *(go'-lan)* {4} *A Levitical city in Manasseh.*
G in Bashan, of the Manassites Deut 4:43 1474
G in Bashan out of the tribe of Josh 20:8 1474
gave *G* in Bashan with her suburbs Josh 21:27 1474
G in Bashan with her suburbs, and 1Chr 6:71 1474

GOLD {419}
land of Havilah, where there is *g* Gen 2:11 2091
the *g* of that land is good Gen 2:12 2091
in cattle, in silver, and in *g* Gen 13:2 2091
hands of ten shekels weight of *g* Gen 24:22 2091
flocks, and herds, and silver, and *g* Gen 24:35 2091
jewels of silver, and jewels of *g* Gen 24:53 2091
put a *g* chain about his neck Gen 41:42 2091
of thy lord's house silver or *g* Gen 44:8 2091
jewels of silver, and jewels of *g* Ex 3:22 2091
jewels of silver, and jewels of *g* Ex 11:2 2091
jewels of silver, and jewels of *g* Ex 12:35 2091
shall ye make unto you gods of *g* Ex 20:23 2091
g, and silver, and brass, Ex 25:3 2091
thou shalt overlay it with pure *g* Ex 25:11 2091
upon it a crown of *g* round about Ex 25:11 2091
shalt cast four rings of *g* for it Ex 25:12 2091
wood, and overlay them with *g* Ex 25:13 2091
shalt make a mercy seat of pure *g* Ex 25:17 2091
shalt make two cherubims of *g* Ex 25:18 2091
thou shalt overlay it with pure *g* Ex 25:24 2091
thereto a crown of *g* round about Ex 25:24 2091
shalt make for it four rings of *g* Ex 25:26 2091
wood, and overlay them with *g* Ex 25:28 2091
of pure *g* shalt thou make them Ex 25:29 2091
make a candlestick of pure *g* Ex 25:31 2091
be one beaten work of pure *g* Ex 25:36 2091
thereof, shall be of pure *g* Ex 25:38 2091
talent of pure *g* shall he make it Ex 25:39 2091
thou shalt make fifty taches of *g* Ex 26:6 2091
shalt overlay the boards with *g* Ex 26:29 2091
make their rings of *g* for places Ex 26:29 2091
shalt overlay the bars with *g* Ex 26:29 2091
of shittim wood overlaid with *g* Ex 26:32 2091
their hooks shall be of *g* Ex 26:32 2091
wood, and overlay them with *g* Ex 26:37 2091
and their hooks shall be of *g* Ex 26:37 2091
And they shall take *g*, and blue, and Ex 28:5 2091
And they shall make the ephod of *g* Ex 28:6 2091
even of *g*, of blue, and purple, and Ex 28:8 2091
them to be set in ouches of *g* Ex 28:11 2091
And thou shalt make ouches of *g* Ex 28:13 2091
two chains of pure *g* at the ends Ex 28:14 2091
of *g*, of blue, and of purple, and Ex 28:15 2091
be set in *g* in their inclosings Ex 28:20 2091
ends of wreathen work of pure *g* Ex 28:22 2091
the breastplate two rings of *g* Ex 28:23 2091
g in the two rings which are on Ex 28:24 2091
And thou shalt make two rings of *g* Ex 28:26 2091
other rings of *g* thou shalt make Ex 28:27 2091
bells of *g* between them round Ex 28:33 2091
thou shalt make a plate of pure *g* Ex 28:36 2091
thou shalt overlay it with pure *g* Ex 30:3 2091
unto it a crown of *g* round about Ex 30:3 2091
wood, and overlay them with *g* Ex 30:5 2091
cunning works, to work in *g* Ex 31:4 2091
unto them, Whosoever hath any *g* Ex 32:24 2091
sin, and have made them gods of *g* Ex 32:31 2091
g, and silver, and brass, Ex 35:5 2091
and tablets, all jewels of *g* Ex 35:22 2091
an offering of *g* unto the LORD Ex 35:22 2091
curious works, to work in *g* Ex 35:32 2091
And he made fifty taches of *g* Ex 36:13 2091
And he overlaid the boards with *g* Ex 36:34 2091
made their rings of *g* to be Ex 36:34 2091
bars, and overlaid the bars with *g* Ex 36:34 2091
wood, and overlaid them with *g* Ex 36:36 2091
their hooks were of *g* Ex 36:36 2091
chapiters and their fillets with *g* Ex 36:38 2091
he overlaid it with pure *g* within Ex 37:2 2091
made a crown of *g* to it round Ex 37:2 2091

And he cast for it four rings of *g*	Ex 37:3	2091
wood, and overlaid them with *g*	Ex 37:4	2091
he made the mercy seat of pure *g*	Ex 37:6	2091
And he made two cherubims of *g*	Ex 37:7	2091
And he overlaid it with pure *g*	Ex 37:11	2091
a crown of *g* round about	Ex 37:11	2091
made a crown of *g* for the border	Ex 37:12	2091
And he cast for it four rings of *g*	Ex 37:13	2091
wood, and overlaid them with *g*	Ex 37:15	2091
covers to cover withal, of pure *g*	Ex 37:16	2091
he made the candlestick of pure *g*	Ex 37:17	2091
it was one beaten work of pure *g*	Ex 37:22	2091
and his snuffdishes, of pure *g*	Ex 37:23	2091
Of a talent of pure *g* made he it	Ex 37:24	2091
And he overlaid it with pure *g*	Ex 37:26	2091
unto it a crown of *g* round about	Ex 37:26	2091
he made two rings of *g* for it	Ex 37:27	2091
wood, and overlaid them with *g*	Ex 37:28	2091
All the *g* that was occupied for	Ex 38:24	2091
even the *g* of the offering, was	Ex 38:24	2091
And he made the ephod of *g*	Ex 39:2	2091
did beat the *g* into thin plates	Ex 39:3	2091
of *g*, blue, and purple, and scarlet	Ex 39:5	2091
stones inclosed in ouches of *g*	Ex 39:6	2091
of *g*, blue, and purple, and scarlet	Ex 39:8	2091
ouches of *g* in their inclosings	Ex 39:13	2091
ends, of wreathen work of pure *g*	Ex 39:15	2091
And they made two ouches of *g*	Ex 39:16	2091
ouches of *g*, and two *g* rings	Ex 39:16	2091
put the two wreathen chains of *g*	Ex 39:17	2091
And they made two rings of *g*	Ex 39:19	2091
And they made bells of pure *g*	Ex 39:25	2091
plate of the holy crown of pure *g*	Ex 39:30	2091
thou shalt set the altar of *g* for	Ex 40:5	2091
One spoon of ten shekels of *g*	Num 7:14	2091
One spoon of *g* of ten shekels,	Num 7:20	2091
silver bowls, twelve spoons of *g*	Num 7:84	2091
all the *g* of the spoons was an	Num 7:86	2091
the candlestick was of beaten *g*	Num 8:4	2091
me his house full of silver and *g*	Num 22:18	2091
me his house full of silver and *g*	Num 24:13	2091
Only the *g*, and the silver, the	Num 31:22	2091
man hath gotten, of jewels of *g*	Num 31:50	2091
the priest took the *g* of them	Num 31:51	2091
all the *g* of the offering that	Num 31:52	2091
Eleazar the priest took the *g* of	Num 31:54	2091
the silver or *g* that is on them	Deut 7:25	2091
thy *g* is multiplied, and all that	Deut 8:13	2091
multiply to himself silver and *g*	Deut 17:17	2091
idols, wood and stone, silver and *g*	Deut 29:17	2091
But all the silver, and *g*, and	Josh 6:19	2091
only the silver, and the *g*	Josh 6:24	2091
a wedge of *g* of fifty shekels	Josh 7:21	2091
and the garment, and the wedge of *g*	Josh 7:24	2091
cattle, with silver, and with *g*	Josh 22:8	2091
and seven hundred shekels of *g*	Judg 8:26	2091
and put the jewels of *g*, which ye	1Sa 6:8	2091
and the coffer with the mice of *g*	1Sa 6:11	2091
it, wherein the jewels of *g* were	1Sa 6:15	2091
ornaments of *g* upon your apparel	2Sa 1:24	2091
David took the shields of *g* that	2Sa 8:7	2091
of silver, and vessels of *g*	2Sa 8:10	2091
g that he had dedicated of all	2Sa 8:11	2091
of *g* with the precious stones	2Sa 12:30	2091
will have no silver nor *g* of Saul	2Sa 21:4	2091
and he overlaid it with pure *g*	1Kin 6:20	2091
the house within with pure *g*	1Kin 6:21	2091
the chains of *g* before the oracle	1Kin 6:21	2091
and he overlaid it with *g*	1Kin 6:21	2091
whole house he overlaid with *g*	1Kin 6:22	2091
by the oracle he overlaid with *g*	1Kin 6:22	2091
he overlaid the cherubims with *g*	1Kin 6:28	2091
of the house he overlaid with *g*	1Kin 6:30	2091
flowers, and overlaid them with *g*	1Kin 6:32	2091
spread *g* upon the cherubims, and	1Kin 6:32	2091
covered them with *g* fitted upon	1Kin 6:35	2091
altar of *g*, and the table of *g*	1Kin 7:48	2091
And the candlesticks of pure *g*	1Kin 7:49	2091
and the lamps, and the tongs of *g*	1Kin 7:49	2091
spoons, and the censers of pure *g*	1Kin 7:50	2091
and the hinges of *g*, both for the	1Kin 7:50	2091
even the silver, and the *g*	1Kin 7:51	2091
trees and fir trees, and with *g*	1Kin 9:11	2091
to the king sixscore talents of *g*	1Kin 9:14	2091
Ophir, and fetched from thence *g*	1Kin 9:28	2091
that bare spices, and very much *g*	1Kin 10:2	2091
an hundred and twenty talents of *g*	1Kin 10:10	2091
Hiram, that brought *g* from Ophir	1Kin 10:11	2091
Now the weight of *g* that came to	1Kin 10:14	2091
threescore and six talents of *g*	1Kin 10:14	2091
two hundred targets of beaten *g*	1Kin 10:16	2091
shekels of *g* went to one target	1Kin 10:16	2091
three hundred shields of beaten *g*	1Kin 10:17	2091
three pound of *g* went to one	1Kin 10:17	2091
and overlaid it with the best *g*	1Kin 10:18	2091
drinking vessels were of *g*	1Kin 10:21	2091
forest of Lebanon were of pure *g*	1Kin 10:21	2091
the navy of Tharshish, bringing *g*	1Kin 10:22	2091
of silver, and vessels of *g*	1Kin 10:25	2091
counsel, and made two calves of *g*	1Kin 12:28	2091
of *g* which Solomon had made	1Kin 14:26	2091
house of the LORD, silver, and *g*	1Kin 15:15	2091
the *g* that were left in the	1Kin 15:18	2091
thee a present of silver and *g*	1Kin 15:19	2091
Thy silver and thy *g* is mine	1Kin 20:3	2091
deliver me thy silver, and thy *g*	1Kin 20:5	2091
and for my silver, and for my *g*	1Kin 20:7	2091
of Tharshish to go to Ophir for *g*	1Kin 22:48	2091
and six thousand pieces of *g*	2Kin 5:5	2091
and carried thence silver, and *g*	2Kin 7:8	2091
trumpets, any vessels of *g*	2Kin 12:13	2091
all the *g* that was found in the	2Kin 12:18	2091
And he took all the *g* and silver,	2Kin 14:14	2091
g that was found in the house of	2Kin 16:8	2091
of silver and thirty talents of *g*	2Kin 18:14	2091
time did Hezekiah cut off the *g*	2Kin 18:16	
things, the silver, and the *g*	2Kin 20:13	2091
of silver, and a talent of *g*	2Kin 23:33	2091
the silver and the *g* to Pharaoh	2Kin 23:35	2091
the *g* of the people of the land,	2Kin 23:35	2091
of *g* which Solomon king of Israel	2Kin 24:13	2091
such things as were of *g*, in *g*	2Kin 25:15	2091
David took the shields of *g* that	1Chr 18:7	2091
him all manner of vessels of *g*	1Chr 18:10	2091
the *g* that he brought from all	1Chr 18:11	2091
found it to weigh a talent of *g*	1Chr 20:2	2091
hundred shekels of *g* by weight	1Chr 21:25	2091
an hundred thousand talents of *g*	1Chr 22:14	2091
Of the *g*, the silver, and the	1Chr 22:16	2091
of *g* by weight for things of *g*	1Chr 28:14	2091
weight for the candlesticks of *g*	1Chr 28:15	2091
and for their lamps of *g*	1Chr 28:15	2091
by weight he gave *g* for the	1Chr 28:16	2091
Also pure *g* for the fleshhooks,	1Chr 28:17	2091
gave *g* by weight for every bason	1Chr 28:17	
of incense refined *g* by weight	1Chr 28:18	2091
g for the pattern of the chariot	1Chr 28:18	2091
g for things to be made of *g*	1Chr 29:2	2091
of mine own proper good, of *g*	1Chr 29:3	2091
Even three thousand talents of *g*	1Chr 29:4	2091
of the *g* of Ophir, and seven	1Chr 29:4	2091
The *g* for things of *g*, and the	1Chr 29:5	2091
of God of *g* five thousand talents	1Chr 29:7	2091
g at Jerusalem as plenteous as	2Chr 1:15	2091
a man cunning to work in *g*	2Chr 2:7	2091
man of Tyre, skilful to work in *g*	2Chr 2:14	2091
he overlaid it within with pure *g*	2Chr 3:4	2091
which he overlaid with fine *g*	2Chr 3:5	2091
and the *g* was *g* of Parvaim	2Chr 3:6	2091
and the doors thereof, with *g*	2Chr 3:7	2091
and he overlaid it with fine *g*	2Chr 3:8	2091
the nails was fifty shekels of *g*	2Chr 3:9	2091
the upper chambers with *g*	2Chr 3:9	2091
work, and overlaid them with *g*	2Chr 3:10	2091
of *g* according to their form	2Chr 4:7	2091
And he made an hundred basons of *g*	2Chr 4:8	2091
before the oracle, of pure *g*	2Chr 4:20	2091
he of *g*, and that perfect *g*	2Chr 4:21	2091
spoons, and the censers, of pure *g*	2Chr 4:22	2091
house of the temple, were of *g*	2Chr 4:22	2091
and the silver, and the *g*, and all	2Chr 5:1	2091
hundred and fifty talents of *g*	2Chr 8:18	2091
g in abundance, and precious	2Chr 9:1	2091
an hundred and twenty talents of *g*	2Chr 9:9	2091
which brought *g* from Ophir	2Chr 9:10	2091
Now the weight of *g* that came to	2Chr 9:13	2091
and threescore and six talents of *g*	2Chr 9:13	2091
of the country brought *g* and	2Chr 9:14	2091
two hundred targets of beaten *g*	2Chr 9:15	2091
of beaten *g* went to one target	2Chr 9:15	2091
shields made he of beaten *g*	2Chr 9:16	2091
shekels of *g* went to one shield	2Chr 9:16	2091
ivory, and overlaid it with pure *g*	2Chr 9:17	2091
the throne, with a footstool of *g*	2Chr 9:18	2091
vessels of king Solomon were of *g*	2Chr 9:20	2091
forest of Lebanon were of pure *g*	2Chr 9:20	2091
the ships of Tarshish bringing *g*	2Chr 9:21	2091
of silver, and vessels of *g*	2Chr 9:24	2091
of *g* which Solomon had made	2Chr 12:9	2091
the candlestick of *g* with the	2Chr 13:11	2091
had dedicated, silver, and *g*	2Chr 15:18	2091
g out of the treasures of the	2Chr 16:2	2091
I have sent thee silver and *g*	2Chr 16:3	2091
great gifts of silver, and of *g*	2Chr 21:3	2091
and spoons, and vessels of *g*	2Chr 24:14	2091
And he took all the *g* and the	2Chr 25:24	2091
treasuries for silver, and for *g*	2Chr 32:27	2091
of silver and a talent of *g*	2Chr 36:3	2091
help him with silver, and with *g*	Ezr 1:4	2091
with vessels of silver, with *g*	Ezr 1:6	2091
thirty chargers of *g*, a thousand	Ezr 1:9	2091
Thirty basons of *g*, silver basons	Ezr 1:10	2091
All the vessels of *g* and of silver	Ezr 1:11	2091
and one thousand drams of *g*	Ezr 2:69	2091
And the vessels also of *g* and	Ezr 5:14	1722
And to carry the silver and *g*	Ezr 7:15	1722
g that thou canst find in all the	Ezr 7:16	1722
the rest of the silver and the *g*	Ezr 7:18	1722
unto them the silver, and the *g*	Ezr 8:25	2091
and of *g* an hundred talents	Ezr 8:26	2091
Also twenty basons of *g*, of a	Ezr 8:27	2091
of fine copper, precious as *g*	Ezr 8:27	2091
the *g* are a freewill offering	Ezr 8:28	2091
weight of the silver, and the *g*	Ezr 8:30	2091
day was the silver and the *g*	Ezr 8:33	2091
treasure a thousand drams of *g*	Neh 7:70	2091
work twenty thousand drams of *g*	Neh 7:71	2091
was twenty thousand drams of *g*	Neh 7:72	2091
the beds were of *g* and silver,	Est 1:6	2091
gave them drink in vessels of *g*	Est 1:7	2091
white, and with a great crown of *g*	Est 8:15	2091
Or with princes that had *g*	Job 3:15	2091
Then shalt thou lay up *g* as dust	Job 22:24	1220
the *g* of Ophir as the stones of	Job 22:24	1220
tried me, I shall come forth as *g*	Job 23:10	2091
a place for *g* where they fine it	Job 28:1	2091
and it hath dust of *g*	Job 28:6	2091
It cannot be gotten for *g*	Job 28:15	5458
be valued with the *g* of Ophir	Job 28:16	3800
The *g* and the crystal cannot equal	Job 28:17	2091
shall not be for jewels of fine *g*	Job 28:17	6337
shall it be valued with pure *g*	Job 28:19	3800
If I have made *g* my hope	Job 31:24	2091
or have said to the fine *g*	Job 31:24	3800
no, not *g*, nor all the forces of	Job 36:19	1222
and every one an earring of *g*	Job 42:11	2091
to be desired are they than *g*	Ps 19:10	2091
yea, than much fine *g*	Ps 19:10	6337
a crown of pure *g* on his head	Ps 21:3	6337
did stand the queen in *g* of Ophir	Ps 45:9	3800
her clothing is of wrought *g*	Ps 45:13	2091
and her feathers with yellow *g*	Ps 68:13	2742
shall be given of the *g* of Sheba	Ps 72:15	2091
them forth also with silver and *g*	Ps 105:37	2091
Their idols are silver and *g*	Ps 115:4	2091
unto me than thousands of *g*	Ps 119:72	2091
I love thy commandments above *g*	Ps 119:127	2091
yea, above fine *g*	Ps 119:127	6337
of the heathen are silver and *g*	Ps 135:15	2091
and the gain thereof than fine *g*	Prov 3:14	2742
and knowledge rather than choice *g*	Prov 8:10	2742
My fruit is better than *g*	Prov 8:19	2742
yea, than fine *g*	Prov 8:19	6337
As a jewel of *g* in a swine's	Prov 11:22	2091
better is it to get wisdom than *g*	Prov 16:16	2742
for silver, and the furnace for *g*	Prov 17:3	2091
There is *g*, and a multitude of	Prov 20:15	2091
favour rather than silver and *g*	Prov 22:1	2091
apples of *g* in pictures of silver	Prov 25:11	2091
As an earring of *g*, and an	Prov 25:12	2091
of *g*, and an ornament of fine *g*	Prov 25:12	3800
for silver, and the furnace for *g*	Prov 27:21	2091
I gathered me also silver and *g*	Eccl 2:8	2091
jewels, thy neck with chains of *g*	Song 1:10	
borders of *g* with studs of silver	Song 1:11	2091
silver, the bottom thereof of *g*	Song 3:10	2091
His head is as the most fine *g*	Song 5:11	6337
His hands are as *g* rings set with	Song 5:14	2091
set upon sockets of fine *g*	Song 5:15	6337
land also is full of silver and *g*	Is 2:7	2091
of silver, and his idols of *g*	Is 2:20	2091
a man more precious than fine *g*	Is 13:12	6337
and as for *g*, they shall not	Is 13:17	2091
of thy molten images of *g*	Is 30:22	2091
of silver, and his idols of *g*	Is 31:7	2091
things, the silver, and the *g*	Is 39:2	2091
spreadeth it over with *g*, and	Is 40:19	2091
They lavish *g* out of the bag, and	Is 46:6	2091
they shall bring *g* and incense	Is 60:6	2091
their *g* with them, unto the name	Is 60:9	2091
For brass I will bring *g*, and for	Is 60:17	2091
deckest thee with ornaments of *g*	Jer 4:30	2091
deck it with silver and with *g*	Jer 10:4	2091
g from Uphaz, the work of the	Jer 10:9	2091
that which was of *g* in *g*	Jer 52:19	2091
How is the *g* become dim	Lam 4:1	2091
how is the most fine *g* changed	Lam 4:1	3800
of Zion, comparable to fine *g*	Lam 4:2	6337
and their *g* shall be removed	Eze 7:19	2091
their *g* shall not be able to	Eze 7:19	2091
Thus wast thou decked with *g*	Eze 16:13	2091
taken thy fair jewels of my *g*	Eze 16:17	2091
and with all precious stones, and *g*	Eze 27:22	2091
thee riches, and hast gotten *g*	Eze 28:4	2091
emerald, and the carbuncle, and *g*	Eze 28:13	2091
to carry away silver and *g*	Eze 38:13	2091
This image's head was of fine *g*	Dan 2:32	1722
the brass, the silver, and the *g*	Dan 2:35	1722
Thou art this head of *g*	Dan 2:38	1722
the clay, the silver, and the *g*	Dan 2:45	1722
the king made an image of *g*	Dan 3:1	1722
wine, and praised the gods of *g*	Dan 5:4	1722
have a chain of *g* about his neck	Dan 5:7	1722
have a chain of *g* about thy neck	Dan 5:16	1722
praised the gods of silver, and *g*	Dan 5:23	1722
put a chain of *g* about his neck	Dan 5:29	1722
were girded with fine *g* of Uphaz	Dan 10:5	3800
vessels of silver and of *g*	Dan 11:8	2091
knew not shall he honour with *g*	Dan 11:38	2091
power over the treasures of *g*	Dan 11:43	2091
and multiplied her silver and *g*	Hos 2:8	2091
their *g* have they made them idols	Hos 8:4	2091
ye have taken my silver and my *g*	Joel 3:5	2091
of silver, take the spoil of *g*	Nah 2:9	2091
Behold, it is laid over with *g*	Hab 2:19	2091
g shall be able to deliver them	Zeph 1:18	2091
the *g* is mine, saith the LORD of	Hag 2:8	2091
and behold a candlestick all of *g*	Zec 4:2	2091
Then take silver and *g*, and make	Zec 6:11	2091
fine *g* as the mire of the streets	Zec 9:3	2742
and will try them as *g* is tried	Zec 13:9	2091
shall be gathered together, *g*	Zec 14:14	2091
sons of Levi, and purge them as *g*	Mal 3:3	2091
g, and frankincense, and myrrh	Mt 2:11	*5557*
Provide neither *g*, nor silver,	Mt 10:9	*5557*
swear by the *g* of the temple	Mt 23:16	*5557*
for whether is greater, the *g*	Mt 23:17	*5557*
the temple that sanctifieth the *g*	Mt 23:17	*5557*
said, Silver and *g* have I none	Acts 3:6	*5553*
that the Godhead is like unto *g*	Acts 17:29	*5557*
coveted no man's silver, or *g*	Acts 20:33	*5553*
man build upon this foundation *g*	1Cor 3:12	*5557*
not with broided hair, or *g*	1Ti 2:9	*5557*
there are not only vessels of *g*	2Ti 2:20	*5552*

overlaid round about with *g* Heb 9:4 *5553*
your assembly a man with a *g* ring Jas 2:2 *5554*
Your *g* and silver is cankered Jas 5:3 *5557*
precious than of *g* that perisheth 1Pet 1:7 *5553*
things, as silver and *g*, from your 1Pet 1:18 *5553*
the hair, and of wearing of *g* 1Pet 3:3 *5553*
to buy of me *g* tried in the fire Rev 3:18 *5553*
had on their heads crowns of *g* Rev 4:4 *5552*
were as it were crowns like *g* Rev 9:7 *5557*
not worship devils, and idols of *g* Rev 9:20 *5552*
scarlet colour, and decked with *g* Rev 17:4 *5557*
The merchandise of *g*, and silver, Rev 18:12 *5557*
and scarlet, and decked with *g* Rev 18:16 *5557*
and the city was pure *g*, like unto Rev 21:18 *5553*
the street of the city was pure *g* Rev 21:21 *5553*

GOLDEN {66}
that the man took a *g* earring of Gen 24:22 2091
thou shalt make a *g* crown to the Ex 25:25 2091
A *g* bell and a pomegranate Ex 28:34 2091
a *g* bell and a pomegranate, upon Ex 28:34 2091
two *g* rings shalt thou make to it Ex 30:4 2091
them, Break off the *g* earrings Ex 32:2 2091
g earrings which were in their Ex 32:3 2091
And they made two other *g* rings Ex 39:20 2091
the *g* altar, and the anointing oil Ex 39:38 2091
he put the *g* altar in the tent of Ex 40:26 2091
forefront, did he put the *g* plate Lev 8:9 2091
upon the *g* altar they shall Num 4:11 2091
One *g* spoon of ten shekels, full Num 7:26 2091
One *g* spoon of ten shekels, full Num 7:32 2091
One *g* spoon of ten shekels, full Num 7:38 2091
One *g* spoon of ten shekels, full Num 7:44 2091
One *g* spoon of ten shekels, full Num 7:50 2091
One *g* spoon of ten shekels, full Num 7:56 2091
One *g* spoon of ten shekels, full Num 7:62 2091
One *g* spoon of ten shekels, full Num 7:68 2091
One *g* spoon of ten shekels, full Num 7:74 2091
One *g* spoon of ten shekels, full Num 7:80 2091
The *g* spoons were twelve, full of Num 7:86 2091
(For they had *g* earrings, because Judg 8:24 2091
the weight of the *g* earrings that Judg 8:26 2091
g emerods, and five *g* mice 1Sa 6:4 2091
these are the *g* emerods which the 1Sa 6:17 2091
the *g* mice, according to the 1Sa 6:18 2091
the *g* calves that were in Beth-el 2Kin 10:29 2091
for the *g* basons he gave gold by 1Chr 28:17 2091
the *g* altar also, and the tables 2Chr 4:19 2091
and there are with you *g* calves 2Chr 13:8 2091
And also let the *g* and silver Ezr 6:5 1722
king shall hold out the *g* sceptre Est 4:11 2091
g sceptre that was in his hand Est 5:2 2091
out the *g* sceptre toward Esther Est 8:4 2091
or the *g* bowl be broken, or the Eccl 12:6 2091
a man than the *g* wedge of Ophir Is 13:12 3800
the *g* city ceased Is 14:4 4062
Babylon hath been a *g* cup in the Jer 51:7 2091
down and worship the *g* image that Dan 3:5 1722
worshipped the *g* image that Dan 3:7 1722
fall down and worship the *g* image Dan 3:10 1722
nor worship the *g* image which Dan 3:12 1722
nor worship the *g* image which I Dan 3:14 1722
nor worship the *g* image which Dan 3:18 1722
wine, commanded to bring the *g* Dan 5:2 1722
Then they brought the *g* vessels Dan 5:3 1722
g pipes empty the *g* oil out Zec 4:12 2091
Which had the *g* censer, and the Heb 9:4 *5552*
wherein was the *g* pot that had Heb 9:4 *5552*
I saw seven *g* candlesticks Rev 1:12 *5552*
about the paps with a *g* girdle Rev 1:13 *5552*
hand, and the seven *g* candlesticks Rev 1:20 *5552*
midst of the seven *g* candlesticks Rev 2:1 *5552*
g vials full of odours, which are Rev 5:8 *5552*
at the altar, having a *g* censer Rev 8:3 *5552*
the *g* altar which was before the Rev 8:3 *5552*
the *g* altar which is before God Rev 9:13 *5552*
man, having on his head a *g* crown Rev 14:14 *5552*
breasts girded with *g* girdles Rev 15:6 *5552*
unto the seven angels seven *g* Rev 15:7 *5552*
having a *g* cup in her hand full Rev 17:4 *5552*
had a *g* reed to measure the city Rev 21:15 *5552*

GOLDSMITH {3}
the *g* spreadeth it over with gold Is 40:19 6884
So the carpenter encouraged the *g* Is 41:7 6884
in the balance, and hire a *g* Is 46:6 6884

GOLDSMITH'S {1}
the *g* son unto the place of the Neh 3:31 6885

GOLDSMITHS {2}
the son of Harhaiah, of the *g* Neh 3:8 6884
the sheep gate repaired the *g* Neh 3:32 6884

GOLGOTHA *(gol'-go-thah)* {3} See CALVARY. *Hill where Jesus was crucified.*
were come unto a place called *G* Mt 27:33 *1115*
they bring him unto the place *G* Mk 15:22 *1115*
which is called in the Hebrew *G* Jn 19:17 *1115*

GOLIATH *(go-li'-ath)* {6} *Philistine warrior killed by David.*
camp of the Philistines, named *G* 1Sa 17:4 1555
G by name, out of the armies of 1Sa 17:23 1555
The sword of *G* the Philistine, 1Sa 21:9 1555
him the sword of *G* the Philistine 1Sa 22:10 1555
slew the brother of *G* the Gittite 2Sa 21:19 1555
the brother of *G* the Gittite 1Chr 20:5 1555

GOMER *(go'-mer)* {6}
1. Son of Japheth.
G, and Magog, and Madai, and Javan, Gen 10:2 1586
And the sons of *G* Gen 10:3 1586
G, and Magog, and Madai, and Javan, 1Chr 1:5 1586
And the sons of *G* 1Chr 1:6 1586
2. Descendants of Gomer 1.
G, and all his bands Eze 38:6 1586
3. Wife of Hosea.
took *G* the daughter of Diblaim Hos 1:3 1586

GOMORRAH *(go-mor'-rah)* {20} See GOMORRHA. *City destroyed by God.*
as thou goest, unto Sodom, and *G* Gen 10:19 6017
the LORD destroyed Sodom and *G* Gen 13:10 6017
Sodom, and with Birsha king of *G* Gen 14:2 6017
king of Sodom, and the king of *G* Gen 14:8 6017
of Sodom and *G* fled, and fell there Gen 14:10 6017
took all the goods of Sodom and *G* Gen 14:11 6017
G is great, and because their sin Gen 18:20 6017
upon *G* brimstone and fire from the Gen 19:24 6017
And he looked toward Sodom and *G* Gen 19:28 6017
like the overthrow of Sodom, and *G* Deut 29:23 6017
of Sodom, and of the fields of *G* Deut 32:32 6017
we should have been like unto *G* Is 1:9 6017
law of our God, ye people of *G* Is 1:10 6017
as when God overthrew Sodom and *G* Is 13:19 6017
and the inhabitants thereof as *G* Jer 23:14 6017
As in the overthrow of Sodom and *G* Jer 49:18 6017
As God overthrew Sodom and *G* Jer 50:40 6017
you, as God overthrew Sodom and *G* Amos 4:11 6017
and the children of Ammon as *G* Zeph 2:9 6017
G into ashes condemned them with 2Pet 2:6 *1116*

GOMORRHA *(go-mor'-rah)* {4} See GOMORRAH. *Greek form of Gomorrah.*
G in the day of judgment, than Mt 10:15 *1116*
G in the day of judgment, than Mk 6:11 *1116*
Sodoma, and been made like unto *G* Rom 9:29 *1116*
Even as Sodom and *G*, and the cities Jude 7 *1116*

GONE {214}
Jacob was yet scarce *g* out from Gen 27:30 3318
mother, and was *g* to Padan-aram Gen 28:7 3212
though thou wouldest needs be *g* Gen 31:30 1980
our daughter, and we will be *g* Gen 34:17 1980
of your households, and be *g* Gen 42:33 3212
when they were *g* out of the city, Gen 44:4 3318
the prey, my son, thou art *g* up Gen 49:9 5927
As soon as I am *g* out of the city Ex 9:29 3318
herds, as ye have said, and be *g* Ex 12:32 3212
And when the dew that lay was *g* up Ex 16:14 5927
the children of Israel were *g* Ex 19:1 3318
Moses, until he was *g* into the Ex 33:8 935
after whom they have *g* a whoring Lev 17:7 2181
if thou hast not *g* aside to Num 5:19 7847
But if thou hast *g* aside to Num 5:20 7847
when Moses was *g* into the Num 7:89 935
which we have *g* to search it Num 13:32 5674
is wrath *g* out from the LORD Num 16:46 3318
there is a fire *g* out of Heshbon Num 21:28 3318
When I was *g* up into the mount to Deut 9:9 5927
are *g* out from among you, and have Deut 13:13 3318
And hath *g* and served other gods, Deut 17:3 3212
That which is *g* out of thy lips Deut 23:23 4161
shall be when ye be *g* over Jordan Deut 27:4 5674
he seeth that their power is *g* Deut 32:36 235
pursued after them were *g* out Josh 2:7 3318
before us, until we were *g* over Josh 4:23 5674
which he commanded you, and have *g* Josh 23:16 1980
When he was *g* out, his servants Judg 3:24 3318
Abinoam was *g* up to mount Tabor Judg 4:12 5927
is not the LORD *g* out before thee Judg 4:14 3318
and the priest, and ye are *g* away Judg 18:24 3212
of Israel were *g* up to Mizpeh Judg 20:3 5927
of the LORD is *g* out against me Ruth 1:13 3318
in law is *g* back unto her people Ruth 1:15 7725
knew not that Jonathan was *g* 1Sa 14:3 1980
now, and see who is *g* from us 1Sa 14:17 1980
is *g* about, and passed on 1Sa 15:12 5437
and *g* down to Gilgal 1Sa 15:12 3381
have *g* the way which the LORD 1Sa 15:20 3212
And as soon as the lad was *g* 1Sa 20:41 935
when the wine was *g* out of Nabal 1Sa 25:37 3318
in the morning the people had *g* 2Sa 2:27 5927
Wherefore hast thou *g* in unto my 2Sa 3:7 935
him away, and he was *g* in peace 2Sa 3:22 3212
him away, and he is *g* in peace 2Sa 3:23 3212
sent him away, and he is quite *g* 2Sa 3:24 3212
ark of the LORD had *g* six paces 2Sa 6:13 6805
Amnon said unto her, Arise, be *g* 2Sa 13:15 3212
They be *g* over the brook of water 2Sa 17:20 5674
them that was not *g* over Jordan 2Sa 17:22 5674
and the men of Israel were *g* away 2Sa 23:9 5927
So when they had *g* through all 2Sa 24:8 7751
For he is *g* down this day, and 1Kin 1:25 3381
had *g* from Jerusalem to Gath 1Kin 2:41 1980
Pharaoh king of Egypt had *g* up 1Kin 9:16 5927
host was *g* up to bury the slain 1Kin 11:15 5927
And when he was *g*, a lion met him 1Kin 13:24 3212
for thou hast *g* and made thee 1Kin 14:9 3212
away dung, till it be all *g* 1Kin 14:10 8552
pass, as soon as I am *g* from thee 1Kin 18:12 3212
was busy here and there, he was *g* 1Kin 20:40 369
whither he is *g* down to possess 1Kin 21:18 3381
the messenger that was *g* to call 1Kin 22:13 1980
that bed on which thou art *g* up 2Kin 1:4 5927
that bed on which thou art *g* up 2Kin 1:6 5927
that bed on which thou art *g* up 2Kin 1:16 5927
to pass, when they were *g* over 2Kin 2:9 5674
And the Syrians had *g* out by 2Kin 5:2 3318
and *g* forth, behold, an host 2Kin 6:15 3318
therefore are they *g* out of the 2Kin 7:12 3318
afore Isaiah was *g* out into the 2Kin 20:4 3318
by which it had *g* down in the 2Kin 20:11 3381
for God is *g* forth before thee to 1Chr 14:15 3318
but have *g* from tent to tent, and 1Chr 17:5 1961
of their feasting were *g* about Job 1:5 5362
shall I arise, and the night be *g* Job 7:4 4059
me on every side, and I am *g* Job 19:10 3212
Neither have I *g* back from the Job 23:12 4185
for a little while, but are *g* Job 24:24 369
up, they are *g* away from men Job 28:4 5128
They are all *g* aside, they are Ps 14:3 5493
Their line is *g* out through all Ps 19:4 3318
iniquities are *g* over mine head Ps 38:4 5674
mine eyes, it also is *g* from me Ps 38:10 369
for I had *g* with the multitude, I Ps 42:4 5674
and thy billows are *g* over me Ps 42:7 5674
God is *g* up with a shout, the Ps 47:5 5927
after he had *g* in to Bath-sheba Ps 51:t 935
Every one of them is *g* back Ps 53:3 5472
as for me, my feet were almost *g* Ps 73:2 5186
Is his mercy clean *g* for ever Ps 77:8 656
thing that is *g* out of my lips Ps 89:34 4161
wind passeth over it, and it is *g* Ps 103:16 369
I am *g* like the shadow when it Ps 109:23 1980
I have *g* astray like a lost sheep Ps 119:176 8582
the stream had *g* over our soul Ps 124:4 5674
proud waters had *g* over our soul Ps 124:5 5674
at home, he is *g* a long journey Prov 7:19 1980
but when he is *g* his way, then he Prov 20:14 235
g from the place of the holy, and Eccl 8:10 1980
is past, the rain is over and *g* Song 2:11 1980
had withdrawn himself, and was *g* Song 5:6 5674
Whither is thy beloved *g*, O thou Song 6:1 1980
My beloved is *g* down into his Song 6:2 3381
anger, they are *g* away backward Is 1:4 2114
my people are *g* into captivity Is 5:13 1540
They are *g* over the passage Is 10:29 5674
He is *g* up to Bajith, and to Dibon Is 15:2 5927
For the cry is *g* round about the Is 15:8 5362
out, they are *g* over the sea Is 16:8 5674
art wholly *g* up to the housetops Is 22:1 5927
the mirth of the land is *g* Is 24:11 1540
which is *g* down in the sun dial Is 38:8 3381
by which degrees it was *g* down Is 38:8 3381
that he had not *g* with his feet Is 41:3 935
the word is *g* out of my mouth in Is 45:23 3318
themselves are *g* into captivity Is 46:2 1980
my salvation is *g* forth, and mine Is 51:5 3318
All we like sheep have *g* astray Is 53:6 8582
to another than me, and art *g* up Is 57:8 5927
me, that they are *g* far from me Jer 2:5 7368
I have not *g* after Baalim Jer 2:23 1980
she is *g* up upon every high Jer 3:6 1980
he is *g* forth from his place to Jer 4:7 3318
they are revolted and *g* Jer 5:23 3212
beast are fled; they are *g* Jer 9:10 1980
my children are *g* forth of me Jer 10:20 3318
and the cry of Jerusalem is *g* up Jer 14:2 5927
the LORD, thou art *g* backward Jer 15:6 3212
her sun is *g* down while it was Jer 15:9 935
g forth into all the land Jer 23:15 3318
of the LORD is *g* forth in fury Jer 23:19 3318
g forth with you into captivity Jer 29:16 3318
army, which are *g* up from you Jer 34:21 5927
Now while he was not yet *g* back Jer 40:5 7725
Egypt, whither ye be *g* to dwell Jer 44:8 935
which are *g* into the land of Jer 44:14 935
that are *g* into the land of Egypt Jer 44:28 935
neither hath he *g* into captivity Jer 48:11 1980
g up out of her cities, and his Jer 48:15 5927
men are *g* down to the slaughter Jer 48:15 3381
thy plants are *g* over the sea Jer 48:32 5674
they have *g* from mountain to hill Jer 50:6 1980
Judah is *g* into captivity because Lam 1:3 1540
her children are *g* into captivity Lam 1:5 1980
they are *g* without strength Lam 1:6 3212
my young men are *g* into captivity Lam 1:18 1980
the morning is *g* forth Eze 7:10 3318
Israel was *g* up from the cherub Eze 9:3 5927
Ye have not *g* up into the gaps, Eze 13:5 5927
fire is *g* out of a rod of her Eze 19:14 3318
because thou hast *g* a whoring Eze 23:30 2181
and whose scum is not *g* out of it Eze 24:6 3318
earth are *g* down from his shadow Eze 31:12 3381
they are *g* down, they lie Eze 32:21 3381
which are *g* down uncircumcised Eze 32:24 3381
which are *g* down to hell with Eze 32:27 3381
which are *g* down with the slain Eze 32:30 3381
are *g* forth out of his land Eze 36:20 3318
the heathen, whither they be *g* Eze 37:21 1980
that are *g* away far from me Eze 44:10 7368
Chaldeans, The thing is *g* from me Dan 2:5 230
ye see the thing is *g* from me Dan 2:8 230
which was *g* forth to slay the Dan 2:14 5312
and when I am *g* forth, lo, the Dan 10:20 3318
they have *g* a whoring from under Hos 4:12 2181
For they are *g* up to Assyria, a Hos 8:9 5927
for thou hast *g* a whoring from Hos 9:1 2181
they are *g* because of destruction Hos 9:6 1980
When will the new moon be *g* Amos 8:5 5674
But Jonah was *g* down into the Jonah 1:5 3381
for they are *g* into captivity Mic 1:16 1540
the gate, and are *g* out by it Mic 2:13 3318
are *g* away from mine ordinances Mal 3:7 5493
Ye shall not have *g* over the Mt 10:23 *5055*

unclean spirit is *g* out of a man Mt 12:43 *1831*
And when they were *g* over, they Mt 14:34 *1276*
sheep, and one of them be *g* astray Mt 18:12 *4105*
and seeketh that which is *g* astray *Mt 18:12* *4105*
for our lamps are *g* out *Mt 25:8* *4570*
when he was *g* out into the porch, *Mt 26:71* *1831*
when he had *g* a little farther Mk 1:19 *4260*
that virtue had *g* out of him Mk 5:30 *1831*
the devil is *g* out of thy Mk 7:29 *1831*
house, she found the devil *g* out Mk 7:30 *1831*
when he was *g* forth into the way, Mk 10:17 *1607*
as the angels were *g* away from Lk 2:15 *565*
the fishermen were *g* out of them Lk 5:2 *576*
that virtue is *g* out of me Lk 8:46 *1831*
to pass, when the devil was *g* out Lk 11:14 *1831*
unclean spirit is *g* out of a man Lk 11:24 *1831*
That he was *g* to be guest with a Lk 19:7 *1525*
as though he would have *g* further Lk 24:28 *4198*
(For his disciples were *g* away Jn 4:8 *565*
his disciples were *g* away alone Jn 6:22 *565*
But when his brethren were *g* up Jn 7:10 *305*
behold, the world is *g* after him Jn 12:19 *565*
Therefore, when he was *g* out Jn 13:31 *1831*
when they had *g* through the isle Acts 13:6 *1330*
when the Jews were *g* out of the Acts 13:42 *1826*
Now when they had *g* throughout Acts 16:6 *1330*
the hope of their gains was *g* Acts 16:19 *1831*
g up, and saluted the church, he Acts 18:22 *305*
when he had *g* over those parts, Acts 20:2 *1330*
among whom I have *g* preaching the Acts 20:25 *1330*
Who also hath *g* about to profane Acts 24:6 *3985*
And when they were *g* aside Acts 26:31 *402*
when they had *g* a little further, Acts 27:28 *1339*
They are all *g* out of the way, Rom 3:12 *1578*
Who is *g* into heaven, and is on 1Pet 3:22 *4198*
are *g* astray, following the way 2Pet 2:15 *4105*
prophets are *g* out into the world 1Jn 4:1 *1831*
for they have *g* in the way of Jude 11 *4198*

GOOD {725}
God saw the light, that it was *g* Gen 1:4 2896
and God saw that it was *g* Gen 1:10 2896
and God saw that it was *g* Gen 1:12 2896
and God saw that it was *g* Gen 1:18 2896
and God saw that it was *g* Gen 1:21 2896
and God saw that it was *g* Gen 1:25 2896
made, and, behold, it was very *g* Gen 1:31 2896
to the sight, and *g* for food Gen 2:9 2896
and the tree of knowledge of *g* Gen 2:9 2896
And the gold of that land is *g* Gen 2:12 2896
of the tree of the knowledge of *g* Gen 2:17 2896
It is not *g* that the man should Gen 2:18 2896
and ye shall be as gods, knowing *g* Gen 3:5 2896
saw that the tree was *g* for food Gen 3:6 2896
is become as one of us, to know *g* Gen 3:22 2896
shalt be buried in a *g* old age Gen 15:15 2896
and fetcht a calf tender and *g* Gen 18:7 2896
ye to them as is *g* in your eyes Gen 19:8 2896
down over against him a *g* way off Gen 21:16 7368
send me *g* speed this day, and shew Gen 24:12
cannot speak unto thee bad or *g* Gen 24:50 2896
the ghost, and died in a *g* old age Gen 25:8 2896
have done unto thee nothing but *g* Gen 26:29 2896
thence two *g* kids of the goats Gen 27:9 2896
what *g* shall my life do me Gen 27:46
God hath endued me with a *g* dowry Gen 30:20 2896
not to Jacob either *g* or bad Gen 31:24 2896
not to Jacob either *g* or bad Gen 31:29 2896
saidst, I will surely do thee *g* Gen 32:12 3190
saw that the interpretation was *g* Gen 40:16 2896
came up upon one stalk, rank and *g* Gen 41:5 2896
came up in one stalk, full and *g* Gen 41:22 2896
ears devoured the seven *g* ears Gen 41:24 2896
The seven *g* kine are seven years Gen 41:26 2896
the seven *g* ears are seven years Gen 41:26 2896
food of those *g* years that come Gen 41:35 2896
the thing was *g* in the eyes of Gen 41:37 3190
servant our father is in *g* health Gen 43:28 7965
have ye rewarded evil for *g* Gen 44:4 2896
I will give you the *g* of the land Gen 45:18 2898
for the *g* of all the land of Gen 45:20 2898
laden with the *g* things of Egypt Gen 45:23 2898
And wept on his neck a *g* while Gen 46:29 5750
And he saw that rest was *g* Gen 49:15 2896
but God meant it unto *g*, to bring Gen 50:20 2896
up out of that land unto a *g* land Ex 3:8 2896
thing that thou doest is not *g* Ex 18:17 2896
owner of the pit shall make it *g* Ex 21:34 7999
and he shall not make it *g* Ex 22:11 7999
he shall not make *g* that which Ex 22:13 7999
it, he shall surely make it *g* Ex 22:14 7999
with it, he shall not make it *g* Ex 22:15 7999
his lips to do evil, or to do *g* Lev 5:4 3190
killeth a beast shall make it *g* Lev 24:18 7999
g for a bad, or a bad for a *g* Lev 27:10 2896
value it, whether it be *g* or bad Lev 27:12 2896
it, whether it be *g* or bad Lev 27:14 2896
not search whether it be *g* or bad Lev 27:33 2896
with us, and we will do thee *g* Num 10:29 2895
hath spoken *g* concerning Israel Num 10:29 2896
dwell in, whether it be *g* or bad Num 13:19 2896
And be ye of *g* courage, and bring Num 13:20
search it, is an exceeding *g* land Num 14:7 2896
to do either *g* or bad of mine own Num 24:13 2896
hast spoken is *g* for us to do Deut 1:14 2896
It is a *g* land which the LORD our Deut 1:25 2896
evil generation see that *g* land Deut 1:35 2896
day had no knowledge between *g* Deut 1:39 2896

take ye *g* heed unto yourselves Deut 2:4 3966
see the *g* land that is beyond Deut 3:25 2896
Take ye therefore *g* heed unto Deut 4:15 3966
should not go in unto that *g* land Deut 4:21 2896
go over, and possess that *g* land Deut 4:22 2896
And houses full of all *g* things Deut 6:11 2898
g in the sight of the LORD Deut 6:18 2896
possess the *g* land which the LORD Deut 6:18 2896
LORD our God, for our *g* always Deut 6:24 2896
God bringeth thee into a *g* land Deut 8:7 2896
g land which he hath given thee Deut 8:10 2896
to do thee *g* at thy latter end Deut 8:16 3190
this *g* land to possess it for thy Deut 9:6 2896
I command thee this day for thy *g* Deut 10:13 2896
g land which the LORD giveth you Deut 11:17 2896
when thou doest that which is *g* Deut 12:28 2896
thou shalt rejoice in every *g* Deut 26:11 2896
open unto thee his *g* treasure Deut 28:12 2896
rejoiced over you to do you *g* Deut 28:63 3190
and he will do thee *g*, and multiply Deut 30:5 3190
in the fruit of thy land, for *g* Deut 30:9 2896
again rejoice over thee for *g* Deut 30:9 2896
before thee this day life and *g* Deut 30:15 2896
of a *g* courage, fear not, nor be Deut 31:6
Be strong and of a *g* courage Deut 31:7
said, Be strong and of a *g* courage Deut 31:23
for the *g* will of him that dwelt Deut 33:16 7522
Be strong and of a *g* courage Josh 1:6
and then thou shalt have *g* success Josh 1:8
Be strong and of a *g* courage Josh 1:9
only be strong and of a *g* courage Josh 1:18
as it seemeth *g* and right unto Josh 9:25 2896
be strong and of *g* courage Josh 10:25
There failed not ought of any *g* Josh 21:45 2896
Take *g* heed therefore unto Josh 23:11 3966
g land which the LORD your God Josh 23:13 2896
thing hath failed of all the *g* Josh 23:14 2896
that as all *g* things are come Josh 23:15 2896
destroyed you from off this *g* Josh 23:15 2896
perish quickly from off the *g* Josh 23:16 2896
after that he hath done you *g* Josh 24:20 3190
son of Joash died in a *g* old age Judg 8:32 2896
my *g* fruit, and go to be promoted Judg 9:11 2896
us whatsoever seemeth *g* unto thee Judg 10:15 2896
know I that the LORD will do me *g* Judg 17:13 3190
land, and, behold, it is very *g* Judg 18:9 2896
when they were a *g* way from the Judg 18:22 7368
with them what seemeth *g* unto you Judg 19:24 2896
Ruth her daughter in law, It is *g* Ruth 2:22 2896
unto her, Do what seemeth thee *g* 1Sa 1:23 2896
for it is no *g* report that I hear 1Sa 2:24 2896
let him do what seemeth him *g* 1Sa 3:18 2896
us all that seemeth *g* unto you 1Sa 11:10 2896
but I will teach you the *g* 1Sa 12:23 2896
Do whatsoever seemeth *g* unto thee 1Sa 14:36 2896
Saul, Do what seemeth *g* unto thee 1Sa 14:40 2896
and the lambs, and all that was *g* 1Sa 15:9 2896
Jonathan spake *g* of David unto 1Sa 19:4 2896
have been to thee-ward very *g* 1Sa 19:4 2896
if there be *g* toward David, and I 1Sa 20:12 2896
him as it shall seem *g* unto thee 1Sa 24:4 3190
for thou hast rewarded me *g* 1Sa 24:17 2896
wherefore the LORD reward thee *g* 1Sa 24:19 2896
was a woman of *g* understanding 1Sa 25:3 2896
for we come in a *g* day 1Sa 25:8 2896
But the men were very *g* unto us 1Sa 25:15 2896
and he hath requited me evil for *g* 1Sa 25:21 2896
g that he hath spoken concerning 1Sa 25:30 2896
This thing is not *g* that thou 1Sa 26:16 2896
me in the host is *g* in my sight 1Sa 29:6 2896
know that thou art *g* in my sight 1Sa 29:9 2896
all that seemed *g* to Israel 2Sa 3:19 2896
that seemed *g* to the whole house 2Sa 3:19
to have brought *g* tidings 2Sa 4:10 1319
a *g* piece of flesh, and a flagon 2Sa 6:19
Be of *g* courage, and let us play 2Sa 10:12
LORD do that which seemeth him *g* 2Sa 10:12 2896
brother Amnon neither *g* nor bad 2Sa 13:22 2896
is my lord the king to discern *g* 2Sa 14:17 2896
it had been *g* for me to have been 2Sa 14:32 2896
unto him, See, thy matters are *g* 2Sa 15:3 2896
do to me as seemeth *g* unto him 2Sa 15:26 2896
me *g* for his cursing this day 2Sa 16:12 2896
hath given is not *g* at this time 2Sa 17:7 2896
the *g* counsel of Ahithophel 2Sa 17:14 2896
And the king said, He is a *g* man 2Sa 18:27 2896
and cometh with *g* tidings 2Sa 18:27 2896
and to do what he thought *g* 2Sa 19:18 2896
therefore what is *g* in thine eyes 2Sa 19:27 2896
and can I discern between *g* 2Sa 19:35 2896
him what shall seem *g* unto thee 2Sa 19:37 2896
that which shall seem *g* unto thee 2Sa 19:38 2896
offer up what seemeth *g* unto him 2Sa 24:22 2896
man, and bringest *g* tidings 1Kin 1:42 2896
unto the king, The saying is *g* 1Kin 2:38 2896
The word that I have heard is *g* 1Kin 2:42 2896
that I may discern between *g* 1Kin 3:9 2896
that thou teach them the *g* way 1Kin 8:36 2896
one word of all his *g* promise 1Kin 8:56 2896
speak *g* words to them, then they 1Kin 12:7 2896
in him there is found some *g* 1Kin 14:13 2896
root up Israel out of this *g* land 1Kin 14:15 2896
or, if it seem *g* to thee, I will 1Kin 21:2 2896
doth not prophesy *g* concerning me 1Kin 22:8 2896
g unto the king with one mouth 1Kin 22:13 2896
of them, and speak that which is *g* 1Kin 22:13 2896
would prophesy no *g* concerning me 1Kin 22:18 2896
city, and shall fell every *g* tree 2Kin 3:19 2896

mar every *g* piece of land with 2Kin 3:19 2896
on every *g* piece of land cast 2Kin 3:25 2896
water, and felled all the *g* trees 2Kin 3:25 2896
this day is a day of *g* tidings 2Kin 7:9
even of every *g* thing of Damascus 2Kin 8:9 2898
that which is *g* in thine eyes 2Kin 10:5 2896
done that which is *g* in thy sight 2Kin 20:3 2896
G is the word of the LORD which 2Kin 20:19 2896
And he said, Is it not *g*, if peace 2Kin 20:19
And they found fat pasture and *g* 1Chr 4:40 2896
of Israel, If it seem *g* unto you 1Chr 13:2 2895
a *g* piece of flesh, and a flagon 1Chr 16:3
for he is *g* 1Chr 16:34 2896
Be of *g* courage, and let us behave 1Chr 19:13
do that which is *g* in his sight 1Chr 19:13 2896
do that which is *g* in his eyes 1Chr 21:23 2896
be strong, and of *g* courage 1Chr 22:13
that ye may possess this *g* land 1Chr 28:8 2896
strong and of *g* courage, and do it 1Chr 28:20
God, I have of mine own proper *g* 1Chr 29:3
And he died in a *g* old age 1Chr 29:28 2896
the LORD, saying, For he is *g* 2Chr 5:13 2896
thou hast taught them the *g* way 2Chr 6:27 2896
the LORD, saying, For he is *g* 2Chr 7:3 2896
speak *g* words to them, they will 2Chr 10:7 2896
And Asa did that which was *g* 2Chr 14:2 2896
for he never prophesied *g* unto me 2Chr 18:7 2896
g to the king with one assent 2Chr 18:12 2896
one of theirs, and speak thou *g* 2Chr 18:12 2896
he would not prophesy *g* unto me 2Chr 18:17 2896
there are *g* things found in thee 2Chr 19:3 2896
and the LORD shall be with the *g* 2Chr 19:11 2896
because he had done *g* in Israel 2Chr 24:16 2896
The *g* LORD pardon every one 2Chr 30:18 2896
the *g* knowledge of the LORD 2Chr 30:22 2896
and wrought that which was *g* 2Chr 31:20 2896
because he is *g*, for his mercy Ezr 3:11 2896
if it seem *g* to the king, let Ezr 5:17 2869
according to the *g* hand of his Ezr 7:9 2896
whatsoever shall seem *g* to thee Ezr 7:18 3191
by the *g* hand of our God upon us Ezr 8:18 2896
upon all them for *g* that seek him Ezr 8:22 2896
eat the *g* of the land, and leave Ezr 9:12 2898
be of *g* courage, and do it Ezr 10:4
according to the *g* hand of my God Neh 2:8 2896
of my God which was *g* upon me Neh 2:18 2896
their hands for this *g* work Neh 2:18 2896
I said, It is not *g* that ye do Neh 5:9 2896
Think upon me, my God, for *g* Neh 5:19 2896
reported his *g* deeds before me Neh 6:19 2896
g statutes and commandments Neh 9:13 2896
Thou gavest also thy *g* spirit to Neh 9:20 2896
the *g* thereof, behold, we are Neh 9:36 2898
wipe not out my *g* deeds that I Neh 13:14 2617
Remember me, O my God, for *g* Neh 13:31 2896
with them as it seemeth *g* to thee Est 3:11 2896
If it seem *g* unto the king, let Est 5:4 2895
who had spoken *g* for the king Est 7:9 2896
and gladness, a feast and a *g* day Est 8:17 2896
a *g* day, and of sending portions Est 9:19 2896
and from mourning into a *g* day Est 9:22 2896
shall we receive *g* at the hand of Job 2:10 2896
it, and know thou it for thy *g* Job 5:27
mine eye shall no more see *g* Job 7:7 2896
they flee away, they see no *g* Job 9:25 2896
Is it *g* unto thee that thou Job 10:3 2896
Is it *g* that he should search you Job 13:9 2896
speeches wherewith he can do no *g* Job 15:3 3276
their *g* is not in their hand Job 21:16 2898
filled their houses with *g* things Job 22:18 2896
thereby *g* shall come unto thee Job 22:21 2896
and doeth not *g* to the widow Job 24:21 3190
When I looked for *g*, then evil Job 30:26 2896
us know among ourselves what is *g* Job 34:4 2896
Their young ones are in *g* liking Job 39:4 2492
that say, Who will shew us any *g* Ps 4:6 2896
works, there is none that doeth *g* Ps 14:1 2896
there is none that doeth *g* Ps 14:3 2896
G and upright is the LORD Ps 25:8 2896
be of *g* courage, and he shall Ps 27:14
Be of *g* courage, and he shall Ps 31:24
O taste and see that the LORD is *g* Ps 34:8 2896
LORD shall not want any *g* thing Ps 34:10 2896
many days, that he may see *g* Ps 34:12 2896
Depart from evil, and do *g* Ps 34:14 2896
They rewarded me evil for *g* to Ps 35:12 2896
left off to be wise, and to do *g* Ps 36:3 3190
himself in a way that is not *g* Ps 36:4 2896
Trust in the LORD, and do *g* Ps 37:3 2896
The steps of a *g* man are ordered Ps 37:23
Depart from evil, and do *g* Ps 37:27 2896
evil for *g* are mine adversaries Ps 38:20 2896
I follow the thing that *g* is Ps 38:20 2896
I held my peace, even from *g* Ps 39:2 2896
My heart is inditing a *g* matter Ps 45:1 2896
Do *g* in thy *g* pleasure unto Ps 51:18 3190
Do *g* in thy *g* pleasure unto Ps 51:18
Thou lovest evil more than *g* Ps 52:3 2896
for it is *g* before thy saints Ps 52:9 2896
there is none that doeth *g* Ps 53:1 2896
there is none that doeth *g* Ps 53:3 2896
for it is *g* Ps 54:6 2896
for thy lovingkindness is *g* Ps 69:16 2896
Truly God is *g* to Israel, even to Ps 73:1 2896
But it is *g* for me to draw near Ps 73:28 2896
no *g* thing will he withhold from Ps 84:11 2896
LORD shall give that which is *g* Ps 85:12 2896
For thou, Lord, art *g*, and ready Ps 86:5 2896

Shew me a token for *g*	Ps 86:17	2896
It is a *g* thing to give thanks	Ps 92:1	2896
For the LORD is *g*	Ps 100:5	2896
thy mouth with *g* things	Ps 103:5	2896
hand, they are filled with *g*	Ps 104:28	2896
for he is *g*	Ps 106:1	2896
I may see the *g* of thy chosen	Ps 106:5	2896
thanks unto the LORD, for he is *g*	Ps 107:1	2896
they have rewarded me evil for *g*	Ps 109:5	2896
because thy mercy is *g*, deliver	Ps 109:21	2896
a *g* understanding have all they	Ps 111:10	2896
A *g* man sheweth favour, and	Ps 112:5	2896
for he is *g*	Ps 118:1	2896
for he is *g*	Ps 118:29	2896
for thy judgments are *g*	Ps 119:39	2896
Teach me *g* judgment and knowledge	Ps 119:66	2898
Thou art *g*, and doest *g*	Ps 119:68	2896
Thou art *g*, and doest *g*	Ps 119:68	2895
It is *g* for me that I have been	Ps 119:71	2896
Be surety for thy servant for *g*	Ps 119:122	2896
LORD our God I will seek thy *g*	Ps 122:9	2896
Do *g*, O LORD, unto those that be	Ps 125:4	2895
O LORD, unto those that be *g*	Ps 125:4	2896
thou shalt see the *g* of Jerusalem	Ps 128:5	2898
Behold, how *g* and how pleasant it	Ps 133:1	2896
for the LORD is *g*	Ps 135:3	2896
for he is *g*	Ps 136:1	2896
thy spirit is *g*	Ps 143:10	2896
The LORD is *g* to all	Ps 145:9	2896
for it is *g* to sing praises unto	Ps 147:1	2896
yea, every *g* path	Prov 2:9	2896
mayest walk in the way of *g* men	Prov 2:20	2896
g understanding in the sight of	Prov 3:4	2896
Withhold not *g* from them to whom	Prov 3:27	2896
For I give you *g* doctrine	Prov 4:2	2896
man doeth *g* to his own soul	Prov 11:17	1580
desire of the righteous is only *g*	Prov 11:23	2896
seeketh *g* procureth favour	Prov 11:27	2896
A *g* man obtaineth favour of the	Prov 12:2	2896
with *g* by the fruit of his mouth	Prov 12:14	2896
but a *g* word maketh it glad	Prov 12:25	2896
A man shall eat *g* by the fruit of	Prov 13:2	2896
G understanding giveth favour	Prov 13:15	2896
the righteous *g* shall be repaid	Prov 13:21	2896
A *g* man leaveth an inheritance to	Prov 13:22	2896
a *g* man shall be satisfied from	Prov 14:14	2896
The evil bow before the *g*	Prov 14:19	2896
shall be to them that devise *g*	Prov 14:22	2896
beholding the evil and the *g*	Prov 15:3	2896
spoken in due season, how *g* is it	Prov 15:23	2896
a *g* report maketh the bones fat	Prov 15:30	2896
a matter wisely shall find *g*	Prov 16:20	2896
him into the way that is not *g*	Prov 16:29	2896
Whoso rewardeth evil for *g*	Prov 17:13	2896
hath a froward heart findeth no *g*	Prov 17:20	2896
heart doeth *g* like a medicine	Prov 17:22	3190
Also to punish the just is not *g*	Prov 17:26	2896
It is not *g* to accept the person	Prov 18:5	2896
findeth a wife findeth a *g* thing	Prov 18:22	2896
be without knowledge, it is not *g*	Prov 19:2	2896
understanding shall find *g*	Prov 19:8	2896
and with *g* advice make war	Prov 20:18	
and a false balance is not *g*	Prov 20:23	2896
A *g* name is rather to be chosen	Prov 22:1	
eat thou honey, because it is *g*	Prov 24:13	2896
It is not *g* to have respect of	Prov 24:23	2896
a *g* blessing shall come upon them	Prov 24:25	2896
so is *g* news from a far country	Prov 25:25	2896
It is not *g* to eat much honey	Prov 25:27	2896
shall have *g* things in possession	Prov 28:10	2896
have respect of persons is not *g*	Prov 28:21	2896
She will do him *g* and not evil all	Prov 31:12	2896
that her merchandise is *g*	Prov 31:18	2896
was that *g* for the sons of men	Eccl 2:3	2896
his soul enjoy *g* in his labour	Eccl 2:24	2896
man that is *g* in his sight wisdom	Eccl 2:26	2896
give to him that is *g* before God	Eccl 2:26	2896
I know that there is no *g* in them	Eccl 3:12	2896
rejoice, and to do *g* in his life	Eccl 3:12	2896
enjoy the *g* of all his labour, it	Eccl 3:13	2896
I labour, and bereave my soul of *g*	Eccl 4:8	2896
because they have a *g* reward for	Eccl 4:9	2896
what *g* is there to the owners	Eccl 5:11	3788
it is *g* and comely for one to eat	Eccl 5:18	2896
to enjoy the *g* of all his labour	Eccl 5:18	2896
and his soul be not filled with *g*	Eccl 6:3	2896
twice told, yet hath he seen no *g*	Eccl 6:6	2896
what is *g* for man in this life	Eccl 6:12	2896
A *g* name is better than precious	Eccl 7:1	
Wisdom is *g* with an inheritance	Eccl 7:11	2896
It is *g* that thou shouldest take	Eccl 7:18	2896
just man upon earth, that doeth *g*	Eccl 7:20	2896
to the *g* and to the clean, and to	Eccl 9:2	2896
as is the *g*, so is the sinner	Eccl 9:2	2896
but one sinner destroyeth much *g*	Eccl 9:18	2896
they both shall be alike *g*	Eccl 11:6	2896
yea, he gave *g* heed, and sought	Eccl 12:9	
secret thing, whether it be *g*	Eccl 12:14	2896
of thy *g* ointments thy name is as	Song 1:3	2896
the tender grape give a *g* smell	Song 2:13	
ye shall eat the *g* of the land	Is 1:19	2898
that call evil *g*, and *g* evil	Is 5:20	2896
refuse the evil, and choose the *g*	Is 7:15	2896
refuse the evil, and choose the *g*	Is 7:16	2896
done that which is *g* in thy sight	Is 38:3	2896
G is the word of the LORD which	Is 39:8	2896
O Zion, that bringest *g* tidings	Is 40:9	1319
that bringest *g* tidings, lift up	Is 40:9	1319
to his brother, Be of *g* courage	Is 41:6	
yea, do *g*, or do evil, that we	Is 41:23	1390
one that bringeth *g* tidings	Is 41:27	1319
of him that bringeth *g* tidings	Is 52:7	1319
that bringeth *g* tidings of *g*,	Is 52:7	2896
me, and eat ye that which is *g*	Is 55:2	2896
to preach *g* tidings unto the meek	Is 61:1	1319
walketh in a way that was not *g*	Is 65:2	2896
do evil, but to do *g* they have no	Jer 4:22	3190
have withholden *g* things from you	Jer 5:25	2896
the old paths, where is the *g* way	Jer 6:16	2896
looked for peace, but no *g* came	Jer 8:15	2896
also is it in them to do *g*	Jer 10:5	3190
girdle, which is *g* for nothing	Jer 13:10	6743
then may ye also do *g*, that are	Jer 13:23	3190
not for this people for their *g*	Jer 14:11	2896
for peace, and there is no *g*	Jer 14:19	2896
and shall not see when *g* cometh	Jer 17:6	2896
as seemed *g* to the potter to make	Jer 18:4	3474
then I will repent of the *g*	Jer 18:10	2896
make your ways and your doings *g*	Jer 18:11	3190
Shall evil be recompensed for *g*	Jer 18:20	2896
before thee to speak *g* for them	Jer 18:20	2896
this city for evil, and not for *g*	Jer 21:10	2896
One basket had very *g* figs	Jer 24:2	2896
the *g* figs, very *g*	Jer 24:3	2896
the *g* figs, very *g*	Jer 24:3	2896
Like these *g* figs, so will I	Jer 24:5	2896
land of the Chaldeans for their *g*	Jer 24:5	2896
set mine eyes upon them for *g*	Jer 24:6	2896
do with me as seemeth *g* and meet	Jer 26:14	2896
perform my *g* word toward you, in	Jer 29:10	2896
neither shall he behold the *g*	Jer 29:32	2896
me for ever, for the *g* of them	Jer 32:39	2896
turn away from them, to do them *g*	Jer 32:40	3190
rejoice over them to do them *g*	Jer 32:41	2895
the *g* that I have promised them	Jer 32:42	2896
all the *g* that I do unto them	Jer 33:9	2896
for the LORD is *g*	Jer 33:11	2896
that I will perform that *g* thing	Jer 33:14	2896
this city for evil, and not for *g*	Jer 39:16	2896
If it seem *g* unto thee to come	Jer 40:4	2896
whither it seemeth *g* and	Jer 40:4	2896
Whether it be *g*, or whether it be	Jer 42:6	2896
over them for evil, and not for *g*	Jer 44:27	2896
The LORD is *g* unto them that wait	Lam 3:25	2896
It is *g* that a man should both	Lam 3:26	2896
It is *g* for a man that he bear	Lam 3:27	2896
High proceedeth not evil and *g*	Lam 3:38	2896
I took them away as I saw *g*	Eze 16:50	
It was planted in a *g* soil by	Eze 17:8	2896
which is not *g* among his people	Eze 18:18	2896
also statutes that were not *g*	Eze 20:25	2896
into it, even every *g* piece	Eze 24:4	2896
I will feed them in a *g* pasture	Eze 34:14	2896
there shall they lie in a *g* fold	Eze 34:14	2896
to have eaten up the *g* pasture	Eze 34:18	2896
and your doings that were not *g*	Eze 36:31	2896
I thought it *g* to shew the signs	Dan 4:2	8232
because the shadow thereof is *g*	Hos 4:13	2896
hath cast off the thing that is *g*	Hos 8:3	2896
Seek *g*, and not evil, that ye may	Amos 5:14	2896
Hate the evil, and love the *g*	Amos 5:15	2896
upon them for evil, and not for *g*	Amos 9:4	2896
of Maroth waited carefully for *g*	Mic 1:12	2896
do not my words do *g* to him that	Mic 2:7	3190
Who hate the *g*, and love the evil	Mic 3:2	2896
shewed thee, O man, what is *g*	Mic 6:8	2896
The *g* man is perished out of the	Mic 7:2	2623
The LORD is *g*, a strong hold in	Nah 1:7	2896
of him that bringeth *g* tidings	Nah 1:15	1319
heart, The LORD will not do *g*	Zeph 1:12	3190
that talked with me with *g* words	Zec 1:13	2896
I said unto them, If ye think *g*	Zec 11:12	2896
it with *g* will at your hand	Mal 2:13	7522
is *g* in the sight of the LORD	Mal 2:17	2896
not forth *g* fruit is hewn down	Mt 3:10	*2570*
it is thenceforth *g* for nothing	Mt 5:13	*2480*
that they may see your *g* works	Mt 5:16	*2570*
do *g* to them that hate you, and	Mt 5:44	*2573*
to rise on the evil and on the *g*	Mt 5:45	*18*
know how to give *g* gifts unto	Mt 7:11	*18*
g things to them that ask him	Mt 7:11	*18*
Even so every *g* tree bringeth	Mt 7:17	*18*
bringeth forth *g* fruit	Mt 7:17	*2570*
A *g* tree cannot bring forth evil	Mt 7:18	*18*
corrupt tree bring forth *g* fruit	Mt 7:18	*2570*
not forth *g* fruit is hewn down	Mt 7:19	*2570*
there was a *g* way off from them	Mt 8:30	*3112*
Son, be of *g* cheer	Mt 9:2	
said, Daughter, be of *g* comfort	Mt 9:22	
for so it seemed *g* in thy sight	Mt 11:26	*2107*
the tree *g*, and his fruit *g*	Mt 12:33	*2570*
ye, being evil, speak *g* things	Mt 12:34	*18*
A *g* man out of the *g* treasure	Mt 12:35	*18*
the heart bringeth forth *g* things	Mt 12:35	*18*
But other fell into *g* ground	Mt 13:8	*2570*
g ground is he that heareth the	Mt 13:23	*2570*
which sowed *g* seed in his field	Mt 13:24	*2570*
not thou sow *g* seed in thy field	Mt 13:27	*2570*
He that soweth the *g* seed is the	Mt 13:37	*2570*
the *g* seed are the children of	Mt 13:38	*2570*
and gathered the *g* into vessels	Mt 13:48	*2570*
unto them, saying, Be of *g* cheer	Mt 14:27	
it is *g* for us to be here	Mt 17:4	*2570*
his wife, it is not *g* to marry	Mt 19:10	*4851*
G Master, what *g* thing shall I	Mt 19:16	*18*
unto him, Why callest thou me *g*	Mt 19:17	*18*
there is none *g* but one, that is,	Mt 19:17	*18*
Is thine eye evil, because I am *g*	Mt 20:15	*18*
many as they found, both bad and *g*	Mt 22:10	*18*
said unto him, Well done, thou *g*	Mt 25:21	*18*
lord said unto him, Well done, *g*	Mt 25:23	*18*
she hath wrought a *g* work upon me	Mt 26:10	*18*
it had been *g* for that man if he	Mt 26:24	*18*
Is it lawful to do *g* on the	Mk 3:4	*15*
And other fell on *g* ground	Mk 4:8	*2570*
they which are sown on *g* ground	Mk 4:20	*2570*
and saith unto them, Be of *g* cheer	Mk 6:50	
it is *g* for us to be here	Mk 9:5	*2750*
Salt is *g*	Mk 9:50	*2750*
G Master, what shall I do that I	Mk 10:17	*18*
unto him, Why callest thou me *g*	Mk 10:18	*18*
there is none *g* but one, that is,	Mk 10:18	*18*
unto him, Be of *g* comfort, rise	Mk 10:49	
she hath wrought a *g* work on me	Mk 14:6	*2570*
ye will ye may do them *g*	Mk 14:7	*2095*
g were it for that man if he had	Mk 14:21	*2570*
It seemed *g* to me also, having	Lk 1:3	
filled the hungry with *g* things	Lk 1:53	*18*
I bring you *g* tidings of great	Lk 2:10	*2097*
on earth peace, *g* will toward men	Lk 2:14	*2107*
not forth *g* fruit is hewn down	Lk 3:9	*2570*
on the sabbath days to do *g*	Lk 6:9	*15*
do *g* to them which hate you,	Lk 6:27	*2573*
do *g* to them which do *g* to you	Lk 6:33	*15*
But love ye your enemies, and do *g*	Lk 6:35	*15*
g measure, pressed down, and	Lk 6:38	*2570*
For a *g* tree bringeth not forth	Lk 6:43	*2570*
corrupt tree bring forth *g* fruit	Lk 6:43	*2570*
A *g* man out of the *g* treasure	Lk 6:45	*18*
bringeth forth that which is *g*	Lk 6:45	*18*
And other fell on *g* ground	Lk 8:8	*18*
But that on the *g* ground are they	Lk 8:15	*2570*
g heart, having heard the word,	Lk 8:15	*18*
her, Daughter, be of *g* comfort	Lk 8:48	
it is *g* for us to be here	Lk 9:33	*2570*
for so it seemed *g* in thy sight	Lk 10:21	*2107*
and Mary hath chosen that *g* part	Lk 10:42	*18*
know how to give *g* gifts unto	Lk 11:13	*18*
for it is your Father's *g*	Lk 12:32	
Salt is *g*	Lk 14:34	*2570*
lifetime receivedst thy *g* things	Lk 16:25	*18*
G Master, what shall I do to	Lk 18:18	*18*
unto him, Why callest thou me *g*	Lk 18:19	*18*
none is *g*, save one, that is, God	Lk 18:19	*18*
unto him, Well, thou *g* servant	Lk 19:17	*18*
and he was a *g* man, and a just	Lk 23:50	*18*
Can there any *g* thing come out of	Jn 1:46	*18*
beginning doth set forth *g* wine	Jn 2:10	*2570*
hast kept the *g* wine until now	Jn 2:10	*2570*
they that have done *g*, unto the	Jn 5:29	*18*
for some said, He is a *g* man	Jn 7:12	*18*
I am the *g* shepherd	Jn 10:11	*2570*
the *g* shepherd giveth his life	Jn 10:11	*2570*
I am the *g* shepherd, and know my	Jn 10:14	*2570*
Many *g* works have I shewed you	Jn 10:32	*2570*
For a *g* work we stone thee not	Jn 10:33	*2570*
but be of *g* cheer	Jn 16:33	
g deed done to the impotent man	Acts 4:9	*2108*
this woman was full of *g* works	Acts 9:36	*18*
of *g* report among all the nation	Acts 10:22	*18*
who went about doing *g*, and	Acts 10:38	*2109*
For he was a *g* man, and full of	Acts 11:24	*18*
without witness, in that he did *g*	Acts 14:17	*15*
ye know how that a *g* while ago	Acts 15:7	*744*
It seemed *g* unto us, being	Acts 15:25	
For it seemed *g* to the Holy Ghost	Acts 15:28	
But Paul thought not *g* to take	Acts 15:38	*515*
this tarried there yet a *g* while	Acts 18:18	*2425*
having a *g* report of all the Jews	Acts 22:12	
I have lived in all *g* conscience	Acts 23:1	*18*
by him, and said, Be of *g* cheer	Acts 23:11	
now I exhort you to be of *g* cheer	Acts 27:22	
Wherefore, sirs, be of *g* cheer	Acts 27:25	
Then were they all of *g* cheer	Acts 27:36	
to every man that worketh *g*	Rom 2:10	*18*
Let us do evil, that *g* may come	Rom 3:8	*18*
there is none that doeth *g*	Rom 3:12	*5544*
yet peradventure for a *g* man some	Rom 5:7	*18*
commandment holy, and just, and *g*	Rom 7:12	*18*
which is *g* made death unto me	Rom 7:13	*18*
death in me by that which is *g*	Rom 7:13	*18*
consent unto the law that it is *g*	Rom 7:16	*2570*
in my flesh,) dwelleth no *g* thing	Rom 7:18	*18*
that which is *g* I find not	Rom 7:18	*2570*
For the *g* that I would I do not	Rom 7:19	*18*
a law, that, when I would do *g*	Rom 7:21	*2570*
for *g* to them that love God	Rom 8:28	*18*
neither having done any *g* or evil	Rom 9:11	*18*
and bring glad tidings of *g* things	Rom 10:15	*18*
to nature into a *g* olive tree	Rom 11:24	*2565*
that ye may prove what is that *g*	Rom 12:2	*18*
cleave to that which is *g*	Rom 12:9	*18*
of evil, but overcome evil with *g*	Rom 12:21	*18*
are not a terror to *g* works	Rom 13:3	*18*
do that which is *g*, and thou shalt	Rom 13:3	*18*
the minister of God to thee for *g*	Rom 13:4	*18*
not then your *g* be evil spoken of	Rom 14:16	*18*
It is *g* neither to eat flesh, nor	Rom 14:21	*2570*
for his *g* to edification	Rom 15:2	*18*
by *g* words and fair speeches	Rom 16:18	*5542*
you wise unto that which is *g*	Rom 16:19	*18*

Your glorying is not *g* ... 1Cor 5:6 2570
It is *g* for a man not to touch a ... 1Cor 7:1 2570
It is *g* for them if they abide ... 1Cor 7:8 2570
is *g* for the present distress ... 1Cor 7:26 2570
that it is *g* for a man so to be ... 1Cor 7:26 2570
communications corrupt *g* manners ... 1Cor 15:33 5543
hath done, whether it be *g* or bad ... 2Cor 5:10 18
by evil report and *g* report ... 2Cor 6:8 2162
may abound to every *g* work ... 2Cor 9:8 18
be of *g* comfort, be of one mind, ... 2Cor 13:11
But it is *g* to be zealously ... Gal 4:18 2570
affected always in a *g* thing ... Gal 4:18 2570
him that teacheth in all *g* things ... Gal 6:6 18
let us do *g* unto all men, ... Gal 6:10 18
according to the *g* pleasure of ... Eph 1:5
according to his *g* pleasure which ... Eph 1:9
in Christ Jesus unto *g* works ... Eph 2:10 18
his hands the thing which is *g* ... Eph 4:28 18
but that which is *g* to the use of ... Eph 4:29 18
With *g* will doing service, as to ... Eph 6:7 2133
whatsoever *g* thing any man doeth ... Eph 6:8 18
that he which hath begun a *g* work ... Phil 1:6 18
and some also of *g* will ... Phil 1:15 2107
will and to do of his *g* pleasure ... Phil 2:13
that I also may be of *g* comfort ... Phil 2:19
whatsoever things are of *g* report ... Phil 4:8 2163
being fruitful in every *g* work ... Col 1:10 18
we thought it *g* to be left at ... 1Th 3:1 2106
brought us *g* tidings of your ... 1Th 3:6 2097
that ye have *g* remembrance of us ... 1Th 3:6 18
but ever follow that which is *g* ... 1Th 5:15 18
hold fast that which is *g* ... 1Th 5:21 2570
fulfil all the *g* pleasure of his ... 2Th 1:11
and *g* hope through grace, ... 2Th 2:16 18
and stablish you in every *g* word ... 2Th 2:17 18
of a *g* conscience, and of faith ... 1Ti 1:5 18
But we know that the law is *g* ... 1Ti 1:8 2570
by them mightest war a *g* warfare ... 1Ti 1:18 2570
Holding faith, and a *g* conscience ... 1Ti 1:19 18
For this is *g* and acceptable in ... 1Ti 2:3 2570
godliness) with *g* works ... 1Ti 2:10 18
of a bishop, he desireth a *g* work ... 1Ti 3:1 2570
sober, of *g* behaviour, given to ... 1Ti 3:2 2887
Moreover he must have a *g* report ... 1Ti 3:7 2570
purchase to themselves a *g* degree ... 1Ti 3:13 2570
For every creature of God is *g* ... 1Ti 4:4 2570
thou shalt be a *g* minister of ... 1Ti 4:6 2570
of *g* doctrine, whereunto thou ... 1Ti 4:6 2570
for that is *g* and acceptable ... 1Ti 5:4 2570
Well reported of for *g* works ... 1Ti 5:10 2570
diligently followed every *g* work ... 1Ti 5:10 18
Likewise also the *g* works of some ... 1Ti 5:25 2570
Fight the *g* fight of faith, lay ... 1Ti 6:12 2570
hast professed a *g* profession ... 1Ti 6:12 2570
Pilate witnessed a *g* confession ... 1Ti 6:13 2570
That they do *g*, that they be rich ... 1Ti 6:18 14
that they be rich in *g* works ... 1Ti 6:18 2570
up in store for themselves a *g* ... 1Ti 6:19 2570
That *g* thing which was committed ... 2Ti 1:14 2570
as a *g* soldier of Jesus Christ ... 2Ti 2:3 2570
and prepared unto every *g* work ... 2Ti 2:21 18
despisers of those that are *g* ... 2Ti 3:3 865
furnished unto all *g* works ... 2Ti 3:17 18
I have fought a *g* fight, I have ... 2Ti 4:7 2570
of hospitality, a lover of *g* men ... Titus 1:8 5358
unto every *g* work reprobate ... Titus 1:16 18
much wine, teachers of *g* things ... Titus 2:3 2567
chaste, keepers at home, *g* ... Titus 2:5 18
thyself a pattern of *g* works ... Titus 2:7 2570
but shewing all *g* fidelity ... Titus 2:10 18
people, zealous of *g* works ... Titus 2:14 2570
to be ready to every *g* work ... Titus 3:1 18
be careful to maintain *g* works ... Titus 3:8 2570
These things are *g* and profitable ... Titus 3:8 2570
g works for necessary uses ... Titus 3:14 2570
by the acknowledging of every *g* ... Philem 6 18
exercised to discern both *g* ... Heb 5:14 2570
And have tasted the *g* word of God ... Heb 6:5 2570
high priest of *g* things to come ... Heb 9:11 18
a shadow of *g* things to come ... Heb 10:1 18
provoke unto love and to *g* works ... Heb 10:24 2570
it the elders obtained a *g* report ... Heb 11:2
him as *g* as dead, so many as the ... Heb 11:12
having obtained a *g* report ... Heb 11:39
For it is a *g* thing that the ... Heb 13:9 2570
But to do *g* and to communicate ... Heb 13:16 2140
we trust we have a *g* conscience ... Heb 13:18 2570
in every *g* work to do his will ... Heb 13:21 18
Every *g* gift and every perfect ... Jas 1:17 18
him, Sit thou here in a *g* place ... Jas 2:3 2573
let him shew out of a *g* ... Jas 3:13 2570
g fruits, without partiality, and ... Jas 3:17 18
to him that knoweth to do *g* ... Jas 4:17 2570
they may by your *g* works ... 1Pet 2:12 2570
not only to the *g* and gentle, but ... 1Pet 2:18 18
see *g* days, let him refrain his ... 1Pet 3:10 18
Let him eschew evil, and do *g* ... 1Pet 3:11 18
be followers of that which is *g* ... 1Pet 3:13 18
Having a *g* conscience ... 1Pet 3:16 18
your *g* conversation in Christ ... 1Pet 3:16 18
but the answer of a *g* conscience ... 1Pet 3:21 18
as *g* stewards of the manifold ... 1Pet 4:10 2570
But whoso hath this world's *g* ... 1Jn 3:17 979
is evil, but that which is *g* ... 3Jn 11 18
He that doeth *g* is of God ... 3Jn 11 15
Demetrius hath *g* report of all ... 3Jn 12

GOODLIER {1}
of Israel a *g* person than he ... 1Sa 9:2 2896

GOODLIEST {2}
your *g* young men, and your asses, ... 1Sa 8:16 2896
also and thy children, even the *g* ... 1Kin 20:3 2896

GOODLINESS {1}
all the *g* thereof is as the ... Is 40:6 2617

GOODLY See APPENDIX.

GOODMAN {6}
For the *g* is not at home, he is ... Prov 7:19 376
against the *g* of the house ... Mt 20:11 3611
that if the *g* of the house had ... Mt 24:43 3611
in, say ye to the *g* of the house ... Mk 14:14 3611
that if the *g* of the house had ... Lk 12:39 3611
shall say unto the *g* of the house ... Lk 22:11 3611

GOODNESS See APPENDIX.

GOODNESS' {1}
remember thou me for thy *g* sake ... Ps 25:7 2898

GOODS {42}
And they took all the *g* of Sodom ... Gen 14:11 7399
son, who dwelt in Sodom, and his *g* ... Gen 14:12 7399
And he brought back all the *g* ... Gen 14:16 7399
again his brother Lot, and his *g* ... Gen 14:16 7399
persons, and take the *g* to thyself ... Gen 14:21 7399
for all the *g* of his master were ... Gen 24:10 2898
all his *g* which he had gotten, ... Gen 31:18 7399
took their cattle, and their *g* ... Gen 46:6 7399
his hand unto his neighbour's *g* ... Ex 22:8 4399
his hand unto his neighbour's *g* ... Ex 22:11 4399
unto Korah, and all their *g* ... Num 16:32 7399
all their flocks, and all their *g* ... Num 31:9 2428
for their cattle, and for their *g* ... Num 35:3 7399
shall make thee plenteous in *g* ... Deut 28:11 2896
and thy wives, and all thy *g* ... 2Chr 21:14 7399
silver, and with gold, and with *g* ... Ezr 1:4 7399
of silver, with gold, with *g* ... Ezr 1:6 7399
that of the king's *g*, even of the ... Ezr 6:8 5232
or to confiscation of *g*, or to ... Ezr 7:26 5232
and possessed houses full of all *g* ... Neh 9:25 2898
his hands shall restore their *g* ... Job 20:10 202
shall no man look for his *g* ... Job 20:21 2898
his *g* shall flow away in the day ... Job 20:28
When *g* increase, they are ... Eccl 5:11 2896
which have gotten cattle and *g* ... Eze 38:12 7075
and gold, to take away cattle and *g* ... Eze 38:13 7075
Therefore their *g* shall become a ... Zeph 1:13 2428
man's house, and spoil his *g* ... Mt 12:29 4632
make him ruler over all his *g* ... Mt 24:47 5224
and delivered unto them his *g* ... Mt 25:14 5224
man's house, and spoil his *g* ... Mk 3:27 4632
away thy *g* ask them not again ... Lk 6:30 4674
his palace, his *g* are in peace ... Lk 11:21 5224
I bestow all my fruits and my *g* ... Lk 12:18 18
thou hast much *g* laid up for many ... Lk 12:19 18
portion of *g* that falleth to me ... Lk 15:12 3776
unto him that he had wasted his *g* ... Lk 16:1 5224
the half of my *g* I give to the ... Lk 19:8 5224
And sold their possessions and *g* ... Acts 2:45 5223
bestow all my *g* to feed the poor ... 1Cor 13:3 5224
joyfully the spoiling of your *g* ... Heb 10:34 5224
I am rich, and increased with *g* ... Rev 3:17 4147

GOPHER {1}
Make thee an ark of *g* wood ... Gen 6:14 1613

GORE {1}
If an ox *g* a man or a woman, that ... Ex 21:28 5055

GORED {2}
Whether he have *g* a son ... Ex 21:31 5055
or have *g* a daughter, according ... Ex 21:31 5055

GORGEOUS {1}
him, and arrayed him in a *g* robe ... Lk 23:11 2986

GORGEOUSLY {2}
captains and rulers clothed most *g* ... Eze 23:12 4358
they which are *g* apparelled ... Lk 7:25 1741

GOSHEN *(go'-shen)* {15}
1. A district of Egypt.
thou shalt dwell in the land of *G* ... Gen 45:10 1657
Joseph, to direct his face unto *G* ... Gen 46:28 1657
and they came into the land of *G* ... Gen 46:28 1657
to meet Israel his father, to *G* ... Gen 46:29 1657
ye may dwell in the land of *G* ... Gen 46:34 1657
behold, they are in the land of *G* ... Gen 47:1 1657
servants dwell in the land of *G* ... Gen 47:4 1657
in the land of *G* let them dwell ... Gen 47:6 1657
of Egypt, in the country of *G* ... Gen 47:27 1657
herds, they left in the land of *G* ... Gen 50:8 1657
sever in that day the land of *G* ... Ex 8:22 1657
Only in the land of *G*, where the ... Ex 9:26 1657
2. A district in southern Palestine.
Gaza, and all the country of *G* ... Josh 10:41 1657
country, and all the land of *G* ... Josh 11:16 1657
3. A town in Judea.
And *G*, and Holon, and Giloh ... Josh 15:51 1657

GOSPEL {101}
preaching the *g* of the kingdom, ... Mt 4:23 2098
preaching the *g* of the kingdom, ... Mt 9:35 2098
poor have the *g* preached to them ... Mt 11:5 2097
this *g* of the kingdom shall be ... Mt 24:14 2098
Wheresoever this *g* shall be ... Mt 26:13 2098
of the *g* of Jesus Christ, the Son ... Mk 1:1 2098
preaching the *g* of the kingdom of ... Mk 1:14 2098
repent ye, and believe the *g* ... Mk 1:15 2098
the *g* must first be published ... Mk 13:10 2098
Wheresoever this *g* shall be ... Mk 14:9 2098
preach the *g* to every creature ... Mk 16:15 2098
me to preach the *g* to the poor ... Lk 4:18 2097
to the poor the *g* is preached ... Lk 7:22 2097
the towns, preaching the *g* ... Lk 9:6 2097
in the temple, and preached the *g* ... Lk 20:1 2097
preached the *g* in many villages ... Acts 8:25 2097
And there they preached the *g* ... Acts 14:7 2097
had preached the *g* to that city ... Acts 14:21 2097
should hear the word of the *g* ... Acts 15:7 2098
us for to preach the *g* unto them ... Acts 16:10 2097
to testify the *g* of the grace of ... Acts 20:24 2098
separated unto the *g* of God ... Rom 1:1 2098
my spirit in the *g* of his Son ... Rom 1:9 2098
I am ready to preach the *g* to you ... Rom 1:15 2097
am not ashamed of the *g* of Christ ... Rom 1:16 2098
by Jesus Christ according to my *g* ... Rom 2:16 2098
them that preach the *g* of peace ... Rom 10:15 2097
they have not all obeyed the *g* ... Rom 10:16 2098
As concerning the *g*, they are ... Rom 11:28 2098
ministering the *g* of God ... Rom 15:16 2098
fully preached the *g* of Christ ... Rom 15:19 2098
so have I strived to preach the *g* ... Rom 15:20 2097
the blessing of the *g* of Christ ... Rom 15:29 2098
to stablish you according to my *g* ... Rom 16:25 2098
to baptize, but to preach the *g* ... 1Cor 1:17 2097
I have begotten you through the *g* ... 1Cor 4:15 2098
we should hinder the *g* of Christ ... 1Cor 9:12 2098
the *g* should live of the *g* ... 1Cor 9:14 2098
For though I preach the *g* ... 1Cor 9:16 2097
is unto me, if I preach not the *g* ... 1Cor 9:16 2097
of the *g* is committed unto me ... 1Cor 9:17
Verily that, when I preach the *g* ... 1Cor 9:18 2097
I may make the *g* of Christ ... 1Cor 9:18 2098
I abuse not my power in the *g* ... 1Cor 9:18 2098
I declare unto you the *g* which I ... 1Cor 15:1 2098
to Troas to preach Christ's *g* ... 2Cor 2:12 2098
But if our *g* be hid, it is hid to ... 2Cor 4:3 2098
light of the glorious *g* of Christ ... 2Cor 4:4 2098
brother, whose praise is in the *g* ... 2Cor 8:18 2098
subjection into the *g* of Christ ... 2Cor 9:13 2098
also in preaching the *g* of Christ ... 2Cor 10:14 2098
To preach the *g* in the regions ... 2Cor 10:16 2097
have not received, or another *g* ... 2Cor 11:4 2098
to you the *g* of God freely ... 2Cor 11:7 2098
grace of Christ unto another *g* ... Gal 1:6 2098
and would pervert the *g* of Christ ... Gal 1:7 2098
preach any other *g* unto you than ... Gal 1:8 2097
g unto you than that ye have ... Gal 1:9 2097
that the *g* which was preached of ... Gal 1:11 2098
that *g* which I preach among the ... Gal 2:2 2098
that the truth of the *g* might ... Gal 2:5 2098
when they saw that the *g* of the ... Gal 2:7 2098
as the *g* of the circumcision was ... Gal 2:7
according to the truth of the *g* ... Gal 2:14 2098
before the *g* unto Abraham ... Gal 3:8 4283
the *g* unto you at the first ... Gal 4:13 2097
of truth, the *g* of your salvation ... Eph 1:13 2098
of his promise in Christ by the *g* ... Eph 3:6 2098
the preparation of the *g* of peace ... Eph 6:15 2098
make known the mystery of the *g* ... Eph 6:19 2098
For your fellowship in the *g* from ... Phil 1:5 2098
defence and confirmation of the *g* ... Phil 1:7 2098
unto the furtherance of the *g* ... Phil 1:12 2098
I am set for the defence of the *g* ... Phil 1:17 2098
be as it becometh the *g* of Christ ... Phil 1:27 2098
together for the faith of the *g* ... Phil 1:27 2098
he hath served with me in the *g* ... Phil 2:22 2098
which laboured with me in the *g* ... Phil 4:3 2098
that in the beginning of the *g* ... Phil 4:15 2098
in the word of the truth of the *g* ... Col 1:5 2098
moved away from the hope of the *g* ... Col 1:23 2098
For our *g* came not unto you in ... 1Th 1:5 2098
the *g* of God with much contention ... 1Th 2:2 2098
God to be put in trust with the *g* ... 1Th 2:4 2098
not the *g* of God only, but also ... 1Th 2:8 2098
we preached unto you the *g* of God ... 1Th 2:9 2098
fellowlabourer in the *g* of Christ ... 1Th 3:2 2098
that obey not the *g* of our Lord ... 2Th 1:8 2098
Whereunto he called you by our *g* ... 2Th 2:14 2098
the glorious *g* of the blessed God ... 1Ti 1:11 2098
of the afflictions of the *g* ... 2Ti 1:8 2098
to light through the *g* ... 2Ti 1:10 2098
from the dead according to my *g* ... 2Ti 2:8 2098
unto me in the bonds of the *g* ... Philem 13 2098
For unto us was the *g* preached ... Heb 4:2 2097
g unto you with the Holy Ghost ... 1Pet 1:12 2097
by the *g* is preached unto you ... 1Pet 1:25 2097
For for this cause was the *g* ... 1Pet 4:6 2097
them that obey not the *g* of God ... 1Pet 4:17 2098
having the everlasting *g* to ... Rev 14:6 2098

GOSPEL'S {3}
his life for my sake and the *g* ... Mk 8:35 2098
or lands, for my sake, and the *g* ... Mk 10:29 2098
And this I do for the *g* sake ... 1Cor 9:23 2098

GOT {7}
which he had *g* in the land of ... Gen 36:6 7408
her hand, and fled, and *g* him out ... Gen 39:12 3318
with me, and fled, and *g* him out ... Gen 39:15 3318
For they *g* not the land in ... Ps 44:3 3423
I *g* me servants and maidens, and ... Eccl 2:7 7069
So I *g* a girdle according to the ... Jer 13:2 7069
Take the girdle that thou hast *g* ... Jer 13:4 7069

GOTTEN See APPENDIX.

GOURD {5}
And the LORD God prepared a *g* ... Jonah 4:6 7021
Jonah was exceeding glad of the *g* ... Jonah 4:6 7021

it smote the g that it withered .... Jonah 4:7 7021
thou well to be angry for the g............. Jonah 4:9 7021
LORD, Thou hast had pity on the g......... Jonah 4:10 7021

GOURDS {1}
thereof wild g his lap full....................... 2Kin 4:39 6498

GOVERN {3}
Dost thou now g the kingdom of............ 1Kin 21:7 6213
Shall even he that hateth right g.......... Job 34:17 2280
and g the nations upon earth .... Ps 67:4 5148

GOVERNMENT {4}
the g shall be upon his shoulder .... Is 9:6 4951
Of the increase of his g and peace .... Is 9:7 4951
I will commit thy g into his hand........... Is 22:21 4475
lust of uncleanness, and despise g 2Pet 2:10 2963

GOVERNMENTS {1}
then gifts of healings, helps, g 1Cor 12:28 2941

GOVERNOR {59}
And Joseph was the g over the land....... Gen 42:6 7989
he is g over all the land of...................... Gen 45:26 4910
which was the g of his house................. 1Kin 18:3 5921
back unto Amon the g of the city............ 1Kin 22:26 8269
gate of Joshua the g of the city 2Kin 23:8 8269
of Babylon had made Gedaliah g............. 2Kin 25:23 6485
unto the LORD to be the chief g.............. 1Chr 29:22 5057
to every g in all Israel, the 2Chr 1:2 5387
back to Amon the g of the city................ 2Chr 18:25 8269
Azrikam the g of the house, and 2Chr 28:7 5057
and Maaseiah the g of the city................ 2Chr 34:8 8269
g on this side the river, and.................... Ezr 5:3 6347
g on this side the river, and...................... Ezr 5:6 6347
Sheshbazzar, whom he had made g......... Ezr 5:14 6347
Tatnai, g beyond the river,....................... Ezr 6:6 6347
let the g of the Jews and the .... Ezr 6:7 6347
g on this side the river,.......................... Ezr 6:13 6347
of the g on this side the river .... Neh 3:7 6346
be their g in the land of Judah................ Neh 5:14 6346
have not eaten the bread of the g........... Neh 5:14 6346
required not I the bread of the g............ Neh 5:18 6346
and in the days of Nehemiah the g .... Neh 12:26 6346
he is the g among the nations .... Ps 22:28 4910
who was also chief g in the house.......... Jer 20:1 5057
their g shall proceed from the............... Jer 30:21 4910
made g over the cities of Judah.............. Jer 40:5 6485
the son of Ahikam g in the land............... Jer 40:7 6485
Babylon had made g over the land.......... Jer 41:2 6485
of Babylon had made g in the land .... Jer 41:18 6485
g of Judah, and to Joshua the son.......... Hag 1:1 6346
g of Judah, and the spirit of.................. Hag 1:14 6346
g of Judah, and to Joshua the son.......... Hag 2:2 6346
g of Judah, saying, I will shake .... Hag 2:21 6346
and he shall be as a g in Judah.............. Zec 9:7 441
offer it now unto thy g............................ Mal 1:8 6346
for out of thee shall come a G................. Mt 2:6 2233
him to Pontius Pilate the g...................... Mt 27:2 2232
And Jesus stood before the g.................. Mt 27:11 2232
the g asked him, saying, Art thou .... Mt 27:11 2232
that the g marvelled greatly .... Mt 27:14 2232
Now at that feast the g was wont .... Mt 27:15 2232
The g answered and said unto them,....... Mt 27:21 2232
the g said, Why, what evil hath............... Mt 27:23 2232
Then the soldiers of the g took............... Mt 27:27 2232
made when Cyrenius was g of Syria .... Lk 2:2 2230
Pontius Pilate being g of Judaea............ Lk 3:1 2230
the power and authority of the g .... Lk 20:20 2230
and bear unto the g of the feast .... Jn 2:8 755
the g of the feast called the..................... Jn 2:9 755
and he made him g over Egypt................ Acts 7:10 2233
bring him safe unto Felix the g............... Acts 23:24 2232
g Felix sendeth greeting .... Acts 23:26 2232
and delivered the epistle to the g .... Acts 23:33 2232
when the g had read the letter, ... Acts 23:34 2232
who informed the g against Paul .... Acts 24:1 2232
after that the g had beckoned .... Acts 24:10 2232
the king rose up, and the g...................... Acts 26:30 2232
In Damascus the g under Aretas............. 2Cor 11:32 1481
helm, whithersoever the g listeth .... Jas 3:4 2116

GOVERNOR'S {1}
And if this come to the g ears .... Mt 28:14 2232

GOVERNORS {22}
heart is toward the g of Israel................. Judg 5:9 2710
out of Machir came down g....................... Judg 5:14 2710
and of the g of the country...................... 1Kin 10:15 6346
for the g of the sanctuary, and 1Chr 24:5 8269
g of the house of God, were of 1Chr 24:5 8269
g of the country brought gold and 2Chr 9:14 6346
the g of the people, and all the 2Chr 23:20 4910
to the g on this side the river .... Ezr 8:36 6346
me to the g beyond the river .... Neh 2:7 6346
I came to the g beyond the river .... Neh 2:9 6346
But the former g that had been............... Neh 5:15 6346
to the g that were over every.................. Est 3:12 6346
chief of the g over all the wise .... Dan 2:48 5461
together the princes, the g...................... Dan 3:2 5461
Then the princes, the g, and................... Dan 3:3 5461
And the princes, g, and captains,............ Dan 3:27 5461
presidents of the kingdom, the g............ Dan 6:7 5461
the g of Judah shall say in their............. Zec 12:5 441
In that day will I make the g of .... Zec 12:6 441
And ye shall be brought before g .... Mt 10:18 2232
g until the time appointed of the .... Gal 4:2 3623
Or unto g, as unto them that are............. 1Pet 2:14 2232

GOYIM See NATIONS.

GOZAN *(go'-zan)* {5} *An Assyrian city.*
and in Habor by the river of G............... 2Kin 17:6 1470
and in Habor by the river of G............... 2Kin 18:11 1470
as G, and Haran, and Rezeph, and the ... 2Kin 19:12 1470
Habor, and Hara, and to the river G........ 1Chr 5:26 1470
my fathers have destroyed, as G............ Is 37:12 1470

GRACE {170}
But Noah found g in the eyes of............. Gen 6:8 2580
servant hath found g in thy sight........... Gen 19:19 2580
that I may find g in thy sight.................. Gen 32:5 2580
These are to find g in the sight .... Gen 33:8 2580
now I have found g in thy sight.............. Gen 33:10 2580
let me find g in the sight of my.............. Gen 33:15 2580
Let me find g in your eyes, and.............. Gen 34:11 2580
And Joseph found g in his sight.............. Gen 39:4 2580
let us find g in the sight of my .... Gen 47:25 2580
now I have found g in thy sight.............. Gen 47:29 2580
now I have found g in your eyes............. Gen 50:4 2580
hast also found g in my sight .... Ex 33:12 2580
if I have found g in thy sight................... Ex 33:13 2580
that I may find g in thy sight.................. Ex 33:13 2580
people have found g in thy sight .... Ex 33:16 2580
for thou hast found g in my sight............ Ex 33:17 2580
now I have found g in thy sight.............. Ex 34:9 2580
if we have found g in thy sight............... Num 32:5 2580
now I have found g in thy sight.............. Judg 6:17 2580
him in whose sight I shall find g............. Ruth 2:2 2580
Why have I found g in thine eyes .... Ruth 2:10 2580
handmaid find g in thy sight.................... 1Sa 1:18 2580
that I have found g in thine eyes............ 1Sa 20:3 2580
I have now found g in thine eyes............ 1Sa 27:5 2580
that I have found g in thy sight.............. 2Sa 14:22 2580
that I may find g in thy sight 2Sa 16:4 2580
now for a little space g hath .... Ezr 9:8 8467
all the women, and she obtained g.......... Est 2:17 2580
g is poured into thy lips .... Ps 45:2 2580
the LORD will give g and glory .... Ps 84:11 2580
be an ornament of g unto thy head......... Prov 1:9 2580
unto thy soul, and g to thy neck............. Prov 3:22 2580
but he giveth g unto the lowly .... Prov 3:34 2580
to thine head an ornament of g.............. Prov 4:9 2580
for the g of his lips the king.................. Prov 22:11 2580
sword found g in the wilderness .... Jer 31:2 2580
crying, G, g unto it .... Zec 4:7 2580
of Jerusalem, the spirit of g................... Zec 12:10 2580
the g of God was upon him .... Lk 2:40 5485
of the Father,) full of g .... Jn 1:14 5485
all we received, and g for g .... Jn 1:16 5485
the law was given by Moses, but g......... Jn 1:17 5485
great g was upon them all .... Acts 4:33 5485
he came, and had seen the g of God .... Acts 11:23 5485
them to continue in the g of God .... Acts 13:43 5485
testimony unto the word of his g .... Acts 14:3 5485
had been recommended to the g of .... Acts 14:26 5485
the g of the Lord Jesus Christ we........... Acts 15:11 5485
by the brethren unto the g of God .... Acts 15:40 5485
much which had believed through g ...... Acts 18:27 5485
the gospel of the g of God .... Acts 20:24 5485
to God, and to the word of his g .... Acts 20:32 5485
By whom we have received g.................. Rom 1:5 5485
G to you and peace from God our........... Rom 1:7 5485
Being justified freely by his g............... Rom 3:24 5485
is the reward not reckoned of g.............. Rom 4:4 5485
of faith, that it might be by g................ Rom 4:16 5485
into this g wherein we stand .... Rom 5:2 5485
g of God, and the gift by g .... Rom 5:15 5485
they which receive abundance of g .... Rom 5:17 5485
abounded, g did much more abound....... Rom 5:20 5485
even so might g reign through................ Rom 5:21 5485
in sin, that g may abound....................... Rom 6:1 5485
not under the law, but under g............... Rom 6:14 5485
not under the law, but under g............... Rom 6:15 5485
according to the election of g............... Rom 11:5 5485
And if by g, then is it no more of........... Rom 11:6 5485
otherwise g is no more g......................... Rom 11:6 5485
be of works, then is it no more g............ Rom 11:6 5485
through the g given unto me, to .... Rom 12:3 5485
to the g that is given to us..................... Rom 12:6 5485
because of the g that is given to............. Rom 15:15 5485
The g of our Lord Jesus Christ be.......... Rom 16:20 5485
The g of our Lord Jesus Christ be.......... Rom 16:24 5485
G be unto you, and peace, from God 1Cor 1:3 5485
for the g of God which is given.............. 1Cor 1:4 5485
According to the g of God which 1Cor 3:10 5485
For if I by g be a partaker, why............. 1Cor 10:30 5485
But by the g of God I am what I 1Cor 15:10 5485
his g which was bestowed upon me 1Cor 15:10 5485
but the g of God which was with............. 1Cor 15:10 5485
The g of our Lord Jesus Christ be.......... 1Cor 16:23 5485
G be to you and peace from God our....... 2Cor 1:2 5485
wisdom, but by the g of God.................. 2Cor 1:12 5485
that the abundant g might through 2Cor 4:15 5485
receive not the g of God in vain 2Cor 6:1 5485
we do you to wit of the g of God 2Cor 8:1 5485
finish in you the same g also................. 2Cor 8:6 5485
see that ye abound in this g also............ 2Cor 8:7 5485
For ye know the g of our Lord 2Cor 8:9 5485
to travel with us with this g.................. 2Cor 8:19 5485
to make all g abound toward you.......... 2Cor 9:8 5485
for the exceeding g of God in you 2Cor 9:14 5485
My g is sufficient for thee 2Cor 12:9 5485
The g of the Lord Jesus Christ, ... 2Cor 13:14 5485
G be to you and peace from God the ...... Gal 1:3 5485
him that called you into the g of........... Gal 1:6 5485
womb, and called me by his g .... Gal 1:15 5485
perceived the g that was given .... Gal 2:9 5485
I do not frustrate the g of God.............. Gal 2:21 5485
ye are fallen from g .... Gal 5:4 5485
the g of our Lord Jesus Christ be........... Gal 6:18 5485
G be to you, and peace, from God.......... Eph 1:2 5485
the praise of the glory of his g .... Eph 1:6 5485
according to the riches of his g .... Eph 1:7 5485
with Christ, (by g ye are saved............... Eph 2:5 5485
his g in his kindness toward us .... Eph 2:7 5485
For by g are ye saved through .... Eph 2:8 5485
of the dispensation of the g of............... Eph 3:2 5485
the g of God given unto me by the......... Eph 3:7 5485
of all saints, is this g given.................... Eph 3:8 5485
unto every one of us is given g .... Eph 4:7 5485
may minister g unto the hearers .... Eph 4:29 5485
G be with all them that love our............ Eph 6:24 5485
G be unto you, and peace, from God ...... Phil 1:2 5485
ye all are partakers of my g.................... Phil 1:7 5485
The g of our Lord Jesus Christ be.......... Phil 4:23 5485
G be unto you, and peace, from God ...... Col 1:2 5485
knew the g of God in truth .... Col 1:6 5485
singing with g in your hearts to............ Col 3:16 5485
Let your speech be alway with g............. Col 4:6 5485
G be with you .... Col 4:18 5485
G be unto you, and peace, from God 1Th 1:1 5485
The g of our Lord Jesus Christ be.......... 1Th 5:28 5485
G unto you, and peace, from God 2Th 1:2 5485
according to the g of our God 2Th 1:12 5485
and good hope through g,...................... 2Th 2:16 5485
The g of our Lord Jesus Christ be.......... 2Th 3:18 5485
G, mercy, and peace, from God our....... 1Ti 1:2 5485
the g of our Lord was exceeding............ 1Ti 1:14 5485
G be with thee 1Ti 6:21 5485
G, mercy, and peace, from God the 2Ti 1:2 5485
according to his own purpose and g 2Ti 1:9 5485
be strong in the g that is in 2Ti 2:1 5485
G be with you 2Ti 4:22 5485
G, mercy, and peace, from God the......... Titus 1:4 5485
For the g of God that bringeth .... Titus 2:11 5485
That being justified by his g .... Titus 3:7 5485
G be with you all..................................... Titus 3:15 5485
G to you, and peace, from God our......... Philem 3 5485
The g of our Lord Jesus Christ be.......... Philem 25 5485
that he by the g of God should............... Heb 2:9 5485
come boldly unto the throne of g............ Heb 4:16 5485
find g to help in time of need................ Heb 4:16 5485
done despite unto the Spirit of g .... Heb 10:29 5485
lest any man fail of the g of God .... Heb 12:15 5485
cannot be moved, let us have g............. Heb 12:28 5485
the heart be established with g .... Heb 13:9 5485
G be with you all..................................... Heb 13:25 5485
the g of the fashion of it......................... Jas 1:11 2143
But he giveth more g .... Jas 4:6 5485
but giveth g unto the humble .... Jas 4:6 5485
G unto you, and peace, be....................... 1Pet 1:2 5485
who prophesied of the g that 1Pet 1:10 5485
hope to the end for the g that is............. 1Pet 1:13 5485
heirs together of the g of life................. 1Pet 3:7 5485
stewards of the manifold g of God.......... 1Pet 4:10 5485
proud, and giveth g to the humble.......... 1Pet 5:5 5485
But the God of all g, who hath 1Pet 5:10 5485
that this is the true g of God.................. 1Pet 5:12 5485
G and peace be multiplied unto you....... 2Pet 1:2 5485
But grow in g, and in the 2Pet 3:18 5485
G be with you, mercy, and peace,........... 2Jn 3 5485
turning the g of our God into................. Jude 4 5485
G be unto you, and peace, from him....... Rev 1:4 5485
The g of our Lord Jesus Christ be.......... Rev 22:21 5485

GRACIOUS {34}
God be g unto thee, my son..................... Gen 43:29 2603
for I am g.. Ex 22:27 2587
be g to whom I will be g.......................... Ex 33:19 2603
LORD, The LORD God, merciful and g ... Ex 34:6 2587
upon thee, and be g unto thee................ Num 6:25 2603
tell whether GOD will be g to me 2Sa 12:22 2603
And the LORD was g unto them.............. 2Kin 13:23 2603
for the LORD your God is g...................... 2Chr 30:9 2587
thou art a God ready to pardon, g .... Neh 9:17 2587
for thou art a g and merciful God.......... Neh 9:31 2587
Then he is g unto him, and saith,........... Job 33:24 2603
Hath God forgotten to be g .... Ps 77:9 2589
a God full of compassion, and g............. Ps 86:15 2587
The LORD is merciful and g.................... Ps 103:8 2587
the LORD is g and full of .... Ps 111:4 2587
he is g, and full of compassion,.............. Ps 112:4 2587
G is the LORD, and righteous.................. Ps 116:5 2587
The LORD is g, and full of .... Ps 145:8 2587
A g woman retaineth honour .... Prov 11:16 2580
words of a wise man's mouth are g......... Eccl 10:12 2580
wait, that he may be g unto you............. Is 30:18 2603
he will be very g unto thee at................. Is 30:19 2603
O LORD, be g unto us.............................. Is 33:2 2603
how g shalt thou be when pangs............ Jer 22:23 2603
for he is g and merciful, slow to............. Joel 2:13 2587
be g unto the remnant of Joseph............ Amos 5:15 2587
for I knew that thou art a g God............ Jonah 4:2 2587
God that he will be g unto us.................. Mal 1:9 2603
wondered at the g words which .... Lk 4:22 5485
ye have tasted that the Lord is g............ 1Pet 2:3 5543

GRACIOUSLY {4}
God hath g given thy servant .... Gen 33:5 2603
because God hath dealt g with me......... Gen 33:11 2603
and grant me thy law g .... Ps 119:29 2603
all iniquity, and receive us g.................. Hos 14:2 2896

GRAFF {1}
God is able to g them in again................ Rom 11:23 1461

GRAFFED {5}
wert g in among them, and with............. Rom 11:17 1461
broken off, that I might be g in.............. Rom 11:19 1461
still in unbelief, shall be g in .... Rom 11:23 1461

G

wert *g* contrary to nature into a Rom 11:24 *1461*
be *g* into their own olive tree Rom 11:24 *1461*

GRAIN {8}
the least *g* fall upon the earth Amos 9:9 6872
is like to a *g* of mustard seed Mt 13:31 *2848*
have faith as a *g* of mustard seed Mt 17:20 *2848*
It is like a *g* of mustard seed, Mk 4:31 *2848*
It is like a *g* of mustard seed, Lk 13:19 *2848*
had faith as a *g* of mustard seed Lk 17:6 *2848*
body that shall be, but bare *g* 1Cor 15:37 *2848*
of wheat, or of some other *g* 1Cor 15:37

GRANDMOTHER {1}
which dwelt first in thy *g* Lois 2Ti 1:5 *3125*

GRANT {22}
shall *g* a redemption for the land Lev 25:24 5414
The LORD *g* you that ye may find Ruth 1:9 5414
the God of Israel *g* thee thy 1Sa 1:17 5414
to Ornan, *G* me the place of this 1Chr 21:22 5414
thou shalt *g* it me for the full 1Chr 21:22 5414
them, but I will *g* them some 2Chr 12:7 5414
according to the *g* that they had Ezr 3:7 7558
g him mercy in the sight of this Neh 1:11 5414
please the king to *g* my petition Est 5:8 5414
that God would *g* me the thing Job 6:8 5414
G thee according to thine own Ps 20:4 5414
O LORD, and *g* us thy salvation Ps 85:7 5414
and *g* me thy law graciously Ps 119:29
G not, O LORD, the desires of the Ps 140:8 5414
G that these my two sons may sit, Mt 20:21 *2036*
G unto us that we may sit, one on Mk 10:37 *1325*
That he would *g* unto us, that we, Lk 1:74 *1325*
g unto thy servants, that with Acts 4:29 *1325*
and consolation *g* you to be Rom 15:5 *1325*
That he would *g* you, according to Eph 3:16 *1325*
The Lord *g* unto him that he may 2Ti 1:18 *1325*
I *g* to sit with me in my throne Rev 3:21 *1325*

GRANTED {15}
God *g* him that which he requested 1Chr 4:10 935
and knowledge is *g* unto thee 2Chr 1:12 5414
the king *g* him all his request, Ezr 7:6 5414
And the king *g* me, according to Neh 2:8 5414
and it shall be *g* thee Est 5:6 5414
and it shall be *g* thee Est 7:2 5414
Wherein the king *g* the Jews which Est 8:11 5414
and it shall be *g* thee Est 9:12 5414
let it be *g* to the Jews which are Est 9:13 5414
Thou hast *g* me life and favour, and Job 10:12 6213
of the righteous shall be *g* Prov 10:24 5414
a murderer to be *g* unto you Acts 3:14 *5483*
Gentiles *g* repentance unto life Acts 11:18 *1325*
g signs and wonders to be done by Acts 14:3 *1325*
to her was *g* that she should be Rev 19:8 *1325*

GRAPE {8}
gather every *g* of thy vineyard Lev 19:10 6528
drink the pure blood of the *g* Deut 32:14 6025
off his unripe *g* as the vine Job 15:33 1154
the tender *g* give a good smell Song 2:13 5563
whether the tender *g* appear Song 7:12 5563
the sour *g* is ripening in the Is 18:5 1155
The fathers have eaten a sour *g* Jer 31:29 1155
every man that eateth the sour *g* Jer 31:30 1155

GRAPEGATHERER {1}
hand as a *g* into the baskets Jer 6:9 1219

GRAPEGATHERERS {2}
If *g* come to thee, would they not Jer 49:9 1219
if the *g* came to thee, would they Obad 5 1219

GRAPEGLEANINGS {1}
fruits, as the *g* of the vintage Mic 7:1 5955

GRAPES {37}
thereof brought forth ripe *g* Gen 40:10 6025
and I took the *g*, and pressed them Gen 40:11 6025
and his clothes in the blood of *g* Gen 49:11 6025
neither gather the *g* of thy vine Lev 25:5 6025
nor gather the *g* in it of thy Lev 25:11
liquor of *g*, nor eat moist *g* Num 6:3 6025
was the time of the firstripe *g* Num 13:20 6025
a branch with one cluster of *g* Num 13:23 6025
because of the cluster of *g* which Num 13:24
then thou mayest eat *g* thy fill Deut 23:24 6025
gatherest the *g* of thy vineyard Deut 24:21
and shalt not gather the *g* thereof Deut 28:30
of the wine, nor gather the *g* Deut 28:39
their *g* are *g* of gall Deut 32:32 6025
the *g* of Ephraim better than the Judg 8:2
their vineyards, and trode the *g* Judg 9:27
as also wine, *g*, and figs, and all Neh 13:15 6025
for our vines have tender *g* Song 2:15 5563
and thy breasts to clusters of *g* Song 7:7
that it should bring forth *g* Is 5:2 6025
and it brought forth wild *g* Is 5:2 891
that it should bring forth *g* Is 5:4 6025
brought it forth wild *g* Is 5:4 891
Yet gleaning *g* shall be left in Is 17:6
as the gleaning *g* when the Is 24:13
there shall be no *g* on the vine Jer 8:13 6025
a shout, as they that tread the *g* Jer 25:30
they not leave some gleaning *g* Jer 49:9
The fathers have eaten sour *g* Eze 18:2 1154
Israel like *g* in the wilderness Hos 9:10 6025
the treader of *g* him that soweth Amos 9:13 6025
thee, would they not leave some *g* Obad 5
Do men gather *g* of thorns Mt 7:16 *4718*
of a bramble bush gather they *g* Lk 6:44 *4718*
for her *g* are fully ripe Rev 14:18 *4718*

GRASS {62}
said, Let the earth bring forth *g* Gen 1:11 1877
And the earth brought forth *g* Gen 1:12 1877
ox licketh up the *g* of the field Num 22:4 3418
I will send *g* in thy fields for Deut 11:15 6212
nor any *g* groweth therein, like Deut 29:23 6212
and as the showers upon the *g* Deut 32:2 6212
as the tender *g* springing out of 2Sa 23:4 1877
we may find *g* to save the horses 1Kin 18:5 2682
they were as the *g* of the field 2Kin 19:26 6212
as the *g* on the house tops, and as 2Kin 19:26 2682
offspring as the *g* of the earth Job 5:25 6212
the wild ass bray when he hath *g* Job 6:5 1877
he eateth *g* as an ox Job 40:15 2682
shall soon be cut down like the *g* Ps 37:2 2682
down like rain upon the mown *g* Ps 72:6
flourish like *g* of the earth Ps 72:16 6212
they are like *g* which groweth up Ps 90:5 2682
When the wicked spring as the *g* Ps 92:7 6212
is smitten, and withered like *g* Ps 102:4 6212
and I am withered like *g* Ps 102:11 6212
As for man, his days are as *g* Ps 103:15 2682
He causeth the *g* to grow for the Ps 104:14 2682
similitude of an ox that eateth *g* Ps 106:20 6212
be as the *g* upon the housetops Ps 129:6 2682
who maketh *g* to grow upon the Ps 147:8 2682
his favour is as dew upon the *g* Prov 19:12 6212
the tender *g* sheweth itself, and Prov 27:25 1877
the *g* faileth, there is no green Is 15:6 1877
shall be *g* with reeds and rushes Is 35:7 2682
they were as the *g* of the field Is 37:27 6212
as the *g* on the housetops, and as Is 37:27 2682
All flesh is *g*, and all the Is 40:6 2682
The *g* withereth, the flower Is 40:7 2682
surely the people is *g* Is 40:7 2682
The *g* withereth, the flower Is 40:8 2682
shall spring up as among the *g* Is 44:4 2682
of man which shall be made as *g* Is 51:12 2682
it, because there was no *g* Jer 14:5 1758
did fail, because there was no *g* Jer 14:6 6212
are grown fat as the heifer at *g* Jer 50:11 1877
in the tender *g* of the field Dan 4:15 1883
the beasts in the *g* of the earth Dan 4:15 6211
in the tender *g* of the field Dan 4:23 1883
shall make thee to eat *g* as oxen Dan 4:25 6211
shall make thee to eat *g* as oxen Dan 4:32 6211
from men, and did eat *g* as oxen Dan 4:33 6211
they fed him with *g* like oxen Dan 5:21 6211
end of eating the *g* of the land Amos 7:2 6212
LORD, as the showers upon the *g* Mic 5:7 6212
rain, to every one *g* in the field Zec 10:1 6212
God so clothe the *g* of the field Mt 6:30 *5528*
multitude to sit down on the *g* Mt 14:19 *5528*
by companies upon the green *g* Mk 6:39 *5528*
If then God so clothe the *g* Lk 12:28 *5528*
Now there was much *g* in the place Jn 6:10 *5528*
of the *g* he shall pass away Jas 1:10 *5528*
heat, but it withereth the *g* Jas 1:11 *5528*
For all flesh is as *g*, and all the 1Pet 1:24 *5528*
glory of man as the flower of *g* 1Pet 1:24 *5528*
The *g* withereth, and the flower 1Pet 1:24 *5528*
up, and all green *g* was burnt up Rev 8:7 *5528*
not hurt the *g* of the earth Rev 9:4 *5528*

GRASSHOPPER {3}
his kind, and the *g* after his kind Lev 11:22 2284
Canst thou make him afraid as a *g* Job 39:20 697
the *g* shall be a burden, and Eccl 12:5 2284

GRASSHOPPERS {7}
and we were in our own sight as *g* Num 13:33 2284
they came as *g* for multitude Judg 6:5 697
the valley like *g* for multitude Judg 7:12 697
the inhabitants thereof are as *g* Is 40:22 2284
because they are more than the *g* Jer 46:23 697
he formed *g* in the beginning of Amos 7:1 1462
and thy captains as the great *g* Nah 3:17 1462

GRATE {6}
for it a *g* of network of brass Ex 27:4 4345
burnt offering, with his brasen *g* Ex 35:16 4345
g of network under the compass Ex 38:4 4345
the four ends of the *g* of brass Ex 38:5 4345
altar, and the brasen *g* for it Ex 38:30 4345
his *g* of brass, his staves, and Ex 39:39 4345

GRAVE {67}
And Jacob set a pillar upon her *g* Gen 35:20 6900
of Rachel's *g* unto this day Gen 35:20 6900
into the *g* unto my son mourning Gen 37:35 7585
gray hairs with sorrow to the *g* Gen 42:38 7585
gray hairs with sorrow to the *g* Gen 44:29 7585
our father with sorrow to the *g* Gen 44:31 7585
in my *g* which I have digged for Gen 50:5 6913
g on them the names of the Ex 28:9 6605
g upon it, like the engravings of Ex 28:36 6605
body, or a bone of a man, or a *g* Num 19:16 6913
or one slain, or one dead, or a *g* Num 19:18 6913
he bringeth down to the *g* 1Sa 2:6 7585
voice, and wept at the *g* of Abner 2Sa 3:32 6913
be buried by the *g* of my father 2Sa 19:37 6913
head go down to the *g* in peace 1Kin 2:6 7585
thou down to the *g* with blood 1Kin 2:9 7585
he laid his carcase in his own *g* 1Kin 13:30 6913
of Jeroboam shall come to the *g* 1Kin 14:13 6913
be gathered into thy *g* in peace 2Kin 22:20 6913
that can skill to *g* with the 2Chr 2:7 6603
also to *g* any manner of graving, 2Chr 2:14 6605
be gathered to thy *g* in peace 2Chr 34:28 6913
glad, when they can find the *g* Job 3:22 6913
shalt come to thy *g* in a full age Job 5:26 6913
to the *g* shall come up no more Job 7:9 7585
carried from the womb to the *g* Job 10:19 6913
thou wouldest hide me in the *g* Job 14:13 7585
If I wait, the *g* is mine house Job 17:13 7585
and in a moment go down to the *g* Job 21:13 7585
Yet shall he be brought to the *g* Job 21:32 6913
so doth the *g* those which have Job 24:19 7585
not stretch out his hand to the *g* Job 30:24 1164
his soul draweth near unto the *g* Job 33:22 7845
in the *g* who shall give thee Ps 6:5 7585
brought up my soul from the *g* Ps 30:3 7585
and let them be silent in the *g* Ps 31:17 7585
Like sheep they are laid in the *g* Ps 49:14 7585
in the *g* from their dwelling Ps 49:14 7585
my soul from the power of the *g* Ps 49:15 7585
my life draweth nigh unto the *g* Ps 88:3 7585
like the slain that lie in the *g* Ps 88:5 6913
be declared in the *g* Ps 88:11 6913
his soul from the hand of the *g* Ps 89:48 7585
us swallow them up alive as the *g* Prov 1:12 7585
The *g*; and the barren Prov 30:16 7585
knowledge, nor wisdom, in the *g* Eccl 9:10 7585
jealousy is cruel as the *g* Song 8:6 7585
Thy pomp is brought down to the *g* Is 14:11 7585
thy *g* like an abominable branch Is 14:19 6913
I shall go to the gates of the *g* Is 38:10 7585
For the *g* cannot praise thee, Is 38:18 7585
he made his *g* with the wicked, and Is 53:9 6913
my mother might have been my *g* Jer 20:17 6913
down to the *g* I caused a mourning Eze 31:15 7585
her company is round about her *g* Eze 32:23 6900
her multitude round about her *g* Eze 32:24 6900
them from the power of the *g* Hos 13:14 7585
O *g*, I will be thy destruction Hos 13:14 7585
I will make thy *g* Nah 1:14 6913
lain in the *g* four days already Jn 11:17 *3419*
goeth unto the *g* to weep there Jn 11:31 *3419*
in himself cometh to the *g* Jn 11:38 *3419*
he called Lazarus out of his *g* Jn 12:17 *3419*
O *g*, where is thy victory 1Cor 15:55 *86*
Likewise must the deacons be *g* 1Ti 3:8 *4586*
Even so must their wives be *g* 1Ti 3:11 *4586*
That the aged men be sober, *g* Titus 2:2 *4586*

GRAVECLOTHES {1}
forth, bound hand and foot with *g* Jn 11:44 *2750*

GRAVED {2}
he *g* cherubims, lions, and palm 1Kin 7:36 6605
and *g* cherubims on the walls 2Chr 3:7 6605

GRAVEL {3}
his mouth shall be filled with *g* Prov 20:17 2687
of thy bowels like the *g* thereof Is 48:19 4579
broken my teeth with *g* stones Lam 3:16 2687

GRAVEN {56}
not make unto thee any *g* image Ex 20:4 6459
writing of God, *g* upon the tables Ex 32:16 2801
inclosed in ouches of gold, *g* Ex 39:6 6605
of gold, *g*, as signets are *g* Ex 39:6 6605
make you no idols nor *g* image Lev 26:1 6459
yourselves, and make you a *g* image Deut 4:16 6459
with you, and make you a *g* image Deut 4:23 6459
yourselves, and make a *g* image Deut 4:25 6459
shalt not make thee any *g* image Deut 5:8 6459
burn their *g* images with fire Deut 7:5 6456
The *g* images of their gods shall Deut 7:25 6456
down the *g* images of their gods Deut 12:3 6456
that maketh any *g* or molten image Deut 27:15 6459
for my son, to make a *g* image Judg 17:3 6459
who made thereof a *g* image Judg 17:4 6459
a *g* image, and a molten image Judg 18:14 6459
in thither, and took the *g* image Judg 18:17 6459
the *g* image, and went in the midst Judg 18:20 6459
of Dan set up the *g* image Judg 18:30 6459
they set them up Micah's *g* image Judg 18:31 6459
LORD, and served their *g* images 2Kin 17:41 6456
he set a *g* image of the grove 2Kin 21:7 6459
g images, before he was humbled 2Chr 33:19 6456
had beaten the *g* images into 2Chr 34:7 6456
That they were *g* with an iron pen Job 19:24 2672
to jealousy with their *g* images Ps 78:58 6456
be all they that serve *g* images Ps 97:7 6459
whose *g* images did excel them of Is 10:10 6456
all the *g* images of her gods he Is 21:9 6456
of thy *g* images of silver Is 30:22 6456
The workman melteth a *g* image Is 40:19 6459
workman to prepare a *g* image Is 40:20 6459
neither my praise to *g* images Is 42:8 6456
ashamed, that trust in *g* images Is 42:17 6459
They that make a *g* image are all Is 44:9 6459
or molten a *g* image that is Is 44:10 6459
he maketh it a *g* image, and Is 44:15 6459
he maketh a god, even his *g* image Is 44:17 6459
set up the wood of their *g* image Is 45:20 6459
my *g* image, and my molten image, Is 48:5 6459
I have *g* thee upon the palms of Is 49:16 2710
me to anger with their *g* images Jer 8:19 6456
is confounded by the *g* image Jer 10:14 6459
it is *g* upon the table of their Jer 17:1 2790
for it is the land of *g* images Jer 50:38 6456
is confounded by the *g* image Jer 51:17 6459
upon the *g* images of Babylon Jer 51:47 6456
do judgment upon her *g* images Jer 51:52 6456
and burned incense to *g* images Hos 11:2 6456
all the *g* images thereof shall be Mic 1:7 6456
Thy *g* images also will I cut off, Mic 5:13 6456
gods will I cut off the *g* image Nah 1:14 6459

What profiteth the *g* image that... Hab 2:18 6459
that the maker thereof hath *g* it... Hab 2:18 6458
stone, *g* by art and man's device... Acts 17:29 *5480*

GRAVE'S {1}
are scattered at the *g* mouth... Ps 141:7 7585

GRAVES {21}
Because there were no *g* in Egypt... Ex 14:11 6913
the powder thereof upon the *g* of... 2Kin 23:6 6913
strowed it upon the *g* of them... 2Chr 34:4 6913
extinct, the *g* are ready for me... Job 17:1 6913
Which remain among the *g*, and... Is 65:4 6913
of Jerusalem, out of their *g*... Jer 8:1 6913
into the *g* of the common people... Jer 26:23 6913
his *g* are about him... Eze 32:22 6913
Whose *g* are set in the sides of... Eze 32:23 6913
her *g* are round about him... Eze 32:25 6913
her *g* are round about him... Eze 32:26 6913
O my people, I will open your *g*... Eze 37:12 6913
you to come up out of your *g*... Eze 37:12 6913
LORD, when I have opened your *g*... Eze 37:13 6913
and brought you up out of your *g*... Eze 37:13 6913
Gog a place there of *g* in Israel... Eze 39:11 6913
And the *g* were opened... Mt 27:52 *3419*
came out of the *g* after his... Mt 27:53 *3419*
for ye are as *g* which appear not,... Lk 11:44 *3419*
are in the *g* shall hear his voice... Jn 5:28 *3419*
their dead bodies to be put in *g*... Rev 11:9 *3418*

GRAVETH {1}
that *g* an habitation for himself... Is 22:16 2710

GRAVING {3}
and fashioned it with a *g* tool... Ex 32:4 2747
also to grave any manner of *g*... 2Chr 2:14 6603
I will engrave the *g* thereof... Zec 3:9 6603

GRAVINGS {1}
of it were *g* with their borders... 1Kin 7:31 4734

GRAVITY {2}
children in subjection with all *g*... 1Ti 3:4 *4587*
doctrine shewing uncorruptness, *g*... Titus 2:7 *4587*

GRAY {5}
then shall ye bring down my *g*... Gen 42:38 7872
ye shall bring down my *g* hairs... Gen 44:29 7872
servants shall bring down the *g*... Gen 44:31 7872
also with the man of *g* hairs... Deut 32:25 7872
g hairs are here and there upon... Hos 7:9 7872

GRAYHEADED {2}
and I am old and *g*... 1Sa 12:2 7867
With us are both the *g* and very... Job 15:10 7867

GREASE {1}
Their heart is as fat as *g*... Ps 119:70 2459

GREAT {968}
And God made two *g* lights... Gen 1:16 1419
And God created *g* whales, and every... Gen 1:21 1419
of man was *g* in the earth... Gen 6:5 7227
fountains of the *g* deep broken up... Gen 7:11 7227
the same is a *g* city... Gen 10:12 1419
And I will make of thee a *g* nation... Gen 12:2 1419
bless thee, and make thy name *g*... Gen 12:2 1431
his house with *g* plagues because... Gen 12:17 1419
for their substance was *g*... Gen 13:6 7227
shield, and thy exceeding *g* reward... Gen 15:1 7235
an horror of *g* darkness fell upon... Gen 15:12 1419
they come out with *g* substance... Gen 15:14 1419
river of Egypt unto the *g* river... Gen 15:18 1419
and I will make him a *g* nation... Gen 17:20 1419
Abraham shall surely become a *g*... Gen 18:18 1419
the cry of Sodom and Gomorrah is *g*... Gen 18:20 7227
with blindness, both small and *g*... Gen 19:11 1419
the cry of them is waxen *g* before... Gen 19:13 1431
on me and on my kingdom a *g* sin... Gen 20:9 1419
Abraham made a *g* feast the same... Gen 21:8 1419
for I will make him a *g* nation... Gen 21:18 1419
and he is become *g*... Gen 24:35 1431
And the man waxed *g*, and went... Gen 26:13 1431
and grew until he became very *g*... Gen 26:13 1431
of herds, and *g* store of servants... Gen 26:14 7227
of his father, he cried with a *g*... Gen 27:34 1419
a *g* stone was upon the well's... Gen 29:2 1419
With *g* wrestlings have I wrestled... Gen 30:8 430
then can I do this *g* wickedness... Gen 39:9 1419
there come seven years of *g*... Gen 41:29 1419
your lives by a *g* deliverance... Gen 45:7 1419
there make of thee a *g* nation... Gen 46:3 1419
a people, and he also shall be *g*... Gen 48:19 1431
and it was a very *g* company... Gen 50:9 3515
and there they mourned with a *g*... Gen 50:10 1419
turn aside, and see this *g* sight... Ex 3:3 1419
out arm, and with *g* judgments... Ex 6:6 1419
the land of Egypt by *g* judgments... Ex 7:4 1419
was very *g* in the land of Egypt... Ex 11:3 1419
there shall be a *g* cry throughout... Ex 11:6 1419
out from Pharaoh in a *g* anger... Ex 11:8 2750
there was a *g* cry in Egypt... Ex 12:30 1419
Israel saw that *g* work which the... Ex 14:31 1419
that every *g* matter they shall... Ex 18:22 1419
upon the *g* toe of their right... Ex 29:20
and I will make of thee a *g* nation... Ex 32:10 1419
of the land of Egypt with *g* power... Ex 32:11 1419
hast brought so *g* a sin upon them... Ex 32:21 1419
people, Ye have sinned a *g* sin... Ex 32:30 1419
this people have sinned a *g* sin... Ex 32:31 1419
upon the *g* toe of his right foot... Lev 8:23
upon the *g* toes of their right... Lev 8:24
and the cormorant, and the *g* owl... Lev 11:17 3244
upon the *g* toe of his right foot... Lev 14:14

upon the *g* toe of his right foot,... Lev 14:17
upon the *g* toe of his right foot... Lev 14:25
upon the *g* toe of his right foot,... Lev 14:28
the people with a very *g* plague... Num 11:33 7227
the cities are walled, and very *g*... Num 13:28 1419
saw in it are men of a *g* stature... Num 13:32
let the power of my LORD be *g*... Num 14:17 1431
of *g* mercy, forgiving iniquity and... Num 14:18 7227
promote thee unto very *g* honour... Num 22:17
people shall rise up as a *g* lion... Num 23:24 3833
down as a lion, and as a *g* lion... Num 24:9 3833
to promote thee unto *g* honour... Num 24:11
had a very *g* multitude of cattle... Num 32:1 6099
even have the *g* sea for a border... Num 34:6 1419
from the *g* sea ye shall point out... Num 34:7 1419
and unto Lebanon, unto the *g* river... Deut 1:7 1419
hear the small as well as the *g*... Deut 1:17 1419
Horeb, we went through all that *g*... Deut 1:19 1419
the cities are *g* and walled up to... Deut 1:28 1419
walking through this *g* wilderness... Deut 2:7 1419
therein in times past, a people *g*... Deut 2:10 1419
A people *g*, and many, and tall, as... Deut 2:21 1419
beside unwalled towns a *g* many... Deut 3:5 3966
Surely this *g* nation is a wise and... Deut 4:6 1419
For what nation is there so *g*... Deut 4:7 1419
And what nation is there so *g*... Deut 4:8 1419
any such thing as this *g* thing is... Deut 4:32 1419
by *g* terrors, according to all... Deut 4:34 1419
earth he shewed thee his *g* fire... Deut 4:36 1419
thick darkness, with a *g* voice... Deut 5:22 1419
for this *g* fire will consume us... Deut 5:25 1419
and to Jacob, to give thee *g*... Deut 6:10 1419
LORD shewed signs and wonders, *g*... Deut 6:22 1419
The *g* temptations which thine... Deut 7:19 1419
Who led thee through that *g*... Deut 8:15 1419
mightier than thyself, cities *g*... Deut 9:1 1419
A people *g* and tall, the children... Deut 9:2 1419
a *g* God, a mighty, and a terrible,... Deut 10:17 1419
that hath done for thee these *g*... Deut 10:21 1419
g acts of the LORD which he did... Deut 11:7 1419
The little owl, and the *g* owl... Deut 14:16 3244
let me see this *g* fire any more... Deut 18:16 1419
in thy bag divers weights, a *g*... Deut 25:13 1419
thine house divers measures, a *g*... Deut 25:14 1419
few, and became there a nation, *g*... Deut 26:5 1419
with *g* terribleness, and with... Deut 26:8 1419
thou shalt set thee up *g* stones... Deut 27:2 1419
even *g* plagues, and of long... Deut 28:59 1419
The *g* temptations which thine... Deut 29:3 1419
the signs, and those *g* miracles... Deut 29:3 1419
meaneth the heat of this *g* anger... Deut 29:24 1419
in *g* indignation, and cast them... Deut 29:28 1419
in all the *g* terror which Moses... Deut 34:12 1419
Lebanon even unto the *g* river... Josh 1:4 1419
unto the *g* sea toward the going... Josh 1:4 1419
people shall shout with a *g* shout... Josh 6:5 1419
the people shouted with a *g* shout... Josh 6:20 1419
what wilt thou do unto thy *g* name... Josh 7:9 1419
they raised over him a *g* heap of... Josh 7:26 1419
raise thereon a *g* heap of stones... Josh 8:29 1419
of the *g* sea over against Lebanon... Josh 9:1 1419
because Gibeon was a *g* city... Josh 10:2 1419
slew them with a *g* slaughter at... Josh 10:10 1419
that the LORD cast down *g* stones... Josh 10:11 1419
Roll *g* stones upon the mouth of... Josh 10:18 1419
them with a very *g* slaughter... Josh 10:20 1419
laid *g* stones in the cave's mouth... Josh 10:27 1419
them, and chased them unto *g* Zidon... Josh 11:8 7227
there, and that the cities were *g*... Josh 14:12 1419
which Arba was a *g* man among the... Josh 14:15 1419
the west border was to the *g* sea... Josh 15:12 1419
the river of Egypt, and the *g* sea... Josh 15:47 1419
inherit, seeing I am a *g* people... Josh 17:14 7227
them, If thou be a *g* people... Josh 17:15 7227
saying, Thou art a *g* people... Josh 17:17 7227
and hast *g* power... Josh 17:17 1419
and Kanah, even unto *g* Zidon... Josh 19:28 7227
by Jordan, a *g* altar to see to... Josh 22:10 1419
off, even unto the *g* sea westward... Josh 23:4 1419
out from before you *g* nations... Josh 23:9 1419
which did those *g* signs in our... Josh 24:17 1419
the law of God, and took a *g* stone... Josh 24:26 1419
cut off his thumbs and his *g* toes... Judg 1:6
their *g* toes cut off, gathered... Judg 1:7
seen all the *g* works of the LORD... Judg 2:7 1419
there were *g* thoughts of heart... Judg 5:15 1419
there were *g* searchings of heart... Judg 5:16 1419
with a very *g* slaughter... Judg 11:33 1419
my people were at *g* strife with... Judg 12:2 3699
hip and thigh with a *g* slaughter... Judg 15:8 1419
and said, Thou hast given this *g*... Judg 15:18 1419
see wherein his *g* strength lieth... Judg 16:5 1419
wherein thy *g* strength lieth, and... Judg 16:6 1419
me wherein thy *g* strength lieth... Judg 16:15 1419
them together for to offer a *g*... Judg 16:23 1419
that they should make a *g* flame... Judg 20:38 7235
For they had made a *g* oath... Judg 21:5 1419
men was very *g* before the LORD... 1Sa 2:17 1419
all Israel shouted with a *g* shout... 1Sa 4:5 1419
this *g* shout in the camp of the... 1Sa 4:6 1419
and there was a very *g* slaughter... 1Sa 4:10 1419
and there hath been also a *g*... 1Sa 4:17 1419
city with a very *g* destruction... 1Sa 5:9 1419
men of the city, both small and *g*... 1Sa 5:9 1419
then he hath done us this *g* evil... 1Sa 6:9 1419
there, where there was a *g* stone... 1Sa 6:14 1419
were, and put them on the *g* stone... 1Sa 6:15 1419

even unto the *g* stone of Abel... 1Sa 6:18 1419
of the people with a *g* slaughter... 1Sa 6:19 1419
a *g* thunder on that day upon the... 1Sa 7:10 1419
stand and see this *g* thing... 1Sa 12:16 1419
and see that your wickedness is *g*... 1Sa 12:17 7227
his people for his *g* name's sake... 1Sa 12:22 1419
for consider how *g* things he hath... 1Sa 12:24 1431
so it was a very *g* trembling... 1Sa 14:15 430
there was a very *g* discomfiture... 1Sa 14:20 1419
roll a *g* stone unto me this day... 1Sa 14:33 1419
this *g* salvation in Israel... 1Sa 14:45 1419
Hath the LORD as *g* delight in... 1Sa 15:22 1419
will enrich him with *g* riches... 1Sa 17:25 1419
the LORD wrought a *g* salvation... 1Sa 19:5 1419
and slew them with a *g* slaughter... 1Sa 19:8 1419
came to a *g* well that is in Sechu... 1Sa 19:22 1419
will do nothing either *g* or small... 1Sa 20:2 1419
and smote them with a *g* slaughter... 1Sa 23:5 1419
and the man was very *g*, and he had... 1Sa 25:2 1419
a *g* space being between them... 1Sa 26:13 7227
thou shalt both do *g* things... 1Sa 26:25
either *g* or small, but carried... 1Sa 30:2 1419
because of all the *g* spoil that... 1Sa 30:16 1419
to them, neither small nor *g*... 1Sa 30:19 1419
brought in a *g* spoil with them... 2Sa 3:22 7227
a *g* man fallen this day in Israel... 2Sa 3:38 1419
And David went on, and grew *g*... 2Sa 5:10 1419
sight, and have made thee a *g* name... 2Sa 7:9 1419
the *g* men that are in the earth... 2Sa 7:9 1419
house for a *g* while to come... 2Sa 7:19 7350
hast thou done all these *g* things... 2Sa 7:21 1420
Wherefore thou art *g*, O LORD God... 2Sa 7:22 1431
a name, and to do for you *g* things... 2Sa 7:23 1420
by this deed thou hast given *g*... 2Sa 12:14 5006
spoil of the city in *g* abundance... 2Sa 12:30 3966
there was there a *g* slaughter... 2Sa 18:7 1419
under the thick boughs of a *g* oak... 2Sa 18:9 1419
cast him into a *g* pit in the wood... 2Sa 18:17 1419
laid a very *g* heap of stones upon... 2Sa 18:17 1419
me thy servant, I saw a *g* tumult... 2Sa 18:29 1419
for he was a very *g* man... 2Sa 19:32 1419
When they were at the *g* stone... 2Sa 20:8 1419
where was a man of *g* stature... 2Sa 21:20
and thy gentleness hath made me *g*... 2Sa 22:36 7235
LORD wrought a *g* victory that day... 2Sa 23:10 1419
and the LORD wrought a *g* victory... 2Sa 23:12 1419
said unto Gad, I am in a *g* strait... 2Sa 24:14 3966
for his mercies are *g*... 2Sa 24:14 7227
pipes, and rejoiced with *g* joy... 1Kin 1:40 1419
for that was the *g* high place... 1Kin 3:4 1419
servant David my father *g* mercy... 1Kin 3:6 1419
hast kept for him this *g* kindness... 1Kin 3:6 1419
a *g* people, that cannot be... 1Kin 3:8 7227
to judge this thy so *g* a people... 1Kin 3:9 3515
threescore *g* cities with walls and... 1Kin 4:13 1419
a wise son over this *g* people... 1Kin 5:7 7227
and they brought *g* stones... 1Kin 5:17 1419
on the outside toward the *g* court... 1Kin 7:9 1419
even *g* stones, stones of ten... 1Kin 7:10 1419
the *g* court round about was with... 1Kin 7:12 1419
For they shall hear of thy *g* name... 1Kin 8:42 1419
a *g* congregation, from the... 1Kin 8:65 1419
to Jerusalem with a very *g* train... 1Kin 10:2 3515
gold, and of spices very *g* store... 1Kin 10:10 7235
Ophir *g* plenty of almug trees... 1Kin 10:11 3966
the king made a *g* throne of ivory... 1Kin 10:18 1419
Hadad found *g* favour in the sight... 1Kin 11:19 3966
as *g* as would contain two... 1Kin 18:32 1004
and wind, and there was a *g* rain... 1Kin 18:45 1419
the journey is too *g* for thee... 1Kin 19:7 7227
the LORD passed by, and a *g*... 1Kin 19:11 1419
thou seen all this *g* multitude... 1Kin 20:13 1419
the Syrians with a *g* slaughter... 1Kin 20:21 1419
will I deliver all this *g*... 1Kin 20:28 1419
Fight neither with small nor *g*... 1Kin 22:31 1419
there was *g* indignation against... 2Kin 3:27 1419
to Shunem, where was a *g* woman... 2Kin 4:8 1419
his servant, Set on the *g* pot... 2Kin 4:38 1419
was a *g* man with his master, and... 2Kin 5:1 1419
had bid thee do some *g* thing... 2Kin 5:13 1419
horses, and chariots, and a *g* host... 2Kin 6:14 3515
he prepared *g* provision for them... 2Kin 6:23 1419
there was a *g* famine in Samaria... 2Kin 6:25 1419
even the noise of a *g* host... 2Kin 7:6 1419
all the *g* things that Elisha hath... 2Kin 8:4 1419
that he should do this *g* thing... 2Kin 8:13 1419
were with the *g* men of the city,... 2Kin 10:6 1419
Ahab in Jezreel, and all his *g* men... 2Kin 10:11 1419
for I have a *g* sacrifice to do to... 2Kin 10:19 1419
Upon the *g* altar burn the morning... 2Kin 16:15 1419
LORD, and made them sin a *g* sin... 2Kin 17:21 1419
of the land of Egypt with *g* power... 2Kin 17:36 1419
with a *g* host against Jerusalem... 2Kin 18:17 3515
Hezekiah, Thus saith the *g* king... 2Kin 18:19 1419
Hear the word of the *g* king... 2Kin 18:28 1419
for *g* is the wrath of the LORD... 2Kin 22:13 1419
all the people, both small and *g*... 2Kin 23:2 1419
the fierceness of his *g* wrath... 2Kin 23:26 1419
every *g* man's house burnt he with... 2Kin 25:9 1419
all the people, both small and *g*... 2Kin 25:26 1419
saved them by a *g* deliverance... 1Chr 11:14 1419
an Egyptian, a man of *g* stature... 1Chr 11:23
help him, until it was a *g* host... 1Chr 12:22 1419
For *g* is the LORD, and greatly to... 1Chr 16:25 1419
the *g* men that are in the earth... 1Chr 17:8 1419
house for a *g* while to come... 1Chr 17:17 7350
making known all these *g* things... 1Chr 17:19 1420

where was a man of *g* stature	1Chr 20:6	
said unto Gad, I am in a *g* strait	1Chr 21:13	3966
for very *g* are his mercies	1Chr 21:13	7227
abundantly, and hast made *g* wars	1Chr 22:8	1419
ward, as well the small as the *g*	1Chr 25:8	1419
lots, as well the small as the *g*	1Chr 26:13	1419
young and tender, and the work is *g*	1Chr 29:1	1419
the king also rejoiced with *g* joy	1Chr 29:9	1419
and in thine hand it is to make *g*	1Chr 29:12	1431
LORD on that day with *g* gladness	1Chr 29:22	1419
Thou hast shewed *g* mercy unto	2Chr 1:8	1419
this thy people, that is so *g*	2Chr 1:10	1419
And the house which I build is *g*	2Chr 2:5	1419
for *g* is our God above all gods	2Chr 2:5	1419
to build shall be wonderful *g*	2Chr 2:9	1419
the *g* court, and doors for the	2Chr 4:9	1419
all these vessels in *g* abundance	2Chr 4:18	3966
far country for thy *g* name's sake	2Chr 6:32	1419
a very *g* congregation, from the	2Chr 7:8	1419
Jerusalem, with a very *g* company	2Chr 9:1	3515
of gold, and of spices *g* abundance	2Chr 9:9	3966
the king made a *g* throne of ivory	2Chr 9:17	1419
ye be a *g* multitude, and there are	2Chr 13:8	7227
slew them with a *g* slaughter	2Chr 13:17	7227
but *g* vexations were upon all the	2Chr 15:5	7227
put to death, whether small or *g*	2Chr 15:13	1419
until his disease was exceeding *g*	2Chr 16:12	
made a very *g* burning for him	2Chr 16:14	1419
Jehoshaphat waxed *g* exceedingly	2Chr 17:12	1432
Fight ye not with small or *g*	2Chr 18:30	1419
There cometh a *g* multitude	2Chr 20:2	1419
we have no might against this *g*	2Chr 20:12	7227
by reason of this *g* multitude	2Chr 20:15	7227
gave them *g* gifts of silver	2Chr 21:3	7227
with a *g* plague will the LORD	2Chr 21:14	1419
thou shalt have *g* sickness by	2Chr 21:15	7227
a very *g* host into their hand	2Chr 24:24	7230
(for they left him in *g* diseases	2Chr 24:25	7227
and they returned home in *g* anger	2Chr 25:10	2750
shoot arrows and *g* stones withal	2Chr 26:15	1419
carried away a *g* multitude of	2Chr 28:5	1419
who smote him with a *g* slaughter	2Chr 28:5	1419
for our trespass is *g*, and there	2Chr 28:13	7227
month, a very *g* congregation	2Chr 30:13	7230
bread seven days with *g* gladness	2Chr 30:21	1419
a *g* number of priests sanctified	2Chr 30:24	7230
So there was *g* joy in Jerusalem	2Chr 30:26	1419
which is left is this *g* store	2Chr 31:10	
as well to the *g* as to the small	2Chr 31:15	1419
and raised it up a very *g* height	2Chr 33:14	
for *g* is the wrath of the LORD	2Chr 34:21	1419
the Levites, and all the people, *g*	2Chr 34:30	1419
vessels of the house of God, *g*	2Chr 36:18	1419
the people shouted with a *g* shout	Ezr 3:11	1419
rest of the nations whom the *g*	Ezr 4:10	7229
Judea, to the house of the *g* God	Ezr 5:8	7229
which is builded with *g* stones	Ezr 5:8	1560
which a *g* king of Israel builded	Ezr 5:11	7229
With three rows of *g* stones	Ezr 6:4	1560
in a *g* trespass unto this day	Ezr 9:7	1419
for our *g* trespass, seeing that	Ezr 9:13	1419
a very *g* congregation of men	Ezr 10:1	7227
of this matter, and for the *g* rain	Ezr 10:9	
the province are in *g* affliction	Neh 1:3	1419
thee, O LORD God of heaven, the *g*	Neh 1:5	1419
thou hast redeemed by thy *g* power	Neh 1:10	1419
over against the *g* tower that	Neh 3:27	1419
took *g* indignation, and mocked the	Neh 4:1	7235
remember the LORD, which is *g*	Neh 4:14	1419
rest of the people, The work is *g*	Neh 4:19	7235
there was a *g* cry of the people	Neh 5:1	1419
I set a *g* assembly against them	Neh 5:7	1419
them, saying, I am doing a *g* work	Neh 6:3	1419
Now the city was large and *g*	Neh 7:4	1419
Ezra blessed the LORD, the *g* God	Neh 8:6	1419
send portions, and to make *g* mirth	Neh 8:12	1419
And there was very *g* gladness	Neh 8:17	1419
of *g* kindness, and forsookest them	Neh 9:17	7227
had wrought *g* provocations	Neh 9:18	1419
themselves in thy *g* goodness	Neh 9:25	1419
and they wrought *g* provocations	Neh 9:26	1419
Nevertheless for thy *g* mercies'	Neh 9:31	7227
Now therefore, our God, the *g*	Neh 9:32	1419
in thy *g* goodness that thou	Neh 9:35	7227
pleasure, and we are in *g* distress	Neh 9:37	1419
the son of one of the *g* men	Neh 11:14	1419
appointed two *g* companies of them	Neh 12:31	1419
day they offered *g* sacrifices	Neh 12:43	1419
had made them rejoice with *g* joy	Neh 12:43	1419
had prepared for him a *g* chamber	Neh 13:5	1419
unto you to do all this *g* evil	Neh 13:27	1419
Shushan the palace, both unto *g*	Est 1:5	1419
all his empire, (for it is *g*	Est 1:20	7227
their husbands honour, both to *g*	Est 1:20	1419
Then the king made a *g* feast unto	Est 2:18	1419
there was *g* mourning among the	Est 4:3	1419
with a *g* crown of gold, and with a	Est 8:15	1419
For Mordecai was *g* in the king's	Est 9:4	1419
g among the Jews, and accepted of	Est 10:3	1419
she asses, and a very *g* household	Job 1:3	7227
there came a *g* wind from the	Job 1:19	1419
saw that his grief was very *g*	Job 2:13	1431
The small and *g* are there	Job 3:19	1419
Which doeth *g* things and	Job 5:9	1419
also that thy seed shall be *g*	Job 5:25	7227
Which doeth *g* things past finding	Job 9:10	1419
Is not thy wickedness *g*	Job 22:5	7227
plead against me with his *g* power	Job 23:6	7227
By the *g* force of my disease is	Job 30:18	7227
rejoiced because my wealth was *g*	Job 31:25	7227
Did I fear a *g* multitude, or did	Job 31:34	7227
G men are not always wise	Job 32:9	7227
he knoweth it not in *g* extremity	Job 35:15	3966
then a *g* ransom cannot deliver	Job 36:18	7227
Behold, God is *g*, and we know him	Job 36:26	7689
g things doeth he, which we	Job 37:5	1419
to the *g* rain of his strength	Job 37:6	4306
the number of thy days is *g*	Job 38:21	7227
him, because his strength is *g*	Job 39:11	7227
There were they in *g* fear	Ps 14:5	6343
and thy gentleness hath made me *g*	Ps 18:35	7235
G deliverance giveth he to his	Ps 18:50	1431
keeping of them there is *g* reward	Ps 19:11	7227
innocent from the *g* transgression	Ps 19:13	7227
His glory is *g* in thy salvation	Ps 21:5	1419
be of thee in the *g* congregation	Ps 22:25	7227
mine iniquity; for it is *g*	Ps 25:11	7227
Oh how *g* is thy goodness, which	Ps 31:19	7227
surely in the floods of *g* waters	Ps 32:6	7227
he deliver any by his *g* strength	Ps 33:17	7230
thee thanks in the *g* congregation	Ps 35:18	7227
is like the *g* mountains	Ps 36:6	410
thy judgments are a *g* deep	Ps 36:6	7227
I have seen the wicked in *g* power	Ps 37:35	
in the *g* congregation	Ps 40:9	7227
thy truth from the *g* congregation	Ps 40:10	7227
he is a *g* King over all the earth	Ps 47:2	1419
G is the LORD, and greatly to be	Ps 48:1	1419
the north, the city of the *g* King	Ps 48:2	7227
There were they in *g* fear	Ps 53:5	
thy mercy is *g* unto the heavens	Ps 57:10	1419
break out the *g* teeth of the	Ps 58:6	4459
g was the company of those that	Ps 68:11	7227
very high, who hast done *g* things	Ps 71:19	1419
Thou, which hast shewed me *g*	Ps 71:20	7229
his name is *g* in Israel	Ps 76:1	1419
who is so *g* a God as our God	Ps 77:13	1419
sea, and thy path in the *g* waters	Ps 77:19	7227
them drink as out of the *g* depths	Ps 78:15	7227
From following the ewes *g* with	Ps 78:71	
them tears to drink in *g* measure	Ps 80:5	7991
For thou art *g*, and doest wondrous	Ps 86:10	1419
For *g* is thy mercy toward me	Ps 86:13	1419
O LORD, how *g* are thy works	Ps 92:5	1431
For the LORD is a *g* God	Ps 95:3	1419
and a *g* King above all gods	Ps 95:3	1419
For the LORD is *g*, and greatly to	Ps 96:4	1419
The LORD is *g* in Zion	Ps 99:2	1419
Let them praise thy *g* and terrible	Ps 99:3	1419
so *g* is his mercy toward them	Ps 103:11	1396
O LORD my God, thou art very *g*	Ps 104:1	1431
So is this *g* and wide sea, wherein	Ps 104:25	1419
both small and *g* beasts	Ps 104:25	1419
which had done *g* things in Egypt	Ps 106:21	1419
that do business in *g* waters	Ps 107:23	7227
For thy mercy is *g* above the	Ps 108:4	1419
The works of the LORD are *g*	Ps 111:2	1419
fear the LORD, both small and *g*	Ps 115:13	1419
merciful kindness is *g* toward us	Ps 117:2	1396
G are thy tender mercies, O LORD	Ps 119:156	7227
word, as one that findeth *g* spoil	Ps 119:162	7227
G peace have they which love thy	Ps 119:165	7227
LORD hath done *g* things for them	Ps 126:2	1431
LORD hath done *g* things for us	Ps 126:3	1431
do I exercise myself in *g* matters	Ps 131:1	1419
For I know that the LORD is *g*	Ps 135:5	1419
Who smote *g* nations, and slew	Ps 135:10	7227
To him who alone doeth *g* wonders	Ps 136:4	1419
To him that made *g* lights	Ps 136:7	1419
To him which smote *g* kings	Ps 136:17	1419
for *g* is the glory of the LORD	Ps 138:5	1419
How *g* is the sum of them	Ps 139:17	6105
me, and deliver me out of *g* waters	Ps 144:7	7227
G is the LORD, and greatly to be	Ps 145:3	1419
the memory of thy *g* goodness	Ps 145:7	7227
slow to anger, and of *g* mercy	Ps 145:8	1419
G is our Lord, and of *g* power	Ps 147:5	1419
G is our Lord, and of *g* power	Ps 147:5	7227
himself poor, yet hath *g* riches	Prov 13:7	7227
to wrath is of *g* understanding	Prov 14:29	7227
fear of the LORD than *g* treasure	Prov 15:16	7227
than *g* revenues without right	Prov 16:8	7230
brother to him that is a *g* waster	Prov 18:9	1167
him, and bringeth him before *g* men	Prov 18:16	1419
A man of *g* wrath shall suffer	Prov 19:19	
rather to be chosen than *g* riches	Prov 22:1	7227
stand not in the place of *g* men	Prov 25:6	1419
The *g* God that formed all things	Prov 26:10	7227
men do rejoice, there is *g* glory	Prov 28:12	7227
is also a *g* oppressor	Prov 28:16	7227
saying, Lo, I am come to *g* estate	Eccl 1:16	1431
my heart had *g* experience of	Eccl 1:16	7235
I made me *g* works	Eccl 2:4	1431
also I had *g* possessions of *g*	Eccl 2:7	7235
also I had *g* possessions of *g*	Eccl 2:7	1241
So I was *g*, and increased more	Eccl 2:9	1431
This also is vanity and a *g* evil	Eccl 2:21	7227
the misery of man is *g* upon him	Eccl 8:6	7227
the sun, and it seemed *g* unto me	Eccl 9:13	1419
there came a *g* king against it,	Eccl 9:14	1419
built *g* bulwarks against it	Eccl 9:14	1419
for yielding pacifieth *g* offences	Eccl 10:4	1419
Folly is set in *g* dignity	Eccl 10:6	7227
under his shadow with *g* delight	Song 2:3	
the *g* man humbleth himself	Is 2:9	
houses shall be desolate, even *g*	Is 5:9	1419
there be a *g* forsaking in the	Is 6:12	7227
said unto me, Take thee a *g* roll	Is 8:1	1419
in darkness have seen a *g* light	Is 9:2	1419
for *g* is the Holy One of Israel	Is 12:6	1419
mountains, like as of a *g* people	Is 13:4	7227
with all that *g* multitude	Is 16:14	7227
a *g* one, and he shall deliver them	Is 19:20	7227
by *g* waters the seed of Sihor,	Is 23:3	7227
day the LORD with his sore and *g*	Is 27:1	1419
that the *g* trumpet shall be blown	Is 27:13	1419
g noise, with storm and tempest,	Is 29:6	1419
in the day of the *g* slaughter	Is 30:25	7227
as the shadow of a *g* rock in a	Is 32:2	3515
is the prey of a *g* spoil divided	Is 33:23	4766
a *g* slaughter in the land of	Is 34:6	1419
There shall the *g* owl make her	Is 34:15	7091
unto king Hezekiah with a *g* army	Is 36:2	3515
Hezekiah, Thus saith the *g* king	Is 36:4	1419
Hear ye the words of the *g* king	Is 36:13	1419
for peace I had *g* bitterness	Is 38:17	
for the *g* abundance of thine	Is 47:9	3966
the sea, the waters of the *g* deep	Is 51:10	7227
I divide him a portion with the *g*	Is 53:12	7227
but with *g* mercies will I gather	Is 54:7	1419
g shall be the peace of thy	Is 54:13	7227
the *g* goodness toward the house	Is 63:7	7227
the north, and a *g* destruction	Jer 4:6	1419
I will get me unto the *g* men	Jer 5:5	1419
therefore they are become *g*	Jer 5:27	1431
of the north, and *g* destruction	Jer 6:1	1419
a *g* nation shall be raised from	Jer 6:22	1419
thou art *g*, and thy name is *g*	Jer 10:6	1419
g, and thy name is *g* in might	Jer 10:6	1419
a *g* commotion out of the north	Jer 10:22	1419
with the noise of a *g* tumult he	Jer 11:16	1419
and the *g* pride of Jerusalem	Jer 13:9	7227
people is broken with a *g* breach	Jer 14:17	1419
Both the *g* and the small shall die	Jer 16:6	1419
all this *g* evil against us	Jer 16:10	1419
her womb to be always *g* with me	Jer 20:17	2030
anger, and in fury, and in *g* wrath	Jer 21:5	1419
they shall die of a *g* pestilence	Jer 21:6	1419
LORD done thus unto this *g* city	Jer 22:8	1419
g kings shall serve themselves of	Jer 25:14	1419
a *g* whirlwind shall be raised up	Jer 25:32	1419
Thus might we procure *g* evil	Jer 26:19	1419
upon the ground, by my *g* power	Jer 27:5	1419
g kings shall serve themselves of	Jer 27:7	1419
against *g* kingdoms, of war, and of	Jer 28:8	1419
for that day is *g*, so that none	Jer 30:7	1419
a *g* company shall return thither	Jer 31:8	1419
and the earth by thy *g* power	Jer 32:17	1419
the *G*, the Mighty God, the LORD	Jer 32:18	1419
G in counsel, and mighty in work	Jer 32:19	1419
out arm, and with *g* terror	Jer 32:21	1419
and in my fury, and in *g* wrath	Jer 32:37	1419
all this *g* evil upon this people	Jer 32:42	1419
will answer thee, and shew thee *g*	Jer 33:3	1419
for *g* is the anger and the fury	Jer 36:7	1419
found him by the *g* waters that	Jer 41:12	7227
Take *g* stones in thine hand, and	Jer 43:9	1419
ye this *g* evil against your souls	Jer 44:7	1419
a *g* multitude, even all the	Jer 44:15	1419
Behold, I have sworn by my *g* name	Jer 44:26	1419
seekest thou *g* things for thyself	Jer 45:5	1419
spoiling and *g* destruction	Jer 48:3	1419
g nations from the north country	Jer 50:9	1419
in the land, and of *g* destruction	Jer 50:22	1419
a *g* nation, and many kings shall	Jer 50:41	1419
g destruction from the land of	Jer 51:54	1419
destroyed out of her the *g* voice	Jer 51:55	1419
her waves do roar like *g* waters	Jer 51:55	7227
and all the houses of the *g* men	Jer 52:13	1419
she that was *g* among the nations,	Lam 1:1	7227
and because of *g* servitude	Lam 1:3	7230
for thy breach is *g* like the sea	Lam 2:13	1419
g is thy faithfulness	Lam 3:23	7227
a *g* cloud, and a fire infolding	Eze 1:4	1419
wings, like the noise of *g* waters	Eze 1:24	7227
behind me a voice of a *g* rushing	Eze 3:12	1419
them, and a noise of a *g* rushing	Eze 3:13	1419
even the *g* abominations that the	Eze 8:6	1419
of Israel and Judah is exceeding *g*	Eze 9:9	1419
O *g* hailstones, shall fall	Eze 13:11	417
g hailstones in my fury to	Eze 13:13	417
and thou hast increased and waxen *g*	Eze 16:7	1431
thy neighbours, *g* of flesh	Eze 16:26	1432
A *g* eagle with *g* wings,	Eze 17:3	1419
he placed it by *g* waters, and set	Eze 17:5	7227
another *g* eagle with *g* wings	Eze 17:7	1419
in a good soil by *g* waters	Eze 17:8	7227
even without *g* power or many	Eze 17:9	1419
g company make for him in the war	Eze 17:17	7227
sword of the *g* men that are slain	Eze 21:14	1419
g lords and renowned, all of them	Eze 23:23	7991
even make the pile for fire *g*	Eze 24:9	1431
her *g* scum went not forth out of	Eze 24:12	7227
I will execute *g* vengeance upon	Eze 25:17	1419
g waters shall cover thee	Eze 26:19	7227
have brought thee into *g* waters	Eze 27:26	7227
By thy *g* wisdom and by thy	Eze 28:5	7230
the *g* dragon that lieth in the	Eze 29:3	1419
serve a *g* service against Tyrus	Eze 29:18	1419
g pain shall be in Ethiopia, when	Eze 30:4	
g pain shall come upon them, as	Eze 30:9	
Sin shall have *g* pain, and No	Eze 30:16	2342
The waters made him *g*, the deep	Eze 31:4	1431

his shadow dwelt all *g* nations ... Eze 31:6 7227
for his root was by *g* waters ... Eze 31:7 7227
and the *g* waters were stayed ... Eze 31:15 7227
thereof from beside the *g* waters ... Eze 32:13 7227
And I will sanctify my *g* name ... Eze 36:23 1419
their feet, an exceeding *g* army ... Eze 37:10 1419
even a *g* company with bucklers and ... Eze 38:4 7227
and goods, to take a *g* spoil ... Eze 38:13 1419
a *g* company, and a mighty army ... Eze 38:15 1419
in that day there shall be a *g* ... Eze 38:19 1419
g hailstones, fire, and brimstone ... Eze 38:22 417
even a *g* sacrifice upon the ... Eze 39:17 1419
were a full reed of six *g* cubits ... Eze 41:8 679
be a very *g* multitude of fish ... Eze 47:9 7227
kinds, as the fish of the *g* sea ... Eze 47:10 1419
the north side, from the *g* sea ... Eze 47:15 1419
in Kadesh, the river to the *g* sea ... Eze 47:19 1419
be the *g* sea from the border ... Eze 47:20 1419
and to the river toward the *g* sea ... Eze 48:28 1419
me gifts and rewards and *g* honour ... Dan 2:6 7690
king, sawest, and behold a *g* image ... Dan 2:31 7690
This *g* image, whose brightness ... Dan 2:31 7229
the image became a *g* mountain ... Dan 2:35 7229
the *g* God hath made known to the ... Dan 2:45 7229
Then the king made Daniel a *g* man ... Dan 2:48 7236
and gave him many *g* gifts ... Dan 2:48 7260
How *g* are his signs ... Dan 4:3 7260
and the height thereof was *g* ... Dan 4:10 7690
and said, Is not this *g* Babylon ... Dan 4:30 7227
a *g* feast to a thousand of his ... Dan 5:1 7227
the heaven strove upon the *g* sea ... Dan 7:2 7227
four *g* beasts came up from the ... Dan 7:3 7260
and it had *g* iron teeth ... Dan 7:7 7260
man, and a mouth speaking *g* things ... Dan 7:8 7260
the *g* words which the horn spake ... Dan 7:11 7260
These *g* beasts, which are four, ... Dan 7:17 7260
a mouth that spake very *g* things ... Dan 7:20 7260
he shall speak *g* words against ... Dan 7:25
to his will, and became *g* ... Dan 8:4 1431
the he goat waxed very *g* ... Dan 8:8 1431
was strong, the *g* horn was broken ... Dan 8:8 1419
horn, which waxed exceeding *g* ... Dan 8:9 1431
And it waxed *g*, even to the host ... Dan 8:10 1431
the *g* horn that is between his ... Dan 8:21 1419
and said, O Lord, the *g* and ... Dan 9:4 1419
us, by bringing upon us a *g* evil ... Dan 9:12 1419
but for thy *g* mercies ... Dan 9:18 7227
I was by the side of the *g* river ... Dan 10:4 1419
but a *g* quaking fell upon them, ... Dan 10:7 1419
left alone, and saw this *g* vision ... Dan 10:8 1419
that shall rule with *g* dominion ... Dan 11:3 7227
dominion shall be a *g* dominion ... Dan 11:5 7227
assemble a multitude of *g* forces ... Dan 11:10 7227
he shall set forth a *g* multitude ... Dan 11:11 7227
after certain years with a *g* army ... Dan 11:13 1419
king of the south with a *g* army ... Dan 11:25 1419
up to battle with a very *g* ... Dan 11:25 1419
into his land with *g* riches ... Dan 11:28 1419
go forth with *g* fury to destroy ... Dan 11:44 1419
the *g* prince which standeth for ... Dan 12:1 1419
land hath committed *g* whoredom ... Hos 1:2
for *g* shall be the day of Jezreel ... Hos 1:11 1419
to him the *g* things of my law ... Hos 8:12 7239
thine iniquity, and the *g* hatred ... Hos 9:7 7227
you because of your *g* wickedness ... Hos 10:15 7451
in the land of *g* drought ... Hos 13:5 8514
hath the cheek teeth of a *g* lion ... Joel 1:6 3833
a *g* people and a strong ... Joel 2:2 7227
for his camp is very *g* ... Joel 2:11 7227
for the day of the LORD is *g* ... Joel 2:11 1419
of *g* kindness, and repenteth him ... Joel 2:13 7227
up, because he hath done *g* things ... Joel 2:20 1431
for the LORD will do *g* things ... Joel 2:21 1431
my *g* army which I sent among you ... Joel 2:25 1419
the moon into blood, before the *g* ... Joel 2:31 1419
for their wickedness is *g* ... Joel 3:13 7227
behold the *g* tumults in the midst ... Amos 3:9 7227
the *g* houses shall have an end, ... Amos 3:15 7227
from thence go ye to Hamath the *g* ... Amos 6:2 7227
he will smite the *g* house with ... Amos 6:11 1419
fire, and it devoured the *g* deep ... Amos 7:4 7227
the ephah small, and the shekel *g* ... Amos 8:5 1431
Arise, go to Nineveh, that *g* city ... Jonah 1:2 1419
sent out a *g* wind into the sea ... Jonah 1:4 1419
sake this *g* tempest is upon you ... Jonah 1:12 1419
a *g* fish to swallow up Jonah ... Jonah 1:17 1419
go unto Nineveh, that *g* city ... Jonah 3:2 1419
g city of three days' journey ... Jonah 3:3 1419
of *g* kindness, and repentest thee ... Jonah 4:2 7227
not I spare Nineveh, that *g* city ... Jonah 4:11 1419
they shall make *g* noise by reason ... Mic 2:12
for now shall he be *g* unto the ... Mic 5:4 1431
and the *g* man, he uttereth his ... Mic 7:3 1419
g in power, and will not at all ... Nah 1:3 1431
slain, and a *g* number of carcases ... Nah 3:3 3514
all her *g* men were bound in ... Nah 3:10 1419
captains as the *g* grasshoppers ... Nah 3:17 1462
through the heap of *g* waters ... Hab 3:15 7227
a *g* crashing from the hills ... Zeph 1:10 1419
The *g* day of the LORD is near, it ... Zeph 1:14 1419
and for Zion with a *g* jealousy ... Zec 1:14 1419
Who art thou, O *g* mountain ... Zec 4:7 1419
therefore came a *g* wrath from the ... Zec 7:12 1419
jealous for Zion with *g* jealousy ... Zec 8:2 1419
I was jealous for her with *g* fury ... Zec 8:2 1419
For how *g* is his goodness ... Zec 9:17
and how *g* is his beauty ... Zec 9:17
be a *g* mourning in Jerusalem ... Zec 12:11 1431
and there shall be a very *g* valley ... Zec 14:4 1419
that a *g* tumult from the LORD ... Zec 14:13 7227
and apparel, in *g* abundance ... Zec 14:14 3966
shall be *g* among the Gentiles ... Mal 1:11 1419
name shall be *g* among the heathen ... Mal 1:11 1419
for I am a *g* King, saith the LORD ... Mal 1:14 1419
before the coming of the *g* ... Mal 4:5 1419
rejoiced with exceeding *g* joy ... Mt 2:10 3173
g mourning, Rachel weeping for ... Mt 2:18 4183
which sat in darkness saw *g* light ... Mt 4:16 3173
there followed him *g* multitudes ... Mt 4:25 4183
for *g* is your reward in heaven ... Mt 5:12 4183
called *g* in the kingdom of heaven ... Mt 5:19 3173
for it is the city of the *g* King ... Mt 5:35 3173
darkness, how *g* is that darkness ... Mt 6:23 4214
and *g* was the fall of it ... Mt 7:27 3173
g multitudes followed him ... Mt 8:1 4183
you, I have not found so *g* faith ... Mt 8:10 5118
Now when Jesus saw *g* multitudes ... Mt 8:18 4183
there arose a *g* tempest in the ... Mt 8:24 3173
and there was a *g* calm ... Mt 8:26 3173
g multitudes followed him, and he ... Mt 12:15 4183
g multitudes were gathered ... Mt 13:2 4183
he had found one pearl of *g* price ... Mt 13:46 4186
saw a *g* multitude, and was moved ... Mt 14:14 4183
unto her, O woman, *g* is thy faith ... Mt 15:28 3173
g multitudes came unto him, ... Mt 15:30 4183
as to fill so *g* a multitude ... Mt 15:33 5118
g multitudes followed him ... Mt 19:2 4183
for he had *g* possessions ... Mt 19:22 4183
them, and they that are *g* exercise ... Mt 20:25 3171
but whosoever will be *g* among you ... Mt 20:26 3173
a *g* multitude followed him ... Mt 20:29 4183
a very *g* multitude spread their ... Mt 21:8 4118
which is the *g* commandment in the ... Mt 22:36 3173
is the first and *g* commandment ... Mt 22:38 3173
For then shall be *g* tribulation ... Mt 24:21 3173
prophets, and shall shew *g* signs ... Mt 24:24 3173
of heaven with power and *g* glory ... Mt 24:30 4183
with a *g* sound of a trumpet ... Mt 24:31 3173
with him a *g* multitude with ... Mt 26:47 4183
he rolled a *g* stone to the door ... Mt 27:60 3173
behold, there was a *g* earthquake ... Mt 28:2 3173
the sepulchre with fear and *g* joy ... Mt 28:8 3173
rising up a *g* while before day ... Mk 1:35 3030
a *g* multitude from Galilee ... Mk 3:7 4183
a *g* multitude, when they had ... Mk 3:8 4183
had heard what *g* things he did ... Mk 3:8 3745
gathered unto him a *g* multitude ... Mk 4:1 4183
herbs, and shooteth out *g* branches ... Mk 4:32 3173
And there arose a *g* storm of wind ... Mk 4:37 3173
ceased, and there was a *g* calm ... Mk 4:39 3173
a *g* herd of swine feeding ... Mk 5:11 3173
tell them how *g* things the Lord ... Mk 5:19 3745
to publish in Decapolis how *g* ... Mk 5:20 3745
astonished with a *g* astonishment ... Mk 5:42 3173
so much the more a *g* deal they ... Mk 7:36 3123
days the multitude being very *g* ... Mk 8:1 3827
he saw a *g* multitude about them, ... Mk 9:14 4183
for he had *g* possessions ... Mk 10:22 4183
their *g* ones exercise authority ... Mk 10:42 3173
but whosoever will be *g* among you ... Mk 10:43 3173
a *g* number of people, blind ... Mk 10:46 2425
but he cried the more a *g* deal ... Mk 10:48 4183
him, Seest thou these *g* buildings ... Mk 13:2 3173
coming in the clouds with *g* power ... Mk 13:26 4183
with him a *g* multitude with ... Mk 14:43 4183
for it was very *g* ... Mk 16:4 3173
For he shall be *g* in the sight of ... Lk 1:15 3173
He shall be *g*, and shall be called ... Lk 1:32 3173
mighty hath done to me *g* things ... Lk 1:49 3167
Lord had shewed *g* mercy upon her ... Lk 1:58 3170
espoused wife, being *g* with child ... Lk 2:5
I bring you good tidings of *g* joy ... Lk 2:10 3173
she was of a *g* age, and had lived ... Lk 2:36 4183
when *g* famine was throughout all ... Lk 4:25 3173
mother was taken with a *g* fever ... Lk 4:38 3173
they inclosed a *g* multitude of ... Lk 5:6 4183
g multitudes came together to ... Lk 5:15 4183
Levi made him a *g* feast in his ... Lk 5:29 3173
and there was a *g* company of ... Lk 5:29 4183
a *g* multitude of people out of ... Lk 6:17 4183
your reward is *g* in heaven ... Lk 6:23 4183
and your reward shall be *g* ... Lk 6:35 4183
and the ruin of that house was *g* ... Lk 6:49 3173
you, I have not found so *g* faith ... Lk 7:9 5118
That a *g* prophet is risen up ... Lk 7:16 3173
for they were taken with *g* fear ... Lk 8:37 3173
shew how *g* things God hath done ... Lk 8:39 3745
throughout the whole city how *g* ... Lk 8:39 3745
you all, the same shall be *g* ... Lk 9:48 3173
unto them, The harvest truly is *g* ... Lk 10:2 4183
they had a *g* while ago repented, ... Lk 10:13 3819
and it grew, and waxed a *g* tree ... Lk 13:19 3173
A certain man made a *g* supper ... Lk 14:16 3173
there went *g* multitudes with him ... Lk 14:25 4183
the other is yet a *g* way off ... Lk 14:32
But when he was yet a *g* way off ... Lk 15:20 3112
us and you there is a *g* gulf fixed ... Lk 16:26 3173
g earthquakes shall be in divers ... Lk 21:11 3173
g signs shall there be from ... Lk 21:11 3173
for there shall be *g* distress in ... Lk 21:23 3173
in a cloud with power and *g* glory ... Lk 21:27 4183
his sweat was as it were *g* drops ... Lk 22:44
him a *g* company of people ... Lk 23:27 4183
returned to Jerusalem with *g* joy ... Lk 24:52 3173
In these lay a *g* multitude of ... Jn 5:3 4183
a *g* multitude followed him, ... Jn 6:2 4183
saw a *g* company come unto him, he ... Jn 6:5 4183
by reason of a *g* wind that blew ... Jn 6:18 3173
that *g* day of the feast, Jesus ... Jn 7:37 3173
the net to land full of *g* fishes ... Jn 21:11 3173
moon into blood, before that *g* ... Acts 2:20 3173
with *g* power gave the apostles ... Acts 4:33 3173
g grace was upon them all ... Acts 4:33 3173
g fear came on all them that ... Acts 5:5 3173
g fear came upon all the church, ... Acts 5:11 3173
a *g* company of the priests were ... Acts 6:7 4183
did *g* wonders and miracles among ... Acts 6:8 3173
Egypt and Chanaan, and *g* affliction ... Acts 7:11 3173
at that time there was a *g* ... Acts 8:1 3173
made *g* lamentation over him ... Acts 8:2 3173
there was *g* joy in that city ... Acts 8:8 3173
out that himself was some *g* one ... Acts 8:9 3173
This man is the *g* power of God ... Acts 8:10 3173
an eunuch of *g* authority under ... Acts 8:27
For I will shew him how *g* things ... Acts 9:16 3745
as it had been a *g* sheet knit at ... Acts 10:11 3173
descend, as it had been a *g* sheet ... Acts 11:5 3173
a *g* number believed, and turned ... Acts 11:21 4183
g dearth throughout all the world ... Acts 11:28 3173
that a *g* multitude both of the ... Acts 14:1 4183
they caused *g* joy unto all the ... Acts 15:3 3173
suddenly there was a *g* earthquake ... Acts 16:26 3173
the devout Greeks a *g* multitude ... Acts 17:4 4183
of the *g* goddess Diana should be ... Acts 19:27 3173
G is Diana of the Ephesians ... Acts 19:28 3173
G is Diana of the Ephesians ... Acts 19:34 3173
worshipper of the *g* goddess Diana ... Acts 19:35 3173
when there was made a *g* silence ... Acts 21:40 4183
heaven a *g* light round about me ... Acts 22:6 2425
With a *g* sum obtained I this ... Acts 22:28 4183
And there arose a *g* cry ... Acts 23:9 3173
when there arose a *g* dissension ... Acts 23:10 4183
bound ourselves under a *g* curse ... Acts 23:14
that by thee we enjoy *g* quietness ... Acts 24:2 4183
with *g* violence took him away out ... Acts 24:7 4183
was come, and Bernice, with *g* pomp ... Acts 25:23 4183
witnessing both to small and *g* ... Acts 26:22 3173
after they had looked a *g* while ... Acts 28:6 4183
had *g* reasoning among themselves ... Acts 28:29 4183
That I have *g* heaviness and ... Rom 9:2 3173
having a *g* desire these many ... Rom 15:23 1974
is it a *g* thing if we shall reap ... 1Cor 9:11 3173
For a *g* door and effectual is ... 1Cor 16:9 3173
delivered us from so *g* a death ... 2Cor 1:10 5082
we use *g* plainness of speech ... 2Cor 3:12 4183
G is my boldness of speech toward ... 2Cor 7:4 4183
you, *g* is my glorying of you ... 2Cor 7:4 4183
How that in a *g* trial of ... 2Cor 8:2 4183
upon the *g* confidence which I ... 2Cor 8:22 4183
Therefore it is no *g* thing if his ... 2Cor 11:15 3173
for his *g* love wherewith he loved ... Eph 2:4 4183
This is a *g* mystery ... Eph 5:32 3173
what *g* conflict I have for you ... Col 2:1 2245
that he hath a *g* zeal for you ... Col 4:13 4183
to see your face with *g* desire ... 1Th 2:17 4183
g boldness in the faith which is ... 1Ti 3:13 4183
without controversy *g* is the ... 1Ti 3:16 3173
with contentment is *g* gain ... 1Ti 6:6 3173
But in a *g* house there are not ... 2Ti 2:20 3173
glorious appearing of the *g* God ... Titus 2:13 3173
For we have *g* joy and consolation ... Philem 7 4183
if we neglect so *g* salvation ... Heb 2:3 5082
then that we have a *g* high priest ... Heb 4:14 3173
Now consider how *g* this man was ... Heb 7:4 4080
ye endured a *g* fight of ... Heb 10:32 4183
which hath *g* recompence of reward ... Heb 10:35 3173
with so *g* a cloud of witnesses ... Heb 12:1 5118
that *g* shepherd of the sheep, ... Heb 13:20 3173
ships, which though they be so *g* ... Jas 3:4 5082
member, and boasteth *g* things ... Jas 3:5 3166
how *g* a matter a little fire ... Jas 3:5 2245
is in the sight of God of *g* price ... 1Pet 3:4 4185
are given unto us exceeding *g* ... 2Pet 1:4 3176
For when they speak *g* swelling ... 2Pet 2:18 5246
shall pass away with a *g* noise ... 2Pet 3:10
unto the judgment of the *g* day ... Jude 6 3173
mouth speaketh *g* swelling words ... Jude 16 5246
day, and heard behind me a *g* voice ... Rev 1:10 3173
with her into *g* tribulation ... Rev 2:22 3173
was given unto him a *g* sword ... Rev 6:4 3173
and, lo, there was a *g* earthquake ... Rev 6:12 3173
kings of the earth, and the *g* men ... Rev 6:15 3175
For the *g* day of his wrath is ... Rev 6:17 3173
a *g* multitude, which no man could ... Rev 7:9 4183
which came out of *g* tribulation ... Rev 7:14 3173
as it were a *g* mountain burning ... Rev 8:8 3173
there fell a *g* star from heaven, ... Rev 8:10 3173
pit, as the smoke of a *g* furnace ... Rev 9:2 3173
bound in the *g* river Euphrates ... Rev 9:14 3173
lie in the street of the *g* city ... Rev 11:8 3173
g fear fell upon them which saw ... Rev 11:11 3173
they heard a *g* voice from heaven ... Rev 11:12 3173
hour was there a *g* earthquake ... Rev 11:13 3173
there were *g* voices in heaven, ... Rev 11:15 3173
hast taken to thee thy *g* power ... Rev 11:17 3173
that fear thy name, small and *g* ... Rev 11:18 3173
and an earthquake, and *g* hail ... Rev 11:19 3173
appeared a *g* wonder in heaven ... Rev 12:1 3173
behold a *g* red dragon, having ... Rev 12:3 3173
the *g* dragon was cast out, that ... Rev 12:9 3173
down unto you, having *g* wrath ... Rev 12:12 3173
were given two wings of a *g* eagle ... Rev 12:14 3173
and his seat, and *g* authority ... Rev 13:2 3173
him a mouth speaking *g* things ... Rev 13:5 3173

And he doeth g wonders, so that he........Rev 13:13 *3173*
he causeth all, both small and g............Rev 13:16 *3173*
and as the voice of a g thunder..............Rev 14:2 *3173*
is fallen, is fallen, that g city..............Rev 14:8 *3173*
cast it into the g winepress of................Rev 14:19 *3173*
I saw another sign in heaven, g................Rev 15:1 *3173*
the song of the Lamb, saying, G..............Rev 15:3 *3173*
I heard a g voice out of the ....Rev 16:1 *3173*
And men were scorched with g heat.......Rev 16:9 *3173*
vial upon the g river Euphrates ....Rev 16:12 *3173*
of that g day of God Almighty ....Rev 16:14 *3173*
there came a g voice out of the ....Rev 16:17 *3173*
and there was a g earthquake ....Rev 16:18 *3173*
so mighty an earthquake, and so g..........Rev 16:18 *3173*
the g city was divided into three............Rev 16:19 *3173*
g Babylon came in remembrance ....Rev 16:19 *3173*
upon men a g hail out of heaven ....Rev 16:21 *3173*
plague thereof was exceeding g ....Rev 16:21 *3173*
g whore that sitteth upon many................Rev 17:1 *3173*
written, MYSTERY, BABYLON THE G..Rev 17:5 *3173*
her, I wondered with g admiration..........Rev 17:6 *3173*
which thou sawest is that g city..............Rev 17:18 *3173*
down from heaven, having g power..........Rev 18:1 *3173*
saying, Babylon the g is fallen ....Rev 18:2 *3173*
alas that g city Babylon, that..................Rev 18:10 *3173*
And saying, Alas, alas that g city...........Rev 18:16 *3173*
For in one hour so g riches is ....Rev 18:17 *5118*
city is like unto this g city.....................Rev 18:18 *3173*
saying, Alas, alas that g city ....Rev 18:19 *3173*
up a stone like a g millstone ....Rev 18:21 *3173*
g city Babylon be thrown down ....Rev 18:21 *3173*
were the g men of the earth ....Rev 18:23 *3175*
after these things I heard a g ....Rev 19:1 *3173*
for he hath judged the g whore................Rev 19:2 *3173*
ye that fear him, both small and g..........Rev 19:5 *3173*
were the voice of a g multitude..............Rev 19:6 *4185*
unto the supper of the g God ....Rev 19:17 *3173*
free and bond, both small and g ....Rev 19:18 *3173*
pit and a g chain in his hand ....Rev 20:1 *3173*
I saw a g white throne, and him..............Rev 20:11 *3173*
And I saw the dead, small and g..............Rev 20:12 *3173*
I heard a g voice out of heaven ....Rev 21:3 *3173*
me away in the spirit to a g......................Rev 21:10 *3173*
and shewed me that g city.......................Rev 21:10 *3173*
And had a wall g and high, and had.......Rev 21:12 *3173*

GREATER See APPENDIX.

GREATEST See APPENDIX.

GREATLY See APPENDIX.

GREATNESS See APPENDIX.

GREAVES {1}
he had g of brass upon his legs,..........1Sa 17:6 4697

GRECIA {3} See GRECIANS, GREECE. *Latin form of Greece.*
the rough goat is the king of G..............Dan 8:21 3120
lo, the prince of G shall come ....Dan 10:20 3120
up all against the realm of G ....Dan 11:2 3120

GRECIANS {4} See GREEKS.
1. Inhabitants of Greece.
Jerusalem have ye sold unto the G..........Joel 3:6 3125
2. Hellenistic Jews.
of the G against the Hebrews..................Acts 6:1 *1675*
Jesus, and disputed against the G...........Acts 9:29 *1675*
come to Antioch, spake unto the G..........Acts 11:20 *1675*

GREECE {2} See GRECIA. *Peninsula south of the Balkans.*
O Zion, against thy sons, O G ....Zec 9:13 3120
much exhortation, he came into G...........Acts 20:2 *1671*

GREEDILY {3}
He coveteth g all the day long.................Prov 21:26 8378
thou hast g gained of thy ....Eze 22:12
ran g after the error of Balaam................Jude 11 *1632*

GREEDINESS {1}
to work all uncleanness with g ....Eph 4:19 *4124*

GREEDY {6}
as a lion that is g of his prey...................Ps 17:12 3700
of every one that is g of gain....................Prov 1:19 1214
He that is g of gain troubleth...................Prov 15:27 1214
they are g dogs which can never .....Is 56:11 5794,5315
no striker, not g of filthy lucre 1Ti 3:3 *866*
much wine, not g of filthy lucre 1Ti 3:8 *146*

GREEK {12} See GREEKS.
1. A native of Greece.
but his father was a G.............................Acts 16:1 *1672*
knew all that his father was a G.............Acts 16:3 *1672*
the Jew first, and also to the G ....Rom 1:16 *1672*
between the Jew and the G ....Rom 10:12 *1672*
Titus, who was with me, being a G.........Gal 2:3 *1672*
There is neither Jew nor G.......................Gal 3:28 *1672*
Where there is neither G nor Jew.............Col 3:11 *1672*
2. A language.
written over him in letters of G ....Lk 23:38 *1673*
and it was written in Hebrew, and G........Jn 19:20 *1676*
Who said, Canst thou speak G..................Acts 21:37 *1676*
but in the G tongue hath his name ....Rev 9:11 *1673*
3. A female.
The woman was a G, a ....Mk 7:26 *1674*

GREEKS {14} See GRECIANS. *Plural of Greek 1.*
there were certain G among them.............Jn 12:20 *1672*
Jews and also of the G believed ....Acts 14:1 *1672*
of the devout G a great multitude............Acts 17:4 *1672*
of honourable women which were G.........Acts 17:12 *1674*
and persuaded the Jews and the G ....Acts 18:4 *1672*
Then all the G took Sosthenes, ...Acts 18:17 *1672*
of the Lord Jesus, both Jews and G ....Acts 19:10 *1672*
G also dwelling at Ephesus......................Acts 19:17 *1672*
to the Jews, and also to the G ....Acts 20:21 *1672*
further brought G also into the..............Acts 21:28 *1672*
I am debtor both to the G ....Rom 1:14 *1672*
sign, and the G seek after wisdom..........1Cor 1:22 *1672*
and unto the G foolishness......................1Cor 1:23 *1672*
which are called, both Jews and G 1Cor 1:24 *1672*

GREEN {41}
have given every g herb for meat ....Gen 1:30 3418
even as the g herb have I given ....Gen 9:3 3418
Jacob took him rods of g poplar...............Gen 30:37 3892
not any g thing in the trees ....Ex 10:15 3418
offering of thy firstfruits g ....Lev 2:14
nor g ears, until the selfsame ....Lev 23:14
the hills, and under every g tree..............Deut 12:2 7488
If they bind me with seven g.....................Judg 16:7 3892
brought up to her seven g withs...............Judg 16:8 3892
high hill, and under every g tree............1Kin 14:23 7488
the hills, and under every g tree.............2Kin 16:4 7488
high hill, and under every g tree............2Kin 17:10 7488
of the field, and as the g herb.................2Kin 19:26 3410
the hills, and under every g tree.............2Chr 28:4 7488
Where were white, g, and blue,................Est 1:6 3768
He is g before the sun, and his ....Job 8:16 7373
and his branch shall not be g...................Job 15:32 7488
he searcheth after every g thing..............Job 39:8 3387
me to lie down in g pastures ....Ps 23:2 1877
grass, and wither as the g herb ....Ps 37:2 3418
himself like a g bay tree ....Ps 37:35 7488
But I am like a g olive tree in..................Ps 52:8 7488
also our bed is g ....Song 1:16 7488
fig tree putteth forth her g figs ....Song 2:13 6291
faileth, there is no g thing.......................Is 15:6 3418
of the field, and as the g herb ....Is 37:27 3419
with idols under every g tree....................Is 57:5 7488
under every g tree thou wanderest...........Jer 2:20 7488
mountain and under every g tree ....Jer 3:6 7488
the strangers under every g tree..............Jer 3:13 7488
A g olive tree, fair, and of.........................Jer 11:16 7488
their groves by the g trees upon ....Jer 17:2 7488
cometh, but her leaf shall be g..................Jer 17:8 7488
mountains, and under every g tree...........Eze 6:13 7488
tree, have dried up the g tree ....Eze 17:24 3892
shall devour every g tree in thee ....Eze 20:47 3892
I am like a g fir tree ....Hos 14:8 7488
by companies upon the g grass ....Mk 6:39 *5515*
they do these things in a g tree ....Lk 23:31 *5200*
up, and all g grass was burnt up..............Rev 8:7 *5515*
of the earth, neither any g thing ....Rev 9:4 *5515*

GREENISH {2}
if the plague be g or reddish in.................Lev 13:49 3422
g or reddish, which in sight are ....Lev 14:37 3422

GREENNESS {1}
Whilst it is yet in his g ....Job 8:12 3

GREET {16}
go to Nabal, and g him.........................1Sa 25:5 7592,7965
G Priscilla and Aquila my helpers...........Rom 16:3 *782*
Likewise g the church that is in...............Rom 16:5 *782*
G Mary, who bestowed much labour.........Rom 16:6 *782*
G Amplias my beloved in the Lord ....Rom 16:8 *782*
G them that be of the household..............Rom 16:11 *782*
All the brethren g you 1Cor 16:20 *782*
G ye one another with an holy.................1Cor 16:20 *782*
G one another with an holy kiss 2Cor 13:12 *782*
brethren which are with me g you ....Phil 4:21 *782*
physician, and Demas, g you ....Col 4:14 *782*
G all the brethren with an holy.................1Th 5:26 *782*
G them that love us in the faith...............Titus 3:15 *782*
G ye one another with a kiss of 1Pet 5:14 *782*
of thy elect sister g thee 2Jn 13 *782*
G the friends by name..............................3Jn 14 *782*

GREETETH {1}
Eubulus g thee, and Pudens, and............2Ti 4:21 *782*

GREETING {3}
brethren send g unto the brethren ....Acts 15:23 *5463*
governor Felix sendeth g ....Acts 23:26 *5463*
which are scattered abroad, g ....Jas 1:1 *5463*

GREETINGS {3}
g in the markets, and to be called............Mt 23:7 *783*
synagogues, and g in the markets ....Lk 11:43 *783*
love g in the markets, and the..................Lk 20:46 *783*

GREW {28}
herb of the field before it g ....Gen 2:5 6779
that which g upon the ground...................Gen 19:25 6780
And the child g, and was weaned ....Gen 21:8 1431
and he g, and dwelt in the........................Gen 21:20 1431
And the boys g...Gen 25:27 1431
g until he became very great....................Gen 26:13 1432
had possessions therein, and g.................Gen 47:27 6509
the more they multiplied and g.................Ex 1:12 6555
And the child g, and she brought.............Ex 2:10 1431
and his wife's sons g up, and they...........Judg 11:2 1431
and the child g, and the LORD.................Judg 13:24 1431
child Samuel g before the LORD..............1Sa 2:21 1431
And the child Samuel g on, and was.......1Sa 2:26 1432
And Samuel g, and the LORD was with..1Sa 3:19 1431
g great, and the LORD God of hosts 2Sa 5:10
it g up together with him, and 2Sa 12:3 1431
And it g, and became a spreading............Eze 17:6 6779
wither in the furrows where it g ....Eze 17:10 6780
The tree g, and was strong, and the ....Dan 4:11 7236
tree that thou sawest, which g ....Dan 4:20 7236
among thorns, and the thorns g up ....Mk 4:7 *305*
bettered, but rather g worse.....................Mk 5:26 *2064*
And the child g, and waxed strong ....Lk 1:80 *837*
And the child g, and waxed strong ....Lk 2:40 *837*
and it g, and waxed a great tree ....Lk 13:19 *837*
sworn to Abraham, the people g ....Acts 7:17 *837*
But the word of God g and.......................Acts 12:24 *837*
So mightily g the word of God and..........Acts 19:20 *837*

GREY {1}
beauty of old men is the g head ....Prov 20:29 7872

GREYHEADED {1}
Now also when I am old and g..................Ps 71:18 7872

GREYHOUND {1}
A g; an he goat also; and a ....Prov 30:31 2223,4975

GRIEF {26}
Which were a g of mind unto Isaac.........Gen 26:35 4786
and g have I spoken hitherto...................1Sa 1:16 3708
That this shall be no g unto thee 1Sa 25:31 6330
know his own sore and his own g 2Chr 6:29 4341
saw that his g was very great...................Job 2:13 3511
O that my g were throughly ....Job 6:2 3708
of my lips should asswage your g............Job 16:5
I speak, my g is not asswaged ....Job 16:6 3511
Mine eye is consumed because of g.........Ps 6:7 3708
mine eye is consumed with g...................Ps 31:9 3708
For my life is spent with g........................Ps 31:10 3015
they talk to the g of those whom ....Ps 69:26 4341
foolish son is a g to his father..................Prov 17:25 3708
For in much wisdom is much g ....Eccl 1:18 3708
are sorrows, and his travail g ....Eccl 2:23 3708
shall be a heap in the day of g ....Is 17:11 2470
of sorrows, and acquainted with g...........Is 53:3 2483
he hath put him to g..................................Is 53:10 2470
before me continually is g ....Jer 6:7 2483
but I said, Truly this is a g ....Jer 10:19 2483
LORD hath added g to my sorrow.............Jer 45:3 3015
But though he cause g, yet will.................Lam 3:32 3013
head, to deliver him from his g ....Jonah 4:6 7451
But if any have caused g, he hath 2Cor 2:5 *3076*
may do it with joy, and not with g ....Heb 13:17 *4727*
conscience toward God endure g..............1Pet 2:19 *3077*

GRIEFS {1}
Surely he hath borne our g........................Is 53:4 2483

GRIEVANCE {1}
iniquity, and cause me to behold g..........Hab 1:3 5999

GRIEVE {5}
thine eyes, and to g thine heart..............1Sa 2:33 109
from evil, that it may not g me 1Chr 4:10 6087
and g him in the desert ....Ps 78:40 6087
nor g the children of men.........................Lam 3:33 3013
g not the holy Spirit of God,.....................Eph 4:30 *3076*

GRIEVED {40}
earth, and it g him at his heart ....Gen 6:6 6087
and the men were g, and they were..........Gen 34:7 6087
Now therefore be not g, nor angry...........Gen 45:5 6087
The archers have sorely g him.................Gen 49:23 4843
they were g because of the ....Ex 1:12 6973
thine heart shall not be g when................Deut 15:10 7489
his soul was g for the misery of...............Judg 10:16 7114
and why is thy heart g..............................1Sa 1:8 7489
And it g Samuel..1Sa 15:11 2734
Jonathan know this, lest he be g...............1Sa 20:3 6087
for he was g for David, because 1Sa 20:34 6087
the soul of all the people was g................1Sa 30:6 4784
how the king was g for his son.................2Sa 19:2 6087
it g them exceedingly that there ....Neh 2:10 7489
neither be ye g ....Neh 8:11 6087
And it g me sore ....Neh 13:8 7489
Then was the queen exceedingly g............Est 4:4 2342
commune with thee, wilt thou be g..........Job 4:2 3811
was not my soul g for the poor.................Job 30:25 5701
Thus my heart was g, and I was...............Ps 73:21 2556
long was I g with this generation.............Ps 95:10 6962
The wicked shall see it, and be g ....Ps 112:10 3707
the transgressors, and was g ....Ps 119:158 6962
am not I g with those that rise.................Ps 139:21 6962
g in spirit, and a wife of youth,................Is 54:6 6087
therefore thou wast not g..........................Is 57:10 2470
them, but they have not g..........................Jer 5:3 2342
I Daniel was g in my spirit in....................Dan 7:15 3735
therefore he shall be g, and.....................Dan 11:30 3512
but they are not g for the ....Amos 6:6 2470
being g for the hardness of their..............Mk 3:5 *4818*
at that saying, and went away g...............Mk 10:22 *3076*
Peter was g because he said unto.............Jn 21:17 *3076*
Being g that they taught the ....Acts 4:2 *1278*
But Paul, being g, turned and said...........Acts 16:18 *1278*
if thy brother be g with thy meat.............Rom 14:15 *3076*
not that ye should be g, but that..............2Cor 2:4 *3076*
caused grief, he hath not g me 2Cor 2:5 *3076*
Wherefore I was g with that.....................Heb 3:10 *4360*
with whom was he g forty years ....Heb 3:17 *4360*

GRIEVETH {2}
for it g me much for your sakes ....Ruth 1:13 4843
it g him to bring it again to his...............Prov 26:15 3811

GRIEVING {1}
nor any g thorn of all that are..................Eze 28:24 3510

GRIEVOUS {38}
for the famine was g in the land ....Gen 12:10 3515
and because their sin is very g ....Gen 18:20 3513
the thing was very g in Abraham's............Gen 21:11 7489
Let it not be g in thy sight ....Gen 21:12 7489
for it shall be very g ....Gen 41:31 3515
This is a g mourning to the ....Gen 50:11 3515
there came a g swarm of flies...................Ex 8:24 3515
there shall be a very g murrain ....Ex 9:3 3515
cause it to rain a very g hail......................Ex 9:18 3515

mingled with the hail, very *g* Ex 9:24 3515
very *g* were they Ex 10:14 3515
which cursed me with a *g* curse in 1Kin 2:8 4834
Thy father made our yoke *g* 1Kin 12:4 7185
thou the *g* service of thy father 1Kin 12:4 7186
Thy father made our yoke *g* 2Chr 10:4 7185
ease thou somewhat the *g* 2Chr 10:4 7186
His ways are always *g* Ps 10:5 2342
which speak *g* things proudly and Ps 31:18 6277
but *g* words stir up anger Prov 15:1 6089
Correction is *g* unto him that Prov 15:10 7451
under the sun is *g* unto me Eccl 2:17 7451
his life shall be *g* unto him Is 15:4 3415
A *g* vision is declared unto me Is 21:2 7186
They are all *g* revolters, walking Jer 6:28 5493
my wound is *g* Jer 10:19 2470
great breach, with a very *g* blow Jer 14:17 2470
They shall die of *g* deaths Jer 16:4 8463
forth in fury, even a *g* whirlwind Jer 23:19 2342
is incurable, and thy wound is *g* Jer 30:12 2470
thy wound is *g* Nah 3:19 2470
g to be borne, and lay them on Mt 23:4 *1418*
men with burdens *g* to be borne Lk 11:46 *1418*
shall *g* wolves enter in among you Acts 20:29 *926*
g complaints against Paul, which Acts 25:7 *926*
to you, to me indeed is not *g* Phil 3:1 *3636*
seemeth to be joyous, but *g* Heb 12:11 *3077*
and his commandments are not *g* 1Jn 5:3 *926*
g sore upon the men which had the Rev 16:2 *4190*

GRIEVOUSLY {7}
afterward did more *g* afflict her Is 9:1 3513
it shall fall *g* upon the head of Jer 23:19 2342
Jerusalem hath *g* sinned Lam 1:8 2399
for I have *g* rebelled Lam 1:20 4784
against me by trespassing *g* Eze 14:13 4604
sick of the palsy, *g* tormented Mt 8:6 *1171*
my daughter is *g* vexed with a Mt 15:22 *2560*

GRIEVOUSNESS {2}
that write *g* which they have Is 10:1 5999
bent bow, and from the *g* of war Is 21:15 3514

GRIND {7}
he did *g* in the prison house Judg 16:21 2912
Then let my wife *g* unto another Job 31:10 2912
and *g* the faces of the poor Is 3:15 2912
Take the millstones, and *g* meal Is 47:2 2912
They took the young men to *g* Lam 5:13 2911
fall, it will *g* him to powder Mt 21:44 *3039*
fall, it will *g* him to powder Lk 20:18 *3039*

GRINDERS {1}
the *g* cease because they are few, Eccl 12:3 2912

GRINDING {3}
when the sound of the *g* is low Eccl 12:4 2913
Two women shall be *g* at the mill Mt 24:41 *229*
Two women shall be *g* together Lk 17:35 *229*

GRISLED {4}
were ringstraked, speckled, and *g* Gen 31:10 1261
are ringstraked, speckled, and *g* Gen 31:12 1261
and in the fourth chariot *g* Zec 6:3 1261
the *g* go forth toward the south Zec 6:6 1261

GROAN {7}
Men *g* from out of the city, and Job 24:12 5008
all her land the wounded shall *g* Jer 51:52 602
he shall *g* before him with the Eze 30:24 5008
How do the beasts *g* Joel 1:18 584
we ourselves *g* within ourselves Rom 8:23 *4727*
For in this we *g*, earnestly 2Cor 5:2 *4727*
that are in this tabernacle do *g* 2Cor 5:4 *4727*

GROANED {1}
he *g* in the spirit, and was Jn 11:33 *1690*

GROANETH {1}
we know that the whole creation *g* Rom 8:22 *4959*

GROANING {9}
And God heard their *g*, and God Ex 2:24 5009
I have also heard the *g* of the Ex 6:5 5009
my stroke is heavier than my *g* Job 23:2 585
I am weary with my *g* Ps 6:6 585
my *g* is not hid from thee Ps 38:9 585
my *g* my bones cleave to my skin Ps 102:5 585
To hear the *g* of the prisoner Ps 102:20 603
Jesus therefore again *g* in Jn 11:38 *1690*
in Egypt, and I have heard their *g* Acts 7:34 *4726*

GROANINGS {3}
of their *g* by reason of them that Judg 2:18 5009
the *g* of a deadly wounded man Eze 30:24 5009
us with *g* which cannot be uttered Rom 8:26 *4726*

GROPE {5}
And thou shalt *g* at noonday Deut 28:29 4959
g in the noonday as in the night Job 5:14 4959
They *g* in the dark without light, Job 12:25 4959
We *g* for the wall like the blind, Is 59:10 1659
we *g* as if we had no eyes Is 59:10 1659

GROPETH {1}
as the blind *g* in darkness Deut 28:29 4959

GROSS {4}
earth, and *g* darkness the people Is 60:2 6205
of death, and make it *g* darkness Jer 13:16 6205
this people's heart is waxed *g* Mt 13:15 *3975*
heart of this people is waxed *g* Acts 28:27 *3975*

GROUND {192}
there was not a man to till the *g* Gen 2:5 127
watered the whole face of the *g* Gen 2:6 127
formed man of the dust of the *g* Gen 2:7 127
out of the *g* made the LORD God to Gen 2:9 127
out of the *g* the LORD God formed Gen 2:19 127
cursed is the *g* for thy sake Gen 3:17 127
till thou return unto the *g* Gen 3:19 127
to till the *g* from whence he was Gen 3:23 127
but Cain was a tiller of the *g* Gen 4:2 127
the *g* an offering unto the LORD Gen 4:3 127
blood crieth unto me from the *g* Gen 4:10 127
When thou tillest the *g*, it shall Gen 4:12 127
because of the *g* which the LORD Gen 5:29 127
which was upon the face of the *g* Gen 7:23 127
abated from off the face of the *g* Gen 8:8 127
behold, the face of the *g* was dry Gen 8:13 127
the *g* any more for man's sake Gen 8:21 127
and bowed himself toward the *g* Gen 18:2 776
with his face toward the *g* Gen 19:1 776
and that which grew upon the *g* Gen 19:25 127
himself to the *g* seven times Gen 33:3 776
wife, that he spilled it on the *g* Gen 38:9 776
down every man his sack to the *g* Gen 44:11 776
and they fell before him on the *g* Gen 44:14 776
whereon thou standest is holy *g* Ex 3:5 127
And he said, Cast it on the *g* Ex 4:3 776
And he cast it on the *g*, and it Ex 4:3 776
also the *g* whereon they are Ex 8:21 127
and the fire ran along upon the *g* Ex 9:23 776
of Israel shall go on dry *g* Ex 14:16
midst of the sea upon the dry *g* Ex 14:22
small as the hoar frost on the *g* Ex 16:14 776
g it to powder, and strawed it Ex 32:20 2912
thing that creepeth on the *g* Lev 20:25 127
g it in mills, or beat it in a Num 11:8 2912
that the *g* clave asunder that was Num 16:31 127
any thing that creepeth on the *g* Deut 4:18 127
g it very small, even until it Deut 9:21 2912
shalt pour it upon the *g* as water Deut 15:23 776
the way in any tree, or on the *g* Deut 22:6 776
thy body, and the fruit of thy *g* Deut 28:4 127
cattle, and in the fruit of thy *g* Deut 28:11 127
foot upon the *g* for delicateness Deut 28:56 776
on dry *g* in the midst of Jordan Josh 3:17
Israelites passed over on dry *g* Josh 3:17
in a parcel of *g* which Jacob Josh 24:32 7704
and fastened it into the *g* Judg 4:21 776
upon all the *g* let there be dew Judg 6:39 776
and there was dew on all the *g* Judg 6:40 776
and fell on their faces to the *g* Judg 13:20 776
destroyed down to the *g* of the Judg 20:21 776
destroyed down to the *g* of the Judg 20:25 776
face, and bowed herself to the *g* Ruth 2:10 776
none of his words fall to the *g* 1Sa 3:19 776
the *g* before the ark of the LORD 1Sa 5:4 776
and will set them to ear his *g* 1Sa 8:12 2758
and there was honey upon the *g* 1Sa 14:25 7704
and calves, and slew them on the *g* 1Sa 14:32 776
hair of his head fall to the *g* 1Sa 14:45 776
son of Jesse liveth upon the *g* 1Sa 20:31 127
and fell on his face to the *g* 1Sa 20:41 776
face, and bowed herself to the *g* 1Sa 25:23 776
stuck in the *g* at his bolster 1Sa 26:7 776
he stooped with his face to the *g* 1Sa 28:14 776
should I smite thee to the *g* 2Sa 2:22 776
line, casting them down to the *g* 2Sa 8:2 776
she fell on her face to the *g* 2Sa 14:4 776
and are as water spilt on the *g* 2Sa 14:14 776
And Joab fell to the *g* on his face 2Sa 14:22 776
his face to the *g* before the king 2Sa 14:33 776
him as the dew falleth on the *g* 2Sa 17:12 127
mouth, and spread *g* corn thereon 2Sa 17:19 7383
thou not smite him there to the *g* 2Sa 18:11 776
and shed out his bowels to the *g* 2Sa 20:10 776
was a piece of *g* full of lentiles 2Sa 23:11 7704
he stood in the midst of the *g* 2Sa 23:12 2513
the king on his face upon the *g* 2Sa 24:20 776
the king with his face to the *g* 1Kin 1:23 776
in the clay *g* between Succoth and 1Kin 7:46 127
that they two went over on dry *g* 2Kin 2:8
themselves to the *g* before him 2Kin 2:15 776
water is naught, and the *g* barren 2Kin 2:19 776
feet, and bowed herself to the *g* 2Kin 4:37 776
and cast him into the plat of *g* 2Kin 9:26
king of Israel, Smite upon the *g* 2Kin 13:18 776
was a parcel of *g* full of barley 1Chr 11:13 7704
to David with his face to the *g* 1Chr 21:21 776
the *g* was Ezri the son of Chelub 1Chr 27:26 127
in the clay *g* between Succoth and 2Chr 4:17 127
faces to the *g* upon the pavement 2Chr 7:3 776
his head with his face to the *g* 2Chr 20:18 776
LORD with their faces to the *g* Neh 8:6 776
to bring the firstfruits of our *g* Neh 10:35 127
tithes of our *g* unto the Levites Neh 10:37 127
his head, and fell down upon the *g* Job 1:20 776
with him upon the *g* seven days Job 2:13 776
doth trouble spring out of the *g* Job 5:6 127
and the stock thereof die in the *g* Job 14:8 6083
he poureth out my gall upon the *g* Job 16:13 776
snare is laid for him in the *g* Job 18:10 776
satisfy the desolate and waste *g* Job 38:27
swalloweth the *g* with fierceness Job 39:24 776
place of thy name to the *g* Ps 74:7 776
his crown by casting it to the *g* Ps 89:39 776
and cast his throne down to the *g* Ps 89:44 776
and devoured the fruit of their *g* Ps 105:35 127
and the watersprings into dry *g* Ps 107:33
water, and dry *g* into watersprings Ps 107:35 127
smitten my life down to the *g* Ps 143:3 776
casteth the wicked down to the *g* Ps 147:6 776
desolate shall sit upon the *g* Is 3:26 776
how art thou cut down to the *g* Is 14:12 776
gods he hath broken unto the *g* Is 21:9 776
down, lay low, and bring to the *g* Is 25:12 776
he layeth it low, even to the *g* Is 26:5 776
open and break the clods of his *g* Is 28:24 127
down, and shalt speak out of the *g* Is 29:4 776
a familiar spirit, out of the *g* Is 29:4 776
that thou shalt sow the *g* withal Is 30:23 127
the *g* shall eat clean provender Is 30:24 127
the parched *g* shall become a pool Is 35:7
thirsty, and floods upon the dry *g* Is 44:3
daughter of Babylon, sit on the *g* Is 47:1 776
thou hast laid thy body as the *g* Is 51:23 776
and as a root out of a dry *g* Is 53:2 776
Jerusalem, Break up your fallow *g* Jer 4:3
field, and upon the fruit of the *g* Jer 7:20 127
they are black unto the *g* Jer 14:2 776
Because the *g* is chapt, for there Jer 14:4 127
they shall be dung upon the *g* Jer 25:33 127
and the beast that are upon the *g* Jer 27:5 776
hath brought them down to the *g* Lam 2:2 776
Her gates are sunk into the *g* Lam 2:9 776
daughter of Zion sit upon the *g* Lam 2:10 776
hang down their heads to the *g* Lam 2:10 776
old lie on the *g* in the streets Lam 2:21 776
thy face, that thou see not the *g* Eze 12:6 776
he see not the *g* with his eyes Eze 12:12 776
morter, and bring it down to the *g* Eze 13:14 776
fury, she was cast down to the *g* Eze 19:12 776
wilderness, in a dry and thirsty *g* Eze 19:13 776
she poured it not upon the *g* Eze 24:7 776
garrisons shall go down to the *g* Eze 26:11 776
they shall sit upon the *g* Eze 26:16 776
I will cast thee to the *g* Eze 28:17 776
and every wall shall fall to the *g* Eze 38:20 776
from the *g* up to the windows, and Eze 41:16 776
From the *g* unto above the door Eze 41:20 776
and the middlemost from the *g* Eze 42:6 776
from the bottom upon the *g* even Eze 43:14 776
whole earth, and touched not the *g* Dan 8:5 776
but he cast him down to the *g* Dan 8:7 776
the host and of the stars to the *g* Dan 8:10 776
it cast down the truth to the *g* Dan 8:12 776
sleep on my face toward the *g* Dan 8:18 776
my face, and my face toward the *g* Dan 10:9 776
me, I set my face toward the *g* Dan 10:15 776
with the creeping things of the *g* Hos 2:18 127
break up your fallow *g* Hos 10:12
be cut off, and fall to the *g* Amos 3:14 776
Who shall bring me down to the *g* Obad 3 776
that which the *g* bringeth forth Hag 1:11 127
the *g* shall give her increase, and Zec 8:12 776
not destroy the fruits of your *g* Mal 3:11 127
fall on the *g* without your Father Mt 10:29 *1093*
But other fell into good *g* Mt 13:8 *1093*
g is he that heareth the word Mt 13:23 *1093*
multitude to sit down on the *g* Mt 15:35 *1093*
And some fell on stony *g*, where it Mk 4:5
And other fell on good *g*, and did Mk 4:8 *1093*
which are sown on stony *g* Mk 4:16
are they which are sown on good *g* Mk 4:20 *1093*
a man should cast seed into the *g* Mk 4:26 *1093*
the people to sit down on the *g* Mk 8:6 *1093*
and he fell on the *g*, and wallowed Mk 9:20 *1093*
a little, and fell on the *g* Mk 14:35 *1093*
And other fell on good *g*, and Lk 8:8 *1093*
But that on the good *g* are they Lk 8:15 *1093*
The *g* of a certain rich man Lk 12:16 *5561*
why cumbereth it the *g* Lk 13:7 *1093*
him, I have bought a piece of *g* Lk 14:18 *68*
And shall lay thee even with the *g* Lk 19:44 *1474*
of blood falling down to the *g* Lk 22:44 *1093*
near to the parcel of *g* that Jn 4:5 *5564*
and with his finger wrote on the *g* Jn 8:6 *1093*
stooped down, and wrote on the *g* Jn 8:8 *1093*
had thus spoken, he spat on the *g* Jn 9:6 *5476*
a corn of wheat fall into the *g* Jn 12:24 *1093*
went backward, and fell to the *g* Jn 18:6 *5476*
where thou standest is holy *g* Acts 7:33 *1093*
And I fell unto the *g*, and heard a Acts 22:7 *1475*
God, the pillar and *g* of the truth 1Ti 3:15 *1477*

GROUNDED {3}
where the *g* staff shall pass Is 30:32 4145
ye, being rooted and *g* in love, Eph 3:17 *2311*
If ye continue in the faith *g* Col 1:23 *2311*

GROVE {17}
Abraham planted a *g* in Beer-sheba Gen 21:33 815
a *g* of any trees near unto the Deut 16:21 842
cut down the *g* that is by it Judg 6:25 842
the *g* which thou shalt cut down Judg 6:26 842
the *g* was cut down that was by it Judg 6:28 842
cut down the *g* that was by it Judg 6:30 842
she had made an idol in a *g* 1Kin 15:13 842
And Ahab made a *g* 1Kin 16:33 842
remained the *g* also in Samaria 2Kin 13:6 842
even two calves, and made a *g* 2Kin 17:16 842
up altars for Baal, and made a *g* 2Kin 21:3 842
he set a graven image of the *g* 2Kin 21:7 842
were made for Baal, and for the *g* 2Kin 23:4 842
he brought out the *g* from the 2Kin 23:6 842
the women wove hangings for the *g* 2Kin 23:7 842
small to powder, and burned the *g* 2Kin 23:15 842
she had made an idol in a *g* 2Chr 15:16 842

GROVES {24}
their images, and cut down their *g* Ex 34:13 842
their images, and cut down their *g* Deut 7:5 842

and burn their *g* with fire ... Deut 12:3 842
God, and served Baalim and the *g* ... Judg 3:7 842
because they have made their *g* ... 1Kin 14:15 842
them high places, and images, and *g* ... 1Kin 14:23 842
prophets of the *g* four hundred ... 1Kin 18:19 842
g in every high hill, and under ... 2Kin 17:10 842
the images, and cut down the *g* ... 2Kin 18:4 842
the images, and cut down the *g* ... 2Kin 23:14 842
the images, and cut down the *g* ... 2Chr 14:3 842
the high places and *g* out of Judah ... 2Chr 17:6 842
taken away the *g* out of the land ... 2Chr 19:3 842
God of their fathers, and served *g* ... 2Chr 24:18 842
in pieces, and cut down the *g* ... 2Chr 31:1 842
up altars for Baalim, and made *g* ... 2Chr 33:3 842
he built high places, and set up *g* ... 2Chr 33:19 842
from the high places, and the *g* ... 2Chr 34:3 842
and the *g*, and the carved images, ... 2Chr 34:4 842
broken down the altars and the *g* ... 2Chr 34:7 842
fingers have made, either the *g* ... Is 17:8 842
that are beaten in sunder, the *g* ... Is 27:9 842
their *g* by the green trees upon ... Jer 17:2 842
I will pluck up thy *g* out of the ... Mic 5:14 842

GROW {38}
g every tree that is pleasant to ... Gen 2:9 6779
let them *g* into a multitude in ... Gen 48:16 1711
locks of the hair of his head *g* ... Num 6:5 1431
to *g* again after he was shaven ... Judg 16:22 6779
although he make it not to *g* ... 2Sa 23:5 6779
such things as *g* of themselves ... 2Kin 19:29 5599
why should damage *g* to the hurt ... Ezr 4:22 7680
Can the rush *g* up without mire ... Job 8:11 1342
can the flag *g* without water ... Job 8:11 6779
out of the earth shall others *g* ... Job 8:19 6779
g out of the dust of the earth ... Job 14:19 5599
Let thistles *g* instead of wheat, ... Job 31:40 3318
good liking, they *g* up with corn ... Job 39:4 7235
he shall *g* like a cedar in ... Ps 92:12 7685
the grass to *g* for the cattle ... Ps 104:14 6779
grass to *g* upon the mountains ... Ps 147:8 6779
nor how the bones do *g* in the ... Eccl 11:5
a Branch shall *g* out of his roots ... Is 11:1 6509
shalt thou make thy plant to *g* ... Is 17:11 7735
For he shall *g* up before him as a ... Is 53:2 5927
they *g*, yea, they bring forth ... Jer 12:2 3212
righteousness to *g* up unto David ... Jer 33:15 6779
nor suffer their locks to *g* long ... Eze 44:20 7971
shall *g* all trees for meat, whose ... Eze 47:12 5927
he shall *g* as the lily, and cast ... Hos 14:5 6524
as the corn, and *g* as the vine ... Hos 14:7 6524
not laboured, neither madest it *g* ... Jonah 4:10 1431
he shall *g* up out of his place, ... Zec 6:12 6779
g up as calves of the stall ... Mal 4:2 6335
lilies of the field, how they *g* ... Mt 6:28 *837*
Let both *g* together until the ... Mt 13:30 *4886*
unto it, Let no fruit *g* on thee ... Mt 21:19 *1096*
and *g* up, he knoweth not how ... Mk 4:27 *3373*
Consider the lilies how they *g* ... Lk 12:27 *837*
of them whereunto this would *g* ... Acts 5:24 *1096*
may *g* up into him in all things, ... Eph 4:15 *837*
the word, that ye may *g* thereby ... 1Pet 2:2 *837*
But *g* in grace, and in the ... 2Pet 3:18 *837*

GROWETH {14}
which *g* for you out of the field ... Ex 10:5 6779
freckled spot that *g* in the skin ... Lev 13:39 6524
That which *g* of its own accord of ... Lev 25:5 5599
reap that which *g* of itself in it ... Lev 25:11 5599
beareth, nor any grass *g* therein ... Deut 29:23 5927
the day *g* to an end, lodge here, ... Judg 19:9 2583
When the dust *g* into hardness ... Job 38:38 3332
they are like grass which *g* up ... Ps 90:5 2498
morning it flourisheth, and *g* up ... Ps 90:6 2498
which withereth afore it *g* up ... Ps 129:6 8025
eat this year such as *g* of itself ... Is 37:30 5599
But when it is sown, it *g* up ... Mk 4:32 *305*
building fitly framed together *g* ... Eph 2:21 *837*
that your faith *g* exceedingly ... 2Th 1:3 *5232*

GROWN {23}
house, till Shelah my son be *g* ... Gen 38:11 1431
for she saw that Shelah was *g* ... Gen 38:14 1431
in those days, when Moses was *g* ... Ex 2:11 1431
for they were not *g* up ... Ex 9:32 648
there is black hair *g* up therein ... Lev 13:37 6779
art waxen fat, thou art *g* thick ... Deut 32:15
tarry for them till they were *g* ... Ruth 1:13 1431
at Jericho until your beards be *g* ... 2Sa 10:5 6779
young men that were *g* up with him ... 1Kin 12:8 1431
the young men that were *g* up with ... 1Kin 12:10 1431
And when the child was *g*, it fell ... 2Kin 4:18 1431
as corn blasted before it be *g* up ... 2Kin 19:26 6965
at Jericho until your beards be *g* ... 1Chr 19:5 6779
our trespass is *g* up unto the ... Ezr 9:6 1431
be as plants *g* up in their youth ... Ps 144:12 1431
it was all *g* over with thorns, and ... Prov 24:31 5927
as corn blasted before it be *g* up ... Is 37:27 6965
because ye are *g* fat as the ... Jer 50:11 6335
are fashioned, and thine hair is *g* ... Eze 16:7 6779
It is thou, O king, that art *g* ... Dan 4:22 7236
for thy greatness is *g*, and ... Dan 4:22 7236
till his hairs were *g* like ... Dan 4:33 7236
but when it is *g*, it is the ... Mt 13:32 *837*

GROWTH {2}
the shooting up of the latter *g* ... Amos 7:1 3954
it was the latter *g* after the ... Amos 7:1 3954

GRUDGE {3}
nor bear any *g* against the ... Lev 19:18 5201
g if they be not satisfied ... Ps 59:15 3885
G not one against another, ... Jas 5:9 *4727*

GRUDGING {1}
one to another without *g* ... 1Pet 4:9 *1112*

GRUDGINGLY {1}
not *g*, or of necessity ... 2Cor 9:7 *1537,3077*

GUARD {50}
of Pharaoh's, and captain of the *g* ... Gen 37:36 2876
of Pharaoh, captain of the *g* ... Gen 39:1 2876
the house of the captain of the *g* ... Gen 40:3 2876
the captain of the *g* charged ... Gen 40:4 2876
servant to the captain of the *g* ... Gen 41:12 2876
And David set him over his *g* ... 2Sa 23:23 4928
the hands of the chief of the *g* ... 1Kin 14:27 7323
that the *g* bare them, and brought ... 1Kin 14:28 7323
them back into the *g* chamber ... 1Kin 14:28 7323
offering, that Jehu said to the *g* ... 2Kin 10:25 7323
and the *g* and the captains cast ... 2Kin 10:25 7323
with the captains and the *g* ... 2Kin 11:4 7323
part at the gate behind the *g* ... 2Kin 11:6 7323
the *g* stood, every man with his ... 2Kin 11:11 7323
Athaliah heard the noise of the *g* ... 2Kin 11:13 7323
and the captains, and the *g* ... 2Kin 11:19 7323
gate of the *g* to the king's house ... 2Kin 11:19 7323
Nebuzar-adan, captain of the *g* ... 2Kin 25:8 2876
were with the captain of the *g* ... 2Kin 25:10 2876
the captain of the *g* carry away ... 2Kin 25:11 2876
But the captain of the *g* left of ... 2Kin 25:12 2876
the captain of the *g* took away ... 2Kin 25:15 2876
the captain of the *g* took Seraiah ... 2Kin 25:18 2876
captain of the *g* took these ... 2Kin 25:20 2876
and David set him over his *g* ... 1Chr 11:25 4928
the hands of the chief of the *g* ... 2Chr 12:10 7323
the *g* came and fetched them, and ... 2Chr 12:11 7323
them again into the *g* chamber ... 2Chr 12:11 7323
the night they may be a *g* to us ... Neh 4:22 4929
men of the *g* which followed me ... Neh 4:23 4929
the *g* carried away captive into ... Jer 39:9 2876
g left of the poor of the people ... Jer 39:10 2876
Nebuzar-adan the captain of the *g* ... Jer 39:11 2876
the captain of the *g* sent ... Jer 39:13 2876
the *g* had let him go from Ramah ... Jer 40:1 2876
captain of the *g* took Jeremiah ... Jer 40:2 2876
of the *g* gave him victuals ... Jer 40:5 2876
g had committed to Gedaliah the ... Jer 41:10 2876
g had left with Gedaliah the son ... Jer 43:6 2876
Nebuzar-adan, captain of the *g* ... Jer 52:12 2876
were with the captain of the *g* ... Jer 52:14 2876
g carried away captive certain of ... Jer 52:15 2876
g left certain of the poor of the ... Jer 52:16 2876
took the captain of the *g* away ... Jer 52:19 2876
the captain of the *g* took Seraiah ... Jer 52:24 2876
the captain of the *g* took them ... Jer 52:26 2876
the *g* carried away captive of the ... Jer 52:30 2876
thee, and be thou a *g* unto them ... Eze 38:7 4929
the captain of the king's *g* ... Dan 2:14 2877
prisoners to the captain of the *g* ... Acts 28:16 *4759*

GUARD'S {1}
in the captain of the *g* house ... Gen 41:10 2876

GUDGODAH *(gud-go'-dah)* {2} See HOR-HAGIDGAD.
A wilderness encampment of Israel.
From thence they journeyed unto *G* ... Deut 10:7 1412
from *G* to Jotbath, a land of ... Deut 10:7 1412

GUEST {1}
That he was gone to be *g* with a ... Lk 19:7 *2647*

GUESTCHAMBER {2}
The Master saith, Where is the *g* ... Mk 14:14 *2646*
saith unto thee, Where is the *g* ... Lk 22:11 *2646*

GUESTS {6}
all the *g* that were with him ... 1Kin 1:41 7121
all the *g* that were with Adonijah ... 1Kin 1:49 7121
that her *g* are in the depths of ... Prov 9:18 7121
a sacrifice, he hath bid his *g* ... Zeph 1:7 7121
the wedding was furnished with *g* ... Mt 22:10 *345*
the king came in to see the *g* ... Mt 22:11 *345*

GUIDE {23}
or canst thou *g* Arcturus with his ... Job 38:32 5148
The meek will he *g* in judgment ... Ps 25:9 1869
thy name's sake lead me, and *g* me ... Ps 31:3 5095
I will *g* thee with mine eye ... Ps 32:8 3289
he will be our *g* even unto death ... Ps 48:14 5090
was thou, a man mine equal, my *g* ... Ps 55:13 441
Thou shalt *g* me with thy counsel, ... Ps 73:24 5148
he will *g* his affairs with ... Ps 112:5 3557
forsaketh the *g* of her youth ... Prov 2:17 441
Which having no *g*, overseer, or ... Prov 6:7 7101
of the upright shall *g* them ... Prov 11:3 5148
wise, and *g* thine heart in the way ... Prov 23:19 833
springs of water shall he *g* them ... Is 49:10 5095
There is none to *g* her among all ... Is 51:18 5095
the LORD shall *g* thee continually ... Is 58:11 5148
thou art the *g* of my youth ... Jer 3:4 441
put ye not confidence in a *g* ... Mic 7:5 441
to *g* our feet into the way of ... Lk 1:79 *2720*
he will *g* you into all truth ... Jn 16:13 *3594*
which was *g* to them that took ... Acts 1:16 *3595*
I, except some man should *g* me ... Acts 8:31 *3594*
thou thyself art a *g* of the blind ... Rom 2:19 *3595*
g the house, give none occasion ... 1Ti 5:14 *3616*

GUIDED {5}
thou hast *g* them in thy strength ... Ex 15:13 5095
other, and *g* them on every side ... 2Chr 32:22 5095
I have *g* her from my mother's ... Job 31:18 5148
g them in the wilderness like a ... Ps 78:52 5090
g them by the skilfulness of his ... Ps 78:72 5148

GUIDES {2}
Woe unto you, ye blind *g*, which ... Mt 23:16 *3595*
Ye blind *g*, which strain at a ... Mt 23:24 *3595*

GUIDING {1}
head, *g* his hands wittingly ... Gen 48:14

GUILE {11}
his neighbour, to slay him with *g* ... Ex 21:14 6195
and in whose spirit there is no *g* ... Ps 32:2 7423
evil, and thy lips from speaking *g* ... Ps 34:13 4820
g depart not from her streets ... Ps 55:11 4820
Israelite indeed, in whom is no *g* ... Jn 1:47 *1388*
being crafty, I caught you with *g* ... 2Cor 12:16 *1388*
nor of uncleanness, nor in *g* ... 1Th 2:3 *1388*
laying aside all malice, and all *g* ... 1Pet 2:1 *1388*
neither was *g* found in his mouth ... 1Pet 2:22 *1388*
and his lips that they speak no *g* ... 1Pet 3:10 *1388*
And in their mouth was found no *g* ... Rev 14:5 *1388*

GUILT {2}
but thou shalt put away the *g* of ... Deut 19:13
So shalt thou put away the *g* of ... Deut 21:9

GUILTINESS {1}
shouldest have brought *g* upon us ... Gen 26:10 817

GUILTLESS {10}
g that taketh his name in vain ... Ex 20:7 5352
shall the man be *g* from iniquity ... Num 5:31 5352
be *g* before the LORD, and before ... Num 32:22 5355
g that taketh his name in vain ... Deut 5:11 5352
be upon his head, and we will be *g* ... Josh 2:19 5355
the LORD's anointed, and be *g* ... 1Sa 26:9 5352
my kingdom are *g* before the LORD ... 2Sa 3:28 5355
and the king and his throne be *g* ... 2Sa 14:9 5355
Now therefore hold him not *g* ... 1Kin 2:9 5352
ye would not have condemned the *g* ... Mt 12:7 *338*

GUILTY {26}
We are verily *g* concerning our ... Gen 42:21 816
that will by no means clear the *g* ... Ex 34:7
should not be done, and are *g* ... Lev 4:13 816
which should not be done, and is *g* ... Lev 4:22 816
ought not to be done, and be *g* ... Lev 4:27 816
he also shall be unclean, and *g* ... Lev 5:2 816
knoweth of it, then he shall be *g* ... Lev 5:3 816
he shall be *g* in one of these ... Lev 5:4 816
when he shall be *g* in one of ... Lev 5:5 816
he wist it not, yet is he *g* ... Lev 5:17 816
because he hath sinned, and is *g* ... Lev 6:4 816
the LORD, and that person be *g* ... Num 5:6 816
and by no means clearing the *g* ... Num 14:18
he shall not be *g* of blood ... Num 35:27
a murderer, which is *g* of death ... Num 35:31 7563
at this time, that ye should be *g* ... Judg 21:22 816
and being *g*, they offered a ram of ... Ezr 10:19 816
he curse thee, and thou be found *g* ... Prov 30:10 816
Thou art become *g* in thy blood ... Eze 22:4 816
them, and hold themselves not *g* ... Zec 11:5 816
the gift that is upon it, he is *g* ... Mt 23:18 *3784*
and said, He is *g* of death ... Mt 26:66 *1777*
condemned him to be *g* of death ... Mk 14:64 *1777*
the world may become *g* before God ... Rom 3:19 *5267*
shall be *g* of the body and blood ... 1Cor 11:27 *1777*
in one point, he is *g* of all ... Jas 2:10 *1777*

GULF {1}
and you there is a great *g* fixed ... Lk 16:26 *5490*

GUNI *(gu'-ni)* {4} See GUNITES.
1. A son of Naphtali.
Jahzeel, and *G*, and Jezer, and ... Gen 46:24 1476
of *G*, the family of the Gunites ... Num 26:48 1476
Jahziel, and *G*, and Jezer, and ... 1Chr 7:13 1476
2. Father of Abdiel.
the son of Abdiel, the son of *G* ... 1Chr 5:15 1476

GUNITES *(gu'-nites)* {1} *Descendants of Guni 1.*
of Guni, the family of the *G* ... Num 26:48 1477

GUR *(gur)* {1} See GUR-BAAL. *A hill near Ibleam.*
they did so at the going up to *G* ... 2Kin 9:27 1483

GUR-BAAL *(gur-ba'-al)* {1} *Place in western Arabia.*
the Arabians that dwelt in *G* ... 2Chr 26:7 1485

GUSH {1}
our eyelids *g* out with waters ... Jer 9:18 5140

GUSHED {5}
till the blood *g* out upon them ... 1Kin 18:28 8210
the rock, that the waters *g* out ... Ps 78:20 2100
the rock, and the waters *g* out ... Ps 105:41 2100
rock also, and the waters *g* out ... Is 48:21 2100
midst, and all his bowels *g* out ... Acts 1:18 *1632*

GUTTER {1}
Whosoever getteth up to the *g* ... 2Sa 5:8 6794

GUTTERS {2}
g in the watering troughs when ... Gen 30:38 7298
the eyes of the cattle in the *g* ... Gen 30:41 7298

H

HA {2}
saith among the trumpets, H, h ... Job 39:25 1889
HAAHASHTARI *(ha-a-hash'-te-ri)* {1} *A son of Naarah.*
and Hepher, and Temeni, and H ... 1Chr 4:6 326
HABAIAH *(hab-ah'-yah)* {2} *A family of exiles.*
the children of H, the children ... Ezr 2:61 2252
the children of H, the children ... Neh 7:63 2252
HABAKKUK *(hab'-ak-kuk)* {2} *A prophet of Judah.*
The burden which H the prophet ... Hab 1:1 2265
A prayer of H the prophet upon ... Hab 3:1 2265
HABAZINIAH *(hab-az-in-i'-ah)* {1} *Head of a Rechabite family.*
the son of Jeremiah, the son of H ... Jer 35:3 2262
HABAZZINIAH See Habaziniah.
HABERGEON {3}
it, as it were the hole of an h ... Ex 28:32 8473
of the robe, as the hole of an h ... Ex 39:23 8473
the spear, the dart, nor the h ... Job 41:26 8302
HABERGEONS {2}
and spears, and helmets, and h ... 2Chr 26:14 8302
shields, and the bows, and the h ... Neh 4:16 8302
HABITABLE {1}
Rejoicing in the h part of his ... Prov 8:31 8398
HABITATION {58}
God, and I will prepare him an h ... Ex 15:2 5115
in thy strength unto thy holy h ... Ex 15:13 5116
without the camp shall his h be ... Lev 13:46 4186
even unto his h shall ye seek ... Deut 12:5 7933
Look down from thy holy h ... Deut 26:15 4583
which I have commanded in my h ... 1Sa 2:29 4583
thou shalt see an enemy in my h ... 1Sa 2:32 4583
and shew me both it, and his h ... 2Sa 15:25 5116
have built an house of h for thee ... 2Chr 6:2 2073
faces from the h of the Lord ... 2Chr 29:6 4908
Israel, whose h is in Jerusalem, ... Ezr 7:15 4907
but suddenly I cursed his h ... Job 5:3 5116
and thou shalt visit thy h ... Job 5:24 5116
make the h of thy righteousness ... Job 8:6 5116
shall be scattered upon his h ... Job 18:15 5116
I have loved the h of thy house ... Ps 26:8 4583
From the place of his h he ... Ps 33:14 3427
the widows, is God in his holy h ... Ps 68:5 4583
Let their h be desolate ... Ps 69:25 2918
Be thou my strong h, whereunto I ... Ps 71:3 4583
judgment are the h of thy throne ... Ps 89:14 4349
refuge, even the most High, thy h ... Ps 91:9 4583
judgment are the h of his throne ... Ps 97:2 4349
fowls of the heaven have their h ... Ps 104:12 7931
that they might go to a city of h ... Ps 107:7 4186
they may prepare a city for h ... Ps 107:36 4186
an h for the mighty God of Jacob ... Ps 132:5 4908
he hath desired it for his h ... Ps 132:13 4186
but he blesseth the h of the just ... Prov 3:33 5116
that graveth an h for himself in ... Is 22:16 4908
the h forsaken, and left like a ... Is 27:10 5116
shall dwell in a peaceable h ... Is 32:18 5116
shall see Jerusalem a quiet h ... Is 33:20 5116
and it shall be an h of dragons ... Is 34:13 5116
in the h of dragons, where each ... Is 35:7 5116
behold from the h of thy holiness ... Is 63:15 2073
Thine h is in the midst of deceit ... Jer 9:6 3427
him, and have made his h desolate ... Jer 10:25 5116
utter his voice from his holy h ... Jer 25:30 4583
he shall mightily roar upon his h ... Jer 25:30 5116
O h of justice, and mountain of ... Jer 31:23 5116
shall be an h of shepherds ... Jer 33:12 5116
and dwelt in the h of Chimham ... Jer 41:17 1628
against the h of the strong ... Jer 49:19 5116
the h of justice, even the Lord, ... Jer 50:7 5116
will bring Israel again to his h ... Jer 50:19 5116
Jordan unto the h of the strong ... Jer 50:44 5116
make their h desolate with them ... Jer 50:45 5116
Pathros, into the land of their h ... Eze 29:14 4351
fowls of the heaven had their h ... Dan 4:21 7932
of the rock, whose h is high ... Obad 3 3427
and moon stood still in their h ... Hab 3:11 2073
he is raised up out of his holy h ... Zec 2:13 4583
Let his h be desolate, and let no ... Acts 1:20 *1886*
and the bounds of their h ... Acts 17:26 *2733*
an h of God through the Spirit ... Eph 2:22 *2732*
estate, but left their own h ... Jude 6 *3613*
and is become the h of devils ... Rev 18:2 *2732*
HABITATIONS {20}
according to their h in the land ... Gen 36:43 4186
of cruelty are in their h ... Gen 49:5 4380
in all your h shall ye eat ... Ex 12:20 4186
your h upon the sabbath day ... Ex 35:3 4186
Ye shall bring out of your h two ... Lev 23:17 4186
be come into the land of your h ... Num 15:2 4186
These were their h, and their ... 1Chr 4:33 4186
the h that were found there, and ... 1Chr 4:41 4583
h were, Beth-el and the towns ... 1Chr 7:28 4186
are full of the h of cruelty ... Ps 74:20 4999
their camp, round about their h ... Ps 78:28 4908
forth the curtains of thine h ... Is 54:2 4908
for the h of the wilderness a ... Jer 9:10 4999
or who shall enter into our h ... Jer 21:13 4585
the peaceable h are cut down ... Jer 25:37 4999
make their h desolate with them ... Jer 49:20 5116
swallowed up all the h of Jacob ... Lam 2:2 4999
toward Diblath, in all their h ... Eze 6:14 4186
the h of the shepherds shall ... Amos 1:2 4999
receive you into everlasting h ... Lk 16:9 *4638*

HABOR *(ha'-bor)* {3} *A Mesopotamian district.*
in H by the river of Gozan, and in ... 2Kin 17:6 2249
in H by the river of Gozan, and in ... 2Kin 18:11 2249
and brought them unto Halah, and H ... 1Chr 5:26 2249
HACALIAH See Hachilah.
HACHALIAH *(hak-a-li'-ah)* {2} *Father of Nehemiah.*
words of Nehemiah the son of H ... Neh 1:1 2446
the Tirshatha, the son of H ... Neh 10:1 2446
HACHILAH *(hak'-i-lah)* {3} *A hill in Judah.*
in the wood, in the hill of H ... 1Sa 23:19 2444
hide himself in the hill of H ... 1Sa 26:1 2444
And Saul pitched in the hill of H ... 1Sa 26:3 2444
HACHMONI *(hak'-mo-ni)* {1} See Hachmonite. *Father of Jehiel.*
Jehiel the son of H was with the ... 1Chr 27:32 2453
HACHMONITE *(hak'-mo-nite)* {1} See Tachmonite. *A descendant of Hachmoni.*
Jashobeam, a H, the chief of the ... 1Chr 11:11 2453
HAD See APPENDIX.
HADAD *(ha'-dad)* {14} See Ben-hadad, Hadadrimmon, Hadar.
1. A son of Bedad.
H the son of Bedad, who smote ... Gen 36:35 1908
H died, and Samlah of Masrekah ... Gen 36:36 1908
H the son of Bedad, which smote ... 1Chr 1:46 1908
when H was dead, Samlah of ... 1Chr 1:47 1908
2. A royal Edomite.
unto Solomon, H the Edomite ... 1Kin 11:14 1908
That H fled, he and certain ... 1Kin 11:17 1908
H being yet a little child ... 1Kin 11:17 1908
H found great favour in the sight ... 1Kin 11:19 1908
when H heard in Egypt that David ... 1Kin 11:21 1908
H said to Pharaoh, Let me depart, ... 1Kin 11:21 1908
beside the mischief that H did ... 1Kin 11:25 1908
3. A son of Ishmael.
Mishma, and Dumah, Massa, H ... 1Chr 1:30 2301
4. An early king of Edom.
was dead, H reigned in his stead ... 1Chr 1:50 1908
H died also ... 1Chr 1:51 1908
HADADEZER *(had-a-de'-zer)* {9} See Hadarezer. *King of Zobah.*
David smote also H, the son of ... 2Sa 8:3 1909
came to succour H king of Zobah ... 2Sa 8:5 1909
that were on the servants of H ... 2Sa 8:7 1909
and from Berothai, cities of H ... 2Sa 8:8 1909
had smitten all the host of H ... 2Sa 8:9 1909
because he had fought against H ... 2Sa 8:10 1909
for H had wars with Toi ... 2Sa 8:10 1909
of Amalek, and of the spoil of H ... 2Sa 8:12 1909
from his lord H king of Zobah ... 1Kin 11:23 1909
HADADRIMMON *(ha'-dad-rim'-mon)* {1} *A place in the valley of Megiddo.*
as the mourning of H in the ... Zec 12:11 1910
HADAR *(ha'-dar)* {2} See Hadad.
1. A son of Ishmael.
H, and Tema, Jetur, Naphish, and ... Gen 25:15 1924
2. An early king of Edom.
died, and H reigned in his stead ... Gen 36:39 1924
HADAREZER *(had-a-re'-zer)* {12} See Hadadezer. *Another name for Hadadezer.*
H sent, and brought out the ... 2Sa 10:16 1928
of the host of H went before them ... 2Sa 10:16 1928
to H saw that they were smitten ... 2Sa 10:19 1928
David smote H king of Zobah unto ... 1Chr 18:3 1928
came to help H king of Zobah ... 1Chr 18:5 1928
that were on the servants of H ... 1Chr 18:7 1928
and from Chun, cities of H ... 1Chr 18:8 1928
all the host of H king of Zobah ... 1Chr 18:9 1928
because he had fought against H ... 1Chr 18:10 1928
for H had war with Tou ... 1Chr 18:10 1928
of the host of H went before them ... 1Chr 19:16 1928
when the servants of H saw that ... 1Chr 19:19 1928
HADASHAH *(had'-a-shah)* {1} *A town in Judah.*
Zenan, and H, and Migdal-gad, ... Josh 15:37 2322
HADASSAH *(ha-das'-sah)* {1} See Esther. *Another name for Esther.*
And he brought up H, that is, ... Est 2:7 1919
HADATTAH *(ha-dat'-tah)* {1} See Hazor-hadattah. *Another name for Hazor.*
And Hazor, H, and Kerioth, and ... Josh 15:25 2675
HADES See Hell.
HADID *(ha'-did)* {3} *A city in Benjamin.*
The children of Lod, H, and Ono, ... Ezr 2:33 2307
The children of Lod, H, and Ono, ... Neh 7:37 2307
H, Zeboim, Neballat, ... Neh 11:34 2307
HADLAI *(had'-la-i)* {1} *Father of Amasa.*
of Shallum, and Amasa the son of H ... 2Chr 28:12 2311
HADORAM *(ha-do'-ram)* {4} See Adoram.
1. A son of Joktan.
And H, and Uzal, and Diklah, ... Gen 10:27 1913
H also, and Uzal, and Diklah, ... 1Chr 1:21 1913
2. A son of Tou.
He sent H his son to king David, ... 1Chr 18:10 1913
3. An officer of Rehoboam.
Then king Rehoboam sent H that ... 2Chr 10:18 1913
HADRACH *(ha'-drak)* {1} *A district in Syria.*
word of the Lord in the land of H ... Zec 9:1 2317

HADST {22}
little which thou h before I came ... Gen 30:30
surely thou h sent me away now ... Gen 31:42
that thou h utterly hated her ... Judg 15:2
thee, except thou h hasted ... 1Sa 25:34
God liveth, unless thou h spoken ... 2Sa 2:27
then h thou smitten Syria till ... 2Kin 13:19
Syria till thou h consumed it ... 2Kin 13:19
with us till thou h consumed us ... Ezr 9:14
which thou h sworn to give them ... Neh 9:15
concerning which thou h promised ... Neh 9:23
because thou h a favour unto them ... Ps 44:3
thou, O God, which h cast us off ... Ps 60:10
or ever thou h formed the earth ... Ps 90:2
thou h removed it far unto all ... Is 26:15
O that thou h hearkened to my ... Is 48:18
thou h a whore's forehead, thou ... Jer 3:3
For thou h cast me into the deep, ... Jonah 2:3
Saying, If thou h known, even ... Lk 19:42
if thou h been here, my brother ... Jn 11:21
if thou h been here, my brother ... Jn 11:32
as if thou h not received it ... 1Cor 4:7
neither h pleasure therein ... Heb 10:8
HA-ELEPH See Eleph.
HAFT {1}
the h also went in after the ... Judg 3:22 5325
HAGAB *(ha'-gab)* {1} See Hagaba. *A family of exiles.*
The children of H, the children ... Ezr 2:46 2285
HAGABA *(hag'-a-bah)* {1} *Same as Hagab.*
of Lebana, the children of H ... Neh 7:48 2286
HAGABAH *(hag'-a-bah)* {1} See Hagaba. *Same as Hagab.*
of Lebanah, the children of H ... Ezr 2:45 2286
HAGAR *(ha'-gar)* {12} *Sarah's handmaid.*
an Egyptian, whose name was H ... Gen 16:1 1904
wife took H her maid the Egyptian ... Gen 16:3 1904
And he went in unto H, and she ... Gen 16:4 1904
And he said, H, Sarai's maid, ... Gen 16:8 1904
And H bare Abram a son ... Gen 16:15 1904
his son's name, which H bare ... Gen 16:15 1904
when H bare Ishmael to Abram ... Gen 16:16 1904
saw the son of H the Egyptian ... Gen 21:9 1904
of water, and gave it unto H ... Gen 21:14 1904
of God called to H out of heaven ... Gen 21:17 1904
unto her, What aileth thee, H ... Gen 21:17 1904
whom H the Egyptian, Sarah's ... Gen 25:12 1904
HAGARENES *(hag-a-renes')* {1} See Hagarites. *A people east of the Jordan.*
of Moab, and the H ... Ps 83:6 1905
HAGARITES *(hag'-a-rites)* {3} *Same as Hagarenes.*
of Saul they made war with the H ... 1Chr 5:10 1905
And they made war with the H ... 1Chr 5:19 1905
the H were delivered into their ... 1Chr 5:20 1905
HAGERITE *(hag'-e-rite)* {1} See Hagarites, Haggeri. *Family of David's herdsmen.*
over the flocks was Jaziz the H ... 1Chr 27:31 1905
HAGGAI *(hag'-ga-i)* {11} *A prophet.*
H the prophet, and Zechariah the ... Ezr 5:1 2292
the prophesying of H the prophet ... Ezr 6:14 2292
came the word of the Lord by H ... Hag 1:1 2292
word of the Lord by H the prophet ... Hag 1:3 2292
and the words of H the prophet ... Hag 1:12 2292
Then spake H the Lord's messenger ... Hag 1:13 2292
word of the Lord by the prophet H ... Hag 2:1 2292
word of the Lord by H the prophet ... Hag 2:10 2292
Then said H, If one that is ... Hag 2:13 2292
Then answered H, and said, So is ... Hag 2:14 2292
the Lord came unto H in the four ... Hag 2:20 2292
HAGGEDOLIM See Neh 12:14.
HAGGERI *(hag'-gher-i)* {1} See Hagerite. *Father of Mibhar.*
of Nathan, Mibhar the son of H ... 1Chr 11:38 1905
HAGGI *(hag'-ghi)* {2} See Haggites. *A son of Gad.*
Ziphion, and H, Shuni, and Ezbon, ... Gen 46:16 2291
of H, the family of the Haggites ... Num 26:15 2291
HAGGIAH *(hag-ghi'-ah)* {1} *A descendant of Merari.*
H his son, Asaiah his son ... 1Chr 6:30 2293
HAGGITES *(hag'-ghites)* {1} See Haggi. *Descendants of Haggi.*
of Haggi, the family of the H ... Num 26:15 2291
HAGGITH *(hag'-ghith)* {5} *A wife of David.*
the fourth, Adonijah the son of H ... 2Sa 3:4 2294
the son of H exalted himself ... 1Kin 1:5 2294
Adonijah the son of H doth reign ... 1Kin 1:11 2294
Adonijah the son of H came to ... 1Kin 2:13 2294
the fourth, Adonijah the son of H ... 1Chr 3:2 2294
HAGRI See Haggeri.
HAGRITE See Hagerite.
HAGRITES See Hagarites.
HAI *(ha'-i)* {2} See Ai. *A form of Ai.*
on the west, and H on the east ... Gen 12:8 5857
beginning, between Beth-el and H ... Gen 13:3 5857
HAIL {38}
it to rain a very grievous h ... Ex 9:18 1259
the h shall come down upon them, ... Ex 9:19 1259
that there may be h in all the ... Ex 9:22 1259
and the Lord sent thunder and h ... Ex 9:23 1259
the Lord rained h upon the land ... Ex 9:23 1259
h, and fire mingled with the h ... Ex 9:24 1259

the *h* smote throughout all the ... Ex 9:25 1259
the *h* smote every herb of the ... Ex 9:25 1259
of Israel were, was there no *h* ... Ex 9:26 1259
no more mighty thunderings and *h* ... Ex 9:28 1259
neither shall there be any more *h* ... Ex 9:29 1259
h ceased, and the rain was not ... Ex 9:33 1259
saw that the rain and the *h* ... Ex 9:34 1259
remaineth unto you from the *h* ... Ex 10:5 1259
even all that the *h* hath left ... Ex 10:12 1259
of the trees which the *h* had left ... Ex 10:15 1259
thou seen the treasures of the *h* ... Job 38:22 1259
h stones and coals of fire ... Ps 18:12 1259
h stones and coals of fire ... Ps 18:13 1259
He destroyed their vines with *h* ... Ps 78:47 1259
up their cattle also to the *h* ... Ps 78:48 1259
He gave them *h* for rain, and ... Ps 105:32 1259
Fire, and *h*; snow, and vapours ... Ps 148:8 1259
one, which as a tempest of *h* ... Is 28:2 1259
the *h* shall sweep away the refuge ... Is 28:17 1259
When it shall *h*, coming down on ... Is 32:19 1258
with *h* in all the labours of your ... Hag 2:17 1259
he came to Jesus, and said, *H* ... Mt 26:49 *5463*
him, and mocked him, saying, *H* ... Mt 27:29 *5463*
Jesus met them, saying, All *h* ... Mt 28:9 *5463*
And began to salute him, *H* ... Mk 15:18 *5463*
came in unto her, and said, *H* ... Lk 1:28 *5463*
And said, *H*, King of the Jews ... Jn 19:3 *5463*
sounded, and there followed *h* ... Rev 8:7 *5464*
and an earthquake, and great *h* ... Rev 11:19 *5464*
upon men a great *h* out of heaven ... Rev 16:21 *5464*
because of the plague of the *h* ... Rev 16:21 *5464*

HAILSTONES {5}
h than they whom the children of ... Josh 10:11 68,1259
scattering, and tempest, and *h* ... Is 30:30 68,1259
and ye, O great *h*, shall fall ... Eze 13:11 68,417
great *h* in my fury to consume it ... Eze 13:13 68,417
and overflowing rain, and great *h* ... Eze 38:22 68,417

HAIR {64}
and fine linen, and goats' *h* ... Ex 25:4
h to be a covering upon the ... Ex 26:7
and fine linen, and goats' *h* ... Ex 35:6
and fine linen, and goats' *h* ... Ex 35:23
them up in wisdom spun goats' *h* ... Ex 35:26
of goats' *h* for the tent over the ... Ex 36:14
when the *h* in the plague is ... Lev 13:3 8181
the *h* thereof be not turned white ... Lev 13:4 8181
and it have turned the *h* white ... Lev 13:10 8181
the *h* thereof be turned white ... Lev 13:20 8181
if the *h* in the bright spot be ... Lev 13:25 8181
there be no white *h* in the bright ... Lev 13:26 8181
and there be in it a yellow thin *h* ... Lev 13:30 8181
and that there is no black *h* in it ... Lev 13:31 8181
and there be in it no yellow *h* ... Lev 13:32 8181
shall not seek for yellow *h* ... Lev 13:36 8181
there is black *h* grown up therein ... Lev 13:37 8181
the man whose *h* is fallen off his ... Lev 13:40 4803
he that hath his *h* fallen off ... Lev 13:41 4803
clothes, and shave off all his *h* ... Lev 14:8 8181
shave all his *h* off his head ... Lev 14:9 8181
even all his *h* he shall shave off ... Lev 14:9 8181
locks of the *h* of his head grow ... Num 6:5 8181
shall take the *h* of the head of ... Num 6:18 8181
after the *h* of his separation is ... Num 6:19
of skins, and all work of goats' *h* ... Num 31:20
Howbeit the *h* of his head began ... Judg 16:22 8181
sling stones at an *h* breadth ... Judg 20:16 8185
there shall not one *h* of his head ... 1Sa 14:45 8185
of goats' *h* for his bolster ... 1Sa 19:13
of goats' *h* for his bolster ... 1Sa 19:16
there shall not one *h* of thy son ... 2Sa 14:11 8185
because the *h* was heavy on him, ... 2Sa 14:26
he weighed the *h* of his head at ... 2Sa 14:26 8181
there shall not an *h* of him fall ... 1Kin 1:52 8185
and plucked off the *h* of my head ... Ezr 9:3 8181
of them, and plucked off their *h* ... Neh 13:25
the *h* of my flesh stood up ... Job 4:15 8185
thy *h* is as a flock of goats, ... Song 4:1 8181
thy *h* is as a flock of goats that ... Song 6:5 8181
the *h* of thine head like purple ... Song 7:5 1803
and instead of well set *h* baldness ... Is 3:24 4748
the head, and the *h* of the feet ... Is 7:20 8181
to them that plucked off the *h* ... Is 50:6
Cut off thine *h*, O Jerusalem, and ... Jer 7:29 5145
to weigh, and divide the *h* ... Eze 5:1
thine *h* is grown, whereas thou ... Eze 16:7 8181
nor was an *h* of their head singed ... Dan 3:27 8177
the *h* of his head like the pure ... Dan 7:9 8177
John had his raiment of camel's *h* ... Mt 3:4 *2359*
not make one *h* white or black ... Mt 5:36 *2359*
John was clothed with camel's *h* ... Mk 1:6 *2359*
not an *h* of your head perish ... Lk 21:18 *2359*
and wiped his feet with her *h* ... Jn 11:2 *2359*
and wiped his feet with her *h* ... Jn 12:3 *2359*
for there shall not an *h* fall ... Acts 27:34 *2359*
you, that, if a man have long *h* ... 1Cor 11:14 *2863*
But if a woman have long *h* ... 1Cor 11:15 *2863*
for her *h* is given her for a ... 1Cor 11:15 *2864*
not with broided *h*, or gold, or ... 1Ti 2:9 *4117*
adorning of plaiting the *h* ... 1Pet 3:3 *2359*
became black as sackcloth of *h* ... Rev 6:12 *5155*
they had *h* as the *h* of women, ... Rev 9:8 *2359*

HAIRS {15}
gray *h* with sorrow to the grave ... Gen 42:38
gray *h* with sorrow to the grave ... Gen 44:29
shall bring down the gray *h* of ... Gen 44:31
there be no white *h* therein ... Lev 13:21 8181
also with the man of gray *h* ... Deut 32:25
are more than the *h* of mine head ... Ps 40:12 8185
are more than the *h* of mine head ... Ps 69:4 8185
even to hoar *h* will I carry you ... Is 46:4
till his *h* were grown like ... Dan 4:33 8177
gray *h* are here and there upon him ... Hos 7:9
But the very *h* of your head are ... Mt 10:30 *2359*
wipe them with the *h* of her head ... Lk 7:38 *2359*
wiped them with the *h* of her head ... Lk 7:44 *2359*
But even the very *h* of your head ... Lk 12:7 *2359*
his *h* were white like wool, as ... Rev 1:14 *2359*

HAIRY {5}
red, all over like an *h* garment ... Gen 25:25 8181
Esau my brother is a *h* man ... Gen 27:11 8163
him not, because his hands were *h* ... Gen 27:23 8163
answered him, He was an *h* man ... 2Kin 1:8 1167,8181
the *h* scalp of such an one as ... Ps 68:21 8181

HAKELDAMA See ACELDAMA.

HAKKATAN *(hak'-ka-tan)* {1} *A family of exiles.*
Johanan the son of *H*, and with him ... Ezr 8:12 6997

HAKKOZ *(hak'-koz)* {1} See KOZ. *A sanctuary servant.*
The seventh to *H*, the eighth to ... 1Chr 24:10 6976

HAKUPHA *(ha-ku'-fah)* {2} *A family of exiles.*
of Bakbuk, the children of *H* ... Ezr 2:51 2709
of Bakbuk, the children of *H* ... Neh 7:53 2709

HALAH *(ha'-lah)* {3} *An Assyrian district.*
into Assyria, and placed them in *H* ... 2Kin 17:6 2477
unto Assyria, and put them in *H* ... 2Kin 18:11 2477
Manasseh, and brought them unto *H* ... 1Chr 5:26 2477

HALAK *(ha'-lak)* {2} *A mountain in southern Canaan.*
Even from the mount *H*, that goeth ... Josh 11:17 2510
of Lebanon even unto the mount *H* ... Josh 12:7 2510

HALE {1}
lest he *h* thee to the judge, and ... Lk 12:58 *2694*

HALF {136}
earring of *h* a shekel weight ... Gen 24:22 1235
Moses took *h* of the blood, and put ... Ex 24:6 2677
h of the blood he sprinkled on ... Ex 24:6 2677
a *h* shall be the length thereof, ... Ex 25:10 2677
a *h* the breadth thereof ... Ex 25:10 2677
a cubit and a *h* the height thereof ... Ex 25:10 2677
a *h* shall be the length thereof, ... Ex 25:17 2677
cubit and a *h* the breadth thereof ... Ex 25:17 2677
a cubit and a *h* the height thereof ... Ex 25:23 2677
the *h* curtain that remaineth, ... Ex 26:12 2677
a *h* shall be the breadth of one ... Ex 26:16 2677
h a shekel after the shekel of ... Ex 30:13 4276
an *h* shekel shall be the ... Ex 30:13 4276
not give less than *h* a shekel ... Ex 30:15 4276
and of sweet cinnamon *h* so much ... Ex 30:23 4276
of a board one cubit and a *h* ... Ex 36:21 2677
a *h* was the length of it, and a ... Ex 37:1 2677
a *h* the breadth of it ... Ex 37:1 2677
a cubit and a *h* the height of it ... Ex 37:1 2677
a *h* was the length thereof, and ... Ex 37:6 2677
cubit and a *h* the breadth thereof ... Ex 37:6 2677
a cubit and a *h* the height thereof ... Ex 37:10 2677
h a shekel, after the shekel of ... Ex 38:26 4276
h of it in the morning, and *h* ... Lev 6:20 4276
of whom the flesh is *h* consumed ... Num 12:12 2677
mingled with *h* an hin of oil ... Num 15:9 2677
a drink offering *h* an hin of wine ... Num 15:10 2677
h an hin of wine unto a bullock ... Num 28:14 2677
Take it of their *h*, and give it ... Num 31:29 4276
And of the children of Israel's *h* ... Num 31:30 4276
And the *h*, which was the portion ... Num 31:36 4275
And of the children of Israel's *h* ... Num 31:42 4276
(Now the *h* that pertained unto ... Num 31:43 4275
of the children of Israel's *h* ... Num 31:47 4276
unto *h* the tribe of Manasseh the ... Num 32:33 2677
nine tribes, and to the *h* tribe ... Num 34:13 2677
h the tribe of Manasseh have ... Num 34:14 2677
the *h* tribe have received their ... Num 34:15 2677
h mount Gilead, and the cities ... Deut 3:12 2677
gave I unto the *h* tribe of ... Deut 3:13 2677
unto the river Arnon *h* the valley ... Deut 3:16 8432
to the *h* tribe of Manasseh ... Deut 29:8 2677
to *h* the tribe of Manasseh, spake ... Josh 1:12 2677
h the tribe of Manasseh, passed ... Josh 4:12 2677
h of them over against mount ... Josh 8:33 2677
h of them over against mount Ebal ... Josh 8:33 2677
from *h* Gilead, even unto the ... Josh 12:2 2677
h Gilead, the border of Sihon ... Josh 12:5 2677
and the *h* tribe of Manasseh ... Josh 12:6 2677
and the *h* tribe of Manasseh, ... Josh 13:7 2677
h the land of the children of ... Josh 13:25 2677
unto the *h* tribe of Manasseh ... Josh 13:29 2677
of the *h* tribe of the children of ... Josh 13:29 2677
h Gilead, and Ashtaroth, and Edrei, ... Josh 13:31 2677
even to the one *h* of the children ... Josh 13:31 2677
nine tribes, and for the *h* tribe ... Josh 14:2 2677
an *h* tribe on the other side ... Josh 14:3 2677
h the tribe of Manasseh, have ... Josh 18:7 2677
out of the *h* tribe of Manasseh, ... Josh 21:5 2677
out of the *h* tribe of Manasseh in ... Josh 21:6 2677
out of the *h* tribe of Manasseh, ... Josh 21:25 4276
out of the other *h* tribe of ... Josh 21:27 2677
and the *h* tribe of Manasseh, ... Josh 22:1 2677
Now to the one *h* of the tribe of ... Josh 22:7 2677
but unto the other *h* thereof gave ... Josh 22:7 2677
the *h* tribe of Manasseh returned, ... Josh 22:9 2677
the *h* tribe of Manasseh built ... Josh 22:10 2677
the *h* tribe of Manasseh have ... Josh 22:11 2677
to the *h* tribe of Manasseh, into ... Josh 22:13 2677
to the *h* tribe of Manasseh, unto ... Josh 22:15 2677
the *h* tribe of Manasseh answered, ... Josh 22:21 2677
as it were an *h* acre of land ... 1Sa 14:14 2677
off the one *h* of their beards ... 2Sa 10:4 2677
neither if *h* of us die, will they ... 2Sa 18:3 2677
also *h* the people of Israel ... 2Sa 19:40 2677
give *h* to the one, and *h* to the ... 1Kin 3:25 2677
work of the base, a cubit and an *h* ... 1Kin 7:31 2677
a wheel was a cubit and *h* a cubit ... 1Kin 7:32 2677
a round compass of *h* a cubit high ... 1Kin 7:35 2677
and, behold, the *h* was not told me ... 1Kin 10:7 2677
thou wilt give me *h* thine house ... 1Kin 13:8 2677
captain of *h* his chariots, ... 1Kin 16:9 4276
h of the people followed Tibni ... 1Kin 16:21 2677
and *h* followed Omri ... 1Kin 16:21 2677
Haroeh, and *h* of the Manahethites ... 1Chr 2:52 2677
h of the Manahethites, the ... 1Chr 2:54 2677
h the tribe of Manasseh, of ... 1Chr 5:18 2677
the children of the *h* tribe of ... 1Chr 5:23 2677
the *h* tribe of Manasseh, and ... 1Chr 5:26 2677
cities given out of the *h* tribe ... 1Chr 6:61 2677
out of the *h* tribe of Manasseh, ... 1Chr 6:61 4276
out of the *h* tribe of Manasseh ... 1Chr 6:70 4276
family of the *h* tribe of Manasseh ... 1Chr 6:71 2677
of the *h* tribe of Manasseh ... 1Chr 12:31 2677
of the *h* tribe of Manasseh, with ... 1Chr 12:37 2677
the *h* tribe of Manasseh, for ... 1Chr 26:32 2677
of the *h* tribe of Manasseh, Joel ... 1Chr 27:20 2677
Of the *h* tribe of Manasseh in ... 1Chr 27:21 2677
the one *h* of the greatness of thy ... 2Chr 9:6 2677
the ruler of the *h* part of ... Neh 3:9 2677
the ruler of the *h* part of ... Neh 3:12 2677
ruler of the *h* part of Beth-zur ... Neh 3:16 2677
the ruler of the *h* part of Keilah ... Neh 3:17 2677
the ruler of the *h* part of Keilah ... Neh 3:18 2677
together unto the *h* thereof ... Neh 4:6 2677
that the *h* of my servants wrought ... Neh 4:16 2677
the other *h* of them held both the ... Neh 4:16 2677
h of them held the spears from ... Neh 4:21 2677
h of the princes of Judah, ... Neh 12:32 2677
the *h* of the people upon the wall ... Neh 12:38 2677
the *h* of the rulers with me ... Neh 12:40 2677
their children spake *h* in the ... Neh 13:24 2677
thee to the *h* of the kingdom ... Est 5:3 2677
even to the *h* of the kingdom it ... Est 5:6 2677
even to the *h* of the kingdom ... Est 7:2 2677
shall not live out *h* their days ... Ps 55:23 2673
Samaria committed *h* of thy sins ... Eze 16:51 2677
an *h* long, and a cubit and an *h* ... Eze 40:42 2677
about it shall be *h* a cubit ... Eze 43:17 2677
be for a time, times, and an *h* ... Dan 12:7 2677
barley, and an *h* homer of barley ... Hos 3:2
h of the city shall go forth into ... Zec 14:2 2677
h of the mountain shall remove ... Zec 14:4 2677
and *h* of it toward the south ... Zec 14:4 2677
h of them toward the former sea, ... Zec 14:8 2677
h of them toward the hinder sea ... Zec 14:8 2677
it thee, unto the *h* of my kingdom ... Mk 6:23 *2255*
and departed, leaving him *h* dead ... Lk 10:30 *2255*
the *h* of my goods I give to the ... Lk 19:8 *2255*
about the space of *h* an hour ... Rev 8:1 *2256*
dead bodies three days and an *h* ... Rev 11:9 *2255*
an *h* the Spirit of life from God ... Rev 11:11 *2255*
h a time, from the face of the ... Rev 12:14 *2255*

HALHUL *(hal'-hul)* {1} *A city in Judah.*
H, Beth-zur, and Gedor, ... Josh 15:58 2478

HALI *(ha'-li)* {1} *A town in Asher.*
And their border was Helkath, and *H* ... Josh 19:25 2482

HALING {1}
h men and women committed them to ... Acts 8:3 *4951*

HALL {8}
took Jesus into the common *h* ... Mt 27:27 *4232*
soldiers led him away into the *h* ... Mk 15:16 *833*
a fire in the midst of the *h* ... Lk 22:55 *833*
Caiaphas unto the *h* of judgment ... Jn 18:28 *4232*
went not into the judgment *h* ... Jn 18:28 *4232*
entered into the judgment *h* again ... Jn 18:33 *4232*
And went again into the judgment *h* ... Jn 19:9 *4232*
to be kept in Herod's judgment *h* ... Acts 23:35 *4232*

HALLOHESH *(hal-lo'-hesh)* {1} See HALOHESH. *Father of Shallum.*
H, Pileha, Shobek, ... Neh 10:24 3873

HALLOW {15}
shall *h* in all their holy gifts ... Ex 28:38 6942
thou shalt do unto them to *h* them ... Ex 29:1 6942
that is therein, and shalt *h* it ... Ex 40:9 6942
h it from the uncleanness of the ... Lev 16:19 6942
those things which they *h* unto me ... Lev 22:2 6942
of Israel *h* unto the LORD ... Lev 22:3 6942
I am the LORD which *h* you ... Lev 22:32 6942
ye shall *h* the fiftieth year, and ... Lev 25:10 6942
shall *h* his head that same day ... Num 6:11 6942
The same day did the king *h* the ... 1Kin 8:64 6942
but *h* ye the sabbath day, as I ... Jer 17:22 6942
but *h* the sabbath day, to do no ... Jer 17:24 6942
unto me to *h* the sabbath day ... Jer 17:27 6942
And *h* my sabbaths ... Eze 20:20 6942
and they shall *h* my sabbaths ... Eze 44:24 6942

HALLOWED {22}
blessed the sabbath day, and *h* it ... Ex 20:11 6942
and he shall be *h*, and his garments ... Ex 29:21 6942
she shall touch no *h* thing ... Lev 12:4 6944
profaned the *h* thing of the LORD ... Lev 19:8 6944
but I will be *h* among the ... Lev 22:32 6942
in the land of Egypt I *h* unto me ... Num 3:13 6942
every man's *h* things shall be his ... Num 5:10 6944
for they are *h* ... Num 16:37 6942

the LORD, therefore they are *h* ... Num 16:38 6942
the *h* things of the children of ... Num 18:8 6944
even the *h* part thereof out of it ... Num 18:29 4720
I have brought away the *h* things ... Deut 26:13 6944
mine hand, but there is *h* bread ... 1Sa 21:4 6944
So the priest gave him *h* bread ... 1Sa 21:6 6944
I have *h* this house, which thou ... 1Kin 9:3 6942
house, which I have *h* for my name ... 1Kin 9:7 6942
all the *h* things that Jehoshaphat ... 2Kin 12:18 6944
dedicated, and his own *h* things ... 2Kin 12:18 6944
Moreover Solomon *h* the middle of ... 2Chr 7:7 6942
LORD which he had *h* in Jerusalem ... 2Chr 36:14 6942
art in heaven, *H* be thy name ... Mt 6:9 *37*
art in heaven, *H* be thy name ... Lk 11:2 *37*

HALOHESH *(ha-lo'-hesh)* {1} See HALLOHESH. *Same as Hallohesh.*
him repaired Shallum the son of *H* ... Neh 3:12 3873

HALT {6}
How long *h* ye between two ... 1Kin 18:21 6452
For I am ready to *h*, and my sorrow ... Ps 38:17 6761
to enter into life *h* or maimed ... Mt 18:8 *5560*
for thee to enter *h* into life ... Mk 9:45 *5560*
the poor, and the maimed, and the *h* ... Lk 14:21 *5560*
of impotent folk, of blind, *h* ... Jn 5:3 *5560*

HALTED {2}
upon him, and he *h* upon his thigh ... Gen 32:31 6761
I will make her that *h* a remnant ... Mic 4:7 6761

HALTETH {2}
LORD, will I assemble her that *h* ... Mic 4:6 6761
and I will save her that *h* ... Zeph 3:19 6761

HALTING {1}
All my familiars watched for my *h* ... Jer 20:10 6761

HAM *(ham)* {17}
1. A son of Noah.
and Noah begat Shem, *H*, and Japheth ... Gen 5:32 2526
And Noah begat three sons, Shem, *H* ... Gen 6:10 2526
day entered Noah, and Shem, and *H* ... Gen 7:13 2526
forth of the ark, were Shem, and *H* ... Gen 9:18 2526
H is the father of Canaan ... Gen 9:18 2526
And *H*, the father of Canaan, saw ... Gen 9:22 2526
of the sons of Noah, Shem, *H* ... Gen 10:1 2526
And the sons of *H* ... Gen 10:6 2526
These are the sons of *H*, after ... Gen 10:20 2526
Karnaim, and the Zuzims in *H* ... Gen 14:5 1990
Noah, Shem, *H*, and Japheth ... 1Chr 1:4 2526
The sons of *H* ... 1Chr 1:8 2526
2. Descendants and land of Ham.
for they of *H* had dwelt there of ... 1Chr 4:40 2526
strength in the tabernacles of *H* ... Ps 78:51 2526
Jacob sojourned in the land of *H* ... Ps 105:23 2526
them, and wonders in the land of *H* ... Ps 105:27 2526
Wondrous works in the land of *H* ... Ps 106:22 2526

HAMAN *(ha'-man)* {50} See HAMAN'S. *Prime minister under King Ahasuerus.*
H the son of Hammedatha the ... Est 3:1 2001
gate, bowed, and reverenced *H* ... Est 3:2 2001
not unto them, that they told *H* ... Est 3:4 2001
when *H* saw that Mordecai bowed ... Est 3:5 2001
then was *H* full of wrath ... Est 3:5 2001
wherefore *H* sought to destroy all ... Est 3:6 2001
before *H* from day to day, and from ... Est 3:7 2001
H said unto king Ahasuerus, There ... Est 3:8 2001
gave it unto *H* the son of ... Est 3:10 2001
And the king said unto *H*, The ... Est 3:11 2001
H had commanded unto the king's ... Est 3:12 2001
the king and *H* sat down to drink ... Est 3:15 2001
that *H* had promised to pay to the ... Est 4:7 2001
H come this day unto the banquet ... Est 5:4 2001
Cause *H* to make haste, that he ... Est 5:5 2001
H came to the banquet that Esther ... Est 5:5 2001
H come to the banquet that I ... Est 5:8 2001
Then went *H* forth that day joyful ... Est 5:9 2001
but when *H* saw Mordecai in the ... Est 5:9 2001
Nevertheless *H* refrained himself ... Est 5:10 2001
H told them of the glory of his ... Est 5:11 2001
H said moreover, Yea, Esther the ... Est 5:12 2001
And the thing pleased *H* ... Est 5:14 2001
Now *H* was come into the outward ... Est 6:4 2001
Behold, *H* standeth in the court ... Est 6:5 2001
So *H* came in ... Est 6:6 2001
Now *H* thought in his heart, To ... Est 6:6 2001
H answered the king, For the man ... Est 6:7 2001
Then the king said to *H*, Make ... Est 6:10 2001
Then took *H* the apparel and the ... Est 6:11 2001
But *H* hasted to his house ... Est 6:12 2001
H told Zeresh his wife and all his ... Est 6:13 2001
hasted to bring *H* unto the ... Est 6:14 2001
H came to banquet with Esther the ... Est 7:1 2001
and enemy is this wicked *H* ... Est 7:6 2001
Then *H* was afraid before the king ... Est 7:6 2001
H stood up to make request for ... Est 7:7 2001
H was fallen upon the bed whereon ... Est 7:8 2001
which *H* had made for Mordecai, ... Est 7:9 2001
king, standeth in the house of *H* ... Est 7:9 2001
So they hanged *H* on the gallows ... Est 7:10 2001
Ahasuerus give the house of *H* the ... Est 8:1 2001
ring, which he had taken from *H* ... Est 8:2 2001
set Mordecai over the house of *H* ... Est 8:2 2001
the mischief of *H* the Agagite ... Est 8:3 2001
by *H* the son of Hammedatha the ... Est 8:5 2001
have given Esther the house of *H* ... Est 8:7 2001
The ten sons of *H* the son of ... Est 9:10 2001
the palace, and the ten sons of *H* ... Est 9:12 2001
Because *H* the son of Hammedatha, ... Est 9:24 2001

HAMAN'S *(ha'-mans)* {3}
king's mouth, they covered *H* face ... Est 7:8 2001
let *H* ten sons be hanged upon the ... Est 9:13 2001
and they hanged *H* ten sons ... Est 9:14 2001

HAMATH *(ha'-math)* {34} See HAMATHITE, HAMATH-ZOBAH, HEMATH. *A capital of Syria.*
Zin unto Rehob, as men come to *H* ... Num 13:21 2574
border unto the entrance of *H* ... Num 34:8 2574
Hermon unto the entering into *H* ... Josh 13:5 2574
unto the entering in of *H* ... Judg 3:3 2574
When Toi king of *H* heard that ... 2Sa 8:9 2574
in of *H* unto the river of Egypt ... 1Kin 8:65 2574
of *H* unto the sea of the plain ... 2Kin 14:25 2574
how he recovered Damascus, and *H* ... 2Kin 14:28 2574
Cuthah, and from Ava, and from *H* ... 2Kin 17:24 2574
the men of *H* made Ashima, ... 2Kin 17:30 2574
Where are the gods of *H*, and of ... 2Kin 18:34 2574
Where is the king of *H*, and the ... 2Kin 19:13 2574
bands at Riblah in the land of *H* ... 2Kin 23:33 2574
them at Riblah in the land of *H* ... 2Kin 25:21 2574
Hadarezer king of Zobah unto *H* ... 1Chr 18:3 2574
Now when Tou king of *H* heard how ... 1Chr 18:9 2574
in of *H* unto the river of Egypt ... 2Chr 7:8 2574
store cities, which he built in *H* ... 2Chr 8:4 2574
is not *H* as Arpad ... Is 10:9 2574
Elam, and from Shinar, and from *H* ... Is 11:11 2574
Where are the gods of *H* and Arphad ... Is 36:19 2574
Where is the king of *H*, and the ... Is 37:13 2574
to Riblah in the land of *H* ... Jer 39:5 2574
H is confounded, and Arpad ... Jer 49:23 2574
to Riblah in the land of *H* ... Jer 52:9 2574
death in Riblah in the land of *H* ... Jer 52:27 2574
H, Berothah, Sibraim, which is ... Eze 47:16 2574
of Damascus and the border of *H* ... Eze 47:16 2574
northward, and the border of *H* ... Eze 47:17 2574
till a man come over against *H* ... Eze 47:20 2574
way of Hethlon, as one goeth to *H* ... Eze 48:1 2574
northward, to the coast of *H* ... Eze 48:1 2574
from thence go ye to *H* the great ... Amos 6:2 2579
H also shall border thereby ... Zec 9:2 2574

HAMATHITE {2}
and the Zemarite, and the *H* ... Gen 10:18 2577
and the Zemarite, and the *H* ... 1Chr 1:16 2577

HAMATH-ZOBAH *(ha'-math-zo'-bah)* {1} *Full name of Hamath.*
And Solomon went to *H*, and ... 2Chr 8:3 2578

HAMITES See HAM.

HAMMATH *(ham'-math)* {1} *A city in Naphtali.*
cities are Ziddim, Zer, and *H* ... Josh 19:35 2575

HAMMEDATHA *(ham-med'a-thah)* {5} *Father of Haman.*
Haman the son of *H* the Agagite ... Est 3:1 4099
Haman the son of *H* the Agagite ... Est 3:10 4099
by Haman the son of *H* the Agagite ... Est 8:5 4099
ten sons of Haman the son of *H* ... Est 9:10 4099
Because Haman the son of *H* ... Est 9:24 4099

HAMMELECH *(ham'-me-lek)* {2} *Father of Jerahmeel*
commanded Jerahmeel the son of *H* ... Jer 36:26 4429
dungeon of Malchiah the son of *H* ... Jer 38:6 4429

HAMMER {7}
took an *h* in her hand, and went ... Judg 4:21 4718
her right hand to the workmen's *h* ... Judg 5:26 1989
with the *h* she smote Sisera, she ... Judg 5:26
so that there was neither *h* nor ... 1Kin 6:7 4717
the *h* him that smote the anvil ... Is 41:7 6360
like a *h* that breaketh the rock ... Jer 23:29 6360
How is the *h* of the whole earth ... Jer 50:23 6360

HAMMERS {3}
thereof at once with axes and *h* ... Ps 74:6 3597
coals, and fashioneth it with *h* ... Is 44:12 4717
fasten it with nails and with *h* ... Jer 10:4 4717

HAMMOLEKETH *(ham-mol'-e-keth)* {1} *Daughter of Machir.*
And his sister *H* bare Ishod ... 1Chr 7:18 4447

HAMMON *(ham'-mon)* {2}
1. A city in Asher.
And Hebron, and Rehob, and *H* ... Josh 19:28 2540
2. A city in Naphtali.
H with her suburbs, and Kirjathaim ... 1Chr 6:76 2540

HAMMOTH-DOR *(ham'-moth-dor')* {1} *Same as Hammon 2.*
H with her suburbs, and Kartan ... Josh 21:32 2576

HAMMUEL See HAMUEL.

HAMONAH *(ha-mo'-nah)* {1} *Place where Gog is buried.*
the name of the city shall be *H* ... Eze 39:16 1997

HAMON-GOG *(ha'-mon-gog)* {2} *Same as Hamonah.*
shall call it The valley of *H* ... Eze 39:11 1996
have buried it in the valley of *H* ... Eze 39:15 1996

HAMOR *(ha'-mor)* {12} See EMMOR, HAMOR'S. *Father of Shechem.*
at the hand of the children of *H* ... Gen 33:19 2544
Shechem the son of *H* the Hivite ... Gen 34:2 2544
Shechem spake unto his father *H* ... Gen 34:4 2544
H the father of Shechem went out ... Gen 34:6 2544
H communed with them, saying, The ... Gen 34:8 2544
H his father deceitfully, and said ... Gen 34:13 2544
And their words pleased *H*, and ... Gen 34:18 2544
And *H* and Shechem his son came unto ... Gen 34:20 2544
And unto *H* and unto Shechem his son ... Gen 34:24 2544
And they slew *H* and Shechem his son ... Gen 34:26 2544
Jacob bought of the sons of *H* the ... Josh 24:32 2544
serve the men of *H* the father of ... Judg 9:28 2544

HAMOR'S *(ha'-mors)* {1}
pleased Hamor, and Shechem *H* son ... Gen 34:18 2544

HAMRAN See AMRAN.

HAMUEL *(ha-mu'-el)* {1} *Son of Mishma.*
H his son, Zacchur his son, ... 1Chr 4:26 2536

HAMUL *(ha'-mul)* {3} See HAMULITES. *A son of Pharez.*
sons of Pharez were Hezron and *H* ... Gen 46:12 2538
of *H*, the family of the Hamulites ... Num 26:21 2538
Hezron, and *H*. ... 1Chr 2:5 2538

HAMULITES *(ha'-mu-lites)* {1} *Descendants of Hamul.*
of Hamul, the family of the *H* ... Num 26:21 2539

HAMUTAL *(ha-mu'-tal)* {3} *Mother of King Jehoahaz.*
And his mother's name was *H* ... 2Kin 23:31 2537
And his mother's name was *H* ... 2Kin 24:18 2537
his mother's name was *H* the ... Jer 52:1 2537

HANAMEAL See HANAMEEL.

HANAMEEL *(ha-nam'-e-el)* {4} *Son of Shallum.*
H the son of Shallum thine uncle ... Jer 32:7 2601
So *H* mine uncle's son came to me ... Jer 32:8 2601
the field of *H* my uncle's son ... Jer 32:9 2601
in the sight of *H* mine uncle's ... Jer 32:12 2601

HANAMEL See HANAMEEL.

HANAN *(ha'-nan)* {12} See BAAL-HANAN, BEN-HANAN, ELON-BETH-HANAN.
1. A son of Shashak.
And Abdon, and Zichri, and *H* ... 1Chr 8:23 2605
2. A son of Azel.
and Sheariah, and Obadiah, and *H* ... 1Chr 8:38 2605
and Sheariah, and Obadiah, and *H* ... 1Chr 9:44 2605
3. A "mighty man" of David.
H the son of Maachah, and ... 1Chr 11:43 2605
4. Family of exiles.
of Shalmai, the children of *H* ... Ezr 2:46 2605
The children of *H*, the children ... Neh 7:49 2605
5. A priest who assisted Ezra.
Kelita, Azariah, Jozabad, *H* ... Neh 8:7 2605
6. A Levite who renewed the covenant.
Hodijah, Kelita, Pelaiah, *H* ... Neh 10:10 2605
next to them was *H* the son of ... Neh 13:13 2605
7. A chief who renewed the covenant.
Pelatiah, *H*, Anaiah, ... Neh 10:22 2605
8. Another chief who renewed the covenant.
And Ahijah, *H*, Anan, ... Neh 10:26 2605
9. Son of Igdaliah.
into the chamber of the sons of *H* ... Jer 35:4 2605

HANANEAL See HANANEEL.

HANANEEL *(ha-nan'-e-el)* {4} *A tower on Jerusalem's wall.*
it, unto the tower of *H* ... Neh 3:1 2606
the fish gate, and the tower of *H* ... Neh 12:39 2606
of *H* unto the gate of the corner ... Jer 31:38 2606
from the tower of *H* unto the ... Zec 14:10 2606

HANANEL See HANANEEL.

HANANI *(ha-na'-ni)* {11}
1. A son of Heman.
Shebuel, and Jerimoth, Hananiah, *H* ... 1Chr 25:4 2607
The eighteenth to *H*, he, his sons ... 1Chr 25:25 2607
2. A prophet.
at that time *H* the seer came to ... 2Chr 16:7 2607
3. Father of Jehu.
Jehu the son of *H* against Baasha ... 1Kin 16:1 2607
of *H* came the word of the LORD ... 1Kin 16:7 2607
Jehu the son of *H* the seer went ... 2Chr 19:2 2607
in the book of Jehu the son of *H* ... 2Chr 20:34 2607
4. Married a foreigner in exile.
of Immer; *H*, and Zebadiah ... Ezr 10:20 2607
5. Brother of Nehemiah.
That *H*, one of my brethren, came, ... Neh 1:2 2607
That I gave my brother *H*, and ... Neh 7:2 2607
6. A priest.
Maai, Nethaneel, and Judah, *H* ... Neh 12:36 2607

HANANIAH *(han-a-ni'-ah)* {29} See SHADRACH.
1. A son of Heman.
Uzziel, Shebuel, and Jerimoth, *H* ... 1Chr 25:4 2608
The sixteenth to *H*, he, his sons, ... 1Chr 25:23 2608
Meraiah; of Jeremiah, *H* ... Neh 12:12 2608
Hear now, *H*, The LORD hath ... Jer 20:15 2608
2. A captain of King Uzziah.
the ruler, under the hand of *H* ... 2Chr 26:11 2608
3. Father of Zedekiah.
Shaphan, and Zedekiah the son of *H* ... Jer 36:12 2608
4. A false prophet.
that *H* the son of Azur the ... Jer 28:1 2608
H in the presence of the priests ... Jer 28:5 2608
Then *H* the prophet took the yoke ... Jer 28:10 2608
H spake in the presence of all ... Jer 28:11 2608
after that *H* the prophet had ... Jer 28:12 2608
Go and tell *H*, saying, Thus saith ... Jer 28:13 2608
Jeremiah unto *H* the prophet ... Jer 28:15 2608
So *H* the prophet died the same ... Jer 28:17 2608
5. Grandfather of Irijah.
son of Shelemiah, the son of *H* ... Jer 37:13 2608
6. Son of Shashak.
And *H*, and Elam, and Antothijah, ... 1Chr 8:24 2608
7. Hebrew form of Shadrach.
the children of Judah, Daniel, *H* ... Dan 1:6 2608
and to *H*, of Shadrach ... Dan 1:7 2608
eunuchs had set over Daniel, *H* ... Dan 1:11 2608
all was found none like Daniel, *H* ... Dan 1:19 2608
and made the thing known to *H* ... Dan 2:17 2608

8. A son of Zerubbabel.
Meshullam, and *H*, and Shelomith ... 1Chr 3:19 2608
And the sons of *H* ... 1Chr 3:21 2608
9. Married a foreigner in exile.
Jehohanan, *H*, Zabbai, and Athlai ... Ezr 10:28 2608
10. A rebuilder of Jerusalem's wall.
repaired *H* the son of one of the ... Neh 3:8 2608
11. Another rebuilder of Jerusalem's wall.
After him repaired *H* the son of ... Neh 3:30 2608
12. A palace servant of Nehemiah.
H the ruler of the palace, charge ... Neh 7:2 2608
13. An Israelite who renewed the covenant.
Hoshea, *H*, Hashub, ... Neh 10:23 2608
14. A priest.
Elioenai, Zechariah, and *H* ... Neh 12:41 2608

HAND {1472}
and now, lest he put forth his *h* ... Gen 3:22 3027
thy brother's blood from thy *h* ... Gen 4:11 3027
then he put forth his *h*, and took ... Gen 8:9 3027
into your *h* are they delivered ... Gen 9:2 3027
at the *h* of every beast will I ... Gen 9:5 3027
I require it, and at the *h* of man ... Gen 9:5 3027
at the *h* of every man's brother ... Gen 9:5 3027
if thou wilt take the left *h* ... Gen 13:9 8041
or if thou depart to the right *h* ... Gen 13:9 3225
is on the left *h* of Damascus ... Gen 14:15 8040
thine enemies into thy *h* ... Gen 14:20 3027
have lift up mine *h* unto the LORD ... Gen 14:22 3027
Behold, thy maid is in thy *h* ... Gen 16:6 3027
his *h* will be against every man, ... Gen 16:12 3027
and every man's *h* against him ... Gen 16:12 3027
But the men put forth their *h* ... Gen 19:10 3027
the men laid hold upon his *h* ... Gen 19:16 3027
upon the *h* of his wife ... Gen 19:16 3027
upon the *h* of his two daughters ... Gen 19:16 3027
the lad, and hold him in thine *h* ... Gen 21:18 3027
ewe lambs shalt thou take of my *h* ... Gen 21:30 3027
and he took the fire in his *h* ... Gen 22:6 3027
And Abraham stretched forth his *h* ... Gen 22:10 3027
Lay not thine *h* upon the lad ... Gen 22:12 3027
I pray thee, thy *h* under my thigh ... Gen 24:2 3027
the servant put his *h* under the ... Gen 24:9 3027
goods of his master were in his *h* ... Gen 24:10 3027
let down her pitcher upon her *h* ... Gen 24:18 3027
that I may turn to the right *h* ... Gen 24:49 3225
his *h* took hold on Esau's heel ... Gen 25:26 3027
into the *h* of her son Jacob ... Gen 27:17 3027
mourning for my father are at *h* ... Gen 27:41 7126
gave them into the *h* of his sons ... Gen 30:35 3027
the power of my *h* to do you hurt ... Gen 31:29 3027
of my *h* didst thou require it, ... Gen 31:39 3027
from the *h* of my brother ... Gen 32:11 3027
from the *h* of Esau ... Gen 32:11 3027
h a present for Esau his brother ... Gen 32:13 3027
them into the *h* of his servants ... Gen 32:16 3027
then receive my present at my *h* ... Gen 33:10 3027
at the *h* of the children of Hamor ... Gen 33:19 3027
gods which were in their *h* ... Gen 35:4 3027
wilderness, and lay no *h* upon him ... Gen 37:22 3027
and let not our *h* be upon him ... Gen 37:27 3027
and thy staff that is in thine *h* ... Gen 38:18 3027
Judah sent the kid by the *h* of ... Gen 38:20 3027
his pledge from the woman's *h* ... Gen 38:20 3027
that the one put out his *h* ... Gen 38:28 3027
bound upon his *h* a scarlet thread ... Gen 38:28 3027
to pass, as he drew back his *h* ... Gen 38:29 3027
had the scarlet thread upon his *h* ... Gen 38:30 3027
that he did to prosper in his *h* ... Gen 39:3 3027
all that he had he put into his *h* ... Gen 39:4 3027
all that he had in Joseph's *h* ... Gen 39:6 3027
all that he hath to my *h* ... Gen 39:8 3027
and he left his garment in her *h* ... Gen 39:12 3027
he had left his garment in her *h* ... Gen 39:13 3027
prison committed to Joseph's *h* ... Gen 39:22 3027
to any thing that was under his *h* ... Gen 39:23 3027
And Pharaoh's cup was in my *h* ... Gen 40:11 3027
I gave the cup into Pharaoh's *h* ... Gen 40:11 3709
deliver Pharaoh's cup into his *h* ... Gen 40:13 3027
he gave the cup into Pharaoh's *h* ... Gen 40:21 3709
up corn under the *h* of Pharaoh ... Gen 41:35 3027
took off his ring from his *h* ... Gen 41:42 3027
h, and put it upon Joseph's *h* ... Gen 41:42 3027
his *h* or foot in all the land of ... Gen 41:44 3027
deliver him into my *h*, and I will ... Gen 42:37 3027
of my *h* shalt thou require him ... Gen 43:9 3027
And take double money in your *h* ... Gen 43:12 3027
sacks, carry it again in your *h* ... Gen 43:12 3027
they took double money in their *h* ... Gen 43:15 3027
we have brought it again in our *h* ... Gen 43:21 3027
was in their *h* into the house ... Gen 43:26 3027
man in whose *h* the cup is found ... Gen 44:17 3027
shall put his *h* upon thine eyes ... Gen 46:4 3027
thy *h* under my thigh, and deal ... Gen 47:29 3027
Ephraim in his right *h* toward ... Gen 48:13 3225
toward Israel's left *h* ... Gen 48:13 8040
Manasseh in his left *h* toward ... Gen 48:13 8040
toward Israel's right *h* ... Gen 48:13 3225
Israel stretched out his right *h* ... Gen 48:14 3225
his left *h* upon Manasseh's head ... Gen 48:14 8040
right *h* upon the head of Ephraim ... Gen 48:17 3225
and he held up his father's *h* ... Gen 48:17 3027
put thy right *h* upon his head ... Gen 48:18 3225
which I took out of the *h* of the ... Gen 48:22 3027
thy *h* shall be in the neck of ... Gen 49:8 3027
us out of the *h* of the shepherds ... Ex 2:19 3027
out of the *h* of the Egyptians ... Ex 3:8 3027
let you go, no, not by a mighty *h* ... Ex 3:19 3027
And I will stretch out my *h* ... Ex 3:20 3027
unto him, What is that in thine *h* ... Ex 4:2 3027
unto Moses, Put forth thine *h* ... Ex 4:4 3027
And he put forth his *h*, and caught ... Ex 4:4 3027
it, and it became a rod in his *h* ... Ex 4:4 3709
Put now thine *h* into thy bosom ... Ex 4:6 3027
he put his *h* into his bosom ... Ex 4:6 3027
his *h* was leprous as snow ... Ex 4:6 3027
Put thine *h* into thy bosom again ... Ex 4:7 3027
he put his *h* into his bosom again ... Ex 4:7 3027
by the *h* of him whom thou wilt ... Ex 4:13 3027
shalt take this rod in thine *h* ... Ex 4:17 3027
took the rod of God in his *h* ... Ex 4:20 3027
which I have put in thine *h* ... Ex 4:21 3027
put a sword in their *h* to slay us ... Ex 5:21 3027
for with a strong *h* shall he let ... Ex 6:1 3027
with a strong *h* shall he drive ... Ex 6:1 3027
that I may lay my *h* upon Egypt ... Ex 7:4 3027
I stretch forth mine *h* upon Egypt ... Ex 7:5 3027
shalt thou take in thine *h* ... Ex 7:15 3027
h upon the waters which are in ... Ex 7:17 3027
stretch out thine *h* upon the ... Ex 7:19 3027
Stretch forth thine *h* with thy ... Ex 8:5 3027
Aaron stretched out his *h* over ... Ex 8:6 3027
stretched out his *h* with his rod ... Ex 8:17 3027
the *h* of the LORD is upon thy ... Ex 9:3 3027
For now I will stretch out my *h* ... Ex 9:15 3027
forth thine *h* toward heaven ... Ex 9:22 3027
Stretch out thine *h* over the land ... Ex 10:12 3027
Stretch out thine *h* toward heaven ... Ex 10:21 3027
forth his *h* toward heaven ... Ex 10:22 3027
feet, and your staff in your *h* ... Ex 12:11 3027
for by strength of *h* the LORD ... Ex 13:3 3027
for a sign unto thee upon thine *h* ... Ex 13:9 3027
for with a strong *h* hath the LORD ... Ex 13:9 3027
By strength of *h* the LORD brought ... Ex 13:14 3027
shall be for a token upon thine *h* ... Ex 13:16 3027
for by strength of *h* the LORD ... Ex 13:16 3027
of Israel went out with an high *h* ... Ex 14:8 3027
stretch out thine *h* over the sea ... Ex 14:16 3027
stretched out his *h* over the sea ... Ex 14:21 3027
a wall unto them on their right *h* ... Ex 14:22 3225
Stretch out thine *h* over the sea ... Ex 14:26 3027
forth his *h* over the sea, and the ... Ex 14:27 3027
a wall unto them on their right *h* ... Ex 14:29 3225
day out of the *h* of the Egyptians ... Ex 14:30 3027
Thy right *h*, O LORD, is become ... Ex 15:6 3225
thy right *h*, O LORD, hath dashed ... Ex 15:6 3225
my sword, my *h* shall destroy them ... Ex 15:9 3027
Thou stretchedst out thy right *h* ... Ex 15:12 3225
of Aaron, took a timbrel in her *h* ... Ex 15:20 3027
the *h* of the LORD in the land of ... Ex 16:3 3027
the river, take in thine *h* ... Ex 17:5 3027
with the rod of God in mine *h* ... Ex 17:9 3027
to pass, when Moses held up his *h* ... Ex 17:11 3027
and when he let down his *h* ... Ex 17:11 3027
out of the *h* of the Egyptians ... Ex 18:9 3027
you out of the *h* of the Egyptians ... Ex 18:10 3027
and out of the *h* of Pharaoh ... Ex 18:10 3027
from under the *h* of the Egyptians ... Ex 18:10 3027
There shall not an *h* touch it ... Ex 19:13 3027
but God deliver him into his *h* ... Ex 21:13 3027
him, or if he be found in his *h* ... Ex 21:16 3027
with a rod, and he die under his *h* ... Ex 21:20 3027
h for *h*, foot for foot, ... Ex 21:24 3027
be certainly found in his *h* alive ... Ex 22:4 3027
his *h* unto his neighbour's goods ... Ex 22:8 3027
that he hath not put his *h* unto ... Ex 22:11 3027
put not thine *h* with the wicked ... Ex 23:1 3027
of the land into your *h* ... Ex 23:31 3027
of Israel he laid not his *h* ... Ex 24:11 3027
of an *h* breadth round about ... Ex 25:25 2948
upon the thumb of their right *h* ... Ex 29:20 3027
And he received them at their *h* ... Ex 32:4 3027
great power, and with a mighty *h* ... Ex 32:11 3027
of the testimony were in his *h* ... Ex 32:15 3027
thee with my *h* while I pass by ... Ex 33:22 3709
And I will take away mine *h* ... Ex 33:23 3709
took in his *h* the two tables of ... Ex 34:4 3027
tables of testimony in Moses' *h* ... Ex 34:29 3027
to be made by the *h* of Moses ... Ex 35:29 3027
gate, on this *h* and that *h* ... Ex 38:15
by the *h* of Ithamar, son to Aaron ... Ex 38:21 3027
he shall put his *h* upon the head ... Lev 1:4 3027
he shall lay his *h* upon the head ... Lev 3:2 3027
he shall lay his *h* upon the head ... Lev 3:8 3027
he shall lay his *h* upon the head ... Lev 3:13 3027
and shall lay his *h* upon the ... Lev 4:4 3027
he shall lay his *h* upon the head ... Lev 4:24 3027
he shall lay his *h* upon the head ... Lev 4:29 3027
he shall lay his *h* upon the head ... Lev 4:33 3027
and upon the thumb of his right *h* ... Lev 8:23 3027
LORD commanded by the *h* of Moses ... Lev 8:36 3027
lifted up his *h* toward the people ... Lev 9:22 3027
unto them by the *h* of Moses ... Lev 10:11 3027
and upon the thumb of his right *h* ... Lev 14:14 3027
into the palm of his own left *h* ... Lev 14:15 8042
in the oil that is in his left *h* ... Lev 14:16 3709
h shall the priest put upon the ... Lev 14:17 3709
and upon the thumb of his right *h* ... Lev 14:17 3027
h he shall pour upon the head of ... Lev 14:18 3709
and upon the thumb of his right *h* ... Lev 14:25 3027
into the palm of his own left *h* ... Lev 14:26 8042
h seven times before the LORD ... Lev 14:27 3709
h upon the tip of the right ear ... Lev 14:28 3709
and upon the thumb of his right *h* ... Lev 14:28 3027
h he shall put upon the head of ... Lev 14:29 3709
whose *h* is not able to get that ... Lev 14:32 3027
by the *h* of a fit man into the ... Lev 16:21 3027
Neither from a stranger's *h* shall ... Lev 22:25 3027
buyest ought of thy neighbour's *h* ... Lev 25:14 3027
the *h* of him that hath bought it ... Lev 25:28 3027
delivered into the *h* of the enemy ... Lev 26:25 3027
in mount Sinai by the *h* of Moses ... Lev 26:46 3027
h of Ithamar the son of Aaron the ... Num 4:28 3027
under the *h* of Ithamar the son of ... Num 4:33 3027
of the LORD by the *h* of Moses ... Num 4:37 3027
of the LORD by the *h* of Moses ... Num 4:45 3027
were numbered by the *h* of Moses ... Num 4:49 3027
the priest shall have in his *h* ... Num 5:18 3027
offering out of the woman's *h* ... Num 5:25 3027
beside that that his *h* shall get ... Num 6:21 3027
under the *h* of Ithamar the son of ... Num 7:8 3027
of the LORD by the *h* of Moses ... Num 9:23 3027
of the LORD by the *h* of Moses ... Num 10:13 3027
kill me, I pray thee, out of *h* ... Num 11:15 2026
Is the LORD's *h* waxed short ... Num 11:23 3027
commanded you by the *h* of Moses ... Num 15:23 3027
said to him by the *h* of Moses ... Num 16:40 3027
And Moses lifted up his *h*, and with ... Num 20:11 3027
to the right *h* nor to the left ... Num 20:17 3225
much people, and with a strong *h* ... Num 20:20 3027
deliver this people into my *h* ... Num 21:2 3027
taken all his land out of his *h* ... Num 21:26 3027
I have delivered him into thy *h* ... Num 21:34 3027
rewards of divination in their *h* ... Num 22:7 3027
way, and his sword drawn in his *h* ... Num 22:23 3027
to the right *h* or to the left ... Num 22:26 3325
there were a sword in mine *h* ... Num 22:29 3027
way, and his sword drawn in his *h* ... Num 22:31 3027
and took a javelin in his *h* ... Num 25:7 3027
spirit, and lay thine *h* upon him ... Num 27:18 3027
LORD commanded by the *h* of Moses ... Num 27:23 3027
and the trumpets to blow in his *h* ... Num 31:6 3027
their armies under the *h* of Moses ... Num 33:1 3027
an high *h* in the sight of all the ... Num 33:3 3027
him with an *h* weapon of wood ... Num 35:18 3027
Or in enmity smite him with his *h* ... Num 35:21 3027
of the *h* of the revenger of blood ... Num 35:25 3027
h of Moses unto the children of ... Num 36:13 3027
us into the *h* of the Amorites ... Deut 1:27 3027
thee in all the works of thy *h* ... Deut 2:7 3027
For indeed the *h* of the LORD was ... Deut 2:15 3027
into thine *h* Sihon the Amorite ... Deut 2:24 3027
unto the right *h* nor to the left ... Deut 2:27 3225
he might deliver him into thy *h* ... Deut 2:30 3027
people, and his land, into thy *h* ... Deut 3:2 3027
of the *h* of the two kings of the ... Deut 3:8 3027
thy greatness, and thy mighty *h* ... Deut 3:24 3027
and by war, and by a mighty *h* ... Deut 4:34 3027
out thence through a mighty *h* ... Deut 5:15 3027
to the right *h* or to the left ... Deut 5:32 3225
bind them for a sign upon thine *h* ... Deut 6:8 3027
us out of Egypt with a mighty *h* ... Deut 6:21 3027
brought you out with a mighty *h* ... Deut 7:8 3027
from the *h* of Pharaoh king of ... Deut 7:8 3027
and the wonders, and the mighty *h* ... Deut 7:19 3027
deliver their kings into thine *h* ... Deut 7:24 3027
the might of mine *h* hath gotten ... Deut 8:17 3027
out of Egypt with a mighty *h* ... Deut 9:26 3027
having the two tables in mine *h* ... Deut 10:3 3027
God, his greatness, his mighty *h* ... Deut 11:2 3027
bind them for a sign upon your *h* ... Deut 11:18 3027
and heave offerings of your *h* ... Deut 12:6 3027
in all that ye put your *h* unto ... Deut 12:7 3027
and the heave offering of your *h* ... Deut 12:11 3027
or heave offering of thine *h* ... Deut 12:17 3027
thine *h* shall be first upon him ... Deut 13:9 3027
afterwards the *h* of all the ... Deut 13:9 3027
of the cursed thing to thine *h* ... Deut 13:17 3027
and bind up the money in thine *h* ... Deut 14:25 3027
work of thine *h* which thou doest ... Deut 14:29 3027
thy brother thine *h* shall release ... Deut 15:3 3027
nor shut thine *h* from thy poor ... Deut 15:7 3027
shalt open thine *h* wide unto him ... Deut 15:8 3027
the year of release, is at *h* ... Deut 15:9 7126
that thou puttest thine *h* unto ... Deut 15:10 3027
thine *h* wide unto thy brother ... Deut 15:11 3027
of a freewill offering of thine *h* ... Deut 16:10 3027
shall shew thee, to the right *h* ... Deut 17:11 3225
the commandment, to the right *h* ... Deut 17:20 3225
his *h* fetcheth a stroke with the ... Deut 19:5 3027
deliver him into the *h* of the ... Deut 19:12 3027
h for *h*, foot for foot ... Deut 19:21 3027
h to in the land whither thou ... Deut 23:20 3027
pluck the ears with thine *h* ... Deut 23:25 3027
divorcement, and give it in her *h* ... Deut 24:1 3027
and giveth it in her *h*, and ... Deut 24:3 3027
of the *h* of him that smiteth him ... Deut 25:11 3027
and putteth forth her *h* ... Deut 25:11 3027
Then thou shalt cut off her *h* ... Deut 25:12 3709
take the basket out of thine *h* ... Deut 26:4 3027
out of Egypt with a mighty *h* ... Deut 26:8 3027
that thou settest thine *h* unto ... Deut 28:8 3027
to bless all the work of thine *h* ... Deut 28:12 3027
thee this day, to the right *h* ... Deut 28:14 3225
settest thine *h* unto for to do ... Deut 28:20 3027
shall be no might in thine *h* ... Deut 28:32 3027
in every work of thine *h*, in the ... Deut 30:9 3027
Our *h* is high, and the LORD hath ... Deut 32:27 3027
the day of their calamity is at *h* ... Deut 32:35 7138
any that can deliver out of my *h* ... Deut 32:39 3027
For I lift up my *h* to heaven ... Deut 32:40 3027
mine *h* take hold on judgment ... Deut 32:41 3027

from his right *h* went a fiery law	Deut 33:2	3225
all his saints are in thy *h*	Deut 33:3	3027
And in all that mighty *h*, and in	Deut 34:12	3027
it to the right *h* or to the left	Josh 1:7	3225
on our head, if any *h* be upon him	Josh 2:19	3027
might know the *h* of the LORD	Josh 4:24	3027
him with his sword drawn in his *h*	Josh 5:13	3027
I have given into thine *h* Jericho	Josh 6:2	3027
us into the *h* of the Amorites	Josh 7:7	3027
given into thy *h* the king of Ai	Josh 8:1	3027
God will deliver it into your *h*	Josh 8:7	3027
spear that is in thy *h* toward Ai	Josh 8:18	3027
for I will give it into thine *h*	Josh 8:18	3027
he had in his *h* toward the city	Josh 8:18	3027
as he had stretched out his *h*	Josh 8:19	3027
For Joshua drew not his *h* back	Josh 8:26	3027
And now, behold, we are in thine *h*	Josh 9:25	3027
the *h* of the children of Israel	Josh 9:26	3027
Slack not thy *h* from thy servants	Josh 10:6	3027
have delivered them into thine *h*	Josh 10:8	3027
hath delivered them into your *h*	Josh 10:19	3027
thereof, into the *h* of Israel	Josh 10:30	3027
Lachish into the *h* of Israel	Josh 10:32	3027
them into the *h* of Israel	Josh 11:8	3027
LORD commanded by the *h* of Moses	Josh 14:2	3027
right *h* unto the inhabitants of	Josh 17:7	3225
goeth out to Cabul on the left *h*	Josh 19:27	8040
spake unto you by the *h* of Moses	Josh 20:2	3027
deliver the slayer up into his *h*	Josh 20:5	3027
not die by the *h* of the avenger	Josh 20:9	3027
The LORD commanded by the *h* of	Josh 21:2	3027
LORD commanded by the *h* of Moses	Josh 21:8	3027
all their enemies into their *h*	Josh 21:44	3027
of the LORD by the *h* of Moses	Josh 22:9	3027
Israel out of the *h* of the LORD	Josh 22:31	3027
to the right *h* or to the left	Josh 23:6	3225
and I gave them into your *h*	Josh 24:8	3027
so I delivered you out of his *h*	Josh 24:10	3027
and I delivered them into your *h*	Josh 24:11	3027
delivered the land into his *h*	Judg 1:2	3027
and the Perizzites into their *h*	Judg 1:4	3027
yet the *h* of the house of Joseph	Judg 1:35	3027
the *h* of the LORD was against	Judg 2:15	3027
the *h* of those that spoiled them	Judg 2:16	3027
delivered them out of the *h* of	Judg 2:18	3027
he them into the *h* of Joshua	Judg 2:23	3027
their fathers by the *h* of Moses	Judg 3:4	3027
he sold them into the *h* of	Judg 3:8	3027
king of Mesopotamia into his *h*	Judg 3:10	3027
and his *h* prevailed against	Judg 3:10	3027
And Ehud put forth his left *h*	Judg 3:21	3027
enemies the Moabites into your *h*	Judg 3:28	3027
that day under the *h* of Israel	Judg 3:30	3027
the *h* of Jabin king of Canaan	Judg 4:2	3027
I will deliver him into thine *h*	Judg 4:7	3027
sell Sisera into the *h* of a woman	Judg 4:9	3027
delivered Sisera into thine *h*	Judg 4:14	3027
tent, and took an hammer in her *h*	Judg 4:21	3027
the *h* of the children of Israel	Judg 4:24	3027
She put her *h* to the nail	Judg 5:26	3027
her right *h* to the workmen's	Judg 5:26	3225
into the *h* of Midian seven years	Judg 6:1	3027
the *h* of Midian prevailed against	Judg 6:2	3027
you out of the *h* of the Egyptians	Judg 6:9	3027
and out of the *h* of all that	Judg 6:9	3027
from the *h* of the Midianites	Judg 6:14	3709
of the staff that was in his *h*	Judg 6:21	3027
thou wilt save Israel by mine *h*	Judg 6:36	3027
thou wilt save Israel by mine *h*	Judg 6:37	3027
saying, Mine own *h* hath saved me	Judg 7:2	3027
putting their *h* to their mouth,	Judg 7:6	3027
the Midianites into thine *h*	Judg 7:7	3027
people took victuals in their *h*	Judg 7:8	3027
I have delivered it into thine *h*	Judg 7:9	3027
for into his *h* hath God delivered	Judg 7:14	3027
into your *h* the host of Midian	Judg 7:15	3027
he put a trumpet in every man's *h*	Judg 7:16	3027
Zebah and Zalmunna now in thine *h*	Judg 8:6	3027
Zebah and Zalmunna into mine *h*	Judg 8:7	3027
Zebah and Zalmunna now in thine *h*	Judg 8:15	3027
delivered us from the *h* of Midian	Judg 8:22	3027
you out of the *h* of Midian	Judg 9:17	3027
God this people were under my *h*	Judg 9:29	3027
and Abimelech took an axe in his *h*	Judg 9:48	3027
and I delivered you out of their *h*	Judg 10:12	3027
his people into the *h* of Israel	Judg 11:21	3027
the LORD delivered them into my *h*	Judg 12:3	3027
LORD delivered them into the *h* of	Judg 13:1	3027
out of the *h* of the Philistines	Judg 13:5	3027
a kid, and he had nothing in his *h*	Judg 14:6	3027
into the *h* of the Philistines	Judg 15:12	3027
and deliver thee into their *h*	Judg 15:13	3027
of an ass, and put forth his *h*	Judg 15:15	3027
away the jawbone out of his *h*	Judg 15:17	3027
into the *h* of thy servant	Judg 15:18	3027
thirst, and fall into the *h* of the	Judg 15:18	3027
her, and brought money in their *h*	Judg 16:18	3027
Samson our enemy into our *h*	Judg 16:23	3027
the lad that held him by the *h*	Judg 16:26	3027
up, of the one with his right *h*	Judg 16:29	
the LORD from my *h* for my son	Judg 17:3	3027
lay thine *h* upon thy mouth, and go	Judg 18:19	3027
I will deliver them into thine *h*	Judg 20:28	3027
the beast, and all that came to *h*	Judg 20:48	4672
h of the LORD is gone out against	Ruth 1:13	3027
the field of the *h* of Naomi	Ruth 4:5	3027
and Mahlon's, of the *h* of Naomi	Ruth 4:9	3027
fleshhook of three teeth in his *h*	1Sa 2:13	3027
us out of the *h* of our enemies	1Sa 4:3	3709
out of the *h* of these mighty Gods	1Sa 4:8	3027
But the *h* of the LORD was heavy	1Sa 5:6	3027
for his *h* is sore upon us, and	1Sa 5:7	3027
the *h* of the LORD was against the	1Sa 5:9	3027
the *h* of God was very heavy there	1Sa 5:11	3027
why his *h* is not removed from you	1Sa 6:3	3027
will lighten his *h* from off you	1Sa 6:5	3027
it is not his *h* that smote us	1Sa 6:9	3027
to the right *h* or to the left	1Sa 6:12	
out of the *h* of the Philistines	1Sa 7:3	3027
out of the *h* of the Philistines	1Sa 7:8	3027
the *h* of the LORD was against the	1Sa 7:13	3027
I have here at *h* the fourth part	1Sa 9:8	3027
out of the *h* of the Philistines	1Sa 9:16	3027
you out of the *h* of the Egyptians	1Sa 10:18	3027
out of the *h* of all kingdoms, and	1Sa 10:18	3027
or of whose *h* have I received any	1Sa 12:3	3027
thou taken ought of any man's *h*	1Sa 12:4	3027
ye have not found ought in my *h*	1Sa 12:5	3027
he sold them into the *h* of Sisera	1Sa 12:9	3027
into the *h* of the Philistines, and	1Sa 12:9	3027
into the *h* of the king of Moab,	1Sa 12:9	3027
us out of the *h* of our enemies	1Sa 12:10	3027
delivered you out of the *h* of	1Sa 12:11	3027
then shall the *h* of the LORD be	1Sa 12:15	3027
sword nor spear found in the *h* of	1Sa 13:22	3027
hath delivered them into our *h*	1Sa 14:10	3027
them into the *h* of Israel	1Sa 14:12	3027
unto the priest, Withdraw thine *h*	1Sa 14:19	3027
but no man put his *h* to his mouth	1Sa 14:26	3027
end of the rod that was in his *h*	1Sa 14:27	3027
and put his *h* to his mouth	1Sa 14:27	3027
deliver them into the *h* of Israel	1Sa 14:37	3027
end of the rod that was in mine *h*	1Sa 14:43	3027
that he shall play with his *h*	1Sa 16:16	3027
an harp, and played with his *h*	1Sa 16:23	3027
h of the keeper of the carriage	1Sa 17:22	3027
out of the *h* of this Philistine	1Sa 17:37	3027
And he took his staff in his *h*	1Sa 17:40	3027
and his sling was in his *h*	1Sa 17:40	3027
the LORD deliver thee into mine *h*	1Sa 17:46	3027
And David put his *h* in his bag	1Sa 17:49	3027
was no sword in the *h* of David	1Sa 17:50	3027
head of the Philistine in his *h*	1Sa 17:57	3027
and David played with his *h*	1Sa 18:10	3027
there was a javelin in Saul's *h*	1Sa 18:10	3027
said, Let not mine *h* be upon him	1Sa 18:17	3027
but let the *h* of the Philistines	1Sa 18:17	3027
that the *h* of the Philistines may	1Sa 18:21	3027
fall by the *h* of the Philistines	1Sa 18:25	3027
For he did put his life in his *h*	1Sa 19:5	3709
house with his javelin in his *h*	1Sa 19:9	3027
and David played with his *h*	1Sa 19:9	3027
it at the *h* of David's enemies	1Sa 20:16	3027
when the business was in *h*	1Sa 20:19	
therefore what is under thine *h*	1Sa 21:3	3027
me five loaves of bread in mine *h*	1Sa 21:3	3027
is no common bread under mine *h*	1Sa 21:4	3027
here under thine *h* spear or sword	1Sa 21:8	3027
Ramah, having his spear in his *h*	1Sa 22:6	3027
because their *h* also is with	1Sa 22:17	3027
king would not put forth their *h*	1Sa 22:17	3027
the Philistines into thine *h*	1Sa 23:4	3027
came down with an ephod in his *h*	1Sa 23:6	3027
hath delivered him into mine *h*	1Sa 23:7	3027
Keilah deliver me up into his *h*	1Sa 23:11	3027
me and my men into the *h* of Saul	1Sa 23:12	3027
God delivered him not into his *h*	1Sa 23:14	3027
and strengthened his *h* in God	1Sa 23:16	3027
for the *h* of Saul my father shall	1Sa 23:17	3027
to deliver him into the king's *h*	1Sa 23:20	3027
deliver thine enemy into thine *h*	1Sa 24:4	3027
stretch forth mine *h* against him	1Sa 24:6	3027
to day into mine *h* in the cave	1Sa 24:10	3027
put forth mine *h* against my lord	1Sa 24:10	3027
see the skirt of thy robe in my *h*	1Sa 24:11	3027
evil nor transgression in mine *h*	1Sa 24:11	3027
but mine *h* shall not be upon thee	1Sa 24:12	3027
but mine *h* shall not be upon thee	1Sa 24:13	3027
and deliver me out of thine *h*	1Sa 24:15	3027
had delivered me into thine *h*	1Sa 24:18	3027
shall be established in thine *h*	1Sa 24:20	3027
to thine *h* unto thy servants	1Sa 25:8	3027
avenging thyself with thine own *h*	1Sa 25:26	3027
avenging myself with mine own *h*	1Sa 25:33	3027
So David received of her *h* that	1Sa 25:35	3027
my reproach from the *h* of Nabal	1Sa 25:39	3027
thine enemy into thine *h* this day	1Sa 26:8	3027
his *h* against the LORD's anointed	1Sa 26:9	3027
h against the LORD's anointed	1Sa 26:11	3027
or what evil is in mine *h*	1Sa 26:18	3027
delivered thee into my *h* to day	1Sa 26:23	3027
h against the LORD's anointed	1Sa 26:23	3027
perish one day by the *h* of Saul	1Sa 27:1	3027
so shall I escape out of his *h*	1Sa 27:1	3027
rent the kingdom out of thine *h*	1Sa 28:17	3027
into the *h* of the Philistines	1Sa 28:19	3027
into the *h* of the Philistines	1Sa 28:19	3027
and I have put my life in my *h*	1Sa 28:21	3709
that came against us into our *h*	1Sa 30:23	3027
afraid to stretch forth thine *h*	2Sa 1:14	3027
he turned not to the right *h* nor	2Sa 2:19	
to thy right *h* or to thy left	2Sa 2:21	
thee into the *h* of David, that	2Sa 3:8	3027
my *h* shall be with thee, to bring	2Sa 3:12	3027
By the *h* of my servant David I	2Sa 3:18	3027
out of the *h* of the Philistines	2Sa 3:18	3027
out of the *h* of all their enemies	2Sa 3:18	3027
now require his blood of your *h*	2Sa 4:11	3027
thou deliver them into mine *h*	2Sa 5:19	3027
the Philistines into thine *h*	2Sa 5:19	3027
put forth his *h* to the ark of God	2Sa 6:6	
out of the *h* of the Philistines	2Sa 8:1	3027
sent to comfort him by the *h* of	2Sa 10:2	3027
into the *h* of Abishai his brother	2Sa 10:10	3027
and sent it by the *h* of Uriah	2Sa 11:14	3027
thee out of the *h* of Saul	2Sa 12:7	3027
he sent by the *h* of Nathan the	2Sa 12:25	3027
I may see it, and eat it at her *h*	2Sa 13:5	3027
my sight, that I may eat at her *h*	2Sa 13:6	3027
that I may eat of thine *h*	2Sa 13:10	3027
laid her *h* on her head, and went	2Sa 13:19	3027
h of the man that would destroy	2Sa 14:16	3709
Is not the *h* of Joab with thee in	2Sa 14:19	3027
none can turn to the right *h* or	2Sa 14:19	
him obeisance, he put forth his *h*	2Sa 15:5	3027
mighty men were on his right *h*	2Sa 16:6	
into the *h* of Absalom thy son	2Sa 16:8	3027
of the people under the *h* of Joab	2Sa 18:2	3027
a third part under the *h* of	2Sa 18:2	3027
under the *h* of Ittai the Gittite	2Sa 18:2	3027
shekels of silver in mine *h*	2Sa 18:12	3709
mine *h* against the king's son	2Sa 18:12	3027
And he took three darts in his *h*	2Sa 18:14	3027
their *h* against my lord the king	2Sa 18:28	3027
us out of the *h* of our enemies	2Sa 19:9	3709
out of the *h* of the Philistines	2Sa 19:9	3709
with the right *h* to kiss him	2Sa 20:9	3027
to the sword that was in Joab's *h*	2Sa 20:10	3027
lifted up his *h* against the king	2Sa 20:21	3027
that had on every *h* six fingers	2Sa 21:20	3027
Gath, and fell by the *h* of David	2Sa 21:22	3027
and by the *h* of his servants	2Sa 21:22	3027
out of the *h* of all his enemies	2Sa 22:1	3709
enemies, and out of the *h* of Saul	2Sa 22:1	3709
Philistines until his *h* was weary	2Sa 23:10	3027
his *h* clave unto the sword	2Sa 23:10	3027
the Egyptian had a spear in his *h*	2Sa 23:21	3027
the spear out of the Egyptian's *h*	2Sa 23:21	3027
fall now into the *h* of the LORD	2Sa 24:14	3027
let me not fall into the *h* of man	2Sa 24:14	3027
the angel stretched out his *h*	2Sa 24:16	3027
stay now thine *h*	2Sa 24:16	3027
let thine *h*, I pray thee, be	2Sa 24:17	3027
and she sat on his right *h*	1Kin 2:19	
king Solomon sent by the *h* of	1Kin 2:25	3027
established in the *h* of Solomon	1Kin 2:46	3027
it was an *h* breadth thick, and the	1Kin 7:26	2947
and hath with his *h* fulfilled it	1Kin 8:15	3027
and hast fulfilled it with thine *h*	1Kin 8:24	3027
great name, and of thy strong *h*	1Kin 8:42	3027
by the *h* of Moses thy servant	1Kin 8:53	3027
by the *h* of Moses his servant	1Kin 8:56	3027
rend it out of the *h* of thy son	1Kin 11:12	3027
lifted up his *h* against the king	1Kin 11:26	3027
lifted up his *h* against the king	1Kin 11:27	3027
kingdom out of the *h* of Solomon	1Kin 11:31	3027
the whole kingdom out of his *h*	1Kin 11:34	3027
the kingdom out of his son's *h*	1Kin 11:35	3027
he put forth his *h* from the altar	1Kin 13:4	3027
And his *h*, which he put forth	1Kin 13:4	3027
that my *h* may be restored me	1Kin 13:6	3027
the king's *h* was restored him	1Kin 13:6	3027
which he spake by the *h* of his	1Kin 14:18	3027
them into the *h* of his servants	1Kin 15:18	3027
also by the *h* of the prophet Jehu	1Kin 16:7	3027
a morsel of bread in thine *h*	1Kin 17:11	3027
thy servant into the *h* of Ahab	1Kin 18:9	3027
out of the sea, like a man's *h*	1Kin 18:44	3709
the *h* of the LORD was on Elijah	1Kin 18:46	3027
they shall put it in their *h*	1Kin 20:6	3027
deliver it into thine *h* this day	1Kin 20:13	3027
this great multitude into thine *h*	1Kin 20:28	3027
thou hast let go out of thy *h* a	1Kin 20:42	3027
out of the *h* of the king of Syria	1Kin 22:3	3027
deliver it into the *h* of the king	1Kin 22:6	3027
deliver it into the king's *h*	1Kin 22:12	3027
deliver it into the *h* of the king	1Kin 22:15	3027
standing by him on his right *h*	1Kin 22:19	
of his chariot, Turn thine *h*	1Kin 22:34	3027
deliver them into the *h* of Moab	2Kin 3:10	3027
deliver them into the *h* of Moab	2Kin 3:13	3027
that the *h* of the LORD came upon	2Kin 3:15	3027
the Moabites also into your *h*	2Kin 3:18	3027
and take my staff in thine *h*	2Kin 4:29	3027
strike his *h* over the place, and	2Kin 5:11	3027
there, and he leaneth on my *h*	2Kin 5:18	3027
tower, he took them from their *h*	2Kin 5:24	3027
And he put out his *h*, and took it	2Kin 6:7	3027
Then a lord on whose *h* the king	2Kin 7:2	3027
appointed the lord on whose *h* he	2Kin 7:17	3027
Hazael, Take a present in thine *h*	2Kin 8:8	3027
from under the *h* of Judah	2Kin 8:20	3027
the *h* of Judah unto this day	2Kin 8:22	3027
take this box of oil in thine *h*	2Kin 9:1	3027
of the LORD, at the *h* of Jezebel	2Kin 9:7	3027
If it be, give me thine *h*	2Kin 10:15	3027
And he gave him his *h*	2Kin 10:15	3027
man with his weapons in his *h*	2Kin 11:8	3027
man with his weapons in his *h*	2Kin 11:11	3027
into whose *h* they delivered the	2Kin 12:15	3027

the *h* of Hazael king of Syria 2Kin 13:3 3027
into the *h* of Ben-hadad the son 2Kin 13:3 3027
from under the *h* of the Syrians 2Kin 13:5 3027
Israel, Put thine *h* upon the bow 2Kin 13:16 3027
And he put his *h* upon it 2Kin 13:16 3027
h of Ben-hadad the son of Hazael 2Kin 13:25 3027
h of Jehoahaz his father by war 2Kin 13:25 3027
kingdom was confirmed in his *h* 2Kin 14:5 3027
by the *h* of his servant Jonah 2Kin 14:25 3027
but he saved them by the *h* of 2Kin 14:27 3027
that his *h* might be with him to 2Kin 15:19 3027
to confirm the kingdom in his *h* 2Kin 15:19 3027
save me out of the *h* of the king 2Kin 16:7 3709
out of the *h* of the king of 2Kin 16:7 3709
from under the *h* of Pharaoh king 2Kin 17:7 3027
them into the *h* of spoilers 2Kin 17:20 3027
out of the *h* of all your enemies 2Kin 17:39 3027
a man lean, it will go into his *h* 2Kin 18:21 3709
able to deliver you out of his *h* 2Kin 18:29 3027
into the *h* of the king of Assyria 2Kin 18:30 3027
of the *h* of the king of Assyria 2Kin 18:33 3027
delivered Samaria out of mine *h* 2Kin 18:34 3027
their country out of mine *h* 2Kin 18:35 3027
deliver Jerusalem out of mine *h* 2Kin 18:35 3027
into the *h* of the king of Assyria 2Kin 19:10 3027
letter of the *h* of the messengers 2Kin 19:14 3027
thee, save thou us out of his *h* 2Kin 19:19 3027
this city out of the *h* of the 2Kin 20:6 3709
them into the *h* of their enemies 2Kin 21:14 3027
to the right *h* or to the left 2Kin 22:2
the *h* of the doers of the work 2Kin 22:5 3027
that was delivered into their *h* 2Kin 22:7 3027
the *h* of them that do the work 2Kin 22:9 3027
left *h* at the gate of the city 2Kin 23:8 3027
which were on the right *h* of the 2Kin 23:13
that thine *h* might be with me, and 1Chr 4:10 3027
Hagarites, who fell by their *h* 1Chr 5:10 3027
were delivered into their *h* 1Chr 5:20 3027
Judah and Jerusalem by the *h* of 1Chr 6:15 3027
Asaph, who stood on his right *h* 1Chr 6:39
of Merari stood on the left *h* 1Chr 6:44
in the Egyptian's *h* was a spear 1Chr 11:23 3027
the spear out of the Egyptian's *h* 1Chr 11:23 3027
and could use both the right *h* 1Chr 12:2
put forth his *h* to hold the ark 1Chr 13:9 3027
because he put his *h* to the ark 1Chr 13:10 3027
thou deliver them into mine *h* 1Chr 14:10 3027
I will deliver them into thine *h* 1Chr 14:10 3027
mine *h* like the breaking forth of 1Chr 14:11 3027
the LORD into the *h* of Asaph 1Chr 16:7 3027
out of the *h* of the Philistines 1Chr 18:1 3027
unto the *h* of Abishai his brother 1Chr 19:11 3027
four and twenty, six on each *h* 1Chr 20:6
and they fell by the *h* of David 1Chr 20:8 3027
and by the *h* of his servants 1Chr 20:8 3027
fall now into the *h* of the LORD 1Chr 21:13 3027
let me not fall into the *h* of man 1Chr 21:13 3027
It is enough, stay now thine *h* 1Chr 21:15 3027
having a drawn sword in his *h* 1Chr 21:16 3027
let thine *h*, I pray thee, O LORD 1Chr 21:17 3027
of the land into mine *h* 1Chr 22:18 3027
it was under the *h* of Shelomith 1Chr 26:28 3027
in writing by his *h* upon me 1Chr 28:19 3027
by the *h* of Jehiel the Gershonite 1Chr 29:8 3027
and in thine *h* is power and might 1Chr 29:12 3027
in thine *h* it is to make great 1Chr 29:12 3027
thine holy name cometh of thine *h* 1Chr 29:16 3027
the temple, one on the right *h* 2Chr 3:17
of that on the right *h* Jachin 2Chr 3:17
and put five on the right *h* 2Chr 4:6
the temple, five on the right *h* 2Chr 4:7
and hast fulfilled it with thine *h* 2Chr 6:15 3027
name's sake, and thy mighty *h* 2Chr 6:32 3027
which he spake by the *h* of Ahijah 2Chr 10:15 3027
also left you in the *h* of Shishak 2Chr 12:5 3027
Jerusalem by the *h* of Shishak 2Chr 12:7 3027
in the *h* of the sons of David 2Chr 13:8 3027
God delivered them into their *h* 2Chr 13:16 3027
of Syria escaped out of thine *h* 2Chr 16:7 3027
he delivered them into thine *h* 2Chr 16:8 3027
stablished the kingdom in his *h* 2Chr 17:5 3027
will deliver it into the king's *h* 2Chr 18:5 3027
deliver it into the *h* of the king 2Chr 18:11 3027
shall be delivered into your *h* 2Chr 18:14 3027
of heaven standing on his right *h* 2Chr 18:18
to his chariot man, Turn thine *h* 2Chr 18:33 3027
in thine *h* is there not power and 2Chr 20:6 3027
the *h* of Judah unto this day 2Chr 21:10 3027
Libnah revolt from under his *h* 2Chr 21:10 3027
man with his weapons in his *h* 2Chr 23:7 3027
man having his weapon in his *h* 2Chr 23:10 3027
the *h* of the priests the Levites 2Chr 23:18 3027
office by the *h* of the Levites 2Chr 24:11 3027
a very great host into their *h* 2Chr 24:24 3027
their own people out of thine *h* 2Chr 25:15 3027
them into the *h* of their enemies 2Chr 25:20 3027
by the *h* of Jeiel the scribe 2Chr 26:11 3027
under the *h* of Hananiah, one of 2Chr 26:11 3027
And under their *h* was an army 2Chr 26:13 3027
a censer in his *h* to burn incense 2Chr 26:19 3027
into the *h* of the king of Syria 2Chr 28:5 3027
into the *h* of the king of Israel 2Chr 28:5 3027
hath delivered them into your *h* 2Chr 28:9 3027
of the *h* of the kings of Assyria 2Chr 30:6 3709
Also in Judah the *h* of God was to 2Chr 30:12 3027
received of the *h* of the Levites 2Chr 30:16 3027
overseers under the *h* of Cononiah 2Chr 31:13 3027
of the *h* of the king of Assyria 2Chr 32:11 3709

deliver their lands out of mine *h* 2Chr 32:13 3027
deliver his people out of mine *h* 2Chr 32:14 3027
able to deliver you out of mine *h* 2Chr 32:14 3027
deliver his people out of mine *h* 2Chr 32:15 3027
out of the *h* of my fathers 2Chr 32:15 3027
God deliver you out of mine *h* 2Chr 32:15 3027
their people out of mine *h* 2Chr 32:17 3027
deliver his people out of mine *h* 2Chr 32:17 3027
of Jerusalem from the *h* of 2Chr 32:22 3027
from the *h* of all other, and 2Chr 32:22 3027
the ordinances by the *h* of Moses 2Chr 33:8 3027
declined neither to the right *h* 2Chr 34:2 3225
had gathered of the *h* of Manasseh 2Chr 34:9 3027
they put it in the *h* of the 2Chr 34:10 3027
it into the *h* of the overseers 2Chr 34:17 3027
and to the *h* of the workmen 2Chr 34:17 3027
of the LORD by the *h* of Moses 2Chr 35:6 3027
he gave them all into his *h* 2Chr 36:17 3027
the *h* of Mithredath the treasurer Ezr 1:8 3027
he gave them into the *h* of Ezr 5:12 3028
shall put to their *h* to alter Ezr 6:12 3028
according to the *h* of the LORD Ezr 7:6 3027
to the good *h* of his God upon him Ezr 7:9 3027
of thy God which is in thine *h* Ezr 7:14 3028
of thy God, that is in thine *h* Ezr 7:25 3028
I was strengthened as the *h* of Ezr 7:28 3027
by the good *h* of our God upon us Ezr 8:18 3027
The *h* of our God is upon all them Ezr 8:22 3027
weighed unto their *h* six hundred Ezr 8:26 3027
the *h* of our God was upon us, and Ezr 8:31 3027
us from the *h* of the enemy Ezr 8:31 3709
h of Meremoth the son of Uriah Ezr 8:33 3027
the *h* of the princes and rulers Ezr 9:2 3027
been delivered into the *h* of the Ezr 9:7 3027
great power, and by thy strong *h* Neh 1:10 3027
to the good *h* of my God upon me Neh 2:8 3027
Then I told them of the *h* of my Neh 2:18 3027
and with the other *h* held a weapon Neh 4:17
time with an open letter in his *h* Neh 6:5 3027
and Maaseiah, on his right *h* Neh 8:4 3225
and on his left *h*, Pedaiah, and Neh 8:4 8040
by the *h* of Moses thy servant Neh 9:14 3027
them into the *h* of their enemies Neh 9:27 3027
out of the *h* of their enemies Neh 9:27 3027
them in the *h* of their enemies Neh 9:28 3027
gavest thou them into the *h* of Neh 9:30 3027
was at the king's *h* in all Neh 11:24 3027
h upon the wall toward the dung Neh 12:31 3225
sought to lay *h* on the king Est 2:21 3027
the king took his ring from his *h* Est 3:10 3027
golden sceptre that was in his *h* Est 5:2 3027
who sought to lay *h* on the king Est 6:2 3027
horse be delivered to the *h* of Est 6:9 3027
he laid his *h* upon the Jews Est 8:7 3027
to lay *h* on such as sought their Est 9:2 3027
the spoil laid they not their *h* Est 9:10 3027
on the prey they laid not their *h* Est 9:15 3027
But put forth thine *h* now Job 1:11 3027
himself put not forth thine *h* Job 1:12 3027
But put forth thine *h* now Job 2:5 3027
Satan, Behold, he is in thine *h* Job 2:6 3027
we receive good at the *h* of God Job 2:10 854
and from the *h* of the mighty Job 5:15 3027
that he would let loose his *h* Job 6:9 3027
Or, Deliver me from the enemy's *h* Job 6:23 3027
me from the *h* of the mighty Job 6:23 3027
is given into the *h* of the wicked Job 9:24 3027
that might lay his *h* upon us both Job 9:33 3027
that can deliver out of thine *h* Job 10:7 3027
If iniquity be in thine *h* Job 11:14 3027
into whose *h* God bringeth Job 12:6 3027
not in all these that the *h* of Job 12:9 3027
In whose *h* is the soul of every Job 12:10 3027
teeth, and put my life in mine *h* Job 13:14 3709
Withdraw thine *h* far from me Job 13:21 3709
day of darkness is ready at his *h* Job 15:23 3027
stretcheth out his *h* against God Job 15:25 3027
for the *h* of God hath touched me Job 19:21 3027
every *h* of the wicked shall come Job 20:22 3027
lay your *h* upon your mouth Job 21:5 3027
Lo, their good is not in their *h* Job 21:16 3027
On the left *h*, where he doth work Job 23:9 8040
he hideth himself on the right *h* Job 23:9 3225
his *h* hath formed the crooked Job 26:13 3027
I will teach you by the *h* of God Job 27:11 3027
he would fain flee out of his *h* Job 27:22 3027
putteth forth his *h* upon the rock Job 28:9 3027
laid their *h* on their mouth Job 29:9 3709
my bow was renewed in my *h* Job 29:20 3027
Upon my right *h* rise the youth Job 30:12 3225
with thy strong *h* thou opposest Job 30:21 3027
stretch out his *h* to the grave Job 30:24 3027
up my *h* against the fatherless Job 31:21 3027
because mine *h* had gotten much Job 31:25 3027
or my mouth hath kissed my *h* Job 31:27 3027
neither shall my *h* be heavy upon Job 33:7 405
shall be taken away without *h* Job 34:20 3027
or what receiveth he of thine *h* Job 35:7 3027
He sealeth up the *h* of every man Job 37:7 3027
I will lay mine *h* upon my mouth Job 40:4 3027
thine own right *h* can save thee Job 40:14 3225
Lay thine *h* upon him, remember Job 41:8 3709
O God, lift up thine *h* Ps 10:12 3027
spite, to requite it with thy *h* Ps 10:14 3027
because he is at my right *h* Ps 16:8 3225
at thy right *h* there are Ps 16:11 3225
h them which put their trust in Ps 17:7 3225
From men which are thy *h*, O LORD, Ps 17:14 3027

him from the *h* of all his enemies Ps 18:*t* 3709
and from the *h* of Saul Ps 18:*t* 3027
thy right *h* hath holden me up, and Ps 18:35 3225
saving strength of his right *h* Ps 20:6 3225
Thine *h* shall find out all thine Ps 21:8 3027
thy right *h* shall find out those Ps 21:8 3225
their right *h* is full of bribes Ps 26:10 3225
Into thine *h* I commit my spirit Ps 31:5 3027
me up into the *h* of the enemy Ps 31:8 3027
My times are in thy *h* Ps 31:15 3027
me from the *h* of mine enemies Ps 31:15 3027
night thy *h* was heavy upon me Ps 32:4 3027
let not the *h* of the wicked Ps 36:11 3027
the LORD upholdeth him with his *h* Ps 37:24 3027
LORD will not leave him in his *h* Ps 37:33 3027
in me, and thy *h* presseth me sore Ps 38:2 3027
consumed by the blow of thine *h* Ps 39:10 3027
drive out the heathen with thy *h* Ps 44:2 3027
but thy right *h*, and thine arm, and Ps 44:3 3225
thy right *h* shall teach thee Ps 45:4 3225
upon thy right *h* did stand the Ps 45:9 3225
thy right *h* is full of Ps 48:10 3225
save with thy right *h*, and hear me Ps 60:5 3225
thy right *h* upholdeth me Ps 63:8 3225
out of the *h* of the wicked Ps 71:4 3027
out of the *h* of the unrighteous Ps 71:4 3709
thou hast holden me by my right *h* Ps 73:23 3027
Why withdrawest thou thy *h* Ps 74:11 3027
even thy right *h* Ps 74:11 3225
For in the *h* of the LORD there is Ps 75:8 3027
of the right *h* of the most High Ps 77:10 3225
like a flock by the *h* of Moses Ps 77:20 3027
They remembered not his *h* Ps 78:42 3027
which his right *h* had purchased Ps 78:54 3225
and his glory into the enemy's *h* Ps 78:61 3027
which thy right *h* hath planted Ps 80:15 3225
Let thy *h* be upon the man of thy Ps 80:17 3027
be upon the man of thy right *h* Ps 80:17 3225
turned my *h* against their Ps 81:14 3027
them out of the *h* of the wicked Ps 82:4 3027
and they are cut off from thy *h* Ps 88:5 3027
thy *h*, and high is thy right *h* Ps 89:13 3225
With whom my *h* shall be Ps 89:21 3027
I will set his *h* also in the sea Ps 89:25 3027
his right *h* in the rivers Ps 89:25 3225
up the right *h* of his adversaries Ps 89:42 3225
his soul from the *h* of the grave Ps 89:48 3027
and ten thousand at thy right *h* Ps 91:7 3225
In his *h* are the deep places of Ps 95:4 3027
pasture, and the sheep of his *h* Ps 95:7 3027
them out of the *h* of the wicked Ps 97:10 3027
his right *h*, and his holy arm, Ps 98:1 3225
thou openest thine *h*, they are Ps 104:28 3027
from the *h* of him that hated them Ps 106:10 3027
them from the *h* of the enemy Ps 106:10 3027
he lifted up his *h* against them Ps 106:26 3027
them into the *h* of the heathen Ps 106:41 3027
into subjection under their *h* Ps 106:42 3027
redeemed from the *h* of the enemy Ps 107:2 3027
save with thy right *h*, and answer Ps 108:6 3225
and let Satan stand at his right *h* Ps 109:6 3225
they may know that this is thy *h* Ps 109:27 3027
stand at the right *h* of the poor Ps 109:31 3225
my Lord, Sit thou at my right *h* Ps 110:1 3225
The LORD at thy right *h* shall Ps 110:5 3225
the right *h* of the LORD doeth Ps 118:15 3225
The right *h* of the LORD is Ps 118:16 3225
the right *h* of the LORD doeth Ps 118:16 3225
My soul is continually in my *h* Ps 119:109 3709
Let thine *h* help me Ps 119:173 3027
is thy shade upon thy right *h* Ps 121:5 3027
look unto the *h* of their masters Ps 123:2 3027
maiden unto the *h* of her mistress Ps 123:2 3027
are in the *h* of a mighty man Ps 127:4 3027
the mower filleth not his *h* Ps 129:7 3709
With a strong *h*, and with a Ps 136:12 3027
let my right *h* forget her cunning Ps 137:5 3225
thine *h* against the wrath of mine Ps 138:7 3027
thy right *h* shall save me Ps 138:7 3225
before, and laid thine *h* upon me Ps 139:5 3709
Even there shall thy *h* lead me Ps 139:10 3027
thy right *h* shall hold me Ps 139:10 3225
I looked on my right *h*, and beheld Ps 142:4 3225
Send thine *h* from above Ps 144:7 3027
from the *h* of strange children Ps 144:7 3027
their right *h* is a right *h* of Ps 144:8 3225
me from the *h* of strange children Ps 144:11 3027
their right *h* is a right *h* of Ps 144:11 3225
Thou openest thine *h*, and Ps 145:16 3027
and a twoedged sword in their *h* Ps 149:6 3027
I have stretched out my *h* Prov 1:24 3027
Length of days is in her right *h* Prov 3:16 3225
and in her left *h* riches and honour Prov 3:16 8040
in the power of thine *h* to do it Prov 3:27 3027
to the right *h* nor to the left Prov 4:27 3227
stricken thy *h* with a stranger Prov 6:1 3709
art come into the *h* of thy friend Prov 6:3 3709
as a roe from the *h* of the hunter Prov 6:5 3027
a bird from the *h* of the fowler Prov 6:5 3027
poor that dealeth with a slack *h* Prov 10:4 3709
but the *h* of the diligent maketh Prov 10:4 3027
Though *h* join in *h*, the wicked Prov 11:21 3027
The *h* of the diligent shall bear Prov 12:24 3027
though *h* join in *h*, he shall Prov 16:5 3027
in the *h* of a fool to get wisdom Prov 17:16 3027
man hideth his *h* in his bosom Prov 19:24 3027
heart is in the *h* of the LORD Prov 21:1 3027
that sendeth a message by the *h* Prov 26:6 3027

goeth up into the *h* of a drunkard ... Prov 26:9 3027
hideth his *h* in his bosom ... Prov 26:15 3027
and the ointment of his right *h* ... Prov 27:16 3225
lay thine *h* upon thy mouth ... Prov 30:32 3027
stretcheth out her *h* to the poor ... Prov 31:20 3709
that it was from the *h* of God ... Eccl 2:24 3027
son, and there is nothing in his *h* ... Eccl 5:14 3027
which he may carry away in his *h* ... Eccl 5:15 3027
from this withdraw not thine *h* ... Eccl 7:18 3027
their works, are in the *h* of God ... Eccl 9:1 3027
Whatsoever thy *h* findeth to do ... Eccl 9:10 3027
man's heart is at his right *h* ... Eccl 10:2 3225
the evening withhold not thine *h* ... Eccl 11:6 3027
His left *h* is under my head, and ... Song 2:6 8040
his right *h* doth embrace me ... Song 2:6 3225
My beloved put in his *h* by the ... Song 5:4 3027
His left *h* should be under my ... Song 8:3 8040
his right *h* should embrace me ... Song 8:3 3225
who hath required this at your *h* ... Is 1:12 3027
And I will turn my *h* upon thee ... Is 1:25 3027
and let this ruin be under thy *h* ... Is 3:6 3027
forth his *h* against them, and hath ... Is 5:25 3027
but his *h* is stretched out still ... Is 5:25 3027
me, having a live coal in his *h* ... Is 6:6 3027
spake thus to me with a strong *h* ... Is 8:11 3027
but his *h* is stretched out still ... Is 9:12 3027
but his *h* is stretched out still ... Is 9:17 3027
And he shall snatch on the right *h* ... Is 9:20 3225
and he shall eat on the left *h* ... Is 9:20 8040
but his *h* is stretched out still ... Is 9:21 3027
but his *h* is stretched out still ... Is 10:4 3027
the staff in their *h* is mine ... Is 10:5 3027
As my *h* hath found the kingdoms ... Is 10:10 3027
strength of my *h* I have done it ... Is 10:13 3027
my *h* hath found as a nest the ... Is 10:14 3027
he shall shake his *h* against the ... Is 10:32 3027
put his *h* on the cockatrice' den ... Is 11:8 3027
his *h* again the second time to ... Is 11:11 3027
they shall lay their *h* upon Edom ... Is 11:14 3027
he shake his *h* over the river ... Is 11:15 3027
the voice unto them, shake the *h* ... Is 13:2 3027
for the day of the LORD is at *h* ... Is 13:6 7138
this is the *h* that is stretched ... Is 14:26 3027
his *h* is stretched out, and who ... Is 14:27 3027
over into the *h* of a cruel lord ... Is 19:4 3027
of the *h* of the LORD of hosts ... Is 19:16 3027
commit thy government into his *h* ... Is 22:21 3027
stretched out his *h* over the sea ... Is 23:11 3027
shall the *h* of the LORD rest ... Is 25:10 3027
when thy *h* is lifted up, they ... Is 26:11 3027
cast down to the earth with the *h* ... Is 28:2 3027
is yet in his *h* he eateth it up ... Is 28:4 3709
it, when ye turn to the right *h* ... Is 30:21 3027
the LORD shall stretch out his *h* ... Is 31:3 3027
his *h* hath divided it unto them ... Is 34:17 3027
a man lean, it will go into his *h* ... Is 36:6 3709
into the *h* of the king of Assyria ... Is 36:15 3027
of the *h* of the king of Assyria ... Is 36:18 3027
delivered Samaria out of my *h* ... Is 36:19 3027
delivered their land out of my *h* ... Is 36:20 3027
deliver Jerusalem out of my *h* ... Is 36:20 3027
into the *h* of the king of Assyria ... Is 37:10 3027
from the *h* of the messengers ... Is 37:14 3027
LORD our God, save us from his *h* ... Is 37:20 3027
this city out of the *h* of the ... Is 38:6 3709
LORD's *h* double for all her sins ... Is 40:2 3027
Lord GOD will come with strong *h* ... Is 40:10
the waters in the hollow of his *h* ... Is 40:12 8168
the right *h* of my righteousness ... Is 41:10 3225
thy God will hold thy right *h* ... Is 41:13 3225
that the *h* of the LORD hath done ... Is 41:20 3027
and will hold thine *h*, and will ... Is 42:6 3027
none that can deliver out of my *h* ... Is 43:13 3027
with his *h* unto the LORD, and ... Is 44:5 3027
Is there not a lie in my right *h* ... Is 44:20 3225
whose right *h* I have holden, to ... Is 45:1 3225
and given them into thine *h* ... Is 47:6 3027
Mine *h* also hath laid the ... Is 48:13 3027
my right *h* hath spanned the ... Is 48:13 3225
shadow of his *h* hath he hid me ... Is 49:2 3027
lift up mine *h* to the Gentiles ... Is 49:22 3027
Is my *h* shortened at all, that it ... Is 50:2 3027
This shall ye have of mine *h* ... Is 50:11 3027
thee in the shadow of mine *h* ... Is 51:16 3027
which hast drunk at the *h* of the ... Is 51:17 3027
any that taketh her by the *h* of ... Is 51:18 3027
of thine *h* the cup of trembling ... Is 51:22 3027
the *h* of them that afflict thee ... Is 51:23 3027
the LORD shall prosper in his *h* ... Is 53:10 3027
shalt break forth on the right *h* ... Is 54:3 3225
keepeth his *h* from doing any evil ... Is 56:2 3027
hast found the life of thine *h* ... Is 57:10 3027
the LORD's *h* is not shortened, ... Is 59:1 3027
of glory in the *h* of the LORD ... Is 62:3 3027
royal diadem in the *h* of thy God ... Is 62:3 3709
LORD hath sworn by his right *h* ... Is 62:8 3225
That led them by the right *h* of ... Is 63:12 3225
and we all are the work of thy *h* ... Is 64:8 3027
all those things hath mine *h* made ... Is 66:2 3027
the *h* of the LORD shall be known ... Is 66:14 3027
Then the LORD put forth his *h* ... Jer 1:9 3027
turn back thine *h* as a ... Jer 6:9 3027
for I will stretch out my *h* upon ... Jer 6:12 3027
LORD, that thou die not by our *h* ... Jer 11:21 3027
my soul into the *h* of her enemies ... Jer 12:7 3709
I stretch out my *h* against thee ... Jer 15:6 3027
I sat alone because of thy *h* ... Jer 15:17 3027
thee out of the *h* of the wicked ... Jer 15:21 3027

thee out of the *h* of the terrible ... Jer 15:21 3709
I will cause them to know mine *h* ... Jer 16:21 3027
was marred in the *h* of the potter ... Jer 18:4 3027
as the clay is in the potter's *h* ... Jer 18:6 3027
so are ye in mine *h* ... Jer 18:6 3027
into the *h* of the king of Babylon ... Jer 20:4 3027
give into the *h* of their enemies ... Jer 20:5 3027
the poor from the *h* of evildoers ... Jer 20:13 3027
you with an outstretched *h* ... Jer 21:5 3027
into the *h* of Nebuchadrezzar king ... Jer 21:7 3027
into the *h* of their enemies, and ... Jer 21:7 3027
into the *h* of those that seek ... Jer 21:7 3027
into the *h* of the king of Babylon ... Jer 21:10 3027
out of the *h* of the oppressor ... Jer 21:12 3027
out of the *h* of the oppressor ... Jer 22:3 3027
were the signet upon my right *h* ... Jer 22:24 3027
I will give thee into the *h* of ... Jer 22:25 3027
into the *h* of them whose face ... Jer 22:25 3027
even into the *h* of Nebuchadrezzar ... Jer 22:25 3027
into the *h* of the Chaldeans ... Jer 22:25 3027
Am I a God at *h*, saith the LORD, ... Jer 23:23 7138
the wine cup of this fury at my *h* ... Jer 25:15 3027
took I the cup at the LORD's *h* ... Jer 25:17 3027
take the cup at thine *h* to drink ... Jer 25:28 3027
As for me, behold, I am in your *h* ... Jer 26:14 3027
Nevertheless the *h* of Ahikam the ... Jer 26:24 3027
the *h* of the people to put him to ... Jer 26:24 3027
by the *h* of the messengers which ... Jer 27:3 3027
h of Nebuchadnezzar the king of ... Jer 27:6 3027
I have consumed them by his *h* ... Jer 27:8 3027
By the *h* of Elasah the son of ... Jer 29:3 3027
the *h* of Nebuchadrezzar king of ... Jer 29:21 3027
ransomed him from the *h* of him ... Jer 31:11 3027
h to bring them out of the land ... Jer 31:32 3027
into the *h* of the king of Babylon ... Jer 32:3 3027
out of the *h* of the Chaldeans ... Jer 32:4 3027
into the *h* of the king of Babylon ... Jer 32:4 3027
with wonders, and with a strong *h* ... Jer 32:21 3027
given into the *h* of the Chaldeans ... Jer 32:24 3027
given into the *h* of the Chaldeans ... Jer 32:25 3027
city into the *h* of the Chaldeans ... Jer 32:28 3027
into the *h* of Nebuchadrezzar king ... Jer 32:28 3027
h of the king of Babylon by the ... Jer 32:36 3027
given into the *h* of the Chaldeans ... Jer 32:43 3027
into the *h* of the king of Babylon ... Jer 34:2 3027
shalt not escape out of his *h* ... Jer 34:3 3027
be taken, and delivered into his *h* ... Jer 34:3 3027
them into the *h* of their enemies ... Jer 34:20 3027
into the *h* of them that seek ... Jer 34:20 3027
give into the *h* of their enemies ... Jer 34:21 3027
into the *h* of them that seek ... Jer 34:21 3027
into the *h* of the king of ... Jer 34:21 3027
Take in thine *h* the roll wherein ... Jer 36:14 3027
of Neriah took the roll in his *h* ... Jer 36:14 3027
into the *h* of the king of Babylon ... Jer 37:17 3027
h of the king of Babylon's army ... Jer 38:3 3027
said, Behold, he is in your *h* ... Jer 38:5 3027
will I give thee into the *h* of ... Jer 38:16 3027
given into the *h* of the Chaldeans ... Jer 38:18 3027
shalt not escape out of their *h* ... Jer 38:18 3027
lest they deliver me into their *h* ... Jer 38:19 3027
shalt not escape out of their *h* ... Jer 38:23 3027
by the *h* of the king of Babylon ... Jer 38:23 3027
the *h* of the men of whom thou art ... Jer 39:17 3027
chains which were upon thine *h* ... Jer 40:4 3027
offerings and incense in their *h* ... Jer 41:5 3027
you, and to deliver you from his *h* ... Jer 42:11 3027
us into the *h* of the Chaldeans ... Jer 43:3 3027
Take great stones in thine *h* ... Jer 43:9 3027
mouths, and fulfilled with your *h* ... Jer 44:25 3027
Egypt into the *h* of his enemies ... Jer 44:30 3027
into the *h* of them that seek his ... Jer 44:30 3027
the *h* of Nebuchadrezzar king of ... Jer 44:30 3027
the *h* of the people of the north ... Jer 46:24 3027
I will deliver them into the *h* of ... Jer 46:26 3027
into the *h* of Nebuchadrezzar king ... Jer 46:26 3027
into the *h* of his servants ... Jer 46:26 3027
she hath given her *h* ... Jer 50:15 3027
been a golden cup in the LORD's *h* ... Jer 51:7 3027
will stretch out mine *h* upon thee ... Jer 51:25 3027
fell into the *h* of the enemy ... Lam 1:7 3027
h upon all her pleasant things ... Lam 1:10 3027
transgressions is bound by his *h* ... Lam 1:14 3027
his right *h* from before the enemy ... Lam 2:3 3225
with his right *h* as an adversary ... Lam 2:4 3225
he hath given up into the *h* of ... Lam 2:7 3027
withdrawn his *h* from destroying ... Lam 2:8 3027
he turneth his *h* against me all ... Lam 3:3 3027
have given the *h* to the Egyptians ... Lam 5:6 3027
doth deliver us out of their *h* ... Lam 5:8 3027
Princes are hanged up by their *h* ... Lam 5:12 3027
the *h* of the LORD was there upon ... Eze 1:3 3027
behold, an *h* was sent unto me ... Eze 2:9 3027
but the *h* of the LORD was strong ... Eze 3:14 3027
blood will I require at thine *h* ... Eze 3:18 3027
blood will I require at thine *h* ... Eze 3:20 3027
the *h* of the LORD was there upon ... Eze 3:22 3027
Smite with thine *h*, and stamp with ... Eze 6:11 3709
will I stretch out my *h* upon them ... Eze 6:14 3027
that the *h* of the Lord GOD fell ... Eze 8:1 3027
And he put forth the form of an *h* ... Eze 8:3 3027
every man his censer in his *h* ... Eze 8:11 3027
his destroying weapon in his *h* ... Eze 9:1 3027
man a slaughter weapon in his *h* ... Eze 9:2 3027
fill thine *h* with coals of fire ... Eze 10:2 2651
one cherub stretched forth his *h* ... Eze 10:7 3027
of a man's *h* under their wings ... Eze 10:8 3027
through the wall with mine *h* ... Eze 12:7 3027

say unto them, The days are at *h* ... Eze 12:23 7126
mine *h* shall be upon the prophets ... Eze 13:9 3027
deliver my people out of your *h* ... Eze 13:21 3027
be no more in your *h* to be hunted ... Eze 13:21 3027
deliver my people out of your *h* ... Eze 13:23 3027
I will stretch out my *h* upon him ... Eze 14:9 3027
will I stretch out mine *h* upon it ... Eze 14:13 3027
have stretched out my *h* over thee ... Eze 16:27 3027
will also give thee into their *h* ... Eze 16:39 3027
that dwell at thy left *h* ... Eze 16:46 8040
that dwelleth at thy right *h* ... Eze 16:46 3225
she strengthen the *h* of the poor ... Eze 16:49 3027
when, lo, he had given his *h* ... Eze 17:18 3027
withdrawn his *h* from iniquity ... Eze 18:8 3027
taken off his *h* from the poor ... Eze 18:17 3027
lifted up mine *h* unto the seed of ... Eze 20:5 3027
when I lifted up mine *h* unto them ... Eze 20:5 3027
that I lifted up mine *h* unto them ... Eze 20:6 3027
Yet also I lifted up my *h* unto ... Eze 20:15 3027
Nevertheless I withdrew mine *h* ... Eze 20:22 3027
I lifted up mine *h* unto them also ... Eze 20:23 3027
up mine *h* to give it to them ... Eze 20:28 3027
Lord GOD, surely with a mighty *h* ... Eze 20:33 3027
ye are scattered, with a mighty *h* ... Eze 20:34 3027
mine *h* to give it to your fathers ... Eze 20:42 3027
give it into the *h* of the slayer ... Eze 21:11 3027
or other, either on the right *h* ... Eze 21:16 3221
At his right *h* was the divination ... Eze 21:22 3225
ye shall be taken with the *h* ... Eze 21:24 3079
thee into the *h* of brutish men ... Eze 21:31 3027
h at thy dishonest gain which ... Eze 22:13 3079
her into the *h* of her lovers ... Eze 23:9 3027
into the *h* of the Assyrians, upon ... Eze 23:9 3027
the *h* of them whom thou hatest ... Eze 23:28 3027
into the *h* of them from whom thy ... Eze 23:28 3027
will I give her cup into thine *h* ... Eze 23:31 3027
will stretch out mine *h* upon thee ... Eze 25:7 3027
also stretch out mine *h* upon Edom ... Eze 25:13 3027
Edom by the *h* of my people Israel ... Eze 25:14 3027
out mine *h* upon the Philistines ... Eze 25:16 3027
were the merchandise of thine *h* ... Eze 27:15 3027
in the *h* of him that slayeth thee ... Eze 28:9 3027
by the *h* of strangers ... Eze 28:10 3027
they took hold of thee by thy *h* ... Eze 29:7 3709
of Egypt to cease by the *h* of ... Eze 30:10 3027
the land into the *h* of the wicked ... Eze 30:12 3027
is therein, by the *h* of strangers ... Eze 30:12 3027
the sword to fall out of his *h* ... Eze 30:22 3027
Babylon, and put my sword in his *h* ... Eze 30:24 3027
into the *h* of the king of Babylon ... Eze 30:25 3027
delivered him into the *h* of the ... Eze 31:11 3027
I require at the watchman's *h* ... Eze 33:6 3027
blood will I require at thine *h* ... Eze 33:8 3027
Now the *h* of the LORD was upon me ... Eze 33:22 3027
will require my flock at their *h* ... Eze 34:10 3027
delivered them out of the *h* of ... Eze 34:27 3027
stretch out mine *h* against thee ... Eze 35:3 3027
I have lifted up mine *h*, Surely ... Eze 36:7 3027
for they are at *h* to come ... Eze 36:8 7126
The *h* of the LORD was upon me, and ... Eze 37:1 3027
they shall become one in thine *h* ... Eze 37:17 3027
which is in the *h* of Ephraim ... Eze 37:19 3027
and they shall be one in mine *h* ... Eze 37:19 3027
be in thine *h* before their eyes ... Eze 37:20 3027
to turn thine *h* upon the desolate ... Eze 38:12 3027
smite thy bow out of thy left *h* ... Eze 39:3 3027
arrows to fall out of thy right *h* ... Eze 39:3 3027
my *h* that I have laid upon them ... Eze 39:21 3027
them into the *h* of their enemies ... Eze 39:23 3027
day the *h* of the LORD was upon me ... Eze 40:1 3027
with a line of flax in his *h* ... Eze 40:3 3027
in the man's *h* a measuring reed ... Eze 40:5 3027
long by the cubit and an *h* breadth ... Eze 40:5 2948
an *h* broad, fastened round about ... Eze 40:43 2948
cubit is a cubit and an *h* breadth ... Eze 43:13 2948
I lifted up mine *h* against them ... Eze 44:12 3027
as his *h* shall attain unto ... Eze 46:7 3027
line in his *h* went forth eastward ... Eze 47:3 3027
the which I lifted up mine *h* to ... Eze 47:14 3027
king of Judah into his *h*, with ... Dan 1:2 3027
heaven hath he given into thine *h* ... Dan 2:38 3028
he will deliver us out of thine *h* ... Dan 3:17 3028
and none can stay his *h*, or say ... Dan 4:35 3028
came forth fingers of a man's *h* ... Dan 5:5 3028
saw the part of the *h* that wrote ... Dan 5:5 3028
the God in whose *h* thy breath is ... Dan 5:23 3028
the part of the *h* sent from him ... Dan 5:24 3028
be given into his *h* until a time ... Dan 7:25 3028
that could deliver out of his *h* ... Dan 8:4 3027
deliver the ram out of his *h* ... Dan 8:7 3027
cause craft to prosper in his *h* ... Dan 8:25 3027
but he shall be broken without *h* ... Dan 8:25 3027
the land of Egypt with a mighty *h* ... Dan 9:15 3027
an *h* touched me, which set me ... Dan 10:10 3027
shall be given into his *h* ... Dan 11:11 3027
which by his *h* shall be consumed ... Dan 11:16 3027
these shall escape out of his *h* ... Dan 11:41 3027
his *h* also upon the countries ... Dan 11:42 3027
when he held up his right *h* ... Dan 12:7 3225
his left *h* unto heaven, and sware ... Dan 12:7 8040
shall deliver her out of mine *h* ... Hos 2:10 3027
stretched out his *h* with scorners ... Hos 7:5 3027
balances of deceit are in his *h* ... Hos 12:7 3027
for the day of the LORD is at *h* ... Joel 1:15 7138
LORD cometh, for it is nigh at *h* ... Joel 2:1
your daughters into the *h* of the ... Joel 3:8 3027
I will turn mine *h* against Ekron ... Amos 1:8 3027
leaned his *h* on the wall, and a ... Amos 5:19 3027

with a plumbline in his *h* ... Amos 7:7 3027
thence shall mine *h* take them ... Amos 9:2 3027
discern between their right *h* ... Jonah 4:11 3235
their right *h* and their left *h* ... Jonah 4:11 8040
it is in the power of their *h* ... Mic 2:1 3027
thee from the *h* of thine enemies ... Mic 4:10 3709
Thine *h* shall be lifted up upon ... Mic 5:9 3027
off witchcrafts out of thine *h* ... Mic 5:12 3027
lay their *h* upon their mouth ... Mic 7:16 3027
right *h* shall be turned unto thee ... Hab 2:16 3225
he had horns coming out of his *h* ... Hab 3:4 3027
stretch out mine *h* upon Judah ... Zeph 1:4 3027
for the day of the LORD is at *h* ... Zeph 1:7 7138
out his *h* against the north ... Zeph 2:13 3027
by her shall hiss, and wag his *h* ... Zeph 2:15 3027
with a measuring line in his *h* ... Zec 2:1 3027
I will shake mine *h* upon them ... Zec 2:9 3027
at his right *h* to resist him ... Zec 3:1 3225
shall see the plummet in the *h* of ... Zec 4:10 3027
his staff in his *h* for very age ... Zec 8:4 3027
every one into his neighbour's *h* ... Zec 11:6 3027
and into the *h* of his king ... Zec 11:6 3027
out of their *h* I will not deliver ... Zec 11:6 3027
round about, on the right *h* ... Zec 12:6 3225
I will turn mine *h* upon the ... Zec 13:7 3027
one on the *h* of his neighbour ... Zec 14:13 3027
his *h* shall rise up against the ... Zec 14:13 3027
up against the *h* of his neighbour ... Zec 14:13 3027
I accept an offering at your *h* ... Mal 1:10 3027
should I accept this of your *h* ... Mal 1:13 3027
it with good will at your *h* ... Mal 2:13 3027
for the kingdom of heaven is at *h* ... Mt 3:2 *1448*
Whose fan is in his *h*, and he will ... Mt 3:12 *5495*
for the kingdom of heaven is at *h* ... Mt 4:17 *1448*
And if thy right *h* offend thee ... Mt 5:30 *5495*
let not thy left *h* know what thy ... Mt 6:3
know what thy right *h* doeth ... Mt 6:3
And Jesus put forth his *h*, and ... Mt 8:3 *5495*
And he touched her *h*, and the fever ... Mt 8:15 *5495*
lay thy *h* upon her, and she shall ... Mt 9:18 *5495*
he went in, and took her by the *h* ... Mt 9:25 *5495*
The kingdom of heaven is at *h* ... Mt 10:7 *1448*
a man which had his *h* withered ... Mt 12:10 *5495*
to the man, Stretch forth thine *h* ... Mt 12:13 *5495*
forth his *h* toward his disciples ... Mt 12:49 *5495*
Jesus stretched forth his *h* ... Mt 14:31 *5495*
Wherefore if thy *h* or thy foot ... Mt 18:8 *5495*
may sit, the one on thy right *h* ... Mt 20:21
but to sit on my right *h*, and on ... Mt 20:23
king to the servants, Bind him *h* ... Mt 22:13 5495
my Lord, Sit thou on my right *h* ... Mt 22:44
set the sheep on his right *h* ... Mt 25:33
King say unto them on his right *h* ... Mt 25:34
say also unto them on the left *h* ... Mt 25:41
The Master saith, My time is at *h* ... Mt 26:18 *1451*
dippeth his *h* with me in the dish ... Mt 26:23 *5495*
behold, the hour is at *h*, and the ... Mt 26:45 *1448*
he is at *h* that doth betray me ... Mt 26:46 *1448*
with Jesus stretched out his *h* ... Mt 26:51 *5495*
sitting on the right *h* of power ... Mt 26:64
head, and a reed in his right *h* ... Mt 27:29
with him, one on the right *h* ... Mt 27:38
and the kingdom of God is at *h* ... Mk 1:15 *1448*
And he came and took her by the *h* ... Mk 1:31 *5495*
with compassion, put forth his *h* ... Mk 1:41 *5495*
man there which had a withered *h* ... Mk 3:1 *5495*
the man which had the withered *h* ... Mk 3:3 *5495*
the man, Stretch forth thine *h* ... Mk 3:5 *5495*
his *h* was restored whole as the ... Mk 3:5 *5495*
And he took the damsel by the *h* ... Mk 5:41 *5495*
beseech him to put his *h* upon him ... Mk 7:32 *5495*
And he took the blind man by the *h* ... Mk 8:23 *5495*
But Jesus took him by the *h* ... Mk 9:27 *5495*
if thy *h* offend thee, cut it off ... Mk 9:43 *5495*
we may sit, one on thy right *h* ... Mk 10:37
and the other on thy left *h* ... Mk 10:37
But to sit on my right *h* and on my ... Mk 10:40
on my left *h* is not mine to give ... Mk 10:40
my Lord, Sit thou on my right *h* ... Mk 12:36
lo, he that betrayeth me is at *h* ... Mk 14:42 *1448*
sitting on the right *h* of power ... Mk 14:62
the one on his right *h*, and the ... Mk 15:27
and sat on the right *h* of God ... Mk 16:19
in *h* to set forth in order a ... Lk 1:1 *2021*
the *h* of the Lord was with him ... Lk 1:66 *5495*
from the *h* of all that hate us ... Lk 1:71 *5495*
being delivered out of the *h* of ... Lk 1:74 *5495*
Whose fan is in his *h*, and he will ... Lk 3:17 *5495*
And he put forth his *h*, and touched ... Lk 5:13 *5495*
a man whose right *h* was withered ... Lk 6:6 *5495*
the man which had the withered *h* ... Lk 6:8 *5495*
unto the man, Stretch forth thy *h* ... Lk 6:10 *5495*
his *h* was restored whole as the ... Lk 6:10 *5495*
all out, and took her by the *h* ... Lk 8:54 *5495*
having put his *h* to the plough ... Lk 9:62 *5495*
and put a ring on his *h*, and shoes ... Lk 15:22 *5495*
my Lord, Sit thou on my right *h* ... Lk 20:42
that summer is now nigh at *h* ... Lk 21:30
the kingdom of God is nigh at *h* ... Lk 21:31
the *h* of him that betrayeth me is ... Lk 22:21 *5495*
the right *h* of the power of God ... Lk 22:69
malefactors, one on the right *h* ... Lk 23:33
And the Jews' passover was at *h* ... Jn 2:13 *1451*
hath given all things into his *h* ... Jn 3:35 *5495*
feast of tabernacles was at *h* ... Jn 7:2 *1451*
any man pluck them out of my *h* ... Jn 10:28 *5495*
pluck them out of my Father's *h* ... Jn 10:29 *5495*
but he escaped out of their *h* ... Jn 10:39 *5495*
that was dead came forth, bound *h* ... Jn 11:44 *5495*
the Jews' passover was nigh at *h* ... Jn 11:55
Jesus with the palm of his *h* ... Jn 18:22
for the sepulchre was nigh at *h* ... Jn 19:42
thrust my *h* into his side, I will ... Jn 20:25 *5495*
and reach hither thy *h*, and thrust ... Jn 20:27 *5495*
my face, for he is on my right *h* ... Acts 2:25
by the right *h* of God exalted ... Acts 2:33
my Lord, Sit thou on my right *h* ... Acts 2:34
And he took him by the right *h* ... Acts 3:7 *5495*
For to do whatsoever thy *h* ... Acts 4:28 *5495*
stretching forth thine *h* to heal ... Acts 4:30 *5495*
with his right *h* to be a Prince ... Acts 5:31
God by his *h* would deliver them ... Acts 7:25 *5495*
a deliverer by the *h* of the angel ... Acts 7:35 *5495*
Hath not my *h* made all these ... Acts 7:50 *5495*
standing on the right *h* of God ... Acts 7:55
standing on the right *h* of God ... Acts 7:56
but they led him by the *h* ... Acts 9:8 *5496*
in, and putting his *h* on him ... Acts 9:12 *5495*
And he gave her his *h*, and lifted ... Acts 9:41 *5495*
the *h* of the Lord was with them ... Acts 11:21 *5495*
me out of the *h* of Herod, and from ... Acts 12:11 *5495*
with the *h* to hold their peace ... Acts 12:17 *5495*
the *h* of the Lord is upon thee ... Acts 13:11 *5495*
seeking some to lead him by the *h* ... Acts 13:11 *5497*
up, and beckoning with his *h* said ... Acts 13:16 *5495*
And Alexander beckoned with the *h* ... Acts 19:33 *5495*
Cyprus, we left it on the left *h* ... Acts 21:3
with the *h* unto the people ... Acts 21:40 *5495*
being led by the *h* of them that ... Acts 22:11 *5496*
chief captain took him by the *h* ... Acts 23:19 *5495*
Then Paul stretched forth the *h* ... Acts 26:1 *5495*
of the heat, and fastened on his *h* ... Acts 28:3 *5495*
the venomous beast hang on his *h* ... Acts 28:4 *5495*
who is even at the right *h* of God ... Rom 8:34
is far spent, the day is at *h* ... Rom 13:12 *1448*
shall say, Because I am not the *h* ... 1Cor 12:15 *5495*
And the eye cannot say unto the *h* ... 1Cor 12:21 *5495*
of me Paul with mine own *h* ... 1Cor 16:21 *5495*
of righteousness on the right *h* ... 2Cor 6:7
of things made ready to our *h* ... 2Cor 10:16
by angels in the *h* of a mediator ... Gal 3:19 *5495*
written unto you with mine own *h* ... Gal 6:11 *5495*
right *h* in the heavenly places ... Eph 1:20
The Lord is at *h* ... Phil 4:5 *1451*
sitteth on the right *h* of God ... Col 3:1
salutation by the *h* of me Paul ... Col 4:18 *5495*
as that the day of Christ is at *h* ... 2Th 2:2 *1764*
of Paul with mine own *h*, which is ... 2Th 3:17 *5495*
the time of my departure is at *h* ... 2Ti 4:6 *2186*
have written it with mine own *h* ... Philem 19 *5495*
sat down on the right *h* of the ... Heb 1:3
at any times, Sit on my right *h* ... Heb 1:13
who is set on the right *h* of the ... Heb 8:1
h to lead them out of the land of ... Heb 8:9 *5495*
sat down on the right *h* of God ... Heb 10:12
the right *h* of the throne of God ... Heb 12:2
and is on the right *h* of God ... 1Pet 3:22
But the end of all things is at *h* ... 1Pet 4:7 *1448*
under the mighty *h* of God ... 1Pet 5:6 *5495*
for the time is at *h* ... Rev 1:3 *1451*
he had in his right *h* seven stars ... Rev 1:16 *5495*
And he laid his right *h* upon me ... Rev 1:17 *5495*
which thou sawest in my right *h* ... Rev 1:20
the seven stars in his right *h* ... Rev 2:1
I saw in the right *h* of him that ... Rev 5:1
took the book out of the right *h* ... Rev 5:7
had a pair of balances in his *h* ... Rev 6:5 *5495*
before God out of the angel's *h* ... Rev 8:4 *5495*
he had in his *h* a little book ... Rev 10:2 *5495*
earth lifted up his *h* to heaven ... Rev 10:5 *5495*
book which is open in the *h* of ... Rev 10:8 *5495*
little book out of the angel's *h* ... Rev 10:10 *5495*
receive a mark in their right *h* ... Rev 13:16 *5495*
mark in his forehead, or in his *h* ... Rev 14:9 *5495*
crown, and in his *h* a sharp sickle ... Rev 14:14 *5495*
cup in her *h* full of abominations ... Rev 17:4 *5495*
blood of his servants at her *h* ... Rev 19:2 *5495*
pit and a great chain in his *h* ... Rev 20:1 *5495*
for the time is at *h* ... Rev 22:10 *1451*

HANDBREADTH {3}
a border of an *h* round about ... Ex 37:12 2948
And the thickness of it was an *h* ... 2Chr 4:5 2947
thou hast made my days as an *h* ... Ps 39:5 2947

HANDED {1}
him while he is weary and weak *h* ... 2Sa 17:2 3027

HANDFUL {9}
his *h* of the flour thereof ... Lev 2:2 4393,7062
the priest shall take his *h* of it ... Lev 5:12 4393,7062
And he shall take of it his *h* ... Lev 6:15 7062
offering, and took an *h* thereof ... Lev 9:17 4390,3709
shall take an *h* of the offering ... Num 5:26 7061
but an *h* of meal in a barrel, and ... 1Kin 17:12 4390,3709
There shall be an *h* of corn in ... Ps 72:16 6451
Better is an *h* with quietness ... Eccl 4:6 4390,3709
as the *h* after the harvestman, and ... Jer 9:22 5995

HANDFULS {5}
the earth brought forth by *h* ... Gen 41:47 7062
Take to you *h* of ashes of the ... Ex 9:8 4393,2651
some of the *h* of purpose for her ... Ruth 2:16 6653
of Samaria shall suffice for *h* ... 1Kin 20:10 8168
among my people for *h* of barley ... Eze 13:19 8168

HANDKERCHIEFS {1}
brought unto the sick *h* or aprons ... Acts 19:12 *4676*

HANDLE {11}
father of all such as *h* the harp ... Gen 4:21 8610
they that *h* the pen of the writer ... Judg 5:14 4900
the battle, that could *h* shield ... 1Chr 12:8 6186
forth to war, that could *h* spear ... 2Chr 25:5 270
They have hands, but they *h* not ... Ps 115:7 4184
they that *h* the law knew me not ... Jer 2:8 8610
and the Libyans, that *h* the shield ... Jer 46:9 8610
and the Lydians, that *h* and bend ... Jer 46:9 8610
And all that *h* the oar, the ... Eze 27:29 8610
h me, and see ... Lk 24:39 *5584*
taste not; *h* not ... Col 2:21 *2345*

HANDLED {3}
to be furbished, that it may be *h* ... Eze 21:11 8610,3709
and sent him away shamefully *h* ... Mk 12:4 *821*
looked upon, and our hands have *h* ... 1Jn 1:1 *5584*

HANDLES {1}
myrrh, upon the *h* of the lock ... Song 5:5 3709

HANDLETH {3}
He that *h* a matter wisely shall ... Prov 16:20 5921
him that *h* the sickle in the time ... Jer 50:16 8610
shall he stand that *h* the bow ... Amos 2:15 8610

HANDLING {2}
and shields, all of them *h* swords ... Eze 38:4 8610
nor *h* the word of God deceitfully ... 2Cor 4:2 *1389*

HANDMAID {45}
and she had an *h*, an Egyptian ... Gen 16:1 8198
Hagar the Egyptian, Sarah's *h* ... Gen 25:12 8198
Leah Zilpah his maid for an *h* ... Gen 29:24 8198
Bilhah his *h* to be her maid ... Gen 29:29 8198
she gave him Bilhah her *h* to wife ... Gen 30:4 8198
And the sons of Bilhah, Rachel's *h* ... Gen 35:25 8198
And the sons of Zilpah, Leah's *h* ... Gen 35:26 8198
ass may rest, and the son of thy *h* ... Ex 23:12 519
and wine also for me, and for thy *h* ... Judg 19:19 519
hast spoken friendly unto thine *h* ... Ruth 2:13 8198
she answered, I am Ruth thine *h* ... Ruth 3:9 519
therefore thy skirt over thine *h* ... Ruth 3:9 519
look on the affliction of thine *h* ... 1Sa 1:11 519
me, and not forget thine *h* ... 1Sa 1:11 519
give unto thine *h* a man child ... 1Sa 1:11 519
Count not thine *h* for a daughter ... 1Sa 1:16 519
Let thine *h* find grace in thy ... 1Sa 1:18 8198
and let thine *h*, I pray thee ... 1Sa 25:24 519
and hear the words of thine *h* ... 1Sa 25:24 519
but I thine *h* saw not the young ... 1Sa 25:25 519
thine *h* hath brought unto my lord ... 1Sa 25:27 8198
forgive the trespass of thine *h* ... 1Sa 25:28 519
my lord, then remember thine *h* ... 1Sa 25:31 519
let thine *h* be a servant to wash ... 1Sa 25:41 519
thine *h* hath obeyed thy voice, and ... 1Sa 28:21 8198
also unto the voice of thine *h* ... 1Sa 28:22 8198
thy *h* had two sons, and they two ... 2Sa 14:6 8198
family is risen against thine *h* ... 2Sa 14:7 8198
Then the woman said, Let thine *h* ... 2Sa 14:12 8198
thy *h* said, I will now speak unto ... 2Sa 14:15 8198
will perform the request of his *h* ... 2Sa 14:15 519
to deliver his *h* out of the hand ... 2Sa 14:16 519
Then thine *h* said, The word of my ... 2Sa 14:17 8198
words in the mouth of thine *h* ... 2Sa 14:19 8198
him, Hear the words of thine *h* ... 2Sa 20:17 519
lord, O king, swear unto thine *h* ... 1Kin 1:13 519
by the LORD thy God unto thine *h* ... 1Kin 1:17 519
beside me, while thine *h* slept ... 1Kin 3:20 519
Thine *h* hath not any thing in the ... 2Kin 4:2 8198
of God, do not lie unto thine *h* ... 2Kin 4:16 8198
and save the son of thine *h* ... Ps 86:16 519
servant, and the son of thine *h* ... Ps 116:16 519
an *h* that is heir to her mistress ... Prov 30:23 8198
his servant, and every man his *h* ... Jer 34:16 8198
said, Behold the *h* of the Lord ... Lk 1:38 *1399*

HANDMAIDEN {1}
regarded the low estate of his *h* ... Lk 1:48 *1399*

HANDMAIDENS {3}
Then the *h* came near, they and ... Gen 33:6 8198
I be not like unto one of thine *h* ... Ruth 2:13 8198
on my *h* I will pour out in those ... Acts 2:18 *1399*

HANDMAIDS {8}
and unto Rachel, and unto the two *h* ... Gen 33:1 8198
And he put the *h* and their children ... Gen 33:2 8198
the eyes of the *h* of his servants ... 2Sa 6:20 519
of the LORD for servants and *h* ... Is 14:2 8198
and caused the servants and the *h* ... Jer 34:11 8198
subjection for servants and for *h* ... Jer 34:11 8198
be unto you for servants and for *h* ... Jer 34:16 8198
upon the *h* in those days will I ... Joel 2:29 8198

HANDS {461}
our work and toil of our *h* ... Gen 5:29 3027
and submit thyself under her *h* ... Gen 16:9 3027
innocency of my *h* have I done ... Gen 20:5 3709
two bracelets for her *h* of ten ... Gen 24:22 3027
and bracelets upon his sister's *h* ... Gen 24:30 3027
face, and the bracelets upon her *h* ... Gen 24:47 3027
the kids of the goats upon his *h* ... Gen 27:16 3027
but the *h* are the *h* of Esau ... Gen 27:22 3027
him not, because his *h* were hairy ... Gen 27:23 3027
as his brother Esau's *h* ... Gen 27:23 3027
affliction and the labour of my *h* ... Gen 31:42 3709
he delivered him out of their *h* ... Gen 37:21 3027
he might rid him out of their *h* ... Gen 37:22 3027
bought him of the *h* of the ... Gen 39:1 3027
brought down in our *h* to buy food ... Gen 43:22 3027
head, guiding his *h* wittingly ... Gen 48:14 3027
the arms of his *h* were made ... Gen 49:24 3027
the *h* of the mighty God of Jacob ... Gen 49:24 3027

spread abroad my *h* unto the LORD........ Ex 9:29 3709
spread abroad his *h* unto the LORD........ Ex 9:33 3709
which thy *h* have established........ Ex 15:17 3027
But Moses' *h* were heavy........ Ex 17:12 3027
and Aaron and Hur stayed up his *h*........ Ex 17:12 3027
his *h* were steady until the going........ Ex 17:12 3027
his sons shall put their *h* upon........ Ex 29:10 3027
their *h* upon the head of the ram........ Ex 29:15 3027
their *h* upon the head of the ram........ Ex 29:19 3027
shalt put all in the *h* of Aaron........ Ex 29:24 3709
and in the *h* of his sons........ Ex 29:24 3027
shalt receive them of their *h*........ Ex 29:25 3027
and his sons shall wash their *h*........ Ex 30:19 3027
So they shall wash their *h*........ Ex 30:21 3027
he cast the tables out of his *h*........ Ex 32:19 3027
hearted did spin with their *h*........ Ex 35:25 3027
Aaron and his sons washed their *h*........ Ex 40:31 3027
h upon the head of the bullock........ Lev 4:15 3027
His own *h* shall bring the........ Lev 7:30 3027
his sons laid their *h* upon the........ Lev 8:14 3027
his sons laid their *h* upon the........ Lev 8:18 3027
his sons laid their *h* upon the........ Lev 8:22 3027
upon the thumbs of their right *h*........ Lev 8:24 3027
And he put all upon Aaron's *h*........ Lev 8:27 3709
and upon his sons' *h*........ Lev 8:27 3709
Moses took them from off their *h*........ Lev 8:28 3709
and hath not rinsed his *h* in water........ Lev 15:11 3027
his *h* full of sweet incense........ Lev 16:12 2651
Aaron shall lay both his *h* upon........ Lev 16:21 3027
him lay their *h* upon his head........ Lev 24:14 3027
the offering of memorial in her *h*........ Num 5:18 3709
them upon the *h* of the Nazarite........ Num 6:19 3709
put their *h* upon the Levites........ Num 8:10 3027
the Levites shall lay their *h*........ Num 8:12 3027
and he smote his *h* together........ Num 24:10 3709
And he laid his *h* upon him........ Num 27:23 3027
the fruit of the land in their *h*........ Deut 1:25 3027
God delivered into our *h* Og also........ Deut 3:3 3027
serve gods, the work of men's *h*........ Deut 4:28 3027
of the covenant were in my two *h*........ Deut 9:15 3027
and cast them out of my two *h*........ Deut 9:17 3027
that thou puttest thine *h* unto........ Deut 12:18 3027
and in all the works of thine *h*........ Deut 16:15 3027
The *h* of the witnesses shall be........ Deut 17:7 3027
afterward the *h* of all the people........ Deut 17:7 3027
hath delivered it into thine *h*........ Deut 20:13 3027
shall wash their *h* over the........ Deut 21:6 3027
Our *h* have not shed this blood,........ Deut 21:7 3027
hath delivered them into thine *h*........ Deut 21:10 3027
thee in all the work of thine *h*........ Deut 24:19 3027
LORD, the work of the *h* of the........ Deut 27:15 3027
anger through the work of your *h*........ Deut 31:29 3027
let his *h* be sufficient for him........ Deut 33:7 3027
and accept the work of his *h*........ Deut 33:11 3027
for Moses had laid his *h* upon him........ Deut 34:9 3027
delivered into our *h* all the land........ Josh 2:24 3027
he delivered them into the *h* of........ Judg 2:14 3027
he sold them into the *h* of their........ Judg 2:14 3027
us into the *h* of the Midianites........ Judg 6:13 3709
give the Midianites into their *h*........ Judg 7:2 3027
afterward shall thine *h* be........ Judg 7:11 3027
the pitchers that were in their *h*........ Judg 7:19 3027
and held the lamps in their left *h*........ Judg 7:20 3027
in their right *h* to blow withal........ Judg 7:20 3027
into your *h* the princes of Midian........ Judg 8:3 3027
Are the *h* of Zebah and Zalmunna........ Judg 8:6 3709
Are the *h* of Zebah and Zalmunna........ Judg 8:15 3709
h of all their enemies on every........ Judg 8:34 3027
to the deserving of his *h*........ Judg 9:16 3027
into the *h* of the Philistines........ Judg 10:7 3027
into the *h* of the children of........ Judg 10:7 3027
the children of Ammon into mine *h*........ Judg 11:30 3027
LORD delivered them into his *h*........ Judg 11:32 3027
delivered me not out of their *h*........ Judg 12:2 3027
me not, I put my life in my *h*........ Judg 12:3 3709
and a meat offering at our *h*........ Judg 13:23 3027
And he took thereof in his *h*........ Judg 14:9 3709
his bands loosed from off his *h*........ Judg 15:14 3027
delivered into our *h* our enemy........ Judg 16:24 3027
for God hath given it into your *h*........ Judg 18:10 3027
her *h* were upon the threshold........ Judg 19:27 3027
both the palms of his *h* were cut........ 1Sa 5:4 3027
out of the *h* of the Philistines........ 1Sa 7:14 3027
thou shalt receive of their *h*........ 1Sa 10:4 3027
of Israel by the *h* of messengers........ 1Sa 11:7 3027
And Jonathan climbed up upon his *h*........ 1Sa 14:13 3027
the *h* of them that spoiled them........ 1Sa 14:48 3027
and he will give you into our *h*........ 1Sa 17:47 3027
and feigned himself mad in their *h*........ 1Sa 21:13 3027
me into the *h* of my master........ 1Sa 30:15 3027
now let your *h* be strengthened........ 2Sa 2:7 3027
Thy *h* were not bound, nor thy........ 2Sa 3:34 3027
his *h* were feeble, and all the........ 2Sa 4:1 3027
slew them, and cut off their *h*........ 2Sa 4:12 3027
then shall the *h* of all that are........ 2Sa 16:21 3027
them into the *h* of the Gibeonites........ 2Sa 21:9 3027
of my *h* hath he recompensed me........ 2Sa 22:21 3027
He teacheth my *h* to war........ 2Sa 22:35 3027
they cannot be taken with *h*........ 2Sa 23:6 3027
spread forth his *h* toward heaven........ 1Kin 8:22 3709
spread forth his *h* toward this........ 1Kin 8:38 3709
with his *h* spread up to heaven........ 1Kin 8:54 3709
committed them unto the *h* of the........ 1Kin 14:27 3027
to anger with the work of his *h*........ 1Kin 16:7 3027
poured water on the *h* of Elijah........ 2Kin 3:11 3027
his eyes, and his *h* upon his *h*........ 2Kin 4:34 3709
at his *h* that which he brought........ 2Kin 5:20 3027
And Joram turned his *h*, and fled,........ 2Kin 9:23 3027

the feet, and the palms of her *h*........ 2Kin 9:35 3027
I have brought into your *h* escape........ 2Kin 10:24 3027
and they clapped their *h*, and said,........ 2Kin 11:12 3709
And they laid *h* on her........ 2Kin 11:16 3027
into the *h* of them that did the........ 2Kin 12:11 3027
put his *h* upon the king's *h*........ 2Kin 13:16 3027
no gods, but the work of men's *h*........ 2Kin 19:18 3027
with all the works of their *h*........ 2Kin 22:17 3027
there is no wrong in mine *h*........ 1Chr 12:17 3709
of Asaph under the *h* of Asaph........ 1Chr 25:2 3027
under the *h* of their father........ 1Chr 25:3 3027
All these were under the *h* of........ 1Chr 25:6 3027
to be made by the *h* of artificers........ 1Chr 29:5 3027
who hath with his *h* fulfilled........ 2Chr 6:4 3027
of Israel, and spread forth his *h*........ 2Chr 6:12 3709
spread forth his *h* toward heaven........ 2Chr 6:13 3709
spread forth his *h* in this house........ 2Chr 6:29 3709
by the *h* of his servants ships........ 2Chr 8:18 3027
committed them to the *h* of the........ 2Chr 12:10 3027
and let not your *h* be weak........ 2Chr 15:7 3027
So they laid *h* on her........ 2Chr 23:15 3027
and they laid their *h* upon them........ 2Chr 29:23 3027
were the work of the *h* of man........ 2Chr 32:19 3027
with all the works of their *h*........ 2Chr 34:25 3027
sprinkled the blood from their *h*........ 2Chr 35:11 3027
their *h* with vessels of silver........ Ezr 1:6 3027
the *h* of the people of Judah........ Ezr 4:4 3027
fast on, and prospereth in their *h*........ Ezr 5:8 3028
to strengthen their *h* in the work........ Ezr 6:22 3027
spread out my *h* unto the LORD my........ Ezr 9:5 3709
they gave their *h* that they would........ Ezr 10:19 3027
their *h* for this good work........ Neh 2:18 3027
one of his *h* wrought in the work........ Neh 4:17 3027
Their *h* shall be weakened from........ Neh 6:9 3027
therefore, O God, strengthen my *h*........ Neh 6:9 3027
Amen, with lifting up their *h*........ Neh 8:6 3027
and gavest them into their *h*........ Neh 9:24 3027
do so again, I will lay *h* on you........ Neh 13:21 3027
scorn to lay *h* on Mordecai alone........ Est 3:6 3027
talents of silver to the *h* of........ Est 3:9 3027
they laid not their *h* on the prey........ Est 9:16 3027
hast blessed the work of his *h*........ Job 1:10 3027
thou hast strengthened the weak *h*........ Job 4:3 3027
so that their *h* cannot perform........ Job 5:12 3027
he woundeth, and his *h* make whole........ Job 5:18 3027
and make my *h* never so clean........ Job 9:30 3709
despise the work of thine *h*........ Job 10:3 3709
Thine *h* have made me and fashioned........ Job 10:8 3027
and stretch out thine *h* toward him........ Job 11:13 3709
a desire to the work of thine *h*........ Job 14:15 3027
me over into the *h* of the wicked........ Job 16:11 3027
Not for any injustice in mine *h*........ Job 16:17 3709
is he that will strike *h* with me........ Job 17:3 3027
hath clean *h* shall be stronger........ Job 17:9 3027
his *h* shall restore their goods........ Job 20:10 3027
by the pureness of thine *h*........ Job 22:30 3709
Men shall clap their *h* at him........ Job 27:23 3709
the strength of their *h* profit me........ Job 30:2 3027
any blot hath cleaved to mine *h*........ Job 31:7 3709
they all are the work of his *h*........ Job 34:19 3027
sin, he clappeth his *h* among us........ Job 34:37
if there be iniquity in my *h*........ Ps 7:3 3709
dominion over the works of thy *h*........ Ps 8:6 3027
snared in the work of his own *h*........ Ps 9:16 3709
of my *h* hath he recompensed me........ Ps 18:20 3027
cleanness of my *h* in his eyesight........ Ps 18:24 3027
He teacheth my *h* to war, so that........ Ps 18:34 3027
they pierced my *h* and my feet........ Ps 22:16 3027
He that hath clean *h*, and a pure........ Ps 24:4 3709
I will wash mine *h* in innocency........ Ps 26:6 3709
In whose *h* is mischief, and their........ Ps 26:10 3027
when I lift up my *h* toward thy........ Ps 28:2 3027
them after the work of their *h*........ Ps 28:4 3027
LORD, nor the operation of his *h*........ Ps 28:5 3027
out our *h* to a strange god........ Ps 44:20 3709
O clap your *h*, all ye people........ Ps 47:1 3709
He hath put forth his *h* against........ Ps 55:20 3027
violence of your *h* in the earth........ Ps 58:2 3027
I will lift up my *h* in thy name........ Ps 63:4 3709
soon stretch out her *h* unto God........ Ps 68:31 3027
vain, and washed my *h* in innocency........ Ps 73:13 3709
men of might have found their *h*........ Ps 76:5 3027
them by the skilfulness of his *h*........ Ps 78:72 3709
his *h* were delivered from the........ Ps 81:6 3709
have stretched out my *h* unto thee........ Ps 88:9 3709
thou the work of our *h* upon us........ Ps 90:17 3027
the work of our *h* establish thou........ Ps 90:17 3027
shall bear thee up in their *h*........ Ps 91:12 3709
triumph in the works of thy *h*........ Ps 92:4 3027
his *h* formed the dry land........ Ps 95:5 3027
Let the floods clap their *h*........ Ps 98:8 3709
the heavens are the work of thy *h*........ Ps 102:25 3027
The works of his *h* are verity........ Ps 111:7 3027
and gold, the work of men's *h*........ Ps 115:4 3027
They have *h*, but they handle not........ Ps 115:7 3027
My *h* also will I lift up unto thy........ Ps 119:48 3709
Thy *h* have made me and fashioned........ Ps 119:73 3027
put forth their *h* unto iniquity........ Ps 125:3 3027
shalt eat the labour of thine *h*........ Ps 128:2 3709
Lift up your *h* in the sanctuary,........ Ps 134:2 3027
and gold, the work of men's *h*........ Ps 135:15 3027
not the works of thine own *h*........ Ps 138:8 3027
O LORD, from the *h* of the wicked........ Ps 140:4 3027
the lifting up of my *h* as the........ Ps 141:2 3709
I muse on the work of thy *h*........ Ps 143:5 3027
I stretch forth my *h* unto thee........ Ps 143:6 3027
which teacheth my *h* to war........ Ps 144:1 3027
little folding of the *h* to sleep........ Prov 6:10 3027

h that shed innocent blood,........ Prov 6:17 3027
the recompence of a man's *h* shall........ Prov 12:14 3027
plucketh it down with her *h*........ Prov 14:1 3027
void of understanding striketh *h*........ Prov 17:18 3709
for his *h* refuse to labour........ Prov 21:25 3027
thou one of them that strike *h*........ Prov 22:26 3709
little folding of the *h* to sleep........ Prov 24:33 3027
The spider taketh hold with her *h*........ Prov 30:28 3027
and worketh willingly with her *h*........ Prov 31:13 3709
with the fruit of her *h* she........ Prov 31:16 3709
She layeth her *h* to the spindle........ Prov 31:19 3027
and her *h* hold the distaff........ Prov 31:19 3709
reacheth forth her *h* to the needy........ Prov 31:20 3027
Give her of the fruit of her *h*........ Prov 31:31 3027
the works that my *h* had wrought........ Eccl 2:11 3027
The fool foldeth his *h* together........ Eccl 4:5 3027
than both the *h* full with travail........ Eccl 4:6 2651
and destroy the work of thine *h*........ Eccl 5:6 3027
snares and nets, and her *h* as bands........ Eccl 7:26 3027
through idleness of the *h* the........ Eccl 10:18 3027
my *h* dropped with myrrh, and my........ Song 5:5 3027
His *h* are as gold rings set with........ Song 5:14 3027
the work of the *h* of a cunning........ Song 7:1 3027
And when ye spread forth your *h*........ Is 1:15 3709
your *h* are full of blood........ Is 1:15 3027
worship the work of their own *h*........ Is 2:8 3027
of his *h* shall be given him........ Is 3:11 3027
consider the operation of his *h*........ Is 5:12 3027
Therefore shall all *h* be faint........ Is 13:7 3027
to the altars, the work of his *h*........ Is 17:8 3027
and Assyria the work of my *h*........ Is 19:25 3027
forth his *h* in the midst of them........ Is 25:11 3027
spreadeth forth his *h* to swim........ Is 25:11
with the spoils of their *h*........ Is 25:11 3027
his children, the work of mine *h*........ Is 29:23 3027
which your own *h* have made unto........ Is 31:7 3027
that shaketh his *h* from holding........ Is 33:15 3709
Strengthen ye the weak *h*, and........ Is 35:3 3027
no gods, but the work of men's *h*........ Is 37:19 3027
or thy work, He hath no *h*........ Is 45:9 3027
the work of my *h* command ye me........ Is 45:11 3027
I, even my *h*, have stretched out........ Is 45:12 3027
thee upon the palms of my *h*........ Is 49:16 3709
of the field shall clap their *h*........ Is 55:12 3709
For your *h* are defiled with blood........ Is 59:3 3709
the act of violence is in their *h*........ Is 59:6 3709
of my planting, the work of my *h*........ Is 60:21 3027
I have spread out my *h* all the........ Is 65:2 3027
long enjoy the work of their *h*........ Is 65:22 3027
the works of their own *h*........ Jer 1:16 3027
him, and thine *h* upon thine head........ Jer 2:37 3027
herself, that spreadeth her *h*........ Jer 4:31 3709
our *h* wax feeble........ Jer 6:24 3027
the work of the *h* of the workman........ Jer 10:3 3027
and of the *h* of the founder........ Jer 10:9 3027
by the *h* of them that seek their........ Jer 19:7 3027
weapons of war that are in your *h*........ Jer 21:4 3027
also the *h* of evildoers, that........ Jer 23:14 3027
to anger with the works of your *h*........ Jer 25:6 3027
works of your *h* to your own hurt........ Jer 25:7 3027
to the works of their own *h*........ Jer 25:14 3027
every man with his *h* on his loins........ Jer 30:6 3027
to anger with the work of their *h*........ Jer 32:30 3027
the *h* of him that telleth them........ Jer 33:13 3027
for thus he weakeneth the *h* of........ Jer 38:4 3027
the *h* of all the people, in........ Jer 38:4 3027
wrath with the works of your *h*........ Jer 44:8 3027
children for feebleness of *h*........ Jer 47:3 3027
upon all the *h* shall be cuttings,........ Jer 48:37 3027
of them, and his *h* waxed feeble........ Jer 50:43 3027
hath delivered me into their *h*........ Lam 1:14 3027
Zion spreadeth forth her *h*........ Lam 1:17 3027
that pass by clap their *h* at thee........ Lam 2:15 3709
lift up thy *h* toward him for the........ Lam 2:19 3709
our *h* unto God in the heavens........ Lam 3:41 3709
according to the work of their *h*........ Lam 3:64 3027
the work of the *h* of the potter........ Lam 4:2 3027
a moment, and no *h* stayed on her........ Lam 4:6 3027
The *h* of the pitiful women have........ Lam 4:10 3027
they had the *h* of a man under........ Eze 1:8 3027
All *h* shall be feeble, and all........ Eze 7:17 3027
I will give it into the *h* of the........ Eze 7:21 3027
the *h* of the people of the land........ Eze 7:27 3027
put it into the *h* of him that was........ Eze 10:7 2651
body, and their backs, and their *h*........ Eze 10:12 3027
the likeness of the *h* of a man........ Eze 10:21 3027
you into the *h* of strangers........ Eze 11:9 3027
strengthened the *h* of the wicked........ Eze 13:22 3027
and I put bracelets upon thy *h*........ Eze 16:11 3027
all *h* shall be feeble, and every........ Eze 21:7 3027
and smite thine *h* together........ Eze 21:14 3709
I will also smite mine *h* together........ Eze 21:17 3709
endure, or can thine *h* be strong........ Eze 22:14 3027
adultery, and blood is in their *h*........ Eze 23:37 3027
which put bracelets upon their *h*........ Eze 23:42 3027
and blood is in their *h*........ Eze 23:45 3027
Because thou hast clapped thine *h*........ Eze 25:6 3027
a stone was cut out without *h*........ Dan 2:34 3028
cut out of the mountain without *h*........ Dan 2:45 3028
shall deliver you out of my *h*........ Dan 3:15 3028
knees and upon the palms of my *h*........ Dan 10:10 3027
say any more to the work of our *h*........ Hos 14:3 3027
nor have laid *h* on their........ Obad 13
the violence that is in their *h*........ Jonah 3:8 3709
more worship the work of thine *h*........ Mic 5:13 3027
may do evil with both *h* earnestly........ Mic 7:3 3709
thee shall clap the *h* over thee........ Nah 3:19 3709
voice, and lifted up his *h* on high........ Hab 3:10 3027

to Zion, Let not thine h be slack Zeph 3:16 3027
and upon all the labour of the h Hag 1:11 3709
and so is every work of their h Hag 2:14 3027
hail in all the labours of your h Hag 2:17 3027
The h of Zerubbabel have laid the Zec 4:9 3027
his h shall also finish it Zec 4:9 3027
Let your h be strong, ye that Zec 8:9 3027
not, but let your h be strong Zec 8:13 3027
What are these wounds in thine h Zec 13:6 3027
in their h they shall bear thee Mt 4:6 5495
not their h when they eat bread Mt 15:2 5495
unwashen h defileth not a man Mt 15:20 5495
be betrayed into the h of men Mt 17:22 5495
rather than having two h or two Mt 18:8 5495
and he laid h on him, and took him Mt 18:28 2902
that he should put his h on them Mt 19:13 5495
And he laid his h on them, and Mt 19:15 5495
when they sought to lay h on him Mt 21:46 2902
is betrayed into the h of sinners Mt 26:45 5495
laid h on Jesus, and took him Mt 26:50 5495
him with the palms of their h Mt 26:67
washed his h before the multitude Mt 27:24 5495
thee, come and lay thy h on her Mk 5:23 5495
mighty works are wrought by his h Mk 6:2 5495
laid his h upon a few sick folk Mk 6:5 5495
that is to say, with unwashen, h Mk 7:2 5495
except they wash their h oft Mk 7:3 5495
but eat bread with unwashen h Mk 7:5 5495
put his h upon him, he asked him Mk 8:23 5495
he put his h again upon his eyes Mk 8:25 5495
is delivered into the h of men Mk 9:31 5495
than having two h to go into hell Mk 9:43 5495
put his h upon them, and blessed Mk 10:16 5495
is betrayed into the h of sinners Mk 14:41 5495
And they laid their h on him Mk 14:46 5495
this temple that is made with h Mk 14:58 5499
will build another made without h Mk 14:58 886
him with the palms of their h Mk 14:65
they shall lay h on the sick Mk 16:18 5495
in their h they shall bear thee Lk 4:11 5495
he laid his h on every one of Lk 4:40 5495
did eat, rubbing them in their h Lk 6:1 5495
be delivered into the h of men Lk 9:44 5495
And he laid his h on her Lk 13:13 5495
same hour sought to lay h on him Lk 20:19 5495
they shall lay their h on you Lk 21:12 5495
stretched forth no h against me Lk 22:53 5495
into thy h I commend my spirit Lk 23:46 5495
into the h of sinful men, and be Lk 24:7 5495
Behold my h and my feet, that it Lk 24:39 5495
thus spoken, he shewed them his h Lk 24:40 5495
to Bethany, and he lifted up his h Lk 24:50 5495
but no man laid h on him, because Jn 7:30 5495
but no man laid h on him Jn 7:44 5495
and no man laid h on him Jn 8:20 4084
had given all things into his h Jn 13:3 5495
not my feet only, but also my h Jn 13:9 5495
and they smote him with their h Jn 19:3 4475
said, he shewed unto them his h Jn 20:20 5495
in his h the print of the nails Jn 20:25 5495
hither thy finger, and behold my h Jn 20:27 5495
thou shalt stretch forth thy h Jn 21:18 5495
by wicked h have crucified and Acts 2:23 5495
And they laid h on them, and put Acts 4:3 5495
by the h of the apostles were Acts 5:12 5495
laid their h on the apostles, and Acts 5:18 5495
prayed, they laid their h on them Acts 6:6 5495
in the works of their own h Acts 7:41 5495
not in temples made with h Acts 7:48 5499
Then laid they their h on them Acts 8:17 5495
h the Holy Ghost was given Acts 8:18 5495
power, that on whomsoever I lay h Acts 8:19 5495
and putting his h on him said Acts 9:17 5495
the elders by the h of Barnabas Acts 11:30 5495
h to vex certain of the church Acts 12:1 5495
And his chains fell off from his h Acts 12:7 5495
prayed, and laid their h on them Acts 13:3 5495
and wonders to be done by their h Acts 14:3 5495
not in temples made with h Acts 17:24 5499
is worshipped with men's h Acts 17:25 5495
Paul had laid his h upon them Acts 19:6 5495
special miracles by the h of Paul Acts 19:11 5495
be no gods, which are made with h Acts 19:26 5495
that these h have ministered unto Acts 20:34 5495
Paul's girdle, and bound his own h Acts 21:11 5495
him into the h of the Gentiles Acts 21:11 5495
all the people, and laid h on him, Acts 21:27 5495
took him away out of our h Acts 24:7 5495
own h the tackling of the ship Acts 27:19 849
and prayed, and laid his h on him Acts 28:8 5495
into the h of the Romans Acts 28:17 5495
forth my h unto a disobedient Rom 10:21 5495
And labour, working with our own h 1Cor 4:12 5495
of God, an house not made with h 2Cor 5:1 886
by the wall, and escaped his h 2Cor 11:33 5495
the right h of fellowship Gal 2:9
in the flesh made by h Eph 2:11 5499
working with his h the thing Eph 4:28 5495
the circumcision made without h Col 2:11 886
and to work with your own h 1Th 4:11 5495
every where, lifting up holy h 1Ti 2:8 5495
on of the h of the presbytery 1Ti 4:14 5495
Lay h suddenly on no man, neither 1Ti 5:22 5495
in thee by the putting on of my h 2Ti 1:6 5495
heavens are the works of thine h Heb 1:10 5495
set him over the works of thy h Heb 2:7 5495
of baptisms, and of laying on of h Heb 6:2 5495
tabernacle, not made with h Heb 9:11 5499
into the holy places made with h Heb 9:24 5499
fall into the h of the living God Heb 10:31 5495
lift up the h which hang down Heb 12:12 5495
Cleanse your h, ye sinners Jas 4:8 5495
our h have handled, of the Word 1Jn 1:1 5495
white robes, and palms in their h Rev 7:9 5495
not of the works of their h Rev 9:20 5495
their foreheads, or in their h Rev 20:4 5495

HANDSTAVES {1}
bows and the arrows, and the h Eze 39:9 4731,3027

HANDWRITING {1}
Blotting out the h of ordinances Col 2:14 5498

HANDYWORK {1}
and the firmament sheweth his h Ps 19:1 4639,3027

HANES *(ha'-nees)* {1} See TAHPANES. *A place in Egypt.*
and his ambassadors came to H Is 30:4 2609

HANG {19}
thee, and shall h thee on a tree Gen 40:19 8518
shall h over the backside of the Ex 26:12 5628
it shall h over the sides of the Ex 26:13 5628
thou shalt h it upon four pillars Ex 26:32 5414
thou shalt h up the vail under Ex 26:33 5414
h up the hanging at the court Ex 40:8 5414
h them up before the LORD against Num 25:4 3363
to death, and thou h him on a tree Deut 21:22 8518
thy life shall h in doubt before Deut 28:66 8511
we will h them up unto the LORD 2Sa 21:6 3363
to speak unto the king to h Est 6:4 8518
Then the king said, H him thereon Est 7:9 8518
whereon there h a thousand Song 4:4 8518
they shall h upon him all the Is 22:24 8518
the virgins of Jerusalem h down Lam 2:10 3381
pin of it to h any vessel thereon Eze 15:3 8518
two commandments h all the law Mt 22:40 2910
the venomous beast h on his hand Acts 28:4 2910
lift up the hands which h down Heb 12:12 3935

HANGED {30}
But he h the chief baker Gen 40:22 8518
unto mine office, and him he h Gen 41:13 8518
(for he that is h is accursed of Deut 21:23 8518
the king of Ai he h on a tree Josh 8:29 8518
them, and h them on five trees Josh 10:26 8518
h them up over the pool in Hebron 2Sa 4:12 8518
h himself, and died, and was buried 2Sa 17:23 2614
Behold, I saw Absalom h in an oak 2Sa 18:10 8518
they h them in the hill before 2Sa 21:9 3363
where the Philistines had h them 2Sa 21:12 8511
the bones of them that were h 2Sa 21:13 3363
set up, let him be h thereon Ezr 6:11 4223
they were both h on a tree Est 2:23 8518
that Mordecai may be h thereon Est 5:14 8518
So they h Haman on the gallows Est 7:10 8518
him they have h upon the gallows, Est 8:7 8518
ten sons be h upon the gallows Est 9:13 8518
and they h Haman's ten sons Est 9:14 8518
sons should be h on the gallows Est 9:25 8518
We h our harps upon the willows Ps 137:2 8518
Princes are h up by their hand Lam 5:12 8518
they h the shield and helmet in Eze 27:10 8518
they h their shields upon thy Eze 27:11 8518
a millstone were h about his neck Mt 18:6 2910
and departed, and went and h himself Mt 27:5 519
a millstone were h about his neck Mk 9:42 4029
a millstone were h about his neck Lk 17:2 4029
which were h railed on him Lk 23:39 2910
whom ye slew and h on a tree Acts 5:30 2910
whom they slew and h on a tree Acts 10:39 2910

HANGETH {2}
and h the earth upon nothing Job 26:7 8518
is every one that h on a tree Gal 3:13 2910

HANGING {18}
thou shalt make an h for the door Ex 26:36 4539
thou shalt make for the h five Ex 26:37 4539
shall be an h of twenty cubits Ex 27:16 4539
the h for the door at the Ex 35:15 4539
the h for the door of the court, Ex 35:17 4539
he made an h for the tabernacle Ex 36:37 4539
the h for the gate of the court Ex 38:18 4539
the h for the tabernacle door, Ex 39:38 4539
the h for the court gate, his Ex 39:40 4539
put the h of the door to the Ex 40:5 4539
hang up the h at the court gate Ex 40:8 4539
he set up the h at the door of Ex 40:28 4539
set up the h of the court gate Ex 40:33 4539
the h for the door of the Num 3:25 4539
wherewith they minister, and the h Num 3:31 4539
the h for the door of the Num 4:25 4539
the h for the door of the gate of Num 4:26 4539
they were h upon the trees until Josh 10:26 8518

HANGINGS {18}
be h for the court of fine twined Ex 27:9 7050
be h of an hundred cubits long Ex 27:11 7050
side shall be h of fifty cubits Ex 27:12 7050
The h of one side of the gate Ex 27:14 7050
side shall be h fifteen cubits Ex 27:15 7050
The h of the court, his pillars, Ex 35:17 7050
the h of the court were of fine Ex 38:9 7050
side the h were an hundred cubits Ex 38:11
west side were h of fifty cubits Ex 38:12 7050
The h of the one side of the gate Ex 38:14 7050
hand, were h of fifteen cubits Ex 38:15 7050
All the h of the court round Ex 38:16 7050
answerable to the h of the court Ex 38:18 7050
The h of the court, his pillars, Ex 39:40 7050
the h of the court, and the Num 3:26 7050
the h of the court, and the Num 4:26 7050
the women wove h for the grove 2Kin 23:7 1004
were white, green, and blue, h Est 1:6

HANIEL *(ha'-ne-el)* {1} See HANNIEL. *A son of Ulla.*
Arah, and H, and Rezia 1Chr 7:39 2592

HANNAH *(han'-nah)* {13} *Mother of Samuel.*
the name of the one was H 1Sa 1:2 2584
children, but H had no children 1Sa 1:2 2584
But unto H he gave a worthy 1Sa 1:5 2584
for he loved H 1Sa 1:5 2584
Elkanah her husband to her, H 1Sa 1:8 2584
So H rose up after they had eaten 1Sa 1:9 2584
Now H, she spake in her heart 1Sa 1:13 2584
H answered and said, No, my lord, 1Sa 1:15 2584
and Elkanah knew H his wife 1Sa 1:19 2584
come about after H had conceived 1Sa 1:20 2584
But H went not up 1Sa 1:22 2584
H prayed, and said, My heart 1Sa 2:1 2584
And the LORD visited H, so that 1Sa 2:21 2584

HANNATHON *(han'-na-thon)* {1} *A city in Zebulun.*
it on the north side to H Josh 19:14 2615

HANNIEL *(han'-ne-el)* {1} See HANIEL. *A prince of Manasseh.*
of Manasseh, H the son of Ephod Num 34:23 2592

HANOCH *(ha'-nok)* {5} See HANOCHITES, HENOCH.
1. A son of Midian.
Ephah, and Epher, and H, and Abidah, Gen 25:4 2585
2. A son of Reuben.
H, and Phallu, and Hezron, and Carmi Gen 46:9 2585
H, and Pallu, Hezron, and Carmi Ex 6:14 2585
H, of whom cometh the family of Num 26:5 2585
the firstborn of Israel were, H 1Chr 5:3 2585

HANOCHITES *(ha'-nok-ites)* {1} *Descendants of Hanoch 2.*
whom cometh the family of the H Num 26:5 2599

HANUN *(ha'-nun)* {11}
1. A king of Ammon.
H his son reigned in his stead 2Sa 10:1 2586
kindness unto H the son of Nahash 2Sa 10:2 2586
of Ammon said unto H their lord 2Sa 10:3 2586
Wherefore H took David's servants 2Sa 10:4 2586
kindness unto H the son of Nahash 1Chr 19:2 2586
of the children of Ammon to H 1Chr 19:2 2586
the children of Ammon said to H 1Chr 19:3 2586
Wherefore H took David's servants 1Chr 19:4 2586
themselves odious to David, H 1Chr 19:6 2586
2. A son of Zalaph.
H the sixth son of Zalaph, Neh 3:30 2586
3. A rebuilder of Jerusalem's wall.
The valley gate repaired H Neh 3:13 2586

HAP {1}
her h was to light on a part of Ruth 2:3 4745

HAPHRAIM *(haf-ra'-im)* {1} *A city in Issachar.*
And H, and Shihon, and Anaharath, Josh 19:19 2663

HAPLY {6}
if h the people had eaten freely 1Sa 14:30 3863
if h he might find any thing Mk 11:13 686
Lest h, after he hath laid the Lk 14:29 3379
lest h ye be found even to fight Acts 5:39 3379
if h they might feel after him, Acts 17:27 686
Lest h if they of Macedonia come 2Cor 9:4 3381

HAPPEN See APPENDIX.

HAPPENED See APPENDIX.

HAPPENETH {6}
also that one event h to them all Eccl 2:14 7136
As it h to the fool Eccl 2:15 4745
so it h even to me Eccl 2:15 7136
unto whom it h according to the Eccl 8:14 5060
to whom it h according to the Eccl 8:14 5060
but time and chance h to them all Eccl 9:11 7136

HAPPIER {1}
But she is h if she so abide, 1Cor 7:40 3107

HAPPIZZEZ See APHSES.

HAPPY {28}
H am I, for the daughters will Gen 30:13 837
H art thou, O Israel Deut 33:29 835
H are thy men, h are these 1Kin 10:8 835
H are thy men, and h are these 2Chr 9:7 835
h is the man whom God correcteth Job 5:17 835
H is the man that hath his quiver Ps 127:5 835
h shalt thou be, and it shall be Ps 128:2 835
h shall he be, that rewardeth Ps 137:8 835
H shall he be, that taketh and Ps 137:9 835
H is that people, that is in such Ps 144:15 835
h is that people, whose God is Ps 144:15 835
H is he that hath the God of Ps 146:5 835
H is the man that findeth wisdom, Prov 3:13 835
h is every one that retaineth her Prov 3:18 833
hath mercy on the poor, h is he Prov 14:21 835
trusteth in the LORD, h is he Prov 16:20 835
H is the man that feareth alway Prov 28:14 835
he that keepeth the law, h is he Prov 29:18 835
wherefore are all they h that Jer 12:1 7951
And now we call the proud h Mal 3:15 833
things, h are ye if ye do them Jn 13:17 3107
I think myself h, king Agrippa, Acts 26:2 3107
H is he that condemneth not Rom 14:22 3107
we count them h which endure Jas 5:11 3106
for righteousness' sake, h are ye 1Pet 3:14 3107
for the name of Christ, h are ye 1Pet 4:14 3107

HARA *(ha'-rah)* {1} *An Assyrian province.*
them unto Halah, and Habor, and *H* 1Chr 5:26 2024

HARADAH *(har'-a-dah)* {2} *A Hebrew encampment in the wilderness.*
mount Shapher, and encamped in *H* .... Num 33:24 2732
And they removed from *H*, and .... Num 33:25 2732

HARAN *(ha'-ran)* {19} See BETH-HARAN, CHARRAN.
1. A son of Terah.
and begat Abram, Nahor, and *H* .... Gen 11:26 2309
Terah begat Abram, Nahor, and *H* .... Gen 11:27 2309
and *H* begat Lot .... Gen 11:27 2309
H died before his father Terah in .... Gen 11:28 2309
wife, Milcah, the daughter of *H* .... Gen 11:29 2309
and Lot the son of *H* his son's son .... Gen 11:31 2309
2. A Levite.
Shelomith, and Haziel, and *H* 1Chr 23:9 2039
3. A son of Caleb.
Ephah, Caleb's concubine, bare *H* 1Chr 2:46 2771
and *H* begat Gazez 1Chr 2:46 2771
4. A city in northern Mesopotamia.
and they came unto *H*, and dwelt .... Gen 11:31 2771
and Terah died in *H* .... Gen 11:32 2771
old when he departed out of *H* .... Gen 12:4 2771
souls that they had gotten in *H* .... Gen 12:5 2771
thou to Laban my brother to *H* .... Gen 27:43 2771
from Beer-sheba, and went toward *H* .... Gen 28:10 2771
And they said, Of *H* are we .... Gen 29:4 2771
as Gozan, and *H*, and Rezeph, and the ... 2Kin 19:12 2771
have destroyed, as Gozan, and *H* .... Is 37:12 2771
H, and Canneh, and Eden, the .... Eze 27:23 2771

HARARITE *(har'-a-rite)* {5} *Native of the hill country of Judah.*
was Shammah the son of Agee the *H* 2Sa 23:11 2043
Shammah the *H*, Ahiam the son of 2Sa 23:33 2043
Ahiam the son of Sharar the *H* 2Sa 23:33 2043
Jonathan the son of Shage the *H* 1Chr 11:34 2043
Ahiam the son of Sacar the *H* 1Chr 11:35 2043

HARBONA *(har-bo'-nah)* {1} See HARBONAH. *A servant of King Ahasuerus.*
he commanded Mehuman, Biztha, *H* .... Est 1:10 2726

HARBONAH *(har-bo'-nah)* {1} See HARBONA. *Same as Harbona.*
And *H*, one of the chamberlains, ... Est 7:9 2726

HARD {45}
Is any thing too *h* for the LORD .... Gen 18:14 6381
travailed, and she had *h* labour .... Gen 35:16 7185
to pass, when she was in *h* labour .... Gen 35:17 7185
their lives bitter with *h* bondage .... Ex 1:14 7186
the *h* causes they brought unto .... Ex 18:26 7186
he take off *h* by the backbone .... Lev 3:9 5980
the cause that is too *h* for you .... Deut 1:17 7185
It shall not seem *h* unto thee .... Deut 15:18 7185
matter too *h* for thee in judgment .... Deut 17:8 6381
us, and laid upon us *h* bondage .... Deut 26:6 7186
went *h* unto the door of the tower .... Judg 9:52 5066
pursued *h* after them unto Gidom, ... Judg 20:45 1692
even they also followed *h* after 1Sa 14:22 1692
Philistines followed *h* upon Saul 1Sa 31:2 1692
and horsemen followed *h* after him 2Sa 1:6 1692
sons of Zeruiah be too *h* for me 2Sa 3:39 7186
Amnon thought it *h* for him to do 2Sa 13:2 6381
to prove him with *h* questions 1Kin 10:1 2420
h by the palace of Ahab king of 1Kin 21:1 681
said, Thou hast asked a *h* thing 2Kin 2:10 7185
Philistines followed *h* after Saul 1Chr 10:2 5221
in the midst *h* by their buttocks 1Chr 19:4
with *h* questions at Jerusalem 2Chr 9:1 2420
as *h* as a piece of the nether .... Job 41:24 3332
hast shewed thy people *h* things .... Ps 60:3 7186
My soul followeth *h* after thee .... Ps 63:8 1692
Thy wrath lieth *h* upon me .... Ps 88:7 5564
they utter and speak *h* things .... Ps 94:4 6277
but the way of transgressors is *h* .... Prov 13:15 386
from the *h* bondage wherein thou .... Is 14:3 7186
there is nothing too *h* for thee .... Jer 32:17 6381
is there any thing too *h* for me .... Jer 32:27 6381
of an *h* language, but to the .... Eze 3:5 3515
of an *h* language, whose words .... Eze 3:6 3515
dreams, and shewing of *h* sentences .... Dan 5:12 280
rowed *h* to bring it to the land .... Jonah 1:13
knew thee that thou art an *h* man .... Mt 25:24 *4642*
how *h* is it for them that trust .... Mk 10:24 *1422*
this, said, This is an *h* saying .... Jn 6:60 *4642*
it is *h* for thee to kick against .... Acts 9:5 *4642*
house joined *h* to the synagogue .... Acts 18:7 *4927*
it is *h* for thee to kick against .... Acts 26:14 *4642*
h to be uttered, seeing ye are .... Heb 5:11 *1421*
some things *h* to be understood 2Pet 3:16 *1425*
of all their *h* speeches which .... Jude 15 *4642*

HARDEN {12}
but I will *h* his heart, that he .... Ex 4:21 2388
I will *h* Pharaoh's heart, and .... Ex 7:3 7185
I will *h* Pharaoh's heart, that he .... Ex 14:4 2388
I will *h* the hearts of the .... Ex 14:17 2388
thou shalt not *h* thine heart .... Deut 15:7 533
was of the LORD to *h* their hearts .... Josh 11:20 2388
then do ye *h* your hearts, as the 1Sa 6:6 5513
I would *h* myself in sorrow .... Job 6:10 5539
H not your heart, as in the .... Ps 95:8 7185
H not your hearts, as in the .... Heb 3:8 *4645*
h not your hearts, as in the .... Heb 3:15 *4645*
hear his voice, *h* not your hearts .... Heb 4:7 *4645*

HARDENED {33}
he *h* Pharaoh's heart, that he .... Ex 7:13 2388
unto Moses, Pharaoh's heart is *h* .... Ex 7:14 3515
and Pharaoh's heart was *h*, neither .... Ex 7:22 2388
he *h* his heart, and hearkened not .... Ex 8:15 3515
and Pharaoh's heart was *h*, and he .... Ex 8:19 2388
Pharaoh *h* his heart at this time .... Ex 8:32 3513
And the heart of Pharaoh was *h* .... Ex 9:7 3515
the LORD *h* the heart of Pharaoh, ... Ex 9:12 2388
h his heart, he and his servants .... Ex 9:34 3513
And the heart of Pharaoh was *h* .... Ex 9:35 2388
for I have *h* his heart, and the .... Ex 10:1 3513
But the LORD *h* Pharaoh's heart, ... Ex 10:20 2388
But the LORD *h* Pharaoh's heart, ... Ex 10:27 2388
the LORD *h* Pharaoh's heart, so .... Ex 11:10 2388
the LORD *h* the heart of Pharaoh .... Ex 14:8 2388
for the LORD thy God *h* his spirit .... Deut 2:30 7185
and Pharaoh *h* their hearts 1Sa 6:6 3513
but *h* their necks, like to the 2Kin 17:14 7185
h his heart from turning unto the 2Chr 36:13 553
h their necks, and hearkened not .... Neh 9:16 7185
but *h* their necks, and in their .... Neh 9:17 7185
h their neck, and would not hear .... Neh 9:29 7185
who hath *h* himself against him, ... Job 9:4 7185
She is *h* against her young ones, ... Job 39:16 7188
h our heart from thy fear .... Is 63:17 7188
their ear, but *h* their neck .... Jer 7:26 7185
because they have *h* their necks .... Jer 19:15 7185
lifted up, and his mind *h* in pride .... Dan 5:20 8631
for their heart was *h* .... Mk 6:52 *4456*
have ye your heart yet *h* .... Mk 8:17 *4456*
their eyes, and *h* their heart .... Jn 12:40 *4456*
But when divers were *h*, and .... Acts 19:9 *4645*
lest any of you be *h* through the .... Heb 3:13 *4645*

HARDENETH {4}
A wicked man *h* his face .... Prov 21:29 5810
but he that *h* his heart shall .... Prov 28:14 7185
being often reproved *h* his neck .... Prov 29:1 7185
have mercy, and whom he will he *h* .... Rom 9:18 *4645*

HARDER {3}
A brother offended is *h* to be won .... Prov 18:19
made their faces *h* than a rock .... Jer 5:3 2388
As an adamant *h* than flint have I .... Eze 3:9 2389

HARDHEARTED {1}
Israel are impudent and *h* .... Eze 3:7 7186,3820

HARDLY {0}
And when Sarai dealt *h* with her .... Gen 16:6 6031
when Pharaoh would *h* let us go .... Ex 13:15 7185
through it, *h* bestead and hungry .... Is 8:21 7185
That a rich man shall *h* enter .... Mt 19:23 *1423*
How *h* shall they that have riches .... Mk 10:23 *1423*
bruising him *h* departeth from him .... Lk 9:39 *3425*
How *h* shall they that have riches .... Lk 18:24 *1423*
h passing it, came unto a place .... Acts 27:8 *3433*

HARDNESS {7}
When the dust groweth into *h* .... Job 38:38 4165
Moses because of the *h* of your .... Mt 19:8 *4641*
grieved for the *h* of their hearts .... Mk 3:5 *4457*
For the *h* of your heart he wrote .... Mk 10:5 *4641*
h of heart, because they believed .... Mk 16:14 *4641*
But after thy *h* and impenitent .... Rom 2:5 *4643*
Thou therefore endure *h*, as a 2Ti 2:3 *2553*

HARE {2}
And the *h*, because he cheweth the .... Lev 11:6 768
as the camel, and the *h*, and the .... Deut 14:7 768

HAREPH *(ha'-ref)* {1} *A son of Caleb.*
H the father of Beth-gader 1Chr 2:51 2780

HARETH *(ha'-reth)* {1} *Forest land in Judah.*
and came into the forest of *H* 1Sa 22:5 2802

HARHAIAH *(har-ha-i'-ah)* {1} *Father of Uzziel.*
him repaired Uzziel the son of *H* .... Neh 3:8 2736

HARHAS *(har'-has)* {1} See HASRAH. *Grandfather of Shallum.*
the son of Tikvah, the son of *H* 2Kin 22:14 2745

HARHUR *(har'-hur)* {2} *A family in exile.*
of Hakupha, the children of *H* .... Ezr 2:51 2744
of Hakupha, the children of *H* .... Neh 7:53 2744

HARIM *(ha'-rim)* {11}
1. A priest.
The third to *H*, the fourth to 1Chr 24:8 2766
The children of *H*, a thousand and .... Ezr 2:39 2766
And of the sons of *H* .... Ezr 10:21 2766
Malchijah the son of *H*, and Hashub .... Neh 3:11 2766
The children of *H*, a thousand and .... Neh 7:42 2766
Of *H*, Adna, of Meraioth .... Neh 12:15 2766
2. A family in exile.
The children of *H*, three hundred .... Ezr 2:32 2766
The children of *H*, three hundred .... Neh 7:35 2766
3. Married a foreigner in exile.
And of the sons of *H* .... Ezr 10:31 2766
4. An Israelite who renewed the covenant.
H, Meremoth, Obadiah, ... Neh 10:5 2766
5. A family who renewed the covenant.
Malluch, *H*, Baanah .... Neh 10:27 2766

HARIPH *(ha'-rif)* {2} See JORAH.
1. A family of exiles.
The children of *H*, an hundred and .... Neh 7:24 2756
2. A family who renewed the covenant.
H, Anathoth, Nebai, ... Neh 10:19 2756

HARLOT {40}
deal with our sister as with an *h* .... Gen 34:31 2181
her, he thought her to be an *h* .... Gen 38:15 2181
place, saying, Where is the *h* .... Gen 38:21 6948
There was no *h* in this place .... Gen 38:21 6948
that there was no *h* in this place .... Gen 38:22 6948
daughter in law hath played the *h* .... Gen 38:24 2181
woman, or profane, or an *h* .... Lev 21:14 2181
only Rahab the *h* shall live .... Josh 6:17 2181
And Joshua saved Rahab the *h* alive .... Josh 6:25 2181
valour, and he was the son of an *h* .... Judg 11:1 2181
Samson to Gaza, and saw there an *h* .... Judg 16:1 2181
a woman with the attire of an *h* .... Prov 7:10 2181
is the faithful city become an *h* .... Is 1:21 2181
years shall Tyre sing as an *h* .... Is 23:15 2181
thou *h* that hast been forgotten .... Is 23:16 2181
thou wanderest, playing the *h* .... Jer 2:20 2181
played the *h* with many lovers .... Jer 3:1 2181
tree, and there hath played the *h* .... Jer 3:6 2181
but went and played the *h* also .... Jer 3:8 2181
playedst the *h* because of thy .... Eze 16:15 2181
and playedst the *h* thereupon .... Eze 16:16 2181
thou hast played the *h* with them .... Eze 16:28 2181
and hast not been as an *h*, in that .... Eze 16:31 2181
Wherefore, O *h*, hear the word of .... Eze 16:35 2181
thee to cease from playing the *h* .... Eze 16:41 2181
played the *h* when she was mine .... Eze 23:5 2181
played the *h* in the land of Egypt .... Eze 23:19 2181
unto a woman that playeth the *h* .... Eze 23:44 2181
their mother hath played the *h* .... Hos 2:5 2181
thou shalt not play the *h* .... Hos 3:3 2181
Though thou, Israel, play the *h* .... Hos 4:15 2181
and have given a boy for an *h* .... Joel 3:3 2181
wife shall be an *h* in the city .... Amos 7:17 2181
gathered it of the hire of an *h* .... Mic 1:7 2181
shall return to the hire of an *h* .... Mic 1:7 2181
whoredoms of the wellfavoured *h* .... Nah 3:4 2181
and make them the members of an *h* 1Cor 6:15 *4204*
is joined to an *h* is one body 1Cor 6:16 *4204*
By faith the *h* Rahab perished not .... Heb 11:31 *4204*
Rahab the *h* justified by works .... Jas 2:25 *4204*

HARLOT'S {2}
went, and came into an *h* house .... Josh 2:1 2181
the country, Go into the *h* house .... Josh 6:22 2181

HARLOTS {7}
came there two women, that were *h* 1Kin 3:16 2181
with *h* spendeth his substance .... Prov 29:3 2181
whores, and they sacrifice with *h* .... Hos 4:14 6948
the *h* go into the kingdom of God .... Mt 21:31 *4204*
publicans and the *h* believed him .... Mt 21:32 *4204*
hath devoured thy living with *h* .... Lk 15:30 *4204*
THE GREAT, THE MOTHER OF *H* .... Rev 17:5 *4204*

HARLOTS' {1}
by troops in the *h* houses .... Jer 5:7 2181

HARM {16}
and this pillar unto me, for *h* .... Gen 31:52 7451
he shall make amends for the *h* .... Lev 5:16 2398
his enemy, neither sought his *h* .... Num 35:23 7451
for I will no more do thee *h* 1Sa 26:21 7489
do us more *h* than did Absalom 2Sa 20:6 3415
And there was no *h* in the pot 2Kin 4:41 1697,7451
anointed, and do my prophets no *h* 1Chr 16:22 7489
anointed, and do my prophets no *h* .... Ps 105:15 7489
cause, if he have done thee no *h* .... Prov 3:30 7451
look well to him, and do him no *h* .... Jer 39:12 7451
voice, saying, Do thyself no *h* .... Acts 16:28 *2556*
Crete, and to have gained this *h* .... Acts 27:21 *5196*
beast into the fire, and felt no *h* .... Acts 28:5 *2556*
saw no *h* come to him, they .... Acts 28:6 *824*
shewed or spake any *h* of thee .... Acts 28:21 *4190*
And who is he that will *h* you 1Pet 3:13 *2559*

HAR-MAGEDON See ARMAGEDDON.

HARMLESS {3}
wise as serpents, and *h* as doves .... Mt 10:16 *185*
That ye may be blameless and *h* .... Phil 2:15 *185*
priest became us, who is holy, *h* .... Heb 7:26 *172*

HARNEPHER *(har-ne'-fur)* {1} *A son of Zophah.*
Suah, and *H*, and Shual, and Beri, and .. 1Chr 7:36 2774

HARNESS {5}
on his *h* boast himself as he that 1Kin 20:11
between the joints of the *h* 1Kin 22:34 8302
and vessels of gold, and raiment, *h* 2Chr 9:24 5402
between the joints of the *h* 2Chr 18:33 8302
H the horses .... Jer 46:4 631

HARNESSED {1}
up *h* out of the land of Egypt .... Ex 13:18 2571

HAROD *(ha'-rod)* {1} See HARODITE. *A spring of water.*
and pitched beside the well of *H* .... Judg 7:1 5878

HARODITE *(ha-ro'-dite)* {2} See HARORITE. *Family name of two of David's "mighty men."*
Shammah the *H*, Elika the *H* 2Sa 23:25 2733

HAROEH *(ha-ro'-eh)* {1} See REAIAH. *A son of Shobal.*
H, and half of the Manahethites 1Chr 2:52 7204

HARORITE *(ha'-ro-rite)* {1} *Family name of a "mighty man."*
Shammoth the *H*, Helez the 1Chr 11:27 2033

HAROSHETH *(har'-o-sheth)* {3} *A city in Galilee.*
which dwelt in *H* of the Gentiles .... Judg 4:2 2800
from *H* of the Gentiles unto the .... Judg 4:13 2800
the host, unto *H* of the Gentiles .... Judg 4:16 2800

HARP {30}
of all such as handle the *h* .... Gen 4:21 3658
songs, with tabret, and with *h* .... Gen 31:27 3658
and a tabret, and a pipe, and a *h* 1Sa 10:5 3658
who is a cunning player on an *h* 1Sa 16:16 3658
upon Saul, that David took an *h* 1Sa 16:23 3658
Jeduthun, who prophesied with a *h* 1Chr 25:3 3658
They take the timbrel and *h* .... Job 21:12 3658
My *h* also is turned to mourning, ... Job 30:31 3658
Praise the LORD with *h* .... Ps 33:2 3658

H

upon the *h* will I praise thee, O.............Ps 43:4 3658
open my dark saying upon the *h*.............Ps 49:4 3658
awake, psaltery and *h*.............................Ps 57:8 3658
unto thee will I sing with the *h*..............Ps 71:22 3658
the pleasant *h* with the psaltery..............Ps 81:2 3658
upon the *h* with a solemn sound.............Ps 92:3 3658
Sing unto the LORD with the *h*................Ps 98:5 3658
with the *h*, and the voice of a.................Ps 98:5 3658
Awake, psaltery and *h*............................Ps 108:2 3658
praise upon the *h* unto our God..............Ps 147:7 3658
unto him with the timbrel and *h*..............Ps 149:3 3658
praise him with the psaltery and *h*.........Ps 150:3 3658
And the *h*, and the viol, the tabret..........Is 5:12 3658
shall sound like an *h* for Moab.................Is 16:11 3658
Take an *h*, go about the city, ...Is 23:16 3658
endeth, the joy of the *h* ceaseth...............Is 24:8 3658
the sound of the cornet, flute, *h*.............Dan 3:5 7030
the sound of the cornet, flute, *h*.............Dan 3:7 7030
the sound of the cornet, flute, *h*.............Dan 3:10 7030
the sound of the cornet, flute, *h*.............Dan 3:15 7030
giving sound, whether pipe or *h*.............1Cor 14:7 *2788*

HARPED {1}
it be known what is piped or *h*...............1Cor 14:7 *2789*

HARPERS {2}
I heard the voice of *h* harping.................Rev 14:2 *2790*
And the voice of *h*, and musicians, ...Rev 18:22 *2790*

HARPING {1}
of harpers *h* with their harps..................Rev 14:2 *2789*

HARPS {20}
made of fir wood, even on *h*....................2Sa 6:5 3658
h also and psalteries for singers.............1Kin 10:12 3658
might, and with singing, and with *h*.......1Chr 13:8 3658
of musick, psalteries and *h*.....................1Chr 15:16 3658
with *h* on the Sheminith to excel.............1Chr 15:21 3658
a noise with psalteries and *h*..................1Chr 15:28 3658
Jeiel with psalteries and with *h*.............1Chr 16:5 3658
who should prophesy with *h*....................1Chr 25:1 3658
with cymbals, psalteries, and *h*..............1Chr 25:6 3658
having cymbals and psalteries and *h*.......2Chr 5:12 3658
and to the king's palace, and *h*...............2Chr 9:11 3658
to Jerusalem with psalteries and *h*.........2Chr 20:28 3658
with psalteries, and with *h*.....................2Chr 29:25 3658
cymbals, psalteries, and with *h*...............Neh 12:27 3658
We hanged our *h* upon the willows............Ps 137:2 3658
it shall be with tabrets and *h*.................Is 30:32 3658
the sound of thy *h* shall be no.................Eze 26:13 3658
Lamb, having every one of them *h*...........Rev 5:8 *2788*
of harpers harping with their *h*..............Rev 14:2 *2788*
sea of glass, having the *h* of God............Rev 15:2 *2788*

HARROW {1}
or will he *h* the valleys after...................Job 39:10 7702

HARROWS {2}
under *h* of iron, and under axes of...........2Sa 12:31 2757
with *h* of iron, and with axes...................1Chr 20:3 2757

HARSHA *(har'-shah)* {2} *A family of exiles.*
of Mehida, the children of *H*...................Ezr 2:52 2797
of Mehida, the children of *H*...................Neh 7:54 2797

HART {9}
as of the roebuck, and as of the *h*...........Deut 12:15 354
the *h* is eaten, so thou shalt eat...............Deut 12:22 354
The *h*, and the roebuck, and the ....Deut 14:5 354
as the roebuck, and as the *h*....................Deut 15:22 354
As the *h* panteth after the water..............Ps 42:1 354
is like a roe or a young *h*.........................Song 2:9 354
h upon the mountains of Bether ....Song 2:17 354
like to a roe or to a young *h*....................Song 8:14 354
shall the lame man leap as an *h*...............Is 35:6 354

HARTS {2}
and an hundred sheep, beside *h*..............1Kin 4:23 354
like *h* that find no pasture ....Lam 1:6 354

HARUM *(ha'-rum)* {1} *Father of Aharhel.*
families of Aharhel the son of *H*...............1Chr 4:8 2037

HARUMAPH *(ha-ru'-maf)* {1} *Father of Jedaiah.*
repaired Jedaiah the son of *H*.................Neh 3:10 2739

HARUPHITE *(ha'-ru-fite)* {1} *A Korhite soldier.*
and Shemariah, and Shephatiah the *H*...1Chr 12:5 2741

HARUZ *(ha'-ruz)* {1} *Father of Meshullemeth.*
the daughter of *H* of Jotbah...................2Kin 21:19 2743

HARVEST {61}
earth remaineth, seedtime and *h*............Gen 8:22 7105
went in the days of wheat *h*.....................Gen 30:14 7105
shall neither be earing nor *h*...................Gen 45:6 7105
And the feast of *h*, the............................Ex 23:16 7105
time and in *h* thou shalt rest...................Ex 34:21 7105
of the firstfruits of wheat *h*....................Ex 34:22 7105
when ye reap the *h* of your land ....Lev 19:9 7105
gather the gleanings of thy *h* ....Lev 19:9 7105
you, and shall reap the *h* thereof ....Lev 23:10 7105
of your *h* unto the priest ....Lev 23:10 7105
when ye reap the *h* of your land ....Lev 23:22 7105
thou gather any gleaning of thy *h*...........Lev 23:22 7105
of thy *h* thou shalt not reap ....Lev 25:5 7105
cuttest down thine *h* in thy field.............Deut 24:19 7105
all his banks all the time of *h* ....Josh 3:15 7105
after, in the time of wheat *h*....................Judg 15:1 7105
in the beginning of barley *h*....................Ruth 1:22 7105
until they have ended all my *h*................Ruth 2:21 7105
of barley *h* and of wheat *h*.....................Ruth 2:23 7105
their wheat *h* in the valley 1Sa 6:13 7105
ear his ground, and to reap his *h* 1Sa 8:12 7105
Is it not wheat *h* to day 1Sa 12:17 7105
put to death in the days of *h*...................2Sa 21:9 7105
in the beginning of barley *h*.....................2Sa 21:9 7105
from the beginning of *h* until...................2Sa 21:10 7105
came to David in the *h* time unto 2Sa 23:13 7105
Whose *h* the hungry eateth up, and ....Job 5:5 7105
and gathereth her food in the *h* ....Prov 6:8 7105
but he that sleepeth in *h* is a...................Prov 10:5 7105
therefore shall he beg in *h*.......................Prov 20:4 7105
the cold of snow in the time of *h* ....Prov 25:13 7105
snow in summer, and as rain in *h* ....Prov 26:1 7105
thee according to the joy in *h*..................Is 9:3 7105
fruits and for thy *h* is fallen....................Is 16:9 7105
but the *h* shall be a heap in the ....Is 17:11 7105
a cloud of dew in the heat of *h* ....Is 18:4 7105
For afore the *h*, when the bud is ....Is 18:5 7105
the *h* of the river, is her ....Is 23:3 7105
And they shall eat up thine *h*...................Jer 5:17 7105
us the appointed weeks of the *h*...............Jer 5:24 7105
The *h* is past, the summer is.....................Jer 8:20 7105
the sickle in the time of *h*........................Jer 50:16 7105
and the time of her *h* shall come..............Jer 51:33 7105
Judah, he hath set an *h* for thee...............Hos 6:11 7105
because the *h* of the field is ....Joel 1:11 7105
in the sickle, for the *h* is ripe ....Joel 3:13 7105
were yet three months to the *h*..................Amos 4:7 7105
The *h* truly is plenteous, but the ....Mt 9:37 *2326*
ye therefore the Lord of the *h* ....Mt 9:38 *2326*
send forth labourers into his *h* ....Mt 9:38 *2326*
both grow together until the *h* ....Mt 13:30 *2326*
in the time of *h* I will say to ....Mt 13:30 *2326*
the *h* is the end of the world ....Mt 13:39 *2326*
the sickle, because the *h* is come ....Mk 4:29 *2326*
The *h* truly is great, but the ....Lk 10:2 *2326*
ye therefore the Lord of the *h* ....Lk 10:2 *2326*
send forth labourers into his *h* ....Lk 10:2 *2326*
yet four months, and then cometh *h* ....Jn 4:35 *2326*
for they are white already to *h* ....Jn 4:35 *2326*
for the *h* of the earth is ripe.....................Rev 14:15 *2326*

HARVESTMAN {2}
as when the *h* gathereth the corn.............Is 17:5 7105
and as the handful after the *h*..................Jer 9:22 7114

HASADIAH *(has-a-di'-ah)* {1} *A son of Zerubbabel.*
and Ohel, and Berechiah, and *H* 1Chr 3:20 2619

HASENUAH *(has-e-nu'-ah)* {1} See SENUAH. *Father of Hodaviah.*
the son of Hodaviah, the son of *H*............1Chr 9:7 5574

HASHABIAH *(hash-a-bi'-ah)* {15}
1. Son of Amaziah.
The son of *H*, the son of Amaziah, ...1Chr 6:45 2811
2. A Merarite Levite.
the son of Azrikam, the son of *H* 1Chr 9:14 2811
3. A son of Jeduthun.
Gedaliah, and Zeri, and Jeshaiah, *H*.......1Chr 25:3 2811
The twelfth to *H*, he, his sons,..................1Chr 25:19 2811
4. A descendant of Hebron.
And of the Hebronites, *H* and his 1Chr 26:30 2811
5. Son of Kemuel.
the Levites, *H* the son of Kemuel............1Chr 27:17 2811
6. A Levite chief.
and Nethaneel, his brethren, and *H*.........2Chr 35:9 2811
7. A Levite in exile.
And *H*, and with him Jeshaiah of the .....Ezr 8:19 2811
8. A chief priest.
of the priests, Sherebiah, *H*.....................Ezr 8:24 2811
9. A rebuilder of Jerusalem's wall.
Next unto him repaired *H*, the..................Neh 3:17 2811
10. A Levite who renewed the covenant.
Micha, Rehob, *H*, ...Neh 10:11 2811
11. Son of Bunni.
the son of Azrikam, the son of *H* ....Neh 11:15 2811
12. Another Levite.
the son of Bani, the son of *H*...................Neh 11:22 2811
13. A priest in Joiakim's time.
Of Hilkiah, *H*..Neh 12:21 2811
14. A chief Levite.
H, Sherebiah, and Jeshua the son ....Neh 12:24 2811

HASHABNAH *(hash-ab'-nah)* {1} *A clan leader who renewed the covenant.*
Rehum, *H*, Maaseiah,.................................Neh 10:25 2812

HASHABNEIAH See HASHABNIAH.

HASHABNIAH *(hash-ab-ni'-ah)* {2}
1. Father of Hattush.
him repaired Hattush the son of *H* ....Neh 3:10 2813
2. A Levite.
Jeshua, and Kadmiel, Bani, *H*...................Neh 9:5 2813

HASHBADANA *(hash-bad'-a-nah)* {1} *A priest.*
and Malchiah, and Hashum, and *H* ....Neh 8:4 2806

HASHBADDANAH See HASHBADANA.

HASHEM *(ha'-shem)* {1} *Father of several "mighty men."*
The sons of *H* the Gizonite,......................1Chr 11:34 2044

HASHMONAH *(hash-mo'-nah)* {2} *A Hebrew encampment in the wilderness.*
from Mithcah, and pitched in *H*..............Num 33:29 2832
And they departed from *H*, and ....Num 33:30 2832

HASHUB *(ha'-shub)* {4} See HASSHUB.
1. Father of Shemaiah.
Shemaiah the son of *H*, the son of ....Neh 11:15 2815
2. Son of Pahath-moab.
H the son of Pahath-moab,.......................Neh 3:11 2815
3. A rebuilder of Jerusalem's wall.
H over against their house ....Neh 3:23 2815
4. A clan leader who renewed the covenant.
Hoshea, Hananiah, *H*, ...Neh 10:23 2815

HASHUBAH *(hash-u'-bah)* {1} *A son of Zerubbabel.*
And *H*, and Ohel, and Berechiah, and 1Chr 3:20 2807

HASHUM *(ha'-shum)* {5}
1. A family of exiles.
The children of *H*, two hundred..............Ezr 2:19 2828
Of the sons of *H*...Ezr 10:33 2828
The children of *H*, three hundred............Neh 7:22 2828
2. A priest.
and Mishael, and Malchiah, and *H* ....Neh 8:4 2828
3. A clan leader who renewed the covenant.
Hodijah, *H*, Bezai, ...Neh 10:18 2828

HASHUPHA *(hash-u'-fah)* {1} See HASUPHA. *A family of exiles.*
of Ziha, the children of *H*.........................Neh 7:46 2817

HASRAH *(has'-rah)* {1} See HARHAS. *Same as Harhas.*
the son of Tikvath, the son of *H*..............2Chr 34:22 2641

HASSENAAH *(has-se-na'-ah)* {1} See SENAAH. *Father of some rebuilders of Jerusalem's wall.*
fish gate did the sons of *H* build.............Neh 3:3 5570

HASSENUAH See SENUAH.

HASSHUB *(hash'-ub)* {1} See HASHUB. *Father of Shemaiah.*
Shemaiah the son of *H*, the son of 1Chr 9:14 2815

HASSPHERETH See SOPHERETH.

HAST {1071}
H thou eaten of the tree, whereof ....Gen 3:11
What is this that thou *h* done ....Gen 3:13
serpent, Because thou *h* done this............Gen 3:14
Because thou *h* hearkened unto the........Gen 3:17
h eaten of the tree, of which I ....Gen 3:17
And he said, What *h* thou done...............Gen 4:10
thou *h* driven me out this day ....Gen 4:14
is this that thou *h* done unto me.............Gen 12:18
to me thou *h* given no seed......................Gen 15:3
they said, So do, as thou *h* said..............Gen 18:5
unto Lot, *H* thou here any besides..........Gen 19:12
and whatsoever thou *h* in the city...........Gen 19:12
thou *h* magnified thy mercy ....Gen 19:19
which thou *h* shewed unto me in ....Gen 19:19
city, for the which thou *h* spoken.............Gen 19:21
for the woman which thou *h* taken ....Gen 20:3
him, What *h* thou done unto us................Gen 20:9
that thou *h* brought on me and on............Gen 20:9
thou *h* done deeds unto me that..............Gen 20:9
that thou *h* done this thing ....Gen 20:10
the land wherein thou *h* sojourned ....Gen 21:23
which thou *h* set by themselves................Gen 21:29
seeing thou *h* not withheld thy ....Gen 22:12
because thou *h* done this thing ....Gen 22:16
h not withheld thy son, thine ....Gen 22:16
because thou *h* obeyed my voice ....Gen 22:18
let the same be she that thou *h* ....Gen 24:14
h shewed kindness unto my master..........Gen 24:14
What is this thou *h* done unto us.............Gen 26:10
that thou *h* found it so quickly ....Gen 27:20
H thou not reserved a blessing.................Gen 27:36
H thou but one blessing, my....................Gen 27:38
that which thou *h* done to him.................Gen 27:45
What is this thou *h* done unto me............Gen 29:25
wherefore then *h* thou beguiled me..........Gen 29:25
that thou *h* taken my husband ....Gen 30:15
What *h* thou done, that thou *h*.................Gen 31:26
that thou *h* stolen away unawares............Gen 31:26
h not suffered me to kiss my sons ....Gen 31:28
thou *h* now done foolishly in so ....Gen 31:28
yet wherefore *h* thou stolen my................Gen 31:30
that thou *h* so hotly pursued ....Gen 31:36
Whereas thou *h* searched all my..............Gen 31:37
what *h* thou found of all thy ....Gen 31:37
thou *h* changed my wages ten times.........Gen 31:41
which thou *h* shewed unto thy ....Gen 32:10
for as a prince *h* thou power with.............Gen 32:28
God and with men, and *h* prevailed..........Gen 32:28
keep that thou *h* unto thyself...................Gen 33:9
is this dream that thou *h* dreamed...........Gen 37:10
this kid, and thou *h* not found her...........Gen 38:23
she said, How *h* thou broken forth...........Gen 38:29
which thou *h* brought unto us,..................Gen 39:17
and thy herds, and all that thou *h* ....Gen 45:10
thy household, and all that thou *h*...........Gen 45:11
they said, Thou *h* saved our lives.............Gen 47:25
he said, I will do as thou *h* said ....Gen 47:30
When thou *h* brought forth the ....Ex 3:12
nor since thou *h* spoken unto thy.............Ex 4:10
Lord, wherefore *h* thou so evil ....Ex 5:22
why is it that thou *h* sent me ....Ex 5:22
neither *h* thou delivered thy......................Ex 5:23
and all that thou *h* in the field.................Ex 9:19
Thou *h* spoken well, I will see...................Ex 10:29
when thou *h* circumcised him, then ....Ex 12:44
cometh of a beast which thou *h* ....Ex 13:12 1961
h thou taken us away to die in ....Ex 14:11
wherefore *h* thou dealt thus with..............Ex 14:11
of thine excellency thou *h* ....Ex 15:7
Thou in thy mercy *h* led forth the ....Ex 15:13
the people which thou *h* redeemed ....Ex 15:13
thou *h* guided them in thy.........................Ex 15:13
pass over, which thou *h* purchased...........Ex 15:16
which thou *h* made for thee to ....Ex 15:17
thou *h* brought us up out of Egypt............Ex 17:3
tool upon it, thou *h* polluted it.................Ex 20:25
which thou *h* sown in the field..................Ex 23:16
when thou *h* gathered in thy ....Ex 23:16
when thou *h* made an atonement for ......Ex 29:36
which thou *h* brought forth out of ....Ex 32:11
that thou *h* brought so great a ....Ex 32:21
of thy book which thou *h* written ....Ex 32:32

the people which thou *h* brought ... Ex 33:1
thou *h* not let me know whom thou ... Ex 33:12
Yet thou *h* said, I know thee by ... Ex 33:12
thou *h* also found grace in my ... Ex 33:12
thing also that thou *h* spoken ... Ex 33:17
for thou *h* found grace in my ... Ex 33:17
if thou *h* not gone aside to ... Num 5:19
But if thou *h* gone aside to ... Num 5:20
Wherefore *h* thou afflicted thy ... Num 11:11
and thou *h* said, I will give them ... Num 11:21
great, according as thou *h* spoken ... Num 14:17
as thou *h* forgiven this people, ... Num 14:19
h brought us up out of a land ... Num 16:13
Moreover thou *h* not brought us ... Num 16:14
that thou *h* smitten me these ... Num 22:28
the ass, Because thou *h* mocked me ... Num 22:29
upon which thou *h* ridden ever ... Num 22:30
Wherefore *h* thou smitten thine ... Num 22:32
Balaam, What *h* thou done unto me ... Num 23:11
thou *h* blessed them altogether ... Num 23:11
thou *h* altogether blessed them ... Num 24:10
And when thou *h* seen it, thou also ... Num 27:13
The thing which thou *h* spoken is ... Deut 1:14
where thou *h* seen how that the ... Deut 1:31
thou *h* lacked nothing ... Deut 2:7
thou *h* begun to shew thy servant ... Deut 3:24
of the fire, as thou *h* heard ... Deut 4:33
When thou *h* eaten and art full, ... Deut 8:10
Lest when thou *h* eaten and art ... Deut 8:12
h built goodly houses, and dwelt ... Deut 8:12
and all that thou *h* is multiplied ... Deut 8:13
and of whom thou *h* heard say ... Deut 9:2
for thy people which thou *h* ... Deut 9:12
which thou *h* redeemed through thy ... Deut 9:26
which thou *h* brought forth out of ... Deut 9:26
Only thy holy things which thou *h* ... Deut 12:26 1961
gods, which thou *h* not known ... Deut 13:2
gods, which thou *h* not known ... Deut 13:6
after that thou *h* gathered in thy ... Deut 16:13
thou *h* heard of it, and enquired ... Deut 17:4
Israel, whom thou *h* redeemed ... Deut 21:8
thou *h* taken them captive, ... Deut 21:10
h a desire unto her, that thou ... Deut 21:11
her, because thou *h* humbled her ... Deut 21:14
thou *h* found, shalt thou do ... Deut 22:3
of thy seed which thou *h* sown ... Deut 22:9
according as thou *h* vowed unto ... Deut 23:23
which thou *h* promised with thy ... Deut 23:23
h forgot a sheaf in the field, ... Deut 24:19
which thou, O LORD, *h* given me ... Deut 26:10
When thou *h* made an end of ... Deut 26:12
h given it unto the Levite, the ... Deut 26:12
which thou *h* commanded me ... Deut 26:13
to all that thou *h* commanded me ... Deut 26:14
and the land which thou *h* given us ... Deut 26:15
Thou *h* avouched the LORD this day ... Deut 26:17
whereby thou *h* forsaken me ... Deut 28:20
h forgotten God that formed thee ... Deut 32:18
oath which thou *h* made us swear ... Josh 2:17
which thou *h* made us to swear ... Josh 2:20
wherefore *h* thou at all brought ... Josh 7:7
and tell me now what thou *h* done ... Josh 7:19
said, Why *h* thou troubled us ... Josh 7:25
because thou *h* wholly followed ... Josh 14:9
for thou *h* given me a south land ... Josh 15:19
Why *h* thou given me but one lot ... Josh 17:14
a great people, and *h* great power ... Josh 17:17
for thou *h* given me a south land ... Judg 1:15
thou *h* trodden down strength ... Judg 5:21
by mine hand, as thou *h* said ... Judg 6:36
by mine hand, as thou *h* said ... Judg 6:37
Why *h* thou served us thus, that ... Judg 8:1
for thou *h* delivered us from the ... Judg 8:22
the people that thou *h* despised ... Judg 9:38
What *h* thou to do with me, that ... Judg 11:12
thou *h* brought me very low, and ... Judg 11:35
if thou *h* opened thy mouth unto ... Judg 11:36
thou *h* put forth a riddle unto ... Judg 14:16
of my people, and *h* not told it me ... Judg 14:16
is this that thou *h* done unto us ... Judg 15:11
and said, Thou *h* given this great ... Judg 15:18
thou *h* mocked me, and told me lies ... Judg 16:10
Samson, Hitherto thou *h* mocked me ... Judg 16:13
thou *h* mocked me these three ... Judg 16:15
h not told me wherein thy great ... Judg 16:15
and what *h* thou here ... Judg 18:3
all that thou *h* done unto thy ... Ruth 2:11
how thou *h* left thy father and thy ... Ruth 2:11
for that thou *h* comforted me ... Ruth 2:13
for that thou *h* spoken friendly ... Ruth 2:13
Where *h* thou gleaned to day ... Ruth 2:19
for thou *h* shewed more kindness ... Ruth 3:10
the vail that thou *h* upon thee ... Ruth 3:15
petition that thou *h* asked of him ... 1Sa 1:17
for thou *h* born a son ... 1Sa 4:20
Thou *h* not defrauded us, nor ... 1Sa 12:4
neither *h* thou taken ought of any ... 1Sa 12:4
And Samuel said, What *h* thou done ... 1Sa 13:11
to Saul, Thou *h* done foolishly ... 1Sa 13:13
thou *h* not kept the commandment ... 1Sa 13:13
because thou *h* not kept that ... 1Sa 13:14
Tell me what thou *h* done ... 1Sa 14:43
Because thou *h* rejected the word ... 1Sa 15:23
for thou *h* rejected the word of ... 1Sa 15:26
with whom *h* thou left those few ... 1Sa 17:28
of Israel, whom thou *h* defied ... 1Sa 17:45
Why *h* thou deceived me so, and ... 1Sa 19:17
for thou *h* brought thy servant ... 1Sa 20:8

when thou *h* stayed three days, ... 1Sa 20:19
do not I know that thou *h* chosen ... 1Sa 20:30
in that thou *h* given him bread, ... 1Sa 22:13
h enquired of God for him, that ... 1Sa 22:13
for thou *h* rewarded me good, ... 1Sa 24:17
thou *h* shewed this day how that ... 1Sa 24:18
that thou *h* dealt well with me ... 1Sa 24:18
that thou *h* done unto me this day ... 1Sa 24:19
and peace be unto all that thou *h* ... 1Sa 25:6
I have heard that thou *h* shearers ... 1Sa 25:7
either that thou *h* shed blood ... 1Sa 25:31
which *h* kept me this day from ... 1Sa 25:33
wherefore then *h* thou not kept ... 1Sa 26:15
is not good that thou *h* done ... 1Sa 26:16
saying, Why *h* thou deceived me ... 1Sa 28:12
Why *h* thou disquieted me, to ... 1Sa 28:15
place which thou *h* appointed him ... 1Sa 29:4
thou *h* been upright, and thy going ... 1Sa 29:6
what *h* thou found in thy servant ... 1Sa 29:8
very pleasant *h* thou been unto me ... 2Sa 1:26
Wherefore *h* thou gone in unto my ... 2Sa 3:7
king, and said, What *h* thou done ... 2Sa 3:24
is it that thou *h* sent him away ... 2Sa 3:24
which thou *h* spoken of, of them ... 2Sa 6:22
that thou *h* brought me hitherto ... 2Sa 7:18
but thou *h* spoken also of thy ... 2Sa 7:19
h thou done all these great ... 2Sa 7:21
For thou *h* confirmed to thyself ... 2Sa 7:24
the word that thou *h* spoken ... 2Sa 7:25
it for ever, and do as thou *h* said ... 2Sa 7:25
h revealed to thy servant, saying ... 2Sa 7:27
thou *h* promised this goodness ... 2Sa 7:28
for thou, O Lord GOD, *h* spoken it ... 2Sa 7:29
When thou *h* made an end of ... 2Sa 11:19
Wherefore *h* thou despised the ... 2Sa 12:9
thou *h* killed Uriah the Hittite ... 2Sa 12:9
h taken his wife to be thy wife, ... 2Sa 12:9
h slain him with the sword of the ... 2Sa 12:9
because thou *h* despised me ... 2Sa 12:10
h taken the wife of Uriah the ... 2Sa 12:10
because by this deed thou *h* given ... 2Sa 12:14
thing is this that thou *h* done ... 2Sa 12:21
Wherefore then *h* thou thought ... 2Sa 14:13
h thou not there with thee Zadok ... 2Sa 15:35
in whose stead thou *h* reigned ... 2Sa 16:8
say, Wherefore *h* thou done so ... 2Sa 16:10
Go tell the king what thou *h* seen ... 2Sa 18:21
that thou *h* no tidings ready ... 2Sa 18:22
said Thou *h* shamed this day the ... 2Sa 19:5
For thou *h* declared this day, ... 2Sa 19:6
Thou *h* also given me the shield ... 2Sa 22:36
Thou *h* enlarged my steps under me ... 2Sa 22:37
For thou *h* girded me with ... 2Sa 22:40
me *h* thou subdued under me ... 2Sa 22:40
Thou *h* also given me the necks of ... 2Sa 22:41
Thou also *h* delivered me from the ... 2Sa 22:44
thou *h* kept me to be head of the ... 2Sa 22:44
thou also *h* lifted me up on high ... 2Sa 22:49
thou *h* delivered me from the ... 2Sa 22:49
in saying, Why *h* thou done so ... 1Kin 1:6
H thou not heard that Adonijah ... 1Kin 1:11
h thou said, Adonijah shall reign ... 1Kin 1:24
thou *h* not shewed it unto thy ... 1Kin 1:27
thou *h* with thee Shimei the son ... 1Kin 2:8
because thou *h* been afflicted in ... 1Kin 2:26
Why then *h* thou not kept the oath ... 1Kin 2:43
Thou *h* shewed unto thy servant ... 1Kin 3:6
thou *h* kept for him this great ... 1Kin 3:6
that thou *h* given him a son to ... 1Kin 3:6
thou *h* made thy servant king ... 1Kin 3:7
of thy people which thou *h* chosen ... 1Kin 3:8
Because thou *h* asked this thing, ... 1Kin 3:11
h not asked for thyself long life ... 1Kin 3:11
neither *h* asked riches for ... 1Kin 3:11
nor *h* asked the life of thine ... 1Kin 3:11
but *h* asked for thyself ... 1Kin 3:11
thee that which thou *h* not asked ... 1Kin 3:13
Who *h* kept with thy servant David ... 1Kin 8:24
h fulfilled it with thine hand, ... 1Kin 8:24
me as thou *h* walked before me ... 1Kin 8:25
the place of which thou *h* said ... 1Kin 8:29
which thou *h* given to thy people ... 1Kin 8:36
the city which thou *h* chosen ... 1Kin 8:44
the city which thou *h* chosen ... 1Kin 8:48
that thou *h* made before me ... 1Kin 9:3
this house, which thou *h* built ... 1Kin 9:3
are these which thou *h* given me ... 1Kin 9:13
thou *h* not kept my covenant and my ... 1Kin 11:11
But what *h* thou lacked with me, ... 1Kin 11:22
Forasmuch as thou *h* disobeyed the ... 1Kin 13:21
h not kept the commandment which ... 1Kin 13:21
h eaten bread and drunk water in ... 1Kin 13:22
yet thou *h* not been as my servant ... 1Kin 14:8 1961
But *h* done evil above all that ... 1Kin 14:9
for thou *h* gone and made thee ... 1Kin 14:9
h cast me behind thy back ... 1Kin 14:9
thou *h* walked in the way of ... 1Kin 16:2
h made my people Israel to sin, ... 1Kin 16:2
go and do as thou *h* said ... 1Kin 17:13
h thou also brought evil upon the ... 1Kin 17:20
LORD, and thou *h* followed Baalim ... 1Kin 18:18
that thou *h* turned their heart ... 1Kin 18:37
H thou seen all this great ... 1Kin 20:13
like the army that thou *h* lost ... 1Kin 20:25
Because thou *h* not obeyed the ... 1Kin 20:36
thyself *h* decided it ... 1Kin 20:40
Because thou *h* let go out of thy ... 1Kin 20:42
H thou killed, and also taken ... 1Kin 21:19

H thou found me, O mine enemy ... 1Kin 21:20
because thou *h* sold thyself to ... 1Kin 21:20
thou *h* provoked me to anger ... 1Kin 21:22
LORD, Forasmuch as thou *h* sent ... 2Kin 1:16
Thou *h* asked a hard thing ... 2Kin 2:10
tell me, what *h* thou in the house ... 2Kin 4:2 3426
thou *h* been careful for us with ... 2Kin 4:13
Wherefore *h* thou rent thy clothes ... 2Kin 5:8
thou smite those whom thou *h* ... 2Kin 6:22
What *h* thou to do with peace ... 2Kin 9:18
What *h* thou to do with peace ... 2Kin 9:19
Because thou *h* done well in ... 2Kin 10:30
h done unto the house of Ahab ... 2Kin 10:30
Thou *h* indeed smitten Edom, and ... 2Kin 14:10
The nations which thou *h* removed ... 2Kin 17:26
of the words which thou *h* heard ... 2Kin 19:6
thou *h* heard what the kings of ... 2Kin 19:11
thou *h* made heaven and earth ... 2Kin 19:15
That which thou *h* prayed to me ... 2Kin 19:20
Whom *h* thou reproached and ... 2Kin 19:22
against whom *h* thou exalted thy ... 2Kin 19:22
thou *h* reproached the Lord ... 2Kin 19:23
h said, With the multitude of my ... 2Kin 19:23
H thou not heard long ago how I ... 2Kin 19:25
of the LORD which thou *h* spoken ... 2Kin 20:19
thou *h* humbled thyself before the ... 2Kin 22:19
h rent thy clothes, and wept ... 2Kin 22:19
these things that thou *h* done ... 2Kin 23:17
thee whithersoever thou *h* walked ... 1Chr 17:8
that thou *h* brought me hitherto ... 1Chr 17:16
for thou *h* also spoken of thy ... 1Chr 17:17
h regarded me according to the ... 1Chr 17:17
h thou done all this greatness, ... 1Chr 17:19
whom thou *h* redeemed out of Egypt ... 1Chr 17:21
let the thing that thou *h* spoken ... 1Chr 17:23
for ever, and do as thou *h* said ... 1Chr 17:23
h told thy servant that thou wilt ... 1Chr 17:25
h promised this goodness unto thy ... 1Chr 17:26
Thou *h* shed blood abundantly ... 1Chr 22:8
and *h* made great wars ... 1Chr 22:8
because thou *h* shed much blood ... 1Chr 22:8
because thou *h* been a man of war, ... 1Chr 28:3
a man of war, and *h* shed blood ... 1Chr 28:3
until thou *h* finished all the ... 1Chr 28:20
h pleasure in uprightness ... 1Chr 29:17
Thou *h* shewed great mercy unto ... 2Chr 1:8
h made me to reign in his stead ... 2Chr 1:8
for thou *h* made me king over a ... 2Chr 1:9
thou *h* not asked riches, wealth, ... 2Chr 1:11
neither yet *h* asked long life ... 2Chr 1:11
but *h* asked wisdom and knowledge ... 2Chr 1:11
Thou which *h* kept with thy ... 2Chr 6:15
that which thou *h* promised him ... 2Chr 6:15
h fulfilled it with thine hand, ... 2Chr 6:15
that which thou *h* promised him ... 2Chr 6:16
as thou *h* walked before me ... 2Chr 6:16
which thou *h* spoken unto thy ... 2Chr 6:17
upon the place whereof thou *h* ... 2Chr 6:20
when thou *h* taught them the good ... 2Chr 6:27
which thou *h* given unto thy ... 2Chr 6:27
this city which thou *h* chosen ... 2Chr 6:34
the city which thou *h* chosen ... 2Chr 6:38
Because thou *h* relied on the king ... 2Chr 16:7
Herein thou *h* done foolishly ... 2Chr 16:9
in that thou *h* taken away the ... 2Chr 19:3
h prepared thine heart to seek ... 2Chr 19:3
which thou *h* given us to inherit ... 2Chr 20:11
Because thou *h* joined thyself ... 2Chr 20:37
Because thou *h* not walked in the ... 2Chr 21:12
But *h* walked in the way of the ... 2Chr 21:13
h made Judah and the inhabitants ... 2Chr 21:13
also *h* slain thy brethren of thy ... 2Chr 21:13
Why *h* thou not required of the ... 2Chr 24:6
Why *h* thou sought after the gods ... 2Chr 25:15
thee, because thou *h* done this ... 2Chr 25:16
h not hearkened unto my counsel ... 2Chr 25:16
thou *h* smitten the Edomites ... 2Chr 25:19
for thou *h* trespassed ... 2Chr 26:18
the words which thou *h* heard ... 2Chr 34:26
Which thou *h* commanded by thy ... Ezr 9:11
seeing that thou our God *h* ... Ezr 9:13
h given us such deliverance as ... Ezr 9:13
with a loud voice, As thou *h* said ... Ezr 10:12
whom thou *h* redeemed by thy great ... Neh 1:10
thou *h* also appointed prophets to ... Neh 6:7
thou *h* made heaven, the heaven of ... Neh 9:6
seed, and *h* performed thy words ... Neh 9:8
for thou *h* done right, but we ... Neh 9:33
unto the kings whom thou *h* set ... Neh 9:37
and the horse, as thou *h* said ... Est 6:10
fail of all that thou *h* spoken ... Est 6:10
before whom thou *h* begun to fall ... Est 6:13
H thou considered my servant Job, ... Job 1:8
H not thou made an hedge about ... Job 1:10
thou *h* blessed the work of his ... Job 1:10
H thou considered my servant Job, ... Job 2:3
thou *h* instructed many ... Job 4:3
thou *h* strengthened the weak ... Job 4:3
thou *h* strengthened the feeble ... Job 4:4
why *h* thou set me as a mark ... Job 7:20
H thou eyes of flesh ... Job 10:4
that thou *h* made me as the clay ... Job 10:9
H thou not poured me out as milk, ... Job 10:10
Thou *h* clothed me with skin and ... Job 10:11
h fenced me with bones and sinews ... Job 10:11
Thou *h* granted me life and favour, ... Job 10:12
these things *h* thou hid in thine ... Job 10:13
Wherefore then *h* thou brought me ... Job 10:18

For thou *h* said, My doctrine is ... Job 11:4
thou *h* appointed his bounds that ... Job 14:5
H thou heard the secret of God ... Job 15:8
thou *h* made desolate all my ... Job 16:7
thou *h* filled me with wrinkles, ... Job 16:8
For thou *h* hid their heart from ... Job 17:4
For thou *h* taken a pledge from ... Job 22:6
Thou *h* not given water to the ... Job 22:7
thou *h* withholden bread from the ... Job 22:7
Thou *h* sent widows away empty, and ... Job 22:9
H thou marked the old way which ... Job 22:15
How *h* thou helped him that is ... Job 26:2
How *h* thou counseled him that ... Job 26:3
how *h* thou plentifully declared ... Job 26:3
To whom *h* thou uttered words ... Job 26:4
Surely thou *h* spoken in mine ... Job 33:8
If thou *h* any thing to say, ... Job 33:32 3426
If now thou *h* understanding, hear ... Job 34:16
But thou *h* fulfilled the judgment ... Job 36:17
for this *h* thou chosen rather ... Job 36:21
can say, Thou *h* wrought iniquity ... Job 36:23
H thou with him spread out the ... Job 37:18
declare, if thou *h* understanding ... Job 38:4
H thou commanded the morning ... Job 38:12
H thou entered into the springs ... Job 38:16
or *h* thou walked in the search of ... Job 38:16
or *h* thou seen the doors of the ... Job 38:17
H thou perceived the breadth of ... Job 38:18
H thou entered into the treasures ... Job 38:22
or *h* thou seen the treasures of ... Job 38:22
h thou clothed his neck with ... Job 39:19
H thou an arm like God ... Job 40:9
for thou *h* smitten all mine ... Ps 3:7
thou *h* broken the teeth of the ... Ps 3:7
thou *h* enlarged me when I was in ... Ps 4:1
Thou *h* put gladness in my heart, ... Ps 4:7
judgment that thou *h* commanded ... Ps 7:6
who *h* set thy glory above the ... Ps 8:1
sucklings *h* thou ordained ... Ps 8:2
the stars, which thou *h* ordained ... Ps 8:3
For thou *h* made him a little ... Ps 8:5
h crowned him with glory and ... Ps 8:5
thou *h* put all things under his ... Ps 8:6
For thou *h* maintained my right and ... Ps 9:4
Thou *h* rebuked the heathen ... Ps 9:5
thou *h* destroyed the wicked ... Ps 9:5
thou *h* put out their name for ... Ps 9:5
and thou *h* destroyed cities ... Ps 9:6
h not forsaken them that seek ... Ps 9:10
Thou *h* seen it ... Ps 10:14
thou *h* heard the desire of the ... Ps 10:17
thou *h* said unto the LORD, Thou ... Ps 16:2
Thou *h* proved mine heart ... Ps 17:3
thou *h* visited me in the night ... Ps 17:3
thou *h* tried me, and shalt find ... Ps 17:3
Thou *h* also given me the shield ... Ps 18:35
Thou *h* enlarged my steps under me ... Ps 18:36
For thou *h* girded me with ... Ps 18:39
thou *h* subdued under me those ... Ps 18:39
Thou *h* also given me the necks of ... Ps 18:40
Thou *h* delivered me from the ... Ps 18:43
thou *h* made me the head of the ... Ps 18:43
thou *h* delivered me from the ... Ps 18:48
Thou *h* given him his heart's ... Ps 21:2
h not withholden the request of ... Ps 21:2
majesty *h* thou laid upon him ... Ps 21:5
For thou *h* made him most blessed ... Ps 21:6
thou *h* made him exceeding glad ... Ps 21:6
my God, why *h* thou forsaken me ... Ps 22:1
thou *h* brought me into the dust ... Ps 22:15
for thou *h* heard me from the ... Ps 22:21
thou *h* been my help ... Ps 27:9 1961
for thou *h* lifted me up, and *h* ... Ps 30:1
unto thee, and thou *h* healed me ... Ps 30:2
thou *h* brought up my soul from ... Ps 30:3
thou *h* kept me alive, that I ... Ps 30:3
by thy favour thou *h* made my ... Ps 30:7
Thou *h* turned for me my mourning ... Ps 30:11
thou *h* put off my sackcloth, and ... Ps 30:11
thou *h* redeemed me, O LORD God of ... Ps 31:5
for thou *h* considered my trouble ... Ps 31:7
thou *h* known my soul in ... Ps 31:7
h not shut me up into the hand of ... Ps 31:8
thou *h* set my feet in a large ... Ps 31:8
which thou *h* laid up for them ... Ps 31:19
which thou *h* wrought for them ... Ps 31:19
This thou *h* seen, O LORD ... Ps 35:22
thou *h* made my days as an ... Ps 39:5
wonderful works which thou *h* done ... Ps 40:5
mine ears *h* thou opened ... Ps 40:6
sin offering *h* thou not required ... Ps 40:6
my rock, Why *h* thou forgotten me ... Ps 42:9
But thou *h* saved us from our ... Ps 44:7
h put them to shame that hated us ... Ps 44:7
But thou *h* cast off, and put us to ... Ps 44:9
Thou *h* given us like sheep ... Ps 44:11
h scattered us among the heathen ... Ps 44:11
Though thou *h* sore broken us in ... Ps 44:19
What *h* thou to do to declare my ... Ps 50:16
h been partaker with adulterers ... Ps 50:18
These things *h* thou done, and I ... Ps 50:21
which thou *h* broken may rejoice ... Ps 51:8
for ever, because thou *h* done it ... Ps 52:9
thou *h* put them to shame, because ... Ps 53:5
For thou *h* delivered my soul from ... Ps 56:13
for thou *h* been my defence and ... Ps 59:16 1961
thou *h* cast us off, thou *h* ... Ps 60:1
us, thou *h* been displeased ... Ps 60:1

Thou *h* made the earth to tremble ... Ps 60:2
thou *h* broken it ... Ps 60:2
Thou *h* shewed thy people hard ... Ps 60:3
thou *h* made us to drink the wine ... Ps 60:3
Thou *h* given a banner to them ... Ps 60:4
For thou *h* been a shelter for me, ... Ps 61:3 1961
For thou, O God, *h* heard my vows ... Ps 61:5
thou *h* given me the heritage of ... Ps 61:5
Because thou *h* been my help ... Ps 63:7 1961
when thou *h* so provided for it ... Ps 65:9
For thou, O God, *h* proved us ... Ps 66:10
thou *h* tried us, as silver is ... Ps 66:10
Thou *h* caused men to ride over ... Ps 66:12
h prepared of thy goodness for ... Ps 68:10
Thou *h* ascended on high ... Ps 68:18
thou *h* led captivity captive ... Ps 68:18
thou *h* received gifts for men ... Ps 68:18
that which thou *h* wrought for us ... Ps 68:28
Thou *h* known my reproach, and my ... Ps 69:19
persecute him whom thou *h* smitten ... Ps 69:26
of those whom thou *h* wounded ... Ps 69:26
thou *h* given commandment to save ... Ps 71:3
thou *h* taught me from my youth ... Ps 71:17
high, who *h* done great things ... Ps 71:19
which *h* shewed me great and sore ... Ps 71:20
and my soul, which thou *h* redeemed ... Ps 71:23
thou *h* holden me by my right hand ... Ps 73:23
thou *h* destroyed all them that go ... Ps 73:27
why *h* thou cast us off for ever ... Ps 74:1
which thou *h* purchased of old ... Ps 74:2
which thou *h* redeemed ... Ps 74:2
mount Zion, wherein thou *h* dwelt ... Ps 74:2
thou *h* prepared the light and the ... Ps 74:16
Thou *h* set all the borders of the ... Ps 74:17
thou *h* made summer and winter ... Ps 74:17
thou *h* declared thy strength ... Ps 77:14
Thou *h* with thine arm redeemed ... Ps 77:15
Thou *h* brought a vine out of ... Ps 80:8
thou *h* cast out the heathen, and ... Ps 80:8
Why *h* thou then broken down her ... Ps 80:12
thou *h* been favourable unto thy ... Ps 85:1
thou *h* brought back the captivity ... Ps 85:1
Thou *h* forgiven the iniquity of ... Ps 85:2
thou *h* covered all their sin ... Ps 85:2
Thou *h* taken away all thy wrath ... Ps 85:3
thou *h* turned thyself from the ... Ps 85:3
whom thou *h* made shall come ... Ps 86:9
thou *h* delivered my soul from the ... Ps 86:13
h holpen me, and comforted me ... Ps 86:17
Thou *h* laid me in the lowest pit, ... Ps 88:6
thou *h* afflicted me with all thy ... Ps 88:7
Thou *h* put away mine acquaintance ... Ps 88:8
thou *h* made me an abomination ... Ps 88:8
friend *h* thou put far from me, and ... Ps 88:18
Thou *h* broken Rahab in pieces, as ... Ps 89:10
thou *h* scattered thine enemies ... Ps 89:10
thereof, thou *h* founded them ... Ps 89:11
and the south thou *h* created them ... Ps 89:12
Thou *h* a mighty arm ... Ps 89:13
But thou *h* cast off and abhorred, ... Ps 89:38
thou *h* been wroth with thine ... Ps 89:38
Thou *h* made void the covenant of ... Ps 89:39
thou *h* profaned his crown by ... Ps 89:39
Thou *h* broken down all his hedges ... Ps 89:40
thou *h* brought his strong holds ... Ps 89:40
Thou *h* set up the right hand of ... Ps 89:42
thou *h* made all his enemies to ... Ps 89:42
Thou *h* also turned the edge of ... Ps 89:43
h not made him to stand in the ... Ps 89:43
Thou *h* made his glory to cease, ... Ps 89:44
of his youth *h* thou shortened ... Ps 89:45
thou *h* covered him with shame ... Ps 89:45
wherefore *h* thou made all men in ... Ps 89:47
thou *h* been our dwelling place in ... Ps 90:1 1961
Thou *h* set our iniquities before ... Ps 90:8
days wherein thou *h* afflicted us ... Ps 90:15
Because thou *h* made the LORD, ... Ps 91:9
h made me glad through thy work ... Ps 92:4
for thou *h* lifted me up, and cast ... Ps 102:10
Of old *h* thou laid the foundation ... Ps 102:25
which thou *h* founded for them ... Ps 104:8
Thou *h* set a bound that they may ... Ps 104:9
In wisdom *h* thou made them all ... Ps 104:24
whom thou *h* made to play therein ... Ps 104:26
thou, O God, who *h* cast us off ... Ps 108:11
that thou, LORD, *h* done it ... Ps 109:27
thou *h* the dew of thy youth ... Ps 110:3
For thou *h* delivered my soul from ... Ps 116:8
thou *h* loosed my bonds ... Ps 116:16
Thou *h* thrust sore at me that I ... Ps 118:13
for thou *h* heard me, and art ... Ps 118:21
Thou *h* commanded us to keep thy ... Ps 119:4
Thou *h* rebuked the proud that are ... Ps 119:21
upon which thou *h* caused me to ... Ps 119:49
Thou *h* dealt well with thy ... Ps 119:65
in faithfulness *h* afflicted me ... Ps 119:75
thou *h* established the earth, and ... Ps 119:90
for with them thou *h* quickened me ... Ps 119:93
Thou through thy commandments *h* ... Ps 119:98
for thou *h* taught me ... Ps 119:102
Thou *h* trodden down all them that ... Ps 119:118
thou *h* commanded are righteous ... Ps 119:138
that thou *h* founded them for ever ... Ps 119:152
when thou *h* taught me thy ... Ps 119:171
thee as thou *h* served us ... Ps 137:8
for thou *h* magnified thy word ... Ps 138:2
thou *h* searched me, and known me ... Ps 139:1
Thou *h* beset me behind and before, ... Ps 139:5

For thou *h* possessed my reins ... Ps 139:13
thou *h* covered me in my mother's ... Ps 139:13
thou *h* covered my head in the day ... Ps 140:7
when thou *h* it by thee ... Prov 3:28 3426
if thou *h* stricken thy hand with ... Prov 6:1
If thou *h* nothing to pay, why ... Prov 22:27
The morsel which thou *h* eaten ... Prov 23:8
when thou *h* found it, then there ... Prov 24:14
H thou found honey ... Prov 25:16
If thou *h* done foolishly in ... Prov 30:32
or if thou *h* thought evil, lay ... Prov 30:32
pay that which thou *h* vowed ... Eccl 5:4
thyself likewise *h* cursed others ... Eccl 7:22
thou *h* doves' eyes ... Song 1:15
thou *h* doves' eyes within thy ... Song 4:1
Thou *h* ravished my heart, my ... Song 4:9
thou *h* ravished my heart with one ... Song 4:9
Therefore thou *h* forsaken thy ... Is 2:6
Thou *h* clothing, be thou our ... Is 3:6
Thou *h* multiplied the nation, and ... Is 9:3
For thou *h* broken the yoke of his ... Is 9:4
For thou *h* said in thine heart, I ... Is 14:13
because thou *h* destroyed thy land ... Is 14:20
Because thou *h* forgotten the God ... Is 17:10
h not been mindful of the rock of ... Is 17:10
What *h* thou here ... Is 22:16
whom *h* thou here, that thou *h* ... Is 22:16
thou harlot that *h* been forgotten ... Is 23:16
for thou *h* done wonderful things ... Is 25:1
For thou *h* made of a city an heap ... Is 25:2
For thou *h* been a strength to the ... Is 25:4
for thou also *h* wrought all our ... Is 26:12
therefore *h* thou visited and ... Is 26:14
Thou *h* increased the nation, O ... Is 26:15
thou *h* increased the nation ... Is 26:15
of the words that thou *h* heard ... Is 37:6
thou *h* heard what the kings of ... Is 37:11
thou *h* made heaven and earth ... Is 37:16
Whereas thou *h* prayed to me ... Is 37:21
Whom *h* thou reproached and ... Is 37:23
against whom *h* thou exalted thy ... Is 37:23
By thy servants *h* thou reproached ... Is 37:24
h said, By the multitude of my ... Is 37:24
H thou not heard long ago, how I ... Is 37:26
but thou *h* in love to my soul ... Is 38:17
for thou *h* cast all my sins ... Is 38:17
of the LORD which thou *h* spoken ... Is 39:8
H thou not known ... Is 40:28
h thou not heard, that the ... Is 40:28
thou *h* been honourable, and I have ... Is 43:4
But thou *h* not called upon me, O ... Is 43:22
but thou *h* been weary of me, O ... Is 43:22
Thou *h* not brought me the small ... Is 43:23
neither *h* thou honoured me with ... Is 43:23
Thou *h* bought me no sweet cane ... Is 43:24
neither *h* thou filled me with the ... Is 43:24
but thou *h* made me to serve with ... Is 43:24
thou *h* wearied me with thine ... Is 43:24
though thou *h* not known me ... Is 45:4
though thou *h* not known me ... Is 45:5
What *h* thou brought forth ... Is 45:10
upon the ancient *h* thou very ... Is 47:6
For thou *h* trusted in thy ... Is 47:10
thou *h* said, None seeth me ... Is 47:10
thou *h* said in thine heart, I am, ... Is 47:10
wherein thou *h* laboured from thy ... Is 47:12
thee with whom thou *h* laboured ... Is 47:15
Thou *h* heard, see all this ... Is 48:6
after thou *h* lost the other, ... Is 49:20
h feared continually every day ... Is 51:13
which *h* drunk at the hand of the ... Is 51:17
thou *h* drunken the dregs of the ... Is 51:17
thou *h* laid thy body as the ... Is 51:23
even to them *h* thou poured a ... Is 57:6
thou *h* offered a meat offering ... Is 57:6
high mountain *h* thou set thy bed ... Is 57:7
the posts *h* thou set up thy ... Is 57:8
for thou *h* discovered thyself to ... Is 57:8
thou *h* enlarged thy bed, and made ... Is 57:8
thou *h* found the life of thine ... Is 57:10
of whom *h* thou been afraid or ... Is 57:11
or feared, that thou *h* lied ... Is 57:11
h not remembered me, nor laid it ... Is 57:11
Whereas thou *h* been forsaken and ... Is 60:15
for the which thou *h* laboured ... Is 62:8
why *h* thou made us to err from ... Is 63:17
for thou *h* hid thy face from us, ... Is 64:7
h consumed us, because of our ... Is 64:7
LORD unto me, Thou *h* well seen ... Jer 1:12
H thou not procured this unto ... Jer 2:17
in that thou *h* forsaken the LORD ... Jer 2:17
now what *h* thou to do in the way ... Jer 2:18
or what *h* thou to do in the way ... Jer 2:18
that thou *h* forsaken the LORD thy ... Jer 2:19
the valley, know what thou *h* done ... Jer 2:23
a stone, Thou *h* brought me forth ... Jer 2:27
thy gods that thou *h* made thee ... Jer 2:28
therefore *h* thou also taught the ... Jer 2:33
but thou *h* played the harlot with ... Jer 3:1
see where thou *h* not been lien ... Jer 3:2
In the ways *h* thou sat for them, ... Jer 3:2
thou *h* polluted the land with thy ... Jer 3:2
thou *h* spoken and done evil things ... Jer 3:5
the king, *H* thou seen that which ... Jer 3:6
that thou *h* transgressed against ... Jer 3:13
h scattered thy ways to the ... Jer 3:13
surely thou *h* greatly deceived ... Jer 4:10
my peace, because thou *h* heard ... Jer 4:19

thou *h* stricken them, but they ... Jer 5:3
thou *h* consumed them, but they ... Jer 5:3
Thou *h* planted them, yea, they ... Jer 12:2
thou *h* seen me, and tried mine ... Jer 12:3
If thou *h* run with the footmen, ... Jer 12:5
Take the girdle that thou *h* got ... Jer 13:4
for thou *h* taught them to be ... Jer 13:21
because thou *h* forgotten me ... Jer 13:25
H thou utterly rejected Judah ... Jer 14:19
why *h* thou smitten us, and there ... Jer 14:19
for thou *h* made all these things ... Jer 14:22
Thou *h* forsaken me, saith the ... Jer 15:6
that thou *h* borne me a man of ... Jer 15:10
for thou *h* filled me with ... Jer 15:17
to whom thou *h* prophesied lies ... Jer 20:6
thou *h* deceived me, and I was ... Jer 20:7
stronger than I, and *h* prevailed ... Jer 20:7
Why *h* thou prophesied in the name ... Jer 26:9
thy words which thou *h* prophesied ... Jer 28:6
Thou *h* broken the yokes of wood ... Jer 28:13
because thou *h* taught rebellion ... Jer 28:16
Because thou *h* sent letters in ... Jer 29:25
Now therefore why *h* thou not ... Jer 29:27
thou *h* no healing medicines ... Jer 30:13
Thou *h* chastised me, and I was ... Jer 31:18
thou *h* made the heaven and the ... Jer 32:17
Which *h* set signs and wonders in ... Jer 32:20
h made thee a name, as at this ... Jer 32:20
h brought forth thy people Israel ... Jer 32:21
h given them this land, which ... Jer 32:22
therefore thou *h* caused all this ... Jer 32:23
what thou *h* spoken is come to ... Jer 32:24
thou *h* said unto me, O Lord GOD, ... Jer 32:25
which thou *h* written from my ... Jer 36:6
hand the roll wherein thou *h* read ... Jer 36:14
Thou *h* burned this roll, saying, ... Jer 36:29
Why *h* thou written therein, ... Jer 36:29
what thou *h* said unto the king ... Jer 38:25
because thou *h* put thy trust in ... Jer 39:18
As for the word that thou *h* ... Jer 44:16
For because thou *h* trusted in thy ... Jer 48:7
because thou *h* striven against ... Jer 50:24
thou *h* spoken against this place, ... Jer 51:62
when thou *h* made an end of ... Jer 51:63
they are glad that thou *h* done it ... Lam 1:21
bring the day that thou *h* called ... Lam 1:21
as thou *h* done unto me for all my ... Lam 1:22
consider to whom thou *h* done this ... Lam 2:20
thou *h* slain them in the day of ... Lam 2:21
thou *h* killed, and not pitied ... Lam 2:21
Thou *h* called as in a solemn day ... Lam 2:22
thou *h* removed my soul far off ... Lam 3:17
thou *h* not pardoned ... Lam 3:42
Thou *h* covered with anger, and ... Lam 3:43
h slain, thou *h* not pitied ... Lam 3:43
Thou *h* covered thyself with a ... Lam 3:44
Thou *h* made us as the offscouring ... Lam 3:45
Thou *h* heard my voice ... Lam 3:56
thou *h* pleaded the causes of my ... Lam 3:58
thou *h* redeemed my life ... Lam 3:58
O LORD, thou *h* seen my wrong ... Lam 3:59
Thou *h* seen all their vengeance ... Lam 3:60
Thou *h* heard their reproach, O ... Lam 3:61
But thou *h* utterly rejected us ... Lam 5:22
but thou *h* delivered thy soul ... Eze 3:19
because thou *h* not given him ... Eze 3:20
also thou *h* delivered thy soul ... Eze 3:21
when thou *h* accomplished them, ... Eze 4:6
till thou *h* ended the days of thy ... Eze 4:8
because thou *h* defiled my ... Eze 5:11
h thou seen what the ancients of ... Eze 8:12
H thou seen this, O son of man ... Eze 8:15
H thou seen this, O son of man ... Eze 8:17
have done as thou *h* commanded me ... Eze 9:11
thou *h* increased and waxen great, ... Eze 16:7
Thou *h* also taken thy fair jewels ... Eze 16:17
thou *h* set mine oil and mine ... Eze 16:18
thou *h* even set it before them ... Eze 16:19
Moreover thou *h* taken thy sons and ... Eze 16:20
whom thou *h* borne unto me, and ... Eze 16:20
these *h* thou sacrificed unto them ... Eze 16:20
That thou *h* slain my children, and ... Eze 16:21
and thy whoredoms thou *h* not ... Eze 16:22
That thou *h* also built unto thee ... Eze 16:24
h made thee an high place in ... Eze 16:24
Thou *h* built thy high place at ... Eze 16:25
h made thy beauty to be abhorred, ... Eze 16:25
h opened thy feet to every one ... Eze 16:25
Thou *h* also committed fornication ... Eze 16:26
h increased thy whoredoms, to ... Eze 16:26
Thou *h* played the whore also with ... Eze 16:28
thou *h* played the harlot with ... Eze 16:28
Thou *h* moreover multiplied thy ... Eze 16:29
h not been as an harlot, in that ... Eze 16:31 1961
with whom thou *h* taken pleasure ... Eze 16:37
and all them that thou *h* loved ... Eze 16:37
with all them that thou *h* hated ... Eze 16:37
Because thou *h* not remembered the ... Eze 16:43
but *h* fretted me in all these ... Eze 16:43
Yet *h* thou not walked after their ... Eze 16:47
nor her daughters, as thou *h* done ... Eze 16:48
but thou *h* multiplied thine ... Eze 16:51
h justified thy sisters in all ... Eze 16:51
abominations which thou *h* done ... Eze 16:51
which *h* judged thy sisters, bear ... Eze 16:52
shame for thy sins that thou *h* ... Eze 16:52
in that thou *h* justified thy ... Eze 16:52
in all that thou *h* done, in that ... Eze 16:54

Thou *h* borne thy lewdness and ... Eze 16:58
deal with thee as thou *h* done ... Eze 16:59
which *h* despised the oath in ... Eze 16:59
thee for all that thou *h* done ... Eze 16:63
in thy blood that thou *h* shed ... Eze 22:4
h defiled thyself in thine idols ... Eze 22:4
in thine idols which thou *h* made ... Eze 22:4
thou *h* caused thy days to draw ... Eze 22:4
Thou *h* despised mine holy things, ... Eze 22:8
and *h* profaned my sabbaths ... Eze 22:8
thou *h* taken usury and increase, ... Eze 22:12
thou *h* greedily gained of thy ... Eze 22:12
h forgotten me, saith the Lord ... Eze 22:12
dishonest gain which thou *h* made ... Eze 22:13
because thou *h* gone a whoring ... Eze 23:30
Thou *h* walked in the way of thy ... Eze 23:31
Because thou *h* forgotten me ... Eze 23:35
whereupon thou *h* set mine incense ... Eze 23:41
Because thou *h* clapped thine ... Eze 25:6
O Tyrus, thou *h* said, I am of ... Eze 27:3
is lifted up, and thou *h* said ... Eze 28:2
thou *h* gotten thee riches ... Eze 28:4
h gotten gold and silver into thy ... Eze 28:4
by thy traffick *h* thou increased ... Eze 28:5
Because thou *h* set thine heart as ... Eze 28:6
Thou *h* been in Eden the garden of ... Eze 28:13 1961
thou *h* walked up and down in the ... Eze 28:14
with violence, and thou *h* sinned ... Eze 28:16
thou *h* corrupted thy wisdom by ... Eze 28:17
Thou *h* defiled thy sanctuaries by ... Eze 28:18
Because thou *h* lifted up thyself ... Eze 31:10
countries which thou *h* not known ... Eze 32:9
but thou *h* delivered thy soul ... Eze 33:9
Because thou *h* had a perpetual ... Eze 35:5 1961
h shed the blood of the children ... Eze 35:5
sith thou *h* not hated blood, even ... Eze 35:6
Because thou *h* said, These two ... Eze 35:10
to thine envy which thou *h* used ... Eze 35:11
all thy blasphemies which thou *h* ... Eze 35:12
up men, and *h* bereaved thy nations ... Eze 36:13
h thou gathered thy company to ... Eze 38:13
When thou *h* made an end of ... Eze 43:23
me, Son of man, *h* thou seen this ... Eze 47:6
who *h* given me wisdom and might, ... Dan 2:23
h made known unto me now what we ... Dan 2:23
for thou *h* now made known unto us ... Dan 2:23
h made a decree, that every man ... Dan 3:10
are certain Jews whom thou *h* set ... Dan 3:12
golden image which thou *h* set up ... Dan 3:12
golden image which thou *h* set up ... Dan 3:18
h not humbled thine heart, though ... Dan 5:22
But *h* lifted up thyself against ... Dan 5:23
thou *h* praised the gods of silver ... Dan 5:23
thy ways, *h* thou not glorified ... Dan 5:23
H thou not signed a decree, that ... Dan 6:12
nor the decree that thou *h* signed ... Dan 6:13
whither thou *h* driven them ... Dan 9:7
that *h* brought thy people forth ... Dan 9:15
h gotten thee renown, as at this ... Dan 9:15
for thou *h* strengthened me ... Dan 10:19
because thou *h* rejected knowledge ... Hos 4:6
seeing thou *h* forgotten the law ... Hos 4:6
for thou *h* gone a whoring from ... Hos 9:1
thou *h* loved a reward upon every ... Hos 9:1
thou *h* sinned from the days of ... Hos 10:9
Israel, thou *h* destroyed thyself ... Hos 13:9
for thou *h* fallen by thine ... Hos 14:1
as thou *h* done, it shall be done ... Obad 15
unto him, Why *h* thou done this ... Jonah 1:10
h done as it pleased thee ... Jonah 1:14
yet *h* thou brought up my life ... Jonah 2:6
Thou *h* had pity on the gourd ... Jonah 4:10
for the which thou *h* not laboured ... Jonah 4:10
which thou *h* sworn unto our ... Mic 7:20
Thou *h* multiplied thy merchants ... Nah 3:16
thou *h* ordained them for judgment ... Hab 1:12
thou *h* established them for ... Hab 1:12
Because thou *h* spoiled many ... Hab 2:8
Thou *h* consulted shame to thy ... Hab 2:10
h sinned against thy soul ... Hab 2:10
wherein thou *h* transgressed ... Zeph 3:11
Judah, against which thou *h* had ... Zec 1:12
ye say, Wherein *h* thou loved us ... Mal 1:2
against whom thou *h* dealt ... Mal 2:14
till thou *h* paid the uttermost ... Mt 5:26
when thou *h* shut thy door, pray ... Mt 6:6
as thou *h* believed, so be it done ... Mt 8:13
because thou *h* hid these things ... Mt 11:25
h revealed them unto babes ... Mt 11:25
when thou *h* opened his mouth, ... Mt 17:27
thou *h* gained thy brother ... Mt 18:15
perfect, go and sell that thou *h* ... Mt 19:21 *5224*
thou *h* made them equal unto us, ... Mt 20:12
sucklings thou *h* perfected praise ... Mt 21:16
thou *h* been faithful over a few ... Mt 25:21
thou *h* been faithful over a few ... Mt 25:23
reaping where thou *h* not sown ... Mt 25:24
where thou *h* not strawed ... Mt 25:24
there thou *h* that is thine ... Mt 25:25 *2192*
He said unto him, Thou *h* said ... Mt 26:25
Jesus saith unto him, Thou *h* said ... Mt 26:64
my God, why *h* thou forsaken me ... Mt 27:46
thy way, sell whatsoever thou *h* ... Mk 10:21 *2192*
Master, thou *h* said the truth ... Mk 12:32
my God, why *h* thou forsaken me ... Mk 15:34
wherein thou *h* been instructed ... Lk 1:4
for thou *h* found favour with God ... Lk 1:30
Which thou *h* prepared before the ... Lk 2:31

why *h* thou thus dealt with us ... Lk 2:48
unto him, Thou *h* rightly judged ... Lk 7:43
that thou *h* hid these things from ... Lk 10:21
h revealed them unto babes ... Lk 10:21
unto him, Thou *h* answered right ... Lk 10:28
and the paps which thou *h* sucked ... Lk 11:27
thou *h* much goods laid up for ... Lk 12:19 *2192*
things be, which thou *h* provided ... Lk 12:20
till thou *h* paid the very last ... Lk 12:59
thou *h* taught in our streets ... Lk 13:26
it is done as thou *h* commanded ... Lk 14:22
thou *h* killed for him the fatted ... Lk 15:30
sell all that thou *h*, and ... Lk 18:22 *2192*
because thou *h* been faithful in a ... Lk 19:17
said, Master, thou *h* well said ... Lk 20:39
h not known the things which are ... Lk 24:18
but thou *h* kept the good wine ... Jn 2:10
thou *h* nothing to draw with, and ... Jn 4:11 *2192*
from whence then *h* thou that ... Jn 4:11 *2192*
Thou *h* well said, I have no ... Jn 4:17
For thou *h* had five husbands ... Jn 4:18 *2192*
he whom thou now *h* is not thy ... Jn 4:18 *2192*
thou *h* the words of eternal life ... Jn 6:68 *2192*
answered and said, Thou *h* a devil ... Jn 7:20 *2192*
art a Samaritan, and *h* a devil ... Jn 8:48 *2192*
Now we know that thou *h* a devil ... Jn 8:52 *2192*
years old, and *h* thou seen Abraham ... Jn 8:57
Thou *h* both seen him, and it is he ... Jn 9:37
I thank thee that thou *h* heard me ... Jn 11:41
may believe that thou *h* sent me ... Jn 11:42
thee not, thou *h* no part with me ... Jn 13:8 *2192*
till thou *h* denied me thrice ... Jn 13:38
yet *h* thou not known me, Philip ... Jn 14:9
As thou *h* given him power over ... Jn 17:2
to as many as thou *h* given him ... Jn 17:2
and Jesus Christ, whom thou *h* sent ... Jn 17:3
thou *h* given me are of thee ... Jn 17:7
for them which thou *h* given me ... Jn 17:9
name those whom thou *h* given me ... Jn 17:11
As thou *h* sent me into the world, ... Jn 17:18
may believe that thou *h* sent me ... Jn 17:21
may know that thou *h* sent me ... Jn 17:23
h loved them, as thou *h* loved ... Jn 17:23
they also, whom thou *h* given me ... Jn 17:24
my glory, which thou *h* given me ... Jn 17:24
have known that thou *h* sent me ... Jn 17:25
thou *h* loved me may be in them ... Jn 17:26
what *h* thou done? ... Jn 18:35
tell me where thou *h* laid him ... Jn 20:15
h seen me, thou *h* believed ... Jn 20:29
of these two thou *h* chosen ... Acts 1:24
Thou *h* made known to me the ways ... Acts 2:28
which *h* made heaven, and earth, and ... Acts 4:24
mouth of thy servant David *h* said ... Acts 4:25
child Jesus, whom thou *h* anointed ... Acts 4:27
why *h* thou conceived this thing ... Acts 5:4
thou *h* not lied unto men, but ... Acts 5:4
because thou *h* thought that the ... Acts 8:20
Thou *h* neither part nor lot in ... Acts 8:21 *2076*
thou *h* well done that thou art ... Acts 10:33
unto all men of what thou *h* seen ... Acts 22:15
for as thou *h* testified of me in ... Acts 23:11
What is that thou *h* to tell me ... Acts 23:19 *2192*
thou *h* shewed these things to me ... Acts 23:22
Forasmuch as I know that thou *h* ... Acts 24:10
H thou appealed unto Caesar ... Acts 25:12
of these things which thou *h* seen ... Acts 26:16
which *h* the form of knowledge and ... Rom 2:20 *2192*
it, Why *h* thou made me thus ... Rom 9:20
H thou faith? ... Rom 14:22 *2192*
what *h* thou that thou didst not ... 1Cor 4:7 *2192*
if thou marry, thou *h* not sinned ... 1Cor 7:28
h knowledge sit at meat in the ... 1Cor 8:10 *2192*
which thou *h* received in the Lord ... Col 4:17
whereunto thou *h* attained ... 1Ti 4:6
h professed a good profession ... 1Ti 6:12
which thou *h* heard of me, in ... 2Ti 1:13
the things that thou *h* heard of ... 2Ti 2:2
But thou *h* fully known my ... 2Ti 3:10
the things which thou *h* learned ... 2Ti 3:14
h been assured of, knowing of ... 2Ti 3:14
of whom thou *h* learned them ... 2Ti 3:14
that from a child thou *h* known ... 2Ti 3:15
which thou *h* toward the Lord ... Philem 5 *2192*
Thou *h* loved righteousness, and ... Heb 1:9
in the beginning *h* laid the ... Heb 1:10
Thou *h* put all things in ... Heb 2:8
but a body *h* thou prepared me ... Heb 10:5
for sin thou *h* had no pleasure ... Heb 10:6
Thou *h* faith, and I have works ... Jas 2:18 *2192*
the things which thou *h* seen ... Rev 1:19
thou *h* tried them which say they ... Rev 2:2
and are not, and *h* found them liars ... Rev 2:2
h borne, and *h* patience, and for ... Rev 2:3
h patience, and for my name's sake ... Rev 2:3 *2192*
h laboured, and *h* not fainted ... Rev 2:3
because thou *h* left thy first ... Rev 2:4
But this thou *h*, that thou hatest ... Rev 2:6 *2192*
h not denied my faith, even in ... Rev 2:13
because thou *h* there them that ... Rev 2:14 *2192*
So *h* thou also them that hold the ... Rev 2:15 *2192*
that thou *h* a name that thou ... Rev 3:1 *2192*
therefore how thou *h* received ... Rev 3:3
Thou *h* a few names even in Sardis ... Rev 3:4 *2192*
for thou *h* a little strength, and ... Rev 3:8 *2192*
h kept my word, and *h* not ... Rev 3:8
Because thou *h* kept the word of ... Rev 3:10
hold that fast which thou *h* ... Rev 3:11 *2192*

for thou *h* created all things, and Rev 4:11
h redeemed us to God by thy blood Rev 5:9
h made us unto our God kings and Rev 5:10
because thou *h* taken to thee thy Rev 11:17
thy great power, and *h* reigned Rev 11:17
be, because thou *h* judged thus Rev 16:5
thou *h* given them blood to drink Rev 16:6

HASTE {55}
H thee, escape thither Gen 19:22 4116
And she made *h*, and let down her Gen 24:46 4116
And Joseph made *h* Gen 43:30 4116
H ye, and go up to my father, and Gen 45:9 4116
and ye shall *h* and bring down my Gen 45:13 4116
called for Moses and Aaron in *h* Ex 10:16 4116
and ye shall eat it in *h* Ex 12:11 2649
send them out of the land in *h* Ex 12:33 4116
And Moses made *h*, and bowed his Ex 34:8 4116
out of the land of Egypt in *h* Deut 16:3 2649
that shall come upon them make *h* Deut 32:35 2363
What ye have seen me do, make *h* Judg 9:48 4116
And the woman made *h*, and ran, and Judg 13:10 4116
make *h* now, for he came to day to 1Sa 9:12 4116
after the lad, Make speed, *h* 1Sa 20:38 2363
the king's business required *h* 1Sa 21:8 5169
David made *h* to get away for fear 1Sa 23:26 2648
Saul, saying, *H* thee, and come 1Sa 23:27 4116
Then Abigail made *h*, and took two 1Sa 25:18 4116
to pass, as she made *h* to flee 2Sa 4:4 2648
Syrians had cast away in their *h* 2Kin 7:15 2648
for God commanded me to make *h* 2Chr 35:21 926
they went up in *h* to Jerusalem Ezr 4:23 924
king said, Cause Haman to make *h* Est 5:5 4116
the king said to Haman, Make *h* Est 6:10 4116
to answer, and for this I make *h* Job 20:2 2363
O my strength, *h* thee to help me Ps 22:19 2363
For I said in my *h*, I am cut off Ps 31:22 2648
Make *h* to help me, O Lord my Ps 38:22 2363
O LORD, make *h* to help me Ps 40:13 2363
Make *h*, O God, to deliver me Ps 70:1
make *h* to help me, O LORD Ps 70:1 2363
make *h* unto me, O God Ps 70:5 2363
O my God, make *h* for my help Ps 71:12 2439
I said in my *h*, All men are liars Ps 116:11 2648
I made *h*, and delayed not to keep Ps 119:60 2363
make *h* unto me Ps 141:1 2363
to evil, and make *h* to shed blood Prov 1:16 4116
but he that maketh *h* to be rich Prov 28:20 213
Make *h*, my beloved, and be thou Song 8:14 1272
that believeth shall not make *h* Is 28:16 2363
Thy children shall make *h* Is 49:17 4116
For ye shall not go out with *h* Is 52:12 2649
they make *h* to shed innocent Is 59:7 4116
And let them make *h*, and take up a Jer 9:18 4116
in Daniel before the king in *h* Dan 2:25 927
was astonied, and rose up in *h* Dan 3:24 927
went in *h* unto the den of lions Dan 6:19 927
they shall make *h* to the wall Nah 2:5 4116
straightway with *h* unto the king Mk 6:25 *4710*
went into the hill country with *h* Lk 1:39 *4710*
And they came with *h*, and found Lk 2:16 *4692*
said unto him, Zacchaeus, make *h* Lk 19:5 *4692*
And he made *h*, and came down, and Lk 19:6 *4692*
And saw him saying unto me, Make *h* Acts 22:18 *4692*

HASTED {24}
and he *h* to dress it Gen 18:7 4116
and she *h*, and let down her pitcher Gen 24:18 4116
And she *h*, and emptied her pitcher Gen 24:20 4116
And the taskmasters *h* them Ex 5:13 213
and the people *h* and passed over Josh 4:10 4116
king of Ai saw it, that they *h* Josh 8:14 4116
into the city, and took it, and *h* Josh 8:19 4116
h not to go down about a whole Josh 10:13 213
And the liers in wait *h*, and rushed Judg 20:37 2363
nigh to meet David, that David *h* 1Sa 17:48 4116
And when Abigail saw David, she *h* 1Sa 25:23 4116
hurting thee, except thou hadst *h* 1Sa 25:34 4116
And Abigail *h*, and arose, and rode 1Sa 25:42 4116
and she *h*, and killed it, and took 1Sa 28:24 4116
which was of Bahurim, *h* and came 2Sa 19:16 4116
And he *h*, and took the ashes away 1Kin 20:41 4116
Then they *h*, and took every man 2Kin 9:13 4116
himself *h* also to go out, because 2Chr 26:20 1765
But Haman *h* to his house mourning Est 6:12 1765
h to bring Haman unto the banquet Est 6:14 926
or if my foot hath *h* to deceit Job 31:5 2363
they were troubled, and *h* away Ps 48:5 2648
voice of thy thunder they *h* away Ps 104:7 2648
for he *h*, if it were possible for Acts 20:16 *4692*

HASTEN {8}
H hither Micaiah the son of Imlah 1Kin 22:9 4116
year, and see that ye *h* the matter 2Chr 24:5 4116
that *h* after another god Ps 16:4 4116
I would *h* my escape from the Ps 55:8 2363
eat, or who else can *h* hereunto Eccl 2:25 2363
h his work, that we may see it Is 5:19 2363
I the LORD will *h* it in his time Is 60:22 2363
for I will *h* my word to perform Jer 1:12 8245

HASTENED {6}
Abraham *h* into the tent unto Gen 18:6 4116
arose, then the angels *h* Lot Gen 19:15 213
Howbeit the Levites *h* it not 2Chr 24:5 4116
being *h* by the king's commandment Est 3:15 1765
mules and camels went out, being *h* Est 8:14 926
I have not *h* from being a pastor Jer 17:16 213

HASTENETH {1}
The captive exile *h* that he may Is 51:14 4116

HASTETH {9}
as the eagle that *h* to the prey Job 9:26 2907
he drinketh up a river, and *h* not Job 40:23 2648
as a bird *h* to the snare, and Prov 7:23 4116
he that *h* with his feet sinneth Prov 19:2 213
He that *h* to be rich hath an evil Prov 28:22 926
h to his place where he arose Eccl 1:5 7602
to come, and his affliction *h* fast Jer 48:16 4116
fly as the eagle that *h* to eat Hab 1:8 2363
h greatly, even the voice of the Zeph 1:14 4116

HASTILY {8}
they brought him *h* out of the Gen 41:14 7323
without driving them out *h* Judg 2:23 4118
Then he called *h* unto the young Judg 9:54 4120
And the man came in *h*, and told Eli 1Sa 4:14 4116
come from him, and did *h* catch it 1Kin 20:33 4116
may be gotten *h* at the beginning Prov 20:21 926
Go not forth *h* to strive, lest Prov 25:8 4118
they saw Mary, that she rose up *h* Jn 11:31 *5030*

HASTING {2}
judgment, and *h* righteousness Is 16:5 4106
h unto the coming of the day of 2Pet 3:12 *4692*

HASTY {9}
but he that is *h* of spirit Prov 14:29 7116
every one that is *h* only to want Prov 21:5 213
thou a man that is *h* in his words Prov 29:20 213
let not thine heart be *h* to utter Eccl 5:2 4116
Be not *h* in thy spirit to be Eccl 7:9 926
Be not *h* to go out of his sight Eccl 8:3 926
as the *h* fruit before the summer Is 28:4 1061
is the decree so *h* from the king Dan 2:15 2685
h nation, which shall march Hab 1:6 4116

HASUPHA *(has-u'-fah)* {1} *A family of exiles.*
of Ziha, the children of *H* Ezr 2:43 2817

HATACH *(ha'-tak)* {4} *A servant of King Ahasuerus.*
Then called Esther for *H*, one of Est 4:5 2047
So *H* went forth to Mordecai unto Est 4:6 2047
H came and told Esther the words Est 4:9 2047
Again Esther spake unto *H* Est 4:10 2047

HATCH {2}
owl make her nest, and lay, and *h* Is 34:15 1234
They *h* cockatrice' eggs, and weave Is 59:5 1234

HATCHETH {1}
sitteth on eggs, and *h* them not Jer 17:11 3205

HATE {87}
the gate of those which *h* them Gen 24:60 8130
come ye to me, seeing ye *h* me Gen 26:27 8130
Joseph will peradventure *h* us Gen 50:15 7852
generation of them that *h* me Ex 20:5 8130
Thou shalt not *h* thy brother in Lev 19:17 8130
they that *h* you shall reign over Lev 26:17 8130
let them that *h* thee flee before Num 10:35 8130
generation of them that *h* me Deut 5:9 8130
them that *h* him to their face Deut 7:10 8130
them upon all them that *h* thee Deut 7:15 8130
But if any man *h* his neighbour Deut 19:11 8130
and go in unto her, and *h* her, Deut 22:13 8130
And if the latter husband *h* her Deut 24:3 8130
enemies, and on them that *h* thee Deut 30:7 8130
and will reward them that *h* me Deut 32:41 8130
him, and of them that *h* him Deut 33:11 8130
elders of Gilead, Did not ye *h* me Judg 11:7 8130
him, and said, Thou dost but *h* me Judg 14:16 8130
I might destroy them that *h* me 2Sa 22:41 8130
but I *h* him 1Kin 22:8 8130
but I *h* him 2Chr 18:7 8130
and love them that *h* the LORD 2Chr 19:2 8130
They that *h* thee shall be clothed Job 8:22 8130
which I suffer of them that *h* me Ps 9:13 8130
I might destroy them that *h* me Ps 18:40 8130
shall find out those that *h* thee Ps 21:8 8130
they *h* me with cruel hatred Ps 25:19 8130
they that *h* the righteous shall Ps 34:21 8130
the eye that *h* me without a cause Ps 35:19 8130
they that *h* me wrongfully are Ps 38:19 8130
All that *h* me whisper together Ps 41:7 8130
they which *h* us spoil for Ps 44:10 8130
upon me, and in wrath they *h* me Ps 55:3 7852
let them also that *h* him flee Ps 68:1 8130
They that *h* me without a cause Ps 69:4 8130
be delivered from them that *h* me Ps 69:14 8130
they that *h* thee have lifted up Ps 83:2 8130
that they which *h* me may see it Ps 86:17 8130
face, and plague them that *h* him Ps 89:23 8130
Ye that love the LORD, *h* evil Ps 97:10 8130
I *h* the work of them that turn Ps 101:3 8130
their heart to *h* his people Ps 105:25 8130
see my desire upon them that *h* me Ps 118:7 8130
therefore I *h* every false way Ps 119:104 8130
I *h* vain thoughts Ps 119:113 8130
and I *h* every false way Ps 119:128 8130
I *h* and abhor lying Ps 119:163 8130
and turned back that *h* Zion Ps 129:5 8130
I *h* them, O LORD, that *h* thee Ps 139:21 8130
I *h* them with perfect hatred Ps 139:22 8130
scorning, and fools *h* knowledge Prov 1:22 8130
These six things doth the LORD *h* Prov 6:16 8130
The fear of the LORD is to *h* evil Prov 8:13 8130
way, and the froward mouth, do I *h* Prov 8:13 8130
all they that *h* me love death Prov 8:36 8130
not a scorner, lest he *h* thee Prov 9:8 8130
the brethren of the poor do *h* him Prov 19:7 8130
he be weary of thee, and so *h* thee Prov 25:17 8130
The bloodthirsty *h* the upright Prov 29:10 8130
A time to love, and a time to *h* Eccl 3:8 8130
I *h* robbery for burnt offering Is 61:8 8130
this abominable thing that I *h* Jer 44:4 8130
unto the will of them that *h* thee Eze 16:27 8130
the dream be to them that *h* thee Dan 4:19 8131
They *h* him that rebuketh in the Amos 5:10 8130
H the evil, and love the good, and Amos 5:15 8130
I *h*, I despise your feast days, Amos 5:21 8130
of Jacob, and *h* his palaces Amos 6:8 8130
Who *h* the good, and love the evil Mic 3:2 8130
for all these are things that I *h* Zec 8:17 8130
thy neighbour, and *h* thine enemy Mt 5:43 *3404*
you, do good to them that *h* you Mt 5:44 *3404*
for either he will *h* the one Mt 6:24 *3404*
another, and shall *h* one another Mt 24:10 *3404*
and from the hand of all that *h* us Lk 1:71 *3404*
are ye, when men shall *h* you Lk 6:22 *3404*
do good to them which *h* you Lk 6:27 *3404*
h not his father, and mother, and Lk 14:26 *3404*
for either he will *h* the one Lk 16:13 *3404*
The world cannot *h* you Jn 7:7 *3404*
If the world *h* you, ye know that Jn 15:18 *3404*
but what I *h*, that do I Rom 7:15 *3404*
my brethren, if the world *h* you 1Jn 3:13 *3404*
the Nicolaitanes, which I also *h* Rev 2:6 *3404*
the Nicolaitanes, which thing I *h* Rev 2:15 *3404*
beast, these shall *h* the whore Rev 17:16 *3404*

HATED {60}
Esau *h* Jacob because of the Gen 27:41 7852
when the LORD saw that Leah was *h* Gen 29:31 8130
the LORD hath heard that I was *h* Gen 29:33 8130
than all his brethren, they *h* him Gen 37:4 8130
and they *h* him yet the more Gen 37:5 8130
they *h* him yet the more for his Gen 37:8 8130
him, and shot at him, and *h* him Gen 49:23 7852
and said, Because the LORD *h* us Deut 1:27 8135
and *h* him not in times past Deut 4:42 8130
them, and because he *h* them Deut 9:28 8135
whom he *h* not in time past Deut 19:4 8130
inasmuch as he *h* him not in time Deut 19:6 8130
wives, one beloved, and another *h* Deut 21:15 8130
both the beloved and the *h* Deut 21:15 8130
firstborn son be hers that was *h* Deut 21:15 8146
firstborn before the son of the *h* Deut 21:16 8130
son of the *h* for the firstborn Deut 21:17 8130
and *h* him not beforetime Josh 20:5 8130
that thou hadst utterly *h* her Judg 15:2 8130
that are *h* of David's soul, he 2Sa 5:8 8130
Then Amnon *h* her exceedingly 2Sa 13:15 8130
h her was greater than the love 2Sa 13:15 8130
for Absalom *h* Amnon, because he 2Sa 13:22 8130
enemy, and from them that *h* me 2Sa 22:18 8130
had rule over them that *h* them Est 9:1 8130
they would unto those that *h* them Est 9:5 8130
the destruction of him that *h* me Job 31:29 8130
enemy, and from them which *h* me Ps 18:17 8130
I have *h* the congregation of Ps 26:5 8130
I have *h* them that regard lying Ps 31:6 8130
hast put them to shame that *h* us Ps 44:7 8130
neither was it he that *h* me that Ps 55:12 8130
from the hand of him that *h* them Ps 106:10 8130
they that *h* them ruled over them Ps 106:41 8130
For that they *h* knowledge Prov 1:29 8130
How have I *h* instruction, and my Prov 5:12 8130
and a man of wicked devices is *h* Prov 14:17 8130
The poor is *h* even of his own Prov 14:20 8130
Therefore I *h* life Eccl 2:17 8130
I *h* all my labour which I had Eccl 2:18 8130
thou hast been forsaken and *h* Is 60:15 8130
Your brethren that *h* you, that Is 66:5 8130
therefore have I *h* it Jer 12:8 8130
with all them that thou hast *h* Eze 16:37 8130
sith thou hast not *h* blood Eze 35:6 8130
for there I *h* them Hos 9:15 8130
I *h* Esau, and laid his mountains Mal 1:3 8130
ye shall be *h* of all men for my Mt 10:22 *3404*
ye shall be *h* of all nations for Mt 24:9 *3404*
ye shall be *h* of all men for my Mk 13:13 *3404*
But his citizens *h* him, and sent a Lk 19:14 *3404*
ye shall be *h* of all men for my Lk 21:17 *3404*
ye know that it *h* me before it Jn 15:18 *3404*
me before it *h* you Jn 15:18
seen and *h* both me and my Father Jn 15:24 *3404*
They *h* me without a cause Jn 15:25 *3404*
and the world hath *h* them, because Jn 17:14 *3404*
have I loved, but Esau have I *h* Rom 9:13 *3404*
no man ever yet *h* his own flesh Eph 5:29 *3404*
righteousness, and *h* iniquity Heb 1:9 *3404*

HATEFUL {3}
his iniquity be found to be *h* Ps 36:2 8130
living in malice and envy, *h* Titus 3:3 *4767*
a cage of every unclean and *h* bird Rev 18:2 *3404*

HATEFULLY {1}
And they shall deal with thee *h* Eze 23:29 8135

HATERS {2}
The *h* of the LORD should have Ps 81:15 8130
h of God, despiteful, proud, Rom 1:30 *2319*

HATEST {6}
thine enemies, and *h* thy friends 2Sa 19:6 8130
thou *h* all workers of iniquity Ps 5:5 8130
righteousness, and *h* wickedness Ps 45:7 8130
Seeing thou *h* instruction Ps 50:17 8130
into the hand of them whom thou *h* Eze 23:28 8130
that thou *h* the deeds of the Rev 2:6 *3404*

HATETH {31}
h thee lying under his burden Ex 23:5 8130
not be slack to him that *h* him Deut 7:10 8130

to the LORD, which he *h*, have ... Deut 12:31 8130
which the LORD thy God *h* ... Deut 16:22 8130
this man to wife, and he *h* her ... Deut 22:16 8130
teareth me in his wrath, who *h* me ... Job 16:9 7852
Shall even he that *h* right govern ... Job 34:17 8130
that loveth violence his soul *h* ... Ps 11:5 8130
long dwelt with him that *h* peace ... Ps 120:6 8130
he that *h* suretiship is sure ... Prov 11:15 8130
but he that *h* reproof is brutish ... Prov 12:1 8130
A righteous man *h* lying ... Prov 13:5 8130
He that spareth his rod *h* his son ... Prov 13:24 8130
he that *h* reproof shall die ... Prov 15:10 8130
but he that *h* gifts shall live ... Prov 15:27 8130
He that *h* dissembleth with his ... Prov 26:24 8130
A lying tongue *h* those that are ... Prov 26:28 8130
but he that *h* covetousness shall ... Prov 28:16 8130
with a thief *h* his own soul ... Prov 29:24 8130
your appointed feasts my soul *h* ... Is 1:14 8130
saith that he *h* putting away ... Mal 2:16 8130
one that doeth evil *h* the light ... Jn 3:20 *3404*
but me it *h*, because I testify of ... Jn 7:7 *3404*
he that *h* his life in this world ... Jn 12:25 *3404*
world, therefore the world *h* you ... Jn 15:19 *3404*
He that *h* me *h* my Father ... Jn 15:23 *3404*
h his brother, is in darkness ... 1Jn 2:9 *3404*
But he that *h* his brother is in ... 1Jn 2:11 *3404*
Whosoever *h* his brother is a ... 1Jn 3:15 *3404*
h his brother, he is a liar ... 1Jn 4:20 *3404*

HATH {2262}

the moving creature that *h* life ... Gen 1:20
h God said, Ye shall not eat of ... Gen 3:1
God *h* said, Ye shall not eat of ... Gen 3:3
which *h* opened her mouth to ... Gen 4:11
h appointed me another seed ... Gen 4:25
ground which the LORD *h* cursed ... Gen 5:29
which *h* delivered thine enemies ... Gen 14:20
the LORD *h* restrained me from ... Gen 16:2
because the LORD *h* heard thy ... Gen 16:11
he *h* broken my covenant ... Gen 17:14
that which he *h* spoken of him ... Gen 18:19
the LORD *h* sent us to destroy it ... Gen 19:13
thy servant *h* found grace in thy ... Gen 19:19
God *h* made me to laugh, so that ... Gen 21:6
all that Sarah *h* said unto thee ... Gen 21:12
for God *h* heard the voice of the ... Gen 21:17
I wot not who *h* done this thing ... Gen 21:26
she *h* also born children unto thy ... Gen 22:20
the cave of Machpelah, which he *h* ... Gen 23:9
who *h* not left destitute my ... Gen 24:27
the LORD *h* blessed my master ... Gen 24:35
he *h* given him flocks, and herds, ... Gen 24:35
him *h* he given all that he *h* ... Gen 24:36
h appointed out for my master's ... Gen 24:44
son's wife, as the LORD *h* spoken ... Gen 24:51
seeing the LORD *h* prospered my ... Gen 24:56
now the LORD *h* made room for us ... Gen 26:22
a field which the LORD *h* blessed ... Gen 27:27
where is he that *h* taken venison ... Gen 27:33
h taken away thy blessing ... Gen 27:35
for he *h* supplanted me these two ... Gen 27:36
now he *h* taken away my blessing ... Gen 27:36
Surely the LORD *h* looked upon my ... Gen 29:32
Because the LORD *h* heard that I ... Gen 29:33
he *h* therefore given me this son ... Gen 29:33
who *h* withheld from thee the ... Gen 30:2
God *h* judged me, and *h* also ... Gen 30:6
my voice, and *h* given me a son ... Gen 30:6
God *h* given me my hire, because I ... Gen 30:18
God *h* endued me with a good dowry ... Gen 30:20
God *h* taken away my reproach ... Gen 30:23
LORD *h* blessed me for thy sake ... Gen 30:27
the LORD *h* blessed thee since my ... Gen 30:30
Jacob *h* taken away all that was ... Gen 31:1
h he gotten all this glory ... Gen 31:1
God of my father *h* been with me ... Gen 31:5 1961
And your father *h* deceived me ... Gen 31:7
Thus God *h* taken away the cattle ... Gen 31:9
for he *h* sold us, and *h* quite ... Gen 31:15
which God *h* taken from our father ... Gen 31:16
whatsoever God *h* said unto thee ... Gen 31:16
God *h* seen mine affliction and the ... Gen 31:42
he said, The children which God *h* ... Gen 33:5
because God *h* dealt graciously ... Gen 33:11
Some evil beast *h* devoured him ... Gen 37:20
an evil beast *h* devoured him ... Gen 37:33
in law *h* played the harlot ... Gen 38:24
She *h* been more righteous than I ... Gen 38:26
he *h* committed all that he ... Gen 39:8
all that he *h* to my hand ... Gen 39:8 3426
neither *h* he kept back any thing ... Gen 39:9
he *h* brought in an Hebrew unto us ... Gen 39:14
God *h* shewed Pharaoh what he is ... Gen 41:25
Forasmuch as God *h* shewed thee ... Gen 41:39
h made me forget all my toil, and ... Gen 41:51
For God *h* caused me to be ... Gen 41:52
is this that God *h* done unto us ... Gen 42:28
h given you treasure in your ... Gen 43:23
God *h* found out the iniquity of ... Gen 44:16
For these two years *h* the famine ... Gen 45:6
he *h* made me a father to Pharaoh, ... Gen 45:8
God *h* made me lord of all Egypt ... Gen 45:9
for their trade *h* been to feed ... Gen 46:32
Thy servants' trade *h* been about ... Gen 46:34 1961
my lord also *h* our herds of ... Gen 47:18 413
whom God *h* given me in this place ... Gen 48:9
God *h* shewed me also thy seed ... Gen 48:11
your fathers *h* sent me unto you ... Ex 3:13
Israel, I AM *h* sent me unto you ... Ex 3:14
God of Jacob, *h* sent me unto you ... Ex 3:15
God of the Hebrews *h* met with us ... Ex 3:18
The LORD *h* not appeared unto thee ... Ex 4:1
of Jacob, *h* appeared unto thee ... Ex 4:5
unto him, Who *h* made man's mouth ... Ex 4:11
God of the Hebrews *h* met with us ... Ex 5:3
he *h* done evil to this people ... Ex 5:23
the Hebrews *h* sent me unto thee ... Ex 7:16
such as *h* not been in Egypt since ... Ex 9:18 1961
even all that the hail *h* left ... Ex 10:12
you, according as he *h* promised ... Ex 12:25
for with a strong hand *h* the LORD ... Ex 13:9
the wilderness *h* shut them in ... Ex 14:3
for he *h* triumphed gloriously ... Ex 15:1
his rider *h* he thrown into the ... Ex 15:1
his host *h* he cast into the sea ... Ex 15:4
h dashed in pieces the enemy ... Ex 15:6
for he *h* triumphed gloriously ... Ex 15:21
his rider *h* he thrown into the ... Ex 15:21
ye shall know that the LORD *h* ... Ex 16:6
for he *h* heard your murmurings ... Ex 16:9
which the LORD *h* given you to eat ... Ex 16:15
thing which the LORD *h* commanded ... Ex 16:16
is that which the LORD *h* said ... Ex 16:23
for that the LORD *h* given you the ... Ex 16:29
Because the LORD *h* sworn that the ... Ex 17:16
who *h* delivered you out of the ... Ex 18:10
who *h* delivered the people from ... Ex 18:10
that the LORD *h* spoken we will do ... Ex 19:8
who *h* betrothed her to himself, ... Ex 21:8
seeing he *h* dealt deceitfully ... Ex 21:8
it *h* been testified to his owner, ... Ex 21:29
he *h* not kept him in ... Ex 21:29
but that he *h* killed a man or a ... Ex 21:29
ox *h* used to push in time past ... Ex 21:36
his owner *h* not kept him in ... Ex 21:36
that he *h* not put his hand unto ... Ex 22:11
which the LORD *h* said will we do ... Ex 24:3
that the LORD *h* said will we do ... Ex 24:7
which the LORD *h* made with you ... Ex 24:8
unto them, Whosoever *h* any gold ... Ex 32:24
Whosoever *h* sinned against me, ... Ex 32:33
words which the LORD *h* commanded ... Ex 35:1
all that the LORD *h* commanded ... Ex 35:10
the LORD *h* called by name ... Ex 35:30
he *h* filled him with the spirit ... Ex 35:31
he *h* put in his heart that he may ... Ex 35:34
Them *h* he filled with wisdom of ... Ex 35:35
for his sin, which he *h* sinned ... Lev 4:3
When a ruler *h* sinned, and done ... Lev 4:22
if his sin, wherein he *h* sinned ... Lev 4:23
Or if his sin, which he *h* sinned ... Lev 4:28
for his sin which he *h* sinned ... Lev 4:28
for his sin that he *h* committed ... Lev 4:35
whether he *h* seen or known of it ... Lev 5:1
that he *h* sinned in that thing ... Lev 5:5
for his sin which he *h* sinned ... Lev 5:6
which he *h* committed, two ... Lev 5:7
him for his sin which he *h* sinned ... Lev 5:10
that he *h* sinned in one of these ... Lev 5:13
that he *h* done in the holy thing ... Lev 5:16
he *h* certainly trespassed against ... Lev 5:19
or *h* deceived his neighbour ... Lev 6:2
it shall be, because he *h* sinned ... Lev 6:4
which he *h* deceitfully gotten ... Lev 6:4
about which he *h* sworn falsely ... Lev 6:5
he *h* done in trespassing therein ... Lev 6:7
fire *h* consumed with the burnt ... Lev 6:10
burnt offering which he *h* offered ... Lev 7:8
As he *h* done this day ... Lev 8:34
so the LORD *h* commanded to do, to ... Lev 8:34
burning which the LORD *h* kindled ... Lev 10:6
h spoken unto them by the hand of ... Lev 10:11
as the LORD *h* commanded ... Lev 10:15
God *h* given it you to bear the ... Lev 10:17
whatsoever *h* fins and scales in ... Lev 11:9
Whatsoever *h* no fins nor scales ... Lev 11:12
or whatsoever *h* more feet among ... Lev 11:42
that *h* born a male or a female ... Lev 12:7
him that *h* the plague seven days ... Lev 13:4
after that he *h* been seen of the ... Lev 13:7
h the plague from his head even ... Lev 13:12
him clean that *h* the plague ... Lev 13:13
him clean that *h* the plague ... Lev 13:17
h the plague of the scall seven ... Lev 13:31
that *h* the scall seven days more ... Lev 13:33
he that *h* his hair fallen off ... Lev 13:41
shut up it that *h* the plague ... Lev 13:50
after that he *h* taken away the ... Lev 14:43
after he *h* scraped the house, and ... Lev 14:43
the plague *h* not spread in the ... Lev 14:48
When any man *h* a running issue ... Lev 15:2 1961
whereon he lieth that *h* the issue ... Lev 15:4
that *h* the issue shall wash his ... Lev 15:6
that *h* the issue shall wash his ... Lev 15:7
if he that *h* the issue spit upon ... Lev 15:8
that *h* the issue shall be unclean ... Lev 15:9
he toucheth that *h* the issue ... Lev 15:11
h not rinsed his hands in water, ... Lev 15:11
he toucheth which *h* the issue ... Lev 15:12
when he that *h* an issue is ... Lev 15:13
is the law of him that *h* an issue ... Lev 15:32
and of him that *h* an issue ... Lev 15:33
And when he *h* made an end of ... Lev 16:20
thing which the LORD *h* commanded ... Lev 17:2
he *h* shed blood ... Lev 17:4
because he *h* profaned the ... Lev 19:8
LORD for his sin which he *h* done ... Lev 19:22
the sin which he *h* done shall be ... Lev 19:22
because he *h* given of his seed ... Lev 20:3
he *h* cursed his father or his ... Lev 20:9
wife *h* uncovered his father's ... Lev 20:11
he *h* uncovered his sister's ... Lev 20:17
he *h* discovered her fountain, and ... Lev 20:18
she *h* uncovered the fountain of ... Lev 20:18
he *h* uncovered his uncle's ... Lev 20:20
he *h* uncovered his brother's ... Lev 20:21
or woman that *h* a familiar spirit ... Lev 20:27 1961
unto him, which *h* had no husband ... Lev 21:3 1961
generations that *h* any blemish ... Lev 21:17 1961
man he be that *h* a blemish ... Lev 21:18
or he that *h* a flat nose, or any ... Lev 21:18
or that *h* a blemish in his eye, ... Lev 21:20
scabbed, or *h* his stones broken ... Lev 21:20
No man that *h* a blemish of the ... Lev 21:21
he *h* a blemish ... Lev 21:21
the altar, because he *h* a blemish ... Lev 21:23
is a leper, or *h* a running issue ... Lev 22:4
whatsoever uncleanness he *h* ... Lev 22:5
The soul which *h* touched any such ... Lev 22:6
But whatsoever *h* a blemish ... Lev 22:20
that *h* any thing superfluous or ... Lev 22:23
Bring forth him that *h* cursed ... Lev 24:14
as he *h* done, so shall it be done ... Lev 24:19
as he *h* caused a blemish in a man ... Lev 24:20
poor, and *h* sold away some of his ... Lev 25:25
h bought it until the year of ... Lev 25:28
LORD a field which he *h* bought ... Lev 27:22
unto the LORD of all that he *h* ... Lev 27:28
and every one that *h* an issue ... Num 5:2
him against whom he *h* trespassed ... Num 5:7
when he *h* made her to drink the ... Num 5:27
he *h* defiled the head of his ... Num 6:9
law of the Nazarite who *h* vowed ... Num 6:21
for the LORD *h* spoken good ... Num 10:29
H the LORD indeed spoken only by ... Num 12:2
h he not spoken also by us ... Num 12:2
wherefore *h* the LORD brought us ... Num 14:3
therefore he *h* slain them in the ... Num 14:16
h followed me fully, him will I ... Num 14:24
place which the LORD *h* promised ... Num 14:40
which the LORD *h* spoken unto ... Num 15:22
Even all that the LORD *h* ... Num 15:23
Because he *h* despised the word of ... Num 15:31
h broken his commandment, that ... Num 15:31
even him whom he *h* chosen will he ... Num 16:5
Israel *h* separated you from the ... Num 16:9
he *h* brought thee near to him, and ... Num 16:10
ye shall know that the LORD *h* ... Num 16:28
then the LORD *h* not sent me ... Num 16:29
law which the LORD *h* commanded ... Num 19:2 125
which *h* no covering bound upon it ... Num 19:15 369
because he *h* defiled the ... Num 19:20
the water of separation *h* not ... Num 19:20
all the travel that *h* befallen us ... Num 20:14
h brought us forth out of Egypt ... Num 20:16
it *h* consumed Ar of Moab, and the ... Num 21:28
he *h* given his sons that escaped, ... Num 21:29
of Moab, *h* sent unto me, saying, ... Num 22:10
of Moab *h* brought me from Aram ... Num 23:7
I curse, whom God *h* not cursed ... Num 23:8
defy, whom the LORD *h* not defied ... Num 23:8
which the LORD *h* put in my mouth ... Num 23:12
unto him, What *h* the LORD spoken ... Num 23:17
h he said, and shall he not do it ... Num 23:19
and he *h* blessed ... Num 23:20
He *h* not beheld iniquity in Jacob ... Num 23:21
neither *h* he seen perverseness in ... Num 23:21
he *h* as it were the strength of a ... Num 23:22
and of Israel, What *h* God wrought ... Num 23:23
Balaam the son of Beor *h* said ... Num 24:3
man whose eyes are open *h* said ... Num 24:3
He *h* said, which heard the words ... Num 24:4
aloes which the LORD *h* planted ... Num 24:6
he *h* as it were the strength of a ... Num 24:8
the LORD *h* kept thee back from ... Num 24:11
Balaam the son of Beor *h* said ... Num 24:15
man whose eyes are open *h* said ... Num 24:15
He *h* said, which heard the words ... Num 24:16
h turned my wrath away from the ... Num 25:11
his family, because he *h* no son ... Num 27:4
thing which the LORD *h* commanded ... Num 30:1
wherewith she *h* bound her soul ... Num 30:4
every bond wherewith she *h* bound ... Num 30:4
wherewith she *h* bound her soul ... Num 30:5
But if her husband *h* utterly made ... Num 30:12
her husband *h* made them void ... Num 30:12
void after that he *h* heard them ... Num 30:15
kill every woman that *h* known man ... Num 31:17
whosoever *h* killed any person, and ... Num 31:19
whosoever *h* touched any slain, ... Num 31:19
the LORD, what every man *h* gotten ... Num 31:50
land which the LORD *h* given them ... Num 32:7
until he *h* driven out his enemies ... Num 32:21
do that which *h* proceeded out of ... Num 32:24
As the LORD *h* said unto thy ... Num 32:31
of the sons of Joseph *h* said well ... Num 36:5
LORD your God *h* multiplied you ... Deut 1:10
bless you, as he *h* promised you ... Deut 1:11
the LORD thy God *h* set the land ... Deut 1:21
of thy fathers *h* said unto thee ... Deut 1:21
he *h* brought us forth out of the ... Deut 1:27
the land that he *h* trodden upon ... Deut 1:36
because he *h* wholly followed the ... Deut 1:36
For the LORD thy God *h* blessed ... Deut 2:7

the LORD thy God *h* been with thee .... Deut 2:7
The LORD your God *h* given you .... Deut 3:18
God *h* given them beyond Jordan........... Deut 3:20
God *h* done unto these two kings........... Deut 3:21
the LORD thy God *h* destroyed them ...... Deut 4:3
who *h* God so nigh unto them, as........... Deut 4:7
that *h* statutes and judgments so .... Deut 4:8
which the LORD thy God *h* divided .... Deut 4:19
But the LORD *h* taken you, and .... Deut 4:20
the LORD thy God *h* forbidden thee .... Deut 4:23
whether there *h* been any such.............. Deut 4:32 1961
thing is, or *h* been heard like it............ Deut 4:32
Or *h* God assayed to go and take .... Deut 4:34
the LORD thy God *h* commanded thee.... Deut 5:12
the LORD thy God *h* commanded thee.... Deut 5:16
the LORD our God *h* shewed us his .... Deut 5:24
that *h* heard the voice of the .... Deut 5:26
the LORD your God *h* commanded you .. Deut 5:32
the LORD your God *h* commanded you .. Deut 5:33
of thy fathers *h* promised thee .... Deut 6:3
which he *h* commanded thee.................... Deut 6:17
before thee, as the LORD *h* spoken .... Deut 6:19
the LORD our God *h* commanded you .... Deut 6:20
our God, as he *h* commanded us .... Deut 6:25
h cast out many nations before .... Deut 7:1
the LORD thy God *h* chosen thee to........ Deut 7:6
h the LORD brought you out with a........ Deut 7:8
good land which he *h* given thee............. Deut 8:10
mine hand *h* gotten me this wealth......... Deut 8:17
as the LORD *h* said unto thee................. Deut 9:3
after that the LORD thy God *h* .... Deut 9:4
h brought me in to possess this.............. Deut 9:4
he *h* brought them out to slay .... Deut 9:28
Wherefore Levi *h* no part nor................. Deut 10:9 1961
that *h* done for thee these great .... Deut 10:21
now the LORD thy God *h* made thee....... Deut 10:22
how the LORD *h* destroyed them............ Deut 11:4
tread upon, as he *h* said unto you .... Deut 11:25
when the LORD thy God *h* brought .... Deut 11:29
the LORD thy God *h* blessed thee .... Deut 12:7
forasmuch as he *h* no part nor .... Deut 12:12
thy God which he *h* given thee............... Deut 12:15
as he *h* promised thee, and thou .... Deut 12:20
place which the LORD thy God *h*............. Deut 12:21
which the LORD *h* given thee................. Deut 12:21
because he *h* spoken to turn you............. Deut 13:5
because he *h* sought to thrust .... Deut 13:10
which the LORD thy God *h* given............ Deut 13:12
as he *h* sworn unto thy fathers................ Deut 13:17
the LORD *h* chosen thee to be a .... Deut 14:2
And whatsoever *h* not fins and .... Deut 14:10
the LORD thy God *h* blessed thee .... Deut 14:24
for he *h* no part nor inheritance............. Deut 14:27
(because he *h* no part nor....................... Deut 14:29
h blessed thee thou shalt give .... Deut 15:14
for he *h* been worth a double .... Deut 15:18
the LORD thy God *h* blessed thee .... Deut 16:10
place which the LORD thy God *h*............. Deut 16:11
thy God which he *h* given thee............... Deut 16:17
that *h* wrought wickedness in the........... Deut 17:2
h gone and served other gods, and.......... Deut 17:3
as the LORD *h* said unto you.................. Deut 17:16
as he *h* said unto them .... Deut 18:2
For the LORD thy God *h* chosen him ...... Deut 18:5
the LORD thy God *h* not suffered........... Deut 18:14
word which the LORD *h* not spoken .... Deut 18:21
thing which the LORD *h* not spoken .... Deut 18:22
but the prophet *h* spoken it.................... Deut 18:22
thy God *h* cut off the nations .... Deut 19:1
as he *h* sworn unto thy fathers,.............. Deut 19:8
h testified falsely against his.................. Deut 19:18
is there that *h* built a new house............ Deut 20:5
and *h* not dedicated it .... Deut 20:5
is he that *h* planted a vineyard .... Deut 20:6
and *h* not yet eaten of it .... Deut 20:6
is there that *h* betrothed a wife.............. Deut 20:7
and *h* not taken her .... Deut 20:7
when the LORD thy God *h* delivered ...... Deut 20:13
the LORD thy God *h* given thee .... Deut 20:14
the LORD thy God *h* commanded thee.... Deut 20:17
it be not known who *h* slain him .... Deut 21:1
which *h* not been wrought with, and ...... Deut 21:3
which *h* not drawn in the yoke............... Deut 21:3
for them the LORD thy God *h*................. Deut 21:5
the LORD thy God *h* delivered them....... Deut 21:10
sons to inherit that which he *h* .... Deut 21:16 1961
a double portion of all that he *h* .... Deut 21:17 4672
of thy brother's, which he *h* lost............ Deut 22:3
he *h* given occasions of speech .... Deut 22:17
because he *h* brought up an evil .... Deut 22:19
because she *h* wrought folly in............... Deut 22:21
the man, because he *h* humbled his .... Deut 22:24
because he *h* humbled her, he may......... Deut 22:29
or *h* his privy member cut off,............... Deut 23:1
When a man *h* taken a wife, and............. Deut 24:1
his eyes, because he *h* found some .... Deut 24:1
When a man *h* taken a new wife, he ...... Deut 24:5
up his wife which he *h* taken .... Deut 24:5
of him that *h* his shoe loosed .... Deut 25:10
when the LORD thy God *h* given............ Deut 25:19
he *h* brought us into this place,............. Deut 26:9
h given us this land, even a land .... Deut 26:9
LORD thy God *h* given unto thee .... Deut 26:11
This day the LORD thy God *h* .... Deut 26:16
the LORD *h* avouched thee this day .... Deut 26:18
as he *h* promised thee, and that .... Deut 26:18
above all nations which he *h* made......... Deut 26:19
the LORD thy God, as he *h* spoken .... Deut 26:19
of thy fathers *h* promised thee .... Deut 27:3
as he *h* sworn unto thee, if thou............. Deut 28:9
the LORD thy God *h* given thee .... Deut 28:52
the LORD thy God *h* given thee .... Deut 28:53
because he *h* nothing left him in............ Deut 28:55
Yet the LORD *h* not given you an........... Deut 29:4
as he *h* said unto thee............................ Deut 29:13
as he *h* sworn unto thy fathers,............... Deut 29:13
which the LORD *h* laid upon it .... Deut 29:22
Wherefore *h* the LORD done thus............ Deut 29:24
the LORD thy God *h* driven thee............ Deut 30:1
the LORD thy God *h* scattered thee .... Deut 30:3
also the LORD *h* said unto me................ Deut 31:2
before thee, as the LORD *h* said.............. Deut 31:3
h sworn unto their fathers to .... Deut 31:7
he thy father that *h* bought thee .... Deut 32:6
H he not made thee, and .... Deut 32:6
the LORD *h* not done all this.................. Deut 32:27
LORD your God *h* given you rest .... Josh 1:13
and *h* given you this land....................... Josh 1:13
as he *h* given you, and they also............. Josh 1:15
the LORD *h* given you the land .... Josh 2:9
when the LORD *h* given us the land......... Josh 2:14
Truly the LORD *h* delivered into .... Josh 2:24
for the LORD *h* given you the city.......... Josh 6:16
the woman, and all that she *h*................ Josh 6:22
Israel *h* sinned, and they have................ Josh 7:11
with fire, he and all that he *h* .... Josh 7:15
because he *h* transgressed the................. Josh 7:15
because he *h* wrought folly in .... Josh 7:15
which no man *h* lift up any iron .... Josh 8:31
for it *h* made peace with Joshua .... Josh 10:4
for the LORD your God *h* delivered .... Josh 10:19
the LORD *h* kept me alive, as he .... Josh 14:10
as the LORD *h* blessed me hitherto......... Josh 17:14
God of your fathers *h* given you............. Josh 18:3
now the LORD your God *h* given .... Josh 22:4
For the LORD *h* made Jordan a .... Josh 22:25
God *h* done unto all these nations .... Josh 23:3
God is he that *h* fought for you.............. Josh 23:3
LORD your God *h* promised unto you..... Josh 23:5
For the LORD *h* driven out from .... Josh 23:9
no man *h* been able to stand .... Josh 23:9
for you, as he *h* promised you .... Josh 23:10
the LORD your God *h* given you .... Josh 23:13
that not one thing *h* failed of .... Josh 23:14
not one thing *h* failed thereof .... Josh 23:14
the LORD your God *h* given you .... Josh 23:15
land which he *h* given unto you .... Josh 23:16
after that he *h* done you good .... Josh 24:20
for it *h* heard all the words of............... Josh 24:27
I have done, so God *h* requited me.......... Judg 1:7
Because that this people *h* .... Judg 2:20
for the LORD *h* delivered your .... Judg 3:28
H not the LORD God of Israel................ Judg 4:6
h delivered Sisera into thine .... Judg 4:14
but now the LORD *h* forsaken us .... Judg 6:13
altar of Baal that thy father *h*................ Judg 6:25
to another, Who *h* done this thing.......... Judg 6:29
son of Joash *h* done this thing................ Judg 6:29
because he *h* cast down the altar .... Judg 6:30
because he *h* cut down the grove .... Judg 6:30
because one *h* cast down his altar........... Judg 6:31
because he *h* thrown down his .... Judg 6:32
saying, Mine own hand *h* saved me......... Judg 7:2
for into his hand *h* God delivered .... Judg 7:14
for the LORD *h* delivered into .... Judg 7:15
God *h* delivered into your hands............. Judg 8:3
when the LORD *h* delivered Zebah .... Judg 8:7
So now the LORD God of Israel *h*........... Judg 11:23
h proceeded out of thy mouth .... Judg 11:36
forasmuch as the LORD *h* taken............. Judg 11:36
the man *h* appeared unto me, that.......... Judg 13:10
Philistines said, Who *h* done this .... Judg 15:6
to do to him as he *h* done to us .... Judg 15:10
There *h* not come a razor upon .... Judg 16:17
for he *h* shewed me all his heart .... Judg 16:18
Our god *h* delivered Samson our............. Judg 16:23
Our god *h* delivered into our .... Judg 16:24
h hired me, and I am his priest .... Judg 18:4
for God *h* given it into your .... Judg 18:10
and every woman that *h* lain by man....... Judg 21:11
for the Almighty *h* dealt very................ Ruth 1:20
the LORD *h* brought me home again....... Ruth 1:21
seeing the LORD *h* testified................... Ruth 1:21
and the Almighty *h* afflicted me .... Ruth 1:21
h continued even from the morning........ Ruth 2:7
It *h* fully been shewed me, all .... Ruth 2:11
who *h* not left off his kindness.............. Ruth 2:20
which *h* not left thee this day .... Ruth 4:14
thee than seven sons, *h* born him........... Ruth 4:15
the LORD *h* given me my petition 1Sa 1:27
so that the barren *h* born seven 1Sa 2:5
she that *h* many children is waxed.......... 1Sa 2:5
he *h* set the world upon them................. 1Sa 2:8
that the LORD *h* said unto thee 1Sa 3:17
Wherefore *h* the LORD smitten us.......... 1Sa 4:3
for there *h* not been such a thing............ 1Sa 4:7 1961
there *h* been also a great 1Sa 4:17 1961
on which there *h* come no yoke 1Sa 6:7
then he *h* done us this great evil 1Sa 6:9
Hitherto *h* the LORD helped us.............. 1Sa 7:12
for unto this time *h* it been kept 1Sa 9:24
Is it not because the LORD *h*................. 1Sa 10:1
thy father *h* left the care of the............. 1Sa 10:2
he *h* hid himself among the stuff 1Sa 10:22
See ye him whom the LORD *h* chosen..... 1Sa 10:24
for to day the LORD *h* wrought.............. 1Sa 11:13
the LORD *h* set a king over you 1Sa 12:13
because it *h* pleased the LORD to 1Sa 12:22
great things he *h* done for you 1Sa 12:24
the LORD *h* sought him a man after 1Sa 13:14
the LORD *h* commanded him to be 1Sa 13:14
for the LORD *h* delivered them 1Sa 14:10
for the LORD *h* delivered them 1Sa 14:12
My father *h* troubled the land................ 1Sa 14:29
wherein this sin *h* been this day............. 1Sa 14:38 1961
die, who *h* wrought this great 1Sa 14:45
for he *h* wrought with God this 1Sa 14:45
h not performed my commandments........ 1Sa 15:11
the LORD *h* said to me this night........... 1Sa 15:16
H the LORD as great delight in.............. 1Sa 15:22
he *h* also rejected thee from 1Sa 15:23
the LORD *h* rejected thee from............... 1Sa 15:26
The LORD *h* rent the kingdom of........... 1Sa 15:28
h given it to a neighbour of 1Sa 15:28
As thy sword *h* made women................. 1Sa 15:33
Neither *h* the LORD chosen this............. 1Sa 16:8
Neither *h* the LORD chosen this............. 1Sa 16:9
The LORD *h* not chosen these 1Sa 16:10
for he *h* found favour in my sight 1Sa 16:22
seeing he *h* defied the armies of............. 1Sa 17:36
Saul *h* slain his thousands, and 1Sa 18:7
the king *h* delight in thee, and............... 1Sa 18:22
because he *h* not sinned against.............. 1Sa 19:4
as he *h* been with my father.................... 1Sa 20:13 1961
not when the LORD *h* cut off the 1Sa 20:15
for the LORD *h* sent thee away 1Sa 20:22
Something *h* befallen him, he is............. 1Sa 20:26
for our family *h* a sacrifice in 1Sa 20:29
he *h* commanded me to be there 1Sa 20:29
what *h* he done?.................................... 1Sa 20:32
The king *h* commanded me a 1Sa 21:2
h said unto me, Let no man know........... 1Sa 21:2
Saul *h* slain his thousands, and 1Sa 21:11
that sheweth me that my son *h* 1Sa 22:8
h stirred up my servant against.............. 1Sa 22:8
God *h* delivered him into mine............... 1Sa 23:7
entering into a town that *h* gates............ 1Sa 23:7
thy servant *h* certainly heard 1Sa 23:10
come down, as thy servant *h* heard 1Sa 23:11
haunt is, and who *h* seen him there 1Sa 23:22
this fellow *h* in the wilderness 1Sa 25:21
he *h* requited me evil for good 1Sa 25:21
seeing the LORD *h* withholden thee........ 1Sa 25:26
handmaid *h* brought unto my lord........... 1Sa 25:27
evil *h* not been found in thee all 1Sa 25:28
that he *h* spoken concerning thee 1Sa 25:30
or that my lord *h* avenged himself 1Sa 25:31
which *h* kept me back from hurting......... 1Sa 25:34
that *h* pleaded the cause of my 1Sa 25:39
h kept his servant from evil 1Sa 25:39
for the LORD *h* returned the 1Sa 25:39
God *h* delivered thine enemy into 1Sa 26:8
He *h* made his people Israel 1Sa 27:12
a woman that *h* a familiar spirit............. 1Sa 28:7 1172
there is a woman that *h* a....................... 1Sa 28:7 1172
thou knowest what Saul *h* done.............. 1Sa 28:9
how he *h* cut off those that have 1Sa 28:9
the LORD *h* done to him, as he 1Sa 28:17
for the LORD *h* rent the kingdom 1Sa 28:17
therefore *h* the LORD done this............. 1Sa 28:18
thine handmaid *h* obeyed thy voice 1Sa 28:21
which *h* been with me these days,........... 1Sa 29:3 1961
that which the LORD *h* given us 1Sa 30:23
who *h* preserved us, and delivered 1Sa 30:23
for thy mouth *h* testified against............. 2Sa 1:16
as the LORD *h* sworn to David,............... 2Sa 3:9
for the LORD *h* spoken of David,............ 2Sa 3:18
he *h* sent him away, and he is gone......... 2Sa 3:23
house of Joab one that *h* an issue............ 2Sa 3:29
the LORD *h* avenged my lord the 2Sa 4:8
who *h* redeemed my soul out of all 2Sa 4:9
The LORD *h* broken forth upon mine...... 2Sa 5:20
The LORD *h* blessed the house of........... 2Sa 6:12
therefore *h* thy servant found in............. 2Sa 7:27
Jonathan *h* yet a son, which is 2Sa 9:3
the king *h* commanded his servant 2Sa 9:11
that he *h* sent comforters unto 2Sa 10:3
h not David rather sent his 2Sa 10:3
the man that *h* done this thing............... 2Sa 12:5
The LORD also *h* put away thy sin.......... 2Sa 12:13
H Amnon thy brother been with 2Sa 13:20
thy servant *h* sheepshearers 2Sa 13:24
Absalom *h* slain all the king's 2Sa 13:30
h been determined from the day 2Sa 13:32
that my lord the king *h* spoken 2Sa 14:19
h thy servant Joab done this.................. 2Sa 14:20
in that the king *h* fulfilled the 2Sa 14:22
near mine, and he *h* barley there 2Sa 14:30
that every man which *h* any suit............. 2Sa 15:4 1961
The LORD *h* returned upon thee all......... 2Sa 16:8
the LORD *h* delivered the kingdom......... 2Sa 16:8
because the LORD *h* said unto him......... 2Sa 16:10
for the LORD *h* bidden him.................... 2Sa 16:11
which he *h* left to keep the house 2Sa 16:21
Ahithophel *h* spoken after this............... 2Sa 17:6
The counsel that Ahithophel *h*............... 2Sa 17:7
for thus *h* Ahithophel counselled........... 2Sa 17:21
how that the LORD *h* avenged him 2Sa 18:19
which *h* delivered up the men that.......... 2Sa 18:28
for the LORD *h* avenged thee this 2Sa 18:31
he *h* slandered thy servant unto.............. 2Sa 19:27
or *h* he given us any gift....................... 2Sa 19:42
h lifted up his hand against the 2Sa 20:21
of my hands *h* he recompensed me.......... 2Sa 22:21

Therefore the LORD *h* recompensed 2Sa 22:25
and thy gentleness *h* made me great 2Sa 22:36
yet he *h* made with me an 2Sa 23:5
he *h* slain oxen and fat cattle and 1Kin 1:19
h called all the sons of the king 1Kin 1:19
thy servant *h* he not called 1Kin 1:19
h slain oxen and fat cattle and 1Kin 1:25
h called all the king's sons, and 1Kin 1:25
servant Solomon, *h* he not called 1Kin 1:26
that *h* redeemed my soul out of 1Kin 1:29
As the LORD *h* been with my lord 1Kin 1:37 1961
king David *h* made Solomon king 1Kin 1:43
the king *h* sent with him Zadok 1Kin 1:44
which *h* given one to sit on my 1Kin 1:48
he *h* caught hold on the horns of 1Kin 1:51
which *h* established me, and set me 1Kin 2:24
who *h* made me an house, as he 1Kin 2:24
said unto him, Do as he *h* said 1Kin 2:31
as my lord the king *h* said 1Kin 2:38
But now the LORD my God *h* given 1Kin 5:4
which *h* given unto David a wise 1Kin 5:7
h with his hand fulfilled it, 1Kin 8:15
the LORD *h* performed his word 1Kin 8:20
that *h* given rest unto his people 1Kin 8:56
there *h* not failed one word of 1Kin 8:56
Why *h* the LORD done thus unto 1Kin 9:8
therefore *h* the LORD brought upon 1Kin 9:9
my father *h* chastised you with 1Kin 12:11
the sign which the LORD *h* spoken 1Kin 13:3
therefore the LORD *h* delivered 1Kin 13:26
which *h* torn him, and slain him, 1Kin 13:26
for the LORD *h* spoken it 1Kin 14:11
Zimri *h* conspired, and *h* also 1Kin 16:16
whither my lord *h* not sent to 1Kin 18:10
mouth which *h* not kissed him 1Kin 19:18
the LORD *h* put a lying spirit in 1Kin 22:23
the LORD *h* spoken evil concerning 1Kin 22:23
the LORD *h* not spoken by me 1Kin 22:28
Thou man of God, the king *h* said 2Kin 1:9
man of God, thus *h* the king said 2Kin 1:11
for the LORD *h* sent me to Beth-el 2Kin 2:2
for the LORD *h* sent me to Jericho 2Kin 2:4
for the LORD *h* sent me to Jordan 2Kin 2:6
Spirit of the LORD *h* taken him up 2Kin 2:16
The king of Moab *h* rebelled 2Kin 3:7
that the LORD *h* called these 2Kin 3:10
for the LORD *h* called these three 2Kin 3:13
Thine handmaid *h* not any thing in 2Kin 4:2
answered, Verily she *h* no child 2Kin 4:14
the LORD *h* hid it from me, and 2Kin 4:27
and *h* not told me 2Kin 4:27
my master *h* spared Naaman this 2Kin 5:20
My master *h* sent me, saying, 2Kin 5:22
and she *h* hid her son 2Kin 6:29
h sent to take away mine head 2Kin 6:32
the king of Israel *h* hired 2Kin 7:6
for the LORD *h* called for a 2Kin 8:1
great things that Elisha *h* done 2Kin 8:4
king of Syria *h* sent me to thee 2Kin 8:9
howbeit the LORD *h* shewed me that 2Kin 8:10
The LORD *h* shewed me that thou 2Kin 8:13
for the LORD *h* done that which he 2Kin 10:10
thine heart *h* lifted thee up 2Kin 14:10
therefore he *h* sent lions among 2Kin 17:26
altars Hezekiah *h* taken away 2Kin 18:22
h said to Judah and Jerusalem, Ye 2Kin 18:22
H my master sent me to thy master 2Kin 18:27
h he not sent me to the men which 2Kin 18:27
H any of the gods of the nations 2Kin 18:33
the king of Assyria his master *h* 2Kin 19:4
which the LORD thy God *h* heard 2Kin 19:4
which *h* sent him to reproach the 2Kin 19:16
the LORD *h* spoken concerning him 2Kin 19:21
daughter of Zion *h* despised thee 2Kin 19:21
h shaken her head at thee 2Kin 19:21
do the thing that he *h* spoken 2Kin 20:9
Judah *h* done these abominations 2Kin 21:11
h done wickedly above all that 2Kin 21:11
h made Judah also to sin with his 2Kin 21:11
Hilkiah the priest *h* delivered me 2Kin 22:10
which the king of Judah *h* read 2Kin 22:16
God *h* broken in upon mine enemies 1Chr 14:11
for them *h* the LORD chosen to 1Chr 15:2
marvellous works that he *h* done 1Chr 16:12
h confirmed the same to Jacob for 1Chr 16:17
therefore thy servant *h* found in 1Chr 17:25
that he *h* sent comforters unto 1Chr 19:3
thy God, as he *h* said of thee 1Chr 22:11
h he not given you rest on every 1Chr 22:18
for he *h* given the inhabitants of 1Chr 22:18
The LORD God of Israel *h* given 1Chr 23:25
for he *h* chosen Judah to be the 1Chr 28:4
(for the LORD *h* given me many 1Chr 28:5
he *h* chosen Solomon my son to 1Chr 28:5
for the LORD *h* chosen thee to 1Chr 28:10
my son, whom alone God *h* chosen 1Chr 29:1
the LORD *h* loved his people 2Chr 2:11
he *h* made thee king over them 2Chr 2:11
who *h* given to David the king a 2Chr 2:12
wine, which my lord *h* spoken of 2Chr 2:15
The LORD *h* said that he would 2Chr 6:1
who *h* with his hands fulfilled 2Chr 6:4
The LORD therefore *h* performed 2Chr 6:10
his word that he *h* spoken 2Chr 6:10
Why *h* the LORD done thus unto 2Chr 7:21
therefore *h* he brought all this 2Chr 7:22
the ark of the LORD *h* come 2Chr 8:11
h rebelled against his lord 2Chr 13:6
he *h* given us rest on every side 2Chr 14:7
h been without the true God 2Chr 15:3
the LORD *h* put a lying spirit in 2Chr 18:22
the LORD *h* spoken evil against 2Chr 18:22
then *h* not the LORD spoken by me 2Chr 18:27
the LORD *h* broken thy works 2Chr 20:37
as the LORD *h* said of the sons of 2Chr 23:3
the LORD, he *h* also forsaken you 2Chr 24:20
for God *h* power to help, and to 2Chr 25:8 3426
I know that God *h* determined to 2Chr 25:16
he *h* delivered them into your 2Chr 28:9
he *h* delivered them to trouble, 2Chr 29:8
for the LORD *h* chosen you to 2Chr 29:11
which he *h* sanctified for ever 2Chr 30:8
for the LORD *h* blessed his people 2Chr 31:10
H not the same Hezekiah taken 2Chr 32:12
the priest *h* given me a book 2Chr 34:18
All the kingdoms of the earth *h* 2Chr 36:23
he *h* charged me to build him an 2Chr 36:23
The LORD God of heaven *h* given me Ezr 1:2
he *h* charged me to build him an Ezr 1:2
the king of Persia *h* commanded us Ezr 4:3
us *h* been plainly read before me Ezr 4:18
search *h* been made, and it is Ezr 4:19
that this city of old time *h* made Ezr 4:19
Who *h* commanded you to build this Ezr 5:3
until now *h* it been in building Ezr 5:16
the God that *h* caused his name to Ezr 6:12
which *h* put such a thing as this Ezr 7:27
h extended mercy unto me before Ezr 7:28
rulers *h* been chief in this Ezr 9:2 1961
now for a little space grace *h* Ezr 9:8 1961
yet our God *h* not forsaken us in Ezr 9:9
but *h* extended mercy unto us in Ezr 9:9
that *h* come upon us, on our kings Neh 9:32
because she *h* not performed the Est 1:15
Vashti the queen *h* not done wrong Est 1:16
that he may do as Esther *h* said Est 5:5
do to morrow as the king *h* said Est 5:8
dignity *h* been done to Mordecai Est 6:3
about all that he *h* on every side Job 1:10
hand now, and touch all that he *h* Job 1:11
all that he *h* is in thy power Job 1:12
h burned up the sheep, and the Job 1:16
gave, and the LORD *h* taken away Job 1:21
all that a man *h* will he give for Job 2:4
is hid, and whom God *h* hedged in Job 3:23
So the poor *h* hope, and iniquity Job 5:16 1961
the wild ass bray when he *h* grass Job 6:5
The eye of him that *h* seen me Job 7:8
who *h* hardened himself against Job 9:4
against him, and *h* prospered Job 9:4
thy visitation *h* preserved my Job 10:12
hand of the LORD *h* wrought this Job 12:9
he *h* counsel and understanding Job 12:13
mine eye *h* seen all this Job 13:1
seen all this, mine ear *h* heard Job 13:1
But now he *h* made me weary Job 16:7
God *h* delivered me to the ungodly Job 16:11
but he *h* broken me asunder Job 16:12
he *h* also taken me by my neck, and Job 16:12
He *h* made me also a byword of the Job 17:6
he that *h* clean hands shall be Job 17:9
Know now that God *h* overthrown me Job 19:6
h compassed me with his net Job 19:6
He *h* fenced up my way that I Job 19:8
he *h* set darkness in my paths Job 19:8
He *h* stripped me of my glory, and Job 19:9
He *h* destroyed me on every side, Job 19:10
mine hope *h* he removed like a Job 19:10
He *h* also kindled his wrath Job 19:11
He *h* put my brethren far from me, Job 19:13
for the hand of God *h* touched me Job 19:21
He *h* swallowed down riches, and he Job 20:15
Because he *h* oppressed and *h* Job 20:19
because he *h* violently taken away Job 20:19
For what pleasure *h* he in his Job 21:21
shall repay him what he *h* done Job 21:31
when he *h* tried me, I shall come Job 23:10
My foot *h* held his steps, his way Job 23:11
neither *h* he covered the darkness Job 23:17
thou the arm that *h* no strength Job 26:2
counseled him that *h* no wisdom Job 26:3
him, and destruction *h* no covering Job 26:6 369
He *h* compassed the waters with Job 26:10
By his spirit he *h* garnished the Job 26:13
his hand *h* formed the crooked Job 26:13
who *h* taken away my judgment Job 27:2
the Almighty, who *h* vexed my soul Job 27:2
the hypocrite, though he *h* gained Job 27:8
and it *h* dust of gold Job 28:6
the vulture's eye *h* not seen Job 28:7
Because he *h* loosed my cord, and Job 30:11
He *h* cast me into the mire, and I Job 30:19
or if my foot *h* hasted to deceit Job 31:5
If my step *h* turned out of the Job 31:7
if any blot *h* cleaved to mine Job 31:7
the fatherless *h* not eaten Job 31:17
my heart *h* been secretly enticed, Job 31:27
or my mouth *h* kissed my hand Job 31:27
Now he *h* not directed his words Job 32:14
belly is as wine which *h* no vent Job 32:19
my tongue *h* spoken in my mouth Job 33:2
The spirit of God *h* made me Job 33:4
of the Almighty *h* given me life Job 33:4
For Job *h* said, I am righteous Job 34:5
God *h* taken away my judgment Job 34:5
For he *h* said, It profiteth a man Job 34:9
Who *h* given him a charge over the Job 34:13
Or who *h* disposed the whole world Job 34:13
Job *h* spoken without knowledge, Job 34:35
he *h* visited in his anger Job 35:15
Who *h* enjoined him his way Job 36:23
Who *h* laid the measures thereof, Job 38:5
or who *h* stretched the line upon Job 38:5
Who *h* divided a watercourse for Job 38:25
H the rain a father Job 38:28 3426
or who *h* begotten the drops of Job 38:28
of heaven, who *h* gendered it Job 38:29
Who *h* put wisdom in the inward Job 38:36
or who *h* given understanding to Job 38:36
Who *h* sent out the wild ass free Job 39:5
or who *h* loosed the bands of the Job 39:5
Because God *h* deprived her of Job 39:17
neither *h* he imparted to her Job 39:17
H thou given the horse strength Job 39:19
Who *h* prevented me, that I should Job 41:11
is right, as my servant Job *h* Job 42:7
The LORD *h* said unto me, Thou art Ps 2:7
But know that the LORD *h* set Ps 4:3
God that *h* pleasure in wickedness Ps 5:4
for the LORD *h* heard the voice of Ps 6:8
The LORD *h* heard my supplication Ps 6:9
he *h* bent his bow, and made it Ps 7:12
He *h* also prepared for him the Ps 7:13
h conceived mischief, and brought Ps 7:14
he *h* prepared his throne for Ps 9:7
He *h* said in his heart, I shall Ps 10:6
He *h* said in his heart, God *h* Ps 10:11
he *h* said in his heart, Thou wilt Ps 10:13
because he *h* dealt bountifully Ps 13:6
The fool *h* said in his heart, Ps 14:1
the LORD, who *h* given me counsel Ps 16:7
of my hands *h* he recompensed me Ps 18:20
Therefore *h* the LORD recompensed Ps 18:24
and thy right hand *h* holden me up Ps 18:35
and thy gentleness *h* made me great Ps 18:35
In them *h* he set a tabernacle for Ps 19:4
For he *h* not despised nor Ps 22:24
neither *h* he hid his face from Ps 22:24
be born, that he *h* done this Ps 22:31
For he *h* founded it upon the seas Ps 24:2
He that *h* clean hands, and a pure Ps 24:4
who *h* not lifted up his soul unto Ps 24:4
because he *h* heard the voice of Ps 28:6
for he *h* shewed me his marvellous Ps 31:21
the people whom he *h* chosen for Ps 33:12
net that he *h* hid catch himself Ps 35:8
said, Aha, aha, our eye *h* seen it Ps 35:21
which *h* pleasure in the Ps 35:27
he *h* left off to be wise, and to Ps 36:3
h is better than the riches of Ps 37:16
he *h* put a new song in my mouth, Ps 40:3
h lifted up his heel against me Ps 41:9
the shame of my face *h* covered me Ps 44:15
therefore God *h* blessed thee for Ps 45:2
h anointed thee with the oil of Ps 45:7
he *h* made in the earth Ps 46:8
h spoken, and called the earth Ps 50:1
of beauty, God *h* shined Ps 50:2
The fool *h* said in his heart, Ps 53:1
for God *h* scattered the bones of Ps 53:5
because God *h* despised them Ps 53:5
For he *h* delivered me out of all Ps 54:7
mine eye *h* seen his desire upon Ps 54:7
me, and horror *h* overwhelmed me Ps 55:5
He *h* delivered my soul in peace Ps 55:18
He *h* put forth his hands against Ps 55:20
he *h* broken his covenant Ps 55:20
God *h* spoken in his holiness Ps 60:6
God *h* spoken once Ps 62:11
uttered, and my mouth *h* spoken Ps 66:14
what he *h* done for my soul Ps 66:16
But verily God *h* heard me Ps 66:19
he *h* attended to the voice of my Ps 66:19
which *h* not turned away my prayer Ps 66:20
Thy congregation *h* dwelt therein Ps 68:10
Thy God *h* commanded thy strength Ps 68:28
shame *h* covered my face Ps 69:7
zeal of thine house *h* eaten me up Ps 69:9
Reproach *h* broken my heart Ps 69:20
an ox or bullock that *h* horns Ps 69:31
Saying, God *h* forsaken him Ps 71:11
also, and him that *h* no helper Ps 72:12
even all that the enemy *h* done Ps 74:3
this, that the enemy *h* reproached Ps 74:18
H God forgotten to be gracious Ps 77:9
h he in anger shut up his tender Ps 77:9
wonderful works that he *h* done Ps 78:4
which he *h* established for ever Ps 78:69
which thy right hand *h* planted Ps 80:15
the sparrow *h* found an house, and Ps 84:3
I am as a man that *h* no strength Ps 88:4 369
Because he *h* set his love upon me Ps 91:14
because he *h* known my name Ps 91:14
wherewith he *h* girded himself Ps 93:1
for he *h* done marvellous things Ps 98:1
arm, *h* gotten him the victory Ps 98:1
The LORD *h* made known his Ps 98:2
his righteousness *h* he openly Ps 98:2
He *h* remembered his mercy and his Ps 98:3
it is he that *h* made us, and not Ps 100:3
him that *h* an high look and a Ps 101:5
For he *h* looked down from the Ps 102:19
He *h* not dealt with us after our Ps 103:10
the west, so far *h* he removed our Ps 103:12

The LORD *h* prepared his throne in ... Ps 103:19
of Lebanon, which he *h* planted ... Ps 104:16
marvellous works that he *h* done ... Ps 105:5
He *h* remembered his covenant for ... Ps 105:8
whom he *h* redeemed from the hand ... Ps 107:2
For he *h* broken the gates of ... Ps 107:16
God *h* spoken in his holiness ... Ps 108:7
extortioner catch all that he *h* ... Ps 109:11
The LORD *h* sworn, and will not ... Ps 110:4
He *h* made his wonderful works to ... Ps 111:4
He *h* given meat unto them that ... Ps 111:5
He *h* shewed his people the power ... Ps 111:6
he *h* commanded his covenant for ... Ps 111:9
He *h* dispersed, he *h* given to ... Ps 112:9
h done whatsoever he *h* pleased ... Ps 115:3
The LORD *h* been mindful of us ... Ps 115:12
but the earth *h* he given to the ... Ps 115:16
because he *h* heard my voice and my ... Ps 116:1
Because he *h* inclined his ear ... Ps 116:2
for the LORD *h* dealt bountifully ... Ps 116:7
The LORD *h* chastened me sore ... Ps 118:18
but he *h* not given me over unto ... Ps 118:18
is the day which the LORD *h* made ... Ps 118:24
the LORD, which *h* shewed us light ... Ps 118:27
for the longing that it *h* unto ... Ps 119:20
for thy word *h* quickened me ... Ps 119:50
Horror *h* taken hold upon me ... Ps 119:53
My zeal *h* consumed me, because ... Ps 119:139
My soul *h* kept thy testimonies ... Ps 119:167
My soul *h* long dwelt with him ... Ps 120:6
who *h* not given us as a prey to ... Ps 124:6
The LORD *h* done great things for ... Ps 126:2
The LORD *h* done great things for ... Ps 126:3
Happy is the man that *h* his ... Ps 127:5
he *h* cut asunder the cords of the ... Ps 129:4
The LORD *h* sworn in truth unto ... Ps 132:11
For the LORD *h* chosen Zion ... Ps 132:13
he *h* desired it for his ... Ps 132:13
For the LORD *h* chosen Jacob unto ... Ps 135:4
h redeemed us from our enemies ... Ps 136:24
yet *h* he respect unto the lowly ... Ps 138:6
For the enemy *h* persecuted my ... Ps 143:3
he *h* smitten my life down to the ... Ps 143:3
he *h* made me to dwell in darkness ... Ps 143:3
Happy is he that *h* the God of ... Ps 146:5
For he *h* strengthened the bars of ... Ps 147:13
he *h* blessed thy children within ... Ps 147:13
He *h* not dealt so with any nation ... Ps 147:20
He *h* also stablished them for ... Ps 148:6
he *h* made a decree which shall ... Ps 148:6
Let every thing that *h* breath ... Ps 150:6
by wisdom *h* founded the earth ... Prov 3:19
by understanding *h* he established ... Prov 3:19
He *h* taken a bag of money with ... Prov 7:20
For she *h* cast down many wounded ... Prov 7:26
Wisdom *h* builded her house ... Prov 9:1
she *h* hewn out her seven pillars ... Prov 9:1
She *h* killed her beasts ... Prov 9:2
she *h* mingled her wine ... Prov 9:2
she *h* also furnished her table ... Prov 9:2
She *h* sent forth her maidens ... Prov 9:3
In the lips of him that *h* ... Prov 10:13
a man of understanding *h* wisdom ... Prov 10:23
h a servant, is better than he ... Prov 12:9
sluggard desireth, and *h* nothing ... Prov 13:4 369
himself rich, yet *h* nothing ... Prov 13:7 369
himself poor, yet *h* great riches ... Prov 13:7
but the rich *h* many friends ... Prov 14:20
but he that *h* mercy on the poor, ... Prov 14:21
honoureth him *h* mercy on the poor ... Prov 14:31
the righteous *h* hope in his death ... Prov 14:32
heart of him that *h* understanding ... Prov 14:33
The heart of him that *h* ... Prov 15:14
a merry heart *h* a continual feast ... Prov 15:15
A man *h* joy by the answer of his ... Prov 15:23
The LORD *h* made all things for ... Prov 16:4
of life unto him that *h* it ... Prov 16:22 1167
in the eyes of him that *h* it ... Prov 17:8 1167
seeing he *h* no heart to it ... Prov 17:16 369
He that *h* a froward heart findeth ... Prov 17:20
he that *h* a perverse tongue ... Prov 17:20
and the father of a fool *h* no joy ... Prov 17:21
before him that *h* understanding ... Prov 17:24
He that *h* knowledge spareth his ... Prov 17:27
A fool *h* no delight in ... Prov 18:2
A man that *h* friends must shew ... Prov 18:24
He that *h* pity upon the poor ... Prov 19:17
that which he *h* given will he pay ... Prov 19:17
and he that *h* it shall abide ... Prov 19:23
reprove one that *h* understanding ... Prov 19:25
the LORD *h* made even both of them ... Prov 20:12
He that *h* a bountiful eye shall ... Prov 22:9
bread of him that *h* an evil eye ... Prov 23:6
Who *h* woe? ... Prov 23:29
who *h* sorrow? ... Prov 23:29
who *h* contentions? ... Prov 23:29
who *h* babbling? ... Prov 23:29
who *h* wounds without ... Prov 23:29
who *h* redness of ... Prov 23:29
do so to him as he *h* done to me ... Prov 24:29
thy neighbour *h* put thee to shame ... Prov 25:8
He that *h* no rule over his own ... Prov 25:28 369
but the poor that *h* understanding ... Prov 28:11
hasteth to be rich *h* an evil eye ... Prov 28:22
Who *h* ascended up into heaven, or ... Prov 30:4
who *h* gathered the wind in his ... Prov 30:4
who *h* bound the waters in a ... Prov 30:4
who *h* established all the ends of ... Prov 30:4

The horseleach *h* two daughters ... Prov 30:15
What profit *h* a man of all his ... Eccl 1:3
The thing that *h* been, it is that ... Eccl 1:9 1961
it *h* been already of old time, ... Eccl 1:10 1961
this sore travail *h* God given to ... Eccl 1:13
even that which *h* been already ... Eccl 2:12
yet to a man that *h* not laboured ... Eccl 2:21
For what *h* man of all his labour, ... Eccl 2:22 1933
wherein he *h* laboured under the ... Eccl 2:22
What profit *h* he that worketh in ... Eccl 3:9
which God *h* given to the sons of ... Eccl 3:10
He *h* made every thing beautiful ... Eccl 3:11
also he *h* set the world in their ... Eccl 3:11
That which *h* been is now ... Eccl 3:15 1961
which is to be *h* already been ... Eccl 3:15 1961
so that a man *h* no preeminence ... Eccl 3:19 369
which *h* not yet been ... Eccl 4:3 1961
who *h* not seen the evil work that ... Eccl 4:3
he *h* neither child nor brother ... Eccl 4:8
for he *h* not another to help him ... Eccl 4:10 369
for he *h* no pleasure in fools ... Eccl 5:4 369
what profit *h* he that *h* ... Eccl 5:16
he *h* much sorrow and wrath with ... Eccl 5:17
also to whom God *h* given riches ... Eccl 5:19
h given him power to eat thereof, ... Eccl 5:19
A man to whom God *h* given riches ... Eccl 6:2
Moreover he *h* not seen the sun, ... Eccl 6:5
this *h* more rest than the other ... Eccl 6:5
twice told, yet *h* he seen no good ... Eccl 6:6
For what *h* the wise more than the ... Eccl 6:8
what *h* the poor, that knoweth to ... Eccl 6:8
That which *h* been is named ... Eccl 6:10 1961
straight, which he *h* made crooked ... Eccl 7:13
God also *h* set the one over ... Eccl 7:14
that God *h* made man upright ... Eccl 7:29
There is no man that *h* power over ... Eccl 8:8
neither *h* he power in the day of ... Eccl 8:8
because a man *h* no better thing ... Eccl 8:15
which he *h* given thee under the ... Eccl 9:9
that which *h* wings shall tell the ... Eccl 10:20 1167
the king *h* brought me into his ... Song 1:4
because the sun *h* looked upon me ... Song 1:6
every man *h* his sword upon his ... Song 3:8
which *h* a most vehement flame ... Song 8:6
sister, and she *h* no breasts ... Song 8:8
for the LORD *h* spoken, I have ... Is 1:2
who *h* required this at your hand, ... Is 1:12
the mouth of the LORD *h* spoken it ... Is 1:20
and as a garden that *h* no water ... Is 1:30
My wellbeloved *h* a vineyard in a ... Is 5:1
Therefore hell *h* enlarged herself ... Is 5:14
he *h* stretched forth his hand ... Is 5:25
against them, and *h* smitten them ... Is 5:25
said, Lo, this *h* touched thy lips ... Is 6:7
the LORD *h* given me are for signs ... Is 8:18
upon them *h* the light shined ... Is 9:2
and it *h* lighted upon Israel ... Is 9:8
As my hand *h* found the kingdoms ... Is 10:10
that when the Lord *h* performed ... Is 10:12
my hand *h* found as a nest the ... Is 10:14
at Michmash he *h* laid up his ... Is 10:28
for he *h* done excellent things ... Is 12:5
How *h* the oppressor ceased ... Is 14:4
The LORD *h* broken the staff of ... Is 14:5
it *h* raised up from their thrones ... Is 14:9
The LORD of hosts *h* sworn ... Is 14:24
For the LORD of hosts *h* purposed ... Is 14:27
That the LORD *h* founded Zion ... Is 14:32
h spoken concerning Moab since ... Is 16:13
But now the LORD *h* spoken ... Is 16:14
of hosts *h* purposed upon Egypt ... Is 19:12
The LORD *h* mingled a perverse ... Is 19:14
which he *h* determined against it ... Is 19:17
my servant Isaiah *h* walked naked ... Is 20:3
the night of my pleasure *h* he ... Is 21:4
For thus *h* the Lord said unto me, ... Is 21:6
gods he *h* broken unto the ground ... Is 21:9
For thus *h* the Lord said unto me, ... Is 21:16
LORD God of Israel *h* spoken it ... Is 21:17
for the LORD *h* spoken it ... Is 22:25
for the sea *h* spoken, even the ... Is 23:4
Who *h* taken this counsel against ... Is 23:8
The LORD of hosts *h* purposed it ... Is 23:9
the LORD *h* given a commandment ... Is 23:11
for the LORD *h* spoken this word ... Is 24:3
Therefore *h* the curse devoured ... Is 24:6
for the LORD *h* spoken it ... Is 25:8
H he smitten him, as he smote ... Is 27:7
Behold, the Lord *h* a mighty ... Is 28:2
When he *h* made plain the face ... Is 28:25
as of one that *h* a familiar ... Is 29:4
is faint, and his soul *h* appetite ... Is 29:8
For the LORD *h* poured out upon ... Is 29:10
deep sleep, and *h* closed your eyes ... Is 29:10
rulers, the seers *h* he covered ... Is 29:10
which *h* been winnowed with the ... Is 30:24
he *h* made it deep and large ... Is 30:33
For thus *h* the LORD spoken unto ... Is 31:4
he *h* filled Zion with judgment and ... Is 33:5
he *h* broken the covenant, he *h* ... Is 33:8
fearfulness *h* surprised the ... Is 33:14
he *h* utterly destroyed them ... Is 34:2
he *h* delivered them to the ... Is 34:2
for the LORD *h* a sacrifice in ... Is 34:6
for my mouth it *h* commanded ... Is 34:16
and his spirit it *h* gathered them ... Is 34:16
he *h* cast the lot for them, and ... Is 34:17
his hand *h* divided it unto them ... Is 34:17

altars Hezekiah *h* taken away ... Is 36:7
H my master sent me to thy master ... Is 36:12
h he not sent me to the men that ... Is 36:12
H any of the gods of the nations ... Is 36:18
the king of Assyria his master *h* ... Is 37:4
which the LORD thy God *h* heard ... Is 37:4
which *h* sent to reproach the ... Is 37:17
the LORD *h* spoken concerning him ... Is 37:22
h despised thee, and laughed thee ... Is 37:22
h shaken her head at thee ... Is 37:22
do this thing that he *h* spoken ... Is 38:7
He *h* both spoken unto me ... Is 38:15
and himself *h* done it ... Is 38:15
for she *h* received of the LORD's ... Is 40:2
the mouth of the LORD *h* spoken it ... Is 40:5
Who *h* measured the waters in the ... Is 40:12
Who *h* directed the Spirit of the ... Is 40:13
being his counsellor *h* taught him ... Is 40:13
he *h* no oblation chooseth a tree ... Is 40:20
h it not been told you from the ... Is 40:21
behold who *h* created these things ... Is 40:26
Who *h* wrought and done it, calling ... Is 41:4
the hand of the LORD *h* done this ... Is 41:20
Holy One of Israel *h* created it ... Is 41:20
Who *h* declared from the beginning ... Is 41:26
Therefore he *h* poured upon him ... Is 42:25
it *h* set him on fire round about, ... Is 42:25
Thy first father *h* sinned ... Is 43:27
Who *h* formed a god, or molten a ... Is 44:10
for he *h* shut their eyes, that ... Is 44:18
deceived heart *h* turned him aside ... Is 44:20
for the LORD *h* done it ... Is 44:23
for the LORD *h* redeemed Jacob, and ... Is 44:23
or thy work, He *h* no hands ... Is 45:9
he *h* established it, he created ... Is 45:18
who *h* declared this from ancient ... Is 45:21
who *h* told it from that time ... Is 45:21
knowledge, it *h* perverted thee ... Is 47:10
say, Mine idol *h* done them ... Is 48:5
my molten image, *h* commanded them ... Is 48:5
Mine hand also *h* laid the ... Is 48:13
my right hand *h* spanned the ... Is 48:13
which among them *h* declared these ... Is 48:14
The LORD *h* loved him ... Is 48:14
GOD, and his Spirit, *h* sent me ... Is 48:16
The LORD *h* redeemed his servant ... Is 48:20
The LORD *h* called me from the ... Is 49:1
h he made mention of my name ... Is 49:1
he *h* made my mouth like a sharp ... Is 49:2
shadow of his hand *h* he hid me ... Is 49:2
in his quiver *h* he hid me ... Is 49:2
for he that *h* mercy on them shall ... Is 49:10
for the LORD *h* comforted his ... Is 49:13
The LORD *h* forsaken me ... Is 49:14
and my Lord *h* forgotten me ... Is 49:14
Who *h* begotten me these, seeing I ... Is 49:21
and who *h* brought up these ... Is 49:21
The Lord GOD *h* given me the ... Is 50:4
The Lord GOD *h* opened mine ear, ... Is 50:5
in darkness, and *h* no light ... Is 50:10
Art thou not it that *h* cut Rahab ... Is 51:9
thou not it which *h* dried the sea ... Is 51:10
that *h* made the depths of the sea ... Is 51:10
that *h* stretched forth the ... Is 51:13
the sons whom she *h* brought forth ... Is 51:18
the sons that she *h* brought up ... Is 51:18
for the LORD *h* comforted his ... Is 52:9
people, he *h* redeemed Jerusalem ... Is 52:9
The LORD *h* made bare his holy arm ... Is 52:10
Who *h* believed our report ... Is 53:1
he *h* no form nor comeliness ... Is 53:2
Surely he *h* borne our griefs, and ... Is 53:4
the LORD *h* laid on him the ... Is 53:6
he *h* put him to grief ... Is 53:10
because he *h* poured out his soul ... Is 53:12
For the LORD *h* called thee as a ... Is 54:6
the LORD that *h* mercy on thee ... Is 54:10
the waters, and he that *h* no money ... Is 55:1
for he *h* glorified thee ... Is 55:5
that *h* joined himself to the LORD ... Is 56:3
The LORD *h* utterly separated me ... Is 56:3
the mouth of the LORD *h* spoken it ... Is 58:14
lies, your tongue *h* muttered ... Is 59:3
because he *h* glorified thee ... Is 60:9
because the LORD *h* anointed me to ... Is 61:1
he *h* sent me to bind up the ... Is 61:1
the seed which the LORD *h* blessed ... Is 61:9
for he *h* clothed me with the ... Is 61:10
he *h* covered me with the robe of ... Is 61:10
The LORD *h* sworn by his right ... Is 62:8
the LORD *h* proclaimed unto the ... Is 62:11
that the LORD *h* bestowed on us ... Is 63:7
which he *h* bestowed on them ... Is 63:7
neither *h* the eye seen, O God, ... Is 64:4
what he *h* prepared for him that ... Is 64:4
man that *h* not filled his days ... Is 65:20
all those things *h* mine hand made ... Is 66:2
Who *h* heard such a thing ... Is 66:8
who *h* seen such things ... Is 66:8
H a nation changed their gods, ... Jer 2:11
your own sword *h* devoured your ... Jer 2:30
for the LORD *h* rejected thy ... Jer 2:37
there *h* been no latter rain ... Jer 3:3 1961
which backsliding Israel *h* done ... Jer 3:6
there *h* played the harlot ... Jer 3:6
h not turned unto me with her ... Jer 3:10
unto me, The backsliding Israel *h* ... Jer 3:11
For shame *h* devoured the labour ... Jer 3:24

because she *h* been rebellious ... Jer 4:17
For thus *h* the LORD said, The ... Jer 4:27
But this people *h* a revolting ... Jer 5:23 1961
For thus *h* the LORD of hosts said ... Jer 6:6
anguish *h* taken hold of us, and ... Jer 6:24
because the LORD *h* rejected them ... Jer 6:30
for the LORD *h* rejected and ... Jer 7:29
LORD our God *h* put us to silence ... Jer 8:14
astonishment *h* taken hold on me ... Jer 8:21
the mouth of the LORD *h* spoken ... Jer 9:12
He *h* made the earth by his power, ... Jer 10:12
he *h* established the world by his ... Jer 10:12
h stretched out the heavens by ... Jer 10:12
What *h* my beloved to do in mine ... Jer 11:15
seeing she *h* wrought lewdness ... Jer 11:15
tumult he *h* kindled fire upon it ... Jer 11:16
h pronounced evil against thee, ... Jer 11:17
the LORD *h* given me knowledge of ... Jer 11:18
for the LORD *h* spoken ... Jer 13:15
h thy soul lothed Zion ... Jer 14:19
She that *h* borne seven ... Jer 15:9
she *h* given up the ghost ... Jer 15:9
she *h* been ashamed and confounded ... Jer 15:9
Wherefore *h* the LORD pronounced ... Jer 16:10
heathen, who *h* heard such things ... Jer 18:13
the virgin of Israel *h* done a ... Jer 18:13
Because my people *h* forgotten me ... Jer 18:15
The LORD *h* not called thy name ... Jer 20:3
for he *h* delivered the soul of ... Jer 20:13
Wherefore *h* the LORD done thus ... Jer 22:8
This *h* been thy manner from thy ... Jer 22:21
like a man whom wine *h* overcome ... Jer 23:9
that despise me, The LORD *h* said ... Jer 23:17
For who *h* stood in the counsel of ... Jer 23:18
h perceived and heard his word ... Jer 23:18
who *h* marked his word, and heard ... Jer 23:18
The prophet that *h* a dream ... Jer 23:28
and he that *h* my word, let him ... Jer 23:28
brother, What *h* the LORD answered ... Jer 23:35
and, What *h* the LORD spoken ... Jer 23:35
What *h* the LORD answered thee ... Jer 23:37
and, What *h* the LORD spoken ... Jer 23:37
word of the LORD *h* come unto me ... Jer 25:3
the LORD *h* sent unto you all his ... Jer 25:4
that the LORD *h* given unto you ... Jer 25:5
which Jeremiah *h* prophesied ... Jer 25:13
for the LORD *h* a controversy with ... Jer 25:31
for the LORD *h* spoiled their ... Jer 25:36
He *h* forsaken his covert, as the ... Jer 25:38
for he *h* prophesied against this ... Jer 26:11
that he *h* pronounced against you ... Jer 26:13
for of a truth the LORD *h* sent me ... Jer 26:15
for he *h* spoken to us in the name ... Jer 26:16
as the LORD *h* spoken against the ... Jer 27:13
that the LORD *h* truly sent him ... Jer 28:9
The LORD *h* not sent thee ... Jer 28:15
The LORD *h* raised us up prophets ... Jer 29:15
The LORD *h* made thee priest in ... Jer 29:26
Shemaiah *h* prophesied unto you ... Jer 29:31
because he *h* taught rebellion ... Jer 29:32
The LORD *h* appeared of old unto ... Jer 31:3
For the LORD *h* redeemed Jacob, and ... Jer 31:11
for the LORD *h* created a new ... Jer 31:22
For this city *h* been to me as a ... Jer 32:31 1961
families which the LORD *h* chosen ... Jer 33:24
he *h* even cast them off ... Jer 33:24
which *h* been sold unto thee ... Jer 34:14
when he *h* served thee six years, ... Jer 34:14
in all that he *h* charged us ... Jer 35:8
but this people *h* not hearkened ... Jer 35:16
unto all that he *h* commanded you ... Jer 35:18
anger and the fury that the LORD *h* ... Jer 36:7
the king of Judah *h* burned ... Jer 36:28
word that the LORD *h* shewed me ... Jer 38:21
The LORD thy God *h* pronounced ... Jer 40:2
Now the LORD *h* brought it ... Jer 40:3
and done according as he *h* said ... Jer 40:3
whom the king of Babylon *h* made ... Jer 40:5
h sent Ishmael the son of ... Jer 40:14
my fury *h* been poured forth upon ... Jer 42:18
The LORD *h* said concerning you, O ... Jer 42:19
the which he *h* sent me unto you ... Jer 42:21
the LORD our God *h* not sent thee ... Jer 43:2
for the LORD *h* added grief to my ... Jer 45:3
hosts *h* a sacrifice in the north ... Jer 46:10
thy cry *h* filled the land ... Jer 46:12
for the mighty man *h* stumbled ... Jer 46:12
he *h* passed the time appointed ... Jer 46:17
seeing the LORD *h* given it a ... Jer 47:7
there *h* he appointed it ... Jer 47:7
destroyed, as the LORD *h* spoken ... Jer 48:8
Moab *h* been at ease from his ... Jer 48:11
he *h* settled on his lees, and *h* ... Jer 48:11
neither *h* he gone into captivity ... Jer 48:11
that he *h* gotten are perished ... Jer 48:36
how *h* Moab turned the back with ... Jer 48:39
because he *h* magnified himself ... Jer 48:42
H Israel no sons? ... Jer 49:1
h he no heir? ... Jer 49:1
Thy terribleness *h* deceived thee ... Jer 49:16
that he *h* taken against Edom ... Jer 49:20
that he *h* purposed against the ... Jer 49:20
to flee, and fear *h* seized on her ... Jer 49:24
h taken counsel against you ... Jer 49:30
h conceived a purpose against you ... Jer 49:30
My people *h* been lost sheep ... Jer 50:6
for she *h* sinned against the LORD ... Jer 50:14
she *h* given her hand ... Jer 50:15

as she *h* done, do unto her ... Jer 50:15
king of Assyria *h* devoured him ... Jer 50:17
of Babylon *h* broken his bones ... Jer 50:17
The LORD *h* opened his armoury, and ... Jer 50:25
h brought forth the weapons of ... Jer 50:25
according to all that she *h* done ... Jer 50:29
for she *h* been proud against the ... Jer 50:29
The king of Babylon *h* heard the ... Jer 50:43
that he *h* taken against Babylon ... Jer 50:45
that he *h* purposed against the ... Jer 50:45
For Israel *h* not been forsaken, ... Jer 51:5
Babylon *h* been a golden cup in ... Jer 51:7
The LORD *h* brought forth our ... Jer 51:10
the LORD *h* raised up the spirit ... Jer 51:11
for the LORD *h* both devised ... Jer 51:12
LORD of hosts *h* sworn by himself ... Jer 51:14
He *h* made the earth by his power, ... Jer 51:15
he *h* established the world by his ... Jer 51:15
h stretched out the heaven by his ... Jer 51:15
their might *h* failed ... Jer 51:30
the king of Babylon *h* devoured me ... Jer 51:34
he *h* crushed me, he *h* made me ... Jer 51:34
he *h* swallowed me up like a ... Jer 51:34
he *h* filled his belly with my ... Jer 51:34
my delicates, he *h* cast me out ... Jer 51:34
that which he *h* swallowed up ... Jer 51:44
As Babylon *h* caused the slain of ... Jer 51:49
shame *h* covered our faces ... Jer 51:51
the LORD *h* spoiled Babylon ... Jer 51:55
lovers she *h* none to comfort her ... Lam 1:2
for the LORD *h* afflicted her for ... Lam 1:5
Jerusalem *h* grievously sinned ... Lam 1:8
for the enemy *h* magnified himself ... Lam 1:9
The adversary *h* spread out his ... Lam 1:10
for she *h* seen that the heathen ... Lam 1:10
wherewith the LORD *h* afflicted me ... Lam 1:12
From above *h* he sent fire into my ... Lam 1:13
he *h* spread a net for my feet ... Lam 1:13
he *h* turned me back ... Lam 1:13
he *h* made me desolate and faint ... Lam 1:13
he *h* made my strength to fall, ... Lam 1:14
the Lord *h* delivered me into ... Lam 1:14
The Lord *h* trodden under foot all ... Lam 1:15
he *h* called an assembly against ... Lam 1:15
the Lord *h* trodden the virgin ... Lam 1:15
the LORD *h* commanded concerning ... Lam 1:17
How *h* the Lord covered the ... Lam 2:1
The Lord *h* swallowed up all the ... Lam 2:2
of Jacob, and *h* not pitied ... Lam 2:2
he *h* thrown down in his wrath the ... Lam 2:2
he *h* brought them down to the ... Lam 2:2
he *h* polluted the kingdom and the ... Lam 2:2
He *h* cut off in his fierce anger ... Lam 2:3
he *h* drawn back his right hand ... Lam 2:3
He *h* bent his bow like an enemy ... Lam 2:4
he *h* swallowed up Israel, he *h* ... Lam 2:5
he *h* destroyed his strong holds, ... Lam 2:5
h increased in the daughter of ... Lam 2:5
he *h* violently taken away his ... Lam 2:6
he *h* destroyed his places of the ... Lam 2:6
the LORD *h* caused the solemn ... Lam 2:6
h despised in the indignation of ... Lam 2:6
The Lord *h* cast off his altar ... Lam 2:7
he *h* abhorred his sanctuary, ... Lam 2:7
he *h* given up into the hand of ... Lam 2:7
The LORD *h* purposed to destroy ... Lam 2:8
he *h* stretched out a line ... Lam 2:8
he *h* not withdrawn his hand from ... Lam 2:8
he *h* destroyed and broken her bars ... Lam 2:9
The LORD *h* done that which he had ... Lam 2:17
he *h* fulfilled his word that he ... Lam 2:17
h thrown down, and *h* not pitied ... Lam 2:17
he *h* caused thine enemy to ... Lam 2:17
he *h* set up the horn of thine ... Lam 2:17
brought up *h* mine enemy consumed ... Lam 2:22
I am the man that *h* seen ... Lam 3:1
He *h* led me, and brought me into ... Lam 3:2
My flesh and my skin *h* he made old ... Lam 3:4
he *h* broken my bones ... Lam 3:4
He *h* builded against me, and ... Lam 3:5
He *h* set me in dark places, as ... Lam 3:6
He *h* hedged me about, that I ... Lam 3:7
he *h* made my chain heavy ... Lam 3:7
He *h* inclosed my ways with hewn ... Lam 3:9
he *h* made my paths crooked ... Lam 3:9
He *h* turned aside my ways, and ... Lam 3:11
he *h* made me desolate ... Lam 3:11
He *h* bent his bow, and set me as a ... Lam 3:12
He *h* caused the arrows of his ... Lam 3:13
He *h* filled me with bitterness, ... Lam 3:15
he *h* made me drunken with ... Lam 3:15
He *h* also broken my teeth with ... Lam 3:16
he *h* covered me with ashes ... Lam 3:16
My soul *h* them still in ... Lam 3:20
because he *h* borne it upon him ... Lam 3:28
The LORD *h* accomplished his fury ... Lam 4:11
he *h* poured out his fierce anger, ... Lam 4:11
h kindled a fire in Zion ... Lam 4:11
it *h* devoured the foundations ... Lam 4:11
anger of the LORD *h* divided them ... Lam 4:16
nation that *h* rebelled against me ... Eze 2:3
there *h* been a prophet among them ... Eze 2:5 1961
his righteousness which he *h* done ... Eze 3:20
my soul *h* not been polluted ... Eze 4:14
she *h* changed my judgments into ... Eze 5:6
which *h* departed from me, and with ... Eze 6:9
the rod *h* blossomed, pride *h* ... Eze 7:10
the LORD *h* forsaken the earth ... Eze 8:12

The LORD *h* forsaken the earth, and ... Eze 9:9
h not the house of Israel, the ... Eze 12:9
and the LORD *h* not sent them ... Eze 13:6
deceived when he *h* spoken a thing ... Eze 14:9
work, when the fire *h* devoured it ... Eze 15:5
GOD, Sodom thy sister *h* not done ... Eze 16:48
Neither *h* Samaria committed half ... Eze 16:51
h taken the king thereof, and the ... Eze 17:12
h taken of the king's seed, and ... Eze 17:13
him, and *h* taken an oath of him ... Eze 17:13
he *h* also taken the mighty of the ... Eze 17:13
h done all these things, he shall ... Eze 17:18
mine oath that he *h* despised ... Eze 17:19
and my covenant that he *h* broken ... Eze 17:19
that he *h* trespassed against me ... Eze 17:20
h not eaten upon the mountains ... Eze 18:6
neither *h* lifted up his eyes to ... Eze 18:6
neither *h* defiled his neighbour's ... Eze 18:6
wife, neither *h* come near to a ... Eze 18:6
h not oppressed any, but *h* ... Eze 18:7
h spoiled none by violence, *h* ... Eze 18:7
h covered the naked with a ... Eze 18:7
He that *h* not given forth upon ... Eze 18:8
neither *h* taken any increase, ... Eze 18:8
that *h* withdrawn his hand from ... Eze 18:8
h executed true judgment between ... Eze 18:8
H walked in my statutes, and *h* ... Eze 18:9
but even *h* eaten upon the ... Eze 18:11
H oppressed the poor and needy, ... Eze 18:12
h spoiled by violence, *h* not ... Eze 18:12
h lifted up his eyes to the idols ... Eze 18:12
h committed abomination ... Eze 18:12
H given forth upon usury, and *h* ... Eze 18:13
he *h* done all these abominations ... Eze 18:13
his father's sins which he *h* done ... Eze 18:14
That *h* not eaten upon the ... Eze 18:15
neither *h* lifted up his eyes to ... Eze 18:15
h not defiled his neighbour's ... Eze 18:15
Neither *h* oppressed any, *h* not ... Eze 18:16
neither *h* spoiled by violence, ... Eze 18:16
but *h* given his bread to the ... Eze 18:16
h covered the naked with a ... Eze 18:16
That *h* taken off his hand from ... Eze 18:17
that *h* not received usury nor ... Eze 18:17
h executed my judgments, *h* ... Eze 18:17
When the son *h* done that which is ... Eze 18:19
h kept all my statutes, and *h* ... Eze 18:19
all his sins that he *h* committed ... Eze 18:21
that he *h* committed, they shall ... Eze 18:22
that he *h* done he shall live ... Eze 18:22
he *h* done shall not be mentioned ... Eze 18:24
his trespass that he *h* trespassed ... Eze 18:24
and in his sin that he *h* sinned ... Eze 18:24
that he *h* done shall he die ... Eze 18:26
wickedness that he *h* committed ... Eze 18:27
that he *h* committed, he shall ... Eze 18:28
which *h* devoured her fruit ... Eze 19:14
so that she *h* no strong rod to be ... Eze 19:14
he *h* given it to be furbished, ... Eze 21:11
one *h* committed abomination with ... Eze 22:11
another *h* lewdly defiled his ... Eze 22:11
another in thee *h* humbled his ... Eze 22:11
at thy blood which *h* been in the ... Eze 22:13 1961
GOD, when the LORD *h* not spoken ... Eze 22:28
She *h* wearied herself with lies, ... Eze 24:12
to all that he *h* done shall ye do ... Eze 24:24
Because that Edom *h* dealt against ... Eze 25:12
h greatly offended, and revenged ... Eze 25:12
because that Tyrus *h* said against ... Eze 26:2
the east wind *h* broken thee in ... Eze 27:26
midst of his rivers, which *h* said ... Eze 29:3
because he *h* said, The river is ... Eze 29:9
he *h* shot up his top among the ... Eze 31:10
his iniquity that he *h* committed ... Eze 33:13
None of his sins that he *h* ... Eze 33:16
he *h* done that which is lawful and ... Eze 33:16
of one that *h* a pleasant voice ... Eze 33:32
that a prophet *h* been among them ... Eze 33:33 1961
the enemy *h* said against you ... Eze 36:2
h entered in by it, therefore it ... Eze 44:2
for sister that *h* had no husband ... Eze 44:25
who *h* appointed your meat and your ... Dan 1:10
The secret which the king *h* ... Dan 2:27
of heaven *h* given thee a kingdom ... Dan 2:37
the fowls of the heaven *h* he ... Dan 2:38
h made thee ruler over them all ... Dan 2:38
the great God *h* made known to the ... Dan 2:45
Nebuchadnezzar the king *h* set up ... Dan 3:5
who *h* sent his angel, and ... Dan 3:28
the high God *h* wrought toward me ... Dan 4:2
God *h* numbered thy kingdom, and ... Dan 5:26
My God *h* sent his angel, and *h* ... Dan 6:22
who *h* delivered Daniel from the ... Dan 6:27
he *h* confirmed his words, which ... Dan 9:12
for under the whole heaven *h* not ... Dan 9:12
as *h* been done upon Jerusalem ... Dan 9:12
Therefore *h* the LORD watched upon ... Dan 9:14
And when he *h* taken away the ... Dan 11:12
for the land *h* committed great ... Hos 1:2
For their mother *h* played the ... Hos 2:5
conceived them *h* done shamefully ... Hos 2:5
her fig trees, whereof she *h* said ... Hos 2:12
for the LORD *h* a controversy with ... Hos 4:1
of whoredoms *h* caused them to err ... Hos 4:12
The wind *h* bound her up in her ... Hos 4:19
he *h* withdrawn himself from them ... Hos 5:6
for he *h* torn, and he will heal us ... Hos 6:1
he *h* smitten, and he will bind us ... Hos 6:1

he *h* set an harvest for thee,	Hos 6:11	
after he *h* kneaded the dough	Hos 7:4	
he *h* mixed himself among the	Hos 7:8	
as their congregation *h* heard	Hos 7:12	
Israel *h* cast off the thing that	Hos 8:3	
calf, O Samaria, *h* cast thee off	Hos 8:5	
it *h* no stalk	Hos 8:7	
Ephraim *h* hired lovers	Hos 8:9	
Because Ephraim *h* made many	Hos 8:11	
For Israel *h* forgotten his Maker,	Hos 8:14	
Judah *h* multiplied fenced cities	Hos 8:14	
fruit he *h* increased the altars	Hos 10:1	
The LORD *h* also a controversy	Hos 12:2	
for she *h* rebelled against her	Hos 13:16	
H this been in your days, or even	Joel 1:2	1961
That which the palmerworm *h* left	Joel 1:4	
that which the locust *h* left *h*	Joel 1:4	
h left *h* the caterpiller eaten	Joel 1:4	
he *h* the cheek teeth of a great	Joel 1:6	
He *h* laid my vine waste, and	Joel 1:7	
he *h* made it clean bare, and cast	Joel 1:7	
for the fire *h* devoured the	Joel 1:19	
the flame *h* burned all the trees	Joel 1:19	
the fire *h* devoured the pastures	Joel 1:20	
there *h* not been ever the like,	Joel 2:2	1961
because he *h* done great things	Joel 2:20	
for he *h* given you the former	Joel 2:23	
the years that the locust *h* eaten	Joel 2:25	
that *h* dealt wondrously with you	Joel 2:26	
deliverance, as the LORD *h* said	Joel 2:32	
for the LORD *h* spoken it	Joel 3:8	
the LORD *h* spoken against you	Amos 3:1	
in the forest, when he *h* no prey	Amos 3:4	
a city, and the LORD *h* not done it	Amos 3:6	
The lion *h* roared, who will not	Amos 3:8	
the Lord GOD *h* spoken, who can	Amos 3:8	
The Lord GOD *h* sworn by his	Amos 4:2	
The Lord GOD *h* sworn by himself,	Amos 6:8	
Thus *h* the Lord GOD shewed unto	Amos 7:1	
Thus *h* the Lord GOD shewed unto	Amos 7:4	
Amos *h* conspired against thee in	Amos 7:10	
Thus *h* the Lord GOD shewed unto	Amos 8:1	
The LORD *h* sworn by the	Amos 8:7	
h founded his troop in the earth	Amos 9:6	
of thine heart *h* deceived thee	Obad 3	
for the LORD *h* spoken it	Obad 18	
which *h* made the sea and the dry	Jonah 1:9	
he *h* changed the portion of my	Mic 2:4	
how *h* he removed it from me	Mic 2:4	
turning away he *h* divided our	Mic 2:4	
of the LORD of hosts *h* spoken it	Mic 4:4	
he *h* laid siege against us	Mic 5:1	
which travaileth *h* brought forth	Mic 5:3	
for the LORD *h* a controversy with	Mic 6:2	
He *h* shewed thee, O man, what is	Mic 6:8	
ye the rod, and who *h* appointed it	Mic 6:9	
the LORD *h* his way in the	Nah 1:3	
the LORD *h* given a commandment	Nah 1:14	
For the LORD *h* turned away the	Nah 2:2	
for upon whom *h* not thy	Nah 3:19	
the maker thereof *h* graven it	Hab 2:18	
for the LORD *h* prepared a	Zeph 1:7	
a sacrifice, he *h* bid his guests	Zeph 1:7	
The LORD *h* taken away thy	Zeph 3:15	
he *h* cast out thine enemy	Zeph 3:15	
olive tree, *h* not brought forth	Hag 2:19	
The LORD *h* been sore displeased	Zec 1:2	
our doings, so *h* he dealt with us	Zec 1:6	
whom the LORD *h* sent to walk to	Zec 1:10	
After the glory *h* he sent me unto	Zec 2:8	
that the LORD of hosts *h* sent me	Zec 2:9	
LORD of hosts *h* sent me unto thee	Zec 2:11	
even the LORD that *h* chosen	Zec 3:2	
LORD of hosts *h* sent me unto you	Zec 4:9	
For who *h* despised the day of	Zec 4:10	
LORD of hosts *h* sent me unto you	Zec 6:15	
h cried by the former prophets	Zec 7:7	
hosts *h* sent in his spirit by the	Zec 7:12	
for the LORD of hosts *h* visited	Zec 10:3	
h made them as his goodly horse	Zec 10:3	
his vision, when he *h* prophesied	Zec 13:4	
the LORD *h* indignation for ever	Mal 1:4	
this *h* been by your means	Mal 1:9	1761
which *h* in his flock a male, and	Mal 1:14	3426
h not one God created us	Mal 2:10	
Judah *h* dealt treacherously, and	Mal 2:11	
for Judah *h* profaned the holiness	Mal 2:11	
h married the daughter of a	Mal 2:11	
Because the LORD *h* been witness	Mal 2:14	
who *h* warned you to flee from the	Mt 3:7	
thy brother *h* ought against thee	Mt 5:23	*2192*
her *h* committed adultery with her	Mt 5:28	
It *h* been said, Whosoever shall	Mt 5:31	
ye have heard that it *h* been said	Mt 5:33	
Ye have heard that it *h* been said	Mt 5:38	
Ye have heard that it *h* been said	Mt 5:43	
but the Son of man *h* not where to	Mt 8:20	*2192*
h power on earth to forgive sins	Mt 9:6	*2192*
thy faith *h* made thee whole	Mt 9:22	
that are born of women there *h*	Mt 11:11	
He that *h* ears to hear, let him	Mt 11:15	*2192*
and they say, He *h* a devil	Mt 11:18	*2192*
Who *h* ears to hear, let him hear	Mt 13:9	*2192*
For whosoever *h*, to him shall be	Mt 13:12	*2192*
but whosoever *h* not, from him	Mt 13:12	*2192*
be taken away even that he *h*	Mt 13:12	*2192*
Yet *h* he not root in himself, but	Mt 13:21	*2192*
from whence then *h* it tares	Mt 13:27	*2192*
unto them, An enemy *h* done this	Mt 13:28	
Who *h* ears to hear, let him hear	Mt 13:43	*2192*
the which when a man *h* found	Mt 13:44	
goeth and selleth all that he *h*	Mt 13:44	*2192*
Whence *h* this man this wisdom, and	Mt 13:54	
Whence then *h* this man all these	Mt 13:56	
my heavenly Father *h* not planted	Mt 15:13	
blood *h* not revealed it unto thee	Mt 16:17	
therefore God *h* joined together	Mt 19:6	
every one that *h* forsaken houses,	Mt 19:29	
him, Because no man *h* hired us	Mt 20:7	
say, The Lord *h* need of them	Mt 21:3	*2192*
whom his lord *h* made ruler over	Mt 24:45	
it unto him which *h* ten talents	Mt 25:28	*2192*
every one that *h* shall be given	Mt 25:29	*2192*
but from him that *h* not shall be	Mt 25:29	*2192*
taken away even that which he *h*	Mt 25:29	*2192*
for she *h* wrought a good work	Mt 26:10	
For in that she *h* poured this	Mt 26:12	
also this, that this woman *h* done	Mt 26:13	
saying, He *h* spoken blasphemy	Mt 26:65	
said, Why, what evil *h* he done	Mt 27:23	
h power on earth to forgive sins	Mk 2:10	*2192*
He *h* Beelzebub, and by the prince	Mk 3:22	*2192*
he cannot stand, but *h* an end	Mk 3:26	*2192*
Holy Ghost *h* never forgiveness	Mk 3:29	*2192*
they said, He *h* an unclean spirit	Mk 3:30	*2192*
He that *h* ears to hear, let him	Mk 4:9	*2192*
For he that *h*, to him shall be	Mk 4:25	*2192*
and he that *h* not, from him shall	Mk 4:25	*2192*
be taken even that which he *h*	Mk 4:25	*2192*
things the Lord *h* done for thee	Mk 5:19	
and *h* had compassion on thee	Mk 5:19	
thy faith *h* made thee whole	Mk 5:34	
From whence *h* this man these	Mk 6:2	
Well *h* Esaias prophesied of you	Mk 7:6	
He *h* done all things well	Mk 7:37	
my son, which *h* a dumb spirit	Mk 9:17	*2192*
ofttimes it *h* cast him into the	Mk 9:22	
therefore God *h* joined together	Mk 10:9	
There is no man that *h* left house	Mk 10:29	
thy faith *h* made thee whole	Mk 10:52	
ye that the Lord *h* need of him	Mk 11:3	*2192*
this poor widow *h* cast more in	Mk 12:43	
elect's sake, whom he *h* chosen	Mk 13:20	
he *h* shortened the days	Mk 13:20	
she *h* wrought a good work on me	Mk 14:6	
She *h* done what she could	Mk 14:8	
this also that she *h* done shall	Mk 14:9	
them, Why, what evil *h* he done	Mk 15:14	
Thus *h* the Lord dealt with me in	Lk 1:25	
she *h* also conceived a son in her	Lk 1:36	
my spirit *h* rejoiced in God my	Lk 1:47	
For he *h* regarded the low estate	Lk 1:48	
For he that is mighty *h* done to	Lk 1:49	
He *h* shewed strength with his arm	Lk 1:51	
he *h* scattered the proud in the	Lk 1:51	
He *h* put down the mighty from	Lk 1:52	
He *h* filled the hungry with good	Lk 1:53	
the rich he *h* sent empty away	Lk 1:53	
He *h* holpen his servant Israel,	Lk 1:54	
for he *h* visited and redeemed his	Lk 1:68	
h raised up an horn of salvation	Lk 1:69	
from on high *h* visited us	Lk 1:78	
which the Lord *h* made known unto	Lk 2:15	
who *h* warned you to flee from the	Lk 3:7	
He that *h* two coats	Lk 3:11	*2192*
let him impart to him that *h* none	Lk 3:11	*2192*
and he that *h* meat, let him do	Lk 3:11	*2192*
because he *h* anointed me to	Lk 4:18	
he *h* sent me to heal the	Lk 4:18	
man *h* power upon earth to forgive	Lk 5:24	*2192*
he *h* built us a synagogue	Lk 7:5	
That God *h* visited his people	Lk 7:16	
John Baptist *h* sent us unto thee,	Lk 7:20	
and ye say, He *h* a devil	Lk 7:33	*2192*
but she *h* washed my feet with	Lk 7:44	
in *h* not ceased to kiss my feet	Lk 7:45	
but this woman *h* anointed my feet	Lk 7:46	
the woman, Thy faith *h* saved thee	Lk 7:50	
He that *h* ears to hear, let him	Lk 8:8	*2192*
when he *h* lighted a candle,	Lk 8:16	
for whosoever *h*, to him shall be	Lk 8:18	*2192*
and whosoever *h* not, from him	Lk 8:18	*2192*
great things God *h* done unto thee	Lk 8:39	
Jesus said, Somebody *h* touched me	Lk 8:46	
thy faith *h* made thee whole	Lk 8:48	
but the Son of man *h* not where to	Lk 9:58	*2192*
sister *h* left me to serve alone	Lk 10:40	
Mary *h* chosen that good part,	Lk 10:42	
when he *h* lighted a candle,	Lk 11:33	*2192*
which after he *h* killed	Lk 12:5	
killed *h* power to cast into hell	Lk 12:5	*2192*
make him ruler over all that he *h*	Lk 12:44	5224
of Abraham, whom Satan *h* bound	Lk 13:16	
h shut to the door, and ye begin	Lk 13:25	
after he *h* laid the foundation,	Lk 14:29	
that forsaketh not all that he *h*	Lk 14:33	5224
He that *h* ears to hear, let him	Lk 14:35	*2192*
when he *h* found it, he layeth it	Lk 15:5	
And when she *h* found it, she	Lk 15:9	
thy father *h* killed the fatted	Lk 15:27	
because he *h* received him safe and	Lk 15:27	
which *h* devoured thy living with	Lk 15:30	
thy faith *h* made thee whole	Lk 17:19	
There is no man that *h* left house	Lk 18:29	
thy faith *h* saved thee	Lk 18:42	
thy pound *h* gained ten pounds	Lk 19:16	
thy pound *h* gained five pounds	Lk 19:18	
give it to him that *h* ten pounds	Lk 19:24	*2192*
unto him, Lord, he *h* ten pounds	Lk 19:25	*2192*
every one which *h* shall be given	Lk 19:26	*2192*
and from him that *h* not	Lk 19:26	*2192*
even that he *h* shall be taken	Lk 19:26	*2192*
Because the Lord *h* need of him	Lk 19:31	*2192*
they said, The Lord *h* need of him	Lk 19:34	*2192*
image and superscription *h* it	Lk 20:24	*2192*
that this poor widow *h* cast in	Lk 21:3	
but she of her penury *h* cast in	Lk 21:4	
as my Father *h* appointed unto me	Lk 22:29	
Satan *h* desired to have you, that	Lk 22:31	
them, But now, he that *h* a purse	Lk 22:36	*2192*
he that *h* no sword, let him sell	Lk 22:36	*2192*
time, Why, what evil *h* he done	Lk 23:22	
but this man *h* done nothing amiss	Lk 23:41	
indeed, and *h* appeared to Simon	Lk 24:34	
for a spirit *h* not flesh and bones	Lk 24:39	*2192*
No man *h* seen God at any time	Jn 1:18	
of the Father, he *h* declared him	Jn 1:18	
zeal of thine house *h* eaten me up	Jn 2:17	
no man *h* ascended up to heaven,	Jn 3:13	
because he *h* not believed in the	Jn 3:18	
He that *h* the bride is the	Jn 3:29	*2192*
And what he *h* seen and heard, that	Jn 3:32	
He that *h* received his testimony	Jn 3:33	
h set to his seal that God is	Jn 3:33	
For he whom God *h* sent speaketh	Jn 3:34	
h given all things into his hand	Jn 3:35	
on the Son *h* everlasting life	Jn 3:36	*2192*
H any man brought him ought to	Jn 4:33	
that a prophet *h* no honour in his	Jn 4:44	*2192*
but *h* committed all judgment unto	Jn 5:22	
not the Father which *h* sent him	Jn 5:23	
h everlasting life, and shall not	Jn 5:24	*2192*
as the Father *h* life in himself	Jn 5:26	*2192*
so *h* he given to the Son to have	Jn 5:26	
h given him authority to execute	Jn 5:27	
of the Father which *h* sent me	Jn 5:30	
the Father *h* given me to finish	Jn 5:36	
of me, that the Father *h* sent me	Jn 5:36	
which *h* sent me, *h* borne	Jn 5:37	
for whom he *h* sent, him ye	Jn 5:38	
which *h* five barley loaves, and	Jn 6:9	*2192*
for him *h* God the Father sealed	Jn 6:27	
ye believe on him whom he *h* sent	Jn 6:29	
the Father's will which *h* sent me	Jn 6:39	
that of all which he *h* given me I	Jn 6:39	
Father which *h* sent me draw him	Jn 6:44	
Every man therefore that *h* heard	Jn 6:45	
h learned of the Father, cometh	Jn 6:45	
that any man *h* seen the Father	Jn 6:46	
is of God, he *h* seen the Father	Jn 6:46	
on me *h* everlasting life	Jn 6:47	*2192*
drinketh my blood, *h* eternal life	Jn 6:54	*2192*
As the living Father *h* sent me	Jn 6:57	
I am from him, and he *h* sent me	Jn 7:29	
than these which this man *h* done	Jn 7:31	
on me, as the scripture *h* said	Jn 7:38	
H not the scripture said, That	Jn 7:42	
h no man condemned thee	Jn 8:10	
but as my Father *h* taught me	Jn 8:28	
the Father *h* not left me alone	Jn 8:29	
because my word *h* no place in you	Jn 8:37	*5562*
a man that *h* told you the truth,	Jn 8:40	
Neither *h* this man sinned, nor	Jn 9:3	
that he *h* opened thine eyes	Jn 9:17	
or who *h* opened his eyes, we know	Jn 9:21	
yet he *h* opened mine eyes	Jn 9:30	
said, He *h* a devil, and is mad	Jn 10:20	*2192*
the words of him that *h* a devil	Jn 10:21	
him, whom the Father *h* sanctified	Jn 10:36	
for he *h* been dead four days	Jn 11:39	
day of my burying *h* she kept this	Jn 12:7	
who *h* believed our report	Jn 12:38	
to whom *h* the arm of the Lord	Jn 12:38	
He *h* blinded their eyes, and	Jn 12:40	
my words, *h* one that judgeth him	Jn 12:48	*2192*
He that eateth bread with me *h*	Jn 13:18	
h seen me *h* seen the Father	Jn 14:9	
He that *h* my commandments, and	Jn 14:21	*2192*
world cometh, and *h* nothing in me	Jn 14:30	*2192*
As the Father *h* loved me, so have	Jn 15:9	
Greater love *h* no man than this,	Jn 15:13	*2192*
sorrow *h* filled your heart	Jn 16:6	
things that the Father *h* are mine	Jn 16:15	*2192*
when she is in travail *h* sorrow	Jn 16:21	*2192*
the world *h* hated them, because	Jn 17:14	
the world *h* not known thee	Jn 17:25	
cup which my Father *h* given me	Jn 18:11	
me unto thee *h* the greater sin	Jn 19:11	*2192*
as my Father *h* sent me, even so	Jn 20:21	
which the Father *h* put in his own	Acts 1:7	
Whom God *h* raised up, having	Acts 2:24	
This Jesus *h* God raised up,	Acts 2:32	
he *h* shed forth this, which ye	Acts 2:33	
that God *h* made that same Jesus,	Acts 2:36	
h glorified his Son Jesus	Acts 3:13	
whom God *h* raised from the dead	Acts 3:15	
his name *h* made this man strong	Acts 3:16	
by him *h* given him this perfect	Acts 3:16	
should suffer, he *h* so fulfilled	Acts 3:18	
which God *h* spoken by the mouth	Acts 3:21	
h been done by them is manifest	Acts 4:16	
why *h* Satan filled thine heart to	Acts 5:3	
Him *h* God exalted with his right	Acts 5:31	
whom God *h* given to them that	Acts 5:32	

H not my hand made all these ... Acts 7:50
h seen in a vision a man named ... Acts 9:12
how much evil he *h* done to thy ... Acts 9:13
here he *h* authority from the ... Acts 9:14 *2192*
h sent me, that thou mightest ... Acts 9:17
second time, What God *h* cleansed ... Acts 10:15
but God *h* shewed me that I should ... Acts 10:28
h at any time entered into my ... Acts 11:8
from heaven, What God *h* cleansed ... Acts 11:9
Then *h* God also to the Gentiles ... Acts 11:18
that the Lord *h* sent his angel, ... Acts 12:11
h delivered me out of the hand of ... Acts 12:11
Of this man's seed *h* God ... Acts 13:23
God *h* fulfilled the same unto us ... Acts 13:33
in that he *h* raised up Jesus ... Acts 13:33
For so *h* the Lord commanded us, ... Acts 13:47
Simeon *h* declared how God at the ... Acts 15:14
For Moses of old time *h* in every ... Acts 15:21 *2192*
Whom Jason *h* received ... Acts 17:7
h made of one blood all nations ... Acts 17:26
h determined the times before ... Acts 17:26
Because he *h* appointed a day, in ... Acts 17:31
by that man whom he *h* ordained ... Acts 17:31
whereof he *h* given assurance unto ... Acts 17:31
in that he *h* raised him from the ... Acts 17:31
all Asia, this Paul *h* persuaded ... Acts 19:26
Holy Ghost *h* made you overseers ... Acts 20:28
which he *h* purchased with his own ... Acts 20:28
h polluted this holy place ... Acts 21:28
God of our fathers *h* chosen thee ... Acts 22:14
or an angel *h* spoken to him ... Acts 23:9
for he *h* a certain thing to tell ... Acts 23:17 *2192*
who *h* something to say unto thee ... Acts 23:18 *2192*
Who also *h* gone about to profane ... Acts 24:6 *2192*
that he himself *h* appealed to ... Acts 25:25
God *h* given thee all them that ... Acts 27:24
though he *h* escaped the sea, yet ... Acts 28:4
for God *h* shewed it unto them ... Rom 1:19
What advantage then *h* the Jew ... Rom 3:1
For if the truth of God *h* more ... Rom 3:7
Whom God *h* set forth to be a ... Rom 3:25
pertaining to the flesh, *h* found ... Rom 4:1
by works, he *h* whereof to glory ... Rom 4:2 *2192*
Christ, *h* abounded unto many ... Rom 5:15
That as sin *h* reigned unto death, ... Rom 5:21
death *h* no more dominion over him ... Rom 6:9
how that the law *h* dominion over ... Rom 7:1
For the woman which *h* an husband ... Rom 7:2 5220
h made me free from the law of ... Rom 8:2
but by reason of him who *h* ... Rom 8:20
word of God *h* taken none effect ... Rom 9:6
Therefore *h* he mercy on whom he ... Rom 9:18
For who *h* resisted his will ... Rom 9:19
H not the potter power over the ... Rom 9:21 *2192*
Even us, whom he *h* called ... Rom 9:24
h not attained to the law of ... Rom 9:31
God *h* raised him from the dead ... Rom 10:9
who *h* believed our report ... Rom 10:16
H God cast away his people ... Rom 11:1
God *h* not cast away his people ... Rom 11:2
Israel *h* not obtained that which ... Rom 11:7
but the election *h* obtained it ... Rom 11:7
God *h* given them the spirit of ... Rom 11:8
For God *h* concluded them all in ... Rom 11:32
For who *h* known the mind of the ... Rom 11:34
or who *h* been his counsellor ... Rom 11:34 *1096*
Or who *h* first given to him, and ... Rom 11:35
according as God *h* dealt to every ... Rom 12:3
another *h* fulfilled the law ... Rom 13:8
for God *h* received him ... Rom 14:3
which Christ *h* not wrought by me ... Rom 15:18
For it *h* pleased them of ... Rom 15:26
It *h* pleased them verily ... Rom 15:27
business she *h* need of you ... Rom 16:2
for she *h* been a succourer of ... Rom 16:2 *1096*
For it *h* been declared unto me of ... 1Cor 1:11
h not God made foolish the wisdom ... 1Cor 1:20
But God *h* chosen the foolish ... 1Cor 1:27
God *h* chosen the weak things of ... 1Cor 1:27
h God chosen, yea, and things ... 1Cor 1:28
Eye *h* not seen, nor ear heard, ... 1Cor 2:9
the things which God *h* prepared ... 1Cor 2:9
But God *h* revealed them unto us ... 1Cor 2:10
For who *h* known the mind of the ... 1Cor 2:16
abide which he *h* built thereupon ... 1Cor 3:14
For I think that God *h* set forth ... 1Cor 4:9
that he that *h* done this deed ... 1Cor 5:2
him that *h* so done this deed ... 1Cor 5:3
God *h* both raised up the Lord, and ... 1Cor 6:14
The wife *h* not power of her own ... 1Cor 7:4 *1850*
h not power of his own body ... 1Cor 7:4 *1850*
But every man *h* his proper gift ... 1Cor 7:7 *2192*
If any brother *h* a wife that ... 1Cor 7:12 *2192*
the woman which *h* an husband that ... 1Cor 7:13 *2192*
but God *h* called us to peace ... 1Cor 7:15
But as God *h* distributed to every ... 1Cor 7:17
as the Lord *h* called every one, ... 1Cor 7:17
as one that *h* obtained mercy of ... 1Cor 7:25
a virgin marry, she *h* not sinned ... 1Cor 7:28
but *h* power over his own will, and ... 1Cor 7:37 *2192*
h so decreed in his heart that he ... 1Cor 7:37
Even so *h* the Lord ordained that ... 1Cor 9:14
There *h* no temptation taken you ... 1Cor 10:13
h many members, and all the ... 1Cor 12:12 *2192*
But now *h* God set the members ... 1Cor 12:18
in the body, as it *h* pleased him ... 1Cor 12:18
but God *h* tempered the body ... 1Cor 12:24
God *h* set some in the church, ... 1Cor 12:28
every one of you *h* a psalm ... 1Cor 14:26 *2192*
h a doctrine, *h* a tongue, *h* ... 1Cor 14:26 *2192*
a revelation, *h* an interpretation ... 1Cor 14:26 *2192*
till he *h* put all enemies under ... 1Cor 15:25
For he *h* put all things under his ... 1Cor 15:27
it a body as it *h* pleased him ... 1Cor 15:38
as God *h* prospered him, that ... 1Cor 16:2
Christ, and *h* anointed us, is God ... 2Cor 1:21
Who *h* also sealed us, and given ... 2Cor 1:22
he *h* not grieved me, but in part ... 2Cor 2:5
Who also *h* made us able ministers ... 2Cor 3:6
In whom the god of this world *h* ... 2Cor 4:4
h shined in our hearts, to give ... 2Cor 4:6
Now he that *h* wrought us for the ... 2Cor 5:5
who also *h* given unto us the ... 2Cor 5:5
body, according to that he *h* done ... 2Cor 5:10
who *h* reconciled us to himself by ... 2Cor 5:18
h given to us the ministry of ... 2Cor 5:18
h committed unto us the word of ... 2Cor 5:19
For he *h* made him to be sin for ... 2Cor 5:21
fellowship *h* righteousness with ... 2Cor 6:14
what communion *h* light with ... 2Cor 6:14
what concord *h* Christ with Belial ... 2Cor 6:15
or what part *h* he that believeth ... 2Cor 6:15
what agreement *h* the temple of ... 2Cor 6:16
as God *h* said, I will dwell in ... 2Cor 6:16
the same epistle *h* made you sorry ... 2Cor 7:8
according to that a man *h* ... 2Cor 8:12 *2192*
and not according to that he *h* not ... 2Cor 8:12 *2192*
your zeal *h* provoked very many ... 2Cor 9:2
is written, He *h* dispersed abroad ... 2Cor 9:9
he *h* given to the poor ... 2Cor 9:9
which the Lord *h* given us for ... 2Cor 10:8
which God *h* distributed to us ... 2Cor 10:13
Lord *h* given me to edification ... 2Cor 13:10
who *h* bewitched you, that ye ... Gal 3:1
Christ *h* been evidently set forth ... Gal 3:1
Christ *h* redeemed us from the ... Gal 3:13
But the scripture *h* concluded all ... Gal 3:22
God *h* sent forth the Spirit of ... Gal 4:6
for the desolate *h* many more ... Gal 4:27
than she which *h* a husband ... Gal 4:27 *2192*
wherewith Christ *h* made us free ... Gal 5:1
who *h* blessed us with all ... Eph 1:3
According as he *h* chosen us in ... Eph 1:4
wherein he *h* made us accepted in ... Eph 1:6
Wherein he *h* abounded toward us ... Eph 1:8
which he *h* purposed in himself ... Eph 1:9
h put all things under his feet, ... Eph 1:22
you *h* he quickened, who were dead ... Eph 2:1
h quickened us together with ... Eph 2:5
h raised us up together, and made ... Eph 2:6
which God *h* before ordained that ... Eph 2:10
who *h* made both one, and *h* ... Eph 2:14
of the world *h* been hid in God ... Eph 3:9
for Christ's sake *h* forgiven you ... Eph 4:32
love, as Christ also *h* loved us ... Eph 5:2
h given himself for us an ... Eph 5:2
h any inheritance in the kingdom ... Eph 5:5 *2192*
that he which *h* begun a good work ... Phil 1:6
God also *h* highly exalted him ... Phil 2:9
he *h* served with me in the gospel ... Phil 2:22
h whereof he might trust in the ... Phil 3:4
care of me *h* flourished again ... Phil 4:10
which *h* made us meet to be ... Col 1:12
Who *h* delivered us from the power ... Col 1:13
h translated us into the kingdom ... Col 1:13
works, yet now *h* he reconciled ... Col 1:21
which *h* been hid from ages ... Col 1:26
who *h* raised him from the dead ... Col 2:12
h he quickened together with him, ... Col 2:13
those things which he *h* not seen ... Col 2:18
for the wrong which he *h* done ... Col 3:25
that he *h* a great zeal for you, ... Col 4:13 *2192*
who *h* called you unto his kingdom ... 1Th 2:12
For God *h* not called us unto ... 1Th 4:7
who *h* also given unto us his holy ... 1Th 4:8
For God *h* not appointed us to ... 1Th 5:9
because God *h* from the beginning ... 2Th 2:13
which *h* loved us, and *h* given ... 2Th 2:16
who *h* enabled me, for that he ... 1Ti 1:12
which God *h* created to be ... 1Ti 4:3
he *h* denied the faith, and is ... 1Ti 5:8
Who only *h* immortality, dwelling ... 1Ti 6:16 *2192*
whom no man *h* seen, nor can see ... 1Ti 6:16
For God *h* not given us the spirit ... 2Ti 1:7
Who *h* saved us, and called us with ... 2Ti 1:9
who *h* abolished death, and *h* ... 2Ti 1:10
who *h* chosen him to be a soldier ... 2Ti 2:4
For Demas *h* forsaken me, having ... 2Ti 4:10
for he *h* greatly withstood our ... 2Ti 4:15
But *h* in due times manifested his ... Titus 1:3
faithful word as he *h* been taught ... Titus 1:9
salvation *h* appeared to all men ... Titus 2:11
If he *h* wronged thee, or oweth ... Philem 18
H in these last days spoken unto ... Heb 1:2
whom he *h* appointed heir of all ... Heb 1:2
as he *h* by inheritance obtained a ... Heb 1:4
h anointed thee with the oil of ... Heb 1:9
For unto the angels *h* he not put ... Heb 2:5
the children which God *h* given me ... Heb 2:13
himself *h* suffered being tempted ... Heb 2:18
inasmuch as he who *h* builded the ... Heb 3:3
h more honour than the house ... Heb 3:3 *2192*
he also *h* ceased from his own ... Heb 4:10
h an unchangeable priesthood ... Heb 7:24 *2192*
But now *h* he obtained a more ... Heb 8:6
covenant, he *h* made the first old ... Heb 8:13
which God *h* enjoined unto you ... Heb 9:20
once in the end of the world *h* he ... Heb 9:26
For by one offering he *h* ... Heb 10:14
which he *h* consecrated for us, ... Heb 10:20
who *h* trodden under foot the Son ... Heb 10:29
h counted the blood of the ... Heb 10:29
h done despite unto the Spirit of ... Heb 10:29
For we know him that *h* said ... Heb 10:30
which *h* great recompence of ... Heb 10:35 *2192*
for a city which *h* foundations ... Heb 11:10 *2192*
for he *h* prepared for them a city ... Heb 11:16
but now he *h* promised, saying, ... Heb 12:26
for he *h* said, I will never leave ... Heb 13:5
which the Lord *h* promised to them ... Jas 1:12
Then when lust *h* conceived ... Jas 1:15
H not God chosen the poor of this ... Jas 2:5
heirs of the kingdom which he *h* ... Jas 2:5
mercy, that *h* shewed no mercy ... Jas 2:13
though a man say he *h* faith ... Jas 2:14 *2192*
if it *h* not works, is dead, being ... Jas 2:17 *2192*
tamed, and *h* been tamed of mankind ... Jas 3:7
h long patience for it, until he ... Jas 5:7
h begotten us again unto a lively ... 1Pet 1:3
But as he which *h* called you is ... 1Pet 1:15
forth the praises of him who *h* ... 1Pet 2:9
For Christ also *h* once suffered ... 1Pet 3:18
Forasmuch then as Christ *h* ... 1Pet 4:1
for he that *h* suffered in the ... 1Pet 4:1
in the flesh *h* ceased from sin ... 1Pet 4:1
As every man *h* received the gift, ... 1Pet 4:10
who *h* called us unto his eternal ... 1Pet 5:10
h given unto us all things that ... 2Pet 1:3
of him that *h* called us to glory ... 2Pet 1:3
h forgotten that he was purged ... 2Pet 1:9
our Lord Jesus Christ *h* shewed me ... 2Pet 1:14
given unto him *h* written unto you ... 2Pet 3:15
that darkness *h* blinded his eyes ... 1Jn 2:11
the same *h* not the Father ... 1Jn 2:23 *2192*
the Son *h* the Father also ... 1Jn 2:23 *2192*
the promise that he *h* promised us ... 1Jn 2:25
lie, and even as it *h* taught you ... 1Jn 2:27
the Father *h* bestowed upon us ... 1Jn 3:1
every man that *h* this hope in him ... 1Jn 3:3 *2192*
whosoever sinneth *h* not seen him ... 1Jn 3:6
ye know that no murderer *h* ... 1Jn 3:15 *2192*
But whoso *h* this world's good, and ... 1Jn 3:17 *2192*
by the Spirit which he *h* given us ... 1Jn 3:24
No man *h* seen God at any time ... 1Jn 4:12
because he *h* given us of his ... 1Jn 4:13
the love that God *h* to us ... 1Jn 4:16 *2192*
because fear *h* torment ... 1Jn 4:18 *2192*
not his brother whom he *h* seen ... 1Jn 4:20
he love God whom he *h* not seen ... 1Jn 4:20
which he *h* testified of his Son ... 1Jn 5:9
of God *h* the witness in himself ... 1Jn 5:10 *2192*
not God *h* made him a liar ... 1Jn 5:10
that God *h* given to us eternal ... 1Jn 5:11
He that *h* the Son *h* life ... 1Jn 5:12 *2192*
he that *h* not the Son of God *h* ... 1Jn 5:12 *2192*
h given us an understanding, that ... 1Jn 5:20
the doctrine of Christ, *h* not God ... 2Jn 9 *2192*
he *h* both the Father and the Son ... 2Jn 9 *2192*
he that doeth evil *h* not seen God ... 3Jn 11
Demetrius *h* good report of all ... 3Jn 12
he *h* reserved in everlasting ... Jude 6
h made us kings and priests unto ... Rev 1:6
He that *h* an ear, let him hear ... Rev 2:7 *2192*
He that *h* an ear, let him hear ... Rev 2:11 *2192*
These things saith he which *h* the ... Rev 2:12 *2192*
He that *h* an ear, let him hear ... Rev 2:17 *2192*
who *h* his eyes like unto a flame ... Rev 2:18 *2192*
He that *h* an ear, let him hear ... Rev 2:29 *2192*
that *h* the seven Spirits of God ... Rev 3:1 *2192*
He that *h* an ear, let him hear ... Rev 3:6 *2192*
he that *h* the key of David, he ... Rev 3:7 *2192*
He that *h* an ear, let him hear ... Rev 3:13 *2192*
He that *h* an ear, let him hear ... Rev 3:22 *2192*
h prevailed to open the book, and ... Rev 5:5
Greek tongue *h* his name Apollyon ... Rev 9:11 *2192*
as he *h* declared to his servants ... Rev 10:7
where she *h* a place prepared of ... Rev 12:6 *2192*
that he *h* but a short time ... Rev 12:12 *2192*
Let him that *h* understanding ... Rev 13:18 *2192*
which *h* power over these plagues ... Rev 16:9 *2192*
which *h* the seven heads and ten ... Rev 17:7 *2192*
here is the mind which *h* wisdom ... Rev 17:9 *2192*
For God *h* put in their hearts to ... Rev 17:17
God *h* remembered her iniquities ... Rev 18:5
in the cup which she *h* filled ... Rev 18:6
How much she *h* glorified herself, ... Rev 18:7
for God *h* avenged you on her ... Rev 18:20
for he *h* judged the great whore, ... Rev 19:2
h avenged the blood of his ... Rev 19:2
his wife *h* made herself ready ... Rev 19:7
he *h* on his vesture and on his ... Rev 19:16 *2192*
holy is he that *h* part in the ... Rev 20:6 *2192*
such the second death *h* no power ... Rev 20:6 *2192*

HATHACH See HATACH.

HATHATH *(ha'-thath)* {1} *Son of Othniel.*
sons of Othniel; *H* ... 1Chr 4:13 2867

HATING {3}
God, men of truth, *h* covetousness ... Ex 18:21 8130
envy, hateful, and *h* one another ... Titus 3:3 *3404*
h even the garment spotted by the ... Jude 23 *3404*

HATIPHA *(hat'-if-ah)* {2} *A family of exiles.*
of Neziah, the children of *H* Ezr 2:54 2412
of Neziah, the children of *H* Neh 7:56 2412

HATITA *(hat'-it-ah)* {2} *A family of exiles.*
of Akkub, the children of *H* Ezr 2:42 2410
of Akkub, the children of *H* Neh 7:45 2410

HATRED {18}
But if he thrust him of *h* Num 35:20 8135
so that the *h* wherewith he hated 2Sa 13:15 8135
and they hate me with cruel *h* Ps 25:19 8135
me about also with words of *h* Ps 109:3 8135
evil for good, and *h* for my love Ps 109:5 8135
I hate them with perfect *h* Ps 139:22 8135
H stirreth up strifes Prov 10:12 8135
He that hideth *h* with lying lips, Prov 10:18 8135
than a stalled ox and *h* therewith Prov 15:17 8135
Whose *h* is covered by deceit, his Prov 26:26 8135
or *h* by all that is before them Eccl 9:1 8135
Also their love, and their *h* Eccl 9:6 8135
to destroy it for the old *h* Eze 25:15 342
thou hast had a perpetual *h* Eze 35:5 342
used out of thy *h* against them Eze 35:11 8135
of thine iniquity, and the great *h* Hos 9:7 4895
h in the house of his God Hos 9:8 4895
Idolatry, witchcraft, *h*, variance Gal 5:20 *2189*

HATS {1}
coats, their hosen, and their *h* Dan 3:21 3737

HATTIL *(hat'-til)* {2} *A family of exiles.*
of Shephatiah, the children of *H* Ezr 2:57 2411
of Shephatiah, the children of *H* Neh 7:59 2411

HATTUSH *(hat'-tush)* {5}
1. A son of Shemaiah.
H, and Igeal, and Bariah, and 1Chr 3:22 2407
2. A son of David.
the sons of David; *H* Ezr 8:2 2407
3. A priest.
Amariah, Malluch, *H*, Neh 12:2 2407
4. A rebuilder of Jerusalem's wall.
repaired *H* the son of Hashabniah Neh 3:10 2407
5. Renewed the covenant.
H, Shebaniah, Malluch, Neh 10:4 2407

HAUGHTILY {1}
neither shall ye go *h* Mic 2:3 7317

HAUGHTINESS {5}
the *h* of men shall be bowed down, Is 2:11 7312
the *h* of men shall be made low Is 2:17 7312
lay low the *h* of the terrible Is 13:11 1346
even of his *h*, and his pride, and Is 16:6 1346
his pride, and the *h* of his heart Jer 48:29 7312

HAUGHTY {10}
but thine eyes are upon the *h* 2Sa 22:28 7311
Lord, my heart is not *h*, nor mine Ps 131:1 1361
an *h* spirit before a fall Prov 16:18 1363
destruction the heart of man is *h* Prov 18:12 1361
h scorner is his name, who Prov 21:24 3093
the daughters of Zion are *h* Is 3:16 1361
down, and the *h* shall be humbled Is 10:33 1364
the *h* people of the earth do Is 24:4 4791
And they were *h*, and committed Eze 16:50 1361
thou shalt no more be *h* because Zeph 3:11 1361

HAUNT {3}
and see his place where his *h* is 1Sa 23:22 7272
himself and his men were wont to *h* 1Sa 30:31 1980
terror to be on all that *h* it Eze 26:17 3427

HAURAN *(hau'-ran)* {2} *A province south of Damascus.*
which is by the coast of *H* Eze 47:16 2362
east side ye shall measure from *H* Eze 47:18 2362

HAVE {3905}
let them *h* dominion over the fish Gen 1:26
h dominion over the fish of the Gen 1:28
I *h* given you every herb bearing Gen 1:29
I *h* given every green herb for Gen 1:30
I *h* gotten a man from the LORD Gen 4:1 1961
in tents, and of such as *h* cattle Gen 4:20
for I *h* slain a man to my Gen 4:23
I will destroy man whom I *h* Gen 6:7
repenteth me that I *h* made them Gen 6:7
for thee *h* I seen righteous Gen 7:1
I *h* made will I destroy from off Gen 7:4
every thing living, as I *h* done Gen 8:21
herb *h* I given you all things Gen 9:3
which I *h* established between me Gen 9:17
one, and they *h* all one language Gen 11:6
which they *h* imagined to do Gen 11:6
so I might *h* taken her to me to Gen 12:19
I *h* lift up mine hand unto the Gen 14:22
say, I *h* made Abram rich Gen 14:23
that which the young men *h* eaten Gen 14:24
Unto thy seed *h* I given this land Gen 15:18
I *h* given my maid into thy bosom Gen 16:5
H I also here looked after him Gen 16:13
of many nations *h* I made thee Gen 17:5
And as for Ishmael, I *h* heard thee Gen 17:20
I *h* blessed him, and will make him Gen 17:20
if now I *h* found favour in thy Gen 18:3
lo, Sarah thy wife shall *h* a son Gen 18:10
I am waxed old shall I *h* pleasure Gen 18:12
of life, and Sarah shall *h* a son Gen 18:14
now, and see whether they *h* done Gen 18:21
I *h* taken upon me to speak unto Gen 18:27
I *h* taken upon me to speak unto Gen 18:31
I *h* two daughters which *h* not Gen 19:8
I *h* accepted thee concerning this Gen 19:21
of my hands *h* I done this Gen 20:5
what *h* I offended thee, that thou Gen 20:9
I *h* given thy brother a thousand Gen 20:16
Who would *h* said unto Abraham, Gen 21:7
that Sarah should *h* given Gen 21:7
for I *h* born him a son in his old Gen 21:7
kindness that I *h* done unto thee Gen 21:23
that I *h* digged this well Gen 21:30
And said, By myself *h* I sworn Gen 22:16
until they *h* done drinking Gen 24:19
We *h* both straw and provender Gen 24:25 5973
for I *h* prepared the house, and Gen 24:31
until I *h* told mine errand Gen 24:33
lightly *h* lien with thy wife Gen 26:10
and thou shouldest *h* brought Gen 26:10
me, and *h* sent me away from you Gen 26:27
as we *h* not touched thee Gen 26:29
as we *h* done unto thee nothing Gen 26:29
h sent thee away in peace Gen 26:29 1961
said unto him, We *h* found water Gen 26:32
I *h* done according as thou badest Gen 27:19
I *h* eaten of all before thou Gen 27:33
thou camest, and *h* blessed him Gen 27:33
I *h* made him thy lord, and all his Gen 27:37
all his brethren *h* I given to him Gen 27:37
corn and wine *h* I sustained him Gen 27:37
when thou shalt *h* the dominion Gen 27:40
until I *h* done that which I *h* Gen 28:15
which I *h* set for a pillar, shall Gen 28:22
because I *h* born him three sons Gen 29:34
that I may also *h* children by her Gen 30:3
With great wrestlings *h* I Gen 30:8
with my sister, and I *h* prevailed Gen 30:8
for surely I *h* hired thee with my Gen 30:16
because I *h* given my maiden to my Gen 30:18
because I *h* born him six sons Gen 30:20
for whom I *h* served thee, and let Gen 30:26
my service which I *h* done thee Gen 30:26
if I *h* found favour in thine eyes Gen 30:27
for I *h* learned by experience Gen 30:27
Thou knowest how I *h* served thee Gen 30:29
my power I *h* served your father Gen 31:6
for I *h* seen all that Laban doeth Gen 31:12
that I might *h* sent thee away Gen 31:27
twenty years *h* I been with thee Gen 31:38
thy she goats *h* not cast their Gen 31:38
rams of thy flock *h* I not eaten Gen 31:38
Thus *h* I been twenty years in thy Gen 31:41
their children which they *h* born Gen 31:43
which I *h* cast betwixt me and thee Gen 31:51
I *h* sojourned with Laban, and Gen 32:4
I *h* oxen, and asses, flocks, and Gen 32:5 1961
I *h* sent to tell my lord, that I Gen 32:5 1961
for I *h* seen God face to face, and Gen 32:30
Esau said, I *h* enough, my brother Gen 33:9 3426
if now I *h* found grace in thy Gen 33:10
for therefore I *h* seen thy face Gen 33:10
with me, and because I *h* enough Gen 33:11 3426
Ye *h* troubled me to make me to Gen 34:30
thou shalt *h* this son also Gen 35:17
you, this dream which I *h* dreamed Gen 37:6
thou indeed *h* dominion over us Gen 37:8
Behold, I *h* dreamed a dream more Gen 37:9
and said, This *h* we found Gen 37:32
We *h* dreamed a dream, and there is Gen 40:8
here also *h* I done nothing that Gen 40:15
I *h* dreamed a dream, and there is Gen 41:15
I *h* heard say of thee, that thou Gen 41:15
which I *h* spoken unto Pharaoh Gen 41:28
I *h* set thee over all the land of Gen 41:41
I *h* heard that there is corn in Gen 42:2
Me *h* ye bereaved of my children Gen 42:36
h ye another brother Gen 43:7 3426
we *h* brought it again in our hand Gen 43:21
other money *h* we brought down in Gen 43:22
Wherefore *h* ye rewarded evil for Gen 44:4
ye *h* done evil in so doing Gen 44:5
What deed is this that ye *h* done Gen 44:15
H ye a father, or a brother Gen 44:19 3426
We *h* a father, an old man, and a Gen 44:20 3426
Egypt, and of all that ye *h* seen Gen 45:13
since I *h* seen thy face, because Gen 46:30
they *h* brought their flocks, and Gen 46:32
their herds, and all that they *h* Gen 46:32
their herds, and all that they *h* Gen 47:1
for thy servants *h* no pasture for Gen 47:4 369
evil *h* the days of the years of Gen 47:9 1961
h not attained unto the days of Gen 47:9
I *h* bought you this day and your Gen 47:23
Pharaoh should *h* the fifth part Gen 47:26
If now I *h* found grace in thy Gen 47:29
Moreover I *h* given to thee one Gen 48:22
I *h* waited for thy salvation, O Gen 49:18
The archers *h* sorely grieved him, Gen 49:23
The blessings of thy father *h* Gen 49:26
If now I *h* found grace in your Gen 50:4
in my grave which I *h* digged for Gen 50:5
Why *h* ye done this thing, and *h* Ex 1:18
why is it that ye *h* left the man Ex 2:20
I *h* been a stranger in a strange Ex 2:22
I *h* surely seen the affliction of Ex 3:7
h heard their cry by reason of Ex 3:7
I *h* also seen the oppression Ex 3:9
unto thee, that I *h* sent thee Ex 3:12
I *h* surely visited you, and seen Ex 3:16
I *h* said, I will bring you up out Ex 3:17
h not I the LORD Ex 4:11
which I *h* put in thine hand Ex 4:21
Wherefore *h* ye not fulfilled your Ex 5:14
because ye *h* made our savour to Ex 5:21
I *h* also established my covenant Ex 6:4
I *h* also heard the groaning of Ex 6:5
I *h* remembered my covenant Ex 6:5
of Israel *h* not hearkened unto me Ex 6:12
I *h* made thee a god to Pharaoh Ex 7:1
for this cause *h* I raised thee up Ex 9:16
unto them, I *h* sinned this time Ex 9:27
for I *h* hardened his heart, and Ex 10:1
what things I *h* wrought in Egypt, Ex 10:2
signs which I *h* done among them Ex 10:2
nor thy fathers' fathers *h* seen Ex 10:6
I *h* sinned against the LORD your Ex 10:16
for in this selfsame day *h* I Ex 12:17
go, serve the LORD, as ye *h* said Ex 12:31
and your herds, as ye *h* said Ex 12:32
Why *h* we done this, that we *h* Ex 14:5
Egyptians whom ye *h* seen to day Ex 14:13
when I *h* gotten me honour upon Ex 14:18
The depths *h* covered them Ex 15:5
which thy hands *h* established Ex 15:17
which I *h* brought upon the Ex 15:26
for ye *h* brought us forth into Ex 16:3
I *h* heard the murmurings of the Ex 16:12
I *h* fed you in the wilderness Ex 16:32
hath sworn that the LORD will *h* Ex 17:16
I *h* been an alien in a strange Ex 18:3 1961
When they *h* a matter, they come Ex 18:16 1961
Ye *h* seen what I did unto the Ex 19:4
which *h* brought thee out of the Ex 20:2
Thou shalt *h* no other gods before Ex 20:3
Ye *h* seen that I *h* talked with Ex 20:22
If his master *h* given him a wife, Ex 21:4
she *h* born him sons or daughters Ex 21:4
nation he shall *h* no power Ex 21:8
if he *h* betrothed her unto his Ex 21:9
Whether he *h* gored a son, or *h* Ex 21:31
if he *h* nothing, then he shall be Ex 22:3
to see whether he *h* put his hand Ex 22:8
in all things that I *h* said unto Ex 23:13
into the place which I *h* prepared Ex 23:20
and commandments which I *h* written Ex 24:12
if any man *h* any matters to do, Ex 24:14
the curtains shall *h* one measure Ex 26:2
whom I *h* filled with the spirit Ex 28:3
It shall *h* the two shoulderpieces Ex 28:7 1961
it shall *h* a binding of woven Ex 28:32 1961
things which I *h* commanded thee Ex 29:35
I *h* called by name Bezaleel the Ex 31:2
I *h* filled him with the spirit of Ex 31:3
I *h* given with him Aholiab, the Ex 31:6
are wise hearted I *h* put wisdom Ex 31:6
make all that I *h* commanded thee Ex 31:6
according to all that I *h* Ex 31:11
of Egypt, *h* corrupted themselves Ex 32:7
They *h* turned aside quickly out Ex 32:8
they *h* made them a molten calf, Ex 32:8
and *h* worshipped it, and *h* Ex 32:8
which *h* brought thee up out of Ex 32:8
I *h* seen this people, and, behold, Ex 32:9
all this land that I *h* spoken of Ex 32:13
people, Ye *h* sinned a great sin Ex 32:30
this people *h* sinned a great sin, Ex 32:31
and *h* made them gods of gold Ex 32:31
of which I *h* spoken unto thee Ex 32:34
if I *h* found grace in thy sight, Ex 33:13
thy people *h* found grace in thy Ex 33:16
If now I *h* found grace in thy Ex 34:9
such as *h* not been done in all Ex 34:10
I *h* made a covenant with thee Ex 34:27
they *h* done somewhat against any Lev 4:13
which they *h* sinned against it, Lev 4:14
Or *h* found that which was lost, Lev 6:3
I *h* given it unto them for their Lev 6:17
atonement therewith shall *h* it Lev 7:7 1961
even the priest shall *h* to Lev 7:8 1961
shall all the sons of Aaron *h* Lev 7:10 1961
shall *h* the right shoulder for Lev 7:33 1961
the heave shoulder *h* I taken of Lev 7:34
h given them unto Aaron the Lev 7:34
Wherefore *h* ye not eaten the sin Lev 10:17
ye should indeed *h* eaten it in Lev 10:18
this day *h* they offered their sin Lev 10:19
and such things *h* befallen me Lev 10:19
should it *h* been accepted in the Lev 10:19
And all that *h* not fins and scales Lev 11:10
but ye shall *h* their carcases in Lev 11:11
these are they which ye shall *h* Lev 11:13
which *h* legs above their feet, to Lev 11:21
which *h* four feet, shall be an Lev 11:23
If a woman *h* conceived seed, and Lev 12:2
When a man shall *h* in the skin of Lev 13:2 1961
it *h* turned the hair white, and Lev 13:10
if the leprosy *h* covered all his Lev 13:13
burneth *h* a white bright spot Lev 13:24 1961
If a man or woman *h* a plague upon Lev 13:29 1961
If a man also or a woman *h* in the Lev 13:38 1961
if the plague *h* not changed his Lev 13:55
And if a woman *h* an issue, and her Lev 15:19 1961
if a woman *h* an issue of her Lev 15:25 1961
he shall *h* the linen breeches Lev 16:4 1961
h made an atonement for himself, Lev 16:17 1961
after whom they *h* gone a whoring Lev 17:7
I *h* given it to you upon the Lev 17:11
h the men of the land done Lev 18:27
shall *h* planted all manner of Lev 19:23
not them that *h* familiar spirits Lev 19:31
ephah, and a just hin, shall ye *h* Lev 19:36 1961

after such as *h* familiar spirits ... Lev 20:6
they *h* wrought confusion ... Lev 20:12
both of them *h* committed an ... Lev 20:13
But I *h* said unto you, Ye shall ... Lev 20:24
which *h* separated you from other ... Lev 20:24
which I *h* separated from you as ... Lev 20:25
h severed you from other people, ... Lev 20:26
h no child, and is returned unto ... Lev 22:13
ye shall *h* an holy convocation ... Lev 23:7 1961
h brought an offering unto your ... Lev 23:14
shall ye *h* a sabbath, a memorial ... Lev 23:24 1961
when ye *h* gathered in the fruit ... Lev 23:39
Ye shall *h* one manner of law, as ... Lev 24:22 1961
if the man *h* none to redeem it, ... Lev 25:26 1961
houses of the villages which *h* no ... Lev 25:31
thy bondmaids, which thou shalt *h* ... Lev 25:44 1961
For I will *h* respect unto you, and ... Lev 26:9
I *h* broken the bands of your yoke ... Lev 26:13
when I *h* broken the staff of your ... Lev 26:26
ye shall *h* no power to stand ... Lev 26:37 1961
that also they *h* walked contrary ... Lev 26:40
that I also *h* walked contrary ... Lev 26:41
h brought them into the land of ... Lev 26:41
or if he *h* sold the field to ... Lev 27:20
I *h* taken the Levites from among ... Num 3:12
h the oversight of them that keep ... Num 3:32
his sons *h* made an end of ... Num 4:15
their sin which they *h* done ... Num 5:7
But if the man *h* no kinsman to ... Num 5:8
the priest shall *h* in his hand ... Num 5:18 1961
If no man *h* lain with thee, and if ... Num 5:19
some man *h* lain with thee beside ... Num 5:20
h done trespass against her ... Num 5:27
of Israel, *h* I taken them unto me ... Num 8:16
I *h* taken the Levites for all the ... Num 8:18
I *h* given the Levites as a gift ... Num 8:19
ye shall *h* one ordinance, both ... Num 9:14 1961
wherefore *h* I not found favour in ... Num 11:11
H I conceived all this people ... Num 11:12
h I begotten them, that thou ... Num 11:12
Whence should I *h* flesh to give ... Num 11:13
if I *h* found favour in thy sight ... Num 11:15
for ye *h* wept in the ears of the ... Num 11:18
because that ye *h* despised the ... Num 11:20
h wept before him, saying, Why ... Num 11:20
wherein we *h* done foolishly ... Num 12:11
and wherein we *h* sinned ... Num 12:11
through which we *h* gone to search ... Num 13:32
signs which I *h* shewed among them ... Num 14:11
for they *h* heard that thou LORD ... Num 14:14
then the nations which *h* heard ... Num 14:15
I *h* pardoned according to thy ... Num 14:20
those men which *h* seen my glory ... Num 14:22
h tempted me now these ten times, ... Num 14:22
h not hearkened to my voice ... Num 14:22
I *h* heard the murmurings of the ... Num 14:27
as ye *h* spoken in mine ears, so ... Num 14:28
which *h* murmured against me, ... Num 14:29
know the land which ye *h* despised ... Num 14:31
I the LORD *h* said, I will surely ... Num 14:35
for we *h* sinned ... Num 14:40
And if ye *h* erred, and not observed ... Num 15:22
Ye shall *h* one law for him that ... Num 15:29 1961
I *h* not taken one ass from them, ... Num 16:15
neither *h* I hurt one of them ... Num 16:15
for I *h* not done them of mine own ... Num 16:28
these men *h* provoked the LORD ... Num 16:30
Ye *h* killed the people of the ... Num 16:41
I *h* taken your brethren the ... Num 18:6
I *h* given your priest's office ... Num 18:7
I also *h* given thee the charge of ... Num 18:8
unto thee *h* I given them by ... Num 18:8
I *h* given them unto thee, and to ... Num 18:11
the LORD, them *h* I given thee ... Num 18:12
h I given thee, and thy sons and ... Num 18:19
Thou shalt *h* no inheritance in ... Num 18:20
neither shalt thou *h* any part ... Num 18:20 1961
I *h* given the children of Levi ... Num 18:21
of Israel they *h* no inheritance ... Num 18:23
I *h* given to the Levites to ... Num 18:24
therefore I *h* said unto them, ... Num 18:24
they shall *h* no inheritance ... Num 18:24
I *h* given you from them for your ... Num 18:26
When ye *h* heaved the best thereof ... Num 18:30
when ye *h* heaved from it the best ... Num 18:32
And why *h* ye brought up the ... Num 20:4
wherefore *h* ye made us to come up ... Num 20:5
the land which I *h* given them ... Num 20:12
we *h* dwelt in Egypt a long time ... Num 20:15
until we *h* passed thy borders ... Num 20:17
I *h* given unto the children of ... Num 20:24
Wherefore *h* ye brought us up out ... Num 21:5
We *h* sinned, for we *h* spoken ... Num 21:7
We *h* shot at them ... Num 21:30
we *h* laid them waste even unto ... Num 21:30
for I *h* delivered him into thy ... Num 21:34
What *h* I done unto thee, that ... Num 22:28
the angel of the LORD, I *h* sinned ... Num 22:34
h I now any power at all to say ... Num 22:38 3201
I *h* prepared seven altars ... Num 23:4
I *h* offered upon every altar a ... Num 23:4
I *h* received commandment to bless ... Num 23:20
come he that shall *h* dominion ... Num 24:19
And he shall *h* it, and his seed ... Num 25:13 1961
wherewith they *h* beguiled you in ... Num 25:18
h no son, then ye shall cause his ... Num 27:8
if he *h* no daughter, then ye ... Num 27:9
if he *h* no brethren, then ye ... Num 27:10

And if his father *h* no brethren ... Num 27:11
see the land which I *h* given unto ... Num 27:12
not as sheep which *h* no shepherd ... Num 27:17
ye shall *h* an holy convocation ... Num 28:25 1961
ye shall *h* an holy convocation ... Num 28:26 1961
ye shall *h* an holy convocation ... Num 29:1 1961
ye shall *h* on the tenth day of ... Num 29:7 1961
ye shall *h* an holy covocation ... Num 29:12 1961
day ye shall *h* a solemn assembly ... Num 29:35 1961
wherewith they *h* bound their ... Num 30:9
H ye saved all the women alive ... Num 31:15
that *h* not known a man by lying ... Num 31:18
Thy servants *h* taken the sum of ... Num 31:49
We *h* therefore brought an ... Num 31:50
cattle, and thy servants *h* cattle ... Num 32:4
if we *h* found grace in thy sight, ... Num 32:5
because they *h* not wholly ... Num 32:11
for they *h* wholly followed the ... Num 32:12
until we *h* brought them unto ... Num 32:17
Israel *h* inherited every man his ... Num 32:18
ye *h* sinned against the LORD ... Num 32:23
they shall *h* possessions among ... Num 32:30 270
for I *h* given you the land to ... Num 33:53
ye shall even *h* the great sea for ... Num 34:6 1961
h received their inheritance ... Num 34:14
h received their inheritance ... Num 34:14
the half tribe *h* received their ... Num 34:15
cities shall they *h* to dwell in ... Num 35:3 1961
from them that *h* many ye shall ... Num 35:8
but from them that *h* few ye shall ... Num 35:8
six cities shall ye *h* for refuge ... Num 35:13 1961
or *h* cast upon him any thing ... Num 35:22
Because he should *h* remained in ... Num 35:28
Ye *h* dwelt long enough in this ... Deut 1:6
I *h* set the land before you ... Deut 1:8
our brethren *h* discouraged our ... Deut 1:28
moreover we *h* seen the sons of ... Deut 1:28
We *h* sinned against the LORD, we ... Deut 1:41
Ye *h* compassed this mountain long ... Deut 2:3
because I *h* given mount Seir unto ... Deut 2:5
because I *h* given Ar unto the ... Deut 2:9
because I *h* given it unto the ... Deut 2:19
I *h* given into thine hand Sihon ... Deut 2:24
I *h* begun to give Sihon and his ... Deut 2:31
(for I know that ye *h* much cattle ... Deut 3:19
your cities which I *h* given you ... Deut 3:19
Until the LORD *h* given rest unto ... Deut 3:20
possession, which I *h* given you ... Deut 3:20
Thine eyes *h* seen all that the ... Deut 3:21
Your eyes *h* seen what the LORD ... Deut 4:3
I *h* taught you statutes and ... Deut 4:5
things which thine eyes *h* seen ... Deut 4:9
ye shall *h* remained long in the ... Deut 4:25
Thou shalt *h* none other gods ... Deut 5:7 1961
we *h* heard his voice out of the ... Deut 5:24
we *h* seen this day that God doth ... Deut 5:24
of the midst of the fire, as we *h* ... Deut 5:26
I *h* heard the voice of the words ... Deut 5:28
which they *h* spoken unto thee ... Deut 5:28
they *h* well said all that they ... Deut 5:28
well said all that they *h* spoken ... Deut 5:28
h brought thee into the land ... Deut 6:10
when thou shalt *h* eaten and be ... Deut 6:11
thine eye shall *h* no pity upon ... Deut 7:16
until thou *h* destroyed them ... Deut 7:24
ye *h* been rebellious against the ... Deut 9:7
angry with you to *h* destroyed you ... Deut 9:8
of Egypt *h* corrupted themselves ... Deut 9:12
they *h* made them a molten image ... Deut 9:12
I *h* seen this people, and, behold, ... Deut 9:13
with Aaron to *h* destroyed him ... Deut 9:20
the land which I *h* given you ... Deut 9:23
Ye *h* been rebellious against the ... Deut 9:24
things, which thine eyes *h* seen ... Deut 10:21
your children which *h* not known ... Deut 11:2
which *h* not seen the chastisement ... Deut 11:2
But your eyes *h* seen all the ... Deut 11:7
other gods, which ye *h* not known ... Deut 11:28
as I *h* commanded thee, and thou ... Deut 12:21
h they done unto their gods ... Deut 12:31
their daughters they *h* burnt in ... Deut 12:31
h withdrawn the inhabitants of ... Deut 13:13
other gods, which ye *h* not known ... Deut 13:13
h compassion upon thee, and ... Deut 13:17
all that *h* fins and scales shall ... Deut 14:9
or *h* any ill blemish, thou shalt ... Deut 15:21
heaven, which I *h* not commanded ... Deut 17:3
which *h* committed that wicked ... Deut 17:5
shall *h* no part nor inheritance ... Deut 18:1
Therefore shall they *h* no ... Deut 18:2
They shall *h* like portions to eat ... Deut 18:8
They *h* well spoken that which ... Deut 18:17
spoken that which they *h* spoken ... Deut 18:17
which I *h* not commanded him to ... Deut 18:20
which they of old time *h* set in ... Deut 19:14
as he had thought to *h* done unto ... Deut 19:19
when the officers *h* made an end ... Deut 20:9
which they *h* done unto their gods ... Deut 20:18
Our hands *h* not shed this blood, ... Deut 21:7
neither *h* our eyes seen it ... Deut 21:7
thou wouldest *h* her to thy wife ... Deut 21:11
if thou *h* no delight in her, then ... Deut 21:14
If a man *h* two wives, one beloved ... Deut 21:15 1961
they *h* born him children, both ... Deut 21:15
If a man *h* a stubborn and ... Deut 21:18 1961
when they *h* chastened him, will ... Deut 21:18
if a man *h* committed a sin worthy ... Deut 21:22
Thou shalt *h* a place also without ... Deut 23:12 1961

thou shalt *h* a paddle upon thy ... Deut 23:13 1961
h no child, the wife of the dead ... Deut 25:5
Thou shalt not *h* in thy bag ... Deut 25:13 1961
Thou shalt not *h* in thine house ... Deut 25:14 1961
But thou shalt *h* a perfect ... Deut 25:15 1961
and just measure shalt thou *h* ... Deut 25:15 1961
I *h* brought the firstfruits of ... Deut 26:10
I *h* brought away the hallowed ... Deut 26:13
also *h* given them unto the Levite ... Deut 26:13
I *h* not transgressed thy ... Deut 26:13
neither *h* I forgotten them ... Deut 26:13
I *h* not eaten thereof in my ... Deut 26:14
neither *h* I taken away ought ... Deut 26:14
but I *h* hearkened to the voice of ... Deut 26:14
h done according to all that thou ... Deut 26:14
until he *h* consumed thee from off ... Deut 28:21
thou shalt *h* none to rescue them ... Deut 28:31
thou nor thy fathers *h* known ... Deut 28:36
Thou shalt *h* olive trees ... Deut 28:40 1961
until he *h* destroyed thee ... Deut 28:48 1961
until he *h* destroyed thee ... Deut 28:51
thou nor thy fathers *h* known ... Deut 28:64
shall the sole of thy foot *h* rest ... Deut 28:65 1961
shalt *h* none assurance of thy ... Deut 28:66
Ye *h* seen all that the LORD did ... Deut 29:2
which thine eyes *h* seen, the ... Deut 29:3
I *h* led you forty years in the ... Deut 29:5
Ye *h* not eaten bread ... Deut 29:6
neither *h* ye drunk wine or strong ... Deut 29:6
(For ye know how we *h* dwelt in ... Deut 29:16
ye *h* seen their abominations, and ... Deut 29:17
heart, saying, I shall *h* peace ... Deut 29:19
Because they *h* forsaken the ... Deut 29:25
which I *h* set before thee, and ... Deut 30:1
h compassion upon thee, and will ... Deut 30:3
I *h* set before thee this day life ... Deut 30:15
that I *h* set before you life and ... Deut 30:19
which I *h* commanded you ... Deut 31:5
which *h* not known any thing, may ... Deut 31:13
covenant which I *h* made with them ... Deut 31:16
evils which they shall *h* wrought ... Deut 31:18
For when I shall *h* brought them ... Deut 31:20
and they shall *h* eaten and filled ... Deut 31:20
before I *h* brought them into the ... Deut 31:21
ye *h* been rebellious against the ... Deut 31:27
the way which I *h* commanded you ... Deut 31:29
They *h* corrupted themselves, ... Deut 32:5
They *h* moved me to jealousy with ... Deut 32:21
they *h* provoked me to anger with ... Deut 32:21
to his mother, I *h* not seen him ... Deut 33:9
for they *h* observed thy word, and ... Deut 33:9
I *h* caused thee to see it with ... Deut 34:4
that I *h* given unto you, as I ... Josh 1:3
and then thou shalt *h* good success ... Josh 1:8
H not I commanded thee ... Josh 1:9
Until the LORD *h* given your ... Josh 1:15
they also *h* possessed the land ... Josh 1:15
For we *h* heard how the LORD dried ... Josh 2:10
since I *h* shewed you kindness, ... Josh 2:12
and my sisters, and all that they *h* ... Josh 2:13
for ye *h* not passed this way ... Josh 3:4
This day *h* I rolled away the ... Josh 5:9
I *h* given into thine hand Jericho ... Josh 6:2
they *h* also transgressed my ... Josh 7:11
for they *h* even taken of the ... Josh 7:11
h also stolen, and dissembled also ... Josh 7:11
they *h* put it even among their ... Josh 7:11
Indeed I *h* sinned against the ... Josh 7:20
Israel, and thus and thus *h* I done ... Josh 7:20
I *h* given into thy hand the king ... Josh 8:1
we *h* drawn them from the city ... Josh 8:6
when ye *h* taken the city, that ye ... Josh 8:8
See, I *h* commanded you ... Josh 8:8
for we *h* heard the fame of him, ... Josh 9:9
We *h* sworn unto them by the LORD ... Josh 9:19
Wherefore *h* ye beguiled us, ... Josh 9:22
of you, and *h* done this thing ... Josh 9:24
for I *h* delivered them into thine ... Josh 10:8
and that they might *h* no favour ... Josh 11:20 1961
as I *h* commanded thee ... Josh 13:6
the Gadites *h* received their ... Josh 13:8
thy feet *h* trodden shall be thine ... Josh 14:9
of the valley *h* chariots of iron ... Josh 17:16
thou shalt not *h* one lot only ... Josh 17:17 1961
though they *h* iron chariots, and ... Josh 17:18
But the Levites *h* no part among ... Josh 18:7
h received their inheritance ... Josh 18:7 1961
Ye *h* kept all that Moses the ... Josh 22:2
h obeyed my voice in all that I ... Josh 22:2
Ye *h* not left your brethren these ... Josh 22:3
but *h* kept the charge of the ... Josh 22:3
the half tribe of Manasseh *h* ... Josh 22:11
ye *h* committed against the God of ... Josh 22:16
in that ye *h* builded you an altar ... Josh 22:16
That we *h* built us an altar to ... Josh 22:23
if we *h* not rather done it for ... Josh 22:24
What *h* ye to do with the LORD God ... Josh 22:24
ye *h* no part in the LORD ... Josh 22:25
to come, Ye *h* no part in the LORD ... Josh 22:27
because ye *h* not committed this ... Josh 22:31
now ye *h* delivered the children ... Josh 22:31
ye *h* seen all that the LORD your ... Josh 23:3
I *h* divided unto you by lot these ... Josh 23:4
all the nations that I *h* cut off ... Josh 23:4
as ye *h* done unto this day ... Josh 23:8
until he *h* destroyed you from off ... Josh 23:15
When ye *h* transgressed the ... Josh 23:16
h gone and served other gods, and ... Josh 23:16

h seen what I *h* done in Egypt ... Josh 24:7
I *h* given you a land for which ye ... Josh 24:13
that ye *h* chosen you the LORD ... Josh 24:22
I *h* delivered the land into his ... Judg 1:2
as I *h* done, so God hath requited ... Judg 1:7
h brought you unto the land which ... Judg 2:1
but ye *h* not obeyed my voice ... Judg 2:2
why *h* ye done this ... Judg 2:2
h not hearkened unto my voice ... Judg 2:20
I *h* a secret errand unto thee, O ... Judg 3:19
I *h* a message from God unto thee ... Judg 3:20
h dominion over the nobles among ... Judg 5:13
the LORD made me *h* dominion over ... Judg 5:13
H they not sped? ... Judg 5:30
h they not divided the prey ... Judg 5:30
but ye *h* not obeyed my voice ... Judg 6:10
h not I sent thee ... Judg 6:14
If now I *h* found grace in thy ... Judg 6:17
for because I *h* seen an angel of ... Judg 6:22
for I *h* delivered it into thine ... Judg 7:9
What *h* I done now in comparison ... Judg 8:2
if ye *h* done truly and sincerely, ... Judg 9:16
in that ye *h* made Abimelech king, ... Judg 9:16
if ye *h* dealt well with Jerubbaal ... Judg 9:16
h done unto him according to the ... Judg 9:16
h slain his sons, threescore and ... Judg 9:18
h made Abimelech, the son of his ... Judg 9:18
If ye then *h* dealt truly and ... Judg 9:19
What ye *h* seen me do, make haste, ... Judg 9:48
and do as I *h* done ... Judg 9:48
We *h* sinned against thee ... Judg 10:10
both because we *h* forsaken our ... Judg 10:10
Yet ye *h* forsaken me, and served ... Judg 10:13
unto the gods which ye *h* chosen ... Judg 10:14
said unto the LORD, We *h* sinned ... Judg 10:15
Wherefore I *h* not sinned against ... Judg 11:27
for I *h* opened my mouth unto the ... Judg 11:35
until we shall *h* made ready a kid ... Judg 13:15
surely die, because we *h* seen God ... Judg 13:22
he would not *h* received a burnt ... Judg 13:23
neither would he *h* shewed us all ... Judg 13:23
nor would as at this time *h* told ... Judg 13:23
I *h* seen a woman in Timnath of ... Judg 14:2
rent him as he would *h* rent a kid ... Judg 14:6
h ye called us to take that we ... Judg 14:15
ye called us to take that we *h* ... Judg 14:15
I *h* not told it my father nor my ... Judg 14:16
unto them, Though ye *h* done this ... Judg 15:7
unto me, so *h* I done unto them ... Judg 15:11
an ass *h* I slain a thousand men ... Judg 15:16
for I *h* been a Nazarite unto God ... Judg 16:17
seeing I *h* a Levite to my priest ... Judg 17:13 1961
for we *h* seen the land, and, ... Judg 18:9
consider what ye *h* to do ... Judg 18:14
Ye *h* taken away my gods which I ... Judg 18:24
and what *h* I more ... Judg 18:24
night, and thought to *h* slain me ... Judg 20:5
and my concubine *h* they forced ... Judg 20:5
for they *h* committed lewdness and ... Judg 20:6
that they *h* wrought in Israel ... Judg 20:10
seeing we *h* sworn by the LORD ... Judg 21:7
the children of Israel *h* sworn ... Judg 21:18
as ye *h* dealt with the dead, and ... Ruth 1:8
for I am too old to *h* an husband ... Ruth 1:12
I *h* hope, if I should *h* an ... Ruth 1:12 3426,1961
h I not charged the young men ... Ruth 2:9
that which the young men *h* drawn ... Ruth 2:9
Why *h* I found grace in thine eyes ... Ruth 2:10
until they *h* ended all my harvest ... Ruth 2:21
man, until he shall *h* done eating ... Ruth 3:3
until he *h* finished the thing ... Ruth 3:18
that I *h* bought all that was ... Ruth 4:9
h I purchased to be my wife, to ... Ruth 4:10
I *h* drunken neither wine nor ... 1Sa 1:15
but *h* poured out my soul before ... 1Sa 1:15
grief *h* I spoken hitherto ... 1Sa 1:16
Because I *h* asked him of the LORD ... 1Sa 1:20
tarry until thou *h* weaned him ... 1Sa 1:23
Therefore also I *h* lent him to ... 1Sa 1:28
They that were full *h* hired out ... 1Sa 2:5
for he will not *h* sodden flesh of ... 1Sa 2:15 3947
which I *h* commanded in my ... 1Sa 2:29
I *h* spoken concerning his house ... 1Sa 3:12
For I *h* told him that I will ... 1Sa 3:13
therefore I *h* sworn unto the ... 1Sa 3:14
Hebrews, as they *h* been to you ... 1Sa 4:9
They *h* brought about the ark of ... 1Sa 5:10
The Philistines *h* brought again ... 1Sa 6:21
We *h* sinned against the LORD ... 1Sa 7:6
for they *h* not rejected thee ... 1Sa 8:7
but they *h* rejected me, that I ... 1Sa 8:7
they *h* done since the day that I ... 1Sa 8:8
day, wherewith they *h* forsaken me ... 1Sa 8:8
king which ye shall *h* chosen you ... 1Sa 8:18
but we will *h* a king over us ... 1Sa 8:19 1961
what *h* we ... 1Sa 9:7
I *h* here at hand the fourth part ... 1Sa 9:8 4672
for I *h* looked upon my people, ... 1Sa 9:16
I said, I *h* invited the people ... 1Sa 9:24
ye *h* this day rejected your God, ... 1Sa 10:19
ye *h* said unto him, Nay, but set ... 1Sa 10:19
the sun be hot, ye shall *h* help ... 1Sa 11:9
I *h* hearkened unto your voice in ... 1Sa 12:1
me, and *h* made a king over you ... 1Sa 12:1
I *h* walked before you from my ... 1Sa 12:2
whose ox *h* I taken ... 1Sa 12:3
or whose ass *h* I taken ... 1Sa 12:3
or whom *h* I defrauded ... 1Sa 12:3
whom *h* I oppressed ... 1Sa 12:3
or of whose hand *h* I received any ... 1Sa 12:3
that ye *h* not found ought in my ... 1Sa 12:5
We *h* sinned, because we *h* ... 1Sa 12:10
h served Baalim and Ashtaroth ... 1Sa 12:10
h chosen, and whom ye *h* desired ... 1Sa 12:13
which ye *h* done in the sight of ... 1Sa 12:17
for we *h* added unto all our sins ... 1Sa 12:19
ye *h* done all this wickedness ... 1Sa 12:20
I *h* not made supplication unto ... 1Sa 13:12
for now would the LORD *h* ... 1Sa 13:13
how mine eyes *h* been enlightened, ... 1Sa 14:29
And he said, Ye *h* transgressed ... 1Sa 14:33
utterly destroy all that they *h* ... 1Sa 15:3
that I *h* set up Saul to be king ... 1Sa 15:11
I *h* performed the commandment of ... 1Sa 15:13
They *h* brought them from the ... 1Sa 15:15
the rest we *h* utterly destroyed ... 1Sa 15:15
I *h* obeyed the voice of the LORD, ... 1Sa 15:20
h gone the way which the LORD ... 1Sa 15:20
h brought Agag the king of Amalek ... 1Sa 15:20
and *h* utterly destroyed the ... 1Sa 15:20
should *h* been utterly destroyed ... 1Sa 15:21
Saul said unto Samuel, I *h* sinned ... 1Sa 15:24
for I *h* transgressed the ... 1Sa 15:24
Then he said, I *h* sinned ... 1Sa 15:30
seeing I *h* rejected him from ... 1Sa 16:1
for I *h* provided me a king among ... 1Sa 16:1
because I *h* refused him ... 1Sa 16:7
I *h* seen a son of Jesse the ... 1Sa 16:18
H ye seen this man that is come ... 1Sa 17:25
And David said, What *h* I now done ... 1Sa 17:29
for I *h* not proved them ... 1Sa 17:39
They *h* ascribed unto David ten ... 1Sa 18:8
to me they *h* ascribed but ... 1Sa 18:8
what can he *h* more but the ... 1Sa 18:8
should *h* been given to David ... 1Sa 18:19
because his works *h* been to ... 1Sa 19:4 1961
before Jonathan, What *h* I done ... 1Sa 20:1
I *h* found grace in thine eyes ... 1Sa 20:3 1961
thy servant shall *h* peace ... 1Sa 20:7
when I *h* sounded my father about ... 1Sa 20:12
I *h* spoken of, behold, the LORD ... 1Sa 20:23
if I *h* found favour in thine eyes ... 1Sa 20:29
forasmuch as we *h* sworn both of ... 1Sa 20:42
thee, and what I *h* commanded thee ... 1Sa 21:2
I *h* appointed my servants to such ... 1Sa 21:2
if the young men *h* kept ... 1Sa 21:4
Of a truth women *h* been kept from ... 1Sa 21:5
for I *h* neither brought my sword ... 1Sa 21:8
wherefore then *h* ye brought him ... 1Sa 21:14
H I need of mad men, that ye *h* ... 1Sa 21:15
That all of you *h* conspired ... 1Sa 22:8
Why *h* ye conspired against me, ... 1Sa 22:13
I *h* occasioned the death of all ... 1Sa 22:22
for ye *h* compassion on me ... 1Sa 23:21
Philistines *h* invaded the land ... 1Sa 23:27
this day thine eyes *h* seen how ... 1Sa 24:10
I *h* not sinned against thee ... 1Sa 24:11
whereas I *h* rewarded thee evil ... 1Sa 24:17
now I *h* heard that thou hast ... 1Sa 25:7
my flesh that I *h* killed for my ... 1Sa 25:11
Surely in vain *h* I kept all that ... 1Sa 25:21
when the LORD shall *h* done to my ... 1Sa 25:30
shall *h* appointed thee ruler over ... 1Sa 25:30
shall *h* dealt well with my lord ... 1Sa 25:31
I *h* hearkened to thy voice ... 1Sa 25:35
and *h* accepted thy person ... 1Sa 25:35
because ye *h* not kept your master ... 1Sa 26:16
for what *h* I done ... 1Sa 26:18
If the LORD *h* stirred thee up ... 1Sa 26:19
for they *h* driven me out this day ... 1Sa 26:19
Then said Saul, I *h* sinned ... 1Sa 26:21
I *h* played the fool, and *h* ... 1Sa 26:21
If I *h* now found grace in thine ... 1Sa 27:5
Whither *h* ye made a road to day ... 1Sa 27:10
off those that *h* familiar spirits ... 1Sa 28:9
therefore I *h* called thee ... 1Sa 28:15
I *h* put my life in my hand, and ... 1Sa 28:21
h hearkened unto thy words which ... 1Sa 28:21
eat, that thou mayest *h* strength ... 1Sa 28:22
I *h* found no fault in him since ... 1Sa 29:3
for I *h* not found evil in thee ... 1Sa 29:6
unto Achish, But what *h* I done ... 1Sa 29:8
in thy servant so long as I *h* ... 1Sa 29:8 1961
princes of the Philistines *h* said ... 1Sa 29:9
the morning, and *h* light, depart ... 1Sa 29:10
of the spoil that we *h* recovered ... 1Sa 30:22
h brought them hither unto my ... 2Sa 1:10
I *h* slain the LORD's anointed ... 2Sa 1:16
that ye *h* shewed this kindness ... 2Sa 2:5
even unto Saul, and *h* buried him ... 2Sa 2:5
because ye *h* done this thing ... 2Sa 2:6
also the house of Judah *h* ... 2Sa 2:7
h not delivered thee into the ... 2Sa 3:8
though they would *h* fetched wheat ... 2Sa 4:6
thinking to *h* brought good ... 2Sa 4:10
who thought that I would *h* given ... 2Sa 4:10
when wicked men *h* slain a ... 2Sa 4:11
Whereas I *h* not dwelt in any ... 2Sa 7:6
but *h* walked in a tent and in a ... 2Sa 7:6
In all the places wherein I *h* ... 2Sa 7:7
h cut off all thine enemies out ... 2Sa 7:9
h made thee a great name, like ... 2Sa 7:9
h caused thee to rest from all ... 2Sa 7:11
all that we *h* heard with our ears ... 2Sa 7:22
I *h* given unto thy master's son ... 2Sa 9:9
master's son may *h* food to eat ... 2Sa 9:10 1961
I would moreover *h* given unto ... 2Sa 12:8
I *h* sinned against the LORD ... 2Sa 12:13
I *h* fought against Rabbah, and ... 2Sa 12:27
h taken the city of waters ... 2Sa 12:27
Amnon said, *H* out all men from me ... 2Sa 13:9 3318
h not I commanded you ... 2Sa 13:28
h slain all the young men the ... 2Sa 13:32
the people *h* made me afraid ... 2Sa 14:15
Behold now, I *h* done this thing ... 2Sa 14:21
that I *h* found grace in thy sight ... 2Sa 14:22
to *h* sent him to the king ... 2Sa 14:29
Wherefore *h* thy servants set my ... 2Sa 14:31
good for me to *h* been there still ... 2Sa 14:32
which I *h* vowed unto the LORD, in ... 2Sa 15:7
thus say, I *h* no delight in thee ... 2Sa 15:26
as I *h* been thy father's servant ... 2Sa 15:34
they *h* there with them their two ... 2Sa 15:36
What *h* I to do with you, ye sons ... 2Sa 16:10
as I *h* served in thy father's ... 2Sa 16:19
and thus and thus *h* I counselled ... 2Sa 17:15
I would *h* given thee ten shekels ... 2Sa 18:11
Otherwise I should *h* wrought ... 2Sa 18:13
thou thyself wouldest *h* set ... 2Sa 18:13
I *h* no son to keep my name in ... 2Sa 18:18
which this day *h* saved thy life ... 2Sa 19:5
servant doth know that I *h* sinned ... 2Sa 19:20
What *h* I to do with you, ye sons ... 2Sa 19:22
What right therefore *h* I yet to ... 2Sa 19:28 3426
I *h* said, Thou and Ziba divide the ... 2Sa 19:29
How long *h* I to live, that I ... 2Sa 19:34
Why *h* our brethren the men of ... 2Sa 19:41
h brought the king, and his ... 2Sa 19:41
h we eaten at all of the king's ... 2Sa 19:42
We *h* ten parts in the king ... 2Sa 19:43
we *h* also more right in David ... 2Sa 19:43
We *h* no part in David ... 2Sa 20:1
neither *h* we inheritance in the ... 2Sa 20:1
We will *h* no silver nor gold of ... 2Sa 21:4
sword, thought to *h* slain David ... 2Sa 21:16
For I *h* kept the ways of the LORD ... 2Sa 22:22
h not wickedly departed from my ... 2Sa 22:22
h kept myself from mine iniquity ... 2Sa 22:24
For by thee I *h* run through a ... 2Sa 22:30
by my God *h* I leaped over a wall ... 2Sa 22:30
I *h* pursued mine enemies, and ... 2Sa 22:38
I *h* consumed them, and wounded ... 2Sa 22:39
I *h* sinned greatly in that I *h* ... 2Sa 24:10
for I *h* done very foolishly ... 2Sa 24:10
h sinned, and I *h* done wickedly ... 2Sa 24:17
but these sheep, what *h* they done ... 2Sa 24:17
I *h* appointed him to be ruler ... 1Kin 1:35
they *h* caused him to ride upon ... 1Kin 1:44
Nathan the prophet *h* anointed him ... 1Kin 1:45
This is the noise that ye *h* heard ... 1Kin 1:45
I *h* somewhat to say unto thee ... 1Kin 2:14
if Adonijah *h* not spoken this ... 1Kin 2:23
The word that I *h* heard is good ... 1Kin 2:42
that I *h* charged thee with ... 1Kin 2:43
I *h* done according to thy words ... 1Kin 3:12
I *h* given thee a wise and an ... 1Kin 3:12
I *h* also given thee that which ... 1Kin 3:13
I *h* considered the things which ... 1Kin 5:8
I *h* surely built thee an house to ... 1Kin 8:13
h built an house for the name of ... 1Kin 8:20
I *h* set there a place for the ark ... 1Kin 8:21
less this house that I *h* builded ... 1Kin 8:27
Yet *h* thou respect unto the ... 1Kin 8:28
because they *h* sinned against ... 1Kin 8:33
because they *h* sinned against ... 1Kin 8:35
this house, which I *h* builded ... 1Kin 8:43
house that I *h* built for thy name ... 1Kin 8:44
We *h* sinned, and *h* done ... 1Kin 8:47
we *h* committed wickedness ... 1Kin 8:47
the house which I *h* built for thy ... 1Kin 8:48
people that *h* sinned against thee ... 1Kin 8:50
they *h* transgressed against thee ... 1Kin 8:50
that they may *h* compassion on ... 1Kin 8:50
wherewith I *h* made supplication ... 1Kin 8:59
I *h* heard thy prayer and thy ... 1Kin 9:3
I *h* hallowed this house, which ... 1Kin 9:3
to all that I *h* commanded thee ... 1Kin 9:4
statutes which I *h* set before you ... 1Kin 9:6
of the land which I *h* given them ... 1Kin 9:7
which I *h* hallowed for my name, ... 1Kin 9:7
h taken hold upon other gods, and ... 1Kin 9:9
h worshipped them, and served them ... 1Kin 9:9
which I *h* commanded thee, I will ... 1Kin 11:11
Jerusalem's sake which I *h* chosen ... 1Kin 11:13
(But he shall *h* one tribe for my ... 1Kin 11:32 1961
the city which I *h* chosen out of ... 1Kin 11:32
Because that they *h* forsaken me ... 1Kin 11:33
h worshipped Ashtoreth the ... 1Kin 11:33
h not walked in my ways, to do ... 1Kin 11:33
that David my servant may *h* a ... 1Kin 11:36
the city which I *h* chosen me to ... 1Kin 11:36
who *h* spoken to me, saying, Make ... 1Kin 12:9
What portion *h* we in David ... 1Kin 12:16
neither *h* we inheritance in the ... 1Kin 12:16
because they *h* made their groves, ... 1Kin 14:15
I *h* sent unto thee a present of ... 1Kin 15:19
I *h* commanded the ravens to feed ... 1Kin 17:4
I *h* commanded a widow woman there ... 1Kin 17:9
I *h* not a cake, but an handful of ... 1Kin 17:12 3426
What *h* I to do with thee, O thou ... 1Kin 17:18
What *h* I sinned, that thou ... 1Kin 18:9
answered, I *h* not troubled Israel ... 1Kin 18:18
in that ye *h* forsaken the ... 1Kin 18:18
that I *h* done all these things at ... 1Kin 18:36

I *h* been very jealous for the 1Kin 19:10
of Israel *h* forsaken thy covenant 1Kin 19:10
I *h* been very jealous for the 1Kin 19:14
of Israel *h* forsaken thy covenant 1Kin 19:14
Yet I *h* left me seven thousand in 1Kin 19:18
knees which *h* not bowed unto Baal 1Kin 19:18
for what *h* I done to thee 1Kin 19:20
I am thine, and all that I *h* 1Kin 20:4
Although I *h* sent unto thee, 1Kin 20:5
LORD, Because the Syrians *h* said 1Kin 20:28
we *h* heard that the kings of the 1Kin 20:31
that I may *h* it for a garden of 1Kin 21:2 1961
And he answered, I *h* found thee 1Kin 21:20
until thou *h* consumed them 1Kin 22:11
as sheep that *h* not a shepherd 1Kin 22:17
the LORD said, These *h* no master 1Kin 22:17
the LORD, I *h* healed these waters 2Kin 2:21
Israel, What *h* I to do with thee 2Kin 3:13
they *h* smitten one another 2Kin 3:23
should *h* reigned in his stead 2Kin 3:27
I *h* therewith sent Naaman my 2Kin 5:6
wouldest thou not *h* done it 2Kin 5:13
you what the Syrians *h* done to us 2Kin 7:12
to *h* the charge of the gate 2Kin 7:17
I *h* anointed thee king over 2Kin 9:3
I *h* an errand to thee, O captain 2Kin 9:5
I *h* anointed thee king over the 2Kin 9:6
I *h* anointed thee king over 2Kin 9:12
Surely I *h* seen yesterday the 2Kin 9:26
They *h* brought the heads of the 2Kin 10:8
for I *h* a great sacrifice to do 2Kin 10:19
If any of the men whom I *h* 2Kin 10:24
H her forth without the ranges 2Kin 11:15 3318
till thou *h* consumed them 2Kin 13:17
Thou shouldest *h* smitten five or 2Kin 13:19
the covenant that I *h* made with 2Kin 17:38
to Lachish, saying, I *h* offended 2Kin 18:14
I *h* counsel and strength for the 2Kin 18:20
h they delivered Samaria out of 2Kin 18:34
that *h* delivered their country 2Kin 18:35
king of Assyria *h* blasphemed me 2Kin 19:6
of Assyria *h* done to all lands 2Kin 19:11
H the gods of the nations 2Kin 19:12
them which my fathers *h* destroyed 2Kin 19:12
the kings of Assyria *h* destroyed 2Kin 19:17
h cast their gods into the fire 2Kin 19:18
therefore they *h* destroyed them 2Kin 19:18
king of Assyria I *h* heard 2Kin 19:20
I *h* digged and drunk strange 2Kin 19:24
with the sole of my feet *h* I 2Kin 19:24
heard long ago how I *h* done it 2Kin 19:25
ancient times that I *h* formed it 2Kin 19:25
now *h* I brought it to pass, that 2Kin 19:25
remember now how I *h* walked 2Kin 20:3
h done that which is good in thy 2Kin 20:3
I *h* heard thy prayer, I *h* seen 2Kin 20:5
sign shalt thou *h* of the LORD 2Kin 20:9
What *h* they seen in thine house 2Kin 20:15
are in mine house *h* they seen 2Kin 20:15
that I *h* not shewed them 2Kin 20:15
that which thy fathers *h* laid up 2Kin 20:17
which I *h* chosen out of all 2Kin 21:7
to all that I *h* commanded them 2Kin 21:8
Because they *h* done that which 2Kin 21:15
h provoked me to anger, since the 2Kin 21:15
the door *h* gathered of the people 2Kin 22:4
that *h* the oversight of the house 2Kin 22:5
I *h* found the book of the law in 2Kin 22:8
Thy servants *h* gathered the money 2Kin 22:9
h delivered it into the hand of 2Kin 22:9
that *h* the oversight of the house 2Kin 22:9
because our fathers *h* not 2Kin 22:13
Because they *h* forsaken me 2Kin 22:17
h burned incense unto other gods, 2Kin 22:17
I also *h* heard thee, saith the 2Kin 22:19
as I *h* removed Israel, and will 2Kin 23:27
city Jerusalem which I *h* chosen 2Kin 23:27
h put their lives in jeopardy 1Chr 11:19
place that I *h* prepared for it 1Chr 15:12
For I *h* not dwelt in an house 1Chr 17:5
but *h* gone from tent to tent, and 1Chr 17:5
Wheresoever I *h* walked with all 1Chr 17:6
Why *h* ye not built me an house of 1Chr 17:6
I *h* been with thee whithersoever 1Chr 17:8 1961
h cut off all thine enemies from 1Chr 17:8
h made thee a name like the name 1Chr 17:8
all that we *h* heard with our ears 1Chr 17:20
I *h* sinned greatly 1Chr 21:8
because I *h* done this thing 1Chr 21:8
for I *h* done very foolishly 1Chr 21:8
even I it is that *h* sinned 1Chr 21:17
for these sheep, what *h* they done 1Chr 21:17
in my trouble I *h* prepared for 1Chr 22:14
timber also and stone *h* I prepared 1Chr 22:14
for I *h* chosen him to be my son, 1Chr 28:6
Now I *h* prepared with all my 1Chr 29:2
because I *h* set my affection to 1Chr 29:3
I *h* of mine own proper good, of 1Chr 29:3 3426
which I *h* given to the house of 1Chr 29:3
above all that I *h* prepared for 1Chr 29:3
of thine own *h* we given thee 1Chr 29:14
all this store that we *h* prepared 1Chr 29:16
I *h* willingly offered all these 1Chr 29:17
now *h* I seen with joy thy people, 1Chr 29:17
for the which I *h* made provision 1Chr 29:19
over whom I *h* made thee king 2Chr 1:11
h had that *h* been before thee 2Chr 1:12 1961
there any after thee *h* the like 2Chr 1:12 1961
now I *h* sent a cunning man, 2Chr 2:13
But I *h* built an house of 2Chr 6:2
But I *h* chosen Jerusalem, that my 2Chr 6:6
h chosen David to be over my 2Chr 6:6
h built the house for the name of 2Chr 6:10
in it *h* I put the ark, wherein is 2Chr 6:11
less this house which I *h* built 2Chr 6:18
H respect therefore to the prayer 2Chr 6:19
because they *h* sinned against 2Chr 6:24
because they *h* sinned against 2Chr 6:26
I *h* built is called by thy name 2Chr 6:33
the house which I *h* built for thy 2Chr 6:34
We *h* sinned, we *h* done amiss, 2Chr 6:37
done amiss, and *h* dealt wickedly 2Chr 6:37
whither they *h* carried them 2Chr 6:38
which I *h* built for thy name 2Chr 6:38
which *h* sinned against thee 2Chr 6:39
I *h* heard thy prayer, and *h* 2Chr 7:12
For now *h* I chosen and sanctified 2Chr 7:16
to all that I *h* commanded thee 2Chr 7:17
according as I *h* covenanted with 2Chr 7:18
which I *h* set before you, and 2Chr 7:19
of my land which I *h* given them 2Chr 7:20
which I *h* sanctified for my name 2Chr 7:20
which *h* spoken to me, saying, 2Chr 10:9
What portion *h* we in David 2Chr 10:16
we *h* none inheritance in the son 2Chr 10:16
Ye *h* forsaken me, and therefore 2Chr 12:5
therefore *h* I also left you in 2Chr 12:5
They *h* humbled themselves 2Chr 12:7
h strengthened themselves against 2Chr 13:7
H ye not cast out the priests of 2Chr 13:9
h made you priests after the 2Chr 13:9
our God, and we *h* not forsaken him 2Chr 13:10
but ye *h* forsaken him 2Chr 13:11
because we *h* sought the LORD our 2Chr 14:7
we *h* sought him, and he hath given 2Chr 14:7
or with them that *h* no power 2Chr 14:11 369
I *h* sent thee silver and gold 2Chr 16:3
from henceforth thou shalt *h* wars 2Chr 16:9 3426
as sheep that *h* no shepherd 2Chr 18:16
the LORD said, These *h* no master 2Chr 18:16
h built thee a sanctuary therein 2Chr 20:8
for we *h* no might against this 2Chr 20:12 369
thou shalt *h* great sickness by 2Chr 21:15
H her forth of the ranges 2Chr 23:14 3318
because ye *h* forsaken the LORD, 2Chr 24:20
I *h* given to the army of Israel 2Chr 25:9
ye *h* slain them in a rage that 2Chr 28:9
which ye *h* taken captive of your 2Chr 28:11
for whereas we *h* offended against 2Chr 28:13
For our fathers *h* trespassed 2Chr 29:6
h forsaken him, and *h* turned 2Chr 29:6
Also they *h* shut up the doors of 2Chr 29:7
h not burned incense nor offered 2Chr 29:7
our fathers *h* fallen by the sword 2Chr 29:9
We *h* cleansed all the house of 2Chr 29:18
h we prepared and sanctified, and, 2Chr 29:19
Now ye *h* consecrated yourselves 2Chr 29:31
we *h* had enough to eat, and *h* 2Chr 31:10
my fathers *h* done unto all the 2Chr 32:13
of the nations of other lands *h* 2Chr 32:17
which I *h* chosen before all the 2Chr 33:7
I *h* appointed for your fathers 2Chr 33:8
to do all that I *h* commanded them 2Chr 33:8
I *h* found the book of the law in 2Chr 34:15
they *h* gathered together the 2Chr 34:17
h delivered it into the hand of 2Chr 34:17
because our fathers *h* not kept 2Chr 34:21
h read before the king of Judah 2Chr 34:24
Because they *h* forsaken me 2Chr 34:25
h burned incense unto other gods, 2Chr 34:25
I *h* even heard thee also, saith 2Chr 34:27
What *h* I to do with thee, thou 2Chr 35:21
the house wherewith I *h* war 2Chr 35:21
said to his servants, *H* me away 2Chr 35:23 5674
Ye *h* nothing to do with us to Ezr 4:3
h set up the walls thereof, and Ezr 4:12
Now because we *h* maintenance from Ezr 4:14
dishonour, therefore *h* we sent Ezr 4:14
that they *h* moved sedition within Ezr 4:15
by this means thou shalt *h* no Ezr 4:16 383
sedition *h* been made therein Ezr 4:19
There *h* been mighty kings also Ezr 4:20 1934
which *h* ruled over all countries Ezr 4:20
And that which they *h* need of Ezr 6:9
Also I *h* made a decree, that Ezr 6:11
I Darius *h* made a decree Ezr 6:12
his counsellors *h* freely offered Ezr 7:15
which thou shalt *h* occasion to Ezr 7:20
h not separated themselves from Ezr 9:1
For they *h* taken of their Ezr 9:2
so that the holy seed *h* mingled Ezr 9:2
h we been in a great trespass Ezr 9:7
and for our iniquities *h* we Ezr 9:7
for we *h* forsaken thy Ezr 9:10
which *h* filled it from one end to Ezr 9:11
We *h* trespassed against our God, Ezr 10:2
h taken strange wives of the Ezr 10:2
Ye *h* transgressed, and *h* taken Ezr 10:10
for we are many that *h* Ezr 10:13
let all them which *h* taken Ezr 10:14
which we *h* sinned against thee Neh 1:6
I and my father's house *h* sinned Neh 1:6
We *h* dealt very corruptly against Neh 1:7
h not kept the commandments, nor Neh 1:7
them unto the place that I *h* Neh 1:9
if thy servant *h* found favour in Neh 2:5
but ye *h* no portion, nor right, Neh 2:20
for they *h* provoked thee to anger Neh 4:5
We *h* mortgaged our lands, Neh 5:3
We *h* borrowed money for the Neh 5:4
for other men *h* our lands Neh 5:5
We after our ability *h* redeemed Neh 5:8
my brethren *h* not eaten the bread Neh 5:14
all that I *h* done for this people Neh 5:19
that they might *h* matter for an Neh 6:13
that would *h* put me in fear Neh 6:14
right, but we *h* done wickedly Neh 9:33
Neither *h* our kings, our princes, Neh 9:34
For they *h* not served thee in Neh 9:35
also they *h* dominion over our Neh 9:37
that the same Levites might *h* the Neh 10:37
I *h* done for the house of my God Neh 13:14
because they *h* defiled the Neh 13:29
which *h* heard of the deed of the Est 1:18
that *h* the charge of the business Est 3:9
but I *h* not been called to come Est 4:11
banquet that I *h* prepared for him Est 5:4
If I *h* found favour in the sight Est 5:8
If I *h* found favour in thy sight, Est 7:3
if I *h* found favour in his sight, Est 8:5
I *h* given Esther the house of Est 8:7
him they *h* hanged upon the Est 8:7
Jews hoped to *h* power over them Est 9:1
the queen, The Jews *h* slain Est 9:12
what *h* they done in the rest of Est 9:12
It may be that my sons *h* sinned Job 1:5
they *h* slain the servants with Job 1:15
h carried them away, yea, and Job 1:17
let it look for light, but *h* none Job 3:9 369
For now should I *h* lain still Job 3:13
and been quiet, I should *h* slept Job 3:13
Thy words *h* upholden him that was Job 4:4
Even as I *h* seen, they that plow Job 4:8
I *h* seen the foolish taking root Job 5:3
we *h* searched it, so it is Job 5:27
Oh that I might *h* my request Job 6:8 935
Then should I yet *h* comfort Job 6:10 1961
for I *h* not concealed the words Job 6:10
My brethren *h* dealt deceitfully Job 6:15
to understand wherein I *h* erred Job 6:24
I *h* sinned Job 7:20
If thy children *h* sinned against Job 8:4
he *h* cast them away for their Job 8:4
him, saying, I *h* not seen thee Job 8:18
Thine hands *h* made me and Job 10:8
I should *h* been as though I had Job 10:19 1961
I should *h* been carried from the Job 10:19
But I *h* understanding as well as Job 12:3
Behold now, I *h* ordered my cause Job 13:18 1961
thou wilt *h* a desire to the work Job 14:15
his flesh upon him shall *h* pain Job 14:22
that which I *h* seen I will Job 15:17
Which wise men *h* told from their Job 15:18
their fathers, and *h* not hid it Job 15:18
I *h* heard many such things Job 16:2
Shall vain words *h* an end Job 16:3
They *h* gaped upon me with their Job 16:10
they *h* smitten me upon the cheek Job 16:10
they *h* gathered themselves Job 16:10
I *h* sewed sackcloth upon my skin, Job 16:15
blood, and let my cry *h* no place Job 16:18 1961
I *h* made my bed in the darkness Job 17:13
I *h* said to corruption, Thou art Job 17:14
he shall *h* no name in the street Job 18:17
He shall neither *h* son nor nephew Job 18:19
These ten times *h* ye reproached Job 19:3
And be it indeed that I *h* erred Job 19:4
My kinsfolk *h* failed, and my Job 19:14
familiar friends *h* forgotten me Job 19:14
H pity upon me, *h* pity upon me Job 19:21
I *h* heard the check of my Job 20:3
they which *h* seen him shall say, Job 20:7
and after that I *h* spoken, mock on Job 21:3
and what profit should we *h* Job 21:15
H ye not asked them that go by Job 21:29
of the fatherless *h* been broken Job 22:9
way which wicked men *h* trodden Job 22:15
thou shalt *h* plenty of silver Job 22:25
For then shalt thou *h* thy delight Job 22:26
held his steps, his way *h* I kept Job 23:11
Neither *h* I gone back from the Job 23:12
I *h* esteemed the words of his Job 23:12
that they *h* no covering in the Job 24:7 369
the grave those which *h* sinned Job 24:19
all ye yourselves *h* seen it Job 27:12
lion's whelps *h* not trodden it Job 28:8
We *h* heard the fame thereof with Job 28:22
younger than I *h* me in derision Job 30:1
I would *h* disdained to *h* set Job 30:1
they also let loose the bridle Job 30:11
my calamity, they *h* no helper Job 30:13
affliction *h* taken hold upon me Job 30:16
If I *h* walked with vanity, or if Job 31:5
If mine heart *h* been deceived by Job 31:9
or if I *h* laid wait at my Job 31:9
If I *h* withheld the poor from Job 31:16
or *h* caused the eyes of the widow Job 31:16
Or *h* eaten my morsel myself alone Job 31:17
I *h* guided her from my mother's Job 31:18
If I *h* seen any perish for want Job 31:19
If his loins *h* not blessed me, and Job 31:20
If I *h* lifted up my hand against Job 31:21
If I *h* made gold my hope, or *h* Job 31:24
for I should *h* denied the God Job 31:28

(Neither *h* I suffered my mouth to ... Job 31:30
If I *h* eaten the fruits thereof ... Job 31:39
or *h* caused the owners thereof to ... Job 31:39
should say, We *h* found out wisdom ... Job 32:13
now I *h* opened my mouth, my ... Job 33:2
I *h* heard the voice of thy words, ... Job 33:8
I *h* found a ransom ... Job 33:24
I *h* sinned, and perverted that ... Job 33:27
ear unto me, ye that *h* knowledge ... Job 34:2
I *h* borne chastisement, I will ... Job 34:31
if I *h* done iniquity, I will do ... Job 34:32
and, What profit shall I *h* ... Job 35:3
I will shew thee that I *h* yet to ... Job 36:2
that they *h* exceeded ... Job 36:9
Even so would he *h* removed thee ... Job 36:16
H the gates of death been opened ... Job 38:17
Which I *h* reserved against the ... Job 38:23
Whose house I *h* made the ... Job 39:6
Once *h* I spoken ... Job 40:5
therefore *h* I uttered that I ... Job 42:3
I *h* heard of thee by the hearing ... Job 42:5
for ye *h* not spoken of me the ... Job 42:7
in that ye *h* not spoken of me the ... Job 42:8
the Lord shall *h* them in derision ... Ps 2:4
Yet *h* I set my king upon my holy ... Ps 2:6
this day *h* I begotten thee ... Ps 2:7
that *h* set themselves against me ... Ps 3:6
h mercy upon me, and hear my ... Ps 4:1
for they *h* rebelled against thee ... Ps 5:10
H mercy upon me, O LORD ... Ps 6:2
O LORD my God, if I *h* done this ... Ps 7:3
If I *h* rewarded evil unto him ... Ps 7:4
I *h* delivered him that without ... Ps 7:4
Thou madest him to *h* dominion ... Ps 8:6
H mercy upon me, O LORD ... Ps 9:13
the devices that they *h* imagined ... Ps 10:2
Who *h* said, With our tongue will ... Ps 12:4
I *h* prevailed against him ... Ps 13:4
But I *h* trusted in thy mercy ... Ps 13:5
they *h* done abominable works, ... Ps 14:1
H all the workers of iniquity no ... Ps 14:4
Ye *h* shamed the counsel of the ... Ps 14:6
yea, I *h* a goodly heritage ... Ps 16:6 5921
I *h* set the LORD always before me ... Ps 16:8
by the word of thy lips I *h* kept ... Ps 17:4
I *h* called upon thee, for thou ... Ps 17:6
They *h* now compassed us in our ... Ps 17:11
they *h* set their eyes bowing down ... Ps 17:11
which *h* their portion in this ... Ps 17:14
For I *h* kept the ways of the LORD ... Ps 18:21
h not wickedly departed from my ... Ps 18:21
For by thee I *h* run through a ... Ps 18:29
by my God *h* I leaped over a wall ... Ps 18:29
I *h* pursued mine enemies, and ... Ps 18:37
I *h* wounded them that they were ... Ps 18:38
a people whom I *h* not known shall ... Ps 18:43
let them not *h* dominion over me ... Ps 19:13
Many bulls *h* compassed me ... Ps 22:12
bulls of Bashan *h* beset me round ... Ps 22:12
For dogs *h* compassed me ... Ps 22:16
of the wicked *h* inclosed me ... Ps 22:16
for they *h* been ever of old ... Ps 25:6
thee unto me, and *h* mercy upon me ... Ps 25:16
for I *h* walked in mine integrity ... Ps 26:1
I *h* trusted also in the LORD ... Ps 26:1
and I *h* walked in thy truth ... Ps 26:3
I *h* not sat with vain persons, ... Ps 26:4
I *h* hated the congregation of ... Ps 26:5
I *h* loved the habitation of thy ... Ps 26:8
One thing *h* I desired of the LORD ... Ps 27:4
h mercy also upon me, and answer ... Ps 27:7
Hear, O LORD, and *h* mercy upon me ... Ps 30:10
that they *h* laid privily for me ... Ps 31:4
I *h* hated them that regard lying ... Ps 31:6
H mercy upon me, O LORD, for I am ... Ps 31:9
For I *h* heard the slander of many ... Ps 31:13
for I *h* called upon thee ... Ps 31:17
and mine iniquity *h* I not hid ... Ps 32:5
mule, which *h* no understanding ... Ps 32:9
because we *h* trusted in his holy ... Ps 33:21
For without cause *h* they hid for ... Ps 35:7
cause they *h* digged for my soul ... Ps 35:7
hearts, Ah, so would we *h* it ... Ps 35:25
not say, We *h* swallowed him up ... Ps 35:25
The wicked *h* drawn out the sword, ... Ps 37:14
h bent their bow, to cast down ... Ps 37:14
I *h* been young, and now am old ... Ps 37:25 1961
yet *h* I not seen the righteous ... Ps 37:25
I *h* seen the wicked in great ... Ps 37:35
I *h* roared by reason of the ... Ps 38:8
I *h* preached righteousness in the ... Ps 40:9
I *h* not refrained my lips, O LORD ... Ps 40:9
I *h* not hid thy righteousness ... Ps 40:10
I *h* declared thy faithfulness and ... Ps 40:10
I *h* not concealed thy ... Ps 40:10
evils *h* compassed me about ... Ps 40:12
mine iniquities *h* taken hold upon ... Ps 40:12
for I *h* sinned against thee ... Ps 41:4
My tears *h* been my meat day and ... Ps 42:3
We *h* heard with our ears, O God, ... Ps 44:1
our fathers *h* told us ... Ps 44:1
yet *h* we not forgotten thee, ... Ps 44:17
neither *h* we dealt falsely in thy ... Ps 44:17
neither *h* our steps declined from ... Ps 44:18
If we *h* forgotten the name of our ... Ps 44:20
which I *h* made touching the king ... Ps 45:1
whereby they *h* made thee glad ... Ps 45:8
As we *h* heard, so *h* we seen in ... Ps 48:8

We *h* thought of thy ... Ps 48:9
the upright shall *h* dominion over ... Ps 49:14
those that *h* made a covenant with ... Ps 50:5
to *h* been continually before me ... Ps 50:8
H mercy upon me, O God, according ... Ps 51:1
h I sinned, and done this evil in ... Ps 51:4
h done abominable iniquity ... Ps 53:1
H the workers of iniquity no ... Ps 53:4
they *h* not called upon God ... Ps 53:4
they *h* not set God before them ... Ps 54:3
for I *h* seen violence and strife ... Ps 55:9
then I could *h* borne it ... Ps 55:12
then I would *h* hid myself from ... Ps 55:12
Because they *h* no changes ... Ps 55:19
his word, in God I *h* put my trust ... Ps 56:4
In God *h* I put my trust ... Ps 56:11
They *h* prepared a net for my ... Ps 57:6
they *h* digged a pit before me, ... Ps 57:6
thou shalt *h* all the heathen in ... Ps 59:8
twice *h* I heard this ... Ps 62:11
so as I *h* seen thee in the ... Ps 63:2
Which my lips *h* uttered, and my ... Ps 66:14
Though ye *h* lien among the pots, ... Ps 68:13
They *h* seen thy goings, O God ... Ps 68:24
for thy sake I *h* borne reproach ... Ps 69:7
that which should *h* been for ... Ps 69:22
there, and *h* it in possession ... Ps 69:35
By thee *h* I been holden up from ... Ps 71:6
hitherto *h* I declared thy ... Ps 71:17
until I *h* shewed thy strength ... Ps 71:18
He shall *h* dominion also from sea ... Ps 72:8
they *h* more than heart could wish ... Ps 73:7
Verily I *h* cleansed my heart in ... Ps 73:13
all the day long *h* I been plagued ... Ps 73:14
Whom *h* I in heaven but thee ... Ps 73:25
I *h* put my trust in the Lord GOD, ... Ps 73:28
They *h* cast fire into thy ... Ps 74:7
they *h* defiled by casting down ... Ps 74:7
they *h* burned up all the ... Ps 74:8
people *h* blasphemed thy name ... Ps 74:18
H respect unto the covenant ... Ps 74:20
spoiled, they *h* slept their sleep ... Ps 76:5
men of might *h* found their hands ... Ps 76:5
I *h* considered the days of old, ... Ps 77:5
Which we *h* heard and known ... Ps 78:3
and our fathers *h* told us ... Ps 78:3
thy holy temple *h* they defiled ... Ps 79:1
they *h* laid Jerusalem on heaps ... Ps 79:1
h they given to be meat unto the ... Ps 79:2
Their blood *h* they shed like ... Ps 79:3
the heathen that *h* not known thee ... Ps 79:6
upon the kingdoms that *h* not ... Ps 79:6
For they *h* devoured Jacob, and ... Ps 79:7
wherewith they *h* reproached thee, ... Ps 79:12
I should soon *h* subdued their ... Ps 81:14
h submitted themselves unto him ... Ps 81:15
time should *h* endured for ever ... Ps 81:15
He should *h* fed them also with ... Ps 81:16
rock should I *h* satisfied thee ... Ps 81:16
I *h* said, Ye are gods ... Ps 82:6
hate thee *h* lifted up the head ... Ps 83:2
They *h* taken crafty counsel ... Ps 83:3
They *h* said, Come, and let us cut ... Ps 83:4
For they *h* consulted together ... Ps 83:5
they *h* holpen the children of Lot ... Ps 83:8
peace *h* kissed each other ... Ps 85:10
men *h* sought after my soul ... Ps 86:14
h not set thee before them ... Ps 86:14
turn unto me, and *h* mercy upon me ... Ps 86:16
I *h* cried day and night before ... Ps 88:1
I *h* called daily upon thee, I ... Ps 88:9
I *h* stretched out my hands unto ... Ps 88:9
But unto thee *h* I cried, O LORD ... Ps 88:13
thy terrors *h* cut me off ... Ps 88:16
For I *h* said, Mercy shall be ... Ps 89:2
I *h* made a covenant with my ... Ps 89:3
I *h* sworn unto David my servant, ... Ps 89:3
I *h* laid help upon one that is ... Ps 89:19
I *h* exalted one chosen out of the ... Ps 89:19
I *h* found David my servant ... Ps 89:20
with my holy oil *h* I anointed him ... Ps 89:20
Once *h* I sworn by my holiness ... Ps 89:35
thine enemies *h* reproached ... Ps 89:51
wherewith they *h* reproached the ... Ps 89:51
the years wherein we *h* seen evil ... Ps 90:15
The floods *h* lifted up, O LORD, ... Ps 93:3
the floods *h* lifted up their ... Ps 93:3
iniquity *h* fellowship with thee ... Ps 94:20
and they *h* not known my ways ... Ps 95:10
all the ends of the earth *h* seen ... Ps 98:3
For I *h* eaten ashes like bread, ... Ps 102:9
shalt arise, and *h* mercy upon Zion ... Ps 102:13
same, and thy years shall *h* no end ... Ps 102:27
of the heaven *h* their habitation ... Ps 104:12
to my God while I *h* my being ... Ps 104:33
We *h* sinned with our fathers ... Ps 106:6
we *h* committed iniquity, we *h* ... Ps 106:6
they *h* spoken against me with a ... Ps 109:2
they *h* rewarded me evil for good, ... Ps 109:5
all them that *h* pleasure therein ... Ps 111:2
h all they that do his ... Ps 111:10
They *h* mouths, but they speak not ... Ps 115:5
eyes *h* they, but they see not ... Ps 115:5
They *h* ears, but they hear not ... Ps 115:6
noses *h* they, but they smell not ... Ps 115:6
They *h* hands, but they handle not ... Ps 115:7
feet *h* they, but they walk not ... Ps 115:7
I believed, therefore *h* I spoken ... Ps 116:10

we *h* blessed you out of the house ... Ps 118:26
when I *h* respect unto all thy ... Ps 119:6
when I shall *h* learned thy ... Ps 119:7
my whole heart *h* I sought thee ... Ps 119:10
Thy word *h* I hid in mine heart, ... Ps 119:11
With my lips *h* I declared all the ... Ps 119:13
I *h* rejoiced in the way of thy ... Ps 119:14
and *h* respect unto thy ways ... Ps 119:15
for I *h* kept thy testimonies ... Ps 119:22
I *h* declared my ways, and thou ... Ps 119:26
I *h* chosen the way of truth ... Ps 119:30
thy judgments *h* I laid before me ... Ps 119:30
I *h* stuck unto thy testimonies ... Ps 119:31
I *h* longed after thy precepts ... Ps 119:40
So shall I *h* wherewith to answer ... Ps 119:42
for I *h* hoped in thy judgments ... Ps 119:43
thy commandments, which I *h* loved ... Ps 119:47
thy commandments, which I *h* loved ... Ps 119:48
The proud *h* had me greatly in ... Ps 119:51
yet *h* I not declined from thy law ... Ps 119:51
and *h* comforted myself ... Ps 119:52
Thy statutes *h* been my songs in ... Ps 119:54 1961
I *h* remembered thy name, O LORD, ... Ps 119:55
in the night, and *h* kept thy law ... Ps 119:55
I *h* said that I would keep thy ... Ps 119:57
bands of the wicked *h* robbed me ... Ps 119:61
but I *h* not forgotten thy law ... Ps 119:61
for I *h* believed thy commandments ... Ps 119:66
but now *h* I kept thy word ... Ps 119:67
The proud *h* forged a lie against ... Ps 119:69
for me that I *h* been afflicted ... Ps 119:71
Thy hands *h* made me and fashioned ... Ps 119:73
because I *h* hoped in thy word ... Ps 119:74
me, and those that *h* known thy ... Ps 119:79
The proud *h* digged pits for me, ... Ps 119:85
I should then *h* perished in mine ... Ps 119:92
for I *h* sought thy precepts ... Ps 119:94
The wicked *h* waited for me to ... Ps 119:95
I *h* seen an end of all perfection ... Ps 119:96
I *h* more understanding than all ... Ps 119:99
I *h* refrained my feet from every ... Ps 119:101
I *h* not departed from thy ... Ps 119:102
I *h* sworn, and I will perform it, ... Ps 119:106
The wicked *h* laid a snare for me ... Ps 119:110
Thy testimonies *h* I taken as an ... Ps 119:111
I *h* inclined mine heart to ... Ps 119:112
I will *h* respect unto thy ... Ps 119:117
I *h* done judgment and justice ... Ps 119:121
for they *h* made void thy law ... Ps 119:126
any iniquity *h* dominion over me ... Ps 119:133
enemies *h* forgotten thy words ... Ps 119:139
anguish *h* taken hold on me ... Ps 119:143
I *h* known of old that thou hast ... Ps 119:152
Princes *h* persecuted me without a ... Ps 119:161
Great peace *h* they which love thy ... Ps 119:165
I *h* hoped for thy salvation, and ... Ps 119:166
I *h* kept thy precepts and thy ... Ps 119:168
for I *h* chosen thy precepts ... Ps 119:173
I *h* longed for thy salvation, O ... Ps 119:174
I *h* gone astray like a lost sheep ... Ps 119:176
until that he *h* mercy upon us ... Ps 123:2
H mercy upon us, O LORD, *h* ... Ps 123:3
Many a time *h* they afflicted me ... Ps 129:1
Many a time *h* they afflicted me ... Ps 129:2
yet they *h* not prevailed against ... Ps 129:2
of the depths *h* I cried unto thee ... Ps 130:1
Surely I *h* behaved and quieted ... Ps 131:2
for I *h* desired it ... Ps 132:14
I *h* ordained a lamp for mine ... Ps 132:17
They *h* mouths, but they speak not ... Ps 135:16
eyes *h* they, but they see not ... Ps 135:16
They *h* ears, but they hear not ... Ps 135:17
They *h* sharpened their tongues ... Ps 140:3
who *h* purposed to overthrow my ... Ps 140:4
The proud *h* hid a snare for me, ... Ps 140:5
they *h* spread a net by the ... Ps 140:5
they *h* set gins for me ... Ps 140:5
snares which they *h* laid for me ... Ps 141:9
In the way wherein I walked *h* ... Ps 142:3
as those that *h* been long dead ... Ps 143:3
unto my God while I *h* any being ... Ps 146:2
judgments, they *h* not known them ... Ps 147:20
this honour *h* all his saints ... Ps 149:9
let us all *h* one purse ... Prov 1:14 1961
Because I *h* called, and ye refused ... Prov 1:24
I *h* stretched out my hand, and no ... Prov 1:24
But ye *h* set at nought all my ... Prov 1:25
if he *h* done thee no harm ... Prov 3:30
I *h* taught thee in the way of ... Prov 4:11
I *h* led thee in right paths ... Prov 4:11
except they *h* done mischief ... Prov 4:16
How *h* I hated instruction, and my ... Prov 5:12
h not obeyed the voice of my ... Prov 5:13
I *h* peace offerings with me ... Prov 7:14
this day *h* I payed my vows ... Prov 7:14
seek thy face, and I *h* found thee ... Prov 7:15
I *h* decked my bed with coverings ... Prov 7:16
I *h* perfumed my bed with myrrh, ... Prov 7:17
many strong men *h* been slain by ... Prov 7:26
I *h* strength ... Prov 8:14
of the wine which I *h* mingled ... Prov 9:5
wide his lips shall *h* destruction ... Prov 13:3
shall *h* a place of refuge ... Prov 14:26 1961
A wise servant shall *h* rule over ... Prov 17:2
shall *h* part of the inheritance ... Prov 17:2
a servant to *h* rule over princes ... Prov 19:10
he beg in harvest, and *h* nothing ... Prov 20:4 369
I *h* made my heart clean, I am ... Prov 20:9

I *h* made known to thee this day, ... Prov 22:19
H not I written to thee excellent ... Prov 22:20
landmark, which thy fathers *h* set ... Prov 22:28
a wise child shall *h* joy of him ... Prov 23:24
They *h* stricken me, shalt thou ... Prov 23:35
they *h* beaten me, and I felt it ... Prov 23:35
It is not good to *h* respect of ... Prov 24:23
the prince whom thine eyes *h* seen ... Prov 25:7
thou shalt *h* goats' milk enough ... Prov 27:27
but the upright shall *h* good ... Prov 28:10
and forsaketh them shall *h* mercy ... Prov 28:13
his land shall *h* plenty of bread ... Prov 28:19
persons shall *h* poverty enough ... Prov 28:19
To *h* respect of persons is not ... Prov 28:21
his eyes shall *h* many a curse ... Prov 28:27
shall *h* him become his son at the ... Prov 29:21 1961
h not the understanding of a man ... Prov 30:2
nor *h* the knowledge of the holy ... Prov 30:3 3045
Two things *h* I required of thee ... Prov 30:7
and saith, I *h* done no wickedness ... Prov 30:20
The locusts *h* no king, yet go ... Prov 30:27
that he shall *h* no need of spoil ... Prov 31:11
Many daughters *h* done virtuously, ... Prov 31:29
I *h* seen all the works that are ... Eccl 1:14
h gotten more wisdom than all ... Eccl 1:16
h been before me in Jerusalem ... Eccl 1:16 1961
yet shall he *h* rule over all my ... Eccl 2:19
my labour wherein I *h* laboured ... Eccl 2:19
wherein I *h* shewed myself wise ... Eccl 2:19
I *h* seen the travail, which God ... Eccl 3:10
yea, they *h* all one breath ... Eccl 3:19
because they *h* a good reward for ... Eccl 4:9 3426
lie together, then they *h* heat ... Eccl 4:11
of all that *h* been before them ... Eccl 4:16 1961
evil which I *h* seen under the sun ... Eccl 5:13
Behold that which I *h* seen ... Eccl 5:18
evil which I *h* seen under the sun ... Eccl 6:1
good, and also that he *h* no burial ... Eccl 6:3 1961
giveth life to them that *h* it ... Eccl 7:12 1167
All things *h* I seen in the days ... Eccl 7:15
All this *h* I proved by wisdom ... Eccl 7:23
this *h* I found, saith the ... Eccl 7:27
man among a thousand *h* I found ... Eccl 7:28
among all those *h* I not found ... Eccl 7:28
Lo, this only *h* I found, that God ... Eccl 7:29
but they *h* sought out many ... Eccl 7:29
All this *h* I seen, and applied my ... Eccl 8:9
neither *h* they any more a reward ... Eccl 9:5
neither *h* they any more a portion ... Eccl 9:6
This wisdom *h* I seen also under ... Eccl 9:13
evil which I *h* seen under the sun ... Eccl 10:5
I *h* seen servants upon horses, and ... Eccl 10:7
say, I *h* no pleasure in them ... Eccl 12:1
mine own vineyard *h* I not kept ... Song 1:6
I *h* compared thee, O my love, to ... Song 1:9
for our vines *h* tender grapes ... Song 2:15
I *h* gathered my myrrh with my ... Song 5:1
I *h* eaten my honeycomb with my ... Song 5:1
I *h* drunk my wine with my milk ... Song 5:1
I *h* put off my coat ... Song 5:3
I *h* washed my feet ... Song 5:3
from me, for they *h* overcome me ... Song 6:5
which I *h* laid up for thee, O my ... Song 7:13
We *h* a little sister, and she hath ... Song 8:8
must *h* a thousand, and those that ... Song 8:12
I *h* nourished and brought up ... Is 1:2
they *h* rebelled against me ... Is 1:2
they *h* forsaken the LORD, they ... Is 1:4
they *h* provoked the Holy One of ... Is 1:4
they *h* not been closed, neither ... Is 1:6
we should *h* been as Sodom ... Is 1:9 1961
we should *h* been like unto ... Is 1:9
of the oaks which ye *h* desired ... Is 1:29
for the gardens that ye *h* chosen ... Is 1:29
which their own fingers *h* made ... Is 2:8
for they *h* rewarded evil unto ... Is 3:9
for ye *h* eaten up the vineyard ... Is 3:14
When the Lord shall *h* washed away ... Is 4:4
shall *h* purged the blood of ... Is 4:4
What could *h* been done more to my ... Is 5:4
vineyard, that I *h* not done in it ... Is 5:4
because they *h* no knowledge ... Is 5:13
because they *h* cast away the law ... Is 5:24
for mine eyes *h* seen the King ... Is 6:5
the LORD *h* removed men far away, ... Is 6:12
h taken evil counsel against thee ... Is 7:5
house, days that *h* not come ... Is 7:17
child shall *h* knowledge to cry ... Is 8:4
unto them that *h* familiar spirits ... Is 8:19
in darkness *h* seen a great light ... Is 9:2
Therefore the Lord shall *h* no joy ... Is 9:17
neither shall *h* mercy on their ... Is 9:17
which they *h* prescribed ... Is 10:1
as I *h* done unto Samaria and her ... Is 10:11
strength of my hand I *h* done it ... Is 10:13
I *h* removed the bounds of the ... Is 10:13
h robbed their treasures ... Is 10:13
I *h* put down the inhabitants like ... Is 10:13
h I gathered all the earth ... Is 10:14
they *h* taken up their lodging at ... Is 10:29
I *h* commanded my sanctified ones, ... Is 13:3
I *h* also called my mighty ones ... Is 13:3
they shall *h* no pity on the fruit ... Is 13:18
the LORD will *h* mercy on Jacob ... Is 14:1
saying, Surely as I *h* thought ... Is 14:24
as I *h* purposed, so shall it ... Is 14:24
the abundance they *h* gotten ... Is 15:7
and that which they *h* laid up ... Is 15:7

We *h* heard of the pride of Moab ... Is 16:6
the lords of the heathen *h* broken ... Is 16:8
I *h* made their vintage shouting ... Is 16:10
his eyes shall *h* respect to the ... Is 17:7
that which his fingers *h* made ... Is 17:8
whose land the rivers *h* spoiled ... Is 18:2
whose land the rivers *h* spoiled ... Is 18:7
to them that *h* familiar spirits, ... Is 19:3
they *h* also seduced Egypt, even ... Is 19:13
they *h* caused Egypt to err in ... Is 19:14
sighing thereof *h* I made to cease ... Is 21:2
pangs *h* taken hold upon me, as ... Is 21:3
that which I *h* heard of the LORD ... Is 21:10
of Israel, *h* I declared unto you ... Is 21:10
together, which *h* fled from far ... Is 22:3
Ye *h* seen also the breaches of ... Is 22:9
ye *h* numbered the houses of ... Is 22:10
the houses *h* ye broken down to ... Is 22:10
but ye *h* not looked unto the ... Is 22:11
pass over the sea, *h* replenished ... Is 23:2
there also shalt thou *h* no rest ... Is 23:12
because they *h* transgressed the ... Is 24:5
of the earth *h* we heard songs ... Is 24:16
dealers *h* dealt treacherously ... Is 24:16
the treacherous dealers *h* dealt ... Is 24:16
we *h* waited for him, and he will ... Is 25:9
we *h* waited for him, we will be ... Is 25:9
We *h* a strong city ... Is 26:1
O LORD, *h* we waited for thee ... Is 26:8
With my soul *h* I desired thee in ... Is 26:9
thee *h* had dominion over us ... Is 26:13
in trouble *h* they visited thee ... Is 26:16
so *h* we been in thy sight, O LORD ... Is 26:17 1961
We *h* been with child ... Is 26:18
we *h* been in pain, we *h* as it ... Is 26:18
we *h* not wrought any deliverance ... Is 26:18
neither *h* the inhabitants of the ... Is 26:18
them will not *h* mercy on them ... Is 27:11
But they also *h* erred through ... Is 28:7
the prophet *h* erred through ... Is 28:7
Because ye *h* said, We *h* made a ... Is 28:15
We *h* made a covenant with death, ... Is 28:15
for we *h* made lies our refuge, and ... Is 28:15
and under falsehood *h* we hid ... Is 28:15
for I *h* heard from the Lord GOD ... Is 28:22
but *h* removed their heart far ... Is 29:13
Egypt, and *h* not asked at my mouth ... Is 30:2
therefore *h* I cried concerning ... Is 30:7
that he may *h* mercy upon you ... Is 30:18
Ye shall *h* a song, as in the ... Is 30:29 1961
of Israel *h* deeply revolted ... Is 31:6
which your own hands *h* made unto ... Is 31:7
we *h* waited for thee ... Is 33:2
that are far off, what I *h* done ... Is 33:13
are but vain words) I *h* counsel ... Is 36:5
h they delivered Samaria out of ... Is 36:19
that *h* delivered their land out ... Is 36:20
king of Assyria *h* blasphemed me ... Is 37:6
h done to all lands by destroying ... Is 37:11
H the gods of the nations ... Is 37:12
them which my fathers *h* destroyed ... Is 37:12
the kings of Assyria *h* laid waste ... Is 37:18
h cast their gods into the fire ... Is 37:19
therefore they *h* destroyed them ... Is 37:19
I *h* digged, and drunk water ... Is 37:25
with the sole of my feet *h* I ... Is 37:25
heard long ago, how I *h* done it ... Is 37:26
ancient times, that I *h* formed it ... Is 37:26
now *h* I brought it to pass, that ... Is 37:26
how I *h* walked before thee in ... Is 38:3
h done that which is good in thy ... Is 38:3
I *h* heard thy prayer, I *h* seen ... Is 38:5
I *h* cut off like a weaver my life ... Is 38:12
What *h* they seen in thine house ... Is 39:4
that is in mine house *h* they seen ... Is 39:4
that I *h* not shewed them ... Is 39:4
that which thy fathers *h* laid up ... Is 39:6
H ye not known? ... Is 40:21
h ye not heard? ... Is 40:21
h ye not understood from the ... Is 40:21
to them that *h* no might he ... Is 40:29
my servant, Jacob whom I *h* chosen ... Is 41:8
Thou whom I *h* taken from the ends ... Is 41:9
I *h* chosen thee, and not cast thee ... Is 41:9
I *h* raised up one from the north, ... Is 41:25
I *h* put my spirit upon him ... Is 42:1
till he *h* set judgment in the ... Is 42:4
I the LORD *h* called thee in ... Is 42:6
I *h* long time holden my peace ... Is 42:14
I *h* been still, and refrained ... Is 42:14
in paths that they *h* not known ... Is 42:16
LORD, he against whom we *h* sinned ... Is 42:24
for I *h* redeemed thee, I *h* ... Is 43:1
honourable, and I *h* loved thee ... Is 43:4
for I *h* created him for my glory, ... Is 43:7
I *h* formed him ... Is 43:7
yea, I *h* made him ... Is 43:7
the blind people that *h* eyes ... Is 43:8 3426
and the deaf that *h* ears ... Is 43:8
and my servant whom I *h* chosen ... Is 43:10
I *h* declared, and *h* saved, and I ... Is 43:12
I *h* shewed, when there was no ... Is 43:12
For your sake I *h* sent to Babylon ... Is 43:14
h brought down all their nobles, ... Is 43:14
This people *h* I formed for myself ... Is 43:21
I *h* not caused thee to serve with ... Is 43:23
thy teachers *h* transgressed ... Is 43:27
Therefore I *h* profaned the ... Is 43:28

h given Jacob to the curse, and ... Is 43:28
and Israel, whom I *h* chosen ... Is 44:1
and thou, Jesurun, whom I *h* chosen ... Is 44:2
h not I told thee from that time, ... Is 44:8
from that time, and *h* declared it ... Is 44:8
Aha, I am warm, I *h* seen the fire ... Is 44:16
They *h* not known nor understood ... Is 44:18
I *h* burned part of it in the fire ... Is 44:19
also I *h* baked bread upon the ... Is 44:19
I *h* roasted flesh, and eaten it ... Is 44:19
I *h* formed thee ... Is 44:21
I *h* blotted out, as a thick cloud ... Is 44:22
for I *h* redeemed thee ... Is 44:22
whose right hand I *h* holden ... Is 45:1
I *h* even called thee by thy name ... Is 45:4
I *h* surnamed thee, though thou ... Is 45:4
I the LORD *h* created it ... Is 45:8
I *h* made the earth, and created ... Is 45:12
h stretched out the heavens ... Is 45:12
and all their host *h* I commanded ... Is 45:12
I *h* raised him up in ... Is 45:13
I *h* not spoken in secret, in a ... Is 45:19
they *h* no knowledge that set up ... Is 45:20
h not I the LORD ... Is 45:21
I *h* sworn by myself, the word is ... Is 45:23
in the LORD *h* I righteousness and ... Is 45:24
I *h* made, and I will bear ... Is 46:4
I *h* spoken it, I will also bring ... Is 46:11
I *h* purposed it, I will also do ... Is 46:11
I *h* polluted mine inheritance, and ... Is 47:6
I *h* declared the former things ... Is 48:3
I *h* even from the beginning ... Is 48:5
I *h* shewed thee new things from ... Is 48:6
I *h* refined thee, but not with ... Is 48:10
I *h* chosen thee in the furnace of ... Is 48:10
I, even I, *h* spoken ... Is 48:15
yea, I *h* called him ... Is 48:15
I *h* brought him, and he shall make ... Is 48:15
I *h* not spoken in secret from the ... Is 48:16
his name should not *h* been cut ... Is 48:19
I *h* laboured in vain, I *h* ... Is 49:4
an acceptable time *h* I heard thee ... Is 49:8
day of salvation *h* I helped thee ... Is 49:8
will *h* mercy upon his afflicted ... Is 49:13
that she should not *h* compassion ... Is 49:15
I *h* graven thee upon the palms of ... Is 49:16
The children which thou shalt *h* ... Is 49:20
seeing I *h* lost my children, and ... Is 49:21
divorcement, whom I *h* put away ... Is 50:1
is it to whom I *h* sold you ... Is 50:1
iniquities *h* ye sold yourselves ... Is 50:1
or *h* I no power to deliver ... Is 50:2
therefore *h* I set my face like a ... Is 50:7
in the sparks that ye *h* kindled ... Is 50:11
This shall ye *h* of mine hand ... Is 50:11 1961
I *h* put my words in thy mouth, and ... Is 51:16
I *h* covered thee in the shadow of ... Is 51:16
Thy sons *h* fainted, they lie at ... Is 51:20
I *h* taken out of thine hand the ... Is 51:22
which *h* said to thy soul, Bow ... Is 51:23
Ye *h* sold yourselves for nought ... Is 52:3
what *h* I here, saith the LORD, ... Is 52:5
All we like sheep *h* gone astray ... Is 53:6
we *h* turned every one to his own ... Is 53:6
a small moment *h* I forsaken thee ... Is 54:7
kindness will I *h* mercy on thee ... Is 54:8
for as I *h* sworn that the waters ... Is 54:9
so *h* I sworn that I would not be ... Is 54:9
I *h* created the smith that ... Is 54:16
I *h* created the waster to destroy ... Is 54:16
I *h* given him for a witness to ... Is 55:4
LORD, and he will *h* mercy upon him ... Is 55:7
dogs which can never *h* enough ... Is 56:11 3045
h not I held my peace even of old ... Is 57:11
me, and the souls which I *h* made ... Is 57:16
I *h* seen his ways, and will heal ... Is 57:18
Wherefore *h* we fasted, say they, ... Is 58:3
wherefore *h* we afflicted our soul ... Is 58:3
Is it such a fast that I *h* chosen ... Is 58:5
not this the fast that I *h* chosen ... Is 58:6
But your iniquities *h* separated ... Is 59:2
your sins *h* hid his face from you ... Is 59:2
your lips *h* spoken lies, your ... Is 59:3
they *h* made them crooked paths ... Is 59:8
words which I *h* put in thy mouth ... Is 59:21
but in my favour *h* I had mercy on ... Is 60:10
For your shame ye shall *h* double ... Is 61:7
I *h* set watchmen upon thy walls, ... Is 62:6
But they that *h* gathered it shall ... Is 62:9
they that *h* brought it together ... Is 62:9
I *h* trodden the winepress alone ... Is 63:3
The people of thy holiness *h* ... Is 63:18
our adversaries *h* trodden down ... Is 63:18
of the world men *h* not heard ... Is 64:4
for we *h* sinned ... Is 64:5
like the wind, *h* taken us away ... Is 64:6
I *h* spread out my hands all the ... Is 65:2
which *h* burned incense upon the ... Is 65:7
for my people that *h* sought me ... Is 65:10
made, and all those things *h* been ... Is 66:2 1961
they *h* chosen their own ways, and ... Is 66:3
that *h* not heard my fame ... Is 66:19
neither *h* seen my glory ... Is 66:19
that *h* transgressed against me ... Is 66:24
I *h* put my words in thy mouth ... Jer 1:9
I *h* this day set thee over the ... Jer 1:10
who *h* forsaken me, and *h* burned ... Jer 1:16
I *h* made thee this day a defenced ... Jer 1:18

H

What iniquity *h* your fathers Jer 2:5
h walked after vanity, and are Jer 2:5
but my people *h* changed their Jer 2:11
For my people *h* committed two Jer 2:13
they *h* forsaken me the fountain Jer 2:13
Tahapanes *h* broken the crown of Jer 2:16
of old time I *h* broken thy yoke Jer 2:20
I *h* not gone after Baalim Jer 2:23
for I *h* loved strangers, and after Jer 2:25
for they *h* turned their back unto Jer 2:27
ye all *h* transgressed against me, Jer 2:29
In vain *h* I smitten your children Jer 2:30
H I been a wilderness unto Israel Jer 2:31
yet my people *h* forgotten me days Jer 2:32
I *h* not found it by secret search Jer 2:34
thou sayest, I *h* not sinned Jer 2:35
the showers *h* been withholden Jer 3:3
ye *h* not obeyed my voice, saith Jer 3:13
I *h* given for an inheritance unto Jer 3:18
so *h* ye dealt treacherously with Jer 3:20
for they *h* perverted their way, Jer 3:21
they *h* forgotten the LORD their Jer 3:21
for we *h* sinned against the LORD Jer 3:25
h not obeyed the voice of the Jer 3:25
saying, Ye shall *h* peace Jer 4:10 1961
thy doings *h* procured these Jer 4:18
is foolish, they *h* not known me Jer 4:22
they *h* none understanding Jer 4:22
to do good they *h* no knowledge Jer 4:22
because I *h* spoken it, I *h* Jer 4:28
For I *h* heard a voice as of a Jer 4:31
them, but they *h* not grieved Jer 5:3
but they *h* refused to receive Jer 5:3
they *h* made their faces harder Jer 5:3
they *h* refused to return Jer 5:3
for they *h* known the way of the Jer 5:5
but these *h* altogether broken the Jer 5:5
thy children *h* forsaken me Jer 5:7
the house of Judah *h* dealt very Jer 5:11
They *h* belied the LORD, and said, Jer 5:12
Like as ye *h* forsaken me, and Jer 5:19
which *h* eyes, and see not Jer 5:21
which *h* ears, and hear not Jer 5:21
which *h* placed the sand for the Jer 5:22
Your iniquities *h* turned away Jer 5:25
your sins *h* withholden good Jer 5:25
and my people love to *h* it so Jer 5:31
I *h* likened the daughter of Zion Jer 6:2
they *h* no delight in it Jer 6:10
They *h* healed also the hurt of Jer 6:14
because they *h* not hearkened unto Jer 6:19
they are cruel, and *h* no mercy Jer 6:23
We *h* heard the fame thereof Jer 6:24
I *h* set thee for a tower and a Jer 6:27
even I *h* seen it, saith the LORD Jer 7:11
because ye *h* done all these works Jer 7:13
fathers, as I *h* done to Shiloh Jer 7:14
as I *h* cast out all your brethren Jer 7:15
the ways that I *h* commanded you Jer 7:23
day I *h* even sent unto you all my Jer 7:25
of Judah *h* done evil in my sight Jer 7:30
they *h* set their abominations in Jer 7:30
they *h* built the high places of Jer 7:31
host of heaven, whom they *h* loved Jer 8:2
and after whom they *h* walked Jer 8:2
and whom they *h* sought Jer 8:2
and whom they *h* worshipped Jer 8:2
places whither I *h* driven them Jer 8:3
wickedness, saying, What *h* I done Jer 8:6
they *h* rejected the word of the Jer 8:9
For they *h* healed the hurt of the Jer 8:11
the things that I *h* given them Jer 8:13
because we *h* sinned against the Jer 8:14
h devoured the land, and all that Jer 8:16
Why *h* they provoked me to anger Jer 8:19
they *h* taught their tongue to Jer 9:5
Because they *h* forsaken my law Jer 9:13
h not obeyed my voice, neither Jer 9:13
But *h* walked after the Jer 9:14
they nor their fathers *h* known Jer 9:16
them, till I *h* consumed them Jer 9:16
because we *h* forsaken the land, Jer 9:19
our dwellings *h* cast us out Jer 9:19
The gods that *h* not made the Jer 10:11
brutish, and *h* not sought the LORD Jer 10:21
for they *h* eaten up Jacob, and Jer 10:25
h made his habitation desolate Jer 10:25
which I *h* sworn unto your fathers Jer 11:5
the house of Judah *h* broken my Jer 11:10
h ye set up altars to that Jer 11:13
which they *h* done against Jer 11:17
for unto thee *h* I revealed my Jer 11:20
them, yea, they *h* taken root Jer 12:2
they *h* wearied thee, then how Jer 12:5
even they *h* dealt treacherously Jer 12:6
they *h* called a multitude after Jer 12:6
I *h* forsaken mine house, I *h* Jer 12:7
I *h* given the dearly beloved of Jer 12:7
therefore *h* I hated it Jer 12:8
Many pastors *h* destroyed my Jer 12:10
they *h* trodden my portion under Jer 12:10
they *h* made my pleasant portion a Jer 12:10
They *h* made it desolate, and being Jer 12:11
no flesh shall *h* peace Jer 12:12
They *h* sown wheat, but shall reap Jer 12:13
they *h* put themselves to pain, Jer 12:13
I *h* caused my people Israel to Jer 12:14
after that I *h* plucked them out I Jer 12:15

h compassion on them, and will Jer 12:15
so *h* I caused to cleave unto me Jer 13:11
nor *h* mercy, but destroy them Jer 13:14
I *h* seen thine adulteries, and thy Jer 13:27
their nobles *h* sent their little Jer 14:3
we *h* sinned against thee Jer 14:7
Thus *h* they loved to wander Jer 14:10
they *h* not refrained their feet, Jer 14:10
sword, neither shall ye *h* famine Jer 14:13
neither *h* I commanded them, Jer 14:14
they shall *h* none to bury them, Jer 14:16
for we *h* sinned against thee Jer 14:20 369
For who shall *h* pity upon thee, O Jer 15:5
I *h* brought upon them against the Jer 15:8
I *h* caused him to fall upon it Jer 15:8
I *h* neither lent on usury, nor Jer 15:10
nor men *h* lent to me on usury Jer 15:10
for thy sake I *h* suffered rebuke Jer 15:15
neither shalt thou *h* sons or Jer 16:2
for I *h* taken away my peace from Jer 16:5
or what is our sin that we *h* Jer 16:10
your fathers *h* forsaken me Jer 16:11
h walked after other gods, and Jer 16:11
h served them, and *h* worshipped Jer 16:11
h forsaken me, and *h* not kept Jer 16:11
ye *h* done worse than your fathers Jer 16:12
because they *h* defiled my land, Jer 16:18
they *h* filled mine inheritance Jer 16:18
our fathers *h* inherited lies Jer 16:19
for ye *h* kindled a fire in mine Jer 17:4
because they *h* forsaken the LORD, Jer 17:13
I *h* not hastened from being a Jer 17:16
neither *h* I desired the woeful Jer 17:16
against whom I *h* pronounced Jer 18:8
they *h* burned incense to vanity, Jer 18:15
they *h* caused them to stumble in Jer 18:15
for they *h* digged a pit for my Jer 18:20
for they *h* digged a pit to take Jer 18:22
Because they *h* forsaken me Jer 19:4
h estranged this place, and *h* Jer 19:4
they nor their fathers *h* known Jer 19:4
h filled this place with the Jer 19:4
They *h* built also the high places Jer 19:5
h burned incense unto all the Jer 19:13
h poured out drink offerings unto Jer 19:13
that I *h* pronounced against it Jer 19:15
because they *h* hardened their Jer 19:15
for unto thee *h* I opened my cause Jer 20:12
my mother might *h* been my grave Jer 20:17
neither *h* pity, nor *h* mercy Jer 21:7
For I *h* set my face against this Jer 21:10
Because they *h* forsaken the Jer 22:9
whither they *h* led him captive Jer 22:12
Ye *h* scattered my flock, and Jer 23:2
them away, and *h* not visited them Jer 23:2
countries whither I *h* driven them Jer 23:3
in my house *h* I found their Jer 23:11
I *h* seen folly in the prophets of Jer 23:13
I *h* seen also in the prophets of Jer 23:14
LORD hath said, Ye shall *h* peace Jer 23:17 1961
not return, until he *h* executed Jer 23:20
till he *h* performed the thoughts Jer 23:20
I *h* not sent these prophets, yet Jer 23:21
I *h* not spoken to them, yet they Jer 23:21
then they should *h* turned them Jer 23:22
I *h* heard what the prophets said, Jer 23:25
I *h* dreamed, I *h* dreamed Jer 23:25
as their fathers *h* forgotten my Jer 23:27
for ye *h* perverted the words of Jer 23:36
I *h* sent unto you, saying, Ye Jer 23:38
whom I *h* sent out of this place Jer 24:5
I *h* spoken unto you, rising early Jer 25:3
but ye *h* not hearkened Jer 25:3
but ye *h* not hearkened, nor Jer 25:4
Yet ye *h* not hearkened unto me, Jer 25:7
Because ye *h* not heard my words, Jer 25:8
which I *h* pronounced against it Jer 25:13
shepherds shall *h* no way to flee Jer 25:35
which I *h* set before you, Jer 26:4
them, but ye *h* not hearkened Jer 26:5
as ye *h* heard with your ears Jer 26:11
all the words that ye *h* heard Jer 26:12
I *h* made the earth, the man and Jer 27:5
h given it unto whom it seemed Jer 27:5
now *h* I given all these lands Jer 27:6
the beasts of the field *h* I given Jer 27:6
until I *h* consumed them by his Jer 27:8
For I *h* not sent them, saith the Jer 27:15
I *h* broken the yoke of the king Jer 28:2
prophets that *h* been before me Jer 28:8 1961
I *h* put a yoke of iron upon the Jer 28:14
I *h* given him the beasts of the Jer 28:14
whom I *h* caused to be carried Jer 29:4
I *h* caused you to be carried away Jer 29:7
peace thereof shall ye *h* peace Jer 29:7
I *h* not sent them, saith the LORD Jer 29:9
the places whither I *h* driven you Jer 29:14
Because ye *h* said, The LORD hath Jer 29:15
nations whither I *h* driven them Jer 29:18
Because they *h* not hearkened to Jer 29:19
whom I *h* sent from Jerusalem to Jer 29:20
Because they *h* committed villany Jer 29:23
h committed adultery with their Jer 29:23
h spoken lying words in my name, Jer 29:23
which I *h* not commanded them Jer 29:23
he shall not *h* a man to dwell Jer 29:32 1961
I *h* spoken unto thee in a book Jer 30:2
We *h* heard a voice of trembling, Jer 30:5

whither I *h* scattered thee Jer 30:11
All thy lovers *h* forgotten thee Jer 30:14
for I *h* wounded thee with the Jer 30:14
I *h* done these things unto thee Jer 30:15
h mercy on his dwellingplaces Jer 30:18
not return, until he *h* done it Jer 30:24
until he *h* performed the intents Jer 30:24
Yea, I *h* loved thee with an Jer 31:3
lovingkindness *h* I drawn thee Jer 31:3
I *h* surely heard Ephraim Jer 31:18
I will surely *h* mercy upon him, Jer 31:20
For I *h* satiated the weary soul, Jer 31:25
I *h* replenished every sorrowful Jer 31:25
that like as I *h* watched over Jer 31:28
The fathers *h* eaten a sour grape, Jer 31:29
Israel for all that they *h* done Jer 31:37
they *h* done nothing of all that Jer 32:23
upon whose roofs they *h* offered Jer 32:29
the children of Judah *h* only done Jer 32:30
for the children of Israel *h* only Jer 32:30
which they *h* done to provoke me Jer 32:32
they *h* turned unto me the back, Jer 32:33
yet they *h* not hearkened to Jer 32:33
whither I *h* driven them in mine Jer 32:37
Like as I *h* brought all this Jer 32:42
the good that I *h* promised them Jer 32:42
whom I *h* slain in mine anger and Jer 33:5
I *h* hid my face from this city Jer 33:5
whereby they *h* sinned against me Jer 33:8
iniquities, whereby they *h* sinned Jer 33:8
whereby they *h* transgressed Jer 33:8
I *h* promised unto the house of Jer 33:14
that he should not *h* a son to Jer 33:21 1961
not what this people *h* spoken Jer 33:24
thus they *h* despised my people, Jer 33:24
and if I *h* not appointed the Jer 33:25
to return, and *h* mercy on them Jer 33:26
for I *h* pronounced the word, Jer 34:5
Ye *h* not hearkened unto me, in Jer 34:17
that *h* transgressed my covenant Jer 34:18
which *h* not performed the words Jer 34:18
nor plant vineyard, nor *h* any Jer 35:7
Thus *h* we obeyed the voice of Jer 35:8
neither *h* we vineyard, nor field, Jer 35:9 1961
But we *h* dwelt in tents, and *h* Jer 35:10
I *h* spoken unto you, rising early Jer 35:14
I *h* sent also unto you all my Jer 35:15
the land which I *h* given to you Jer 35:15
but ye *h* not inclined your ear, Jer 35:15
h performed the commandment of Jer 35:16
that I *h* pronounced against them Jer 35:17
because I *h* spoken unto them Jer 35:17
but they *h* not heard Jer 35:17
I *h* called unto them Jer 35:17
but they *h* not answered Jer 35:17
Because ye *h* obeyed the Jer 35:18
therein all the words that I *h* Jer 36:2
He shall *h* none to sit upon the Jer 36:30 1961
all the evil that I *h* pronounced Jer 36:31
What *h* I offended against thee, Jer 37:18
that ye *h* put me in prison Jer 37:18
for he shall *h* his life for a Jer 38:2
these men *h* done evil in all that Jer 38:9
h done to Jeremiah the prophet Jer 38:9
whom they *h* cast into the dungeon Jer 38:9
say, Thy friends *h* set thee on Jer 38:22
and *h* prevailed against thee Jer 38:22
hear that I *h* talked with thee Jer 38:25
because ye *h* sinned against the Jer 40:3
h not obeyed his voice, therefore Jer 40:3
in your cities that ye *h* taken Jer 40:10
for we *h* treasures in the field, Jer 41:8 3426
said unto them, I *h* heard you Jer 42:4
the evil that I *h* done unto you Jer 42:10
that he may *h* mercy upon you, and Jer 42:12
trumpet, nor *h* hunger of bread Jer 42:14
know certainly that I *h* Jer 42:19
now I *h* this day declared it to Jer 42:21
but ye *h* not obeyed the voice of Jer 42:21
upon these stones that I *h* hid Jer 43:10
Ye *h* seen all the evil that I Jer 44:2
that I *h* brought upon Jerusalem Jer 44:2
they *h* committed to provoke me to Jer 44:3
H ye forgotten the wickedness of Jer 44:9
which they *h* committed in the Jer 44:9
neither *h* they feared, nor walked Jer 44:10
that *h* set their faces to go into Jer 44:12
as I *h* punished Jerusalem, by the Jer 44:13
to the which they *h* a desire to Jer 44:14 5375
offerings unto her, as we *h* done Jer 44:17
we *h* wanted all things, and *h* Jer 44:18
abominations which ye *h* committed Jer 44:22
Because ye *h* burned incense, and Jer 44:23
because ye *h* sinned against the Jer 44:23
h not obeyed the voice of the Jer 44:23
your wives *h* both spoken with Jer 44:25
perform our vows that we *h* vowed Jer 44:25
I *h* sworn by my great name, saith Jer 44:26
that which I *h* built will I break Jer 45:4
that which I *h* planted I will Jer 45:4
Wherefore *h* I seen them dismayed Jer 46:5
The nations *h* heard of thy shame, Jer 46:12
nations whither I *h* driven thee Jer 46:28
in Heshbon they *h* devised evil Jer 48:2
her little ones *h* caused a cry to Jer 48:4
h heard a cry of destruction Jer 48:5
We *h* heard the pride of Moab, (he Jer 48:29
I *h* caused wine to fail from the Jer 48:33

h they uttered their voice, from ... Jer 48:34
for I *h* broken Moab like a vessel ... Jer 48:38
will destroy till they *h* enough ... Jer 49:9
But I *h* made Esau bare, I *h* ... Jer 49:10
of the cup *h* assuredly drunken ... Jer 49:12
For I *h* sworn by myself, saith ... Jer 49:13
I *h* heard a rumour from the LORD, ... Jer 49:14
for they *h* heard evil tidings ... Jer 49:23
sorrows *h* taken her, as a woman ... Jer 49:24
which *h* neither gates nor bars, ... Jer 49:31
them, till I *h* consumed them ... Jer 49:37
their shepherds *h* caused them to ... Jer 50:6
they *h* turned them away on the ... Jer 50:6
they *h* gone from mountain to hill ... Jer 50:6
they *h* forgotten their ... Jer 50:6
that found them *h* devoured them ... Jer 50:7
because they *h* sinned against the ... Jer 50:7
the lions *h* driven him away ... Jer 50:17
as I *h* punished the king of ... Jer 50:18
to all that I *h* commanded thee ... Jer 50:21
I *h* laid a snare for thee, and ... Jer 50:24
the nations *h* drunken of her wine ... Jer 51:7
We would *h* healed Babylon, but ... Jer 51:9
all their evil that they *h* done ... Jer 51:24
men of Babylon *h* forborn to fight ... Jer 51:30
they *h* remained in their holds ... Jer 51:30
they *h* burned her dwellingplaces ... Jer 51:30
the reeds they *h* burned with fire ... Jer 51:32
Ye that *h* escaped the sword, go ... Jer 51:50
because we *h* heard reproach ... Jer 51:51
all her friends *h* dealt ... Lam 1:2
because they *h* seen her nakedness ... Lam 1:8
they *h* given their pleasant ... Lam 1:11
for I *h* rebelled against his ... Lam 1:18
for I *h* grievously rebelled ... Lam 1:20
They *h* heard that I sigh ... Lam 1:21
all mine enemies *h* heard of my ... Lam 1:21
they *h* made a noise in the house ... Lam 2:7
they *h* cast up dust upon their ... Lam 2:10
they *h* girded themselves with ... Lam 2:10
Thy prophets *h* seen vain and ... Lam 2:14
they *h* not discovered thine ... Lam 2:14
but *h* seen for thee false burdens ... Lam 2:14
All thine enemies *h* opened their ... Lam 2:16
they say, We *h* swallowed her up ... Lam 2:16
we *h* found, we *h* seen it ... Lam 2:16
those that I *h* swaddled and ... Lam 2:22
to my mind, therefore *h* I hope ... Lam 3:21
grief, yet will he *h* compassion ... Lam 3:32
h transgressed and *h* rebelled ... Lam 3:42
All our enemies *h* opened their ... Lam 3:46
They *h* cut off my life in the ... Lam 3:53
women *h* sodden their own children ... Lam 4:10
would not *h* believed that the ... Lam 4:12
the enemy should *h* entered into ... Lam 4:12
that *h* shed the blood of the just ... Lam 4:13
They *h* wandered as blind men in ... Lam 4:14
they *h* polluted themselves with ... Lam 4:14
in our watching we *h* watched for ... Lam 4:17
We *h* drunken our water for money ... Lam 5:4
we labour, and *h* no rest ... Lam 5:5
We *h* given the hand to the ... Lam 5:6
Our fathers *h* sinned, and are not ... Lam 5:7
we *h* borne their iniquities ... Lam 5:7
Servants *h* ruled over us ... Lam 5:8
The elders *h* ceased from the gate ... Lam 5:14
woe unto us, that we *h* sinned ... Lam 5:16
their fathers *h* transgressed ... Eze 2:3
they would *h* hearkened unto thee ... Eze 3:6
I *h* made thy face strong against ... Eze 3:8
than flint *h* I made thy forehead ... Eze 3:9
I *h* made thee a watchman unto the ... Eze 3:17
For I *h* laid upon thee the years ... Eze 4:5
I *h* appointed thee each day for a ... Eze 4:6
from my youth up even till now *h* ... Eze 4:14
I *h* given thee cow's dung for ... Eze 4:15
I *h* set it in the midst of the ... Eze 5:5
for they *h* refused my judgments ... Eze 5:6
they *h* not walked in them ... Eze 5:6
h not walked in my statutes, ... Eze 5:7
neither *h* kept my judgments, ... Eze 5:7
neither *h* done according to the ... Eze 5:7
in thee that which I *h* not done ... Eze 5:9
spare, neither will I *h* any pity ... Eze 5:11
I the LORD *h* spoken it in my zeal ... Eze 5:13
when I *h* accomplished my fury in ... Eze 5:13
I the LORD *h* spoken it ... Eze 5:15
I the LORD *h* spoken it ... Eze 5:17
that ye may *h* some that shall ... Eze 6:8 1961
they *h* committed in all their ... Eze 6:9
that I *h* not said in vain that I ... Eze 6:10
spare thee, neither will I *h* pity ... Eze 7:4
not spare, neither will I *h* pity ... Eze 7:9
They *h* blown the trumpet, even to ... Eze 7:14
therefore *h* I set it far from ... Eze 7:20
for they *h* filled the land with ... Eze 8:17
h returned to provoke me to anger ... Eze 8:17
not spare, neither will I *h* pity ... Eze 8:18
Cause them that *h* charge over the ... Eze 9:1
your eye spare, neither *h* ye pity ... Eze 9:5
not spare, neither will I *h* pity ... Eze 9:10
I *h* done as thou hast commanded ... Eze 9:11
Thus *h* ye said, O house of Israel ... Eze 11:5
Ye *h* multiplied your slain in ... Eze 11:6
ye *h* filled the streets thereof ... Eze 11:6
Your slain whom ye *h* laid in the ... Eze 11:7
Ye *h* feared the sword ... Eze 11:8
for ye *h* not walked in my ... Eze 11:12

but *h* done after the manners of ... Eze 11:12
inhabitants of Jerusalem *h* said ... Eze 11:15
Although I *h* cast them far off ... Eze 11:16
although I *h* scattered them among ... Eze 11:16
where ye *h* been scattered ... Eze 11:17
which *h* eyes to see, and see not ... Eze 12:2
they *h* ears to hear, and hear not ... Eze 12:2
for I *h* set thee for a sign unto ... Eze 12:6
like as I *h* done, so shall it be ... Eze 12:11
that ye *h* in the land of Israel ... Eze 12:22
which I *h* spoken shall be done ... Eze 12:28
own spirit, and *h* seen nothing ... Eze 13:3
Ye *h* not gone up into the gaps, ... Eze 13:5
They *h* seen vanity and lying ... Eze 13:6
they *h* made others to hope that ... Eze 13:6
H ye not seen a vain vision ... Eze 13:7
and *h* ye not spoken a lying ... Eze 13:7
albeit I *h* not spoken ... Eze 13:7
Because ye *h* spoken vanity, and ... Eze 13:8
because they *h* seduced my people ... Eze 13:10
daubing wherewith ye *h* daubed it ... Eze 13:12
h daubed with untempered morter ... Eze 13:14
upon them that *h* daubed it with ... Eze 13:15
Because with lies ye *h* made the ... Eze 13:22
sad, whom I *h* not made sad ... Eze 13:22
these men *h* set up their idols in ... Eze 14:3
I the LORD *h* deceived that ... Eze 14:9
that I *h* brought upon Jerusalem ... Eze 14:22
all that I *h* brought upon it ... Eze 14:22
ye shall know that I *h* not done ... Eze 14:23
cause all that I *h* done in it ... Eze 14:23
which I *h* given to the fire for ... Eze 15:6
because they *h* committed a ... Eze 15:8
to *h* compassion upon thee ... Eze 16:5
I *h* caused thee to multiply as ... Eze 16:7
therefore I *h* stretched out my ... Eze 16:27
h diminished thine ordinary food, ... Eze 16:27
know that I the LORD *h* spoken it ... Eze 17:21
LORD *h* brought down the high tree ... Eze 17:24
h exalted the low tree, *h* ... Eze 17:24
h made the dry tree to flourish ... Eze 17:24
the LORD *h* spoken and *h* done it ... Eze 17:24
The fathers *h* eaten sour grapes, ... Eze 18:2
ye shall not *h* occasion any more ... Eze 18:3
H I any pleasure at all that the ... Eze 18:23
whereby ye *h* transgressed ... Eze 18:31
For I *h* no pleasure in the death ... Eze 18:32
this your fathers *h* blasphemed me ... Eze 20:27
in that they *h* committed a ... Eze 20:27
wherein ye *h* been scattered ... Eze 20:41
wherein ye *h* been defiled ... Eze 20:43
your evils that ye *h* committed ... Eze 20:43
when I *h* wrought with you for my ... Eze 20:44
see that I the LORD *h* kindled it ... Eze 20:48
flesh may know that I the LORD *h* ... Eze 21:5
I *h* set the point of the sword ... Eze 21:15
I the LORD *h* said it ... Eze 21:17
sight, to them that *h* sworn oaths ... Eze 21:23
Because ye *h* made your iniquity ... Eze 21:24
when iniquity shall *h* an end ... Eze 21:25
their iniquity shall *h* an end ... Eze 21:29
for I the LORD *h* spoken it ... Eze 21:32
therefore *h* I made thee a ... Eze 22:4
In thee *h* they set light by ... Eze 22:7
in the midst of thee *h* they dealt ... Eze 22:7
in thee *h* they vexed the ... Eze 22:7
In thee *h* they discovered their ... Eze 22:10
in thee *h* they humbled her that ... Eze 22:10
In thee *h* they taken gifts to ... Eze 22:12
therefore I *h* smitten mine hand ... Eze 22:13
I the LORD *h* spoken it, and will ... Eze 22:14
h poured out my fury upon you ... Eze 22:22
they *h* devoured souls ... Eze 22:25
they *h* taken the treasure and ... Eze 22:25
they *h* made her many widows in ... Eze 22:25
Her priests *h* violated my law, and ... Eze 22:26
h profaned mine holy things ... Eze 22:26
they *h* put no difference between ... Eze 22:26
neither *h* they shewed difference ... Eze 22:26
h hid their eyes from my sabbaths ... Eze 22:26
her prophets *h* daubed them with ... Eze 22:28
of the land *h* used oppression ... Eze 22:29
h vexed the poor and needy ... Eze 22:29
they *h* oppressed the stranger ... Eze 22:29
Therefore *h* I poured out mine ... Eze 22:31
I *h* consumed them with the fire ... Eze 22:31
their own way *h* I recompensed ... Eze 22:31
Wherefore I *h* delivered her into ... Eze 23:9
for I *h* spoken it, saith the Lord ... Eze 23:34
That they *h* committed adultery, ... Eze 23:37
with their idols *h* they committed ... Eze 23:37
h also caused their sons, whom ... Eze 23:37
Moreover this they *h* done unto me ... Eze 23:38
they *h* defiled my sanctuary in ... Eze 23:38
day, and *h* profaned my sabbaths ... Eze 23:38
thus *h* they done in the midst of ... Eze 23:39
that ye *h* sent for men to come ... Eze 23:40
I *h* set her blood upon the top of ... Eze 24:8
because I *h* purged thee, and thou ... Eze 24:13
till I *h* caused my fury to rest ... Eze 24:13
I the LORD *h* spoken it ... Eze 24:14
your daughters whom ye *h* left ... Eze 24:21
And ye shall do as I *h* done ... Eze 24:22
Philistines *h* dealt by revenge ... Eze 25:15
and *h* taken vengeance with a ... Eze 25:15
for I *h* spoken it, saith the Lord ... Eze 26:5
for I the LORD *h* spoken it ... Eze 26:14
thy builders *h* perfected thy ... Eze 27:4

They *h* made all thy ship boards ... Eze 27:5
they *h* taken cedars from Lebanon ... Eze 27:5
of Bashan *h* they made thine oars ... Eze 27:6
h made thy benches of ivory ... Eze 27:6
they *h* made thy beauty perfect ... Eze 27:11
Thy rowers *h* brought thee into ... Eze 27:26
for I *h* spoken it, saith the Lord ... Eze 28:10
and I *h* set thee so ... Eze 28:14
of thy merchandise they *h* filled ... Eze 28:16
when I shall *h* executed judgments ... Eze 28:22
When I shall *h* gathered the house ... Eze 28:25
I *h* given to my servant Jacob ... Eze 28:25
when I *h* executed judgments upon ... Eze 28:26
own, and I *h* made it for myself ... Eze 29:3
I *h* given thee for meat to the ... Eze 29:5
because they *h* been a staff of ... Eze 29:6 1961
The river is mine, and I *h* made it ... Eze 29:9
I *h* given him the land of Egypt ... Eze 29:20
when I *h* set a fire in Egypt, and ... Eze 30:8
I the LORD *h* spoken it ... Eze 30:12
Sin shall *h* great pain, and No ... Eze 30:16
Noph shall *h* distresses daily ... Eze 30:16
I *h* broken the arm of Pharaoh ... Eze 30:21
I *h* made him fair by the ... Eze 31:9
I *h* therefore delivered him into ... Eze 31:11
I *h* driven him out for his ... Eze 31:11
h cut him off, and *h* left him ... Eze 31:12
from his shadow, and *h* left him ... Eze 31:12
yet *h* they borne their shame with ... Eze 32:24
They *h* set her a bed in the midst ... Eze 32:25
yet *h* they borne their shame with ... Eze 32:25
they *h* laid their swords under ... Eze 32:27
For I *h* caused my terror in the ... Eze 32:32
I *h* set thee a watchman unto the ... Eze 33:7
I *h* no pleasure in the death of ... Eze 33:11
when I *h* laid the land most ... Eze 33:29
which they *h* committed ... Eze 33:29
The diseased *h* ye not ... Eze 34:4
neither *h* ye healed that which ... Eze 34:4
neither *h* ye bound up that which ... Eze 34:4
neither *h* ye brought again that ... Eze 34:4
neither *h* ye sought that which ... Eze 34:4
with cruelty *h* ye ruled them ... Eze 34:4
h been scattered in the cloudy ... Eze 34:12
to *h* eaten up the good pasture ... Eze 34:18
to *h* drunk of the deep waters, ... Eze 34:18
which ye *h* trodden with your feet ... Eze 34:19
which ye *h* fouled with your feet ... Eze 34:19
Because ye *h* thrust with side and ... Eze 34:21
till ye *h* scattered them abroad ... Eze 34:21
I the LORD *h* spoken it ... Eze 34:24
when I *h* broken the bands of ... Eze 34:27
among them, when I *h* judged thee ... Eze 35:11
LORD, and that I *h* heard all thy ... Eze 35:12
mouth ye *h* boasted against me ... Eze 35:13
h multiplied your words against ... Eze 35:13
I *h* heard them ... Eze 35:13
Because they *h* made you desolate, ... Eze 36:3
in the fire of my jealousy *h* I ... Eze 36:5
which *h* appointed my land into ... Eze 36:5
I *h* spoken in my jealousy and in ... Eze 36:6
because ye *h* borne the shame of ... Eze 36:6
I *h* lifted up mine hand, Surely ... Eze 36:7
which ye *h* profaned among the ... Eze 36:22
which ye *h* profaned in the midst ... Eze 36:23
In the day that I shall *h* ... Eze 36:33
I the LORD *h* spoken it, and I will ... Eze 36:36
when I *h* opened your graves, O my ... Eze 37:13
know that I the LORD *h* spoken it ... Eze 37:14
wherein they *h* sinned, and will ... Eze 37:23
and they all shall *h* one shepherd ... Eze 37:24 1961
I *h* given unto Jacob my servant ... Eze 37:25
wherein your fathers *h* dwelt ... Eze 37:25
which *h* been always waste ... Eze 38:8
which *h* gotten cattle and goods, ... Eze 38:12
Art thou he of whom I *h* spoken in ... Eze 38:17
the fire of my wrath *h* I spoken ... Eze 38:19
for I *h* spoken it, saith the Lord ... Eze 39:5
is the day whereof I *h* spoken ... Eze 39:8
till the buriers *h* buried it in ... Eze 39:15
which I *h* sacrificed for you ... Eze 39:19
see my judgment that I *h* executed ... Eze 39:21
my hand that I *h* laid upon them ... Eze 39:21
transgressions *h* I done unto them ... Eze 39:24
h mercy upon the whole house of ... Eze 39:25
After that they *h* borne their ... Eze 39:26
they *h* trespassed against me ... Eze 39:26
When I *h* brought them again from ... Eze 39:27
but I *h* gathered them unto their ... Eze 39:28
h left none of them any more ... Eze 39:28
for I *h* poured out my spirit upon ... Eze 39:29
about, that they might *h* hold ... Eze 41:6 1961
they *h* even defiled my holy name ... Eze 43:8
that they *h* committed ... Eze 43:8
wherefore I *h* consumed them in ... Eze 43:8
ashamed of all that they *h* done ... Eze 43:11
In that ye *h* brought into my ... Eze 44:7
they *h* broken my covenant because ... Eze 44:7
ye *h* not kept the charge of mine ... Eze 44:8
but ye *h* set keepers of my charge ... Eze 44:8
therefore *h* I lifted up mine hand ... Eze 44:12
which they *h* committed ... Eze 44:13
They shall *h* linen bonnets upon ... Eze 44:18 1961
shall *h* linen breeches upon their ... Eze 44:18 1961
house, *h* for themselves, for a ... Eze 45:5 1961
Ye shall *h* just balances, and a ... Eze 45:10 1961
ye shall *h* the passover, a feast ... Eze 45:21 1961
Joseph shall *h* two portions ... Eze 47:13

they shall *h* inheritance with you ... Eze 47:22 5307
which *h* kept my charge, which ... Eze 48:11
priests the Levites shall *h* five ... Eze 48:13
side, Benjamin shall *h* a portion ... Eze 48:23
side, Simeon shall *h* a portion ... Eze 48:24
I *h* dreamed a dream, and my spirit ... Dan 2:3
for ye *h* prepared lying and ... Dan 2:9
I *h* found a man of the captives ... Dan 2:25
unto me the dream which I *h* seen ... Dan 2:26
that I *h* more than any living ... Dan 2:30 383
men, O king, *h* not regarded thee ... Dan 3:12
the golden image which I *h* set up ... Dan 3:14
worship the image which I *h* made ... Dan 3:15
of the fire, and they *h* no hurt ... Dan 3:25 383
h changed the king's word, and ... Dan 3:28
visions of my dream that I *h* seen ... Dan 4:9
I king Nebuchadnezzar *h* seen ... Dan 4:18
after that thou shalt *h* known ... Dan 4:26
that I *h* built for the house of ... Dan 4:30
h a chain of gold about his neck, ... Dan 5:7
I *h* even heard of thee, that the ... Dan 5:14
h been brought in before me, that ... Dan 5:15
I *h* heard of thee, that thou ... Dan 5:16
h a chain of gold about thy neck, ... Dan 5:16
they *h* brought the vessels of his ... Dan 5:23
concubines, *h* drunk wine in them ... Dan 5:23
and the king should *h* no damage ... Dan 6:2 1934
h consulted together to establish ... Dan 6:7
mouths, that they *h* not hurt me ... Dan 6:22
thee, O king, *h* I done no hurt ... Dan 6:22
We *h* sinned, and *h* committed ... Dan 9:5
h done wickedly, and *h* rebelled ... Dan 9:5
Neither *h* we hearkened unto thy ... Dan 9:6
they *h* trespassed against thee ... Dan 9:7
because we *h* sinned against thee ... Dan 9:8
though we *h* rebelled against him ... Dan 9:9
Neither *h* we obeyed the voice of ... Dan 9:10
all Israel *h* transgressed thy law ... Dan 9:11
because we *h* sinned against him ... Dan 9:11
h sinned, we *h* done wickedly ... Dan 9:15
me, and I *h* retained no strength ... Dan 10:16
strong above him, and *h* dominion ... Dan 11:5
that which his fathers *h* not done ... Dan 11:24
h indignation against the holy ... Dan 11:30
h intelligence with them that ... Dan 11:30
But he shall *h* power over the ... Dan 11:43
when he shall *h* accomplished to ... Dan 12:7
for I will no more *h* mercy upon ... Hos 1:6
But I will *h* mercy upon the house ... Hos 1:7
I will not *h* mercy upon her ... Hos 2:4
rewards that my lovers *h* given me ... Hos 2:12
I will *h* mercy upon her that had ... Hos 2:23
they shall eat, and not *h* enough ... Hos 4:10
because they *h* left off to take ... Hos 4:10
they *h* gone a whoring from under ... Hos 4:12
they *h* committed whoredom ... Hos 4:18
because ye *h* been a snare on ... Hos 5:1 1961
though I *h* been a rebuker of them ... Hos 5:2
they *h* not known the LORD ... Hos 5:4
They *h* dealt treacherously ... Hos 5:7
for they *h* begotten strange ... Hos 5:7
among the tribes of Israel *h* I ... Hos 5:9
Therefore *h* I hewed them by the ... Hos 6:5
I *h* slain them by the words of my ... Hos 6:5
But they like men *h* transgressed ... Hos 6:7
there *h* they dealt treacherously ... Hos 6:7
I *h* seen an horrible thing in the ... Hos 6:10
When I would *h* healed Israel, ... Hos 7:1
own doings *h* beset them about ... Hos 7:2
h made him sick with bottles of ... Hos 7:5
For they *h* made ready their heart ... Hos 7:6
oven, and *h* devoured their judges ... Hos 7:7
Strangers *h* devoured his strength ... Hos 7:9
for they *h* fled from me ... Hos 7:13
because they *h* transgressed ... Hos 7:13
though I *h* redeemed them ... Hos 7:13
yet they *h* spoken lies against me ... Hos 7:13
they *h* not cried unto me with ... Hos 7:14
Though I *h* bound and strengthened ... Hos 7:15
because they *h* transgressed my ... Hos 8:1
They *h* set up kings, but not by ... Hos 8:4
they *h* made princes, and I knew it ... Hos 8:4
their gold *h* they made them idols ... Hos 8:4
For they *h* sown the wind, and they ... Hos 8:7
though they *h* hired among the ... Hos 8:10
I *h* written to him the great ... Hos 8:12
They *h* deeply corrupted ... Hos 9:9
land they *h* made goodly images ... Hos 10:1
We *h* no king, because we feared ... Hos 10:3
They *h* spoken words, swearing ... Hos 10:4
Ye *h* plowed wickedness, ye *h* ... Hos 10:13
ye *h* eaten the fruit of lies ... Hos 10:13
I *h* found me out substance ... Hos 12:8
I *h* also spoken by the prophets, ... Hos 12:10
I *h* multiplied visions, and used ... Hos 12:10
h made them molten images of ... Hos 13:2
therefore *h* they forgotten me ... Hos 13:6
What *h* I to do any more with ... Hos 14:8
I *h* heard him, and observed him ... Hos 14:8
because they *h* no pasture ... Joel 1:18
whom they *h* scattered among the ... Joel 3:2
they *h* cast lots for my people ... Joel 3:3
h given a boy for an harlot, and ... Joel 3:3
what *h* ye to do with me, O Tyre, ... Joel 3:4
Because ye *h* taken my silver and ... Joel 3:5
h carried into your temples my ... Joel 3:5
h ye sold unto the Grecians ... Joel 3:6
the place whither ye *h* sold them ... Joel 3:7
because they *h* shed innocent ... Joel 3:19
their blood that I *h* not cleansed ... Joel 3:21
because they *h* threshed Gilead ... Amos 1:3
because they *h* ripped up the ... Amos 1:13
because they *h* despised the law ... Amos 2:4
h not kept his commandments, and ... Amos 2:4
the which their fathers *h* walked ... Amos 2:4
You only *h* I known of all the ... Amos 3:2
of his den, if he *h* taken nothing ... Amos 3:4
earth, and *h* taken nothing at all ... Amos 3:5
the great houses shall *h* an end ... Amos 3:15
I also *h* given you cleanness of ... Amos 4:6
yet *h* ye not returned unto me, ... Amos 4:6
also I *h* withholden the rain from ... Amos 4:7
yet *h* ye not returned unto me, ... Amos 4:8
I *h* smitten you with blasting and ... Amos 4:9
yet *h* ye not returned unto me, ... Amos 4:9
I *h* sent among you the pestilence ... Amos 4:10
your young men *h* I slain with the ... Amos 4:10
and *h* taken away your horses ... Amos 4:10
I *h* made the stink of your camps ... Amos 4:10
yet *h* ye not returned unto me, ... Amos 4:10
I *h* overthrown some of you, as ... Amos 4:11
yet *h* ye not returned unto me, ... Amos 4:11
ye *h* built houses of hewn stone, ... Amos 5:11
ye *h* planted pleasant vineyards, ... Amos 5:11
shall be with you, as ye *h* spoken ... Amos 5:14
H ye offered unto me sacrifices ... Amos 5:25
But ye *h* borne the tabernacle of ... Amos 5:26
for ye *h* turned judgment into ... Amos 6:12
H we not taken to us horns by our ... Amos 6:13
H not I brought up Israel out of ... Amos 9:7
their land which I *h* given them ... Amos 9:15
We *h* heard a rumour from the LORD ... Obad 1
I *h* made thee small among the ... Obad 2
would they not *h* stolen till ... Obad 5
All the men of thy confederacy *h* ... Obad 7
peace with thee *h* deceived thee ... Obad 7
bread *h* laid a wound under thee ... Obad 7
But thou shouldest not *h* looked ... Obad 12
neither shouldest thou *h* rejoiced ... Obad 12
neither shouldest thou *h* spoken ... Obad 12
Thou shouldest not *h* entered into ... Obad 13
thou shouldest not *h* looked on ... Obad 13
nor *h* laid hands on their ... Obad 13
thou *h* stood in the crossway ... Obad 14
neither shouldest thou *h* ... Obad 14
For as ye *h* drunk upon my holy ... Obad 16
I will pay that that I *h* vowed ... Jonah 2:9
Therefore thou shalt *h* none that ... Mic 2:5 1961
The women of my people *h* ye cast ... Mic 2:9
from their children *h* ye taken ... Mic 2:9
they *h* broken up, and *h* passed ... Mic 2:13
as they *h* behaved themselves ill ... Mic 3:4
you, that ye shall not *h* a vision ... Mic 3:6
out, and her that I *h* afflicted ... Mic 4:6
for pangs *h* taken thee as a woman ... Mic 4:9
goings forth *h* been from of old ... Mic 5:2
thou shalt *h* no more soothsayers ... Mic 5:12 1961
heathen, such as they *h* not heard ... Mic 5:15
people, what *h* I done unto thee ... Mic 6:3
and wherein *h* I wearied thee ... Mic 6:3
inhabitants thereof *h* spoken lies ... Mic 6:12
for I am as when they *h* gathered ... Mic 7:1
because I *h* sinned against him, ... Mic 7:9
he will *h* compassion upon us ... Mic 7:19
Though I *h* afflicted thee, I will ... Nah 1:12
the emptiers *h* emptied them out ... Nah 2:2
that *h* no ruler over them ... Hab 1:14
I *h* heard thy speech, and was ... Hab 3:2
those that *h* not sought the LORD, ... Zeph 1:6
because they *h* sinned against the ... Zeph 1:17
which *h* wrought his judgment ... Zeph 2:3
I *h* heard the reproach of Moab, ... Zeph 2:8
whereby they *h* reproached my ... Zeph 2:8
This shall they *h* for their pride ... Zeph 2:10
because they *h* reproached ... Zeph 2:10
her priests *h* polluted the ... Zeph 3:4
they *h* done violence to the law ... Zeph 3:4
I *h* cut off the nations ... Zeph 3:6
where they *h* been put to shame ... Zeph 3:19
Ye *h* sown much, and bring in ... Hag 1:6
ye eat, but ye *h* not enough ... Hag 1:6
for I *h* chosen thee, saith the ... Hag 2:23
whom the former prophets *h* cried ... Zec 1:4
We *h* walked to and fro through the ... Zec 1:11
thou not *h* mercy on Jerusalem ... Zec 1:12
the horns which *h* scattered Judah ... Zec 1:19
the horns which *h* scattered Judah ... Zec 1:21
for I *h* spread you abroad as the ... Zec 2:6
I *h* caused thine iniquity to pass ... Zec 3:4
stone that I *h* laid before Joshua ... Zec 3:9
I said, I *h* looked, and behold a ... Zec 4:2
The hands of Zerubbabel *h* laid ... Zec 4:9
go toward the north country *h* ... Zec 6:8
as I *h* done these so many years ... Zec 7:3
So again *h* I thought in these ... Zec 8:15
for we *h* heard that God is with ... Zec 8:23
for now *h* I seen with mine eyes ... Zec 9:8
by the blood of thy covenant I *h* ... Zec 9:11
When I *h* bent Judah for me, ... Zec 9:13
For the idols *h* spoken vanity ... Zec 10:2
and the diviners *h* seen a lie ... Zec 10:2
and *h* told false dreams ... Zec 10:2
for I *h* mercy upon them ... Zec 10:6
for I *h* redeemed them ... Zec 10:8
increase as they *h* increased ... Zec 10:8
look upon me whom they *h* pierced ... Zec 12:10
that *h* fought against Jerusalem ... Zec 14:12
up, and come not, that *h* no rain ... Zec 14:18
I *h* loved you, saith the LORD ... Mal 1:2
Wherein *h* we despised thy name ... Mal 1:6
Wherein *h* we polluted thee ... Mal 1:7
I *h* no pleasure in you, saith the ... Mal 1:10
But ye *h* profaned it, in that ye ... Mal 1:12
ye *h* snuffed at it, saith the ... Mal 1:13
I *h* cursed them already, because ... Mal 2:2
ye shall know that I *h* sent this ... Mal 2:4
ye *h* caused many to stumble at ... Mal 2:8
ye *h* corrupted the covenant of ... Mal 2:8
Therefore *h* I also made you ... Mal 2:9
according as ye *h* not kept my ... Mal 2:9
but *h* been partial in the law ... Mal 2:9
H we not all one father ... Mal 2:10
this *h* ye done again, covering ... Mal 2:13
Ye *h* wearied the LORD with your ... Mal 2:17
ye say, Wherein *h* we wearied him ... Mal 2:17
ordinances, and *h* not kept them ... Mal 3:7
Yet ye *h* robbed me ... Mal 3:8
ye say, Wherein *h* we robbed thee ... Mal 3:8
for ye *h* robbed me, even this ... Mal 3:9
Your words *h* been stout against ... Mal 3:13
What *h* we spoken so much against ... Mal 3:13
Ye *h* said, It is vain to serve ... Mal 3:14
it that we *h* kept his ordinance ... Mal 3:14
that we *h* walked mournfully ... Mal 3:14
for we *h* seen his star in the ... Mt 2:2
when ye *h* found him, bring me ... Mt 2:8
Out of Egypt *h* I called my son ... Mt 2:15
We *h* Abraham to our father ... Mt 3:9 *2192*
I *h* need to be baptized of thee, ... Mt 3:14 *2192*
but if the salt *h* lost his savour ... Mt 5:13
Ye *h* heard that it was said by ... Mt 5:21
Ye *h* heard that it was said by ... Mt 5:27
ye *h* heard that it hath been said ... Mt 5:33
Ye *h* heard that it hath been said ... Mt 5:38
coat, let him *h* thy cloke also ... Mt 5:40 *863*
Ye *h* heard that it hath been said ... Mt 5:43
which love you, what reward *h* ye ... Mt 5:46 *2192*
otherwise ye *h* no reward of your ... Mt 6:1 *2192*
that they may *h* glory of men ... Mt 6:2
say unto you, They *h* their reward ... Mt 6:2 *568*
say unto you, They *h* their reward ... Mt 6:5 *568*
knoweth what things ye *h* need of ... Mt 6:8 *2192*
say unto you, They *h* their reward ... Mt 6:16 *568*
ye *h* need of all these things ... Mt 6:32
h we not prophesied in thy name ... Mt 7:22
in thy name *h* cast out devils ... Mt 7:22
I *h* not found so great faith, no, ... Mt 8:10
saith unto him, The foxes *h* holes ... Mt 8:20 *2192*
and the birds of the air *h* nests ... Mt 8:20
What *h* we to do with thee, Jesus, ... Mt 8:29
what that meaneth, I will *h* mercy ... Mt 9:13 *2309*
Thou son of David, *h* mercy on us ... Mt 9:27
freely ye *h* received, freely give ... Mt 10:8
Ye shall not *h* gone over the ... Mt 10:23
If they *h* called the master of ... Mt 10:25
the poor *h* the gospel preached to ... Mt 11:5
We *h* piped unto you, and ye *h* ... Mt 11:17
we *h* mourned unto you, and ye *h* ... Mt 11:17
they would *h* repented long ago in ... Mt 11:21
which *h* been done in thee, had ... Mt 11:23
it would *h* remained until this ... Mt 11:23
H ye not read what David did, ... Mt 12:3
Or *h* ye not read in the law, how ... Mt 12:5
what this meaneth, I will *h* mercy ... Mt 12:7 *2309*
ye would not *h* condemned the ... Mt 12:7
among you, that shall *h* one sheep ... Mt 12:11 2192
my servant, whom I *h* chosen ... Mt 12:18
he shall *h* more abundance ... Mt 13:12
and their eyes they *h* closed ... Mt 13:15
righteous men *h* desired to see ... Mt 13:17
which ye see, and *h* not seen them ... Mt 13:17
ye hear, and *h* not heard them ... Mt 13:17
which *h* been kept secret from the ... Mt 13:35
H ye understood all these things ... Mt 13:51
is not lawful for thee to *h* her ... Mt 14:4 *2192*
when he would *h* put him to death, ... Mt 14:5
We *h* here but five loaves, and two ... Mt 14:17 *2192*
Thus *h* ye made the commandment of ... Mt 15:6
H mercy on me, O Lord, thou son ... Mt 15:22
I *h* compassion on the multitude, ... Mt 15:32
three days, and *h* nothing to eat ... Mt 15:32 *2192*
Whence should we *h* so much bread ... Mt 15:33
unto them, How many loaves *h* ye ... Mt 15:34 *2192*
It is because we *h* taken no bread ... Mt 16:7
because ye *h* brought no bread ... Mt 16:8
but *h* done unto him whatsoever ... Mt 17:12
Lord, *h* mercy on my son ... Mt 17:15
If ye *h* faith as a grain of ... Mt 17:20 *2192*
if a man *h* an hundred sheep, and ... Mt 18:12 *1099*
h patience with me, and I will pay ... Mt 18:26
H patience with me, and I will pay ... Mt 18:29
thou also *h* had compassion on thy ... Mt 18:33
H ye not read, that he which made ... Mt 19:4
which *h* made themselves eunuchs ... Mt 19:12
that I may *h* eternal life ... Mt 19:16 *2192*
All these things *h* I kept from my ... Mt 19:20
thou shalt *h* treasure in heaven ... Mt 19:21 *2192*
we *h* forsaken all, and followed ... Mt 19:27
what shall we *h* therefore ... Mt 19:27 *2701*
you, That ye which *h* followed me ... Mt 19:28
that they should *h* received more ... Mt 20:10
These last *h* wrought but one hour ... Mt 20:12
which *h* borne the burden and heat ... Mt 20:12
H mercy on us, O Lord, thou son ... Mt 20:30

H mercy on us, O Lord, thou son .... Mt 20:31
but ye *h* made it a den of thieves .... Mt 21:13
h ye never read, Out of the mouth .... Mt 21:16
I say unto you, If ye *h* faith .... Mt 21:21 *2192*
Behold, I *h* prepared my dinner .... Mt 22:4
h ye not read that which was .... Mt 22:31
h omitted the weightier matters .... Mt 23:23
these ought ye to *h* done, and not .... Mt 23:23
we would not *h* been partakers .... Mt 23:30
how often would I *h* gathered thy .... Mt 23:37
Behold, I *h* told you before .... Mt 24:25
would come, he would *h* watched .... Mt 24:43
would not *h* suffered his house to .... Mt 24:43
I *h* gained beside them five .... Mt 25:20
I *h* gained two other talents .... Mt 25:22
and gather where I *h* not strawed .... Mt 25:26
Thou oughtest therefore to *h* put .... Mt 25:27
then at my coming I should *h* .... Mt 25:27
be given, and he shall *h* abundance .... Mt 25:29
Inasmuch as ye *h* done it unto one .... Mt 25:40
my brethren, ye *h* done it unto me .... Mt 25:40
might *h* been sold for much .... Mt 26:9
For ye *h* the poor always with you .... Mt 26:11 *2192*
but me ye *h* not always .... Mt 26:11 *2192*
further need *h* we of witnesses .... Mt 26:65 *2192*
now ye *h* heard his blasphemy .... Mt 26:65
I *h* sinned in that I *h* .... Mt 27:4
H thou nothing to do with that .... Mt 27:19
for I *h* suffered many things this .... Mt 27:19
deliver him now, if he will *h* him .... Mt 27:43 *2309*
said unto them, Ye *h* a watch .... Mt 27:65 *2192*
lo, I *h* told you .... Mt 28:7
whatsoever I *h* commanded you .... Mt 28:20
I indeed *h* baptized you with .... Mk 1:8
what *h* we to do with thee, thou .... Mk 1:24
They that are whole *h* no need of .... Mk 2:17 *2192*
as long as they *h* the bridegroom .... Mk 2:19 *2192*
H ye never read what David did .... Mk 2:25
to *h* power to heal sicknesses, and .... Mk 3:15 *2192*
but when they *h* heard, Satan .... Mk 4:15
when they *h* heard the word .... Mk 4:16
h no root in themselves, and so .... Mk 4:17 *2192*
If any man *h* ears to hear, let .... Mk 4:23 *2192*
how is it that ye *h* no faith .... Mk 4:40 *2192*
What *h* I to do with thee, Jesus .... Mk 5:7
for thee to *h* thy brother's wife .... Mk 6:18 *2192*
him, and would *h* killed him .... Mk 6:19
for they *h* nothing to eat .... Mk 6:36 *2192*
unto them, How many loaves *h* ye .... Mk 6:38 *2192*
sea, and would *h* passed by them .... Mk 6:48
which they *h* received to hold, as .... Mk 7:4
tradition, which ye *h* delivered .... Mk 7:13
If any man *h* ears to hear, let .... Mk 7:16 *2192*
house, and would *h* no man know it .... Mk 7:24
I *h* compassion on the multitude .... Mk 8:2
because they *h* now been with me .... Mk 8:2
three days, and *h* nothing to eat .... Mk 8:2 *2192*
asked them, How many loaves *h* ye .... Mk 8:5 *2192*
It is because we *h* no bread .... Mk 8:16 *2192*
reason ye, because ye *h* no bread .... Mk 8:17 *2192*
h ye your heart yet hardened .... Mk 8:17 *2192*
till they *h* seen the kingdom of .... Mk 9:1
they *h* done unto him whatsoever .... Mk 9:13
I *h* brought unto thee my son .... Mk 9:17
h compassion on us, and help us .... Mk 9:22
but if the salt *h* lost his .... Mk 9:50
H salt in yourselves .... Mk 9:50 *2192*
and *h* peace one with another .... Mk 9:50
all these *h* I observed from my .... Mk 10:20
thou shalt *h* treasure in heaven .... Mk 10:21 *2192*
How hardly shall they that *h* .... Mk 10:23 *2192*
we *h* left all .... Mk 10:28 *2192*
and *h* followed thee .... Mk 10:28
thou son of David, *h* mercy on me .... Mk 10:47
Thou son of David, *h* mercy on me .... Mk 10:48
but ye *h* made it a den of thieves .... Mk 11:17
saith unto them, *H* faith in God .... Mk 11:22 *2192*
he shall *h* whatsoever he saith .... Mk 11:23 *2071*
receive them, and ye shall *h* them .... Mk 11:24 *2071*
if ye *h* ought against any .... Mk 11:25 *2192*
h ye not read this scripture .... Mk 12:10
h ye not read in the book of .... Mk 12:26
than all they which *h* cast into .... Mk 12:43
I *h* foretold you all things .... Mk 13:23
For it might *h* been sold for more .... Mk 14:5
and *h* been given to the poor .... Mk 14:5
For ye *h* the poor with you always .... Mk 14:7 *3103*
but me ye *h* not always .... Mk 14:7 *2192*
Ye *h* heard the blasphemy .... Mk 14:64
Forasmuch as many *h* taken in hand .... Lk 1:1
And thou shalt *h* joy and gladness .... Lk 1:14 *2071*
father, how he would *h* him called .... Lk 1:62
which *h* been since the world .... Lk 1:70
For mine eyes *h* seen thy .... Lk 2:30
supposing him to *h* been in the .... Lk 2:44
I *h* sought thee sorrowing .... Lk 2:48
We *h* Abraham to our father .... Lk 3:8 *2192*
whatsoever we *h* heard done in .... Lk 4:23
what *h* we to do with thee, thou .... Lk 4:34
we *h* toiled all the night .... Lk 5:5
and *h* taken nothing .... Lk 5:5
We *h* seen strange things to day .... Lk 5:26
H ye not read so much as this .... Lk 6:3
for ye *h* received your .... Lk 6:24
which love you, what thank *h* ye .... Lk 6:32 *2076*
do good to you, what thank *h* ye .... Lk 6:33 *2076*
hope to receive, what thank *h* ye .... Lk 6:34 *2076*
I *h* not found so great faith, no .... Lk 7:9
tell John what things ye *h* seen .... Lk 7:22
We *h* piped unto you, and ye *h* .... Lk 7:32
we *h* mourned to you, and ye *h* .... Lk 7:32
would *h* known who and what .... Lk 7:39
I *h* somewhat to say unto thee .... Lk 7:40 *2192*
these *h* no root, which for a .... Lk 8:13 *2192*
they, which, when they *h* heard .... Lk 8:14
even that which he seemeth to *h* .... Lk 8:18 *2192*
What *h* I to do with thee, Jesus .... Lk 8:28
neither *h* two coats apiece .... Lk 9:3 *2192*
And Herod said, John *h* I beheaded .... Lk 9:9
We *h* no more but five loaves and .... Lk 9:13 *2076*
said unto him, Foxes *h* holes .... Lk 9:58 *2192*
and birds of the air *h* nests .... Lk 9:58
which *h* been done in you, they .... Lk 10:13
kings *h* desired to see those .... Lk 10:24
which ye see, and *h* not seen them .... Lk 10:24
ye hear, and *h* not heard them .... Lk 10:24
Which of you shall *h* a friend .... Lk 11:5 *2192*
I *h* nothing to set before him .... Lk 11:6 *2192*
give alms of such things as ye *h* .... Lk 11:41 *1751*
these ought ye to *h* done, and not .... Lk 11:42
for ye *h* taken away the key of .... Lk 11:52
Therefore whatsoever ye *h* spoken .... Lk 12:3
that which ye *h* spoken in the ear .... Lk 12:3
after that *h* no more that they .... Lk 12:4 *2192*
because I *h* no room where to .... Lk 12:17 *2192*
which neither *h* storehouse nor .... Lk 12:24 *2076*
that ye *h* need of these things .... Lk 12:30
Sell that ye *h*, and give alms .... Lk 12:33 *5224*
would come, he would *h* watched .... Lk 12:39
not *h* suffered his house to be .... Lk 12:39
to whom men *h* committed much, of .... Lk 12:48
But I *h* a baptism to be baptized .... Lk 12:50 *2192*
We *h* eaten and drunk in thy .... Lk 13:26
how often would I *h* gathered thy .... Lk 13:34
Which of you shall *h* an ass or an .... Lk 14:5
then shalt thou *h* worship in the .... Lk 14:10 *2071*
I *h* bought a piece of ground, and .... Lk 14:18
I pray thee *h* me excused .... Lk 14:18 *2192*
I *h* bought five yoke of oxen, and .... Lk 14:19
I pray thee *h* me excused .... Lk 14:19 *2192*
I *h* married a wife, and therefore .... Lk 14:20
whether he *h* sufficient to finish .... Lk 14:28 *2192*
but if the salt *h* lost his savour .... Lk 14:34
for I *h* found my sheep which was .... Lk 15:6
for I *h* found the piece which I .... Lk 15:9
he would fain *h* filled his belly .... Lk 15:16
of my father's *h* bread enough .... Lk 15:17 *4052*
I *h* sinned against heaven, and .... Lk 15:18
I *h* sinned against heaven, and in .... Lk 15:21
with me, and all that I *h* is thine .... Lk 15:31 *1699*
If therefore ye *h* not been .... Lk 16:11
if ye *h* not been faithful in that .... Lk 16:12
h mercy on me, and send Lazarus .... Lk 16:24
For I *h* five brethren .... Lk 16:28 *2192*
They *h* Moses and the prophets .... Lk 16:29 2192
and serve me, till I *h* eaten .... Lk 17:8
when ye shall *h* done all those .... Lk 17:10
we *h* done that which was our duty .... Lk 17:10
Jesus, Master, *h* mercy on us .... Lk 17:13
All these *h* I kept from my youth .... Lk 18:21
thou shalt *h* treasure in heaven .... Lk 18:22 *2192*
How hardly shall they that *h* .... Lk 18:24 *2192*
we *h* left all, and followed thee .... Lk 18:28
thou son of David, *h* mercy on me .... Lk 18:38
Thou son of David, *h* mercy on me .... Lk 18:39
if I *h* taken any thing from any .... Lk 19:8
We will not *h* this man to reign .... Lk 19:14
h thou authority over ten cities .... Lk 19:17 *2192*
which I *h* kept laid up in a .... Lk 19:20
that at my coming I might *h* .... Lk 19:23
but ye *h* made it a den of thieves .... Lk 19:46
For all these *h* of their .... Lk 21:4
With desire I *h* desired to eat .... Lk 22:15
Ye are they which *h* continued .... Lk 22:28
Satan hath desired to *h* you .... Lk 22:31
But I *h* prayed for thee, that thy .... Lk 22:32
the things concerning me *h* an end .... Lk 22:37 *2192*
for we ourselves *h* heard of his .... Lk 22:71
he hoped to *h* seen some miracle .... Lk 23:8
Ye *h* brought this man unto me, as .... Lk 23:14
h found no fault in this man .... Lk 23:14
I *h* found no cause of death in .... Lk 23:22
these that ye *h* one to another .... Lk 24:17 *474*
to death, and *h* crucified him .... Lk 24:20
he which should *h* redeemed Israel .... Lk 24:21
all that the prophets *h* spoken .... Lk 24:25
Ought not Christ to *h* suffered .... Lk 24:26
as though he would *h* gone further .... Lk 24:28
flesh and bones, as ye see me *h* .... Lk 24:39 *2192*
unto them, *H* ye here any meat .... Lk 24:41 *2192*
of his fulness *h* all we received .... Jn 1:16
We *h* found the Messias, which is .... Jn 1:41
We *h* found him, of whom Moses in .... Jn 1:45
saith unto him, They *h* no wine .... Jn 2:3 *2192*
Woman, what *h* I to do with thee .... Jn 2:4
when men *h* well drunk, then that .... Jn 2:10
know, and testify that we *h* seen .... Jn 3:11
If I *h* told you earthly things .... Jn 3:12
not perish, but *h* eternal life .... Jn 3:15 *2192*
perish, but *h* everlasting life .... Jn 3:16 *2192*
for the Jews *h* no dealings with .... Jn 4:9
thou wouldest *h* asked of him .... Jn 4:10
he would *h* given thee living .... Jn 4:10
answered and said, I *h* no husband .... Jn 4:17 *2192*
hast well said, I *h* no husband .... Jn 4:17 *2192*
I *h* meat to eat that ye know not .... Jn 4:32 *2192*
for we *h* heard him ourselves, and .... Jn 4:42
I *h* no man, when the water is .... Jn 5:7 *2192*
to the Son to *h* life in himself .... Jn 5:26 *2192*
they that *h* done good, unto the .... Jn 5:29
and they that *h* done evil, unto .... Jn 5:29
But I *h* greater witness than that .... Jn 5:36 *2192*
Ye *h* neither heard his voice at .... Jn 5:37
ye *h* not his word abiding in you .... Jn 5:38 *2192*
them ye think ye *h* eternal life .... Jn 5:39 *2192*
come to me, that ye might *h* life .... Jn 5:40 *2192*
that ye *h* not the love of God in .... Jn 5:42 *2192*
Moses, ye would *h* believed me .... Jn 5:46
unto you, That ye also *h* seen me .... Jn 6:36
on him, may *h* everlasting life .... Jn 6:40 *2192*
his blood, ye *h* no life in you .... Jn 6:53 *2192*
H not I chosen you twelve, and one .... Jn 6:70
I *h* done one work, and ye all .... Jn 7:21
because I *h* made a man every whit .... Jn 7:23
And some of them would *h* taken him .... Jn 7:44
them, Why *h* ye not brought him .... Jn 7:45
H any of the rulers or of the .... Jn 7:48
that they might *h* to accuse him .... Jn 8:6 *2192*
but shall *h* the light of life .... Jn 8:12 *2192*
ye should *h* known my Father also .... Jn 8:19
I *h* many things to say and to .... Jn 8:26 *2192*
things which I *h* heard of him .... Jn 8:26
When ye *h* lifted up the Son of .... Jn 8:28
which I *h* seen with my Father .... Jn 8:38
ye do that which ye *h* seen with .... Jn 8:38
the truth, which I *h* heard of God .... Jn 8:40
we *h* one Father, even God .... Jn 8:41 *2192*
Jesus answered, I *h* not a devil .... Jn 8:49 *2192*
Yet ye *h* not known him .... Jn 8:55
I *h* told you already, and ye did .... Jn 9:27
ye were blind, ye should *h* no sin .... Jn 9:41 *2192*
I am come that they might *h* life .... Jn 10:10 *2192*
that they might *h* it more .... Jn 10:10 *2192*
And other sheep I *h*, which are not .... Jn 10:16 *2192*
I *h* power to lay it down .... Jn 10:18 *2192*
I *h* power to take it again .... Jn 10:18 *2192*
This commandment *h* I received of .... Jn 10:18
Many good works *h* I shewed you .... Jn 10:32
And said, Where *h* ye laid him .... Jn 11:34
h caused that even this man .... Jn 11:37
even this man should not *h* died .... Jn 11:37
For the poor always ye *h* with you .... Jn 12:8 *2192*
but me ye *h* not always .... Jn 12:8 *2192*
I *h* both glorified it, and will .... Jn 12:28
We *h* heard out of the law that .... Jn 12:34
Walk while ye *h* the light .... Jn 12:35 *2192*
While ye *h* light, believe in the .... Jn 12:36 *2192*
the word that I *h* spoken, the .... Jn 12:48
For I *h* not spoken of myself .... Jn 12:49
Know ye what I *h* done to you .... Jn 13:12
and Master, *h* washed your feet .... Jn 13:14
For I *h* given you an example .... Jn 13:15
ye should do as I *h* done to you .... Jn 13:15
I know whom I *h* chosen .... Jn 13:18
give a sop, when I *h* dipped it .... Jn 13:26
Buy those things that we *h* need .... Jn 13:29 *2192*
as I *h* loved you, that ye also .... Jn 13:34
if ye *h* love one to another .... Jn 13:35 *2192*
were not so, I would *h* told you .... Jn 14:2
ye should *h* known my Father also .... Jn 14:7
ye know him, and *h* seen him .... Jn 14:7
H I been so long time with you .... Jn 14:9 *1510*
These things *h* I spoken unto you .... Jn 14:25
whatsoever I *h* said unto you .... Jn 14:26
Ye *h* heard how I said unto you, I .... Jn 14:28
now I *h* told you before it come .... Jn 14:29
word which I *h* spoken unto you .... Jn 15:3
hath loved me, so *h* I loved you .... Jn 15:9
even as I *h* kept my Father's .... Jn 15:10
These things *h* I spoken unto you .... Jn 15:11
one another, as I *h* loved you .... Jn 15:12
but I *h* called you friends .... Jn 15:15
for all things that I *h* heard of .... Jn 15:15
my Father I *h* made known unto you .... Jn 15:15
Ye *h* not chosen me, but I *h* .... Jn 15:16
but I *h* chosen you out of the .... Jn 15:19
If they *h* persecuted me, they .... Jn 15:20
if they *h* kept my saying, they .... Jn 15:20
but now they *h* no cloke for their .... Jn 15:22 2192
but now *h* they both seen and hated .... Jn 15:24
because ye *h* been with me from .... Jn 15:27 *2075*
These things *h* I spoken unto you .... Jn 16:1
because they *h* not known the .... Jn 16:3
But these things *h* I told you .... Jn 16:4
But because I *h* said these things .... Jn 16:6
I *h* yet many things to say unto .... Jn 16:12 2192
And ye now therefore *h* sorrow .... Jn 16:22 2192
Hitherto *h* ye asked nothing in my .... Jn 16:24
These things *h* I spoken unto you .... Jn 16:25
loveth you, because ye *h* loved me .... Jn 16:27
h believed that I came out from .... Jn 16:27
These things I *h* spoken unto you .... Jn 16:33
that in me ye might *h* peace .... Jn 16:33 *2192*
the world ye shall *h* tribulation .... Jn 16:33 *2192*
I *h* overcome the world .... Jn 16:33
I *h* glorified thee on the earth .... Jn 17:4
I *h* finished the work which thou .... Jn 17:4
I *h* manifested thy name unto the .... Jn 17:6
and they *h* kept thy word .... Jn 17:6
Now they *h* known that all things .... Jn 17:7
For I *h* given unto them the words .... Jn 17:8
they *h* received them, and *h* .... Jn 17:8
they *h* believed that thou didst .... Jn 17:8
that thou gavest me I *h* kept .... Jn 17:12

world, that they might *h* my joy ... Jn 17:13 2192
I *h* given them thy word ... Jn 17:14
even so *h* I also sent them into ... Jn 17:18
thou gavest me I *h* given them ... Jn 17:22
but I *h* known thee, and these *h* ... Jn 17:25
I *h* declared unto them thy name, ... Jn 17:26
I *h* told you that I am he ... Jn 18:8
thou gavest me *h* I lost none ... Jn 18:9
in secret *h* I said nothing ... Jn 18:20
heard me, what I *h* said unto them ... Jn 18:21
If I *h* spoken evil, bear witness ... Jn 18:23
we would not *h* delivered him up ... Jn 18:30
the chief priests *h* delivered ... Jn 18:35
But ye *h* a custom, that I should ... Jn 18:39 2076
We *h* a law, and by our law he ... Jn 19:7 2192
that I *h* power to crucify thee ... Jn 19:10 2192
and *h* power to release thee ... Jn 19:10 2192
Thou couldest *h* no power at all ... Jn 19:11 2192
answered, We *h* no king but Caesar ... Jn 19:15 2192
What I *h* written I *h* written ... Jn 19:22
They *h* taken away the Lord out of ... Jn 20:2
we know not where they *h* laid him ... Jn 20:2
Because they *h* taken away my Lord ... Jn 20:13
I know not where they *h* laid him ... Jn 20:13
if thou *h* borne him hence, tell ... Jn 20:15
said unto him, We *h* seen the Lord ... Jn 20:25
blessed are they that *h* not seen ... Jn 20:29
and yet *h* believed ... Jn 20:29
ye might *h* life through his name ... Jn 20:31 2192
them, Children, *h* ye any meat ... Jn 21:5 2192
of the fish which ye *h* now caught ... Jn 21:10
The former treatise *h* I made ... Acts 1:1
which, saith he, ye *h* heard of me ... Acts 1:4
as ye *h* seen him go into heaven ... Acts 1:11
must needs *h* been fulfilled ... Acts 1:16
Wherefore of these men which *h* ... Acts 1:21
ye *h* taken, and by wicked hands ... Acts 2:23
and by wicked hands *h* crucified ... Acts 2:23
whom ye *h* crucified, both Lord and ... Acts 2:36
said, Silver and gold *h* I none ... Acts 3:6 5225
but such as I *h* give I thee ... Acts 3:6 2192
follow after, as many as *h* spoken ... Acts 3:24
h likewise foretold of these days ... Acts 3:24
or by what name, *h* ye done this ... Acts 4:7
speak the things which we *h* seen ... Acts 4:20
How is it that ye *h* agreed ... Acts 5:9
the feet of them which *h* buried ... Acts 5:9
to the prison to *h* them brought ... Acts 5:21
lest they should *h* been stoned ... Acts 5:26
ye *h* filled Jerusalem with your ... Acts 5:28
We *h* heard him speak blasphemous ... Acts 6:11
For we *h* heard him say, that this ... Acts 6:14
h understood how that God by his ... Acts 7:25
would *h* set them at one again, ... Acts 7:26
I *h* seen, I *h* seen the ... Acts 7:34
I *h* heard their groaning, and am ... Acts 7:34
h ye offered to me slain beasts ... Acts 7:42
Which of the prophets *h* not your ... Acts 7:52
they *h* slain them which shewed ... Acts 7:52
of whom ye *h* been now the ... Acts 7:52 1096
Who *h* received the law by the ... Acts 7:53
of angels, and *h* not kept it ... Acts 7:53
which ye *h* spoken come upon me ... Acts 8:24
Lord, what wilt thou *h* me to do ... Acts 9:6
I *h* heard by many of this man, ... Acts 9:13
very hungry, and would *h* eaten ... Acts 10:10
for I *h* never eaten any thing ... Acts 10:14
for I *h* sent them ... Acts 10:20
for what intent ye *h* sent for me ... Acts 10:29
which *h* received the Holy Ghost ... Acts 10:47
when Herod would *h* brought him ... Acts 12:6
work whereunto I *h* called them ... Acts 13:2
if ye *h* any word of exhortation ... Acts 13:15 2076
I *h* found David the son of Jesse, ... Acts 13:22
day, they *h* fulfilled them in ... Acts 13:27
this day *h* I begotten thee ... Acts 13:33
should first *h* been spoken to you ... Acts 13:46
I *h* set thee to be a light of the ... Acts 13:47
would *h* done sacrifice with the ... Acts 14:13
Forasmuch as we *h* heard, that ... Acts 15:24
from us *h* troubled you with words ... Acts 15:24
Men that *h* hazarded their lives ... Acts 15:26
We *h* sent therefore Judas and ... Acts 15:27
h preached the word of the Lord ... Acts 15:36
Him would Paul *h* to go forth with ... Acts 16:3
If ye *h* judged me to be faithful ... Acts 16:15
would *h* killed himself, supposing ... Acts 16:27
The magistrates *h* sent to let you ... Acts 16:36
them, They *h* beaten us openly ... Acts 16:37
Romans, and *h* cast us into prison ... Acts 16:37
that Christ must needs *h* suffered ... Acts 17:3
These that *h* turned the world ... Acts 17:6
we live, and move, and *h* our being ... Acts 17:28 2070
also of your own poets *h* said ... Acts 17:28
for I *h* much people in this city ... Acts 18:10 2076
H ye received the Holy Ghost ... Acts 19:2
We *h* not so much as heard whether ... Acts 19:2
After I *h* been there, I must also ... Acts 19:21 1096
by this craft we *h* our wealth ... Acts 19:25 2076
when Paul would *h* entered in unto ... Acts 19:30
would *h* made his defence unto the ... Acts 19:33
For ye *h* brought hither these men ... Acts 19:37
h a matter against any man, the ... Acts 19:38 2192
after what manner I *h* been with ... Acts 20:18 1096
but *h* shewed you, and *h* taught ... Acts 20:20
which I *h* received of the Lord ... Acts 20:24
among whom I *h* gone preaching the ... Acts 20:25
For I *h* not shunned to declare ... Acts 20:27

I *h* coveted no man's silver, or ... Acts 20:33
that these hands *h* ministered ... Acts 20:34
I *h* shewed you all things, how ... Acts 20:35
We *h* four men which ... Acts 21:23 1526
four men which *h* a vow on them ... Acts 21:23 2192
we *h* written and concluded that ... Acts 21:25
him which should *h* examined him ... Acts 22:29
because he would *h* known the ... Acts 22:30
I *h* lived in all good conscience ... Acts 23:1
fearing lest Paul should *h* been ... Acts 23:10
We *h* bound ourselves under a ... Acts 23:14
eat nothing until we *h* slain Paul ... Acts 23:14
The Jews *h* agreed to desire thee ... Acts 23:20
which *h* bound themselves with an ... Acts 23:21
nor drink till they *h* killed him ... Acts 23:21
should *h* been killed of them ... Acts 23:27
when I would *h* known the cause ... Acts 23:28
but to *h* nothing laid to his ... Acts 23:29 2192
For we *h* found this man a ... Acts 24:5
would *h* judged according to our ... Acts 24:6
h hope toward God, which they ... Acts 24:15 2192
to *h* always a conscience void of ... Acts 24:16 2192
Who ought to *h* been here before ... Acts 24:19
if they *h* found any evil doing in ... Acts 24:20
Paul, and to let him *h* liberty ... Acts 24:23 2192
when I *h* a convenient season, I ... Acts 24:25 3335
should *h* been given him of Paul ... Acts 24:26
h I offended any thing at all ... Acts 25:8
to the Jews *h* I done no wrong, as ... Acts 25:10
or *h* committed any thing worthy ... Acts 25:11
desiring to *h* judgment against ... Acts 25:15
h the accusers face to face ... Acts 25:16 2192
h licence to answer for himself ... Acts 25:16 2983
of the Jews *h* dealt with me ... Acts 25:24
I *h* determined to send him ... Acts 25:25
Of whom I *h* no certain thing to ... Acts 25:26 2192
Wherefore I *h* brought him forth ... Acts 25:26
I might *h* somewhat to write ... Acts 25:26 2192
for I *h* appeared unto thee for ... Acts 26:16
This man might *h* been set at ... Acts 26:32
ye should *h* hearkened unto me, and ... Acts 27:21
not *h* loosed from Crete ... Acts 27:21
to *h* gained this harm and loss ... Acts 27:21
we should *h* fallen upon rocks ... Acts 27:29
would *h* cast anchors out of the ... Acts 27:30
fourteenth day that ye *h* tarried ... Acts 27:33
looked when he should *h* swollen ... Acts 28:6
though I *h* committed nothing ... Acts 28:17
would *h* let me go, because there ... Acts 28:18
therefore *h* I called for you ... Acts 28:20
and their eyes *h* they closed ... Acts 28:27
By whom we *h* received grace and ... Rom 1:5
h a prosperous journey by the ... Rom 1:10
Now I would not *h* you ignorant ... Rom 1:13 2309
that I might *h* some fruit among ... Rom 1:13 2192
but *h* pleasure in them that do ... Rom 1:32
For as many as *h* sinned without ... Rom 2:12
as many as *h* sinned in the law ... Rom 2:12
which *h* not the law, do by nature ... Rom 2:14 2192
for we *h* before proved both Jews ... Rom 3:9
their tongues they *h* used deceit ... Rom 3:13
the way of peace *h* they not known ... Rom 3:17
For all *h* sinned, and come short ... Rom 3:23
I *h* made thee a father of many ... Rom 4:17
we *h* peace with God through our ... Rom 5:1 2192
By whom also we *h* access by faith ... Rom 5:2 2192
by whom we *h* now received the ... Rom 5:11
all men, for that all *h* sinned ... Rom 5:12
For if we *h* been planted together ... Rom 6:5
sin shall not *h* dominion over you ... Rom 6:14
but ye *h* obeyed from the heart ... Rom 6:17
for as ye *h* yielded your members ... Rom 6:19
ye *h* your fruit unto holiness, and ... Rom 6:22 2192
Now if any man *h* not the Spirit ... Rom 8:9 2192
For ye *h* not received the spirit ... Rom 8:15
but ye *h* received the Spirit of ... Rom 8:15
which *h* the firstfruits of the ... Rom 8:23 2192
That I *h* great heaviness and ... Rom 9:2 2076
I come, and Sarah shall *h* a son ... Rom 9:9 2071
Jacob *h* I loved ... Rom 9:13
Esau *h* I hated ... Rom 9:13
h mercy on whom I will *h* mercy ... Rom 9:15
I will *h* compassion on whom I ... Rom 9:15
on whom I will *h* compassion ... Rom 9:15
same purpose *h* I raised thee up ... Rom 9:17
he mercy on whom he will *h* mercy ... Rom 9:18
h attained to righteousness, even ... Rom 9:30
record that they *h* a zeal of God ... Rom 10:2 2192
h not submitted themselves unto ... Rom 10:3
him in whom they *h* not believed ... Rom 10:14
in him of whom they *h* not heard ... Rom 10:14
But they *h* not all obeyed the ... Rom 10:16
But I say, *H* they not heard ... Rom 10:18
All day long I *h* stretched forth ... Rom 10:21
they *h* killed thy prophets, and ... Rom 11:3
I *h* reserved to myself seven ... Rom 11:4
who *h* not bowed the knee to the ... Rom 11:4
H they stumbled that they should ... Rom 11:11
in times past *h* not believed God ... Rom 11:30
yet *h* now obtained mercy through ... Rom 11:30
Even so *h* these also now not ... Rom 11:31
that he might *h* mercy upon all ... Rom 11:32
For as we *h* many members in one ... Rom 12:4 2192
all members *h* not the same office ... Rom 12:4 2192
thou shalt *h* praise of the same ... Rom 13:3 2192
h it to thyself before God ... Rom 14:22 2192
of the scriptures might *h* hope ... Rom 15:4 2192
I *h* written the more boldly unto ... Rom 15:15

I *h* therefore whereof I may glory ... Rom 15:17 2192
I *h* fully preached the gospel of ... Rom 15:19
so *h* I strived to preach the ... Rom 15:20
they that *h* not heard shall ... Rom 15:21
For which cause also I *h* been ... Rom 15:22
For if the Gentiles *h* been made ... Rom 15:27
When therefore I *h* performed this ... Rom 15:28
h sealed to them this fruit, I ... Rom 15:28
that my service which I *h* for ... Rom 15:31
Who *h* for my life laid down their ... Rom 16:4
the doctrine which ye *h* learned ... Rom 16:17
but yet I would *h* you wise unto ... Rom 16:19 2309
they would not *h* crucified the ... 1Cor 2:8
neither *h* entered into the heart ... 1Cor 2:9
Now we *h* received, not the spirit ... 1Cor 2:12
But we *h* the mind of Christ ... 1Cor 2:16 2192
I *h* fed you with milk, and not ... 1Cor 3:2
I *h* planted, Apollos watered ... 1Cor 3:6
I *h* laid the foundation, and ... 1Cor 3:10
shall every man *h* praise of God ... 1Cor 4:5 1096
I *h* in a figure transferred to ... 1Cor 4:6
ye *h* reigned as kings without us ... 1Cor 4:8
h no certain dwellingplace ... 1Cor 4:11
For though ye *h* ten thousand ... 1Cor 4:15 2192
yet *h* ye not many fathers ... 1Cor 4:15
for in Christ Jesus I *h* begotten ... 1Cor 4:15 2192
For this cause *h* I sent unto you ... 1Cor 4:17
that one should *h* his father's ... 1Cor 5:1 2192
h not rather mourned, that he ... 1Cor 5:2
h judged already, as though I ... 1Cor 5:3
But now I *h* written unto you not ... 1Cor 5:11
For what *h* I to do to judge them ... 1Cor 5:12
If then ye *h* judgments of things ... 1Cor 6:4 2192
is in you, which ye *h* of God ... 1Cor 6:19 2192
let every man *h* his own wife ... 1Cor 7:2 2192
let every woman *h* her own husband ... 1Cor 7:2 2192
Now concerning virgins I *h* no ... 1Cor 7:25 2192
such shall *h* trouble in the flesh ... 1Cor 7:28 2192
that both they that *h* wives be as ... 1Cor 7:29 2192
But I would *h* you without ... 1Cor 7:32 2309
also that I *h* the Spirit of God ... 1Cor 7:40 2192
we know that we all *h* knowledge ... 1Cor 8:1 2192
h I not seen Jesus Christ our ... 1Cor 9:1
H we not power to eat and to drink ... 1Cor 9:4 2192
H we not power to lead about a ... 1Cor 9:5 2192
h not we power to forbear working ... 1Cor 9:6 2192
If we *h* sown unto you spiritual ... 1Cor 9:11
Nevertheless we *h* not used this ... 1Cor 9:12
But I *h* used none of these things ... 1Cor 9:15
neither *h* I written these things, ... 1Cor 9:15
gospel, I *h* nothing to glory of ... 1Cor 9:16 2076
thing willingly, I *h* a reward ... 1Cor 9:17 2192
yet *h* I made myself servant unto ... 1Cor 9:19
when I *h* preached to others, I ... 1Cor 9:27
should *h* fellowship with devils ... 1Cor 10:20 1096
But I would *h* you know, that the ... 1Cor 11:3
to *h* power on her head because of ... 1Cor 11:10 2192
if a man *h* long hair, it is a ... 1Cor 11:14
But if a woman *h* long hair ... 1Cor 11:15
we *h* no such custom, neither the ... 1Cor 11:16 2192
h ye not houses to eat and to ... 1Cor 11:22 2192
of God, and shame them that *h* not ... 1Cor 11:22 2192
For I *h* received of the Lord that ... 1Cor 11:23
I would not *h* you ignorant ... 1Cor 12:1 2309
h been all made to drink into one ... 1Cor 12:13
the hand, I *h* no need of thee ... 1Cor 12:21 2192
to the feet, I *h* no need of you ... 1Cor 12:21 2192
our uncomely parts *h* more ... 1Cor 12:23 2192
For our comely parts *h* no need ... 1Cor 12:24 2192
but that the members should *h* the ... 1Cor 12:25
H all the gifts of healing ... 1Cor 12:30 2192
h not charity, I am become as ... 1Cor 13:1 2192
though I *h* the gift of prophecy, ... 1Cor 13:2 2192
though I *h* all faith, so that I ... 1Cor 13:2 2192
h not charity, I am nothing ... 1Cor 13:2 2192
h not charity, it profiteth me ... 1Cor 13:3 2192
you, which also ye *h* received ... 1Cor 15:1
unless ye *h* believed in vain ... 1Cor 15:2
because we *h* testified of God ... 1Cor 15:15
life only we *h* hope in Christ ... 1Cor 15:19 2070
when he shall *h* delivered up the ... 1Cor 15:24
when he shall *h* put down all rule ... 1Cor 15:24
I *h* in Christ Jesus our Lord ... 1Cor 15:31 2192
If after the manner of men I *h* ... 1Cor 15:32
for some *h* not the knowledge of ... 1Cor 15:34 2192
as we *h* borne the image of the ... 1Cor 15:49
shall *h* put on incorruption ... 1Cor 15:54
this mortal shall *h* put on ... 1Cor 15:54
as I *h* given order to the ... 1Cor 16:1
when he shall *h* convenient time ... 1Cor 16:12
that they *h* addicted themselves ... 1Cor 16:15
on your part they *h* supplied ... 1Cor 16:17
For they *h* refreshed my spirit and ... 1Cor 16:18
h you ignorant of our trouble ... 2Cor 1:8 2309
we *h* had our conversation in the ... 2Cor 1:12
As also ye *h* acknowledged us in ... 2Cor 1:14
that ye might *h* a second benefit ... 2Cor 1:15 2192
Not for that we *h* dominion over ... 2Cor 1:24
I should *h* sorrow from them of ... 2Cor 2:3 2192
I *h* more abundantly unto you ... 2Cor 2:4 2192
But if any *h* caused grief, he ... 2Cor 2:5
such trust *h* we through Christ to ... 2Cor 3:4 2192
Seeing then that we *h* such hope ... 2Cor 3:12 2192
seeing we *h* this ministry ... 2Cor 4:1 2192
as we *h* received mercy, we faint ... 2Cor 4:1
But *h* renounced the hidden things ... 2Cor 4:2
But we *h* this treasure in earthen ... 2Cor 4:7 2192
believed, and therefore *h* I spoken ... 2Cor 4:13

we *h* a building of God, an house	2Cor 5:1	2192
that ye may *h* somewhat to answer	2Cor 5:12	2192
though we *h* known Christ after	2Cor 5:16	
I *h* heard thee in a time accepted	2Cor 6:2	
of salvation *h* I succoured thee	2Cor 6:2	
we *h* wronged no man, we *h*	2Cor 7:2	
no man, we *h* defrauded no man	2Cor 7:2	
for I *h* said before, that ye are	2Cor 7:3	
In all things ye *h* approved	2Cor 7:11	
For if I *h* boasted any thing to	2Cor 7:14	
I rejoice therefore that I *h*	2Cor 7:16	
who *h* begun before, not only to	2Cor 8:10	
also out of that which ye *h*	2Cor 8:11	2192
we *h* sent with him the brother,	2Cor 8:18	
we *h* sent with them our brother,	2Cor 8:22	
whom we *h* oftentimes proved	2Cor 8:22	
great confidence which I *h* in you	2Cor 8:22	
Yet *h* I sent the brethren, lest	2Cor 9:3	
for I *h* espoused you to one	2Cor 11:2	
whom we *h* not preached, or if ye	2Cor 11:4	
which ye *h* not received, or	2Cor 11:4	
which ye *h* not accepted, ye might	2Cor 11:4	
but we *h* been throughly made	2Cor 11:6	
H I committed an offence in	2Cor 11:7	
because I *h* preached to you the	2Cor 11:7	
in all things I *h* kept myself	2Cor 11:9	
a day I *h* been in the deep	2Cor 11:25	4160
ye *h* compelled me	2Cor 12:11	
for I ought to *h* been commended	2Cor 12:11	
many which *h* sinned already	2Cor 12:21	
h not repented of the uncleanness	2Cor 12:21	
which they *h* committed	2Cor 12:21	
to them which heretofore *h* sinned	2Cor 13:2	
that which we *h* preached unto you	Gal 1:8	
unto you than that ye *h* received	Gal 1:9	
For ye *h* heard of my conversation	Gal 1:13	
which we *h* in Christ Jesus	Gal 2:4	2192
even we *h* believed in Jesus	Gal 2:16	
H ye suffered so many things in	Gal 3:4	
given which could *h* given life	Gal 3:21	
should *h* been by the law	Gal 3:21	2258
For as many of you as *h* been	Gal 3:27	
into Christ *h* put on Christ	Gal 3:27	
now, after that ye *h* known God	Gal 4:9	
lest I *h* bestowed upon you labour	Gal 4:11	
ye *h* not injured me at all	Gal 4:12	
ye would *h* plucked out your own	Gal 4:15	
and *h* given them to me	Gal 4:15	
I *h* confidence in you through the	Gal 5:10	
ye *h* been called unto liberty	Gal 5:13	
as I *h* also told you in time past	Gal 5:21	
And they that are Christ's *h*	Gal 5:24	
then shall he *h* rejoicing in	Gal 6:4	2192
As we *h* therefore opportunity,	Gal 6:10	2192
Ye see how large a letter I *h*	Gal 6:11	
but desire to *h* you circumcised,	Gal 6:13	
In whom we *h* redemption through	Eph 1:7	2192
In whom also we *h* obtained an	Eph 1:11	
For through him we both *h* access	Eph 2:18	2192
If ye *h* heard of the dispensation	Eph 3:2	
In whom we *h* boldness and access	Eph 3:12	2192
Who being past feeling *h* given	Eph 4:19	
But ye *h* not so learned Christ	Eph 4:20	
If so be that ye *h* heard him	Eph 4:21	
h been taught by him, as the	Eph 4:21	
that he may *h* to give to him that	Eph 4:28	2192
And *h* no fellowship with the	Eph 5:11	
Whom I *h* sent unto you for the	Eph 6:22	
because I *h* you in my heart	Phil 1:7	2192
me *h* fallen out rather unto the	Phil 1:12	
as ye *h* always obeyed, not as in	Phil 2:12	
that I *h* not run in vain, neither	Phil 2:16	
For I *h* no man likeminded, who	Phil 2:20	2192
lest I should *h* sorrow upon	Phil 2:27	2192
h no confidence in the flesh	Phil 3:3	
Though I might also *h* confidence	Phil 3:4	2192
for whom I *h* suffered the loss of	Phil 3:8	
count not myself to *h* apprehended	Phil 3:13	
whereto we *h* already attained,	Phil 3:16	
so as ye *h* us for an ensample	Phil 3:17	2192
of whom I *h* told you often, and	Phil 3:18	
which ye *h* both learned, and	Phil 4:9	
for I *h* learned, in whatsoever	Phil 4:11	
Notwithstanding ye *h* well done	Phil 4:14	
But I *h* all, and abound	Phil 4:18	568
love which ye *h* to all the saints	Col 1:4	
In whom we *h* redemption through	Col 1:14	2192
things he might *h* the preeminence	Col 1:18	1096
of the gospel, which ye *h* heard	Col 1:23	
what great conflict I *h* for you	Col 2:1	2192
for as many as *h* not seen my face	Col 2:1	
As ye *h* therefore received Christ	Col 2:6	
as ye *h* been taught, abounding	Col 2:7	
Which things *h* indeed a shew of	Col 2:23	2192
seeing that ye *h* put off the old	Col 3:9	
h put on the new man, which is	Col 3:10	
if any man *h* a quarrel against	Col 3:13	2192
that ye also *h* a Master in heaven	Col 4:1	2192
Whom I *h* sent unto you for the	Col 4:8	
which *h* been a comfort unto me	Col 4:11	1096
when we might *h* been burdensome,	1Th 2:6	1511
willing to *h* imparted unto you	1Th 2:8	
for ye also *h* suffered like	1Th 2:14	
even as they *h* of the Jews	1Th 2:14	
own prophets, and *h* persecuted us	1Th 2:15	
we would *h* come unto you, even I	1Th 2:18	
means the tempter *h* tempted you	1Th 3:5	
that ye *h* good remembrance of us	1Th 3:6	2192

that as ye *h* received of us how	1Th 4:1	
as we also *h* forewarned you and	1Th 4:6	
that ye may *h* lack of nothing	1Th 4:12	2192
But I would not *h* you to be	1Th 4:13	2309
even as others which *h* no hope	1Th 4:13	2192
ye *h* no need that I write unto	1Th 5:1	2192
traditions which ye *h* been taught	2Th 2:15	
of the Lord may *h* free course	2Th 3:1	
for all men *h* not faith	2Th 3:2	
we *h* confidence in the Lord	2Th 3:4	
Not because we *h* not power	2Th 3:9	2192
h no company with him, that he	2Th 3:14	
From which some having swerved *h*	1Ti 1:6	
concerning faith *h* made shipwreck	1Ti 1:19	
whom I *h* delivered unto Satan,	1Ti 1:20	
Who will *h* all men to be saved,	1Ti 2:4	2309
Moreover he must *h* a good report	1Ti 3:7	2192
For they that *h* used the office	1Ti 3:13	
But if any widow *h* children or	1Ti 5:4	2192
if she *h* brought up children	1Ti 5:10	
if she *h* lodged strangers	1Ti 5:10	
if she *h* washed the saints' feet,	1Ti 5:10	
if she *h* relieved the afflicted,	1Ti 5:10	
if she *h* diligently followed	1Ti 5:10	
for when they *h* begun to wax	1Ti 5:11	
because they *h* cast off their	1Ti 5:12	
or woman that believeth *h* widows	1Ti 5:16	2192
they that *h* believing masters,	1Ti 6:2	2192
they *h* erred from the faith, and	1Ti 6:10	
Which some professing *h* erred	1Ti 6:21	
that without ceasing I *h*	2Ti 1:3	2192
for I know whom I *h* believed	2Ti 1:12	
h committed unto him against that	2Ti 1:12	
Who concerning the truth *h* erred	2Ti 2:18	
I *h* fought a good fight, I *h*	2Ti 4:7	
my course, I *h* kept the faith	2Ti 4:7	
Tychicus *h* I sent to Ephesus	2Ti 4:12	
but Trophimus *h* I left at Miletum	2Ti 4:20	
of righteousness which we *h* done	Titus 3:5	
that they which *h* believed in God	Titus 3:8	
for I *h* determined there to	Titus 3:12	
For we *h* great joy and consolation	Philem 7	2192
whom I *h* begotten in my bonds	Philem 10	
Whom I *h* sent again	Philem 12	
Whom I would *h* retained with me,	Philem 13	
that in thy stead he might *h*	Philem 13	
I Paul *h* written it with mine own	Philem 19	
let me *h* joy of thee in the Lord	Philem 20	
this day *h* I begotten thee	Heb 1:5	
to the things which we *h* heard	Heb 2:1	
and they *h* not known my ways	Heb 3:10	
For we which *h* believed do enter	Heb 4:3	
As I *h* sworn in my wrath, if they	Heb 4:3	
afterward *h* spoken of another day	Heb 4:8	
eyes of him with whom we *h* to do	Heb 4:13	
that we *h* a great high priest	Heb 4:14	2192
For we *h* not an high priest which	Heb 4:15	2192
Who can *h* compassion on the	Heb 5:2	
my Son, to day *h* I begotten thee	Heb 5:5	
Of whom we *h* many things to say,	Heb 5:11	
ye *h* need that one teach you	Heb 5:12	2192
are become such as *h* need of milk	Heb 5:12	2192
use *h* their senses exercised to	Heb 5:14	2192
h tasted of the heavenly gift, and	Heb 6:4	
h tasted the good word of God, and	Heb 6:5	
which ye *h* shewed toward his name	Heb 6:10	
in that ye *h* ministered to the	Heb 6:10	
we might *h* a strong consolation,	Heb 6:18	2192
who *h* fled for refuge to lay hold	Heb 6:18	
Which hope we *h* as an anchor of	Heb 6:19	2192
h a commandment to take tithes of	Heb 7:5	2192
high priests which *h* infirmity	Heb 7:28	2192
which we *h* spoken this is the sum	Heb 8:1	
We *h* such an high priest, who is	Heb 8:1	2192
this man *h* somewhat also to offer	Heb 8:3	2192
then should no place *h* been	Heb 8:7	
For then must he often *h* suffered	Heb 9:26	
they not *h* ceased to be offered	Heb 10:2	
h had no more conscience of sins	Heb 10:2	2192
h received the knowledge of the	Heb 10:26	
that ye *h* in heaven a better	Heb 10:34	2192
For ye *h* need of patience, that,	Heb 10:36	
after ye *h* done the will of God,	Heb 10:36	
my soul shall *h* no pleasure in	Heb 10:38	
they might *h* had opportunity to	Heb 11:15	2192
had opportunity to *h* returned	Heb 11:15	
Ye *h* not yet resisted unto blood,	Heb 12:4	
ye *h* forgotten the exhortation	Heb 12:5	
Furthermore we *h* had fathers of	Heb 12:9	2192
when he would *h* inherited the	Heb 12:17	
cannot be moved, let us *h* grace	Heb 12:28	2192
for thereby some *h* entertained	Heb 13:2	
content with such things as ye *h*	Heb 13:5	3918
them which *h* the rule over you	Heb 13:7	
who *h* spoken unto you the word of	Heb 13:7	
which *h* not profited them that	Heb 13:9	
them that *h* been occupied therein	Heb 13:9	
We *h* an altar, whereof they *h*	Heb 13:10	2192
For here *h* we no continuing city,	Heb 13:14	2192
Obey them that *h* the rule over	Heb 13:17	
for we trust we *h* a good	Heb 13:18	2192
for I *h* written a letter unto you	Heb 13:22	
all them that *h* the rule over you	Heb 13:24	
let patience *h* her perfect work	Jas 1:4	2192
h not the faith of our Lord Jesus	Jas 2:1	2192
ye *h* respect to him that weareth	Jas 2:3	
But ye *h* despised the poor	Jas 2:6	
But if ye *h* respect to persons,	Jas 2:9	

For he shall *h* judgment without	Jas 2:13	
say he hath faith, and *h* not works	Jas 2:14	2192
Thou hast faith, and I *h* works	Jas 2:18	2192
But if ye *h* bitter envying and	Jas 3:14	2192
Ye lust, and *h* not	Jas 4:2	2192
ye kill, and desire to *h*, and	Jas 4:2	2192
ye fight and war, yet ye *h* not	Jas 4:2	2192
Ye *h* heaped treasure together for	Jas 5:3	
who *h* reaped down your fields	Jas 5:4	2192
the cries of them which *h* reaped	Jas 5:4	
Ye *h* lived in pleasure on the	Jas 5:5	
ye *h* nourished your hearts, as in	Jas 5:5	
Ye *h* condemned and killed the just	Jas 5:6	
who *h* spoken in the name of the	Jas 5:10	
Ye *h* heard of the patience of Job	Jas 5:11	
h seen the end of the Lord	Jas 5:11	
if he *h* committed sins, they	Jas 5:15	
salvation the prophets *h* enquired	1Pet 1:10	
h preached the gospel unto you	1Pet 1:12	
Seeing ye *h* purified your souls	1Pet 1:22	
If so be ye *h* tasted that the	1Pet 2:3	
mercy, but now *h* obtained mercy	1Pet 2:10	
us to *h* wrought the will of the	1Pet 4:3	
above all things *h* fervent	1Pet 4:8	2192
after that ye *h* suffered a while,	1Pet 5:10	
I *h* written briefly, exhorting,	1Pet 5:12	
to them that *h* obtained like	2Pet 1:1	
to *h* these things always in	2Pet 1:15	2192
For we *h* not followed cunningly	2Pet 1:16	
We *h* also a more sure word of	2Pet 1:19	2192
an heart they *h* exercised with	2Pet 2:14	2192
Which *h* forsaken the right way,	2Pet 2:15	
For if after they *h* escaped the	2Pet 2:20	
h known the way of righteousness	2Pet 2:21	
than, after they *h* known it	2Pet 2:21	
the beginning, which we *h* heard	1Jn 1:1	
which we *h* seen with our eyes,	1Jn 1:1	
which we *h* looked upon	1Jn 1:1	
and our hands *h* handled	1Jn 1:1	
we *h* seen it, and bear witness, and	1Jn 1:2	
That which we *h* seen and heard	1Jn 1:3	
that ye also may *h* fellowship	1Jn 1:3	2192
message which we *h* heard of him	1Jn 1:5	
If we say that we *h* fellowship	1Jn 1:6	2192
we *h* fellowship one with another,	1Jn 1:7	2192
If we say that we *h* no sin	1Jn 1:8	2192
If we say that we *h* not sinned	1Jn 1:10	
we *h* an advocate with the Father,	1Jn 2:1	2192
is the word which ye *h* heard from	1Jn 2:7	
because ye *h* known him that is	1Jn 2:13	
because ye *h* overcome the wicked	1Jn 2:13	
because ye *h* known the Father	1Jn 2:13	
I *h* written unto you, fathers,	1Jn 2:14	
because ye *h* known him that is	1Jn 2:14	
I *h* written unto you, young men,	1Jn 2:14	
ye *h* overcome the wicked one	1Jn 2:14	
as ye *h* heard that antichrist	1Jn 2:18	
no doubt *h* continued with us	1Jn 2:19	
But ye *h* an unction from the Holy	1Jn 2:20	2192
I *h* not written unto you because	1Jn 2:21	
which ye *h* heard from the	1Jn 2:24	
If that which ye *h* heard from the	1Jn 2:24	
These things *h* I written unto you	1Jn 2:26	
But the anointing which ye *h*	1Jn 2:27	
we may *h* confidence, and not be	1Jn 2:28	2192
We know that we *h* passed from	1Jn 3:14	
good, and seeth his brother *h* need	1Jn 3:17	2192
then *h* we confidence toward God	1Jn 3:21	2192
whereof ye *h* heard that it should	1Jn 4:3	
children, and *h* overcome them	1Jn 4:4	
we *h* seen and do testify that the	1Jn 4:14	
we *h* known and believed the love	1Jn 4:16	
that we may *h* boldness in the day	1Jn 4:17	2192
And this commandment *h* we	1Jn 4:21	2192
These things *h* I written unto you	1Jn 5:13	
may know that ye *h* eternal life	1Jn 5:13	2192
the confidence that we *h* in him	1Jn 5:14	2192
we know that we *h* the petitions	1Jn 5:15	2192
all they that *h* known the truth	2Jn 1	
as we *h* received a commandment	2Jn 4	
as ye *h* heard from the beginning,	2Jn 6	
those things which we *h* wrought	2Jn 8	
I *h* no greater joy than to hear	3Jn 4	2192
Which *h* borne witness of thy	3Jn 6	
who loveth to *h* the preeminence	3Jn 9	
for they *h* gone in the way of	Jude 11	
which they *h* ungodly committed	Jude 15	
sinners *h* spoken against him	Jude 15	
of some *h* compassion, making a	Jude 22	
h the keys of hell and of death	Rev 1:18	2192
Nevertheless I *h* somewhat against	Rev 2:4	2192
ye shall *h* tribulation ten days	Rev 2:10	2192
But I *h* a few things against thee	Rev 2:14	2192
Notwithstanding I *h* a few things	Rev 2:20	2192
as many as *h* not this doctrine,	Rev 2:24	2192
which *h* not known the depths of	Rev 2:24	2192
But that which ye *h* already hold	Rev 2:25	2192
for I *h* not found thy works	Rev 3:2	
h not defiled their garments	Rev 3:4	
I *h* set before thee an open door,	Rev 3:8	
and to know that I *h* loved thee	Rev 3:9	
with goods, and *h* need of nothing	Rev 3:17	2192
till we *h* sealed the servants of	Rev 7:3	
h washed their robes, and made	Rev 7:14	
scorpions of the earth *h* power	Rev 9:3	2192
but only those men which *h* not	Rev 9:4	2192
These *h* power to shut heaven,	Rev 11:6	2192
h power over waters to turn them	Rev 11:6	2192

when they shall *h* finished their .... Rev 11:7
h the testimony of Jesus Christ .... Rev 12:17 *2192*
If any man *h* an ear, let him hear .... Rev 13:9 *2192*
they *h* no rest day nor night, who .... Rev 14:11 *2192*
For they *h* shed the blood of .... Rev 16:6
the earth *h* committed fornication .... Rev 17:2
the inhabitants of the earth *h* .... Rev 17:2
which *h* received no kingdom as .... Rev 17:12
These *h* one mind, and shall give .... Rev 17:13 *2192*
For all nations *h* drunk of the .... Rev 18:3
and the kings of the earth *h* .... Rev 18:3
For her sins *h* reached unto .... Rev 18:5
who *h* committed fornication and .... Rev 18:9
of thy brethren that *h* the .... Rev 19:10 *2192*
shall *h* their part in the lake .... Rev 21:8
that they may *h* right to the tree .... Rev 22:14 *2071*
I Jesus *h* sent mine angel to .... Rev 22:16

HAVEN {5}
shall dwell at the *h* of the sea .... Gen 49:13 2348
and he shall be for an *h* of ships .... Gen 49:13 2348
them unto their desired *h* .... Ps 107:30 4231
because the *h* was not commodious .... Acts 27:12 *3040*
which is an *h* of Crete, and lieth .... Acts 27:12 *3040*

HAVENS {1}
place which is called The fair *h* .... Acts 27:8 *2568*

HAVILAH *(hav'-il-ah)* {7}
1. A son of Cush.
and *H*, and Sabtah, and Raamah, ... Gen 10:7 2341
Seba, and *H*, and Sabta, and Raamah, ... 1Chr 1:9 2341
2. A son of Joktan.
And Ophir, and *H*, and Jobab .... Gen 10:29 2341
And Ophir, and *H*, and Jobab 1Chr 1:23 2341
3. A land west of Ural.
compasseth the whole land of *H* .... Gen 2:11 2341
4. A district east of Amalek.
And they dwelt from *H* unto Shur .... Gen 25:18 2341
from *H* until thou comest to Shur 1Sa 15:7 2341

HAVING {193}
h Beth-el on the west, and Hai on .... Gen 12:8
h his uncleanness upon him, even .... Lev 7:20
lie with a woman *h* her sickness .... Lev 20:18
h his uncleanness upon him, that .... Lev 22:3
or *h* a wen, or scurvy, or scabbed .... Lev 22:22
a trance, but *h* his eyes open .... Num 24:4
a trance, but *h* his eyes open .... Num 24:16
h the two tables in mine hand .... Deut 10:3
h their thumbs and their great .... Judg 1:7
h his servant with him, and a .... Judg 19:3
ye stay for them from *h* husbands .... Ruth 1:13
h his spear in his hand, and all 1Sa 22:6
h three thousand chosen men of 1Sa 26:2
h put on their robes, in a void 1Kin 22:10
h for their captains Pelatiah, and 1Chr 4:42
h a drawn sword in his hand 1Chr 21:16
h wards one against another, to 1Chr 26:12
h cymbals and psalteries and harps, ... 2Chr 5:12
h Judah and Benjamin on his side 2Chr 11:12
every man *h* his weapon in his 2Chr 23:10
h rent my garment and my mantle, I .... Ezr 9:5
h knowledge, and *h* understanding .... Neh 10:28
h the oversight of the chamber of .... Neh 13:4 5414
mourning, and *h* his head covered .... Est 6:12
h sorrow in my heart daily .... Ps 13:2
Which *h* no guide, overseer, or .... Prov 6:7
h separated himself, seeketh and .... Prov 18:1
h a live coal in his hand, which .... Is 6:6
threshing instrument *h* teeth .... Is 41:15 1167
h their beards shaven, and their .... Jer 41:5
h cut themselves, with offerings .... Jer 41:5
h neither bars nor gates, ... Eze 38:11
at the side of the east gate *h* .... Eze 40:44
h charge at the gates of the .... Eze 44:11
The ram which thou sawest *h* two .... Dan 8:20 1167
of Saphir, *h* thy shame naked .... Mic 1:11
he is just, and *h* salvation .... Zec 9:9
he taught them as one *h* authority .... Mt 7:29 *2192*
authority, *h* soldiers under me .... Mt 8:9 *2192*
abroad, as sheep *h* no shepherd .... Mt 9:36 *2192*
h with them those that were lame, ... Mt 15:30 *2192*
rather than *h* two hands or two .... Mt 18:8 *2192*
rather than *h* two eyes to be cast .... Mt 18:9 *2192*
in hither not *h* a wedding garment .... Mt 22:12 *2192*
h no children, his brother shall .... Mt 22:24 *2192*
h no issue, left his wife unto .... Mt 22:25 *2192*
woman *h* an alabaster box of very .... Mt 26:7 *2192*
were as sheep not *h* a shepherd .... Mk 6:34 *2192*
h nothing to eat, Jesus called .... Mk 8:1 *2192*
H eyes, see ye not .... Mk 8:18 *2192*
and *h* ears, hear ye not .... Mk 8:18 *2192*
than *h* two hands to go into hell, ... Mk 9:43 *2192*
than *h* two feet to be cast into .... Mk 9:45 *2192*
than *h* two eyes to be cast into .... Mk 9:47 *2192*
a fig tree afar off *h* leaves .... Mk 11:13 *2192*
H yet therefore one son, his .... Mk 12:6 *2192*
h heard them reasoning together, ... Mk 12:28
there came a woman *h* an alabaster .... Mk 14:3 *2192*
h a linen cloth cast about his .... Mk 14:51
h had perfect understanding of .... Lk 1:3
No man also *h* drunk old wine .... Lk 5:39
h under me soldiers, and I say .... Lk 7:8 *2192*
h heard the word, keep it, and .... Lk 8:15
a woman *h* an issue of blood .... Lk 8:43
h put his hand to the plough, and .... Lk 9:62
h no part dark, the whole shall .... Lk 11:36 *2192*
h an hundred sheep, if he lose .... Lk 15:4 *2192*
Either what woman *h* ten pieces of .... Lk 15:8 *2192*
h a servant plowing or feeding .... Lk 17:7 *2192*
h received the kingdom, then he .... Lk 19:15
h a wife, and he die without .... Lk 20:28 *2192*
h examined him before you, have .... Lk 23:14
h said thus, he gave up the ghost .... Lk 23:46
h seen all the things that he did .... Jn 4:45
tongue Bethesda, *h* five porches .... Jn 5:2 *2192*
this man letters, *h* never learned .... Jn 7:15
h loved his own which were in the .... Jn 13:1
the devil *h* now put into the .... Jn 13:2
He then *h* received the sop went .... Jn 13:30
h received a band of men and .... Jn 18:3
Simon Peter *h* a sword drew it .... Jn 18:10 *2192*
h loosed the pains of death .... Acts 2:24
h received of the Father the .... Acts 2:33
h favour with all the people .... Acts 2:47 *2192*
h raised up his Son Jesus, sent .... Acts 3:26
H land, sold it, and brought the .... Acts 4:37 *5225*
h made Blastus the king's .... Acts 12:20
h stoned Paul, drew him out of .... Acts 14:19
h received such a charge, thrust .... Acts 16:24
h shorn his head in Cenchrea .... Acts 18:18
Paul *h* passed through the upper .... Acts 19:1
h caught Gaius and Aristarchus, ... Acts 19:29
h a good report of all the Jews .... Acts 22:12
h understood that he was a Roman .... Acts 23:27
h more perfect knowledge of that .... Acts 24:22
h received authority from the .... Acts 26:10
H therefore obtained help of God, ... Acts 26:22
fasting, *h* taken nothing .... Acts 27:33
h not the law, are a law unto .... Rom 2:14 *2192*
neither *h* done any good or evil, ... Rom 9:11
H then gifts differing according .... Rom 12:6 *2192*
But now *h* no more place in these .... Rom 15:23 *2192*
h a great desire these many years .... Rom 15:23 *2192*
h a matter against another, go to 1Cor 6:1 *2192*
h no necessity, but hath power 1Cor 7:37 *2192*
h his head covered, dishonoureth 1Cor 11:4 *2192*
h given more abundant honour to 1Cor 12:24
h confidence in you all, that my 2Cor 2:3
We *h* the same spirit of faith, ... 2Cor 4:13 *2192*
as *h* nothing, and yet possessing 2Cor 6:10 *2192*
H therefore these promises dearly 2Cor 7:1 *2192*
always *h* all sufficiency in all 2Cor 9:8 *2192*
h in a readiness to revenge all 2Cor 10:6 *2192*
but *h* hope, when your faith is 2Cor 10:15 *2192*
h begun in the Spirit, are ye now .... Gal 3:3
H predestinated us unto the .... Eph 1:5
H made known unto us the mystery .... Eph 1:9
h no hope, and without God in the .... Eph 2:12 *2192*
H abolished in his flesh the .... Eph 2:15
h slain the enmity thereby .... Eph 2:16
H the understanding darkened, ... Eph 4:18
not *h* spot, or wrinkle, or any .... Eph 5:27 *2192*
evil day, and *h* done all, to stand .... Eph 6:13
h your loins girt about with .... Eph 6:14
truth, and *h* on the breastplate of .... Eph 6:14 *1746*
h a desire to depart, and to be .... Phil 1:23 *2192*
h this confidence, I know that I .... Phil 1:25
H the same conflict which ye saw .... Phil 1:30 *2192*
h the same love, being of one .... Phil 2:2 *2192*
not *h* mine own righteousness, ... Phil 3:9 *2192*
h received of Epaphroditus the .... Phil 4:18
h made peace through the blood of .... Col 1:20
h forgiven you all trespasses .... Col 2:13
h spoiled principalities and .... Col 2:15
bands *h* nourishment ministered, ... Col 2:19
h received the word in much 1Th 1:6
From which some *h* swerved have 1Ti 1:6
which some *h* put away concerning 1Ti 1:19
h his children in subjection with 1Ti 3:4 *2192*
h their conscience seared with a 1Ti 4:2
h promise of the life that now is 1Ti 4:8 *2192*
h been the wife of one man, ... 1Ti 5:9
H damnation, because they have 1Ti 5:12 *2192*
h food and raiment let us be 1Ti 6:8 *2192*
h this seal, The Lord knoweth 2Ti 2:19 *2192*
H a form of godliness, but 2Ti 3:5 *2192*
teachers, *h* itching ears 2Ti 4:3
h loved this present world, and is 2Ti 4:10
h faithful children not accused .... Titus 1:6 *2192*
h no evil thing to say of you .... Titus 2:8 *2192*
H confidence in thy obedience I .... Philem 21
h neither beginning of days, nor .... Heb 7:3 *2192*
h obtained eternal redemption for .... Heb 9:12
For the law *h* a shadow of good .... Heb 10:1 *2192*
H therefore, brethren, boldness .... Heb 10:19 *2192*
h an high priest over the house .... Heb 10:21
h our hearts sprinkled from an .... Heb 10:22
not *h* received the promises .... Heb 11:13
but *h* seen them afar off, and were .... Heb 11:13
h obtained a good report through .... Heb 11:39
God *h* provided some better thing .... Heb 11:40
Whom *h* not seen, ye love 1Pet 1:8
H your conversation honest among 1Pet 2:12 *2192*
h compassion one of another, love 1Pet 3:8
H a good conscience 1Pet 3:16 *2192*
h escaped the corruption that is 2Pet 1:4
H eyes full of adultery, and that 2Pet 2:14 *2192*
H many things to write unto you, ... 2Jn 12 *2192*
h saved the people out of the .... Jude 5
h men's persons in admiration .... Jude 16
sensual, *h* not the Spirit .... Jude 19 *2192*
h seven horns and seven eyes, ... Rev 5:6 *2192*
h every one of them harps, and .... Rev 5:8 *2192*
h the seal of the living God .... Rev 7:2 *2192*
at the altar, *h* a golden censer .... Rev 8:3 *2192*
h breastplates of fire, and of .... Rev 9:17 *2192*
h seven heads and ten horns, and .... Rev 12:3 *2192*
h great wrath, because he knoweth .... Rev 12:12 *2192*
h seven heads and ten horns, and .... Rev 13:1 *2192*
h his Father's name written in .... Rev 14:1 *2192*
h the everlasting gospel to .... Rev 14:6 *2192*
h on his head a golden crown, and .... Rev 14:14 *2192*
heaven, he also *h* a sharp sickle .... Rev 14:17 *2192*
seven angels *h* the seven last .... Rev 15:1 *2192*
sea of glass, *h* the harps of God .... Rev 15:2 *2192*
h the seven plagues, clothed in .... Rev 15:6 *2192*
h their breasts girded with .... Rev 15:6 *2192*
h seven heads and ten horns .... Rev 17:3 *2192*
h a golden cup in her hand full .... Rev 17:4 *2192*
down from heaven, *h* great power .... Rev 18:1 *2192*
h the key of the bottomless pit .... Rev 20:1 *2192*
H the glory of God .... Rev 21:11 *2192*

HAVOCK {1}
he made *h* of the church, entering .... Acts 8:3 *3075*

HAVOTH-JAIR *(ha'-voth-ja'-ir)* {2} See BASHAN-HAVOTH. *Villages in Gilead.*
towns thereof, and called them *H* .... Num 32:41 2334
which are called *H* unto this day .... Judg 10:4 2334

HAWK {5}
And the owl, and the night *h* .... Lev 11:16 8464
cuckow, and the *h* after his kind, ... Lev 11:16 5322
And the owl, and the night *h* .... Deut 14:15 8464
cuckow, and the *h* after his kind, ... Deut 14:15 5322
Doth the *h* fly by thy wisdom, and .... Job 39:26 5322

HAY {3}
The *h* appeareth, and the tender .... Prov 27:25 2682
for the *h* is withered away, the .... Is 15:6 2682
silver, precious stones, wood, *h* 1Cor 3:12 *5528*

HAZAEL *(ha'-za-el)* {23} *A king of Syria.*
anoint *H* to be king over Syria 1Kin 19:15 2371
the sword of *H* shall Jehu slay 1Kin 19:17 2371
And the king said unto *H*, Take a 2Kin 8:8 2371
So *H* went to meet him, and took a 2Kin 8:9 2371
H said, Why weepeth my lord 2Kin 8:12 2371
H said, But what, is thy servant 2Kin 8:13 2371
and *H* reigned in his stead 2Kin 8:15 2371
H king of Syria in Ramoth-gilead 2Kin 8:28 2371
he fought against *H* king of Syria 2Kin 8:29 2371
because of *H* king of Syria 2Kin 9:14 2371
he fought with *H* king of Syria 2Kin 9:15 2371
H smote them in all the coasts of 2Kin 10:32 2371
Then *H* king of Syria went up, and 2Kin 12:17 2371
H set his face to go up to 2Kin 12:17 2371
sent it to *H* king of Syria 2Kin 12:18 2371
into the hand of *H* king of Syria 2Kin 13:3 2371
hand of Ben-hadad the son of *H* 2Kin 13:3 2371
But *H* king of Syria oppressed 2Kin 13:22 2371
So *H* king of Syria died 2Kin 13:24 2371
Ben-hadad the son of *H* the cities 2Kin 13:25 2371
king of Israel to war against *H* 2Chr 22:5 2371
he fought with *H* king of Syria 2Chr 22:6 2371
send a fire into the house of *H* .... Amos 1:4 2371

HAZAIAH *(ha-za-i'-ah)* {1} *Son of Adaiah.*
the son of Colhozeh, the son of *H* .... Neh 11:5 2382

HAZAR-ADDAR *(ha'-zar-ad'-dar)* {1} See ADDAR. *A place in southern Palestine.*
and shall go on to *H*, and pass on .... Num 34:4 2692

HAZARDED {1}
Men that have *h* their lives for .... Acts 15:26 *3860*

HAZAR-ENAN *(ha'-zar-e'-nan)* {4} *A village in northeastern Palestine.*
goings out of it shall be at *H* .... Num 34:9 2704
east border from *H* to Shepham .... Num 34:10 2704
border from the sea shall be *H* .... Eze 47:17 2703
as one goeth to Hamath, *H* .... Eze 48:1 2704

HAZAR-GADDAH *(ha'-zar-gad'-dah)* {1} *A town in Judah.*
And *H*, and Heshmon, and Beth-palet, ... Josh 15:27 2693

HAZAR-HATTICON *(ha'-zar-hat'-ti-con)* {1} *A place in Hauran.*
H, which is by the coast of .... Eze 47:16 2694

HAZARMAVETH *(ha-zar-ma'-veth)* {2} *A son of Joktan.*
begat Almodad, and Sheleph, and *H* .... Gen 10:26 2700
begat Almodad, and Sheleph, and *H* 1Chr 1:20 2700

HAZAR-SHUAL *(ha'-zar-shoo'-al)* {4} *A town in Judah.*
And *H*, and Beer-sheba, and .... Josh 15:28 2705
And *H*, and Balah, and Azem, ... Josh 19:3 2705
at Beer-sheba, and Moladah, and *H* 1Chr 4:28 2705
And at *H*, and at Beer-sheba, and in .... Neh 11:27 2705

HAZAR-SUSAH *(ha'-zar-soo'-sah)* {1} See HAZAR-SUSIM. *A city in Judah.*
Ziklag, and Beth-marcaboth, and *H* .... Josh 19:5 2701

HAZAR-SUSIM *(ha'-zar-soo'-sim)* {1} See HAZAR-SUSAH. *Same as Hazar-susah.*
And at Beth-marcaboth, and *H* 1Chr 4:31 2702

HAZAZON-TAMAR *(haz'-a-zon-ta'-mar)* {1} See HAZEZON-TAMAR. *A name for En-gedi.*
and, behold, they be in *H*, which 2Chr 20:2 2688

HAZEL {1}
rods of green poplar, and of the *h* .... Gen 30:37 3869

HAZELELPONI *(haz-el-el-po'-ni)* {1} *Sister of the sons of Etam.*
and the name of their sister was *H* 1Chr 4:3 6753

HAZER-HATTICON See HAZAR-HATTICON.

HAZERIM *(haz'-e-rim)* {1} *A district near Gaza.*
And the Avims which dwelt in *H* .... Deut 2:23 2699

HAZEROTH *(haz'-e-roth)* {6} *A Hebrew encampment in the wilderness.*
from Kibroth-hattaavah unto *H* .... Num 11:35 2698
and abode at *H* .... Num 11:35 2698
the people removed from *H* .... Num 12:16 2698
and encamped at *H* .... Num 33:17 2698
And they departed from *H*, and .... Num 33:18 2698
Paran, and Tophel, and Laban, and *H* .... Deut 1:1 2698

HAZEZON-TAMAR *(haz'-e-zon-ta'-mar)* {1} See EN-GEDI, HAZAZON-TAMAR. *Same as Hazazon-tamar.*
the Amorites, that dwelt in *H* .... Gen 14:7 2688

HAZIEL *(ha'-ze-el)* {1} *A Levite.*
Shelomith, and *H*, and Haran, three 1Chr 23:9 2381

HAZO *(ha'-zo)* {1} *A son of Nahor.*
And Chesed, and *H*, and Pildash, and .... Gen 22:22 2375

HAZOBEBAH See HAZELELPONI.

HAZOR *(ha'-zor)* {19} See BAAL-HAZOR, EN-HAZOR, HEZRON.
1. A fortified city in Naphtali.
when Jabin king of *H* had heard .... Josh 11:1 2674
that time turned back, and took *H* .... Josh 11:10 2674
for *H* beforetime was the head of .... Josh 11:10 2674
and he burnt *H* with fire .... Josh 11:11 2674
burned none of them, save *H* only .... Josh 11:13 2674
the king of *H*, one .... Josh 12:19 2674
And Adamah, and Ramah, and *H* .... Josh 19:36 2674
king of Canaan, that reigned in *H* .... Judg 4:2 2674
peace between Jabin the king of *H* .... Judg 4:17 2674
Sisera, captain of the host of *H* 1Sa 12:9 2674
and the wall of Jerusalem, and *H* 1Kin 9:15 2674
H, Ramah, Gittaim, ... Neh 11:33 2674
2. A city in Judah.
And Kedesh, and *H*, and Ithnan, ... Josh 15:23 2674
and Janoah, and Kedesh, and *H* 2Kin 15:29 2674
3. Another town in Judah.
And *H*, Hadattah, and Kerioth, and .... Josh 15:25 2675
and Kerioth, and Hezron, which is *H* ..... Josh 15:25 2674
4. Where the Benjamites lived after the Exile.
and concerning the kingdoms of *H* .... Jer 49:28 2674
5. An area in eastern Arabia.
dwell deep, O ye inhabitants of *H* .... Jer 49:30 2674
H shall be a dwelling for dragons .... Jer 49:33 2674

HAZZELELPONI See HAZELELPONI.

HE *(hay)* See APPENDIX. *A Hebrew letter.*

HEAD {363}
it shall bruise thy *h*, and thou .... Gen 3:15 7218
And the man bowed down his *h* .... Gen 24:26
And I bowed down my *h*, and .... Gen 24:48
shall Pharaoh lift up thine *h* .... Gen 40:13 7218
I had three white baskets on my *h* .... Gen 40:16 7218
them out of the basket upon my *h* .... Gen 40:17 7218
lift up thy *h* from off thee .... Gen 40:19 7218
he lifted up the *h* of the chief .... Gen 40:20 7218
bowed himself upon the bed's *h* .... Gen 47:31 7218
hand, and laid it upon Ephraim's *h* .... Gen 48:14 7218
his left hand upon Manasseh's *h* .... Gen 48:14 7218
right hand upon the *h* of Ephraim .... Gen 48:17 7218
Ephraim's *h* unto Manasseh's *h* .... Gen 48:17 7218
put thy right hand upon his *h* .... Gen 48:18 7218
they shall be on the *h* of Joseph .... Gen 49:26 7218
on the crown of the *h* of him that .... Gen 49:26 6936
his *h* with his legs, and with the .... Ex 12:9 7218
And the people bowed the *h* .... Ex 12:27
above the *h* of it unto one ring .... Ex 26:24 7218
shalt put the mitre upon his *h* .... Ex 29:6 7218
oil, and pour it upon his *h* .... Ex 29:7 7218
hands upon the *h* of the bullock .... Ex 29:10 7218
their hands upon the *h* of the ram .... Ex 29:15 7218
unto his pieces, and unto his *h* .... Ex 29:17 7218
their hands upon the *h* of the ram .... Ex 29:19 7218
bowed his *h* toward the earth, and .... Ex 34:8
coupled together at the *h* thereof .... Ex 36:29 7218
upon the *h* of the burnt offering .... Lev 1:4 7218
sons, shall lay the parts, the *h* .... Lev 1:8 7218
it into his pieces, with his *h* .... Lev 1:12 7218
the altar, and wring off his *h* .... Lev 1:15 7218
hand upon the *h* of his offering .... Lev 3:2 7218
hand upon the *h* of his offering .... Lev 3:8 7218
lay his hand upon the *h* of it .... Lev 3:13 7218
lay his hand upon the bullock's *h* .... Lev 4:4 7218
and all his flesh, with his *h* .... Lev 4:11 7218
h of the bullock before the LORD .... Lev 4:15 7218
his hand upon the *h* of the goat .... Lev 4:24 7218
upon the *h* of the sin offering .... Lev 4:29 7218
upon the *h* of the sin offering .... Lev 4:33 7218
and wring off his *h* from his neck .... Lev 5:8 7218
And he put the mitre upon his *h* .... Lev 8:9 7218
the anointing oil upon Aaron's *h* .... Lev 8:12 7218
the *h* of the bullock for the sin .... Lev 8:14 7218
their hands upon the *h* of the ram .... Lev 8:18 7218
and Moses burnt the *h*, and the .... Lev 8:20 7218
their hands upon the *h* of the ram .... Lev 8:22 7218
with the pieces thereof, and the *h* .... Lev 9:13 7218
from his *h* even to his foot .... Lev 13:12 7218
a plague upon the *h* or the beard .... Lev 13:29 7218
a leprosy upon the *h* or beard .... Lev 13:30 7218
whose hair is fallen off his *h* .... Lev 13:40 7218
the part of his *h* toward his face .... Lev 13:41 7218
And if there be in the bald *h* .... Lev 13:42
a leprosy sprung up in his bald *h* .... Lev 13:42
be white reddish in his bald *h* .... Lev 13:43
his plague is in his *h* .... Lev 13:44 7218
his *h* bare, and he shall put a .... Lev 13:45 7218
shave all his hair off his *h* .... Lev 14:9 7218
hand he shall pour upon the *h* of .... Lev 14:18 7218
hand he shall put upon the *h* of .... Lev 14:29 7218
hands upon the *h* of the live goat .... Lev 16:21 7218
them upon the *h* of the goat .... Lev 16:21 7218
shalt rise up before the hoary *h* .... Lev 19:32
not make baldness upon their *h* .... Lev 21:5 7218
upon whose *h* the anointing oil .... Lev 21:10 7218
garments, shall not uncover his *h* .... Lev 21:10 7218
him lay their hands upon his *h* .... Lev 24:14 7218
every one *h* of the house of his .... Num 1:4 7218
LORD, and uncover the woman's *h* .... Num 5:18 7218
shall no razor come upon his *h* .... Num 6:5 7218
locks of the hair of his *h* grow .... Num 6:5 7218
of his God is upon his *h* .... Num 6:7 7218
defiled the *h* of his consecration .... Num 6:9 7218
then he shall shave his *h* in the .... Num 6:9 7218
shall hallow his *h* that same day .... Num 6:11 7218
the Nazarite shall shave the *h* of .... Num 6:18 7218
hair of the *h* of his separation .... Num 6:18 7218
for one rod shall be for the *h* of .... Num 17:3 7218
and he bowed down his *h*, and fell .... Num 22:31
he was *h* over a people, and of a .... Num 25:15 7218
the *h* slippeth from the helve, and .... Deut 19:5 1270
and she shall shave her *h*, and pare .... Deut 21:12 7218
And the LORD shall make thee the *h* .... Deut 28:13 7218
that is over thy *h* shall be brass .... Deut 28:23 7218
of thy foot unto the top of thy *h* .... Deut 28:35 6936
he shall be the *h*, and thou shalt .... Deut 28:44 7218
come upon the *h* of Joseph .... Deut 33:16 7218
upon the top of the *h* of him that .... Deut 33:16 6936
the arm with the crown of the *h* .... Deut 33:20 6936
his blood shall be upon his *h* .... Josh 2:19 7218
his blood shall be on our *h* .... Josh 2:19 7218
was the *h* of all those kingdoms .... Josh 11:10 7218
each one was an *h* of the house of .... Josh 22:14 7218
smote Sisera, she smote off his *h* .... Judg 5:26 7218
of a millstone upon Abimelech's *h* .... Judg 9:53 7218
he shall be *h* over all the .... Judg 10:18 7218
be our *h* over all the inhabitants .... Judg 11:8 7218
them before me, shall I be your *h* .... Judg 11:9 7218
Gilead, and the people made him *h* .... Judg 11:11 7218
and no razor shall come on his *h* .... Judg 13:5 7218
seven locks of my *h* with the web .... Judg 16:13 7218
hath not come a razor upon mine *h* .... Judg 16:17 7218
off the seven locks of his *h* .... Judg 16:19 7218
Howbeit the hair of his *h* began .... Judg 16:22 7218
shall no razor come upon his *h* 1Sa 1:11 7218
rent, and with earth upon his *h* 1Sa 4:12 7218
the *h* of Dagon and both the palms 1Sa 5:4 7218
of oil, and poured it upon his *h* 1Sa 10:1 7218
hair of his *h* fall to the ground 1Sa 14:45 7218
wast thou not made the *h* of the 1Sa 15:17 7218
had an helmet of brass upon his *h* 1Sa 17:5 7218
his spear's *h* weighed six hundred 1Sa 17:7 3852
put an helmet of brass upon his *h* 1Sa 17:38 7218
thee, and take thine *h* from thee 1Sa 17:46 7218
him, and cut off his *h* therewith 1Sa 17:51 7218
And David took the *h* of the 1Sa 17:54 7218
him before Saul with the *h* of the 1Sa 17:57 7218
of Nabal upon his own *h* 1Sa 25:39 7218
thee keeper of mine *h* for ever 1Sa 28:2 7218
And they cut off his *h*, and 1Sa 31:9 7218
clothes rent, and earth upon his *h* 2Sa 1:2 7218
the crown that was upon his *h* 2Sa 1:10 7218
unto him, Thy blood be upon thy *h* 2Sa 1:16 7218
every one his fellow by the *h* 2Sa 2:16 7218
and said, Am I a dog's *h*, which 2Sa 3:8 7218
Let it rest on the *h* of Joab 2Sa 3:29 7218
and beheaded him, and took his *h* 2Sa 4:7 7218
they brought the *h* of Ish-bosheth 2Sa 4:8 7218
Behold the *h* of Ish-bosheth the 2Sa 4:8 7218
they took the *h* of Ish-bosheth 2Sa 4:12 7218
their king's crown from off his *h* 2Sa 12:30 7218
and it was set on David's *h* 2Sa 12:30 7218
And Tamar put ashes on her *h* 2Sa 13:19 7218
on her, and laid her hand on her *h* 2Sa 13:19 7218
his *h* there was no blemish in him 2Sa 14:25 6936
And when he polled his *h*, (for it 2Sa 14:26 7218
he weighed the hair of his *h* at 2Sa 14:26 7218
he went up, and had his *h* covered 2Sa 15:30 7218
with him covered every man his *h* 2Sa 15:30 7218
coat rent, and earth upon his *h* 2Sa 15:32 7218
I pray thee, and take off his *h* 2Sa 16:9 7218
his *h* caught hold of the oak, and 2Sa 18:9 7218
his *h* shall be thrown to thee 2Sa 20:21 7218
they cut off the *h* of Sheba the 2Sa 20:22 7218
kept me to be *h* of the heathen 2Sa 22:44 7218
let not his hoar *h* go down to the 1Kin 2:6
but his hoar *h* bring thou down to 1Kin 2:9
return his blood upon his own *h* 1Kin 2:32 7218
return upon the *h* of Joab 1Kin 2:33 7218
upon the *h* of his seed for ever 1Kin 2:33 7218
blood shall be upon thine own *h* 1Kin 2:37 7218
thy wickedness upon thine own *h* 1Kin 2:44 7218
to bring his way upon his *h* 1Kin 8:32 7218
and a cruse of water at his *h* 1Kin 19:6 4763
away thy master from thy *h* to day 2Kin 2:3 7218
away thy master from thy *h* to day 2Kin 2:5 7218
said unto him, Go up, thou bald *h* 2Kin 2:23
go up, thou bald *h* 2Kin 2:23
unto his father, My *h*, my *h* 2Kin 4:19 7218
the ax *h* fell into the water 2Kin 6:5 1270
until an ass's *h* was sold for 2Kin 6:25 7218
if the *h* of Elisha the son of 2Kin 6:31 7218
hath sent to take away mine *h* 2Kin 6:32 7218
box of oil, and pour it on his *h* 2Kin 9:3 7218
and he poured the oil on his *h* 2Kin 9:6 7218
painted her face, and tired her *h* 2Kin 9:30 7218
hath shaken her *h* at thee 2Kin 19:21 7218
began to reign did lift up the *h* 2Kin 25:27 7218
had stripped him, they took his *h* 1Chr 10:9 7218
fastened his *h* in the temple of 1Chr 10:10 1538
of their king from off his *h* 1Chr 20:2 7218
and it was set upon David's *h* 1Chr 20:2 7218
thou art exalted as *h* above all 1Chr 29:11 7218
his way upon his own *h* 2Chr 6:23 7218
Jehoshaphat bowed his *h* with his 2Chr 20:18
and plucked off the hair of my *h* .... Ezr 9:3 7218
are increased over our *h*, and our .... Ezr 9:6 7218
their reproach upon their own *h* .... Neh 4:4 7218
he set the royal crown upon her *h* .... Est 2:17 7218
royal which is set upon his *h* .... Est 6:8 7218
mourning, and having his *h* covered .... Est 6:12 7218
should return upon his own *h* .... Est 9:25 7218
rent his mantle, and shaved his *h* .... Job 1:20 7218
yet will I not lift up my *h* .... Job 10:15 7218
you, and shake mine *h* at you .... Job 16:4 7218
and taken the crown from my *h* .... Job 19:9 7218
his *h* reach unto the clouds .... Job 20:6 7218
When his candle shined upon my *h* .... Job 29:3 7218
or his *h* with fish spears .... Job 41:7 7218
glory, and the lifter up of mine *h* .... Ps 3:3 7218
shall return upon his own *h* .... Ps 7:16 7218
hast made me the *h* of the heathen .... Ps 18:43 7218
a crown of pure gold on his *h* .... Ps 21:3 7218
out the lip, they shake the *h* .... Ps 22:7 7218
thou anointest my *h* with oil .... Ps 23:5 7218
now shall mine *h* be lifted up .... Ps 27:6 7218
iniquities are gone over mine *h* .... Ps 38:4 7218
are more than the hairs of mine *h* .... Ps 40:12 7218
shaking of the *h* among the people .... Ps 44:14 7218
also is the strength of mine *h* .... Ps 60:7 7218
shall wound the *h* of his enemies .... Ps 68:21 7218
are more than the hairs of mine *h* .... Ps 69:4 7218
hate thee have lifted up the *h* .... Ps 83:2 7218
also is the strength of mine *h* .... Ps 108:8 7218
therefore shall he lift up the *h* .... Ps 110:7 7218
become the *h* stone of the corner .... Ps 118:22 7218
the precious ointment upon the *h* .... Ps 133:2 7218
covered my *h* in the day of battle .... Ps 140:7 7218
As for the *h* of those that .... Ps 140:9 7218
oil, which shall not break my *h* .... Ps 141:5 7218
an ornament of grace unto thy *h* .... Prov 1:9 7218
to thine *h* an ornament of grace .... Prov 4:9 7218
are upon the *h* of the just .... Prov 10:6 7218
upon the *h* of him that selleth it .... Prov 11:26 7218
The hoary *h* is a crown of glory, ... Prov 16:31
beauty of old men is the grey *h* .... Prov 20:29
heap coals of fire upon his *h* .... Prov 25:22 7218
The wise man's eyes are in his *h* .... Eccl 2:14 7218
let thy *h* lack no ointment .... Eccl 9:8 7218
His left hand is under my *h* .... Song 2:6 7218
for my *h* is filled with dew, and .... Song 5:2 7218
His *h* is as the most fine gold, ... Song 5:11 7218
Thine *h* upon thee is like Carmel, ... Song 7:5 7218
the hair of thine *h* like purple .... Song 7:5 7218
left hand should be under my *h* .... Song 8:3 7218
the whole *h* is sick, and the whole .... Is 1:5 7218
the *h* there is no soundness in it .... Is 1:6 7218
of the *h* of the daughters of Zion .... Is 3:17 6936
For the *h* of Syria is Damascus, ... Is 7:8 7218
the *h* of Damascus is Rezin .... Is 7:8 7218
the *h* of Ephraim is Samaria, and .... Is 7:9 7218
the *h* of Samaria is Remaliah's .... Is 7:9 7218
by the king of Assyria, the *h* .... Is 7:20 7218
LORD will cut off from Israel *h* .... Is 9:14 7218
and honourable, he is the *h* .... Is 9:15 7218
for Egypt, which the *h* or tail .... Is 19:15 7218
which are on the *h* of the fat .... Is 28:1 7218
which is on the *h* of the fat .... Is 28:4 7218
hath shaken her *h* at thee .... Is 37:22 7218
joy shall be upon their *h* .... Is 51:11 7218
they lie at the *h* of all the .... Is 51:20 7218
it to bow down his *h* as a bulrush .... Is 58:5 7218
an helmet of salvation upon his *h* .... Is 59:17 7218
have broken the crown of thy *h* .... Jer 2:16 6936
him, and thine hands upon thine *h* .... Jer 2:37 7218
Oh that my *h* were waters, and mine .... Jer 9:1 7218
shall be astonished, and wag his *h* .... Jer 18:16 7218
unto me, and the *h* of Lebanon .... Jer 22:6 7218
upon the *h* of the wicked .... Jer 23:19 7218
pain upon the *h* of the wicked .... Jer 30:23 7218
For every *h* shall be bald, and .... Jer 48:37 7218
the crown of the *h* of the .... Jer 48:45 6936
the *h* of Jehoiachin king of Judah .... Jer 52:31 7218
wag their *h* at the daughter of .... Lam 2:15 7218
Waters flowed over mine *h* .... Lam 3:54 7218
The crown is fallen from our *h* .... Lam 5:16 7218
and cause it to pass upon thine *h* .... Eze 5:1 7218
and took me by a lock of mine *h* .... Eze 8:3 7218
recompense their way upon their *h* .... Eze 9:10 7218
firmament that was above the *h* of .... Eze 10:1 7218
the *h* looked they followed it .... Eze 10:11 7218
make kerchiefs upon the *h* of .... Eze 13:18 7218
and a beautiful crown upon thine *h* .... Eze 16:12 7218
high place at every *h* of the way .... Eze 16:25 7218
place in the *h* of every way .... Eze 16:31 7218
recompense thy way upon thine *h* .... Eze 16:43 7218
will I recompense upon his own *h* .... Eze 17:19 7218
choose it at the *h* of the way to .... Eze 21:19 7218
at the *h* of the two ways, to use .... Eze 21:21 7218
the tire of thine *h* upon thee .... Eze 24:17
every *h* was made bald, and every .... Eze 29:18 7218
his blood shall be upon his own *h* .... Eze 33:4 7218
was a door in the *h* of the way .... Eze 42:12 7218
make me endanger my *h* to the king .... Dan 1:10 7218
the visions of thy *h* upon thy bed .... Dan 2:28 7217

This image's *h* was of fine gold, Dan 2:32 7217
Thou art this *h* of gold Dan 2:38 7217
nor was an hair of their *h* singed Dan 3:27 7217
the visions of my *h* troubled me Dan 4:5 7217
the visions of mine *h* in my bed Dan 4:10 7217
the visions of my *h* upon my bed Dan 4:13 7217
and visions of his *h* upon his bed Dan 7:1 7217
the hair of his *h* like the pure Dan 7:9 7217
the visions of my *h* troubled me Dan 7:15 7217
the ten horns that were in his *h* Dan 7:20 7217
and appoint themselves one *h* Hos 1:11 7218
your recompence upon your own *h* Joel 3:4 7218
your recompence upon your own *h* Joel 3:7 7218
of the earth on the *h* of the poor Amos 2:7 7218
loins, and baldness upon every *h* Amos 8:10 7218
and cut them in the *h*, all of them Amos 9:1 7218
shall return upon thine own *h* Obad 15 7218
the weeds were wrapped about my *h* Jonah 2:5 7218
it might be a shadow over his *h* Jonah 4:6 7218
the sun beat upon the *h* of Jonah Jonah 4:8 7218
and the LORD on the *h* of them Mic 2:13 7218
thou woundedst the *h* out of the Hab 3:13 7218
his staves the *h* of his villages Hab 3:14 7218
so that no man did lift up his *h* Zec 1:21 7218
them set a fair mitre upon his *h* Zec 3:5 7218
they set a fair mitre upon his *h* Zec 3:5 7218
set them upon the *h* of Joshua the Zec 6:11 7218
Neither shalt thou swear by thy *h* Mt 5:36 *2776*
when thou fastest, anoint thine *h* Mt 6:17 *2776*
man hath not where to lay his *h* Mt 8:20 *2776*
hairs of your *h* are all numbered Mt 10:30 *2776*
John Baptist's *h* in a charger Mt 14:8 *2776*
his *h* was brought in a charger, Mt 14:11 *2776*
is become the *h* of the corner Mt 21:42 *2776*
ointment, and poured it on his *h* Mt 26:7 *2776*
of thorns, they put it upon his *h* Mt 27:29 *2776*
the reed, and smote him on the *h* Mt 27:30 *2776*
set up over his *h* his accusation Mt 27:37 *2776*
The *h* of John the Baptist Mk 6:24 *2776*
charger the *h* of John the Baptist Mk 6:25 *2776*
and commanded his *h* to be brought Mk 6:27 *2776*
brought his *h* in a charger, and Mk 6:28 *2776*
stones, and wounded him in the *h* Mk 12:4 *2775*
is become the *h* of the corner Mk 12:10 *2776*
the box, and poured it on his *h* Mk 14:3 *2776*
of thorns, and put it about his *h* Mk 15:17 *2776*
smote him on the *h* with a reed Mk 15:19 *2776*
wipe them with the hairs of her *h* Lk 7:38 *2776*
them with the hairs of her *h* Lk 7:44 *2776*
My *h* with oil thou didst not Lk 7:46 *2776*
man hath not where to lay his *h* Lk 9:58 *2776*
hairs of your *h* are all numbered Lk 12:7 *2776*
is become the *h* of the corner Lk 20:17 *2776*
not an hair of your *h* perish Lk 21:18 *2776*
only, but also my hands and my *h* Jn 13:9 *2776*
of thorns, and put it on his *h* Jn 19:2 *2776*
and he bowed his *h*, and gave up the Jn 19:30 *2776*
the napkin, that was about his *h* Jn 20:7 *2776*
white sitting, the one at the *h* Jn 20:12 *2776*
is become the *h* of the corner Acts 4:11 *2776*
having shorn his *h* in Cenchrea Acts 18:18 *2776*
fall from the *h* of any of you Acts 27:34 *2776*
shalt heap coals of fire on his *h* Rom 12:20 *2776*
that the *h* of every man is Christ 1Cor 11:3 *2776*
the *h* of the woman is the man 1Cor 11:3 *2776*
and the *h* of Christ is God 1Cor 11:3 *2776*
prophesying, having his *h* covered 1Cor 11:4 *2776*
h uncovered dishonoureth her *h* 1Cor 11:5 *2776*
indeed ought not to cover his *h* 1Cor 11:7 *2776*
on her *h* because of the angels 1Cor 11:10 *2776*
nor again the *h* to the feet 1Cor 12:21 *2776*
gave him to be the *h* over all Eph 1:22 *2776*
him in all things, which is the *h* Eph 4:15 *2776*
the husband is the *h* of the wife Eph 5:23 *2776*
as Christ is the *h* of the church Eph 5:23 *2776*
he is the *h* of the body, the Col 1:18 *2776*
in him, which is the *h* of all Col 2:10 *2776*
And not holding the *H*, from which Col 2:19 *2776*
same is made the *h* of the corner 1Pet 2:7 *2776*
His *h* and his hairs were white Rev 1:14 *2776*
and a rainbow was upon his *h* Rev 10:1 *2776*
upon her *h* a crown of twelve Rev 12:1 *2776*
having on his *h* a golden crown, Rev 14:14 *2776*
on his *h* were many crowns Rev 19:12 *2776*

HEADBANDS {1}

ornaments of the legs, and the *h* Is 3:20 7196

HEADLONG {3}

of the froward is carried *h* Job 5:13
that they might cast him down *h* Lk 4:29 *2630*
and falling *h*, he burst asunder in Acts 1:18 *4248*

HEADS {110}

was parted, and became into four *h* Gen 2:10 7218
And they bowed down their *h* Gen 43:28
then they bowed their *h* and Ex 4:31
These be the *h* of their fathers' Ex 6:14 7218
these are the *h* of the fathers of Ex 6:25 7218
made them *h* over the people, Ex 18:25 7218
his sons, Uncover not your *h* Lev 10:6 7218
not round the corners of your *h* Lev 19:27 7218
fathers, *h* of thousands in Israel Num 1:16 7218
h of the house of their fathers, Num 7:2 7218
hands upon the *h* of the bullocks Num 8:12 7218
which are *h* of the thousands of Num 10:4 7218
all those men were *h* of the Num 13:3 7218
Take all the *h* of the people, and Num 25:4 7218
Moses spake unto the *h* of the Num 30:1 7218
and known, and made them *h* over you Deut 1:15 7218
even all the *h* of your tribes, and Deut 5:23 7218
when the *h* of the people and the Deut 33:5 7218
he came with the *h* of the people Deut 33:21 7218
Israel, and put dust upon their *h* Josh 7:6 7218
the *h* of the fathers of the Josh 14:1 7218
the *h* of the fathers of the Josh 19:51 7218
Then came near the *h* of the Josh 21:1 7218
unto the *h* of the fathers of the Josh 21:1 7218
said unto the *h* of the thousands Josh 22:21 7218
h of the thousands of Israel Josh 22:30 7218
for their elders, and for their *h* Josh 23:2 7218
elders of Israel, and for their *h* Josh 24:1 7218
Midian, and brought the *h* of Oreb Judg 7:25 7218
they lifted up their *h* no more Judg 8:28 7218
did God render upon their *h* Judg 9:57 7218
it not be with the *h* of these men 1Sa 29:4 7218
all the *h* of the tribes, the 1Kin 8:1 7218
on our loins, and ropes upon our *h* 1Kin 20:31 7218
loins, and put ropes on their *h* 1Kin 20:32 7218
take ye the *h* of the men your 2Kin 10:6 7218
put their *h* in baskets, and sent 2Kin 10:7 7218
brought the *h* of the king's sons 2Kin 10:8 7218
these were the *h* of the house of 1Chr 5:24 7218
h of the house of their fathers 1Chr 5:24 7218
h of their father's house, to wit 1Chr 7:2 7218
h of the house of their fathers, 1Chr 7:7 7218
h of the house of their fathers, 1Chr 7:9 7218
by the *h* of their fathers, mighty 1Chr 7:11 7218
h of their father's house, choice 1Chr 7:40 7218
these are the *h* of the fathers of 1Chr 8:6 7218
were his sons, *h* of the fathers 1Chr 8:10 7218
who were *h* of the fathers of the 1Chr 8:13 7218
These were *h* of the fathers, by 1Chr 8:28 7218
h of the house of their fathers, 1Chr 9:13 7218
Saul to the jeopardy of our *h* 1Chr 12:19 7218
the *h* of them were two hundred 1Chr 12:32
fathers, and bowed down their *h* 1Chr 29:20
put them on the *h* of the pillars 2Chr 3:16 7218
all the *h* of the tribes, the 2Chr 5:2 7218
Then certain of the *h* of the 2Chr 28:12
gladness, and they bowed their *h* 2Chr 29:30
and they bowed their *h*, and Neh 8:6
dust upon their *h* toward heaven Job 2:12 7218
Lift up your *h*, O ye gates Ps 24:7 7218
Lift up your *h*, O ye gates Ps 24:9 7218
caused men to ride over our *h* Ps 66:12 7218
thou brakest the *h* of the dragons Ps 74:13 7218
Thou brakest the *h* of leviathan Ps 74:14 7218
upon me they shaked their *h* Ps 109:25 7218
he shall wound the *h* over many Ps 110:6 7218
on all their *h* shall be baldness, Is 15:2 7218
and everlasting joy upon their *h* Is 35:10 7218
and confounded, and covered their *h* Jer 14:3 7218
ashamed, they covered their *h* Jer 14:4 7218
have cast up dust upon their *h* Lam 2:10 7218
hang down their *h* to the ground Lam 2:10 7218
of the firmament upon the *h* of Eze 1:22 7218
forth over their *h* above Eze 1:22 7218
firmament that was over their *h* Eze 1:25 7218
h was the likeness of a throne Eze 1:26 7218
and baldness upon all their *h* Eze 7:18 7218
their way upon their own *h* Eze 11:21 7218
have I recompensed upon their *h* Eze 22:31 7218
in dyed attire upon their *h* Eze 23:15 7218
and beautiful crowns upon their *h* Eze 23:42 7218
your tires shall be upon your *h* Eze 24:23 7218
shall cast up dust upon their *h* Eze 27:30 7218
laid their swords under their *h* Eze 32:27 7218
have linen bonnets upon their *h* Eze 44:18 7218
Neither shall they shave their *h* Eze 44:20 7218
they shall only poll their *h* Eze 44:20 7218
the beast had also four *h* Dan 7:6 7217
O *h* of Jacob, and ye princes of Mic 3:1 7218
ye *h* of the house of Jacob, and Mic 3:9 7218
The *h* thereof judge for reward, Mic 3:11 7218
by reviled him, wagging their *h* Mt 27:39 *2776*
by railed on him, wagging their *h* Mk 15:29 *2776*
then look up, and lift up your *h* Lk 21:28 *2776*
Your blood be upon your own *h* Acts 18:6 *2776*
them, that they may shave their *h* Acts 21:24 *2776*
had on their *h* crowns of gold Rev 4:4 *2776*
on their *h* were as it were crowns Rev 9:7 *2776*
the *h* of the horses were as the Rev 9:17 *2776*
the horses were as the *h* of lions Rev 9:17 *2776*
were like unto serpents, and had *h* Rev 9:19 *2776*
great red dragon, having seven *h* Rev 12:3 *2776*
horns, and seven crowns upon his *h* Rev 12:3 *2776*
up out of the sea, having seven *h* Rev 13:1 *2776*
upon his *h* the name of blasphemy Rev 13:1 *2776*
I saw one of his *h* as it were Rev 13:3 *2776*
of blasphemy, having seven *h* Rev 17:3 *2776*
her, which hath the seven *h* Rev 17:7 *2776*
The seven *h* are seven mountains, Rev 17:9 *2776*
And they cast dust on their *h* Rev 18:19 *2776*

HEADSTONE {1}

the *h* thereof with shoutings Zec 4:7 68,7222

HEADY {1}

Traitors, *h*, highminded, lovers 2Ti 3:4 *4312*

HEAL {40}

H her now, O God, I beseech thee Num 12:13 7495
I wound, and I *h* Deut 32:39 7495
behold, I will *h* thee 2Kin 20:5 7495
the sign that the LORD will *h* me 2Kin 20:8 7495
their sin, and will *h* their land 2Chr 7:14 7495
O LORD, *h* me Ps 6:2 7495
h my soul Ps 41:4 7495
h the breaches thereof Ps 60:2 7495
A time to kill, and a time to *h* Eccl 3:3 7495
he shall smite and *h* it Is 19:22 7495
of them, and shall *h* them Is 19:22 7495
have seen his ways, and will *h* him Is 57:18 7495
and I will *h* him Is 57:19 7495
I will *h* your backslidings Jer 3:22 7495
H me, O LORD, and I shall be Jer 17:14 7495
I will *h* thee of thy wounds, Jer 30:17 7495
who can *h* thee? Lam 2:13 7495
yet could he not *h* you, nor cure Hos 5:13 7495
for he hath torn, and he will *h* us Hos 6:1 7495
I will *h* their backsliding, I Hos 14:4 7495
nor *h* that that is broken, nor Zec 11:16 7495
unto him, I will come and *h* him Mt 8:7 *2323*
to *h* all manner of sickness and Mt 10:1 *2323*
H the sick, cleanse the lepers, Mt 10:8 *2323*
Is it lawful to *h* on the sabbath Mt 12:10 *2323*
be converted, and I should *h* them Mt 13:15 *2390*
whether he would *h* him on the Mk 3:2 *2323*
And to have power to *h* sicknesses Mk 3:15 *2323*
sent me to *h* the brokenhearted Lk 4:18 *2390*
proverb, Physician, *h* thyself Lk 4:23 *2323*
of the Lord was present to *h* them Lk 5:17 *2390*
whether he would *h* on the sabbath Lk 6:7 *2323*
he would come and *h* his servant Lk 7:3 *1295*
kingdom of God, and to *h* the sick Lk 9:2 *2390*
h the sick that are therein, and Lk 10:9 *2323*
Is it lawful to *h* on the sabbath Lk 14:3 *2323*
he would come down, and *h* his son Jn 4:47 *2390*
be converted, and I should *h* them Jn 12:40 *2390*
stretching forth thine hand to *h* Acts 4:30 *2392*
be converted, and I should *h* them Acts 28:27 *2392*

HEALED {79}

God *h* Abimelech, and his wife, and Gen 20:17 7495
cause him to be thoroughly *h* Ex 21:19 7495
skin thereof, was a boil, and is *h* Lev 13:18 7495
the scall is *h*, he is clean Lev 13:37 7495
of leprosy be *h* in the leper Lev 14:3 7495
clean, because the plague is *h* Lev 14:48 7495
itch, whereof thou canst not be *h* Deut 28:27 7495
a sore botch that cannot be *h* Deut 28:35 7495
then ye shall be *h*, and it shall 1Sa 6:3 7495
the LORD, I have *h* these waters 2Kin 2:21 7495
the waters were *h* unto this day 2Kin 2:22 7495
king Joram went back to be *h* in 2Kin 8:29 7495
king Joram was returned to be *h* 2Kin 9:15 7495
he returned to be *h* in Jezreel 2Chr 22:6 7495
to Hezekiah, and *h* the people 2Chr 30:20 7495
unto thee, and thou hast *h* me Ps 30:2 7495
h them, and delivered them from Ps 107:20 7495
their heart, and convert, and be *h* Is 6:10 7495
and with his stripes we are *h* Is 53:5 7495
They have *h* also the hurt of the Jer 6:14 7495
For they have *h* the hurt of the Jer 8:11 7495
incurable, which refuseth to be *h* Jer 15:18 7495
Heal me, O LORD, and I shall be *h* Jer 17:14 7495
her pain, if so be she may be *h* Jer 51:8 7495
h Babylon, but she is not *h* Jer 51:9 7495
it shall not be bound up to be *h* Eze 30:21 5414,7499
neither have ye *h* that which was Eze 34:4 7495
the sea, the waters shall be *h* Eze 47:8 7495
for they shall be *h* Eze 47:9 7495
marishes thereof shall not be *h* Eze 47:11 7495
When I would have *h* Israel Hos 7:1 7495
but they knew not that I *h* them Hos 11:3 7495
and he *h* them Mt 4:24 *2323*
only, and my servant shall be *h* Mt 8:8 *2390*
his servant was *h* in the selfsame Mt 8:13 *2390*
his word, and *h* all that were sick Mt 8:16 *2323*
followed him, and he *h* them all Mt 12:15 *2323*
he *h* him, insomuch that the blind Mt 12:22 *2323*
toward them, and he *h* their sick Mt 14:14 *2323*
and he *h* them Mt 15:30 *2323*
and he *h* them there Mt 19:2 *2323*
and he *h* them Mt 21:14 *2323*
he *h* many that were sick of Mk 1:34 *2323*
For he had *h* many Mk 3:10 *2323*
hands on her, that she may be *h* Mk 5:23 *4982*
that she was *h* of that plague Mk 5:29 *2390*
upon a few sick folk, and *h* them Mk 6:5 *2323*
many that were sick, and *h* them Mk 6:13 *2323*
on every one of them, and *h* them Lk 4:40 *2323*
hear, and to be *h* by him of their Lk 5:15 *2323*
to be *h* of their diseases Lk 6:17 *2390*
and they were *h* Lk 6:18 *2323*
virtue out of him, and *h* them all Lk 6:19 *2390*
a word, and my servant shall be *h* Lk 7:7 *2390*
which had been *h* of evil spirits Lk 8:2 *2390*
was possessed of the devils was *h* Lk 8:36 *4982*
neither could be *h* of any Lk 8:43 *2323*
him, and how she was *h* immediately Lk 8:47 *2390*
h them that had need of healing Lk 9:11 *2390*
h the child, and delivered him Lk 9:42 *2390*
Jesus had *h* on the sabbath day Lk 13:14 *2323*
in them therefore come and be *h* Lk 13:14 *2323*
took him, and *h* him, and let him go Lk 14:4 *2323*
them, when he saw that he was *h* Lk 17:15 *2390*
And he touched his ear, and *h* him Lk 22:51 *2390*
he that was *h* wist not who it was Jn 5:13 *2390*
lame man which was *h* held Peter Acts 3:11 *2390*
which was *h* standing with them Acts 4:14 *2323*
and they were *h* every one Acts 5:16 *2323*
and that were lame, were *h* Acts 8:7 *2323*
that he had faith to be *h* Acts 14:9 *4982*
laid his hands on him, and *h* him Acts 28:8 *2390*
in the island, came, and were *h* Acts 28:9 *2323*
but let it rather be *h* Heb 12:13 *2390*

one for another, that ye may be *h*.......... Jas 5:16 2390
by whose stripes ye were *h*.......... 1Pet 2:24 2390
and his deadly wound was *h*.......... Rev 13:3 2323
beast, whose deadly wound was *h*.......... Rev 13:12 2323

HEALER {1}
swear, saying, I will not be an *h*.......... Is 3:7 2280

HEALETH {4}
for I am the LORD that *h* thee.......... Ex 15:26 7495
who *h* all thy diseases.......... Ps 103:3 7495
He *h* the broken in heart, and.......... Ps 147:3 7495
h the stroke of their wound.......... Is 30:26 7495

HEALING {14}
us, and there is no *h* for us.......... Jer 14:19 4832
and for the time of *h*, and behold.......... Jer 14:19 4832
thou hast no *h* medicines.......... Jer 30:13 8585
There is no *h* of thy bruise.......... Nah 3:19 3545
arise with *h* in his wings.......... Mal 4:2 4832
h all manner of sickness and all.......... Mt 4:23 2323
h every sickness and every disease.......... Mt 9:35 2323
the gospel, and *h* every where.......... Lk 9:6 2323
and healed them that had need of *h*.......... Lk 9:11 2322
whom this miracle of *h* was shewed.......... Acts 4:22 2392
h all that were oppressed of the.......... Acts 10:38 2390
the gifts of *h* by the same Spirit.......... 1Cor 12:9 2386
Have all the gifts of *h*.......... 1Cor 12:30 2386
were for the *h* of the nations.......... Rev 22:2 2322

HEALINGS {1}
that miracles, then gifts of *h*.......... 1Cor 12:28 2386

HEALTH {17}
servant our father is in good *h*.......... Gen 43:28 7965
Joab said to Amasa, Art thou in *h*.......... 2Sa 20:9 7965
who is the *h* of my countenance,.......... Ps 42:11 3444
who is the *h* of my countenance,.......... Ps 43:5 3444
thy saving *h* among all nations.......... Ps 67:2
It shall be *h* to thy navel, and.......... Prov 3:8 7500
them, and *h* to all their flesh.......... Prov 4:22 4832
but the tongue of the wise is *h*.......... Prov 12:18 4832
but a faithful ambassador is *h*.......... Prov 13:17 4832
to the soul, and *h* to the bones.......... Prov 16:24 4832
thine *h* shall spring forth.......... Is 58:8 724
and for a time of *h*, and behold.......... Jer 8:15 4832
why then is not the *h* of the.......... Jer 8:22 724
For I will restore *h* unto thee.......... Jer 30:17 724
Behold, I will bring it *h*.......... Jer 33:6 724
for this is for your *h*.......... Acts 27:34 4491
thou mayest prosper and be in *h*.......... 3Jn 2 5198

HEAP {38}
and they took stones, and made an *h*.......... Gen 31:46 1530
and they did eat there upon the *h*.......... Gen 31:46 1530
This *h* is a witness between me and.......... Gen 31:48 1530
said to Jacob, Behold this *h*.......... Gen 31:51 1530
This *h* be witness, and this pillar.......... Gen 31:52 1530
will not pass over this *h* to thee.......... Gen 31:52 1530
thou shalt not pass over this *h*.......... Gen 31:52 1530
the floods stood upright as an *h*.......... Ex 15:8 5067
and it shall be an *h* for ever.......... Deut 13:16 8510
I will *h* mischiefs upon them.......... Deut 32:23 5595
and they shall stand upon an *h*.......... Josh 3:13 5067
rose up upon an *h* very far from.......... Josh 3:16 5067
a great *h* of stones unto this day.......... Josh 7:26 1530
Ai, and made it an *h* for ever.......... Josh 8:28 8510
raise thereon a great *h* of stones.......... Josh 8:29 1530
down at the end of the *h* of corn.......... Ruth 3:7 6194
laid a very great *h* of stones.......... 2Sa 18:17 1530
His roots are wrapped about the *h*.......... Job 8:17 1530
I could *h* up words against you,.......... Job 16:4 2266
Though he *h* up silver as the dust.......... Job 27:16 6651
hypocrites in heart *h* up wrath.......... Job 36:13 7760
of the sea together as an *h*.......... Ps 33:7 5067
made the waters to stand as an *h*.......... Ps 78:13 5067
For thou shalt *h* coals of fire.......... Prov 25:22 2846
travail, to gather and to *h* up.......... Eccl 2:26 3664
thy belly is like an *h* of wheat.......... Song 7:2 6194
city, and it shall be a ruinous *h*.......... Is 17:1 4596
shall be a *h* in the day of grief.......... Is 17:11 5067
For thou hast made of a city an *h*.......... Is 25:2 1530
shall be builded upon her own *h*.......... Jer 30:18 8510
and it shall be a desolate *h*.......... Jer 49:2 8510
H on wood, kindle the fire,.......... Eze 24:10 7235
make Samaria as an *h* of the field.......... Mic 1:6 5856
for they shall *h* dust, and take it.......... Hab 1:10 6651
through the *h* of great waters.......... Hab 3:15 2563
came to an *h* of twenty measures.......... Hag 2:16 6194
shalt *h* coals of fire on his head.......... Rom 12:20 4987
they *h* to themselves teachers.......... 2Ti 4:3 2002

HEAPED {2}
h up silver as the dust, and fine.......... Zec 9:3 6651
Ye have *h* treasure together for.......... Jas 5:3 2343

HEAPETH {2}
he *h* up riches, and knoweth not.......... Ps 39:6 6651
nations, and *h* unto him all people.......... Hab 2:5 6908

HEAPS {20}
gathered them together upon *h*.......... Ex 8:14 2563
h upon *h*, with the jaw of an.......... Judg 15:16 2565
Lay ye them in two *h* at the.......... 2Kin 10:8 6632
fenced cities into ruinous *h*.......... 2Kin 19:25 1530
LORD their God, and laid them by *h*.......... 2Chr 31:6 6194
to lay the foundation of the *h*.......... 2Chr 31:7 6194
and the princes came and saw the *h*.......... 2Chr 31:8 6194
and the Levites concerning the *h*.......... 2Chr 31:9 6194
revive the stones out of the *h* of.......... Neh 4:2 6194
which are ready to become *h*.......... Job 15:28 1530
they have laid Jerusalem on *h*.......... Ps 79:1 5856
defenced cities into ruinous *h*.......... Is 37:26 1530
And I will make Jerusalem *h*.......... Jer 9:11 1530
and Jerusalem shall become *h*.......... Jer 26:18 5856
up waymarks, make thee high *h*.......... Jer 31:21 8564
cast her up as *h*, and destroy her.......... Jer 50:26 6194
And Babylon shall become *h*.......... Jer 51:37 1530
their altars are as *h* in the.......... Hos 12:11 1530
and Jerusalem shall become *h*.......... Mic 3:12 5856

HEAR {550}
wives, Adah and Zillah, *H* my voice.......... Gen 4:23 8085
so that all that *h* will laugh.......... Gen 21:6 8085
H us, my lord.......... Gen 23:6 8085
h me, and intreat for me to Ephron.......... Gen 23:8 8085
Nay, my lord, *h* me.......... Gen 23:11 8085
wilt give it, I pray thee, *h* me.......... Gen 23:13 8085
And he said unto them, *H*, I pray.......... Gen 37:6 8085
he besought us, and we would not *h*.......... Gen 42:21 8085
and ye would not *h*.......... Gen 42:22 8085
Gather yourselves together, and *h*.......... Gen 49:2 8085
how then shall Pharaoh *h* me.......... Ex 6:12 8085
hitherto thou wouldest not *h*.......... Ex 7:16 8085
The people shall *h*, and be afraid.......... Ex 15:14 8085
that the people may *h* when I.......... Ex 19:9 8085
Speak thou with us, and we will *h*.......... Ex 20:19 8085
me, I will surely *h* their cry.......... Ex 22:23 8085
he crieth unto me, that I will *h*.......... Ex 22:27 8085
noise of them that sing do I *h*.......... Ex 32:18 8085
h the voice of swearing, and is a.......... Lev 5:1 8085
I will *h* what the LORD will.......... Num 9:8 8085
And he said, *H* now my words.......... Num 12:6 8085
Then the Egyptians shall *h* it.......... Num 14:13 8085
And Moses said unto Korah, *H*.......... Num 16:8 8085
said unto them, *H* now, ye rebels.......... Num 20:10 8085
and said, Rise up, Balak, and *h*.......... Num 23:18 8085
And her father *h* her vow, and her.......... Num 30:4 8085
H the causes between your.......... Deut 1:16 8085
but ye shall *h* the small as well.......... Deut 1:17 8085
bring it unto me, and I will *h* it.......... Deut 1:17 8085
and ye would not *h*, but rebelled.......... Deut 1:43 8085
who shall *h* report of thee, and.......... Deut 2:25 8085
for your sakes, and would not *h* me.......... Deut 3:26 8085
which shall *h* all these statutes,.......... Deut 4:6 8085
and I will make them *h* my words.......... Deut 4:10 8085
stone, which neither see, nor *h*.......... Deut 4:28 8085
Did ever people *h* the voice of.......... Deut 4:33 8085
he made thee to *h* his voice.......... Deut 4:36 8085
all Israel, and said unto them, *H*.......... Deut 5:1 8085
if we *h* the voice of the LORD our.......... Deut 5:25 8085
h all that the LORD our God shall.......... Deut 5:27 8085
and we will *h* it, and do it.......... Deut 5:27 8085
H therefore, O Israel, and observe.......... Deut 6:3 8085
H, O Israel.......... Deut 6:4 8085
H, O Israel.......... Deut 9:1 8085
h all these words which I command.......... Deut 12:28 8085
And all Israel shall *h*, and fear,.......... Deut 13:11 8085
If thou shalt *h* say in one of thy.......... Deut 13:12 8085
And all the people shall *h*.......... Deut 17:13 8085
Let me not *h* again the voice of.......... Deut 18:16 8085
And those which remain shall *h*.......... Deut 19:20 8085
And shall say unto them, *H*.......... Deut 20:3 8085
and all Israel shall *h*, and fear.......... Deut 21:21 8085
and eyes to see, and ears to *h*.......... Deut 29:4 8085
it unto us, that we may *h* it.......... Deut 30:12 8085
it unto us, that we may *h* it.......... Deut 30:13 8085
away, so that thou wilt not *h*.......... Deut 30:17 8085
within thy gates, that they may *h*.......... Deut 31:12 8085
have not known any thing, may *h*.......... Deut 31:13 8085
and *h*, O earth, the words of my.......... Deut 32:1 8085
and he said, *H*, LORD, the voice of.......... Deut 33:7 8085
h the words of the LORD your God.......... Josh 3:9 8085
when ye *h* the sound of the.......... Josh 6:5 8085
of the land shall *h* of it.......... Josh 7:9 8085
H, O ye kings.......... Judg 5:3 8085
to *h* the bleatings of the flocks.......... Judg 5:16 8085
thou shalt *h* what they say.......... Judg 7:11 8085
thy riddle, that we may *h* it.......... Judg 14:13 8085
for I *h* of your evil dealings by.......... 1Sa 2:23 8085
for it is no good report that I *h*.......... 1Sa 2:24 8085
LORD will not *h* you in that day.......... 1Sa 8:18 6030
land, saying, Let the Hebrews *h*.......... 1Sa 13:3 8085
the lowing of the oxen which I *h*.......... 1Sa 15:14 8085
if Saul *h* it, he will kill me.......... 1Sa 16:2 8085
about him, *H* now, ye Benjamites.......... 1Sa 22:7 8085
H now, thou son of Ahitub.......... 1Sa 22:12 8085
h the words of thine handmaid.......... 1Sa 25:24 8085
let my lord the king *h* the words.......... 1Sa 26:19 8085
For the king will *h*, to deliver.......... 2Sa 14:16 8085
man deputed of the king to *h* thee.......... 2Sa 15:3 8085
As soon as ye *h* the sound of the.......... 2Sa 15:10 8085
shalt *h* out of the king's house.......... 2Sa 15:35 8085
unto me every thing that ye can *h*.......... 2Sa 15:36 8085
all Israel shall *h* that thou art.......... 2Sa 16:21 8085
let us *h* likewise what he saith.......... 2Sa 17:5 8085
can I *h* any more the voice of.......... 2Sa 19:35 8085
woman out of the city, *H*, *h*.......... 2Sa 20:16 8085
H the words of thine handmaid.......... 2Sa 20:17 8085
And he answered, I do *h*.......... 2Sa 20:17 8085
he did *h* my voice out of his.......... 2Sa 22:7 8085
as soon as they *h*, they shall be.......... 2Sa 22:45 8085
people to *h* the wisdom of Solomon.......... 1Kin 4:34 8085
h thou in heaven thy dwelling.......... 1Kin 8:30 8085
Then *h* thou in heaven, and do, and.......... 1Kin 8:32 8085
Then *h* thou in heaven, and forgive.......... 1Kin 8:34 8085
Then *h* thou in heaven, and forgive.......... 1Kin 8:36 8085
Then *h* thou in heaven thy.......... 1Kin 8:39 8085
(For they shall *h* of thy great.......... 1Kin 8:42 8085
H thou in heaven thy dwelling.......... 1Kin 8:43 8085
Then *h* thou in heaven their.......... 1Kin 8:45 8085
Then *h* thou their prayer and their.......... 1Kin 8:49 8085
before thee, and that *h* thy wisdom.......... 1Kin 10:8 8085
to *h* his wisdom, which God had.......... 1Kin 10:24 8085
until noon, saying, O Baal, *h* us.......... 1Kin 18:26 6030
H me, O LORD, *h* me, that this.......... 1Kin 18:37 6030
H thou therefore the word of the.......... 1Kin 22:19 8085
H ye the word of the LORD.......... 2Kin 7:1 8085
Syrians to *h* a noise of chariots.......... 2Kin 7:6 8085
But Amaziah would not *h*.......... 2Kin 14:11 8085
Notwithstanding they would not *h*.......... 2Kin 17:14 8085
commanded, and would not *h* them.......... 2Kin 18:12 8085
H the word of the great king, the.......... 2Kin 18:28 8085
h all the words of Rab-shakeh.......... 2Kin 19:4 8085
upon him, and he shall *h* a rumour.......... 2Kin 19:7 8085
LORD, bow down thine ear, and *h*.......... 2Kin 19:16 8085
h the words of Sennacherib, which.......... 2Kin 19:16 8085
Hezekiah, *H* the word of the LORD.......... 2Kin 20:16 8085
when thou shalt *h* a sound of.......... 1Chr 14:15 8085
H me, my brethren, and my people.......... 1Chr 28:2 8085
h thou from thy dwelling place,.......... 2Chr 6:21 8085
Then *h* thou from heaven, and do,.......... 2Chr 6:23 8085
Then *h* thou from the heavens, and.......... 2Chr 6:25 8085
Then *h* thou from heaven, and.......... 2Chr 6:27 8085
Then *h* thou from heaven thy.......... 2Chr 6:30 8085
Then *h* thou from the heavens,.......... 2Chr 6:33 8085
Then *h* thou from the heavens.......... 2Chr 6:35 8085
Then *h* thou from the heavens,.......... 2Chr 6:39 8085
then will I *h* from heaven.......... 2Chr 7:14 8085
before thee, and *h* thy wisdom.......... 2Chr 9:7 8085
to *h* his wisdom, that God had put.......... 2Chr 9:23 8085
H me, thou Jeroboam, and all.......... 2Chr 13:4 8085
H ye me, Asa, and all Judah and.......... 2Chr 15:2 8085
Therefore *h* the word of the LORD.......... 2Chr 18:18 8085
our affliction, then thou wilt *h*.......... 2Chr 20:9 8085
H me, O Judah, and ye inhabitants.......... 2Chr 20:20 8085
But Amaziah would not *h*.......... 2Chr 25:20 8085
Now *h* me therefore, and deliver.......... 2Chr 28:11 8085
H me, ye Levites, sanctify now.......... 2Chr 29:5 8085
that thou mayest *h* the prayer of.......... Neh 1:6 8085
H, O our God.......... Neh 4:4 8085
ye *h* the sound of the trumpet.......... Neh 4:20 8085
women, and all that could *h* with.......... Neh 8:2 8085
their neck, and would not *h*.......... Neh 9:29 8085
they *h* not the voice of the.......... Job 3:18 8085
h it, and know thou it for thy.......... Job 5:27 8085
H now my reasoning, and hearken to.......... Job 13:6 8085
H diligently my speech, and my.......... Job 13:17 8085
I will shew thee, *h* me.......... Job 15:17 8085
H diligently my speech, and let.......... Job 21:2 8085
unto him, and he shall *h* thee.......... Job 22:27 8085
Will God *h* his cry when trouble.......... Job 27:9 8085
unto thee, and thou dost not *h* me.......... Job 30:20 6030
Oh that one would *h* me.......... Job 31:35 8085
h my speeches, and hearken to all.......... Job 33:1 8085
H my words, O ye wise men.......... Job 34:2 8085
thou hast understanding, *h* this.......... Job 34:16 8085
Surely God will not *h* vanity.......... Job 35:13 8085
H attentively the noise of his.......... Job 37:2 8085
H, I beseech thee, and I will.......... Job 42:4 8085
H me when I call, O God of my.......... Ps 4:1 6030
mercy upon me, and *h* my prayer.......... Ps 4:1 8085
the LORD will *h* when I call unto.......... Ps 4:3 8085
voice shalt thou *h* in the morning.......... Ps 5:3 8085
thou wilt cause thine ear to *h*.......... Ps 10:17 7181
Consider and *h* me, O LORD my God.......... Ps 13:3 6030
H the right, O LORD, attend unto.......... Ps 17:1 8085
upon thee, for thou wilt *h* me.......... Ps 17:6 6030
thine ear unto me, and *h* my speech.......... Ps 17:6 8085
As soon as they *h* of me, they.......... Ps 18:44 8085
The LORD *h* thee in the day of.......... Ps 20:1 6030
he will *h* him from his holy.......... Ps 20:6 6030
let the king *h* us when we call.......... Ps 20:9 6030
H, O LORD, when I cry with my.......... Ps 27:7 8085
H the voice of my supplications,.......... Ps 28:2 8085
H, O LORD, and have mercy upon me.......... Ps 30:10 8085
the humble shall *h* thereof.......... Ps 34:2 8085
thou wilt *h*, O Lord my God.......... Ps 38:15 6030
H me, lest otherwise they should.......... Ps 38:16
H my prayer, O LORD, and give ear.......... Ps 39:12 8085
H this, all ye people.......... Ps 49:1 8085
H, O my people, and I will speak.......... Ps 50:7 8085
Make me to *h* joy and gladness.......... Ps 51:8 8085
H my prayer, O God.......... Ps 54:2 8085
Attend unto me, and *h* me.......... Ps 55:2 6030
and he shall *h* my voice.......... Ps 55:17 8085
God shall *h*, and afflict them,.......... Ps 55:19 8085
for who, say they, doth *h*.......... Ps 59:7 8085
save with thy right hand, and *h* me.......... Ps 60:5 6030
H my cry, O God.......... Ps 61:1 8085
H my voice, O God, in my prayer.......... Ps 64:1 8085
Come and *h*, all ye that fear God,.......... Ps 66:16 8085
my heart, the Lord will not *h* me.......... Ps 66:18 8085
the multitude of thy mercy *h* me.......... Ps 69:13 6030
H me, O LORD.......... Ps 69:16 6030
h me speedily.......... Ps 69:17 6030
H, O my people, and I will testify.......... Ps 81:8 8085
O LORD God of hosts, *h* my prayer.......... Ps 84:8 8085
I will *h* what God the LORD will.......... Ps 85:8 8085
Bow down thine ear, O LORD, *h* me.......... Ps 86:1 6030
mine ears shall *h* my desire of.......... Ps 92:11 8085
planted the ear, shall he not *h*.......... Ps 94:9 8085
To day if ye will *h* his voice.......... Ps 95:7 8085
H my prayer, O LORD, and let my.......... Ps 102:1 8085
To *h* the groaning of the prisoner.......... Ps 102:20 8085
They have ears, but they *h* not.......... Ps 115:6 8085
h me, O LORD.......... Ps 119:145 6030
H my voice according unto thy.......... Ps 119:149 8085
Lord, *h* my voice.......... Ps 130:2 8085
They have ears, but they *h* not.......... Ps 135:17 238

H

Context	Reference	Strong's
when they *h* the words of thy	Ps 138:4	8085
h the voice of my supplications,	Ps 140:6	238
places, they shall *h* my words	Ps 141:6	8085
H my prayer, O LORD, give ear to	Ps 143:1	8085
H me speedily, O LORD	Ps 143:7	6030
Cause me to *h* thy lovingkindness	Ps 143:8	8085
he also will *h* their cry, and will	Ps 145:19	8085
A wise man will *h*, and will	Prov 1:5	8085
h the instruction of thy father,	Prov 1:8	8085
H, ye children, the instruction	Prov 4:1	8085
H, O my son, and receive my	Prov 4:10	8085
H me now therefore, O ye children	Prov 5:7	8085
H; for I will speak	Prov 8:6	8085
H instruction, and be wise, and	Prov 8:33	8085
H counsel, and receive instruction	Prov 19:20	8085
to *h* the instruction that causeth	Prov 19:27	8085
h the words of the wise, and apply	Prov 22:17	8085
H thou, my son, and be wise, and	Prov 23:19	8085
of God, and be more ready to *h*	Eccl 5:1	8085
It is better to *h* the rebuke of	Eccl 7:5	8085
for a man to *h* the song of fools	Eccl 7:5	8085
lest thou *h* thy servant curse	Eccl 7:21	8085
Let us *h* the conclusion of the	Eccl 12:13	8085
countenance, let me *h* thy voice	Song 2:14	8085
cause me to *h* it	Song 8:13	8085
H, O heavens, and give ear, O	Is 1:2	8085
H the word of the LORD, ye rulers	Is 1:10	8085
make many prayers, I will not *h*	Is 1:15	8085
H ye indeed, but understand not	Is 6:9	8085
h with their ears, and understand	Is 6:10	8085
H ye now, O house of David	Is 7:13	8085
when he bloweth a trumpet, *h* ye	Is 18:3	8085
yet they would not *h*	Is 28:12	8085
Wherefore *h* the word of the LORD,	Is 28:14	8085
Give ye ear, and *h* my voice	Is 28:23	8085
hearken, and *h* my speech	Is 28:23	8085
the deaf *h* the words of the book	Is 29:18	8085
will not *h* the law of the LORD	Is 30:9	8085
when he shall *h* it, he will	Is 30:19	8085
thine ears shall *h* a word behind	Is 30:21	8085
ears of them that *h* shall hearken	Is 32:3	8085
h my voice, ye careless daughters	Is 32:9	8085
H, ye that are far off, what I	Is 33:13	8085
Come near, ye nations, to *h*	Is 34:1	8085
let the earth *h*, and all that is	Is 34:1	8085
H ye the words of the great king,	Is 36:13	8085
God will *h* the words of Rabshakeh	Is 37:4	8085
upon him, and he shall *h* a rumour	Is 37:7	8085
Incline thine ear, O LORD, and *h*	Is 37:17	8085
h all the words of Sennacherib,	Is 37:17	8085
H the word of the LORD of hosts	Is 39:5	8085
thirst, I the LORD will *h* them	Is 41:17	6030
H, ye deaf	Is 42:18	8085
hearken and *h* for the time to come	Is 42:23	8085
or let them *h*, and say, It is	Is 43:9	8085
Yet now *h*, O Jacob my servant	Is 44:1	8085
Therefore *h* now this, thou that	Is 47:8	8085
H ye this, O house of Jacob,	Is 48:1	8085
All ye, assemble yourselves, and *h*	Is 48:14	8085
Come ye near unto me, *h* ye this	Is 48:16	8085
mine ear to *h* as the learned	Is 50:4	8085
Therefore *h* now this, thou	Is 51:21	8085
h, and your soul shall live	Is 55:3	8085
his ear heavy, that it cannot *h*	Is 59:1	8085
face from you, that he will not *h*	Is 59:2	8085
when I spake, ye did not *h*	Is 65:12	8085
they are yet speaking, I will *h*	Is 65:24	8085
when I spake, they did not *h*	Is 66:4	8085
H the word of the LORD, ye that	Is 66:5	8085
H ye the word of the LORD, O	Jer 2:4	8085
h the sound of the trumpet	Jer 4:21	8085
H now this, O foolish people, and	Jer 5:21	8085
which have ears, and *h* not	Jer 5:21	8085
and give warning, that they may *h*	Jer 6:10	8085
Therefore *h*, ye nations, and know,	Jer 6:18	8085
H, O earth	Jer 6:19	8085
H the word of the LORD, all ye of	Jer 7:2	8085
for I will not *h* thee	Jer 7:16	8085
neither can men *h* the voice of	Jer 9:10	8085
Yet *h* the word of the LORD, O ye	Jer 9:20	8085
H ye the word which the LORD	Jer 10:1	8085
H ye the words of this covenant,	Jer 11:2	8085
H ye the words of this covenant,	Jer 11:6	8085
which refused to *h* my words	Jer 11:10	8085
for I will not *h* them in the time	Jer 11:14	8085
which refuse to *h* my words	Jer 13:10	8085
but they would not *h*	Jer 13:11	8085
H ye, and give ear	Jer 13:15	8085
But if ye will not *h* it, my soul	Jer 13:17	8085
they fast, I will not *h* their cry	Jer 14:12	8085
H ye the word of the LORD, ye	Jer 17:20	8085
neck stiff, that they might not *h*	Jer 17:23	8085
I will cause thee to *h* my words	Jer 18:2	8085
H ye the word of the LORD, O	Jer 19:3	8085
that they might not *h* my words	Jer 19:15	8085
let him *h* the cry in the morning,	Jer 20:16	8085
H ye the word of the LORD	Jer 21:11	8085
H the word of the LORD, O king of	Jer 22:2	8085
But if ye will not *h* these words	Jer 22:5	8085
but thou saidst, I will not *h*	Jer 22:21	8085
earth, *h* the word of the LORD	Jer 22:29	8085
caused my people to *h* my words	Jer 23:22	8085
nor inclined your ear to *h*	Jer 25:4	8085
Nevertheless *h* thou now this word	Jer 28:7	8085
the prophet, *H* now, Hananiah	Jer 28:15	8085
but ye would not *h*, saith the	Jer 29:19	8085
H ye therefore the word of the	Jer 29:20	8085
H the word of the LORD, O ye	Jer 31:10	8085
which shall *h* all the good that I	Jer 33:9	8085
Yet *h* the word of the LORD, O	Jer 34:4	8085
h all the evil which I purpose to	Jer 36:3	8085
but he would not *h* them	Jer 36:25	8085
Therefore *h* now, I pray thee, O	Jer 37:20	8085
But if the princes *h* that I have	Jer 38:25	8085
nor *h* the sound of the trumpet,	Jer 42:14	8085
now therefore *h* the word of the	Jer 42:15	8085
H the word of the LORD, all Judah	Jer 44:24	8085
Therefore *h* ye the word of the	Jer 44:26	8085
Therefore *h* the counsel of the	Jer 49:20	8085
Therefore *h* ye the counsel of the	Jer 50:45	8085
h, I pray you, all people, and	Lam 1:18	8085
And they, whether they will *h*	Eze 2:5	8085
unto them, whether they will *h*	Eze 2:7	8085
of man, *h* what I say unto thee	Eze 2:8	8085
thine heart, and *h* with thine ears	Eze 3:10	8085
whether they will *h*, or whether	Eze 3:11	8085
therefore *h* the word at my mouth,	Eze 3:17	8085
He that heareth, let him *h*	Eze 3:27	8085
h the word of the Lord GOD	Eze 6:3	8085
loud voice, yet will I not *h* them	Eze 8:18	8085
they have ears to *h*, and *h* not	Eze 12:2	8085
H ye the word of the LORD	Eze 13:2	8085
to my people that *h* your lies	Eze 13:19	8085
O harlot, *h* the word of the LORD	Eze 16:35	8085
H now, O house of Israel	Eze 18:25	8085
the south, *H* the word of the LORD	Eze 20:47	8085
to cause thee to *h* it with thine	Eze 24:26	2045
H the word of the Lord GOD	Eze 25:3	8085
thou shalt *h* the word at my mouth	Eze 33:7	8085
h what is the word that cometh	Eze 33:30	8085
they *h* thy words, but they will	Eze 33:31	8085
for they *h* thy words, but they do	Eze 33:32	8085
shepherds, *h* the word of the LORD	Eze 34:7	8085
shepherds, *h* the word of the LORD	Eze 34:9	8085
of Israel, *h* the word of the LORD	Eze 36:1	8085
h the word of the Lord GOD	Eze 36:4	8085
men to *h* in thee the shame of the	Eze 36:15	8085
dry bones, *h* the word of the LORD	Eze 37:4	8085
h with thine ears, and set thine	Eze 40:4	8085
h with thine ears all that I say	Eze 44:5	8085
That at what time ye *h* the sound	Dan 3:5	8086
shall *h* the sound of the cornet	Dan 3:10	8086
time ye *h* the sound of the cornet	Dan 3:15	8086
and stone, which see not, nor *h*	Dan 5:23	8086
h the prayer of thy servant, and	Dan 9:17	8085
O my God, incline thine ear, and *h*	Dan 9:18	8085
O Lord, *h*; O Lord	Dan 9:19	8085
to pass in that day, I will *h*	Hos 2:21	6030
I will *h* the heavens	Hos 2:21	6030
and they shall *h* the earth	Hos 2:21	6030
And the earth shall *h* the corn	Hos 2:22	6030
and they shall *h* Jezreel	Hos 2:22	6030
H the word of the LORD, ye	Hos 4:1	8085
H ye this, O priests	Hos 5:1	8085
H this, ye old men, and give ear,	Joel 1:2	8085
H this word that the LORD hath	Amos 3:1	8085
H ye, and testify in the house of	Amos 3:13	8085
H this word, ye kine of Bashan,	Amos 4:1	8085
H ye this word which I take up	Amos 5:1	8085
for I will not *h* the melody of	Amos 5:23	8085
Now therefore *h* thou the word of	Amos 7:16	8085
H this, O ye that swallow up the	Amos 8:4	8085
H, all ye people	Mic 1:2	8085
And I said, *H*, I pray you, O heads	Mic 3:1	8085
the LORD, but he will not *h* them	Mic 3:4	6030
H this, I pray you, ye heads of	Mic 3:9	8085
H ye now what the LORD saith	Mic 6:1	8085
and let the hills *h* thy voice	Mic 6:1	8085
H ye, O mountains, the LORD's	Mic 6:2	8085
h ye the rod, and who hath	Mic 6:9	8085
my God will *h* me	Mic 7:7	8085
all that *h* the bruit of thee	Nah 3:19	8085
shall I cry, and thou wilt not *h*	Hab 1:2	8085
but they did not *h*, nor hearken	Zec 1:4	8085
H now, O Joshua the high priest,	Zec 3:8	8085
Should ye not *h* the words which	Zec 7:7	
ears, that they should not *h*	Zec 7:11	8085
stone, lest they should *h* the law	Zec 7:12	8085
as he cried, and they would not *h*	Zec 7:13	8085
so they cried, and I would not *h*	Zec 7:13	8085
ye that *h* in these days these	Zec 8:9	8085
LORD their God, and will *h* them	Zec 10:6	6030
call on my name, and I will *h* them	Zec 13:9	6030
If ye will not *h*, and if ye will	Mal 2:2	8085
nor *h* your words, when ye depart	Mt 10:14	*191*
what ye *h* in the ear, that preach	Mt 10:27	*191*
again those things which ye do *h*	Mt 11:4	*191*
are cleansed, and the deaf *h*	Mt 11:5	*191*
that hath ears to *h*, let him *h*	Mt 11:15	*191*
neither shall any man *h* his voice	Mt 12:19	*191*
earth to *h* the wisdom of Solomon	Mt 12:42	*191*
Who hath ears to *h*, let him *h*	Mt 13:9	*191*
and hearing they *h* not, neither do	Mt 13:13	*191*
saith, By hearing ye shall *h*	Mt 13:14	*191*
h with their ears, and should	Mt 13:15	*191*
and your ears, for they *h*	Mt 13:16	*191*
to *h* those things which ye *h*	Mt 13:17	*191*
H ye therefore the parable of the	Mt 13:18	*191*
Who hath ears to *h*, let him *h*	Mt 13:43	*191*
multitude, and said unto them, *H*	Mt 15:10	*191*
h ye him	Mt 17:5	*191*
if he shall *h* thee, thou hast	Mt 18:15	*191*
But if he will not *h* thee	Mt 18:16	*191*
And if he shall neglect to *h* them	Mt 18:17	*3878*
but if he neglect to *h* the church	Mt 18:17	*3878*
H another parable	Mt 21:33	*191*
And ye shall *h* of wars and rumours	Mt 24:6	*191*
that hath ears to *h*, let him *h*	Mk 4:9	*191*
and hearing they may *h*, and not	Mk 4:12	*191*
such as *h* the word,	Mk 4:18	*191*
such as *h* the word, and receive it	Mk 4:20	*191*
man have ears to *h*, let him *h*	Mk 4:23	*191*
unto them, Take heed what ye *h*	Mk 4:24	*191*
unto you that *h* shall more be	Mk 4:24	*191*
them, as they were able to *h* it	Mk 4:33	*191*
shall not receive you, nor *h* you	Mk 6:11	*191*
man have ears to *h*, let him *h*	Mk 7:16	*191*
he maketh both the deaf to *h*	Mk 7:37	*191*
and having ears, *h* ye not	Mk 8:18	*191*
h him	Mk 9:7	*191*
of all the commandments is, *H*	Mk 12:29	*191*
And when ye shall *h* of wars	Mk 13:7	*191*
upon him to *h* the word of God	Lk 5:1	*191*
multitudes came together to *h*	Lk 5:15	*191*
and Sidon, which came to *h* him	Lk 6:17	*191*
But I say unto you which *h*	Lk 6:27	*191*
lepers are cleansed, the deaf *h*	Lk 7:22	*191*
that hath ears to *h*, let him *h*	Lk 8:8	*191*
by the way side are they that *h*	Lk 8:12	*191*
rock are they, which, when they *h*	Lk 8:13	*191*
Take heed therefore how ye *h*	Lk 8:18	*191*
are these which *h* the word of God	Lk 8:21	*191*
is this, of whom I *h* such things	Lk 9:9	*191*
h him	Lk 9:35	*191*
to *h* those things which ye *h*	Lk 10:24	*191*
are they that *h* the word of God	Lk 11:28	*191*
earth to *h* the wisdom of Solomon	Lk 11:31	*191*
that hath ears to *h*, let him *h*	Lk 14:35	*191*
publicans and sinners for to *h* him	Lk 15:1	*191*
How is it that I *h* this of thee	Lk 16:2	*191*
let them *h* them	Lk 16:29	*191*
If they *h* not Moses and the	Lk 16:31	*191*
H what the unjust judge saith	Lk 18:6	*191*
were very attentive to *h* him	Lk 19:48	*191*
But when ye shall *h* of wars	Lk 21:9	*191*
him in the temple, for to *h* him	Lk 21:38	*191*
when the dead shall *h* the voice	Jn 5:25	*191*
and they that *h* shall live	Jn 5:25	*191*
in the graves shall *h* his voice	Jn 5:28	*191*
as I *h*, I judge	Jn 5:30	*191*
who can *h* it?	Jn 6:60	*191*
judge any man, before it *h* him	Jn 7:51	*191*
even because ye cannot *h* my word	Jn 8:43	*191*
ye therefore *h* them not, because	Jn 8:47	*191*
told you already, and ye did not *h*	Jn 9:27	*191*
wherefore would ye *h* it again	Jn 9:27	*191*
and the sheep *h* his voice	Jn 10:3	*191*
but the sheep did not *h* them	Jn 10:8	*191*
bring, and they shall *h* my voice	Jn 10:16	*191*
why *h* ye him?	Jn 10:20	*191*
My sheep *h* my voice, and I know	Jn 10:27	*191*
And if any man *h* my words, and	Jn 12:47	*191*
the word which ye *h* is not mine	Jn 14:24	*191*
but whatsoever he shall *h*	Jn 16:13	*191*
how *h* we every man in our own	Acts 2:8	*191*
we do *h* them speak in our tongues	Acts 2:11	*191*
Ye men of Israel, *h* these words	Acts 2:22	*191*
forth this, which ye now see and *h*	Acts 2:33	*191*
him shall ye *h* in all things	Acts 3:22	*191*
which will not *h* that prophet	Acts 3:23	*191*
him shall ye *h*	Acts 7:37	*191*
his house, and to *h* words of thee	Acts 10:22	*191*
God, to *h* all things that are	Acts 10:33	*191*
desired to *h* the word of God	Acts 13:7	*191*
together to *h* the word of God	Acts 13:44	*191*
should *h* the word of the gospel	Acts 15:7	*191*
to tell, or to *h* some new thing	Acts 17:21	*191*
We will *h* thee again of this	Acts 17:32	*191*
Moreover ye see and *h*, that not	Acts 19:26	*191*
for they will *h* that thou art	Acts 21:22	*191*
h ye my defence which I make now	Acts 22:1	*191*
shouldest *h* the voice of his	Acts 22:14	*191*
I will *h* thee, said he, when	Acts 23:35	*1251*
h us of thy clemency a few words	Acts 24:4	*191*
I would also *h* the man myself	Acts 25:22	*191*
morrow, said he, thou shalt *h* him	Acts 25:22	*191*
I beseech thee to *h* me patiently	Acts 26:3	*191*
but also all that *h* me this day	Acts 26:29	*191*
But we desire to *h* of thee what	Acts 28:22	*191*
and say, Hearing ye shall *h*	Acts 28:26	*191*
h with their ears, and understand	Acts 28:27	*191*
Gentiles, and that they will *h* it	Acts 28:28	*191*
how shall they *h* without a	Rom 10:14	*191*
and ears that they should not *h*	Rom 11:8	*191*
I *h* that there be divisions among	1Cor 11:18	*191*
for all that will they not *h* me	1Cor 14:21	*1522*
the law, do ye not *h* the law	Gal 4:21	*191*
I may *h* of your affairs, that ye	Phil 1:27	*191*
saw in me, and now *h* to be in me	Phil 1:30	*191*
For we *h* that there are some	2Th 3:11	*191*
save thyself, and them that *h* thee	1Ti 4:16	*191*
and that all the Gentiles might *h*	2Ti 4:17	*191*
To day if ye will *h* his voice	Heb 3:7	*191*
To day if ye will *h* his voice	Heb 3:15	*191*
To day if ye will *h* his voice	Heb 4:7	*191*
let every man be swift to *h*	Jas 1:19	*191*
And if we know that he *h* us	1Jn 5:15	*191*
I have no greater joy than to *h*	3Jn 4	*191*
they that *h* the words of this	Rev 1:3	*191*
let him *h* what the Spirit saith	Rev 2:7	*191*
let him *h* what the Spirit saith	Rev 2:11	*191*
let him *h* what the Spirit saith	Rev 2:17	*191*
let him *h* what the Spirit saith	Rev 2:29	*191*
let him *h* what the Spirit saith	Rev 3:6	*191*

let him *h* what the Spirit saith	Rev 3:13	*191*
if any man *h* my voice, and open	Rev 3:20	*191*
let him *h* what the Spirit saith	Rev 3:22	*191*
which neither can see, nor *h*	Rev 9:20	*191*
If any man have an ear, let him *h*	Rev 13:9	*191*

HEARD {641}

they *h* the voice of the LORD God	Gen 3:8	8085
I *h* thy voice in the garden, and I	Gen 3:10	8085
when Abram *h* that his brother was	Gen 14:14	8085
the LORD hath *h* thy affliction	Gen 16:11	8085
And as for Ishmael, I have *h* thee	Gen 17:20	8085
Sarah *h* it in the tent door,	Gen 18:10	8085
God *h* the voice of the lad	Gen 21:17	8085
for God hath *h* the voice of the	Gen 21:17	8085
tell me, neither yet *h* I of it	Gen 21:26	8085
when he *h* the words of Rebekah	Gen 24:30	8085
Abraham's servant *h* their words	Gen 24:52	8085
Rebekah *h* when Isaac spake to	Gen 27:5	8085
I *h* thy father speak unto Esau	Gen 27:6	8085
when Esau *h* the words of his	Gen 27:34	8085
when Laban *h* the tidings of Jacob	Gen 29:13	8085
the LORD hath *h* that I was hated	Gen 29:33	8085
me, and hath also *h* my voice	Gen 30:6	8085
he *h* the words of Laban's sons,	Gen 31:1	8085
Jacob *h* that he had defiled Dinah	Gen 34:5	8085
out of the field when they *h* it	Gen 34:7	8085
and Israel *h* it	Gen 35:22	8085
for I *h* them say, Let us go to	Gen 37:17	8085
And Reuben *h* it, and he delivered	Gen 37:21	8085
when he *h* that I lifted up my	Gen 39:15	8085
when his master *h* the words of	Gen 39:19	8085
I have *h* say of thee, that thou	Gen 41:15	8085
I have *h* that there is corn in	Gen 42:2	8085
for they *h* that they should eat	Gen 43:25	8085
and the house of Pharaoh *h*	Gen 45:2	8085
thereof was *h* in Pharaoh's house	Gen 45:16	8085
Now when Pharaoh *h* this thing	Ex 2:15	8085
God *h* their groaning, and God	Ex 2:24	8085
have *h* their cry by reason of	Ex 3:7	8085
when they *h* that the LORD had	Ex 4:31	8085
I have also *h* the groaning of the	Ex 6:5	8085
for he hath *h* your murmurings	Ex 16:9	8085
I have *h* the murmurings of the	Ex 16:12	8085
h of all that God had done for	Ex 18:1	8085
let it be *h* out of thy mouth	Ex 23:13	8085
his sound shall be *h* when he	Ex 28:35	8085
when Joshua *h* the noise of the	Ex 32:17	8085
when the people *h* these evil	Ex 33:4	8085
And when Moses *h* that, he was	Lev 10:20	8085
let all that *h* him lay their	Lev 24:14	8085
then he *h* the voice of one	Num 7:89	8085
and the LORD *h* it	Num 11:1	8085
Then Moses *h* the people weep	Num 11:10	8085
And the LORD *h* it	Num 12:2	8085
for they have *h* that thou LORD	Num 14:14	8085
h the fame of thee will speak	Num 14:15	8085
I have *h* the murmurings of the	Num 14:27	8085
And when Moses *h* it, he fell upon	Num 16:4	8085
he *h* our voice, and sent an angel,	Num 20:16	8085
h tell that Israel came by the	Num 21:1	8085
when Balak *h* that Balaam was come	Num 22:36	8085
which *h* the words of God, which	Num 24:4	8085
which *h* the words of God, and knew	Num 24:16	8085
And her husband *h* it, and held his	Num 30:7	8085
at her in the day that he *h* it	Num 30:7	8085
her on the day that he *h* it	Num 30:8	8085
And her husband *h* it, and held his	Num 30:11	8085
them void on the day he *h* them	Num 30:12	8085
at her in the day that he *h* them	Num 30:14	8085
void after that he hath *h* them	Num 30:15	8085
h of the coming of the children	Num 33:40	8085
the LORD *h* the voice of your	Deut 1:34	8085
ye *h* the voice of the words, but	Deut 4:12	8085
only ye *h* a voice	Deut 4:12	8085
thing is, or hath been *h* like it	Deut 4:32	8085
midst of the fire, as thou hast *h*	Deut 4:33	8085
when ye *h* the voice out of the	Deut 5:23	8085
we have *h* his voice out of the	Deut 5:24	8085
that hath *h* the voice of the	Deut 5:26	8085
the LORD *h* the voice of your	Deut 5:28	8085
I have *h* the voice of the words	Deut 5:28	8085
and of whom thou hast *h* say	Deut 9:2	8085
told thee, and thou hast *h* of it	Deut 17:4	8085
the LORD *h* our voice, and looked	Deut 26:7	8085
For we have *h* how the LORD dried	Josh 2:10	8085
as soon as we had *h* these things	Josh 2:11	8085
h that the LORD had dried up the	Josh 5:1	8085
when the people *h* the sound of	Josh 6:20	8085
and the Jebusite, *h* thereof	Josh 9:1	8085
h what Joshua had done unto	Josh 9:3	8085
for we have *h* the fame of him, and	Josh 9:9	8085
that they *h* that they were their	Josh 9:16	8085
king of Jerusalem had *h* how	Josh 10:1	8085
king of Hazor had *h* those things	Josh 11:1	8085
And the children of Israel *h* say	Josh 22:11	8085
the children of Israel *h* of it	Josh 22:12	8085
h the words that the children of	Josh 22:30	8085
for it hath *h* all the words of	Josh 24:27	8085
when Gideon *h* the telling of the	Judg 7:15	8085
Zebul the ruler of the city *h* the	Judg 9:30	8085
of the tower of Shechem *h* that	Judg 9:46	8085
Let not thy voice be *h* among us	Judg 18:25	8085
h that the children of Israel	Judg 20:3	8085
for she had *h* in the country of	Ruth 1:6	8085
moved, but her voice was not *h*	1Sa 1:13	8085
h all that his sons did unto all	1Sa 2:22	8085
when the Philistines *h* the noise	1Sa 4:6	8085
when Eli *h* the noise of the	1Sa 4:14	8085
when she *h* the tidings that the	1Sa 4:19	8085
when the Philistines *h* that the	1Sa 7:7	8085
when the children of Israel *h* it	1Sa 7:7	8085
and the LORD *h* him	1Sa 7:9	6030
Samuel *h* all the words of the	1Sa 8:21	8085
upon Saul when he *h* those tidings	1Sa 11:6	8085
Geba, and the Philistines *h* of it	1Sa 13:3	8085
all Israel *h* say that Saul had	1Sa 13:4	8085
when they *h* that the Philistines	1Sa 14:22	8085
But Jonathan *h* not when his	1Sa 14:27	8085
all Israel *h* those words of the	1Sa 17:11	8085
and David *h* them	1Sa 17:23	8085
Eliab his eldest brother *h* when	1Sa 17:28	8085
words were *h* which David spake	1Sa 17:31	8085
and all his father's house *h* it	1Sa 22:1	8085
When Saul *h* that David was	1Sa 22:6	8085
thy servant hath certainly *h* that	1Sa 23:10	8085
come down, as thy servant hath *h*	1Sa 23:11	8085
And when Saul *h* that, he pursued	1Sa 23:25	8085
David *h* in the wilderness that	1Sa 25:4	8085
now I have *h* that thou hast	1Sa 25:7	8085
when David *h* that Nabal was dead,	1Sa 25:39	8085
inhabitants of Jabesh-gilead *h* of	1Sa 31:11	8085
And afterward when David *h* it	2Sa 3:28	8085
when Saul's son *h* that Abner was	2Sa 4:1	8085
But when the Philistines *h* that	2Sa 5:17	8085
and David *h* of it, and went down to	2Sa 5:17	8085
all that we have *h* with our ears	2Sa 7:22	8085
When Toi king of Hamath *h* that	2Sa 8:9	8085
And when David *h* of it, he sent	2Sa 10:7	8085
when the wife of Uriah *h* that	2Sa 11:26	8085
king David *h* of all these things	2Sa 13:21	8085
all the people *h* when the king	2Sa 18:5	8085
for the people *h* say that day how	2Sa 19:2	8085
Hast thou not *h* that Adonijah the	1Kin 1:11	8085
h it as they had made an end of	1Kin 1:41	8085
when Joab *h* the sound of the	1Kin 1:41	8085
This is the noise that ye have *h*	1Kin 1:45	8085
The word that I have *h* is good	1Kin 2:42	8085
all Israel *h* of the judgment	1Kin 3:28	8085
which had *h* of his wisdom	1Kin 4:34	8085
for he had *h* that they had	1Kin 5:1	8085
when Hiram *h* the words of Solomon	1Kin 5:7	8085
any tool of iron *h* in the house	1Kin 6:7	8085
I have *h* thy prayer and thy	1Kin 9:3	8085
of Sheba *h* of the fame of Solomon	1Kin 10:1	8085
It was a true report that I *h* in	1Kin 10:6	8085
exceedeth the fame which I *h*	1Kin 10:7	8085
when Hadad *h* in Egypt that David	1Kin 11:21	8085
h of it, (for he was fled from	1Kin 12:2	8085
when all Israel *h* that Jeroboam	1Kin 12:20	8085
when king Jeroboam *h* the saying	1Kin 13:4	8085
him back from the way *h* thereof	1Kin 13:26	8085
when Ahijah *h* the sound of her	1Kin 14:6	8085
to pass, when Baasha *h* thereof	1Kin 15:21	8085
people that were encamped *h* say	1Kin 16:16	8085
the LORD *h* the voice of Elijah	1Kin 17:22	8085
And it was so, when Elijah *h* it	1Kin 19:13	8085
when Ben-hadad *h* this message	1Kin 20:12	8085
we have *h* that the kings of the	1Kin 20:31	8085
when Jezebel *h* that Naboth was	1Kin 21:15	8085
when Ahab *h* that Naboth was dead,	1Kin 21:16	8085
when Ahab *h* those words, that he	1Kin 21:27	8085
when all the Moabites *h* that the	2Kin 3:21	8085
had *h* that the king of Israel had	2Kin 5:8	8085
when the king *h* the words of the	2Kin 6:30	8085
come to Jezreel, Jezebel *h* of it	2Kin 9:30	8085
when Athaliah *h* the noise of the	2Kin 11:13	8085
to pass, when king Hezekiah *h* it	2Kin 19:1	8085
which the LORD thy God hath *h*	2Kin 19:4	8085
of the words which thou hast *h*	2Kin 19:6	8085
for he had *h* that he was departed	2Kin 19:8	8085
when he *h* say of Tirhakah king of	2Kin 19:9	8085
thou hast *h* what the kings of	2Kin 19:11	8085
king of Assyria I have *h*	2Kin 19:20	8085
Hast thou not *h* long ago how I	2Kin 19:25	8085
I have *h* thy prayer, I have seen	2Kin 20:5	8085
for he had *h* that Hezekiah had	2Kin 20:12	8085
when the king had *h* the words of	2Kin 22:11	8085
the words which thou hast *h*	2Kin 22:18	8085
I also have *h* thee, saith the	2Kin 22:19	8085
h that the king of Babylon had	2Kin 25:23	8085
when all Jabesh-gilead *h* all that	1Chr 10:11	8085
when the Philistines *h* that David	1Chr 14:8	8085
And David *h* of it, and went out	1Chr 14:8	8085
all that we have *h* with our ears	1Chr 17:20	8085
Now when Tou king of Hamath *h* how	1Chr 18:9	8085
And when David *h* of it, he sent	1Chr 19:8	8085
one sound to be *h* in praising	2Chr 5:13	8085
I have *h* thy prayer, and have	2Chr 7:12	8085
of Sheba *h* of the fame of Solomon	2Chr 9:1	8085
It was a true report which I *h* in	2Chr 9:5	8085
thou exceedest the fame that I *h*	2Chr 9:6	8085
h it, that Jeroboam returned out	2Chr 10:2	8085
when Asa *h* these words, and the	2Chr 15:8	8085
it came to pass, when Baasha *h* it	2Chr 16:5	8085
when they had *h* that the LORD	2Chr 20:29	8085
Now when Athaliah *h* the noise of	2Chr 23:12	8085
and their voice was *h*, and their	2Chr 30:27	8085
h his supplication, and brought	2Chr 33:13	8085
when the king had *h* the words of	2Chr 34:19	8085
the words which thou hast *h*	2Chr 34:26	8085
I have even *h* thee also, saith	2Chr 34:27	8085
and the noise was *h* afar off	Ezr 3:13	8085
Benjamin *h* that the children of	Ezr 4:1	8085
when I *h* this thing, I rent my	Ezr 9:3	8085
when I *h* these words, that I sat	Neh 1:4	8085
h of it, it grieved them	Neh 2:10	8085
h it, they laughed us to scorn,	Neh 2:19	8085
that when Sanballat *h* that we	Neh 4:1	8085
h that the walls of Jerusalem	Neh 4:7	8085
when our enemies *h* that it was	Neh 4:15	8085
was very angry when I *h* their cry	Neh 5:6	8085
h that I had builded the wall, and	Neh 6:1	8085
when all our enemies *h* thereof	Neh 6:16	8085
when they *h* the words of the law	Neh 8:9	8085
of Jerusalem was *h* even afar off	Neh 12:43	8085
to pass, when they had *h* the law	Neh 13:3	8085
which have *h* of the deed of the	Est 1:18	8085
commandment and his decree was *h*	Est 2:8	8085
Now when Job's three friends *h* of	Job 2:11	8085
silence, and I *h* a voice, saying,	Job 4:16	8085
seen all this, mine ear hath *h*	Job 13:1	8085
Hast thou *h* the secret of God	Job 15:8	8085
I have *h* many such things	Job 16:2	8085
cry out of wrong, but I am not *h*	Job 19:7	6030
I have *h* the check of my reproach	Job 20:3	8085
how little a portion is *h* of him	Job 26:14	8085
We have *h* the fame thereof with	Job 28:22	8085
When the ear *h* me, then it	Job 29:11	8085
I have *h* the voice of thy words,	Job 33:8	8085
not stay them when his voice is *h*	Job 37:4	8085
I have *h* of thee by the hearing	Job 42:5	8085
he *h* me out of his holy hill	Ps 3:4	6030
for the LORD hath *h* the voice of	Ps 6:8	8085
The LORD hath *h* my supplication	Ps 6:9	8085
thou hast *h* the desire of the	Ps 10:17	8085
he *h* my voice out of his temple,	Ps 18:6	8085
where their voice is not *h*	Ps 19:3	8085
for thou hast *h* me from the horns	Ps 22:21	6030
but when he cried unto him, he *h*	Ps 22:24	8085
because he hath *h* the voice of my	Ps 28:6	8085
For I have *h* the slander of many	Ps 31:13	8085
I sought the LORD, and he *h* me	Ps 34:4	6030
poor man cried, and the LORD *h* him	Ps 34:6	8085
But I, as a deaf man, *h* not	Ps 38:13	8085
he inclined unto me, and *h* my cry	Ps 40:1	8085
We have *h* with our ears, O God,	Ps 44:1	8085
As we have *h*, so have we seen in	Ps 48:8	8085
For thou, O God, hast *h* my vows	Ps 61:5	8085
twice have I *h* this	Ps 62:11	8085
the voice of his praise to be *h*	Ps 66:8	8085
But verily God hath *h* me	Ps 66:19	8085
judgment to be *h* from heaven	Ps 76:8	8085
Which we have *h* and known, and our	Ps 78:3	8085
Therefore the LORD *h* this	Ps 78:21	8085
When God *h* this, he was wroth, and	Ps 78:59	8085
where I *h* a language that I	Ps 81:5	8085
Zion *h*, and was glad	Ps 97:8	8085
affliction, when he *h* their cry	Ps 106:44	8085
LORD, because he hath *h* my voice	Ps 116:1	8085
for thou hast *h* me, and art become	Ps 118:21	6030
I cried unto the LORD, and he *h* me	Ps 120:1	6030
Lo, we *h* of it at Ephratah	Ps 132:6	8085
cry himself, but shall not be *h*	Prov 21:13	6030
despised, and his words are not *h*	Eccl 9:16	8085
The words of wise men are *h* in	Eccl 9:17	8085
of the turtle is *h* in our land	Song 2:12	8085
Also I *h* the voice of the Lord,	Is 6:8	8085
cause it to be *h* unto Laish	Is 10:30	7181
voice shall be *h* even unto Jahaz	Is 15:4	8085
We have *h* of the pride of Moab	Is 16:6	8085
that which I have *h* of the LORD	Is 21:10	8085
part of the earth have we *h* songs	Is 24:16	8085
for I have *h* from the Lord GOD of	Is 28:22	8085
cause his glorious voice to be *h*	Is 30:30	8085
to pass, when king Hezekiah *h* it	Is 37:1	8085
which the LORD thy God hath *h*	Is 37:4	8085
of the words that thou hast *h*	Is 37:6	8085
for he had *h* that he was departed	Is 37:8	8085
he *h* say concerning Tirhakah king	Is 37:9	8085
And when he *h* it, he sent	Is 37:9	8085
thou hast *h* what the kings of	Is 37:11	8085
Hast thou not *h* long ago, how I	Is 37:26	8085
I have *h* thy prayer, I have seen	Is 38:5	8085
for he had *h* that he had been	Is 39:1	8085
have ye not *h*?	Is 40:21	8085
hast thou not *h*, that the	Is 40:28	8085
his voice to be *h* in the street	Is 42:2	8085
Thou hast *h*, see all this	Is 48:6	8085
an acceptable time have I *h* thee	Is 49:8	6030
had not *h* shall they consider	Is 52:15	8085
make your voice to be *h* on high	Is 58:4	8085
shall no more be *h* in thy land	Is 60:18	8085
of the world men have not *h*	Is 64:4	8085
weeping shall be no more *h* in her	Is 65:19	8085
Who hath *h* such a thing	Is 66:8	8085
afar off, that have not *h* my fame	Is 66:19	8085
A voice was *h* upon the high	Jer 3:21	8085
my peace, because thou hast *h*	Jer 4:19	8085
For I have *h* a voice as of a	Jer 4:31	8085
violence and spoil is *h* in her	Jer 6:7	8085
We have *h* the fame thereof	Jer 6:24	8085
early and speaking, but ye *h* not	Jer 7:13	8085
I hearkened and *h*, but they spake	Jer 8:6	8085
of his horses was *h* from Dan	Jer 8:16	8085
voice of wailing is *h* out of Zion	Jer 9:19	8085
heathen, who hath *h* such things	Jer 18:13	8085
Let a cry be *h* from their houses,	Jer 18:22	8085
h that Jeremiah prophesied these	Jer 20:1	8085
For I *h* the defaming of many,	Jer 20:10	8085
and hath perceived and *h* his word	Jer 23:18	8085
who hath marked his word, and *h* it	Jer 23:18	8085
I have *h* what the prophets said,	Jer 23:25	8085
Because ye have not *h* my words	Jer 25:8	8085

H

of the flock, shall be *h*	Jer 25:36	8085
all the people *h* Jeremiah	Jer 26:7	8085
princes of Judah *h* these things	Jer 26:10	8085
as ye have *h* with your ears	Jer 26:11	8085
city all the words that ye have *h*	Jer 26:12	8085
h his words, the king sought to	Jer 26:21	8085
but when Urijah *h* it, he was	Jer 26:21	8085
We have *h* a voice of trembling,	Jer 30:5	8085
A voice was *h* in Ramah,	Jer 31:15	8085
I have surely *h* Ephraim bemoaning	Jer 31:18	8085
there shall be *h* in this place	Jer 33:10	8085
h that every one should let his	Jer 34:10	8085
unto them, but they have not *h*	Jer 35:17	8085
had *h* out of the book all the	Jer 36:11	8085
them all the words that he had *h*	Jer 36:13	8085
when they had *h* all the words	Jer 36:16	8085
servants that *h* all these words	Jer 36:24	8085
Jerusalem *h* tidings of them	Jer 37:5	8085
h the words that Jeremiah had	Jer 38:1	8085
h that they had put Jeremiah in	Jer 38:7	8085
h that the king of Babylon had	Jer 40:7	8085
h that the king of Babylon had	Jer 40:11	8085
h of all the evil that Ishmael	Jer 41:11	8085
said unto them, I have *h* you	Jer 42:4	8085
The nations have *h* of thy shame	Jer 46:12	8085
ones have caused a cry to be *h*	Jer 48:4	8085
have *h* a cry of destruction	Jer 48:5	8085
We have *h* the pride of Moab, (he	Jer 48:29	8085
be *h* in Rabbah of the Ammonites	Jer 49:2	8085
I have *h* a rumour from the LORD,	Jer 49:14	8085
thereof was *h* in the Red sea	Jer 49:21	8085
for they have *h* evil tidings	Jer 49:23	8085
Babylon hath *h* the report of them	Jer 50:43	8085
the cry is *h* among the nations	Jer 50:46	8085
that shall be *h* in the land	Jer 51:46	8085
because we have *h* reproach	Jer 51:51	8085
They have *h* that I sigh	Lam 1:21	8085
mine enemies have *h* of my trouble	Lam 1:21	8085
Thou hast *h* my voice	Lam 3:56	8085
Thou hast *h* their reproach, O	Lam 3:61	8085
I *h* the noise of their wings,	Eze 1:24	8085
I *h* a voice of one that spake	Eze 1:28	8085
that I *h* him that spake unto me	Eze 2:2	8085
I *h* behind me a voice of a great	Eze 3:12	8085
I *h* also the noise of the wings	Eze 3:13	
was *h* even to the outer court	Eze 10:5	8085
The nations also *h* of him	Eze 19:4	8085
his voice should no more be *h*	Eze 19:9	8085
of thy harps shall be no more *h*	Eze 26:13	8085
their voice to be *h* against thee	Eze 27:30	8085
He *h* the sound of the trumpet, and	Eze 33:5	8085
that I have *h* all thy blasphemies	Eze 35:12	8085
I have *h* them	Eze 35:13	8085
I *h* him speaking unto me out of	Eze 43:6	8085
when all the people *h* the sound	Dan 3:7	8086
I have even *h* of thee, that the	Dan 5:14	8086
I have *h* of thee, that thou canst	Dan 5:16	8086
when he *h* these words, was sore	Dan 6:14	8086
Then I *h* one saint speaking, and	Dan 8:13	8085
I *h* a man's voice between the	Dan 8:16	8085
Yet *h* I the voice of his words	Dan 10:9	8085
when I *h* the voice of his words,	Dan 10:9	8085
before thy God, thy words were *h*	Dan 10:12	8085
I *h* the man clothed in linen,	Dan 12:7	8085
And I *h*, but I understood not	Dan 12:8	8085
as their congregation hath *h*	Hos 7:12	8085
I have *h* him, and observed him	Hos 14:8	6030
We have *h* a rumour from the LORD,	Obad 1	8085
unto the LORD, and he *h* me	Jonah 2:2	6030
heathen, such as they have not *h*	Mic 5:15	8085
thy messengers shall no more be *h*	Nah 2:13	8085
I have *h* thy speech, and was	Hab 3:2	8085
When I *h*, my belly trembled	Hab 3:16	8085
I have *h* the reproach of Moab, and	Zeph 2:8	8085
for we have *h* that God is with	Zec 8:23	8085
h it, and a book of remembrance	Mal 3:16	8085
Herod the king had *h* these things	Mt 2:3	*191*
When they had *h* the king, they	Mt 2:9	*191*
In Rama was there a voice *h*	Mt 2:18	*191*
But when he *h* that Archelaus did	Mt 2:22	*191*
Now when Jesus had *h* that John	Mt 4:12	*191*
Ye have *h* that it was said by	Mt 5:21	*191*
Ye have *h* that it was said by	Mt 5:27	*191*
ye have *h* that it hath been said	Mt 5:33	*191*
Ye have *h* that it hath been said,	Mt 5:38	*191*
Ye have *h* that it hath been said,	Mt 5:43	*191*
be *h* for their much speaking	Mt 6:7	*1522*
When Jesus *h* it, he marvelled, and	Mt 8:10	*191*
But when Jesus *h* that, he said	Mt 9:12	*191*
Now when John had *h* in the prison	Mt 11:2	*191*
But when the Pharisees *h* it	Mt 12:24	*191*
which ye hear, and have not *h* them	Mt 13:17	*191*
tetrarch *h* of the fame of Jesus	Mt 14:1	*191*
When Jesus *h* of it, he departed	Mt 14:13	*191*
and when the people had *h* thereof	Mt 14:13	*191*
after they *h* this saying	Mt 15:12	*191*
And when the disciples *h* it	Mt 17:6	*191*
when the young man *h* that saying	Mt 19:22	*191*
When his disciples *h* it, they	Mt 19:25	*191*
And when the ten *h* it, they were	Mt 20:24	*191*
when they *h* that Jesus passed by,	Mt 20:30	*191*
and Pharisees had *h* his parables	Mt 21:45	*191*
But when the king *h* thereof	Mt 22:7	*191*
When they had *h* these words	Mt 22:22	*191*
And when the multitude *h* this	Mt 22:33	*191*
But when the Pharisees had *h* that	Mt 22:34	*191*
now ye have *h* his blasphemy	Mt 26:65	*191*
stood there, when they *h* that	Mt 27:47	*191*
When Jesus *h* it, he saith unto	Mk 2:17	*191*
when they had *h* what great things	Mk 3:8	*191*
And when his friends *h* of it	Mk 3:21	*191*
but when they have *h*, Satan	Mk 4:15	*191*
who, when they have *h* the word	Mk 4:16	*191*
When she had *h* of Jesus, came in	Mk 5:27	*191*
As soon as Jesus *h* the word that	Mk 5:36	*191*
And king Herod *h* of him	Mk 6:14	*191*
But when Herod *h* thereof, he said	Mk 6:16	*191*
and when he *h* him, he did many	Mk 6:20	*191*
did many things, and *h* him gladly	Mk 6:20	*191*
And when his disciples *h* of it	Mk 6:29	*191*
were sick, where they *h* he was	Mk 6:55	*191*
h of him, and came and fell at his	Mk 7:25	*191*
And when the ten *h* it, they began	Mk 10:41	*191*
when he *h* that it was Jesus of	Mk 10:47	*191*
And his disciples *h* it	Mk 11:14	*191*
the scribes and chief priests *h* it	Mk 11:18	*191*
having *h* them reasoning together,	Mk 12:28	*191*
And the common people *h* him gladly	Mk 12:37	*191*
And when they *h* it, they were glad	Mk 14:11	*191*
We *h* him say, I will destroy this	Mk 14:58	*191*
Ye have *h* the blasphemy	Mk 14:64	*191*
stood by, when they *h* it said	Mk 15:35	*191*
when they had *h* that he was alive	Mk 16:11	*191*
for thy prayer is *h*	Lk 1:13	*1522*
when Elisabeth *h* the salutation	Lk 1:41	*191*
her cousins *h* how the Lord had	Lk 1:58	*191*
all they that *h* them laid them up	Lk 1:66	*191*
all they that *h* it wondered at	Lk 2:18	*191*
all the things that they had *h*	Lk 2:20	*191*
all that *h* him were astonished at	Lk 2:47	*191*
we have *h* done in Capernaum	Lk 4:23	*191*
when they *h* these things, were	Lk 4:28	*191*
when he *h* of Jesus, he sent unto	Lk 7:3	*191*
When Jesus *h* these things, he	Lk 7:9	*191*
what things ye have seen and *h*	Lk 7:22	*191*
And all the people that *h* him	Lk 7:29	*191*
are they, which, when they have *h*	Lk 8:14	*191*
having *h* the word, keep it, and	Lk 8:15	*191*
But when Jesus *h* it, he answered	Lk 8:50	*191*
Now Herod the tetrarch *h* of all	Lk 9:7	*191*
which ye hear, and have not *h* them	Lk 10:24	*191*
sat at Jesus' feet, and *h* his word	Lk 10:39	*191*
darkness shall be *h* in the light	Lk 12:3	*191*
at meat with him *h* these things	Lk 14:15	*191*
the house, he *h* musick and dancing	Lk 15:25	*191*
were covetous, *h* all these things	Lk 16:14	*191*
Now when Jesus *h* these things	Lk 18:22	*191*
And when he *h* this, he was very	Lk 18:23	*191*
And they that *h* it said, Who then	Lk 18:26	*191*
as they *h* these things, he added	Lk 19:11	*191*
And when they *h* it, they said, God	Lk 20:16	*191*
ourselves have *h* of his own mouth	Lk 22:71	*191*
When Pilate *h* of Galilee, he	Lk 23:6	*191*
because he had *h* many things of	Lk 23:8	*191*
And the two disciples *h* him speak	Jn 1:37	*191*
One of the two which *h* John speak	Jn 1:40	*191*
And what he hath seen and *h*	Jn 3:32	*191*
Pharisees had *h* that Jesus made	Jn 4:1	*191*
for we have *h* him ourselves, and	Jn 4:42	*191*
When he *h* that Jesus was come out	Jn 4:47	*191*
Ye have neither *h* his voice at	Jn 5:37	*191*
Every man therefore that hath *h*	Jn 6:45	*191*
disciples, when they had *h* this	Jn 6:60	*191*
The Pharisees *h* that the people	Jn 7:32	*191*
when they *h* this saying, said, Of	Jn 7:40	*191*
ground, as though he *h* them not	Jn 8:6	
And they which *h* it, being	Jn 8:9	*191*
things which I have *h* of him	Jn 8:26	*191*
the truth, which I have *h* of God	Jn 8:40	*191*
the world began was it not *h* that	Jn 9:32	*191*
Jesus *h* that they had cast him	Jn 9:35	*191*
which were with him *h* these words	Jn 9:40	*191*
When Jesus *h* that, he said, This	Jn 11:4	*191*
When he had *h* therefore that he	Jn 11:6	*191*
as soon as she *h* that Jesus was	Jn 11:20	*191*
As soon as she *h* that, she arose	Jn 11:29	*191*
I thank thee that thou hast *h* me	Jn 11:41	*191*
when they *h* that Jesus was coming	Jn 12:12	*191*
for that they *h* that he had done	Jn 12:18	*191*
h it, said that it thundered	Jn 12:29	*191*
We have *h* out of the law that	Jn 12:34	*191*
Ye have *h* how I said unto you, I	Jn 14:28	*191*
for all things that I have *h* of	Jn 15:15	*191*
ask them which *h* me, what I have	Jn 18:21	*191*
Pilate therefore *h* that saying	Jn 19:8	*191*
Pilate therefore *h* that saying	Jn 19:13	*191*
Peter *h* that it was the Lord	Jn 21:7	*191*
which, saith he, ye have *h* of me	Acts 1:4	*191*
because that every man *h* them	Acts 2:6	*191*
Now when they *h* this, they were	Acts 2:37	*191*
of them which *h* the word believed	Acts 4:4	*191*
things which we have seen and *h*	Acts 4:20	*191*
And when they *h* that, they lifted	Acts 4:24	*191*
on all them that *h* these things	Acts 5:5	*191*
and upon as many as *h* these things	Acts 5:11	*191*
And when they *h* that, they entered	Acts 5:21	*191*
the chief priests *h* these things	Acts 5:24	*191*
When they *h* that, they were cut	Acts 5:33	*191*
We have *h* him speak blasphemous	Acts 6:11	*191*
For we have *h* him say, that this	Acts 6:14	*191*
But when Jacob *h* that there was	Acts 7:12	*191*
I have *h* their groaning, and am	Acts 7:34	*191*
When they *h* these things, they	Acts 7:54	*191*
which were at Jerusalem *h* that	Acts 8:14	*191*
h him read the prophet Esaias, and	Acts 8:30	*191*
h a voice saying unto him, Saul,	Acts 9:4	*191*
I have *h* by many of this man, how	Acts 9:13	*191*
But all that *h* him were amazed,	Acts 9:21	*191*
the disciples had *h* that Peter	Acts 9:38	*191*
said, Cornelius, thy prayer is *h*	Acts 10:31	*1522*
fell on all them which *h* the word	Acts 10:44	*191*
For they *h* them speak with	Acts 10:46	*191*
h that the Gentiles had also	Acts 11:1	*191*
I *h* a voice saying unto me, Arise	Acts 11:7	*191*
When they *h* these things, they	Acts 11:18	*191*
And when the Gentiles *h* this	Acts 13:48	*191*
The same *h* Paul speak	Acts 14:9	*191*
h of, they rent their clothes, and	Acts 14:14	*191*
Forasmuch as we have *h*, that	Acts 15:24	*191*
which worshipped God, *h* us	Acts 16:14	*191*
and the prisoners *h* them	Acts 16:25	*1874*
when they *h* that they were Romans	Acts 16:38	*191*
city, when they *h* these things	Acts 17:8	*191*
when they *h* of the resurrection	Acts 17:32	*191*
when Aquila and Priscilla had *h*	Acts 18:26	*191*
We have not so much as *h* whether	Acts 19:2	*191*
When they *h* this, they were	Acts 19:5	*191*
Asia *h* the word of the Lord Jesus	Acts 19:10	*191*
when they *h* these sayings, they	Acts 19:28	*191*
when we *h* these things, both we,	Acts 21:12	*191*
And when they *h* it, they glorified	Acts 21:20	*191*
when they *h* that he spake in the	Acts 22:2	*191*
h a voice saying unto me, Saul,	Acts 22:7	*191*
but they *h* not the voice of him	Acts 22:9	*191*
men of what thou hast seen and *h*	Acts 22:15	*191*
When the centurion *h* that	Acts 22:26	*191*
son *h* of their lying in wait	Acts 23:16	*191*
when Felix *h* these things, having	Acts 24:22	*191*
h him concerning the faith in	Acts 24:24	*191*
I *h* a voice speaking unto me, and	Acts 26:14	*191*
thence, when the brethren *h* of us	Acts 28:15	*191*
in him of whom they have not *h*	Rom 10:14	*191*
But I say, Have they not *h*	Rom 10:18	*191*
that have not *h* shall understand	Rom 15:21	*191*
Eye hath not seen, nor ear *h*	1Cor 2:9	*191*
I have *h* thee in a time accepted,	2Cor 6:2	*1873*
h unspeakable words, which it is	2Cor 12:4	*191*
For ye have *h* of my conversation	Gal 1:13	*191*
But they had *h* only, That he	Gal 1:23	*191*
after that ye *h* the word of truth	Eph 1:13	*191*
after I *h* of your faith in the	Eph 1:15	*191*
If ye have *h* of the dispensation	Eph 3:2	*191*
If so be that ye have *h* him	Eph 4:21	*191*
because that ye had *h* that he had	Phil 2:26	*191*
both learned, and received, and *h*	Phil 4:9	*191*
Since we *h* of your faith in	Col 1:4	*191*
whereof ye *h* before in the word	Col 1:5	*4257*
in you, since the day ye *h* of it	Col 1:6	*191*
we also, since the day we *h* it	Col 1:9	*191*
of the gospel, which ye have *h*	Col 1:23	*191*
the word of God which ye *h* of us	1Th 2:13	*189*
words, which thou hast *h* of me	2Ti 1:13	*191*
the things that thou hast *h* of me	2Ti 2:2	*191*
to the things which we have *h*	Heb 2:1	*191*
unto us by them that *h* him	Heb 2:3	*191*
For some, when they had *h*	Heb 3:16	*191*
with faith in them that *h* it	Heb 4:2	*191*
death, and was *h* in that he feared	Heb 5:7	*1522*
which voice they that *h* intreated	Heb 12:19	*191*
Ye have *h* of the patience of Job,	Jas 5:11	*191*
voice which came from heaven we *h*	2Pet 1:18	*191*
the beginning, which we have *h*	1Jn 1:1	*191*
h declare we unto you, that ye	1Jn 1:3	*191*
message which we have *h* of him	1Jn 1:5	*191*
ye have *h* from the beginning	1Jn 2:7	*191*
as ye have *h* that antichrist	1Jn 2:18	*191*
in you, which ye have *h* from the	1Jn 2:24	*191*
If that which ye have *h* from the	1Jn 2:24	*191*
that ye *h* from the beginning	1Jn 3:11	*191*
whereof ye have *h* that it should	1Jn 4:3	*191*
as ye have *h* from the beginning,	2Jn 6	*191*
h behind me a great voice, as of	Rev 1:10	*191*
how thou hast received and *h*	Rev 3:3	*191*
the first voice which I *h* was as	Rev 4:1	*191*
I *h* the voice of many angels	Rev 5:11	*191*
h I saying, Blessing, and honour,	Rev 5:13	*191*
opened one of the seals, and I *h*	Rev 6:1	*191*
I *h* the second beast say, Come and	Rev 6:3	*191*
I *h* the third beast say, Come and	Rev 6:5	*191*
I *h* a voice in the midst of the	Rev 6:6	*191*
I *h* the voice of the fourth beast	Rev 6:7	*191*
I *h* the number of them which were	Rev 7:4	*191*
h an angel flying through the	Rev 8:13	*191*
I *h* a voice from the four horns	Rev 9:13	*191*
and I *h* the number of them	Rev 9:16	*191*
I *h* a voice from heaven saying	Rev 10:4	*191*
the voice which I *h* from heaven	Rev 10:8	*191*
they *h* a great voice from heaven	Rev 11:12	*191*
I *h* a loud voice saying in heaven	Rev 12:10	*191*
I *h* a voice from heaven, as the	Rev 14:2	*191*
I *h* the voice of harpers harping	Rev 14:2	*191*
I *h* a voice from heaven saying	Rev 14:13	*191*
I *h* a great voice out of the	Rev 16:1	*191*
I *h* the angel of the waters say,	Rev 16:5	*191*
I *h* another out of the altar say,	Rev 16:7	*191*
I *h* another voice from heaven,	Rev 18:4	*191*
shall be *h* no more at all in thee	Rev 18:22	*191*
shall be *h* no more at all in thee	Rev 18:22	*191*
of the bride shall be *h* no more	Rev 18:23	*191*
after these things I *h* a great	Rev 19:1	*191*
I *h* as it were the voice of a	Rev 19:6	*191*
I *h* a great voice out of heaven	Rev 21:3	*191*
John saw these things, and *h* them	Rev 22:8	*191*
And when I had *h* and seen, I fell	Rev 22:8	*191*

HEARDEST {12}

thou *h* his words out of the midst	Deut 4:36	8085
for thou *h* in that day how the	Josh 14:12	8085
when thou *h* what I spake against	2Kin 22:19	8085
when thou *h* his words against	2Chr 34:27	8085
h their cry by the Red sea	Neh 9:9	8085
thee, thou *h* them from heaven	Neh 9:27	8085
thee, thou *h* them from heaven	Neh 9:28	8085
nevertheless thou *h* the voice of	Ps 31:22	8085
declared my ways, and thou *h* me	Ps 119:26	6030
the day when thou *h* them not	Is 48:7	8085
Yea, thou *h* not	Is 48:8	8085
hell cried I, and thou *h* my voice	Jonah 2:2	8085

HEARER {2}

For if any be a *h* of the word	Jas 1:23	*202*
he being not a forgetful *h*	Jas 1:25	*202*

HEARERS {4}

(For not the *h* of the law are	Rom 2:13	*202*
it may minister grace unto the *h*	Eph 4:29	*191*
but to the subverting of the *h*	2Ti 2:14	*191*
not *h* only, deceiving your own	Jas 1:22	*202*

HEAREST {11}

Ruth, *H* thou not, my daughter	Ruth 2:8	8085
Wherefore *h* thou men's words,	1Sa 24:9	8085
when thou *h* the sound of a going	2Sa 5:24	8085
and when thou *h*, forgive	1Kin 8:30	8085
and when thou *h*, forgive	2Chr 6:21	8085
in the daytime, but thou *h* not	Ps 22:2	6030
O thou that *h* prayer, unto thee	Ps 65:2	8085
unto him, *H* thou what these say	Mt 21:16	*191*
H thou not how many things they	Mt 27:13	*191*
thou *h* the sound thereof, but	Jn 3:8	*191*
And I knew that thou *h* me always	Jn 11:42	*191*

HEARETH {52}

for that he *h* your murmurings	Ex 16:7	8085
for that the LORD *h* your	Ex 16:8	8085
disallow her in the day that he *h*	Num 30:5	8085
when he *h* the words of this curse	Deut 29:19	8085
for thy servant *h*	1Sa 3:9	8085
for thy servant *h*	1Sa 3:10	8085
every one that *h* it shall tingle	1Sa 3:11	8085
that whosoever *h* it will say	2Sa 17:9	8085
and Judah, that whosoever *h* of it	2Kin 21:12	8085
he *h* the cry of the afflicted	Job 34:28	8085
The righteous cry, and the LORD *h*	Ps 34:17	8085
Thus I was as a man that *h* not	Ps 38:14	8085
For the LORD *h* the poor, and	Ps 69:33	8085
Blessed is the man that *h* me	Prov 8:34	8085
A wise son *h* his father's	Prov 13:1	8085
but a scorner *h* not rebuke	Prov 13:1	8085
but the poor *h* not rebuke	Prov 13:8	8085
but he *h* the prayer of the	Prov 15:29	8085
The ear that *h* the reproof of	Prov 15:31	8085
but he that *h* reproof getteth	Prov 15:32	8085
answereth a matter before he *h* it	Prov 18:13	8085
but the man that *h* speaketh	Prov 21:28	8085
Lest he that *h* it put thee to	Prov 25:10	8085
he *h* cursing, and bewrayeth it not	Prov 29:24	8085
there is none that *h* your words	Is 41:26	8085
opening the ears, but he *h* not	Is 42:20	8085
this place, the which whosoever *h*	Jer 19:3	8085
He that *h*, let him hear	Eze 3:27	8085
Then whosoever *h* the sound of the	Eze 33:4	8085
Therefore whosoever *h* these	Mt 7:24	*191*
every one that *h* these sayings of	Mt 7:26	*191*
When any one *h* the word of the	Mt 13:19	*191*
the same is he that *h* the word	Mt 13:20	*191*
the thorns is he that *h* the word	Mt 13:22	*191*
good ground is he that *h* the word	Mt 13:23	*191*
h my sayings, and doeth them, I	Lk 6:47	*191*
But he that *h*, and doeth not, is	Lk 6:49	*191*
He that *h* you *h* me	Lk 10:16	*191*
h him, rejoiceth greatly because	Jn 3:29	*191*
I say unto you, He that *h* my word	Jn 5:24	*191*
He that is of God *h* God's words	Jn 8:47	*191*
we know that God *h* not sinners	Jn 9:31	*191*
God, and doeth his will, him he *h*	Jn 9:31	*191*
that is of the truth *h* my voice	Jn 18:37	*191*
me to be, or that he *h* of me	2Cor 12:6	*191*
of the world, and the world *h* them	1Jn 4:5	*191*
he that knoweth God *h* us	1Jn 4:6	*191*
he that is not of God *h* not us	1Jn 4:6	*191*
according to his will, he *h* us	1Jn 5:14	*191*
And let him that *h* say, Come	Rev 22:17	*191*
h the words of the prophecy of	Rev 22:18	*191*

HEARING {39}

law before all Israel in their *h*	Deut 31:11	241
for in our *h* the king charged	2Sa 18:12	241
there was neither voice, nor *h*	2Kin 4:31	7182
Surely thou hast spoken in mine *h*	Job 33:8	241
heard of thee by the *h* of the ear	Job 42:5	8088
The *h* ear, and the seeing eye, the	Prov 20:12	8085
away his ear from *h* the law	Prov 28:9	8085
seeing, nor the ear filled with *h*	Eccl 1:8	8085
reprove after the *h* of his ears	Is 11:3	4926
I was bowed down at the *h* of it	Is 21:3	8085
stoppeth his ears from *h* of blood	Is 33:15	8085
to the others he said in mine *h*	Eze 9:5	241
it was cried unto them in my *h*	Eze 10:13	241
but of the *h* the words of the LORD	Amos 8:11	8085
h they hear not, neither do they	Mt 13:13	*191*
By *h* ye shall hear, and shall not	Mt 13:14	*189*
and their ears are dull of *h*	Mt 13:15	*191*
and *h* they may hear, and not	Mk 4:12	*191*
many *h* him were astonished,	Mk 6:2	*191*
midst of the doctors, both *h* them	Lk 2:46	*191*
h they might not understand	Lk 8:10	*191*
h the multitude pass by, he asked	Lk 18:36	*191*
Ananias *h* these words fell down,	Acts 5:5	*191*
things which Philip spake, *h*	Acts 8:6	*191*
h a voice, but seeing no man	Acts 9:7	*191*
of the Corinthians *h* believed	Acts 18:8	*191*
reserved unto the *h* of Augustus	Acts 25:21	*1233*
was entered into the place of *h*	Acts 25:23	*201*
H ye shall hear, and shall not	Acts 28:26	*189*
and their ears are dull of *h*	Acts 28:27	*191*
So then faith cometh by *h*	Rom 10:17	*189*
and *h* by the word of God	Rom 10:17	*189*
were an eye, where were the *h*	1Cor 12:17	*189*
If the whole were *h*, where were	1Cor 12:17	*189*
of the law, or by the *h* of faith	Gal 3:2	*189*
of the law, or by the *h* of faith	Gal 3:5	*189*
H of thy love and faith, which	Philem 5	*191*
uttered, seeing ye are dull of *h*	Heb 5:11	*189*
among them, in seeing and *h*	2Pet 2:8	*189*

HEARKEN {153}

wives of Lamech, *h* unto my speech	Gen 4:23	238
said unto thee, *h* unto her voice	Gen 21:12	8085
My lord, *h* unto me	Gen 23:15	8085
But if ye will not *h* unto us	Gen 34:17	8085
h unto Israel your father	Gen 49:2	8085
they shall *h* to thy voice	Ex 3:18	8085
believe me, nor *h* unto my voice	Ex 4:1	8085
neither *h* to the voice of the	Ex 4:8	8085
neither *h* unto thy voice, that	Ex 4:9	8085
and how shall Pharaoh *h* unto me	Ex 6:30	8085
But Pharaoh shall not *h* unto you	Ex 7:4	8085
neither did he *h* unto them	Ex 7:22	8085
Pharaoh shall not *h* unto you	Ex 11:9	8085
If thou wilt diligently *h* to the	Ex 15:26	8085
H now unto my voice, I will give	Ex 18:19	8085
But if ye will not *h* unto me	Lev 26:14	8085
not yet for all this *h* unto me	Lev 26:18	8085
unto me, and will not *h* unto me	Lev 26:21	8085
will not for all this *h* unto me	Lev 26:27	8085
h unto me, thou son of Zippor	Num 23:18	238
LORD would not *h* to your voice	Deut 1:45	8085
Now therefore *h*, O Israel, unto	Deut 4:1	8085
if ye *h* to these judgments, and	Deut 7:12	8085
if ye shall *h* diligently unto my	Deut 11:13	8085
Thou shalt not *h* unto the words	Deut 13:3	8085
consent unto him, nor *h* unto him	Deut 13:8	8085
When thou shalt *h* to the voice of	Deut 13:18	8085
Only if thou carefully *h* unto the	Deut 15:5	8085
will not *h* unto the priest that	Deut 17:12	8085
unto him ye shall *h*	Deut 18:15	8085
that whosoever will not *h* unto my	Deut 18:19	8085
him, will not *h* unto them	Deut 21:18	8085
thy God would not *h* unto Balaam	Deut 23:5	8085
judgments, and to *h* unto his voice	Deut 26:17	8085
Israel, saying, Take heed, and *h*	Deut 27:9	8085
if thou shalt *h* diligently unto	Deut 28:1	8085
if thou shalt *h* unto the voice of	Deut 28:2	8085
if that thou *h* unto the	Deut 28:13	8085
if thou wilt not *h* unto the voice	Deut 28:15	8085
If thou shalt *h* unto the voice of	Deut 30:10	8085
things, so will we *h* unto thee	Josh 1:17	8085
will not *h* unto thy words in all	Josh 1:18	8085
But I would not *h* unto Balaam	Josh 24:10	8085
would not *h* unto their judges	Judg 2:17	8085
to know whether they would *h* unto	Judg 3:4	8085
H unto me, ye men of Shechem,	Judg 9:7	8085
that God may *h* unto you	Judg 9:7	8085
king of Edom would not *h* thereto	Judg 11:17	8085
But the men would not *h* to him	Judg 19:25	8085
h to the voice of their brethren	Judg 20:13	8085
H unto the voice of the people in	1Sa 8:7	8085
Now therefore *h* unto their voice	1Sa 8:9	8085
H unto their voice, and make them	1Sa 8:22	8085
now therefore *h* thou unto the	1Sa 15:1	8085
to *h* than the fat of rams	1Sa 15:22	7181
h thou also unto the voice of	1Sa 28:22	8085
For who will *h* unto you in this	1Sa 30:24	8085
he would not *h* unto our voice	2Sa 12:18	8085
he would not *h* unto her voice	2Sa 13:14	8085
But he would not *h* unto her	2Sa 13:16	8085
to *h* unto the cry and to the	1Kin 8:28	8085
that thou mayest *h* unto the	1Kin 8:29	8085
h thou to the supplication of thy	1Kin 8:30	8085
to *h* unto them in all that they	1Kin 8:52	8085
if thou wilt *h* unto all that I	1Kin 11:38	8085
H not unto him, nor consent	1Kin 20:8	8085
And he said, *H*, O people, every	1Kin 22:28	8085
if ye will *h* unto my voice, take	2Kin 10:6	8085
Howbeit they did not *h*, but they	2Kin 17:40	8085
H not to Hezekiah	2Kin 18:31	8085
h not unto Hezekiah, when he	2Kin 18:32	8085
to *h* unto the cry and the prayer	2Chr 6:19	8085
to *h* unto the prayer which thy	2Chr 6:20	8085
H therefore unto the	2Chr 6:21	8085
the king would not *h* unto them	2Chr 10:16	8085
And he said, *H*, all ye people	2Chr 18:27	8085
he said, *H* ye, all Judah, and ye	2Chr 20:15	7181
but they would not *h*	2Chr 33:10	7181
Shall we then *h* unto you to do	Neh 13:27	8085
h to the pleadings of my lips	Job 13:6	7181
Therefore I said, *H* to me	Job 32:10	8085
my speeches, and *h* to all my words	Job 33:1	238
Mark well, O Job, *h* unto me	Job 33:31	8085
If not, *h* unto me	Job 33:33	8085
Therefore *h* unto me, ye men of	Job 34:10	8085
h to the voice of my words	Job 34:16	238
me, and let a wise man *h* unto me	Job 34:34	8085
H unto this, O Job	Job 37:14	238
H unto the voice of my cry, my	Ps 5:2	7181
Come, ye children, *h* unto me	Ps 34:11	8085
H, O daughter, and consider, and	Ps 45:10	8085
Which will not *h* to the voice of	Ps 58:5	8085
O Israel, if thou wilt *h* unto me	Ps 81:8	8085
my people would not *h* to my voice	Ps 81:11	8085
H unto me now therefore, O ye	Prov 7:24	8085
Now therefore *h* unto me, O ye	Prov 8:32	8085
H unto thy father that begat thee	Prov 23:22	8085
If a ruler *h* to lies, all his	Prov 29:12	7181
the companions *h* to thy voice	Song 8:13	7181
h, and hear my speech	Is 28:23	7181
ears of them that hear shall *h*	Is 32:3	7181
and *h*, ye people	Is 34:1	7181
H not to Hezekiah	Is 36:16	8085
who will *h* and hear for the time	Is 42:23	7181
H unto me, O house of Jacob, and	Is 46:3	8085
H unto me, ye stouthearted, that	Is 46:12	8085
H unto me, O Jacob and Israel, my	Is 48:12	8085
and *h*, ye people, from far	Is 49:1	7181
H to me, ye that follow after	Is 51:1	8085
H unto me, my people	Is 51:4	7181
H unto me, ye that know	Is 51:7	8085
h diligently unto me, and eat ye	Is 55:2	8085
uncircumcised, and they cannot *h*	Jer 6:10	7181
H to the sound of the trumpet	Jer 6:17	7181
But they said, We will not *h*	Jer 6:17	7181
but they will not *h* to thee	Jer 7:27	8085
unto me, I will not *h* unto them	Jer 11:11	8085
that they may not *h* unto me	Jer 16:12	8085
pass, if ye diligently *h* unto me	Jer 17:24	8085
But if ye will not *h* unto me to	Jer 17:27	8085
h to the voice of them that	Jer 18:19	8085
H not unto the words of the	Jer 23:16	8085
If so be they will *h*, and turn	Jer 26:3	8085
If ye will not *h* to me, to walk	Jer 26:4	8085
To *h* to the words of my servants	Jer 26:5	8085
Therefore *h* not ye to your	Jer 27:9	8085
Therefore *h* not unto the words of	Jer 27:14	8085
H not to the words of your	Jer 27:16	8085
H not unto them	Jer 27:17	8085
neither *h* to your dreams which ye	Jer 29:8	8085
unto me, and I will *h* unto you	Jer 29:12	8085
instruction to *h* to my words	Jer 35:13	8085
did *h* unto the words of the LORD,	Jer 37:2	8085
counsel, wilt thou not *h* unto me	Jer 38:15	8085
the LORD, we will not *h* unto thee	Jer 44:16	8085
of Israel will not *h* unto thee	Eze 3:7	8085
for they will not *h* unto me	Eze 3:7	8085
me, and would not *h* unto me	Eze 20:8	8085
also, if ye will not *h* unto me	Eze 20:39	8085
O Lord, *h* and do	Dan 9:19	7181
and *h*, ye house of Israel	Hos 5:1	7181
because they did not *h* unto him	Hos 9:17	8085
h, O earth, and all that therein	Mic 1:2	7181
nor *h* unto me, saith the LORD	Zec 1:4	7181
But they refused to *h*, and pulled	Zec 7:11	7181
H; Behold, there went	Mk 4:3	*191*
H unto me every one of you, and	Mk 7:14	*191*
known unto you, and *h* to my words	Acts 2:14	*1801*
to *h* unto you more than unto God	Acts 4:19	*191*
Men, brethren, and fathers, *h*	Acts 7:2	*191*
of the gate, a damsel came to *h*	Acts 12:13	*5219*
Men and brethren, *h* unto me	Acts 15:13	*191*
H, my beloved brethren, Hath not	Jas 2:5	*191*

HEARKENED {81}

Because thou hast *h* unto the	Gen 3:17	8085
Abram *h* to the voice of Sarai	Gen 16:2	8085
And Abraham *h* unto Ephron	Gen 23:16	8085
God *h* unto Leah, and she conceived	Gen 30:17	8085
God *h* to her, and opened her womb	Gen 30:22	8085
unto Shechem his son *h* all that	Gen 34:24	8085
that he *h* not unto her, to lie by	Gen 39:10	8085
but they *h* not unto Moses for	Ex 6:9	8085
of Israel have not *h* unto me	Ex 6:12	8085
heart, that he *h* not unto them	Ex 7:13	8085
his heart, and *h* not unto them	Ex 8:15	8085
hardened, and he *h* not unto them	Ex 8:19	8085
of Pharaoh, and he *h* not unto them	Ex 9:12	8085
they *h* not unto Moses	Ex 16:20	8085
So Moses *h* to the voice of his	Ex 18:24	8085
times, and have not *h* to my voice	Num 14:22	8085
the LORD *h* to the voice of Israel	Num 21:3	8085
But the LORD *h* unto me at that	Deut 9:19	8085
him not, nor *h* to his voice	Deut 9:23	8085
the LORD *h* unto me at that time	Deut 10:10	8085
h unto observers of times, and	Deut 18:14	8085
but I have *h* to the voice of the	Deut 26:14	8085
the children of Israel *h* unto him	Deut 34:9	8085
According as we *h* unto Moses in	Josh 1:17	8085
that the LORD *h* unto the voice of	Josh 10:14	8085
and have not *h* unto my voice	Judg 2:20	8085
king of the children of Ammon *h*	Judg 11:28	8085
God *h* to the voice of Manoah	Judg 13:9	8085
Notwithstanding they *h* not unto	1Sa 2:25	8085
I have *h* unto your voice in all	1Sa 12:1	8085
Saul *h* unto the voice of Jonathan	1Sa 19:6	8085
I have *h* to thy voice, and have	1Sa 25:35	8085
have *h* unto thy words which thou	1Sa 28:21	8085
and he *h* unto their voice	1Sa 28:23	8085
Wherefore the king *h* not unto the	1Kin 12:15	8085
saw that the king *h* not unto them	1Kin 12:16	8085
They *h* therefore to the word of	1Kin 12:24	8085
So Ben-hadad *h* unto king Asa, and	1Kin 15:20	8085
he *h* unto their voice, and did so	1Kin 20:25	8085
the LORD, and the LORD *h* unto him	2Kin 13:4	8085

H

And the king of Assyria *h* unto him........ 2Kin 16:9 8085
Hezekiah *h* unto them, and shewed 2Kin 20:13 8085
But they *h* not.. 2Kin 21:9 8085
not *h* unto the words of this book........... 2Kin 22:13 8085
So the king *h* not unto the people........... 2Chr 10:15 8085
Ben-hadad *h* unto king Asa, and 2Chr 16:4 8085
Then the king *h* unto them...................... 2Chr 24:17 8085
hast not *h* unto my counsel 2Chr 25:16 8085
the LORD *h* to Hezekiah, and healed...... 2Chr 30:20 8085
h not unto the words of Necho................ 2Chr 35:22 8085
h not unto thy commandments,................ Neh 9:16 8085
h not unto thy commandments, but .... Neh 9:29 8085
nor *h* unto thy commandments and .... Neh 9:34 7181
he *h* not unto them, that they .... Est 3:4 8085
that he had *h* unto my voice.................... Job 9:16 238
Oh that my people had *h* unto me........... Ps 81:13 8085
h not unto the voice of the LORD .... Ps 106:25 8085
he *h* diligently with much heed............... Is 21:7 7181
O that thou hadst *h* to my........................ Is 48:18 7181
they have not *h* unto my words.................. Jer 6:19 7181
But they *h* not, nor inclined..................... Jer 7:24 8085
Yet they *h* not unto me, nor...................... Jer 7:26 8085
I *h* and heard, but they spake not........... Jer 8:6 8085
but ye have not *h*...................................... Jer 25:3 8085
but ye have not *h*, nor inclined .... Jer 25:4 8085
Yet ye have not *h* unto me .... Jer 25:7 8085
sending them, but ye have not *h* .... Jer 26:5 8085
they have not *h* to my words.................... Jer 29:19 8085
yet they have not *h* to receive.................. Jer 32:33 8085
but your fathers *h* not unto me .... Jer 34:14 8085
Ye have not *h* unto me, in....................... Jer 34:17 8085
but ye *h* not unto me .... Jer 35:14 8085
inclined your ear, nor *h* unto me .... Jer 35:15 8085
this people hath not *h* unto me .... Jer 35:16 8085
but they *h* not.. Jer 36:31 8085
But he *h* not to him .... Jer 37:14 8085
But they *h* not, nor inclined.................... Jer 44:5 8085
them, they would have *h* unto thee......... Eze 3:6 8085
Neither have we *h* unto thy...................... Dan 9:6 8085
and the LORD *h*, and heard it, and a ...... Mal 3:16 7181
Sirs, ye should have *h* unto me .... Acts 27:21 *3980*

HEARKENEDST {1}
because thou *h* not unto the voice........... Deut 28:45 8085

HEARKENETH {2}
But whoso *h* unto me shall dwell .... Prov 1:33 8085
but he that *h* unto counsel is.................. Prov 12:15 8085

HEARKENING {1}
h unto the voice of his word.................... Ps 103:20 8085

HEART {830}
of the thoughts of his *h* was only .... Gen 6:5 3820
earth, and it grieved him at his *h*........... Gen 6:6 3820
and the LORD said in his *h* .... Gen 8:21 3820
of man's *h* is evil from his youth .... Gen 8:21 3820
and laughed, and said in his *h* .... Gen 17:17 3820
in the integrity of my *h* and .... Gen 20:5 3824
this in the integrity of thy *h*.................. Gen 20:6 3824
I had done speaking in mine *h*............... Gen 24:45 3820
and Esau said in his *h*, The days........... Gen 27:41 3820
their *h* failed them, and they were.......... Gen 42:28 3820
And Jacob's *h* fainted, for he.................. Gen 45:26 3820
thee, he will be glad in his *h* .... Ex 4:14 3820
but I will harden his *h*, that he .... Ex 4:21 3820
And I will harden Pharaoh's *h* .... Ex 7:3 3820
And he hardened Pharaoh's *h* .... Ex 7:13 3820
Pharaoh's *h* is hardened, he .... Ex 7:14 3820
Pharaoh's *h* was hardened, neither .... Ex 7:22 3820
did he set his *h* to this also .... Ex 7:23 3820
was respite, he hardened his *h* .... Ex 8:15 3820
Pharaoh's *h* was hardened, and he.......... Ex 8:19 3820
hardened his *h* at this time also............. Ex 8:32 3820
the *h* of Pharaoh was hardened, and....... Ex 9:7 3820
LORD hardened the *h* of Pharaoh........... Ex 9:12 3820
send all my plagues upon thine *h*........... Ex 9:14 3820
yet more, and hardened his *h* .... Ex 9:34 3820
the *h* of Pharaoh was hardened,.............. Ex 9:35 3820
for I have hardened his *h* .... Ex 10:1 3820
the *h* of his servants, that I .... Ex 10:1 3820
But the LORD hardened Pharaoh's *h* ...... Ex 10:20 3820
But the LORD hardened Pharaoh's *h* ...... Ex 10:27 3820
and the LORD hardened Pharaoh's *h*...... Ex 11:10 3820
And I will harden Pharaoh's *h* .... Ex 14:4 3820
the *h* of Pharaoh and of his..................... Ex 14:5 3824
the LORD hardened the *h* of .... Ex 14:8 3820
congealed in the *h* of the sea.................. Ex 15:8 3820
for ye know the *h* of a stranger .... Ex 23:9 5315
his *h* ye shall take my offering .... Ex 25:2 3820
of judgment upon his *h*, when he............ Ex 28:29 3820
and they shall be upon Aaron's *h*............ Ex 28:30 3820
his *h* before the LORD continually........... Ex 28:30 3820
whosoever is of a willing *h*..................... Ex 35:5 3820
every one whose *h* stirred him up .... Ex 35:21 3820
all the women whose *h* stirred .... Ex 35:26 3820
whose *h* made them willing to .... Ex 35:29 3820
put in his *h* that he may teach .... Ex 35:34 3820
hath he filled with wisdom of *h* .... Ex 35:35 3820
in whose *h* the LORD had put.................. Ex 36:2 3820
even every one whose *h* stirred .... Ex 36:2 3820
not hate thy brother in thine *h*............... Lev 19:17 3824
the eyes, and cause sorrow of *h*.............. Lev 26:16 5315
that ye seek not after your own *h* .... Num 15:39 3824
wherefore discourage ye the *h* of .... Num 32:7 3820
they discouraged the *h* of the.................. Num 32:9 3820
brethren have discouraged our *h*............. Deut 1:28 3824
made his *h* obstinate, that he.................. Deut 2:30 3824
thy *h* all the days of thy life .... Deut 4:9 3824
if thou seek him with all thy *h*................ Deut 4:29 3824
day, and consider it in thine *h*................ Deut 4:39 3824
that there were such an *h* in them .... Deut 5:29 3824
the LORD thy God with all thine *h*......... Deut 6:5 3824
this day, shall be in thine *h* .... Deut 6:6 3824
If thou shalt say in thine *h*..................... Deut 7:17 3824
thee, to know what was in thine *h* .... Deut 8:2 3824
shalt also consider in thine *h* .... Deut 8:5 3824
Then thine *h* be lifted up, and................. Deut 8:14 3824
And thou say in thine *h*, My power......... Deut 8:17 3824
Speak not thou in thine *h* .... Deut 9:4 3824
or for the uprightness of thine *h* .... Deut 9:5 3824
the LORD thy God with all thy *h* .... Deut 10:12 3824
therefore the foreskin of your *h* .... Deut 10:16 3824
and to serve him with all your *h*............. Deut 11:13 3824
that your *h* be not deceived, and............. Deut 11:16 3824
lay up these my words in your *h* .... Deut 11:18 3824
the LORD your God with all your *h*......... Deut 13:3 3824
thou shalt not harden thine *h* .... Deut 15:7 3824
be not a thought in thy wicked *h* .... Deut 15:9 3824
thine *h* shall not be grieved when........... Deut 15:10 3824
himself, that his *h* turn not away............ Deut 17:17 3824
That his *h* be not lifted up above........... Deut 17:20 3824
And if thou say in thine *h* .... Deut 18:21 3824
the slayer, while his *h* is hot.................. Deut 19:6 3824
h faint as well as his *h* .... Deut 20:8 3824
is poor, and setteth his *h* upon it............. Deut 24:15 5315
keep and do them with all thine *h* .... Deut 26:16 3824
blindness, and astonishment of *h*............. Deut 28:28 3824
joyfulness, and with gladness of *h* .... Deut 28:47 3824
give thee there a trembling *h* .... Deut 28:65 3820
for the fear of thine *h* wherewith............ Deut 28:67 3824
not given you an *h* to perceive................. Deut 29:4 3820
whose *h* turneth away this day................ Deut 29:18 3824
that he bless himself in his *h* .... Deut 29:19 3824
walk in the imagination of mine *h*.......... Deut 29:19 3820
and thy children, with all thine *h* .... Deut 30:2 3824
thy God will circumcise thine *h* .... Deut 30:6 3824
the *h* of thy seed, to love the .... Deut 30:6 3824
the LORD thy God with all thine *h*......... Deut 30:6 3824
the LORD thy God with all thine *h*......... Deut 30:10 3824
thee, in thy mouth, and in thy *h*............. Deut 30:14 3824
But if thine *h* turn away, so that .... Deut 30:17 3824
passed over, that their *h* melted .... Josh 5:1 3824
word again as it was in mine *h* .... Josh 14:7 3824
me made the *h* of the people melt........... Josh 14:8 3820
and to serve him with all your *h*............. Josh 22:5 3824
incline your *h* unto the LORD God .... Josh 24:23 3824
My *h* is toward the governors of .... Judg 5:9 3820
there were great thoughts of *h* .... Judg 5:15 3820
there were great searchings of *h* .... Judg 5:16 3820
when thine *h* is not with me.................... Judg 16:15 3820
That he told her all his *h*....................... Judg 16:17 3820
that he had told her all his *h* .... Judg 16:18 3820
for he hath shewed me all his *h* .... Judg 16:18 3820
And the priest's *h* was glad .... Judg 18:20 3820
Comfort thine *h* with a morsel of............. Judg 19:5 3820
night, and let thine *h* be merry .... Judg 19:6 3820
father said, Comfort thine *h*................... Judg 19:8 3824
that thine *h* may be merry....................... Judg 19:9 3824
his *h* was merry, he went to lie............... Ruth 3:7 3820
and why is thy *h* grieved 1Sa 1:8 3824
Now Hannah, she spake in her *h* 1Sa 1:13 3820
My *h* rejoiceth in the LORD, mine.......... 1Sa 2:1 3820
thine eyes, and to grieve thine *h* 1Sa 2:33 5315
to that which is in mine *h* 1Sa 2:35 3824
for his *h* trembled for the ark of 1Sa 4:13 3820
tell thee all that is in thine *h* 1Sa 9:19 3824
Samuel, God gave him another *h*............ 1Sa 10:9 3820
serve the LORD with all your *h*.............. 1Sa 12:20 3824
him in truth with all your *h*.................... 1Sa 12:24 3824
sought him a man after his own *h* 1Sa 13:14 3824
him, Do all that is in thine *h*.................. 1Sa 14:7 3824
I am with thee according to thy *h* 1Sa 14:7 3824
but the LORD looketh on the *h* 1Sa 16:7 3824
and the naughtiness of thine *h*................ 1Sa 17:28 3824
Let no man's *h* fail because of................ 1Sa 17:32 3820
laid up these words in his *h* 1Sa 21:12 3824
that David's *h* smote him 1Sa 24:5 3820
nor offence of *h* unto my lord................. 1Sa 25:31 3820
Nabal's *h* was merry within him 1Sa 25:36 3820
that his *h* died within him, and he.......... 1Sa 25:37 3820
And David said in his *h*, I shall 1Sa 27:1 3820
afraid, and his *h* greatly trembled........... 1Sa 28:5 3820
over all that thine *h* desireth.................. 2Sa 3:21 5315
and she despised him in her *h*................ 2Sa 6:16 3820
Go, do all that is in thine *h*................... 2Sa 7:3 3824
sake, and according to thine own *h* 2Sa 7:21 3820
h to pray this prayer unto thee................ 2Sa 7:27 3820
when Amnon's *h* is merry with wine....... 2Sa 13:28 3820
the king take the thing to his *h*.............. 2Sa 13:33 3820
the king's *h* was toward Absalom 2Sa 14:1 3820
whose *h* is as the *h* of a lion................... 2Sa 17:10 3820
them through the *h* of Absalom 2Sa 18:14 3820
he bowed the *h* of all the men of............. 2Sa 19:14 3824
Judah, even as the *h* of one man 2Sa 19:14
the king should take it to his *h*............... 2Sa 19:19 3820
David's *h* smote him after that he........... 2Sa 24:10 3820
me in truth with all their *h*.................... 1Kin 2:4 3824
which thine *h* is privy to 1Kin 2:44 3824
and in uprightness of *h* with thee 1Kin 3:6 3824
h to judge thy people, that I may 1Kin 3:9 3820
thee a wise and an understanding *h* 1Kin 3:12 3820
exceeding much, and largeness of *h* 1Kin 4:29 3820
it was in the *h* of David my.................... 1Kin 8:17 3824
Whereas it was in thine *h* to 1Kin 8:18 3824
didst well that it was in thine *h*............. 1Kin 8:18 3824
walk before thee with all their *h*............ 1Kin 8:23 3820
every man the plague of his own *h* 1Kin 8:38 3824
to his ways, whose *h* thou knowest 1Kin 8:39 3824
return unto thee with all their *h*............ 1Kin 8:48 3824
Let your *h* therefore be perfect 1Kin 8:61 3824
glad of *h* for all the goodness.................. 1Kin 8:66 3824
mine *h* shall be there perpetually............ 1Kin 9:3 3824
father walked, in integrity of *h*.............. 1Kin 9:4 3824
with him of all that was in her *h* 1Kin 10:2 3824
which God had put in his *h*..................... 1Kin 10:24 3820
turn away your *h* after their gods 1Kin 11:2 3824
and his wives turned away his *h* 1Kin 11:3 3820
away his *h* after other gods..................... 1Kin 11:4 3824
his *h* was not perfect with the.................. 1Kin 11:4 3824
as was the *h* of David his father 1Kin 11:4 3824
because his *h* was turned from the.......... 1Kin 11:9 3824
And Jeroboam said in his *h*.................... 1Kin 12:26 3820
then shall the *h* of this people................. 1Kin 12:27 3820
which he had devised of his own *h* 1Kin 12:33 3820
and who followed me with all his *h*........ 1Kin 14:8 3824
his *h* was not perfect with the................. 1Kin 15:3 3824
as the *h* of David his father..................... 1Kin 15:3 3824
nevertheless Asa's *h* was perfect 1Kin 15:14 3824
hast turned their *h* back again................. 1Kin 18:37 3820
bread, and let thine *h* be merry............... 1Kin 21:7 3820
him, Went not mine *h* with thee.............. 2Kin 5:26 3820
Therefore the *h* of the king of 2Kin 6:11 3820
and the arrow went out at his *h*............... 2Kin 9:24 3820
and said to him, Is thine *h* right 2Kin 10:15 3824
as my *h* is with thy *h* 2Kin 10:15 3824
to all that was in mine *h* 2Kin 10:30 3824
LORD God of Israel with all his *h*.......... 2Kin 10:31 3824
that cometh into any man's *h* to.............. 2Kin 12:4 3820
thine *h* hath lifted thee up 2Kin 14:10 3820
thee in truth and with a perfect *h*.......... 2Kin 20:3 3824
Because thine *h* was tender...................... 2Kin 22:19 3824
and his statutes with all their *h*............. 2Kin 23:3 3820
turned to the LORD with all his *h*.......... 2Kin 23:25 3824
mine *h* shall be knit unto you 1Chr 12:17 3824
they were not of double *h*........................ 1Chr 12:33 3820
came with a perfect *h* to Hebron 1Chr 12:38 3824
were of one *h* to make David king 1Chr 12:38 3824
and she despised him in her *h*................ 1Chr 15:29 3820
let the *h* of them rejoice that.................. 1Chr 16:10 3820
David, Do all that is in thine *h* 1Chr 17:2 3824
sake, and according to thine own *h* 1Chr 17:19 3820
in his *h* to pray before thee 1Chr 17:25
Now set your *h* and your soul to............ 1Chr 22:19 3824
I had in mine *h* to build an house.......... 1Chr 28:2 3824
and serve him with a perfect *h*.............. 1Chr 28:9 3820
because with perfect *h* they 1Chr 29:9 3820
my God, that thou triest the *h* 1Chr 29:17 3824
in the uprightness of mine *h* I................. 1Chr 29:17 3824
thoughts of the *h* of thy people 1Chr 29:18 3824
and prepare their *h* unto thee 1Chr 29:18 3824
unto Solomon my son a perfect *h*............ 1Chr 29:19 3824
Because this was in thine *h*..................... 2Chr 1:11 3824
Now it was in the *h* of David my 2Chr 6:7 3824
Forasmuch as it was in thine *h* to 2Chr 6:8 3824
well in that it was in thine *h*.................. 2Chr 6:8 3824
his ways, whose *h* thou knowest 2Chr 6:30 3824
return to thee with all their *h* 2Chr 6:38 3820
merry in *h* for the goodness that.............. 2Chr 7:10 3820
h to make in the house of the.................. 2Chr 7:11 3820
mine *h* shall be there perpetually............ 2Chr 7:16 3820
with him of all that was in her *h* 2Chr 9:1 3824
wisdom, that God had put in his *h*.......... 2Chr 9:23 3820
not his *h* to seek the LORD...................... 2Chr 12:14 3820
of their fathers with all their *h*............... 2Chr 15:12 3824
they had sworn with all their *h*............... 2Chr 15:15 3824
nevertheless the *h* of Asa was 2Chr 15:17 3824
whose *h* is perfect toward him................ 2Chr 16:9 3820
his *h* was lifted up in the ways................ 2Chr 17:6 3820
hast prepared thine *h* to seek God 2Chr 19:3 3824
faithfully, and with a perfect *h* 2Chr 19:9 3824
sought the LORD with all his *h*.............. 2Chr 22:9 3824
LORD, but not with a perfect *h*............... 2Chr 25:2 3824
thine *h* lifteth thee up to boast 2Chr 25:19 3820
his *h* was lifted up to his......................... 2Chr 26:16 3820
Now it is in mine *h* to make a 2Chr 29:10 3824
were of a free *h* burnt offerings 2Chr 29:31 3820
Levites were more upright in *h* to........... 2Chr 29:34 3824
of God was to give them one *h* to............ 2Chr 30:12 3820
That prepareth his *h* to seek God............ 2Chr 30:19 3824
his God, he did it with all his *h* 2Chr 31:21 3824
for his *h* was lifted up 2Chr 32:25 3820
himself for the pride of his *h* 2Chr 32:26 3820
might know all that was in his *h* 2Chr 32:31 3824
Because thine *h* was tender..................... 2Chr 34:27 3824
and his statutes, with all his *h*............... 2Chr 34:31 3824
hardened his *h* from turning unto............ 2Chr 36:13 3824
turned the *h* of the king of .... Ezr 6:22 3820
For Ezra had prepared his *h* to .... Ezr 7:10 3824
a thing as this in the king's *h*................. Ezr 7:27 3820
is nothing else but sorrow of *h*................ Neh 2:2 3820
put in my *h* to do at Jerusalem................. Neh 2:12
feignest them out of thine own *h* .... Neh 6:8
my God put into mine *h* to gather............ Neh 7:5 3820
foundest his *h* faithful before.................. Neh 9:8 3824
when the *h* of the king was merry........... Est 1:10 3820
that day joyful and with a glad *h*............ Est 5:9 3820
Now Haman thought in his *h* .... Est 6:6 3820
durst presume in his *h* to do so .... Est 7:5 3820
shouldest set thine *h* upon him................ Job 7:17 3820
and utter words out of their *h*................. Job 8:10 3820
He is wise in *h*, and mighty in .... Job 9:4 3824
things hast thou hid in thine *h*................ Job 10:13 3824
If thou prepare thine *h*, and .... Job 11:13 3820
He taketh away the *h* of the chief........... Job 12:24 3820
Why doth thine *h* carry thee away .... Job 15:12 3820

hid their *h* from understanding	Job 17:4	3820
off, even the thoughts of my *h*	Job 17:11	3824
and lay up his words in thine *h*	Job 22:22	3824
For God maketh my *h* soft, and the	Job 23:16	3820
my *h* shall not reproach me so	Job 27:6	3824
the widow's *h* to sing for joy	Job 29:13	3820
mine *h* walked after mine eyes, and	Job 31:7	3820
If mine *h* have been deceived by a	Job 31:9	3820
my *h* hath been secretly enticed,	Job 31:27	3820
be of the uprightness of my *h*	Job 33:3	3820
If he set his *h* upon man, if he	Job 34:14	3820
the hypocrites in *h* heap up wrath	Job 36:13	3820
At this also my *h* trembleth	Job 37:1	3820
not any that are wise of *h*	Job 37:24	3820
hath given understanding to the *h*	Job 38:36	7907
His *h* is as firm as a stone	Job 41:24	3820
with your own *h* upon your bed	Ps 4:4	3824
Thou hast put gladness in my *h*	Ps 4:7	3820
which saveth the upright in *h*	Ps 7:10	3820
thee, O LORD, with my whole *h*	Ps 9:1	3820
He hath said in his *h*, I shall	Ps 10:6	3820
He hath said in his *h*, God hath	Ps 10:11	3820
he hath said in his *h*, Thou wilt	Ps 10:13	3820
thou wilt prepare their *h*	Ps 10:17	3820
privily shoot at the upright in *h*	Ps 11:2	3820
and with a double *h* do they speak	Ps 12:2	3820
soul, having sorrow in my *h* daily	Ps 13:2	3824
my *h* shall rejoice in thy	Ps 13:5	3820
The fool hath said in his *h*	Ps 14:1	3820
and speaketh the truth in his *h*	Ps 15:2	3824
Therefore my *h* is glad, and my	Ps 16:9	3820
Thou hast proved mine *h*	Ps 17:3	3820
LORD are right, rejoicing the *h*	Ps 19:8	3820
mouth, and the meditation of my *h*	Ps 19:14	3820
thee according to thine own *h*	Ps 20:4	3824
my *h* is like wax	Ps 22:14	3820
your *h* shall live for ever	Ps 22:26	3824
hath clean hands, and a pure *h*	Ps 24:4	3824
The troubles of my *h* are enlarged	Ps 25:17	3824
try my reins and my *h*	Ps 26:2	3820
against me, my *h* shall not fear	Ps 27:3	3820
my *h* said unto thee, Thy face,	Ps 27:8	3820
and he shall strengthen thine *h*	Ps 27:14	3820
my *h* trusted in him, and I am	Ps 28:7	3820
therefore my *h* greatly rejoiceth	Ps 28:7	3820
and he shall strengthen your *h*	Ps 31:24	3824
joy, all ye that are upright in *h*	Ps 32:11	3820
of his *h* to all generations	Ps 33:11	3820
For our *h* shall rejoice in him,	Ps 33:21	3820
unto them that are of a broken *h*	Ps 34:18	3820
of the wicked saith within my *h*	Ps 36:1	3820
righteousness to the upright in *h*	Ps 36:10	3820
give thee the desires of thine *h*	Ps 37:4	3820
shall enter into their own *h*	Ps 37:15	3820
The law of his God is in his *h*	Ps 37:31	3820
of the disquietness of my *h*	Ps 38:8	3820
My *h* panteth, my strength faileth	Ps 38:10	3820
My *h* was hot within me	Ps 39:3	3820
yea, thy law is within my *h*	Ps 40:8	4578
hid thy righteousness within my *h*	Ps 40:10	3820
therefore my *h* faileth me	Ps 40:12	3820
his *h* gathereth iniquity to	Ps 41:6	3820
Our *h* is not turned back, neither	Ps 44:18	3820
he knoweth the secrets of the *h*	Ps 44:21	3820
My *h* is inditing a good matter	Ps 45:1	3820
in the *h* of the king's enemies	Ps 45:5	3820
the meditation of my *h* shall be	Ps 49:3	3820
Create in me a clean *h*, O God	Ps 51:10	3820
a broken and a contrite *h*, O God,	Ps 51:17	3820
The fool hath said in his *h*	Ps 53:1	3820
My *h* is sore pained within me	Ps 55:4	3820
than butter, but war was in his *h*	Ps 55:21	3820
My *h* is fixed, O God, my *h* is	Ps 57:7	3820
Yea, in *h* ye work wickedness	Ps 58:2	3820
thee, when my *h* is overwhelmed	Ps 61:2	3820
pour out your *h* before him	Ps 62:8	3824
set not your *h* upon them	Ps 62:10	3820
of every one of them, and the *h*	Ps 64:6	3820
all the upright in *h* shall glory	Ps 64:10	3820
If I regard iniquity in my *h*	Ps 66:18	3820
Reproach hath broken my *h*	Ps 69:20	3820
your *h* shall live that seek God	Ps 69:32	3824
even to such as are of a clean *h*	Ps 73:1	3824
they have more than *h* could wish	Ps 73:7	3824
I have cleansed my *h* in vain	Ps 73:13	3824
Thus my *h* was grieved, and I was	Ps 73:21	3824
My flesh and my *h* faileth	Ps 73:26	3824
but God is the strength of my *h*	Ps 73:26	3824
I commune with mine own *h*	Ps 77:6	3824
that set not their *h* aright	Ps 78:8	3820
they tempted God in their *h* by	Ps 78:18	3824
For their *h* was not right with	Ps 78:37	3820
to the integrity of his *h*	Ps 78:72	3824
my *h* and my flesh crieth out for	Ps 84:2	3820
in whose *h* are the ways of them	Ps 84:5	3824
unite my *h* to fear thy name	Ps 86:11	3824
O Lord my God, with all my *h*	Ps 86:12	3824
the upright in *h* shall follow it	Ps 94:15	3820
Harden not your *h*, as in the	Ps 95:8	3824
a people that do err in their *h*	Ps 95:10	3824
and gladness for the upright in *h*	Ps 97:11	3820
within my house with a perfect *h*	Ps 101:2	3824
A froward *h* shall depart from me	Ps 101:4	3820
a proud *h* will not I suffer	Ps 101:5	3824
My *h* is smitten, and withered like	Ps 102:4	3820
that maketh glad the *h* of man	Ps 104:15	3824
bread which strengtheneth man's *h*	Ps 104:15	3824
let the *h* of them rejoice that	Ps 105:3	3820

He turned their *h* to hate his	Ps 105:25	3820
brought down their *h* with labour	Ps 107:12	3820
O God, my *h* is fixed	Ps 108:1	3820
might even slay the broken in *h*	Ps 109:16	3824
my *h* is wounded within me	Ps 109:22	3820
praise the LORD with my whole *h*	Ps 111:1	3824
his *h* is fixed, trusting in the	Ps 112:7	3820
His *h* is established, he shall	Ps 112:8	3820
and that seek him with the whole *h*	Ps 119:2	3820
praise thee with uprightness of *h*	Ps 119:7	3824
With my whole *h* have I sought	Ps 119:10	3820
Thy word have I hid in mine *h*	Ps 119:11	3820
when thou shalt enlarge my *h*	Ps 119:32	3820
shall observe it with my whole *h*	Ps 119:34	3820
Incline my *h* unto thy testimonies	Ps 119:36	3820
thy favour with my whole *h*	Ps 119:58	3820
keep thy precepts with my whole *h*	Ps 119:69	3820
Their *h* is as fat as grease	Ps 119:70	3820
Let my *h* be sound in thy statutes	Ps 119:80	3820
they are the rejoicing of my *h*	Ps 119:111	3820
I have inclined mine *h* to perform	Ps 119:112	3820
I cried with my whole *h*	Ps 119:145	3820
but my *h* standeth in awe of thy	Ps 119:161	3820
my *h* is not haughty, nor mine	Ps 131:1	3820
will praise thee with my whole *h*	Ps 138:1	3820
Search me, O God, and know my *h*	Ps 139:23	3824
imagine mischiefs in their *h*	Ps 140:2	3820
Incline not my *h* to any evil	Ps 141:4	3820
my *h* within me is desolate	Ps 143:4	3820
He healeth the broken in *h*	Ps 147:3	3820
apply thine *h* to understanding	Prov 2:2	3820
When wisdom entereth into thine *h*	Prov 2:10	3820
but let thine *h* keep my	Prov 3:1	3820
them upon the table of thine *h*	Prov 3:3	3820
in the LORD with all thine *h*	Prov 3:5	3820
Let thine *h* retain my words	Prov 4:4	3820
keep them in the midst of thine *h*	Prov 4:21	3824
Keep thy *h* with all diligence	Prov 4:23	3820
and my *h* despised reproof	Prov 5:12	3820
Frowardness is in his *h*, he	Prov 6:14	3820
An *h* that deviseth wicked	Prov 6:18	3820
them continually upon thine *h*	Prov 6:21	3820
not after her beauty in thine *h*	Prov 6:25	3824
them upon the table of thine *h*	Prov 7:3	3820
of an harlot, and subtil of *h*	Prov 7:10	3820
Let not thine *h* decline to her	Prov 7:25	3820
be ye of an understanding *h*	Prov 8:5	3820
The wise in *h* will receive	Prov 10:8	3820
the *h* of the wicked is little	Prov 10:20	3820
They that are of a froward *h* are	Prov 11:20	3820
shall be servant to the wise of *h*	Prov 11:29	3820
of a perverse *h* shall be despised	Prov 12:8	3820
Deceit is in the *h* of them that	Prov 12:20	3820
but the *h* of fools proclaimeth	Prov 12:23	3820
Heaviness in the *h* of man maketh	Prov 12:25	3820
Hope deferred maketh the *h* sick	Prov 13:12	3820
The *h* knoweth his own bitterness	Prov 14:10	3820
in laughter the *h* is sorrowful	Prov 14:13	3820
The backslider in *h* shall be	Prov 14:14	3820
A sound *h* is the life of the	Prov 14:30	3820
Wisdom resteth in the *h* of him	Prov 14:33	3820
but the *h* of the foolish doeth	Prov 15:7	3820
A merry *h* maketh a cheerful	Prov 15:13	3820
of the *h* the spirit is broken	Prov 15:13	3820
The *h* of him that hath	Prov 15:14	3820
a merry *h* hath a continual feast	Prov 15:15	3820
The *h* of the righteous studieth	Prov 15:28	3820
light of the eyes rejoiceth the *h*	Prov 15:30	3820
The preparations of the *h* in man	Prov 16:1	3820
Every one that is proud in *h* is	Prov 16:5	3820
A man's *h* deviseth his way	Prov 16:9	3820
The wise in *h* shall be called	Prov 16:21	3820
The *h* of the wise teacheth his	Prov 16:23	3820
wisdom, seeing he hath no *h* to it	Prov 17:16	3820
hath a froward *h* findeth no good	Prov 17:20	3820
A merry *h* doeth good like a	Prov 17:22	3820
but that his *h* may discover	Prov 18:2	3820
the *h* of man is haughty	Prov 18:12	3820
The *h* of the prudent getteth	Prov 18:15	3820
his *h* fretteth against the LORD	Prov 19:3	3820
are many devices in a man's *h*	Prov 19:21	3820
Counsel in the *h* of man is like	Prov 20:5	3820
can say, I have made my *h* clean	Prov 20:9	3820
The king's *h* is in the hand of	Prov 21:1	3820
An high look, and a proud *h*	Prov 21:4	3820
He that loveth pureness of *h*	Prov 22:11	3820
is bound in the *h* of a child	Prov 22:15	3820
apply thine *h* unto my knowledge	Prov 22:17	3820
For as he thinketh in his *h*	Prov 23:7	5315
but his *h* is not with thee	Prov 23:7	3820
Apply thine *h* unto instruction,	Prov 23:12	3820
My son, if thine *h* be wise	Prov 23:15	3820
my *h* shall rejoice, even mine	Prov 23:15	3820
Let not thine *h* envy sinners	Prov 23:17	3820
wise, and guide thine *h* in the way	Prov 23:19	3820
My son, give me thine *h*, and let	Prov 23:26	3820
thine *h* shall utter perverse	Prov 23:33	3820
For their *h* studieth destruction,	Prov 24:2	3820
that pondereth the *h* consider it	Prov 24:12	3826
let not thine *h* be glad when he	Prov 24:17	3820
the *h* of kings is unsearchable	Prov 25:3	3820
that singeth songs to an heavy *h*	Prov 25:20	3820
a wicked *h* are like a potsherd	Prov 26:23	3820
are seven abominations in his *h*	Prov 26:25	3820
Ointment and perfume rejoice the *h*	Prov 27:9	3820
son, be wise, and make my *h* glad	Prov 27:11	3820
to face, so the *h* of man to man	Prov 27:19	3820
his *h* shall fall into mischief	Prov 28:14	3820

of a proud *h* stirreth up strife	Prov 28:25	5315
trusteth in his own *h* is a fool	Prov 28:26	3820
The *h* of her husband doth safely	Prov 31:11	3820
And I gave my *h* to seek and search	Eccl 1:13	3820
I communed with mine own *h*	Eccl 1:16	3820
my *h* had great experience of	Eccl 1:16	3820
I gave my *h* to know wisdom, and to	Eccl 1:17	3820
I said in mine *h*, Go to now, I	Eccl 2:1	3820
I sought in mine *h* to give myself	Eccl 2:3	3820
acquainting mine *h* with wisdom	Eccl 2:3	3820
I withheld not my *h* from any joy	Eccl 2:10	3820
for my *h* rejoiced in all my	Eccl 2:10	3820
Then said I in my *h*, As it	Eccl 2:15	3820
Then I said in my *h*, that this	Eccl 2:15	3820
I went about to cause my *h* to	Eccl 2:20	3820
and of the vexation of his *h*	Eccl 2:22	3820
his *h* taketh not rest in the	Eccl 2:23	3820
he hath set the world in their *h*	Eccl 3:11	3820
I said in mine *h*, God shall judge	Eccl 3:17	3820
I said in mine *h* concerning the	Eccl 3:18	3820
let not thine *h* be hasty to utter	Eccl 5:2	3820
answereth him in the joy of his *h*	Eccl 5:20	3820
the living will lay it to his *h*	Eccl 7:2	3820
countenance the *h* is made better	Eccl 7:3	3820
The *h* of the wise is in the house	Eccl 7:4	3820
but the *h* of fools is in the	Eccl 7:4	3820
and a gift destroyeth the *h*	Eccl 7:7	3820
own *h* knoweth that thou thyself	Eccl 7:22	3820
I applied mine *h* to know, and to	Eccl 7:25	3820
whose *h* is snares and nets, and her	Eccl 7:26	3820
a wise man's *h* discerneth both	Eccl 8:5	3820
applied my *h* unto every work that	Eccl 8:9	3820
therefore the *h* of the sons of	Eccl 8:11	3820
I applied mine *h* to know wisdom	Eccl 8:16	3820
in my *h* even to declare all this	Eccl 9:1	3820
also the *h* of the sons of men is	Eccl 9:3	3820
is in their *h* while they live	Eccl 9:3	3824
and drink thy wine with a merry *h*	Eccl 9:7	3820
A wise man's *h* is at his right	Eccl 10:2	3820
but a fool's *h* at his left	Eccl 10:2	3820
let thy *h* cheer thee in the days	Eccl 11:9	3820
and walk in the ways of thine *h*	Eccl 11:9	3820
remove sorrow from thy *h*, and put	Eccl 11:10	3820
the day of the gladness of his *h*	Song 3:11	3820
Thou hast ravished my *h*, my	Song 4:9	3823
thou hast ravished my *h* with one	Song 4:9	3823
I sleep, but my *h* waketh	Song 5:2	3820
Set me as a seal upon thine *h*	Song 8:6	3820
is sick, and the whole *h* faint	Is 1:5	3824
Make the *h* of this people fat, and	Is 6:10	3820
ears, and understand with their *h*	Is 6:10	3824
his *h* was moved, and the *h* of	Is 7:2	3824
in the pride and stoutness of *h*	Is 9:9	3824
so, neither doth his *h* think so	Is 10:7	3824
but it is in his *h* to destroy	Is 10:7	3824
stout *h* of the king of Assyria	Is 10:12	3824
and every man's *h* shall melt	Is 13:7	3824
For thou hast said in thine *h*	Is 14:13	3824
My *h* shall cry out for Moab	Is 15:5	3820
the *h* of Egypt shall melt in the	Is 19:1	3824
My *h* panted, fearfulness	Is 21:4	3824
have removed their *h* far from me	Is 29:13	3820
and gladness of *h*, as when one	Is 30:29	3824
The *h* also of the rash shall	Is 32:4	3824
his *h* will work iniquity, to	Is 32:6	3820
Thine *h* shall meditate terror	Is 33:18	3820
to them that are of a fearful *h*	Is 35:4	3820
thee in truth and with a perfect *h*	Is 38:3	3820
him, yet he laid it not to *h*	Is 42:25	3820
And none considereth in his *h*	Is 44:19	3820
a deceived *h* hath turned him	Is 44:20	3820
not lay these things to thy *h*	Is 47:7	3820
that sayest in thine *h*, I am, and	Is 47:8	3824
and thou hast said in thine *h*	Is 47:10	3820
Then shalt thou say in thine *h*	Is 49:21	3824
the people in whose *h* is my law	Is 51:7	3820
and no man layeth it to *h*	Is 57:1	3820
me, nor laid it to thy *h*	Is 57:11	3820
to revive the *h* of the contrite	Is 57:15	3820
on frowardly in the way of his *h*	Is 57:17	3820
uttering from the *h* words of	Is 59:13	3820
thine *h* shall fear, and be	Is 60:5	3824
the day of vengeance is in mine *h*	Is 63:4	3820
hardened our *h* from thy fear	Is 63:17	3820
servants shall sing for joy of *h*	Is 65:14	3820
but ye shall cry for sorrow of *h*	Is 65:14	3820
your *h* shall rejoice, and your	Is 66:14	3820
turned unto me with her whole *h*	Jer 3:10	3820
you pastors according to mine *h*	Jer 3:15	3820
the imagination of their evil *h*	Jer 3:17	3820
take away the foreskins of your *h*	Jer 4:4	3824
that the *h* of the king shall	Jer 4:9	3820
perish, and the *h* of the princes	Jer 4:9	3820
wash thine *h* from wickedness,	Jer 4:14	3820
because it reacheth unto thine *h*	Jer 4:18	3820
I am pained at my very *h*	Jer 4:19	3820
my *h* maketh a noise in me	Jer 4:19	3820
a revolting and a rebellious *h*	Jer 5:23	3820
Neither say they in their *h*	Jer 5:24	3824
the imagination of their evil *h*	Jer 7:24	3820
not, neither came it into my *h*	Jer 7:31	3820
sorrow, my *h* is faint in me	Jer 8:18	3820
but in *h* he layeth his wait	Jer 9:8	7130
the imagination of their own *h*	Jer 9:14	3820
Israel are uncircumcised in the *h*	Jer 9:26	3820
the imagination of their evil *h*	Jer 11:8	3820
that triest the reins and the *h*	Jer 11:20	3820
me, and tried mine *h* toward thee	Jer 12:3	3820

because no man layeth it to *h* Jer 12:11 3820
in the imagination of their *h* Jer 13:10 3820
And if thou say in thine *h* Jer 13:22 3824
nought, and the deceit of their *h* Jer 14:14 3820
me the joy and rejoicing of mine *h* Jer 15:16 3824
the imagination of his evil *h* Jer 16:12 3820
graven upon the table of their *h* Jer 17:1 3820
whose *h* departeth from the LORD Jer 17:5 3820
The *h* is deceitful above all Jer 17:9 3820
I the LORD search the *h*, I try Jer 17:10 3820
do the imagination of his evil *h* Jer 18:12 3820
But his word was in mine *h* as a Jer 20:9 3820
and seest the reins and the *h* Jer 20:12 3820
thine *h* are not but for thy Jer 22:17 3820
Mine *h* within me is broken Jer 23:9 3820
speak a vision of their own *h* Jer 23:16 3820
the imagination of his own *h* Jer 23:17 3820
performed the thoughts of his *h* Jer 23:20 3820
h of the prophets that prophesy Jer 23:26 3820
of the deceit of their own *h* Jer 23:26 3820
I will give them an *h* to know me Jer 24:7 3820
return unto me with their whole *h* Jer 24:7 3820
search for me with all your *h* Jer 29:13 3824
engaged his *h* to approach unto me Jer 30:21 3820
performed the intents of his *h* Jer 30:24 3820
set thine *h* toward the highway, Jer 31:21 3820
And I will give them one *h* Jer 32:39 3820
land assuredly with my whole *h* Jer 32:41 3820
and the haughtiness of his *h* Jer 48:29 3820
mine *h* shall mourn for the men of Jer 48:31
Therefore mine *h* shall sound for Jer 48:36 3820
mine *h* shall sound like pipes for Jer 48:36 3820
as the *h* of a woman in her pangs Jer 48:41 3820
thee, and the pride of thine *h* Jer 49:16 3820
at that day shall the *h* of the Jer 49:22 3820
as the *h* of a woman in her pangs Jer 49:22 3820
And lest your *h* faint, and ye fear Jer 51:46 3824
mine *h* is turned within me Lam 1:20 3820
sighs are many, and my *h* is faint Lam 1:22 3820
Their *h* cried unto the Lord, O Lam 2:18 3820
h like water before the face of Lam 2:19 3820
Let us lift up our *h* with our Lam 3:41 3824
Mine eye affecteth mine *h* because Lam 3:51 5315
Give them sorrow of *h*, thy curse Lam 3:65 3820
The joy of our *h* is ceased Lam 5:15 3820
For this our *h* is faint Lam 5:17 3820
unto thee receive in thine *h* Eze 3:10 3824
I am broken with their whorish *h* Eze 6:9 3820
And I will give them one *h* Eze 11:19 3820
the stony *h* out of their flesh Eze 11:19 3820
and will give them an *h* of flesh Eze 11:19 3820
But as for them whose *h* walketh Eze 11:21 3820
the *h* of their detestable things Eze 11:21 3820
which prophesy out of their own *h* Eze 13:17 3820
made the *h* of the righteous sad Eze 13:22 3820
set up their idols in their *h* Eze 14:3 3820
setteth up his idols in his *h* Eze 14:4 3820
house of Israel in their own *h* Eze 14:5 3820
and setteth up his idols in his *h* Eze 14:7 3820
How weak is thine *h*, saith the Eze 16:30 3826
and make you a new *h* and a new Eze 18:31 3820
for their *h* went after their Eze 20:16 3820
every *h* shall melt, and all hands Eze 21:7 3820
gates, that their *h* may faint Eze 21:15 3820
Can thine *h* endure, or can thine Eze 22:14 3820
rejoiced in *h* with all thy Eze 25:6 5315
vengeance with a despiteful *h* Eze 25:15 5315
for thee with bitterness of *h* Eze 27:31 5315
Because thine *h* is lifted up Eze 28:2 3820
set thine *h* as the *h* of God Eze 28:2 3820
thine *h* is lifted up because of Eze 28:5 3824
set thine *h* as the *h* of God Eze 28:6 3820
Thine *h* was lifted up because of Eze 28:17 3820
his *h* is lifted up in his height Eze 31:10 3824
but their *h* goeth after their Eze 33:31 3820
with the joy of all their *h* Eze 36:5 3824
A new *h* also will I give you, and Eze 36:26 3820
the stony *h* out of your flesh Eze 36:26 3820
and I will give you an *h* of flesh Eze 36:26 3820
set thine *h* upon all that I shall Eze 40:4 3820
strangers, uncircumcised in *h* Eze 44:7 3820
No stranger, uncircumcised in *h* Eze 44:9 3820
in his *h* that he would not defile Dan 1:8 3820
know the thoughts of thy *h* Dan 2:30 3825
Let his *h* be changed from man's, Dan 4:16 3825
let a beast's *h* be given unto him Dan 4:16 3825
But when his *h* was lifted up, and Dan 5:20 3825
his *h* was made like the beasts, Dan 5:21 3825
hast not humbled thine *h* Dan 5:22 3825
set his *h* on Daniel to deliver Dan 6:14 1079
a man's *h* was given to it Dan 7:4 3825
but I kept the matter in my *h* Dan 7:28 3821
he shall magnify himself in his *h* Dan 8:25 3824
didst set thine *h* to understand Dan 10:12 3820
his *h* shall be lifted up Dan 11:12 3824
his *h* shall be against the holy Dan 11:28 3824
they set their *h* on their Hos 4:8 5315
wine and new wine take away the *h* Hos 4:11 3820
made ready their *h* like an oven Hos 7:6 3820
is like a silly dove without *h* Hos 7:11 3820
not cried unto me with their *h* Hos 7:14
Their *h* is divided Hos 10:2 3820
mine *h* is turned within me, my Hos 11:8 3820
filled, and their *h* was exalted Hos 13:6 3820
and will rend the caul of their *h* Hos 13:8 3820
ye even to me with all your *h* Joel 2:12 3824
And rend your *h*, and not your Joel 2:13 3824
of thine *h* hath deceived thee Obad 3 3820

that saith in his *h*, Who shall Obad 3 3820
the *h* melteth, and the knees smite Nah 2:10 3820
that say in their *h*, The LORD Zeph 1:12 3824
carelessly, that said in her *h* Zeph 2:15 3824
be glad and rejoice with all the *h* Zeph 3:14 3820
against his brother in your *h* Zec 7:10 3824
their *h* shall rejoice as through Zec 10:7 3820
their *h* shall rejoice in the LORD Zec 10:7 3820
of Judah shall say in their *h* Zec 12:5 3820
and if ye will not lay it to *h* Mal 2:2 3820
because ye do not lay it to *h* Mal 2:2 3820
he shall turn the *h* of the Mal 4:6 3820
the *h* of the children to their Mal 4:6 3820
Blessed are the pure in *h* Mt 5:8 *2588*
with her already in his *h* Mt 5:28 *2588*
is, there will your *h* be also Mt 6:21 *2588*
for I am meek and lowly in *h* Mt 11:29 *2588*
of the *h* the mouth speaketh Mt 12:34 *2588*
the *h* bringeth forth good things Mt 12:35 *2588*
nights in the *h* of the earth Mt 12:40 *2588*
this people's *h* is waxed gross Mt 13:15 *2588*
and should understand with their *h* Mt 13:15 *2588*
away that which was sown in his *h* Mt 13:19 *2588*
but their *h* is far from me Mt 15:8 *2588*
the mouth come forth from the *h* Mt 15:18 *2588*
For out of the *h* proceed evil Mt 15:19 *2588*
the Lord thy God with all thy *h* Mt 22:37 *2588*
evil servant shall say in his *h* Mt 24:48 *2588*
for their *h* was hardened Mk 6:52 *2588*
but their *h* is far from me Mk 7:6 *2588*
it entereth not into his *h* Mk 7:19 *2588*
from within, out of the *h* of men Mk 7:21 *2588*
have ye your *h* yet hardened Mk 8:17 *2588*
For the hardness of your *h* he Mk 10:5 *4641*
and shall not doubt in his *h* Mk 11:23 *2588*
the Lord thy God with all thy *h* Mk 12:30 *2588*
And to love him with all the *h* Mk 12:33 *2588*
their unbelief and hardness of *h* Mk 16:14 *4641*
things, and pondered them in her *h* Lk 2:19 *2588*
kept all these sayings in her *h* Lk 2:51 *2588*
h bringeth forth that which is Lk 6:45 *2588*
h bringeth forth that which is Lk 6:45 *2588*
of the *h* his mouth speaketh Lk 6:45 *2588*
which in an honest and good *h* Lk 8:15 *2588*
perceiving the thought of their *h* Lk 9:47 *2588*
the Lord thy God with all thy *h* Lk 10:27 *2588*
is, there will your *h* be also Lk 12:34 *2588*
and if that servant say in his *h* Lk 12:45 *2588*
slow of *h* to believe all that the Lk 24:25 *2588*
Did not our *h* burn within us, Lk 24:32 *2588*
their eyes, and hardened their *h* Jn 12:40 *2588*
eyes, nor understand with their *h* Jn 12:40 *2588*
put into the *h* of Judas Iscariot Jn 13:2 *2588*
Let not your *h* be troubled Jn 14:1 *2588*
Let not your *h* be troubled Jn 14:27 *2588*
you, sorrow hath filled your *h* Jn 16:6 *2588*
your *h* shall rejoice, and your joy Jn 16:22 *2588*
Therefore did my *h* rejoice Acts 2:26 *2588*
they were pricked in their *h* Acts 2:37 *2588*
with gladness and singleness of *h* Acts 2:46 *2588*
them that believed were of one *h* Acts 4:32 *2588*
thine *h* to lie to the Holy Ghost Acts 5:3 *2588*
conceived this thing in thine *h* Acts 5:4 *2588*
that, they were cut to the *h* Acts 5:33 2588
it came into his *h* to visit his Acts 7:23 2588
stiffnecked and uncircumcised in *h* Acts 7:51 2588
things, they were cut to the *h* Acts 7:54 2588
for thy *h* is not right in the Acts 8:21 *2588*
of thine *h* may be forgiven thee Acts 8:22 *2588*
thou believest with all thine *h* Acts 8:37 *2588*
that with purpose of *h* they would Acts 11:23 *2588*
of Jesse, a man after mine own *h* Acts 13:22 *2588*
whose *h* the Lord opened, that she Acts 16:14 *2588*
ye to weep and to break mine *h* Acts 21:13 *2588*
For the *h* of this people is waxed Acts 28:27 *2588*
ears, and understand with their *h* Acts 28:27 *2588*
and their foolish *h* was darkened Rom 1:21 *2588*
impenitent *h* treasurest up unto Rom 2:5 *2588*
and circumcision is that of the *h* Rom 2:29 *2588*
but ye have obeyed from the *h* Rom 6:17 *2588*
and continual sorrow in my *h* Rom 9:2 *2588*
on this wise, Say not in thine *h* Rom 10:6 *2588*
even in thy mouth, and in thy *h* Rom 10:8 *2588*
shalt believe in thine *h* that God Rom 10:9 *2588*
For with the *h* man believeth unto Rom 10:10 *2588*
have entered into the *h* of man 1Cor 2:9 *2588*
that standeth stedfast in his *h* 1Cor 7:37 *2588*
hath so decreed in his *h* that he 1Cor 7:37 *2588*
secrets of his *h* made manifest 1Cor 14:25 *2588*
anguish of *h* I wrote unto you 2Cor 2:4 *2588*
but in fleshly tables of the *h* 2Cor 3:3 *2588*
is read, the vail is upon their *h* 2Cor 3:15 *2588*
glory in appearance, and not in *h* 2Cor 5:12 *2588*
open unto you, our *h* is enlarged 2Cor 6:11 *2588*
care into the *h* of Titus for you 2Cor 8:16 *2588*
as he purposeth in his *h*, so let 2Cor 9:7 *2588*
of the blindness of their *h* Eph 4:18 *2588*
melody in your *h* to the Lord Eph 5:19 *2588*
in singleness of your *h*, as unto Eph 6:5 *2588*
doing the will of God from the *h* Eph 6:6 *5590*
all, because I have you in my *h* Phil 1:7 *2588*
but in singleness of *h*, fearing Col 3:22 *2588*
short time in presence, not in *h* 1Th 2:17 *2588*
is charity out of a pure *h* 1Ti 1:5 *2588*
call on the Lord out of a pure *h* 2Ti 2:22 *2588*
They do alway err in their *h* Heb 3:10 *2588*
any of you an evil *h* of unbelief Heb 3:12 *2588*
the thoughts and intents of the *h* Heb 4:12 *2588*

true *h* in full assurance of faith Heb 10:22 *2588*
the *h* be established with grace Heb 13:9 *2588*
tongue, but deceiveth his own *h* Jas 1:26 *2588*
another with a pure *h* fervently 1Pet 1:22 *2588*
let it be the hidden man of the *h* 1Pet 3:4 *2588*
an *h* they have exercised with 2Pet 2:14 *2588*
For if our *h* condemn 1Jn 3:20 *2588*
God is greater than our *h* 1Jn 3:20 *2588*
if our *h* condemn us not, then 1Jn 3:21 *2588*
for she saith in her *h*, I sit a Rev 18:7 *2588*

HEARTED {8}

speak unto all that are wise *h* Ex 28:3 3820
that are wise *h* I have put wisdom Ex 31:6 3820
every wise *h* among you shall come Ex 35:10 3820
women, as many as were willing *h* Ex 35:22 3820
wise *h* did spin with their hands Ex 35:25 3820
and Aholiab, and every wise *h* man Ex 36:1 3820
and Aholiab, and every wise *h* man Ex 36:2 3820
every wise *h* man among them that Ex 36:8 3820

HEARTH {7}

it, and make cakes upon the *h* Gen 18:6
and my bones are burned as an *h* Ps 102:3 4168
a sherd to take fire from the *h* Is 30:14 3344
fire on the *h* burning before him Jer 36:22 254
into the fire that was on the *h* Jer 36:23 254
in the fire that was on the *h* Jer 36:23 254
like an *h* of fire among the wood Zec 12:6 3595

HEARTILY {1}

And whatsoever ye do, do it *h* Col 3:23 *1537,5590*

HEART'S {3}

wicked boasteth of his *h* desire Ps 10:3 5315
Thou hast given him his *h* desire Ps 21:2 3820
my *h* desire and prayer to God for Rom 10:1 *2588*

HEARTS {112}

of bread, and comfort ye your *h* Gen 18:5 3820
harden the *h* of the Egyptians Ex 14:17 3820
in the *h* of all that are wise Ex 31:6 3820
send a faintness into their *h* in Lev 26:36 3824
their uncircumcised *h* be humbled Lev 26:41 3824
let not your *h* faint, fear not, Deut 20:3 3824
Set your *h* unto all the words Deut 32:46 3824
our *h* did melt, neither did there Josh 2:11 3824
wherefore the *h* of the people Josh 7:5 3824
was of the LORD to harden their *h* Josh 11:20 3820
and ye know in all your *h* and in Josh 23:14 3824
their *h* inclined to follow Judg 9:3 3820
to pass, when their *h* were merry Judg 16:25 3820
as they were making their *h* merry Judg 19:22 3820
then do ye harden your *h*, as the 1Sa 6:6 3824
and Pharaoh hardened their *h* 1Sa 6:6 3820
unto the LORD with all your *h* 1Sa 7:3 3824
prepare your *h* unto the LORD, and 1Sa 7:3 3824
of men, whose *h* God had touched 1Sa 10:26 3820
stole the *h* of the men of Israel 2Sa 15:6 3820
The *h* of the men of Israel are 2Sa 15:13 3820
knowest the *h* of all the children 1Kin 8:39 3824
he may incline our *h* unto him 1Kin 8:58 3824
for the LORD searcheth all *h* 1Chr 28:9 3824
walk before thee with all their *h* 2Chr 6:14 3820
the *h* of the children of men 2Chr 6:30 3824
of Israel such as set their *h* to 2Chr 11:16 3824
h unto the God of their fathers 2Chr 20:33 3824
sinned, and cursed God in their *h* Job 1:5 3824
the righteous God trieth the *h* Ps 7:9 3826
but mischief is in their *h* Ps 28:3 3824
He fashioneth their *h* alike Ps 33:15 3820
Let them not say in their *h* Ps 35:25 3820
They said in their *h*, Let us Ps 74:8 3820
we may apply our *h* unto wisdom Ps 90:12 3824
them that are upright in their *h* Ps 125:4 3826
then the *h* of the children of men Prov 15:11 3826
but the LORD trieth the *h* Prov 17:3 3826
but the LORD pondereth the *h* Prov 21:2 3826
unto those that be of heavy *h* Prov 31:6 5315
and their *h*, that they cannot Is 44:18 3826
parts, and write it in their *h* Jer 31:33 3820
but I will put my fear in their *h* Jer 32:40 3824
For ye dissembled in your *h* Jer 42:20 5315
the mighty men's *h* in Moab at Jer 48:41 3820
that prophesy out of their own *h* Eze 13:2 3820
also vex the *h* of many people Eze 32:9 3820
both these kings' *h* shall be to Dan 11:27 3824
their *h* that I remember all their Hos 7:2 3824
they made their *h* as an adamant Zec 7:12 3820
in your *h* against his neighbour Zec 8:17 3820
Wherefore think ye evil in your *h* Mt 9:4 *2588*
if ye from your *h* forgive not Mt 18:35 *2588*
h suffered you to put away your Mt 19:8 *4641*
there, and reasoning in their *h* Mk 2:6 *2588*
reason ye these things in your *h* Mk 2:8 *2588*
for the hardness of their *h* Mk 3:5 *2588*
the word that was sown in their *h* Mk 4:15 *2588*
to turn the *h* of the fathers to Lk 1:17 *2588*
in the imagination of their *h* Lk 1:51 *2588*
them laid them up in their *h* Lk 1:66 *2588*
of many *h* may be revealed Lk 2:35 *2588*
all men mused in their *h* of John Lk 3:15 *2588*
them, What reason ye in your *h* Lk 5:22 *2588*
away the word out of their *h* Lk 8:12 *2588*
but God knoweth your *h* Lk 16:15 *2588*
Settle it therefore in your *h* Lk 21:14 *2588*
Men's *h* failing them for fear, and Lk 21:26 *674*
lest at any time your *h* be Lk 21:34 *2588*
why do thoughts arise in your *h* Lk 24:38 *2588*
which knowest the *h* of all men Acts 1:24 *2589*
in their *h* turned back again into Acts 7:39 *2588*

seasons, filling our *h* with food	Acts 14:17	*2588*
And God, which knoweth the *h*	Acts 15:8	*2589*
them, purifying their *h* by faith	Acts 15:9	*2588*
through the lusts of their own *h*	Rom 1:24	*2588*
of the law written in their *h*	Rom 2:15	*2588*
our *h* by the Holy Ghost which is	Rom 5:5	*2588*
he that searcheth the *h* knoweth	Rom 8:27	*2588*
deceive the *h* of the simple	Rom 16:18	*2588*
manifest the counsels of the *h*	1Cor 4:5	*2588*
earnest of the Spirit in our *h*	2Cor 1:22	*2588*
are our epistle written in our *h*	2Cor 3:2	*2588*
of darkness, hath shined in our *h*	2Cor 4:6	*2588*
that ye are in our *h* to die	2Cor 7:3	*2588*
the Spirit of his Son into your *h*	Gal 4:6	*2588*
may dwell in your *h* by faith	Eph 3:17	*2588*
and that he might comfort your *h*	Eph 6:22	*2588*
understanding, shall keep your *h*	Phil 4:7	*2588*
That their *h* might be comforted,	Col 2:2	*2588*
the peace of God rule in your *h*	Col 3:15	*2588*
with grace in your *h* to the Lord	Col 3:16	*2588*
your estate, and comfort your *h*	Col 4:8	*2588*
men, but God, which trieth our *h*	1Th 2:4	*2588*
h unblameable in holiness before	1Th 3:13	*2588*
Comfort your *h*, and stablish you	2Th 2:17	*2588*
your *h* into the love of God	2Th 3:5	*2588*
Harden not your *h*, as in the	Heb 3:8	*2588*
hear his voice, harden not your *h*	Heb 3:15	*2588*
hear his voice, harden not your *h*	Heb 4:7	*2588*
mind, and write them in their *h*	Heb 8:10	*2588*
I will put my laws into their *h*	Heb 10:16	*2588*
having our *h* sprinkled from an	Heb 10:22	*2588*
envying and strife in your *h*	Jas 3:14	*2588*
and purify your *h*, ye double	Jas 4:8	*2588*
ye have nourished your *h*, as in a	Jas 5:5	*2588*
ye also patient; stablish your *h*	Jas 5:8	*2588*
sanctify the Lord God in your *h*	1Pet 3:15	*2588*
and the day star arise in your *h*	2Pet 1:19	*2588*
and shall assure our *h* before him	1Jn 3:19	*2588*
he which searcheth the reins and *h*	Rev 2:23	*2588*
put in their *h* to fulfil his will	Rev 17:17	*2588*

HEARTS' {1}

them up unto their own *h* lust	Ps 81:12	3820

HEARTY {1}

of a man's friend by *h* counsel	Prov 27:9	5315

HEAT {32}

seedtime and harvest, and cold and *h*	Gen 8:22	2527
the tent door in the *h* of the day	Gen 18:1	2527
what meaneth the *h* of this great	Deut 29:24	2750
and devoured with burning *h*	Deut 32:24	7565
Ammonites until the *h* of the day	1Sa 11:11	2527
came about the *h* of the day to	2Sa 4:5	2527
him with clothes, but he gat no *h*	1Kin 1:1	3179
that my lord the king may get *h*	1Kin 1:2	2552
h consume the snow waters	Job 24:19	2527
me, and my bones are burned with *h*	Job 30:30	2721
is nothing hid from the *h* thereof	Ps 19:6	2535
lie together, then they have *h*	Eccl 4:11	2552
shadow in the daytime from the *h*	Is 4:6	2721
place like a clear *h* upon herbs	Is 18:4	2527
cloud of dew in the *h* of harvest	Is 18:4	2527
the storm, a shadow from the *h*	Is 25:4	2721
as the *h* in a dry place	Is 25:5	2721
even the *h* with the shadow of a	Is 25:5	2721
neither shall the *h* nor sun smite	Is 49:10	8273
and shall not see when *h* cometh	Jer 17:8	2527
be cast out in the day to the *h*	Jer 36:30	2721
In their *h* I will make their	Jer 51:39	2527
bitterness, in the *h* of my spirit	Eze 3:14	2534
commanded that they should *h* the	Dan 3:19	228
borne the burden and *h* of the day	Mt 20:12	*2742*
blow, ye say, There will be *h*	Lk 12:55	*2742*
there came a viper out of the *h*	Acts 28:3	*2329*
no sooner risen with a burning *h*	Jas 1:11	*2742*
shall melt with fervent *h*	2Pet 3:10	*2741*
shall melt with fervent *h*	2Pet 3:12	*2741*
the sun light on them, nor any *h*	Rev 7:16	*2738*
And men were scorched with great *h*	Rev 16:9	*2738*

HEATED {2}

more than it was wont to be *h*	Dan 3:19	228
as an oven *h* by the baker, who	Hos 7:4	1197

HEATH {2}

shall be like the *h* in the desert	Jer 17:6	6176
be like the *h* in the wilderness	Jer 48:6	6176

HEATHEN {150}

shall be of the *h* that are round	Lev 25:44	1471
And I will scatter you among the *h*	Lev 26:33	1471
And ye shall perish among the *h*	Lev 26:38	1471
of Egypt in the sight of the *h*	Lev 26:45	1471
be left few in number among the *h*	Deut 4:27	1471
hast kept me to be head of the *h*	2Sa 22:44	1471
unto thee, O LORD, among the *h*	2Sa 22:50	1471
to the abominations of the *h*	2Kin 16:3	1471
walked in the statutes of the *h*	2Kin 17:8	1471
as did the *h* whom the LORD	2Kin 17:11	1471
went after the *h* that were round	2Kin 17:15	1471
after the abominations of the *h*	2Kin 21:2	1471
Declare his glory among the *h*	1Chr 16:24	1471
and deliver us from the *h*	1Chr 16:35	1471
over all the kingdoms of the *h*	2Chr 20:6	1471
the *h* whom the LORD had cast out	2Chr 28:3	1471
unto the abominations of the *h*	2Chr 33:2	1471
to err, and to do worse than the *h*	2Chr 33:9	1471
all the abominations of the *h*	2Chr 36:14	1471
filthiness of the *h* of the land	Ezr 6:21	1471
Jews, which were sold unto the *h*	Neh 5:8	1471
the reproach of the *h* our enemies	Neh 5:9	1471
among the *h* that are about us	Neh 5:17	1471
It is reported among the *h*	Neh 6:6	1471
all the *h* that were about us saw	Neh 6:16	1471
Why do the *h* rage, and the people	Ps 2:1	1471
thee the *h* for thine inheritance	Ps 2:8	1471
Thou hast rebuked the *h*, thou	Ps 9:5	1471
The *h* are sunk down in the pit	Ps 9:15	1471
let the *h* be judged in thy sight	Ps 9:19	1471
the *h* are perished out of his	Ps 10:16	1471
hast made me the head of the *h*	Ps 18:43	1471
unto thee, O LORD, among the *h*	Ps 18:49	1471
the counsel of the *h* to nought	Ps 33:10	1471
drive out the *h* with thy hand	Ps 44:2	1471
and hast scattered us among the *h*	Ps 44:11	1471
makest us a byword among the *h*	Ps 44:14	1471
The *h* raged, the kingdoms were	Ps 46:6	1471
I will be exalted among the *h*	Ps 46:10	1471
God reigneth over the *h*	Ps 47:8	1471
Israel, awake to visit all the *h*	Ps 59:5	1471
shalt have all the *h* in derision	Ps 59:8	1471
He cast out the *h* also before	Ps 78:55	1471
the *h* are come into thine	Ps 79:1	1471
the *h* that have not known thee	Ps 79:6	1471
Wherefore should the *h* say	Ps 79:10	1471
let him be known among the *h* in	Ps 79:10	1471
thou hast cast out the *h*, and	Ps 80:8	1471
He that chastiseth the *h*, shall	Ps 94:10	1471
Declare his glory among the *h*	Ps 96:3	1471
Say among the *h* that the LORD	Ps 96:10	1471
shewed in the sight of the *h*	Ps 98:2	1471
So the *h* shall fear the name of	Ps 102:15	1471
And gave them the lands of the *h*	Ps 105:44	1471
But were mingled among the *h*	Ps 106:35	1471
gave them into the hand of the *h*	Ps 106:41	1471
and gather us from among the *h*	Ps 106:47	1471
He shall judge among the *h*	Ps 110:6	1471
give them the heritage of the *h*	Ps 111:6	1471
Wherefore should the *h* say	Ps 115:2	1471
then said they among the *h*	Ps 126:2	1471
The idols of the *h* are silver	Ps 135:15	1471
To execute vengeance upon the *h*	Ps 149:7	1471
the lords of the *h* have broken	Is 16:8	1471
scatter them also among the *h*	Jer 9:16	1471
LORD, Learn not the way of the *h*	Jer 10:2	1471
for the *h* are dismayed at them	Jer 10:2	1471
upon the *h* that know thee not	Jer 10:25	1471
Ask ye now among the *h*, who hath	Jer 18:13	1471
an ambassador is sent unto the *h*	Jer 49:14	1471
will make thee small among the *h*	Jer 49:15	1471
she dwelleth among the *h*, she	Lam 1:3	1471
the *h* entered into her sanctuary	Lam 1:10	1471
wandered, they said among the *h*	Lam 4:15	1471
shadow we shall live among the *h*	Lam 4:20	1471
I will bring the worst of the *h*	Eze 7:24	1471
of the *h* that are round about you	Eze 11:12	1471
cast them far off among the *h*	Eze 11:16	1471
among the *h* whither they come	Eze 12:16	1471
forth among the *h* for thy beauty	Eze 16:14	1471
not be polluted before the *h*	Eze 20:9	1471
not be polluted before the *h*	Eze 20:14	1471
be polluted in the sight of the *h*	Eze 20:22	1471
I would scatter them among the *h*	Eze 20:23	1471
that ye say, We will be as the *h*	Eze 20:32	1471
be sanctified in you before the *h*	Eze 20:41	1471
I made thee a reproach unto the *h*	Eze 22:4	1471
I will scatter thee among the *h*	Eze 22:15	1471
in thyself in the sight of the *h*	Eze 22:16	1471
hast gone a whoring after the *h*	Eze 23:30	1471
deliver thee for a spoil to the *h*	Eze 25:7	1471
of Judah is like unto all the *h*	Eze 25:8	1471
in them in the sight of the *h*	Eze 28:25	1471
it shall be the time of the *h*	Eze 30:3	1471
hand of the mighty one of the *h*	Eze 31:11	1471
his shadow in the midst of the *h*	Eze 31:17	1471
shall no more be a prey to the *h*	Eze 34:28	1471
bear the shame of the *h* any more	Eze 34:29	1471
unto the residue of the *h*	Eze 36:3	1471
of the *h* that are round about	Eze 36:4	1471
against the residue of the *h*	Eze 36:5	1471
ye have borne the shame of the *h*	Eze 36:6	1471
Surely the *h* that are about you,	Eze 36:7	1471
thee the shame of the *h* any more	Eze 36:15	1471
And I scattered them among the *h*	Eze 36:19	1471
And when they entered unto the *h*	Eze 36:20	1471
Israel had profaned among the *h*	Eze 36:21	1471
ye have profaned among the *h*	Eze 36:22	1471
which was profaned among the *h*	Eze 36:23	1471
the *h* shall know that I am the	Eze 36:23	1471
I will take you from among the *h*	Eze 36:24	1471
reproach of famine among the *h*	Eze 36:30	1471
Then the *h* that are left round	Eze 36:36	1471
of Israel from among the *h*	Eze 37:21	1471
the *h* shall know that I the LORD	Eze 37:28	1471
that the *h* may know me, when I	Eze 38:16	1471
the *h* shall know that I am the	Eze 39:7	1471
I will set my glory among the *h*	Eze 39:21	1471
all the *h* shall see my judgment	Eze 39:21	1471
the *h* shall know that the house	Eze 39:23	1471
be led into captivity among the *h*	Eze 39:28	1471
that the *h* should rule over them	Joel 2:17	1471
make you a reproach among the *h*	Joel 2:19	1471
yourselves, and come, all ye *h*	Joel 3:11	1471
Let the *h* be wakened, and come up	Joel 3:12	1471
to judge all the *h* round about	Joel 3:12	1471
remnant of Edom, and of all the *h*	Amos 9:12	1471
an ambassador is sent among the *h*	Obad 1	1471
have made thee small among the *h*	Obad 2	1471
the LORD is near upon all the *h*	Obad 15	1471
so shall all the *h* drink	Obad 16	1471
in anger and fury upon the *h*	Mic 5:15	1471
Behold ye among the *h*, and regard,	Hab 1:5	1471
thou didst thresh the *h* in anger	Hab 3:12	1471
even all the isles of the *h*	Zeph 2:11	1471
strength of the kingdoms of the *h*	Hag 2:22	1471
with the *h* that are at ease	Zec 1:15	1471
as ye were a curse among the *h*	Zec 8:13	1471
he shall speak peace unto the *h*	Zec 9:10	1471
the wealth of all the *h* round	Zec 14:14	1471
the LORD will smite the *h* that	Zec 14:18	1471
name shall be great among the *h*	Mal 1:11	1471
my name is dreadful among the *h*	Mal 1:14	1471
not vain repetitions, as the *h* do	Mt 6:7	*1482*
let him be unto thee as an *h* man	Mt 18:17	*1482*
hast said, Why did the *h* rage	Acts 4:25	*1484*
countrymen, in perils by the *h*	2Cor 11:26	*1484*
I might preach him among the *h*	Gal 1:16	*1484*
that we should go unto the *h*	Gal 2:9	*1484*
would justify the *h* through faith	Gal 3:8	*1484*

HEAVE {29}

and the shoulder of the *h* offering	Ex 29:27	8641
for it is an *h* offering	Ex 29:28	8641
it shall be an *h* offering from	Ex 29:28	8641
even their *h* offering unto the	Ex 29:28	8641
for an *h* offering unto the LORD	Lev 7:14	8641
h offering of the sacrifices of	Lev 7:32	8641
the *h* shoulder have I taken of	Lev 7:34	8641
h shoulder shall ye eat in a	Lev 10:14	8641
The *h* shoulder and the wave breast	Lev 10:15	8641
the wave breast and *h* shoulder	Num 6:20	8641
ye shall offer up an *h* offering	Num 15:19	8641
of your dough for an *h* offering	Num 15:20	8641
as ye do the *h* offering of the	Num 15:20	8641
threshingfloor, so shall ye *h* it	Num 15:20	7311
an *h* offering in your generations	Num 15:21	8641
h offerings of all the hallowed	Num 18:8	8641
the *h* offering of their gift,	Num 18:11	8641
All the *h* offerings of the holy	Num 18:19	8641
as an *h* offering unto the LORD	Num 18:24	8641
then ye shall offer up an *h*	Num 18:26	8641
this your *h* offering shall be	Num 18:27	8641
Thus ye also shall offer an *h*	Num 18:28	8641
h offering to Aaron the priest	Num 18:28	8641
every *h* offering of the LORD	Num 18:29	8641
for an *h* offering of the LORD	Num 31:29	8641
which was the LORD's *h* offering	Num 31:41	8641
h offerings of your hand, and your	Deut 12:6	8641
the *h* offering of your hand, and	Deut 12:11	8641
or *h* offering of thine hand	Deut 12:17	8641

HEAVED {3}

which is waved, and which is *h* up	Ex 29:27	7311
When ye have *h* the best thereof	Num 18:30	7311
when ye have *h* from it the best	Num 18:32	7311

HEAVEN {582}

the beginning God created the *h*	Gen 1:1	8064
And God called the firmament *H*	Gen 1:8	8064
Let the waters under the *h* be	Gen 1:9	8064
the *h* to divide the day from the	Gen 1:14	8064
h to give light upon the earth	Gen 1:15	8064
h to give light upon the earth	Gen 1:17	8064
earth in the open firmament of *h*	Gen 1:20	8064
the breath of life, from under *h*	Gen 6:17	8064
and the windows of *h* were opened	Gen 7:11	8064
that were under the whole *h*	Gen 7:19	8064
things, and the fowl of the *h*	Gen 7:23	8064
and the windows of *h* were stopped	Gen 8:2	8064
the rain from *h* was restrained	Gen 8:2	8064
tower, whose top may reach unto *h*	Gen 11:4	8064
the most high God, possessor of *h*	Gen 14:19	8064
most high God, the possessor of *h*	Gen 14:22	8064
and said, Look now toward *h*	Gen 15:5	8064
and fire from the LORD out of *h*	Gen 19:24	8064
of God called to Hagar out of *h*	Gen 21:17	8064
the LORD called unto him out of *h*	Gen 22:11	8064
Abraham out of *h* the second time	Gen 22:15	8064
thy seed as the stars of the *h*	Gen 22:17	8064
swear by the LORD, the God of *h*	Gen 24:3	8064
The LORD God of *h*, which took me	Gen 24:7	8064
to multiply as the stars of *h*	Gen 26:4	8064
God give thee of the dew of *h*	Gen 27:28	8064
and of the dew of *h* from above	Gen 27:39	8064
and the top of it reached to *h*	Gen 28:12	8064
of God, and this is the gate of *h*	Gen 28:17	8064
thee with blessings of *h* above	Gen 49:25	8064
the *h* in the sight of Pharaoh	Ex 9:8	8064
and Moses sprinkled it up toward *h*	Ex 9:10	8064
Stretch forth thine hand toward *h*	Ex 9:22	8064
stretched forth his rod toward *h*	Ex 9:23	8064
Stretch out thine hand toward *h*	Ex 10:21	8064
stretched forth his hand toward *h*	Ex 10:22	8064
I will rain bread from *h* for you	Ex 16:4	8064
of Amalek from under *h*	Ex 17:14	8064
of any thing that is in *h* above	Ex 20:4	8064
For in six days the LORD made *h*	Ex 20:11	8064
I have talked with you from *h*	Ex 20:22	8064
the body of *h* in his clearness	Ex 24:10	8064
for in six days the LORD made *h*	Ex 31:17	8064
your seed as the stars of *h*	Ex 32:13	8064
and I will make your *h* as iron	Lev 26:19	8064
as the stars of *h* for multitude	Deut 1:10	8064
are great and walled up to *h*	Deut 1:28	8064
that are under the whole *h*	Deut 2:25	8064
God is there in *h* or in earth	Deut 3:24	8064
with fire unto the midst of *h*	Deut 4:11	8064
thou lift up thine eyes unto *h*	Deut 4:19	8064
the stars, even all the host of *h*	Deut 4:19	8064

all nations under the whole *h*	Deut 4:19	8064
I call *h* and earth to witness	Deut 4:26	8064
the one side of *h* unto the other	Deut 4:32	8064
Out of *h* he made thee to hear his	Deut 4:36	8064
the LORD he is God in *h* above	Deut 4:39	8064
of any thing that is in *h* above	Deut 5:8	8064
destroy their name from under *h*	Deut 7:24	8064
cities great and fenced up to *h*	Deut 9:1	8064
blot out their name from under *h*	Deut 9:14	8064
Behold, the *h* and the *h* of	Deut 10:14	8064
as the stars of *h* for multitude	Deut 10:22	8064
drinketh water of the rain of *h*	Deut 11:11	8064
against you, and he shut up the *h*	Deut 11:17	8064
as the days of *h* upon the earth	Deut 11:21	8064
or moon, or any of the host of *h*	Deut 17:3	8064
of Amalek from under *h*	Deut 25:19	8064
from thy holy habitation, from *h*	Deut 26:15	8064
the *h* to give the rain unto thy	Deut 28:12	8064
thy *h* that is over thy head shall	Deut 28:23	8064
from *h* shall it come down upon	Deut 28:24	8064
as the stars of *h* for multitude	Deut 28:62	8064
blot out his name from under *h*	Deut 29:20	8064
out unto the outmost parts of *h*	Deut 30:4	8064
It is not in *h*, that thou	Deut 30:12	8064
say, Who shall go up for us to *h*	Deut 30:12	8064
I call *h* and earth to record this	Deut 30:19	8064
words in their ears, and call *h*	Deut 31:28	8064
For I lift up my hand to *h*	Deut 32:40	8064
for the precious things of *h*	Deut 33:13	8064
who rideth upon the *h* in thy help	Deut 33:26	8064
your God, he is God in *h* above	Josh 2:11	8064
of the city ascended up to *h*	Josh 8:20	8064
from *h* upon them unto Azekah	Josh 10:11	8064
sun stood still in the midst of *h*	Josh 10:13	8064
They fought from *h*	Judg 5:20	8064
up toward *h* from off the altar	Judg 13:20	8064
of the city ascended up to *h*	Judg 20:40	8064
out of *h* shall he thunder upon	1Sa 2:10	8064
the cry of the city went up to *h*	1Sa 5:12	8064
and he was taken up between the *h*	2Sa 18:9	8064
water dropped upon them out of *h*	2Sa 21:10	8064
the foundations of *h* moved	2Sa 22:8	8064
The LORD thundered from *h*	2Sa 22:14	8064
spread forth his hands toward *h*	1Kin 8:22	8064
in *h* above, or on earth beneath,	1Kin 8:23	8064
behold, the *h* and *h* of	1Kin 8:27	8064
hear thou in *h* thy dwelling place	1Kin 8:30	8064
Then hear thou in *h*, and do, and	1Kin 8:32	8064
Then hear thou in *h*, and forgive	1Kin 8:34	8064
When *h* is shut up, and there is no	1Kin 8:35	8064
Then hear thou in *h*, and forgive	1Kin 8:36	8064
Then hear thou in *h* thy dwelling	1Kin 8:39	8064
Hear thou in *h* thy dwelling place	1Kin 8:43	8064
Then hear thou in *h* their prayer	1Kin 8:45	8064
in *h* thy dwelling place, and	1Kin 8:49	8064
with his hands spread up to *h*	1Kin 8:54	8064
that the *h* was black with clouds	1Kin 18:45	8064
all the host of *h* standing by him	1Kin 22:19	8064
then let fire come down from *h*	2Kin 1:10	8064
And there came down fire from *h*	2Kin 1:10	8064
of God, let fire come down from *h*	2Kin 1:12	8064
the fire of God came down from *h*	2Kin 1:12	8064
there came fire down from *h*	2Kin 1:14	8064
up Elijah into *h* by a whirlwind	2Kin 2:1	8064
went up by a whirlwind into *h*	2Kin 2:11	8064
the LORD would make windows in *h*	2Kin 7:2	8064
the LORD should make windows in *h*	2Kin 7:19	8064
the name of Israel from under *h*	2Kin 14:27	8064
and worshipped all the host of *h*	2Kin 17:16	8064
thou hast made *h* and earth	2Kin 19:15	8064
and worshipped all the host of *h*	2Kin 21:3	8064
altars for all the host of *h* in	2Kin 21:5	8064
grove, and for all the host of *h*	2Kin 23:4	8064
planets, and to all the host of *h*	2Kin 23:5	8064
stand between the earth and the *h*	1Chr 21:16	8064
he answered him from *h* by fire	1Chr 21:26	8064
for all that is in the *h* and in	1Chr 29:11	8064
build him an house, seeing the *h*	2Chr 2:6	8064
h of heavens cannot contain him	2Chr 2:6	8064
LORD God of Israel, that made *h*	2Chr 2:12	8064
spread forth his hands toward *h*	2Chr 6:13	8064
is no God like thee in the *h*	2Chr 6:14	8064
behold, *h* and the *h* of	2Chr 6:18	8064
thy dwelling place, even from *h*	2Chr 6:21	8064
Then hear thou from *h*, and do, and	2Chr 6:23	8064
When the *h* is shut up, and there	2Chr 6:26	8064
Then hear thou from *h*, and forgive	2Chr 6:27	8064
thou from *h* thy dwelling place	2Chr 6:30	8064
the fire came down from *h*	2Chr 7:1	8064
If I shut up *h* that there be no	2Chr 7:13	8064
then will I hear from *h*, and will	2Chr 7:14	8064
all the host of *h* standing on his	2Chr 18:18	8064
fathers, art not thou God in *h*	2Chr 20:6	8064
in a rage that reacheth up unto *h*	2Chr 28:9	8064
holy dwelling place, even unto *h*	2Chr 30:27	8064
son of Amoz, prayed and cried to *h*	2Chr 32:20	8064
and worshipped all the host of *h*	2Chr 33:3	8064
altars for all the host of *h* in	2Chr 33:5	8064
hath the LORD God of *h* given me	2Chr 36:23	8064
The LORD God of *h* hath given me	Ezr 1:2	8064
are the servants of the God of *h*	Ezr 5:11	8065
provoked the God of *h* unto wrath	Ezr 5:12	8065
burnt offerings of the God of *h*	Ezr 6:9	8065
sweet savours unto the God of *h*	Ezr 6:10	8065
scribe of the law of the God of *h*	Ezr 7:12	8065
scribe of the law of the God of *h*	Ezr 7:21	8065
is commanded by the God of *h*	Ezr 7:23	8065
for the house of the God of *h*	Ezr 7:23	8065
and prayed before the God of *h*	Neh 1:4	8064
I beseech thee, O LORD God of *h*	Neh 1:5	8064
unto the uttermost part of the *h*	Neh 1:9	8064
So I prayed to the God of *h*	Neh 2:4	8064
and said unto them, The God of *h*	Neh 2:20	8064
thou hast made *h*, the *h* of	Neh 9:6	8064
the host of *h* worshippeth thee	Neh 9:6	8064
and spakest with them from *h*	Neh 9:13	8064
bread from *h* for their hunger	Neh 9:15	8064
thou as the stars of *h*, and	Neh 9:23	8064
thee, thou heardest them from *h*	Neh 9:27	8064
thee, thou heardest them from *h*	Neh 9:28	8064
The fire of God is fallen from *h*	Job 1:16	8064
dust upon their heads toward *h*	Job 2:12	8064
It is as high as *h*	Job 11:8	8064
now, behold, my witness is in *h*	Job 16:19	8064
The *h* shall reveal his iniquity	Job 20:27	8064
Is not God in the height of *h*	Job 22:12	8064
and he walketh in the circuit of *h*	Job 22:14	8064
The pillars of *h* tremble, and are	Job 26:11	8064
earth, and seeth under the whole *h*	Job 28:24	8064
us wiser than the fowls of *h*	Job 35:11	8064
He directeth it under the whole *h*	Job 37:3	8064
and the hoary frost of *h*, who hath	Job 38:29	8064
Knowest thou the ordinances of *h*	Job 38:33	8064
or who can stay the bottles of *h*	Job 38:37	8064
is under the whole *h* is mine	Job 41:11	8064
temple, the LORD's throne is in *h*	Ps 11:4	8064
from *h* upon the children of men	Ps 14:2	8064
forth is from the end of the *h*	Ps 19:6	8064
he will hear him from his holy *h*	Ps 20:6	8064
The LORD looketh from *h*	Ps 33:13	8064
God looked down from *h* upon the	Ps 53:2	8064
He shall send from *h*, and save me	Ps 57:3	8064
Let the *h* and earth praise him,	Ps 69:34	8064
Whom have I in *h* but thee	Ps 73:25	8064
cause judgment to be heard from *h*	Ps 76:8	8064
voice of thy thunder was in the *h*	Ps 77:18	1534
above, and opened the doors of *h*	Ps 78:23	8064
had given them of the corn of *h*	Ps 78:24	8064
an east wind to blow in the *h*	Ps 78:26	8064
be meat unto the fowls of the *h*	Ps 79:2	8064
look down from *h*, and behold, and	Ps 80:14	8064
shall look down from *h*	Ps 85:11	8064
For who in the *h* can be compared	Ps 89:6	7834
and his throne as the days of *h*	Ps 89:29	8064
and as a faithful witness in *h*	Ps 89:37	7834
from *h* did the LORD behold the	Ps 102:19	8064
For as the *h* is high above the	Ps 103:11	8064
of the *h* have their habitation	Ps 104:12	8064
them with the bread of *h*	Ps 105:40	8064
They mount up to the *h*, they go	Ps 107:26	8064
behold the things that are in *h*	Ps 113:6	8064
blessed of the LORD which made *h*	Ps 115:15	8064
The *h*, even the heavens, are the	Ps 115:16	8064
O LORD, thy word is settled in *h*	Ps 119:89	8064
from the LORD, which made *h*	Ps 121:2	8064
the name of the LORD, who made *h*	Ps 124:8	8064
The LORD that made *h* and earth	Ps 134:3	8064
LORD pleased, that did he in *h*	Ps 135:6	8064
O give thanks unto the God of *h*	Ps 136:26	8064
If I ascend up into *h*, thou art	Ps 139:8	8064
Which made *h*, and earth, the sea,	Ps 146:6	8064
Who covereth the *h* with clouds	Ps 147:8	8064
his glory is above the earth and *h*	Ps 148:13	8064
fly away as an eagle toward *h*	Prov 23:5	8064
The *h* for height, and the earth	Prov 25:3	8064
Who hath ascended up into *h*	Prov 30:4	8064
all things that are done under *h*	Eccl 1:13	8064
the *h* all the days of their life	Eccl 2:3	8064
time to every purpose under the *h*	Eccl 3:1	8064
for God is in *h*, and thou upon	Eccl 5:2	8064
a far country, from the end of *h*	Is 13:5	8064
For the stars of *h* and the	Is 13:10	8064
How art thou fallen from *h*	Is 14:12	8064
thine heart, I will ascend into *h*	Is 14:13	8064
all the host of *h* shall be	Is 34:4	8064
For my sword shall be bathed in *h*	Is 34:5	8064
thou hast made *h* and earth	Is 37:16	8064
meted out *h* with the span, and	Is 40:12	8064
cometh down, and the snow from *h*	Is 55:10	8064
Look down from *h*, and behold from	Is 63:15	8064
The *h* is my throne, and the earth	Is 66:1	8064
to make cakes to the queen of *h*	Jer 7:18	8064
be meat for the fowls of the *h*	Jer 7:33	8064
and the moon, and all the host of *h*	Jer 8:2	8064
the stork in the *h* knoweth her	Jer 8:7	8064
be not dismayed at the signs of *h*	Jer 10:2	8064
to tear, and the fowls of the *h*	Jer 15:3	8064
shall be meat for the fowls of *h*	Jer 16:4	8064
to be meat for the fowls of the *h*	Jer 19:7	8064
incense unto all the host of *h*	Jer 19:13	8064
Do not I fill *h* and earth	Jer 23:24	8064
If *h* above can be measured, and	Jer 31:37	8064
behold, thou hast made the *h*	Jer 32:17	8064
As the host of *h* cannot be	Jer 33:22	8064
not appointed the ordinances of *h*	Jer 33:25	8064
for meat unto the fowls of the *h*	Jer 34:20	8064
burn incense unto the queen of *h*	Jer 44:17	8064
to burn incense to the queen of *h*	Jer 44:18	8064
burned incense to the queen of *h*	Jer 44:19	8064
to burn incense to the queen of *h*	Jer 44:25	8064
winds from the four quarters of *h*	Jer 49:36	8064
for her judgment reacheth unto *h*	Jer 51:9	8064
out the *h* by his understanding	Jer 51:15	8064
Then the *h* and the earth, and all	Jer 51:48	8064
Babylon should mount up to *h*	Jer 51:53	8064
cast down from *h* unto the earth	Lam 2:1	8064
LORD look down, and behold from *h*	Lam 3:50	8064
swifter than the eagles of the *h*	Lam 4:19	8064
me up between the earth and the *h*	Eze 8:3	8064
field and to the fowls of the *h*	Eze 29:5	8064
All the fowls of *h* made their	Eze 31:6	8064
all the fowls of the *h* remain	Eze 31:13	8064
of the *h* to remain upon thee	Eze 32:4	8064
put thee out, I will cover the *h*	Eze 32:7	8064
All the bright lights of *h* will I	Eze 32:8	8064
of the sea, and the fowls of the *h*	Eze 38:20	8064
God of *h* concerning this secret	Dan 2:18	8065
Then Daniel blessed the God of *h*	Dan 2:19	8065
But there is a God in *h* that	Dan 2:28	8065
for the God of *h* hath given thee	Dan 2:37	8065
the fowls of the *h* hath he given	Dan 2:38	8065
the God of *h* set up a kingdom	Dan 2:44	8065
the height thereof reached unto *h*	Dan 4:11	8065
the fowls of the *h* dwelt in the	Dan 4:12	8065
and an holy one came down from *h*	Dan 4:13	8065
let it be wet with the dew of *h*	Dan 4:15	8065
whose height reached unto the *h*	Dan 4:20	8065
of the *h* had their habitation	Dan 4:21	8065
is grown, and reacheth unto *h*	Dan 4:22	8065
and an holy one coming down from *h*	Dan 4:23	8065
let it be wet with the dew of *h*	Dan 4:23	8065
shall wet thee with the dew of *h*	Dan 4:25	8065
mouth, there fell a voice from *h*	Dan 4:31	8065
body was wet with the dew of *h*	Dan 4:33	8065
lifted up mine eyes unto *h*	Dan 4:34	8065
to his will in the army of *h*	Dan 4:35	8065
and extol and honour the King of *h*	Dan 4:37	8065
body was wet with the dew of *h*	Dan 5:21	8065
up thyself against the Lord of *h*	Dan 5:23	8065
he worketh signs and wonders in *h*	Dan 6:27	8065
the four winds of the *h* strove	Dan 7:2	8065
of man came with the clouds of *h*	Dan 7:13	8065
of the kingdom under the whole *h*	Dan 7:27	8065
ones toward the four winds of *h*	Dan 8:8	8064
great, even to the host of *h*	Dan 8:10	8064
for under the whole *h* hath not	Dan 9:12	8064
toward the four winds of *h*	Dan 11:4	8064
hand and his left hand unto *h*	Dan 12:7	8064
the field, and with the fowls of *h*	Hos 2:18	8064
the field, and with the fowls of *h*	Hos 4:3	8064
them down as the fowls of the *h*	Hos 7:12	8064
though they climb up to *h*	Amos 9:2	8064
buildeth his stories in the *h*	Amos 9:6	8064
and I fear the LORD, the God of *h*	Jonah 1:9	8064
merchants above the stars of *h*	Nah 3:16	8064
I will consume the fowls of the *h*	Zeph 1:3	8064
the host of *h* upon the housetops	Zeph 1:5	8064
Therefore the *h* over you is	Hag 1:10	8064
abroad as the four winds of the *h*	Zec 2:6	8064
ephah between the earth and the *h*	Zec 5:9	8064
not open you the windows of *h*	Mal 3:10	8064
for the kingdom of *h* is at hand	Mt 3:2	3772
And lo a voice from *h*, saying,	Mt 3:17	3772
for the kingdom of *h* is at hand	Mt 4:17	3772
for theirs is the kingdom of *h*	Mt 5:3	3772
for theirs is the kingdom of *h*	Mt 5:10	3772
for great is your reward in *h*	Mt 5:12	3772
glorify your Father which is in *h*	Mt 5:16	3772
For verily I say unto you, Till *h*	Mt 5:18	3772
the least in the kingdom of *h*	Mt 5:19	3772
called great in the kingdom of *h*	Mt 5:19	3772
case enter into the kingdom of *h*	Mt 5:20	3772
Swear not at all; neither by *h*	Mt 5:34	3772
of your Father which is in *h*	Mt 5:45	3772
Father which is in *h* is perfect	Mt 5:48	3772
of your Father which is in *h*	Mt 6:1	3772
Our Father which art in *h*	Mt 6:9	3772
be done in earth, as it is in *h*	Mt 6:10	3772
up for yourselves treasures in *h*	Mt 6:20	3772
h give good things to them that	Mt 7:11	3772
shall enter into the kingdom of *h*	Mt 7:21	3772
will of my Father which is in *h*	Mt 7:21	3772
and Jacob, in the kingdom of *h*	Mt 8:11	3772
The kingdom of *h* is at hand	Mt 10:7	3772
before my Father which is in *h*	Mt 10:32	3772
before my Father which is in *h*	Mt 10:33	3772
kingdom of *h* is greater than he	Mt 11:11	3772
kingdom of *h* suffereth violence	Mt 11:12	3772
which art exalted unto *h*	Mt 11:23	3772
I thank thee, O Father, Lord of *h*	Mt 11:25	3772
will of my Father which is in *h*	Mt 12:50	3772
the mysteries of the kingdom of *h*	Mt 13:11	3772
The kingdom of *h* is likened unto	Mt 13:24	3772
The kingdom of *h* is like to a	Mt 13:31	3772
The kingdom of *h* is like unto	Mt 13:33	3772
the kingdom of *h* is like unto	Mt 13:44	3772
the kingdom of *h* is like unto a	Mt 13:45	3772
the kingdom of *h* is like unto a	Mt 13:47	3772
h is like unto a man that is an	Mt 13:52	3772
two fishes, and looking up to *h*	Mt 14:19	3772
he would shew them a sign from *h*	Mt 16:1	3772
thee, but my Father which is in *h*	Mt 16:17	3772
thee the keys of the kingdom of *h*	Mt 16:19	3772
bind on earth shall be bound in *h*	Mt 16:19	3772
on earth shall be loosed in *h*	Mt 16:19	3772
the greatest in the kingdom of *h*	Mt 18:1	3772
not enter into the kingdom of *h*	Mt 18:3	3772
is greatest in the kingdom of *h*	Mt 18:4	3772
That in *h* their angels do always	Mt 18:10	3772
face of my Father which is in *h*	Mt 18:10	3772
will of your Father which is in *h*	Mt 18:14	3772
bind on earth shall be bound in *h*	Mt 18:18	3772
on earth shall be loosed in *h*	Mt 18:18	3772
them of my Father which is in *h*	Mt 18:19	3772

of *h* likened unto a certain king Mt 18:23 *3772*
for of such is the kingdom of *h* Mt 19:14 *3772*
and thou shalt have treasure in *h* Mt 19:21 *3772*
enter into the kingdom of *h* Mt 19:23 *3772*
For the kingdom of *h* is like unto Mt 20:1 *3772*
from *h*, or of men Mt 21:25 *3772*
saying, If we shall say, From *h* Mt 21:25 *3772*
The kingdom of *h* is like unto a Mt 22:2 *3772*
but are as the angels of God in *h* Mt 22:30 *3772*
one is your Father, which is in *h* Mt 23:9 *3772*
up the kingdom of *h* against men Mt 23:13 *3772*
And he that shall swear by *h* Mt 23:22 *3772*
and the stars shall fall from *h* Mt 24:29 *3772*
the sign of the Son of man in *h* Mt 24:30 *3772*
in the clouds of *h* with power Mt 24:30 *3772*
from one end of *h* to the other Mt 24:31 *3772*
H and earth shall pass away, but Mt 24:35 *3772*
no man, no, not the angels of *h* Mt 24:36 *3772*
Then shall the kingdom of *h* be Mt 25:1 *3772*
For the kingdom of *h* is as a man Mt 25:14
and coming in the clouds of *h* Mt 26:64 *3772*
of the Lord descended from *h* Mt 28:2 *3772*
All power is given unto me in *h* Mt 28:18 *3772*
And there came a voice from *h* Mk 1:11 *3772*
the two fishes, he looked up to *h* Mk 6:41 *3772*
And looking up to *h*, he sighed, and Mk 7:34 *3772*
him, seeking of him a sign from *h* Mk 8:11 *3772*
and thou shalt have treasure in *h* Mk 10:21 *3772*
your Father also which is in *h* Mk 11:25 *3772*
is in *h* forgive your trespasses Mk 11:26 *3772*
baptism of John, was it from *h* Mk 11:30 *3772*
saying, If we shall say, From *h* Mk 11:31 *3772*
are as the angels which are in *h* Mk 12:25 *3772*
And the stars of *h* shall fall Mk 13:25 *3772*
that are in *h* shall be shaken Mk 13:25 *3772*
earth to the uttermost part of *h* Mk 13:27 *3772*
H and earth shall pass away Mk 13:31 *3772*
no, not the angels which are in *h* Mk 13:32 *3772*
and coming in the clouds of *h* Mk 14:62 *3772*
them, he was received up into *h* Mk 16:19 *3772*
were gone away from them into *h* Lk 2:15 *3772*
and praying, the *h* was opened Lk 3:21 *3772*
upon him, and a voice came from *h* Lk 3:22 *3772*
when the *h* was shut up three Lk 4:25 *3772*
behold, your reward is great in *h* Lk 6:23 *3772*
two fishes, and looking up to *h* Lk 9:16 *3772*
command fire to come down from *h* Lk 9:54 *3772*
Capernaum, which art exalted to *h* Lk 10:15 *3772*
Satan as lightning fall from *h* Lk 10:18 *3772*
your names are written in *h* Lk 10:20 *3772*
I thank thee, O Father, Lord of *h* Lk 10:21 *3772*
say, Our Father which art in *h* Lk 11:2 *3772*
Thy will be done, as in *h* Lk 11:2 *3772*
him, sought of him a sign from *h* Lk 11:16 *3772*
that likewise joy shall be in *h* Lk 15:7 *3772*
Father, I have sinned against *h* Lk 15:18 *3772*
Father, I have sinned against *h* Lk 15:21 *3772*
And it is easier for *h* and earth to Lk 16:17 *3772*
out of the one part under *h* Lk 17:24 *3772*
unto the other part under *h* Lk 17:24 *3772*
rained fire and brimstone from *h* Lk 17:29 *3772*
up so much as his eyes unto *h* Lk 18:13 *3772*
and thou shalt have treasure in *h* Lk 18:22 *3772*
peace in *h*, and glory in the Lk 19:38 *3772*
baptism of John, was it from *h* Lk 20:4 *3772*
saying, If we shall say, From *h* Lk 20:5 *3772*
great signs shall there be from *h* Lk 21:11 *3772*
the powers of *h* shall be shaken Lk 21:26 *3772*
H and earth shall pass away Lk 21:33 *3772*
appeared an angel unto him from *h* Lk 22:43 *3772*
from them, and carried up into *h* Lk 24:51 *3772*
descending from *h* like a dove Jn 1:32 *3772*
Hereafter ye shall see *h* open Jn 1:51 *3772*
And no man hath ascended up to *h* Jn 3:13 *3772*
but he that came down from *h* Jn 3:13 *3772*
even the Son of man which is in *h* Jn 3:13 *3772*
except it be given him from *h* Jn 3:27 *3772*
that cometh from *h* is above all Jn 3:31 *3772*
He gave them bread from *h* to eat Jn 6:31 *3772*
gave you not that bread from *h* Jn 6:32 *3772*
giveth you the true bread from *h* Jn 6:32 *3772*
is he which cometh down from *h* Jn 6:33 *3772*
For I came down from *h*, not to do Jn 6:38 *3772*
the bread which came down from *h* Jn 6:41 *3772*
that he saith, I came down from *h* Jn 6:42 *3772*
bread which cometh down from *h* Jn 6:50 *3772*
bread which came down from *h* Jn 6:51 *3772*
that bread which came down from *h* Jn 6:58 *3772*
Then came there a voice from *h* Jn 12:28 *3772*
Jesus, and lifted up his eyes to *h* Jn 17:1 *3772*
stedfastly toward *h* as he went up Acts 1:10 *3772*
why stand ye gazing up into *h* Acts 1:11 *3772*
which is taken up from you into *h* Acts 1:11 *3772*
as ye have seen him go into *h* Acts 1:11 *3772*
there came a sound from *h* as of a Acts 2:2 *3772*
men, out of every nation under *h* Acts 2:5 *3772*
And I will shew wonders in *h* above Acts 2:19 *3772*
Whom the *h* must receive until the Acts 3:21 *3772*
name under *h* given among men Acts 4:12 *3772*
thou art God, which hast made *h* Acts 4:24 *3772*
them up to worship the host of *h* Acts 7:42 *3772*
H is my throne, and earth is my Acts 7:49 *3772*
looked up stedfastly into *h* Acts 7:55 *3772*
round about him a light from *h* Acts 9:3 *3772*
saw *h* opened, and a certain vessel Acts 10:11 *3772*
was received up again into *h* Acts 10:16 *3772*
let down from *h* by four corners Acts 11:5 *3772*
voice answered me again from *h* Acts 11:9 *3772*
and all were drawn up again into *h* Acts 11:10 *3772*
unto the living God, which made *h* Acts 14:15 *3772*
did good, and gave us rain from *h* Acts 14:17 *3771*
seeing that he is Lord of *h* Acts 17:24 *3772*
suddenly there shone from *h* a Acts 22:6 *3772*
I saw in the way a light from *h* Acts 26:13 *3771*
from *h* against all ungodliness Rom 1:18 *3772*
heart, Who shall ascend into *h* Rom 10:6 *3772*
whether in *h* or in earth, (as 1Cor 8:5 *3772*
the second man is the Lord from *h* 1Cor 15:47 *3772*
with our house which is from *h* 2Cor 5:2 *3772*
an one caught up to the third *h* 2Cor 12:2 *3772*
But though we, or an angel from *h* Gal 1:8 *3772*
in Christ, both which are in *h* Eph 1:10 *3772*
Of whom the whole family in *h* Eph 3:15 *3772*
that your Master also is in *h* Eph 6:9 *3772*
knee should bow, of things in *h* Phil 2:10 *2032*
For our conversation is in *h* Phil 3:20 *3772*
which is laid up for you in *h* Col 1:5 *3772*
all things created, that are in *h* Col 1:16 *3772*
things in earth, or things in *h* Col 1:20 *3772*
every creature which is under *h* Col 1:23 *3772*
that ye also have a Master in *h* Col 4:1 *3772*
And to wait for his Son from *h* 1Th 1:10 *3772*
shall descend from *h* with a shout 1Th 4:16 *3772*
from *h* with his mighty angels 2Th 1:7 *3772*
but into *h* itself, now to appear Heb 9:24 *3772*
that ye have in *h* a better Heb 10:34 *3772*
firstborn, which are written in *h* Heb 12:23 *3772*
from him that speaketh from *h* Heb 12:25 *3772*
not the earth only, but also *h* Heb 12:26 *3772*
brethren, swear not, neither by *h* Jas 5:12 *3772*
the *h* gave rain, and the earth Jas 5:18 *3772*
not away, reserved in *h* for you 1Pet 1:4 *3772*
the Holy Ghost sent down from *h* 1Pet 1:12 *3772*
Who is gone into *h*, and is on the 1Pet 3:22 *3772*
voice which came from *h* we heard 2Pet 1:18 *3772*
are three that bear record in *h* 1Jn 5:7 *3772*
cometh down out of *h* from my God Rev 3:12 *3772*
behold, a door was opened in *h* Rev 4:1 *3772*
and, behold, a throne was set in *h* Rev 4:2 *3772*
And no man in *h*, nor in earth, Rev 5:3 *3772*
And every creature which is in *h* Rev 5:13 *3772*
the stars of *h* fell unto the Rev 6:13 *3772*
the *h* departed as a scroll when Rev 6:14 *3772*
there was silence in *h* about the Rev 8:1 *3772*
and there fell a great star from *h* Rev 8:10 *3772*
flying through the midst of *h* Rev 8:13 *3321*
a star fall from *h* unto the earth Rev 9:1 *3772*
mighty angel come down from *h* Rev 10:1 *3772*
a voice from *h* saying unto me Rev 10:4 *3772*
the earth lifted up his hand to *h* Rev 10:5 *3772*
for ever and ever, who created *h* Rev 10:6 *3772*
heard from *h* spake unto me again Rev 10:8 *3772*
These have power to shut *h* Rev 11:6 *3772*
voice from *h* saying unto them Rev 11:12 *3772*
they ascended up to *h* in a cloud Rev 11:12 *3772*
and gave glory to the God of *h* Rev 11:13 *3772*
and there were great voices in *h* Rev 11:15 *3772*
the temple of God was opened in *h* Rev 11:19 *3772*
appeared a great wonder in *h* Rev 12:1 *3772*
appeared another wonder in *h* Rev 12:3 *3772*
the third part of the stars of *h* Rev 12:4 *3772*
And there was war in *h* Rev 12:7 *3772*
their place found any more in *h* Rev 12:8 *3772*
I heard a loud voice saying in *h* Rev 12:10 *3772*
and them that dwell in *h* Rev 13:6 *3772*
h on the earth in the sight of Rev 13:13 *3772*
And I heard a voice from *h* Rev 14:2 *3772*
angel fly in the midst of *h* Rev 14:6 *3321*
and worship him that made *h* Rev 14:7 *3772*
a voice from *h* saying unto me Rev 14:13 *3772*
out of the temple which is in *h* Rev 14:17 *3772*
And I saw another sign in *h* Rev 15:1 *3772*
of the testimony in *h* was opened Rev 15:5 *3772*
blasphemed the God of *h* because Rev 16:11 *3772*
voice out of the temple of *h* Rev 16:17 *3772*
upon men a great hail out of *h* Rev 16:21 *3772*
another angel come down from *h* Rev 18:1 *3772*
And I heard another voice from *h* Rev 18:4 *3772*
For her sins have reached unto *h* Rev 18:5 *3772*
Rejoice over her, thou *h*, and ye Rev 18:20 *3772*
a great voice of much people in *h* Rev 19:1 *3772*
I saw *h* opened, and behold a white Rev 19:11 *3772*
the armies which were in *h* Rev 19:14 *3772*
fowls that fly in the midst of *h* Rev 19:17 *3321*
I saw an angel come down from *h* Rev 20:1 *3772*
fire came down from God out of *h* Rev 20:9 *3772*
face the earth and the *h* fled away Rev 20:11 *3772*
And I saw a new *h* and a new earth Rev 21:1 *3772*
for the first *h* and the first Rev 21:1 *3772*
coming down from God out of *h* Rev 21:2 *3772*
a great voice out of *h* saying Rev 21:3 *3772*
descending out of *h* from God Rev 21:10 *3772*

HEAVENLY {23}

your *h* Father will also forgive Mt 6:14 *3770*
yet your *h* Father feedeth them Mt 6:26 *3770*
for your *h* Father knoweth that Mt 6:32 *3770*
which my *h* Father hath not Mt 15:13 *3770*
So likewise shall my *h* Father do Mt 18:35 *2032*
of the *h* host praising God Lk 2:13 *3770*
much more shall your *h* Father Lk 11:13 *1537,3772*
if I tell you of *h* things Jn 3:12 *2032*
not disobedient unto the *h* vision Acts 26:19 *3770*
and as is the *h*, such are they 1Cor 15:48 *2032*
such are they also that are *h* 1Cor 15:48 *2032*
also bear the image of the *h* 1Cor 15:49 *2032*
blessings in *h* places in Christ Eph 1:3 *2032*
own right hand in the *h* places Eph 1:20 *2032*
in *h* places in Christ Jesus Eph 2:6 *2032*
powers in *h* places might be known Eph 3:10 *2032*
preserve me unto his *h* kingdom 2Ti 4:18 *2032*
partakers of the *h* calling Heb 3:1 *2032*
and have tasted of the *h* gift Heb 6:4 *2032*
the example and shadow of *h* things Heb 8:5 *2032*
but the *h* things themselves with Heb 9:23 *2032*
a better country, that is, an *h* Heb 11:16 *2032*
the *h* Jerusalem, and to an Heb 12:22 *2032*

HEAVEN'S {1}

eunuchs for the kingdom of *h* sake Mt 19:12 *3772*

HEAVENS {133}

Thus the *h* and the earth were Gen 2:1 8064
are the generations of the *h* Gen 2:4 8064
LORD God made the earth and the *h* Gen 2:4 8064
the heaven of *h* is the LORD's thy Deut 10:14 8064
Give ear, O ye *h*, and I will speak Deut 32:1 8064
also his *h* shall drop down dew Deut 33:28 8064
the *h* dropped, the clouds also Judg 5:4 8064
He bowed the *h* also, and came down 2Sa 22:10 8064
heaven of *h* cannot contain thee 1Kin 8:27 8064
but the LORD made the *h* 1Chr 16:26 8064
Let the *h* be glad, and let the 1Chr 16:31 8064
Israel like to the stars of the *h* 1Chr 27:23 8064
heaven of *h* cannot contain him 2Chr 2:6 8064
the heaven of *h* cannot contain 2Chr 6:18 8064
Then hear thou from the *h* 2Chr 6:25 8064
Then hear thou from the *h* 2Chr 6:33 8064
hear thou from the *h* their prayer 2Chr 6:35 8064
Then hear thou from the *h* 2Chr 6:39 8064
trespass is grown up unto the *h* Ezr 9:6 8064
hast made heaven, the heaven of *h* Neh 9:6 8064
Which alone spreadeth out the *h* Job 9:8 8064
till the *h* be no more, they shall Job 14:12 8064
the *h* are not clean in his sight Job 15:15 8064
his excellency mount up to the *h* Job 20:6 8064
spirit he hath garnished the *h* Job 26:13 8064
Look unto the *h*, and see Job 35:5 8064
that sitteth in the *h* shall laugh Ps 2:4 8064
hast set thy glory above the *h* Ps 8:1 8064
When I consider thy *h*, the work Ps 8:3 8064
He bowed the *h* also, and came down Ps 18:9 8064
The LORD also thundered in the *h* Ps 18:13 8064
The *h* declare the glory of God Ps 19:1 8064
word of the LORD were the *h* made Ps 33:6 8064
Thy mercy, O LORD, is in the *h* Ps 36:5 8064
He shall call to the *h* from above Ps 50:4 8064
And the *h* shall declare his Ps 50:6 8064
thou exalted, O God, above the *h* Ps 57:5 8064
For thy mercy is great unto the *h* Ps 57:10 8064
thou exalted, O God, above the *h* Ps 57:11 8064
rideth upon the *h* by his name JAH Ps 68:4 6160
the *h* also dropped at the Ps 68:8 8064
that rideth upon the *h* of *h* Ps 68:33 8064
set their mouth against the *h* Ps 73:9 8064
thou establish in the very *h* Ps 89:2 8064
the *h* shall praise thy wonders, O Ps 89:5 8064
The *h* are thine, the earth also Ps 89:11 8064
but the LORD made the *h* Ps 96:5 8064
Let the *h* rejoice, and let the Ps 96:11 8064
The *h* declare his righteousness, Ps 97:6 8064
the *h* are the work of thy hands Ps 102:25 8064
hath prepared his throne in the *h* Ps 103:19 8064
out the *h* like a curtain Ps 104:2 8064
thy mercy is great above the *h* Ps 108:4 8064
thou exalted, O God, above the *h* Ps 108:5 8064
nations, and his glory above the *h* Ps 113:4 8064
But our God is in the *h* Ps 115:3 8064
The heaven, even the *h*, are the Ps 115:16 8064
O thou that dwellest in the *h* Ps 123:1 8064
To him that by wisdom made the *h* Ps 136:5 8064
Bow thy *h*, O LORD, and come down Ps 144:5 8064
Praise ye the LORD from the *h* Ps 148:1 8064
Praise him, ye *h* of *h* Ps 148:4 8064
and ye waters that be above the *h* Ps 148:4 8064
hath he established the *h* Prov 3:19 8064
When he prepared the *h*, I was Prov 8:27 8064
Hear, O *h*, and give ear, O earth Is 1:2 8064
is darkened in the *h* thereof Is 5:30 6183
Therefore I will shake the *h* Is 13:13 8064
the *h* shall be rolled together as Is 34:4 8064
stretcheth out the *h* as a curtain Is 40:22 8064
the LORD, he that created the *h* Is 42:5 8064
Sing, O ye *h* Is 44:23 8064
that stretcheth forth the *h* alone Is 44:24 8064
Drop down, ye *h*, from above, and Is 45:8 8064
hands, have stretched out the *h* Is 45:12 8064
saith the LORD that created the *h* Is 45:18 8064
my right hand hath spanned the *h* Is 48:13 8064
Sing, O *h* Is 49:13 8064
I clothe the *h* with blackness, and Is 50:3 8064
Lift up your eyes to the *h* Is 51:6 8064
for the *h* shall vanish away like Is 51:6 8064
that hath stretched forth the *h* Is 51:13 8064
mine hand, that I may plant the *h* Is 51:16 8064
For as the *h* are higher than the Is 55:9 8064
Oh that thou wouldest rend the *h* Is 64:1 8064
For, behold, I create new *h* Is 65:17 8064
For as the new *h* and the new earth Is 66:22 8064
Be astonished, O ye *h*, at this, Jer 2:12 8064
and the *h*, and they had no light Jer 4:23 8064
all the birds of the *h* were fled Jer 4:25 8064
mourn, and the *h* above be black Jer 4:28 8064
both the fowl of the *h* and the Jer 9:10 8064
The gods that have not made the *h* Jer 10:11 8065

H

the earth, and from under these *h* ... Jer 10:11 8065
out the *h* by his discretion ... Jer 10:12 8064
is a multitude of waters in the *h* ... Jer 10:13 8064
or can the *h* give showers ... Jer 14:22 8064
is a multitude of waters in the *h* ... Jer 51:16 8064
with our hands unto God in the *h* ... Lam 3:41 8064
from under the *h* of the LORD ... Lam 3:66 8064
that the *h* were opened, and I saw ... Eze 1:1 8064
have known that the *h* do rule ... Dan 4:26 8065
saith the LORD, I will hear the *h* ... Hos 2:21 8064
the *h* shall tremble ... Joel 2:10 8064
And I will shew wonders in the *h* ... Joel 2:30 8064
and the *h* and the earth shall shake ... Joel 3:16 8064
His glory covered the *h*, and the ... Hab 3:3 8064
while, and I will shake the *h* ... Hag 2:6 8064
Judah, saying, I will shake the *h* ... Hag 2:21 8064
are the four spirits of the *h* ... Zec 6:5 8064
the *h* shall give their dew ... Zec 8:12 8064
which stretcheth forth the *h* ... Zec 12:1 8064
the *h* were opened unto him, and he ... Mt 3:16 *3772*
powers of the *h* shall be shaken ... Mt 24:29 *3772*
of the water, he saw the *h* opened ... Mk 1:10 *3772*
in the *h* that faileth not ... Lk 12:33 *3772*
David is not ascended into the *h* ... Acts 2:34 *3772*
said, Behold, I see the *h* opened ... Acts 7:56 *3772*
made with hands, eternal in the *h* ... 2Cor 5:1 *3772*
that ascended up far above all *h* ... Eph 4:10 *3772*
the *h* are the works of thine ... Heb 1:10 *3772*
priest, that is passed into the *h* ... Heb 4:14 *3772*
and made higher than the *h* ... Heb 7:26 *3772*
throne of the Majesty in the *h* ... Heb 8:1 *3772*
h should be purified with these ... Heb 9:23 *3772*
the word of God the *h* were of old ... 2Pet 3:5 *3772*
But the *h* and the earth, which are ... 2Pet 3:7 *3772*
in the which the *h* shall pass ... 2Pet 3:10 *3772*
wherein the *h* being on fire shall ... 2Pet 3:12 *3772*
to his promise, look for new *h* ... 2Pet 3:13 *3772*
Therefore rejoice, ye *h*, and ye ... Rev 12:12 *3772*

HEAVIER {3}
For now it would be *h* than the ... Job 6:3 3513
my stroke is *h* than my groaning ... Job 23:2 3513
fool's wrath is *h* than them both ... Prov 27:3 3513

HEAVILY {3}
wheels, that they drave them *h* ... Ex 14:25 3517
I bowed down *h*, as one that ... Ps 35:14 6957
hast thou very *h* laid thy yoke ... Is 47:6 3513

HEAVINESS {14}
sacrifice I arose up from my *h* ... Ezr 9:5 8589
complaint, I will leave off my *h* ... Job 9:27 6440
and I am full of *h* ... Ps 69:20 5136
My soul melteth for *h* ... Ps 119:28 8424
son is the *h* of his mother ... Prov 10:1 8424
H in the heart of man maketh it ... Prov 12:25 1674
and the end of that mirth is *h* ... Prov 14:13 8424
Ariel, and there shall be *h* ... Is 29:2 8386
of praise for the spirit of *h* ... Is 61:3 3544
That I have great *h* and continual ... Rom 9:2 *3077*
would not come again to you in *h* ... 2Cor 2:1 *3077*
after you all, and was full of *h* ... Phil 2:26 *85*
to mourning, and your joy to *h* ... Jas 4:9 *2726*
ye are in *h* through manifold ... 1Pet 1:6 *3076*

HEAVY {41}
But Moses' hands were *h* ... Ex 17:12 3515
for this thing is too *h* for thee ... Ex 18:18 3515
alone, because it is too *h* for me ... Num 11:14 3515
for he was an old man, and *h* ... 1Sa 4:18 3513
LORD was *h* upon them of Ashdod ... 1Sa 5:6 3513
the hand of God was very *h* there ... 1Sa 5:11 3513
because the hair was *h* on him ... 2Sa 14:26 3513
his *h* yoke which he put upon us, ... 1Kin 12:4 3515
Thy father made our yoke *h* ... 1Kin 12:10 3513
father did lade you with a *h* yoke ... 1Kin 12:11 3515
My father made your yoke *h* ... 1Kin 12:14 3513
I am sent to thee with *h* tidings ... 1Kin 14:6 7186
of Israel went to his house *h* ... 1Kin 20:43 5620
And Ahab came into his house *h* ... 1Kin 21:4 5620
his *h* yoke that he put upon us, ... 2Chr 10:4 3515
Thy father made our yoke *h* ... 2Chr 10:10 3513
my father put a *h* yoke upon you ... 2Chr 10:11 3515
My father made your yoke *h* ... 2Chr 10:14 3513
bondage was *h* upon this people ... Neh 5:18 3513
shall my hand be *h* upon thee ... Job 33:7 3513
and night thy hand was *h* upon me ... Ps 32:4 3513
as an *h* burden they are too *h* ... Ps 38:4 3515
burden they are too *h* for me ... Ps 38:4 3513
that singeth songs to an *h* heart ... Prov 25:20 7451
A stone is *h*, and the sand weighty ... Prov 27:3 3514
unto those that be of *h* hearts ... Prov 31:6 4751
people fat, and make their ears *h* ... Is 6:10 3513
thereof shall be *h* upon it ... Is 24:20 3513
anger, and the burden thereof is *h* ... Is 30:27 3514
your carriages were *h* loaden ... Is 46:1
wickedness, to undo the *h* burdens ... Is 58:6 4133
neither his ear *h*, that it cannot ... Is 59:1 3513
he hath made my chain *h* ... Lam 3:7 3513
are *h* laden, and I will give you ... Mt 11:28
For they bind *h* burdens and ... Mt 23:4 *926*
began to be sorrowful and very *h* ... Mt 26:37 *85*
for their eyes were *h* ... Mt 26:43 *916*
be sore amazed, and to be very *h* ... Mk 14:33 *85*
again, (for their eyes were *h* ... Mk 14:40 *916*
were with him were *h* with sleep ... Lk 9:32 *916*

HEBER *(he'-bur)* {13} See EBER, HEBER'S, HEBERITES.
1. A son of Beriah.
H, and Malchiel ... Gen 46:17 2268
of *H*, the family of the Heberites ... Num 26:45 2268
H, and Malchiel, who is the father ... 1Chr 7:31 2268
H begat Japhlet, and Shomer, and ... 1Chr 7:32 2268
of Phalec, which was the son of *H* ... Lk 3:35 *1443*
2. Husband of Jael.
Now *H* the Kenite, which was of ... Judg 4:11 2268
of Jael the wife of *H* the Kenite ... Judg 4:17 2268
and the house of *H* the Kenite ... Judg 4:17 2268
Jael the wife of *H* the Kenite be ... Judg 5:24 2268
3. A son of Ezra.
H the father of Socho, and ... 1Chr 4:18 2268
4. A son of Elpaal.
and Meshullam, and Hezeki, and *H* ... 1Chr 8:17 2268
5. A head of a Gadite family.
and Jorai, and Jachan, and Zia, and *H* ... 1Chr 5:13 5677
6. A son of Shashak.
And Ishpan, and *H*, and Eliel, ... 1Chr 8:22 5677

HEBERITES *(he'-bur-ites)* {1} *Descendants of Heber.*
of Heber, the family of the *H* ... Num 26:45 2277

HEBER'S *(he'-burs)* {1} *Refers to Heber 2.*
Then Jael *H* wife took a nail of ... Judg 4:21 2268

HEBREW *(he'-broo)* {26} See HEBREWESS, HEBREWS.
1. Descendants of Jacob.
had escaped, and told Abram the *H* ... Gen 14:13 5680
in an *H* unto us to mock us ... Gen 39:14 5680
The *H* servant, which thou hast ... Gen 39:17 5680
there with us a young man, an *H* ... Gen 41:12 5680
of Egypt spake to the *H* midwives ... Ex 1:15 5680
of a midwife to the *H* women ... Ex 1:16 5680
Because the *H* women are not as ... Ex 1:19 5680
to thee a nurse of the *H* women ... Ex 2:7 5680
he spied an Egyptian smiting an *H* ... Ex 2:11 5680
If thou buy an *H* servant, six ... Ex 21:2 5680
an *H* man, or an *H* woman, be ... Deut 15:12 5680
being an *H* or an Hebrewess, go ... Jer 34:9 5680
ye go every man his brother an *H* ... Jer 34:14 5680
And he said unto them, I am an *H* ... Jonah 1:9 5680
of Benjamin, an *H* of the Hebrews ... Phil 3:5 *1446*
2. A language.
letters of Greek, and Latin, and *H* ... Lk 23:38 *1444*
called in the *H* tongue Bethesda ... Jn 5:2 *1447*
called the Pavement, but in the *H* ... Jn 19:13 *1447*
which is called in the *H* Golgotha ... Jn 19:17 *1447*
and it was written in *H*, and Greek, ... Jn 19:20 *1447*
spake unto them in the *H* tongue ... Acts 21:40 *1446*
he spake in the *H* tongue to them ... Acts 22:2 *1446*
me, and saying in the *H* tongue ... Acts 26:14 *1446*
name in the *H* tongue is Abaddon ... Rev 9:11 *1447*
called in the *H* tongue Armageddon ... Rev 16:16 *1447*

HEBREWESS *(he'-broo-ess)* {1}
being an Hebrew or an *H*, go free ... Jer 34:9 5680

HEBREWS *(he'-brooz)* {21} See HEBREWS'.
away out of the land of the *H* ... Gen 40:15 5680
might not eat bread with the *H* ... Gen 43:32 5680
two men of the *H* strove together ... Ex 2:13 5680
God of the *H* hath met with us ... Ex 3:18 5680
The God of the *H* hath met with us ... Ex 5:3 5680
The LORD God of the *H* hath sent ... Ex 7:16 5680
Thus saith the LORD God of the *H* ... Ex 9:1 5680
Thus saith the LORD God of the *H* ... Ex 9:13 5680
Thus saith the LORD God of the *H* ... Ex 10:3 5680
great shout in the camp of the *H* ... 1Sa 4:6 5680
ye be not servants unto the *H* ... 1Sa 4:9 5680
the land, saying, Let the *H* hear ... 1Sa 13:3 5680
some of the *H* went over Jordan to ... 1Sa 13:7 5680
Lest the *H* make them swords or ... 1Sa 13:19 5680
the *H* come forth out of the holes ... 1Sa 14:11 5680
Moreover the *H* that were with the ... 1Sa 14:21 5680
Philistines, What do these *H* here ... 1Sa 29:3 5680
of the Grecians against the *H* ... Acts 6:1 *1445*
Are they *H* ... 2Cor 11:22 *1445*
of Benjamin, an Hebrew of the *H* ... Phil 3:5 *1445*
Written to the *H* from Italy by ... Heb *s*

HEBREWS' *(he'-brooz)* {1}
This is one of the *H* children ... Ex 2:6 5680

HEBRON *(he'-brun)* {73} See HEBRONITES.
1. A city in Asher.
And *H*, and Rehob, and Hammon, and ... Josh 19:28 2275
2. A city in Judah.
the plain of Mamre, which is in *H* ... Gen 13:18 2275
the same is *H* in the land of ... Gen 23:2 2275
the same is *H* in the land of ... Gen 23:19 2275
the city of Arbah, which is *H* ... Gen 35:27 2275
he sent him out of the vale of *H* ... Gen 37:14 2275
by the south, and came unto *H* ... Num 13:22 2275
(Now *H* was built seven years ... Num 13:22 2275
sent unto Hoham king of *H* ... Josh 10:3 2275
king of Jerusalem, the king of *H* ... Josh 10:5 2275
king of Jerusalem, the king of *H* ... Josh 10:23 2275
and all Israel with him, unto *H* ... Josh 10:36 2275
as he had done to *H*, so he did to ... Josh 10:39 2275
from the mountains, from *H* ... Josh 11:21 2275
the king of *H*, one ... Josh 12:10 2275
of Jephunneh *H* for an inheritance ... Josh 14:13 2275
H therefore became the ... Josh 14:14 2275
And the name of *H* before was ... Josh 14:15 2275
father of Anak, which city is *H* ... Josh 15:13 2275
and Kirjath-arba, which is *H* ... Josh 15:54 2275
and Kirjath-arba, which is *H* ... Josh 20:7 2275
father of Anak, which city is *H* ... Josh 21:11 2275
the priest *H* with her suburbs ... Josh 21:13 2275
the Canaanites that dwelt in *H* ... Judg 1:10 2275
(now the name of *H* before was ... Judg 1:10 2275
they gave *H* unto Caleb, as Moses ... Judg 1:20 2275
top of an hill that is before *H* ... Judg 16:3 2275
And to them which were in *H* ... 1Sa 30:31 2275
And he said, Unto *H* ... 2Sa 2:1 2275
and they dwelt in the cities of *H* ... 2Sa 2:3 2275
in *H* over the house of Judah was ... 2Sa 2:11 2275
they came to *H* at break of day ... 2Sa 2:32 2275
And unto David were sons born in *H* ... 2Sa 3:2 2275
These were born to David in *H* ... 2Sa 3:5 2275
speak in the ears of David in *H* ... 2Sa 3:19 2275
So Abner came to David to *H* ... 2Sa 3:20 2275
but Abner was not with David in *H* ... 2Sa 3:22 2275
And when Abner was returned to *H* ... 2Sa 3:27 2275
And they buried Abner in *H* ... 2Sa 3:32 2275
heard that Abner was dead in *H* ... 2Sa 4:1 2275
of Ish-bosheth unto David to *H* ... 2Sa 4:8 2275
hanged them up over the pool in *H* ... 2Sa 4:12 2275
it in the sepulchre of Abner in *H* ... 2Sa 4:12 2275
tribes of Israel to David unto *H* ... 2Sa 5:1 2275
of Israel came to the king to *H* ... 2Sa 5:3 2275
with them in *H* before the LORD ... 2Sa 5:3 2275
In *H* he reigned over Judah seven ... 2Sa 5:5 2275
after he was come from *H* ... 2Sa 5:13 2275
I have vowed unto the LORD, in *H* ... 2Sa 15:7 2275
So he arose, and went to *H* ... 2Sa 15:9 2275
shall say, Absalom reigneth in *H* ... 2Sa 15:10 2275
seven years reigned he in *H* ... 1Kin 2:11 2275
which were born unto him in *H* ... 1Chr 3:1 2275
These six were born unto him in *H* ... 1Chr 3:4 2275
they gave them *H* in the land of ... 1Chr 6:55 2275
the cities of Judah, namely, *H* ... 1Chr 6:57 2275
themselves to David unto *H* ... 1Chr 11:1 2275
elders of Israel to the king to *H* ... 1Chr 11:3 2275
with them in *H* before the LORD ... 1Chr 11:3 2275
to the war, and came to David to *H* ... 1Chr 12:23 2275
came with a perfect heart to *H* ... 1Chr 12:38 2275
seven years reigned he in *H* ... 1Chr 29:27 2275
And Zorah, and Aijalon, and *H* ... 2Chr 11:10 2275
3. A son of Kohath.
Amram, and Izhar, and *H*, and Uzziel ... Ex 6:18 2275
Amram, and Izehar, *H*, and Uzziel ... Num 3:19 2275
Amram, Izhar, and *H*, and Uzziel ... 1Chr 6:2 2275
were, Amram, and Izhar, and *H* ... 1Chr 6:18 2275
Amram, Izhar, *H*, and Uzziel, four ... 1Chr 23:12 2275
Of the sons of *H* ... 1Chr 23:19 2275
And the sons of *H* ... 1Chr 24:23
4. A son of Mareshah.
sons of Mareshah the father of *H* ... 1Chr 2:42 2275
And the sons of *H* ... 1Chr 2:43 2275
Of the sons of *H* ... 1Chr 15:9 2275

HEBRONITES *(he'-brun-ites)* {6} *Descendants of Hebron 3.*
and the family of the *H*, and the ... Num 3:27 2276
the Libnites, the family of the *H* ... Num 26:58 2276
and the Izharites, the *H*, and the ... 1Chr 26:23 2276
And of the *H*, Hashabiah and his ... 1Chr 26:30 2276
Among the *H* was Jerijah the chief ... 1Chr 26:31 2276
even among the *H*, according to the ... 1Chr 26:31 2276

HEDGE {9}
Hast not thou made an *h* about him ... Job 1:10 7753
slothful man is as an *h* of thorns ... Prov 15:19 4881
and whoso breaketh an *h*, a serpent ... Eccl 10:8 1447
I will take away the *h* thereof ... Is 5:5 4881
neither made up the *h* for the ... Eze 13:5 1447
them, that should make up the *h* ... Eze 22:30 1447
I will *h* up thy way with thorns, ... Hos 2:6 7753
upright is sharper than a thorn *h* ... Mic 7:4 4534
set an *h* about it, and digged a ... Mk 12:1 *5418*

HEDGED {3}
way is hid, and whom God hath *h* in ... Job 3:23 5526
He hath *h* me about, that I cannot ... Lam 3:7 1443
h it round about, and digged a ... Mt 21:33 *5418,4060*

HEDGES {6}
that dwelt among plants and *h* ... 1Chr 4:23 1448
hast thou then broken down her *h* ... Ps 80:12 1447
Thou hast broken down all his *h* ... Ps 89:40 1448
lament, and run to and fro by the *h* ... Jer 49:3 1448
camp in the *h* in the cold day ... Nah 3:17 1448
Go out into the highways and *h* ... Lk 14:23 *5418*

HEED {80}
Take *h* that thou speak not to ... Gen 31:24 8104
Take thou *h* that thou speak not ... Gen 31:29 8104
take *h* to thyself, see my face no ... Ex 10:28 8104
Take *h* to yourselves, that ye go ... Ex 19:12 8104
Take *h* to thyself, lest thou make ... Ex 34:12 8104
Must I not take *h* to speak that ... Num 23:12 8104
take ye good *h* unto yourselves ... Deut 2:4 8104
Only take *h* to thyself, and keep ... Deut 4:9 8104
therefore good *h* unto yourselves ... Deut 4:15 8104
Take *h* unto yourselves, lest ye ... Deut 4:23 8104
Take *h* to yourselves, that your ... Deut 11:16 8104
Take *h* to thyself that thou offer ... Deut 12:13 8104
Take *h* to thyself that thou ... Deut 12:19 8104
Take *h* to thyself that thou be ... Deut 12:30 8104
Take *h* in the plague of leprosy, ... Deut 24:8 8104
unto all Israel, saying, Take *h* ... Deut 27:9 5535
But take diligent *h* to do the ... Josh 22:5 8104
Take good *h* therefore unto ... Josh 23:11 8104
take *h* to thyself until the ... 1Sa 19:2 8104
But Amasa took no *h* to the sword ... 2Sa 20:10 8104
thy children take *h* to their way ... 1Kin 2:4 8104
thy children take *h* to their way ... 1Kin 8:25 8104
But Jehu took no *h* to walk in the ... 2Kin 10:31 8104
if thou takest *h* to fulfil the ... 1Chr 22:13 8104
Take *h* now ... 1Chr 28:10 7200
yet so that thy children take *h* ... 2Chr 6:16 8104
to the judges, Take *h* what ye do ... 2Chr 19:6 7200
take *h* and do it ... 2Chr 19:7 8104
so that they will take *h* to do ... 2Chr 33:8 8104

Take *h* now that ye fail not to do .... Ezr 4:22 2095
Take *h*, regard not iniquity........................ Job 36:21 8104
I said, I will take *h* to my ways .... Ps 39:1 8104
by taking *h* thereto according to............. Ps 119:9 8104
doer giveth *h* to false lips........................ Prov 17:4 7181
Also take no *h* unto all words .... Eccl 7:21 5414,3820
yea, he gave good *h*, and sought............. Eccl 12:9 238
And say unto him, Take *h*, and be............ Is 7:4 8104
hearkened diligently with much *h* .... Is 21:7 7182
Take ye *h* every one of his .... Jer 9:4 8104
Take *h* to yourselves, and bear no........... Jer 17:21 8104
let us not give *h* to any of his.................. Jer 18:18 7181
Give *h* to me, O LORD, and hearken .... Jer 18:19 7181
left off to take *h* to the LORD .... Hos 4:10 8104
Therefore take *h* to your spirit................. Mal 2:15 8104
therefore take *h* to your spirit................. Mal 2:16 8104
Take *h* that ye do not your alms.............. Mt 6:1 *4337*
Then Jesus said unto them, Take *h* .... Mt 16:6 *3708*
Take *h* that ye despise not one of............ Mt 18:10 *3708*
Take *h* that no man deceive you.............. Mt 24:4 *991*
unto them, Take *h* what ye hear.............. Mk 4:24 *991*
he charged them, saying, Take *h* .... Mk 8:15 *3708*
Take *h* lest any man deceive you............. Mk 13:5 *991*
But take *h* to yourselves.......................... Mk 13:9 *991*
But take ye *h* .... Mk 13:23 *991*
Take ye *h*, watch and pray .... Mk 13:33 *991*
Take *h* therefore how ye hear................... Lk 8:18 *991*
Take *h* therefore that the light................. Lk 11:35 *4648*
And he said unto them, Take *h* .... Lk 12:15 *3708*
Take *h* to yourselves................................. Lk 17:3 *4337*
Take *h* that ye be not deceived................. Lk 21:8 *991*
take *h* to yourselves, lest at any.............. Lk 21:34 *4337*
he gave *h* unto them, expecting to .... Acts 3:5 *1907*
take *h* to yourselves what ye .... Acts 5:35 *4337*
h unto those things which Philip .... Acts 8:6 *4337*
To whom they all gave *h*, from the............ Acts 8:10 *4337*
Take *h* therefore unto yourselves,............. Acts 20:28 *4337*
saying, Take *h* what thou doest............... Acts 22:26 *3708*
take *h* lest he also spare not.................... Rom 11:21
But let every man take *h* how he............. 1Cor 3:10 *991*
But take *h* lest by any means this 1Cor 8:9 *991*
he standeth take *h* lest he fall................ 1Cor 10:12 *991*
take *h* that ye be not consumed .... Gal 5:15 *991*
take *h* to the ministry which thou .... Col 4:17 *991*
Neither give *h* to fables and 1Ti 1:4 *4337*
giving *h* to seducing spirits, and 1Ti 4:1 *4337*
Take *h* unto thyself, and unto the 1Ti 4:16 *1907*
Not giving *h* to Jewish fables, and.......... Titus 1:14 *4337*
h to the things which we have................. Heb 2:1 *4337*
Take *h*, brethren, lest there be................. Heb 3:12 *991*
ye do well that ye take *h* 2Pet 1:19 *433*

HEEL {6}
head, and thou shalt bruise his *h*............ Gen 3:15 6119
and his hand took hold on Esau's *h* .... Gen 25:26 6119
The gin shall take him by the *h*............... Job 18:9 6119
hath lifted up his *h* against me .... Ps 41:9 6119
his brother by the *h* in the womb .... Hos 12:3 6117
hath lifted up his *h* against me .... Jn 13:18 *4418*

HEELS {4}
the path, that biteth the horse *h* .... Gen 49:17 6119
a print upon the *h* of my feet .... Job 13:27 8328
of my *h* shall compass me about .... Ps 49:5 6120
discovered, and thy *h* made bare............. Jer 13:22 6119

HEGAI *(he'-gahee)* {3} See HEGE. *Servant of King Ahasuerus.*
the palace, to the custody of *H*................. Est 2:8 1896
king's house, to the custody of *H* .... Est 2:8 1896
but what *H* the king's chamberlain........... Est 2:15 1896

HEGE *(he'-ghe)* {1} See HEGAI. *Same as Hegai.*
unto the custody of *H* the king's .... Est 2:3 1896

HEIFER {19}
Take me an *h* of three years old, ... Gen 15:9 5697
bring thee a red *h* without spot.............. Num 19:2 6510
one shall burn the *h* in his sight .... Num 19:5 6510
the midst of the burning of the *h*............ Num 19:6 6510
gather up the ashes of the *h*................... Num 19:9 6510
of the *h* shall wash his clothes .... Num 19:10 6510
burnt *h* of purification for sin.................. Num 19:17
of that city shall take an *h* .... Deut 21:3 5697
down the *h* unto a rough valley .... Deut 21:4 5697
h that is beheaded in the valley .... Deut 21:6 5697
If ye had not plowed with my *h* .... Judg 14:18 5697
Take an *h* with thee, and say, I am.......... 1Sa 16:2 5697
Zoar, an *h* of three years old .... Is 15:5 5697
Egypt is like a very fair *h*....................... Jer 46:20 5697
as an *h* of three years old........................ Jer 48:34 5697
are grown fat as the *h* at grass................ Jer 50:11 5697
slideth back as a backsliding *h* .... Hos 4:16 6510
Ephraim is as an *h* that is taught............. Hos 10:11 5697
the ashes of an *h* sprinkling the.............. Heb 9:13 *1151*

HEIFER'S {1}
shall strike off the *h* neck there .... Deut 21:4 5697

HEIGHT {63}
the *h* of it thirty cubits.......................... Gen 6:15 6967
a cubit and a half the *h* thereof .... Ex 25:10 6967
a cubit and a half the *h* thereof .... Ex 25:23 6967
the *h* thereof shall be three .... Ex 27:1 6967
the *h* five cubits of fine twined .... Ex 27:18 6967
two cubits shall be the *h* thereof.............. Ex 30:2 6967
and a cubit and a half the *h* of it............. Ex 37:1 6967
a cubit and a half the *h* thereof .... Ex 37:10 6967
and two cubits was the *h* of it.................. Ex 37:25 6967
and three cubits the *h* thereof.................. Ex 38:1 6967
the *h* in the breadth was five.................... Ex 38:18 6967
or on the *h* of his stature 1Sa 16:7 1364
whose *h* was six cubits and a span 1Sa 17:4 1363
the *h* thereof thirty cubits 1Kin 6:2 6967
and twenty cubits in the *h* thereof........... 1Kin 6:20 6967
The *h* of the one cherub was ten 1Kin 6:26 6967
the *h* thereof thirty cubits, upon 1Kin 7:2 6967
the *h* of the one chapiter was.................. 1Kin 7:16 6967
the *h* of the other chapiter was 1Kin 7:16 6967
about, and his *h* was five cubits.............. 1Kin 7:23 6967
and three cubits the *h* of it..................... 1Kin 7:27 6967
the *h* of a wheel was a cubit and 1Kin 7:32 6967
come up to the *h* of the mountains 2Kin 19:23 4791
The *h* of the one pillar was 2Kin 25:17 6967
the *h* of the chapiter three...................... 2Kin 25:17 6967
the *h* was an hundred and twenty........... 2Chr 3:4 1363
and ten cubits the *h* thereof.................... 2Chr 4:1 6967
and five cubits the *h* thereof 2Chr 4:2 6967
and raised it up a very great *h* 2Chr 33:14 1361
the *h* thereof threescore cubits,.............. Ezr 6:3 7312
Is not God in the *h* of heaven.................. Job 22:12 1363
behold the *h* of the stars, how................. Job 22:12 7218
down from the *h* of his sanctuary .... Ps 102:19 4791
The heaven for *h*, and the earth .... Prov 25:3 7312
in the depth, or in the *h* above............... Is 7:11 1361
come up to the *h* of the mountains .... Is 37:24 4791
enter into the *h* of his border .... Is 37:24 4791
come and sing in the *h* of Zion .... Jer 31:12 4791
that holdest the *h* of the hill .... Jer 49:16 4791
fortify the *h* of her strength .... Jer 51:53 4791
the *h* of one pillar was eighteen.............. Jer 52:21 6967
the *h* of one chapiter was five .... Jer 52:22 6967
In the mountain of the *h* of...................... Eze 17:23 4791
she appeared in her *h* with the .... Eze 19:11 1363
the mountain of the *h* of Israel .... Eze 20:40 4791
Therefore his *h* was exalted above.......... Eze 31:5 6967
thou hast lifted up thyself in *h*............... Eze 31:10 6967
his heart is lifted up in his *h*.................. Eze 31:10 1363
exalt themselves for their *h*.................... Eze 31:14 6967
their trees stand up in their *h* .... Eze 31:14 1363
and fill the valleys with thy *h* .... Eze 32:5 7419
and the *h*, one reed .... Eze 40:5 6967
I saw also the *h* of the house.................. Eze 41:8 1364
whose *h* was threescore cubits, and .... Dan 3:1 7314
earth, and the *h* thereof was great .... Dan 4:10 7314
the *h* thereof reached unto heaven......... Dan 4:11 7314
whose *h* reached unto the heaven,.......... Dan 4:20 7314
whose *h* was like the *h* of...................... Amos 2:9 1363
was like the *h* of the cedars.................... Amos 2:9 1363
Nor *h*, nor depth, nor any other.............. Rom 8:39 *5313*
and length, and depth, and *h* .... Eph 3:18 *5311*
breadth and the *h* of it are equal .... Rev 21:16 *5311*

HEIGHTS {2}
praise him in the *h* .... Ps 148:1 4791
ascend above the *h* of the clouds............ Is 14:14 1116

HEINOUS {1}
For this is an *h* crime.............................. Job 31:11 2154

HEIR {18}
one born in my house is mine *h* .... Gen 15:3 3423
saying, This shall not be thine *h* .... Gen 15:4 3423
thine own bowels shall be thine *h*........... Gen 15:4 3423
shall not be *h* with my son .... Gen 21:10 3423
and we will destroy the *h* also................. 2Sa 14:7 3423
that is *h* to her mistress.......................... Prov 30:23 3423
hath he no *h*? .... Jer 49:1 3423
then shall Israel be *h* unto them .... Jer 49:2 3423
Yet will I bring an *h* unto thee................. Mic 1:15 3423
among themselves, This is the *h*.............. Mt 21:38 *2818*
among themselves, This is the *h*.............. Mk 12:7 *2818*
themselves, saying, This is the *h* .... Lk 20:14 *2818*
he should be the *h* of the world .... Rom 4:13 *2818*
Now I say, That the *h*, as long as............. Gal 4:1 *2818*
then an *h* of God through Christ.............. Gal 4:7 *2818*
of the bondwoman shall not be *h*............. Gal 4:30 *2816*
he hath appointed *h* of all things............. Heb 1:2 *2818*
became *h* of the righteousness .... Heb 11:7 *2818*

HEIRS {11}
be heir unto them that were his *h*............ Jer 49:2 3423
if they which are of the law be *h* .... Rom 4:14 *2818*
And if children, then *h* .... Rom 8:17 *2818*
h of God, and joint-heirs with .... Rom 8:17 *2818*
h according to the promise..................... Gal 3:29 *2818*
we should be made *h* according to........... Titus 3:7 *2818*
them who shall be *h* of salvation .... Heb 1:14 *2816*
abundantly to shew unto the *h* of............ Heb 6:17 *2818*
the *h* with him of the same .... Heb 11:9 *4789*
h of the kingdom which he hath .... Jas 2:5 *2818*
as being *h* together of the grace.............. 1Pet 3:7 *4789*

HELAH *(he'-lah)* {2} *A wife of Asher.*
father of Tekoa had two wives, *H* 1Chr 4:5 2458
And the sons of *H* were, Zereth, and 1Chr 4:7 2458

HELAM *(he'-lam)* {2} *A place east of the Jordan.*
and they came to *H* 2Sa 10:16 2431
passed over Jordan, and came to *H*.......... 2Sa 10:17 2431

HELBAH *(hel'-bah)* {1} *A town in Asher.*
of Ahlab, nor of Achzib, nor of *H* .... Judg 1:31 2462

HELBON *(hel'-bon)* {1} *A city near Damascus.*
in the wine of *H*, and white wool............ Eze 27:18 2463

HELD {52}
man wondering at her *h* his peace .... Gen 24:21 2790
Jacob *h* his peace until they were .... Gen 34:5 2790
he *h* up his father's hand, to................... Gen 48:17 8557
when Moses *h* up his hand, that.............. Ex 17:11 7311
the loops *h* one curtain to .... Ex 36:12 6901
And Aaron *h* his peace .... Lev 10:3 1826
h his peace at her in the day .... Num 30:7 2790
h his peace at her, and disallowed .... Num 30:11 2790
because he *h* his peace at her in.............. Num 30:14 2790
h the lamps in their left hands,............... Judg 7:20 2388
the lad that *h* him by the hand .... Judg 16:26 2388
And when she *h* it, he measured six .... Ruth 3:15 270
But he *h* his peace 1Sa 10:27 2790
he *h* a feast in his house, like.................. 1Sa 25:36
for Joab *h* back the people 2Sa 18:16 2820
And at that time Solomon *h* a feast........ 1Kin 8:65 6213
But the people *h* their peace 2Kin 18:36 2790
and *h* three thousand baths...................... 2Chr 4:5 3557
half of them *h* both the spears .... Neh 4:16 2388
and with the other hand *h* a weapon...... Neh 4:17 2388
half of them *h* the spears from............... Neh 4:21 2388
Then *h* they their peace, and found .... Neh 5:8 2790
the king *h* out to Esther the................... Est 5:2 3447
I had *h* my tongue, although the............ Est 7:4 2790
Then the king *h* out the golden .... Est 8:4 3447
My foot hath *h* his steps, his way........... Job 23:11 270
The nobles *h* their peace, and .... Job 29:10 2244
whose mouth must be *h* in with bit .... Ps 32:9 1102
I *h* my peace, even from good.................. Ps 39:2 2814
thy mercy, O LORD, *h* me up .... Ps 94:18 5582
I *h* him, and would not let him go,.......... Song 3:4 270
the king is *h* in the galleries................... Song 7:5 631
But they *h* their peace, and..................... Is 36:21 2790
have not I *h* my peace even of old............ Is 57:11 2814
took them captives *h* them fast............... Jer 50:33 2388
when he *h* up his right hand and............ Dan 12:7 7311
h a council against him, how they .... Mt 12:14 *2983*
But Jesus *h* his peace.............................. Mt 26:63 *4623*
h him by the feet, and worshipped.......... Mt 28:9 *2902*
But they *h* their peace .... Mk 3:4 *4623*
But they *h* their peace .... Mk 9:34 *4623*
But he *h* his peace, and answered .... Mk 14:61 *4623*
the morning the chief priests *h* a .... Mk 15:1 *4160*
And they *h* their peace............................ Lk 14:4 *2270*
at his answer, and *h* their peace............. Lk 20:26 *4601*
the men that *h* Jesus mocked him,.......... Lk 22:63 *4912*
lame man which was healed *h* Peter....... Acts 3:11 *2902*
they *h* their peace, and glorified .... Acts 11:18 *2270*
part *h* with the Jews, and part................ Acts 14:4 *2258*
And after they had *h* their peace .... Acts 15:13 *4601*
that being dead wherein we were *h* .... Rom 7:6 *2722*
and for the testimony which they *h* .... Rev 6:9 *2192*

HELDAI *(hel'-dahee)* {2} See HELED, HELEM.
1. A sanctuary servant.
month was *H* the Netophathite............... 1Chr 27:15 2469
2. An honored exile.
them of the captivity, even of *H* .... Zec 6:10 2469

HELEB *(he'-leb)* {1} See HELED. *A "mighty man" of David.*
H the son of Baanah, a 2Sa 23:29 2460

HELECH See HELEK.

HELED *(he'-led)* {1} See HELEB, HELDAI. *Same as Heleb.*
H the son of Baanah the.......................... 1Chr 11:30 2466

HELEK *(he'-lek)* {2} See HELEKITES. *A son of Gilead.*
of *H*, the family of the Helekites............. Num 26:30 2507
Abiezer, and for the children of *H* .... Josh 17:2 2507

HELEKITES *(he'-lek-ites)* {1} *Descendants of Helek.*
of Helek, the family of the *H*................... Num 26:30 2516

HELEM *(he'-lem)* {2}
1. A descendant of Asher.
And the sons of his brother *H* 1Chr 7:35 2494
2. Same as Heldai 2.
And the crowns shall be to *H*.................... Zec 6:14 2494

HELEPH *(he'-lef)* {1} *A town in Naphtali.*
And their coast was from *H* .... Josh 19:33 2501

HELEZ *(he'-lez)* {5}
1. A "mighty man" of David.
H the Paltite, Ira the son of...................... 2Sa 23:26 2503
the Harorite, *H* the Pelonite,.................... 1Chr 11:27 2503
seventh month was *H* the Pelonite......... 1Chr 27:10 2503
2. A son of Azariah.
And Azariah begat *H*, and Helez 1Chr 2:39 2503
begat Helez, and *H* begat Eleasah,.......... 1Chr 2:39 2503

HELI *(he'-li)* {1} See ELI. *Father of Joseph; ancestor of Jesus.*
of Joseph, which was the son of *H*.......... Lk 3:23 *2242*

HELKAI *(hel'-kahee)* {1} *A priest.*
Adna; of Meraioth, *H* .... Neh 12:15 2517

HELKATH *(hel'-kath)* {2} See HELKATH-HAZZURIM, HUKOK. *A town in Asher.*
And their border was *H*, and Hali,......... Josh 19:25 2520
H with her suburbs, and Rehob with....... Josh 21:31 2520

HELKATH-HAZZURIM *(hel'-kath-haz'-zu-rim)* {1} *A plain near the pool of Gibeon.*
wherefore that place was called *H*.......... 2Sa 2:16 2521

HELL {54}
and shall burn unto the lowest *h* .... Deut 32:22 7585
The sorrows of *h* compassed me.............. 2Sa 22:6 7585
deeper than *h*.. Job 11:8 7585
H is naked before him, and .... Job 26:6 7585
The wicked shall be turned into *h* .... Ps 9:17 7585
thou wilt not leave my soul in *h*.............. Ps 16:10 7585
The sorrows of *h* compassed me.............. Ps 18:5 7585
and let them go down quick into *h* .... Ps 55:15 7585
my soul from the lowest *h* .... Ps 86:13 7585
the pains of *h* gat hold upon me .... Ps 116:3 7585
if I make my bed in *h*, behold, ... Ps 139:8 7585
her steps take hold on *h* .... Prov 5:5 7585
Her house is the way to *h*........................ Prov 7:27 7585
her guests are in the depths of *h*............. Prov 9:18 7585

H and destruction are before the ... Prov 15:11 7585
that he may depart from *h* beneath ... Prov 15:24 7585
and shalt deliver his soul from *h* ... Prov 23:14 7585
H and destruction are never full ... Prov 27:20 7585
Therefore *h* hath enlarged herself ... Is 5:14 7585
H from beneath is moved for thee ... Is 14:9 7585
thou shalt be brought down to *h* ... Is 14:15 7585
with *h* are we at agreement ... Is 28:15 7585
agreement with *h* shall not stand ... Is 28:18 7585
didst debase thyself even unto *h* ... Is 57:9 7585
when I cast him down to *h* with ... Eze 31:16 7585
They also went down into *h* with ... Eze 31:17 7585
of *h* with them that help him ... Eze 32:21 7585
which are gone down to *h* with ... Eze 32:27 7585
Though they dig into *h*, thence ... Amos 9:2 7585
out of the belly of *h* cried I ... Jonah 2:2 7585
who enlargeth his desire as *h* ... Hab 2:5 7585
shall be in danger of *h* fire ... Mt 5:22 *1067*
whole body should be cast into *h* ... Mt 5:29 *1067*
whole body should be cast into *h* ... Mt 5:30 *1067*
to destroy both soul and body in *h* ... Mt 10:28 *1067*
shalt be brought down to *h* ... Mt 11:23 *86*
the gates of *h* shall not prevail ... Mt 16:18 *86*
two eyes to be cast into *h* fire ... Mt 18:9 *1067*
the child of *h* than yourselves ... Mt 23:15 *1067*
can ye escape the damnation of *h* ... Mt 23:33 *1067*
having two hands to go into *h* ... Mk 9:43 *1067*
having two feet to be cast into *h* ... Mk 9:45 *1067*
two eyes to be cast into *h* fire ... Mk 9:47 *1067*
heaven, shalt be thrust down to *h* ... Lk 10:15 *86*
killed hath power to cast into *h* ... Lk 12:5 *1067*
in *h* he lift up his eyes, being ... Lk 16:23 *86*
thou wilt not leave my soul in *h* ... Acts 2:27 *86*
that his soul was not left in *h* ... Acts 2:31 *86*
and it is set on fire of *h* ... Jas 3:6 *1067*
sinned, but cast them down to *h* ... 2Pet 2:4 *5020*
and have the keys of *h* and of death ... Rev 1:18 *86*
was Death, and *H* followed with him ... Rev 6:8 *86*
h delivered up the dead which ... Rev 20:13 *86*
h were cast into the lake of fire ... Rev 20:14 *86*

HELLENISTS See GRECIANS.

HELM {1}
turned about with a very small *h* ... Jas 3:4 *4079*

HELMET {8}
he had an *h* of brass upon his ... 1Sa 17:5 3553
he put an *h* of brass upon his ... 1Sa 17:38 6959
an *h* of salvation upon his head ... Is 59:17 3553
and shield and *h* round about ... Eze 23:24 6959
hanged the shield and *h* in thee ... Eze 27:10 3553
all of them with shield and *h* ... Eze 38:5 3553
take the *h* of salvation, and the ... Eph 6:17 *4030*
and for an *h*, the hope of ... 1Th 5:8 *4030*

HELMETS {2}
the host shields, and spears, and *h* ... 2Chr 26:14 3553
and stand forth with your *h* ... Jer 46:4 3553

HELON *(he'-lon)* {5} *Father of Eliab.*
Eliab the son of *H* ... Num 1:9 2497
Eliab the son of *H* shall be ... Num 2:7 2497
the third day Eliab the son of *H* ... Num 7:24 2497
offering of Eliab the son of *H* ... Num 7:29 2497
of Zebulun was Eliab the son of *H* ... Num 10:16 2497

HELP {126}
I will make him an *h* meet for him ... Gen 2:18 5828
was not found an *h* meet for him ... Gen 2:20 5828
of thy father, who shall *h* thee ... Gen 49:25 5826
of my father, said he, was mine *h* ... Ex 18:4 5828
and wouldest forbear to *h* him ... Ex 23:5 5800
thou shalt surely *h* with him ... Ex 23:5 5800
thou shalt surely *h* him to lift ... Deut 22:4 6965
h you, and be your protection ... Deut 32:38 5826
be thou an *h* to him from his ... Deut 33:7 5828
rideth upon the heaven in thy *h* ... Deut 33:26 5828
by the LORD, the shield of thy *h* ... Deut 33:29 5828
mighty men of valour, and *h* them ... Josh 1:14 5826
h me, that we may smite Gibeon ... Josh 10:4 5826
us quickly, and save us, and *h* us ... Josh 10:6 5826
of Gezer came up to *h* Lachish ... Josh 10:33 5826
came not to the *h* of the LORD ... Judg 5:23 5833
to the *h* of the LORD against the ... Judg 5:23 5833
the sun be hot, ye shall have *h* ... 1Sa 11:9 8668
for me, then thou shalt *h* me ... 2Sa 10:11 3447
thee, then I will come and *h* thee ... 2Sa 10:11 3467
So the Syrians feared to *h* the ... 2Sa 10:19 3467
and did obeisance, and said, *H* ... 2Sa 14:4 3467
cried a woman unto him, saying, *H* ... 2Kin 6:26 3467
h thee, whence shall I *h* thee ... 2Kin 6:27 3467
be come peaceably unto me to *h* me ... 1Chr 12:17 5826
day there came to David to *h* him ... 1Chr 12:22 5826
came to *h* Hadarezer king of Zobah ... 1Chr 18:5 5826
for me, then thou shalt *h* me ... 1Chr 19:12 8668
for thee, then I will *h* thee ... 1Chr 19:12 3467
neither would the Syrians *h* the ... 1Chr 19:19 3467
of Israel to *h* Solomon his son ... 1Chr 22:17 5826
it is nothing with thee to *h* ... 2Chr 14:11 5826
h us, O LORD our God ... 2Chr 14:11 5826
Shouldest thou *h* the ungodly ... 2Chr 19:2 5826
together, to ask *h* of the LORD ... 2Chr 20:4
then thou wilt hear and *h* ... 2Chr 20:9 3467
for God hath power to *h*, and to ... 2Chr 25:8 5826
to *h* the king against the enemy ... 2Chr 26:13 5826
the kings of Assyria to *h* him ... 2Chr 28:16 5826
gods of the kings of Syria *h* them ... 2Chr 28:23 5826
to them, that they may *h* me ... 2Chr 28:23 5826
brethren the Levites did *h* them ... 2Chr 29:34 2388
and they did *h* him ... 2Chr 32:3 5826
us is the LORD our God to *h* us ... 2Chr 32:8 5826
of his place *h* him with silver ... Ezr 1:4 5375
horsemen to *h* us against the ... Ezr 8:22 5826
Is not my *h* in me ... Job 6:13 5833
neither will he *h* the evil doers ... Job 8:20 2388
and him that had none to *h* him ... Job 29:12 5826
when I saw my *h* in the gate ... Job 31:21 5833
There is no *h* for him in God ... Ps 3:2 3444
H, LORD; for the godly ... Ps 12:1 3467
Send thee *h* from the sanctuary, ... Ps 20:2 5828
for there is none to *h* ... Ps 22:11 5826
O my strength, haste thee to *h* me ... Ps 22:19 5833
thou hast been my *h* ... Ps 27:9 5833
he is our *h* and our shield ... Ps 33:20 5828
buckler, and stand up for mine *h* ... Ps 35:2 5833
And the LORD shall *h* them, and ... Ps 37:40 5826
Make haste to *h* me, O Lord my ... Ps 38:22 5833
O LORD, make haste to *h* me ... Ps 40:13 5833
thou art my *h* and my deliverer ... Ps 40:17 5833
him for the *h* of his countenance ... Ps 42:5 3444
Arise for our *h*, and redeem us for ... Ps 44:26 5833
a very present *h* in trouble ... Ps 46:1 5833
God shall *h* her, and that right ... Ps 46:5 5826
awake to *h* me, and behold ... Ps 59:4 7125
Give us *h* from trouble ... Ps 60:11 5833
for vain is the *h* of man ... Ps 60:11 8668
Because thou hast been my *h* ... Ps 63:7 5833
make haste to *h* me, O LORD ... Ps 70:1 5833
thou art my *h* and my deliverer ... Ps 70:5 5828
O my God, make haste for my *h* ... Ps 71:12 5833
H us, O God of our salvation, for ... Ps 79:9 5826
I have laid *h* upon one that is ... Ps 89:19 5828
Unless the LORD had been my *h* ... Ps 94:17 5833
fell down, and there was none to *h* ... Ps 107:12 5826
Give us *h* from trouble ... Ps 108:12 5833
for vain is the *h* of man ... Ps 108:12 8668
H me, O LORD my God ... Ps 109:26 5826
he is their *h* and their shield ... Ps 115:9 5828
he is their *h* and their shield ... Ps 115:10 5828
he is their *h* and their shield ... Ps 115:11 5828
my part with them that *h* me ... Ps 118:7 5826
h thou me ... Ps 119:86 5826
Let thine hand *h* me ... Ps 119:173 5826
and let thy judgments *h* me ... Ps 119:175 5826
hills, from whence cometh my *h* ... Ps 121:1 5828
My *h* cometh from the LORD, which ... Ps 121:2 5828
Our *h* is in the name of the LORD, ... Ps 124:8 5828
son of man, in whom there is no *h* ... Ps 146:3 8668
hath the God of Jacob for his *h* ... Ps 146:5 5828
he hath not another to *h* him up ... Eccl 4:10 6965
to whom will ye flee for *h* ... Is 10:3 5833
whither we flee for *h* to be ... Is 20:6 5833
nor be an *h* nor profit, but a ... Is 30:5 5828
For the Egyptians shall *h* in vain ... Is 30:7 5826
them that go down to Egypt for *h* ... Is 31:1 5833
against the *h* of them that work ... Is 31:2 5833
yea, I will *h* thee ... Is 41:10 5826
I will *h* thee ... Is 41:13 5826
I will *h* thee, saith the LORD, and ... Is 41:14 5826
from the womb, which will *h* thee ... Is 44:2 5826
For the Lord GOD will *h* me ... Is 50:7 5826
Behold, the Lord GOD will *h* me ... Is 50:9 5826
I looked, and there was none to *h* ... Is 63:5 5826
which is come forth to *h* you ... Jer 37:7 5833
of the enemy, and none did *h* her ... Lam 1:7 5826
eyes as yet failed for our vain *h* ... Lam 4:17 5833
all that are about him to *h* him ... Eze 12:14 5828
of hell with them that *h* him ... Eze 32:21 5826
the chief princes, came to *h* me ... Dan 10:13 5826
shall be holpen with a little *h* ... Dan 11:34 5828
to his end, and none shall *h* him ... Dan 11:45 5826
but in me is thine *h* ... Hos 13:9 5828
him, saying, Lord, *h* me ... Mt 15:25 *997*
have compassion on us, and *h* us ... Mk 9:22 *997*
h thou mine unbelief ... Mk 9:24 *997*
that they should come and *h* them ... Lk 5:7 *4815*
bid her therefore that she *h* me ... Lk 10:40 *4878*
Come over into Macedonia, and *h* us ... Acts 16:9 *997*
Crying out, Men of Israel, *h* ... Acts 21:28 *997*
therefore obtained *h* of God ... Acts 26:22 *1947*
h those women which laboured with ... Phil 4:3 *4815*
find grace to *h* in time of need ... Heb 4:16 *996*

HELPED {24}
h them, and watered their flock ... Ex 2:17 3467
Hitherto hath the LORD *h* us ... 1Sa 7:12 5826
and they following Adonijah *h* him ... 1Kin 1:7 5826
thirty and two kings that *h* him ... 1Kin 20:16 5826
they were *h* against them, and the ... 1Chr 5:20 5826
but they *h* them not ... 1Chr 12:19 5826
they *h* David against the band of ... 1Chr 12:21 5826
when God *h* the Levites that bare ... 1Chr 15:26 5826
cried out, and the LORD *h* him ... 2Chr 18:31 5826
every one *h* to destroy another ... 2Chr 20:23 5826
God *h* him against the Philistines ... 2Chr 26:7 5826
for he was marvellously *h* ... 2Chr 26:15 5826
but he *h* him not ... 2Chr 28:21 5833
and Shabbethai the Levite *h* them ... Ezr 10:15 5826
officers of the king, *h* the Jews ... Est 9:3 5375
How hast thou *h* him that is ... Job 26:2 5826
heart trusted in him, and I am *h* ... Ps 28:7 5826
I was brought low, and he *h* me ... Ps 116:6 3467
but the LORD *h* me ... Ps 118:13 5826
They *h* every one his neighbour ... Is 41:6 5826
a day of salvation have I *h* thee ... Is 49:8 5826
they *h* forward the affliction ... Zec 1:15 5826
h them much which had believed ... Acts 18:27 *4820*
And the earth *h* the woman, and the ... Rev 12:16 *997*

HELPER {9}
any left, nor any *h* for Israel ... 2Kin 14:26 5826
my calamity, they have no *h* ... Job 30:13 5826
thou art the *h* of the fatherless ... Ps 10:14 5826
LORD, be thou my *h* ... Ps 30:10 5826
Behold, God is mine *h* ... Ps 54:4 5826
poor also, and him that hath no *h* ... Ps 72:12 5826
Zidon every *h* that remaineth ... Jer 47:4 5826
our *h* in Christ, and Stachys my ... Rom 16:9 *4904*
may boldly say, The Lord is my *h* ... Heb 13:6 *998*

HELPERS {7}
the mighty men, *h* of the war ... 1Chr 12:1 5826
unto thee, and peace be to thine *h* ... 1Chr 12:18 5826
the proud *h* do stoop under him ... Job 9:13 5826
when all her *h* shall be destroyed ... Eze 30:8 5826
Put and Lubim were thy *h* ... Nah 3:9 5833
Aquila my *h* in Christ Jesus ... Rom 16:3 *4904*
your faith, but are *h* of your joy ... 2Cor 1:24 *4904*

HELPETH {4}
for thy God *h* thee ... 1Chr 12:18 5826
hand, both he that *h* shall fall ... Is 31:3 5826
the Spirit also *h* our infirmities ... Rom 8:26 *4878*
and to every one that *h* with us ... 1Cor 16:16 *4903*

HELPING {3}
were the prophets of God *h* them ... Ezr 5:2 5582
why art thou so far from *h* me ... Ps 22:1 3467
Ye also *h* together by prayer for ... 2Cor 1:11 *4943*

HELPS {2}
they had taken up, they used *h* ... Acts 27:17 *996*
then gifts of healings, *h* ... 1Cor 12:28 *484*

HELVE {1}
and the head slippeth from the *h* ... Deut 19:5 6086

HEM {7}
beneath upon the *h* of it thou ... Ex 28:33 7757
round about the *h* thereof ... Ex 28:33 7757
upon the *h* of the robe round ... Ex 28:34 7757
upon the *h* of the robe, round ... Ex 39:25 7757
round about the *h* of the robe to ... Ex 39:26 7757
touched the *h* of his garment ... Mt 9:20 *2899*
only touch the *h* of his garment ... Mt 14:36 *2899*

HEMAM *(he'-mam)* {1} See HOMAM. *A son of Lotan.*
children of Lotan were Hori and *H* ... Gen 36:22 1967

HEMAN *(he'-man)* {17}
1. *A son of Zerah.*
than Ethan the Ezrahite, and *H* ... 1Kin 4:31 1968
Zimri, and Ethan, and *H*, and Calcol, ... 1Chr 2:6 1968
Of *H*: the sons of *H* ... 1Chr 25:4 1968
2. *A son of Joel.*
H a singer, the son of Joel, the ... 1Chr 6:33 1968
appointed *H* the son of Joel ... 1Chr 15:17 1968
So the singers, *H*, Asaph, and ... 1Chr 15:19 1968
And with them *H* and Jeduthun, and ... 1Chr 16:41 1968
And with them *H* and Jeduthun with ... 1Chr 16:42 1968
of the sons of Asaph, and of *H* ... 1Chr 25:1 1968
All these were the sons of *H* the ... 1Chr 25:5 1968
God gave to *H* fourteen sons and ... 1Chr 25:5 1968
order to Asaph, Jeduthun, and *H* ... 1Chr 25:6 1968
all of them of Asaph, of *H* ... 2Chr 5:12 1968
And of the sons of *H* ... 2Chr 29:14 1968
of David, and Asaph, and *H*, and ... 2Chr 35:15 1968
Maschil of *H* the Ezrahite ... Ps 88:*t* 1968

HEMATH *(he'-math)* {3} See HAMATH.
1. *Same as Hamath.*
Egypt even unto the entering of *H* ... 1Chr 13:5 2574
in of *H* unto the river of the ... Amos 6:14 2574
2. *Father of the Kenites and Rechabites.*
are the Kenites that came of *H* ... 1Chr 2:55 2574

HEMDAN *(hem'-dan)* {1} See AMRAM. *Son of Dishon.*
H, and Eshban, and Ithran, and ... Gen 36:26 2533

HEMLOCK {2}
as *h* in the furrows of the field ... Hos 10:4 7219
the fruit of righteousness into *h* ... Amos 6:12 3939

HEMS {1}
they made upon the *h* of the robe ... Ex 39:24 7757

HEN *(hen)* {3} *A son of Zephaniah.*
to *H* the son of Zephaniah, for a ... Zec 6:14 2581
even as a *h* gathereth her ... Mt 23:37 *3733*
as a *h* doth gather her brood ... Lk 13:34 *3733*

HENA *(he'-nah)* {3} *A city on the Euphrates.*
are the gods of Sepharvaim, *H* ... 2Kin 18:34 2012
of the city of Sepharvaim, *H* ... 2Kin 19:13 2012
king of the city of Sepharvaim, *H* ... Is 37:13 2012

HENADAD *(hen'-a-dad)* {4} *A Levite.*
the sons of *H*, with their sons and ... Ezr 3:9 2582
brethren, Bavai the son of *H* ... Neh 3:18 2582
Binnui the son of *H* another piece ... Neh 3:24 2582
Azaniah, Binnui the of sons of *H* ... Neh 10:9 2582

HENCE {30}
the man said, They are departed *h* ... Gen 37:17 2088
Pharaoh ye shall not go forth *h* ... Gen 42:15 2088
ye shall carry up my bones from *h* ... Gen 50:25 2088
afterwards he will let you go *h* ... Ex 11:1 2088
thrust you out *h* altogether ... Ex 11:1 2088
carry up my bones away *h* with you ... Ex 13:19 2088
unto Moses, Depart, and go up *h* ... Ex 33:1 2088
go not with me, carry us not up *h* ... Ex 33:15 2088
get thee down quickly from *h* ... Deut 9:12 2088
Take you *h* out of the midst of ... Josh 4:3 2088
Depart not *h*, I pray thee, until ... Judg 6:18 2088
another field, neither go from *h* ... Ruth 2:8 2088
Get thee *h*, and turn thee eastward ... 1Kin 17:3 2088
recover strength, before I go *h* ... Ps 39:13 2088
shalt say unto it, Get thee *h* ... Is 30:22 3318

Take from *h* thirty men with thee, Jer 38:10 2088
and he said, Get you *h*, walk to and Zec 6:7 3212
saith Jesus unto him, Get thee *h* Mt 4:10 *5217*
Remove *h* to yonder place Mt 17:20 *1782*
of God, cast thyself down from *h* Lk 4:9 *1782*
him, Get thee out, and depart *h* Lk 13:31 *1782*
would pass from *h* to you cannot Lk 16:26 *1782*
sold doves, Take these things *h* Jn 2:16 *1782*
therefore said unto him, Depart *h* Jn 7:3 *1782*
Arise, let us go *h* Jn 14:31 *1782*
but now is my kingdom not from *h* Jn 18:36 *1782*
Sir, if thou have borne him *h* Jn 20:15
the Holy Ghost not many days *h* Acts 1:5 *3226,5025*
send thee far *h* unto the Gentiles Acts 22:21 *1821*
come they not *h*, even of your Jas 4:1 *1782*

HENCEFORTH {33}
it shall not *h* yield unto thee Gen 4:12 3254
must the children of Israel *h* Num 18:22 5750
Ye shall *h* return no more that Deut 17:16 3254
shall *h* commit no more any such Deut 19:20 3254
I also will not *h* drive out any Judg 2:21 3254
for thy servant will *h* offer 2Kin 5:17 5750
therefore from *h* thou shalt have 2Chr 16:9 6258
his people from *h* even for ever Ps 125:2 6258
Israel hope in the LORD from *h* Ps 131:3 6258
with justice from *h* even for ever Is 9:7 6258
for *h* there shall no more come Is 52:1 6258
seed, saith the LORD, from *h* Is 59:21 3254
thou shalt no more *h* bereave them Eze 36:12
over them in mount Zion from *h* Mic 4:7
unto you, Ye shall not see me *h* Mt 23:39 *575,737*
I will not drink *h* of this fruit Mt 26:29 *575,737*
from *h* all generations shall call Lk 1:48 *3568*
from *h* thou shalt catch men Lk 5:10 *3568*
For from *h* there shall be five in Lk 12:52 *3568*
from *h* ye know him, and have seen Jn 14:7 *737*
H I call you not servants Jn 15:15 *3765*
that they speak *h* to no man in Acts 4:17 *3371*
from *h* I will go unto the Acts 18:6 *3568*
that *h* we should not serve sin Rom 6:6 *3371*
should not *h* live unto themselves 2Cor 5:15 *3371*
h know we no man after 2Cor 5:16 *575,3588,3568*
yet now *h* know we him no more 2Cor 5:16 *2089*
From *h* let no man trouble me Gal 6:17 *3063*
That we *h* be no more children, Eph 4:14 *3063*
that ye *h* walk not as other Eph 4:17 *3371*
H there is laid up for me a crown 2Ti 4:8 *3063*
From *h* expecting till his enemies Heb 10:13 *3063*
dead which die in the Lord from *h* Rev 14:13 *534*

HENCEFORWARD {2}
and *h* among your generations Num 15:23 1973
no fruit grow on thee *h* for ever Mt 21:19 *3371*

HENNA See CAMPHIRE.

HENOCH *(he'-nok)* {2} See ENOCH. *Same as Enoch.*
H, Methuselah, Lamech, 1Chr 1:3 2585
Ephah, and Epher, and *H*, and Abida, 1Chr 1:33 2585

HEPHER *(he'-fer)* {9} See GATH-HEPHER, HEPHERITES.
1. A son of Gilead.
and of *H*, the family of the Num 26:32 2660
the son of *H* had no sons, but Num 26:33 2660
of Zelophehad, the son of *H* Num 27:1 2660
Shechem, and for the children of *H* Josh 17:2 2660
But Zelophehad, the son of *H* Josh 17:3 2660
2. A son of Naarah.
And Naarah bare him Ahuzam, and *H* 1Chr 4:6 2660
3. A "mighty man" of David.
H the Mecherathite, Ahijah the 1Chr 11:36 2660
4. A Canaanite city.
the king of *H*, one Josh 12:17 2660
Sochoh, and all the land of *H* 1Kin 4:10 2660

HEPHERITES *(he'-fer-ites)* {1} *Descendants of Hepher 1.*
and of Hepher, the family of the *H* Num 26:32 2662

HEPHZI-BAH *(hef'-zi-bah)* {2}
1. Wife of King Hezekiah.
And his mother's name was *H* 2Kin 21:1 2657
2. A symbolic name for Jerusalem.
but thou shalt be called *H* Is 62:4 2657

HER See APPENDIX.

HERALD {1}
Then an *h* cried aloud, To you it Dan 3:4 3744

HERB {19}
the *h* yielding seed, and the fruit Gen 1:11 6212
h yielding seed after his kind, Gen 1:12 6212
given you every *h* bearing seed Gen 1:29 6212
have given every green *h* for meat Gen 1:30 6212
every *h* of the field before it Gen 2:5 6212
thou shalt eat the *h* of the field Gen 3:18 6212
even as the green *h* have I given Gen 9:3 6212
upon every *h* of the field, Ex 9:22 6212
hail smote every *h* of the field Ex 9:25 6212
eat every *h* of the land, even all Ex 10:12 6212
they did eat every *h* of the land Ex 10:15 6212
the small rain upon the tender *h* Deut 32:2 1877
of the field, and as the green *h* 2Kin 19:26 1877
it withereth before any other *h* Job 8:12 2682
of the tender *h* to spring forth Job 38:27 1877
grass, and wither as the green *h* Ps 37:2 1877
and *h* for the service of man Ps 104:14 6212
of the field, and as the green *h* Is 37:27 1877
bones shall flourish like an *h* Is 66:14 1877

HERBS {18}
or in the *h* of the field, through Ex 10:15 6212
with bitter *h* they shall eat it Ex 12:8
with unleavened bread and bitter *h* Num 9:11
with thy foot, as a garden of *h* Deut 11:10 3419
I may have it for a garden of *h* 1Kin 21:2 3419
out into the field to gather *h* 2Kin 4:39 219
eat up all the *h* in their land Ps 105:35 6212
is a dinner of *h* where love is Prov 15:17 3419
h of the mountains are gathered Prov 27:25 6212
place like a clear heat upon *h* Is 18:4 216
for thy dew is as the dew of *h* Is 26:19 219
and hills, and dry up all their *h* Is 42:15 6212
the *h* of every field wither, for Jer 12:4 6212
grown, it is the greatest among *h* Mt 13:32 *3001*
and becometh greater than all *h* Mk 4:32 *3001*
mint and rue and all manner of *h* Lk 11:42 *3001*
another, who is weak, eateth *h* Rom 14:2 *3001*
bringeth forth *h* meet for them by Heb 6:7 *1008*

HERD {22}
And Abraham ran unto the *h* Gen 18:7 1241
of the cattle, even of the *h* Lev 1:2 1241
be a burnt sacrifice of the *h* Lev 1:3 1241
offering, if he offer it of the *h* Lev 3:1 1241
And concerning the tithe of the *h* Lev 27:32 1241
savour unto the LORD, of the *h* Num 15:3 1241
then thou shalt kill of thy *h* Deut 12:21 1241
males that come of thy *h* and of Deut 15:19 1241
thy God, of the flock and the *h* Deut 16:2 1241
came after the *h* out of the field 1Sa 11:5 1241
of his own flock and of his own *h* 2Sa 12:4 1241
young of the flock and of the *h* Jer 31:12 1241
h nor flock, taste any thing Jonah 3:7 1241
there shall be no *h* in the stalls Hab 3:17 1241
them an *h* of many swine feeding Mt 8:30 *34*
us to go away into the *h* of swine Mt 8:31 *34*
they went into the *h* of swine Mt 8:32 *34*
behold, the whole *h* of swine ran Mt 8:32 *34*
a great *h* of swine feeding Mk 5:11 *34*
the *h* ran violently down a steep Mk 5:13 *34*
there was there an *h* of many Lk 8:32 *34*
the *h* ran violently down a steep Lk 8:33 *34*

HERDMAN {1}
but I was an *h*, and a gatherer of Amos 7:14 951

HERDMEN {8}
between the *h* of Abram's cattle Gen 13:7 7462
cattle and the *h* of Lot's cattle Gen 13:7 7462
and between my *h* and thy *h* Gen 13:8 7462
the *h* of Gerar did strive with Gen 26:20 7462
Gerar did strive with Isaac's *h* Gen 26:20 7462
the chiefest of the *h* that 1Sa 21:7 7462
who was among the *h* of Tekoa Amos 1:1 5349

HERDS {3}
went with Abram, had flocks, and *h* Gen 13:5 1241
and he hath given him flocks, and *h* Gen 24:35 1241
of flocks, and possession of *h* Gen 26:14 1241
was with him, and the flocks, and *h* Gen 32:7 1241
and *h* with young are with me Gen 33:13 1241
children, and thy flocks, and thy *h* Gen 45:10 1241
brought their flocks, and their *h* Gen 46:32 1241
and their flocks, and their *h* Gen 47:1 1241
and for the cattle of the *h* Gen 47:17 1241
my lord also hath our *h* of cattle Gen 47:18 4735
ones, and their flocks, and their *h* Gen 50:8 1241
flocks and with our *h* will we go Ex 10:9 1241
your flocks and your *h* be stayed Ex 10:24 1241
Also take your flocks and your *h* Ex 12:32 1241
and flocks, and *h*, even very much Ex 12:38 1241
nor *h* feed before that mount Ex 34:3 1241
the *h* be slain for them, to Num 11:22 1241
And when thy *h* and thy flocks Deut 8:13 1241
and the firstlings of your *h* Deut 12:6 1241
of thy *h* or of thy flock, nor any Deut 12:17 1241
oil, and the firstlings of thy *h* Deut 14:23 1241
took all the flocks and the *h* 1Sa 30:20 1241
had exceeding many flocks and *h* 2Sa 12:2 1241
over the *h* that fed in Sharon was 1Chr 27:29 1241
over the *h* that were in the 1Chr 27:29 1241
of flocks and *h* in abundance 2Chr 32:29 1241
law, and the firstlings of our *h* Neh 10:36 1241
thy flocks, and look well to thy *h* Prov 27:23 5739
a place for the *h* to lie down in Is 65:10 1241
their flocks and their *h*, their Jer 3:24 1241
eat up thy flocks and thine *h* Jer 5:17 1241
with their *h* to seek the LORD Hos 5:6 1241
the *h* of cattle are perplexed, Joel 1:18 5739

HERE See APPENDIX.

HEREAFTER See APPENDIX.

HEREBY {13}
H ye shall be proved Gen 42:15 2063
H shall I know that ye are true Gen 42:33 2063
H ye shall know that the LORD Num 16:28 2063
H ye shall know that the living Josh 3:10 2063
yet am I not *h* justified 1Cor 4:4 *1722,5129*
h we do know that we know him, if 1Jn 2:3 *1722,5129*
h know we that we are in him 1Jn 2:5 *1722,5129*
H perceive we the love of God, 1Jn 3:16 *1722,5129*
h we know that we are of the 1Jn 3:19 *1722,5129*
h we know that he abideth in us, 1Jn 3:24 *1722,5129*
H know ye the Spirit of God 1Jn 4:2 *1722,5129*
H know we the spirit of truth, and 1Jn 4:6 *1537,5124*
H know we that we dwell in him, 1Jn 4:13 *1722,5129*

HEREIN {9}
Only *h* will the men consent unto Gen 34:22 2063
H thou hast done foolishly 2Chr 16:9 5921,2063
h is that saying true, One soweth Jn 4:37 *1722,5129*
Why *h* is a marvellous thing, that Jn 9:30 *1722,5129*
H is my Father glorified, that ye Jn 15:8 *1722,5129*
h do I exercise myself, to have Acts 24:16 *1722,5129*
And *h* I give my advice 2Cor 8:10 *1722,5129*
H is love, not that we loved God, 1Jn 4:10 *1722,5129*
H is our love made perfect, that 1Jn 4:17 *1722,5129*

HEREOF {2}
the fame *h* went abroad into all Mt 9:26 *3778*
And by reason *h* he ought, as for Heb 5:3 *5026*

HERES *(he'-res)* {1} See KIR-HERES, TIMMATH-HERES. *A mountain in Judah.*
would dwell in mount *H* in Aijalon Judg 1:35 2776

HERESH *(he'-resh)* {1} *A Levite.*
And Bakbakkar, *H*, and Galal, and 1Chr 9:15 2792

HERESIES {3}
there must be also *h* among you 1Cor 11:19 *139*
wrath, strife, seditions, *h* Gal 5:20 *139*
privily shall bring in damnable *h* 2Pet 2:1 *139*

HERESY {1}
after the way which they call *h* Acts 24:14 *139*

HERETH See HARETH.

HERETICK {1}
man that is an *h* after the first Titus 3:10 *141*

HERETOFORE {8}
I am not eloquent, neither *h* Ex 4:10 8543
people straw to make brick, as *h* Ex 5:7 8543
the bricks, which they did make *h* Ex 5:8 8543
both yesterday and to day, as *h* Ex 5:14 8543
for ye have not passed this way *h* Josh 3:4 8543
a people which thou knewest not *h* Ruth 2:11 8543
hath not been such a thing *h* 1Sa 4:7 865
write to them which *h* have sinned 2Cor 13:2 *4258*

HEREUNTO {2}
can eat, or who else can hasten *h* Eccl 2:25
For even *h* were ye called 1Pet 2:21 *1519,5124*

HEREWITH {2}
and yet thou wast not satisfied *h* Eze 16:29 2063
in mine house, and prove me now *h* Mal 3:10 2063

HERITAGE {30}
and I will give it you for an *h* Ex 6:8 4181
the *h* appointed unto him by God Job 20:29 5159
the *h* of oppressors, which they Job 27:13 5159
yea, I have a goodly *h* Ps 16:6 5159
thou hast given me the *h* of those Ps 61:5 3425
O LORD, and afflict thine *h* Ps 94:5 5159
give them the *h* of the heathen Ps 111:6 5159
have I taken as an *h* for ever Ps 119:111 5157
Lo, children are an *h* of the LORD Ps 127:3 5159
And gave their land for an *h* Ps 135:12 5159
an *h* unto Israel his people Ps 135:12 5159
And gave their land for an *h* Ps 136:21 5159
Even an *h* unto Israel his servant Ps 136:22 5159
This is the *h* of the servants of Is 54:17 5159
feed thee with the *h* of Jacob thy Is 58:14 5159
made mine *h* an abomination Jer 2:7 5159
a goodly *h* of the hosts of Jer 3:19 5159
mine house, I have left mine *h* Jer 12:7 5159
Mine *h* is unto me as a lion in Jer 12:8 5159
Mine *h* is unto me as a speckled Jer 12:9 5159
them again, every man to his *h* Jer 12:15 5159
from thine *h* that I gave thee Jer 17:4 5159
O ye destroyers of mine *h* Jer 50:11 5159
and give not thine *h* to reproach Joel 2:17 5159
for my people and for my *h* Israel Joel 3:2 5159
and his house, even a man and his *h* Mic 2:2 5159
thy rod, the flock of thine *h* Mic 7:14 5159
of the remnant of his *h* Mic 7:18 5159
his *h* waste for the dragons of Mal 1:3 5159
as being lords over God's *h* 1Pet 5:3 *2819*

HERITAGES {1}
cause to inherit the desolate *h* Is 49:8 5159

HERMAS *(her'-mas)* {1} *A Christian acquaintance of Paul.*
Salute Asyncritus, Phlegon, *H* Rom 16:14 *2057*

HERMES *(her'-mees)* {1} *A Christian acquaintance of Paul.*
Phlegon, Hermas, Patrobas, *H* Rom 16:14 *2060*

HERMOGENES *(her-mog'-e-nees)* {1} *A false Christian teacher.*
of whom are Phygellus and *H* 2Ti 1:15 *2061*

HERMON {13}
the river of Arnon unto mount *H* Deut 3:8 2768
(Which *H* the Sidonians call Deut 3:9 2768
even unto mount Sion which is *H* Deut 4:48 2768
to the Hivite under *H* in the land Josh 11:3 2768
valley of Lebanon under mount *H* Josh 11:17 2768
from the river Arnon unto mount *H* Josh 12:1 2768
And reigned in mount *H*, and in Josh 12:5 2768
from Baal-gad under mount *H* unto Josh 13:5 2768
and Maachathites, and all mount *H* Josh 13:11 2768
and Senir, and unto mount *H* 1Chr 5:23 2768
H shall rejoice in thy name Ps 89:12 2768
As the dew of *H*, and as the dew Ps 133:3 2768
from the top of Shenir and of *H* Song 4:8 2768

HERMONITES *(her'-mon-ites)* {1} See HERMON. *Inhabitants of Mt. Hermon.*
the land of Jordan, and of the *H* Ps 42:6 2769

HEROD *(her'-od)* {40} See HERODIANS, HEROD'S.
1. Herod the Great.
Judaea in the days of *H* the king Mt 2:1 *2264*
When *H* the king had heard these Mt 2:3 *2264*

Then *H*, when he had privily ... Mt 2:7 *2264*
that they should not return to *H* ... Mt 2:12 *2264*
for *H* will seek the young child ... Mt 2:13 *2264*
And was there until the death of *H* ... Mt 2:15 *2264*
Then *H*, when he saw that he was ... Mt 2:16 *2264*
But when *H* was dead, behold, an ... Mt 2:19 *2264*
in the room of his father *H* ... Mt 2:22 *2264*
There was in the days of *H* ... Lk 1:5 *2264*
No, nor yet *H*: for I sent ... Lk 23:15 *2264*
2. Herod Antipas.
At that time *H* the tetrarch heard ... Mt 14:1 *2264*
For *H* had laid hold on John, and ... Mt 14:3 *2264*
danced before them, and pleased *H* ... Mt 14:6 *2264*
And king *H* heard of him ... Mk 6:14 *2264*
But when *H* heard thereof, he said ... Mk 6:16 *2264*
For *H* himself had sent forth and ... Mk 6:17 *2264*
For John had said unto *H*, It is ... Mk 6:18 *2264*
For *H* feared John, knowing that ... Mk 6:20 *2264*
that *H* on his birthday made a ... Mk 6:21 *2264*
came in, and danced, and pleased *H* ... Mk 6:22 *2264*
Pharisees, and of the leaven of *H* ... Mk 8:15 *2264*
H being tetrarch of Galilee, and ... Lk 3:1 *2264*
But *H* the tetrarch, being ... Lk 3:19 *2264*
all the evils which *H* had done ... Lk 3:19 *2264*
Now *H* the tetrarch heard of all ... Lk 9:7 *2264*
H said, John have I beheaded ... Lk 9:9 *2264*
for *H* will kill thee ... Lk 13:31 *2264*
jurisdiction, he sent him to *H* ... Lk 23:7 *2264*
And when *H* saw Jesus, he was ... Lk 23:8 *2264*
H with his men of war set him at ... Lk 23:11 *2264*
H were made friends together ... Lk 23:12 *2264*
whom thou hast anointed, both *H* ... Acts 4:27 *2264*
brought up with *H* the tetrarch ... Acts 13:1 *2264*
3. Herod Agrippa I.
Now about that time *H* the king ... Acts 12:1 *2264*
when *H* would have brought him ... Acts 12:6 *2264*
delivered me out of the hand of *H* ... Acts 12:11 *2264*
when *H* had sought for him, and ... Acts 12:19 *2264*
H was highly displeased with them ... Acts 12:20 *2264*
And upon a set day *H*, arrayed in ... Acts 12:21 *2264*

HERODIANS *(he-ro'-de-uns)* {3} *Hellenizing Jews.*
him their disciples with the *H* ... Mt 22:16 *2265*
counsel with the *H* against him ... Mk 3:6 *2265*
of the Pharisees and of the *H* ... Mk 12:13 *2265*

HERODIAS *(he-ro'-de-as)* {4} See HERODIAS'. *Granddaughter of Herod 1.*
the daughter of *H* danced before ... Mt 14:6 *2266*
Therefore *H* had a quarrel against ... Mk 6:19 *2266*
daughter of the said *H* came in ... Mk 6:22 *2266*
for *H* his brother Philip's wife ... Lk 3:19 *2266*

HERODIAS' *(he-ro'-de-as)* {2}
and put him in prison for *H* sake ... Mt 14:3 *2266*
and bound him in prison for *H* sake ... Mk 6:17 *2266*

HERODION *(he-ro'-de-on)* {1} *A relative of Paul.*
Salute *H* my kinsman ... Rom 16:11 *2267*

HEROD'S *(her'-ods)* {4}
1. Refers to Herod 2.
But when *H* birthday was kept, the ... Mt 14:6 *2264*
the wife of Chuza *H* steward ... Lk 8:3 *2264*
he belonged unto *H* jurisdiction ... Lk 23:7 *2264*
2. Refers to Herod 3.
him to be kept in *H* judgment hall ... Acts 23:35 *2264*

HERON {2}
the *h* after her kind, and the ... Lev 11:19 601
the *h* after her kind, and the ... Deut 14:18 601

HERS See APPENDIX.

HERSELF See APPENDIX.

HESED *(he'-sed)* {1} See JUSHAB-HESED. *Father of an officer of Solomon.*
The son of *H*, in Aruboth ... 1Kin 4:10 2618

HESHBON *(hesh'-bon)* {38} *A Levitical city in Reuben and Gad.*
the cities of the Amorites, in *H* ... Num 21:25 2809
For *H* was the city of Sihon the ... Num 21:26 2809
in proverbs say, Come into *H* ... Num 21:27 2809
For there is a fire gone out of *H* ... Num 21:28 2809
H is perished even unto Dibon, and ... Num 21:30 2809
of the Amorites, which dwelt at *H* ... Num 21:34 2809
Dibon, and Jazer, and Nimrah, and *H* ... Num 32:3 2809
And the children of Reuben built *H* ... Num 32:37 2809
of the Amorites, which dwelt in *H* ... Deut 1:4 2809
hand Sihon the Amorite, king of *H* ... Deut 2:24 2809
king of *H* with words of peace ... Deut 2:26 2809
But Sihon king of *H* would not let ... Deut 2:30 2809
of the Amorites, which dwelt at *H* ... Deut 3:2 2809
as we did unto Sihon king of *H* ... Deut 3:6 2809
of the Amorites, who dwelt at *H* ... Deut 4:46 2809
this place, Sihon the king of *H* ... Deut 29:7 2809
beyond Jordan, to Sihon king of *H* ... Josh 9:10 2809
of the Amorites, who dwelt in *H* ... Josh 12:2 2809
the border of Sihon king of *H* ... Josh 12:5 2809
the Amorites, which reigned in *H* ... Josh 13:10 2809
H, and all her cities that are in ... Josh 13:17 2809
the Amorites, which reigned in *H* ... Josh 13:21 2809
from *H* unto Ramath-mizpeh, and ... Josh 13:26 2809
of the kingdom of Sihon king of *H* ... Josh 13:27 2809
H with her suburbs, Jazer with ... Josh 21:39 2809
of the Amorites, the king of *H* ... Judg 11:19 2809
While Israel dwelt in *H* and her ... Judg 11:26 2809
H with her suburbs, and Jazer with ... 1Chr 6:81 2809
and the land of the king of *H* ... Neh 9:22 2809
eyes like the fishpools in *H* ... Song 7:4 2809
And *H* shall cry, and Elealeh ... Is 15:4 2809
For the fields of *H* languish ... Is 16:8 2809
water thee with my tears, O *H* ... Is 16:9 2809
in *H* they have devised evil ... Jer 48:2 2809
From the cry of *H* even unto ... Jer 48:34 2809
shadow of *H* because of the force ... Jer 48:45 2809
a fire shall come forth out of *H* ... Jer 48:45 2809
Howl, O *H*, for Ai is spoiled ... Jer 49:3 2809

HESHMON *(hesh'-mon)* {1} See AZMON. *A town in Judah.*
And Hazar-gaddah, and *H*, and ... Josh 15:27 2829

HESLI See ESLI.

HETH *(heth)* {14} *Son of Canaan.*
begat Sidon his firstborn, and *H* ... Gen 10:15 2845
dead, and spake unto the sons of *H* ... Gen 23:3 2845
the children of *H* answered ... Gen 23:5 2845
land, even to the children of *H* ... Gen 23:7 2845
dwelt among the children of *H* ... Gen 23:10 2845
the audience of the children of *H* ... Gen 23:10 2845
in the audience of the sons of *H* ... Gen 23:16 2845
the presence of the children of *H* ... Gen 23:18 2845
a buryingplace by the sons of *H* ... Gen 23:20 2845
purchased of the sons of *H* ... Gen 25:10 2845
because of the daughters of *H* ... Gen 27:46 2845
take a wife of the daughters of *H* ... Gen 27:46 2845
was from the children of *H* ... Gen 49:32 2845
begat Zidon his firstborn, and *H* ... 1Chr 1:13 2845

HETHLON *(heth'-lon)* {2} *A place in northern Palestine.*
from the great sea, the way of *H* ... Eze 47:15 2855
end to the coast of the way of *H* ... Eze 48:1 2855

HEW {12}
H thee two tables of stone like ... Ex 34:1 6458
H thee two tables of stone like ... Deut 10:1 6458
ye shall *h* down the graven images ... Deut 12:3 1438
wood with his neighbour to *h* wood ... Deut 19:5 2404
command thou that they *h* me cedar ... 1Kin 5:6 3772
h timber like unto the Sidonians ... 1Kin 5:6 3772
and Hiram's builders did *h* them ... 1Kin 5:18 6458
he set masons to *h* wrought stones ... 1Chr 22:2 2672
thousand to *h* in the mountain ... 2Chr 2:2 2672
H ye down trees, and cast a mount ... Jer 6:6 3772
H down the tree, and cut off his ... Dan 4:14 1414
H the tree down, and destroy it ... Dan 4:23 1414

HEWED {13}
he *h* two tables of stone like ... Ex 34:4 6458
h two tables of stone like unto ... Deut 10:3 6458
h them in pieces, and sent them ... 1Sa 11:7 5408
Samuel *h* Agag in pieces before ... 1Sa 15:33 8158
h stones, to lay the foundation ... 1Kin 5:17 1496
court with three rows of *h* stone ... 1Kin 6:36 1496
to the measures of *h* stones ... 1Kin 7:9 1496
after the measures of *h* stones ... 1Kin 7:11 1496
was with three rows of *h* stones ... 1Kin 7:12 1496
h stone to repair the breaches of ... 2Kin 12:12 4274
that thou hast *h* thee out a ... Is 22:16 2672
h them out cisterns, broken ... Jer 2:13 2672
Therefore have I *h* them by the ... Hos 6:5 2672

HEWER {1}
from the *h* of thy wood unto the ... Deut 29:11 2404

HEWERS {9}
but let them be *h* of wood ... Josh 9:21 2404
h of wood and drawers of water for ... Josh 9:23 2404
made them that day *h* of wood ... Josh 9:27 2404
thousand *h* in the mountains ... 1Kin 5:15 2672
h of stone, and to buy timber and ... 2Kin 12:12 2672
workmen with thee in abundance, *h* ... 1Chr 22:15 2672
the *h* that cut timber, twenty ... 2Chr 2:10 2404
thousand to be *h* in the mountain ... 2Chr 2:18 2672
her with axes, as *h* of wood ... Jer 46:22 2404

HEWETH {3}
against him that *h* therewith ... Is 10:15 2672
as he that *h* him out an sepulchre ... Is 22:16 2672
He *h* him down cedars, and taketh ... Is 44:14 3772

HEWN {17}
shalt not build it of *h* stone ... Ex 20:25 1496
h stone to repair the house ... 2Kin 22:6 4274
gave they it, to buy *h* stone ... 2Chr 34:11 4274
she hath *h* out her seven pillars ... Prov 9:1 2672
but we will build with *h* stones ... Is 9:10 1496
ones of stature shall be *h* down ... Is 10:33 1438
Lebanon is ashamed and *h* down ... Is 33:9 7060
unto the rock whence ye are *h* ... Is 51:1 2672
inclosed my ways with *h* stone ... Lam 3:9 1496
the four tables were of *h* stone ... Eze 40:42 1496
ye have built houses of *h* stone ... Amos 5:11 1496
not forth good fruit is *h* down ... Mt 3:10 *1581*
not forth good fruit is *h* down ... Mt 7:19 *1581*
which he had *h* out in the rock ... Mt 27:60 *2998*
which was *h* out of a rock ... Mk 15:46 *2998*
not forth good fruit is *h* down ... Lk 3:9 *1581*
a sepulchre that was *h* in stone ... Lk 23:53 *2991*

HEZEKI *(hez'-e-ki)* {1} *A Benjamite.*
And Zebadiah, and Meshullam, and *H* ... 1Chr 8:17 2395

HEZEKIAH *(hez-e-ki'-ah)* {128} See EZEKIAS, HIZKIAH.
1. Son of King Ahaz.
H his son reigned in his stead ... 2Kin 16:20 2396
that *H* the son of Ahaz king of ... 2Kin 18:1 2396
pass in the fourth year of king *H* ... 2Kin 18:9 2396
even in the sixth year of *H* ... 2Kin 18:10 2396
in the fourteenth year of king *H* ... 2Kin 18:13 2396
H king of Judah sent to the king ... 2Kin 18:14 2396
H king of Judah three hundred ... 2Kin 18:14 2396
H gave him all the silver that ... 2Kin 18:15 2396
At that time did *H* cut off the ... 2Kin 18:16 2396
from the pillars which *H* king of ... 2Kin 18:16 2396
king *H* with a great host against ... 2Kin 18:17 2396
said unto them, Speak ye now to *H* ... 2Kin 18:19 2396
whose altars *H* hath taken away, ... 2Kin 18:22 2396
the king, Let not *H* deceive you ... 2Kin 18:29 2396
Neither let *H* make you trust in ... 2Kin 18:30 2396
Hearken not to *H* ... 2Kin 18:31 2396
and hearken not unto *H*, when he ... 2Kin 18:32 2396
to *H* with their clothes rent, and ... 2Kin 18:37 2396
to pass, when king *H* heard it ... 2Kin 19:1 2396
they said unto him, Thus saith *H* ... 2Kin 19:3 2396
servants of king *H* came to Isaiah ... 2Kin 19:5 2396
he sent messengers again unto *H* ... 2Kin 19:9 2396
shall ye speak to *H* king of Judah ... 2Kin 19:10 2396
H received the letter of the hand ... 2Kin 19:14 2396
H went up into the house of the ... 2Kin 19:14 2396
H prayed before the LORD, and said ... 2Kin 19:15 2396
Isaiah the son of Amoz sent to *H* ... 2Kin 19:20 2396
those days was *H* sick unto death ... 2Kin 20:1 2396
And *H* wept sore ... 2Kin 20:3 2396
tell *H* the captain of my people, ... 2Kin 20:5 2396
H said unto Isaiah, What shall be ... 2Kin 20:8 2396
H answered, It is a light thing ... 2Kin 20:10 2396
sent letters and a present unto *H* ... 2Kin 20:12 2396
he had heard that *H* had been sick ... 2Kin 20:12 2396
H hearkened unto them, and shewed ... 2Kin 20:13 2396
dominion, that *H* shewed them not ... 2Kin 20:13 2396
Isaiah the prophet unto king *H* ... 2Kin 20:14 2396
H said, They are come from a far ... 2Kin 20:14 2396
H answered, All the things that ... 2Kin 20:15 2396
And Isaiah said unto *H*, Hear the ... 2Kin 20:16 2396
Then said *H* unto Isaiah, Good is ... 2Kin 20:19 2396
And the rest of the acts of *H* ... 2Kin 20:20 2396
And *H* slept with his fathers ... 2Kin 20:21 2396
which *H* his father had destroyed ... 2Kin 21:3 2396
H his son, Manasseh his son, ... 1Chr 3:13 2396
in the days of *H* king of Judah ... 1Chr 4:41 2396
H his son reigned in his stead ... 2Chr 28:27 2396
H began to reign when he was five ... 2Chr 29:1 2396
Then they went in to *H* the king ... 2Chr 29:18 2396
Then *H* the king rose early, and ... 2Chr 29:20 2396
H commanded to offer the burnt ... 2Chr 29:27 2396
Moreover *H* the king and the ... 2Chr 29:30 2396
Then *H* answered and said, Now ye ... 2Chr 29:31 2396
H rejoiced, and all the people, ... 2Chr 29:36 2396
H sent to all Israel and Judah, and ... 2Chr 30:1 2396
But *H* prayed for them, saying, ... 2Chr 30:18 2396
And the LORD hearkened to *H* ... 2Chr 30:20 2396
H spake comfortably unto all the ... 2Chr 30:22 2396
For *H* king of Judah did give to ... 2Chr 30:24 2396
H appointed the courses of the ... 2Chr 31:2 2396
And when *H* and the princes came and ... 2Chr 31:8 2396
Then *H* questioned with the ... 2Chr 31:9 2396
Then *H* commanded to prepare ... 2Chr 31:11 2396
at the commandment of *H* the king ... 2Chr 31:13 2396
thus did *H* throughout all Judah, ... 2Chr 31:20 2396
when *H* saw that Sennacherib was ... 2Chr 32:2 2396
upon the words of *H* king of Judah ... 2Chr 32:8 2396
unto *H* king of Judah, and unto ... 2Chr 32:9 2396
Doth not *H* persuade you to give ... 2Chr 32:11 2396
Hath not the same *H* taken away ... 2Chr 32:12 2396
therefore let not *H* deceive you ... 2Chr 32:15 2396
God, and against his servant *H* ... 2Chr 32:16 2396
so shall not the God of *H* deliver ... 2Chr 32:17 2396
And for this cause *H* the king ... 2Chr 32:20 2396
Thus the LORD saved *H* and the ... 2Chr 32:22 2396
presents to *H* king of Judah ... 2Chr 32:23 2396
In those days *H* was sick to the ... 2Chr 32:24 2396
But *H* rendered not again ... 2Chr 32:25 2396
Notwithstanding *H* humbled himself ... 2Chr 32:26 2396
not upon them in the days of *H* ... 2Chr 32:26 2396
H had exceeding much riches and ... 2Chr 32:27 2396
This same *H* also stopped the ... 2Chr 32:30 2396
H prospered in all his works ... 2Chr 32:30 2396
Now the rest of the acts of *H* ... 2Chr 32:32 2396
H slept with his fathers, and they ... 2Chr 32:33 2396
H his father had broken down ... 2Chr 33:3 2396
which the men of *H* king of Judah ... Prov 25:1 2396
of Uzziah, Jotham, Ahaz, and *H* ... Is 1:1 2396
in the fourteenth year of king *H* ... Is 36:1 2396
unto king *H* with a great army ... Is 36:2 2396
said unto them, Say ye now to *H* ... Is 36:4 2396
whose altars *H* hath taken away, ... Is 36:7 2396
the king, Let not *H* deceive you ... Is 36:14 2396
Neither let *H* make you trust in ... Is 36:15 2396
Hearken not to *H* ... Is 36:16 2396
Beware lest *H* persuade you, ... Is 36:18 2396
to *H* with their clothes rent, and ... Is 36:22 2396
to pass, when king *H* heard it ... Is 37:1 2396
they said unto him, Thus saith *H* ... Is 37:3 2396
servants of king *H* came to Isaiah ... Is 37:5 2396
heard it, he sent messengers to *H* ... Is 37:9 2396
shall ye speak to *H* king of Judah ... Is 37:10 2396
H received the letter from the ... Is 37:14 2396
H went up unto the house of the ... Is 37:14 2396
H prayed unto the LORD, saying, ... Is 37:15 2396
the son of Amoz sent unto *H* ... Is 37:21 2396
those days was *H* sick unto death ... Is 38:1 2396
Then *H* turned his face toward the ... Is 38:2 2396
And *H* wept sore ... Is 38:3 2396
Go, and say to *H*, Thus saith the ... Is 38:5 2396
The writing of *H* king of Judah ... Is 38:9 2396
H also had said, What is the sign ... Is 38:22 2396
sent letters and a present to *H* ... Is 39:1 2396
H was glad of them, and shewed ... Is 39:2 2396
dominion, that *H* shewed them not ... Is 39:2 2396
Isaiah the prophet unto king *H* ... Is 39:3 2396
H said, They are come from a far ... Is 39:3 2396
H answered, All that is in mine ... Is 39:4 2396

Then said Isaiah to *H*, Hear the .... Is 39:5 2396
Then said *H* to Isaiah, Good is .... Is 39:8 2396
the son of *H* king of Judah .... Jer 15:4 2396
in the days of *H* king of Judah .... Jer 26:18 2396
Did *H* king of Judah and all Judah .... Jer 26:19 2396
of Uzziah, Jotham, Ahaz, and *H* .... Hos 1:1 2396
in the days of Jotham, Ahaz, and *H* .... Mic 1:1 2396
2. A son of Neariah.
Elioenai, and *H*, and Azrikam, three 1Chr 3:23 2396
3. A family of exiles.
The children of Ater of *H* .... Ezr 2:16 2396
The children of Ater of *H* .... Neh 7:21 2396

HEZION *(he'-zi-on)* {1} *Grandfather of King Ben-hadad of Syria.*
the son of Tabrimon, the son of *H* 1Kin 15:18 2383

HEZIR *(he'-zir)* {2}
1. A sanctuary servant.
The seventeenth to *H*, the 1Chr 24:15 2387
2. An Israelite who renewed the covenant.
Magpiash, Meshullam, *H*, ... Neh 10:20 2387

HEZRAI *(hez'-rahee)* {1} See HEZRO. *A "mighty man" of David.*
H the Carmelite, Paarai the 2Sa 23:35 2695

HEZRO *(hez'-ro)* {1} See HEZRAI. *Same as Hezrai.*
H the Carmelite, Naarai the son 1Chr 11:37 2695

HEZRON *(hez'-ron)* {17} See HAZOR, HEZRONITES, HEZBON'S.
1. Son of Pharez.
And the sons of Pharez were *H* .... Gen 46:12 2696
Of *H*, the family of the .... Num 26:6 2696
of *H*, the family of the .... Num 26:21 2696
Pharez begat *H*, ... Ruth 4:18 2696
H begat Ram, and Ram begat .... Ruth 4:19 2696
of Pharez; *H*, and Hamul 1Chr 2:5 2696
The sons also of *H*, that were 1Chr 2:9 2696
Caleb the son of *H* begat children 1Chr 2:18 2696
afterward *H* went in to the 1Chr 2:21 2696
And after that *H* was dead in 1Chr 2:24 2696
Jerahmeel the firstborn of *H* were 1Chr 2:25 2696
Pharez, *H*, and Carmi, and Hur, and 1Chr 4:1 2696
2. A son of Reuben.
and Phallu, and *H*, and Carmi .... Gen 46:9 2696
Hanoch, and Pallu, *H*, and Carmi .... Ex 6:14 2696
Israel were, Hanoch, and Pallu, *H* 1Chr 5:3 2696
3. A town in Judah.
and passed along to *H*, and went up .... Josh 15:3 2696
Hazor, Hadattah, and Kerioth, and *H* .... Josh 15:25 2696

HEZRONITES *(hez'-ron-ites)* {2} *Descendants of Hezron 2.*
Of Hezron, the family of the *H* .... Num 26:6 2697
of Hezron, the family of the *H* .... Num 26:21 2697

HEZRON'S *(hez'-ronz)* {1} *Refers to Hezron 2.*
then Abiah *H* wife bare him Ashur 1Chr 2:24 2696

HID {129}
his wife *h* themselves from the .... Gen 3:8 2244
and I *h* myself .... Gen 3:10 2244
and from thy face shall I be *h* .... Gen 4:14 5641
Jacob *h* them under the oak which .... Gen 35:4 2934
child, she *h* him three months .... Ex 2:2 6845
Egyptian, and *h* him in the sand .... Ex 2:12 2934
And Moses *h* his face .... Ex 3:6 5641
the thing be *h* from the eyes of .... Lev 4:13 5956
withal, and it be *h* from him .... Lev 5:3 5956
with an oath, and it be *h* from him .... Lev 5:4 5956
it be *h* from the eyes of her .... Num 5:13 5956
and of treasures *h* in the sand .... Deut 33:19 2934
h them, and said thus, There came .... Josh 2:4 6845
h them with the stalks of flax, ... Josh 2:6 2934
because she *h* the messengers that .... Josh 6:17 2244
because she *h* the messengers, ... Josh 6:25 2244
they are *h* in the earth in the .... Josh 7:21 2934
it was *h* in his tent, and the .... Josh 7:22 2934
h themselves in a cave at .... Josh 10:16 2244
are found *h* in a cave at Makkedah .... Josh 10:17 2244
the cave wherein they had been *h* .... Josh 10:27 2244
for he *h* himself .... Judg 9:5 2244
every whit, and *h* nothing from him 1Sa 3:18 3582
he hath *h* himself among the stuff 1Sa 10:22 2244
holes where they had *h* themselves 1Sa 14:11 2244
had *h* themselves in mount Ephraim 1Sa 14:22 2244
So David *h* himself in the field 1Sa 20:24 5641
he is *h* now in some pit, or in 2Sa 17:9 2244
is no matter *h* from the king 2Sa 18:13 3582
was not any thing *h* from the king 1Kin 10:3 5956
h them by fifty in a cave, and fed 1Kin 18:4 2244
how I *h* an hundred men of the 1Kin 18:13 2244
and the LORD hath *h* it from me 2Kin 4:27 5956
and she hath *h* her son 2Kin 6:29 2244
gold, and raiment, and went and *h* it 2Kin 7:8 2934
thence also, and went and *h* it 2Kin 7:8 2934
and they *h* him, even him and his 2Kin 11:2 5641
he was with her *h* in the house of 2Kin 11:3 2244
four sons with him *h* themselves 1Chr 21:20 2244
there was nothing *h* from Solomon 2Chr 9:2 5956
him, (for he was *h* in Samaria 2Chr 22:9 2244
h him from Athaliah, so that she 2Chr 22:11 5641
he was with them *h* in the house 2Chr 22:12 2244
nor *h* sorrow from mine eyes .... Job 3:10 5641
for it more than for *h* treasures .... Job 3:21 4301
given to a man whose way is *h* .... Job 3:23 5641
Thou shalt be *h* from the scourge .... Job 5:21 2244
the ice, and wherein the snow is *h* .... Job 6:16 5956
things hast thou *h* in thine heart .... Job 10:13 6845
their fathers, and have not *h* it .... Job 15:18 3582
For thou hast *h* their heart from .... Job 17:4 6845
shall be *h* in his secret places .... Job 20:26 2244
the thing that is *h* bringeth he .... Job 28:11 8587
Seeing it is *h* from the eyes of .... Job 28:21 5956
young men saw me, and *h* themselves .... Job 29:8 2244
The waters are *h* as with a stone, ... Job 38:30 2244
in the net which they *h* is their .... Ps 9:15 2934
thou fillest with thy *h* treasure .... Ps 17:14 6845
there is nothing *h* from the heat .... Ps 19:6 5641
neither hath he *h* his face from .... Ps 22:24 5641
and mine iniquity have I not *h* .... Ps 32:5 3680
they *h* for me their net in a pit .... Ps 35:7 2934
net that he hath *h* catch himself .... Ps 35:8 2934
and my groaning is not *h* from thee .... Ps 38:9 5641
I have not *h* thy righteousness .... Ps 40:10 3680
I would have *h* myself from him .... Ps 55:12 5641
and my sins are not *h* from thee .... Ps 69:5 3582
Thy word have I *h* in mine heart .... Ps 119:11 6845
My substance was not *h* from thee .... Ps 139:15 3582
The proud have *h* a snare for me .... Ps 140:5 2934
for her as for *h* treasures .... Prov 2:4 4301
falsehood have we *h* ourselves .... Is 28:15 5641
of their prudent men shall be *h* .... Is 29:14 5641
My way is *h* from the LORD, and my .... Is 40:27 5641
they are *h* in prison houses .... Is 42:22 2244
shadow of his hand hath he *h* me .... Is 49:2 2244
in his quiver hath he *h* me .... Is 49:2 5641
I *h* not my face from shame and .... Is 50:6 5641
we *h* as it were our faces from .... Is 53:3 5641
In a little wrath I *h* my face .... Is 54:8 5641
I *h* me, and was wroth, and he went .... Is 57:17 5641
your sins have *h* his face from .... Is 59:2 5641
for thou hast *h* thy face from us, ... Is 64:7 5641
because they are *h* from mine eyes .... Is 65:16 5641
h it by Euphrates, as the LORD .... Jer 13:5 2934
from the place where I had *h* it .... Jer 13:7 2934
they are not *h* from my face .... Jer 16:17 5641
their iniquity *h* from mine eyes .... Jer 16:17 6845
take me, and *h* snares for my feet .... Jer 18:22 2934
I have *h* my face from this city .... Jer 33:5 5641
but the LORD *h* them .... Jer 36:26 5641
upon these stones that I have *h* .... Jer 43:10 2934
have *h* their eyes from my .... Eze 22:26 5956
therefore *h* I my face from them, ... Eze 39:23 5641
unto them, and *h* my face from them .... Eze 39:24 5641
and Israel is not *h* from me .... Hos 5:3 3582
his sin is *h* .... Hos 13:12 6845
shall be *h* from mine eyes .... Hos 13:14 5641
though they be *h* from my sight in .... Amos 9:3 5641
thou shalt be *h*, thou also shalt .... Nah 3:11 5956
it may be ye shall be *h* in the .... Zeph 2:3 5641
is set on an hill cannot be *h* .... Mt 5:14 *2928*
and *h*, that shall not be known .... Mt 10:26 *2927*
because thou hast *h* these things .... Mt 11:25 *613*
h in three measures of meal, till .... Mt 13:33 *1470*
like unto treasure *h* in a field .... Mt 13:44 *2928*
the earth, and *h* his lord's money .... Mt 25:18 *613*
h thy talent in the earth .... Mt 25:25 *2928*
For there is nothing *h*, which .... Mk 4:22 *2927*
but he could not be *h* .... Mk 7:24 *2990*
h herself five months, saying, ... Lk 1:24 *4032*
neither any thing *h*, that shall .... Lk 8:17 *614*
the woman saw that she was not *h* .... Lk 8:47 *2990*
it was *h* from them, that they .... Lk 9:45 *3871*
that thou hast *h* these things .... Lk 10:21 *613*
neither *h*, that shall not be .... Lk 12:2 *2927*
h in three measures of meal, till .... Lk 13:21 *1470*
and this saying was *h* from them .... Lk 18:34 *2928*
now they are *h* from thine eyes .... Lk 19:42 *2928*
but Jesus *h* himself, and went out .... Jn 8:59 *2928*
But if our gospel be *h*, it is *h* 2Cor 4:3 *2572*
of the world hath been *h* in God .... Eph 3:9 *613*
which hath been *h* from ages .... Col 1:26 *613*
In whom are *h* all the treasures .... Col 2:3 *614*
your life is *h* with Christ in God .... Col 3:3 *2928*
that are otherwise cannot be *h* 1Ti 5:25 *2928*
was *h* three months of his parents .... Heb 11:23 *2928*
h themselves in the dens and in .... Rev 6:15 *2928*

HIDDAI *(hid'-dahee)* {1} See HURAI. *A "mighty man" of David.*
H of the brooks of Gaash, ... 2Sa 23:30 1914

HIDDEKEL *(hid'-de-kel)* {2} *A name for the Tigris River.*
the name of the third river is *H* .... Gen 2:14 2313
of the great river, which is *H* .... Dan 10:4 2313

HIDDEN {17}
things, and if it be *h* from him .... Lev 5:2 5956
this day, it is not *h* from thee .... Deut 30:11 6381
Or as an *h* untimely birth I had .... Job 3:16 2934
of years is *h* to the oppressor .... Job 15:20 6845
times are not *h* from the Almighty .... Job 24:1 6845
in the *h* part thou shalt make me .... Ps 51:6 5640
and consulted against thy *h* ones .... Ps 83:3 6845
when the wicked rise, a man is *h* .... Prov 28:12 2664
h riches of secret places, that .... Is 45:3 4301
even *h* things, and thou didst not .... Is 48:6 5341
how are his *h* things sought up .... Obad 6 4710
of these things are *h* from him .... Acts 26:26 *2990*
in a mystery, even the *h* wisdom 1Cor 2:7 *613*
to light the *h* things of darkness 1Cor 4:5 *2927*
the *h* things of dishonesty 2Cor 4:2 *2927*
let it be the *h* man of the heart 1Pet 3:4 *2927*
will I give to eat of the *h* manna .... Rev 2:17 *2928*

HIDE {83}
Shall I *h* from Abraham that thing .... Gen 18:17 3680
We will not *h* it from my lord, ... Gen 47:18 3582
when she could not longer *h* him .... Ex 2:3 6845
But the bullock, and his *h* .... Lev 8:17 5785
the *h* he burnt with fire without .... Lev 9:11 5785
ways *h* their eyes from the man .... Lev 20:4 5956
h themselves from thee, be .... Deut 7:20 5641
go astray, and *h* thyself from them .... Deut 22:1 5956
thou mayest not *h* thyself .... Deut 22:3 5956
the way, and *h* thyself from them .... Deut 22:4 5956
I will *h* my face from them, and .... Deut 31:17 5641
I will surely *h* my face in that .... Deut 31:18 5641
I will *h* my face from them, I .... Deut 32:20 5641
h yourselves there three days, ... Josh 2:16 2247
h it not from me .... Josh 7:19 3582
to *h* it from the Midianites .... Judg 6:11 5127
I pray thee *h* it not from me 1Sa 3:17 3582
if thou *h* any thing from me of 1Sa 3:17 3582
people did *h* themselves in caves 1Sa 13:6 2244
in a secret place, and *h* thyself 1Sa 19:2 2244
my father *h* this thing from me 1Sa 20:2 5641
that I may *h* myself in the field 1Sa 20:5 5641
h thyself when the business was 1Sa 20:19 5641
Doth not David *h* himself with us 1Sa 23:19 5641
Doth not David *h* himself in the 1Sa 26:1 5641
H not from me, I pray thee, the 2Sa 14:18 3582
h thyself by the brook Cherith, ... 1Kin 17:3 5641
an inner chamber to *h* thyself 1Kin 22:25 2247
camp to *h* themselves in the field 2Kin 7:12 2247
an inner chamber to *h* thyself 2Chr 18:24 2244
then I will not *h* myself from .... Job 13:20 5641
thou wouldest *h* me in the grave .... Job 14:13 6845
though he *h* it under his tongue .... Job 20:12 3582
the earth *h* themselves together .... Job 24:4 2244
his purpose, and *h* pride from man .... Job 33:17 3680
of iniquity may *h* themselves .... Job 34:22 5641
H them in the dust together .... Job 40:13 2934
long wilt thou *h* thy face from me .... Ps 13:1 5641
h me under the shadow of thy .... Ps 17:8 5641
he shall *h* me in his pavilion .... Ps 27:5 6845
of his tabernacle shall he *h* me .... Ps 27:5 5641
H not thy face far from me .... Ps 27:9 5641
thou didst *h* thy face, and I was .... Ps 30:7 5641
Thou shalt *h* them in the secret .... Ps 31:20 5641
H thy face from my sins, and blot .... Ps 51:9 5641
Doth not David *h* himself with us .... Ps 54:*t* 5641
and *h* not thyself from my .... Ps 55:1 5956
they *h* themselves, they mark my .... Ps 56:6 6845
H me from the secret counsel of .... Ps 64:2 5641
h not thy face from thy servant .... Ps 69:17 5641
We will not *h* them from their .... Ps 78:4 3582
wilt thou *h* thyself for ever .... Ps 89:46 5641
H not thy face from me in the day .... Ps 102:2 5641
h not thy commandments from me .... Ps 119:19 5641
h not thy face from me, lest I be .... Ps 143:7 5641
I flee unto thee to *h* me .... Ps 143:9 3680
h my commandments with thee .... Prov 2:1 6845
the wicked rise, men *h* themselves .... Prov 28:28 5641
I will *h* mine eyes from you .... Is 1:15 5956
h thee in the dust, for fear of .... Is 2:10 2934
their sin as Sodom, they *h* it not .... Is 3:9 3582
h the outcasts .... Is 16:3 5641
h thyself as it were for a little .... Is 26:20 2247
to *h* their counsel from the LORD .... Is 29:15 5641
that thou *h* not thyself from .... Is 58:7 5956
h it there in a hole of the rock .... Jer 13:4 2934
which I commanded thee to *h* there .... Jer 13:6 2934
Can any *h* himself in secret .... Jer 23:24 5641
Go, *h* thee, thou and Jeremiah .... Jer 36:19 5641
h nothing from me .... Jer 38:14 3582
h it not from us, and we will not .... Jer 38:25 3582
h them in the clay in the .... Jer 43:9 2934
he shall not be able to *h* himself .... Jer 49:10 2247
h not thine ear at my breathing, ... Lam 3:56 5956
secret that they can *h* from thee .... Eze 28:3 6004
the garden of God could not *h* him .... Eze 31:8 6004
Neither will I *h* my face any more .... Eze 39:29 5641
so that they fled to *h* themselves .... Dan 10:7 2244
though they *h* themselves in the .... Amos 9:3 2244
he will even *h* his face from them .... Mic 3:4 5641
and did *h* himself from them .... Jn 12:36 *2928*
shall *h* a multitude of sins .... Jas 5:20 *2572*
h us from the face of him that .... Rev 6:16 *2928*

HIDEST {6}
Wherefore *h* thou thy face, and .... Job 13:24 5641
why *h* thou thyself in times of .... Ps 10:1 5956
Wherefore *h* thou thy face, and .... Ps 44:24 5641
why *h* thou thy face from me .... Ps 88:14 5641
Thou *h* thy face, they are .... Ps 104:29 5641
thou art a God that *h* thyself .... Is 45:15 5641

HIDETH {16}
lurking places where he *h* himself 1Sa 23:23 2244
he *h* himself on the right hand, ... Job 23:9 5848
when he *h* his face, who then can .... Job 34:29 5641
Who is he that *h* counsel without .... Job 42:3 5956
he *h* his face .... Ps 10:11 5641
the darkness *h* not from thee .... Ps 139:12 2821
He that *h* hatred with lying lips, ... Prov 10:18 3680
A slothful man *h* his hand in his .... Prov 19:24 2934
foreseeth the evil, and *h* himself .... Prov 22:3 5641
The slothful *h* his hand in his .... Prov 26:15 2934
foreseeth the evil, and *h* himself .... Prov 27:12 5641
Whosoever *h* her *h* the wind, ... Prov 27:16 6845
but he that *h* his eyes shall have .... Prov 28:27 5956
that *h* his face from the house of .... Is 8:17 5641
which when a man hath found, he *h* .... Mt 13:44 *2928*

HIDING {6}
by *h* mine iniquity in my bosom .... Job 31:33 2934
Thou art my *h* place .... Ps 32:7 5643
Thou art my *h* place and my shield .... Ps 119:114 5643

waters shall overflow the *h* place Is 28:17 5643
be as an *h* place from the wind Is 32:2 4224
and there was the *h* of his power Hab 3:4 2253

HIEL *(hi'-el)* {1} *A Bethelite.*
In his days did *H* the Beth-elite 1Kin 16:34 2419

HIERAPOLIS *(hi-e-rap'-o-lis)* {1} *A city in Phrygia.*
are in Laodicea, and them in *H* Col 4:13 *2404*

HIGGAION *(hig-gah'-yon)* {1} *A musical notation.*
work of his own hands. *H.* Ps 9:16 1902

HIGH See APPENDIX.

HIGHER {21}
and his king shall be *h* than Agag Num 24:7 7311
upward he was *h* than any of the 1Sa 9:2 1364
he was *h* than any of the people 1Sa 10:23 1361
He built the *h* gate of the house 2Kin 15:35 5945
the wall, and on the *h* places Neh 4:13 6706
the clouds which are *h* than thou Job 35:5 1361
me to the rock that is *h* than I Ps 61:2 7311
h than the kings of the earth Ps 89:27 5945
for he that is *h* than the highest Eccl 5:8 1364
and there be *h* than they Eccl 5:8 1364
the heavens are *h* than the earth Is 55:9 1361
so are my ways *h* than your ways Is 55:9 1361
the scribe, in the *h* court Jer 36:10 5945
came from the way of the *h* gate Eze 9:2 5945
the galleries were *h* than these Eze 42:5 3201
this shall be the *h* place of the Eze 43:13 1354
but one was *h* than the other Dan 8:3 1364
and the *h* came up last Dan 8:3 1364
say unto thee, Friend, go up *h* Lk 14:10 *511*
soul be subject unto the *h* powers Rom 13:1 *5242*
and made *h* than the heavens Heb 7:26 *5308*

HIGHEST {18}
heavens, and the *H* gave his voice Ps 18:13 5945
the *h* himself shall establish her Ps 87:5 5945
nor the *h* part of the dust of the Prov 8:26 7218
upon the *h* places of the city Prov 9:3 4791
is higher than the *h* regardeth Eccl 5:8 1364
took the *h* branch of the cedar Eze 17:3 6788
I will also take of the *h* branch Eze 17:22 6788
chamber to the *h* by the midst Eze 41:7 5945
Hosanna in the *h* Mt 21:9 *5310*
Hosanna in the *h* Mk 11:10 *5310*
shall be called the Son of the *H* Lk 1:32 *5310*
thee, and the power of the *H* shall Lk 1:35 *5310*
be called the prophet of the *H* Lk 1:76 *5310*
Glory to God in the *h*, and on Lk 2:14 *5310*
ye shall be the children of the *H* Lk 6:35 *5310*
sit not down in the *h* room Lk 14:8 *4411*
in heaven, and glory in the *h* Lk 19:38 *5310*
the *h* seats in the synagogues, and Lk 20:46 *4410*

HIGHLY {6}
Hail, thou that art *h* favoured Lk 1:28
for that which is *h* esteemed Lk 16:15 *5308*
Herod was *h* displeased with them Acts 12:20 *2371*
more *h* than he ought to think Rom 12:3 *5252*
God also hath *h* exalted him Phil 2:9 *5251*
to esteem them very *h* in love for 1Th 5:13 *1537,4053*

HIGHMINDED {3}
Be not *h*, but fear Rom 11:20 *5309*
in this world, that they be not *h* 1Ti 6:17 *5309*
Traitors, heady, *h*, lovers of 2Ti 3:4 *5187*

HIGHNESS {2}
by reason of his *h* I could not Job 31:23 7613
even them that rejoice in my *h* Is 13:3 1346

HIGHWAY {15}
on the east side of the *h* that Judg 21:19 4546
Beth-shemesh, and went along the *h* 1Sa 6:12 4546
in blood in the midst of the *h* 2Sa 20:12 4546
Amasa out of the *h* into the field 2Sa 20:12 4546
When he was removed out of the *h* 2Sa 20:13 4546
which is in the *h* of the fuller's 2Kin 18:17 4546
The *h* of the upright is to depart Prov 16:17 4546
in the *h* of the fuller's field Is 7:3 4546
there shall be an *h* for the Is 11:16 4546
be a *h* out of Egypt to Assyria Is 19:23 4546
an *h* shall be there, and a way, and Is 35:8 4547
in the *h* of the fuller's field Is 36:2 4546
in the desert a *h* for our God Is 40:3 4546
set thine heart toward the *h* Jer 31:21 4546
sat by the *h* side begging Mk 10:46 *3598*

HIGHWAYS {11}
the *h* were unoccupied, and the Judg 5:6 734
kill, as at other times, in the *h* Judg 20:31 4546
them from the city unto the *h* Judg 20:32 4546
them in the *h* five thousand men Judg 20:45 4546
The *h* lie waste, the wayfaring Is 33:8 4546
a way, and my *h* shall be exalted Is 49:11 4546
cast up, cast up the *h* Is 62:10 4546
and they shall say in all the *h* Amos 5:16 2351
Go ye therefore into the *h* Mt 22:9 *1327,3598*
servants went out into the *h* Mt 22:10 *3598*
the servant, Go out into the *h* Lk 14:23 *3598*

HILEN *(hi'-len)* {1} See HOLON. *A Levitical city in Judah.*
H with her suburbs, Debir with 1Chr 6:58 2432

HILKIAH *(hil-ki'-ah)* {33} See HELKAI, HILKIAH'S.
1. Father of Eliakim.
out to them Eliakim the son of *H* 2Kin 18:18 2518
Then said Eliakim the son of *H* 2Kin 18:26 2518
Then came Eliakim the son of *H* 2Kin 18:37 2518
And Shallum begat *H* 1Chr 6:13 2518
and *H* begat Azariah 1Chr 6:13 2518
Of *H*, Hashabiah; of Jedaiah Neh 12:21 2518
my servant Eliakim the son of *H* Is 22:20 2518
Then came Eliakim, the son of *H* Is 36:22 2518
2. A high priest.
Go up to *H* the high priest, that 2Kin 22:4 2518
H the high priest said unto 2Kin 22:8 2518
H gave the book to Shaphan, and he 2Kin 22:8 2518
H the priest hath delivered me a 2Kin 22:10 2518
the king commanded *H* the priest 2Kin 22:12 2518
So *H* the priest, and Ahikam, and 2Kin 22:14 2518
king commanded *H* the high priest 2Kin 23:4 2518
H the priest found in the house 2Kin 23:24 2518
And Azariah the son of *H*, the son 1Chr 9:11 2518
they came to *H* the high priest 2Chr 34:9 2518
H the priest found a book of the 2Chr 34:14 2518
H answered and said to Shaphan the 2Chr 34:15 2518
H delivered the book to Shaphan 2Chr 34:15 2518
H the priest hath given me a book 2Chr 34:18 2518
And the king commanded *H*, and 2Chr 34:20 2518
And *H*, and they that the king had 2Chr 34:22 2518
H and Zechariah and Jehiel, rulers 2Chr 35:8 2518
the son of Azariah, the son of *H* Ezr 7:1 2518
Shaphan, and Gemariah the son of *H* Jer 29:3 2518
3. A descendant of Merari.
the son of Amaziah, the son of *H* 1Chr 6:45 2518
4. A son of Hosah.
H the second, Tebaliah the third, 1Chr 26:11 2518
5. A priest who assisted Ezra.
Anaiah, and Urijah, and *H* Neh 8:4 2518
Seraiah the son of *H*, the son of Neh 11:11 2518
Sallu, Amok, *H*, Jedaiah Neh 12:7 2518
6. Father of Jeremiah.
words of Jeremiah the son of *H* Jer 1:1 2518

HILKIAH'S *(hil-ki'-ahs)* {1} *Refers to Hilkiah 1.*
H son, which was over the house, Is 36:3 2518

HILL {76}
the *h* with the rod of God in mine Ex 17:9 1389
Hur went up to the top of the *h* Ex 17:10 1389
and builded an altar under the *h* Ex 24:4 2022
presumed to go up unto the *h* top Num 14:44 2022
Canaanites which dwelt in that *h* Num 14:45 2022
ye were ready to go up into the *h* Deut 1:41 2022
went presumptuously up into the *h* Deut 1:43 2022
Israel at the *h* of the foreskins Josh 5:3 1389
the *h* country from Lebanon unto Josh 13:6 2022
was drawn from the top of the *h* Josh 15:9 2022
The *h* is not enough for us Josh 17:16 2022
near the *h* that lieth on the Josh 18:13 2022
from the *h* that lieth before Josh 18:14 2022
in the *h* country of Judah, with Josh 21:11 2022
the north side of the *h* of Gaash Josh 24:30 2022
they buried him in a *h* that Josh 24:33 1389
on the north side of the *h* Gaash Judg 2:9 2022
by the *h* of Moreh, in the valley Judg 7:1 1389
top of an *h* that is before Hebron Judg 16:3 2022
the house of Abinadab in the *h* 1Sa 7:1 1389
as they went up the *h* to the city 1Sa 9:11 4608
thou shalt come to the *h* of God 1Sa 10:5 1389
when they came thither to the *h* 1Sa 10:10 1389
in the *h* of Hachilah, which is on 1Sa 23:19 1389
came down by the covert of the *h* 1Sa 25:20 2022
hide himself in the *h* of Hachilah 1Sa 26:1 1389
Saul pitched in the *h* of Hachilah 1Sa 26:3 1389
stood on the top of an *h* afar off 1Sa 26:13 2022
they were come to the *h* of Ammah 2Sa 2:24 1389
and stood on the top of an *h* 2Sa 2:25 1389
the way of the *h* side behind him 2Sa 13:34 2022
a little past the top of the *h* 2Sa 16:1
them in the *h* before the LORD 2Sa 21:9 2022
in the *h* that is before Jerusalem 1Kin 11:7 2022
and groves, on every high *h* 1Kin 14:23 1389
he bought the *h* Samaria of Shemer 1Kin 16:24 2022
of silver, and built on the *h* 1Kin 16:24 2022
name of Shemer, owner of the *h* 1Kin 16:24 2022
behold, he sat on the top of an *h* 2Kin 1:9 2022
came to the man of God to the *h* 2Kin 4:27 2022
images and groves in every high *h* 2Kin 17:10 1389
my king upon my holy *h* of Zion Ps 2:6 2022
and he heard me out of his holy *h* Ps 3:4 2022
who shall dwell in thy holy *h* Ps 15:1 2022
ascend into the *h* of the LORD Ps 24:3 2022
the Hermonites, from the *h* Mizar Ps 42:6 2022
let them bring me unto thy holy *h* Ps 43:3 2022
h of God is as the *h* of Bashan Ps 68:15 2022
an high *h* as the *h* of Bashan Ps 68:15 2022
this is the *h* which God desireth Ps 68:16 2022
our God, and worship at his holy *h* Ps 99:9 2022
and to the *h* of frankincense Song 4:6 1389
a vineyard in a very fruitful *h* Is 5:1 7161
of Zion, the *h* of Jerusalem Is 10:32 1389
mountain, and as an ensign on an *h* Is 30:17 1389
mountain, and upon every high *h* Is 30:25 1389
mount Zion, and for the *h* thereof Is 31:4 1389
mountain and *h* shall be made low Is 40:4 1389
when upon every high *h* and under Jer 2:20 1389
every mountain, and from every *h* Jer 16:16 1389
over against it upon the *h* Gareb Jer 31:39 1389
that holdest the height of the *h* Jer 49:16 1389
they have gone from mountain to *h* Jer 50:6 1389
their altars, upon every high *h* Eze 6:13 1389
them, then they saw every high *h* Eze 20:28 1389
mountains, and upon every high *h* Eze 34:6 1389
round about my *h* a blessing Eze 34:26 1389
that is set on an *h* cannot be hid Mt 5:14 *3735*
went into the *h* country with Lk 1:39 *3714*
all the *h* country of Judaea Lk 1:65 *3714*
and *h* shall be brought low Lk 3:5 *1015*
h whereon their city was built Lk 4:29 *3735*
they were come down from the *h* Lk 9:37 *3735*
stood in the midst of Mars' *h* Acts 17:22 *697*

HILLEL *(hil'-lel)* {2} *Father of Abdon.*
And after him Abdon the son of *H* Judg 12:13 1985
And Abdon the son of *H* the Judg 12:15 1985

HILL'S {1}
on the *h* side over against him 2Sa 16:13 2022

HILLS {65}
and all the high *h*, that were Gen 7:19 2022
utmost bound of the everlasting *h* Gen 49:26 1389
him, and from the *h* I behold him Num 23:9 1389
thereunto, in the plain, in the *h* Deut 1:7 2022
that spring out of valleys and *h* Deut 8:7 2022
out of whose *h* thou mayest dig Deut 8:9 2042
go to possess it, is a land of *h* Deut 11:11 2022
the high mountains, and upon the *h* Deut 12:2 1389
precious things of the lasting *h* Deut 33:15 1389
on this side Jordan, in the *h* Josh 9:1 2022
smote all the country of the *h* Josh 10:40 2022
Joshua took all that land, the *h* Josh 11:16 2022
him, Their gods are gods of the *h* 1Kin 20:23 2022
said, The LORD is God of the *h* 1Kin 20:28 2022
all Israel scattered upon the *h* 1Kin 22:17 2022
in the high places, and on the *h* 2Kin 16:4 1389
in the high places, and on the *h* 2Chr 28:4 1389
or wast thou made before the *h* Job 15:7 1389
foundations also of the *h* moved Ps 18:7 2022
and the cattle upon a thousand *h* Ps 50:10 2042
the little *h* rejoice on every Ps 65:12 1389
Why leap ye, ye high *h* Ps 68:16 2022
to the people, and the little *h* Ps 72:3 1389
The *h* were covered with the Ps 80:10 2022
the strength of the *h* is his also Ps 95:4 2022
The *h* melted like wax at the Ps 97:5 2022
let the *h* be joyful together Ps 98:8 2022
valleys, which run among the *h* Ps 104:10 2022
He watereth the *h* from his Ps 104:13 2022
The high *h* are a refuge for the Ps 104:18 2022
he toucheth the *h*, and they smoke Ps 104:32 2022
rams, and the little *h* like lambs Ps 114:4 1389
and ye little *h*, like lambs Ps 114:6 1389
will lift up mine eyes unto the *h* Ps 121:1 2022
Mountains, and all *h* Ps 148:9 1389
before the *h* was I brought forth Prov 8:25 1389
mountains, skipping upon the *h* Song 2:8 1389
and shall be exalted above the *h* Is 2:2 1389
upon all the *h* that are lifted up Is 2:14 1389
the *h* did tremble, and their Is 5:25 2022
on all *h* that shall be digged Is 7:25 2022
in scales, and the *h* in a balance Is 40:12 1389
and shalt make the *h* as chaff Is 41:15 1389
I will make waste mountains and *h* Is 42:15 1389
shall depart, and the *h* be removed Is 54:10 1389
the *h* shall break forth before Is 55:12 1389
and blasphemed me upon the *h* Is 65:7 1389
is salvation hoped for from the *h* Jer 3:23 1389
and all the *h* moved lightly Jer 4:24 1389
on the *h* in the fields Jer 13:27 1389
the green trees upon the high *h* Jer 17:2 1389
GOD to the mountains, and to the *h* Eze 6:3 1389
in thy *h*, and in thy valleys, and Eze 35:8 1389
GOD to the mountains, and to the *h* Eze 36:4 1389
unto the mountains, and to the *h* Eze 36:6 1389
and burn incense upon the *h* Hos 4:13 1389
and to the *h*, Fall on us Hos 10:8 1389
the *h* shall flow with milk, and Joel 3:18 1389
wine, and all the *h* shall melt Amos 9:13 1389
it shall be exalted above the *h* Mic 4:1 1389
and let the *h* hear thy voice Mic 6:1 1389
the *h* melt, and the earth is Nah 1:5 1389
the perpetual *h* did bow Hab 3:6 1389
and a great crashing from the *h* Zeph 1:10 1389
and to the *h*, Cover us Lk 23:30 *1015*

HIM See APPENDIX.

HIMSELF See APPENDIX.

HIN {22}
fourth part of an *h* of beaten oil Ex 29:40 1969
the fourth part of an *h* of wine Ex 29:40 1969
sanctuary, and of oil olive an *h* Ex 30:24 1969
a just ephah, and a just *h* Lev 19:36 1969
of wine, the fourth part of a *h* Lev 23:13 1969
the fourth part of an *h* of oil Num 15:4 1969
the fourth part of an *h* of wine Num 15:5 1969
the third part of an *h* of oil Num 15:6 1969
the third part of an *h* of wine Num 15:7 1969
mingled with half an *h* of oil Num 15:9 1969
drink offering half an *h* of wine Num 15:10 1969
fourth part of an *h* of beaten oil Num 28:5 1969
part of an *h* for the one lamb Num 28:7 1969
half an *h* of wine unto a bullock Num 28:14 1969
the third part of an *h* unto a ram Num 28:14 1969
a fourth part of an *h* unto a lamb Num 28:14 1969
measure, the sixth part of an *h* Eze 4:11 1969
ram, and an *h* of oil for an ephah Eze 45:24 1969
give, and an *h* of oil to an ephah Eze 46:5 1969
unto, and an *h* of oil to an ephah Eze 46:7 1969
give, and an *h* of oil to an ephah Eze 46:11 1969
and the third part of an *h* of oil Eze 46:14 1969

HIND {3}
Naphtali is a *h* let loose Gen 49:21 355
Let her be as the loving *h* Prov 5:19 365
the *h* also calved in the field, Jer 14:5 365

HINDER {16}
H me not, seeing the LORD hath Gen 24:56 309
h thee from coming unto me Num 22:16 4513

wherefore Abner with the *h* end of........ 2Sa 2:23 310
all their *h* parts were inward 1Kin 7:25 268
all their *h* parts were inward 2Chr 4:4 268
against Jerusalem, and to *h* it .... Neh 4:8 6213,8442
he taketh away, who can *h* him.............. Job 9:12 7725
together, then who can *h* him................ Job 11:10 7725
smote his enemies in the *h* parts............ Ps 78:66 268
his *h* part toward the utmost sea,............ Joel 2:20 5490
and half of them toward the *h* sea .... Zec 14:8 314
he was in the *h* part of the ship,............. Mk 4:38 *4403*
what doth *h* me to be baptized .... Acts 8:36 *2967*
the *h* part was broken with.................... Acts 27:41 *4403*
lest we should *h* the gospel of... 1Cor 9:12 *5100,1464,1325*
who did *h* you that ye should not .... Gal 5:7 *348*

HINDERED {5}
these men, that they be not *h*................. Ezr 6:8 989
them that were entering in ye *h* .... Lk 11:52 *2967*
been much *h* from coming to you........... Rom 15:22 *1465*
but Satan *h* us... 1Th 2:18 *1465*
that your prayers be not *h*..................... 1Pet 3:7 *1581*

HINDERETH {1}
anger, is persecuted, and none *h* .... Is 14:6 2820

HINDERMOST {2}
after, and Rachel and Joseph *h*............... Gen 33:2 314
the *h* of the nations shall be a................ Jer 50:12 319

HINDMOST {3}
They shall go *h* with their .... Num 2:31 314
the way, and smote the *h* of thee............ Deut 25:18 2179
enemies, and smite the *h* of them............ Josh 10:19 2179

HINDS {4}
thou mark when the *h* do calve................ Job 39:1 355
of the LORD maketh the *h* to calve.......... Ps 29:9 355
by the *h* of the field, that ye................... Song 2:7 355
by the *h* of the field, that ye................... Song 3:5 355

HINDS' {3}
He maketh my feet like *h* feet 2Sa 22:34 355
He maketh my feet like *h* feet .... Ps 18:33 355
he will make my feet like *h* feet............. Hab 3:19 355

HINGES {2}
the *h* of gold, both for the doors 1Kin 7:50 6596
As the door turneth upon his *h*................ Prov 26:14 6735

HINNOM *(hin'-nom)* {13} *A valley near Jerusalem.*
of *H* unto the south side of the .... Josh 15:8 2011
before the valley of *H* westward .... Josh 15:8 2011
before the valley of the son of *H*............. Josh 18:16 2011
and descended to the valley of *H*............. Josh 18:16 2011
the valley of the children of *H* 2Kin 23:10 2011
in the valley of the son of *H*.................... 2Chr 28:3 2011
in the valley of the son of *H*.................... 2Chr 33:6 2011
Beer-sheba unto the valley of *H*............... Neh 11:30 2011
is in the valley of the son of *H* .... Jer 7:31 2011
nor the valley of the son of *H*.................. Jer 7:32 2011
unto the valley of the son of *H*................. Jer 19:2 2011
nor The valley of the son of *H*.................. Jer 19:6 2011
are in the valley of the son of *H*.............. Jer 32:35 2011

HIP {1}
And he smote them *h* and thigh with...... Judg 15:8 7785

HIRAH *(hi'-rah)* {2} *A friend of Judah.*
Adullamite, whose name was *H*.............. Gen 38:1 2437
his friend *H* the Adullamite .... Gen 38:12 2437

HIRAM *(hi'-ram)* {22} See HIRAM'S, HURAM.
1. A king of Tyre.
H king of Tyre sent messengers to........... 2Sa 5:11 2438
H king of Tyre sent his servants.............. 1Kin 5:1 2438
for *H* was ever a lover of David 1Kin 5:1 2438
And Solomon sent to *H*, saying,............... 1Kin 5:2 2438
when *H* heard the words of Solomon...... 1Kin 5:7 2438
H sent to Solomon, saying, I have 1Kin 5:8 2438
So *H* gave Solomon cedar trees and......... 1Kin 5:10 2438
Solomon gave *H* twenty thousand............ 1Kin 5:11 2438
gave Solomon to *H* year by year............... 1Kin 5:11 2438
and there was peace between *H*............... 1Kin 5:12 2438
(Now *H* the king of Tyre had.................... 1Kin 9:11 2438
H twenty cities in the land of.................. 1Kin 9:11 2438
H came out from Tyre to see the 1Kin 9:12 2438
H sent to the king sixscore...................... 1Kin 9:14 2438
H sent in the navy his servants, ... 1Kin 9:27 2438
And the navy also of *H*, that 1Kin 10:11 2438
of Tharshish with the navy of *H* 1Kin 10:22 2438
Now *H* king of Tyre sent.......................... 1Chr 14:1 2438
2. An architect.
sent and fetched *H* out of Tyre................. 1Kin 7:13 2438
H made the lavers, and the shovels 1Kin 7:40 2438
So *H* made an end of doing all the........... 1Kin 7:40 2438
which *H* made to king Solomon for 1Kin 7:45 2438

HIRAM'S *(hi'-rams)* {1} *Refers to Hiram 1.*
H builders did hew them, and the........... 1Kin 5:18 2438

HIRE {23}
Leah said, God hath given me my *h*........ Gen 30:18 7939
and of such shall be my *h*....................... Gen 30:32 7939
come for my *h* before thy face................. Gen 30:33 7939
The ringstraked shall be thy *h* .... Gen 31:8 7939
an hired thing, it came for his *h*............. Ex 22:15 7939
shalt not bring the *h* of a whore .... Deut 23:18 868
his day thou shalt give him his *h* .... Deut 24:15 7939
unto thee will I give *h* for thy................. 1Kin 5:6 7939
of silver to *h* them chariots 1Chr 19:6 7936
Tyre, and she shall turn to her *h* .... Is 23:17 868
her *h* shall be holiness to the .... Is 23:18 868
in the balance, and *h* a goldsmith........... Is 46:6 7936
harlot, in that thou scornest *h* .... Eze 16:31 868
also shalt give no *h* any more.................. Eze 16:41 868
gathered it of the *h* of an harlot.............. Mic 1:7 868
return to the *h* of an harlot .... Mic 1:7 868
the priests thereof teach for *h*................ Mic 3:11 4242
h for man, nor any *h* for beast .... Zec 8:10 7939
to *h* labourers into his vineyard .... Mt 20:1 *3409*
labourers, and give them their *h* .... Mt 20:8 *3408*
the labourer is worthy of his *h*................ Lk 10:7 *3408*
the *h* of the labourers who have.............. Jas 5:4 *3408*

HIRED {34}
for surely I have *h* thee with my............. Gen 30:16 7936
an *h* servant shall not eat........................ Ex 12:45 7916
if it be an *h* thing, it came for................. Ex 22:15 7916
the wages of him that is *h* shall .... Lev 19:13 7916
or an *h* servant, shall not eat of .... Lev 22:10 7916
thy maid, and for thy *h* servant............... Lev 25:6 7916
But as an *h* servant, and as a .... Lev 25:40 7916
according to the time of an *h* .... Lev 25:50 7916
as a yearly *h* servant shall he be .... Lev 25:53 7916
worth a double *h* servant to thee .... Deut 15:18 7916
because they *h* against thee..................... Deut 23:4 7936
oppress an *h* servant that is poor .... Deut 24:14 7916
wherewith Abimelech *h* vain.................... Judg 9:4 7936
Micah with me, and hath *h* me .... Judg 18:4 7936
have *h* out themselves for bread.............. 1Sa 2:5 7936
h the Syrians of Beth-rehob, and 2Sa 10:6 7936
the king of Israel hath *h* against............. 2Kin 7:6 7936
So they *h* thirty and two thousand 1Chr 19:7 7936
h masons and carpenters to repair.......... 2Chr 24:12 7936
He *h* also an hundred thousand 2Chr 25:6 7936
h counsellors against them, to................ Ezr 4:5 7936
for Tobiah and Sanballat had *h* him........ Neh 6:12 7936
Therefore was he *h*, that I should............ Neh 6:13 7936
but *h* Balaam against them, that.............. Neh 13:2 7936
Lord shave with a razor that is *h*............. Is 7:20 7917
Also her *h* men are in the midst.............. Jer 46:21 7916
Ephraim hath *h* lovers.............................. Hos 8:9 8566
though they have *h* among the .... Hos 8:10 8566
him, Because no man hath *h* us .... Mt 20:7 *3409*
were *h* about the eleventh hour.............. Mt 20:9
in the ship with the *h* servants............... Mk 1:20 *3411*
How many *h* servants of my .... Lk 15:17 *3407*
make me as one of thy *h* servants .... Lk 15:19 *3407*
whole years in his own *h* house.............. Acts 28:30 *3410*

HIRELING {9}
days also like the days of a *h* .... Job 7:1 7916
as a *h* looketh for the reward of .... Job 7:2 7916
till he shall accomplish, as an *h*.............. Job 14:6 7916
three years, as the years of an *h*............. Is 16:14 7916
according to the years of an *h*................. Is 21:16 7916
that oppress the *h* in his wages.............. Mal 3:5 7916
But he that is an *h*, and not the .... Jn 10:12 *3411*
h fleeth, because he is an *h* .... Jn 10:13 *3411*

HIRES {1}
all the *h* thereof shall be burned............ Mic 1:7 868

HIREST {1}
h them, that they may come unto............ Eze 16:33 7806

HIS See APPENDIX.

HISS {12}
shall be astonished, and shall *h* 1Kin 9:8 8319
shall *h* him out of his place.................... Job 27:23 8319
will *h* unto them from the end of............ Is 5:26 8319
that the LORD shall *h* for the fly .... Is 7:18 8319
h because of all the plagues .... Jer 19:8 8319
shall *h* at all the plagues .... Jer 49:17 8319
and *h* at all her plagues........................... Jer 50:13 8319
they *h* and wag their head at the .... Lam 2:15 8319
they *h* and gnash the teeth...................... Lam 2:16 8319
among the people shall *h* at thee .... Eze 27:36 8319
one that passeth by her shall *h* .... Zeph 2:15 8319
I will *h* for them, and gather them.......... Zec 10:8 8319

HISSING {8}
trouble, to astonishment, and to *h* 2Chr 29:8 8322
land desolate, and a perpetual *h*.............. Jer 18:16 8292
make this city desolate, and an *h*............. Jer 19:8 8322
them an astonishment, and an *h* .... Jer 25:9 8322
desolation, an astonishment, an *h* .... Jer 25:18 8322
and an astonishment, and an *h* .... Jer 29:18 8322
dragons, an astonishment, and an *h* .... Jer 51:37 8322
and the inhabitants thereof an *h*............. Mic 6:16 8322

HIT {2}
Saul, and the archers *h* him 1Sa 31:3 4672
Saul, and the archers *h* him 1Chr 10:3 4672

HITHER {66}
they shall come *h* again.......................... Gen 15:16 2008
your youngest brother come *h*................. Gen 42:15
yourselves, that ye sold me *h*................... Gen 45:5
now it was not you that sent me *h*.......... Gen 45:8
haste and bring down my father *h*........... Gen 45:13
And he said, Draw not nigh *h* .... Ex 3:5 1988
there came men in *h* to night of .... Josh 2:2
the children of Israel, Come *h* .... Josh 3:9 5066
and bring the description *h* to me........... Josh 18:6
Gazites, saying, Samson is come *h*........... Judg 16:2
said unto him, Who brought thee *h*......... Judg 18:3 1988
We will not turn aside *h* into the .... Judg 19:12
unto her, At mealtime come thou *h*......... Ruth 2:14 1988
Bring *h* a burnt offering to me,................ 1Sa 13:9 5066
Ahiah, Bring *h* the ark of God 1Sa 14:18 5066
Bring me *h* every man his ox, and........... 1Sa 14:34 5066
Let us draw near *h* unto God................... 1Sa 14:36 1988
And Saul said, Draw ye near *h* 1Sa 14:38 1988
Bring ye *h* to me Agag the king of 1Sa 15:32 5066
will not sit down till he come *h* 1Sa 16:11 6311
he said, Why camest thou down *h*............ 1Sa 17:28
the priest, Bring *h* the ephod 1Sa 23:9 5066
I pray thee, bring me *h* the ephod........... 1Sa 30:7 5066
have brought them *h* unto my lord.......... 2Sa 1:10
lame, thou shalt not come in *h*................ 2Sa 5:6
I sent unto thee, saying, Come *h* 2Sa 14:32
pray you, unto Joab, Come near *h*............ 2Sa 20:16
Hasten *h* Micaiah the son of Imlah......... 1Kin 22:9
waters, and they were divided *h*............. 2Kin 2:8
smitten the waters, they parted *h* 2Kin 2:14
saying, The man of God is come *h* 2Kin 8:7 2008
to David, Thou shalt not come *h*............. 1Chr 11:5
shall not bring in the captives *h*............. 2Chr 28:13
of Assur, which brought us up *h* .... Ezr 4:2
Therefore his people return *h*................. Ps 73:10 1988
bring *h* the timbrel, the pleasant .... Ps 81:2
is simple, let him turn in *h*...................... Prov 9:4
is simple, let him turn in *h*...................... Prov 9:16
it be said unto thee, Come up *h* .... Prov 25:7
But draw near *h*, ye sons of the............... Is 57:3
them unto thee art thou brought *h*.......... Eze 40:4
high God, come forth, and come *h* .... Dan 3:26
art thou come *h* to torment us................ Mt 8:29 *5602*
He said, Bring them *h* to me .... Mt 14:18 *5602*
bring him *h* to me.................................. Mt 17:17 *5602*
how camest thou in *h* not having a .... Mt 22:12 *5602*
and straightway he will send him *h*......... Mk 11:3 *5602*
Bring thy son *h* .... Lk 9:41 *5602*
the city, and bring in *h* the poor .... Lk 14:21 *5602*
bring *h* the fatted calf, and kill............... Lk 15:23
I should reign over them, bring *h*............ Lk 19:27 *5602*
loose him, and bring him *h* .... Lk 19:30
not, neither come *h* to draw .... Jn 4:15 *1759*
Go, call thy husband, and come *h* .... Jn 4:16 *1759*
him, Rabbi, when camest thou *h*.............. Jn 6:25 *5602*
Reach *h* thy finger, and behold my.......... Jn 20:27 *5602*
reach *h* thy hand, and thrust it .... Jn 20:27 *5602*
came *h* for that intent, that he............... Acts 9:21 *5602*
call *h* Simon, whose surname is .... Acts 10:32 *3333*
world upside down are come *h* also......... Acts 17:6 *1759*
For ye have brought *h* these men .... Acts 19:37
Therefore, when they were come *h*.......... Acts 25:17 *1759*
which said, Come up *h*, and I will .... Rev 4:1 *5602*
saying unto them, Come up *h* .... Rev 11:12 *5602*
with me, saying unto me, Come *h* .... Rev 17:1 *1204*
and talked with me, saying, Come *h* .... Rev 21:9 *1204*

HITHERTO {19}
behold, *h* thou wouldest not hear.... Ex 7:16 5704,3541
as the LORD hath blessed me *h*....... Josh 17:14 5704,3541
H thou hast mocked me, and told ... Judg 16:13 5704,2008
and grief have I spoken *h* 1Sa 1:16 5704,2008
H hath the LORD helped us 1Sa 7:12 5704,2008
that thou hast brought me *h* 2Sa 7:18 1988
have been thy father's servant *h*............ 2Sa 15:34 227
Who *h* waited in the king's gate...... 1Chr 9:18 5704,2008
for *h* the greatest part of them........ 1Chr 12:29 5704,2008
that thou hast brought me *h* 1Chr 17:16 1988
H shalt thou come, but no further... Job 38:11 5704,6311
h have I declared thy wondrous ...... Ps 71:17 5704,2008
terrible from their beginning *h* .... Is 18:2 1973
terrible from their beginning *h* .... Is 18:7 1973
H is the end of the matter .... Dan 7:28 5705,3542
them, My Father worketh *h* .... Jn 5:17 *2193,737*
H have ye asked nothing in my .... Jn 16:24 *2193,737*
to come unto you, (but was let *h*..... Rom 1:13 *891,1204*
for *h* ye were not able to bear it............ 1Cor 3:2 *3768*

HITTITE *(hit'-tite)* {26} See HITTITES. *A descendant of Heth.*
Ephron the *H* answered Abraham in ...... Gen 23:10 2850
of Ephron the son of Zohar the *H*.......... Gen 25:9 2850
the daughter of Beeri the *H* .... Gen 26:34 2850
the daughter of Elon the *H*................... Gen 26:34 2850
Adah the daughter of Elon the *H*........... Gen 36:2 2850
is in the field of Ephron the *H*............... Gen 49:29 2850
the *H* for a possession of a .... Gen 49:30 2850
of a buryingplace of Ephron the *H* .... Gen 50:13 2850
Hivite, the Canaanite, and the *H* .... Ex 23:28 2850
Canaanite, the Amorite, and the *H* .... Ex 33:2 2850
and the Canaanite, and the *H* .... Ex 34:11 2850
sea over against Lebanon, the *H*............ Josh 9:1 2850
west, and to the Amorite, and the *H*....... Josh 11:3 2850
David and said to Ahimelech the *H* 1Sa 26:6 2850
of Eliam, the wife of Uriah the *H*........... 2Sa 11:3 2850
Joab, saying, Send me Uriah the *H*.......... 2Sa 11:6 2850
and Uriah the *H* died also...................... 2Sa 11:17 2850
servant Uriah the *H* is dead also............ 2Sa 11:21 2850
servant Uriah the *H* is dead also............ 2Sa 11:24 2850
killed Uriah the *H* with the sword 2Sa 12:9 2850
of Uriah the *H* to be thy wife.................. 2Sa 12:10 2850
Uriah the *H*: thirty and seven 2Sa 23:39 2850
only in the matter of Uriah the *H* 1Kin 15:5 2850
Uriah the *H*, Zabad the son of 1Chr 11:41 2850
an Amorite, and thy mother an *H* .... Eze 16:3 2850
your mother was an *H*, and your............. Eze 16:45 2850

HITTITES *(hit'-tites)* {22}
And the *H*, and the Perizzites, and .... Gen 15:20 2850
place of the Canaanites, and the *H* .... Ex 3:8 2850
land of the Canaanites, and the *H* .... Ex 3:17 2850
land of the Canaanites, and the *H* .... Ex 13:5 2850
in unto the Amorites, and the *H* .... Ex 23:23 2850
and the *H*, and the Jebusites, and.......... Num 13:29 2850
many nations before thee, the *H* .... Deut 7:1 2850
namely, the *H*, and the Amorites,............ Deut 20:17 2850
Euphrates, all the land of the *H*............. Josh 1:4 2850
you the Canaanites, and the *H*............... Josh 3:10 2850
the *H*, the Amorites, and the.................. Josh 12:8 2850
and the Canaanites, and the *H*............... Josh 24:11 2850
man went into the land of the *H*............. Judg 1:26 2850
dwelt among the Canaanites, *H* .... Judg 3:5 2850
that were left of the Amorites, *H* 1Kin 9:20 2850
and so for all the kings of the *H* 1Kin 10:29 2850

Edomites, Zidonians, and *H* 1Kin 11:1 2850
against us the kings of the *H* 2Kin 7:6 2850
horses for all the kings of the *H* 2Chr 1:17 2850
people that were left of the *H* 2Chr 8:7 2850
even of the Canaanites, the *H* Ezr 9:1 2850
the land of the Canaanites, the *H* Neh 9:8 2850

HIVITE *(hi'-vite)* {9} *A descendant of Canaan.*
And the *H*, and the Arkite, and the Gen 10:17 2340
Shechem the son of Hamor the *H* Gen 34:2 2340
Anah the daughter of Zibeon the *H* Gen 36:2 2340
thee, which shall drive out the *H* Ex 23:28 2340
Hittite, and the Perizzite, the *H* Ex 33:2 2340
and the Perizzite, and the *H* Ex 34:11 2340
Canaanite, the Perizzite, the *H* Josh 9:1 2340
to the *H* under Hermon in the land Josh 11:3 2340
And the *H*, and the Arkite, and the 1Chr 1:15 2340

HIVITES *(hi'-vites)* {6}
and the Perizzites, and the *H* Ex 3:8 2340
and the Perizzites, and the *H* Ex 3:17 2340
and the Amorites, and the *H* Ex 13:5 2340
and the Canaanites, the *H* Ex 23:23 2340
and the Perizzites, and the *H* Deut 7:1 2340
and the Perizzites, the *H* Deut 20:17 2340
and the Hittites, and the *H* Josh 3:10 2340
the men of Israel said unto the *H* Josh 9:7 2340
save the *H* the inhabitants of Josh 11:19 2340
Canaanites, the Perizzites, the *H* Josh 12:8 2340
and the Girgashites, the *H* Josh 24:11 2340
the *H* that dwelt in mount Lebanon Judg 3:3 2340
and Amorites, and Perizzites, and *H* Judg 3:5 2340
and to all the cities of the *H* 2Sa 24:7 2340
Amorites, Hittites, Perizzites, *H* 1Kin 9:20 2340
and the Perizzites, and the *H* 2Chr 8:7 2340

HIZKI See HEZEKI.

HIZKIAH *(hiz-ki'-ah)* {1} See HEZEKIAH, HIZKIJAH. *An ancestor of Zephaniah.*
the son of Amariah, the son of *H* Zeph 1:1 2396

HIZKIJAH *(hiz-ki'-jah)* {1} See HIZKIAH. *An Israelite who renewed the covenant.*
Ater, *H*, Azzur, Neh 10:17 2396

HO {4}
unto whom he said, *H*, such a one Ruth 4:1 1945
H, every one that thirsteth, come Is 55:1 1945
H, *h*, come forth, and flee from Zec 2:6 1945

HOAR {5}
as small as the *h* frost on the Ex 16:14 3713
let not his *h* head go down to the 1Kin 2:6 7872
but his *h* head bring thou down to 1Kin 2:9 7872
scattereth the *h* frost like ashes Ps 147:16 3713
even to *h* hairs will I carry you Is 46:4 7872

HOARY {4}
shalt rise up before the *h* head Lev 19:32 7872
the *h* frost of heaven, who hath Job 38:29 3713
one would think the deep to be *h* Job 41:32 7872
The *h* head is a crown of glory, Prov 16:31 7872

HOBAB *(ho'-bab)* {2} See JETHRO. *Another name for Jethro.*
And Moses said unto *H*, the son of Num 10:29 2246
of *H* the father in law of Moses Judg 4:11 2246

HOBAH *(ho'-bah)* {1} *Place where Abraham pursued the five kings.*
them, and pursued them unto *H* Gen 14:15 2327

HOBAIAH See HABAIAH.

HOD *(hod)* {1} *A son of Zophah.*
Bezer, and *H*, and Shamma, and 1Chr 7:37 1963

HODAIAH *(ho-da-i'-ah)* {1} See HODAVIAH. *A royal descendant of Judah.*
And the sons of Elioenai were, *H* 1Chr 3:24 1939

HODAVIAH *(ho-da-vi'-ah)* {3} See HODAIAH, HODEVAH.
1. A chief of Manasseh.
and Azriel, and Jeremiah, and *H* 1Chr 5:24 1938
2. Son of Hassenuah.
son of Meshullam, the son of *H* 1Chr 9:7 1938
3. A family of exiles.
and Kadmiel, of the children of *H* Ezr 2:40 1938

HODESH *(ho'-desh)* {1} *Wife of Shaharaim.*
And he begat of *H* his wife 1Chr 8:9 2321

HODEVAH *(ho-de'-vah)* {1} See HODAVIAH. *A family of exiles.*
Kadmiel, and of the children of *H* Neh 7:43 1937

HODIAH *(ho-di'-ah)* {1} See HODIJAH. *A wife of Mered.*
of his wife *H* the sister of Naham 1Chr 4:19 1940

HODIJAH *(ho-di'-jah)* {5} See HODIAH.
1. A Levite.
Jamin, Akkub, Shabbethai, *H* Neh 8:7 1940
Bani, Hashabniah, Sherebiah, *H* Neh 9:5 1940
And their brethren, Shebaniah, *H* Neh 10:10 1940
H, Bani, Beninu Neh 10:13 1940
2. A leader of the people.
H, Hashum, Bezai, Neh 10:18 1940

HOGLAH *(hog'-lah)* {4} See BETH-HOGLAH. *A daughter of Zelophehad.*
were Mahlah, and Noah, *H*, Milcah, Num 26:33 2295
Mahlah, Noah, and *H*, and Milcah, Num 27:1 2295
For Mahlah, Tirzah, and *H*, and Num 36:11 2295
his daughters, Mahlah, and Noah, *H* Josh 17:3 2295

HOHAM *(ho'-ham)* {1} *An Amorite king.*
sent unto *H* king of Hebron Josh 10:3 1944

HOISED {1}
h up the mainsail to the wind, and Acts 27:40 *1869*

HOLD {185}
the men laid *h* upon his hand, and Gen 19:16 2388
the lad, and *h* him in thine hand Gen 21:18 2388
his hand took *h* on Esau's heel Gen 25:26 270
that they may *h* a feast unto me Ex 5:1
them go, and wilt *h* them still, Ex 9:2 2388
for we must *h* a feast unto the Ex 10:9
for you, and ye shall *h* your peace Ex 14:14 2790
sorrow shall take *h* on the Ex 15:14 270
trembling shall take *h* upon them Ex 15:15 270
for the LORD will not *h* him Ex 20:7
loops may take *h* one of another Ex 26:5 6901
father shall *h* his peace at her Num 30:4 2790
h his peace at her from day to Num 30:14 2790
for the LORD will not *h* him Deut 5:11
father and his mother lay *h* on him Deut 21:19 8610
lay *h* on her, and lie with her, and Deut 22:28 8610
and mine hand take *h* on judgment Deut 32:41 270
they entered into an *h* of the Judg 9:46 6877
Abimelech, and put them to the *h* Judg 9:49 6877
set the *h* on fire upon them Judg 9:49 6877
Samson took *h* of the two middle Judg 16:29 3943
H thy peace, lay thine hand upon Judg 18:19 2790
laid *h* on his concubine, and Judg 19:29 2388
that thou hast upon thee, and *h* it Ruth 3:15 270
he laid *h* upon the skirt of his 1Sa 15:27 2388
the while that David was in the *h* 1Sa 22:4 4686
unto David, Abide not in the *h* 1Sa 22:5 4686
and his men gat them up unto the *h* 1Sa 24:22 4686
Then David took *h* on his clothes 2Sa 1:11 2388
lay thee *h* on one of the young 2Sa 2:21 270
how then should I *h* up my face to 2Sa 2:22 5375
good tidings, I took *h* of him 2Sa 4:10 270
David took the strong *h* of Zion 2Sa 5:7 4686
of it, and went down to the *h* 2Sa 5:17 4686
the ark of God, and took *h* of it 2Sa 6:6 270
unto him to eat, he took *h* of her 2Sa 13:11 2388
but *h* now thy peace, my sister 2Sa 13:20 2790
and his head caught *h* of the oak 2Sa 18:9 2388
And David was then in an *h* 2Sa 23:14 4686
And came to the strong *h* of Tyre 2Sa 24:7 4013
caught *h* on the horns of the 1Kin 1:50 2388
he hath caught *h* on the horns of 1Kin 1:51 270
Now therefore *h* him not guiltless 1Kin 2:9
caught *h* on the horns of the 1Kin 2:28 2388
have taken *h* upon other gods, and 1Kin 9:9 2388
the altar, saying, Lay *h* on him 1Kin 13:4 8610
h ye your peace 2Kin 2:3 2814
h ye your peace 2Kin 2:5 2814
he took *h* of his own clothes, and 2Kin 2:12 2388
door, and *h* him fast at the door 2Kin 6:32 3905
good tidings, and we *h* our peace 2Kin 7:9 2814
And David was then in the *h* 1Chr 11:16 4686
h to the wilderness men of might 1Chr 12:8 4679
and Judah to the *h* unto David 1Chr 12:16 4679
put forth his hand to *h* the ark 1Chr 13:9 270
and laid *h* on other gods, and 2Chr 7:22 2388
H your peace, for the day is holy Neh 8:11 2013
shall *h* out the golden sceptre Est 4:11 3447
Teach me, and I will *h* my tongue Job 6:24 2790
he shall *h* it fast, but it shall Job 8:15 2388
that thou wilt not *h* me innocent Job 9:28
thy lies make men *h* their peace Job 11:3 2790
ye would altogether *h* your peace Job 13:5 2790
H your peace, let me alone, that Job 13:13 2790
if I *h* my tongue, I shall give up Job 13:19 2790
righteous also shall *h* on his way Job 17:9 270
and trembling taketh *h* on my flesh Job 21:6 270
My righteousness I *h* fast Job 27:6 2388
Terrors take *h* on him as waters, Job 27:20 5381
affliction have taken *h* upon me Job 30:16 270
h thy peace, and I will speak Job 33:31 2790
h thy peace, and I shall teach Job 33:33 2790
and justice take *h* on thee Job 36:17 8551
That it might take *h* of the ends Job 38:13 270
him that layeth at him cannot *h* Job 41:26 6965
H up my goings in thy paths, that Ps 17:5 8551
Take *h* of shield and buckler, and Ps 35:2 2388
h not thy peace at my tears Ps 39:12 2790
iniquities have taken *h* upon me Ps 40:12 5381
Fear took *h* upon them there, and Ps 48:6 270
thy wrathful anger take *h* of them Ps 69:24 5381
h not thy peace, and be not still, Ps 83:1 2790
H not thy peace, O God of my Ps 109:1 2790
the pains of hell gat *h* upon me Ps 116:3 4672
Horror hath taken *h* upon me Ps 119:53 270
H thou me up, and I shall be safe Ps 119:117 5582
and anguish have taken *h* on me Ps 119:143 4672
me, and thy right hand shall *h* me Ps 139:10 270
neither take they *h* of the paths Prov 2:19 5381
life to them that lay *h* upon her Prov 3:18 2388
Take fast *h* of instruction Prov 4:13 2388
her steps take *h* on hell Prov 5:5 8551
spider taketh *h* with her hands Prov 30:28 8610
and her hands *h* the distaff Prov 31:19 8551
to lay *h* on folly, till I might Eccl 2:3 270
thou shouldest take *h* of this Eccl 7:18 270
They all *h* swords, being expert Song 3:8 270
I will take *h* of the boughs Song 7:8 270
When a man shall take *h* of his Is 3:6 8610
women shall take *h* of one man Is 4:1 2388
lay *h* of the prey, and shall carry Is 5:29 270
and sorrows shall take *h* of them Is 13:8 270
pangs have taken *h* upon me Is 21:3 270
Or let him take *h* of my strength Is 27:5 2388
over to his strong *h* for fear Is 31:9 5553
thy God will *h* thy right hand Is 41:13 2388
will *h* thine hand, and will keep Is 42:6 2388
son of man that layeth *h* on it Is 56:2 2388
me, and take *h* of my covenant Is 56:4 2388
it, and taketh *h* of my covenant Is 56:6 2388
Zion's sake will I not *h* my peace Is 62:1 2814
which shall never *h* their peace Is 62:6 2814
up himself to take *h* of thee Is 64:7 2388
wilt thou *h* thy peace, and afflict Is 64:12 2814
cisterns, that can *h* no water Jer 2:13 3557
I cannot *h* my peace, because thou Jer 4:19 2790
They shall lay *h* on bow and spear Jer 6:23 2388
anguish hath taken *h* of us Jer 6:24 2388
they *h* fast deceit, they refuse Jer 8:5 2388
astonishment hath taken *h* on me Jer 8:21 2388
They shall *h* the bow and the lance Jer 50:42 2388
anguish took *h* of him, and pangs Jer 50:43 2388
When they took *h* of thee by thy Eze 29:7 8610
to make it strong to *h* the sword Eze 30:21 8610
about, that they might have *h* Eze 41:6 270
but they had not *h* in the wall of Eze 41:6 270
Then shall he say, *H* thy tongue Amos 6:10 2013
the strong *h* of the daughter of Mic 4:8 6076
and thou shalt take *h*, but shalt Mic 6:14 5253
a strong *h* in the day of trouble Nah 1:7 4581
they shall deride every strong *h* Hab 1:10 4013
H thy peace at the presence of Zeph 1:7
they not take *h* of your fathers Zec 1:6 5381
that ten men shall take *h* out of Zec 8:23 2388
even shall take *h* of the skirt of Zec 8:23 2388
did build herself a strong *h* Zec 9:3 4692
Turn you to the strong *h*, ye Zec 9:12 1225
them, and *h* themselves not guilty Zec 11:5 816
they shall lay *h* every one on the Zec 14:13 2388
or else he will *h* to the one Mt 6:24 *472*
day, will he not lay *h* on it Mt 12:11 *2902*
For Herod had laid *h* on John Mt 14:3 *2902*
because they should *h* their peace Mt 20:31 *4623*
for all *h* John as a prophet Mt 21:26 *2192*
same is he: *h* him fast Mt 26:48 *2902*
the temple, and ye laid no *h* on me Mt 26:55 *2902*
they that had laid *h* on Jesus led Mt 26:57 *2902*
H thy peace, and come out of him Mk 1:25 *5392*
it, they went out to lay *h* on him Mk 3:21 *2902*
laid *h* upon John, and bound him in Mk 6:17 *2902*
be, which they have received to *h* Mk 7:4 *2902*
ye *h* the tradition of men, as the Mk 7:8 *2902*
him that he should *h* his peace Mk 10:48 *4623*
And they sought to lay *h* on him Mk 12:12 *2902*
and the young men laid *h* on him Mk 14:51 *2902*
H thy peace, and come out of him Lk 4:35 *5392*
or else he will *h* to the one Lk 16:13 *472*
him, that he should *h* his peace Lk 18:39 *4623*
if these should *h* their peace Lk 19:40 *4623*
they might take *h* of his words Lk 20:20 *1949*
they could not take *h* of his Lk 20:26 *1949*
they laid *h* upon one Simon, a Lk 23:26 *1949*
put them in *h* unto the next day Acts 4:3 *5084*
with the hand to *h* their peace Acts 12:17 *4601*
but speak, and *h* not thy peace Acts 18:9 *4623*
of men, who *h* the truth in Rom 1:18 *2722*
by, let the first *h* his peace 1Cor 14:30 *4601*
and *h* such in reputation Phil 2:29 *2192*
h fast that which is good 1Th 5:21 *2722*
h the traditions which ye have 2Th 2:15 *2902*
lay *h* on eternal life, whereunto 1Ti 6:12 *1949*
they may lay *h* on eternal life 1Ti 6:19 *1949*
H fast the form of sound words, 2Ti 1:13 *2192*
if we *h* fast the confidence and Heb 3:6 *2722*
if we *h* the beginning of our Heb 3:14 *2722*
let us *h* fast our profession Heb 4:14 *2902*
lay *h* upon the hope set before us Heb 6:18 *2902*
Let us *h* fast the profession of Heb 10:23 *2722*
that *h* the doctrine of Balaam Rev 2:14 *2902*
them that *h* the doctrine of the Rev 2:15 *2902*
have already *h* fast till I come Rev 2:25 *2902*
and heard, and *h* fast, and repent Rev 3:3 *5083*
h that fast which thou hast, that Rev 3:11 *2902*
the *h* of every foul spirit, and a Rev 18:2 *5438*
he laid *h* on the dragon, that old Rev 20:2 *2902*

HOLDEN {12}
Surely there was not *h* such a 2Kin 23:22 6213
was *h* to the LORD in Jerusalem 2Kin 23:23 6213
be *h* in cords of affliction Job 36:8 3920
and thy right hand hath *h* me up Ps 18:35 5582
have I been *h* up from the womb Ps 71:6 5564
thou hast *h* me by my right hand Ps 73:23 270
he shall be *h* with the cords of Prov 5:22 8551
I have long time *h* my peace Is 42:14 2814
Cyrus, whose right hand I have *h* Is 45:1 2388
But their eyes were *h* that they Lk 24:16 *2902*
that he should be *h* of it Acts 2:24 *2902*
Yea, he shall be *h* up Rom 14:4

HOLDEST {6}
h thy peace at this time, then Est 4:14 2790
thy face, and *h* me for thine enemy Job 13:24 2803
Thou *h* mine eyes waking Ps 77:4 270
that *h* the height of the hill Jer 49:16 8610
h thy tongue when the wicked Hab 1:13 2790
thou *h* fast my name, and hast not Rev 2:13 *2902*

HOLDETH {9}
still he *h* fast his integrity, Job 2:3 2388
He *h* back the face of his throne, Job 26:9 270
Which *h* our soul in life, and Ps 66:9 7760
man of understanding *h* his peace Prov 11:12 2790
when he *h* his peace, is counted Prov 17:28 2790
there is none that *h* with me in Dan 10:21 2388
him that *h* the sceptre from the Amos 1:5 8551

him that *h* the sceptre from ... Amos 1:8 8551
These things saith he that *h* the ... Rev 2:1 *2902*

HOLDING {9}
his hands from *h* of bribes ... Is 33:15 8551
I am weary with *h* in ... Jer 6:11 3557
h the tradition of the elders ... Mk 7:3 *2902*
H forth the word of life ... Phil 2:16 *1907*
not *h* the Head, from which all ... Col 2:19 *2902*
H faith, and a good conscience ... 1Ti 1:19 *2192*
H the mystery of the faith in a ... 1Ti 3:9 *2192*
H fast the faithful word as he ... Titus 1:9 *472*
h the four winds of the earth, ... Rev 7:1 *2902*

HOLDS {21}
whether in tents, or in strong *h* ... Num 13:19 4013
mountains, and caves, and strong *h* ... Judg 6:2 4679
In the wilderness in strong *h* ... 1Sa 23:14 4679
with us in strong *h* in the wood ... 1Sa 23:19 4679
and dwelt in strong *h* at En-gedi ... 1Sa 23:29 4679
their strong *h* wilt thou set on ... 2Kin 8:12 4013
And he fortified the strong *h* ... 2Chr 11:11 4694
hast brought his strong *h* to ruin ... Ps 89:40 4013
to destroy the strong *h* thereof ... Is 23:11 4581
and he shall destroy thy strong *h* ... Jer 48:18 4013
the strong *h* are surprised, and ... Jer 48:41 4679
they have remained in their *h* ... Jer 51:30 4679
strong *h* of the daughter of Judah ... Lam 2:2 4013
he hath destroyed his strong *h* ... Lam 2:5 4013
they brought him into *h*, that his ... Eze 19:9 4686
his devices against the strong *h* ... Dan 11:24 4013
most strong *h* with a strange god ... Dan 11:39 4013
and throw down all thy strong *h* ... Mic 5:11 4013
All thy strong *h* shall be like ... Nah 3:12 4013
the siege, fortify thy strong *h* ... Nah 3:14 4013
to the pulling down of strong *h* ... 2Cor 10:4

HOLE {12}
shall be an *h* in the top of it ... Ex 28:32 6310
work round about the *h* of it ... Ex 28:32 6310
as it were the *h* of an habergeon, ... Ex 28:32 6310
there was an *h* in the midst of ... Ex 39:23 6310
as the *h* of an habergeon, with a ... Ex 39:23 6310
with a band round about the *h* ... Ex 39:23 6310
bored a *h* in the lid of it, and ... 2Kin 12:9 2356
in his hand by the *h* of the door ... Song 5:4 2356
shall play on the *h* of the asp ... Is 11:8 2356
to the *h* of the pit whence ye are ... Is 51:1 4718
hide it there in a *h* of the rock ... Jer 13:4 5357
I looked, behold a *h* in the wall ... Eze 8:7 2356

HOLE'S {1}
nest in the sides of the *h* mouth ... Jer 48:28 6354

HOLES {11}
h where they had hid themselves ... 1Sa 14:11 2356
shall go into the *h* of the rocks ... Is 2:19 4631
in the *h* of the rocks, and upon ... Is 7:19 5357
they are all of them snared in *h* ... Is 42:22 2356
out of the *h* of the rocks ... Jer 16:16 5357
their *h* like worms of the earth ... Mic 7:17 4526
and filled his *h* with prey ... Nah 2:12 2356
wages to put it into a bag with *h* ... Hag 1:6 5344
shall consume away in their *h* ... Zec 14:12 2356
saith unto him, The foxes have *h* ... Mt 8:20 *5454*
Jesus said unto him, Foxes have *h* ... Lk 9:58 *5454*

HOLIER {1}
for I am *h* than thou ... Is 65:5 6942

HOLIEST {3}
which is called the *H* of all ... Heb 9:3 *39*
that the way into the *h* of all ... Heb 9:8 *39*
into the *h* by the blood of Jesus ... Heb 10:19 *39*

HOLILY {1}
are witnesses, and God also, how *h* ... 1Th 2:10 *3743*

HOLINESS {43}
Who is like thee, glorious in *h* ... Ex 15:11 6944
of a signet, *H* TO THE LORD ... Ex 28:36 6944
of a signet, *H* TO THE LORD ... Ex 39:30 6944
the LORD in the beauty of *h* ... 1Chr 16:29 6944
should praise the beauty of *h* ... 2Chr 20:21 6944
they sanctified themselves in *h* ... 2Chr 31:18 6944
the LORD in the beauty of *h* ... Ps 29:2 6944
at the remembrance of his *h* ... Ps 30:4 6944
sitteth upon the throne of his *h* ... Ps 47:8 6944
our God, in the mountain of his *h* ... Ps 48:1 6944
God hath spoken in his *h* ... Ps 60:6 6944
Once have I sworn by my *h* that I ... Ps 89:35 6944
h becometh thine house, O LORD, ... Ps 93:5 6944
the LORD in the beauty of *h* ... Ps 96:9 6944
at the remembrance of his *h* ... Ps 97:12 6944
God hath spoken in his *h* ... Ps 108:7 6944
in the beauties of *h* from the ... Ps 110:3 6944
her hire shall be *h* to the LORD ... Is 23:18 6944
it shall be called The way of *h* ... Is 35:8 6944
drink it in the courts of my *h* ... Is 62:9 6944
from the habitation of thy *h* ... Is 63:15 6944
The people of thy *h* have ... Is 63:18 6944
Israel was *h* unto the LORD, and ... Jer 2:3 6944
and because of the words of his *h* ... Jer 23:9 6944
of justice, and mountain of *h* ... Jer 31:23 6944
The Lord GOD hath sworn by his *h* ... Amos 4:2 6944
deliverance, and there shall be *h* ... Obad 17 6944
of the horses, *H* UNTO THE LORD ... Zec 14:20 6944
in Judah shall be *h* unto the LORD ... Zec 14:21 6944
the *h* of the LORD which he loved ... Mal 2:11 6944
In *h* and righteousness before him, ... Lk 1:75 *3742*
or *h* we had made this man to walk ... Acts 3:12 *2150*
according to the spirit of *h* ... Rom 1:4 *42*
servants to righteousness unto *h* ... Rom 6:19 *38*
to God, ye have your fruit unto *h* ... Rom 6:22 *38*
perfecting *h* in the fear of God ... 2Cor 7:1 *42*
in righteousness and true *h* ... Eph 4:24 *3742*
unblameable in *h* before God ... 1Th 3:13 *42*
us unto uncleanness, but unto *h* ... 1Th 4:7 *38*
and charity and *h* with sobriety ... 1Ti 2:15 *38*
be in behaviour as becometh *h* ... Titus 2:3 *2412*
we might be partakers of his *h* ... Heb 12:10 *41*
Follow peace with all men, and *h* ... Heb 12:14 *38*

HOLLOW {10}
he touched the *h* of his thigh ... Gen 32:25 3709
the *h* of Jacob's thigh was out of ... Gen 32:25 3709
which is upon the *h* of the thigh ... Gen 32:32 3709
because he touched the *h* of ... Gen 32:32 3709
H with boards shalt thou make it ... Ex 27:8 5014
he made the altar *h* with boards ... Ex 38:7 5014
walls of the house with *h* strakes ... Lev 14:37 8258
But God clave an *h* place that was ... Judg 15:19 4388
the waters in the *h* of his hand ... Is 40:12 8168
was four fingers: it was *h* ... Jer 52:21 5014

HOLON (*ho'-lon*) {3} See HILEN.
1. A Levitical city in Judah.
And Goshen, and *H*, and Giloh ... Josh 15:51 2473
H with her suburbs, and Debir with ... Josh 21:15 2473
2. A Moabite city.
upon *H*, and upon Jahazah, and upon ... Jer 48:21 2473

HOLPEN {5}
they have *h* the children of Lot ... Ps 83:8 2220
because thou, LORD, hast *h* me ... Ps 86:17 5826
he that is *h* shall fall down, and ... Is 31:3 5826
they shall be *h* with a little ... Dan 11:34 5826
He hath *h* his servant Israel, in ... Lk 1:54 *482*

HOLY {611}
whereon thou standest is *h* ground ... Ex 3:5 6944
there shall be an *h* convocation ... Ex 12:16 6944
shall be an *h* convocation to you ... Ex 12:16 6944
strength unto thy *h* habitation ... Ex 15:13 6944
of the *h* sabbath unto the LORD ... Ex 16:23 6944
of priests, and an *h* nation ... Ex 19:6 6918
the sabbath day, to keep it *h* ... Ex 20:8 6942
And ye shall be *h* men unto me ... Ex 22:31 6944
the *h* place and the most *h* ... Ex 26:33 6944
the testimony in the most *h* place ... Ex 26:34 6944
thou shalt make *h* garments for ... Ex 28:2 6944
they shall make *h* garments for ... Ex 28:4 6944
when he goeth in unto the *h* place ... Ex 28:29 6944
unto the *h* place before the LORD ... Ex 28:35 6944
bear the iniquity of the *h* things ... Ex 28:38 6944
shall hallow in all their *h* gifts ... Ex 28:38 6944
altar to minister in the *h* place ... Ex 28:43 6944
put the *h* crown upon the mitre ... Ex 29:6 6944
the *h* garments of Aaron shall be ... Ex 29:29 6944
to minister in the *h* place ... Ex 29:30 6944
seethe his flesh in the *h* place ... Ex 29:31 6918
eat thereof, because they are *h* ... Ex 29:33 6944
not be eaten, because it is *h* ... Ex 29:34 6944
and it shall be an altar most *h* ... Ex 29:37 6944
toucheth the altar shall be *h* ... Ex 29:37 6944
it is most *h* unto the LORD ... Ex 30:10 6944
make it an oil of *h* ointment ... Ex 30:25 6944
it shall be an *h* anointing oil ... Ex 30:25 6944
them, that they may be most *h* ... Ex 30:29 6944
toucheth them shall be *h* ... Ex 30:29 6942
This shall be an *h* anointing oil ... Ex 30:31 6944
it is *h*, and it shall be *h* unto ... Ex 30:32 6944
tempered together, pure and *h* ... Ex 30:35 6944
it shall be unto you most *h* ... Ex 30:36 6944
shall be unto thee *h* for the LORD ... Ex 30:37 6944
the *h* garments for Aaron the ... Ex 31:10 6944
and sweet incense for the *h* place ... Ex 31:11 6944
for it is *h* unto you ... Ex 31:14 6944
sabbath of rest, *h* to the LORD ... Ex 31:15 6944
there shall be to you an *h* day ... Ex 35:2 6944
to do service in the *h* place ... Ex 35:19 6944
the *h* garments for Aaron the ... Ex 35:19 6944
service, and for the *h* garments ... Ex 35:21 6944
he made the *h* anointing oil, and ... Ex 37:29 6944
in all the work of the *h* place ... Ex 38:24 6944
to do service in the *h* place ... Ex 39:1 6944
made the *h* garments for Aaron ... Ex 39:1 6944
plate of the *h* crown of pure gold ... Ex 39:30 6944
to do service in the *h* place ... Ex 39:41 6944
the *h* garments for Aaron the ... Ex 39:41 6944
and it shall be *h* ... Ex 40:9 6944
and it shall be an altar most *h* ... Ex 40:10 6944
put upon Aaron the *h* garments ... Ex 40:13 6944
it is a thing most *h* of the ... Lev 2:3 6944
it is a thing most *h* of the ... Lev 2:10 6944
in the *h* things of the LORD ... Lev 5:15 6944
that he hath done in the *h* thing ... Lev 5:16 6944
shall it be eaten in the *h* place ... Lev 6:16 6918
it is most *h*, as is the sin ... Lev 6:17 6944
one that toucheth them shall be *h* ... Lev 6:18 6942
it is most *h* ... Lev 6:25 6944
in the *h* place shall it be eaten, ... Lev 6:26 6918
the flesh thereof shall be *h* ... Lev 6:27 6942
it was sprinkled in the *h* place ... Lev 6:27 6918
it is most *h* ... Lev 6:29 6944
reconcile withal in the *h* place ... Lev 6:30 6944
it is most *h* ... Lev 7:1 6944
it shall be eaten in the *h* place ... Lev 7:6 6918
it is most *h* ... Lev 7:6 6944
put the golden plate, the *h* crown ... Lev 8:9 6944
ye may put difference between *h* ... Lev 10:10 6944
for it is most *h* ... Lev 10:12 6944
And ye shall eat it in the *h* place ... Lev 10:13 6918
h place, seeing it is most *h* ... Lev 10:17 6944
not brought in within the *h* place ... Lev 10:18 6944
have eaten it in the *h* place ... Lev 10:18 6944
yourselves, and ye shall be *h* ... Lev 11:44 6918
for I am *h* ... Lev 11:44 6918
therefore be *h*, for I am *h* ... Lev 11:45 6918
burnt offering, in the *h* place ... Lev 14:13 6944
it is most *h* ... Lev 14:13 6944
h place within the vail before ... Lev 16:2 6944
shall Aaron come into the *h* place ... Lev 16:3 6944
He shall put on the *h* linen coat ... Lev 16:4 6944
these are *h* garments ... Lev 16:4 6944
make an atonement for the *h* place ... Lev 16:16 6944
make an atonement in the *h* place ... Lev 16:17 6944
an end of reconciling the *h* place ... Lev 16:20 6944
on when he went into the *h* place ... Lev 16:23 6944
flesh with water in the *h* place ... Lev 16:24 6918
to make atonement in the *h* place ... Lev 16:27 6944
clothes, even the *h* garments ... Lev 16:32 6944
an atonement for the *h* sanctuary ... Lev 16:33 6944
and say unto them, Ye shall be *h* ... Lev 19:2 6918
for I the LORD your God am *h* ... Lev 19:2 6918
be *h* to praise the LORD withal ... Lev 19:24 6944
and to profane my *h* name ... Lev 20:3 6944
yourselves therefore, and be ye *h* ... Lev 20:7 6918
And ye shall be *h* unto me ... Lev 20:26 6918
for I the LORD am *h*, and have ... Lev 20:26 6918
They shall be *h* unto their God, ... Lev 21:6 6918
therefore they shall be *h* ... Lev 21:6 6944
for he is *h* unto his God ... Lev 21:7 6918
he shall be *h* unto thee ... Lev 21:8 6918
LORD, which sanctify you, am *h* ... Lev 21:8 6918
of the most *h*, and of the *h* ... Lev 21:22 6944
the *h* things of the children of ... Lev 22:2 6944
that they profane not my *h* name ... Lev 22:2 6944
that goeth unto the *h* things ... Lev 22:3 6944
he shall not eat of the *h* things ... Lev 22:4 6944
and shall not eat of the *h* things ... Lev 22:6 6944
afterward eat of the *h* things ... Lev 22:7 6944
no stranger eat of the *h* thing ... Lev 22:10 6944
shall not eat of the *h* thing ... Lev 22:10 6944
of an offering of the *h* things ... Lev 22:12 6944
eat of the *h* thing unwittingly ... Lev 22:14 6944
unto the priest with the *h* thing ... Lev 22:14 6944
the *h* things of the children of ... Lev 22:15 6944
when they eat their *h* things ... Lev 22:16 6944
shall ye profane my *h* name ... Lev 22:32 6944
proclaim to be *h* convocations ... Lev 23:2 6944
sabbath of rest, an *h* convocation ... Lev 23:3 6944
even *h* convocations, which ye ... Lev 23:4 6944
ye shall have an *h* convocation ... Lev 23:7 6944
seventh day is an *h* convocation ... Lev 23:8 6944
they shall be *h* to the LORD for ... Lev 23:20 6944
that it may be an *h* convocation ... Lev 23:21 6944
of trumpets, an *h* convocation ... Lev 23:24 6944
it shall be an *h* convocation unto ... Lev 23:27 6944
day shall be an *h* convocation ... Lev 23:35 6944
be an *h* convocation unto you ... Lev 23:36 6944
proclaim to be *h* convocations ... Lev 23:37 6944
they shall eat it in the *h* place ... Lev 24:9 6918
for it is most *h* unto him of the ... Lev 24:9 6944
it shall be *h* unto you ... Lev 25:12 6944
of such unto the LORD shall be *h* ... Lev 27:9 6944
the exchange thereof shall be *h* ... Lev 27:10 6944
his house to be *h* unto the LORD ... Lev 27:14 6944
shall be *h* unto the LORD, as a ... Lev 27:21 6944
as a *h* thing unto the LORD ... Lev 27:23 6944
thing is most *h* unto the LORD ... Lev 27:28 6944
it is *h* unto the LORD ... Lev 27:30 6944
tenth shall be *h* unto the LORD ... Lev 27:32 6944
and the change thereof shall be *h* ... Lev 27:33 6944
about the most *h* things ... Num 4:4 6944
they shall not touch any *h* thing ... Num 4:15 6944
approach unto the most *h* things ... Num 4:19 6944
see when the *h* things are covered ... Num 4:20 6944
the *h* things of the children of ... Num 5:9 6944
the priest shall take *h* water in ... Num 5:17 6918
unto the LORD, he shall be *h* ... Num 6:5 6918
separation he is *h* unto the LORD ... Num 6:8 6918
this is *h* for the priest, with ... Num 6:20 6944
and be *h* unto your God ... Num 15:40 6918
seeing all the congregation are *h* ... Num 16:3 6918
shew who are his, and who is *h* ... Num 16:5 6918
LORD doth choose, he shall be *h* ... Num 16:7 6918
be thine of the most *h* things ... Num 18:9 6944
unto me, shall be most *h* for thee ... Num 18:9 6944
In the most *h* place shalt thou ... Num 18:10 6944
it shall be *h* unto thee ... Num 18:10 6944
they are *h* ... Num 18:17 6944
heave offerings of the *h* things ... Num 18:19 6944
the *h* things of the children of ... Num 18:32 6944
in the *h* place shalt thou cause ... Num 28:7 6944
day shall be an *h* convocation ... Num 28:18 6944
ye shall have an *h* convocation ... Num 28:25 6944
ye shall have an *h* convocation ... Num 28:26 6944
ye shall have an *h* convocation ... Num 29:1 6944
seventh month an *h* convocation ... Num 29:7 6944
ye shall have an *h* convocation ... Num 29:12 6944
with the *h* instruments, and the ... Num 31:6 6944
which was anointed with the *h* oil ... Num 35:25 6944
For thou art an *h* people unto the ... Deut 7:6 6918
Only thy *h* things which thou hast ... Deut 12:26 6944
For thou art an *h* people unto the ... Deut 14:2 6918
for thou art an *h* people unto the ... Deut 14:21 6918
therefore shall thy camp be *h* ... Deut 23:14 6918
Look down from thy *h* habitation ... Deut 26:15 6944
that thou mayest be an *h* people ... Deut 26:19 6918
thee an *h* people unto himself ... Deut 28:9 6918
and thy Urim be with thy *h* one ... Deut 33:8 2623

place whereon thou standest is *h* ... Josh 5:15 6944
for he is an *h* God ... Josh 24:19 6918
There is none *h* as the LORD ... 1Sa 2:2 6918
to stand before this *h* LORD God ... 1Sa 6:20 6918
vessels of the young men are *h* ... 1Sa 21:5 6944
oracle, even for the most *h* place ... 1Kin 6:16 6944
the inner house, the most *h* place ... 1Kin 7:50 6944
all the *h* vessels that were in ... 1Kin 8:4 6944
of the house, to the most *h* place ... 1Kin 8:6 6944
in the *h* place before the oracle ... 1Kin 8:8 6944
were come out of the *h* place ... 1Kin 8:10 6944
that this is an *h* man of God ... 2Kin 4:9 6918
even against the *H* One of Israel ... 2Kin 19:22 6918
all the work of the place most *h* ... 1Chr 6:49 6944
Glory ye in his *h* name ... 1Chr 16:10 6944
we may give thanks to thy *h* name ... 1Chr 16:35 6944
the *h* vessels of God, into the ... 1Chr 22:19 6944
should sanctify the most *h* things ... 1Chr 23:13 6944
in the purifying of all *h* things ... 1Chr 23:28 6944
and the charge of the *h* place ... 1Chr 23:32 6944
I have prepared for the *h* house ... 1Chr 29:3 6944
thine *h* name cometh of thine hand ... 1Chr 29:16 6944
And he made the most *h* house ... 2Chr 3:8 6944
in the most *h* house he made two ... 2Chr 3:10 6944
thereof for the most *h* place ... 2Chr 4:22 6944
all the *h* vessels that were in ... 2Chr 5:5 6944
the house, into the most *h* place ... 2Chr 5:7 6944
were come out of the *h* place ... 2Chr 5:11 6944
Israel, because the places are *h* ... 2Chr 8:11 6944
they shall go in, for they are *h* ... 2Chr 23:6 6944
the filthiness out of the *h* place ... 2Chr 29:5 6944
h place unto the God of Israel ... 2Chr 29:7 6944
came up to his *h* dwelling place ... 2Chr 30:27 6944
the tithe of *h* things which were ... 2Chr 31:6 6944
of the LORD, and the most *h* things ... 2Chr 31:14 6944
which were *h* unto the LORD ... 2Chr 35:3 6918
Put the *h* ark in the house which ... 2Chr 35:3 6944
stand in the *h* place according to ... 2Chr 35:5 6944
but the other *h* offerings sod ... 2Chr 35:13 6944
not eat of the most *h* things ... Ezr 2:63 6944
unto them, Ye are *h* unto the LORD ... Ezr 8:28 6944
the vessels are *h* also ... Ezr 8:28 6944
so that the *h* seed have mingled ... Ezr 9:2 6944
to give us a nail in his *h* place ... Ezr 9:8 6944
not eat of the most *h* things ... Neh 7:65 6944
This day is *h* unto the LORD your ... Neh 8:9 6918
for this day is *h* unto our Lord ... Neh 8:10 6918
Hold your peace, for the day is *h* ... Neh 8:11 6918
known unto them thy *h* sabbath ... Neh 9:14 6944
on the sabbath, or on the *h* day ... Neh 10:31 6944
set feasts, and for the *h* things ... Neh 10:33 6944
to dwell in Jerusalem the *h* city ... Neh 11:1 6944
All the Levites in the *h* city ... Neh 11:18 6944
they sanctified *h* things unto the ... Neh 12:47
concealed the words of the *H* One ... Job 6:10 6918
my king upon my *h* hill of Zion ... Ps 2:6 6944
and he heard me out of his *h* hill ... Ps 3:4 6944
I worship toward thy *h* temple ... Ps 5:7 6944
The LORD is in his *h* temple ... Ps 11:4 6944
who shall dwell in thy *h* hill ... Ps 15:1 6944
thine *H* One to see corruption ... Ps 16:10 2623
he will hear him from his *h* ... Ps 20:6 6944
But thou art *h*, O thou that ... Ps 22:3 6918
or who shall stand in his *h* place ... Ps 24:3 6944
up my hands toward thy *h* oracle ... Ps 28:2 6944
we have trusted in his *h* name ... Ps 33:21 6944
let them bring me unto thy *h* hill ... Ps 43:3 6944
the *h* place of the tabernacles of ... Ps 46:4 6918
take not thy *h* spirit from me ... Ps 51:11 6944
thy house, even of thy *h* temple ... Ps 65:4 6918
is God in his *h* habitation ... Ps 68:5 6944
them, as in Sinai, in the *h* place ... Ps 68:17 6944
art terrible out of thy *h* places ... Ps 68:35 4720
the harp, O thou *H* One of Israel ... Ps 71:22 6918
limited the *H* One of Israel ... Ps 78:41 6918
thy *h* temple have they defiled ... Ps 79:1 6944
for I am *h* ... Ps 86:2 2623
foundation is in the *h* mountains ... Ps 87:1 6944
the *H* One of Israel is our king ... Ps 89:18 6918
spakest in vision to thy *h* one ... Ps 89:19 2623
with my *h* oil have I anointed him ... Ps 89:20 6944
his right hand, and his *h* arm ... Ps 98:1 6944
for it is *h* ... Ps 99:3 6918
for he is *h* ... Ps 99:5 6918
our God, and worship at his *h* hill ... Ps 99:9 6944
for the LORD our God is *h* ... Ps 99:9 6918
is within me, bless his *h* name ... Ps 103:1 6944
Glory ye in his *h* name ... Ps 105:3 6944
For he remembered his *h* promise ... Ps 105:42 6944
to give thanks unto thy *h* name ... Ps 106:47 6944
h and reverend is his name ... Ps 111:9 6918
will worship toward thy *h* temple ... Ps 138:2 6944
his ways, and *h* in all his works ... Ps 145:17 2623
flesh bless his *h* name for ever ... Ps 145:21 6944
of the *h* is understanding ... Prov 9:10 6918
man who devoureth that which is *h* ... Prov 20:25 6944
nor have the knowledge of the *h* ... Prov 30:3 6918
and gone from the place of the *h* ... Eccl 8:10 6918
they have provoked the *H* One of ... Is 1:4 6918
in Jerusalem, shall be called *h* ... Is 4:3 6918
God that is *h* shall be sanctified ... Is 5:16 6918
let the counsel of the *H* One of ... Is 5:19 6918
the word of the *H* One of Israel ... Is 5:24 6918
another, and said, *H*, *h*, *h* ... Is 6:3 6918
so the *h* seed shall be the ... Is 6:13 6944
a fire, and his *H* One for a flame ... Is 10:17 6918
the *H* One of Israel, in truth ... Is 10:20 6918
nor destroy in all my *h* mountain ... Is 11:9 6944

for great is the *H* One of Israel ... Is 12:6 6918
respect to the *H* One of Israel ... Is 17:7 6918
LORD in the *h* mount at Jerusalem ... Is 27:13 6944
rejoice in the *H* One of Israel ... Is 29:19 6918
and sanctify the *H* One of Jacob ... Is 29:23 6918
cause the *H* One of Israel to ... Is 30:11 6918
thus saith the *H* One of Israel ... Is 30:12 6918
the Lord GOD, the *H* One of Israel ... Is 30:15 6918
night when a *h* solemnity is kept ... Is 30:29 6942
look not unto the *H* One of Israel ... Is 31:1 6918
even against the *H* One of Israel ... Is 37:23 6918
I be equal? saith the *H* One ... Is 40:25 6918
thy redeemer, the *H* One of Israel ... Is 41:14 6918
glory in the *H* One of Israel ... Is 41:16 6918
the *H* One of Israel hath created ... Is 41:20 6918
the *H* One of Israel, thy Saviour ... Is 43:3 6918
redeemer, the *H* One of Israel ... Is 43:14 6918
I am the LORD, your *H* One ... Is 43:15 6918
the *H* One of Israel, and his Maker ... Is 45:11 6918
is his name, the *H* One of Israel ... Is 47:4 6918
call themselves of the *h* city ... Is 48:2 6944
thy Redeemer, the *H* One of Israel ... Is 48:17 6918
Redeemer of Israel, and his *H* One ... Is 49:7 6918
the *H* One of Israel, and he shall ... Is 49:7 6918
garments, O Jerusalem, the *h* city ... Is 52:1 6944
his *h* arm in the eyes of all the ... Is 52:10 6944
thy Redeemer the *H* One of Israel ... Is 54:5 6918
God, and for the *H* One of Israel ... Is 55:5 6918
will I bring to my *h* mountain ... Is 56:7 6944
and shall inherit my *h* mountain ... Is 57:13 6944
eternity, whose name is *H* ... Is 57:15 6918
h place, with him also that is of ... Is 57:15 6918
doing thy pleasure on my *h* day ... Is 58:13 6944
the *h* of the LORD, honourable ... Is 58:13 6918
to the *H* One of Israel, because ... Is 60:9 6918
The Zion of the *H* One of Israel ... Is 60:14 6918
The *h* people, The redeemed of the ... Is 62:12 6944
rebelled, and vexed his *h* Spirit ... Is 63:10 6944
that put his *h* Spirit within him ... Is 63:11 6944
Thy *h* cities are a wilderness, ... Is 64:10 6944
Our *h* and our beautiful house, ... Is 64:11 6944
LORD, that forget my *h* mountain ... Is 65:11 6944
nor destroy in all my *h* mountain ... Is 65:25 6944
to my *h* mountain Jerusalem, saith ... Is 66:20 6944
the *h* flesh is passed from thee ... Jer 11:15 6944
his voice from his *h* habitation ... Jer 25:30 6944
east, shall be *h* unto the LORD ... Jer 31:40 6944
against the *H* One of Israel ... Jer 50:29 6918
sin against the *H* One of Israel ... Jer 51:5 6918
their *h* places shall be defiled ... Eze 7:24 6942
but pollute ye my *h* name no more ... Eze 20:39 6944
For in mine *h* mountain, in the ... Eze 20:40 6944
oblations, with all your *h* things ... Eze 20:40
drop thy word toward the *h* places ... Eze 21:2 4720
Thou hast despised mine *h* things ... Eze 22:8 6944
and have profaned mine *h* things ... Eze 22:26 6944
put no difference between the *h* ... Eze 22:26 6944
wast upon the *h* mountain of God ... Eze 28:14 6944
went, they profaned my *h* name ... Eze 36:20 6944
But I had pity for mine *h* name ... Eze 36:21 6944
but for mine *h* name's sake ... Eze 36:22 6944
As the *h* flock, as the flock of ... Eze 36:38 6944
So will I make my *h* name known in ... Eze 39:7 6944
them pollute my *h* name any more ... Eze 39:7 6944
am the LORD, the *H* One in Israel ... Eze 39:7 6918
and will be jealous for my *h* name ... Eze 39:25 6944
unto me, This is the most *h* place ... Eze 41:4 6944
they be *h* chambers, where the ... Eze 42:13 6944
LORD shall eat the most *h* things ... Eze 42:13 6944
shall they lay the most *h* things ... Eze 42:13 6944
for the place is *h* ... Eze 42:13 6918
the *h* place into the utter court ... Eze 42:14 6944
for they are *h* ... Eze 42:14
my *h* name, shall the house of ... Eze 43:7 6944
they have even defiled my *h* name ... Eze 43:8 6944
round about shall be most *h* ... Eze 43:12 6944
kept the charge of mine *h* things ... Eze 44:8 6944
h things, in the most *h* place ... Eze 44:13 6944
and lay them in the *h* chambers ... Eze 44:19 6944
the difference between the *h* ... Eze 44:23 6944
LORD, an *h* portion of the land ... Eze 45:1 6944
This shall be *h* in all the ... Eze 45:1 6944
the sanctuary and the most *h* place ... Eze 45:3 6944
The *h* portion of the land shall ... Eze 45:4 6944
an *h* place for the sanctuary ... Eze 45:4 4720
the oblation of the *h* portion ... Eze 45:6 6944
of the oblation of the *h* portion ... Eze 45:7 6944
the oblation of the *h* portion ... Eze 45:7 6944
into the *h* chambers of the ... Eze 46:19 6944
priests, shall be this *h* oblation ... Eze 48:10 6944
h by the border of the Levites ... Eze 48:12 6944
for it is *h* unto the LORD ... Eze 48:14 6944
against the oblation of the *h* ... Eze 48:18 6944
the oblation of the *h* portion ... Eze 48:18 6944
ye shall offer the *h* oblation ... Eze 48:20 6944
and on the other of the *h* oblation ... Eze 48:21 6944
and it shall be the *h* oblation ... Eze 48:21 6944
whom is the spirit of the *h* gods ... Dan 4:8 6922
spirit of the *h* gods is in thee ... Dan 4:9 6922
an *h* one came down from heaven ... Dan 4:13 6922
demand by the word of the *h* ones ... Dan 4:17 6922
spirit of the *h* gods is in thee ... Dan 4:18 6922
an *h* one coming down from heaven, ... Dan 4:23 6922
whom is the spirit of the *h* gods ... Dan 5:11 6922
the mighty and the *h* people ... Dan 8:24 6918
city Jerusalem, thy *h* mountain ... Dan 9:16 6944
God for the *h* mountain of my God ... Dan 9:20 6944
thy people and upon thy *h* city ... Dan 9:24 6944

prophecy, and to anoint the most *H* ... Dan 9:24 6944
shall be against the *h* covenant ... Dan 11:28 6944
against the *h* covenant ... Dan 11:30 6944
them that forsake the *h* covenant ... Dan 11:30 6944
seas in the glorious *h* mountain ... Dan 11:45 6944
scatter the power of the *h* people ... Dan 12:7 6944
the *H* One in the midst of thee ... Hos 11:9 6918
sound an alarm in my *h* mountain ... Joel 2:1 6944
dwelling in Zion, my *h* mountain ... Joel 3:17 6944
then shall Jerusalem be *h* ... Joel 3:17 6944
same maid, to profane my *h* name ... Amos 2:7 6944
ye have drunk upon my *h* mountain ... Obad 16 6944
look again toward thy *h* temple ... Jonah 2:4 6944
in unto thee, into thine *h* temple ... Jonah 2:7 6944
you, the Lord from his *h* temple ... Mic 1:2 6944
O LORD my God, mine *H* One ... Hab 1:12 6918
But the LORD is in his *h* temple ... Hab 2:20 6944
the *H* One from mount Paran ... Hab 3:3 6918
haughty because of my *h* mountain ... Zeph 3:11 6944
If one bear *h* flesh in the skirt ... Hag 2:12 6944
oil, or any meat, shall it be *h* ... Hag 2:12 6942
Judah his portion in the *h* land ... Zec 2:12 6944
raised up out of his *h* habitation ... Zec 2:13 6944
the LORD of hosts the *h* mountain ... Zec 8:3 6944
found with child of the *H* Ghost ... Mt 1:18 *40*
in her is of the *H* Ghost ... Mt 1:20 *40*
baptize you with the *H* Ghost ... Mt 3:11 *40*
taketh him up into the *h* city ... Mt 4:5 *40*
not that which is *h* unto the dogs ... Mt 7:6 *40*
the *H* Ghost shall not be forgiven ... Mt 12:31
speaketh against the *H* Ghost ... Mt 12:32 *40*
the prophet, stand in the *h* place ... Mt 24:15 *40*
all the *h* angels with him, then ... Mt 25:31 *40*
and went into the *h* city, and ... Mt 27:53 *40*
and of the Son, and of the *H* Ghost ... Mt 28:19 *40*
baptize you with the *H* Ghost ... Mk 1:8 *40*
who thou art, the *H* One of God ... Mk 1:24 *40*
shall blaspheme against the *H* ... Mk 3:29 *40*
that he was a just man and an *h* ... Mk 6:20 *40*
of his Father with the *h* angels ... Mk 8:38 *40*
David himself said by the *H* Ghost ... Mk 12:36 *40*
ye that speak, but the *H* Ghost ... Mk 13:11 *40*
shall be filled with the *H* Ghost ... Lk 1:15 *40*
The *H* Ghost shall come upon thee, ... Lk 1:35 *40*
therefore also that *h* thing which ... Lk 1:35 *40*
was filled with the *H* Ghost ... Lk 1:41 *40*
and *h* is his name ... Lk 1:49 *40*
was filled with the *H* Ghost ... Lk 1:67 *40*
by the mouth of his *h* prophets ... Lk 1:70 *40*
and to remember his *h* covenant ... Lk 1:72 *40*
shall be called *h* to the Lord ... Lk 2:23 *40*
and the *H* Ghost was upon him ... Lk 2:25 *40*
revealed unto him by the *H* Ghost ... Lk 2:26 *40*
baptize you with the *H* Ghost ... Lk 3:16 *40*
the *H* Ghost descended in a bodily ... Lk 3:22 *40*
Jesus being full of the *H* Ghost ... Lk 4:1 *40*
the *H* One of God ... Lk 4:34 *40*
his Father's, and of the *h* angels ... Lk 9:26 *40*
the *H* Spirit to them that ask him ... Lk 11:13 *40*
that blasphemeth against the *H* ... Lk 12:10 *40*
For the *H* Ghost shall teach you ... Lk 12:12 *40*
which baptizeth with the *H* Ghost ... Jn 1:33 *40*
for the *H* Ghost was not yet given ... Jn 7:39 *40*
Comforter, which is the *H* Ghost ... Jn 14:26 *40*
H Father, keep through thine own ... Jn 17:11 *40*
unto them, Receive ye the *H* Ghost ... Jn 20:22 *40*
after that he through the *H* Ghost ... Acts 1:2 *40*
the *H* Ghost not many days hence ... Acts 1:5 *40*
after that the *H* Ghost is come ... Acts 1:8 *40*
which the *H* Ghost by the mouth of ... Acts 1:16 *40*
were all filled with the *H* Ghost ... Acts 2:4 *40*
thine *H* One to see corruption ... Acts 2:27 *3741*
Father the promise of the *H* Ghost ... Acts 2:33 *40*
receive the gift of the *H* Ghost ... Acts 2:38 *40*
But ye denied the *H* One and the ... Acts 3:14 *40*
h prophets since the world began ... Acts 3:21 *40*
Peter, filled with the *H* Ghost ... Acts 4:8 *40*
a truth against thy *h* child Jesus ... Acts 4:27 *40*
by the name of thy *h* child Jesus ... Acts 4:30 *40*
were all filled with the *H* Ghost ... Acts 4:31 *40*
thine heart to lie to the *H* Ghost ... Acts 5:3 *40*
and so is also the *H* Ghost ... Acts 5:32 *40*
report, full of the *H* Ghost ... Acts 6:3 *40*
full of faith and of the *H* Ghost ... Acts 6:5 *40*
words against this *h* place ... Acts 6:13 *40*
where thou standest is *h* ground ... Acts 7:33 *40*
ye do always resist the *H* Ghost ... Acts 7:51 *40*
But he, being full of the *H* Ghost ... Acts 7:55 *40*
they might receive the *H* Ghost ... Acts 8:15 *40*
and they received the *H* Ghost ... Acts 8:17 *40*
hands the *H* Ghost was given ... Acts 8:18 *40*
hands, he may receive the *H* Ghost ... Acts 8:19 *40*
and be filled with the *H* Ghost ... Acts 9:17 *40*
and in the comfort of the *H* Ghost ... Acts 9:31 *40*
was warned from God by an *h* angel ... Acts 10:22 *40*
of Nazareth with the *H* Ghost ... Acts 10:38 *40*
the *H* Ghost fell on all them ... Acts 10:44 *40*
out the gift of the *H* Ghost ... Acts 10:45 *40*
the *H* Ghost as well as we ... Acts 10:47 *40*
the *H* Ghost fell on them, as on ... Acts 11:15 *40*
be baptized with the *H* Ghost ... Acts 11:16 *40*
good man, and full of the *H* Ghost ... Acts 11:24 *40*
the *H* Ghost said, Separate me ... Acts 13:2 *40*
being sent forth by the *H* Ghost ... Acts 13:4 *40*
Paul,) filled with the *H* Ghost ... Acts 13:9 *40*
thine *H* One to see corruption ... Acts 13:35 *3741*
with joy, and with the *H* Ghost ... Acts 13:52 *40*
witness, giving them the *H* Ghost ... Acts 15:8 *40*

For it seemed good to the *H* Ghost ... Acts 15:28 ... 40
were forbidden of the *H* Ghost to ... Acts 16:6 ... 40
Have ye received the *H* Ghost ... Acts 19:2 ... 40
whether there be any *H* Ghost ... Acts 19:2 ... 40
them, the *H* Ghost came on them ... Acts 19:6 ... 40
Save that the *H* Ghost witnesseth ... Acts 20:23 ... 40
over the which the *H* Ghost hath ... Acts 20:28 ... 40
and said, Thus saith the *H* Ghost ... Acts 21:11 ... 40
and hath polluted this *h* place ... Acts 21:28 ... 40
Well spake the *H* Ghost by Esaias ... Acts 28:25 ... 40
his prophets in the *h* scriptures ... Rom 1:2 ... 40
abroad in our hearts by the *H* ... Rom 5:5 ... 40
law is *h*, and the commandment *h* ... Rom 7:12 ... 40
bearing me witness in the *H* Ghost ... Rom 9:1 ... 40
be *h*, the lump is also *h* ... Rom 11:16 ... 40
and if the root be *h*, so are the ... Rom 11:16 ... 40
your bodies a living sacrifice, *h* ... Rom 12:1 ... 40
and peace, and joy in the *H* Ghost ... Rom 14:17 ... 40
through the power of the *H* Ghost ... Rom 15:13 ... 40
being sanctified by the *H* Ghost ... Rom 15:16 ... 40
Salute one another with an *h* kiss ... Rom 16:16 ... 40
but which the *H* Ghost teacheth ... 1Cor 2:13 ... 40
for the temple of God is *h* ... 1Cor 3:17 ... 40
of the *H* Ghost which is in you ... 1Cor 6:19 ... 40
but now are they *h* ... 1Cor 7:14 ... 40
that she may be *h* both in body ... 1Cor 7:34 ... 40
h things live of the things of ... 1Cor 9:13 ... 2413
is the Lord, but by the *H* Ghost ... 1Cor 12:3 ... 40
ye one another with an *h* kiss ... 1Cor 16:20 ... 40
by kindness, by the *H* Ghost ... 2Cor 6:6 ... 40
Greet one another with an *h* kiss ... 2Cor 13:12 ... 40
and the communion of the *H* Ghost ... 2Cor 13:14 ... 40
of the world, that we should be *h* ... Eph 1:4 ... 40
with that *h* Spirit of promise ... Eph 1:13 ... 40
unto an *h* temple in the Lord ... Eph 2:21 ... 40
now revealed unto his *h* apostles ... Eph 3:5 ... 40
And grieve not the *h* Spirit of God ... Eph 4:30 ... 40
but that it should be *h* and ... Eph 5:27 ... 40
through death, to present you *h* ... Col 1:22 ... 40
therefore, as the elect of God, *h* ... Col 3:12 ... 40
also in power, and in the *H* Ghost ... 1Th 1:5 ... 40
with joy of the *H* Ghost ... 1Th 1:6 ... 40
also given unto us his *h* Spirit ... 1Th 4:8 ... 40
all the brethren with an *h* kiss ... 1Th 5:26 ... 40
be read unto all the *h* brethren ... 1Th 5:27 ... 40
every where, lifting up *h* hands ... 1Ti 2:8 ... 3741
and called us with an *h* calling ... 2Ti 1:9 ... 40
the *H* Ghost which dwelleth in us ... 2Ti 1:14 ... 40
thou hast known the *h* scriptures ... 2Ti 3:15 ... 2413
lover of good men, sober, just, *h* ... Titus 1:8 ... 3741
and renewing of the *H* Ghost ... Titus 3:5 ... 40
miracles, and gifts of the *H* Ghost ... Heb 2:4 ... 40
h brethren, partakers of the ... Heb 3:1 ... 40
Wherefore (as the *H* Ghost saith ... Heb 3:7 ... 40
made partakers of the *H* Ghost ... Heb 6:4 ... 40
high priest became us, who is *h* ... Heb 7:26 ... 3741
The *H* Ghost this signifying, that ... Heb 9:8 ... 40
entered in once into the *h* place ... Heb 9:12 ... 39
into the *h* places made with hands ... Heb 9:24 ... 39
high priest entereth into the *h* ... Heb 9:25 ... 39
Whereof the *H* Ghost also is a ... Heb 10:15 ... 40
the *H* Ghost sent down from heaven ... 1Pet 1:12 ... 40
as he which hath called you is *h* ... 1Pet 1:15 ... 40
so be ye *h* in all manner of ... 1Pet 1:15 ... 40
Be ye *h*; for I am *h* ... 1Pet 1:16 ... 40
an *h* priesthood, to offer up ... 1Pet 2:5 ... 40
an *h* nation, a peculiar people ... 1Pet 2:9 ... 40
in the old time the *h* women also ... 1Pet 3:5 ... 40
we were with him in the *h* mount ... 2Pet 1:18 ... 40
but *h* men of God spake as they ... 2Pet 1:21 ... 40
as they were moved by the *H* Ghost ... 2Pet 1:21 ... 40
to turn from the *h* commandment ... 2Pet 2:21 ... 40
spoken before by the *h* prophets ... 2Pet 3:2 ... 40
ye to be in all *h* conversation ... 2Pet 3:11 ... 40
ye have an unction from the *H* One ... 1Jn 2:20 ... 40
Father, the Word, and the *H* Ghost ... 1Jn 5:7 ... 40
yourselves on your most *h* faith ... Jude 20 ... 40
praying in the *H* Ghost ... Jude 20 ... 40
These things saith he that is *h* ... Rev 3:7 ... 40
and night, saying, *H*, *h*, *h* ... Rev 4:8 ... 40
saying, How long, O Lord, *h* ... Rev 6:10 ... 40
the *h* city shall they tread under ... Rev 11:2 ... 40
in the presence of the *h* angels ... Rev 14:10 ... 40
for thou only art *h* ... Rev 15:4 ... 3741
ye *h* apostles and prophets ... Rev 18:20 ... 40
h is he that hath part in the ... Rev 20:6 ... 40
And I John saw the *h* city, new ... Rev 21:2 ... 40
the *h* Jerusalem, descending out ... Rev 21:10 ... 40
the Lord God of the *h* prophets ... Rev 22:6 ... 40
that is *h*, let him be *h* still ... Rev 22:11 ... 37
of life, and out of the *h* city ... Rev 22:19 ... 40

HOLYDAY {2}
with a multitude that kept *h* ... Ps 42:4 ... 2287
in drink, or in respect of an *h* ... Col 2:16 ... 1859

HOMAM *(ho'-mam)* {1} See HEMAM. *A son of Lotan.*
of Lotan; Hori, and *H* ... 1Chr 1:39 ... 1950

HOME {51}
by her, until his lord came *h* ... Gen 39:16 ... 1004
of his house, Bring these men *h* ... Gen 43:16 ... 1004
And when Joseph came *h*, they ... Gen 43:26 ... 1004
field, and shall not be brought *h* ... Ex 9:19 ... 1004
mother, whether she be born at *h* ... Lev 18:9 ... 1004
shalt bring her *h* to thine house ... Deut 21:12 ... 8432
he shall be free at *h* one year ... Deut 24:5 ... 1004
father's household, *h* unto thee ... Josh 2:18 ... 1004
If ye bring me *h* again to fight ... Judg 11:9 ... 7725
your way, that thou mayest go *h* ... Judg 19:9 ... 168
hath brought me *h* again empty ... Ruth 1:21 ... 7725
And they went unto their own *h* ... 1Sa 2:20 ... 4725
and bring their calves *h* from them ... 1Sa 6:7 ... 1004
and shut up their calves at *h* ... 1Sa 6:10 ... 1004
And Saul also went *h* to Gibeah ... 1Sa 10:26 ... 1004
no more *h* to his father's house ... 1Sa 18:2 ... 7725
And Saul went *h* ... 1Sa 24:22 ... 1004
Then David sent *h* to Tamar ... 2Sa 13:7 ... 1004
not fetch *h* again his banished ... 2Sa 14:13 ... 7725
gat him *h* to his house, to his ... 2Sa 17:23 ... 1004
in Lebanon, and two months at *h* ... 1Kin 5:14 ... 1004
Come *h* with me, and refresh ... 1Kin 13:7 ... 1004
Come *h* with me, and eat bread ... 1Kin 13:15 ... 1004
glory of this, and tarry at *h* ... 2Kin 14:10 ... 1004
I bring the ark of God *h* to me ... 1Chr 13:12
So David brought not the ark *h* to ... 1Chr 13:13
him out of Ephraim, to go *h* again ... 2Chr 25:10 ... 4725
they returned *h* in great anger ... 2Chr 25:10 ... 4725
abide now at *h* ... 2Chr 25:19 ... 1004
and when he came *h*, he sent and ... Est 5:10 ... 1004
that he will bring *h* thy seed ... Job 39:12 ... 7725
tarried at *h* divided the spoil ... Ps 68:12 ... 1004
For the goodman is not at *h* ... Prov 7:19 ... 1004
will come *h* at the day appointed ... Prov 7:20 ... 1004
because man goeth to his long *h* ... Eccl 12:5 ... 1004
that he should carry him *h* ... Jer 39:14 ... 1004
bereaveth, at *h* there is as death ... Lam 1:20 ... 1004
a proud man, neither keepeth at *h* ... Hab 2:5 ... 5115
and when ye brought it *h*, I did ... Hag 1:9 ... 1004
lieth at *h* sick of the palsy ... Mt 8:6 ... 3614
Go *h* to thy friends, and tell them ... Mk 5:19 ... 3624
which are at *h* at my house ... Lk 9:61
And when he cometh *h*, he calleth ... Lk 15:6 ... 3624
disciple took her unto his own *h* ... Jn 19:27
went away again unto their own *h* ... Jn 20:10 ... 1438
and they returned *h* again ... Acts 21:6 ... 2398
any man hunger, let him eat at *h* ... 1Cor 11:34 ... 3624
let them ask their husbands at *h* ... 1Cor 14:35 ... 3624
whilst we are at *h* in the body ... 2Cor 5:6 ... 1736
learn first to shew piety at *h* ... 1Ti 5:4 ... 2398
be discreet, chaste, keepers at *h* ... Titus 2:5 ... 3626

HOMEBORN {2}
One law shall be to him that is *h* ... Ex 12:49 ... 249
is he a *h* slave? ... Jer 2:14 ... 1004

HOMER {11}
a *h* of barley seed shall be ... Lev 27:16 ... 2563
the seed of an *h* shall yield an ... Is 5:10 ... 2563
contain the tenth part of an *h* ... Eze 45:11 ... 2563
the ephah the tenth part of an *h* ... Eze 45:11 ... 2563
thereof shall be after the *h* ... Eze 45:11 ... 2563
part of an ephah of an *h* of wheat ... Eze 45:13 ... 2563
of an ephah of an *h* of barley ... Eze 45:13 ... 2563
which is an *h* of ten baths ... Eze 45:14 ... 2563
for ten baths are an *h* ... Eze 45:14 ... 2563
an *h* of barley, and an half *h* ... Hos 3:2 ... 2563

HOMERS {1}
gathered least gathered ten *h* ... Num 11:32 ... 2563

HONEST {7}
ground are they, which in an *h* ... Lk 8:15 ... 2570
among you seven men of *h* report ... Acts 6:3
Provide things *h* in the sight of ... Rom 12:17 ... 2570
Providing for *h* things, not only ... 2Cor 8:21 ... 2570
that ye should do that which is *h* ... 2Cor 13:7 ... 2570
are true, whatsoever things are *h* ... Phil 4:8 ... 4586
conversation *h* among the Gentiles ... 1Pet 2:12 ... 2570

HONESTLY {3}
Let us walk *h*, as in the day ... Rom 13:13 ... 2156
That ye may walk *h* toward them ... 1Th 4:12 ... 2156
in all things willing to live *h* ... Heb 13:18 ... 2573

HONESTY {1}
life in all godliness and *h* ... 1Ti 2:2 ... 4587

HONEY {56}
a little balm, and a little *h* ... Gen 43:11 ... 1706
a land flowing with milk and *h* ... Ex 3:8 ... 1706
a land flowing with milk and *h* ... Ex 3:17 ... 1706
a land flowing with milk and *h* ... Ex 13:5 ... 1706
of it was like wafers made with *h* ... Ex 16:31 ... 1706
a land flowing with milk and *h* ... Ex 33:3 ... 1706
shall burn no leaven, nor any *h* ... Lev 2:11 ... 1706
land that floweth with milk and *h* ... Lev 20:24 ... 1706
surely it floweth with milk and *h* ... Num 13:27 ... 1706
land which floweth with milk and *h* ... Num 14:8 ... 1706
land that floweth with milk and *h* ... Num 16:13 ... 1706
land that floweth with milk and *h* ... Num 16:14 ... 1706
land that floweth with milk and *h* ... Deut 6:3 ... 1706
a land of oil olive, and *h* ... Deut 8:8 ... 1706
land that floweth with milk and *h* ... Deut 11:9 ... 1706
land that floweth with milk and *h* ... Deut 26:9 ... 1706
land that floweth with milk and *h* ... Deut 26:15 ... 1706
land that floweth with milk and *h* ... Deut 27:3 ... 1706
that floweth with milk and *h* ... Deut 31:20 ... 1706
him to suck *h* out of the rock ... Deut 32:13 ... 1706
land that floweth with milk and *h* ... Josh 5:6 ... 1706
h in the carcase of the lion ... Judg 14:8 ... 1706
h out of the carcase of the lion ... Judg 14:9 ... 1706
went down, What is sweeter than *h* ... Judg 14:18 ... 1706
there was *h* upon the ground ... 1Sa 14:25 ... 1706
the wood, behold, the *h* dropped ... 1Sa 14:26 ... 1706
I tasted a little of this *h* ... 1Sa 14:29 ... 1706
I did but taste a little *h* with ... 1Sa 14:43 ... 1706
And *h*, and butter, and sheep, and ... 2Sa 17:29 ... 1706
and cracknels, and a cruse of *h* ... 1Kin 14:3 ... 1706
a land of oil olive and of *h* ... 2Kin 18:32 ... 1706
of corn, wine, and oil, and *h* ... 2Chr 31:5 ... 1706
the floods, the brooks of *h* ... Job 20:17 ... 1706
sweeter also than *h* and the ... Ps 19:10 ... 1706
with *h* out of the rock should I ... Ps 81:16 ... 1706
yea, sweeter than *h* to my mouth ... Ps 119:103 ... 1706
My son, eat thou *h*, because it is ... Prov 24:13 ... 1706
Hast thou found *h*? ... Prov 25:16 ... 1706
It is not good to eat much *h* ... Prov 25:27 ... 1706
h and milk are under thy tongue ... Song 4:11 ... 1706
have eaten my honeycomb with my *h* ... Song 5:1 ... 1706
h shall he eat, that he may know ... Is 7:15 ... 1706
h shall every one eat that is ... Is 7:22 ... 1706
a land flowing with milk and *h* ... Jer 11:5 ... 1706
a land flowing with milk and *h* ... Jer 32:22 ... 1706
and of barley, and of oil, and of *h* ... Jer 41:8 ... 1706
in my mouth as *h* for sweetness ... Eze 3:3 ... 1706
thou didst eat fine flour, and *h* ... Eze 16:13 ... 1706
thee, fine flour, and oil, and *h* ... Eze 16:19 ... 1706
for them, flowing with milk and *h* ... Eze 20:6 ... 1706
them, flowing with milk and *h* ... Eze 20:15 ... 1706
wheat of Minnith, and Pannag, and *h* ... Eze 27:17 ... 1706
and his meat was locusts and wild *h* ... Mt 3:4 ... 3192
and he did eat locusts and wild *h* ... Mk 1:6 ... 3192
shall be in thy mouth sweet as *h* ... Rev 10:9 ... 3192
and it was in my mouth sweet as *h* ... Rev 10:10 ... 3192

HONEYCOMB {9}
in his hand, and dipped it in an *h* ... 1Sa 14:27 ... 3295,1706
sweeter also than honey and the *h* ... Ps 19:10 ... 5317,6688
of a strange woman drop as an *h* ... Prov 5:3 ... 5317
Pleasant words are as an *h* ... Prov 16:24 ... 6688,1706
and the *h*, which is sweet to thy ... Prov 24:13 ... 5317
The full soul loatheth an *h* ... Prov 27:7 ... 5317
lips, O my spouse, drop as the *h* ... Song 4:11 ... 5317
I have eaten my *h* with my honey ... Song 5:1 ... 3293
of a broiled fish, and of an *h* ... Lk 24:42 ... 3193,2781

HONOUR {146}
unto their assembly, mine *h* ... Gen 49:6 ... 3519
and I will get me *h* upon Pharaoh ... Ex 14:17 ... 3513
I have gotten me *h* upon Pharaoh ... Ex 14:18 ... 3513
H thy father and thy mother ... Ex 20:12 ... 3513
nor *h* the person of the mighty ... Lev 19:15 ... 1921
h the face of the old man, and ... Lev 19:32 ... 1921
promote thee unto very great *h* ... Num 22:17 ... 3513
able indeed to promote thee to *h* ... Num 22:37 ... 3513
to promote thee unto great *h* ... Num 24:11 ... 3513
LORD hath kept thee back from *h* ... Num 24:11 ... 3519
put some of thine *h* upon him ... Num 27:20 ... 1935
H thy father and thy mother, as ... Deut 5:16 ... 3513
in praise, and in name, and in *h* ... Deut 26:19 ... 8597
takest shall not be for thine *h* ... Judg 4:9 ... 8597
wherewith by me they *h* God ... Judg 9:9 ... 3513
come to pass we may do thee *h* ... Judg 13:17 ... 3513
for them that *h* me I will *h* ... 1Sa 2:30 ... 3513
yet *h* me now, I pray thee, before ... 1Sa 15:30 ... 3513
of, of them shall I be had in *h* ... 2Sa 6:22 ... 3513
thou that David doth *h* thy father ... 2Sa 10:3 ... 3513
hast not asked, both riches, and *h* ... 1Kin 3:13 ... 3519
Glory and *h* are in his presence ... 1Chr 16:27 ... 1926
to thee for the *h* of thy servant ... 1Chr 17:18 ... 3519
thou that David doth *h* thy father ... 1Chr 19:3 ... 3513
h come of thee, and thou reignest ... 1Chr 29:12 ... 3519
age, full of days, riches, and *h* ... 1Chr 29:28 ... 3519
not asked riches, wealth, or *h* ... 2Chr 1:11 ... 3519
give thee riches, and wealth, and *h* ... 2Chr 1:12 ... 3519
he had riches and *h* in abundance ... 2Chr 17:5 ... 3519
h in abundance, and joined ... 2Chr 18:1 ... 3519
be for thine *h* from the LORD God ... 2Chr 26:18 ... 3519
had exceeding much riches and *h* ... 2Chr 32:27 ... 3519
Jerusalem did him *h* at his death ... 2Chr 32:33 ... 3519
the *h* of his excellent majesty ... Est 1:4 ... 3366
shall give to their husbands *h* ... Est 1:20 ... 3366
And the king said, What *h* and ... Est 6:3 ... 3366
man whom the king delighteth to *h* ... Est 6:6 ... 3366
to do *h* more than to myself ... Est 6:6 ... 3366
man whom the king delighteth to *h* ... Est 6:7 ... 3366
whom the king delighteth to *h* ... Est 6:9 ... 3366
man whom the king delighteth to *h* ... Est 6:9 ... 3366
man whom the king delighteth to *h* ... Est 6:11 ... 3366
light, and gladness, and joy, and *h* ... Est 8:16 ... 3366
His sons come to *h*, and he knoweth ... Job 14:21 ... 3513
earth, and lay mine *h* in the dust ... Ps 7:5 ... 3519
hast crowned him with glory and *h* ... Ps 8:5 ... 1926
h and majesty hast thou laid upon ... Ps 21:5 ... 1935
the place where thine *h* dwelleth ... Ps 26:8 ... 3519
man being in *h* abideth not ... Ps 49:12 ... 3366
Man that is in *h*, and ... Ps 49:20 ... 3366
Sing forth the *h* of his name ... Ps 66:2 ... 3519
praise and with thy *h* all the day ... Ps 71:8 ... 8597
I will deliver him, and *h* him ... Ps 91:15 ... 3515
H and majesty are before him ... Ps 96:6 ... 1935
thou art clothed with *h* and ... Ps 104:1 ... 1935
his horn shall be exalted with *h* ... Ps 112:9 ... 3519
of the glorious *h* of thy majesty ... Ps 145:5 ... 1926
this *h* have all his saints ... Ps 149:9 ... 1926
H the LORD with thy substance, and ... Prov 3:9 ... 3513
and in her left hand riches and *h* ... Prov 3:16 ... 3519
she shall bring thee to *h* ... Prov 4:8 ... 3513
thou give thine *h* unto others ... Prov 5:9 ... 1935
Riches and *h* are with me ... Prov 8:18 ... 3519
A gracious woman retaineth *h* ... Prov 11:16 ... 3519
of people is the king's *h* ... Prov 14:28 ... 1927
and before *h* is humility ... Prov 15:33 ... 3519
and before *h* is humility ... Prov 18:12 ... 3519
It is an *h* for a man to cease ... Prov 20:3 ... 3519
findeth life, righteousness, and *h* ... Prov 21:21 ... 3519
fear of the LORD are riches, and *h* ... Prov 22:4 ... 3519
but the *h* of kings is to search ... Prov 25:2 ... 3519
so *h* is not seemly for a fool ... Prov 26:1 ... 3519
so is he that giveth *h* to a fool ... Prov 26:8 ... 3519

H

but *h* shall uphold the humble in ... Prov 29:23 3519
Strength and *h* are her clothing ... Prov 31:25 1926
hath given riches, wealth, and *h* ... Eccl 6:2 3519
is in reputation for wisdom and *h* ... Eccl 10:1 3519
mouth, and with their lips do *h* me ... Is 29:13 3513
The beast of the field shall *h* me ... Is 43:20 3513
and shalt *h* him, not doing thine ... Is 58:13 3513
an *h* before all the nations of ... Jer 33:9 8597
of me gifts and rewards and great *h* ... Dan 2:6 3367
power, and for the *h* of my majesty ... Dan 4:30 3367
the glory of my kingdom, mine *h* ... Dan 4:36 1923
h the King of heaven, all whose ... Dan 4:37 1922
and majesty, and glory, and *h* ... Dan 5:18 1923
not give the *h* of the kingdom ... Dan 11:21 1935
shall he *h* the God of forces ... Dan 11:38 3513
knew not shall he *h* with gold ... Dan 11:38 3513
I be a father, where is mine *h* ... Mal 1:6 3519
them, A prophet is not without *h* ... Mt 13:57 *820*
saying, *H* thy father and mother ... Mt 15:4 *5091*
h not his father or his mother, ... Mt 15:6 *5091*
H thy father and thy mother ... Mt 19:19 *5091*
them, A prophet is not without *h* ... Mk 6:4 *820*
H thy father and thy mother ... Mk 7:10 *5091*
not, *H* thy father and mother ... Mk 10:19 *5091*
H thy father and thy mother ... Lk 18:20 *5091*
hath no *h* in his own country ... Jn 4:44 *5092*
That all men should *h* the Son ... Jn 5:23 *5091*
even as they *h* the Father ... Jn 5:23 *5091*
I receive not *h* from men ... Jn 5:41 *1391*
which receive *h* one of another, ... Jn 5:44 *1391*
seek not the *h* that cometh from ... Jn 5:44 *1391*
but I *h* my Father, and ye do ... Jn 8:49 *5091*
I *h* myself, my *h* is nothing ... Jn 8:54 *1391*
serve me, him will my Father *h* ... Jn 12:26 *5091*
in well doing seek for glory and *h* ... Rom 2:7 *5092*
But glory, *h*, and peace, to every ... Rom 2:10 *5092*
lump to make one vessel unto *h* ... Rom 9:21 *5092*
in *h* preferring one another ... Rom 12:10 *5092*
to whom fear; *h* to whom *h* ... Rom 13:7 *5092*
these we bestow more abundant *h* ... 1Cor 12:23 *5092*
h to that part which lacked ... 1Cor 12:24 *5092*
By *h* and dishonour, by evil report ... 2Cor 6:8 *1391*
H thy father and mother ... Eph 6:2 *5091*
not in any *h* to the satisfying of ... Col 2:23 *5092*
his vessel in sanctification and *h* ... 1Th 4:4 *5092*
the only wise God, be *h* and glory ... 1Ti 1:17 *5092*
H widows that are widows indeed ... 1Ti 5:3 *5091*
be counted worthy of double *h* ... 1Ti 5:17 *5092*
their own masters worthy of all *h* ... 1Ti 6:1 *5092*
to whom be *h* and power everlasting ... 1Ti 6:16 *5092*
and some to *h*, and some to ... 2Ti 2:20 *5092*
he shall be a vessel unto *h* ... 2Ti 2:21 *5092*
crownedst him with glory and *h* ... Heb 2:7 *5092*
of death, crowned with glory and *h* ... Heb 2:9 *5092*
house hath more *h* than the house ... Heb 3:3 *5092*
no man taketh this *h* unto himself ... Heb 5:4 *5092*
might be found unto praise and *h* ... 1Pet 1:7 *5092*
H all men ... 1Pet 2:17 *5091*
H the king ... 1Pet 2:17 *5091*
giving *h* unto the wife, as unto ... 1Pet 3:7 *5092*
he received from God the Father *h* ... 2Pet 1:17 *5092*
when those beasts give glory and *h* ... Rev 4:9 *5092*
O Lord, to receive glory and *h* ... Rev 4:11 *5092*
and wisdom, and strength, and *h* ... Rev 5:12 *5092*
heard I saying, Blessing, and *h* ... Rev 5:13 *5092*
and wisdom, and thanksgiving, and *h* ... Rev 7:12 *5092*
Salvation, and glory, and *h* ... Rev 19:1 *5092*
glad and rejoice, and give *h* to him ... Rev 19:7 *1391*
do bring their glory and *h* into it ... Rev 21:24 *5092*
glory and *h* of the nations into it ... Rev 21:26 *5092*

HONOURABLE {30}
he was more *h* than all the house ... Gen 34:19 3513
more, and more *h* than they ... Num 22:15 3513
a man of God, and he is an *h* man ... 1Sa 9:6 3513
bidding, and is *h* in thine house ... 1Sa 22:14 3513
Was he not most *h* of three ... 2Sa 23:19 3513
He was more *h* than the thirty, ... 2Sa 23:23 3513
great man with his master, and *h* ... 2Kin 5:1 5375,6440
Jabez was more *h* than his ... 1Chr 4:9 3513
he was more *h* than the two ... 1Chr 11:21 3513
he was *h* among the thirty, but ... 1Chr 11:25 3513
and the *h* man dwelt in it ... Job 22:8 5375,6440
daughters were among thy *h* women ... Ps 45:9 3368
His work is *h* and glorious ... Ps 111:3 1935
captain of fifty, and the *h* man ... Is 3:3 5375,6440
and the base against the *h* ... Is 3:5 3519
their *h* men are famished, and ... Is 5:13 3519
The ancient and *h*, he is the head ... Is 9:15 5375,6440
are the *h* of the earth ... Is 23:8 1935
contempt all the *h* of the earth ... Is 23:9 3513
magnify the law, and make it *h* ... Is 42:21 142
in my sight, thou hast been *h* ... Is 43:4 3513
delight, the holy of the LORD, *h* ... Is 58:13 3513
and they cast lots for her *h* men ... Nah 3:10 3513
an *h* counsellor, which also ... Mk 15:43 *2158*
lest a more *h* man than thou be ... Lk 14:8 *1784*
h women, and the chief men of the ... Acts 13:50 *2158*
also of *h* women which were Greeks ... Acts 17:12 *2158*
ye are *h*, but we are despised ... 1Cor 4:10 *1741*
body, which we think to be less *h* ... 1Cor 12:23 *820*
Marriage is *h* in all, and the bed ... Heb 13:4 *5093*

HONOURED {9}
I will be *h* upon Pharaoh, and upon ... Ex 14:4 3513
that regardeth reproof shall be *h* ... Prov 13:18 3513
waiteth on his master shall be *h* ... Prov 27:18 3513
neither hast thou *h* me with thy ... Is 43:23 3513
all that *h* her despise her, ... Lam 1:8 3513
the faces of elders were not *h* ... Lam 5:12 1921
h him that liveth for ever, whose ... Dan 4:34 1922
Who also *h* us with many honours ... Acts 28:10 *5092*
or one member be *h*, all the ... 1Cor 12:26 *1392*

HONOUREST {1}
h thy sons above me, to make ... 1Sa 2:29 3513

HONOURETH {9}
but he *h* them that fear the LORD ... Ps 15:4 3513
is better than he that *h* himself ... Prov 12:9 3513
but he that *h* him hath mercy on ... Prov 14:31 3513
A son *h* his father, and a servant ... Mal 1:6 3513
mouth, and *h* me with their lips ... Mt 15:8 *5091*
This people *h* me with their lips, ... Mk 7:6 *5091*
He that *h* not the Son *h* not ... Jn 5:23 *5091*
it is my Father that *h* me ... Jn 8:54 *1392*

HONOURS {1}
Who also honoured us with many *h* ... Acts 28:10 *5091*

HOODS {1}
and the fine linen, and the *h* ... Is 3:23 6797

HOOF {12}
shall not an *h* be left behind ... Ex 10:26 6541
Whatsoever parteth the *h*, and is ... Lev 11:3 6541
cud, or of them that divide the *h* ... Lev 11:4 6541
the cud, but divideth not the *h* ... Lev 11:4 6541
the cud, but divideth not the *h* ... Lev 11:5 6541
the cud, but divideth not the *h* ... Lev 11:6 6541
the swine, though he divide the *h* ... Lev 11:7 6541
every beast which divideth the *h* ... Lev 11:26 6541
And every beast that parteth the *h* ... Deut 14:6 6541
of them that divide the cloven *h* ... Deut 14:7 6541
the cud, but divide not the *h* ... Deut 14:7 6541
swine, because it divideth the *h* ... Deut 14:8 6541

HOOFS {6}
or bullock that hath horns and *h* ... Ps 69:31 6536
their horses' *h* shall be counted ... Is 5:28 6541
of the *h* of his strong horses ... Jer 47:3 6541
With the *h* of his horses shall he ... Eze 26:11 6541
nor the *h* of beasts trouble them ... Eze 32:13 6541
iron, and I will make thy *h* brass ... Mic 4:13 6541

HOOK {5}
I will put my *h* in thy nose ... 2Kin 19:28 2397
thou draw out leviathan with an *h* ... Job 41:1 100
Canst thou put an *h* into his nose ... Job 41:2 2443
will I put my *h* in thy nose ... Is 37:29 2397
go thou to the sea, and cast an *h* ... Mt 17:27 *44*

HOOKS {17}
their *h* shall be of gold, upon ... Ex 26:32 2053
gold, and their *h* shall be of gold ... Ex 26:37 2053
the *h* of the pillars and their ... Ex 27:10 2053
the *h* of the pillars and their ... Ex 27:11 2053
their *h* shall be of silver, and ... Ex 27:17 2053
their *h* were of gold ... Ex 36:36 2053
five pillars of it with their *h* ... Ex 36:38 2053
the *h* of the pillars and their ... Ex 38:10 2053
the *h* of the pillars and their ... Ex 38:11 2053
the *h* of the pillars and their ... Ex 38:12 2053
the *h* of the pillars and their ... Ex 38:17 2053
their *h* of silver, and the ... Ex 38:19 2053
shekels he made *h* for the pillars ... Ex 38:28 2053
But I will put *h* in thy jaws ... Eze 29:4 2397
put *h* into thy jaws, and I will ... Eze 38:4 2397
And within were *h*, an hand broad, ... Eze 40:43 8240
that he will take you away with *h* ... Amos 4:2 6793

HOPE {132}
If I should say, I have *h* ... Ruth 1:12 8615
yet now there is *h* in Israel ... Ezr 10:2 4723
thy fear, thy confidence, thy *h* ... Job 4:6 8615
So the poor hath *h*, and iniquity ... Job 5:16 8615
is my strength, that I should *h* ... Job 6:11 3176
shuttle, and are spent without *h* ... Job 7:6 8615
and the hypocrite's *h* shall perish ... Job 8:13 8615
Whose *h* shall be cut off, and ... Job 8:14 3689
be secure, because there is *h* ... Job 11:18 8615
their *h* shall be as the giving up ... Job 11:20 8615
For there is *h* of a tree, if it ... Job 14:7 8615
and thou destroyest the *h* of man ... Job 14:19 8615
And where is now my *h* ... Job 17:15 8615
as for my *h*, who shall see it ... Job 17:15 8615
mine *h* hath he removed like a ... Job 19:10 8615
For what is the *h* of the ... Job 27:8 8615
If I have made gold my *h*, or have ... Job 31:24 3689
Behold, the *h* of him is in vain ... Job 41:9 8431
my flesh also shall rest in *h* ... Ps 16:9 983
thou didst make me *h* when I was ... Ps 22:9 982
heart, all ye that *h* in the LORD ... Ps 31:24 3176
upon them that *h* in his mercy ... Ps 33:18 3176
us, according as we *h* in thee ... Ps 33:22 3176
For in thee, O LORD, do I *h* ... Ps 38:15 3176
my *h* is in thee ... Ps 39:7 8431
h thou in God ... Ps 42:5 3176
h thou in God ... Ps 42:11 3176
h in God ... Ps 43:5 3176
For thou art my *h*, O Lord GOD ... Ps 71:5 8615
But I will *h* continually, and will ... Ps 71:14 3176
they might set their *h* in God ... Ps 78:7 3689
which thou hast caused me to *h* ... Ps 119:49 3176
but I *h* in thy word ... Ps 119:81 3176
I *h* in thy word ... Ps 119:114 3176
and let me not be ashamed of my *h* ... Ps 119:116 7664
doth wait, and in his word do I *h* ... Ps 130:5 3176
Let Israel *h* in the LORD ... Ps 130:7 3176
Let Israel *h* in the LORD from ... Ps 131:3 3176
whose *h* is in the LORD his God ... Ps 146:5 7664
him, in those that *h* in his mercy ... Ps 147:11 3176
The *h* of the righteous shall be ... Prov 10:28 8431
the *h* of unjust men perisheth ... Prov 11:7 8431
H deferred maketh the heart sick, ... Prov 13:12 8431
the righteous hath *h* in his death ... Prov 14:32 2620
Chasten thy son while there is *h* ... Prov 19:18 8615
there is more *h* of a fool than of ... Prov 26:12 8615
there is more *h* of a fool than of ... Prov 29:20 8615
to all the living there is *h* ... Eccl 9:4 986
the pit cannot *h* for thy truth ... Is 38:18 7663
saidst thou not, There is no *h* ... Is 57:10 2976
but thou saidst, There is no *h* ... Jer 2:25 2976
O the *h* of Israel, the saviour ... Jer 14:8 4723
the LORD, and whose *h* the LORD is ... Jer 17:7 4009
the *h* of Israel, all that forsake ... Jer 17:13 4723
thou art my *h* in the day of evil ... Jer 17:17 4268
And they said, There is no *h* ... Jer 18:12 2976
there is *h* in thine end, saith ... Jer 31:17 8615
the LORD, the *h* of their fathers ... Jer 50:7 4723
my *h* is perished from the LORD ... Lam 3:18 8431
to my mind, therefore have I *h* ... Lam 3:21 3176
therefore will I *h* in him ... Lam 3:24 3176
is good that a man should both *h* ... Lam 3:26 2342
if so be there may be *h* ... Lam 3:29 8615
they have made others to *h* that ... Eze 13:6 3176
her *h* was lost, then she took ... Eze 19:5 8615
bones are dried, and our *h* is lost ... Eze 37:11 8615
valley of Achor for a door of *h* ... Hos 2:15 8615
LORD will be the *h* of his people ... Joel 3:16 4268
strong hold, ye prisoners of *h* ... Zec 9:12 8615
to them of whom ye *h* to receive ... Lk 6:34 *1679*
also my flesh shall rest in *h* ... Acts 2:26 *1680*
the *h* of their gains was gone ... Acts 16:19 *1680*
of the *h* and resurrection of the ... Acts 23:6 *1680*
have *h* toward God, which they ... Acts 24:15 *1680*
am judged for the *h* of the ... Acts 26:6 *1680*
God day and night, *h* to come ... Acts 26:7 *1679*
all *h* that we should be saved was ... Acts 27:20 *1680*
because that for the *h* of Israel ... Acts 28:20 *1680*
Who against *h* believed in *h*, ... Rom 4:18 *1680*
Who against *h* believed in *h* ... Rom 4:18 *1680*
rejoice in *h* of the glory of God ... Rom 5:2 *1680*
experience; and experience, *h* ... Rom 5:4 *1680*
And *h* maketh not ashamed ... Rom 5:5 *1680*
who hath subjected the same in *h* ... Rom 8:20 *1680*
For we are saved by *h* ... Rom 8:24 *1680*
but *h* that is seen is not *h* ... Rom 8:24 *1680*
man seeth, why doth he yet *h* for ... Rom 8:24 *1679*
But if we *h* for that we see not, ... Rom 8:25 *1679*
Rejoicing in *h* ... Rom 12:12 *1680*
of the scriptures might have *h* ... Rom 15:4 *1680*
Now the God of *h* fill you with ... Rom 15:13 *1680*
that ye may abound in *h*, through ... Rom 15:13 *1680*
he that ploweth should plow in *h* ... 1Cor 9:10 *1680*
that he that thresheth in *h* ... 1Cor 9:10 *1680*
h should be partaker of his *h* ... 1Cor 9:10 *1680*
And now abideth faith, *h*, charity, ... 1Cor 13:13 *1680*
life only we have *h* in Christ ... 1Cor 15:19 *1679*
our *h* of you is stedfast, knowing ... 2Cor 1:7 *1680*
Seeing then that we have such *h* ... 2Cor 3:12 *1680*
but having *h*, when your faith is ... 2Cor 10:15 *1680*
the *h* of righteousness by faith ... Gal 5:5 *1680*
know what is the *h* of his calling ... Eph 1:18 *1680*
covenants of promise, having no *h* ... Eph 2:12 *1680*
called in one *h* of your calling ... Eph 4:4 *1680*
to my earnest expectation and my *h* ... Phil 1:20 *1680*
Him therefore I *h* to send ... Phil 2:23 *1679*
For the *h* which is laid up for ... Col 1:5 *1680*
away from the *h* of the gospel ... Col 1:23 *1680*
is Christ in you, the *h* of glory ... Col 1:27 *1680*
patience of *h* in our Lord Jesus ... 1Th 1:3 *1680*
For what is our *h*, or joy, or ... 1Th 2:19 *1680*
even as others which have no *h* ... 1Th 4:13 *1680*
for an helmet, the *h* of salvation ... 1Th 5:8 *1680*
and good *h* through grace, ... 2Th 2:16 *1680*
Lord Jesus Christ, which is our *h* ... 1Ti 1:1 *1680*
In *h* of eternal life, which God, ... Titus 1:2 *1680*
Looking for that blessed *h* ... Titus 2:13 *1680*
to the *h* of eternal life ... Titus 3:7 *1680*
of the *h* firm unto the end ... Heb 3:6 *1680*
full assurance of *h* unto the end ... Heb 6:11 *1680*
lay hold upon the *h* set before us ... Heb 6:18 *1680*
Which *h* we have as an anchor of ... Heb 6:19
the bringing in of a better *h* did ... Heb 7:19 *1680*
h by the resurrection of Jesus ... 1Pet 1:3 *1680*
h to the end for the grace that ... 1Pet 1:13 *1679*
your faith and *h* might be in God ... 1Pet 1:21 *1680*
h that is in you with meekness ... 1Pet 3:15 *1680*
this *h* in him purifieth himself ... 1Jn 3:3 *1680*

HOPED {11}
Jews *h* to have power over them ... Est 9:1 7663
confounded because they had *h* ... Job 6:20 982
for I have *h* in thy judgments ... Ps 119:43 3176
because I have *h* in thy word ... Ps 119:74 3176
I *h* in thy word ... Ps 119:147 3176
I have *h* for thy salvation, and ... Ps 119:166 7663
is salvation *h* for from the hills ... Jer 3:23
he *h* to have seen some miracle ... Lk 23:8 *1679*
He *h* also that money should have ... Acts 24:26 *1679*
And this they did, not as we *h* ... 2Cor 8:5 *1679*
is the substance of things *h* for ... Heb 11:1 *1679*

HOPE'S {1}
For which *h* sake, king Agrippa, I ... Acts 26:7 *1679*

HOPETH {1}
h all things, endureth all things ... 1Cor 13:7 *1679*

HOPHNI *(hof'-ni)* {5} *A son of Eli.*
And the two sons of Eli, *H* ... 1Sa 1:3 2652
come upon thy two sons, on *H* ... 1Sa 2:34 2652

and the two sons of Eli, *H* ... 1Sa 4:4 2652
and the two sons of Eli, *H* ... 1Sa 4:11 2652
people, and thy two sons also, *H* ... 1Sa 4:17 2652

HOPING {2}
and lend, *h* for nothing again ... Lk 6:35 *560*
h to come unto thee shortly ... 1Ti 3:14 *1679*

HOR *(hor)* {12} See HOR-HAGIDGAD.
1. A mountain in Moab.
from Kadesh, and came unto mount *H* ... Num 20:22 2023
unto Moses and Aaron in mount *H* ... Num 20:23 2023
and bring them up unto mount *H* ... Num 20:25 2023
mount *H* in the sight of all the ... Num 20:27 2023
mount *H* by the way of the Red sea ... Num 21:4 2023
Kadesh, and pitched in mount *H* ... Num 33:37 2023
the priest went up into mount *H* ... Num 33:38 2023
years old when he died in mount *H* ... Num 33:39 2023
And they departed from mount *H* ... Num 33:41 2023
Aaron thy brother died in mount *H* ... Deut 32:50 2023
2. A hill in northern Israel.
shall point out for you mount *H* ... Num 34:7 2023
From mount *H* ye shall point out ... Num 34:8 2023

HORAM *(ho'-ram)* {1} *A Canaanite king.*
Then *H* king of Gezer came up to ... Josh 10:33 2036

HOREB *(ho'-reb)* {17} See SINAI. *A mountain range in Sinai.*
to the mountain of God, even to *H* ... Ex 3:1 2722
thee there upon the rock in *H* ... Ex 17:6 2722
of their ornaments by the mount *H* ... Ex 33:6 2722
H by the way of mount Seir unto ... Deut 1:2 2722
LORD our God spake unto us in *H* ... Deut 1:6 2722
And when we departed from *H* ... Deut 1:19 2722
before the LORD thy God in *H* ... Deut 4:10 2722
in *H* out of the midst of the fire ... Deut 4:15 2722
God made a covenant with us in *H* ... Deut 5:2 2722
Also in *H* ye provoked the LORD to ... Deut 9:8 2722
of the LORD thy God in *H* in the ... Deut 18:16 2722
which he made with them in *H* ... Deut 29:1 2722
stone, which Moses put there at *H* ... 1Kin 8:9 2722
nights unto *H* the mount of God ... 1Kin 19:8 2722
which Moses put therein at *H* ... 2Chr 5:10 2722
They made a calf in *H*, and ... Ps 106:19 2722
unto him in *H* for all Israel ... Mal 4:4 2722

HOREM *(ho'-rem)* {1} *A city in Naphtali.*
And Iron, and Migdal-el, *H*, and ... Josh 19:38 2765

HORESH See ZIPH.

HOR-HAGIDGAD *(hor-hag-id'-gad)* {2} *An encampment of Israel in the wilderness.*
Bene-jaakan, and encamped at *H* ... Num 33:32 2735
And they went from *H*, and pitched ... Num 33:33 2735

HORI *(ho'-ri)* {4} See HORITE.
1. Son of Lotan.
And the children of Lotan were *H* ... Gen 36:22 2753
are the dukes that came of *H* ... Gen 36:30 2753
H, and Homam ... 1Chr 1:39 2753
2. Father of Shapat.
of Simeon, Shaphat the son of *H* ... Num 13:5 2753

HORIMS *(ho'-rims)* {2} See HORITES. *Inhabitants of Mt. Seir.*
The *H* also dwelt in Seir ... Deut 2:12 2752
destroyed the *H* from before them ... Deut 2:22 2752

HORITE *(ho'-rite)* {1} See HORI, HORITES. *An inhabitant of Mt. Seir.*
These are the sons of Seir the *H* ... Gen 36:20 2752

HORITES *(ho'-rites)* {3} See HORIMS. *Same as Horims.*
the *H* in their mount Seir, unto ... Gen 14:6 2752
these are the dukes of the *H* ... Gen 36:21 2752
are the dukes that came of the *H* ... Gen 36:29 2752

HORMAH *(hor'-mah)* {9} See ZEPHATH. *A Canaanite royal town.*
and discomfited them, even unto *H* ... Num 14:45 2767
he called the name of the place *H* ... Num 21:3 2767
you in Seir, even unto *H* ... Deut 1:44 2767
The king of *H*, one ... Josh 12:14 2767
And Eltolad, and Chesil, and *H* ... Josh 15:30 2767
And Eltolad, and Bethul, and *H* ... Josh 19:4 2767
the name of the city was called *H* ... Judg 1:17 2767
And to them which were in *H* ... 1Sa 30:30 2767
And at Bethuel, and at *H*, and at ... 1Chr 4:30 2767

HORN {36}
to push with his *h* in time past ... Ex 21:29
a long blast with the ram's *h* ... Josh 6:5 7161
mine *h* is exalted in the LORD ... 1Sa 2:1 7161
exalt the *h* of his anointed ... 1Sa 2:10 7161
fill thine *h* with oil, and go, I ... 1Sa 16:1 7161
Then Samuel took the *h* of oil ... 1Sa 16:13 7161
the *h* of my salvation, my high ... 2Sa 22:3 7161
Zadok the priest took an *h* of oil ... 1Kin 1:39 7161
words of God, to lift up the *h* ... 1Chr 25:5 7161
skin, and defiled my *h* in the dust ... Job 16:15 7161
the *h* of my salvation, and my high ... Ps 18:2 7161
to the wicked, Lift not up the *h* ... Ps 75:4 7161
Lift not up your *h* on high ... Ps 75:5 7161
thy favour our *h* shall be exalted ... Ps 89:17 7161
in my name shall his *h* be exalted ... Ps 89:24 7161
But my *h* shalt thou exalt like ... Ps 92:10 7161
exalt like the *h* of an unicorn ... Ps 92:10
his *h* shall be exalted with ... Ps 112:9 7161
will I make the *h* of David to bud ... Ps 132:17 7161
also exalteth the *h* of his people ... Ps 148:14 7161
The *h* of Moab is cut off, and his ... Jer 48:25 7161
fierce anger all the *h* of Israel ... Lam 2:3 7161
he hath set up the *h* of thine ... Lam 2:17 7161
In that day will I cause the *h* of ... Eze 29:21 7161
up among them another little *h* ... Dan 7:8 7162
in this *h* were eyes like the eyes ... Dan 7:8 7162
the great words which the *h* spake ... Dan 7:11 7162
even of that *h* that had eyes, and ... Dan 7:20 7162
the same *h* made war with the ... Dan 7:21 7162
had a notable *h* between his eyes ... Dan 8:5 7161
strong, the great *h* was broken ... Dan 8:8 7161
one of them came forth a little *h* ... Dan 8:9 7161
the great *h* that is between his ... Dan 8:21 7161
for I will make thine *h* iron ... Mic 4:13 7161
which lifted up their *h* over the ... Zec 1:21 7161
hath raised up an *h* of salvation ... Lk 1:69 *2768*

HORNET {2}
God will send the *h* among them ... Deut 7:20 6880
And I sent the *h* before you ... Josh 24:12 6880

HORNETS {1}
And I will send *h* before thee ... Ex 23:28 6880

HORNS {67}
ram caught in a thicket by his *h* ... Gen 22:13 7161
thou shalt make the *h* of it upon ... Ex 27:2 7161
his *h* shall be of the same ... Ex 27:2 7161
put it upon the *h* of the altar ... Ex 29:12 7161
the *h* thereof shall be of the ... Ex 30:2 7161
round about, and the *h* thereof ... Ex 30:3 7161
make an atonement upon the *h* of ... Ex 30:10 7161
the *h* thereof were of the same ... Ex 37:25 7161
round about, and the *h* of it ... Ex 37:26 7161
he made the *h* thereof on the four ... Ex 38:2 7161
the *h* thereof were of the same ... Ex 38:2 7161
h of the altar of sweet incense ... Lev 4:7 7161
h of the altar which is before ... Lev 4:18 7161
put it upon the *h* of the altar of ... Lev 4:25 7161
put it upon the *h* of the altar of ... Lev 4:30 7161
put it upon the *h* of the altar of ... Lev 4:34 7161
put it upon the *h* of the altar ... Lev 8:15 7161
and put it upon the *h* of the altar ... Lev 9:9 7161
put it upon the *h* of the altar ... Lev 16:18 7161
h are like the *h* of unicorns ... Deut 33:17 7161
the ark seven trumpets of rams' *h* ... Josh 6:4 3104
h before the ark of the LORD ... Josh 6:6 3104
rams' *h* passed on before the LORD ... Josh 6:8
h before the ark of the LORD went ... Josh 6:13 3104
caught hold on the *h* of the altar ... 1Kin 1:50 7161
caught hold on the *h* of the altar ... 1Kin 1:51 7161
caught hold on the *h* of the altar ... 1Kin 2:28 7161
of Chenaanah made him *h* of iron ... 1Kin 22:11 7161
Chenaanah had made him *h* of iron ... 2Chr 18:10 7161
me from the *h* of the unicorns ... Ps 22:21 7161
than an ox or bullock that hath *h* ... Ps 69:31 7160
All the *h* of the wicked also will ... Ps 75:10 7161
but the *h* of the righteous shall ... Ps 75:10 7161
even unto the *h* of the altar ... Ps 118:27 7161
upon the *h* of your altars ... Jer 17:1 7161
thee for a present *h* of ivory ... Eze 27:15 7161
all the diseased with your *h* ... Eze 34:21 7161
altar and upward shall be four *h* ... Eze 43:15 7161
and put it on the four *h* of it ... Eze 43:20 7161
and it had ten *h* ... Dan 7:7 7162
I considered the *h*, and, behold, ... Dan 7:8 7162
first *h* plucked up by the roots ... Dan 7:8 7162
of the ten *h* that were in his ... Dan 7:20 7162
the ten *h* out of this kingdom are ... Dan 7:24 7162
the river a ram which had two *h* ... Dan 8:3 7161
and the two *h* were high ... Dan 8:3 7161
he came to the ram that had two *h* ... Dan 8:6 7161
smote the ram, and brake his two *h* ... Dan 8:7 7161
two *h* are the kings of Media ... Dan 8:20 7161
the *h* of the altar shall be cut ... Amos 3:14 7161
taken to us *h* by our own strength ... Amos 6:13 7161
he had *h* coming out of his hand ... Hab 3:4 7161
eyes, and saw, and behold four *h* ... Zec 1:18 7161
These are the *h* which have ... Zec 1:19 7161
These are the *h* which have ... Zec 1:21 7161
to cast out the *h* of the Gentiles ... Zec 1:21 7161
it had been slain, having seven *h* ... Rev 5:6 *2768*
h of the golden altar which is ... Rev 9:13 *2768*
having seven heads and ten *h* ... Rev 12:3 *2768*
sea, having seven heads and ten *h* ... Rev 13:1 *2768*
upon his *h* ten crowns, and upon ... Rev 13:1 *2768*
he had two *h* like a lamb, and he ... Rev 13:11 *2768*
having seven heads and ten *h* ... Rev 17:3 *2768*
hath the seven heads and ten *h* ... Rev 17:7 *2768*
the ten *h* which thou sawest are ... Rev 17:12 *2768*
the ten *h* which thou sawest upon ... Rev 17:16 *2768*

HORONAIM *(hor-o-na'-im)* {4} See HOLON. *A Moabite city.*
for in the way of *H* they shall ... Is 15:5 2773
A voice of crying shall be from *H* ... Jer 48:3 2773
for in the going down of *H* the ... Jer 48:5 2773
voice, from Zoar even unto *H* ... Jer 48:34 2773

HORONITE *(ho'-ron-ite)* {3} *A native of Horonaim.*
When Sanballat the *H*, and Tobiah ... Neh 2:10 2772
But when Sanballat the *H*, and ... Neh 2:19 2772
was son in law to Sanballat the *H* ... Neh 13:28 2772

HORRIBLE {6}
and brimstone, and an *h* tempest ... Ps 11:6 2152
me up also out of an *h* pit ... Ps 40:2 7588
h thing is committed in the land ... Jer 5:30 8186
Israel hath done a very *h* thing ... Jer 18:13 8186
prophets of Jerusalem an *h* thing ... Jer 23:14 8186
I have seen an *h* thing in the ... Hos 6:10 8186

HORRIBLY {2}
be *h* afraid, be ye very desolate, ... Jer 2:12 8175
kings shall be *h* afraid for thee ... Eze 32:10 8178

HORROR {4}
an *h* of great darkness fell upon ... Gen 15:12 367
upon me, and *h* hath overwhelmed me ... Ps 55:5 6427
H hath taken hold upon me because ... Ps 119:53 2152
sackcloth, and *h* shall cover them ... Eze 7:18 6427

HORSE {45}
the path, that biteth the *h* heels ... Gen 49:17 5483
the *h* and his rider hath he thrown ... Ex 15:1 5483
For the *h* of Pharaoh went in with ... Ex 15:19 5483
the *h* and his rider hath he thrown ... Ex 15:21 5483
an *h* for an hundred and fifty ... 1Kin 10:29 5483
escaped on an *h* with the horsemen ... 1Kin 20:20 5483
h for *h*, and chariot for ... 1Kin 20:25 5483
that thou hast lost, *h* for *h* ... 1Kin 20:25 5483
an *h* for an hundred and fifty ... 2Chr 1:17 5483
of the *h* gate by the king's house ... 2Chr 23:15 5483
From above the *h* gate repaired ... Neh 3:28 5483
the *h* that the king rideth upon, ... Est 6:8 5483
h be delivered to the hand of one ... Est 6:9 5483
and take the apparel and the *h* ... Est 6:10 5483
took Haman the apparel and the *h* ... Est 6:11 5483
on high, she scorneth the *h* ... Job 39:18 5483
Hath thou given the *h* strength ... Job 39:19 5483
Be ye not as the *h*, or as the ... Ps 32:9 5483
An *h* is a vain thing for safety ... Ps 33:17 5483
h are cast into a dead sleep ... Ps 76:6 5483
not in the strength of the *h* ... Ps 147:10 5483
The *h* is prepared against the day ... Prov 21:31 5483
A whip for the *h*, a bridle for ... Prov 26:3 5483
bringeth forth the chariot and *h* ... Is 43:17 5483
as an *h* in the wilderness, that ... Is 63:13 5483
as the *h* rusheth into the battle ... Jer 8:6 5483
of the *h* gate toward the east ... Jer 31:40 5483
thee will I break in pieces the *h* ... Jer 51:21 5483
that rideth the *h* deliver himself ... Amos 2:15 5483
behold a man riding upon a red *h* ... Zec 1:8 5483
the *h* from Jerusalem, and the ... Zec 9:10 5483
as his goodly *h* in the battle ... Zec 10:3 5483
smite every *h* with astonishment ... Zec 12:4 5483
will smite every *h* of the people ... Zec 12:4 5483
so shall be the plague of the *h* ... Zec 14:15 5483
And I saw, and behold a white *h* ... Rev 6:2 *2462*
went out another *h* that was red ... Rev 6:4 *2462*
And I beheld, and lo a black *h* ... Rev 6:5 *2462*
And I looked, and behold a pale *h* ... Rev 6:8 *2462*
even unto the *h* bridles, by the ... Rev 14:20 *2462*
opened, and behold a white *h* ... Rev 19:11 *2462*
war against him that sat on the *h* ... Rev 19:19 *2462*
sword of him that sat upon the *h* ... Rev 19:21 *2462*

HORSEBACK {5}
there went one on *h* to meet him ... 2Kin 9:18 7392,5483
Then he sent out a second on *h* ... 2Kin 9:19 7392,5483
bring him on *h* through the street ... Est 6:9 7392
brought him on *h* through the ... Est 6:11 7392
and sent letters by posts on *h* ... Est 8:10 5483

HORSEHOOFS {1}
Then were the *h* broken by the ... Judg 5:22 6119,5483

HORSELEACH {1}
The *h* hath two daughters, crying, ... Prov 30:15 5936

HORSEMAN {2}
And Joram said, Take an *h*, and send ... 2Kin 9:17 7395
The *h* lifteth up both the bright ... Nah 3:3 6571

HORSEMEN {59}
up with him both chariots and *h* ... Gen 50:9 6571
and chariots of Pharaoh, and his *h* ... Ex 14:9 6571
upon his chariots, and upon his *h* ... Ex 14:17 6571
upon his chariots, and upon his *h* ... Ex 14:18 6571
horses, his chariots, and his *h* ... Ex 14:23 6571
their chariots, and upon their *h* ... Ex 14:26 6571
and covered the chariots, and the *h* ... Ex 14:28 6571
with his *h* into the sea, and the ... Ex 15:19 6571
chariots and *h* unto the Red sea ... Josh 24:6 6571
for his chariots, and to be his *h* ... 1Sa 8:11 6571
chariots, and six thousand *h* ... 1Sa 13:5 6571
h followed hard after him ... 2Sa 1:6 6571
chariots, and seven hundred *h* ... 2Sa 8:4 6571
the Syrians, and forty thousand *h* ... 2Sa 10:18 6571
and he prepared him chariots and *h* ... 1Kin 1:5 6571
chariots, and twelve thousand *h* ... 1Kin 4:26 6571
his chariots, and cities for his *h* ... 1Kin 9:19 6571
rulers of his chariots, and his *h* ... 1Kin 9:22 6571
gathered together chariots and *h* ... 1Kin 10:26 6571
chariots, and twelve thousand *h* ... 1Kin 10:26 6571
escaped on an horse with the *h* ... 1Kin 20:20 6571
of Israel, and the *h* thereof ... 2Kin 2:12 6571
people to Jehoahaz but fifty *h* ... 2Kin 13:7 6571
of Israel, and the *h* thereof ... 2Kin 13:14 6571
on Egypt for chariots and for *h* ... 2Kin 18:24 6571
chariots, and seven thousand *h* ... 1Chr 18:4 6571
h out of Mesopotamia, and out of ... 1Chr 19:6 6571
And Solomon gathered chariots and *h* ... 2Chr 1:14 6571
chariots, and twelve thousand *h* ... 2Chr 1:14 6571
cities, and the cities of the *h* ... 2Chr 8:6 6571
and captains of his chariots and *h* ... 2Chr 8:9 6571
and chariots, and twelve thousand *h* ... 2Chr 9:25 6571
and threescore thousand *h* ... 2Chr 12:3 6571
with very many chariots and *h* ... 2Chr 16:8 6571
h to help us against the enemy in ... Ezr 8:22 6571
captains of the army and *h* with me ... Neh 2:9 6571
saw a chariot with a couple of *h* ... Is 21:7 6571
of men, with a couple of *h* ... Is 21:9 6571
quiver with chariots of men and *h* ... Is 22:6 6571
the *h* shall set themselves in ... Is 22:7 6571
cart, nor bruise it with his *h* ... Is 28:28 6571
and in *h*, because they are very ... Is 31:1 6571
on Egypt for chariots and for *h* ... Is 36:9 6571

H

shall flee for the noise of the *h* ... Jer 4:29 6571
and get up, ye *h*, and stand forth ... Jer 46:4 6571
young men, *h* riding upon horses ... Eze 23:6 6571
h riding upon horses, all of them ... Eze 23:12 6571
and with chariots, and with *h* ... Eze 26:7 6571
shall shake at the noise of the *h* ... Eze 26:10 6571
in thy fairs with horses and *h* ... Eze 27:14 6571
and all thine army, horses and *h* ... Eze 38:4 6571
with chariots, and with *h* ... Dan 11:40 6571
by battle, by horses, nor by *h* ... Hos 1:7 6571
and as *h*, so shall they run ... Joel 2:4 6571
their *h* shall spread themselves, ... Hab 1:8 6571
their *h* shall come from far ... Hab 1:8 6571
h threescore and ten, and spearmen ... Acts 23:23 *2460*
they left the *h* to go with him ... Acts 23:32 *2460*
the *h* were two hundred thousand ... Rev 9:16 *2461*

HORSES {109}
gave them bread in exchange for *h* ... Gen 47:17 5483
which is in the field, upon the *h* ... Ex 9:3 5483
pursued after them, all the *h* ... Ex 14:9 5483
of the sea, even all Pharaoh's *h* ... Ex 14:23 5483
the army of Egypt, unto their *h* ... Deut 11:4 5483
shall not multiply *h* to himself ... Deut 17:16 5483
the end that he should multiply *h* ... Deut 17:16 5483
against thine enemies, and seest *h* ... Deut 20:1 5483
sea shore in multitude, with *h* ... Josh 11:4 5483
thou shalt hough their *h*, and burn ... Josh 11:6 5483
he houghed their *h*, and burnt ... Josh 11:9 5483
David houghed all the chariot *h* ... 2Sa 8:4
prepared him chariots and *h* ... 2Sa 15:1 5483
stalls of *h* for his chariots ... 1Kin 4:26 5483
Barley also and straw for the *h* ... 1Kin 4:28 5483
garments, and armour, and spices, *h* ... 1Kin 10:25 5483
Solomon had *h* brought out of ... 1Kin 10:28 5483
we may find grass to save the *h* ... 1Kin 18:5 5483
and two kings with him, and *h* ... 1Kin 20:1 5483
Israel went out, and smote the *h* ... 1Kin 20:21 5483
as thy people, my *h* as thy *h* ... 1Kin 22:4 5483
h of fire, and parted them both ... 2Kin 2:11 5483
thy people, and my *h* as thy *h* ... 2Kin 3:7 5483
So Naaman came with his *h* ... 2Kin 5:9 5483
Therefore sent he thither *h* ... 2Kin 6:14 5483
compassed the city both with *h* ... 2Kin 6:15 5483
the mountain was full of *h* ... 2Kin 6:17 5483
of chariots, and a noise of *h* ... 2Kin 7:6 5483
and left their tents, and their *h* ... 2Kin 7:7 5483
but *h* tied, and asses tied, and the ... 2Kin 7:10 5483
thee, five of the *h* that remain ... 2Kin 7:13 5483
They took therefore two chariot *h* ... 2Kin 7:14 5483
on the wall, and on the *h* ... 2Kin 9:33 5483
there are with you chariots and *h* ... 2Kin 10:2 5483
the *h* came into the king's house ... 2Kin 11:16 5483
And they brought him on *h* ... 2Kin 14:20 5483
will deliver thee two thousand *h* ... 2Kin 18:23 5483
he took away the *h* that the kings ... 2Kin 23:11 5483
also houghed all the chariot *h* ... 1Chr 18:4
Solomon had *h* brought out of ... 2Chr 1:16 5483
so brought they out *h* for all the ... 2Chr 1:17 5483
and raiment, harness, and spices, *h* ... 2Chr 9:24 5483
had four thousand stalls for *h* ... 2Chr 9:25 5483
unto Solomon *h* out of Egypt ... 2Chr 9:28 5483
And they brought him upon *h* ... 2Chr 25:28 5483
Their *h* were seven hundred thirty ... Ezr 2:66 5483
Their *h*, seven hundred thirty and ... Neh 7:68 5483
trust in chariots, and some in *h* ... Ps 20:7 5483
I have seen servants upon *h* ... Eccl 10:7 5483
to a company of *h* in Pharaoh's ... Song 1:9 5484
their land is also full of *h* ... Is 2:7 5483
for we will flee upon *h* ... Is 30:16 5483
and stay on *h*, and trust in ... Is 31:1 5483
and their *h* flesh, and not spirit ... Is 31:3 5483
I will give thee two thousand *h* ... Is 36:8 5483
LORD out of all nations upon *h* ... Is 66:20 5483
his *h* are swifter than eagles ... Jer 4:13 5483
They were as fed *h* in the morning ... Jer 5:8 5483
and they ride upon *h*, set in array ... Jer 6:23 5483
of his *h* was heard from Dan ... Jer 8:16 5483
how canst thou contend with *h* ... Jer 12:5 5483
David, riding in chariots and on *h* ... Jer 17:25 5483
David, riding in chariots and on *h* ... Jer 22:4 5483
Harness the *h* ... Jer 46:4 5483
Come up, ye *h* ... Jer 46:9 5483
of the hoofs of his strong *h* ... Jer 47:3
A sword is upon their *h*, and upon ... Jer 50:37 5483
sea, and they shall ride upon *h* ... Jer 50:42 5483
cause the *h* to come up as the ... Jer 51:27 5483
Egypt, that they might give him *h* ... Eze 17:15 5483
young men, horsemen riding upon *h* ... Eze 23:6 5483
horsemen riding upon *h*, all of ... Eze 23:12 5483
issue is like the issue of *h* ... Eze 23:20 5483
all of them riding upon *h* ... Eze 23:23 5483
of kings, from the north, with *h* ... Eze 26:7 5483
his *h* their dust shall cover thee ... Eze 26:10 5483
With the hoofs of his *h* shall he ... Eze 26:11 5483
traded in thy fairs with *h* ... Eze 27:14 5483
thee forth, and all thine army, *h* ... Eze 38:4 5483
thee, all of them riding upon *h* ... Eze 38:15 5483
be filled at my table with *h* ... Eze 39:20 5483
nor by sword, nor by battle, by *h* ... Hos 1:7 5483
we will not ride upon *h* ... Hos 14:3 5483
of them is as the appearance of *h* ... Joel 2:4 5483
sword, and have taken away your *h* ... Amos 4:10 5483
Shall *h* run upon the rock ... Amos 6:12 5483
that I will cut off thy *h* out of ... Mic 5:10 5483
the wheels, and of the pransing *h* ... Nah 3:2 5483
Their *h* also are swifter than the ... Hab 1:8 5483
that thou didst ride upon thine *h* ... Hab 3:8 5483
walk through the sea with thine *h* ... Hab 3:15 5483
and the *h* and their riders shall ... Hag 2:22 5483
and behind him were there red *h* ... Zec 1:8 5483
In the first chariot were red *h* ... Zec 6:2 5483
and in the second chariot black *h* ... Zec 6:2 5483
And in the third chariot white *h* ... Zec 6:3 5483
fourth chariot grisled and bay *h* ... Zec 6:3 5483
The black *h* which are therein go ... Zec 6:6 5483
them, and the riders on *h* shall be ... Zec 10:5 5483
there be upon the bells of the *h* ... Zec 14:20 5483
like unto *h* prepared unto battle ... Rev 9:7 *2462*
of many *h* running to battle ... Rev 9:9 *2462*
And thus I saw the *h* in the vision ... Rev 9:17 *2462*
the heads of the *h* were as the ... Rev 9:17 *2462*
wheat, and beasts, and sheep, and *h* ... Rev 18:13 *2462*
heaven followed him upon white *h* ... Rev 19:14 *2462*
of mighty men, and the flesh of *h* ... Rev 19:18 *2462*

HORSES' {2}
their *h* hoofs shall be counted ... Is 5:28 5483
we put bits in the *h* mouths ... Jas 3:3 *2462*

HOSAH *(ho'-sah)* {5}
1. A city in Asher.
and the coast turneth to *H* ... Josh 19:29 2621
2. A Levite.
of Jeduthun and *H* to be porters ... 1Chr 16:38 2621
Also *H*, of the children of Merari ... 1Chr 26:10 2621
brethren of *H* were thirteen ... 1Chr 26:11 2621
H the lot came forth westward, ... 1Chr 26:16 2621

HOSANNA {6}
saying, *H* to the son of David ... Mt 21:9 *5614*
H in the highest ... Mt 21:9 *5614*
and saying, *H* to the son of David ... Mt 21:15 *5614*
that followed, cried, saying, *H* ... Mk 11:9 *5614*
H in the highest ... Mk 11:10 *5614*
forth to meet him, and cried, *H* ... Jn 12:13 *5614*

HOSEA *(ho-se'-ah)* {3} See HOSHEA, OSEE, OSHEA. *A prophet.*
word of the LORD that came unto *H* ... Hos 1:1 1954
of the word of the LORD by *H* ... Hos 1:2 1954
And the LORD said to *H*, Go, take ... Hos 1:2 1954

HOSEN {1}
bound in their coats, their *h* ... Dan 3:21 6361

HOSHAIAH *(ho-sha-i'-ah)* {3}
1. Helped dedicate the wall.
And after them went *H*, and half of ... Neh 12:32 1955
2. Father of Jezaniah.
Kareah, and Jezaniah the son of *H* ... Jer 42:1 1955
Then spake Azariah the son of *H* ... Jer 43:2 1955

HOSHAMA *(ho-sha'-mah)* {1} *Father of Jeconiah.*
Pedaiah, and Shenazar, Jecamiah, *H* ... 1Chr 3:18 1953

HOSHEA *(ho-she'-ah)* {11} See HOSEA.
1. Original name of Joshua.
people, he, and *H* the son of Nun ... Deut 32:44 1954
2. An Ephramite ruler.
of Ephraim, *H* the son of Azaziah ... 1Chr 27:20 1954
3. Last king of Israel.
And *H* the son of Elah made a ... 2Kin 15:30 1954
H the son of Elah to reign in ... 2Kin 17:1 1954
H became his servant, and gave him ... 2Kin 17:3 1954
of Assyria found conspiracy in *H* ... 2Kin 17:4 1954
In the ninth year of *H* the king ... 2Kin 17:6 1954
of *H* son of Elah king of Israel ... 2Kin 18:1 1954
of *H* son of Elah king of Israel ... 2Kin 18:9 1954
ninth year of *H* king of Israel ... 2Kin 18:10 1954
4. An Israelite who renewed the covenant.
H, Hananiah, Hashub, ... Neh 10:23 1954

HOSPITALITY {4}
given to *h* ... Rom 12:13 *5381*
of good behaviour, given to *h* ... 1Ti 3:2 *5382*
But a lover of *h*, a lover of good ... Titus 1:8 *5382*
Use *h* one to another without ... 1Pet 4:9 *5382*

HOST {192}
finished, and all the *h* of them ... Gen 2:1 6635
of his *h* spake unto Abraham ... Gen 21:22 6635
the chief captain of his *h* ... Gen 21:32 6635
them, he said, This is God's *h* ... Gen 32:2 4264
upon Pharaoh, and upon all his *h* ... Ex 14:4 2428
upon Pharaoh, and upon all his *h* ... Ex 14:17 2428
h of the Egyptians through the ... Ex 14:24 4264
troubled the *h* of the Egyptians, ... Ex 14:24 4264
all the *h* of Pharaoh that came ... Ex 14:28 2428
his *h* hath he cast into the sea ... Ex 15:4 2428
the dew lay round about the *h* ... Ex 16:13 4264
And his *h*, and those that were ... Num 2:4 6635
And his *h*, and those that were ... Num 2:6 6635
And his *h*, and those that were ... Num 2:8 6635
And his *h*, and those that were ... Num 2:11 6635
And his *h*, and those that were ... Num 2:13 6635
And his *h*, and those that were ... Num 2:15 6635
And his *h*, and those that were ... Num 2:19 6635
And his *h*, and those that were ... Num 2:21 6635
And his *h*, and those that were ... Num 2:23 6635
And his *h*, and those that were ... Num 2:26 6635
And his *h*, and those that were ... Num 2:28 6635
And his *h*, and those that were ... Num 2:30 6635
old, all that enter into the *h* ... Num 4:3 6635
over his *h* was Nahshon the son of ... Num 10:14
over the *h* of the tribe of the ... Num 10:15 6635
over the *h* of the tribe of the ... Num 10:16 6635
over his *h* was Elizur the son of ... Num 10:18 6635
over the *h* of the tribe of the ... Num 10:19 6635
over the *h* of the tribe of the ... Num 10:20 6635
over his *h* was Elishama the son ... Num 10:22 6635
over the *h* of the tribe of the ... Num 10:23 6635
over the *h* of the tribe of the ... Num 10:24 6635
over his *h* was Ahiezer the son of ... Num 10:25 6635
over the *h* of the tribe of the ... Num 10:26 6635
over the *h* of the tribe of the ... Num 10:27 6635
wroth with the officers of the *h* ... Num 31:14 2428
were over thousands of the *h* ... Num 31:48 6635
were wasted out from among the *h* ... Deut 2:14 4264
to destroy them from among the *h* ... Deut 2:15 4264
stars, even all the *h* of heaven ... Deut 4:19 6635
moon, or any of the *h* of heaven ... Deut 17:3 6635
When the *h* goeth forth against ... Deut 23:9 4264
Pass through the *h*, and command ... Josh 1:11 4264
the officers went through the *h* ... Josh 3:2 4264
but as captain of the *h* of the ... Josh 5:14 6635
of the LORD's *h* said unto Joshua ... Josh 5:15 6635
even all the *h* that was on the ... Josh 8:13 4264
to Joshua to the *h* at Shiloh ... Josh 18:9 4264
the captain of whose *h* was Sisera ... Judg 4:2 6635
and all his chariots, and all his *h* ... Judg 4:15 4264
the chariots, and after the *h* ... Judg 4:16 4264
all the *h* of Sisera fell upon the ... Judg 4:16 4264
so that the *h* of the Midianites ... Judg 7:1 4264
the *h* of Midian was beneath him ... Judg 7:8 4264
Arise, get thee down unto the *h* ... Judg 7:9 4264
Phurah thy servant down to the *h* ... Judg 7:10 4264
to go down unto the *h* ... Judg 7:11 4264
the armed men that were in the *h* ... Judg 7:11 4264
tumbled into the *h* of Midian ... Judg 7:13 4264
delivered Midian, and all the *h* ... Judg 7:14 4264
and returned into the *h* of Israel ... Judg 7:15 4264
into your hand the *h* of Midian ... Judg 7:15 4264
and all the *h* ran, and cried, and ... Judg 7:21 4264
fellow, even throughout all the *h* ... Judg 7:22 4264
the *h* fled to Beth-shittah in ... Judg 7:22 4264
Nobah and Jogbehah, and smote the *h* ... Judg 8:11 4264
for the *h* was secure ... Judg 8:11 4264
and discomfited all the *h* ... Judg 8:12 4264
of the *h* in the morning watch ... 1Sa 11:11 4264
Sisera, captain of the *h* of Hazor ... 1Sa 12:9 6635
And there was trembling in the *h* ... 1Sa 14:15 4264
the *h* of the Philistines went on ... 1Sa 14:19 4264
And he gathered an *h*, and smote the ... 1Sa 14:48 2428
of the captain of his *h* was Abner ... 1Sa 14:50 6635
as the *h* was going forth to the ... 1Sa 17:20 2428
the *h* of the Philistines this day ... 1Sa 17:46 4264
unto Abner, the captain of the *h* ... 1Sa 17:55 6635
son of Ner, the captain of his *h* ... 1Sa 26:5 6635
when Saul saw the *h* of the ... 1Sa 28:5 4264
h of Israel into the hand of the ... 1Sa 28:19 4264
me in the *h* is good in my sight ... 1Sa 29:6 4264
son of Ner, captain of Saul's *h* ... 2Sa 2:8 6635
all the *h* that was with him were ... 2Sa 3:23 6635
to smite the *h* of the Philistines ... 2Sa 5:24 4264
smitten all the *h* of Hadadezer ... 2Sa 8:9 2428
the son of Zeruiah was over the *h* ... 2Sa 8:16 6635
all the *h* of the mighty men ... 2Sa 10:7 6635
Shobach the captain of the *h* of ... 2Sa 10:16 6635
Shobach the captain of their *h* ... 2Sa 10:18 6635
captain of the *h* instead of Joab ... 2Sa 17:25 6635
h before me continually in the ... 2Sa 19:13 6635
Joab was over all the *h* of Israel ... 2Sa 20:23 6635
through the *h* of the Philistines ... 2Sa 23:16 4264
said to Joab the captain of the *h* ... 2Sa 24:2 2428
and against the captains of the *h* ... 2Sa 24:4 2428
the captains of the *h* went out ... 2Sa 24:4 2428
and Joab the captain of the *h* ... 1Kin 1:19 6635
sons, and the captains of the *h* ... 1Kin 1:25 6635
Ner, captain of the *h* of Israel ... 1Kin 2:32 6635
Jether, captain of the *h* of Judah ... 1Kin 2:32 6635
Jehoiada in his room over the *h* ... 1Kin 2:35 6635
son of Jehoiada was over the *h* ... 1Kin 4:4 6635
Joab the captain of the *h* was ... 1Kin 11:15 6635
the captain of the *h* was dead ... 1Kin 11:21 6635
made Omri, the captain of the *h* ... 1Kin 16:16 6635
Syria gathered all his *h* together ... 1Kin 20:1 2428
all the *h* of heaven standing by ... 1Kin 22:19 6635
hand, and carry me out of the *h* ... 1Kin 22:34 4264
a proclamation throughout the *h* ... 1Kin 22:36 4264
and there was no water for the *h* ... 2Kin 3:9 4264
king, or to the captain of the *h* ... 2Kin 4:13 6635
captain of the *h* of the king of ... 2Kin 5:1 6635
horses, and chariots, and a great *h* ... 2Kin 6:14 2428
an *h* compassed the city both with ... 2Kin 6:15 2428
king of Syria gathered all his *h* ... 2Kin 6:24
us fall unto the *h* of the Syrians ... 2Kin 7:4 4264
For the LORD had made the *h* of ... 2Kin 7:6 4264
even the noise of a great *h* ... 2Kin 7:6 2428
sent after the *h* of the Syrians ... 2Kin 7:14 4264
captains of the *h* were sitting ... 2Kin 9:5 2428
hundreds, the officers of the *h* ... 2Kin 11:15 2428
and worshipped all the *h* of heaven ... 2Kin 17:16 6635
with a great *h* against Jerusalem ... 2Kin 18:17 2426
and worshipped all the *h* of heaven ... 2Kin 21:3 6635
he built altars for all the *h* of ... 2Kin 21:5 6635
grove, and for all the *h* of heaven ... 2Kin 23:4 6635
and to all the *h* of heaven ... 2Kin 23:5 6635
of Babylon came, he, and all his *h* ... 2Kin 25:1 2428
and the principal scribe of the *h* ... 2Kin 25:19 6635
being over the *h* of the LORD ... 1Chr 9:19 4264
the *h* of the Philistines encamped ... 1Chr 11:15 4264
through the *h* of the Philistines ... 1Chr 11:18 4264
sons of Gad, captains of the *h* ... 1Chr 12:14 6635
valour, and were captains in the *h* ... 1Chr 12:21 6635
a great *h*, like the *h* of God ... 1Chr 12:22 4264
to smite the *h* of the Philistines ... 1Chr 14:15 4264
and they smote the *h* of the ... 1Chr 14:16 4264
the *h* of Hadarezer king of Zobah ... 1Chr 18:9 2428
the son of Zeruiah was over the *h* ... 1Chr 18:15 6635

all the *h* of the mighty men 1Chr 19:8 6635
Shophach the captain of the *h* of 1Chr 19:16 6635
Shophach the captain of the *h* 1Chr 19:18 6635
the captains of the *h* separated 1Chr 25:1 6635
and the captains of the *h* 1Chr 26:26 6635
of the *h* for the first month 1Chr 27:3 6635
The third captain of the *h* for 1Chr 27:5 6635
with an *h* of a thousand thousand 2Chr 14:9 2428
before the LORD, and before his *h* 2Chr 14:13 4264
therefore is the *h* of the king of 2Chr 16:7 2428
Ethiopians and the Lubims a huge *h* 2Chr 16:8 2428
all the *h* of heaven standing on 2Chr 18:18 6635
thou mayest carry me out of the *h* 2Chr 18:33 6635
hundreds that were set over the *h* 2Chr 23:14 2428
that the *h* of Syria came up 2Chr 24:23 2428
a very great *h* into their hand 2Chr 24:24 2428
Uzziah had an *h* of fighting men 2Chr 26:11 2428
them throughout all the *h* shields 2Chr 26:14 6635
before the *h* that came to Samaria 2Chr 28:9 6635
and worshipped all the *h* of heaven 2Chr 33:3 6635
he built altars for all the *h* of 2Chr 33:5 6635
of the *h* of the king of Assyria 2Chr 33:11 6635
of heavens, with all their *h* Neh 9:6 6635
the *h* of heaven worshippeth thee Neh 9:6 6635
Though an *h* should encamp against Ps 27:3 4264
all the *h* of them by the breath Ps 33:6 6635
saved by the multitude of an *h* Ps 33:16 2428
Pharaoh and his *h* in the Red sea Ps 136:15 2428
mustereth the *h* of the battle Is 13:4 6635
h of the high ones that are on Is 24:21 6635
all the *h* of heaven shall be Is 34:4 6635
all their *h* shall fall down, as Is 34:4 6635
bringeth out their *h* by number Is 40:26 6635
all their *h* have I commanded Is 45:12 6635
all the *h* of heaven, whom they Jer 8:2 6635
incense unto all the *h* of heaven Jer 19:13 6635
As the *h* of heaven cannot be Jer 33:22 6635
destroy ye utterly all her *h* Jer 51:3 6635
and the principal scribe of the *h* Jer 52:25 6635
of speech, as the noise of an *h* Eze 1:24 4264
great, even to the *h* of heaven Dan 8:10 6635
and it cast down some of the *h* Dan 8:10 6635
even to the prince of the *h* Dan 8:11 6635
an *h* was given him against the Dan 8:12 6635
the *h* to be trodden under foot Dan 8:13 6635
the captivity of this *h* of the Obad 20 2426
them that worship the *h* of heaven Zeph 1:5 6635
of the heavenly *h* praising God Lk 2:13 *4756*
two pence, and gave them to the *h* Lk 10:35 *3830*
up to worship the *h* of heaven Acts 7:42 *4756*
Gaius mine *h*, and of the whole Rom 16:23 *3581*

HOSTAGES {2}

of the king's house, and *h* 2Kin 14:14 1121,8594
the *h* also, and returned to 2Chr 25:24 1121,8594

HOSTS {299}

that all the *h* of the LORD went Ex 12:41 6635
own standard, throughout their *h* Num 1:52 6635
their *h* were six hundred thousand Num 2:32 6635
all the camps throughout their *h* Num 10:25 6635
and went up, they and all their *h* Josh 10:5 4264
they and all their *h* with them Josh 11:4 4264
their *h* with them, about fifteen Judg 8:10 4264
the *h* of the children of the east Judg 8:10 4264
unto the LORD of *h* in Shiloh 1Sa 1:3 6635
vowed a vow, and said, O LORD of *h* 1Sa 1:11 6635
of the covenant of the LORD of *h* 1Sa 4:4 6635
Thus saith the LORD of *h*, I 1Sa 15:2 6635
thee in the name of the LORD of *h* 1Sa 17:45 6635
and the LORD God of *h* was with him 2Sa 5:10 6635
of *h* that dwelleth between the 2Sa 6:2 6635
in the name of the LORD of *h* 2Sa 6:18 6635
David, Thus saith the LORD of *h* 2Sa 7:8 6635
The LORD of *h* is the God over 2Sa 7:26 6635
For thou, O LORD of *h*, God of 2Sa 7:27 6635
two captains of the *h* of Israel 1Kin 2:5 6635
sent the captains of the *h* which 1Kin 15:20 2428
said, As the LORD of *h* liveth 1Kin 18:15 6635
jealous for the LORD God of *h* 1Kin 19:10 6635
jealous for the LORD God of *h* 1Kin 19:14 6635
said, As the LORD of *h* liveth 2Kin 3:14 6635
of the LORD of *h* shall do this 2Kin 19:31
for the LORD of *h* was with him 1Chr 11:9 6635
David, Thus saith the LORD of *h* 1Chr 17:7 6635
The LORD of *h* is the God of 1Chr 17:24 6635
The LORD of *h*, he is the King of Ps 24:10 6635
The LORD of *h* is with us Ps 46:7 6635
The LORD of *h* is with us Ps 46:11 6635
seen in the city of the LORD of *h* Ps 48:8 6635
Thou therefore, O LORD God of *h* Ps 59:5 6635
wait on thee, O Lord GOD of *h* Ps 69:6 6635
O LORD God of *h*, how long wilt Ps 80:4 6635
Turn us again, O God of *h* Ps 80:7 6635
we beseech thee, O God of *h* Ps 80:14 6635
Turn us again, O LORD God of *h* Ps 80:19 6635
are thy tabernacles, O LORD of *h* Ps 84:1 6635
even thine altars, O LORD of *h* Ps 84:3 6635
O LORD God of *h*, hear my prayer Ps 84:8 6635
O LORD of *h*, blessed is the man Ps 84:12 6635
O LORD God of *h*, who is a strong Ps 89:8 6635
Bless ye the LORD, all ye his *h* Ps 103:21 6635
thou, O God, go forth with our *h* Ps 108:11 6635
praise ye him, all his *h* Ps 148:2 6635
Except the LORD of *h* had left Is 1:9 6635
saith the Lord, the LORD of *h* Is 1:24 6635
For the day of the LORD of *h* Is 2:12 6635
behold, the Lord, the LORD of *h* Is 3:1 6635
saith the Lord GOD of *h* Is 3:15 6635
LORD of *h* is the house of Israel Is 5:7 6635
In mine ears said the LORD of *h* Is 5:9 6635
But the LORD of *h* shall be Is 5:16 6635
away the law of the LORD of *h* Is 5:24 6635
holy, holy, is the LORD of *h* Is 6:3 6635
have seen the King, the LORD of *h* Is 6:5 6635
Sanctify the LORD of *h* himself Is 8:13 6635
in Israel from the LORD of *h* Is 8:18 6635
the LORD of *h* will perform this Is 9:7 6635
do they seek the LORD of *h* Is 9:13 6635
LORD of *h* is the land darkened Is 9:19 6635
shall the Lord, the Lord of *h* Is 10:16 6635
For the Lord GOD of *h* shall make Is 10:23 6635
thus saith the Lord GOD of *h* Is 10:24 6635
the LORD of *h* shall stir up a Is 10:26 6635
Behold, the Lord, the LORD of *h* Is 10:33 6635
the LORD of *h* mustereth the host Is 13:4 6635
in the wrath of the LORD of *h* Is 13:13 6635
against them, saith the LORD of *h* Is 14:22 6635
destruction, saith the LORD of *h* Is 14:23 6635
The LORD of *h* hath sworn, saying, Is 14:24 6635
For the LORD of *h* hath purposed Is 14:27 6635
of Israel, saith the LORD of *h* Is 17:3 6635
LORD of *h* of a people scattered Is 18:7 6635
of the name of the LORD of *h* Is 18:7 6635
saith the Lord, the LORD of *h* Is 19:4 6635
of *h* hath purposed upon Egypt Is 19:12 6635
of the hand of the LORD of *h* Is 19:16 6635
of the counsel of the LORD of *h* Is 19:17 6635
Canaan, and swear to the LORD of *h* Is 19:18 6635
LORD of *h* in the land of Egypt Is 19:20 6635
Whom the LORD of *h* shall bless Is 19:25 6635
I have heard of the LORD of *h* Is 21:10 6635
GOD of *h* in the valley of vision Is 22:5 6635
the Lord GOD of *h* call to weeping Is 22:12 6635
in mine ears by the LORD of *h* Is 22:14 6635
ye die, saith the Lord GOD of *h* Is 22:14 6635
Thus saith the Lord GOD of *h* Is 22:15 6635
In that day, saith the LORD of *h* Is 22:25 6635
The LORD of *h* hath purposed it, Is 23:9 6635
when the LORD of *h* shall reign in Is 24:23 6635
h make unto all people a feast of Is 25:6 6635
LORD of *h* be for a crown of glory Is 28:5 6635
the Lord GOD of *h* a consumption Is 28:22 6635
cometh forth from the LORD of *h* Is 28:29 6635
of the LORD of *h* with thunder Is 29:6 6635
so shall the LORD of *h* come down Is 31:4 6635
the LORD of *h* defend Jerusalem Is 31:5 6635
O LORD of *h*, God of Israel, that Is 37:16 6635
of the LORD of *h* shall do this Is 37:32 6635
Hear the word of the LORD of *h* Is 39:5 6635
and his redeemer the LORD of *h* Is 44:6 6635
nor reward, saith the LORD of *h* Is 45:13 6635
the LORD of *h* is his name Is 47:4 6635
The LORD of *h* is his name Is 48:2 6635
The LORD of *h* is his name Is 51:15 6635
the LORD of *h* is his name Is 54:5 6635
in thee, saith the Lord GOD of *h* Jer 2:19 6635
heritage of the *h* of nations Jer 3:19 6635
thus saith the LORD God of *h* Jer 5:14 6635
For thus hath the LORD of *h* said Jer 6:6 6635
Thus saith the LORD of *h*, They Jer 6:9 6635
Thus saith the LORD of *h*, the God Jer 7:3 6635
Thus saith the LORD of *h*, the God Jer 7:21 6635
driven them, saith the LORD of *h* Jer 8:3 6635
thus saith the LORD of *h*, Behold, Jer 9:7 6635
thus saith the LORD of *h*, the God Jer 9:15 6635
Thus saith the LORD of *h*, Jer 9:17 6635
The LORD of *h* is his name Jer 10:16 6635
For the LORD of *h*, that planted Jer 11:17 6635
But, O LORD of *h*, that judgest Jer 11:20 6635
thus saith the LORD of *h*, Behold, Jer 11:22 6635
by thy name, O LORD God of *h* Jer 15:16 6635
For thus saith the LORD of *h* Jer 16:9 6635
Thus saith the LORD of *h*, the God Jer 19:3 6635
them, Thus saith the LORD of *h* Jer 19:11 6635
Thus saith the LORD of *h*, the God Jer 19:15 6635
But, O LORD of *h*, that triest the Jer 20:12 6635
thus saith the LORD of *h* Jer 23:15 6635
Thus saith the LORD of *h*, Hearken Jer 23:16 6635
God, of the LORD of *h* our God Jer 23:36 6635
thus saith the LORD of *h* Jer 25:8 6635
them, Thus saith the LORD of *h* Jer 25:27 6635
them, Thus saith the LORD of *h* Jer 25:28 6635
of the earth, saith the LORD of *h* Jer 25:29 6635
Thus saith the LORD of *h*, Behold, Jer 25:32 6635
saying, Thus saith the LORD of *h* Jer 26:18 6635
masters, Thus saith the LORD of *h* Jer 27:4 6635
intercession to the LORD of *h* Jer 27:18 6635
LORD of *h* concerning the pillars Jer 27:19 6635
Yea, thus saith the LORD of *h* Jer 27:21 6635
Thus speaketh the LORD of *h* Jer 28:2 6635
For thus saith the LORD of *h* Jer 28:14 6635
Thus saith the LORD of *h*, the God Jer 29:4 6635
For thus saith the LORD of *h* Jer 29:8 6635
Thus saith the LORD of *h* Jer 29:17 6635
Thus saith the LORD of *h*, the God Jer 29:21 6635
Thus speaketh the LORD of *h* Jer 29:25 6635
in that day, saith the LORD of *h* Jer 30:8 6635
Thus saith the LORD of *h*, the God Jer 31:23 6635
The LORD of *h* is his name Jer 31:35 6635
Thus saith the LORD of *h*, the God Jer 32:14 6635
For thus saith the LORD of *h* Jer 32:15 6635
the Mighty God, the LORD of *h* Jer 32:18 6635
shall say, Praise the LORD of *h* Jer 33:11 6635
Thus saith the LORD of *h* Jer 33:12 6635
Thus saith the LORD of *h*, the God Jer 35:13 6635
thus saith the LORD God of *h* Jer 35:17 6635
Thus saith the LORD of *h* Jer 35:18 6635
thus saith the LORD of *h*, the God Jer 35:19 6635
Thus saith the LORD, the God of *h* Jer 38:17 6635
saying, Thus saith the LORD of *h* Jer 39:16 6635
Thus saith the LORD of *h*, the God Jer 42:15 6635
For thus saith the LORD of *h* Jer 42:18 6635
them, Thus saith the LORD of *h* Jer 43:10 6635
Thus saith the LORD of *h*, the God Jer 44:2 6635
thus saith the LORD, the God of *h* Jer 44:7 6635
thus saith the LORD of *h*, the God Jer 44:11 6635
Thus saith the LORD of *h*, the God Jer 44:25 6635
is the day of the Lord GOD of *h* Jer 46:10 6635
for the Lord GOD of *h* hath a Jer 46:10 6635
King, whose name is the LORD of *h* Jer 46:18 6635
The LORD of *h*, the God of Israel, Jer 46:25 6635
Moab thus saith the LORD of *h* Jer 48:1 6635
King, whose name is the LORD of *h* Jer 48:15 6635
thee, saith the Lord GOD of *h* Jer 49:5 6635
Edom, thus saith the LORD of *h* Jer 49:7 6635
in that day, saith the LORD of *h* Jer 49:26 6635
Thus saith the LORD of *h* Jer 49:35 6635
thus saith the LORD of *h*, the God Jer 50:18 6635
of *h* in the land of the Chaldeans Jer 50:25 6635
proud, saith the Lord GOD of *h* Jer 50:31 6635
Thus saith the LORD of *h* Jer 50:33 6635
the LORD of *h* is his name Jer 50:34 6635
of his God, of the LORD of *h* Jer 51:5 6635
The LORD of *h* hath sworn by Jer 51:14 6635
the LORD of *h* is his name Jer 51:19 6635
For thus saith the LORD of *h* Jer 51:33 6635
King, whose name is the LORD of *h* Jer 51:57 6635
Thus saith the LORD of *h* Jer 51:58 6635
Even the LORD God of *h* Hos 12:5 6635
saith the Lord GOD, the God of *h* Amos 3:13 6635
the earth, The LORD, The God of *h* Amos 4:13 6635
and so the LORD, the God of *h* Amos 5:14 6635
of *h* will be gracious unto the Amos 5:15 6635
Therefore the LORD, the God of *h* Amos 5:16 6635
LORD, whose name is The God of *h* Amos 5:27 6635
saith the LORD the God of *h* Amos 6:8 6635
saith the LORD the God of *h* Amos 6:14 6635
the Lord GOD of *h* is he that Amos 9:5 6635
of the LORD of *h* hath spoken it Mic 4:4 6635
against thee, saith the LORD of *h* Nah 2:13 6635
against thee, saith the LORD of *h* Nah 3:5 6635
is it not of the LORD of *h* that Hab 2:13 6635
as I live, saith the LORD of *h* Zeph 2:9 6635
the people of the LORD of *h* Zeph 2:10 6635
Thus speaketh the LORD of *h* Hag 1:2 6635
thus saith the LORD of *h* Hag 1:5 6635
Thus saith the LORD of *h* Hag 1:7 6635
saith the LORD of *h* Hag 1:9 6635
in the house of the LORD of *h* Hag 1:14 6635
am with you, saith the LORD of *h* Hag 2:4 6635
For thus saith the LORD of *h* Hag 2:6 6635
with glory, saith the LORD of *h* Hag 2:7 6635
gold is mine, saith the LORD of *h* Hag 2:8 6635
the former, saith the LORD of *h* Hag 2:9 6635
I give peace, saith the LORD of *h* Hag 2:9 6635
Thus saith the LORD of *h* Hag 2:11 6635
In that day, saith the LORD of *h* Hag 2:23 6635
chosen thee, saith the LORD of *h* Hag 2:23 6635
them, Thus saith the LORD of *h* Zec 1:3 6635
ye unto me, saith the LORD of *h* Zec 1:3 6635
unto you, saith the LORD of *h* Zec 1:3 6635
saying, Thus saith the LORD of *h* Zec 1:4 6635
Like as the LORD of *h* thought to Zec 1:6 6635
answered and said, O LORD of *h* Zec 1:12 6635
saying, Thus saith the LORD of *h* Zec 1:14 6635
built in it, saith the LORD of *h* Zec 1:16 6635
saying, Thus saith the LORD of *h* Zec 1:17 6635
For thus saith the LORD of *h* Zec 2:8 6635
that the LORD of *h* hath sent me Zec 2:9 6635
LORD of *h* hath sent me unto thee Zec 2:11 6635
Thus saith the LORD of *h* Zec 3:7 6635
thereof, saith the LORD of *h* Zec 3:9 6635
In that day, saith the LORD of *h* Zec 3:10 6635
by my spirit, saith the LORD of *h* Zec 4:6 6635
LORD of *h* hath sent me unto you Zec 4:9 6635
it forth, saith the LORD of *h* Zec 5:4 6635
Thus speaketh the LORD of *h* Zec 6:12 6635
LORD of *h* hath sent me unto you Zec 6:15 6635
in the house of the LORD of *h* Zec 7:3 6635
the word of the LORD of *h* unto me Zec 7:4 6635
Thus speaketh the LORD of *h* Zec 7:9 6635
the words which the LORD of *h* Zec 7:12 6635
a great wrath from the LORD of *h* Zec 7:12 6635
not hear, saith the LORD of *h* Zec 7:13 6635
word of the LORD of *h* came to me Zec 8:1 6635
Thus saith the LORD of *h* Zec 8:2 6635
the LORD of *h* the holy mountain Zec 8:3 6635
Thus saith the LORD of *h* Zec 8:4 6635
Thus saith the LORD of *h* Zec 8:6 6635
saith the LORD of *h* Zec 8:6 6635
Thus saith the LORD of *h* Zec 8:7 6635
Thus saith the LORD of *h* Zec 8:9 6635
house of the LORD of *h* was laid Zec 8:9 6635
former days, saith the LORD of *h* Zec 8:11 6635
For thus saith the LORD of *h* Zec 8:14 6635
me to wrath, saith the LORD of *h* Zec 8:14 6635
of the LORD of *h* came unto me Zec 8:18 6635
Thus saith the LORD of *h* Zec 8:19 6635
Thus saith the LORD of *h* Zec 8:20 6635
LORD, and to seek the LORD of *h* Zec 8:21 6635
seek the LORD of *h* in Jerusalem Zec 8:22 6635
Thus saith the LORD of *h* Zec 8:23 6635
The LORD of *h* shall defend them Zec 9:15 6635
for the LORD of *h* hath visited Zec 10:3 6635

H

in the LORD of *h* their God ... Zec 12:5 6635
in that day, saith the LORD of *h* ... Zec 13:2 6635
is my fellow, saith the LORD of *h* ... Zec 13:7 6635
worship the King, the LORD of *h* ... Zec 14:16 6635
worship the King, the LORD of *h* ... Zec 14:17 6635
be holiness unto the LORD of *h* ... Zec 14:21 6635
in the house of the LORD of *h* ... Zec 14:21 6635
thus saith the LORD of *h*, They ... Mal 1:4 6635
saith the LORD of *h* unto you ... Mal 1:6 6635
saith the LORD of *h* ... Mal 1:8 6635
saith the LORD of *h* ... Mal 1:9 6635
in you, saith the LORD of *h* ... Mal 1:10 6635
the heathen, saith the LORD of *h* ... Mal 1:11 6635
at it, saith the LORD of *h* ... Mal 1:13 6635
a great King, saith the LORD of *h* ... Mal 1:14 6635
unto my name, saith the LORD of *h* ... Mal 2:2 6635
be with Levi, saith the LORD of *h* ... Mal 2:4 6635
is the messenger of the LORD of *h* ... Mal 2:7 6635
of Levi, saith the LORD of *h* ... Mal 2:8 6635
an offering unto the LORD of *h* ... Mal 2:12 6635
his garment, saith the LORD of *h* ... Mal 2:16 6635
shall come, saith the LORD of *h* ... Mal 3:1 6635
fear not me, saith the LORD of *h* ... Mal 3:5 6635
unto you, saith the LORD of *h* ... Mal 3:7 6635
now herewith, saith the LORD of *h* ... Mal 3:10 6635
in the field, saith the LORD of *h* ... Mal 3:11 6635
land, saith the LORD of *h* ... Mal 3:12 6635
mournfully before the LORD of *h* ... Mal 3:14 6635
be mine, saith the LORD of *h* ... Mal 3:17 6635
burn them up, saith the LORD of *h* ... Mal 4:1 6635
do this, saith the LORD of *h* ... Mal 4:3 6635

HOT {31}
and when the sun waxed *h*, it ... Ex 16:21 2552
And my wrath shall wax *h*, and I ... Ex 22:24 2734
my wrath may wax *h* against them ... Ex 32:10 2734
wrath wax *h* against thy people ... Ex 32:11 2734
and Moses' anger waxed *h*, and he ... Ex 32:19 2734
not the anger of my lord wax *h* ... Ex 32:22 2734
skin whereof there is a *h* burning ... Lev 13:24 784
h displeasure, wherewith the LORD ... Deut 9:19 2534
the slayer, while his heart is *h* ... Deut 19:6 3179
This our bread we took *h* for our ... Josh 9:12 2525
of the LORD was *h* against Israel ... Judg 2:14 2734
of the LORD was *h* against Israel ... Judg 2:20 2734
of the LORD was *h* against Israel ... Judg 3:8 2734
not thine anger be *h* against me ... Judg 6:39 2734
of the LORD was *h* against Israel ... Judg 10:7 2734
morrow, by that time the sun be *h* ... 1Sa 11:9 2527
to put *h* bread in the day when it ... 1Sa 21:6 2527
be opened until the sun be *h* ... Neh 7:3 2527
when it is *h*, they are consumed ... Job 6:17 2527
chasten me in thy *h* displeasure ... Ps 6:1 2534
chasten me in thy *h* displeasure ... Ps 38:1 2534
My heart was *h* within me ... Ps 39:3 2552
and their flocks to *h* thunderbolts ... Ps 78:48 7565
Can one go upon *h* coals, and his ... Prov 6:28 3179
that the brass of it may be *h* ... Eze 24:11 3179
and the furnace exceeding *h* ... Dan 3:22 228
They are all *h* as an oven ... Hos 7:7 2552
conscience seared with a *h* iron ... 1Ti 4:2 *2743*
that thou art neither cold nor *h* ... Rev 3:15 *2200*
I would thou wert cold or *h* ... Rev 3:15 *2200*
lukewarm, and neither cold nor *h* ... Rev 3:16 *2200*

HOTHAM *(ho'-tham)* {1} See HOTHAN. *A son of Heber.*
begat Japhlet, and Shomer, and *H* ... 1Chr 7:32 2369

HOTHAN *(ho'-than)* {1} See HOTHAM. *Father of Shama and Jehiel.*
Jehiel the sons of *H* the Aroerite ... 1Chr 11:44 2369

HOTHIR *(ho'-thir)* {2} *A son of Heman.*
Joshbekashah, Mallothi, *H* ... 1Chr 25:4 1956
The one and twentieth to *H* ... 1Chr 25:28 1956

HOTLY {1}
thou hast so *h* pursued after me ... Gen 31:36 1814

HOTTEST {1}
in the forefront of the *h* battle ... 2Sa 11:15 2389

HOUGH {1}
thou shalt *h* their horses, and ... Josh 11:6 6131

HOUGHED {3}
he *h* their horses, and burnt their ... Josh 11:9 6131
David *h* all the chariot horses, ... 2Sa 8:4 6131
David also *h* all the chariot ... 1Chr 18:4 6131

HOUR {94}
worshippeth shall the same *h* be ... Dan 3:6 8160
ye shall be cast the same *h* into ... Dan 3:15 8160
was astonied for one *h*, and his ... Dan 4:19 8160
The same *h* was the thing ... Dan 4:33 8160
In the same *h* came forth fingers ... Dan 5:5 8160
was healed in the selfsame *h* ... Mt 8:13 *5610*
woman was made whole from that *h* ... Mt 9:22 *5610*
that same *h* what ye shall speak ... Mt 10:19 *5610*
was made whole from that very *h* ... Mt 15:28 *5610*
child was cured from that very *h* ... Mt 17:18 *5610*
And he went out about the third *h* ... Mt 20:3 *5610*
out about the sixth and ninth *h* ... Mt 20:5 *5610*
about the eleventh *h* he went out ... Mt 20:6 *5610*
were hired about the eleventh *h* ... Mt 20:9 *5610*
These last have wrought but one *h* ... Mt 20:12 *5610*
h knoweth no man, no, not the ... Mt 24:36 *5610*
not what *h* your Lord doth come ... Mt 24:42 *5610*
for in such an *h* as ye think not ... Mt 24:44 *5610*
in an *h* that he is not aware of, ... Mt 24:50 *5610*
h wherein the Son of man cometh ... Mt 25:13 *5610*
could ye not watch with me one *h* ... Mt 26:40 *5610*
the *h* is at hand, and the Son of ... Mt 26:45 *5610*
In that same *h* said Jesus to the ... Mt 26:55 *5610*
Now from the sixth *h* there was ... Mt 27:45 *5610*
all the land unto the ninth *h* ... Mt 27:45 *5610*
about the ninth *h* Jesus cried ... Mt 27:46 *5610*
shall be given you in that *h* ... Mk 13:11 *5610*
that *h* knoweth no man, no, not ... Mk 13:32 *5610*
the *h* might pass from him ... Mk 14:35 *5610*
couldest not thou watch one *h* ... Mk 14:37 *5610*
it is enough, the *h* is come ... Mk 14:41 *5610*
And it was the third *h*, and they ... Mk 15:25 *5610*
And when the sixth *h* was come ... Mk 15:33 *5610*
the whole land until the ninth *h* ... Mk 15:33 *5610*
at the ninth *h* Jesus cried with a ... Mk 15:34 *5610*
in that same *h* he cured many of ... Lk 7:21 *5610*
In that *h* Jesus rejoiced in ... Lk 10:21 *5610*
the same *h* what ye ought to say ... Lk 12:12 *5610*
known what *h* the thief would come ... Lk 12:39 *5610*
cometh at an *h* when ye think not ... Lk 12:40 *5610*
at an *h* when he is not aware, and ... Lk 12:46 *5610*
the scribes the same *h* sought to ... Lk 20:19 *5610*
And when the *h* was come, he sat ... Lk 22:14 *5610*
but this is your *h*, and the power ... Lk 22:53 *5610*
about the space of one *h* after ... Lk 22:59 *5610*
And it was about the sixth *h* ... Lk 23:44 *5610*
all the earth until the ninth *h* ... Lk 23:44 *5610*
And they rose up the same *h* ... Lk 24:33 *5610*
for it was about the tenth *h* ... Jn 1:39 *5610*
mine *h* is not yet come ... Jn 2:4 *5610*
and it was about the sixth *h* ... Jn 4:6 *5610*
the *h* cometh, when ye shall ... Jn 4:21 *5610*
But the *h* cometh, and now is, when ... Jn 4:23 *5610*
them the *h* when he began to amend ... Jn 4:52 *5610*
the seventh *h* the fever left him ... Jn 4:52 *5610*
knew that it was at the same *h* ... Jn 4:53 *5610*
The *h* is coming, and now is, when ... Jn 5:25 *5610*
for the *h* is coming, in the which ... Jn 5:28 *5610*
because his *h* was not yet come ... Jn 7:30 *5610*
for his *h* was not yet come ... Jn 8:20 *5610*
The *h* is come, that the Son of ... Jn 12:23 *5610*
Father, save me from this *h* ... Jn 12:27 *5610*
for this cause came I unto this *h* ... Jn 12:27 *5610*
when Jesus knew that his *h* was ... Jn 13:1 *5610*
sorrow, because her *h* is come ... Jn 16:21 *5610*
the *h* cometh, yea, is now come, ... Jn 16:32 *5610*
and said, Father, the *h* is come ... Jn 17:1 *5610*
passover, and about the sixth *h* ... Jn 19:14 *5610*
from that *h* that disciple took ... Jn 19:27 *5610*
it is but the third *h* of the day ... Acts 2:15 *5610*
h of prayer, being the ninth *h* ... Acts 3:1
evidently about the ninth *h* of ... Acts 10:3 *5610*
to pray about the sixth *h* ... Acts 10:9 *5610*
ago I was fasting until this *h* ... Acts 10:30 *5610*
at the ninth *h* I prayed in my ... Acts 10:30 *5610*
And he came out the same *h* ... Acts 16:18 *5610*
took them the same *h* of the night ... Acts 16:33 *5610*
the same *h* I looked up upon him ... Acts 22:13 *5610*
at the third *h* of the night ... Acts 23:23 *5610*
this present *h* we both hunger ... 1Cor 4:11 *5610*
of the idol unto this *h* eat it as ... 1Cor 8:7 *734*
why stand we in jeopardy every *h* ... 1Cor 15:30 *5610*
by subjection, no, not for an *h* ... Gal 2:5 *5610*
know what *h* I will come upon thee ... Rev 3:3 *5610*
thee from the *h* of temptation ... Rev 3:10 *5610*
about the space of half an *h* ... Rev 8:1 *2256*
which were prepared for an *h* ... Rev 9:15 *5610*
the same *h* was there a great ... Rev 11:13 *5610*
for the *h* of his judgment is come ... Rev 14:7 *5610*
as kings one *h* with the beast ... Rev 17:12 *5610*
for in one *h* is thy judgment come ... Rev 18:10 *5610*
For in one *h* so great riches is ... Rev 18:17 *5610*
for in one *h* is she made desolate ... Rev 18:19 *5610*

HOURS {3}
Are there not twelve *h* in the day ... Jn 11:9 *5610*
about the space of three *h* after ... Acts 5:7 *5610*
the space of two *h* cried out ... Acts 19:34 *5610*

HOUSE {2030}
thou and all thy *h* into the ark ... Gen 7:1 1004
kindred, and from thy father's *h* ... Gen 12:1 1004
woman was taken into Pharaoh's *h* ... Gen 12:15 1004
his *h* with great plagues because ... Gen 12:17 1004
servants, born in his own *h* ... Gen 14:14 1004
the steward of my *h* is this ... Gen 15:2 1004
lo, one born in my *h* is mine heir ... Gen 15:3 1004
he that is born in the *h* ... Gen 17:12 1004
He that is born in thy *h*, and he ... Gen 17:13 1004
and all that were born in his *h* ... Gen 17:23 1004
male among the men of Abraham's *h* ... Gen 17:23 1004
men of his *h*, born in the *h* ... Gen 17:27 1004
I pray you, into your servant's *h* ... Gen 19:2 1004
unto him, and entered into his *h* ... Gen 19:3 1004
of Sodom, compassed the *h* round ... Gen 19:4 1004
and pulled Lot into the *h* to them ... Gen 19:10 1004
the door of the *h* with blindness ... Gen 19:11 1004
me to wander from my father's *h* ... Gen 20:13 1004
the wombs of the *h* of Abimelech ... Gen 20:18 1004
unto his eldest servant of his *h* ... Gen 24:2 1004
which took me from my father's *h* ... Gen 24:7 1004
thy father's *h* for us to lodge in ... Gen 24:23 1004
the LORD led me to the *h* of my ... Gen 24:27 1004
of her mother's *h* these things ... Gen 24:28 1004
for I have prepared the *h* ... Gen 24:31 1004
And the man came into the *h* ... Gen 24:32 1004
thou shalt go unto my father's *h* ... Gen 24:38 1004
my kindred, and of my father's *h* ... Gen 24:40 1004
which were with her in the *h* ... Gen 27:15 1004
to the *h* of Bethuel thy mother's ... Gen 28:2 1004
is none other but the *h* of God ... Gen 28:17 1004
again to my father's *h* in peace ... Gen 28:21 1004
for a pillar, shall be God's *h* ... Gen 28:22 1004
him, and brought him to his *h* ... Gen 29:13 1004
I provide for mine own *h* also ... Gen 30:30 1004
for us in our father's *h* ... Gen 31:14 1004
longedst after thy father's *h* ... Gen 31:30 1004
have I been twenty years in thy *h* ... Gen 31:41 1004
to Succoth, and built him an *h* ... Gen 33:17 1004
than all the *h* of his father ... Gen 34:19 1004
and took Dinah out of Shechem's *h* ... Gen 34:26 1004
even all that was in the *h* ... Gen 34:29 1004
I shall be destroyed, I and my *h* ... Gen 34:30 1004
and all the persons of his *h* ... Gen 36:6 1004
Remain a widow at thy father's *h* ... Gen 38:11 1004
went and dwelt in her father's *h* ... Gen 38:11 1004
he was in the *h* of his master the ... Gen 39:2 1004
he made him overseer over his *h* ... Gen 39:4 1004
he had made him overseer in his *h* ... Gen 39:5 1004
Egyptian's *h* for Joseph's sake ... Gen 39:5 1004
was upon all that he had in the *h* ... Gen 39:5 1004
not what is with me in the *h* ... Gen 39:8 1004
is none greater in this *h* than I ... Gen 39:9 1004
into the *h* to do his business ... Gen 39:11 1004
of the men of the *h* there within ... Gen 39:11 1004
she called unto the men of her *h* ... Gen 39:14 1004
he put them in ward in the *h* of ... Gen 40:3 1004
him in the ward of his lord's *h* ... Gen 40:7 1004
and bring me out of this *h* ... Gen 40:14 1004
in the captain of the guard's *h* ... Gen 41:10 1004
Thou shalt be over my *h*, and ... Gen 41:40 1004
all my toil, and all my father's *h* ... Gen 41:51 1004
be bound in the *h* of your prison ... Gen 42:19 1004
he said to the ruler of his *h* ... Gen 43:16 1004
brought the men into Joseph's *h* ... Gen 43:17 1004
they were brought into Joseph's *h* ... Gen 43:18 1004
near to the steward of Joseph's *h* ... Gen 43:19 1004
with him at the door of the *h* ... Gen 43:19 1004
brought the men into Joseph's *h* ... Gen 43:24 1004
was in their hand into the *h* ... Gen 43:26 1004
he commanded the steward of his *h* ... Gen 44:1 1004
of thy lord's *h* silver or gold ... Gen 44:8 1004
his brethren came to Joseph's *h* ... Gen 44:14 1004
and the *h* of Pharaoh heard ... Gen 45:2 1004
to Pharaoh, and lord of all his *h* ... Gen 45:8 1004
thereof was heard in Pharaoh's *h* ... Gen 45:16 1004
all the souls of the *h* of Jacob ... Gen 46:27 1004
brethren, and unto his father's *h* ... Gen 46:31 1004
My brethren, and my father's *h* ... Gen 46:31 1004
the money into Pharaoh's *h* ... Gen 47:14 1004
spake unto the *h* of Pharaoh ... Gen 50:4 1004
of Pharaoh, the elders of his *h* ... Gen 50:7 1004
all the *h* of Joseph, and his ... Gen 50:8 1004
his brethren, and his father's *h* ... Gen 50:8 1004
in Egypt, he, and his father's *h* ... Gen 50:22 1004
there went a man of the *h* of Levi ... Ex 2:1 1004
of her that sojourneth in her *h* ... Ex 3:22 1004
Pharaoh turned and went into his *h* ... Ex 7:23 1004
shall go up and come into thine *h* ... Ex 8:3 1004
into the *h* of thy servants, and ... Ex 8:3 1004
of flies into the *h* of Pharaoh ... Ex 8:24 1004
to the *h* of their fathers ... Ex 12:3 1004
of their fathers, a lamb for an *h* ... Ex 12:3 1004
his neighbour next unto his *h* ... Ex 12:4 1004
door of his *h* until the morning ... Ex 12:22 1004
for there was not a *h* where there ... Ex 12:30 1004
In one *h* shall it be eaten ... Ex 12:46 1004
of the flesh abroad out of the *h* ... Ex 12:46 1004
Egypt, out of the *h* of bondage ... Ex 13:3 1004
from Egypt, from the *h* of bondage ... Ex 13:14 1004
the *h* of Israel called the name ... Ex 16:31 1004
shalt thou say to the *h* of Jacob ... Ex 19:3 1004
of Egypt, out of the *h* of bondage ... Ex 20:2 1004
shalt not covet thy neighbour's *h* ... Ex 20:17 1004
it be stolen out of the man's *h* ... Ex 22:7 1004
then the master of the *h* shall be ... Ex 22:8 1004
into the *h* of the LORD thy God ... Ex 23:19 1004
unto the *h* of the LORD thy God ... Ex 34:26 1004
the sight of all the *h* of Israel ... Ex 40:38 1004
brethren, the whole *h* of Israel ... Lev 10:6 1004
h of the land of your possession ... Lev 14:34 1004
he that owneth the *h* shall come ... Lev 14:35 1004
is as it were a plague in the *h* ... Lev 14:35 1004
command that they empty the *h* ... Lev 14:36 1004
is in the *h* be not made unclean ... Lev 14:36 1004
priest shall go in to see the *h* ... Lev 14:36 1004
of the *h* with hollow strakes ... Lev 14:37 1004
of the *h* to the door of the *h* ... Lev 14:38 1004
and shut up the *h* seven days ... Lev 14:38 1004
be spread in the walls of the *h* ... Lev 14:39 1004
he shall cause the *h* to be ... Lev 14:41 1004
morter, and shall plaister the *h* ... Lev 14:42 1004
come again, and break out in the *h* ... Lev 14:43 1004
and after he hath scraped the *h* ... Lev 14:43 1004
if the plague be spread in the *h* ... Lev 14:44 1004
it is a fretting leprosy in the *h* ... Lev 14:44 1004
And he shall break down the *h* ... Lev 14:45 1004
and all the morter of the *h* ... Lev 14:45 1004
h all the while that it is shut ... Lev 14:46 1004
he that lieth in the *h* shall wash ... Lev 14:47 1004
he that eateth in the *h* shall ... Lev 14:47 1004
plague hath not spread in the *h* ... Lev 14:48 1004
after the *h* was plaistered ... Lev 14:48 1004
shall pronounce the *h* clean ... Lev 14:48 1004
take to cleanse the *h* two birds ... Lev 14:49 1004
and sprinkle the *h* seven times ... Lev 14:51 1004
he shall cleanse the *h* with the ... Lev 14:52 1004
and make an atonement for the *h* ... Lev 14:53 1004
leprosy of a garment, and of a *h* ... Lev 14:55 1004
for himself, and for his *h* ... Lev 16:6 1004

for himself, and for his *h* Lev 16:11 1004
there be of the *h* of Israel Lev 17:3 1004
man there be of the *h* of Israel Lev 17:8 1004
man there be of the *h* of Israel Lev 17:10 1004
it, and he that is born in his *h* Lev 22:11 1004
is returned unto her father's *h* Lev 22:13 1004
he be of the *h* of Israel, or of Lev 22:18 1004
a dwelling *h* in a walled city Lev 25:29 1004
then the *h* that is in the walled Lev 25:30 1004
then the *h* that was sold, and the Lev 25:33 1004
his *h* to be holy unto the LORD Lev 27:14 1004
sanctified it will redeem his *h* Lev 27:15 1004
by the *h* of their fathers, with Num 1:2 1004
one head of the *h* of his fathers Num 1:4 1004
by the *h* of their fathers, Num 1:18 1004
by the *h* of their fathers, Num 1:20 1004
by the *h* of their fathers, those Num 1:22 1004
by the *h* of their fathers, Num 1:24 1004
by the *h* of their fathers, Num 1:26 1004
by the *h* of their fathers, Num 1:28 1004
by the *h* of their fathers, Num 1:30 1004
by the *h* of their fathers, Num 1:32 1004
by the *h* of their fathers, Num 1:34 1004
by the *h* of their fathers, Num 1:36 1004
by the *h* of their fathers, Num 1:38 1004
by the *h* of their fathers, Num 1:40 1004
by the *h* of their fathers, Num 1:42 1004
one was for the *h* of his fathers Num 1:44 1004
by the *h* of their fathers, from Num 1:45 1004
the ensign of their father's *h* Num 2:2 1004
Israel by the *h* of their fathers Num 2:32 1004
to the *h* of their fathers Num 2:34 1004
Levi after the *h* of their fathers Num 3:15 1004
to the *h* of their fathers Num 3:20 1004
the chief of the *h* of the father Num 3:24 1004
the chief of the *h* of the father Num 3:30 1004
the chief of the *h* of the father Num 3:35 1004
by the *h* of their fathers, Num 4:2 1004
by the *h* of their fathers Num 4:29 1004
after the *h* of their fathers, Num 4:34 1004
by the *h* of their fathers, Num 4:38 1004
by the *h* of their fathers, were Num 4:40 1004
by the *h* of their fathers, Num 4:42 1004
after the *h* of their fathers, Num 4:46 1004
heads of the *h* of their fathers Num 7:2 1004
so, who is faithful in all mine *h* Num 12:7 1004
to the *h* of their fathers Num 17:2 1004
h of their fathers twelve rods Num 17:2 1004
head of the *h* of their fathers Num 17:3 1004
for the *h* of Levi was budded Num 17:8 1004
thy father's *h* with thee shall Num 18:1 1004
is clean in thy *h* shall eat of it Num 18:11 1004
clean in thine *h* shall eat of it Num 18:13 1004
days, even all the *h* of Israel Num 20:29 1004
give me his *h* full of silver Num 22:18 1004
give me his *h* full of silver Num 24:13 1004
a prince of a chief *h* among the Num 25:14 1004
people, and of a chief *h* in Midian Num 25:15 1004
throughout their fathers' *h* Num 26:2 1004
in her father's *h* in her youth Num 30:3 1004
if she vowed in her husband's *h* Num 30:10 1004
in her youth in her father's *h* Num 30:16 1004
to the *h* of their fathers Num 34:14 1004
to the *h* of their fathers Num 34:14 1004
of Egypt, from the *h* of bondage Deut 5:6 1004
thou covet thy neighbour's *h* Deut 5:21 1004
them when thou sittest in thine *h* Deut 6:7 1004
them upon the posts of thy *h* Deut 6:9 1004
of Egypt, from the *h* of bondage Deut 6:12 1004
you out of the *h* of bondmen Deut 7:8 1004
bring an abomination into thine *h* Deut 7:26 1004
of Egypt, from the *h* of bondage Deut 8:14 1004
them when thou sittest in thine *h* Deut 11:19 1004
upon the door posts of thine *h* Deut 11:20 1004
you out of the *h* of bondage Deut 13:5 1004
of Egypt, from the *h* of bondage Deut 13:10 1004
because he loveth thee and thine *h* Deut 15:16 1004
is there that hath built a new *h* Deut 20:5 1004
let him go and return to his *h* Deut 20:5 1004
him also go and return unto his *h* Deut 20:6 1004
let him go and return unto his *h* Deut 20:7 1004
let him go and return unto his *h* Deut 20:8 1004
shalt bring her home to thine *h* Deut 21:12 1004
her, and shall remain in thine *h* Deut 21:13 1004
shalt bring it unto thine own *h* Deut 22:2 1004
When thou buildest a new *h* Deut 22:8 1004
thou bring not blood upon thine *h* Deut 22:8 1004
to the door of her father's *h* Deut 22:21 1004
play the whore in her father's *h* Deut 22:21 1004
into the *h* of the LORD thy God Deut 23:18 1004
hand, and send her out of his *h* Deut 24:1 1004
when she is departed out of his *h* Deut 24:2 1004
hand, and sendeth her out of his *h* Deut 24:3 1004
go into his *h* to fetch his pledge Deut 24:10 1004
will not build up his brother's *h* Deut 25:9 1004
The *h* of him that hath his shoe Deut 25:10 1004
have in thine *h* divers measures Deut 25:14 1004
given unto thee, and unto thine *h* Deut 26:11 1004
the hallowed things out of mine *h* Deut 26:13 1004
thou shalt build an *h*, and thou Deut 28:30 1004
went, and came into an harlot's *h* Josh 2:1 1004
which are entered into thine *h* Josh 2:3 1004
them up to the roof of the *h* Josh 2:6
shew kindness unto my father's *h* Josh 2:12 1004
for her *h* was upon the town wall, Josh 2:15 1004
doors of thy *h* into the street Josh 2:19 1004
shall be with thee in the *h* Josh 2:19 1004
and all that are with her in the *h* Josh 6:17 1004

country, Go into the harlot's *h* Josh 6:22 1004
the treasury of the *h* of the LORD Josh 6:24 1004
of water for the *h* of my God Josh 9:23 1004
Joshua spake unto the *h* of Joseph Josh 17:17 1004
the *h* of Joseph shall abide in Josh 18:5 1004
his own city, and unto his own *h* Josh 20:6 1004
had spoken unto the *h* of Israel Josh 21:45 1004
princes, of each chief *h* a prince Josh 22:14 1004
the *h* of their fathers among the Josh 22:14 1004
but as for me and my *h*, we will Josh 24:15 1004
from the *h* of bondage, and which Josh 24:17 1004
the *h* of Joseph, they also went Judg 1:22 1004
the *h* of Joseph sent to descry Judg 1:23 1004
hand of the *h* of Joseph prevailed Judg 1:35 1004
the *h* of Heber the Kenite Judg 4:17 1004
you forth out of the *h* of bondage Judg 6:8 1004
I am the least in my father's *h* Judg 6:15 1004
a snare unto Gideon, and to his *h* Judg 8:27 1004
Joash went and dwelt in his own *h* Judg 8:29 1004
kindness to the *h* of Jerubbaal Judg 8:35 1004
of the *h* of his mother's father Judg 9:1 1004
out of the *h* of Baal-berith Judg 9:4 1004
unto his father's *h* at Ophrah Judg 9:5 1004
all the *h* of Millo, and went, and Judg 9:6 1004
well with Jerubbaal and his *h* Judg 9:16 1004
up against my father's *h* this day Judg 9:18 1004
Jerubbaal and with his *h* this day Judg 9:19 1004
men of Shechem, and the *h* of Millo Judg 9:20 1004
Shechem, and from the *h* of Millo Judg 9:20 1004
and went into the *h* of their god Judg 9:27 1004
hold of the *h* of the god Berith Judg 9:46 1004
and against the *h* of Ephraim Judg 10:9 1004
not inherit in our father's *h* Judg 11:2 1004
and expel me out of my father's *h* Judg 11:7 1004
of the doors of my *h* to meet me Judg 11:31 1004
came to Mizpeh unto his *h* Judg 11:34 1004
we will burn thine *h* upon thee Judg 12:1 1004
thee and thy father's *h* with fire Judg 14:15 1004
and he went up to his father's *h* Judg 14:19 1004
and he did grind in the prison *h* Judg 16:21 1004
for Samson out of the prison *h* Judg 16:25 1004
pillars whereupon the *h* standeth Judg 16:26 1004
Now the *h* was full of men and Judg 16:27 1004
pillars upon which the *h* stood Judg 16:29 1004
the *h* fell upon the lords, and Judg 16:30 1004
all the *h* of his father came down Judg 16:31 1004
and they were in the *h* of Micah Judg 17:4 1004
And the man Micah had an *h* of gods Judg 17:5 1004
mount Ephraim to the *h* of Micah Judg 17:8 1004
priest, and was in the *h* of Micah Judg 17:12 1004
to the *h* of Micah, they lodged Judg 18:2 1004
When they were by the *h* of Micah Judg 18:3 1004
and came unto the *h* of Micah Judg 18:13 1004
came to the *h* of the young man Judg 18:15 1004
Levite, even unto the *h* of Micah Judg 18:15 1004
And these went into Micah's *h* Judg 18:18 1004
be a priest unto the *h* of one man Judg 18:19 1004
a good way from the *h* of Micah Judg 18:22 1004
Micah's *h* were gathered together Judg 18:22 1004
he turned and went back unto his *h* Judg 18:26 1004
that the *h* of God was in Shiloh Judg 18:31 1004
father's *h* to Beth-lehem-judah Judg 19:2 1004
brought him into her father's *h* Judg 19:3 1004
took them into his *h* to lodging Judg 19:15 1004
am now going to the *h* of the LORD Judg 19:18 1004
is no man that receiveth me to *h* Judg 19:18 1004
So he brought him into his *h* Judg 19:21 1004
beset the *h* round about, and beat Judg 19:22 1004
and spake to the master of the *h* Judg 19:22 1004
the man that came into thine *h* Judg 19:22 1004
And the man, the master of the *h* Judg 19:23 1004
that this man is come into mine *h* Judg 19:23 1004
of the man's *h* where her lord was Judg 19:26 1004
and opened the doors of the *h* Judg 19:27 1004
fallen down at the door of the *h* Judg 19:27 1004
And when he was come into his *h* Judg 19:29 1004
beset the *h* round about upon me Judg 20:5 1004
will we any of us turn into his *h* Judg 20:8 1004
arose, and went up to the *h* of God Judg 20:18 1008
up, and came unto the *h* of God Judg 20:26 1008
one goeth up to the *h* of God Judg 20:31 1008
the people came to the *h* of God Judg 21:2 1008
Go, return each to her mother's *h* Ruth 1:8 1004
of you in the *h* of her husband Ruth 1:9 1004
she tarried a little in the *h* Ruth 2:7 1004
is come into thine *h* like Rachel Ruth 4:11 1004
two did build the *h* of Israel Ruth 4:11 1004
thy *h* be like the *h* of Pharez Ruth 4:12 1004
she went up to the *h* of the LORD 1Sa 1:7 1004
and came to their *h* to Ramah 1Sa 1:19 1004
And the man Elkanah, and all his *h* 1Sa 1:21 1004
brought him unto the *h* of the 1Sa 1:24 1004
And Elkanah went to Ramah to his *h* 1Sa 2:11 1004
appear unto the *h* of thy father 1Sa 2:27 1004
they were in Egypt in Pharaoh's *h* 1Sa 2:27 1004
did I give unto the *h* of thy 1Sa 2:28 1004
saith, I said indeed that thy *h* 1Sa 2:30 1004
the *h* of thy father, should walk 1Sa 2:30 1004
arm, and the arm of thy father's *h* 1Sa 2:31 1004
not be an old man in thine *h* 1Sa 2:31 1004
be an old man in thine *h* for ever 1Sa 2:32 1004
all the increase of thine *h* shall 1Sa 2:33 1004
and I will build him a sure *h* 1Sa 2:35 1004
is left in thine *h* shall come 1Sa 2:36 1004
I have spoken concerning his *h* 1Sa 3:12 1004
told him that I will judge his *h* 1Sa 3:13 1004
I have sworn unto the *h* of Eli 1Sa 3:14 1004
Eli's *h* shall not be purged with 1Sa 3:14 1004

the doors of the *h* of the LORD 1Sa 3:15 1004
brought it into the *h* of Dagon 1Sa 5:2 1004
nor any that come into Dagon's *h* 1Sa 5:5 1004
brought it into the *h* of Abinadab 1Sa 7:1 1004
all the *h* of Israel lamented 1Sa 7:2 1004
spake unto all the *h* of Israel 1Sa 7:3 1004
for there was his *h* 1Sa 7:17 1004
pray thee, where the seer's *h* is 1Sa 9:18 1004
on thee, and on all thy father's *h* 1Sa 9:20 1004
with Saul upon the top of the *h* 1Sa 9:25
called Saul to the top of the *h* 1Sa 9:26
people away, every man to his *h* 1Sa 10:25 1004
up to his *h* to Gibeah of Saul 1Sa 15:34 1004
his father's *h* free in Israel 1Sa 17:25 1004
go no more home to his father's *h* 1Sa 18:2 1004
prophesied in the midst of the *h* 1Sa 18:10 1004
as he sat in his *h* with his 1Sa 19:9 1004
sent messengers unto David's *h* 1Sa 19:11 1004
thy kindness from my *h* for ever 1Sa 20:15 1004
a covenant with the *h* of David 1Sa 20:16 1004
shall this fellow come into my *h* 1Sa 21:15 1004
and all his father's *h* heard it 1Sa 22:1 1004
of Ahitub, and all his father's *h* 1Sa 22:11 1004
and is honourable in thine *h* 1Sa 22:14 1004
nor to all the *h* of my father 1Sa 22:15 1004
thou, and all thy father's *h* 1Sa 22:16 1004
all the persons of thy father's *h* 1Sa 22:22 1004
wood, and Jonathan went to his *h* 1Sa 23:18 1004
my name out of my father's *h* 1Sa 24:21 1004
and buried him in his *h* at Ramah 1Sa 25:1 1004
and he was of the *h* of Caleb 1Sa 25:3 1004
to thee, and peace be to thine *h* 1Sa 25:6 1004
certainly make my lord a sure *h* 1Sa 25:28 1004
her, Go up in peace to thine *h* 1Sa 25:35 1004
behold, he held a feast in his *h* 1Sa 25:36 1004
the woman had a fat calf in the *h* 1Sa 28:24 1004
it in the *h* of their idols 1Sa 31:9 1004
his armour in the *h* of Ashtaroth 1Sa 31:10 1004
the LORD, and for the *h* of Israel 2Sa 1:12 1004
David king over the *h* of Judah 2Sa 2:4 1004
also the *h* of Judah have anointed 2Sa 2:7 1004
But the *h* of Judah followed David 2Sa 2:10 1004
the *h* of Judah was seven years 2Sa 2:11 1004
h of Saul and the *h* of David 2Sa 3:1 1004
the *h* of Saul waxed weaker and 2Sa 3:1 1004
was war between the *h* of Saul 2Sa 3:6 1004
the *h* of David, that Abner made 2Sa 3:6 1004
himself strong for the *h* of Saul 2Sa 3:6 1004
day unto the *h* of Saul thy father 2Sa 3:8 1004
the kingdom from the *h* of Saul 2Sa 3:10 1004
good to the whole *h* of Benjamin 2Sa 3:19 1004
of Joab, and on all his father's *h* 2Sa 3:29 1004
let there not fail from the *h* of 2Sa 3:29 1004
the day to the *h* of Ish-bosheth 2Sa 4:5 1004
thither into the midst of the *h* 2Sa 4:6 1004
For when they came into the *h* 2Sa 4:7 1004
person in his own *h* upon his bed 2Sa 4:11 1004
lame shall not come into the *h* 2Sa 5:8 1004
and they built David an *h* 2Sa 5:11 1004
brought it out of the *h* of 2Sa 6:3 1004
they brought it out of the *h* of 2Sa 6:4 1004
all the *h* of Israel played before 2Sa 6:5 1004
the *h* of Obed-edom the Gittite 2Sa 6:10 1004
of the LORD continued in the *h* of 2Sa 6:11 1004
hath blessed the *h* of Obed-edom 2Sa 6:12 1004
up the ark of God from the *h* of 2Sa 6:12 1004
all the *h* of Israel brought up 2Sa 6:15 1004
departed every one to his *h* 2Sa 6:19 1004
thy father, and before all his *h* 2Sa 6:21 1004
pass, when the king sat in his *h* 2Sa 7:1 1004
See now, I dwell in an *h* of cedar 2Sa 7:2 1004
build me an *h* for me to dwell in 2Sa 7:5 1004
h since the time that I brought 2Sa 7:6 1004
Why build ye not me an *h* of cedar 2Sa 7:7 1004
thee that he will make thee an *h* 2Sa 7:11 1004
He shall build an *h* for my name 2Sa 7:13 1004
And thine *h* and thy kingdom shall 2Sa 7:16 1004
and what is my *h*, that thou hast 2Sa 7:18 1004
h for a great while to come 2Sa 7:19 1004
thy servant, and concerning his *h* 2Sa 7:25 1004
let the *h* of thy servant David be 2Sa 7:26 1004
saying, I will build thee an *h* 2Sa 7:27 1004
to bless the *h* of thy servant 2Sa 7:29 1004
with thy blessing let the *h* of 2Sa 7:29 1004
any that is left of the *h* of Saul 2Sa 9:1 1004
there was of the *h* of Saul a 2Sa 9:2 1004
not yet any of the *h* of Saul 2Sa 9:3 1004
Behold, he is in the *h* of Machir 2Sa 9:4 1004
him out of the *h* of Machir 2Sa 9:5 1004
pertained to Saul and to all his *h* 2Sa 9:9 1004
all that dwelt in the *h* of Ziba 2Sa 9:12 1004
upon the roof of the king's *h* 2Sa 11:2 1004
and she returned unto her *h* 2Sa 11:4 1004
said to Uriah, Go down to thy *h* 2Sa 11:8 1004
departed out of the king's *h* 2Sa 11:8 1004
h with all the servants of his 2Sa 11:9 1004
lord, and went not down to his *h* 2Sa 11:9 1004
Uriah went not down unto his *h* 2Sa 11:10 1004
thou not go down unto thine *h* 2Sa 11:10 1004
shall I then go into mine *h* 2Sa 11:11 1004
lord, but went not down to his *h* 2Sa 11:13 1004
sent and fetched her to his *h* 2Sa 11:27 1004
And I gave thee thy master's *h* 2Sa 12:8 1004
and gave thee the *h* of Israel 2Sa 12:8 1004
shall never depart from thine *h* 2Sa 12:10 1004
against thee out of thine own *h* 2Sa 12:11 1004
And Nathan departed unto his *h* 2Sa 12:15 1004
And the elders of his *h* arose 2Sa 12:17 1004

H

and came into the *h* of the LORD 2Sa 12:20 1004
then he came to his own *h* 2Sa 12:20 1004
Go now to thy brother Amnon's *h* 2Sa 13:7 1004
went to her brother Amnon's *h* 2Sa 13:8 1004
in her brother Absalom's *h* 2Sa 13:20 1004
unto the woman, Go to thine *h* 2Sa 14:8 1004
be on me, and on my father's *h* 2Sa 14:9 1004
said, Let him turn to his own *h* 2Sa 14:24 1004
So Absalom returned to his own *h* 2Sa 14:24 1004
and came to Absalom unto his *h* 2Sa 14:31 1004
were concubines, to keep the *h* 2Sa 15:16 1004
shalt hear out of the king's *h* 2Sa 15:35 1004
Today shall the *h* of Israel 2Sa 16:3 1004
of the family of the *h* of Saul 2Sa 16:5 1004
all the blood of the *h* of Saul 2Sa 16:8 1004
which he hath left to keep the *h* 2Sa 16:21 1004
a tent upon the top of the *h* 2Sa 16:22 1004
and came to a man's *h* in Bahurim 2Sa 17:18 1004
came to the woman to the *h* 2Sa 17:20 1004
arose, and gat him home to his *h* 2Sa 17:23 1004
Joab came into the *h* to the king 2Sa 19:5 1004
to bring the king back to his *h* 2Sa 19:11 1004
come to the king, even to his *h* 2Sa 19:11 1004
Ziba the servant of the *h* of Saul 2Sa 19:17 1004
the first this day of all the *h* 2Sa 19:20 1004
For all of my father's *h* were but 2Sa 19:28 1004
again in peace unto his own *h* 2Sa 19:30 1004
David came to his *h* at Jerusalem 2Sa 20:3 1004
whom he had left to keep the *h* 2Sa 20:3 1004
is for Saul, and for his bloody *h* 2Sa 21:1 1004
nor gold of Saul, nor of his *h* 2Sa 21:4 1004
Although my *h* be not so with God 2Sa 23:5 1004
me, and against my father's *h* 2Sa 24:17 1004
said unto him, Go to thine *h* 1Kin 1:53 1004
father, and who hath made me an *h* 1Kin 2:24 1004
concerning the *h* of Eli in Shiloh 1Kin 2:27 1004
me, and from the *h* of my father 1Kin 2:31 1004
and upon his seed, and upon his *h* 1Kin 2:33 1004
in his own *h* in the wilderness 1Kin 2:34 1004
him, Build thee an *h* in Jerusalem 1Kin 2:36 1004
made an end of building his own *h* 1Kin 3:1 1004
the *h* of the LORD, and the wall of 1Kin 3:1 1004
because there was no *h* built unto 1Kin 3:2 1004
I and this woman dwell in one *h* 1Kin 3:17 1004
of a child with her in the *h* 1Kin 3:17 1004
was no stranger with us in the *h* 1Kin 3:18 1004
save we two in the *h* 1Kin 3:18 1004
my father could not build an *h* 1Kin 5:3 1004
I purpose to build an *h* unto the 1Kin 5:5 1004
he shall build an *h* unto my name 1Kin 5:5 1004
to lay the foundation of the *h* 1Kin 5:17 1004
timber and stones to build the *h* 1Kin 5:18 1004
began to build the *h* of the LORD 1Kin 6:1 1004
the *h* which king Solomon built 1Kin 6:2 1004
porch before the temple of the *h* 1Kin 6:3 1004
according to the breadth of the *h* 1Kin 6:3 1004
the breadth thereof before the *h* 1Kin 6:3 1004
for the *h* he made windows of 1Kin 6:4 1004
against the wall of the *h* he 1Kin 6:5 1004
the walls of the *h* round about 1Kin 6:5 1004
h he made narrowed rests round 1Kin 6:6 1004
be fastened in the walls of the *h* 1Kin 6:6 1004
And the *h*, when it was in building 1Kin 6:7 1004
any tool of iron heard in the *h* 1Kin 6:7 1004
was in the right side of the *h* 1Kin 6:8 1004
So he built the *h*, and finished it 1Kin 6:9 1004
and covered the *h* with beams 1Kin 6:9 1004
built chambers against all the *h* 1Kin 6:10 1004
they rested on the *h* with timber 1Kin 6:10 1004
Concerning this *h* which thou art 1Kin 6:12 1004
So Solomon built the *h*, and 1Kin 6:14 1004
he built the walls of the *h* 1Kin 6:15 1004
of cedar, both the floor of the *h* 1Kin 6:15 1004
floor of the *h* with planks of fir 1Kin 6:15 1004
cubits on the sides of the *h* 1Kin 6:16 1004
And the *h*, that is, the temple 1Kin 6:17 1004
the cedar of the *h* within was 1Kin 6:18 1004
he prepared in the *h* within 1Kin 6:19 1004
the *h* within with pure gold 1Kin 6:21 1004
the whole *h* he overlaid with gold 1Kin 6:22 1004
until he had finished all the *h* 1Kin 6:22 1004
the cherubims within the inner *h* 1Kin 6:27 1004
one another in the midst of the *h* 1Kin 6:27 1004
he carved all the walls of the *h* 1Kin 6:29 1004
the floor of the *h* he overlaid 1Kin 6:30 1004
of the *h* of the LORD laid 1Kin 6:37 1004
was the *h* finished throughout all 1Kin 6:38 1004
building his own *h* thirteen years 1Kin 7:1 1004
and he finished all his *h* 1Kin 7:1 1004
He built also the *h* of the forest 1Kin 7:2 1004
his *h* where he dwelt had another 1Kin 7:8 1004
Solomon made also an *h* for 1Kin 7:8 1004
inner court of the *h* of the LORD 1Kin 7:12 1004
and for the porch of the *h* 1Kin 7:12 1004
bases on the right side of the *h* 1Kin 7:39 1004
and five on the left side of the *h* 1Kin 7:39 1004
sea on the right side of the *h* 1Kin 7:39 1004
Solomon for the *h* of the LORD 1Kin 7:40 1004
Solomon for the *h* of the LORD 1Kin 7:45 1004
pertained unto the *h* of the LORD 1Kin 7:48 1004
both for the doors of the inner *h* 1Kin 7:50 1004
place, and for the doors of the *h* 1Kin 7:50 1004
made for the *h* of the LORD 1Kin 7:51 1004
treasures of the *h* of the LORD 1Kin 7:51 1004
place, into the oracle of the *h* 1Kin 8:6 1004
cloud filled the *h* of the LORD 1Kin 8:10 1004
LORD had filled the *h* of the LORD 1Kin 8:11 1004
built thee an *h* to dwell in 1Kin 8:13 1004

tribes of Israel to build an *h* 1Kin 8:16 1004
of David my father to build an *h* 1Kin 8:17 1004
heart to build an *h* unto my name 1Kin 8:18 1004
thou shalt not build the *h* 1Kin 8:19 1004
he shall build the *h* unto my name 1Kin 8:19 1004
have built an *h* for the name of 1Kin 8:20 1004
how much less this *h* that I have 1Kin 8:27 1004
may be open toward this *h* night 1Kin 8:29 1004
come before thine altar in this *h* 1Kin 8:31 1004
supplication unto thee in this *h* 1Kin 8:33 1004
forth his hands toward this *h* 1Kin 8:38 1004
shall come and pray toward this *h* 1Kin 8:42 1004
and that they may know that this *h* 1Kin 8:43 1004
toward the *h* that I have built 1Kin 8:44 1004
the *h* which I have built for thy 1Kin 8:48 1004
dedicated the *h* of the LORD 1Kin 8:63 1004
that was before the *h* of the LORD 1Kin 8:64 1004
the building of the *h* of the LORD 1Kin 9:1 1004
of the LORD, and the king's *h* 1Kin 9:1 1004
I have hallowed this *h*, which 1Kin 9:3 1004
and this *h*, which I have hallowed 1Kin 9:7 1004
And at this *h*, which is high, 1Kin 9:8 1004
thus unto this land, and to this *h* 1Kin 9:8 1004
the *h* of the LORD, and the king's 1Kin 9:10 1004
of the LORD, and the king's *h* 1Kin 9:10 1004
h of the LORD, and his own *h* 1Kin 9:15 1004
of the city of David unto her *h* 1Kin 9:24 1004
So he finished the *h* 1Kin 9:25 1004
and the *h* that he had built, 1Kin 10:4 1004
he went up unto the *h* of the LORD 1Kin 10:5 1004
pillars for the *h* of the LORD 1Kin 10:12 1004
of the LORD, and for the king's *h* 1Kin 10:12 1004
in the *h* of the forest of Lebanon 1Kin 10:17 1004
all the vessels of the *h* of the 1Kin 10:21 1004
which gave him an *h*, and appointed 1Kin 11:18 1004
Tahpenes weaned in Pharaoh's *h* 1Kin 11:20 1004
all the charge of the *h* of Joseph 1Kin 11:28 1004
with thee, and build thee a sure *h* 1Kin 11:38 1004
now see to thine own *h*, David 1Kin 12:16 1004
the *h* of David unto this day 1Kin 12:19 1004
none that followed the *h* of David 1Kin 12:20 1004
he assembled all the *h* of Judah 1Kin 12:21 1004
to fight against the *h* of Israel 1Kin 12:21 1004
Judah, and unto all the *h* of Judah 1Kin 12:23 1004
return every man to his *h* 1Kin 12:24 1004
kingdom return to the *h* of David 1Kin 12:26 1004
in the *h* of the LORD at Jerusalem 1Kin 12:27 1004
he made an *h* of high places, and 1Kin 12:31 1004
shall be born unto the *h* of David 1Kin 13:2 1004
If thou wilt give me half thine *h* 1Kin 13:8 1004
him back with thee into thine *h* 1Kin 13:18 1004
him, and did eat bread in his *h* 1Kin 13:19 1004
became sin unto the *h* of Jeroboam 1Kin 13:34 1004
and came to the *h* of Ahijah 1Kin 14:4 1004
kingdom away from the *h* of David 1Kin 14:8 1004
bring evil upon the *h* of Jeroboam 1Kin 14:10 1004
the remnant of the *h* of Jeroboam 1Kin 14:10 1004
get thee to thine own *h* 1Kin 14:12 1004
of Israel in the *h* of Jeroboam 1Kin 14:13 1004
off the *h* of Jeroboam that day 1Kin 14:14 1004
treasures of the *h* of the LORD 1Kin 14:26 1004
and the treasures of the king's *h* 1Kin 14:26 1004
kept the door of the king's *h* 1Kin 14:27 1004
king went into the *h* of the LORD 1Kin 14:28 1004
into the *h* of the LORD, silver, 1Kin 15:15 1004
treasures of the *h* of the LORD 1Kin 15:18 1004
and the treasures of the king's *h* 1Kin 15:18 1004
of the *h* of Issachar, conspired 1Kin 15:27 1004
he smote all the *h* of Jeroboam 1Kin 15:29 1004
Baasha, and the posterity of his *h* 1Kin 16:3 1004
thy *h* like the *h* of Jeroboam 1Kin 16:3 1004
against Baasha, and against his *h* 1Kin 16:7 1004
in being like the *h* of Jeroboam 1Kin 16:7 1004
drinking himself drunk in the *h* 1Kin 16:9 1004
Arza steward of his *h* in Tirzah 1Kin 16:9 1004
that he slew all the *h* of Baasha 1Kin 16:11 1004
Zimri destroy all the *h* of Baasha 1Kin 16:12 1004
into the palace of the king's *h* 1Kin 16:18 1004
burnt the king's *h* over him with 1Kin 16:18 1004
altar for Baal in the *h* of Baal 1Kin 16:32 1004
and she, and he, and her *h*, did eat 1Kin 17:15 1004
the woman, the mistress of the *h* 1Kin 17:17 1004
out of the chamber into the *h* 1Kin 17:23 1004
which was the governor of his *h* 1Kin 18:3 1004
but thou, and thy father's *h* 1Kin 18:18 1004
and they shall search thine *h* 1Kin 20:6 1004
heard that the kings of the *h* of 1Kin 20:31 1004
of Israel went to his *h* heavy 1Kin 20:43 1004
because it is near unto my *h* 1Kin 21:2 1004
And Ahab came into his *h* heavy 1Kin 21:4 1004
will make thine *h* like the *h* 1Kin 21:22 1004
h of Jeroboam the son of Nebat 1Kin 21:22 1004
like the *h* of Baasha the son of 1Kin 21:22 1004
will I bring the evil upon his *h* 1Kin 21:29 1004
every man to his *h* in peace 1Kin 22:17 1004
the ivory *h* which he made, and all 1Kin 22:39 1004
tell me, what hast thou in the *h* 2Kin 4:2 1004
hath not any thing in the *h* 2Kin 4:2 1004
when Elisha was come into the *h* 2Kin 4:32 1004
returned, and walked in the *h* to 2Kin 4:35 1004
at the door of the *h* of Elisha 2Kin 5:9 1004
the *h* of Rimmon to worship there 2Kin 5:18 1004
I bow myself in the *h* of Rimmon 2Kin 5:18 1004
down myself in the *h* of Rimmon 2Kin 5:18 1004
hand, and bestowed them in the *h* 2Kin 5:24 1004
But Elisha sat in his *h*, and the 2Kin 6:32 1004
told it to the king's *h* within 2Kin 7:11 1004
to cry unto the king for her *h* 2Kin 8:3 1004

life, cried to the king for her *h* 2Kin 8:5 1004
of Israel, as did the *h* of Ahab 2Kin 8:18 1004
in the way of the *h* of Ahab 2Kin 8:27 1004
of the LORD, as did the *h* of Ahab 2Kin 8:27 1004
the son in law of the *h* of Ahab 2Kin 8:27 1004
And he arose, and went into the *h* 2Kin 9:6 1004
smite the *h* of Ahab thy master 2Kin 9:7 1004
For the whole *h* of Ahab shall 2Kin 9:8 1004
I will make the *h* of Ahab like 2Kin 9:9 1004
h of Jeroboam the son of Nebat 2Kin 9:9 1004
like the *h* of Baasha the son of 2Kin 9:9 1004
fled by the way of the garden *h* 2Kin 9:27 1004
and fight for your master's *h* 2Kin 10:3 1004
And he that was over the *h* 2Kin 10:5 1004
spake concerning the *h* of Ahab 2Kin 10:10 1004
of the *h* of Ahab in Jezreel 2Kin 10:11 1004
was at the shearing *h* in the way 2Kin 10:12 1004
them at the pit of the shearing *h* 2Kin 10:14 1004
And they came into the *h* of Baal 2Kin 10:21 1004
the *h* of Baal was full from one 2Kin 10:21 1004
son of Rechab, into the *h* of Baal 2Kin 10:23 1004
went to the city of the *h* of Baal 2Kin 10:25 1004
the images out of the *h* of Baal 2Kin 10:26 1004
Baal, and brake down the *h* of Baal 2Kin 10:27 1004
made it a draught *h* unto this day 2Kin 10:27
hast done unto the *h* of Ahab 2Kin 10:30 1004
in the *h* of the LORD six years 2Kin 11:3 1004
to him into the *h* of the LORD 2Kin 11:4 1004
oath of them in the *h* of the LORD 2Kin 11:4 1004
of the watch of the king's *h* 2Kin 11:5 1004
shall ye keep the watch of the *h* 2Kin 11:6 1004
the *h* of the LORD about the king 2Kin 11:7 1004
not be slain in the *h* of the LORD 2Kin 11:15 1004
the horses came into the king's *h* 2Kin 11:16 1004
the land went into the *h* of Baal 2Kin 11:18 1004
officers over the *h* of the LORD 2Kin 11:18 1004
the king from the *h* of the LORD 2Kin 11:19 1004
gate of the guard to the king's *h* 2Kin 11:19 1004
the sword beside the king's *h* 2Kin 11:20 1004
is brought into the *h* of the LORD 2Kin 12:4 1004
to bring into the *h* of the LORD 2Kin 12:4 1004
them repair the breaches of the *h* 2Kin 12:5 1004
repaired the breaches of the *h* 2Kin 12:6 1004
ye not the breaches of the *h* 2Kin 12:7 1004
it for the breaches of the *h* 2Kin 12:7 1004
to repair the breaches of the *h* 2Kin 12:8 1004
one cometh into the *h* of the LORD 2Kin 12:9 1004
brought into the *h* of the LORD 2Kin 12:9 1004
was found in the *h* of the LORD 2Kin 12:10 1004
oversight of the *h* of the LORD 2Kin 12:11 1004
wrought upon the *h* of the LORD 2Kin 12:11 1004
the breaches of the *h* of the LORD 2Kin 12:12 1004
laid out for the *h* to repair it 2Kin 12:12 1004
the *h* of the LORD bowls of silver 2Kin 12:13 1004
brought into the *h* of the LORD 2Kin 12:13 1004
therewith the *h* of the LORD 2Kin 12:14 1004
brought into the *h* of the LORD 2Kin 12:16 1004
treasures of the *h* of the LORD 2Kin 12:18 1004
of the LORD, and in the king's *h* 2Kin 12:18 1004
and slew Joash in the *h* of Millo 2Kin 12:20 1004
the sins of the *h* of Jeroboam 2Kin 13:6 1004
were found in the *h* of the LORD 2Kin 14:14 1004
in the treasures of the king's *h* 2Kin 14:14 1004
death, and dwelt in a several *h* 2Kin 15:5 1004
the king's son was over the *h* 2Kin 15:5 1004
in the palace of the king's *h* 2Kin 15:25 1004
higher gate of the *h* of the LORD 2Kin 15:35 1004
was found in the *h* of the LORD 2Kin 16:8 1004
in the treasures of the king's *h* 2Kin 16:8 1004
LORD, from the forefront of the *h* 2Kin 16:14 1004
the *h* of the LORD, and put it on 2Kin 16:14 1004
that they had built in the *h* 2Kin 16:18 1004
turned he from the *h* of the LORD 2Kin 16:18 1004
rent Israel from the *h* of David 2Kin 17:21 1004
was found in the *h* of the LORD 2Kin 18:15 1004
in the treasures of the king's *h* 2Kin 18:15 1004
and went into the *h* of the LORD 2Kin 19:1 1004
went up into the *h* of the LORD 2Kin 19:14 1004
herb, as the grass on the *h* tops 2Kin 19:26
h of Judah shall yet again take 2Kin 19:30 1004
in the *h* of Nisroch his god 2Kin 19:37 1004
the LORD, Set thine *h* in order 2Kin 20:1 1004
go up unto the *h* of the LORD 2Kin 20:5 1004
the *h* of the LORD the third day 2Kin 20:8 1004
shewed them all the *h* of his 2Kin 20:13 1004
all the *h* of his armour, and all 2Kin 20:13 1004
there was nothing in his *h* 2Kin 20:13 1004
What have they seen in thine *h* 2Kin 20:15 1004
that are in mine *h* have they seen 2Kin 20:15 1004
come, that all that is in thine *h* 2Kin 20:17 1004
built altars in the *h* of the LORD 2Kin 21:4 1004
two courts of the *h* of the LORD 2Kin 21:5 1004
grove that he had made in the *h* 2Kin 21:7 1004
and to Solomon his son, In this *h* 2Kin 21:7 1004
and the plummet of the *h* of Ahab 2Kin 21:13 1004
buried in the garden of his own *h* 2Kin 21:18 1004
and slew the king in his own *h* 2Kin 21:23 1004
to the *h* of the LORD, saying, 2Kin 22:3 1004
is brought into the *h* of the LORD 2Kin 22:4 1004
oversight of the *h* of the LORD 2Kin 22:5 1004
which is in the *h* of the LORD 2Kin 22:5 1004
to repair the breaches of the *h* 2Kin 22:5 1004
and hewn stone to repair the *h* 2Kin 22:6 1004
of the law in the *h* of the LORD 2Kin 22:8 1004
the money that was found in the *h* 2Kin 22:9 1004
oversight of the *h* of the LORD 2Kin 22:9 1004
went up into the *h* of the LORD 2Kin 23:2 1004
was found in the *h* of the LORD 2Kin 23:2 1004

the grove from the *h* of the LORD	2Kin 23:6	1004
that were by the *h* of the LORD	2Kin 23:7	1004
entering in of the *h* of the LORD	2Kin 23:11	1004
two courts of the *h* of the LORD	2Kin 23:12	1004
priest found in the *h* of the LORD	2Kin 23:24	1004
the *h* of which I said, My name	2Kin 23:27	1004
treasures of the *h* of the LORD	2Kin 24:13	1004
and the treasures of the king's *h*	2Kin 24:13	1004
And he burnt the *h* of the LORD	2Kin 25:9	1004
of the LORD, and the king's *h*	2Kin 25:9	1004
every great man's *h* burnt he with	2Kin 25:9	1004
that were in the *h* of the LORD	2Kin 25:13	1004
sea that was in the *h* of the LORD	2Kin 25:13	1004
had made for the *h* of the LORD	2Kin 25:16	1004
the *h* of Joab, and half of the	1Chr 2:54	5854
the father of the *h* of Rechab	1Chr 2:55	1004
the families of the *h* of them	1Chr 4:21	1004
fine linen, of the *h* of Ashbea,	1Chr 4:21	1004
the *h* of their fathers increased	1Chr 4:38	1004
of the *h* of their fathers were	1Chr 5:13	1004
chief of the *h* of their fathers	1Chr 5:15	1004
heads of the *h* of their fathers	1Chr 5:24	1004
heads of the *h* of their fathers	1Chr 5:24	1004
of song in the *h* of the LORD	1Chr 6:31	1004
the *h* of the LORD in Jerusalem	1Chr 6:32	1004
of the tabernacle of the *h* of God	1Chr 6:48	1004
heads of their father's *h*	1Chr 7:2	1004
after the *h* of their fathers,	1Chr 7:4	1004
heads of the *h* of their fathers,	1Chr 7:7	1004
heads of the *h* of their fathers,	1Chr 7:9	1004
because it went evil with his *h*	1Chr 7:23	1004
Asher, heads of their father's *h*	1Chr 7:40	1004
fathers in the *h* of their fathers	1Chr 9:9	1004
Ahitub, the ruler of the *h* of God	1Chr 9:11	1004
heads of the *h* of their fathers,	1Chr 9:13	1004
of the service of the *h* of God	1Chr 9:13	1004
of the *h* of his father, the	1Chr 9:19	1004
of the gates of the *h* of the LORD	1Chr 9:23	1004
the *h* of the tabernacle, by wards	1Chr 9:23	1004
and treasures of the *h* of God	1Chr 9:26	1004
lodged round about the *h* of God	1Chr 9:27	1004
sons, and all his *h* died together	1Chr 10:6	1004
his armour in the *h* of their gods	1Chr 10:10	1004
and of his father's *h* twenty	1Chr 12:28	1004
kept the ward of the *h* of Saul	1Chr 12:29	1004
throughout the *h* of their fathers	1Chr 12:30	1004
new cart out of the *h* of Abinadab	1Chr 13:7	1004
the *h* of Obed-edom the Gittite	1Chr 13:13	1004
Obed-edom in his *h* three months	1Chr 13:14	1004
LORD blessed the *h* of Obed-edom	1Chr 13:14	1004
and carpenters, to build him an *h*	1Chr 14:1	1004
of the *h* of Obed-edom with joy	1Chr 15:25	1004
departed every man to his *h*	1Chr 16:43	1004
and David returned to bless his *h*	1Chr 16:43	1004
to pass, as David sat in his *h*	1Chr 17:1	1004
Lo, I dwell in an *h* of cedars	1Chr 17:1	1004
not build me an *h* to dwell in	1Chr 17:4	1004
For I have not dwelt in an *h*	1Chr 17:5	1004
ye not built me an *h* of cedars	1Chr 17:6	1004
the LORD will build thee an *h*	1Chr 17:10	1004
He shall build me an *h*, and I will	1Chr 17:12	1004
But I will settle him in mine *h*	1Chr 17:14	1004
I, O LORD God, and what is mine *h*	1Chr 17:16	1004
h for a great while to come	1Chr 17:17	1004
concerning his *h* be established	1Chr 17:23	1004
let the *h* of David thy servant be	1Chr 17:24	1004
that thou wilt build him an *h*	1Chr 17:25	1004
to bless the *h* of thy servant	1Chr 17:27	1004
be on me, and on my father's *h*	1Chr 21:17	1004
This is the *h* of the LORD God, and	1Chr 22:1	1004
stones to build the *h* of God	1Chr 22:2	1004
the *h* that is to be builded for	1Chr 22:5	1004
charged him to build an *h* for the	1Chr 22:6	1004
an *h* unto the name of the LORD my	1Chr 22:7	1004
shalt not build an *h* unto my name	1Chr 22:8	1004
He shall build an *h* for my name	1Chr 22:10	1004
build the *h* of the LORD thy God,	1Chr 22:11	1004
h of the LORD an hundred thousand	1Chr 22:14	1004
into the *h* that is to be built to	1Chr 22:19	1004
the work of the *h* of the LORD	1Chr 23:4	1004
according to their father's *h*	1Chr 23:11	1004
Levi after the *h* of their fathers	1Chr 23:24	1004
the service of the *h* of the LORD	1Chr 23:24	1004
the service of the *h* of the LORD	1Chr 23:28	1004
of the service of the *h* of God	1Chr 23:28	1004
the service of the *h* of the LORD	1Chr 23:32	1004
men of the *h* of their fathers	1Chr 24:4	1004
to the *h* of their fathers	1Chr 24:4	1004
and governors of the *h* of God	1Chr 24:5	
to come into the *h* of the LORD	1Chr 24:19	1004
after the *h* of their fathers	1Chr 24:30	1004
for song in the *h* of the LORD	1Chr 25:6	1004
for the service of the *h* of God	1Chr 25:6	1004
throughout the *h* of their father	1Chr 26:6	1004
to minister in the *h* of the LORD	1Chr 26:12	1004
to the *h* of their fathers	1Chr 26:13	1004
and to his sons the *h* of Asuppim	1Chr 26:15	1004
the treasures of the *h* of God	1Chr 26:20	1004
treasures of the *h* of the LORD	1Chr 26:22	1004
to maintain the *h* of the LORD	1Chr 26:27	1004
an *h* of rest for the ark of the	1Chr 28:2	1004
shalt not build an *h* for my name	1Chr 28:3	1004
h of my father to be king over	1Chr 28:4	1004
h of Judah, the *h* of my father	1Chr 28:4	1004
thy son, he shall build my *h*	1Chr 28:6	1004
to build an *h* for the sanctuary	1Chr 28:10	1004
the courts of the *h* of the LORD	1Chr 28:12	1004
of the treasuries of the *h* of God	1Chr 28:12	1004
the service of the *h* of the LORD	1Chr 28:13	1004
of service in the *h* of the LORD	1Chr 28:13	1004
the service of the *h* of the LORD	1Chr 28:20	1004
all the service of the *h* of God	1Chr 28:21	1004
with all my might for the *h* of my	1Chr 29:2	1004
my affection to the *h* of my God	1Chr 29:3	1004
I have given to the *h* of my God	1Chr 29:3	1004
I have prepared for the holy *h*	1Chr 29:3	1004
gave for the service of the *h* of	1Chr 29:7	1004
the treasure of the *h* of the LORD	1Chr 29:8	1004
h for thine holy name cometh of	1Chr 29:16	1004
an *h* for the name of the LORD	2Chr 2:1	1004
the LORD, and an *h* for his kingdom	2Chr 2:1	1004
build him an *h* to dwell therein	2Chr 2:3	1004
I build an *h* to the name of the	2Chr 2:4	1004
the *h* which I build is great	2Chr 2:5	1004
But who is able to build him an *h*	2Chr 2:6	1004
that I should build him an *h*	2Chr 2:6	1004
for the *h* which I am about to	2Chr 2:9	1004
might build an *h* for the LORD	2Chr 2:12	1004
and an *h* for his kingdom	2Chr 2:12	1004
the *h* of the LORD at Jerusalem in	2Chr 3:1	1004
for the building of the *h* of God	2Chr 3:3	1004
that was in the front of the *h*	2Chr 3:4	
according to the breadth of the *h*	2Chr 3:4	1004
the greater *h* he cieled with fir	2Chr 3:5	1004
he garnished the *h* with precious	2Chr 3:6	1004
He overlaid also the *h*, the beams	2Chr 3:7	1004
And he made the most holy *h*	2Chr 3:8	1004
according to the breadth of the *h*	2Chr 3:8	1004
in the most holy *h* he made two	2Chr 3:10	1004
reaching to the wall of the *h*	2Chr 3:11	1004
reaching to the wall of the *h*	2Chr 3:12	1004
the *h* two pillars of thirty	2Chr 3:15	1004
for king Solomon for the *h* of God	2Chr 4:11	1004
the *h* of the LORD of bright brass	2Chr 4:16	1004
that were for the *h* of God	2Chr 4:19	1004
and the entry of the *h*, the inner	2Chr 4:22	1004
the doors of the *h* of the temple	2Chr 4:22	1004
the *h* of the LORD was finished	2Chr 5:1	1004
the treasures of the *h* of God	2Chr 5:1	1004
his place, to the oracle of the *h*	2Chr 5:7	1004
that then the *h* was filled with a	2Chr 5:13	1004
a cloud, even the *h* of the LORD	2Chr 5:13	1004
the LORD had filled the *h* of God	2Chr 5:14	1004
But I have built an *h* of	2Chr 6:2	1004
tribes of Israel to build an *h* in	2Chr 6:5	1004
of David my father to build an *h*	2Chr 6:7	1004
heart to build an *h* for my name	2Chr 6:8	1004
thou shalt not build the *h*	2Chr 6:9	1004
he shall build the *h* for my name	2Chr 6:9	1004
have built the *h* for the name of	2Chr 6:10	1004
less this *h* which I have built	2Chr 6:18	1004
eyes may be open upon this *h* day	2Chr 6:20	1004
come before thine altar in this *h*	2Chr 6:22	1004
before thee in this *h*	2Chr 6:24	1004
spread forth his hands in this *h*	2Chr 6:29	1004
if they come and pray in this *h*	2Chr 6:32	1004
may know that this *h* which I have	2Chr 6:33	1004
the *h* which I have built for thy	2Chr 6:34	1004
toward the *h* which I have built	2Chr 6:38	1004
glory of the LORD filled the *h*	2Chr 7:1	1004
not enter into the *h* of the LORD	2Chr 7:2	1004
the LORD had filled the LORD's *h*	2Chr 7:2	1004
the glory of the LORD upon the *h*	2Chr 7:3	1004
the people dedicated the *h* of God	2Chr 7:5	1004
that was before the *h* of the LORD	2Chr 7:7	1004
finished the *h* of the LORD	2Chr 7:11	1004
of the LORD, and the king's *h*	2Chr 7:11	1004
to make in the *h* of the LORD	2Chr 7:11	1004
of the LORD, and in his own *h*	2Chr 7:11	1004
to myself for an *h* of sacrifice	2Chr 7:12	1004
I chosen and sanctified this *h*	2Chr 7:16	1004
and this *h*, which I have	2Chr 7:20	1004
And this *h*, which is high, shall	2Chr 7:21	1004
unto this land, and unto this *h*	2Chr 7:21	1004
h of the LORD, and his own *h*	2Chr 8:1	1004
the *h* that he had built for her	2Chr 8:11	1004
in the *h* of David king of Israel	2Chr 8:11	1004
foundation of the *h* of the LORD	2Chr 8:16	1004
So the *h* of the LORD was	2Chr 8:16	1004
and the *h* that he had built,	2Chr 9:3	1004
he went up into the *h* of the LORD	2Chr 9:4	1004
terraces to the *h* of the LORD	2Chr 9:11	1004
in the *h* of the forest of Lebanon	2Chr 9:16	1004
all the vessels of the *h* of the	2Chr 9:20	1004
and now, David, see to thine own *h*	2Chr 10:16	1004
the *h* of David unto this day	2Chr 10:19	1004
he gathered of the *h* of Judah	2Chr 11:1	1004
return every man to his *h*	2Chr 11:4	1004
treasures of the *h* of the LORD	2Chr 12:9	1004
and the treasures of the king's *h*	2Chr 12:9	1004
kept the entrance of the king's *h*	2Chr 12:10	1004
entered into the *h* of the LORD	2Chr 12:11	1004
he brought into the *h* of God the	2Chr 15:18	1004
treasures of the *h* of the LORD	2Chr 16:2	1004
of the LORD and of the king's *h*	2Chr 16:2	1004
seer, and put him in a prison *h*	2Chr 16:10	1004
to the *h* of their fathers	2Chr 17:14	1004
every man to his *h* in peace	2Chr 18:16	1004
to his *h* in peace to Jerusalem	2Chr 19:1	1004
the ruler of the *h* of Judah	2Chr 19:11	1004
in the *h* of the LORD, before the	2Chr 20:5	1004
or famine, we stand before this *h*	2Chr 20:9	1004
(for thy name is in this *h*	2Chr 20:9	1004
trumpets unto the *h* of the LORD	2Chr 20:28	1004
Israel, like as did the *h* of Ahab	2Chr 21:6	1004
would not destroy the *h* of David	2Chr 21:7	1004
to the whoredoms of the *h* of Ahab	2Chr 21:13	1004
thy brethren of thy father's *h*	2Chr 21:13	1004
that was found in the king's *h*	2Chr 21:17	1004
in the ways of the *h* of Ahab	2Chr 22:3	1004
of the LORD like the *h* of Ahab	2Chr 22:4	1004
anointed to cut off the *h* of Ahab	2Chr 22:7	1004
judgment upon the *h* of Ahab	2Chr 22:8	1004
So the *h* of Ahaziah had no power	2Chr 22:9	1004
the seed royal of the *h* of Judah	2Chr 22:10	1004
hid in the *h* of God six years	2Chr 22:12	1004
with the king in the *h* of God	2Chr 23:3	1004
part shall be at the king's *h*	2Chr 23:5	1004
the courts of the *h* of the LORD	2Chr 23:5	1004
none come into the *h* of the LORD	2Chr 23:6	1004
whosoever else cometh into the *h*	2Chr 23:7	1004
which were in the *h* of God	2Chr 23:9	1004
the people into the *h* of the LORD	2Chr 23:12	1004
Slay her not in the *h* of the LORD	2Chr 23:14	1004
of the horse gate by the king's *h*	2Chr 23:15	1004
the people went to the *h* of Baal	2Chr 23:17	1004
appointed the offices of the *h* of	2Chr 23:18	1004
distributed in the *h* of the LORD	2Chr 23:18	1004
at the gates of the *h* of the LORD	2Chr 23:19	1004
the king from the *h* of the LORD	2Chr 23:20	1004
the high gate into the king's *h*	2Chr 23:20	1004
to repair the *h* of the LORD	2Chr 24:4	1004
h of your God from year to year	2Chr 24:5	1004
woman, had broken up the *h* of God	2Chr 24:7	1004
the *h* of the LORD did they bestow	2Chr 24:7	1004
at the gate of the *h* of the LORD	2Chr 24:8	1004
the service of the *h* of the LORD	2Chr 24:12	1004
to repair the *h* of the LORD	2Chr 24:12	1004
brass to mend the *h* of the LORD	2Chr 24:12	1004
they set the *h* of God in his	2Chr 24:13	1004
vessels for the *h* of the LORD	2Chr 24:14	1004
offered burnt offerings in the *h*	2Chr 24:14	1004
both toward God, and toward his *h*	2Chr 24:16	1004
they left the *h* of the LORD God	2Chr 24:18	1004
in the court of the *h* of the LORD	2Chr 24:21	1004
and the repairing of the *h* of God	2Chr 24:27	1004
in the *h* of God with Obed-edom	2Chr 25:24	1004
and the treasures of the king's *h*	2Chr 25:24	1004
the priests in the *h* of the LORD	2Chr 26:19	1004
death, and dwelt in a several *h*	2Chr 26:21	1004
cut off from the *h* of the LORD	2Chr 26:21	1004
his son was over the king's *h*	2Chr 26:21	1004
high gate of the *h* of the LORD	2Chr 27:3	1004
and Azrikam the governor of the *h*	2Chr 28:7	1004
portion out of the *h* of the LORD	2Chr 28:21	1004
out of the *h* of the king, and of	2Chr 28:21	1004
the vessels of the *h* of God	2Chr 28:24	1004
the vessels of the *h* of God	2Chr 28:24	1004
up the doors of the *h* of the LORD	2Chr 28:24	1004
the doors of the *h* of the LORD	2Chr 29:3	1004
sanctify the *h* of the LORD God of	2Chr 29:5	1004
to cleanse the *h* of the LORD	2Chr 29:15	1004
inner part of the *h* of the LORD	2Chr 29:16	1004
the court of the *h* of the LORD	2Chr 29:16	1004
so they sanctified the *h* of the	2Chr 29:17	1004
cleansed all the *h* of the LORD	2Chr 29:18	1004
and went up to the *h* of the LORD	2Chr 29:20	1004
in the *h* of the LORD with cymbals	2Chr 29:25	1004
offerings into the *h* of the LORD	2Chr 29:31	1004
So the service of the *h* of the	2Chr 29:35	1004
to the *h* of the LORD at Jerusalem	2Chr 30:1	1004
offerings into the *h* of the LORD	2Chr 30:15	1004
of the *h* of Zadok answered him	2Chr 31:10	1004
offerings into the *h* of the LORD	2Chr 31:10	1004
chambers in the *h* of the LORD	2Chr 31:11	1004
Azariah the ruler of the *h* of God	2Chr 31:13	1004
entereth into the *h* of the LORD	2Chr 31:16	1004
priests by the *h* of their fathers	2Chr 31:17	1004
in the service of the *h* of God	2Chr 31:21	1004
he was come into the *h* of his god	2Chr 32:21	1004
built altars in the *h* of the LORD	2Chr 33:4	1004
two courts of the *h* of the LORD	2Chr 33:5	1004
he had made, in the *h* of God	2Chr 33:7	1004
and to Solomon his son, In this *h*	2Chr 33:7	1004
the idol out of the *h* of the LORD	2Chr 33:15	1004
in the mount of the *h* of the LORD	2Chr 33:15	1004
and they buried him in his own *h*	2Chr 33:20	1004
him, and slew him in his own *h*	2Chr 33:24	1004
he had purged the land, and the *h*	2Chr 34:8	1004
to repair the *h* of the LORD his	2Chr 34:8	1004
was brought into the *h* of God	2Chr 34:9	1004
oversight of the *h* of the LORD	2Chr 34:10	1004
that wrought in the *h* of the LORD	2Chr 34:10	1004
LORD, to repair and amend the *h*	2Chr 34:10	1004
brought into the *h* of the LORD	2Chr 34:14	1004
of the law in the *h* of the LORD	2Chr 34:15	1004
was found in the *h* of the LORD	2Chr 34:17	1004
went up into the *h* of the LORD	2Chr 34:30	1004
was found in the *h* of the LORD	2Chr 34:30	1004
the service of the *h* of the LORD	2Chr 35:2	1004
Put the holy ark in the *h* which	2Chr 35:3	1004
and Jehiel, rulers of the *h* of God	2Chr 35:8	1004
but against the *h* wherewith I	2Chr 35:21	1004
of the *h* of the LORD to Babylon	2Chr 36:7	1004
vessels of the *h* of the LORD	2Chr 36:10	1004
polluted the *h* of the LORD which	2Chr 36:14	1004
sword in the *h* of their sanctuary	2Chr 36:17	1004
all the vessels of the *h* of God	2Chr 36:18	1004
treasures of the *h* of the LORD	2Chr 36:18	1004
And they burnt the *h* of God	2Chr 36:19	1004
me to build him an *h* in Jerusalem	2Chr 36:23	1004
me to build him an *h* at Jerusalem	Ezr 1:2	1004
build the *h* of the LORD God of	Ezr 1:3	1004
the *h* of God that is in Jerusalem	Ezr 1:4	1004

to go up to build the *h* of the ... Ezr 1:5 1004
the vessels of the *h* of the LORD ... Ezr 1:7 1004
had put them in the *h* of his gods ... Ezr 1:7 1004
of the *h* of Jeshua, nine hundred ... Ezr 2:36 1004
could not shew their father's *h* ... Ezr 2:59 1004
when they came to the *h* of the ... Ezr 2:68 1004
offered freely for the *h* of God ... Ezr 2:68 1004
unto the *h* of God at Jerusalem ... Ezr 3:8 1004
the work of the *h* of the LORD ... Ezr 3:8 1004
the workmen in the *h* of God ... Ezr 3:9 1004
of the *h* of the LORD was laid ... Ezr 3:11 1004
men, that had seen the first *h* ... Ezr 3:12 1004
this *h* was laid before their eyes ... Ezr 3:12 1004
us to build an *h* unto our God ... Ezr 4:3 1004
Then ceased the work of the *h* of ... Ezr 4:24 1005
began to build the *h* of God which ... Ezr 5:2 1005
commanded you to build this *h* ... Ezr 5:3 1005
to the *h* of the great God, which ... Ezr 5:8 1005
Who commanded you to build this *h* ... Ezr 5:9 1005
build the *h* that was builded ... Ezr 5:11 1005
Chaldean, who destroyed this *h* ... Ezr 5:12 1005
a decree to build this *h* of God ... Ezr 5:13 1005
of gold and silver of the *h* of God ... Ezr 5:14 1005
let the *h* of God be builded in ... Ezr 5:15 1005
laid the foundation of the *h* of ... Ezr 5:16 1005
made in the king's treasure *h* ... Ezr 5:17 1005
build this *h* of God at Jerusalem ... Ezr 5:17 1005
was made in the *h* of the rolls ... Ezr 6:1 1005
the *h* of God at Jerusalem ... Ezr 6:3 1005
Let the *h* be builded, the place ... Ezr 6:3 1005
be given out of the king's *h* ... Ezr 6:4 1004
and silver vessels of the *h* of God ... Ezr 6:5 1005
and place them in the *h* of God ... Ezr 6:5 1005
the work of this *h* of God alone ... Ezr 6:7 1005
build this *h* of God in his place ... Ezr 6:7 1005
for the building of this *h* of God ... Ezr 6:8 1005
timber be pulled down from his *h* ... Ezr 6:11 1005
let his *h* be made a dunghill for ... Ezr 6:11 1005
to destroy this *h* of God which is ... Ezr 6:12 1005
this *h* was finished on the third ... Ezr 6:15 1005
of this *h* of God with joy ... Ezr 6:16 1005
at the dedication of this *h* of ... Ezr 6:17 1005
hands in the work of the *h* of God ... Ezr 6:22 1004
the *h* of their God which is in ... Ezr 7:16 1005
of the *h* of your God which is in ... Ezr 7:17 1005
the service of the *h* of thy God ... Ezr 7:19 1005
be needful for the *h* of thy God ... Ezr 7:20 1005
it out of the king's treasure *h* ... Ezr 7:20 1005
for the *h* of the God of heaven ... Ezr 7:23 1005
or ministers of this *h* of God ... Ezr 7:24 1005
to beautify the *h* of the LORD ... Ezr 7:27 1004
us ministers for the *h* of our God ... Ezr 8:17 1004
the offering of the *h* of our God ... Ezr 8:25 1004
the chambers of the *h* of the LORD ... Ezr 8:29 1004
Jerusalem unto the *h* of our God ... Ezr 8:30 1004
the *h* of our God by the hand of ... Ezr 8:33 1004
the people, and the *h* of God ... Ezr 8:36 1004
to set up the *h* of our God ... Ezr 9:9 1004
himself down before the *h* of God ... Ezr 10:1 1004
rose up from before the *h* of God ... Ezr 10:6 1004
sat in the street of the *h* of God ... Ezr 10:9 1004
after the *h* of their fathers, and ... Ezr 10:16 1004
I and my father's *h* have sinned ... Neh 1:6 1004
palace which appertained to the *h* ... Neh 2:8 1004
for the *h* that I shall enter into ... Neh 2:8 1004
Harumaph, even over against his *h* ... Neh 3:10 1004
made, and unto the *h* of the mighty ... Neh 3:16 1004
the *h* of Eliashib the high priest ... Neh 3:20 1004
from the door of the *h* of ... Neh 3:21 1004
to the end of the *h* of Eliashib ... Neh 3:21 1004
and Hashub over against their *h* ... Neh 3:23 1004
the son of Ananiah by his *h* ... Neh 3:23 1004
from the *h* of Azariah unto the ... Neh 3:24 1004
lieth out from the king's high *h* ... Neh 3:25 1004
every one over against his *h* ... Neh 3:28 1004
son of Immer over against his *h* ... Neh 3:29 1004
were behind all the *h* of Judah ... Neh 4:16 1004
shake out every man from his *h* ... Neh 5:13 1004
Afterward I came unto the *h* of ... Neh 6:10 1004
us meet together in the *h* of God ... Neh 6:10 1004
one to be over against his *h* ... Neh 7:3
of the *h* of Jeshua, nine hundred ... Neh 7:39
could not shew their father's *h* ... Neh 7:61
every one upon the roof of his *h* ... Neh 8:16
and in the courts of the *h* of God ... Neh 8:16 1004
the service of the *h* of our God ... Neh 10:32 1004
all the work of the *h* of our God ... Neh 10:33 1004
to bring it into the *h* of our God ... Neh 10:34 1004
by year, unto the *h* of the LORD ... Neh 10:35 1004
to bring to the *h* of our God ... Neh 10:36 1004
that minister in the *h* of our God ... Neh 10:36 1004
the chambers of the *h* of our God ... Neh 10:37 1004
the tithes unto the *h* of our God ... Neh 10:38 1004
the chambers, into the treasure *h* ... Neh 10:38 1004
will not forsake the *h* of our God ... Neh 10:39 1004
was the ruler of the *h* of God ... Neh 11:11 1004
that did the work of the *h* were ... Neh 11:12 1004
outward business of the *h* of God ... Neh 11:16 1004
over the business of the *h* of God ... Neh 11:22 1004
Also from the *h* of Gilgal ... Neh 12:29 1004
of the wall, above the *h* of David ... Neh 12:37 1004
that gave thanks in the *h* of God ... Neh 12:40 1004
the chamber of the *h* of our God ... Neh 13:4 1004
in the courts of the *h* of God ... Neh 13:7 1004
again the vessels of the *h* of God ... Neh 13:9 1004
Why is the *h* of God forsaken ... Neh 13:11 1004
I have done for the *h* of my God ... Neh 13:14 1004
to all the officers of his *h* ... Est 1:8 1004
royal *h* which belonged to king ... Est 1:9 1004
man should bear rule in his own *h* ... Est 1:22 1004
to the *h* of the women, unto the ... Est 2:3 1004
brought also unto the king's *h* ... Est 2:8 1004
be given her, out of the king's *h* ... Est 2:9 1004
best place of the *h* of the women ... Est 2:9 1004
before the court of the women's *h* ... Est 2:11 1004
h of the women unto the king's ... Est 2:13 1004
of the women unto the king's *h* ... Est 2:13 1004
into the second *h* of the women ... Est 2:14 1004
his *h* royal in the tenth month ... Est 2:16 1004
thou shalt escape in the king's *h* ... Est 4:13 1004
thy father's *h* shall be destroyed ... Est 4:14 1004
the inner court of the king's *h* ... Est 5:1 1004
h, over against the king's *h* ... Est 5:1 1004
his royal throne in the royal *h* ... Est 5:1 1004
over against the gate of the *h* ... Est 5:1 1004
the outward court of the king's *h* ... Est 6:4 1004
Haman hasted to his *h* mourning ... Est 6:12 1004
the queen also before me in the *h* ... Est 7:8 1004
king, standeth in the *h* of Haman ... Est 7:9 1004
h of Haman the Jews' enemy unto ... Est 8:1 1004
set Mordecai over the *h* of Haman ... Est 8:2 1004
have given Esther the *h* of Haman ... Est 8:7 1004
was great in the king's *h* ... Est 9:4 1004
hedge about him, and about his *h* ... Job 1:10 1004
wine in their eldest brother's *h* ... Job 1:13 1004
wine in their eldest brother's *h* ... Job 1:18 1004
smote the four corners of the *h* ... Job 1:19 1004
He shall return no more to his *h* ... Job 7:10 1004
He shall lean upon his *h*, but it ... Job 8:15 1004
If I wait, the grave is mine *h* ... Job 17:13 1004
They that dwell in mine *h* ... Job 19:15 1004
away an *h* which he builded not ... Job 20:19 1004
increase of his *h* shall depart ... Job 20:28 1004
hath he in his *h* after him ... Job 21:21 1004
Where is the *h* of the prince ... Job 21:28 1004
He buildeth his *h* as a moth ... Job 27:18 1004
to the *h* appointed for all living ... Job 30:23 1004
know the paths to the *h* thereof ... Job 38:20 1004
Whose *h* I have made the ... Job 39:6 1004
did eat bread with him in his *h* ... Job 42:11 1004
I will come into thy *h* in the ... Ps 5:7 1004
I will dwell in the *h* of the LORD ... Ps 23:6 1004
loved the habitation of thy *h* ... Ps 26:8 1004
that I may dwell in the *h* of the ... Ps 27:4 1004
the dedication of the *h* of David ... Ps 30:*t* 1004
for an *h* of defence to save me ... Ps 31:2 1004
with the fatness of thy *h* ... Ps 36:8 1004
I went with them to the *h* of God ... Ps 42:4 1004
own people, and thy father's *h* ... Ps 45:10 1004
the glory of his *h* is increased ... Ps 49:16 1004
will take no bullock out of thy *h* ... Ps 50:9 1004
is come to the *h* of Ahimelech ... Ps 52:*t* 1004
green olive tree in the *h* of God ... Ps 52:8 1004
walked unto the *h* of God in ... Ps 55:14 1004
and they watched the *h* to kill him ... Ps 59:*t* 1004
with the goodness of thy *h* ... Ps 65:4 1004
I will go into thy *h* with burnt ... Ps 66:13 1004
zeal of thine *h* hath eaten me up ... Ps 69:9 1004
Yea, the sparrow hath found an *h* ... Ps 84:3 1004
are they that dwell in thy *h* ... Ps 84:4 1004
a doorkeeper in the *h* of my God ... Ps 84:10 1004
Those that be planted in the *h* of ... Ps 92:13 1004
holiness becometh thine *h* ... Ps 93:5 1004
his truth toward the *h* of Israel ... Ps 98:3 1004
within my *h* with a perfect heart ... Ps 101:2 1004
shall not dwell within my *h* ... Ps 101:7 1004
as a sparrow alone upon the *h* top ... Ps 102:7
stork, the fir trees are her *h* ... Ps 104:17 1004
He made him lord of his *h* ... Ps 105:21 1004
and riches shall be in his *h* ... Ps 112:3 1004
maketh the barren woman to keep *h* ... Ps 113:9 1004
the *h* of Jacob from a people of ... Ps 114:1 1004
O *h* of Aaron, trust in the LORD ... Ps 115:10 1004
he will bless the *h* of Israel ... Ps 115:12 1004
he will bless the *h* of Aaron ... Ps 115:12 1004
In the courts of the LORD's *h* ... Ps 116:19 1004
Let the *h* of Aaron now say, that ... Ps 118:3 1004
you out of the *h* of the LORD ... Ps 118:26 1004
songs in the *h* of my pilgrimage ... Ps 119:54 1004
Let us go into the *h* of the LORD ... Ps 122:1 1004
the thrones of the *h* of David ... Ps 122:5 1004
Because of the *h* of the LORD our ... Ps 122:9 1004
Except the LORD build the *h* ... Ps 127:1 1004
vine by the sides of thine *h* ... Ps 128:3 1004
come into the tabernacle of my *h* ... Ps 132:3 1004
night stand in the *h* of the LORD ... Ps 134:1 1004
that stand in the *h* of the LORD ... Ps 135:2 1004
in the courts of the *h* of our God ... Ps 135:2 1004
Bless the LORD, O *h* of Israel ... Ps 135:19 1004
bless the LORD, O *h* of Aaron ... Ps 135:19 1004
Bless the LORD, O *h* of Levi ... Ps 135:20 1004
For her *h* inclineth unto death ... Prov 2:18 1004
LORD is in the *h* of the wicked ... Prov 3:33 1004
come not nigh the door of her *h* ... Prov 5:8 1004
labours be in the *h* of a stranger ... Prov 5:10 1004
give all the substance of his *h* ... Prov 6:31 1004
For at the window of my *h* I ... Prov 7:6 1004
and he went the way to her *h* ... Prov 7:8 1004
her feet abide not in her *h* ... Prov 7:11 1004
Her *h* is the way to hell, going ... Prov 7:27 1004
Wisdom hath builded her *h* ... Prov 9:1 1004
she sitteth at the door of her *h* ... Prov 9:14 1004
his own *h* shall inherit the wind ... Prov 11:29 1004
but the *h* of the righteous shall ... Prov 12:7 1004
Every wise woman buildeth her *h* ... Prov 14:1 1004
The *h* of the wicked shall be ... Prov 14:11 1004
In the *h* of the righteous is much ... Prov 15:6 1004
will destroy the *h* of the proud ... Prov 15:25 1004
of gain troubleth his own *h* ... Prov 15:27 1004
than an *h* full of sacrifices with ... Prov 17:1 1004
evil shall not depart from his *h* ... Prov 17:13 1004
H and riches are the inheritance ... Prov 19:14 1004
a brawling woman and in a wide *h* ... Prov 21:9 1004
considereth the *h* of the wicked ... Prov 21:12 1004
Through wisdom is an *h* builded ... Prov 24:3 1004
and afterwards build thine *h* ... Prov 24:27 1004
thy foot from thy neighbour's *h* ... Prov 25:17 1004
a brawling woman and in a wide *h* ... Prov 25:24 1004
h in the day of thy calamity ... Prov 27:10 1004
and had servants born in my *h* ... Eccl 2:7 1004
when thou goest to the *h* of God ... Eccl 5:1 1004
better to go to the *h* of mourning ... Eccl 7:2 1004
than to go to the *h* of feasting ... Eccl 7:2 1004
the wise is in the *h* of mourning ... Eccl 7:4 1004
of fools is in the *h* of mirth ... Eccl 7:4 1004
the hands the *h* droppeth through ... Eccl 10:18 1004
keepers of the *h* shall tremble ... Eccl 12:3 1004
The beams of our *h* are cedar ... Song 1:17 1004
He brought me to the banqueting *h* ... Song 2:4 1004
brought him into my mother's *h* ... Song 3:4 1004
and bring thee into my mother's *h* ... Song 8:2 1004
the substance of his *h* for love ... Song 8:7 1004
h shall be established in the top ... Is 2:2 1004
to the *h* of the God of Jacob ... Is 2:3 1004
O *h* of Jacob, come ye, and let us ... Is 2:5 1004
thy people the *h* of Jacob ... Is 2:6 1004
brother of the *h* of his father ... Is 3:6 1004
for in my *h* is neither bread nor ... Is 3:7 1004
LORD of hosts is the *h* of Israel ... Is 5:7 1004
unto them that join *h* to *h* ... Is 5:8 1004
the *h* was filled with smoke ... Is 6:4 1004
And it was told the *h* of David ... Is 7:2 1004
said, Hear ye now, O *h* of David ... Is 7:13 1004
people, and upon thy father's *h* ... Is 7:17 1004
his face from the *h* of Jacob ... Is 8:17 1004
as are escaped of the *h* of Jacob ... Is 10:20 1004
shall cleave to the *h* of Jacob ... Is 14:1 1004
the *h* of Israel shall possess ... Is 14:2 1004
opened not the *h* of his prisoners ... Is 14:17 1004
in glory, every one in his own *h* ... Is 14:18 1004
the armour of the *h* of the forest ... Is 22:8 1004
unto Shebna, which is over the *h* ... Is 22:15 1004
be the shame of thy lord's *h* ... Is 22:18 1004
Jerusalem, and to the *h* of Judah ... Is 22:21 1004
the key of the *h* of David will I ... Is 22:22 1004
glorious throne to his father's *h* ... Is 22:23 1004
all the glory of his father's *h* ... Is 22:24 1004
laid waste, so that there is no *h* ... Is 23:1 1004
every *h* is shut up, that no man ... Is 24:10 1004
concerning the *h* of Jacob ... Is 29:22 1004
against the *h* of the evildoers ... Is 31:2 1004
son, which was over the *h* ... Is 36:3 1004
and went into the *h* of the LORD ... Is 37:1 1004
went up unto the *h* of the LORD ... Is 37:14 1004
h of Judah shall again take root ... Is 37:31 1004
in the *h* of Nisroch his god ... Is 37:38 1004
the LORD, Set thine *h* in order ... Is 38:1 1004
of our life in the *h* of the LORD ... Is 38:20 1004
shall go up to the *h* of the LORD ... Is 38:22 1004
shewed them the *h* of his precious ... Is 39:2 1004
all the *h* of his armour, and all ... Is 39:2 1004
there was nothing in his *h* ... Is 39:2 1004
What have they seen in thine *h* ... Is 39:4 1004
that is in mine *h* have they seen ... Is 39:4 1004
come, that all that is in thine *h* ... Is 39:6 1004
in darkness out of the prison *h* ... Is 42:7 1004
that it may remain in the *h* ... Is 44:13 1004
O *h* of Jacob, and all the remnant ... Is 46:3 1004
the remnant of the *h* of Israel ... Is 46:3 1004
O *h* of Jacob, which are called by ... Is 48:1 1004
unto them will I give in mine *h* ... Is 56:5 1004
them joyful in my *h* of prayer ... Is 56:7 1004
for mine *h* shall be called an ... Is 56:7 1004
an *h* of prayer for all people ... Is 56:7 1004
the *h* of Jacob their sins ... Is 58:1 1004
poor that are cast out to thy *h* ... Is 58:7 1004
I will glorify the *h* of my glory ... Is 60:7 1004
goodness toward the *h* of Israel ... Is 63:7 1004
Our holy and our beautiful *h* ... Is 64:11 1004
where is the *h* that ye build unto ... Is 66:1 1004
vessel into the *h* of the LORD ... Is 66:20 1004
O *h* of Jacob, and all the families ... Jer 2:4 1004
the families of the *h* of Israel ... Jer 2:4 1004
so is the *h* of Israel ashamed ... Jer 2:26 1004
In those days the *h* of Judah ... Jer 3:18 1004
shall walk with the *h* of Israel ... Jer 3:18 1004
O *h* of Israel, saith the LORD ... Jer 3:20 1004
h of Israel and the *h* of Judah ... Jer 5:11 1004
O *h* of Israel, saith the LORD ... Jer 5:15 1004
Declare this in the *h* of Jacob ... Jer 5:20 1004
Stand in the gate of the LORD's *h* ... Jer 7:2 1004
come and stand before me in this *h* ... Jer 7:10 1004
Is this *h*, which is called by my ... Jer 7:11 1004
Therefore will I do unto this *h* ... Jer 7:14 1004
the *h* which is called by my name ... Jer 7:30 1004
and all the *h* of Israel are ... Jer 9:26 1004
speaketh unto you, O *h* of Israel ... Jer 10:1 1004
h of Israel and the *h* of Judah ... Jer 11:10 1004
hath my beloved to do in mine *h* ... Jer 11:15 1004
for the evil of the *h* of Israel ... Jer 11:17 1004
of the *h* of Judah, which they ... Jer 11:17 1004
the *h* of thy father, even they ... Jer 12:6 1004
I have forsaken mine *h*, I have ... Jer 12:7 1004
pluck out the *h* of Judah from ... Jer 12:14 1004

Context	Reference	Strong's
unto me the whole *h* of Israel	Jer 13:11	1004
of Israel and the whole *h* of Judah	Jer 13:11	1004
Enter not into the *h* of mourning	Jer 16:5	1004
also go into the *h* of feasting	Jer 16:8	1004
of praise, unto the *h* of the LORD	Jer 17:26	1004
and go down to the potter's *h*	Jer 18:2	1004
I went down to the potter's *h*	Jer 18:3	1004
O *h* of Israel, cannot I do with	Jer 18:6	1004
ye in mine hand, O *h* of Israel	Jer 18:6	1004
in the court of the LORD's *h*	Jer 19:14	1004
governor in the *h* of the LORD	Jer 20:1	1004
which was by the *h* of the LORD	Jer 20:2	1004
thine *h* shall go into captivity	Jer 20:6	1004
touching the *h* of the king of	Jer 21:11	1004
O *h* of David, thus saith the LORD	Jer 21:12	1004
Go down to the *h* of the king of	Jer 22:1	1004
h kings sitting upon the throne	Jer 22:4	1004
that this *h* shall become a	Jer 22:5	1004
LORD unto the king's *h* of Judah	Jer 22:6	1004
buildeth his *h* by unrighteousness	Jer 22:13	1004
saith, I will build me a wide *h*	Jer 22:14	1004
which led the seed of the *h* of	Jer 23:8	1004
in my *h* have I found their	Jer 23:11	1004
even punish that man and his *h*	Jer 23:34	1004
in the court of the LORD's *h*	Jer 26:2	1004
come to worship in the LORD's *h*	Jer 26:2	1004
will I make this *h* like Shiloh	Jer 26:6	1004
these words in the *h* of the LORD	Jer 26:7	1004
This *h* shall be like Shiloh, and	Jer 26:9	1004
Jeremiah in the *h* of the LORD	Jer 26:9	1004
h unto the *h* of the LORD	Jer 26:10	1004
of the new gate of the LORD's *h*	Jer 26:10	
me to prophesy against this *h*	Jer 26:12	1004
the mountain of the *h* as the high	Jer 26:18	1004
the vessels of the LORD's *h* shall	Jer 27:16	1004
are left in the *h* of the LORD	Jer 27:18	1004
in the *h* of the king of Judah, and	Jer 27:18	1004
that remain in the *h* of the LORD	Jer 27:21	1004
in the *h* of the king of Judah and	Jer 27:21	1004
unto me in the *h* of the LORD	Jer 28:1	1004
all the vessels of the LORD's *h*	Jer 28:3	1004
that stood in the *h* of the LORD	Jer 28:5	1004
again the vessels of the LORD's *h*	Jer 28:6	1004
be officers in the *h* of the LORD	Jer 29:26	1004
that I will sow the *h* of Israel	Jer 31:27	1004
the *h* of Judah with the seed of	Jer 31:27	1004
new covenant with the *h* of Israel	Jer 31:31	1004
and with the *h* of Judah	Jer 31:31	1004
I will make with the *h* of Israel	Jer 31:33	1004
was in the king of Judah's *h*	Jer 32:2	1004
set their abominations in the *h*	Jer 32:34	1004
of praise into the *h* of the LORD	Jer 33:11	1004
promised unto the *h* of Israel	Jer 33:14	1004
of Israel and to the *h* of Judah	Jer 33:14	1004
the throne of the *h* of Israel	Jer 33:17	1004
of Egypt, out of the *h* of bondmen	Jer 34:13	1004
the *h* which is called by my name	Jer 34:15	1004
Go unto the *h* of the Rechabites,	Jer 35:2	1004
bring them into the *h* of the LORD	Jer 35:2	1004
the whole *h* of the Rechabites	Jer 35:3	1004
them into the *h* of the LORD	Jer 35:4	1004
I set before the sons of the *h* of	Jer 35:5	1004
Neither shall ye build *h*, nor sow	Jer 35:7	1004
said unto the *h* of the Rechabites	Jer 35:18	1004
It may be that the *h* of Judah	Jer 36:3	1004
cannot go into the *h* of the LORD	Jer 36:5	1004
the LORD's *h* upon the fasting day	Jer 36:6	1004
words of the LORD in the LORD's *h*	Jer 36:8	1004
of Jeremiah in the *h* of the LORD	Jer 36:10	1004
of the new gate of the LORD's *h*	Jer 36:10	1004
he went down into the king's *h*	Jer 36:12	1004
in the *h* of Jonathan the scribe	Jer 37:15	1004
king asked him secretly in his *h*	Jer 37:17	1004
to the *h* of Jonathan the scribe	Jer 37:20	1004
eunuchs which was in the king's *h*	Jer 38:7	1004
went forth out of the king's *h*	Jer 38:8	1004
went into the *h* of the king under	Jer 38:11	1004
that is in the *h* of the LORD	Jer 38:14	1004
and thou shalt live, and thine *h*	Jer 38:17	1004
h shall be brought forth to the	Jer 38:22	1004
me to return to Jonathan's *h*	Jer 38:26	1004
the Chaldeans burned the king's *h*	Jer 39:8	1004
bring them to the *h* of the LORD	Jer 41:5	1004
entry of Pharaoh's *h* in Tahpanhes	Jer 43:9	1004
as the *h* of Israel was ashamed of	Jer 48:13	1004
the sanctuaries of the LORD's *h*	Jer 51:51	1004
h of the LORD, and the king's *h*	Jer 52:13	1004
that were in the *h* of the LORD	Jer 52:17	1004
sea that was in the *h* of the LORD	Jer 52:17	1004
had made in the *h* of the LORD	Jer 52:20	1004
made a noise in the *h* of the LORD	Lam 2:7	1004
(for they are a rebellious *h*	Eze 2:5	1004
though they be a rebellious *h*	Eze 2:6	
rebellious like that rebellious *h*	Eze 2:8	1004
and go speak unto the *h* of Israel	Eze 3:1	1004
go, get thee unto the *h* of Israel	Eze 3:4	1004
language, but to the *h* of Israel	Eze 3:5	1004
But the *h* of Israel will not	Eze 3:7	1004
for all the *h* of Israel are	Eze 3:7	1004
though they be a rebellious *h*	Eze 3:9	1004
a watchman unto the *h* of Israel	Eze 3:17	1004
Go, shut thyself within thine *h*	Eze 3:24	1004
for they are a rebellious *h*	Eze 3:26	1004
for they are a rebellious *h*	Eze 3:27	1004
be a sign to the *h* of Israel	Eze 4:3	1004
of the *h* of Israel upon it	Eze 4:4	1004
the iniquity of the *h* of Israel	Eze 4:5	1004
of the *h* of Judah forty days	Eze 4:6	1004
forth into all the *h* of Israel	Eze 5:4	1004
abominations of the *h* of Israel	Eze 6:11	1004
of the month, as I sat in mine *h*	Eze 8:1	1004
the *h* of Israel committeth here	Eze 8:6	1004
all the idols of the *h* of Israel	Eze 8:10	1004
the ancients of the *h* of Israel	Eze 8:11	1004
of the *h* of Israel do in the dark	Eze 8:12	1004
h which was toward the north	Eze 8:14	1004
the inner court of the LORD's *h*	Eze 8:16	1004
Is it a light thing to the *h* of	Eze 8:17	1004
he was, to the threshold of the *h*	Eze 9:3	1004
men which were before the *h*	Eze 9:6	1004
he said unto them, Defile the *h*	Eze 9:7	1004
The iniquity of the *h* of Israel	Eze 9:9	1004
stood on the right side of the *h*	Eze 10:3	1004
stood over the threshold of the *h*	Eze 10:4	1004
the *h* was filled with the cloud,	Eze 10:4	1004
from off the threshold of the *h*	Eze 10:18	1004
of the east gate of the LORD's *h*	Eze 10:19	1004
the east gate of the LORD's *h*	Eze 11:1	1004
Thus have ye said, O *h* of Israel	Eze 11:5	1004
all the *h* of Israel wholly, are	Eze 11:15	1004
in the midst of a rebellious *h*	Eze 12:2	1004
for they are a rebellious *h*	Eze 12:2	1004
though they be a rebellious *h*	Eze 12:3	1004
for a sign unto the *h* of Israel	Eze 12:6	1004
h of Israel, the rebellious *h*	Eze 12:9	1004
all the *h* of Israel that are	Eze 12:10	1004
divination within the *h* of Israel	Eze 12:24	1004
for in your days, O rebellious *h*	Eze 12:25	1004
they of the *h* of Israel say, The	Eze 12:27	1004
the *h* of Israel to stand in the	Eze 13:5	1004
in the writing of the *h* of Israel	Eze 13:9	1004
Every man of the *h* of Israel that	Eze 14:4	1004
That I may take the *h* of Israel	Eze 14:5	1004
say unto the *h* of Israel, Thus	Eze 14:6	1004
For every one of the *h* of Israel	Eze 14:7	1004
That the *h* of Israel may go no	Eze 14:11	1004
a parable unto the *h* of Israel	Eze 17:2	1004
Say now to the rebellious *h*	Eze 17:12	1004
to the idols of the *h* of Israel	Eze 18:6	1004
to the idols of the *h* of Israel	Eze 18:15	1004
Hear now, O *h* of Israel	Eze 18:25	1004
Yet saith the *h* of Israel	Eze 18:29	1004
O *h* of Israel, are not my ways	Eze 18:29	1004
you, O *h* of Israel, every one	Eze 18:30	1004
why will ye die, O *h* of Israel	Eze 18:31	1004
unto the seed of the *h* of Jacob	Eze 20:5	1004
But the *h* of Israel rebelled	Eze 20:13	1004
man, speak unto the *h* of Israel	Eze 20:27	1004
say unto the *h* of Israel, Thus	Eze 20:30	1004
enquired of by you, O *h* of Israel	Eze 20:31	1004
O *h* of Israel, thus saith the	Eze 20:39	1004
there shall all the *h* of Israel	Eze 20:40	1004
O ye *h* of Israel, saith the Lord	Eze 20:44	1004
the *h* of Israel is to me become	Eze 22:18	1004
they done in the midst of mine *h*	Eze 23:39	1004
a parable unto the rebellious *h*	Eze 24:3	1004
Speak unto the *h* of Israel	Eze 24:21	1004
and against the *h* of Judah	Eze 25:3	1004
the *h* of Judah is like unto all	Eze 25:8	1004
Edom hath dealt against the *h* of	Eze 25:12	1004
They of the *h* of Togarmah traded	Eze 27:14	1004
brier unto the *h* of Israel	Eze 28:24	1004
When I shall have gathered the *h*	Eze 28:25	1004
staff of reed to the *h* of Israel	Eze 29:6	1004
the confidence of the *h* of Israel	Eze 29:16	1004
of the *h* of Israel to bud forth	Eze 29:21	1004
a watchman unto the *h* of Israel	Eze 33:7	1004
man, speak unto the *h* of Israel	Eze 33:10	1004
why will ye die, O *h* of Israel	Eze 33:11	1004
O ye *h* of Israel, I will judge	Eze 33:20	1004
even the *h* of Israel, are my	Eze 34:30	1004
inheritance of the *h* of Israel	Eze 35:15	1004
all the *h* of Israel, even all of	Eze 36:10	1004
when the *h* of Israel dwelt in	Eze 36:17	1004
which the *h* of Israel had	Eze 36:21	1004
say unto the *h* of Israel, Thus	Eze 36:22	1004
O *h* of Israel, but for mine holy	Eze 36:22	1004
for your own ways, O *h* of Israel	Eze 36:32	1004
be enquired of by the *h* of Israel	Eze 36:37	1004
bones are the whole *h* of Israel	Eze 37:11	1004
for all the *h* of Israel his	Eze 37:16	1004
the *h* of Togarmah of the north	Eze 38:6	1004
seven months shall the *h* of	Eze 39:12	1004
So the *h* of Israel shall know	Eze 39:22	1004
h of Israel went into captivity	Eze 39:23	1004
mercy upon the whole *h* of Israel	Eze 39:25	1004
my spirit upon the *h* of Israel	Eze 39:29	1004
thou seest to the *h* of Israel	Eze 40:4	1004
the outside of the *h* round about	Eze 40:5	1004
keepers of the charge of the *h*	Eze 40:45	1004
the altar that was before the *h*	Eze 40:47	1004
brought me to the porch of the *h*	Eze 40:48	1004
he measured the wall of the *h*	Eze 41:5	1004
round about the *h* on every side	Eze 41:5	1004
the *h* for the side chambers round	Eze 41:6	1004
had not hold in the wall of the *h*	Eze 41:6	1004
for the winding about of the *h*	Eze 41:7	1004
still upward round about the *h*	Eze 41:7	1004
breadth of the *h* was still upward	Eze 41:7	1004
the height of the *h* round about	Eze 41:8	1004
round about the *h* on every side	Eze 41:10	1004
So he measured the *h*, an hundred	Eze 41:13	1004
the breadth of the face of the *h*	Eze 41:14	1004
the door, even unto the inner *h*	Eze 41:17	1004
through all the *h* round about	Eze 41:19	1004
upon the side chambers of the *h*	Eze 41:26	1004
an end of measuring the inner *h*	Eze 42:15	1004
h by the way of the gate whose	Eze 43:4	1004
glory of the LORD filled the *h*	Eze 43:5	1004
him speaking unto me out of the *h*	Eze 43:6	1004
shall the *h* of Israel no more	Eze 43:7	1004
shew the *h* to the *h* of Israel	Eze 43:10	1004
done, shew them the form of the *h*	Eze 43:11	1004
This is the law of the *h*	Eze 43:12	1004
Behold, this is the law of the *h*	Eze 43:12	1004
in the appointed place of the *h*	Eze 43:21	1004
of the north gate before the *h*	Eze 44:4	1004
the LORD filled the *h* of the LORD	Eze 44:4	1004
ordinances of the *h* of the LORD	Eze 44:5	1004
well the entering in of the *h*	Eze 44:5	1004
even to the *h* of Israel, Thus	Eze 44:6	1004
O ye *h* of Israel, let it suffice	Eze 44:6	1004
to pollute it, even my *h*	Eze 44:7	1004
charge at the gates of the *h*	Eze 44:11	1004
h, and ministering to the *h*	Eze 44:11	1004
caused the *h* of Israel to fall	Eze 44:12	1004
keepers of the charge of the *h*	Eze 44:14	1004
of the seed of the *h* of Israel	Eze 44:22	1004
the blessing to rest in thine *h*	Eze 44:30	1004
Levites, the ministers of the *h*	Eze 45:5	1004
be for the whole *h* of Israel	Eze 45:6	1004
h of Israel according to their	Eze 45:8	1004
solemnities of the *h* of Israel	Eze 45:17	1004
for the *h* of Israel	Eze 45:17	1004
and put it upon the posts of the *h*	Eze 45:19	1004
so shall ye reconcile the *h*	Eze 45:20	1004
where the ministers of the *h*	Eze 46:24	1004
me again unto the door of the *h*	Eze 47:1	1004
the threshold of the *h* eastward	Eze 47:1	1004
of the *h* stood toward the east	Eze 47:1	1004
from the right side of the *h*	Eze 47:1	1004
the sanctuary of the *h* shall be	Eze 48:21	1004
of the vessels of the *h* of God	Dan 1:2	1004
of Shinar to the *h* of his god	Dan 1:2	1004
into the treasure *h* of his god	Dan 1:2	1004
Then Daniel went to his *h*	Dan 2:17	1005
was at rest in mine *h*, and	Dan 4:4	1005
that I have built for the *h* of	Dan 4:30	1005
h of God which was at Jerusalem	Dan 5:3	1005
lords, came into the banquet *h*	Dan 5:10	1005
the vessels of his *h* before thee	Dan 5:23	1005
was signed, he went into his *h*	Dan 6:10	1005
of Jezreel upon the *h* of Jehu	Hos 1:4	1004
the kingdom of the *h* of Israel	Hos 1:4	1004
have mercy upon the *h* of Israel	Hos 1:6	1004
have mercy upon the *h* of Judah	Hos 1:7	1004
and hearken, ye *h* of Israel	Hos 5:1	1004
and give ye ear, O *h* of the king	Hos 5:1	1004
to the *h* of Judah as rottenness	Hos 5:12	1004
as a young lion to the *h* of Judah	Hos 5:14	1004
horrible thing in the *h* of Israel	Hos 6:10	1004
eagle against the *h* of the LORD	Hos 8:1	1004
not come into the *h* of the LORD	Hos 9:4	1004
and hatred in the *h* of his God	Hos 9:8	1004
I will drive them out of mine *h*	Hos 9:15	1004
the *h* of Israel with deceit	Hos 11:12	1004
is cut off from the *h* of the LORD	Joel 1:9	1004
withholden from the *h* of your God	Joel 1:13	1004
into the *h* of the LORD your God	Joel 1:14	1004
and gladness from the *h* of our God	Joel 1:16	1004
come forth of the *h* of the LORD	Joel 3:18	1004
send a fire into the *h* of Hazael	Amos 1:4	1004
the sceptre from the *h* of Eden	Amos 1:5	1004
condemned in the *h* of their god	Amos 2:8	1004
ye, and testify in the *h* of Jacob	Amos 3:13	1004
winter *h* with the summer *h*	Amos 3:15	1004
even a lamentation, O *h* of Israel	Amos 5:1	1004
leave ten, to the *h* of Israel	Amos 5:3	1004
the LORD unto the *h* of Israel	Amos 5:4	1004
out like fire in the *h* of Joseph	Amos 5:6	1004
or went into the *h*, and leaned his	Amos 5:19	1004
forty years, O *h* of Israel	Amos 5:25	1004
to whom the *h* of Israel came	Amos 6:1	1004
if there remain ten men in one *h*	Amos 6:9	1004
bring out the bones out of the *h*	Amos 6:10	1004
him that is by the sides of the *h*	Amos 6:10	1004
smite the great *h* with breaches	Amos 6:11	1004
and the little *h* with clefts	Amos 6:11	1004
O *h* of Israel, saith the LORD the	Amos 6:14	1004
I will rise against the *h* of	Amos 7:9	1004
in the midst of the *h* of Israel	Amos 7:10	1004
thy word against the *h* of Isaac	Amos 7:16	1004
utterly destroy the *h* of Jacob	Amos 9:8	1004
I will sift the *h* of Israel among	Amos 9:9	1004
the *h* of Jacob shall possess	Obad 17	1004
the *h* of Jacob shall be a fire,	Obad 18	1004
the *h* of Joseph a flame, and the	Obad 18	1004
the *h* of Esau for stubble, and	Obad 18	1004
be any remaining of the *h* of Esau	Obad 18	1004
for the sins of the *h* of Israel	Mic 1:5	1004
in the *h* of Aphrah roll thyself	Mic 1:10	1035
so they oppress a man and his *h*	Mic 2:2	1004
that art named the *h* of Jacob	Mic 2:7	1004
and ye princes of the *h* of Israel	Mic 3:1	1004
you, ye heads of the *h* of Jacob	Mic 3:9	1004
and princes of the *h* of Israel	Mic 3:9	1004
the mountain of the *h* as the high	Mic 3:12	1004
of the *h* of the LORD shall be	Mic 4:1	1004
to the *h* of the God of Jacob	Mic 4:2	1004
thee out of the *h* of servants	Mic 6:4	1004
wickedness in the *h* of the wicked	Mic 6:10	1004
and all the works of the *h* of Ahab	Mic 6:16	1004
enemies are the men of his own *h*	Mic 7:6	1004
out of the *h* of thy gods will I	Nah 1:14	1004

H

an evil covetousness to his *h* ... Hab 2:9 1004
thy *h* by cutting off many people ... Hab 2:10 1004
head out of the *h* of the wicked ... Hab 3:13 1004
for the remnant of the *h* of Judah ... Zeph 2:7 1004
that the LORD's *h* should be built ... Hag 1:2 1004
houses, and this *h* lie waste ... Hag 1:4 1004
and bring wood, and build the *h* ... Hag 1:8 1004
Because of mine *h* that is waste ... Hag 1:9 1004
ye run every man unto his own *h* ... Hag 1:9 1004
did work in the *h* of the LORD of ... Hag 1:14 1004
saw this *h* in her first glory ... Hag 2:3 1004
and I will fill this *h* with glory ... Hag 2:7 1004
The glory of this latter *h* shall ... Hag 2:9 1004
my *h* shall be built in it, saith ... Zec 1:16 1004
then thou shalt also judge my *h* ... Zec 3:7 1004
laid the foundation of this *h* ... Zec 4:9 1004
enter into the *h* of the thief ... Zec 5:4 1004
into the *h* of him that sweareth ... Zec 5:4 1004
remain in the midst of his *h* ... Zec 5:4 1004
To build it an *h* in the land of ... Zec 5:11 1004
go into the *h* of Josiah the son ... Zec 6:10 1004
sent unto the *h* of God Sherezer ... Zec 7:2 1008
in the *h* of the LORD of hosts ... Zec 7:3 1004
h of the LORD of hosts was laid ... Zec 8:9 1004
O *h* of Judah, and *h* of Israel ... Zec 8:13 1004
Jerusalem and to the *h* of Judah ... Zec 8:15 1004
shall be to the *h* of Judah joy ... Zec 8:19 1004
about mine *h* because of the army ... Zec 9:8 1004
visited his flock the *h* of Judah ... Zec 10:3 1004
I will strengthen the *h* of Judah ... Zec 10:6 1004
and I will save the *h* of Joseph ... Zec 10:6 1004
the potter in the *h* of the LORD ... Zec 11:13 1004
mine eyes upon the *h* of Judah ... Zec 12:4 1004
that the glory of the *h* of David ... Zec 12:7 1004
the *h* of David shall be as God, ... Zec 12:8 1004
I will pour upon the *h* of David ... Zec 12:10 1004
family of the *h* of David apart ... Zec 12:12 1004
family of the *h* of Nathan apart ... Zec 12:12 1004
The family of the *h* of Levi apart ... Zec 12:13 1004
fountain opened to the *h* of David ... Zec 13:1 1004
wounded in the *h* of my friends ... Zec 13:6 1004
the pots in the LORD's *h* shall be ... Zec 14:20 1004
in the *h* of the LORD of hosts ... Zec 14:21 1004
that there may be meat in mine *h* ... Mal 3:10 1004
And when they were come into the *h* ... Mt 2:11 3614
light unto all that are in the *h* ... Mt 5:15 3614
which built his *h* upon a rock ... Mt 7:24 3614
winds blew, and beat upon that *h* ... Mt 7:25 3614
which built his *h* upon the sand ... Mt 7:26 3614
winds blew, and beat upon that *h* ... Mt 7:27 3614
Jesus was come into Peter's *h* ... Mt 8:14 3614
up thy bed, and go unto thine *h* ... Mt 9:6 3624
And he arose, and departed to his *h* ... Mt 9:7 3624
as Jesus sat at meat in the *h* ... Mt 9:10 3614
Jesus came into the ruler's *h* ... Mt 9:23 3614
And when he was come into the *h* ... Mt 9:28 3614
the lost sheep of the *h* of Israel ... Mt 10:6 3624
And when ye come into an *h* ... Mt 10:12 3614
if the *h* be worthy, let your ... Mt 10:13 3614
ye depart out of that *h* or city ... Mt 10:14 3614
the master of the *h* Beelzebub ... Mt 10:25 3617
How he entered into the *h* of God ... Mt 12:4 3624
every city or *h* divided against ... Mt 12:25 3614
one enter into a strong man's *h* ... Mt 12:29 3614
and then he will spoil his *h* ... Mt 12:29 3614
I will return into my *h* from ... Mt 12:44 3624
same day went Jesus out of the *h* ... Mt 13:1 3614
away, and went into the *h* ... Mt 13:36 3614
his own country, and in his own *h* ... Mt 13:57 3614
the lost sheep of the *h* of Israel ... Mt 15:24 3624
And when he was come into the *h* ... Mt 17:25 3614
against the goodman of the *h* ... Mt 20:11 3617
My *h* shall be called the *h* of ... Mt 21:13 3624
your *h* is left unto you desolate ... Mt 23:38 3624
to take any thing out of his *h* ... Mt 24:17 3614
that if the goodman of the *h* had ... Mt 24:43 3617
suffered his *h* to be broken up ... Mt 24:43 3614
in the *h* of Simon the leper, ... Mt 26:6 3614
at thy *h* with my disciples ... Mt 26:18
they entered into the *h* of Simon ... Mk 1:29 3614
was noised that he was in the *h* ... Mk 2:1 3624
bed, and go thy way into thine *h* ... Mk 2:11 3624
as Jesus sat at meat in his *h* ... Mk 2:15 3614
How he went into the *h* of God in ... Mk 2:26 3624
and they went into an *h* ... Mk 3:19 3624
if a *h* be divided against itself, ... Mk 3:25 3614
that *h* cannot stand ... Mk 3:25 3614
can enter into a strong man's *h* ... Mk 3:27 3614
and then he will spoil his *h* ... Mk 3:27 3614
synagogue's *h* certain which said ... Mk 5:35
he cometh to the *h* of the ruler ... Mk 5:38 3624
his own kin, and in his own *h* ... Mk 6:4 3614
place soever ye enter into a *h* ... Mk 6:10 3614
into the *h* from the people ... Mk 7:17 3624
and Sidon, and entered into an *h* ... Mk 7:24 3614
And when she was come to her *h* ... Mk 7:30 3624
And he sent him away to his *h* ... Mk 8:26 3624
And when he was come into the *h* ... Mk 9:28 3624
being in the *h* he asked them, ... Mk 9:33 3614
in the *h* his disciples asked him ... Mk 10:10 3614
There is no man that hath left *h* ... Mk 10:29 3614
My *h* shall be called of all ... Mk 11:17 3624
of all nations the *h* of prayer ... Mk 11:17 3624
housetop not go down into the *h* ... Mk 13:15 3614
to take any thing out of his *h* ... Mk 13:15 3614
a far journey, who left his *h* ... Mk 13:34 3614
when the master of the *h* cometh ... Mk 13:35 3614
in the *h* of Simon the leper ... Mk 14:3 3614
say ye to the goodman of the *h* ... Mk 14:14 3617
he departed to his own *h* ... Lk 1:23 3624
was Joseph, of the *h* of David ... Lk 1:27 3624
over the *h* of Jacob for ever ... Lk 1:33 3624
entered into the *h* of Zacharias ... Lk 1:40 3624
months, and returned to her own *h* ... Lk 1:56 3624
us in the *h* of his servant David ... Lk 1:69 3624
(because he was of the *h* and ... Lk 2:4 3624
and entered into Simon's *h* ... Lk 4:38 3614
up thy couch, and go into thine *h* ... Lk 5:24 3624
he lay, and departed to his own *h* ... Lk 5:25 3624
him a great feast in his own *h* ... Lk 5:29 3614
How he went into the *h* of God ... Lk 6:4 3624
He is like a man which built an *h* ... Lk 6:48 3614
beat vehemently upon that *h* ... Lk 6:48 3614
built an *h* upon the earth ... Lk 6:49 3614
and the ruin of that *h* was great ... Lk 6:49 3614
he was now not far from the *h* ... Lk 7:6 3614
were sent, returning to the *h* ... Lk 7:10 3624
And he went into the Pharisee's *h* ... Lk 7:36 3614
sat at meat in the Pharisee's *h* ... Lk 7:37 3614
I entered into thine *h*, thou ... Lk 7:44 3614
clothes, neither abode in any *h* ... Lk 8:27 3614
Return to thine own *h*, and shew ... Lk 8:39 3624
him that he would come into his *h* ... Lk 8:41 3624
the ruler of the synagogue's *h* ... Lk 8:49
And when he came into the *h* ... Lk 8:51 3614
whatsoever *h* ye enter into, there ... Lk 9:4 3614
which are at home at my *h* ... Lk 9:61 3624
And into whatsoever *h* ye enter ... Lk 10:5 3614
first say, Peace be to this *h* ... Lk 10:5 3624
And in the same *h* remain, eating ... Lk 10:7 3614
Go not from *h* to *h* ... Lk 10:7 3614
Martha received him into her *h* ... Lk 10:38 3624
h divided against a *h* falleth ... Lk 11:17 3624
unto my *h* whence I came out ... Lk 11:24 3624
that if the goodman of the *h* had ... Lk 12:39 3617
his *h* to be broken through ... Lk 12:39 3624
shall be five in one *h* divided ... Lk 12:52 3624
the master of the *h* is risen up ... Lk 13:25 3617
your *h* is left unto you desolate ... Lk 13:35 3624
as he went into the *h* of one of ... Lk 14:1 3624
Then the master of the *h* being ... Lk 14:21 3617
come in, that my *h* may be filled ... Lk 14:23 3624
light a candle, and sweep the *h* ... Lk 15:8 3614
as he came and drew nigh to the *h* ... Lk 15:25 3614
send him to my father's *h* ... Lk 16:27 3624
housetop, and his stuff in the *h* ... Lk 17:31 3614
this man went down to his *h* ... Lk 18:14 3624
There is no man that hath left *h* ... Lk 18:29 3614
for to day I must abide at thy *h* ... Lk 19:5 3624
day is salvation come to this *h* ... Lk 19:9 3624
My *h* is the *h* of prayer ... Lk 19:46 3624
follow him into the *h* where he ... Lk 22:10 3614
say unto the goodman of the *h* ... Lk 22:11 3614
him into the high priest's *h* ... Lk 22:54 3624
h an *h* of merchandise ... Jn 2:16 3624
zeal of thine *h* hath eaten me up ... Jn 2:17 3624
himself believed, and his whole *h* ... Jn 4:53 3614
And every man went unto his own *h* ... Jn 7:53 3624
abideth not in the *h* for ever ... Jn 8:35 3614
but Mary sat still in the *h* ... Jn 11:20 3624
then which were with her in the *h* ... Jn 11:31 3614
the *h* was filled with the odour ... Jn 12:3 3614
In my Father's *h* are many ... Jn 14:2 3614
it filled all the *h* where they ... Acts 2:2 3624
Therefore let all the *h* of Israel ... Acts 2:36 3624
and breaking bread from *h* to *h* ... Acts 2:46 3624
in the temple, and in every *h* ... Acts 5:42 3624
governor over Egypt and all his *h* ... Acts 7:10 3624
up in his father's *h* three months ... Acts 7:20 3624
O ye *h* of Israel, have ye offered ... Acts 7:42 3624
But Solomon built him an *h* ... Acts 7:47 3624
what *h* will ye build me ... Acts 7:49 3624
the church, entering into every *h* ... Acts 8:3 3624
enquire in the *h* of Judas for one ... Acts 9:11 3614
his way, and entered into the *h* ... Acts 9:17 3614
that feared God with all his *h* ... Acts 10:2 3624
whose *h* is by the sea side ... Acts 10:6 3614
had made enquiry for Simon's *h* ... Acts 10:17 3614
angel to send for thee into his *h* ... Acts 10:22 3624
the ninth hour I prayed in my *h* ... Acts 10:30 3624
he is lodged in the *h* of one ... Acts 10:32 3614
come unto the *h* where I was ... Acts 11:11 3614
and we entered into the man's *h* ... Acts 11:12 3624
how he had seen an angel in his *h* ... Acts 11:13 3624
thou and all thy *h* shall be saved ... Acts 11:14 3624
he came to the *h* of Mary the ... Acts 12:12 3614
to the Lord, come into my *h* ... Acts 16:15 3624
and thou shalt be saved, and thy *h* ... Acts 16:31 3624
and to all that were in his *h* ... Acts 16:32 3614
he had brought them into his *h* ... Acts 16:34 3624
believing in God with all his *h* ... Acts 16:34 3832
and entered into the *h* of Lydia ... Acts 16:40
and assaulted the *h* of Jason ... Acts 17:5 3614
and entered into a certain man's *h* ... Acts 18:7 3614
whose *h* joined hard to the ... Acts 18:7 3614
on the Lord with all his *h* ... Acts 18:8 3624
they fled out of that *h* naked ... Acts 19:16 3624
publickly, and from *h* to *h*, ... Acts 20:20 3624
we entered into the *h* of Philip ... Acts 21:8 3624
whole years in his own hired *h* ... Acts 28:30
the church that is in their *h* ... Rom 16:5 3624
them which are of the *h* of Chloe ... 1Cor 1:11
(ye know the *h* of Stephanas ... 1Cor 16:15 3614
the church that is in their *h* ... 1Cor 16:19 3624
earthly *h* of this tabernacle were ... 2Cor 5:1 3614
an *h* not made with hands, eternal ... 2Cor 5:1 3614
with our *h* which is from heaven ... 2Cor 5:2 3613
and the church which is in his *h* ... Col 4:15 3624
One that ruleth well his own *h* ... 1Ti 3:4 3624
know not how to rule his own *h* ... 1Ti 3:5 3624
to behave thyself in the *h* of God ... 1Ti 3:15 3624
specially for those of his own *h* ... 1Ti 5:8 3609
wandering about from *h* to *h* ... 1Ti 5:13 3614
marry, bear children, guide the *h* ... 1Ti 5:14 3616
mercy unto the *h* of Onesiphorus ... 2Ti 1:16 3624
But in a great *h* there are not ... 2Ti 2:20 3614
and to the church in thy *h* ... Philem 2 3624
Moses was faithful in all his *h* ... Heb 3:2 3624
h hath more honour than the *h* ... Heb 3:3 3624
For every *h* is builded by some ... Heb 3:4 3624
verily was faithful in all his *h* ... Heb 3:5 3624
Christ as a son over his own *h* ... Heb 3:6 3624
whose *h* are we, if we hold fast ... Heb 3:6 3624
new covenant with the *h* of Israel ... Heb 8:8 3624
of Israel and with the *h* of Judah ... Heb 8:8 3624
that I will make with the *h* of ... Heb 8:10 3624
an high priest over the *h* of God ... Heb 10:21 3624
an ark to the saving of his *h* ... Heb 11:7 3624
are built up a spiritual *h* ... 1Pet 2:5 3624
must begin at the *h* of God ... 1Pet 4:17 3624
receive him not into your *h* ... 2Jn 10 3614

HOUSEHOLD {61}

his *h* after him, and they shall ... Gen 18:19 1004
thou found of all thy *h* stuff ... Gen 31:37 1004
Then Jacob said unto his *h* ... Gen 35:2 1004
lest thou, and thy *h*, and all that ... Gen 45:11 1004
brethren, and all his father's *h* ... Gen 47:12 1004
man and his *h* came with Jacob ... Ex 1:1 1004
if the *h* be too little for the ... Ex 12:4 1004
for himself, and for his *h* ... Lev 16:17 1004
upon Pharaoh, and upon all his *h* ... Deut 6:22 1004
shalt rejoice, thou, and thine *h* ... Deut 14:26 1004
LORD shall choose, thou and thy *h* ... Deut 15:20 1004
brethren, and all thy father's *h* ... Josh 2:18 1004
harlot alive, and her father's *h* ... Josh 6:25 1004
the *h* which the LORD shall take ... Josh 7:14 1004
And he brought his *h* man by man ... Josh 7:18 1004
because he feared his father's *h* ... Judg 6:27 1004
thy life, with the lives of thy *h* ... Judg 18:25 1004
our master, and against all his *h* ... 1Sa 25:17 1004
and his men, every man with his *h* ... 1Sa 27:3 1004
bring up, every man with his *h* ... 2Sa 2:3 1004
blessed Obed-edom, and all his *h* ... 2Sa 6:11 1004
David returned to bless his *h* ... 2Sa 6:20 1004
forth, and all his *h* after him ... 2Sa 15:16 1004
be for the king's *h* to ride on ... 2Sa 16:2 1004
put his *h* in order, and hanged ... 2Sa 17:23 1004
boat to carry over the king's *h* ... 2Sa 19:18 1004
have brought the king, and his *h* ... 2Sa 19:41 1004
And Ahishar was over the *h* ... 1Kin 4:6 1004
victuals for the king and his *h* ... 1Kin 4:7 1004
desire, in giving food for my *h* ... 1Kin 5:9 1004
of wheat for food to his *h* ... 1Kin 5:11 1004
h among the sons of Pharaoh ... 1Kin 11:20 1004
we may go and tell the king's *h* ... 2Kin 7:9 1004
Arise, and go thou and thine *h* ... 2Kin 8:1 1004
and she went with her *h*, and ... 2Kin 8:2 1004
of Hilkiah, which was over the *h* ... 2Kin 18:18 1004
of Hilkiah, which was over the *h* ... 2Kin 18:37 1004
Eliakim, which was over the *h* ... 2Kin 19:2 1004
one principal *h* being taken for ... 1Chr 24:6 1004
the *h* stuff of Tobiah out of the ... Neh 13:8 1004
she asses, and a very great *h* ... Job 1:3 5657
thy food, for the food of thy *h* ... Prov 27:27 1004
night, and giveth meat to her *h* ... Prov 31:15 1004
not afraid of the snow for her *h* ... Prov 31:21 1004
for all her *h* are clothed with ... Prov 31:21 1004
looketh well to the ways of her *h* ... Prov 31:27 1004
of Hilkiah, that was over the *h* ... Is 36:22 1004
sent Eliakim, who was over the *h* ... Is 37:2 1004
shall they call them of his *h* ... Mt 10:25 3615
foes shall be they of his own *h* ... Mt 10:36 3615
lord hath made ruler over his *h* ... Mt 24:45 2322
lord shall make ruler over his *h* ... Lk 12:42 2322
he called two of his *h* servants ... Acts 10:7 3610
when she was baptized, and her *h* ... Acts 16:15 3624
them which are of Aristobulus' *h* ... Rom 16:10
that be of the *h* of Narcissus ... Rom 16:11
baptized also the *h* of Stephanas ... 1Cor 1:16 3624
them who are of the *h* of faith ... Gal 6:10 3609
the saints, and of the *h* of God ... Eph 2:19 3609
they that are of Caesar's *h* ... Phil 4:22 3614
Aquila, and the *h* of Onesiphorus ... 2Ti 4:19 3624

HOUSEHOLDER {4}

So the servants of the *h* came ... Mt 13:27 3617
is like unto a man that is an *h* ... Mt 13:52 3617
is like unto a man that is an *h* ... Mt 20:1 3617
There was a certain *h*, which ... Mt 21:33 3617

HOUSEHOLDS {7}

food for the famine of your *h* ... Gen 42:33 1004
And take your father and your *h* ... Gen 45:18 1004
your food, and for them of your *h* ... Gen 47:24 1004
it in every place, ye and your *h* ... Num 18:31 1004
and swallowed them up, and their *h* ... Deut 11:6 1004
put your hand unto, ye and your *h* ... Deut 12:7 1004
LORD shall take shall come by *h* ... Josh 7:14 1004

HOUSES {136}

corn for the famine of your *h* ... Gen 42:19 1004
feared God, that he made them *h* ... Ex 1:21 1004
be the heads of their fathers' *h* ... Ex 6:14 1004
the frogs from thee and thy *h* ... Ex 8:9 1004
depart from thee, and from thy *h* ... Ex 8:11 1004

and the frogs died out of the *h* Ex 8:13 1004
and upon thy people, and into thy *h* Ex 8:21 1004
the *h* of the Egyptians shall be Ex 8:21 1004
Pharaoh, and into his servants' *h* Ex 8:24 1004
and his cattle flee into the *h* Ex 9:20 1004
And they shall fill thy *h* Ex 10:6 1004
the *h* of all thy servants Ex 10:6 1004
the *h* of all the Egyptians Ex 10:6 1004
on the upper door post of the *h* Ex 12:7 1004
a token upon the *h* where ye are Ex 12:13 1004
put away leaven out of your *h* Ex 12:15 1004
be no leaven found in your *h* Ex 12:19 1004
come in unto your *h* to smite you Ex 12:23 1004
who passed over the *h* of the Ex 12:27 1004
the Egyptians, and delivered our *h* Ex 12:27 1004
But the *h* of the villages which Lev 25:31 1004
the *h* of the cities of their Lev 25:32 1004
for the *h* of the cities of the Lev 25:33 1004
throughout the *h* of their fathers Num 4:22 1004
and swallowed them up, and their *h* Num 16:32 1004
according to their fathers' *h* Num 17:6 1004
We will not return unto our *h* Num 32:18 1004
h full of all good things, which Deut 6:11 1004
art full, and hast built goodly *h* Deut 8:12 1004
in their cities, and in their *h* Deut 19:1 1004
for our provision out of our *h* on Josh 9:12 1004
that there is in these *h* an ephod Judg 18:14 1004
the men that were in the *h* near Judg 18:22 1004
when Solomon had built the two *h* 1Kin 9:10 1004
against all the *h* of the high 1Kin 13:32 1004
house, and the *h* of thy servants 1Kin 20:6 1004
put them in the *h* of the high 2Kin 17:29 1004
them in the *h* of the high places 2Kin 17:32 1004
brake down the *h* of the sodomites 2Kin 23:7 1004
all the *h* also of the high places 2Kin 23:19 1004
all the *h* of Jerusalem, and every 2Kin 25:9 1004
David made him *h* in the city of 1Chr 15:1 1004
of the *h* thereof, and of the 1Chr 28:11 1004
overlay the walls of the *h* withal 1Chr 29:4 1004
to the *h* of their fathers 2Chr 25:5 1004
to floor the *h* which the kings of 2Chr 34:11 1004
by the *h* of your fathers, after 2Chr 35:4 1004
daughters, your wives, and your *h* Neh 4:14 1004
our lands, vineyards, and *h* Neh 5:3 1004
their oliveyards, and their *h* Neh 5:11 1004
and the *h* were not builded Neh 7:4 1004
possessed *h* full of all goods, Neh 9:25 1004
after the *h* of our fathers, at Neh 10:34 1004
sons went and feasted in their *h* Job 1:4 1004
who filled their *h* with silver Job 3:15 1004
in them that dwell in *h* of clay Job 4:19 1004
in *h* which no man inhabiteth, Job 15:28 1004
Their *h* are safe from fear, Job 21:9 1004
filled their *h* with good things Job 22:18 1004
In the dark they dig through *h* Job 24:16 1004
that their *h* shall continue for Ps 49:11 1004
the *h* of God in possession Ps 83:12 4999
we shall fill our *h* with spoil Prov 1:13 1004
make they their *h* in the rocks Prov 30:26
I builded me *h* Eccl 2:4 1004
spoil of the poor is in your *h* Is 3:14 1004
Of a truth many *h* shall be Is 5:9 1004
the *h* without man, and the land be Is 6:11 1004
offence to both the *h* of Israel Is 8:14 1004
their *h* shall be spoiled, and Is 13:16 1004
their *h* shall be full of doleful Is 13:21 1004
shall cry in their desolate *h* Is 13:22 490
on the tops of their *h*, and in Is 15:3
have numbered the *h* of Jerusalem Is 22:10 1004
the *h* have ye broken down to Is 22:10 1004
upon all the *h* of joy in the Is 32:13 1004
and they are hid in prison *h* Is 42:22 1004
And they shall build *h*, and inhabit Is 65:21 1004
by troops in the harlots' *h* Jer 5:7 1004
so are their *h* full of deceit Jer 5:27 1004
their *h* shall be turned unto Jer 6:12 1004
out of your *h* on the sabbath day Jer 17:22 1004
Let a cry be heard from their *h* Jer 18:22 1004
the *h* of Jerusalem Jer 19:13 1004
the *h* of the kings of Judah, Jer 19:13 1004
because of all the *h* upon whose Jer 19:13 1004
Build ye *h*, and dwell in them Jer 29:5 1004
build ye *h*, and dwell in them Jer 29:28 1004
H and fields and vineyards shall be Jer 32:15 1004
this city, and burn it with the *h* Jer 32:29 1004
concerning the *h* of this city Jer 33:4 1004
concerning the *h* of the kings of Jer 33:4 1004
Nor to build *h* for us to dwell in Jer 35:9 1004
the *h* of the people, with fire, Jer 39:8 1004
in the *h* of the gods of Egypt Jer 43:12 1004
and the *h* of the gods of the Jer 43:13 1004
all the *h* of Jerusalem, and all Jer 52:13 1004
all the *h* of the great men, Jer 52:13 1004
to strangers, our *h* to aliens Lam 5:2 1004
and they shall possess their *h* Eze 7:24 1004
let us build *h* Eze 11:3 1004
they shall burn thine *h* with fire Eze 16:41 1004
and burn up their *h* with fire Eze 23:47 1004
walls, and destroy thy pleasant *h* Eze 26:12 1004
safely therein, and shall build *h* Eze 28:26 1004
walls and in the doors of the *h* Eze 33:30 1004
it shall be a place for their *h* Eze 45:4 1004
your *h* shall be made a dunghill Dan 2:5 1005
their *h* shall be made a dunghill Dan 3:29 1005
and I will place them in their *h* Hos 11:11 1004
they shall climb up upon the *h* Joel 2:9 1004
the *h* of ivory shall perish, and Amos 3:15 1004
the great *h* shall have an end, Amos 3:15 1004
ye have built *h* of hewn stone Amos 5:11 1004
the *h* of Achzib shall be a lie to Mic 1:14 1004
and *h*, and take them away Mic 2:2 1004
ye cast out from their pleasant *h* Mic 2:9 1004
their masters' *h* with violence Zeph 1:9 1004
a booty, and their *h* a desolation Zeph 1:13 1004
they shall also build *h*, but not Zeph 1:13 1004
in the *h* of Ashkelon shall they Zeph 2:7 1004
O ye, to dwell in your cieled *h* Hag 1:4 1004
the *h* rifled, and the women Zec 14:2 1004
soft clothing are in kings' *h* Mt 11:8 *3624*
And every one that hath forsaken *h* Mt 19:29 *3614*
for ye devour widows' *h*, and for a Mt 23:14 *3614*
them away fasting to their own *h* Mk 8:3 *3624*
hundredfold now in this time, *h* Mk 10:30 *3614*
Which devour widows' *h*, and for a Mk 12:40 *3614*
they may receive me into their *h* Lk 16:4 *3624*
Which devour widows' *h*, and for a Lk 20:47 *3614*
of lands or *h* sold them, and Acts 4:34 *3614*
have ye not *h* to eat and to drink 1Cor 11:22 *3614*
children and their own *h* well 1Ti 3:12 *3624*
sort are they which creep into *h* 2Ti 3:6 *3614*
be stopped, who subvert whole *h* Titus 1:11 *3624*

HOUSETOP {7}
to dwell in a corner of the *h* Prov 21:9 1406
to dwell in the corner of the *h* Prov 25:24 1406
Let him which is on the *h* not Mt 24:17 *1430*
let him that is on the *h* not go Mk 13:15 *1430*
multitude, they went upon the *h* Lk 5:19 *1430*
day, he which shall be upon the *h* Lk 17:31 *1430*
Peter went up upon the *h* to pray Acts 10:9 *1430*

HOUSETOPS {7}
them be as the grass upon the *h* Ps 129:6 1406
thou art wholly gone up to the *h* Is 22:1 1406
green herb, as the grass on the *h* Is 37:27 1406
generally upon all the *h* of Moab Jer 48:38 1406
the host of heaven upon the *h* Zeph 1:5 1406
ear, that preach ye upon the *h* Mt 10:27 *1430*
shall be proclaimed upon the *h* Lk 12:3 *1430*

HOW See APPENDIX.

HOWBEIT {64}
H Sisera fled away on his feet to Judg 4:17
H the king of the children of Judg 11:28
H the hair of his head began to Judg 16:22
h the name of the city was Laish Judg 18:29 199
H we may not give them wives of Judg 21:18
h there is a kinsman nearer than Ruth 3:12
h yet protest solemnly unto them, 1Sa 8:9 389
H he refused to turn aside 2Sa 2:23
H, because by this deed thou hast 2Sa 12:14 657
H he would not hearken unto her 2Sa 13:14
h he would not go, but blessed 2Sa 13:25
h he attained not unto the first 2Sa 23:19
h the kingdom is turned about, and 1Kin 2:15
H I believed not the words, until 1Kin 10:7
H I will not rend away all the 1Kin 11:13 7535
h let me go in any wise 1Kin 11:22
H I will not take the whole 1Kin 11:34
h the slingers went about it, and 2Kin 3:25
h the LORD hath shewed me that he 2Kin 8:10
H from the sins of Jeroboam the 2Kin 10:29
H there were not made for the 2Kin 12:13
H the high places were not taken 2Kin 14:4
H the high places were not 2Kin 15:35
H every nation made gods of their 2Kin 17:29
H they did not hearken, but they 2Kin 17:40
H there was no reckoning made 2Kin 22:7
h he attained not to the first 1Chr 11:21
H the LORD God of Israel chose me 1Chr 28:4
H I believed not their words, 2Chr 9:6
h the king of Israel stayed 2Chr 18:34
H the high places were not taken 2Chr 20:33
H the LORD would not destroy the 2Chr 21:7
H they buried him in the city of 2Chr 21:20
H the Levites hastened it not 2Chr 24:5
h he entered not into the temple 2Chr 27:2
H in the business of the 2Chr 32:31 3651
H thou art just in all that is Neh 9:33
h our God turned the curse into a Neh 13:2
H he will not stretch out his Job 30:24
H he meaneth not so, neither doth Is 10:7
H I sent unto you all my servants Jer 44:4
H this kind goeth not out but by Mt 17:21
H Jesus suffered him not, but Mk 5:19
H in vain do they worship me, Mk 7:7
(*H* there came other boats from Jn 6:23 *1161*
H no man spake openly of him for Jn 7:13 *3305*
H we know this man whence he is Jn 7:27 *235*
H Jesus spake of his death Jn 11:13
H when he, the Spirit of truth, Jn 16:13
H many of them which heard the Acts 4:4
H the most High dwelleth not in Acts 7:48 *235*
H, as the disciples stood round Acts 14:20
H certain men clave unto him, and Acts 17:34
H we must be cast upon a certain Acts 27:26
H they looked when he should have Acts 28:6
H we speak wisdom among them that 1Cor 2:6
H there is not in every man that 1Cor 8:7 *235*
h in the spirit he speaketh 1Cor 14:2
h in malice be ye children, but 1Cor 14:20 *235*
H that was not first which is 1Cor 15:46 *235*
H whereinsoever any is bold, 2Cor 11:21
H then, when ye knew not God, ye Gal 4:8 *235*
H for this cause I obtained mercy 1Ti 1:16 *235*
h not all that came out of Egypt Heb 3:16 *235*

HOWL {29}
H ye; for the day of the LORD Is 13:6 3213
H, O gate Is 14:31 3213
Moab shall *h* over Nebo, and over Is 15:2 3213
their streets, every one shall *h* Is 15:3 3213
h for Moab, every one shall *h* Is 16:7 3213
H, ye ships of Tarshish Is 23:1 3213
h, ye inhabitants of the isle Is 23:6 3213
H, ye ships of Tarshish Is 23:14 3213
rule over them make them to *h* Is 52:5 3213
shall *h* for vexation of spirit Is 65:14 3213
you with sackcloth, lament and *h* Jer 4:8 3213
H, ye shepherds, and cry Jer 25:34 3213
inhabitants of the land shall *h* Jer 47:2 3213
h and cry; tell ye it Jer 48:20 3213
Therefore will I *h* for Moab Jer 48:31 3213
They shall *h*, saying, How is it Jer 48:39 3213
H, O Heshbon, for Ai is spoiled Jer 49:3 3213
h for her; take balm Jer 51:8 3213
Cry and *h*, son of man Eze 21:12 3213
H ye, Woe worth the day Eze 30:2 3213
and *h*, all ye drinkers of wine, Joel 1:5 3213
h, O ye vinedressers, for the Joel 1:11 3213
h, ye ministers of the altar Joel 1:13 3213
Therefore I will wail and *h* Mic 1:8 3213
H, ye inhabitants of Maktesh, for Zeph 1:11 3213
H, fir tree; for the cedar Zec 11:2 3213
h, O ye oaks of Bashan Zec 11:2 3213
h for your miseries that shall Jas 5:1 *3649*

HOWLED {1}
when they *h* upon their beds Hos 7:14 3213

HOWLING {6}
and in the waste *h* wilderness Deut 32:10 3214
the *h* thereof unto Eglaim, and the Is 15:8 3213
the *h* thereof unto Beer-elim Is 15:8 3213
an *h* of the principal of the Jer 25:36 3213
an *h* from the second, and a great Zeph 1:10 3213
a voice of the *h* of the shepherds Zec 11:3 3213

HOWLINGS {1}
the temple shall be *h* in that day Amos 8:3 3213

HOWSOEVER {4}
h let all thy wants lie upon me Judg 19:20 7535
of Zadok yet again to Joab, But *h* 2Sa 18:22 1961,4101
But *h*, said he, let me run 2Sa 18:23
not be cut off, *h* I punished them Zeph 3:7 3605,834

HOZAI See SEERS.

HUBBAH See JUHUBBAH.

HUGE {1}
Ethiopians and the Lubims a *h* host 2Chr 16:8 7230

HUKKOK *(huk'-kok)* {1} See HELKATH, HUKOK.
A place in Naphtali.
and goeth out from thence to *H* Josh 19:34 2712

HUKOK *(hu'-kok)* {1} See HUKKOK. *A city in Asher.*
H with her suburbs, and Rehob with 1Chr 6:75 2712

HUL *(hul)* {2} *A son of Aram.*
Uz, and *H*, and Gether, and Mash Gen 10:23 2343
and Lud, and Aram, and Uz, and *H* 1Chr 1:17 2343

HULDAH *(hul'-dah)* {2} *A prophetess.*
went unto *H* the prophetess, the 2Kin 22:14 2468
went to *H* the prophetess, the 2Chr 34:22 2468

HUMBLE {25}
refuse to *h* thyself before me Ex 10:3 6031
to *h* thee, and to prove thee, to Deut 8:2 6031
knew not, that he might *h* thee Deut 8:16 6031
h ye them, and do with them what Judg 19:24 6031
shall *h* themselves, and pray, and 2Chr 7:14 3665
thou didst *h* thyself before God, 2Chr 34:27 3665
and he shall save the *h* person Job 22:29 7807,5869
forgetteth not the cry of the *h* Ps 9:12 6041
forget not the *h* Ps 10:12 6041
hast heard the desire of the *h* Ps 10:17 6041
the *h* shall hear thereof, and be Ps 34:2 6041
The *h* shall see this, and be glad Ps 69:32 6041
h thyself, and make sure thy Prov 6:3 7511
be of an *h* spirit with the lowly Prov 16:19 8213
shall uphold the *h* in spirit Prov 29:23 8217
that is of a contrite and *h* spirit Is 57:15 8217
to revive the spirit of the *h* Is 57:15 8217
the queen, *H* yourselves, sit down Jer 13:18 8213
Whosoever therefore shall *h* Mt 18:4 *5013*
he that shall *h* himself shall be Mt 23:12 *5013*
my God will *h* me among you, and 2Cor 12:21 *5013*
but giveth grace unto the *h* Jas 4:6 *5011*
H yourselves in the sight of the Jas 4:10 *5013*
proud, and giveth grace to the *h* 1Pet 5:5 *5011*
H yourselves therefore under the 1Pet 5:6 *5013*

HUMBLED {28}
their uncircumcised hearts be *h* Lev 26:41 3665
he *h* thee, and suffered thee to Deut 8:3 6031
of her, because thou hast *h* her Deut 21:14 6031
because he hath *h* his neighbour's Deut 22:24 6031
because he hath *h* her, he may not Deut 22:29 6031
thou hast *h* thyself before the 2Kin 22:19 3665
Israel and the king *h* themselves 2Chr 12:6 3665
LORD saw that they *h* themselves 2Chr 12:7 3665
saying, They have *h* themselves 2Chr 12:7 3665
And when he *h* himself, the wrath 2Chr 12:12 3665
and of Zebulun *h* themselves 2Chr 30:11 3665
Notwithstanding Hezekiah *h* 2Chr 32:26 3665
h himself greatly before the God 2Chr 33:12 3665
and graven images, before he was *h* 2Chr 33:19 3665
h not himself before the LORD, as 2Chr 33:23 3665
Manasseh his father had *h* himself 2Chr 33:23 3665
h not himself before Jeremiah the 2Chr 36:12 3665

H

I *h* my soul with fasting ... Ps 35:13 6031
The lofty looks of man shall be *h* ... Is 2:11 8213
and the mighty man shall be *h* ... Is 5:15 8213
the eyes of the lofty shall be *h* ... Is 5:15 8213
down, and the haughty shall be *h* ... Is 10:33 8213
They are not *h* even unto this day ... Jer 44:10 1792
in remembrance, and is *h* in me ... Lam 3:20 7743
in thee have they *h* her that was ... Eze 22:10 6031
another in thee hath *h* his sister ... Eze 22:11 6031
hast not *h* thine heart, though ... Dan 5:22 8214
he *h* himself, and became obedient ... Phil 2:8 *5013*

HUMBLEDST {1}
h thyself before me, and didst ... 2Chr 34:27 3665

HUMBLENESS {1}
kindness, *h* of mind, meekness, ... Col 3:12 *5012*

HUMBLETH {7}
thou how Ahab *h* himself before me ... 1Kin 21:29 3665
because he *h* himself before me, I ... 1Kin 21:29 3665
h himself, that the poor may fall ... Ps 10:10 7817
Who *h* himself to behold the ... Ps 113:6 8213
down, and the great man *h* himself ... Is 2:9 8213
he that *h* himself shall be ... Lk 14:11 *5013*
he that *h* himself shall be ... Lk 18:14 *5013*

HUMBLY {2}
I *h* beseech thee that I may find ... 2Sa 16:4 7812
mercy, and to walk *h* with thy God ... Mic 6:8 6800

HUMILIATION {1}
In his *h* his judgment was taken ... Acts 8:33 *5014*

HUMILITY {7}
and before honour is *h* ... Prov 15:33 6038
and before honour is *h* ... Prov 18:12 6038
By *h* and the fear of the LORD are ... Prov 22:4 6038
the Lord with all *h* of mind ... Acts 20:19 *5012*
of your reward in a voluntary *h* ... Col 2:18 *5012*
of wisdom in will worship, and *h* ... Col 2:23 *5012*
to another, and be clothed with *h* ... 1Pet 5:5 *5012*

HUMTAH *(hum'-tah)* {1} *A city in Judah.*
And *H*, and Kirjath-arba, which is ... Josh 15:54 2457

HUNDRED See APPENDIX.

HUNDREDFOLD {7}
received in the same year an *h* ... Gen 26:12 3967,8180
how many soever they be, an *h* ... 2Sa 24:3
and brought forth fruit, some an *h* ... Mt 13:8 *1540*
and bringeth forth, some an *h* ... Mt 13:23 *1540*
name's sake, shall receive an *h* ... Mt 19:29 *1542*
receive an *h* now in this time ... Mk 10:30 *1542*
and sprang up, and bare fruit an *h* ... Lk 8:8 *1542*

HUNDREDS {28}
of thousands, and rulers of *h* ... Ex 18:21 3967
rulers of thousands, rulers of *h* ... Ex 18:25 3967
thousands, and captains over *h* ... Num 31:14 3967
of thousands, and captains of *h* ... Num 31:48 3967
and of the captains of *h*, was ... Num 31:52 3967
the captains of thousands and of *h* ... Num 31:54 3967
thousands, and captains over *h* ... Deut 1:15 3967
of thousands, and captains of *h* ... 1Sa 22:7 3967
of the Philistines passed on by *h* ... 1Sa 29:2 3967
and captains of *h* over them ... 2Sa 18:1 3967
and all the people came out by *h* ... 2Sa 18:4 3967
sent and fetched the rulers over *h* ... 2Kin 11:4 3967
the captains over the *h* did ... 2Kin 11:9 3967
to the captains over *h* did the ... 2Kin 11:10 3967
commanded the captains of the *h* ... 2Kin 11:15 3967
And he took the rulers over *h* ... 2Kin 11:19 3967
the captains of thousands and *h* ... 1Chr 13:1 3967
the captains over thousands and *h* ... 1Chr 26:26 3967
and captains of thousands and *h* ... 1Chr 27:1 3967
thousands, and captains over the *h* ... 1Chr 28:1 3967
the captains of thousands and of *h* ... 1Chr 29:6 3967
the captains of thousands and of *h* ... 2Chr 1:2 3967
and took the captains of *h* ... 2Chr 23:1 3967
to the captains of *h* spears ... 2Chr 23:9 3967
of *h* that were set over the host ... 2Chr 23:14 3967
And he took the captains of *h* ... 2Chr 23:20 3967
thousands, and captains over *h* ... 2Chr 25:5 3967
And they sat down in ranks, by *h* ... Mk 6:40 *1540*

HUNDREDTH {3}
In the six *h* year of Noah's life, ... Gen 7:11 3967
And it came to pass in the six *h* ... Gen 8:13 3967
also the *h* part of the money, and ... Neh 5:11 3967

HUNGER {24}
kill this whole assembly with *h* ... Ex 16:3 7457
thee, and suffered thee to *h* ... Deut 8:3 7456
shall send against thee, in *h* ... Deut 28:48 7457
They shall be burnt with *h* ... Deut 32:24 7457
bread from heaven for their *h* ... Neh 9:15 7457
young lions do lack, and suffer *h* ... Ps 34:10 7456
and an idle soul shall suffer *h* ... Prov 19:15 7456
They shall not *h* nor thirst ... Is 49:10 7456
he is like to die for *h* in the ... Jer 38:9 7457
the trumpet, nor have *h* of bread ... Jer 42:14 7456
that faint for *h* in the top of ... Lam 2:19 7457
than they that be slain with *h* ... Lam 4:9 7457
more consumed with *h* in the land ... Eze 34:29 7457
Blessed are they which do *h* ... Mt 5:6 *3983*
Blessed are ye that *h* now ... Lk 6:21 *3983*
for ye shall *h* ... Lk 6:25 *3983*
and to spare, and I perish with *h* ... Lk 15:17 *3042*
that cometh to me shall never *h* ... Jn 6:35 *3983*
Therefore if thine enemy *h* ... Rom 12:20 *3983*
unto this present hour we both *h* ... 1Cor 4:11 *3983*
And if any man *h*, let him eat at ... 1Cor 11:34 *3983*
in watchings often, in *h* ... 2Cor 11:27 *3042*
to kill with sword, and with *h* ... Rev 6:8 *3042*
They shall *h* no more, neither ... Rev 7:16 *3983*

HUNGERBITTEN {1}
His strength shall be *h*, and ... Job 18:12 7457

HUNGERED {2}
he returned into the city, he *h* ... Mt 21:18 *3983*
they were ended, he afterward *h* ... Lk 4:2 *3983*

HUNGRED {9}
nights, he was afterward an *h* ... Mt 4:2 *3983*
and his disciples were an *h* ... Mt 12:1 *3983*
what David did, when he was an *h* ... Mt 12:3 *3983*
For I was an *h*, and ye gave me ... Mt 25:35 *3983*
Lord, when saw we thee an *h* ... Mt 25:37 *3983*
For I was an *h*, and ye gave me no ... Mt 25:42 *3983*
Lord, when saw we thee an *h* ... Mt 25:44 *3983*
when he had need, and was an *h* ... Mk 2:25 *3983*
David did, when himself was an *h* ... Lk 6:3 *3983*

HUNGRY {30}
and they that were *h* ceased ... 1Sa 2:5 7456
for they said, The people is *h* ... 2Sa 17:29 7456
They know that we be *h* ... 2Kin 7:12 7456
Whose harvest the *h* eateth up ... Job 5:5 7456
hast withholden bread from the *h* ... Job 22:7 7456
take away the sheaf from the *h* ... Job 24:10 7456
If I were *h*, I would not tell ... Ps 50:12 7456
H and thirsty, their soul fainted ... Ps 107:5 7456
filleth the *h* soul with goodness ... Ps 107:9 7456
And there he maketh the *h* to dwell ... Ps 107:36 7456
which giveth food to the *h* ... Ps 146:7 7456
to satisfy his soul when he is *h* ... Prov 6:30 7456
If thine enemy be *h*, give him ... Prov 25:21 7456
but to the *h* soul every bitter ... Prov 27:7 7456
through it, hardly bestead and *h* ... Is 8:21 7456
pass, that when they shall be *h* ... Is 8:21 7456
snatch on the right hand, and be *h* ... Is 9:20 7456
even be as when an *h* man dreameth ... Is 29:8 7456
to make empty the soul of the *h* ... Is 32:6 7456
yea, he is *h*, and his strength ... Is 44:12 7456
it not to deal thy bread to the *h* ... Is 58:7 7456
thou draw out thy soul to the *h* ... Is 58:10 7456
shall eat, but ye shall be *h* ... Is 65:13 7456
hath given his bread to the *h* ... Eze 18:7 7456
but hath given his bread to the *h* ... Eze 18:16 7456
were come from Bethany, he was *h* ... Mk 11:12 *3983*
filled the *h* with good things ... Lk 1:53 *3983*
And he became very *h*, and would ... Acts 10:10 *4361*
and one is *h*, and another is ... 1Cor 11:21 *3983*
both to be full and to be *h* ... Phil 4:12 *3983*

HUNT {12}
to the field to *h* for venison ... Gen 27:5 6679
as when one doth *h* a partridge in ... 1Sa 26:20 7291
Wilt thou *h* the prey for the lion ... Job 38:39 6679
evil shall *h* the violent man to ... Ps 140:11 6679
the adulteress will *h* for the ... Prov 6:26 6679
they shall *h* them from every ... Jer 16:16 6679
They *h* our steps, that we cannot ... Lam 4:18 6679
head of every stature to *h* souls ... Eze 13:18 6679
Will ye *h* the souls of my people, ... Eze 13:18 6679
wherewith ye there *h* the souls to ... Eze 13:20 6679
souls that ye *h* to make them fly ... Eze 13:20 6679
they *h* every man his brother with ... Mic 7:2 6679

HUNTED {1}
be no more in your hand to be *h* ... Eze 13:21 4686

HUNTER {4}
He was a mighty *h* before the LORD ... Gen 10:9 6718
the mighty *h* before the LORD ... Gen 10:9 6718
and Esau was a cunning *h*, a man of ... Gen 25:27 6718
as a roe from the hand of the *h* ... Prov 6:5 6718

HUNTERS {1}
and after will I send for many *h* ... Jer 16:16 6719

HUNTEST {2}
yet thou *h* my soul to take it ... 1Sa 24:11 6658
Thou *h* me as a fierce lion ... Job 10:16 6679

HUNTETH {1}
that sojourn among you, which *h* ... Lev 17:13 6679

HUNTING {2}
his brother came in from his *h* ... Gen 27:30 6718
not that which he took in *h* ... Prov 12:27 6718

HUPHAM *(hu'-fam)* {1} See HUPPIM, HUPHAMITES. *A son of Benjamin.*
of *H*, the family of the ... Num 26:39 2349

HUPHAMITES *(hu'-fam-ites)* {1} *Descendants of Hupham.*
of Hupham, the family of the *H* ... Num 26:39 2350

HUPPAH *(hup'-pah)* {1} *A priest.*
The thirteenth to *H*, the ... 1Chr 24:13 2647

HUPPIM *(hup'-pim)* {3} See HUPHAM. *Head of a Benjamite family.*
Ehi, and Rosh, Muppim, and *H* ... Gen 46:21 2650
Shuppim also, and *H*, the children ... 1Chr 7:12 2650
took to wife the sister of *H* ... 1Chr 7:15 2650

HUPPITES See HUPPIM.

HUR *(hur)* {16}
1. Assisted Moses at Rephidim.
H went up to the top of the hill ... Ex 17:10 2354
H stayed up his hands, the one on ... Ex 17:12 2354
behold, Aaron and *H* are with you ... Ex 24:14 2354
2. A son of Caleb.
the son of Uri, the son of *H* ... Ex 31:2 2354
the son of Uri, the son of *H* ... Ex 35:30 2354
the son of Uri, the son of *H* ... Ex 38:22 2354
him Ephrath, which bare him *H* ... 1Chr 2:19 2354
H begat Uri, and Uri begat ... 1Chr 2:20 2354
the son of Uri, the son of *H* ... 2Chr 1:5 2354
3. A Midianite king.
Evi, and Rekem, and Zur, and *H* ... Num 31:8 2354
Evi, and Rekem, and Zur, and *H* ... Josh 13:21 2354
4. An officer of Solomon.
The son of *H*, in mount Ephraim ... 1Kin 4:8 2354
5. Father of Caleb.
the sons of Caleb the son of *H* ... 1Chr 2:50 2354
These are the sons of *H*, the ... 1Chr 4:4 2354
6. A descendant of Judah.
Pharez, Hezron, and Carmi, and *H* ... 1Chr 4:1 2354
7. A rebuilder of Jerusalem's wall.
repaired Rephaiah the son of *H* ... Neh 3:9 2354

HURAI *(hu'-rahee)* {1} See HIDDAI. *A "mighty man" of David.*
H of the brooks of Gaash, Abiel ... 1Chr 11:32 2360

HURAM *(hu'-ram)* {12} See HIRAM.
1. Son of Bela.
And Gera, and Shephuphan, and *H* ... 1Chr 8:5 2361
2. Same as Hiram 1.
Solomon sent to *H* the king of ... 2Chr 2:3 2361
Then *H* the king of Tyre answered ... 2Chr 2:11 2438
H said moreover, Blessed be the ... 2Chr 2:12 2361
understanding, of *H* my father's, ... 2Chr 2:13 2438
That the cities which *H* had ... 2Chr 8:2 2438
H sent him by the hands of his ... 2Chr 8:18 2438
And the servants also of *H* ... 2Chr 9:10 2438
Tarshish with the servants of *H* ... 2Chr 9:21 2438
3. Same as Hiram 2.
H made the pots, and the shovels, ... 2Chr 4:11 2361
H finished the work that he was ... 2Chr 4:11 2361
did *H* his father make to king ... 2Chr 4:16 2361

HURAM-ABI See HURAM.

HURI *(hu'-ri)* {1} *Father of Abihail.*
children of Abihail the son of *H* ... 1Chr 5:14 2359

HURL {1}
or *h* at him by laying of wait, ... Num 35:20 7993

HURLETH {1}
as a storm *h* him out of his place ... Job 27:21 8175

HURLING {1}
hand and the left in *h* stones ... 1Chr 12:2

HURT {63}
wounding, and a young man to my *h* ... Gen 4:23 2250
That thou wilt do us no *h* ... Gen 26:29 7451
but God suffered him not to *h* me ... Gen 31:7 7489
the power of my hand to do you *h* ... Gen 31:29 7451
h a woman with child, so that her ... Ex 21:22 5062
And if one man's ox *h* another's ... Ex 21:35 5062
and it die, or be *h*, or driven ... Ex 22:10 7665
of his neighbour, and it be *h* ... Ex 22:14 7665
neither have I *h* one of them ... Num 16:15 7489
then he will turn and do you *h* ... Josh 24:20 7489
there is peace to thee, and no *h* ... 1Sa 20:21 1697
Behold, David seeketh thy *h* ... 1Sa 24:9 7451
we *h* them not, neither was there ... 1Sa 25:7 3637
good unto us, and we were not *h* ... 1Sa 25:15 3637
rise against thee to do thee *h* ... 2Sa 18:32 7451
shouldest thou meddle to thy *h* ... 2Kin 14:10 7451
shouldest thou meddle to thine *h* ... 2Chr 25:19 7451
damage grow to the *h* of the kings ... Ezr 4:22 5142
hand on such as sought their *h* ... Est 9:2 7451
may *h* a man as thou art ... Job 35:8
He that sweareth to his own *h* ... Ps 15:4 7489
to confusion that devise my *h* ... Ps 35:4 7451
together that rejoice at mine *h* ... Ps 35:26 7451
they that seek my *h* speak ... Ps 38:12 7451
against me do they devise my *h* ... Ps 41:7 7451
to confusion, that desire my *h* ... Ps 70:2 7451
and dishonour that seek my *h* ... Ps 71:13 7451
unto shame, that seek my *h* ... Ps 71:24 7451
Whose feet they *h* with fetters ... Ps 105:18 6031
for the owners thereof to their *h* ... Eccl 5:13 7451
ruleth over another to his own *h* ... Eccl 8:9 7451
stones shall be *h* therewith ... Eccl 10:9 6087
They shall not *h* nor destroy in ... Is 11:9 7489
lest any *h* it, I will keep it ... Is 27:3 6485
They shall not *h* nor destroy in ... Is 65:25 7489
They have healed also the *h* of ... Jer 6:14 7667
walk after other gods to your *h* ... Jer 7:6 7451
For they have healed the *h* of the ... Jer 8:11 7667
For the *h* of the daughter of my ... Jer 8:21 7667
the daughter of my people am I *h* ... Jer 8:21 7665
Woe is me for my *h* ... Jer 10:19 7667
kingdoms of the earth for their *h* ... Jer 24:9 7451
and I will do you no *h* ... Jer 25:6 7489
works of your hands to your own *h* ... Jer 25:7 7451
welfare of this people, but the *h* ... Jer 38:4 7451
of the fire, and they have no *h* ... Dan 3:25 2257
mouths, that they have not *h* me ... Dan 6:22 2255
thee, O king, have I done no *h* ... Dan 6:22 2248
no manner of *h* was found upon him ... Dan 6:23 2257
deadly thing, it shall not *h* them ... Mk 16:18 *984*
he came out of him, and *h* him not ... Lk 4:35 *984*
nothing shall by any means *h* you ... Lk 10:19 *91*
man shall set on thee to *h* thee ... Acts 18:10 *2559*
that this voyage will be with *h* ... Acts 27:10 *5196*
not be *h* of the second death ... Rev 2:11 *91*
see thou *h* not the oil and the ... Rev 6:6 *91*
whom it was given to *h* the earth ... Rev 7:2 *91*
H not the earth, neither the sea, ... Rev 7:3 *91*

not *h* the grass of the earth ... Rev 9:4 *91*
power was to *h* men five months ... Rev 9:10 *91*
had heads, and with them they do *h* ... Rev 9:19 *91*
And if any man will *h* them ... Rev 11:5 *91*
and if any man will *h* them ... Rev 11:5 *91*

HURTFUL {3}
h unto kings and provinces, and ... Ezr 4:15 5142
his servant from the *h* sword ... Ps 144:10 7451
h lusts, which drown men in ... 1Ti 6:9 *983*

HURTING {1}
hath kept me back from *h* thee ... 1Sa 25:34 7489

HUSBAND {120}
and gave also unto her *h* with her ... Gen 3:6 376
and thy desire shall be to thy *h* ... Gen 3:16 376
gave her to her *h* Abram to be his ... Gen 16:3 376
now therefore my *h* will love me ... Gen 29:32 376
time will my *h* be joined unto me ... Gen 29:34 376
matter that thou hast taken my *h* ... Gen 30:15 376
I have given my maiden to my *h* ... Gen 30:18 376
now will my *h* dwell with me, ... Gen 30:20 376
Surely a bloody *h* art thou to me ... Ex 4:25 2860
she said, A bloody *h* thou art ... Ex 4:26 2860
the woman's *h* will lay upon him ... Ex 21:22 1167
is a bondmaid, betrothed to an *h* ... Lev 19:20 376
unto him, which hath had no *h* ... Lev 21:3 376
take a woman put away from her *h* ... Lev 21:7 376
it be hid from the eyes of her *h* ... Num 5:13 376
with another instead of thy *h* ... Num 5:19 376
aside to another instead of thy *h* ... Num 5:20 376
lain with thee beside thine *h* ... Num 5:20 376
have done trespass against her *h* ... Num 5:27 376
aside to another instead of her *h* ... Num 5:29 376
And if she had at all an *h* ... Num 30:6 376
her *h* heard it, and held his peace ... Num 30:7 376
But if her *h* disallowed her on ... Num 30:8 376
her *h* heard it, and held his peace ... Num 30:11 376
But if her *h* hath utterly made ... Num 30:12 376
her *h* hath made them void ... Num 30:12 376
her *h* may establish it ... Num 30:13 376
or her *h* may make it void ... Num 30:13 376
But if her *h* altogether hold his ... Num 30:14 376
shalt go in unto her, and be her *h* ... Deut 21:13 1167
with a woman married to an *h* ... Deut 22:22 1167
a virgin be betrothed unto an *h* ... Deut 22:23 376
And if the latter *h* hate her ... Deut 24:3 376
or if the latter *h* die, which ... Deut 24:3 376
Her former *h*, which sent her away ... Deut 24:4 1167
her *h* out of the hand of him that ... Deut 25:11 376
be evil toward the *h* of her bosom ... Deut 28:56 376
Then the woman came and told her *h* ... Judg 13:6 376
but Manoah her *h* was not with her ... Judg 13:9 376
haste, and ran, and shewed her *h* ... Judg 13:10 376
unto Samson's wife, Entice thy *h* ... Judg 14:15 376
her *h* arose, and went after her, ... Judg 19:3 376
the *h* of the woman that was slain ... Judg 20:4 376
And Elimelech Naomi's *h* died ... Ruth 1:3 376
was left of her two sons and her *h* ... Ruth 1:5 376
each of you in the house of her *h* ... Ruth 1:9 376
for I am too old to have an *h* ... Ruth 1:12 376
I should have an *h* also to night ... Ruth 1:12 376
in law since the death of thine *h* ... Ruth 2:11 376
Then said Elkanah her *h* to her ... 1Sa 1:8 376
for she said unto her *h*, I will ... 1Sa 1:22 376
Elkanah her *h* said unto her, Do ... 1Sa 1:23 376
when she came up with her *h* to ... 1Sa 2:19 376
her *h* were dead, she bowed ... 1Sa 4:19 376
of her father in law and her *h* ... 1Sa 4:21 376
But she told not her *h* Nabal ... 1Sa 25:19 376
sent, and took her from her *h* ... 2Sa 3:15 376
her *h* went with her along weeping ... 2Sa 3:16 376
heard that Uriah her *h* was dead ... 2Sa 11:26 376
she mourned for her *h* ... 2Sa 11:26 1167
a widow woman, and mine *h* is dead ... 2Sa 14:5 376
shall not leave to my *h* neither ... 2Sa 14:7 376
saying, Thy servant my *h* is dead ... 2Kin 4:1 376
And she said unto her *h*, Behold ... 2Kin 4:9 376
hath no child, and her *h* is old ... 2Kin 4:14 376
And she called unto her *h*, and said ... 2Kin 4:22 376
is it well with thy *h* ... 2Kin 4:26 376
woman is a crown to her *h* ... Prov 12:4 1167
The heart of her *h* doth safely ... Prov 31:11 1167
Her *h* is known in the gates, when ... Prov 31:23 1167
her *h* also, and he praiseth her ... Prov 31:28 1167
For thy Maker is thine *h* ... Is 54:5 1167
departeth from her *h*, so have ye ... Jer 3:20 1167
for even the *h* with the wife ... Jer 6:11 376
although I was an *h* unto them ... Jer 31:32 1167
taketh strangers instead of her *h* ... Eze 16:32 376
daughter, that lotheth her *h* ... Eze 16:45 376
or for sister that hath had no *h* ... Eze 44:25 376
not my wife, neither am I her *h* ... Hos 2:2 376
I will go and return to my first *h* ... Hos 2:7 376
sackcloth for the *h* of her youth ... Joel 1:8 1167
Jacob begat Joseph the *h* of Mary ... Mt 1:16 *435*
Then Joseph her *h*, being a just ... Mt 1:19 *435*
if a woman shall put away her *h* ... Mk 10:12 *435*
had lived with an *h* seven years ... Lk 2:36 *435*
from her *h* committeth adultery ... Lk 16:18 *435*
saith unto her, Go, call thy *h* ... Jn 4:16 *435*
answered and said, I have no *h* ... Jn 4:17 *435*
Thou hast well said, I have no *h* ... Jn 4:17 *435*
whom thou now hast is not thy *h* ... Jn 4:18 *435*
have buried thy *h* are at the door ... Acts 5:9 *435*
her forth, buried her by her *h* ... Acts 5:10 *435*
an *h* is bound by the law to her ... Rom 7:2 *5220*
law to her *h* so long as he liveth ... Rom 7:2 *435*
but if the *h* be dead, she is ... Rom 7:2 *435*
is loosed from the law of her *h* ... Rom 7:2 *435*
So then if, while her *h* liveth ... Rom 7:3 *435*
but if her *h* be dead, she is free ... Rom 7:3 *435*
and let every woman have her own *h* ... 1Cor 7:2 *435*
Let the *h* render unto the wife ... 1Cor 7:3 *435*
likewise also the wife unto the *h* ... 1Cor 7:3 *435*
power of her own body, but the *h* ... 1Cor 7:4 *435*
likewise also the *h* hath not ... 1Cor 7:4 *435*
not the wife depart from her *h* ... 1Cor 7:10 *435*
or be reconciled to her *h* ... 1Cor 7:11 *435*
let not the *h* put away his wife ... 1Cor 7:11 *435*
hath an *h* that believeth not ... 1Cor 7:13 *435*
For the unbelieving *h* is ... 1Cor 7:14 *435*
wife is sanctified by the *h* ... 1Cor 7:14 *435*
whether thou shalt save thy *h* ... 1Cor 7:16 *435*
world, how she may please her *h* ... 1Cor 7:34 *435*
the law as long as her *h* liveth ... 1Cor 7:39 *435*
but if her *h* be dead, she is at ... 1Cor 7:39 *435*
for I have espoused you to one *h* ... 2Cor 11:2 *435*
children than she which hath a *h* ... Gal 4:27 *435*
For the *h* is the head of the wife ... Eph 5:23 *435*
wife see that she reverence her *h* ... Eph 5:33 *435*
the *h* of one wife, vigilant, ... 1Ti 3:2 *435*
the *h* of one wife, having ... Titus 1:6 *435*
as a bride adorned for her *h* ... Rev 21:2 *435*

HUSBANDMAN {7}
Noah began to be an *h*, and he ... Gen 9:20 376,127
thee will I break in pieces the *h* ... Jer 51:23 406
they shall call the *h* to mourning ... Amos 5:16 406
say, I am no prophet, I am an *h* ... Zec 13:5 5647
true vine, and my Father is the *h* ... Jn 15:1 *1092*
The *h* that laboureth must be ... 2Ti 2:6 *1092*
the *h* waiteth for the precious ... Jas 5:7 *1092*

HUSBANDMEN {21}
the land to be vinedressers and *h* ... 2Kin 25:12 1461
h also, and vine dressers in the ... 2Chr 26:10 406
the cities thereof together, *h* ... Jer 31:24 406
land for vinedressers and for *h* ... Jer 52:16 3009
Be ye ashamed, O ye *h* ... Joel 1:11 406
built a tower, and let it out to *h* ... Mt 21:33 *1092*
he sent his servants to the *h* ... Mt 21:34 *1092*
the *h* took his servants, and beat ... Mt 21:35 *1092*
But when the *h* saw the son ... Mt 21:38 *1092*
what will he do unto those *h* ... Mt 21:40 *1092*
let out his vineyard unto other *h* ... Mt 21:41 *1092*
built a tower, and let it out to *h* ... Mk 12:1 *1092*
season he sent to the *h* a servant ... Mk 12:2 *1092*
h of the fruit of the vineyard ... Mk 12:2 *1092*
But those *h* said among themselves ... Mk 12:7 *1092*
he will come and destroy the *h* ... Mk 12:9 *1092*
a vineyard, and let it forth to *h* ... Lk 20:9 *1092*
season he sent a servant to the *h* ... Lk 20:10 *1092*
but the *h* beat him, and sent him ... Lk 20:10 *1092*
But when the *h* saw him, they ... Lk 20:14 *1092*
He shall come and destroy these *h* ... Lk 20:16 *1092*

HUSBANDRY {2}
for he loved *h* ... 2Chr 26:10 127
ye are God's *h*, ye are God's ... 1Cor 3:9 *1091*

HUSBAND'S {6}
And if she vowed in her *h* house ... Num 30:10 376
her *h* brother shall go in unto ... Deut 25:5 2993
the duty of an *h* brother unto her ... Deut 25:5 2992
My *h* brother refuseth to raise up ... Deut 25:7 2993
perform the duty of my *h* brother ... Deut 25:7 2992
And Naomi had a kinsman of her *h* ... Ruth 2:1 376

HUSBANDS {19}
my womb, that they may be your *h* ... Ruth 1:11 582
ye stay for them from having *h* ... Ruth 1:13 376
despise their *h* in their eyes ... Est 1:17 1167
shall give to their *h* honour ... Est 1:20 1167
sons, and give your daughters to *h* ... Jer 29:6 582
thy sisters, which lothed their *h* ... Eze 16:45 582
For thou hast had five *h* ... Jn 4:18 *435*
let them ask their *h* at home ... 1Cor 14:35 *435*
submit yourselves unto your own *h* ... Eph 5:22 *435*
be to their own *h* in every thing ... Eph 5:24 *435*
H, love your wives, even as ... Eph 5:25 *435*
submit yourselves unto your own *h* ... Col 3:18 *435*
H, love your wives, and be not ... Col 3:19 *435*
the deacons be the *h* of one wife ... 1Ti 3:12 *435*
to be sober, to love their *h* ... Titus 2:4 *5362*
good, obedient to their own *h* ... Titus 2:5 *435*
be in subjection to your own *h* ... 1Pet 3:1 *435*
in subjection unto their own *h* ... 1Pet 3:5 *435*
Likewise, ye *h*, dwell with them ... 1Pet 3:7 *435*

HUSHAH *(hu'-shah)* {1} See HUSHATHITE, SHUAH.
A son of Ezer.
of Gedor, and Ezer the father of *H* ... 1Chr 4:4 2364

HUSHAI *(hu'-shahee)* {14} *Friend and advisor of David.*
H the Archite came to meet him ... 2Sa 15:32 2365
So *H* David's friend came into the ... 2Sa 15:37 2365
when *H* the Archite, David's ... 2Sa 16:16 2365
that *H* said unto Absalom, God ... 2Sa 16:16 2365
And Absalom said to *H*, Is this thy ... 2Sa 16:17 2365
And *H* said unto Absalom, Nay ... 2Sa 16:18 2365
Call now *H* the Archite also, and ... 2Sa 17:5 2365
when *H* was come to Absalom, ... 2Sa 17:6 2365
H said unto Absalom, The counsel ... 2Sa 17:7 2365
For, said *H*, thou knowest thy ... 2Sa 17:8 2365
The counsel of *H* the Archite is ... 2Sa 17:14 2365
Then said *H* unto Zadok and to ... 2Sa 17:15 2365
Baanah the son of *H* was in Asher ... 1Kin 4:16 2365
H the Archite was the king's ... 1Chr 27:33 2365

HUSHAM *(hu'-sham)* {4} *A king of Edom.*
H of the land of Temani reigned ... Gen 36:34 2367
H died, and Hadad the son of Bedad ... Gen 36:35 2367
H of the land of the Temanites ... 1Chr 1:45 2367
when *H* was dead, Hadad the son of ... 1Chr 1:46 2367

HUSHATHITE *(hu'-shath-ite)* {5} *A descendant of Hushah.*
then Sibbechai the *H* slew Saph ... 2Sa 21:18 2843
the Anethothite, Mebunnai the *H* ... 2Sa 23:27 2843
Sibbecai the *H*, Ilai the Ahohite, ... 1Chr 11:29 2843
time Sibbechai the *H* slew Sippai ... 1Chr 20:4 2843
eighth month was Sibbecai the *H* ... 1Chr 27:11 2843

HUSHIM *(hu'-shim)* {4} See SHUHAM.
1. A son of Dan.
the sons of Dan; *H* ... Gen 46:23 2366
2. Son of Aher.
Huppim, the children of Ir, and *H* ... 1Chr 7:12 2366
3. A wife of Shaharaim.
H and Baara were his wives ... 1Chr 8:8 2366
of *H* he begat Abitub, and Elpaal ... 1Chr 8:11 2366

HUSHITES See HUSHIM.

HUSK {2}
from the kernels even to the *h* ... Num 6:4 2085
ears of corn in the *h* thereof ... 2Kin 4:42 6861

HUSKS {1}
with the *h* that the swine did eat ... Lk 15:16 *2769*

HUZ *(huz)* {1} *A son of Nabor.*
H his firstborn, and Buz his ... Gen 22:21 5780

HUZZAB *(huz'-zab)* {1} *A region in Assyria.*
H shall be led away captive, she ... Nah 2:7 5324

HYMENAEUS *(hy-men-e'-us)* {2} *A false Christian teacher.*
Of whom is *H* and Alexander ... 1Ti 1:20 *5211*
of whom is *H* and Philetus ... 2Ti 2:17 *5211*

HYMN {2}
And when they had sung an *h* ... Mt 26:30 *5214*
And when they had sung an *h* ... Mk 14:26

HYMNS {2}
to yourselves in psalms and *h* ... Eph 5:19 *5215*
one another in psalms and *h* ... Col 3:16 *5215*

HYPOCRISIES {1}
all malice, and all guile, and *h* ... 1Pet 2:1 *5272*

HYPOCRISY {6}
will work iniquity, to practise *h* ... Is 32:6 2612
men, but within ye are full of *h* ... Mt 23:28 *5272*
But he, knowing their *h*, said ... Mk 12:15 *5272*
of the Pharisees, which is *h* ... Lk 12:1 *5272*
Speaking lies in *h* ... 1Ti 4:2 *5272*
without partiality, and without *h* ... Jas 3:17 *505*

HYPOCRITE {10}
for an *h* shall not come before ... Job 13:16 2611
stir up himself against the *h* ... Job 17:8 2611
the joy of the *h* but for a moment ... Job 20:5 2611
For what is the hope of the *h* ... Job 27:8 2611
That the *h* reign not, lest the ... Job 34:30 120,2611
An *h* with his mouth destroyeth ... Prov 11:9 2611
for every one is an *h* and an ... Is 9:17 2611
Thou *h*, first cast out the beam ... Mt 7:5 *5273*
Thou *h*, cast out first the beam ... Lk 6:42 *5273*
answered him, and said, Thou *h* ... Lk 13:15 *5273*

HYPOCRITE'S {1}
and the *h* hope shall perish ... Job 8:13 2611

HYPOCRITES {20}
of the *h* shall be desolate, and fire ... Job 15:34 2611
But the *h* in heart heap up wrath ... Job 36:13 2611
fearfulness hath surprised the *h* ... Is 33:14 120,2611
as the *h* do in the synagogues and ... Mt 6:2 *5273*
thou shalt not be as the *h* are ... Mt 6:5 *5273*
when ye fast, be not, as the *h* ... Mt 6:16 *5273*
Ye *h*, well did Esaias prophesy of ... Mt 15:7 *5273*
O ye *h*, ye can discern the face ... Mt 16:3 *5273*
and said, Why tempt ye me, ye *h* ... Mt 22:18 *5273*
unto you, scribes and Pharisees, *h* ... Mt 23:13 *5273*
unto you, scribes and Pharisees, *h* ... Mt 23:14 *5273*
unto you, scribes and Pharisees, *h* ... Mt 23:15 *5273*
unto you, scribes and Pharisees, *h* ... Mt 23:23 *5273*
unto you, scribes and Pharisees, *h* ... Mt 23:25 *5273*
unto you, scribes and Pharisees, *h* ... Mt 23:27 *5273*
unto you, scribes and Pharisees, *h* ... Mt 23:29 *5273*
him his portion with the *h* ... Mt 24:51 *5273*
hath Esaias prophesied of you *h* ... Mk 7:6 *5273*
unto you, scribes and Pharisees, *h* ... Lk 11:44 *5273*
Ye *h*, ye can discern the face of ... Lk 12:56 *5273*

HYPOCRITICAL {2}
With *h* mockers in feasts, they ... Ps 35:16 2611
will send him against an *h* nation ... Is 10:6 2611

HYSSOP {12}
And ye shall take a bunch of *h* ... Ex 12:22 231
and cedar wood, and scarlet, and *h* ... Lev 14:4 231
wood, and the scarlet, and the *h* ... Lev 14:6 231
and cedar wood, and scarlet, and *h* ... Lev 14:49 231
take the cedar wood, and the *h* ... Lev 14:51 231
the cedar wood, and with the *h* ... Lev 14:52 231
shall take cedar wood, and *h* ... Num 19:6 231
And a clean person shall take *h* ... Num 19:18 231
is in Lebanon even unto the *h* ... 1Kin 4:33 231
Purge me with *h*, and I shall be ... Ps 51:7 231
with vinegar, and put it upon *h* ... Jn 19:29 *5301*
with water, and scarlet wool, and *h* ... Heb 9:19 *5301*

H

I

I See APPENDIX.

IBHAR *(ib'-har)* {3} *A son of David.*
I also, and Elishua, and Nepheg, and 2Sa 5:15 2984
I also, and Elishama, and Eliphelet 1Chr 3:6 2984
And *I*, and Elishua, and Elpalet,............. 1Chr 14:5 2984

IBLEAM *(ib'-le-am)* {3} *A city in Asher.*
Beth-shean and her towns, and *I*........... Josh 17:11 2991
towns, nor the inhabitants of *I*.............. Judg 1:27 2991
going up to Gur, which is by *I*................ 2Kin 9:27 2991

IBNEIAH *(ib-ne-i'-ah)* {1} *A son of Jeroham.*
I the son of Jeroham, and Elah the 1Chr 9:8 2997

IBNIJAH *(ib-ni'-jah)* {1} *A family of exiles.*
the son of Reuel, the son of *I*................. 1Chr 9:8 2998

IBRI *(ib'-ri)* {1} *A descendant of Levi.*
Beno, and Shoham, and Zaccur, and *I*.... 1Chr 24:27 5681

IBSAM See JIBSAM.

IBZAN *(ib'-zan)* {2} *A judge of Israel.*
after him *I* of Beth-lehem judged........... Judg 12:8 78
Then died *I*, and was buried at .... Judg 12:10 78

ICE {3}
are blackish by reason of the *i* .... Job 6:16 7140
Out of whose womb came the *i*............... Job 38:29 7140
casteth forth his *i* like morsels................ Ps 147:17 7140

I-CHABOD *(ik'-a-bod)* {1} See I-CHABOD'S. *Son of Phinehas.*
And she named the child *I*, saying, ... 1Sa 4:21 350

ICHABOD See I-CHABOD.

I-CHABOD'S *(ik'-a-bods)* {1}
I brother, the son of Phinehas, ... 1Sa 14:3 350

ICONIUM *(i-co'-ne-um)* {6} *A city in Asia Minor.*
feet against them, and came unto *I*......... Acts 13:51 *2430*
And it came to pass in *I*, that................. Acts 14:1 *2430*
certain Jews from Antioch and *I*.............. Acts 14:19 *2430*
returned again to Lystra, and to *I*.......... Acts 14:21 *2430*
brethren that were at Lystra and *I*.......... Acts 16:2 *2430*
came unto me at Antioch, at *I*................. 2Ti 3:11 *2430*

IDALAH *(id'-a-lah)* {1} *A town in Zebulun.*
and Nahallal, and Shimron, and *I*........... Josh 19:15 3030

IDBASH *(id'-bash)* {1} *A son of Abi-etam.*
Jezreel, and Ishma, and *I*........................ 1Chr 4:3 3031

IDDO *(id'-do)* {14}
1. Father of Ahinadab.
the son of *I* had Mahanaim 1Kin 4:14 5714
2. A descendant of Gershom.
I his son, Zerah his son, ... 1Chr 6:21 5714
3. A son of Zechariah.
in Gilead, *I* the son of Zechariah 1Chr 27:21 3035
4. A seer.
in the visions of *I* the seer 2Chr 9:29 3260
and of *I* the seer concerning...................... 2Chr 12:15 5714
in the story of the prophet *I*..................... 2Chr 13:22 5714
5. An ancestor of Zechariah.
and Zechariah the son of *I*......................... Ezr 5:1 5714
prophet and Zechariah the son of *I*........... Ezr 6:14 5714
the son of *I* the prophet, saying,.............. Zec 1:1 5714
the son of *I* the prophet, saying,.............. Zec 1:7 5714
6. A Nethinim chief in exile.
I the chief at the place Casiphia .... Ezr 8:17 112
them what they should say unto *I*........... Ezr 8:17 112
7. A priest.
I, Ginnetho, Abijah,.................................. Neh 12:4 5714
Of *I*, Zechariah .... Neh 12:16 5714

IDLE {11}
for they be *i* .... Ex 5:8 7504
he said, Ye are *i*, ye are *i*........................ Ex 5:17 7504
an *i* soul shall suffer hunger.................... Prov 19:15 7423
That every *i* word that men shall .... Mt 12:36 *692*
standing *i* in the marketplace .... Mt 20:3 *692*
out, and found others standing *i*.............. Mt 20:6 *692*
Why stand ye here all the day *i*................ Mt 20:6 *692*
words seemed to them as *i* tales.............. Lk 24:11 *3026*
And withal they learn to be *i*.................... 1Ti 5:13 *692*
and not only *i*, but tattlers also............... 1Ti 5:13 *692*

IDLENESS {3}
and eateth not the bread of *i*.................... Prov 31:27 6104
through *i* of the hands the house .... Eccl 10:18 8220
and abundance of *i* was in her .... Eze 16:49 8252

IDOL {15}
she had made an *i* in a grove................... 1Kin 15:13 4656
and Asa destroyed her *i*, and burnt......... 1Kin 15:13 4656
she had made an *i* in a grove................... 2Chr 15:16 4656
and Asa cut down her *i*, and stamped..... 2Chr 15:16 4656
the *i* which he had made, in the................ 2Chr 33:7 5566
the *i* out of the house of the 2Chr 33:15 5566
Mine *i* hath done them, and my .... Is 48:5 6090
incense, as if he blessed an *i* .... Is 66:3 205
man Coniah a despised broken *i* .... Jer 22:28 6089
Woe to the *i* shepherd that .... Zec 11:17 457
and offered sacrifice unto the *i*................ Acts 7:41 *1497*
we know that an *i* is nothing in 1Cor 8:4 *1497*
the *i* unto this hour eat it as a................ 1Cor 8:7 *1497*
it as a thing offered unto an *i*.................. 1Cor 8:7 *1494*
that the *i* is any thing, or that................. 1Cor 10:19 *1497*

IDOLATER {2}
fornicator, or covetous, or an *i* 1Cor 5:11 *1496*
nor covetous man, who is an *i*.................. Eph 5:5 *1496*

IDOLATERS {5}
or extortioners, or with *i*......................... 1Cor 5:10 *1496*
neither fornicators, nor *i* 1Cor 6:9 *1496*
Neither be ye *i*, as were some of.............. 1Cor 10:7 *1496*
whoremongers, and sorcerers, and *i*......... Rev 21:8 *1496*
whoremongers, and murderers, and *i*....... Rev 22:15 *1496*

IDOLATRIES {1}
banquetings, and abominable *i* 1Pet 4:3 *1495*

IDOLATROUS {1}
And he put down the *i* priests.................. 2Kin 23:5 3649

IDOLATRY {5}
stubbornness is as iniquity and *i* 1Sa 15:23 8655
he saw the city wholly given to *i*............. Acts 17:16 *2712*
my dearly beloved, flee from *i*................. 1Cor 10:14 *1495*
I, witchcraft, hatred, variance,................ Gal 5:20 *1495*
and covetousness, which is *i*.................... Col 3:5 *1495*

IDOL'S {1}
sit at meat in the *i* temple 1Cor 8:10 *1493*

IDOLS {101}
Turn ye not unto *i*, nor make to .... Lev 19:4 457
make you no *i* nor graven image .... Lev 26:1 457
upon the carcases of your *i* .... Lev 26:30 1544
their abominations, and their *i* .... Deut 29:17 1544
it in the house of their *i*.......................... 1Sa 31:9 6091
removed all the *i* that his 1Kin 15:12 1544
very abominably in following *i* 1Kin 21:26 1544
For they served *i*, whereof the 2Kin 17:12 1544
made Judah also to sin with his *i*............ 2Kin 21:11 1544
served the *i* that his father 2Kin 21:21 1544
wizards, and the images, and the *i*.......... 2Kin 23:24 1544
to carry tidings unto their *i*.................... 1Chr 10:9 6091
all the gods of the people are *i*................ 1Chr 16:26 457
put away the abominable *i* out of 2Chr 15:8 8251
fathers, and served groves and *i*.............. 2Chr 24:18 6091
cut down all the *i* throughout all 2Chr 34:7 2553
all the gods of the nations are *i*.............. Ps 96:5 457
that boast themselves of *i*........................ Ps 97:7 457
And they served their *i*............................ Ps 106:36 6091
sacrificed unto the *i* of Canaan................ Ps 106:38 6091
Their *i* are silver and gold, the................. Ps 115:4 6091
The *i* of the heathen are silver .... Ps 135:15 6091
Their land also is full of *i*........................ Is 2:8 457
the *i* he shall utterly abolish .... Is 2:18 457
a man shall cast his *i* of silver.................. Is 2:20 457
his *i* of gold, which they made .... Is 2:20 457
hath found the kingdoms of the *i*............. Is 10:10 457
I have done unto Samaria and her *i*......... Is 10:11 457
so do to Jerusalem and her *i*.................... Is 10:11 6091
the *i* of Egypt shall be moved at .... Is 19:1 457
and they shall seek to the *i* .... Is 19:3 457
shall cast away his *i* of silver .... Is 31:7 457
his *i* of gold, which your own.................. Is 31:7 457
together that are makers of *i*.................. Is 45:16 6736
their *i* were upon the beasts, and............ Is 46:1 6091
with *i* under every green tree .... Is 57:5 410
her *i* are confounded, her images .... Jer 50:2 6091
and they are mad upon their *i*.................. Jer 50:38 367
down your slain men before your *i* .... Eze 6:4 1544
children of Israel before their *i* .... Eze 6:5 1544
your *i* may be broken and cease, and...... Eze 6:6 1544
which go a whoring after their *i* .... Eze 6:9 1544
their *i* round about their altars .... Eze 6:13 1544
offer sweet savour to all their *i* .... Eze 6:13 1544
all the *i* of the house of Israel, ... Eze 8:10 1544
set up their *i* in their heart...................... Eze 14:3 1544
setteth up his *i* in his heart .... Eze 14:4 1544
to the multitude of his *i* .... Eze 14:4 1544
estranged from me through their *i*.......... Eze 14:5 1544
and turn yourselves from your *i*............... Eze 14:6 1544
and setteth up his *i* in his heart .... Eze 14:7 1544
lovers, and with all the *i* of thy............... Eze 16:36 1544
to the *i* of the house of Israel .... Eze 18:6 1544
hath lifted up his eyes to the *i* .... Eze 18:12 1544
to the *i* of the house of Israel .... Eze 18:15 1544
yourselves with the *i* of Egypt................... Eze 20:7 1544
did they forsake the *i* of Egypt................. Eze 20:8 1544
their heart went after their *i* .... Eze 20:16 1544
defile yourselves with their *i*.................. Eze 20:18 1544
eyes were after their fathers' *i* .... Eze 20:24 1544
yourselves with all your *i* .... Eze 20:31 1544
Go ye, serve ye every one his *i*................. Eze 20:39 1544
with your gifts, and with your *i*.............. Eze 20:39 1544
maketh *i* against herself to....................... Eze 22:3 1544
in thine *i* which thou hast made .... Eze 22:4 1544
with all their *i* she defiled....................... Eze 23:7 1544
thou art polluted with their *i*................... Eze 23:30 1544
with their *i* have they committed............ Eze 23:37 1544
slain their children to their *i*................. Eze 23:39 1544
ye shall bear the sins of your *i* .... Eze 23:49 1544
I will also destroy the *i*........................... Eze 30:13 1544
lift up your eyes toward your *i*............... Eze 33:25 1544
for their *i* wherewith they had................ Eze 36:18 1544
filthiness, and from all your *i*................. Eze 36:25 1544
themselves any more with their *i* .... Eze 37:23 1544
astray away from me after their *i*........... Eze 44:10 1544
unto them before their *i*, and.................. Eze 44:12 1544
Ephraim is joined to *i*............................... Hos 4:17 6091
their gold have they made them *i*............. Hos 8:4 6091
and *i* according to their own.................... Hos 13:2 6091
What have I to do any more with *i*........... Hos 14:8 6091
all the *i* thereof will I lay .... Mic 1:7 6091
trusteth therein, to make dumb *i* .... Hab 2:18 457
For the *i* have spoken vanity, and........... Zec 10:2 8655
names of the *i* out of the land .... Zec 13:2 6091
they abstain from pollutions of *i*............. Acts 15:20 *1497*
abstain from meats offered to *i*................ Acts 15:29 *1494*
from things offered to *i*, and from........... Acts 21:25 *1494*
thou that abhorrest *i*, dost thou .... Rom 2:22 *1497*
as touching things offered unto *i* 1Cor 8:1 *1494*
are offered in sacrifice unto *i* 1Cor 8:4 *1494*
things which are offered to *i* 1Cor 8:10 *1494*
in sacrifice to *i* is any thing..................... 1Cor 10:19 *1494*
is offered in sacrifice unto *i* 1Cor 10:28 *1494*
carried away unto these dumb *i*............... 1Cor 12:2 *1497*
hath the temple of God with *i*.................. 2Cor 6:16 *1497*
to God from *i* to serve the living.............. 1Th 1:9 *1497*
children, keep yourselves from *i*.............. 1Jn 5:21 *1497*
to eat things sacrificed unto *i* .... Rev 2:14 *1494*
to eat things sacrificed unto *i* .... Rev 2:20 *1494*
i of gold, and silver, and brass, ... Rev 9:20 *1497*

IDUMAEA *(i-doo-me'-ah)* {1} See IDUMEA. *Greek form of Edom.*
And from Jerusalem, and from *I* .... Mk 3:8 *2401*

IDUMEA *(i-doo-me'-ah)* {4} See EDOM, IDUMAEA. *Same as Edom.*
behold, it shall come down upon *I*........... Is 34:5 123
great slaughter in the land of *I*............... Is 34:6 123
desolate, O mount Seir, and all *I*............. Eze 35:15 123
of the heathen, and against all *I* .... Eze 36:5 123

IEZERITES See JEEZERITES.

IF See APPENDIX.

IGAL *(i'-gal)* {2} See IGEAL.
1. One of the twelve spies.
of Issachar, *I* the son of Joseph................ Num 13:7 3008
2. A "mighty man" of David.
I the son of Nathan of Zobah,.................. 2Sa 23:36 3008

IGDALIAH *(ig-da-li'-ah)* {1} *Father of Hanan.*
the sons of Hanan, the son of *I* .... Jer 35:4 3012

IGEAL *(ig'-e-al)* {1} See IGAL. *A royal descendant of Judah.*
Hattush, and *I*, and Bariah, and 1Chr 3:22 3008

IGNOMINY {1}
also contempt, and with *i* reproach......... Prov 18:3 7036

IGNORANCE {18}
If a soul shall sin through *i*..................... Lev 4:2 7684
of Israel sin through *i*, and the................ Lev 4:13 7686
done somewhat through *i* against .... Lev 4:22 7684
the common people sin through *i*............. Lev 4:27 7684
a trespass, and sin through *i* .... Lev 5:15 7684
concerning his *i* wherein he erred........... Lev 5:18 7684
if ought be committed by *i* .... Num 15:24 7684
for it is *i*.. Num 15:25 7684
before the LORD, for their *i*...................... Num 15:25 7684
seeing all the people were in *i*.................. Num 15:26 7684
And if any soul sin through *i* .... Num 15:27 7684
he sinneth by *i* before the LORD .... Num 15:28 7684
for him that sinneth through *i* .... Num 15:29 7684
I wot that through *i* ye did it .... Acts 3:17 *52*
the times of this *i* God winked at............ Acts 17:30 *52*
God through the *i* that is in them........... Eph 4:18 *52*
to the former lusts in your *i* 1Pet 1:14 *52*
to silence the *i* of foolish men 1Pet 2:15 *56*

IGNORANT {17}
So foolish was I, and *i*.............................. Ps 73:22 3808,3045
they are all *i*, they are all dumb...... Is 56:10 3808,3045
father, though Abraham be *i* of us.. Is 63:16 3808,3045
and *i* men, they marvelled........................ Acts 4:13 *2399*
Now I would not have you *i* .... Rom 1:13 *50*
For they being *i* of God's .... Rom 10:3 *50*
ye should be *i* of this mystery.................. Rom 11:25 *50*
I would not that ye should be *i* 1Cor 10:1 *50*
brethren, I would not have you *i* 1Cor 12:1 *50*
any man be *i*, let him be *i*........................ 1Cor 14:38 *50*
have you *i* of our trouble which 2Cor 1:8 *50*
for we are not *i* of his devices 2Cor 2:11 *50*
But I would not have you to be *i*.............. 1Th 4:13 *50*
Who can have compassion on the *i* .... Heb 5:2 *50*
For this they willingly are *i* of................. 2Pet 3:5 *2990*
be not *i* of this one thing, that 2Pet 3:8 *2990*

IGNORANTLY {4}
for the soul that sinneth *i*....................... Num 15:28 7683
Whoso killeth his neighbour *i* .... Deut 19:4 1097,1847
Whom therefore ye *i* worship .... Acts 17:23 *50*
because I did it *i* in unbelief 1Ti 1:13 *50*

IIM *(i'-im)* {2} See IJE-ABARIM.
1. A Hebrew encampment in the wilderness.
And they departed from *I*, and................. Num 33:45 5864
2. A town in Judah.
Baalah, and *I*, and Azem,......................... Josh 15:29 5864

IJE-ABARIM *(i'-je-ab'-a-rim)* {2} See IIM. *Same as Iim 1.*
from Oboth, and pitched at *I* .... Num 21:11 5863
from Oboth, and pitched in *I* .... Num 33:44 5863

IJON *(i'-jon)* {3} *A town in Naphtali.*
the cities of Israel, and smote *I*............... 1Kin 15:20 5859
king of Assyria, and took *I*....................... 2Kin 15:29 5859
and they smote *I*, and Dan, and............... 2Chr 16:4 5859

IKKESH *(ik'-kesh)* {3} *Father of Ira.*
Ira the son of *I* the Tekoite...................... 2Sa 23:26 6142
Ira the son of *I* the Tekoite...................... 1Chr 11:28 6142
was Ira the son of *I* the Tekoite............... 1Chr 27:9 6142

ILAI *(i'-lahee)* {1} See ZALMON. *A "mighty man" of David.*
the Hushathite, *I* the Ahohite,.................. 1Chr 11:29 5866

ILL {15}
i favoured and leanfleshed .... Gen 41:3 7451
the *i* favoured and leanfleshed .... Gen 41:4 7451

very *i* favoured and leanfleshed, Gen 41:19 7451
the *i* favoured kine did eat up Gen 41:20 7451
but they were still *i* favoured Gen 41:21 7451
i favoured kine that came up Gen 41:27 7451
Wherefore dealt ye so *i* with me Gen 43:6 7489
or blind, or have any *i* blemish Deut 15:21 7451
it shall go *i* with him that is Job 20:26 3415
so that it went *i* with Moses for Ps 106:32 3415
it shall be *i* with him Is 3:11 7451
but if it seem *i* unto thee to Jer 40:4 7489
his *i* savour shall come up, Joel 2:20 6709
themselves *i* in their doings Mic 3:4 7489
Love worketh no *i* to his Rom 13:10 *2556*

ILLUMINATED {1}
days, in which, after ye were *i* Heb 10:32 *5461*

ILLYRICUM *(il-lir'-ic-um)* {1} *A Roman Adriatic province.*
Jerusalem, and round about unto *I* Rom 15:19 *2437*

IMAGE {102}
said, Let us make man in our *i* Gen 1:26 6754
So God created man in his own *i* Gen 1:27 6754
in the *i* of God created he him Gen 1:27 6754
in his own likeness, after his *i* Gen 5:3 6754
for in the *i* of God made he man Gen 9:6 6754
not make unto thee any graven *i* Ex 20:4
make you no idols nor graven *i* Lev 26:1
neither rear you up a standing *i* Lev 26:1 6676
up any *i* of stone in your land Lev 26:1 4906
and make you a graven *i*, the Deut 4:16
with you, and make you a graven *i* Deut 4:23
yourselves, and make a graven *i* Deut 4:25
shalt not make thee any graven *i* Deut 5:8
they have made them a molten *i* Deut 9:12
shalt thou set thee up any *i* Deut 16:22 4676
maketh any graven or molten *i* Deut 27:15
make a graven *i* and a molten *i* Judg 17:3
a graven *i* and a molten *i* Judg 17:4
and a graven *i*, and a molten *i* Judg 18:14
in thither, and took the graven *i* Judg 18:17
and the teraphim, and the molten *i* Judg 18:17
house, and fetched the carved *i* Judg 18:18
and the teraphim, and the molten *i* Judg 18:18
and the teraphim, and the graven *i* Judg 18:20
of Dan set up the graven *i* Judg 18:30
they set them up Micah's graven *i* Judg 18:31
And Michal took an *i*, and laid it 1Sa 19:13 8655
behold, there was an *i* in the bed 1Sa 19:16 8655
for he put away the *i* of Baal 2Kin 3:2 4676
And they brake down the *i* of Baal 2Kin 10:27 4676
he set a graven *i* of the grove 2Kin 21:7
he made two cherubims of *i* work 2Chr 3:10 6816
And he set a carved *i*, the idol 2Chr 33:7
an *i* was before mine eyes, there Job 4:16 8544
thou shalt despise their *i* Ps 73:20 6754
Horeb, and worshipped the molten *i* Ps 106:19
The workman melteth a graven *i* Is 40:19
workman to prepare a graven *i* Is 40:20
a graven *i* are all of them vanity Is 44:9
or molten a graven *i* that is Is 44:10
he maketh it a graven *i*, and Is 44:15
maketh a god, even his graven *i* Is 44:17
set up the wood of their graven *i* Is 45:20
hath done them, and my graven *i* Is 48:5
my graven *i*, and my molten *i* Is 48:5
is confounded by the graven *i* Jer 10:14 6459
for his molten *i* is falsehood Jer 10:14
is confounded by the graven *i* Jer 51:17 6459
for his molten *i* is falsehood Jer 51:17
was the seat of the *i* of jealousy Eze 8:3 5566
this *i* of jealousy in the entry Eze 8:5 5566
king, sawest, and behold a great *i* Dan 2:31 6755
This great *i*, whose brightness Dan 2:31 6755
which smote the *i* upon his feet Dan 2:34 6755
the *i* became a great mountain Dan 2:35 6755
the king made an *i* of gold Dan 3:1 6755
i which Nebuchadnezzar the king Dan 3:2 6755
unto the dedication of the *i* that Dan 3:3 6755
they stood before the *i* that Dan 3:3 6755
worship the golden *i* that Dan 3:5 6755
worshipped the golden *i* that Dan 3:7 6755
fall down and worship the golden *i* Dan 3:10 6755
golden *i* which thou hast set up Dan 3:12 6755
the golden *i* which I have set up Dan 3:14 6755
worship the *i* which I have made Dan 3:15 6755
golden *i* which thou hast set up Dan 3:18 6755
a sacrifice, and without an *i* Hos 3:4 6755
gods will I cut off the graven *i* Nah 1:14
the graven *i* and the molten *i* Nah 1:14
What profiteth the graven *i* that Hab 2:18
the molten *i*, and a teacher of Hab 2:18
saith unto them, Whose is this *i* Mt 22:20 *1504*
saith unto them, Whose is this *i* Mk 12:16 *1504*
Whose *i* and superscription hath it Lk 20:24 *1504*
of the *i* which fell down from Acts 19:35
an *i* made like to corruptible man Rom 1:23 *1504*
be conformed to the *i* of his Son Rom 8:29 *1504*
bowed the knee to the *i* of Baal Rom 11:4
head, forasmuch as he is the *i* 1Cor 11:7 *1504*
we have borne the *i* of the earthy 1Cor 15:49 *1504*
also bear the *i* of the heavenly 1Cor 15:49
the same *i* from glory to glory 2Cor 3:18 *1504*
of Christ, who is the *i* of God 2Cor 4:4 *1504*
Who is the *i* of the invisible God Col 1:15 *1504*
the *i* of him that created him Col 3:10 *1504*
the express *i* of his person, and Heb 1:3 *5481*
not the very *i* of the things, can Heb 10:1 *1504*
should make an *i* to the beast Rev 13:14 *1504*
give life unto the *i* of the beast Rev 13:15 *1504*
that the *i* of the beast should Rev 13:15 *1504*
i of the beast should be killed Rev 13:15 *1504*
man worship the beast and his *i* Rev 14:9 *1504*
who worship the beast and his *i* Rev 14:11 *1504*
over the beast, and over his *i* Rev 15:2 *1504*
upon them which worshipped his *i* Rev 16:2 *1504*
and them that worshipped his *i* Rev 19:20 *1504*
the beast, neither his *i*, neither Rev 20:4 *1504*

IMAGERY {1}
man in the chambers of his *i* Eze 8:12 4906

IMAGE'S {1}
This *i* head was of fine gold, his Dan 2:32 6755

IMAGES {72}
Rachel had stolen the *i* that were Gen 31:19 8655
Now Rachel had taken the *i* Gen 31:34 8655
he searched, but found not the *i* Gen 31:35 8655
them, and quite break down their *i* Ex 23:24 4676
their altars, break their *i* Ex 34:13 4676
high places, and cut down your *i* Lev 26:30 2553
and destroy all their molten *i* Num 33:52
altars, and break down their *i* Deut 7:5 4676
and burn their graven *i* with fire Deut 7:5
The graven *i* of their gods shall Deut 7:25
down the graven *i* of their gods Deut 12:3
ye shall make *i* of your emerods 1Sa 6:5 6754
i of your mice that mar the land 1Sa 6:5 6754
of gold and the *i* of their emerods 1Sa 6:11 6754
And there they left their *i* 2Sa 5:21 6091
made thee other gods, and molten *i* 1Kin 14:9
also built them high places, and *i* 1Kin 14:23 4676
they brought forth the *i* out of 2Kin 10:26 4676
his *i* brake they in pieces 2Kin 11:18 6754
And they set them up *i* and groves 2Kin 17:10 4676
their God, and made them molten *i* 2Kin 17:16
LORD, and served their graven *i* 2Kin 17:41
the high places, and brake the *i* 2Kin 18:4 4676
And he brake in pieces the *i* 2Kin 23:14 4676
spirits, and the wizards, and the *i* 2Kin 23:24 8655
high places, and brake down the *i* 2Chr 14:3 4676
of Judah the high places and the *i* 2Chr 14:5
his *i* in pieces, and slew Mattan 2Chr 23:17 6754
and made also molten *i* for Baalim 2Chr 28:2
Judah, and brake the *i* in pieces 2Chr 31:1 4676
and set up groves and graven *i* 2Chr 33:19
i which Manasseh his father had 2Chr 33:22
carved *i*, and the molten *i* 2Chr 34:3
and the *i*, that were on high above 2Chr 34:4 2553
carved *i*, and the molten *i* 2Chr 34:4
beaten the graven *i* into powder 2Chr 34:7 6456
to jealousy with their graven *i* Ps 78:58 6456
be all they that serve graven *i* Ps 97:7
whose graven *i* did excel them of Is 10:10
made, either the groves, or the *i* Is 17:8 2553
all the graven *i* of her gods he Is 21:9
groves and *i* shall not stand up Is 27:9 2553
of thy graven *i* of silver Is 30:22
ornament of thy molten *i* of gold Is 30:22
their molten *i* are wind and Is 41:29
neither my praise to graven *i* Is 42:8
ashamed, that trust in graven *i* Is 42:17
i, that say to the molten *i* Is 42:17
me to anger with their graven *i* Jer 8:19
break also the *i* of Beth-shemesh Jer 43:13 4676
her *i* are broken in pieces Jer 50:2 1544
for it is the land of graven *i* Jer 50:38
upon the graven *i* of Babylon Jer 51:47
do judgment upon her graven *i* Jer 51:52
and your *i* shall be broken Eze 6:4 2553
your *i* may be cut down, and your Eze 6:6 2553
but they made the *i* of their Eze 7:20 6754
and madest to thyself *i* of men Eze 16:17 6754
bright, he consulted with *i* Eze 21:21 8655
the *i* of the Chaldeans pourtrayed Eze 23:14 6754
I will cause their *i* to cease out Eze 30:13 457
his land they have made goodly *i* Hos 10:1 4676
altars, he shall spoil their *i* Hos 10:2 4676
and burned incense to graven *i* Hos 11:2
them molten *i* of their silver Hos 13:2
of your Moloch and Chiun your *i* Amos 5:26 6754
all the graven *i* thereof shall be Mic 1:7
Thy graven *i* also will I cut off, Mic 5:13 4676
thy standing *i* out of the midst Mic 5:13

IMAGINATION {14}
that every *i* of the thoughts of Gen 6:5 3336
for the *i* of man's heart is evil Gen 8:21 3336
I walk in the *i* of mine heart Deut 29:19 8307
for I know their *i* which they go Deut 31:21 3336
keep this for ever in the *i* of 1Chr 29:18 3336
after the *i* of their evil heart Jer 3:17 8307
in the *i* of their evil heart, and Jer 7:24 8307
after the *i* of their own heart Jer 9:14 8307
one in the *i* of their evil heart Jer 11:8 8307
walk in the *i* of their heart Jer 13:10 8307
one after the *i* of his evil heart Jer 16:12 8307
one do the *i* of his evil heart Jer 18:12 8307
after the *i* of his own heart Jer 23:17 8307
proud in the *i* of their hearts Lk 1:51 *1271*

IMAGINATIONS {6}
all the *i* of the thoughts 1Chr 28:9 3336
An heart that deviseth wicked *i* Prov 6:18 4284
and all their *i* against me Lam 3:60 4284
O LORD, and all their *i* against me Lam 3:61 4284
but became vain in their *i* Rom 1:21 *1261*
Casting down *i*, and every high 2Cor 10:5 *3053*

IMAGINE {12}
Do ye *i* to reprove words, and the Job 6:26 2803
which ye wrongfully *i* against me Job 21:27 2554
the people *i* a vain thing Ps 2:1 1897
i deceits all the day long Ps 38:12 1897
How long will ye *i* mischief Ps 62:3 2050
Which *i* mischiefs in their heart Ps 140:2 2803
in the heart of them that *i* evil Prov 12:20 2790
yet do they *i* mischief against me Hos 7:15 2803
What do ye *i* against the LORD Nah 1:9 2803
let none of you *i* evil against Zec 7:10 2803
let none of you *i* evil in your Zec 8:17
rage, and the people *i* vain things Acts 4:25 *3191*

IMAGINED {3}
them, which they have *i* to do Gen 11:6 2161
in the devices that they have *i* Ps 10:2 2803
they *i* a mischievous device, Ps 21:11 2803

IMAGINETH {1}
that *i* evil against the LORD, a Nah 1:11 2803

IMLA *(im'-lah)* {2} See IMLAH. *Father of Michaiah.*
the same is Micaiah the son of *I* 2Chr 18:7 3229
quickly Micaiah the son of *I* 2Chr 18:8 3229

IMLAH *(im'-lah)* {2} See IMLA. *Same as Imla.*
yet one man, Micaiah the son of *I* 1Kin 22:8 3229
hither Micaiah the son of *I* 1Kin 22:9 3229

IMMANUEL *(im-man'-u-el)* {1} See EMMANUEL. *A Messianic name.*
a son, and shall call his name *I* Is 7:14 6005
fill the breadth of thy land, O *I* Is 8:8 6005

IMMEDIATELY {55}
they *i* left the ship and their Mt 4:22 *2112*
i his leprosy was cleansed Mt 8:3 *2112*
i Jesus stretched forth his hand, Mt 14:31 *2112*
i their eyes received sight, and Mt 20:34 *2112*
I after the tribulation of those Mt 24:29 *2112*
And *i* the cock crew Mt 26:74 *2112*
i the spirit driveth him into the Mk 1:12 *2117*
And *i* his fame spread abroad Mk 1:28 *2117*
i the fever left her, and she Mk 1:31 *2112*
i the leprosy departed from him, Mk 1:42 *2112*
i when Jesus perceived in his Mk 2:8 *2112*
i he arose, took up the bed, and Mk 2:12 *2112*
i it sprang up, because it had no Mk 4:5 *2112*
they have heard, Satan cometh *i* Mk 4:15 *2112*
i receive it with gladness Mk 4:16 *2112*
word's sake, *i* they are offended Mk 4:17 *2112*
i he putteth in the sickle, Mk 4:29 *2112*
i there met him out of the tombs Mk 5:2 *2112*
i knowing in himself that virtue Mk 5:30 *2112*
i the king sent an executioner, Mk 6:27 *2112*
i he talked with them, and saith Mk 6:50 *2112*
i he received his sight, and Mk 10:52 *2112*
And *i*, while he yet spake, cometh Mk 14:43 *2112*
And his mouth was opened *i* Lk 1:64 *3916*
i she arose and ministered unto Lk 4:39 *3916*
i the leprosy departed from him Lk 5:13 *2112*
i he rose up before them, and took Lk 5:25 *3916*
did beat vehemently, and *i* it fell Lk 6:49 *2112*
i her issue of blood stanched Lk 8:44 *3916*
him, and how she was healed *i* Lk 8:47 *3916*
they may open unto him *i* Lk 12:36 *2112*
i she was made straight, and Lk 13:13 *3916*
i he received his sight, and Lk 18:43 *3916*
kingdom of God should *i* appear Lk 19:11 *3916*
peace, the stones would *i* cry out Lk 19:40
And *i*, while he yet spake, the Lk 22:60 *3916*
i the man was made whole, and took Jn 5:9 *2112*
i the ship was at the land Jn 6:21 *2112*
received the sop went *i* out Jn 13:30 *2112*
and *i* the cock crew Jn 18:27 *2112*
forth, and entered into a ship *i* Jn 21:3 *2117*
i his feet and ancle bones Acts 3:7 *3916*
i there fell from his eyes as it Acts 9:18 *2112*
And he arose *i* Acts 9:34 *2112*
I therefore I sent to thee Acts 10:33 *1824*
i there were three men already Acts 11:11 *1824*
i the angel of the Lord smote him Acts 12:23 *3916*
i there fell on him a mist and a Acts 13:11 *3916*
i we endeavoured to go into Acts 16:10 *2112*
i all the doors were opened, and Acts 16:26 *3916*
the brethren *i* sent away Paul and Acts 17:10 *2112*
then *i* the brethren sent away Acts 17:14 *2112*
Who *i* took soldiers and centurions Acts 21:32 *1824*
i I conferred not with flesh and Gal 1:16 *2112*
And *i* I was in the spirit Rev 4:2 *2112*

IMMER *(im'-mur)* {10}
1. Father of Meshillemeth.
son of Meshillemith, the son of *I* 1Chr 9:12 564
The children of *I*, a thousand Ezr 2:37 564
And of the sons of *I* Ezr 10:20 564
The children of *I*, a thousand Neh 7:40 564
son of Meshillemoth, the son of *I* Neh 11:13 564
2. A sanctuary servant.
to Bilgah, the sixteenth to *I* 1Chr 24:14 564
3. An exile.
Tel-harsa, Cherub, Addan, and *I* Ezr 2:59 564
Tel-haresha, Cherub, Addon, and *I* Neh 7:61 564
4. Father of Zadok.
son of *I* over against his house Neh 3:29 564
5. A priest.
Pashur the son of *I* the priest Jer 20:1 564

IMMORTAL {1}
Now unto the King eternal, *i* 1Ti 1:17 *862*

IMMORTALITY {5}
- seek for glory and honour and *i* ... Rom 2:7 *861*
- and this mortal must put on *i* ... 1Cor 15:53 *110*
- this mortal shall have put on *i* ... 1Cor 15:54 *110*
- Who only hath *i*, dwelling in the ... 1Ti 6:16 *110*
- *i* to light through the gospel ... 2Ti 1:10 *861*

IMMUTABILITY {1}
- of promise the *i* of his counsel ... Heb 6:17 *276*

IMMUTABLE {1}
- That by two *i* things, in which it ... Heb 6:18 *276*

IMNA *(im'-nah)* {1} See IMNAH, JIMNA. *A son of Helem.*
- Zophah, and *I*, and Shelesh, and Amal ... 1Chr 7:35 3234

IMNAH *(im'-nah)* {2} See IMNA, JIMNAH.
- *1. Son of Asher.*
- *I*, and Isuah, and Ishuai, and Beriah ... 1Chr 7:30 3232
- *2. Father of Kore.*
- And Kore the son of *I* the Levite ... 2Chr 31:14 3232

IMPART {2}
- let him *i* to him that hath none ... Lk 3:11 *3330*
- that I may *i* unto you some ... Rom 1:11 *3330*

IMPARTED {2}
- wisdom, neither hath he *i* to her ... Job 39:17 2505
- were willing to have *i* unto you ... 1Th 2:8 *3330*

IMPEDIMENT {1}
- deaf, and had an *i* in his speech ... Mk 7:32 *3424*

IMPENITENT {1}
- *i* heart treasurest up unto ... Rom 2:5 *279*

IMPERIOUS {1}
- the work of an *i* whorish woman ... Eze 16:30 7986

IMPLACABLE {1}
- without natural affection, *i* ... Rom 1:31 *786*

IMPLEAD {1}
- let them *i* one another ... Acts 19:38 *1458*

IMPORTUNITY {1}
- yet because of his *i* he will rise ... Lk 11:8 *335*

IMPOSE {1}
- it shall not be lawful to *i* toll ... Ezr 7:24 7412

IMPOSED {1}
- *i* on them until the time of ... Heb 9:10 *1942*

IMPOSSIBLE {9}
- and nothing shall be *i* unto you ... Mt 17:20 *101*
- unto them, With men this is *i* ... Mt 19:26 *102*
- upon them saith, With men it is *i* ... Mk 10:27 *102*
- For with God nothing shall be *i* ... Lk 1:37 *101*
- It is *i* but that offences will ... Lk 17:1 *418*
- The things which are *i* with men ... Lk 18:27 *102*
- For it is *i* for those who were ... Heb 6:4 *102*
- in which it was *i* for God to lie ... Heb 6:18 *102*
- faith it is *i* to please him ... Heb 11:6 *102*

IMPOTENT {4}
- lay a great multitude of *i* folk ... Jn 5:3 *770*
- The *i* man answered him, Sir, I ... Jn 5:7 *770*
- the good deed done to the *i* man ... Acts 4:9 *772*
- *i* in his feet, being a cripple ... Acts 14:8 *102*

IMPOVERISH {1}
- they shall *i* thy fenced cities, ... Jer 5:17 7567

IMPOVERISHED {3}
- Israel was greatly *i* because of ... Judg 6:6 1809
- He that is so *i* that he hath no ... Is 40:20 5533
- Whereas Edom saith, We are *i* ... Mal 1:4 7567

IMPRISONED {1}
- I said, Lord, they know that I *i* ... Acts 22:19 *5439*

IMPRISONMENT {2}
- to confiscation of goods, or to *i* ... Ezr 7:26 613
- yea, moreover of bonds and *i* ... Heb 11:36 *5438*

IMPRISONMENTS {1}
- In stripes, in *i*, in tumults, in ... 2Cor 6:5 *5438*

IMPUDENT {3}
- with an *i* face said unto him, ... Prov 7:13 5810
- For they are *i* children and ... Eze 2:4 7186,6440
- for all the house of Israel are *i* ... Eze 3:7 2389,4696

IMPUTE {3}
- let not the king *i* any thing unto ... 1Sa 22:15 7760
- Let not my lord *i* iniquity unto ... 2Sa 19:19 2803
- to whom the Lord will not *i* sin ... Rom 4:8 *3049*

IMPUTED {8}
- neither shall it be *i* unto him ... Lev 7:18 2803
- blood shall be *i* unto that man ... Lev 17:4 2803
- might be *i* unto them also ... Rom 4:11 *3049*
- therefore it was *i* to him for ... Rom 4:22 *3049*
- sake alone, that it was *i* to him ... Rom 4:23 *3049*
- us also, to whom it shall be *i* ... Rom 4:24 *3049*
- but sin is not *i* when there is no ... Rom 5:13 *1677*
- God, and it was *i* unto him for ... Jas 2:23 *3049*

IMPUTETH {2}
- unto whom the LORD *i* not iniquity ... Ps 32:2 2803
- unto whom God *i* righteousness ... Rom 4:6 *3049*

IMPUTING {2}
- *i* this his power unto his god ... Hab 1:11
- not *i* their trespasses unto them ... 2Cor 5:19 *3049*

IMRAH *(im'-rah)* {1} *A chief of Asher.*
- and Shual, and Beri, and *I*, ... 1Chr 7:36 3236

IMRI *(im'-ri)* {2}
- *1. Son of Bani.*
- the son of Omri, the son of *I* ... 1Chr 9:4 556
- *2. Father of Zaccur.*
- them builded Zaccur the son of *I* ... Neh 3:2 556

IN See APPENDIX.

INASMUCH See APPENDIX.

INCENSE {129}
- for anointing oil, and for sweet *i* ... Ex 25:6 7004
- make an altar to burn *i* upon ... Ex 30:1 7004
- thereon sweet *i* every morning ... Ex 30:7 7004
- lamps, he shall burn *i* upon it ... Ex 30:7
- at even, he shall burn *i* upon it ... Ex 30:8 6999
- a perpetual *i* before the LORD ... Ex 30:8 7004
- shall offer no strange *i* thereon ... Ex 30:9 7004
- and his vessels, and the altar of *i* ... Ex 30:27 7004
- his furniture, and the altar of *i* ... Ex 31:8 7004
- sweet *i* for the holy place ... Ex 31:11 7004
- anointing oil, and for the sweet *i* ... Ex 35:8 7004
- the *i* altar, and his staves, and ... Ex 35:15 7004
- the anointing oil, and the sweet *i* ... Ex 35:15 7004
- anointing oil, and for the sweet *i* ... Ex 35:28 7004
- he made the *i* altar of shittim ... Ex 37:25 7004
- the pure *i* of sweet spices, ... Ex 37:29 7004
- the anointing oil, and the sweet *i* ... Ex 39:38 7004
- set the altar of gold for the *i* ... Ex 40:5 7004
- And he burnt sweet *i* thereon ... Ex 40:27 7004
- altar of sweet *i* before the LORD ... Lev 4:7 7004
- put *i* thereon, and offered strange ... Lev 10:1 7004
- full of sweet *i* beaten small ... Lev 16:12 7004
- he shall put the *i* upon the fire ... Lev 16:13 7004
- that the cloud of the *i* may cover ... Lev 16:13 7004
- oil for the light, and the sweet *i* ... Num 4:16 7004
- of ten shekels of gold, full of *i* ... Num 7:14 7004
- of gold of ten shekels, full of *i* ... Num 7:20 7004
- spoon of ten shekels, full of *i* ... Num 7:26 7004
- spoon of ten shekels, full of *i* ... Num 7:32 7004
- spoon of ten shekels, full of *i* ... Num 7:38 7004
- spoon of ten shekels, full of *i* ... Num 7:44 7004
- spoon of ten shekels, full of *i* ... Num 7:50 7004
- spoon of ten shekels, full of *i* ... Num 7:56 7004
- spoon of ten shekels, full of *i* ... Num 7:62 7004
- spoon of ten shekels, full of *i* ... Num 7:68 7004
- spoon of ten shekels, full of *i* ... Num 7:74 7004
- spoon of ten shekels, full of *i* ... Num 7:80 7004
- spoons were twelve, full of *i* ... Num 7:86 7004
- put *i* in them before the LORD to ... Num 16:7 7004
- put *i* in them, and bring ye before ... Num 16:17 7004
- laid *i* thereon, and stood in the ... Num 16:18 7004
- and fifty men that offered *i* ... Num 16:35 7004
- near to offer *i* before the LORD ... Num 16:40 7004
- from off the altar, and put on *i* ... Num 16:46 7004
- and he put on *i*, and made an ... Num 16:47 7004
- they shall put *i* before thee ... Deut 33:10 7004
- offer upon mine altar, to burn *i* ... 1Sa 2:28 7004
- and burnt *i* in high places ... 1Kin 3:3 6999
- he burnt *i* upon the altar that ... 1Kin 9:25 6999
- his strange wives, which burnt *i* ... 1Kin 11:8 6999
- upon the altar, and burnt *i* ... 1Kin 12:33 6999
- stood by the altar to burn *i* ... 1Kin 13:1 6999
- high places that burn *i* upon thee ... 1Kin 13:2 6999
- burnt *i* yet in the high places ... 1Kin 22:43 6999
- burnt *i* in the high places ... 2Kin 12:3 6999
- burnt *i* on the high places ... 2Kin 14:4 6999
- burnt *i* still on the high places ... 2Kin 15:4 6999
- burned *i* still in the high places ... 2Kin 15:35 6999
- burnt *i* in the high places, and on ... 2Kin 16:4 6999
- there they burnt *i* in all the ... 2Kin 17:11 6999
- of Israel did burn *i* to it ... 2Kin 18:4 6999
- have burned *i* unto other gods, ... 2Kin 22:17 6999
- burn *i* in the high places in the ... 2Kin 23:5 6999
- them also that burned *i* unto Baal ... 2Kin 23:5 6999
- where the priests had burned *i* ... 2Kin 23:8 6999
- offering, and on the altar of *i* ... 1Chr 6:49 7004
- to burn *i* before the LORD, to ... 1Chr 23:13 6999
- for the altar of *i* refined gold ... 1Chr 28:18 7004
- and to burn before him sweet *i* ... 2Chr 2:4 7004
- burnt sacrifices and sweet *i* ... 2Chr 13:11 7004
- them, and burned *i* unto them ... 2Chr 25:14 6999
- burn *i* upon the altar of *i* ... 2Chr 26:16 6999
- to burn *i* unto the LORD, but to ... 2Chr 26:18 6999
- that are consecrated to burn *i* ... 2Chr 26:18 6999
- a censer in his hand to burn *i* ... 2Chr 26:19 6999
- the LORD, from beside the *i* altar ... 2Chr 26:19 7004
- Moreover he burnt *i* in the valley ... 2Chr 28:3 6999
- burnt *i* in the high places, and on ... 2Chr 28:4 6999
- places to burn *i* unto other gods ... 2Chr 28:25 6999
- have not burned *i* nor offered ... 2Chr 29:7 7004
- minister unto him, and burn *i* ... 2Chr 29:11 6999
- the altars for *i* took they away ... 2Chr 30:14 6999
- one altar, and burn *i* upon it ... 2Chr 32:12 6999
- have burned *i* unto other gods, ... 2Chr 34:25 6999
- of fatlings, with the *i* of rams ... Ps 66:15 7004
- be set forth before thee as *i* ... Ps 141:2 7004
- *i* is an abomination unto me ... Is 1:13 7004
- offering, nor wearied thee with *i* ... Is 43:23 3828
- they shall bring gold and *i* ... Is 60:6 3828
- burneth *i* upon altars of brick ... Is 65:3 6999
- which have burned *i* upon the ... Is 65:7 6999
- he that burneth *i*, as if he ... Is 66:3 3828
- have burned *i* unto other gods, and ... Jer 1:16 6999
- cometh there to me *i* from Sheba ... Jer 6:20 3828
- burn *i* unto Baal, and walk after ... Jer 7:9 6999
- the gods unto whom they offer *i* ... Jer 11:12 6999
- even altars to burn *i* unto Baal ... Jer 11:13 6999
- to anger in offering *i* unto Baal ... Jer 11:17 6999
- and meat offerings, and *i*, and ... Jer 17:26 3828
- me, they have burned *i* to vanity ... Jer 18:15 6999
- have burned *i* in it unto other ... Jer 19:4 6999
- *i* unto all the host of heaven ... Jer 19:13 6999
- they have offered *i* unto Baal ... Jer 32:29 6999
- *i* in their hand, to bring them to ... Jer 41:5 3828
- in that they went to burn *i* ... Jer 44:3 6999
- to burn no *i* unto other gods ... Jer 44:5 6999
- burning *i* unto other gods in the ... Jer 44:8 6999
- had burned *i* unto other gods ... Jer 44:15 6999
- to burn *i* unto the queen of ... Jer 44:17 6999
- to burn *i* to the queen of heaven ... Jer 44:18 6999
- when we burned *i* to the queen of ... Jer 44:19 6999
- The *i* that ye burned in the ... Jer 44:21 7002
- Because ye have burned *i*, and ... Jer 44:23 6999
- to burn *i* to the queen of heaven, ... Jer 44:25 6999
- and him that burneth *i* to his gods ... Jer 48:35 6999
- and a thick cloud of *i* went up ... Eze 8:11 7004
- mine oil and mine *i* before them ... Eze 16:18 7004
- whereupon thou hast set mine *i* ... Eze 23:41 7004
- wherein she burned *i* to them ... Hos 2:13 6999
- burn *i* upon the hills, under oaks ... Hos 4:13 6999
- burned *i* to graven images ... Hos 11:2 6999
- net, and burn *i* unto their drag ... Hab 1:16 6999
- in every place *i* shall be offered ... Mal 1:11 6999
- his lot was to burn *i* when he ... Lk 1:9 *2370*
- praying without at the time of *i* ... Lk 1:10 *2368*
- the right side of the altar of *i* ... Lk 1:11 *2368*
- there was given unto him much *i* ... Rev 8:3 *2368*
- And the smoke of the *i*, which came ... Rev 8:4 *2368*

INCENSED {2}
- all they that were *i* against thee ... Is 41:11 2734
- all that are *i* against him shall ... Is 45:24 2734

INCLINE {16}
- *i* your heart unto the LORD God of ... Josh 24:23 5186
- That he may *i* our hearts unto him ... 1Kin 8:58 5186
- *i* thine ear unto me, and hear my ... Ps 17:6 5186
- and consider, and *i* thine ear ... Ps 45:10 5186
- I will *i* mine ear to a parable ... Ps 49:4 5186
- *i* thine ear unto me, and save me ... Ps 71:2 5186
- *i* your ears to the words of my ... Ps 78:1 5186
- *i* thine ear unto my cry ... Ps 88:2 5186
- *i* thine ear unto me ... Ps 102:2 5186
- *I* my heart unto thy testimonies, ... Ps 119:36 5186
- *I* not my heart to any evil thing, ... Ps 141:4 5186
- So that thou *i* thine ear unto ... Prov 2:2 7181
- *i* thine ear unto my sayings ... Prov 4:20 5186
- *I* thine ear, O LORD, and hear ... Is 37:17 5186
- *I* your ear, and come unto me ... Is 55:3 5186
- O my God, *i* thine ear, and hear ... Dan 9:18 5186

INCLINED {13}
- and their hearts *i* to follow ... Judg 9:3 5186
- he *i* unto me, and heard my cry ... Ps 40:1 5186
- Because he hath *i* his ear unto me ... Ps 116:2 5186
- I have *i* mine heart to perform ... Ps 119:112 5186
- nor *i* mine ear to them that ... Prov 5:13 5186
- nor *i* their ear, but walked in ... Jer 7:24 5186
- nor *i* their ear, but hardened ... Jer 7:26 5186
- nor *i* their ear, but walked every ... Jer 11:8 5186
- neither *i* their ear, but made ... Jer 17:23 5186
- hearkened, nor *i* your ear to hear ... Jer 25:4 5186
- not unto me, neither *i* their ear ... Jer 34:14 5186
- but ye have not *i* your ear ... Jer 35:15 5186
- nor *i* their ear to turn from ... Jer 44:5 5186

INCLINETH {1}
- For her house *i* unto death ... Prov 2:18 7743

INCLOSE {1}
- we will *i* her with boards of ... Song 8:9 6696

INCLOSED {8}
- onyx stones *i* in ouches of gold ... Ex 39:6 4142
- they were *i* in ouches of gold in ... Ex 39:13 4142
- Thus they *i* the Benjamites round ... Judg 20:43 3803
- They are *i* in their own fat ... Ps 17:10 5462
- assembly of the wicked have *i* me ... Ps 22:16 5362
- A garden *i* is my sister, my ... Song 4:12 5274
- He hath *i* my ways with hewn stone ... Lam 3:9 1443
- they *i* a great multitude of ... Lk 5:6 *4788*

INCLOSINGS {2}
- shall be set in gold in their *i* ... Ex 28:20 4396
- in ouches of gold in their *i* ... Ex 39:13 4396

INCONTINENCY {1}
- Satan tempt you not for your *i* ... 1Cor 7:5 *192*

INCONTINENT {1}
- trucebreakers, false accusers, *i* ... 2Ti 3:3 *193*

INCORRUPTIBLE {4}
- but we an *i* ... 1Cor 9:25 *862*
- and the dead shall be raised *i* ... 1Cor 15:52 *862*
- To an inheritance *i*, and undefiled ... 1Pet 1:4 *862*
- not of corruptible seed, but of *i* ... 1Pet 1:23 *862*

INCORRUPTION {4}
- it is raised in *i* ... 1Cor 15:42 *861*
- neither doth corruption inherit *i* ... 1Cor 15:50 *861*
- this corruptible must put on *i* ... 1Cor 15:53 *861*
- corruptible shall have put on *i* ... 1Cor 15:54 *861*

INCREASE {88}
- And it shall come to pass in the *i* ... Gen 47:24 8393
- may yield unto you the *i* thereof ... Lev 19:25 8393
- shall all the *i* thereof be meat ... Lev 25:7 8393
- ye shall eat the *i* thereof out of ... Lev 25:12 8393
- thou shalt *i* the price thereof ... Lev 25:16 7235
- not sow, nor gather in our *i* ... Lev 25:20 8393
- Take thou no usury of him, or *i* ... Lev 25:36 8635
- nor lend him thy victuals for *i* ... Lev 25:37 4768
- and the land shall yield her *i* ... Lev 26:4 2981
- your land shall not yield her *i* ... Lev 26:20 2981
- as the *i* of the threshingfloor ... Num 18:30 8393
- as the *i* of the winepress ... Num 18:30 8393
- an *i* of sinful men, to augment ... Num 32:14 8635
- thee, and that ye may *i* mightily ... Deut 6:3 7235
- the *i* of thy kine, and the flocks ... Deut 7:13 7698
- beasts of the field *i* upon thee ... Deut 7:22 7235

truly tithe all the *i* of thy seed ... Deut 14:22 8393
tithe of thine *i* the same year ... Deut 14:28 8393
shall bless thee in all thine *i* ... Deut 16:15 8393
tithes of thine *i* the third year ... Deut 26:12 8393
the *i* of thy kine, and the flocks ... Deut 28:4 7698
the *i* of thy kine, and the flocks ... Deut 28:18 7698
or the *i* of thy kine, or flocks ... Deut 28:51 7698
he might eat the *i* of the fields ... Deut 32:13 8570
consume the earth with her *i* ... Deut 32:22 2981
and destroyed the *i* of the earth ... Judg 6:4 2981
I thine army, and come out ... Judg 9:29 7239
all the *i* of thine house shall ... 1Sa 2:33 4768
the LORD had said he would *i* ... 1Chr 27:23 7235
over the *i* of the vineyards for ... 1Chr 27:27
of all the *i* of the field ... 2Chr 31:5 8393
also for the *i* of corn, and wine, ... 2Chr 32:28 8393
to *i* the trespass of Israel ... Ezr 10:10 3254
it yieldeth much *i* unto the kings ... Neh 9:37 8393
thy latter end should greatly *i* ... Job 8:7 7685
The *i* of his house shall depart, ... Job 20:28 2981
and would root out all mine *i* ... Job 31:12 8393
dost not *i* thy wealth by their ... Ps 44:12 7235
if riches *i*, set not your heart ... Ps 62:10 5107
Then shall the earth yield her *i* ... Ps 67:6 2981
Thou shalt *i* my greatness, and ... Ps 71:21 7235
they *i* in riches ... Ps 73:12 7685
He gave also their *i* unto the ... Ps 78:46 2981
and our land shall yield her *i* ... Ps 85:12 2981
which may yield fruits of *i* ... Ps 107:37 8393
The LORD shall *i* you more ... Ps 115:14 3254
man will hear, and will *i* learning ... Prov 1:5 3254
the firstfruits of all thine *i* ... Prov 3:9 8393
man, and he will *i* in learning ... Prov 9:9 3254
that gathereth by labour shall *i* ... Prov 13:11 7235
but much *i* is by the strength of ... Prov 14:4 8393
with the *i* of his lips shall he ... Prov 18:20 8393
the poor to *i* his riches, and he ... Prov 22:16 7235
when they perish, the righteous *i* ... Prov 28:28 7235
he that loveth abundance with *i* ... Eccl 5:10 8393
When goods *i*, they are increased ... Eccl 5:11 7235
be many things that *i* vanity ... Eccl 6:11 7235
Of the *i* of his government and ... Is 9:7 4768
The meek also shall *i* their joy ... Is 29:19 3254
and bread of the *i* of the earth ... Is 30:23 8393
didst *i* thy perfumes, and didst ... Is 57:9 7235
LORD, and the firstfruits of his *i* ... Jer 2:3 8393
and they shall be fruitful and *i* ... Jer 23:3 7235
I will *i* the famine upon you, and ... Eze 5:16 3254
usury, neither hath taken any *i* ... Eze 18:8 8635
forth upon usury, and hath taken *i* ... Eze 18:13 8635
hath not received usury nor *i* ... Eze 18:17 8635
thou hast taken usury and *i* ... Eze 22:12 8635
and the earth shall yield her *i* ... Eze 34:27 2981
and they shall *i* and bring fruit ... Eze 36:11 7235
call for the corn, and will *i* it ... Eze 36:29 7235
the *i* of the field, that ye shall ... Eze 36:30 8570
I will *i* them with men like a ... Eze 36:37 7235
the *i* thereof shall be for food ... Eze 48:18 8393
shall acknowledge and *i* with glory ... Dan 11:39 7235
commit whoredom, and shall not *i* ... Hos 4:10 6555
and the ground shall give her *i* ... Zec 8:12 2981
they shall *i* as they have ... Zec 10:8 7235
said unto the Lord, *I* our faith ... Lk 17:5 *4369*
He must *i*, but I must decrease ... Jn 3:30 *837*
but God gave the *i* ... 1Cor 3:6 *837*
but God that giveth the *i* ... 1Cor 3:7 *837*
sown, and *i* the fruits of your ... 2Cor 9:10 *837*
maketh *i* of the body unto the ... Eph 4:16 *838*
increaseth with the *i* of God ... Col 2:19 *838*
And the Lord make you to *i* ... 1Th 3:12 *4121*
you, brethren, that ye *i* more ... 1Th 4:10 *4052*
for they will *i* unto more ... 2Ti 2:16 *4298*

INCREASED {49}
and the waters *i*, and bare up the ... Gen 7:17 7235
were *i* greatly upon the earth ... Gen 7:18 7235
it is now *i* unto a multitude ... Gen 30:30 6555
the man *i* exceedingly, and had ... Gen 30:43 6555
i abundantly, and multiplied, and ... Ex 1:7 8317
from before thee, until thou be *i* ... Ex 23:30 6509
of the Philistines went on and *i* ... 1Sa 14:19 7227
for the people *i* continually with ... 2Sa 15:12 7227
And the battle *i* that day ... 1Kin 22:35 5927
house of their fathers *i* greatly ... 1Chr 4:38 6555
they *i* from Bashan unto ... 1Chr 5:23 7235
And the battle *i* that day ... 2Chr 18:34 5927
iniquities are *i* over our head ... Ezr 9:6 7235
and his substance is *i* in the land ... Job 1:10 6555
how are they *i* that trouble me ... Ps 3:1 7231
that their corn and their wine *i* ... Ps 4:7 7231
when the glory of his house is *i* ... Ps 49:16 7235
And he *i* his people greatly ... Ps 105:24 6509
the years of thy life shall be *i* ... Prov 9:11 3254
i more than all that were before ... Eccl 2:9 3254
they are *i* that eat them ... Eccl 5:11 7231
the nation, and not *i* the joy ... Is 9:3 1431
Thou hast *i* the nation, O LORD, ... Is 26:15 3254
thou hast *i* the nation ... Is 26:15 3254
alone, and blessed him, and *i* him ... Is 51:2 7235
i in the land, in those days, ... Jer 3:16 6509
many, and their backslidings are *i* ... Jer 5:6 6105
Their widows are *i* to me above ... Jer 15:8 6105
that ye may be *i* there, and not ... Jer 29:6 7235
because thy sins were *i* ... Jer 30:14 6105
because thy sins were *i*, I have ... Jer 30:15 6105
hath *i* in the daughter of Judah ... Lam 2:5 7235
bud of the field, and thou hast *i* ... Eze 16:7 7235
hast *i* thy whoredoms, to provoke ... Eze 16:26 7235
And that she *i* her whoredoms ... Eze 23:14 3254
traffick hast thou *i* thy riches ... Eze 28:5 7235
so *i* from the lowest chamber to ... Eze 41:7 5927
and fro, and knowledge shall be *i* ... Dan 12:4 7235
As they were *i*, so they sinned ... Hos 4:7 7230
of his fruit he hath *i* the altars ... Hos 10:1 7235
fig trees and your olive trees *i* ... Amos 4:9 7235
shall increase as they have *i* ... Zec 10:8 7235
yield fruit that sprang up and *i* ... Mk 4:8 *837*
Jesus *i* in wisdom and stature, and ... Lk 2:52 *4298*
And the word of God *i* ... Acts 6:7 *837*
But Saul *i* the more in strength, ... Acts 9:22 *1743*
the faith, and *i* in number daily ... Acts 16:5 *4052*
having hope, when your faith is *i* ... 2Cor 10:15 *837*
i with goods, and have need of ... Rev 3:17 *4147*

INCREASEST {1}
i thine indignation upon me ... Job 10:17 7235

INCREASETH {15}
For it *i*. Thou huntest me ... Job 10:16 1342
He *i* the nations, and destroyeth ... Job 12:23 7679
up against thee *i* continually ... Ps 74:23 5927
is that scattereth, and yet *i* ... Prov 11:24 3254
sweetness of the lips *i* learning ... Prov 16:21 3254
i the transgressors among men ... Prov 23:28 3254
a man of knowledge *i* strength ... Prov 24:5 553
unjust gain *i* his substance, he ... Prov 28:8 7235
are multiplied, transgression *i* ... Prov 29:16 7235
he that *i* knowledge *i* sorrow ... Eccl 1:18 3254
that have no might he *i* strength ... Is 40:29 7235
he daily *i* lies and desolation ... Hos 12:1 7235
Woe to him that *i* that which is ... Hab 2:6 7235
i with the increase of God ... Col 2:19 *837*

INCREASING {1}
i in the knowledge of God ... Col 1:10 *837*

INCREDIBLE {1}
it be thought a thing *i* with you ... Acts 26:8 *571*

INCURABLE {6}
in his bowels with an *i* disease ... 2Chr 21:18 369,4832
my wound is *i* without ... Job 34:6 605
my pain perpetual, and my wound *i* ... Jer 15:18 605
saith the LORD, Thy bruise is *i* ... Jer 30:12 605
thy sorrow is *i* for the multitude ... Jer 30:15 605
For her wound is *i* ... Mic 1:9 605

INDEBTED {1}
forgive every one that is *i* to us ... Lk 11:4 *3784*

INDEED See APPENDIX.

INDIA *(in'-de-ah)* {2} *Eastern boundary of the Persian Empire.*
reigned from *I* even unto Ethiopia ... Est 1:1 1912
which are from *I* unto Ethiopia ... Est 8:9 1912

INDIGNATION {41}
anger, and in wrath, and in great *i* ... Deut 29:28 7110
there was great *i* against Israel ... 2Kin 3:27 7110
he was wroth, and took great *i* ... Neh 4:1 3707
he was full of *i* against Mordecai ... Est 5:9 2534
me, and increasest thine *i* upon me ... Job 10:17 3708
Pour out thine *i* upon them ... Ps 69:24 2195
of his anger, wrath, and *i* ... Ps 78:49 2195
Because of thine *i* and thy wrath ... Ps 102:10 2195
the staff in their hand is mine *i* ... Is 10:5 2195
the *i* shall cease, and mine anger ... Is 10:25 2195
the LORD, and the weapons of his *i* ... Is 13:5 2195
moment, until the *i* be overpast ... Is 26:20 2195
his lips are full of *i*, and his ... Is 30:27 2195
with the *i* of his anger, and with ... Is 30:30 2197
For the *i* of the LORD is upon all ... Is 34:2 7110
and his *i* toward his enemies ... Is 66:14 2194
shall not be able to abide his *i* ... Jer 10:10 2195
for thou hast filled me with *i* ... Jer 15:17 2195
forth the weapons of his *i* ... Jer 50:25 2195
hath despised in the *i* of his ... Lam 2:6 2195
I will pour out mine *i* upon thee ... Eze 21:31 2195
nor rained upon in the day of *i* ... Eze 22:24 2195
I poured out mine *i* upon them ... Eze 22:31 2195
shall be in the last end of the *i* ... Dan 8:19 2195
have *i* against the holy covenant ... Dan 11:30 2194
till the *i* be accomplished ... Dan 11:36 2195
I will bear the *i* of the LORD ... Mic 7:9 2197
Who can stand before his *i* ... Nah 1:6 2195
didst march through the land in *i* ... Hab 3:12 2195
to pour upon them mine *i* ... Zeph 3:8 2195
thou hast had *i* these threescore ... Zec 1:12 2194
whom the LORD hath *i* for ever ... Mal 1:4 2194
they were moved with *i* against ... Mt 20:24 *23*
his disciples saw it, they had *i* ... Mt 26:8 *23*
some that had *i* within themselves ... Mk 14:4 *23*
of the synagogue answered with *i* ... Lk 13:14 *23*
Sadducees,) and were filled with *i* ... Acts 5:17 *2205*
but obey unrighteousness, *i* ... Rom 2:8 *2372*
of yourselves, yea, what *i* ... 2Cor 7:11 *24*
for of judgment and fiery *i* ... Heb 10:27 *2205*
mixture into the cup of his *i* ... Rev 14:10 *3709*

INDITING {1}
My heart is *i* a good matter ... Ps 45:1 7370

INDUSTRIOUS {1}
the young man that he was *i* ... 1Kin 11:28 6213,4399

INEXCUSABLE {1}
Therefore thou art *i*, O man, ... Rom 2:1 *379*

INFALLIBLE {1}
his passion by many *i* proofs ... Acts 1:3

INFAMOUS {1}
shall mock thee, which art *i* ... Eze 22:5 2931,8034

INFAMY {2}
shame, and thine *i* turn not away ... Prov 25:10 1681
and are an *i* of the people ... Eze 36:3 1681

INFANT {2}
but slay both man and woman, *i* ... 1Sa 15:3 5768
be no more thence an *i* of days ... Is 65:20 5764

INFANTS {3}
as *i* which never saw light ... Job 3:16 5768
their *i* shall be dashed in pieces ... Hos 13:16 5768
And they brought unto him also *i* ... Lk 18:15 *1025*

INFERIOR {4}
I am not *i* to you ... Job 12:3 5307
I am not *i* unto you ... Job 13:2 5307
arise another kingdom *i* to thee ... Dan 2:39 772
ye were *i* to other churches ... 2Cor 12:13 *2274*

INFIDEL {2}
hath he that believeth with an *i* ... 2Cor 6:15 *571*
the faith, and is worse than an *i* ... 1Ti 5:8 *571*

INFINITE {3}
and thine iniquities *i* ... Job 22:5 369,7093
his understanding is *i* ... Ps 147:5 369,4557
were her strength, and it was *i* ... Nah 3:9 369,7093

INFIRMITIES {12}
saying, Himself took our *i* ... Mt 8:17 *769*
and to be healed by him of their *i* ... Lk 5:15 *769*
hour he cured many of their *i* ... Lk 7:21 *3554*
been healed of evil spirits and *i* ... Lk 8:2 *769*
the Spirit also helpeth our *i* ... Rom 8:26 *769*
ought to bear the *i* of the weak ... Rom 15:1 *771*
the things which concern mine *i* ... 2Cor 11:30 *769*
I will not glory, but in mine *i* ... 2Cor 12:5 *769*
will I rather glory in my *i* ... 2Cor 12:9 *769*
Therefore I take pleasure in *i* ... 2Cor 12:10 *769*
stomach's sake and thine often *i* ... 1Ti 5:23 *769*
touched with the feeling of our *i* ... Heb 4:15 *769*

INFIRMITY {10}
for her *i* shall she be unclean ... Lev 12:2 1738
And I said, This is my *i* ... Ps 77:10 2470
of a man will sustain his *i* ... Prov 18:14 4245
had a spirit of *i* eighteen years ... Lk 13:11 *769*
thou art loosed from thine *i* ... Lk 13:12 *769*
was there, which had an *i* thirty ... Jn 5:5 *769*
because of the *i* of your flesh ... Rom 6:19 *769*
Ye know how through *i* of the ... Gal 4:13 *769*
himself also is compassed with *i* ... Heb 5:2 *769*
men high priests which have *i* ... Heb 7:28 *769*

INFLAME {1}
until night, till wine *i* them ... Is 5:11 1814

INFLAMMATION {2}
for it is an *i* of the burning ... Lev 13:28 6867
and with a fever, and with an *i* ... Deut 28:22 1816

INFLICTED {1}
punishment, which was *i* of many ... 2Cor 2:6

INFLUENCES {1}
thou bind the sweet *i* of Pleiades ... Job 38:31 4575

INFOLDING {1}
a great cloud, and a fire *i* itself ... Eze 1:4 3947

INFORM {1}
according to all that they *i* thee ... Deut 17:10 3384

INFORMED {6}
And he *i* me, and talked with me, and ... Dan 9:22 995
And they are *i* of thee, that thou ... Acts 21:21 *2727*
they were *i* concerning thee ... Acts 21:24 *2727*
who *i* the governor against Paul ... Acts 24:1 *1718*
of the Jews *i* him against Paul ... Acts 25:2 *1718*
and the elders of the Jews *i* me ... Acts 25:15 *1718*

INGATHERING {2}
and the feast of *i*, which is in ... Ex 23:16 614
the feast of *i* at the year's end ... Ex 34:22 614

INHABIT {10}
the land which ye shall *i* ... Num 35:34 3427
the wicked shall not *i* the earth ... Prov 10:30 7931
the villages that Kedar doth *i* ... Is 42:11 3427
shall build houses, and *i* them ... Is 65:21 3427
shall not build, and another *i* ... Is 65:22 3427
but shall *i* the parched places in ... Jer 17:6 7931
Thou daughter that dost *i* Dibon ... Jer 48:18 3427
they that *i* those wastes of the ... Eze 33:24 3427
build the waste cities, and *i* them ... Amos 9:14 3427
also build houses, but not *i* them ... Zeph 1:13 3427

INHABITANT {33}
The flood breaketh out from the *i* ... Job 28:4 1481
even great and fair, without *i* ... Is 5:9 3427
the cities be wasted without *i* ... Is 6:11 3427
the *i* of Samaria, that say in the ... Is 9:9 3427
Cry out and shout, thou *i* of Zion ... Is 12:6 3427
the *i* of this isle shall say in ... Is 20:6 3427
are upon thee, O *i* of the earth ... Is 24:17 3427
the *i* shall not say, I am sick ... Is 33:24 7934
his cities are burned without *i* ... Jer 2:15 3427
shall be laid waste, without an *i* ... Jer 4:7 3427
of Judah desolate, without an *i* ... Jer 9:11 3427
of the land, O *i* of the fortress ... Jer 10:17 3427
O *i* of the valley, and rock of the ... Jer 21:13 3427
O *i* of Lebanon, that makest thy ... Jer 22:23 3427
shall be desolate without an *i* ... Jer 26:9 3427
without man, and without *i* ... Jer 33:10 3427
Judah a desolation without an *i* ... Jer 34:22 3427
and a curse, without an *i* ... Jer 44:22 3427
be waste and desolate without an *i* ... Jer 46:19 3427
O *i* of Aroer, stand by the way, ... Jer 48:19 3427
O *i* of Moab, saith the LORD ... Jer 48:43 3427

I

Babylon a desolation without an *i* Jer 51:29 3427
Babylon, shall the *i* of Zion say Jer 51:35 3427
and an hissing, without an *i* Jer 51:37 3427
cut off the *i* from the plain of Amos 1:5 3427
I will cut off the *i* from Ashdod Amos 1:8 3427
thou *i* of Saphir, having thy Mic 1:11 3427
the *i* of Zaanan came not forth in Mic 1:11 3427
For the *i* of Maroth waited Mic 1:12 3427
O thou *i* of Lachish, bind the Mic 1:13 3427
heir unto thee, O *i* of Mareshah Mic 1:15 3427
thee, that there shall be no *i* Zeph 2:5 3427
is no man, that there is none *i* Zeph 3:6 3427

INHABITANTS {202}

all the *i* of the cities, and that Gen 19:25 3427
to stink among the *i* of the land Gen 34:30 3427
when the *i* of the land, the Gen 50:11 3427
take hold on the *i* of Palestina Ex 15:14 3427
all the *i* of Canaan shall melt Ex 15:15 3427
for I will deliver the *i* of the Ex 23:31 3427
thou make a covenant with the *i* Ex 34:12 3427
a covenant with the *i* of the land Ex 34:15 3427
land itself vomiteth out her *i* Lev 18:25 3427
the land unto all the *i* thereof Lev 25:10 3427
land that eateth up the *i* thereof Num 13:32 3427
tell it to the *i* of this land Num 14:14 3427
because of the *i* of the land Num 32:17 3427
the *i* of the land from before you Num 33:52 3427
dispossess the *i* of the land Num 33:53
the *i* of the land from before you Num 33:55 3427
withdrawn the *i* of their city Deut 13:13 3427
Thou shalt surely smite the *i* of Deut 13:15 3427
that all the *i* of the land faint Josh 2:9 3427
for even all the *i* of the country Josh 2:24 3427
all the *i* of the land shall hear Josh 7:9 3427
all the *i* of Ai in the field Josh 8:24 3427
utterly destroyed all the *i* of Ai Josh 8:26 3427
when the *i* of Gibeon heard what Josh 9:3 3427
all the *i* of our country spake to Josh 9:11 3427
to destroy all the *i* of the land Josh 9:24 3427
how the *i* of Gibeon had made Josh 10:1 3427
save the Hivites the *i* of Gibeon Josh 11:19 3427
All the *i* of the hill country Josh 13:6 3427
went up thence to the *i* of Debir Josh 15:15 3427
the Jebusites the *i* of Jerusalem Josh 15:63 3427
hand unto the *i* of En-tappuah Josh 17:7 3427
the *i* of Dor and her towns Josh 17:11 3427
the *i* of En-dor and her towns, and Josh 17:11 3427
the *i* of Taanach and her towns, and Josh 17:11 3427
the *i* of Megiddo and her towns, Josh 17:11 3427
drive out the *i* of those cities Josh 17:12
he went against the *i* of Debir Judg 1:11 3427
drave out the *i* of the mountain Judg 1:19
not drive out the *i* of the valley Judg 1:19 3427
drive out the *i* of Beth-shean Judg 1:27
and her towns, nor the *i* of Dor Judg 1:27 3427
nor the *i* of Ibleam and her towns, Judg 1:27 3427
nor the *i* of Megiddo and her towns Judg 1:27 3427
Zebulun drive out the *i* of Kitron Judg 1:30 3427
nor the *i* of Nahalol Judg 1:30 3427
Asher drive out the *i* of Accho Judg 1:31 3427
nor the *i* of Zidon, nor of Ahlab, Judg 1:31 3427
the Canaanites, the *i* of the land Judg 1:32 3427
drive out the *i* of Beth-shemesh Judg 1:33 3427
nor the *i* of Beth-anath Judg 1:33 3427
the Canaanites, the *i* of the land Judg 1:33 3427
the *i* of Beth-shemesh and of Judg 1:33 3427
no league with the *i* of this land Judg 2:2 3427
The *i* of the villages ceased, Judg 5:7
the *i* of his villages in Israel Judg 5:11
curse ye bitterly the *i* thereof Judg 5:23 3427
be head over all the *i* of Gilead Judg 10:18 3427
our head over all the *i* of Gilead Judg 11:8 3427
Amorites, the *i* of that country Judg 11:21 3427
sword, beside the *i* of Gibeah Judg 20:15 3427
of the *i* of Jabesh-gilead there Judg 21:9 3427
smite the *i* of Jabesh-gilead with Judg 21:10 3427
they found among the *i* of Judg 21:12 3427
thee, saying, Buy it before the *i* Ruth 4:4 3427
to the *i* of Kirjath-jearim 1Sa 6:21 3427
So David saved the *i* of Keilah 1Sa 23:5 3427
were of old the *i* of the land 1Sa 27:8 3427
when the *i* of Jabesh-gilead heard 1Sa 31:11 3427
the Jebusites, the *i* of the land 2Sa 5:6 3427
who was of the *i* of Gilead 1Kin 17:1 8453
nobles who were the *i* in his city 1Kin 21:11 3427
Therefore their *i* were of small 2Kin 19:26 3427
this place, and upon the *i* thereof 2Kin 22:16 3427
place, and against the *i* thereof 2Kin 22:19 3427
all the *i* of Jerusalem with him, 2Kin 23:2 3427
of the fathers of the *i* of Geba 1Chr 8:6 3427
the fathers of the *i* of Aijalon 1Chr 8:13 3427
who drove away the *i* of Gath 1Chr 8:13 3427
Now the first *i* that dwelt in 1Chr 9:2 3427
Jebusites were, the *i* of the land 1Chr 11:4 3427
the *i* of Jebus said to David, 1Chr 11:5 3427
for he hath given the *i* of the 1Chr 22:18 3427
upon all the *i* of the countries 2Chr 15:5 3427
who didst drive out the *i* of this 2Chr 20:7 3427
ye *i* of Jerusalem, and thou king 2Chr 20:15 3427
the *i* of Jerusalem fell before 2Chr 20:18 3427
me, O Judah, and ye *i* of Jerusalem 2Chr 20:20 3427
up against the *i* of mount Seir 2Chr 20:23 3427
had made an end of the *i* of Seir 2Chr 20:23 3427
caused the *i* of Jerusalem to 2Chr 21:11 3427
the *i* of Jerusalem to go a 2Chr 21:13 3427
the *i* of Jerusalem made Ahaziah 2Chr 22:1 3427
the *i* of Jerusalem from the hand 2Chr 32:22 3427
the *i* of Jerusalem, so that the 2Chr 32:26 3427
the *i* of Jerusalem did him honour 2Chr 32:33 3427
the *i* of Jerusalem to err, and to 2Chr 33:9 3427
this place, and upon the *i* thereof 2Chr 34:24 3427
place, and against the *i* thereof 2Chr 34:27 3427
place, and upon the *i* of the same 2Chr 34:28 3427
the *i* of Jerusalem, and the 2Chr 34:30 3427
the *i* of Jerusalem did according 2Chr 34:32 3427
present, and the *i* of Jerusalem 2Chr 35:18 3427
accusation against the *i* of Judah Ezr 4:6 3427
Hanun, and the *i* of Zanoah Neh 3:13 3427
watches of the *i* of Jerusalem Neh 7:3 3427
before them the *i* of the land Neh 9:24 3427
the waters, and the *i* thereof Job 26:5 7934
let all the *i* of the world stand Ps 33:8 3427
upon all the *i* of the earth Ps 33:14 3427
give ear, all ye *i* of the world Ps 49:1 3427
all the *i* thereof are dissolved Ps 75:3 3427
Philistines with the *i* of Tyre Ps 83:7 3427
O *i* of Jerusalem, and men of Judah Is 5:3 3427
for a snare to the *i* of Jerusalem Is 8:14 3427
put down the *i* like a valiant man Is 10:13 3427
the *i* of Gebim gather themselves Is 10:31 3427
All ye *i* of the world, and Is 18:3 3427
The *i* of the land of Tema brought Is 21:14 3427
be a father to the *i* of Jerusalem Is 22:21 3427
Be still, ye *i* of the isle Is 23:2 3427
howl, ye *i* of the isle Is 23:6 3427
scattereth abroad the *i* thereof Is 24:1 3427
is defiled under the *i* thereof Is 24:5 3427
therefore the *i* of the earth are Is 24:6 3427
the *i* of the world will learn Is 26:9 3427
neither have the *i* of the world Is 26:18 3427
out of his place to punish the *i* Is 26:21 3427
Therefore their *i* were of small Is 37:27 3427
no more with the *i* of the world Is 38:11 3427
the *i* thereof are as grasshoppers Is 40:22 3427
the isles, and the *i* thereof Is 42:10 3427
let the *i* of the rock sing, let Is 42:11 3427
be too narrow by reason of the *i* Is 49:19 3427
forth upon all the *i* of the land Jer 1:14 3427
ye men of Judah and *i* of Jerusalem Jer 4:4 3427
my hand upon the *i* of the land Jer 6:12 3427
the bones of the *i* of Jerusalem Jer 8:1 3427
I will sling out the *i* of the Jer 10:18 3427
Judah, and to the *i* of Jerusalem Jer 11:2 3427
and among the *i* of Jerusalem Jer 11:9 3427
i of Jerusalem go, and cry unto Jer 11:12 3427
will fill all the *i* of this land Jer 13:13 3427
all the *i* of Jerusalem, with Jer 13:13 3427
all the *i* of Jerusalem, that Jer 17:20 3427
of Judah, and the *i* of Jerusalem Jer 17:25 3427
to the *i* of Jerusalem, saying, Jer 18:11 3427
kings of Judah, and *i* of Jerusalem Jer 19:3 3427
to the *i* thereof, and even make Jer 19:12 3427
I will smite the *i* of this city Jer 21:6 3427
the *i* thereof as Gomorrah Jer 23:14 3427
to all the *i* of Jerusalem, saying Jer 25:2 3427
land, and against the *i* thereof Jer 25:9 3427
sword upon all the *i* of the earth Jer 25:29 3427
against all the *i* of the earth Jer 25:30 3427
this city, and upon the *i* thereof Jer 26:15 3427
of Judah, and the *i* of Jerusalem Jer 32:32 3427
the *i* of Jerusalem, Will ye not Jer 35:13 3427
upon all the *i* of Jerusalem all Jer 35:17 3427
upon the *i* of Jerusalem, and upon Jer 36:31 3427
forth upon the *i* of Jerusalem Jer 42:18 3427
destroy the city and the *i* thereof Jer 46:8 3427
all the *i* of the land shall howl Jer 47:2 3427
back, dwell deep, O *i* of Dedan Jer 49:8 3427
purposed against the *i* of Teman Jer 49:20 3427
O ye *i* of Hazor, saith the LORD Jer 49:30 3427
it, and against the *i* of Pekod Jer 50:21 3427
and disquiet the *i* of Babylon Jer 50:34 3427
upon the *i* of Babylon, and upon Jer 50:35 3427
he spake against the *i* of Babylon Jer 51:12 3427
to all the *i* of Chaldea all their Jer 51:24 3427
and my blood upon the *i* of Chaldea Jer 51:35 3427
all the *i* of the world, would not Lam 4:12 3427
whom the *i* of Jerusalem have said Eze 11:15 3427
Lord GOD of the *i* of Jerusalem Eze 12:19 3427
so will I give the *i* of Jerusalem Eze 15:6 3427
strong in the sea, she and her *i* Eze 26:17 3427
The *i* of Zidon and Arvad were thy Eze 27:8 3427
All the *i* of the isles shall be Eze 27:35 3427
all the *i* of Egypt shall know Eze 29:6 3427
all the *i* of the earth are Dan 4:35 1753
and among the *i* of the earth Dan 4:35 1753
to the *i* of Jerusalem, and unto Dan 9:7 3427
with the *i* of the land, because Hos 4:1 3427
The *i* of Samaria shall fear Hos 10:5 7934
and give ear, all ye *i* of the land Joel 1:2 3427
all the *i* of the land into the Joel 1:14 3427
let all the *i* of the land tremble Joel 2:1 3427
the *i* thereof have spoken lies, Mic 6:12 3427
and the *i* thereof an hissing Mic 6:16 3427
and upon all the *i* of Jerusalem Zeph 1:4 3427
ye *i* of Maktesh, for all the Zeph 1:11 3427
Woe unto the *i* of the sea coast, Zeph 2:5 3427
people, and the *i* of many cities Zec 8:20 3427
the *i* of one city shall go to Zec 8:21 3427
no more pity the *i* of the land Zec 11:6 3427
The *i* of Jerusalem shall be my Zec 12:5 3427
the glory of the *i* of Jerusalem Zec 12:7 3427
LORD defend the *i* of Jerusalem Zec 12:8 3427
upon the *i* of Jerusalem, the Zec 12:10 3427
to the *i* of Jerusalem for sin and Zec 13:1 3427
the *i* of the earth have been made Rev 17:2 *2730*

INHABITED {32}

Seir the Horite, who *i* the land Gen 36:20 3427
until they came to a land *i* Ex 16:35 3427
iniquities unto a land not *i* Lev 16:22 1509
the Canaanites that *i* Zephath Judg 1:17 3427
the Jebusites that *i* Jerusalem Judg 1:21 3427
eastward he *i* unto the entering 1Chr 5:9 3427
It shall never be *i*, neither Is 13:20 3427
to Jerusalem, Thou shalt be *i* Is 44:26 3427
not in vain, he formed it to be *i* Is 45:18 3427
make the desolate cities to be *i* Is 54:3 3427
make thee desolate, a land not *i* Jer 6:8 3427
in a salt land and not *i* Jer 17:6 3427
and cities which are not *i* Jer 22:6 3427
and afterward it shall be *i* Jer 46:26 7931
of the LORD it shall not be *i* Jer 50:13 3427
and it shall be no more *i* for ever Jer 50:39 3427
that are *i* shall be laid waste Eze 12:20 3427
that wast *i* of seafaring men, the Eze 26:17 3427
like the cities that are not *i* Eze 26:19 3427
to the pit, that thou be not *i* Eze 26:20 3427
neither shall it be *i* forty years Eze 29:11 3427
in all the *i* places of the Eze 34:13 4186
and the cities shall be *i*, and the Eze 36:10 3427
are become fenced, and are *i* Eze 36:35 3427
desolate places that are now *i* Eze 38:12 3427
Jerusalem shall be *i* as towns Zec 2:4 3427
prophets, when Jerusalem was *i* Zec 7:7 3427
when men *i* the south and the plain Zec 7:7 3427
Gaza, and Ashkelon shall not be *i* Zec 9:5 3427
Jerusalem shall be *i* again in her Zec 12:6 3427
i in her place, from Benjamin's Zec 14:10 3427
but Jerusalem shall be safely *i* Zec 14:11 3427

INHABITERS {2}

to the *i* of the earth by reason Rev 8:13 *2730*
Woe to the *i* of the earth and of Rev 12:12 *2730*

INHABITEST {1}

O thou that *i* the praises of Ps 22:3 3427

INHABITETH {2}

and in houses which no man *i* Job 15:28 3427
high and lofty One that *i* eternity Is 57:15 7931

INHABITING {1}

to the people *i* the wilderness Ps 74:14 6728

INHERIT {62}

to give thee this land to *i* it Gen 15:7 3423
shall I know that I shall *i* it Gen 15:8 3423
that thou mayest *i* the land Gen 28:4 3423
thou be increased, and *i* the land Ex 23:30 5157
seed, and they shall *i* it for ever Ex 32:13 5157
Ye shall *i* their land, and I will Lev 20:24 3423
to *i* them for a possession Lev 25:46 3423
I have given to the Levites to *i* Num 18:24 5159
of their fathers they shall *i* Num 26:55 5157
For we will not *i* with them on Num 32:19 5157
tribes of your fathers ye shall *i* Num 33:54 5157
the land which ye shall *i* by lot Num 34:13 5157
for he shall cause Israel to *i* it Deut 1:38 5157
that thou mayest *i* his land Deut 2:31 3423
he shall cause them to *i* the land Deut 3:28 5157
the LORD your God giveth you to *i* Deut 12:10 5157
i the land which the LORD thy God Deut 16:20 3423
the LORD thy God giveth thee to *i* Deut 19:3 5157
which thou shalt *i* in the land Deut 19:14 5157
his sons to *i* that which he hath Deut 21:16 5157
and thou shalt cause them to *i* it Deut 31:7 5157
but one lot and one portion to *i* Josh 17:14 5159
Thou shalt not *i* in our father's Judg 11:2 5157
to make them *i* the throne of 1Sa 2:8 5157
which thou hast given us to *i* 2Chr 20:11 3423
and his seed shall *i* the earth Ps 25:13 3423
the LORD, they shall *i* the earth Ps 37:9 3423
But the meek shall *i* the earth Ps 37:11 3423
blessed of him shall *i* the earth Ps 37:22 3423
The righteous shall *i* the land Ps 37:29 3423
he shall exalt thee to *i* the land Ps 37:34 3423
also of his servants shall *i* it Ps 69:36 5157
for thou shalt *i* all nations Ps 82:8 5157
The wise shall *i* glory Prov 3:35 5157
those that love me to *i* substance Prov 8:21 5157
his own house shall *i* the wind Prov 11:29 5157
The simple *i* folly Prov 14:18 5157
to cause to *i* the desolate Is 49:8 5157
and thy seed shall *i* the Gentiles Is 54:3 3423
land, and shall *i* my holy mountain Is 57:13 3423
they shall *i* the land for ever, Is 60:21 3423
and mine elect shall *i* it, and my Is 65:9 3423
fields to them that shall *i* them Jer 8:10 3423
have caused my people Israel to *i* Jer 12:14 5157
why then doth their king *i* Gad Jer 49:1 3423
whereby ye shall *i* the land Eze 47:13 5157
And ye shall *i* it, one as well as Eze 47:14 3423
the LORD shall *i* Judah his Zec 2:12 5157
for they shall *i* the earth Mt 5:5 *2816*
and shall *i* everlasting life Mt 19:29 *2816*
i the kingdom prepared for you Mt 25:34 *2816*
I do that I may *i* eternal life Mk 10:17 *2816*
what shall I do to *i* eternal life Lk 10:25 *2816*
what shall I do to *i* eternal life Lk 18:18 *2816*
shall not *i* the kingdom of God 1Cor 6:9 *2816*
shall *i* the kingdom of God 1Cor 6:10 *2816*
blood cannot *i* the kingdom of God 1Cor 15:50 *2816*
doth corruption *i* incorruption 1Cor 15:50 *2816*
shall not *i* the kingdom of God Gal 5:21 *2816*
faith and patience *i* the promises Heb 6:12 *2816*
that ye should *i* a blessing 1Pet 3:9 *2816*
overcometh shall *i* all things Rev 21:7 *2816*

INHERITANCE {239}

Is there yet any portion or *i* for	Gen 31:14	5159
name of their brethren in their *i*	Gen 48:6	5159
them in the mountain of thine *i*	Ex 15:17	5159
our sin, and take us for thine *i*	Ex 34:9	5157
ye shall take them as an *i* for	Lev 25:46	5157
and honey, or given us *i* of fields	Num 16:14	5159
shalt have no *i* in their land	Num 18:20	5157
thine *i* among the children of	Num 18:20	5159
all the tenth in Israel for an *i*	Num 18:21	5159
children of Israel they have no *i*	Num 18:23	5159
of Israel they shall have no *i*	Num 18:24	5159
given you from them for your *i*	Num 18:26	5159
an *i* according to the number of	Num 26:53	5159
many thou shalt give the more *i*	Num 26:54	5159
to few thou shalt give the less *i*	Num 26:54	5159
to every one shall his *i* be given	Num 26:54	5159
because there was no *i* given them	Num 26:62	5159
give them a possession of an *i*	Num 27:7	5159
thou shalt cause the *i* of their	Num 27:7	5159
then ye shall cause his *i* to pass	Num 27:8	5159
give his *i* unto his brethren	Num 27:9	5159
then ye shall give his *i* unto his	Num 27:10	5159
then ye shall give his *i* unto his	Num 27:11	5159
have inherited every man his *i*	Num 32:18	5159
because our *i* is fallen to us on	Num 32:19	5159
that the possession of our *i* on	Num 32:32	5159
lot for an *i* among your families	Num 33:54	5157
the more ye shall give the more *i*	Num 33:54	5159
fewer ye shall give the less *i*	Num 33:54	5159
every man's *i* shall be in the	Num 33:54	
that shall fall unto you for an *i*	Num 34:2	5159
fathers, have received their *i*	Num 34:14	
of Manasseh have received their *i*	Num 34:14	5159
their *i* on this side Jordan near	Num 34:15	5159
tribe, to divide the land by *i*	Num 34:18	5157
LORD commanded to divide the *i*	Num 34:29	5157
give unto the Levites of the *i* of	Num 35:2	5159
to his *i* which he inheriteth	Num 35:8	5159
an *i* by lot to the children of	Num 36:2	5159
by the LORD to give the *i* of	Num 36:2	5159
then shall their *i* be taken from	Num 36:3	5159
taken from the *i* of our fathers	Num 36:3	5159
shall be put to the *i* of the	Num 36:3	5159
it be taken from the lot of our *i*	Num 36:3	5159
i be put unto the *i* of	Num 36:4	5159
so shall their *i* be taken away	Num 36:4	5159
be taken away from the *i* of the	Num 36:4	5159
So shall not the *i* of the	Num 36:7	5159
shall keep himself to the *i* of	Num 36:7	5159
that possesseth an *i* in any tribe	Num 36:8	5159
every man the *i* of his fathers	Num 36:8	5159
Neither shall the *i* remove from	Num 36:9	5159
shall keep himself to his own *i*	Num 36:9	5159
their *i* remained in the tribe of	Num 36:12	5159
to be unto him a people of *i*	Deut 4:20	5159
LORD thy God giveth thee for an *i*	Deut 4:21	5159
to give thee their land for an *i*	Deut 4:38	5159
destroy not thy people and thine *i*	Deut 9:26	5159
they are thy people and thine *i*	Deut 9:29	5159
no part nor *i* with his brethren	Deut 10:9	5159
the LORD is his *i*, according as	Deut 10:9	5159
yet come to the rest and to the *i*	Deut 12:9	5159
as he hath no part nor *i* with you	Deut 12:12	5159
he hath no part nor *i* with thee	Deut 14:27	5159
he hath no part nor *i* with thee	Deut 14:29	5159
thee for an *i* to possess it	Deut 15:4	5159
have no part nor *i* with Israel	Deut 18:1	5159
the LORD made by fire, and his *i*	Deut 18:1	5159
have no *i* among their brethren	Deut 18:2	5159
the LORD is their *i*, as he hath	Deut 18:2	5159
LORD thy God giveth thee for an *i*	Deut 19:10	5159
of old time have set in thine *i*	Deut 19:14	5159
thy God doth give thee for an *i*	Deut 20:16	5159
LORD thy God giveth thee for an *i*	Deut 21:23	5159
LORD thy God giveth thee for an *i*	Deut 24:4	5159
thee for an *i* to possess it	Deut 25:19	5159
LORD thy God giveth thee for an *i*	Deut 26:1	5159
gave it for an *i* unto the	Deut 29:8	5159
divided to the nations their *i*	Deut 32:8	5157
Jacob is the lot of his *i*	Deut 32:9	5159
even the *i* of the congregation of	Deut 33:4	4181
thou divide for an *i* the land	Josh 1:6	5157
Joshua gave it for an *i* unto	Josh 11:23	5159
lot unto the Israelites for an *i*	Josh 13:6	5159
for an *i* unto the nine tribes	Josh 13:7	5159
the Gadites have received their *i*	Josh 13:8	5159
the tribe of Levi he gave none *i*	Josh 13:14	5159
Israel made by fire are their *i*	Josh 13:14	5159
i according to their families	Josh 13:15	
This was the *i* of the children of	Josh 13:23	5159
Moses gave *i* unto the tribe of	Josh 13:24	
This is the *i* of the children of	Josh 13:28	5159
Moses gave *i* unto the half tribe	Josh 13:29	
for *i* in the plains of Moab	Josh 13:32	5157
of Levi Moses gave not any *i*	Josh 13:33	5159
LORD God of Israel was their *i*	Josh 13:33	5159
Israel, distributed for *i* to them	Josh 14:1	5157
By lot was their *i*, as the LORD	Josh 14:2	5159
had given the *i* of two tribes	Josh 14:3	5159
Levites he gave none *i* among them	Josh 14:3	5159
have trodden shall be thine *i*	Josh 14:9	5159
son of Jephunneh Hebron for an *i*	Josh 14:13	5159
Hebron therefore became the *i* of	Josh 14:14	5159
This is the *i* of the tribe of the	Josh 15:20	5159
Manasseh and Ephraim, took their *i*	Josh 16:4	5157
of their *i* on the east side was	Josh 16:5	5159
This is the *i* of the tribe of the	Josh 16:8	5159
of Ephraim were among the *i* of	Josh 16:9	5159
give us an *i* among our brethren	Josh 17:4	5159
an *i* among the brethren of their	Josh 17:4	5159
Manasseh had an *i* among his sons	Josh 17:6	5157
had not yet received their *i*	Josh 18:2	5159
it according to the *i* of them	Josh 18:4	5159
priesthood of the LORD is their *i*	Josh 18:7	5159
have received their *i* beyond	Josh 18:7	5159
This was the *i* of the children of	Josh 18:20	5159
This is the *i* of the children of	Josh 18:28	5159
and their *i* was within the	Josh 19:1	5159
the *i* of the children of Judah	Josh 19:1	5159
And they had in their *i* Beer-sheba	Josh 19:2	5159
This is the *i* of the tribe of the	Josh 19:8	5159
the *i* of the children of Simeon	Josh 19:9	5159
i within the *i* of them	Josh 19:9	5159
border of their *i* was unto Sarid	Josh 19:10	5159
This is the *i* of the children of	Josh 19:16	5159
This is the *i* of the tribe of the	Josh 19:23	5159
This is the *i* of the tribe of the	Josh 19:31	5159
This is the *i* of the tribe of the	Josh 19:39	5159
And the coast of their *i* was Zorah	Josh 19:41	5159
This is the *i* of the tribe of the	Josh 19:48	5159
the land for *i* by their coasts	Josh 19:49	5157
i to Joshua the son of Nun among	Josh 19:49	5159
divided for an *i* by lot in Shiloh	Josh 19:51	5157
unto the Levites out of their *i*	Josh 21:3	5159
to be an *i* for your tribes, from	Josh 23:4	5159
depart, every man unto his *i*	Josh 24:28	5159
border of his *i* in Timnath-serah	Josh 24:30	5159
it became the *i* of the children	Josh 24:32	5159
unto his *i* to possess the land	Judg 2:6	5159
border of his *i* in Timnath-heres	Judg 2:9	5159
sought them an *i* to dwell in	Judg 18:1	5159
for unto that day all their *i* had	Judg 18:1	5159
the country of the *i* of Israel	Judg 20:6	5159
There must be an *i* for them that	Judg 21:17	3425
went and returned unto their *i*	Judg 21:23	5159
from thence every man to his *i*	Judg 21:24	5159
the name of the dead upon his *i*	Ruth 4:5	5159
for myself, lest I mar mine own *i*	Ruth 4:6	5159
the name of the dead upon his *i*	Ruth 4:10	5159
thee to be captain over his *i*	1Sa 10:1	5159
from abiding in the *i* of the LORD	1Sa 26:19	5159
son together out of the *i* of God	2Sa 14:16	5159
neither have we *i* in the son of	2Sa 20:1	5159
thou swallow up the *i* of the LORD	2Sa 20:19	5159
ye may bless the *i* of the LORD	2Sa 21:3	5159
hast given to thy people for an *i*	1Kin 8:36	5159
they be thy people, and thine *i*	1Kin 8:51	5159
of the earth, to be thine *i*	1Kin 8:53	5159
neither have we *i* in the son of	1Kin 12:16	5159
that I should give the *i* of my	1Kin 21:3	5159
not give thee the *i* of my fathers	1Kin 21:4	5159
forsake the remnant of mine *i*	2Kin 21:14	5159
land of Canaan, the lot of your *i*	1Chr 16:18	5159
leave it for an *i* for your	1Chr 28:8	5157
given unto thy people for an *i*	2Chr 6:27	5159
we have none *i* in the son of	2Chr 10:16	5159
leave it for an *i* to your	Ezr 9:12	3423
of Judah, every one in his *i*	Neh 11:20	5159
what *i* of the Almighty from on	Job 31:2	5159
gave them *i* among their brethren	Job 42:15	5159
give thee the heathen for thine *i*	Ps 2:8	5159
The LORD is the portion of mine *i*	Ps 16:5	2506
Save thy people, and bless thine *i*	Ps 28:9	5159
whom he hath chosen for his own *i*	Ps 33:12	5159
their *i* shall be for ever	Ps 37:18	5159
He shall choose our *i* for us	Ps 47:4	5159
thou didst confirm thine *i*	Ps 68:9	5159
the rod of thine *i*, which thou	Ps 74:2	5159
and divided them an *i* by line	Ps 78:55	5159
and was wroth with his *i*	Ps 78:62	5159
Jacob his people, and Israel his *i*	Ps 78:71	5159
the heathen are come into thine *i*	Ps 79:1	5159
neither will he forsake his *i*	Ps 94:14	5159
land of Canaan, the lot of your *i*	Ps 105:11	5159
that I may glory with thine *i*	Ps 106:5	5159
that he abhorred his own *i*	Ps 106:40	5159
A good man leaveth an *i* to his	Prov 13:22	5157
part of the *i* among the brethren	Prov 17:2	5159
and riches are the *i* of fathers	Prov 19:14	5159
An *i* may be gotten hastily at the	Prov 20:21	5159
Wisdom is good with an *i*	Eccl 7:11	5159
of my hands, and Israel mine *i*	Is 19:25	5159
my people, I have polluted mine *i*	Is 47:6	5159
sake, the tribes of thine *i*	Is 63:17	5159
given for an *i* unto your fathers	Jer 3:18	5157
and Israel is the rod of his *i*	Jer 10:16	5159
that touch the *i* which I have	Jer 12:14	5159
they have filled mine *i* with the	Jer 16:18	5159
for the right of *i* is thine	Jer 32:8	3425
and Israel is the rod of his *i*	Jer 51:19	5159
Our *i* is turned to strangers, our	Lam 5:2	5159
thou shalt take thine *i* in	Eze 22:16	2490
the land is given us for *i*	Eze 33:24	4181
at the *i* of the house of Israel	Eze 35:15	5159
thee, and thou shalt be their *i*	Eze 36:12	5159
And it shall be unto them for an *i*	Eze 44:28	5159
I am their *i*	Eze 44:28	5159
divide by lot the land for *i*	Eze 45:1	5159
the *i* thereof shall be his sons'	Eze 46:16	5159
it shall be their possession by *i*	Eze 46:16	5159
of his *i* to one of his servants	Eze 46:17	5159
but his *i* shall be his sons' for	Eze 46:17	5159
of the people's *i* by oppression	Eze 46:18	5159
sons *i* out of his own possession	Eze 46:18	5157
land shall fall unto you for *i*	Eze 47:14	5159
it by lot for an *i* unto you	Eze 47:22	5159
they shall have *i* with you among	Eze 47:22	5159
there shall ye give him his *i*	Eze 47:23	5159
unto the tribes of Israel for *i*	Eze 48:29	5159
him, and let us seize on his *i*	Mt 21:38	*2817*
kill him, and the *i* shall be ours	Mk 12:7	*2817*
that he divide the *i* with me	Lk 12:13	*2817*
kill him, that the *i* may be ours	Lk 20:14	*2817*
And he gave him none *i* in it	Acts 7:5	*2817*
to give you an *i* among all them	Acts 20:32	*2817*
i among them which are sanctified	Acts 26:18	*2819*
For if the *i* be of the law, it is	Gal 3:18	*2817*
whom also we have obtained an *i*	Eph 1:11	*2820*
our *i* until the redemption of the	Eph 1:14	*2817*
the glory of his *i* in the saints	Eph 1:18	*2817*
hath any *i* in the kingdom of	Eph 5:5	*2817*
of the *i* of the saints in light	Col 1:12	*2819*
shall receive the reward of the *i*	Col 3:24	*2817*
as he hath by *i* obtained a more	Heb 1:4	*2820*
receive the promise of eternal *i*	Heb 9:15	*2817*
he should after receive for an *i*	Heb 11:8	*2817*
To an *i* incorruptible, and	1Pet 1:4	*2817*

INHERITANCES {1}

These are the *i*, which Eleazar	Josh 19:51	5159

INHERITED {6}

have *i* every man his inheritance	Num 32:18	5157
of Israel *i* in the land of Canaan	Josh 14:1	5157
they *i* the labour of the people	Ps 105:44	3423
Surely our fathers have *i* lies	Jer 16:19	5157
Abraham was one, and he *i* the land	Eze 33:24	3423
when he would have *i* the blessing	Heb 12:17	*2816*

INHERITETH {1}

to his inheritance which he *i*	Num 35:8	5157

INHERITOR {1}

out of Judah an *i* of my mountains	Is 65:9	3423

INIQUITIES {56}

confess over him all the *i* of the	Lev 16:21	5771
their *i* unto a land not inhabited	Lev 16:22	5771
also in the *i* of their fathers	Lev 26:39	5771
for a year, shall ye bear your *i*	Num 14:34	5771
for our *i* are increased over our	Ezr 9:6	5771
and for our *i* have we, our kings,	Ezr 9:7	5771
us less than our *i* deserve	Ezr 9:13	5771
sins, and the *i* of their fathers	Neh 9:2	5771
How many are mine *i* and sins	Job 13:23	5771
me to possess the *i* of my youth	Job 13:26	5771
and thine *i* infinite	Job 22:5	5771
For mine *i* are gone over mine	Ps 38:4	5771
mine *i* have taken hold upon me,	Ps 40:12	5771
my sins, and blot out all mine *i*	Ps 51:9	5771
They search out *i*	Ps 64:6	5766
I prevail against me	Ps 65:3	1647,5771
remember not against us former *i*	Ps 79:8	5771
Thou hast set our *i* before thee	Ps 90:8	5771
Who forgiveth all thine *i*	Ps 103:3	5771
rewarded us according to our *i*	Ps 103:10	5771
and because of their *i*, are	Ps 107:17	5771
If thou, LORD, shouldest mark *i*	Ps 130:3	5771
redeem Israel from all his *i*	Ps 130:8	5771
His own *i* shall take the wicked	Prov 5:22	5771
thou hast wearied me with thine *i*	Is 43:24	5771
Behold, for your *i* have ye sold	Is 50:1	5771
he was bruised for our *i*	Is 53:5	5771
for he shall bear their *i*	Is 53:11	5771
But your *i* have separated between	Is 59:2	5771
and as for our *i*, we know them	Is 59:12	5771
and our *i*, like the wind, have	Is 64:6	5771
consumed us, because of our *i*	Is 64:7	5771
Your *i*, and the *i* of your	Is 65:7	5771
Your *i* have turned away these	Jer 5:25	5771
to the *i* of their forefathers	Jer 11:10	5771
though our *i* testify against us,	Jer 14:7	5771
and I will pardon all their *i*	Jer 33:8	5771
the *i* of her priests, that have	Lam 4:13	5771
and we have borne their *i*	Lam 5:7	5771
but ye shall pine away for your *i*	Eze 24:23	5771
by the multitude of thine *i*	Eze 28:18	5771
but their *i* shall be upon their	Eze 32:27	5771
in your own sight for your *i*	Eze 36:31	5771
i I will also cause you to dwell	Eze 36:33	5771
they may be ashamed of their *i*	Eze 43:10	5771
thine *i* by shewing mercy to the	Dan 4:27	5758
that we might turn from our *i*	Dan 9:13	5771
for the *i* of our fathers,	Dan 9:16	5771
I will punish you for all your *i*	Amos 3:2	5771
he will subdue our *i*	Mic 7:19	5771
away every one of you from his *i*	Acts 3:26	*4189*
are they whose *i* are forgiven	Rom 4:7	*458*
their *i* will I remember no more	Heb 8:12	*458*
i will I remember no more	Heb 10:17	*458*
and God hath remembered her *i*	Rev 18:5	*92*

INIQUITY {278}

for the *i* of the Amorites is not	Gen 15:16	5771
be consumed in the *i* of the city	Gen 19:15	5771
found out the *i* of thy servants	Gen 44:16	5771
visiting the *i* of the fathers	Ex 20:5	5771
may bear the *i* of the holy things	Ex 28:38	5771
that they bear not *i*, and die	Ex 28:43	5771
mercy for thousands, forgiving *i*	Ex 34:7	5771
visiting the *i* of the fathers	Ex 34:7	5771
and pardon our *i* and our sin, and	Ex 34:9	5771
it, then he shall bear his *i*	Lev 5:1	5771
is he guilty, and shall bear his *i*	Lev 5:17	5771
eateth of it shall bear his *i*	Lev 7:18	5771
to bear the *i* of the congregation	Lev 10:17	5771
then he shall bear his *i*	Lev 17:16	5771

I do visit the *i* thereof upon it ... Lev 18:25 5771
that eateth it shall bear his *i* ... Lev 19:8 5771
he shall bear his *i* ... Lev 20:17 5771
they shall bear their *i* ... Lev 20:19 5771
them to bear the *i* of trespass ... Lev 22:16 5771
in their *i* in your enemies' lands ... Lev 26:39 5771
If they shall confess their *i* ... Lev 26:40 5771
the *i* of their fathers, with ... Lev 26:40 5771
of the punishment of their *i* ... Lev 26:41 5771
of the punishment of their *i* ... Lev 26:43 5771
bringing *i* to remembrance ... Num 5:15 5771
shall the man be guiltless from *i* ... Num 5:31 5771
and this woman shall bear her *i* ... Num 5:31 5771
and of great mercy, forgiving *i* ... Num 14:18 5771
visiting the *i* of the fathers ... Num 14:18 5771
the *i* of this people according ... Num 14:19 5771
his *i* shall be upon him ... Num 15:31 5771
shall bear the *i* of the sanctuary ... Num 18:1 5771
bear the *i* of your priesthood ... Num 18:1 5771
and they shall bear their *i* ... Num 18:23 5771
He hath not beheld *i* in Jacob ... Num 23:21 205
then he shall bear her *i* ... Num 30:15 5771
visiting the *i* of the fathers ... Deut 5:9 5771
rise up against a man for any *i* ... Deut 19:15 5771
a God of truth and without *i* ... Deut 32:4 5766
Is the *i* of Peor too little for ... Josh 22:17 5771
man perished not alone in his *i* ... Josh 22:20 5771
ever for the *i* which he knoweth ... 1Sa 3:13 5771
that the *i* of Eli's house shall ... 1Sa 3:14 5771
and stubbornness is as *i* and ... 1Sa 15:23 205
what is mine *i*? ... 1Sa 20:1 5771
if there be in me *i*, slay me ... 1Sa 20:8 5771
my lord, upon me let this *i* be ... 1Sa 25:24 5771
If he commit *i*, I will chasten ... 2Sa 7:14 5753
the *i* be on me, and on my father's ... 2Sa 14:9 5771
and if there be any *i* in me ... 2Sa 14:32 5771
Let not my lord impute *i* unto me ... 2Sa 19:19 5771
and have kept myself from mine *i* ... 2Sa 22:24 5771
take away the *i* of thy servant ... 2Sa 24:10 5771
do away the *i* of thy servant ... 1Chr 21:8 5771
for there is no *i* with the LORD ... 2Chr 19:7 5766
And cover not their *i*, and let not ... Neh 4:5 5771
as I have seen, they that plow *i* ... Job 4:8 205
hope, and *i* stoppeth her mouth ... Job 5:16 5766
I pray you, let it not be *i* ... Job 6:29 5766
Is there *i* in my tongue ... Job 6:30 5766
and take away mine *i* ... Job 7:21 5771
That thou enquirest after mine *i* ... Job 10:6 5771
wilt not acquit me from mine *i* ... Job 10:14 5771
thee less than thine *i* deserveth ... Job 11:6 5771
If *i* be in thine hand, put it far ... Job 11:14 205
a bag, and thou sewest up mine *i* ... Job 14:17 5771
For thy mouth uttereth thine *i* ... Job 15:5 5771
man, which drinketh *i* like water ... Job 15:16 5766
The heaven shall reveal his *i* ... Job 20:27 5771
layeth up his *i* for his children ... Job 21:19 205
thou shalt put away *i* far from ... Job 22:23 5766
punishment to the workers of *i* ... Job 31:3 205
it is an *i* to be punished by the ... Job 31:11 5771
This also were an *i* to be ... Job 31:28 5771
by hiding mine *i* in my bosom ... Job 31:33 5771
neither is there *i* in me ... Job 33:9 5771
in company with the workers of *i* ... Job 34:8 205
Almighty, that he should commit *i* ... Job 34:10 5766
workers of *i* may hide themselves ... Job 34:22 205
if I have done *i*, I will do no ... Job 34:32 5766
that they return from *i* ... Job 36:10 205
Take heed, regard not *i* ... Job 36:21 205
who can say, Thou hast wrought *i* ... Job 36:23 5766
thou hatest all workers of *i* ... Ps 5:5 205
from me, all ye workers of *i* ... Ps 6:8 205
if there be *i* in my hands ... Ps 7:3 5766
Behold, he travaileth with *i* ... Ps 7:14 205
all the workers of *i* no knowledge ... Ps 14:4 205
him, and I kept myself from mine *i* ... Ps 18:23 5771
sake, O LORD, pardon mine *i* ... Ps 25:11 5771
wicked, and with the workers of *i* ... Ps 28:3 205
faileth because of mine *i* ... Ps 31:10 5771
unto whom the LORD imputeth not *i* ... Ps 32:2 5771
thee, and mine *i* have I not hid ... Ps 32:5 5771
and thou forgavest the *i* of my sin ... Ps 32:5 5771
until his *i* be found to be ... Ps 36:2 5771
The words of his mouth are *i* ... Ps 36:3 205
There are the workers of *i* fallen ... Ps 36:12 205
envious against the workers of *i* ... Ps 37:1 5766
For I will declare mine *i* ... Ps 38:18 5771
rebukes dost correct man for *i* ... Ps 39:11 5771
his heart gathereth *i* to itself ... Ps 41:6 205
when the *i* of my heels shall ... Ps 49:5 5771
Wash me throughly from mine *i* ... Ps 51:2 5771
Behold, I was shapen in *i* ... Ps 51:5 5771
they, and have done abominable *i* ... Ps 53:1 5766
the workers of *i* no knowledge ... Ps 53:4 205
for they cast *i* upon me, and in ... Ps 55:3 205
Shall they escape by *i* ... Ps 56:7 205
Deliver me from the workers of *i* ... Ps 59:2 205
insurrection of the workers of *i* ... Ps 64:2 205
If I regard *i* in my heart ... Ps 66:18 205
Add *i* unto their *i* ... Ps 69:27 5771
of compassion, forgave their *i* ... Ps 78:38 5771
hast forgiven the *i* of thy people ... Ps 85:2 5771
the rod, and their *i* with stripes ... Ps 89:32 5771
all the workers of *i* do flourish ... Ps 92:7 205
workers of *i* shall be scattered ... Ps 92:9 205
the workers of *i* boast themselves ... Ps 94:4 205
for me against the workers of *i* ... Ps 94:16 205
Shall the throne of *i* have ... Ps 94:20 1942
shall bring upon them their own *i* ... Ps 94:23 205
our fathers, we have committed *i* ... Ps 106:6 5753
and were brought low for their *i* ... Ps 106:43 5771
all *i* shall stop her mouth ... Ps 107:42 5766
Let the *i* of his fathers be ... Ps 109:14 5771
They also do no *i* ... Ps 119:3 5766
let not any *i* have dominion over ... Ps 119:133 205
put forth their hands unto *i* ... Ps 125:3 5766
them forth with the workers of *i* ... Ps 125:5 205
wicked works with men that work *i* ... Ps 141:4 205
and the gins of the workers of *i* ... Ps 141:9 205
shall be to the workers of *i* ... Prov 10:29 205
By mercy and truth *i* is purged ... Prov 16:6 5771
mouth of the wicked devoureth *i* ... Prov 19:28 205
shall be to the workers of *i* ... Prov 21:15 205
He that soweth *i* shall reap ... Prov 22:8 5766
righteousness, that *i* was there ... Eccl 3:16 7562
nation, a people laden with *i* ... Is 1:4 5771
it is *i*, even the solemn meeting ... Is 1:13 205
that draw *i* with cords of vanity ... Is 5:18 5771
thine *i* is taken away, and thy sin ... Is 6:7 5771
evil, and the wicked for their *i* ... Is 13:11 5771
for the *i* of their fathers ... Is 14:21 5771
Surely this *i* shall not be purged ... Is 22:14 5771
of the earth for their *i* ... Is 26:21 5771
shall the *i* of Jacob be purged ... Is 27:9 5771
all that watch for *i* are cut off ... Is 29:20 205
Therefore this *i* shall be to you ... Is 30:13 5771
the help of them that work *i* ... Is 31:2 205
villany, and his heart will work *i* ... Is 32:6 205
therein shall be forgiven their *i* ... Is 33:24 5771
that her *i* is pardoned ... Is 40:2 5771
hath laid on him the *i* of us all ... Is 53:6 5771
For the *i* of his covetousness was ... Is 57:17 5771
blood, and your fingers with *i* ... Is 59:3 5771
mischief, and bring forth *i* ... Is 59:4 205
their works are works of *i* ... Is 59:6 205
their thoughts are thoughts of *i* ... Is 59:7 205
LORD, neither remember *i* for ever ... Is 64:9 5771
What *i* have your fathers found in ... Jer 2:5 5766
yet thine *i* is marked before me, ... Jer 2:22 5771
Only acknowledge thine *i*, that ... Jer 3:13 5771
and weary themselves to commit *i* ... Jer 9:5 5753
thine *i* are thy skirts discovered ... Jer 13:22 5771
he will now remember their *i* ... Jer 14:10 5771
and the *i* of our fathers ... Jer 14:20 5771
or what is our *i* ... Jer 16:10 5771
neither is their *i* hid from mine ... Jer 16:17 5771
first I will recompense their *i* ... Jer 16:18 5771
forgive not their *i*, neither blot ... Jer 18:23 5771
saith the LORD, for their *i* ... Jer 25:12 5771
one, for the multitude of thine *i* ... Jer 30:14 5771
for the multitude of thine *i* ... Jer 30:15 5771
every one shall die for his own *i* ... Jer 31:30 5771
for I will forgive their *i* ... Jer 31:34 5771
recompensest the *i* of the fathers ... Jer 32:18 5771
cleanse them from all their *i* ... Jer 33:8 5771
that I may forgive their *i* ... Jer 36:3 5771
seed and his servants for their *i* ... Jer 36:31 5771
the *i* of Israel shall be sought ... Jer 50:20 5771
be not cut off in her *i* ... Jer 51:6 5771
they have not discovered thine *i* ... Lam 2:14 5771
For the punishment of the *i* of ... Lam 4:6 5771
of thine *i* is accomplished ... Lam 4:22 5771
he will visit thine *i*, O daughter ... Lam 4:22 5771
wicked man shall die in his *i* ... Eze 3:18 5771
wicked way, he shall die in his *i* ... Eze 3:19 5771
his righteousness, and commit *i* ... Eze 3:20 5766
lay the *i* of the house of Israel ... Eze 4:4 5771
upon it thou shalt bear their *i* ... Eze 4:4 5771
upon thee the years of their *i* ... Eze 4:5 5771
bear the *i* of the house of Israel ... Eze 4:5 5771
thou shalt bear the *i* of the ... Eze 4:6 5771
and consume away for their *i* ... Eze 4:17 5771
himself in the *i* of his life ... Eze 7:13 5771
mourning, every one for his *i* ... Eze 7:16 5771
is the stumblingblock of their *i* ... Eze 7:19 5771
The *i* of the house of Israel and ... Eze 9:9 5771
of their *i* before their face ... Eze 14:3 5771
of his *i* before his face, and ... Eze 14:4 5771
of his *i* before his face, and ... Eze 14:7 5771
bear the punishment of their *i* ... Eze 14:10 5771
this was the *i* of thy sister ... Eze 16:49 5771
hath withdrawn his hand from *i* ... Eze 18:8 5766
not die for the *i* of his father ... Eze 18:17 5771
lo, even he shall die in his *i* ... Eze 18:18 5771
the son bear the *i* of the father ... Eze 18:19 5771
not bear the *i* of the father ... Eze 18:20 5771
the father bear the *i* of the son ... Eze 18:20 5771
righteousness, and committeth *i* ... Eze 18:24 5766
righteousness, and committeth *i* ... Eze 18:26 5766
for his *i* that he hath done shall ... Eze 18:26 5766
so *i* shall not be your ruin ... Eze 18:30 5771
he will call to remembrance the *i* ... Eze 21:23 5771
have made your *i* to be remembered ... Eze 21:24 5771
when *i* shall have an end, ... Eze 21:25 5771
when their *i* shall have an end ... Eze 21:29 5771
created, till *i* was found in thee ... Eze 28:15 5766
by the *i* of thy traffick ... Eze 28:18 5766
bringeth their *i* to remembrance ... Eze 29:16 5771
them, he is taken away in his *i* ... Eze 33:6 5771
wicked man shall die in his *i* ... Eze 33:8 5771
his way, he shall die in his *i* ... Eze 33:9
own righteousness, and commit *i* ... Eze 33:13 5766
but for his *i* that he hath ... Eze 33:13 5766
of life, without committing *i* ... Eze 33:15 5766
righteousness, and committeth *i* ... Eze 33:18 5766
the time that their *i* had an end ... Eze 35:5 5771
went into captivity for their *i* ... Eze 39:23 5771
they shall even bear their *i* ... Eze 44:10 5771
house of Israel to fall into *i* ... Eze 44:12 5771
GOD, and they shall bear their *i* ... Eze 44:12 5771
have sinned, and have committed *i* ... Dan 9:5 5753
and to make reconciliation for *i* ... Dan 9:24 5771
they set their heart on their *i* ... Hos 4:8 5771
Israel and Ephraim fall in their *i* ... Hos 5:5 5771
is a city of them that work *i* ... Hos 6:8 205
then the *i* of Ephraim was ... Hos 7:1 5771
now will he remember their *i* ... Hos 8:13 5771
mad, for the multitude of thine *i* ... Hos 9:7 5771
he will remember their *i*, he will ... Hos 9:9 5771
of *i* did not overtake them ... Hos 10:9 5932
wickedness, ye have reaped *i* ... Hos 10:13 5766
find none *i* in me that were sin ... Hos 12:8 5771
Is there *i* in Gilead ... Hos 12:11 205
The *i* of Ephraim is bound up ... Hos 13:12 5771
for thou hast fallen by thine *i* ... Hos 14:1 5771
say unto him, Take away all *i* ... Hos 14:2 5771
Woe to them that devise *i* ... Mic 2:1 205
with blood, and Jerusalem with *i* ... Mic 3:10 5766
like unto thee, that pardoneth *i* ... Mic 7:18 5771
Why dost thou shew me *i*, and cause ... Hab 1:3 205
evil, and canst not look on *i* ... Hab 1:13 5999
blood, and stablisheth a city by *i* ... Hab 2:12 5766
he will not do *i* ... Zeph 3:5 5766
remnant of Israel shall not do *i* ... Zeph 3:13 5766
caused thine *i* to pass from thee ... Zec 3:4 5771
I will remove the *i* of that land ... Zec 3:9 5771
i was not found in his lips ... Mal 2:6 5766
and did turn many away from *i* ... Mal 2:6 5771
depart from me, ye that work *i* ... Mt 7:23 *458*
that offend, and them which do *i* ... Mt 13:41 *458*
ye are full of hypocrisy and *i* ... Mt 23:28 *458*
because *i* shall abound, the love ... Mt 24:12 *458*
from me, all ye workers of *i* ... Lk 13:27 *93*
a field with the reward of *i* ... Acts 1:18 *93*
bitterness, and in the bond of *i* ... Acts 8:23 *93*
uncleanness and to *i* unto *i* ... Rom 6:19 *458*
Rejoiceth not in *i*, but rejoiceth ... 1Cor 13:6 *93*
mystery of *i* doth already work ... 2Th 2:7 *458*
the name of Christ depart from *i* ... 2Ti 2:19 *93*
he might redeem us from all *i* ... Titus 2:14 *458*
loved righteousness, and hated *i* ... Heb 1:9 *458*
tongue is a fire, a world of *i* ... Jas 3:6 *93*
But was rebuked for his *i* ... 2Pet 2:16 *3892*

INJURED {1}
ye have not *i* me at all ... Gal 4:12 *91*

INJURIOUS {1}
blasphemer, and a persecutor, and *i* ... 1Ti 1:13 *5197*

INJUSTICE {1}
Not for any *i* in mine hands ... Job 16:17 2555

INK {4}
I wrote them with *i* in the book ... Jer 36:18 1773
by us, written not with *i* ... 2Cor 3:3 *3188*
I would not write with paper and *i* ... 2Jn 12 *3188*
to write, but I will not with *i* ... 3Jn 13 *3188*

INKHORN {3}
with a writer's *i* by his side ... Eze 9:2 7083
had the writer's *i* by his side ... Eze 9:3 7083
which had the *i* by his side ... Eze 9:11 7083

INN {5}
give his ass provender in the *i* ... Gen 42:27 4411
to pass, when we came to the *i* ... Gen 43:21 4411
came to pass by the way in the *i* ... Ex 4:24 4411
was no room for them in the *i* ... Lk 2:7 *2646*
own beast, and brought him to an *i* ... Lk 10:34 *3829*

INNER {37}
the cherubims within the *i* house ... 1Kin 6:27 6442
he built the *i* court with three ... 1Kin 6:36 6442
both for the *i* court of the house ... 1Kin 7:12 6442
both for the doors of the *i* house ... 1Kin 7:50 6442
into the city, into an *i* chamber ... 1Kin 20:30 2315
into an *i* chamber to hide thyself ... 1Kin 22:25 2315
and carry him to an *i* chamber ... 2Kin 9:2 2315
of the *i* parlours thereof, and of ... 1Chr 28:11 6442
the *i* doors thereof for the most ... 2Chr 4:22 6442
into an *i* chamber to hide thyself ... 2Chr 18:24 2315
the priests went into the *i* part ... 2Chr 29:16 6441
unto the king into the *i* court ... Est 4:11 6442
stood in the *i* court of the ... Est 5:1 6442
to the door of the *i* gate ... Eze 8:3 6442
he brought me into the *i* court of ... Eze 8:16 6442
and the cloud filled the *i* court ... Eze 10:3 6442
of the *i* gate were fifty cubits ... Eze 40:15 6442
forefront of the *i* court without ... Eze 40:19 6442
the gate of the *i* court was over ... Eze 40:23 6442
in the *i* court toward the south ... Eze 40:27 6442
he brought me to the *i* court by ... Eze 40:28 6442
into the *i* court toward the east ... Eze 40:32 6442
without the *i* gate were the ... Eze 40:44 6442
of the singers in the *i* court ... Eze 40:44 6442
hundred cubits, with the *i* temple ... Eze 41:15 6442
the door, even unto the *i* house ... Eze 41:17 6442
cubits which were for the *i* court ... Eze 42:3 6442
an end of measuring the *i* house ... Eze 42:15 6442
and brought me into the *i* court ... Eze 43:5 6442
in at the gates of the *i* court ... Eze 44:17 6442
in the gates of the *i* court ... Eze 44:17 6442
when they enter into the *i* court ... Eze 44:21 6442
the sanctuary, unto the *i* court ... Eze 44:27 6442
posts of the gate of the *i* court ... Eze 45:19 6442
The gate of the *i* court that ... Eze 46:1 6442
thrust them into the *i* prison ... Acts 16:24 *2082*
might by his Spirit in the *i* man ... Eph 3:16 *2080*

INNERMOST {2}
into the *i* parts of the belly ... Prov 18:8 2315
into the *i* parts of the belly ... Prov 26:22 2315

INNOCENCY {5}
i of my hands have I done this ... Gen 20:5 5356
I will wash mine hands in *i* ... Ps 26:6 5356
in vain, and washed my hands in *i* ... Ps 73:13 5356
as before him *i* was found in me ... Dan 6:22 2136
will it be ere they attain to *i* ... Hos 8:5 5356

INNOCENT {38}
and the *i* and righteous slay thou ... Ex 23:7 5355
That *i* blood be not shed in thy ... Deut 19:10 5355
the guilt of *i* blood from Israel ... Deut 19:13 5355
lay not *i* blood unto thy people ... Deut 21:8 5355
guilt of *i* blood from among you ... Deut 21:9 5355
taketh reward to slay an *i* person ... Deut 27:25 5355
wilt thou sin against *i* blood ... 1Sa 19:5 5355
thou mayest take away the *i* blood ... 1Kin 2:31 2600
Manasseh shed *i* blood very much ... 2Kin 21:16 5355
also for the *i* blood that he shed ... 2Kin 24:4 5355
he filled Jerusalem with *i* blood ... 2Kin 24:4 5355
thee, who ever perished, being *i* ... Job 4:7 5355
will laugh at the trial of the *i* ... Job 9:23 5355
know that thou wilt not hold me *i* ... Job 9:28 5352
the *i* shall stir up himself ... Job 17:8 5355
the *i* laugh them to scorn ... Job 22:19 5355
shall deliver the island of the *i* ... Job 22:30 5355
the *i* shall divide the silver ... Job 27:17 5355
without transgression, I am *i* ... Job 33:9 2643
places doth he murder the *i* ... Ps 10:8 5355
nor taketh reward against the *i* ... Ps 15:5 5355
I shall be *i* from the great ... Ps 19:13 5352
righteous, and condemn the *i* blood ... Ps 94:21 5355
shed *i* blood, even the blood of ... Ps 106:38 5355
privily for the *i* without cause ... Prov 1:11 5355
and hands that shed *i* blood ... Prov 6:17 5355
toucheth her shall not be *i* ... Prov 6:29 5352
haste to be rich shall not be *i* ... Prov 28:20 5352
they make haste to shed *i* blood ... Is 59:7 5355
Yet thou sayest, Because I am *i* ... Jer 2:35 5352
shed not *i* blood in this place, ... Jer 7:6 5355
neither shed *i* blood in this ... Jer 22:3 5355
and for to shed *i* blood, and for ... Jer 22:17 5355
bring *i* blood upon yourselves ... Jer 26:15 5355
have shed *i* blood in their land ... Joel 3:19 5355
life, and lay not upon us *i* blood ... Jonah 1:14 5355
that I have betrayed the *i* blood ... Mt 27:4 *121*
I am *i* of the blood of this just ... Mt 27:24 *121*

INNOCENTS {2}
blood of the souls of the poor *i* ... Jer 2:34 5355
this place with the blood of *i* ... Jer 19:4 5355

INNUMERABLE {7}
him, as there are *i* before him ... Job 21:33 369,4557
For *i* evils have compassed me ... Ps 40:12 369,4557
wherein are things creeping *i* ... Ps 104:25 369,4557
than the grasshoppers, and are *i* ... Jer 46:23 369,4557
together an *i* multitude of people ... Lk 12:1 *3461*
sand which is by the sea shore *i* ... Heb 11:12 *382*
to an *i* company of angels, ... Heb 12:22 *3461*

INORDINATE {2}
corrupt in her *i* love than she ... Eze 23:11 5691
i affection, evil concupiscence, ... Col 3:5 *3806*

INQUIRE See ENQUIRE.

INQUISITION {3}
the judges shall make diligent *i* ... Deut 19:18 1875
when *i* was made of the matter, it ... Est 2:23 1245
When he maketh *i* for blood ... Ps 9:12 1875

INSCRIPTION {1}
I found an altar with this *i* ... Acts 17:23 *1924*

INSIDE See APPENDIX.

INSOMUCH See APPENDIX.

INSPIRATION {2}
the *i* of the Almighty giveth them ... Job 32:8 5397
scripture is given by *i* of God ... 2Ti 3:16 *2315*

INSTANT {8}
yea, it shall be at an *i* suddenly ... Is 29:5 6621
breaking cometh suddenly at an *i* ... Is 30:13 6621
At what *i* I shall speak ... Jer 18:7 7281
And at what *i* I shall speak ... Jer 18:9 7281
she coming in that *i* gave thanks ... Lk 2:38 *5610*
they were *i* with loud voices, ... Lk 23:23 *1945*
continuing *i* in prayer ... Rom 12:12 *4342*
be *i* in season, out of season ... 2Ti 4:2 *2186*

INSTANTLY {2}
to Jesus, they besought him *i* ... Lk 7:4 *4705*
i serving God day and night, hope .. Acts 26:7 *1722,1616*

INSTEAD See APPENDIX.

INSTRUCT {9}
his voice, that he might *i* thee ... Deut 4:36 3256
also thy good spirit to *i* them ... Neh 9:20 7919
with the Almighty *i* him ... Job 40:2 3250
my reins also *i* me in the night ... Ps 16:7 3256
I will *i* thee and teach thee in ... Ps 32:8 7919
my mother's house, who would *i* me ... Song 8:2 3925
For his God doth *i* him to ... Is 28:26 3256
among the people shall *i* many ... Dan 11:33 995
of the Lord, that he may *i* him ... 1Cor 2:16 *4822*

INSTRUCTED {19}
he *i* him, he kept him as the ... Deut 32:10 995
wherein Jehoiada the priest *i* him ... 2Kin 12:2 3384
he *i* about the song, because he ... 1Chr 15:22 3256
were *i* in the songs of the LORD ... 1Chr 25:7 3925
i for the building of the house ... 2Chr 3:3 3245
Behold, thou hast *i* many, and thou ... Job 4:3 3256
be *i*, ye judges of the earth ... Ps 2:10 3256
mine ear to them that *i* me ... Prov 5:13 3925
and when the wise is *i*, he ... Prov 21:11 7919
i me that I should not walk in ... Is 8:11 3256
took he counsel, and who *i* him ... Is 40:14 995
Be thou *i*, O Jerusalem, lest my ... Jer 6:8 3256
and after that I was *i*, I smote ... Jer 31:19 3045
i unto the kingdom of heaven is ... Mt 13:52 *3100*
being before *i* of her mother, ... Mt 14:8 *4264*
things, wherein thou hast been *i* ... Lk 1:4 *2727*
This man was *i* in the way of the ... Acts 18:25 *2727*
excellent, being *i* out of the law ... Rom 2:18 *2727*
all things I am *i* both to be full ... Phil 4:12 *3453*

INSTRUCTER {1}
an *i* of every artificer in brass ... Gen 4:22 3913

INSTRUCTERS {1}
ye have ten thousand *i* in Christ ... 1Cor 4:15 *3807*

INSTRUCTING {1}
In meekness *i* those that oppose ... 2Ti 2:25 *3811*

INSTRUCTION {33}
ears of men, and sealeth their *i* ... Job 33:16 4561
Seeing thou hatest *i*, and castest ... Ps 50:17 4148
To know wisdom and *i* ... Prov 1:2 4148
To receive the *i* of wisdom ... Prov 1:3 4148
but fools despise wisdom and *i* ... Prov 1:7 4148
hear the *i* of thy father, and ... Prov 1:8 4148
the *i* of a father, and attend to ... Prov 4:1 4148
Take fast hold of *i* ... Prov 4:13 4148
And say, How have I hated *i* ... Prov 5:12 4148
He shall die without *i* ... Prov 5:23 4148
reproofs of *i* are the way of life ... Prov 6:23 4148
Receive my *i*, and not silver ... Prov 8:10 4148
Hear *i*, and be wise, and refuse it not ... Prov 8:33 4148
Give *i* to a wise man, and he will ... Prov 9:9
in the way of life that keepeth *i* ... Prov 10:17 4148
Whoso loveth *i* loveth knowledge ... Prov 12:1 4148
A wise son heareth his father's *i* ... Prov 13:1 4148
shall be to him that refuseth *i* ... Prov 13:18 4148
A fool despiseth his father's *i* ... Prov 15:5 4148
He that refuseth *i* despiseth his ... Prov 15:32 4148
of the LORD is the *i* of wisdom ... Prov 15:33 4148
but the *i* of fools is folly ... Prov 16:22 4148
Hear counsel, and receive *i* ... Prov 19:20 4148
to hear the *i* that causeth to err ... Prov 19:27 4148
Apply thine heart unto *i*, and ... Prov 23:12 4148
also wisdom, and *i*, and ... Prov 23:23 4148
I looked upon it, and received *i* ... Prov 24:32 4148
might not hear, nor receive *i* ... Jer 17:23 4148
have not hearkened to receive *i* ... Jer 32:33 4148
Will ye not receive *i* to hearken ... Jer 35:13 4148
be a reproach and a taunt, an *i* ... Eze 5:15 4148
wilt fear me, thou wilt receive *i* ... Zeph 3:7 4148
for *i* in righteousness ... 2Ti 3:16 *3809*

INSTRUCTOR {1}
An *i* of the foolish, a teacher of ... Rom 2:20 *3810*

INSTRUMENT {8}
if he smite him with an *i* of iron ... Num 35:16 3627
psaltery and an *i* of ten strings ... Ps 33:2
Upon an *i* of ten strings, and upon ... Ps 92:3
an *i* of ten strings will I sing ... Ps 144:9
not threshed with a threshing *i* ... Is 28:27
sharp threshing *i* having teeth ... Is 41:15
bringeth forth an *i* for his work ... Is 54:16 3627
voice, and can play well on an *i* ... Eze 33:32

INSTRUMENTS {51}
i of cruelty are in their ... Gen 49:5 3627
the pattern of all the *i* thereof ... Ex 25:9 3627
they shall keep all the *i* of the ... Num 3:8 3627
shall take all the *i* of ministry ... Num 4:12 3627
all the *i* of their service, and ... Num 4:26 3627
and their cords, with all their *i* ... Num 4:32 3627
by name ye shall reckon the *i* of ... Num 4:32 3627
it, and all the *i* thereof, both ... Num 7:1 3627
to the war, with the holy *i* ... Num 31:6 3627
harvest, and to make his *i* of war ... 1Sa 8:12 3627
and *i* of his chariots ... 1Sa 8:12 3627
with joy, and with *i* of musick ... 1Sa 18:6 7991
all manner of *i* made of fir wood ... 2Sa 6:5
burnt sacrifice, and threshing *i* ... 2Sa 24:22
other *i* of the oxen for wood ... 2Sa 24:22 3627
flesh with the *i* of the oxen ... 1Kin 19:21 3627
all the *i* of the sanctuary, and ... 1Chr 9:29 3627
expert in war, with all *i* of war ... 1Chr 12:33 3627
with all manner of *i* of war for ... 1Chr 12:37 3627
be the singers with *i* of musick ... 1Chr 15:16 3627
a sound, and with musical *i* of God ... 1Chr 16:42 3627
and the threshing *i* for wood ... 1Chr 21:23
the LORD with the *i* which I made ... 1Chr 23:5 3627
for all *i* of all manner of ... 1Chr 28:14 3627
for all *i* of silver by weight ... 1Chr 28:14 3627
for all *i* of every kind of ... 1Chr 28:14 3627
and the fleshhooks, and all their *i* ... 2Chr 4:16 3627
silver, and the gold, and all the *i* ... 2Chr 5:1 3627
i of musick, and praised the LORD, ... 2Chr 5:13 3627
also with *i* of musick of the LORD ... 2Chr 7:6 3627
also the singers with *i* of musick ... 2Chr 23:13 3627
Levites stood with the *i* of David ... 2Chr 29:26 3627
with the *i* ordained by David king ... 2Chr 29:27 3627
singing with loud *i* unto the LORD ... 2Chr 30:21 3627
that could skill of *i* of musick ... 2Chr 34:12 3627
with the musical *i* of David the ... Neh 12:36 3627
prepared for him the *i* of death ... Ps 7:13 3627
the players on *i* followed after ... Ps 68:25
the players on *i* shall be there ... Ps 87:7
praise him with stringed *i* ... Ps 150:4 4482
of the sons of men, as musical *i* ... Eccl 2:8
The *i* also of the churl are evil ... Is 32:7 3627
sing my songs to the stringed *i* ... Is 38:20
whereupon also they laid the *i* ... Eze 40:42 3627
neither were *i* of musick brought ... Dan 6:18 1761
Gilead with threshing *i* of iron ... Amos 1:3
invent to themselves *i* of musick ... Amos 6:5 3627
the chief singer on my stringed *i* ... Hab 3:19
yet the *i* of a foolish shepherd ... Zec 11:15 3627
yield ye your members as *i* of ... Rom 6:13 *3696*
the dead, and your members as *i* of ... Rom 6:13 *3696*

INSURRECTION {5}
time hath made *i* against kings ... Ezr 4:19 5376
from the *i* of the workers of ... Ps 64:2 7285
them that had made *i* with him ... Mk 15:7 *4955*
who had committed murder in the *i* ... Mk 15:7 *4714*
the Jews made *i* with one accord ... Acts 18:12 *2721*

INTEGRITY {16}
in the *i* of my heart and innocency ... Gen 20:5 8537
didst this in the *i* of thy heart ... Gen 20:6 8537
in *i* of heart, and in uprightness, ... 1Kin 9:4 8537
and still he holdeth fast his *i* ... Job 2:3 8538
Dost thou still retain thine *i* ... Job 2:9 8538
I will not remove mine *i* from me ... Job 27:5 8538
balance, that God may know mine *i* ... Job 31:6 8538
according to mine *i* that is in me ... Ps 7:8 8537
Let *i* and uprightness preserve me ... Ps 25:21 8537
for I have walked in mine *i* ... Ps 26:1 8537
as for me, I will walk in mine *i* ... Ps 26:11 8537
me, thou upholdest me in mine *i* ... Ps 41:12 8537
according to the *i* of his heart ... Ps 78:72 8537
The *i* of the upright shall guide ... Prov 11:3 8538
is the poor that walketh in his *i* ... Prov 19:1 8537
The just man walketh in his *i* ... Prov 20:7 8537

INTELLIGENCE {1}
have *i* with them that forsake the ... Dan 11:30 995

INTEND {4}
did not *i* to go up against them ... Josh 22:33 559
ye *i* to add more to our sins and ... 2Chr 28:13 559
i to bring this man's blood upon ... Acts 5:28 *1014*
ye *i* to do as touching these men ... Acts 5:35 *3195*

INTENDED {1}
For they *i* evil against thee ... Ps 21:11 5186

INTENDEST {1}
i thou to kill me, as thou ... Ex 2:14 559

INTENDING {3}
i to build a tower, sitteth not ... Lk 14:28 *2309*
i after Easter to bring him forth ... Acts 12:4 *1011*
Assos, there *i* to take in Paul ... Acts 20:13 *3195*

INTENT {11}
to the *i* that the LORD might ... 2Sa 17:14 5668
to the *i* that he might destroy ... 2Kin 10:19 4616
to the *i* that he might let none ... 2Chr 16:1
for to the *i* that I might shew ... Eze 40:4 4616
to the *i* that the living may know ... Dan 4:17 1701
there, to the *i* ye may believe ... Jn 11:15 *2443*
for what *i* he spake this unto him ... Jn 13:28
and came hither for that *i* ... Acts 9:21
for what *i* ye have sent for me ... Acts 10:29 *3056*
to the *i* we should not lust after ... 1Cor 10:6
To the *i* that now unto the ... Eph 3:10 *2443*

INTENTS {2}
have performed the *i* of his heart ... Jer 30:24 4209
of the thoughts and *i* of the heart ... Heb 4:12 *1771*

INTERCESSION {9}
made *i* for the transgressors ... Is 53:12 6293
for them, neither make *i* to me ... Jer 7:16 6293
let them now make *i* to the LORD ... Jer 27:18 6293
Gemariah had made *i* to the king ... Jer 36:25 6293
i for us with groanings which ... Rom 8:26 *5241*
because he maketh *i* for the ... Rom 8:27 *1793*
of God, who also maketh *i* for us ... Rom 8:34 *1793*
how he maketh *i* to God against ... Rom 11:2 *1793*
he ever liveth to make *i* for them ... Heb 7:25 *1793*

INTERCESSIONS {1}
of all, supplications, prayers, *i* ... 1Ti 2:1 *1783*

INTERCESSOR {1}
and wondered that there was no *i* ... Is 59:16 6293

INTERMEDDLE {1}
stranger doth not *i* with his joy ... Prov 14:10 6148

INTERMEDDLETH {1}
seeketh and *i* with all wisdom ... Prov 18:1 1566

INTERMISSION {1}
and ceaseth not, without any *i* ... Lam 3:49 2014

INTERPRET {8}
that could *i* them unto Pharaoh ... Gen 41:8 6622
according to his dream he did *i* ... Gen 41:12 6622
and there is none that can *i* it ... Gen 41:15 6622
canst understand a dream to *i* it ... Gen 41:15 6622
do all *i*? ... 1Cor 12:30 *1329*
with tongues, except he *i* ... 1Cor 14:5 *1329*
unknown tongue pray that he may *i* ... 1Cor 14:13 *1329*
and let one *i* ... 1Cor 14:27 *1329*

INTERPRETATION {46}
according to the *i* of his dream ... Gen 40:5 6623
unto him, This is the *i* of it ... Gen 40:12 6623
baker saw that the *i* was good ... Gen 40:16 6623
and said, This is the *i* thereof ... Gen 40:18 6623
according to the *i* of his dream ... Gen 41:11 6623
the *i* thereof, that he worshipped ... Judg 7:15 7667
To understand a proverb, and the *i* ... Prov 1:6 4426

I

and who knoweth the *i* of a thing ... Eccl 8:1 6592
the dream, and we will shew the *i* ... Dan 2:4 6591
me the dream, with the *i* thereof ... Dan 2:5 6591
the *i* thereof, ye shall receive ... Dan 2:6 6591
me the dream, and the *i* thereof ... Dan 2:6 6591
and we will shew the *i* of it ... Dan 2:7 6591
that ye can shew me the *i* thereof ... Dan 2:9 6591
that he would shew the king the *i* ... Dan 2:16 6591
I will shew unto the king the *i* ... Dan 2:24 6591
make known unto the king the *i* ... Dan 2:25 6591
I have seen, and the *i* thereof ... Dan 2:26 6591
make known the *i* to the king ... Dan 2:30 6591
we will tell the *i* thereof before ... Dan 2:36 6591
is certain, and the *i* thereof sure ... Dan 2:45 6591
known unto me the *i* of the dream ... Dan 4:6 6591
make known unto me the *i* thereof ... Dan 4:7 6591
I have seen, and the *i* thereof ... Dan 4:9 6591
declare the *i* thereof, forasmuch ... Dan 4:18 6591
able to make known unto me the *i* ... Dan 4:18 6591
or the *i* thereof, trouble thee ... Dan 4:19 6591
the *i* thereof to thine enemies ... Dan 4:19 6591
This is the *i*, O king, and this is ... Dan 4:24 6591
writing, and shew me the *i* thereof ... Dan 5:7 6591
known to the king the *i* thereof ... Dan 5:8 6591
be called, and he will shew the *i* ... Dan 5:12 6591
make known unto me the *i* thereof ... Dan 5:15 6591
could not shew the *i* of the thing ... Dan 5:15 6591
and make known to me the *i* thereof ... Dan 5:16 6591
king, and make known to him the *i* ... Dan 5:17 6591
This is the *i* of the thing ... Dan 5:26 6591
made me know the *i* of the things ... Dan 7:16 6591
be called Cephas, which is by *i* ... Jn 1:42 *2059*
pool of Siloam, (which is by *i* ... Jn 9:7 *2059*
which by *i* is called Dorcas ... Acts 9:36 *1329*
is his name by *i*) withstood them ... Acts 13:8 *3177*
to another the *i* of tongues ... 1Cor 12:10 *2058*
hath a revelation, hath an *i* ... 1Cor 14:26 *2058*
first being by *i* King of ... Heb 7:2 *2059*
the scripture is of any private *i* ... 2Pet 1:20 *1955*

INTERPRETATIONS {2}
unto them, Do not *i* belong to God ... Gen 40:8 6623
of thee, that thou canst make *i* ... Dan 5:16 6591

INTERPRETED {11}
as Joseph had *i* to them ... Gen 40:22 6622
him, and he *i* to us our dreams ... Gen 41:12 6622
And it came to pass, as he *i* to us ... Gen 41:13 6622
tongue, and *i* in the Syrian tongue ... Ezr 4:7 8638
name Emmanuel, which being *i* is ... Mt 1:23 *3177*
which is, being *i*, Damsel, I say ... Mk 5:41 *3177*
place Golgotha, which is, being *i* ... Mk 15:22 *3177*
which is, being *i*, My God, my God ... Mk 15:34 *3177*
Rabbi, (which is to say, being *i* ... Jn 1:38 *2059*
the Messias, which is, being *i* ... Jn 1:41 *3177*
Barnabas, (which is, being *i* ... Acts 4:36 *3177*

INTERPRETER {4}
a dream, and there is no *i* of it ... Gen 40:8 6622
for he spake unto them by an *i* ... Gen 42:23 3887
be a messenger with him, an *i* ... Job 33:23 3887
But if there be no *i*, let him ... 1Cor 14:28 *1328*

INTERPRETING {1}
i of dreams, and shewing of hard ... Dan 5:12 6591

INTO See APPENDIX.

INTREAT {15}
i for me to Ephron the son of ... Gen 23:8 6293
I the LORD, that he may take away ... Ex 8:8 6279
when shall I *i* for thee, and for ... Ex 8:9 6279
very far away: *i* for me ... Ex 8:28 6279
I will *i* the LORD that the swarms ... Ex 8:29 6279
I the LORD (for it is enough) ... Ex 9:28 6279
i the LORD your God, that he may ... Ex 10:17 6279
I me not to leave thee, or to ... Ruth 1:16 6293
the LORD, who shall *i* for him ... 1Sa 2:25 6419
I now the face of the LORD thy ... 1Kin 13:6 2470
the people shall *i* thy favour ... Ps 45:12 2470
Many will *i* the favour of the ... Prov 19:6 2470
Being defamed, we *i* ... 1Cor 4:13 *3870*
I *i* thee also, true yokefellow, ... Phil 4:3 *2065*
an elder, but *i* him as a father ... 1Ti 5:1 *3870*

INTREATED {18}
Isaac *i* the LORD for his wife, ... Gen 25:21 6279
and the LORD was *i* of him, and ... Gen 25:21 6279
out from Pharaoh, and *i* the LORD ... Ex 8:30 6279
out from Pharaoh, and *i* the LORD ... Ex 10:18 6279
Then Manoah *i* the LORD, and said, ... Judg 13:8 6279
after that God was *i* for the land ... 2Sa 21:14 6279
So the LORD was *i* for the land ... 2Sa 24:25 6279
the battle, and he was *i* of them ... 1Chr 5:20 6279
and he was *i* of him, and heard his ... 2Chr 33:13 6279
also, and how God was *i* of him ... 2Chr 33:19 6279
and he was *i* of us ... Ezr 8:23 6279
I *i* him with my mouth ... Job 19:16 2603
though I *i* for the children's ... Job 19:17 2589
I *i* thy favour with my whole ... Ps 119:58 2470
LORD, and he shall be *i* of them ... Is 19:22 6279
came his father out, and *i* him ... Lk 15:28 *3870*
i that the word should not be ... Heb 12:19 *3862*
gentle, and easy to be *i*, full of ... Jas 3:17 *2138*

INTREATIES {1}
The poor useth *i* ... Prov 18:23 8469

INTREATY {1}
Praying us with much *i* that we ... 2Cor 8:4 *3874*

INTRUDING {1}
i into those things which he hath ... Col 2:18 *1687*

INVADE {2}
thou wouldest not let Israel *i* ... 2Chr 20:10 935
he will *i* them with his troops ... Hab 3:16 1464

INVADED {5}
the Philistines have *i* the land ... 1Sa 23:27 6584
i the Geshurites, and the Gezrites ... 1Sa 27:8 6584
the Amalekites had *i* the south ... 1Sa 30:1 6584
the bands of the Moabites *i* the ... 2Kin 13:20 935
The Philistines also had *i* the ... 2Chr 28:18 6584

INVASION {1}
We made an *i* upon the south of ... 1Sa 30:14 6584

INVENT {1}
i to themselves instruments of ... Amos 6:5 2803

INVENTED {1}
i by cunning men, to be on the ... 2Chr 26:15 2803

INVENTIONS {5}
thou tookest vengeance of their *i* ... Ps 99:8 5949
him to anger with their *i* ... Ps 106:29 4611
went a whoring with their own *i* ... Ps 106:39 4611
and find out knowledge of witty *i* ... Prov 8:12 4209
but they have sought out many *i* ... Eccl 7:29 2810

INVENTORS {1}
i of evil things, disobedient to ... Rom 1:30 *2182*

INVISIBLE {5}
For the *i* things of him from the ... Rom 1:20 *517*
Who is the image of the *i* God ... Col 1:15 *517*
that are in earth, visible and *i* ... Col 1:16 *517*
the King eternal, immortal, *i* ... 1Ti 1:17 *517*
endured, as seeing him who is *i* ... Heb 11:27 *517*

INVITED {3}
since I said, I have *i* the people ... 1Sa 9:24 7121
Absalom *i* all the king's sons ... 2Sa 13:23 7121
to morrow am I *i* unto her also ... Est 5:12 7121

INWARD {25}
is in the side of the ephod *i* ... Ex 28:26 1004
was on the side of the ephod *i* ... Ex 39:19 1004
it is fret *i*, whether it be bare ... Lev 13:55
built round about from Millo and *i* ... 2Sa 5:9 1004
and all their hinder parts were *i* ... 1Kin 7:25 1004
their feet, and their faces were *i* ... 2Chr 3:13 1004
and all their hinder parts were *i* ... 2Chr 4:4 1004
All my *i* friends abhorred me ... Job 19:19 5475
hath put wisdom in the *i* parts ... Job 38:36 2910
their *i* part is very wickedness ... Ps 5:9 7130
Their *i* thought is, that their ... Ps 49:11 7130
desirest truth in the *i* parts ... Ps 51:6 2910
both the *i* thought of every one ... Ps 64:6 7130
searching all the *i* parts of the ... Prov 20:27 2315
so do stripes the *i* parts of the ... Prov 20:30 2315
mine *i* parts for Kir-haresh ... Is 16:11 7130
will put my law in their *i* parts ... Jer 31:33 7130
and the porch of the gate was *i* ... Eze 40:9 1004
and windows were round about *i* ... Eze 40:16 6441
Then went he *i*, and measured the ... Eze 41:3 6441
a walk of ten cubits breadth *i* ... Eze 42:4 6442
but your *i* part is full of ... Lk 11:39 *2081*
in the law of God after the *i* man ... Rom 7:22 *2080*
yet the *i* man is renewed day by ... 2Cor 4:16 *2081*
his *i* affection is more abundant ... 2Cor 7:15 *4698*

INWARDLY {3}
their mouth, but they curse *i* ... Ps 62:4 7130
but *i* they are ravening wolves ... Mt 7:15 *2081*
But he is a Jew, which is one *i* ... Rom 2:29 *1722,2927*

INWARDS {20}
all the fat that covereth the *i* ... Ex 29:13 7130
in pieces, and wash the *i* of him ... Ex 29:17 7130
and the fat that covereth the *i* ... Ex 29:22 7130
But his *i* and his legs shall he ... Lev 1:9 7130
But he shall wash the *i* and the ... Lev 1:13 7130
the fat that covereth the *i* ... Lev 3:3 7130
and all the fat that is upon the *i* ... Lev 3:3 7130
and the fat that covereth the *i* ... Lev 3:9 7130
and all the fat that is upon the *i* ... Lev 3:9 7130
the fat that covereth the *i* ... Lev 3:14 7130
and all the fat that is upon the *i* ... Lev 3:14 7130
the fat that covereth the *i* ... Lev 4:8 7130
and all the fat that is upon the *i* ... Lev 4:8 7130
head, and with his legs, and his *i* ... Lev 4:11 7130
and the fat that covereth the *i* ... Lev 7:3 7130
all the fat that was upon the *i* ... Lev 8:16 7130
And he washed the *i* and the legs in ... Lev 8:21 7130
all the fat that was upon the *i* ... Lev 8:25 7130
And he did wash the *i* and the legs, ... Lev 9:14 7130
and that which covereth the *i* ... Lev 9:19

IOB See JOB.

IPHEDEIAH *(if-e-di'-ah)* {1} *A son of Shashak.*
And *I*, and Penuel, the sons of ... 1Chr 8:25 3301

IPHTAH See JIPHTAH.

IPHTAH EL See JIPHTHAH-EL.

IR *(ur)* {1} See IR-NAHASH, IR-SHEMESH. *Father of Machir.*
and Huppim, the children of *I* ... 1Chr 7:12 5893

IRA *(i'-rah)* {6}
1. An officer of David.
I also the Jairite was a chief ... 2Sa 20:26 5896
2. A mighty man of David.
I the son of Ikkesh the Tekoite, ... 2Sa 23:26 5896
I an Ithrite, Gareb an Ithrite, ... 2Sa 23:38 5896
I the son of Ikkesh the Tekoite, ... 1Chr 11:28 5896
I the Ithrite, Gareb the Ithrite, ... 1Chr 11:40 5896
I the son of Ikkesh the Tekoite ... 1Chr 27:9 5896

IRAD *(i'-rad)* {2} *Son of Enoch.*
And unto Enoch was born *I* ... Gen 4:18 5897
and *I* begat Mehujael ... Gen 4:18 5897

IRAM *(i'-ram)* {2} *An Edomite leader.*
Duke Magdiel, duke *I* ... Gen 36:43 5902
Duke Magdiel, duke *I* ... 1Chr 1:54 5902

IRI *(i'-ri)* {1} *A son of Bela.*
and Uzziel, and Jerimoth, and *I* ... 1Chr 7:7 5901

IRIJAH *(i-ri'-jah)* {2} *A captain of the guard.*
ward was there, whose name was *I* ... Jer 37:13 3376
so *I* took Jeremiah, and brought ... Jer 37:14 3376

IR-NAHASH *(ur-na'-hash)* {1} *A descendant of Chelub.*
and Tehinnah the father of *I* ... 1Chr 4:12 5904

IRON *(i'-ron)* {99} *A city in Naphtali.*
And *I*, and Migdal-el, Horem, and ... Josh 19:38 3375
of every artificer in brass and *i* ... Gen 4:22 1270
and I will make your heaven as *i* ... Lev 26:19 1270
and the silver, the brass, the *i* ... Num 31:22 1270
smite him with an instrument of *i* ... Num 35:16 1270
his bedstead was a bedstead of *i* ... Deut 3:11 1270
you forth out of the *i* furnace ... Deut 4:20 1270
a land whose stones are *i* ... Deut 8:9 1270
not lift up any *i* tool upon them ... Deut 27:5 1270
that is under thee shall be *i* ... Deut 28:23 1270
put a yoke of *i* upon thy neck ... Deut 28:48 1270
Thy shoes shall be *i* and brass ... Deut 33:25 1270
and gold, and vessels of brass and *i* ... Josh 6:19 1270
and the vessels of brass and of *i* ... Josh 6:24 1270
which no man hath lift up any *i* ... Josh 8:31 1270
of the valley have chariots of *i* ... Josh 17:16 1270
though they have *i* chariots ... Josh 17:18 1270
gold, and with brass, and with *i* ... Josh 22:8 1270
because they had chariots of *i* ... Judg 1:19 1270
he had nine hundred chariots of *i* ... Judg 4:3 1270
even nine hundred chariots of *i* ... Judg 4:13 1270
weighed six hundred shekels of *i* ... 1Sa 17:7 1270
of iron, and under axes of *i* ... 2Sa 12:31 1270
touch them must be fenced with *i* ... 2Sa 23:7 1270
any tool of *i* heard in the house ... 1Kin 6:7 1270
the midst of the furnace of *i* ... 1Kin 8:51 1270
of Chenaanah made him horns of *i* ... 1Kin 22:11 1270
and the *i* did swim ... 2Kin 6:6 1270
with saws, and with harrows of *i* ... 1Chr 20:3 1270
David prepared *i* in abundance for ... 1Chr 22:3 1270
and of brass and *i* without weight ... 1Chr 22:14 1270
silver, and the brass, and the *i* ... 1Chr 22:16 1270
the *i* for things of iron, and wood ... 1Chr 29:2 1270
brass, the iron for things of *i* ... 1Chr 29:2 1270
one hundred thousand talents of *i* ... 1Chr 29:7 1270
in silver, and in brass, and in *i* ... 2Chr 2:7 1270
and in silver, in brass, in *i* ... 2Chr 2:14 1270
Chenaanah had made him horns of *i* ... 2Chr 18:10 1270
LORD, and also such as wrought *i* ... 2Chr 24:12 1270
they were graven with an *i* pen ... Job 19:24 1270
He shall flee from the *i* weapon ... Job 20:24 1270
I is taken out of the earth, and ... Job 28:2 1270
his bones are like bars of *i* ... Job 40:18 1270
He esteemeth *i* as straw, and brass ... Job 41:27 1270
shalt break them with a rod of *i* ... Ps 2:9 1270
he was laid in *i* ... Ps 105:18 1270
being bound in affliction and *i* ... Ps 107:10 1270
and cut the bars of *i* in sunder ... Ps 107:16 1270
and their nobles with fetters of *i* ... Ps 149:8 1270
I sharpeneth iron ... Prov 27:17 1270
Iron sharpeneth *i* ... Prov 27:17 1270
If the *i* be blunt, and he do not ... Eccl 10:10 1270
the thickets of the forest with *i* ... Is 10:34 1270
and cut in sunder the bars of *i* ... Is 45:2 1270
and thy neck is an *i* sinew ... Is 48:4 1270
for *i* I will bring silver, and for ... Is 60:17 1270
for wood brass, and for stones *i* ... Is 60:17 1270
an *i* pillar, and brasen walls ... Jer 1:18 1270
they are brass and *i* ... Jer 6:28 1270
land of Egypt, from the *i* furnace ... Jer 11:4 1270
Shall *i* break the northern iron ... Jer 15:12 1270
Shall iron break the northern *i* ... Jer 15:12 1270
Judah is written with a pen of *i* ... Jer 17:1 1270
shalt make for them yokes of *i* ... Jer 28:13 1270
I have put a yoke of *i* upon the ... Jer 28:14 1270
take thou unto thee an *i* pan ... Eze 4:3 1270
it for a wall of *i* between thee ... Eze 4:3 1270
all they are brass, and tin, and *i* ... Eze 22:18 1270
gather silver, and brass, and *i* ... Eze 22:20 1270
with silver, *i*, tin, and lead, ... Eze 27:12 1270
bright *i*, cassia, and calamus, ... Eze 27:19 1270
legs of iron, his feet part of *i* ... Dan 2:33 6523
upon his feet that were of *i* ... Dan 2:34 6523
Then was the *i*, the clay, the ... Dan 2:35 6523
kingdom shall be strong as *i* ... Dan 2:40 6523
forasmuch as *i* breaketh in pieces ... Dan 2:40 6523
as *i* that breaketh all these, ... Dan 2:40 6523
of potters' clay, and part of *i* ... Dan 2:41 6523
be in it of the strength of the *i* ... Dan 2:41 6523
sawest the *i* mixed with miry clay ... Dan 2:41 6523
toes of the feet were part of *i* ... Dan 2:42 6523
whereas thou sawest *i* mixed with ... Dan 2:43 6523
even as *i* is not mixed with clay ... Dan 2:43 6523
and that it brake in pieces the *i* ... Dan 2:45 6523
the earth, even with a band of *i* ... Dan 4:15 6523
the earth, even with a band of *i* ... Dan 4:23 6523
and of silver, of brass, of *i* ... Dan 5:4 6523
of silver, and gold, of brass, *i* ... Dan 5:23 6523
and it had great *i* teeth ... Dan 7:7 6523
dreadful, whose teeth were of *i* ... Dan 7:19 6523
with threshing instruments of *i* ... Amos 1:3 1270
for I will make thine horn *i* ... Mic 4:13 1270

they came unto the *i* gate that ... Acts 12:10 *4603*
conscience seared with a hot *i* ... 1Ti 4:2
shall rule them with a rod of *i* ... Rev 2:27 *4603*
as it were breastplates of *i* ... Rev 9:9 *4603*
rule all nations with a rod of *i* ... Rev 12:5 *4603*
precious wood, and of brass, and *i* ... Rev 18:12 *4604*
shall rule them with a rod of *i* ... Rev 19:15 *4603*

IRONS {1}
thou fill his skin with barbed *i* ... Job 41:7 7905

IRPEEL *(ur'-pe-el)* {1} *A city in Benjamin.*
And Rekem, and *I*, and Taralah, ... Josh 18:27 3416

IR-SHEMESH *(ur-she'-mesh)* {1} *A city in Dan.*
was Zorah, and Eshtaol, and *I* ... Josh 19:41 5905

IRU *(i'-ru)* {1} *A son of Caleb.*
I, Elah, and Naam ... 1Chr 4:15 5902

IS See APPENDIX.

ISAAC *(i'-za-ak)* {128} See ISAAC'S. *Son of Abraham and Sarah.*
and thou shalt call his name *I* ... Gen 17:19 3327
covenant will I establish with *I* ... Gen 17:21 3327
him, whom Sarah bare to him, *I* ... Gen 21:3 3327
his son *I* being eight days old ... Gen 21:4 3327
when his son *I* was born unto him ... Gen 21:5 3327
the same day that *I* was weaned ... Gen 21:8 3327
be heir with my son, even with *I* ... Gen 21:10 3327
for in *I* shall thy seed be called ... Gen 21:12 3327
now thy son, thine only son *I* ... Gen 22:2 3327
I his son, and clave the wood for ... Gen 22:3 3327
and laid it upon *I* his son ... Gen 22:6 3327
I spake unto Abraham his father, ... Gen 22:7 3327
bound *I* his son, and laid him on ... Gen 22:9 3327
and take a wife unto my son *I* ... Gen 24:4 3327
hast appointed for thy servant *I* ... Gen 24:14 3327
I came from the way of the well ... Gen 24:62 3327
I went out to meditate in the ... Gen 24:63 3327
up her eyes, and when she saw *I* ... Gen 24:64 3327
the servant told *I* all things ... Gen 24:66 3327
I brought her into his mother ... Gen 24:67 3327
I was comforted after his ... Gen 24:67 3327
gave all that he had unto *I* ... Gen 25:5 3327
and sent them away from *I* his son ... Gen 25:6 3327
And his sons *I* and Ishmael buried ... Gen 25:9 3327
that God blessed his son *I* ... Gen 25:11 3327
I dwelt by the well Lahai-roi ... Gen 25:11 3327
And these are the generations of *I* ... Gen 25:19 3327
Abraham begat *I* ... Gen 25:19 3327
I was forty years old when he ... Gen 25:20 3327
I intreated the LORD for his wife ... Gen 25:21 3327
I was threescore years old when ... Gen 25:26 3327
I loved Esau, because he did eat ... Gen 25:28 3327
I went unto Abimelech king of the ... Gen 26:1 3327
And *I* dwelt in Gerar ... Gen 26:6 3327
I was sporting with Rebekah his ... Gen 26:8 3327
And Abimelech called *I*, and said, ... Gen 26:9 3327
I said unto him, Because I said, ... Gen 26:9 3327
Then *I* sowed in that land, and ... Gen 26:12 3327
And Abimelech said unto *I*, Go from ... Gen 26:16 3327
I departed thence, and pitched his ... Gen 26:17 3327
I digged again the wells of water ... Gen 26:18 3327
I said unto them, Wherefore come ... Gen 26:27 3327
I sent them away, and they ... Gen 26:31 3327
Which were a grief of mind unto *I* ... Gen 26:35 3327
came to pass, that when *I* was old ... Gen 27:1 3327
Rebekah heard when *I* spake to ... Gen 27:5 3327
I said unto his son, How is it ... Gen 27:20 3327
I said unto Jacob, Come near, I ... Gen 27:21 3327
Jacob went near unto *I* his father ... Gen 27:22 3327
his father *I* said unto him, Come ... Gen 27:26 3327
as soon as *I* had made an end of ... Gen 27:30 3327
from the presence of *I* his father ... Gen 27:30 3327
I his father said unto him, Who ... Gen 27:32 3327
I trembled very exceedingly, and ... Gen 27:33 3327
I answered and said unto Esau, ... Gen 27:37 3327
I his father answered and said ... Gen 27:39 3327
And Rebekah said to *I*, I am weary ... Gen 27:46 3327
I called Jacob, and blessed him, ... Gen 28:1 3327
And *I* sent away Jacob ... Gen 28:5 3327
Esau saw that *I* had blessed Jacob ... Gen 28:6 3327
Canaan pleased not *I* his father ... Gen 28:8 3327
thy father, and the God of *I* ... Gen 28:13 3327
for to go to *I* his father in the ... Gen 31:18 3327
God of Abraham, and the fear of *I* ... Gen 31:42 3327
sware by the fear of his father *I* ... Gen 31:53 3327
Abraham, and God of my father *I* ... Gen 32:9 3327
land which I gave Abraham and *I* ... Gen 35:12 3327
Jacob came unto *I* his father unto ... Gen 35:27 3327
where Abraham and *I* sojourned ... Gen 35:27 3327
the days of *I* were an hundred and ... Gen 35:28 3327
I gave up the ghost, and died, and ... Gen 35:29 3327
unto the God of his father *I* ... Gen 46:1 3327
I did walk, the God which fed me ... Gen 48:15 3327
name of my fathers Abraham and *I* ... Gen 48:16 3327
there they buried *I* and Rebekah ... Gen 49:31 3327
which he sware to Abraham, to *I* ... Gen 50:24 3327
his covenant with Abraham, with *I* ... Ex 2:24 3327
the God of Abraham, the God of *I* ... Ex 3:6 3327
the God of Abraham, the God of *I* ... Ex 3:15 3327
fathers, the God of Abraham, of *I* ... Ex 3:16 3327
the God of Abraham, the God of *I* ... Ex 4:5 3327
I appeared unto Abraham, unto *I* ... Ex 6:3 3327
swear to give it to Abraham, to *I* ... Ex 6:8 3327
Remember Abraham, *I*, and Israel, ... Ex 32:13 3327
which I sware unto Abraham, to *I* ... Ex 33:1 3327
Jacob, and also my covenant with *I* ... Lev 26:42 3327
I sware unto Abraham, unto *I* ... Num 32:11 3327
unto your fathers, Abraham, *I* ... Deut 1:8 3327
thy fathers, to Abraham, to *I* ... Deut 6:10 3327
unto thy fathers, Abraham, *I* ... Deut 9:5 3327
Remember thy servants, Abraham, *I* ... Deut 9:27 3327
thy fathers, to Abraham, to *I* ... Deut 29:13 3327
thy fathers, to Abraham, to *I* ... Deut 30:20 3327
I sware unto Abraham, unto *I* ... Deut 34:4 3327
his seed, and gave him *I* ... Josh 24:3 3327
And I gave unto *I* Jacob and Esau ... Josh 24:4 3327
and said, LORD God of Abraham, *I* ... 1Kin 18:36 3327
of his covenant with Abraham, *I* ... 2Kin 13:23 3327
I, and Ishmael ... 1Chr 1:28 3327
And Abraham begat *I* ... 1Chr 1:34 3327
The sons of *I* ... 1Chr 1:34 3327
Abraham, and of his oath unto *I* ... 1Chr 16:16 3327
O LORD God of Abraham, *I*, and of ... 1Chr 29:18 3327
unto the LORD God of Abraham, *I* ... 2Chr 30:6 3327
with Abraham, and his oath unto *I* ... Ps 105:9 3446
over the seed of Abraham, *I* ... Jer 33:26 3446
places of *I* shall be desolate ... Amos 7:9 3446
thy word against the house of *I* ... Amos 7:16 3446
Abraham begat *I* ... Mt 1:2 *2464*
and *I* begat Jacob ... Mt 1:2 *2464*
shall sit down with Abraham, and *I* ... Mt 8:11 *2464*
God of Abraham, and the God of *I* ... Mt 22:32 *2464*
God of Abraham, and the God of *I* ... Mk 12:26 *2464*
of Jacob, which was the son of *I* ... Lk 3:34 *2464*
when ye shall see Abraham, and *I* ... Lk 13:28 *2464*
God of Abraham, and the God of *I* ... Lk 20:37 *2464*
The God of Abraham, and of *I* ... Acts 3:13 *2464*
and so Abraham begat *I* ... Acts 7:8 *2464*
and *I* begat Jacob ... Acts 7:8 *2464*
God of Abraham, and the God of *I* ... Acts 7:32 *2464*
In *I* shall thy seed be called ... Rom 9:7 *2464*
by one, even by our father *I* ... Rom 9:10 *2464*
as *I* was, are the children of ... Gal 4:28 *2464*
dwelling in tabernacles with *I* ... Heb 11:9 *2464*
when he was tried, offered up *I* ... Heb 11:17 *2464*
That in *I* shall thy seed be ... Heb 11:18 *2464*
By faith *I* blessed Jacob and Esau ... Heb 11:20 *2464*
when he had offered *I* his son ... Jas 2:21 *2464*

ISAAC'S *(i'-za-aks)* {4}
I servants digged in the valley, ... Gen 26:19 3327
Gerar did strive with *I* herdmen ... Gen 26:20 3327
there *I* servants digged a well ... Gen 26:25 3327
that *I* servants came, and told him ... Gen 26:32 3327

ISAIAH *(i-za'-yah)* {32} See ESAIAS. *A prophet.*
to *I* the prophet the son of Amoz ... 2Kin 19:2 3470
of king Hezekiah came to *I* ... 2Kin 19:5 3470
I said unto them, Thus shall ye ... 2Kin 19:6 3470
Then *I* the son of Amoz sent to ... 2Kin 19:20 3470
the prophet *I* the son of Amoz ... 2Kin 20:1 3470
afore *I* was gone out into the ... 2Kin 20:4 3470
I said, Take a lump of figs ... 2Kin 20:7 3470
And Hezekiah said unto *I*, What ... 2Kin 20:8 3470
I said, This sign shalt thou have ... 2Kin 20:9 3470
I the prophet cried unto the LORD ... 2Kin 20:11 3470
Then came *I* the prophet unto king ... 2Kin 20:14 3470
I said unto Hezekiah, Hear the ... 2Kin 20:16 3470
Then said Hezekiah unto *I* ... 2Kin 20:19 3470
did *I* the prophet, the son of ... 2Chr 26:22 3470
the prophet *I* the son of Amoz, ... 2Chr 32:20 3470
in the vision of *I* the prophet ... 2Chr 32:32 3470
The vision of *I* the son of Amoz, ... Is 1:1 3470
The word that *I* the son of Amoz ... Is 2:1 3470
Then said the LORD unto *I* ... Is 7:3 3470
which *I* the son of Amoz did see ... Is 13:1 3470
the LORD by *I* the son of Amoz ... Is 20:2 3470
as my servant *I* hath walked naked ... Is 20:3 3470
unto *I* the prophet the son of ... Is 37:2 3470
of king Hezekiah came to *I* ... Is 37:5 3470
I said unto them, Thus shall ye ... Is 37:6 3470
Then *I* the son of Amoz sent unto ... Is 37:21 3470
I the prophet the son of Amoz ... Is 38:1 3470
came the word of the LORD to *I* ... Is 38:4 3470
For *I* had said, Let them take a ... Is 38:21 3470
Then came *I* the prophet unto king ... Is 39:3 3470
Then said *I* to Hezekiah, Hear the ... Is 39:5 3470
Then said Hezekiah to *I*, Good is ... Is 39:8 3470

ISCAH *(is'-cah)* {1} See SARAH. *A daughter of Haran.*
of Milcah, and the father of *I* ... Gen 11:29 3252

ISCARIOT *(is-car'-e-ot)* {11} See JUDAS. *Disciple who betrayed Jesus.*
Simon the Canaanite, and Judas *I* ... Mt 10:4 *2469*
one of the twelve, called Judas *I* ... Mt 26:14 *2469*
And Judas *I*, which also betrayed ... Mk 3:19 *2469*
And Judas *I*, one of the twelve, ... Mk 14:10 *2469*
the brother of James, and Judas *I* ... Lk 6:16 *2469*
Satan into Judas surnamed *I* ... Lk 22:3 *2469*
spake of Judas *I* the son of Simon ... Jn 6:71 *2469*
one of his disciples, Judas *I* ... Jn 12:4 *2469*
now put into the heart of Judas *I* ... Jn 13:2 *2469*
the sop, he gave it to Judas *I* ... Jn 13:26 *2469*
Judas saith unto him, not *I* ... Jn 14:22 *2469*

ISHBAH *(ish'-bah)* {1} *Father of Eshtemoa.*
and *I* the father of Eshtemoa ... 1Chr 4:17 3431

ISHBAK *(ish'-bak)* {2} *A son of Abraham.*
and Medan, and Midian, and *I* ... Gen 25:2 3435
and Medan, and Midian, and *I* ... 1Chr 1:32 3435

ISHBI-BENOB *(ish'-bi-be'-nob)* {1} *A Philistine giant.*
And *I*, which was of the sons of ... 2Sa 21:16 3430

ISH-BOSHETH *(ish-bo'-sheth)* {12} See ESH-BAAL. *Son of Saul.*
took *I* the son of Saul, and ... 2Sa 2:8 378
I Saul's son was forty years old ... 2Sa 2:10 378
the servants of *I* the son of Saul ... 2Sa 2:12 378
pertained to *I* the son of Saul ... 2Sa 2:15 378
I said to Abner, Wherefore hast ... 2Sa 3:7
very wroth for the words of *I* ... 2Sa 3:8 378
sent messengers to *I* Saul's son ... 2Sa 3:14 378
I sent, and took her from her ... 2Sa 3:15 378
heat of the day to the house of *I* ... 2Sa 4:5 378
head of *I* unto David to Hebron ... 2Sa 4:8 378
Behold the head of *I* the son of ... 2Sa 4:8 378
But they took the head of *I* ... 2Sa 4:12 378

ISHI *(i'-shi)* {6}
1. A descendant of Pharez.
sons of Appaim; *I* ... 1Chr 2:31 3469
And the sons of *I* ... 1Chr 2:31 3469
2. A descendant of Judah.
And the sons of *I* were, Zoheth, and ... 1Chr 4:20 3469
3. A Simeonite.
and Uzziel, the sons of *I* ... 1Chr 4:42 3469
4. A chief of Manasseh.
their fathers, even Epher, and *I* ... 1Chr 5:24 3469
5. A symbolic name for Israel.
LORD, that thou shalt call me *I* ... Hos 2:16 376

ISHIAH *(i-shi'-ah)* {1} See ISHIJAH, ISSHIAH. *A son of Izrahiah.*
Michael, and Obadiah, and Joel, *I* ... 1Chr 7:3 3449

ISHIJAH *(i-shi'-jah)* {1} See ISHIAH, JESIAH. *Married a foreigner in exile.*
Eliezer, *I*, Malchiah, Shemaiah, ... Ezr 10:31 3449

ISHMA *(ish'-mah)* {1} *A descendant of Caleb.*
Jezreel, and *I*, and Idbash ... 1Chr 4:3 3457

ISHMAEL *(ish'-ma-el)* {47} See ISHMAELITE, ISHMAEL'S.
1. Son of Abraham and Hagar.
a son, and shalt call his name *I* ... Gen 16:11 3458
son's name, which Hagar bare, *I* ... Gen 16:15 3458
old, when Hagar bare *I* to Abram ... Gen 16:16 3458
O that *I* might live before thee ... Gen 17:18 3458
And as for *I*, I have heard thee ... Gen 17:20 3458
And Abraham took *I* his son ... Gen 17:23 3458
I his son was thirteen years old, ... Gen 17:25 3458
Abraham circumcised, and *I* his son ... Gen 17:26 3458
I buried him in the cave of ... Gen 25:9 3458
these are the generations of *I* ... Gen 25:12 3458
are the names of the sons of *I* ... Gen 25:13 3458
the firstborn of *I*, Nebajoth ... Gen 25:13 3458
These are the sons of *I*, and these ... Gen 25:16 3458
are the years of the life of *I* ... Gen 25:17 3458
Then went Esau unto *I*, and took ... Gen 28:9 3458
the daughter of *I* Abraham's son ... Gen 28:9 3458
Isaac, and *I* ... 1Chr 1:28 3458
The firstborn of *I*, Nebaioth ... 1Chr 1:29 3458
These are the sons of *I* ... 1Chr 1:31 3458
2. A ruler of Judah.
and Zebadiah the son of *I*, the ... 2Chr 19:11 3458
3. Son of Azel.
are these, Azrikam, Bocheru, and *I* ... 1Chr 8:38 3458
are these, Azrikam, Bocheru, and *I* ... 1Chr 9:44 3458
4. A captain who aided Joash.
I the son of Jehohanan, and ... 2Chr 23:1 3458
5. Married a foreigner in exile.
Elioenai, Maaseiah, *I*, Nethaneel, ... Ezr 10:22 3458
6. The son of Nethaniah.
even *I* the son of Nethaniah, and ... 2Kin 25:23 3458
that *I* the son of Nethaniah, the ... 2Kin 25:25 3458
even *I* the son of Nethaniah, and ... Jer 40:8 3458
I the son of Nethaniah to slay ... Jer 40:14 3458
thee, and I will slay *I* the son of ... Jer 40:15 3458
for thou speakest falsely of *I* ... Jer 40:16 3458
that *I* the son of Nethaniah the ... Jer 41:1 3458
Then arose *I* the son of Nethaniah ... Jer 41:2 3458
I also slew all the Jews that ... Jer 41:3 3458
I the son of Nethaniah went forth ... Jer 41:6 3458
that *I* the son of Nethaniah slew ... Jer 41:7 3458
found among them that said unto *I* ... Jer 41:8 3458
Now the pit wherein *I* had cast ... Jer 41:9 3458
I the son of Nethaniah filled it ... Jer 41:9 3458
Then *I* carried away captive all ... Jer 41:10 3458
I the son of Nethaniah carried ... Jer 41:10 3458
heard of all the evil that *I* the ... Jer 41:11 3458
went to fight with *I* the son of ... Jer 41:12 3458
I saw Johanan the son of Kareah ... Jer 41:13 3458
So all the people that *I* had ... Jer 41:14 3458
But *I* the son of Nethaniah ... Jer 41:15 3458
from *I* the son of Nethaniah ... Jer 41:16 3458
because *I* the son of Nethaniah ... Jer 41:18 3458

ISHMAELITE *(ish'-ma-el-ite)* {1} *Descendants of Ishmael 1.*
the camels also was Obil the *I* ... 1Chr 27:30 3458

ISHMAELITES *(ish'-ma-el-lites)* {2} See ISHMEELITES.
earrings, because they were *I* ... Judg 8:24 3459
The tabernacles of Edom, and the *I* ... Ps 83:6 3459

ISHMAEL'S *(ish'-ma-els)* {1} *Refers to Ishmael 1.*
And Bashemath *I* daughter, sister ... Gen 36:3 3458

ISHMAIAH *(ish-ma-i'-ah)* {1} See ISMAIAH. *A prince of Zebulun.*
Of Zebulun, *I* the son of Obadiah ... 1Chr 27:19 3460

ISHMEELITE *(ish'-me-el-ite)* {1} See ISHMAELITE, ISHMEELITES. *Same as Ishmaelite.*
father of Amasa was Jether the *I* ... 1Chr 2:17 3459

ISHMEELITES *(ish'-me-el-ites)* {4} See ISHMAELITES.
a company of *I* came from Gilead ... Gen 37:25 3459
Come, and let us sell him to the *I* ... Gen 37:27 3459
sold Joseph to the *I* for twenty ... Gen 37:28 3459
bought him of the hands of the *I* ... Gen 39:1 3459

ISHMERAI *(ish'-me-rahee)* {1} *A chief of Benjamin.*
I also, and Jezliah, and Jobab, the 1Chr 8:18 3461

ISHOD *(i'-shod)* {1} *A son of Hammoleketh.*
And his sister Hammoleketh bare *I*......... 1Chr 7:18 379

ISHPAH See ISPAH.

ISHPAN *(ish'-pan)* {1} *A son of Shashak.*
And *I*, and Heber, and Eliel,.................... 1Chr 8:22 3473

ISH-TOB *(ish'-tob)* {2} *A district of Aram.*
men, and of *I* twelve thousand men 2Sa 10:6 382
of Zoba, and of Rehob, and *I*.................. 2Sa 10:8 382

ISHUAH *(ish'-u-ah)* {1} See ISUAH. *A son of Asher.*
Jimnah, and *I*, and Isui, and Beriah,....... Gen 46:17 3438

ISHUAI {1}
Imnah, and Isuah, and *I*, and Beriah, ... 1Chr 7:30 3440

ISHUI *(ish'-u-i)* {1} See ISHUAI, JESUI. *A son of Saul.*
sons of Saul were Jonathan, and *I* 1Sa 14:49 3440

ISLAND {9}
deliver the *i* of the innocent .... Job 22:30 336
with the wild beasts of the *i*..................... Is 34:14 338
certain *i* which is called Clauda.............. Acts 27:16 *3519*
we must be cast upon a certain *i*............. Acts 27:26 *3520*
knew that the *i* was called Melita .... Acts 28:1 *3520*
of the chief man of the *i*........................ Acts 28:7 *3520*
also, which had diseases in the *i* .... Acts 28:9 *3520*
i were moved out of their places .... Rev 6:14 *3520*
every *i* fled away, and the......................... Rev 16:20 *3520*

ISLANDS {7}
Hamath, and from the *i* of the sea .... Is 11:11 339
the wild beasts of the *i* shall .... Is 13:22 338
Keep silence before me, O *i* .... Is 41:1 339
and declare his praise in the *i*................. Is 42:12 339
and I will make the rivers *i* .... Is 42:15 339
to the *i* he will repay recompence .... Is 59:18 339
beasts of the *i* shall dwell there............... Jer 50:39 339

ISLE {6}
of this *i* shall say in that day.................. Is 20:6 339
Be still, ye inhabitants of the *i*.................. Is 23:2 339
howl, ye inhabitants of the *i* .... Is 23:6 339
gone through the *i* unto Paphos .... Acts 13:6 *3520*
which had wintered in the *i* .... Acts 28:11 *3520*
was in the *i* that is called .... Rev 1:9 *3520*

ISLES {27}
By these were the *i* of the........................ Gen 10:5 339
land, and upon the *i* of the sea................ Est 10:1 339
of the *i* shall bring presents .... Ps 72:10 339
multitude of *i* be glad thereof .... Ps 97:1 339
God of Israel in the *i* of the sea............... Is 24:15 339
he taketh up the *i* as a very .... Is 40:15 339
The *i* saw it, and feared............................ Is 41:5 339
the *i* shall wait for his law .... Is 42:4 339
the *i*, and the inhabitants thereof .... Is 42:10 339
Listen, O *i*, unto me.................................. Is 49:1 339
the *i* shall wait upon me, and on.............. Is 51:5 339
Surely the *i* shall wait for me,.................. Is 60:9 339
to the *i* afar off, that have not................. Is 66:19 339
For pass over the *i* of Chittim.................. Jer 2:10 339
the kings of the *i* which are...................... Jer 25:22 339
and declare it in the *i* afar off .... Jer 31:10 339
Shall not the *i* shake at the .... Eze 26:15 339
Now shall the *i* tremble in the .... Eze 26:18 339
the *i* that are in the sea shall.................... Eze 26:18 339
merchant of the people for many *i*.......... Eze 27:3 339
brought out of the *i* of Chittim .... Eze 27:6 339
purple from the *i* of Elishah was............. Eze 27:7 339
many *i* were the merchandise of............... Eze 27:15 339
All the inhabitants of the *i*...................... Eze 27:35 339
that dwell carelessly in the *i* .... Eze 39:6 339
shall he turn his face unto the *i* .... Dan 11:18 339
even all the *i* of the heathen .... Zeph 2:11 339

ISMACHIAH *(is-ma-ki'-ah)* {1} *A temple servant.*
and Jozabad, and Eliel, and *I*................. 2Chr 31:13 3253

ISMAIAH *(is-ma-i'-ah)* {1} See ISHMAIAH. *A warrior in David's army.*
I the Gibeonite, a mighty man 1Chr 12:4 3460

ISPAH *(is'-pah)* {1} *A son of Beriah.*
And Michael, and *I*, and Joha, the 1Chr 8:16 3472

ISRAEL *(iz'-ra-el)* {2563} See EL-ELOHE-ISRAEL, ISRAELITE, ISRAEL'S, JACOB, JESHURUN.
1. Name given to Jacob.
be called no more Jacob, but *I* .... Gen 32:28 3478
Jacob, but *I* shall be thy name................. Gen 35:10 3478
and he called his name *I*.......................... Gen 35:10 3478
I journeyed, and spread his tent............... Gen 35:21 3478
when *I* dwelt in that land, that .... Gen 35:22 3478
and *I* heard it.. Gen 35:22 3478
Now *I* loved Joseph more than all .... Gen 37:3 3478
I said unto Joseph, Do not thy .... Gen 37:13 3478
the sons of *I* came to buy corn .... Gen 42:5 3478
I said, Wherefore dealt ye so ill.............. Gen 43:6 3478
And Judah said unto *I* his father .... Gen 43:8 3478
their father *I* said unto them, If .... Gen 43:11 3478
And the children of *I* did so .... Gen 45:21 3478
And *I* said, It is enough........................... Gen 45:28 3478
I took his journey with all that .... Gen 46:1 3478
God spake unto *I* in the visions............... Gen 46:2 3478
the sons of *I* carried Jacob their............. Gen 46:5 3478
the names of the children of *I* .... Gen 46:8 3478
and went up to meet *I* his father............. Gen 46:29 3478
I said unto Joseph, Now let me .... Gen 46:30 3478
I dwelt in the land of Egypt, in .... Gen 47:27 3478
time drew nigh that *I* must die .... Gen 47:29 3478
I bowed himself upon the bed's.............. Gen 47:31 3478
I strengthened himself, and sat.............. Gen 48:2 3478
I beheld Joseph's sons, and said, ... Gen 48:8 3478
Now the eyes of *I* were dim for .... Gen 48:10 3478
I said unto Joseph, I had not .... Gen 48:11 3478
I stretched out his right hand,................. Gen 48:14 3478
saying, In thee shall *I* bless .... Gen 48:20 3478
I said unto Joseph, Behold, I die .... Gen 48:21 3478
and hearken unto *I* your father .... Gen 49:2 3478
and the physicians embalmed *I*............... Gen 50:2 3478
the names of the children of *I* .... Ex 1:1 3478
the children of *I* were fruitful .... Ex 1:7 3478
sons of Reuben the firstborn of *I* .... Ex 6:14 3478
Remember Abraham, Isaac, and *I* .... Ex 32:13 3478
Reuben, the eldest son of *I*...................... Num 26:5 3478
their father, who was born unto *I* .... Judg 18:29 3478
came, saying, *I* shall be thy name........... 1Kin 18:31 3478
God of Abraham, Isaac, and of *I*.............. 1Kin 18:36 3478
of Jacob, whom he named *I*....................... 2Kin 17:34 3478
The sons of Isaac; Esau and *I*.................. 1Chr 1:34 3478
These are the sons of *I*............................. 1Chr 2:1 3478
sons of Reuben the firstborn of *I* 1Chr 5:1 3478
the sons of Joseph the son of *I* 1Chr 5:1 3478
of Reuben the firstborn of *I* were............ 1Chr 5:3 3478
the son of Levi, the son of *I*.................... 1Chr 6:38 3478
children of Joseph the son of *I* 1Chr 7:29 3478
be thou, LORD God of *I* our father 1Chr 29:10 3478
God of Abraham, Isaac, and of *I*.............. 1Chr 29:18 3478
LORD God of Abraham, Isaac, and *I* 2Chr 30:6 3478
the son of Levi, the son of *I*..................... Ezr 8:18 3478
2. People descended from Jacob.
Therefore the children of *I* eat .... Gen 32:32 3478
I in lying with Jacob's daughter .... Gen 34:7 3478
any king over the children of *I*................. Gen 36:31 3478
in Jacob, and scatter them in *I*................. Gen 49:7 3478
people, as one of the tribes of *I*.............. Gen 49:16 3478
is the shepherd, the stone of *I* .... Gen 49:24 3478
these are the twelve tribes of *I*............... Gen 49:28 3478
took an oath of the children of *I*............. Gen 50:25 3478
of the children of *I* are more .... Ex 1:9 3478
because of the children of *I*..................... Ex 1:12 3478
of *I* to serve with rigour .... Ex 1:13 3478
the children of *I* sighed by....................... Ex 2:23 3478
God looked upon the children of *I*............ Ex 2:25 3478
the children of *I* is come unto me............ Ex 3:9 3478
the children of *I* out of Egypt.................. Ex 3:10 3478
the children of *I* out of Egypt.................. Ex 3:11 3478
I come unto the children of *I*................... Ex 3:13 3478
thou say unto the children of *I*................. Ex 3:14 3478
thou say unto the children of *I*................. Ex 3:15 3478
gather the elders of *I* together................ Ex 3:16 3478
come, thou and the elders of *I*................. Ex 3:18 3478
I is my son, even my firstborn .... Ex 4:22 3478
the elders of the children of *I*................. Ex 4:29 3478
had visited the children of *I*................... Ex 4:31 3478
Thus saith the LORD God of *I*................... Ex 5:1 3478
should obey his voice to let *I* go............... Ex 5:2 3478
the LORD, neither will I let *I* go................ Ex 5:2 3478
the officers of the children of *I*.............. Ex 5:14 3478
of the children of *I* came .... Ex 5:15 3478
I did see that they were in evil................ Ex 5:19 3478
the groaning of the children of *I* .... Ex 6:5 3478
say unto the children of *I* .... Ex 6:6 3478
spake so unto the children of *I*................ Ex 6:9 3478
children of *I* go out of his land................ Ex 6:11 3478
the children of *I* have not .... Ex 6:12 3478
a charge unto the children of *I*................ Ex 6:13 3478
of *I* out of the land of Egypt .... Ex 6:13 3478
of *I* from the land of Egypt .... Ex 6:26 3478
out the children of *I* from Egypt .... Ex 6:27 3478
the children of *I* out of his land .... Ex 7:2 3478
and my people the children of *I* .... Ex 7:4 3478
the children of *I* from among them .... Ex 7:5 3478
sever between the cattle of *I* .... Ex 9:4 3478
all that is the children's of *I*................... Ex 9:4 3478
of the children of *I* died not one.............. Ex 9:6 3478
where the children of *I* were .... Ex 9:26 3478
would he let the children of *I* go.............. Ex 9:35 3478
not let the children of *I* go .... Ex 10:20 3478
but all the children of *I* had.................... Ex 10:23 3478
against any of the children of *I*............... Ex 11:7 3478
between the Egyptians and *I*................... Ex 11:7 3478
children of *I* go out of his land............... Ex 11:10 3478
ye unto all the congregation of *I* .... Ex 12:3 3478
of *I* shall kill it in the evening................ Ex 12:6 3478
that soul shall be cut off from *I* .... Ex 12:15 3478
off from the congregation of *I*................. Ex 12:19 3478
called for all the elders of *I*................... Ex 12:21 3478
of the children of *I* in Egypt.................... Ex 12:27 3478
And the children of *I* went away.............. Ex 12:28 3478
both ye and the children of *I*................... Ex 12:31 3478
the children of *I* did according................ Ex 12:35 3478
the children of *I* journeyed from .... Ex 12:37 3478
sojourning of the children of *I* .... Ex 12:40 3478
of *I* in their generations.......................... Ex 12:42 3478
congregation of *I* shall keep it................. Ex 12:47 3478
Thus did all the children of *I* .... Ex 12:50 3478
of *I* out of the land of Egypt by............... Ex 12:51 3478
the womb among the children of *I*........... Ex 13:2 3478
the children of *I* went up......................... Ex 13:18 3478
straitly sworn the children of *I*............... Ex 13:19 3478
Speak unto the children of *I* .... Ex 14:2 3478
will say of the children of *I* .... Ex 14:3 3478
that we have let *I* go from .... Ex 14:5 3478
pursued after the children of *I*............... Ex 14:8 3478
the children of *I* went out with .... Ex 14:8 3478
the children of *I* lifted up their .... Ex 14:10 3478
the children of *I* cried out unto.............. Ex 14:10 3478
speak unto the children of *I*.................... Ex 14:15 3478
the children of *I* shall go on dry............. Ex 14:16 3478
which went before the camp of *I*............. Ex 14:19 3478
of the Egyptians and the camp of *I*......... Ex 14:20 3478
the children of *I* went into the .... Ex 14:22 3478
Let us flee from the face of *I*.................. Ex 14:25 3478
But the children of *I* walked upon .... Ex 14:29 3478
Thus the LORD saved *I* that day .... Ex 14:30 3478
I saw the Egyptians dead upon the.......... Ex 14:30 3478
I saw that great work which the .... Ex 14:31 3478
the children of *I* this song unto.............. Ex 15:1 3478
but the children of *I* went on dry............ Ex 15:19 3478
Moses brought *I* from the Red sea........... Ex 15:22 3478
I came unto the wilderness of Sin........... Ex 16:1 3478
of *I* murmured against Moses.................. Ex 16:2 3478
the children of *I* said unto them............. Ex 16:3 3478
said unto all the children of *I*................. Ex 16:6 3478
congregation of the children of *I*............ Ex 16:9 3478
congregation of the children of *I*............ Ex 16:10 3478
murmurings of the children of *I*.............. Ex 16:12 3478
And when the children of *I* saw it............ Ex 16:15 3478
And the children of *I* did so .... Ex 16:17 3478
the house of *I* called the name .... Ex 16:31 3478
the children of *I* did eat manna.............. Ex 16:35 3478
I journeyed from the wilderness............. Ex 17:1 3478
take with thee of the elders of *I*............. Ex 17:5 3478
in the sight of the elders of *I*.................. Ex 17:6 3478
the chiding of the children of *I* .... Ex 17:7 3478
and fought with *I* in Rephidim................. Ex 17:8 3478
up his hand, that *I* prevailed................... Ex 17:11 3478
for *I* his people, and that the.................. Ex 18:1 3478
LORD had brought *I* out of Egypt............. Ex 18:1 3478
which the LORD had done to *I*.................. Ex 18:9 3478
came, and all the elders of *I*................... Ex 18:12 3478
Moses chose able men out of all *I* .... Ex 18:25 3478
when the children of *I* were gone............ Ex 19:1 3478
there *I* camped before the mount .... Ex 19:2 3478
Jacob, and tell the children of *I* .... Ex 19:3 3478
speak unto the children of *I*.................... Ex 19:6 3478
shalt say unto the children of *I*............... Ex 20:22 3478
and seventy of the elders of *I*................. Ex 24:1 3478
to the twelve tribes of *I* .... Ex 24:4 3478
young men of the children of *I*................ Ex 24:5 3478
and seventy of the elders of *I*................. Ex 24:9 3478
And they saw the God of *I* .... Ex 24:10 3478
of *I* he laid not his hand......................... Ex 24:11 3478
in the eyes of the children of *I* .... Ex 24:17 3478
Speak unto the children of *I* .... Ex 25:2 3478
unto the children of *I* .... Ex 25:22 3478
shalt command the children of *I*............. Ex 27:20 3478
the behalf of the children of *I*................. Ex 27:21 3478
him, from among the children of *I*........... Ex 28:1 3478
the names of the children of *I*................. Ex 28:9 3478
the names of the children of *I*................. Ex 28:11 3478
memorial unto the children of *I*.............. Ex 28:12 3478
the names of the children of *I*................. Ex 28:21 3478
the names of the children of *I* in .... Ex 28:29 3478
I upon his heart before the LORD .... Ex 28:30 3478
which the children of *I* shall .... Ex 28:38 3478
for ever from the children of *I*................ Ex 29:28 3478
offering from the children of *I* .... Ex 29:28 3478
will meet with the children of *I* .... Ex 29:43 3478
dwell among the children of *I* .... Ex 29:45 3478
children of *I* after their number............. Ex 30:12 3478
money of the children of *I*....................... Ex 30:16 3478
the children of *I* before the LORD............ Ex 30:16 3478
speak unto the children of *I* .... Ex 30:31 3478
thou also unto the children of *I*.............. Ex 31:13 3478
of *I* shall keep the sabbath .... Ex 31:16 3478
me and the children of *I* for ever............. Ex 31:17 3478
they said, These be thy gods, O *I*............ Ex 32:4 3478
and said, These be thy gods, O *I*............ Ex 32:8 3478
the children of *I* drink of it .... Ex 32:20 3478
Thus saith the LORD God of *I*.................. Ex 32:27 3478
Moses, Say unto the children of *I*............ Ex 33:5 3478
the children of *I* stripped .... Ex 33:6 3478
before the Lord GOD, the God of *I*........... Ex 34:23 3478
a covenant with thee and with *I* .... Ex 34:27 3478
all the children of *I* saw Moses............... Ex 34:30 3478
all the children of *I* came nigh .... Ex 34:32 3478
spake unto the children of *I* that............ Ex 34:34 3478
the children of *I* saw the face of............. Ex 34:35 3478
of the children of *I* together .... Ex 35:1 3478
congregation of the children of *I*............ Ex 35:4 3478
I departed from the presence of .... Ex 35:20 3478
The children of *I* brought a .... Ex 35:29 3478
Moses said unto the children of *I*............ Ex 35:30 3478
which the children of *I* had...................... Ex 36:3 3478
the names of the children of *I* .... Ex 39:6 3478
a memorial to the children of *I* .... Ex 39:7 3478
to the names of the children of *I*............. Ex 39:14 3478
the children of *I* did according................ Ex 39:32 3478
children of *I* made all the work.............. Ex 39:42 3478
the children of *I* went onward in............. Ex 40:36 3478
the sight of all the house of *I* .... Ex 40:38 3478
Speak unto the children of *I* .... Lev 1:2 3478
Speak unto the children of *I* .... Lev 4:2 3478
of *I* sin through ignorance....................... Lev 4:13 3478
Speak unto the children of *I* .... Lev 7:23 3478
Speak unto the children of *I* .... Lev 7:29 3478
of *I* from off the sacrifices of.................. Lev 7:34 3478
ever from among the children of *I*........... Lev 7:34 3478
given them of the children of *I*............... Lev 7:36 3478
he commanded the children of *I* to .... Lev 7:38 3478
and his sons, and the elders of *I*.............. Lev 9:1 3478
children of *I* thou shalt speak .... Lev 9:3 3478
brethren, the whole house of *I* .... Lev 10:6 3478
ye may teach the children of *I*................. Lev 10:11 3478
offerings of the children of *I* .... Lev 10:14 3478
Speak unto the children of *I* .... Lev 11:2 3478

Speak unto the children of *I* ... Lev 12:2 3478
Speak unto the children of *I* ... Lev 15:2 3478
of *I* from their uncleanness ... Lev 15:31 3478
I two kids of the goats for a sin ... Lev 16:5 3478
uncleanness of the children of *I* ... Lev 16:16 3478
and for all the congregation of *I* ... Lev 16:17 3478
uncleanness of the children of *I* ... Lev 16:19 3478
iniquities of the children of *I* ... Lev 16:21 3478
atonement for the children of *I* ... Lev 16:34 3478
and unto all the children of *I* ... Lev 17:2 3478
soever there be of the house of *I* ... Lev 17:3 3478
of *I* may bring their sacrifices ... Lev 17:5 3478
man there be of the house of *I* ... Lev 17:8 3478
man there be of the house of *I* ... Lev 17:10 3478
I said unto the children of *I* ... Lev 17:12 3478
man there be of the children of *I* ... Lev 17:13 3478
I said unto the children of *I* ... Lev 17:14 3478
Speak unto the children of *I* ... Lev 18:2 3478
congregation of the children of *I* ... Lev 19:2 3478
shalt say to the children of *I* ... Lev 20:2 3478
he be of the children of *I* ... Lev 20:2 3478
the strangers that sojourn in *I* ... Lev 20:2 3478
and unto all the children of *I* ... Lev 21:24 3478
holy things of the children of *I* ... Lev 22:2 3478
of *I* hallow unto the LORD ... Lev 22:3 3478
holy things of the children of *I* ... Lev 22:15 3478
and unto all the children of *I* ... Lev 22:18 3478
he be of the house of *I* ... Lev 22:18 3478
or of the strangers in *I* ... Lev 22:18 3478
hallowed among the children of *I* ... Lev 22:32 3478
Speak unto the children of *I* ... Lev 23:2 3478
Speak unto the children of *I* ... Lev 23:10 3478
Speak unto the children of *I* ... Lev 23:24 3478
Speak unto the children of *I* ... Lev 23:34 3478
children of *I* to dwell in booths ... Lev 23:43 3478
of *I* the feasts of the LORD ... Lev 23:44 3478
Command the children of *I* ... Lev 24:2 3478
of *I* by an everlasting covenant ... Lev 24:8 3478
went out among the children of *I* ... Lev 24:10 3481
a man of *I* strove together in the ... Lev 24:10 3478
speak unto the children of *I* ... Lev 24:15 3478
Moses spake to the children of *I* ... Lev 24:23 3478
the children of *I* did as the LORD ... Lev 24:23 3478
Speak unto the children of *I* ... Lev 25:2 3478
among the children of *I* ... Lev 25:33 3478
your brethren the children of *I* ... Lev 25:46 3478
me the children of *I* are servants ... Lev 25:55 3478
the children of *I* in mount Sinai ... Lev 26:46 3478
Speak unto the children of *I* ... Lev 27:2 3478
the children of *I* in mount Sinai ... Lev 27:34 3478
congregation of the children of *I* ... Num 1:2 3478
are able to go forth to war in *I* ... Num 1:3 3478
fathers, heads of thousands in *I* ... Num 1:16 3478
numbered, and the princes of *I* ... Num 1:44 3478
numbered of the children of *I* ... Num 1:45 3478
were able to go forth to war in *I* ... Num 1:45 3478
of them among the children of *I* ... Num 1:49 3478
the children of *I* shall pitch ... Num 1:52 3478
congregation of the children of *I* ... Num 1:53 3478
the children of *I* did according ... Num 1:54 3478
Every man of the children of *I* ... Num 2:2 3478
numbered of the children of *I* by ... Num 2:32 3478
numbered among the children of *I* ... Num 2:33 3478
the children of *I* did according ... Num 2:34 3478
the charge of the children of *I* ... Num 3:8 3478
unto him out of the children of *I* ... Num 3:9 3478
from among the children of *I* ... Num 3:12 3478
matrix among the children of *I* ... Num 3:12 3478
unto me all the firstborn in *I* ... Num 3:13 3478
the charge of the children of *I* ... Num 3:38 3478
children of *I* from a month old ... Num 3:40 3478
firstborn among the children of *I* ... Num 3:41 3478
the cattle of the children of *I* ... Num 3:41 3478
firstborn among the children of *I* ... Num 3:42 3478
firstborn among the children of *I* ... Num 3:45 3478
firstborn of the children of *I* ... Num 3:46 3478
children of *I* took he the money ... Num 3:50 3478
Aaron and the chief of *I* numbered ... Num 4:46 3478
Command the children of *I* ... Num 5:2 3478
And the children of *I* did so ... Num 5:4 3478
Moses, so did the children of *I* ... Num 5:4 3478
Speak unto the children of *I* ... Num 5:6 3478
holy things of the children of *I* ... Num 5:9 3478
Speak unto the children of *I* ... Num 5:12 3478
Speak unto the children of *I* ... Num 6:2 3478
ye shall bless the children of *I* ... Num 6:23 3478
my name upon the children of *I* ... Num 6:27 3478
That the princes of *I*, heads of ... Num 7:2 3478
was anointed, by the princes of *I* ... Num 7:84 3478
from among the children of *I* ... Num 8:6 3478
of the children of *I* together ... Num 8:9 3478
the children of *I* shall put their ... Num 8:10 3478
an offering of the children of *I* ... Num 8:11 3478
from among the children of *I* ... Num 8:14 3478
me from among the children of *I* ... Num 8:16 3478
of all the children of *I*, have I ... Num 8:16 3478
of the children of *I* are mine ... Num 8:17 3478
firstborn of the children of *I* ... Num 8:18 3478
sons from among the children of *I* ... Num 8:19 3478
of *I* in the tabernacle of the ... Num 8:19 3478
atonement for the children of *I* ... Num 8:19 3478
no plague among the children of *I* ... Num 8:19 3478
when the children of *I* come nigh ... Num 8:19 3478
congregation of the children of *I* ... Num 8:20 3478
did the children of *I* unto them ... Num 8:20 3478
Let the children of *I* also keep ... Num 9:2 3478
spake unto the children of *I* ... Num 9:4 3478
Moses, so did the children of *I* ... Num 9:5 3478

season among the children of *I* ... Num 9:7 3478
Speak unto the children of *I* ... Num 9:10 3478
that the children of *I* journeyed ... Num 9:17 3478
children of *I* pitched their tents ... Num 9:17 3478
LORD the children of *I* journeyed ... Num 9:18 3478
then the children of *I* kept the ... Num 9:19 3478
the children of *I* abode in their ... Num 9:22 3478
are heads of the thousands of *I* ... Num 10:4 3478
the children of *I* took their ... Num 10:12 3478
of *I* according to their armies ... Num 10:28 3478
hath spoken good concerning *I* ... Num 10:29 3478
unto the many thousands of *I* ... Num 10:36 3478
the children of *I* also wept again ... Num 11:4 3478
me seventy men of the elders of *I* ... Num 11:16 3478
the camp, he and the elders of *I* ... Num 11:30 3478
I give unto the children of *I* ... Num 13:2 3478
were heads of the children of *I* ... Num 13:3 3478
of *I* cut down from thence ... Num 13:24 3478
congregation of the children of *I* ... Num 13:26 3478
searched unto the children of *I* ... Num 13:32 3478
all the children of *I* murmured ... Num 14:2 3478
congregation of the children of *I* ... Num 14:5 3478
the company of the children of *I* ... Num 14:7 3478
before all the children of *I* ... Num 14:10 3478
murmurings of the children of *I* ... Num 14:27 3478
unto all the children of *I* ... Num 14:39 3478
Speak unto the children of *I* ... Num 15:2 3478
Speak unto the children of *I* ... Num 15:18 3478
congregation of the children of *I* ... Num 15:25 3478
congregation of the children of *I* ... Num 15:26 3478
is born among the children of *I* ... Num 15:29 3478
while the children of *I* were in ... Num 15:32 3478
Speak unto the children of *I* ... Num 15:38 3478
with certain of the children of *I* ... Num 16:2 3478
that the God of *I* hath separated ... Num 16:9 3478
you from the congregation of *I* ... Num 16:9 3478
and the elders of *I* followed him ... Num 16:25 3478
all *I* that were round about them ... Num 16:34 3478
be a sign unto the children of *I* ... Num 16:38 3478
a memorial unto the children of *I* ... Num 16:40 3478
of *I* murmured against Moses ... Num 16:41 3478
Speak unto the children of *I* ... Num 17:2 3478
murmurings of the children of *I* ... Num 17:5 3478
spake unto the children of *I* ... Num 17:6 3478
LORD unto all the children of *I* ... Num 17:9 3478
the children of *I* spake unto ... Num 17:12 3478
any more upon the children of *I* ... Num 18:5 3478
from among the children of *I* ... Num 18:6 3478
things of the children of *I* ... Num 18:8 3478
offerings of the children of *I* ... Num 18:11 3478
thing devoted in *I* shall be thine ... Num 18:14 3478
children of *I* offer unto the LORD ... Num 18:19 3478
among the children of *I* ... Num 18:20 3478
the tenth in *I* for an inheritance ... Num 18:21 3478
of *I* henceforth come nigh the ... Num 18:22 3478
of *I* they have no inheritance ... Num 18:23 3478
the tithes of the children of *I* ... Num 18:24 3478
Among the children of *I* they ... Num 18:24 3478
I the tithes which I have given ... Num 18:26 3478
ye receive of the children of *I* ... Num 18:28 3478
holy things of the children of *I* ... Num 18:32 3478
Speak unto the children of *I* ... Num 19:2 3478
of *I* for a water of separation ... Num 19:9 3478
shall be unto the children of *I* ... Num 19:10 3478
that soul shall be cut off from *I* ... Num 19:13 3478
Then came the children of *I* ... Num 20:1 3478
in the eyes of the children of *I* ... Num 20:12 3478
of *I* strove with the LORD ... Num 20:13 3478
of Edom, Thus saith thy brother *I* ... Num 20:14 3478
the children of *I* said unto him ... Num 20:19 3478
Thus Edom refused to give *I* ... Num 20:21 3478
wherefore *I* turned away from him ... Num 20:21 3478
And the children of *I*, even the ... Num 20:22 3478
have given unto the children of *I* ... Num 20:24 3478
days, even all the house of *I* ... Num 20:29 3478
heard tell that *I* came by the way ... Num 21:1 3478
then he fought against *I*, and took ... Num 21:1 3478
I vowed a vow unto the LORD, and ... Num 21:2 3478
LORD hearkened to the voice of *I* ... Num 21:3 3478
and much people of *I* died ... Num 21:6 3478
And the children of *I* set forward ... Num 21:10 3478
Then *I* sang this song, Spring up, ... Num 21:17 3478
I sent messengers unto Sihon king ... Num 21:21 3478
Sihon would not suffer *I* to pass ... Num 21:23 3478
went out against *I* into the ... Num 21:23 3478
to Jahaz, and fought against *I* ... Num 21:23 3478
I smote him with the edge of the ... Num 21:24 3478
And *I* took all these cities ... Num 21:25 3478
I dwelt in all the cities of the ... Num 21:25 3478
Thus *I* dwelt in the land of the ... Num 21:31 3478
And the children of *I* set forward ... Num 22:1 3478
that *I* had done to the Amorites ... Num 22:2 3478
because of the children of *I* ... Num 22:3 3478
curse me Jacob, and come, defy *I* ... Num 23:7 3478
number of the fourth part of *I* ... Num 23:10 3478
hath he seen perverseness in *I* ... Num 23:21 3478
is there any divination against *I* ... Num 23:23 3478
it shall be said of Jacob and of *I* ... Num 23:23 3478
it pleased the LORD to bless *I* ... Num 24:1 3478
he saw *I* abiding in his tents ... Num 24:2 3478
O Jacob, and thy tabernacles, O *I* ... Num 24:5 3478
and a Sceptre shall rise out of *I* ... Num 24:17 3478
and *I* shall do valiantly ... Num 24:18 3478
I abode in Shittim, and the people ... Num 25:1 3478
I joined himself unto Baal-peor ... Num 25:3 3478
of the LORD was kindled against *I* ... Num 25:3 3478
LORD may be turned away from *I* ... Num 25:4 3478
Moses said unto the judges of *I* ... Num 25:5 3478

one of the children of *I* came ... Num 25:6 3478
congregation of the children of *I* ... Num 25:6 3478
after the man of *I* into the tent ... Num 25:8 3478
of them through, the man of *I* ... Num 25:8 3478
was stayed from the children of *I* ... Num 25:8 3478
wrath away from the children of *I* ... Num 25:11 3478
the children of *I* in my jealousy ... Num 25:11 3478
atonement for the children of *I* ... Num 25:13 3478
congregation of the children of *I* ... Num 26:2 3478
that are able to go to war in *I* ... Num 26:2 3478
Moses and the children of *I* ... Num 26:4 3478
the numbered of the children of *I* ... Num 26:51 3478
numbered among the children of *I* ... Num 26:62 3478
them among the children of *I* ... Num 26:62 3478
who numbered the children of *I* in ... Num 26:63 3478
of *I* in the wilderness of Sinai ... Num 26:64 3478
speak unto the children of *I* ... Num 27:8 3478
of *I* a statute of judgment ... Num 27:11 3478
have given unto the children of *I* ... Num 27:12 3478
the children of *I* may be obedient ... Num 27:20 3478
and all the children of *I* with him ... Num 27:21 3478
Command the children of *I* ... Num 28:2 3478
Moses told the children of *I* ... Num 29:40 3478
concerning the children of *I* ... Num 30:1 3478
children of *I* of the Midianites ... Num 31:2 3478
throughout all the tribes of *I* ... Num 31:4 3478
out of the thousands of *I* ... Num 31:5 3478
the children of *I* took all the ... Num 31:9 3478
congregation of the children of *I* ... Num 31:12 3478
these caused the children of *I* ... Num 31:16 3478
the children of *I* before the LORD ... Num 31:54 3478
before the congregation of *I* ... Num 32:4 3478
I from going over into the land ... Num 32:7 3478
the heart of the children of *I* ... Num 32:9 3478
anger was kindled against *I* ... Num 32:13 3478
fierce anger of the LORD toward *I* ... Num 32:14 3478
armed before the children of *I* ... Num 32:17 3478
until the children of *I* have ... Num 32:18 3478
before the LORD, and before *I* ... Num 32:22 3478
the tribes of the children of *I* ... Num 32:28 3478
the journeys of the children of *I* ... Num 33:1 3478
the passover the children of *I* ... Num 33:3 3478
the children of *I* removed from ... Num 33:5 3478
year after the children of *I* were ... Num 33:38 3478
the coming of the children of *I* ... Num 33:40 3478
Speak unto the children of *I* ... Num 33:51 3478
Command the children of *I* ... Num 34:2 3478
Moses commanded the children of *I* ... Num 34:13 3478
unto the children of *I* in the ... Num 34:29 3478
Command the children of *I* ... Num 35:2 3478
possession of the children of *I* ... Num 35:8 3478
Speak unto the children of *I* ... Num 35:10 3478
both for the children of *I* ... Num 35:15 3478
dwell among the children of *I* ... Num 35:34 3478
fathers of the children of *I* ... Num 36:1 3478
by lot to the children of *I* ... Num 36:2 3478
other tribes of the children of *I* ... Num 36:3 3478
of the children of *I* shall be ... Num 36:4 3478
of *I* according to the word of the ... Num 36:5 3478
of *I* remove from tribe to tribe ... Num 36:7 3478
of *I* shall keep himself to the ... Num 36:7 3478
in any tribe of the children of *I* ... Num 36:8 3478
that the children of *I* may enjoy ... Num 36:8 3478
I shall keep himself to his own ... Num 36:9 3478
of Moses unto the children of *I* ... Num 36:13 3478
all *I* on this side Jordan in the ... Deut 1:1 3478
spake unto the children of *I* ... Deut 1:3 3478
he shall cause *I* to inherit it ... Deut 1:38 3478
as *I* did unto the land of his ... Deut 2:12 3478
your brethren the children of *I* ... Deut 3:18 3478
Now therefore hearken, O *I* ... Deut 4:1 3478
set before the children of *I* ... Deut 4:44 3478
spake unto the children of *I* ... Deut 4:45 3478
Moses and the children of *I* smote ... Deut 4:46 3478
And Moses called all *I* ... Deut 5:1 3478
and said unto them, Hear, O *I* ... Deut 5:1 3478
Hear therefore, O *I*, and observe ... Deut 6:3 3478
Hear, O *I*: The LORD our God ... Deut 6:4 3478
Hear, O *I*: Thou art to pass ... Deut 9:1 3478
the children of *I* took their ... Deut 10:6 3478
And now, *I*, what doth the LORD thy ... Deut 10:12 3478
possession, in the midst of all *I* ... Deut 11:6 3478
all *I* shall hear, and fear, and ... Deut 13:11 3478
such abomination is wrought in *I* ... Deut 17:4 3478
shalt put away the evil from *I* ... Deut 17:12 3478
his children, in the midst of *I* ... Deut 17:20 3478
no part nor inheritance with *I* ... Deut 18:1 3478
any of thy gates out of all *I* ... Deut 18:6 3478
guilt of innocent blood from *I* ... Deut 19:13 3478
And shall say unto them, Hear, O *I* ... Deut 20:3 3478
O LORD, unto thy people *I* ... Deut 21:8 3478
all *I* shall hear, and fear ... Deut 21:21 3478
an evil name upon a virgin of *I* ... Deut 22:19 3478
she hath wrought folly in *I* ... Deut 22:21 3478
shalt thou put away evil from *I* ... Deut 22:22 3478
be no whore of the daughters of *I* ... Deut 23:17 3478
nor a sodomite of the sons of *I* ... Deut 23:17 3478
his brethren of the children of *I* ... Deut 24:7 3478
that his name be not put out of *I* ... Deut 25:6 3478
up unto his brother a name in *I* ... Deut 25:7 3478
And his name shall be called in *I* ... Deut 25:10 3478
heaven, and bless thy people *I* ... Deut 26:15 3478
elders of *I* commanded the people ... Deut 27:1 3478
the Levites spake unto all *I* ... Deut 27:9 3478
Take heed, and hearken, O *I* ... Deut 27:9 3478
the men of *I* with a loud voice ... Deut 27:14 3478
children of *I* in the land of Moab ... Deut 29:1 3478
And Moses called unto all *I* ... Deut 29:2 3478

I

officers, with all the men of *I*	Deut 29:10	3478
evil out of all the tribes of *I*	Deut 29:21	3478
and spake these words unto all *I*	Deut 31:1	3478
unto him in the sight of all *I*	Deut 31:7	3478
LORD, and unto all the elders of *I*	Deut 31:9	3478
When all *I* is come to appear	Deut 31:11	3478
law before all *I* in their hearing	Deut 31:11	3478
and teach it the children of *I*	Deut 31:19	3478
for me against the children of *I*	Deut 31:19	3478
and taught it the children of *I*	Deut 31:22	3478
of *I* into the land which I sware	Deut 31:23	3478
of *I* the words of this song	Deut 31:30	3478
the number of the children of *I*	Deut 32:8	3478
speaking all these words to all *I*	Deut 32:45	3478
children of *I* for a possession	Deut 32:49	3478
me among the children of *I* at the	Deut 32:51	3478
in the midst of the children of *I*	Deut 32:51	3478
which I give the children of *I*	Deut 32:52	3478
children of *I* before his death	Deut 33:1	3478
the tribes of *I* were gathered	Deut 33:5	3478
Jacob thy judgments, and *I* thy law	Deut 33:10	3478
the LORD, and his judgments with *I*	Deut 33:21	3478
I then shall dwell in safety	Deut 33:28	3478
Happy art thou, O *I*	Deut 33:29	3478
the children of *I* wept for Moses	Deut 34:8	3478
the children of *I* hearkened unto	Deut 34:9	3478
since in *I* like unto Moses	Deut 34:10	3478
shewed in the sight of all *I*	Deut 34:12	3478
them, even to the children of *I*	Josh 1:2	3478
of *I* to search out the country	Josh 2:2	3478
he and all the children of *I*	Josh 3:1	3478
thee in the sight of all *I*	Josh 3:7	3478
said unto the children of *I*	Josh 3:9	3478
twelve men out of the tribes of *I*	Josh 3:12	3478
had prepared of the children of *I*	Josh 4:4	3478
the tribes of the children of *I*	Josh 4:5	3478
unto the children of *I* for ever	Josh 4:7	3478
the children of *I* did so as	Josh 4:8	3478
the tribes of the children of *I*	Josh 4:8	3478
armed before the children of *I*	Josh 4:12	3478
Joshua in the sight of all *I*	Josh 4:14	3478
he spake unto the children of *I*	Josh 4:21	3478
I came over this Jordan on dry	Josh 4:22	3478
from before the children of *I*	Josh 5:1	3478
because of the children of *I*	Josh 5:1	3478
the children of *I* the second time	Josh 5:2	3478
circumcised the children of *I* at	Josh 5:3	3478
For the children of *I* walked	Josh 5:6	3478
the children of *I* encamped in	Josh 5:10	3478
the children of *I* manna any more	Josh 5:12	3478
up because of the children of *I*	Josh 6:1	3478
and make the camp of *I* a curse	Josh 6:18	3478
left them without the camp of *I*	Josh 6:23	3478
she dwelleth in *I* even unto this	Josh 6:25	3478
But the children of *I* committed a	Josh 7:1	3478
kindled against the children of *I*	Josh 7:1	3478
eventide, he and the elders of *I*	Josh 7:6	3478
when *I* turneth their backs before	Josh 7:8	3478
I hath sinned, and they have also	Josh 7:11	3478
Therefore the children of *I* could	Josh 7:12	3478
for thus saith the LORD God of *I*	Josh 7:13	3478
thing in the midst of thee, O *I*	Josh 7:13	3478
he hath wrought folly in *I*	Josh 7:15	3478
brought *I* by their tribes	Josh 7:16	3478
thee, glory to the LORD God of *I*	Josh 7:19	3478
sinned against the LORD God of *I*	Josh 7:20	3478
and unto all the children of *I*	Josh 7:23	3478
all *I* with him, took Achan the	Josh 7:24	3478
all *I* stoned him with stones, and	Josh 7:25	3478
and went up, he and the elders of *I*	Josh 8:10	3478
city went out against *I* to battle	Josh 8:14	3478
all *I* made as if they were beaten	Josh 8:15	3478
that went not out after *I*	Josh 8:17	3478
the city open, and pursued after *I*	Josh 8:17	3478
all *I* saw that the ambush had	Josh 8:21	3478
so they were in the midst of *I*	Josh 8:22	3478
when *I* had made an end of slaying	Josh 8:24	3478
the spoil of that city *I* took for	Josh 8:27	3478
the LORD God of *I* in mount Ebal	Josh 8:30	3478
LORD commanded the children of *I*	Josh 8:31	3478
the presence of the children of *I*	Josh 8:32	3478
And all *I*, and their elders, and	Josh 8:33	3478
they should bless the people of *I*	Josh 8:33	3478
before all the congregation of *I*	Josh 8:35	3478
to fight with Joshua and with *I*	Josh 9:2	3478
said unto him, and to the men of *I*	Josh 9:6	3478
the men of *I* said unto the	Josh 9:7	3478
And the children of *I* journeyed	Josh 9:17	3478
the children of *I* smote them not	Josh 9:18	3478
unto them by the LORD God of *I*	Josh 9:18	3478
unto them by the LORD God of *I*	Josh 9:19	3478
of the hand of the children of *I*	Josh 9:26	3478
of Gibeon had made peace with *I*	Josh 10:1	3478
Joshua and with the children of *I*	Josh 10:4	3478
LORD discomfited them before *I*	Josh 10:10	3478
pass, as they fled from before *I*	Josh 10:11	3478
children of *I* slew with the sword	Josh 10:11	3478
Amorites before the children of *I*	Josh 10:12	3478
and he said in the sight of *I*	Josh 10:12	3478
for the LORD fought for *I*	Josh 10:14	3478
all *I* with him, unto the camp to	Josh 10:15	3478
the children of *I* had made an end	Josh 10:20	3478
against any of the children of *I*	Josh 10:21	3478
called for all the men of *I*	Josh 10:24	3478
all *I* with him, unto Libnah, and	Josh 10:29	3478
king thereof, into the hand of *I*	Josh 10:30	3478
all *I* with him, unto Lachish, and	Josh 10:31	3478
Lachish into the hand of *I*	Josh 10:32	3478
unto Eglon, and all *I* with him	Josh 10:34	3478
all *I* with him, unto Hebron	Josh 10:36	3478
and all *I* with him, to Debir	Josh 10:38	3478
as the LORD God of *I* commanded	Josh 10:40	3478
LORD God of *I* fought for Israel	Josh 10:42	3478
LORD God of Israel fought for *I*	Josh 10:42	3478
all *I* with him, unto the camp to	Josh 10:43	3478
of Merom, to fight against *I*	Josh 11:5	3478
them up all slain before *I*	Josh 11:6	3478
delivered them into the hand of *I*	Josh 11:8	3478
I burned none of them, save Hazor	Josh 11:13	3478
the children of *I* took for a prey	Josh 11:14	3478
the plain, and the mountain of *I*	Josh 11:16	3478
made peace with the children of *I*	Josh 11:19	3478
should come against *I* in battle	Josh 11:20	3478
and from all the mountains of *I*	Josh 11:21	3478
in the land of the children of *I*	Josh 11:22	3478
I according to their divisions by	Josh 11:23	3478
which the children of *I* smote	Josh 12:1	3478
LORD and the children of *I* smite	Josh 12:6	3478
the children of *I* smote on this	Josh 12:7	3478
I for a possession according to	Josh 12:7	3478
out from before the children of *I*	Josh 13:6	3478
of *I* expelled not the Geshurites	Josh 13:13	3478
God of *I* made by fire are their	Josh 13:14	3478
did the children of *I* slay with	Josh 13:22	3478
the LORD God of *I* was their	Josh 13:33	3478
I inherited in the land of Canaan	Josh 14:1	3478
the tribes of the children of *I*	Josh 14:1	3478
Moses, so the children of *I* did	Josh 14:5	3478
while the children of *I* wandered	Josh 14:10	3478
wholly followed the LORD God of *I*	Josh 14:14	3478
children of *I* were waxen strong	Josh 17:13	3478
of *I* assembled together at Shiloh	Josh 18:1	3478
the children of *I* seven tribes	Josh 18:2	3478
said unto the children of *I*	Josh 18:3	3478
of *I* according to their divisions	Josh 18:10	3478
the children of *I* gave an	Josh 19:49	3478
the tribes of the children of *I*	Josh 19:51	3478
Speak to the children of *I*	Josh 20:2	3478
for all the children of *I*	Josh 20:9	3478
the tribes of the children of *I*	Josh 21:1	3478
the children of *I* gave unto the	Josh 21:3	3478
the children of *I* gave by lot	Josh 21:8	3478
of the children of *I* were forty	Josh 21:41	3478
the LORD gave unto *I* all the land	Josh 21:43	3478
had spoken unto the house of *I*	Josh 21:45	3478
the children of *I* out of Shiloh	Josh 22:9	3478
And the children of *I* heard say	Josh 22:11	3478
the passage of the children of *I*	Josh 22:11	3478
the children of *I* heard of it	Josh 22:12	3478
I gathered themselves together at	Josh 22:12	3478
the children of *I* sent unto the	Josh 22:13	3478
throughout all the tribes of *I*	Josh 22:14	3478
fathers among the thousands of *I*	Josh 22:14	3478
committed against the God of *I*	Josh 22:16	3478
with the whole congregation of *I*	Josh 22:18	3478
fell on all the congregation of *I*	Josh 22:20	3478
the heads of the thousands of *I*	Josh 22:21	3478
he knoweth, and *I* he shall know	Josh 22:22	3478
ye to do with the LORD God of *I*	Josh 22:24	3478
of *I* which were with him, heard	Josh 22:30	3478
of *I* out of the hand of the LORD	Josh 22:31	3478
of Canaan, to the children of *I*	Josh 22:32	3478
thing pleased the children of *I*	Josh 22:33	3478
and the children of *I* blessed God	Josh 22:33	3478
I from all their enemies round	Josh 23:1	3478
And Joshua called for all *I*	Josh 23:2	3478
all the tribes of *I* to Shechem	Josh 24:1	3478
and called for the elders of *I*	Josh 24:1	3478
Thus saith the LORD God of *I*	Josh 24:2	3478
Moab, arose and warred against *I*	Josh 24:9	3478
your heart unto the LORD God of *I*	Josh 24:23	3478
I served the LORD all the days of	Josh 24:31	3478
the LORD, that he had done for *I*	Josh 24:31	3478
which the children of *I* brought	Josh 24:32	3478
the children of *I* asked the LORD	Judg 1:1	3478
when *I* was strong, that they put	Judg 1:28	3478
words unto all the children of *I*	Judg 2:4	3478
the children of *I* went every man	Judg 2:6	3478
of the LORD, that he did for *I*	Judg 2:7	3478
the works which he had done for *I*	Judg 2:10	3478
the children of *I* did evil in the	Judg 2:11	3478
of the LORD was hot against *I*	Judg 2:14	3478
of the LORD was hot against *I*	Judg 2:20	3478
That through them I may prove *I*	Judg 2:22	3478
the LORD left, to prove *I* by them	Judg 3:1	3478
even as many of *I* as had not	Judg 3:1	3478
of the children of *I* might know	Judg 3:2	3478
And they were to prove *I* by them	Judg 3:4	3478
the children of *I* dwelt among the	Judg 3:5	3478
the children of *I* did evil in the	Judg 3:7	3478
of the LORD was hot against *I*	Judg 3:8	3478
and the children of *I* served	Judg 3:8	3478
children of *I* cried unto the LORD	Judg 3:9	3478
a deliverer to the children of *I*	Judg 3:9	3478
came upon him, and he judged *I*	Judg 3:10	3478
the children of *I* did evil again	Judg 3:12	3478
Eglon the king of Moab against *I*	Judg 3:12	3478
and Amalek, and went and smote *I*	Judg 3:13	3478
So the children of *I* served Eglon	Judg 3:14	3478
children of *I* cried unto the LORD	Judg 3:15	3478
by him the children of *I* sent a	Judg 3:15	3478
the children of *I* went down with	Judg 3:27	3478
that day under the hand of *I*	Judg 3:30	3478
and he also delivered *I*	Judg 3:31	3478
the children of *I* again did evil	Judg 4:1	3478
the children of *I* cried unto the	Judg 4:3	3478
oppressed the children of *I*	Judg 4:3	3478
she judged *I* at that time	Judg 4:4	3478
the children of *I* came up to her	Judg 4:5	3478
not the LORD God of *I* commanded	Judg 4:6	3478
Canaan before the children of *I*	Judg 4:23	3478
of the children of *I* prospered	Judg 4:24	3478
ye the LORD for the avenging of *I*	Judg 5:2	3478
sing praise to the LORD God of *I*	Judg 5:3	3478
from before the LORD God of *I*	Judg 5:5	3478
villages ceased, they ceased in *I*	Judg 5:7	3478
arose, that I arose a mother in *I*	Judg 5:7	3478
seen among forty thousand in *I*	Judg 5:8	3478
is toward the governors of *I*	Judg 5:9	3478
inhabitants of his villages in *I*	Judg 5:11	3478
the children of *I* did evil in the	Judg 6:1	3478
of Midian prevailed against *I*	Judg 6:2	3478
the Midianites the children of *I*	Judg 6:2	3478
when *I* had sown, that the	Judg 6:3	3478
Gaza, and left no sustenance for *I*	Judg 6:4	3478
I was greatly impoverished	Judg 6:6	3478
the children of *I* cried unto the	Judg 6:6	3478
when the children of *I* cried unto	Judg 6:7	3478
a prophet unto the children of *I*	Judg 6:8	3478
Thus saith the LORD God of *I*	Judg 6:8	3478
thou shalt save *I* from the hand	Judg 6:14	3478
my Lord, wherewith shall I save *I*	Judg 6:15	3478
If thou wilt save *I* by mine hand	Judg 6:36	3478
thou wilt save *I* by mine hand	Judg 6:37	3478
lest *I* vaunt themselves against	Judg 7:2	3478
rest of *I* every man unto his tent	Judg 7:8	3478
the son of Joash, a man of *I*	Judg 7:14	3478
and returned into the host of *I*	Judg 7:15	3478
the men of *I* gathered themselves	Judg 7:23	3478
Then the men of *I* said unto	Judg 8:22	3478
all *I* went thither a whoring	Judg 8:27	3478
subdued before the children of *I*	Judg 8:28	3478
the children of *I* turned again	Judg 8:33	3478
the children of *I* remembered not	Judg 8:34	3478
which he had shewed unto *I*	Judg 8:35	3478
had reigned three years over *I*	Judg 9:22	3478
when the men of *I* saw that	Judg 9:55	3478
to defend *I* Tola the son of Puah	Judg 10:1	3478
And he judged *I* twenty and three	Judg 10:2	3478
a Gileadite, and judged *I* twenty	Judg 10:3	3478
the children of *I* did evil again	Judg 10:6	3478
of the LORD was hot against *I*	Judg 10:7	3478
and oppressed the children of *I*	Judg 10:8	3478
all the children of *I* that were	Judg 10:8	3478
so that *I* was sore distressed	Judg 10:9	3478
the children of *I* cried unto the	Judg 10:10	3478
LORD said unto the children of *I*	Judg 10:11	3478
the children of *I* said unto the	Judg 10:15	3478
was grieved for the misery of *I*	Judg 10:16	3478
the children of *I* assembled	Judg 10:17	3478
of Ammon made war against *I*	Judg 11:4	3478
of Ammon made war against *I*	Judg 11:5	3478
Because *I* took away my land, when	Judg 11:13	3478
I took not away the land of Moab,	Judg 11:15	3478
But when *I* came up from Egypt, and	Judg 11:16	3478
Then *I* sent messengers unto the	Judg 11:17	3478
and *I* abode in Kadesh	Judg 11:17	3478
I sent messengers unto Sihon king	Judg 11:19	3478
I said unto him, Let us pass, we	Judg 11:19	3478
But Sihon trusted not *I* to pass	Judg 11:20	3478
in Jahaz, and fought against *I*	Judg 11:20	3478
the LORD God of *I* delivered Sihon	Judg 11:21	3478
all his people into the hand of *I*	Judg 11:21	3478
so *I* possessed all the land of	Judg 11:21	3478
So now the LORD God of *I* hath	Judg 11:23	3478
Amorites from before his people *I*	Judg 11:23	3478
did he ever strive against *I*	Judg 11:25	3478
While *I* dwelt in Heshbon and her	Judg 11:26	3478
day between the children of *I*	Judg 11:27	3478
subdued before the children of *I*	Judg 11:33	3478
And it was a custom in *I*,	Judg 11:39	3478
That the daughters of *I* went	Judg 11:40	3478
And Jephthah judged *I* six years	Judg 12:7	3478
him Ibzan of Beth-lehem judged *I*	Judg 12:8	3478
And he judged *I* seven years	Judg 12:9	3478
him Elon, a Zebulonite, judged *I*	Judg 12:11	3478
and he judged *I* ten years	Judg 12:11	3478
Hillel, a Pirathonite, judged *I*	Judg 12:13	3478
and he judged *I* eight years	Judg 12:14	3478
the children of *I* did evil again	Judg 13:1	3478
deliver *I* out of the hand of the	Judg 13:5	3478
Philistines had dominion over *I*	Judg 14:4	3478
he judged *I* in the days of the	Judg 15:20	3478
And he judged *I* twenty years	Judg 16:31	3478
those days there was no king in *I*	Judg 17:6	3478
those days there was no king in *I*	Judg 18:1	3478
unto them among the tribes of *I*	Judg 18:1	3478
unto a tribe and a family in *I*	Judg 18:19	3478
days, when there was no king in *I*	Judg 19:1	3478
that is not of the children of *I*	Judg 19:12	3478
sent her into all the coasts of *I*	Judg 19:29	3478
of *I* came up out of the land of	Judg 19:30	3478
all the children of *I* went out	Judg 20:1	3478
even of all the tribes of *I*	Judg 20:2	3478
of *I* were gone up to Mizpeh	Judg 20:3	3478
Then said the children of *I*	Judg 20:3	3478
country of the inheritance of *I*	Judg 20:6	3478
committed lewdness and folly in *I*	Judg 20:6	3478
Behold, ye are all children of *I*	Judg 20:7	3478
throughout all the tribes of *I*	Judg 20:10	3478
folly that they have wrought in *I*	Judg 20:10	3478
So all the men of *I* were gathered	Judg 20:11	3478
the tribes of *I* sent men through	Judg 20:12	3478
to death, and put away evil from *I*	Judg 20:13	3478

their brethren the children of *I* Judg 20:13 3478
battle against the children of *I* Judg 20:14 3478
And the men of *I*, beside Benjamin, Judg 20:17 3478
And the children of *I* arose Judg 20:18 3478
the children of *I* rose up in the Judg 20:19 3478
the men of *I* went out to battle Judg 20:20 3478
the men of *I* put themselves in Judg 20:20 3478
men of *I* encouraged themselves Judg 20:22 3478
(And the children of *I* went up Judg 20:23 3478
the children of *I* came near Judg 20:24 3478
of *I* again eighteen thousand men Judg 20:25 3478
Then all the children of *I* Judg 20:26 3478
the children of *I* enquired of the Judg 20:27 3478
I set liers in wait round about Judg 20:29 3478
the children of *I* went up against Judg 20:30 3478
the field, about thirty men of *I* Judg 20:31 3478
But the children of *I* said Judg 20:32 3478
all the men of *I* rose up out of Judg 20:33 3478
the liers in wait of *I* came forth Judg 20:33 3478
thousand chosen men out of all *I* Judg 20:34 3478
the LORD smote Benjamin before *I* Judg 20:35 3478
the children of *I* destroyed of Judg 20:35 3478
for the men of *I* gave place to Judg 20:36 3478
sign between the men of *I* Judg 20:38 3478
when the men of *I* retired in the Judg 20:39 3478
kill of the men of *I* about thirty Judg 20:39 3478
And when the men of *I* turned again Judg 20:41 3478
their backs before the men of *I* Judg 20:42 3478
the men of *I* turned again upon Judg 20:48 3478
Now the men of *I* had sworn in Judg 21:1 3478
And said, O LORD God of *I* Judg 21:3 3478
why is this come to pass in *I* Judg 21:3 3478
be to day one tribe lacking in *I* Judg 21:3 3478
And the children of *I* said Judg 21:5 3478
of *I* that came not up with the Judg 21:5 3478
the children of *I* repented them Judg 21:6 3478
one tribe cut off from *I* this day Judg 21:6 3478
I that came not up to Mizpeh to Judg 21:8 3478
made a breach in the tribes of *I* Judg 21:15 3478
a tribe be not destroyed out of *I* Judg 21:17 3478
for the children of *I* have sworn Judg 21:18 3478
the children of *I* departed thence Judg 21:24 3478
those days there was no king in *I* Judg 21:25 3478
given thee of the LORD God of *I* Ruth 2:12 3478
time in *I* concerning redeeming Ruth 4:7 3478
and this was a testimony in *I* Ruth 4:7 3478
two did build the house of *I* Ruth 4:11 3478
that his name may be famous in *I* Ruth 4:14 3478
the God of *I* grant thee thy 1Sa 1:17 3478
all that his sons did unto all *I* 1Sa 2:22 3478
the tribes of *I* to be my priest 1Sa 2:28 3478
made by fire of the children of *I* 1Sa 2:28 3478
all the offerings of *I* my people 1Sa 2:29 3478
Wherefore the LORD God of *I* saith 1Sa 2:30 3478
the wealth which God shall give *I* 1Sa 2:32 3478
Behold, I will do a thing in *I* 1Sa 3:11 3478
all *I* from Dan even to Beer-sheba 1Sa 3:20 3478
the word of Samuel came to all *I* 1Sa 4:1 3478
Now *I* went out against the 1Sa 4:1 3478
put themselves in array against *I* 1Sa 4:2 3478
battle, *I* was smitten before the 1Sa 4:2 3478
the camp, the elders of *I* said 1Sa 4:3 3478
all *I* shouted with a great shout, 1Sa 4:5 3478
I was smitten, and they fled every 1Sa 4:10 3478
for there fell of *I* thirty 1Sa 4:10 3478
I is fled before the Philistines, 1Sa 4:17 3478
And he had judged *I* forty years 1Sa 4:18 3478
The glory is departed from *I* 1Sa 4:21 3478
The glory is departed from *I* 1Sa 4:22 3478
The ark of the God of *I* shall not 1Sa 5:7 3478
do with the ark of the God of *I* 1Sa 5:8 3478
Let the ark of the God of *I* be 1Sa 5:8 3478
ark of the God of *I* about thither 1Sa 5:8 3478
the ark of the God of *I* to us 1Sa 5:10 3478
Send away the ark of the God of *I* 1Sa 5:11 3478
send away the ark of the God of *I* 1Sa 6:3 3478
give glory unto the God of *I* 1Sa 6:5 3478
all the house of *I* lamented after 1Sa 7:2 3478
spake unto all the house of *I* 1Sa 7:3 3478
children of *I* did put away Baalim 1Sa 7:4 3478
said, Gather all *I* to Mizpeh 1Sa 7:5 3478
the children of *I* in Mizpeh 1Sa 7:6 3478
of *I* were gathered together to 1Sa 7:7 3478
the Philistines went up against *I* 1Sa 7:7 3478
when the children of *I* heard it 1Sa 7:7 3478
the children of *I* said to Samuel 1Sa 7:8 3478
Samuel cried unto the LORD for *I* 1Sa 7:9 3478
drew near to battle against *I* 1Sa 7:10 3478
and they were smitten before *I* 1Sa 7:10 3478
the men of *I* went out of Mizpeh, 1Sa 7:11 3478
came no more into the coast of *I* 1Sa 7:13 3478
from *I* were restored to Israel 1Sa 7:14 3478
the coasts thereof did *I* deliver 1Sa 7:14 3478
And there was peace between *I* 1Sa 7:14 3478
Samuel judged *I* all the days of 1Sa 7:15 3478
judged *I* in all those places 1Sa 7:16 3478
and there he judged *I* 1Sa 7:17 3478
he made his sons judges over *I* 1Sa 8:1 3478
Then all the elders of *I* gathered 1Sa 8:4 3478
And Samuel said unto the men of *I* 1Sa 8:22 3478
of *I* a goodlier person than he 1Sa 9:2 3478
(Beforetime in *I*, when a man went 1Sa 9:9 3478
to be captain over my people *I* 1Sa 9:16 3478
And on whom is all the desire of *I* 1Sa 9:20 3478
the smallest of the tribes of *I* 1Sa 9:21 3478
And said unto the children of *I* 1Sa 10:18 3478
Thus saith the LORD God of *I* 1Sa 10:18 3478
I brought up *I* out of Egypt 1Sa 10:18 3478

all the tribes of *I* to come near 1Sa 10:20 3478
lay it for a reproach upon all *I* 1Sa 11:2 3478
unto all the coasts of *I* 1Sa 11:3 3478
of *I* by the hands of messengers 1Sa 11:7 3478
the children of *I* were three 1Sa 11:8 3478
LORD hath wrought salvation in *I* 1Sa 11:13 3478
all the men of *I* rejoiced greatly 1Sa 11:15 3478
And Samuel said unto all *I* 1Sa 12:1 3478
he had reigned two years over *I* 1Sa 13:1 3478
chose him three thousand men of *I* 1Sa 13:2 3478
all *I* heard say that Saul had 1Sa 13:4 3478
and that *I* also was had in 1Sa 13:4 3478
together to fight with *I*, thirty 1Sa 13:5 3478
When the men of *I* saw that they 1Sa 13:6 3478
thy kingdom upon *I* for ever 1Sa 13:13 3478
throughout all the land of *I* 1Sa 13:19 3478
delivered them into the hand of *I* 1Sa 14:12 3478
that time with the children of *I* 1Sa 14:18 3478
Likewise all the men of *I* which 1Sa 14:22 3478
So the LORD saved *I* that day 1Sa 14:23 3478
the men of *I* were distressed that 1Sa 14:24 3478
deliver them into the hand of *I* 1Sa 14:37 3478
the LORD liveth, which saveth *I* 1Sa 14:39 3478
Then said he unto all *I*, Be ye on 1Sa 14:40 3478
Saul said unto the LORD God of *I* 1Sa 14:41 3478
wrought this great salvation in *I* 1Sa 14:45 3478
So Saul took the kingdom over *I* 1Sa 14:47 3478
delivered *I* out of the hands of 1Sa 14:48 3478
be king over his people, over *I* 1Sa 15:1 3478
that which Amalek did to *I* 1Sa 15:2 3478
kindness to all the children of *I* 1Sa 15:6 3478
made the head of the tribes of *I* 1Sa 15:17 3478
LORD anointed thee king over *I* 1Sa 15:17 3478
thee from being king over *I* 1Sa 15:26 3478
kingdom of *I* from thee this day 1Sa 15:28 3478
also the Strength of *I* will not 1Sa 15:29 3478
elders of my people, and before *I* 1Sa 15:30 3478
that he had made Saul king over *I* 1Sa 15:35 3478
rejected him from reigning over *I* 1Sa 16:1 3478
the men of *I* were gathered 1Sa 17:2 3478
I stood on a mountain on the 1Sa 17:3 3478
and cried unto the armies of *I* 1Sa 17:8 3478
I defy the armies of *I* this day 1Sa 17:10 3478
all *I* heard those words of the 1Sa 17:11 3478
and they, and all the men of *I* 1Sa 17:19 3478
For *I* and the Philistines had put 1Sa 17:21 3478
And all the men of *I*, when they 1Sa 17:24 3478
And the men of *I* said, Have ye 1Sa 17:25 3478
surely to defy *I* is he come up 1Sa 17:25 3478
make his father's house free in *I* 1Sa 17:25 3478
taketh away the reproach from *I* 1Sa 17:26 3478
hosts, the God of the armies of *I* 1Sa 17:45 3478
may know that there is a God in *I* 1Sa 17:46 3478
And the men of *I* and of Judah arose 1Sa 17:52 3478
the children of *I* returned from 1Sa 17:53 3478
women came out of all cities of *I* 1Sa 18:6 3478
But all *I* and Judah loved David, 1Sa 18:16 3478
life, or my father's family in *I* 1Sa 18:18 3478
a great salvation for all *I* 1Sa 19:5 3478
said unto David, O LORD God of *I* 1Sa 20:12 3478
Then said David, O LORD God of *I* 1Sa 23:10 3478
O LORD God of *I*, I beseech thee, 1Sa 23:11 3478
and thou shalt be king over *I* 1Sa 23:17 3478
thousand chosen men out of all *I* 1Sa 24:2 3478
whom is the king of *I* come out 1Sa 24:14 3478
that the kingdom of *I* shall be 1Sa 24:20 3478
have appointed thee ruler over *I* 1Sa 25:30 3478
Blessed be the LORD God of *I* 1Sa 25:32 3478
deed, as the LORD God of *I* liveth 1Sa 25:34 3478
thousand chosen men of *I* with him 1Sa 26:2 3478
and who is like to thee in *I* 1Sa 26:15 3478
for the king of *I* is come out to 1Sa 26:20 3478
me any more in any coast of *I* 1Sa 27:1 3478
his people *I* utterly to abhor him 1Sa 27:12 3478
for warfare, to fight with *I* 1Sa 28:1 3478
all *I* had lamented him, and buried 1Sa 28:3 3478
and Saul gathered all *I* together 1Sa 28:4 3478
the LORD will also deliver *I* with 1Sa 28:19 3478
host of *I* into the hand of the 1Sa 28:19 3478
the servant of Saul the king of *I* 1Sa 29:3 3478
an ordinance for *I* unto this day 1Sa 30:25 3478
the Philistines fought against *I* 1Sa 31:1 3478
the men of *I* fled from before the 1Sa 31:1 3478
when the men of *I* that were on 1Sa 31:7 3478
saw that the men of *I* fled 1Sa 31:7 3478
Out of the camp of *I* am I escaped 2Sa 1:3 3478
the LORD, and for the house of *I* 2Sa 1:12 3478
The beauty of *I* is slain upon thy 2Sa 1:19 3478
Ye daughters of *I*, weep over Saul 2Sa 1:24 3478
and over Benjamin, and over all *I* 2Sa 2:9 3478
old when he began to reign over *I* 2Sa 2:10 3478
Abner was beaten, and the men of *I* 2Sa 2:17 3478
still, and pursued after *I* no more 2Sa 2:28 3478
set up the throne of David over *I* 2Sa 3:10 3478
to bring about all *I* unto thee 2Sa 3:12 3478
with the elders of *I*, saying, Ye 2Sa 3:17 3478
people *I* out of the hand of the 2Sa 3:18 3478
Hebron all that seemed good to *I* 2Sa 3:19 3478
will gather all *I* unto my lord 2Sa 3:21 3478
all *I* understood that day that it 2Sa 3:37 3478
a great man fallen this day in *I* 2Sa 3:38 3478
tribes of *I* to David unto Hebron 2Sa 5:1 3478
leddest out and broughtest in *I* 2Sa 5:2 3478
thee, Thou shalt feed my people *I* 2Sa 5:2 3478
and thou shalt be a captain over *I* 2Sa 5:2 3478
So all the elders of *I* came to 2Sa 5:3 3478
they anointed David king over *I* 2Sa 5:3 3478
thirty and three years over all *I* 2Sa 5:5 3478

had established him king over *I* 2Sa 5:12 3478
had anointed David king over *I* 2Sa 5:17 3478
together all the chosen men of *I* 2Sa 6:1 3478
all the house of *I* played before 2Sa 6:5 3478
all the house of *I* brought up the 2Sa 6:15 3478
among the whole multitude of *I* 2Sa 6:19 3478
glorious was the king of *I* today 2Sa 6:20 3478
the people of the LORD, over *I* 2Sa 6:21 3478
up the children of *I* out of Egypt 2Sa 7:6 3478
I spake I a word with any of the 2Sa 7:7 3478
word with any of the tribes of *I* 2Sa 7:7 3478
I commanded to feed my people *I* 2Sa 7:7 3478
be ruler over my people, over *I* 2Sa 7:8 3478
appoint a place for my people *I* 2Sa 7:10 3478
judges to be over my people *I* 2Sa 7:11 3478
is like thy people, even like *I* 2Sa 7:23 3478
I to be a people unto thee for 2Sa 7:24 3478
LORD of hosts is the God over *I* 2Sa 7:26 3478
thou, O LORD of hosts, God of *I* 2Sa 7:27 3478
And David reigned over all *I* 2Sa 8:15 3478
chose of all the choice men of *I* 2Sa 10:9 3478
that they were smitten before *I* 2Sa 10:15 3478
David, he gathered all *I* together 2Sa 10:17 3478
And the Syrians fled before *I* 2Sa 10:18 3478
that they were smitten before *I* 2Sa 10:19 3478
Israel, they made peace with *I* 2Sa 10:19 3478
his servants with him, and all *I* 2Sa 11:1 3478
said unto David, The ark, and *I* 2Sa 11:11 3478
Thus saith the LORD God of *I* 2Sa 12:7 3478
I anointed thee king over *I* 2Sa 12:7 3478
and gave thee the house of *I* 2Sa 12:8 3478
I will do this thing before all *I* 2Sa 12:12 3478
such thing ought to be done in *I* 2Sa 13:12 3478
shalt be as one of the fools in *I* 2Sa 13:13 3478
But in all *I* there was none to be 2Sa 14:25 3478
is of one of the tribes of *I* 2Sa 15:2 3478
all *I* that came to the king for 2Sa 15:6 3478
stole the hearts of the men of *I* 2Sa 15:6 3478
throughout all the tribes of *I* 2Sa 15:10 3478
of the men of *I* are after Absalom 2Sa 15:13 3478
Today shall the house of *I* 2Sa 16:3 3478
and all the people the men of *I* 2Sa 16:15 3478
this people, and all the men of *I* 2Sa 16:18 3478
all *I* shall hear that thou art 2Sa 16:21 3478
concubines in the sight of all *I* 2Sa 16:22 3478
well, and all the elders of *I* 2Sa 17:4 3478
for all *I* knoweth that thy father 2Sa 17:10 3478
Therefore I counsel that all *I* be 2Sa 17:11 3478
then shall all *I* bring ropes to 2Sa 17:13 3478
Absalom and all the men of *I* said 2Sa 17:14 3478
Absalom and the elders of *I* 2Sa 17:15 3478
he and all the men of *I* with him 2Sa 17:24 3478
So *I* and Absalom pitched in the 2Sa 17:26 3478
went out into the field against *I* 2Sa 18:6 3478
Where the people of *I* were slain 2Sa 18:7 3478
returned from pursuing after *I* 2Sa 18:16 3478
all *I* fled every one to his tent 2Sa 18:17 3478
for *I* had fled every man to his 2Sa 19:8 3478
throughout all the tribes of *I* 2Sa 19:9 3478
of all *I* is come to the king 2Sa 19:11 3478
man be put to death this day in *I* 2Sa 19:22 3478
that I am this day king over *I* 2Sa 19:22 3478
and also half the people of *I* 2Sa 19:40 3478
all the men of *I* came to the king 2Sa 19:41 3478
of Judah answered the men of *I* 2Sa 19:42 3478
the men of *I* answered the men of 2Sa 19:43 3478
than the words of the men of *I* 2Sa 19:43 3478
every man to his tents, O *I* 2Sa 20:1 3478
So every man of *I* went up from 2Sa 20:2 3478
all the tribes of *I* unto Abel 2Sa 20:14 3478
are peaceable and faithful in *I* 2Sa 20:19 3478
destroy a city and a mother in *I* 2Sa 20:19 3478
Joab was over all the host of *I* 2Sa 20:23 3478
were not of the children of *I* 2Sa 21:2 3478
the children of *I* had sworn unto 2Sa 21:2 3478
in his zeal to the children of *I* 2Sa 21:2 3478
us shalt thou kill any man in *I* 2Sa 21:4 3478
in any of the coasts of *I* 2Sa 21:5 3478
had yet war again with *I* 2Sa 21:15 3478
thou quench not the light of *I* 2Sa 21:17 3478
And when he defied *I*, Jonathan the 2Sa 21:21 3478
Jacob, and the sweet psalmist of *I* 2Sa 23:1 3478
The God of *I* said, the Rock of 2Sa 23:3 3478
said, the Rock of *I* spake to me 2Sa 23:3 3478
the men of *I* were gone away 2Sa 23:9 3478
of the LORD was kindled against *I* 2Sa 24:1 3478
against them to say, Go, number *I* 2Sa 24:1 3478
now through all the tribes of *I* 2Sa 24:2 3478
king, to number the people of *I* 2Sa 24:4 3478
there were in *I* eight hundred 2Sa 24:9 3478
I from the morning even to the 2Sa 24:15 3478
and the plague was stayed from *I* 2Sa 24:25 3478
throughout all the coasts of *I* 1Kin 1:3 3478
the eyes of all *I* are upon thee 1Kin 1:20 3478
unto thee by the LORD God of *I* 1Kin 1:30 3478
anoint him there king over *I* 1Kin 1:34 3478
appointed him to be ruler over *I* 1Kin 1:35 3478
Blessed be the LORD God of *I* 1Kin 1:48 3478
said he) a man on the throne of *I* 1Kin 2:4 3478
two captains of the hosts of *I* 1Kin 2:5 3478
reigned over *I* were forty years 1Kin 2:11 3478
that all *I* set their faces on me, 1Kin 2:15 3478
of Ner, captain of the host of *I* 1Kin 2:32 3478
all *I* heard of the judgment which 1Kin 3:28 3478
king Solomon was king over all *I* 1Kin 4:1 3478
had twelve officers over all *I* 1Kin 4:7 3478
raised a levy out of all *I* 1Kin 5:13 3478
year after the children of *I* were 1Kin 6:1 3478

year of Solomon's reign over *I*	1Kin 6:1	3478
dwell among the children of *I*	1Kin 6:13	3478
and will not forsake my people *I*	1Kin 6:13	3478
Solomon assembled the elders of *I*	1Kin 8:1	3478
the fathers of the children of *I*	1Kin 8:1	3478
all the men of *I* assembled	1Kin 8:2	3478
And all the elders of *I* came	1Kin 8:3	3478
and all the congregation of *I*	1Kin 8:5	3478
a covenant with the children of *I*	1Kin 8:9	3478
blessed all the congregation of *I*	1Kin 8:14	3478
all the congregation of *I* stood	1Kin 8:14	3478
Blessed be the LORD God of *I*	1Kin 8:15	3478
forth my people *I* out of Egypt	1Kin 8:16	3478
the tribes of *I* to build an house	1Kin 8:16	3478
David to be over my people *I*	1Kin 8:16	3478
for the name of the LORD God of *I*	1Kin 8:17	3478
father, and sit on the throne of *I*	1Kin 8:20	3478
for the name of the LORD God of *I*	1Kin 8:20	3478
of all the congregation of *I*	1Kin 8:22	3478
And he said, LORD God of *I*	1Kin 8:23	3478
Therefore now, LORD God of *I*	1Kin 8:25	3478
sight to sit on the throne of *I*	1Kin 8:25	3478
And now, O God of *I*, let thy word,	1Kin 8:26	3478
thy servant, and of thy people *I*	1Kin 8:30	3478
When thy people *I* be smitten down	1Kin 8:33	3478
forgive the sin of thy people *I*	1Kin 8:34	3478
thy servants, and of thy people *I*	1Kin 8:36	3478
any man, or by all thy people *I*	1Kin 8:38	3478
that is not of thy people *I*	1Kin 8:41	3478
to fear thee, as do thy people *I*	1Kin 8:43	3478
the supplication of thy people *I*	1Kin 8:52	3478
of *I* with a loud voice, saying,	1Kin 8:55	3478
hath given rest unto his people *I*	1Kin 8:56	3478
of his people *I* at all times	1Kin 8:59	3478
all *I* with him, offered sacrifice	1Kin 8:62	3478
all the children of *I* dedicated	1Kin 8:63	3478
feast, and all *I* with him, a great	1Kin 8:65	3478
his servant, and for *I* his people	1Kin 8:66	3478
of thy kingdom upon *I* for ever	1Kin 9:5	3478
thee a man upon the throne of *I*	1Kin 9:5	3478
Then will I cut off *I* out of the	1Kin 9:7	3478
I shall be a proverb and a byword	1Kin 9:7	3478
were not of the children of *I*	1Kin 9:20	3478
whom the children of *I* also were	1Kin 9:21	3478
But of the children of *I* did	1Kin 9:22	3478
to set thee on the throne of *I*	1Kin 10:9	3478
because the LORD loved *I* for ever	1Kin 10:9	3478
LORD said unto the children of *I*	1Kin 11:2	3478
was turned from the LORD God of *I*	1Kin 11:9	3478
did Joab remain there with all *I*	1Kin 11:16	3478
he was an adversary to *I* all the	1Kin 11:25	3478
and he abhorred *I*, and reigned over	1Kin 11:25	3478
thus saith the LORD, the God of *I*	1Kin 11:31	3478
chosen out of all the tribes of *I*	1Kin 11:32	3478
desireth, and shalt be king over *I*	1Kin 11:37	3478
David, and will give *I* unto thee	1Kin 11:38	3478
over all *I* was forty years	1Kin 11:42	3478
for all *I* were come to Shechem to	1Kin 12:1	3478
and all the congregation of *I* came	1Kin 12:3	3478
So when all *I* saw that the king	1Kin 12:16	3478
to your tents, O *I*	1Kin 12:16	3478
So *I* departed unto their tents	1Kin 12:16	3478
But as for the children of *I*	1Kin 12:17	3478
Thus saith the LORD God of *I*	1Kin 14:7	3478
made thee prince over my people *I*	1Kin 14:7	3478
choose out of all the tribes of *I*	1Kin 14:21	3478
cast out before the children of *I*	1Kin 14:24	3478
sin wherewith he made *I* to sin	1Kin 15:34	3478
I to anger than all the kings of	1Kin 16:33	3478
Ahab, As the LORD God of *I* liveth	1Kin 17:1	3478
For thus saith the LORD God of *I*	1Kin 17:14	3478
this day that thou art God in *I*	1Kin 18:36	3478
to anger the LORD God of *I*	1Kin 22:53	3478
my father, the chariot of *I*	2Kin 2:12	3478
him, Thus saith the LORD God of *I*	2Kin 9:6	3478
LORD God of *I* with all his heart	2Kin 10:31	3478
He restored the coast of *I* from	2Kin 14:25	3478
to the word of the LORD God of *I*	2Kin 14:25	3478
of *I* did burn incense to it	2Kin 18:4	3478
He trusted in the LORD God of *I*	2Kin 18:5	3478
LORD, and said, O LORD God of *I*	2Kin 19:15	3478
Thus saith the LORD God of *I*	2Kin 19:20	3478
even against the Holy One of *I*	2Kin 19:22	3478
cast out before the children of *I*	2Kin 21:2	3478
a grove, as did Ahab king of *I*	2Kin 21:3	3478
chosen out of all tribes of *I*	2Kin 21:7	3478
I move any more out of the land	2Kin 21:8	3478
before the children of *I*	2Kin 21:9	3478
thus saith the LORD God of *I*	2Kin 21:12	3478
Thus saith the LORD God of *I*	2Kin 22:15	3478
him, Thus saith the LORD God of *I*	2Kin 22:18	3478
which Solomon the king of *I* had	2Kin 23:13	3478
days of the judges that judged *I*	2Kin 23:22	3478
I had made in the temple of the	2Kin 24:13	3478
reigned over the children of *I*	1Chr 1:43	3478
Achar, the troubler of *I*, who	1Chr 2:7	3478
And Jabez called on the God of *I*	1Chr 4:10	3478
the God of *I* stirred up the	1Chr 5:26	3478
and to make an atonement for *I*	1Chr 6:49	3478
the children of *I* gave to the	1Chr 6:64	3478
So all *I* were reckoned by	1Chr 9:1	3478
the Philistines fought against *I*	1Chr 10:1	3478
the men of *I* fled from before the	1Chr 10:1	3478
when all the men of *I* that were	1Chr 10:7	3478
Then all *I* gathered themselves to	1Chr 11:1	3478
leddest out and broughtest in *I*	1Chr 11:2	3478
thee, Thou shalt feed my people *I*	1Chr 11:2	3478
shalt be ruler over my people *I*	1Chr 11:2	3478
elders of *I* to the king to Hebron	1Chr 11:3	3478
they anointed David king over *I*	1Chr 11:3	3478
all *I* went to Jerusalem, which is	1Chr 11:4	3478
him in his kingdom, and with all *I*	1Chr 11:10	3478
the word of the LORD concerning *I*	1Chr 11:10	3478
times, to know what *I* ought to do	1Chr 12:32	3478
to make David king over all *I*	1Chr 12:38	3478
all the rest also of *I* were of	1Chr 12:38	3478
for there was joy in *I*	1Chr 12:40	3478
unto all the congregation of *I*	1Chr 13:2	3478
are left in all the land of *I*	1Chr 13:2	3478
So David gathered all *I* together	1Chr 13:5	3478
And David went up, and all *I*	1Chr 13:6	3478
all *I* played before God with all	1Chr 13:8	3478
had confirmed him king over *I*	1Chr 14:2	3478
on high, because of his people *I*	1Chr 14:2	3478
was anointed king over all *I*	1Chr 14:8	3478
David gathered all *I* together to	1Chr 15:3	3478
of *I* unto the place that I have	1Chr 15:12	3478
up the ark of the LORD God of *I*	1Chr 15:14	3478
So David, and the elders of *I*	1Chr 15:25	3478
Thus all *I* brought up the ark of	1Chr 15:28	3478
And he dealt to every one of *I*	1Chr 16:3	3478
thank and praise the LORD God of *I*	1Chr 16:4	3478
O ye seed of *I* his servant	1Chr 16:13	3478
to *I* for an everlasting covenant,	1Chr 16:17	3478
be the LORD God of *I* for ever	1Chr 16:36	3478
of the LORD, which he commanded *I*	1Chr 16:40	3478
that I brought up *I* unto this day	1Chr 17:5	3478
I have walked with all *I*, spake I	1Chr 17:6	3478
a word to any of the judges of *I*	1Chr 17:6	3478
be ruler over my people *I*	1Chr 17:7	3478
ordain a place for my people *I*	1Chr 17:9	3478
judges to be over my people *I*	1Chr 17:10	3478
in the earth is like thy people *I*	1Chr 17:21	3478
For thy people *I* didst thou make	1Chr 17:22	3478
God of Israel, even a God to *I*	1Chr 17:24	3478
So David reigned over all *I*	1Chr 18:14	3478
chose out of all the choice of *I*	1Chr 19:10	3478
were put to the worse before *I*	1Chr 19:16	3478
and he gathered all *I*, and passed	1Chr 19:17	3478
But the Syrians fled before *I*	1Chr 19:18	3478
were put to the worse before *I*	1Chr 19:19	3478
But when he defied *I*, Jonathan	1Chr 20:7	3478
And Satan stood up against *I*	1Chr 21:1	3478
and provoked David to number *I*	1Chr 21:1	3478
number *I* from Beer-sheba even to	1Chr 21:2	3478
he be a cause of trespass to *I*	1Chr 21:3	3478
and went throughout all *I*	1Chr 21:4	3478
all they of *I* were a thousand	1Chr 21:5	3478
therefore he smote *I*	1Chr 21:7	3478
throughout all the coasts of *I*	1Chr 21:12	3478
the LORD sent pestilence upon *I*	1Chr 21:14	3478
there fell of *I* seventy thousand	1Chr 21:14	3478
Then David and the elders of *I*	1Chr 21:16	
altar of the burnt offering for *I*	1Chr 22:1	3478
that were in the land of *I*	1Chr 22:2	3478
an house for the LORD God of *I*	1Chr 22:6	3478
and quietness unto *I* in his days	1Chr 22:9	3478
of his kingdom over *I* for ever	1Chr 22:10	3478
and give thee charge concerning *I*	1Chr 22:12	3478
charged Moses with concerning *I*	1Chr 22:13	3478
of *I* to help Solomon his son	1Chr 22:17	3478
made Solomon his son king over *I*	1Chr 23:1	3478
together all the princes of *I*	1Chr 23:2	3478
The LORD God of *I* hath given rest	1Chr 23:25	3478
LORD God of *I* had commanded him	1Chr 24:19	3478
for the outward business over *I*	1Chr 26:29	3478
were officers among them of *I* on	1Chr 26:30	3478
children of *I* after their number	1Chr 27:1	3478
Furthermore over the tribes of *I*	1Chr 27:16	3478
the princes of the tribes of *I*	1Chr 27:22	3478
I like to the stars of the	1Chr 27:23	3478
there fell wrath for it against *I*	1Chr 27:24	3478
assembled all the princes of *I*	1Chr 28:1	3478
Howbeit the LORD God of *I* chose	1Chr 28:4	3478
father to be king over *I* for ever	1Chr 28:4	3478
me to make me king over all *I*	1Chr 28:4	3478
of the kingdom of the LORD over *I*	1Chr 28:5	3478
in the sight of all *I* the	1Chr 28:8	3478
and princes of the tribes of *I*	1Chr 29:6	3478
sacrifices in abundance for all *I*	1Chr 29:21	3478
and all *I* obeyed him	1Chr 29:23	3478
exceedingly in the sight of all *I*	1Chr 29:25	3478
been on any king before him in *I*	1Chr 29:25	3478
son of Jesse reigned over all *I*	1Chr 29:26	3478
he reigned over *I* was forty years	1Chr 29:27	3478
that went over him, and over *I*	1Chr 29:30	3478
Then Solomon spake unto all *I*	2Chr 1:2	3478
and to every governor in all *I*	2Chr 1:2	3478
congregation, and reigned over *I*	2Chr 1:13	3478
is an ordinance for ever to *I*	2Chr 2:4	3478
Blessed be the LORD God of *I*	2Chr 2:12	3478
that were in the land of *I*	2Chr 2:17	3478
Solomon assembled the elders of *I*	2Chr 5:2	3478
the fathers of the children of *I*	2Chr 5:2	3478
Wherefore all the men of *I*	2Chr 5:3	3478
And all the elders of *I* came	2Chr 5:4	3478
all the congregation of *I* that	2Chr 5:6	3478
a covenant with the children of *I*	2Chr 5:10	3478
the whole congregation of *I*	2Chr 6:3	3478
all the congregation of *I* stood	2Chr 6:3	3478
Blessed be the LORD God of *I*	2Chr 6:4	3478
tribes of *I* to build an house in	2Chr 6:5	3478
to be a ruler over my people *I*	2Chr 6:5	3478
David to be over my people *I*	2Chr 6:6	3478
for the name of the LORD God of *I*	2Chr 6:7	3478
and am set on the throne of *I*	2Chr 6:10	3478
for the name of the LORD God of *I*	2Chr 6:10	3478
he made with the children of *I*	2Chr 6:11	3478
of all the congregation of *I*	2Chr 6:12	3478
before all the congregation of *I*	2Chr 6:13	3478
And said, O LORD God of *I*, there	2Chr 6:14	3478
Now therefore, O LORD God of *I*	2Chr 6:16	3478
sight to sit upon the throne of *I*	2Chr 6:16	3478
Now then, O LORD God of *I*	2Chr 6:17	3478
thy servant, and of thy people *I*	2Chr 6:21	3478
if thy people *I* be put to the	2Chr 6:24	3478
forgive the sin of thy people *I*	2Chr 6:25	3478
thy servants, and of thy people *I*	2Chr 6:27	3478
any man, or of all thy people *I*	2Chr 6:29	3478
which is not of thy people *I*	2Chr 6:32	3478
fear thee, as doth thy people *I*	2Chr 6:33	3478
when all the children of *I* saw	2Chr 7:3	3478
before them, and all *I* stood	2Chr 7:6	3478
all *I* with him, a very great	2Chr 7:8	3478
and to Solomon, and to *I* his people	2Chr 7:10	3478
fail thee a man to be ruler in *I*	2Chr 7:18	3478
the children of *I* to dwell there	2Chr 8:2	3478
Jebusites, which were not of *I*	2Chr 8:7	3478
the children of *I* consumed not	2Chr 8:8	3478
But of the children of *I* did	2Chr 8:9	3478
in the house of David king of *I*	2Chr 8:11	3478
because thy God loved *I*, to	2Chr 9:8	3478
Jerusalem over all *I* forty years	2Chr 9:30	3478
were all *I* come to make him king	2Chr 10:1	3478
all *I* came and spake to Rehoboam,	2Chr 10:3	3478
when all *I* saw that the king	2Chr 10:16	3478
every man to your tents, O *I*	2Chr 10:16	3478
So all *I* went to their tents	2Chr 10:16	3478
But as for the children of *I* that	2Chr 10:17	3478
to all *I* in Judah and Benjamin,	2Chr 11:3	3478
LORD God of *I* came to Jerusalem	2Chr 11:16	3478
of the LORD, and all *I* with him	2Chr 12:1	3478
Whereupon the princes of *I*	2Chr 12:6	3478
chosen out of all the tribes of *I*	2Chr 12:13	3478
to know that the LORD God of *I*	2Chr 13:5	3478
kingdom over *I* to David for ever	2Chr 13:5	3478
Now for a long season *I* hath been	2Chr 15:3	3478
did turn unto the LORD God of *I*	2Chr 15:4	3478
God of *I* should be put to death	2Chr 15:13	3478
of the chief of the fathers of *I*	2Chr 19:8	3478
of this land before thy people *I*	2Chr 20:7	3478
thou wouldest not let *I* invade	2Chr 20:10	3478
of *I* with a loud voice on high	2Chr 20:19	3478
fought against the enemies of *I*	2Chr 20:29	3478
and the chief of the fathers of *I*	2Chr 23:2	3478
gather of all *I* money to repair	2Chr 24:5	3478
LORD, and of the congregation of *I*	2Chr 24:6	3478
God laid upon *I* in the wilderness	2Chr 24:9	3478
because he had done good in *I*	2Chr 24:16	3478
cast out before the children of *I*	2Chr 28:3	3478
were the ruin of him, and of all *I*	2Chr 28:23	3478
book of the kings of Judah and *I*	2Chr 28:26	3478
the sepulchres of the kings of *I*	2Chr 28:27	3478
the holy place unto the God of *I*	2Chr 29:7	3478
a covenant with the LORD God of *I*	2Chr 29:10	3478
to make an atonement for all *I*	2Chr 29:24	3478
offering should be made for all *I*	2Chr 29:24	3478
ordained by David king of *I*	2Chr 29:27	3478
And Hezekiah sent to all *I*	2Chr 30:1	3478
passover unto the LORD God of *I*	2Chr 30:1	3478
proclamation throughout all *I*	2Chr 30:5	3478
the LORD God of *I* at Jerusalem	2Chr 30:5	3478
king, saying, Ye children of *I*	2Chr 30:6	3478
the son of David king of *I* there	2Chr 30:26	3478
all *I* that were present went out	2Chr 31:1	3478
all the children of *I* returned	2Chr 31:1	3478
the children of *I* brought in	2Chr 31:5	3478
blessed the LORD, and his people *I*	2Chr 31:8	3478
to rail on the LORD God of *I*	2Chr 32:17	3478
cast out before the children of *I*	2Chr 33:2	3478
chosen before all the tribes of *I*	2Chr 33:7	3478
of *I* from out of the land which I	2Chr 33:8	3478
before the children of *I*	2Chr 33:9	3478
Judah to serve the LORD God of *I*	2Chr 33:16	3478
in the name of the LORD God of *I*	2Chr 33:18	3478
in the book of the kings of *I*	2Chr 33:18	3478
throughout all the land of *I*	2Chr 34:7	3478
Thus saith the LORD God of *I*	2Chr 34:23	3478
Thus saith the LORD God of *I*	2Chr 34:26	3478
pertained to the children of *I*	2Chr 34:33	3478
that were present in *I* to serve	2Chr 34:33	3478
the Levites that taught all *I*	2Chr 35:3	3478
son of David king of *I* did build	2Chr 35:3	3478
LORD your God, and his people *I*	2Chr 35:3	3478
to the writing of David king of *I*	2Chr 35:4	3478
the children of *I* that were	2Chr 35:17	3478
in *I* from the days of Samuel the	2Chr 35:18	3478
and made them an ordinance in *I*	2Chr 35:25	3478
turning unto the LORD God of *I*	2Chr 36:13	3478
the house of the LORD God of *I*	Ezr 1:3	3478
of the men of the people of *I*	Ezr 2:2	3478
seed, whether they were of *I*	Ezr 2:59	3478
cities, and all *I* in their cities	Ezr 2:70	3478
the children of *I* were in the	Ezr 3:1	3478
builded the altar of the God of *I*	Ezr 3:2	3478
the ordinance of David king of *I*	Ezr 3:10	3478
mercy endureth for ever toward *I*	Ezr 3:11	3478
the temple unto the LORD God of *I*	Ezr 4:1	3478
of the chief of the fathers of *I*	Ezr 4:3	3478
will build unto the LORD God of *I*	Ezr 4:3	3478

in the name of the God of *I* ..... Ezr 5:1 3479
which a great king of *I* builded ..... Ezr 5:11 3479
the commandment of the God of *I* ..... Ezr 6:14 3479
And the children of *I*, the priests ..... Ezr 6:16 3479
and for a sin offering for all *I* ..... Ezr 6:17 3479
to the number of the tribes of *I* ..... Ezr 6:17 3479
And the children of *I*, which were ..... Ezr 6:21 3478
land, to seek the LORD God of *I* ..... Ezr 6:21 3478
of the house of God, the God of *I* ..... Ezr 6:22 3478
which the LORD God of *I* had given ..... Ezr 7:6 3478
went up some of the children of *I* ..... Ezr 7:7 3478
do it, and to teach in *I* statutes ..... Ezr 7:10 3478
the LORD, and of his statutes to *I* ..... Ezr 7:11 3478
that all they of the people of *I* ..... Ezr 7:13 3479
freely offered unto the God of *I* ..... Ezr 7:15 3479
of *I* chief men to go up with me ..... Ezr 7:28 3478
all *I* there present, had offered ..... Ezr 8:25 3478
and chief of the fathers of *I* ..... Ezr 8:29 3478
burnt offerings unto the God of *I* ..... Ezr 8:35 3478
twelve bullocks for all *I* ..... Ezr 8:35 3478
to me, saying, The people of *I* ..... Ezr 9:1 3478
at the words of the God of *I* ..... Ezr 9:4 3478
O LORD God of *I*, thou art ..... Ezr 9:15 3478
of *I* a very great congregation of ..... Ezr 10:1 3478
hope in *I* concerning this thing ..... Ezr 10:2 3478
priests, the Levites, and all *I* ..... Ezr 10:5 3478
to increase the trespass of *I* ..... Ezr 10:10 3478
Moreover of *I*: of the sons of ..... Ezr 10:25 3478
the children of *I* thy servants ..... Neh 1:6 3478
the sins of the children of *I* ..... Neh 1:6 3478
the welfare of the children of *I* ..... Neh 2:10 3478
men of the people of *I* was this ..... Neh 7:7 3478
seed, whether they were of *I* ..... Neh 7:61 3478
and the Nethinims, and all *I* ..... Neh 7:73 3478
the children of *I* were in their ..... Neh 7:73 3478
which the LORD had commanded to *I* ..... Neh 8:1 3478
that the children of *I* should ..... Neh 8:14 3478
had not the children of *I* done so ..... Neh 8:17 3478
of *I* were assembled with fasting ..... Neh 9:1 3478
And the seed of *I* separated ..... Neh 9:2 3478
to make an atonement for *I* ..... Neh 10:33 3478
For the children of *I* and the ..... Neh 10:39 3478
in their cities, to wit, *I* ..... Neh 11:3 3478
And the residue of *I*, of the ..... Neh 11:20 3478
all *I* in the days of Zerubbabel, ... Neh 12:47 3478
not the children of *I* with bread ..... Neh 13:2 3478
from *I* all the mixed multitude ..... Neh 13:3 3478
upon *I* by profaning the sabbath ..... Neh 13:18 3478
king of *I* sin by these things ..... Neh 13:26 3478
and God made him king over all *I* ..... Neh 13:26 3478
of *I* were come out of Zion ..... Ps 14:7 3478
shall rejoice, and *I* shall be glad ..... Ps 14:7 3478
that inhabitest the praises of *I* ..... Ps 22:3 3478
and fear him, all ye the seed of *I* ..... Ps 22:23 3478
Redeem *I*, O God, out of all his ..... Ps 25:22 3478
LORD God of *I* from everlasting ..... Ps 41:13 3478
O *I*, and I will testify against ..... Ps 50:7 3478
of *I* were come out of Zion ..... Ps 53:6 3478
shall rejoice, and *I* shall be glad ..... Ps 53:6 3478
O LORD God of hosts, the God of *I* ..... Ps 59:5 3478
the presence of God, the God of *I* ..... Ps 68:8 3478
the Lord, from the fountain of *I* ..... Ps 68:26 3478
his excellency is over *I*, and his ..... Ps 68:34 3478
the God of *I* is he that giveth ..... Ps 68:35 3478
for my sake, O God of *I* ..... Ps 69:6 3478
the harp, O thou Holy One of *I* ..... Ps 71:22 3478
be the LORD God, the God of *I* ..... Ps 72:18 3478
Truly God is good to *I*, even to ..... Ps 73:1 3478
his name is great in *I* ..... Ps 76:1 3478
in Jacob, and appointed a law in *I* ..... Ps 78:5 3478
and anger also came up against *I* ..... Ps 78:21 3478
and smote down the chosen men of *I* ..... Ps 78:31 3478
God, and limited the Holy One of *I* ..... Ps 78:41 3478
made the tribes of *I* to dwell in ..... Ps 78:55 3478
was wroth, and greatly abhorred *I* ..... Ps 78:59 3478
his people, and *I* his inheritance ..... Ps 78:71 3478
Give ear, O Shepherd of *I* ..... Ps 80:1 3478
For this was a statute for *I* ..... Ps 81:4 3478
O *I*, if thou wilt hearken unto me ..... Ps 81:8 3478
and *I* would none of me ..... Ps 81:11 3478
me, and *I* had walked in my ways ..... Ps 81:13 3478
that the name of *I* may be no more ..... Ps 83:4 3478
and the Holy One of *I* is our king ..... Ps 89:18 3478
his truth toward the house of *I* ..... Ps 98:3 3478
his acts unto the children of *I* ..... Ps 103:7 3478
to *I* for an everlasting covenant ..... Ps 105:10 3478
I also came into Egypt ..... Ps 105:23 3478
Blessed be the LORD God of *I* from ..... Ps 106:48 3478
When *I* went out of Egypt, the ..... Ps 114:1 3478
his sanctuary, and *I* his dominion ..... Ps 114:2 3478
O *I*, trust thou in the LORD ..... Ps 115:9 3478
he will bless the house of *I* ..... Ps 115:12 3478
Let *I* now say, that his mercy ..... Ps 118:2 3478
he that keepeth *I* shall neither ..... Ps 121:4 3478
the LORD, unto the testimony of *I* ..... Ps 122:4 3478
was on our side, now may *I* say ..... Ps 124:1 3478
but peace shall be upon *I* ..... Ps 125:5 3478
children, and peace upon *I* ..... Ps 128:6 3478
me from my youth, may *I* now say ..... Ps 129:1 3478
Let *I* hope in the LORD ..... Ps 130:7 3478
he shall redeem *I* from all his ..... Ps 130:8 3478
Let *I* hope in the LORD from ..... Ps 131:3 3478
I for his peculiar treasure ..... Ps 135:4 3478
an heritage unto *I* his people ..... Ps 135:12 3478
Bless the LORD, O house of *I* ..... Ps 135:19 3478
brought out *I* from among them ..... Ps 136:11 3478
made *I* to pass through the midst ..... Ps 136:14 3478
an heritage unto *I* his servant ..... Ps 136:22 3478
together the outcasts of *I* ..... Ps 147:2 3478
statutes and his judgments unto *I* ..... Ps 147:19 3478
even of the children of *I* ..... Ps 148:14 3478
Let *I* rejoice in him that made ..... Ps 149:2 3478
the son of David, king of *I* ..... Prov 1:1 3478
was king over *I* in Jerusalem ..... Eccl 1:12 3478
are about it, of the valiant of *I* ..... Song 3:7 3478
but *I* doth not know, my people ..... Is 1:3 3478
the Holy One of *I* unto anger ..... Is 1:4 3478
of hosts, the mighty One of *I* ..... Is 1:24 3478
for them that are escaped of *I* ..... Is 4:2 3478
LORD of hosts is the house of *I* ..... Is 5:7 3478
of the Holy One of *I* draw nigh ..... Is 5:19 3478
the word of the Holy One of *I* ..... Is 5:24 3478
offence to both the houses of *I* ..... Is 8:14 3478
for wonders in *I* from the LORD of ..... Is 8:18 3478
Jacob, and it hath lighted upon *I* ..... Is 9:8 3478
shall devour *I* with open mouth ..... Is 9:12 3478
the LORD will cut off from *I* head ..... Is 9:14 3478
the light of *I* shall be for a ..... Is 10:17 3478
that day, that the remnant of *I* ..... Is 10:20 3478
upon the LORD, the Holy One of *I* ..... Is 10:20 3478
For though thy people *I* be as the ..... Is 10:22 3478
shall assemble the outcasts of *I* ..... Is 11:12 3478
like as it was to *I* in the day ..... Is 11:16 3478
One of *I* in the midst of thee ..... Is 12:6 3478
on Jacob, and will yet choose *I* ..... Is 14:1 3478
the house of *I* shall possess them ..... Is 14:2 3478
as the glory of the children of *I* ..... Is 17:3 3478
thereof, saith the LORD God of *I* ..... Is 17:6 3478
have respect to the Holy One of *I* ..... Is 17:7 3478
left because of the children of *I* ..... Is 17:9 3478
In that day shall *I* be the third ..... Is 19:24 3478
my hands, and *I* mine inheritance ..... Is 19:25 3478
the LORD of hosts, the God of *I* ..... Is 21:10 3478
the LORD God of *I* hath spoken it ..... Is 21:17 3478
God of *I* in the isles of the sea ..... Is 24:15 3478
I shall blossom and bud, and fill ..... Is 27:6 3478
one by one, O ye children of *I* ..... Is 27:12 3478
rejoice in the Holy One of *I* ..... Is 29:19 3478
Jacob, and shall fear the God of *I* ..... Is 29:23 3478
cause the Holy One of *I* to cease ..... Is 30:11 3478
thus saith the Holy One of *I* ..... Is 30:12 3478
the Lord GOD, the Holy One of *I* ..... Is 30:15 3478
the LORD, to the mighty One of *I* ..... Is 30:29 3478
look not unto the Holy One of *I* ..... Is 31:1 3478
of *I* have deeply revolted ..... Is 31:6 3478
O LORD of hosts, God of *I* ..... Is 37:16 3478
Thus saith the LORD God of *I* ..... Is 37:21 3478
even against the Holy One of *I* ..... Is 37:23 3478
thou, O Jacob, and speakest, O *I* ..... Is 40:27 3478
But thou, *I*, art my servant, ... Is 41:8 3478
thou worm Jacob, and ye men of *I* ..... Is 41:14 3478
thy redeemer, the Holy One of *I* ..... Is 41:14 3478
shalt glory in the Holy One of *I* ..... Is 41:16 3478
I the God of *I* will not forsake ..... Is 41:17 3478
the Holy One of *I* hath created it ..... Is 41:20 3478
for a spoil, and *I* to the robbers ..... Is 42:24 3478
and he that formed thee, O *I* ..... Is 43:1 3478
LORD thy God, the Holy One of *I* ..... Is 43:3 3478
your redeemer, the Holy One of *I* ..... Is 43:14 3478
your Holy One, the creator of *I* ..... Is 43:15 3478
thou hast been weary of me, O *I* ..... Is 43:22 3478
to the curse, and *I* to reproaches ..... Is 43:28 3478
and *I*, whom I have chosen ..... Is 44:1 3478
surname himself by the name of *I* ..... Is 44:5 3478
Thus saith the LORD the King of *I* ..... Is 44:6 3478
Remember these, O Jacob and *I* ..... Is 44:21 3478
O *I*, thou shalt not be forgotten ..... Is 44:21 3478
Jacob, and glorified himself in *I* ..... Is 44:23 3478
thee by thy name, am the God of *I* ..... Is 45:3 3478
I mine elect, I have even called ..... Is 45:4 3478
saith the LORD, the Holy One of *I* ..... Is 45:11 3478
that hidest thyself, O God of *I* ..... Is 45:15 3478
But *I* shall be saved in the LORD ..... Is 45:17 3478
all the seed of *I* be justified ..... Is 45:25 3478
all the remnant of the house of *I* ..... Is 46:3 3478
salvation in Zion for *I* my glory ..... Is 46:13 3478
is his name, the Holy One of *I* ..... Is 47:4 3478
which are called by the name of *I* ..... Is 48:1 3478
and make mention of the God of *I* ..... Is 48:1 3478
stay themselves upon the God of *I* ..... Is 48:2 3478
Hearken unto me, O Jacob and *I* ..... Is 48:12 3478
thy Redeemer, the Holy One of *I* ..... Is 48:17 3478
unto me, Thou art my servant, O *I* ..... Is 49:3 3478
Though *I* be not gathered, yet ..... Is 49:5 3478
and to restore the preserved of *I* ..... Is 49:6 3478
saith the LORD, the Redeemer of *I* ..... Is 49:7 3478
is faithful, and the Holy One of *I* ..... Is 49:7 3478
the God of *I* will be your ..... Is 52:12 3478
and thy Redeemer the Holy One of *I* ..... Is 54:5 3478
thy God, and for the Holy One of *I* ..... Is 55:5 3478
gathereth the outcasts of *I* saith ..... Is 56:8 3478
thy God, and to the Holy One of *I* ..... Is 60:9 3478
The Zion of the Holy One of *I* ..... Is 60:14 3478
goodness toward the house of *I* ..... Is 63:7 3478
of us, and *I* acknowledge us not ..... Is 63:16 3478
as the children of *I* bring an ..... Is 66:20 3478
I was holiness unto the LORD, and ..... Jer 2:3 3478
the families of the house of *I* ..... Jer 2:4 3478
Is *I* a servant? ..... Jer 2:14 3478
with me, O house of *I*, saith the ..... Jer 3:20 3478
of the children of *I* ..... Jer 3:21 3478
our God is the salvation of *I* ..... Jer 3:23 3478
If thou wilt return, O *I*, saith ..... Jer 4:1 3478
upon you from far, O house of *I* ..... Jer 5:15 3478
glean the remnant of *I* as a vine ..... Jer 6:9 3478
the LORD of hosts, the God of *I* ..... Jer 7:3 3478
for the wickedness of my people *I* ..... Jer 7:12 3478
the LORD of hosts, the God of *I* ..... Jer 7:21 3478
the LORD of hosts, the God of *I* ..... Jer 9:15 3478
speaketh unto you, O house of *I* ..... Jer 10:1 3478
I is the rod of his inheritance ..... Jer 10:16 3478
Thus saith the LORD God of *I* ..... Jer 11:3 3478
caused my people *I* to inherit ..... Jer 12:14 3478
unto me the whole house of *I* ..... Jer 13:11 3478
Thus saith the LORD God of *I* ..... Jer 13:12 3478
O the hope of *I*, the saviour ..... Jer 14:8 3478
the LORD of hosts, the God of *I* ..... Jer 16:9 3478
of *I* out of the land of Egypt ..... Jer 16:14 3478
of *I* from the land of the north ..... Jer 16:15 3478
O LORD, the hope of *I*, all that ..... Jer 17:13 3478
O house of *I*, cannot I do with ..... Jer 18:6 3478
are ye in mine hand, O house of *I* ..... Jer 18:6 3478
the virgin of *I* hath done a very ..... Jer 18:13 3478
the LORD of hosts, the God of *I* ..... Jer 19:3 3478
the LORD of hosts, the God of *I* ..... Jer 19:15 3478
Thus saith the LORD God of *I* ..... Jer 21:4 3478
thus saith the LORD God of *I* ..... Jer 23:2 3478
of *I* out of the land of Egypt ..... Jer 23:7 3478
of *I* out of the north country ..... Jer 23:8 3478
and caused my people *I* to err ..... Jer 23:13 3478
Thus saith the LORD, the God of *I* ..... Jer 24:5 3478
saith the LORD God of *I* unto me ..... Jer 25:15 3478
the LORD of hosts, the God of *I* ..... Jer 25:27 3478
the LORD of hosts, the God of *I* ..... Jer 27:4 3478
the LORD of hosts, the God of *I* ..... Jer 27:21 3478
the LORD of hosts, the God of *I* ..... Jer 28:2 3478
the LORD of hosts, the God of *I* ..... Jer 28:14 3478
the LORD of hosts, the God of *I* ..... Jer 29:4 3478
the LORD of hosts, the God of *I* ..... Jer 29:8 3478
the LORD of hosts, the God of *I* ..... Jer 29:21 3478
they have committed villany in *I* ..... Jer 29:23 3478
the LORD of hosts, the God of *I* ..... Jer 29:25 3478
Thus speaketh the LORD God of *I* ..... Jer 30:2 3478
the captivity of my people *I* ..... Jer 30:3 3478
that the LORD spake concerning *I* ..... Jer 30:4 3478
neither be dismayed, O *I* ..... Jer 30:10 3478
the God of all the families of *I* ..... Jer 31:1 3478
even *I*, when I went to cause him ..... Jer 31:2 3478
shalt be built, O virgin of *I* ..... Jer 31:4 3478
save thy people, the remnant of *I* ..... Jer 31:7 3478
for I am a father to *I*, and ..... Jer 31:9 3478
that scattered *I* will gather him ..... Jer 31:10 3478
turn again, O virgin of *I* ..... Jer 31:21 3478
the LORD of hosts, the God of *I* ..... Jer 31:23 3478
I will make with the house of *I* ..... Jer 31:33 3478
then the seed of *I* also shall ..... Jer 31:36 3478
of *I* for all that they have done ..... Jer 31:37 3478
the LORD of hosts, the God of *I* ..... Jer 32:14 3478
the LORD of hosts, the God of *I* ..... Jer 32:15 3478
even unto this day, and in *I* ..... Jer 32:20 3478
I out of the land of Egypt with ..... Jer 32:21 3478
for the children of *I* have only ..... Jer 32:30 3478
thus saith the LORD, the God of *I* ..... Jer 32:36 3478
thus saith the LORD, the God of *I* ..... Jer 33:4 3478
and the captivity of *I* to return ..... Jer 33:7 3478
have promised unto the house of *I* ..... Jer 33:14 3478
upon the throne of the house of *I* ..... Jer 33:17 3478
Thus saith the LORD, the God of *I* ..... Jer 34:2 3478
Thus saith the LORD, the God of *I* ..... Jer 34:13 3478
the LORD of hosts, the God of *I* ..... Jer 35:13 3478
LORD God of hosts, the God of *I* ..... Jer 35:17 3478
the LORD of hosts, the God of *I* ..... Jer 35:18 3478
the LORD of hosts, the God of *I* ..... Jer 35:19 3478
I have spoken unto thee against *I* ..... Jer 36:2 3478
Thus saith the LORD, the God of *I* ..... Jer 37:7 3478
the God of hosts, the God of *I* ..... Jer 38:17 3478
the LORD of hosts, the God of *I* ..... Jer 39:16 3478
Thus saith the LORD, the God of *I* ..... Jer 42:9 3478
the LORD of hosts, the God of *I* ..... Jer 42:15 3478
the LORD of hosts, the God of *I* ..... Jer 42:18 3478
the LORD of hosts, the God of *I* ..... Jer 43:10 3478
the LORD of hosts, the God of *I* ..... Jer 44:2 3478
the God of hosts, the God of *I* ..... Jer 44:7 3478
the LORD of hosts, the God of *I* ..... Jer 44:11 3478
the LORD of hosts, the God of *I* ..... Jer 44:25 3478
Thus saith the LORD, the God of *I* ..... Jer 45:2 3478
The LORD of hosts, the God of *I* ..... Jer 46:25 3478
Jacob, and be not dismayed, O *I* ..... Jer 46:27 3478
the LORD of hosts, the God of *I* ..... Jer 48:1 3478
For was not *I* a derision unto ..... Jer 48:27 3478
Hath *I* no sons? ..... Jer 49:1 3478
then shall *I* be heir unto them ..... Jer 49:2 3478
the children of *I* shall come ..... Jer 50:4 3478
I is a scattered sheep ..... Jer 50:17 3478
the LORD of hosts, the God of *I* ..... Jer 50:18 3478
I will bring *I* again to his ..... Jer 50:19 3478
the iniquity of *I* shall be sought ..... Jer 50:20 3478
LORD, against the Holy One of *I* ..... Jer 50:29 3478
For *I* hath not been forsaken, nor ..... Jer 51:5 3478
sin against the Holy One of *I* ..... Jer 51:5 3478
I is the rod of his inheritance ..... Jer 51:19 3478
the LORD of hosts, the God of *I* ..... Jer 51:33 3478
caused the slain of *I* to fall ..... Jer 51:49 3478
unto the earth the beauty of *I* ..... Lam 2:1 3478
fierce anger all the horn of *I* ..... Lam 2:3 3478
he hath swallowed up *I*, he hath ..... Lam 2:5 3478
I send thee to the children of *I* ..... Eze 2:3 3478
and go speak unto the house of *I* ..... Eze 3:1 3478
go, get thee unto the house of *I* ..... Eze 3:4 3478
language, but to the house of *I* ..... Eze 3:5 3478
But the house of *I* will not ..... Eze 3:7 3478
all the house of *I* are impudent ..... Eze 3:7 3478

Context	Reference	Strong's No.
a watchman unto the house of *I*	Eze 3:17	3478
shall be a sign to the house of *I*	Eze 4:3	3478
I eat their defiled bread among	Eze 4:13	3478
forth into all the house of *I*	Eze 5:4	3478
face toward the mountains of *I*	Eze 6:2	3478
And say, Ye mountains of *I*	Eze 6:3	3478
children of *I* before their idols	Eze 6:5	3478
abominations of the house of *I*	Eze 6:11	3478
the Lord GOD unto the land of *I*	Eze 7:2	3478
glory of the God of *I* was there	Eze 8:4	3478
the house of *I* committeth here	Eze 8:6	3478
all the idols of the house of *I*	Eze 8:10	3478
of the ancients of the house of *I*	Eze 8:11	3478
of the house of *I* do in the dark	Eze 8:12	3478
the glory of the God of *I* was	Eze 9:3	3478
I in thy pouring out of thy fury	Eze 9:8	3478
the God of *I* was over them above	Eze 10:19	3478
God of *I* by the river of Chebar	Eze 10:20	3478
Thus have ye said, O house of *I*	Eze 11:5	3478
will judge you in the border of *I*	Eze 11:10	3478
will judge you in the border of *I*	Eze 11:11	3478
a full end of the remnant of *I*	Eze 11:13	3478
and all the house of *I* wholly	Eze 11:15	3478
and I will give you the land of *I*	Eze 11:17	3478
the God of *I* was over them above	Eze 11:22	3478
for a sign unto the house of *I*	Eze 12:6	3478
of man, hath not the house of *I*	Eze 12:9	3478
all the house of *I* that are among	Eze 12:10	3478
of Jerusalem, and of the land of *I*	Eze 12:19	3478
that ye have in the land of *I*	Eze 12:22	3478
no more use it as a proverb in *I*	Eze 12:23	3478
divination within the house of *I*	Eze 12:24	3478
they of the house of *I* say	Eze 12:27	3478
the prophets of *I* that prophesy	Eze 13:2	3478
O *I*, thy prophets are like the	Eze 13:4	3478
I to stand in the battle in the	Eze 13:5	3478
in the writing of the house of *I*	Eze 13:9	3478
they enter into the land of *I*	Eze 13:9	3478
the prophets of *I* which prophesy	Eze 13:16	3478
of the elders of *I* unto me	Eze 14:1	3478
Every man of the house of *I* that	Eze 14:4	3478
the house of *I* in their own heart	Eze 14:5	3478
Therefore say unto the house of *I*	Eze 14:6	3478
For every one of the house of *I*	Eze 14:7	3478
the stranger that sojourneth in *I*	Eze 14:7	3478
him from the midst of my people *I*	Eze 14:9	3478
That the house of *I* may go no	Eze 14:11	3478
a parable unto the house of *I*	Eze 17:2	3478
the height of *I* will I plant it	Eze 17:23	3478
proverb concerning the land of *I*	Eze 18:2	3478
any more to use this proverb in *I*	Eze 18:3	3478
to the idols of the house of *I*	Eze 18:6	3478
to the idols of the house of *I*	Eze 18:15	3478
Hear now, O house of *I*	Eze 18:25	3478
Yet saith the house of *I*, The way	Eze 18:29	3478
O house of *I*, are not my ways	Eze 18:29	3478
I will judge you, O house of *I*	Eze 18:30	3478
for why will ye die, O house of *I*	Eze 18:31	3478
lamentation for the princes of *I*	Eze 19:1	3478
be heard upon the mountains of *I*	Eze 19:9	3478
of *I* came to enquire of the LORD	Eze 20:1	3478
man, speak unto the elders of *I*	Eze 20:3	3478
In the day when I chose *I*	Eze 20:5	3478
But the house of *I* rebelled	Eze 20:13	3478
of man, speak unto the house of *I*	Eze 20:27	3478
Wherefore say unto the house of *I*	Eze 20:30	3478
enquired of by you, O house of *I*	Eze 20:31	3478
not enter into the land of *I*	Eze 20:38	3478
As for you, O house of *I*, thus	Eze 20:39	3478
the mountain of the height of *I*	Eze 20:40	3478
there shall all the house of *I*	Eze 20:40	3478
bring you into the land of *I*	Eze 20:42	3478
corrupt doings, O ye house of *I*	Eze 20:44	3478
and prophesy against the land of *I*	Eze 21:2	3478
And say to the land of *I*, Thus	Eze 21:3	3478
be upon all the princes of *I*	Eze 21:12	3478
thou, profane wicked prince of *I*	Eze 21:25	3478
Behold, the princes of *I*, every	Eze 22:6	3478
the house of *I* is to me become	Eze 22:18	3478
Speak unto the house of *I*	Eze 24:21	3478
and against the land of *I*, when it	Eze 25:3	3478
thy despite against the land of *I*	Eze 25:6	3478
Edom by the hand of my people *I*	Eze 25:14	3478
brier unto the house of *I*	Eze 28:24	3478
have gathered the house of *I* from	Eze 28:25	3478
a staff of reed to the house of *I*	Eze 29:6	3478
the confidence of the house of *I*	Eze 29:16	3478
of the house of *I* to bud forth	Eze 29:21	3478
a watchman unto the house of *I*	Eze 33:7	3478
of man, speak unto the house of *I*	Eze 33:10	3478
for why will ye die, O house of *I*	Eze 33:11	3478
O ye house of *I*, I will judge you	Eze 33:20	3478
wastes of the land of *I* speak	Eze 33:24	3478
the mountains of *I* shall be	Eze 33:28	3478
against the shepherds of *I*	Eze 34:2	3478
of *I* that do feed themselves	Eze 34:2	3478
the mountains of *I* by the rivers	Eze 34:13	3478
of *I* shall their fold be	Eze 34:14	3478
they feed upon the mountains of *I*	Eze 34:14	3478
and that they, even the house of *I*	Eze 34:30	3478
of *I* by the force of the sword in	Eze 35:5	3478
spoken against the mountains of *I*	Eze 35:12	3478
the inheritance of the house of *I*	Eze 35:15	3478
prophesy unto the mountains of *I*	Eze 36:1	3478
and say, Ye mountains of *I*	Eze 36:1	3478
Therefore, ye mountains of *I*	Eze 36:4	3478
concerning the land of *I*, and say	Eze 36:6	3478
But ye, O mountains of *I*, ye	Eze 36:8	3478
your fruit to my people of *I*	Eze 36:8	3478
men upon you, all the house of *I*	Eze 36:10	3478
walk upon you, even my people *I*	Eze 36:12	3478
when the house of *I* dwelt in	Eze 36:17	3478
which the house of *I* had profaned	Eze 36:21	3478
Therefore say unto the house of *I*	Eze 36:22	3478
this for your sakes, O house of *I*	Eze 36:22	3478
for your own ways, O house of *I*	Eze 36:32	3478
be enquired of by the house of *I*	Eze 36:37	3478
bones are the whole house of *I*	Eze 37:11	3478
and bring you into the land of *I*	Eze 37:12	3478
all the house of *I* his companions	Eze 37:16	3478
and the tribes of *I* his fellows	Eze 37:19	3478
of *I* from among the heathen	Eze 37:21	3478
the land upon the mountains of *I*	Eze 37:22	3478
that I the LORD do sanctify *I*	Eze 37:28	3478
against the mountains of *I*	Eze 38:8	3478
my people of *I* dwelleth safely	Eze 38:14	3478
come up against my people of *I*	Eze 38:16	3478
by my servants the prophets of *I*	Eze 38:17	3478
shall come against the land of *I*	Eze 38:18	3478
a great shaking in the land of *I*	Eze 38:19	3478
thee upon the mountains of *I*	Eze 39:2	3478
fall upon the mountains of *I*	Eze 39:4	3478
known in the midst of my people *I*	Eze 39:7	3478
I am the LORD, the Holy One in *I*	Eze 39:7	3478
in the cities of *I* shall go forth	Eze 39:9	3478
Gog a place there of graves in *I*	Eze 39:11	3478
the house of *I* be burying of them	Eze 39:12	3478
sacrifice upon the mountains of *I*	Eze 39:17	3478
So the house of *I* shall know that	Eze 39:22	3478
shall know that the house of *I*	Eze 39:23	3478
mercy upon the whole house of *I*	Eze 39:25	3478
out my spirit upon the house of *I*	Eze 39:29	3478
brought he me into the land of *I*	Eze 40:2	3478
that thou seest to the house of *I*	Eze 40:4	3478
the glory of the God of *I* came	Eze 43:2	3478
of the children of *I* for ever	Eze 43:7	3478
the house of *I* no more defile	Eze 43:7	3478
shew the house to the house of *I*	Eze 43:10	3478
because the LORD, the God of *I*	Eze 44:2	3478
even to the house of *I*, Thus	Eze 44:6	3478
O ye house of *I*, let it suffice	Eze 44:6	3478
that is among the children of *I*	Eze 44:9	3478
when *I* went astray, which went	Eze 44:10	3478
caused the house of *I* to fall	Eze 44:12	3478
of the seed of the house of *I*	Eze 44:22	3478
give them no possession in *I*	Eze 44:28	3478
thing in *I* shall be their's	Eze 44:29	3478
shall be for the whole house of *I*	Eze 45:6	3478
land shall be his possession in *I*	Eze 45:8	3478
of *I* according to their tribes	Eze 45:8	3478
it suffice you, O princes of *I*	Eze 45:9	3478
out of the fat pastures of *I*	Eze 45:15	3478
this oblation for the prince in *I*	Eze 45:16	3478
all solemnities of the house of *I*	Eze 45:17	3478
reconciliation for the house of *I*	Eze 45:17	3478
to the twelve tribes of *I*	Eze 47:13	3478
and from the land of *I* by Jordan	Eze 47:18	3478
you according to the tribes of *I*	Eze 47:21	3478
country among the children of *I*	Eze 47:22	3478
with you among the tribes of *I*	Eze 47:22	3478
the children of *I* went astray	Eze 48:11	3478
it out of all the tribes of *I*	Eze 48:19	3478
the tribes of *I* for inheritance	Eze 48:29	3478
the names of the tribes of *I*	Eze 48:31	3478
certain of the children of *I*	Dan 1:3	3478
of Jerusalem, and unto all *I*	Dan 9:7	3478
all *I* have transgressed thy law,	Dan 9:11	3478
my sin and the sin of my people *I*	Dan 9:20	3478
the son of Joash, king of *I*	Hos 1:1	3478
the kingdom of the house of *I*	Hos 1:4	3478
bow of *I* in the valley of Jezreel	Hos 1:5	3478
have mercy upon the house of *I*	Hos 1:6	3478
the number of the children of *I*	Hos 1:10	3478
the children of *I* be gathered	Hos 1:11	3478
the LORD toward the children of *I*	Hos 3:1	3478
For the children of *I* shall abide	Hos 3:4	3478
shall the children of *I* return	Hos 3:5	3478
of the LORD, ye children of *I*	Hos 4:1	3478
Though thou, *I*, play the harlot,	Hos 4:15	3478
For *I* slideth back as a	Hos 4:16	3478
and hearken, ye house of *I*	Hos 5:1	3478
Ephraim, and *I* is not hid from me	Hos 5:3	3478
whoredom, and *I* is defiled	Hos 5:3	3478
the pride of *I* doth testify to	Hos 5:5	3478
therefore shall *I* and Ephraim fall	Hos 5:5	3478
among the tribes of *I* have I made	Hos 5:9	3478
horrible thing in the house of *I*	Hos 6:10	3478
whoredom of Ephraim, *I* is defiled	Hos 6:10	3478
When I would have healed *I*	Hos 7:1	3478
the pride of *I* testifieth to his	Hos 7:10	3478
I shall cry unto me, My God, we	Hos 8:2	3478
I hath cast off the thing that is	Hos 8:3	3478
For from *I* was it also	Hos 8:6	3478
I is swallowed up	Hos 8:8	3478
For *I* hath forgotten his Maker,	Hos 8:14	3478
Rejoice not, O *I*, for joy, as	Hos 9:1	3478
I shall know it	Hos 9:7	3478
I found *I* like grapes in the	Hos 9:10	3478
I is an empty vine, he bringeth	Hos 10:1	3478
I shall be ashamed of his own	Hos 10:6	3478
places also of Aven, the sin of *I*	Hos 10:8	3478
O *I*, thou hast sinned from the	Hos 10:9	3478
the king of *I* utterly be cut off	Hos 10:15	3478
When *I* was a child, then I loved	Hos 11:1	3478
how shall I deliver thee, *I*	Hos 11:8	3478
and the house of *I* with deceit	Hos 11:12	3478
I served for a wife, and for a	Hos 12:12	3478
the LORD brought *I* out of Egypt	Hos 12:13	3478
he exalted himself in *I*	Hos 13:1	3478
O *I*, thou hast destroyed thyself	Hos 13:9	3478
O *I*, return unto the LORD thy God	Hos 14:1	3478
I will be as the dew unto *I*	Hos 14:5	3478
know that I am in the midst of *I*	Joel 2:27	3478
my people and for my heritage *I*	Joel 3:2	3478
the strength of the children of *I*	Joel 3:16	3478
which he saw concerning *I* in the	Amos 1:1	3478
the son of Joash king of *I*	Amos 1:1	3478
For three transgressions of *I*	Amos 2:6	3478
not even thus, O ye children of *I*	Amos 2:11	3478
against you, O children of *I*	Amos 3:1	3478
so shall the children of *I* be	Amos 3:12	3478
visit the transgressions of *I*	Amos 3:14	3478
liketh you, O ye children of *I*	Amos 4:5	3478
thus will I do unto thee, O *I*	Amos 4:12	3478
prepare to meet thy God, O *I*	Amos 4:12	3478
even a lamentation, O house of *I*	Amos 5:1	3478
The virgin of *I* is fallen	Amos 5:2	3478
leave ten, to the house of *I*	Amos 5:3	3478
the LORD unto the house of *I*	Amos 5:4	3478
forty years, O house of *I*	Amos 5:25	3478
to whom the house of *I* came	Amos 6:1	3478
you a nation, O house of *I*	Amos 6:14	3478
in the midst of my people *I*	Amos 7:8	3478
the sanctuaries of *I* shall be	Amos 7:9	3478
sent to Jeroboam king of *I*	Amos 7:10	3478
in the midst of the house of *I*	Amos 7:10	3478
I shall surely be led away	Amos 7:11	3478
me, Go, prophesy unto my people *I*	Amos 7:15	3478
sayest, Prophesy not against *I*	Amos 7:16	3478
I shall surely go into captivity	Amos 7:17	3478
end is come upon my people of *I*	Amos 8:2	3478
unto me, O children of *I*	Amos 9:7	3478
Have not I brought up *I* out of	Amos 9:7	3478
the house of *I* among all nations	Amos 9:9	3478
the captivity of my people of *I*	Amos 9:14	3478
of *I* shall possess that of the	Obad 20	3478
and for the sins of the house of *I*	Mic 1:5	3478
of *I* were found in thee	Mic 1:13	3478
shall be a lie to the kings of *I*	Mic 1:14	3478
come unto Adullam the glory of *I*	Mic 1:15	3478
surely gather the remnant of *I*	Mic 2:12	3478
and ye princes of the house of *I*	Mic 3:1	3478
transgression, and to *I* his sin	Mic 3:8	3478
and princes of the house of *I*	Mic 3:9	3478
of *I* with a rod upon the cheek	Mic 5:1	3478
unto me that is to be ruler in *I*	Mic 5:2	3478
return unto the children of *I*	Mic 5:3	3478
people, and he will plead with *I*	Mic 6:2	3478
of Jacob, as the excellency of *I*	Nah 2:2	3478
the LORD of hosts, the God of *I*	Zeph 2:9	3478
The remnant of *I* shall not do	Zeph 3:13	3478
shout, O *I*	Zeph 3:14	3478
the king of *I*, even the LORD, is	Zeph 3:15	3478
of man, as of all the tribes of *I*	Zec 9:1	3478
of the word of the LORD for *I*	Zec 12:1	3478
word of the LORD to *I* by Malachi	Mal 1:1	3478
be magnified from the border of *I*	Mal 1:5	3478
For the LORD, the God of *I*	Mal 2:16	3478
unto him in Horeb for all *I*	Mal 4:4	3478
that shall rule my people *I*	Mt 2:6	*2474*
mother, and go into the land of *I*	Mt 2:20	*2474*
and came into the land of *I*	Mt 2:21	*2474*
so great faith, no, not in *I*	Mt 8:10	*2474*
saying, It was never so seen in *I*	Mt 9:33	*2474*
the lost sheep of the house of *I*	Mt 10:6	*2474*
have gone over the cities of *I*	Mt 10:23	*2474*
the lost sheep of the house of *I*	Mt 15:24	*2474*
and they glorified the God of *I*	Mt 15:31	*2474*
judging the twelve tribes of *I*	Mt 19:28	*2474*
of the children of *I* did value	Mt 27:9	*2474*
If he be the King of *I*, let him	Mt 27:42	*2474*
the commandments is, Hear, O *I*	Mk 12:29	*2474*
Let Christ the King of *I* descend	Mk 15:32	*2474*
many of the children of *I* shall	Lk 1:16	*2474*
He hath holpen his servant *I*	Lk 1:54	*2474*
Blessed be the Lord God of *I*	Lk 1:68	*2474*
the day of his shewing unto *I*	Lk 1:80	*2474*
waiting for the consolation of *I*	Lk 2:25	*2474*
and the glory of thy people *I*	Lk 2:32	*2474*
fall and rising again of many in *I*	Lk 2:34	*2474*
many widows were in *I* in the days	Lk 4:25	*2474*
many lepers were in *I* in the time	Lk 4:27	*2474*
so great faith, no, not in *I*	Lk 7:9	*2474*
judging the twelve tribes of *I*	Lk 22:30	*2474*
he which should have redeemed *I*	Lk 24:21	*2474*
he should be made manifest to *I*	Jn 1:31	*2474*
thou art the King of *I*	Jn 1:49	*2474*
unto him, Art thou a master of *I*	Jn 3:10	*2474*
Blessed is the King of *I* that	Jn 12:13	*2474*
restore again the kingdom to *I*	Acts 1:6	*2474*
Ye men of *I*, hear these words	Acts 2:22	*2475*
all the house of *I* know assuredly	Acts 2:36	*2474*
unto the people, Ye men of *I*	Acts 3:12	*2475*
of the people, and elders of *I*	Acts 4:8	*2474*
all, and to all the people of *I*	Acts 4:10	*2474*
the Gentiles, and the people of *I*	Acts 4:27	*2474*
the senate of the children of *I*	Acts 5:21	*2474*
for to give repentance to *I*	Acts 5:31	*2474*
And said unto them, Ye men of *I*	Acts 5:35	*2475*
his brethren the children of *I*	Acts 7:23	*2474*
which said unto the children of *I*	Acts 7:37	*2474*

of the prophets, O ye house of *I*	Acts 7:42	*2474*
and kings, and the children of *I*	Acts 9:15	*2474*
God sent unto the children of *I*	Acts 10:36	*2474*
with his hand said, Men of *I*	Acts 13:16	*2475*
people of *I* chose our fathers	Acts 13:17	*2474*
promise raised unto *I* a Saviour	Acts 13:23	*2474*
repentance to all the people of *I*	Acts 13:24	*2474*
Crying out, Men of *I*, help	Acts 21:28	*2475*
of *I* I am bound with this chain	Acts 28:20	*2474*
For they are not all *I*, which are	Rom 9:6	*2474*
not all Israel, which are of *I*	Rom 9:6	*2474*
Esaias also crieth concerning *I*	Rom 9:27	*2474*
of *I* be as the sand of the sea	Rom 9:27	*2474*
But *I*, which followed after the	Rom 9:31	*2474*
desire and prayer to God for *I* is	Rom 10:1	*2474*
But I say, Did not *I* know	Rom 10:19	*2474*
But to *I* he saith, All day long I	Rom 10:21	*2474*
intercession to God against *I*	Rom 11:2	*2474*
I hath not obtained that which he	Rom 11:7	*2474*
in part is happened to *I*, until	Rom 11:25	*2474*
And so all *I* shall be saved	Rom 11:26	*2474*
Behold *I* after the flesh	1Cor 10:18	*2474*
so that the children of *I* could	2Cor 3:7	*2474*
that the children of *I* could not	2Cor 3:13	*2474*
and mercy, and upon the *I* of God	Gal 6:16	*2474*
aliens from the commonwealth of *I*	Eph 2:12	*2474*
the eighth day, of the stock of *I*	Phil 3:5	*2474*
new covenant with the house of *I*	Heb 8:8	*2474*
the house of *I* after those days	Heb 8:10	*2474*
departing of the children of *I*	Heb 11:22	*2474*
before the children of *I*, to eat	Rev 2:14	*2474*
the tribes of the children of *I*	Rev 7:4	*2474*
tribes of the children of *I*	Rev 21:12	*2474*
3. *The ten northern tribes.*		
I were many, as the sand which is	1Kin 4:20	3478
I dwelt safely, every man under	1Kin 4:25	3478
all *I* stoned him with stones,	1Kin 12:18	3478
So *I* rebelled against the house	1Kin 12:19	3478
when all *I* heard that Jeroboam	1Kin 12:20	3478
and made him king over all *I*	1Kin 12:20	3478
to fight against the house of *I*	1Kin 12:21	3478
your brethren the children of *I*	1Kin 12:24	3478
behold thy gods, O *I*, which	1Kin 12:28	3478
a feast unto the children of *I*	1Kin 12:33	3478
him that is shut up and left in *I*	1Kin 14:10	3478
all *I* shall mourn for him, and	1Kin 14:13	3478
God of *I* in the house of Jeroboam	1Kin 14:13	3478
shall raise him up a king over *I*	1Kin 14:14	3478
For the LORD shall smite *I*	1Kin 14:15	3478
he shall root up *I* out of this	1Kin 14:15	3478
he shall give *I* up because of the	1Kin 14:16	3478
who did sin, and who made *I* to sin	1Kin 14:16	3478
all *I* mourned for him, according	1Kin 14:18	3478
the chronicles of the kings of *I*	1Kin 14:19	3478
king of *I* reigned Asa over Judah	1Kin 15:9	3478
Baasha king of *I* all their days	1Kin 15:16	3478
Baasha king of *I* went up against	1Kin 15:17	3478
thy league with Baasha king of *I*	1Kin 15:19	3478
he had against the cities of *I*	1Kin 15:20	3478
I in the second year of Asa king	1Kin 15:25	3478
and reigned over *I* two years	1Kin 15:25	3478
sin wherewith he made *I* to sin	1Kin 15:26	3478
all *I* laid siege to Gibbethon	1Kin 15:27	3478
he sinned, and which he made *I* sin	1Kin 15:30	3478
the LORD God of *I* to anger	1Kin 15:30	3478
the chronicles of the kings of *I*	1Kin 15:31	3478
Baasha king of *I* all their days	1Kin 15:32	3478
to reign over all *I* in Tirzah	1Kin 15:33	3478
made thee prince over my people *I*	1Kin 16:2	3478
and hast made my people *I* to sin	1Kin 16:2	3478
the chronicles of the kings of *I*	1Kin 16:5	3478
Baasha to reign over *I* in Tirzah	1Kin 16:8	3478
and by which they made *I* to sin	1Kin 16:13	3478
of *I* to anger with their vanities	1Kin 16:13	3478
the chronicles of the kings of *I*	1Kin 16:14	3478
wherefore all *I* made Omri	1Kin 16:16	3478
king over *I* that day in the camp	1Kin 16:16	3478
all *I* with him, and they besieged	1Kin 16:17	3478
which he did, to make *I* to sin	1Kin 16:19	3478
the chronicles of the kings of *I*	1Kin 16:20	3478
of *I* divided into two parts	1Kin 16:21	3478
Judah began Omri to reign over *I*	1Kin 16:23	3478
sin wherewith he made *I* to sin	1Kin 16:26	3478
to provoke the LORD God of *I* to	1Kin 16:26	3478
the chronicles of the kings of *I*	1Kin 16:27	3478
the son of Omri to reign over *I*	1Kin 16:29	3478
reigned over *I* in Samaria twenty	1Kin 16:29	3478
kings of *I* that were before him	1Kin 16:33	3478
him, Art thou he that troubleth *I*	1Kin 18:17	3478
answered, I have not troubled *I*	1Kin 18:18	3478
gather to me all *I* unto mount	1Kin 18:19	3478
sent unto all the children of *I*	1Kin 18:20	3478
for the children of *I* have	1Kin 19:10	3478
because the children of *I* have	1Kin 19:14	3478
thou anoint to be king over *I*	1Kin 19:16	3478
have left me seven thousand in *I*	1Kin 19:18	3478
to Ahab king of *I* into the city	1Kin 20:2	3478
And the king of *I* answered	1Kin 20:4	3478
Then the king of *I* called all the	1Kin 20:7	3478
And the king of *I* answered	1Kin 20:11	3478
a prophet unto Ahab king of *I*	1Kin 20:13	3478
even all the children of *I*	1Kin 20:15	3478
and *I* pursued them	1Kin 20:20	3478
And the king of *I* went out	1Kin 20:21	3478
the prophet came to the king of *I*	1Kin 20:22	3478
up to Aphek, to fight against *I*	1Kin 20:26	3478
the children of *I* were numbered	1Kin 20:27	3478
the children of *I* pitched before	1Kin 20:27	3478
God, and spake unto the king of *I*	1Kin 20:28	3478
the children of *I* slew of the	1Kin 20:29	3478
the house of *I* are merciful kings	1Kin 20:31	3478
heads, and go out to the king of *I*	1Kin 20:31	3478
heads, and came to the king of *I*	1Kin 20:32	3478
the king of *I* said unto him, So	1Kin 20:40	3478
the king of *I* discerned him that	1Kin 20:41	3478
the king of *I* went to his house	1Kin 20:43	3478
thou now govern the kingdom of *I*	1Kin 21:7	3478
go down to meet Ahab king of *I*	1Kin 21:18	3478
him that is shut up and left in *I*	1Kin 21:21	3478
me to anger, and made *I* to sin	1Kin 21:22	3478
cast out before the children of *I*	1Kin 21:26	3478
without war between Syria and *I*	1Kin 22:1	3478
Judah came down to the king of *I*	1Kin 22:2	3478
the king of *I* said unto his	1Kin 22:3	3478
Jehoshaphat said to the king of *I*	1Kin 22:4	3478
said unto the king of *I*, Enquire,	1Kin 22:5	3478
Then the king of *I* gathered the	1Kin 22:6	3478
And the king of *I* said unto	1Kin 22:8	3478
Then the king of *I* called an	1Kin 22:9	3478
And the king of *I* and Jehoshaphat	1Kin 22:10	3478
I saw all *I* scattered upon the	1Kin 22:17	3478
And the king of *I* said unto	1Kin 22:18	3478
And the king of *I* said, Take	1Kin 22:26	3478
So the king of *I* and Jehoshaphat	1Kin 22:29	3478
And the king of *I* said unto	1Kin 22:30	3478
the king of *I* disguised himself,	1Kin 22:30	3478
save only with the king of *I*	1Kin 22:31	3478
said, Surely it is the king of *I*	1Kin 22:32	3478
that it was not the king of *I*	1Kin 22:33	3478
smote the king of *I* between the	1Kin 22:34	3478
the chronicles of the kings of *I*	1Kin 22:39	3478
the fourth year of Ahab king of *I*	1Kin 22:41	3478
made peace with the king of *I*	1Kin 22:44	3478
I in Samaria the seventeenth year	1Kin 22:51	3478
and reigned two years over *I*	1Kin 22:51	3478
son of Nebat, who made *I* to sin	1Kin 22:52	3478
against *I* after the death of Ahab	2Kin 1:1	3478
because there is not a God in *I*	2Kin 1:3	3478
because there is not a God in *I*	2Kin 1:6	3478
God in *I* to enquire of his word	2Kin 1:16	3478
the chronicles of the kings of *I*	2Kin 1:18	3478
I in Samaria the eighteenth year	2Kin 3:1	3478
son of Nebat, which made *I* to sin	2Kin 3:3	3478
of *I* an hundred thousand lambs	2Kin 3:4	3478
rebelled against the king of *I*	2Kin 3:5	3478
the same time, and numbered all *I*	2Kin 3:6	3478
So the king of *I* went, and the	2Kin 3:9	3478
And the king of *I* said, Alas	2Kin 3:10	3478
So the king of *I* and Jehoshaphat	2Kin 3:12	3478
And Elisha said unto the king of *I*	2Kin 3:13	3478
the king of *I* said unto him, Nay	2Kin 3:13	3478
when they came to the camp of *I*	2Kin 3:24	3478
was great indignation against *I*	2Kin 3:27	3478
of the land of *I* a little maid	2Kin 5:2	3478
the maid that is of the land of *I*	2Kin 5:4	3478
send a letter unto the king of *I*	2Kin 5:5	3478
the letter to the king of *I*	2Kin 5:6	3478
when the king of *I* had read the	2Kin 5:7	3478
king of *I* had rent his clothes	2Kin 5:8	3478
know that there is a prophet in *I*	2Kin 5:8	3478
better than all the waters of *I*	2Kin 5:12	3478
no God in all the earth, but in *I*	2Kin 5:15	3478
king of Syria warred against *I*	2Kin 6:8	3478
of God sent unto the king of *I*	2Kin 6:9	3478
the king of *I* sent to the place	2Kin 6:10	3478
which of us is for the king of *I*	2Kin 6:11	3478
Elisha, the prophet that is in *I*	2Kin 6:12	3478
telleth the king of *I* the words	2Kin 6:12	3478
the king of *I* said unto Elisha,	2Kin 6:21	3478
came no more into the land of *I*	2Kin 6:23	3478
as the king of *I* was passing by	2Kin 6:26	3478
the king of *I* hath hired against	2Kin 7:6	3478
of *I* that are left in it	2Kin 7:13	3478
wilt do unto the children of *I*	2Kin 8:12	3478
Joram the son of Ahab king of *I*	2Kin 8:16	3478
in the way of the kings of *I*	2Kin 8:18	3478
Joram the son of Ahab king of *I*	2Kin 8:25	3478
the daughter of Omri king of *I*	2Kin 8:26	3478
I have anointed thee king over *I*	2Kin 9:3	3478
people of the LORD, even over *I*	2Kin 9:6	3478
him that is shut up and left in *I*	2Kin 9:8	3478
I have anointed thee king over *I*	2Kin 9:12	3478
kept Ramoth gilead, he and all *I*	2Kin 9:14	3478
And Joram king of *I* and Ahaziah	2Kin 9:21	3478
And Jehu sent through all *I*	2Kin 10:21	3478
Thus Jehu destroyed Baal out of *I*	2Kin 10:28	3478
son of Nebat, who made *I* to sin	2Kin 10:29	3478
shall sit on the throne of *I*	2Kin 10:30	3478
of Jeroboam, which made *I* to sin	2Kin 10:31	3478
the LORD began to cut *I* short	2Kin 10:32	3478
smote them in all the coasts of *I*	2Kin 10:32	3478
the chronicles of the kings of *I*	2Kin 10:34	3478
over *I* in Samaria was twenty	2Kin 10:36	3478
began to reign over *I* in Samaria	2Kin 13:1	3478
son of Nebat, which made *I* to sin	2Kin 13:2	3478
of the LORD was kindled against *I*	2Kin 13:3	3478
for he saw the oppression of *I*	2Kin 13:4	3478
(And the LORD gave *I* a saviour	2Kin 13:5	3478
the children of *I* dwelt in their	2Kin 13:5	3478
house of Jeroboam, who made *I* sin	2Kin 13:6	3478
the chronicles of the kings of *I*	2Kin 13:8	3478
to reign over *I* in Samaria	2Kin 13:10	3478
the son of Nebat, who made *I* sin	2Kin 13:11	3478
the chronicles of the kings of *I*	2Kin 13:12	3478
in Samaria with the kings of *I*	2Kin 13:13	3478
Joash the king of *I* came down	2Kin 13:14	3478
my father, the chariot of *I*	2Kin 13:14	3478
And he said to the king of *I*	2Kin 13:16	3478
And he said unto the king of *I*	2Kin 13:18	3478
I all the days of Jehoahaz	2Kin 13:22	3478
him, and recovered the cities of *I*	2Kin 13:25	3478
of *I* reigned Amaziah the son of	2Kin 14:1	3478
Jehoahaz son of Jehu, king of *I*	2Kin 14:8	3478
Jehoash the king of *I* sent to	2Kin 14:9	3478
Jehoash king of *I* went up	2Kin 14:11	3478
was put to the worse before *I*	2Kin 14:12	3478
Jehoash king of *I* took Amaziah	2Kin 14:13	3478
the chronicles of the kings of *I*	2Kin 14:15	3478
in Samaria with the kings of *I*	2Kin 14:16	3478
Jehoahaz king of *I* fifteen years	2Kin 14:17	3478
the son of Joash king of *I* began	2Kin 14:23	3478
son of Nebat, who made *I* to sin	2Kin 14:24	3478
the LORD saw the affliction of *I*	2Kin 14:26	3478
any left, nor any helper for *I*	2Kin 14:26	3478
the name of *I* from under heaven	2Kin 14:27	3478
which belonged to Judah, for *I*	2Kin 14:28	3478
the chronicles of the kings of *I*	2Kin 14:28	3478
fathers, even with the kings of *I*	2Kin 14:29	3478
year of Jeroboam king of *I* began	2Kin 15:1	3478
over *I* in Samaria six months	2Kin 15:8	3478
son of Nebat, who made *I* to sin	2Kin 15:9	3478
the chronicles of the kings of *I*	2Kin 15:11	3478
of *I* unto the fourth generation	2Kin 15:12	3478
the chronicles of the kings of *I*	2Kin 15:15	3478
the son of Gadi to reign over *I*	2Kin 15:17	3478
son of Nebat, who made *I* to sin	2Kin 15:18	3478
And Menahem exacted the money of *I*	2Kin 15:20	3478
the chronicles of the kings of *I*	2Kin 15:21	3478
began to reign over *I* in Samaria	2Kin 15:23	3478
son of Nebat, who made *I* to sin	2Kin 15:24	3478
the chronicles of the kings of *I*	2Kin 15:26	3478
began to reign over *I* in Samaria	2Kin 15:27	3478
son of Nebat, who made *I* to sin	2Kin 15:28	3478
of *I* came Tiglath-pileser king of	2Kin 15:29	3478
the chronicles of the kings of *I*	2Kin 15:31	3478
the son of Remaliah king of *I*	2Kin 15:32	3478
in the way of the kings of *I*	2Kin 16:3	3478
out from before the children of *I*	2Kin 16:3	3478
of *I* came up to Jerusalem to war	2Kin 16:5	3478
out of the hand of the king of *I*	2Kin 16:7	3478
in Samaria over *I* nine years	2Kin 17:1	3478
kings of *I* that were before him	2Kin 17:2	3478
carried *I* away into Assyria, and	2Kin 17:6	3478
that the children of *I* had sinned	2Kin 17:7	3478
out from before the children of *I*	2Kin 17:8	3478
and of the kings of *I*	2Kin 17:8	3478
the children of *I* did secretly	2Kin 17:9	3478
Yet the LORD testified against *I*	2Kin 17:13	3478
the LORD was very angry with *I*	2Kin 17:18	3478
the statutes of *I* which they made	2Kin 17:19	3478
LORD rejected all the seed of *I*	2Kin 17:20	3478
For he rent *I* from the house of	2Kin 17:21	3478
Jeroboam drave *I* from following	2Kin 17:21	3478
For the children of *I* walked in	2Kin 17:22	3478
LORD removed *I* out of his sight	2Kin 17:23	3478
So was *I* carried away out of	2Kin 17:23	3478
instead of the children of *I*	2Kin 17:24	3478
of Hoshea son of Elah king of *I*	2Kin 18:1	3478
of Hoshea son of Elah king of *I*	2Kin 18:9	3478
ninth year of Hoshea king of *I*	2Kin 18:10	3478
did carry away *I* unto Assyria	2Kin 18:11	3478
son of Nebat, who made *I* to sin	2Kin 23:15	3478
which the kings of *I* had made to	2Kin 23:19	3478
in all the days of the kings of *I*	2Kin 23:22	3478
of my sight, as I have removed *I*	2Kin 23:27	3478
in the days of Jeroboam king of *I*	1Chr 5:17	3478
in the book of the kings of *I*	1Chr 9:1	3478
the children of *I* stoned him with	2Chr 10:18	3478
I rebelled against the house of	2Chr 10:19	3478
were warriors, to fight against *I*	2Chr 11:1	3478
all *I* resorted to him out of all	2Chr 11:13	3478
of *I* such as set their hearts to	2Chr 11:16	3478
Hear me, thou Jeroboam, and all *I*	2Chr 13:4	3478
O children of *I*, fight ye not	2Chr 13:12	3478
all *I* before Abijah and Judah	2Chr 13:15	3478
the children of *I* fled before	2Chr 13:16	3478
so there fell down slain of *I*	2Chr 13:17	3478
Thus the children of *I* were	2Chr 13:18	3478
fell to him out of *I* in abundance	2Chr 15:9	3478
were not taken away out of *I*	2Chr 15:17	3478
king of *I* came up against Judah	2Chr 16:1	3478
thy league with Baasha king of *I*	2Chr 16:3	3478
armies against the cities of *I*	2Chr 16:4	3478
book of the kings of Judah and *I*	2Chr 16:11	3478
and strengthened himself against *I*	2Chr 17:1	3478
and not after the doings of *I*	2Chr 17:4	3478
And Ahab king of *I* said unto	2Chr 18:3	3478
said unto the king of *I*, Enquire,	2Chr 18:4	3478
Therefore the king of *I* gathered	2Chr 18:5	3478
And the king of *I* said unto	2Chr 18:7	3478
the king of *I* called for one of	2Chr 18:8	3478
And the king of *I* and Jehoshaphat	2Chr 18:9	3478
I did see all *I* scattered upon	2Chr 18:16	3478
the king of *I* said to Jehoshaphat	2Chr 18:17	3478
Who shall entice Ahab king of *I*	2Chr 18:19	3478
Then the king of *I* said, Take ye	2Chr 18:25	3478
So the king of *I* and Jehoshaphat	2Chr 18:28	3478
And the king of *I* said unto	2Chr 18:29	3478
So the king of *I* disguised	2Chr 18:29	3478
save only with the king of *I*	2Chr 18:30	3478

they said, It is the king of *I* 2Chr 18:31 3478
that it was not the king of *I* 2Chr 18:32 3478
smote the king of *I* between the 2Chr 18:33 3478
howbeit the king of *I* stayed 2Chr 18:34 3478
in the book of the kings of *I* 2Chr 20:34 3478
himself with Ahaziah king of *I* 2Chr 20:35 3478
the sons of Jehoshaphat king of *I* 2Chr 21:2 3478
divers also of the princes of *I* 2Chr 21:4 3478
in the way of the kings of *I* 2Chr 21:6 3478
in the way of the kings of *I* 2Chr 21:13 3478
I to war against Hazael king of 2Chr 22:5 3478
of *I* for an hundred talents of 2Chr 25:6 3478
not the army of *I* go with thee 2Chr 25:7 3478
for the LORD is not with *I* 2Chr 25:7 3478
I have given to the army of *I* 2Chr 25:9 3478
the son of Jehu, king of *I* 2Chr 25:17 3478
Joash king of *I* sent to Amaziah 2Chr 25:18 3478
So Joash the king of *I* went up 2Chr 25:21 3478
was put to the worse before *I* 2Chr 25:22 3478
Joash the king of *I* took Amaziah 2Chr 25:23 3478
Jehoahaz king of *I* fifteen years 2Chr 25:25 3478
book of the kings of Judah and *I* 2Chr 25:26 3478
in the book of the kings of *I* 2Chr 27:7 3478
in the ways of the kings of *I* 2Chr 28:2 3478
into the hand of the king of *I* 2Chr 28:5 3478
the children of *I* carried away 2Chr 28:8 3478
there is fierce wrath against *I* 2Chr 28:13 3478
low because of Ahaz king of *I* 2Chr 28:19 3478
and his princes throughout all *I* 2Chr 30:6 3478
the children of *I* that were 2Chr 30:21 3478
congregation that came out of *I* 2Chr 30:25 3478
that came out of the land of *I* 2Chr 30:25 3478
And concerning the children of *I* 2Chr 31:6 3478
book of the kings of Judah and *I* 2Chr 32:32 3478
and of all the remnant of *I* 2Chr 34:9 3478
and for them that are left in *I* 2Chr 34:21 3478
neither did all the kings of *I* 2Chr 35:18 3478
I that were present, and the 2Chr 35:18 3478
in the book of the kings of *I* 2Chr 35:27 3478
in the book of the kings of *I* 2Chr 36:8 3478
the son of Remaliah, king of *I* Is 7:1 3478
so is the house of *I* ashamed Jer 2:26 3478
Have I been a wilderness unto *I* Jer 2:31 3478
which backsliding *I* hath done Jer 3:6 3478
I committed adultery I had put Jer 3:8 3478
The backsliding *I* hath justified Jer 3:11 3478
say, Return, thou backsliding *I* Jer 3:12 3478
shall walk with the house of *I* Jer 3:18 3478
For the house of *I* and the house Jer 5:11 3478
and all the house of *I* are Jer 9:26 3478
the house of *I* and the house of Jer 11:10 3478
for the evil of the house of *I* Jer 11:17 3478
be saved, and *I* shall dwell safely Jer 23:6 3478
that I will sow the house of *I* Jer 31:27 3478
new covenant with the house of *I* Jer 31:31 3478
For the children of *I* and the Jer 32:30 3478
all the evil of the children of *I* Jer 32:32 3478
made for fear of Baasha king of *I* Jer 41:9 3478
as the house of *I* was ashamed of Jer 48:13 3478
The children of *I* and the children Jer 50:33 3478
of the house of *I* upon it Eze 4:4 3478
the iniquity of the house of *I* Eze 4:5 3478
The iniquity of the house of *I* Eze 9:9 3478
Judah, and the land of *I*, they Eze 27:17 3478
the children of *I* his companions Eze 37:16 3478
children of *I* went astray from me Eze 44:15 3478
which have scattered Judah, *I* Zec 1:19 3478
O house of Judah, and house of *I* Zec 8:13 3478
brotherhood between Judah and *I* Zec 11:14 3478
an abomination is committed in *I* Mal 2:11 3478

ISRAELITE *(iz'-ra-el-ite)* {4} See ISRAELITES, ISRAELITISH. *A member of Israel 3.*
the name of the *I* that was slain Num 25:14 1121,3478
son, whose name was Ithra an *I* 2Sa 17:25 3481
saith of him, Behold an *I* indeed Jn 1:47 *2475*
For I also am an *I*, of the seed Rom 11:1 *2475*

ISRAELITES *(iz'-ra-el-ites)* {18}
one of the cattle of the *I* dead Ex 9:7 3478
all that are *I* born shall dwell Lev 23:42 3478
all the *I* passed over on dry Josh 3:17 3478
that all the *I* returned unto Ai, Josh 8:24 3478
lot unto the *I* for an inheritance Josh 13:6 3478
dwell among the *I* until this day Josh 13:13 3478
ground of the *I* that day twenty Judg 20:21 3478
unto all the *I* that came thither 1Sa 2:14 3478
But all the *I* went down to the 1Sa 13:20 3478
be with the *I* that were with Saul 1Sa 14:21 3478
all the *I* were gathered together, 1Sa 25:1 3478
the *I* pitched by a fountain which 1Sa 29:1 3478
and all the *I* were troubled 2Sa 4:1 3478
the *I* rose up and smote the 2Kin 3:24 3478
of the *I* that are consumed 2Kin 7:13 3478
in their cities were, the *I* 1Chr 9:2 3478
Who are *I* Rom 9:4 *2475*
Are they *I* 2Cor 11:22 *2475*

ISRAELITISH {3}
And the son of an *I* woman, whose Lev 24:10 3482
and this son of the *I* woman Lev 24:10 3482
the *I* woman's son blasphemed the Lev 24:11 3482

ISRAEL'S *(iz'-ra-els)* {10}
1. Refers to Israel 1.
his right hand toward *I* left hand Gen 48:13 3478
his left hand toward *I* right hand Gen 48:13 3478
of Reuben, *I* eldest son, by their Num 1:20 3478
2. Refers to Israel 2.
and to the Egyptians for *I* sake Ex 18:8 3478
And of the children of *I* half Num 31:30 3478
And of the children of *I* half Num 31:42 3478
Even of the children of *I* half Num 31:47 3478
blood unto thy people of *I* charge Deut 21:8 3478
his kingdom for his people *I* sake 2Sa 5:12 3478
3. Refers to Israel 3.
the king of *I* servants answered 2Kin 3:11 3478

ISSACHAR *(is'-sa-kar)* {44}
1. A son of Jacob.
and she called his name *I* Gen 30:18 3485
Simeon, and Levi, and Judah, and *I* Gen 35:23 3485
And the sons of *I* Gen 46:13 3485
I is a strong ass couching down Gen 49:14 3485
I, Zebulun, and Benjamin, Ex 1:3 3485
Reuben, Simeon, Levi, and Judah, *I* 1Chr 2:1 3485
Now the sons of *I* were, Tola, and 1Chr 7:1 3485
2. Descendants of Issachar 1.
Of *I* Num 1:8 3485
Of the children of *I*, by their Num 1:28 3485
of them, even of the tribe of *I* Num 1:29 3485
unto him shall be the tribe of *I* Num 2:5 3485
be captain of the children of *I* Num 2:5 3485
the son of Zuar, prince of *I* Num 7:18 3485
I was Nethaneel the son of Zuar Num 10:15 3485
Of the tribe of *I*, Igal the son Num 13:7 3485
Of the sons of *I* after their Num 26:23 3485
These are the families of *I* Num 26:25 3485
of the tribe of the children of *I* Num 34:26 3485
Simeon, and Levi, and Judah, and *I* Deut 27:12 3485
and, *I*, in thy tents Deut 33:18 3485
on the north, and in *I* on the east Josh 17:10 3485
And Manasseh had in *I* and in Asher Josh 17:11 3485
And the fourth lot came out to *I* Josh 19:17 3485
for the children of *I* according Josh 19:17 3485
of *I* according to their families Josh 19:23 3485
of the families of the tribe of *I* Josh 21:6 3485
And out of the tribe of *I*, Kishon Josh 21:28 3485
the princes of *I* were with Judg 5:15 3485
even *I*, and also Barak Judg 5:15 3485
Puah, the son of Dodo, a man of *I* Judg 10:1 3485
the son of Paruah, in *I* 1Kin 4:17 3485
son of Ahijah, of the house of *I* 1Kin 15:27 3485
families out of the tribe of *I* 1Chr 6:62 3485
And out of the tribe of *I* 1Chr 6:72 3485
of *I* were valiant men of might 1Chr 7:5 3485
And of the children of *I*, which 1Chr 12:32 3485
that were nigh them, even unto *I* 1Chr 12:40 3485
of *I*, Omri the son of Michael 1Chr 27:18 3485
many of Ephraim, and Manasseh, *I* 2Chr 30:18 3485
unto the west side, *I* a portion Eze 48:25 3485
And by the border of *I*, from the Eze 48:26 3485
one gate of Simeon, one gate of *I* Eze 48:33 3485
Of the tribe of *I* were sealed Rev 7:7 *2466*
3. A porter of the tabernacle.
I the seventh, Peulthai the 1Chr 26:5 3485

ISSHIAH *(is-shi'-ah)* {3} See ISAIAH, JESIAH.
1. A descendant of Moses.
sons of Rehabiah, the first was *I* 1Chr 24:21 3449
2. A Levite.
The brother of Michah was *I* 1Chr 24:25 3449
of the sons of *I* 1Chr 24:25

ISSHIJAH See ISHIJAH.

ISSHOD See ISHOD.

ISSUE {41}
And thy *i*, which thou begettest Gen 48:6 4138
cleansed from the *i* of her blood Lev 12:7 4726
hath a running *i* out of his flesh Lev 15:2 2100
because of his *i* he is unclean Lev 15:2 2101
this shall be his uncleanness in his *i* Lev 15:3 2101
whether his flesh run with his *i* Lev 15:3 2101
his flesh be stopped from his *i* Lev 15:3 2101
whereon he lieth that hath the *i* Lev 15:4 2100
hath the *i* shall wash his clothes Lev 15:6 2100
hath the *i* shall wash his clothes Lev 15:7 2100
if he that hath the *i* spit upon Lev 15:8 2100
that hath the *i* shall be unclean Lev 15:9 2100
he toucheth that hath the *i* Lev 15:11 2100
that he toucheth which hath the *i* Lev 15:12 2100
when he that hath an *i* is Lev 15:13 2100
an *i* is cleansed of his *i* Lev 15:13 2101
for him before the LORD for his *i* Lev 15:15 2101
And if a woman have an *i* Lev 15:19 2100
her *i* in her flesh be blood, she Lev 15:19 2101
if a woman have an *i* of her blood Lev 15:25 2100
all the days of the *i* of her Lev 15:25 2101
she lieth all the days of her *i* Lev 15:26 2101
But if she be cleansed of her *i* Lev 15:28 2101
LORD for the *i* of her uncleanness Lev 15:30 2101
is the law of him that hath an *i* Lev 15:32 2100
flowers, and of him that hath an *i* Lev 15:33 2100
is a leper, or hath a running *i* Lev 22:4 2100
and every one that hath an *i* Num 5:2 2100
house of Joab one that hath an *i* 2Sa 3:29 2100
thy sons that shall *i* from thee 2Kin 20:18 3318
house, the offspring and the *i* Is 22:24 6849
thy sons that shall *i* from thee Is 39:7 3318
i is like the *i* of horses Eze 23:20 2231
These waters *i* out toward the Eze 47:8 3318
with an *i* of blood twelve years Mt 9:20 *131*
a wife, deceased, and, having no *i* Mt 22:25 *4690*
which had an *i* of blood twelve Mk 5:25 *4511*
a woman having an *i* of blood Lk 8:43 *4511*
immediately her *i* of blood Lk 8:44 *4511*

ISSUED {7}
the other *i* out of the city Josh 8:22 3318
as if it had *i* out of the womb Job 38:8 3318
waters *i* out from under the Eze 47:1 3318
they they *i* out of the sanctuary Eze 47:12 3318
A fiery stream *i* and came forth Dan 7:10 5047
and out of their mouths *i* fire Rev 9:17 *1607*
which *i* out of their mouths Rev 9:18 *1607*

ISSUES {2}
the Lord belong the *i* from death Ps 68:20 8444
for out of it are the *i* of life Prov 4:23 8444

ISUAH *(is'-u-ah)* {1} See ISHUAH. *A son of Asher.*
Imnah, and *I*, and Ishuai, and Beriah 1Chr 7:30 3440

ISUI *(is'-u-i)* {1} See ISHUI. *A son of Asher.*
Jimnah, and Ishuah, and *I*, and Gen 46:17 3440

IT See APPENDIX.

ITALIAN *(it-al'-yan)* {1}
of the band called the *I* band Acts 10:1 *2483*

ITALY *(it'-a-lee)* {5} *Homeland of most Roman citizens.*
in Pontus, lately come from *I* Acts 18:2 *2482*
that we should sail into *I* Acts 27:1 *2482*
ship of Alexandria sailing into *I* Acts 27:6 *2482*
They of *I* salute you Heb 13:24 *2482*
to the Hebrews from *I* by Timothy Heb *s*

ITCH {1}
and with the scab, and with the *i* Deut 28:27 2775

ITCHING {1}
teachers, having *i* ears 2Ti 4:3 *2833*

ITHAI *(ith'-a-i)* {1} See ITTAI. *A mighty man of David.*
I the son of Ribai of Gibeah, 1Chr 11:31 863

ITHAMAR *(ith'-a-mar)* {21} *A son of Aaron.*
Nadab, and Abihu, Eleazar, and *I* Ex 6:23 385
Nadab and Abihu, Eleazar and *I* Ex 28:1 385
of the Levites, by the hand of *I* Ex 38:21 385
Aaron, and unto Eleazar and unto *I* Lev 10:6 385
Aaron, and unto Eleazar and unto *I* Lev 10:12 385
and he was angry with Eleazar and *I* Lev 10:16 385
and Abihu, Eleazar, and *I* Num 3:2 385
I ministered in the priest's Num 3:4 385
shall be under the hand of *I* the Num 4:28 385
under the hand of *I* the son of Num 4:33 385
under the hand of *I* the son of Num 7:8 385
Nadab, and Abihu, Eleazar, and *I* Num 26:60 385
Nadab, and Abihu, Eleazar, and *I* 1Chr 6:3 385
Nadab, and Abihu, Eleazar, and *I* 1Chr 24:1 385
I executed the priest's office 1Chr 24:2 385
and Ahimelech of the sons of *I* 1Chr 24:3 385
of Eleazar than of the sons of *I* 1Chr 24:4 385
eight among the sons of *I* 1Chr 24:4 385
of Eleazar, and of the sons of *I* 1Chr 24:5 385
for Eleazar, and one taken for *I* 1Chr 24:6 385
of the sons of *I* Ezr 8:2 385

ITHIEL *(ith'-e-el)* {3}
1. Son of Jesaiah.
the son of Maaseiah, the son of *I* Neh 11:7 384
2. Person mentioned in Proverbs.
the man spake unto *I*, even unto Prov 30:1 384
spake unto Ithiel, even unto *I* Prov 30:1 384

ITHLAH See JETHLAH.

ITHMAH *(ith'-mah)* {1} *A mighty man of David.*
sons of Elnaam, and *I* the Moabite, 1Chr 11:46 3495

ITHNAN *(ith'-nan)* {1} *A town in Judah.*
And Kedesh, and Hazor, and *I* Josh 15:23 3497

ITHRA *(ith'-rah)* {1} See JETHER. *Father of Amasa.*
whose name was *I* an Israelite 2Sa 17:25 3501

ITHRAN *(ith'-ran)* {3}
1. A son of Dishon.
Hemdan, and Eshban, and *I*, and Gen 36:26 3506
Amram, and Eshban, and *I*, and Cheran. 1Chr 1:41 3506
2. A son of Zophah.
Hod, and Shamma, and Shilshah, and *I*. 1Chr 7:37 3506

ITHREAM *(ith'-re-am)* {2} *A son of David.*
And the sixth, *I*, by Eglah David's 2Sa 3:5 3507
the sixth, *I* by Eglah his wife 1Chr 3:3 3507

ITHRITE *(ith'-rite)* {8} See ITHRITES. *A descendant of Jether.*
Ira an *I*, Gareb an *I*, 2Sa 23:38 3505
Ira an *I*, Gareb an *I* 2Sa 23:38 3505
Ira the *I*, Gareb the *I*, 1Chr 11:40 3505
Ira the *I*, Gareb the *I* 1Chr 11:40 3505

ITHRITES *(ith'-rites)* {1}
the *I*, and the Puhites, and the 1Chr 2:53 3505

ITS See APPENDIX.

ITSELF See APPENDIX.

ITTAH-KAZIN *(it'-tah-ka'-zin)* {1} *A city in Zebulun.*
the east to Gittah-hepher, to *I* Josh 19:13 6278

ITTAI *(it'-ta-i)* {8} See ITHAI.
1. A Philistine in David's army.
said the king to *I* the Gittite 2Sa 15:19 863
I answered the king, and said, As 2Sa 15:21 863
And David said to *I*, Go and pass 2Sa 15:22 863
I the Gittite passed over, and all 2Sa 15:22 863
under the hand of *I* the Gittite 2Sa 18:2 863
commanded Joab and Abishai and *I* 2Sa 18:5 863
king charged thee and Abishai and *I* 2Sa 18:12 863

2. A mighty man of David.
I the son of Ribai out of Gibeah............2Sa 23:29 863

ITURAEA *(i-tu-re'-ah)* {1} *A province near Mt. Hermon.*
his brother Philip tetrarch of *I*...............Lk 3:1 *2434*

IVAH *(i'-vah)* {3} See AHAVA, AVA. *A Mesopotamian district.*
gods of Sepharvaim, Hena, and *I*..........2Kin 18:34 5755
city of Sepharvaim, of Hena, and *I*.........2Kin 19:13 5755
city of Sepharvaim, Hena, and *I*............Is 37:13 5755

IVORY {13}
the king made a great throne of *i*...........1Kin 10:18 8127
bringing gold, and silver, *i*...................1Kin 10:22 8143
the *i* house which he made, and all.........1Kin 22:39 8127
the king made a great throne of *i*...........2Chr 9:17 8127
bringing gold, and silver, *i*....................2Chr 9:21 8143
and cassia, out of the *i* palaces..............Ps 45:8 8127
his belly is as bright *i* overlaid...............Song 5:14 8127
Thy neck is as a tower of *i*......................Song 7:4 8127
have made thy benches of *i*......................Eze 27:6 8127
thee for a present horns of *i*....................Eze 27:15 8127
and the houses of *i* shall perish..............Amos 3:15 8127
That lie upon beds of *i*, and ....Amos 6:4 8127
wood, and all manner vessels of *i*.............Rev 18:12 *1661*

IZEHAR *(iz'-e-har)* {1} See IZEHARITES, IZHAR. *A son of Kohath.*
Amram, and *I*, Hebron, and Uzziel.........Num 3:19 3324

IZEHARITES *(iz'-e-har-ites)* {1} See IZHARITE. *Descendants of Izehar.*
Amramites, and the family of the *I*.........Num 3:27 3325

IZHAR *(iz'-har)* {8} See IZEHAB, IZHARITES. *Same as Izehar.*
Amram, and *I*, and Hebron, and Uzziel..Ex 6:18 3324
And the sons of *I*...................................Ex 6:21 3324
Now Korah, the son of *I*, the son ....Num 16:1 3324
Amram, *I*, and Hebron, and Uzziel.........1Chr 6:2 3324
sons of Kohath were, Amram, and *I*.........1Chr 6:18 3324
The son of *I*, the son of Kohath,..............1Chr 6:38 3324
Amram, *I*, Hebron, and Uzziel, four........1Chr 23:12 3324
Of the sons of *I*.......................................1Chr 23:18 3324

IZHARITES *(iz'-har-ites)* {1} See IZEHARITES. *Same as Izeharites.*
Of the *I*; Shelomoth 1Chr 24:22 3325
Of the Amramites, and the *I*....................1Chr 26:23 3325
Of the *I*, Chenaniah and his sons 1Chr 26:29 3325

IZLIAH See JEZLIAH.

IZRAHIAH *(iz-ra-hi'-ah)* {2} See JEZRAHIAH. *Grandson of Tola.*
the sons of Uzzi; *I*...................................1Chr 7:3 3156
and the sons of *I*......................................1Chr 7:3 3156

IZRAHITE *(iz'-ra-hite)* {1} See EZRAHITE. *Family name of Shamhuth.*
fifth month was Shamhuth the *I*.............1Chr 27:8 3155

IZRI *(iz'-ri)* {1} See ZERI. *A sanctuary servant.*
The fourth to *I*, he, his sons, and............1Chr 25:11 3342

IZZIAH See JEZIAH.

J

JAAKAN *(ja'-a-kan)* {1} See AKAN, BENE-JAAKAN. *A son of Ezer.*
of the children of *J* to Mosera ....Deut 10:6 3292

JAAKOBAH *(ja-ak'-o-bah)* {1} *A descendant of Simeon.*
And Elioenai, and *J*, and Jeshohaiah, ...1Chr 4:36 3291

JAALA *(ja'-a-lah)* {1} See JAALAH. *A family of exiles.*
The children of *J*, the children ....Neh 7:58 3279

JAALAH *(ja'-a-lah)* {1} See JAALA. *Same as Jaala.*
The children of *J*, the children ....Ezr 2:56 3279

JAALAM *(ja'-a-lam)* {4} *A son of Esau.*
And Aholibamah bare Jeush, and *J*.........Gen 36:5 3281
and she bare to Esau Jeush, and *J*.........Gen 36:14 3281
duke Jeush, duke *J*, duke Korah.............Gen 36:18 3281
Eliphaz, Reuel, and Jeush, and *J*............1Chr 1:35 3281

JAANAI *(ja'-a-nahee)* {1} *A Gadite.*
chief, and Shapham the next, and *J*........1Chr 5:12 3285

JAAR See WOOD.

JAARE-OREGIM *(ja'-a-re-or'-eg-im)* {1} See JAIR. *Father of Elhanan.*
where Elhanan the son of *J*.....................2Sa 21:19 3296

JAASAU *(ja-a'-saw)* {1} *Married a foreigner in exile.*
Mattaniah, Mattenai, and *J*....................Ezr 10:37 3299

JAASIEL *(ja-a'-se-el)* {1} *A son of Abner.*
of Benjamin, *J* the son of Abner.............1Chr 27:21 3300

JAASU See JAASAU.

JAAZANIAH *(ja-az-a-ni'-ah)* {4} See JEZANIAH.
1. A son of a Maachathite.
J the son of a Maachathite, they 2Kin 25:23 2970
2. A chief Rechabite.
Then I took *J* the son of Jeremiah ....Jer 35:3 2970
3. Son of Shaphan.
them stood *J* the son of Shaphan............Eze 8:11 2970
4. Son of Azur.
whom I saw *J* the son of Azur.................Eze 11:1 2970

JAAZER *(ja-a'-zer)* {2} See JAZER. *A city in Gilead.*
And Moses sent to spy out *J*...................Num 21:32 3270
And Atroth, Shophan, and *J*, and.............Num 32:35 3270

JAAZIAH *(ja-a-zi'-ah)* {2} *A descendant of Merari.*
the sons of *J*; Beno..................................1Chr 24:26 3269
The sons of Merari by *J*...........................1Chr 24:27 3269

JA-AZIEL See BEN.

JAAZIEL *(ja-a'-ze-el)* {1} See AZIEL. *A priest.*
degree, Zechariah, Ben, and *J*................1Chr 15:18 3268

JABAL *(ja'-bal)* {1} *A son of Adah.*
And Adah bare *J*.......................................Gen 4:20 2989

JABBOK *(jab'-bok)* {7} *A brook in Bashan.*
sons, and passed over the ford *J*.............Gen 32:22 2999
his land from Arnon unto *J*......................Num 21:24 2999
nor unto any place of the river *J*.............Deut 2:37 2999
the border even unto the river *J*..............Deut 3:16 2999
Gilead, even unto the river *J*...................Josh 12:2 2999
of Egypt, from Arnon even unto *J*............Judg 11:13 2999
Amorites, from Arnon even unto *J*...........Judg 11:22 2999

JABESH *(ja'-besh)* {12} See JABESH-GILEAD.
1. A city in Gad.
all the men of *J* said unto Nahash 1Sa 11:1 3003
And the elders of *J* said unto him...........1Sa 11:3 3003
him the tidings of the men of *J*................1Sa 11:5 3003
came and shewed it to the men of *J*........1Sa 11:9 3003
Therefore the men of *J* said.....................1Sa 11:10 3003
wall of Beth-shan, and came to *J*............1Sa 31:12 3003
and buried them under a tree at *J*...........1Sa 31:13 3003
of his sons, and brought them to *J*..........1Chr 10:12 3003
their bones under the oak in *J*.................1Chr 10:12 3003
2. Father of Shallum.
Shallum the son of *J* conspired...............2Kin 15:10 3003
Shallum the son of *J* began to.................2Kin 15:13 3003
Shallum the son of *J* in Samaria.............2Kin 15:14 3003

JABESH-GILEAD *(ja'-besh-ghil'-e-ad)* {12} *Same as Jabesh 1.*
the camp from *J* to the assembly.....Judg 21:8 3003,1568
of the inhabitants of *J* there...........Judg 21:9 3003,1568
smite the inhabitants of *J* with ....Judg 21:10 3003,1568
of *J* four hundred young virgins......Judg 21:12 3003,1568
had saved alive of the women of *J*...Judg 21:14 3003,1568
came up, and encamped against *J*...1Sa 11:1 3003,1568
shall ye say unto the men of *J*.........1Sa 11:9 3003,1568
of *J* heard of that which the............1Sa 31:11 3003,1568
That the men of *J* were they that....2Sa 2:4 3003,1568
sent messengers unto the men of *J*..2Sa 2:5 3003,1568
his son from the men of *J*................2Sa 21:12 3003,1568
when all *J* heard all that the...........1Chr 10:11 3003,1568

JABEZ *(ja'-bez)* {4}
1. A city in Judah.
of the scribes which dwelt at *J*...............1Chr 2:55 3258
2. Head of a family of Judah.
J was more honourable than his 1Chr 4:9 3258
and his mother called his name *J*...........1Chr 4:9 3258
J called on the God of Israel, ...1Chr 4:10 3258

JABIN *(ja'-bin)* {7} See JABIN'S.
1. A king of Hazor.
when *J* king of Hazor had heard............Josh 11:1 2985
2. Another king of Hazor.
into the hand of *J* king of Canaan ....Judg 4:2 2985
peace between *J* the king of Hazor ....Judg 4:17 2985
So God subdued on that day *J* the..........Judg 4:23 2985
prevailed against *J* the king of...............Judg 4:24 2985
had destroyed *J* king of Canaan..............Judg 4:24 2985
as to Sisera, as to *J*, at the.......................Ps 83:9 2985

JABIN'S {1}
Sisera, the captain of *J* army ....Judg 4:7 2985

JABNEEL *(jab'-ne-el)* {2} See JABNEH.
1. A city in Judah.
mount Baalah, and went out unto *J*........Josh 15:11 2995
2. A city in Naphtali.
Zaanannim, and Adami, Nekeb, and *J*....Josh 19:33 2995

JABNEH *(jab'-neh)* {1} See JABNEEL. *A Philistine city.*
wall of Gath, and the wall of *J*...............2Chr 26:6 2996

JACAN See JACHAN.

JACHAN *(ja'-kan)* {1} See AKAN. *Head of a Gadite family.*
and Sheba, and Jorai, and *J*.....................1Chr 5:13 3275

JACHIN *(ja'-kin)* {8} See JACHINITES, JARIB.
1. A son of Simeon.
Jemuel, and Jamin, and Ohad, and *J*......Gen 46:10 3199
Jemuel, and Jamin, and Ohad, and *J*......Ex 6:15 3199
of *J*, the family of the ....Num 26:12 3199
2. A pillar of Solomon's Temple.
and called the name thereof *J*.................1Kin 7:21 3199
name of that on the right hand *J*.............2Chr 3:17 3199
3. A family of exiles.
Jedaiah, and Jehoiarib, and *J*..................1Chr 9:10 3199
Jedaiah the son of Joiarib, *J*....................Neh 11:10 3199
4. A sanctuary servant.
The one and twentieth to *J*.......................1Chr 24:17 3199

JACHINITES *(ja'-kin-ites)* {1} *Descendants of Jachin 1.*
of Jachin, the family of the *J*...................Num 26:12 3200

JACINTH {2}
breastplates of fire, and of *j*....................Rev 9:17 *5191*
the eleventh, a *j*...Rev 21:20 *5192*

JACOB *(ja'-cub)* {358} See ISRAEL, JACOB'S, JAMES.
1. Son of Isaac and Rebekah.
and his name was called *J*.......................Gen 25:26 3290
J was a plain man, dwelling in.................Gen 25:27 3290
but Rebekah loved *J*..................................Gen 25:28 3290
And *J* sod pottage.......................................Gen 25:29 3290
And Esau said to *J*, Feed me, I..................Gen 25:30 3290
J said, Sell me this day thy ....Gen 25:31 3290
J said, Swear to me this day.......................Gen 25:33 3290
and he sold his birthright unto *J*................Gen 25:33 3290
Then *J* gave Esau bread and pottage ....Gen 25:34 3290
And Rebekah spake unto *J* her son............Gen 27:6 3290
J said to Rebekah his mother, ...Gen 27:11 3290
put them upon *J* her younger son................Gen 27:15 3290
into the hand of her son *J*..........................Gen 27:17 3290
J said unto his father, I am Esau.................Gen 27:19 3290
And Isaac said unto *J*, Come near, ...Gen 27:21 3290
J went near unto Isaac his father................Gen 27:22 3290
had made an end of blessing *J*.....................Gen 27:30 3290
J was yet scarce gone out from ....Gen 27:30 3290
said, Is not he rightly named *J*....................Gen 27:36 3290
Esau hated *J* because of the........................Gen 27:41 3290
then will I slay my brother *J*.......................Gen 27:41 3290
called *J* her younger son, and said..............Gen 27:42 3290
if *J* take a wife of the daughters ....Gen 27:46 3290
And Isaac called *J*, and blessed him...........Gen 28:1 3290
And Isaac sent away *J*...............................Gen 28:5 3290
Esau saw that Isaac had blessed *J* ....Gen 28:6 3290
that *J* obeyed his father and his.................Gen 28:7 3290
J went out from Beer-sheba, and.................Gen 28:10 3290
J awaked out of his sleep, and he...............Gen 28:16 3290
J rose up early in the morning, ...Gen 28:18 3290
J vowed a vow, saying, If God ....Gen 28:20 3290
Then *J* went on his journey, and ....Gen 29:1 3290
J said unto them, My brethren, ...Gen 29:4 3290
when *J* saw Rachel the daughter of ....Gen 29:10 3290
that *J* went near, and rolled the ....Gen 29:10 3290
J kissed Rachel, and lifted up his.................Gen 29:11 3290
J told Rachel that he was her.......................Gen 29:12 3290
the tidings of *J* his sister's son ....Gen 29:13 3290
And Laban said unto *J*, Because ....Gen 29:15 3290
And *J* loved Rachel......................................Gen 29:18 3290
J served seven years for Rachel ....Gen 29:20 3290
J said unto Laban, Give me my....................Gen 29:21 3290
J did so, and fulfilled her week....................Gen 29:28 3290
saw that she bare *J* no children....................Gen 30:1 3290
and said unto *J*, Give me children,...............Gen 30:1 3290
and *J* went in unto her ....Gen 30:4 3290
Bilhah conceived, and bare *J* a son ....Gen 30:5 3290
again, and bare *J* a second son....................Gen 30:7 3290
her maid, and gave her *J* to wife..................Gen 30:9 3290
Zilpah Leah's maid bare *J* a son ....Gen 30:10 3290
Leah's maid bare *J* a second son.................Gen 30:12 3290
J came out of the field in the ....Gen 30:16 3290
and bare *J* the fifth son ....Gen 30:17 3290
again, and bare *J* the sixth son ....Gen 30:19 3290
that *J* said unto Laban, Send me ....Gen 30:25 3290
J said, Thou shalt not give me.....................Gen 30:31 3290
journey betwixt himself and *J* ....Gen 30:36 3290
J fed the rest of Laban's flocks ....Gen 30:36 3290
J took him rods of green poplar, ...Gen 30:37 3290
J did separate the lambs, and set..................Gen 30:40 3290
that *J* laid the rods before the ....Gen 30:41 3290
J hath taken away all that was ....Gen 31:1 3290
J beheld the countenance of Laban ....Gen 31:2 3290
And the LORD said unto *J*, Return.................Gen 31:3 3290
J sent and called Rachel and Leah................Gen 31:4 3290
unto me in a dream, saying, *J* ....Gen 31:11 3290
Then *J* rose up, and set his sons...................Gen 31:17 3290
J stole away unawares to Laban ....Gen 31:20 3290
on the third day that *J* was fled ....Gen 31:22 3290
speak not to *J* either good or bad..................Gen 31:24 3290
Then Laban overtook *J*...............................Gen 31:25 3290
Now *J* had pitched his tent in the.................Gen 31:25 3290
And Laban said to *J*, What hast....................Gen 31:26 3290
speak not to *J* either good or bad.................Gen 31:29 3290
J answered and said to Laban,......................Gen 31:31 3290
For *J* knew not that Rachel had...................Gen 31:32 3290
J was wroth, and chode with Laban ....Gen 31:36 3290
J answered and said to Laban, What ....Gen 31:36 3290
And Laban answered and said unto *J*............Gen 31:43 3290
J took a stone, and set it up for ....Gen 31:45 3290
J said unto his brethren, Gather ....Gen 31:46 3290
but *J* called it Galeed ....Gen 31:47 3290
And Laban said to *J*, Behold this ....Gen 31:51 3290
J sware by the fear of his father...................Gen 31:53 3290
Then *J* offered sacrifice upon the..................Gen 31:54 3290
J went on his way, and the angels ....Gen 32:1 3290
when *J* saw them, he said, This is..................Gen 32:2 3290
J sent messengers before him to ....Gen 32:3 3290
Thy servant *J* saith thus, I have ....Gen 32:4 3290
And the messengers returned to *J*..................Gen 32:6 3290
Then *J* was greatly afraid and........................Gen 32:7 3290
J said, O God of my father ....Gen 32:9 3290
thy servant *J* is behind us..............................Gen 32:20 3290
And *J* was left alone ....Gen 32:24 3290
And he said, *J*..Gen 32:27 3290
name shall be called no more *J*......................Gen 32:28 3290

J

J asked him, and said, Tell me, I Gen 32:29 3290
J called the name of the place Gen 32:30 3290
J lifted up his eyes, and looked, Gen 33:1 3290
J said, Nay, I pray thee, if now Gen 33:10 3290
J journeyed to Succoth, and built Gen 33:17 3290
J came to Shalem, a city of Gen 33:18 3290
of Leah, which she bare unto *J* Gen 34:1 3290
unto Dinah the daughter of *J* Gen 34:3 3290
J heard that he had defiled Dinah Gen 34:5 3290
J held his peace until they were Gen 34:5 3290
out unto *J* to commune with him Gen 34:6 3290
the sons of *J* came out of the Gen 34:7 3290
the sons of *J* answered Shechem and Gen 34:13 3290
sore, that two of the sons of *J* Gen 34:25 3290
The sons of *J* came upon the slain Gen 34:27 3290
J said to Simeon and Levi, Ye have Gen 34:30 3290
And God said unto *J*, Arise, go up Gen 35:1 3290
Then *J* said unto his household, Gen 35:2 3290
they gave unto *J* all the strange Gen 35:4 3290
J hid them under the oak which Gen 35:4 3290
not pursue after the sons of *J* Gen 35:5 3290
So *J* came to Luz, which is in the Gen 35:6 3290
And God appeared unto *J* again Gen 35:9 3290
God said unto him, Thy name is *J* Gen 35:10 3290
shall not be called any more *J* Gen 35:10 3290
J set up a pillar in the place Gen 35:14 3290
J called the name of the place Gen 35:15 3290
J set a pillar upon her grave Gen 35:20 3290
Now the sons of *J* were twelve Gen 35:22 3290
these are the sons of *J*, which Gen 35:26 3290
J came unto Isaac his father unto Gen 35:27 3290
and his sons Esau and *J* buried him Gen 35:29 3290
from the face of his brother *J* Gen 36:6 3290
J dwelt in the land wherein his Gen 37:1 3290
These are the generations of *J* Gen 37:2 3290
J rent his clothes, and put Gen 37:34 3290
Now when *J* saw that there was Gen 42:1 3290
J said unto his sons, Why do ye Gen 42:1 3290
J sent not with his brethren Gen 42:4 3290
they came unto *J* their father Gen 42:29 3290
J their father said unto them, Me Gen 42:36 3290
of Canaan unto *J* their father Gen 45:25 3290
the spirit of *J* their father Gen 45:27 3290
of the night, and said, *J*, *J* Gen 46:2 3290
J rose up from Beer-sheba Gen 46:5 3290
of Israel carried *J* their father Gen 46:5 3290
of Canaan, and came into Egypt, *J* Gen 46:6 3290
Israel, which came into Egypt, *J* Gen 46:8 3290
she bare unto *J* in Padan-aram Gen 46:15 3290
and these she bare unto *J* Gen 46:18 3290
of Rachel, which were born to *J* Gen 46:22 3290
and she bare these unto *J* Gen 46:25 3290
souls that came with *J* into Egypt Gen 46:26 3290
all the souls of the house of *J* Gen 46:27 3290
And Joseph brought in *J* his father Gen 47:7 3290
and *J* blessed Pharaoh Gen 47:7 3290
And Pharaoh said unto *J*, How old Gen 47:8 3290
J said unto Pharaoh, The days of Gen 47:9 3290
J blessed Pharaoh, and went out Gen 47:10 3290
J lived in the land of Egypt Gen 47:28 3290
so the whole age of *J* was an Gen 47:28 3290
And one told *J*, and said, Behold, Gen 48:2 3290
J said unto Joseph, God Almighty Gen 48:3 3290
J called unto his sons, and said, Gen 49:1 3290
together, and hear, ye sons of *J* Gen 49:2 3290
I will divide them in *J*, and Gen 49:7 3290
the hands of the mighty God of *J* Gen 49:24 3290
when *J* had made an end of Gen 49:33 3290
to Abraham, to Isaac, and to *J* Gen 50:24 3290
man and his household came with *J* Ex 1:1 3290
the loins of *J* were seventy souls Ex 1:5 3290
Abraham, with Isaac, and with *J* Ex 2:24 3290
the God of Isaac, and the God of *J* Ex 3:6 3290
the God of Isaac, and the God of *J* Ex 3:15 3290
God of Abraham, of Isaac, and of *J* Ex 3:16 3290
the God of Isaac, and the God of *J* Ex 4:5 3290
Abraham, unto Isaac, and unto *J* Ex 6:3 3290
it to Abraham, to Isaac, and to *J* Ex 6:8 3290
shalt thou say to the house of *J* Ex 19:3 3290
unto Abraham, to Isaac, and to *J* Ex 33:1 3290
I remember my covenant with *J* Lev 26:42 3290
Abraham, unto Isaac, and unto *J* Num 32:11 3290
fathers, Abraham, Isaac, and *J* Deut 1:8 3290
to Abraham, to Isaac, and to *J* Deut 6:10 3290
thy fathers, Abraham, Isaac, and *J* Deut 9:5 3290
servants, Abraham, Isaac, and *J* Deut 9:27 3290
to Abraham, to Isaac, and to *J* Deut 29:13 3290
to Abraham, to Isaac, and to *J* Deut 30:20 3290
Abraham, unto Isaac, and unto *J* Deut 34:4 3290
And I gave unto Isaac *J* and Esau Josh 24:4 3290
but *J* and his children went down Josh 24:4 3290
in a parcel of ground which *J* Josh 24:32 3290
When *J* was come into Egypt, and 1Sa 12:8 3290
with Abraham, Isaac, and *J* 2Kin 13:23 3290
yet I loved *J*, Mal 1:2 3290
and Isaac begat *J* Mt 1:2 *2384*
J begat Judas and his brethren Mt 1:2 *2384*
down with Abraham, and Isaac, and *J* Mt 8:11 *2384*
the God of Isaac, and the God of *J* Mt 22:32 *2384*
the God of Isaac, and the God of *J* Mk 12:26 *2384*
over the house of *J* for ever Lk 1:33 *2384*
Which was the son of *J*, which was Lk 3:34 *2384*
shall see Abraham, and Isaac, and *J* Lk 13:28 *2384*
the God of Isaac, and the God of *J* Lk 20:37 *2384*
that *J* gave to his son Joseph Jn 4:5 *2384*
thou greater than our father *J* Jn 4:12 *2384*
of Abraham, and of Isaac, and of *J* Acts 3:13 *2384*
and Isaac begat *J* Acts 7:8 *2384*
J begat the twelve patriarchs Acts 7:8 *2384*
But when *J* heard that there was Acts 7:12 *2384*
and called his father *J* to him Acts 7:14 *2384*
So *J* went down into Egypt, and Acts 7:15 *2384*
the God of Isaac, and the God of *J* Acts 7:32 *2384*
a tabernacle for the God of *J* Acts 7:46 *2384*
J have I loved, but Esau have I Rom 9:13 *2384*
turn away ungodliness from *J* Rom 11:26 *2384*
in tabernacles with Isaac and *J* Heb 11:9 *2384*
By faith Isaac blessed *J* and Esau Heb 11:20 *2384*
By faith *J*, when he was a dying, Heb 11:21 *2384*

2. Father of Joseph; ancestor of Jesus.

and Matthan begat *J* Mt 1:15 *2384*
J begat Joseph the husband of Mt 1:16 *2384*

3. Descendants of Jacob.

east, saying, Come, curse me *J* Num 23:7 3290
Who can count the dust of *J* Num 23:10 3290
He hath not beheld iniquity in *J* Num 23:21 3290
there is no enchantment against *J* Num 23:23 3290
this time it shall be said of *J* Num 23:23 3290
How goodly are thy tents, O *J* Num 24:5 3290
there shall come a Star out of *J* Num 24:17 3290
Out of *J* shall come he that shall Num 24:19 3290
J is the lot of his inheritance Deut 32:9 3290
of the congregation of *J* Deut 33:4 3290
They shall teach *J* thy judgments Deut 33:10 3290
the fountain of *J* shall be upon a Deut 33:28 3290
the anointed of the God of *J* 2Sa 23:1 3290
of the tribes of the sons of *J* 1Kin 18:31 3290
LORD commanded the children of *J* 2Kin 17:34 3290
his servant, ye children of *J* 1Chr 16:13 3290
confirmed the same to *J* for a law 1Chr 16:17 3290
J shall rejoice, and Israel shall Ps 14:7 3290
name of the God of *J* defend thee Ps 20:1 3290
all ye the seed of *J*, glorify him Ps 22:23 3290
seek him, that seek thy face, O *J* Ps 24:6 3290
command deliverances for *J* Ps 44:4 3290
the God of *J* is our refuge Ps 46:7 3290
the God of *J* is our refuge Ps 46:11 3290
the excellency of *J* whom he loved Ps 47:4 3290
J shall rejoice, and Israel shall Ps 53:6 3290
in *J* unto the ends of the earth Ps 59:13 3290
will sing praises to the God of *J* Ps 75:9 3290
At thy rebuke, O God of *J* Ps 76:6 3290
thy people, the sons of *J* Ps 77:15 3290
he established a testimony in *J* Ps 78:5 3290
so a fire was kindled against *J* Ps 78:21 3290
brought him to feed *J* his people Ps 78:71 3290
For they have devoured *J*, and laid Ps 79:7 3290
a joyful noise unto the God of *J* Ps 81:1 3290
Israel, and a law of the God of *J* Ps 81:4 3290
give ear, O God of *J* Ps 84:8 3290
brought back the captivity of *J* Ps 85:1 3290
more than all the dwellings of *J* Ps 87:2 3290
shall the God of *J* regard it Ps 94:7 3290
judgment and righteousness in *J* Ps 99:4 3290
ye children of *J* his chosen Ps 105:6 3290
the same unto *J* for a law Ps 105:10 3290
J sojourned in the land of Ham Ps 105:23 3290
the house of *J* from a people of Ps 114:1 3290
at the presence of the God of *J* Ps 114:7 3290
and vowed unto the mighty God of *J* Ps 132:2 3290
for the mighty God of *J* Ps 132:5 3290
LORD hath chosen *J* unto himself Ps 135:4 3290
hath the God of *J* for his help Ps 146:5 3290
He sheweth his word unto *J* Ps 147:19 3290
to the house of the God of *J* Is 2:3 3290
O house of *J*, come ye, and let us Is 2:5 3290
thy people the house of *J* Is 2:6 3290
his face from the house of *J* Is 8:17 3290
The Lord sent a word into *J* Is 9:8 3290
as are escaped of the house of *J* Is 10:20 3290
return, even the remnant of *J* Is 10:21 3290
For the LORD will have mercy on *J* Is 14:1 3290
shall cleave to the house of *J* Is 14:1 3290
that the glory of *J* shall be made Is 17:4 3290
them that come of *J* to take root Is 27:6 3290
shall the iniquity of *J* be purged Is 27:9 3290
concerning the house of *J* Is 29:22 3290
J shall not now be ashamed, Is 29:22 3290
and sanctify the Holy One of *J* Is 29:23 3290
Why sayest thou, O *J*, and speakest Is 40:27 3290
J whom I have chosen, the seed of Is 41:8 3290
Fear not, thou worm *J*, and ye men Is 41:14 3290
reasons, saith the King of *J* Is 41:21 3290
Who gave *J* for a spoil, and Israel Is 42:24 3290
the LORD that created thee, O *J* Is 43:1 3290
thou hast not called upon me, O *J* Is 43:22 3290
have given *J* to the curse, and Is 43:28 3290
Yet now hear, O *J* my servant Is 44:1 3290
Fear not, O *J*, my servant Is 44:2 3290
call himself by the name of *J* Is 44:5 3290
Remember these, O *J* and Israel Is 44:21 3290
for the LORD hath redeemed *J* Is 44:23 3290
For *J* my servant's sake, and Is 45:4 3290
I said not unto the seed of *J* Is 45:19 3290
Hearken unto me, O house of *J* Is 46:3 3290
Hear ye this, O house of *J* Is 48:1 3290
Hearken unto me, O *J* and Israel, Is 48:12 3290
LORD hath redeemed his servant *J* Is 48:20 3290
to bring *J* again to him, Though Is 49:5 3290
to raise up the tribes of *J* Is 49:6 3290
thy Redeemer, the mighty One of *J* Is 49:26 3290
and the house of *J* their sins Is 58:1 3290
with the heritage of *J* thy father Is 58:14 3290
that turn from transgression in *J* Is 59:20 3290
thy Redeemer, the mighty One of *J* Is 60:16 3290
will bring forth a seed out of *J* Is 65:9 3290
word of the LORD, O house of *J* Jer 2:4 3290
Declare this in the house of *J* Jer 5:20 3290
The portion of *J* is not like them Jer 10:16 3290
for they have eaten up *J*, and Jer 10:25 3290
fear thou not, O my servant *J* Jer 30:10 3290
J shall return, and shall be in Jer 30:10 3290
Sing with gladness for *J*, and Jer 31:7 3290
For the LORD hath redeemed *J* Jer 31:11 3290
will I cast away the seed of *J* Jer 33:26 3290
the seed of Abraham, Isaac, and *J* Jer 33:26 3290
But fear not thou, O my servant *J* Jer 46:27 3290
J shall return, and be in rest and Jer 46:27 3290
O *J* my servant, saith the LORD Jer 46:28 3290
The portion of *J* is not like them Jer 51:19 3290
LORD hath commanded concerning *J* Lam 1:17 3290
up all the habitations of *J* Lam 2:2 3290
he burned against *J* like a Lam 2:3 3290
unto the seed of the house of *J* Eze 20:5 3290
that I have given to my servant *J* Eze 28:25 3290
I have given unto *J* my servant Eze 37:25 3290
I bring again the captivity of *J* Eze 39:25 3290
plow, and *J* shall break his clods Hos 10:11 3290
will punish *J* according to his Hos 12:2 3290
J fled into the country of Syria, Hos 12:12 3290
ye, and testify in the house of *J* Amos 3:13 3290
I abhor the excellency of *J* Amos 6:8 3290
by whom shall *J* arise Amos 7:2 3290
by whom shall *J* arise Amos 7:5 3290
hath sworn by the excellency of *J* Amos 8:7 3290
utterly destroy the house of *J* Amos 9:8 3290
brother *J* shame shall cover thee Obad 10 3290
the house of *J* shall possess Obad 17 3290
the house of *J* shall be a fire, Obad 18 3290
transgression of *J* is all this Mic 1:5 3290
What is the transgression of *J* Mic 1:5 3290
that art named the house of *J* Mic 2:7 3290
I will surely assemble, O *J* Mic 2:12 3290
Hear, I pray you, O heads of *J* Mic 3:1 3290
of might, to declare unto *J* his Mic 3:8 3290
you, ye heads of the house of *J* Mic 3:9 3290
and to the house of the God of *J* Mic 4:2 3290
the remnant of *J* shall be in the Mic 5:7 3290
the remnant of *J* shall be among Mic 5:8 3290
Thou wilt perform the truth to *J* Mic 7:20 3290
turned away the excellency of *J* Nah 2:2 3290
out of the tabernacles of *J* Mal 2:12 3290
ye sons of *J* are not consumed Mal 3:6 3290

JACOB'S *(ja'-cubs)* {19}

1. Refers to Jacob 1.

and said, The voice is *J* voice Gen 27:22 3290
Syrian, the brother of Rebekah, *J* Gen 28:5 3290
J anger was kindled against Gen 30:2 3290
were Laban's, and the stronger *J* Gen 30:42 3290
And Laban went into *J* tent Gen 31:33 3290
shalt say, They be thy servant *J* Gen 32:18 3290
the hollow of *J* thigh was out of Gen 32:25 3290
he touched the hollow of *J* thigh Gen 32:32 3290
Israel in lying with *J* daughter Gen 34:7 3290
he had delight in *J* daughter Gen 34:19 3290
J firstborn, and Simeon, and Levi, Gen 35:23 3290
J heart fainted, for he believed Gen 45:26 3290
Reuben, *J* firstborn Gen 46:8 3290
The sons of Rachel *J* wife Gen 46:19 3290
besides *J* sons' wives, all the Gen 46:26 3290
Was not Esau *J* brother Mal 1:2 3290
Now *J* well was there Jn 4:6 *2384*

2. Refers to Jacob 3.

it is even the time of *J* trouble Jer 30:7 3290
again the captivity of *J* tents Jer 30:18 3290

JADA *(ja'-dah)* {2} *A grandson of Jerahmeel.*
sons of Onam were, Shammai, and *J* 1Chr 2:28 3047
the sons of *J* the brother of 1Chr 2:32 3047

JADAH See JARAH.

JADAI See JADAU.

JADAU *(ja'-daw)* {1} *Married a foreigner in exile.*
Mattithiah, Zabad, Zebina, *J* Ezr 10:43 3035

JADDAI See JADAU.

JADDUA *(jad'-du-ah)* {3}

1. A Levite.

Meshezabeel, Zadok, *J*, Neh 10:21 3037

2. A priest.

Jonathan, and Jonathan begat *J* Neh 12:11 3037
Joiada, and Johanan, and *J* Neh 12:22 3037

JADON *(ja'-don)* {1} *A repairer of Jerusalem's wall.*
J the Meronothite, the men of Neh 3:7 3036

JAEL *(ja'-el)* {6} *The wife of Heber.*
of *J* the wife of Heber the Kenite Judg 4:17 3278
J went out to meet Sisera, and Judg 4:18 3278
Then *J* Heber's wife took a nail Judg 4:21 3278
J came out to meet him, and said Judg 4:22 3278
son of Anath, in the days of *J* Judg 5:6 3278
Blessed above women shall *J* the Judg 5:24 3278

JAGUR *(ja'-gur)* {1} *A town in Judah.*
were Kabzeel, and Eder, and *J* Josh 15:21 3017

JAH *(jah)* {1} See JEHOVAH. *A shortened form of Jehovah.*
upon the heavens by his name *J* Ps 68:4 3050

JAHALALEEL See JAHLEEL.

JAHATH *(ja'-hath)* {8}

1. A descendant of Shobal.

Reaiah the son of Shobal begat *J* 1Chr 4:2 3189
and *J* begat Ahumai, and Lahad 1Chr 4:2 3189

2. A descendant of Gershom.
J his son, Zimmah his son, ... 1Chr 6:20 3189
The son of *J*, the son of Gershom, ... 1Chr 6:43 3189
3. Another descendant of Gershom.
And the sons of Shimei were, *J* ... 1Chr 23:10 3189
J was the chief, and Zizah the ... 1Chr 23:11 3189
4. A descendant of Kohath.
of the sons of Shelomoth; *J* ... 1Chr 24:22 3189
5. A descendant of Merari.
and the overseers of them were *J* ... 2Chr 34:12 3189

JAHAZ *(ja'-haz)* {5} See Jahaza, Jahazah, Jahzah. *A Levitical city in Reuben.*
and he came to *J*, and fought ... Num 21:23 3096
and all his people, to fight at *J* ... Deut 2:32 3096
people together, and pitched in *J* ... Judg 11:20 3096
voice shall be heard even unto *J* ... Is 15:4 3096
even unto Elealeh, and even unto *J* ... Jer 48:34 3096

JAHAZA *(ja-ha'-zah)* {1} See Jahaz. *Same as Jahaz.*
And *J*, and Kedemoth, and Mephaath, ... Josh 13:18 3096

JAHAZAH *(ja-ha'-zah)* {2} See Jahaz. *Same as Jahaz.*
suburbs, and *J* with her suburbs, ... Josh 21:36 3096
upon Holon, and upon *J*, and upon ... Jer 48:21 3096

JAHAZIAH *(ja-ha-zi'-ah)* {1} *Son of Tikvah.*
J the son of Tikvah were employed ... Ezr 10:15 3167

JAHAZIEL *(ja-ha'-ze-el)* {6}
1. A captain in David's army.
Jeremiah, and *J*, and Johanan, and ... 1Chr 12:4 3166
2. A priest.
J the priests with trumpets ... 1Chr 16:6 3166
3. A son of Hebron.
J the third, and Jekameam the ... 1Chr 23:19 3166
J the third, Jekameam the fourth ... 1Chr 24:23 3166
4. A Levite.
Then upon *J* the son of Zechariah, ... 2Chr 20:14 3166
5. A family of exiles.
the son of *J*, and with him three ... Ezr 8:5 3166

JAHDAI *(jah'-dahee)* {1} *A descendant of Caleb.*
And the sons of *J* ... 1Chr 2:47 3056

JAHDIEL *(jah'-de-el)* {1} *Head of a family of Manasseh.*
and Jeremiah, and Hodaviah, and *J* ... 1Chr 5:24 3164

JAHDO *(jah'-do)* {1} *Son of Buz.*
son of Jeshishai, the son of *J* ... 1Chr 5:14 3163

JAHLEEL *(jah'-le-el)* {2} See Jahleelites. *A son of Zebulun.*
Sered, and Elon, and *J* ... Gen 46:14 3177
of *J*, the family of the ... Num 26:26 3177

JAHLEELITES *(jah'-le-el-ites)* {1} *Descendants of Jahleel.*
of Jahleel, the family of the *J* ... Num 26:26 3178

JAHMAI *(jah'-mahee)* {1} *A son of Tola.*
and Rephaiah, and Jeriel, and *J* ... 1Chr 7:2 3181

JAHZAH *(jah'-zah)* {1} See Jahaz. *A Levitical city in Reuben.*
suburbs, and *J* with her suburbs, ... 1Chr 6:78 3096

JAHZEEL *(jah'-ze-el)* {2} See Jahzeelites, Jahziel. *A son of Naphtali.*
J, and Guni, and Jezer, and Shillem ... Gen 46:24 3183
of *J*, the family of the ... Num 26:48 3183

JAHZEELITES *(jah'-ze-el-ites)* {1} *Descendants of Jahzeel.*
of Jahzeel, the family of the *J* ... Num 26:48 3184

JAHZEIAH See Jahaziah.

JAHZERAH *(jah'-ze-rah)* {1} See Ahazai. *The son of Meshullam.*
the son of Adiel, the son of *J* ... 1Chr 9:12 3170

JAHZIEL *(jah'-ze-el)* {1} See Jahzeel. *Same as Jahzeel.*
J, and Guni, and Jezer, and Shallum, ... 1Chr 7:13 3185

JAILER {1}
charging the *j* to keep them ... Acts 16:23 *1200*

JAIR *(ja'-ur)* {10} See Havoth-jair, Jaare-oregim, Jairite.
1. A descendant of Judah and Manasseh.
J the son of Manasseh went and ... Num 32:41 2971
J the son of Manasseh took all ... Deut 3:14 2971
towns of *J* the son of Manasseh ... 1Kin 4:13 2971
And Segub begat *J*, who had three ... 1Chr 2:22 2971
2. A judge.
And after him arose *J*, a Gileadite ... Judg 10:3 2971
J died, and was buried in Camon ... Judg 10:5 2971
3. A district in Bashan.
of Bashan, and all the towns of *J* ... Josh 13:30 2971
and Aram, with the towns of *J* ... 1Chr 2:23 2971
4. Father of Mordecai.
name was Mordecai, the son of *J* ... Est 2:5 2971
5. Father of Elhanan.
Elhanan the son of *J* slew Lahmi ... 1Chr 20:5 2971

JAIRITE *(ja'-ur-ite)* {1} *A descendant of Jair 1.*
Ira also the *J* was a chief ruler ... 2Sa 20:26 2972

JAIRUS *(ja-i'-rus)* {2} *A ruler of a synagogue.*
of the synagogue, *J* by name ... Mk 5:22 *2383*
behold, there came a man named *J* ... Lk 8:41 *2383*

JAKAN *(ja'-kan)* {1} See Akan, Jaakan. *A son of Ezer.*
Bilhan, and Zavan, and *J* ... 1Chr 1:42 3292

JAKEH *(ja'-keh)* {1} *Father of Agur.*
The words of Agur the son of *J* ... Prov 30:1 3348

JAKIM *(ja'-kim)* {2}
1. Son of Shimhi.
And *J*, and Zichri, and Zabdi, ... 1Chr 8:19 3356
2. A sanctuary servant.
to Eliashib, the twelfth to *J* ... 1Chr 24:12 3356

JAKIN See Jachinites.

JAKINITE See Jachinites.

JALAM See Jaalam.

JALON *(ja'-lon)* {1} *A son of Ezra.*
Jether, and Mered, and Epher, and *J* ... 1Chr 4:17 3210

JAMBRES *(jam'-brees)* {1} *An opponent of Moses.*
J withstood Moses, so do these ... 2Ti 3:8 *2387*

JAMES *(james)* {42} See Jacob.
1. Son of Zebedee.
J the son of Zebedee, and John his ... Mt 4:21 *2385*
J the son of Zebedee, and John his ... Mt 10:2 *2385*
six days Jesus taketh Peter, *J* ... Mt 17:1 *2385*
he saw *J* the son of Zebedee, and ... Mk 1:19 *2385*
house of Simon and Andrew, with *J* ... Mk 1:29 *2385*
And *J* the son of ... Mk 3:17 *2385*
and John the brother of *J* ... Mk 3:17 *2385*
J, and John the brother of *J* ... Mk 5:37 *2385*
Jesus taketh with him Peter, and *J* ... Mk 9:2 *2385*
And *J* and John, the sons of Zebedee ... Mk 10:35 *2385*
to be much displeased with *J* ... Mk 10:41 *2385*
against the temple, Peter and *J* ... Mk 13:3 *2385*
And he taketh with him Peter and *J* ... Mk 14:33 *2385*
And so was also *J*, and John, the ... Lk 5:10 *2385*
Peter,) and Andrew his brother, *J* ... Lk 6:14 *2385*
no man to go in, save Peter, and *J* ... Lk 8:51 *2385*
he took Peter and John and *J* ... Lk 9:28 *2385*
And when his disciples *J* and John ... Lk 9:54 *2385*
where abode both Peter, and *J* ... Acts 1:13 *2385*
he killed *J* the brother of John ... Acts 12:2 *2385*
2. Son of Alphaeus.
J the son of Alphaeus, and ... Mt 10:3 *2385*
J the son of Alphaeus, and ... Mk 3:18 *2385*
J the son of Alphaeus, and Simon ... Lk 6:15 *2385*
J the son of Alphaeus, and Simon ... Acts 1:13 *2385*
3. Brother of Jesus.
and his brethren, *J*, and Joses, and ... Mt 13:55 *2385*
and Mary the mother of *J* and Joses ... Mt 27:56 *2385*
the son of Mary, the brother of *J* ... Mk 6:3 *2385*
and Mary the mother of *J* the less ... Mk 15:40 *2385*
and Mary the mother of *J*, and ... Mk 16:1 *2385*
And Judas the brother of *J* ... Lk 6:16 *2385*
Joanna, and Mary the mother of *J* ... Lk 24:10 *2385*
and Judas the brother of *J* ... Acts 1:13 *2385*
said, Go shew these things unto *J* ... Acts 12:17 *2385*
J answered, saying, Men and ... Acts 15:13 *2385*
Paul went in with us unto *J* ... Acts 21:18 *2385*
After that, he was seen of *J* ... 1Cor 15:7 *2385*
save *J* the Lord's brother ... Gal 1:19 *2385*
And when *J*, Cephas, and John, who ... Gal 2:9 *2385*
before that certain came from *J* ... Gal 2:12 *2385*
J, a servant of God and of the ... Jas 1:1 *2385*
of Jesus Christ, and brother of *J* ... Jude 1 *2385*

JAMIN *(ja'-min)* {6} See Jaminites.
1. A son of Simeon.
Jemuel, and *J*, and Ohad, and Jachin, ... Gen 46:10 3226
Jemuel, and *J*, and Ohad, and Jachin, ... Ex 6:15 3226
of *J*, the family of the Jaminites ... Num 26:12 3226
sons of Simeon were, Nemuel, and *J* ... 1Chr 4:24 3226
2. A descendant of Hezron.
of Jerahmeel were, Maaz, and *J* ... 1Chr 2:27 3226
3. A priest.
Jeshua, and Bani, and Sherebiah, *J* ... Neh 8:7 3226

JAMINITES *(ja'-min-ites)* {1} *Descendants of Jamin.*
of Jamin, the family of the *J* ... Num 26:12 3228

JAMLECH *(jam'-lek)* {1} *A royal descendant of Simeon.*
And Meshobab, and *J*, and Joshah the ... 1Chr 4:34 3230

JANAI See Jaanai.

JANGLING {1}
have turned aside unto vain *j* ... 1Ti 1:6 *3150*

JANIM See Janum.

JANNA *(jan'-nah)* {1} *Father of Melchi; ancestor of Jesus.*
of Melchi, which was the son of *J* ... Lk 3:24 *2388*

JANNAI See Janna.

JANNES *(jan'-nees)* {1} *An opponent of Moses.*
Now as *J* and Jambres withstood ... 2Ti 3:8 *2389*

JANOAH *(ja-no'-ah)* {1} See Janohah. *A city in Naphtali.*
Ijon, and Abel-beth-maachah, and *J* ... 2Kin 15:29 3239

JANOHAH *(ja-no'-hah)* {2} See Janoah. *A city between Ephraim and Manasseh.*
and passed by it on the east to *J* ... Josh 16:6 3239
And it went down from *J* to Ataroth ... Josh 16:7 3239

JANUM *(ja'-num)* {1} *A city in Judah.*
J, and Beth-tappuah, and Aphekah ... Josh 15:53 3241

JAPHETH *(ja'-feth)* {11} *A son of Noah.*
and Noah begat Shem, Ham, and *J* ... Gen 5:32 3315
begat three sons, Shem, Ham, and *J* ... Gen 6:10 3315
Noah, and Shem, and Ham, and *J* ... Gen 7:13 3315
the ark, were Shem, and Ham, and *J* ... Gen 9:18 3315
J took a garment, and laid it upon ... Gen 9:23 3315
God shall enlarge *J*, and he shall ... Gen 9:27 3315
the sons of Noah, Shem, Ham, and *J* ... Gen 10:1 3315
The sons of *J*; Gomer ... Gen 10:2 3315
Eber, the brother of *J* the elder ... Gen 10:21 3315
Noah, Shem, Ham, and *J* ... 1Chr 1:4 3315
The sons of *J*; Gomer ... 1Chr 1:5 3315

JAPHIA *(ja-fi'-ah)* {5}
1. An Amorite king.
unto *J* king of Lachish, and unto ... Josh 10:3 3309
2. A town in Zebulun.
out to Daberath, and goeth up to *J* ... Josh 19:12 3309
3. A son of David.
also, and Elishua, and Nepheg, and *J* ... 2Sa 5:15 3309
And Nogah, and Nepheg, and *J* ... 1Chr 3:7 3309
And Nogah, and Nepheg, and *J* ... 1Chr 14:6 3309

JAPHLET *(jaf'-let)* {3} See Japhleti. *A grandson of Beriah.*
And Heber begat *J*, and Shomer, and ... 1Chr 7:32 3310
And the sons of *J* ... 1Chr 7:33 3310
These are the children of *J* ... 1Chr 7:33 3310

JAPHLETI *(jaf'-let-i)* {1} See Japhlet. *A landmark in Ephraim.*
down westward to the coast of *J* ... Josh 16:3 3311

JAPHLETITES See Japhleti.

JAPHO *(ja'-fo)* {1} See Joppa. *A city in Dan.*
Rakkon, with the border before *J* ... Josh 19:46 3305

JARAH *(ja'-rah)* {2} See Jehoadah. *A son of Ahaz.*
And Ahaz begat *J* ... 1Chr 9:42 3294
J begat Alemeth, and Azmaveth, and ... 1Chr 9:42 3294

JAREB *(ja'-reb)* {2} *An Assyrian king.*
the Assyrian, and sent to king *J* ... Hos 5:13 3377
Assyria for a present to king *J* ... Hos 10:6 3377

JARED *(ja'-red)* {6} See Jered.
1. A descendant of Seth.
sixty and five years, and begat *J* ... Gen 5:15 3382
after he begat *J* eight hundred ... Gen 5:16 3382
J lived an hundred sixty and two ... Gen 5:18 3382
J lived after he begat Enoch ... Gen 5:19 3382
all the days of *J* were nine ... Gen 5:20 3382
2. Father of Enoch; ancestor of Jesus.
of Enoch, which was the son of *J* ... Lk 3:37 *2391*

JARESIAH *(ja-re-si'-ah)* {1} *A descendant of Benjamin.*
And *J*, and Eliah, and Zichri, the ... 1Chr 8:27 3298

JARHA *(jar'-hah)* {2} *An Egyptian servant.*
an Egyptian, whose name was *J* ... 1Chr 2:34 3398
daughter to *J* his servant to wife ... 1Chr 2:35 3398

J

JARIB *(ja'-rib)* {3} See Jachin.
1. A son of Simeon.
Simeon were, Nemuel, and Jamin, *J* ... 1Chr 4:24 3402
2. A family of exiles.
and for Elnathan, and for *J* ... Ezr 8:16 3402
3. Married a foreigner.
Maaseiah, and Eliezer, and *J* ... Ezr 10:18 3402

JARMUTH *(jar'-muth)* {7} See Remeth.
1. A city in Judah.
Hebron, and unto Piram king of *J* ... Josh 10:3 3412
the king of Hebron, the king of *J* ... Josh 10:5 3412
the king of Hebron, the king of *J* ... Josh 10:23 3412
The king of *J*, one ... Josh 12:11 3412
J, and Adullam, Socoh, and Azekah, ... Josh 15:35 3412
J with her suburbs, En-gannim ... Josh 21:29 3412
En-rimmon, and at Zareah, and at *J* ... Neh 11:29 3412

JAROAH *(ja-ro'-ah)* {1} *A descendant of Gad.*
the son of Huri, the son of *J* ... 1Chr 5:14 3386

JASHAR See Jasher.

JASHEN *(ja'-shen)* {1} See Hashem. *Father of several "mighty men" of David.*
the Shaalbonite, of the sons of *J* ... 2Sa 23:32 3464

JASHER *(ja'-shur)* {2} *A book of songs.*
not this written in the book of *J* ... Josh 10:13 3477
it is written in the book of *J* ... 2Sa 1:18 3477

JASHOBEAM *(jash-o'-be-am)* {3}
1. A "mighty man" of David.
J, a Hachmonite, the chief of the ... 1Chr 11:11 3434
month was *J* the son of Zabdiel ... 1Chr 27:2 3434
2. Another "mighty man" of David.
and Azareel, and Joezer, and *J* ... 1Chr 12:6 3434

JASHUB *(ja'-shub)* {3} See Jashubi-lehem, Job, Jashubites, Shear-jashub.
1. A son of Issachar.
Of *J*, the family of the ... Num 26:24 3437
Issachar were, Tola, and Puah, *J* ... 1Chr 7:1 3437
2. Married a foreigner in exile.
Meshullam, Malluch, and Adaiah, *J* ... Ezr 10:29 3437

JASHUBI-LAHEM See Jashubi-lehem.

JASHUBI-LEHEM *(jash'-u-bi-le'-hem)* {1} *A descendant of Shelah.*
had the dominion in Moab, and *J* ... 1Chr 4:22 3433

JASHUBITES *(jash'-u-bites)* {1} *Descendants of Jashub.*
Of Jashub, the family of the *J* ... Num 26:24 3432

JASIEL *(ja'-se-el)* {1} *A "mighty man" of David.*
and Obed, and *J* the Mesobaite ... 1Chr 11:47 3300

JASON *(ja'-sun)* {5}
1. A Christian in Thessalonica.
and assaulted the house of *J* ... Acts 17:5 *2394*
they found them not, they drew *J* ... Acts 17:6 *2394*
Whom *J* hath received: ... Acts 17:7 *2394*
when they had taken security of *J* ... Acts 17:9 *2394*
2. A relative of Paul.
my workfellow, and Lucius, and *J* ... Rom 16:21 *2394*

JASPER {7}
row a beryl, and an onyx, and a *j* ... Ex 28:20 3471
row, a beryl, an onyx, and a *j* ... Ex 39:13 3471
the beryl, the onyx, and the *j* ... Eze 28:13 3471
sat was to look upon like a *j* ... Rev 4:3 *2393*
precious, even like a *j* stone ... Rev 21:11 *2393*
of the wall of it was of *j* ... Rev 21:18 *2393*
The first foundation was *j* ... Rev 21:19 *2393*

JATHNIEL *(jath'-ne-el)* {1} *A son of Meshelemiah.*
Zebadiah the third, *J* the fourth, ... 1Chr 26:2 3496

JATTIR *(jat'-tur)* {4} *A Levitical city in Judah.*
And in the mountains, Shamir, and *J* ... Josh 15:48 3492
J with her suburbs, and Eshtemoa ... Josh 21:14 3492
and to them which were in *J* ... 1Sa 30:27 3492
and Libnah with her suburbs, and *J* ... 1Chr 6:57 3492

JAVAN *(ja'-van)* {7}
1. A son of Joktan.
Gomer, and Magog, and Madai, and *J* ... Gen 10:2 3120
And the sons of *J* ... Gen 10:4 3120
Gomer, and Magog, and Madai, and *J* ... 1Chr 1:5 3120
And the sons of *J* ... 1Chr 1:7 3120
2. Descendants of Javan 1.
that draw the bow, to Tubal, and *J* ... Is 66:19 3120
3. A city in southern Arabia.
J, Tubal, and Meshech, they were ... Eze 27:13 3120
J going to and fro occupied in thy ... Eze 27:19 3120

JAVELIN {7}
and took a *j* in his hand ... Num 25:7 7420
there was a *j* in Saul's hand ... 1Sa 18:10 2595
And Saul cast the *j* ... 1Sa 18:11 2595
his house with his *j* in his hand ... 1Sa 19:9 2595
David even to the wall with the *j* ... 1Sa 19:10 2595
he smote the *j* into the wall ... 1Sa 19:10 2595
Saul cast a *j* at him to smite him ... 1Sa 20:33 2595

JAW {4}
with the *j* of an ass have I slain ... Judg 15:16 3895
an hollow place that was in the *j* ... Judg 15:19 3895
or bore his *j* through with a ... Job 41:2 3895
their *j* teeth as knives, to ... Prov 30:14 4973

JAWBONE {3}
And he found a new *j* of an ass ... Judg 15:15 3895
With the *j* of an ass, heaps upon ... Judg 15:16 3895
cast away the *j* out of his hand ... Judg 15:17 3895

JAWS {6}
I brake the *j* of the wicked, and ... Job 29:17 4973
and my tongue cleaveth to my *j* ... Ps 22:15 4455
a bridle in the *j* of the people ... Is 30:28 3895
But I will put hooks in thy *j* ... Eze 29:4 3895
back, and put hooks into thy *j* ... Eze 38:4 3895
that take off the yoke on their *j* ... Hos 11:4 3895

JAZER *(ja'-zur)* {11} See JAAZER. *A Levitical city in Gad.*
and when they saw the land of *J* ... Num 32:1 3270
Ataroth, and Dibon, and *J*, and ... Num 32:3 3270
And their coast was *J*, and all the ... Josh 13:25 3270
her suburbs, *J* with her suburbs ... Josh 21:39 3270
of the river of Gad, and toward *J* ... 2Sa 24:5 3270
suburbs, and *J* with her suburbs ... 1Chr 6:81 3270
men of valour at *J* of Gilead ... 1Chr 26:31 3270
they are come even unto *J* ... Is 16:8 3270
weeping of *J* the vine of Sibmah ... Is 16:9 3270
for thee with the weeping of *J* ... Jer 48:32 3270
they reach even to the sea of *J* ... Jer 48:32 3270

JAZIZ *(ja'-ziz)* {1} *Overseer of David's flocks.*
the flocks was *J* the Hagerite ... 1Chr 27:31 3151

JEALOUS {19}
for I the LORD thy God am a *j* God ... Ex 20:5 7067
whose name is *J*, is a *j* God ... Ex 34:14 7065
he be *j* of his wife, and she be ... Num 5:14 7065
he be *j* of his wife, and she be ... Num 5:14 7065
he be *j* over his wife, and shall ... Num 5:30 7065
is a consuming fire, even a *j* God ... Deut 4:24 7067
for I the LORD thy God am a *j* God ... Deut 5:9 7067
(For the LORD thy God is a *j* God ... Deut 6:15 7067
he is a *j* God ... Josh 24:19 7072
I have been very *j* for the LORD ... 1Kin 19:10 7065
I have been very *j* for the LORD ... 1Kin 19:14 7065
will be *j* for my holy name ... Eze 39:25 7065
will the LORD be *j* for his land ... Joel 2:18 7065
God is *j*, and the LORD revengeth ... Nah 1:2 7072
I am *j* for Jerusalem and for Zion ... Zec 1:14 7065
I was *j* for Zion with great ... Zec 8:2 7065
I was *j* for her with great fury ... Zec 8:2 7065
For I am *j* over you with godly ... 2Cor 11:2 *2206*

JEALOUSIES {1}
This is the law of *j*, when a wife ... Num 5:29 7068

JEALOUSY {34}
And the spirit of *j* come upon him ... Num 5:14 7068
if the spirit of *j* come upon him ... Num 5:14 7068
for it is an offering of *j* ... Num 5:15 7068
hands, which is the *j* offering ... Num 5:18 7068
the *j* offering out of the woman's ... Num 5:25 7068
the spirit of *j* cometh upon him ... Num 5:30 7068
the children of Israel in my *j* ... Num 25:11 7068
his *j* shall smoke against that ... Deut 29:20 7068
him to *j* with strange gods ... Deut 32:16 7065
They have moved me to *j* with that ... Deut 32:21 7065
I will move them to *j* with those ... Deut 32:21 7065
they provoked him to *j* with their ... 1Kin 14:22 7065
moved him to *j* with their graven ... Ps 78:58 7065
shall thy *j* burn like fire ... Ps 79:5 7068
For *j* is the rage of a man ... Prov 6:34 7068
j is cruel as the grave ... Song 8:6 7068
he shall stir up *j* like a man of ... Is 42:13 7068
of *j*, which provoketh to *j* ... Eze 8:3 7069
this image of *j* in the entry ... Eze 8:5 7068
will give thee blood in fury and *j* ... Eze 16:38 7068
my *j* shall depart from thee, and I ... Eze 16:42 7068
And I will set my *j* against thee ... Eze 23:25 7068
Surely in the fire of my *j* have I ... Eze 36:5 7068
Behold, I have spoken in my *j* ... Eze 36:6 7068
For in my *j* and in the fire of my ... Eze 38:19 7068
be devoured by the fire of his *j* ... Zeph 1:18 7068
be devoured with the fire of my *j* ... Zeph 3:8 7068
and for Zion with a great *j* ... Zec 1:14 7068
was jealous for Zion with great *j* ... Zec 8:2 7068
I will provoke you to *j* by them ... Rom 10:19
for to provoke them to *j* ... Rom 11:11
Do we provoke the Lord to *j* ... 1Cor 10:22
am jealous over you with godly *j* ... 2Cor 11:2 *2205*

JEARIM *(je'-a-rim)* {1} See KIRJATH-JEARIM. *A mountain in Judah.*
along unto the side of mount *J* ... Josh 15:10 3297

JEATERAI *(je-at'-e-rahee)* {1} *A descendant of Gershom.*
his son, Zerah his son, *J* his son ... 1Chr 6:21 2979

JEATHERAI See JEATERAI.

JEBERECHIAH *(je-ber'-e-ki'-ah)* {1} *Father of Zechariah.*
priest, and Zechariah the son of *J* ... Is 8:2 3000

JEBEREKIAH See JEBERECHIAH.

JEBUS *(je'-bus)* {4} See JEBUSI, JEBUSITE, JERUSALEM. *Original name of Jerusalem.*
departed, and came over against *J* ... Judg 19:10 2982
And when they were by *J*, the day ... Judg 19:11 2982
went to Jerusalem, which is *J* ... 1Chr 11:4 2982
inhabitants of *J* said to David ... 1Chr 11:5 2982

JEBUSI *(jeb'-u-si)* {2} See JEBUSITE. *Same as Jebus.*
to the side of *J* on the south ... Josh 18:16 2983
And Zelah, Eleph, and *J*, which is ... Josh 18:28 2983

JEBUSITE *(jeb'-u-site)* {14} See JEBUSITES. *Descendant of Canaan.*
And the *J*, and the Amorite, and the ... Gen 10:16 2983
Perizzite, the Hivite, and the *J* ... Ex 33:2 2983
and the Hivite, and the *J* ... Ex 34:11 2983
Perizzite, the Hivite, and the *J* ... Josh 9:1 2983
the *J* in the mountains, and to the ... Josh 11:3 2983
unto the south side of the *J* ... Josh 15:8 2983
threshingplace of Araunah the *J* ... 2Sa 24:16 2983
threshingfloor of Araunah the *J* ... 2Sa 24:18 2983
The *J* also, and the Amorite, and ... 1Chr 1:14 2983
the threshingfloor of Ornan the *J* ... 1Chr 21:15 2983
the threshingfloor of Ornan the *J* ... 1Chr 21:18 2983
the threshingfloor of Ornan the *J* ... 1Chr 21:28 2983
the threshingfloor of Ornan the *J* ... 2Chr 3:1 2983
in Judah, and Ekron as a *J* ... Zec 9:7 2983

JEBUSITES *(jeb'-u-sites)* {25}
and the Girgashites, and the *J* ... Gen 15:21 2983
and the Hivites, and the *J* ... Ex 3:8 2983
and the Hivites, and the *J* ... Ex 3:17 2983
and the Hivites, and the *J* ... Ex 13:5 2983
Canaanites, the Hivites, and the *J* ... Ex 23:23 2983
and the Hittites, and the *J* ... Num 13:29 2983
and the Hivites, and the *J* ... Deut 7:1 2983
Perizzites, the Hivites, and the *J* ... Deut 20:17 2983
and the Amorites, and the *J* ... Josh 3:10 2983
Perizzites, the Hivites, and the *J* ... Josh 12:8 2983
As for the *J* the inhabitants of ... Josh 15:63 2983
but the *J* dwell with the children ... Josh 15:63 2983
the Hivites, and the *J* ... Josh 24:11 2983
the *J* that inhabited Jerusalem ... Judg 1:21 2983
but the *J* dwell with the children ... Judg 1:21 2983
and Perizzites, and Hivites, and *J* ... Judg 3:5 2983
turn in into this city of the *J* ... Judg 19:11 2983
men went to Jerusalem unto the *J* ... 2Sa 5:6 2983
to the gutter, and smiteth the *J* ... 2Sa 5:8 2983
Perizzites, Hivites, and *J* ... 1Kin 9:20 2983
where the *J* were, the inhabitants ... 1Chr 11:4 2983
the *J* first shall be chief ... 1Chr 11:6 2983
and the Hivites, and the *J* ... 2Chr 8:7 2983
Hittites, the Perizzites, the *J* ... Ezr 9:1 2983
and the Perizzites, and the *J* ... Neh 9:8 2983

JECAMIAH *(jek-a-mi'-ah)* {1} See JEKAMIAH. *A son of Jeconiah.*
also, and Pedaiah, and Shenazar, *J* ... 1Chr 3:18 3359

JECHILIAH See JECHOLIAH.

JECHOLIAH *(jek-o-li'-ah)* {1} See JECOLIAH. *Mother of Uzziah.*
mother's name was *J* of Jerusalem ... 2Kin 15:2 3203

JECHONIAS *(jek-o-ni'-as)* {2} See JECONIAH. *Greek form of Jeconiah.*
And Josias begat *J* and his brethren ... Mt 1:11 *2423*
to Babylon, *J* begat Salathiel ... Mt 1:12 *2423*

JECOLIAH *(jek-o-li'-ah)* {1} See JECHOLIAH. *Same as Jecholiah.*
name also was *J* of Jerusalem ... 2Chr 26:3 3203

JECONIAH *(jek-o-ni'-ah)* {7} See CONIAH, JECHONIAS, JEHOIACHIN. *A king of Judah.*
J his son, Zedekiah his son ... 1Chr 3:16 3204
And the sons of *J* ... 1Chr 3:17 3204
carried away with *J* king of Judah ... Est 2:6 3204
had carried away captive *J* the ... Jer 24:1 3204
J the son of Jehoiakim king of ... Jer 27:20 3204
J the son of Jehoiakim king of ... Jer 28:4 3204
(After that *J* the king, and the ... Jer 29:2 3204

JEDAIAH *(jed-a-i'-ah)* {13}
1. A descendant of Simeon.
the son of Allon, the son of *J* ... 1Chr 4:37 3042
2. A rebuilder of Jerusalem's wall.
repaired *J* the son of Harumaph ... Neh 3:10 3042
3. A priest in Jerusalem.
J, and Jehoiarib, and Jachin ... 1Chr 9:10 3048
to Jehoiarib, the second to *J* ... 1Chr 24:7 3048
the children of *J*, of the house ... Ezr 2:36 3048
the children of *J*, of the house ... Neh 7:39 3048
4. A family of exiles.
J the son of Joiarib, Jachin ... Neh 11:10 3048
Shemaiah, and Joiarib, *J*, ... Neh 12:6 3048
Mattenai; of Joiarib, Uzzi ... Neh 12:19 3048
of Heldai, of Tobijah, and of *J* ... Zec 6:10 3048
to Helem, and to Tobijah, and to *J* ... Zec 6:14 3048
5. A priest.
Sallu, Amok, Hilkiah, *J* ... Neh 12:7 3048
of *J*, Nethaneel ... Neh 12:21 3048

JEDIAEL *(jed-e-a'-el)* {6}
1. A son of Benjamin.
Bela, and Becher, and *J*, three ... 1Chr 7:6 3043
The sons also of *J* ... 1Chr 7:10 3043
All these the sons of *J*, by the ... 1Chr 7:11 3043
2. A "mighty man" of David.
J the son of Shimri, and Joha his ... 1Chr 11:45 3043
3. A warrior in David's army.
Manasseh, Adnah, and Jozabad, and *J* ... 1Chr 12:20 3043
4. Son of Meshelemiah.
J the second, Zebadiah the third, ... 1Chr 26:2 3043

JEDIDAH *(je-di'-dah)* {1} *Mother of King Josiah.*
And his mother's name was *J* ... 2Kin 22:1 3040

JEDIDIAH *(jed-id-i'-ah)* {1} *Another name for Solomon.*
and he called his name *J*, because ... 2Sa 12:25 3041

JEDUTHUN *(jed'-u-thun)* {17} *A Levite.*
the son of Galal, the son of *J* ... 1Chr 9:16 3038
Obed-edom also the son of *J* ... 1Chr 16:38 3038
And with them Heman and *J*, and the ... 1Chr 16:41 3038
J with trumpets and cymbals for ... 1Chr 16:42 3038
the sons of *J* were porters ... 1Chr 16:42 3038
of Asaph, and of Heman, and of *J* ... 1Chr 25:1 3038
Of *J*: the sons of *J* ... 1Chr 25:3 3038
under the hands of their father *J* ... 1Chr 25:3 3038
to the king's order to Asaph, *J* ... 1Chr 25:6 3038
of them of Asaph, of Heman, of *J* ... 2Chr 5:12 3038
and of the sons of *J* ... 2Chr 29:14 3038
and Heman, and *J* the king's seer ... 2Chr 35:15 3038
the son of Galal, the son of *J* ... Neh 11:17 3038
To the chief Musician, even to *J* ... Ps 39:*t* 3038
To the chief Musician, to *J* ... Ps 62:*t* 3038
To the chief Musician, to *J* ... Ps 77:*t* 3038

JEEZER *(je-e'-zur)* {1} See ABIEZER, JEEZERITES. *A son of Gilead.*
of *J*, the family of the ... Num 26:30 372

JEEZERITES *(je-e'-zur-ites)* {1} *Descendants of Jeezer.*
of Jeezer, the family of the *J* ... Num 26:30 373

JEGAR-SAHADUTHA {1}
And Laban called it *J* ... Gen 31:47 3026

JEHALELEEL *(je-hal-e'-le-el)* {1} See JEHALELEL. *A descendant of Judah.*
And the sons of *J* ... 1Chr 4:16 3094

JEHALELEL *(je-hal'-e-lel)* {1} See JEHALELEEL. *A descendant of Merari.*
of Abdi, and Azariah the son of *J* ... 2Chr 29:12 3094

JEHALLELEL See JEHALELEL.

JEHDEIAH *(jeh-di'-ah)* {2}
1. A sanctuary servant.
the sons of Shubael; *J* ... 1Chr 24:20 3165
2. A herdsman of David.
the asses was *J* the Meronothite ... 1Chr 27:30 3165

JEHEZEKEL *(je-hez'-e-kel)* {1} See EZEKIEL. *A sanctuary servant.*
to Pethahiah, the twentieth to *J* ... 1Chr 24:16 3168

JEHEZEL See JEHEZEKEL.

JEHIAH *(je-hi'-ah)* {1} See JEHIEL. *A priest.*
J were doorkeepers for the ark ... 1Chr 15:24 3174

JEHIEL *(je-hi'-el)* {16} See JEHIAH, JEIEL, JEHIELI.
1. A Levite.
and Jaaziel, and Shemiramoth, and *J* ... 1Chr 15:18 3171
and Aziel, and Shemiramoth, and *J* ... 1Chr 15:20 3171
Jeiel, and Shemiramoth, and *J* ... 1Chr 16:5 3171
2. A Gershonite.
the chief was *J*, and Zetham, and ... 1Chr 23:8 3171
by the hand of *J* the Gershonite ... 1Chr 29:8 3171
3. A friend of David's son.
J the son of Hachmoni was with ... 1Chr 27:32 3171
4. Son of King Jehoshaphat.
of Jehoshaphat, Azariah, and *J* ... 2Chr 21:2 3171
5. A son of Heman.
sons of Heman; *J*, and Shimei ... 2Chr 29:14 3171
6. A Levite in Hezekiah's time.
And *J*, and Azaziah, and Nahath, and ... 2Chr 31:13 3171
7. A chief priest.
Hilkiah and Zechariah and *J* ... 2Chr 35:8 3171
8. A family of exiles.
Obadiah the son of *J*, and with him ... Ezr 8:9 3171
9. The father of Shechaniah.
And Shechaniah the son of *J* ... Ezr 10:2 3171
10. A son of Harim.
and Elijah, and Shemaiah, and *J* ... Ezr 10:21 3171
11. A man of Elam's family who married a foreigner.
Mattaniah, Zechariah, and *J* ... Ezr 10:26 3171
12. Father of Gibeon.
dwelt the father of Gibeon, *J* ... 1Chr 9:35 3273
13. A "mighty man" of David.
J the sons of Hothan the Aroerite ... 1Chr 11:44 3273

JEHIELI *(je-hi'-el-i)* {2} See JEHIEL. *A sanctuary servant.*
of Laadan the Gershonite, were *J* ... 1Chr 26:21 3172
The sons of *J*; Zetham, and ... 1Chr 26:22 3172

JEHIELITES See JEHIEL.

JEHIZKIAH *(je-hiz-ki'-ah)* {1} See HEZEKIAH. *A son of Shallum.*
J the son of Shallum, and Amasa ... 2Chr 28:12 3169

JEHOADAH *(je-ho'-a-dah)* {2} See JARAH. *Son of Ahaz.*
And Ahaz begat *J* ... 1Chr 8:36 3085
J begat Alemeth, and Azmaveth, and ... 1Chr 8:36 3085

JEHOADDAH See JEHOADAH.

JEHOADDAN *(je-ho-ad'-dan)* {2} *Mother of King Amaziah.*
mother's name was *J* of Jerusalem ... 2Kin 14:2 3086
mother's name was *J* of Jerusalem ... 2Chr 25:1 3086

JEHOADDIN See JEHOADDAN.

JEHOAHAZ *(je-ho'-a-haz)* {22} See AHAZIAH, JOAHAZ, SHALLUM.
1. Son of King Jehu.
J his son reigned in his stead ... 2Kin 10:35 3059
son of Ahaziah king of Judah *J* ... 2Kin 13:1 3059
J besought the LORD, and the LORD ... 2Kin 13:4 3059
people to *J* but fifty horsemen ... 2Kin 13:7 3059
Now the rest of the acts of *J* ... 2Kin 13:8 3059
And *J* slept with his fathers ... 2Kin 13:9 3059
Judah began Jehoash the son of *J* ... 2Kin 13:10 3059
Israel all the days of *J* ... 2Kin 13:22 3059
Jehoash the son of *J* took again ... 2Kin 13:25 3059
the hand of *J* his father by war ... 2Kin 13:25 3059
J king of Israel reigned Amaziah ... 2Kin 14:1 3099
the son of *J* son of Jehu, king of ... 2Kin 14:8 3059
the death of Jehoash son of *J* ... 2Kin 14:17 3059
and sent to Joash, the son of *J* ... 2Chr 25:17 3059
of *J* king of Israel fifteen years ... 2Chr 25:25 3059
2. Son of King Josiah.
the land took *J* the son of Josiah ... 2Kin 23:30 3059
J was twenty and three years old ... 2Kin 23:31 3059
name to Jehoiakim, and took *J* away ... 2Kin 23:34 3059
J was twenty and three years old ... 2Chr 36:2 3059
Necho took *J* his brother, and ... 2Chr 36:4 3059
3. A son of King Jehoram.
was never a son left him, save *J* ... 2Chr 21:17 3059
the son of Joash, the son of *J* ... 2Chr 25:23 3059

JEHOASH *(je-ho'-ash)* {17} See JOASH.
1. A king of Judah.
Seven years old was *J* when he ... 2Kin 11:21 3060
year of Jehu *J* began to reign ... 2Kin 12:1 3060
J did that which was right in the ... 2Kin 12:2 3060
J said to the priests, All the ... 2Kin 12:4 3060
twentieth year of king *J* the ... 2Kin 12:6 3060
Then king *J* called for Jehoiada ... 2Kin 12:7 3060
J king of Judah took all the ... 2Kin 12:18 3060
the son of *J* the son of Ahaziah, ... 2Kin 14:13 3060
2. A king of Israel.
J the son of Jehoahaz to reign ... 2Kin 13:10 3060
J the son of Jehoahaz took again ... 2Kin 13:25 3060
Then Amaziah sent messengers to *J* ... 2Kin 14:8 3060
J the king of Israel sent to ... 2Kin 14:9 3060
Therefore *J* king of Israel went ... 2Kin 14:11 3060
J king of Israel took Amaziah ... 2Kin 14:13 3060
of the acts of *J* which he did ... 2Kin 14:15 3060
J slept with his fathers, and was ... 2Kin 14:16 3060
J son of Jehoahaz king of Israel ... 2Kin 14:17 3060

JEHOHANAN *(je-ho'-ha-nan)* {6}
1. A sanctuary servant.
J the sixth, Elioenai the seventh ... 1Chr 26:3 3076
2. A chief captain.
And next to him was *J* the captain ... 2Chr 17:15 3076
3. Father of Ishmael.
Jeroham, and Ishmael the son of *J* ... 2Chr 23:1 3076
4. Married a foreigner in exile.
J, Hananiah, Zabbai, and Athlai ... Ezr 10:28 3076
5. A priest in exile.
Meshullam; of Amariah, *J* ... Neh 12:13 3076
6. A priest who dedicated the wall.
and Eleazar, and Uzzi, and *J* ... Neh 12:42 3076

JEHOIACHIN *(je-hoy'-a-kin)* {10} See CONIAH, JECONIAH, JECONIAS, JEHOIACHIN'S. *A king of Judah.*
J his son reigned in his stead ... 2Kin 24:6 3078
J was eighteen years old when he ... 2Kin 24:8 3078
J the king of Judah went out to ... 2Kin 24:12 3078
And he carried away *J* to Babylon ... 2Kin 24:15 3078
the captivity of *J* king of Judah ... 2Kin 25:27 3078
of *J* king of Judah out of prison ... 2Kin 25:27 3078
J his son reigned in his stead ... 2Chr 36:8 3078
J was eight years old when he ... 2Chr 36:9 3078
the captivity of *J* king of Judah ... Jer 52:31 3078
up the head of *J* king of Judah ... Jer 52:31 3078

JEHOIACHIN'S *(je-hoy'-a-kins)* {1}
fifth year of king *J* captivity ... Eze 1:2 3112

JEHOIADA *(je-hoy'-a-dah)* {52} See BERECHIAS, JOIADA.
1. Father of Benaiah.
Benaiah the son of *J* was over ... 2Sa 8:18 3111
Benaiah the son of *J* was over the ... 2Sa 20:23 3111
And Benaiah the son of *J*, the son ... 2Sa 23:20 3111
things did Benaiah the son of *J* ... 2Sa 23:22 3111
priest, and Benaiah the son of *J* ... 1Kin 1:8 3111
priest, and Benaiah the son of *J* ... 1Kin 1:26 3111
prophet, and Benaiah the son of *J* ... 1Kin 1:32 3111
the son of *J* answered the king ... 1Kin 1:36 3111
prophet, and Benaiah the son of *J* ... 1Kin 1:38 3111
prophet, and Benaiah the son of *J* ... 1Kin 1:44 3111
the hand of Benaiah the son of *J* ... 1Kin 2:25 3111
Solomon sent Benaiah the son of *J* ... 1Kin 2:29 3111
So Benaiah the son of *J* went up ... 1Kin 2:34 3111
of *J* in his room over the host ... 1Kin 2:35 3111
commanded Benaiah the son of *J* ... 1Kin 2:46 3111
the son of *J* was over the host ... 1Kin 4:4 3111
Benaiah the son of *J*, the son of ... 1Chr 11:22 3111
things did Benaiah the son of *J* ... 1Chr 11:24 3111
Benaiah the son of *J* was over the ... 1Chr 18:17 3111
month was Benaiah the son of *J* ... 1Chr 27:5 3111
2. A high priest.
And the seventh year *J* sent ... 2Kin 11:4 3111
that *J* the priest commanded ... 2Kin 11:9 3111
sabbath, and came to *J* the priest ... 2Kin 11:9 3111
But *J* the priest commanded the ... 2Kin 11:15 3111
J made a covenant between the ... 2Kin 11:17 3111
J the priest instructed him ... 2Kin 12:2 3111
Jehoash called for *J* the priest ... 2Kin 12:7 3111
But *J* the priest took a chest, and ... 2Kin 12:9 3111
Jehoram, the wife of *J* the priest ... 2Chr 22:11 3111
And in the seventh year *J* ... 2Chr 23:1 3111
that *J* the priest had commanded ... 2Chr 23:8 3111
for *J* the priest dismissed not ... 2Chr 23:8 3111
Moreover *J* the priest delivered ... 2Chr 23:9 3111
And *J* and his sons anointed him, and ... 2Chr 23:11 3111
Then *J* the priest brought out the ... 2Chr 23:14 3111
J made a covenant between him, and ... 2Chr 23:16 3111
Also *J* appointed the offices of ... 2Chr 23:18 3111
LORD all the days of *J* the priest ... 2Chr 24:2 3111
And *J* took for him two wives ... 2Chr 24:3 3111
the king called for *J* the chief ... 2Chr 24:6 3111
J gave it to such as did the work ... 2Chr 24:12 3111
of the money before the king and *J* ... 2Chr 24:14 3111
continually all the days of *J* ... 2Chr 24:14 3111
But *J* waxed old, and was full of ... 2Chr 24:15 3111
Now after the death of *J* came the ... 2Chr 24:17 3111
Zechariah the son of *J* the priest ... 2Chr 24:20 3111
not the kindness which *J* his ... 2Chr 24:22 3111
blood of the sons of *J* the priest ... 2Chr 24:25 3111
3. A captain in David's army.
J was the leader of the Aaronites ... 1Chr 12:27 3111
4. Son of Benaiah.
was *J* the son of Benaiah, and ... 1Chr 27:34 3111
5. A rebuilder of Jerusalem's wall.
gate repaired *J* the son of Paseah ... Neh 3:6 3111
6. A pre-exilic priest.
in the stead of *J* the priest ... Jer 29:26 3111

JEHOIAKIM *(je-hoy'-a-kim)* {37} See ELIAKIM, JOIAKIM. *A king of Judah.*
father, and turned his name to *J* ... 2Kin 23:34 3079
J gave the silver and the gold to ... 2Kin 23:35 3079
J was twenty and five years old ... 2Kin 23:36 3079
J became his servant three years ... 2Kin 24:1 3079
Now the rest of the acts of *J* ... 2Kin 24:5 3079
So *J* slept with his fathers ... 2Kin 24:6 3079
according to all that *J* had done ... 2Kin 24:19 3079
firstborn Johanan, the second *J* ... 1Chr 3:15 3079
And the sons of *J* ... 1Chr 3:16 3079
and turned his name to *J* ... 2Chr 36:4 3079
J was twenty and five years old ... 2Chr 36:5 3079
Now the rest of the acts of *J* ... 2Chr 36:8 3079
It came also in the days of *J* the ... Jer 1:3 3079
thus saith the LORD concerning *J* ... Jer 22:18 3079
though Coniah the son of *J* king ... Jer 22:24 3079
the son of *J* king of Judah ... Jer 24:1 3079
of Judah in the fourth year of *J* ... Jer 25:1 3079
the beginning of the reign of *J* ... Jer 26:1 3079
when *J* the king, with all his ... Jer 26:21 3079
J the king sent men into Egypt, ... Jer 26:22 3079
and brought him unto *J* the king ... Jer 26:23 3079
the beginning of the reign of *J* ... Jer 27:1 3079
captive Jeconiah the son of *J* ... Jer 27:20 3079
the son of *J* king of Judah ... Jer 28:4 3079
from the LORD in the days of *J* ... Jer 35:1 3079
to pass in the fourth year of *J* ... Jer 36:1 3079
to pass in the fifth year of *J* ... Jer 36:9 3079
which *J* the king of Judah hath ... Jer 36:28 3079
thou shalt say to *J* king of Judah ... Jer 36:29 3079
saith the LORD of *J* king of Judah ... Jer 36:30 3079
J king of Judah had burned in the ... Jer 36:32 3079
instead of Coniah the son of *J* ... Jer 37:1 3079
in the fourth year of *J* the son ... Jer 45:1 3079
smote in the fourth year of *J* the ... Jer 46:2 3079
according to all that *J* had done ... Jer 52:2 3079
the reign of *J* king of Judah came ... Dan 1:1 3079
the Lord gave *J* king of Judah ... Dan 1:2 3079

JEHOIARIB *(je-hoy'-a-rib)* {2} See JOIARIB.
1. A priest.
Jedaiah, and *J*, and Jachin, ... 1Chr 9:10 3080
2. A sanctuary servant.
Now the first lot came forth to *J* ... 1Chr 24:7 3080

JEHONADAB *(je-hon'-a-dab)* {3} See JONADAB. *A son of Rechab.*
he lighted on *J* the son of Rechab ... 2Kin 10:15 3082
And *J* answered, It is ... 2Kin 10:15 3082
J the son of Rechab, into the ... 2Kin 10:23 3082

JEHONATHAN *(je-hon'-a-than)* {3} See JONATHAN.
1. A storehouse servant.
castles, was *J* the son of Uzziah ... 1Chr 27:25 3083
2. A Levite teacher.
and Asahel, and Shemiramoth, and *J* ... 2Chr 17:8 3083
3. A priest.
of Shemaiah, *J* ... Neh 12:18 3083

JEHORAM *(je-ho'-ram)* {23} See HADORAM, JORAM.
1. A king of Judah.
J his son reigned in his stead ... 1Kin 22:50 3088
J the son of Jehoshaphat king of ... 2Kin 1:17 3088
J the son of Jehoshaphat king of ... 2Kin 8:16 3088
of *J* king of Judah begin to reign ... 2Kin 8:25 3088
Ahaziah the son of *J* king of ... 2Kin 8:29 3088
things that Jehoshaphat, and *J* ... 2Kin 12:18 3088
J his son reigned in his stead ... 2Chr 21:1 3088
but the kingdom gave he to *J* ... 2Chr 21:3 3088
Now when *J* was risen up to the ... 2Chr 21:4 3088
J was thirty and two years old ... 2Chr 21:5 3088
Then *J* went forth with his ... 2Chr 21:9 3088
the LORD stirred up against *J* the ... 2Chr 21:16 3088
son of *J* king of Judah reigned ... 2Chr 22:1 3088
Azariah the son of *J* king of ... 2Chr 22:6 3088
the daughter of king *J*, the wife ... 2Chr 22:11 3088
2. A son of Ahab.
J reigned in his stead in the ... 2Kin 1:17 3088
Now *J* the son of Ahab began to ... 2Kin 3:1 3088
king *J* went out of Samaria the ... 2Kin 3:6 3088
smote *J* between his arms, and the ... 2Kin 9:24 3088
went with *J* the son of Ahab king ... 2Chr 22:5 3088
see *J* the son of Ahab at Jezreel ... 2Chr 22:6 3088
he went out with *J* against Jehu ... 2Chr 22:7 3088
3. A priest.
and with them Elishama and *J* ... 2Chr 17:8 3088

JEHOSHABEATH *(je-ho-shab'-e-ath)* {2} See JEHOSHEBA. *A daughter of King Jehoram.*
But *J*, the daughter of the king, ... 2Chr 22:11 3090
So *J*, the daughter of king ... 2Chr 22:11 3090

JEHOSHAPHAT *(je-hosh'-a-fat)* {85} See JOSAPHAT, JOSHAPHAT.
1. David's recorder.
J the son of Ahilud was recorder ... 2Sa 8:16 3092
J the son of Ahilud was recorder ... 2Sa 20:24 3092
J the son of Ahilud, the recorder ... 1Kin 4:3 3092
J the son of Ahilud, recorder ... 1Chr 18:15 3092
2. An officer of Solomon.
J the son of Paruah, in Issachar ... 1Kin 4:17 3092
3. A king of Judah.
J his son reigned in his stead ... 1Kin 15:24 3092
that *J* the king of Judah came ... 1Kin 22:2 3092
And he said unto *J*, Wilt thou go ... 1Kin 22:4 3092
J said to the king of Israel, I ... 1Kin 22:4 3092
J said unto the king of Israel, ... 1Kin 22:5 3092
J said, Is there not here a ... 1Kin 22:7 3092
And the king of Israel said unto *J* ... 1Kin 22:8 3092
J said, Let not the king say so ... 1Kin 22:8 3092
J the king of Judah sat each on ... 1Kin 22:10 3092
And the king of Israel said unto *J* ... 1Kin 22:18 3092
J the king of Judah went up to ... 1Kin 22:29 3092
And the king of Israel said unto *J* ... 1Kin 22:30 3092
captains of the chariots saw *J* ... 1Kin 22:32 3092
and *J* cried out ... 1Kin 22:32 3092
J the son of Asa began to reign ... 1Kin 22:41 3092
J was thirty and five years old ... 1Kin 22:42 3092
J made peace with the king of ... 1Kin 22:44 3092
Now the rest of the acts of *J* ... 1Kin 22:45 3092
J made ships of Tharshish to go ... 1Kin 22:48 3092
Ahaziah the son of Ahab unto *J* ... 1Kin 22:49 3092
But *J* would not ... 1Kin 22:49 3092
J slept with his fathers, and was ... 1Kin 22:50 3092
year of *J* king of Judah, and ... 1Kin 22:51 3092
the son of *J* king of Judah ... 2Kin 1:17 3092
year of *J* king of Judah, and ... 2Kin 3:1 3092
sent to *J* the king of Judah, ... 2Kin 3:7 3092
But *J* said, Is there not here a ... 2Kin 3:11 3092
J said, The word of the LORD is ... 2Kin 3:12 3092
So the king of Israel and *J* ... 2Kin 3:12 3092
presence of *J* the king of Judah ... 2Kin 3:14 3092
J being then king of Judah, ... 2Kin 8:16 3092
Jehoram the son of *J* king of ... 2Kin 8:16 3092
all the hallowed things that *J* ... 2Kin 12:18 3092
his son, Asa his son, *J* his son, ... 1Chr 3:10 3092
J his son reigned in his stead, ... 2Chr 17:1 3092
And the LORD was with *J*, because ... 2Chr 17:3 3092
all Judah brought to *J* presents ... 2Chr 17:5 3092
that they made no war against *J* ... 2Chr 17:10 3092
Philistines brought *J* presents ... 2Chr 17:11 3092
J waxed great exceedingly ... 2Chr 17:12 3092
Now *J* had riches and honour in ... 2Chr 18:1 3092
Israel said unto *J* king of Judah ... 2Chr 18:3 3092
J said unto the king of Israel, ... 2Chr 18:4 3092
But *J* said, Is there not here a ... 2Chr 18:6 3092
And the king of Israel said unto *J* ... 2Chr 18:7 3092
J said, Let not the king say so ... 2Chr 18:7 3092
J king of Judah sat either of ... 2Chr 18:9 3092
And the king of Israel said to *J* ... 2Chr 18:17 3092
J the king of Judah went up to ... 2Chr 18:28 3092
And the king of Israel said unto *J* ... 2Chr 18:29 3092
captains of the chariots saw *J* ... 2Chr 18:31 3092
but *J* cried out, and the LORD ... 2Chr 18:31 3092
J the king of Judah returned to ... 2Chr 19:1 3092
to meet him, and said to king *J* ... 2Chr 19:2 3092
And *J* dwelt at Jerusalem ... 2Chr 19:4 3092
did *J* set of the Levites, and of ... 2Chr 19:8 3092
came against *J* to battle ... 2Chr 20:1 3092
Then there came some that told *J* ... 2Chr 20:2 3092
J feared, and set himself to seek ... 2Chr 20:3 3092
J stood in the congregation of ... 2Chr 20:5 3092
of Jerusalem, and thou king *J* ... 2Chr 20:15 3092
J bowed his head with his face to ... 2Chr 20:18 3092
J stood and said, Hear me, O Judah ... 2Chr 20:20 3092
And when *J* and his people came to ... 2Chr 20:25 3092
J in the forefront of them, to go ... 2Chr 20:27 3092
So the realm of *J* was quiet ... 2Chr 20:30 3092
And *J* reigned over Judah ... 2Chr 20:31 3092
Now the rest of the acts of *J* ... 2Chr 20:34 3092
after this did *J* king of Judah ... 2Chr 20:35 3092
of Mareshah prophesied against *J* ... 2Chr 20:37 3092
Now *J* slept with his fathers, and ... 2Chr 21:1 3092
And he had brethren the sons of *J* ... 2Chr 21:2 3092
were the sons of *J* king of Israel ... 2Chr 21:2 3092
in the ways of *J* thy father ... 2Chr 21:12 3092
said they, he is the son of *J* ... 2Chr 22:9 3092

4. Father of Jehu.
the son of *J* the son of Nimshi............... 2Kin 9:2 3092
So Jehu the son of *J* the son of............... 2Kin 9:14 3092
5. A priest.
And Shebaniah, and *J*, and Nethaneel, ... 1Chr 15:24 3046
6. A valley near Jerusalem.
them down into the valley of *J*............... Joel 3:2 3092
and come up to the valley of *J*............... Joel 3:12 3092

JEHOSHEBA *(je-hosh'-e-bah)* {1} See JEHOSHABEATH. *Same as Jehoshabeath.*
But *J*, the daughter of king Joram............... 2Kin 11:2 3089

JEHOSHUA *(je-hosh'-u-ah)* {1} See JEHOSHUAH, JOSHUA. *Same as Joshua, son of Nun.*
called Oshea the son of Nun *J*............... Num 13:16 3091

JEHOSHUAH *(je-hosh'-u-ah)* {1} *Same as Joshua, son of Nun.*
Non his son, *J* his son............................ 1Chr 7:27 3091

JEHOVAH *(je-ho'-vah)* {4} See GOD, JAH, JEHOVAH-JIREH, JEHOVAH-NISSI, JEHOVAH-SHALOM, LORD. *A name for God.*
but by my name *J* was I not known .... Ex 6:3 3068
that thou, whose name alone is *J*............ Ps 83:18 3068
for the LORD *J* is my strength and.......... Is 12:2 3068
for in the LORD *J* is everlasting .... Is 26:4 3068

JEHOVAH-JIREH *(je-ho'-vah-ji'-reh)* {1} *Mt. Moriah.*
called the name of that place *J*.............. Gen 22:14 3070

JEHOVAH-NISSI *(je-ho'-vah-nis'-si)* {1} *An altar built by Moses.*
altar, and called the name of it *J* .... Ex 17:15 3071

JEHOVAH-SHALOM *(je-ho'-vah-sha'-lom)* {1} *An altar built by Gideon.*
unto the LORD, and called it *J*............... Judg 6:24 3073

JEHOZABAD *(je-hoz'-a-bad)* {4} See JOZABAD.
1. Son of Shomer.
J the son of Shomer, his servants........... 2Kin 12:21 3075
J the son of Shimrith a Moabitess.......... 2Chr 24:26 3075
2. A son of Obed-edom.
J the second, Joah the third, and 1Chr 26:4 3075
3. A general of Jehoshaphat.
And next him was *J*, and with him an 2Chr 17:18 3075

JEHOZADAK *(je-hoz'-a-dak)* {2} *Great-grandson of Hilkiah.*
begat Seraiah, and Seraiah begat *J* 1Chr 6:14 3087
J went into captivity, when the 1Chr 6:15 3087

JEHU *(je-hu)* {58}
1. A son of Hanani.
to *J* the son of Hanani against 1Kin 16:1 3058
J the son of Hanani came the word.......... 1Kin 16:7 3058
against Baasha by *J* the prophet 1Kin 16:12 3058
J the son of Hanani the seer went........... 2Chr 19:2 3058
the book of *J* the son of Hanani.............. 2Chr 20:34 3058
2. A king of Israel.
J the son of Nimshi shalt thou 1Kin 19:16 3058
the sword of Hazael shall *J* slay............. 1Kin 19:17 3058
the sword of *J* shall Elisha slay.............. 1Kin 19:17 3058
look out there *J* the son of...................... 2Kin 9:2 3058
J said, Unto which of all us..................... 2Kin 9:5 3058
Then *J* came forth to the servants.......... 2Kin 9:11 3058
with trumpets, saying, *J* is king 2Kin 9:13 3058
So *J* the son of Jehoshaphat the.............. 2Kin 9:14 3058
J said, If it be your minds, then 2Kin 9:15 3058
So *J* rode in a chariot, and went.............. 2Kin 9:16 3058
spied the company of *J* as he came 2Kin 9:17 3058
J said, What hast thou to do with 2Kin 9:18 3058
J answered, What hast thou to do 2Kin 9:19 3058
driving of *J* the son of Nimshi................. 2Kin 9:20 3058
and they went out against *J* 2Kin 9:21 3058
it came to pass, when Joram saw *J* 2Kin 9:22 3058
that he said, Is it peace, *J*...................... 2Kin 9:22 3058
J drew a bow with his full 2Kin 9:24 3058
Then said *J* to Bidkar his captain 2Kin 9:25
J followed after him, and said,............... 2Kin 9:27 3058
when *J* was come to Jezreel,.................... 2Kin 9:30 3058
as *J* entered in at the gate, she.............. 2Kin 9:31 3058
J wrote letters, and sent to..................... 2Kin 10:1 3058
up of the children, sent to *J* 2Kin 10:5 3058
So *J* slew all that remained of................. 2Kin 10:11 3058
J met with the brethren of 2Kin 10:13 3058
J gathered all the people 2Kin 10:18 3058
but *J* shall serve him much....................... 2Kin 10:18 3058
But *J* did it in subtilty, to the................. 2Kin 10:19 3058
J said, Proclaim a solemn......................... 2Kin 10:20 3058
J sent through all Israel 2Kin 10:21 3058
J went, and Jehonadab the son of 2Kin 10:23 3058
J appointed fourscore men without 2Kin 10:24 3058
that *J* said to the guard and to................ 2Kin 10:25 3058
Thus *J* destroyed Baal out of 2Kin 10:28 3058
J departed not from after them,............... 2Kin 10:29 3058
And the LORD said unto *J*, Because......... 2Kin 10:30 3058
But *J* took no heed to walk in the........... 2Kin 10:31 3058
Now the rest of the acts of *J* 2Kin 10:34 3058
And *J* slept with his fathers 2Kin 10:35 3058
the time that *J* reigned over 2Kin 10:36 3058
year of *J* Jehoash began to reign 2Kin 12:1 3058
of Judah Jehoahaz the son of *J*................. 2Kin 13:1 3058
the son of Jehoahaz son of *J*.................... 2Kin 14:8 3058
of the LORD which he spake unto *J*.......... 2Kin 15:12 3058
against *J* the son of Nimshi..................... 2Chr 22:7 3058
when *J* was executing judgment 2Chr 22:8 3058
in Samaria,) and brought him to *J*........... 2Chr 22:9 3058
the son of Jehoahaz, the son of *J*............ 2Chr 25:17 3058
of Jezreel upon the house of *J*................. Hos 1:4 3058
3. A son of Obed.
begat Jehu, and *J* begat Azariah, ... 1Chr 2:38 3058
4. A son of Josibiah.
J the son of Josibiah, the son of 1Chr 4:35 3058
5. A warrior in David's army.
and Berachah, and *J* the Antothite, ... 1Chr 12:3 3058

JEHUBBAH *(je-hub'-bah)* {1} *A descendant of Shamer.*
Ahi, and Rohgah, *J*, and Aram 1Chr 7:34 3160

JEHUCAL *(je-hu'-kal)* {1} See JUCAL. *A son of Shelemiah.*
king sent *J* the son of Shelemiah .... Jer 37:3 3081

JEHUD *(je'-hud)* {1} *A city in Dan.*
And *J*, and Bene-berak, and.................... Josh 19:45 3055

JEHUDI *(je-hu'-di)* {4} *Son of Nethaniah.*
sent *J* the son of Nethaniah..................... Jer 36:14 3065
So the king sent *J* to fetch the .... Jer 36:21 3065
J read it in the ears of the king.............. Jer 36:21 3065
that when *J* had read three or .... Jer 36:23 3065

JEHUDIJAH *(je-hu-di'-jah)* {1} See HODIAH. *A descendant of Judah.*
his wife *J* bare Jered the father.............. 1Chr 4:18 3057

JEHUSH *(je'-hush)* {1} See JEUSH. *A descendant of King Saul.*
J the second, and Eliphelet the 1Chr 8:39 3266

JEIEL *(je-i'-el)* {11} See JEHIEL, JEUEL.
1. A chief Reubenite.
was reckoned, were the chief, *J*............. 1Chr 5:7 3273
2. A Levite gatekeeper.
and Mikneiah, and Obed-edom, and *J*.... 1Chr 15:18 3273
and Mikneiah, and Obed-edom, and *J*.... 1Chr 15:21 3273
and next to him Zechariah, *J*.................. 1Chr 16:5 3273
J with psalteries and with harps............. 1Chr 16:5 3273
3. A Levite of the Asaph family.
the son of Benaiah, the son of *J*............. 2Chr 20:14 3273
4. A scribe.
by the hand of *J* the scribe..................... 2Chr 26:11 3273
5. A Levite in Hezekiah's time.
Shimri, and *J*: and of the sons............... 2Chr 29:13 3273
6. A chief Levite.
his brethren, and Hashabiah and *J*.......... 2Chr 35:9 3273
7. An exile.
names are these, Eliphelet, *J*.................. Ezr 8:13 3273
8. Married a foreigner in exile.
J, Mattithiah, Zabad, Zebina,.................. Ezr 10:43 3273

JEKABZEEL *(je-kab'-ze-el)* {1} See KABZEEL. *A city in Judah.*
in the villages thereof, and at *J*............. Neh 11:25 3343

JEKAMEAM *(je-kam'-e-am)* {2} *Son of Hebron.*
the third, and *J* the fourth..................... 1Chr 23:19 3360
Jahaziel the third, *J* the fourth............... 1Chr 24:23 3360

JEKAMIAH *(jek-a-mi'-ah)* {2} See JECAMIAH. *A descendant of Shallum.*
And Shallum begat *J*............................... 1Chr 2:41 3359
and *J* begat Elishama 1Chr 2:41 3359

JEKUTHIEL *(je-ku'-the-el)* {1} *A descendant of Ezra.*
Socho, and *J* the father of Zanoah.......... 1Chr 4:18 3354

JEMIMA *(je-mi'-mah)* {1} *A daughter of Job.*
called the name of the first, *J* .... Job 42:14 3224

JEMIMAH See JEMIMA.

JEMUEL *(je-mu'-el)* {2} See NEMUEL. *A son of Simeon.*
J, and Jamin, and Ohad, and Jachin,....... Gen 46:10 3223
J, and Jamin, and Ohad, and Jachin,....... Ex 6:15 3223

JEOPARDED {1}
Naphtali were a people that *j*.................. Judg 5:18 2778

JEOPARDY {6}
men that went in *j* of their lives............. 2Sa 23:17
that have put their lives in *j*.................... 1Chr 11:19
for with the *j* of their lives 1Chr 11:19
master Saul to the *j* of our heads............ 1Chr 12:19
filled with water, and were in *j* .... Lk 8:23 *2793*
And why stand we in *j* every hour 1Cor 15:30 *2793*

JEPHTHAE *(jef'-thah-e)* {1} See JEPHTHAH. *Same as Jephthah.*
of Barak, and of Samson, and of *J*.......... Heb 11:32 *2422*

JEPHTHAH *(jef'-thah)* {29} See JEPHTHAE, JIPHTHAH-EL. *A judge.*
Now *J* the Gileadite was a mighty.......... Judg 11:1 3316
and Gilead begat *J* .... Judg 11:1 3316
grew up, and they thrust out *J*................ Judg 11:2 3316
Then *J* fled from his brethren, and .... Judg 11:3 3316
there were gathered vain men to *J*.......... Judg 11:3 3316
to fetch *J* out of the land of Tob............. Judg 11:5 3316
And they said unto *J*, Come, and be........ Judg 11:6 3316
J said unto the elders of Gilead, ... Judg 11:7 3316
the elders of Gilead said unto *J* .... Judg 11:8 3316
J said unto the elders of Gilead, ... Judg 11:9 3316
the elders of Gilead said unto *J* .... Judg 11:10 3316
Then *J* went with the elders of................. Judg 11:11 3316
J uttered all his words before................. Judg 11:11 3316
J sent messengers unto the king............. Judg 11:12 3316
answered unto the messengers of *J* .... Judg 11:13 3316
J sent messengers again unto the .... Judg 11:14 3316
And said unto him, Thus saith *J* .... Judg 11:15 3316
the words of *J* which he sent him............ Judg 11:28 3316
Spirit of the LORD came upon *J* .... Judg 11:29 3316
J vowed a vow unto the LORD, and .... Judg 11:30 3316
So *J* passed over unto the....................... Judg 11:32 3316
J came to Mizpeh unto his house, ... Judg 11:34 3316
to lament the daughter of *J* the.............. Judg 11:40 3316
and went northward, and said unto *J*..... Judg 12:1 3316
J said unto them, I and my people .... Judg 12:2 3316
Then *J* gathered together all the .... Judg 12:4 3316
J judged Israel six years .... Judg 12:7 3316
Then died *J* the Gileadite, and was......... Judg 12:7 3316
sent Jerubbaal, and Bedan, and *J* 1Sa 12:11 3316

JEPHUNNEH *(je-fun'-neh)* {16}
1. Father of Caleb.
of Judah, Caleb the son of *J* .... Num 13:6 3312
son of Nun, and Caleb the son of *J* .... Num 14:6 3312
therein, save Caleb the son of *J*.............. Num 14:30 3312
son of Nun, and Caleb the son of *J* .... Num 14:38 3312
of them, save Caleb the son of *J*............. Num 26:65 3312
Caleb the son of *J* the Kenezite................ Num 32:12 3312
of Judah, Caleb the son of *J* .... Num 34:19 3312
Save Caleb the son of *J* .... Deut 1:36 3312
Caleb the son of *J* the Kenezite............... Josh 14:6 3312
of *J* Hebron for an inheritance................ Josh 14:13 3312
of *J* the Kenezite unto this day .... Josh 14:14 3312
unto Caleb the son of *J* he gave a............ Josh 15:13 3312
the son of *J* for his possession .... Josh 21:12 3312
And the sons of Caleb the son of *J*.......... 1Chr 4:15 3312
they gave to Caleb the son of *J* 1Chr 6:56 3312
2. Head of an Asherite family.
J, and Pispah, and Ara 1Chr 7:38 3312

JERAH *(je'-rah)* {2} *A son of Joktan.*
and Sheleph, and Hazarmaveth, and *J* ... Gen 10:26 3392
and Sheleph, and Hazarmaveth, and *J* ... 1Chr 1:20 3392

JERAHMEEL *(je-rah'-me-el)* {8} See JERAHMEELITES.
1. A son of Hezron.
J, and Ram, and Chelubai 1Chr 2:9 3396
the sons of *J* the firstborn of 1Chr 2:25 3396
J had also another wife, whose 1Chr 2:26 3396
of Ram the firstborn of *J* were 1Chr 2:27 3396
These were the sons of *J*......................... 1Chr 2:33 3396
of Caleb the brother of *J* were................. 1Chr 2:42 3396
2. A son of Kish.
the son of Kish was *J* 1Chr 24:29 3396
3. An officer of Jehoiakim.
commanded *J* the son of Hammelech...... Jer 36:26 3396

JERAHMEELITES *(je-rah'-me-el-ites)* {2} *Descendants of Jerahmeel.*
and against the south of the *J* 1Sa 27:10 3397
which were in the cities of the *J* 1Sa 30:29 3397

JERED *(je'-red)* {2} See JARED.
1. A descendant of Seth.
Kenan, Mahalaleel, *J*, ... 1Chr 1:2 3382
2. A descendant of Ezra.
bare *J* the father of Gedor....................... 1Chr 4:18 3382

JEREMAI *(jer'-e-mahee)* {1} *Married a foreigner in exile.*
Mattathah, Zabad, Eliphelet, *J* .... Ezr 10:33 3413

JEREMIAH *(jer-e-mi'-ah)* {146} See JEREMIAH'S, JEREMIAS, JEREMY.
1. Father of Hamutal.
the daughter of *J* of Libnah 2Kin 23:31 3414
the daughter of *J* of Libnah 2Kin 24:18 3414
the daughter of *J* of Libnah .... Jer 52:1 3414
2. Head of a Manassite family.
Ishi, and Eliel, and Azriel, and *J*............. 1Chr 5:24 3414
3. A warrior in David's army.
and *J*, and Jahaziel, and Johanan, and.... 1Chr 12:4 3414
4. A Gadite warrior.
the fourth, *J* the fifth,............................ 1Chr 12:10 3414
5. Another Gadite warrior.
J the tenth, Machbanai the..................... 1Chr 12:13 3414
6. A prophet.
And *J* lamented for Josiah....................... 2Chr 35:25 3414
humbled not himself before *J* the........... 2Chr 36:12 3414
of the LORD by the mouth of *J* 2Chr 36:21 3414
mouth of *J* might be accomplished 2Chr 36:22 3414
the mouth of *J* might be fulfilled............ Ezr 1:1 3414
The words of *J* the son of Hilkiah............ Jer 1:1 3414
the LORD came unto me, saying, *J*.......... Jer 1:11 3414
word that came to *J* from the LORD .... Jer 7:1 3414
word that came to *J* from the LORD .... Jer 11:1 3414
came to *J* concerning the dearth .... Jer 14:1 3414
which came to *J* from the LORD .... Jer 18:1 3414
let us devise devices against *J*............... Jer 18:18 3414
Then came *J* from Tophet, whither .... Jer 19:14 3414
heard that *J* prophesied these .... Jer 20:1 3414
Then Pashur smote *J* the prophet............ Jer 20:2 3414
brought forth *J* out of the stocks............ Jer 20:3 3414
Then said *J* unto him, The LORD .... Jer 20:3 3414
which came unto *J* from the LORD .... Jer 21:1 3414
Then said *J* unto them, Thus shall .... Jer 21:3 3414
LORD unto me, What seest thou, *J*........... Jer 24:3 3414
The word that came to *J* .... Jer 25:1 3414
The which *J* the prophet spake .... Jer 25:2 3414
which *J* hath prophesied against............. Jer 25:13 3414
all the people heard *J* speaking.............. Jer 26:7 3414
when *J* had made an end of .... Jer 26:8 3414
J in the house of the LORD .... Jer 26:9 3414
Then spake *J* unto all the princes .... Jer 26:12 3414
according to all the words of *J*................ Jer 26:20 3414
the son of Shaphan was with *J* .... Jer 26:24 3414
this word unto *J* from the LORD .... Jer 27:1 3414
Then the prophet *J* said unto the .... Jer 28:5 3414
Even the prophet *J* said, Amen .... Jer 28:6 3414
the prophet *J* went his way .... Jer 28:11 3414
the LORD came unto *J* the prophet........... Jer 28:12 3414
off the neck of the prophet *J* .... Jer 28:12 3414
Then said the prophet *J* unto .... Jer 28:15 3414
the words of the letter that *J*.................. Jer 29:1 3414
thou not reproved *J* of Anathoth............. Jer 29:27 3414
in the ears of *J* the prophet .... Jer 29:29 3414
came the word of the LORD unto *J*........... Jer 29:30 3414
word that came to *J* from the LORD .... Jer 30:1 3414
The word that came to *J* from the........... Jer 32:1 3414
J the prophet was shut up in the............ Jer 32:2 3414

J said, The word of the LORD came .... Jer 32:6 3414
came the word of the LORD unto J .... Jer 32:26 3414
LORD came unto J the second time .... Jer 33:1 3414
the word of the LORD came unto J .... Jer 33:19 3414
the word of the LORD came to J .... Jer 33:23 3414
which came unto J from the LORD .... Jer 34:1 3414
Then J the prophet spake all .... Jer 34:6 3414
that came unto J from the LORD .... Jer 34:8 3414
the LORD came to J from the LORD .... Jer 34:12 3414
The word which came unto J from .... Jer 35:1 3414
I took Jaazaniah the son of J .... Jer 35:3 3414
came the word of the LORD unto J .... Jer 35:12 3414
J said unto the house of the .... Jer 35:18 3414
word came unto J from the LORD .... Jer 36:1 3414
Then J called Baruch the son of .... Jer 36:4 3414
of J all the words of the LORD .... Jer 36:4 3414
J commanded Baruch, saying, I am .... Jer 36:5 3414
that J the prophet commanded him .... Jer 36:8 3414
of J in the house of the LORD .... Jer 36:10 3414
Baruch, Go, hide thee, thou and J .... Jer 36:19 3414
the scribe and J the prophet .... Jer 36:26 3414
the word of the LORD came to J .... Jer 36:27 3414
Baruch wrote at the mouth of J .... Jer 36:27 3414
Then took J another roll, and gave .... Jer 36:32 3414
J all the words of the book which .... Jer 36:32 3414
which he spake by the prophet J .... Jer 37:2 3414
the priest to the prophet J .... Jer 37:3 3414
Now J came in and went out among .... Jer 37:4 3414
of the LORD unto the prophet J .... Jer 37:6 3414
Then J went forth out of .... Jer 37:12 3414
he took J the prophet, saying, ... Jer 37:13 3414
Then said J, It is false .... Jer 37:14 3414
so Irijah took J, and brought him .... Jer 37:14 3414
the princes were wroth with J .... Jer 37:15 3414
When J was entered into the .... Jer 37:16 3414
J had remained there many days .... Jer 37:16 3414
And J said, There is .... Jer 37:17 3414
Moreover J said unto king .... Jer 37:18 3414
that they should commit J into .... Jer 37:21 3414
Thus J remained in the court of .... Jer 37:21 3414
heard the words that J had spoken .... Jer 38:1 3414
Then took they J, and cast him .... Jer 38:6 3414
and they let down J with cords .... Jer 38:6 3414
so J sunk in the mire .... Jer 38:6 3414
they had put J in the dungeon .... Jer 38:7 3414
they have done to J the prophet .... Jer 38:9 3414
take up J the prophet out of the .... Jer 38:10 3414
by cords into the dungeon to J .... Jer 38:11 3414
the Ethiopian said unto J .... Jer 38:12 3414
And J did so .... Jer 38:12 3414
So they drew up J with cords .... Jer 38:13 3414
J remained in the court of the .... Jer 38:13 3414
took J the prophet unto him into .... Jer 38:14 3414
and the king said unto J, I will .... Jer 38:14 3414
Then J said unto Zedekiah, If I .... Jer 38:15 3414
the king sware secretly unto J .... Jer 38:16 3414
Then said J unto Zedekiah, Thus .... Jer 38:17 3414
And Zedekiah the king said unto J .... Jer 38:19 3414
But J said, They shall not .... Jer 38:20 3414
Then said Zedekiah unto J .... Jer 38:24 3414
Then came all the princes unto J .... Jer 38:27 3414
So J abode in the court of the .... Jer 38:28 3414
J to Nebuzar-adan the captain of .... Jer 39:11 3414
took J out of the court of the .... Jer 39:14 3414
the word of the LORD came unto J .... Jer 39:15 3414
word that came to J from the LORD .... Jer 40:1 3414
the captain of the guard took J .... Jer 40:2 3414
Then went J unto Gedaliah the son .... Jer 40:6 3414
said unto J the prophet, Let, we .... Jer 42:2 3414
Then J the prophet said unto them .... Jer 42:4 3414
Then they said to J, The LORD be .... Jer 42:5 3414
the word of the LORD came unto J .... Jer 42:7 3414
that when J had made an end of .... Jer 43:1 3414
all the proud men, saying unto J .... Jer 43:2 3414
J the prophet, and Baruch the son .... Jer 43:6 3414
of the LORD unto J in Tahpanhes .... Jer 43:8 3414
The word that came to J .... Jer 44:1 3414
of Egypt, in Pathros, answered J .... Jer 44:15 3414
Then J said unto all the people, ... Jer 44:20 3414
Moreover J said unto all the .... Jer 44:24 3414
The word that J the prophet spake .... Jer 45:1 3414
words in a book at the mouth of J .... Jer 45:1 3414
came to J the prophet against the .... Jer 46:1 3414
the LORD spake to J the prophet .... Jer 46:13 3414
came to J the prophet against the .... Jer 47:1 3414
word of the LORD that came to J .... Jer 49:34 3414
of the Chaldeans by J the prophet .... Jer 50:1 3414
The word which J the prophet .... Jer 51:59 3414
So J wrote in a book all the evil .... Jer 51:60 3414
J said to Seraiah, When thou .... Jer 51:61 3414
Thus far are the words of J .... Jer 51:64 3414
of the LORD came to J the prophet .... Dan 9:2 3414

7. A priest.

Seraiah, Azariah, J, ... Neh 10:2 3414
Seraiah, J, Ezra, ... Neh 12:1 3414
of J, Hananiah .... Neh 12:12 3414
and Benjamin, and Shemaiah, and J .... Neh 12:34 3414

JEREMIAH'S *(jer-e-mi'-ahz)* {1} *Refers to Jeremiah 6.*

yoke from off the prophet J neck .... Jer 28:10 3414

JEREMIAS *(jer-e-mi'-as)* {1} See JEREMIAH. *Greek form of Jeremiah.*

and others, J, or one of the .... Mt 16:14 *2408*

JEREMOTH *(jer'-e-moth)* {5} See JERIMOTH.

1. A son of Beriah.

And Ahio, Shashak, and J, ... 1Chr 8:14 3406

2. A son of Elam.

and Jehiel, and Abdi, and J .... Ezr 10:26 3406

3. Another who married a foreigner in exile.

Eliashib, Mattaniah, and J .... Ezr 10:27 3406

4. A son of Mushi.

Mahli, and Eder, and J, three 1Chr 23:23 3406

5. A sanctuary servant.

The fifteenth to J, he, his sons, ... 1Chr 25:22 3406

JEREMY *(jer'-e-mee)* {2} See JEREMIAH. *Latin form of Jeremiah.*

which was spoken by J the prophet .... Mt 2:17 *2408*
which was spoken by J the prophet .... Mt 27:9 *2408*

JERIAH *(je-ri'-ah)* {2} See JERIJAH. *A descendant of Hebron.*

J the first, Amariah the second, ... 1Chr 23:19 3404
J the first, Amariah the second, ... 1Chr 24:23 3404

JERIBAI *(jer'-ib-ahee)* {1} *A "mighty man" of David.*

Eliel the Mahavite, and J, and 1Chr 11:46 3403

JERICHO *(jer'-ik-o)* {64} *A city in Benjamin.*

of Moab on this side Jordan by J .... Num 22:1 3405
plains of Moab by Jordan near J .... Num 26:3 3405
plains of Moab by Jordan near J .... Num 26:63 3405
Moab, which are by Jordan near J .... Num 31:12 3405
plains of Moab by Jordan near J .... Num 33:48 3405
plains of Moab by Jordan, near J .... Num 33:50 3405
this side Jordan near J eastward .... Num 34:15 3405
plains of Moab by Jordan near J .... Num 35:1 3405
plains of Moab by Jordan near J .... Num 36:13 3405
of Moab, that is over against J .... Deut 32:49 3405
of Pisgah, that is over against J .... Deut 34:1 3405
and the plain of the valley of J .... Deut 34:3 3405
saying, Go view the land, even J .... Josh 2:1 3405
And it was told the king of J .... Josh 2:2 3405
the king of J sent unto Rahab, ... Josh 2:3 3405
passed over right against J .... Josh 3:16 3405
unto battle, to the plains of J .... Josh 4:13 3405
Gilgal, in the east border of J .... Josh 4:19 3405
month at even in the plains of J .... Josh 5:10 3405
to pass, when Joshua was by J .... Josh 5:13 3405
Now J was straitly shut up .... Josh 6:1 3405
I have given into thine hand J .... Josh 6:2 3405
which Joshua sent to spy out J .... Josh 6:25 3405
riseth up and buildeth this city J .... Josh 6:26 3405
And Joshua sent men from J to Ai .... Josh 7:2 3405
and her king as thou didst unto J .... Josh 8:2 3405
heard what Joshua had done unto J .... Josh 9:3 3405
as he had done to J and her king, ... Josh 10:1 3405
as he did unto the king of J .... Josh 10:28 3405
as he did unto the king of J .... Josh 10:30 3405
The king of J, one .... Josh 12:9 3405
on the other side Jordan, by J .... Josh 13:32 3405
of Joseph fell from Jordan by J .... Josh 16:1 3405
unto the water of J on the east .... Josh 16:1 3405
from J throughout mount Beth-el .... Josh 16:1 3405
and to Naarath, and came to J .... Josh 16:7 3405
the side of J on the north side .... Josh 18:12 3405
to their families were J, and .... Josh 18:21 3405
other side Jordan by J eastward .... Josh 20:8 3405
went over Jordan, and came unto J .... Josh 24:11 3405
the men of J fought against you, ... Josh 24:11 3405
Tarry at J until your beards be 2Sa 10:5 3405
did Hiel the Beth-elite build J 1Kin 16:34 3405
for the LORD hath sent me to J 2Kin 2:4 3405
So they came to J 2Kin 2:4 3405
that were at J came to Elisha 2Kin 2:5 3405
which were to view at J saw him 2Kin 2:15 3405
to him, (for he tarried at J 2Kin 2:18 3405
overtook him in the plains of J 2Kin 25:5 3405
And on the other side Jordan by J 1Chr 6:78 3405
Tarry at J until your beards be 1Chr 19:5 3405
upon asses, and brought them to J 2Chr 28:15 3405
The children of J, three hundred .... Ezr 2:34 3405
unto him builded the men of J .... Neh 3:2 3405
The children of J, three hundred .... Neh 7:36 3405
Zedekiah in the plains of J .... Jer 39:5 3405
Zedekiah in the plains of J .... Jer 52:8 3405
And as they departed from J .... Mt 20:29 *2410*
And they came to J .... Mk 10:46 *2410*
as he went out of J with his .... Mk 10:46 *2410*
man went down from Jerusalem to J .... Lk 10:30 *2410*
that as he was come nigh unto J .... Lk 18:35 *2410*
Jesus entered and passed through J .... Lk 19:1 *2410*
By faith the walls of J fell down .... Heb 11:30 *2410*

JERIEL *(je-ri'-el)* {1} *A son of Tola.*

Uzzi, and Rephaiah, and J, and 1Chr 7:2 3400

JERIJAH *(je-ri'-jah)* {1} *Same as Jeriah.*

the Hebronites was J the chief 1Chr 26:31 3404

JERIMOTH *(jer'-im-oth)* {8} See JEREMOTH.

1. A son of Bela.

Ezbon, and Uzzi, and Uzziel, and J 1Chr 7:7 3406

2. A son of Becher.

and Elioenai, and Omri, and J 1Chr 7:8 3406

3. A warrior in David's army.

Eluzai, and J, and Bealiah, and 1Chr 12:5 3406

4. A son of Mushi.

Mahli, and Eder, and J 1Chr 24:30 3406

5. A sanctuary servant.

Mattaniah, Uzziel, Shebuel, and J 1Chr 25:4 3406

6. A Naphtalite ruler.

of Naphtali, J the son of Azriel 1Chr 27:19 3406

7. A son of David.

of J the son of David to wife 2Chr 11:18 3406

8. A Temple servant.

and Nahath, and Asahel, and J 2Chr 31:13 3406

JERIOTH *(je'-re-oth)* {1} *A wife of Caleb.*

of Azubah his wife, and of J 1Chr 2:18 3408

JEROBOAM *(jer-o-bo'-am)* {102} See JEROBOAM'S.

1. A king of Israel.

J the son of Nebat, an Ephrathite 1Kin 11:26 3379
the man J was a mighty man of 1Kin 11:28 3379
time when J went out of Jerusalem 1Kin 11:29 3379
And he said to J, Take thee ten 1Kin 11:31 3379
sought therefore to kill J 1Kin 11:40 3379
J arose, and fled into Egypt, unto 1Kin 11:40 3379
when J the son of Nebat, who was 1Kin 12:2 3379
king Solomon, and J dwelt in Egypt 1Kin 12:2 3379
And J and all the congregation of 1Kin 12:3 3379
So J and all the people came to 1Kin 12:12 3379
Shilonite unto J the son of Nebat 1Kin 12:15 3379
heard that J was come again 1Kin 12:20 3379
Then J built Shechem in mount 1Kin 12:25 3379
J said in his heart, Now shall 1Kin 12:26 3379
J ordained a feast in the eighth 1Kin 12:32 3379
J stood by the altar to burn 1Kin 13:1 3379
when king J heard the saying of 1Kin 13:4 3379
After this thing J returned not 1Kin 13:33 3379
became sin unto the house of J 1Kin 13:34 3379
Abijah the son of J fell sick 1Kin 14:1 3379
J said to his wife, Arise, I pray 1Kin 14:2 3379
be not known to be the wife of J 1Kin 14:2 3379
the wife of J cometh to ask a 1Kin 14:5 3379
he said, Come in, thou wife of J 1Kin 14:6 3379
Go, tell J, Thus saith the LORD 1Kin 14:7 3379
bring evil upon the house of J 1Kin 14:10 3379
will cut off from J him that 1Kin 14:10 3379
the remnant of the house of J 1Kin 14:10 3379
Him that dieth of J in the city 1Kin 14:11 3379
for he only of J shall come to 1Kin 14:13 3379
God of Israel in the house of J 1Kin 14:13 3379
cut off the house of J that day 1Kin 14:14 3379
up because of the sins of J 1Kin 14:16 3379
And the rest of the acts of J 1Kin 14:19 3379
the days which J reigned were two 1Kin 14:20 3379
Rehoboam and J all their days 1Kin 14:30 3379
in the eighteenth year of king J 1Kin 15:1 3379
J all the days of his life 1Kin 15:6 3379
there was war between Abijam and J 1Kin 15:7 3379
in the twentieth year of J king 1Kin 15:9 3379
Nadab the son of J began to reign 1Kin 15:25 3379
that he smote all the house of J 1Kin 15:29 3379
he left not to J any that 1Kin 15:29 3379
of the sins of J which he sinned 1Kin 15:30 3379
LORD, and walked in the way of J 1Kin 15:34 3379
thou hast walked in the way of J 1Kin 16:2 3379
the house of J the son of Nebat 1Kin 16:3 3379
in being like the house of J 1Kin 16:7 3379
LORD, in walking in the way of J 1Kin 16:19 3379
all the way of J the son of Nebat 1Kin 16:26 3379
in the sins of J the son of Nebat 1Kin 16:31 3379
the house of J the son of Nebat 1Kin 21:22 3379
in the way of J the son of Nebat, ... 1Kin 22:52 3379
the sins of J the son of Nebat 2Kin 3:3 3379
the house of J the son of Nebat 2Kin 9:9 3379
the sins of J the son of Nebat 2Kin 10:29 3379
departed not from the sins of J 2Kin 10:31 3379
the sins of J the son of Nebat 2Kin 13:2 3379
from the sins of the house of J 2Kin 13:6 3379
the sins of J the son of Nebat 2Kin 13:11 3379
the sins of J the son of Nebat 2Kin 14:24 3379
the sins of J the son of Nebat 2Kin 15:9 3379
the sins of J the son of Nebat 2Kin 15:18 3379
the sins of J the son of Nebat 2Kin 15:24 3379
the sins of J the son of Nebat 2Kin 15:28 3379
they made J the son of Nebat king 2Kin 17:21 3379
J drave Israel from following the 2Kin 17:21 3379
in all the sins of J which he did 2Kin 17:22 3379
place which J the son of Nebat 2Kin 23:15 3379
seer against J the son of Nebat 2Chr 9:29 3379
when J the son of Nebat, who was 2Chr 10:2 3379
that J returned out of Egypt 2Chr 10:2 3379
So J and all Israel came and spake 2Chr 10:3 3379
So J and all the people came to 2Chr 10:12 3379
Shilonite to J the son of Nebat 2Chr 10:15 3379
and returned from going against J 2Chr 11:4 3379
for J and his sons had cast them 2Chr 11:14 3379
between Rehoboam and J continually 2Chr 12:15 3379
king J began Abijah to reign over 2Chr 13:1 3379
there was war between Abijah and J 2Chr 13:2 3379
J also set the battle in array 2Chr 13:3 3379
Ephraim, and said, Hear me, thou J 2Chr 13:4 3379
Yet J the son of Nebat, the 2Chr 13:6 3379
which J made you for gods 2Chr 13:8 3379
But J caused an ambushment to 2Chr 13:13 3379
it came to pass, that God smote J 2Chr 13:15 3379
And Abijah pursued after J 2Chr 13:19 3379
Neither did J recover strength 2Chr 13:20 3379

2. Another king of Israel, son of Jehoash.

and J sat upon his throne 2Kin 13:13 3379
J his son reigned in his stead 2Kin 14:16 3379
the son of Joash king of Judah J 2Kin 14:23 3379
by the hand of J the son of Joash 2Kin 14:27 3379
Now the rest of the acts of J 2Kin 14:28 3379
J slept with his fathers, even 2Kin 14:29 3379
seventh year of J king of Israel 2Kin 15:1 3379
of J reign over Israel in Samaria 2Kin 15:8 3379
in the days of J king of Israel 1Chr 5:17 3379
in the days of J the son of Joash .... Hos 1:1 3379
in the days of J the son of Joash .... Amos 1:1 3379
the house of J with the sword .... Amos 7:9 3379
Beth-el sent to J king of Israel .... Amos 7:10 3379
J shall die by the sword, and .... Amos 7:11 3379

JEROBOAM'S *(jer-o-bo'-ams)* {2} *Refers to Jeroboam 1.*
J wife did so, and arose, and went 1Kin 14:4 3379
J wife arose, and departed, and 1Kin 14:17 3379

JEROHAM *(je-ro'-ham)* {10}
1. Grandfather of Samuel.
name was Elkanah, the son of *J* 1Sa 1:1 3395
J his son, Elkanah his son 1Chr 6:27 3395
The son of Elkanah, the son of *J* 1Chr 6:34 3395
2. Head of a Benjamite family.
Eliah, and Zichri, the sons of *J* 1Chr 8:27 3395
3. A descendant of Benjamin.
And Ibneiah the son of *J*, and Elah 1Chr 9:8 3395
4. A family of exiles.
And Adaiah the son of *J*, the son 1Chr 9:12 3395
and Adaiah the son of *J*, the son Neh 11:12 3395
5. A warrior in David's army.
Zebadiah, the sons of *J* of Gedor 1Chr 12:7 3395
6. Father of Azareel.
Of Dan, Azareel the son of *J* 1Chr 27:22 3395
7. Father of Azariah.
of hundreds, Azariah the son of *J* 2Chr 23:1 3395

JERUBBAAL *(je-rub'-ba-al)* {14} See GIDEON, JERUBBESHETH. *Another name for Gideon.*
on that day he called him *J* Judg 6:32 3378
Then *J*, who is Gideon, and all the Judg 7:1 3378
J the son of Joash went and dwelt Judg 8:29 3378
they kindness to the house of *J* Judg 8:35 3378
Abimelech the son of *J* went to Judg 9:1 3378
either that all the sons of *J* Judg 9:2 3378
slew his brethren the sons of *J* Judg 9:5 3378
the youngest son of *J* was left Judg 9:5 3378
and if ye have dealt well with *J* Judg 9:16 3378
dealt truly and sincerely with *J* Judg 9:19 3378
and ten sons of *J* might come Judg 9:24 3378
is not he the son of *J* Judg 9:28 3378
the curse of Jotham the son of *J* Judg 9:57 3378
And the LORD sent *J*, and Bedan, and 1Sa 12:11 3378

JERUBBESHETH *(je-rubb'-be-sheth)* {1} See JERUBBAAL. *Another name for Gideon.*
Who smote Abimelech the son of *J* 2Sa 11:21 3380

JERUEL *(je-ru'-el)* {1} *A wilderness in Judah.*
brook, before the wilderness of *J* 2Chr 20:16 3385

JERUSALEM *(je-ru'-sa-lem)* {811} See JERUSALEM'S, SALEM. *City where the Temple was located.*
when Adoni-zedek king of *J* had Josh 10:1 3389
Wherefore Adoni-zedek king of *J* Josh 10:3 3389
of the Amorites, the king of *J* Josh 10:5 3389
out of the cave, the king of *J* Josh 10:23 3389
The king of *J*, one Josh 12:10 3389
Jebusite; the same is *J* Josh 15:8 3389
Jebusites the inhabitants of *J* Josh 15:63 3389
of Judah at *J* unto this day Josh 15:63 3389
Eleph, and Jebusi, which is *J* Josh 18:28 3389
And they brought him to *J*, and Judg 1:7 3389
of Judah had fought against *J* Judg 1:8 3389
the Jebusites that inhabited *J* Judg 1:21 3389
of Benjamin in *J* unto this day Judg 1:21 3389
over against Jebus, which is *J* Judg 19:10 3389
Philistine, and brought it to *J* 1Sa 17:54 3389
in *J* he reigned thirty and three 2Sa 5:5 3389
his men went to *J* unto the 2Sa 5:6 3389
more concubines and wives out of *J* 2Sa 5:13 3389
that were born unto him in *J* 2Sa 5:14 3389
Hadadezer, and brought them to *J* 2Sa 8:7 3389
So Mephibosheth dwelt in *J* 2Sa 9:13 3389
children of Ammon, and came to *J* 2Sa 10:14 3389
But David tarried still at *J* 2Sa 11:1 3389
So Uriah abode in *J* that day 2Sa 11:12 3389
and all the people returned unto *J* 2Sa 12:31 3389
Geshur, and brought Absalom to *J* 2Sa 14:23 3389
Absalom dwelt two full years in *J* 2Sa 14:28 3389
shall bring me again indeed to *J* 2Sa 15:8 3389
went two hundred men out of *J* 2Sa 15:11 3389
servants that were with him at *J* 2Sa 15:14 3389
carried the ark of God again to *J* 2Sa 15:29 3389
the city, and Absalom came into *J* 2Sa 15:37 3389
the king, Behold, he abideth at *J* 2Sa 16:3 3389
the men of Israel, came to *J* 2Sa 16:15 3389
not find them, they returned to *J* 2Sa 17:20 3389
my lord the king went out of *J* 2Sa 19:19 3389
he was come to *J* to meet the king 2Sa 19:25 3389
and I will feed thee with me in *J* 2Sa 19:33 3389
should go up with the king unto *J* 2Sa 19:34 3389
their king, from Jordan even to *J* 2Sa 20:2 3389
And David came to his house at *J* 2Sa 20:3 3389
and they went out of *J*, to pursue 2Sa 20:7 3389
Joab returned to *J* unto the king 2Sa 20:22 3389
they came to *J* at the end of nine 2Sa 24:8 3389
out his hand upon *J* to destroy it 2Sa 24:16 3389
and three years reigned he in *J* 1Kin 2:11 3389
him, Build thee an house in *J* 1Kin 2:36 3389
And Shimei dwelt in *J* many days 1Kin 2:38 3389
Shimei had gone from *J* to Gath 1Kin 2:41 3389
and the wall of *J* round about 1Kin 3:1 3389
And he came to *J*, and stood before 1Kin 3:15 3389
of Israel, unto king Solomon in *J* 1Kin 8:1 3389
house, and Millo, and the wall of *J* 1Kin 9:15 3389
Solomon desired to build in *J* 1Kin 9:19 3389
she came to *J* with a very great 1Kin 10:2 3389
chariots, and with the king at *J* 1Kin 10:26 3389
made silver to be in *J* as stones 1Kin 10:27 3389
in the hill that is before *J* 1Kin 11:7 3389
time when Jeroboam went out of *J* 1Kin 11:29 3389
have a light alway before me in *J* 1Kin 11:36 3389
time that Solomon reigned in *J* 1Kin 11:42 3389
up to his chariot, to flee to *J* 1Kin 12:18 3389
And when Rehoboam was come to *J* 1Kin 12:21 3389
in the house of the LORD at *J* 1Kin 12:27 3389
is too much for you to go up to *J* 1Kin 12:28 3389
he reigned seventeen years in *J* 1Kin 14:21 3389
king of Egypt came up against *J* 1Kin 14:25 3389
Three years reigned he in *J* 1Kin 15:2 3389
LORD his God give him a lamp in *J* 1Kin 15:4 3389
son after him, and to establish *J* 1Kin 15:4 3389
and one years reigned he in *J* 1Kin 15:10 3389
reigned twenty and five years in *J* 1Kin 22:42 3389
and he reigned eight years in *J* 2Kin 8:17 3389
and he reigned one year in *J* 2Kin 8:26 3389
carried him in a chariot to *J* 2Kin 9:28 3389
and forty years reigned he in *J* 2Kin 12:1 3389
Hazael set his face to go up to *J* 2Kin 12:17 3389
and he went away from *J* 2Kin 12:18 3389
reigned twenty and nine years in *J* 2Kin 14:2 3389
mother's name was Jehoaddan of *J* 2Kin 14:2 3389
at Beth-shemesh, and came to *J* 2Kin 14:13 3389
brake down the wall of *J* from the 2Kin 14:13 3389
a conspiracy against him in *J* 2Kin 14:19 3389
he was buried at *J* with his 2Kin 14:20 3389
reigned two and fifty years in *J* 2Kin 15:2 3389
mother's name was Jecholiah of *J* 2Kin 15:2 3389
and he reigned sixteen years in *J* 2Kin 15:33 3389
and reigned sixteen years in *J* 2Kin 16:2 3389
of Israel came up to *J* to war 2Kin 16:5 3389
reigned twenty and nine years in *J* 2Kin 18:2 3389
with a great host against *J* 2Kin 18:17 3389
And they went up and came to *J* 2Kin 18:17 3389
away, and hath said to Judah and *J* 2Kin 18:22 3389
worship before this altar in *J* 2Kin 18:22 3389
should deliver *J* out of mine hand 2Kin 18:35 3389
J shall not be delivered into the 2Kin 19:10 3389
the daughter of *J* hath shaken her 2Kin 19:21 3389
For out of *J* shall go forth a 2Kin 19:31 3389
reigned fifty and five years in *J* 2Kin 21:1 3389
said, In *J* will I put my name 2Kin 21:4 3389
his son, In this house, and in *J* 2Kin 21:7 3389
I am bringing such evil upon *J* 2Kin 21:12 3389
over *J* the line of Samaria 2Kin 21:13 3389
I will wipe *J* as a man wipeth a 2Kin 21:13 3389
till he had filled *J* from one end 2Kin 21:16 3389
and he reigned two years in *J* 2Kin 21:19 3389
reigned thirty and one years in *J* 2Kin 22:1 3389
now she dwelt in *J* in the college 2Kin 22:14 3389
all the elders of Judah and of *J* 2Kin 23:1 3389
all the inhabitants of *J* with him 2Kin 23:2 3389
he burned them without *J* in the 2Kin 23:4 3389
and in the places round about *J* 2Kin 23:5 3389
the house of the LORD, without *J* 2Kin 23:6 3389
up to the altar of the LORD in *J* 2Kin 23:9 3389
high places that were before *J* 2Kin 23:13 3389
bones upon them, and returned to *J* 2Kin 23:20 3389
was holden to the LORD in *J* 2Kin 23:23 3389
in the land of Judah and in *J* 2Kin 23:24 3389
this city *J* which I have chosen 2Kin 23:27 3389
from Megiddo, and brought him to *J* 2Kin 23:30 3389
and he reigned three months in *J* 2Kin 23:31 3389
that he might not reign in *J* 2Kin 23:33 3389
and he reigned eleven years in *J* 2Kin 23:36 3389
for he filled *J* with innocent 2Kin 24:4 3389
and he reigned in *J* three months 2Kin 24:8 3389
the daughter of Elnathan of *J* 2Kin 24:8 3389
king of Babylon came up against *J* 2Kin 24:10 3389
And he carried away all *J*, and all 2Kin 24:14 3389
into captivity from *J* to Babylon 2Kin 24:15 3389
and he reigned eleven years in *J* 2Kin 24:18 3389
of the LORD it came to pass in *J* 2Kin 24:20 3389
he, and all his host, against *J* 2Kin 25:1 3389
of the king of Babylon, unto *J* 2Kin 25:8 3389
house, and all the houses of *J* 2Kin 25:9 3389
down the walls of *J* round about 2Kin 25:10 3389
in *J* he reigned thirty and three 1Chr 3:4 3389
And these were born unto him in *J* 1Chr 3:5 3389
temple that Solomon built in *J* 1Chr 6:10 3389
J by the hand of Nebuchadnezzar 1Chr 6:15 3389
built the house of the LORD in *J* 1Chr 6:32 3389
These dwelt in *J* 1Chr 8:28 3389
dwelt with their brethren in *J* 1Chr 8:32 3389
in *J* dwelt of the children of 1Chr 9:3 3389
these dwelt at *J* 1Chr 9:34 3389
dwelt with their brethren at *J* 1Chr 9:38 3389
And David and all Israel went to *J* 1Chr 11:4 3389
And David took more wives at *J* 1Chr 14:3 3389
of his children which he had in *J* 1Chr 14:4 3389
gathered all Israel together to *J* 1Chr 15:3 3389
Hadarezer, and brought them to *J* 1Chr 18:7 3389
Then Joab came to *J* 1Chr 19:15 3389
But David tarried at *J* 1Chr 20:1 3389
and all the people returned to *J* 1Chr 20:3 3389
all Israel, and came to *J* 1Chr 21:4 3389
an angel unto *J* to destroy it 1Chr 21:15 3389
in his hand stretched out over *J* 1Chr 21:16 3389
that they may dwell in *J* for ever 1Chr 23:25 3389
with all the valiant men, unto *J* 1Chr 28:1 3389
and three years reigned he in *J* 1Chr 29:27 3389
he had pitched a tent for it at *J* 2Chr 1:4 3389
place that was at Gibeon to *J* 2Chr 1:13 3389
cities, and with the king at *J* 2Chr 1:14 3389
gold at *J* as plenteous as stones 2Chr 1:15 3389
that are with me in Judah and in *J* 2Chr 2:7 3389
and thou shalt carry it up to *J* 2Chr 2:16 3389
of the LORD at *J* in mount Moriah 2Chr 3:1 3389
of the children of Israel, unto *J* 2Chr 5:2 3389
But I have chosen *J*, that my name 2Chr 6:6 3389
Solomon desired to build in *J* 2Chr 8:6 3389
Solomon with hard questions at *J* 2Chr 9:1 3389
cities, and with the king at *J* 2Chr 9:25 3389
king made silver in *J* as stones 2Chr 9:27 3389
Solomon reigned in *J* over all 2Chr 9:30 3389
up to his chariot, to flee to *J* 2Chr 10:18 3389
And when Rehoboam was come to *J* 2Chr 11:1 3389
And Rehoboam dwelt in *J*, and built 2Chr 11:5 3389
possession, and came to Judah and *J* 2Chr 11:14 3389
the LORD God of Israel came to *J* 2Chr 11:16 3389
king of Egypt came up against *J* 2Chr 12:2 3389
pertained to Judah, and came to *J* 2Chr 12:4 3389
together to *J* because of Shishak 2Chr 12:5 3389
out upon *J* by the hand of Shishak 2Chr 12:7 3389
king of Egypt came up against *J* 2Chr 12:9 3389
strengthened himself in *J* 2Chr 12:13 3389
he reigned seventeen years in *J* 2Chr 12:13 3389
He reigned three years in *J* 2Chr 13:2 3389
in abundance, and returned to *J* 2Chr 14:15 3389
together at *J* in the third month 2Chr 15:10 3389
mighty men of valour, were in *J* 2Chr 17:13 3389
to his house in peace to *J* 2Chr 19:1 3389
And Jehoshaphat dwelt at *J* 2Chr 19:4 3389
Moreover in *J* did Jehoshaphat set 2Chr 19:8 3389
when they returned to *J* 2Chr 19:8 3389
in the congregation of Judah and *J* 2Chr 20:5 3389
all Judah, and ye inhabitants of *J* 2Chr 20:15 3389
the LORD with you, O Judah and *J* 2Chr 20:17 3389
the inhabitants of *J* fell before 2Chr 20:18 3389
O Judah, and ye inhabitants of *J* 2Chr 20:20 3389
returned, every man of Judah and *J* 2Chr 20:27 3389
them, to go again to *J* with joy 2Chr 20:27 3389
they came to *J* with psalteries and 2Chr 20:28 3389
reigned twenty and five years in *J* 2Chr 20:31 3389
and he reigned eight years in *J* 2Chr 21:5 3389
of *J* to commit fornication 2Chr 21:11 3389
inhabitants of *J* to go a whoring 2Chr 21:13 3389
and he reigned in *J* eight years 2Chr 21:20 3389
the inhabitants of *J* made Ahaziah 2Chr 22:1 3389
and he reigned one year in *J* 2Chr 22:2 3389
of Israel, and they came to *J* 2Chr 23:2 3389
and he reigned forty years in *J* 2Chr 24:1 3389
Judah and out of *J* the collection, 2Chr 24:6 3389
a proclamation through Judah and *J* 2Chr 24:9 3389
J for this their trespass 2Chr 24:18 3389
and they came to Judah and *J* 2Chr 24:23 3389
reigned twenty and nine years in *J* 2Chr 25:1 3389
mother's name was Jehoaddan of *J* 2Chr 25:1 3389
Beth-shemesh, and brought him to *J* 2Chr 25:23 3389
brake down the wall of *J* from the 2Chr 25:23 3389
a conspiracy against him in *J* 2Chr 25:27 3389
reigned fifty and two years in *J* 2Chr 26:3 3389
name also was Jecoliah of *J* 2Chr 26:3 3389
towers in *J* at the corner gate 2Chr 26:9 3389
And he made in *J* engines, invented 2Chr 26:15 3389
and he reigned sixteen years in *J* 2Chr 27:1 3389
and reigned sixteen years in *J* 2Chr 27:8 3389
and he reigned sixteen years in *J* 2Chr 28:1 3389
J for bondmen and bondwomen unto 2Chr 28:10 3389
him altars in every corner of *J* 2Chr 28:24 3389
buried him in the city, even in *J* 2Chr 28:27 3389
reigned nine and twenty years in *J* 2Chr 29:1 3389
of the LORD was upon Judah and *J* 2Chr 29:8 3389
to the house of the LORD at *J* 2Chr 30:1 3389
and all the congregation in *J* 2Chr 30:2 3389
gathered themselves together to *J* 2Chr 30:3 3389
unto the LORD God of Israel at *J* 2Chr 30:5 3389
humbled themselves, and came to *J* 2Chr 30:11 3389
there assembled at *J* much people 2Chr 30:13 3389
away the altars that were in *J* 2Chr 30:14 3389
at *J* kept the feast of unleavened 2Chr 30:21 3389
So there was great joy in *J* 2Chr 30:26 3389
there was not the like in *J* 2Chr 30:26 3389
the people that dwelt in *J* to 2Chr 31:4 3389
was purposed to fight against *J* 2Chr 32:2 3389
of Assyria send his servants to *J* 2Chr 32:9 3389
and unto all Judah that were at *J* 2Chr 32:9 3389
that ye abide in the siege in *J* 2Chr 32:10 3389
altars, and commanded Judah and *J* 2Chr 32:12 3389
people of *J* that were on the wall 2Chr 32:18 3389
they spake against the God of *J* 2Chr 32:19 3389
the inhabitants of *J* from the 2Chr 32:22 3389
brought gifts unto the LORD to *J* 2Chr 32:23 3389
upon him, and upon Judah and *J* 2Chr 32:25 3389
both he and the inhabitants of *J* 2Chr 32:26 3389
the inhabitants of *J* did him 2Chr 32:33 3389
reigned fifty and five years in *J* 2Chr 33:1 3389
In *J* shall my name be for ever 2Chr 33:4 3389
his son, In this house, and in *J* 2Chr 33:7 3389
and the inhabitants of *J* to err 2Chr 33:9 3389
him again to *J* into his kingdom 2Chr 33:13 3389
of the house of the LORD, and in *J* 2Chr 33:15 3389
reign, and reigned two years in *J* 2Chr 33:21 3389
to reign, and he reigned in *J* one 2Chr 34:1 3389
J from the high places, and the 2Chr 34:3 3389
altars, and cleansed Judah and *J* 2Chr 34:5 3389
land of Israel, he returned to *J* 2Chr 34:7 3389
and they returned to *J* 2Chr 34:9 3389
now she dwelt in *J* in the college 2Chr 34:22 3389
all the elders of Judah and *J* 2Chr 34:29 3389
of Judah, and the inhabitants of *J* 2Chr 34:30 3389
caused all that were present in *J* 2Chr 34:32 3389
And the inhabitants of *J* did 2Chr 34:32 3389
a passover unto the LORD in *J* 2Chr 35:1 3389
present, and the inhabitants of *J* 2Chr 35:18 3389
and they brought him to *J*, and he 2Chr 35:24 3389
all Judah and *J* mourned for Josiah 2Chr 35:24 3389
king in his father's stead in *J* 2Chr 36:1 3389
and he reigned three months in *J* 2Chr 36:2 3389
king of Egypt put him down at *J* 2Chr 36:3 3389

his brother king over Judah and *J*	2Chr 36:4	3389
and he reigned eleven years in *J*	2Chr 36:5	3389
three months and ten days in *J*	2Chr 36:9	3389
his brother king over Judah and *J*	2Chr 36:10	3389
and reigned eleven years in *J*	2Chr 36:11	3389
LORD which he had hallowed in *J*	2Chr 36:14	3389
God, and brake down the wall of *J*	2Chr 36:19	3389
me to build him an house in *J*	2Chr 36:23	3389
me to build him an house at *J*	Ezr 1:2	3389
with him, and let him go up to *J*	Ezr 1:3	3389
(he is the God,) which is in *J*	Ezr 1:3	3389
for the house of God that is in *J*	Ezr 1:4	3389
house of the LORD which is in *J*	Ezr 1:5	3389
had brought forth out of *J*	Ezr 1:7	3389
brought up from Babylon unto *J*	Ezr 1:11	3389
Babylon, and came again unto *J*	Ezr 2:1	3389
house of the LORD which is at *J*	Ezr 2:68	3389
together as one man to *J*	Ezr 3:1	3389
coming unto the house of God at *J*	Ezr 3:8	3389
come out of the captivity unto *J*	Ezr 3:8	3389
the inhabitants of Judah and *J*	Ezr 4:6	3389
scribe wrote a letter against *J*	Ezr 4:8	3390
from thee to us are come unto *J*	Ezr 4:12	3390
been mighty kings also over *J*	Ezr 4:20	3390
up in haste to *J* unto the Jews	Ezr 4:23	3390
of the house of God which is at *J*	Ezr 4:24	3390
J in the name of the God of	Ezr 5:1	3390
the house of God which is at *J*	Ezr 5:2	3390
out of the temple that was in *J*	Ezr 5:14	3390
them into the temple that is in *J*	Ezr 5:15	3390
of the house of God which is in *J*	Ezr 5:16	3390
to build this house of God at *J*	Ezr 5:17	3390
concerning the house of God at *J*	Ezr 6:3	3390
out of the temple which is at *J*	Ezr 6:5	3390
unto the temple which is at *J*	Ezr 6:5	3390
of the priests which are at *J*	Ezr 6:9	3390
this house of God which is at *J*	Ezr 6:12	3390
the service of God, which is at *J*	Ezr 6:18	3390
porters, and the Nethinims, unto *J*	Ezr 7:7	3389
he came to *J* in the fifth month,	Ezr 7:8	3389
of the fifth month came he to *J*	Ezr 7:9	3389
their own freewill to go up to *J*	Ezr 7:13	3390
to enquire concerning Judah and *J*	Ezr 7:14	3390
Israel, whose habitation is in *J*	Ezr 7:15	3390
house of their God which is in *J*	Ezr 7:16	3390
house of your God which is in *J*	Ezr 7:17	3390
deliver thou before the God of *J*	Ezr 7:19	3390
house of the LORD which is in *J*	Ezr 7:27	3389
of the fathers of Israel, at *J*	Ezr 8:29	3389
to bring them to *J* unto the house	Ezr 8:30	3389
of the first month, to go unto *J*	Ezr 8:31	3389
And we came to *J*, and abode there	Ezr 8:32	3389
give us a wall in Judah and in *J*	Ezr 9:9	3389
J unto all the children of the	Ezr 10:7	3389
gather themselves together unto *J*	Ezr 10:7	3389
together unto *J* within three days	Ezr 10:9	3389
of the captivity, and concerning *J*	Neh 1:2	3389
the wall of *J* also is broken down	Neh 1:3	3389
So I came to *J*, and was there	Neh 2:11	3389
had put in my heart to do at *J*	Neh 2:12	3389
port, and viewed the walls of *J*	Neh 2:13	3389
how *J* lieth waste, and the gates	Neh 2:17	3389
and let us build up the wall of *J*	Neh 2:17	3389
nor right, nor memorial, in *J*	Neh 2:20	3389
they fortified *J* unto the broad	Neh 3:8	3389
the ruler of the half part of *J*	Neh 3:9	3389
the ruler of the half part of *J*	Neh 3:12	3389
that the walls of *J* were made up	Neh 4:7	3389
to come and to fight against *J*	Neh 4:8	3389
with his servant lodge within *J*	Neh 4:22	3389
prophets to preach of thee at *J*	Neh 6:7	3389
of the palace, charge over *J*	Neh 7:2	3389
Let not the gates of *J* be opened	Neh 7:3	3389
watches of the inhabitants of *J*	Neh 7:3	3389
carried away, and came again to *J*	Neh 7:6	3389
in all their cities, and in *J*	Neh 8:15	3389
rulers of the people dwelt at *J*	Neh 11:1	3389
ten to dwell in *J* the holy city	Neh 11:1	3389
offered themselves to dwell at *J*	Neh 11:2	3389
of the province that dwelt in *J*	Neh 11:3	3389
at *J* dwelt certain of the	Neh 11:4	3389
at *J* were four hundred threescore	Neh 11:6	3389
at *J* was Uzzi the son of Bani	Neh 11:22	3389
the dedication of the wall of *J*	Neh 12:27	3389
their places, to bring them to *J*	Neh 12:27	3389
the plain country round about *J*	Neh 12:28	3389
them villages round about *J*	Neh 12:29	3389
so that the joy of *J* was heard	Neh 12:43	3389
in all this time was not I at *J*	Neh 13:6	3389
And I came to *J*, and understood of	Neh 13:7	3389
brought into *J* on the sabbath day	Neh 13:15	3389
the children of Judah, and in *J*	Neh 13:16	3389
that when the gates of *J* began to	Neh 13:19	3389
lodged without *J* once or twice	Neh 13:20	3389
J with the captivity which had	Est 2:6	3389
build thou the walls of *J*	Ps 51:18	3389
Because of thy temple at *J* shall	Ps 68:29	3389
they have laid *J* on heaps	Ps 79:1	3389
shed like water round about *J*	Ps 79:3	3389
LORD in Zion, and his praise in *J*	Ps 102:21	3389
house, in the midst of thee, O *J*	Ps 116:19	3389
shall stand within thy gates, O *J*	Ps 122:2	3389
J is builded as a city that is	Ps 122:3	3389
Pray for the peace of *J*	Ps 122:6	3389
the mountains are round about *J*	Ps 125:2	3389
of *J* all the days of thy life	Ps 128:5	3389
out of Zion, which dwelleth at *J*	Ps 135:21	3389
If I forget thee, O *J*, let my	Ps 137:5	3389
if I prefer not *J* above my chief	Ps 137:6	3389
children of Edom in the day of *J*	Ps 137:7	3389
The LORD doth build up *J*	Ps 147:2	3389
Praise the LORD, O *J*	Ps 147:12	3389
the son of David, king in *J*	Eccl 1:1	3389
was king over Israel in *J*	Eccl 1:12	3389
that have been before me in *J*	Eccl 1:16	3389
all that were in *J* before me	Eccl 2:7	3389
than all that were before me in *J*	Eccl 2:9	3389
but comely, O ye daughters of *J*	Song 1:5	3389
I charge you, O ye daughters of *J*	Song 2:7	3389
I charge you, O ye daughters of *J*	Song 3:5	3389
with love, for the daughters of *J*	Song 3:10	3389
I charge you, O daughters of *J*	Song 5:8	3389
is my friend, O daughters of *J*	Song 5:16	3389
O my love, as Tirzah, comely as *J*	Song 6:4	3389
I charge you, O daughters of *J*	Song 8:4	3389
J in the days of Uzziah, Jotham,	Is 1:1	3389
of Amoz saw concerning Judah and *J*	Is 2:1	3389
and the word of the LORD from *J*	Is 2:3	3389
of hosts, doth take away from *J*	Is 3:1	3389
For *J* is ruined, and Judah is	Is 3:8	3389
Zion, and he that remaineth in *J*	Is 4:3	3389
is written among the living in *J*	Is 4:3	3389
J from the midst thereof by the	Is 4:4	3389
And now, O inhabitants of *J*	Is 5:3	3389
went up toward *J* to war against	Is 7:1	3389
a snare to the inhabitants of *J*	Is 8:14	3389
graven images did excel them of *J*	Is 10:10	3389
Samaria and her idols, so do to *J*	Is 10:11	3389
work upon mount Zion and on *J*	Is 10:12	3389
daughter of Zion, the hill of *J*	Is 10:32	3389
ye have numbered the houses of *J*	Is 22:10	3389
a father to the inhabitants of *J*	Is 22:21	3389
reign in mount Zion, and in *J*	Is 24:23	3389
the LORD in the holy mount at *J*	Is 27:13	3389
rule this people which is in *J*	Is 28:14	3389
people shall dwell in Zion at *J*	Is 30:19	3389
will the LORD of hosts defend *J*	Is 31:5	3389
is in Zion, and his furnace in *J*	Is 31:9	3389
shall see *J* a quiet habitation	Is 33:20	3389
sent Rabshakeh from Lachish to *J*	Is 36:2	3389
away, and said to Judah and to *J*	Is 36:7	3389
should deliver *J* out of my hand	Is 36:20	3389
J shall not be given into the	Is 37:10	3389
the daughter of *J* hath shaken her	Is 37:22	3389
For out of *J* shall go forth a	Is 37:32	3389
Speak ye comfortably to *J*	Is 40:2	3389
O *J*, that bringest good tidings,	Is 40:9	3389
I will give to *J* one that	Is 41:27	3389
that saith to *J*, Thou shalt be	Is 44:26	3389
even saying to *J*, Thou shalt be	Is 44:28	3389
Awake, awake, stand up, O *J*	Is 51:17	3389
on thy beautiful garments, O *J*	Is 52:1	3389
arise, and sit down, O *J*	Is 52:2	3389
together, ye waste places of *J*	Is 52:9	3389
his people, he hath redeemed *J*	Is 52:9	3389
set watchmen upon thy walls, O *J*	Is 62:6	3389
till he make *J* a praise in the	Is 62:7	3389
is a wilderness, *J* a desolation	Is 64:10	3389
I create *J* a rejoicing, and her	Is 65:18	3389
And I will rejoice in *J*, and joy in	Is 65:19	3389
Rejoice ye with *J*, and be glad	Is 66:10	3389
and ye shall be comforted in *J*	Is 66:13	3389
beasts, to my holy mountain *J*	Is 66:20	3389
unto the carrying away of *J*	Jer 1:3	3389
at the entering of the gates of *J*	Jer 1:15	3389
Go and cry in the ears of *J*	Jer 2:2	3389
call *J* the throne of the LORD	Jer 3:17	3389
it, to the name of the LORD, to *J*	Jer 3:17	3389
the LORD to the men of Judah and *J*	Jer 4:3	3389
men of Judah and inhabitants of *J*	Jer 4:4	3389
ye in Judah, and publish in *J*	Jer 4:5	3389
greatly deceived this people and *J*	Jer 4:10	3389
it be said to this people and to *J*	Jer 4:11	3389
O *J*, wash thine heart from	Jer 4:14	3389
behold, publish against *J*	Jer 4:16	3389
and fro through the streets of *J*	Jer 5:1	3389
to flee out of the midst of *J*	Jer 6:1	3389
trees, and cast a mount against *J*	Jer 6:6	3389
Be thou instructed, O *J*, lest my	Jer 6:8	3389
of Judah and in the streets of *J*	Jer 7:17	3389
Cut off thine hair, O *J*, and cast	Jer 7:29	3389
Judah, and from the streets of *J*	Jer 7:34	3389
the bones of the inhabitants of *J*	Jer 8:1	3389
Why then is this people of *J*	Jer 8:5	3389
And I will make *J* heaps, and a den	Jer 9:11	3389
Judah, and to the inhabitants of *J*	Jer 11:2	3389
of Judah, and in the streets of *J*	Jer 11:6	3389
and among the inhabitants of *J*	Jer 11:9	3389
of Judah and inhabitants of *J* go	Jer 11:12	3389
J have ye set up altars to that	Jer 11:13	3389
of Judah, and the great pride of *J*	Jer 13:9	3389
and all the inhabitants of *J*	Jer 13:13	3389
Woe unto thee, O *J*	Jer 13:27	3389
and the cry of *J* is gone up	Jer 14:2	3389
of *J* because of the famine	Jer 14:16	3389
Judah, for that which he did in *J*	Jer 15:4	3389
shall have pity upon thee, O *J*	Jer 15:5	3389
go out, and in all the gates of *J*	Jer 17:19	3389
and all the inhabitants of *J*	Jer 17:20	3389
nor bring it in by the gates of *J*	Jer 17:21	3389
of Judah, and the inhabitants of *J*	Jer 17:25	3389
Judah, and from the places about *J*	Jer 17:26	3389
the gates of *J* on the sabbath day	Jer 17:27	3389
it shall devour the palaces of *J*	Jer 17:27	3389
Judah, and to the inhabitants of *J*	Jer 18:11	3389
of Judah, and inhabitants of *J*	Jer 19:3	3389
of Judah and *J* in this place	Jer 19:7	3389
And the houses of *J*, and the houses	Jer 19:13	3389
cast forth beyond the gates of *J*	Jer 22:19	3389
prophets of *J* an horrible thing	Jer 23:14	3389
for from the prophets of *J* is	Jer 23:15	3389
the carpenters and smiths, from *J*	Jer 24:1	3389
his princes, and the residue of *J*	Jer 24:8	3389
and to all the inhabitants of *J*	Jer 25:2	3389
To wit, *J*, and the cities of Judah	Jer 25:18	3389
J shall become heaps, and the	Jer 26:18	3389
to *J* unto Zedekiah king of Judah	Jer 27:3	3389
of the king of Judah, and at *J*	Jer 27:18	3389
king of Judah from *J* to Babylon	Jer 27:20	3389
and all the nobles of Judah and *J*	Jer 27:20	3389
of the king of Judah and of *J*	Jer 27:21	3389
J unto the residue of the elders	Jer 29:1	3389
away captive from *J* to Babylon	Jer 29:1	3389
the princes of Judah and *J*	Jer 29:2	3389
the smiths, were departed from *J*	Jer 29:2	3389
carried away from *J* unto Babylon	Jer 29:4	3389
I have sent from *J* to Babylon	Jer 29:20	3389
unto all the people that are at *J*	Jer 29:25	3389
king of Babylon's army besieged *J*	Jer 32:2	3389
of Judah, and the inhabitants of *J*	Jer 32:32	3389
and in the places about *J*	Jer 32:44	3389
of Judah, and in the streets of *J*	Jer 33:10	3389
and in the places about *J*	Jer 33:13	3389
be saved, and *J* shall dwell safely	Jer 33:16	3389
all the people, fought against *J*	Jer 34:1	3389
unto Zedekiah king of Judah in *J*	Jer 34:6	3389
Babylon's army fought against *J*	Jer 34:7	3389
all the people which were at *J*	Jer 34:8	3389
of Judah, and the princes of *J*	Jer 34:19	3389
let us go to *J* for fear of the	Jer 35:11	3389
so we dwell at *J*	Jer 35:11	3389
of Judah and the inhabitants of *J*	Jer 35:13	3389
of *J* all the evil that I have	Jer 35:17	3389
the LORD to all the people in *J*	Jer 36:9	3389
from the cities of Judah unto *J*	Jer 36:9	3389
and upon the inhabitants of *J*	Jer 36:31	3389
besieged *J* heard tidings of them	Jer 37:5	3389
of them, they departed from *J*	Jer 37:5	3389
from *J* for fear of Pharaoh's army	Jer 37:11	3389
J to go into the land of Benjamin	Jer 37:12	3389
until the day that *J* was taken	Jer 38:28	3389
and he was there when *J* was taken	Jer 38:28	3389
Babylon and all his army against *J*	Jer 39:1	3389
and brake down the walls of *J*	Jer 39:8	3389
were carried away captive of *J*	Jer 40:1	3389
forth upon the inhabitants of *J*	Jer 42:18	3389
evil that I have brought upon *J*	Jer 44:2	3389
of Judah and in the streets of *J*	Jer 44:6	3389
of Judah, and in the streets of *J*	Jer 44:9	3389
of Egypt, as I have punished *J*	Jer 44:13	3389
of Judah, and in the streets of *J*	Jer 44:17	3389
of Judah, and in the streets of *J*	Jer 44:21	3389
of Chaldea, shall *J* say	Jer 51:35	3389
let *J* come into your mind	Jer 51:50	3389
and he reigned eleven years in *J*	Jer 52:1	3389
of the LORD it came to pass in *J*	Jer 52:3	3389
he and all his army, against *J*	Jer 52:4	3389
the king of Babylon, into *J*	Jer 52:12	3389
and all the houses of *J*, and all	Jer 52:13	3389
all the walls of *J* round about	Jer 52:14	3389
from *J* eight hundred thirty	Jer 52:29	3389
J remembered in the days of her	Lam 1:7	3389
J hath grievously sinned	Lam 1:8	3389
J is as a menstruous woman among	Lam 1:17	3389
the virgins of *J* hang down their	Lam 2:10	3389
I liken to thee, O daughter of *J*	Lam 2:13	3389
their head at the daughter of *J*	Lam 2:15	3389
have entered into the gates of *J*	Lam 4:12	3389
pourtray upon it the city, even *J*	Eze 4:1	3389
thy face toward the siege of *J*	Eze 4:7	3389
break the staff of bread in *J*	Eze 4:16	3389
This is *J*	Eze 5:5	3389
me in the visions of God to *J*	Eze 8:3	3389
the city, through the midst of *J*	Eze 9:4	3389
pouring out of thy fury upon *J*	Eze 9:8	3389
the inhabitants of *J* have said	Eze 11:15	3389
burden concerneth the prince in *J*	Eze 12:10	3389
Lord GOD of the inhabitants of *J*	Eze 12:19	3389
which prophesy concerning *J*	Eze 13:16	3389
my four sore judgments upon *J*	Eze 14:21	3389
evil that I have brought upon *J*	Eze 14:22	3389
will I give the inhabitants of *J*	Eze 15:6	3389
cause *J* to know her abominations,	Eze 16:2	3389
Thus saith the Lord GOD unto *J*	Eze 16:3	3389
the king of Babylon is come to *J*	Eze 17:12	3389
Son of man, set thy face toward *J*	Eze 21:2	3389
to Judah in *J* the defenced	Eze 21:20	3389
hand was the divination for *J*	Eze 21:22	3389
gather you into the midst of *J*	Eze 22:19	3389
Samaria is Aholah, and *J* Aholibah	Eze 23:4	3389
himself against *J* this same day	Eze 24:2	3389
that Tyrus hath said against *J*	Eze 26:2	3389
had escaped out of *J* came unto me	Eze 33:21	3389
as the flock of *J* in her solemn	Eze 36:38	3389
king of Babylon unto *J*, and	Dan 1:1	3389
out of the temple which was in *J*	Dan 5:2	3390
the house of God which was at *J*	Dan 5:3	3390
open in his chamber toward *J*	Dan 6:10	3390
years in the desolations of *J*	Dan 9:2	3389
Judah, and to the inhabitants of *J*	Dan 9:7	3389
done as hath been done upon *J*	Dan 9:12	3389
be turned away from thy city *J*	Dan 9:16	3389
the iniquities of our fathers, *J*	Dan 9:16	3389
to build *J* unto the Messiah the	Dan 9:25	3389

in *J* shall be deliverance, as the ... Joel 2:32 3389
again the captivity of Judah and *J* ... Joel 3:1 3389
the children of *J* have ye sold ... Joel 3:6 3389
Zion, and utter his voice from *J* ... Joel 3:16 3389
then shall *J* be holy, and there ... Joel 3:17 3389
J from generation to generation ... Joel 3:20 3389
Zion, and utter his voice from *J* ... Amos 1:2 3389
it shall devour the palaces of *J* ... Amos 2:5 3389
his gates, and cast lots upon *J* ... Obad 11 3389
and the captivity of *J*, which is ... Obad 20 3389
he saw concerning Samaria and *J* ... Mic 1:1 3389
are they not *J*? ... Mic 1:5 3389
the gate of my people, even to *J* ... Mic 1:9 3389
from the LORD unto the gate of *J* ... Mic 1:12 3389
with blood, and *J* with iniquity ... Mic 3:10 3389
J shall become heaps, and the ... Mic 3:12 3389
and the word of the LORD from *J* ... Mic 4:2 3389
shall come to the daughter of *J* ... Mic 4:8 3389
and upon all the inhabitants of *J* ... Zeph 1:4 3389
that I will search *J* with candles ... Zeph 1:12 3389
all the heart, O daughter of *J* ... Zeph 3:14 3389
In that day it shall be said to *J* ... Zeph 3:16 3389
wilt thou not have mercy on *J* ... Zec 1:12 3389
I am jealous for *J* and for Zion ... Zec 1:14 3389
I am returned to *J* with mercies ... Zec 1:16 3389
shall be stretched forth upon *J* ... Zec 1:16 3389
Zion, and shall yet choose *J* ... Zec 1:17 3389
scattered Judah, Israel, and *J* ... Zec 1:19 3389
And he said unto me, To measure *J* ... Zec 2:2 3389
J shall be inhabited as towns ... Zec 2:4 3389
land, and shall choose *J* again ... Zec 2:12 3389
that hath chosen *J* rebuke thee ... Zec 3:2 3389
when *J* was inhabited and in ... Zec 7:7 3389
and will dwell in the midst of *J* ... Zec 8:3 3389
J shall be called a city of truth ... Zec 8:3 3389
women dwell in the streets of *J* ... Zec 8:4 3389
shall dwell in the midst of *J* ... Zec 8:8 3389
in these days to do well unto *J* ... Zec 8:15 3389
to seek the LORD of hosts in *J* ... Zec 8:22 3389
shout, O daughter of *J* ... Zec 9:9 3389
from Ephraim, and the horse from *J* ... Zec 9:10 3389
I will make *J* a cup of trembling ... Zec 12:2 3389
both against Judah and against *J* ... Zec 12:2 3389
in that day will I make *J* a ... Zec 12:3 3389
The inhabitants of *J* shall be my ... Zec 12:5 3389
J shall be inhabited again in her ... Zec 12:6 3389
again in her own place, even in *J* ... Zec 12:6 3389
of *J* do not magnify themselves ... Zec 12:7 3389
LORD defend the inhabitants of *J* ... Zec 12:8 3389
the nations that come against *J* ... Zec 12:9 3389
and upon the inhabitants of *J* ... Zec 12:10 3389
there be a great mourning in *J* ... Zec 12:11 3389
to the inhabitants of *J* for sin ... Zec 13:1 3389
all nations against *J* to battle ... Zec 14:2 3389
which is before *J* on the east ... Zec 14:4 3389
living waters shall go out from *J* ... Zec 14:8 3389
from Geba to Rimmon south of *J* ... Zec 14:10 3389
but *J* shall be safely inhabited ... Zec 14:11 3389
people that have fought against *J* ... Zec 14:12 3389
And Judah also shall fight at *J* ... Zec 14:14 3389
J shall even go up from year to ... Zec 14:16 3389
earth unto *J* to worship the King ... Zec 14:17 3389
Yea, every pot in *J* and in Judah ... Zec 14:21 3389
is committed in Israel and in *J* ... Mal 2:11 3389
J be pleasant unto the LORD, as ... Mal 3:4 3389
came wise men from the east to *J* ... Mt 2:1 *2414*
was troubled, and all *J* with him ... Mt 2:3 *2414*
Then went out to him *J*, and all ... Mt 3:5 *2414*
and from Decapolis, and from *J* ... Mt 4:25 *2414*
neither by *J*; for it is the city ... Mt 5:35 *2414*
and Pharisees, which were of *J* ... Mt 15:1 *2414*
how that he must go unto *J* ... Mt 16:21 *2414*
Jesus going up to *J* took the ... Mt 20:17 *2414*
Behold, we go up to *J* ... Mt 20:18 *2414*
And when they drew nigh unto *J* ... Mt 21:1 *2414*
And when he was come into *J* ... Mt 21:10 *2414*
O *J*, *J*, thou that killest ... Mt 23:37 *2419*
the land of Judaea, and they of *J* ... Mk 1:5 *2414*
And from *J*, and from Idumaea, and ... Mk 3:8 *2414*
which came down from *J* said ... Mk 3:22 *2414*
of the scribes, which came from *J* ... Mk 7:1 *2414*
were in the way going up to *J* ... Mk 10:32 *2414*
Saying, Behold, we go up to *J* ... Mk 10:33 *2414*
And when they came nigh to *J* ... Mk 11:1 *2419*
And Jesus entered into *J*, and into ... Mk 11:11 *2414*
And they come to *J* ... Mk 11:15 *2414*
And they come again to *J* ... Mk 11:27 *2414*
which came up with him unto *J* ... Mk 15:41 *2414*
they brought him to *J*, to ... Lk 2:22 *2414*
And, behold, there was a man in *J* ... Lk 2:25 *2419*
that looked for redemption in *J* ... Lk 2:38 *2419*
Now his parents went to *J* every ... Lk 2:41 *2419*
they went up to *J* after the ... Lk 2:42 *2414*
child Jesus tarried behind in *J* ... Lk 2:43 *2419*
not, they turned back again to *J* ... Lk 2:45 *2419*
And he brought him to *J*, and set ... Lk 4:9 *2419*
town of Galilee, and Judaea, and *J* ... Lk 5:17 *2419*
of people out of all Judaea and *J* ... Lk 6:17 *2419*
which he should accomplish at *J* ... Lk 9:31 *2419*
set his face to go to *J* ... Lk 9:51 *2419*
was as though he would go to *J* ... Lk 9:53 *2419*
man went down from *J* to Jericho ... Lk 10:30 *2419*
above all men that dwelt in *J* ... Lk 13:4 *2419*
teaching, and journeying toward *J* ... Lk 13:22 *2419*
be that a prophet perish out of *J* ... Lk 13:33 *2419*
O *J*, *J*, which killest the ... Lk 13:34 *2419*
it came to pass, as he went to *J* ... Lk 17:11 *2419*
unto them, Behold, we go up to *J* ... Lk 18:31 *2414*
parable, because he was nigh to *J* ... Lk 19:11 *2419*
he went before, ascending up to *J* ... Lk 19:28 *2414*
when ye shall see *J* compassed ... Lk 21:20 *2419*
J shall be trodden down of the ... Lk 21:24 *2419*
also was at *J* at that time ... Lk 23:7 *2414*
unto them said, Daughters of *J* ... Lk 23:28 *2419*
which was from *J* about threescore ... Lk 24:13 *2419*
Art thou only a stranger in *J* ... Lk 24:18 *2419*
the same hour, and returned to *J* ... Lk 24:33 *2419*
among all nations, beginning at *J* ... Lk 24:47 *2419*
but tarry ye in the city of *J* ... Lk 24:49 *2419*
returned to *J* with great joy ... Lk 24:52 *2419*
and Levites from *J* to ask him ... Jn 1:19 *2414*
at hand, and Jesus went up to *J* ... Jn 2:13 *2414*
when he was in *J* at the passover ... Jn 2:23 *2414*
that in *J* is the place where men ... Jn 4:20 *2414*
in this mountain, nor yet at *J* ... Jn 4:21 *2414*
that he did at *J* at the feast ... Jn 4:45 *2414*
and Jesus went up to *J* ... Jn 5:1 *2414*
Now there is at *J* by the sheep ... Jn 5:2 *2414*
Then said some of them of *J* ... Jn 7:25 *2414*
it was at *J* the feast of the ... Jn 10:22 *2414*
Now Bethany was nigh unto *J* ... Jn 11:18 *2414*
up to *J* before the passover ... Jn 11:55 *2414*
heard that Jesus was coming to *J* ... Jn 12:12 *2414*
they should not depart from *J* ... Acts 1:4 *2414*
be witnesses unto me both in *J* ... Acts 1:8 *2419*
Then returned they unto *J* from ... Acts 1:12 *2419*
which is from *J* a sabbath day's ... Acts 1:12 *2419*
known unto all the dwellers at *J* ... Acts 1:19 *2419*
And there were dwelling at *J* Jews ... Acts 2:5 *2419*
Judaea, and all ye that dwell at *J* ... Acts 2:14 *2419*
were gathered together at *J* ... Acts 4:6 *2419*
to all them that dwell in *J* ... Acts 4:16 *2419*
of the cities round about unto *J* ... Acts 5:16 *2419*
ye have filled *J* with your ... Acts 5:28 *2419*
disciples multiplied in *J* greatly ... Acts 6:7 *2419*
against the church which was at *J* ... Acts 8:1 *2414*
J heard that Samaria had received ... Acts 8:14 *2414*
word of the Lord, returned to *J* ... Acts 8:25 *2419*
that goeth down from *J* unto Gaza ... Acts 8:26 *2419*
had come to *J* for to worship ... Acts 8:27 *2419*
he might bring them bound unto *J* ... Acts 9:2 *2419*
he hath done to thy saints at *J* ... Acts 9:13 *2419*
which called on this name in *J* ... Acts 9:21 *2419*
And when Saul was come to *J* ... Acts 9:26 *2419*
them coming in and going out at *J* ... Acts 9:28 *2419*
in the land of the Jews, and in *J* ... Acts 10:39 *2419*
And when Peter was come up to *J* ... Acts 11:2 *2414*
ears of the church which was in *J* ... Acts 11:22 *2414*
came prophets from *J* unto Antioch ... Acts 11:27 *2414*
Barnabas and Saul returned from *J* ... Acts 12:25 *2419*
departing from them returned to *J* ... Acts 13:13 *2414*
For they that dwell at *J*, and ... Acts 13:27 *2419*
up with him from Galilee to *J* ... Acts 13:31 *2419*
should go up to *J* unto the ... Acts 15:2 *2419*
And when they were come to *J* ... Acts 15:4 *2419*
and elders which were at *J* ... Acts 16:4 *2419*
keep this feast that cometh in *J* ... Acts 18:21 *2414*
Macedonia and Achaia, to go to *J* ... Acts 19:21 *2414*
to be at *J* the day of Pentecost ... Acts 20:16 *2414*
I go bound in the spirit unto *J* ... Acts 20:22 *2419*
that he should not go up to *J* ... Acts 21:4 *2419*
So shall the Jews at *J* bind the ... Acts 21:11 *2419*
besought him not to go up to *J* ... Acts 21:12 *2419*
but also to die at *J* for the name ... Acts 21:13 *2419*
up our carriages, and went up to *J* ... Acts 21:15 *2419*
And when we were come to *J* ... Acts 21:17 *2414*
that all *J* was in an uproar ... Acts 21:31 *2419*
which were there bound unto *J* ... Acts 22:5 *2419*
that, when I was come again to *J* ... Acts 22:17 *2419*
and get thee quickly out of *J* ... Acts 22:18 *2419*
as thou hast testified of me in *J* ... Acts 23:11 *2419*
I went up to *J* for to worship ... Acts 24:11 *2419*
he ascended from Caesarea to *J* ... Acts 25:1 *2414*
that he would send for him to *J* ... Acts 25:3 *2419*
down from *J* stood round about ... Acts 25:7 *2414*
and said, Wilt thou go up to *J* ... Acts 25:9 *2414*
About whom, when I was at *J* ... Acts 25:15 *2414*
him whether he would go to *J* ... Acts 25:20 *2419*
have dealt with me, both at *J* ... Acts 25:24 *2414*
first among mine own nation at *J* ... Acts 26:4 *2414*
Which thing I also did in *J* ... Acts 26:10 *2414*
unto them of Damascus, and at *J* ... Acts 26:20 *2414*
J into the hands of the Romans ... Acts 28:17 *2414*
so that from *J*, and round about ... Rom 15:19 *2419*
But now I go unto *J* to minister ... Rom 15:25 *2419*
the poor saints which are at *J* ... Rom 15:26 *2419*
my service which I have for *J* may ... Rom 15:31 *2419*
to bring your liberality unto *J* ... 1Cor 16:3 *2419*
Neither went I up to *J* to them ... Gal 1:17 *2414*
years I went up to *J* to see Peter ... Gal 1:18 *2414*
went up again to *J* with Barnabas ... Gal 2:1 *2414*
and answereth to *J* which now is ... Gal 4:25 *2419*
But *J* which is above is free ... Gal 4:26 *2419*
of the living God, the heavenly *J* ... Heb 12:22 *2419*
city of my God, which is new *J* ... Rev 3:12 *2419*
I John saw the holy city, new *J* ... Rev 21:2 *2419*
me that great city, the holy *J* ... Rev 21:10 *2419*

JERUSALEM'S *(je-ru'-sa-lems)* {3}
for *J* sake which I have chosen ... 1Kin 11:13 3389
for *J* sake, the city which I have ... 1Kin 11:32 3389
for *J* sake I will not rest, until ... Is 62:1 3389

JERUSHA *(je-ru'-shah)* {1} See JERUSHAH. *Mother of King Jotham of Judah.*
And his mother's name was *J* ... 2Kin 15:33 3388

JERUSHAH *(je-ru'-shah)* {1} See JERUSHA. *Same as Jerusha.*
His mother's name also was *J* ... 2Chr 27:1 3388

JESAIAH *(jes-a-i'-ah)* {2} See ISAIAH, JESHAIAH.
1. Grandson of Zerubbabel.
Hananiah; Pelatiah, and *J* ... 1Chr 3:21 3470
2. A family of exiles.
the son of Ithiel, the son of *J* ... Neh 11:7 3470

JESHAIAH *(jesh-a-i'-ah)* {5} See JESAIAH.
1. A sanctuary servant.
Gedaliah, and Zeri, and *J*, ... 1Chr 25:3 3740
The eighth to *J*, he, his sons, and ... 1Chr 25:15 3740
2. A grandson of Eliezer.
J his son, and Joram his son, and ... 1Chr 26:25 3740
3. An Elamite exile.
J the son of Athaliah, and with ... Ezr 8:7 3740
4. A Merarite exile.
with him *J* of the sons of Merari, ... Ezr 8:19 3740

JESHANAH *(je-sha'-nah)* {1} *A city near Bethel.*
J with the towns thereof, and ... 2Chr 13:19 3466

JESHARELAH *(je-shar'-e-lah)* {1} See ASARELAH. *A sanctuary servant.*
The seventh to *J*, he, his sons, ... 1Chr 25:14 3480

JESHEBEAB *(je-sheb'-e-ab)* {1} *A sanctuary servant.*
to Huppah, the fourteenth to *J* ... 1Chr 24:13 3434

JESHER *(je'-shur)* {1} *A son of Caleb.*
J, and Shobab, and Ardon ... 1Chr 2:18 3475

JESHIMON *(jesh'-im-on)* {6}
1. A place in the Sinai.
of Pisgah, which looketh toward *J* ... Num 21:20 3452
of Peor, that looketh toward *J* ... Num 23:28 3452
2. A place in the wilderness of Judah.
which is on the south of *J* ... 1Sa 23:19 3452
in the plain on the south of *J* ... 1Sa 23:24 3452
of Hachilah, which is before *J* ... 1Sa 26:1 3452
of Hachilah, which is before *J* ... 1Sa 26:3

JESHISHAI *(jesh'-i-shahee)* {1} *Ancestor of a Gadite family.*
the son of Michael, the son of *J* ... 1Chr 5:14 3454

JESHOHAIAH *(je-sho-ha-i'-ah)* {1} *A descendant of Simeon.*
And Elioenai, and Jaakobah, and *J* ... 1Chr 4:36 3439

JESHUA *(jesh'-u-ah)* {30} See JESHUAH, JOSHUA.
1. A sanctuary servant.
of Jedaiah, of the house of *J* ... Ezr 2:36 3442
of Jedaiah, of the house of *J* ... Neh 7:39 3442
2. A Levite in Hezekiah's time.
The ninth to *J*, the tenth to ... 1Chr 24:11 3442
him were Eden, and Miniamin, and *J* ... 2Chr 31:15 3442
the children of *J* and Kadmiel, of ... Ezr 2:40 3442
the children of *J*, of Kadmiel, and ... Neh 7:43 3442
3. A priest in exile.
J, Nehemiah, Seraiah, Reelaiah, ... Ezr 2:2 3442
Then stood up *J* the son of ... Ezr 3:2 3442
J the son of Jozadak, and the ... Ezr 3:8 3442
Then stood *J* with his sons and his ... Ezr 3:9 3442
But Zerubbabel, and *J*, and the rest ... Ezr 4:3 3442
J the son of Jozadak, and began to ... Ezr 5:2 3443
of the sons of *J* the son of ... Ezr 10:18 3442
Who came with Zerubbabel, *J* ... Neh 7:7 3442
the son of Shealtiel, and *J* ... Neh 12:1 3442
their brethren in the days of *J* ... Neh 12:7 3442
J begat Joiakim, Joiakim also ... Neh 12:10 3442
the days of Joiakim the son of *J* ... Neh 12:26 3442
4. Father of Jozabad.
them was Jozabad the son of *J* ... Ezr 8:33 3443
5. A family of exiles.
Pahath-moab, of the children of *J* ... Ezr 2:6 3442
Pahath-moab, of the children of *J* ... Neh 7:11 3442
6. Father of Ezer.
to him repaired Ezer the son of *J* ... Neh 3:19 3442
7. A priest who assisted Ezra.
Also *J*, and Bani, and Sherebiah, ... Neh 8:7 3442
the stairs, of the Levites, *J* ... Neh 9:4 3442
Then the Levites, *J*, and Kadmiel, ... Neh 9:5 3442
J, Binnui, Kadmiel, Sherebiah, ... Neh 12:8 3442
J the son of Kadmiel, with their ... Neh 12:24 3442
8. Same as Joshua, son of Nun.
for since the days of *J* the son ... Neh 8:17 3442
9. A Levite who renewed the covenant.
both *J* the son of Azaniah, Binnui ... Neh 10:9 3442
10. A city in Benjamin.
And at *J*, and at Moladah, and at ... Neh 11:26 3442

JESHURUN *(jesh'-u-run)* {3} *Another name for the people Israel.*
But *J* waxed fat, and kicked ... Deut 32:15 3484
And he was king in *J*, when the ... Deut 33:5 3484
is none like unto the God of *J* ... Deut 33:26 3484

JESIAH *(je-si'-ah)* {2} See ISHIAH.
1. A warrior in David's army.
Elkanah, and *J*, and Azareel, and ... 1Chr 12:6 3449
2. A descendant of Uzziel.
Micah the first, and *J* the second ... 1Chr 23:20 3449

JESIMIEL *(je-sim'-e-el)* {1} *A descendant of Simeon.*
and Asaiah, and Adiel, and *J* ... 1Chr 4:36 3450

JESSE *(jes'-se)* {47} *Father of David.*
he is the father of *J*, the father ... Ruth 4:17 3448
begat *J*, and *J* begat David ... Ruth 4:22 3448
send thee to *J* the Beth-lehemite ... 1Sa 16:1 3448
call *J* to the sacrifice, and I ... 1Sa 16:3 3448
And he sanctified *J* and his sons, ... 1Sa 16:5 3448
Then *J* called Abinadab, and made ... 1Sa 16:8 3448
Then *J* made Shammah to pass by ... 1Sa 16:9 3448

J made seven of his sons to pass ... 1Sa 16:10 3448
And Samuel said unto *J*, The LORD ... 1Sa 16:10 3448
And Samuel said unto *J*, Are here ... 1Sa 16:11 3448
And Samuel said unto *J*, Send and ... 1Sa 16:11 3448
seen a son of *J* the Beth-lehemite ... 1Sa 16:18 3448
Saul sent messengers unto *J* ... 1Sa 16:19 3448
J took an ass laden with bread, ... 1Sa 16:20 3448
And Saul sent to *J*, saying, Let ... 1Sa 16:22 3448
whose name was *J*; and he had ... 1Sa 17:12 3448
the three eldest sons of *J* went ... 1Sa 17:13 3448
J said unto David his son, Take ... 1Sa 17:17 3448
and went, as *J* had commanded him ... 1Sa 17:20 3448
thy servant *J* the Beth-lehemite ... 1Sa 17:58 3448
cometh not the son of *J* to meat ... 1Sa 20:27 3448
son of *J* to thine own confusion ... 1Sa 20:30 3448
son of *J* liveth upon the ground ... 1Sa 20:31 3448
will the son of *J* give every one ... 1Sa 22:7 3448
made a league with the son of *J* ... 1Sa 22:8 3448
I saw the son of *J* coming to Nob ... 1Sa 22:9 3448
against me, thou and the son of *J* ... 1Sa 22:13 3448
and who is the son of *J* ... 1Sa 25:10 3448
we inheritance in the son of *J* ... 2Sa 20:1 3448
David the son of *J* said, and the ... 2Sa 23:1 3448
we inheritance in the son of *J* ... 1Kin 12:16 3448
Boaz begat Obed, and Obed begat *J* ... 1Chr 2:12 3448
J begat his firstborn Eliab, and ... 1Chr 2:13 3448
kingdom unto David the son of *J* ... 1Chr 10:14 3448
and on thy side, thou son of *J* ... 1Chr 12:18 3448
Thus David the son of *J* reigned ... 1Chr 29:26 3448
none inheritance in the son of *J* ... 2Chr 10:16 3448
daughter of Eliab the son of *J* ... 2Chr 11:18 3448
of David the son of *J* are ended ... Ps 72:20 3448
forth a rod out of the stem of *J* ... Is 11:1 3448
day there shall be a root of *J* ... Is 11:10 3448
and Obed begat *J* ... Mt 1:5 *2421*
And *J* begat David the king ... Mt 1:6 *2421*
Which was the son of *J*, which was ... Lk 3:32 *2421*
I have found David the son of *J* ... Acts 13:22 *2421*
saith, There shall be a root of *J* ... Rom 15:12 *2421*

JESSHIAH See JESIAH.

JESTING {1}
nor foolish talking, nor *j* ... Eph 5:4 *2160*

JESUI *(jes'-u-i)* {1} See ISHUI, JESUITES. *A descendant of Asher.*
of *J*, the family of the Jesuites ... Num 26:44 3440

JESUITES *(jes'-u-ites)* {1} *Descendants of Jesui.*
of Jesui, the family of the *J* ... Num 26:44 3441

JESURUN *(jes'-u-run)* {1} See JESHURUN. *Same as Jeshurun.*
and thou, *J*, whom I have chosen ... Is 44:2 3484

JESUS *(je'-zus)* {971} See BAR-JESUS, CHRIST, JESUS', JOSHUA, JUSTUS.
1. The Christ.
of the generation of *J* Christ ... Mt 1:1 *2424*
of Mary, of whom was born *J* ... Mt 1:16 *2424*
Now the birth of *J* Christ was on ... Mt 1:18 *2424*
and thou shalt call his name *J* ... Mt 1:21 *2424*
and he called his name *J* ... Mt 1:25 *2424*
Now when *J* was born in Bethlehem ... Mt 2:1 *2424*
Then cometh *J* from Galilee to ... Mt 3:13 *2424*
J answering said unto him, Suffer ... Mt 3:15 *2424*
And *J*, when he was baptized, went ... Mt 3:16 *2424*
Then was *J* led up of the spirit ... Mt 4:1 *2424*
J said unto him, It is written ... Mt 4:7 *2424*
Then saith *J* unto him, Get thee ... Mt 4:10 *2424*
Now when *J* had heard that John ... Mt 4:12 *2424*
From that time *J* began to preach, ... Mt 4:17 *2424*
And *J*, walking by the sea of ... Mt 4:18 *2424*
J went about all Galilee, ... Mt 4:23 *2424*
when *J* had ended these sayings, ... Mt 7:28 *2424*
J put forth his hand, and touched ... Mt 8:3 *2424*
J saith unto him, See thou tell ... Mt 8:4 *2424*
when *J* was entered into Capernaum ... Mt 8:5 *2424*
J saith unto him, I will come and ... Mt 8:7 *2424*
When *J* heard it, he marvelled, and ... Mt 8:10 *2424*
J said unto the centurion, Go thy ... Mt 8:13 *2424*
when *J* was come into Peter's ... Mt 8:14 *2424*
Now when *J* saw great multitudes ... Mt 8:18 *2424*
J saith unto him, The foxes have ... Mt 8:20 *2424*
But *J* said unto him, Follow me ... Mt 8:22 *2424*
What have we to do with thee, *J* ... Mt 8:29 *2424*
the whole city came out to meet *J* ... Mt 8:34 *2424*
J seeing their faith said unto ... Mt 9:2 *2424*
J knowing their thoughts said, ... Mt 9:4 *2424*
as *J* passed forth from thence, he ... Mt 9:9 *2424*
as *J* sat at meat in the house, ... Mt 9:10 *2424*
But when *J* heard that, he said ... Mt 9:12 *2424*
J said unto them, Can the ... Mt 9:15 *2424*
J arose, and followed him, and so ... Mt 9:19 *2424*
But *J* turned him about, and when ... Mt 9:22 *2424*
when *J* came into the ruler's ... Mt 9:23 *2424*
when *J* departed thence, two blind ... Mt 9:27 *2424*
J saith unto them, Believe ye ... Mt 9:28 *2424*
J straitly charged them, saying, ... Mt 9:30 *2424*
J went about all the cities and ... Mt 9:35 *2424*
These twelve *J* sent forth ... Mt 10:5 *2424*
when *J* had made an end of ... Mt 11:1 *2424*
J answered and said unto them, Go ... Mt 11:4 *2424*
departed, *J* began to say unto the ... Mt 11:7 *2424*
At that time *J* answered and said, ... Mt 11:25 *2424*
At that time *J* went on the ... Mt 12:1 *2424*
But when *J* knew it, he withdrew ... Mt 12:15 *2424*
J knew their thoughts, and said ... Mt 12:25 *2424*
same day went *J* out of the house ... Mt 13:1 *2424*
All these things spake *J* unto the ... Mt 13:34 *2424*
Then *J* sent the multitude away, ... Mt 13:36 *2424*
J saith unto them, Have ye ... Mt 13:51 *2424*
that when *J* had finished these ... Mt 13:53 *2424*
But *J* said unto them, A prophet ... Mt 13:57 *2424*
tetrarch heard of the fame of *J* ... Mt 14:1 *2424*
and buried it, and went and told *J* ... Mt 14:12 *2424*
When *J* heard of it, he departed ... Mt 14:13 *2424*
J went forth, and saw a great ... Mt 14:14 *2424*
But *J* said unto them, They need ... Mt 14:16 *2424*
straightway *J* constrained his ... Mt 14:22 *2424*
of the night *J* went unto them ... Mt 14:25 *2424*
But straightway *J* spake unto them ... Mt 14:27 *2424*
walked on the water, to go to *J* ... Mt 14:29 *2424*
immediately *J* stretched forth his ... Mt 14:31 *2424*
Then came to *J* scribes and ... Mt 15:1 *2424*
J said, Are ye also yet without ... Mt 15:16 *2424*
Then *J* went thence, and departed ... Mt 15:21 *2424*
Then *J* answered and said unto her, ... Mt 15:28 *2424*
J departed from thence, and came ... Mt 15:29 *2424*
Then *J* called his disciples unto ... Mt 15:32 *2424*
J saith unto them, How many ... Mt 15:34 *2424*
Then *J* said unto them, Take heed ... Mt 16:6 *2424*
Which when *J* perceived, he said ... Mt 16:8 *2424*
When *J* came into the coasts of ... Mt 16:13 *2424*
J answered and said unto him, ... Mt 16:17 *2424*
no man that he was *J* the Christ ... Mt 16:20 *2424*
J to shew unto his disciples ... Mt 16:21 *2424*
Then said *J* unto his disciples, ... Mt 16:24 *2424*
And after six days *J* taketh Peter ... Mt 17:1 *2424*
answered Peter, and said unto *J* ... Mt 17:4 *2424*
J came and touched them, and said, ... Mt 17:7 *2424*
they saw no man, save *J* only ... Mt 17:8 *2424*
J charged them, saying, Tell the ... Mt 17:9 *2424*
J answered and said unto them, ... Mt 17:11 *2424*
Then *J* answered and said, O ... Mt 17:17 *2424*
And *J* rebuked the devil ... Mt 17:18 *2424*
came the disciples to *J* apart ... Mt 17:19 *2424*
J said unto them, Because of your ... Mt 17:20 *2424*
J said unto them, The Son of man ... Mt 17:22 *2424*
J prevented him, saying, What ... Mt 17:25 *2424*
J saith unto him, Then are the ... Mt 17:26 *2424*
time came the disciples unto *J* ... Mt 18:1 *2424*
J called a little child unto him, ... Mt 18:2 *2424*
J saith unto him, I say not unto ... Mt 18:22 *2424*
that when *J* had finished these ... Mt 19:1 *2424*
But *J* said, Suffer little ... Mt 19:14 *2424*
J said, Thou shalt do no murder, ... Mt 19:18 *2424*
J said unto him, If thou wilt be ... Mt 19:21 *2424*
Then said *J* unto his disciples, ... Mt 19:23 *2424*
But *J* beheld them, and said unto ... Mt 19:26 *2424*
J said unto them, Verily I say ... Mt 19:28 *2424*
J going up to Jerusalem took the ... Mt 20:17 *2424*
But *J* answered and said, Ye know ... Mt 20:22 *2424*
But *J* called them unto him, and ... Mt 20:25 *2424*
when they heard that *J* passed by ... Mt 20:30 *2424*
J stood still, and called them, and ... Mt 20:32 *2424*
So *J* had compassion on them, and ... Mt 20:34 *2424*
then sent *J* two disciples, ... Mt 21:1 *2424*
went, and did as *J* commanded them, ... Mt 21:6 *2424*
This is *J* the prophet of Nazareth ... Mt 21:11 *2424*
J went into the temple of God, and ... Mt 21:12 *2424*
And *J* saith unto them, Yea ... Mt 21:16 *2424*
J answered and said unto them, ... Mt 21:21 *2424*
J answered and said unto them, I ... Mt 21:24 *2424*
And they answered *J*, and said, We ... Mt 21:27 *2424*
J saith unto them, Verily I say ... Mt 21:31 *2424*
J saith unto them, Did ye never ... Mt 21:42 *2424*
J answered and spake unto them ... Mt 22:1 *2424*
But *J* perceived their wickedness, ... Mt 22:18 *2424*
J answered and said unto them, Ye ... Mt 22:29 *2424*
J said unto him, Thou shalt love ... Mt 22:37 *2424*
gathered together, *J* asked them, ... Mt 22:41 *2424*
Then spake *J* to the multitude, and ... Mt 23:1 *2424*
J went out, and departed from the ... Mt 24:1 *2424*
J said unto them, See ye not all ... Mt 24:2 *2424*
J answered and said unto them, ... Mt 24:4 *2424*
when *J* had finished all these ... Mt 26:1 *2424*
they might take *J* by subtilty ... Mt 26:4 *2424*
Now when *J* was in Bethany, in the ... Mt 26:6 *2424*
When *J* understood it, he said ... Mt 26:10 *2424*
bread the disciples came to *J* ... Mt 26:17 *2424*
did as *J* had appointed them ... Mt 26:19 *2424*
J took bread, and blessed it, and ... Mt 26:26 *2424*
Then saith *J* unto them, All ye ... Mt 26:31 *2424*
J said unto him, Verily I say ... Mt 26:34 *2424*
Then cometh *J* with them unto a ... Mt 26:36 *2424*
And forthwith he came to *J* ... Mt 26:49 *2424*
And *J* said unto him, Friend, ... Mt 26:50 *2424*
came they, and laid hands on *J* ... Mt 26:50 *2424*
with *J* stretched out his hand ... Mt 26:51 *2424*
Then said *J* unto him, Put up ... Mt 26:52 *2424*
hour said *J* to the multitudes ... Mt 26:55 *2424*
they that had laid hold on *J* led ... Mt 26:57 *2424*
sought false witness against *J* ... Mt 26:59 *2424*
But *J* held his peace ... Mt 26:63 *2424*
J saith unto him, Thou hast said ... Mt 26:64 *2424*
Thou also wast with *J* of Galilee ... Mt 26:69 *2424*
was also with *J* of Nazareth ... Mt 26:71 *2424*
And Peter remembered the word of *J* ... Mt 26:75 *2424*
against *J* to put him to death ... Mt 27:1 *2424*
J stood before the governor ... Mt 27:11 *2424*
J said unto him, Thou sayest ... Mt 27:11 *2424*
or *J* which is called Christ ... Mt 27:17 *2424*
should ask Barabbas, and destroy *J* ... Mt 27:20 *2424*
with *J* which is called Christ ... Mt 27:22 *2424*
and when he had scourged *J* ... Mt 27:26 *2424*
took *J* into the common hall ... Mt 27:27 *2424*
THIS IS J THE KING OF THE JEWS ... Mt 27:37 *2424*
about the ninth hour *J* cried with ... Mt 27:46 *2424*
J, when he had cried again with a ... Mt 27:50 *2424*
that were with him, watching *J* ... Mt 27:54 *2424*
which followed *J* from Galilee ... Mt 27:55 *2424*
Pilate, and begged the body of *J* ... Mt 27:58 *2424*
for I know that ye seek *J* ... Mt 28:5 *2424*
J met them, saying, All hail ... Mt 28:9 *2424*
Then said *J* unto them, Be not ... Mt 28:10 *2424*
where *J* had appointed them ... Mt 28:16 *2424*
J came and spake unto them, saying ... Mt 28:18 *2424*
of the gospel of *J* Christ ... Mk 1:1 *2424*
that *J* came from Nazareth of ... Mk 1:9 *2424*
J came into Galilee, preaching ... Mk 1:14 *2424*
J said unto them, Come ye after ... Mk 1:17 *2424*
do with thee, thou *J* of Nazareth ... Mk 1:24 *2424*
J rebuked him, saying, Hold thy ... Mk 1:25 *2424*
And *J*, moved with compassion, put ... Mk 1:41 *2424*
insomuch that *J* could no more ... Mk 1:45 *2424*
When *J* saw their faith, he said ... Mk 2:5 *2424*
immediately when *J* perceived in ... Mk 2:8 *2424*
as *J* sat at meat in his house, ... Mk 2:15 *2424*
sinners sat also together with *J* ... Mk 2:15 *2424*
When *J* heard it, he saith unto ... Mk 2:17 *2424*
J said unto them, Can the ... Mk 2:19 *2424*
But *J* withdrew himself with his ... Mk 3:7 *2424*
But when he saw *J* afar off ... Mk 5:6 *2424*
What have I to do with thee, *J* ... Mk 5:7 *2424*
forthwith *J* gave them leave ... Mk 5:13 *2424*
And they come to *J*, and see him ... Mk 5:15 *2424*
Howbeit *J* suffered him not, but ... Mk 5:19 *2424*
great things *J* had done for him ... Mk 5:20 *2424*
when *J* was passed over again by ... Mk 5:21 *2424*
And *J* went with him ... Mk 5:24
When she had heard of *J*, came in ... Mk 5:27 *2424*
And *J*, immediately knowing in ... Mk 5:30 *2424*
As soon as *J* heard the word that ... Mk 5:36 *2424*
But *J* said unto them, A prophet ... Mk 6:4 *2424*
themselves together unto *J* ... Mk 6:30 *2424*
And *J*, when he came out, saw much ... Mk 6:34 *2424*
But *J* said unto her, Let the ... Mk 7:27 *2424*
J called his disciples unto him, ... Mk 8:1 *2424*
when *J* knew it, he saith unto ... Mk 8:17 *2424*
J went out, and his disciples, ... Mk 8:27 *2424*
after six days *J* taketh with him ... Mk 9:2 *2424*
and they were talking with *J* ... Mk 9:4 *2424*
And Peter answered and said to *J* ... Mk 9:5 *2424*
save *J* only with themselves ... Mk 9:8 *2424*
J said unto him, If thou canst ... Mk 9:23 *2424*
When *J* saw that the people came ... Mk 9:25 *2424*
But *J* took him by the hand, and ... Mk 9:27 *2424*
But *J* said, Forbid him not ... Mk 9:39 *2424*
J answered and said unto them, For ... Mk 10:5 *2424*
But when *J* saw it, he was much ... Mk 10:14 *2424*
J said unto him, Why callest thou ... Mk 10:18 *2424*
Then *J* beholding him loved him, ... Mk 10:21 *2424*
J looked round about, and saith ... Mk 10:23 *2424*
But *J* answereth again, and saith ... Mk 10:24 *2424*
J looking upon them saith, With ... Mk 10:27 *2424*
J answered and said, Verily I say ... Mk 10:29 *2424*
and *J* went before them ... Mk 10:32 *2424*
But *J* said unto them, Ye know not ... Mk 10:38 *2424*
J said unto them, Ye shall indeed ... Mk 10:39 *2424*
But *J* called them to him, and ... Mk 10:42 *2424*
heard that it was *J* of Nazareth ... Mk 10:47 *2424*
he began to cry out, and say, *J* ... Mk 10:47 *2424*
J stood still, and commanded him ... Mk 10:49 *2424*
his garment, rose, and came to *J* ... Mk 10:50 *2424*
J answered and said unto him, What ... Mk 10:51 *2424*
J said unto him, Go thy way ... Mk 10:52 *2424*
sight, and followed *J* in the way ... Mk 10:52 *2424*
unto them even as *J* had commanded ... Mk 11:6 *2424*
And they brought the colt to *J* ... Mk 11:7 *2424*
J entered into Jerusalem, and into ... Mk 11:11 *2424*
J answered and said unto it, No ... Mk 11:14 *2424*
J went into the temple, and began ... Mk 11:15 *2424*
J answering saith unto them, Have ... Mk 11:22 *2424*
J answered and said unto them, I ... Mk 11:29 *2424*
And they answered and said unto *J* ... Mk 11:33 *2424*
J answering saith unto them, ... Mk 11:33 *2424*
J answering said unto them, ... Mk 12:17 *2424*
J answering said unto them, Do ye ... Mk 12:24 *2424*
J answered him, The first of all ... Mk 12:29 *2424*
when *J* saw that he answered ... Mk 12:34 *2424*
J answered and said, while he ... Mk 12:35 *2424*
J sat over against the treasury, ... Mk 12:41 *2424*
J answering said unto him, Seest ... Mk 13:2 *2424*
J answering them began to say, ... Mk 13:5 *2424*
And *J* said, Let her alone ... Mk 14:6 *2424*
J said, Verily I say unto you, ... Mk 14:18 *2424*
J took bread, and blessed, and ... Mk 14:22 *2424*
J saith unto them, All ye shall ... Mk 14:27 *2424*
J saith unto him, Verily I say ... Mk 14:30 *2424*
J answered and said unto them, Are ... Mk 14:48 *2424*
they led *J* away to the high ... Mk 14:53 *2424*
against *J* to put him to death ... Mk 14:55 *2424*
stood up in the midst, and asked *J* ... Mk 14:60 *2424*
And *J* said, I am ... Mk 14:62 *2424*
thou also wast with *J* of Nazareth ... Mk 14:67 *2424*
the word that *J* said unto him ... Mk 14:72 *2424*
and the whole council, and bound *J* ... Mk 15:1 *2424*
But *J* yet answered nothing ... Mk 15:5 *2424*
unto them, and delivered *J* ... Mk 15:15 *2424*
at the ninth hour *J* cried with a ... Mk 15:34 *2424*
J cried with a loud voice, and ... Mk 15:37 *2424*
Pilate, and craved the body of *J* ... Mk 15:43 *2424*
Ye seek *J* of Nazareth, which was ... Mk 16:6 *2424*
Now when *J* was risen early the ... Mk 16:9
a son, and shalt call his name *J* ... Lk 1:31 *2424*
the child, his name was called *J* ... Lk 2:21 *2424*

parents brought in the child *J* Lk 2:27 *2424*
the child *J* tarried behind in Lk 2:43 *2424*
J increased in wisdom and stature, Lk 2:52 *2424*
that *J* also being baptized, and Lk 3:21 *2424*
J himself began to be about Lk 3:23 *2424*
J being full of the Holy Ghost Lk 4:1 *2424*
J answered him, saying, It is Lk 4:4 *2424*
J answered and said unto him, Get Lk 4:8 *2424*
J answering said unto him, It is Lk 4:12 *2424*
J returned in the power of the Lk 4:14 *2424*
do with thee, thou *J* of Nazareth Lk 4:34 *2424*
J rebuked him, saying, Hold thy Lk 4:35 *2424*
J said unto Simon, Fear not Lk 5:10 *2424*
who seeing *J* fell on his face, and Lk 5:12 *2424*
his couch into the midst before *J* Lk 5:19 *2424*
But when *J* perceived their Lk 5:22 *2424*
J answering said unto them, They Lk 5:31 *2424*
J answering them said, Have ye Lk 6:3 *2424*
Then said *J* unto them, I will ask Lk 6:9 *2424*
another what they might do to *J* Lk 6:11 *2424*
And when he heard of *J*, he sent Lk 7:3 *2424*
And when they came to *J*, they Lk 7:4 *2424*
Then *J* went with them Lk 7:6 *2424*
When *J* heard these things, he Lk 7:9 *2424*
of his disciples sent them to *J* Lk 7:19 *2424*
Then *J* answering said unto them, Lk 7:22 *2424*
when she knew that *J* sat at meat Lk 7:37
J answering said unto him, Simon, Lk 7:40 *2424*
When he saw *J*, he cried out, and Lk 8:28 *2424*
What have I to do with thee, *J* Lk 8:28 *2424*
J asked him, saying, What is thy Lk 8:30 *2424*
and came to *J*, and found the man, Lk 8:35 *2424*
sitting at the feet of *J* Lk 8:35 *2424*
but *J* sent him away, saying, Lk 8:38 *2424*
great things *J* had done unto him Lk 8:39 *2424*
when *J* was returned, the people Lk 8:40 *2424*
And *J* said, Who touched me Lk 8:45 *2424*
J said, Somebody hath touched me Lk 8:46 *2424*
But when *J* heard it, he answered Lk 8:50 *2424*
from him, Peter said unto *J* Lk 9:33 *2424*
voice was past, *J* was found alone Lk 9:36 *2424*
J answering said, O faithless and Lk 9:41 *2424*
J rebuked the unclean spirit, and Lk 9:42 *2424*
one at all things which *J* did Lk 9:43 *2424*
And *J*, perceiving the thought of Lk 9:47 *2424*
J said unto him, Forbid him not Lk 9:50 *2424*
J said unto him, Foxes have holes Lk 9:58 *2424*
J said unto him, Let the dead Lk 9:60 *2424*
J said unto him, No man, having Lk 9:62 *2424*
In that hour *J* rejoiced in spirit Lk 10:21 *2424*
to justify himself, said unto *J* Lk 10:29 *2424*
J answering said, A certain man Lk 10:30 *2424*
Then said *J* unto him, Go, and do Lk 10:37 *2424*
J answered and said unto her, Lk 10:41 *2424*
J answering said unto them, Lk 13:2 *2424*
when *J* saw her, he called her to Lk 13:12 *2424*
because that *J* had healed on the Lk 13:14 *2424*
J answering spake unto the Lk 14:3 *2424*
up their voices, and said, *J* Lk 17:13 *2424*
J answering said, Were there not Lk 17:17 *2424*
But *J* called them unto him, and Lk 18:16 *2424*
J said unto him, Why callest thou Lk 18:19 *2424*
Now when *J* heard these things, he Lk 18:22 *2424*
when *J* saw that he was very Lk 18:24 *2424*
that *J* of Nazareth passeth by Lk 18:37 *2424*
And he cried, saying, *J*, thou son Lk 18:38 *2424*
J stood, and commanded him to be Lk 18:40 *2424*
J said unto him, Receive thy Lk 18:42 *2424*
J entered and passed through Lk 19:1
And he sought to see *J* who he was Lk 19:3 *2424*
when *J* came to the place, he Lk 19:5 *2424*
J said unto him, This day is Lk 19:9 *2424*
And they brought him to *J* Lk 19:35 *2424*
the colt, and they set *J* thereon Lk 19:35 *2424*
J said unto them, Neither tell I Lk 20:8 *2424*
J answering said unto them, The Lk 20:34 *2424*
and drew near unto *J* to kiss him Lk 22:47 *2424*
But *J* said unto him, Judas, Lk 22:48 *2424*
J answered and said, Suffer ye Lk 22:51 *2424*
Then *J* said unto the chief Lk 22:52 *2424*
And the men that held *J* mocked him Lk 22:63 *2424*
And when Herod saw *J*, he was Lk 23:8 *2424*
therefore, willing to release *J* Lk 23:20 *2424*
but he delivered *J* to their will Lk 23:25 *2424*
that he might bear it after *J* Lk 23:26 *2424*
But *J* turning unto them said, Lk 23:28 *2424*
Then said *J*, Father, forgive them Lk 23:34 *2424*
And he said unto *J*, Lord, remember Lk 23:42 *2424*
J said unto him, Verily I say Lk 23:43 *2424*
when *J* had cried with a loud Lk 23:46 *2424*
Pilate, and begged the body of *J* Lk 23:52 *2424*
found not the body of the Lord *J* Lk 24:3 *2424*
J himself drew near, and went with Lk 24:15 *2424*
Concerning *J* of Nazareth, which Lk 24:19 *2424*
J himself stood in the midst of Lk 24:36 *2424*
grace and truth came by *J* Christ Jn 1:17 *2424*
day John seeth *J* coming unto him Jn 1:29 *2424*
And looking upon *J* as he walked Jn 1:36 *2424*
him speak, and they followed *J* Jn 1:37 *2424*
Then *J* turned, and saw them Jn 1:38 *2424*
And he brought him to *J* Jn 1:42 *2424*
when *J* beheld him, he said, Thou Jn 1:42 *2424*
The day following *J* would go Jn 1:43 *2424*
J of Nazareth, the son of Joseph Jn 1:45 *2424*
J saw Nathanael coming to him, and Jn 1:47 *2424*
J answered and said unto him, Jn 1:48 *2424*
J answered and said unto him, Jn 1:50 *2424*
and the mother of *J* was there Jn 2:1 *2424*
both *J* was called, and his Jn 2:2 *2424*
the mother of *J* saith unto him, Jn 2:3 *2424*
J saith unto her, Woman, what Jn 2:4 *2424*
J saith unto them, Fill the Jn 2:7 *2424*
miracles did *J* in Cana of Galilee Jn 2:11 *2424*
hand, and *J* went up to Jerusalem, Jn 2:13 *2424*
J answered and said unto them, Jn 2:19 *2424*
and the word which *J* had said Jn 2:22 *2424*
But *J* did not commit himself unto Jn 2:24 *2424*
The same came to *J* by night Jn 3:2 *2424*
J answered and said unto him, Jn 3:3 *2424*
J answered, Verily, verily, I say Jn 3:5 *2424*
J answered and said unto him, Art Jn 3:10 *2424*
After these things came *J* Jn 3:22 *2424*
Pharisees had heard that *J* made Jn 4:1 *2424*
(Though *J* himself baptized not, Jn 4:2 *2424*
J therefore, being wearied with Jn 4:6 *2424*
J saith unto her, Give me to Jn 4:7 *2424*
J answered and said unto her, If Jn 4:10 *2424*
J answered and said unto her, Jn 4:13 *2424*
J saith unto her, Go, call thy Jn 4:16 *2424*
J said unto her, Thou hast well Jn 4:17 *2424*
J saith unto her, Woman, believe Jn 4:21 *2424*
J saith unto her, I that speak Jn 4:26 *2424*
J saith unto them, My meat is to Jn 4:34 *2424*
For *J* himself testified, that a Jn 4:44 *2424*
So *J* came again into Cana of Jn 4:46
When he heard that *J* was come out Jn 4:47 *2424*
Then said *J* unto him, Except ye Jn 4:48 *2424*
J saith unto him, Go thy way Jn 4:50 *2424*
word that *J* had spoken unto him Jn 4:50 *2424*
in the which *J* said unto him, Thy Jn 4:53 *2424*
the second miracle that *J* did Jn 4:54 *2424*
and *J* went up to Jerusalem Jn 5:1 *2424*
When *J* saw him lie, and knew that Jn 5:6 *2424*
J saith unto him, Rise, take up Jn 5:8 *2424*
for *J* had conveyed himself away, Jn 5:13 *2424*
Afterward *J* findeth him in the Jn 5:14 *2424*
and told the Jews that it was *J* Jn 5:15 *2424*
did the Jews persecute *J*, and Jn 5:16 *2424*
But *J* answered them, My Father Jn 5:17 *2424*
Then answered *J* and said unto them Jn 5:19 *2424*
After these things *J* went over Jn 6:1 *2424*
J went up into a mountain, and Jn 6:3 *2424*
When *J* then lifted up his eyes, Jn 6:5 *2424*
J said, Make the men sit down Jn 6:10 *2424*
And *J* took the loaves Jn 6:11 *2424*
had seen the miracle that *J* did Jn 6:14 *2424*
When *J* therefore perceived that Jn 6:15 *2424*
dark, and *J* was not come to them Jn 6:17 *2424*
they see *J* walking on the sea, and Jn 6:19 *2424*
and that *J* went not with his Jn 6:22 *2424*
saw that *J* was not there, neither Jn 6:24 *2424*
came to Capernaum, seeking for *J* Jn 6:24 *2424*
J answered them and said, Verily, Jn 6:26 *2424*
J answered and said unto them, Jn 6:29 *2424*
Then *J* said unto them, Verily, Jn 6:32 *2424*
J said unto them, I am the bread Jn 6:35 *2424*
And they said, Is not this *J* Jn 6:42 *2424*
J therefore answered and said unto Jn 6:43 *2424*
Then *J* said unto them, Verily, Jn 6:53 *2424*
When *J* knew in himself that his Jn 6:61 *2424*
For *J* knew from the beginning who Jn 6:64 *2424*
Then said *J* unto the twelve, Will Jn 6:67 *2424*
J answered them, Have not I Jn 6:70 *2424*
these things *J* walked in Galilee Jn 7:1 *2424*
Then *J* said unto them, My time is Jn 7:6 *2424*
feast *J* went up into the temple Jn 7:14 *2424*
J answered them, and said, My Jn 7:16 *2424*
J answered and said unto them, I Jn 7:21 *2424*
Then cried *J* in the temple as he Jn 7:28 *2424*
Then said *J* unto them, Yet a Jn 7:33 *2424*
J stood and cried, saying, If any Jn 7:37 *2424*
because that *J* was not yet Jn 7:39 *2424*
them, (he that came to *J* by night Jn 7:50 *846*
J went unto the mount of Olives Jn 8:1 *2424*
But *J* stooped down, and with his Jn 8:6 *2424*
J was left alone, and the woman Jn 8:9 *2424*
When *J* had lifted up himself, and Jn 8:10 *2424*
J said unto her, Neither do I Jn 8:11 *2424*
Then spake *J* again unto them, Jn 8:12 *2424*
J answered and said unto them, Jn 8:14 *2424*
J answered, Ye neither know me, Jn 8:19 *2424*
words spake *J* in the treasury Jn 8:20 *2424*
Then said *J* again unto them, I go Jn 8:21 *2424*
J saith unto them, Even the same Jn 8:25 *2424*
Then said *J* unto them, When ye Jn 8:28 *2424*
Then said *J* to those Jews which Jn 8:31 *2424*
J answered them, Verily, verily, Jn 8:34 *2424*
J saith unto them, If ye were Jn 8:39 *2424*
J said unto them, If God were Jn 8:42 *2424*
J answered, I have not a devil Jn 8:49 *2424*
J answered, If I honour myself, Jn 8:54 *2424*
J said unto them, Verily, verily, Jn 8:58 *2424*
but *J* hid himself, and went out of Jn 8:59 *2424*
as *J* passed by, he saw a man Jn 9:1
J answered, Neither hath this man Jn 9:3 *2424*
A man that is called *J* made clay Jn 9:11 *2424*
sabbath day when *J* made the clay Jn 9:14 *2424*
J heard that they had cast him Jn 9:35 *2424*
J said unto him, Thou hast both Jn 9:37 *2424*
J said, For judgment I am come Jn 9:39 *2424*
J said unto them, If ye were Jn 9:41 *2424*
This parable spake *J* unto them Jn 10:6 *2424*
Then said *J* unto them again, Jn 10:7 *2424*
J walked in the temple in Jn 10:23 *2424*
J answered them, I told you, and Jn 10:25 *2424*
J answered them, Many good works Jn 10:32 *2424*
J answered them, Is it not Jn 10:34 *2424*
When *J* heard that, he said, This Jn 11:4 *2424*
Now *J* loved Martha, and her sister Jn 11:5 *2424*
J answered, Are there not twelve Jn 11:9 *2424*
Howbeit *J* spake of his death Jn 11:13 *2424*
Then said *J* unto them plainly, Jn 11:14 *2424*
Then when *J* came, he found that Jn 11:17 *2424*
as she heard that *J* was coming Jn 11:20 *2424*
Then said Martha unto *J*, Lord, if Jn 11:21 *2424*
J saith unto her, Thy brother Jn 11:23 *2424*
J said unto her, I am the Jn 11:25 *2424*
Now *J* was not yet come into the Jn 11:30 *2424*
when Mary was come where *J* was Jn 11:32 *2424*
When *J* therefore saw her weeping, Jn 11:33 *2424*
J wept Jn 11:35 *2424*
J therefore again groaning in Jn 11:38 *2424*
J said, Take ye away the stone Jn 11:39 *2424*
J saith unto her, Said I not unto Jn 11:40 *2424*
J lifted up his eyes, and said, Jn 11:41 *2424*
J saith unto them, Loose him, and Jn 11:44 *2424*
had seen the things which *J* did Jn 11:45 *2424*
told them what things *J* had done Jn 11:46 *2424*
he prophesied that *J* should die Jn 11:51 *2424*
J therefore walked no more openly Jn 11:54 *2424*
Then sought they for *J*, and spake Jn 11:56 *2424*
Then *J* six days before the Jn 12:1 *2424*
costly, and anointed the feet of *J* Jn 12:3 *2424*
Then said *J*, Let her alone Jn 12:7 *2424*
Jews went away, and believed on *J* Jn 12:11 *2424*
when they heard that *J* was coming Jn 12:12 *2424*
And *J*, when he had found a young Jn 12:14 *2424*
but when *J* was glorified, then Jn 12:16 *2424*
him, saying, Sir, we would see *J* Jn 12:21 *2424*
and again Andrew and Philip tell *J* Jn 12:22 *2424*
J answered them, saying, The hour Jn 12:23 *2424*
J answered and said, This voice Jn 12:30 *2424*
Then *J* said unto them, Yet a Jn 12:35 *2424*
These things spake *J*, and departed Jn 12:36 *2424*
J cried and said, He that Jn 12:44 *2424*
when *J* knew that his hour was Jn 13:1 *2424*
J knowing that the Father had Jn 13:3 *2424*
J answered and said unto him, What Jn 13:7 *2424*
J answered him, If I wash thee Jn 13:8 *2424*
J saith to him, He that is washed Jn 13:10 *2424*
When *J* had thus said, he was Jn 13:21 *2424*
of his disciples, whom *J* loved Jn 13:23 *2424*
J answered, He it is, to whom I Jn 13:26 *2424*
Then said *J* unto him, That thou Jn 13:27 *2424*
that *J* had said unto him, Buy Jn 13:29 *2424*
J said, Now is the Son of man Jn 13:31 *2424*
J answered him, Whither I go, Jn 13:36 *2424*
J answered him, Wilt thou lay Jn 13:38 *2424*
J saith unto him, I am the way, Jn 14:6 *2424*
J saith unto him, Have I been so Jn 14:9 *2424*
J answered and said unto him, If a Jn 14:23 *2424*
Now *J* knew that they were Jn 16:19 *2424*
J answered them, Do ye now Jn 16:31 *2424*
These words spake *J*, and lifted up Jn 17:1 *2424*
J Christ, whom thou hast sent Jn 17:3 *2424*
When *J* had spoken these words, he Jn 18:1 *2424*
for *J* ofttimes resorted thither Jn 18:2 *2424*
J therefore, knowing all things Jn 18:4 *2424*
They answered him, *J* of Nazareth Jn 18:5 *2424*
J saith unto them, I am he Jn 18:5 *2424*
And they said, *J* of Nazareth Jn 18:7 *2424*
J answered, I have told you that Jn 18:8 *2424*
Then said *J* unto Peter, Put up Jn 18:11 *2424*
and officers of the Jews took *J* Jn 18:12 *2424*
And Simon Peter followed *J* Jn 18:15 *2424*
went in with *J* into the palace of Jn 18:15 *2424*
then asked *J* of his disciples Jn 18:19 *2424*
J answered him, I spake openly to Jn 18:20 *2424*
J with the palm of his hand Jn 18:22 *2424*
J answered him, If I have spoken Jn 18:23 *2424*
Then led they *J* from Caiaphas Jn 18:28 *2424*
saying of *J* might be fulfilled Jn 18:32 *2424*
judgment hall again, and called *J* Jn 18:33 *2424*
J answered him, Sayest thou this Jn 18:34 *2424*
J answered, My kingdom is not of Jn 18:36 *2424*
J answered, Thou sayest that I am Jn 18:37 *2424*
Then Pilate therefore took *J* Jn 19:1 *2424*
Then came *J* forth, wearing the Jn 19:5 *2424*
judgment hall, and saith unto *J* Jn 19:9 *2424*
But *J* gave him no answer Jn 19:9 *2424*
J answered, Thou couldest have no Jn 19:11 *2424*
that saying, he brought *J* forth Jn 19:13 *2424*
And they took *J*, and led him away Jn 19:16 *2424*
side one, and *J* in the midst Jn 19:18 *2424*
J OF NAZARETH THE KING OF THE Jn 19:19 *2424*
for the place where *J* was Jn 19:20 *2424*
when they had crucified *J* Jn 19:23 *2424*
by the cross of *J* his mother Jn 19:25 *2424*
When *J* therefore saw his mother, Jn 19:26 *2424*
J knowing that all things were Jn 19:28 *2424*
When *J* therefore had received the Jn 19:30 *2424*
But when they came to *J*, and saw Jn 19:33 *2424*
Arimathaea, being a disciple of *J* Jn 19:38 *2424*
he might take away the body of *J* Jn 19:38 *2424*
therefore, and took the body of *J* Jn 19:38 *2424*
at the first came to *J* by night Jn 19:39 *2424*
Then took they the body of *J* Jn 19:40 *2424*
There laid they *J* therefore Jn 19:42 *2424*
whom *J* loved, and saith unto them, Jn 20:2 *2424*
where the body of *J* had lain Jn 20:12 *2424*
saw *J* standing, and knew not that Jn 20:14 *2424*
and knew not that it was *J* Jn 20:14 *2424*
J saith unto her, Woman, why Jn 20:15 *2424*
J saith unto her, Mary Jn 20:16 *2424*

J saith unto her, Touch me not ... Jn 20:17 2424
for fear of the Jews, came J ... Jn 20:19 2424
Then said J to them again, Peace ... Jn 20:21 2424
was not with them when J came ... Jn 20:24 2424
then came J, the doors being shut ... Jn 20:26 2424
J saith unto him, Thomas, because ... Jn 20:29 2424
did J in the presence of his ... Jn 20:30 2424
believe that J is the Christ ... Jn 20:31 2424
After these things J shewed ... Jn 21:1 2424
now come, J stood on the shore ... Jn 21:4 2424
disciples knew not that it was J ... Jn 21:4 2424
Then J saith unto them, Children, ... Jn 21:5 2424
whom J loved saith unto Peter ... Jn 21:7 2424
J saith unto them, Bring of the ... Jn 21:10 2424
J saith unto them, Come and dine ... Jn 21:12 2424
J then cometh, and taketh bread, ... Jn 21:13 2424
J shewed himself to his disciples ... Jn 21:14 2424
J saith to Simon Peter, Simon, ... Jn 21:15 2424
J saith unto him, Feed my sheep ... Jn 21:17 2424
disciple whom J loved following ... Jn 21:20 2424
Peter seeing him saith to J ... Jn 21:21 2424
J saith unto him, If I will that ... Jn 21:22 2424
yet J said not unto him, He shall ... Jn 21:23 2424
many other things which J did ... Jn 21:25 2424
of all that J began both to do and ... Acts 1:1 2424
this same J, which is taken up ... Acts 1:11 2424
women, and Mary the mother of J ... Acts 1:14 2424
was guide to them that took J ... Acts 1:16 2424
the time that the Lord J went in ... Acts 1:21 2424
J of Nazareth, a man approved of ... Acts 2:22 2424
This J hath God raised up, ... Acts 2:32 2424
that God hath made that same J ... Acts 2:36 2424
of J Christ for the remission of ... Acts 2:38 2424
In the name of J Christ of ... Acts 3:6 2424
fathers, hath glorified his Son J ... Acts 3:13 2424
And he shall send J Christ ... Acts 3:20 2424
God, having raised up his Son J ... Acts 3:26 2424
people, and preached through J the ... Acts 4:2 2424
the name of J Christ of Nazareth ... Acts 4:10 2424
them, that they had been with J ... Acts 4:13 2424
at all nor teach in the name of J ... Acts 4:18 2424
a truth against thy holy child J ... Acts 4:27 2424
by the name of thy holy child J ... Acts 4:30 2424
of the resurrection of the Lord J ... Acts 4:33 2424
God of our fathers raised up J ... Acts 5:30 2424
should not speak in the name of J ... Acts 5:40 2424
not to teach and preach J Christ ... Acts 5:42 2424
that this J of Nazareth shall ... Acts 6:14 2424
with J into the possession of the ... Acts 7:45 2424
J standing on the right hand of ... Acts 7:55 2424
upon God, and saying, Lord J ... Acts 7:59 2424
of God, and the name of J Christ ... Acts 8:12 2424
in the name of the Lord J ... Acts 8:16 2424
scripture, and preached unto him J ... Acts 8:35 2424
I believe that J Christ is the ... Acts 8:37 2424
I am J whom thou persecutest ... Acts 9:5 2424
Brother Saul, the Lord, even J ... Acts 9:17 2424
at Damascus in the name of J ... Acts 9:27 2424
boldly in the name of the Lord J ... Acts 9:29 2424
J Christ maketh thee whole ... Acts 9:34 2424
preaching peace by J Christ ... Acts 10:36 2424
How God anointed J of Nazareth ... Acts 10:38 2424
who believed on the Lord J Christ ... Acts 11:17 2424
Grecians, preaching the Lord J ... Acts 11:20 2424
raised unto Israel a Saviour, J ... Acts 13:23 2424
in that he hath raised up J again ... Acts 13:33 2424
Lord J Christ we shall be saved ... Acts 15:11 2424
for the name of our Lord J Christ ... Acts 15:26 2424
of J Christ to come out of her ... Acts 16:18 2424
Believe on the Lord J Christ ... Acts 16:31 2424
and that this J, whom I preach ... Acts 17:3 2424
that there is another king, one J ... Acts 17:7 2424
because he preached unto them J ... Acts 17:18 2424
to the Jews that J was Christ ... Acts 18:5 2424
the scriptures that J was Christ ... Acts 18:28 2424
after him, that is, on Christ J ... Acts 19:4 2424
in the name of the Lord J ... Acts 19:5 2424
Asia heard the word of the Lord J ... Acts 19:10 2424
spirits the name of the Lord J ... Acts 19:13 2424
We adjure you by J whom Paul ... Acts 19:13 2424
and said, J I know, and Paul I know ... Acts 19:15 2424
name of the Lord J was magnified ... Acts 19:17 2424
and faith toward our Lord J Christ ... Acts 20:21 2424
I have received of the Lord J ... Acts 20:24 2424
remember the words of the Lord J ... Acts 20:35 2424
for the name of the Lord J ... Acts 21:13 2424
I am J of Nazareth, whom thou ... Acts 22:8 2424
own superstition, and of one J ... Acts 25:19 2424
to the name of J of Nazareth ... Acts 26:9 2424
I am J whom thou persecutest ... Acts 26:15 2424
God, persuading them concerning J ... Acts 28:23 2424
which concern the Lord J Christ ... Acts 28:31 2424
Paul, a servant of J Christ ... Rom 1:1 2424
his Son J Christ our Lord ... Rom 1:3 2424
ye also the called of J Christ ... Rom 1:6 2424
our Father, and the Lord J Christ ... Rom 1:7 2424
God through J Christ for you all ... Rom 1:8 2424
judge the secrets of men by J ... Rom 2:16 2424
is by faith of J Christ unto all ... Rom 3:22 2424
redemption that is in Christ J ... Rom 3:24 2424
of him which believeth in J ... Rom 3:26 2424
up J our Lord from the dead ... Rom 4:24 2424
God through our Lord J Christ ... Rom 5:1 2424
in God through our Lord J Christ ... Rom 5:11 2424
J Christ, hath abounded unto many ... Rom 5:15 2424
reign in life by one, J Christ ... Rom 5:17 2424
eternal life by J Christ our Lord ... Rom 5:21 2424
of us as were baptized into J ... Rom 6:3 2424
God through J Christ our Lord ... Rom 6:11 2424
life through J Christ our Lord ... Rom 6:23 2424
God through J Christ our Lord ... Rom 7:25 2424
to them which are in Christ J ... Rom 8:1 2424
the Spirit of life in Christ J ... Rom 8:2 2424
up J from the dead dwell in you ... Rom 8:11 2424
which is in Christ J our Lord ... Rom 8:39 2424
confess with thy mouth the Lord J ... Rom 10:9 2424
But put ye on the Lord J Christ ... Rom 13:14 2424
and am persuaded by the Lord J ... Rom 14:14 2424
another according to Christ J ... Rom 15:5 2424
the Father of our Lord J Christ ... Rom 15:6 2424
Now I say that J Christ was a ... Rom 15:8 2424
of J Christ to the Gentiles ... Rom 15:16 2424
whereof I may glory through J ... Rom 15:17 2424
for the Lord J Christ's sake, and ... Rom 15:30 2424
and Aquila my helpers in Christ J ... Rom 16:3 2424
such serve not our Lord J Christ ... Rom 16:18 2424
of our Lord J Christ be with you ... Rom 16:20 2424
The grace of our Lord J Christ be ... Rom 16:24 2424
and the preaching of J Christ ... Rom 16:25 2424
glory through J Christ for ever ... Rom 16:27 2424
called to be an apostle of J ... 1Cor 1:1 2424
that are sanctified in Christ J ... 1Cor 1:2 2424
the name of J Christ our Lord ... 1Cor 1:2 2424
Father, and from the Lord J Christ ... 1Cor 1:3 2424
which is given you by J Christ ... 1Cor 1:4 2424
the coming of our Lord J Christ ... 1Cor 1:7 2424
in the day of our Lord J Christ ... 1Cor 1:8 2424
of his Son J Christ our Lord ... 1Cor 1:9 2424
by the name of our Lord J Christ ... 1Cor 1:10 2424
But of him are ye in Christ J ... 1Cor 1:30 2424
save J Christ, and him crucified ... 1Cor 2:2 2424
that is laid, which is J Christ ... 1Cor 3:11 2424
for in Christ J I have begotten ... 1Cor 4:15 2424
In the name of our Lord J Christ ... 1Cor 5:4 2424
the power of our Lord J Christ ... 1Cor 5:4 2424
be saved in the day of the Lord J ... 1Cor 5:5 2424
in the name of the Lord J ... 1Cor 6:11 2424
and one Lord J Christ, by whom are ... 1Cor 8:6 2424
have I not seen J Christ our Lord ... 1Cor 9:1 2424
That the Lord J the same night in ... 1Cor 11:23 2424
Spirit of God calleth J accursed ... 1Cor 12:3 2424
no man can say that J is the Lord ... 1Cor 12:3 2424
which I have in Christ J our Lord ... 1Cor 15:31 2424
victory through our Lord J Christ ... 1Cor 15:57 2424
man love not the Lord J Christ ... 1Cor 16:22 2424
of our Lord J Christ be with you ... 1Cor 16:23 2424
love be with you all in Christ J ... 1Cor 16:24 2424
an apostle of J Christ by the ... 2Cor 1:1 2424
Father, and from the Lord J Christ ... 2Cor 1:2 2424
the Father of our Lord J Christ ... 2Cor 1:3 2424
are ours in the day of the Lord J ... 2Cor 1:14 2424
J Christ, who was preached among ... 2Cor 1:19 2424
ourselves, but Christ J the Lord ... 2Cor 4:5 2424
of God in the face of J Christ ... 2Cor 4:6 2424
the body the dying of the Lord J ... 2Cor 4:10 2424
that the life also of J might be ... 2Cor 4:10 2424
that the life also of J might be ... 2Cor 4:11 2424
he which raised up the Lord J ... 2Cor 4:14 2424
shall raise up us also by J ... 2Cor 4:14 2424
us to himself by J Christ ... 2Cor 5:18 2424
the grace of our Lord J Christ ... 2Cor 8:9 2424
that cometh preacheth another J ... 2Cor 11:4 2424
and Father of our Lord J Christ ... 2Cor 11:31 2424
how that J Christ is in you, ... 2Cor 13:5 2424
The grace of the Lord J Christ ... 2Cor 13:14 2424
neither by man, but by J Christ ... Gal 1:1 2424
Father, and from our Lord J Christ ... Gal 1:3 2424
but by the revelation of J Christ ... Gal 1:12 2424
liberty which we have in Christ J ... Gal 2:4 2424
law, but by the faith of J Christ ... Gal 2:16 2424
even we have believed in J Christ ... Gal 2:16 2424
before whose eyes J Christ hath ... Gal 3:1 2424
on the Gentiles through J Christ ... Gal 3:14 2424
that the promise by faith of J ... Gal 3:22 2424
of God by faith in Christ J ... Gal 3:26 2424
for ye are all one in Christ J ... Gal 3:28 2424
an angel of God, even as Christ J ... Gal 4:14 2424
For in J Christ neither ... Gal 5:6 2424
in the cross of our Lord J Christ ... Gal 6:14 2424
For in Christ J neither ... Gal 6:15 2424
my body the marks of the Lord J ... Gal 6:17 2424
the grace of our Lord J Christ be ... Gal 6:18 2424
an apostle of J Christ by the ... Eph 1:1 2424
and to the faithful in Christ J ... Eph 1:1 2424
Father, and from the Lord J Christ ... Eph 1:2 2424
and Father of our Lord J Christ ... Eph 1:3 2424
children by J Christ to himself ... Eph 1:5 2424
heard of your faith in the Lord J ... Eph 1:15 2424
That the God of our Lord J Christ ... Eph 1:17 2424
in heavenly places in Christ J ... Eph 2:6 2424
toward us through Christ J ... Eph 2:7 2424
in Christ J unto good works ... Eph 2:10 2424
But now in Christ J ye who ... Eph 2:13 2424
J Christ himself being the chief ... Eph 2:20 2424
the prisoner of J Christ for you ... Eph 3:1 2424
created all things by J Christ ... Eph 3:9 2424
he purposed in Christ J our Lord ... Eph 3:11 2424
the Father of our Lord J Christ ... Eph 3:14 2424
by Christ J throughout all ages ... Eph 3:21 2424
by him, as the truth is in J ... Eph 4:21 2424
in the name of our Lord J Christ ... Eph 5:20 2424
the Father and the Lord J Christ ... Eph 6:23 2424
our Lord J Christ in sincerity ... Eph 6:24 2424
the servants of J Christ ... Phil 1:1 2424
in Christ J which are at Philippi ... Phil 1:1 2424
Father, and from the Lord J Christ ... Phil 1:2 2424
it until the day of J Christ ... Phil 1:6 2424
you all in the bowels of J Christ ... Phil 1:8 2424
which are by J Christ, unto the ... Phil 1:11 2424
supply of the Spirit of J Christ ... Phil 1:19 2424
may be more abundant in J Christ ... Phil 1:26 2424
you, which was also in Christ J ... Phil 2:5 2424
That at the name of J every knee ... Phil 2:10 2424
confess that J Christ is Lord ... Phil 2:11 2424
But I trust in the Lord J to send ... Phil 2:19 2424
the things which are J Christ's ... Phil 2:21 2424
spirit, and rejoice in Christ J ... Phil 3:3 2424
the knowledge of Christ J my Lord ... Phil 3:8 2424
also I am apprehended of Christ J ... Phil 3:12 2424
high calling of God in Christ J ... Phil 3:14 2424
the Saviour, the Lord J Christ ... Phil 3:20 2424
hearts and minds through Christ J ... Phil 4:7 2424
his riches in glory by Christ J ... Phil 4:19 2424
Salute every saint in Christ J ... Phil 4:21 2424
The grace of our Lord J Christ be ... Phil 4:23 2424
an apostle of J Christ by the ... Col 1:1 2424
our Father and the Lord J Christ ... Col 1:2 2424
the Father of our Lord J Christ ... Col 1:3 2424
heard of your faith in Christ J ... Col 1:4 2424
every man perfect in Christ J ... Col 1:28 2424
received Christ J the Lord ... Col 2:6 2424
do all in the name of the Lord J ... Col 3:17 2424
Father and in the Lord J Christ ... 1Th 1:1 2424
our Father, and the Lord J Christ ... 1Th 1:1 2424
of hope in our Lord J Christ ... 1Th 1:3 2424
he raised from the dead, even J ... 1Th 1:10 2424
which in Judaea are in Christ J ... 1Th 2:14 2424
Who both killed the Lord J ... 1Th 2:15 2424
our Lord J Christ at his coming ... 1Th 2:19 2424
our Father, and our Lord J Christ ... 1Th 3:11 2424
at the coming of our Lord J ... 1Th 3:13 2424
and exhort you by the Lord J ... 1Th 4:1 2424
we gave you by the Lord J ... 1Th 4:2 2424
For if we believe that J died ... 1Th 4:14 2424
in J will God bring with him ... 1Th 4:14 2424
salvation by our Lord J Christ ... 1Th 5:9 2424
of God in Christ J concerning you ... 1Th 5:18 2424
the coming of our Lord J Christ ... 1Th 5:23 2424
of our Lord J Christ be with you ... 1Th 5:28 2424
our Father and the Lord J Christ ... 2Th 1:1 2424
our Father and the Lord J Christ ... 2Th 1:2 2424
when the Lord J shall be revealed ... 2Th 1:7 2424
the gospel of our Lord J Christ ... 2Th 1:8 2424
That the name of our Lord J ... 2Th 1:12 2424
of our God and the Lord J Christ ... 2Th 1:12 2424
the coming of our Lord J Christ ... 2Th 2:1 2424
of the glory of our Lord J Christ ... 2Th 2:14 2424
Now our Lord J Christ himself, and ... 2Th 2:16 2424
in the name of our Lord J Christ ... 2Th 3:6 2424
and exhort by our Lord J Christ ... 2Th 3:12 2424
The grace of our Lord J Christ be ... 2Th 3:18 2424
an apostle of J Christ by the ... 1Ti 1:1 2424
Lord J Christ, which is our hope ... 1Ti 1:1 2424
our Father and J Christ our Lord ... 1Ti 1:2 2424
And I thank Christ J our Lord ... 1Ti 1:12 2424
and love which is in Christ J ... 1Ti 1:14 2424
that Christ J came into the world ... 1Ti 1:15 2424
that in me first J Christ might ... 1Ti 1:16 2424
God and men, the man Christ J ... 1Ti 2:5 2424
in the faith which is in Christ J ... 1Ti 3:13 2424
be a good minister of J Christ ... 1Ti 4:6 2424
before God, and the Lord J Christ ... 1Ti 5:21 2424
the words of our Lord J Christ ... 1Ti 6:3 2424
all things, and before Christ J ... 1Ti 6:13 2424
appearing of our Lord J Christ ... 1Ti 6:14 2424
an apostle of J Christ by the ... 2Ti 1:1 2424
of life which is in Christ J ... 2Ti 1:1 2424
the Father and Christ J our Lord ... 2Ti 1:2 2424
Christ J before the world began ... 2Ti 1:9 2424
appearing of our Saviour J Christ ... 2Ti 1:10 2424
and love which is in Christ J ... 2Ti 1:13 2424
in the grace that is in Christ J ... 2Ti 2:1 2424
as a good soldier of J Christ ... 2Ti 2:3 2424
Remember that J Christ of the ... 2Ti 2:8 2424
is in Christ J with eternal glory ... 2Ti 2:10 2424
Christ J shall suffer persecution ... 2Ti 3:12 2424
faith which is in Christ J ... 2Ti 3:15 2424
before God, and the Lord J Christ ... 2Ti 4:1 2424
The Lord J Christ be with thy ... 2Ti 4:22 2424
of God, and an apostle of J Christ ... Titus 1:1 2424
the Lord J Christ our Saviour ... Titus 1:4 2424
great God and our Saviour J Christ ... Titus 2:13 2424
through J Christ our Saviour ... Titus 3:6 2424
Paul, a prisoner of J Christ ... Philem 1 2424
our Father and the Lord J Christ ... Philem 3 2424
which thou hast toward the Lord J ... Philem 5 2424
thing which is in you in Christ J ... Philem 6 2424
now also a prisoner of J Christ ... Philem 9 2424
my fellowprisoner in Christ J ... Philem 23 2424
The grace of our Lord J Christ be ... Philem 25 2424
But we see J, who was made a ... Heb 2:9 2424
of our profession, Christ J ... Heb 3:1 2424
J the Son of God, let us hold ... Heb 4:14 2424
is for us entered, even J ... Heb 6:20 2424
By so much was J made a surety of ... Heb 7:22 2424
the body of J Christ once for all ... Heb 10:10 2424
the holiest by the blood of J ... Heb 10:19 2424
Looking unto J the author ... Heb 12:2 2424
to J the mediator of the new ... Heb 12:24 2424
J Christ the same yesterday, and ... Heb 13:8 2424
Wherefore J also, that he might ... Heb 13:12 2424
again from the dead our Lord J ... Heb 13:20 2424
in his sight, through J Christ ... Heb 13:21 2424
of God and of the Lord J Christ ... Jas 1:1 2424

the faith of our Lord *J* Christ ... Jas 2:1 *2424*
Peter, an apostle of *J* Christ ... 1Pet 1:1 *2424*
of the blood of *J* Christ ... 1Pet 1:2 *2424*
and Father of our Lord *J* Christ ... 1Pet 1:3 *2424*
of *J* Christ from the dead ... 1Pet 1:3 *2424*
at the appearing of *J* Christ ... 1Pet 1:7 *2424*
you at the revelation of *J* Christ ... 1Pet 1:13 *2424*
acceptable to God by *J* Christ ... 1Pet 2:5 *2424*
by the resurrection of *J* Christ ... 1Pet 3:21 *2424*
may be glorified through *J* Christ ... 1Pet 4:11 *2424*
his eternal glory by Christ *J* ... 1Pet 5:10 *2424*
with you all that are in Christ *J* ... 1Pet 5:14 *2424*
servant and an apostle of *J* Christ ... 2Pet 1:1 *2424*
of God and our Saviour *J* Christ ... 2Pet 1:1 *2424*
of God, and of *J* our Lord, ... 2Pet 1:2 *2424*
knowledge of our Lord *J* Christ ... 2Pet 1:8 *2424*
of our Lord and Saviour *J* Christ ... 2Pet 1:11 *2424*
even as our Lord *J* Christ hath ... 2Pet 1:14 *2424*
and coming of our Lord *J* Christ ... 2Pet 1:16 *2424*
of the Lord and Saviour *J* Christ ... 2Pet 2:20 *2424*
of our Lord and Saviour *J* Christ ... 2Pet 3:18 *2424*
Father, and with his Son *J* Christ ... 1Jn 1:3 *2424*
the blood of *J* Christ his Son ... 1Jn 1:7 *2424*
Father, *J* Christ the righteous ... 1Jn 2:1 *2424*
that denieth that *J* is the Christ ... 1Jn 2:22 *2424*
on the name of his Son *J* Christ ... 1Jn 3:23 *2424*
spirit that confesseth that *J* ... 1Jn 4:2 *2424*
J Christ is come in the flesh is ... 1Jn 4:3 *2424*
confess that *J* is the Son of God ... 1Jn 4:15 *2424*
Whosoever believeth that *J* is the ... 1Jn 5:1 *2424*
that *J* is the Son of God ... 1Jn 5:5 *2424*
by water and blood, even *J* Christ ... 1Jn 5:6 *2424*
is true, even in his Son *J* Christ ... 1Jn 5:20 *2424*
Father, and from the Lord *J* Christ ... 2Jn 3 *2424*
who confess not that *J* Christ is ... 2Jn 7 *2424*
Jude, the servant of *J* Christ ... Jude 1 *2424*
Father, and preserved in *J* Christ ... Jude 1 *2424*
Lord God, and our Lord *J* Christ ... Jude 4 *2424*
the apostles of our Lord *J* Christ ... Jude 17 *2424*
Lord *J* Christ unto eternal life ... Jude 21 *2424*
The Revelation of *J* Christ ... Rev 1:1 *2424*
and of the testimony of *J* Christ ... Rev 1:2 *2424*
from *J* Christ, who is the ... Rev 1:5 *2424*
kingdom and patience of *J* Christ ... Rev 1:9 *2424*
and for the testimony of *J* Christ ... Rev 1:9 *2424*
and have the testimony of *J* Christ ... Rev 12:17 *2424*
of God, and the faith of *J* ... Rev 14:12 *2424*
the blood of the martyrs of *J* ... Rev 17:6 *2424*
that have the testimony of *J* ... Rev 19:10 *2424*
for the testimony of *J* is the ... Rev 19:10 *2424*
beheaded for the witness of *J* ... Rev 20:4 *2424*
I *J* have sent mine angel to ... Rev 22:16 *2424*
Even so, come, Lord *J* ... Rev 22:20 *2424*
The grace of our Lord *J* Christ be ... Rev 22:21 *2424*
2. Joshua, son of Nun.
For if *J* had given them rest, ... Heb 4:8 *2424*
3. Justus, a Roman Christian.
And *J*, which is called Justus, who ... Col 4:11 *2424*

JESUS' *(je'-zus)* {10} *Refers to the Christ.*
and cast them down at *J* feet ... Mt 15:30 *2424*
who also himself was *J* disciple ... Mt 27:57 *2424*
saw it, he fell down at *J* knees ... Lk 5:8 *2424*
and he fell down at *J* feet ... Lk 8:41 *2424*
Mary, which also sat at *J* feet ... Lk 10:39 *2424*
and they came not for *J* sake only ... Jn 12:9 *2424*
Now there was leaning on *J* bosom ... Jn 13:23 *2424*
He then lying on *J* breast saith ... Jn 13:25 *2424*
your servants for *J* sake ... 2Cor 4:5 *2424*
delivered unto death for *J* sake ... 2Cor 4:11 *2424*

JETHER *(je'-thur)* {8} See HOBAB, ITHRA, ITHRITES, JETHRO, RAGUEL.
1. A son of Gideon.
he said unto *J* his firstborn, Up, ... Judg 8:20 3500
2. Father of Amasa.
Ner, and unto Amasa the son of *J* ... 1Kin 2:5 3500
of Israel, and Amasa the son of *J* ... 1Kin 2:32 3500
of Amasa was *J* the Ishmeelite ... 1Chr 2:17 3500
3. A son of Jerahmeel.
J, and Jonathan ... 1Chr 2:32 3500
and *J* died without children ... 1Chr 2:32 3500
4. A son of Ezra.
And the sons of Ezra were, *J* ... 1Chr 4:17 3500
5. A descendant of Asher.
And the sons of *J* ... 1Chr 7:38 3500

JETHETH *(je'-theth)* {2} *A prince of Edom.*
duke Timnah, duke Alvah, duke *J* ... Gen 36:40 3509
duke Timnah, duke Aliah, duke *J* ... 1Chr 1:51 3509

JETHLAH *(jeth'-lah)* {1} *A city in Dan.*
And Shaalabbin, and Ajalon, and *J* ... Josh 19:42 3494

JETHRO *(je'-thro)* {10} See JETHER. *Father-in-law of Moses.*
the flock of *J* his father in law ... Ex 3:1 3503
returned to *J* his father in law, ... Ex 4:18 3503
J said to Moses, Go in peace ... Ex 4:18 3503
When *J*, the priest of Midian, ... Ex 18:1 3503
Then *J*, Moses' father in law, ... Ex 18:2 3503
And *J*, Moses' father in law, came ... Ex 18:5 3503
father in law *J* am come unto thee ... Ex 18:6 3503
J rejoiced for all the goodness ... Ex 18:9 3503
J said, Blessed be the LORD, who ... Ex 18:10 3503
And *J*, Moses' father in law, took ... Ex 18:12 3503

JETUR *(je'-tur)* {3}
1. A son of Ishmael.
Hadar, and Tema, *J*, Naphish, and ... Gen 25:15 3195
J, Naphish, and Kedemah ... 1Chr 1:31 3195
2. Descendants of Jetur.
war with the Hagarites, with *J* ... 1Chr 5:19 3195

JEUEL *(je-u'-el)* {1} See JEIEL. *A descendant of Zerah.*
J, and their brethren, six hundred ... 1Chr 9:6 3262

JEUSH *(je'-ush)* {8} See JEHUSH.
1. A son of Esau.
And Aholibamah bare *J*, and Jaalam, ... Gen 36:5 3266
and she bare to Esau *J*, and Jaalam, ... Gen 36:14 3266
duke *J*, duke Jaalam, duke Korah ... Gen 36:18 3266
Eliphaz, Reuel, and *J*, and Jaalam, ... 1Chr 1:35 3266
2. Grandson of Jediael.
J, and Benjamin, and Ehud, and ... 1Chr 7:10 3266
3. A sanctuary servant.
Shimei were, Jahath, Zina, and *J* ... 1Chr 23:10 3266
but *J* and Beriah had not many sons ... 1Chr 23:11 3266
4. A son of Rehoboam.
J, and Shamariah, and Zaham ... 2Chr 11:19 3266

JEUZ *(je'-uz)* {1} *Son of Shaharaim.*
And *J*, and Shachia, and Mirma ... 1Chr 8:10 3263

JEW *(jew)* {32} See JEWESS, JEWISH, JEWS. *Post-exilic term for the Israelites.*
the palace there was a certain *J* ... Est 2:5 3064
he had told them that he was a *J* ... Est 3:4 3064
the *J* sitting at the king's gate ... Est 5:13 3064
and do even so to Mordecai the *J* ... Est 6:10 3064
the queen and to Mordecai the *J* ... Est 8:7 3064
of Abihail, and Mordecai the *J* ... Est 9:29 3064
according as Mordecai the *J* ... Est 9:31 3064
For Mordecai the *J* was next unto ... Est 10:3 3064
them, to wit, of a *J* his brother ... Jer 34:9 3064
of the skirt of him that is a *J* ... Zec 8:23 3064
How is it that thou, being a *J* ... Jn 4:9 *2453*
Pilate answered, Am I a *J* ... Jn 18:35 *2453*
a man that is a *J* to keep company ... Acts 10:28 *2453*
sorcerer, a false prophet, a *J* ... Acts 13:6 *2453*
And found a certain *J* named Aquila ... Acts 18:2 *2453*
a certain *J* named Apollos, born ... Acts 18:24 *2453*
were seven sons of one Sceva, a *J* ... Acts 19:14 *2453*
when they knew that he was a *J* ... Acts 19:34 *2453*
I am a man which am a *J* of Tarsus ... Acts 21:39 *2453*
I am verily a man which am a *J* ... Acts 22:3 *2453*
to the *J* first, and also to the ... Rom 1:16 *2453*
that doeth evil, of the *J* first ... Rom 2:9 *2453*
that worketh good, to the *J* first ... Rom 2:10 *2453*
Behold, thou art called a *J* ... Rom 2:17 *2453*
For he is not a *J*, which is one ... Rom 2:28 *2453*
But he is a *J*, which is one ... Rom 2:29 *2453*
What advantage then hath the *J* ... Rom 3:1 *2453*
is no difference between the *J* ... Rom 10:12 *2453*
And unto the Jews I became as a *J* ... 1Cor 9:20 *2453*
them all, If thou, being a *J* ... Gal 2:14 *2453*
There is neither *J* nor Greek ... Gal 3:28 *2453*
there is neither Greek nor *J* ... Col 3:11 *2453*

JEWEL {3}
As a *j* of gold in a swine's snout ... Prov 11:22 5141
of knowledge are a precious *j* ... Prov 20:15 3627
I put a *j* on thy forehead, and ... Eze 16:12 5141

JEWELS {25}
servant brought forth *j* of silver ... Gen 24:53 3627
j of gold, and raiment, and gave ... Gen 24:53 3627
j of silver, and *j* of gold, ... Ex 3:22 3627
j of silver, and *j* of gold ... Ex 11:2 3627
of the Egyptians *j* of silver ... Ex 12:35 3627
and *j* of gold, and raiment ... Ex 12:35 3627
rings, and tablets, all *j* of gold ... Ex 35:22 3627
gotten, of *j* of gold, chains, and ... Num 31:50 3627
gold of them, even all wrought *j* ... Num 31:51 3627
and put the *j* of gold, which ye ... 1Sa 6:8 3627
wherein the *j* of gold were, and ... 1Sa 6:15 3627
the dead bodies, and precious *j* ... 2Chr 20:25 3627
and for all manner of pleasant *j* ... 2Chr 32:27 3627
shall not be for *j* of fine gold ... Job 28:17 3627
cheeks are comely with rows of *j* ... Song 1:10
joints of thy thighs are like *j* ... Song 7:1 2484
The rings, and nose *j*, ... Is 3:21 5141
bride adorneth herself with her *j* ... Is 61:10 3627
also taken thy fair *j* of my gold ... Eze 16:17 3627
clothes, and shall take thy fair *j* ... Eze 16:39 3627
clothes, and take away thy fair *j* ... Eze 23:26 3627
with her earrings and her *j* ... Hos 2:13 2484
in that day when I make up my *j* ... Mal 3:17 5459

JEWESS *(jew'-ess)* {2} *A female Jew.*
of a certain woman, which was a *J* ... Acts 16:1 *2453*
his wife Drusilla, which was a *J* ... Acts 24:24 *2453*

JEWISH *(jew'-ish)* {1} *Of or relating to the Jews.*
Not giving heed to *J* fables ... Titus 1:14 *2451*

JEWRY *(jew'-ree)* {3} See JUDEA. *Of or relating to the Jews.*
king my father brought out of *J* ... Dan 5:13 3061
people, teaching throughout all *J* ... Lk 23:5 *2449*
for he would not walk in *J* ... Jn 7:1 *2449*

JEWS *(jews)* {243} See JEWS'.
Syria, and drave the *J* from Elath ... 2Kin 16:6 3064
Gedaliah, that he died, and the *J* ... 2Kin 25:25 3064
that the *J* which came up from ... Ezr 4:12 3062
in haste to Jerusalem unto the *J* ... Ezr 4:23 3062
unto the *J* that were in Judah ... Ezr 5:1 3062
God was upon the elders of the *J* ... Ezr 5:5 3062
let the governor of the *J* ... Ezr 6:7 3062
the elders of the *J* build this ... Ezr 6:7 3062
J for the building of this house ... Ezr 6:8 3062
And the elders of the *J* builded ... Ezr 6:14 3062
concerning the *J* that had escaped ... Neh 1:2 3064
had I as yet told it to the *J* ... Neh 2:16 3064
indignation, and mocked the *J* ... Neh 4:1 3064
and said, What do these feeble *J* ... Neh 4:2 3064
that when the *J* which dwelt by ... Neh 4:12 3064
against their brethren the *J* ... Neh 5:1 3064
have redeemed our brethren the *J* ... Neh 5:8 3064
an hundred and fifty of the *J* ... Neh 5:17 3064
that thou and the *J* think to rebel ... Neh 6:6 3064
In those days also saw I *J* that ... Neh 13:23 3064
J that were throughout the whole ... Est 3:6 3064
and to cause to perish, all *J* ... Est 3:13 3064
was great mourning among the *J* ... Est 4:3 3064
the king's treasuries for the *J* ... Est 4:7 3064
king's house, more than all the *J* ... Est 4:13 3064
arise to the *J* from another place ... Est 4:14 3064
gather together all the *J* that ... Est 4:16 3064
Mordecai be of the seed of the *J* ... Est 6:13 3064
that he had devised against the *J* ... Est 8:3 3064
the *J* which are in all the king's ... Est 8:5 3064
he laid his hand upon the *J* ... Est 8:7 3064
Write ye also for the *J*, as it ... Est 8:8 3064
Mordecai commanded unto the *J* ... Est 8:9 3064
to the *J* according to their ... Est 8:9 3064
the *J* which were in every city to ... Est 8:11 3064
that the *J* should be ready ... Est 8:13 3064
The *J* had light, and gladness, and ... Est 8:16 3064
the *J* had joy and gladness, a ... Est 8:17 3064
the people of the land became *J* ... Est 8:17 3054
the fear of the *J* fell upon them ... Est 8:17 3064
J hoped to have power over them ... Est 9:1 3064
that the *J* had rule over them ... Est 9:1 3064
The *J* gathered themselves ... Est 9:2 3064
of the king, helped the *J* ... Est 9:3 3064
Thus the *J* smote all their ... Est 9:5 3064
in Shushan the palace the *J* slew ... Est 9:6 3064
of Hammedatha, the enemy of the *J* ... Est 9:10 3064
The *J* have slain and destroyed ... Est 9:12 3064
let it be granted to the *J* which ... Est 9:13 3064
For the *J* that were in Shushan ... Est 9:15 3064
But the other *J* that were in the ... Est 9:16 3064
But the *J* that were at Shushan ... Est 9:18 3064
Therefore the *J* of the villages, ... Est 9:19 3064
sent letters unto all the *J* that ... Est 9:20 3064
As the days wherein the *J* rested ... Est 9:22 3064
the *J* undertook to do as they had ... Est 9:23 3064
Agagite, the enemy of all the *J* ... Est 9:24 3064
against the *J* to destroy them ... Est 9:24 3064
which he devised against the *J* ... Est 9:25 3064
The *J* ordained, and took upon them ... Est 9:27 3064
should not fail from among the *J* ... Est 9:28 3064
sent the letters unto all the *J* ... Est 9:30 3064
Ahasuerus, and great among the *J* ... Est 10:3 3064
before all the *J* that sat in the ... Jer 32:12 3064
I am afraid of the *J* that are ... Jer 38:19 3064
when all the *J* that were in Moab ... Jer 40:11 3064
Even all the *J* returned out of ... Jer 40:12 3064
that all the *J* which are gathered ... Jer 40:15 3064
slew all the *J* that were with him ... Jer 41:3 3064
the *J* which dwell in the land of ... Jer 44:1 3064
the seventh year three thousand *J* ... Jer 52:28 3064
of the *J* seven hundred forty ... Jer 52:30 3064
came near, and accused the *J* ... Dan 3:8 3064
There are certain *J* whom thou ... Dan 3:12 3064
is he that is born King of the *J* ... Mt 2:2 *2453*
Art thou the King of the *J* ... Mt 27:11 *2453*
him, saying, Hail, King of the *J* ... Mt 27:29 *2453*
THIS IS JESUS THE KING OF THE *J* ... Mt 27:37 *2453*
among the *J* until this day ... Mt 28:15 *2453*
For the Pharisees, and all the *J* ... Mk 7:3 *2453*
him, Art thou the King of the *J* ... Mk 15:2 *2453*
unto you the King of the *J* ... Mk 15:9 *2453*
whom ye call the King of the *J* ... Mk 15:12 *2453*
salute him, Hail, King of the *J* ... Mk 15:18 *2453*
written over, THE KING OF THE *J* ... Mk 15:26 *2453*
sent unto him the elders of the *J* ... Lk 7:3 *2453*
Art thou the King of the *J* ... Lk 23:3 *2453*
If thou be the king of the *J* ... Lk 23:37 *2453*
THIS IS THE KING OF THE *J* ... Lk 23:38 *2453*
of Arimathaea, a city of the *J* ... Lk 23:51 *2453*
when the *J* sent priests and ... Jn 1:19 *2453*
manner of the purifying of the *J* ... Jn 2:6 *2453*
Then answered the *J* and said unto ... Jn 2:18 *2453*
Then said the *J*, Forty and six ... Jn 2:20 *2453*
named Nicodemus, a ruler of the *J* ... Jn 3:1 *2453*
and the *J* about purifying ... Jn 3:25 *2453*
for the *J* have no dealings with ... Jn 4:9 *2453*
for salvation is of the *J* ... Jn 4:22 *2453*
this there was a feast of the *J* ... Jn 5:1 *2453*
The *J* therefore said unto him ... Jn 5:10 *2453*
told the *J* that it was Jesus, ... Jn 5:15 *2453*
did the *J* persecute Jesus ... Jn 5:16 *2453*
Therefore the *J* sought the more ... Jn 5:18 *2453*
And the passover, a feast of the *J* ... Jn 6:4 *2453*
The *J* then murmured at him, ... Jn 6:41 *2453*
The *J* therefore strove among ... Jn 6:52 *2453*
because the *J* sought to kill him ... Jn 7:1 *2453*
Then the *J* sought him at the ... Jn 7:11 *2453*
openly of him for fear of the *J* ... Jn 7:13 *2453*
the *J* marvelled, saying, How ... Jn 7:15 *2453*
Then said the *J* among themselves, ... Jn 7:35 *2453*
Then said the *J*, Will he kill ... Jn 8:22 *2453*
to those *J* which believed on him ... Jn 8:31 *2453*
Then answered the *J*, and said unto ... Jn 8:48 *2453*
Then said the *J* unto him, Now we ... Jn 8:52 *2453*
Then said the *J* unto him, Thou ... Jn 8:57 *2453*
But the *J* did not believe ... Jn 9:18 *2453*
because they feared the *J* ... Jn 9:22 *2453*
for the *J* had agreed already, ... Jn 9:22 *2453*
among the *J* for these sayings ... Jn 10:19 *2453*

Then came the *J* round about him, ... Jn 10:24 2453
Then the *J* took up stones again............ Jn 10:31 2453
The *J* answered him, saying, For a .... Jn 10:33 2453
the *J* of late sought to stone .... Jn 11:8 2453
many of the *J* came to Martha and .... Jn 11:19 2453
The *J* then which were with her in .... Jn 11:31 2453
the *J* also weeping which came .... Jn 11:33 2453
Then said the *J*, Behold how he.............. Jn 11:36 2453
Then many of the *J* which came to .... Jn 11:45 2453
walked no more openly among the *J*....... Jn 11:54 2453
Much people of the *J* therefore................ Jn 12:9 2453
of him many of the *J* went away .... Jn 12:11 2453
and as I said unto the *J*, Whither .... Jn 13:33 2453
and officers of the *J* took Jesus .... Jn 18:12 2453
he, which gave counsel to the *J* .... Jn 18:14 2453
whither the *J* always resort .... Jn 18:20 2453
The *J* therefore said unto him, It............. Jn 18:31 2453
him, Art thou the King of the *J*.............. Jn 18:33 2453
should not be delivered to the *J* .... Jn 18:36 2453
he went out again unto the *J*................... Jn 18:38 2453
unto you the King of the *J*...................... Jn 18:39 2453
And said, Hail, King of the *J* .... Jn 19:3 2453
The *J* answered him, We have a law........ Jn 19:7 2453
but the *J* cried out, saying, If .... Jn 19:12 2453
and he saith unto the *J*, Behold................ Jn 19:14 2453
OF NAZARETH THE KING OF THE *J*.. Jn 19:19 2453
title then read many of the *J*.................. Jn 19:20 2453
chief priests of the *J* to Pilate .... Jn 19:21 2453
Write not, The King of the *J*.................... Jn 19:21 2453
that he said, I am King of the *J* .... Jn 19:21 2453
The *J* therefore, because it was .... Jn 19:31 2453
but secretly for fear of the *J*................... Jn 19:38 2453
as the manner of the *J* is to bury .... Jn 19:40 2453
were assembled for fear of the *J* .... Jn 20:19 2453
were dwelling at Jerusalem *J* .... Acts 2:5 2453
Cyrene, and strangers of Rome, *J*.......... Acts 2:10 2453
confounded the *J* which dwelt at .... Acts 9:22 2453
the *J* took counsel to kill him................. Acts 9:23 2453
among all the nation of the *J* .... Acts 10:22 2453
he did both in the land of the *J*............. Acts 10:39 2453
word to none but unto the *J* only........... Acts 11:19 2453
because he saw it pleased the *J*............. Acts 12:3 2453
of the people of the *J*............................ Acts 12:11 2453
of God in the synagogues of the *J*........... Acts 13:5 2453
when the *J* were gone out of the .... Acts 13:42 2453
was broken up, many of the *J* .... Acts 13:43 2453
But when the *J* saw the multitudes........ Acts 13:45 2453
But the *J* stirred up the devout .... Acts 13:50 2453
into the synagogue of the *J* .... Acts 14:1 2453
a great multitude both of the *J* .... Acts 14:1 2453
But the unbelieving *J* stirred up .... Acts 14:2 2453
and part held with the *J*, and part .... Acts 14:4 2453
also of the *J* with their rulers,............... Acts 14:5 2453
thither certain *J* from Antioch .... Acts 14:19 2453
J which were in those quarters .... Acts 16:3 2453
saying, These men, being *J*.................... Acts 16:20 2453
where was a synagogue of the *J*.............. Acts 17:1 2453
But the *J* which believed not,................. Acts 17:5 2453
went into the synagogue of the *J* .... Acts 17:10 2453
But when the *J* of Thessalonica .... Acts 17:13 2453
he in the synagogue with the *J*............... Acts 17:17 2453
all *J* to depart from Rome .... Acts 18:2 2453
every sabbath, and persuaded the *J*........ Acts 18:4 2453
testified to the *J* that Jesus was .... Acts 18:5 2453
the *J* made insurrection with one........... Acts 18:12 2453
his mouth, Gallio said unto the *J*........... Acts 18:14 2453
wrong or wicked lewdness, O ye *J* .... Acts 18:14 2453
synagogue, and reasoned with the *J*........ Acts 18:19 2453
For he mightily convinced the *J* .... Acts 18:28 2453
word of the Lord Jesus, both *J*.............. Acts 19:10 2453
Then certain of the vagabond *J*.............. Acts 19:13 2453
And this was known to all the *J*............. Acts 19:17 2453
the *J* putting him forward .... Acts 19:33 2453
when the *J* laid wait for him, as............. Acts 20:3 2453
me by the lying in wait of the *J* .... Acts 20:19 2453
Testifying both to the *J*, and also .... Acts 20:21 2453
So shall the *J* at Jerusalem bind .... Acts 21:11 2453
how many thousands of *J* there are......... Acts 21:20 2453
that thou teachest all the *J*................... Acts 21:21 2453
the *J* which were of Asia, when .... Acts 21:27 2453
of all the *J* which dwelt there................. Acts 22:12 2453
wherefore he was accused of the *J*......... Acts 22:30 2453
certain of the *J* banded together,............. Acts 23:12 2453
The *J* have agreed to desire thee .... Acts 23:20 2453
This man was taken of the *J* .... Acts 23:27 2453
that the *J* laid wait for the man .... Acts 23:30 2453
all the *J* throughout the world .... Acts 24:5 2453
the *J* also assented, saying that............. Acts 24:9 2453
Whereupon certain *J* from Asia.............. Acts 24:18 2453
willing to shew the *J* a pleasure............. Acts 24:27 2453
the chief of the *J* informed him............. Acts 25:2 2453
the *J* which came down from .... Acts 25:7 2453
Neither against the law of the *J*............. Acts 25:8 2453
willing to do the *J* a pleasure................ Acts 25:9 2453
to the *J* have I done no wrong, as........... Acts 25:10 2453
the elders of the *J* informed me............. Acts 25:15 2453
of the *J* have dealt with me .... Acts 25:24 2453
whereof I am accused of the *J*................ Acts 26:2 2453
questions which are among the *J* .... Acts 26:3 2453
at Jerusalem, know all the *J* .... Acts 26:4 2453
Agrippa, I am accused of the *J*.............. Acts 26:7 2453
For these causes the *J* caught me .... Acts 26:21 2453
the chief of the *J* together .... Acts 28:17 2453
But when the *J* spake against it,............. Acts 28:19 2453
the *J* departed, and had great .... Acts 28:29 2453
for we have before proved both *J*........... Rom 3:9 2453
Is he the God of the *J* only .... Rom 3:29 2453
he hath called, not of the *J* only............. Rom 9:24 2453
For the *J* require a sign, and the 1Cor 1:22 2453
unto the *J* a stumblingblock, and............ 1Cor 1:23 2453
them which are called, both *J* 1Cor 1:24 2453
unto the *J* I became as a Jew, ... 1Cor 9:20 2453
as a Jew, that I might gain the *J* 1Cor 9:20 2453
none offence, neither to the *J*................. 1Cor 10:32 2453
body, whether we be *J* or Gentiles 1Cor 12:13 2453
Of the *J* five times received I................. 2Cor 11:24 2453
the other *J* dissembled likewise .... Gal 2:13 2453
of Gentiles, and not as do the *J*.............. Gal 2:14 2452
the Gentiles to live as do the *J*.............. Gal 2:14 2450
We who are *J* by nature, and not............. Gal 2:15 2453
even as they have of the *J*....................... 1Th 2:14 2453
of them which say they are *J*.................. Rev 2:9 2453
of Satan, which say they are *J* .... Rev 3:9 2453

JEWS' *(jews)* {14}
talk not with us in the *J*........................... 2Kin 18:26 3066
a loud voice in the *J* language................. 2Kin 18:28 3066
the *J* speech unto the people of............... 2Chr 32:18 3066
could not speak in the *J* language........... Neh 13:24 3066
the Agagite, the *J* enemy .... Est 3:10 3064
the *J* enemy unto Esther the queen......... Est 8:1 3064
speak not to us in the *J* language............ Is 36:11 3064
a loud voice in the *J* language................. Is 36:13 3064
the *J* passover was at hand, and.............. Jn 2:13 2453
Now the *J* feast of tabernacles................ Jn 7:2 2453
the *J* passover was nigh at hand .... Jn 11:55 2453
because of the *J* preparation day .... Jn 19:42 2453
in time past in the *J* religion .... Gal 1:13 2454
profited in the *J* religion above .... Gal 1:14 2454

JEZANIAH *(jez-a-ni'-ah)* {2} See JAAZANIAH. *A Jewish captain.*
J the son of a Maachathite, they .... Jer 40:8 3153
J the son of Hoshaiah, and all the........... Jer 42:1 3153

JEZEBEL *(jez'-e-bel)* {22} See JEZEBEL'S. *Wife of King Ahab.*
that he took to wife *J* the......................... 1Kin 16:31 348
when *J* cut off the prophets of 1Kin 18:4 348
told my lord what I did when *J*............... 1Kin 18:13 348
Ahab told *J* all that Elijah had 1Kin 19:1 348
Then *J* sent a messenger unto 1Kin 19:2 348
But *J* his wife came to him, and.............. 1Kin 21:5 348
J his wife said unto him, Dost................. 1Kin 21:7 348
did as *J* had sent unto them, and 1Kin 21:11 348
Then they sent to *J*, saying, ... 1Kin 21:14 348
when *J* heard that Naboth was 1Kin 21:15 348
that *J* said to Ahab, Arise, take............... 1Kin 21:15 348
of *J* also spake the LORD, saying, ... 1Kin 21:23 348
The dogs shall eat *J* by the wall.............. 1Kin 21:23 348
whom *J* his wife stirred up..................... 1Kin 21:25 348
of the LORD, at the hand of *J* 2Kin 9:7 348
the dogs shall eat *J* in the 2Kin 9:10 348
as the whoredoms of thy mother *J*.......... 2Kin 9:22 348
come to Jezreel, *J* heard of it.................. 2Kin 9:30 348
shall dogs eat the flesh of *J*.................... 2Kin 9:36 348
the carcase of *J* shall be as dung............ 2Kin 9:37 348
they shall not say, This is *J*.................... 2Kin 9:37 348
thou sufferest that woman *J*.................... Rev 2:20 2403

JEZEBEL'S *(jez'-e-bels)* {1}
hundred, which eat at *J* table.................. 1Kin 18:19 348

JEZER *(je'-zur)* {3} See JEZERITES. *A son of Naphtali.*
Jahzeel, and Guni, and *J*, and .... Gen 46:24 3337
Of *J*, the family of the Jezerites............... Num 26:49 3337
Jahziel, and Guni, and *J*, and.................. 1Chr 7:13 3337

JEZERITES *(je'-zur-ites)* {1} *Descendants of Jezer.*
Of Jezer, the family of the *J*.................... Num 26:49 3339

JEZIAH *(je-zi'-ah)* {1} *Married a foreigner in exile.*
Ramiah, and *J*, and Malchiah, and.......... Ezr 10:25 3150

JEZIEL *(je'-ze-el)* {1} *A warrior in David's army.*
and *J*, and Pelet, the sons of.................... 1Chr 12:3 3149

JEZLIAH *(jez-li'-ah)* {1} *A son of Elpaal.*
Ishmerai also, and *J*, and Jobab, ... 1Chr 8:18 3152

JEZOAR *(je-zo'-ar)* {1} See ZOAR. *A son of Helah.*
sons of Helah were, Zereth, and *J*........... 1Chr 4:7 3328

JEZRAHIAH *(jez-ra-hi'-ah)* {1} See IZRAHIAH. *A priest.*
sang loud, with *J* their overseer .... Neh 12:42 3156

JEZREEL *(jez'-re-el)* {36} See JEZREELITE.
1. A city in Judah.
And *J*, and Jokdeam, and Zanoah, ... Josh 15:56 3157
and pitched in the valley of *J*.................. Judg 6:33 3157
David also took Ahinoam of *J*.................. 1Sa 25:43 3157
by a fountain which is in *J*...................... 1Sa 29:1 3157
And the Philistines went up to *J*............. 1Sa 29:11 3157
2. A city in Issachar.
And their border was toward *J* .... Josh 19:18 3157
and over the Ashurites, and over *J*.......... 2Sa 2:9 3157
came of Saul and Jonathan out of *J*......... 2Sa 4:4 3157
which is by Zartanah beneath *J*.............. 1Kin 4:12 3157
And Ahab rode, and went to *J* 1Kin 18:45 3157
before Ahab to the entrance of *J*............ 1Kin 18:46 3157
had a vineyard, which was in *J*............... 1Kin 21:1 3157
eat Jezebel by the wall of *J* 1Kin 21:23 3157
J of the wounds which the Syrians 2Kin 8:29 3157
to see Joram the son of Ahab in *J* 2Kin 8:29 3157
eat Jezebel in the portion of *J* 2Kin 9:10 3157
was returned to be healed in *J* of............ 2Kin 9:15 3157
of the city to go to tell it in *J* 2Kin 9:15 3157
rode in a chariot, and went to *J* 2Kin 9:16 3157
a watchman on the tower in *J*.................. 2Kin 9:17 3157
And when Jehu was come to *J* 2Kin 9:30 3157
In the portion of *J* shall dogs 2Kin 9:36 3157
of the field in the portion of *J*................ 2Kin 9:37 3157
to Samaria, unto the rulers of *J* 2Kin 10:1 3157
come to me to *J* by to morrow this.......... 2Kin 10:6 3157
in baskets, and sent him them to *J*.......... 2Kin 10:7 3157
of the house of Ahab in *J* 2Kin 10:11 3157
in *J* because of the wounds which............ 2Chr 22:6 3157
see Jehoram the son of Ahab at *J*............ 2Chr 22:6 3157
3. A plain.
they who are of the valley of *J*................ Josh 17:16 3157
bow of Israel in the valley of *J*............... Hos 1:5 3157
and they shall hear *J* .... Hos 2:22 3157
4. A descendant of Etam.
J, and Ishma, and Idbash........................ 1Chr 4:3 3157
5. Symbolic name for Hosea's eldest son.
said unto him, Call his name *J*................ Hos 1:4 3157
blood of *J* upon the house of Jehu........... Hos 1:4 3157
for great shall be the day of *J* .... Hos 1:11 3157

JEZREELITE *(jez'-re-el-ite)* {8} See JEZREELITESS. *An inhabitant of Jezreel.*
that Naboth the *J* had a vineyard 1Kin 21:1 3158
Naboth the *J* had spoken to him 1Kin 21:4 3158
Because I spake unto Naboth the *J*.......... 1Kin 21:6 3158
thee the vineyard of Naboth the *J*........... 1Kin 21:7 3158
of the vineyard of Naboth the *J*............... 1Kin 21:15 3158
to the vineyard of Naboth the *J*............... 1Kin 21:16 3158
in the portion of Naboth the *J* 2Kin 9:21 3158
of the field of Naboth the *J*..................... 2Kin 9:25 3158

JEZREELITESS *(jez'-re-el-i-tess)* {5} *A female Jezreelite.*
with his two wives, Ahinoam the *J* 1Sa 27:3 3159
taken captives, Ahinoam the *J* 1Sa 30:5 3159
his two wives also, Ahinoam the *J* 2Sa 2:2 3159
was Amnon, of Ahinoam the *J* 2Sa 3:2 3159
firstborn Amnon, of Ahinoam the *J* 1Chr 3:1 3159

JIBSAM *(jib'-sam)* {1} *A son of Tola.*
and Jeriel, and Jahmai, and *J*.................. 1Chr 7:2 3005

JIDLAPH *(jid'-laf)* {1} *A son of Nahor.*
Chesed, and Hazo, and Pildash, and *J* .... Gen 22:22 3044

JIMNA *(jim'-nah)* {1} See IMNA, JIMNAH, JIMNITES. *A son of Asher.*
of *J*, the family of the Jimnites................ Num 26:44 3232

JIMNAH *(jim'-nah)* {1} See JIMNA. *Same as Jimna.*
J, and Ishuah, and Isui, and Beriah,......... Gen 46:17 3232

JIMNITES *(jim'-nites)* {1} *Descendants of Jimna.*
of Jimna, the family of the *J* .... Num 26:44 3232

JIPHTAH *(jif'-tah)* {1} See JEPHTHAH, JIPHTHAH-EL. *A city in Judah.*
And *J*, and Ashnah, and Nezib, ... Josh 15:43 3316

JIPHTHAH-EL *(jif'-thah-el)* {2} *A valley in Zebulun.*
thereof are in the valley of *J* .... Josh 19:14 3317
to the valley of *J* toward the .... Josh 19:27 3317

JOAB *(jo'-ab)* {138} See ATAROTH, HOUSE, JOAB'S.
1. Commander of David's army.
the son of Zeruiah, brother to *J*.............. 1Sa 26:6 3097
J the son of Zeruiah, and the 2Sa 2:13 3097
And Abner said to *J*, Let the young 2Sa 2:14 3097
And *J* said, Let them arise 2Sa 2:14 3097
three sons of Zeruiah there, *J*................. 2Sa 2:18 3097
hold up my face to *J* thy brother............. 2Sa 2:22 3097
J also and Abishai pursued after 2Sa 2:24 3097
Then Abner called to *J*, and said,............ 2Sa 2:26 3097
J said, As God liveth, unless 2Sa 2:27 3097
So *J* blew a trumpet, and all the............. 2Sa 2:28 3097
J returned from following Abner 2Sa 2:30 3097
And *J* and his men went all night,........... 2Sa 2:32 3097
J came from pursuing a troop, and 2Sa 3:22 3097
When *J* and all the host that was............ 2Sa 3:23 3097
with him were come, they told *J*............. 2Sa 3:23 3097
Then *J* came to the king, and said,.......... 2Sa 3:24 3097
when *J* was come out from David, ... 2Sa 3:26 3097
J took him aside in the gate to................ 2Sa 3:27 3097
Let it rest on the head of *J* 2Sa 3:29 3097
house of *J* one that hath an issue 2Sa 3:29 3097
So *J* and Abishai his brother slew 2Sa 3:30 3097
And David said to *J*, and to all the 2Sa 3:31 3097
J the son of Zeruiah was over the........... 2Sa 8:16 3097
when David heard of it, he sent *J* 2Sa 10:7 3097
When *J* saw that the front of the 2Sa 10:9 3097
J drew nigh, and the people that 2Sa 10:13 3097
So *J* returned from the children.............. 2Sa 10:14 3097
to battle, that David sent *J* 2Sa 11:1 3097
And David sent to *J*, saying, Send............ 2Sa 11:6 3097
And *J* sent Uriah to David 2Sa 11:6 3097
David demanded of him how *J* did 2Sa 11:7 3097
and my lord *J*, and the servants of 2Sa 11:11 3097
that David wrote a letter to *J*................. 2Sa 11:14 3097
when *J* observed the city, that he............ 2Sa 11:16 3097
city went out, and fought with *J*............. 2Sa 11:17 3097
Then *J* sent and told David all the.......... 2Sa 11:18 3097
David all that *J* had sent him for............ 2Sa 11:22 3097
Thus shalt thou say unto *J* 2Sa 11:25 3097
J fought against Rabbah of the 2Sa 12:26 3097
J sent messengers to David, and 2Sa 12:27 3097
Now *J* the son of Zeruiah........................ 2Sa 14:1 3097
J sent to Tekoah, and fetched.................. 2Sa 14:2 3097
So *J* put the words in her mouth............. 2Sa 14:3 3097
Is not the hand of *J* with thee in............. 2Sa 14:19 3097
for thy servant *J*, he bade me, and 2Sa 14:19 3097
thy servant *J* done this thing.................. 2Sa 14:20 3097
And the king said unto *J*, Behold............ 2Sa 14:21 3097
J fell to the ground on his face,.............. 2Sa 14:22 3097
J said, Today thy servant knoweth......... 2Sa 14:22 3097
So *J* arose and went to Geshur, and......... 2Sa 14:23 3097
Therefore Absalom sent for *J* 2Sa 14:29 3097
Then *J* arose, and came to Absalom......... 2Sa 14:31 3097
And Absalom answered *J*, Behold, I......... 2Sa 14:32 3097
So *J* came to the king, and told............... 2Sa 14:33 3097

captain of the host instead of *J* 2Sa 17:25 3097
of the people under the hand of *J* 2Sa 18:2 3097
And the king commanded *J* and 2Sa 18:5 3097
a certain man saw it, and told *J* 2Sa 18:10 3097
J said unto the man that told him 2Sa 18:11 3097
And the man said unto *J*, Though I 2Sa 18:12 3097
Then said *J*, I may not tarry thus 2Sa 18:14 3097
J blew the trumpet, and the people 2Sa 18:16 3097
for *J* held back the people 2Sa 18:16 3097
J said unto him, Thou shalt not 2Sa 18:20 3097
Then said *J* to Cushi, Go tell the 2Sa 18:21 3097
And Cushi bowed himself unto *J* 2Sa 18:21 3097
the son of Zadok yet again to *J* 2Sa 18:22 3097
J said, Wherefore wilt thou run, ... 2Sa 18:22 3097
When *J* sent the king's servant, ... 2Sa 18:29 3097
And it was told *J*, Behold, the 2Sa 19:1 3097
J came into the house to the king 2Sa 19:5 3097
me continually in the room of *J* 2Sa 19:13 3097
J said to Amasa, Art thou in 2Sa 20:9 3097
J took Amasa, by the beard with 2Sa 20:9 3097
So *J* and Abishai his brother 2Sa 20:10 3097
him, and said, He that favoureth *J* 2Sa 20:11 3097
is for David, let him go after *J* 2Sa 20:11 3097
all the people went on after *J* 2Sa 20:13 3097
were with *J* battered the wall 2Sa 20:15 3097
say, I pray you, unto *J*, Come 2Sa 20:16 3097
her, the woman said, Art thou *J* 2Sa 20:17 3097
J answered and said, Far be it, ... 2Sa 20:20 3097
And the woman said unto *J*, Behold, ... 2Sa 20:21 3097
of Bichri, and cast it out to *J* 2Sa 20:22 3097
J returned to Jerusalem unto the 2Sa 20:22 3097
Now *J* was over all the host of 2Sa 20:23 3097
And Abishai, the brother of *J* 2Sa 23:18 3097
of *J* was one of the thirty 2Sa 23:24 3097
armourbearer to *J* the son of 2Sa 23:37 3097
For the king said to *J* the 2Sa 24:2 3097
J said unto the king, Now the 2Sa 24:3 3097
king's word prevailed against *J* 2Sa 24:4 3097
And *J* and the captains of the host 2Sa 24:4 3097
J gave up the sum of the number 2Sa 24:9 3097
he conferred with *J* the son of 1Kin 1:7 3097
J the captain of the host 1Kin 1:19 3097
when *J* heard the sound of the 1Kin 1:41 3097
J the son of Zeruiah did to me 1Kin 2:5 3097
and for *J* the son of Zeruiah 1Kin 2:22 3097
Then tidings came to *J* 1Kin 2:28 3097
for *J* had turned after Adonijah, ... 1Kin 2:28 3097
J fled unto the tabernacle of the 1Kin 2:28 3097
it was told king Solomon that *J* 1Kin 2:29 3097
word again, saying, Thus said *J* 1Kin 2:30 3097
the innocent blood, which *J* shed 1Kin 2:31 3097
return upon the head of *J* 1Kin 2:33 3097
J the captain of the host was 1Kin 11:15 3097
(For six months did *J* remain 1Kin 11:16 3097
that *J* the captain of the host 1Kin 11:21 3097
Abishai, and *J*, and Asahel, three 1Chr 2:16 3097
So *J* the son of Zeruiah went 1Chr 11:6 3097
J repaired the rest of the city 1Chr 11:8 3097
And Abishai the brother of *J* 1Chr 11:20 3097
were, Asahel the brother of *J* 1Chr 11:26 3097
of *J* the son of Zeruiah, ... 1Chr 11:39 3097
J the son of Zeruiah was over the 1Chr 18:15 3097
when David heard of it, he sent *J* 1Chr 19:8 3097
Now when *J* saw that the battle 1Chr 19:10 3097
So *J* and the people that were with 1Chr 19:14 3097
Then *J* came to Jerusalem 1Chr 19:15 3097
J led forth the power of the army 1Chr 20:1 3097
J smote Rabbah, and destroyed it 1Chr 20:1 3097
And David said to *J* and to the 1Chr 21:2 3097
J answered, The LORD make his 1Chr 21:3 3097
king's word prevailed against *J* 1Chr 21:4 3097
Wherefore *J* departed, and went 1Chr 21:4 3097
J gave the sum of the number of 1Chr 21:5 3097
king's word was abominable to *J* 1Chr 21:6 3097
J the son of Zeruiah, had 1Chr 26:28 3097
month was Asahel the brother of *J* 1Chr 27:7 3097
J the son of Zeruiah began to 1Chr 27:24 3097
general of the king's army was *J* 1Chr 27:34 3097
when *J* returned, and smote of Edom .... Ps 60:*t* 3097
2. A descendant of Caleb.
Ataroth, the house of *J*, and half 1Chr 2:54 5854
3. A grandson of Kenaz.
and Seraiah begat *J*, the father of 1Chr 4:14 3097
4. A family of exiles with Zerubbabel.
of the children of Jeshua and *J* .... Ezr 2:6 3097
of the children of Jeshua and *J* .... Neh 7:11 3097
5. A family of exiles with Ezra.
Of the sons of *J* .... Ezr 8:9 3097

JOAB'S *(jo'-abs)* {8} *Refers to Joab 1.*
J field is near mine, and he hath 2Sa 14:30 3097
sister to Zeruiah *J* mother 2Sa 17:25 3097
J brother, and a third part under 2Sa 18:2 3097
bare *J* armour compassed about 2Sa 18:15 3097
And there went out after him *J* men 2Sa 20:7 3097
J garment that he had put on was 2Sa 20:8 3097
to the sword that was in *J* hand 2Sa 20:10 3097
one of *J* men stood by him, and 2Sa 20:11 3097

JOAH *(jo'-ah)* {11} See ETHAN.
1. A son of Asaph.
J the son of Asaph the recorder 2Kin 18:18 3098
son of Hilkiah, and Shebna, and *J* 2Kin 18:26 3098
J the son of Asaph the recorder, ... 2Kin 18:37 3098
house, and Shebna the scribe, and *J* .... Is 36:3 3098
J unto Rabshakeh, Speak, I pray .... Is 36:11 3098
and Shebna the scribe, and *J* .... Is 36:22 3098
2. A descendant of Gershom.
J his son, Iddo his son, Zerah 1Chr 6:21 3098
J the son of Zimmah 2Chr 29:12 3098
and Eden the son of *J* 2Chr 29:12 3098
3. A sanctuary servant.
J the third, and Sacar the fourth, ... 1Chr 26:4 3098
4. A Levite.
J the son of Joahaz the recorder, ... 2Chr 34:8 3098

JOAHAZ *(jo'-a-haz)* {1} See JEHOAHAZ. *Father of Joah.*
and Joah the son of *J* the recorder 2Chr 34:8 3098

JOANAN See JOANNA.

JOANNA *(jo-an'-nah)* {3}
1. A female disciple.
J the wife of Chuza Herod's .... Lk 8:3 *2489*
It was Mary Magdalene, and *J* .... Lk 24:10 *2489*
2. An ancestor of Jesus.
Which was the son of *J*, which was .... Lk 3:27 *2489*

JOASH *(jo'-ash)* {49} See JEHOASH.
1. A son of Becher.
Zemira, and *J*, and Eliezer, and 1Chr 7:8 3135
2. A sanctuary servant.
and over the cellars of oil was *J* 1Chr 27:28 3135
3. Father of Gideon.
pertained unto *J* the Abi-ezrite .... Judg 6:11 3101
Gideon the son of *J* hath done .... Judg 6:29 3101
the men of the city said unto *J* .... Judg 6:30 3101
J said unto all that stood .... Judg 6:31 3101
the sword of Gideon the son of *J* .... Judg 7:14 3101
Gideon the son of *J* returned from .... Judg 8:13 3101
And Jerubbaal the son of *J* went .... Judg 8:29 3101
Gideon the son of *J* died in a .... Judg 8:32 3101
in the sepulchre of *J* his father .... Judg 8:32 3101
4. A son of King Ahab.
the city, and to *J* the king's son 1Kin 22:26 3101
the city, and to *J* the king's son 2Chr 18:25 3101
5. A son of King Ahaziah.
took *J* the son of Ahaziah, and 2Kin 11:2 3101
And the rest of the acts of *J* 2Kin 12:19 3101
slew *J* in the house of Millo, ... 2Kin 12:20 3101
twentieth year of *J* the son of 2Kin 13:1 3101
seventh year of *J* king of Judah 2Kin 13:10 3101
the son of *J* king of Judah 2Kin 14:1 3101
to all things as *J* his father did 2Kin 14:3 3101
Amaziah the son of *J* king of 2Kin 14:17 3101
year of Amaziah the son of *J* king 2Kin 14:23 3101
son, Ahaziah his son, *J* his son, ... 1Chr 3:11 3101
took *J* the son of Ahaziah, and 2Chr 22:11 3101
J was seven years old when he 2Chr 24:1 3101
J did that which was right in the 2Chr 24:2 3101
that *J* was minded to repair the 2Chr 24:4 3101
Thus *J* the king remembered not 2Chr 24:22 3101
they executed judgment against *J* 2Chr 24:24 3101
king of Judah, the son of *J* 2Chr 25:23 3101
Amaziah the son of *J* king of 2Chr 25:25 3101
6. A king of Israel.
J his son reigned in his stead 2Kin 13:9 3101
And the rest of the acts of *J* 2Kin 13:12 3101
And *J* slept with his fathers 2Kin 13:13 3101
J was buried in Samaria with the 2Kin 13:13 3101
J the king of Israel came down 2Kin 13:14 3101
Three times did *J* beat him 2Kin 13:25 3101
In the second year of *J* son of 2Kin 14:1 3101
of Judah Jeroboam the son of *J* 2Kin 14:23 3101
the hand of Jeroboam the son of *J* 2Kin 14:27 3101
Judah took advice, and sent to *J* 2Chr 25:17 3101
J king of Israel sent to Amaziah 2Chr 25:18 3101
So *J* the king of Israel went up 2Chr 25:21 3101
J the king of Israel took Amaziah 2Chr 25:23 3101
J son of Jehoahaz king of Israel 2Chr 25:25 3101
the days of Jeroboam the son of *J* .... Hos 1:1 3101
the son of *J* king of Israel .... Amos 1:1 3101
7. A descendant of Shelah.
and the men of Chozeba, and *J* 1Chr 4:22 3101
8. A captain in David's army.
The chief was Ahiezer, then *J* 1Chr 12:3 3101

JOATHAM *(jo'-a-tham)* {2} See JOTHAM. *Ancestor of Joseph, husband of Mary.*
And Ozias begat *J* .... Mt 1:9 *2488*
and *J* begat Achaz .... Mt 1:9 *2488*

JOAZCAR See JOZACHAR.

JOB *(jobe)* {59} See JASHUB, JOB'S.
1. A descendant of Issachar.
Tola, and Phuvah, and *J*, and Shimron ... Gen 46:13 3102
2. A righteous sufferer.
the land of Uz, whose name was *J* .... Job 1:1 347
were gone about, that *J* sent .... Job 1:5 347
for *J* said, It may be that my .... Job 1:5 347
Thus did *J* continually .... Job 1:5 347
Hast thou considered my servant *J* .... Job 1:8 347
Doth *J* fear God for nought .... Job 1:9 347
And there came a messenger unto *J* .... Job 1:14 347
Then *J* arose, and rent his mantle, ... Job 1:20 347
In all this *J* sinned not, nor .... Job 1:22 347
Hast thou considered my servant *J* .... Job 2:3 347
smote *J* with sore boils from the .... Job 2:7 347
this did not *J* sin with his lips .... Job 2:10 347
After this opened *J* his mouth .... Job 3:1 347
And *J* spake, and said, ... Job 3:2 347
But *J* answered and said, ... Job 6:1 347
Then *J* answered and said, ... Job 9:1 347
And *J* answered and said, ... Job 12:1 347
Then *J* answered and said, ... Job 16:1 347
Then *J* answered and said, ... Job 19:1 347
But *J* answered and said, ... Job 21:1 347
Then *J* answered and said, ... Job 23:1 347
But *J* answered and said, ... Job 26:1 347
Moreover *J* continued his parable, ... Job 27:1 347
Moreover *J* continued his parable, ... Job 29:1 347
The words of *J* are ended .... Job 31:40 347
three men ceased to answer *J* .... Job 32:1 347
against *J* was his wrath kindled, ... Job 32:2 347
no answer, and yet had condemned *J* .... Job 32:3 347
had waited till *J* had spoken .... Job 32:4 347
was none of you that convinced *J* .... Job 32:12 347
Wherefore, *J*, I pray thee, hear .... Job 33:1 347
Mark well, O *J*, hearken unto me .... Job 33:31 347
For *J* hath said, I am righteous .... Job 34:5 347
What man is like *J*, who drinketh .... Job 34:7 347
J hath spoken without knowledge, ... Job 34:35 347
My desire is that *J* may be tried .... Job 34:36 347
Therefore doth *J* open his mouth .... Job 35:16 347
Hearken unto this, O *J* .... Job 37:14 347
answered *J* out of the whirlwind .... Job 38:1 347
Moreover the LORD answered *J* .... Job 40:1 347
Then *J* answered the LORD, and said .... Job 40:3 347
LORD unto *J* out of the whirlwind .... Job 40:6 347
Then *J* answered the LORD, and said .... Job 42:1 347
had spoken these words unto *J* .... Job 42:7 347
is right, as my servant *J* hath .... Job 42:7 347
seven rams, and go to my servant *J* .... Job 42:8 347
my servant *J* shall pray for you .... Job 42:8 347
which is right, like my servant *J* .... Job 42:8 347
the LORD also accepted *J* .... Job 42:9 347
LORD turned the captivity of *J* .... Job 42:10 347
also the LORD gave *J* twice as .... Job 42:10 347
end of *J* more than his beginning .... Job 42:12 347
so fair as the daughters of *J* .... Job 42:15 347
After this lived *J* an hundred .... Job 42:16 347
So *J* died, being old and full of .... Job 42:17 347
three men, Noah, Daniel, and *J* .... Eze 14:14 347
Though Noah, Daniel, and *J* .... Eze 14:20 347
have heard of the patience of *J* .... Jas 5:11 *2492*

JOBAB *(jo'-bab)* {9}
1. A son of Joktan.
And Ophir, and Havilah, and *J* .... Gen 10:29 3103
And Ophir, and Havilah, and *J* 1Chr 1:23 3103
2. A king of Edom.
J the son of Zerah of Bozrah .... Gen 36:33 3103
J died, and Husham of the land of .... Gen 36:34 3103
J the son of Zerah of Bozrah 1Chr 1:44 3103
when *J* was dead, Husham of the 1Chr 1:45 3103
3. A Canaanite king.
that he sent to *J* king of Madon .... Josh 11:1 3103
4. A son of Shaharaim.
And he begat of Hodesh his wife, *J* 1Chr 8:9 3103
5. A son of Elpaal.
Ishmerai also, and Jezliah, and *J* 1Chr 8:18 3103

JOB'S *(jobes)* {1} *Refers to Job 2.*
Now when *J* three friends heard of .... Job 2:11 347

JOCHEBED *(jok'-e-bed)* {2} *Wife of Amram.*
Amram took him *J* his father's .... Ex 6:20 3115
And the name of Amram's wife was *J* ..... Num 26:59 3115

JODA See JUDA.

JOED *(jo'-ed)* {1} *A son of Pedaiah.*
son of Meshullam, the son of *J* .... Neh 11:7 3133

JOEL *(jo'-el)* {20}
1. A son of Samuel.
the name of his firstborn was *J* 1Sa 8:2 3100
Heman a singer, the son of *J* 1Chr 6:33 3100
appointed Heman the son of *J* 1Chr 15:17 3100
2. A Simeonite.
And *J*, and Jehu the son of Josibiah 1Chr 4:35 3100
3. Father of Shemaiah.
The sons of *J* 1Chr 5:4 3100
the son of Shema, the son of *J* 1Chr 5:8 3100
4. A chief Gadite.
J the chief, and Shapham the next, ... 1Chr 5:12 3100
5. A Kohathite.
The son of Elkanah, the son of *J* 1Chr 6:36 3100
6. A descendant of Tola.
Michael, and Obadiah, and *J* 1Chr 7:3 3100
7. A "mighty man" of David.
J the brother of Nathan, Mibhar 1Chr 11:38 3100
8. A Gershomite.
J the chief, and his brethren an 1Chr 15:7 3100
Levites, for Uriel, Asaiah, and *J* 1Chr 15:11 3100
chief was Jehiel, and Zetham, and *J* 1Chr 23:8 3100
9. A treasurer of the Temple.
J his brother, which were over 1Chr 26:22 3100
10. A prince of Manasseh.
of Manasseh, *J* the son of Pedaiah 1Chr 27:20 3100
11. A Kohathite who cleansed the Temple.
J the son of Azariah, of the sons 2Chr 29:12 3100
12. Married a foreigner in exile.
Zabad, Zebina, Jadau, and *J* .... Ezr 10:43 3100
13. An overseer of the Benjamites.
J the son of Zichri was their .... Neh 11:9 3100
14. A prophet.
that came to *J* the son of Pethuel .... Joel 1:1 3100
which was spoken by the prophet *J* .... Acts 2:16 *2493*

JOELAH *(jo-e'-lah)* {1} *A member of David's band.*
And *J*, and Zebadiah, the sons of 1Chr 12:7 3132

JOEZER *(jo-e'-zer)* {1} *A warrior in David's army.*
and Jesiah, and Azareel, and *J* 1Chr 12:6 3134

JOGBEHAH *(jog'-be-hah)* {2} *A place in Gad.*
Atroth, Shophan, and Jaazer, and *J* .... Num 32:35 3011
tents on the east of Nobah and *J* .... Judg 8:11 3011

JOGLI *(jog'-li)* {1} *A Danite prince.*
of Dan, Bukki the son of *J* .... Num 34:22 3020

JOHA *(jo'-hah)* {2}
1. Son of Beriah.
And Michael, and Ispah, and *J* 1Chr 8:16 3109
2. A "mighty man" of David.
J his brother, the Tizite, 1Chr 11:45 3109

JOHANAN *(jo-ha'-nan)* {27} See JEHOHANAN, JOHN.
1. A son of Kareah.
J the son of Careah, and Seraiah 2Kin 25:23 3110
the son of Nethaniah, and *J* Jer 40:8 3110
Moreover *J* the son of Kareah, and Jer 40:13 3110
Then *J* the son of Kareah spake to Jer 40:15 3110
said unto *J* the son of Kareah Jer 40:16 3110
But when *J* the son of Kareah, and Jer 41:11 3110
Ishmael saw *J* the son of Kareah Jer 41:13 3110
went unto *J* the son of Kareah Jer 41:14 3110
escaped from *J* with eight men Jer 41:15 3110
Then took *J* the son of Kareah, and Jer 41:16 3110
J the son of Kareah, and Jezaniah Jer 42:1 3110
Then called he *J* the son of Jer 42:8 3110
J the son of Kareah, and all the Jer 43:2 3110
So *J* the son of Kareah, and all Jer 43:4 3110
But *J* the son of Kareah, and all Jer 43:5 3110
2. A son of King Josiah.
of Josiah were, the firstborn *J* 1Chr 3:15 3110
3. A son of Elioenai.
and Pelaiah, and Akkub, and *J* 1Chr 3:24 3110
4. A grandson of Ahimaaz.
begat Azariah, and Azariah begat *J* 1Chr 6:9 3110
J begat Azariah, (he it is that 1Chr 6:10 3110
5. A warrior in David's army.
and Jeremiah, and Jahaziel, and *J* 1Chr 12:4 3110
6. A Gadite warrior in David's army.
J the eighth, Elzabad the ninth, 1Chr 12:12 3110
7. An Ephraimite.
of Ephraim, Azariah the son of *J* 2Chr 28:12 3076
8. An exile with Ezra.
J the son of Hakkatan, and with Ezr 8:12 3110
9. A priest in exile with Ezra.
chamber of *J* the son of Eliashib Ezr 10:6 3076
10. A son of Tobiah.
his son *J* had taken the daughter Neh 6:18 3076
11. A priest in exile with Zerubbabel.
days of Eliashib, Joiada, and *J* Neh 12:22 3110
the days of *J* the son of Eliashib Neh 12:23 3110

JOHN *(jon)* {131} See BAPTIST, JEHOHANAN, JOHN'S, MARK.
1. The Baptizer.
In those days came *J* the Baptist Mt 3:1 *2491*
the same *J* had his raiment of Mt 3:4 *2491*
from Galilee to Jordan unto *J* Mt 3:13 *2491*
But *J* forbad him, saying, I have Mt 3:14 *2491*
heard that *J* was cast into prison Mt 4:12 *2491*
came to him the disciples of *J* Mt 9:14 *2491*
Now when *J* had heard in the Mt 11:2 *2491*
shew *J* again those things which Mt 11:4 *2491*
unto the multitudes concerning *J* Mt 11:7 *2491*
a greater than *J* the Baptist Mt 11:11 *2491*
from the days of *J* the Baptist Mt 11:12 *2491*
and the law prophesied until *J* Mt 11:13 *2491*
For *J* came neither eating nor Mt 11:18 *2491*
servants, This is *J* the Baptist Mt 14:2 *2491*
For Herod had laid hold on *J* Mt 14:3 *2491*
For *J* said unto him, It is not Mt 14:4 *2491*
Give me here *J* Baptist's head in Mt 14:8 *2491*
sent, and beheaded *J* in the prison Mt 14:10 *2491*
say that thou art *J* the Baptist Mt 16:14 *2491*
spake unto them of *J* the Baptist Mt 17:13 *2491*
The baptism of *J*, whence was it Mt 21:25 *2491*
for all hold *J* as a prophet Mt 21:26 *2491*
For *J* came unto you in the way of Mt 21:32 *2491*
J did baptize in the wilderness, Mk 1:4 *2491*
J was clothed with camel's hair, Mk 1:6 *2491*
and was baptized of *J* in Jordan Mk 1:9 *2491*
Now after that *J* was put in Mk 1:14 *2491*
And the disciples of *J* and of the Mk 2:18 *2491*
him, Why do the disciples of *J* Mk 2:18 *2491*
That *J* the Baptist was risen from Mk 6:14 *2491*
heard thereof, he said, It is *J* Mk 6:16 *2491*
sent forth and laid hold upon *J* Mk 6:17 *2491*
For *J* had said unto Herod, It is Mk 6:18 *2491*
For Herod feared *J*, knowing that Mk 6:20 *2491*
said, The head of *J* the Baptist Mk 6:24 *2491*
charger the head of *J* the Baptist Mk 6:25 *2491*
And they answered, *J* the Baptist Mk 8:28 *2491*
The baptism of *J*, was it from Mk 11:30 *2491*
for all men counted *J*, that he Mk 11:32 *2491*
and thou shalt call his name *J* Lk 1:13 *2491*
but he shall be called *J* Lk 1:60 *2491*
and wrote, saying, His name is *J* Lk 1:63 *2491*
the word of God came unto *J* the Lk 3:2 *2491*
men mused in their hearts of *J* Lk 3:15 *2491*
J answered, saying unto them all, Lk 3:16 *2491*
all, that he shut up *J* in prison Lk 3:20 *2491*
do the disciples of *J* fast often Lk 5:33 *2491*
the disciples of *J* shewed him of Lk 7:18 *2491*
J calling unto him two of his Lk 7:19 *2491*
J Baptist hath sent us unto thee, Lk 7:20 *2491*
tell *J* what things ye have seen Lk 7:22 *2491*
the messengers of *J* were departed Lk 7:24 *2491*
unto the people concerning *J* Lk 7:24 *2491*
prophet than *J* the Baptist Lk 7:28 *2491*
baptized with the baptism of *J* Lk 7:29 *2491*
For *J* the Baptist came neither Lk 7:33 *2491*
that *J* was risen from the dead Lk 9:7 *2491*
And Herod said, *J* have I beheaded Lk 9:9 *2491*
answering said, *J* the Baptist Lk 9:19 *2491*
as *J* also taught his disciples Lk 11:1 *2491*
law and the prophets were until *J* Lk 16:16 *2491*
The baptism of *J*, was it from Lk 20:4 *2491*
be persuaded that *J* was a prophet Lk 20:6 *2491*
sent from God, whose name was *J* Jn 1:6 *2491*
J bare witness of him, and cried, Jn 1:15 *2491*
And this is the record of *J* Jn 1:19 *2491*
J answered them, saying, I Jn 1:26 *2491*
Jordan, where *J* was baptizing Jn 1:28 *2491*
The next day *J* seeth Jesus coming Jn 1:29 *2491*
J bare record, saying, I saw the Jn 1:32 *2491*
Again the next day after *J* stood Jn 1:35 *2491*
of the two which heard *J* speak Jn 1:40 *2491*
J also was baptizing in Aenon Jn 3:23 *2491*
For *J* was not yet cast into Jn 3:24 *2491*
And they came unto *J*, and said unto Jn 3:26 *2491*
J answered and said, A man can Jn 3:27 *2491*
and baptized more disciples than *J* Jn 4:1 *2491*
Ye sent unto *J*, and he bare Jn 5:33 *2491*
greater witness than that of *J* Jn 5:36 *2491*
place where *J* at first baptized Jn 10:40 *2491*
him, and said, *J* did no miracle Jn 10:41 *2491*
but all things that *J* spake of Jn 10:41 *2491*
For *J* truly baptized with water Acts 1:5 *2491*
Beginning from the baptism of *J* Acts 1:22 *2491*
the baptism which *J* preached Acts 10:37 *2491*
J indeed baptized with water Acts 11:16 *2491*
When *J* had first preached before Acts 13:24 *2491*
as *J* fulfilled his course, he Acts 13:25 *2491*
knowing only the baptism of *J* Acts 18:25 *2491*
J verily baptized with the Acts 19:4 *2491*
2. Son of Zebedee.
J his brother, in a ship with Mt 4:21 *2491*
son of Zebedee, and *J* his brother Mt 10:2 *2491*
J his brother, and bringeth them Mt 17:1 *2491*
J his brother, who also were in Mk 1:19 *2491*
Simon and Andrew, with James and *J* Mk 1:29 *2491*
and *J* the brother of James Mk 3:17 *2491*
James, and *J* the brother of James Mk 5:37 *2491*
with him Peter, and James, and *J* Mk 9:2 *2491*
J answered him, saying, Master, Mk 9:38 *2491*
And James and *J*, the sons of Mk 10:35 *2491*
much displeased with James and *J* Mk 10:41 *2491*
the temple, Peter and James and *J* Mk 13:3 *2491*
with him Peter and James and *J* Mk 14:33 *2491*
And so was also James, and *J* Lk 5:10 *2491*
and Andrew his brother, James and *J* Lk 6:14 *2491*
go in, save Peter, and James, and *J* Lk 8:51 *2491*
these sayings, he took Peter and *J* Lk 9:28 *2491*
J answered and said, Master, we Lk 9:49 *2491*
J saw this, they said, Lord, wilt Lk 9:54 *2491*
And he sent Peter and *J*, saying, Go Lk 22:8 *2491*
abode both Peter, and James, and *J* Acts 1:13 *2491*
J went up together into the Acts 3:1 *2491*
J about to go into the temple Acts 3:3 *2491*
his eyes upon him with *J*, said, Acts 3:4 *2491*
which was healed held Peter and *J* Acts 3:11 *2491*
saw the boldness of Peter and *J* Acts 4:13 *2491*
J answered and said unto them, Acts 4:19 *2491*
they sent unto them Peter and *J* Acts 8:14 *2491*
the brother of *J* with the sword Acts 12:2 *2491*
And when James, Cephas, and *J* Gal 2:9 *2491*
by his angel unto his servant *J* Rev 1:1 *2491*
J to the seven churches which are Rev 1:4 *2491*
I *J*, who also am your brother, and Rev 1:9 *2491*
I *J* saw the holy city, new Rev 21:2 *2491*
I *J* saw these things, and heard Rev 22:8 *2491*
3. A relative of Annas the priest.
high priest, and Caiaphas, and *J* Acts 4:6 *2491*
4. Surnamed Mark.
the house of Mary the mother of *J* Acts 12:12 *2491*
ministry, and took with them *J* Acts 12:25 *2491*
they had also *J* to their minister Acts 13:5 *2491*
J departing from them returned to Acts 13:13 *2491*
determined to take with them *J* Acts 15:37 *2491*

JOHN'S *(jonz)* {2} *Refers to John 1.*
between some of *J* disciples Jn 3:25 *2491*
And they said, Unto *J* baptism Acts 19:3 *2491*

JOIADA *(joy'-a-dah)* {4} See JEHOIADA. *A priest with Zerubbabel.*
Eliashib, and Eliashib begat *J* Neh 12:10 3111
J begat Jonathan, and Jonathan Neh 12:11 3111
in the days of Eliashib, *J* Neh 12:22 3111
And one of the sons of *J*, the son Neh 13:28 3111

JOIAKIM *(joy'-a-kim)* {4} See JEHOIAKIM. *Another priest with Zerubbabel.*
And Jeshua begat *J* Neh 12:10 3113
J also begat Eliashib Neh 12:10 3113
And in the days of *J* were priests Neh 12:12 3113
the days of *J* the son of Jeshua Neh 12:26 3113

JOIARIB *(joy'-a-rib)* {5} See JEHOIARIB.
1. A messenger for Ezra.
also for *J*, and for Elnathan, men Ezr 8:16 3114
2. A descendant of Perez.
the son of Adaiah, the son of *J* Neh 11:5 3114
3. Father of Jedaiah.
Jedaiah the son of *J*, Jachin Neh 11:10 3114
Shemaiah, and *J*, Jedaiah, Neh 12:6 3114
And of *J*, Mattenai Neh 12:19 3114

JOIN {14}
they *j* also unto our enemies, and Ex 1:10 3254
j himself with Ahaziah king of 2Chr 20:35 2266
j in affinity with the people of Ezr 9:14 2859
Though hand *j* in hand, the wicked Prov 11:21
though hand *j* in hand, he shall Prov 16:5
unto them that *j* house to house Is 5:8 5060
him, and *j* his enemies together Is 9:11 5526
that *j* themselves to the LORD, to Is 56:6 3867
let us *j* ourselves to the LORD in Jer 50:5 3867
j them one to another into one Eze 37:17 7126
they shall *j* themselves together Dan 11:6 2266
durst no man *j* himself to them Acts 5:13 *2853*
j thyself to this chariot Acts 8:29 *2853*
he assayed to *j* himself to the Acts 9:26 *2853*

JOINED {43}
All these were *j* together in the Gen 14:3 2266
they *j* battle with them in the Gen 14:8 6186
time will my husband be *j* unto me Gen 29:34 3867
j at the two edges thereof Ex 28:7 2266
and so it shall be *j* together Ex 28:7 2266
that they may be *j* unto thee Num 18:2 3867
And they shall be *j* unto thee Num 18:4 3867
Israel *j* himself unto Baal-peor Num 25:3 6775
men that were *j* unto Baal-peor Num 25:5 6775
and when they *j* battle, Israel was 1Sa 4:2 5208
of the wheels were *j* to the base 1Kin 7:32
the seventh day the battle was *j* 1Kin 20:29 7126
and *j* affinity with Ahab 2Chr 18:1 2859
he *j* himself with him to make 2Chr 20:36 2266
Because thou hast *j* thyself with 2Chr 20:37 2266
thereof, and *j* the foundations Ezr 4:12 2338
all the wall was *j* together unto Neh 4:6 7194
upon all such as *j* themselves Est 9:27 3867
let it not be *j* unto the days of Job 3:6 2302
They are *j* one to another, they Job 41:17 1692
of his flesh are *j* together Job 41:23 1692
Assur also is *j* with them Ps 83:8 3867
They *j* themselves also unto Ps 106:28 6775
For to him that is *j* to all the Eccl 9:4 977
every one that is *j* unto them Is 13:15 5595
strangers shall be *j* with them Is 14:1 3867
Thou shalt not be *j* with them in Is 14:20 3161
that hath *j* himself to the LORD, Is 56:3 3867
Their wings were *j* one to another Eze 1:9 2266
every one were *j* one to another Eze 1:11 2266
courts *j* of forty cubits long Eze 46:22 7000
Ephraim is *j* to idols Hos 4:17 2266
many nations shall be *j* to the Zec 2:11 3867
therefore God hath *j* together Mt 19:6 *4801*
therefore God hath *j* together Mk 10:9 *4801*
j himself to a citizen of that Lk 15:15 *2853*
about four hundred, *j* themselves Acts 5:36 *4347*
whose house *j* hard to the Acts 18:7 *4927*
but that ye be perfectly *j* 1Cor 1:10 *2675*
is *j* to an harlot is one body 1Cor 6:16 *2853*
But he that is *j* unto the Lord is 1Cor 6:17 *2853*
the whole body fitly *j* together Eph 4:16 *4883*
shall be *j* unto his wife, and they Eph 5:31 *4347*

JOINING {1}
j to the wing of the other cherub 2Chr 3:12 1692

JOININGS {1}
doors of the gates, and for the *j* 1Chr 22:3 4226

JOINT {4}
of Jacob's thigh was out of *j* Gen 32:25 3363
and all my bones are out of *j* Ps 22:14 6504
broken tooth, and a foot out of *j* Prov 25:19 4154
by that which every *j* supplieth Eph 4:16 *860*

JOINT-HEIRS {1}
heirs of God, and *j* with Christ Rom 8:17 *4789*

JOINTS {6}
between the *j* of the harness 1Kin 22:34 1694
between the *j* of the harness 2Chr 18:33 1694
the *j* of thy thighs are like Song 7:1 2542
so that the *j* of his loins were Dan 5:6 7001
from which all the body by *j* Col 2:19 *860*
of soul and spirit, and of the *j* Heb 4:12 *719*

JOKDEAM *(jok'-de-am)* {1} *A city in Judah.*
And Jezreel, and *J*, and Zanoah, Josh 15:56 3347

JOKIM *(jo'-kim)* {1} *A descendant of Shelah.*
And *J*, and the men of Chozeba, and 1Chr 4:22 3137

JOKMEAM *(jok'-me-am)* {1} See JOKNEAM. *A Levitical city in Ephraim.*
J with her suburbs, and Beth-horon 1Chr 6:68 3361

JOKNEAM *(jok'-ne-am)* {4} See JOKMEAM, KIBZAIM.
1. A Levitical city in Zebulun.
the king of *J* of Carmel, one Josh 12:22 3362
to the river that is before *J* Josh 19:11 3362
J with her suburbs, and Kartah Josh 21:34 3362
2. A Levitical city in Ephraim.
unto the place that is beyond *J* 1Kin 4:12 3362

JOKSHAN *(jok'-shan)* {4} *A son of Abraham.*
And she bare him Zimran, and *J* Gen 25:2 3370
And *J* begat Sheba, and Dedan Gen 25:3 3370
she bare Zimran, and *J*, and Medan, 1Chr 1:32 3370
And the sons of *J* 1Chr 1:32 3370

JOKTAN *(jok'-tan)* {6} *A son of Eber.*
and his brother's name was *J* Gen 10:25 3355
J begat Almodad, and Sheleph, and Gen 10:26 3355
all these were the sons of *J* Gen 10:29 3355
and his brother's name was *J* 1Chr 1:19 3355
J begat Almodad, and Sheleph, and 1Chr 1:20 3355
All these were the sons of *J* 1Chr 1:23 3355

JOKTHEEL *(jok'-the-el)* {2} See SELAH.
1. A city in Judah.
And Dilean, and Mizpeh, and *J* Josh 15:38 3371
2. Another name for Petra in Edom.
the name of it *J* unto this day 2Kin 14:7 3371

JONA *(jo'-nah)* {1} See BAR-JONA, JONAH, JONAS. *Greek form of Jonah.*
said, Thou art Simon the son of *J* Jn 1:42 *2495*

J

JONADAB *(jon'-a-dab)* {12} See JEHONADAB.
1. A son of Shimeah.
had a friend, whose name was J ... 2Sa 13:3 3122
and J was a very subtil man ... 2Sa 13:3 3122
J said unto him, Lay thee down on ... 2Sa 13:5 3122
And J, the son of Shimeah David's ... 2Sa 13:32 3122
J said unto the king, Behold, the ... 2Sa 13:35 3122
2. A son of Rechab.
for J the son of Rechab our ... Jer 35:6 3122
have we obeyed the voice of J the ... Jer 35:8 3082
that J our father commanded us ... Jer 35:10 3122
The words of J the son of Rechab, ... Jer 35:14 3082
Because the sons of J the son of ... Jer 35:16 3082
the commandment of J your father ... Jer 35:18 3082
J the son of Rechab shall not ... Jer 35:19 3122

JONAH *(jo'-nah)* {19} See JONA, JONAS. *A prophet.*
by the hand of his servant J ... 2Kin 14:25 3124
came unto J the son of Amittai ... Jonah 1:1 3124
But J rose up to flee unto ... Jonah 1:3 3124
But J was gone down into the ... Jonah 1:5 3124
cast lots, and the lot fell upon J ... Jonah 1:7 3124
So they took up J, and cast him ... Jonah 1:15 3124
a great fish to swallow up J ... Jonah 1:17 3124
J was in the belly of the fish ... Jonah 1:17 3124
Then J prayed unto the LORD his ... Jonah 2:1 3124
it vomited out J upon the dry ... Jonah 2:10 3124
LORD came unto J the second time ... Jonah 3:1 3124
So J arose, and went unto Nineveh, ... Jonah 3:3 3124
J began to enter into the city a ... Jonah 3:4 3124
But it displeased J exceedingly ... Jonah 4:1 3124
So J went out of the city, and sat ... Jonah 4:5 3124
and made it to come up over J ... Jonah 4:6 3124
So J was exceeding glad of the ... Jonah 4:6 3124
the sun beat upon the head of J ... Jonah 4:8 3124
And God said to J, Doest thou well ... Jonah 4:9 3124

JONAM See JONAN.

JONAN *(jo'-nan)* {1} *Ancestor of Joseph, husband of Mary.*
of Joseph, which was the son of J ... Lk 3:30 *2494*

JONAS *(jo'-nas)* {12} See JONA, JONAH.
1. Same as Jonah.
it, but the sign of the prophet J ... Mt 12:39 *2495*
For as J was three days and three ... Mt 12:40 *2495*
repented at the preaching of J ... Mt 12:41 *2495*
behold, a greater than J is here ... Mt 12:41 *2495*
it, but the sign of the prophet J ... Mt 16:4 *2495*
it, but the sign of J the prophet ... Lk 11:29 *2495*
For as J was a sign unto the ... Lk 11:30 *2495*
repented at the preaching of J ... Lk 11:32 *2495*
behold, a greater than J is here ... Lk 11:32 *2495*
2. Father of Peter.
to Simon Peter, Simon, son of J ... Jn 21:15 *2495*
the second time, Simon, son of J ... Jn 21:16 *2495*
the third time, Simon, son of J ... Jn 21:17 *2495*

JONATHAN *(jon'-a-than)* {118} See JEHONATHAN, JONATHAN'S.
1. A Levite.
and J, the son of Gershom, the son ... Judg 18:30 3129
2. Son of Saul.
a thousand were with J in Gibeah ... 1Sa 13:2 3129
J smote the garrison of the ... 1Sa 13:3 3129
J his son, and the people that ... 1Sa 13:16 3129
people that were with Saul and J ... 1Sa 13:22 3129
with J his son was there found ... 1Sa 13:22 3129
that J the son of Saul said unto ... 1Sa 14:1 3129
people knew not that J was gone ... 1Sa 14:3 3129
by which J sought to go over unto ... 1Sa 14:4 3129
J said to the young man that bare ... 1Sa 14:6 3083
Then said J, Behold, we will pass ... 1Sa 14:8 3083
men of the garrison answered J ... 1Sa 14:12 3129
J said unto his armourbearer, ... 1Sa 14:12 3129
J climbed up upon his hands and ... 1Sa 14:13 3129
and they fell before J ... 1Sa 14:13 3129
And that first slaughter, which J ... 1Sa 14:14 3129
when they had numbered, behold, J ... 1Sa 14:17 3129
that were with Saul and J ... 1Sa 14:21 3129
But J heard not when his father ... 1Sa 14:27 3129
Then said J, My father hath ... 1Sa 14:29 3129
Israel, though it be in J my son ... 1Sa 14:39 3129
J my son will be on the other ... 1Sa 14:40 3129
And Saul and J were taken ... 1Sa 14:41 3129
Cast lots between me and J my son ... 1Sa 14:42 3129
And J was taken ... 1Sa 14:42 3129
Then Saul said to J, Tell me what ... 1Sa 14:43 3129
J told him, and said, I did but ... 1Sa 14:43 3129
for thou shalt surely die, J ... 1Sa 14:44 3129
said unto Saul, Shall J die ... 1Sa 14:45 3129
So the people rescued J, that he ... 1Sa 14:45 3129
Now the sons of Saul were J ... 1Sa 14:49 3129
that the soul of J was knit with ... 1Sa 18:1 3083
J loved him as his own soul ... 1Sa 18:1 3083
Then J and David made a covenant, ... 1Sa 18:3 3083
J stripped himself of the robe ... 1Sa 18:4 3083
And Saul spake to J his son ... 1Sa 19:1 3129
But J Saul's son delighted much ... 1Sa 19:2 3083
J told David, saying, Saul my ... 1Sa 19:2 3083
J spake good of David unto Saul ... 1Sa 19:4 3083
hearkened unto the voice of J ... 1Sa 19:6 3083
J called David, and Jonathan ... 1Sa 19:7 3083
J shewed him all those things ... 1Sa 19:7 3083
J brought David to Saul, and he ... 1Sa 19:7 3083
Ramah, and came and said before J ... 1Sa 20:1 3083
Let not J know this, lest he be ... 1Sa 20:3 3083
Then said J unto David, ... 1Sa 20:4 3083
And David said unto J, Behold, to ... 1Sa 20:5 3083
J said, Far be it from thee ... 1Sa 20:9 3083
Then said David to J, Who shall ... 1Sa 20:10 3083
J said unto David, Come, and let ... 1Sa 20:11 3083
J said unto David, O LORD God of ... 1Sa 20:12 3083
The LORD do so and much more to J ... 1Sa 20:13 3083
So J made a covenant with the ... 1Sa 20:16 3083
J caused David to swear again, ... 1Sa 20:17 3083
Then J said to David, To morrow ... 1Sa 20:18 3083
J arose, and Abner sat by Saul's ... 1Sa 20:25 3083
and Saul said unto J his son ... 1Sa 20:27 3083
J answered Saul, David earnestly ... 1Sa 20:28 3083
anger was kindled against J ... 1Sa 20:30 3083
J answered Saul his father, and ... 1Sa 20:32 3083
whereby J knew that it was ... 1Sa 20:33 3083
So J arose from the table in ... 1Sa 20:34 3083
that J went out into the field at ... 1Sa 20:35 3083
of the arrow which J had shot ... 1Sa 20:37 3083
J cried after the lad, and said, ... 1Sa 20:37 3083
J cried after the lad, Make speed ... 1Sa 20:38 3083
only J and David knew the matter ... 1Sa 20:39 3083
J gave his artillery unto his lad ... 1Sa 20:40 3083
J said to David, Go in peace, ... 1Sa 20:42 3083
and J went into the city ... 1Sa 20:42 3083
J Saul's son arose, and went to ... 1Sa 23:16 3083
the wood, and J went to his house ... 1Sa 23:18 3083
and the Philistines slew J ... 1Sa 31:2 3083
Saul and J his son are dead also ... 2Sa 1:4 3083
that Saul and J his son be dead ... 2Sa 1:5 3083
for J his son, and for the people ... 2Sa 1:12 3083
over Saul and over J his son ... 2Sa 1:17 3083
the bow of J turned not back, and ... 2Sa 1:22 3083
J were lovely and pleasant in ... 2Sa 1:23 3083
O J, thou wast slain in thine ... 2Sa 1:25 3083
distressed for thee, my brother J ... 2Sa 1:26 3083
And J, Saul's son, had a son that ... 2Sa 4:4 3083
J out of Jezreel, and his nurse ... 2Sa 4:4 3083
J hath yet a son, which is lame ... 2Sa 9:3 3083
when Mephibosheth, the son of J ... 2Sa 9:6 3083
kindness for J thy father's sake ... 2Sa 9:7 3083
the son of J the son of Saul, ... 2Sa 21:7 3083
David and J the son of Saul ... 2Sa 21:7 3083
the bones of J his son from the ... 2Sa 21:12 3083
of Saul and the bones of J his son ... 2Sa 21:13 3083
J his son buried they in the ... 2Sa 21:14 3083
Kish begat Saul, and Saul begat J ... 1Chr 8:33 3083
the son of J was Merib-baal ... 1Chr 8:34 3083
and Saul begat J, and Malchi-shua, ... 1Chr 9:39 3083
the son of J was Merib-baal ... 1Chr 9:40 3083
and the Philistines slew J ... 1Chr 10:2 3129
3. A son of Abiathar.
thy son, and J the son of Abiathar ... 2Sa 15:27 3083
Zadok's son, and J Abiathar's son ... 2Sa 15:36 3083
Now J and Ahimaaz stayed by ... 2Sa 17:17 3083
they said, Where is Ahimaaz and J ... 2Sa 17:20 3083
J the son of Abiathar the priest ... 1Kin 1:42 3129
J answered and said to Adonijah, ... 1Kin 1:43 3129
4. A son of Shimea.
J the son of Shimeah the brother ... 2Sa 21:21 3083
J the son of Shimea David's ... 1Chr 20:7 3083
5. A "mighty man" of David.
of the sons of Jashen, J ... 2Sa 23:32 3083
J the son of Shage the Hararite, ... 1Chr 11:34 3129
6. A son of Jada.
Shammai; Jether, and J ... 1Chr 2:32 3129
And the sons of J ... 1Chr 2:33 3129
7. An uncle of David.
Also J David's uncle was a ... 1Chr 27:32 3083
8. A family of exiles.
Ebed the son of J, and with him ... Ezr 8:6 3083
9. Son of Asahel.
Only J the son of Asahel and ... Ezr 10:15 3083
10. A descendant of Jeshua.
And Joiada begat J ... Neh 12:11 3083
and J begat Jaddua ... Neh 12:11 3083
11. A priest descended from Melicu.
Of Melicu, J ... Neh 12:14 3083
12. A priest descended from Shemaiah.
namely, Zechariah the son of J ... Neh 12:35 3083
13. A scribe.
in the house of J the scribe ... Jer 37:15 3083
to the house of J the scribe ... Jer 37:20 3083
14. A son of Kareah.
J the sons of Kareah, and Seraiah ... Jer 40:8 3129

JONATHAN'S *(jon'-a-thans)* {3} *Refers to Jonathan 2.*
J lad gathered up the arrows, and ... 1Sa 20:38 3129
may shew him kindness for J sake ... 2Sa 9:1 3129
not cause me to return to J house ... Jer 38:26 3129

JONATH-ELEM-RECHOKIM *(jo'-nath-e'-lem-re-ko'-kim)* {1} *A musical notation.*
To the chief Musician upon J ... Ps 56:*t* 3128

JOPPA *(jop'-pah)* {13} *A seaport in Dan.*
it to thee in flotes by sea to J ... 2Chr 2:16 3305
from Lebanon to the sea of J ... Ezr 3:7 3305
of the LORD, and went down to J ... Jonah 1:3 3305
Now there was at J a certain ... Acts 9:36 *2445*
forasmuch as Lydda was nigh to J ... Acts 9:38 *2445*
And it was known throughout all J ... Acts 9:42 *2445*
days in J with one Simon a tanner ... Acts 9:43 *2445*
And now send men to J, and call for ... Acts 10:5 *2445*
unto them, he sent them to J ... Acts 10:8 *2445*
brethren from J accompanied him ... Acts 10:23 *2445*
Send therefore to J, and call ... Acts 10:32 *2445*
I was in the city of J praying ... Acts 11:5 *2445*
and said unto him, Send men to J ... Acts 11:13 *2445*

JORAH *(jo'-rah)* {1} See HARIPH. *A family of exiles.*
The children of J, an hundred and ... Ezr 2:18 3139

JORAI *(jo'-rahee)* {1} *Head of a Gadite family.*
and Meshullam, and Sheba, and J ... 1Chr 5:13 3140

JORAM *(jo'-ram)* {29} See JEHORAM.
1. A son of Toi.
Then Toi sent J his son unto king ... 2Sa 8:10 3141
J brought with him vessels of ... 2Sa 8:10
2. Same as Jehoram.
So J went over to Zair, and all ... 2Kin 8:21 3141
And the rest of the acts of J ... 2Kin 8:23 3141
J slept with his fathers, and was ... 2Kin 8:24 3141
Jehosheba, the daughter of king J ... 2Kin 11:2 3141
J his son, Ahaziah his son, Joash ... 1Chr 3:11 3141
and Josaphat begat J ... Mt 1:8 *2496*
and J begat Ozias ... Mt 1:8 *2496*
3. A son of Ahab.
in the fifth year of J the son of ... 2Kin 8:16 3141
In the twelfth year of J the son ... 2Kin 8:25 3141
he went with J the son of Ahab to ... 2Kin 8:28 3141
and the Syrians wounded J ... 2Kin 8:28 3141
king J went back to be healed in ... 2Kin 8:29 3141
see J the son of Ahab in Jezreel ... 2Kin 8:29 3141
son of Nimshi conspired against J ... 2Kin 9:14 3141
(Now J had kept Ramoth-gilead, he ... 2Kin 9:14 3141
But king J was returned to be ... 2Kin 9:15 3188
for J lay there ... 2Kin 9:16 3141
of Judah was come down to see J ... 2Kin 9:16 3141
J said, Take an horseman, and send ... 2Kin 9:17 3188
And J said, Make ready ... 2Kin 9:21 3188
J king of Israel and Ahaziah king ... 2Kin 9:21 3188
when J saw Jehu, that he said, Is ... 2Kin 9:22 3188
J turned his hands, and fled, and ... 2Kin 9:23 3188
in the eleventh year of J the son ... 2Kin 9:29 3188
and the Syrians smote J ... 2Chr 22:5 3141
Ahaziah was of God by coming to J ... 2Chr 22:7 3141
4. A descendant of Eliezer.
J his son, and Zichri his son, and ... 1Chr 26:25 3141

JORDAN *(jor'-dan)* {198} *A river that runs from the Sea of Galilee to the Dead Sea.*
and beheld all the plain of J ... Gen 13:10 3383
Lot chose him all the plain of J ... Gen 13:11 3383
my staff I passed over this J ... Gen 32:10 3383
of Atad, which is beyond J ... Gen 50:10 3383
Abel-mizraim, which is beyond J ... Gen 50:11 3383
by the sea, and by the coast of J ... Num 13:29 3383
of Moab on this side J by Jericho ... Num 22:1 3383
plains of Moab by J near Jericho ... Num 26:3 3383
plains of Moab by J near Jericho ... Num 26:63 3383
Moab, which are by J near Jericho ... Num 31:12 3383
and bring us not over J ... Num 32:5 3383
with them on yonder side J ... Num 32:19 3383
to us on this side J eastward ... Num 32:19 3383
you armed over J before the LORD ... Num 32:21 3383
Reuben will pass with you over J ... Num 32:29 3383
on this side J may be ours ... Num 32:32 3383
plains of Moab by J near Jericho ... Num 33:48 3383
And they pitched by J, from ... Num 33:49 3383
Moses in the plains of Moab by J ... Num 33:50 3383
over J into the land of Canaan ... Num 33:51 3383
And the border shall go down to J ... Num 34:12 3383
this side J near Jericho eastward ... Num 34:15 3383
plains of Moab by J near Jericho ... Num 35:1 3383
When ye be come over J into the ... Num 35:10 3383
give three cities on this side J ... Num 35:14 3383
plains of Moab by J near Jericho ... Num 36:13 3383
on this side J in the wilderness ... Deut 1:1 3383
On this side J, in the land of ... Deut 1:5 3383
until I shall pass over J into ... Deut 2:29 3383
the land that was on this side J ... Deut 3:8 3383
The plain also, and J, and the ... Deut 3:17 3383
your God hath given them beyond J ... Deut 3:20 3383
the good land that is beyond J ... Deut 3:25 3383
for thou shalt not go over this J ... Deut 3:27 3383
sware that I should not go over J ... Deut 4:21 3383
this land, I must not go over J ... Deut 4:22 3383
ye go over J to possess it ... Deut 4:26 3383
this side J toward the sunrising ... Deut 4:41 3383
On this side J, in the valley ... Deut 4:46 3383
this side J toward the sunrising ... Deut 4:47 3383
the plain on this side J eastward ... Deut 4:49 3383
Thou art to pass over J this day ... Deut 9:1 3383
Are they not on the other side J ... Deut 11:30 3383
For ye shall pass over J to go in ... Deut 11:31 3383
But when ye go over J, and dwell ... Deut 12:10 3383
J unto the land which the LORD ... Deut 27:2 3383
shall be when ye be gone over J ... Deut 27:4 3383
people, when ye are come over J ... Deut 27:12 3383
over J to go to possess it ... Deut 30:18 3383
me, Thou shalt not go over this J ... Deut 31:2 3383
ye go over J to possess it ... Deut 31:13 3383
ye go over J to possess it ... Deut 32:47 3383
therefore arise, go over this J ... Josh 1:2 3383
days ye shall pass over this J ... Josh 1:11 3383
Moses gave you on this side J ... Josh 1:14 3383
this side J toward the sunrising ... Josh 1:15 3383
them the way to J unto the fords ... Josh 2:7 3383
that were on the other side J ... Josh 2:10 3383
from Shittim, and came to J ... Josh 3:1 3383
to the brink of the water of J ... Josh 3:8 3383
J, ye shall stand still in J ... Josh 3:8 3383
passeth over before you into J ... Josh 3:11 3383
shall rest in the waters of J ... Josh 3:13 3383
that the waters of J shall be cut ... Josh 3:13 3383
from their tents, to pass over J ... Josh 3:14 3383
bare the ark were come unto J ... Josh 3:15 3383
(for J overfloweth all his banks ... Josh 3:15 3383
on dry ground in the midst of J ... Josh 3:17 3383
people were passed clean over J ... Josh 3:17 3383

people were clean passed over J ... Josh 4:1 3383
you hence out of the midst of J ... Josh 4:3 3383
LORD your God into the midst of J ... Josh 4:5 3383
That the waters of J were cut off ... Josh 4:7 3383
when it passed over J ... Josh 4:7 3383
the waters of J were cut off ... Josh 4:7 3383
stones out of the midst of J ... Josh 4:8 3383
twelve stones in the midst of J ... Josh 4:9 3383
the ark stood in the midst of J ... Josh 4:10 3383
that they come up out of J ... Josh 4:16 3383
saying, Come ye up out of J ... Josh 4:17 3383
come up out of the midst of J ... Josh 4:18 3383
that the waters of J returned ... Josh 4:18 3383
the people came up out of J on ... Josh 4:19 3383
stones, which they took out of J ... Josh 4:20 3383
came over this J on dry land ... Josh 4:22 3383
the waters of J from before you ... Josh 4:23 3383
were on the side of J westward ... Josh 5:1 3383
of J from before the children of ... Josh 5:1 3383
at all brought this people over J ... Josh 7:7 3383
and dwelt on the other side J ... Josh 7:7 3383
kings which were on this side J ... Josh 9:1 3383
the Amorites, that were beyond J ... Josh 9:10 3383
J toward the rising of the sun ... Josh 12:1 3383
smote on this side J on the west ... Josh 12:7 3383
beyond J eastward, even as Moses ... Josh 13:8 3383
of the children of Reuben was J ... Josh 13:23 3383
of Sihon king of Heshbon, J ... Josh 13:27 3383
on the other side J eastward ... Josh 13:27 3383
of Moab, on the other side J ... Josh 13:32 3383
an half tribe on the other side J ... Josh 14:3 3383
salt sea, even unto the end of J ... Josh 15:5 3383
sea at the uttermost part of J ... Josh 15:5 3383
of Joseph fell from J by Jericho ... Josh 16:1 3383
came to Jericho, and went out at J ... Josh 16:7 3383
which were on the other side J ... Josh 17:5 3383
inheritance beyond J on the east ... Josh 18:7 3383
on the north side was from J ... Josh 18:12 3383
salt sea at the south end of J ... Josh 18:19 3383
J was the border of it on the ... Josh 18:20 3383
of their border were at J ... Josh 19:22 3383
the outgoings thereof were at J ... Josh 19:33 3383
to Judah upon J toward the ... Josh 19:34 3383
on the other side J by Jericho ... Josh 20:8 3383
LORD gave you on the other side J ... Josh 22:4 3383
brethren on this side J westward ... Josh 22:7 3383
they came unto the borders of J ... Josh 22:10 3383
built there an altar by J ... Josh 22:10 3383
of Canaan, in the borders of J ... Josh 22:11 3383
hath made J a border between us ... Josh 22:25 3383
for your tribes, from J, with all ... Josh 23:4 3383
which dwelt on the other side J ... Josh 24:8 3383
And ye went over J, and came unto ... Josh 24:11 3383
took the fords of J toward Moab ... Judg 3:28 3383
Gilead abode beyond J ... Judg 5:17 3383
the waters unto Beth-barah and J ... Judg 7:24 3383
the waters unto Beth-barah and J ... Judg 7:24 3383
to Gideon on the other side J ... Judg 7:25 3383
And Gideon came to J, and passed ... Judg 8:4 3383
J in the land of the Amorites ... Judg 10:8 3383
J to fight also against Judah ... Judg 10:9 3383
Arnon even unto Jabbok, and unto J ... Judg 11:13 3383
from the wilderness even unto J ... Judg 11:22 3383
of J before the Ephraimites ... Judg 12:5 3383
and slew him at the passages of J ... Judg 12:6 3383
went over J to the land of Gad ... 1Sa 13:7 3383
that were on the other side J ... 1Sa 31:7 3383
the plain, and passed over J ... 2Sa 2:29 3383
Israel together, and passed over J ... 2Sa 10:17 3383
with him, and they passed over J ... 2Sa 17:22 3383
of them that was not gone over J ... 2Sa 17:22 3383
And Absalom passed over J, he and ... 2Sa 17:24 3383
the king returned, and came to J ... 2Sa 19:15 3383
king, to conduct the king over J ... 2Sa 19:15 3383
they went over J before the king ... 2Sa 19:17 3383
the king, as he was come over J ... 2Sa 19:18 3383
went over J with the king ... 2Sa 19:31 3383
to conduct him over J ... 2Sa 19:31 3383
a little way over J with the king ... 2Sa 19:36 3383
And all the people went over J ... 2Sa 19:39 3383
all David's men with him, over J ... 2Sa 19:41 3383
king, from J even to Jerusalem ... 2Sa 20:2 3383
And they passed over J, and pitched ... 2Sa 24:5 3383
but he came down to meet me at J ... 1Kin 2:8 3383
In the plain of J did the king ... 1Kin 7:46 3383
brook Cherith, that is before J ... 1Kin 17:3 3383
brook Cherith, that is before J ... 1Kin 17:5 3383
for the LORD hath sent me to J ... 2Kin 2:6 3383
and they two stood by J ... 2Kin 2:7 3383
back, and stood by the bank of J ... 2Kin 2:13 3383
wash in J seven times, and thy ... 2Kin 5:10 3383
dipped himself seven times in J ... 2Kin 5:14 3383
Let us go, we pray thee, unto J ... 2Kin 6:2 3383
And when they came to J, they cut ... 2Kin 6:4 3383
And they went after them unto J ... 2Kin 7:15 3383
From J eastward, all the land of ... 2Kin 10:33 3383
And on the other side J by Jericho ... 1Chr 6:78 3383
on the east side of J ... 1Chr 6:78 3383
went over J in the first month ... 1Chr 12:15 3383
And on the other side of J ... 1Chr 12:37 3383
all Israel, and passed over J ... 1Chr 19:17 3383
them of Israel on this side J ... 1Chr 26:30 3383
In the plain of J did the king ... 2Chr 4:17 3383
he can draw up J into his mouth ... Job 40:23 3383
remember thee from the land of J ... Ps 42:6 3383
J was driven back ... Ps 114:3 3383
thou J, that thou wast driven ... Ps 114:5 3383
by the way of the sea, beyond J ... Is 9:1 3383
wilt thou do in the swelling of J ... Jer 12:5 3383
a lion from the swelling of J ... Jer 49:19 3383
of J unto the habitation of the ... Jer 50:44 3383
and from the land of Israel by J ... Eze 47:18 3383
for the pride of J is spoiled ... Zec 11:3 3383
and all the region round about J ... Mt 3:5 *2446*
And were baptized of him in J ... Mt 3:6 *2446*
Jesus from Galilee to J unto John ... Mt 3:13 *2446*
by the way of the sea, beyond J ... Mt 4:15 *2446*
and from Judaea, and from beyond J ... Mt 4:25 *2446*
the coasts of Judaea beyond J ... Mt 19:1 *2446*
baptized of him in the river of J ... Mk 1:5 *2446*
and was baptized of John in J ... Mk 1:9 *2446*
and from Idumaea, and from beyond J ... Mk 3:8 *2446*
Judaea by the farther side of J ... Mk 10:1 *2446*
came into all the country about J ... Lk 3:3 *2446*
of the Holy Ghost returned from J ... Lk 4:1 *2446*
were done in Bethabara beyond J ... Jn 1:28 *2446*
he that was with thee beyond J ... Jn 3:26 *2446*
went away again beyond J into the ... Jn 10:40 *2446*

JORIM *(jo'-rim)* {1} *Son of Matthat; ancestor of Jesus.*
Eliezer, which was the son of J ... Lk 3:29 *2497*

JORKEAM See JORKOAM.

JORKOAM *(jor'-ko-am)* {1} *A descendant of Hebron.*
begat Raham, the father of J ... 1Chr 2:44 3421

JOSABAD *(jos'-a-bad)* {1} See JOZABAD. *A warrior in David's army.*
and Johanan, and J the Gederathite, ... 1Chr 12:4 3107

JOSAPHAT *(jos'-a-fat)* {2} See JEHOSHAPHAT. *Son of Asa; ancestor of Jesus.*
And Asa begat J ... Mt 1:8 *2498*
and J begat Joram ... Mt 1:8 *2498*

JOSE *(jo'-ze)* {1} See JOSES. *Son of Eliezer; ancestor of Jesus.*
Which was the son of J, which was ... Lk 3:29 *2499*

JOSECH See JOSEPH.

JOSEDECH *(jos'-e-dek)* {6} See JOZADAK. *Father of Joshua, the priest.*
Judah, and to Joshua the son of J ... Hag 1:1 3087
Shealtiel, and Joshua the son of J ... Hag 1:12 3087
the spirit of Joshua the son of J ... Hag 1:14 3087
Judah, and to Joshua the son of J ... Hag 2:2 3087
and be strong, O Joshua, son of J ... Hag 2:4 3087
the head of Joshua the son of J ... Zec 6:11 3087

JOSEPH *(jo'-zef)* {228} See BARSABAS, JOSEPH'S.
1. Son of Jacob and Rachel.
And she called his name J ... Gen 30:24 3130
to pass, when Rachel had born J ... Gen 30:25 3130
after, and Rachel and J hindermost ... Gen 33:2 3130
and after came J near and Rachel, ... Gen 33:7 3130
sons of Rachel; J, and Benjamin ... Gen 35:24 3130
J, being seventeen years old, was ... Gen 37:2 3130
J brought unto his father their ... Gen 37:2 3130
Now Israel loved J more than all ... Gen 37:3 3130
J dreamed a dream, and he told it ... Gen 37:5 3130
And Israel said unto J, Do not thy ... Gen 37:13 3130
J went after his brethren, and ... Gen 37:17 3130
when J was come unto his brethren ... Gen 37:23 3130
they stript J out of his coat ... Gen 37:23 3130
lifted up J out of the pit, and ... Gen 37:28 3130
sold J to the Ishmeelites for ... Gen 37:28 3130
and they brought J into Egypt ... Gen 37:28 3130
and, behold, J was not in the pit ... Gen 37:29 3130
J is without doubt rent in pieces ... Gen 37:33 3130
J was brought down to Egypt ... Gen 39:1 3130
And the LORD was with J, and he was ... Gen 39:2 3130
J found grace in his sight, and he ... Gen 39:4 3130
J was a goodly person, and well ... Gen 39:6 3130
wife cast her eyes upon J ... Gen 39:7 3130
as she spake to J day by day ... Gen 39:10 3130
that J went into the house to do ... Gen 39:11 3130
But the LORD was with J, and ... Gen 39:21 3130
the place where J was bound ... Gen 40:3 3130
of the guard charged J with them ... Gen 40:4 3130
J came in unto them in the ... Gen 40:6 3130
And J said unto them, Do not ... Gen 40:8 3130
chief butler told his dream to J ... Gen 40:9 3130
J said unto him, This is the ... Gen 40:12 3130
was good, he said unto J, I also ... Gen 40:16 3130
J answered and said, This is the ... Gen 40:18 3130
as J had interpreted to them ... Gen 40:22 3130
not the chief butler remember J ... Gen 40:23 3130
Then Pharaoh sent and called J ... Gen 41:14 3130
And Pharaoh said unto J, I have ... Gen 41:15 3130
J answered Pharaoh, saying, It is ... Gen 41:16 3130
And Pharaoh said unto J, In my ... Gen 41:17 3130
J said unto Pharaoh, The dream of ... Gen 41:25 3130
And Pharaoh said unto J, Forasmuch ... Gen 41:39 3130
And Pharaoh said unto J, See, I ... Gen 41:41 3130
And Pharaoh said unto J, I am ... Gen 41:44 3130
J went out over all the land of ... Gen 41:45 3130
J was thirty years old when he ... Gen 41:46 3130
J went out from the presence of ... Gen 41:46 3130
J gathered corn as the sand of ... Gen 41:49 3130
unto J were born two sons before ... Gen 41:50 3130
And J called the name of the ... Gen 41:51 3130
to come, according as J had said ... Gen 41:54 3130
unto all the Egyptians, Go unto J ... Gen 41:55 3130
J opened all the storehouses, and ... Gen 41:56 3130
into Egypt to J for to buy corn ... Gen 41:57 3130
J was the governor over the land, ... Gen 42:6 3130
J saw his brethren, and he knew ... Gen 42:7 3130
J knew his brethren, but they ... Gen 42:8 3130
J remembered the dreams which he ... Gen 42:9 3130
J said unto them, That is it that ... Gen 42:14 3130
J said unto them the third day, ... Gen 42:18 3130
knew not that J understood them ... Gen 42:23 3130
Then J commanded to fill their ... Gen 42:25 3130
J is not, and Simeon is not, and ye ... Gen 42:36 3130
down to Egypt, and stood before J ... Gen 43:15 3130
when J saw Benjamin with them, he ... Gen 43:16 3130
And the man did as J bade ... Gen 43:17 3130
present against J came at noon ... Gen 43:25 3130
when J came home, they brought ... Gen 43:26 3130
And J made haste ... Gen 43:30 3130
to the word that J had spoken ... Gen 44:2 3130
J said unto his steward, Up, ... Gen 44:4 3130
J said unto them, What deed is ... Gen 44:15 3130
Then J could not refrain himself ... Gen 45:1 3130
while J made himself known unto ... Gen 45:1 3130
J said unto his brethren ... Gen 45:3 3130
I am J; doth my father yet ... Gen 45:3 3130
J said unto his brethren, Come ... Gen 45:4 3130
I am J your brother, whom ye sold ... Gen 45:4 3130
unto him, Thus saith thy son J ... Gen 45:9 3130
And Pharaoh said unto J, Say unto ... Gen 45:17 3130
J gave them wagons, according to ... Gen 45:21 3130
J is yet alive, and he is governor ... Gen 45:26 3130
they told him all the words of J ... Gen 45:27 3130
which J had sent to carry him ... Gen 45:27 3130
J my son is yet alive ... Gen 45:28 3130
J shall put his hand upon thine ... Gen 46:4 3130
Jacob's wife; J, and Benjamin ... Gen 46:19 3130
unto J in the land of Egypt were ... Gen 46:20 3130
And the sons of J, which were born ... Gen 46:27 3130
he sent Judah before him unto J ... Gen 46:28 3130
J made ready his chariot, and went ... Gen 46:29 3130
And Israel said unto J, Now let me ... Gen 46:30 3130
J said unto his brethren, and unto ... Gen 46:31 3130
Then J came and told Pharaoh, and ... Gen 47:1 3130
And Pharaoh spake unto J, saying, ... Gen 47:5 3130
J brought in Jacob his father, and ... Gen 47:7 3130
J placed his father and his ... Gen 47:11 3130
J nourished his father, and his ... Gen 47:12 3130
J gathered up all the money that ... Gen 47:14 3130
and J brought the money into ... Gen 47:14 3130
all the Egyptians came unto J ... Gen 47:15 3130
And J said, Give your cattle ... Gen 47:16 3130
they brought their cattle unto J ... Gen 47:17 3130
J gave them bread in exchange for ... Gen 47:17 3130
J bought all the land of Egypt ... Gen 47:20 3130
Then J said unto the people, ... Gen 47:23 3130
J made it a law over the land of ... Gen 47:26 3130
and he called his son J, and said ... Gen 47:29 3130
these things, that one told J ... Gen 48:1 3130
thy son J cometh unto thee ... Gen 48:2 3130
And Jacob said unto J, God ... Gen 48:3 3130
J said unto his father, They are ... Gen 48:9 3130
And Israel said unto J, I had not ... Gen 48:11 3130
J brought them out from between ... Gen 48:12 3130
J took them both, Ephraim in his ... Gen 48:13 3130
And he blessed J, and said, God, ... Gen 48:15 3130
when J saw that his father laid ... Gen 48:17 3130
J said unto his father, Not so, ... Gen 48:18 3130
And Israel said unto J, Behold, I ... Gen 48:21 3130
J is a fruitful bough, even a ... Gen 49:22 3130
they shall be on the head of J ... Gen 49:26 3130
J fell upon his father's face, and ... Gen 50:1 3130
J commanded his servants the ... Gen 50:2 3130
J spake unto the house of Pharaoh ... Gen 50:4 3130
J went up to bury his father ... Gen 50:7 3130
And all the house of J, and his ... Gen 50:8 3130
J returned into Egypt, he, and his ... Gen 50:14 3130
J will peradventure hate us, and ... Gen 50:15 3130
And they sent a messenger unto J ... Gen 50:16 3130
So shall ye say unto J, Forgive, ... Gen 50:17 3130
J wept when they spake unto him ... Gen 50:17 3130
J said unto them, Fear not ... Gen 50:19 3130
J dwelt in Egypt, he, and his ... Gen 50:22 3130
J lived an hundred and ten years ... Gen 50:22 3130
J saw Ephraim's children of the ... Gen 50:23 3130
J said unto his brethren, I die ... Gen 50:24 3130
J took an oath of the children of ... Gen 50:25 3130
So J died, being an hundred and ... Gen 50:26 3130
for J was in Egypt already ... Ex 1:5 3130
J died, and all his brethren, and ... Ex 1:6 3130
king over Egypt, which knew not J ... Ex 1:8 3130
took the bones of J with him ... Ex 13:19 3130
families of Manasseh the son of J ... Num 27:1 3130
tribe of Manasseh the son of J ... Num 32:33 3130
The prince of the children of J ... Num 34:23 3130
the sons of Manasseh the son of J ... Num 36:12 3130
Levi, and Judah, and Issachar, and J ... Deut 27:12 3130
the children of J were two tribes ... Josh 14:4 3130
the lot of the children of J fell ... Josh 16:1 3130
So the children of J, Manasseh and ... Josh 16:4 3130
for he was the firstborn of J ... Josh 17:1 3130
the son of J by their families ... Josh 17:2 3130
the children of J spake unto ... Josh 17:14 3130
And the children of J said ... Josh 17:16 3130
And the bones of J, which the ... Josh 24:32 3130
Dan, J, and Benjamin, Naphtali, ... 1Chr 2:2 3130
He sent a man before them, even J ... Ps 105:17 3130
that Jacob gave to his son J ... Jn 4:5 *2501*
with envy, sold J into Egypt ... Acts 7:9 *2501*
at the second time J was made ... Acts 7:13 *2501*
Then sent J, and called his father ... Acts 7:14 *2501*
king arose, which knew not J ... Acts 7:18 *2501*
dying, blessed both the sons of J ... Heb 11:21 *2501*
By faith J, when he died, made ... Heb 11:22 *2501*
2. Descendants of Joseph 1.
Of the children of J ... Num 1:10 3130
Of the children of J, namely, of ... Num 1:32 3130

Of the tribe of *J*, namely, of the ... Num 13:11 3130
The sons of *J* after their ... Num 26:28 3130
sons of *J* after their families ... Num 26:37 3130
of the families of the sons of *J* ... Num 36:1 3130
of the sons of *J* hath said well ... Num 36:5 3130
of *J* he said, Blessed of the LORD ... Deut 33:13 3130
blessing come upon the head of *J* ... Deut 33:16 3130
Joshua spake unto the house of *J* ... Josh 17:17 3130
the house of *J* shall abide in ... Josh 18:5 3130
of Judah and the children of *J* ... Josh 18:11 3130
inheritance of the children of *J* ... Josh 24:32 3130
And the house of *J*, they also went ... Judg 1:22 3130
the house of *J* sent to descry ... Judg 1:23 3130
hand of the house of *J* prevailed ... Judg 1:35 3130
this day of all the house of *J* to ... 2Sa 19:20 3130
all the charge of the house of *J* ... 1Kin 11:28 3130
the sons of *J* the son of Israel ... 1Chr 5:1 3130
children of *J* the son of Israel ... 1Chr 7:29 3130
people, the sons of Jacob and *J* ... Ps 77:15 3130
he refused the tabernacle of *J* ... Ps 78:67 3130
thou that leadest *J* like a flock ... Ps 80:1 3130
he ordained in *J* for a testimony ... Ps 81:5 3084
stick, and write upon it, For *J* ... Eze 37:16 3130
I will take the stick of *J* ... Eze 37:19 3130
J shall have two portions ... Eze 47:13 3130
and one gate of *J*, one gate of ... Eze 48:32 3130
out like fire in the house of *J* ... Amos 5:6 3130
be gracious unto the remnant of *J* ... Amos 5:15 3130
grieved for the affliction of *J* ... Amos 6:6 3130
a fire, and the house of *J* a flame ... Obad 18 3130
and I will save the house of *J* ... Zec 10:6 3130
Of the tribe of *J* were sealed ... Rev 7:8 *2501*

3. A spy sent to the Promised Land.
of Issachar, Igal the son of *J* ... Num 13:7 3130

4. A son of Asaph.
Zaccur, and *J*, and Nethaniah, and ... 1Chr 25:2 3130
lot came forth for Asaph to *J* ... 1Chr 25:9 3130

5. Married a foreigner in exile.
Shallum, Amariah, and *J* ... Ezr 10:42 3130

6. A priest.
Jonathan; of Shebaniah, *J* ... Neh 12:14 3130

7. Husband of Mary, the mother of Jesus.
Jacob begat *J* the husband of Mary ... Mt 1:16 *2501*
his mother Mary was espoused to *J* ... Mt 1:18 *2501*
Then *J* her husband, being a just ... Mt 1:19 *2501*
unto him in a dream, saying, *J* ... Mt 1:20 *2501*
Then *J* being raised from sleep ... Mt 1:24 *2501*
Lord appeareth to *J* in a dream ... Mt 2:13 *2501*
in a dream to *J* in Egypt, ... Mt 2:19 *2501*
to a man whose name was *J* ... Lk 1:27 *2501*
J also went up from Galilee, out ... Lk 2:4 *2501*
with haste, and found Mary, and *J* ... Lk 2:16 *2501*
And *J* and his mother marvelled at ... Lk 2:33 *2501*
and *J* and his mother knew not of it ... Lk 2:43 *2501*
(as was supposed) the son of *J* ... Lk 3:23 *2501*
Jesus of Nazareth, the son of *J* ... Jn 1:45 *2501*
Is not this Jesus, the son of *J* ... Jn 6:42 *2501*

8. A disciple of Jesus.
a rich man of Arimathaea, named *J* ... Mt 27:57 *2501*
when *J* had taken the body, he ... Mt 27:59 *2501*
J of Arimathaea, an honourable ... Mk 15:43 *2501*
centurion, he gave the body to *J* ... Mk 15:45 *2501*
behold, there was a man named *J* ... Lk 23:50 *2501*
after this *J* of Arimathaea, being ... Jn 19:38 *2501*

9. Son of Mattathias; ancestor of Jesus.
of Janna, which was the son of *J* ... Lk 3:24 *2501*

10. Son of Juda; ancestor of Jesus.
of Semei, which was the son of *J* ... Lk 3:26 *2501*

11. Son of Jonan; ancestor of Jesus.
of Juda, which was the son of *J* ... Lk 3:30 *2501*

12. A nominee for Judas' apostleship.
J called Barsabas, who was ... Acts 1:23 *2501*

JOSEPH'S *(jo'-zefs)* {22}
1. Refers to Joseph 1.
And they took *J* coat, and killed a ... Gen 37:31 3130
the Egyptian's house for *J* sake ... Gen 39:5 3130
he left all that he had in *J* hand ... Gen 39:6 3130
J master took him, and put him ... Gen 39:20 3130
of the prison committed to *J* hand ... Gen 39:22 3130
his hand, and put it upon *J* hand ... Gen 41:42 3130
And Pharaoh called *J* name ... Gen 41:45 3130
J ten brethren went down to buy ... Gen 42:3 3130
J brother, Jacob sent not with ... Gen 42:4 3130
J brethren came, and bowed down ... Gen 42:6 3130
man brought the men into *J* house ... Gen 43:17 3130
they were brought into *J* house ... Gen 43:18 3130
near to the steward of *J* house ... Gen 43:19 3130
man brought the men into *J* house ... Gen 43:24 3130
and his brethren came to *J* house ... Gen 44:14 3130
saying, *J* brethren are come ... Gen 45:16 3130
And Israel beheld *J* sons, and said, ... Gen 48:8 3130
when *J* brethren saw that their ... Gen 50:15 3130
were brought up upon *J* knees ... Gen 50:23 3130
but the birthright was *J* ... 1Chr 5:2 3130
J kindred was made known unto ... Acts 7:13 *2501*

2. Refers to Joseph 7.
And they said, Is not this *J* son ... Lk 4:22 *2501*

JOSES *(jo'-zez)* {6} See JOSE.
1. A brother of Jesus.
and his brethren, James, and *J* ... Mt 13:55 *2500*
Mary, the brother of James, and *J* ... Mk 6:3 *2500*

2. Brother of James the younger.
and Mary the mother of James and *J* ... Mt 27:56 *2500*
mother of James the less and of *J* ... Mk 15:40 *2500*
Mary the mother of *J* beheld where ... Mk 15:47 *2500*

3. Same as Barnabas.
And *J*, who by the apostles was ... Acts 4:36 *2500*

JOSHAH *(jo'-shah)* {1} *A descendant of Simeon.*
Jamlech, and *J* the son of Amaziah, ... 1Chr 4:34 3144

JOSHAPHAT *(josh'-a-fat)* {1} See JEHOSHAPHAT, JOSAPHAT. *A "mighty man" of David.*
of Maachah, and *J* the Mithnite, ... 1Chr 11:43 3146

JOSHAVIAH *(josh-a-vi'-ah)* {1} *A "mighty man" of David.*
the Mahavite, and Jeribai, and *J* ... 1Chr 11:46 3145

JOSHBEKASHAH *(josh-bek'-a-shah)* {2} *A sanctuary servant.*
Giddalti, and Romamti-ezer, *J* ... 1Chr 25:4 3436
The seventeenth to *J*, he, his ... 1Chr 25:24 3436

JOSHEB-BASSHEBETH See ADINO.

JOSHUA *(josh'-u-ah)* {216} See HOSEA, HOSHEA, JEHOSHUAH, JESHUA, JESHUAH, JESUS, OSEA, OSHEA.
1. Son of Nun.
And Moses said unto *J*, Choose us ... Ex 17:9 3091
So *J* did as Moses had said to him ... Ex 17:10 3091
J discomfited Amalek and his ... Ex 17:13 3091
and rehearse it in the ears of *J* ... Ex 17:14 3091
Moses rose up, and his minister *J* ... Ex 24:13 3091
when *J* heard the noise of the ... Ex 32:17 3091
but his servant *J*, the son of Nun ... Ex 33:11 3091
J the son of Nun, the servant of ... Num 11:28 3091
J the son of Nun, and Caleb the ... Num 14:6 3091
of Jephunneh, and *J* the son of Nun ... Num 14:30 3091
But *J* the son of Nun, and Caleb ... Num 14:38 3091
of Jephunneh, and *J* the son of Nun ... Num 26:65 3091
Take thee *J* the son of Nun, a man ... Num 27:18 3091
and he took *J*, and set him before ... Num 27:22 3091
the Kenezite, and *J* the son of Nun ... Num 32:12 3091
J the son of Nun, and the chief ... Num 32:28 3091
the priest, and *J* the son of Nun ... Num 34:17 3091
But *J* the son of Nun, which ... Deut 1:38 3091
I commanded *J* at that time, ... Deut 3:21 3091
But charge *J*, and encourage him, ... Deut 3:28 3091
and *J*, he shall go over before ... Deut 31:3 3091
And Moses called unto *J*, and said ... Deut 31:7 3091
call *J*, and present yourselves in ... Deut 31:14 3091
J went, and presented themselves ... Deut 31:14 3091
he gave *J* the son of Nun a charge ... Deut 31:23 3091
J the son of Nun was full of the ... Deut 34:9 3091
LORD spake unto *J* the son of Nun ... Josh 1:1 3091
Then *J* commanded the officers of ... Josh 1:10 3091
the tribe of Manasseh, spake *J* ... Josh 1:12 3091
And they answered *J*, saying, All ... Josh 1:16 3091
J the son of Nun sent out of ... Josh 2:1 3091
came to *J* the son of Nun, and told ... Josh 2:23 3091
And they said unto *J*, Truly the ... Josh 2:24 3091
J rose early in the morning ... Josh 3:1 3091
J said unto the people, Sanctify ... Josh 3:5 3091
J spake unto the priests, saying, ... Josh 3:6 3091
And the LORD said unto *J*, This day ... Josh 3:7 3091
J said unto the children of ... Josh 3:9 3091
J said, Hereby ye shall know that ... Josh 3:10 3091
that the LORD spake unto *J* ... Josh 4:1 3091
Then *J* called the twelve men, ... Josh 4:4 3091
J said unto them, Pass over ... Josh 4:5 3091
of Israel did so as *J* commanded ... Josh 4:8 3091
Jordan, as the LORD spake unto *J* ... Josh 4:8 3091
J set up twelve stones in the ... Josh 4:9 3091
that the LORD commanded *J* to ... Josh 4:10 3091
to all that Moses commanded *J* ... Josh 4:10 3091
J in the sight of all Israel ... Josh 4:14 3091
And the LORD spake unto *J*, saying, ... Josh 4:15 3091
J therefore commanded the priests ... Josh 4:17 3091
of Jordan, did *J* pitch in Gilgal ... Josh 4:20 3091
At that time the LORD said unto *J* ... Josh 5:2 3091
J made him sharp knives, and ... Josh 5:3 3091
is the cause why *J* did circumcise ... Josh 5:4 3091
their stead, them *J* circumcised ... Josh 5:7 3091
And the LORD said unto *J*, This day ... Josh 5:9 3091
when *J* was by Jericho, that he ... Josh 5:13 3091
J went unto him, and said unto him ... Josh 5:13 3091
J fell on his face to the earth, ... Josh 5:14 3091
of the LORD's host said unto *J* ... Josh 5:15 3091
And *J* did so ... Josh 5:15 3091
And the LORD said unto *J*, See, I ... Josh 6:2 3091
J the son of Nun called the ... Josh 6:6 3091
when *J* had spoken unto the people ... Josh 6:8 3091
J had commanded the people, ... Josh 6:10 3091
J rose early in the morning, and ... Josh 6:12 3091
J said unto the people, Shout ... Josh 6:16 3091
But *J* had said unto the two men ... Josh 6:22 3091
J saved Rahab the harlot alive, ... Josh 6:25 3091
which *J* sent to spy out Jericho ... Josh 6:25 3091
J adjured them at that time, ... Josh 6:26 3091
So the LORD was with *J* ... Josh 6:27 3091
J sent men from Jericho to Ai, ... Josh 7:2 3091
And they returned to *J*, and said ... Josh 7:3 3091
J rent his clothes, and fell to ... Josh 7:6 3091
J said, Alas, O Lord GOD, ... Josh 7:7 3091
And the LORD said unto *J*, Get thee ... Josh 7:10 3091
So *J* rose up early in the morning ... Josh 7:16 3091
J said unto Achan, My son, give, ... Josh 7:19 3091
And Achan answered *J*, and said, ... Josh 7:20 3091
So *J* sent messengers, and they ran ... Josh 7:22 3091
the tent, and brought them unto *J* ... Josh 7:23 3091
And *J*, and all Israel with him, ... Josh 7:24 3091
J said, Why hast thou troubled us ... Josh 7:25 3091
And the LORD said unto *J*, Fear not ... Josh 8:1 3091
So *J* arose, and all the people of ... Josh 8:3 3091
J chose out thirty thousand ... Josh 8:3 3091
J therefore sent them forth ... Josh 8:9 3091
but *J* lodged that night among the ... Josh 8:9 3091
J rose up early in the morning, ... Josh 8:10 3091
J went that night into the midst ... Josh 8:13 3091
And *J* and all Israel made as if ... Josh 8:15 3091
and they pursued after *J*, and were ... Josh 8:16 3091
And the LORD said unto *J*, Stretch ... Josh 8:18 3091
J stretched out the spear that he ... Josh 8:18 3091
And when *J* and all Israel saw that ... Josh 8:21 3091
took alive, and brought him to *J* ... Josh 8:23 3091
For *J* drew not his hand back, ... Josh 8:26 3091
of the LORD which he commanded *J* ... Josh 8:27 3091
J burnt Ai, and made it an heap ... Josh 8:28 3091
J commanded that they should take ... Josh 8:29 3091
Then *J* built an altar unto the ... Josh 8:30 3091
which *J* read not before all the ... Josh 8:35 3091
together, to fight with *J* ... Josh 9:2 3091
of Gibeon heard what *J* had done ... Josh 9:3 3091
they went to *J* unto the camp at ... Josh 9:6 3091
And they said unto *J*, We are thy ... Josh 9:8 3091
J said unto them, Who are ye ... Josh 9:8 3091
J made peace with them, and made a ... Josh 9:15 3091
J called for them, and he spake ... Josh 9:22 3091
And they answered *J*, and said, ... Josh 9:24 3091
J made them that day hewers of ... Josh 9:27 3091
had heard how *J* had taken Ai ... Josh 10:1 3091
for it hath made peace with *J* ... Josh 10:4 3091
sent unto *J* to the camp to Gilgal ... Josh 10:6 3091
So *J* ascended from Gilgal, he, and ... Josh 10:7 3091
And the LORD said unto *J*, Fear ... Josh 10:8 3091
J therefore came unto them ... Josh 10:9 3091
Then spake *J* to the LORD in the ... Josh 10:12 3091
J returned, and all Israel with ... Josh 10:15 3091
And it was told *J*, saying, The ... Josh 10:17 3091
J said, Roll great stones upon ... Josh 10:18 3091
And it came to pass, when *J* ... Josh 10:20 3091
camp to *J* at Makkedah in peace ... Josh 10:21 3091
Then said *J*, Open the mouth of ... Josh 10:22 3091
brought out those kings unto *J* ... Josh 10:24 3091
that *J* called for all the men of ... Josh 10:24 3091
J said unto them, Fear not, nor ... Josh 10:25 3091
afterward *J* smote them, and slew ... Josh 10:26 3091
that *J* commanded, and they took ... Josh 10:27 3091
that day *J* took Makkedah, and ... Josh 10:28 3091
Then *J* passed from Makkedah, and ... Josh 10:29 3091
J passed from Libnah, and all ... Josh 10:31 3091
J smote him and his people, until ... Josh 10:33 3091
from Lachish *J* passed unto Eglon, ... Josh 10:34 3091
J went up from Eglon, and all ... Josh 10:36 3091
J returned, and all Israel with ... Josh 10:38 3091
So *J* smote all the country of the ... Josh 10:40 3091
J smote them from Kadesh-barnea ... Josh 10:41 3091
their land did *J* take at one time ... Josh 10:42 3091
J returned, and all Israel with ... Josh 10:43 3091
And the LORD said unto *J*, Be not ... Josh 11:6 3091
So *J* came, and all the people of ... Josh 11:7 3091
J did unto them as the LORD bade ... Josh 11:9 3091
J at that time turned back, and ... Josh 11:10 3091
did *J* take, and smote them with ... Josh 11:12 3091
that did *J* burn ... Josh 11:13 3091
Moses command *J*, and so did *J* ... Josh 11:15 3091
So *J* took all that land, the ... Josh 11:16 3091
J made war a long time with all ... Josh 11:18 3091
And at that time came *J*, and cut ... Josh 11:21 3091
J destroyed them utterly with ... Josh 11:21 3091
So *J* took the whole land, ... Josh 11:23 3091
J gave it for an inheritance unto ... Josh 11:23 3091
the kings of the country which *J* ... Josh 12:7 3091
which *J* gave unto the tribes of ... Josh 12:7 3091
Now *J* was old and stricken in ... Josh 13:1 3091
J the son of Nun, and the heads of ... Josh 14:1 3091
of Judah came unto *J* in Gilgal ... Josh 14:6 3091
J blessed him, and gave unto Caleb ... Josh 14:13 3091
the commandment of the LORD to *J* ... Josh 15:13 3091
before *J* the son of Nun, and ... Josh 17:4 3091
children of Joseph spake unto *J* ... Josh 17:14 3091
J answered them, If thou be a ... Josh 17:15 3091
J spake unto the house of Joseph, ... Josh 17:17 3091
J said unto the children of ... Josh 18:3 3091
J charged them that went to ... Josh 18:8 3091
came again to *J* to the host at ... Josh 18:9 3091
J cast lots for them in Shiloh ... Josh 18:10 3091
there *J* divided the land unto the ... Josh 18:10 3091
to *J* the son of Nun among them ... Josh 19:49 3091
J the son of Nun, and the heads of ... Josh 19:51 3091
The LORD also spake unto *J* ... Josh 20:1 3091
unto *J* the son of Nun, and unto ... Josh 21:1 3091
Then *J* called the Reubenites, and ... Josh 22:1 3091
So *J* blessed them, and sent them ... Josh 22:6 3091
the other half thereof gave *J* ... Josh 22:7 3091
when *J* sent them away also unto ... Josh 22:7 3091
that *J* waxed old and stricken in ... Josh 23:1 3091
J called for all Israel, and for ... Josh 23:2 3091
J gathered all the tribes of ... Josh 24:1 3091
J said unto all the people, Thus ... Josh 24:2 3091
J said unto the people, Ye cannot ... Josh 24:19 3091
And the people said unto *J* ... Josh 24:21 3091
J said unto the people, Ye are ... Josh 24:22 3091
And the people said unto *J* ... Josh 24:24 3091
So *J* made a covenant with the ... Josh 24:25 3091
J wrote these words in the book ... Josh 24:26 3091
J said unto all the people, ... Josh 24:27 3091
So *J* let the people depart, every ... Josh 24:28 3091
that *J* the son of Nun, the ... Josh 24:29 3091
served the LORD all the days of *J* ... Josh 24:31 3091
of the elders that overlived *J* ... Josh 24:31 3091
the death of *J* it came to pass ... Judg 1:1 3091
when *J* had let the people go, the ... Judg 2:6 3091
served the LORD all the days of *J* ... Judg 2:7 3091
of the elders that outlived *J* ... Judg 2:7 3091
J the son of Nun, the servant of ... Judg 2:8 3091

nations which J left when he died .... Judg 2:21 3091
he them into the hand of J .... Judg 2:23 3091
he spake by J the son of Nun 1Kin 16:34 3091
2. A Bethshemite.
the cart came into the field of J 1Sa 6:14 3091
unto this day in the field of J 1Sa 6:18 3091
3. A governor of Jerusalem.
of J the governor of the city 2Kin 23:8 3091
4. A High Priest.
to J the son of Josedech, the .... Hag 1:1 3091
J the son of Josedech, the high .... Hag 1:12 3091
the spirit of J the son of .... Hag 1:14 3091
to J the son of Josedech, the .... Hag 2:2 3091
and be strong, O J, son of .... Hag 2:4 3091
he shewed me J the high priest .... Zec 3:1 3091
Now J was clothed with filthy .... Zec 3:3 3091
of the LORD protested unto J .... Zec 3:6 3091
O J the high priest, thou, and thy .... Zec 3:8 3091
stone that I have laid before J .... Zec 3:9 3091
the head of J the son of Josedech .... Zec 6:11 3091

JOSIAH *(jo-si'-ah)* {53} See JOSIAS.
1. A king of Judah.
the house of David, J by name 1Kin 13:2 2977
made J his son king in his stead 2Kin 21:24 2977
J his son reigned in his stead 2Kin 21:26 2977
J was eight years old when he 2Kin 22:1 2977
in the eighteenth year of king J 2Kin 22:3 2977
as J turned himself, he spied the 2Kin 23:16 2977
J took away, and did to them 2Kin 23:19 2977
in the eighteenth year of king J 2Kin 23:23 2977
did J put away, that he might 2Kin 23:24 2977
Now the rest of the acts of J 2Kin 23:28 2977
and king J went against him 2Kin 23:29 2977
land took Jehoahaz the son of J 2Kin 23:30 2977
made Eliakim the son of J king in 2Kin 23:34 2977
king in the room of J his father 2Kin 23:34 2977
Amon his son, J his son 1Chr 3:14 2977
And the sons of J were, the 1Chr 3:15 2977
made J his son king in his stead 2Chr 33:25 2977
J was eight years old when he 2Chr 34:1 2977
J took away all the abominations 2Chr 34:33 2977
Moreover J kept a passover unto 2Chr 35:1 2977
J gave to the people, of the 2Chr 35:7 2977
to the commandment of king J 2Chr 35:16 2977
keep such a passover as J kept 2Chr 35:18 2977
reign of J was this passover kept 2Chr 35:19 2977
when J had prepared the temple, ... 2Chr 35:20 2977
and J went out against him 2Chr 35:20 2977
Nevertheless J would not turn his 2Chr 35:22 2977
And the archers shot at king J 2Chr 35:23 2977
Judah and Jerusalem mourned for J 2Chr 35:24 2977
And Jeremiah lamented for J 2Chr 35:25 2977
the singing women spake of J in 2Chr 35:25 2977
Now the rest of the acts of J 2Chr 35:26 2977
land took Jehoahaz the son of J 2Chr 36:1 2977
J the son of Amon king of Judah .... Jer 1:2 2977
the son of J king of Judah .... Jer 1:3 2977
the son of J king of Judah .... Jer 1:3 2977
unto me in the days of J the king .... Jer 3:6 2977
the son of J king of Judah .... Jer 22:11 2977
reigned instead of J his father .... Jer 22:11 2977
the son of J king of Judah .... Jer 22:18 2977
the son of J king of Judah .... Jer 25:1 2977
From the thirteenth year of J the .... Jer 25:3 2977
of J king of Judah came this word .... Jer 26:1 2977
of J king of Judah came this word .... Jer 27:1 2977
the son of J king of Judah .... Jer 35:1 2977
the son of J king of Judah .... Jer 36:1 2977
unto thee, from the days of J .... Jer 36:2 2977
the son of J king of Judah .... Jer 36:9 2977
king Zedekiah the son of J .... Jer 37:1 2977
the son of J king of Judah .... Jer 45:1 2977
the son of J king of Judah .... Jer 46:2 2977
in the days of J the son of Amon, ... Zeph 1:1 2977
2. A son of Zephaniah.
house of J the son of Zephaniah .... Zec 6:10 2977

JOSIAS *(jo-si'-as)* {2} See JOSIAH. *Son of Amon; ancestor of Jesus.*
and Amon begat J .... Mt 1:10 *2502*
J begat Jechonias and his brethren .... Mt 1:11 *2502*

JOSIBIAH *(jos-ib-i'-ah)* {1} *A Simeonite.*
And Joel, and Jehu the son of J 1Chr 4:35 3143

JOSIPHIAH *(jos-if-i'-ah)* {1} *A family of exiles.*
the son of J, and with him an .... Ezr 8:10 3131

JOT {1}
one j or one tittle shall in no .... Mt 5:18 *2503*

JOTBAH *(jot'-bah)* {1} *A place near Hebron.*
the daughter of Haruz of J 2Kin 21:19 3192

JOTBATH *(jot'-bath)* {1} See JOTBATHAH. *An encampment during the Exodus.*
and from Gudgodah to J, a land of .... Deut 10:7 3193

JOTBATHAH *(jot'-ba-thah)* {2} See JOTBATH. *Same as Jotbath.*
Hor-hagidgad, and pitched in J .... Num 33:33 3193
And they removed from J, and .... Num 33:34 3193

JOTHAM *(jo'-tham)* {24} See JOATHAM.
1. A son of Gideon.
notwithstanding yet J the .... Judg 9:5 3147
And when they told it to J .... Judg 9:7 3147
J ran away, and fled, and went to .... Judg 9:21 3147
curse of J the son of Jerubbaal .... Judg 9:57 3147
2. Father of King Ahaz.
J the king's son was over the 2Kin 15:5 3147
J his son reigned in his stead 2Kin 15:7 3147
year of J the son of Uzziah 2Kin 15:30 3147
Remaliah king of Israel began J 2Kin 15:32 3147
Now the rest of the acts of J 2Kin 15:36 3147
J slept with his fathers, and was 2Kin 15:38 3147
of J king of Judah began to reign 2Kin 16:1 3147
son, Azariah his son, J his son, ... 1Chr 3:12 3147
in the days of J king of Judah 1Chr 5:17 3147
J his son was over the king's 2Chr 26:21 3147
J his son reigned in his stead 2Chr 26:23 3147
J was twenty and five years old 2Chr 27:1 3147
So J became mighty, because he 2Chr 27:6 3147
Now the rest of the acts of J 2Chr 27:7 3147
J slept with his fathers, and they 2Chr 27:9 3147
in the days of Uzziah, J, Ahaz, ... Is 1:1 3147
in the days of Ahaz the son of J .... Is 7:1 3147
Beeri, in the days of Uzziah, J .... Hos 1:1 3147
the Morasthite in the days of J .... Mic 1:1 3147
3. A descendant of Caleb.
Regem, and J, and Gesham, and Pelet, ... 1Chr 2:47 3147

JOURNEY {60}
had made his j prosperous or not .... Gen 24:21 1870
Jacob went on his j, and came .... Gen 29:1 5575,7272
set three days' j betwixt himself .... Gen 30:36 1870
pursued after him seven days' j .... Gen 31:23 1870
And he said, Let us take our j .... Gen 33:12 5265
Israel took his j with all that .... Gen 46:1 5265
three days' j into the wilderness .... Ex 3:18 1870
three days' j into the desert, and .... Ex 5:3 1870
three days' j into the wilderness .... Ex 8:27 1870
And they took their j from Succoth .... Ex 13:20 5265
And they took their j from Elim .... Ex 16:1 5265
dead body, or be in a j afar off .... Num 9:10 1870
that is clean, and is not in a j .... Num 9:13 1870
the south side shall take their j .... Num 10:6 5265
they first took their j according .... Num 10:13 5265
mount of the LORD three days' j .... Num 10:33 1870
before them in the three days' j .... Num 10:33 1870
as it were a day's j on this side .... Num 11:31 1870
were a day's j on the other side .... Num 11:31 1870
went three days' j in the .... Num 33:8 1870
they took their j out of the .... Num 33:12 5265
(There are eleven days' j from .... Deut 1:2
Turn you, and take your j, and go .... Deut 1:7 5265
take your j into the wilderness .... Deut 1:40 5265
took our j into the wilderness by .... Deut 2:1 5265
Rise ye up, take your j, and pass .... Deut 2:24 5265
children of Israel took their j .... Deut 10:6 5265
take thy j before the people, ... Deut 10:11 4550
Take victuals with you for the j .... Josh 9:11 1870
old by reason of the very long j .... Josh 9:13 1870
notwithstanding the j that thou .... Judg 4:9 1870
And the LORD sent thee on a j 1Sa 15:18 1870
Uriah, Camest thou not from thy j 2Sa 11:10 1870
he is pursuing, or he is in a j 1Kin 18:27 1870
a day's j into the wilderness 1Kin 19:4 1870
because the j is too great for 1Kin 19:7 1870
a compass of seven days' j 2Kin 3:9 1870
Then Solomon came from his j to 2Chr 1:13
him,) For how long shall thy j be .... Neh 2:6 4109
not at home, he is gone a long j .... Prov 7:19 1870
great city of three days' j .... Jonah 3:3 4109
to enter into the city a day's j .... Jonah 3:4 4109
Nor scrip for your j, neither two .... Mt 10:10 *3598*
and straightway took his j .... Mt 25:15 *589*
should take nothing for their j .... Mk 6:8 *3598*
of man is as a man taking a far j .... Mk 13:34 *590*
in the company, went a day's j .... Lk 2:44 *3598*
them, Take nothing for your j .... Lk 9:3 *3598*
of mine in his j is come to me .... Lk 11:6 *3598*
took his j into a far country, and .... Lk 15:13 *589*
being wearied with his j .... Jn 4:6 *3597*
from Jerusalem a sabbath day's j .... Acts 1:12 *3598*
morrow, as they went on their j .... Acts 10:9 *3596*
to pass, that, as I made my j .... Acts 22:6 *4198*
I might have a prosperous j by .... Rom 1:10 *2137*
Whensoever I take my j into Spain .... Rom 15:24 *4198*
for I trust to see you in my j .... Rom 15:24 *1279*
me on my j whithersoever I go 1Cor 16:6
and Apollos on their j diligently .... Titus 3:13
on their j after a godly sort 3Jn 6

JOURNEYED {33}
as they j from the east, that .... Gen 11:2 5265
And Abram j, going on still toward .... Gen 12:9 5265
and Lot j east .... Gen 13:11 5265
Abraham j from thence toward the .... Gen 20:1 5265
Jacob j to Succoth, and built him .... Gen 33:17 5265
And they j: and the terror .... Gen 35:5 5265
And they j from Beth-el .... Gen 35:16 5265
And Israel j, and spread his tent .... Gen 35:21 5265
the children of Israel j from .... Ex 12:37 5265
of the children of Israel j from .... Ex 17:1 5265
then they j not till the day that .... Ex 40:37 5265
that the children of Israel j .... Num 9:17 5265
the LORD the children of Israel j .... Num 9:18 5265
the charge of the LORD, and j not .... Num 9:19 5265
commandment of the LORD they j .... Num 9:20 5265
up in the morning, then they j .... Num 9:21 5265
the cloud was taken up, they j .... Num 9:21 5265
abode in their tents, and j not .... Num 9:22 5265
but when it was taken up, they j .... Num 9:22 5265
commandment of the LORD they j .... Num 9:23 5265
And the people j from .... Num 11:35 5265
the people j not till Miriam was .... Num 12:15 5265
j from Kadesh, and came unto mount .... Num 20:22 5265
they j from mount Hor by the way .... Num 21:4 5265
they j from Oboth, and pitched at .... Num 21:11 5265
they j from Rissah, and pitched in .... Num 33:22 5265
From thence they j unto Gudgodah .... Deut 10:7 5265
And the children of Israel j .... Josh 9:17 5265
to the house of Micah, as he j .... Judg 17:8 6213,1870
But a certain Samaritan, as he j .... Lk 10:33 *3593*
And as he j, he came near Damascus .... Acts 9:3 *4198*
the men which j with him stood .... Acts 9:7 *4922*
about me and them which j with me .... Acts 26:13 *4198*

JOURNEYING {3}
and for the j of the camps .... Num 10:2 4550
We are j unto the place of which .... Num 10:29 5265
teaching, and j toward Jerusalem .... Lk 13:22 *4197,4160*

JOURNEYINGS {2}
Thus were the j of the children .... Num 10:28 4550
In j often, in perils of waters, ... 2Cor 11:26 *3597*

JOURNEYS {9}
he went on his j from the south .... Gen 13:3 4550
wilderness of Sin, after their j .... Ex 17:1 4550
Israel went onward in all their j .... Ex 40:36 4550
of Israel, throughout all their j .... Ex 40:38 4550
shall blow an alarm for their j .... Num 10:6 4550
children of Israel took their j .... Num 10:12 4550
These are the j of the children .... Num 33:1 4550
goings out according to their j .... Num 33:2 4550
these are their j according to .... Num 33:2 4550

JOY {169}
king Saul, with tabrets, with j 1Sa 18:6 8057
pipes, and rejoiced with great j 1Kin 1:40 8057
for there was j in Israel 1Chr 12:40 8057
by lifting up the voice with j 1Chr 15:16 8057
of the house of Obed-edom with j 1Chr 15:25 8057
king also rejoiced with great j 1Chr 29:9 8057
now have I seen with j thy people 1Chr 29:17 8057
to go again to Jerusalem with j 2Chr 20:27 8057
So there was great j in Jerusalem 2Chr 30:26 8057
and many shouted aloud for j .... Ezr 3:12 8057
the noise of the shout of j from .... Ezr 3:13 8057
of this house of God with j .... Ezr 6:16 2305
bread seven days with j .... Ezr 6:22 8057
for the j of the LORD is your .... Neh 8:10 2304
made them rejoice with great j .... Neh 12:43 8057
so that the j of Jerusalem was .... Neh 12:43 8057
Jews had light, and gladness, and j .... Est 8:16 8342
his decree came, the Jews had j .... Est 8:17 8057
turned unto them from sorrow to j .... Est 9:22 8057
make them days of feasting and j .... Est 9:22 8057
Behold, this is the j of his way .... Job 8:19 4885
the j of the hypocrite but for a .... Job 20:5 8057
the widow's heart to sing for j .... Job 29:13 7442
and he shall see his face with j .... Job 33:26 8643
all the sons of God shouted for j .... Job 38:7
is turned into j before him .... Job 41:22
let them ever shout for j .... Ps 5:11
in thy presence is fulness of j .... Ps 16:11 8057
The king shall j in thy strength, ... Ps 21:1 8055
in his tabernacle sacrifices of j .... Ps 27:6 8643
but j cometh in the morning .... Ps 30:5 7440
and shout for j, all ye that are .... Ps 32:11
Let them shout for j, and be glad, ... Ps 35:27
house of God, with the voice of j .... Ps 42:4 7440
of God, unto God my exceeding j .... Ps 43:4 1524
the j of the whole earth, is .... Ps 48:2 4885
Make me to hear j and gladness .... Ps 51:8 8342
unto me the j of thy salvation .... Ps 51:12 8342
they shout for j, they also sing .... Ps 65:13
the nations be glad and sing for j .... Ps 67:4
brought forth his people with j .... Ps 105:43 8342
that sow in tears shall reap in j .... Ps 126:5 7440
and let thy saints shout for j .... Ps 132:9 7442
saints shall shout aloud for j .... Ps 132:16 7442
not Jerusalem above my chief j .... Ps 137:6 8057
to the counsellors of peace is j .... Prov 12:20 8057
doth not intermeddle with his j .... Prov 14:10 8057
Folly is j to him that is .... Prov 15:21 8057
A man hath j by the answer of his .... Prov 15:23 8057
and the father of a fool hath no j .... Prov 17:21 8056
It is j to the just to do .... Prov 21:15 8057
a wise child shall have j of him .... Prov 23:24 8056
withheld not my heart from any j .... Eccl 2:10 8057
sight wisdom, and knowledge, and j .... Eccl 2:26 8057
him in the j of his heart .... Eccl 5:20 8057
Go thy way, eat thy bread with j .... Eccl 9:7 8057
nation, and not increased the j .... Is 9:3 8057
they j before thee according to .... Is 9:3 8055
according to the j in harvest .... Is 9:3 8057
have no j in their young men .... Is 9:17 8055
Therefore with j shall ye draw .... Is 12:3 8342
j out of the plentiful field .... Is 16:10 1524
And behold j and gladness, slaying .... Is 22:13 8342
the j of the harp ceaseth .... Is 24:8 4885
all j is darkened, the mirth of .... Is 24:11 8057
increase their j in the LORD .... Is 29:19 8057
houses of j in the joyous city .... Is 32:13 4885
a j of wild asses, a pasture of .... Is 32:14 4885
and rejoice even with j and .... Is 35:2 1525
everlasting j upon their heads .... Is 35:10 8057
they shall obtain j and gladness, ... Is 35:10 8057
j and gladness shall be found .... Is 51:3 8342
everlasting j shall be upon their .... Is 51:11 8057
they shall obtain gladness and j .... Is 51:11 8057
Break forth into j, sing together .... Is 52:9
For ye shall go out with j .... Is 55:12 8057
a j of many generations .... Is 60:15 4885
the oil of j for mourning, the .... Is 61:3 8342
everlasting j shall be unto them .... Is 61:7 8057
shall sing for j of heart .... Is 65:14 2898
a rejoicing, and her people a j .... Is 65:18 4885
in Jerusalem, and j in my people .... Is 65:19 7796

but he shall appear to your *j* ... Is 66:5 8057
rejoice for *j* with her, all ye ... Is 66:10 4885
and thy word was unto me the *j* ... Jer 15:16 8342
I will turn their mourning into *j* ... Jer 31:13 8342
And it shall be to me a name of *j* ... Jer 33:9 8342
The voice of *j*, and the voice of ... Jer 33:11 8342
of him, thou skippedst for *j* ... Jer 48:27
And *j* and gladness is taken from ... Jer 48:33 8057
praise not left, the city of my *j* ... Jer 49:25 4885
beauty, The *j* of the whole earth ... Lam 2:15 4885
The *j* of our heart is ceased ... Lam 5:15 4885
the *j* of their glory, the desire ... Eze 24:25 4885
with the *j* of all their heart ... Eze 36:5 8057
Rejoice not, O Israel, for *j* ... Hos 9:1 1524
because *j* is withered away from ... Joel 1:12 8342
cut off before our eyes, yea, *j* ... Joel 1:16 8057
I will *j* in the God of my ... Hab 3:18 1523
he will rejoice over thee with *j* ... Zeph 3:17 8057
he will *j* over thee with singing ... Zeph 3:17 1523
shall be to the house of Judah *j* ... Zec 8:19 8342
rejoiced with exceeding great *j* ... Mt 2:10 *5479*
word, and anon with *j* receiveth it ... Mt 13:20 *5479*
for *j* thereof goeth and selleth ... Mt 13:44 *5479*
enter thou into the *j* of thy lord ... Mt 25:21 *5479*
enter thou into the *j* of thy lord ... Mt 25:23 *5479*
sepulchre with fear and great *j* ... Mt 28:8 *5479*
And thou shalt have *j* and gladness ... Lk 1:14 *5479*
the babe leaped in my womb for *j* ... Lk 1:44 *20*
bring you good tidings of great *j* ... Lk 2:10 *5479*
ye in that day, and leap for *j* ... Lk 6:23
hear, receive the word with *j* ... Lk 8:13 *5479*
the seventy returned again with *j* ... Lk 10:17 *5479*
that likewise *j* shall be in ... Lk 15:7 *5479*
there is *j* in the presence of the ... Lk 15:10 *5479*
while they yet believed not for *j* ... Lk 24:41 *5479*
to Jerusalem with great *j* ... Lk 24:52 *5479*
this my *j* therefore is fulfilled ... Jn 3:29 *5479*
that my *j* might remain in you, and ... Jn 15:11 *5479*
that your *j* might be full ... Jn 15:11 *5479*
sorrow shall be turned into *j* ... Jn 16:20 *5479*
for *j* that a man is born into the ... Jn 16:21 *5479*
your *j* no man taketh from you ... Jn 16:22 *5479*
receive, that your *j* may be full ... Jn 16:24 *5479*
have my *j* fulfilled in themselves ... Jn 17:13 *5479*
me full of *j* with thy countenance ... Acts 2:28 *2167*
And there was great *j* in that city ... Acts 8:8 *5479*
the disciples were filled with *j* ... Acts 13:52 *5479*
they caused great *j* unto all the ... Acts 15:3 *5479*
I might finish my course with *j* ... Acts 20:24 *5479*
but we also *j* in God through our ... Rom 5:11 *2744*
and peace, and *j* in the Holy Ghost ... Rom 14:17 *5479*
God of hope fill you with all *j* ... Rom 15:13 *5479*
you with *j* by the will of God ... Rom 15:32 *5479*
faith, but are helpers of your *j* ... 2Cor 1:24 *5479*
that my *j* is the *j* of you all ... 2Cor 2:3 *5479*
that my *j* is the *j* of you all ... 2Cor 2:3
more joyed we for the *j* of Titus ... 2Cor 7:13 *5479*
the abundance of their *j* and their ... 2Cor 8:2 *5479*
fruit of the Spirit is love, *j* ... Gal 5:22 *5479*
for you all making request with *j* ... Phil 1:4 *5479*
your furtherance and *j* of faith ... Phil 1:25 *5479*
Fulfil ye my *j*, that ye be ... Phil 2:2 *5479*
and service of your faith, I *j* ... Phil 2:17 *5468*
For the same cause also do ye *j* ... Phil 2:18 *5468*
beloved and longed for, my *j* ... Phil 4:1 *5479*
with *j* of the Holy Ghost ... 1Th 1:6 *5479*
For what is our hope, or *j* ... 1Th 2:19 *5479*
For ye are our glory and *j* ... 1Th 2:20 *5479*
for all the *j* wherewith we *j* ... 1Th 3:9 *5479*
for all the *j* wherewith we *j* ... 1Th 3:9 *5468*
that I may be filled with *j* ... 2Ti 1:4 *5479*
For we have great *j* and ... Philem 7 *5485*
let me have *j* of thee in the Lord ... Philem 20 *3685*
who for the *j* that was set before ... Heb 12:2 *5479*
that they may do it with *j* ... Heb 13:17 *5479*
count it all *j* when ye fall into ... Jas 1:2 *5479*
mourning, and your *j* to heaviness ... Jas 4:9 *5479*
ye rejoice with *j* unspeakable ... 1Pet 1:8 *5479*
may be glad also with exceeding *j* ... 1Pet 4:13 *21*
unto you, that your *j* may be full ... 1Jn 1:4 *5479*
to face, that our *j* may be full ... 2Jn 12 *5479*
I have no greater *j* than to hear ... 3Jn 4 *5479*
of his glory with exceeding *j* ... Jude 24 *20*

JOYED {1}
exceedingly the more *j* we for the ... 2Cor 7:13 *5463*

JOYFUL {25}
king, and went unto their tents *j* ... 1Kin 8:66 8056
for the LORD had made them *j* ... Ezr 6:22 8055
Then went Haman forth that day *j* ... Est 5:9 8056
let no *j* voice come therein ... Job 3:7 7445
that love thy name be *j* in thee ... Ps 5:11 5970
And my soul shall be *j* in the LORD ... Ps 35:9 1523
shall praise thee with *j* lips ... Ps 63:5 7445
Make a *j* noise unto God, all ye ... Ps 66:1
make a *j* noise unto the God of ... Ps 81:1
the people that know the *j* sound ... Ps 89:15 8643
let us make a *j* noise to the rock ... Ps 95:1
make a *j* noise unto him with ... Ps 95:2
Let the field be *j*, and all that ... Ps 96:12 5937
Make a *j* noise unto the LORD, all ... Ps 98:4
make a *j* noise before the LORD ... Ps 98:6
let the hills be *j* together ... Ps 98:8 7442
Make a *j* noise unto the LORD, all ... Ps 100:1
to be a *j* mother of children ... Ps 113:9 8056
of Zion be *j* in their King ... Ps 149:2 1523
Let the saints be *j* in glory ... Ps 149:5 5937
In the day of prosperity be *j* ... Eccl 7:14 2896
and be *j*, O earth ... Is 49:13 1523
make them *j* in my house of prayer ... Is 56:7 8055
my soul shall be *j* in my God ... Is 61:10 1523
I am exceeding *j* in all our ... 2Cor 7:4 *5479*

JOYFULLY {3}
Live *j* with the wife whom thou ... Eccl 9:9 2416
and came down, and received him *j* ... Lk 19:6 *5463*
took *j* the spoiling of your goods ... Heb 10:34 *3326,5479*

JOYFULNESS {2}
not the LORD thy God with *j* ... Deut 28:47 8057
patience and longsuffering with *j* ... Col 1:11 *5479*

JOYING {1}
am I with you in the spirit, *j* ... Col 2:5 *5463*

JOYOUS {4}
a tumultuous city, a *j* city ... Is 22:2 5947
Is this your *j* city, whose ... Is 23:7 5947
the houses of joy in the *j* city ... Is 32:13 5947
for the present seemeth to be *j* ... Heb 12:11 *5479*

JOZABAD *(joz'-a-bad)* {9}
1. Another warrior in David's army.
to him of Manasseh, Adnah, and *J* ... 1Chr 12:20 3107
and Jediael, and Michael, and *J* ... 1Chr 12:20 3107
2. A Chief Levite in Josiah's time.
and Asahel, and Jerimoth, and *J* ... 2Chr 31:13 3107
3. An exile with Ezra.
and Hashabiah and Jeiel and *J* ... 2Chr 35:9 3107
4. A priest.
with them was *J* the son of Jeshua ... Ezr 8:33 3107
5. A Levite.
Maaseiah, Ishmael, Nethaneel, *J* ... Ezr 10:22 3107
6. A priest who helped Ezra.
J, and Shimei, and Kelaiah, (the ... Ezr 10:23 3107
7. A chief Levite in exile.
Maaseiah, Kelita, Azariah, *J* ... Neh 8:7 3107
8. A chief Levite in exile.
And Shabbethai and *J*, of the chief ... Neh 11:16 3107

JOZACHAR *(joz'-a-kar)* {1} See ZABAD. *Son of Shimeath.*
For *J* the son of Shimeath, and ... 2Kin 12:21 3108

JOZADAK *(joz'-a-dak)* {5} See JEHOZADAK, JOSEDECH. *A priest with Zerubbabel.*
Then stood up Jeshua the son of *J* ... Ezr 3:2 3136
Shealtiel, and Jeshua the son of *J* ... Ezr 3:8 3136
Shealtiel, and Jeshua the son of *J* ... Ezr 5:2 3136
the sons of Jeshua the son of *J* ... Ezr 10:18 3136
the son of Jeshua, the son of *J* ... Neh 12:26 3136

JUBAL *(ju'-bal)* {1} *Son of Adah.*
And his brother's name was *J* ... Gen 4:21 3106

JUBILE {22}
j to sound on the tenth day of ... Lev 25:9 8643
it shall be a *j* unto you ... Lev 25:10 3104
A *j* shall that fiftieth year be ... Lev 25:11 3104
For it is the *j* ... Lev 25:12 3104
In the year of this *j* ye shall ... Lev 25:13 3104
the number of years after the *j* ... Lev 25:15 3104
bought it until the year of *j* ... Lev 25:28 3104
in the *j* it shall go out, and he ... Lev 25:28 3104
it shall not go out in the *j* ... Lev 25:30 3104
and they shall go out in the *j* ... Lev 25:31 3104
shall go out in the year of *j* ... Lev 25:33 3104
serve thee unto the year of *j* ... Lev 25:40 3104
sold to him unto the year of *j* ... Lev 25:50 3104
but few years unto the year of *j* ... Lev 25:52 3104
he shall go out in the year of *j* ... Lev 25:54 3104
his field from the year of *j* ... Lev 27:17 3104
he sanctify his field after the *j* ... Lev 27:18 3104
even unto the year of the *j* ... Lev 27:18 3104
field, when it goeth out in the *j* ... Lev 27:21 3104
even unto the year of the *j* ... Lev 27:23 3104
In the year of the *j* the field ... Lev 27:24 3104
when the *j* of the children of ... Num 36:4 3104

JUCAL *(ju'-kal)* {1} See JEHUCAL. *An enemy of Jeremiah.*
J the son of Shelemiah, and Pashur ... Jer 38:1 3116

JUDA *(ju'-dah)* {8} See JUDAH.
1. Greek form of Judah, the tribe.
thou Bethlehem, in the land of *J* ... Mt 2:6 *2455*
the least among the princes of *J* ... Mt 2:6 *2455*
with haste, into a city of *J* ... Lk 1:39 *2448*
that our Lord sprang out of *J* ... Heb 7:14 *2455*
the Lion of the tribe of *J* ... Rev 5:5 *2455*
Of the tribe of *J* were sealed ... Rev 7:5 *2455*
2. A brother of Jesus.
of James, and Joses, and of *J* ... Mk 6:3 *2455*
3. An ancestor of Jesus.
of Joseph, which was the son of *J* ... Lk 3:26 *2455*
of Phares, which was the son of *J* ... Lk 3:33 *2455*

JUDAEA {43} *A Roman province.*
J in the days of Herod the king ... Mt 2:1 *2449*
said unto him, In Bethlehem of *J* ... Mt 2:5 *2449*
that Archelaus did reign in *J* in ... Mt 2:22 *2499*
preaching in the wilderness of *J* ... Mt 3:1 *2449*
out to him Jerusalem, and all *J* ... Mt 3:5 *2449*
and from Jerusalem, and from *J* ... Mt 4:25 *2449*
the coasts of *J* beyond Jordan ... Mt 19:1 *2449*
be in *J* flee into the mountains ... Mt 24:16 *2449*
out unto him all the land of *J* ... Mk 1:5 *2449*
Galilee followed him, and from *J* ... Mk 3:7 *2449*
cometh into the coasts of *J* by ... Mk 10:1 *2449*
be in *J* flee to the mountains ... Mk 13:14 *2449*
the days of Herod, the king of *J* ... Lk 1:5 *2449*
all the hill country of *J* ... Lk 1:65 *2449*
of the city of Nazareth, into *J* ... Lk 2:4 *2449*
Pilate being governor of *J* ... Lk 3:1 *2449*
of every town of Galilee, and *J* ... Lk 5:17 *2449*
multitude of people out of all *J* ... Lk 6:17 *2449*
him went forth throughout all *J* ... Lk 7:17 *2449*
are in *J* flee to the mountains ... Lk 21:21 *2449*
his disciples into the land of *J* ... Jn 3:22 *2449*
He left *J*, and departed again into ... Jn 4:3 *2449*
was come out of *J* into Galilee ... Jn 4:47 *2449*
he was come out of *J* into Galilee ... Jn 4:54 *2449*
him, Depart hence, and go into *J* ... Jn 7:3 *2449*
disciples, Let us go into *J* again ... Jn 11:7 *2449*
me both in Jerusalem, and in all *J* ... Acts 1:8 *2449*
dwellers in Mesopotamia, and in *J* ... Acts 2:9 *2449*
and said unto them, Ye men of *J* ... Acts 2:14 *2453*
throughout the regions of *J* ... Acts 8:1 *2449*
churches rest throughout all *J* ... Acts 9:31 *2449*
was published throughout all *J* ... Acts 10:37 *2449*
brethren that were in *J* heard ... Acts 11:1 *2449*
the brethren which dwelt in *J* ... Acts 11:29 *2449*
he went down from *J* to Caesarea ... Acts 12:19 *2449*
down from *J* taught the brethren ... Acts 15:1 *2449*
down from *J* a certain prophet ... Acts 21:10 *2449*
and throughout all the coasts of *J* ... Acts 26:20 *2449*
letters out of *J* concerning thee ... Acts 28:21 *2449*
them that do not believe in *J* ... Rom 15:31 *2449*
to be brought on my way toward *J* ... 2Cor 1:16 *2449*
of *J* which were in Christ ... Gal 1:22 *2449*
which in *J* are in Christ Jesus ... 1Th 2:14 *2449*

JUDAH *(ju'-dah)* {813} See BETHLEHEM-JUDAH, JUDA, JUDAH'S, JUDAS, JUDEA, JUDE.
1. Son of Jacob and Leah.
therefore she called his name *J* ... Gen 29:35 3063
and Simeon, and Levi, and *J* ... Gen 35:23 3063
J said unto his brethren, What ... Gen 37:26 3063
that *J* went down from his ... Gen 38:1 3063
J saw there a daughter of a ... Gen 38:2 3063
And *J* took a wife for Er his ... Gen 38:6 3063
J said unto Onan, Go in unto thy ... Gen 38:8 3063
Then said *J* to Tamar his daughter ... Gen 38:11 3063
J was comforted, and went up unto ... Gen 38:12 3063
When *J* saw her, he thought her to ... Gen 38:15 3063
J sent the kid by the hand of his ... Gen 38:20 3063
And he returned to *J*, and said, I ... Gen 38:22 3063
J said, Let her take it to her ... Gen 38:23 3063
months after, that it was told *J* ... Gen 38:24 3063
J said, Bring her forth, and let ... Gen 38:24 3063
J acknowledged them, and said, She ... Gen 38:26 3063
J spake unto him, saying, The man ... Gen 43:3 3063
J said unto Israel his father ... Gen 43:8 3063
And *J* and his brethren came to ... Gen 44:14 3063
J said, What shall we say unto my ... Gen 44:16 3063
Then *J* came near unto him, and ... Gen 44:18 3063
And the sons of *J* ... Gen 46:12 3063
he sent *J* before him unto Joseph ... Gen 46:28 3063
J, thou art he whom thy brethren ... Gen 49:8 3063
J is a lion's whelp ... Gen 49:9 3063
Reuben, Simeon, Levi, and *J* ... Ex 1:2 3063
The sons of *J* were Er and Onan ... Num 26:19 3063
of Pharez, whom Tamar bare unto *J* ... Ruth 4:12 3063
Reuben, Simeon, Levi, and *J* ... 1Chr 2:1 3063
The sons of *J*; Er, and ... 1Chr 2:3 3063
And Er, the firstborn of *J* ... 1Chr 2:3 3063
All the sons of *J* were five ... 1Chr 2:4 3063
prince of the children of *J* ... 1Chr 2:10 3063
The sons of *J*; Pharez ... 1Chr 4:1 3063
sons of Shelah the son of *J* were ... 1Chr 4:21 3063
like to the children of *J* ... 1Chr 4:27 3063
For *J* prevailed above his ... 1Chr 5:2 3063
children of Pharez the son of *J* ... 1Chr 9:4 3063
children of Zerah the son of *J* ... Neh 11:24 3063
2. The tribe and its land.
sceptre shall not depart from *J* ... Gen 49:10 3063
the son of Hur, of the tribe of *J* ... Ex 31:2 3063
the son of Hur, of the tribe of *J* ... Ex 35:30 3063
the son of Hur, of the tribe of *J* ... Ex 38:22 3063
Of *J*; Nashon the son ... Num 1:7 3063
Of the children of *J*, by their ... Num 1:26 3063
of them, even of the tribe of *J* ... Num 1:27 3063
J pitch throughout their armies ... Num 2:3 3063
be captain of the children of *J* ... Num 2:3 3063
of *J* were an hundred thousand ... Num 2:9 3063
of Amminadab, of the tribe of *J* ... Num 7:12 3063
of *J* according to their armies ... Num 10:14 3063
Of the tribe of *J*, Caleb the son ... Num 13:6 3063
the sons of *J* after their ... Num 26:20 3063
These are the families of *J* ... Num 26:22 3063
Of the tribe of *J*, Caleb the son ... Num 34:19 3063
Simeon, and Levi, and *J*, and ... Deut 27:12 3063
And this is the blessing of *J* ... Deut 33:7 3063
said, Hear, LORD, the voice of *J* ... Deut 33:7 3063
and Manasseh, and all the land of *J* ... Deut 34:2 3063
son of Zerah, of the tribe of *J* ... Josh 7:1 3063
and the tribe of *J* was taken ... Josh 7:16 3063
And he brought the family of *J* ... Josh 7:17 3063
son of Zerah, of the tribe of *J* ... Josh 7:18 3063
and from all the mountains of *J* ... Josh 11:21 3063
Then the children of *J* came unto ... Josh 14:6 3063
children of *J* by their families ... Josh 15:1 3063
J round about according to their ... Josh 15:12 3063
a part among the children of *J* ... Josh 15:13 3063
of *J* according to their families ... Josh 15:20 3063
of *J* toward the coast of Edom ... Josh 15:21 3063
the children of *J* could not drive ... Josh 15:63 3063
of *J* at Jerusalem unto this day ... Josh 15:63 3063
J shall abide in their coast on ... Josh 18:5 3063
forth between the children of *J* ... Josh 18:11 3063
a city of the children of *J* ... Josh 18:14 3063
inheritance of the children of *J* ... Josh 19:1 3063

of *J* was the inheritance of the	Josh 19:9	3063
of *J* was too much for them	Josh 19:9	3063
to *J* upon Jordan toward the	Josh 19:34	3063
is Hebron, in the mountain of *J*	Josh 20:7	3063
had by lot out of the tribe of *J*	Josh 21:4	3063
of the tribe of the children of *J*	Josh 21:9	3063
Hebron, in the hill country of *J*	Josh 21:11	3063
And the LORD said, *J* shall go up	Judg 1:2	3063
J said unto Simeon his brother,	Judg 1:3	3063
And *J* went up	Judg 1:4	3063
Now the children of *J* had fought	Judg 1:8	3063
afterward the children of *J* went	Judg 1:9	3063
J went against the Canaanites	Judg 1:10	3063
of *J* into the wilderness of Judah	Judg 1:16	3063
of Judah into the wilderness of *J*	Judg 1:16	3063
J went with Simeon his brother,	Judg 1:17	3063
Also *J* took Gaza with the coast	Judg 1:18	3063
And the LORD was with *J*	Judg 1:19	3063
Jordan to fight also against *J*	Judg 10:9	3063
went up, and pitched in *J*, and	Judg 15:9	3063
And the men of *J* said, Why are ye	Judg 15:10	3063
Then three thousand men of *J* went	Judg 15:11	3063
of the family of *J*, who was a	Judg 17:7	3063
pitched in Kirjath-jearim, in *J*	Judg 18:12	3063
LORD said, *J* shall go up first	Judg 20:18	3063
way to return unto the land of *J*	Ruth 1:7	3063
the men of *J* thirty thousand	1Sa 11:8	3063
footmen, and ten thousand men of *J*	1Sa 15:4	3063
at Shochoh, which belongeth to *J*	1Sa 17:1	3063
of *J* arose, and shouted, and	1Sa 17:52	3063
J loved David, because he went	1Sa 18:16	3063
and get thee into the land of *J*	1Sa 22:5	3063
Behold, we be afraid here in *J*	1Sa 23:3	3063
throughout all the thousands of *J*	1Sa 23:23	3063
unto the kings of *J* unto this day	1Sa 27:6	3063
said, Against the south of *J*	1Sa 27:10	3063
the coast which belongeth to *J*	1Sa 30:14	3063
and out of the land of *J*	1Sa 30:16	3063
of the spoil unto the elders of *J*	1Sa 30:26	3063
children of *J* the use of the bow	2Sa 1:18	3063
go up into any of the cities of *J*	2Sa 2:1	3063
And the men of *J* came, and there	2Sa 2:4	3063
David king over the house of *J*	2Sa 2:4	3063
also the house of *J* have anointed	2Sa 2:7	3063
But the house of *J* followed David	2Sa 2:10	3063
the house of *J* was seven years	2Sa 2:11	3063
which against *J* do shew kindness	2Sa 3:8	3063
of David over Israel and over *J*	2Sa 3:10	3063
he reigned over *J* seven years	2Sa 5:5	3063
three years over all Israel and *J*	2Sa 5:5	3063
were with him from Baale of *J*	2Sa 6:2	3063
David, The ark, and Israel, and *J*	2Sa 11:11	3063
thee the house of Israel and of *J*	2Sa 12:8	3063
Speak unto the elders of *J*	2Sa 19:11	3063
the heart of all the men of *J*	2Sa 19:14	3063
J came to Gilgal, to go to meet	2Sa 19:15	3063
the men of *J* to meet king David	2Sa 19:16	3063
all the people of *J* conducted the	2Sa 19:40	3063
the men of *J* stolen thee away	2Sa 19:41	3063
all the men of *J* answered the men	2Sa 19:42	3063
of Israel answered the men of *J*	2Sa 19:43	3063
the words of the men of *J* were	2Sa 19:43	3063
but the men of *J* clave unto their	2Sa 20:2	3063
me the men of *J* within three days	2Sa 20:4	3063
went to assemble the men of *J*	2Sa 20:5	3063
to the children of Israel and *J*	2Sa 21:2	3063
to say, Go, number Israel and *J*	2Sa 24:1	3063
they went out to the south of *J*	2Sa 24:7	3063
the men of *J* were five hundred	2Sa 24:9	3063
all the men of *J* the king's	1Kin 1:9	3063
to be ruler over Israel and over *J*	1Kin 1:35	3063
Jether, captain of the host of *J*	1Kin 2:32	3063
J and Israel were many, as the	1Kin 4:20	3063
And *J* and Israel dwelt safely,	1Kin 4:25	3063
gave them Hebron in the land of *J*	1Chr 6:55	3063
Aaron they gave the cities of *J*	1Chr 6:57	3063
of the tribe of the children of *J*	1Chr 6:65	3063
dwelt of the children of *J*	1Chr 9:3	3063
and *J* to the hold unto David	1Chr 12:16	3063
The children of *J* that bare	1Chr 12:24	3063
which belonged to *J*, to bring up	1Chr 13:6	3063
Of *J*, Elihu, one of the brethren	1Chr 27:18	3063
he hath chosen *J* to be the ruler	1Chr 28:4	3063
and of the house of *J*, the house	1Chr 28:4	3063
cunning men that are with me in *J*	2Chr 2:7	3063
such seen before in the land of *J*	2Chr 9:11	3063
house at Jerusalem, which is in *J*	Ezr 1:2	3063
go up to Jerusalem, which is in *J*	Ezr 1:3	3063
up the chief of the fathers of *J*	Ezr 1:5	3063
unto Sheshbazzar, the prince of *J*	Ezr 1:8	3063
the hands of the people of *J*	Ezr 4:4	3063
against the inhabitants of *J*	Ezr 4:6	3063
unto the Jews that were in *J*	Ezr 5:1	3061
to enquire concerning *J* and	Ezr 7:14	3061
and to give us a wall in *J*	Ezr 9:9	3063
made proclamation throughout *J*	Ezr 10:7	3063
Then all the men of *J* and Benjamin	Ezr 10:9	3063
came, he and certain men of *J*	Neh 1:2	3063
that thou wouldest send me unto *J*	Neh 2:5	3063
convey me over till I come into *J*	Neh 2:7	3063
J said, The strength of the	Neh 4:10	3063
were behind all the house of *J*	Neh 4:16	3063
their governor in the land of *J*	Neh 5:14	3063
saying, There is a king in *J*	Neh 6:7	3063
in those days the nobles of *J*	Neh 6:17	3063
were many in *J* sworn unto him	Neh 6:18	3063
came again to Jerusalem and to *J*	Neh 7:6	3063
but in the cities of *J* dwelt	Neh 11:3	3063
certain of the children of *J*	Neh 11:4	3063
Of the children of *J*	Neh 11:4	3063
were in all the cities of *J*	Neh 11:20	3063
of *J* dwelt at Kirjath-arba	Neh 11:25	3063
the Levites were divisions in *J*	Neh 11:36	3063
up the princes of *J* upon the wall	Neh 12:31	3063
and half of the princes of *J*	Neh 12:32	3063
for *J* rejoiced for the priests and	Neh 12:44	3063
Then brought all *J* the tithe of	Neh 13:12	3063
In those days saw I in *J* some	Neh 13:15	3063
sabbath unto the children of *J*	Neh 13:16	3063
I contended with the nobles of *J*	Neh 13:17	3063
away with Jeconiah king of *J*	Est 2:6	3063
let the daughters of *J* be glad	Ps 48:11	3063
J is my lawgiver	Ps 60:7	3063
he was in the wilderness of *J*	Ps 63:*t*	3063
their ruler, the princes of *J*	Ps 68:27	3063
and will build the cities of *J*	Ps 69:35	3063
In *J* is God known	Ps 76:1	3063
But chose the tribe of *J*, the	Ps 78:68	3063
the daughters of *J* rejoiced	Ps 97:8	3063
J is my lawgiver	Ps 108:8	3063
J was his sanctuary, and Israel	Ps 114:2	3063
of Israel and with the house of *J*	Heb 8:8	*2455*

3. The southern kingdom after the revolt of the ten northern tribes.

which dwelt in the cities of *J*	1Kin 12:17	3063
of David, but the tribe of *J* only	1Kin 12:20	3063
he assembled all the house of *J*	1Kin 12:21	3063
the son of Solomon, king of *J*	1Kin 12:23	3063
Judah, and unto all the house of *J*	1Kin 12:23	3063
even unto Rehoboam king of *J*	1Kin 12:27	3063
and go again to Rehoboam king of *J*	1Kin 12:27	3063
like unto the feast that is in *J*	1Kin 12:32	3063
of *J* by the word of the LORD unto	1Kin 13:1	3063
of God went, which came from *J*	1Kin 13:12	3063
the man of God that camest from *J*	1Kin 13:14	3063
the man of God that came from *J*	1Kin 13:21	3063
the son of Solomon reigned in *J*	1Kin 14:21	3063
J did evil in the sight of the	1Kin 14:22	3063
the chronicles of the kings of *J*	1Kin 14:29	3063
of Nebat reigned Abijam over *J*	1Kin 15:1	3063
the chronicles of the kings of *J*	1Kin 15:7	3063
king of Israel reigned Asa over *J*	1Kin 15:9	3063
king of Israel went up against *J*	1Kin 15:17	3063
out or come in to Asa king of *J*	1Kin 15:17	3063
a proclamation throughout all *J*	1Kin 15:22	3063
the chronicles of the kings of *J*	1Kin 15:23	3063
the second year of Asa king of *J*	1Kin 15:25	3063
Asa king of *J* did Baasha slay him	1Kin 15:28	3063
the third year of Asa king of *J*	1Kin 15:33	3063
sixth year of Asa king of *J* began	1Kin 16:8	3063
and seventh year of Asa king of *J*	1Kin 16:10	3063
seventh year of Asa king of *J* did	1Kin 16:15	3063
first year of Asa king of *J* began	1Kin 16:23	3063
eighth year of Asa king of *J*	1Kin 16:29	3063
Beer-sheba, which belongeth to *J*	1Kin 19:3	3063
that Jehoshaphat the king of *J*	1Kin 22:2	3063
king of *J* sat each on his throne	1Kin 22:10	3063
Jehoshaphat the king of *J* went up	1Kin 22:29	3063
son of Asa began to reign over *J*	1Kin 22:41	3063
the chronicles of the kings of *J*	1Kin 22:45	3063
year of Jehoshaphat king of *J*	1Kin 22:51	3063
the son of Jehoshaphat king of *J*	2Kin 1:17	3063
year of Jehoshaphat king of *J*	2Kin 3:1	3063
sent to Jehoshaphat the king of *J*	2Kin 3:7	3063
of Israel went, and the king of *J*	2Kin 3:9	3063
of Jehoshaphat the king of *J*	2Kin 3:14	3063
Jehoshaphat being then king of *J*	2Kin 8:16	3063
king of *J* began to reign	2Kin 8:16	3063
J for David his servant's sake	2Kin 8:19	3063
revolted from under the hand of *J*	2Kin 8:20	3063
under the hand of *J* unto this day	2Kin 8:22	3063
the chronicles of the kings of *J*	2Kin 8:23	3063
Jehoram king of *J* begin to reign	2Kin 8:25	3063
the son of Jehoram king of *J* went	2Kin 8:29	3063
Ahaziah king of *J* was come down	2Kin 9:16	3063
and Ahaziah king of *J* went out	2Kin 9:21	3063
Ahaziah the king of *J* saw this	2Kin 9:27	3063
began Ahaziah to reign over *J*	2Kin 9:29	3063
the brethren of Ahaziah king of *J*	2Kin 10:13	3063
Jehoash king of *J* took all the	2Kin 12:18	3063
Ahaziah, his fathers, kings of *J*	2Kin 12:18	3063
the chronicles of the kings of *J*	2Kin 12:19	3063
the son of Ahaziah king of *J*	2Kin 13:1	3063
of *J* began Jehoash the son of	2Kin 13:10	3063
fought against Amaziah king of *J*	2Kin 13:12	3063
the son of Joash king of *J*	2Kin 14:1	3063
Israel sent to Amaziah king of *J*	2Kin 14:9	3063
fall, even thou, and *J* with thee	2Kin 14:10	3063
Amaziah king of *J* looked one	2Kin 14:11	3063
which belongeth to *J*	2Kin 14:11	3063
J was put to the worse before	2Kin 14:12	3063
of Israel took Amaziah king of *J*	2Kin 14:13	3063
he fought with Amaziah king of *J*	2Kin 14:15	3063
of *J* lived after the death of	2Kin 14:17	3063
the chronicles of the kings of *J*	2Kin 14:18	3063
all the people of *J* took Azariah	2Kin 14:21	3063
built Elath, and restored it to *J*	2Kin 14:22	3063
the son of Joash king of *J*	2Kin 14:23	3063
and Hamath, which belonged to *J*	2Kin 14:28	3063
son of Amaziah king of *J* to reign	2Kin 15:1	3063
the chronicles of the kings of *J*	2Kin 15:6	3063
of *J* did Zachariah the son of	2Kin 15:8	3063
year of Uzziah king of *J*	2Kin 15:13	3063
year of Azariah king of *J* began	2Kin 15:17	3063
year of Azariah king of *J*	2Kin 15:23	3063
year of Azariah king of *J* Pekah	2Kin 15:27	3063
son of Uzziah king of *J* to reign	2Kin 15:32	3063
the chronicles of the kings of *J*	2Kin 15:36	3063
against *J* Rezin the king of Syria	2Kin 15:37	3063
Jotham king of *J* began to reign	2Kin 16:1	3063
the chronicles of the kings of *J*	2Kin 16:19	3063
twelfth year of Ahaz king of *J*	2Kin 17:1	3063
against Israel, and against *J*	2Kin 17:13	3063
none left but the tribe of *J* only	2Kin 17:18	3063
Also *J* kept not the commandments	2Kin 17:19	3063
of Ahaz king of *J* began to reign	2Kin 18:1	3063
like him among all the kings of *J*	2Kin 18:5	3063
all the fenced cities of *J*	2Kin 18:13	3063
Hezekiah king of *J* sent to the	2Kin 18:14	3063
J three hundred talents of silver	2Kin 18:14	3063
Hezekiah king of *J* had overlaid	2Kin 18:16	3063
taken away, and hath said to *J*	2Kin 18:22	3063
ye speak to Hezekiah king of *J*	2Kin 19:10	3063
of *J* shall yet again take root	2Kin 19:30	3063
the chronicles of the kings of *J*	2Kin 20:20	3063
Because Manasseh king of *J* hath	2Kin 21:11	3063
hath made *J* also to sin with his	2Kin 21:11	3063
such evil upon Jerusalem and *J*	2Kin 21:12	3063
sin wherewith he made *J* to sin	2Kin 21:16	3063
the chronicles of the kings of *J*	2Kin 21:17	3063
the chronicles of the kings of *J*	2Kin 21:25	3063
and for the people, and for all *J*	2Kin 22:13	3063
which the king of *J* hath read	2Kin 22:16	3063
But to the king of *J* which sent	2Kin 22:18	3063
unto him all the elders of *J*	2Kin 23:1	3063
of the LORD, and all the men of *J*	2Kin 23:2	3063
whom the kings of *J* had ordained	2Kin 23:5	3063
high places in the cities of *J*	2Kin 23:5	3063
priests out of the cities of *J*	2Kin 23:8	3063
kings of *J* had given to the sun	2Kin 23:11	3063
which the kings of *J* had made	2Kin 23:12	3063
the man of God, which came from *J*	2Kin 23:17	3063
of Israel, nor of the kings of *J*	2Kin 23:22	3063
that were spied in the land of *J*	2Kin 23:24	3063
his anger was kindled against *J*	2Kin 23:26	3063
I will remove *J* also out of my	2Kin 23:27	3063
the chronicles of the kings of *J*	2Kin 23:28	3063
sent them against *J* to destroy it	2Kin 24:2	3063
of the LORD came this upon *J*	2Kin 24:3	3063
the chronicles of the kings of *J*	2Kin 24:5	3063
Jehoiachin the king of *J* went out	2Kin 24:12	3063
it came to pass in Jerusalem and *J*	2Kin 24:20	3063
So *J* was carried away out of	2Kin 25:21	3063
that remained in the land of *J*	2Kin 25:22	3063
captivity of Jehoiachin king of *J*	2Kin 25:27	3063
king of *J* out of prison	2Kin 25:27	3063
in the days of Hezekiah king of *J*	1Chr 4:41	3063
in the days of Jotham king of *J*	1Chr 5:17	3063
when the LORD carried away *J*	1Chr 6:15	3063
book of the kings of Israel and *J*	1Chr 9:1	3063
J was four hundred threescore and	1Chr 21:5	3063
that dwelt in the cities of *J*	2Chr 10:17	3063
he gathered of the house of *J*	2Chr 11:1	3063
the son of Solomon, king of *J*	2Chr 11:3	3063
of Judah, and to all Israel in *J*	2Chr 11:3	3063
and built cities for defence in *J*	2Chr 11:5	3063
and Hebron, which are in *J*	2Chr 11:10	3063
them exceeding strong, having *J*	2Chr 11:12	3063
and their possession, and came to *J*	2Chr 11:14	3063
strengthened the kingdom of *J*	2Chr 11:17	3063
throughout all the countries of *J*	2Chr 11:23	3063
cities which pertained to *J*	2Chr 12:4	3063
Rehoboam, and to the princes of *J*	2Chr 12:5	3063
also in *J* things went well	2Chr 12:12	3063
began Abijah to reign over *J*	2Chr 13:1	3063
so they were before *J*, and the	2Chr 13:13	3063
when *J* looked back, behold, the	2Chr 13:14	3063
Then the men of *J* gave a shout	2Chr 13:15	3063
and as the men of *J* shouted	2Chr 13:15	3063
and all Israel before Abijah and *J*	2Chr 13:15	3063
children of Israel fled before *J*	2Chr 13:16	3063
and the children of *J* prevailed	2Chr 13:18	3063
commanded *J* to seek the LORD God	2Chr 14:4	3063
the cities of *J* the high places	2Chr 14:5	3063
And he built fenced cities in *J*	2Chr 14:6	3063
Therefore he said unto *J*, Let us	2Chr 14:7	3063
out of *J* three hundred thousand	2Chr 14:8	3063
before Asa, and before *J*	2Chr 14:12	3063
him, Hear ye me, Asa, and all *J*	2Chr 15:2	3063
idols out of all the land of *J*	2Chr 15:8	3063
And he gathered all *J* and Benjamin,	2Chr 15:9	3063
all *J* rejoiced at the oath	2Chr 15:15	3063
king of Israel came up against *J*	2Chr 16:1	3063
out or come in to Asa king of *J*	2Chr 16:1	3063
Then Asa the king took all *J*	2Chr 16:6	3063
the seer came to Asa king of *J*	2Chr 16:7	3063
in the book of the kings of *J*	2Chr 16:11	3063
in all the fenced cities of *J*	2Chr 17:2	3063
and set garrisons in the land of *J*	2Chr 17:2	3063
all *J* brought to Jehoshaphat	2Chr 17:5	3063
high places and groves out of *J*	2Chr 17:6	3063
to teach in the cities of *J*	2Chr 17:7	3063
And they taught in *J*, and had the	2Chr 17:9	3063
throughout all the cities of *J*	2Chr 17:9	3063
the lands that were round about *J*	2Chr 17:10	3063
and he built in *J* castles, and	2Chr 17:12	3063
much business in the cities of *J*	2Chr 17:13	3063
Of *J*, the captains of thousands	2Chr 17:14	3063
fenced cities throughout all *J*	2Chr 17:19	3063
said unto Jehoshaphat king of *J*	2Chr 18:3	3063
Jehoshaphat king of *J* sat either	2Chr 18:9	3063
Jehoshaphat the king of *J* went up	2Chr 18:28	3063
Jehoshaphat the king of *J*	2Chr 19:1	3063
all the fenced cities of *J*	2Chr 19:5	3063

the ruler of the house of J 2Chr 19:11 3063
a fast throughout all J 2Chr 20:3 3063
J gathered themselves together, ... 2Chr 20:4 3063
of J they came to seek the LORD 2Chr 20:4 3063
stood in the congregation of J 2Chr 20:5 3063
all J stood before the LORD, with 2Chr 20:13 3063
And he said, Hearken ye, all J 2Chr 20:15 3063
of the LORD with you, O J 2Chr 20:17 3063
and all J and the inhabitants of 2Chr 20:18 3063
stood and said, Hear me, O J 2Chr 20:20 3063
Seir, which were come against J 2Chr 20:22 3063
when J came toward the watch 2Chr 20:24 3063
they returned, every man of J 2Chr 20:27 3063
And Jehoshaphat reigned over J 2Chr 20:31 3063
this did Jehoshaphat king of J 2Chr 20:35 3063
things, with fenced cities in J 2Chr 21:3 3063
from under the dominion of J 2Chr 21:8 3063
under the hand of J unto this day 2Chr 21:10 3063
high places in the mountains of J 2Chr 21:11 3063
and compelled J thereto 2Chr 21:11 3063
nor in the ways of Asa king of J 2Chr 21:12 3063
kings of Israel, and hast made J 2Chr 21:13 3063
And they came up into J, and brake 2Chr 21:17 3063
son of Jehoram king of J reigned 2Chr 22:1 3063
the son of Jehoram king of J went 2Chr 22:6 3063
Ahab, and found the princes of J 2Chr 22:8 3063
the seed royal of the house of J 2Chr 22:10 3063
And they went about in J, and 2Chr 23:2 3063
out of all the cities of J 2Chr 23:2 3063
all J did according to all things 2Chr 23:8 3063
them, Go out unto the cities of J 2Chr 24:5 3063
the Levites to bring in out of J 2Chr 24:6 3063
made a proclamation through J 2Chr 24:9 3063
of Jehoiada came the princes of J 2Chr 24:17 3063
and wrath came upon J and Jerusalem 2Chr 24:18 3063
and they came to J and Jerusalem, ... 2Chr 24:23 3063
Amaziah gathered J together 2Chr 25:5 3063
their fathers, throughout all J 2Chr 25:5 3063
was greatly kindled against J 2Chr 25:10 3063
children of J carry away captive 2Chr 25:12 3063
battle, fell upon the cities of J 2Chr 25:13 3063
Amaziah king of J took advice 2Chr 25:17 3063
Israel sent to Amaziah king of J 2Chr 25:18 3063
fall, even thou, and J with thee 2Chr 25:19 3063
both he and Amaziah king of J 2Chr 25:21 3063
which belongeth to J 2Chr 25:21 3063
J was put to the worse before 2Chr 25:22 3063
of Israel took Amaziah king of J 2Chr 25:23 3063
the son of Joash king of J lived 2Chr 25:25 3063
in the book of the kings of J 2Chr 25:26 3063
with his fathers in the city of J 2Chr 25:28 3063
all the people of J took Uzziah 2Chr 26:1 3063
built Eloth, and restored it to J 2Chr 26:2 3063
cities in the mountains of J 2Chr 27:4 3063
book of the kings of Israel and J 2Chr 27:7 3063
of Remaliah slew in J an hundred 2Chr 28:6 3063
of your fathers was wroth with J 2Chr 28:9 3063
to keep under the children of J 2Chr 28:10 3063
Edomites had come and smitten J 2Chr 28:17 3063
low country, and of the south of J 2Chr 28:18 3063
For the LORD brought J low 2Chr 28:19 3063
for he made J naked, and 2Chr 28:19 3063
in every several city of J he 2Chr 28:25 3063
in the book of the kings of J 2Chr 28:26 3063
the wrath of the LORD was upon J 2Chr 29:8 3063
and for the sanctuary, and for J 2Chr 29:21 3063
Hezekiah sent to all Israel and J 2Chr 30:1 3063
throughout all Israel and J 2Chr 30:6 3063
Also in J the hand of God was to 2Chr 30:12 3063
For Hezekiah king of J did give 2Chr 30:24 3063
And all the congregation of J 2Chr 30:25 3063
of Israel, and that dwelt in J 2Chr 30:25 3063
went out to the cities of J 2Chr 31:1 3063
places and the altars out of all J 2Chr 31:1 3063
the children of Israel and J 2Chr 31:6 3063
that dwelt in the cities of J 2Chr 31:6 3063
did Hezekiah throughout all J 2Chr 31:20 3063
Assyria came, and entered into J 2Chr 32:1 3063
the words of Hezekiah king of J 2Chr 32:8 3063
him,) unto Hezekiah king of J 2Chr 32:9 3063
unto all J that were at Jerusalem 2Chr 32:9 3063
and his altars, and commanded J 2Chr 32:12 3063
and presents to Hezekiah king of J 2Chr 32:23 3063
was wrath upon him, and upon J 2Chr 32:25 3063
and in the book of the kings of J 2Chr 32:32 3063
and all J and the inhabitants of 2Chr 32:33 3063
So Manasseh made J and the 2Chr 33:9 3063
war in all the fenced cities of J 2Chr 33:14 3063
commanded J to serve the LORD God 2Chr 33:16 3063
twelfth year he began to purge J 2Chr 34:3 3063
upon their altars, and cleansed J 2Chr 34:5 3063
remnant of Israel, and of all J 2Chr 34:9 3063
the kings of J had destroyed 2Chr 34:11 3063
that are left in Israel and in J 2Chr 34:21 3063
have read before the king of J 2Chr 34:24 3063
And as for the king of J, who sent 2Chr 34:26 3063
together all the elders of J 2Chr 34:29 3063
of the LORD, and all the men of J 2Chr 34:30 3063
priests, and the Levites, and all J 2Chr 35:18 3063
I to do with thee, thou king of J 2Chr 35:21 3063
And all J and Jerusalem mourned for 2Chr 35:24 3063
book of the kings of Israel and J 2Chr 35:27 3063
Eliakim his brother king over J 2Chr 36:4 3063
book of the kings of Israel and J 2Chr 36:8 3063
Zedekiah his brother king over J 2Chr 36:10 3063
house in Jerusalem, which is in J 2Chr 36:23 3063
and came again unto Jerusalem and J .... Ezr 2:1 3063
Now when the adversaries of J .... Ezr 4:1 3063

of Hezekiah king of J copied out .... Prov 25:1 3063
Amoz, which he saw concerning J .... Is 1:1 3063
Ahaz, and Hezekiah, kings of J .... Is 1:1 3063
the son of Amoz saw concerning J .... Is 2:1 3063
from J the stay and the staff, the .... Is 3:1 3063
is ruined, and J is fallen .... Is 3:8 3063
of Jerusalem, and men of J .... Is 5:3 3063
the men of J his pleasant plant .... Is 5:7 3063
the son of Uzziah, king of J .... Is 7:1 3063
Let us go up against J, and vex it .... Is 7:6 3063
day that Ephraim departed from J .... Is 7:17 3063
And he shall pass through J .... Is 8:8 3063
they together shall be against J .... Is 9:21 3063
together the dispersed of J from .... Is 11:12 3063
adversaries of J shall be cut off .... Is 11:13 3063
Ephraim shall not envy J, and .... Is 11:13 3063
Judah, and J shall not vex Ephraim .... Is 11:13 3063
the land of J shall be a terror .... Is 19:17 3063
he discovered the covering of J .... Is 22:8 3063
Jerusalem, and to the house of J .... Is 22:21 3063
song be sung in the land of J .... Is 26:1 3063
all the defenced cities of J .... Is 36:1 3063
hath taken away, and said to J .... Is 36:7 3063
ye speak to Hezekiah king of J .... Is 37:10 3063
J shall again take root downward .... Is 37:31 3063
The writing of Hezekiah king of J .... Is 38:9 3063
say unto the cities of J, Behold .... Is 40:9 3063
and to the cities of J, Ye shall .... Is 44:26 3063
come forth out of the waters of J .... Is 48:1 3063
out of J an inheritor of my .... Is 65:9 3063
Josiah the son of Amon king of J .... Jer 1:2 3063
the son of Josiah king of J .... Jer 1:3 3063
the son of Josiah king of J .... Jer 1:3 3063
and against all the cities of J .... Jer 1:15 3063
land, against the kings of J .... Jer 1:18 3063
of thy cities are thy gods, O J .... Jer 2:28 3063
her treacherous sister J saw it .... Jer 3:7 3063
treacherous sister J feared not .... Jer 3:8 3063
J hath not turned unto me with .... Jer 3:10 3063
herself more than treacherous J .... Jer 3:11 3063
In those days the house of J .... Jer 3:18 3063
saith the LORD to the men of J .... Jer 4:3 3063
of your heart, ye men of J .... Jer 4:4 3063
Declare ye in J, and publish in .... Jer 4:5 3063
voice against the cities of J .... Jer 4:16 3063
the house of J have dealt very .... Jer 5:11 3063
of Jacob, and publish it in J .... Jer 5:20 3063
the word of the LORD, all ye of J .... Jer 7:2 3063
what they do in the cities of J .... Jer 7:17 3063
For the children of J have done .... Jer 7:30 3063
to cease from the cities of J .... Jer 7:34 3063
out the bones of the kings of J .... Jer 8:1 3063
make the cities of J desolate .... Jer 9:11 3063
Egypt, and J, and Edom, and the .... Jer 9:26 3063
to make the cities of J desolate .... Jer 10:22 3063
and speak unto the men of J .... Jer 11:2 3063
these words in the cities of J .... Jer 11:6 3063
is found among the men of J .... Jer 11:9 3063
the house of J have broken my .... Jer 11:10 3063
Then shall the cities of J .... Jer 11:12 3063
of thy cities were thy gods, O J .... Jer 11:13 3063
of Israel and of the house of J .... Jer 11:17 3063
the house of J from among them .... Jer 12:14 3063
manner will I mar the pride of J .... Jer 13:9 3063
of Israel and the whole house of J .... Jer 13:11 3063
J shall be carried away captive .... Jer 13:19 3063
J mourneth, and the gates thereof .... Jer 14:2 3063
Hast thou utterly rejected J .... Jer 14:19 3063
the son of Hezekiah king of J .... Jer 15:4 3063
The sin of J is written with a .... Jer 17:1 3063
whereby the kings of J come in .... Jer 17:19 3063
word of the LORD, ye kings of J .... Jer 17:20 3063
LORD, ye kings of Judah, and all J .... Jer 17:20 3063
and their princes, the men of J .... Jer 17:25 3063
shall come from the cities of J .... Jer 17:26 3063
go to, speak to the men of J .... Jer 18:11 3063
word of the LORD, O kings of J .... Jer 19:3 3063
have known, nor the kings of J .... Jer 19:4 3063
I will make void the counsel of J .... Jer 19:7 3063
and the houses of the kings of J .... Jer 19:13 3063
I will give all J into the hand .... Jer 20:4 3063
of J will I give into the hand of .... Jer 20:5 3063
I will deliver Zedekiah king of J .... Jer 21:7 3063
the house of the king of J .... Jer 21:11 3063
to the house of the king of J .... Jer 22:1 3063
the word of the LORD, O king of J .... Jer 22:2 3063
LORD unto the king's house of J .... Jer 22:6 3063
the son of Josiah king of J .... Jer 22:11 3063
the son of Josiah king of J .... Jer 22:18 3063
the son of Jehoiakim king of J .... Jer 22:24 3063
of David, and ruling any more in J .... Jer 22:30 3063
In his days J shall be saved, and .... Jer 23:6 3063
the son of Jehoiakim king of J .... Jer 24:1 3063
and the princes of J .... Jer 24:1 3063
are carried away captive of J .... Jer 24:5 3063
I give Zedekiah the king of J .... Jer 24:8 3063
concerning all the people of J in .... Jer 25:1 3063
the son of Josiah king of J .... Jer 25:1 3063
spake unto all the people of J .... Jer 25:2 3063
Josiah the son of Amon king of J .... Jer 25:3 3063
Jerusalem, and the cities of J .... Jer 25:18 3063
the son of Josiah king of J came .... Jer 26:1 3063
and speak unto all the cities of J .... Jer 26:2 3063
princes of J heard these things .... Jer 26:10 3063
in the days of Hezekiah king of J .... Jer 26:18 3063
and spake to all the people of J .... Jer 26:18 3063
Did Hezekiah king of J and all .... Jer 26:19 3063
all J put him at all to death .... Jer 26:19 3063

the son of Josiah king of J came .... Jer 27:1 3063
Jerusalem unto Zedekiah king of J .... Jer 27:3 3063
of J according to all these words .... Jer 27:12 3063
and in the house of the king of J .... Jer 27:18 3063
of J from Jerusalem to Babylon .... Jer 27:20 3063
and all the nobles of J .... Jer 27:20 3063
and in the house of the king of J .... Jer 27:21 3063
the reign of Zedekiah king of J .... Jer 28:1 3063
the son of Jehoiakim king of J .... Jer 28:4 3063
Judah, with all the captives of J .... Jer 28:4 3063
and the eunuchs, the princes of J .... Jer 29:2 3063
king of J sent unto Babylon to .... Jer 29:3 3063
of J which are in Babylon .... Jer 29:22 3063
of my people Israel and J, saith .... Jer 30:3 3063
concerning Israel and concerning J .... Jer 30:4 3063
use this speech in the land of J .... Jer 31:23 3063
And there shall dwell in J itself .... Jer 31:24 3063
the house of J with the seed of .... Jer 31:27 3063
of Israel, and with the house of J .... Jer 31:31 3063
tenth year of Zedekiah king of J .... Jer 32:1 3063
king of J had shut him up .... Jer 32:3 3063
Zedekiah king of J shall not .... Jer 32:4 3063
the children of J have only done .... Jer 32:30 3063
of Israel and of the children of J .... Jer 32:32 3063
their prophets, and the men of J .... Jer 32:32 3063
abomination, to cause J to sin .... Jer 32:35 3063
Jerusalem, and in the cities of J .... Jer 32:44 3063
the houses of the kings of J .... Jer 33:4 3063
I will cause the captivity of J .... Jer 33:7 3063
beast, even in the cities of J .... Jer 33:10 3063
Jerusalem, and in the cities of J .... Jer 33:13 3063
of Israel and to the house of J .... Jer 33:14 3063
In those days shall J be saved .... Jer 33:16 3063
Go and speak to Zedekiah king of J .... Jer 34:2 3063
of the LORD, O Zedekiah king of J .... Jer 34:4 3063
Zedekiah king of J in Jerusalem .... Jer 34:6 3063
the cities of J that were left .... Jer 34:7 3063
remained of the cities of J .... Jer 34:7 3063
The princes of J, and the princes .... Jer 34:19 3063
And Zedekiah king of J and his .... Jer 34:21 3063
of J a desolation without an .... Jer 34:22 3063
the son of Josiah king of J .... Jer 35:1 3063
Go and tell the men of J and the .... Jer 35:13 3063
Behold, I will bring upon J .... Jer 35:17 3063
the son of Josiah king of J .... Jer 36:1 3063
thee against Israel, and against J .... Jer 36:2 3063
It may be that the house of J .... Jer 36:3 3063
read them in the ears of all J .... Jer 36:6 3063
the son of Josiah king of J .... Jer 36:9 3063
the cities of J unto Jerusalem .... Jer 36:9 3063
the king of J hath burned .... Jer 36:28 3063
shalt say to Jehoiakim king of J .... Jer 36:29 3063
the LORD of Jehoiakim king of J .... Jer 36:30 3063
Jerusalem, and upon the men of J .... Jer 36:31 3063
king of J had burned in the fire .... Jer 36:32 3063
made king in the land of J .... Jer 37:1 3063
shall ye say to the king of J .... Jer 37:7 3063
ninth year of Zedekiah king of J .... Jer 39:1 3063
Zedekiah the king of J saw them .... Jer 39:4 3063
Babylon slew all the nobles of J .... Jer 39:6 3063
had nothing, in the land of J .... Jer 39:10 3063
away captive of Jerusalem and J .... Jer 40:1 3063
governor over the cities of J .... Jer 40:5 3063
Babylon had left a remnant of J .... Jer 40:11 3063
driven, and came to the land of J .... Jer 40:12 3063
and the remnant in J perish .... Jer 40:15 3063
word of the LORD, ye remnant of J .... Jer 42:15 3063
concerning you, O ye remnant of J .... Jer 42:19 3063
LORD, to dwell in the land of J .... Jer 43:4 3063
forces, took all the remnant of J .... Jer 43:5 3063
driven, to dwell in the land of J .... Jer 43:5 3063
in the sight of the men of J .... Jer 43:9 3064
and upon all the cities of J .... Jer 44:2 3063
and was kindled in the cities of J .... Jer 44:6 3063
child and suckling, out of J .... Jer 44:7 3063
the wickedness of the kings of J .... Jer 44:9 3063
have committed in the land of J .... Jer 44:9 3063
you for evil, and to cut off all J .... Jer 44:11 3063
And I will take the remnant of J .... Jer 44:12 3063
So that none of the remnant of J .... Jer 44:14 3063
should return into the land of J .... Jer 44:14 3063
our princes, in the cities of J .... Jer 44:17 3063
that ye burned in the cities of J .... Jer 44:21 3063
all J that are in the land of .... Jer 44:24 3063
all J that dwell in the land of .... Jer 44:26 3063
man of J in all the land of Egypt .... Jer 44:26 3063
all the men of J that are in the .... Jer 44:27 3063
land of Egypt into the land of J .... Jer 44:28 3063
and all the remnant of J .... Jer 44:28 3063
as I gave Zedekiah king of J into .... Jer 44:30 3063
the son of Josiah king of J .... Jer 45:1 3063
the son of Josiah king of J .... Jer 46:2 3063
the reign of Zedekiah king of J .... Jer 49:34 3063
and the children of J together .... Jer 50:4 3063
and the sins of J, and they shall .... Jer 50:20 3063
the children of J were oppressed .... Jer 50:33 3063
nor J of his God, of the LORD of .... Jer 51:5 3063
went with Zedekiah the king of J .... Jer 51:59 3063
it came to pass in Jerusalem and J .... Jer 52:3 3063
all the princes of J in Riblah .... Jer 52:10 3063
Thus J was carried away captive .... Jer 52:27 3063
captivity of Jehoiachin king of J .... Jer 52:31 3063
the head of Jehoiachin king of J .... Jer 52:31 3063
J is gone into captivity because .... Lam 1:3 3063
the virgin, the daughter of J .... Lam 1:15 3063
strong holds of the daughter of J .... Lam 2:2 3063
in the daughter of J mourning .... Lam 2:5 3063
and the maids in the cities of J .... Lam 5:11 3063

of the house of J forty days ... Eze 4:6 3063
and the elders of J sat before me ... Eze 8:1 3063
house of J that they commit the ... Eze 8:17 3063
J is exceeding great, and the land ... Eze 9:9 3063
to J in Jerusalem the defenced ... Eze 21:20 3063
and against the house of J ... Eze 25:3 3063
the house of J is like unto all ... Eze 25:8 3063
house of J by taking vengeance ... Eze 25:12 3063
J, and the land of Israel, they ... Eze 27:17 3063
stick, and write upon it, For J ... Eze 37:16 3063
him, even with the stick of J ... Eze 37:19 3063
the west side, a portion for J ... Eze 48:7 3063
And by the border of J, from the ... Eze 48:8 3063
prince's, between the border of J ... Eze 48:22 3063
one gate of Reuben, one gate of J ... Eze 48:31 3063
of J came Nebuchadnezzar king of ... Dan 1:1 3063
Jehoiakim king of J into his hand ... Dan 1:2 3063
these were of the children of J ... Dan 1:6 3063
found a man of the captives of J ... Dan 2:25 3061
children of the captivity of J ... Dan 5:13 3061
children of the captivity of J ... Dan 6:13 3061
to the men of J, and to the ... Dan 9:7 3063
Ahaz, and Hezekiah, kings of J ... Hos 1:1 3063
have mercy upon the house of J ... Hos 1:7 3063
Then shall the children of J ... Hos 1:11 3063
the harlot, yet let not J offend ... Hos 4:15 3063
J also shall fall with them ... Hos 5:5 3063
The princes of J were like them ... Hos 5:10 3063
to the house of J as rottenness ... Hos 5:12 3063
J saw his wound, then went ... Hos 5:13 3063
as a young lion to the house of J ... Hos 5:14 3063
O J, what shall I do unto thee ... Hos 6:4 3063
Also, O J, he hath set an harvest ... Hos 6:11 3063
J hath multiplied fenced cities ... Hos 8:14 3063
J shall plow, and Jacob shall ... Hos 10:11 3063
but J yet ruleth with God, and is ... Hos 11:12 3063
hath also a controversy with J ... Hos 12:2 3063
bring again the captivity of J ... Joel 3:1 3063
The children also of J and the ... Joel 3:6 3063
the hand of the children of J ... Joel 3:8 3063
all the rivers of J shall flow ... Joel 3:18 3063
against the children of J ... Joel 3:19 3063
But J shall dwell for ever, and ... Joel 3:20 3063
in the days of Uzziah king of J ... Amos 1:1 3063
For three transgressions of J ... Amos 2:4 3063
But I will send a fire upon J ... Amos 2:5 3063
flee thee away into the land of J ... Amos 7:12 3063
rejoiced over the children of J ... Obad 12 3063
Ahaz, and Hezekiah, kings of J ... Mic 1:1 3063
and what are the high places of J ... Mic 1:5 3063
for it is come unto J ... Mic 1:9 3063
little among the thousands of J ... Mic 5:2 3063
O J, keep thy solemn feasts ... Nah 1:15 3063
Josiah the son of Amon, king of J ... Zeph 1:1 3063
also stretch out mine hand upon J ... Zeph 1:4 3063
for the remnant of the house of J ... Zeph 2:7 3063
son of Shealtiel, governor of J ... Hag 1:1 3063
son of Shealtiel, governor of J ... Hag 1:14 3063
son of Shealtiel, governor of J ... Hag 2:2 3063
to Zerubbabel, governor of J ... Hag 2:21 3063
Jerusalem and on the cities of J ... Zec 1:12 3063
the horns which have scattered J ... Zec 1:19 3063
the horns which have scattered J ... Zec 1:21 3063
over the land of J to scatter it ... Zec 1:21 3063
the LORD shall inherit J his ... Zec 2:12 3063
among the heathen, O house of J ... Zec 8:13 3063
Jerusalem and to the house of J ... Zec 8:15 3063
shall be to the house of J joy ... Zec 8:19 3063
and he shall be as a governor in J ... Zec 9:7 3063
When I have bent J for me ... Zec 9:13 3063
visited his flock the house of J ... Zec 10:3 3063
I will strengthen the house of J ... Zec 10:6 3063
break the brotherhood between J ... Zec 11:14 3063
be in the siege both against J ... Zec 12:2 3063
mine eyes upon the house of J ... Zec 12:4 3063
the governors of J shall say in ... Zec 12:5 3063
of J like an hearth of fire among ... Zec 12:6 3063
shall save the tents of J first ... Zec 12:7 3063
not magnify themselves against J ... Zec 12:7 3063
in the days of Uzziah king of J ... Zec 14:5 3063
J also shall fight at Jerusalem ... Zec 14:14 3063
in J shall be holiness unto the ... Zec 14:21 3063
J hath dealt treacherously, and an ... Mal 2:11 3063
for J hath profaned the holiness ... Mal 2:11 3063
Then shall the offering of J ... Mal 3:4 3063
4. A Levite.
and his sons, the sons of J ... Ezr 3:9 3063
5. A Levite who married a foreigner.
the same is Kelita,) Pethahiah, J ... Ezr 10:23 3063
6. An overseer.
J the son of Senuah was second ... Neh 11:9 3063
7. A Levite with Zerubbabel.
Binnui, Kadmiel, Sherebiah, J ... Neh 12:8 3063
8. An exile.
J, and Benjamin, and Shemaiah, and ... Neh 12:34 3063
9. A musician in exile.
Gilalai, Maai, Nethaneel, and J ... Neh 12:36 3063

JUDAH'S *(ju'-dahs)* {4}
1. Refers to Judah 1.
J firstborn, was wicked in the ... Gen 38:7 3063
the daughter of Shuah J wife died ... Gen 38:12 3063
which was in the king of J house ... Jer 32:2 3063
that are left in the king of J ... Jer 38:22 3063

JUDAISM See JEWS, PROSELYTES.

JUDAS *(ju'-das)* {33} See BARSABAS, ISCARIOT, JUDAH, JUDE, LEBBAEUS, THADDAEUS.
1. Betrayer of Jesus.
J Iscariot, who also betrayed him ... Mt 10:4 2455
called J Iscariot, went unto the ... Mt 26:14 2455
Then J, which betrayed him, ... Mt 26:25 2455
And while he yet spake, lo, J, ... Mt 26:47 2455
Then J, which had betrayeth him, ... Mt 27:3 2455
J Iscariot, which also betrayed ... Mk 3:19 2455
J Iscariot, one of the twelve, ... Mk 14:10 2455
while he yet spake, cometh J ... Mk 14:43 2455
J Iscariot, which also was the ... Lk 6:16 2455
Satan into J surnamed Iscariot ... Lk 22:3 2455
and he that was called J, one of ... Lk 22:47 2455
But Jesus said unto him, J ... Lk 22:48 2455
He spake of J Iscariot the son of ... Jn 6:71 2455
J Iscariot, Simon's son, which ... Jn 12:4 2455
put into the heart of J Iscariot ... Jn 13:2 2455
the sop, he gave it to J Iscariot ... Jn 13:26 2455
because J had the bag, that Jesus ... Jn 13:29 2455
J also, which betrayed him, knew ... Jn 18:2 2455
J then, having received a band of ... Jn 18:3 2455
J also, which betrayed him, stood ... Jn 18:5 2455
David spake before concerning J ... Acts 1:16 2455
from which J by transgression ... Acts 1:25 2455
2. A brother of Jesus.
James, and Joses, and Simon, and J ... Mt 13:55 2455
3. A disciple of Jesus.
J the brother of James, and Judas ... Lk 6:16 2455
J saith unto him, not Iscariot, ... Jn 14:22 2455
and J the brother of James ... Acts 1:13 2455
4. A seditious Galilean.
After this man rose up J of ... Acts 5:37 2455
5. Lodged Paul in Damascus.
house of J for one called Saul ... Acts 9:11 2455
6. Surnamed Barsabas.
J surnamed Barsabas, and Silas, ... Acts 15:22 2455
We have sent therefore J and Silas ... Acts 15:27 2455
And J and Silas, being prophets ... Acts 15:32 2455
7. A Greek form of Joseph.
and Jacob begat J and his brethren ... Mt 1:2 2455
J begat Phares and Zara of Thamar ... Mt 1:3 2455

JUDE *(good)* {1} See JUDAS. *A brother of Jesus.*
J, the servant of Jesus Christ, ... Jude 1 2455

JUDEA *(ju-de'-ah)* {1} See JEWRY, JUDAH. *Southern portion of Israel.*
we went into the province of J ... Ezr 5:8 3061

JUDGE {191}
whom they shall serve, will I j ... Gen 15:14 1777
the LORD j between me and thee ... Gen 16:5 8199
Shall not the J of all the earth ... Gen 18:25 8199
sojourn, and he will needs be a j ... Gen 19:9 8199
that they may j betwixt us both ... Gen 31:37 3198
God of their father, j betwixt us ... Gen 31:53 8199
Dan shall j his people, as one of ... Gen 49:16 1777
made thee a prince and a j over us ... Ex 2:14 8199
The LORD look upon you, and j ... Ex 5:21 8199
that Moses sat to j the people ... Ex 18:13 8199
I j between one and another, and I ... Ex 18:16 8199
let them j the people at all ... Ex 18:22 8199
every small matter they shall j ... Ex 18:22 8199
shalt thou j thy neighbour ... Lev 19:15 8199
shall j between the slayer ... Num 35:24 8199
j righteously between every man ... Deut 1:16 8199
they shall j the people with just ... Deut 16:18 8199
unto the j that shall be in those ... Deut 17:9 8199
the LORD thy God, or unto the j ... Deut 17:12 8199
that the judges may j them ... Deut 25:1 8199
that the j shall cause him to lie ... Deut 25:2 8199
For the LORD shall j his people ... Deut 32:36 1777
then the LORD was with the j ... Judg 2:18 8199
enemies all the days of the j ... Judg 2:18 8199
came to pass, when the j was dead ... Judg 2:19 8199
the LORD the J be j this day ... Judg 11:27 8199
the LORD shall j the ends of the ... 1Sa 2:10 1777
another, the j shall j him ... 1Sa 2:25 430
will j his house for ever for the ... 1Sa 3:13 8199
now make us a king to j us like ... 1Sa 8:5 8199
they said, Give us a king to j us ... 1Sa 8:6 8199
and that our king may j us ... 1Sa 8:20 8199
The LORD j between me and thee, and ... 1Sa 24:12 8199
The LORD therefore be j ... 1Sa 24:15 1784
j between me and thee, and see, and ... 1Sa 24:15 8199
Oh that I were made j in the land ... 2Sa 15:4 8199
heart to j thy people, that I may ... 1Kin 3:9 8199
for who is able to j this thy so ... 1Kin 3:9 8199
for the throne where he might j ... 1Kin 7:7 8199
j thy servants, condemning the ... 1Kin 8:32 8199
because he cometh to j the earth ... 1Chr 16:33 8199
for who can j this thy people, ... 2Chr 1:10 8199
that thou mayest j my people ... 2Chr 1:11 8199
j thy servants, by requiting the ... 2Chr 6:23 8199
for ye j not for man, but for the ... 2Chr 19:6 8199
O our God, wilt thou not j them ... 2Chr 20:12 8199
which may j all the people that ... Ezr 7:25
I would make supplication to my j ... Job 9:15 8199
can he j through the dark cloud ... Job 22:13 8199
I be delivered for ever from my j ... Job 23:7 8199
iniquity to be punished by the j ... Job 31:28 6416
The LORD shall j the people ... Ps 7:8 1777
j me, O LORD, according to my ... Ps 7:8 8199
And he shall j the world in ... Ps 9:8 8199
To j the fatherless and the ... Ps 10:18 8199
J me, O LORD ... Ps 26:1 8199
J me, O LORD my God, according to ... Ps 35:24 8199
J me, O God, and plead my cause ... Ps 43:1 8199
earth, that he may j his people ... Ps 50:4 1777
for God is j himself ... Ps 50:6 8199
thy name, and j me by thy strength ... Ps 54:1 1777
do ye j uprightly, O ye sons of ... Ps 58:1 8199
for thou shalt j the people ... Ps 67:4 8199
a j of the widows, is God in his ... Ps 68:5 1781
He shall j thy people with ... Ps 72:2 1777
He shall j the poor of the people ... Ps 72:4 8199
congregation I will j uprightly ... Ps 75:2 8199
But God is the j ... Ps 75:7 8199
How long will ye j unjustly ... Ps 82:2 8199
Arise, O God, j the earth ... Ps 82:8 8199
up thyself, thou j of the earth ... Ps 94:2 8199
he shall j the people righteously ... Ps 96:10 1777
for he cometh to j the earth ... Ps 96:13 8199
he shall j the world with ... Ps 96:13 8199
for he cometh to j the earth ... Ps 98:9 8199
shall he j the world, and the ... Ps 98:9 8199
He shall j among the heathen, he ... Ps 110:6 1777
For the LORD will j his people ... Ps 135:14 1777
j righteously, and plead the cause ... Prov 31:9 8199
God shall j the righteous and the ... Eccl 3:17 8199
j the fatherless, plead for the ... Is 1:17 8199
they j not the fatherless, ... Is 1:23 8199
he shall j among the nations, and ... Is 2:4 8199
man, and the man of war, the j ... Is 3:2 8199
and standeth to j the people ... Is 3:13 1777
of Jerusalem, and men of Judah, j ... Is 5:3 8199
he shall not j after the sight of ... Is 11:3 8199
righteousness shall he j the poor ... Is 11:4 8199
For the LORD is our j, the LORD ... Is 33:22 8199
and mine arms shall j the people ... Is 51:5 8199
they j not the cause, the cause ... Jer 5:28 1777
right of the needy do they not j ... Jer 5:28 8199
j thou my cause ... Lam 3:59 8199
will j thee according to thy ways ... Eze 7:3 8199
I will j thee according to thy ... Eze 7:8 8199
to their deserts will I j them ... Eze 7:27 8199
I will j you in the border of ... Eze 11:10 8199
but I will j you in the border of ... Eze 11:11 8199
And I will j thee, as women that ... Eze 16:38 8199
Therefore I will j you, O house ... Eze 18:30 8199
Wilt thou j them, son of man, ... Eze 20:4 8199
son of man, wilt thou j them ... Eze 20:4 8199
I will j thee in the place where ... Eze 21:30 8199
Now, thou son of man, wilt thou j ... Eze 22:2 8199
wilt thou j the bloody city ... Eze 22:2 8199
they shall j thee according to ... Eze 23:24 8199
Son of man, wilt thou j Aholah ... Eze 23:36 8199
they shall j them after the ... Eze 23:45 8199
to thy doings, shall they j thee ... Eze 24:14 8199
I will j you every one after his ... Eze 33:20 8199
I j between cattle and cattle, ... Eze 34:17 8199
will j between the fat cattle and ... Eze 34:20 8199
I will j between cattle and cattle ... Eze 34:22 8199
they shall j it according to my ... Eze 44:24 8199
for there will I sit to j all the ... Joel 3:12 8199
I will cut off the j from the ... Amos 2:3 8199
mount Zion to j the mount of Esau ... Obad 21 8199
The heads thereof j for reward ... Mic 3:11 8199
he shall j among many people, and ... Mic 4:3 8199
they shall smite the j of Israel ... Mic 5:1 8199
the j asketh for a reward ... Mic 7:3 8199
then thou shalt also j my house ... Zec 3:7 1777
adversary deliver thee to the j ... Mt 5:25 2923
the j deliver thee to the officer ... Mt 5:25 2923
J not, that ye be not judged ... Mt 7:1 2919
For with what judgment ye j ... Mt 7:2 2919
J not, and ye shall not be judged ... Lk 6:37 2919
who made me a j or a divider over ... Lk 12:14 1348
yourselves j ye not what is right ... Lk 12:57 2919
lest he hale thee to the j ... Lk 12:58 2923
the j deliver thee to the officer ... Lk 12:58 2923
Saying, There was in a city a j ... Lk 18:2 2923
Hear what the unjust j saith ... Lk 18:6 2923
of thine own mouth will I j thee ... Lk 19:22 2919
as I hear, I j ... Jn 5:30 2919
J not according to the appearance ... Jn 7:24 2919
but j righteous judgment ... Jn 7:24 2919
Doth our law j any man, before it ... Jn 7:51 2919
Ye j after the flesh ... Jn 8:15 2919
I j no man ... Jn 8:15 2919
And yet if I j, my judgment is ... Jn 8:16 2919
many things to say and to j of you ... Jn 8:26 2919
and believe not, I j him not ... Jn 12:47 2919
for I came not to j the world ... Jn 12:47 2919
the same shall j him in the last ... Jn 12:48 2919
j him according to your law ... Jn 18:31 2919
unto you more than unto God, j ye ... Acts 4:19 2919
they shall be in bondage will I j ... Acts 7:7 2919
made thee a ruler and a j over us ... Acts 7:27 1348
Who made thee a ruler and a j ... Acts 7:35 1348
of God to be the J of quick ... Acts 10:42 2923
you, and j yourselves unworthy of ... Acts 13:46 2919
in the which he will j the world ... Acts 17:31 2919
I will be no j of such matters ... Acts 18:15 2923
thou to j me after the law ... Acts 23:3 2919
many years a j unto this nation ... Acts 24:10 2923
In the day when God shall j the ... Rom 2:16 2919
j thee, who by the letter and ... Rom 2:27 2919
then how shall God j the world ... Rom 3:6 2919
eateth not j him that eateth ... Rom 14:3 2919
But why dost thou j thy brother ... Rom 14:10 2919
therefore j one another any more ... Rom 14:13 2919
but j this rather, that no man ... Rom 14:13 2919
yea, I j not mine own self ... 1Cor 4:3 350
Therefore j nothing before the ... 1Cor 4:5 2919
For what have I to do to j them ... 1Cor 5:12 2919
do not ye j them that are within ... 1Cor 5:12 2919

that the saints shall j the world 1Cor 6:2 2919
are ye unworthy to j the smallest 1Cor 6:2 2922
ye not that we shall j angels 1Cor 6:3 2919
set them to j who are least 1Cor 6:4
be able to j between his brethren 1Cor 6:5 1252
j ye what I say 1Cor 10:15 2919
J in yourselves 1Cor 11:13 2919
For if we would j ourselves 1Cor 11:31 1252
two or three, and let the other j 1Cor 14:29 1252
because we thus j, that if one 2Cor 5:14 2919
no man therefore j you in meat Col 2:16 2919
Christ, who shall j the quick 2Ti 4:1 2919
which the Lord, the righteous j 2Ti 4:8 2923
The Lord shall j his people Heb 10:30 2919
in heaven, and to God the J of all Heb 12:23 2923
and adulterers God will j Heb 13:4 2919
but if thou j the law, thou art Jas 4:11 2919
not a doer of the law, but a j Jas 4:11 2923
the j standeth before the door Jas 5:9 2923
him that is ready to j the quick 1Pet 4:5 2919
holy and true, dost thou not j Rev 6:10 2919
and in righteousness he doth j Rev 19:11 2919

JUDGED {63}

And Rachel said, God hath j me Gen 30:6 1777
they j the people at all seasons Ex 18:26 8199
small matter they j themselves Ex 18:26 8199
he j Israel, and went out to war Judg 3:10 8199
she j Israel at that time Judg 4:4 8199
he j Israel twenty and three years Judg 10:2 8199
j Israel twenty and two years Judg 10:3 8199
Jephthah j Israel six years Judg 12:7 8199
him Ibzan of Beth-lehem j Israel Judg 12:8 8199
And he j Israel seven years Judg 12:9 8199
him Elon, a Zebulonite, j Israel Judg 12:11 8199
and he j Israel ten years Judg 12:11 8199
Hillel, a Pirathonite, j Israel Judg 12:13 8199
and he j Israel eight years Judg 12:14 8199
he j Israel in the days of the Judg 15:20 8199
And he j Israel twenty years Judg 16:31 8199
he had j Israel forty years 1Sa 4:18 8199
Samuel j the children of Israel 1Sa 7:6 8199
Samuel j Israel all the days of 1Sa 7:15 8199
j Israel in all those places 1Sa 7:16 8199
and there he j Israel 1Sa 7:17 8199
the judgment which the king had j 1Kin 3:28 8199
days of the judges that j Israel 2Kin 23:22 8199
let the heathen be j in thy sight Ps 9:19 8199
nor condemn him when he is j Ps 37:33 8199
When he shall be j, let him be Ps 109:7 8199
He j the cause of the poor and Jer 22:16 1777
break wedlock and shed blood are j Eze 16:38 4941
which hast j thy sisters, bear Eze 16:52 6419
the wounded shall be j in the Eze 28:23 5307
among them, when I have j thee Eze 35:11 8199
to their doings I j them Eze 36:19 8199
and against our judges that j us Dan 9:12 8199
Judge not, that ye be not j Mt 7:1 2919
judgment ye judge, ye shall be j Mt 7:2 2919
Judge not, and ye shall not be j Lk 6:37 2919
unto him, Thou hast rightly j Lk 7:43 2919
the prince of this world is j Jn 16:11 2919
If ye have j me to be faithful to Acts 16:15 2919
would have j according to our law Acts 24:6 2919
there be j of these things before Acts 25:9 2919
seat, where I ought to be j Acts 25:10 2919
there be j of these matters Acts 25:20 2919
am j for the hope of the promise Acts 26:6 2919
in the law shall be j by the law Rom 2:12 2919
mightest overcome when thou art j Rom 3:4 2919
why yet am I also j as a sinner Rom 3:7 2919
yet he himself is j of no man 1Cor 2:15 350
thing that I should be j of you 1Cor 4:3 350
have j already, as though I were 1Cor 5:3 2919
and if the world shall be j by you 1Cor 6:2 2919
for why is my liberty j of 1Cor 10:29 2919
ourselves, we should not be j 1Cor 11:31 2919
But when we are j, we are 1Cor 11:32 2919
convinced of all, he is j of all 1Cor 14:24 350
because she j him faithful who Heb 11:11 2233
shall be j by the law of liberty Jas 2:12 2919
that they might be j according to 1Pet 4:6 2919
the dead, that they should be j Rev 11:18 2919
be, because thou hast j thus Rev 16:5 2919
for he hath j the great whore, Rev 19:2 2919
the dead were j out of those Rev 20:12 2919
they were j every man according Rev 20:13 2919

JUDGES {52}

master shall bring him unto the j Ex 21:6 430
he shall pay as the j determine Ex 21:22 6414
house shall be brought unto the j Ex 22:8 430
parties shall come before the j Ex 22:9 430
whom the j shall condemn, he Ex 22:9 430
Moses said unto the j of Israel Num 25:5 8199
And I charged your j at that time Deut 1:16 8199
J and officers shalt thou make Deut 16:18 8199
LORD, before the priests and the j Deut 19:17 8199
the j shall make diligent Deut 19:18 8199
thy j shall come forth, and they Deut 21:2 8199
that the j may judge them Deut 25:1 8199
our enemies themselves being j Deut 32:31 6414
elders, and officers, and their j Josh 8:33 8199
for their heads, and for their j Josh 23:2 8199
for their heads, and for their j Josh 24:1 8199
Nevertheless the LORD raised up j Judg 2:16 8199
would not hearken unto their j Judg 2:17 8199
And when the LORD raised them up j Judg 2:18 8199
pass in the days when the j ruled Ruth 1:1 8199
he made his sons j over Israel 1Sa 8:1 8199
they were j in Beer-sheba 1Sa 8:2 8199
j to be over my people Israel 2Sa 7:11 8199
days of the j that judged Israel 2Kin 23:22 8199
a word to any of the j of Israel 1Chr 17:6 8199
j to be over my people Israel 1Chr 17:10 8199
six thousand were officers and j 1Chr 23:4 8199
over Israel, for officers and j 1Chr 26:29 8199
and of hundreds, and to the j 2Chr 1:2 8199
he set j in the land throughout 2Chr 19:5 8199
And said to the j, Take heed what 2Chr 19:6 8199
thine hand, set magistrates and j Ezr 7:25 1782
the j thereof, until the fierce Ezr 10:14 8199
the faces of the j thereof Job 9:24 8199
spoiled, and maketh the j fools Job 12:17 8199
iniquity to be punished by the j Job 31:11 6414
be instructed, ye j of the earth Ps 2:10 8199
When their j are overthrown in Ps 141:6 8199
princes, and all j of the earth Ps 148:11 8199
even all the j of the earth Prov 8:16 8199
restore thy j as at the first Is 1:26 8199
he maketh the j of the earth as Is 40:23 8199
governors, and the captains, the j Dan 3:2 148
the governors, and captains, the j Dan 3:3 148
against our j that judged us, by Dan 9:12 8199
an oven, and have devoured their j Hos 7:7 8199
thy j of whom thou saidst, Give Hos 13:10 8199
her j are evening wolves Zeph 3:3 8199
therefore they shall be your j Mt 12:27 2923
therefore shall they be your j Lk 11:19 2923
after that he gave unto them j Acts 13:20 2923
are become j of evil thoughts Jas 2:4 2923

JUDGEST {8}

speakest, and be clear when thou j Ps 51:4 8199
that j righteously, that triest Jer 11:20 8199
O man, whosoever thou art that j Rom 2:1 2919
for wherein thou j another Rom 2:1 2919
for thou that j doest the same Rom 2:1 2919
that j them which do such things, Rom 2:3 2919
Who art thou that j another man's Rom 14:4 2919
who art thou that j another Jas 4:12 2919

JUDGETH {17}

seeing he j those that are high Job 21:22 8199
For by them j he the people Job 36:31 1777
God j the righteous, and God is Ps 7:11 8199
he is a God that j in the earth Ps 58:11 8199
he j among the gods Ps 82:1 8199
king that faithfully j the poor Prov 29:14 8199
For the Father j no man, but hath Jn 5:22 2919
there is one that seeketh and j Jn 8:50 2919
not my words, hath one that j him Jn 12:48 2919
he that is spiritual j all things 1Cor 2:15 350
but he that j me is the Lord 1Cor 4:4 2919
But them that are without God j 1Cor 5:13 2919
j his brother, speaketh evil of Jas 4:11 2919
evil of the law, and j the law Jas 4:11 2919
j according to every man's work 1Pet 1:17 2919
himself to him that j righteously 1Pet 2:23 2919
strong is the Lord God who j her Rev 18:8 2919

JUDGING {6}

house, j the people of the land 2Kin 15:5 8199
house, j the people of the land 2Chr 26:21 8199
thou satest in the throne j right Ps 9:4 8199
in the tabernacle of David, j Is 16:5 8199
j the twelve tribes of Israel Mt 19:28 2919
sit on thrones j the twelve Lk 22:30 2919

JUDGMENT {294}

of the LORD, to do justice and j Gen 18:19 4941
gods of Egypt I will execute j Ex 12:12 8201
according to this j shall it be Ex 21:31 4941
to decline after many to wrest j Ex 23:2
the j of thy poor in his cause Ex 23:6 4941
of j with cunning work Ex 28:15 4941
breastplate of j upon his heart Ex 28:29 4941
in the breastplate of j the Urim Ex 28:30 4941
Aaron shall bear the j of the Ex 28:30 4941
shall do no unrighteousness in j Lev 19:15 4941
shall do no unrighteousness in j Lev 19:35 4941
children of Israel a statute of j Num 27:11 4941
the j of Urim before the LORD Num 27:21 4941
before the congregation in j Num 35:12 4941
of j unto you throughout your Num 35:29 4941
Ye shall not respect persons in j Deut 1:17 4941
for the j is God's Deut 1:17 4941
execute the j of the fatherless Deut 10:18 4941
judge the people with just j Deut 16:18 4941
Thou shalt not wrest j Deut 16:19 4941
a matter too hard for thee in j Deut 17:8 4941
shall shew thee the sentence of j Deut 17:9 4941
according to the j which they Deut 17:11 4941
not pervert the j of the stranger Deut 24:17 4941
between men, and they come unto j Deut 25:1 4941
perverteth the j of the stranger Deut 27:19 4941
for all his ways are j Deut 32:4 4941
and mine hand take hold on j Deut 32:41 4941
before the congregation for j Josh 20:6 4941
of Israel came up to her for j Judg 4:5 4941
on white asses, ye that sit in j Judg 5:10 4055
and took bribes, and perverted j 1Sa 8:3 4941
and David executed j and justice 2Sa 8:15 4941
came to the king for j, then 2Sa 15:2 4941
that came to the king for j 2Sa 15:6 4941
understanding to discern j 1Kin 3:11 4941
all Israel heard of the j which 1Kin 3:28 4941
wisdom of God was in him, to do j 1Kin 3:28 4941
might judge, even the porch of j 1Kin 7:7 4941
made he thee king, to do j 1Kin 10:9 4941
said unto him, So shall thy j be 1Kin 20:40 4941
and they gave j upon him 2Kin 25:6 4941
over all Israel, and executed j 1Chr 18:14 4941
he thee king over them, to do j 2Chr 9:8 4941
LORD, who is with you in the j 2Chr 19:6
for the j of the LORD, and for 2Chr 19:8 4941
cometh upon us, as the sword, j 2Chr 20:9 8196
j upon the house of Ahab, and 2Chr 22:8 8199
So they executed j against Joash 2Chr 24:24 8201
let j be executed speedily upon Ezr 7:26 1780
toward all that knew law and j Est 1:13 1779
Doth God pervert j? Job 8:3 4941
and if of j, who shall set me a Job 9:19 4941
and we should come together in j Job 9:32 4941
and bringest me into j with thee Job 14:3 4941
I cry aloud, but there is no j Job 19:7 4941
that ye may know there is a j Job 19:29 1779
will he enter with thee into j Job 22:4 4941
liveth, who hath taken away my j Job 27:2 4941
my j was as a robe and a diadem Job 29:14 4941
neither do the aged understand j Job 32:9 4941
Let us choose to us j Job 34:4 4941
and God hath taken away my j Job 34:5 4941
will the Almighty pervert j Job 34:12 4941
he should enter into j with God Job 34:23 4941
not see him, yet j is before him Job 35:14 1779
fulfilled the j of the wicked Job 36:17 1779
j and justice take hold on thee Job 36:17 1779
he is excellent in power, and in j Job 37:23 4941
Wilt thou also disannul my j Job 40:8 4941
ungodly shall not stand in the j Ps 1:5 4941
awake for me to the j that thou Ps 7:6 4941
he hath prepared his throne for j Ps 9:7 4941
he shall minister j to the people Ps 9:8 1777
known by the j which he executeth Ps 9:16 4941
The meek will he guide in j Ps 25:9 4941
He loveth righteousness and j Ps 33:5 4941
Stir up thyself, and awake to my j Ps 35:23 4941
light, and thy j as the noonday Ps 37:6 4941
For the LORD loveth j, and Ps 37:28 4941
and his tongue talketh of j Ps 37:30 4941
righteousness and thy poor with j Ps 72:2 4941
Thou didst cause j to be heard Ps 76:8 1779
When God arose to j, to save all Ps 76:9 4941
j are the habitation of thy Ps 89:14 4941
But j shall return unto Ps 94:15 4941
j are the habitation of his Ps 97:2 4941
The king's strength also loveth j Ps 99:4 4941
equity, thou executest j and Ps 99:4 4941
I will sing of mercy and j Ps 101:1 4941
j for all that are oppressed Ps 103:6 4941
Blessed are they that keep j Ps 106:3 4941
stood up Phinehas, and executed j Ps 106:30 6419
of his hands are verity and j Ps 111:7 4941
Teach me good j and knowledge Ps 119:66 2940
when wilt thou execute j on them Ps 119:84 4941
I have done j and justice Ps 119:121 4941
quicken me according to thy j Ps 119:149 4941
For there are set thrones of j Ps 122:5 4941
enter not into j with thy servant Ps 143:2 4941
Which executeth j for the Ps 146:7 4941
execute upon them the j written Ps 149:9 4941
of wisdom, justice, and j, and Prov 1:3 4941
He keepeth the paths of j Prov 2:8 4941
understand righteousness, and j Prov 2:9 4941
in the midst of the paths of j Prov 8:20 4941
that is destroyed for want of j Prov 13:23 4941
his mouth transgresseth not in j Prov 16:10 4941
bosom to pervert the ways of j Prov 17:23 4941
to overthrow the righteous in j Prov 18:5 4941
An ungodly witness scorneth j Prov 19:28 4941
j scattereth away all evil with Prov 20:8 1779
j is more acceptable to the LORD Prov 21:3 4941
because they refuse to do j Prov 21:7 4941
It is joy to the just to do j Prov 21:15 4941
to have respect of persons in j Prov 24:23 4941
Evil men understand not j Prov 28:5 4941
The king by j establisheth the Prov 29:4 4941
but every man's j cometh from the Prov 29:26 4941
pervert the j of any of the Prov 31:5 1779
saw under the sun the place of j Eccl 3:16 4941
poor, and violent perverting of j Eccl 5:8 4941
heart discerneth both time and j Eccl 8:5 4941
every purpose there is time and j Eccl 8:6 4941
things God will bring thee into j Eccl 11:9 4941
God shall bring every work into j Eccl 12:14 4941
seek j, relieve the oppressed, Is 1:17 4941
it was full of j Is 1:21 4941
Zion shall be redeemed with j Is 1:27 4941
The LORD will enter into j with Is 3:14 4941
midst thereof by the spirit of j Is 4:4 4941
and he looked for j, but behold Is 5:7 4941
of hosts shall be exalted in j Is 5:16 4941
it, and to establish it with j Is 9:7 4941
To turn aside the needy from j Is 10:2 1779
Take counsel, execute j Is 16:3 6415
of David, judging, and seeking j Is 16:5 4941
j to him that sitteth in j Is 28:6 4941
err in vision, they stumble in j Is 28:7 6417
J also will I lay to the line, and Is 28:17 4941
for the LORD is a God of j Is 30:18 4941
and princes shall rule in j Is 32:1 4941
Then j shall dwell in the Is 32:16 4941
he hath filled Zion with j Is 33:5 4941
upon the people of my curse, to j Is 34:5 4941
and taught him in the path of j Is 40:14 4941
my j is passed over from my God Is 40:27 4941

let us come near together to *j* ... Is 41:1 4941
bring forth *j* to the Gentiles ... Is 42:1 4941
he shall bring forth *j* unto truth ... Is 42:3 4941
till he have set *j* in the earth ... Is 42:4 4941
yet surely my *j* is with the LORD, ... Is 49:4 4941
I will make my *j* to rest for a ... Is 51:4 4941
was taken from prison and from *j* ... Is 53:8 4941
thee in *j* thou shalt condemn ... Is 54:17 4941
Thus saith the LORD, Keep ye *j* ... Is 56:1 4941
there is no *j* in their goings ... Is 59:8 4941
Therefore is *j* far from us ... Is 59:9 4941
we look for *j*, but there is none ... Is 59:11 4941
j is turned away backward, and ... Is 59:14 4941
him that there was no *j* ... Is 59:15 4941
For I the LORD love *j*, I hate ... Is 61:8 4941
The LORD liveth, in truth, in *j* ... Jer 4:2 4941
if there be any that executeth *j* ... Jer 5:1 4941
the LORD, nor the *j* of their God ... Jer 5:4 4941
the LORD, and the *j* of their God ... Jer 5:5 4941
throughly execute *j* between a man ... Jer 7:5 4941
people know not the *j* of the LORD ... Jer 8:7 4941
which exercise lovingkindness, *j* ... Jer 9:24 4941
O LORD, correct me, but with *j* ... Jer 10:24 4941
Execute *j* in the morning, and ... Jer 21:12 4941
Execute ye *j* and righteousness, and ... Jer 22:3 4941
thy father eat and drink, and do *j* ... Jer 22:15 4941
and prosper, and shall execute *j* ... Jer 23:5 4941
and he shall execute *j* and ... Jer 33:15 4941
Hamath, where he gave *j* upon him ... Jer 39:5 4941
j is come upon the plain country ... Jer 48:21 4941
Thus far is the *j* of Moab ... Jer 48:47 4941
they whose *j* was not to drink of ... Jer 49:12 4941
for her *j* reacheth unto heaven, ... Jer 51:9 4941
that I will do *j* upon the graven ... Jer 51:47 6485
that I will do *j* upon her graven ... Jer 51:52 6485
where he gave *j* upon him ... Jer 52:9 4941
hath executed true *j* between man ... Eze 18:8 4941
for they had executed *j* upon her ... Eze 23:10 8196
I will set *j* before them, and they ... Eze 23:24 4941
I will feed them with *j* ... Eze 34:16 4941
see my *j* that I have executed ... Eze 39:21 4941
controversy they shall stand in *j* ... Eze 44:24 8199
violence and spoil, and execute *j* ... Eze 45:9 4941
works are truth, and his ways *j* ... Dan 4:37 1780
the *j* was set, and the books were ... Dan 7:10 1780
j was given to the saints of the ... Dan 7:22 1780
But the *j* shall sit, and they ... Dan 7:26 1780
unto me in righteousness, and in *j* ... Hos 2:19 4941
for *j* is toward you, because ye ... Hos 5:1 4941
is oppressed and broken in *j* ... Hos 5:11 4941
thus *j* springeth up as hemlock in ... Hos 10:4 4941
keep mercy and *j*, and wait on thy ... Hos 12:6 4941
Ye who turn *j* to wormwood ... Amos 5:7 4941
good, and establish *j* in the gate ... Amos 5:15 4941
But let *j* run down as waters, and ... Amos 5:24 4941
for ye have turned *j* into gall ... Amos 6:12 4941
Is it not for you to know *j* ... Mic 3:1 4941
the spirit of the LORD, and of *j* ... Mic 3:8 4941
the house of Israel, that abhor *j* ... Mic 3:9 4941
my cause, and execute *j* for me ... Mic 7:9 4941
slacked, and *j* doth never go forth ... Hab 1:4 4941
therefore wrong *j* proceedeth ... Hab 1:4 4941
their *j* and their dignity shall ... Hab 1:7 4941
thou hast ordained them for *j* ... Hab 1:12 4941
earth, which have wrought his *j* ... Zeph 2:3 4941
doth he bring his *j* to light ... Zeph 3:5 4941
of hosts, saying, Execute true *j* ... Zec 7:9 4941
execute the *j* of truth and peace ... Zec 8:16 4941
or, Where is the God of *j* ... Mal 2:17 4941
And I will come near to you to *j* ... Mal 3:5 4941
kill shall be in danger of the *j* ... Mt 5:21 *2920*
cause shall be in danger of the *j* ... Mt 5:22 *2920*
For with what *j* ye judge, ye ... Mt 7:2 *2917*
Sodom and Gomorrha in the day of *j* ... Mt 10:15 *2920*
for Tyre and Sidon at the day of *j* ... Mt 11:22 *2920*
the land of Sodom in the day of *j* ... Mt 11:24 *2920*
he shall shew *j* to the Gentiles ... Mt 12:18 *2920*
till he send forth *j* unto victory ... Mt 12:20 *2920*
account thereof in the day of *j* ... Mt 12:36 *2920*
rise in *j* with this generation ... Mt 12:41 *2920*
up in the *j* with this generation ... Mt 12:42 *2920*
weightier matters of the law, *j* ... Mt 23:23 *2920*
he was set down on the *j* seat ... Mt 27:19 *968*
Sodom and Gomorrha in the day of *j* ... Mk 6:11 *2920*
for Tyre and Sidon at the *j* ... Lk 10:14 *2920*
the south shall rise up in the *j* ... Lk 11:31 *2920*
up in the *j* with this generation ... Lk 11:32 *2920*
manner of herbs, and pass over *j* ... Lk 11:42 *2920*
hath committed all *j* unto the Son ... Jn 5:22 *2920*
him authority to execute *j* also ... Jn 5:27 *2920*
and my *j* is just ... Jn 5:30 *2920*
appearance, but judge righteous *j* ... Jn 7:24 *2920*
And yet if I judge, my *j* is true ... Jn 8:16 *2920*
For *j* I am come into this world, ... Jn 9:39 *2917*
Now is the *j* of this world ... Jn 12:31 *2920*
sin, and of righteousness, and of *j* ... Jn 16:8 *2920*
Of *j*, because the prince of this ... Jn 16:11 *2920*
from Caiaphas unto the hall of *j* ... Jn 18:28 *4232*
went not into the *j* hall, lest ... Jn 18:28 *4232*
entered into the *j* hall again ... Jn 18:33 *4232*
And went again into the *j* hall ... Jn 19:9 *4232*
sat down in the *j* seat in a place ... Jn 19:13 *968*
humiliation his *j* was taken away ... Acts 8:33 *2920*
and brought him to the *j* seat ... Acts 18:12 *968*
And he drave them from the *j* seat ... Acts 18:16 *968*
and beat him before the *j* seat ... Acts 18:17 *968*
him to be kept in Herod's *j* hall ... Acts 23:35 *4232*
j to come, Felix trembled, and ... Acts 24:25 *2917*
the *j* seat commanded Paul to be ... Acts 25:6 *968*
Paul, I stand at Caesar's *j* seat ... Acts 25:10 *968*
desiring to have *j* against him ... Acts 25:15 *1349*
on the morrow I sat on the *j* seat ... Acts 25:17 *968*
Who knowing the *j* of God, that ... Rom 1:32 *1345*
But we are sure that the *j* of God ... Rom 2:2 *2917*
thou shalt escape the *j* of God ... Rom 2:3 *2917*
of the righteous *j* of God ... Rom 2:5 *1341*
for the *j* was by one to ... Rom 5:16 *2917*
of one *j* came upon all men to ... Rom 5:18
stand before the *j* seat of Christ ... Rom 14:10 *968*
in the same mind and in the same *j* ... 1Cor 1:10 *1106*
be judged of you, or of man's *j* ... 1Cor 4:3 *2250*
yet I give my *j*, as one that hath ... 1Cor 7:25 *1106*
if she so abide, after my *j* ... 1Cor 7:40 *1106*
before the *j* seat of Christ ... 2Cor 5:10 *968*
troubleth you shall bear his *j* ... Gal 5:10 *2917*
and more in knowledge and in all *j* ... Phil 1:9 *144*
token of the righteous *j* of God ... 2Th 1:5 *2920*
beforehand, going before to *j* ... 1Ti 5:24 *2920*
of the dead, and of eternal *j* ... Heb 6:2 *2917*
once to die, but after this the *j* ... Heb 9:27 *2920*
certain fearful looking for of *j* ... Heb 10:27 *2920*
and draw you before the *j* seats ... Jas 2:6 *2922*
For he shall have *j* without mercy ... Jas 2:13 *2920*
and mercy rejoiceth against *j* ... Jas 2:13 *2920*
For the time is come that *j* must ... 1Pet 4:17 *2917*
whose *j* now of a long time ... 2Pet 2:3 *2917*
darkness, to be reserved unto *j* ... 2Pet 2:4 *2920*
unto the day of *j* to be punished ... 2Pet 2:9 *2920*
unto fire against the day of *j* ... 2Pet 3:7 *2920*
may have boldness in the day of *j* ... 1Jn 4:17 *2920*
unto the *j* of the great day ... Jude 6 *2920*
To execute *j* upon all, and to ... Jude 15 *2920*
for the hour of his *j* is come ... Rev 14:7 *2920*
I will shew unto thee the *j* of ... Rev 17:1 *2917*
for in one hour is thy *j* come ... Rev 18:10 *2920*
them, and *j* was given unto them ... Rev 20:4 *2917*

JUDGMENTS {127}
out arm, and with great *j* ... Ex 6:6 8201
of the land of Egypt by great *j* ... Ex 7:4 8201
Now these are the *j* which thou ... Ex 21:1 4941
words of the LORD, and all the *j* ... Ex 24:3 4941
Ye shall do my *j*, and keep mine ... Lev 18:4 4941
keep my statutes, and my *j* ... Lev 18:5 4941
keep my statutes and my *j*, and ... Lev 18:26 4941
all my statutes, and all my *j* ... Lev 19:37 4941
keep all my statutes, and all my *j* ... Lev 20:22 4941
do my statutes, and keep my *j* ... Lev 25:18 4941
or if your soul abhor my *j* ... Lev 26:15 4941
even because they despised my *j* ... Lev 26:43 4941
These are the statutes and *j* ... Lev 26:46 4941
gods also the LORD executed *j* ... Num 33:4 8201
of blood according to these *j* ... Num 35:24 4941
are the commandments and the *j* ... Num 36:13 4941
unto the statutes and unto the *j* ... Deut 4:1 4941
I have taught you statutes and *j* ... Deut 4:5 4941
j so righteous as all this law, ... Deut 4:8 4941
time to teach you statutes and *j* ... Deut 4:14 4941
and the statutes, and the *j* ... Deut 4:45 4941
j which I speak in your ears this ... Deut 5:1 4941
and the statutes, and the *j* ... Deut 5:31 4941
the statutes, and the *j*, which ... Deut 6:1 4941
and the statutes, and the *j* ... Deut 6:20 4941
and the statutes, and the *j* ... Deut 7:11 4941
to pass, if ye hearken to these *j* ... Deut 7:12 4941
his commandments, and his *j* ... Deut 8:11 4941
charge, and his statutes, and his *j* ... Deut 11:1 4941
j which I set before you this day ... Deut 11:32 4941
These are the statutes and *j* ... Deut 12:1 4941
thee to do these statutes and *j* ... Deut 26:16 4941
and his commandments, and his *j* ... Deut 26:17 4941
and his statutes and his *j*, that ... Deut 30:16 4941
They shall teach Jacob thy *j* ... Deut 33:10 4941
of the LORD, and his *j* with Israel ... Deut 33:21 4941
For all his *j* were before me ... 2Sa 22:23 4941
and his commandments, and his *j* ... 1Kin 2:3 4941
in my statutes, and execute my *j* ... 1Kin 6:12 4941
and his statutes, and his *j* ... 1Kin 8:58 4941
and wilt keep my statutes and my *j* ... 1Kin 9:4 4941
and to keep my statutes and my *j* ... 1Kin 11:33 4941
wonders, and the *j* of his mouth ... 1Chr 16:12 4941
his *j* are in all the earth ... 1Chr 16:14 4941
j which the LORD charged Moses ... 1Chr 22:13 4941
to do my commandments and my *j* ... 1Chr 28:7 4941
shalt observe my statutes and my *j* ... 2Chr 7:17 4941
law and commandment, statutes and *j* ... 2Chr 19:10 4941
to teach in Israel statutes and *j* ... Ezr 7:10 4941
nor the statutes, nor the *j* ... Neh 1:7 4941
heaven, and gavest them right *j* ... Neh 9:13 4941
but sinned against thy *j* ... Neh 9:29 4941
of the LORD our Lord, and his *j* ... Neh 10:29 4941
thy *j* are far above out of his ... Ps 10:5 4941
For all his *j* were before me, and ... Ps 18:22 4941
the *j* of the LORD are true and ... Ps 19:9 4941
thy *j* are a great deep ... Ps 36:6 4941
Judah be glad, because of thy *j* ... Ps 48:11 4941
Give the king thy *j*, O God, and ... Ps 72:1 4941
my law, and walk not in my *j* ... Ps 89:30 4941
Judah rejoiced because of thy *j* ... Ps 97:8 4941
wonders, and the *j* of his mouth ... Ps 105:5 4941
his *j* are in all the earth ... Ps 105:7 4941
have learned thy righteous *j* ... Ps 119:7 4941
I declared all the *j* of thy mouth ... Ps 119:13 4941
it hath unto thy *j* at all times ... Ps 119:20 4941
thy *j* have I laid before me ... Ps 119:30 4941
for thy *j* are good ... Ps 119:39 4941
for I have hoped in thy *j* ... Ps 119:43 4941
I remembered thy *j* of old ... Ps 119:52 4941
thee because of thy righteous *j* ... Ps 119:62 4941
that thy *j* are right, and that ... Ps 119:75 4941
I have not departed from thy *j* ... Ps 119:102 4941
that I will keep thy righteous *j* ... Ps 119:106 4941
mouth, O LORD, and teach me thy *j* ... Ps 119:108 4941
and I am afraid of thy *j* ... Ps 119:120 4941
O LORD, and upright are thy *j* ... Ps 119:137 4941
quicken me according to thy *j* ... Ps 119:156 4941
thy righteous *j* endureth for ever ... Ps 119:160 4941
thee because of thy righteous *j* ... Ps 119:164 4941
and let thy *j* help me ... Ps 119:175 4941
his statutes and his *j* unto Israel ... Ps 147:19 4941
and as for his *j*, they have not ... Ps 147:20 4941
J are prepared for scorners, and ... Prov 19:29 8201
Yea, in the way of thy *j*, O LORD, ... Is 26:8 4941
for when thy *j* are in the earth, ... Is 26:9 4941
I will utter my *j* against them ... Jer 1:16 4941
let me talk with thee of thy *j* ... Jer 12:1 4941
she hath changed my *j* into ... Eze 5:6 4941
for they have refused my *j* ... Eze 5:6 4941
statutes, neither have kept my *j* ... Eze 5:7 4941
have done according to the *j* of ... Eze 5:7 4941
will execute *j* in the midst of ... Eze 5:8 4941
and I will execute *j* in thee ... Eze 5:10 8201
shall execute *j* in thee in anger ... Eze 5:15 8201
and will execute *j* among you ... Eze 11:9 8201
statutes, neither executed my *j* ... Eze 11:12 4941
my four sore *j* upon Jerusalem ... Eze 14:21 8201
execute *j* upon thee in the sight ... Eze 16:41 8201
in my statutes, and hath kept my *j* ... Eze 18:9 4941
nor increase, hath executed my *j* ... Eze 18:17 4941
my statutes, and shewed them my *j* ... Eze 20:11 4941
statutes, and they despised my *j* ... Eze 20:13 4941
Because they despised my *j* ... Eze 20:16 4941
fathers, neither observe their *j* ... Eze 20:18 4941
walk in my statutes, and keep my *j* ... Eze 20:19 4941
neither kept my *j* to do them ... Eze 20:21 4941
they had not executed my *j* ... Eze 20:24 4941
j whereby they should not live ... Eze 20:25 4941
judge thee according to their *j* ... Eze 23:24 4941
And I will execute *j* upon Moab ... Eze 25:11 8201
I shall have executed *j* in her ... Eze 28:22 8201
when I have executed *j* upon all ... Eze 28:26 8201
in Zoan, and will execute *j* in No ... Eze 30:14 8201
Thus will I execute *j* in Egypt ... Eze 30:19 8201
statutes, and ye shall keep my *j* ... Eze 36:27 4941
they shall also walk in my *j* ... Eze 37:24 4941
shall judge it according to my *j* ... Eze 44:24 4941
from thy precepts and from thy *j* ... Dan 9:5 4941
thy *j* are as the light that goeth ... Hos 6:5 4941
The LORD hath taken away thy *j* ... Zeph 3:15 4941
Israel, with the statutes and *j* ... Mal 4:4 4941
how unsearchable are his *j* ... Rom 11:33 *2917*
If then ye have *j* of things ... 1Cor 6:4 *2922*
for thy *j* are made manifest ... Rev 15:4 *1345*
true and righteous are thy *j* ... Rev 16:7 *2920*
For true and righteous are his *j* ... Rev 19:2 *2920*

JUDITH *(ju'-dith)* {1} *A wife of Esau.*
wife *J* the daughter of Beeri the ... Gen 26:34 3067

JUICE {1}
wine of the *j* of my pomegranate ... Song 8:2 6071

JULIA *(ju'-le-ah)* {1} *A Christian acquaintance of Paul.*
Salute Philologus, and *J*, Nereus, ... Rom 16:15 *2456*

JULIUS *(ju'-le-us)* {2} *A Roman centurion.*
other prisoners unto one named *J* ... Acts 27:1 *2457*
J courteously entreated Paul, and ... Acts 27:3 *2457*

JUMPING {1}
horses, and of the *j* chariots ... Nah 3:2 7540

JUNIA *(ju'-ne-ah)* {1} *A Christian acquaintance of Paul.*
Salute Andronicus and *J*, my ... Rom 16:7 *2458*

JUNIPER {4}
came and sat down under a *j* tree ... 1Kin 19:4 7574
as he lay and slept under a *j* tree ... 1Kin 19:5 7574
bushes, and *j* roots for their meat ... Job 30:4 7574
of the mighty, with coals of *j* ... Ps 120:4 7574

JUPITER *(ju'-pit-ur)* {3} *Chief god of the Romans.*
And they called Barnabas, *J* ... Acts 14:12 *2203*
Then the priest of *J*, which was ... Acts 14:13 *2203*
the image which fell down from *J* ... Acts 19:35 *1356*

JURISDICTION {1}
that he belonged unto Herod's *j* ... Lk 23:7 *1849*

JUSHAB-HESED *(ju'-shab-he'-sed)* {1} *A son of Zerubbabel.*
and Berechiah, and Hasadiah, *J* ... 1Chr 3:20 3142

JUST {94}
Noah was a *j* man and perfect in ... Gen 6:9 6662
J balances, *j* weights ... Lev 19:36 6664
a *j* ephah, and a *j* hin, shall ... Lev 19:36 6664
judge the people with *j* judgment ... Deut 16:18 6664
is altogether *j* shalt thou follow ... Deut 16:20 6664
j weight, a perfect and ... Deut 25:15 6664
j measure shalt thou have ... Deut 25:15 6664
of truth and without iniquity, *j* ... Deut 32:4 6662
He that ruleth over men must be *j* ... 2Sa 23:3 6662
Howbeit thou art *j* in all that is ... Neh 9:33 6662
mortal man be more *j* than God ... Job 4:17 6663
but how should man be *j* with God ... Job 9:2 6663
the *j* upright man is laughed to ... Job 12:4 6662
but the *j* shall put it on, and the ... Job 27:17 6662
Behold, in this thou art not *j* ... Job 33:12 6663
thou condemn him that is most *j* ... Job 34:17 6662
but establish the *j* ... Ps 7:9 6662

J

The wicked plotteth against the *j* ... Ps 37:12 6662
blesseth the habitation of the *j* ... Prov 3:33 6662
But the path of the *j* is as the ... Prov 4:18 6662
teach a *j* man, and he will ... Prov 9:9 6662
are upon the head of the *j* ... Prov 10:6 6662
The memory of the *j* is blessed ... Prov 10:7 6662
The tongue of the *j* is as choice ... Prov 10:20 6662
The mouth of the *j* bringeth forth ... Prov 10:31 6662
but a *j* weight is his delight ... Prov 11:1 8003
shall the *j* be delivered ... Prov 11:9 6662
but the *j* shall come out of ... Prov 12:13 6662
shall no evil happen to the *j* ... Prov 12:21 6662
the sinner is laid up for the *j* ... Prov 13:22 6662
A *j* weight and balance are the ... Prov 16:11 4941
and he that condemneth the *j* ... Prov 17:15 6662
Also to punish the *j* is not good ... Prov 17:26 6662
first in his own cause seemeth *j* ... Prov 18:17 6662
The *j* man walketh in his ... Prov 20:7 6662
It is joy to the *j* to do judgment ... Prov 21:15 6662
For a *j* man falleth seven times, ... Prov 24:16 6662
but the *j* seek his soul ... Prov 29:10 3477
man is an abomination to the *j* ... Prov 29:27 6662
there is a *j* man that perisheth ... Eccl 7:15 6662
there is not a *j* man upon earth ... Eccl 7:20 6662
that there be *j* men, unto whom it ... Eccl 8:14 6662
The way of the *j* is uprightness ... Is 26:7 6662
dost weigh the path of the *j* ... Is 26:7 6662
turn aside the *j* for a thing of ... Is 29:21 6662
a *j* God and a Saviour ... Is 45:21 6662
of the *j* in the midst of her ... Lam 4:13 6662
But if a man be *j*, and do that ... Eze 18:5 6662
he is *j*, he shall surely live, ... Eze 18:9 6662
Ye shall have *j* balances, and a ... Eze 45:10 6664
a *j* ephah, and a *j* bath ... Eze 45:10 6664
and the *j* shall walk in them ... Hos 14:9 6662
they afflict the *j*, they take a ... Amos 5:12 6662
but the *j* shall live by his faith ... Hab 2:4 6662
The *j* LORD is in the midst ... Zeph 3:5 6662
he is *j*, and having salvation ... Zec 9:9 6662
Joseph her husband, being a *j* man ... Mt 1:19 *1342*
good, and sendeth rain on the *j* ... Mt 5:45 *1342*
sever the wicked from among the *j* ... Mt 13:49 *1342*
nothing to do with that *j* man ... Mt 27:19 *1342*
of the blood of this *j* person ... Mt 27:24 *1342*
John, knowing that he was a *j* man ... Mk 6:20 *1342*
to the wisdom of the *j* ... Lk 1:17 *1342*
and the same man was *j* and devout, ... Lk 2:25 *1342*
at the resurrection of the *j* ... Lk 14:14 *1342*
nine *j* persons, which need no ... Lk 15:7 *1342*
should feign themselves *j* men ... Lk 20:20 *1342*
and he was a good man, and a *j* ... Lk 23:50 *1342*
and my judgment is *j* ... Jn 5:30 *1342*
ye denied the Holy One and the *J* ... Acts 3:14 *1342*
before of the coming of the *J* One ... Acts 7:52 *1342*
a *j* man, and one that feareth God, ... Acts 10:22 *1342*
know his will, and see that *J* One ... Acts 22:14 *1342*
of the dead, both of the *j* ... Acts 24:15 *1342*
The *j* shall live by faith ... Rom 1:17 *1342*
of the law are *j* before God ... Rom 2:13 *1342*
whose damnation is *j* ... Rom 3:8 *1738*
that he might be *j*, and the ... Rom 3:26 *1342*
and the commandment holy, and *j* ... Rom 7:12 *1342*
The *j* shall live by faith ... Gal 3:11 *1342*
honest, whatsoever things are *j* ... Phil 4:8 *1342*
your servants that which is *j* ... Col 4:1 *1342*
a lover of good men, sober, *j* ... Titus 1:8 *1342*
received a *j* recompence of reward ... Heb 2:2 *1738*
Now the *j* shall live by faith ... Heb 10:38 *1342*
the spirits of *j* men made perfect ... Heb 12:23 *1342*
Ye have condemned and killed the *j* ... Jas 5:6 *1342*
the *j* for the unjust, that he ... 1Pet 3:18 *1342*
And delivered *j* Lot, vexed with ... 2Pet 2:7 *1342*
j to forgive us our sins, and to ... 1Jn 1:9 *1342*
j and true are thy ways, thou King ... Rev 15:3 *1342*

JUSTICE {28}
keep the way of the LORD, to do *j* ... Gen 18:19 6666
he executed the *j* of the LORD ... Deut 33:21 6666
judgment and *j* unto all his people ... 2Sa 8:15 6666
come unto me, and I would do him *j* ... 2Sa 15:4 6663
he thee king, to do judgment and *j* ... 1Kin 10:9 6666
and *j* among all his people ... 1Chr 18:14 6666
over them, to do judgment and *j* ... 2Chr 9:8 6666
or doth the Almighty pervert *j* ... Job 8:3 6664
judgment and *j* take hold on thee ... Job 36:17 4941
and in judgment, and in plenty of *j* ... Job 37:23 6666
do *j* to the afflicted and needy ... Ps 82:3 6663
J and judgment are the habitation ... Ps 89:14 6664
I have done judgment and *j* ... Ps 119:121 6664
the instruction of wisdom, *j* ... Prov 1:3 6664
kings reign, and princes decree *j* ... Prov 8:15 6664
To do *j* and judgment is more ... Prov 21:3 6666
j in a province, marvel not at ... Eccl 5:8 6664
with *j* from henceforth even for ... Is 9:7 6666
LORD, Keep ye judgment, and do *j* ... Is 56:1 6666
ask of me the ordinances of *j* ... Is 58:2 6664
None calleth for *j*, nor any ... Is 59:4 6664
us, neither doth *j* overtake us ... Is 59:9 6666
backward, and *j* standeth afar off ... Is 59:14 6666
eat and drink, and do judgment and *j* ... Jer 22:15 6666
judgment and *j* in the earth ... Jer 23:5 6666
bless thee, O habitation of *j* ... Jer 31:23 6664
the LORD, the habitation of *j* ... Jer 50:7 6664
spoil, and execute judgment and *j* ... Eze 45:9 6666

JUSTIFICATION {3}
and was raised again for our *j* ... Rom 4:25 *1347*
gift is of many offences unto *j* ... Rom 5:16 *1345*
came upon all men unto *j* of life ... Rom 5:18 *1347*

JUSTIFIED {43}
and should a man full of talk be *j* ... Job 11:2 6663
I know that I shall be *j* ... Job 13:18 6663
How then can man be *j* with God ... Job 25:4 6663
because he *j* himself rather than ... Job 32:2 6663
mightest be *j* when thou speakest ... Ps 51:4 6663
sight shall no man living be *j* ... Ps 143:2 6663
witnesses, that they may be *j* ... Is 43:9 6663
thou, that thou mayest be *j* ... Is 43:26 6663
shall all the seed of Israel be *j* ... Is 45:25 6663
The backsliding Israel hath *j* ... Jer 3:11 6663
hast *j* thy sisters in all thine ... Eze 16:51 6663
in that thou hast *j* thy sisters ... Eze 16:52 6663
But wisdom is *j* of her children ... Mt 11:19 *1344*
For by thy words thou shalt be *j* ... Mt 12:37 *1344*
j God, being baptized with the ... Lk 7:29 *1344*
But wisdom is *j* of all her ... Lk 7:35 *1344*
his house *j* rather than the other ... Lk 18:14 *1344*
believe are *j* from all things ... Acts 13:39 *1344*
not be *j* by the law of Moses ... Acts 13:39 *1344*
the doers of the law shall be *j* ... Rom 2:13 *1344*
thou mightest be *j* in thy sayings ... Rom 3:4 *1344*
shall no flesh be *j* in his sight ... Rom 3:20 *1344*
Being *j* freely by his grace ... Rom 3:24 *1344*
we conclude that a man is *j* by ... Rom 3:28 *1344*
For if Abraham were *j* by works ... Rom 4:2 *1344*
Therefore being *j* by faith ... Rom 5:1 *1344*
being now *j* by his blood, we ... Rom 5:9 *1344*
and whom he called, them he also *j* ... Rom 8:30 *1344*
and whom he *j*, them he also ... Rom 8:30 *1344*
yet am I not hereby *j* ... 1Cor 4:4 *1344*
but ye are *j* in the name of the ... 1Cor 6:11 *1344*
is not *j* by the works of the law ... Gal 2:16 *1344*
that we might be *j* by the faith ... Gal 2:16 *1344*
of the law shall no flesh be *j* ... Gal 2:16 *1344*
while we seek to be *j* by Christ ... Gal 2:17 *1344*
But that no man is *j* by the law ... Gal 3:11 *1344*
that we might be *j* by faith ... Gal 3:24 *1344*
whosoever of you are *j* by the law ... Gal 5:4 *1344*
j in the Spirit, seen of angels, ... 1Ti 3:16 *1344*
That being *j* by his grace, we ... Titus 3:7 *1344*
not Abraham our father *j* by works ... Jas 2:21 *1344*
then how that by works a man is *j* ... Jas 2:24 *1344*
not Rahab the harlot *j* by works ... Jas 2:25 *1344*

JUSTIFIER {1}
the *j* of him which believeth in ... Rom 3:26 *1344*

JUSTIFIETH {4}
He that *j* the wicked, and he that ... Prov 17:15 6663
He is near that *j* me ... Is 50:8 6663
on him that *j* the ungodly ... Rom 4:5 *1344*
It is God that *j* ... Rom 8:33 *1344*

JUSTIFY {11}
for I will not *j* the wicked ... Ex 23:7 6663
then they shall *j* the righteous ... Deut 25:1 6663
If I *j* myself, mine own mouth ... Job 9:20 6663
God forbid that I should *j* you ... Job 27:5 6663
speak, for I desire to *j* thee ... Job 33:32 6663
Which *j* the wicked for reward, and ... Is 5:23 6663
shall my righteous servant *j* many ... Is 53:11 6663
But he, willing to *j* himself ... Lk 10:29 *1344*
Ye are they which *j* yourselves ... Lk 16:15 *1344*
which shall *j* the circumcision by ... Rom 3:30 *1344*
would *j* the heathen through faith ... Gal 3:8 *1344*

JUSTIFYING {2}
j the righteous, to give him ... 1Kin 8:32 6663
by *j* the righteous, by giving him ... 2Chr 6:23 6663

JUSTLE {1}
they shall *j* one against another ... Nah 2:4 8264

JUSTLY {3}
LORD require of thee, but to do *j* ... Mic 6:8 4941
And we indeed *j*; for we receive ... Lk 23:41 *1346*
and God also, how holily and *j* ... 1Th 2:10 *1346*

JUSTUS *(jus'-tus)* {3} See BARSABAS, JESUS.
1. Surname for Barsabas.
Barsabas, who was surnamed *J* ... Acts 1:23 *2459*
2. A Corinthian Christian.
a certain man's house, named *J* ... Acts 18:7 *2459*
3. A Christian acquaintance of Paul.
And Jesus, which is called *J* ... Col 4:11 *2459*

JUTTAH *(jut'-tah)* {2} *A city in Judah.*
Maon, Carmel, and Ziph, and *J* ... Josh 15:55 3194
and *J* with her suburbs, and ... Josh 21:16 3194

K

KABZEEL *(kab'-ze-el)* {3} See JEKABZEEL. *A city in Judah.*
coast of Edom southward were *K* ... Josh 15:21 6909
the son of a valiant man, of *K* ... 2Sa 23:20 6909
the son of a valiant man of *K* ... 1Chr 11:22 6909

KADESH *(ka'-desh)* {17} See EN-MISHPAT, KADESH-BARNEA, KEDESH. *A place in the wilderness, south of Judah.*
and came to En=mishpat, which is *K* ... Gen 14:7 6946
behold, it is between *K* and Bered ... Gen 16:14 6946
country, and dwelled between *K* ... Gen 20:1 6946
the wilderness of Paran, to *K* ... Num 13:26 6946
and the people abode in *K* ... Num 20:1 6946
from *K* unto the king of Edom ... Num 20:14 6946
and, behold, we are in *K*, a city ... Num 20:16 6946
congregation, journeyed from *K* ... Num 20:22 6946
in *K* in the wilderness of Zin ... Num 27:14 6946
the wilderness of Zin, which is *K* ... Num 33:36 6946
And they removed from *K*, and ... Num 33:37 6946
So ye abode in *K* many days ... Deut 1:46 6946
unto the Red sea, and came to *K* ... Judg 11:16 6946
and Israel abode in *K* ... Judg 11:17 6946
LORD shaketh the wilderness of *K* ... Ps 29:8 6946
even to the waters of strife in *K* ... Eze 47:19 6946
unto the waters of strife in *K* ... Eze 48:28 6946

KADESH-BARNEA *(ka'-desh-bar'-ne-ah)* {10} See KADESH. *Same as Kadesh.*
sent them from *K* to see the land ... Num 32:8 6947
shall be from the south to *K* ... Num 34:4 6947
by the way of mount Seir unto *K* ... Deut 1:2 6947
and we came to *K* ... Deut 1:19 6947
the space in which we came from *K* ... Deut 2:14 6947
when the LORD sent you from *K* ... Deut 9:23 6947
smote them from *K* even unto Gaza ... Josh 10:41 6947
of God concerning me and thee in *K* ... Josh 14:6 6947
me from *K* to espy out the land ... Josh 14:7 6947
up on the south side unto *K* ... Josh 15:3 6947

KADMIEL *(kad'-me-el)* {8}
1. An exile.
the children of Jeshua and *K* ... Ezr 2:40 6934
the children of Jeshua, of *K* ... Neh 7:43 6934
2. A rebuilder of the Temple.
with his sons and his brethren, *K* ... Ezr 3:9 6934
3. A Levite with Nehemiah.
the Levites, Jeshua, and Bani, *K* ... Neh 9:4 6934
Then the Levites, Jeshua, and *K* ... Neh 9:5 6934
Binnui of the sons of Henadad, *K* ... Neh 10:9 6934
Jeshua, Binnui, *K*, Sherebiah, ... Neh 12:8 6934
Sherebiah, and Jeshua the son of *K* ... Neh 12:24 6934

KADMONITES *(kad'-mo-nites)* {1} *A Phoenician tribe.*
and the Kenizzites, and the *K* ... Gen 15:19 6935

KAIN See CAIN.

KAIWAN See CHIUN.

KALLAI *(kal'-la-i)* {1} *A priest.*
Of Sallai, *K*; of Amok ... Neh 12:20 7040

KAMON See CAMON.

KANAH *(ka'-nah)* {3}
1. A brook between Ephraim and Manasseh.
Tappuah westward unto the river *K* ... Josh 16:8 7071
coast descended unto the river *K* ... Josh 17:9 7071
2. A city in Asher.
and Rehob, and Hammon, and *K* ... Josh 19:28 7071

KAREAH *(ka'-re-ah)* {13} See CAREAH. *A captain of the Jews.*
Johanan and Jonathan the sons of *K* ... Jer 40:8 7143
Moreover Johanan the son of *K* ... Jer 40:13 7143
Then Johanan the son of *K* spake ... Jer 40:15 7143
said unto Johanan the son of *K* ... Jer 40:16 7143
But when Johanan the son of *K* ... Jer 41:11 7143
Ishmael saw Johanan the son of *K* ... Jer 41:13 7143
and went unto Johanan the son of *K* ... Jer 41:14 7143
Then took Johanan the son of *K* ... Jer 41:16 7143
forces, and Johanan the son of *K* ... Jer 42:1 7143
called he Johanan the son of *K* ... Jer 42:8 7143
Hoshaiah, and Johanan the son of *K* ... Jer 43:2 7143
So Johanan the son of *K*, and all ... Jer 43:4 7143
But Johanan the son of *K*, and all ... Jer 43:5 7143

KARKA See KARKAA.

KARKAA *(kar'-ka-ah)* {1} *A city in Judah.*
Adar, and fetched a compass to *K* ... Josh 15:3 7173

KARKOR *(kar'-kor)* {1} *A Gadite city.*
Now Zebah and Zalmunna were in *K* ... Judg 8:10 7174

KARNAIM *(kar'-na-im)* {1} See ASHTEROTH. *A city in Og.*
smote the Rephaims in Ashteroth *K* ... Gen 14:5

KARTAH *(kar'-tah)* {1} See KATTATH. *A Levitical city in Zebulun.*
suburbs, and *K* with her suburbs, ... Josh 21:34 7177

KARTAN *(kar'-tan)* {1} See KIRJATHAIM. *A Levitical city in Naphtali.*
suburbs, and *K* with her suburbs ... Josh 21:32 7178

KATTATH *(kat'-tath)* {1} See KARTAH, KITRON. *A city in Zebulun.*
And *K*, and Nahallal, and Shimron, ... Josh 19:15 7005

KEBAR See CHEBAR.

KEDAR *(ke'-dar)* {12}
1. A son of Ishmael.
and *K*, and Adbeel, and Mibsam, ... Gen 25:13 6938
then *K*, and Adbeel, and Mibsam, ... 1Chr 1:29 6938

2. The tribe.
that I dwell in the tents of *K* Ps 120:5 6938
of Jerusalem, as the tents of *K* Song 1:5 6938
and all the glory of *K* shall fail Is 21:16 6938
mighty men of the children of *K* Is 21:17 6938
the villages that *K* doth inhabit Is 42:11 6938
All the flocks of *K* shall be Is 60:7 6938
and send unto *K*, and consider Jer 2:10 6938
Concerning *K*, and concerning the Jer 49:28 6938
Arise ye, go up to *K*, and spoil Jer 49:28 6938
Arabia, and all the princes of *K* Eze 27:21 6938

KEDEMAH *(ked'-e-mah)* {2} *A son of Ishmael.*
and Tema, Jetur, Naphish, and *K* Gen 25:15 6929
Jetur, Naphish, and *K* 1Chr 1:31 6929

KEDEMOTH *(ked'-e-moth)* {4}
1. A wilderness in Reuben.
out of the wilderness of *K* unto Deut 2:26 6932
2. A Levitical city in Reuben.
And Jahaza, and *K*, and Mephaath, Josh 13:18 6932
K with her suburbs, and Mephaath Josh 21:37 6932
K also with her suburbs, and 1Chr 6:79 6932

KEDESH *(ke'-desh)* {11} See KADESH, KEDESH-NAPHTALI, KISHION.
1. A Canaanite city.
The king of *K*, one Josh 12:22 6943
And *K*, and Edrei, and En-hazor, Josh 19:37 6943
2. A city of refuge in Naphtali.
they appointed *K* in Galilee in Josh 20:7 6943
K in Galilee with her suburbs, to Josh 21:32 6943
arose, and went with Barak to *K* Judg 4:9 6943
called Zebulun and Naphtali to *K* Judg 4:10 6943
plain of Zaanaim, which is by *K* Judg 4:11 6943
and Janoah, and *K*, and Hazor, and 2Kin 15:29 6943
K in Galilee with her suburbs, and 1Chr 6:76 6943
3. A Levitical city in Naphtali.
K with her suburbs, Daberath with 1Chr 6:72 6943
4. A city in Judah.
And *K*, and Hazor, and Ithnan, Josh 15:23 6943

KEDESH-NAPHTALI *(ke'-desh-naf'-ta-li)* {1} *Same as Kedesh 2.*
Barak the son of Abinoam out of *K* Judg 4:6 6943,5321

KEDOLAOMER See CHEDORLAOMER.

KEEP {362}
of Eden to dress it and to *k* it Gen 2:15 8104
to *k* the way of the tree of life Gen 3:24 8104
to *k* them alive with thee Gen 6:19 8104
come unto thee, to *k* them alive Gen 6:20 8104
to *k* seed alive upon the face of Gen 7:3
Abraham, Thou shalt *k* my covenant Gen 17:9 8104
is my covenant, which ye shall *k* Gen 17:10 8104
they shall *k* the way of the LORD, Gen 18:19 8104
will *k* thee in all places whither Gen 28:15 8104
will *k* me in this way that I go, Gen 28:20 8104
I will again feed and *k* thy flock Gen 30:31 8104
k that thou hast unto thyself Gen 33:9 1961
let them *k* food in the cities Gen 41:35 8104
whom the Egyptians *k* in bondage Ex 6:5
ye shall *k* it up until the Ex 12:6 4931
ye shall *k* it a feast to the LORD Ex 12:14 2287
ye shall *k* it a feast by an Ex 12:14 2287
that ye shall *k* this service Ex 12:25 8104
congregation of Israel shall *k* it Ex 12:47 6213
will *k* the passover to the LORD, Ex 12:48 6213
and then let him come near and *k* it Ex 12:48 6213
that thou shalt *k* this service in Ex 13:5 5647
Thou shalt therefore *k* this Ex 13:10 8104
k all his statutes, I will put Ex 15:26 8104
refuse ye to *k* my commandments Ex 16:28 8104
k my covenant, then ye shall be a Ex 19:5 8104
love me, and *k* my commandments Ex 20:6 8104
the sabbath day, to *k* it holy Ex 20:8 6942
his neighbour money or stuff to *k* Ex 22:7 8104
or a sheep, or any beast, to *k* Ex 22:10 8104
K thee far from a false matter Ex 23:7 7368
Three times thou shalt *k* a feast Ex 23:14 2287
Thou shalt *k* the feast of Ex 23:15 8104
to *k* thee in the way, and to bring Ex 23:20 8104
Verily my sabbaths ye shall *k* Ex 31:13 8104
Ye shall *k* the sabbath therefore Ex 31:14 8104
of Israel shall *k* the sabbath Ex 31:16 8104
of unleavened bread shalt thou *k* Ex 34:18 8104
that which was delivered him to *k* Lev 6:2
that which was delivered him to *k* Lev 6:4 6485
k the charge of the LORD, that ye Lev 8:35 8104
k mine ordinances, to walk Lev 18:4 8104
Ye shall therefore *k* my statutes Lev 18:5 8104
Ye shall therefore *k* my statutes Lev 18:26 8104
shall ye *k* mine ordinance Lev 18:30 8104
and his father, and *k* my sabbaths Lev 19:3 8104
Ye shall *k* my statutes Lev 19:19 8104
Ye shall *k* my sabbaths, and Lev 19:30 8104
ye shall *k* my statutes, and do Lev 20:8 8104
shall therefore *k* all my statutes Lev 20:22 8104
shall therefore *k* mine ordinance Lev 22:9 8104
shall ye *k* my commandments Lev 22:31 8104
ye shall *k* a feast unto the LORD Lev 23:39 2287
ye shall *k* it a feast unto the LORD Lev 23:41 2287
then shall the land *k* a sabbath Lev 25:2
k my judgments, and do them Lev 25:18 8104
Ye shall *k* my sabbaths, and Lev 26:2 8104
k my commandments, and do them Lev 26:3 8104
the Levites shall *k* the charge of Num 1:53 8104
And they shall *k* his charge Num 3:7 8104
they shall *k* all the instruments Num 3:8 8104
k the charge of the sanctuary Num 3:32 8104
The LORD bless thee, and *k* thee Num 6:24 8104
to *k* the charge, and shall do no Num 8:26 8104
k the passover at his appointed Num 9:2 6213
ye shall *k* it in his appointed Num 9:3 6213
ceremonies thereof, shall ye *k* it Num 9:3 6213
that they should *k* the passover Num 9:4 6213
that they could not *k* the Num 9:6 6213
yet he shall *k* the passover unto Num 9:10 6213
month at even they shall *k* it Num 9:11 6213
of the passover they shall *k* it Num 9:12 6213
and forbeareth to *k* the passover Num 9:13 6213
will *k* the passover unto the LORD Num 9:14 6213
And they shall *k* thy charge Num 18:3 8104
k the charge of the tabernacle of Num 18:4 8104
ye shall *k* the charge of the Num 18:5 8104
thy sons with thee shall *k* your Num 18:7 8104
ye shall *k* a feast unto the LORD Num 29:12 2287
with him, *k* alive for yourselves Num 31:18
which *k* the charge of the Num 31:30 8104
k himself to the inheritance of Num 36:7 1692
k himself to his own inheritance Num 36:9 1692
that ye may *k* the commandments of Deut 4:2 8104
K therefore and do them Deut 4:6 8104
k thy soul diligently, lest thou Deut 4:9 8104
Thou shalt *k* therefore his Deut 4:40 8104
day, that ye may learn them, and *k* Deut 5:1 8104
that love me and *k* my commandments Deut 5:10 8104
K the sabbath day to sanctify it, Deut 5:12 8104
thee to *k* the sabbath day Deut 5:15 6213
k all my commandments always, Deut 5:29 8104
to *k* all his statutes and his Deut 6:2 8104
Ye shall diligently *k* the Deut 6:17 8104
because he would *k* the oath which Deut 7:8 8104
k his commandments to a thousand Deut 7:9 8104
therefore *k* the commandments Deut 7:11 8104
hearken to these judgments, and *k* Deut 7:12 8104
shall *k* unto thee the covenant Deut 7:12 8104
thou wouldest *k* his commandments Deut 8:2 8104
Therefore thou shalt *k* the Deut 8:6 8104
To *k* the commandments of the LORD Deut 10:13 8104
k his charge, and his statutes, and Deut 11:1 8104
Therefore shall ye *k* all the Deut 11:8 8104
For if ye shall diligently *k* all Deut 11:22 8104
k his commandments, and obey his Deut 13:4 8104
to *k* all his commandments which I Deut 13:18 8104
k the passover unto the LORD thy Deut 16:1 6213
thou shalt *k* the feast of weeks Deut 16:10 6213
Seven days shalt thou *k* a solemn Deut 16:15 2287
to *k* all the words of this law and Deut 17:19 8104
If thou shalt *k* all these Deut 19:9 8104
then *k* thee from every wicked Deut 23:9 8104
gone out of thy lips thou shalt *k* Deut 23:23 8104
thou shalt therefore *k* and do them Deut 26:16 8104
to *k* his statutes, and his Deut 26:17 8104
that thou shouldest *k* all his Deut 26:18 8104
K all the commandments which I Deut 27:1 8104
if thou shalt *k* the commandments Deut 28:9 8104
to *k* his commandments and his Deut 28:45 8104
K therefore the words of this Deut 29:9 8104
to *k* his commandments and his Deut 30:10 8104
to *k* his commandments and his Deut 30:16 8104
in any wise *k* yourselves from the Josh 6:18 8104
and set men by it for to *k* them Josh 10:18 8104
to *k* his commandments, and to Josh 22:5 8104
ye therefore very courageous to *k* Josh 23:6 8104
whether they will *k* the way of Judg 2:22 8104
as their fathers did *k* it Judg 2:22 8104
who said, *K* silence Judg 3:19
Thou shalt *k* fast by my young men Ruth 2:21 1692
He will *k* the feet of his saints, 1Sa 2:9 8104
his son to *k* the ark of the LORD 1Sa 7:1 8104
and with one full line to *k* alive 2Sa 8:2
were concubines, to *k* the house 2Sa 15:16 8104
which he hath left to *k* the house 2Sa 16:21 8104
I have no son to *k* my name in 2Sa 18:18
whom he had left to *k* the house 2Sa 20:3 8104
k the charge of the LORD thy God, 1Kin 2:3 8104
to *k* his statutes, and his 1Kin 2:3 8104
my ways, to *k* my statutes and my 1Kin 3:14 8104
k all my commandments to walk in 1Kin 6:12 8104
k with thy servant David my 1Kin 8:25 8104
to *k* his commandments, and his 1Kin 8:58 8104
to *k* his commandments, as at this 1Kin 8:61 8104
thee, and wilt *k* my statutes and my 1Kin 9:4 8104
will not *k* my commandments and my 1Kin 9:6 8104
to *k* my statutes and my judgments, 1Kin 11:33
my sight, to *k* my statutes and my 1Kin 11:38 8104
man unto me, and said, *K* this man 1Kin 20:39 8104
so shall ye *k* the watch of the 2Kin 11:6 8104
even they shall *k* the watch of 2Kin 11:7 8104
k my commandments and my statutes, 2Kin 17:13 8104
to *k* his commandments and his 2Kin 23:3 8104
K the passover unto the LORD your 2Kin 23:21 6213
that thou wouldest *k* me from evil 1Chr 4:10 6213
thousand, which could *k* rank 1Chr 12:33 5737
men of war, that could *k* rank 1Chr 12:38 5737
that thou mayest *k* the law of the 1Chr 22:12 8104
that they should *k* the charge of 1Chr 23:32 8104
and in the audience of our God, *k* 1Chr 28:8 8104
fathers, *k* this for ever in the 1Chr 29:18 8104
to *k* thy commandments, thy 1Chr 29:19 8104
k with thy servant David my 2Chr 6:16 8104
for we *k* the charge of the LORD 2Chr 13:11 8104
no power to *k* still the kingdom 2Chr 22:9 6113
shall *k* the watch of the LORD 2Chr 23:6 8104
now ye purpose to *k* under the 2Chr 28:10 3533
to *k* the passover unto the LORD 2Chr 30:1 6213
to *k* the passover in the second 2Chr 30:2 6213
they could not *k* it at that time 2Chr 30:3 6213
that they should come to *k* the 2Chr 30:5 6213
at Jerusalem much people to *k* the 2Chr 30:13 6213
counsel to *k* other seven days 2Chr 30:23 6213
to *k* his commandments, and his 2Chr 34:31 8104
to *k* the passover, and to offer 2Chr 35:16 6213
did all the kings of Israel *k* 2Chr 35:18 6213
k them, until ye weigh them Ezr 8:29 8104
k my commandments, and do them Neh 1:9 8104
to *k* the dedication with gladness Neh 12:27 6213
k the gates, to sanctify the Neh 13:22 8104
neither *k* they the king's laws Est 3:8 6213
that they should *k* the fourteenth Est 9:21 6213
that they would *k* these two days Est 9:27 6213
that thou wouldest *k* me secret Job 14:13
but *k* it still within his mouth Job 20:13 4513
Thou shalt *k* them, O LORD, thou Ps 12:7 8104
K me as the apple of the eye Ps 17:8 8104
K back thy servant also from Ps 19:13 2820
none can *k* alive his own soul Ps 22:29
truth unto such as *k* his covenant Ps 25:10 5341
O *k* my soul, and deliver me Ps 25:20 8104
thou shalt *k* them secretly in a Ps 31:20
to *k* them alive in famine Ps 33:19
K thy tongue from evil, and thy Ps 34:13 5341
k not silence Ps 35:22
k his way, and he shall exalt thee Ps 37:34 8104
I will *k* my mouth with a bridle, Ps 39:1 8104
will preserve him, and *k* him alive Ps 41:2
come, and shall not *k* silence Ps 50:3
of God, but *k* his commandments Ps 78:7 5341
K not thou silence, O God Ps 83:1
My mercy will I *k* for him for Ps 89:28 8104
and *k* not my commandments Ps 89:31 8104
to *k* thee in all thy ways Ps 91:11 8104
neither will he *k* his anger for Ps 103:9 5201
To such as *k* his covenant, and to Ps 103:18 8104
his statutes, and *k* his laws Ps 105:45 5341
Blessed are they that *k* judgment Ps 106:3 8104
the barren woman to *k* house Ps 113:9
are they that *k* his testimonies Ps 119:2 5341
us to *k* thy precepts diligently Ps 119:4 8104
were directed to *k* thy statutes Ps 119:5 8104
I will *k* thy statutes Ps 119:8 8104
that I may live, and *k* thy word Ps 119:17 8104
I shall *k* it unto the end Ps 119:33 5341
and I shall *k* thy law Ps 119:34 5341
So shall I *k* thy law continually Ps 119:44 8104
said that I would *k* thy words Ps 119:57 8104
delayed not to *k* thy commandments Ps 119:60 8104
and of them that *k* thy precepts Ps 119:63 8104
but I will *k* thy precepts with my Ps 119:69 5341
so shall I *k* the testimony of thy Ps 119:88 8104
because I *k* thy precepts Ps 119:100 5341
evil way, that I might *k* thy word Ps 119:101 8104
that I will *k* thy righteous Ps 119:106 8104
for I will *k* the commandments of Ps 119:115 5341
therefore doth my soul *k* them Ps 119:129 5341
so will I *k* thy precepts Ps 119:134 8104
eyes, because they *k* not thy law Ps 119:136 8104
I will *k* thy statutes Ps 119:145 5341
I shall *k* thy testimonies Ps 119:146 8104
except the LORD *k* the city Ps 127:1 8104
thy children will *k* my covenant Ps 132:12 8104
K me, O LORD, from the hands of Ps 140:4 8104
K the door of my lips Ps 141:3 5341
K me from the snares which they Ps 141:9 8104
thee, understanding shall *k* thee Prov 2:11 5341
k the paths of the righteous Prov 2:20 8104
let thine heart *k* my commandments Prov 3:1 5341
k sound wisdom and discretion Prov 3:21 5341
shall *k* thy foot from being taken Prov 3:26 8104
k my commandments, and live Prov 4:4 8104
love her, and she shall *k* thee Prov 4:6 5341
let her not go: *k* her Prov 4:13 5341
k them in the midst of thine Prov 4:21 8104
K thy heart with all diligence Prov 4:23 5341
and that thy lips may *k* knowledge Prov 5:2 5341
k thy father's commandment, and Prov 6:20 5341
thou sleepest, it shall *k* thee Prov 6:22 8104
To *k* thee from the evil woman, Prov 6:24 8104
My son, *k* my words, and lay up my Prov 7:1 8104
K my commandments, and live Prov 7:2 8104
That they may *k* thee from the Prov 7:5 8104
blessed are they that *k* my ways Prov 8:32 8104
he that doth *k* his soul shall be Prov 22:5 8104
thing if thou *k* them within thee Prov 22:18 8104
but such as *k* the law contend Prov 28:4 8104
a time to *k*, and a time to cast Eccl 3:6 8104
a time to *k* silence, and a time to Eccl 3:7
K thy foot when thou goest to the Eccl 5:1 8104
I counsel thee to *k* the king's Eccl 8:2 8104
Fear God, and *k* his commandments Eccl 12:13 8104
those that *k* the fruit thereof Song 8:12 5201
Thou wilt *k* him in perfect peace, Is 26:3 5341
I the LORD do *k* it Is 27:3 5341
hurt it, I will *k* it night and day Is 27:3 5341
K silence before me, O islands Is 41:1
hold thine hand, and will *k* thee Is 42:6 5341
and to the south, *K* not back Is 43:6 3607
K ye judgment, and do justice Is 56:1 8104
the eunuchs that *k* my sabbaths Is 56:4 8104
of the LORD, *k* not silence, Is 62:6
I will not *k* silence, but will Is 65:6
will he *k* it to the end Jer 3:5 8104
I will not *k* anger for ever Jer 3:12 5201
k him, as a shepherd doth his Jer 31:10 8104
I will *k* nothing back from you Jer 42:4 4513
sit upon the ground, and *k* silence Lam 2:10

k mine ordinances, and do them ... Eze 11:20 8104
k all my statutes, and do that ... Eze 18:21 8104
k my judgments, and do them ... Eze 20:19 8104
ye shall *k* my judgments, and do ... Eze 36:27 8104
that they may *k* the whole form ... Eze 43:11 8104
me, and they shall *k* my charge ... Eze 44:16 8104
and they shall *k* my laws and my ... Eze 44:24 8104
to them that *k* his commandments ... Dan 9:4 8104
k mercy and judgment, and wait on ... Hos 12:6 8104
shall *k* silence in that time ... Amos 5:13
k the doors of thy mouth from her ... Mic 7:5 8104
k thy solemn feasts, perform thy ... Nah 1:15 2287
k the munition, watch the way, ... Nah 2:1 5341
let all the earth *k* silence ... Hab 2:20
ways, and if thou wilt *k* my charge ... Zec 3:7 8104
house, and shalt also *k* my courts ... Zec 3:7 8104
me to *k* cattle from my youth ... Zec 13:5 7069
to *k* the feast of tabernacles ... Zec 14:16 2287
up to *k* the feast of tabernacles ... Zec 14:18 2287
up to *k* the feast of tabernacles ... Zec 14:19 2287
priest's lips should *k* knowledge ... Mal 2:7 8104
into life, *k* the commandments ... Mt 19:17 *5083*
I will *k* the passover at thy ... Mt 26:18 *4160*
that ye may *k* your own tradition ... Mk 7:9 *5083*
charge over thee, to *k* thee ... Lk 4:10 *1314*
k it, and bring forth fruit with ... Lk 8:15 *2722*
hear the word of God, and *k* it ... Lk 11:28 *5442*
and *k* thee in on every side, ... Lk 19:43 *4912*
If a man *k* my saying, he shall ... Jn 8:51 *5083*
If a man *k* my saying, he shall ... Jn 8:52 *5083*
but I know him, and *k* his saying ... Jn 8:55 *5083*
shall *k* it unto life eternal ... Jn 12:25 *5442*
If ye love me, *k* my commandments ... Jn 14:15 *5083*
a man love me, he will *k* my words ... Jn 14:23 *5083*
If ye *k* my commandments, ye shall ... Jn 15:10 *5083*
my saying, they will *k* yours also ... Jn 15:20 *5083*
k through thine own name those ... Jn 17:11 *5083*
shouldest *k* them from the evil ... Jn 17:15 *5083*
to *k* back part of the price of ... Acts 5:3 *3557*
a man that is a Jew to *k* company ... Acts 10:28 *2853*
quaternions of soldiers to *k* him ... Acts 12:4 *5442*
them to *k* the law of Moses ... Acts 15:5 *5083*
must be circumcised, and *k* the law ... Acts 15:24 *5083*
from which if ye *k* yourselves ... Acts 15:29 *1301*
them the decrees for to *k* ... Acts 16:4 *5442*
the jailer to *k* them safely ... Acts 16:23 *5083*
I must by all means *k* this feast ... Acts 18:21 *4160*
save only that they *k* themselves ... Acts 21:25 *5442*
commanded a centurion to *k* Paul ... Acts 24:23 *5083*
profiteth, if thou *k* the law ... Rom 2:25 *4238*
k the righteousness of the law ... Rom 2:26 *5442*
Therefore let us *k* the feast ... 1Cor 5:8 *1858*
written unto you not to *k* company ... 1Cor 5:11 *4874*
heart that he will *k* his virgin ... 1Cor 7:37 *5083*
But I *k* under my body, and bring ... 1Cor 9:27 *5299*
k the ordinances, as I delivered ... 1Cor 11:2 *2722*
let him *k* silence in the church ... 1Cor 14:28 *4601*
Let your women *k* silence in the ... 1Cor 14:34 *4601*
if ye *k* in memory what I preached ... 1Cor 15:2 *2722*
unto you, and so will I *k* myself ... 2Cor 11:9 *5083*
who are circumcised *k* the law ... Gal 6:13 *5442*
Endeavouring to *k* the unity of ... Eph 4:3 *5083*
shall *k* your hearts and minds ... Phil 4:7 *5432*
stablish you, and *k* you from evil ... 2Th 3:3 *5442*
k thyself pure ... 1Ti 5:22 *5083*
That thou *k* this commandment ... 1Ti 6:14 *5083*
k that which is committed to thy ... 1Ti 6:20 *5442*
to *k* that which I have committed ... 2Ti 1:12 *5442*
thee *k* by the Holy Ghost which ... 2Ti 1:14 *5442*
to *k* himself unspotted from the ... Jas 1:27 *5083*
whosoever shall *k* the whole law ... Jas 2:10 *5083*
him, if we *k* his commandments ... 1Jn 2:3 *5083*
because we *k* his commandments, and ... 1Jn 3:22 *5083*
love God, and *k* his commandments ... 1Jn 5:2 *5083*
that we *k* his commandments ... 1Jn 5:3 *5083*
children, *k* yourselves from idols ... 1Jn 5:21 *5442*
K yourselves in the love of God, ... Jude 21 *5083*
is able to *k* you from falling ... Jude 24 *5442*
k those things which are written ... Rev 1:3 *5083*
I also will *k* thee from the hour ... Rev 3:10 *5083*
which *k* the commandments of God, ... Rev 12:17 *5083*
here are they that *k* the ... Rev 14:12 *5083*
of them which *k* the sayings of ... Rev 22:9 *5083*

KEEPER {21}
And Abel was a *k* of sheep, but ... Gen 4:2 7462
Am I my brother's *k* ... Gen 4:9 8104
the sight of the *k* of the prison ... Gen 39:21 8269
the *k* of the prison committed to ... Gen 39:22 8269
The *k* of the prison looked not to ... Gen 39:23 8269
and left the sheep with a *k* ... 1Sa 17:20 8104
the hand of the *k* of the carriage ... 1Sa 17:22 8104
make thee *k* of mine head for ever ... 1Sa 28:2 8104
son of Harhas, *k* of the wardrobe ... 2Kin 22:14 8104
son of Hasrah, *k* of the wardrobe ... 2Chr 34:22 8104
Asaph the *k* of the king's forest ... Neh 2:8 8104
the *k* of the east gate ... Neh 3:29 8104
chamberlain, *k* of the women ... Est 2:3 8104
custody of Hegai, *k* of the women ... Est 2:8 8104
the *k* of the women, appointed ... Est 2:15 8104
and as a booth that the *k* maketh ... Job 27:18 5341
The LORD is thy *k* ... Ps 121:5 8104
made me the *k* of the vineyards ... Song 1:6 5201
son of Shallum, the *k* of the door ... Jer 35:4 8104
the *k* of the prison awaking out ... Acts 16:27 *1200*
the *k* of the prison told this ... Acts 16:36 *1200*

KEEPERS {21}
be *k* of the watch of the king's ... 2Kin 11:5 8104
which the *k* of the door have ... 2Kin 22:4 8104
the *k* of the door, to bring forth ... 2Kin 23:4 8104
and the three *k* of the door ... 2Kin 25:18 8104
k of the gates of the tabernacle ... 1Chr 9:19 8104
of the LORD, were *k* of the entry ... 1Chr 9:19 8104
the *k* of the door, who sought to ... Est 6:2 8104
In the day when the *k* of the ... Eccl 12:3 8104
the *k* of the walls took away my ... Song 5:7 8104
he let out the vineyard unto *k* ... Song 8:11 5201
As *k* of a field, are they against ... Jer 4:17 8104
and the three *k* of the door ... Jer 52:24 8104
the *k* of the charge of the house ... Eze 40:45 8104
the *k* of the charge of the altar ... Eze 40:46 8104
but ye have set *k* of my charge in ... Eze 44:8 8104
But I will make them *k* of the ... Eze 44:14 8104
for fear of him the *k* did shake ... Mt 28:4 *5083*
the *k* standing without before the ... Acts 5:23 *5441*
the *k* before the door kept the ... Acts 12:6 *5441*
found him not, he examined the *k* ... Acts 12:19 *5441*
k at home, good, obedient to ... Titus 2:5 *3626*

KEEPEST {4}
who *k* covenant and mercy with thy ... 1Kin 8:23 8104
which *k* covenant, and shewest ... 2Chr 6:14 8104
who *k* covenant and mercy, let not ... Neh 9:32 8104
walkest orderly, and *k* the law ... Acts 21:24 *5442*

KEEPETH {48}
and he die not, but *k* his bed ... Ex 21:18 5307
which *k* covenant and mercy with ... Deut 7:9 8104
and, behold, he *k* the sheep ... 1Sa 16:11 7462
that *k* covenant and mercy for them ... Neh 1:5 8104
He *k* back his soul from the pit, ... Job 33:18 2820
He *k* all his bones ... Ps 34:20 8104
he that *k* thee will not slumber ... Ps 121:3 8104
he that *k* Israel shall neither ... Ps 121:4 8104
which *k* truth for ever ... Ps 146:6 8104
He *k* the paths of judgment, and ... Prov 2:8 5341
way of life that *k* instruction ... Prov 10:17 8104
He that *k* his mouth *k* his ... Prov 13:3 5341
that *k* his mouth *k* his life ... Prov 13:3 8104
Righteousness *k* him that is ... Prov 13:6 5341
he that *k* his way preserveth his ... Prov 16:17 5341
he that *k* understanding shall ... Prov 19:8 8104
He that *k* the commandment *k* ... Prov 19:16 8104
Whoso *k* his mouth and his tongue ... Prov 21:23 8104
his tongue *k* his soul from ... Prov 21:23 8104
he that *k* thy soul, doth not he ... Prov 24:12 5341
Whoso *k* the fig tree shall eat ... Prov 27:18 5341
Whoso *k* the law is a wise son ... Prov 28:7 5341
but he that *k* company with ... Prov 29:3
but a wise man *k* it in till ... Prov 29:11 7623
but he that *k* the law, happy is ... Prov 29:18 8104
Whoso *k* the commandment shall ... Eccl 8:5 8104
which *k* the truth may enter in ... Is 26:2 8104
that *k* the sabbath from polluting ... Is 56:2 8104
k his hand from doing any evil ... Is 56:2 8104
every one that *k* the sabbath from ... Is 56:6 8104
cursed be he that *k* back his ... Jer 48:10 4513
k silence, because he hath borne ... Lam 3:28
is a proud man, neither *k* at home ... Hab 2:5
a strong man armed *k* his palace ... Lk 11:21 *5442*
law, and yet none of you *k* the law ... Jn 7:19 *4160*
because he *k* not the sabbath day ... Jn 9:16 *5083*
k them, he it is that loveth me ... Jn 14:21 *5083*
loveth me not *k* not my sayings ... Jn 14:24 *5083*
k not his commandments, is a liar ... 1Jn 2:4 *5083*
But whoso *k* his word, in him ... 1Jn 2:5 *5083*
he that *k* his commandments ... 1Jn 3:24 *5083*
that is begotten of God *k* himself ... 1Jn 5:18 *5083*
k my works unto the end, to him ... Rev 2:26 *5083*
k his garments, lest he walk ... Rev 16:15 *5083*
blessed is he that *k* the sayings ... Rev 22:7 *5083*

KEEPING {12}
K mercy for thousands, forgiving ... Ex 34:7 5341
k the charge of the sanctuary ... Num 3:28 8104
k the charge of the sanctuary for ... Num 3:38 8104
in not *k* his commandments, and his ... Deut 8:11 8104
we were with them *k* the sheep ... 1Sa 25:16 7462
were porters *k* the ward at the ... Neh 12:25 8104
in *k* of them there is great ... Ps 19:11 8104
but that by *k* of his covenant it ... Eze 17:14 8104
k the covenant and mercy to them ... Dan 9:4 8104
k watch over their flock by night ... Lk 2:8 *5442*
but the *k* of the commandments of ... 1Cor 7:19 *5084*
k of their souls to him in well ... 1Pet 4:19

KEHELATHAH *(ke-hel'-a-thah)* {2} *An Israelite encampment in the wilderness.*
from Rissah, and pitched in *K* ... Num 33:22 6954
And they went from *K*, and pitched ... Num 33:23 6954

KEILAH *(ki'-lah)* {18}
1. A city in Judah.
And *K*, and Achzib, and Mareshah ... Josh 15:44 7084
the Philistines fight against *K* ... 1Sa 23:1 7084
smite the Philistines, and save *K* ... 1Sa 23:2 7084
to *K* against the armies of the ... 1Sa 23:3 7084
him and said, Arise, go down to *K* ... 1Sa 23:4 7084
So David and his men went to *K* ... 1Sa 23:5 7084
David saved the inhabitants of *K* ... 1Sa 23:5 7084
of Ahimelech fled to David to *K* ... 1Sa 23:6 7084
Saul that David was come to *K* ... 1Sa 23:7 7084
together to war, to go down to *K* ... 1Sa 23:8 7084
that Saul seeketh to come to *K* ... 1Sa 23:10 7084
Will the men of *K* deliver me up ... 1Sa 23:11 7084
Will the men of *K* deliver me ... 1Sa 23:12 7084
arose and departed out of *K* ... 1Sa 23:13 7084
that David was escaped from *K* ... 1Sa 23:13 7084
the ruler of the half part of *K* ... Neh 3:17 7084
the ruler of the half part of *K* ... Neh 3:18 7084
2. A descendant of Caleb.
the father of *K* the Garmite ... 1Chr 4:19 7084

KELAIAH *(kel-ah'-yah)* {1} See KELITA. *Married a foreigner in exile.*
Jozabad, and Shimei, and *K*, (the ... Ezr 10:23 7041

KELAL See CHELAL.

KELITA *(kel'-i-tah)* {3} See KELAIAH.
1. Married a foreigner in exile.
and Kelaiah, (the same is *K* ... Ezr 10:23 7042
2. A priest who assisted Ezra.
Shabbethai, Hodijah, Maaseiah, *K* ... Neh 8:7 7042
3. A Levite who renewed the covenant.
brethren, Shebaniah, Hodijah, *K* ... Neh 10:10 7042

KELUB See CHELUB.

KELUHI See CHELLUH.

KEMUEL *(kem-u'-el)* {3}
1. A son of Nahor.
brother, and *K* the father of Aram, ... Gen 22:21 7055
2. An Ephraimite prince.
of Ephraim, *K* the son of Shiphtan ... Num 34:24 7055
3. Father of Hashabiah.
Levites, Hashabiah the son of *K* ... 1Chr 27:17 7055

KENAANAH See CHENAANAH.

KENAN *(ke'-nan)* {1} See CAINAN. *Son of Enosh.*
K, Mahalaleel, Jered, ... 1Chr 1:2 7018

KENANI See CHENANI.

KENANIAH See CHENANIAH.

KENATH *(ke'-nath)* {2} See NOBAH. *A city in Bashan.*
And Nobah went and took *K*, and the ... Num 32:42 7079
towns of Jair, from them, with *K* ... 1Chr 2:23 7079

KENAZ *(ke'-naz)* {11} See KENEZITE.
1. A son of Eliphaz.
Omar, Zepho, and Gatam, and *K* ... Gen 36:11 7073
duke Omar, duke Zepho, duke *K* ... Gen 36:15 7073
and Omar, Zephi, and Gatam, *K* ... 1Chr 1:36 7073
2. A duke of Edom.
Duke *K*, duke Teman, duke Mibzar, ... Gen 36:42 7073
Duke *K*, duke Teman, duke Mibzar, ... 1Chr 1:53 7073
3. Brother of Caleb.
And Othniel the son of *K*, the ... Josh 15:17 7073
And Othniel the son of *K*, Caleb's ... Judg 1:13 7073
them, even Othniel the son of *K* ... Judg 3:9 7073
And Othniel the son of *K* died ... Judg 3:11 7073
And the sons of *K* ... 1Chr 4:13 7073
4. A grandson of Caleb.
and the sons of Elah, even *K* ... 1Chr 4:15 7073

KENEZITE *(ken'-e-zite)* {3} See KENIZZITES. *Descendants of Jephunneh.*
Caleb the son of Jephunneh the *K* ... Num 32:12 7074
of Jephunneh the *K* said unto him ... Josh 14:6 7074
of Jephunneh the *K* unto this day ... Josh 14:14 7074

KENITE *(ken'-ite)* {6} See KENITES. *A member of a Canaanite tribe.*
the *K* shall be wasted, until ... Num 24:22 7014
And the children of the *K*, Moses' ... Judg 1:16 7017
Now Heber the *K*, which was of the ... Judg 4:11 7014
of Jael the wife of Heber the *K* ... Judg 4:17 7017
Hazor and the house of Heber the *K* ... Judg 4:17 7017
Jael the wife of Heber the *K* be ... Judg 5:24 7017

KENITES *(ken'-ites)* {8} See MIDIANITES.
The *K*, and the Kenizzites, and the ... Gen 15:19 7017
And he looked on the *K*, and took up ... Num 24:21 7017
had severed himself from the *K* ... Judg 4:11 7017
And Saul said unto the *K*, Go, ... 1Sa 15:6 7017
So the *K* departed from among the ... 1Sa 15:6 7017
and against the south of the *K* ... 1Sa 27:10 7017
which were in the cities of the *K* ... 1Sa 30:29 7017
These are the *K* that came of ... 1Chr 2:55 7017

KENIZZITE See KENIZZITES.

KENIZZITES *(ken'-iz-zites)* {1} See KENEZITE. *A Canaanite tribe in Abraham's time.*
The Kenites, and the *K*, and the ... Gen 15:19 7074

KENNIZZITE See KENIZZITES.

KEPHER AMMONI See CHEPHAR-HAAMMONAI.

KEPHIRAH See CHEPHIRAH.

KEPT {175}
k my charge, my commandments, my ... Gen 26:5 8104
father's sheep: for she *k* them ... Gen 29:9 7462
neither hath he *k* back any thing ... Gen 39:9 2820
and ye shall be *k* in prison ... Gen 42:16 631
Now Moses *k* the flock of Jethro ... Ex 3:1 7462
for you to be *k* until the morning ... Ex 16:23 4931
it to be *k* for your generations ... Ex 16:32 4931
to be *k* for your generations ... Ex 16:33 4931
up before the Testimony, to be *k* ... Ex 16:34 4931
owner, and he hath not *k* him in ... Ex 21:29 8104
and his owner hath not *k* him in ... Ex 21:36 8104
be *k* close, and she be defiled, and ... Num 5:13 5641
they *k* the passover on the ... Num 9:5 6213
wherefore are we *k* back, that we ... Num 9:7 1639
Israel *k* the charge of the LORD ... Num 9:19 8104
they *k* the charge of the LORD, at ... Num 9:23 8104
to be *k* for a token against the ... Num 17:10 4931
place, and it shall be *k* for the ... Num 19:9 4931
the LORD hath *k* thee back from ... Num 24:11 4513
which *k* the charge of the ... Num 31:47 8104
he *k* him as the apple of his eye ... Deut 32:10 5341
thy word, and *k* thy covenant ... Deut 33:9 5341

k the passover on the fourteenth ... Josh 5:10 6213
behold, the LORD hath *k* me alive ... Josh 14:10
Ye have *k* all that Moses the ... Josh 22:2 8104
but have *k* the charge of the ... Josh 22:3 8104
So she *k* fast by the maidens of ... Ruth 2:23 1692
it been *k* for thee since I said ... 1Sa 9:24 8104
thou hast not *k* the commandment ... 1Sa 13:13 8104
because thou hast not *k* that ... 1Sa 13:14 8104
Thy servant *k* his father's sheep, ... 1Sa 17:34 7462
if the young men have *k* ... 1Sa 21:4 8104
Of a truth women have been *k* from ... 1Sa 21:5 6113
Surely in vain have I *k* all that ... 1Sa 25:21 8104
which hast *k* me this day from ... 1Sa 25:33 3607
which hath *k* me back from hurting ... 1Sa 25:34 4513
hath *k* his servant from evil ... 1Sa 25:39 2820
hast thou not *k* thy lord the king ... 1Sa 26:15 8104
because ye have not *k* your master ... 1Sa 26:16 8104
the young man that *k* the watch ... 2Sa 13:34
For I have *k* the ways of the LORD ... 2Sa 22:22 8104
have *k* myself from mine iniquity ... 2Sa 22:24 8104
thou hast *k* me to be head of the ... 2Sa 22:44 8104
thou not *k* the oath of the LORD ... 1Kin 2:43 8104
thou hast *k* for him this great ... 1Kin 3:6 8104
Who hast *k* with thy servant David ... 1Kin 8:24 8104
but he *k* not that which the LORD ... 1Kin 11:10 8104
and thou hast not *k* my covenant ... 1Kin 11:11 8104
because he *k* my commandments and ... 1Kin 11:34 8104
hast not *k* the commandment which ... 1Kin 13:21 8104
who *k* my commandments, and who ... 1Kin 14:8 8104
which *k* the door of the king's ... 1Kin 14:27 8104
(Now Joram had *k* Ramoth-gilead ... 2Kin 9:14 8104
the priests that *k* the door put ... 2Kin 12:9 8104
Also Judah *k* not the commandments ... 2Kin 17:19 8104
but *k* his commandments, which the ... 2Kin 18:6 8104
word of the LORD, which he *k* not ... 1Chr 10:13 8104
while he yet *k* himself close ... 1Chr 12:1 6113
k the ward of the house of Saul ... 1Chr 12:29 8104
Thou which hast *k* with thy ... 2Chr 6:15 8104
Solomon *k* the feast seven days ... 2Chr 7:8 6213
for they *k* the dedication of the ... 2Chr 7:9 6213
that *k* the entrance of the king's ... 2Chr 12:10 8104
k the feast of unleavened bread ... 2Chr 30:21 6213
they *k* other seven days with ... 2Chr 30:23 6213
which the Levites that *k* the ... 2Chr 34:9 8104
have not *k* the word of the LORD ... 2Chr 34:21 8104
Moreover Josiah *k* a passover unto ... 2Chr 35:1 6213
k the passover at that time ... 2Chr 35:17 6213
that *k* in Israel from the days of ... 2Chr 35:18 6213
keep such a passover as Josiah *k* ... 2Chr 35:18 6213
of Josiah was this passover *k* ... 2Chr 35:19 6213
as she lay desolate she *k* sabbath ... 2Chr 36:21 7673
They *k* also the feast of ... Ezr 3:4 6213
k the dedication of this house of ... Ezr 6:16 5648
captivity *k* the passover upon the ... Ezr 6:19 6213
k the feast of unleavened bread ... Ezr 6:22 6213
have not *k* the commandments, nor ... Neh 1:7 8104
they *k* the feast seven days ... Neh 8:18 6213
k thy law, nor hearkened unto thy ... Neh 9:34 6213
their brethren that *k* the gates ... Neh 11:19 8104
the porters *k* the ward of their ... Neh 12:45 8104
which *k* the concubines ... Est 2:14 8104
Teresh, of those which *k* the door ... Est 2:21 8104
k throughout every generation, ... Est 9:28 6213
held his steps, his way have I *k* ... Job 23:11 8104
k close from the fowls of the air ... Job 28:21 5641
and *k* silence at my counsel ... Job 29:21
that I *k* silence, and went not out ... Job 31:34
I have *k* me from the paths of the ... Ps 17:4 8104
For I have *k* the ways of the LORD ... Ps 18:21 8104
I *k* myself from mine iniquity ... Ps 18:23 8104
thou hast *k* me alive, that I ... Ps 30:3
When I *k* silence, my bones waxed ... Ps 32:3 2790
with a multitude that *k* holyday ... Ps 42:4 2287
hast thou done, and I *k* silence ... Ps 50:21 2790
They *k* not the covenant of God, ... Ps 78:10 8104
God, and *k* not his testimonies ... Ps 78:56 8104
they *k* his testimonies, and the ... Ps 99:7 8104
for I have *k* thy testimonies ... Ps 119:22 5341
in the night, and have *k* thy law ... Ps 119:55 8104
I had, because I *k* thy precepts ... Ps 119:56 5341
but now have I *k* thy word ... Ps 119:67 8104
because they *k* not thy word ... Ps 119:158 8104
My soul hath *k* thy testimonies ... Ps 119:167 8104
I have *k* thy precepts and thy ... Ps 119:168 8104
eyes desired I *k* not from them ... Eccl 2:10 680
riches *k* for the owners thereof ... Eccl 5:13 8104
mine own vineyard have I not *k* ... Song 1:6 5201
night when a holy solemnity is *k* ... Is 30:29 6942
forsaken me, and have not *k* my law ... Jer 16:11 8104
k all his precepts, and done ... Jer 35:18 8104
neither have *k* my judgments ... Eze 5:7 6213
hath *k* my judgments, to deal ... Eze 18:9 8104
hath *k* all my statutes, and hath ... Eze 18:19 8104
neither *k* my judgments to do them ... Eze 20:21 8104
ye have not *k* the charge of mine ... Eze 44:8 8104
that *k* the charge of my sanctuary ... Eze 44:15 8104
which have *k* my charge, which ... Eze 48:11 8104
and whom he would he *k* alive ... Dan 5:19
but I *k* the matter in my heart ... Dan 7:28 5202
a wife, and for a wife he *k* sheep ... Hos 12:12 8104
and he *k* his wrath for ever ... Amos 1:11 8104
have not *k* his commandments, and ... Amos 2:4 8104
For the statutes of Omri are *k* ... Mic 6:16 8104
as ye have not *k* my ways, but ... Mal 2:9 8104
ordinances, and have not *k* them ... Mal 3:7 8104
it that we have *k* his ordinance ... Mal 3:14 8104
And they that *k* them fled, and went ... Mt 8:33 *1006*
utter things which have been *k* ... Mt 13:35

But when Herod's birthday was *k* ... Mt 14:6 *71*
things have I *k* from my youth up ... Mt 19:20 *5442*
neither was any thing *k* secret ... Mk 4:22 *1096*
And they *k* that saying with ... Mk 9:10 *2902*
But Mary *k* all these things, and ... Lk 2:19 *4933*
but his mother *k* all these ... Lk 2:51 *1301*
he was *k* bound with chains and in ... Lk 8:29 *5442*
they *k* it close, and told no man ... Lk 9:36 *4601*
these have I *k* from my youth up ... Lk 18:21 *5442*
which I have *k* laid up in a ... Lk 19:20 *2192*
but thou hast *k* the good wine ... Jn 2:10 *5083*
day of my burying hath she *k* this ... Jn 12:7 *5083*
even as I have *k* my Father's ... Jn 15:10 *5083*
if they have *k* my saying, they ... Jn 15:20 *5083*
and they have *k* thy word ... Jn 17:6 *5083*
the world, I *k* them in thy name ... Jn 17:12 *5083*
that thou gavest me I have *k* ... Jn 17:12 *5442*
and spake unto her that *k* the door ... Jn 18:16 *2377*
damsel that *k* the door unto Peter ... Jn 18:17 *2377*
k back part of the price, his ... Acts 5:2 *3557*
of angels, and have not *k* it ... Acts 7:53 *5442*
which had *k* his bed eight years, ... Acts 9:33 *2621*
Peter therefore was *k* in prison ... Acts 12:5 *5083*
before the door *k* the prison ... Acts 12:6 *5083*
Then all the multitude *k* silence ... Acts 15:12 *4601*
how I *k* back nothing that was ... Acts 20:20 *5288*
to them, they *k* the more silence ... Acts 22:2 *3930*
k the raiment of them that slew ... Acts 22:20 *5442*
he commanded him to be *k* in ... Acts 23:35 *5442*
that Paul should be *k* at Caesarea ... Acts 25:4 *5083*
I commanded him to be *k* till I ... Acts 25:21 *5083*
k them from their purpose ... Acts 27:43 *2967*
himself with a soldier that *k* him ... Acts 28:16 *5442*
which was *k* secret since the ... Rom 16:25
in all things I have *k* myself ... 2Cor 11:9 *5083*
governor under Aretas the king *k* ... 2Cor 11:32 *5432*
we were *k* under the law, shut up ... Gal 3:23 *5432*
my course, I have *k* the faith ... 2Ti 4:7 *5083*
Through faith he *k* the passover ... Heb 11:28 *4160*
which is of you *k* back by fraud ... Jas 5:4 *650*
Who are *k* by the power of God ... 1Pet 1:5 *5432*
by the same word are *k* in store ... 2Pet 3:7 *2343*
the angels which *k* not their ... Jude 6 *5083*
hast *k* my word, and hast not ... Rev 3:8 *5083*
Because thou hast *k* the word of ... Rev 3:10 *5083*

KERAN See CHERAN.

KERCHIEFS {2}
make *k* upon the head of every ... Eze 13:18 4556
Your *k* also will I tear, and ... Eze 13:21 4556

KEREN-HAPPUCH *(ke'-ren-hap'-puk)* {1} *A daughter of Job.*
and the name of the third, *K*. ... Job 42:14 7163

KERETHITE See CHERETHITES.

KERETHITES See CHERETHITES.

KERIOTH *(ke'-re-oth)* {3} See ISCARIOT, KIRIOTH.
1. A city in Judah.
And Hazor, Hadattah, and *K*, and ... Josh 15:25 7152
2. A city in Moab.
And upon *K*, and upon Bozrah, and ... Jer 48:24 7152
K is taken, and the strong holds ... Jer 48:41 7152

KERIOTH HEZRON See KERIOTH.

KERITH See CHERITH.

KERNELS {1}
from the *k* even to the husk ... Num 6:4 2785

KEROS *(ke'-ros)* {2} *A family of exiles.*
The children of *K*, the children ... Ezr 2:44 7026
The children of *K*, the children ... Neh 7:47 7026

KERUB See CHERUB.

KESALON See CHESALON.

KESED See CHESED.

KESIL See CHESIL.

KESULLOTH See CHESULLOTH.

KETTLE {1}
he struck it into the pan, or *k* ... 1Sa 2:14 1731

KETURAH *(ket-u'-rah)* {4} *A wife of Abraham.*
took a wife, and her name was *K*. ... Gen 25:1 6989
All these were the children of *K* ... Gen 25:4 6989
Now the sons of *K*, Abraham's ... 1Chr 1:32 6989
All these are the sons of *K* ... 1Chr 1:33 6989

KEY {6}
therefore they took a *k*, and ... Judg 3:25 4668
the *k* of the house of David will ... Is 22:22 4668
taken away the *k* of knowledge ... Lk 11:52 *2807*
true, he that hath the *k* of David ... Rev 3:7 *2807*
to him was given the *k* of the ... Rev 9:1 *2807*
having the *k* of the bottomless ... Rev 20:1 *2807*

KEYS {2}
the *k* of the kingdom of heaven ... Mt 16:19 *2807*
and have the *k* of hell and of death ... Rev 1:18 *2807*

KEZIA *(ke-zi'-ah)* {1} *A daughter of Job.*
and the name of the second, *K* ... Job 42:14 7103

KEZIAH See KEZIA.

KEZIB See CHEZIB.

KEZIZ *(ke'-ziz)* {1} *A valley in Benjamin.*
Beth-hoglah, and the valley of *K* ... Josh 18:21 7104

KIBROTH-HATTAAVAH *(kib'-roth-hat-ta'-a-vah)* {5} *A Hebrew encampment in the wilderness.*
called the name of that place *K* ... Num 11:34 6914
journeyed from *K* unto Hazeroth ... Num 11:35 6914
desert of Sinai, and pitched at *K* ... Num 33:16 6914

And they departed from *K*, and ... Num 33:17 6914
at Taberah, and at Massah, and at *K* ... Deut 9:22 6914

KIBZAIM *(kib-za'-im)* {1} See JOKMEAM. *A Levitical city in Ephraim.*
K with her suburbs, and Beth-horon ... Josh 21:22 6911

KICK {3}
Wherefore *k* ye at my sacrifice and ... 1Sa 2:29 1163
for thee to *k* against the pricks ... Acts 9:5 *2979*
for thee to *k* against the pricks ... Acts 26:14 *2979*

KICKED {1}
But Jeshurun waxed fat, and *k* ... Deut 32:15 1163

KID {43}
killed a *k* of the goats, and ... Gen 37:31 8163
will send thee a *k* from the flock ... Gen 38:17 1423
Judah sent the *k* by the hand of ... Gen 38:20 1423
behold, I sent this *k*, and thou ... Gen 38:23 1423
seethe a *k* in his mother's milk ... Ex 23:19 1423
seethe a *k* in his mother's milk ... Ex 34:26 1423
a *k* of the goats, a male without ... Lev 4:23 8163
a *k* of the goats, a female ... Lev 4:28 8166
a lamb or a *k* of the goats, for a ... Lev 5:6 8166
Take ye a *k* of the goats for a ... Lev 9:3 8163
Then ye shall sacrifice one *k* of ... Lev 23:19 8163
One *k* of the goats for a sin ... Num 7:16 8163
One *k* of the goats for a sin ... Num 7:22 8163
One *k* of the goats for a sin ... Num 7:28 8163
One *k* of the goats for a sin ... Num 7:34 8163
One *k* of the goats for a sin ... Num 7:40 8163
One *k* of the goats for a sin ... Num 7:46 8163
One *k* of the goats for a sin ... Num 7:52 8163
One *k* of the goats for a sin ... Num 7:58 8163
One *k* of the goats for a sin ... Num 7:64 8163
One *k* of the goats for a sin ... Num 7:70 8163
One *k* of the goats for a sin ... Num 7:76 8163
One *k* of the goats for a sin ... Num 7:82 8163
one ram, or for a lamb, or a *k* ... Num 15:11 5795
one *k* of the goats for a sin ... Num 15:24 8163
one *k* of the goats for a sin ... Num 28:15 8163
one *k* of the goats, to make an ... Num 28:30 8163
one *k* of the goats for a sin ... Num 29:5 8163
One *k* of the goats for a sin ... Num 29:11 8163
one *k* of the goats for a sin ... Num 29:16 8163
one *k* of the goats for a sin ... Num 29:19 8163
one *k* of the goats for a sin ... Num 29:25 8163
seethe a *k* in his mother's milk ... Deut 14:21 1423
went in, and made ready a *k* ... Judg 6:19 1423,5795
have made ready a *k* for thee ... Judg 13:15 1423,5795
So Manoah took a *k* with a meat ... Judg 13:19 1423,5795
him as he would have rent a *k* ... Judg 14:6 1423
Samson visited his wife with a *k* ... Judg 15:1 1423,5795
and a bottle of wine, and a *k* ... 1Sa 16:20 1423,5795
leopard shall lie down with the *k* ... Is 11:6 1423
a *k* of the goats without blemish ... Eze 43:22 8163
a *k* of the goats daily for a sin ... Eze 45:23 8163
and yet thou never gavest me a *k* ... Lk 15:29 *2056*

KIDNEYS {18}
is above the liver, and the two *k* ... Ex 29:13 3629
above the liver, and the two *k* ... Ex 29:22 3629
And the two *k*, and the fat that is ... Lev 3:4 3629
caul above the liver, with the *k* ... Lev 3:4 3629
And the two *k*, and the fat that is ... Lev 3:10 3629
caul above the liver, with the *k* ... Lev 3:10 3629
And the two *k*, and the fat that is ... Lev 3:15 3629
caul above the liver, with the *k* ... Lev 3:15 3629
And the two *k*, and the fat that is ... Lev 4:9 3629
caul above the liver, with the *k* ... Lev 4:9 3629
And the two *k*, and the fat that is ... Lev 7:4 3629
is above the liver, with the *k* ... Lev 7:4 3629
above the liver, and the two *k* ... Lev 8:16 3629
above the liver, and the two *k* ... Lev 8:25 3629
But the fat, and the *k*, and the ... Lev 9:10 3629
covereth the inwards, and the *k* ... Lev 9:19 3629
goats, with the fat of *k* of wheat ... Deut 32:14 3629
with the fat of the *k* of rams ... Is 34:6 3629

KIDRON *(kid'-ron)* {11} *A brook near Jerusalem.*
himself passed over the brook *K* ... 2Sa 15:23 6939
out, and passest over the brook *K* ... 1Kin 2:37 6939
idol, and burnt it by the brook *K* ... 1Kin 15:13 6939
Jerusalem in the fields of *K* ... 2Kin 23:4 6939
Jerusalem, unto the brook *K* ... 2Kin 23:6 6939
and burned it at the brook *K* ... 2Kin 23:6 6939
the dust of them into the brook *K* ... 2Kin 23:12 6939
it, and burnt it at the brook *K* ... 2Chr 15:16 6939
it out abroad into the brook *K* ... 2Chr 29:16 6939
and cast them into the brook *K* ... 2Chr 30:14 6939
the fields unto the brook of *K* ... Jer 31:40 6939

KIDS {8}
thence two good *k* of the goats ... Gen 27:9 1423
she put the skins of the *k* of the ... Gen 27:16 1423
of the children of Israel two *k* ... Lev 16:5 8163
the *k* of the goats for sin ... Num 7:87 8163
to Beth-el, one carrying three *k* ... 1Sa 10:3 1423
them like two little flocks of *k* ... 1Kin 20:27 5795
people, of the flock, lambs and *k* ... 2Chr 35:7
feed thy *k* beside the shepherds' ... Song 1:8 1423

KILEAB See CHILEAB.

KILION See CHILION.

KILION'S See CHILION'S.

KILL {126}
lest any finding him should *k* him ... Gen 4:15 5221
and they will *k* me, but they will ... Gen 12:12 2026
the place should *k* me for Rebekah ... Gen 26:7 2026
himself, purposing to *k* thee ... Gen 27:42 2026
and said, Let us not *k* him ... Gen 37:21 5221

it be a son, then ye shall *k* him ... Ex 1:16 4191
intendest thou to *k* me, as thou ... Ex 2:14 2026
LORD met him, and sought to *k* him ... Ex 4:24 4191
Israel shall *k* it in the evening ... Ex 12:6 7819
your families, and *k* the passover ... Ex 12:21 7819
to *k* this whole assembly with ... Ex 16:3 4191
us up out of Egypt, to *k* us ... Ex 17:3 4191
Thou shalt not *k* ... Ex 20:13 7523
or a sheep, and *k* it, or sell it ... Ex 22:1 2873
I will *k* you with the sword ... Ex 22:24 2026
thou shalt *k* the bullock before ... Ex 29:11 7819
Then shalt thou *k* the ram ... Ex 29:20 7819
he shall *k* the bullock before the ... Lev 1:5 7819
he shall *k* it on the side of the ... Lev 1:11 7819
and *k* it at the door of the ... Lev 3:2 7819
k it before the tabernacle of the ... Lev 3:8 7819
k it before the tabernacle of the ... Lev 3:13 7819
k the bullock before the LORD ... Lev 4:4 7819
k it in the place where they *k* ... Lev 4:24 7819
where they *k* the burnt offering ... Lev 4:33 7819
In the place where they *k* the ... Lev 7:2 7819
they *k* the trespass offering ... Lev 7:2 7819
where he shall *k* the sin offering ... Lev 14:13 7819
he shall *k* the burnt offering ... Lev 14:19 7819
he shall *k* the lamb of the ... Lev 14:25 7819
he shall *k* the one of the birds ... Lev 14:50 7819
shall *k* the bullock of the sin ... Lev 16:11 7819
Then shall he *k* the goat of the ... Lev 16:15 7819
seed unto Molech, and *k* him not ... Lev 20:4 4191
thereto, thou shalt *k* the woman ... Lev 20:16 2026
be cow or ewe, ye shall not *k* it ... Lev 22:28 7819
k me, I pray thee, out of hand, ... Num 11:15 2026
Now if thou shalt *k* all this ... Num 14:15 4191
to *k* us in the wilderness, except ... Num 16:13 4191
mine hand, for now would I *k* thee ... Num 22:29 2026
Now therefore *k* every male among ... Num 31:17 2026
k every woman that hath known man ... Num 31:17 2026
revenger of blood *k* the slayer ... Num 35:27 7523
which should *k* his neighbour ... Deut 4:42 7523
Thou shalt not *k* ... Deut 5:17 7523
Notwithstanding thou mayest *k* ... Deut 12:15 2076
then thou shalt *k* of thy herd ... Deut 12:21 2076
But thou shalt surely *k* him ... Deut 13:9 2026
I *k*, and I make alive ... Deut 32:39 4191
If the LORD were pleased to *k* us ... Judg 13:23 4191
but surely we will not *k* thee ... Judg 15:13 4191
when it is day, we shall *k* him ... Judg 16:2 2026
to smite of the people, and *k* ... Judg 20:31 2491
k of the men of Israel about ... Judg 20:39 2491
if Saul hear it, he will *k* me ... 1Sa 16:2 2026
able to fight with me, and to *k* me ... 1Sa 17:9 5221
k him, then shall ye be our ... 1Sa 17:9 5221
that they should *k* David ... 1Sa 19:1 4191
Saul my father seeketh to *k* thee ... 1Sa 19:2 4191
why should I *k* thee ... 1Sa 19:17 4191
and some bade me *k* thee ... 1Sa 24:10 2026
God, that thou wilt neither *k* me ... 1Sa 30:15 4191
then *k* him, fear not ... 2Sa 13:28 4191
his brother, that we may *k* him ... 2Sa 14:7 4191
any iniquity in me, let him *k* me ... 2Sa 14:32 4191
us shalt thou *k* any man in Israel ... 2Sa 21:4 4191
sought therefore to *k* Jeroboam ... 1Kin 11:40 4191
king of Judah, and they shall *k* me ... 1Kin 12:27 2026
clothes, and said, Am I God, to *k* ... 2Kin 5:7 4191
and if they *k* us, we shall but die ... 2Kin 7:4 4191
followeth her *k* with the sword ... 2Kin 11:15 4191
So *k* the passover, and sanctify ... 2Chr 35:6 7819
provinces, to destroy, to *k* ... Est 3:13 2026
they watched the house to *k* him ... Ps 59:*t* 4191
A time to *k*, and a time to heal ... Eccl 3:3 2026
I will *k* thy root with famine, and ... Is 14:30 4191
let them *k* sacrifices ... Is 29:1 5362
the wool, ye *k* them that are fed ... Eze 34:3 2076
of old time, Thou shalt not *k* ... Mt 5:21 *5407*
whosoever shall *k* shall be in ... Mt 5:21 *5407*
And fear not them which *k* the body ... Mt 10:28 *615*
but are not able to *k* the soul ... Mt 10:28 *615*
And they shall *k* him, and the third ... Mt 17:23 *615*
come, let us *k* him, and let us ... Mt 21:38 *615*
and some of them ye shall *k* ... Mt 23:34 *615*
to be afflicted, and shall *k* you ... Mt 24:9 *615*
take Jesus by subtilty, and *k* him ... Mt 26:4 *615*
to save life, or to *k* ... Mk 3:4 *615*
hands of men, and they shall *k* him ... Mk 9:31 *615*
Do not commit adultery, Do not *k* ... Mk 10:19 *5407*
spit upon him, and shall *k* him ... Mk 10:34 *615*
come, let us *k* him, and the ... Mk 12:7 *615*
afraid of them that *k* the body ... Lk 12:4 *615*
for Herod will *k* thee ... Lk 13:31 *615*
hither the fatted calf, and *k* it ... Lk 15:23 *2380*
Do not commit adultery, Do not *k* ... Lk 18:20 *5407*
come, let us *k* him, that the ... Lk 20:14 *615*
sought how they might *k* him ... Lk 22:2 *337*
the Jews sought the more to *k* him ... Jn 5:18 *615*
because the Jews sought to *k* him ... Jn 7:1 *615*
Why go ye about to *k* me ... Jn 7:19 *615*
who goeth about to *k* thee ... Jn 7:20 *615*
not this he, whom they seek to *k* ... Jn 7:25 *615*
said the Jews, Will he *k* himself ... Jn 8:22 *615*
but ye seek to *k* me, because my ... Jn 8:37 *615*
But now ye seek to *k* me, a man ... Jn 8:40 *615*
not, but for to steal, and to *k* ... Jn 10:10 *2380*
Wilt thou *k* me, as thou diddest ... Acts 7:28 *337*
the Jews took counsel to *k* him ... Acts 9:23 *337*
the gates day and night to *k* him ... Acts 9:24 *337*
Rise, Peter; *k*, and eat ... Acts 10:13 *2380*
And as they went about to *k* him ... Acts 21:31 *615*
he come near, are ready to *k* him ... Acts 23:15 *337*
laying wait in the way to *k* him ... Acts 25:3 *337*
the temple, and went about to *k* me ... Acts 26:21 *1315*
counsel was to *k* the prisoners ... Acts 27:42 *615*
commit adultery, Thou shalt not *k* ... Rom 13:9 *5407*
adultery, said also, Do not *k* ... Jas 2:11 *5407*
commit no adultery, yet if thou *k* ... Jas 2:11 *5407*
ye *k*, and desire to have, and ... Jas 4:2 *5407*
I will *k* her children with death ... Rev 2:23 *615*
and that they should *k* one another ... Rev 6:4 *4969*
to *k* with sword, and with hunger, ... Rev 6:8 *615*
given that they should not *k* them ... Rev 9:5 *615*
and shall overcome them, and *k* them ... Rev 11:7 *615*

KILLED {67}

k a kid of the goats, and dipped ... Gen 37:31 7819
that he hath *k* a man or a woman ... Ex 21:29 4191
shall be *k* before the LORD ... Lev 4:15 7819
is *k* shall the sin offering be ... Lev 6:25 7819
sin offering be *k* before the LORD ... Lev 6:25 7819
And he *k* it; and Moses ... Lev 8:19 7819
that one of the birds be *k* in an ... Lev 14:5 7819
that was *k* over the running water ... Lev 14:6 7819
Ye have *k* the people of the LORD ... Num 16:41 4191
whosoever hath *k* any person ... Num 31:19 2026
k thee not, know thou and see that ... 1Sa 24:11 2026
that I have *k* for my shearers ... 1Sa 25:11 2873
k it, and took flour, and kneaded ... 1Sa 28:24 2076
thou hast *k* Uriah the Hittite ... 2Sa 12:9 5221
and smote the Philistine, and *k* him ... 2Sa 21:17 4191
and because he *k* him ... 1Kin 16:7 5221
k him, in the twenty and seventh ... 1Kin 16:10 4191
Thus saith the LORD, Hast thou *k* ... 1Kin 21:19 7523
he *k* him, and reigned in his room ... 2Kin 15:25 4191
k Shophach the captain of the ... 1Chr 19:18 4191
Ahab *k* sheep and oxen for him in ... 2Chr 18:2 3076
that had *k* the king his father ... 2Chr 25:3 5221
So they *k* the bullocks, and the ... 2Chr 29:22 7819
when they had *k* the rams ... 2Chr 29:22 7819
they *k* also the lambs, and they ... 2Chr 29:22 7819
And the priests *k* them, and they ... 2Chr 29:24 7819
Then they *k* the passover on the ... 2Chr 30:15 7819
they *k* the passover on the ... 2Chr 35:1 7819
they *k* the passover, and the ... 2Chr 35:11 7819
k the passover for all the ... Ezr 6:20 7819
sake are we *k* all the day long ... Ps 44:22 2026
She hath *k* her beasts ... Prov 9:2 2873
thou hast *k*, and not pitied ... Lam 2:21 2873
chief priests and scribes, and be *k* ... Mt 16:21 *615*
k another, and stoned another ... Mt 21:35 *615*
my oxen and my fatlings are *k* ... Mt 22:4 *2380*
of them which *k* the prophets ... Mt 23:31 *5407*
against him, and would have *k* him ... Mk 6:19 *615*
priests, and scribes, and be *k* ... Mk 8:31 *615*
and after that he is *k*, he shall ... Mk 9:31 *615*
and him they *k*, and many others ... Mk 12:5 *615*
k him, and cast him out of the ... Mk 12:8 *615*
when they *k* the passover, his ... Mk 14:12 *2380*
prophets, and your fathers *k* them ... Lk 11:47 *615*
for they indeed *k* them, and ye ... Lk 11:48 *615*
which after he hath *k* hath power ... Lk 12:5 *615*
thy father hath *k* the fatted calf ... Lk 15:27 *2380*
thou hast *k* for him the fatted ... Lk 15:30 *2380*
him out of the vineyard, and *k* him ... Lk 20:15 *615*
when the passover must be *k* ... Lk 22:7 *2380*
k the Prince of life, whom God ... Acts 3:15 *615*
he *k* James the brother of John ... Acts 12:2 *337*
sword, and would have *k* himself ... Acts 16:27 *337*
nor drink till they had *k* Paul ... Acts 23:12 *615*
nor drink till they have *k* him ... Acts 23:21 *337*
and should have been *k* of them ... Acts 23:27 *615*
sake we are *k* all the day long ... Rom 8:36 *2289*
they have *k* thy prophets, and ... Rom 11:3 *615*
as chastened, and not *k* ... 2Cor 6:9 *2289*
Who both *k* the Lord Jesus, and ... 1Th 2:15 *615*
Ye have condemned and *k* the just ... Jas 5:6 *5407*
that should be *k* as they were ... Rev 6:11 *615*
three was the third part of men *k* ... Rev 9:18 *615*
k by these plagues yet repented ... Rev 9:20 *615*
them, he must in this manner be *k* ... Rev 11:5 *615*
sword must be *k* with the sword ... Rev 13:10 *615*
image of the beast should be *k* ... Rev 13:15 *615*

KILLEDST {2}

kill me, as thou *k* the Egyptian ... Ex 2:14 2026
me into thine hand, thou *k* me not ... 1Sa 24:18 2026

KILLEST {2}

thou that *k* the prophets, and ... Mt 23:37 *615*
which *k* the prophets, and stonest ... Lk 13:34 *615*

KILLETH {23}

that *k* an ox, or lamb, or goat, ... Lev 17:3 7819
or that *k* it out of the camp, ... Lev 17:3 7819
he that *k* any man shall surely be ... Lev 24:17 5221
he that *k* a beast shall make it ... Lev 24:18 5221
And he that *k* a beast, he shall ... Lev 24:21 5221
and he that *k* a man, he shall be ... Lev 24:21 5221
which *k* any person at unawares ... Num 35:11 5221
that every one that *k* any person ... Num 35:15 5221
Whoso *k* any person, the murderer ... Num 35:30 5221
Whoso *k* his neighbour ignorantly, ... Deut 19:4 5221
slayer that *k* any person unawares ... Josh 20:3 5221
that whosoever *k* any person at ... Josh 20:9 5221
The LORD *k*, and maketh alive ... 1Sa 2:6 4191
shall be, that the man who *k* him ... 1Sa 17:25 5221
to the man that *k* this Philistine ... 1Sa 17:26 5221
it be done to the man that *k* him ... 1Sa 17:27 5221
For wrath *k* the foolish man, and ... Job 5:2 2026
rising with the light *k* the poor ... Job 24:14 6991
The desire of the slothful *k* him ... Prov 21:25 4191
He that *k* an ox is as if he slew ... Is 66:3 7819
that whosoever *k* you will think ... Jn 16:2 *615*
for the letter *k*, but the spirit ... 2Cor 3:6 *615*
he that *k* with the sword must be ... Rev 13:10 *615*

KILLING {5}

him in the *k* of his brethren ... Judg 9:24 2026
Levites had the charge of the *k* ... 2Chr 30:17 7821
k sheep, eating flesh, and ... Is 22:13 7819
By swearing, and lying, and *k* ... Hos 4:2 7523
beating some, and *k* some ... Mk 12:5 *615*

KILMAD See CHILMAD.

KIMHAM See CHIMHAM.

KIN {8}

to any that is near of *k* to him ... Lev 18:6 1320
for he uncovereth his near *k* ... Lev 20:19 7607
But for his *k*, that is near unto ... Lev 21:2 7607
if any of his *k* come to redeem it ... Lev 25:25 7138
or any that is nigh of *k* unto him ... Lev 25:49 1320
her, The man is near of *k* unto us ... Ruth 2:20
the king is near of *k* to us ... 2Sa 19:42
own country, and among his own *k* ... Mk 6:4 *4773*

KINAH *(ki'-nah)* {1} *A city in Judah.*

And *K*, and Dimonah, and Adadah, ... Josh 15:22 7016

KIND {45}

tree yielding fruit after his *k* ... Gen 1:11 4327
and herb yielding seed after his *k* ... Gen 1:12 4327
seed was in itself, after his *k* ... Gen 1:12 4327
forth abundantly, after their *k* ... Gen 1:21 4327
and every winged fowl after his *k* ... Gen 1:21 4327
the living creature after his *k* ... Gen 1:24 4327
and beast of the earth after his *k* ... Gen 1:24 4327
his *k*, and cattle after their *k* ... Gen 1:25 4327
upon the earth after his *k* ... Gen 1:25 4327
Of fowls after their *k* ... Gen 6:20 4327
and of cattle after their *k* ... Gen 6:20 4327
thing of the earth after his *k* ... Gen 6:20 4327
They, and every beast after his *k* ... Gen 7:14 4327
and all the cattle after their *k* ... Gen 7:14 4327
upon the earth after his *k* ... Gen 7:14 4327
and every fowl after his *k* ... Gen 7:14 4327
vulture, and the kite after his *k* ... Lev 11:14 4327
Every raven after his *k* ... Lev 11:15 4327
cuckow, and the hawk after his *k* ... Lev 11:16 4327
the stork, the heron after her *k* ... Lev 11:19 4327
the locust after his *k* ... Lev 11:22 4327
and the bald locust after his *k* ... Lev 11:22 4327
and the beetle after his *k* ... Lev 11:22 4327
and the grasshopper after his *k* ... Lev 11:22 4327
and the tortoise after his *k* ... Lev 11:29 4327
cattle gender with a diverse *k* ... Lev 19:19
kite, and the vulture after his *k* ... Deut 14:13 4327
And every raven after his *k* ... Deut 14:14 4327
cuckow, and the hawk after his *k* ... Deut 14:15 4327
stork, and the heron after her *k* ... Deut 14:18 4327
instruments of every *k* of service ... 1Chr 28:14
If thou be *k* to this people, and ... 2Chr 10:7 2896
sellers of all *k* of ware lodged ... Neh 13:20
trees in them of all *k* of fruits ... Eccl 2:5
the multitude of all *k* of riches ... Eze 27:12
the sea, and gathered of every *k* ... Mt 13:47 *1085*
Howbeit this *k* goeth not out but ... Mt 17:21 *1085*
This *k* can come forth by nothing, ... Mk 9:29 *1085*
for he is *k* unto the unthankful ... Lk 6:35 *5543*
Charity suffereth long, and is *k* ... 1Cor 13:4 *5541*
there is one *k* of flesh of men ... 1Cor 15:39
And be ye *k* one to another, ... Eph 4:32 *5543*
truth, that we should be a *k* of ... Jas 1:18 *5100*
For every *k* of beasts, and of ... Jas 3:7 *5449*

KINDLE {19}

Ye shall *k* no fire throughout ... Ex 35:3 1197
is a contentious man to *k* strife ... Prov 26:21 2787
shall *k* in the thickets of the ... Is 9:18 3341
under his glory he shall *k* a ... Is 10:16 3344
a stream of brimstone, doth *k* it ... Is 30:33 1197
shall the flame *k* upon thee ... Is 43:2 1197
Behold, all ye that *k* a fire ... Is 50:11 6919
wood, and the fathers *k* the fire ... Jer 7:18 1197
then will I *k* a fire in the gates ... Jer 17:27 3341
I will *k* a fire in the forest ... Jer 21:14 3341
to *k* meat offerings, and to do ... Jer 33:18 6999
I will *k* a fire in the houses of ... Jer 43:12 3341
I will *k* a fire in the wall of ... Jer 49:27 3341
I will *k* a fire in his cities, and ... Jer 50:32 3341
I will *k* a fire in thee, and it ... Eze 20:47 3341
k the fire, consume the flesh, and ... Eze 24:10 1814
But I will *k* a fire in the wall ... Amos 1:14 3341
stubble, and they shall *k* in them ... Obad 18 1814
neither do ye *k* fire on mine ... Mal 1:10 215

KINDLED {66}

anger was *k* against Rachel ... Gen 30:2 2734
that his wrath was *k* ... Gen 39:19 2734
of the LORD was *k* against Moses ... Ex 4:14 2734
he that *k* the fire shall surely ... Ex 22:6 1197
the burning which the LORD hath *k* ... Lev 10:6 8313
and his anger was *k* ... Num 11:1 2734
anger of the LORD was *k* greatly ... Num 11:10 2734
the LORD was *k* against the people ... Num 11:33 2734
of the LORD was *k* against them ... Num 12:9 2734
God's anger was *k* because he went ... Num 22:22 2734
and Balaam's anger was *k*, and he ... Num 22:27 2734
anger was *k* against Balaam ... Num 24:10 2734
of the LORD was *k* against Israel ... Num 25:3 2734
LORD's anger was *k* the same time ... Num 32:10 2734
LORD's anger was *k* against Israel ... Num 32:13 2734
LORD thy God be *k* against thee ... Deut 6:15 2734

of the LORD be *k* against you .... Deut 7:4 2734
the LORD's wrath be *k* against you .... Deut 11:17 2734
the LORD was *k* against this land .... Deut 29:27 2734
Then my anger shall be *k* against .... Deut 31:17 2734
For a fire is *k* in mine anger .... Deut 32:22 6919
the anger of the LORD was *k* .... Josh 7:1 2734
of the LORD be *k* against you .... Josh 23:16 2734
the son of Ebed, his anger was *k* .... Judg 9:30 2734
And his anger was *k*, and he went up ..... Judg 14:19 2734
and his anger was *k* greatly 1Sa 11:6 2734
Eliab's anger was *k* against David 1Sa 17:28 2734
anger was *k* against Jonathan 1Sa 20:30 2734
of the LORD was *k* against Uzzah 2Sa 6:7 2734
was greatly *k* against the man 2Sa 12:5 2734
coals were *k* by it 2Sa 22:9 1197
before him were coals of fire *k* 2Sa 22:13 1197
of the LORD was *k* against Israel 2Sa 24:1 2734
of the LORD was *k* against Israel 2Kin 13:3 2734
of the LORD that is *k* against us 2Kin 22:13 3341
shall be *k* against this place 2Kin 22:17 3341
his anger was *k* against Judah 2Kin 23:26 2734
of the LORD was *k* against Uzza 1Chr 13:10 2734
anger was greatly *k* against Judah 2Chr 25:10 2734
of the LORD was *k* against Amaziah 2Chr 25:15 2734
He hath also *k* his wrath against .... Job 19:11 2734
Then was *k* the wrath of Elihu the .... Job 32:2 2734
against Job was his wrath *k* .... Job 32:2 2734
his three friends was his wrath *k* .... Job 32:3 2734
three men, then his wrath was *k* .... Job 32:5 2734
My wrath is *k* against thee, and .... Job 42:7 2734
when his wrath is *k* but a little .... Ps 2:12 1197
coals were *k* by it .... Ps 18:8 1197
so a fire was *k* against Jacob .... Ps 78:21 5400
a fire was *k* in their company .... Ps 106:18 1197
of the LORD *k* against his people .... Ps 106:40 2734
when their wrath was *k* against us .... Ps 124:3 2734
of the LORD *k* against his people .... Is 5:25 2734
and in the sparks that ye have *k* .... Is 50:11 1197
tumult he hath *k* fire upon it .... Jer 11:16 3341
for a fire is *k* in mine anger .... Jer 15:14 6919
for ye have *k* a fire in mine .... Jer 17:4 6919
was *k* in the cities of Judah and .... Jer 44:6 1197
hath *k* a fire in Zion, and it hath .... Lam 4:11 3341
see that I the LORD have *k* it .... Eze 20:48 1197
mine anger is *k* against them .... Hos 8:5 2734
me, my repentings are *k* together .... Hos 11:8 3648
Mine anger was *k* against the .... Zec 10:3 2734
what will I, if it be already *k* .... Lk 12:49 *381*
when they had *k* a fire in the .... Lk 22:55 *681*
for they *k* a fire, and received us .... Acts 28:2 *381*

KINDLETH {3}

His breath *k* coals, and a flame .... Job 41:21 3857
yea, he *k* it, and baketh bread .... Is 44:15 5400
great a matter a little fire *k* .... Jas 3:5 *381*

KINDLY {10}

And now if ye will deal *k* and truly .... Gen 24:49 2617
and spake *k* unto the damsel .... Gen 34:3 5921,3820
hand under my thigh, and deal *k* .... Gen 47:29 2617
them, and spake *k* unto them .... Gen 50:21 5921,3820
us the land, that we will deal *k* .... Josh 2:14 2617
the LORD deal *k* with you, as ye .... Ruth 1:8 2617
shalt deal *k* with thy servant 1Sa 20:8 2617
And he spake *k* to him, and set his 2Kin 25:28 2896
spake *k* unto him, and set his .... Jer 52:32 2896
Be *k* affectioned one to another .... Rom 12:10 *5387*

KINDNESS {48}

This is thy *k* which thou shalt .... Gen 20:13 2617
but according to the *k* that I .... Gen 21:23 2617
shew *k* unto my master Abraham .... Gen 24:12 2617
thou hast shewed *k* unto my master .... Gen 24:14 2617
be well with thee, and shew *k* .... Gen 40:14 2617
LORD, since I have shewed you *k* .... Josh 2:12 2617
shew *k* unto my father's house .... Josh 2:12 2617
Neither shewed they *k* to the .... Judg 8:35 2617
not left off his *k* to the living .... Ruth 2:20 2617
for thou hast shewed more *k* in .... Ruth 3:10 2617
for ye shewed *k* to all the 1Sa 15:6 2617
I live shew me the *k* of the LORD 1Sa 20:14 2617
off thy *k* from my house for ever 1Sa 20:15 2617
have shewed this *k* unto your lord 2Sa 2:5 2617
And now the LORD shew *k* and truth 2Sa 2:6 2617
and I also will requite you this *k* 2Sa 2:6 2896
which against Judah do shew *k* 2Sa 3:8 2617
shew him *k* for Jonathan's sake 2Sa 9:1 2617
I may shew the *k* of God unto him 2Sa 9:3 2617
for I will surely shew thee *k* for 2Sa 9:7 2617
I will shew *k* unto Hanun the son 2Sa 10:2 2617
as his father shewed *k* unto me 2Sa 10:2 2617
Is this thy *k* to thy friend 2Sa 16:17 2617
But shew *k* unto the sons of 1Kin 2:7 2617
hast kept for him this great *k* 1Kin 3:6 2617
I will shew *k* unto Hanun the son 1Chr 19:2 2617
because his father shewed *k* to me 1Chr 19:2 2617
the king remembered not the *k* 2Chr 24:22 2617
slow to anger, and of great *k* .... Neh 9:17 2617
him, and she obtained *k* of him .... Est 2:9 2617
his marvellous *k* in a strong city .... Ps 31:21 2617
For his merciful *k* is great .... Ps 117:2 2617
thy merciful *k* be for my comfort, ... Ps 119:76 2617
it shall be a *k* .... Ps 141:5 2617
The desire of a man is his *k* .... Prov 19:22 2617
and in her tongue is the law of *k* .... Prov 31:26 2617
but with everlasting *k* will I .... Is 54:8 2617
but my *k* shall not depart from .... Is 54:10 2617
the *k* of thy youth, the love of .... Jer 2:2 2617
slow to anger, and of great *k* .... Joel 2:13 2617
slow to anger, and of great *k* .... Jonah 4:2 2617

people shewed us no little *k* .... Acts 28:2 *5363*
knowledge, by longsuffering, by *k* 2Cor 6:6 *5544*
riches of his grace in his *k* .... Eph 2:7 *5544*
and beloved, bowels of mercies, *k* .... Col 3:12 *5544*
But after that the *k* and love of .... Titus 3:4 *5544*
And to godliness brotherly *k* 2Pet 1:7 *5360*
and to brotherly *k* charity 2Pet 1:7 *5360*

KINDRED {28}

out of thy country, and from thy *k* .... Gen 12:1 4138
go unto my country, and to my *k* .... Gen 24:4 4138
house, and from the land of my *k* .... Gen 24:7 4138
my father's house, and to my *k* .... Gen 24:38 4940
take a wife for my son of my *k* .... Gen 24:40 4940
my oath, when thou comest to my *k* .... Gen 24:41 4940
land of thy fathers, and to thy *k* .... Gen 31:3 4138
and return unto the land of thy *k* .... Gen 31:13 4138
unto thy country, and to thy *k* .... Gen 32:9 4138
of our state, and of our *k* .... Gen 43:7 4138
to mine own land, and to my *k* .... Num 10:30 4138
and they brought out all her *k* .... Josh 6:23 4940
who was of the *k* of Elimelech .... Ruth 2:3 4940
And now is not Boaz of our *k* .... Ruth 3:2 4130
the *k* of Saul, three thousand 1Chr 12:29 250
not shewed her people nor her *k* .... Est 2:10 4138
yet shewed her *k* nor her people .... Est 2:20 4138
to see the destruction of my *k* .... Est 8:6 4138
the Buzite, of the *k* of Ram .... Job 32:2 4940
thy brethren, the men of thy *k* .... Eze 11:15 1353
There is none of thy *k* that is .... Lk 1:61 *4772*
were of the *k* of the high priest .... Acts 4:6 *1085*
out of thy country, and from thy *k* .... Acts 7:3 *4772*
Joseph's *k* was made known unto .... Acts 7:13 *1085*
father Jacob to him, and all his *k* .... Acts 7:14 *4772*
same dealt subtilly with our *k* .... Acts 7:19 *1085*
God by thy blood out of every *k* .... Rev 5:9 *5443*
earth, and to every nation, and *k* .... Rev 14:6 *5443*

KINDREDS {8}

ye *k* of the people, give unto the 1Chr 16:28 4940
all the *k* of the nations shall .... Ps 22:27 4940
O ye *k* of the people, give unto .... Ps 96:7 4940
all the *k* of the earth be blessed .... Acts 3:25 *3965*
all *k* of the earth shall wail .... Rev 1:7 *5443*
number, of all nations, and *k* .... Rev 7:9 *5443*
And they of the people and *k* .... Rev 11:9 *5443*
and power was given him over all *k* .... Rev 13:7 *5443*

KINDS {10}

upon the earth, after their *k* .... Gen 8:19 4940
divers *k* of spices prepared by 2Chr 16:14 2177
I will appoint over them four *k* .... Jer 15:3 4940
shall be according to their *k* .... Eze 47:10 4327
all *k* of musick, ye fall down and .... Dan 3:5 2177
all *k* of musick, all the people, ... Dan 3:7 2177
all *k* of musick, shall fall down .... Dan 3:10 2177
all *k* of musick, ye fall down and .... Dan 3:15 2177
to another divers *k* of tongues 1Cor 12:10 *1085*
so many *k* of voices in the world, ... 1Cor 14:10 *1085*

KINE {24}

camels with their colts, forty *k* .... Gen 32:15 6510
the river seven well favoured *k* .... Gen 41:2 6510
seven other *k* came up after them .... Gen 41:3 6510
stood by the other *k* upon the .... Gen 41:3 6510
leanfleshed *k* did eat up the .... Gen 41:4 6510
the seven well favoured and fat *k* .... Gen 41:4 6510
came up out of the river seven *k* .... Gen 41:18 6510
seven other *k* came up after them, ... Gen 41:19 6510
the ill favoured *k* did eat up the .... Gen 41:20 6510
did eat up the first seven fat *k* .... Gen 41:20 6510
The seven good *k* are seven years .... Gen 41:26 6510
ill favoured *k* that came up after .... Gen 41:27 6510
thine oil, the increase of thy *k* .... Deut 7:13 504
thy cattle, the increase of thy *k* .... Deut 28:4 504
thy land, the increase of thy *k* .... Deut 28:18 504
or oil, or the increase of thy *k* .... Deut 28:51 504
Butter of *k*, and milk of sheep, ... Deut 32:14 1241
a new cart, and take two milch *k* 1Sa 6:7 6510
tie the *k* to the cart, and bring 1Sa 6:7 6510
and took two milch *k*, and tied them 1Sa 6:10 6510
the *k* took the straight way to 1Sa 6:12 6510
offered the *k* a burnt offering 1Sa 6:14 6510
butter, and sheep, and cheese of *k* 2Sa 17:29 1241
ye *k* of Bashan, that are in the .... Amos 4:1 6510

KING {2259}

the days of Amraphel *k* of Shinar .... Gen 14:1 4428
Arioch *k* of Ellasar, Chedorlaomer .... Gen 14:1 4428
Ellasar, Chedorlaomer *k* of Elam .... Gen 14:1 4428
of Elam, and Tidal *k* of nations .... Gen 14:1 4428
made war with Bera *k* of Sodom .... Gen 14:2 4428
and with Birsha *k* of Gomorrah .... Gen 14:2 4428
Shinab *k* of Admah .... Gen 14:2 4428
Shemeber *k* of Zeboiim .... Gen 14:2 4428
the *k* of Bela, which is Zoar .... Gen 14:2 4428
And there went out the *k* of Sodom .... Gen 14:8 4428
the *k* of Gomorrah .... Gen 14:8 4428
the *k* of Admah .... Gen 14:8 4428
the *k* of Zeboiim .... Gen 14:8 4428
the *k* of Bela (the same is Zoar .... Gen 14:8 4428
With Chedorlaomer the *k* of Elam .... Gen 14:9 4428
and with Tidal *k* of nations .... Gen 14:9 4428
Amraphel *k* of Shinar, and Arioch .... Gen 14:9 4428
of Shinar, and Arioch *k* of Ellasar .... Gen 14:9 4428
the *k* of Sodom went out to meet .... Gen 14:17 4428
Melchizedek *k* of Salem brought .... Gen 14:18 4428
the *k* of Sodom said unto Abram, ... Gen 14:21 4428
And Abram said to the *k* of Sodom .... Gen 14:22 4428
Abimelech *k* of Gerar sent, and .... Gen 20:2 4428
Isaac went unto Abimelech *k* of .... Gen 26:1 4428

time, that Abimelech *k* of the .... Gen 26:8 4428
before there reigned any *k* over .... Gen 36:31 4428
that the butler of the *k* of Egypt .... Gen 40:1 4428
their lord the *k* of Egypt .... Gen 40:1 4428
and the baker of the *k* of Egypt .... Gen 40:5 4428
stood before Pharaoh *k* of Egypt .... Gen 41:46 4428
there arose up a new *k* over Egypt .... Ex 1:8 4428
the *k* of Egypt spake to the .... Ex 1:15 4428
did not as the *k* of Egypt .... Ex 1:17 4428
the *k* of Egypt called for the .... Ex 1:18 4428
of time, that the *k* of Egypt died .... Ex 2:23 4428
of Israel, unto the *k* of Egypt .... Ex 3:18 4428
I am sure that the *k* of Egypt .... Ex 3:19 4428
the *k* of Egypt said unto them, ... Ex 5:4 4428
in, speak unto Pharaoh *k* of Egypt .... Ex 6:11 4428
and unto Pharaoh *k* of Egypt .... Ex 6:13 4428
which spake to Pharaoh *k* of Egypt .... Ex 6:27 4428
speak thou unto Pharaoh *k* of .... Ex 6:29 4428
it was told the *k* of Egypt that .... Ex 14:5 4428
the heart of Pharaoh *k* of Egypt .... Ex 14:8 4428
from Kadesh unto the *k* of Edom .... Num 20:14 4428
when *k* Arad the Canaanite, which .... Num 21:1 4428
unto Sihon *k* of the Amorites .... Num 21:21 4428
of Sihon the *k* of the Amorites .... Num 21:26 4428
against the former *k* of Moab .... Num 21:26 4428
unto Sihon *k* of the Amorites .... Num 21:29 4428
Og the *k* of Bashan went out .... Num 21:33 4428
unto Sihon *k* of the Amorites .... Num 21:34 4428
Balak the son of Zippor was *k* of .... Num 22:4 4428
k of Moab, hath sent unto me, ... Num 22:10 4428
Balak the *k* of Moab hath brought .... Num 23:7 4428
and the shout of a *k* is among them .... Num 23:21 4428
his *k* shall be higher than Agag, ... Num 24:7 4428
of Sihon *k* of the Amorites .... Num 32:33 4428
and the kingdom of Og *k* of Bashan .... Num 32:33 4428
k Arad the Canaanite, which dwelt .... Num 33:40 4428
slain Sihon the *k* of the Amorites .... Deut 1:4 4428
Og the *k* of Bashan, which dwelt .... Deut 1:4 4428
k of Heshbon, and his land .... Deut 2:24 4428
of Kedemoth unto Sihon *k* of .... Deut 2:26 4428
But Sihon *k* of Heshbon would not .... Deut 2:30 4428
Og the *k* of Bashan came out .... Deut 3:1 4428
unto Sihon *k* of the Amorites .... Deut 3:2 4428
the *k* of Bashan, and all his .... Deut 3:3 4428
as we did unto Sihon *k* of Heshbon .... Deut 3:6 4428
For only Og *k* of Bashan remained .... Deut 3:11 4428
land of Sihon *k* of the Amorites .... Deut 4:46 4428
and the land of Og *k* of Bashan .... Deut 4:47 4428
the hand of Pharaoh *k* of Egypt .... Deut 7:8 4428
Egypt unto Pharaoh the *k* of Egypt .... Deut 11:3 4428
shalt say, I will set a *k* over me .... Deut 17:14 4428
in any wise set him *k* over thee .... Deut 17:15 4428
shalt thou set *k* over thee .... Deut 17:15 4428
thy *k* which thou shalt set over .... Deut 28:36 4428
Sihon the *k* of Heshbon .... Deut 29:7 4428
Og the *k* of Bashan, came out .... Deut 29:7 4428
he was *k* in Jeshurun, when the .... Deut 33:5 4428
And it was told the *k* of Jericho .... Josh 2:2 4428
the *k* of Jericho sent unto Rahab, ... Josh 2:3 4428
the *k* thereof, and the mighty men .... Josh 6:2 4428
given into thy hand the *k* of Ai .... Josh 8:1 4428
her *k* as thou didst unto Jericho .... Josh 8:2 4428
thou didst unto Jericho and her *k* .... Josh 8:2 4428
when the *k* of Ai saw it, that .... Josh 8:14 4428
the *k* of Ai they took alive, and .... Josh 8:23 4428
the *k* of Ai he hanged on a tree .... Josh 8:29 4428
to Sihon *k* of Heshbon .... Josh 9:10 4428
to Og *k* of Bashan, which was at .... Josh 9:10 4428
when Adoni-zedek *k* of Jerusalem .... Josh 10:1 4428
he had done to Jericho and her *k* .... Josh 10:1 4428
so he had done to Ai and her *k* .... Josh 10:1 4428
Wherefore Adoni-zedek *k* of .... Josh 10:3 4428
sent unto Hoham *k* of Hebron .... Josh 10:3 4428
and unto Piram *k* of Jarmuth .... Josh 10:3 4428
and unto Japhia *k* of Lachish .... Josh 10:3 4428
and unto Debir *k* of Eglon .... Josh 10:3 4428
the *k* of Jerusalem .... Josh 10:5 4428
the *k* of Hebron .... Josh 10:5 4428
the *k* of Jarmuth .... Josh 10:5 4428
the *k* of Lachish .... Josh 10:5 4428
the *k* of Eglon, gathered .... Josh 10:5 4428
the *k* of Jerusalem .... Josh 10:23 4428
the *k* of Hebron .... Josh 10:23 4428
the *k* of Jarmuth .... Josh 10:23 4428
the *k* of Lachish .... Josh 10:23 4428
and the *k* of Eglon .... Josh 10:23 4428
and the *k* thereof he utterly .... Josh 10:28 4428
he did to the *k* of Makkedah as he .... Josh 10:28 4428
as he did unto the *k* of Jericho .... Josh 10:28 4428
the *k* thereof, into the hand of .... Josh 10:30 4428
but did unto the *k* thereof as he .... Josh 10:30 4428
as he did unto the *k* of Jericho .... Josh 10:30 4428
Then Horam *k* of Gezer came up to .... Josh 10:33 4428
the *k* thereof, and all the cities .... Josh 10:37 4428
the *k* thereof, and all the cities .... Josh 10:39 4428
did to Debir, and to the *k* thereof .... Josh 10:39 4428
done also to Libnah, and to her *k* .... Josh 10:39 4428
when Jabin *k* of Hazor had heard .... Josh 11:1 4428
that he sent to Jobab *k* of Madon .... Josh 11:1 4428
to the *k* of Shimron .... Josh 11:1 4428
and to the *k* of Achshaph .... Josh 11:1 4428
smote the *k* thereof with the .... Josh 11:10 4428
Sihon *k* of the Amorites, who .... Josh 12:2 4428
And the coast of Og *k* of Bashan .... Josh 12:4 4428
the border of Sihon *k* of Heshbon .... Josh 12:5 4428
The *k* of Jericho, one .... Josh 12:9 4428
the *k* of Ai, which is beside .... Josh 12:9 4428
The *k* of Jerusalem, one .... Josh 12:10 4428

K

the *k* of Hebron, one	Josh 12:10	4428
The *k* of Jarmuth, one	Josh 12:11	4428
the *k* of Lachish, one	Josh 12:11	4428
The *k* of Eglon, one	Josh 12:12	4428
the *k* of Gezer, one	Josh 12:12	4428
The *k* of Debir, one	Josh 12:13	4428
the *k* of Geder, one	Josh 12:13	4428
The *k* of Hormah, one	Josh 12:14	4428
the *k* of Arad, one	Josh 12:14	4428
The *k* of Libnah, one	Josh 12:15	4428
the *k* of Adullam, one	Josh 12:15	4428
The *k* of Makkedah, one	Josh 12:16	4428
the *k* of Beth-el, one	Josh 12:16	4428
The *k* of Tappuah, one	Josh 12:17	4428
the *k* of Hepher, one	Josh 12:17	4428
The *k* of Aphek, one	Josh 12:18	4428
the *k* of Lasharon, one	Josh 12:18	4428
The *k* of Madon, one	Josh 12:19	4428
the *k* of Hazor, one	Josh 12:19	4428
The *k* of Shimron-meron, one	Josh 12:20	4428
the *k* of Achshaph, one	Josh 12:20	4428
The *k* of Taanach, one	Josh 12:21	4428
the *k* of Megiddo, one	Josh 12:21	4428
The *k* of Kedesh, one	Josh 12:22	4428
the *k* of Jokneam of Carmel, one	Josh 12:22	4428
The *k* of Dor in the coast of Dor,	Josh 12:23	4428
the *k* of the nations of Gilgal,	Josh 12:23	4428
The *k* of Tirzah, one	Josh 12:24	4428
cities of Sihon *k* of the Amorites	Josh 13:10	4428
of Sihon *k* of the Amorites	Josh 13:21	4428
the kingdom of Sihon *k* of Heshbon	Josh 13:27	4428
all the kingdom of Og *k* of Bashan	Josh 13:30	4428
k of Moab, arose and warred	Josh 24:9	4428
k of Mesopotamia	Judg 3:8	4428
k of Mesopotamia into his hand	Judg 3:10	4428
the *k* of Moab against Israel	Judg 3:12	4428
the *k* of Moab eighteen years	Judg 3:14	4428
present unto Eglon the *k* of Moab	Judg 3:15	4428
the present unto Eglon *k* of Moab	Judg 3:17	4428
a secret errand unto thee, O *k*	Judg 3:19	4428
the hand of Jabin *k* of Canaan	Judg 4:2	4428
between Jabin the *k* of Hazor	Judg 4:17	4428
k of Canaan before the children	Judg 4:23	4428
against Jabin the *k* of Canaan	Judg 4:24	4428
had destroyed Jabin *k* of Canaan	Judg 4:24	4428
one resembled the children of a *k*	Judg 8:18	4428
and went, and made Abimelech *k*	Judg 9:6	4428
on a time to anoint a *k* over them	Judg 9:8	4428
in truth ye anoint me *k* over you	Judg 9:15	4428
in that ye have made Abimelech *k*	Judg 9:16	4427
k over the men of Shechem,	Judg 9:18	4427
the *k* of the children of Ammon	Judg 11:12	4428
the *k* of the children of Ammon	Judg 11:13	4428
the *k* of the children of Ammon	Judg 11:14	4428
messengers unto the *k* of Edom	Judg 11:17	4428
but the *k* of Edom would not	Judg 11:17	4428
they sent unto the *k* of Moab	Judg 11:17	4428
unto Sihon *k* of the Amorites	Judg 11:19	4428
of the Amorites, the *k* of Heshbon	Judg 11:19	4428
the son of Zippor, *k* of Moab	Judg 11:25	4428
Howbeit the *k* of the children of	Judg 11:28	4428
days there was no *k* in Israel	Judg 17:6	4428
days there was no *k* in Israel	Judg 18:1	4428
when there was no *k* in Israel	Judg 19:1	4428
days there was no *k* in Israel	Judg 21:25	4428
he shall give strength unto his *k*	1Sa 2:10	4428
now make us a *k* to judge us like	1Sa 8:5	4428
said, Give us a *k* to judge us	1Sa 8:6	4428
the *k* that shall reign over them	1Sa 8:9	4428
the people that asked of him a *k*	1Sa 8:10	4428
the *k* that shall reign over you	1Sa 8:11	4428
k which ye shall have chosen you	1Sa 8:18	4428
but we will have a *k* over us	1Sa 8:19	4428
that our *k* may judge us, and go	1Sa 8:20	4428
their voice, and make them a *k*	1Sa 8:22	4428
him, Nay, but set a *k* over us	1Sa 10:19	4428
shouted, and said, God save the *k*	1Sa 10:24	4428
there they made Saul *k* before the	1Sa 11:15	4427
me, and have made a *k* over you	1Sa 12:1	4428
behold, the *k* walketh before you	1Sa 12:2	4428
and into the hand of the *k* of Moab	1Sa 12:9	4428
when ye saw that Nahash the *k* of	1Sa 12:12	4428
but a *k* shall reign over us	1Sa 12:12	4428
when the LORD your God was your *k*	1Sa 12:12	4428
behold the *k* whom ye have chosen	1Sa 12:13	4428
the LORD hath set a *k* over you	1Sa 12:13	4428
also the *k* that reigneth over you	1Sa 12:14	4428
of the LORD, in asking you a *k*	1Sa 12:17	4428
our sins this evil, to ask us a *k*	1Sa 12:19	4428
be consumed, both ye and your *k*	1Sa 12:25	4428
thee to be *k* over his people	1Sa 15:1	4428
he took Agag the *k* of the	1Sa 15:8	4428
that I have set up Saul to be *k*	1Sa 15:11	4428
LORD anointed thee *k* over Israel	1Sa 15:17	4428
have brought Agag the *k* of Amalek	1Sa 15:20	4428
also rejected thee from being *k*	1Sa 15:23	4428
thee from being *k* over Israel	1Sa 15:26	4428
me Agag the *k* of the Amalekites	1Sa 15:32	4428
he had made Saul *k* over Israel	1Sa 15:35	4427
provided me a *k* among his sons	1Sa 16:1	4428
the *k* will enrich him with great	1Sa 17:25	4428
said, As thy soul liveth, O *k*	1Sa 17:55	4428
the *k* said, Enquire thou whose	1Sa 17:56	4428
and dancing, to meet *k* Saul	1Sa 18:6	4428
I should be son in law to the *k*	1Sa 18:18	4428
the *k* hath delight in thee, and	1Sa 18:22	4428
The *k* desireth not any dowry, but	1Sa 18:25	4428
gave them in full tale to the *k*	1Sa 18:27	4428
Let not the *k* sin against his	1Sa 19:4	4428
fail to sit with the *k* at meat	1Sa 20:5	4428
the *k* sat him down to eat meat	1Sa 20:24	4428
the *k* sat upon his seat, as at	1Sa 20:25	4428
The *k* hath commanded me a	1Sa 21:2	4428
and went to Achish the *k* of Gath	1Sa 21:10	4428
not this David the *k* of the land	1Sa 21:11	4428
afraid of Achish the *k* of Gath	1Sa 21:12	4428
and he said unto the *k* of Moab	1Sa 22:3	4428
brought them before the *k* of Moab	1Sa 22:4	4428
Then the *k* sent to call Ahimelech	1Sa 22:11	4428
and they came all of them to the *k*	1Sa 22:11	4428
Then Ahimelech answered the *k*	1Sa 22:14	4428
let not the *k* impute any thing	1Sa 22:15	4428
the *k* said, Thou shalt surely die	1Sa 22:16	4428
the *k* said unto the footmen that	1Sa 22:17	4428
But the servants of the *k* would	1Sa 22:17	4428
the *k* said to Doeg, Turn thou, and	1Sa 22:18	4428
and thou shalt be *k* over Israel	1Sa 23:17	4427
Now therefore, O *k*, come down	1Sa 23:20	4428
after Saul, saying, My lord the *k*	1Sa 24:8	4428
After whom is the *k* of Israel	1Sa 24:14	4428
well that thou shalt surely be *k*	1Sa 24:20	4428
his house, like the feast of a *k*	1Sa 25:36	4428
Who art thou that criest to the *k*	1Sa 26:14	4428
hast thou not kept thy lord the *k*	1Sa 26:15	4428
in to destroy the *k* thy lord	1Sa 26:15	4428
It is my voice, my lord, O *k*	1Sa 26:17	4428
let my lord the *k* hear the words	1Sa 26:19	4428
for the *k* of Israel is come out	1Sa 26:20	4428
the son of Maoch, *k* of Gath	1Sa 27:2	4428
the *k* said unto her, Be not	1Sa 28:13	4428
servant of Saul the *k* of Israel	1Sa 29:3	4428
the enemies of my lord the *k*	1Sa 29:8	4428
David *k* over the house of Judah	2Sa 2:4	4428
have anointed me *k* over them	2Sa 2:7	4428
made him *k* over Gilead, and over	2Sa 2:9	4427
the time that David was *k* in	2Sa 2:11	4428
daughter of Talmai *k* of Geshur	2Sa 3:3	4428
in times past to be *k* over you	2Sa 3:17	4428
all Israel unto my lord the *k*	2Sa 3:21	4428
the son of Ner came to the *k*	2Sa 3:23	4428
Then Joab came to the *k*, and said,	2Sa 3:24	4428
k David himself followed the bier	2Sa 3:31	4428
the *k* lifted up his voice, and	2Sa 3:32	4428
the *k* lamented over Abner, and	2Sa 3:33	4428
as whatsoever the *k* did pleased	2Sa 3:36	4428
k to slay Abner the son of Ner	2Sa 3:37	4428
the *k* said unto his servants,	2Sa 3:38	4428
this day weak, though anointed *k*	2Sa 3:39	4428
David to Hebron, and said to the *k*	2Sa 4:8	4428
my lord the *k* this day of Saul	2Sa 4:8	4428
past, when Saul was *k* over us	2Sa 5:2	4428
of Israel came to the *k* to Hebron	2Sa 5:3	4428
k David made a league with them	2Sa 5:3	4428
they anointed David *k* over Israel	2Sa 5:3	4428
And the *k* and his men went to	2Sa 5:6	4428
Hiram *k* of Tyre sent messengers	2Sa 5:11	4428
had established him *k* over Israel	2Sa 5:12	4428
had anointed David *k* over Israel	2Sa 5:17	4428
And it was told *k* David, saying,	2Sa 6:12	4428
saw *k* David leaping and dancing	2Sa 6:16	4428
was the *k* of Israel today	2Sa 6:20	4428
when the *k* sat in his house, and	2Sa 7:1	4428
That the *k* said unto Nathan the	2Sa 7:2	4428
And Nathan said to the *k*, Go, do	2Sa 7:3	4428
Then went *k* David in, and sat	2Sa 7:18	4428
k of Zobah, as he went to recover	2Sa 8:3	4428
to succour Hadadezer *k* of Zobah	2Sa 8:5	4428
k David took exceeding much brass	2Sa 8:8	4428
When Toi *k* of Hamath heard that	2Sa 8:9	4428
sent Joram his son unto *k* David	2Sa 8:10	4428
Which also *k* David did dedicate	2Sa 8:11	4428
son of Rehob, *k* of Zobah	2Sa 8:12	4428
the *k* said unto him, Art thou	2Sa 9:2	4428
the *k* said, is there not yet any	2Sa 9:3	4428
And Ziba said unto the *k*, Jonathan	2Sa 9:3	4428
the *k* said unto him, Where is he	2Sa 9:4	4428
And Ziba said unto the *k*, Behold,	2Sa 9:4	4428
Then *k* David sent, and fetched him	2Sa 9:5	4428
Then the *k* called to Ziba, Saul's	2Sa 9:9	4428
Then said Ziba unto the *k*	2Sa 9:11	4428
to all that my lord the *k* hath	2Sa 9:11	4428
As for Mephibosheth, said the *k*	2Sa 9:11	4428
that the *k* of the children of	2Sa 10:1	4428
the *k* said, Tarry at Jericho	2Sa 10:5	4428
of *k* Maacah a thousand men, and of	2Sa 10:6	4428
him a mess of meat from the *k*	2Sa 11:8	4428
the matters of the war unto the *k*	2Sa 11:19	4428
I anointed thee *k* over Israel	2Sa 12:7	4428
when the *k* was come to see him,	2Sa 13:6	4428
to see him, Amnon said unto the *k*	2Sa 13:6	4428
I pray thee, speak unto the *k*	2Sa 13:13	4428
But when *k* David heard of all	2Sa 13:21	4428
And Absalom came to the *k*, and said	2Sa 13:24	4428
let the *k*, I beseech thee, and his	2Sa 13:24	4428
the *k* said to Absalom, Nay, my	2Sa 13:25	4428
the *k* said unto him, Why should	2Sa 13:26	4428
Then the *k* arose, and tare his	2Sa 13:31	4428
the *k* take the thing to his heart	2Sa 13:33	4428
And Jonadab said unto the *k*	2Sa 13:35	4428
the *k* also and all his servants	2Sa 13:36	4428
the son of Ammihud, *k* of Geshur	2Sa 13:37	4428
the soul of *k* David longed to go	2Sa 13:39	4428
And come to the *k*, and speak on	2Sa 14:3	4428
woman of Tekoah spake to the *k*	2Sa 14:4	4428
did obeisance, and said, Help, O *k*	2Sa 14:4	4428
the *k* said unto her, What aileth	2Sa 14:5	4428
the *k* said unto the woman, Go to	2Sa 14:8	4428
said unto the *k*, My lord, O *k*	2Sa 14:9	4428
and the *k* and his throne be	2Sa 14:9	4428
the *k* said, Whosoever saith ought	2Sa 14:10	4428
let the *k* remember the LORD thy	2Sa 14:11	4428
speak one word unto my lord the *k*	2Sa 14:12	4428
for the *k* doth speak this thing	2Sa 14:13	4428
in that the *k* doth not fetch home	2Sa 14:13	4428
of this thing unto my lord the *k*	2Sa 14:15	4428
said, I will now speak unto the *k*	2Sa 14:15	4428
it may be that the *k* will perform	2Sa 14:15	4428
For the *k* will hear, to deliver	2Sa 14:16	4428
The word of my lord the *k* shall	2Sa 14:17	4428
is my lord the *k* to discern good	2Sa 14:17	4428
Then the *k* answered and said unto	2Sa 14:18	4428
said, Let my lord the *k* now speak	2Sa 14:18	4428
the *k* said, Is not the hand of	2Sa 14:19	4428
As thy soul liveth, my lord the *k*	2Sa 14:19	4428
that my lord the *k* hath spoken	2Sa 14:19	4428
the *k* said unto Joab, Behold now,	2Sa 14:21	4428
bowed himself, and thanked the *k*	2Sa 14:22	4428
grace in thy sight, my lord, O *k*	2Sa 14:22	4428
in that the *k* hath fulfilled the	2Sa 14:22	4428
the *k* said, Let him turn to his	2Sa 14:24	4428
Joab, to have sent him to the *k*	2Sa 14:29	4428
that I may send thee to the *k*	2Sa 14:32	4428
So Joab came to the *k*, and told	2Sa 14:33	4428
for Absalom, he came to the *k*	2Sa 14:33	4428
face to the ground before the *k*	2Sa 14:33	4428
and the *k* kissed Absalom	2Sa 14:33	4428
came to the *k* for judgment	2Sa 15:2	4428
man deputed of the *k* to hear thee	2Sa 15:3	4428
that came to the *k* for judgment	2Sa 15:6	4428
that Absalom said unto the *k*	2Sa 15:7	4428
the *k* said unto him, Go in peace	2Sa 15:9	4428
king's servants said unto the *k*	2Sa 15:15	4428
my lord the *k* shall appoint	2Sa 15:15	4428
the *k* went forth, and all his	2Sa 15:16	4428
the *k* left ten women, which were	2Sa 15:16	4428
the *k* went forth, and all the	2Sa 15:17	4428
from Gath, passed on before the *k*	2Sa 15:18	4428
Then said the *k* to Ittai the	2Sa 15:19	4428
to thy place, and abide with the *k*	2Sa 15:19	4428
And Ittai answered the *k*, and said,	2Sa 15:21	4428
and as my lord the *k* liveth	2Sa 15:21	4428
what place my lord the *k* shall be	2Sa 15:21	4428
the *k* also himself passed over	2Sa 15:23	4428
the *k* said unto Zadok, Carry back	2Sa 15:25	4428
The *k* said also unto Zadok the	2Sa 15:27	4428
I will be thy servant, O *k*	2Sa 15:34	4428
the *k* said unto Ziba, What	2Sa 16:2	4428
the *k* said, And where is thy	2Sa 16:3	4428
And Ziba said unto the *k*, Behold,	2Sa 16:3	4428
Then said the *k* to Ziba, Behold,	2Sa 16:4	4428
grace in thy sight, my lord, O *k*	2Sa 16:4	4428
when *k* David came to Bahurim,	2Sa 16:5	4428
and at all the servants of *k* David	2Sa 16:6	4428
the son of Zeruiah unto the *k*	2Sa 16:9	4428
this dead dog curse my lord the *k*	2Sa 16:9	4428
the *k* said, What have I to do	2Sa 16:10	4428
And the *k*, and all the people that	2Sa 16:14	4428
God save the *k*, God save the *k*	2Sa 16:16	4428
and I will smite the *k* only	2Sa 17:2	4428
lest the *k* be swallowed up, and	2Sa 17:16	4428
and they went and told *k* David	2Sa 17:17	4428
told *k* David, and said unto David,	2Sa 17:21	4428
the *k* said unto the people, I	2Sa 18:2	4428
the *k* said unto them, What	2Sa 18:4	4428
the *k* stood by the gate side, and	2Sa 18:4	4428
the *k* commanded Joab and Abishai	2Sa 18:5	4428
k gave all the captains charge	2Sa 18:5	4428
in our hearing the *k* charged thee	2Sa 18:12	4428
there is no matter hid from the *k*	2Sa 18:13	4428
me now run, and bear the *k* tidings	2Sa 18:19	4428
Go tell the *k* what thou hast seen	2Sa 18:21	4428
the watchman cried, and told the *k*	2Sa 18:25	4428
the *k* said, If he be alone, there	2Sa 18:25	4428
the *k* said, He also bringeth	2Sa 18:26	4428
the *k* said, He is a good man, and	2Sa 18:27	4428
called, and said unto the *k*	2Sa 18:28	4428
earth upon his face before the *k*	2Sa 18:28	4428
their hand against my lord the *k*	2Sa 18:28	4428
the *k* said, Is the young man	2Sa 18:29	4428
the *k* said unto him, Turn aside,	2Sa 18:30	4428
said, Tidings, my lord the *k*	2Sa 18:31	4428
the *k* said unto Cushi, Is the	2Sa 18:32	4428
The enemies of my lord the *k*	2Sa 18:32	4428
the *k* was much moved, and went up	2Sa 18:33	4428
the *k* weepeth and mourneth for	2Sa 19:1	4428
how the *k* was grieved for his son	2Sa 19:2	4428
But the *k* covered his face, and	2Sa 19:4	4428
the *k* cried with a loud voice, O	2Sa 19:4	4428
Joab came into the house to the *k*	2Sa 19:5	4428
Then the *k* arose, and sat in the	2Sa 19:8	4428
the *k* doth sit in the gate	2Sa 19:8	4428
all the people came before the *k*	2Sa 19:8	4428
The *k* saved us out of the hand of	2Sa 19:9	4428
not a word of bringing the *k* back	2Sa 19:10	4428
k David sent to Zadok and to	2Sa 19:11	4428
to bring the *k* back to his house	2Sa 19:11	4428
of all Israel is come to the *k*	2Sa 19:11	4428
ye the last to bring back the *k*	2Sa 19:12	4428
they sent this word unto the *k*	2Sa 19:14	4428
So the *k* returned, and came to	2Sa 19:15	4428
to Gilgal, to go to meet the *k*	2Sa 19:15	4428
to conduct the *k* over Jordan	2Sa 19:15	4428
the men of Judah to meet *k* David	2Sa 19:16	4428
went over Jordan before the *k*	2Sa 19:17	4428

of Gera fell down before the *k* 2Sa 19:18 4428
And said unto the *k*, Let not my 2Sa 19:19 4428
lord the *k* went out of Jerusalem 2Sa 19:19 4428
that the *k* should take it to his 2Sa 19:19 4428
to go down to meet my lord the *k* 2Sa 19:20 4428
that I am this day *k* over Israel 2Sa 19:22 4428
Therefore the *k* said unto Shimei, 2Sa 19:23 4428
And the *k* sware unto him 2Sa 19:23 4428
of Saul came down to meet the *k* 2Sa 19:24 4428
from the day the *k* departed until 2Sa 19:24 4428
come to Jerusalem to meet the *k* 2Sa 19:25 4428
that the *k* said unto him, 2Sa 19:25 4428
And he answered, My lord, O *k* 2Sa 19:26 4428
may ride thereon, and go to the *k* 2Sa 19:26 4428
thy servant unto my lord the *k* 2Sa 19:27 4428
but my lord the *k* is as an angel 2Sa 19:27 4428
but dead men before my lord the *k* 2Sa 19:28 4428
I yet to cry any more unto the *k* 2Sa 19:28 4428
the *k* said unto him, Why speakest 2Sa 19:29 4428
And Mephibosheth said unto the *k* 2Sa 19:30 4428
forasmuch as my lord the *k* is 2Sa 19:30 4428
and went over Jordan with the *k* 2Sa 19:31 4428
and he had provided the *k* of 2Sa 19:32 4428
the *k* said unto Barzillai, Come 2Sa 19:33 4428
And Barzillai said unto the *k* 2Sa 19:34 4428
go up with the *k* unto Jerusalem 2Sa 19:34 4428
yet a burden unto my lord the *k* 2Sa 19:35 4428
little way over Jordan with the *k* 2Sa 19:36 4428
why should the *k* recompense it me 2Sa 19:36 4428
him go over with my lord the *k* 2Sa 19:37 4428
the *k* answered, Chimham shall go 2Sa 19:38 4428
when the *k* was come over 2Sa 19:39 4428
the *k* kissed Barzillai, and 2Sa 19:39 4428
Then the *k* went on to Gilgal, and 2Sa 19:40 4428
people of Judah conducted the *k* 2Sa 19:40 4428
to the *k*, and said unto the *k* 2Sa 19:41 4428
thee away, and have brought the *k* 2Sa 19:41 4428
Because the *k* is near of kin to 2Sa 19:42 4428
said, We have ten parts in the *k* 2Sa 19:43 4428
first had in bringing back our *k* 2Sa 19:43 4428
men of Judah clave unto their *k* 2Sa 20:2 4428
the *k* took the ten women his 2Sa 20:3 4428
Then said the *k* to Amasa, 2Sa 20:4 4428
lifted up his hand against the *k* 2Sa 20:21 4428
returned to Jerusalem unto the *k* 2Sa 20:22 4428
the *k* called the Gibeonites, and 2Sa 21:2 4428
And they answered the *k*, The man 2Sa 21:5 4428
the *k* said, I will give them 2Sa 21:6 4428
But the *k* spared Mephibosheth, 2Sa 21:7 4428
But the *k* took the two sons of 2Sa 21:8 4428
all that the *k* commanded 2Sa 21:14 4428
the tower of salvation for his *k* 2Sa 22:51 4428
For the *k* said to Joab the 2Sa 24:2 4428
And Joab said unto the *k*, Now the 2Sa 24:3 4428
eyes of my lord the *k* may see it 2Sa 24:3 4428
lord the *k* delight in this thing 2Sa 24:3 4428
out from the presence of the *k* 2Sa 24:4 4428
number of the people unto the *k* 2Sa 24:9 4428
And Araunah looked, and saw the *k* 2Sa 24:20 4428
bowed himself before the *k* on his 2Sa 24:20 4428
my lord the *k* come to his servant 2Sa 24:21 4428
David, Let my lord the *k* take 2Sa 24:22 4428
as a *k*, give unto the *k* 2Sa 24:23 4428
And Araunah said unto the *k* 2Sa 24:23 4428
the *k* said unto Araunah, Nay 2Sa 24:24 4428
Now *k* David was old and stricken 1Kin 1:1 4428
for my lord the *k* a young virgin 1Kin 1:2 4428
and let her stand before the *k* 1Kin 1:2 4428
that my lord the *k* may get heat 1Kin 1:2 4428
and brought her to the *k* 1Kin 1:3 4428
was very fair, and cherished the *k* 1Kin 1:4 4428
but the *k* knew her not 1Kin 1:4 4428
himself, saying, I will be *k* 1Kin 1:5 4427
Go and get thee in unto *k* David 1Kin 1:13 4428
him, Didst not thou, my lord, O *k* 1Kin 1:13 4428
thou yet talkest there with the *k* 1Kin 1:14 4428
in unto the *k* into the chamber 1Kin 1:15 4428
and the *k* was very old 1Kin 1:15 4428
Shunammite ministered unto the *k* 1Kin 1:15 4428
and did obeisance unto the *k* 1Kin 1:16 4428
the *k* said, What wouldest thou 1Kin 1:16 4428
and now, my lord the *k*, thou 1Kin 1:18 4428
hath called all the sons of the *k* 1Kin 1:19 4428
And thou, my lord, O *k*, the eyes 1Kin 1:20 4428
throne of my lord the *k* after him 1Kin 1:20 4428
when my lord the *k* shall sleep 1Kin 1:21 4428
while she yet talked with the *k* 1Kin 1:22 4428
And they told the *k*, saying, 1Kin 1:23 4428
when he was come in before the *k* 1Kin 1:23 4428
the *k* with his face to the ground 1Kin 1:23 4428
And Nathan said, My lord, O *k* 1Kin 1:24 4428
him, and say, God save *k* Adonijah 1Kin 1:25 4428
this thing done by my lord the *k* 1Kin 1:27 4428
throne of my lord the *k* after him 1Kin 1:27 4428
Then *k* David answered and said, 1Kin 1:28 4428
presence, and stood before the *k* 1Kin 1:28 4428
the *k* sware, and said, As the LORD 1Kin 1:29 4428
earth, and did reverence to the *k* 1Kin 1:31 4428
Let my lord *k* David live for ever 1Kin 1:31 4428
k David said, Call me Zadok the 1Kin 1:32 4428
And they came before the *k* 1Kin 1:32 4428
The *k* also said unto them, Take 1Kin 1:33 4428
anoint him there *k* over Israel 1Kin 1:34 4428
and say, God save *k* Solomon 1Kin 1:34 4428
for he shall be *k* in my stead 1Kin 1:35 4427
son of Jehoiada answered the *k* 1Kin 1:36 4428
God of my lord the *k* say so too 1Kin 1:36 4428
LORD hath been with my lord the *k* 1Kin 1:37 4428

the throne of my lord *k* David 1Kin 1:37 4428
to ride upon *k* David's mule 1Kin 1:38 4428
people said, God save *k* Solomon 1Kin 1:39 4428
k David hath made Solomon *k* 1Kin 1:43 4427
the *k* hath sent with him Zadok 1Kin 1:44 4428
have anointed him *k* in Gihon 1Kin 1:45 4428
came to bless our lord *k* David 1Kin 1:47 4428
the *k* bowed himself upon the bed 1Kin 1:47 4428
And also thus said the *k*, Blessed 1Kin 1:48 4428
Adonijah feareth *k* Solomon 1Kin 1:51 4428
Let *k* Solomon swear unto me to 1Kin 1:51 4428
So *k* Solomon sent, and they 1Kin 1:53 4428
and bowed himself to *k* Solomon 1Kin 1:53 4428
I pray thee, unto Solomon the *k* 1Kin 2:17 4428
I will speak for thee unto the *k* 1Kin 2:18 4428
therefore went unto *k* Solomon 1Kin 2:19 4428
the *k* rose up to meet her, and 1Kin 2:19 4428
the *k* said unto her, Ask on, my 1Kin 2:20 4428
k Solomon answered and said unto 1Kin 2:22 4428
Then *k* Solomon sware by the LORD, 1Kin 2:23 4428
k Solomon sent by the hand of 1Kin 2:25 4428
Abiathar the priest said the *k* 1Kin 2:26 4428
it was told *k* Solomon that Joab 1Kin 2:29 4428
said unto him, Thus saith the *k* 1Kin 2:30 4428
Benaiah brought the *k* word again 1Kin 2:30 4428
the *k* said unto him, Do as he 1Kin 2:31 4428
the *k* put Benaiah the son of 1Kin 2:35 4428
Zadok the priest did the *k* put in 1Kin 2:35 4428
the *k* sent and called for Shimei, 1Kin 2:36 4428
And Shimei said unto the *k* 1Kin 2:38 4428
as my lord the *k* hath said 1Kin 2:38 4428
Achish son of Maachah *k* of Gath 1Kin 2:39 4428
the *k* sent and called for Shimei, 1Kin 2:42 4428
The *k* said moreover to Shimei, 1Kin 2:44 4428
k Solomon shall be blessed, and 1Kin 2:45 4428
So the *k* commanded Benaiah the 1Kin 2:46 4428
affinity with Pharaoh *k* of Egypt 1Kin 3:1 4428
the *k* went to Gibeon to sacrifice 1Kin 3:4 4428
k instead of David my father 1Kin 3:7 4427
that were harlots, unto the *k* 1Kin 3:16 4428
Thus they spake before the *k* 1Kin 3:22 4428
Then said the *k*, The one saith, 1Kin 3:23 4428
the *k* said, Bring me a sword 1Kin 3:24 4428
they brought a sword before the *k* 1Kin 3:24 4428
the *k* said, Divide the living 1Kin 3:25 4428
the living child was unto the *k* 1Kin 3:26 4428
Then the *k* answered and said, Give 1Kin 3:27 4428
judgment which the *k* had judged 1Kin 3:28 4428
and they feared the *k* 1Kin 3:28 4428
So *k* Solomon was *k* over all 1Kin 4:1 4428
which provided victuals for the *k* 1Kin 4:7 4428
of Sihon *k* of the Amorites 1Kin 4:19 4428
and of Og *k* of Bashan 1Kin 4:19 4428
provided victual for *k* Solomon 1Kin 4:27 4428
that came unto *k* Solomon's table 1Kin 4:27 4428
Hiram *k* of Tyre sent his servants 1Kin 5:1 4428
him *k* in the room of his father 1Kin 5:1 4428
k Solomon raised a levy out of 1Kin 5:13 4428
the *k* commanded, and they brought 1Kin 5:17 4428
the house which *k* Solomon built 1Kin 6:2 4428
k Solomon sent and fetched Hiram 1Kin 7:13 4428
And he came to *k* Solomon, and 1Kin 7:14 4428
k Solomon for the house of the 1Kin 7:40 4428
which Hiram made to *k* Solomon for 1Kin 7:45 4428
of Jordan did the *k* cast them 1Kin 7:46 4428
k Solomon made for the house of 1Kin 7:51 4428
unto *k* Solomon in Jerusalem, that 1Kin 8:1 4428
assembled themselves unto *k* 1Kin 8:2 4428
And *k* Solomon, and all the 1Kin 8:5 4428
the *k* turned his face about, and 1Kin 8:14 4428
And the *k*, and all Israel with him, 1Kin 8:62 4428
So the *k* and all the children of 1Kin 8:63 4428
The same day did the *k* hallow the 1Kin 8:64 4428
and they blessed the *k*, and went 1Kin 8:66 4428
(Now Hiram the *k* of Tyre had 1Kin 9:11 4428
that then *k* Solomon gave Hiram 1Kin 9:11 4428
Hiram sent to the *k* sixscore 1Kin 9:14 4428
the levy which *k* Solomon raised 1Kin 9:15 4428
For Pharaoh *k* of Egypt had gone 1Kin 9:16 4428
k Solomon made a navy of ships in 1Kin 9:26 4428
and brought it to *k* Solomon 1Kin 9:28 4428
was not any thing hid from the *k* 1Kin 10:3 4428
And she said to the *k*, It was a 1Kin 10:6 4428
ever, therefore made he thee *k* 1Kin 10:9 4428
And she gave the *k* an hundred 1Kin 10:10 4428
queen of Sheba gave to *k* Solomon 1Kin 10:10 4428
the *k* made of the almug trees 1Kin 10:12 4428
k Solomon gave unto the queen of 1Kin 10:13 4428
k Solomon made two hundred 1Kin 10:16 4428
the *k* put them in the house of 1Kin 10:17 4428
Moreover the *k* made a great 1Kin 10:18 4428
all *k* Solomon's drinking vessels 1Kin 10:21 4428
For the *k* had at sea a navy of 1Kin 10:22 4428
So *k* Solomon exceeded all the 1Kin 10:23 4428
and with the *k* at Jerusalem 1Kin 10:26 4428
the *k* made silver to be in 1Kin 10:27 4428
But *k* Solomon loved many strange 1Kin 11:1 4428
to Egypt, unto Pharaoh *k* of Egypt 1Kin 11:18 4428
his lord Hadadezer *k* of Zobah 1Kin 11:23 4428
lifted up his hand against the *k* 1Kin 11:26 4428
lifted up his hand against the *k* 1Kin 11:27 4428
and shalt be *k* over Israel 1Kin 11:37 4428
Egypt, unto Shishak *k* of Egypt 1Kin 11:40 4428
come to Shechem to make him *k* 1Kin 12:1 4427
from the presence of *k* Solomon 1Kin 12:2 4428
k Rehoboam consulted with the old 1Kin 12:6 4428
as the *k* had appointed, saying, 1Kin 12:12 4428
the *k* answered the people roughly 1Kin 12:13 4428

Wherefore the *k* hearkened not 1Kin 12:15 4428
the *k* hearkened not unto them 1Kin 12:16 4428
the people answered the *k* 1Kin 12:16 4428
Then *k* Rehoboam sent Adoram, who 1Kin 12:18 4428
Therefore *k* Rehoboam made speed 1Kin 12:18 4428
made him *k* over all Israel 1Kin 12:20 4427
k of Judah, and unto all the house 1Kin 12:23 4428
even unto Rehoboam *k* of Judah 1Kin 12:27 4428
go again to Rehoboam *k* of Judah 1Kin 12:27 4428
Whereupon the *k* took counsel 1Kin 12:28 4428
when *k* Jeroboam heard the saying 1Kin 13:4 4428
the *k* answered and said unto the 1Kin 13:6 4428
the *k* said unto the man of God, 1Kin 13:7 4428
And the man of God said unto the *k* 1Kin 13:8 4428
which he had spoken unto the *k* 1Kin 13:11 4428
I should be *k* over this people 1Kin 14:2 4428
raise him up a *k* over Israel 1Kin 14:14 4428
in the fifth year of *k* Rehoboam 1Kin 14:25 4428
that Shishak *k* of Egypt came up 1Kin 14:25 4428
k Rehoboam made in their stead 1Kin 14:27 4428
when the *k* went into the house of 1Kin 14:28 4428
of *k* Jeroboam the son of Nebat 1Kin 15:1 4428
k of Israel reigned Asa over 1Kin 15:9 4428
Baasha *k* of Israel all their days 1Kin 15:16 4428
Baasha *k* of Israel went up 1Kin 15:17 4428
out or come in to Asa *k* of Judah 1Kin 15:17 4428
k Asa sent them to Ben-hadad, the 1Kin 15:18 4428
k of Syria, that dwelt at 1Kin 15:18 4428
league with Baasha *k* of Israel 1Kin 15:19 4428
So Ben-hadad hearkened unto *k* Asa 1Kin 15:20 4428
Then *k* Asa made a proclamation 1Kin 15:22 4428
k Asa built with them Geba of 1Kin 15:22 4428
the second year of Asa *k* of Judah 1Kin 15:25 4428
k of Judah did Baasha slay him 1Kin 15:28 4428
Baasha *k* of Israel all their days 1Kin 15:32 4428
In the third year of Asa *k* of 1Kin 15:33 4428
sixth year of Asa *k* of Judah 1Kin 16:8 4428
and seventh year of Asa *k* of Judah 1Kin 16:10 4428
seventh year of Asa *k* of Judah 1Kin 16:15 4428
and hath also slain the *k* 1Kin 16:16 4428
k over Israel that day in the 1Kin 16:16 4427
the son of Ginath, to make him *k* 1Kin 16:21 4427
first year of Asa *k* of Judah 1Kin 16:23 4428
eighth year of Asa *k* of Judah 1Kin 16:29 4428
of Ethbaal *k* of the Zidonians 1Kin 16:31 4428
anoint Hazael to be *k* over Syria 1Kin 19:15 4428
thou anoint to be *k* over Israel 1Kin 19:16 4428
Ben-hadad the *k* of Syria gathered 1Kin 20:1 4428
to Ahab *k* of Israel into the city 1Kin 20:2 4428
the *k* of Israel answered and said, 1Kin 20:4 4428
answered and said, My lord, O *k* 1Kin 20:4 4428
Then the *k* of Israel called all 1Kin 20:7 4428
of Ben-hadad, Tell my lord the *k* 1Kin 20:9 4428
the *k* of Israel answered and said, 1Kin 20:11 4428
a prophet unto Ahab *k* of Israel 1Kin 20:13 4428
Ben-hadad the *k* of Syria escaped 1Kin 20:20 4428
the *k* of Israel went out, and 1Kin 20:21 4428
prophet came to the *k* of Israel 1Kin 20:22 4428
k of Syria will come up against 1Kin 20:22 4428
the servants of the *k* of Syria 1Kin 20:23 4428
and spake unto the *k* of Israel 1Kin 20:28 4428
and go out to the *k* of Israel 1Kin 20:31 4428
heads, and came to the *k* of Israel 1Kin 20:32 4428
and waited for the *k* by the way 1Kin 20:38 4428
as the *k* passed by, he cried unto 1Kin 20:39 4428
passed by, he cried unto the *k* 1Kin 20:39 4428
the *k* of Israel said unto him, So 1Kin 20:40 4428
the *k* of Israel discerned him 1Kin 20:41 4428
the *k* of Israel went to his house 1Kin 20:43 4428
the palace of Ahab *k* of Samaria 1Kin 21:1 4428
Thou didst blaspheme God and the *k* 1Kin 21:10 4428
Naboth did blaspheme God and the *k* 1Kin 21:13 4428
go down to meet Ahab *k* of Israel 1Kin 21:18 4428
that Jehoshaphat the *k* of Judah 1Kin 22:2 4428
came down to the *k* of Israel 1Kin 22:2 4428
the *k* of Israel said unto his 1Kin 22:3 4428
out of the hand of the *k* of Syria 1Kin 22:3 4428
said to the *k* of Israel, I am as 1Kin 22:4 4428
said unto the *k* of Israel 1Kin 22:5 4428
Then the *k* of Israel gathered the 1Kin 22:6 4428
deliver it into the hand of the *k* 1Kin 22:6 4428
the *k* of Israel said unto 1Kin 22:8 4428
said, Let not the *k* say so 1Kin 22:8 4428
Then the *k* of Israel called an 1Kin 22:9 4428
the *k* of Israel and Jehoshaphat 1Kin 22:10 4428
Jehoshaphat the *k* of Judah sat 1Kin 22:10 4428
good unto the *k* with one mouth 1Kin 22:13 4428
So he came to the *k* 1Kin 22:15 4428
the *k* said unto him, Micaiah, 1Kin 22:15 4428
deliver it into the hand of the *k* 1Kin 22:15 4428
the *k* said unto him, How many 1Kin 22:16 4428
the *k* of Israel said unto 1Kin 22:18 4428
the *k* of Israel said, Take 1Kin 22:26 4428
And say, Thus saith the *k*, Put 1Kin 22:27 4428
So the *k* of Israel and Jehoshaphat 1Kin 22:29 4428
Jehoshaphat the *k* of Judah went 1Kin 22:29 4428
the *k* of Israel said unto 1Kin 22:30 4428
the *k* of Israel disguised himself 1Kin 22:30 4428
But the *k* of Syria commanded his 1Kin 22:31 4428
save only with the *k* of Israel 1Kin 22:31 4428
Surely it is the *k* of Israel 1Kin 22:32 4428
that it was not the *k* of Israel 1Kin 22:33 4428
smote the *k* of Israel between the 1Kin 22:34 4428
the *k* was stayed up in his 1Kin 22:35 4428
So the *k* died, and was brought to 1Kin 22:37 4428
and they buried the *k* in Samaria 1Kin 22:37 4428
fourth year of Ahab *k* of Israel 1Kin 22:41 4428
made peace with the *k* of Israel 1Kin 22:44 4428

There was then no *k* in Edom 1Kin 22:47 4428
a deputy was *k* 1Kin 22:47 4428
year of Jehoshaphat *k* of Judah 1Kin 22:51 4428
messengers of the *k* of Samaria 2Kin 1:3 4428
again unto the *k* that sent you 2Kin 1:6 4428
Then the *k* sent unto him a 2Kin 1:9 4428
the *k* hath said, Come down 2Kin 1:9 4428
man of God, thus hath the *k* said 2Kin 1:11 4428
and went down with him unto the *k* 2Kin 1:15 4428
the son of Jehoshaphat *k* of Judah 2Kin 1:17 4428
year of Jehoshaphat *k* of Judah 2Kin 3:1 4428
Mesha *k* of Moab was a sheepmaster 2Kin 3:4 4428
rendered unto the *k* of Israel an 2Kin 3:4 4428
that the *k* of Moab rebelled 2Kin 3:5 4428
rebelled against the *k* of Israel 2Kin 3:5 4428
k Jehoram went out of Samaria the 2Kin 3:6 4428
to Jehoshaphat the *k* of Judah 2Kin 3:7 4428
The *k* of Moab hath rebelled 2Kin 3:7 4428
So the *k* of Israel went 2Kin 3:9 4428
k of Judah, and the *k* of Edom 2Kin 3:9 4428
the *k* of Israel said, Alas 2Kin 3:10 4428
one of the *k* of Israel's servants 2Kin 3:11 4428
So the *k* of Israel and Jehoshaphat 2Kin 3:12 4428
the *k* of Edom went down to him 2Kin 3:12 4428
Elisha said unto the *k* of Israel 2Kin 3:13 4428
the *k* of Israel said unto him, 2Kin 3:13 4428
of Jehoshaphat the *k* of Judah 2Kin 3:14 4428
when the *k* of Moab saw that the 2Kin 3:26 4428
through even unto the *k* of Edom 2Kin 3:26 4428
thou be spoken for to the *k* 2Kin 4:13 4428
of the host of the *k* of Syria 2Kin 5:1 4428
the *k* of Syria said, Go to, go, 2Kin 5:5 4428
a letter unto the *k* of Israel 2Kin 5:5 4428
the letter to the *k* of Israel 2Kin 5:6 4428
when the *k* of Israel had read the 2Kin 5:7 4428
man of God had heard that the *k* 2Kin 5:8 4428
clothes, that he sent to the *k* 2Kin 5:8 4428
Then the *k* of Syria warred 2Kin 6:8 4428
of God sent unto the *k* of Israel 2Kin 6:9 4428
the *k* of Israel sent to the place 2Kin 6:10 4428
Therefore the heart of the *k* of 2Kin 6:11 4428
of us is for the *k* of Israel 2Kin 6:11 4428
servants said, None, my lord, O *k* 2Kin 6:12 4428
telleth the *k* of Israel the words 2Kin 6:12 4428
the *k* of Israel said unto Elisha, 2Kin 6:21 4428
that Ben-hadad *k* of Syria 2Kin 6:24 4428
as the *k* of Israel was passing by 2Kin 6:26 4428
him, saying, Help, my lord, O *k* 2Kin 6:26 4428
the *k* said unto her, What aileth 2Kin 6:28 4428
when the *k* heard the words of the 2Kin 6:30 4428
the *k* sent a man from before him 2Kin 6:32
Then a lord on whose hand the *k* 2Kin 7:2 4428
the *k* of Israel hath hired 2Kin 7:6 4428
the *k* arose in the night, and said 2Kin 7:12 4428
the *k* sent after the host of the 2Kin 7:14 4428
returned, and told the *k* 2Kin 7:15 4428
the *k* appointed the lord on whose 2Kin 7:17 4428
spake when the *k* came down to him 2Kin 7:17 4428
man of God had spoken to the *k* 2Kin 7:18 4428
to cry unto the *k* for her house 2Kin 8:3 4428
the *k* talked with Gehazi the 2Kin 8:4 4428
as he was telling the *k* how he 2Kin 8:5 4428
cried to the *k* for her house and 2Kin 8:5 4428
And Gehazi said, My lord, O *k* 2Kin 8:5 4428
when the *k* asked the woman, she 2Kin 8:6 4428
So the *k* appointed unto her a 2Kin 8:6 4428
Ben-hadad the *k* of Syria was sick 2Kin 8:7 4428
the *k* said unto Hazael, Take a 2Kin 8:8 4428
Thy son Ben-hadad *k* of Syria hath 2Kin 8:9 4428
that thou shalt be *k* over Syria 2Kin 8:13 4428
Joram the son of Ahab *k* of Israel 2Kin 8:16 4428
Jehoshaphat being then *k* of Judah 2Kin 8:16 4428
k of Judah began to reign 2Kin 8:16 4428
and made a *k* over themselves 2Kin 8:20 4428
k of Israel did Ahaziah the son 2Kin 8:25 4428
Jehoram *k* of Judah begin to reign 2Kin 8:25 4428
the daughter of Omri *k* of Israel 2Kin 8:26 4428
k of Syria in Ramoth-gilead 2Kin 8:28 4428
k Joram went back to be healed in 2Kin 8:29 4428
fought against Hazael *k* of Syria 2Kin 8:29 4428
Ahaziah the son of Jehoram *k* of 2Kin 8:29 4428
have anointed thee *k* over Israel 2Kin 9:3 4428
I have anointed thee *k* over the 2Kin 9:6 4428
have anointed thee *k* over Israel 2Kin 9:12 4428
with trumpets, saying, Jehu is *k* 2Kin 9:13 4427
because of Hazael *k* of Syria 2Kin 9:14 4428
But *k* Joram was returned to be 2Kin 9:15 4428
he fought with Hazael *k* of Syria 2Kin 9:15 4428
Ahaziah *k* of Judah was come down 2Kin 9:16 4428
him, and said, Thus saith the *k* 2Kin 9:18 4428
them, and said, Thus saith the *k* 2Kin 9:19 4428
Joram *k* of Israel and Ahaziah *k* 2Kin 9:21 4428
Ahaziah the *k* of Judah saw this 2Kin 9:27 4428
we will not make any *k* 2Kin 10:5 4427
brethren of Ahaziah *k* of Judah 2Kin 10:13 4428
to salute the children of the *k* 2Kin 10:13 4428
the daughter of *k* Joram, sister 2Kin 11:2 4428
the house of the LORD about the *k* 2Kin 11:7 4428
shall compass the *k* round about 2Kin 11:8 4428
be ye with the *k* as he goeth out 2Kin 11:8 4428
the priest give *k* David's spears 2Kin 11:10 4428
in his hand, round about the *k* 2Kin 11:11 4428
and they made him *k*, and anointed 2Kin 11:12 4427
hands, and said, God save the *k* 2Kin 11:12 4428
the *k* stood by a pillar, as the 2Kin 11:14 4428
and the trumpeters by the *k* 2Kin 11:14 4428
between the LORD and the *k* 2Kin 11:17 4428
between the *k* also and the people 2Kin 11:17 4428
they brought down the *k* from the 2Kin 11:19 4428
twentieth year of *k* Jehoash the 2Kin 12:6 4428
Then *k* Jehoash called for 2Kin 12:7 4428
Then Hazael *k* of Syria went up, 2Kin 12:17 4428
Jehoash *k* of Judah took all the 2Kin 12:18 4428
and sent it to Hazael *k* of Syria 2Kin 12:18 4428
of Joash the son of Ahaziah *k* of 2Kin 13:1 4428
the hand of Hazael *k* of Syria 2Kin 13:3 4428
because the *k* of Syria oppressed 2Kin 13:4 4428
for the *k* of Syria had destroyed 2Kin 13:7 4428
seventh year of Joash *k* of Judah 2Kin 13:10 4428
fought against Amaziah *k* of Judah 2Kin 13:12 4428
Joash the *k* of Israel came down 2Kin 13:14 4428
And he said to the *k* of Israel 2Kin 13:16 4428
And he said unto the *k* of Israel 2Kin 13:18 4428
But Hazael *k* of Syria oppressed 2Kin 13:22 4428
So Hazael *k* of Syria died 2Kin 13:24 4428
k of Israel reigned Amaziah the 2Kin 14:1 4428
the son of Joash *k* of Judah 2Kin 14:1 4428
which had slain the *k* his father 2Kin 14:5 4428
k of Israel, saying, Come, let us 2Kin 14:8 4428
Jehoash the *k* of Israel sent to 2Kin 14:9 4428
Israel sent to Amaziah *k* of Judah 2Kin 14:9 4428
Jehoash *k* of Israel went up 2Kin 14:11 4428
Amaziah *k* of Judah looked one 2Kin 14:11 4428
Jehoash *k* of Israel took Amaziah 2Kin 14:13 4428
of Israel took Amaziah *k* of Judah 2Kin 14:13 4428
he fought with Amaziah *k* of Judah 2Kin 14:15 4428
Amaziah the son of Joash *k* of 2Kin 14:17 4428
k of Israel fifteen years 2Kin 14:17 4428
made him *k* instead of his father 2Kin 14:21 4427
after that the *k* slept with his 2Kin 14:22 4428
of Amaziah the son of Joash *k* of 2Kin 14:23 4428
k of Israel began to reign in 2Kin 14:23 4428
seventh year of Jeroboam *k* of 2Kin 15:1 4428
of Amaziah *k* of Judah to reign 2Kin 15:1 4428
And the LORD smote the *k*, so that 2Kin 15:5 4428
eighth year of Azariah *k* of Judah 2Kin 15:8 4428
year of Uzziah *k* of Judah 2Kin 15:13 4428
thirtieth year of Azariah *k* of 2Kin 15:17 4428
Pul the *k* of Assyria came against 2Kin 15:19 4428
to give to the *k* of Assyria 2Kin 15:20 4428
So the *k* of Assyria turned back, 2Kin 15:20 4428
k of Judah Pekahiah the son of 2Kin 15:23 4428
fiftieth year of Azariah *k* of 2Kin 15:27 4428
In the days of Pekah *k* of Israel 2Kin 15:29 4428
came Tiglath-pileser *k* of Assyria 2Kin 15:29 4428
of Pekah the son of Remaliah *k* of 2Kin 15:32 4428
son of Uzziah *k* of Judah to reign 2Kin 15:32 4428
Judah Rezin the *k* of Syria 2Kin 15:37 4428
Jotham *k* of Judah began to reign 2Kin 16:1 4428
Then Rezin *k* of Syria and Pekah 2Kin 16:5 4428
Pekah son of Remaliah *k* of Israel 2Kin 16:5 4428
At that time Rezin *k* of Syria 2Kin 16:6 4428
to Tiglath-pileser *k* of Assyria 2Kin 16:7 4428
out of the hand of the *k* of Syria 2Kin 16:7 4428
of the hand of the *k* of Israel 2Kin 16:7 4428
for a present to the *k* of Assyria 2Kin 16:8 4428
the *k* of Assyria hearkened unto 2Kin 16:9 4428
for the *k* of Assyria went up 2Kin 16:9 4428
k Ahaz went to Damascus to meet 2Kin 16:10 4428
meet Tiglath-pileser *k* of Assyria 2Kin 16:10 4428
k Ahaz sent to Urijah the priest 2Kin 16:10 4428
k Ahaz had sent from Damascus 2Kin 16:11 4428
against *k* Ahaz came from Damascus 2Kin 16:11 4428
when the *k* was come from Damascus 2Kin 16:12 4428
the *k* saw the altar 2Kin 16:12 4428
the *k* approached to the altar, and 2Kin 16:12 4428
k Ahaz commanded Urijah the 2Kin 16:15 4428
to all that *k* Ahaz commanded 2Kin 16:16 4428
k Ahaz cut off the borders of the 2Kin 16:17 4428
of the LORD for the *k* of Assyria 2Kin 16:18 4428
In the twelfth year of Ahaz *k* of 2Kin 17:1 4428
came up Shalmaneser *k* of Assyria 2Kin 17:3 4428
the *k* of Assyria found conspiracy 2Kin 17:4 4428
sent messengers to So *k* of Egypt 2Kin 17:4 4428
no present to the *k* of Assyria 2Kin 17:4 4428
therefore the *k* of Assyria shut 2Kin 17:4 4428
Then the *k* of Assyria came up 2Kin 17:5 4428
the *k* of Assyria took Samaria 2Kin 17:6 4428
the hand of Pharaoh *k* of Egypt 2Kin 17:7 4428
made Jeroboam the son of Nebat *k* 2Kin 17:21 4427
the *k* of Assyria brought men from 2Kin 17:24 4428
they spake to the *k* of Assyria 2Kin 17:26 4428
Then the *k* of Assyria commanded, 2Kin 17:27 4428
of Hoshea son of Elah *k* of Israel 2Kin 18:1 4428
of Ahaz *k* of Judah began to reign 2Kin 18:1 4428
rebelled against the *k* of Assyria 2Kin 18:7 4428
in the fourth year of *k* Hezekiah 2Kin 18:9 4428
of Hoshea son of Elah *k* of Israel 2Kin 18:9 4428
that Shalmaneser *k* of Assyria 2Kin 18:9 4428
ninth year of Hoshea *k* of Israel 2Kin 18:10 4428
the *k* of Assyria did carry away 2Kin 18:11 4428
k Hezekiah did Sennacherib *k* 2Kin 18:13 4428
Hezekiah *k* of Judah sent to the 2Kin 18:14 4428
to the *k* of Assyria to Lachish 2Kin 18:14 4428
the *k* of Assyria appointed unto 2Kin 18:14 4428
k of Judah three hundred talents 2Kin 18:14 4428
Hezekiah *k* of Judah had overlaid 2Kin 18:16 4428
and gave it to the *k* of Assyria 2Kin 18:16 4428
the *k* of Assyria sent Tartan and 2Kin 18:17 4428
to *k* Hezekiah with a great host 2Kin 18:17 4428
And when they had called to the *k* 2Kin 18:18 4428
Hezekiah, Thus saith the great *k* 2Kin 18:19 4428
the *k* of Assyria, What confidence 2Kin 18:19 4428
so is Pharaoh *k* of Egypt unto all 2Kin 18:21 4428
to my lord the *k* of Assyria 2Kin 18:23 4428
the great *k*, the *k* of Assyria 2Kin 18:28 4428
Thus saith the *k*, Let not 2Kin 18:29 4428
into the hand of the *k* of Assyria 2Kin 18:30 4428
for thus saith the *k* of Assyria 2Kin 18:31 4428
of the hand of the *k* of Assyria 2Kin 18:33 4428
when *k* Hezekiah heard it, that he 2Kin 19:1 4428
whom the *k* of Assyria his master 2Kin 19:4 4428
So the servants of *k* Hezekiah 2Kin 19:5 4428
k of Assyria have blasphemed me 2Kin 19:6 4428
found the *k* of Assyria warring 2Kin 19:8 4428
say of Tirhakah *k* of Ethiopia 2Kin 19:9 4428
ye speak to Hezekiah *k* of Judah 2Kin 19:10 4428
into the hand of the *k* of Assyria 2Kin 19:10 4428
Where is the *k* of Hamath 2Kin 19:13 4428
the *k* of Arpad 2Kin 19:13 4428
the *k* of the city of Sepharvaim, 2Kin 19:13 4428
k of Assyria I have heard 2Kin 19:20 4428
LORD concerning the *k* of Assyria 2Kin 19:32 4428
So Sennacherib *k* of Assyria 2Kin 19:36 4428
of the hand of the *k* of Assyria 2Kin 20:6 4428
k of Babylon, sent letters and a 2Kin 20:12 4428
the prophet unto *k* Hezekiah 2Kin 20:14 4428
in the palace of the *k* of Babylon 2Kin 20:18 4428
a grove, as did Ahab *k* of Israel 2Kin 21:3 4428
Because Manasseh *k* of Judah hath 2Kin 21:11 4428
slew the *k* in his own house 2Kin 21:23 4428
that had conspired against *k* Amon 2Kin 21:24 4428
Josiah his son *k* in his stead 2Kin 21:24 4427
the eighteenth year of *k* Josiah 2Kin 22:3 4428
that the *k* sent Shaphan the son 2Kin 22:3 4428
Shaphan the scribe came to the *k* 2Kin 22:9 4428
and brought the *k* word again 2Kin 22:9 4428
Shaphan the scribe shewed the *k* 2Kin 22:10 4428
And Shaphan read it before the *k* 2Kin 22:10 4428
when the *k* had heard the words of 2Kin 22:11 4428
the *k* commanded Hilkiah the 2Kin 22:12 4428
which the *k* of Judah hath read 2Kin 22:16 4428
But to the *k* of Judah which sent 2Kin 22:18 4428
And they brought the *k* word again 2Kin 22:20 4428
the *k* sent, and they gathered unto 2Kin 23:1 4428
the *k* went up into the house of 2Kin 23:2 4428
the *k* stood by a pillar, and made 2Kin 23:3 4428
the *k* commanded Hilkiah the high 2Kin 23:4 4428
did the *k* beat down, and brake 2Kin 23:12 4428
which Solomon the *k* of Israel had 2Kin 23:13 4428
of Ammon, did the *k* defile 2Kin 23:13 4428
the *k* commanded all the people, 2Kin 23:21 4428
the eighteenth year of *k* Josiah 2Kin 23:23 4428
him was there no *k* before him 2Kin 23:25 4428
In his days Pharaoh-nechoh *k* of 2Kin 23:29 4428
the *k* of Assyria to the river 2Kin 23:29 4428
k Josiah went against him 2Kin 23:29 4428
made him *k* in his father's stead 2Kin 23:30 4427
k in the room of Josiah his 2Kin 23:34 4427
k of Babylon came up, and 2Kin 24:1 4428
the *k* of Egypt came not again any 2Kin 24:7 4428
for the *k* of Babylon had taken 2Kin 24:7 4428
that pertained to the *k* of Egypt 2Kin 24:7 4428
k of Babylon came up against 2Kin 24:10 4428
Nebuchadnezzar *k* of Babylon came 2Kin 24:11 4428
Jehoiachin the *k* of Judah went 2Kin 24:12 4428
went out to the *k* of Babylon 2Kin 24:12 4428
the *k* of Babylon took him in the 2Kin 24:12 4428
k of Israel had made in the 2Kin 24:13 4428
even them the *k* of Babylon 2Kin 24:16 4428
the *k* of Babylon made Mattaniah 2Kin 24:17 4428
father's brother *k* in his stead 2Kin 24:17 4427
rebelled against the *k* of Babylon 2Kin 24:20 4428
Nebuchadnezzar *k* of Babylon came 2Kin 25:1 4428
the eleventh year of *k* Zedekiah 2Kin 25:2 4428
the *k* went the way toward the 2Kin 25:4
the Chaldees pursued after the *k* 2Kin 25:5 4428
So they took the *k*, and brought 2Kin 25:6 4428
up to the *k* of Babylon to Riblah 2Kin 25:6 4428
k Nebuchadnezzar *k* of Babylon 2Kin 25:8 4428
a servant of the *k* of Babylon 2Kin 25:8 4428
fell away to the *k* of Babylon 2Kin 25:11 4428
brought them to the *k* of Babylon 2Kin 25:20 4428
the *k* of Babylon smote them, and 2Kin 25:21 4428
k of Babylon had left, even over 2Kin 25:22 4428
heard that the *k* of Babylon had 2Kin 25:23 4428
land, and serve the *k* of Babylon 2Kin 25:24 4428
of Jehoiachin *k* of Judah, in the 2Kin 25:27 4428
that Evil-merodach *k* of Babylon 2Kin 25:27 4428
k of Judah out of prison 2Kin 25:27 4428
allowance given him of the *k* 2Kin 25:30 4428
k reigned over the children of 1Chr 1:43 4428
daughter of Talmai *k* of Geshur 1Chr 3:2 4428
dwelt with the *k* for his work 1Chr 4:23 4428
the days of Hezekiah *k* of Judah 1Chr 4:41 4428
whom Tilgath-pilneser *k* of 1Chr 5:6 4428
in the days of Jotham *k* of Judah 1Chr 5:17 4428
the days of Jeroboam *k* of Israel 1Chr 5:17 4428
up the spirit of Pul *k* of Assyria 1Chr 5:26 4428
of Tilgath-pilneser *k* of Assyria 1Chr 5:26 4428
time past, even when Saul was *k* 1Chr 11:2 4428
of Israel to the *k* to Hebron 1Chr 11:3 4428
they anointed David *k* over Israel 1Chr 11:3 4428
and with all Israel, to make him *k* 1Chr 11:10 4427
by name, to come and make David *k* 1Chr 12:31 4427
to make David *k* over all Israel 1Chr 12:38 4427
were of one heart to make David *k* 1Chr 12:38 4427
Now Hiram *k* of Tyre sent 1Chr 14:1 4428
had confirmed him *k* over Israel 1Chr 14:2 4428
was anointed *k* over all Israel 1Chr 14:8 4428
at a window saw *k* David dancing 1Chr 15:29 4428
And David the *k* came and sat before 1Chr 17:16 4428
Hadarezer *k* of Zobah unto Hamath 1Chr 18:3 4428
came to help Hadarezer *k* of Zobah 1Chr 18:5 4428

Now when Tou *k* of Hamath heard 1Chr 18:9 4428
the host of Hadarezer *k* of Zobah 1Chr 18:9 4428
sent Hadoram his son to *k* David 1Chr 18:10 4428
Them also *k* David dedicated unto 1Chr 18:11 4428
of David were chief about the *k* 1Chr 18:17 4428
that Nahash the *k* of the children 1Chr 19:1 4428
the *k* said, Tarry at Jericho 1Chr 19:5 4428
the *k* of Maachah and his people 1Chr 19:7 4428
of their *k* from off his head 1Chr 20:2 4428
but, my lord the *k*, are they not 1Chr 21:3 4428
let my lord the *k* do that which 1Chr 21:23 4428
k David said to Ornan, Nay 1Chr 21:24 4428
Solomon his son *k* over Israel 1Chr 23:1 4427
Levites, wrote them before the *k* 1Chr 24:6 4428
in the presence of David the *k* 1Chr 24:31 4428
according to the order of the *k* 1Chr 25:2 4428
things, which David the *k* 1Chr 26:26 4428
LORD, and in the service of the *k* 1Chr 26:30 4428
whom *k* David made rulers over the 1Chr 26:32 4428
to God, and affairs of the *k* 1Chr 26:32 4428
k in any matter of the courses 1Chr 27:1 4428
of the Chronicles of *k* David 1Chr 27:24 4428
the substance which was *k* David's 1Chr 27:31 4428
ministered to the *k* by course 1Chr 28:1 4428
substance and possession of the *k* 1Chr 28:1 4428
Then David the *k* stood up upon 1Chr 28:2 4428
to be *k* over Israel for ever 1Chr 28:4 4428
me to make me *k* over all Israel 1Chr 28:4 4427
Furthermore David the *k* said unto 1Chr 29:1 4428
David the *k* also rejoiced with 1Chr 29:9 4428
and worshipped the LORD, and the *k* 1Chr 29:20 4428
son of David *k* the second time 1Chr 29:22 4428
as *k* instead of David his father 1Chr 29:23 4428
all the sons likewise of *k* David 1Chr 29:24 4428
themselves unto Solomon the *k* 1Chr 29:24 4428
on any *k* before him in Israel 1Chr 29:25 4428
Now the acts of David the *k* 1Chr 29:29 4428
for thou hast made me *k* over a 2Chr 1:9 4427
over whom I have made thee *k* 2Chr 1:11 4427
and with the *k* at Jerusalem 2Chr 1:14 4428
the *k* made silver and gold at 2Chr 1:15 4428
sent to Huram the *k* of Tyre 2Chr 2:3 4428
Then Huram the *k* of Tyre answered 2Chr 2:11 4428
he hath made thee *k* over them 2Chr 2:11 4427
given to David the *k* a wise son 2Chr 2:12 4428
k Solomon for the house of God 2Chr 4:11 4428
to *k* Solomon for the house of the 2Chr 4:16 4428
of Jordan did the *k* cast them 2Chr 4:17 4428
k in the feast which was in the 2Chr 5:3 4428
Also *k* Solomon, and all the 2Chr 5:6 4428
the *k* turned his face, and blessed 2Chr 6:3 4428
Then the *k* and all the people 2Chr 7:4 4428
k Solomon offered a sacrifice of 2Chr 7:5 4428
so the *k* and all the people 2Chr 7:5 4428
which David the *k* had made to 2Chr 7:6 4428
the chief of *k* Solomon's officers 2Chr 8:10 4428
in the house of David *k* of Israel 2Chr 8:11 4428
of the *k* unto the priests 2Chr 8:15 4428
and brought them to *k* Solomon 2Chr 8:18 4428
And she said to the *k*, It was a 2Chr 9:5 4428
to be *k* for the LORD thy God 2Chr 9:8 4428
made he thee *k* over them, to do 2Chr 9:8 4428
And she gave the *k* an hundred 2Chr 9:9 4428
the queen of Sheba gave *k* Solomon 2Chr 9:9 4428
the *k* made of the algum trees 2Chr 9:11 4428
k Solomon gave to the queen of 2Chr 9:12 4428
which she had brought unto the *k* 2Chr 9:12 4428
k Solomon made two hundred 2Chr 9:15 4428
the *k* put them in the house of 2Chr 9:16 4428
Moreover the *k* made a great 2Chr 9:17 4428
vessels of *k* Solomon were of gold 2Chr 9:20 4428
k Solomon passed all the kings of 2Chr 9:22 4428
and with the *k* at Jerusalem 2Chr 9:25 4428
the *k* made silver in Jerusalem as 2Chr 9:27 4428
all Israel come to make him *k* 2Chr 10:1 4427
the presence of Solomon the *k* 2Chr 10:2 4428
k Rehoboam took counsel with the 2Chr 10:6 4428
on the third day, as the *k* bade 2Chr 10:12 4428
the *k* answered them roughly 2Chr 10:13 4428
k Rehoboam forsook the counsel of 2Chr 10:13 4428
So the *k* hearkened not unto the 2Chr 10:15 4428
the *k* would not hearken unto them 2Chr 10:16 4428
the people answered the *k* 2Chr 10:16 4428
Then *k* Rehoboam sent Hadoram that 2Chr 10:18 4428
But *k* Rehoboam made speed to get 2Chr 10:18 4428
k of Judah, and to all Israel in 2Chr 11:3 4428
for he thought to make him *k* 2Chr 11:22 4427
that in the fifth year of *k* 2Chr 12:2 4428
k of Egypt came up against 2Chr 12:2 4428
and the *k* humbled themselves 2Chr 12:6 4428
So Shishak *k* of Egypt came up 2Chr 12:9 4428
Instead of which *k* Rehoboam made 2Chr 12:10 4428
when the *k* entered into the house 2Chr 12:11 4428
So *k* Rehoboam strengthened 2Chr 12:13 4428
Now in the eighteenth year of *k* 2Chr 13:1 4428
Maachah the mother of Asa the *k* 2Chr 15:16 4428
k of Israel came up against Judah 2Chr 16:1 4428
out or come in to Asa *k* of Judah 2Chr 16:1 4428
and sent to Ben-hadad *k* of Syria 2Chr 16:2 4428
league with Baasha *k* of Israel 2Chr 16:3 4428
And Ben-hadad hearkened unto *k* Asa 2Chr 16:4 4428
Then Asa the *k* took all Judah 2Chr 16:6 4428
the seer came to Asa *k* of Judah 2Chr 16:7 4428
hast relied on the *k* of Syria 2Chr 16:7 4428
therefore is the host of the *k* of 2Chr 16:7 4428
These waited on the *k* 2Chr 17:19 4428
beside those whom the *k* put in 2Chr 17:19 4428
Ahab *k* of Israel said unto 2Chr 18:3 4428
said unto Jehoshaphat *k* of Judah 2Chr 18:3 4428
said unto the *k* of Israel 2Chr 18:4 4428
Therefore the *k* of Israel 2Chr 18:5 4428
the *k* of Israel said unto 2Chr 18:7 4428
said, Let not the *k* say so 2Chr 18:7 4428
the *k* of Israel called for one of 2Chr 18:8 4428
the *k* of Israel and Jehoshaphat 2Chr 18:9 4428
Jehoshaphat *k* of Judah sat either 2Chr 18:9 4428
deliver it into the hand of the *k* 2Chr 18:11 4428
good to the *k* with one assent 2Chr 18:12 4428
And when he was come to the *k* 2Chr 18:14 4428
the *k* said unto him, Micaiah, ... 2Chr 18:14 4428
the *k* said to him, How many times 2Chr 18:15 4428
And the *k* of Israel said to 2Chr 18:17 4428
Who shall entice Ahab *k* of Israel 2Chr 18:19 4428
Then the *k* of Israel said, Take 2Chr 18:25 4428
And say, Thus saith the *k*, Put 2Chr 18:26 4428
So the *k* of Israel and Jehoshaphat 2Chr 18:28 4428
Jehoshaphat the *k* of Judah went 2Chr 18:28 4428
the *k* of Israel said unto 2Chr 18:29 4428
So the *k* of Israel disguised 2Chr 18:29 4428
Now the *k* of Syria had commanded 2Chr 18:30 4428
save only with the *k* of Israel 2Chr 18:30 4428
they said, It is the *k* of Israel 2Chr 18:31 4428
that it was not the *k* of Israel 2Chr 18:32 4428
smote the *k* of Israel between the 2Chr 18:33 4428
howbeit the *k* of Israel stayed 2Chr 18:34 4428
Jehoshaphat the *k* of Judah 2Chr 19:1 4428
said to *k* Jehoshaphat, Shouldest 2Chr 19:2 4428
thou *k* Jehoshaphat, Thus saith 2Chr 20:15 4428
k of Judah join himself with 2Chr 20:35 4428
himself with Ahaziah *k* of Israel 2Chr 20:35 4428
sons of Jehoshaphat *k* of Israel 2Chr 21:2 4428
of Judah, and made themselves a *k* 2Chr 21:8 4428
nor in the ways of Asa *k* of Judah 2Chr 21:12 4428
his youngest son *k* in his stead 2Chr 22:1 4427
son of Jehoram *k* of Judah reigned 2Chr 22:1 4428
with Jehoram the son of Ahab *k* of 2Chr 22:5 4428
k of Syria at Ramoth-gilead 2Chr 22:5 4428
he fought with Hazael *k* of Syria 2Chr 22:6 4428
k of Judah went down to see 2Chr 22:6 4428
the daughter of the *k*, took 2Chr 22:11 4428
the daughter of *k* Jehoram 2Chr 22:11 4428
with the *k* in the house of God 2Chr 23:3 4428
shall compass the *k* round about 2Chr 23:7 4428
ye with the *k* when he cometh in 2Chr 23:7 4428
shields, that had been *k* David's 2Chr 23:9 4428
the temple, by the *k* round about 2Chr 23:10 4428
him the testimony, and made him *k* 2Chr 23:11 4427
him, and said, God save the *k* 2Chr 23:11 4428
people running and praising the *k* 2Chr 23:12 4428
the *k* stood at his pillar at the 2Chr 23:13 4428
princes and the trumpets by the *k* 2Chr 23:13 4428
all the people, and between the *k* 2Chr 23:16 4428
brought down the *k* from the house 2Chr 23:20 4428
set the *k* upon the throne of the 2Chr 23:20 4428
the *k* called for Jehoiada the 2Chr 24:6 4428
And the *k* and Jehoiada gave it to 2Chr 24:12 4428
rest of the money before the *k* 2Chr 24:14 4428
Judah, and made obeisance to the *k* 2Chr 24:17 4428
Then the *k* hearkened unto them 2Chr 24:17 4428
at the commandment of the *k* in 2Chr 24:21 4428
Thus Joash the *k* remembered not 2Chr 24:22 4428
of them unto the *k* of Damascus 2Chr 24:23 4428
that had killed the *k* his father 2Chr 25:3 4428
a man of God to him, saying, O *k* 2Chr 25:7 4428
that the *k* said unto him, Art 2Chr 25:16
Then Amaziah *k* of Judah took 2Chr 25:17 4428
k of Israel, saying, Come, let us 2Chr 25:17 4428
Joash *k* of Israel sent to Amaziah 2Chr 25:18 4428
Israel sent to Amaziah *k* of Judah 2Chr 25:18 4428
So Joash the *k* of Israel went up 2Chr 25:21 4428
both he and Amaziah *k* of Judah, at 2Chr 25:21 4428
Joash the *k* of Israel took 2Chr 25:23 4428
of Israel took Amaziah *k* of Judah 2Chr 25:23 4428
Amaziah the son of Joash *k* of 2Chr 25:25 4428
k of Israel fifteen years 2Chr 25:25 4428
made him *k* in the room of his 2Chr 26:1 4427
after that the *k* slept with his 2Chr 26:2 4428
to help the *k* against the enemy 2Chr 26:13 4428
And they withstood Uzziah the *k* 2Chr 26:18 4428
Uzziah the *k* was a leper unto the 2Chr 26:21 4428
also with the *k* of the Ammonites 2Chr 27:5 4428
into the hand of the *k* of Syria 2Chr 28:5 4428
into the hand of the *k* of Israel 2Chr 28:5 4428
and Elkanah that was next to the *k* 2Chr 28:7 4428
At that time did *k* Ahaz send unto 2Chr 28:16 4428
low because of Ahaz *k* of Israel 2Chr 28:19 4428
Tilgath-pilneser *k* of Assyria 2Chr 28:20 4428
and out of the house of the *k* 2Chr 28:21 4428
and gave it unto the *k* of Assyria 2Chr 28:21 4428
this is that *k* Ahaz 2Chr 28:22 4428
to the commandment of the *k* 2Chr 29:15 4428
they went in to Hezekiah the *k* 2Chr 29:18 4428
which *k* Ahaz in his reign did 2Chr 29:19 4428
Then Hezekiah the *k* rose early 2Chr 29:20 4428
for the sin offering before the *k* 2Chr 29:23 4428
for the *k* commanded that the 2Chr 29:24 4428
ordained by David *k* of Israel 2Chr 29:27 4428
made an end of offering, the *k* 2Chr 29:29 4428
Moreover Hezekiah the *k* and the 2Chr 29:30 4428
For the *k* had taken counsel, and 2Chr 30:2 4428
And the thing pleased the *k* 2Chr 30:4 4428
went with the letters from the *k* 2Chr 30:6 4428
to the commandment of the *k* 2Chr 30:6 4428
to do the commandment of the *k* 2Chr 30:12 4428
For Hezekiah *k* of Judah did give 2Chr 30:24 4428
k of Israel there was not the 2Chr 30:26 4428
the commandment of Hezekiah the *k* 2Chr 31:13 4428
Sennacherib *k* of Assyria came, and 2Chr 32:1 4428
nor dismayed for the *k* of Assyria 2Chr 32:7 4428
the words of Hezekiah *k* of Judah 2Chr 32:8 4428
After this did Sennacherib *k* of 2Chr 32:9 4428
him,) unto Hezekiah *k* of Judah 2Chr 32:9 4428
saith Sennacherib *k* of Assyria 2Chr 32:10 4428
of the hand of the *k* of Assyria 2Chr 32:11 4428
And for this cause Hezekiah the *k* 2Chr 32:20 4428
in the camp of the *k* of Assyria 2Chr 32:21 4428
of Sennacherib the *k* of Assyria 2Chr 32:22 4428
presents to Hezekiah *k* of Judah 2Chr 32:23 4428
of the host of the *k* of Assyria 2Chr 33:11 4428
that had conspired against *k* Amon 2Chr 33:25 4428
Josiah his son *k* in his stead 2Chr 33:25 4427
Shaphan carried the book to the *k* 2Chr 34:16 4428
brought the *k* word back again, ... 2Chr 34:16 4428
Shaphan the scribe told the *k* 2Chr 34:18 4428
And Shaphan read it before the *k* 2Chr 34:18 4428
when the *k* had heard the words of 2Chr 34:19 4428
the *k* commanded Hilkiah, and 2Chr 34:20 4428
and they that the *k* had appointed 2Chr 34:22 4428
have read before the *k* of Judah 2Chr 34:24 4428
And as for the *k* of Judah, who 2Chr 34:26 4428
So they brought the *k* word again 2Chr 34:28 4428
Then the *k* sent and gathered 2Chr 34:29 4428
the *k* went up into the house of 2Chr 34:30 4428
the *k* stood in his place, and made 2Chr 34:31 4428
of David *k* of Israel did build 2Chr 35:3 4428
the writing of David *k* of Israel 2Chr 35:4 4428
to the commandment of *k* Josiah 2Chr 35:16 4428
Necho *k* of Egypt came up to fight 2Chr 35:20 4428
to do with thee, thou *k* of Judah 2Chr 35:21 4428
And the archers shot at *k* Josiah 2Chr 35:23 4428
the *k* said to his servants, Have 2Chr 35:23 4428
made him *k* in his father's stead 2Chr 36:1 4427
the *k* of Egypt put him down at 2Chr 36:3 4428
the *k* of Egypt made Eliakim his 2Chr 36:4 4428
Eliakim his brother *k* over Judah 2Chr 36:4 4427
up Nebuchadnezzar *k* of Babylon 2Chr 36:6 4428
k Nebuchadnezzar sent, and brought 2Chr 36:10 4428
Zedekiah his brother *k* over Judah 2Chr 36:10 4427
rebelled against *k* Nebuchadnezzar 2Chr 36:13 4428
upon them the *k* of the Chaldees 2Chr 36:17 4428
LORD, and the treasures of the *k* 2Chr 36:18 4428
first year of Cyrus *k* of Persia 2Chr 36:22 4428
the spirit of Cyrus *k* of Persia 2Chr 36:22 4428
Thus saith Cyrus *k* of Persia 2Chr 36:23 4428
first year of Cyrus *k* of Persia .... Ezr 1:1 4428
the spirit of Cyrus *k* of Persia .... Ezr 1:1 4428
Thus saith Cyrus *k* of Persia .... Ezr 1:2 4428
Also Cyrus the *k* brought forth .... Ezr 1:7 4428
Even those did Cyrus *k* of Persia .... Ezr 1:8 4428
whom Nebuchadnezzar the *k* of .... Ezr 2:1 4428
they had of Cyrus *k* of Persia .... Ezr 3:7 4428
ordinance of David *k* of Israel .... Ezr 3:10 4428
days of Esar-haddon *k* of Assur .... Ezr 4:2 4428
as *k* Cyrus the *k* of Persia .... Ezr 4:3 4428
all the days of Cyrus *k* of Persia .... Ezr 4:5 4428
the reign of Darius *k* of Persia .... Ezr 4:5 4428
unto Artaxerxes *k* of Persia .... Ezr 4:7 4428
to Artaxerxes the *k* in this sort .... Ezr 4:8 4430
him, even unto Artaxerxes the *k* .... Ezr 4:11 4430
Be it known unto the *k*, that the .... Ezr 4:12 4430
Be it known now unto the *k* .... Ezr 4:13 4430
have we sent and certified the *k* .... Ezr 4:14 4430
We certify the *k* that, if this .... Ezr 4:16 4430
Then sent the *k* an answer unto .... Ezr 4:17 4430
Now when the copy of *k* .... Ezr 4:23 4430
the reign of Darius *k* of Persia .... Ezr 4:24 4430
the river, sent unto Darius the *k* .... Ezr 5:6 4430
Unto Darius the *k*, all peace .... Ezr 5:7 4430
Be it known unto the *k*, that we .... Ezr 5:8 4430
which a great *k* of Israel builded .... Ezr 5:11 4430
Nebuchadnezzar the *k* of Babylon .... Ezr 5:12 4430
k of Babylon the same *k* Cyrus .... Ezr 5:13 4430
those did Cyrus the *k* take out of .... Ezr 5:14 4430
if it seem good to the *k* .... Ezr 5:17 4430
k to build this house of God at .... Ezr 5:17 4430
let the *k* send his pleasure to us .... Ezr 5:17 4430
Then Darius the *k* made a decree .... Ezr 6:1 4430
the *k* the same Cyrus the *k* .... Ezr 6:3 4430
and pray for the life of the *k* .... Ezr 6:10 4430
that which Darius the *k* had sent .... Ezr 6:13 4430
Darius, and Artaxerxes *k* of Persia .... Ezr 6:14 4430
year of the reign of Darius the *k* .... Ezr 6:15 4430
of the *k* of Assyria unto them .... Ezr 6:22 4428
reign of Artaxerxes *k* of Persia .... Ezr 7:1 4428
the *k* granted him all his request .... Ezr 7:6 4428
seventh year of Artaxerxes the *k* .... Ezr 7:7 4428
was in the seventh year of the *k* .... Ezr 7:8 4428
k Artaxerxes gave unto Ezra the .... Ezr 7:11 4428
k of kings, unto Ezra the priest, ... Ezr 7:12 4430
as thou art sent of the *k* .... Ezr 7:14 4430
the silver and gold, which the *k* .... Ezr 7:15 4430
And I, even I Artaxerxes the *k* .... Ezr 7:21 4430
wrath against the realm of the *k* .... Ezr 7:23 4430
of thy God, and the law of the *k* .... Ezr 7:26 4430
mercy unto me before the *k* .... Ezr 7:28 4428
in the reign of Artaxerxes the *k* .... Ezr 8:1 4428
of the *k* a band of soldiers .... Ezr 8:22 4428
because we had spoken unto the *k* .... Ezr 8:22 4428
the house of our God, which the *k* .... Ezr 8:25 4428
year of Artaxerxes the *k*, that .... Neh 2:1 4428
the wine, and gave it unto the *k* .... Neh 2:1 4428
Wherefore the *k* said unto me .... Neh 2:2 4428
the *k*, Let the *k* live for ever .... Neh 2:3 4428
Then the *k* said unto me, For what .... Neh 2:4 4428

unto the *k*, If it please the *k*	Neh 2:5	4428
the *k* said unto me, (the queen	Neh 2:6	4428
So it pleased the *k* to send me	Neh 2:6	4428
unto the *k*, If it please the *k*	Neh 2:7	4428
the *k* granted me, according to	Neh 2:8	4428
Now the *k* had sent captains of	Neh 2:9	4428
will ye rebel against the *k*	Neh 2:19	4428
year of Artaxerxes the *k*, that is	Neh 5:14	4428
wall, that thou mayest be their *k*	Neh 6:6	4428
saying, There is a *k* in Judah	Neh 6:7	4428
to the *k* according to these words	Neh 6:7	4428
whom Nebuchadnezzar the *k* of	Neh 7:6	4428
and the land of the *k* of Heshbon	Neh 9:22	4428
and the land of Og *k* of Bashan	Neh 9:22	4428
k of Babylon came I unto the *k*	Neh 13:6	4428
days obtained I leave of the *k*	Neh 13:6	4428
Did not Solomon *k* of Israel sin	Neh 13:26	4428
nations was there no *k* like him	Neh 13:26	4428
God made him *k* over all Israel	Neh 13:26	4428
when the *k* Ahasuerus sat on the	Est 1:2	4428
the *k* made a feast unto all the	Est 1:5	4428
according to the state of the *k*	Est 1:7	4428
for so the *k* had appointed to all	Est 1:8	4428
which belonged to *k* Ahasuerus	Est 1:9	4428
of the *k* was merry with wine	Est 1:10	4428
the presence of Ahasuerus the *k*	Est 1:10	4428
before the *k* with the crown royal	Est 1:11	4428
therefore was the *k* very wroth	Est 1:12	4428
Then the *k* said to the wise men,	Est 1:13	4428
the commandment of the *k*	Est 1:15	4428
And Memucan answered before the *k*	Est 1:16	4428
hath not done wrong to the *k* only	Est 1:16	4428
the provinces of the *k* Ahasuerus	Est 1:16	4428
The *k* Ahasuerus commanded Vashti	Est 1:17	4428
If it please the *k*, let there go	Est 1:19	4428
come no more before *k* Ahasuerus	Est 1:19	4428
let the *k* give her royal estate	Est 1:19	4428
And the saying pleased the *k*	Est 1:21	4428
the *k* did according to the word	Est 1:21	4428
When the wrath of *k* Ahasuerus was	Est 2:1	4428
young virgins sought for the *k*	Est 2:2	4428
let the *k* appoint officers in all	Est 2:3	4428
the *k* be queen instead of Vashti	Est 2:4	4428
And the thing pleased the *k*	Est 2:4	4428
away with Jeconiah *k* of Judah	Est 2:6	4428
whom Nebuchadnezzar the *k* of	Est 2:6	4428
was come to go in to *k* Ahasuerus	Est 2:12	4428
thus came every maiden unto the *k*	Est 2:13	4428
she came in unto the *k* no more	Est 2:14	4428
except the *k* delighted in her, and	Est 2:14	4428
was come to go in unto the *k*	Est 2:15	4428
So Esther was taken unto *k*	Est 2:16	4428
the *k* loved Esther above all the	Est 2:17	4428
Then the *k* made a great feast	Est 2:18	4428
according to the state of the *k*	Est 2:18	4428
to lay hand on the *k* Ahasuerus	Est 2:21	4428
Esther certified the *k* thereof in	Est 2:22	4428
of the chronicles before the *k*	Est 2:23	4428
After these things did *k*	Est 3:1	4428
for the *k* had so commanded	Est 3:2	4428
the twelfth year of *k* Ahasuerus	Est 3:7	4428
And Haman said unto *k* Ahasuerus	Est 3:8	4428
If it please the *k*, let it be	Est 3:9	4428
the *k* took his ring from his hand	Est 3:10	4428
the *k* said unto Haman, The silver	Est 3:11	4428
in the name of *k* Ahasuerus was it	Est 3:12	4428
And the *k* and Haman sat down to	Est 3:15	4428
that she should go in unto the *k*	Est 4:8	4428
shall come unto the *k* into the	Est 4:11	4428
except such to whom the *k* shall	Est 4:11	4428
in unto the *k* these thirty days	Est 4:11	4428
and so will I go in unto the *k*	Est 4:16	4428
the *k* sat upon his royal throne	Est 5:1	4428
when the *k* saw Esther the queen	Est 5:2	4428
the *k* held out to Esther the	Est 5:2	4428
Then said the *k* unto her, What	Est 5:3	4428
good unto the *k*, let the *k*	Est 5:4	4428
Then the *k* said, Cause Haman to	Est 5:5	4428
So the *k* and Haman came to the	Est 5:5	4428
the *k* said unto Esther at the	Est 5:6	4428
favour in the sight of the *k*	Est 5:8	4428
if it please the *k* to grant my	Est 5:8	4428
to perform my request, let the *k*	Est 5:8	4428
do to morrow as the *k* hath said	Est 5:8	4428
wherein the *k* had promoted him	Est 5:11	4428
the princes and servants of the *k*	Est 5:11	4428
k unto the banquet that she had	Est 5:12	4428
invited unto her also with the *k*	Est 5:12	4428
the *k* that Mordecai may be hanged	Est 5:14	4428
with the *k* unto the banquet	Est 5:14	4428
that night could not the *k* sleep	Est 6:1	4428
and they were read before the *k*	Est 6:1	4428
to lay hand on the *k* Ahasuerus	Est 6:2	4428
the *k* said, What honour and	Est 6:3	4428
the *k* said, Who is in the court	Est 6:4	4428
to speak unto the *k* to hang	Est 6:4	4428
the *k* said, Let him come in	Est 6:5	4428
the *k* said unto him, What shall	Est 6:6	4428
whom the *k* delighteth to honour	Est 6:6	4428
To whom would the *k* delight to do	Est 6:6	4428
And Haman answered the *k*, For the	Est 6:7	4428
whom the *k* delighteth to honour	Est 6:7	4428
brought which the *k* useth to wear	Est 6:8	4428
the horse that the *k* rideth upon	Est 6:8	4428
whom the *k* delighteth to honour	Est 6:9	4428
whom the *k* delighteth to honour	Est 6:9	4428
Then the *k* said to Haman, Make	Est 6:10	4428
whom the *k* delighteth to honour	Est 6:11	4428
So the *k* and Haman came to banquet	Est 7:1	4428
the *k* said again unto Esther on	Est 7:2	4428
O *k*, and if it please the *k*	Est 7:3	4428
Then the *k* Ahasuerus answered and	Est 7:5	4428
Haman was afraid before the *k*	Est 7:6	4428
the *k* arising from the banquet of	Est 7:7	4428
determined against him by the *k*	Est 7:7	4428
Then the *k* returned out of the	Est 7:8	4428
Then said the *k*, Will he force	Est 7:8	4428
chamberlains, said before the *k*	Est 7:9	4428
who had spoken good for the *k*	Est 7:9	4428
Then the *k* said, Hang him thereon	Est 7:9	4428
On that day did the *k* Ahasuerus	Est 8:1	4428
And Mordecai came before the *k*	Est 8:1	4428
the *k* took off his ring, which he	Est 8:2	4428
spake yet again before the *k*	Est 8:3	4428
Then the *k* held out the golden	Est 8:4	4428
arose, and stood before the *k*	Est 8:4	4428
And said, If it please the *k*	Est 8:5	4428
the thing seem right before the *k*	Est 8:5	4428
Then the *k* Ahasuerus said unto	Est 8:7	4428
he wrote in the *k* Ahasuerus' name	Est 8:10	4428
Wherein the *k* granted the Jews	Est 8:11	4428
all the provinces of *k* Ahasuerus	Est 8:12	4428
of the *k* in royal apparel of blue	Est 8:15	4428
the provinces of the *k* Ahasuerus	Est 9:2	4428
deputies, and officers of the *k*	Est 9:3	4428
palace was brought before the *k*	Est 9:11	4428
the *k* said unto Esther the queen,	Est 9:12	4428
said Esther, If it please the *k*	Est 9:13	4428
the *k* commanded it so to be done	Est 9:14	4428
the provinces of the *k* Ahasuerus	Est 9:20	4428
But when Esther came before the *k*	Est 9:25	4428
the *k* Ahasuerus laid a tribute	Est 10:1	4428
whereunto the *k* advanced him	Est 10:2	4428
the Jew was next unto *k* Ahasuerus	Est 10:3	4428
as a *k* ready to the battle	Job 15:24	4428
bring him to the *k* of terrors	Job 18:14	4428
dwelt as a *k* in the army, as one	Job 29:25	4428
Is it fit to say to a *k*, Thou art	Job 34:18	4428
he is a *k* over all the children	Job 41:34	4428
Yet have I set my *k* upon my holy	Ps 2:6	4428
unto the voice of my cry, my *K*	Ps 5:2	4428
The LORD is *K* for ever and ever	Ps 10:16	4428
deliverance giveth he to his *k*	Ps 18:50	4428
let the *k* hear us when we call	Ps 20:9	4428
The *k* shall joy in thy strength,	Ps 21:1	4428
For the *k* trusteth in the LORD,	Ps 21:7	4428
the *K* of glory shall come in	Ps 24:7	4428
Who is this *K* of glory	Ps 24:8	4428
the *K* of glory shall come in	Ps 24:9	4428
Who is this *K* of glory	Ps 24:10	4428
of hosts, he is the *K* of glory	Ps 24:10	4428
yea, the LORD sitteth *K* for ever	Ps 29:10	4428
There is no *k* saved by the	Ps 33:16	4428
Thou art my *K*, O God	Ps 44:4	4428
which I have made touching the *k*	Ps 45:1	4428
So shall the *k* greatly desire thy	Ps 45:11	4428
the *k* in raiment of needlework	Ps 45:14	4428
he is a great *K* over all the	Ps 47:2	4428
sing praises unto our *K*, sing	Ps 47:6	4428
For God is the *K* of all the earth	Ps 47:7	4428
north, the city of the great *K*	Ps 48:2	4428
But the *k* shall rejoice in God	Ps 63:11	4428
even the goings of my God, my *K*	Ps 68:24	4428
Give the *k* thy judgments, O God,	Ps 72:1	4428
For God is my *K* of old, working	Ps 74:12	4428
altars, O LORD of hosts, my *K*	Ps 84:3	4428
the Holy One of Israel is our *k*	Ps 89:18	4428
God, and a great *K* above all gods	Ps 95:3	4428
noise before the LORD, the *K*	Ps 98:6	4428
The *k* sent and loosed him	Ps 105:20	4428
Sihon *k* of the Amorites	Ps 135:11	4428
Og *k* of Bashan, and all the	Ps 135:11	4428
Sihon *k* of the Amorites	Ps 136:19	4428
And Og the *k* of Bashan	Ps 136:20	4428
I will extol thee, my God, O *k*	Ps 145:1	4428
of Zion be joyful in their *K*	Ps 149:2	4428
the son of David, *k* of Israel	Prov 1:1	4428
sentence is in the lips of the *k*	Prov 16:10	4428
The wrath of a *k* is as messengers	Prov 16:14	4428
The fear of a *k* is as the roaring	Prov 20:2	4428
A *k* that sitteth in the throne of	Prov 20:8	4428
A wise *k* scattereth the wicked,	Prov 20:26	4428
Mercy and truth preserve the *k*	Prov 20:28	4428
lips the *k* shall be his friend	Prov 22:11	4428
son, fear thou the LORD and the *k*	Prov 24:21	4428
of Hezekiah *k* of Judah copied out	Prov 25:1	4428
away the wicked from before the *k*	Prov 25:5	4428
thyself in the presence of the *k*	Prov 25:6	4428
The *k* by judgment establisheth	Prov 29:4	4428
The *k* that faithfully judgeth the	Prov 29:14	4428
The locusts have no *k*, yet go	Prov 30:27	4428
and a *k*, against whom there is no	Prov 30:31	4428
The words of *k* Lemuel, the	Prov 31:1	4428
the son of David, *k* in Jerusalem	Eccl 1:1	4428
I the Preacher was *k* over Israel	Eccl 1:12	4428
man do that cometh after the *k*	Eccl 2:12	4428
child than an old and foolish *k*	Eccl 4:13	4428
the *k* himself is served by the	Eccl 5:9	4428
Where the word of a *k* is, there	Eccl 8:4	4428
there came a great *k* against it	Eccl 9:14	4428
when thy *k* is a child, and thy	Eccl 10:16	4428
when thy *k* is the son of nobles,	Eccl 10:17	4428
Curse not the *k*, no not in thy	Eccl 10:20	4428
the *k* hath brought me into his	Song 1:4	4428
While the *k* sitteth at his table,	Song 1:12	4428
K Solomon made himself a chariot	Song 3:9	4428
behold *k* Solomon with the crown	Song 3:11	4428
the *k* is held in the galleries	Song 7:5	4428
In the year that *k* Uzziah died I	Is 6:1	4428
for mine eyes have seen the *K*	Is 6:5	4428
k of Judah, that Rezin the *k*	Is 7:1	4428
Judah, that Rezin the *k* of Syria	Is 7:1	4428
k of Israel, went up toward	Is 7:1	4428
set a *k* in the midst of it, even	Is 7:6	4428
even the *k* of Assyria	Is 7:17	4428
by the *k* of Assyria, the head, and	Is 7:20	4428
away before the *k* of Assyria	Is 8:4	4428
even the *k* of Assyria, and all his	Is 8:7	4428
fret themselves, and curse their *k*	Is 8:21	4428
stout heart of the *k* of Assyria	Is 10:12	4428
proverb against the *k* of Babylon	Is 14:4	4428
In the year that *k* Ahaz died was	Is 14:28	4428
a fierce *k* shall rule over them,	Is 19:4	4428
(when Sargon the *k* of Assyria	Is 20:1	4428
So shall the *k* of Assyria lead	Is 20:4	4428
delivered from the *k* of Assyria	Is 20:6	4428
according to the days of one *k*	Is 23:15	4428
yea, for the *k* it is prepared	Is 30:33	4428
a *k* shall reign in righteousness,	Is 32:1	4428
shall see the *k* in his beauty	Is 33:17	4428
our lawgiver, the LORD is our *k*	Is 33:22	4428
the fourteenth year of *k* Hezekiah	Is 36:1	4428
that Sennacherib *k* of Assyria	Is 36:1	4428
the *k* of Assyria sent Rabshakeh	Is 36:2	4428
unto *k* Hezekiah with a great army	Is 36:2	4428
Hezekiah, Thus saith the great *k*	Is 36:4	4428
the *k* of Assyria, What confidence	Is 36:4	4428
so is Pharaoh *k* of Egypt to all	Is 36:6	4428
to my master the *k* of Assyria	Is 36:8	4428
the great *k*, the *k* of Assyria	Is 36:13	4428
Thus saith the *k*, Let not	Is 36:14	4428
into the hand of the *k* of Assyria	Is 36:15	4428
for thus saith the *k* of Assyria	Is 36:16	4428
of the hand of the *k* of Assyria	Is 36:18	4428
when *k* Hezekiah heard it, that he	Is 37:1	4428
whom the *k* of Assyria his master	Is 37:4	4428
So the servants of *k* Hezekiah	Is 37:5	4428
k of Assyria have blasphemed me	Is 37:6	4428
found the *k* of Assyria warring	Is 37:8	4428
concerning Tirhakah *k* of Ethiopia	Is 37:9	4428
ye speak to Hezekiah *k* of Judah	Is 37:10	4428
into the hand of the *k* of Assyria	Is 37:10	4428
Where is the *k* of Hamath	Is 37:13	4428
the *k* of Arphad	Is 37:13	4428
the *k* of the city of Sepharvaim,	Is 37:13	4428
against Sennacherib *k* of Assyria	Is 37:21	4428
LORD concerning the *k* of Assyria	Is 37:33	4428
So Sennacherib *k* of Assyria	Is 37:37	4428
of the hand of the *k* of Assyria	Is 38:6	4428
writing of Hezekiah *k* of Judah	Is 38:9	4428
k of Babylon, sent letters and a	Is 39:1	4428
the prophet unto *k* Hezekiah	Is 39:3	4428
in the palace of the *k* of Babylon	Is 39:7	4428
reasons, saith the *K* of Jacob	Is 41:21	4428
the creator of Israel, your *K*	Is 43:15	4428
saith the LORD the *K* of Israel	Is 44:6	4428
wentest to the *k* with ointment	Is 57:9	4428
Josiah the son of Amon *k* of Judah	Jer 1:2	4428
the son of Josiah *k* of Judah	Jer 1:3	4428
the son of Josiah *k* of Judah	Jer 1:3	4428
me in the days of Josiah the *k*	Jer 3:6	4428
the heart of the *k* shall perish	Jer 4:9	4428
is not her *k* in her	Jer 8:19	4428
not fear thee, O *K* of nations	Jer 10:7	4428
living God, and an everlasting *k*	Jer 10:10	4428
Say unto the *k* and to the queen,	Jer 13:18	4428
the son of Hezekiah *k* of Judah	Jer 15:4	4428
into the hand of the *k* of Babylon	Jer 20:4	4428
when *k* Zedekiah sent unto him	Jer 21:1	4428
for Nebuchadrezzar *k* of Babylon	Jer 21:2	4428
ye fight against the *k* of Babylon	Jer 21:4	4428
will deliver Zedekiah *k* of Judah	Jer 21:7	4428
of Nebuchadrezzar *k* of Babylon	Jer 21:7	4428
into the hand of the *k* of Babylon	Jer 21:10	4428
the house of the *k* of Judah	Jer 21:11	4428
to the house of the *k* of Judah	Jer 22:1	4428
O *k* of Judah, that sittest upon	Jer 22:2	4428
the son of Josiah *k* of Judah	Jer 22:11	4428
the son of Josiah *k* of Judah	Jer 22:18	4428
Coniah the son of Jehoiakim *k* of	Jer 22:24	4428
of Nebuchadrezzar *k* of Babylon	Jer 22:25	4428
a *K* shall reign and prosper, and	Jer 23:5	4428
after that Nebuchadrezzar *k* of	Jer 24:1	4428
the son of Jehoiakim *k* of Judah	Jer 24:1	4428
I give Zedekiah the *k* of Judah	Jer 24:8	4428
the son of Josiah *k* of Judah	Jer 25:1	4428
of Nebuchadrezzar *k* of Babylon	Jer 25:1	4428
Josiah the son of Amon *k* of Judah	Jer 25:3	4428
Nebuchadrezzar the *k* of Babylon	Jer 25:9	4428
the *k* of Babylon seventy years	Jer 25:11	4428
I will punish the *k* of Babylon	Jer 25:12	4428
Pharaoh *k* of Egypt, and his	Jer 25:19	4428
the *k* of Sheshach shall drink	Jer 25:26	4428
k of Judah came this word from	Jer 26:1	4428
the days of Hezekiah *k* of Judah	Jer 26:18	4428
Did Hezekiah *k* of Judah and all	Jer 26:19	4428
And when Jehoiakim the *k*, with all	Jer 26:21	4428
the *k* sought to put him to death	Jer 26:21	4428
Jehoiakim the *k* sent men into	Jer 26:22	4428
brought him unto Jehoiakim the *k*	Jer 26:23	4428
k of Judah came this word unto	Jer 27:1	4428
And send them to the *k* of Edom	Jer 27:3	4428
to the *k* of Moab	Jer 27:3	4428
to the *k* of the Ammonites	Jer 27:3	4428

to the *k* of Tyrus	Jer 27:3	4428
to the *k* of Zidon	Jer 27:3	4428
unto Zedekiah *k* of Judah	Jer 27:3	4428
Nebuchadnezzar the *k* of Babylon	Jer 27:6	4428
Nebuchadnezzar the *k* of Babylon	Jer 27:8	4428
the yoke of the *k* of Babylon	Jer 27:8	4428
shall not serve the *k* of Babylon	Jer 27:9	4428
the yoke of the *k* of Babylon	Jer 27:11	4428
I spake also to Zedekiah *k* of	Jer 27:12	4428
the yoke of the *k* of Babylon	Jer 27:12	4428
will not serve the *k* of Babylon	Jer 27:13	4428
shall not serve the *k* of Babylon	Jer 27:14	4428
serve the *k* of Babylon, and live	Jer 27:17	4428
and in the house of the *k* of Judah	Jer 27:18	4428
k of Babylon took not, when he	Jer 27:20	4428
k of Judah from Jerusalem to	Jer 27:20	4428
and in the house of the *k* of Judah	Jer 27:21	4428
the reign of Zedekiah *k* of Judah	Jer 28:1	4428
the yoke of the *k* of Babylon	Jer 28:2	4428
that Nebuchadnezzar *k* of Babylon	Jer 28:3	4428
the son of Jehoiakim *k* of Judah	Jer 28:4	4428
the yoke of the *k* of Babylon	Jer 28:4	4428
the yoke of Nebuchadnezzar *k* of	Jer 28:11	4428
serve Nebuchadnezzar *k* of Babylon	Jer 28:14	4428
(After that Jeconiah the *k*	Jer 29:2	4428
(whom Zedekiah *k* of Judah sent	Jer 29:3	4428
k of Babylon) saying,	Jer 29:3	4428
k that sitteth upon the throne of	Jer 29:16	4428
of Nebuchadrezzar *k* of Babylon	Jer 29:21	4428
whom the *k* of Babylon roasted in	Jer 29:22	4428
LORD their God, and David their *k*	Jer 30:9	4428
tenth year of Zedekiah *k* of Judah	Jer 32:1	4428
For then the *k* of Babylon's army	Jer 32:2	4428
was in the *k* of Judah's house	Jer 32:2	4428
For Zedekiah *k* of Judah had shut	Jer 32:3	4428
into the hand of the *k* of Babylon	Jer 32:3	4428
Zedekiah *k* of Judah shall not	Jer 32:4	4428
into the hand of the *k* of Babylon	Jer 32:4	4428
of Nebuchadrezzar *k* of Babylon	Jer 32:28	4428
of the *k* of Babylon by the sword	Jer 32:36	4428
when Nebuchadnezzar *k* of Babylon	Jer 34:1	4428
and speak to Zedekiah *k* of Judah	Jer 34:2	4428
into the hand of the *k* of Babylon	Jer 34:2	4428
the eyes of the *k* of Babylon	Jer 34:3	4428
the LORD, O Zedekiah *k* of Judah	Jer 34:4	4428
Zedekiah *k* of Judah in Jerusalem	Jer 34:6	4428
When the *k* of Babylon's army	Jer 34:7	4428
after that the *k* Zedekiah had	Jer 34:8	4428
And Zedekiah *k* of Judah and his	Jer 34:21	4428
hand of the *k* of Babylon's army	Jer 34:21	4428
the son of Josiah *k* of Judah	Jer 35:1	4428
when Nebuchadrezzar *k* of Babylon	Jer 35:11	4428
the son of Josiah *k* of Judah	Jer 36:1	4428
the son of Josiah *k* of Judah	Jer 36:9	4428
tell the *k* of all these words	Jer 36:16	4428
went in to the *k* into the court	Jer 36:20	4428
the words in the ears of the *k*	Jer 36:20	4428
So the *k* sent Jehudi to fetch the	Jer 36:21	4428
read it in the ears of the *k*	Jer 36:21	4428
princes which stood beside the *k*	Jer 36:21	4428
Now the *k* sat in the winterhouse	Jer 36:22	4428
their garments, neither the *k*	Jer 36:24	4428
had made intercession to the *k*	Jer 36:25	4428
But the *k* commanded Jerahmeel the	Jer 36:26	4428
after that the *k* had burned the	Jer 36:27	4428
which Jehoiakim the *k* of Judah	Jer 36:28	4428
shalt say to Jehoiakim *k* of Judah	Jer 36:29	4428
The *k* of Babylon shall certainly	Jer 36:29	4428
the LORD of Jehoiakim *k* of Judah	Jer 36:30	4428
of the book which Jehoiakim *k* of	Jer 36:32	4428
k Zedekiah the son of Josiah	Jer 37:1	4428
whom Nebuchadrezzar *k* of Babylon	Jer 37:1	4428
made *k* in the land of Judah	Jer 37:1	4428
Zedekiah the *k* sent Jehucal the	Jer 37:3	4428
shall ye say to the *k* of Judah	Jer 37:7	4428
Then Zedekiah the *k* sent, and took	Jer 37:17	4428
the *k* asked him secretly in his	Jer 37:17	4428
into the hand of the *k* of Babylon	Jer 37:17	4428
Jeremiah said unto *k* Zedekiah	Jer 37:18	4428
The *k* of Babylon shall not come	Jer 37:19	4428
now, I pray thee, O my lord the *k*	Jer 37:20	4428
Then Zedekiah the *k* commanded	Jer 37:21	4428
hand of the *k* of Babylon's army	Jer 38:3	4428
the princes said unto the *k*	Jer 38:4	4428
Then Zedekiah the *k* said, Behold	Jer 38:5	4428
for the *k* is not he that can do	Jer 38:5	4428
the *k* then sitting in the gate of	Jer 38:7	4428
king's house, and spake to the *k*	Jer 38:8	4428
My lord the *k*, these men have	Jer 38:9	4428
Then the *k* commanded Ebed-melech	Jer 38:10	4428
house of the *k* under the treasury	Jer 38:11	4428
Then Zedekiah the *k* sent, and took	Jer 38:14	4428
the *k* said unto Jeremiah, I will	Jer 38:14	4428
So Zedekiah the *k* sware secretly	Jer 38:16	4428
unto the *k* of Babylon's princes	Jer 38:17	4428
to the *k* of Babylon's princes	Jer 38:18	4428
Zedekiah the *k* said unto Jeremiah	Jer 38:19	4428
the *k* of Judah's house shall be	Jer 38:22	4428
to the *k* of Babylon's princes	Jer 38:22	4428
by the hand of the *k* of Babylon	Jer 38:23	4428
what thou hast said unto the *k*	Jer 38:25	4428
also what the *k* said unto thee	Jer 38:25	4428
my supplication before the *k*	Jer 38:26	4428
words that the *k* had commanded	Jer 38:27	4428
ninth year of Zedekiah *k* of Judah	Jer 39:1	4428
came Nebuchadrezzar *k* of Babylon	Jer 39:1	4428
of the *k* of Babylon came in	Jer 39:3	4428
the princes of the *k* of Babylon	Jer 39:3	4428
Zedekiah the *k* of Judah saw them	Jer 39:4	4428
him up to Nebuchadnezzar *k* of	Jer 39:5	4428
Then the *k* of Babylon slew the	Jer 39:6	4428
also the *k* of Babylon slew all	Jer 39:6	4428
Now Nebuchadrezzar *k* of Babylon	Jer 39:11	4428
all the *k* of Babylon's princes	Jer 39:13	4428
whom the *k* of Babylon hath made	Jer 40:5	4428
heard that the *k* of Babylon had	Jer 40:7	4428
serve the *k* of Babylon, and it	Jer 40:9	4428
heard that the *k* of Babylon had	Jer 40:11	4428
the *k* of the Ammonites hath sent	Jer 40:14	4428
royal, and the princes of the *k*	Jer 41:1	4428
whom the *k* of Babylon had made	Jer 41:2	4428
was it which Asa the *k* had made	Jer 41:9	4428
for fear of Baasha *k* of Israel	Jer 41:9	4428
whom the *k* of Babylon made	Jer 41:18	4428
Be not afraid of the *k* of Babylon	Jer 42:11	4428
Nebuchadrezzar the *k* of Babylon	Jer 43:10	4428
I will give Pharaoh-hophra *k* of	Jer 44:30	4428
as I gave Zedekiah *k* of Judah	Jer 44:30	4428
of Nebuchadrezzar *k* of Babylon	Jer 44:30	4428
the son of Josiah *k* of Judah	Jer 45:1	4428
army of Pharaoh-necho *k* of Egypt	Jer 46:2	4428
which Nebuchadrezzar *k* of Babylon	Jer 46:2	4428
the son of Josiah *k* of Judah	Jer 46:2	4428
how Nebuchadrezzar *k* of Babylon	Jer 46:13	4428
Pharaoh *k* of Egypt is but a noise	Jer 46:17	4428
As I live, saith the *K*, whose	Jer 46:18	4428
of Nebuchadrezzar *k* of Babylon	Jer 46:26	4428
to the slaughter, saith the *K*	Jer 48:15	4428
why then doth their *k* inherit Gad	Jer 49:1	4428
for their *k* shall go into	Jer 49:3	4428
which Nebuchadrezzar *k* of Babylon	Jer 49:28	4428
for Nebuchadrezzar *k* of Babylon	Jer 49:30	4428
the reign of Zedekiah *k* of Judah	Jer 49:34	4428
and will destroy from thence the *k*	Jer 49:38	4428
first the *k* of Assyria hath	Jer 50:17	4428
last this Nebuchadrezzar *k* of	Jer 50:17	4428
I will punish the *k* of Babylon	Jer 50:18	4428
I have punished the *k* of Assyria	Jer 50:18	4428
The *k* of Babylon hath heard the	Jer 50:43	4428
to shew the *k* of Babylon that his	Jer 51:31	4428
Nebuchadrezzar the *k* of Babylon	Jer 51:34	4428
sleep, and not wake, saith the *K*	Jer 51:57	4428
k of Judah into Babylon in the	Jer 51:59	4428
rebelled against the *k* of Babylon	Jer 52:3	4428
Nebuchadrezzar *k* of Babylon came	Jer 52:4	4428
the eleventh year of *k* Zedekiah	Jer 52:5	4428
the Chaldeans pursued after the *k*	Jer 52:8	4428
Then they took the *k*	Jer 52:9	4428
carried him up unto the *k* of	Jer 52:9	4428
the *k* of Babylon slew the sons of	Jer 52:10	4428
the *k* of Babylon bound him in	Jer 52:11	4428
of Nebuchadrezzar *k* of Babylon	Jer 52:12	4428
which served the *k* of Babylon	Jer 52:12	4428
that fell to the *k* of Babylon	Jer 52:15	4428
which *k* Solomon had made in the	Jer 52:20	4428
brought them to the *k* of Babylon	Jer 52:26	4428
the *k* of Babylon smote them, and	Jer 52:27	4428
of Jehoiachin *k* of Judah, in the	Jer 52:31	4428
that Evil-merodach *k* of Babylon	Jer 52:31	4428
the head of Jehoiachin *k* of Judah	Jer 52:31	4428
given him of the *k* of Babylon	Jer 52:34	4428
indignation of his anger the *k*	Lam 2:6	4428
her *k* and her princes are among	Lam 2:9	4428
year of *k* Jehoiachin's captivity	Eze 1:2	4428
The *k* shall mourn, and the prince	Eze 7:27	4428
the *k* of Babylon is come to	Eze 17:12	4428
and hath taken the *k* thereof	Eze 17:12	4428
the *k* dwelleth that made him *k*	Eze 17:16	4428
the *k* dwelleth that made him *k*	Eze 17:16	4427
brought him to the *k* of Babylon	Eze 19:9	4428
of the *k* of Babylon may come	Eze 21:19	4428
For the *k* of Babylon stood at the	Eze 21:21	4428
the *k* of Babylon set himself	Eze 24:2	4428
Tyrus Nebuchadrezzar *k* of Babylon	Eze 26:7	4428
a *k* of kings, from the north,	Eze 26:7	4428
a lamentation upon the *k* of Tyrus	Eze 28:12	4428
face against Pharaoh *k* of Egypt	Eze 29:2	4428
Pharaoh *k* of Egypt, the great	Eze 29:3	4428
Nebuchadrezzar *k* of Babylon	Eze 29:18	4428
unto Nebuchadrezzar *k* of Babylon	Eze 29:19	4428
of Nebuchadrezzar *k* of Babylon	Eze 30:10	4428
the arm of Pharaoh *k* of Egypt	Eze 30:21	4428
I am against Pharaoh *k* of Egypt	Eze 30:22	4428
the arms of the *k* of Babylon	Eze 30:24	4428
the arms of the *k* of Babylon	Eze 30:25	4428
into the hand of the *k* of Babylon	Eze 30:25	4428
speak unto Pharaoh *k* of Egypt	Eze 31:2	4428
for Pharaoh *k* of Egypt, and say	Eze 32:2	4428
The sword of the *k* of Babylon	Eze 32:11	4428
one *k* shall be *k* to them all	Eze 37:22	4428
my servant shall be *k* over them	Eze 37:24	4428
k of Judah came Nebuchadnezzar	Dan 1:1	4428
k of Babylon unto Jerusalem	Dan 1:1	4428
k of Judah into his hand, with	Dan 1:2	4428
the *k* spake unto Ashpenaz the	Dan 1:3	4428
the *k* appointed them a daily	Dan 1:5	4428
they might stand before the *k*	Dan 1:5	4428
unto Daniel, I fear my lord the *k*	Dan 1:10	4428
make me endanger my head to the *k*	Dan 1:10	4428
k had said he should bring them	Dan 1:18	4428
And the *k* communed with them	Dan 1:19	4428
therefore stood they before the *k*	Dan 1:19	4428
that the *k* enquired of them, he	Dan 1:20	4428
unto the first year of *k* Cyrus	Dan 1:21	4428
Then the *k* commanded to call the	Dan 2:2	4428
for to shew the *k* his dreams	Dan 2:2	4428
they came and stood before the *k*	Dan 2:2	4428
the *k* said unto them, I have	Dan 2:3	4428
the Chaldeans to the *k* in Syriack	Dan 2:4	4428
O *k*, live for ever	Dan 2:4	4430
The *k* answered and said to the	Dan 2:5	4430
Let the *k* tell his servants the	Dan 2:7	4430
The *k* answered and said, I know of	Dan 2:8	4430
Chaldeans answered before the *k*	Dan 2:10	4430
therefore there is no *k*, lord,	Dan 2:10	4430
a rare thing that the *k* requireth	Dan 2:11	4430
that can shew it before the *k*	Dan 2:11	4430
For this cause the *k* was angry	Dan 2:12	4430
is the decree so hasty from the *k*	Dan 2:15	4430
desired of the *k* that he would	Dan 2:16	4430
shew the *k* the interpretation	Dan 2:16	4430
whom the *k* had ordained to	Dan 2:24	4430
bring me in before the *k*, and I	Dan 2:24	4430
unto the *k* the interpretation	Dan 2:24	4430
in Daniel before the *k* in haste	Dan 2:25	4430
unto the *k* the interpretation	Dan 2:25	4430
The *k* answered and said to Daniel,	Dan 2:26	4430
answered in the presence of the *k*	Dan 2:27	4430
The secret which the *k* hath	Dan 2:27	4430
the soothsayers, shew unto the *k*	Dan 2:27	4430
secrets, and maketh known to the *k*	Dan 2:28	4430
As for thee, O *k*, thy thoughts	Dan 2:29	4430
known the interpretation to the *k*	Dan 2:30	4430
Thou, O *k*, sawest, and behold a	Dan 2:31	4430
thereof before the *k*	Dan 2:36	4430
Thou, O *k*, art a *k* of kings	Dan 2:37	4430
to the *k* what shall come to pass	Dan 2:45	4430
Then the *k* Nebuchadnezzar fell	Dan 2:46	4430
The *k* answered unto Daniel, and	Dan 2:47	4430
Then the *k* made Daniel a great	Dan 2:48	4430
Then Daniel requested of the *k*	Dan 2:49	4430
Daniel sat in the gate of the *k*	Dan 2:49	4430
Nebuchadnezzar the *k* made an	Dan 3:1	4430
Then Nebuchadnezzar the *k* sent to	Dan 3:2	4430
Nebuchadnezzar the *k* had set up	Dan 3:2	4430
Nebuchadnezzar the *k* had set up	Dan 3:3	4430
Nebuchadnezzar the *k* hath set up	Dan 3:5	4430
Nebuchadnezzar the *k* had set up	Dan 3:7	4430
to the *k* Nebuchadnezzar, O *k*	Dan 3:9	4430
Thou, O *k*, hast made a decree,	Dan 3:10	4430
these men, O *k*, have not regarded	Dan 3:12	4430
brought these men before the *k*	Dan 3:13	4430
answered and said to the *k*	Dan 3:16	4430
deliver us out of thine hand, O *k*	Dan 3:17	4430
not, be it known unto thee, O *k*	Dan 3:18	4430
Nebuchadnezzar the *k* was astonied	Dan 3:24	4430
and said unto the *k*, True, O *k*	Dan 3:24	4430
Then the *k* promoted Shadrach,	Dan 3:30	4430
Nebuchadnezzar the *k*, unto all	Dan 4:1	4430
This dream I *k* Nebuchadnezzar	Dan 4:18	4430
The *k* spake, and said,	Dan 4:19	4430
It is thou, O *k*, that art grown	Dan 4:22	4430
whereas the *k* saw a watcher and an	Dan 4:23	4430
This is the interpretation, O *k*	Dan 4:24	4430
which is come upon my lord the *k*	Dan 4:24	4430
Wherefore, O *k*, let my counsel be	Dan 4:27	4430
came upon the *k* Nebuchadnezzar	Dan 4:28	4430
The *k* spake, and said, Is not this	Dan 4:30	4430
O *k* Nebuchadnezzar, to thee it is	Dan 4:31	4430
extol and honour the *K* of heaven	Dan 4:37	4430
Belshazzar the *k* made a great	Dan 5:1	4430
that the *k*, and his princes, his	Dan 5:2	4430
and the *k*, and his princes, his	Dan 5:3	4430
the *k* saw the part of the hand	Dan 5:5	4430
The *k* cried aloud to bring in the	Dan 5:7	4430
the *k* spake, and said to the wise	Dan 5:7	4430
nor make known to the *k* the	Dan 5:8	4430
Then was *k* Belshazzar greatly	Dan 5:9	4430
by reason of the words of the *k*	Dan 5:10	4430
and the queen spake and said, O *k*	Dan 5:10	4430
whom the *k* Nebuchadnezzar thy	Dan 5:11	4430
Nebuchadnezzar thy father, the *k*	Dan 5:11	4430
whom the *k* named Belteshazzar	Dan 5:12	4430
Daniel brought in before the *k*	Dan 5:13	4430
the *k* spake and said unto Daniel,	Dan 5:13	4430
whom the *k* my father brought out	Dan 5:13	4430
answered and said before the *k*	Dan 5:17	4430
will read the writing unto the *k*	Dan 5:17	4430
O thou *k*, the most high God gave	Dan 5:18	4430
the *k* of the Chaldeans slain	Dan 5:30	4430
the *k* should have no damage	Dan 6:2	4430
the *k* thought to set him over the	Dan 6:3	4430
assembled together to the *k*	Dan 6:6	4430
unto him, *K* Darius, live for ever	Dan 6:6	4430
thirty days, save of thee, O *k*	Dan 6:7	4430
Now, O *k*, establish the decree,	Dan 6:8	4430
Wherefore *k* Darius signed the	Dan 6:9	4430
spake before the *k* concerning the	Dan 6:12	4430
thirty days, save of thee, O *k*	Dan 6:12	4430
The *k* answered and said, The thing	Dan 6:12	4430
they and said before the *k*	Dan 6:13	4430
of Judah, regardeth not thee, O *k*	Dan 6:13	4430
Then the *k*, when he heard these	Dan 6:14	4430
these men assembled unto the *k*	Dan 6:15	4430
and said unto the *k*, Know, O *k*	Dan 6:15	4430
the *k* establisheth may be changed	Dan 6:15	4430
Then the *k* commanded, and they	Dan 6:16	4430
Now the *k* spake and said unto	Dan 6:16	4430
the *k* sealed it with his own	Dan 6:17	4430
Then the *k* went to his palace, and	Dan 6:18	4430
Then the *k* arose very early in	Dan 6:19	4430
the *k* spake and said to Daniel, O	Dan 6:20	4430
said Daniel unto the *k*, O *k*	Dan 6:21	4430
and also before thee, O *k*, have I	Dan 6:22	4430

Then was the *k* exceeding glad for	Dan 6:23	4430
the *k* commanded, and they brought	Dan 6:24	4430
Then *k* Darius wrote unto all	Dan 6:25	4430
k of Babylon Daniel had a dream	Dan 7:1	4430
of *k* Belshazzar a vision appeared	Dan 8:1	4428
the rough goat is the *k* of Grecia	Dan 8:21	4428
between his eyes is the first *k*	Dan 8:21	4428
a *k* of fierce countenance, and	Dan 8:23	4428
which was made *k* over the realm	Dan 9:1	4427
In the third year of Cyrus *k* of	Dan 10:1	4428
a mighty *k* shall stand up, that	Dan 11:3	4428
the *k* of the south shall be	Dan 11:5	4428
to the *k* of the north to make an	Dan 11:6	4428
fortress of the *k* of the north	Dan 11:7	4428
years than the *k* of the north	Dan 11:8	4428
So the *k* of the south shall come	Dan 11:9	4428
the *k* of the south shall be moved	Dan 11:11	4428
him, even with the *k* of the north	Dan 11:11	4428
For the *k* of the north shall	Dan 11:13	4428
up against the *k* of the south	Dan 11:14	4428
So the *k* of the north shall come,	Dan 11:15	4428
his courage against the *k* of the	Dan 11:25	4428
the *k* of the south shall be	Dan 11:25	4428
the *k* shall do according to his	Dan 11:36	4428
the *k* of the south push at him	Dan 11:40	4428
the *k* of the north shall come	Dan 11:40	4428
the son of Joash, *k* of Israel	Hos 1:1	4428
shall abide many days without a *k*	Hos 3:4	4428
LORD their God, and David their *k*	Hos 3:5	4428
and give ye ear, O house of the *k*	Hos 5:1	4428
the Assyrian, and sent to *k* Jareb	Hos 5:13	4428
They make the *k* glad with their	Hos 7:3	4428
In the day of our *k* the princes	Hos 7:5	4428
the burden of the *k* of princes	Hos 8:10	4428
now they shall say, We have no *k*	Hos 10:3	4428
what then should a *k* do to us	Hos 10:3	4428
Assyria for a present to *k* Jareb	Hos 10:6	4428
her *k* is cut off as the foam upon	Hos 10:7	4428
in a morning shall the *k* of	Hos 10:15	4428
but the Assyrian shall be his *k*	Hos 11:5	4428
I will be thy *k*	Hos 13:10	4428
of whom thou saidst, Give me a *k*	Hos 13:10	4428
I gave thee a *k* in mine anger	Hos 13:11	4428
in the days of Uzziah *k* of Judah	Amos 1:1	4428
the son of Joash *k* of Israel	Amos 1:1	4428
their *k* shall go into captivity,	Amos 1:15	4428
bones of the *k* of Edom into lime	Amos 2:1	4428
sent to Jeroboam *k* of Israel	Amos 7:10	4428
word came unto the *k* of Nineveh	Jonah 3:6	4428
Nineveh by the decree of the *k*	Jonah 3:7	4428
their *k* shall pass before them,	Mic 2:13	4428
is there no *k* in thee	Mic 4:9	4428
what Balak *k* of Moab consulted	Mic 6:5	4428
shepherds slumber, O *k* of Assyria	Nah 3:18	4428
the son of Amon, *k* of Judah	Zeph 1:1	4428
the *k* of Israel, even the LORD,	Zeph 3:15	4428
the second year of Darius the *k*	Hag 1:1	4428
the second year of Darius the *k*	Hag 1:15	4428
in the fourth year of *k* Darius	Zec 7:1	4428
the *k* shall perish from Gaza, and	Zec 9:5	4428
behold, thy *K* cometh unto thee	Zec 9:9	4428
hand, and into the hand of his *k*	Zec 11:6	4428
in the days of Uzziah *k* of Judah	Zec 14:5	4428
the LORD shall be *k* over all the	Zec 14:9	4428
year to year to worship the *K*	Zec 14:16	4428
unto Jerusalem to worship the *K*	Zec 14:17	4428
for I am a great *K*, saith the	Mal 1:14	4428
And Jesse begat David the *k*	Mt 1:6	*935*
David the *k* begat Solomon of her	Mt 1:6	*935*
Judaea in the days of Herod the *k*	Mt 2:1	*935*
is he that is born *K* of the Jews	Mt 2:2	*935*
When Herod the *k* had heard these	Mt 2:3	*935*
When they had heard the *k*	Mt 2:9	*935*
for it is the city of the great *K*	Mt 5:35	*935*
And the *k* was sorry	Mt 14:9	*935*
heaven likened unto a certain *k*	Mt 18:23	*935*
thy *K* cometh unto thee, meek, and	Mt 21:5	*935*
heaven is like unto a certain *k*	Mt 22:2	*935*
But when the *k* heard thereof, he	Mt 22:7	*935*
when the *k* came in to see the	Mt 22:11	*935*
Then said the *k* to the servants,	Mt 22:13	*935*
Then shall the *K* say unto them on	Mt 25:34	*935*
the *K* shall answer and say unto	Mt 25:40	*935*
Art thou the *K* of the Jews	Mt 27:11	*935*
him, saying, Hail, *K* of the Jews	Mt 27:29	*935*
JESUS THE *K* OF THE JEWS	Mt 27:37	*935*
If he be the *K* of Israel, let him	Mt 27:42	*935*
And *k* Herod heard of him	Mk 6:14	*935*
the *k* said unto the damsel, Ask	Mk 6:22	*935*
straightway with haste unto the *k*	Mk 6:25	*935*
the *k* was exceeding sorry	Mk 6:26	*935*
immediately the *k* sent an	Mk 6:27	*935*
him, Art thou the *K* of the Jews	Mk 15:2	*935*
unto you the *K* of the Jews	Mk 15:9	*935*
whom ye call the *K* of the Jews	Mk 15:12	*935*
salute him, Hail, *K* of the Jews	Mk 15:18	*935*
written over, THE *K* OF THE JEWS	Mk 15:26	*935*
Let Christ the *K* of Israel	Mk 15:32	*935*
the *k* of Judaea, a certain priest	Lk 1:5	*935*
Or what *k*, going to make war	Lk 14:31	*935*
to make war against another *k*	Lk 14:31	*935*
Blessed be the *K* that cometh in	Lk 19:38	*935*
that he himself is Christ a *K*	Lk 23:2	*935*
Art thou the *K* of the Jews	Lk 23:3	*935*
If thou be the *k* of the Jews	Lk 23:37	*935*
THIS IS THE *K* OF THE JEWS	Lk 23:38	*935*
thou art the *K* of Israel	Jn 1:49	*935*
him by force, to make him a *k*	Jn 6:15	*935*
Blessed is the *K* of Israel that	Jn 12:13	*935*
thy *K* cometh, sitting on an ass's	Jn 12:15	*935*
him, Art thou the *K* of the Jews	Jn 18:33	*935*
said unto him, Art thou a *k* then	Jn 18:37	*935*
Thou sayest that I am a *k*	Jn 18:37	*935*
unto you the *K* of the Jews	Jn 18:39	*935*
And said, Hail, *K* of the Jews	Jn 19:3	*935*
a *k* speaketh against Caesar	Jn 19:12	*935*
unto the Jews, Behold your *K*	Jn 19:14	*935*
unto them, Shall I crucify your *K*	Jn 19:15	*935*
answered, We have no *k* but Caesar	Jn 19:15	*935*
NAZARETH THE *K* OF THE JEWS	Jn 19:19	*935*
Write not, The *K* of the Jews	Jn 19:21	*935*
that he said, I am *K* of the Jews	Jn 19:21	*935*
the sight of Pharaoh *k* of Egypt	Acts 7:10	*935*
Till another *k* arose, which knew	Acts 7:18	*935*
k stretched forth his hands to	Acts 12:1	*935*
And afterward they desired a *k*	Acts 13:21	*935*
up unto them David to be their *k*	Acts 13:22	*935*
saying that there is another *k*	Acts 17:7	*935*
And after certain days *k* Agrippa	Acts 25:13	*935*
declared Paul's cause unto the *k*	Acts 25:14	*935*
K Agrippa, and all men which are	Acts 25:24	*935*
thee, O *k* Agrippa, that, after	Acts 25:26	*935*
k Agrippa, because I shall answer	Acts 26:2	*935*
k Agrippa, I am accused of the	Acts 26:7	*935*
At midday, O *k*, I saw in the way	Acts 26:13	*935*
Whereupon, O *k* Agrippa, I was not	Acts 26:19	*935*
For the *k* knoweth of these things	Acts 26:26	*935*
K Agrippa, believest thou the	Acts 26:27	*935*
the *k* rose up, and the governor,	Acts 26:30	*935*
the governor under Aretas the *k*	2Cor 11:32	*935*
Now unto the *K* eternal, immortal,	1Ti 1:17	*935*
the *K* of kings, and Lord of lords	1Ti 6:15	*935*
k of Salem, priest of the most	Heb 7:1	*935*
interpretation *K* of righteousness	Heb 7:2	*935*
and after that also *K* of Salem	Heb 7:2	*935*
of Salem, which is, *K* of peace	Heb 7:2	*935*
not fearing the wrath of the *k*	Heb 11:27	*935*
whether it be to the *k*, as	1Pet 2:13	*935*
Honour the *k*	1Pet 2:17	*935*
And they had a *k* over them	Rev 9:11	*935*
are thy ways, thou *K* of saints	Rev 15:3	*935*
is Lord of lords, and *K* of kings	Rev 17:14	*935*
K OF KINGS, AND LORD OF LORDS	Rev 19:16	*935*

KINGDOM {342}

the beginning of his *k* was Babel	Gen 10:10	4467
on me and on my *k* a great sin	Gen 20:9	4467
shall be unto me a *k* of priests	Ex 19:6	4467
Agag, and his *k* shall be exalted	Num 24:7	4438
the *k* of Sihon king of the	Num 32:33	4467
the *k* of Og king of Bashan, the	Num 32:33	4467
of Argob, the *k* of Og in Bashan	Deut 3:4	4467
cities of the *k* of Og in Bashan	Deut 3:10	4467
and all Bashan, being the *k* of Og	Deut 3:13	4467
sitteth upon the throne of his *k*	Deut 17:18	4467
he may prolong his days in his *k*	Deut 17:20	4467
All the *k* of Og in Bashan, which	Josh 13:12	4468
all the *k* of Sihon king of the	Josh 13:21	4468
the rest of the *k* of Sihon king	Josh 13:27	4468
all the *k* of Og king of Bashan,	Josh 13:30	4468
cities of the *k* of Og in Bashan,	Josh 13:31	4468
But of the matter of the *k*	1Sa 10:16	4410
the people the manner of the *k*	1Sa 10:25	4410
to Gilgal, and renew the *k* there	1Sa 11:14	4410
thy *k* upon Israel for ever	1Sa 13:13	4467
But now thy *k* shall not continue	1Sa 13:14	4467
So Saul took the *k* over Israel	1Sa 14:47	4410
The LORD hath rent the *k* of	1Sa 15:28	4468
what can he have more but the *k*	1Sa 18:8	4410
not be established, nor thy *k*	1Sa 20:31	4438
that the *k* of Israel shall be	1Sa 24:20	4467
hath rent the *k* out of thine hand	1Sa 28:17	4467
To translate the *k* from the house	2Sa 3:10	4467
my *k* are guiltless before the	2Sa 3:28	4467
that he had exalted his *k* for his	2Sa 5:12	4467
bowels, and I will establish his *k*	2Sa 7:12	4467
the throne of his *k* for ever	2Sa 7:13	4467
thy *k* shall be established for	2Sa 7:16	4467
restore me the *k* of my father	2Sa 16:3	4468
the LORD hath delivered the *k*	2Sa 16:8	4410
sitteth on the throne of the *k*	1Kin 1:46	4410
his *k* was established greatly	1Kin 2:12	4438
Thou knowest that the *k* was mine	1Kin 2:15	4410
howbeit the *k* is turned about, and	1Kin 2:15	4410
ask for him the *k* also	1Kin 2:22	4410
the *k* was established in the hand	1Kin 2:46	4467
of thy *k* upon Israel for ever	1Kin 9:5	4467
was not the like made in any *k*	1Kin 10:20	4467
will surely rend the *k* from thee	1Kin 11:11	4467
I will not rend away all the *k*	1Kin 11:13	4467
I will rend the *k* out of the hand	1Kin 11:31	4467
take the whole *k* out of his hand	1Kin 11:34	4467
But I will take the *k* out of his	1Kin 11:35	4410
to bring the *k* again to Rehoboam	1Kin 12:21	4410
Now shall the *k* return to the	1Kin 12:26	4467
rent the *k* away from the house of	1Kin 14:8	4467
liveth, there is no nation or *k*	1Kin 18:10	4467
he took an oath of the *k* and	1Kin 18:10	4467
thou now govern the *k* of Israel	1Kin 21:7	4410
as soon as the *k* was confirmed in	2Kin 14:5	4467
him to confirm the *k* in his hand	2Kin 15:19	4467
turned the *k* unto David the son	1Chr 10:14	4410
themselves with him in his *k*	1Chr 11:10	4438
to turn the *k* of Saul to him,	1Chr 12:23	4438
for his *k* was lifted up on high,	1Chr 14:2	4438
from one *k* to another people	1Chr 16:20	4467
and I will establish his *k*	1Chr 17:11	4438
in mine house and in my *k* for ever	1Chr 17:14	4438
of his *k* over Israel for ever	1Chr 22:10	4438
of the *k* of the LORD over Israel	1Chr 28:5	4438
I will establish his *k* for ever	1Chr 28:7	4438
thine is the *k*, O LORD, and thou	1Chr 29:11	4467
David was strengthened in his *k*	2Chr 1:1	4438
the LORD, and an house for his *k*	2Chr 2:1	4438
the LORD, and an house for his *k*	2Chr 2:12	
I stablish the throne of thy *k*	2Chr 7:18	4438
was not the like made in any *k*	2Chr 9:19	4467
bring the *k* again to Rehoboam	2Chr 11:1	4467
they strengthened the *k* of Judah	2Chr 11:17	4438
Rehoboam had established the *k*	2Chr 12:1	4438
k over Israel to David for ever	2Chr 13:5	4467
now ye think to withstand the *k*	2Chr 13:8	4467
the *k* was quiet before him	2Chr 14:5	4467
LORD stablished the *k* in his hand	2Chr 17:5	4467
but the *k* gave he to Jehoram	2Chr 21:3	4467
risen up to the *k* of his father	2Chr 21:4	4467
had no power to keep still the *k*	2Chr 22:9	4467
the king upon the throne of the *k*	2Chr 23:20	4467
when the *k* was established to him	2Chr 25:3	4467
for a sin offering for the *k*	2Chr 29:21	4467
for no god of any nation or *k* was	2Chr 32:15	4467
him again to Jerusalem into his *k*	2Chr 33:13	4438
the reign of the *k* of Persia	2Chr 36:20	4438
proclamation throughout all his *k*	2Chr 36:22	4438
proclamation throughout all his *k*	Ezr 1:1	4438
have not served thee in their *k*	Neh 9:35	4438
sat on the throne of his *k*	Est 1:2	4438
the riches of his glorious *k*	Est 1:4	4438
and which sat the first in the *k*	Est 1:14	4438
in all the provinces of his *k*	Est 2:3	4438
the whole *k* of Ahasuerus, even	Est 3:6	4438
in all the provinces of thy *k*	Est 3:8	4438
to the *k* for such a time as this	Est 4:14	4438
given thee to the half of the *k*	Est 5:3	4438
of the *k* it shall be performed	Est 5:6	4438
even to the half of the *k*	Est 7:2	4438
provinces of the *k* of Ahasuerus	Est 9:30	4438
For the *k* is the LORD's	Ps 22:28	4410
of thy *k* is a right sceptre	Ps 45:6	4438
and his *k* ruleth over all	Ps 103:19	4438
from one *k* to another people	Ps 105:13	4467
shall speak of the glory of thy *k*	Ps 145:11	4438
and the glorious majesty of his *k*	Ps 145:12	4438
Thy *k* is an everlasting *k*,	Ps 145:13	4438
is born in his *k* becometh poor	Eccl 4:14	4438
throne of David, and upon his *k*	Is 9:7	4467
the *k* from Damascus, and the	Is 17:3	4467
city, and *k* against *k*	Is 19:2	4467
call the nobles thereof to the *k*	Is 34:12	4410
k that will not serve thee shall	Is 60:12	4467
a nation, and concerning a *k*	Jer 18:7	4467
a nation, and concerning a *k*	Jer 18:9	4467
k which will not serve the same	Jer 27:8	4467
he hath polluted the *k* and the	Lam 2:2	4467
and thou didst prosper into a *k*	Eze 16:13	4410
That the *k* might be base, that it	Eze 17:14	4467
and they shall be there a base *k*	Eze 29:14	4467
God of heaven hath given thee a *k*	Dan 2:37	4437
arise another *k* inferior to thee	Dan 2:39	4437
and another third *k* of brass	Dan 2:39	4437
the fourth *k* shall be strong as	Dan 2:40	4437
of iron, the *k* shall be divided	Dan 2:41	4437
so the *k* shall be partly strong,	Dan 2:42	4437
the God of heaven set up a *k*	Dan 2:44	4437
the *k* shall not be left to other	Dan 2:44	4437
his *k* is an everlasting *k*	Dan 4:3	4437
most High ruleth in the *k* of men	Dan 4:17	4437
as all the wise men of my *k* are	Dan 4:18	4437
most High ruleth in the *k* of men	Dan 4:25	4437
thy *k* shall be sure unto thee,	Dan 4:26	4437
in the palace of the *k* of Babylon	Dan 4:29	4437
of the *k* by the might of my power	Dan 4:30	4437
The *k* is departed from thee	Dan 4:31	4437
most High ruleth in the *k* of men	Dan 4:32	4437
his *k* is from generation to	Dan 4:34	4437
and for the glory of my *k*, mine	Dan 4:36	4437
and I was established in my *k*	Dan 4:36	4437
shall be the third ruler in the *k*	Dan 5:7	4437
There is a man in thy *k*, in whom	Dan 5:11	4437
shalt be the third ruler in the *k*	Dan 5:16	4437
Nebuchadnezzar thy father a *k*	Dan 5:18	4437
high God ruled in the *k* of men	Dan 5:21	4437
God hath numbered thy *k*, and	Dan 5:26	4437
Thy *k* is divided, and given to the	Dan 5:28	4437
be the third ruler in the *k*	Dan 5:29	4437
And Darius the Median took the *k*	Dan 5:31	4437
to set over the *k* an hundred	Dan 6:1	4437
which should be over the whole *k*	Dan 6:1	4437
against Daniel concerning the *k*	Dan 6:4	4437
All the presidents of the *k*	Dan 6:7	4437
dominion of my *k* men tremble	Dan 6:26	4437
his *k* that which shall not be	Dan 6:26	4437
him dominion, and glory, and a *k*	Dan 7:14	4437
his *k* that which shall not be	Dan 7:14	4437
of the most High shall take the *k*	Dan 7:18	4437
and possess the *k* for ever	Dan 7:18	4437
that the saints possessed the *k*	Dan 7:22	4437
shall be the fourth *k* upon earth	Dan 7:23	4437
the ten horns out of this *k* are	Dan 7:24	4437
And the *k* and dominion	Dan 7:27	4437
the greatness of the *k* under the	Dan 7:27	4437
whose *k* is an everlasting *k*	Dan 7:27	4437
And in the latter time of their *k*	Dan 8:23	4438
But the prince of the *k* of Persia	Dan 10:13	4438

his *k* shall be broken, and shall	Dan 11:4	4438
for his *k* shall be plucked up,	Dan 11:4	4438
the south shall come into his *k*	Dan 11:9	4438
with the strength of his whole *k*	Dan 11:17	4438
of taxes in the glory of the *k*	Dan 11:20	4438
not give the honour of the *k*	Dan 11:21	4438
obtain the *k* by flatteries	Dan 11:21	4438
the *k* of the house of Israel	Hos 1:4	4468
Lord GOD are upon the sinful *k*	Amos 9:8	4467
the *k* shall be the LORD's	Obad 21	4410
the *k* shall come to the daughter	Mic 4:8	4467
for the *k* of heaven is at hand	Mt 3:2	*932*
for the *k* of heaven is at hand	Mt 4:17	*932*
and preaching the gospel of the *k*	Mt 4:23	*932*
for theirs is the *k* of heaven	Mt 5:3	*932*
for theirs is the *k* of heaven	Mt 5:10	*932*
the least in the *k* of heaven	Mt 5:19	*932*
called great in the *k* of heaven	Mt 5:19	*932*
case enter into the *k* of heaven	Mt 5:20	*932*
Thy *k* come	Mt 6:10	*932*
For thine is the *k*, and the power,	Mt 6:13	*932*
But seek ye first the *k* of God	Mt 6:33	*932*
shall enter into the *k* of heaven	Mt 7:21	*932*
and Jacob, in the *k* of heaven	Mt 8:11	*932*
But the children of the *k* shall	Mt 8:12	*932*
and preaching the gospel of the *k*	Mt 9:35	*932*
The *k* of heaven is at hand	Mt 10:7	*932*
he that is least in the *k* of	Mt 11:11	*932*
k of heaven suffereth violence	Mt 11:12	*932*
Every *k* divided against itself is	Mt 12:25	*932*
how shall then his *k* stand	Mt 12:26	*932*
then the *k* of God is come unto	Mt 12:28	*932*
the mysteries of the *k* of heaven	Mt 13:11	*932*
any one heareth the word of the *k*	Mt 13:19	*932*
The *k* of heaven is likened unto a	Mt 13:24	*932*
The *k* of heaven is like to a	Mt 13:31	*932*
The *k* of heaven is like unto	Mt 13:33	*932*
seed are the children of the *k*	Mt 13:38	*932*
of his *k* all things that offend	Mt 13:41	*932*
the sun in the *k* of their Father	Mt 13:43	*932*
the *k* of heaven is like unto	Mt 13:44	*932*
the *k* of heaven is like unto a	Mt 13:45	*932*
the *k* of heaven is like unto a	Mt 13:47	*932*
k of heaven is like unto a man	Mt 13:52	*932*
thee the keys of the *k* of heaven	Mt 16:19	*932*
the Son of man coming in his *k*	Mt 16:28	*932*
the greatest in the *k* of heaven	Mt 18:1	*932*
not enter into the *k* of heaven	Mt 18:3	*932*
is greatest in the *k* of heaven	Mt 18:4	*932*
Therefore is the *k* of heaven	Mt 18:23	*932*
for the *k* of heaven's sake	Mt 19:12	*932*
for of such is the *k* of heaven	Mt 19:14	*932*
hardly enter into the *k* of heaven	Mt 19:23	*932*
man to enter into the *k* of God	Mt 19:24	*932*
For the *k* of heaven is like unto	Mt 20:1	*932*
the other on the left, in thy *k*	Mt 20:21	*932*
go into the *k* of God before you	Mt 21:31	*932*
The *k* of God shall be taken from	Mt 21:43	*932*
The *k* of heaven is like unto a	Mt 22:2	*932*
for ye shut up the *k* of heaven	Mt 23:13	*932*
nation, and *k* against *k*	Mt 24:7	*932*
this gospel of the *k* shall be	Mt 24:14	*932*
Then shall the *k* of heaven be	Mt 25:1	*932*
For the *k* of heaven is as a man	Mt 25:14	*932*
inherit the *k* prepared for you	Mt 25:34	*932*
it new with you in my Father's *k*	Mt 26:29	*932*
the gospel of the *k* of God	Mk 1:14	*932*
and the *k* of God is at hand	Mk 1:15	*932*
if a *k* be divided against itself,	Mk 3:24	*932*
that *k* cannot stand	Mk 3:24	*932*
know the mystery of the *k* of God	Mk 4:11	*932*
And he said, So is the *k* of God	Mk 4:26	*932*
shall we liken the *k* of God	Mk 4:30	*932*
it thee, unto the half of my *k*	Mk 6:23	*932*
seen the *k* of God come with power	Mk 9:1	*932*
into the *k* of God with one eye	Mk 9:47	*932*
for of such is the *k* of God	Mk 10:14	*932*
the *k* of God as a little child	Mk 10:15	*932*
riches enter into the *k* of God	Mk 10:23	*932*
riches to enter into the *k* of God	Mk 10:24	*932*
man to enter into the *k* of God	Mk 10:25	*932*
Blessed be the *k* of our father	Mk 11:10	*932*
art not far from the *k* of God	Mk 12:34	*932*
nation, and *k* against *k*	Mk 13:8	*932*
I drink it new in the *k* of God	Mk 14:25	*932*
also waited for the *k* of God	Mk 15:43	*932*
of his *k* there shall be no end	Lk 1:33	*932*
I must preach the *k* of God to	Lk 4:43	*932*
for yours is the *k* of God	Lk 6:20	*932*
the *k* of God is greater than he	Lk 7:28	*932*
the glad tidings of the *k* of God	Lk 8:1	*932*
the mysteries of the *k* of God	Lk 8:10	*932*
sent them to preach the *k* of God	Lk 9:2	*932*
spake unto them of the *k* of God	Lk 9:11	*932*
death, till they see the *k* of God	Lk 9:27	*932*
go thou and preach the *k* of God	Lk 9:60	*932*
back, is fit for the *k* of God	Lk 9:62	*932*
The *k* of God is come nigh unto	Lk 10:9	*932*
that the *k* of God is come nigh	Lk 10:11	*932*
Thy *k* come	Lk 11:2	*932*
Every *k* divided against itself is	Lk 11:17	*932*
himself, how shall his *k* stand	Lk 11:18	*932*
no doubt the *k* of God is come	Lk 11:20	*932*
But rather seek ye the *k* of God	Lk 12:31	*932*
good pleasure to give you the *k*	Lk 12:32	*932*
Unto what is the *k* of God like	Lk 13:18	*932*
shall I liken the *k* of God	Lk 13:20	*932*
all the prophets, in the *k* of God	Lk 13:28	*932*
and shall sit down in the *k* of God	Lk 13:29	*932*
shall eat bread in the *k* of God	Lk 14:15	*932*
time the *k* of God is preached	Lk 16:16	*932*
when the *k* of God should come, he	Lk 17:20	*932*
The *k* of God cometh not with	Lk 17:20	*932*
the *k* of God is within you	Lk 17:21	*932*
for of such is the *k* of God	Lk 18:16	*932*
k of God as a little child shall	Lk 18:17	*932*
riches enter into the *k* of God	Lk 18:24	*932*
man to enter into the *k* of God	Lk 18:25	*932*
for the *k* of God's sake,	Lk 18:29	*932*
the *k* of God should immediately	Lk 19:11	*932*
to receive for himself a *k*	Lk 19:12	*932*
returned, having received the *k*	Lk 19:15	*932*
nation, and *k* against *k*	Lk 21:10	*932*
know ye that the *k* of God is nigh	Lk 21:31	*932*
it be fulfilled in the *k* of God	Lk 22:16	*932*
until the *k* of God shall come	Lk 22:18	*932*
And I appoint unto you a *k*	Lk 22:29	*932*
eat and drink at my table in my *k*	Lk 22:30	*932*
me when thou comest into thy *k*	Lk 23:42	*932*
himself waited for the *k* of God	Lk 23:51	*932*
again, he cannot see the *k* of God	Jn 3:3	*932*
he cannot enter into the *k* of God	Jn 3:5	*932*
My *k* is not of this world	Jn 18:36	*932*
if my *k* were of this world, then	Jn 18:36	*932*
but now is my *k* not from hence	Jn 18:36	*932*
things pertaining to the *k* of God	Acts 1:3	*932*
restore again the *k* to Israel	Acts 1:6	*932*
things concerning the *k* of God	Acts 8:12	*932*
enter into the *k* of God	Acts 14:22	*932*
things concerning the *k* of God	Acts 19:8	*932*
have gone preaching the *k* of God	Acts 20:25	*932*
and testified the *k* of God	Acts 28:23	*932*
Preaching the *k* of God, and	Acts 28:31	*932*
For the *k* of God is not meat and	Rom 14:17	*932*
For the *k* of God is not in word,	1Cor 4:20	*932*
shall not inherit the *k* of God	1Cor 6:9	*932*
shall inherit the *k* of God	1Cor 6:10	*932*
have delivered up the *k* to God	1Cor 15:24	*932*
blood cannot inherit the *k* of God	1Cor 15:50	*932*
shall not inherit the *k* of God	Gal 5:21	*932*
inheritance in the *k* of Christ	Eph 5:5	*932*
us into the *k* of his dear Son	Col 1:13	*932*
fellow workers unto the *k* of God	Col 4:11	*932*
who hath called you unto his *k*	1Th 2:12	*932*
be counted worthy of the *k* of God	2Th 1:5	*932*
dead at his appearing and his *k*	2Ti 4:1	*932*
preserve me unto his heavenly *k*	2Ti 4:18	*932*
is the sceptre of thy *k*	Heb 1:8	*932*
a *k* which cannot be moved	Heb 12:28	*932*
heirs of the *k* which he hath	Jas 2:5	*932*
the everlasting *k* of our Lord	2Pet 1:11	*932*
in tribulation, and in the *k*	Rev 1:9	*932*
the *k* of our God, and the power of	Rev 12:10	*932*
his *k* was full of darkness	Rev 16:10	*932*
which have received no *k* as yet	Rev 17:12	*932*
give their *k* unto the beast,	Rev 17:17	*932*

KINGDOMS {57}

all the *k* whither thou passest	Deut 3:21	4467
into all the *k* of the earth	Deut 28:25	4467
was the head of all those *k*	Josh 11:10	4467
and out of the hand of all *k*	1Sa 10:18	4467
Solomon reigned over all *k* from	1Kin 4:21	4467
of all the *k* of the earth	2Kin 19:15	4467
that all the *k* of the earth may	2Kin 19:19	4467
over all the *k* of the countries	1Chr 29:30	4467
service of the *k* of the countries	2Chr 12:8	4467
k of the lands that were round	2Chr 17:10	4467
over all the *k* of the heathen	2Chr 20:6	4467
on all the *k* of those countries	2Chr 20:29	4467
All the *k* of the earth hath the	2Chr 36:23	4467
given me all the *k* of the earth	Ezr 1:2	4467
Moreover thou gavest them *k*	Neh 9:22	4467
heathen raged, the *k* were moved	Ps 46:6	4467
Sing unto God, ye *k* of the earth	Ps 68:32	4467
upon the *k* that have not called	Ps 79:6	4467
are gathered together, and the *k*	Ps 102:22	4467
of Bashan, and all the *k* of Canaan	Ps 135:11	4467
hath found the *k* of the idols	Is 10:10	4467
a tumultuous noise of the *k* of	Is 13:4	4467
And Babylon, the glory of *k*	Is 13:19	4467
to tremble, that did shake *k*	Is 14:16	4467
hand over the sea, he shook the *k*	Is 23:11	4467
k of the world upon the face of	Is 23:17	4467
of all the *k* of the earth	Is 37:16	4467
that all the *k* of the earth may	Is 37:20	4467
no more be called, The lady of *k*	Is 47:5	4467
over the nations and over the *k*	Jer 1:10	4467
families of the *k* of the north	Jer 1:15	4467
of the nations, and in all their *k*	Jer 10:7	4467
removed into all *k* of the earth	Jer 15:4	4467
the *k* of the earth for their hurt	Jer 24:9	4467
all the *k* of the world, which are	Jer 25:26	4467
countries, and against great *k*	Jer 28:8	4467
removed to all the *k* of the earth	Jer 29:18	4467
all the *k* of the earth of his	Jer 34:1	4467
into all the *k* of the earth	Jer 34:17	4467
and concerning the *k* of Hazor	Jer 49:28	4467
and with thee will I destroy *k*	Jer 51:20	4467
against her the *k* of Ararat	Jer 51:27	4467
It shall be the basest of the *k*	Eze 29:15	4467
into two *k* any more at all	Eze 37:22	4467
in pieces and consume all these *k*	Dan 2:44	4437
which shall be diverse from all *k*	Dan 7:23	4437
four *k* shall stand up out of the	Dan 8:22	4438
be they better than these *k*	Amos 6:2	4467
thy nakedness, and the *k* thy shame	Nah 3:5	4467
that I may assemble the *k*	Zeph 3:8	4467
I will overthrow the throne of *k*	Hag 2:22	4467
strength of the *k* of the heathen	Hag 2:22	4467
him all the *k* of the world	Mt 4:8	*932*
shewed unto him all the *k* of the	Lk 4:5	*932*
Who through faith subdued *k*	Heb 11:33	*932*
The *k* of this world are become	Rev 11:15	*932*
are become the *k* of our Lord	Rev 11:15	*932*

KINGLY {1}

he was deposed from his *k* throne	Dan 5:20	4437

KING'S {284}

of Shaveh, which is the *k* dale	Gen 14:17	4428
a place where the *k* prisoners	Gen 39:20	4428
we will go by the *k* high way	Num 20:17	4428
will go along by the *k* high way	Num 21:22	4428
now therefore be the *k* son in law	1Sa 18:22	4428
light thing to be a *k* son in law	1Sa 18:23	4428
to be avenged of the *k* enemies	1Sa 18:25	4428
David well to be the *k* son in law	1Sa 18:26	4428
that he might be the *k* son in law	1Sa 18:27	4428
he cometh not unto the *k* table	1Sa 20:29	4428
because the *k* business required	1Sa 21:8	4428
David, which is the *k* son in law	1Sa 22:14	4428
be to deliver him into the *k* hand	1Sa 23:20	4428
And now see where the *k* spear is	1Sa 26:16	4428
and said, Behold the *k* spear	1Sa 26:22	4428
at my table, as one of the *k* sons	2Sa 9:11	4428
eat continually at the *k* table	2Sa 9:13	4428
upon the roof of the *k* house	2Sa 11:2	4428
Uriah departed out of the *k* house	2Sa 11:8	4428
k house with all the servants of	2Sa 11:9	4428
if so be that the *k* wrath arise	2Sa 11:20	4428
some of the *k* servants be dead,	2Sa 11:24	4428
he took their *k* crown from off	2Sa 12:30	4428
Why art thou, being the *k* son	2Sa 13:4	4428
the *k* daughters that were virgins	2Sa 13:18	4428
and Absalom invited all the *k* sons	2Sa 13:23	4428
all the *k* sons go with him	2Sa 13:27	4428
Then all the *k* sons arose	2Sa 13:29	4428
Absalom hath slain all the *k* sons	2Sa 13:30	4428
all the young men the *k* sons	2Sa 13:32	4428
that all the *k* sons are dead	2Sa 13:33	4428
the king, Behold, the *k* sons come	2Sa 13:35	4428
the *k* sons came, and lifted up	2Sa 13:36	4428
the *k* heart was toward Absalom	2Sa 14:1	4428
own house, and saw not the *k* face	2Sa 14:24	4428
shekels after the *k* weight	2Sa 14:26	4428
Jerusalem, and saw not the *k* face	2Sa 14:28	4428
therefore let me see the *k* face	2Sa 14:32	4428
the *k* servants said unto the king	2Sa 15:15	4428
shalt hear out of the *k* house	2Sa 15:35	4428
be for the *k* household to ride on	2Sa 16:2	4428
forth mine hand against the *k* son	2Sa 18:12	4428
a pillar, which is in the *k* dale	2Sa 18:18	4428
because the *k* son is dead	2Sa 18:20	4428
When Joab sent the *k* servant	2Sa 18:29	4428
to carry over the *k* household	2Sa 19:18	4428
we eaten at all of the *k* cost	2Sa 19:42	4428
Notwithstanding the *k* word	2Sa 24:4	4428
all his brethren the *k* sons	1Kin 1:9	4428
the men of Judah the *k* servants	1Kin 1:9	4428
and hath called all the *k* sons	1Kin 1:25	4428
And she came into the *k* presence	1Kin 1:28	4428
him to ride upon the *k* mule	1Kin 1:44	4428
moreover the *k* servants came to	1Kin 1:47	4428
a seat to be set for the *k* mother	1Kin 2:19	4428
officer, and the *k* friend	1Kin 4:5	4428
the *k* house, and all Solomon's	1Kin 9:1	4428
of the LORD, and the *k* house,	1Kin 9:10	4428
of the LORD, and for the *k* house	1Kin 10:12	4428
the *k* merchants received the	1Kin 10:28	4428
he was of the *k* seed in Edom	1Kin 11:14	4428
the *k* hand was restored him again	1Kin 13:6	4428
and the treasures of the *k* house	1Kin 14:26	4428
kept the door of the *k* house	1Kin 14:27	4428
and the treasures of the *k* house	1Kin 15:18	4428
into the palace of the *k* house	1Kin 16:18	4428
burnt the *k* house over him with	1Kin 16:18	4428
shall deliver it into the *k* hand	1Kin 22:12	4428
the city, and to Joash the *k* son	1Kin 22:26	4428
we may go and tell the *k* household	2Kin 7:9	4428
told it to the *k* house within	2Kin 7:11	4428
for she is a *k* daughter	2Kin 9:34	4428
Now the *k* sons, being seventy	2Kin 10:6	4428
them, that they took the *k* sons	2Kin 10:7	4428
brought the heads of the *k* sons	2Kin 10:8	4428
among the *k* sons which were slain	2Kin 11:2	4428
LORD, and shewed them the *k* son	2Kin 11:4	4428
of the watch of the *k* house	2Kin 11:5	4428
And he brought forth the *k* son	2Kin 11:12	4428
the horses came into the *k* house	2Kin 11:16	4428
gate of the guard to the *k* house	2Kin 11:19	4428
with the sword beside the *k* house	2Kin 11:20	4428
in the chest, that the *k* scribe	2Kin 12:10	4428
of the LORD, and in the *k* house	2Kin 12:18	4428
put his hands upon the *k* hands	2Kin 13:16	4428
in the treasures of the *k* house	2Kin 14:14	4428
Jotham the *k* son was over the	2Kin 15:5	4428
in the palace of the *k* house	2Kin 15:25	4428
in the treasures of the *k* house	2Kin 16:8	4428
the *k* burnt sacrifice, and his	2Kin 16:15	4428
the *k* entry without, turned he	2Kin 16:18	4428
in the treasures of the *k* house	2Kin 18:15	4428
for the *k* commandment was, saying	2Kin 18:36	4428
and Asahiah a servant of the *k*	2Kin 22:12	4428
and the treasures of the *k* house	2Kin 24:13	4428

K

the *k* mother, and the *k* wives	2Kin 24:15	4428
walls, which is by the *k* garden	2Kin 25:4	4428
the *k* house, and all the houses of	2Kin 25:9	4428
them that were in the *k* presence	2Kin 25:19	4428
waited in the *k* gate eastward	1Chr 9:18	4428
Nevertheless the *k* word prevailed	1Chr 21:4	4428
for the *k* word was abominable to	1Chr 21:6	4428
the *k* seer in the words of God	1Chr 25:5	4428
according to the *k* order to Asaph	1Chr 25:6	4428
over the *k* treasures was Azmaveth	1Chr 27:25	4428
of Hachmoni was with the *k* sons	1Chr 27:32	4428
Ahithophel was the *k* counsellor	1Chr 27:33	4428
the Archite was the *k* companion	1Chr 27:33	4428
general of the *k* army was Joab	1Chr 27:34	4428
with the rulers of the *k* work	1Chr 29:6	4428
the *k* merchants received the	2Chr 1:16	4428
house of the LORD, and the *k* house	2Chr 7:11	4428
of the LORD, and to the *k* palace	2Chr 9:11	4428
For the *k* ships went to Tarshish	2Chr 9:21	4428
and the treasures of the *k* house	2Chr 12:9	4428
kept the entrance of the *k* house	2Chr 12:10	4428
of the LORD and of the *k* house	2Chr 16:2	4428
will deliver it into the *k* hand	2Chr 18:5	4428
the city, and to Joash the *k* son	2Chr 18:25	4428
of Judah, for all the *k* matters	2Chr 19:11	4428
that was found in the *k* house	2Chr 21:17	4428
among the *k* sons that were slain	2Chr 22:11	4428
the *k* son shall reign, as the	2Chr 23:3	4428
part shall be at the *k* house	2Chr 23:5	4428
Then they brought out the *k* son	2Chr 23:11	4428
of the horse gate by the *k* house	2Chr 23:15	4428
the high gate into the *k* house	2Chr 23:20	4428
at the *k* commandment they made a	2Chr 24:8	4428
the *k* office by the hand of the	2Chr 24:11	4428
the *k* scribe and the high priest's	2Chr 24:11	4428
Art thou made of the *k* counsel	2Chr 25:16	4428
and the treasures of the *k* house	2Chr 25:24	4428
Hananiah, one of the *k* captains	2Chr 26:11	4428
his son was over the *k* house	2Chr 26:21	4428
Ephraim, slew Maaseiah the *k* son	2Chr 28:7	4428
of David, and of Gad the *k* seer	2Chr 29:25	4428
He appointed also the *k* portion	2Chr 31:3	4428
and Asaiah a servant of the *k*	2Chr 34:20	4428
these were of the *k* substance	2Chr 35:7	4428
according to the *k* commandment	2Chr 35:10	4428
and Heman, and Jeduthun the *k* seer	2Chr 35:15	4428
maintenance from the *k* palace	Ezr 4:14	4430
for us to see the *k* dishonour	Ezr 4:14	4430
made in the *k* treasure house	Ezr 5:17	4430
be given out of the *k* house	Ezr 6:4	4430
that of the *k* goods, even of the	Ezr 6:8	4430
it out of the *k* treasure house	Ezr 7:20	4430
a thing as this in the *k* heart	Ezr 7:27	4428
before all the *k* mighty princes	Ezr 7:28	4428
they delivered the *k* commissions	Ezr 8:36	4428
unto the *k* lieutenants, and to the	Ezr 8:36	4428
For I was the *k* cupbearer	Neh 1:11	4428
Asaph the keeper of the *k* forest	Neh 2:8	4428
river, and gave them the *k* letters	Neh 2:9	4428
of the fountain, and to the *k* pool	Neh 2:14	4428
as also the *k* words that he had	Neh 2:18	4428
pool of Siloah by the *k* garden	Neh 3:15	4428
lieth out from the *k* high house	Neh 3:25	4428
borrowed money for the *k* tribute	Neh 5:4	4428
For it was the *k* commandment	Neh 11:23	4428
was at the *k* hand in all matters	Neh 11:24	4428
of the garden of the *k* palace	Est 1:5	4428
Vashti refused to come at the *k*	Est 1:12	4428
(for so was the *k* manner toward	Est 1:13	4428
and Media, which saw the *k* face	Est 1:14	4428
this day unto all the *k* princes	Est 1:18	4428
when the *k* decree which he shall	Est 1:20	4428
letters into all the *k* provinces	Est 1:22	4428
Then said the *k* servants that	Est 2:2	4428
custody of Hege the *k* chamberlain	Est 2:3	4428
when the *k* commandment and his	Est 2:8	4428
was brought also unto the *k* house	Est 2:8	4428
be given her, out of the *k* house	Est 2:9	4428
of the women unto the *k* house	Est 2:13	4428
the *k* chamberlain, which kept the	Est 2:14	4428
but what Hegai the *k* chamberlain	Est 2:15	4428
then Mordecai sat in the *k* gate	Est 2:19	4428
while Mordecai sat in the *k* gate	Est 2:21	4428
two of the *k* chamberlains,	Est 2:21	4428
all the *k* servants, that were in	Est 3:2	4428
servants, that were in the *k* gate	Est 3:2	4428
Then the *k* servants, which were	Est 3:3	4428
which were in the *k* gate	Est 3:3	4428
thou the *k* commandment	Est 3:3	4428
neither keep they the *k* laws	Est 3:8	4428
for the *k* profit to suffer them	Est 3:8	4428
to bring it into the *k* treasuries	Est 3:9	4428
Then were the *k* scribes called on	Est 3:12	4428
commanded unto the *k* lieutenants	Est 3:12	4428
and sealed with the *k* ring	Est 3:12	4428
by posts into all the *k* provinces	Est 3:13	4428
hastened by the *k* commandment	Est 3:15	4428
And came even before the *k* gate	Est 4:2	4428
the *k* gate clothed with sackcloth	Est 4:2	4428
whithersoever the *k* commandment	Est 4:3	4428
one of the *k* chamberlains, whom	Est 4:5	4428
city, which was before the *k* gate	Est 4:6	4428
to the *k* treasuries for the Jews	Est 4:7	4428
All the *k* servants, and the people	Est 4:11	4428
and the people of the *k* provinces	Est 4:11	4428
thou shalt escape in the *k* house	Est 4:13	4428
in the inner court of the *k* house	Est 5:1	4428
over against the *k* house	Est 5:1	4428
Haman saw Mordecai in the *k* gate	Est 5:9	4428
the Jew sitting at the *k* gate	Est 5:13	4428
two of the *k* chamberlains, the	Est 6:2	4428
Then said the *k* servants that	Est 6:3	4428
the outward court of the *k* house	Est 6:4	4428
the *k* servants said unto him,	Est 6:5	4428
one of the *k* most noble princes	Est 6:9	4428
Jew, that sitteth at the *k* gate	Est 6:10	4428
Mordecai came again to the *k* gate	Est 6:12	4428
came the *k* chamberlains, and	Est 6:14	4428
not countervail the *k* damage	Est 7:4	4428
the word went out of the *k* mouth	Est 7:8	4428
Then was the *k* wrath pacified	Est 7:10	4428
which are in all the *k* provinces	Est 8:5	4428
as it liketh you, in the *k* name	Est 8:8	4428
and seal it with the *k* ring	Est 8:8	4428
which is written in the *k* name	Est 8:8	4428
and sealed with the *k* ring	Est 8:8	4428
Then were the *k* scribes called at	Est 8:9	4428
and sealed it with the *k* ring	Est 8:10	4428
pressed on by the *k* commandment	Est 8:14	4428
whithersoever the *k* commandment	Est 8:17	4428
when the *k* commandment and his	Est 9:1	4428
Mordecai was great in the *k* house	Est 9:4	4428
in the rest of the *k* provinces	Est 9:12	4428
k provinces gathered themselves	Est 9:16	4428
in the heart of the *k* enemies	Ps 45:5	4428
The *k* daughter is all glorious	Ps 45:13	4428
shall enter into the *k* palace	Ps 45:15	4428
Thou wilt prolong the *k* life	Ps 61:6	4428
thy righteousness unto the *k* son	Ps 72:1	4428
The *k* strength also loveth	Ps 99:4	4428
of people is the *k* honour	Prov 14:28	4428
The *k* favour is toward a wise	Prov 14:35	4428
of the *k* countenance is life	Prov 16:15	4428
The *k* wrath is as the roaring of	Prov 19:12	4428
The *k* heart is in the hand of the	Prov 21:1	4428
thee to keep the *k* commandment	Eccl 8:2	4428
for the *k* commandment was, saying	Is 36:21	4428
LORD unto the *k* house of Judah	Jer 22:6	4428
then they came up from the *k*	Jer 26:10	4428
he went down into the *k* house	Jer 36:12	4428
eunuchs which was in the *k* house	Jer 38:7	4428
went forth out of the *k* house	Jer 38:8	4428
night, by the way of the *k* garden	Jer 39:4	4428
the Chaldeans burned the *k* house	Jer 39:8	4428
even the *k* daughters, and all the	Jer 41:10	4428
the *k* daughters, and every person	Jer 43:6	4428
walls, which was by the *k* garden	Jer 52:7	4428
house of the LORD, and the *k* house	Jer 52:13	4428
them that were near the *k* person	Jer 52:25	4428
And hath taken of the *k* seed	Eze 17:13	4410
of Israel, and of the *k* seed	Dan 1:3	4410
in them to stand in the *k* palace	Dan 1:4	4428
a daily provision of the *k* meat	Dan 1:5	4428
with the portion of the *k* meat	Dan 1:8	4428
eat of the portion of the *k* meat	Dan 1:13	4428
did eat the portion of the *k* meat	Dan 1:15	4428
earth that can shew the *k* matter	Dan 2:10	4430
Arioch the captain of the *k* guard	Dan 2:14	4430
and said to Arioch the *k* captain	Dan 2:15	4430
made known unto us the *k* matter	Dan 2:23	4430
Therefore because the *k*	Dan 3:22	4430
the *k* counsellors, being gathered	Dan 3:27	4430
him, and have changed the *k* word	Dan 3:28	4430
While the word was in the *k* mouth	Dan 4:31	4430
of the wall of the *k* palace	Dan 5:5	4430
Then the *k* countenance was	Dan 5:6	4430
Then came in all the *k* wise men	Dan 5:8	4430
the king concerning the *k* decree	Dan 6:12	4430
I rose up, and did the *k* business	Dan 8:27	4428
for the *k* daughter of the south	Dan 11:6	4428
latter growth after the *k* mowings	Amos 7:1	4428
for it is the *k* chapel	Amos 7:13	4428
and it is the *k* court	Amos 7:13	4467
the *k* children, and all such as	Zeph 1:8	4428
Hananeel unto the *k* winepresses	Zec 14:10	4428
having made Blastus the *k*	Acts 12:20	*935*
was nourished by the *k* country	Acts 12:20	*937*
not afraid of the *k* commandment	Heb 11:23	*935*

KINGS {329}

the *k* that were with him, and	Gen 14:5	4428
four *k* with five	Gen 14:9	4428
the *k* of Sodom and Gomorrah fled,	Gen 14:10	4428
of the *k* that were with him, at	Gen 14:17	4428
thee, and *k* shall come out of thee	Gen 17:6	4428
k of people shall be of her	Gen 17:16	4428
k shall come out of thy loins	Gen 35:11	4428
these are the *k* that reigned in	Gen 36:31	4428
And they slew the *k* of Midian	Num 31:8	4428
and Hur, and Reba, five *k* of Midian	Num 31:8	4428
k of the Amorites the land that	Deut 3:8	4428
God hath done unto these two *k*	Deut 3:21	4428
two *k* of the Amorites, which were	Deut 4:47	4428
deliver their *k* into thine hand	Deut 7:24	4428
k of the Amorites, and unto the	Deut 31:4	4428
unto the two *k* of the Amorites	Josh 2:10	4428
when all the *k* of the Amorites,	Josh 5:1	4428
all the *k* of the Canaanites,	Josh 5:1	4428
when all the *k* which were on this	Josh 9:1	4428
did to the two *k* of the Amorites	Josh 9:10	4428
the five *k* of the Amorites	Josh 10:5	4428
for all the *k* of the Amorites	Josh 10:6	4428
But these five *k* fled, and hid	Josh 10:16	4428
The five *k* are found hid in a	Josh 10:17	4428
bring out those five *k* unto me	Josh 10:22	4428
five *k* unto him out of the cave	Josh 10:23	4428
brought out those *k* unto Joshua	Josh 10:24	4428
feet upon the necks of these *k*	Josh 10:24	4428
and of the springs, and all their *k*	Josh 10:40	4428
And all these *k* and their land did	Josh 10:42	4428
to the *k* that were on the north	Josh 11:2	4428
when all these *k* were met	Josh 11:5	4428
those *k*, and all the *k* of them	Josh 11:12	4428
and all their *k* he took, and smote	Josh 11:17	4428
war a long time with all those *k*	Josh 11:18	4428
Now these are the *k* of the land	Josh 12:1	4428
these are the *k* of the country	Josh 12:7	4428
all the *k* thirty and one	Josh 12:24	4428
even the two *k* of the Amorites	Josh 24:12	4428
said, Threescore and ten *k*	Judg 1:7	4428
Hear, O ye *k*	Judg 5:3	4428
The *k* came and fought	Judg 5:19	4428
then fought the *k* of Canaan in	Judg 5:19	4428
Zebah and Zalmunna, *k* of Midian	Judg 8:5	4428
them, and took the two *k* of Midian	Judg 8:12	4428
that was on the *k* of Midian	Judg 8:26	4428
Edom, and against the *k* of Zobah	1Sa 14:47	4428
unto the *k* of Judah unto this day	1Sa 27:6	4428
when all the *k* that were servants	2Sa 10:19	4428
at the time when *k* go forth to	2Sa 11:1	4428
shall not be any among the *k* like	1Kin 3:13	4428
over all the *k* on this side the	1Kin 4:24	4428
from all *k* of the earth, which	1Kin 4:34	4428
and of all the *k* of Arabia	1Kin 10:15	4428
all the *k* of the earth for riches	1Kin 10:23	4428
so for all the *k* of the Hittites,	1Kin 10:29	4428
for the *k* of Syria, did they	1Kin 10:29	4428
the chronicles of the *k* of Israel	1Kin 14:19	4428
the chronicles of the *k* of Judah	1Kin 14:29	4428
the chronicles of the *k* of Judah	1Kin 15:7	4428
the chronicles of the *k* of Judah	1Kin 15:23	4428
the chronicles of the *k* of Israel	1Kin 15:31	4428
the chronicles of the *k* of Israel	1Kin 16:5	4428
the chronicles of the *k* of Israel	1Kin 16:14	4428
the chronicles of the *k* of Israel	1Kin 16:20	4428
the chronicles of the *k* of Israel	1Kin 16:27	4428
k of Israel that were before him	1Kin 16:33	4428
two *k* with him, and horses, and	1Kin 20:1	4428
the *k* in the pavilions, that he	1Kin 20:12	4428
in the pavilions, he and the *k*	1Kin 20:16	4428
thirty and two *k* that helped him	1Kin 20:16	4428
And do this thing, Take the *k* away	1Kin 20:24	4428
we have heard that the *k* of the	1Kin 20:31	4428
house of Israel are merciful *k*	1Kin 20:31	4428
the chronicles of the *k* of Israel	1Kin 22:39	4428
the chronicles of the *k* of Judah	1Kin 22:45	4428
the chronicles of the *k* of Israel	2Kin 1:18	4428
called these three *k* together	2Kin 3:10	4428
called these three *k* together	2Kin 3:13	4428
k were come up to fight against	2Kin 3:21	4428
the *k* are surely slain, and they	2Kin 3:23	4428
against us the *k* of the Hittites	2Kin 7:6	4428
the *k* of the Egyptians, to come	2Kin 7:6	4428
in the way of the *k* of Israel	2Kin 8:18	4428
the chronicles of the *k* of Judah	2Kin 8:23	4428
two *k* stood not before him	2Kin 10:4	4428
the chronicles of the *k* of Israel	2Kin 10:34	4428
And he sat on the throne of the *k*	2Kin 11:19	4428
k of Judah, had dedicated, and his	2Kin 12:18	4428
the chronicles of the *k* of Judah	2Kin 12:19	4428
the chronicles of the *k* of Israel	2Kin 13:8	4428
the chronicles of the *k* of Israel	2Kin 13:12	4428
in Samaria with the *k* of Israel	2Kin 13:13	4428
the chronicles of the *k* of Israel	2Kin 14:15	4428
in Samaria with the *k* of Israel	2Kin 14:16	4428
the chronicles of the *k* of Judah	2Kin 14:18	4428
the chronicles of the *k* of Israel	2Kin 14:28	4428
even with the *k* of Israel	2Kin 14:29	4428
the chronicles of the *k* of Judah	2Kin 15:6	4428
the chronicles of the *k* of Israel	2Kin 15:11	4428
the chronicles of the *k* of Israel	2Kin 15:15	4428
the chronicles of the *k* of Israel	2Kin 15:21	4428
the chronicles of the *k* of Israel	2Kin 15:26	4428
the chronicles of the *k* of Israel	2Kin 15:31	4428
the chronicles of the *k* of Judah	2Kin 15:36	4428
in the way of the *k* of Israel	2Kin 16:3	4428
the chronicles of the *k* of Judah	2Kin 16:19	4428
but not as the *k* of Israel that	2Kin 17:2	4428
of the *k* of Israel, which they	2Kin 17:8	4428
like him among all the *k* of Judah	2Kin 18:5	4428
thou hast heard what the *k* of	2Kin 19:11	4428
the *k* of Assyria have destroyed	2Kin 19:17	4428
the chronicles of the *k* of Judah	2Kin 20:20	4428
the chronicles of the *k* of Judah	2Kin 21:17	4428
the chronicles of the *k* of Judah	2Kin 21:25	4428
whom the *k* of Judah had ordained	2Kin 23:5	4428
k of Judah had given to the sun	2Kin 23:11	4428
which the *k* of Judah had made, and	2Kin 23:12	4428
which the *k* of Israel had made to	2Kin 23:19	4428
all the days of the *k* of Israel	2Kin 23:22	4428
nor of the *k* of Judah	2Kin 23:22	4428
the chronicles of the *k* of Judah	2Kin 23:28	4428
the chronicles of the *k* of Judah	2Kin 24:5	4428
k that were with him in Babylon	2Kin 25:28	4428
Now these are the *k* that reigned	1Chr 1:43	4428
in the book of the *k* of Israel	1Chr 9:1	4428
he reproved *k* for their sakes,	1Chr 16:21	4428
the *k* that were come were by	1Chr 19:9	4428
the time that *k* go out to battle	1Chr 20:1	4428
such as none of the *k* have had	2Chr 1:12	4428
for all the *k* of the Hittites	2Chr 1:17	4428
for the *k* of Syria, by their	2Chr 1:17	4428
all the *k* of Arabia and governors	2Chr 9:14	4428
all the *k* of the earth in riches	2Chr 9:22	4428

all the *k* of the earth sought the ... 2Chr 9:23 4428
he reigned over all the *k* from ... 2Chr 9:26 4428
in the book of the *k* of Judah ... 2Chr 16:11 4428
in the book of the *k* of Israel ... 2Chr 20:34 4428
in the way of the *k* of Israel ... 2Chr 21:6 4428
in the way of the *k* of Israel ... 2Chr 21:13 4428
not in the sepulchres of the *k* ... 2Chr 21:20 4428
in the city of David among the *k* ... 2Chr 24:16 4428
not in the sepulchres of the *k* ... 2Chr 24:25 4428
in the story of the book of the *k* ... 2Chr 24:27 4428
in the book of the *k* of Judah ... 2Chr 25:26 4428
burial which belonged to the *k* ... 2Chr 26:23 4428
in the book of the *k* of Israel ... 2Chr 27:7 4428
in the ways of the *k* of Israel ... 2Chr 28:2 4428
unto the *k* of Assyria to help him ... 2Chr 28:16 4428
gods of the *k* of Syria help them ... 2Chr 28:23 4428
in the book of the *k* of Judah ... 2Chr 28:26 4428
the sepulchres of the *k* of Israel ... 2Chr 28:27 4428
of the hand of the *k* of Assyria ... 2Chr 30:6 4428
Why should the *k* of Assyria come, ... 2Chr 32:4 4428
and in the book of the *k* of Judah ... 2Chr 32:32 4428
in the book of the *k* of Israel ... 2Chr 33:18 4428
the *k* of Judah had destroyed ... 2Chr 34:11 4428
neither did all the *k* of Israel ... 2Chr 35:18 4428
in the book of the *k* of Israel ... 2Chr 35:27 4428
in the book of the *k* of Israel ... 2Chr 36:8 4428
endamage the revenue of the *k* ... Ezr 4:13 4430
city, and hurtful unto *k* and ... Ezr 4:15 4430
hath made insurrection against *k* ... Ezr 4:19 4430
been mighty *k* also over Jerusalem ... Ezr 4:20 4430
damage grow to the hurt of the *k* ... Ezr 4:22 4430
name to dwell there destroy all *k* ... Ezr 6:12 4430
Artaxerxes, king of *k*, unto Ezra ... Ezr 7:12 4428
for our iniquities have we, our *k* ... Ezr 9:7 4428
the hand of the *k* of the lands ... Ezr 9:7 4428
in the sight of the *k* of Persia ... Ezr 9:9 4428
into their hands, with their *k* ... Neh 9:24 4428
that hath come upon us, on our *k* ... Neh 9:32 4428
since the time of the *k* of ... Neh 9:32 4428
Neither have our *k*, our princes, ... Neh 9:34 4428
the *k* whom thou hast set over us ... Neh 9:37 4428
the chronicles of the *k* of Media ... Est 10:2 4428
With *k* and counsellors of the ... Job 3:14 4428
He looseth the bond of *k*, and ... Job 12:18 4428
but with *k* are they on the throne ... Job 36:7 4428
The *k* of the earth set themselves ... Ps 2:2 4428
Be wise now therefore, O ye *k* ... Ps 2:10 4428
the *k* were assembled, they passed ... Ps 48:4 4428
K of armies did flee apace ... Ps 68:12 4428
the Almighty scattered *k* in it ... Ps 68:14 4428
shall *k* bring presents unto thee ... Ps 68:29 4428
The *k* of Tarshish and of the isles ... Ps 72:10 4428
the *k* of Sheba and Seba shall ... Ps 72:10 4428
all *k* shall fall down before him ... Ps 72:11 4428
is terrible to the *k* of the earth ... Ps 76:12 4428
higher than the *k* of the earth ... Ps 89:27 4428
all the *k* of the earth thy glory ... Ps 102:15 4428
he reproved *k* for their sakes ... Ps 105:14 4428
in the chambers of their *k* ... Ps 105:30 4428
through *k* in the day of his wrath ... Ps 110:5 4428
of thy testimonies also before *k* ... Ps 119:46 4428
great nations, and slew mighty *k* ... Ps 135:10 4428
To him which smote great *k* ... Ps 136:17 4428
And slew famous *k* ... Ps 136:18 4428
All the *k* of the earth shall ... Ps 138:4 4428
he that giveth salvation unto *k* ... Ps 144:10 4428
K of the earth, and all people ... Ps 148:11 4428
To bind their *k* with chains ... Ps 149:8 4428
By me *k* reign, and princes decree ... Prov 8:15 4428
to *k* to commit wickedness ... Prov 16:12 4428
lips are the delight of *k* ... Prov 16:13 4428
he shall stand before *k* ... Prov 22:29 4428
but the honour of *k* is to search ... Prov 25:2 4428
the heart of *k* is unsearchable ... Prov 25:3 4428
ways to that which destroyeth *k* ... Prov 31:3 4428
It is not for *k*, O Lemuel, it is ... Prov 31:4 4428
it is not for *k* to drink wine ... Prov 31:4 4428
and the peculiar treasure of *k* ... Eccl 2:8 4428
Ahaz, and Hezekiah, *k* of Judah ... Is 1:1 4428
shall be forsaken of both her *k* ... Is 7:16 4428
Are not my princes altogether *k* ... Is 10:8 4428
thrones all the *k* of the nations ... Is 14:9 4428
All the *k* of the nations, even ... Is 14:18 4428
of the wise, the son of ancient *k* ... Is 19:11 4428
the *k* of the earth upon the earth ... Is 24:21 4428
thou hast heard what the *k* of ... Is 37:11 4428
the *k* of Assyria have laid waste ... Is 37:18 4428
him, and made him rule over *k* ... Is 41:2 4428
and I will loose the loins of *k* ... Is 45:1 4428
K shall see and arise, princes ... Is 49:7 4428
k shall be thy nursing fathers, ... Is 49:23 4428
the *k* shall shut their mouths at ... Is 52:15 4428
k to the brightness of thy rising ... Is 60:3 4428
their *k* shall minister unto thee ... Is 60:10 4428
that their *k* may be brought ... Is 60:11 4428
and shalt suck the breast of *k* ... Is 60:16 4428
righteousness, and all *k* thy glory ... Is 62:2 4428
land, against the *k* of Judah ... Jer 1:18 4428
they, their *k*, their princes, and ... Jer 2:26 4428
out the bones of the *k* of Judah ... Jer 8:1 4428
even the *k* that sit upon David's ... Jer 13:13 4428
whereby the *k* of Judah come in, ... Jer 17:19 4428
ye *k* of Judah, and all Judah, and ... Jer 17:20 4428
into the gates of this city *k* ... Jer 17:25 4428
O *k* of Judah, and inhabitants of ... Jer 19:3 4428
nor the *k* of Judah, and have ... Jer 19:4 4428
and the houses of the *k* of Judah ... Jer 19:13 4428
all the treasures of the *k* of ... Jer 20:5 4428

k sitting upon the throne of ... Jer 22:4 4428
great *k* shall serve themselves of ... Jer 25:14 4428
the *k* thereof, and the princes ... Jer 25:18 4428
all the *k* of the land of Uz, and ... Jer 25:20 4428
all the *k* of the land of the ... Jer 25:20 4428
all the *k* of Tyrus ... Jer 25:22 4428
all the *k* of Zidon ... Jer 25:22 4428
the *k* of the isles which are ... Jer 25:22 4428
all the *k* of Arabia ... Jer 25:24 4428
all the *k* of the mingled people ... Jer 25:24 4428
all the *k* of Zimri ... Jer 25:25 4428
and all the *k* of Elam ... Jer 25:25 4428
and all the *k* of the Medes ... Jer 25:25 4428
all the *k* of the north, far and ... Jer 25:26 4428
great *k* shall serve themselves of ... Jer 27:7 4428
me to anger, they, their *k* ... Jer 32:32 4428
the houses of the *k* of Judah ... Jer 33:4 4428
the former *k* which were before ... Jer 34:5 4428
the wickedness of the *k* of Judah ... Jer 44:9 4428
done, we, and our fathers, our *k* ... Jer 44:17 4428
ye, and your fathers, your *k* ... Jer 44:21 4428
with their gods, and their *k* ... Jer 46:25 4428
many *k* shall be raised up from ... Jer 50:41 4428
the spirit of the *k* of the Medes ... Jer 51:11 4428
nations with the *k* of the Medes ... Jer 51:28 4428
k that were with him in Babylon ... Jer 52:32 4428
The *k* of the earth, and all the ... Lam 4:12 4428
king of Babylon, a king of *k* ... Eze 26:7 4428
thou didst enrich the *k* of the ... Eze 27:33 4428
their *k* shall be sore afraid, ... Eze 27:35 4428
ground, I will lay thee before *k* ... Eze 28:17 4428
their *k* shall be horribly afraid ... Eze 32:10 4428
There is Edom, her *k*, and all her ... Eze 32:29 4428
defile, neither they, nor their *k* ... Eze 43:7 4428
of their *k* in their high places ... Eze 43:7 4428
and the carcases of their *k* ... Eze 43:9 4428
removeth *k*, and setteth up *k* ... Dan 2:21 4430
Thou, O king, art a king of *k* ... Dan 2:37 4430
in the days of these *k* shall the ... Dan 2:44 4430
is a God of gods, and a LORD of *k* ... Dan 2:47 4430
which are four, are four *k* ... Dan 7:17 4430
are ten *k* that shall arise ... Dan 7:24 4430
first, and he shall subdue three *k* ... Dan 7:24 4430
two horns are the *k* of Media ... Dan 8:20 4428
which spake in thy name to our *k* ... Dan 9:6 4428
confusion of face, to our *k* ... Dan 9:8 4428
there with the *k* of Persia ... Dan 10:13 4428
stand up yet three *k* in Persia ... Dan 11:2 4428
k of Judah, and in the days of ... Hos 1:1 4428
all their *k* are fallen ... Hos 7:7 4428
They have set up *k*, but not by me ... Hos 8:4 4428
k of Judah, which he saw ... Mic 1:1 4428
shall be a lie to the *k* of Israel ... Mic 1:14 4428
And they shall scoff at the *k* ... Hab 1:10 4428
k for my sake, for a testimony ... Mt 10:18 *935*
of whom do the *k* of the earth ... Mt 17:25 *935*
k for my sake, for a testimony ... Mk 13:9 *935*
k have desired to see those ... Lk 10:24 *935*
prisons, being brought before *k* ... Lk 21:12 *935*
The *k* of the Gentiles exercise ... Lk 22:25 *935*
The *k* of the earth stood up, and ... Acts 4:26 *935*
my name before the Gentiles, and *k* ... Acts 9:15 *935*
ye have reigned as *k* without us ... 1Cor 4:8
For *k*, and for all that are in ... 1Ti 2:2 *935*
and only Potentate, the King of *k* ... 1Ti 6:15 *936*
from the slaughter of the *k* ... Heb 7:1 *935*
the prince of the *k* of the earth ... Rev 1:5 *935*
And hath made us *k* and priests unto ... Rev 1:6 *935*
And hast made us unto our God *k* ... Rev 5:10 *935*
the *k* of the earth, and the great ... Rev 6:15 *935*
and nations, and tongues, and *k* ... Rev 10:11 *935*
that the way of the *k* of the east ... Rev 16:12 *935*
go forth unto the *k* of the earth ... Rev 16:14 *935*
With whom the *k* of the earth have ... Rev 17:2 *935*
And there are seven *k* ... Rev 17:10 *935*
horns which thou sawest are ten *k* ... Rev 17:12 *935*
but receive power as *k* one hour ... Rev 17:12 *935*
he is Lord of lords, and King of *k* ... Rev 17:14 *935*
reigneth over the *k* of the earth ... Rev 17:18 *935*
the *k* of the earth have committed ... Rev 18:3 *935*
the *k* of the earth, who have ... Rev 18:9 *935*
thigh a name written, KING OF *K* ... Rev 19:16 *935*
That ye may eat the flesh of *k* ... Rev 19:18 *935*
the *k* of the earth, and their ... Rev 19:19 *935*
the *k* of the earth do bring their ... Rev 21:24 *935*

KINGS' {5}
K daughters were among thy ... Ps 45:9 4428
her hands, and is in *k* palaces ... Prov 30:28 4428
both these *k* hearts shall be to ... Dan 11:27 4428
soft clothing are in *k* houses ... Mt 11:8 *935*
live delicately, are in *k* courts ... Lk 7:25 *933*

KINNERETH See CINNEROTH.

KINSFOLK {2}
My *k* have failed, and my familiar ... Job 19:14 7138
and they sought him among their *k* ... Lk 2:44 *4773*

KINSFOLKS {3}
against a wall, neither of his *k* ... 1Kin 16:11 1350
and all his great men, and his *k* ... 2Kin 10:11 3045
by parents, and brethren, and *k* ... Lk 21:16 *4773*

KINSMAN {16}
But if the man have no *k* to ... Num 5:8 1350
his *k* that is next to him of his ... Num 27:11 7607
Naomi had a *k* of her husband's, a ... Ruth 2:1 3045
for thou art a near *k* ... Ruth 3:9 1350
it is true that I am thy near *k* ... Ruth 3:12 1350
there is a *k* nearer than I ... Ruth 3:12 1350
perform unto thee the part of a *k* ... Ruth 3:13 1350
not do the part of a *k* to thee ... Ruth 3:13 1350
will I do the part of a *k* to thee ... Ruth 3:13 1350
the *k* of whom Boaz spake came by ... Ruth 4:1 1350
And he said unto the *k*, Naomi, ... Ruth 4:3 1350
the *k* said, I cannot redeem it ... Ruth 4:6 1350
Therefore the *k* said unto Boaz, ... Ruth 4:8 1350
left thee this day without a *k* ... Ruth 4:14 1350
being his *k* whose ear Peter cut ... Jn 18:26 *4773*
Salute Herodion my *k* ... Rom 16:11 *4773*

KINSMAN'S {1}
let him do the *k* part ... Ruth 3:13 1350

KINSMEN {7}
of kin unto us, one of our next *k* ... Ruth 2:20 1350
and my *k* stand afar off ... Ps 38:11 7138
nor thy brethren, neither thy *k* ... Lk 14:12 *4773*
and had called together his *k* ... Acts 10:24 *4773*
my *k* according to the flesh ... Rom 9:3 *4773*
Salute Andronicus and Junia, my *k* ... Rom 16:7 *4773*
and Jason, and Sosipater, my *k* ... Rom 16:21 *4773*

KINSWOMAN {3}
she is thy father's near *k* ... Lev 18:12 7607
for she is thy mother's near *k* ... Lev 18:13 7607
and call understanding thy *k* ... Prov 7:4 4129

KINSWOMEN {1}
for they are her near *k* ... Lev 18:17 7608

KIOS See CHIOS.

KIR *(kur)* {5} See KIR-HARESH.
1. An Assyrian district on the Kur River.
the people of it captive to *K* ... 2Kin 16:9 7024
shall go into captivity unto *K* ... Amos 1:5 7024
Caphtor, and the Syrians from *K* ... Amos 9:7 7024
2. A Moabite city.
because in the night *K* of Moab is ... Is 15:1 7024
3. Inhabitants of Kir 1.
and *K* uncovered the shield ... Is 22:6 7024

KIR-HARASETH *(kur-har'-a-seth)* {1} See KIR-HARESETH. *A Moabite city.*
only in *K* left they the stones ... 2Kin 3:25 7025

KIR-HARESETH *(kur-har'-e-seth)* {1} See KIR-HARESH. *Same as Kir-haraseth.*
foundations of *K* shall ye mourn ... Is 16:7 7025

KIR-HARESH *(kur-ha'-resh)* {1} See KIR-HARASETH, KIR-HARESETH, KIR-HERES. *Same as Kir-haraseth.*
Moab, and mine inward parts for *K* ... Is 16:11 7025

KIR-HERES *(kur-he'-res)* {2} See KIR-HARESH. *Same as Kir-haraseth.*
shall mourn for the men of *K* ... Jer 48:31 7025
sound like pipes for the men of *K* ... Jer 48:36 7025

KIRIATH See KIRJATH.

KIRIATHAIM *(kir-e-a-thay'-im)* {4} See KIRJATHAIM.
1. A town east of the Jordan.
in Ham, and the Emims in Shaveh *K* ... Gen 14:5 7741
2. A city in Reuben.
K is confounded and taken ... Jer 48:1 7156
And upon *K*, and upon Beth-gamul, ... Jer 48:23 7156
Beth-jeshimoth, Baal-meon, and *K* ... Eze 25:9 7156

KIRIATH-ARBA See KIRJATH-ARBA.

KIRIATH-ARIM See KIRJATH-ARIM.

KIRIATH-BAAL See KIRJATH-BAAL.

KIRIATH-JEARIM See KIRJATH.

KIRIATH-SANNAH See KIRJATH-SANNAH.

KIRIATH-SEPHER See KIRJATH-SEPHER.

KIRIOTH *(kir'-e-oth)* {1} See KERIOTH. *A Moabite city.*
it shall devour the palaces of *K* ... Amos 2:2 7152

KIRJATH *(kur'-jath)* {1} See KIRJATH-ARIM, KIRJATH-BAAL, KIRJATH-JEARIM. *Short form of Kirjath-jearim.*
which is Jerusalem, Gibeath, and *K* ... Josh 18:28 7157

KIRJATHAIM *(jur'-jath-a'-im)* {3}
1. A city in Reuben.
built Heshbon, and Elealeh, and *K* ... Num 32:37 7156
K, and Sibmah, and Zareth-shahar ... Josh 13:19 7156
2. A Levitical city in Naphtali.
suburbs, and *K* with her suburbs ... 1Chr 6:76 7156

KIRJATH-ARBA *(kur'-jath-ar'-bah)* {6} See HEBRON. *A city in Judah.*
And Sarah died in *K* ... Gen 23:2 7153
the name of Hebron before was *K* ... Josh 14:15 7153
And Humtah, and *K*, which is Hebron ... Josh 15:54 7153
in mount Ephraim, and *K* ... Josh 20:7 7153
the name of Hebron before was *K* ... Judg 1:10 7153
the children of Judah dwelt at *K* ... Neh 11:25 7153

KIRJATH-ARIM *(kur'-jath-a'-rim)* {1} See KIRJATH-JEARIM. *Same as Kirjath-jearim.*
The children of *K*, Chephirah, and ... Ezr 2:25 7157

KIRJATH-BAAL *(kur'-jath-ba'-al)* {2} See BAALAH, KIRJATH-JEARIM. *Same as Kirjath-jearim.*
K, which is Kirjath-jearim, and ... Josh 15:60 7154
the goings out thereof were at *K* ... Josh 18:14 7154

KIRJATH-HUZOTH *(kur'-jath-hu'-zoth)* {1} *Residence of Balak, king of Edom.*
with Balak, and they came unto *K* ... Num 22:39 7155

KIRJATH-JEARIM *(kur'-jath-je'-a-rim)* {18} See KIRJATH, KIRJATH-ARIM, KIRJATH-BAAL.
1. A city in Judah.
and Chephirah, and Beeroth, and *K* ... Josh 9:17 7157
was drawn to Baalah, which is *K* ... Josh 15:9 7157
Kirjath-baal, which is *K*, and ... Josh 15:60 7157
were at Kirjath-baal, which is *K* ... Josh 18:14 7157

quarter was from the end of *K*........ Josh 18:15 7157
And they went up, and pitched in *K*....... Judg 18:12 7157
behold, it is behind *K*........ Judg 18:12 7157
to the inhabitants of *K*, saying,........ 1Sa 6:21 7157
And the men of *K* came, and brought..... 1Sa 7:1 7157
to pass, while the ark abode in *K*........ 1Sa 7:2 7157
to bring the ark of God from *K*........ 1Chr 13:5 7157
Israel, to Baalah, that is, to *K*........ 1Chr 13:6 7157
K to the place which David had........ 2Chr 1:4 7157
The men of *K*, Chephirah, and........ Neh 7:29 7157
Urijah the son of Shemaiah of *K*........ Jer 26:20 7157
2. A descendant of Caleb.
Shobal the father of *K*,........ 1Chr 2:50 7157
Shobal the father of *K* had sons........ 1Chr 2:52 7157
And the families of *K*........ 1Chr 2:53 7157

KIRJATH-SANNAH *(kur'-jath-san'-nah)* {1} *A city in Judah.*
And Dannah, and *K*, which is Debir,...... Josh 15:49 7158

KIRJATH-SEPHER *(kur'-jath-se'-fer)* {4} See DEBIR, KIRJATH-SANNAH. *Same as Kirjath-sannah.*
and the name of Debir before was *K*........ Josh 15:15 7158
And Caleb said, He that smiteth *K*........ Josh 15:16 7158
and the name of Debir before was *K*...... Judg 1:11 7158
And Caleb said, He that smiteth *K*........ Judg 1:12 7158

KISH *(kish)* {20}
1. Father of King Saul.
man of Benjamin, whose name was *K*.... 1Sa 9:1 7027
the asses of *K* Saul's father were........ 1Sa 9:3 7027
K said to Saul his son, Take now........ 1Sa 9:3 7027
that is come unto the son of *K*........ 1Sa 10:11 7027
and Saul the son of *K* was taken........ 1Sa 10:21 7027
And *K* was the father of Saul........ 1Sa 14:51 7027
in the sepulchre of *K* his father........ 2Sa 21:14 7027
And Ner begat *K*........ 1Chr 8:33 7027
K begat Saul........ 1Chr 8:33 7027
And Ner begat *K*........ 1Chr 9:39 7027
and *K* begat Saul........ 1Chr 9:39 7027
because of Saul the son of *K*........ 1Chr 12:1 7027
the seer, and Saul the son of *K*........ 1Chr 26:28 7027
2. Son of Abi-Gibeon.
firstborn son Abdon, and Zur, and *K*...... 1Chr 8:30 7027
son Abdon, then Zur, and *K*........ 1Chr 9:36 7027
3. A sanctuary servant.
of Mahli; Eleazar, and *K*........ 1Chr 23:21 7027
brethren the sons of *K* took them........ 1Chr 23:22 7027
Concerning *K*: the son of Kish........ 1Chr 24:29 7027
4. A Levite.
K the son of Abdi, and Azariah the........ 2Chr 29:12 7027
5. An ancestor of Mordecai.
the son of Shimei, the son of *K*........ Est 2:5 7027

KISHI *(kish'-i)* {1} See KUSHAIAH. *Father of Ethan.*
Ethan the son of *K*, the son of........ 1Chr 6:44 7029

KISHION *(kish'-e-on)* {1} See KEDESH, KISHON. *A Levitical city in Issachar.*
And Rabbith, and *K*, and Abez,........ Josh 19:20 7191

KISHON *(ki'-shon)* {6} See KISHION, KISON.
1. Same as Kishion.
K with her suburbs, Dabareh with........ Josh 21:28 7191
the Gentiles unto the river of *K*........ Judg 4:13 7028
The river of *K* swept them away,........ Judg 5:21 7028
that ancient river, the river *K*,........ Judg 5:21 7028
brought them down to the brook *K*........ 1Kin 18:40 7028
2. A brook near Mt. Tabor.
draw unto thee to the river *K*........ Judg 4:7 7028

KISLEV See CHISLEU.

KISLON See CHISLON.

KISLOTH TABOR See CHISLOTH-TABOR.

KISON *(ki'-son)* {1} See KISHON. *Same as Kishon 2.*
as to Jabin, at the brook of *K*........ Ps 83:9 7028

KISS {20}
Come near now, and *k* me, my son........ Gen 27:26 5401
hast not suffered me to *k* my sons........ Gen 31:28 5401
with the right hand to *k* him........ 2Sa 20:9 5401
k my father and my mother, and then..... 1Kin 19:20 5401
K the Son, lest he be angry, and........ Ps 2:12 5401
Every man shall *k* his lips that........ Prov 24:26 5401
Let him *k* me with the kisses of........ Song 1:2 5401
find thee without, I would *k* thee........ Song 8:1 5401
men that sacrifice *k* the calves........ Hos 13:2 5401
saying, Whomsoever I shall *k*........ Mt 26:48 *5368*
saying, Whomsoever I shall *k*........ Mk 14:44 *5368*
Thou gavest me no *k*........ Lk 7:45 *5370*
in hath not ceased to *k* my feet........ Lk 7:45 *2705*
and drew near unto Jesus to *k* him........ Lk 22:47 *5368*
thou the Son of man with a *k*........ Lk 22:48 *5370*
Salute one another with an holy *k*........ Rom 16:16 *5370*
ye one another with an holy *k*........ 1Cor 16:20 *5370*
Greet one another with an holy *k*........ 2Cor 13:12 *5370*
all the brethren with an holy *k*........ 1Th 5:26 *5370*
one another with a *k* of charity........ 1Pet 5:14 *5370*

KISSED {26}
And he came near, and *k* him........ Gen 27:27 5401
Jacob *k* Rachel, and lifted up his........ Gen 29:11 5401
k him, and brought him to his........ Gen 29:13 5401
k his sons and his daughters, and........ Gen 31:55 5401
and fell on his neck, and *k* him........ Gen 33:4 5401
Moreover he *k* all his brethren,........ Gen 45:15 5401
he *k* them, and embraced them........ Gen 48:10 5401
face, and wept upon him, and *k* him...... Gen 50:1 5401
him in the mount of God, and *k* him...... Ex 4:27 5401
law, and did obeisance, and *k* him........ Ex 18:7 5401
Then she *k* them........ Ruth 1:9 5401
Orpah *k* her mother in law........ Ruth 1:14 5401
k him, and said, Is it not because........ 1Sa 10:1 5401
they *k* one another, and wept one........ 1Sa 20:41 5401
and the king *k* Absalom........ 2Sa 14:33 5401
his hand, and took him, and *k* him........ 2Sa 15:5 5401
the king *k* Barzillai, and blessed........ 2Sa 19:39 5401
every mouth which hath not *k* him........ 1Kin 19:18 5401
or my mouth hath *k* my hand........ Job 31:27 5401
and peace have *k* each other........ Ps 85:10 5401
k him, and with an impudent face........ Prov 7:13 5401
master; and *k* him........ Mt 26:49 *2705*
Master, master; and *k* him........ Mk 14:45 *2705*
k his feet, and anointed them with........ Lk 7:38 *2705*
and fell on his neck, and *k* him........ Lk 15:20 *2705*
and fell on Paul's neck, and *k* him,........ Acts 20:37 *2705*

KISSES {2}
but the *k* of an enemy are........ Prov 27:6 5390
kiss me with the *k* of his mouth........ Song 1:2 5390

KITE {2}
vulture, and the *k* after his kind........ Lev 11:14 344
And the glede, and the *k*, and the........ Deut 14:13 344

KITHLISH *(kith'-lish)* {1} *A city in Judah.*
And Cabbon, and Lahmam, and *K*........ Josh 15:40 3798

KITRON *(ki'-tron)* {1} See KATTAH. *A city in Zebulun.*
drive out the inhabitants of *K*........ Judg 1:30 7003

KITTIM *(kit'-tim)* {2} See CHITTIM. *A son of Javan.*
Elishah, and Tarshish, *K*, and........ Gen 10:4 3794
Elishah, and Tarshish, *K*, and........ 1Chr 1:7 3794

KIYYUN See CHIUN.

KNEAD {2}
k it, and make cakes upon the........ Gen 18:6 3888
the women *k* their dough, to make........ Jer 7:18 3888

KNEADED {3}
k it, and did bake unleavened........ 1Sa 28:24 3888
k it, and made cakes in his sight,........ 2Sa 13:8 3888
raising after he hath *k* the dough........ Hos 7:4 3888

KNEADINGTROUGHS {2}
into thine ovens, and into thy *k*........ Ex 8:3 4863
their *k* being bound up in their........ Ex 12:34 4863

KNEE {6}
they cried before him, Bow the *k*........ Gen 41:43
That unto me every *k* shall bow........ Is 45:23 1290
and they bowed the *k* before him........ Mt 27:29
bowed the *k* to the image of Baal........ Rom 11:4 *1119*
every *k* shall bow to me, and every........ Rom 14:11 *1119*
name of Jesus every *k* should bow........ Phil 2:10 *1119*

KNEEL {2}
he made his camels to *k* down........ Gen 24:11 1288
let us *k* before the LORD our........ Ps 95:6 1288

KNEELED {8}
k down upon his knees before all........ 2Chr 6:13 1288
he *k* upon his knees three times a........ Dan 6:10 1289
k to him, and asked him, Good........ Mk 10:17 *1120*
cast, and *k* down, and prayed,........ Lk 22:41 *5087,1119*
he *k* down, and cried with a loud.... Acts 7:60 *5087,1119*
all forth, and *k* down, and prayed... Acts 9:40 *5087,1119*
he *k* down, and prayed with them... Acts 20:36 *5087,1119*
k down on the shore, and prayed.... Acts 21:5 *5087,1119*

KNEELING {3}
from *k* on his knees with his........ 1Kin 8:54 3766
k down to him, and saying,........ Mt 17:14 *1120*
k down to him, and saying unto him...... Mk 1:40 *1120*

KNEES {30}
and she shall bear upon my *k*........ Gen 30:3 1290
them out from between his *k*........ Gen 48:12 1290
were brought up upon Joseph's *k*........ Gen 50:23 1290
LORD shall smite thee in the *k*........ Deut 28:35 1290
boweth down upon his *k* to drink........ Judg 7:5 1290
down upon their *k* to drink water........ Judg 7:6 1290
And she made him sleep upon her *k*........ Judg 16:19 1290
from kneeling on his *k* with his........ 1Kin 8:54 1290
and put his face between his *k*........ 1Kin 18:42 1290
all the *k* which have not bowed........ 1Kin 19:18 1290
fell on his *k* before Elijah, and........ 2Kin 1:13 1290
mother, he sat on her *k* till noon........ 2Kin 4:20 1290
kneeled down upon his *k* before........ 2Chr 6:13 1290
and my mantle, I fell upon my *k*........ Ezr 9:5 1290
Why did the *k* prevent me........ Job 3:12 1290
hast strengthened the feeble *k*........ Job 4:4 1290
My *k* are weak through fasting........ Ps 109:24 1290
hands, and confirm the feeble *k*........ Is 35:3 1290
sides, and be dandled upon her *k*........ Is 66:12 1290
all *k* shall be weak as water........ Eze 7:17 1290
all *k* shall be weak as water........ Eze 21:7 1290
the waters were to the *k*........ Eze 47:4 1290
his *k* smote one against another........ Dan 5:6 755
upon his *k* three times a day........ Dan 6:10 1291
me, which set me upon my *k*........ Dan 10:10 1290
the *k* smite together, and much........ Nah 2:10 1290
bowing their *k* worshipped him........ Mk 15:19 *1119*
saw it, he fell down at Jesus' *k*........ Lk 5:8 *1119*
For this cause I bow my *k* unto........ Eph 3:14 *1119*
which hang down, and the feeble *k*........ Heb 12:12 *1119*

KNEW {169}
they *k* that they were naked........ Gen 3:7 3045
And Adam *k* Eve his wife........ Gen 4:1 3045
And Cain *k* his wife........ Gen 4:17 3045
And Adam *k* his wife again........ Gen 4:25 3045
so Noah *k* that the waters were........ Gen 8:11 3045
k what his younger son had done........ Gen 9:24 3045
and I *k* it not........ Gen 28:16 3045
For Jacob *k* not that Rachel had........ Gen 31:32 3045
And he *k* it, and said, It is my........ Gen 37:33 5234
Onan *k* that the seed should not........ Gen 38:9 3045
(for he *k* not that she was his........ Gen 38:16 3045
And he *k* her again no more........ Gen 38:26 3045
he *k* not ought he had, save the........ Gen 39:6 3045
he *k* them, but made himself........ Gen 42:7 5234
Joseph *k* his brethren........ Gen 42:8 5234
his brethren, but they *k* not him........ Gen 42:8 3045
they *k* not that Joseph understood........ Gen 42:23 3045
over Egypt, which *k* not Joseph........ Ex 1:8 3045
for I *k* not that thou stoodest in........ Num 22:34 3045
k the knowledge of the most High,........ Num 24:16 3045
manna, which thy fathers *k* not........ Deut 8:16 3045
LORD from the day that I *k* you........ Deut 9:24 3045
them, gods whom they *k* not........ Deut 29:26 3045
to gods whom they *k* not, to new........ Deut 32:17 3045
brethren, nor *k* his own children........ Deut 33:9 3045
whom the LORD *k* face to face........ Deut 34:10 3045
which *k* not the LORD, nor yet the........ Judg 2:10 3045
such as before *k* nothing thereof........ Judg 3:2 3045
and she *k* no man........ Judg 11:39 3045
For Manoah *k* not that he was an........ Judg 13:16 3045
Then Manoah *k* that he was an........ Judg 13:21 3045
his mother *k* not that it was of........ Judg 14:4 3045
they *k* the voice of the young man........ Judg 18:3 5234
and they *k* her, and abused her all........ Judg 19:25 3045
but they *k* not that evil was near........ Judg 20:34 3045
Elkanah *k* Hannah his wife........ 1Sa 1:19 3045
they *k* not the LORD........ 1Sa 2:12 3045
from Dan even to Beer-sheba *k*........ 1Sa 3:20 3045
when all that *k* him beforetime........ 1Sa 10:11 3045
the people *k* not that Jonathan........ 1Sa 14:3 3045
k that the LORD was with David,........ 1Sa 18:28 3045
for if I *k* certainly that evil........ 1Sa 20:9 3045
whereby Jonathan *k* that it was........ 1Sa 20:33 3045
But the lad *k* not any thing........ 1Sa 20:39 3045
Jonathan and David *k* the matter........ 1Sa 20:39 3045
for thy servant *k* nothing of all........ 1Sa 22:15 3045
and because they *k* when he fled........ 1Sa 22:17 3045
I *k* it that day, when Doeg the........ 1Sa 22:22 3045
David *k* that Saul secretly........ 1Sa 23:9 3045
away, and no man saw it, nor *k* it........ 1Sa 26:12 3045
Saul *k* David's voice, and said, Is........ 1Sa 26:17 5234
but David *k* it not........ 2Sa 3:26 3045
where he *k* that valiant men were........ 2Sa 11:16 3045
k ye not that they would shoot........ 2Sa 11:20 3045
and they *k* not any thing........ 2Sa 15:11 3045
tumult, but I *k* not what it was........ 2Sa 18:29 3045
a people which I *k* not shall........ 2Sa 22:44 3045
but the king *k* her not........ 1Kin 1:4 3045
he *k* him, and fell on his face, and........ 1Kin 18:7 5234
for they *k* them not........ 2Kin 4:39 3045
Then Manasseh *k* that the LORD he........ 2Chr 33:13 3045
the rulers *k* not whither I went,........ Neh 2:16 3045
which *k* the times, (for so was........ Est 1:13 5234
manner toward all that *k* law........ Est 1:13 5234
k him not, they lifted up their........ Job 2:12 5234
Oh that I *k* where I might find........ Job 23:3 3045
the cause which I *k* not I........ Job 29:16 3045
wonderful for me, which I *k* not........ Job 42:3 3045
to my charge things that I *k* not........ Ps 35:11 3045
against me, and I *k* it not........ Ps 35:15 3045
thou sayest, Behold, we *k* it not........ Prov 24:12 3045
blind by a way that they *k* not........ Is 42:16 3045
on fire round about, yet he *k* not........ Is 42:25 3045
Because I *k* that thou art........ Is 48:4 1847
shouldest say, Behold, I *k* them........ Is 48:7 3045
for I *k* that thou wouldest deal........ Is 48:8 3045
nations that *k* not thee shall run........ Is 55:5 3045
formed thee in the belly I *k* thee........ Jer 1:5 3045
they that handle the law *k* me not........ Jer 2:8 3045
I *k* not that they had devised........ Jer 11:19 3045
Then I *k* that this was the word........ Jer 32:8 3045
slain Gedaliah, and no man *k* it........ Jer 41:4 3045
serve other gods, whom they *k* not........ Jer 44:3 3045
Then all the men which *k* that........ Jer 44:15 3045
I *k* that they were the cherubims........ Eze 10:20 3045
he *k* their desolate palaces, and........ Eze 19:7 3045
till he *k* that the most high God........ Dan 5:21 3046
Now when Daniel *k* that the........ Dan 6:10 3046
a god whom his fathers *k* not........ Dan 11:38 3045
have made princes, and I *k* it not........ Hos 8:4 3045
but they *k* not that I healed them........ Hos 11:3 3045
For the men *k* that he fled from........ Jonah 1:10 3045
for I *k* that thou art a gracious........ Jonah 4:2 3045
all the nations whom they *k* not........ Zec 7:14 3045
me *k* that it was the word of the........ Zec 11:11 3045
k her not till she had brought........ Mt 1:25 *1097*
profess unto them, I never *k* you........ Mt 7:23 *1097*
But when Jesus *k* it, he withdrew........ Mt 12:15 *1097*
Jesus *k* their thoughts, and said........ Mt 12:25 *1492*
they *k* him not, but have done........ Mt 17:12 *1912*
k not until the flood came, and........ Mt 24:39 *1097*
I *k* thee that thou art an hard........ Mt 25:24 *1097*
For he *k* that for envy they had........ Mt 27:18 *1492*
to speak, because they *k* him........ Mk 1:34 *1492*
saw them departing, and many *k* him........ Mk 6:33 *1921*
And when they *k*, they say, Five,........ Mk 6:38 *1097*
the ship, straightway they *k* him........ Mk 6:54 *1921*
And when Jesus *k* it, he saith unto........ Mk 8:17 *1097*
for they *k* that he had spoken the........ Mk 12:12 *1097*
For he *k* that the chief priests........ Mk 15:10 *1097*
when he *k* it of the centurion, he........ Mk 15:45 *1097*
Joseph and his mother *k* not of it........ Lk 2:43 *1097*
for they *k* that he was Christ........ Lk 4:41
But he *k* their thoughts, and said........ Lk 6:8 *1492*
when she *k* that Jesus sat at meat........ Lk 7:37 *1921*
And the people, when they *k* it........ Lk 9:11 *1097*
which *k* his lord's will, and........ Lk 12:47 *1097*
But he that *k* not, and did commit........ Lk 12:48 *1097*
neither *k* they the things which........ Lk 18:34 *1097*

as soon as he *k* that he belonged ... Lk 23:7 1921
eyes were opened, and they *k* him ... Lk 24:31 1921
by him, and the world *k* him not ... Jn 1:10 1097
And I *k* him not ... Jn 1:31 1492
And I *k* him not ... Jn 1:33 1492
made wine, and *k* not whence it was ... Jn 2:9 1492
servants which drew the water *k* ... Jn 2:9 1492
unto them, because he *k* all men ... Jn 2:24 1097
for he *k* what was in man ... Jn 2:25 1097
When therefore the Lord *k* how the ... Jn 4:1 1097
So the father *k* that it was at ... Jn 4:53 1097
k that he had been now a long ... Jn 5:6 1097
for he himself *k* what he would do ... Jn 6:6 1492
When Jesus *k* in himself that his ... Jn 6:61 1492
For Jesus *k* from the beginning ... Jn 6:64 1492
I *k* that thou hearest me always ... Jn 11:42 1492
if any man *k* where he were, he ... Jn 11:57 1097
therefore *k* that he was there ... Jn 12:9 1097
when Jesus *k* that his hour was ... Jn 13:1 1492
For he *k* who should betray him ... Jn 13:11 1492
Now no man at the table *k* for ... Jn 13:28 1097
Now Jesus *k* that they were ... Jn 16:19 1097
which betrayed him, *k* the place ... Jn 18:2 1492
For as yet they *k* not the ... Jn 20:9 1492
and *k* not that it was Jesus ... Jn 20:14 1492
but the disciples *k* not that it ... Jn 21:4 1492
they *k* that it was he which sat ... Acts 3:10 1921
king arose, which *k* not Joseph ... Acts 7:18 1492
Which when the brethren *k* ... Acts 9:30 1921
when she *k* Peter's voice, she ... Acts 12:14 1921
rulers, because they *k* him not ... Acts 13:27 50
for they *k* all that his father ... Acts 16:3 1492
the more part *k* not wherefore ... Acts 19:32 1492
But when they *k* that he was a Jew ... Acts 19:34 1921
after he *k* that he was a Roman, ... Acts 22:29 1921
Which *k* me from the beginning, if ... Acts 26:5 4267
it was day, they *k* not the land ... Acts 27:39 1921
then they *k* that the island was ... Acts 28:1 1921
Because that, when they *k* God ... Rom 1:21 1097
God the world by wisdom *k* not God ... 1Cor 1:21 1097
of the princes of this world *k* ... 1Cor 2:8 1097
to be sin for us, who *k* no sin ... 2Cor 5:21 1097
I *k* a man in Christ above ... 2Cor 12:2 1492
I *k* such a man, (whether in the ... 2Cor 12:3 1492
Howbeit then, when ye *k* not God ... Gal 4:8 1492
k the grace of God in truth ... Col 1:6 1921
For I would that ye *k* what great ... Col 2:1 1492
us not, because it *k* him not ... 1Jn 3:1 1097
though ye once *k* this, how that ... Jude 5 1492
had a name written, that no man *k* ... Rev 19:12 1492

KNEWEST {10}
thee with manna, which thou *k* not ... Deut 8:3 3045
which thou *k* not heretofore ... Ruth 2:11 3045
for thou *k* that they dealt ... Neh 9:10 3045
within me, then thou *k* my path ... Ps 142:3 3045
yea, thou *k* not ... Is 48:8 3045
heart, though thou *k* all this ... Dan 5:22 3046
thou *k* that I reap where I sowed ... Mt 25:26 1492
Thou *k* that I was an austere man, ... Lk 19:22 1492
because thou *k* not the time of ... Lk 19:44 1097
If thou *k* the gift of God, and who ... Jn 4:10 1492

KNIFE {6}
took the fire in his hand, and a *k* ... Gen 22:6 3979
took the *k* to slay his son ... Gen 22:10 3979
come into his house, he took a *k* ... Judg 19:29 3979
put a *k* to thy throat, if thou be ... Prov 23:2 7915
son of man, take thee a sharp *k* ... Eze 5:1 2719
part, and smite about it with a *k* ... Eze 5:2 2719

KNIT {6}
the city, *k* together as one man ... Judg 20:11 2270
was *k* with the soul of David ... 1Sa 18:1 7194
mine heart shall be *k* unto you ... 1Chr 12:17 3162
great sheet *k* at the four corners ... Acts 10:11 1210
being *k* together in love, and unto ... Col 2:2 4822
k together, increaseth with the ... Col 2:19 4822

KNIVES {5}
unto Joshua, Make thee sharp *k* ... Josh 5:2 2719
And Joshua made him sharp *k* ... Josh 5:3 2719
after their manner with *k* ... 1Kin 18:28 2719
of silver, nine and twenty *k* ... Ezr 1:9 4252
swords, and their jaw teeth as *k* ... Prov 30:14 3979

KNOCK {4}
k, and it shall be opened unto you ... Mt 7:7 2925
k, and it shall be opened unto you ... Lk 11:9 2925
to *k* at the door, saying, Lord, ... Lk 13:25 2925
Behold, I stand at the door, and *k* ... Rev 3:20 2925

KNOCKED {1}
as Peter *k* at the door of the ... Acts 12:13 2925

KNOCKETH {4}
is the voice of my beloved that *k* ... Song 5:2 1849
to him that *k* it shall be opened ... Mt 7:8 2925
to him that *k* it shall be opened ... Lk 11:10 2925
that when he cometh and *k*, they ... Lk 12:36 2925

KNOCKING {1}
But Peter continued *k* ... Acts 12:16 2925

KNOP {10}
made like unto almonds, with a *k* ... Ex 25:33 3730
in the other branch, with a *k* ... Ex 25:33 3730
there shall be a *k* under two ... Ex 25:35 3730
a *k* under two branches of the ... Ex 25:35 3730
a *k* under two branches of the ... Ex 25:35 3730
of almonds in one branch, a *k* ... Ex 37:19 3730
almonds in another branch, a *k* ... Ex 37:19 3730
a *k* under two branches of the ... Ex 37:21 3730
a *k* under two branches of the ... Ex 37:21 3730
a *k* under two branches of the ... Ex 37:21 3730

KNOPS {9}
and his branches, his bowls, his *k* ... Ex 25:31 3730
like unto almonds, with their *k* ... Ex 25:34 3730
Their *k* and their branches shall ... Ex 25:36 3730
and his branch, his bowls, his *k* ... Ex 37:17 3730
bowls made like almonds, his *k* ... Ex 37:20 3730
Their *k* and their branches were of ... Ex 37:22 3730
house within was carved with *k* ... 1Kin 6:18 6497
about there were *k* compassing it ... 1Kin 7:24 6497
the *k* were cast in two rows, when ... 1Kin 7:24 6497

KNOW {767}
For God doth *k* that in the day ye ... Gen 3:5 3045
as one of us, to *k* good and evil ... Gen 3:22 3045
And he said, I *k* not ... Gen 4:9 3045
I *k* that thou art a fair woman to ... Gen 12:11 3045
whereby shall I *k* that I shall ... Gen 15:8 3045
K of a surety that thy seed shall ... Gen 15:13 3045
For I *k* him, that he will command ... Gen 18:19 3045
and if not, I will *k* ... Gen 18:21 3045
out unto us, that we may *k* them ... Gen 19:5 3045
I *k* that thou didst this in the ... Gen 20:6 3045
k thou that thou shalt surely die ... Gen 20:7 3045
for now I *k* that thou fearest God ... Gen 22:12 3045
thereby shall I *k* that thou hast ... Gen 24:14 3045
I *k* not the day of my death ... Gen 27:2 3045
K ye Laban the son of Nahor ... Gen 29:5 3045
And they said, We *k* him ... Gen 29:5 3045
ye *k* that with all my power I ... Gen 31:6 3045
k now whether it be thy son's ... Gen 37:32 5234
Hereby shall I *k* that ye are true ... Gen 42:33 3045
then shall I *k* that ye are no ... Gen 42:34 3045
we certainly *k* that he would say ... Gen 43:7 3045
Ye *k* that my wife bare me two ... Gen 44:27 3045
I *k* it, my son, I *k* it ... Gen 48:19 3045
for I *k* their sorrows ... Ex 3:7 3045
I *k* that he can speak well ... Ex 4:14 3045
I *k* not the LORD, neither will I ... Ex 5:2 3045
ye shall *k* that I am the LORD ... Ex 6:7 3045
shall *k* that I am the LORD ... Ex 7:5 3045
thou shalt *k* that I am the LORD ... Ex 7:17 3045
that thou mayest *k* that there is ... Ex 8:10 3045
to the end thou mayest *k* that I ... Ex 8:22 3045
that thou mayest *k* that there is ... Ex 9:14 3045
that thou mayest *k* how that the ... Ex 9:29 3045
I *k* that ye will not yet fear the ... Ex 9:30 3045
that ye may *k* how that I am the ... Ex 10:2 3045
we *k* not with what we must serve ... Ex 10:26 3045
that ye may *k* how that the LORD ... Ex 11:7 3045
may *k* that I am the LORD ... Ex 14:4 3045
shall *k* that I am the LORD ... Ex 14:18 3045
then ye shall *k* that the LORD ... Ex 16:6 3045
ye shall *k* that I am the LORD ... Ex 16:12 3045
Now I *k* that the LORD is greater ... Ex 18:11 3045
I do make them *k* the statutes of ... Ex 18:16 3045
for ye *k* the heart of a stranger, ... Ex 23:9 3045
they shall *k* that I am the LORD ... Ex 29:46 3045
that ye may *k* that I am the LORD ... Ex 31:13 3045
that I may *k* what to do unto thee ... Ex 33:5 3045
thou hast not let me *k* whom thou ... Ex 33:12 3045
I *k* thee by name, and thou hast ... Ex 33:12 3045
me now thy way, that I may *k* thee ... Ex 33:13 3045
in my sight, and I *k* thee by name ... Ex 33:17 3045
understanding to *k* how to work ... Ex 36:1 3045
That your generations may *k* that ... Lev 23:43 3045
they shall *k* the land which ye ... Num 14:31 3045
ye shall *k* my breach of promise ... Num 14:34 3045
Hereby ye shall *k* that the LORD ... Num 16:28 3045
that I may *k* what the LORD will ... Num 22:19 3045
(for I *k* that ye have much cattle ... Deut 3:19 3045
that thou mightest *k* that the ... Deut 4:35 3045
K therefore this day, and consider ... Deut 4:39 3045
K therefore that the LORD thy God ... Deut 7:9 3045
to *k* what was in thine heart, ... Deut 8:2 3045
not, neither did thy fathers *k* ... Deut 8:3 3045
that he might make thee *k* that ... Deut 8:3 3045
And *k* ye this day ... Deut 11:2 3045
to *k* whether ye love the LORD ... Deut 13:3 3045
How shall we *k* the word which the ... Deut 18:21 3045
unto thee, or if thou *k* him not ... Deut 22:2 3045
that ye might *k* that I am the ... Deut 29:6 3045
(For ye *k* how we have dwelt in ... Deut 29:16 3045
for I *k* their imagination which ... Deut 31:21 3045
For I *k* thy rebellion, and thy ... Deut 31:27 3045
For I *k* that after my death ye ... Deut 31:29 3045
I *k* that the LORD hath given you ... Josh 2:9 3045
that ye may *k* the way by which ye ... Josh 3:4 3045
all Israel, that they may *k* that ... Josh 3:7 3045
Hereby ye shall *k* that the living ... Josh 3:10 3045
Then ye shall let your children *k* ... Josh 4:22 3045
might *k* the hand of the LORD ... Josh 4:24 3045
he knoweth, and Israel he shall *k* ... Josh 22:22 3045
K for a certainty that the LORD ... Josh 23:13 3045
ye *k* in all your hearts and in all ... Josh 23:14 3045
of the children of Israel might *k* ... Judg 3:2 3045
to *k* whether they would hearken ... Judg 3:4 3045
then shall I *k* that thou wilt ... Judg 6:37 3045
Now *k* I that the LORD will do me ... Judg 17:13 3045
that we may *k* whether our way ... Judg 18:5 3045
Do ye *k* that there is in these ... Judg 18:14 3045
thine house, that we may *k* him ... Judg 19:22 3045
k that thou art a virtuous woman ... Ruth 3:11 3045
up before one could *k* another ... Ruth 3:14 5234
until thou *k* how the matter will ... Ruth 3:18 3045
it, then tell me, that I may *k* ... Ruth 4:4 3045
Now Samuel did not yet *k* the LORD ... 1Sa 3:7 3045
then we shall *k* that it is not ... 1Sa 6:9 3045
and *k* and see wherein this sin hath ... 1Sa 14:38 3045
I *k* thy pride, and the naughtiness ... 1Sa 17:28 3045
that all the earth may *k* that ... 1Sa 17:46 3045
all this assembly shall *k* that ... 1Sa 17:47 3045
he saith, Let not Jonathan *k* this ... 1Sa 20:3 3045
do not I *k* that thou hast chosen ... 1Sa 20:30 3045
Let no man *k* any thing of the ... 1Sa 21:2 3045
till I *k* what God will do for me ... 1Sa 22:3 3045
Go, I pray you, prepare yet, and *k* ... 1Sa 23:22 3045
k thou and see that there is ... 1Sa 24:11 3045
I *k* well that thou shalt surely ... 1Sa 24:20 3045
whom I *k* not whence they be ... 1Sa 25:11 3045
Now therefore *k* and consider what ... 1Sa 25:17 3045
K thou assuredly, that thou shalt ... 1Sa 28:1 3045
Surely thou shalt *k* what thy ... 1Sa 28:2 3045
I *k* that thou art good in my ... 1Sa 29:9 3045
to *k* thy going out and thy coming ... 2Sa 3:25 3045
in, and to *k* all that thou doest ... 2Sa 3:25 3045
K ye not that there is a prince ... 2Sa 3:38 3045
to make thy servant *k* them ... 2Sa 7:21 3045
to *k* all things that are in the ... 2Sa 14:20 3045
servant doth *k* that I have sinned ... 2Sa 19:20 3045
for do not I *k* that I am this day ... 2Sa 19:22 3045
that I may *k* the number of the ... 2Sa 24:2 3045
thou shalt *k* for certain that ... 1Kin 2:37 3045
K for a certain, on the day thou ... 1Kin 2:42 3045
I *k* not how to go out or come in ... 1Kin 3:7 3045
which shall *k* every man the ... 1Kin 8:38 3045
of the earth may *k* thy name ... 1Kin 8:43 3045
that they may *k* that this house, ... 1Kin 8:43 3045
earth may *k* that the LORD is God ... 1Kin 8:60 3045
Now by this I *k* that thou art a ... 1Kin 17:24 3045
shall carry thee whither I *k* not ... 1Kin 18:12 3045
that this people may *k* that thou ... 1Kin 18:37 3045
thou shalt *k* that I am the LORD ... 1Kin 20:13 3045
ye shall *k* that I am the LORD ... 1Kin 20:28 3045
K ye that Ramoth in Gilead is ... 1Kin 22:3 3045
And he said, Yea, I *k* it ... 2Kin 2:3 3045
And he answered, Yea, I *k* it ... 2Kin 2:5 3045
he shall *k* that there is a ... 2Kin 5:8 3045
now I *k* that there is no God in ... 2Kin 5:15 3045
They *k* that we be hungry ... 2Kin 7:12 3045
Because I *k* the evil that thou ... 2Kin 8:12 3045
unto them, Ye *k* the man, and his ... 2Kin 9:11 3045
K now that there shall fall unto ... 2Kin 10:10 3045
k not the manner of the God of ... 2Kin 17:26 3045
because they *k* not the manner of ... 2Kin 17:26 3045
may *k* that thou art the LORD God ... 2Kin 19:19 3045
But I *k* thy abode, and thy going ... 2Kin 19:27 3045
to *k* what Israel ought to do ... 1Chr 12:32 3045
of them to me, that I may *k* it ... 1Chr 21:2 3045
k thou the God of thy father, and ... 1Chr 28:9 3045
I *k* also, my God, that thou ... 1Chr 29:17 3045
for I *k* that thy servants can ... 2Chr 2:8 3045
every one shall *k* his own sore ... 2Chr 6:29 3045
of the earth may *k* thy name ... 2Chr 6:33 3045
may *k* that this house which I ... 2Chr 6:33 3045
that they may *k* my service ... 2Chr 12:8 3045
Ought ye not to *k* that the LORD ... 2Chr 13:5 3045
neither *k* we what to do ... 2Chr 20:12 3045
I *k* that God hath determined to ... 2Chr 25:16 3045
K ye not what I and my fathers ... 2Chr 32:13 3045
that he might *k* all that was in ... 2Chr 32:31 3045
k that this city is a rebellious ... Ezr 4:15 3046
all such as *k* the laws of thy God ... Ezr 7:25 3046
and teach ye them that *k* them not ... Ezr 7:25 3046
said, They shall not *k*, neither ... Neh 4:11 3045
to *k* how Esther did, and what ... Est 2:11 3045
to *k* what it was, and why it was ... Est 4:5 3045
of the king's provinces, do *k* ... Est 4:11 3045
thou shalt *k* that thy tabernacle ... Job 5:24 3045
Thou shalt *k* also that thy seed ... Job 5:25 3045
it, and *k* thou it for thy good ... Job 5:27 3045
shall his place *k* him any more ... Job 7:10 5234
k nothing, because our days upon ... Job 8:9 3045
I *k* it is so of a truth ... Job 9:2 3045
the mountains, and they *k* not ... Job 9:5 3045
yet would I not *k* my soul ... Job 9:21 3045
I *k* that thou wilt not hold me ... Job 9:28 3045
I *k* that this is with thee ... Job 10:13 3045
K therefore that God exacteth of ... Job 11:6 3045
what canst thou *k* ... Job 11:8 3045
What ye *k*, the same do I *k* ... Job 13:2 1847
ye *k*, the same do I *k* also ... Job 13:2 3045
I *k* that I shall be justified ... Job 13:18 3045
make me to *k* my transgression and ... Job 13:23 3045
What knowest thou, that we *k* not ... Job 15:9 3045
K now that God hath overthrown me ... Job 19:6 3045
For I *k* that my redeemer liveth, ... Job 19:25 3045
that ye may *k* there is a judgment ... Job 19:29 3045
rewardeth him, and he shall *k* it ... Job 21:19 3045
I *k* your thoughts, and the devices ... Job 21:27 3045
do ye not *k* their tokens, ... Job 21:29 5234
And thou sayest, How doth God *k* ... Job 22:13 3045
I would *k* the words which he ... Job 23:5 3045
do they that *k* him not see his ... Job 24:1 3045
they *k* not the ways thereof, nor ... Job 24:13 5234
they *k* not the light ... Job 24:16 3045
if one *k* them, they are in the ... Job 24:17 5234
For I *k* that thou wilt bring me ... Job 30:23 3045
that God may *k* mine integrity ... Job 31:6 3045
For I *k* not to give flattering ... Job 32:22 3045
let us *k* among ourselves what is ... Job 34:4 3045
we *k* him not, neither can the ... Job 36:26 3045
that all men may *k* his work ... Job 37:7 3045
Dost thou *k* when God disposed ... Job 37:15 3045
Dost thou *k* the balancings of the ... Job 37:16 3045

the dayspring to *k* his place ... Job 38:12 3045
that thou shouldest *k* the paths ... Job 38:20 995
I *k* that thou canst do every ... Job 42:2 3045
But *k* that the LORD hath set ... Ps 4:3 3045
they that *k* thy name will put ... Ps 9:10 3045
that the nations may *k* themselves ... Ps 9:20 3045
Now *k* I that the LORD saveth his ... Ps 20:6 3045
unto them that *k* thee ... Ps 36:10 3045
LORD, make me to *k* mine end ... Ps 39:4 3045
that I may *k* how frail I am ... Ps 39:4 3045
By this I *k* that thou favourest ... Ps 41:11 3045
Be still, and *k* that I am God ... Ps 46:10 3045
I *k* all the fowls of the ... Ps 50:11 3045
thou shalt make me to *k* wisdom ... Ps 51:6 3045
enemies turn back: this I *k* ... Ps 56:9 3045
let them *k* that God ruleth in ... Ps 59:13 3045
for I *k* not the numbers thereof ... Ps 71:15 3045
And they say, How doth God *k* ... Ps 73:11 3045
When I thought to *k* this, it was ... Ps 73:16 3045
generation to come might *k* them ... Ps 78:6 3045
They *k* not, neither will they ... Ps 82:5 3045
That men may *k* that thou, whose ... Ps 83:18 3045
and Babylon to them that *k* me ... Ps 87:4 3045
people that *k* the joyful sound ... Ps 89:15 3045
man knowledge, shall not he *k* ... Ps 94:10
K ye that the LORD he is God ... Ps 100:3 3045
I will not *k* a wicked person ... Ps 101:4
place thereof shall *k* it no more ... Ps 103:16 5234
That they may *k* that this is thy ... Ps 109:27 3045
I *k*, O LORD, that thy judgments ... Ps 119:75 3045
that I may *k* thy testimonies ... Ps 119:125 3045
For I *k* that the LORD is great, ... Ps 135:5 3045
Search me, O God, and *k* my heart ... Ps 139:23 3045
try me, and *k* my thoughts ... Ps 139:23 3045
I *k* that the LORD will maintain ... Ps 140:12 3045
there was no man that would *k* me ... Ps 142:4 5234
cause me to *k* the way wherein I ... Ps 143:8 3045
To *k* wisdom and instruction ... Prov 1:2 3045
attend to *k* understanding ... Prov 4:1 3045
they *k* not at what they stumble ... Prov 4:19 3045
that thou canst not *k* them ... Prov 5:6 3045
righteous *k* what is acceptable ... Prov 10:32 3045
That I might make thee *k* the ... Prov 22:21 3045
thy soul, doth not he *k* it ... Prov 24:12 3045
lest thou *k* not what to do in the ... Prov 25:8
Be thou diligent to *k* the state ... Prov 27:23 3045
the wicked regardeth not to *k* it ... Prov 29:7 1847
for me, yea, four which I *k* not ... Prov 30:18 3045
And I gave my heart to *k* wisdom ... Eccl 1:17 3045
and to *k* madness and folly ... Eccl 1:17 3045
I *k* that there is no good in them ... Eccl 3:12 3045
I *k* that, whatsoever God doeth, ... Eccl 3:14 3045
I applied mine heart to *k* ... Eccl 7:25 3045
to *k* the wickedness of folly, ... Eccl 7:25 3045
yet surely I *k* that it shall be ... Eccl 8:12 3045
I applied mine heart to *k* wisdom ... Eccl 8:16 3045
though a wise man think to *k* it ... Eccl 8:17 3045
For the living *k* that they shall ... Eccl 9:5 3045
but the dead *k* not any thing, ... Eccl 9:5 3045
but *k* thou, that for all these ... Eccl 11:9 3045
If thou *k* not, O thou fairest ... Song 1:8 3045
but Israel doth not *k*, my people ... Is 1:3 3045
nigh and come, that we may *k* it ... Is 5:19 3045
that he may *k* to refuse the evil, ... Is 7:15 3045
child shall *k* to refuse the evil ... Is 7:16 3045
And all the people shall *k* ... Is 9:9 3045
let them *k* what the LORD of hosts ... Is 19:12 3045
the Egyptians shall *k* the LORD in ... Is 19:21 3045
may *k* that thou art the LORD ... Is 37:20 3045
But I *k* thy abode, and thy going ... Is 37:28 3045
That they may see, and *k*, and ... Is 41:20 3045
them, and *k* the latter end of them ... Is 41:22 3045
that we may *k* that ye are gods ... Is 41:23 3045
from the beginning, that we may *k* ... Is 41:26 3045
that ye may *k* and believe me, and ... Is 43:10 3045
shall ye not *k* it ... Is 43:19 3045
I *k* not any ... Is 44:8 3045
they see not, nor *k* ... Is 44:9 3045
places, that thou mayest *k* that I ... Is 45:3 3045
That they may *k* from the rising ... Is 45:6 3045
neither shall I *k* the loss of ... Is 47:8 3045
thou shalt not *k* from whence it ... Is 47:11 3045
suddenly, which thou shalt not *k* ... Is 47:11 3045
things, and thou didst not *k* them ... Is 48:6 3045
thou shalt *k* that I am the LORD ... Is 49:23 3045
all flesh shall *k* that I the LORD ... Is 49:26 3045
that I should *k* how to speak a ... Is 50:4 3045
I *k* that I shall not be ashamed ... Is 50:7 3045
ye that *k* righteousness, the ... Is 51:7 3045
my people shall *k* my name ... Is 52:6 3045
therefore they shall *k* in that ... Is 52:6
me daily, and delight to *k* my ways ... Is 58:2 1847
The way of peace they *k* not ... Is 59:8 3045
goeth therein shall not *k* peace ... Is 59:8 3045
as for our iniquities, we *k* them ... Is 59:12 3045
thou shalt *k* that I the LORD am ... Is 60:16 3045
For I *k* their works and their ... Is 66:18
k therefore and see that it is an ... Jer 2:19 3045
the valley, *k* what thou hast done ... Jer 2:23 3045
of Jerusalem, and see now, and *k* ... Jer 5:1 3045
for they *k* not the way of the ... Jer 5:4 3045
Therefore hear, ye nations, and *k* ... Jer 6:18 3045
my people, that thou mayest *k* ... Jer 6:27 3045
after other gods whom ye *k* not ... Jer 7:9 3045
but my people *k* not the judgment ... Jer 8:7 3045
they *k* not me, saith the LORD ... Jer 9:3 3045
deceit they refuse to *k* me ... Jer 9:6 3045

I *k* that the way of man is not in ... Jer 10:23 3045
upon the heathen that *k* thee not ... Jer 10:25 3045
me knowledge of it, and I *k* it ... Jer 11:18 3045
Do we not certainly *k* that every ... Jer 13:12 3045
about into a land that they *k* not ... Jer 14:18 3045
k that for thy sake I have ... Jer 15:15 3045
land into a land that ye *k* not ... Jer 16:13 3045
I will this once cause them to *k* ... Jer 16:21 3045
I will cause them to *k* mine hand ... Jer 16:21 3045
they shall *k* that my name is The ... Jer 16:21 3045
who can *k* it? ... Jer 17:9 3045
was not this to *k* me ... Jer 22:16 1847
cast into a land which they *k* not ... Jer 22:28 3045
I will give them an heart to *k* me ... Jer 24:7 3045
But *k* ye for certain, that if ye ... Jer 26:15 3045
For I *k* the thoughts that I think ... Jer 29:11 3045
K that thus saith the LORD of the ... Jer 29:16
even I *k*, and am a witness, saith ... Jer 29:23 3045
his brother, saying, *K* the LORD ... Jer 31:34 3045
for they shall all *k* me, from the ... Jer 31:34 3045
and let no man *k* where ye be ... Jer 36:19 3045
Let no man *k* of these words, and ... Jer 38:24 3045
Dost thou certainly *k* that Baalis ... Jer 40:14 3045
Nethaniah, and no man shall *k* it ... Jer 40:15 3045
k certainly that I have ... Jer 42:19 3045
Now therefore *k* certainly that ye ... Jer 42:22 3045
shall *k* whose words shall stand, ... Jer 44:28 3045
that ye may *k* that my words shall ... Jer 44:29 3045
and all ye that *k* his name ... Jer 48:17 3045
I *k* his wrath, saith the LORD ... Jer 48:30 3045
yet shall *k* that there hath been ... Eze 2:5 3045
they shall *k* that I the LORD have ... Eze 5:13 3045
ye shall *k* that I am the LORD ... Eze 6:7 3045
they shall *k* that I am the LORD, ... Eze 6:10 3045
Then shall ye *k* that I am the ... Eze 6:13 3045
they shall *k* that I am the LORD ... Eze 6:14 3045
ye shall *k* that I am the LORD ... Eze 7:4 3045
ye shall *k* that I am the LORD ... Eze 7:9 3045
they shall *k* that I am the LORD ... Eze 7:27 3045
for I *k* the things that come into ... Eze 11:5 3045
ye shall *k* that I am the LORD ... Eze 11:10 3045
ye shall *k* that I am the LORD ... Eze 11:12 3045
they shall *k* that I am the LORD, ... Eze 12:15 3045
they shall *k* that I am the LORD ... Eze 12:16 3045
ye shall *k* that I am the LORD ... Eze 12:20 3045
ye shall *k* that I am the Lord GOD ... Eze 13:9 3045
ye shall *k* that I am the LORD ... Eze 13:14 3045
ye shall *k* that I am the LORD ... Eze 13:21 3045
ye shall *k* that I am the LORD ... Eze 13:23 3045
ye shall *k* that I am the LORD ... Eze 14:8 3045
ye shall *k* that I have not done ... Eze 14:23 3045
ye shall *k* that I am the LORD, ... Eze 15:7 3045
Jerusalem to *k* her abominations ... Eze 16:2 3045
thou shalt *k* that I am the LORD ... Eze 16:62 3045
K ye not what these things mean ... Eze 17:12 3045
ye shall *k* that I the LORD have ... Eze 17:21 3045
k that I the LORD have brought ... Eze 17:24 3045
cause them to *k* the abominations ... Eze 20:4 3045
that they might *k* that I am the ... Eze 20:12 3045
that ye may *k* that I am the LORD ... Eze 20:20 3045
they might *k* that I am the LORD ... Eze 20:26 3045
ye shall *k* that I am the LORD ... Eze 20:38 3045
ye shall *k* that I am the LORD, ... Eze 20:42 3045
ye shall *k* that I am the LORD, ... Eze 20:44 3045
That all flesh may *k* that I the ... Eze 21:5 3045
thou shalt *k* that I am the LORD ... Eze 22:16 3045
ye shall *k* that I the LORD have ... Eze 22:22 3045
ye shall *k* that I am the Lord GOD ... Eze 23:49 3045
ye shall *k* that I am the Lord GOD ... Eze 24:24 3045
they shall *k* that I am the LORD ... Eze 24:27 3045
ye shall *k* that I am the LORD ... Eze 25:5 3045
thou shalt *k* that I am the LORD ... Eze 25:7 3045
they shall *k* that I am the LORD ... Eze 25:11 3045
they shall *k* my vengeance, saith ... Eze 25:14 3045
they shall *k* that I am the LORD, ... Eze 25:17 3045
they shall *k* that I am the LORD ... Eze 26:6 3045
All they that *k* thee among the ... Eze 28:19 3045
they shall *k* that I am the LORD, ... Eze 28:22 3045
they shall *k* that I am the LORD ... Eze 28:23 3045
they shall *k* that I am the Lord ... Eze 28:24 3045
they shall *k* that I am the LORD ... Eze 28:26 3045
Egypt shall *k* that I am the LORD ... Eze 29:6 3045
they shall *k* that I am the LORD ... Eze 29:9 3045
but they shall *k* that I am the ... Eze 29:16 3045
they shall *k* that I am the LORD ... Eze 29:21 3045
they shall *k* that I am the LORD, ... Eze 30:8 3045
they shall *k* that I am the LORD ... Eze 30:19 3045
they shall *k* that I am the LORD, ... Eze 30:25 3045
they shall *k* that I am the LORD ... Eze 30:26 3045
then shall they *k* that I am the ... Eze 32:15 3045
Then shall they *k* that I am the ... Eze 33:29 3045
then shall they *k* that a prophet ... Eze 33:33 3045
shall *k* that I am the LORD, when ... Eze 34:27 3045
Thus shall they *k* that I the LORD ... Eze 34:30 3045
thou shalt *k* that I am the LORD ... Eze 35:4 3045
ye shall *k* that I am the LORD ... Eze 35:9 3045
thou shalt *k* that I am the LORD, ... Eze 35:12 3045
they shall *k* that I am the LORD ... Eze 35:15 3045
ye shall *k* that I am the Lord ... Eze 36:11 3045
the heathen shall *k* that I am the ... Eze 36:23 3045
shall *k* that I the LORD build the ... Eze 36:36 3045
they shall *k* that I am the LORD ... Eze 36:38 3045
ye shall *k* that I am the LORD ... Eze 37:6 3045
ye shall *k* that I am the LORD, ... Eze 37:13 3045
then shall ye *k* that I the LORD ... Eze 37:14 3045
the heathen shall *k* that I the ... Eze 37:28 3045
safely, shalt thou not *k* it ... Eze 38:14 3045

land, that the heathen may *k* me ... Eze 38:16 3045
they shall *k* that I am the LORD ... Eze 38:23 3045
they shall *k* that I am the LORD ... Eze 39:6 3045
the heathen shall *k* that I am the ... Eze 39:7 3045
k that I am the LORD their God ... Eze 39:22 3045
the heathen shall *k* that the ... Eze 39:23 3045
Then shall they *k* that I am the ... Eze 39:28 3045
was troubled to *k* the dream ... Dan 2:3 3045
I *k* of certainty that ye would ... Dan 2:8 3046
I shall *k* that ye can shew me the ... Dan 2:9 3046
to them that *k* understanding ... Dan 2:21 3046
that thou mightest *k* the thoughts ... Dan 2:30 3046
because I *k* that the spirit of ... Dan 4:9 3046
k that the most High ruleth in ... Dan 4:17 3046
till thou *k* that the most High ... Dan 4:25 3046
until thou *k* that the most High ... Dan 4:32 3046
which see not, nor hear, nor *k* ... Dan 5:23 3046
king, and said unto the king, *K* ... Dan 6:15 3046
made me *k* the interpretation of ... Dan 7:16 3046
Then I would *k* the truth of the ... Dan 7:19 3046
I will make thee *k* what shall be ... Dan 8:19 3045
K therefore and understand, that ... Dan 9:25 3045
but the people that do *k* their ... Dan 11:32 3045
For she did not *k* that I gave her ... Hos 2:8 3045
and thou shalt *k* the LORD ... Hos 2:20 3045
I *k* Ephraim, and Israel is not hid ... Hos 5:3 3045
Then shall we *k*, if we follow on ... Hos 6:3 3045
if we follow on to *k* the LORD ... Hos 6:3 3045
cry unto me, My God, we *k* thee ... Hos 8:2 3045
Israel shall *k* it ... Hos 9:7 3045
thou shalt *k* no god but me ... Hos 13:4 3045
I did *k* thee in the wilderness, ... Hos 13:5 3045
prudent, and he shall *k* them ... Hos 14:9 3045
ye shall *k* that I am in the midst ... Joel 2:27 3045
So shall ye *k* that I am the LORD ... Joel 3:17 3045
For they *k* not to do right, saith ... Amos 3:10 3045
For I *k* your manifold ... Amos 5:12 3045
that we may *k* for whose cause ... Jonah 1:7 3045
for I *k* that for my sake this ... Jonah 1:12 3045
Is it not for you to *k* judgment ... Mic 3:1 3045
But they *k* not the thoughts of ... Mic 4:12 3045
that ye may *k* the righteousness ... Mic 6:5 3045
ye shall *k* that the LORD of hosts ... Zec 2:9 3045
thou shalt *k* that the LORD of ... Zec 2:11 3045
thou shalt *k* that the LORD of ... Zec 4:9 3045
ye shall *k* that the LORD of hosts ... Zec 6:15 3045
ye shall *k* that I have sent this ... Mal 2:4 3045
let not thy left hand *k* what thy ... Mt 6:3 *1097*
k how to give good gifts unto ... Mt 7:11 *1492*
Ye shall *k* them by their fruits ... Mt 7:16 *1921*
by their fruits ye shall *k* them ... Mt 7:20 *1921*
But that ye may *k* that the Son of ... Mt 9:6 *1492*
saying, See that no man *k* it ... Mt 9:30 *1097*
k the mysteries of the kingdom of ... Mt 13:11 *1097*
and said, Ye *k* not what ye ask ... Mt 20:22 *1492*
Ye *k* that the princes of the ... Mt 20:25 *1492*
we *k* that thou art true, and ... Mt 22:16 *1492*
leaves, ye *k* that summer is nigh ... Mt 24:32 *1097*
k that it is near, even at the ... Mt 24:33 *1097*
for ye *k* not what hour your Lord ... Mt 24:42 *1492*
But *k* this, that if the goodman ... Mt 24:43 *1097*
I say unto you, I *k* you not ... Mt 25:12 *1492*
for ye *k* neither the day nor the ... Mt 25:13 *1492*
Ye *k* that after two days is the ... Mt 26:2 *1492*
saying, I *k* not what thou sayest ... Mt 26:70 *1492*
with an oath, I do not *k* the man ... Mt 26:72 *1492*
to swear, saying, I *k* not the man ... Mt 26:74 *1492*
for I *k* that ye seek Jesus, which ... Mt 28:5 *1492*
I *k* thee who thou art, the Holy ... Mk 1:24 *1492*
But that ye may *k* that the Son of ... Mk 2:10 *1492*
Unto you it is given to *k* the ... Mk 4:11 *1097*
unto them, *K* ye not this parable ... Mk 4:13 *1492*
how then will ye *k* all parables ... Mk 4:13 *1097*
straitly that no man should *k* it ... Mk 5:43 *1097*
house, and would have no man *k* it ... Mk 7:24 *1097*
not that any man should *k* it ... Mk 9:30 *1097*
unto them, Ye *k* not what ye ask ... Mk 10:38 *1492*
them, Ye *k* that they which are ... Mk 10:42 *1492*
we *k* that thou art true, and ... Mk 12:14 *1492*
because ye *k* not the scriptures, ... Mk 12:24 *1492*
leaves, ye *k* that summer is near ... Mk 13:28 *1097*
k that it is nigh, even at the ... Mk 13:29 *1097*
for ye *k* not when the time is ... Mk 13:33 *1492*
for ye *k* not when the master of ... Mk 13:35 *1492*
I *k* not, neither understand I ... Mk 14:68 *1492*
I *k* not this man of whom ye speak ... Mk 14:71 *1492*
That thou mightest *k* the ... Lk 1:4 *1921*
the angel, Whereby shall I *k* this ... Lk 1:18 *1097*
this be, seeing I *k* not a man ... Lk 1:34 *1097*
I *k* thee who thou art ... Lk 4:34 *1492*
But that ye may *k* that the Son of ... Lk 5:24 *1492*
Unto you it is given to *k* the ... Lk 8:10 *1097*
Ye *k* not what manner of spirit ye ... Lk 9:55 *1492*
k how to give good gifts unto ... Lk 11:13 *1492*
And this *k*, that if the goodman of ... Lk 12:39 *1097*
I *k* you not whence ye are ... Lk 13:25 *1492*
I *k* you not whence ye are ... Lk 13:27 *1492*
that he might *k* how much every ... Lk 19:15 *1097*
we *k* that thou sayest and teachest ... Lk 20:21 *1492*
then *k* that the desolation ... Lk 21:20 *1097*
k of your own selves that summer ... Lk 21:30 *1097*
k ye that the kingdom of God is ... Lk 21:31 *1097*
him, saying, Woman, I *k* him not ... Lk 22:57 *1492*
Man, I *k* not what thou sayest ... Lk 22:60 *1492*
for they *k* not what they do ... Lk 23:34 *1492*
holden that they should not *k* him ... Lk 24:16 *1921*
one among you, whom ye *k* not ... Jn 1:26 *1492*

we *k* that thou art a teacher come ... Jn 3:2 1492
unto thee, We speak that we do *k* ... Jn 3:11 1492
Ye worship ye *k* not what ... Jn 4:22 1492
we *k* what we worship ... Jn 4:22 1492
I *k* that Messias cometh, which is ... Jn 4:25 1492
have meat to eat that ye *k* not of ... Jn 4:32 1492
k that this is indeed the Christ, ... Jn 4:42 1492
I *k* that the witness which he ... Jn 5:32 1492
But I *k* you, that ye have not the ... Jn 5:42 1097
whose father and mother we *k* ... Jn 6:42 1492
he shall *k* of the doctrine, ... Jn 7:17 1097
Do the rulers *k* indeed that this ... Jn 7:26 1097
Howbeit we *k* this man whence he ... Jn 7:27 1492
both *k* me, and ye *k* whence I am ... Jn 7:28 1492
sent me is true, whom ye *k* not ... Jn 7:28 1492
But I *k* him ... Jn 7:29 1492
it hear him, and *k* what he doeth ... Jn 7:51 1097
for I *k* whence I came, and whither ... Jn 8:14 1492
Jesus answered, Ye neither *k* me ... Jn 8:19 1492
man, then shall ye *k* that I am he ... Jn 8:28 1097
ye shall *k* the truth, and the ... Jn 8:32 1097
I *k* that ye are Abraham's seed ... Jn 8:37 1097
Now we *k* that thou hast a devil ... Jn 8:52 1492
but I *k* him ... Jn 8:55 1492
I *k* him not, I shall be a liar ... Jn 8:55 1492
but I *k* him, and keep his saying ... Jn 8:55 1492
He said, I *k* not ... Jn 9:12 1492
We *k* that this is our son, and ... Jn 9:20 1492
what means he now seeth, we *k* not ... Jn 9:21 1492
hath opened his eyes, we *k* not ... Jn 9:21 1492
we *k* that this man is a sinner ... Jn 9:24 1492
he be a sinner or no, I *k* not ... Jn 9:25 1492
one thing I *k*, that, whereas I ... Jn 9:25 1492
We *k* that God spake unto Moses ... Jn 9:29 1492
we *k* not from whence he is ... Jn 9:29 1492
that ye *k* not from whence he is, ... Jn 9:30 1492
Now we *k* that God heareth not ... Jn 9:31 1492
for they *k* his voice ... Jn 10:4 1492
for they *k* not the voice of ... Jn 10:5 1492
k my sheep, and am known of mine ... Jn 10:14 1097
me, even so *k* I the Father ... Jn 10:15 1097
I *k* them, and they follow me ... Jn 10:27 1097
that ye may *k*, and believe, that ... Jn 10:38 1097
But I *k*, that even now, ... Jn 11:22 1492
I *k* that he shall rise again in ... Jn 11:24 1492
unto them, Ye *k* nothing at all, ... Jn 11:49 1492
I *k* that his commandment is life ... Jn 12:50 1492
but thou shalt *k* hereafter ... Jn 13:7 1097
K ye what I have done to you ... Jn 13:12 1097
If ye *k* these things, happy are ... Jn 13:17 1492
I *k* whom I have chosen ... Jn 13:18 1492
By this shall all men *k* that ye ... Jn 13:35 1097
I go ye *k*, and the way ye *k* ... Jn 14:4 1492
we *k* not whither thou goest ... Jn 14:5 1492
and how can we *k* the way ... Jn 14:5
and from henceforth ye *k* him ... Jn 14:7 1097
but ye *k* him ... Jn 14:17 1492
At that day ye shall *k* that I am ... Jn 14:20 1097
may *k* that I love the Father ... Jn 14:31 1097
ye *k* that it hated me before it ... Jn 15:18 1097
because they *k* not him that sent ... Jn 15:21 1492
that they might *k* thee the only ... Jn 17:3 1097
that the world may *k* that thou ... Jn 17:23 1097
behold, they *k* what I said ... Jn 18:21 1492
that ye may *k* that I find no ... Jn 19:4 1097
we *k* not where they have laid him ... Jn 20:2 1492
I *k* not where they have laid him ... Jn 20:13 1492
we *k* that his testimony is true ... Jn 21:24 1492
It is not for you to *k* the times ... Acts 1:7 1097
of you, as ye yourselves also *k* ... Acts 2:22 1492
the house of Israel *k* assuredly ... Acts 2:36 1097
this man strong, whom ye see and *k* ... Acts 3:16 1492
Ye *k* how that it is an unlawful ... Acts 10:28 1987
That word, I say, ye *k*, which was ... Acts 10:37 1492
Now I *k* of a surety, that the ... Acts 12:11 1492
ye *k* how that a good while ago ... Acts 15:7 1987
May we *k* what this new doctrine, ... Acts 17:19 1097
we would *k* therefore what these ... Acts 17:20 1097
said, Jesus I *k*, and Paul I *k* ... Acts 19:15 1987
ye *k* that by this craft we have ... Acts 19:25 1987
to him, he said unto them, Ye *k* ... Acts 20:18 1987
I *k* that ye all, among whom I ... Acts 20:25 1492
For I *k* this, that after my ... Acts 20:29 1492
Yea, ye yourselves *k*, that these ... Acts 20:34 1097
all may *k* that those things, ... Acts 21:24 1097
when he could not *k* the certainty ... Acts 21:34 1097
that thou shouldest *k* his will ... Acts 22:14 1097
they *k* that I imprisoned and beat ... Acts 22:19 1987
that he might *k* wherefore they ... Acts 22:24 1921
Forasmuch as I *k* that thou hast ... Acts 24:10 1987
I will *k* the uttermost of your ... Acts 24:22 1231
Especially because I *k* thee to be ... Acts 26:3
at Jerusalem, *k* all the Jews ... Acts 26:4 2467
I *k* that thou believest ... Acts 26:27 1492
we *k* that every where it is ... Acts 28:22 1110
Now we *k* that what things soever ... Rom 3:19 1492
K ye not, that so many of us as ... Rom 6:3 50
K ye not, that to whom ye yield ... Rom 6:16 1492
K ye not, brethren, (for I speak ... Rom 7:1 50
I speak to them that *k* the law ... Rom 7:1 1097
For we *k* that the law is ... Rom 7:14 1492
For I *k* that in me (that is, in ... Rom 7:18 1492
For we *k* that the whole creation ... Rom 8:22 1492
for we *k* not what we should pray ... Rom 8:26 1492
we *k* that all things work ... Rom 8:28 1492
But I say, Did not Israel *k* ... Rom 10:19 1097
I *k*, and am persuaded by the Lord ... Rom 14:14 1492

I *k* not whether I baptized any ... 1Cor 1:16 1492
not to *k* any thing among you ... 1Cor 2:2 1492
that we might *k* the things that ... 1Cor 2:12 1492
neither can he *k* them, because ... 1Cor 2:14 1097
K ye not that ye are the temple ... 1Cor 3:16 1492
For I *k* nothing by myself ... 1Cor 4:4 4892
if the Lord will, and will *k* ... 1Cor 4:19 1097
K ye not that a little leaven ... 1Cor 5:6 1492
Do ye not *k* that the saints shall ... 1Cor 6:2 1492
K ye not that we shall judge ... 1Cor 6:3 1492
K ye not that the unrighteous ... 1Cor 6:9 1492
K ye not that your bodies are the ... 1Cor 6:15 1492
k ye not that he which is joined ... 1Cor 6:16 1492
k ye not that your body is the ... 1Cor 6:19 1492
we *k* that we all have knowledge ... 1Cor 8:1 1492
nothing yet as he ought to *k* ... 1Cor 8:2 1097
we *k* that an idol is nothing in ... 1Cor 8:4 1492
Do ye not *k* that they which ... 1Cor 9:13 1492
K ye not that they which run in a ... 1Cor 9:24 1492
But I would have you *k*, that the ... 1Cor 11:3 1492
Ye *k* that ye were Gentiles, ... 1Cor 12:2 1492
For we *k* in part, and we prophesy ... 1Cor 13:9 1097
now I *k* in part ... 1Cor 13:12 1097
but then shall I *k* even as also I ... 1Cor 13:12 1921
Therefore if I *k* not the meaning ... 1Cor 14:11 1492
forasmuch as ye *k* that your ... 1Cor 15:58 1492
(ye *k* the house of Stephanas, ... 1Cor 16:15 1492
but that ye might *k* the love ... 2Cor 2:4 1097
that I might *k* the proof of you, ... 2Cor 2:9 1097
For we *k* that if our earthly ... 2Cor 5:1 1492
Wherefore henceforth *k* we no man ... 2Cor 5:16 1492
now henceforth *k* we him no more ... 2Cor 5:16 1097
For ye *k* the grace of our Lord ... 2Cor 8:9 1097
For I *k* the forwardness of your ... 2Cor 9:2 1492
K ye not your own selves, how ... 2Cor 13:5 1921
But I trust that ye shall *k* that ... 2Cor 13:6 1097
K ye therefore that they which ... Gal 3:7 1097
Ye *k* how through infirmity of the ... Gal 4:13 1492
that ye may *k* what is the hope of ... Eph 1:18 1492
to *k* the love of Christ, which ... Eph 3:19 1097
For this ye *k*, that no ... Eph 5:5 1097
But that ye also may *k* my affairs ... Eph 6:21 1492
that ye might *k* our affairs ... Eph 6:22 1097
For I *k* that this shall turn to ... Phil 1:19 1492
I *k* that I shall abide and ... Phil 1:25 1492
good comfort, when I *k* your state ... Phil 2:19 1097
But ye *k* the proof of him, that, ... Phil 2:22 1097
That I may *k* him, and the power of ... Phil 3:10 1097
I *k* both how to be abased ... Phil 4:12 1492
and I *k* how to abound ... Phil 4:12 1492
Now ye Philippians *k* also ... Phil 4:15 1492
that ye may *k* how ye ought to ... Col 4:6 1492
that he might *k* your estate ... Col 4:8 1097
as ye *k* what manner of men we ... 1Th 1:5 1492
k our entrance in unto you, that ... 1Th 2:1 1492
shamefully entreated, as ye *k* ... 1Th 2:2 1492
used we flattering words, as ye *k* ... 1Th 2:5 1492
As ye *k* how we exhorted and ... 1Th 2:11 1492
for yourselves *k* that we are ... 1Th 3:3 1492
even as it came to pass, and ye *k* ... 1Th 3:4 1492
I sent to *k* your faith, lest by ... 1Th 3:5 1097
For ye *k* what commandments we ... 1Th 4:2 1492
k how to possess his vessel in ... 1Th 4:4 1492
as the Gentiles which *k* not God ... 1Th 4:5 1492
For yourselves *k* perfectly that ... 1Th 5:2 1492
to *k* them which labour among you, ... 1Th 5:12 1492
vengeance on them that *k* not God ... 2Th 1:8 1492
now ye *k* what withholdeth that he ... 2Th 2:6 1492
For yourselves *k* how ye ought to ... 2Th 3:7 1492
But we *k* that the law is good, if ... 1Ti 1:8 1492
(For if a man *k* not how to rule ... 1Ti 3:5 1492
that thou mayest *k* how thou ... 1Ti 3:15 1492
them which believe and *k* the truth ... 1Ti 4:3 1921
for I *k* whom I have believed, and ... 2Ti 1:12 1492
This *k* also, that in the last ... 2Ti 3:1 1097
They profess that they *k* God ... Titus 1:16 1492
his brother, saying, *K* the Lord ... Heb 8:11 1097
for all shall *k* me, from the ... Heb 8:11 1492
For we *k* him that hath said, ... Heb 10:30 1492
For ye *k* how that afterward, when ... Heb 12:17 2467
K ye that our brother Timothy is ... Heb 13:23 1097
But wilt thou *k*, O vain man, that ... Jas 2:20 1097
k ye not that the friendship of ... Jas 4:4 1492
Whereas ye *k* not what shall be on ... Jas 4:14 1987
Let him *k*, that he which ... Jas 5:20 1097
Forasmuch as ye *k* that ye were ... 1Pet 1:18 1492
of these things, though ye *k* them ... 2Pet 1:12 1492
seeing ye *k* these things before, ... 2Pet 3:17 4267
hereby we do *k* that we *k* him, ... 1Jn 2:3 1097
hereby we do *k* that we *k* him ... 1Jn 2:3 1097
I *k* him, and keepeth not his ... 1Jn 2:4 1097
hereby *k* we that we are in him ... 1Jn 2:5 1097
whereby we *k* that it is the last ... 1Jn 2:18 1097
the Holy One, and ye *k* all things ... 1Jn 2:20 1492
you because ye *k* not the truth ... 1Jn 2:21 1492
but because ye *k* it ... 1Jn 2:21 1492
If ye *k* that he is righteous ... 1Jn 2:29 1492
ye *k* that every one that doeth ... 1Jn 2:29 1097
but we *k* that, when he shall ... 1Jn 3:2 1492
ye *k* that he was manifested to ... 1Jn 3:5 1492
We *k* that we have passed from ... 1Jn 3:14 1492
ye *k* that no murderer hath ... 1Jn 3:15 1492
hereby we *k* that we are of the ... 1Jn 3:19 1097
hereby we *k* that he abideth in us ... 1Jn 3:24 1097
Hereby *k* ye the Spirit of God ... 1Jn 4:2 1097
Hereby *k* we the spirit of truth, ... 1Jn 4:6 1097

Hereby *k* we that we dwell in him, ... 1Jn 4:13 1097
By this we *k* that we love the ... 1Jn 5:2 1097
that ye may *k* that ye have ... 1Jn 5:13 1492
And if we *k* that he hear us, ... 1Jn 5:15 1492
we *k* that we have the petitions ... 1Jn 5:15 1492
We *k* that whosoever is born of ... 1Jn 5:18 1492
we *k* that we are of God, and the ... 1Jn 5:19 1492
we *k* that the Son of God is come, ... 1Jn 5:20 1492
that we may *k* him that is true, ... 1Jn 5:20 1097
ye *k* that our record is true ... 3Jn 12 1492
of those things which they *k* not ... Jude 10 1492
but what they *k* naturally ... Jude 10 1987
I *k* thy works, and thy labour, and ... Rev 2:2 1492
I *k* thy works, and tribulation, and ... Rev 2:9 1492
I *k* the blasphemy of them which ... Rev 2:9
I *k* thy works, and where thou ... Rev 2:13 1492
I *k* thy works, and charity, and ... Rev 2:19 1492
all the churches shall *k* that I ... Rev 2:23 1097
I *k* thy works, that thou hast a ... Rev 3:1 1492
thou shalt not *k* what hour I will ... Rev 3:3 1097
I *k* thy works ... Rev 3:8 1492
to *k* that I have loved thee ... Rev 3:9 1097
I *k* thy works, that thou art ... Rev 3:15 1492

KNOWEST {89}

for thou *k* my service which I ... Gen 30:26 3045
Thou *k* how I have served thee, and ... Gen 30:29 3045
if thou *k* any men of activity ... Gen 47:6 3045
k thou not yet that Egypt is ... Ex 10:7 3045
thou *k* the people, that they are ... Ex 32:22 3045
forasmuch as thou *k* how we are to ... Num 10:31 3045
whom thou *k* to be the elders of ... Num 11:16 3045
Thou *k* all the travel that hath ... Num 20:14 3045
diseases of Egypt, which thou *k* ... Deut 7:15 3045
of the Anakims, whom thou *k* ... Deut 9:2 3045
Only the trees which thou *k* that ... Deut 20:20 3045
a nation which thou *k* not eat up ... Deut 28:33 3045
Thou *k* the thing that the LORD ... Josh 14:6 3045
K thou not that the Philistines ... Judg 15:11 3045
thou *k* what Saul hath done, how ... 1Sa 28:9 3045
How *k* thou that Saul and Jonathan ... 2Sa 1:5 3045
k thou not that it will be ... 2Sa 2:26 3045
Thou *k* Abner the son of Ner, that ... 2Sa 3:25 3045
for thou, Lord GOD, *k* thy servant ... 2Sa 7:20 3045
thou *k* thy father and his men, ... 2Sa 17:8 3045
my lord the king, thou *k* it not ... 1Kin 1:18 3045
Moreover thou *k* also what Joab ... 1Kin 2:5 3045
k what thou oughtest to do unto ... 1Kin 2:9 3045
Thou *k* that the kingdom was mine, ... 1Kin 2:15 3045
Thou *k* all the wickedness which ... 1Kin 2:44 3045
Thou *k* how that David my father ... 1Kin 5:3 3045
for thou *k* that there is not ... 1Kin 5:6 3045
to his ways, whose heart thou *k* ... 1Kin 8:39 3045
k the hearts of all the children ... 1Kin 8:39 3045
K thou that the LORD will take ... 2Kin 2:3 3045
K thou that the LORD will take ... 2Kin 2:5 3045
thou *k* that thy servant did fear ... 2Kin 4:1 3045
for thou *k* thy servant ... 1Chr 17:18 3045
all his ways, whose heart thou *k* ... 2Chr 6:30 3045
(for thou only *k* the hearts of ... 2Chr 6:30 3045
Thou *k* that I am not wicked ... Job 10:7 1847
What *k* thou, that we know not ... Job 15:9 3045
K thou not this of old, since man ... Job 20:4 3045
therefore speak what thou *k* ... Job 34:33 3045
the measures thereof, if thou *k* ... Job 38:5 3045
declare if thou *k* it all ... Job 38:18 3045
K thou it, because thou wast then ... Job 38:21 3045
K thou the ordinances of heaven ... Job 38:33 3045
K thou the time when the wild ... Job 39:1 3045
or *k* thou the time when they ... Job 39:2 3045
refrained my lips, O LORD, thou *k* ... Ps 40:9 3045
O God, thou *k* my foolishness ... Ps 69:5 3045
Thou *k* my downsitting and mine ... Ps 139:2 3045
lo, O LORD, thou *k* it altogether ... Ps 139:4 3045
for thou *k* not what a day may ... Prov 27:1 3045
for thou *k* not what evil shall be ... Eccl 11:2 3045
As thou *k* not what is the way of ... Eccl 11:5 3045
even so thou *k* not the works of ... Eccl 11:5 3045
for thou *k* not whether shall ... Eccl 11:6 3045
call a nation that thou *k* not ... Is 55:5 3045
nation whose language thou *k* not ... Jer 5:15 3045
But thou, O LORD, *k* me ... Jer 12:3 3045
into a land which thou *k* not ... Jer 15:14 3045
O LORD, thou *k* ... Jer 15:15 3045
in the land which thou *k* not ... Jer 17:4 3045
thou *k*: that which came ... Jer 17:16 3045
thou *k* all their counsel against ... Jer 18:23 3045
mighty things, which thou *k* not ... Jer 33:3 3045
And I answered, O Lord GOD, thou *k* ... Eze 37:3 3045
K thou wherefore I come unto thee ... Dan 10:20 3045
unto me, *K* thou not what these be ... Zec 4:5 3045
and said, *K* thou not what these be ... Zec 4:13 3045
K thou that the Pharisees were ... Mt 15:12 1492
Thou *k* the commandments, Do not ... Mk 10:19 1492
Thou *k* the commandments, Do not ... Lk 18:20 1492
shalt thrice deny that thou *k* me ... Lk 22:34 1492
saith unto him, Whence *k* thou me ... Jn 1:48 1097
of Israel, and *k* not these things ... Jn 3:10 1097
him, What I do thou *k* not now ... Jn 13:7 1492
we sure that thou *k* all things ... Jn 16:30 1492
k thou not that I have power to ... Jn 19:10 1492
thou *k* that I love thee ... Jn 21:15 1492
thou *k* that I love thee ... Jn 21:16 1492
unto him, Lord, thou *k* all things ... Jn 21:17 1492
thou *k* that I love thee ... Jn 21:17 1097
which *k* the hearts of all men, ... Acts 1:24 2589
no wrong, as thou very well *k* ... Acts 25:10 1921
k his will, and approvest the ... Rom 2:18 1097

K

For what *k* thou, O wife, whether	1Cor 7:16	*1492*
or how *k* thou, O man, whether	1Cor 7:16	*1492*
This thou *k*, that all they which	2Ti 1:15	*1492*
me at Ephesus, thou *k* very well	2Ti 1:18	*1097*
k not that thou art wretched, and	Rev 3:17	*1492*
And I said unto him, Sir, thou *k*	Rev 7:14	*1492*

KNOWETH {104}

My lord *k* that the children are	Gen 33:13	3045
when he *k* of it, then he shall be	Lev 5:3	3045
when he *k* of it, then he shall be	Lev 5:4	3045
he *k* thy walking through this	Deut 2:7	3045
but no man *k* of his sepulchre	Deut 34:6	3045
gods, the LORD God of gods, he *k*	Josh 22:22	3045
ever for the iniquity which he *k*	1Sa 3:13	3045
Thy father certainly *k* that I	1Sa 20:3	3045
and that also Saul my father *k*	1Sa 23:17	3045
Today thy servant *k* that I have	2Sa 14:22	3045
for all Israel *k* that thy father	2Sa 17:10	3045
reign, and David our lord *k* it not	1Kin 1:11	3045
who *k* whether thou art come to	Est 4:14	3045
For he *k* vain men	Job 11:11	3045
who *k* not such things as these	Job 12:3	854
Who *k* not in all these that the	Job 12:9	3045
come to honour, and he *k* it not	Job 14:21	3045
he *k* that the day of darkness is	Job 15:23	3045
the place of him that *k* not God	Job 18:21	3045
But he *k* the way that I take	Job 23:10	3045
There is a path which no fowl *k*	Job 28:7	3045
Man *k* not the price thereof	Job 28:13	3045
and he *k* the place thereof	Job 28:23	3045
Therefore he *k* their works	Job 34:25	5234
yet he *k* it not in great	Job 35:15	3045
For the LORD *k* the way of the	Ps 1:6	3045
The LORD *k* the days of the	Ps 37:18	3045
k not who shall gather them	Ps 39:6	3045
for he *k* the secrets of the heart	Ps 44:21	3045
among us any that *k* how long	Ps 74:9	3045
Who *k* the power of thine anger	Ps 90:11	3045
A brutish man *k* not	Ps 92:6	3045
The LORD *k* the thoughts of man,	Ps 94:11	3045
For he *k* our frame	Ps 103:14	3045
the sun *k* his going down	Ps 104:19	3045
but the proud he *k* afar off	Ps 138:6	3045
and that my soul *k* right well	Ps 139:14	3045
k not that it is for his life	Prov 7:23	3045
she is simple, and *k* nothing	Prov 9:13	3045
But he *k* not that the dead are	Prov 9:18	3045
The heart *k* his own bitterness	Prov 14:10	3045
who *k* the ruin of them both	Prov 24:22	3045
who *k* whether he shall be a wise	Eccl 2:19	3045
Who *k* the spirit of man that	Eccl 3:21	3045
that *k* to walk before the living	Eccl 6:8	3045
For who *k* what is good for man in	Eccl 6:12	3045
k that thou thyself likewise hast	Eccl 7:22	3045
who *k* the interpretation of a	Eccl 8:1	3045
For he *k* not that which shall be	Eccl 8:7	3045
no man *k* either love or hatred by	Eccl 9:1	3045
For man also *k* not his time	Eccl 9:12	3045
because he *k* not how to go to the	Eccl 10:15	3045
The ox *k* his owner, and the ass	Is 1:3	3045
and who *k* us?	Is 29:15	3045
the heaven *k* her appointed times	Jer 8:7	3045
k me, that I am the LORD which	Jer 9:24	3045
he *k* what is in the darkness, and	Dan 2:22	3046
his strength, and he *k* it not	Hos 7:9	3045
and there upon him, yet he *k* not	Hos 7:9	3045
Who *k* if he will return and repent	Joel 2:14	3045
he *k* them that trust in him	Nah 1:7	3045
but the unjust *k* no shame	Zeph 3:5	3045
for your Father *k* what things ye	Mt 6:8	*1492*
for your heavenly Father *k* that	Mt 6:32	*1492*
no man *k* the Son, but the Father	Mt 11:27	*1921*
neither *k* any man the Father,	Mt 11:27	*1921*
hour *k* no man, no, not the angels	Mt 24:36	*1492*
spring and grow up, he *k* not how	Mk 4:27	*1492*
of that day and that hour *k* no man	Mk 13:32	*1492*
no man *k* who the Son is, but the	Lk 10:22	*1097*
your Father *k* that ye have need	Lk 12:30	*1492*
but God *k* your hearts	Lk 16:15	*1097*
How *k* this man letters, having	Jn 7:15	*1492*
cometh, no man *k* whence he is	Jn 7:27	*1097*
But this people who *k* not the law	Jn 7:49	*1097*
As the Father *k* me, even so know	Jn 10:15	*1097*
darkness *k* not whither he goeth	Jn 12:35	*1492*
it seeth him not, neither *k* him	Jn 14:17	*1097*
for the servant *k* not what his	Jn 15:15	*1492*
he *k* that he saith true, that ye	Jn 19:35	*1492*
which *k* the hearts, bare them	Acts 15:8	*2589*
what man is there that *k* not how	Acts 19:35	*1097*
For the king *k* of these things,	Acts 26:26	*1987*
he that searcheth the hearts *k*	Rom 8:27	*1492*
For what man *k* the things of a	1Cor 2:11	*1492*
so the things of God *k* no man	1Cor 2:11	*1492*
The Lord *k* the thoughts of the	1Cor 3:20	*1097*
any man think that he *k* any thing	1Cor 8:2	*1492*
he *k* nothing yet as he ought to	1Cor 8:2	*1097*
I love you not? God *k*	2Cor 11:11	*1492*
for evermore, *k* that I lie not	2Cor 11:31	*1492*
I cannot tell: God *k*	2Cor 12:2	*1492*
I cannot tell: God *k*	2Cor 12:3	*1492*
The Lord *k* them that are his	2Ti 2:19	*1097*
to him that *k* to do good, and	Jas 4:17	*1492*
The Lord *k* how to deliver the	2Pet 2:9	*1492*
k not whither he goeth, because	1Jn 2:11	*1492*
therefore the world *k* us not	1Jn 3:1	*1097*
than our heart, and *k* all things	1Jn 3:20	*1097*
he that *k* God heareth us	1Jn 4:6	*1097*
loveth is born of God, and *k* God	1Jn 4:7	*1097*
He that loveth not *k* not God	1Jn 4:8	*1097*
which no man *k* saving he that	Rev 2:17	*1097*
because he *k* that he hath but a	Rev 12:12	*1492*

KNOWING {51}

shall be as gods, *k* good and evil	Gen 3:5	3045
my father David not *k* thereof	1Kin 2:32	3045
Jesus *k* their thoughts said,	Mt 9:4	*1492*
not *k* the scriptures, nor the	Mt 22:29	*1492*
immediately *k* in himself that	Mk 5:30	*1921*
k what was done in her, came and	Mk 5:33	*1492*
k that he was a just man and an	Mk 6:20	*1492*
k their hypocrisy, said unto them	Mk 12:15	*1492*
him to scorn, *k* that she was dead	Lk 8:53	*1492*
not *k* what he said	Lk 9:33	*1492*
k their thoughts, said unto them,	Lk 11:17	*1492*
Jesus *k* that the Father had given	Jn 13:3	*1492*
k all things that should come	Jn 18:4	*1492*
Jesus *k* that all things were now	Jn 19:28	*1492*
k that it was the Lord	Jn 21:12	*1492*
k that God had sworn with an oath	Acts 2:30	*1492*
not *k* what was done, came in	Acts 5:7	*1492*
k only the baptism of John	Acts 18:25	*1987*
not *k* the things that shall	Acts 20:22	*1492*
Who *k* the judgment of God, that	Rom 1:32	*1921*
not *k* that the goodness of God	Rom 2:4	*50*
k that tribulation worketh	Rom 5:3	*1492*
K this, that our old man is	Rom 6:6	*1097*
K that Christ being raised from	Rom 6:9	*1492*
k the time, that now it is high	Rom 13:11	*1492*
And our hope of you is stedfast, *k*	2Cor 1:7	*1492*
K that he which raised up the	2Cor 4:14	*1492*
k that, whilst we are at home in	2Cor 5:6	*1492*
K therefore the terror of the	2Cor 5:11	*1492*
K that a man is not justified by	Gal 2:16	*1492*
K that whatsoever good thing any	Eph 6:8	*1492*
k that your Master also is in	Eph 6:9	*1492*
k that I am set for the defence	Phil 1:17	*1492*
K that of the Lord ye shall	Col 3:24	*1492*
k that ye also have a Master in	Col 4:1	*1492*
K, brethren beloved, your	1Th 1:4	*1492*
K this, that the law is not made	1Ti 1:9	*1492*
k nothing, but doting about	1Ti 6:4	*1987*
k that they do gender strifes	2Ti 2:23	*1492*
k of whom thou hast learned them	2Ti 3:14	*1492*
K that he that is such is	Titus 3:11	*1492*
k that thou wilt also do more	Philem 21	*1492*
k in yourselves that ye have in	Heb 10:34	*1097*
went out, not *k* whither he went	Heb 11:8	*1987*
K this, that the trying of your	Jas 1:3	*1097*
k that we shall receive the	Jas 3:1	*1492*
k that ye are thereunto called,	1Pet 3:9	*1492*
k that the same afflictions are	1Pet 5:9	*1492*
K that shortly I must put off	2Pet 1:14	*1492*
K this first, that no prophecy of	2Pet 1:20	*1097*
K this first, that there shall	2Pet 3:3	*1097*

KNOWLEDGE {172}

garden, and the tree of *k* of good	Gen 2:9	1847
But of the tree of the *k* of good	Gen 2:17	1847
and in understanding, and in *k*	Ex 31:3	1847
wisdom, in understanding, and in *k*	Ex 35:31	1847
he hath sinned, come to his *k*	Lev 4:23	3045
he hath sinned, come to his *k*	Lev 4:28	3045
without the *k* of the congregation	Num 15:24	5869
knew the *k* of the most High,	Num 24:16	1847
in that day had no *k* between good	Deut 1:39	3045
that thou shouldest take *k* of me	Ruth 2:10	5234
be he that did take *k* of thee	Ruth 2:19	5234
for the LORD is a God of *k*	1Sa 2:3	1844
take *k* of all the lurking places	1Sa 23:23	3045
shipmen that had *k* of the sea	1Kin 9:27	3045
Give me now wisdom and *k*, that I	2Chr 1:10	4093
k for thyself, that thou mayest	2Chr 1:11	4093
Wisdom and *k* is granted unto thee	2Chr 1:12	4093
and servants that had *k* of the sea	2Chr 8:18	3045
taught the good *k* of the LORD	2Chr 30:22	7922
daughters, every one having *k*	Neh 10:28	3045
Should a wise man utter vain *k*	Job 15:2	1847
we desire not the *k* of thy ways	Job 21:14	1847
Shall any teach God *k*	Job 21:22	1847
and my lips shall utter *k* clearly	Job 33:3	1847
give ear unto me, ye that have *k*	Job 34:2	3045
Job hath spoken without *k*	Job 34:35	1847
he multiplieth words without *k*	Job 35:16	1847
I will fetch my *k* from afar	Job 36:3	1843
that is perfect in *k* is with thee	Job 36:4	1844
and they shall die without *k*	Job 36:12	1847
of him which is perfect in *k*	Job 37:16	1843
counsel by words without *k*	Job 38:2	1847
he that hideth counsel without *k*	Job 42:3	1847
all the workers of iniquity no *k*	Ps 14:4	3045
and night unto night sheweth *k*	Ps 19:2	1847
Have the workers of iniquity no *k*	Ps 53:4	3045
is there *k* in the most High	Ps 73:11	1844
he that teacheth man *k*, shall not	Ps 94:10	1847
Teach me good judgment and *k*	Ps 119:66	1847
Such *k* is too wonderful for me	Ps 139:6	1847
is man, that thou takest *k* of him	Ps 144:3	3045
to the simple, to the young man *k*	Prov 1:4	1847
of the LORD is the beginning of *k*	Prov 1:7	1847
their scorning, and fools hate *k*	Prov 1:22	1847
For that they hated *k*, and did not	Prov 1:29	1847
Yea, if thou criest after *k*	Prov 2:3	998
of the LORD, and find the *k* of God	Prov 2:5	1847
out of his mouth cometh *k*	Prov 2:6	1847
k is pleasant unto thy soul	Prov 2:10	1847
By his *k* the depths are broken up	Prov 3:20	1847
and that thy lips may keep *k*	Prov 5:2	1847
and right to them that find *k*	Prov 8:9	1847
k rather than choice gold	Prov 8:10	1847
find out *k* of witty inventions	Prov 8:12	1847
and the *k* of the holy is	Prov 9:10	1847
Wise men lay up *k*	Prov 10:14	1847
but through *k* shall the just be	Prov 11:9	1847
Whoso loveth instruction loveth *k*	Prov 12:1	1847
A prudent man concealeth *k*	Prov 12:23	1847
Every prudent man dealeth with *k*	Prov 13:16	1847
but *k* is easy unto him that	Prov 14:6	1847
not in him the lips of *k*	Prov 14:7	1847
the prudent are crowned with *k*	Prov 14:18	1847
tongue of the wise useth *k* aright	Prov 15:2	1847
The lips of the wise disperse *k*	Prov 15:7	1847
that hath understanding seeketh *k*	Prov 15:14	1847
He that hath *k* spareth his words	Prov 17:27	1847
heart of the prudent getteth *k*	Prov 18:15	1847
and the ear of the wise seeketh *k*	Prov 18:15	1847
Also, that the soul be without *k*	Prov 19:2	1847
and he will understand *k*	Prov 19:25	1847
to err from the words of *k*	Prov 19:27	1847
but the lips of *k* are a precious	Prov 20:15	1847
is instructed, he receiveth *k*	Prov 21:11	1847
The eyes of the LORD preserve *k*	Prov 22:12	1847
and apply thine heart unto my *k*	Prov 22:17	1847
excellent things in counsels and *k*	Prov 22:20	1847
and thine ears to the words of *k*	Prov 23:12	1847
by *k* shall the chambers be filled	Prov 24:4	1847
a man of *k* increaseth strength	Prov 24:5	1847
So shall the *k* of wisdom be unto	Prov 24:14	3045
k the state thereof shall be	Prov 28:2	3045
nor have the *k* of the holy	Prov 30:3	1847
great experience of wisdom and *k*	Eccl 1:16	1847
increaseth *k* increaseth sorrow	Eccl 1:18	1847
labour is in wisdom, and in *k*	Eccl 2:21	1847
is good in his sight wisdom, and *k*	Eccl 2:26	1847
but the excellency of *k* is	Eccl 7:12	1847
is no work, nor device, nor *k*	Eccl 9:10	1847
he still taught the people *k*	Eccl 12:9	1847
captivity, because they have no *k*	Is 5:13	1847
the child shall have *k* to cry	Is 8:4	3045
counsel and might, the spirit of *k*	Is 11:2	1847
be full of the *k* of the LORD	Is 11:9	1844
Whom shall he teach *k*	Is 28:9	1844
of the rash shall understand *k*	Is 32:4	1847
k shall be the stability of thy	Is 33:6	1847
path of judgment, and taught him *k*	Is 40:14	1847
his heart, neither is there *k* nor	Is 44:19	1847
and maketh their *k* foolish	Is 44:25	1847
they have no *k* that set up the	Is 45:20	3045
Thy wisdom and thy *k*, it hath	Is 47:10	1847
by his *k* shall my righteous	Is 53:11	1847
our soul, and thou takest no *k*	Is 58:3	3045
which shall feed you with *k*	Jer 3:15	1844
but to do good they have no *k*	Jer 4:22	3045
Every man is brutish in his *k*	Jer 10:14	1847
And the LORD hath given me *k* of it	Jer 11:18	3045
Every man is brutish by his *k*	Jer 51:17	1847
in all wisdom, and cunning in *k*	Dan 1:4	1847
four children, God gave them *k*	Dan 1:17	4093
k to them that know understanding	Dan 2:21	998
as an excellent spirit, and *k*	Dan 5:12	998
and fro, and *k* shall be increased	Dan 12:4	1847
mercy, nor *k* of God in the land	Hos 4:1	1847
are destroyed for lack of *k*	Hos 4:6	1847
because thou hast rejected *k*	Hos 4:6	1847
the *k* of God more than burnt	Hos 6:6	1847
the *k* of the glory of the LORD	Hab 2:14	3045
the priest's lips should keep *k*	Mal 2:7	1847
men of that place had *k* of him	Mt 14:35	*1921*
To give *k* of salvation unto his	Lk 1:77	*1108*
ye have taken away the key of *k*	Lk 11:52	*1108*
and they took *k* of them, that they	Acts 4:13	*1921*
had *k* that the word of God was	Acts 17:13	*1097*
mayest take *k* of all these things	Acts 24:8	*1921*
having more perfect *k* of that way	Acts 24:22	*1492*
not like to retain God in their *k*	Rom 1:28	*1922*
babes, which hast the form of *k*	Rom 2:20	*1108*
for by the law is the *k* of sin	Rom 3:20	*1922*
of God, but not according to *k*	Rom 10:2	*1922*
both of the wisdom and *k* of God	Rom 11:33	*1108*
of goodness, filled with all *k*	Rom 15:14	*1108*
in all utterance, and in all *k*	1Cor 1:5	*1108*
idols, we know that we all have *k*	1Cor 8:1	*1108*
K puffeth up, but charity	1Cor 8:1	*1108*
there is not in every man that *k*	1Cor 8:7	*1108*
hast *k* sit at meat in the idol's	1Cor 8:10	*1108*
through thy *k* shall the weak	1Cor 8:11	*1108*
the word of *k* by the same Spirit	1Cor 12:8	*1108*
all mysteries, and all *k*	1Cor 13:2	*1108*
whether there be *k*, it shall	1Cor 13:8	*1108*
you either by revelation, or by *k*	1Cor 14:6	*1108*
for some have not the *k* of God	1Cor 15:34	*56*
of his *k* by us in every place	2Cor 2:14	*1108*
to give the light of the *k* of the	2Cor 4:6	*1108*
By pureness, by *k*, by	2Cor 6:6	*1108*
in faith, and utterance, and *k*	2Cor 8:7	*1108*
itself against the *k* of God	2Cor 10:5	*1108*
I be rude in speech, yet not in *k*	2Cor 11:6	*1108*
and revelation in the *k* of him	Eph 1:17	*1922*
ye may understand my *k* in the	Eph 3:4	*4907*
love of Christ, which passeth *k*	Eph 3:19	*1108*
of the *k* of the Son of God, unto	Eph 4:13	*1922*
may abound yet more and more in *k*	Phil 1:9	*1922*
of the *k* of Christ Jesus my Lord	Phil 3:8	*1108*
the *k* of his will in all wisdom	Col 1:9	*1922*

and increasing in the *k* of God Col 1:10 *1922*
all the treasures of wisdom and *k* Col 2:3 *1108*
which is renewed in *k* after the Col 3:10 *1922*
to come unto the *k* of the truth 1Ti 2:4 *1922*
to come to the *k* of the truth 2Ti 3:7 *1922*
have received the *k* of the truth Heb 10:26 *1922*
man and endued with *k* among you Jas 3:13 *1990*
dwell with them according to *k* 1Pet 3:7 *1108*
unto you through the *k* of God 2Pet 1:2 *1922*
through the *k* of him that hath 2Pet 1:3 *1922*
and to virtue *k* 2Pet 1:5 *1108*
And to *k* temperance 2Pet 1:6 *1108*
in the *k* of our Lord Jesus Christ 2Pet 1:8 *1922*
world through the *k* of the Lord 2Pet 2:20 *1922*
in the *k* of our Lord and Saviour 2Pet 3:18 *1108*

KNOWN {222}
daughters which have not *k* man Gen 19:8 3045
virgin, neither had any man *k* her Gen 24:16 3045
it could not be *k* that they had Gen 41:21 3045
the plenty shall not be *k* in the Gen 41:31 3045
made himself *k* unto his brethren Gen 45:1 3045
and said, Surely this thing is *k* Ex 2:14 3045
name JEHOVAH was I not *k* to them Ex 6:3 3045
Or if it be *k* that the ox hath Ex 21:36 3045
wherein shall it be *k* here that I Ex 33:16 3045
they have sinned against it, is *k* Lev 4:14 3045
whether he hath seen or *k* of it Lev 5:1 3045
myself *k* unto him in a vision Num 12:6 3045
that hath *k* man by lying with him Num 31:17 3045
that have not *k* a man by lying Num 31:18 3045
had not *k* man by lying with him Num 31:35 3045
k among your tribes, and I will Deut 1:13 3045
of your tribes, wise men, and *k* Deut 1:15 3045
your children which have not *k* Deut 11:2 3045
other gods, which ye have not *k* Deut 11:28 3045
other gods, which thou hast not *k* Deut 13:2 3045
other gods, which thou hast not *k* Deut 13:6 3045
other gods, which ye have not *k* Deut 13:13 3045
it be not *k* who hath slain him Deut 21:1 3045
thou nor thy fathers have *k* Deut 28:36 3045
thou nor thy fathers have *k* Deut 28:64 3045
which have not *k* any thing Deut 31:13 3045
which had *k* all the works of the Josh 24:31 3045
had not *k* all the wars of Canaan Judg 3:1 3045
So his strength was not *k* Judg 16:9 3045
that had *k* no man by lying with Judg 21:12 3045
make not thyself *k* unto the man Ruth 3:3 3045
Let it not be *k* that a woman came Ruth 3:14 3045
it shall be *k* to you why his hand 1Sa 6:3 3045
that thou mayest make *k* unto me 1Sa 28:15 3045
and the thing was not *k* 2Sa 17:19 3045
that thou be not *k* to be the wife 1Kin 14:2 3045
let it be *k* this day that thou 1Kin 18:36 3045
make *k* his deeds among the people 1Chr 16:8 3045
in making *k* all these great 1Chr 17:19 3045
Be it *k* unto the king, that the Ezr 4:12 3046
Be it *k* now unto the king, that, Ezr 4:13 3046
Be it *k* unto the king, that we Ezr 5:8 3046
heard that it was *k* unto us Neh 4:15 3045
madest *k* unto them thy holy Neh 9:14 3045
And the thing was *k* to Mordecai Est 2:22 3045
The LORD is *k* by the judgment Ps 9:16 3045
whom I have not *k* shall serve me Ps 18:43 3045
thou hast *k* my soul in Ps 31:7 3045
God is *k* in her palaces for a Ps 48:3 3045
That thy way may be *k* upon earth Ps 67:2 3045
Thou hast *k* my reproach, and my Ps 69:19 3045
In Judah is God *k* Ps 76:1 3045
and thy footsteps are not *k* Ps 77:19 3045
Which we have heard and *k*, and our Ps 78:3 3045
make them *k* to their children Ps 78:5 3045
the heathen that have not *k* thee Ps 79:6 3045
let him be *k* among the heathen in Ps 79:10 3045
thy wonders be *k* in the dark Ps 88:12 3045
I make *k* thy faithfulness to all Ps 89:1 3045
high, because he hath *k* my name Ps 91:14 3045
heart, and they have not *k* my ways Ps 95:10 3045
LORD hath made *k* his salvation Ps 98:2 3045
He made *k* his ways unto Moses, Ps 103:7 3045
make *k* his deeds among the people Ps 105:1 3045
make his mighty power to be *k* Ps 106:8 3045
those that have *k* thy testimonies Ps 119:79 3045
I have *k* of old that thou hast Ps 119:152 3045
thou hast searched me, and *k* me Ps 139:1 3045
To make *k* to the sons of men his Ps 145:12 3045
judgments, they have not *k* them Ps 147:20 3045
I will make *k* my words unto you Prov 1:23 3045
perverteth his ways shall be *k* Prov 10:9 3045
A fool's wrath is presently *k* Prov 12:16 3045
in the midst of fools is made *k* Prov 14:33 3045
Even a child is *k* by his doings Prov 20:11 5234
I have made *k* to thee this day, Prov 22:19 3045
Her husband is *k* in the gates Prov 31:23 3045
a fool's voice is *k* by multitude Eccl 5:3
not seen the sun, nor *k* any thing Eccl 6:5 3045
and it is *k* that it is man Eccl 6:10 3045
this is *k* in all the earth Is 12:5 3045
And the LORD shall be *k* to Egypt Is 19:21 3045
children shall make *k* thy truth Is 38:19 3045
Have ye not *k*? Is 40:21 3045
Hast thou not *k*? Is 40:28 3045
in paths that they have not *k* Is 42:16 3045
They have not *k* nor understood Is 44:18 3045
thee, though thou hast not *k* me Is 45:4 3045
thee, though thou hast not *k* me Is 45:5 3045
shall be *k* among the Gentiles Is 61:9 3045
to make thy name *k* to thine Is 64:2 3045
shall be *k* toward his servants Is 66:14 3045
is foolish, they have not *k* me Jer 4:22 3045
for they have *k* the way of the Jer 5:5 3045
they nor their fathers have *k* Jer 9:16 3045
they nor their fathers have *k* Jer 19:4 3045
pass, then shall the prophet be *k* Jer 28:9 3045
they are not *k* in the streets Lam 4:8 5234
made myself *k* unto them in the Eze 20:5 3045
sight I made myself *k* unto them Eze 20:9 3045
countries which thou hast not *k* Eze 32:9 3045
I will make myself *k* among them Eze 35:11 3045
the Lord GOD, be it *k* unto you Eze 36:32 3045
I will be *k* in the eyes of many Eze 38:23 3045
name *k* in the midst of my people Eze 39:7 3045
will not make *k* unto me the dream Dan 2:5 3046
will not make *k* unto me the dream Dan 2:9 3046
Arioch made the thing *k* to Daniel Dan 2:15 3046
and made the thing *k* to Hananiah Dan 2:17 3046
hast made *k* unto me now what we Dan 2:23 3046
for thou hast now made *k* unto us Dan 2:23 3046
that will make *k* unto the king Dan 2:25 3046
Art thou able to make *k* unto me Dan 2:26 3046
secrets, and maketh *k* to the king Dan 2:28 3046
that revealeth secrets maketh *k* Dan 2:29 3046
k the interpretation to the king Dan 2:30 3046
the great God hath made *k* to the Dan 2:45 3046
be it *k* unto thee, O king, that Dan 3:18 3046
that they might make *k* unto me Dan 4:6 3046
but they did not make *k* unto me Dan 4:7 3046
make *k* unto me the interpretation Dan 4:18 3046
have *k* that the heavens do rule Dan 4:26 3046
nor make *k* to the king the Dan 5:8 3046
make *k* unto me the interpretation Dan 5:15 3046
make *k* to me the interpretation Dan 5:16 3046
make *k* to him the interpretation Dan 5:17 3046
them, and they have not *k* the LORD Hos 5:4 3045
made *k* that which shall surely be Hos 5:9 3045
You only have I *k* of all the Amos 3:2 3045
place is not *k* where they are Nah 3:17 3045
in the midst of the years make *k* Hab 3:2 3045
day which shall be *k* to the LORD Zec 14:7 3045
and hid, that shall not be *k* Mt 10:26 *1097*
But if ye had *k* what this meaneth Mt 12:7 *1097*
that they should not make him *k* Mt 12:16 *5318*
for the tree is *k* by his fruit Mt 12:33 *1097*
k in what watch the thief would Mt 24:43 *1492*
that they should not make him *k* Mk 3:12 *5318*
the Lord hath made *k* unto us Lk 2:15 *1107*
they made *k* abroad the saying Lk 2:17 *1232*
every tree is *k* by his own fruit Lk 6:44 *1097*
were a prophet, would have *k* who Lk 7:39 *1097*
thing hid, that shall not be *k* Lk 8:17 *1097*
neither hid, that shall not be *k* Lk 12:2 *1097*
k what hour the thief would come Lk 12:39 *1492*
Saying, If thou hadst *k*, even Lk 19:42 *1097*
hast not *k* the things which are Lk 24:18 *1097*
how he was *k* of them in breaking Lk 24:35 *1097*
he himself seeketh to be *k* openly Jn 7:4 *1097*
if ye had *k* me, ye should have Jn 8:19 *1492*
ye should have *k* my Father also Jn 8:19 *1492*
Yet ye have not *k* him Jn 8:55 *1097*
my sheep, and am *k* of mine Jn 10:14 *1097*
If ye had *k* me, ye should have Jn 14:7 *1097*
ye should have *k* my Father also Jn 14:7 *1097*
you, and yet hast thou not *k* me Jn 14:9 *1097*
my Father I have made *k* unto you Jn 15:15 *1107*
they have not *k* the Father Jn 16:3 *1097*
Now they have *k* that all things Jn 17:7 *1097*
have *k* surely that I came out Jn 17:8 *1097*
Father, the world hath not *k* thee Jn 17:25 *1097*
but I have *k* thee, and these have Jn 17:25 *1097*
these have *k* that thou hast sent Jn 17:25 *1097*
that disciple was *k* unto the high Jn 18:15 *1110*
which was *k* unto the high priest, Jn 18:16 *1110*
it was *k* unto all the dwellers at Acts 1:19 *1110*
be this *k* unto you, and hearken to Acts 2:14 *1110*
Thou hast made *k* to me the ways Acts 2:28 *1107*
Be it *k* unto you all, and to all Acts 4:10 *1110*
Joseph was made *k* to his brethren Acts 7:13 *319*
kindred was made *k* unto Pharaoh Acts 7:13 *5318*
their laying await was *k* of Saul Acts 9:24 *1097*
it was *k* throughout all Joppa Acts 9:42 *1110*
Be it *k* unto you therefore, men Acts 13:38 *1110*
K unto God are all his works from Acts 15:18 *1110*
this was *k* to all the Jews and Acts 19:17 *1110*
because he would have *k* the Acts 22:30 *1097*
when I would have *k* the cause Acts 23:28 *1097*
Be it *k* therefore unto you, that Acts 28:28 *1110*
Because that which may be *k* of Rom 1:19 *1110*
the way of peace have they not *k* Rom 3:17 *1097*
Nay, I had not *k* sin, but by the Rom 7:7 *1097*
for I had not *k* lust, except the Rom 7:7 *1492*
his wrath, and to make his power *k* Rom 9:22 *1107*
that he might make *k* the riches Rom 9:23 *1107*
For who hath *k* the mind of the Rom 11:34 *1097*
made *k* to all nations for the Rom 16:26 *1107*
for had they *k* it, they would not 1Cor 2:8 *1097*
For who hath *k* the mind of the 1Cor 2:16 *1097*
love God, the same is *k* of him 1Cor 8:3 *1097*
shall I know even as also I am *k* 1Cor 13:12 *1921*
how shall it be *k* what is piped 1Cor 14:7 *1097*
how shall it be *k* what is spoken 1Cor 14:9 *1097*
epistle written in our hearts, *k* 2Cor 3:2 *1097*
though we have *k* Christ after the 2Cor 5:16 *1097*
As unknown, and yet well *k* 2Cor 6:9 *1921*
But now, after that ye have *k* God Gal 4:9 *1097*
or rather are *k* of God Gal 4:9 *1097*
Having made *k* unto us the mystery Eph 1:9 *1107*
he made *k* unto me the mystery Eph 3:3 *1107*
not made *k* unto the sons of men Eph 3:5 *1107*
be *k* by the church the manifold Eph 3:10 *1107*
to make *k* the mystery of the Eph 6:19 *1107*
shall make *k* to you all things Eph 6:21 *1107*
your moderation be *k* unto all men Phil 4:5 *1097*
your requests be made *k* unto God Phil 4:6 *1107*
To whom God would make *k* what is Col 1:27 *1107*
They shall make *k* unto you all Col 4:9 *1107*
But thou hast fully *k* my doctrine 2Ti 3:10 *3877*
thou hast *k* the holy scriptures 2Ti 3:15 *1492*
me the preaching might be fully *k* 2Ti 4:17 *4135*
and they have not *k* my ways Heb 3:10 *1097*
when we made *k* unto you the power 2Pet 1:16 *1107*
have *k* the way of righteousness 2Pet 2:21 *1921*
than, after they have *k* it 2Pet 2:21 *1921*
because ye have *k* him that is 1Jn 2:13 *1097*
because ye have *k* the Father 1Jn 2:13 *1097*
because ye have *k* him that is 1Jn 2:14 *1097*
hath not seen him, neither *k* him 1Jn 3:6 *1097*
And we have *k* and believed the love 1Jn 4:16 *1097*
all they that have *k* the truth 2Jn 1 *1097*
which have not *k* the depths of Rev 2:24 *1097*

KOA *(ko'-ah)* {1} *An obscure tribe.*
Chaldeans, Pekod, and Shoa, and *K* Eze 23:23 6970

KOHATH *(ko'-hath)* {32} See KOHATHITES. *A son of Levi.*
Gershon, *K*, and Merari Gen 46:11 6955
Gershon, and *K*, and Merari Ex 6:16 6955
And the sons of *K* Ex 6:18 6955
life of *K* were an hundred thirty Ex 6:18 6955
Gershon, and *K*, and Merari Num 3:17 6955
the sons of *K* by their families Num 3:19 6955
of *K* was the family of the Num 3:27 6955
The families of the sons of *K* Num 3:29 6955
of *K* from among the sons of Levi Num 4:2 6955
of *K* in the tabernacle of the Num 4:4 6955
the sons of *K* shall come to bear Num 4:15 6955
of *K* in the tabernacle of the Num 4:15 6955
unto the sons of *K* he gave none Num 7:9 6955
the son of Izhar, the son of *K* Num 16:1 6955
of *K*, the family of the Num 26:57 6955
And *K* begat Amram Num 26:58 6955
the rest of the children of *K* had Josh 21:5 6955
the families of the children of *K* Josh 21:20 6955
remained of the children of *K* Josh 21:20 6955
the children of *K* that remained Josh 21:26 6955
Gershon, *K*, and Merari 1Chr 6:1 6955
And the sons of *K* 1Chr 6:2 6955
Gershom, *K*, and Merari 1Chr 6:16 6955
And the sons of *K* were, Amram, and 1Chr 6:18 6955
The sons of *K* 1Chr 6:22 6955
The son of Izhar, the son of *K* 1Chr 6:38 6955
And unto the sons of *K*, which were 1Chr 6:61 6955
K had cities of their coasts out 1Chr 6:66 6955
of the remnant of the sons of *K* 1Chr 6:70 6955
Of the sons of *K* 1Chr 15:5 6955
sons of Levi, namely, Gershon, *K* 1Chr 23:6 6955
The sons of *K* 1Chr 23:12 6955

KOHATHITES *(ko'-hath-ites)* {15} *Descendants of Kohath.*
these are the families of the *K* Num 3:27 6956
K shall be Elizaphan the son of Num 3:30 6956
of the *K* from among the Levites Num 4:18 6956
of the *K* after their families Num 4:34 6956
numbered of the families of the *K* Num 4:37 6956
the *K* set forward, bearing the Num 10:21 6956
of Kohath, the family of the *K* Num 26:57 6956
out for the families of the *K* Josh 21:4 6956
being of the families of the *K* Josh 21:10 6956
Of the sons of the *K* 1Chr 6:33 6956
Aaron, of the families of the *K* 1Chr 6:54 6956
brethren, of the sons of the *K* 1Chr 9:32 6956
Levites, of the children of the *K* 2Chr 20:19 6956
of Azariah, of the sons of the *K* 2Chr 29:12 6956
Meshullam, of the sons of the *K* 2Chr 34:12 6956

KOLAIAH *(ko-la-i'-ah)* {2}
1. *A family of exiles.*
the son of Pedaiah, the son of *K* Neh 11:7 6964
2. *Father of Ahab.*
of Israel, of Ahab the son of *K* Jer 29:21 6964

KORAH *(ko'-rah)* {37} See CORE, KORAHITE, KORE.
1. *A son of Esau.*
bare Jeush, and Jaalam, and *K* Gen 36:5 7141
to Esau Jeush, and Jaalam, and *K* Gen 36:14 7141
duke Jeush, duke Jaalam, duke *K* Gen 36:18 7141
Reuel, and Jeush, and Jaalam, and *K* 1Chr 1:35 7141
2. *A son of Eliphaz.*
Duke *K*, duke Gatam, and duke Gen 36:16 7141
3. *A conspirator against Moses.*
K, and Nepheg, and Zichri Ex 6:21 7141
And the sons of *K* Ex 6:24 7141
Now *K*, the son of Izhar, the son Num 16:1 7141
And he spake unto *K* and unto all Num 16:5 7141
Take you censers, *K*, and all his Num 16:6 7141
And Moses said unto *K*, Hear, I Num 16:8 7141
And Moses said unto *K*, Be thou and Num 16:16 7141
K gathered all the congregation Num 16:19 7141
up from about the tabernacle of *K* Num 16:24 7141
gat up from the tabernacle of *K* Num 16:27 7141
the men that appertained unto *K* Num 16:32 7141
that he be not as *K*, and as his Num 16:40 7141
that died about the matter of *K* Num 16:49 7141
against Aaron in the company of *K* Num 26:9 7141
swallowed them up together with *K* Num 26:10 7141
the children of *K* died not Num 26:11 7141

the LORD in the company of *K* ... Num 27:3 7141
the son of Ebiasaph, the son of *K* ... 1Chr 6:37 7141
the son of Ebiasaph, the son of *K* ... 1Chr 9:19 7141
4. A son of Hebron.
K, and Tappuah, and Rekem ... 1Chr 2:43 7141
5. A grandson of Kohath.
K his son, Assir his son, ... 1Chr 6:22 7141
Maschil, for the sons of *K* ... Ps 42:*t* 7141
chief Musician for the sons of *K* ... Ps 44:*t* 7141
Shoshannim, for the sons of *K* ... Ps 45:*t* 7141
chief Musician for the sons of *K* ... Ps 46:*t* 7141
A Psalm for the sons of *K* ... Ps 47:*t* 7141
A Song and Psalm for the sons of *K* ... Ps 48:*t* 7141
A Psalm for the sons of *K* ... Ps 49:*t* 7141
A Psalm for the sons of *K* ... Ps 84:*t* 7141
A Psalm for the sons of *K* ... Ps 85:*t* 7141
A Psalm or Song for the sons of *K* ... Ps 87:*t* 7141
of *K* to the chief Musician upon ... Ps 88:*t* 7141

KORAHITE *(ko'-ra-hite)* {1} See KORAHITES, KORE. *A descendant of Korah.*
the firstborn of Shallum the *K* ... 1Chr 9:31 7145

KORAHITES *(ko'-ra-hites)* {1} See KORATHITES, KORHITES.
of the house of his father, the *K* ... 1Chr 9:19 7145

KORATHITES *(ko'-ra-thites)* {1} See KORAHITES. *Same as Korahites.*
the Mushites, the family of the *K* ... Num 26:58 7145

KORAZIN See CHORAZIN.

KORE *(ko'-re)* {4} See KORAH, KORAHITE.
1. Father of Shallum.
And Shallum the son of *K*, the son ... 1Chr 9:19 6981
was Meshelemiah the son of *K* ... 1Chr 26:1 6981
the porters among the sons of *K* ... 1Chr 26:19 7145
2. A Temple servant.
K the son of Imnah the Levite, ... 2Chr 31:14 6981

KORHITES *(kor'-hites)* {4} See KORAHITES. *Same as Korahites.*
these are the families of the *K* ... Ex 6:24 7145
and Joezer, and Jashobeam, the *K* ... 1Chr 12:6 7145
Of the *K* was Meshelemiah the son ... 1Chr 26:1 7145
and of the children of the *K* ... 2Chr 20:19 7145

KOUM See CUMI.

KOZ *(coz)* {4} See HAKKOZ.
1. A family of exiles.
of Habaiah, the children of *K* ... Ezr 2:61 6976
of Habaiah, the children of *K* ... Neh 7:63 6976
2. Father of two rebuilders of the wall.
the son of Urijah, the son of *K* ... Neh 3:4 6976
Urijah the son of *K* another piece ... Neh 3:21 6976

KUSHAIAH *(cu-shah'-yah)* {1} See KISHI. *Father of Ethan.*
brethren, Ethan the son of *K* ... 1Chr 15:17 6984

L

LAADAH *(la'-a-dah)* {1} *Son of Shelah.*
L the father of Mareshah, and the ... 1Chr 4:21 3935

LAADAN *(la'-a-dan)* {7} See LIBNI.
1. A descendant of Ephraim.
L his son, Ammihud his son, ... 1Chr 7:26 3936
2. A descendant of Gershon.
Of the Gershonites were, *L* ... 1Chr 23:7 3936
The sons of *L* ... 1Chr 23:8 3936
the chief of the fathers of *L* ... 1Chr 23:9 3936
As concerning the sons of *L* ... 1Chr 26:21 3936
the sons of the Gershonite *L* ... 1Chr 26:21 3936
even of *L* the Gershonite, were ... 1Chr 26:21 3936

LABAN *(la'-ban)* {51} See LABAN'S, LIBNAH.
1. Father of Rachel.
had a brother, and his name was *L* ... Gen 24:29 3837
L ran out unto the man, unto the ... Gen 24:29 3837
Then *L* and Bethuel answered and ... Gen 24:50 3837
the sister to *L* the Syrian ... Gen 25:20 3837
flee thou to *L* my brother to ... Gen 27:43 3837
of *L* thy mother's brother ... Gen 28:2 3837
and he went to Padan-aram unto *L* ... Gen 28:5 3837
Know ye *L* the son of Nahor ... Gen 29:5 3837
of *L* his mother's brother ... Gen 29:10 3837
the sheep of *L* his mother's ... Gen 29:10 3837
flock of *L* his mother's brother ... Gen 29:10 3837
when *L* heard the tidings of Jacob ... Gen 29:13 3837
he told *L* all these things ... Gen 29:13 3837
L said to him, Surely thou art my ... Gen 29:14 3837
L said unto Jacob, Because thou ... Gen 29:15 3837
And *L* had two daughters ... Gen 29:16 3837
L said, It is better that I give ... Gen 29:19 3837
And Jacob said unto *L*, Give me my ... Gen 29:21 3837
L gathered together all the men ... Gen 29:22 3837
L gave unto his daughter Leah ... Gen 29:24 3837
and he said to *L*, What is this ... Gen 29:25 3837
L said, It must not be so done in ... Gen 29:26 3837
L gave to Rachel his daughter ... Gen 29:29 3837
Joseph, that Jacob said unto *L* ... Gen 30:25 3837
L said unto him, I pray thee, if ... Gen 30:27 3837
L said, Behold, I would it might ... Gen 30:34 3837
all the brown in the flock of *L* ... Gen 30:40 3837
Jacob beheld the countenance of *L* ... Gen 31:2 3837
seen all that *L* doeth unto thee ... Gen 31:12 3837
L went to shear his sheep ... Gen 31:19 3837
away unawares to *L* the Syrian ... Gen 31:20 3837
it was told *L* on the third day ... Gen 31:22 3837
God came to *L* the Syrian in a ... Gen 31:24 3837
Then *L* overtook Jacob ... Gen 31:25 3837
L with his brethren pitched in ... Gen 31:25 3837
L said to Jacob, What hast thou ... Gen 31:26 3837
And Jacob answered and said to *L* ... Gen 31:31 3837
L went into Jacob's tent, and into ... Gen 31:33 3837
L searched all the tent, but ... Gen 31:34 3837
Jacob was wroth, and chode with *L* ... Gen 31:36 3837
and Jacob answered and said to *L* ... Gen 31:36 3837
L answered and said unto Jacob, ... Gen 31:43 3837
L called it Jegar-sahadutha ... Gen 31:47 3837
L said, This heap is a witness ... Gen 31:48 3837
L said to Jacob, Behold this heap ... Gen 31:51 3837
And early in the morning *L* rose up ... Gen 31:55 3837
L departed, and returned unto his ... Gen 31:55 3837
thus, I have sojourned with *L* ... Gen 32:4 3837
whom *L* gave to Leah his daughter, ... Gen 46:18 3837
which *L* gave unto Rachel his ... Gen 46:25 3837
2. A Hebrew encampment in the wilderness.
between Paran, and Tophel, and *L* ... Deut 1:1 3837

LABAN'S *(la'-bans)* {4} *Refers to Laban 1.*
and Jacob fed the rest of *L* flocks ... Gen 30:36 3837
and put them not unto *L* cattle ... Gen 30:40 3837
so the feebler were *L*, and the ... Gen 30:42 3837
And he heard the words of *L* sons ... Gen 31:1 3837

LABOUR {89}
the *l* of my hands, and rebuked ... Gen 31:42 3018
travailed, and she had hard *l* ... Gen 35:16 3205
to pass, when she was in hard *l* ... Gen 35:17 3205
the men, that they may *l* therein ... Ex 5:9 6213
Six days shalt thou *l*, and do all ... Ex 20:9 5647
Six days thou shalt *l*, and do all ... Deut 5:13 5647
on our affliction, and our *l* ... Deut 26:7 5999
not all the people to *l* thither ... Josh 7:3 3021
you a land for which ye did not *l* ... Josh 24:13 3021
be a guard to us, and *l* on the day ... Neh 4:22 4399
man from his house, and from his *l* ... Neh 5:13 3018
I be wicked, why then *l* I in vain ... Job 9:29 3021
or wilt thou leave thy *l* to him ... Job 39:11 3018
her *l* is in vain without fear ... Job 39:16 3018
and their *l* unto the locust ... Ps 78:46 3018
years, yet is their strength *l* ... Ps 90:10 5999
to his *l* until the evening ... Ps 104:23 5656
inherited the *l* of the people ... Ps 105:44 5999
brought down their heart with *l* ... Ps 107:12 5999
and let the strangers spoil his *l* ... Ps 109:11 3018
they *l* in vain that build it ... Ps 127:1 5998
shalt eat the *l* of thine hands ... Ps 128:2 3018
That our oxen may be strong to *l* ... Ps 144:14 5445
The *l* of the righteous tendeth to ... Prov 10:16 6468
gathereth by *l* shall increase ... Prov 13:11 3027
In all *l* there is profit ... Prov 14:23 6089
for his hands refuse to *l* ... Prov 21:25 6213
L not to be rich ... Prov 23:4 3021
profit hath a man of all his *l* ... Eccl 1:3 5999
All things are full of *l* ... Eccl 1:8 3023
for my heart rejoiced in all my *l* ... Eccl 2:10 5999
this was my portion of all my *l* ... Eccl 2:10 5999
on the *l* that I had laboured to ... Eccl 2:11 5999
I hated all my *l* which I had ... Eccl 2:18 5999
all my *l* wherein I have laboured ... Eccl 2:19 5999
the *l* which I took under the sun ... Eccl 2:20 5999
is a man whose *l* is in wisdom ... Eccl 2:21 5999
For what hath man of all his *l* ... Eccl 2:22 5999
make his soul enjoy good in his *l* ... Eccl 2:24 5999
and enjoy the good of all his *l* ... Eccl 3:13 5999
yet is there no end of all his *l* ... Eccl 4:8 5999
neither saith he, For whom do I *l* ... Eccl 4:8 6001
have a good reward for their *l* ... Eccl 4:9 5999
and shall take nothing of his *l* ... Eccl 5:15 5999
l that he taketh under the sun ... Eccl 5:18 5999
portion, and to rejoice in his *l* ... Eccl 5:19 5999
All the *l* of man is for his mouth ... Eccl 6:7 5999
him of his *l* the days of his life ... Eccl 8:15 5999
though a man *l* to seek it out ... Eccl 8:17 5998
in thy *l* which thou takest under ... Eccl 9:9 5999
The *l* of the foolish wearieth ... Eccl 10:15 5999
l not to comfort me, because of ... Is 22:4 213
The *l* of Egypt, and merchandise of ... Is 45:14 3018
your *l* for that which satisfieth ... Is 55:2 3018
They shall not *l* in vain, nor ... Is 65:23 3021
For shame hath devoured the *l* of ... Jer 3:24 3018
I forth out of the womb to see *l* ... Jer 20:18 5999
and the people shall *l* in vain ... Jer 51:58 3021
we *l*, and have no rest ... Lam 5:5 3021
and shall take away all thy *l* ... Eze 23:29 3018
him the land of Egypt for his *l* ... Eze 29:20 6468
l to bring forth, O daughter of ... Mic 4:10 1518
people shall *l* in the very fire ... Hab 2:13 3021
the *l* of the olive shall fail, and ... Hab 3:17 4639
and upon all the *l* of the hands ... Hag 1:11 3018
Come unto me, all ye that *l* ... Mt 11:28 *2872*
that whereon ye bestowed no *l* ... Jn 4:38 *2872*
L not for the meat which ... Jn 6:27 *2038*
Mary, who bestowed much *l* on us ... Rom 16:6 *2872*
and Tryphosa, who *l* in the Lord ... Rom 16:12 *2872*
own reward according to his own *l* ... 1Cor 3:8 *2873*
And *l*, working with our own hands ... 1Cor 4:12 *2872*
your *l* is not in vain in the Lord ... 1Cor 15:58 *2873*
Wherefore we *l*, that, whether ... 2Cor 5:9 *5389*
have bestowed upon you *l* in vain ... Gal 4:11 *2872*
but rather let him *l*, working ... Eph 4:28 *2872*
flesh, this is the fruit of my *l* ... Phil 1:22 *2041*
my brother, and companion in *l* ... Phil 2:25 *4904*
Whereunto I also *l*, striving ... Col 1:29 *2872*
l of love, and patience of hope in ... 1Th 1:3 *2873*
For ye remember, brethren, our *l* ... 1Th 2:9 *2873*
tempted you, and our *l* be in vain ... 1Th 3:5 *2873*
to know them which *l* among you ... 1Th 5:12 *2872*
but wrought with *l* and travail ... 2Th 3:8 *2873*
For therefore we both *l* and suffer ... 1Ti 4:10 *2872*
especially they who *l* in the word ... 1Ti 5:17 *2872*
Let us *l* therefore to enter into ... Heb 4:11 *4704*
l of love, which ye have shewed ... Heb 6:10 *2873*
I know thy works, and thy *l* ... Rev 2:2 *2873*

LABOURED {19}
So we *l* in the work ... Neh 4:21 6213
That which he *l* for shall he ... Job 20:18 3022
on the labour that I had *l* to do ... Eccl 2:11 5998
all my labour wherein I have *l* ... Eccl 2:19 5998
yet to a man that hath not *l* ... Eccl 2:21 5998
wherein he hath *l* under the sun ... Eccl 2:22 6001
hath he that hath *l* for the wind ... Eccl 5:16 5998
thou hast *l* from thy youth ... Is 47:12 3021
unto thee with whom thou hast *l* ... Is 47:15 3021
I have *l* in vain, I have spent my ... Is 49:4 3021
wine, for the which thou hast *l* ... Is 62:8 3021
he *l* till the going down of the ... Dan 6:14 7712
for the which thou hast not *l* ... Jonah 4:10 5998
other men *l*, and ye are entered ... Jn 4:38 *2872*
Persis, which *l* much in the Lord ... Rom 16:12 *2872*
but I *l* more abundantly than they ... 1Cor 15:10 *2872*
run in vain, neither *l* in vain ... Phil 2:16 *2872*
which *l* with me in the gospel ... Phil 4:3 *4866*
and for my name's sake hast *l* ... Rev 2:3 *2872*

LABOURER {2}
for the *l* is worthy of his hire ... Lk 10:7 *2040*
The *l* is worthy of his reward ... 1Ti 5:18 *2040*

LABOURERS {9}
is plenteous, but the *l* are few ... Mt 9:37 *2040*
send forth *l* into his harvest ... Mt 9:38 *2040*
to hire *l* into his vineyard ... Mt 20:1 *2040*
with the *l* for a penny a day ... Mt 20:2 *2040*
unto his steward, Call the *l* ... Mt 20:8 *2040*
truly is great, but the *l* are few ... Lk 10:2 *2040*
send forth *l* into his harvest ... Lk 10:2 *2040*
For we are *l* together with God ... 1Cor 3:9 *4904*
the hire of the *l* who have reaped ... Jas 5:4 *2040*

LABOURETH {7}
He that *l l* for himself ... Prov 16:26 6001
He that *l l* for himself ... Prov 16:26 5998
that worketh in that wherein he *l* ... Eccl 3:9 6001
one that helpeth with us, and *l* ... 1Cor 16:16 *2872*
The husbandman that *l* must be ... 2Ti 2:6 *2872*

LABOURING {4}
The sleep of a *l* man is sweet ... Eccl 5:12 5647
how that so *l* ye ought to support ... Acts 20:35 *2872*
always *l* fervently for you in ... Col 4:12 75
for *l* night and day, because we ... 1Th 2:9 *2873*

LABOURS {13}
harvest, the firstfruits of thy *l* ... Ex 23:16 4639
in thy *l* out of the field ... Ex 23:16 4639
fruit of thy land, and all thy *l* ... Deut 28:33 3018
thy *l* be in the house of a ... Prov 5:10 6089
pleasure, and exact all your *l* ... Is 58:3 6092
this city, and all the *l* thereof ... Jer 20:5 3018
in all my *l* they shall find none ... Hos 12:8 3018
hail in all the *l* of your hands ... Hag 2:17 4639
and ye are entered into their *l* ... Jn 4:38 *2873*
imprisonments, in tumults, in *l* ... 2Cor 6:5 *2873*
that is, of other men's *l* ... 2Cor 10:15 *2873*
in *l* more abundant, in stripes ... 2Cor 11:23 *2873*
that they may rest from their *l* ... Rev 14:13 *2873*

LACE {4}
of the ephod with a *l* of blue ... Ex 28:28 6616
And thou shalt put it on a blue *l* ... Ex 28:37 6616
of the ephod with a *l* of blue ... Ex 39:21 6616
And they tied unto it a *l* of blue ... Ex 39:31 6616

LACHISH *(la'-kish)* {24} *An Amorite city.*
Jarmuth, and unto Japhia king of *L* ... Josh 10:3 3923
king of Jarmuth, the king of *L* ... Josh 10:5 3923
king of Jarmuth, the king of *L* ... Josh 10:23 3923
and all Israel with him, unto *L* ... Josh 10:31 3923
the LORD delivered *L* into the ... Josh 10:32 3923
king of Gezer came up to help *L* ... Josh 10:33 3923
from *L* Joshua passed unto Eglon, ... Josh 10:34 3923
to all that he had done to *L* ... Josh 10:35 3923
the king of *L*, one ... Josh 12:11 3923
L, and Bozkath, and Eglon, ... Josh 15:39 3923
and he fled to *L* ... 2Kin 14:19 3923
but they sent after him to *L* ... 2Kin 14:19 3923
sent to the king of Assyria to *L* ... 2Kin 18:14 3923
Rab-shakeh from *L* to king ... 2Kin 18:17 3923
heard that he was departed from *L* ... 2Kin 19:8 3923

And Adoraim, and *L*, and Azekah, ... 2Chr 11:9 3923
and he fled to *L* ... 2Chr 25:27 3923
but they sent to *L* after him ... 2Chr 25:27 3923
he himself laid siege against *L* ... 2Chr 32:9 3923
and in their villages, at *L* ... Neh 11:30 3923
of Assyria sent Rabshakeh from *L* ... Is 36:2 3923
heard that he was departed from *L* ... Is 37:8 3923
Judah that were left, against *L* ... Jer 34:7 3923
O thou inhabitant of *L*, bind the ... Mic 1:13 3923

LACK {15}
Peradventure there shall *l* five ... Gen 18:28 2637
all the city for *l* of five ... Gen 18:28
he that gathered little had no *l* ... Ex 16:18 2637
thou shalt not *l* any thing in it ... Deut 8:9 2637
old lion perisheth for *l* of prey ... Job 4:11 1097
God, they wander for *l* of meat ... Job 38:41 1097
The young lions do *l*, and suffer ... Ps 34:10 7326
giveth unto the poor shall not *l* ... Prov 28:27 4270
and let thy head *l* no ointment ... Eccl 9:8 2637
are destroyed for *l* of knowledge ... Hos 4:6 1097
what *l* I yet ... Mt 19:20 *5302*
that had gathered little had no *l* ... 2Cor 8:15 *1641*
to supply your *l* of service ... Phil 2:30 *5303*
and that ye may have *l* of nothing ... 1Th 4:12 *5532*
If any of you *l* wisdom, let him ... Jas 1:5 *3007*

LACKED {11}
thou hast *l* nothing ... Deut 2:7 2637
there *l* of David's servants ... 2Sa 2:30 6485
by the morning light there *l* not ... 2Sa 17:22 5737
they *l* nothing ... 1Kin 4:27 5737
him, But what hast thou *l* with me ... 1Kin 11:22 2638
so that they *l* nothing ... Neh 9:21 2637
away, because it *l* moisture ... Lk 8:6 *3361,2192*
scrip, and shoes, *l* ye any thing ... Lk 22:35 *5302*
was there any among them that *l* ... Acts 4:34 *1729*
honour to that part which *l* ... 1Cor 12:24 *5302*
careful, but ye *l* opportunity ... Phil 4:10 *170*

LACKEST {2}
said unto him, One thing thou *l* ... Mk 10:21 *5302*
unto him, Yet *l* thou one thing ... Lk 18:22 *3007*

LACKETH {5}
there *l* not one man of us ... Num 31:49 6485
on the sword, or that *l* bread ... 2Sa 3:29 2638
with a woman *l* understanding ... Prov 6:32 2638
honoureth himself, and *l* bread ... Prov 12:9 2638
But he that *l* these things is ... 2Pet 1:9 *3361,3918*

LACKING {8}
to be *l* from thy meat offering ... Lev 2:13 7673
superfluous or *l* in his parts ... Lev 22:23 7038
be to day one tribe *l* in Israel ... Judg 21:3 6485
And there was nothing *l* to them ... 1Sa 30:19 5737
dismayed, neither shall they be *l* ... Jer 23:4 6485
for that which was *l* on your part ... 1Cor 16:17 *5303*
for that which was *l* to me the ... 2Cor 11:9 *5303*
that which is *l* in your faith ... 1Th 3:10 *5303*

LAD {33}
in thy sight because of the *l* ... Gen 21:12 5288
And God heard the voice of the *l* ... Gen 21:17 5288
the voice of the *l* where he is ... Gen 21:17 5288
Arise, lift up the *l*, and hold him ... Gen 21:18 5288
with water, and gave the *l* drink ... Gen 21:19 5288
And God was with the *l* ... Gen 21:20 5288
the *l* will go yonder and worship, ... Gen 22:5 5288
Lay not thine hand upon the *l* ... Gen 22:12 5288
the *l* was with the sons of Bilhah ... Gen 37:2 5288
his father, Send the *l* with me ... Gen 43:8 5288
The *l* cannot leave his father ... Gen 44:22 5288
father, and the *l* be not with us ... Gen 44:30 5288
seeth that the *l* is not with us ... Gen 44:31 5288
surety for the *l* unto my father ... Gen 44:32 5288
of the *l* a bondman to my lord ... Gen 44:33 5288
let the *l* go up with his brethren ... Gen 44:33 5288
father, and the *l* be not with me ... Gen 44:34 5288
Samson said unto the *l* that held ... Judg 16:26 5288
And, behold, I will send a *l* ... 1Sa 20:21 5288
If I expressly say unto the *l* ... 1Sa 20:21 5288
David, and a little *l* with him ... 1Sa 20:35 5288
And he said unto his *l*, Run, find ... 1Sa 20:36 5288
And as the *l* ran, he shot an arrow ... 1Sa 20:36 5288
when the *l* was come to the place ... 1Sa 20:37 5288
shot, Jonathan cried after the *l* ... 1Sa 20:37 5288
And Jonathan cried after the *l* ... 1Sa 20:38 5288
Jonathan's *l* gathered up the ... 1Sa 20:38 5288
But the *l* knew not any thing ... 1Sa 20:39 5288
gave his artillery unto his *l* ... 1Sa 20:40 5288
And as soon as the *l* was gone ... 1Sa 20:41 5288
Nevertheless a *l* saw them ... 2Sa 17:18 5288
And he said to a *l*, Carry him to ... 2Kin 4:19 5288
There is a *l* here, which hath ... Jn 6:9 *3808*

LADAN See LAADAN.

LADDER {1}
behold a *l* set up on the earth, ... Gen 28:12 5551

LADE {3}
l your beasts, and go, get you ... Gen 45:17 2943
did *l* you with a heavy yoke ... 1Kin 12:11 6006
for ye *l* men with burdens ... Lk 11:46 *5412*

LADED {4}
they *l* their asses with the corn, ... Gen 42:26 5375
l every man his ass, and returned ... Gen 44:13 6006
bare burdens, with those that *l* ... Neh 4:17 6006
they *l* us with such things as ... Acts 28:10 *2007*

LADEN {6}
ten asses *l* with the good things ... Gen 45:23 5375
and ten she asses *l* with corn ... Gen 45:23 5375
And Jesse took an ass *l* with bread ... 1Sa 16:20
a people *l* with iniquity, a seed ... Is 1:4 3515
all ye that labour and are heavy *l* ... Mt 11:28 *5412*
captive silly women *l* with sins ... 2Ti 3:6 *4987*

LADETH {1}
to him that *l* himself with thick ... Hab 2:6 3515

LADIES {2}
Her wise *l* answered her, yea, she ... Judg 5:29 8282
Likewise shall the *l* of Persia ... Est 1:18 8282

LADING {2}
bringing in sheaves, and *l* asses ... Neh 13:15 6006
and much damage, not only of the *l* ... Acts 27:10 *5414*

LAD'S {1}
life is bound up in the *l* life ... Gen 44:30 5288

LADS {1}
me from all evil, bless the *l* ... Gen 48:16 5288

LADY {4}
more be called, The *l* of kingdoms ... Is 47:5 1404
saidst, I shall be a *l* for ever ... Is 47:7 1404
The elder unto the elect *l* ... 2Jn 1 *2959*
And now I beseech thee, *l*, not as ... 2Jn 5 *2959*

LAEL *(la'-el)* {1} *A Levite.*
shall be Eliasaph the son of *L* ... Num 3:24 3815

LAHAD *(la'-had)* {1} *Great-grandson of Shobal.*
and Jahath begat Ahumai, and *L* ... 1Chr 4:2 3854

LAHAI-ROI *(la-hah'-ee-roy)* {2} See BEER-LAHAI-ROI. *A well in Paran.*
came from the way of the well *L* ... Gen 24:62 883
and Isaac dwelt by the well *L* ... Gen 25:11 883

LAHMAM *(lah'-mam)* {1} *A city in Judah.*
And Cabbon, and *L*, and Kithlish, ... Josh 15:40 3903

LAHMAS See LAHMAM.

LAHMI *(lah'-mi)* {1} See BETHLEHEMITE. *A brother of Goliath.*
slew *L* the brother of Goliath the ... 1Chr 20:5 3902

LAID {279}
l it upon both their shoulders, ... Gen 9:23 7760
l each piece one against another ... Gen 15:10 5414
the men *l* hold upon his hand, and ... Gen 19:16
and *l* it upon Isaac his son ... Gen 22:6 7760
l the wood in order, and bound ... Gen 22:9
l him on the altar upon the wood ... Gen 22:9 7760
that Jacob *l* the rods before the ... Gen 30:41 7760
l by her vail from her, and put on ... Gen 38:19 5493
she *l* up his garment by her, ... Gen 39:16 3241
l up the food in the cities ... Gen 41:40 5414
every city, *l* he up in the same ... Gen 41:48 5414
l it upon Ephraim's head, who was ... Gen 48:14 7896
l his right hand upon the head of ... Gen 48:17 7896
she *l* it in the flags by the ... Ex 2:3 7760
there more work be *l* upon the men ... Ex 5:9 3515
they *l* it up till the morning, as ... Ex 16:24 3241
so Aaron *l* it up before the ... Ex 16:34 3241
l before their faces all these ... Ex 19:7 7760
If there be *l* on him a sum of ... Ex 21:30 7896
his life whatsoever is *l* upon him ... Ex 21:30 7896
of Israel he *l* not his hand ... Ex 24:11 7971
his sons *l* their hands upon the ... Lev 8:14 5564
his sons *l* their hands upon the ... Lev 8:18 5564
his sons *l* their hands upon the ... Lev 8:22 5564
l incense thereon, and stood in ... Num 16:18 7760
Moses *l* up the rods before the ... Num 17:7 3241
we have *l* them waste even unto ... Num 21:30
he *l* his hands upon him, and gave ... Num 27:23 5564
us, and *l* upon us hard bondage ... Deut 26:6 5414
which the LORD hath *l* upon it ... Deut 29:22 2470
Is not this *l* up in store with me ... Deut 32:34 3647
for Moses had *l* his hands upon ... Deut 34:9 5564
which she had *l* in order upon the ... Josh 2:6
And before they were *l* down ... Josh 2:8 7901
they lodged, and *l* them down there ... Josh 4:8 3241
l them out before the LORD ... Josh 7:23 3332
l great stones in the cave's ... Josh 10:27 7760
their blood be *l* upon Abimelech ... Judg 9:24 7760
they *l* wait against Shechem in ... Judg 9:34
l wait in the field, and looked, ... Judg 9:43
l it on his shoulder, and said ... Judg 9:48 7760
l wait for him all night in the ... Judg 16:2
l hold on his concubine, and ... Judg 19:29
uncovered his feet, and *l* her down ... Ruth 3:7 7901
of barley, and *l* it on her ... Ruth 3:15 7896
l it in her bosom, and became ... Ruth 4:16 7896
when Eli was *l* down in his place, ... 1Sa 3:2 7901
Samuel was *l* down to sleep ... 1Sa 3:3 7901
they *l* the ark of the LORD upon ... 1Sa 6:11 7760
book, and *l* it up before the LORD ... 1Sa 10:25 3241
how he *l* wait for him in the way, ... 1Sa 15:2 7760
Amalek, and *l* wait in the valley ... 1Sa 15:5
he *l* hold upon the skirt of his ... 1Sa 15:27
l it in the bed, and put a pillow ... 1Sa 19:13 7760
David *l* up these words in his ... 1Sa 21:12 7760
cakes of figs, and *l* them on asses ... 1Sa 25:18 7760
and he was *l* down ... 2Sa 13:8 7901
l her hand on her head, and went ... 2Sa 13:19 7760
l a very great heap of stones ... 2Sa 18:17 5324
l it in her bosom ... 1Kin 3:20 7901
l her dead child in my bosom ... 1Kin 3:20 7901
of the house of the LORD *l* ... 1Kin 6:37
an oath be *l* upon him to cause ... 1Kin 8:31 5375
l it upon the ass, and brought it ... 1Kin 13:29 3241
he *l* his carcase in his own grave ... 1Kin 13:30 3241
all Israel *l* siege to Gibbethon ... 1Kin 15:27
he *l* the foundation thereof in ... 1Kin 16:34
abode, and *l* him upon his own bed ... 1Kin 17:19 7901
l him on the wood, and said, Fill ... 1Kin 18:33 7760
eat and drink, and *l* him down again ... 1Kin 19:6 7901
he *l* him down upon his bed, and ... 1Kin 21:4 7901
l him on the bed of the man of ... 2Kin 4:21 7901
l the staff upon the face of the ... 2Kin 4:31 7760
child was dead, and *l* upon his bed ... 2Kin 4:32 7901
l them upon two of his servants ... 2Kin 5:23 5414
the LORD *l* this burden upon him ... 2Kin 9:25 5375
And they *l* hands on her ... 2Kin 11:16 7760
they *l* it out to the carpenters ... 2Kin 12:11 3318
for all that was *l* out for the ... 2Kin 12:12 3318
l it on the boil, and he recovered ... 2Kin 20:7 7760
have *l* up in store unto this day ... 2Kin 20:17
an oath be *l* upon him to make him ... 2Chr 6:22 5375
and *l* hold on other gods, and ... 2Chr 7:22
l him in the bed which was filled ... 2Chr 16:14 7901
So they *l* hands on her ... 2Chr 23:15 7760
l upon Israel in the wilderness ... 2Chr 24:9
of the burdens *l* upon him ... 2Chr 24:27
they *l* their hands upon them ... 2Chr 29:23 5564
their God, and *l* them by heaps ... 2Chr 31:6 5414
(but he himself *l* siege against ... 2Chr 32:9
temple of the LORD was not yet *l* ... Ezr 3:6
And when the builders *l* the ... Ezr 3:10
of the house of the LORD was *l* ... Ezr 3:11
house was *l* before their eyes ... Ezr 3:12
timber is *l* in the walls, and this ... Ezr 5:8 7760
l the foundation of the house of ... Ezr 5:16 3052
treasures were *l* up in Babylon ... Ezr 6:1 5182
foundations thereof be strongly *l* ... Ezr 6:3 5446
who also *l* the beams thereof, and ... Neh 3:3
they *l* the beams thereof, and set ... Neh 3:6
they *l* the meat offerings ... Neh 13:5 5414
because he *l* his hand upon the ... Est 8:7 7971
but on the spoil *l* they not their ... Est 9:10 7971
on the prey they *l* not their hand ... Est 9:15 7971
but they *l* not their hands on the ... Est 9:16 7971
the king Ahasuerus *l* a tribute ... Est 10:1 7760
my calamity *l* in the balances ... Job 6:2 5375
The snare is *l* for him in the ... Job 18:10
l their hand on their mouth ... Job 29:9 7760
or if I have *l* wait at my ... Job 31:9
Where wast thou when I *l* the ... Job 38:4
Who hath *l* the measures thereof, ... Job 38:5 7760
or who *l* the corner stone thereof ... Job 38:6 3384
I *l* me down and slept ... Ps 3:5 7901
and majesty hast thou *l* upon him ... Ps 21:5 7737
that they have *l* privily for me ... Ps 31:4 2934
which thou hast *l* up for them ... Ps 31:19 6845
they *l* to my charge things that I ... Ps 35:11
sheep they are *l* in the grave ... Ps 49:14 8371
to be *l* in the balance, they are ... Ps 62:9 5927
they have *l* Jerusalem on heaps ... Ps 79:1 7760
l waste his dwelling place ... Ps 79:7
Thou hast *l* me in the lowest pit, ... Ps 88:6 7896
I have *l* help upon one that is ... Ps 89:19 7737
Of old hast thou *l* the foundation ... Ps 102:25
Who *l* the foundations of the ... Ps 104:5
he was *l* in iron ... Ps 105:18 935
thy judgments have I *l* before me ... Ps 119:30 7737
The wicked have *l* a snare for me ... Ps 119:110 5414
before, and *l* thine hand upon me ... Ps 139:5 7896
snares which they have *l* for me ... Ps 141:9 3369
they privily *l* a snare for me ... Ps 142:3 2934
the sinner is *l* up for the just ... Prov 13:22 6845
old, which I have *l* up for thee ... Song 7:13 6845
he *l* it upon my mouth, and said, ... Is 6:7 5060
he hath *l* up his carriages ... Is 10:28 6485
saying, Since thou art *l* down ... Is 14:8 7901
the night Ar of Moab is *l* waste ... Is 15:1
the night Kir of Moab is *l* waste ... Is 15:1
and that which they have *l* up ... Is 15:7 6486
for it is *l* waste, so that there ... Is 23:1
for your strength is *l* waste ... Is 23:14
shall not be treasured nor *l* up ... Is 23:18 2630
have *l* waste all the nations ... Is 37:18
have *l* up in store until this day ... Is 39:6
him, yet he *l* it not to heart ... Is 42:25 7760
temple, Thy foundation shall be *l* ... Is 44:28
hast thou very heavily *l* thy yoke ... Is 47:6
Mine hand also hath *l* the ... Is 48:13
l the foundations of the earth ... Is 51:13
thou hast *l* thy body as the ... Is 51:23 7760
the LORD hath *l* on him the ... Is 53:6 6293
me, nor *l* it to thy heart ... Is 57:11 7760
our pleasant things are *l* waste ... Is 64:11
and thy cities shall be *l* waste ... Jer 4:7
should this city be *l* waste ... Jer 27:17
but they *l* up the roll in the ... Jer 36:20 6485
I have *l* a snare for thee, and ... Jer 50:24
they *l* wait for us in the ... Lam 4:19
For I have *l* upon thee the years ... Eze 4:5 5414
the cities shall be *l* waste ... Eze 6:6
that your altars may be *l* waste ... Eze 6:6
whom ye have *l* in the midst of it ... Eze 11:7 7760
are inhabited shall be *l* waste ... Eze 12:20
and he *l* waste their cities ... Eze 19:7
replenished, now she is *l* waste ... Eze 26:2
among the cities that are *l* waste ... Eze 29:12
be thou *l* with the uncircumcised ... Eze 32:19 7901
they have *l* their swords under ... Eze 32:27 5414
which with their might are *l* by ... Eze 32:29 5414
he shall be *l* in the midst of the ... Eze 32:32 7901
when I have *l* the land most ... Eze 33:29 5414
saying, They are *l* desolate ... Eze 35:12
my hand that I have *l* upon them ... Eze 39:21 7760
whereupon also they *l* the ... Eze 40:42 3240
l upon the mouth of the den ... Dan 6:17 7760

L

their jaws, and I *l* meat unto them Hos 11:4 5186
He hath *l* my vine waste, and Joel 1:7 7760
clods, the garners are *l* desolate Joel 1:17
l to pledge by every altar Amos 2:8
of Israel shall be *l* waste Amos 7:9
bread have *l* a wound under thee Obad 7 7760
nor have *l* hands on their Obad 13 7971
he *l* his robe from him, and Jonah 3:6 5674
he hath *l* siege against us Mic 5:1 7760
thee, and say, Nineveh is *l* waste Nah 3:7
it is *l* over with gold and silver, Hab 2:19 8610
from before a stone was *l* upon a Hag 2:15 7760
of the LORD's temple was *l* Hag 2:18
stone that I have *l* before Joshua Zec 3:9 5414
l the foundation of this house Zec 4:9
for they *l* the pleasant land Zec 7:14 7760
house of the LORD of hosts was *l* Zec 8:9
l his mountains and his heritage Mal 1:3 7760
now also the ax is *l* unto the Mt 3:10 *2749*
house, he saw his wife's mother *l* Mt 8:14 *906*
For Herod had *l* hold on John Mt 14:3
he *l* hands on him, and took him by Mt 18:28
he *l* his hands on them, and Mt 19:15 *2007*
l hands on Jesus, and took him Mt 26:50 *1911*
the temple, and ye *l* no hold on me Mt 26:55
they that had *l* hold on Jesus led Mt 26:57
l it in his own new tomb, which Mt 27:60 *5087*
save that he *l* his hands upon a Mk 6:5 *2007*
l hold upon John, and bound him in Mk 6:17
up his corpse, and *l* it in a tomb Mk 6:29 *5087*
they *l* the sick in the streets, Mk 6:56 *5087*
and her daughter *l* upon the bed Mk 7:30 *906*
they *l* their hands on him, and Mk 14:46 *1911*
and the young men *l* hold on him Mk 14:51
l him in a sepulchre which was Mk 15:46 *2698*
of Joses beheld where he was *l* Mk 15:47 *5087*
behold the place where they *l* him Mk 16:6 *5087*
them *l* them up in their hearts Lk 1:66 *5087*
clothes, and *l* him in a manger Lk 2:7 *347*
now also the axe is *l* unto the Lk 3:9 *2749*
he *l* his hands on every one of Lk 4:40 *2007*
l the foundation on a rock Lk 6:48 *5087*
much goods *l* up for many years Lk 12:19 *2749*
And he *l* his hands on her Lk 13:13 *2007*
after he hath *l* the foundation, Lk 14:29 *5087*
which was *l* at his gate, full of Lk 16:20 *906*
I have kept *l* up in a napkin Lk 19:20 *606*
man, taking up that I *l* not down Lk 19:22 *5087*
they *l* hold upon one Simon, a Lk 23:26
and on him they *l* the cross Lk 23:26 *2007*
l it in a sepulchre that was hewn Lk 23:53 *5087*
wherein never man before was *l* Lk 23:53 *2749*
sepulchre, and how his body was *l* Lk 23:55 *5087*
the linen clothes *l* by themselves Lk 24:12 *2749*
but no man *l* hands on him, Jn 7:30 *1911*
but no man *l* hands on him Jn 7:44 *1911*
and no man *l* hands on him Jn 8:20
And said, Where have ye *l* him Jn 11:34 *5087*
the place where the dead was *l* Jn 11:41 *2749*
supper, and *l* aside his garments Jn 13:4 *5087*
wherein was never man yet *l* Jn 19:41 *5087*
There *l* they Jesus therefore Jn 19:42 *5087*
we know not where they have *l* him Jn 20:2 *5087*
I know not where they have *l* him Jn 20:13 *5087*
tell me where thou hast *l* him Jn 20:15 *5087*
and fish *l* thereon, and bread Jn 21:9 *1945*
whom they *l* daily at the gate of Acts 3:2 *5087*
they *l* hands on them, and put them Acts 4:3 *1911*
l them down at the apostles' feet Acts 4:35 *5087*
l it at the apostles' feet Acts 4:37 *5087*
l it at the apostles' feet Acts 5:2 *5087*
l them on beds and couches, that Acts 5:15 *5087*
l their hands on the apostles, and Acts 5:18 *1911*
they *l* their hands on them Acts 6:6 *2007*
l in the sepulchre that Abraham Acts 7:16 *5087*
the witnesses *l* down their Acts 7:58 *659*
Then *l* they their hands on them, Acts 8:17 *2007*
they *l* her in an upper chamber Acts 9:37 *5087*
l their hands on them, they sent Acts 13:3 *2007*
the tree, and *l* him in a sepulchre Acts 13:29 *5087*
was *l* unto his fathers, and saw Acts 13:36 *4369*
when they had *l* many stripes upon Acts 16:23 *2007*
when Paul had *l* his hands upon Acts 19:6 *2007*
And when the Jews *l* wait for him Acts 20:3 *1096*
the people, and *l* hands on him, Acts 21:27 *1911*
but to have nothing *l* to his Acts 23:29 *1462*
that the Jews *l* wait for the man Acts 23:30 *2071*
l many and grievous complaints Acts 25:7 *5342*
the crime *l* against him Acts 25:16 *1462*
signify the crimes *l* against him Acts 25:27
l them on the fire, there came a Acts 28:3 *2007*
l his hands on him, and healed him Acts 28:8 *2007*
my life *l* down their own necks Rom 16:4 *5294*
I have *l* the foundation, and 1Cor 3:10 *5087*
can no man lay than that is *l* 1Cor 3:11 *5087*
for necessity is *l* upon me 1Cor 9:16 *1945*
which is *l* up for you in heaven Col 1:5 *606*
Henceforth there is *l* up for me a 2Ti 4:8 *606*
it may not be *l* to their charge 2Ti 4:16 *3049*
in the beginning hast *l* the Heb 1:10
because he *l* down his life for us 1Jn 3:16 *5087*
he *l* his right hand upon me, Rev 1:17 *2007*
he *l* hold on the dragon, that old Rev 20:2

LAIDST {1}
thou *l* affliction upon our loins Ps 66:11 7760

LAIN {6}
woman, If no man have *l* with thee Num 5:19 7901
some man have *l* with thee beside Num 5:20 5414,7903
every woman that hath *l* by man Judg 21:11 3045,4904
For now should I have *l* still Job 3:13 7901
he found that he had *l* in the Jn 11:17
where the body of Jesus had *l* Jn 20:12 *2749*

LAISH *(la'-ish)* {7} See DAN, LESHEM.
1. Same as the city of Dan.
five men departed, and came to *L* Judg 18:7 3919
went to spy out the country of *L* Judg 18:14 3919
which he had, and came unto *L* Judg 18:27 3919
of the city was *L* at the first Judg 18:29 3919
cause it to be heard unto *L* Is 10:30 3919
2. Father of Phaltiel.
wife, to Phalti the son of *L* 1Sa 25:44 3919
even from Phaltiel the son of *L* 2Sa 3:15 3919

LAKE {10}
he stood by the *l* of Gennesaret Lk 5:1 *3041*
saw two ships standing by the *l* Lk 5:2 *3041*
over unto the other side of the *l* Lk 8:22 *3041*
down a storm of wind on the *l* Lk 8:23 *3041*
down a steep place into the *l* Lk 8:33 *3041*
both were cast alive into a *l* of Rev 19:20 *3041*
them was cast into the *l* of fire Rev 20:10 *3041*
hell were cast into the *l* of fire Rev 20:14 *3041*
life was cast into the *l* of fire Rev 20:15 *3041*
in the *l* which burneth with fire Rev 21:8 *3041*

LAKKUM See LAKUM.

LAKUM *(la'-kum)* {1} *A city in Naphtali.*
Adami, Nekeb, and Jabneel, unto *L* Josh 19:33 3946

LAMA {2}
saying, Eli, Eli, *l* sabachthani Mt 27:46 *2982*
saying, Eloi, Eloi, *l* sabachthani Mk 15:34 *2982*

LAMB {105}
but where is the *l* for a burnt Gen 22:7 7716
himself a *l* for a burnt offering Gen 22:8 7716
shall take to them every man a *l* Ex 12:3 7716
their fathers, a *l* for an house Ex 12:3 7716
household be too little for the *l* Ex 12:4 7716
shall make your count for the *l* Ex 12:4 7716
Your *l* shall be without blemish, Ex 12:5 7716
take you a *l* according to your Ex 12:21 6629
an ass thou shalt redeem with a *l* Ex 13:13 7716
The one *l* thou shalt offer in the Ex 29:39 3532
the other *l* thou shalt offer at Ex 29:39 3532
with the one *l* a tenth deal of Ex 29:40 3532
the other *l* thou shalt offer at Ex 29:41 3532
an ass thou shalt redeem with a *l* Ex 34:20 7716
If he offer a *l* for his offering, Lev 3:7 3775
if he bring a *l* for a sin Lev 4:32 3532
as the fat of the *l* is taken away Lev 4:35 3775
a *l* or a kid of the goats, for a Lev 5:6 3776
And if he be not able to bring a *l* Lev 5:7 7716
and a calf and a *l*, both of the Lev 9:3 3532
she shall bring a *l* of the first Lev 12:6 3532
if she be not able to bring a *l* Lev 12:8 7716
one ewe *l* of the first year Lev 14:10 3535
And the priest shall take one he *l* Lev 14:12 3532
he shall slay the *l* in the place Lev 14:13 3532
then he shall take one *l* for a Lev 14:21 3532
the *l* of the trespass offering Lev 14:24 3532
he shall kill the *l* of the Lev 14:25 3532
Israel, that killeth an ox, or *l* Lev 17:3 3775
Either a bullock or a *l* that hath Lev 22:23 7716
he *l* without blemish of the first Lev 23:12 3532
shall bring a *l* of the first year Num 6:12 3532
one he *l* of the first year Num 6:14 3532
one ewe *l* of the first year Num 6:14 3535
one *l* of the first year, for a Num 7:15 3532
one *l* of the first year, for a Num 7:21 3532
one *l* of the first year, for a Num 7:27 3532
one *l* of the first year, for a Num 7:33 3532
one *l* of the first year, for a Num 7:39 3532
one *l* of the first year, for a Num 7:45 3532
one *l* of the first year, for a Num 7:51 3532
one *l* of the first year, for a Num 7:57 3532
one *l* of the first year, for a Num 7:63 3532
one *l* of the first year, for a Num 7:69 3532
one *l* of the first year, for a Num 7:75 3532
one *l* of the first year, for a Num 7:81 3532
offering or sacrifice, for one *l* Num 15:5 3532
or for one ram, or for a *l* Num 15:11 7716
The one *l* shalt thou offer in the Num 28:4 3532
the other *l* shalt thou offer at Num 28:4 3532
part of an hin for the one *l* Num 28:7 3532
the other *l* shalt thou offer at Num 28:8 3532
for a meat offering unto one *l* Num 28:13 3532
a fourth part of an hin unto a *l* Num 28:14 3532
deal shalt thou offer for every *l* Num 28:21 3532
A several tenth deal unto one *l* Num 28:29 3532
And one tenth deal for one *l* Num 29:4 3532
A several tenth deal for one *l* Num 29:10 3532
to each *l* of the fourteen lambs Num 29:15 3532
And Samuel took a sucking *l* 1Sa 7:9 2924
took a *l* out of the flock 1Sa 17:34 7716
nothing, save one little ewe *l* 2Sa 12:3 3535
but took the poor man's *l* 2Sa 12:4 3535
he shall restore the *l* fourfold 2Sa 12:6 3535
wolf also shall dwell with the *l* Is 11:6 3532
Send ye the *l* to the ruler of the Is 16:1 3733
brought as a *l* to the slaughter Is 53:7 7716
the *l* shall feed together, and the Is 65:25 2924
he that sacrificeth a *l*, as if he Is 66:3 7716
But I was like a *l* or an ox that Jer 11:19 3532
one *l* out of the flock, out of Eze 45:15 7716
of a *l* of the first year without Eze 46:13 3532
Thus shall they prepare the *l* Eze 46:15 3532
feed them as a *l* in a large place Hos 4:16 3532
and saith, Behold the *L* of God Jn 1:29 *286*
he saith, Behold the *L* of God Jn 1:36 *286*
like a *l* dumb before his shearer, Acts 8:32 *286*
as of a *l* without blemish and 1Pet 1:19 *286*
stood a *L* as it had been slain, Rev 5:6 *721*
elders fell down before the *L* Rev 5:8 *721*
Worthy is the *L* that was slain to Rev 5:12 *721*
throne, and unto the *L* for ever Rev 5:13 *721*
I saw when the *L* opened one of Rev 6:1 *721*
and from the wrath of the *L* Rev 6:16 *721*
the throne, and before the *L* Rev 7:9 *721*
upon the throne, and unto the *L* Rev 7:10 *721*
them white in the blood of the *L* Rev 7:14 *721*
For the *L* which is in the midst Rev 7:17 *721*
him by the blood of the *L* Rev 12:11 *721*
in the book of life of the *L* Rev 13:8 *721*
and he had two horns like a *l* Rev 13:11 *721*
a *L* stood on the mount Sion, and Rev 14:1 *721*
the *L* whithersoever he goeth Rev 14:4 *721*
firstfruits unto God and to the *L* Rev 14:4 *721*
and in the presence of the *L* Rev 14:10 *721*
of God, and the song of the *L* Rev 15:3 *721*
These shall make war with the *L* Rev 17:14 *721*
the *L* shall overcome them Rev 17:14 *721*
for the marriage of the *L* is come Rev 19:7 *721*
unto the marriage supper of the *L* Rev 19:9 *721*
of the twelve apostles of the *L* Rev 21:14 *721*
the *L* are the temple of it Rev 21:22 *721*
the *L* is the light thereof Rev 21:23 *721*
of the throne of God and of the *L* Rev 22:1 *721*
of God and of the *L* shall be in it Rev 22:3 *721*

LAMB'S {2}
shew thee the bride, the *L* wife Rev 21:9 *721*
are written in the *L* book of life Rev 21:27 *721*

LAMBS {81}
Abraham set seven ewe *l* of the Gen 21:28 3535
ewe *l* which thou hast set by Gen 21:29 3535
For these seven ewe *l* shalt thou Gen 21:30 3535
And Jacob did separate the *l* Gen 30:40 3775
two *l* of the first year day by Ex 29:38 3532
take two he *l* without blemish Lev 14:10 3532
offer with the bread seven *l* Lev 23:18 3532
two *l* of the first year for a Lev 23:19 3532
before the LORD, with the two *l* Lev 23:20 3532
goats, five *l* of the first year Num 7:17 3532
goats, five *l* of the first year Num 7:23 3532
goats, five *l* of the first year Num 7:29 3532
goats, five *l* of the first year Num 7:35 3532
goats, five *l* of the first year Num 7:41 3532
goats, five *l* of the first year Num 7:47 3532
goats, five *l* of the first year Num 7:53 3532
goats, five *l* of the first year Num 7:59 3532
goats, five *l* of the first year Num 7:65 3532
goats, five *l* of the first year Num 7:71 3532
goats, five *l* of the first year Num 7:77 3532
goats, five *l* of the first year Num 7:83 3532
the *l* of the first year twelve, Num 7:87 3532
the *l* of the first year sixty Num 7:88 3532
two *l* of the first year without Num 28:3 3532
on the sabbath day two *l* of the Num 28:9 3532
seven *l* of the first year without Num 28:11 3532
seven *l* of the first year Num 28:19 3532
lamb, throughout the seven *l* Num 28:21 3532
seven *l* of the first year Num 28:27 3532
one lamb, throughout the seven *l* Num 28:29 3532
seven *l* of the first year without Num 29:2 3532
one lamb, throughout the seven *l* Num 29:4 3532
seven *l* of the first year Num 29:8 3532
one lamb, throughout the seven *l* Num 29:10 3532
fourteen *l* of the first year Num 29:13 3532
to each lamb of the fourteen *l* Num 29:15 3532
fourteen *l* of the first year Num 29:17 3532
for the rams, and for the *l* Num 29:18 3532
fourteen *l* of the first year Num 29:20 3532
for the rams, and for the *l* Num 29:21 3532
fourteen *l* of the first year Num 29:23 3532
for the rams, and for the *l* Num 29:24 3532
fourteen *l* of the first year Num 29:26 3532
for the rams, and for the *l* Num 29:27 3532
fourteen *l* of the first year Num 29:29 3532
for the rams, and for the *l* Num 29:30 3532
fourteen *l* of the first year Num 29:32 3532
for the rams, and for the *l* Num 29:33 3532
seven *l* of the first year without Num 29:36 3532
for the ram, and for the *l* Num 29:37 3532
and milk of sheep, with fat of *l* Deut 32:14 3733
and of the fatlings, and the *l* 1Sa 15:9 3733
of Israel an hundred thousand *l* 2Kin 3:4 3733
a thousand rams, and a thousand *l* 1Chr 29:21 3532
and seven rams, and seven *l* 2Chr 29:21 3532
they killed also the *l*, and they 2Chr 29:22 3532
an hundred rams, and two hundred *l* 2Chr 29:32 3532
to the people, of the flock, *l* 2Chr 35:7 3532
young bullocks, and rams, and *l* Ezr 6:9 563
two hundred rams, four hundred *l* Ezr 6:17 563
with this money bullocks, rams, *l* Ezr 7:17 563
and six rams, seventy and seven *l* Ezr 8:35 3532
the LORD shall be as the fat of *l* Ps 37:20 3733
rams, and the little hills like *l* Ps 114:4 1121,6629
and ye little hills, like *l* Ps 114:6 1121,6629
The *l* are for thy clothing, and Prov 27:26 3532
in the blood of bullocks, or of *l* Is 1:11 3532
Then shall the *l* feed after their Is 5:17 3532
fatness, and with the blood of *l* Is 34:6 3733

shall gather the *l* with his arm ... Is 40:11 2922
them down like *l* to the slaughter ... Jer 51:40 3733
they occupied with thee in *l* ... Eze 27:21 3733
of the earth, of rams, of *l* ... Eze 39:18 3733
shall be six *l* without blemish ... Eze 46:4 3532
the meat offering for the *l* as he ... Eze 46:5 3532
bullock without blemish, and six *l* ... Eze 46:6 3532
for the *l* according as his hand ... Eze 46:7 3532
to the *l* as he is able to give, ... Eze 46:11 3532
eat the *l* out of the flock, and ... Amos 6:4 3733
send you forth as *l* among wolves ... Lk 10:3 *704*
He saith unto him, Feed my *l* ... Jn 21:15 *721*

LAME {27}
a blind man, or a *l*, or he that ... Lev 21:18 6455
blemish therein, as if it be *l* ... Deut 15:21 6455
had a son that was *l* of his feet ... 2Sa 4:4 5223
flee, that he fell, and became *l* ... 2Sa 4:4 6452
thou take away the blind and the *l* ... 2Sa 5:6 6455
smiteth the Jebusites, and the *l* ... 2Sa 5:8 6455
the *l* shall not come into the ... 2Sa 5:8 6455
yet a son, which is *l* on his feet ... 2Sa 9:3 5223
and was *l* on both his feet ... 2Sa 9:13 6455
because thy servant is *l* ... 2Sa 19:26 6455
the blind, and feet was I to the *l* ... Job 29:15 6455
The legs of the *l* are not equal ... Prov 26:7 6455
the *l* take the prey ... Is 33:23 6455
Then shall the *l* man leap as an ... Is 35:6 6455
and with them the blind and the *l* ... Jer 31:8 6455
and if ye offer the *l* and sick, is ... Mal 1:8 6455
that which was torn, and the *l* ... Mal 1:13 6455
the *l* walk, the lepers are ... Mt 11:5 *5560*
with them those that were *l* ... Mt 15:30 *5560*
the *l* to walk, and the blind to ... Mt 15:31 *5560*
the *l* came to him in the temple ... Mt 21:14 *5560*
the *l* walk, the lepers are ... Lk 7:22 *5560*
call the poor, the maimed, the *l* ... Lk 14:13 *5560*
a certain man *l* from his mother's ... Acts 3:2 *5560*
as the *l* man which was healed ... Acts 3:11 *5560*
with palsies, and that were *l* ... Acts 8:7 *5560*
lest that which is *l* be turned ... Heb 12:13 *5560*

LAMECH *(la'-mek)* {12} *A son of Methuselah.*
and Methusael begat *L* ... Gen 4:18 3929
L took unto him two wives ... Gen 4:19 3929
L said unto his wives, Adah and ... Gen 4:23 3929
ye wives of *L*, hearken unto my ... Gen 4:23 3929
truly *L* seventy and sevenfold ... Gen 4:24 3929
eighty and seven years, and begat *L* ... Gen 5:25 3929
he begat *L* seven hundred eighty ... Gen 5:26 3929
L lived an hundred eighty and two ... Gen 5:28 3929
L lived after he begat Noah five ... Gen 5:30 3929
all the days of *L* were seven ... Gen 5:31 3929
Henoch, Methuselah, *L*, ... 1Chr 1:3 3929
of Noe, which was the son of *L* ... Lk 3:36 *2984*

LAMENT {21}
of Israel went yearly to *l* the ... Judg 11:40 8567
And her gates shall *l* and mourn ... Is 3:26 578
angle into the brooks shall *l* ... Is 19:8 56
They shall *l* for the teats, for ... Is 32:12 5594
this gird you with sackcloth, *l* ... Jer 4:8 5594
neither go to *l* nor bemoan them ... Jer 16:5 5594
neither shall men *l* for them ... Jer 16:6 5594
They shall not *l* for him, saying ... Jer 22:18 5594
they shall not *l* for him, saying, ... Jer 22:18 5594
and they will *l* thee, saying, Ah ... Jer 34:5 5594
l, and run to and fro by the hedges ... Jer 49:3 5594
made the rampart and the wall to *l* ... Lam 2:8 56
l over thee, saying, What city is ... Eze 27:32 6969
wherewith they shall *l* her ... Eze 32:16 6969
of the nations shall *l* her ... Eze 32:16 6969
they shall *l* for her, even for ... Eze 32:16 6969
L like a virgin girded with ... Joel 1:8 421
Gird yourselves, and *l*, ye priests ... Joel 1:13 5594
l with a doleful lamentation, and ... Mic 2:4 5091
unto you, That ye shall weep and *l* ... Jn 16:20 *2354*
l for her, when they shall see ... Rev 18:9 *2875*

LAMENTABLE {1}
he cried with a *l* voice unto ... Dan 6:20 6088

LAMENTATION {25}
with a great and very sore *l* ... Gen 50:10 4553
lamented with this *l* over Saul ... 2Sa 1:17 7015
and their widows made no *l* ... Ps 78:64 1058
as for an only son, most bitter *l* ... Jer 6:26 4553
take up a *l* on high places ... Jer 7:29 7015
habitations of the wilderness a *l* ... Jer 9:10 7015
and every one her neighbour *l* ... Jer 9:20 7015
A voice was heard in Ramah, *l* ... Jer 31:15 5092
There shall be *l* generally upon ... Jer 48:38 4553
daughter of Judah mourning and *l* ... Lam 2:5 592
Moreover take thou up a *l* for the ... Eze 19:1 7015
is a *l*, and shall be for a *l* ... Eze 19:14 7015
they shall take up a *l* for thee ... Eze 26:17 7015
son of man, take up a *l* for Tyrus ... Eze 27:2 7015
they shall take up a *l* for thee ... Eze 27:32 7015
take up a *l* upon the king of ... Eze 28:12 7015
take up a *l* for Pharaoh king of ... Eze 32:2 7015
This is the *l* wherewith they ... Eze 32:16 7015
I take up against you, even a *l* ... Amos 5:1 7015
as are skilful of *l* to wailing ... Amos 5:16 5092
and all your songs into *l* ... Amos 8:10 7015
you, and lament with a doleful *l* ... Mic 2:4 5092
Rama was there a voice heard, *l* ... Mt 2:18 *2355*
burial, and made great *l* over him ... Acts 8:2 *2870*

LAMENTATIONS {3}
of Josiah in their *l* to this day ... 2Chr 35:25 7015
behold, they are written in the *l* ... 2Chr 35:25 7015
and there was written therein *l* ... Eze 2:10 7015

LAMENTED {11}
and the people *l*, because the LORD ... 1Sa 6:19 56
house of Israel *l* after the LORD ... 1Sa 7:2 5091
l him, and buried him in his house ... 1Sa 25:1 5594
was dead, and all Israel had *l* him ... 1Sa 28:3 5594
David *l* with this lamentation ... 2Sa 1:17 6969
the king *l* over Abner, and said, ... 2Sa 3:33 6969
And Jeremiah *l* for Josiah ... 2Chr 35:25 6969
they shall not be *l* ... Jer 16:4 5594
they shall not be *l*, neither ... Jer 25:33 5594
unto you, and ye have not *l* ... Mt 11:17 *2875*
which also bewailed and *l* him ... Lk 23:27 *2354*

LAMP {13}
a burning *l* that passed between ... Gen 15:17 3940
to cause the *l* to burn always ... Ex 27:20 5216
ere the *l* of God went out in the ... 1Sa 3:3 5216
For thou art my *l*, O LORD ... 2Sa 22:29 5216
his God give him a *l* in Jerusalem ... 1Kin 15:4 5216
to slip with his feet is as a *l* ... Job 12:5 3940
Thy word is a *l* unto my feet ... Ps 119:105 5216
ordained a *l* for mine anointed ... Ps 132:17 5216
For the commandment is a *l* ... Prov 6:23 5216
but the *l* of the wicked shall be ... Prov 13:9 5216
his *l* shall be put out in obscure ... Prov 20:20 5216
thereof as a *l* that burneth ... Is 62:1 3940
heaven, burning as it were a *l* ... Rev 8:10 *2985*

LAMPS {37}
shalt make the seven *l* thereof ... Ex 25:37 5216
and they shall light the *l* thereof ... Ex 25:37 5216
when he dresseth the *l*, he shall ... Ex 30:7 5216
when Aaron lighteth the *l* at even ... Ex 30:8 5216
light, and his furniture, and his *l* ... Ex 35:14 5216
And he made his seven *l*, and his ... Ex 37:23 5216
candlestick, with the *l* thereof ... Ex 39:37 5216
even with the *l* to be set in ... Ex 39:37 5216
and light the *l* thereof ... Ex 40:4 5216
he lighted the *l* before the LORD ... Ex 40:25 5216
the light, to cause the *l* to burn ... Lev 24:2 5216
He shall order the *l* upon the ... Lev 24:4 5216
of the light, and his *l*, and his ... Num 4:9 5216
him, When thou lightest the *l* ... Num 8:2 5216
the seven *l* shall give light over ... Num 8:2 5216
he lighted the *l* thereof over ... Num 8:3 5216
and *l* within the pitchers ... Judg 7:16 3940
held the *l* in their left hands, ... Judg 7:20 3940
with the flowers, and the *l* ... 1Kin 7:49 5216
of gold, and for their *l* of gold ... 1Chr 28:15 5216
candlestick, and for the *l* thereof ... 1Chr 28:15 5216
and also for the *l* thereof ... 1Chr 28:15 5216
the candlesticks with their *l* ... 2Chr 4:20 5216
And the flowers, and the *l*, and the ... 2Chr 4:21 5216
of gold with the *l* thereof ... 2Chr 13:11 5216
of the porch, and put out the *l* ... 2Chr 29:7 5216
Out of his mouth go burning *l* ... Job 41:19 3940
fire, and like the appearance of *l* ... Eze 1:13 3940
and his eyes as *l* of fire ... Dan 10:6 3940
top of it, and his seven *l* thereon ... Zec 4:2 5216
and seven pipes to the seven *l* ... Zec 4:2 5216
ten virgins, which took their *l* ... Mt 25:1 *2985*
that were foolish took their *l* ... Mt 25:3 *2985*
oil in their vessels with their *l* ... Mt 25:4 *2985*
virgins arose, and trimmed their *l* ... Mt 25:7 *2985*
for our *l* are gone out ... Mt 25:8 *2985*
there were seven *l* of fire ... Rev 4:5 *2985*

LANCE {1}
They shall hold the bow and the *l* ... Jer 50:42 3591

LANCETS {1}
their manner with knives and *l* ... 1Kin 18:28 7420

LAND {1717}
place, and let the dry *l* appear ... Gen 1:9
And God called the dry *l* Earth ... Gen 1:10
compasseth the whole *l* of Havilah ... Gen 2:11 776
And the gold of that *l* is good ... Gen 2:12 776
the whole *l* of Ethiopia ... Gen 2:13 776
LORD, and dwelt in the *l* of Nod ... Gen 4:16 776
of all that was in the dry *l* ... Gen 7:22
and Calneh, in the *l* of Shinar ... Gen 10:10 776
Out of that *l* went forth Asshur, ... Gen 10:11 776
found a plain in the *l* of Shinar ... Gen 11:2 776
Terah in the *l* of his nativity ... Gen 11:28 776
to go into the *l* of Canaan ... Gen 11:31 776
unto a *l* that I will shew thee ... Gen 12:1 776
forth to go into the *l* of Canaan ... Gen 12:5 776
into the *l* of Canaan they came ... Gen 12:5 776
the *l* unto the place of Sichem ... Gen 12:6 776
the Canaanite was then in the *l* ... Gen 12:6 776
Unto thy seed will I give this *l* ... Gen 12:7 776
And there was a famine in the *l* ... Gen 12:10 776
the famine was grievous in the *l* ... Gen 12:10 776
the *l* was not able to bear them, ... Gen 13:6 776
Perizzite dwelled then in the *l* ... Gen 13:7 776
Is not the whole *l* before thee ... Gen 13:9 776
of the LORD, like the *l* of Egypt ... Gen 13:10 776
Abram dwelled in the *l* of Canaan ... Gen 13:12 776
For all the *l* which thou seest, ... Gen 13:15 776
walk through the *l* in the length ... Gen 13:17 776
to give thee this *l* to inherit it ... Gen 15:7 776
in a *l* that is not theirs ... Gen 15:13 776
Unto thy seed have I given this *l* ... Gen 15:18 776
ten years in the *l* of Canaan ... Gen 16:3 776
the *l* wherein thou art a stranger ... Gen 17:8 776
all the *l* of Canaan, for an ... Gen 17:8 776
and toward all the *l* of the plain ... Gen 19:28 776
said, Behold, my *l* is before thee ... Gen 20:15 776
him a wife out of the *l* of Egypt ... Gen 21:21 776
to the *l* wherein thou hast ... Gen 21:23 776
into the *l* of the Philistines ... Gen 21:32 776
in the Philistines' *l* many days ... Gen 21:34 776
and get thee into the *l* of Moriah ... Gen 22:2 776
same is Hebron in the *l* of Canaan ... Gen 23:2 776
himself to the people of the *l* ... Gen 23:7 776
before the people of the *l* ... Gen 23:12 776
audience of the people of the *l* ... Gen 23:13 776
the *l* is worth four hundred ... Gen 23:15 776
same is Hebron in the *l* of Canaan ... Gen 23:19 776
willing to follow me unto this *l* ... Gen 24:5 776
the *l* from whence thou camest ... Gen 24:5 776
from the *l* of my kindred, and ... Gen 24:7 776
Unto thy seed will I give this *l* ... Gen 24:7 776
Canaanites, in whose *l* I dwell ... Gen 24:37 776
And there was a famine in the *l* ... Gen 26:1 776
dwell in the *l* which I shall tell ... Gen 26:2 776
Sojourn in this *l*, and I will be ... Gen 26:3 776
Then Isaac sowed in that *l* ... Gen 26:12 776
and we shall be fruitful in the *l* ... Gen 26:22 776
are of the daughters of the *l* ... Gen 27:46 776
the *l* wherein thou art a stranger ... Gen 28:4 776
the *l* whereon thou liest, to thee ... Gen 28:13 776
will bring thee again into this *l* ... Gen 28:15 127
came into the *l* of the people of ... Gen 29:1 776
Return unto the *l* of thy fathers ... Gen 31:3 776
arise, get thee out from this *l* ... Gen 31:13 776
return unto the *l* of thy kindred ... Gen 31:13 776
his father in the *l* of Canaan ... Gen 31:18 776
his brother unto the *l* of Seir ... Gen 32:3 776
which is in the *l* of Canaan ... Gen 33:18 776
out to see the daughters of the *l* ... Gen 34:1 776
the *l* shall be before you ... Gen 34:10 776
therefore let them dwell in the *l* ... Gen 34:21 776
for the *l*, behold, it is large ... Gen 34:21 776
among the inhabitants of the *l* ... Gen 34:30 776
Luz, which is in the *l* of Canaan ... Gen 35:6 776
the *l* which I gave Abraham and ... Gen 35:12 776
seed after thee will I give the *l* ... Gen 35:12 776
pass, when Israel dwelt in that *l* ... Gen 35:22 776
born unto him in the *l* of Canaan ... Gen 36:5 776
he had got in the *l* of Canaan ... Gen 36:6 776
the *l* wherein they were strangers ... Gen 36:7 776
came of Eliphaz in the *l* of Edom ... Gen 36:16 776
came of Reuel in the *l* of Edom ... Gen 36:17 776
the Horite, who inhabited the *l* ... Gen 36:20 776
children of Seir in the *l* of Edom ... Gen 36:21 776
their dukes in the *l* of Seir ... Gen 36:30 776
that reigned in the *l* of Edom ... Gen 36:31 776
Husham of the *l* of Temani reigned ... Gen 36:34 776
in the *l* of their possession ... Gen 36:43 776
Jacob dwelt in the *l* wherein his ... Gen 37:1 776
a stranger, in the *l* of Canaan ... Gen 37:1 776
away out of the *l* of the Hebrews ... Gen 40:15 776
in all the *l* of Egypt for badness ... Gen 41:19 776
throughout all the *l* of Egypt ... Gen 41:29 776
be forgotten in the *l* of Egypt ... Gen 41:30 776
and the famine shall consume the *l* ... Gen 41:30 776
in the *l* by reason of that famine ... Gen 41:31 776
and set him over the *l* of Egypt ... Gen 41:33 776
him appoint officers over the *l* ... Gen 41:34 776
take up the fifth part of the *l* ... Gen 41:34 776
the *l* against the seven years of ... Gen 41:36 776
which shall be in the *l* of Egypt ... Gen 41:36 776
that the *l* perish not through the ... Gen 41:36 776
set thee over all the *l* of Egypt ... Gen 41:41 776
him ruler over all the *l* of Egypt ... Gen 41:43 776
or foot in all the *l* of Egypt ... Gen 41:44 776
went out over all the *l* of Egypt ... Gen 41:45 776
throughout all the *l* of Egypt ... Gen 41:46 776
which were in the *l* of Egypt ... Gen 41:48 776
in the *l* of my affliction ... Gen 41:52 776
that was in the *l* of Egypt ... Gen 41:53 776
but in all the *l* of Egypt there ... Gen 41:54 776
when all the *l* of Egypt was ... Gen 41:55 776
waxed sore in the *l* of Egypt ... Gen 41:56 776
the famine was in the *l* of Canaan ... Gen 42:5 776
was the governor over the *l* ... Gen 42:6 776
sold to all the people of the *l* ... Gen 42:6 776
From the *l* of Canaan to buy food ... Gen 42:7 776
nakedness of the *l* ye are come ... Gen 42:9 776
nakedness of the *l* ye are come ... Gen 42:12 776
of one man in the *l* of Canaan ... Gen 42:13 776
their father unto the *l* of Canaan ... Gen 42:29 776
The man, who is the lord of the *l* ... Gen 42:30 776
our father in the *l* of Canaan ... Gen 42:32 776
and ye shall traffick in the *l* ... Gen 42:34 776
And the famine was sore in the *l* ... Gen 43:1 776
fruits in the *l* in your vessels ... Gen 43:11 776
unto thee out of the *l* of Canaan ... Gen 44:8 776
hath the famine been in the *l* ... Gen 45:6 776
throughout all the *l* of Egypt ... Gen 45:8 776
shalt dwell in the *l* of Goshen ... Gen 45:10 776
go, get you unto the *l* of Canaan ... Gen 45:17 776
you the good of the *l* of Egypt ... Gen 45:18 776
and ye shall eat the fat of the *l* ... Gen 45:18 776
take you wagons out of the *l* of ... Gen 45:19 776
of all the *l* of Egypt is yours ... Gen 45:20 776
came into the *l* of Canaan unto ... Gen 45:25 776
governor over all the *l* of Egypt ... Gen 45:26 776
had gotten in the *l* of Canaan ... Gen 46:6 776
and Onan died in the *l* of Canaan ... Gen 46:12 776
unto Joseph in the *l* of Egypt ... Gen 46:20 776
and they came into the *l* of Goshen ... Gen 46:28 776
which were in the *l* of Canaan ... Gen 46:31 776
ye may dwell in the *l* of Goshen ... Gen 46:34 776
are come out of the *l* of Canaan ... Gen 47:1 776
they are in the *l* of Goshen ... Gen 47:1 776
to sojourn in the *l* are we come ... Gen 47:4 776

famine is sore in the *l* of Canaan	Gen 47:4	776
servants dwell in the *l* of Goshen	Gen 47:4	776
The *l* of Egypt is before thee	Gen 47:6	776
the best of the *l* make thy father	Gen 47:6	776
in the *l* of Goshen let them dwell	Gen 47:6	776
a possession in the *l* of Egypt	Gen 47:11	776
in the best of the *l*	Gen 47:11	776
in the *l* of Rameses, as Pharaoh	Gen 47:11	776
there was no bread in all the *l*	Gen 47:13	776
very sore, so that the *l* of Egypt	Gen 47:13	776
all the *l* of Canaan fainted by	Gen 47:13	776
that was found in the *l* of Egypt	Gen 47:14	776
in the *l* of Canaan, for the corn	Gen 47:14	776
money failed in the *l* of Egypt	Gen 47:15	776
in the *l* of Canaan, all the	Gen 47:15	776
thine eyes, both we and our *l*	Gen 47:19	127
our *l* for bread, and we and our	Gen 47:19	127
our *l* will be servants unto	Gen 47:19	127
that the *l* be not desolate	Gen 47:19	127
all the *l* of Egypt for Pharaoh	Gen 47:20	127
so the *l* became Pharaoh's	Gen 47:20	776
Only the *l* of the priests bought	Gen 47:22	127
this day and your *l* for Pharaoh	Gen 47:23	127
for you, and ye shall sow the *l*	Gen 47:23	127
over the *l* of Egypt unto this day	Gen 47:26	127
except the *l* of the priests only,	Gen 47:26	127
And Israel dwelt in the *l* of Egypt	Gen 47:27	776
Jacob lived in the *l* of Egypt	Gen 47:28	776
unto me at Luz in the *l* of Canaan	Gen 48:3	776
will give this *l* to thy seed	Gen 48:4	776
were born unto thee in the *l* of	Gen 48:5	776
me in the *l* of Canaan in the way	Gen 48:7	776
again unto the *l* of your fathers	Gen 48:21	776
the *l* that it was pleasant	Gen 49:15	776
in the *l* of Canaan, which Abraham	Gen 49:30	776
digged for me in the *l* of Canaan	Gen 50:5	776
all the elders of the *l* of Egypt	Gen 50:7	776
they left in the *l* of Goshen	Gen 50:8	776
And when the inhabitants of the *l*	Gen 50:11	776
carried him into the *l* of Canaan	Gen 50:13	776
bring you out of this *l* unto the	Gen 50:24	776
the *l* which he sware to Abraham	Gen 50:24	776
the *l* was filled with them	Ex 1:7	776
and so get them up out of the *l*	Ex 1:10	776
and dwelt in the *l* of Midian	Ex 2:15	776
been a stranger in a strange *l*	Ex 2:22	776
up out of that *l* unto a good *l*	Ex 3:8	776
unto a *l* flowing with milk and	Ex 3:8	776
unto the *l* of the Canaanites	Ex 3:17	776
unto a *l* flowing with milk and	Ex 3:17	776
river, and pour it upon the dry *l*	Ex 4:9	
shall become blood upon the dry *l*	Ex 4:9	
and he returned to the *l* of Egypt	Ex 4:20	776
the people of the *l* now are many	Ex 5:5	776
abroad throughout all the *l* of	Ex 5:12	776
shall he drive them out of his *l*	Ex 6:1	776
to give them the *l* of Canaan	Ex 6:4	776
the *l* of their pilgrimage,	Ex 6:4	776
And I will bring you in unto the *l*	Ex 6:8	776
of Israel go out of his *l*	Ex 6:11	776
of Israel out of the *l* of Egypt	Ex 6:13	776
the *l* of Egypt according to their	Ex 6:26	776
unto Moses in the *l* of Egypt	Ex 6:28	776
children of Israel out of his *l*	Ex 7:2	776
and my wonders in the *l* of Egypt	Ex 7:3	776
out of the *l* of Egypt by great	Ex 7:4	776
throughout all the *l* of Egypt	Ex 7:19	776
throughout all the *l* of Egypt	Ex 7:21	776
to come up upon the *l* of Egypt	Ex 8:5	776
up, and covered the *l* of Egypt	Ex 8:6	776
up frogs upon the *l* of Egypt	Ex 8:7	776
and the *l* stank	Ex 8:14	776
rod, and smite the dust of the *l*	Ex 8:16	776
throughout all the *l* of Egypt	Ex 8:16	776
all the dust of the *l* became lice	Ex 8:17	776
throughout all the *l* of Egypt	Ex 8:17	776
sever in that day the *l* of Goshen	Ex 8:22	776
and into all the *l* of Egypt	Ex 8:24	776
the *l* was corrupted by reason of	Ex 8:24	776
sacrifice to your God in the *l*	Ex 8:25	776
LORD shall do this thing in the *l*	Ex 9:5	776
small dust in all the *l* of Egypt	Ex 9:9	776
throughout all the *l* of Egypt	Ex 9:9	776
may be hail in all the *l* of Egypt	Ex 9:22	776
field, throughout the *l* of Egypt	Ex 9:22	776
rained hail upon the *l* of Egypt	Ex 9:23	776
the *l* of Egypt since it became a	Ex 9:24	776
l of Egypt all that was in the	Ex 9:25	776
Only in the *l* of Goshen, where	Ex 9:26	776
the *l* of Egypt for the locusts	Ex 10:12	776
may come up upon the *l* of Egypt	Ex 10:12	776
and eat every herb of the *l*	Ex 10:12	776
forth his rod over the *l* of Egypt	Ex 10:13	776
east wind upon the *l* all that day	Ex 10:13	776
went up over all the *l* of Egypt	Ex 10:14	776
so that the *l* was darkened	Ex 10:15	776
they did eat every herb of the *l*	Ex 10:15	776
field, through all the *l* of Egypt	Ex 10:15	776
be darkness over the *l* of Egypt	Ex 10:21	776
in all the *l* of Egypt three days	Ex 10:22	776
was very great in the *l* of Egypt	Ex 11:3	776
in the *l* of Egypt shall die	Ex 11:5	776
cry throughout all the *l* of Egypt	Ex 11:6	776
be multiplied in the *l* of Egypt	Ex 11:9	776
of Israel go out of his *l*	Ex 11:10	776
Moses and Aaron in the *l* of Egypt	Ex 12:1	776
through the *l* of Egypt this night	Ex 12:12	776
the firstborn in the *l* of Egypt	Ex 12:12	776
you, when I smite the *l* of Egypt	Ex 12:13	776
your armies out of the *l* of Egypt	Ex 12:17	776
be a stranger, or born in the *l*	Ex 12:19	776
when ye be come to the *l* which	Ex 12:25	776
the firstborn in the *l* of Egypt	Ex 12:29	776
send them out of the *l* in haste	Ex 12:33	776
LORD went out from the *l* of Egypt	Ex 12:41	776
them out from the *l* of Egypt	Ex 12:42	776
be as one that is born in the *l*	Ex 12:48	776
of the *l* of Egypt by their armies	Ex 12:51	776
thee into the *l* of the Canaanites	Ex 13:5	776
a *l* flowing with milk and honey,	Ex 13:5	776
thee into the *l* of the Canaanites	Ex 13:11	776
the firstborn in the *l* of Egypt	Ex 13:15	776
way of the *l* of the Philistines	Ex 13:17	776
harnessed out of the *l* of Egypt	Ex 13:18	776
They are entangled in the *l*	Ex 14:3	776
that night, and made the sea dry *l*	Ex 14:21	
dry *l* in the midst of the sea	Ex 14:29	
on dry *l* in the midst of the sea	Ex 15:19	
departing out of the *l* of Egypt	Ex 16:1	776
of the LORD in the *l* of Egypt	Ex 16:3	776
you out from the *l* of Egypt	Ex 16:6	776
you forth from the *l* of Egypt	Ex 16:32	776
until they came to a *l* inhabited	Ex 16:35	776
the borders of the *l* of Canaan	Ex 16:35	776
have been an alien in a strange *l*	Ex 18:3	776
and he went his way into his own *l*	Ex 18:27	776
gone forth out of the *l* of Egypt	Ex 19:1	776
thee out of the *l* of Egypt	Ex 20:2	776
l which the LORD thy God giveth	Ex 20:12	127
were strangers in the *l* of Egypt	Ex 22:21	776
were strangers in the *l* of Egypt	Ex 23:9	776
And six years thou shalt sow thy *l*	Ex 23:10	776
l thou shalt bring into the house	Ex 23:19	127
young, nor be barren, in thy *l*	Ex 23:26	776
lest the *l* become desolate, and	Ex 23:29	776
be increased, and inherit the *l*	Ex 23:30	776
of the *l* into your hand	Ex 23:31	776
They shall not dwell in thy *l*	Ex 23:33	776
them forth out of the *l* of Egypt	Ex 29:46	776
us up out of the *l* of Egypt	Ex 32:1	776
thee up out of the *l* of Egypt	Ex 32:4	776
broughtest out of the *l* of Egypt	Ex 32:7	776
thee up out of the *l* of Egypt	Ex 32:8	776
the *l* of Egypt with great power	Ex 32:11	776
all this *l* that I have spoken of	Ex 32:13	776
us up out of the *l* of Egypt	Ex 32:23	776
brought up out of the *l* of Egypt	Ex 33:1	776
unto the *l* which I sware unto	Ex 33:1	776
Unto a *l* flowing with milk and	Ex 33:3	776
of the *l* whither thou goest	Ex 34:12	776
with the inhabitants of the *l*	Ex 34:15	776
shall any man desire thy *l*	Ex 34:24	776
l thou shalt bring unto the house	Ex 34:26	127
you up out of the *l* of Egypt	Lev 11:45	776
ye be come into the *l* of Canaan	Lev 14:34	776
house of the *l* of your possession	Lev 14:34	776
iniquities unto a *l* not inhabited	Lev 16:22	776
the doings of the *l* of Egypt	Lev 18:3	776
the doings of the *l* of Canaan	Lev 18:3	776
And the *l* is defiled	Lev 18:25	776
the *l* itself vomiteth out her	Lev 18:25	776
have the men of the *l* done	Lev 18:27	776
before you, and the *l* is defiled	Lev 18:27	776
That the *l* spue not you out also,	Lev 18:28	776
ye reap the harvest of your *l*	Lev 19:9	776
And when ye shall come into the *l*	Lev 19:23	776
lest the *l* fall to whoredom, and	Lev 19:29	776
the *l* become full of wickedness	Lev 19:29	776
sojourn with thee in your *l*	Lev 19:33	776
were strangers in the *l* of Egypt	Lev 19:34	776
brought you out of the *l* of Egypt	Lev 19:36	776
the people of the *l* shall stone	Lev 20:2	776
if the people of the *l* do any	Lev 20:4	776
that the *l*, whither I bring you	Lev 20:22	776
you, Ye shall inherit their *l*	Lev 20:24	127
a *l* that floweth with milk and	Lev 20:24	776
any offering thereof in your *l*	Lev 22:24	776
brought you out of the *l* of Egypt	Lev 22:33	776
into the *l* which I give unto you	Lev 23:10	776
ye reap the harvest of your *l*	Lev 23:22	776
gathered in the fruit of the *l*	Lev 23:39	776
them out of the *l* of Egypt	Lev 23:43	776
as he that is born in the *l*	Lev 24:16	249
come into the *l* which I give you	Lev 25:2	776
then shall the *l* keep a sabbath	Lev 25:2	776
be a sabbath of rest unto the *l*	Lev 25:4	776
it is a year of rest unto the *l*	Lev 25:5	776
the sabbath of the *l* shall be	Lev 25:6	776
for the beast that are in thy *l*	Lev 25:7	776
sound throughout all your *l*	Lev 25:9	776
the *l* unto all the inhabitants	Lev 25:10	776
ye shall dwell in the *l* in safety	Lev 25:18	776
the *l* shall yield her fruit, and	Lev 25:19	776
The *l* shall not be sold for ever	Lev 25:23	776
for the *l* is mine	Lev 25:23	776
in all the *l* of your possession	Lev 25:24	776
grant a redemption for the *l*	Lev 25:24	776
you forth out of the *l* of Egypt	Lev 25:38	776
to give you the *l* of Canaan	Lev 25:38	776
forth out of the *l* of Egypt	Lev 25:42	776
you, which they begat in your *l*	Lev 25:45	776
forth out of the *l* of Egypt	Lev 25:55	776
up any image of stone in your *l*	Lev 26:1	776
the *l* shall yield her increase,	Lev 26:4	776
full, and dwell in your *l* safely	Lev 26:5	776
And I will give peace in the *l*	Lev 26:6	776
will rid evil beasts out of the *l*	Lev 26:6	776
shall the sword go through your *l*	Lev 26:6	776
you forth out of the *l* of Egypt	Lev 26:13	776
for your *l* shall not yield her	Lev 26:20	776
trees of the *l* yield their fruits	Lev 26:20	776
will bring the *l* into desolation	Lev 26:32	776
your *l* shall be desolate, and your	Lev 26:33	776
Then shall the *l* enjoy her	Lev 26:34	776
and ye be in your enemies' *l*	Lev 26:34	776
even then shall the *l* rest	Lev 26:34	776
the *l* of your enemies shall eat	Lev 26:38	776
them into the *l* of their enemies	Lev 26:41	776
and I will remember the *l*	Lev 26:42	776
The *l* also shall be left of them,	Lev 26:43	776
they be in the *l* of their enemies	Lev 26:44	776
l of Egypt in the sight of the	Lev 26:45	776
possession of the *l* did belong	Lev 27:24	776
And all the tithe of the *l*	Lev 27:30	776
whether of the seed of the *l*	Lev 27:30	776
were come out of the *l* of Egypt	Num 1:1	776
smote all the firstborn in the *l*	Num 3:13	776
l of Egypt I sanctified them for	Num 8:17	776
were come out of the *l* of Egypt	Num 9:1	776
and for him that was born in the *l*	Num 9:14	776
in your *l* against the enemy that	Num 10:9	776
but I will depart to mine own *l*	Num 10:30	776
unto the *l* which thou swarest	Num 11:12	127
they may search the *l* of Canaan	Num 13:2	776
which Moses sent to spy out the *l*	Num 13:16	776
them to spy out the *l* of Canaan	Num 13:17	776
And see the *l*, what it is	Num 13:18	776
what the *l* is that they dwell in,	Num 13:19	776
And what the *l* is, whether it be	Num 13:20	776
and bring of the fruit of the *l*	Num 13:20	776
up, and searched the *l* from the	Num 13:21	776
of the *l* after forty days	Num 13:25	776
and shewed them the fruit of the *l*	Num 13:26	776
We came unto the *l* whither thou	Num 13:27	776
be strong that dwell in the *l*	Num 13:28	776
dwell in the *l* of the south	Num 13:29	776
up an evil report of the *l* which	Num 13:32	776
children of Israel, saying, The *l*	Num 13:32	776
is a *l* that eateth up the	Num 13:32	776
we had died in the *l* of Egypt	Num 14:2	776
the LORD brought us unto this *l*	Num 14:3	776
were of them that searched the *l*	Num 14:6	776
children of Israel, saying, The *l*	Num 14:7	776
search it, is an exceeding good *l*	Num 14:7	776
then he will bring us into this *l*	Num 14:8	776
a *l* which floweth with milk and	Num 14:8	776
fear ye the people of the *l*	Num 14:9	776
it to the inhabitants of this *l*	Num 14:14	776
the *l* which he sware unto them	Num 14:16	776
the *l* which I sware unto their	Num 14:23	776
into the *l* whereinto he went	Num 14:24	776
ye shall not come into the *l*	Num 14:30	776
they shall know the *l* which ye	Num 14:31	776
days in which ye searched the *l*	Num 14:34	776
which Moses sent to search the *l*	Num 14:36	776
bringing up a slander upon the *l*	Num 14:36	776
up the evil report upon the *l*	Num 14:37	776
the men that went to search the *l*	Num 14:38	776
into the *l* of your habitations	Num 15:2	776
into the *l* whither I bring you	Num 15:18	776
when ye eat of the bread of the *l*	Num 15:19	776
whether he be born in the *l*	Num 15:30	249
brought you out of the *l* of Egypt	Num 15:41	776
out of a *l* that floweth with milk	Num 16:13	776
into a *l* that floweth with milk	Num 16:14	776
whatsoever is first ripe in the *l*	Num 18:13	776
have no inheritance in their *l*	Num 18:20	776
the *l* which I have given them	Num 20:12	776
by the coast of the *l* of Edom	Num 20:23	776
the *l* which I have given unto the	Num 20:24	776
Red sea, to compass the *l* of Edom	Num 21:4	776
Let me pass through thy *l*	Num 21:22	776
possessed his *l* from Arnon unto	Num 21:24	776
taken all his *l* out of his hand,	Num 21:26	776
dwelt in the *l* of the Amorites	Num 21:31	776
hand, and all his people, and his *l*	Num 21:34	776
and they possessed his *l*	Num 21:35	776
which is by the river of the *l* of	Num 22:5	776
I may drive them out of the *l*	Num 22:6	776
of Balak, Get you into your *l*	Num 22:13	776
went forth out of the *l* of Egypt	Num 26:4	776
and Onan died in the *l* of Canaan	Num 26:19	776
Unto these the *l* shall be divided	Num 26:53	776
Notwithstanding the *l* shall be	Num 26:55	776
see the *l* which I have given unto	Num 27:12	776
and when they saw the *l* of Jazer	Num 32:1	776
the *l* of Gilead, that, behold,	Num 32:1	776
is a *l* for cattle, and thy	Num 32:4	776
let this *l* be given unto thy	Num 32:5	776
l which the LORD hath given them	Num 32:7	776
from Kadesh-barnea to see the *l*	Num 32:8	776
valley of Eshcol, and saw the *l*	Num 32:9	776
they should not go into the *l*	Num 32:9	776
shall see the *l* which I sware	Num 32:11	127
of the inhabitants of the *l*	Num 32:17	776
the *l* be subdued before the LORD	Num 32:22	776
this *l* shall be your possession	Num 32:22	776
the *l* shall be subdued before you	Num 32:29	776
the *l* of Gilead for a possession	Num 32:29	776
among you in the *l* of Canaan	Num 32:30	776
the LORD into the *l* of Canaan	Num 32:32	776
of Og king of Bashan, the *l*	Num 32:33	776
the *l* of Egypt with their armies	Num 33:1	776
Hor, in the edge of the *l* of Edom	Num 33:37	776

were come out of the *l* of Egypt ... Num 33:38 776
in the south in the *l* of Canaan ... Num 33:40 776
over Jordan into the *l* of Canaan ... Num 33:51 776
of the *l* from before you, and ... Num 33:52 776
the inhabitants of the *l*, and ... Num 33:53 776
given you the *l* to possess it ... Num 33:53 776
ye shall divide the *l* by lot for ... Num 33:54 776
of the *l* from before you ... Num 33:55 776
vex you in the *l* wherein ye dwell ... Num 33:55 776
When ye come into the *l* of Canaan ... Num 34:2 776
(this is the *l* that shall fall ... Num 34:2 776
even the *l* of Canaan with the ... Num 34:2 776
this shall be your *l* with the ... Num 34:12 776
This is the *l* which ye shall ... Num 34:13 776
which shall divide the *l* unto you ... Num 34:17 776
to divide the *l* by inheritance ... Num 34:18 776
of Israel in the *l* of Canaan ... Num 34:29 776
over Jordan into the *l* of Canaan ... Num 35:10 776
shall ye give in the *l* of Canaan ... Num 35:14 776
into the *l* of his possession ... Num 35:28 776
come again to dwell in the *l* ... Num 35:32 776
not pollute the *l* wherein ye are ... Num 35:33 776
for blood it defileth the *l* ... Num 35:33 776
the *l* cannot be cleansed of the ... Num 35:33 776
the *l* which ye shall inhabit ... Num 35:34 776
l for an inheritance by lot to ... Num 36:2 776
in the *l* of Moab, began Moses to ... Deut 1:5 776
to the *l* of the Canaanites, and ... Deut 1:7 776
I have set the *l* before you ... Deut 1:8 776
possess the *l* which the LORD ... Deut 1:8 776
God hath set the *l* before thee ... Deut 1:21 776
and they shall search us out the *l* ... Deut 1:22 776
the fruit of the *l* in their hands ... Deut 1:25 776
It is a good *l* which the LORD our ... Deut 1:25 776
us forth out of the *l* of Egypt ... Deut 1:27 776
evil generation see that good *l* ... Deut 1:35 776
to him will I give the *l* that he ... Deut 1:36 776
I will not give you of their *l* ... Deut 2:5 776
thee of their *l* for a possession ... Deut 2:9 776
did unto the *l* of his possession ... Deut 2:12 776
l of the children of Ammon any ... Deut 2:19 776
also was accounted a *l* of giants ... Deut 2:20 776
king of Heshbon, and his *l* ... Deut 2:24 776
Let me pass through thy *l* ... Deut 2:27 776
l which the LORD our God giveth ... Deut 2:29 776
give Sihon and his *l* before thee ... Deut 2:31 776
that thou mayest inherit his *l* ... Deut 2:31 776
Only unto the *l* of the children ... Deut 2:37 776
him, and all his people, and his *l* ... Deut 3:2 776
l that was on this side Jordan ... Deut 3:8 776
And this *l*, which we possessed at ... Deut 3:12 776
which was called the *l* of giants ... Deut 3:13 776
given you this *l* to possess it ... Deut 3:18 776
until they also possess the *l* ... Deut 3:20 776
see the good *l* that is beyond ... Deut 3:25 776
the *l* which thou shalt see ... Deut 3:28 776
possess the *l* which the LORD God ... Deut 4:1 776
the *l* whither ye go to possess it ... Deut 4:5 776
that ye might do them in the *l* ... Deut 4:14 776
should not go in unto that good *l* ... Deut 4:21 776
But I must die in this *l*, I must ... Deut 4:22 776
go over, and possess that good *l* ... Deut 4:22 776
shall have remained long in the *l* ... Deut 4:25 776
utterly perish from off the *l* ... Deut 4:26 776
thee their *l* for an inheritance ... Deut 4:38 776
in the *l* of Sihon king of the ... Deut 4:46 776
And they possessed his *l* ... Deut 4:47 776
the *l* of Og king of Bashan, two ... Deut 4:47 776
thee out of the *l* of Egypt ... Deut 5:6 776
wast a servant in the *l* of Egypt ... Deut 5:15 776
in the *l* which the LORD thy God ... Deut 5:16 127
that they may do them in the *l* ... Deut 5:31 776
in the *l* which ye shall possess ... Deut 5:33 776
the *l* whither ye go to possess it ... Deut 6:1 776
in the *l* that floweth with milk ... Deut 6:3 776
have brought thee into the *l* ... Deut 6:10 776
thee forth out of the *l* of Egypt ... Deut 6:12 776
possess the good *l* which the LORD ... Deut 6:18 776
to give us the *l* which he sware ... Deut 6:23 776
l whither thou goest to possess ... Deut 7:1 776
thy womb, and the fruit of thy *l* ... Deut 7:13 127
in the *l* which he sware unto thy ... Deut 7:13 127
possess the *l* which the LORD ... Deut 8:1 776
God bringeth thee into a good *l* ... Deut 8:7 776
a *l* of brooks of water, of ... Deut 8:7 776
A *l* of wheat, and barley, and vines ... Deut 8:8 776
a *l* of oil olive, and honey ... Deut 8:8 776
A *l* wherein thou shalt eat bread ... Deut 8:9 776
a *l* whose stones are iron, and out ... Deut 8:9 776
good *l* which he hath given thee ... Deut 8:10 776
thee forth out of the *l* of Egypt ... Deut 8:14 776
brought me in to possess this *l* ... Deut 9:4 776
dost thou go to possess their *l* ... Deut 9:5 776
this good *l* to possess it for thy ... Deut 9:6 776
depart out of the *l* of Egypt ... Deut 9:7 776
possess the *l* which I have given ... Deut 9:23 776
Lest the *l* whence thou broughtest ... Deut 9:28 776
into the *l* which he promised them ... Deut 9:28 776
Jotbath, a *l* of rivers of waters ... Deut 10:7 776
they may go in and possess the *l* ... Deut 10:11 776
were strangers in the *l* of Egypt ... Deut 10:19 776
king of Egypt, and unto all his *l* ... Deut 11:3 776
strong, and go in and possess the *l* ... Deut 11:8 776
ye may prolong your days in the *l* ... Deut 11:9 127
a *l* that floweth with milk and ... Deut 11:9 776
For the *l*, whither thou goest in ... Deut 11:10 776
it, is not as the *l* of Egypt ... Deut 11:10 776
But the *l*, whither ye go to ... Deut 11:11 776
is a *l* of hills and valleys, and ... Deut 11:11 776
A *l* which the LORD thy God careth ... Deut 11:12 776
rain of your *l* in his due season ... Deut 11:14 776
that the *l* yield not her fruit ... Deut 11:17 127
good *l* which the LORD giveth you ... Deut 11:17 776
in the *l* which the LORD sware ... Deut 11:21 127
the *l* that ye shall tread upon ... Deut 11:25 776
l whither thou goest to possess ... Deut 11:29 776
in the *l* of the Canaanites, which ... Deut 11:30 776
l which the LORD your God giveth ... Deut 11:31 776
ye shall observe to do in the *l* ... Deut 12:1 776
dwell in the *l* which the LORD ... Deut 12:10 776
them, and dwellest in their *l* ... Deut 12:29 776
brought you out of the *l* of Egypt ... Deut 13:5 776
thee out of the *l* of Egypt ... Deut 13:10 776
l which the LORD thy God giveth ... Deut 15:4 776
l which the LORD thy God giveth ... Deut 15:7 776
shall never cease out of the *l* ... Deut 15:11 776
poor, and to thy needy, in thy *l* ... Deut 15:11 776
wast a bondman in the *l* of Egypt ... Deut 15:15 776
out of the *l* of Egypt in haste ... Deut 16:3 776
l of Egypt all the days of thy ... Deut 16:3 776
inherit the *l* which the LORD thy ... Deut 16:20 776
When thou art come unto the *l* ... Deut 17:14 776
When thou art come into the *l* ... Deut 18:9 776
whose *l* the LORD thy God giveth ... Deut 19:1 776
for thee in the midst of thy *l* ... Deut 19:2 776
and divide the coasts of thy *l* ... Deut 19:3 776
give thee all the *l* which he ... Deut 19:8 776
blood be not shed in thy *l* ... Deut 19:10 776
l that the LORD thy God giveth ... Deut 19:14 776
thee up out of the *l* of Egypt ... Deut 20:1 776
If one be found slain in the *l* ... Deut 21:1 127
that thy *l* be not defiled, which ... Deut 21:23 127
thou wast a stranger in his *l* ... Deut 23:7 776
settest thine hand to in the *l* ... Deut 23:20 776
thou shalt not cause the *l* to sin ... Deut 24:4 776
are in thy *l* within thy gates ... Deut 24:14 776
wast a bondman in the *l* of Egypt ... Deut 24:22 776
l which the LORD thy God giveth ... Deut 25:15 127
in the *l* which the LORD thy God ... Deut 25:19 776
l which the LORD thy God giveth ... Deut 26:1 776
l that the LORD thy God giveth ... Deut 26:2 776
place, and hath given us this *l* ... Deut 26:9 776
even a *l* that floweth with milk ... Deut 26:9 776
brought the firstfruits of the *l* ... Deut 26:10 127
the *l* which thou hast given us, ... Deut 26:15 127
a *l* that floweth with milk and ... Deut 26:15 776
l which the LORD thy God giveth ... Deut 27:2 776
l which the LORD thy God giveth ... Deut 27:3 776
a *l* that floweth with milk and ... Deut 27:3 776
he shall bless thee in the *l* ... Deut 28:8 776
in the *l* which the LORD sware ... Deut 28:11 127
the rain unto thy *l* in his season ... Deut 28:12 776
thy body, and the fruit of thy *l* ... Deut 28:18 127
have consumed thee from off the *l* ... Deut 28:21 127
make the rain of thy *l* powder ... Deut 28:24 776
The fruit of thy *l*, and all thy ... Deut 28:33 127
fruit of thy *l* shall the locust ... Deut 28:42 127
thy cattle, and the fruit of thy *l* ... Deut 28:51 127
trustedst, throughout all thy *l* ... Deut 28:52 776
thy gates throughout all thy *l* ... Deut 28:52 776
l whither thou goest to possess ... Deut 28:63 127
of Israel in the *l* of Moab ... Deut 29:1 776
in the *l* of Egypt unto Pharaoh ... Deut 29:2 776
his servants, and unto all his *l* ... Deut 29:2 776
And we took their *l*, and gave it ... Deut 29:8 776
we have dwelt in the *l* of Egypt ... Deut 29:16 776
that shall come from a far *l* ... Deut 29:22 776
they see the plagues of that *l* ... Deut 29:22 776
that the whole *l* thereof is ... Deut 29:23 776
the LORD done thus unto this *l* ... Deut 29:24 776
them forth out of the *l* of Egypt ... Deut 29:25 776
LORD was kindled against this *l* ... Deut 29:27 776
them out of their *l* in anger ... Deut 29:28 127
and cast them into another *l* ... Deut 29:28 776
the *l* which thy fathers possessed ... Deut 30:5 776
cattle, and in the fruit of thy *l* ... Deut 30:9 127
l whither thou goest to possess ... Deut 30:16 776
not prolong your days upon the *l* ... Deut 30:18 127
l which the LORD sware unto thy ... Deut 30:20 127
Amorites, and unto the *l* of them ... Deut 31:4 776
go with this people unto the *l* ... Deut 31:7 776
as long as ye live in the *l* ... Deut 31:13 127
gods of the strangers of the *l* ... Deut 31:16 776
the *l* which I sware unto their ... Deut 31:20 127
them into the *l* which I sware ... Deut 31:21 776
the *l* which I sware unto them ... Deut 31:23 776
He found him in a desert *l* ... Deut 32:10 776
and will be merciful unto his *l* ... Deut 32:43 127
shall prolong your days in the *l* ... Deut 32:47 127
Nebo, which is in the *l* of Moab ... Deut 32:49 776
and behold the *l* of Canaan ... Deut 32:49 776
thou shalt see the *l* before thee ... Deut 32:52 776
l which I give the children of ... Deut 32:52 776
Blessed of the LORD be his *l* ... Deut 33:13 776
Jacob shall be upon a *l* of corn ... Deut 33:28 776
shewed him all the *l* of Gilead ... Deut 34:1 776
the *l* of Ephraim, and Manasseh, and ... Deut 34:2 776
all the *l* of Judah, unto the ... Deut 34:2 776
This is the *l* which I sware unto ... Deut 34:4 776
LORD died there in the *l* of Moab ... Deut 34:5 776
him in a valley in the *l* of Moab ... Deut 34:6 776
do in the *l* of Egypt to Pharaoh ... Deut 34:11 776
all his servants, and to all his *l* ... Deut 34:11 776
unto the *l* which I do give to ... Josh 1:2 776
all the *l* of the Hittites, and ... Josh 1:4 776
divide for an inheritance the *l* ... Josh 1:6 776
Jordan, to go in to possess the *l* ... Josh 1:11 776
rest, and hath given you this *l* ... Josh 1:13 776
shall remain in the *l* which Moses ... Josh 1:14 776
they also have possessed the *l* ... Josh 1:15 776
unto the *l* of your possession ... Josh 1:15 776
secretly, saying, Go view the *l* ... Josh 2:1 776
the LORD hath given you the *l* ... Josh 2:9 776
of the *l* faint because of you ... Josh 2:9 776
when the LORD hath given us the *l* ... Josh 2:14 776
Behold, when we come into the *l* ... Josh 2:18 776
into our hands all the *l* ... Josh 2:24 776
were lifted up unto the dry *l* ... Josh 4:18
came over this Jordan on dry *l* ... Josh 4:22
that he would not shew them the *l* ... Josh 5:6 776
a *l* that floweth with milk and ... Josh 5:6 776
of the *l* on the morrow after the ... Josh 5:11 776
eaten of the old corn of the *l* ... Josh 5:12 776
of the *l* of Canaan that year ... Josh 5:12 776
of the *l* shall hear of it ... Josh 7:9 776
his people, and his city, and his *l* ... Josh 8:1 776
Moses to give you all the *l* ... Josh 9:24 776
of the *l* from before you, ... Josh 9:24 776
their *l* did Joshua take at one ... Josh 10:42 776
under Hermon in the *l* of Mizpeh ... Josh 11:3 776
So Joshua took all that *l* ... Josh 11:16 776
all the *l* of Goshen, and the ... Josh 11:16 776
the *l* of the children of Israel ... Josh 11:22 776
So Joshua took the whole *l* ... Josh 11:23 776
And the *l* rested from war ... Josh 11:23 776
Now these are the kings of the *l* ... Josh 12:1 776
possessed their *l* on the other ... Josh 12:1 776
yet very much *l* to be possessed ... Josh 13:1 776
This is the *l* that yet remaineth ... Josh 13:2 776
all the *l* of the Canaanites, and ... Josh 13:4 776
the *l* of the Giblites, and all ... Josh 13:5 776
Now therefore divide this *l* for ... Josh 13:7 776
half the *l* of the children of ... Josh 13:25 776
inherited in the *l* of Canaan ... Josh 14:1 776
no part unto the Levites in the *l* ... Josh 14:4 776
Israel did, and they divided the *l* ... Josh 14:5 776
Kadesh-barnea to espy out the *l* ... Josh 14:7 776
Surely the *l* whereon thy feet ... Josh 14:9 776
And the *l* had rest from war ... Josh 14:15 776
for thou hast given me a south *l* ... Josh 15:19 776
Manasseh, beside the *l* of Gilead ... Josh 17:5 776
sons had the *l* of Gilead ... Josh 17:6 776
Now Manasseh had the *l* of Tappuah ... Josh 17:8 776
Canaanites would dwell in that *l* ... Josh 17:12 776
there in the *l* of the Perizzites ... Josh 17:15 776
Canaanites that dwell in the *l* of ... Josh 17:16 776
the *l* was subdued before them ... Josh 18:1 776
ye slack to go to possess the *l* ... Josh 18:3 776
shall rise, and go through the *l* ... Josh 18:4 776
describe the *l* into seven parts ... Josh 18:6 776
them that went to describe the *l* ... Josh 18:8 776
saying, Go and walk through the *l* ... Josh 18:8 776
men went and passed through the *l* ... Josh 18:9 776
there Joshua divided the *l* unto ... Josh 18:10 776
l for inheritance by their coasts ... Josh 19:49 776
them at Shiloh in the *l* of Canaan ... Josh 21:2 776
the *l* which he sware to give unto ... Josh 21:43 776
unto the *l* of your possession, ... Josh 22:4 776
which is in the *l* of Canaan ... Josh 22:9 776
to the *l* of their possession, ... Josh 22:9 776
that are in the *l* of Canaan ... Josh 22:10 776
over against the *l* of Canaan ... Josh 22:11 776
into the *l* of Gilead, Phinehas ... Josh 22:13 776
unto the *l* of Gilead, and they ... Josh 22:15 776
if the *l* of your possession be ... Josh 22:19 776
then pass ye over unto the *l* of ... Josh 22:19 776
of Gad, out of the *l* of Gilead ... Josh 22:32 776
unto the *l* of Canaan, to the ... Josh 22:32 776
to destroy the *l* wherein the ... Josh 22:33 776
and ye shall possess their *l* ... Josh 23:5 776
l which the LORD your God hath ... Josh 23:13 127
you from off this good *l* which ... Josh 23:15 127
quickly from off the good *l* which ... Josh 23:16 776
throughout all the *l* of Canaan ... Josh 24:3 776
you into the *l* of the Amorites ... Josh 24:8 776
that ye might possess their *l* ... Josh 24:8 776
I have given you a *l* for which ye ... Josh 24:13 776
the Amorites, in whose *l* ye dwell ... Josh 24:15 776
our fathers out of the *l* of Egypt ... Josh 24:17 776
the Amorites which dwelt in the *l* ... Josh 24:18 776
delivered the *l* into his hand ... Judg 1:2 776
for thou hast given me a south *l* ... Judg 1:15 776
went into the *l* of the Hittites ... Judg 1:26 776
Canaanites would dwell in that *l* ... Judg 1:27 776
the inhabitants of the *l* ... Judg 1:32 776
the inhabitants of the *l* ... Judg 1:33 776
have brought you unto the *l* which ... Judg 2:1 776
with the inhabitants of this *l* ... Judg 2:2 776
his inheritance to possess the *l* ... Judg 2:6 776
them out of the *l* of Egypt ... Judg 2:12 776
the *l* had rest forty years ... Judg 3:11 776
the *l* had rest fourscore years ... Judg 3:30 776
the *l* had rest forty years ... Judg 5:31 776
entered into the *l* to destroy it ... Judg 6:5 776
before you, and gave you their *l* ... Judg 6:9 776
the Amorites, in whose *l* ye dwell ... Judg 6:10 776
down by the middle of the *l* ... Judg 9:37 776
day, which are in the *l* of Gilead ... Judg 10:4 776
Jordan in the *l* of the Amorites ... Judg 10:8 776
and dwelt in the *l* of Tob ... Judg 11:3 776
Jephthah out of the *l* of Tob ... Judg 11:5 776
come against me to fight in my *l* ... Judg 11:12 776
Because Israel took away my *l* ... Judg 11:13 776
took not away the *l* of Moab ... Judg 11:15 776

nor the *l* of the children of ... Judg 11:15 776
I pray thee, pass through thy *l* ... Judg 11:17 776
and compassed the *l* of Edom ... Judg 11:18 776
the *l* of Moab, and came by the ... Judg 11:18 776
by the east side of the *l* of Moab ... Judg 11:18 776
through thy *l* into my place ... Judg 11:19 776
all the *l* of the Amorites ... Judg 11:21 776
in Pirathon in the *l* of Ephraim ... Judg 12:15 776
and from Eshtaol, to spy out the *l* ... Judg 18:2 776
said unto them, Go, search the *l* ... Judg 18:2 776
there was no magistrate in the *l* ... Judg 18:7 776
for we have seen the *l*, and, ... Judg 18:9 776
go, and to enter to possess the *l* ... Judg 18:9 776
a people secure, and to a large *l* ... Judg 18:10 776
went to spy out the *l* went up ... Judg 18:17 776
the day of the captivity of the *l* ... Judg 18:30 776
of the *l* of Egypt unto this day ... Judg 19:30 776
with the *l* of Gilead, unto the ... Judg 20:1 776
which is in the *l* of Canaan ... Judg 21:12 776
and go to the *l* of Benjamin ... Judg 21:21 776
that there was a famine in the *l* ... Ruth 1:1 776
way to return unto the *l* of Judah ... Ruth 1:7 776
the *l* of thy nativity, and art ... Ruth 2:11 776
of Moab, selleth a parcel of *l* ... Ruth 4:3 7704
of your mice that mar the *l* ... 1Sa 6:5 776
off your gods, and from off your *l* ... 1Sa 6:5 776
passed through the *l* of Shalisha ... 1Sa 9:4 776
passed through the *l* of Shalim ... 1Sa 9:4 776
through the *l* of the Benjamites ... 1Sa 9:4 776
they were come to the *l* of Zuph ... 1Sa 9:5 776
a man out of the *l* of Benjamin ... 1Sa 9:16 776
fathers up out of the *l* of Egypt ... 1Sa 12:6 776
the trumpet throughout all the *l* ... 1Sa 13:3 776
went over Jordan to the *l* of Gad ... 1Sa 13:7 776
to Ophrah, unto the *l* of Shual ... 1Sa 13:17 776
throughout all the *l* of Israel ... 1Sa 13:19 776
as it were an half acre of *l* ... 1Sa 14:14 7704
all they of the *l* came to a wood ... 1Sa 14:25 776
My father hath troubled the *l* ... 1Sa 14:29 776
not this David the king of the *l* ... 1Sa 21:11 776
and get thee into the *l* of Judah ... 1Sa 22:5 776
come to pass, if he be in the *l* ... 1Sa 23:23 776
Philistines have invaded the *l* ... 1Sa 23:27 776
into the *l* of the Philistines ... 1Sa 27:1 776
of old the inhabitants of the *l* ... 1Sa 27:8 776
to Shur, even unto the *l* of Egypt ... 1Sa 27:8 776
And David smote the *l*, and left ... 1Sa 27:9 776
and the wizards, out of the *l* ... 1Sa 28:3 776
and the wizards, out of the *l* ... 1Sa 28:9 776
into the *l* of the Philistines ... 1Sa 29:11 776
out of the *l* of the Philistines ... 1Sa 30:16 776
and out of the *l* of Judah ... 1Sa 30:16 776
armour, and sent into the *l* of the ... 1Sa 31:9 776
behalf, saying, Whose is the *l* ... 2Sa 3:12 776
the inhabitants of the *l* ... 2Sa 5:6 776
things and terrible, for thy *l* ... 2Sa 7:23 776
thee all the *l* of Saul thy father ... 2Sa 9:7 7704
shall till the *l* for him ... 2Sa 9:10 127
the *l* of the children of Ammon ... 2Sa 10:2 776
that I were made judge in the *l* ... 2Sa 15:4 776
pitched in the *l* of Gilead ... 2Sa 17:26 776
is fled out of the *l* for Absalom ... 2Sa 19:9 776
said, Thou and Ziba divide the *l* ... 2Sa 19:29 7704
that God was intreated for the *l* ... 2Sa 21:14 776
to the *l* of Tahtim-hodshi ... 2Sa 24:6 776
they had gone through all the *l* ... 2Sa 24:8 776
of famine come unto thee in thy *l* ... 2Sa 24:13 776
three days' pestilence in thy *l* ... 2Sa 24:13 776
the LORD was intreated for the *l* ... 2Sa 24:25 776
Sochoh, and all the *l* of Hepher ... 1Kin 4:10 776
only officer which was in the *l* ... 1Kin 4:19 776
unto the *l* of the Philistines ... 1Kin 4:21 776
were come out of the *l* of Egypt ... 1Kin 6:1 776
they came out of the *l* of Egypt ... 1Kin 8:9 776
them out of the *l* of Egypt ... 1Kin 8:21 776
bring them again unto the *l* which ... 1Kin 8:34 127
walk, and give rain upon thy *l* ... 1Kin 8:36 776
If there be in the *l* famine ... 1Kin 8:37 776
them in the *l* of their cities ... 1Kin 8:37 776
the *l* which thou gavest unto our ... 1Kin 8:40 127
captives unto the *l* of the enemy ... 1Kin 8:46 776
the *l* whither they were carried ... 1Kin 8:47 776
the *l* of them that carried them ... 1Kin 8:47 776
in the *l* of their enemies, which ... 1Kin 8:48 776
and pray unto thee toward their *l* ... 1Kin 8:48 776
of the *l* which I have given them ... 1Kin 9:7 127
the LORD done thus unto this *l* ... 1Kin 9:8 776
fathers out of the *l* of Egypt ... 1Kin 9:9 776
twenty cities in the *l* of Galilee ... 1Kin 9:11 776
he called them the *l* of Cabul ... 1Kin 9:13 776
in the wilderness, in the *l* ... 1Kin 9:18 776
in all the *l* of his dominion ... 1Kin 9:19 776
were left after them in the *l* ... 1Kin 9:21 776
of the Red sea, in the *l* of Edom ... 1Kin 9:26 776
I heard in mine own *l* of thy acts ... 1Kin 10:6 776
him victuals, and gave him *l* ... 1Kin 11:18 776
thee up out of the *l* of Egypt ... 1Kin 12:28 776
root up Israel out of this good *l* ... 1Kin 14:15 127
were also sodomites in the *l* ... 1Kin 14:24 776
away the sodomites out of the *l* ... 1Kin 15:12 776
with all the *l* of Naphtali ... 1Kin 15:20 776
there had been no rain in the *l* ... 1Kin 17:7 776
said unto Obadiah, Go into the *l* ... 1Kin 18:5 776
So they divided the *l* between ... 1Kin 18:6 776
called all the elders of the *l* ... 1Kin 20:7 776
father Asa, he took out of the *l* ... 1Kin 22:46 776
thence any more death or barren *l* ... 2Kin 2:21
every good piece of *l* with stones ... 2Kin 3:19
on every good piece of *l* cast ... 2Kin 3:25
him, and returned to their own *l* ... 2Kin 3:27 776
and there was a dearth in the *l* ... 2Kin 4:38 776
of the *l* of Israel a little maid ... 2Kin 5:2 776
maid that is of the *l* of Israel ... 2Kin 5:4 776
came no more into the *l* of Israel ... 2Kin 6:23 776
also come upon the *l* seven years ... 2Kin 8:1 776
sojourned in the *l* of the ... 2Kin 8:2 776
out of the *l* of the Philistines ... 2Kin 8:3 776
king for her house and for her *l* ... 2Kin 8:3 7704
king for her house and for her *l* ... 2Kin 8:5 7704
since the day that she left the *l* ... 2Kin 8:6 776
all the *l* of Gilead, the Gadites, ... 2Kin 10:33 776
And Athaliah did reign over the *l* ... 2Kin 11:3 776
all the people of the *l* rejoiced ... 2Kin 11:14 776
all the people of the *l* went into ... 2Kin 11:18 776
guard, and all the people of the *l* ... 2Kin 11:19 776
all the people of the *l* rejoiced ... 2Kin 11:20 776
of the Moabites invaded the *l* at ... 2Kin 13:20 776
judging the people of the *l* ... 2Kin 15:5 776
of Assyria came against the *l* ... 2Kin 15:19 776
and stayed not there in the *l* ... 2Kin 15:20 776
all the *l* of Naphtali, and carried ... 2Kin 15:29 776
of all the people of the *l* ... 2Kin 16:15 776
came up throughout all the *l* ... 2Kin 17:5 776
them up out of the *l* of Egypt ... 2Kin 17:7 776
own *l* to Assyria unto this day ... 2Kin 17:23 127
the manner of the God of the *l* ... 2Kin 17:26 776
the manner of the God of the *l* ... 2Kin 17:26 776
the manner of the God of the *l* ... 2Kin 17:27 776
the *l* of Egypt with great power ... 2Kin 17:36 776
said to me, Go up against this *l* ... 2Kin 18:25 776
away to a *l* like your own *l* ... 2Kin 18:32 776
a *l* of corn and wine ... 2Kin 18:32 776
a *l* of bread and vineyards ... 2Kin 18:32 776
a *l* of oil olive and of honey ... 2Kin 18:32 776
nations delivered at all his *l* ... 2Kin 18:33 776
and shall return to his own *l* ... 2Kin 19:7 776
to fall by the sword in his own *l* ... 2Kin 19:7 776
escaped into the *l* of Armenia ... 2Kin 19:37 776
the *l* which I gave their fathers ... 2Kin 21:8 127
the people of the *l* slew all them ... 2Kin 21:24 776
the people of the *l* made Josiah ... 2Kin 21:24 776
that were spied in the *l* of Judah ... 2Kin 23:24 776
the people of the *l* took Jehoahaz ... 2Kin 23:30 776
at Riblah in the *l* of Hamath ... 2Kin 23:33 776
put the *l* to a tribute of an ... 2Kin 23:33 776
but he taxed the *l* to give the ... 2Kin 23:35 776
the gold of the people of the *l* ... 2Kin 23:35 776
not again any more out of his *l* ... 2Kin 24:7 776
sort of the people of the *l* ... 2Kin 24:14 776
officers, and the mighty of the *l* ... 2Kin 24:15 776
no bread for the people of the *l* ... 2Kin 25:3 776
poor of the *l* to be vinedressers ... 2Kin 25:12 776
mustered the people of the *l* ... 2Kin 25:19 776
men of the people of the *l* that ... 2Kin 25:19 776
them at Riblah in the *l* of Hamath ... 2Kin 25:21 776
was carried away out of their *l* ... 2Kin 25:21 127
that remained in the *l* of Judah ... 2Kin 25:22 776
dwell in the *l*, and serve the king ... 2Kin 25:24 776
the kings that reigned in the *l* ... 1Chr 1:43 776
Husham of the *l* of the Temanites ... 1Chr 1:45 776
twenty cities in the *l* of Gilead ... 1Chr 2:22 776
the *l* was wide, and quiet, and ... 1Chr 4:40 776
multiplied in the *l* of Gilead ... 1Chr 5:9 776
all the east *l* of Gilead ... 1Chr 5:10
in the *l* of Bashan unto Salchah ... 1Chr 5:11 776
tribe of Manasseh dwelt in the *l* ... 1Chr 5:23 776
the gods of the people of the *l* ... 1Chr 5:25 776
them Hebron in the *l* of Judah ... 1Chr 6:55 776
that were born in that *l* slew ... 1Chr 7:21 776
armour, and sent into the *l* of the ... 1Chr 10:9 776
were, the inhabitants of the *l* ... 1Chr 11:4 776
are left in all the *l* of Israel ... 1Chr 13:2 776
thee will I give the *l* of Canaan ... 1Chr 16:18 776
the *l* of the children of Ammon to ... 1Chr 19:2 776
to overthrow, and to spy out the *l* ... 1Chr 19:3 776
even the pestilence, in the *l* ... 1Chr 21:12 776
that were in the *l* of Israel ... 1Chr 22:2 776
of the *l* into mine hand ... 1Chr 22:18 776
the *l* is subdued before the LORD, ... 1Chr 22:18 776
that ye may possess this good *l* ... 1Chr 28:8 776
that were in the *l* of Israel ... 2Chr 2:17 776
forth my people out of the *l* of ... 2Chr 6:5 776
the *l* which thou gavest to them ... 2Chr 6:25 127
and send rain upon thy *l*, which ... 2Chr 6:27 776
If there be dearth in the *l* ... 2Chr 6:28 776
them in the cities of their *l* ... 2Chr 6:28 776
the *l* which thou gavest unto our ... 2Chr 6:31 127
captives unto a *l* far off or near ... 2Chr 6:36 776
in the *l* whither they are carried ... 2Chr 6:37 776
thee in the *l* of their captivity ... 2Chr 6:37 776
soul in the *l* of their captivity ... 2Chr 6:38 776
captives, and pray toward their *l* ... 2Chr 6:38 776
the locusts to devour the *l* ... 2Chr 7:13 776
their sin, and will heal their *l* ... 2Chr 7:14 776
of my *l* which I have given them ... 2Chr 7:20 127
the LORD done thus unto this *l* ... 2Chr 7:21 776
them forth out of the *l* of Egypt ... 2Chr 7:22 776
all the *l* of his dominion ... 2Chr 8:6 776
who were left after them in the *l* ... 2Chr 8:8 776
at the sea side in the *l* of Edom ... 2Chr 8:17 776
heard in mine own *l* of thine acts ... 2Chr 9:5 776
seen before in the *l* of Judah ... 2Chr 9:11 776
turned, and went away to her own *l* ... 2Chr 9:12 776
unto the *l* of the Philistines ... 2Chr 9:26 776
In his days the *l* was quiet ten ... 2Chr 14:1 776
for the *l* had rest, and he had no ... 2Chr 14:6 776
while the *l* is yet before us ... 2Chr 14:7 776
idols out of all the *l* of Judah ... 2Chr 15:8 776
set garrisons in the *l* of Judah ... 2Chr 17:2 776
away the groves out of the *l* ... 2Chr 19:3 776
he set judges in the *l* throughout ... 2Chr 19:5 776
this *l* before thy people Israel ... 2Chr 20:7 776
they came out of the *l* of Egypt ... 2Chr 20:10 776
and Athaliah reigned over the *l* ... 2Chr 22:12 776
all the people of the *l* rejoiced ... 2Chr 23:13 776
and all the people of the *l* ... 2Chr 23:20 776
all the people of the *l* rejoiced ... 2Chr 23:21 776
judging the people of the *l* ... 2Chr 26:21 776
they shall come again into this *l* ... 2Chr 30:9 776
that came out of the *l* of Israel ... 2Chr 30:25 776
ran through the midst of the *l* ... 2Chr 32:4 776
with shame of face to his own *l* ... 2Chr 32:21 776
the wonder that was done in the *l* ... 2Chr 32:31 776
foot of Israel from out of the *l* ... 2Chr 33:8 127
But the people of the *l* slew all ... 2Chr 33:25 776
the people of the *l* made Josiah ... 2Chr 33:25 776
throughout all the *l* of Israel ... 2Chr 34:7 776
reign, when he had purged the *l* ... 2Chr 34:8 776
Then the people of the *l* took ... 2Chr 36:1 776
condemned the *l* in an hundred ... 2Chr 36:3 776
until the *l* had enjoyed her ... 2Chr 36:21 776
Then the people of the *l* weakened ... Ezr 4:4 776
of the heathen of the *l*, to seek ... Ezr 6:21 776
the prophets, saying, The *l* ... Ezr 9:11 776
it, is an unclean *l* with the ... Ezr 9:11 776
strong, and eat the good of the *l* ... Ezr 9:12 776
wives of the people of the *l* ... Ezr 10:2 776
from the people of the *l*, and from ... Ezr 10:11 776
for a prey in the *l* of captivity ... Neh 4:4 776
their governor in the *l* of Judah ... Neh 5:14 776
wall, neither bought we any *l* ... Neh 5:16 7704
to give the *l* of the Canaanites ... Neh 9:8 776
and on all the people of his *l* ... Neh 9:10 776
the midst of the sea on the dry *l* ... Neh 9:11
should go in to possess the *l* ... Neh 9:15 776
so they possessed the *l* of Sihon ... Neh 9:22 776
the *l* of the king of Heshbon, and ... Neh 9:22 776
the *l* of Og king of Bashan ... Neh 9:22 776
and broughtest them into the *l* ... Neh 9:23 776
went in and possessed the *l* ... Neh 9:24 776
them the inhabitants of the *l* ... Neh 9:24 776
kings, and the people of the *l* ... Neh 9:24 776
took strong cities, and a fat *l* ... Neh 9:25 127
fat *l* which thou gavest before ... Neh 9:35 776
for the *l* that thou gavest unto ... Neh 9:36 776
unto the people of the *l*, nor ... Neh 10:30 776
if the people of the *l* bring ware ... Neh 10:31 776
the people of the *l* became Jews ... Est 8:17 776
laid a tribute upon the *l* ... Est 10:1 776
There was a man in the *l* of Uz ... Job 1:1 776
substance is increased in the *l* ... Job 1:10 776
return, even to the *l* of darkness ... Job 10:21 776
A *l* of darkness, as darkness ... Job 10:22 776
it found in the *l* of the living ... Job 28:13 776
If my *l* cry against me, or that ... Job 31:38 127
for correction, or for his *l* ... Job 37:13 776
the barren *l* his dwellings ... Job 39:6
in all the *l* were no women found ... Job 42:15 776
heathen are perished out of his *l* ... Ps 10:16 776
the LORD in the *l* of the living ... Ps 27:13 776
them that are quiet in the *l* ... Ps 35:20 776
so shalt thou dwell in the *l* ... Ps 37:3 776
The righteous shall inherit the *l* ... Ps 37:29 776
shall exalt thee to inherit the *l* ... Ps 37:34 776
thee from the *l* of Jordan ... Ps 42:6 776
For they got not the *l* in ... Ps 44:3 776
thee out of the *l* of the living ... Ps 52:5 776
for thee in a dry and thirsty *l* ... Ps 63:1 776
He turned the sea into dry *l* ... Ps 66:6 776
the rebellious dwell in a dry *l* ... Ps 68:6
the synagogues of God in the *l* ... Ps 74:8 776
in the *l* of Egypt, in the field ... Ps 78:12 776
deep root, and it filled the *l* ... Ps 80:9 776
went out through the *l* of Egypt ... Ps 81:5 776
thee out of the *l* of Egypt ... Ps 81:10 776
hast been favourable unto thy *l* ... Ps 85:1 776
that glory may dwell in our *l* ... Ps 85:9 776
our *l* shall yield her increase ... Ps 85:12 776
in the *l* of forgetfulness ... Ps 88:12 776
and his hands formed the dry *l* ... Ps 95:5
be upon the faithful of the *l* ... Ps 101:6 776
destroy all the wicked of the *l* ... Ps 101:8 776
thee will I give the *l* of Canaan ... Ps 105:11 776
he called for a famine upon the *l* ... Ps 105:16 776
Jacob sojourned in the *l* of Ham ... Ps 105:23 776
them, and wonders in the *l* of Ham ... Ps 105:27 776
Their *l* brought forth frogs in ... Ps 105:30 776
rain, and flaming fire in their *l* ... Ps 105:32 776
eat up all the herbs in their *l* ... Ps 105:35 776
also all the firstborn in their *l* ... Ps 105:36 776
Wondrous works in the *l* of Ham ... Ps 106:22 776
Yea, they despised the pleasant *l* ... Ps 106:24 776
the *l* was polluted with blood ... Ps 106:38 776
A fruitful *l* into barrenness, for ... Ps 107:34 776
the LORD in the *l* of the living ... Ps 116:9 776
gave their *l* for an heritage, an ... Ps 135:12 776
gave their *l* for an heritage ... Ps 136:21 776
the LORD's song in a strange *l* ... Ps 137:4 127
my portion in the *l* of the living ... Ps 142:5 776
after thee, as a thirsty *l* ... Ps 143:6 776
lead me into the *l* of uprightness ... Ps 143:10 776
the upright shall dwell in the *l* ... Prov 2:21 776
He that tilleth his *l* shall be ... Prov 12:11 127
For the transgression of a *l* many ... Prov 28:2 776

He that tilleth his *l* shall have	Prov 28:19	127
by judgment establisheth the *l*	Prov 29:4	776
sitteth among the elders of the *l*	Prov 31:23	776
Woe to thee, O *l*, when thy king	Eccl 10:16	776
Blessed art thou, O *l*, when thy	Eccl 10:17	776
of the turtle is heard in our *l*	Song 2:12	776
your *l*, strangers devour it in	Is 1:7	127
ye shall eat the good of the *l*	Is 1:19	776
Their *l* also is full of silver and	Is 2:7	776
their *l* is also full of horses,	Is 2:7	776
Their *l* also is full of idols	Is 2:8	776
and if one look unto the *l*	Is 5:30	776
the *l* be utterly desolate,	Is 6:11	127
forsaking in the midst of the *l*	Is 6:12	776
the *l* that thou abhorrest shall	Is 7:16	127
bee that is in the *l* of Assyria	Is 7:18	776
one that is left in the *l*	Is 7:22	776
because all the *l* shall become	Is 7:24	776
shall fill the breadth of thy *l*	Is 8:8	776
afflicted the *l* of Zebulun	Is 9:1	776
the *l* of Naphtali, and afterward	Is 9:1	776
in the *l* of the shadow of death	Is 9:2	776
LORD of hosts is the *l* darkened	Is 9:19	776
in the midst of all the *l*	Is 10:23	776
he came up out of the *l* of Egypt	Is 11:16	776
to destroy the whole *l*	Is 13:5	776
anger, to lay the *l* desolate	Is 13:9	776
and flee every one into his own *l*	Is 13:14	776
and set them in their own *l*	Is 14:1	127
in the *l* of the LORD for servants	Is 14:2	127
because thou hast destroyed thy *l*	Is 14:20	776
do not rise, nor possess the *l*	Is 14:21	776
I will break the Assyrian in my *l*	Is 14:25	776
and upon the remnant of the *l*	Is 15:9	127
the *l* from Sela to the wilderness	Is 16:1	776
are consumed out of the *l*	Is 16:4	776
Woe to the *l* shadowing with wings	Is 18:1	776
whose *l* the rivers have spoiled	Is 18:2	776
whose *l* the rivers have spoiled,	Is 18:7	776
the *l* of Judah shall be a terror	Is 19:17	127
day shall five cities in the *l* of	Is 19:18	776
in the midst of the *l* of Egypt	Is 19:19	776
LORD of hosts in the *l* of Egypt	Is 19:20	776
a blessing in the midst of the *l*	Is 19:24	776
the desert, from a terrible *l*	Is 21:1	776
The inhabitants of the *l* of Tema	Is 21:14	776
from the *l* of Chittim it is	Is 23:1	776
Pass through thy *l* as a river	Is 23:10	776
Behold the *l* of the Chaldeans	Is 23:13	776
The *l* shall be utterly emptied,	Is 24:3	776
the mirth of the *l* is gone	Is 24:11	776
midst of the *l* among the people	Is 24:13	776
song be sung in the *l* of Judah	Is 26:1	776
in the *l* of uprightness will he	Is 26:10	776
to perish in the *l* of Assyria	Is 27:13	776
and the outcasts in the *l* of Egypt	Is 27:13	776
into the *l* of trouble and anguish,	Is 30:6	776
of a great rock in a weary *l*	Is 32:2	776
Upon the *l* of my people shall	Is 32:13	127
behold the *l* that is very far off	Is 33:17	776
slaughter in the *l* of Idumea	Is 34:6	776
their *l* shall be soaked with	Is 34:7	776
the *l* thereof shall become	Is 34:9	776
the thirsty *l* springs of water	Is 35:7	776
LORD against this *l* to destroy it	Is 36:10	776
unto me, Go up against this *l*	Is 36:10	776
away to a *l* like your own *l*	Is 36:17	776
a *l* of corn and wine	Is 36:17	776
a *l* of bread and vineyards	Is 36:17	776
of the nations delivered his *l*	Is 36:18	776
delivered their *l* out of my hand	Is 36:20	776
a rumour, and return to his own *l*	Is 37:7	776
to fall by the sword in his own *l*	Is 37:7	776
escaped into the *l* of Armenia	Is 37:38	776
the LORD, in the *l* of the living	Is 38:11	776
the dry *l* springs of water	Is 41:18	776
and these from the *l* of Sinim	Is 49:12	776
the *l* of thy destruction, shall	Is 49:19	776
off out of the *l* of the living	Is 53:8	776
trust in me shall possess the *l*	Is 57:13	776
shall no more be heard in thy *l*	Is 60:18	776
they shall inherit the *l* for ever	Is 60:21	776
therefore in their *l* they shall	Is 61:7	776
neither shall thy *l* any more be	Is 62:4	776
Hephzi-bah, and thy *l* Beulah	Is 62:4	776
thee, and thy *l* shall be married	Is 62:4	776
in Anathoth in the *l* of Benjamin	Jer 1:1	776
upon all the inhabitants of the *l*	Jer 1:14	776
brasen walls against the whole *l*	Jer 1:18	776
and against the people of the *l*	Jer 1:18	776
in a *l* that was not sown	Jer 2:2	776
us up out of the *l* of Egypt	Jer 2:6	776
through a *l* of deserts and of pits	Jer 2:6	776
through a *l* of drought, and of the	Jer 2:6	776
through a *l* that no man passed	Jer 2:6	776
when ye entered, ye defiled my *l*	Jer 2:7	776
yelled, and they made his *l* waste	Jer 2:15	776
a *l* of darkness	Jer 2:31	776
shall not that *l* be greatly	Jer 3:1	776
polluted the *l* with thy whoredoms	Jer 3:2	776
whoredom, that she defiled the *l*	Jer 3:9	776
multiplied and increased in the *l*	Jer 3:16	776
shall come together out of the *l*	Jer 3:18	776
to the *l* that I have given for an	Jer 3:18	776
and give thee a pleasant *l*	Jer 3:19	776
say, Blow ye the trumpet in the *l*	Jer 4:5	776
his place to make thy *l* desolate	Jer 4:7	776
for the whole *l* is spoiled	Jer 4:20	776
The whole *l* shall be desolate	Jer 4:27	776
and served strange gods in your *l*	Jer 5:19	776
in a *l* that is not yours	Jer 5:19	776
thing is committed in the *l*	Jer 5:30	776
thee desolate, a *l* not inhabited	Jer 6:8	776
upon the inhabitants of the *l*	Jer 6:12	776
in the *l* that I gave to your	Jer 7:7	776
them out of the *l* of Egypt	Jer 7:22	776
l of Egypt unto this day I have	Jer 7:25	776
for the *l* shall be desolate	Jer 7:34	776
the whole *l* trembled at the sound	Jer 8:16	776
are come, and have devoured the *l*	Jer 8:16	776
it, for what the *l* perisheth	Jer 9:12	776
because we have forsaken the *l*	Jer 9:19	776
Gather up thy wares out of the *l*	Jer 10:17	776
inhabitants of the *l* at this once	Jer 10:18	776
them forth out of the *l* of Egypt	Jer 11:4	776
to give them a *l* flowing with	Jer 11:5	776
them up out of the *l* of Egypt	Jer 11:7	776
him off from the *l* of the living	Jer 11:19	776
How long shall the *l* mourn	Jer 12:4	776
and if in the *l* of peace, wherein	Jer 12:5	776
the whole *l* is made desolate,	Jer 12:11	776
l even to the other end of the	Jer 12:12	776
even to the other end of the *l*	Jer 12:12	776
I will pluck them out of their *l*	Jer 12:14	127
heritage, and every man to his *l*	Jer 12:15	776
all the inhabitants of this *l*	Jer 13:13	776
thou be as a stranger in the *l*	Jer 14:8	776
and famine shall not be in this *l*	Jer 14:15	776
about into a *l* that they know not	Jer 14:18	776
with a fan in the gates of the *l*	Jer 15:7	776
into a *l* which thou knowest not	Jer 15:14	776
fathers that begat them in this *l*	Jer 16:3	776
and the small shall die in this *l*	Jer 16:6	776
will I cast you out of this *l*	Jer 16:13	776
into a *l* that ye know not	Jer 16:13	776
of Israel out of the *l* of Egypt	Jer 16:14	776
of Israel from the *l* of the north	Jer 16:15	776
bring them again into their *l*	Jer 16:15	127
because they have defiled my *l*	Jer 16:18	776
in the *l* which thou knowest not	Jer 17:4	776
in the wilderness, in a salt *l*	Jer 17:6	776
from the *l* of Benjamin, and from	Jer 17:26	776
To make their *l* desolate, and a	Jer 18:16	776
and shall see this *l* no more	Jer 22:12	776
But to the *l* whereunto they	Jer 22:27	776
are cast into a *l* which they know	Jer 22:28	776
of Israel out of the *l* of Egypt	Jer 23:7	776
they shall dwell in their own *l*	Jer 23:8	127
For the *l* is full of adulterers	Jer 23:10	776
of swearing the *l* mourneth	Jer 23:10	776
gone forth into all the *l*	Jer 23:15	776
l of the Chaldeans for their good	Jer 24:5	776
I will bring them again to this *l*	Jer 24:6	776
Jerusalem, that remain in this *l*	Jer 24:8	776
them that dwell in the *l* of Egypt	Jer 24:8	776
off the *l* that I gave unto them	Jer 24:10	127
dwell in the *l* that the LORD hath	Jer 25:5	127
and will bring them against this *l*	Jer 25:9	776
And this whole *l* shall be a	Jer 25:11	776
the *l* of the Chaldeans, and will	Jer 25:12	776
I will bring upon that *l* all my	Jer 25:13	776
and all the kings of the *l* of Uz	Jer 25:20	776
kings of the *l* of the Philistines	Jer 25:20	776
for their *l* is desolate because	Jer 25:38	776
up certain of the elders of the *l*	Jer 26:17	776
against this *l* according to all	Jer 26:20	776
until the very time of his *l* come	Jer 27:7	776
to remove you far from your *l*	Jer 27:10	127
I let remain still in their own *l*	Jer 27:11	127
cause them to return to the *l*	Jer 30:3	776
thy seed from the *l* of their	Jer 30:10	776
again from the *l* of the enemy	Jer 31:16	776
use this speech in the *l* of Judah	Jer 31:23	776
bring them out of the *l* of Egypt	Jer 31:32	776
be possessed again in this *l*	Jer 32:15	776
and wonders in the *l* of Egypt	Jer 32:20	776
out of the *l* of Egypt with signs	Jer 32:21	776
And hast given them this *l*	Jer 32:22	776
a *l* flowing with milk and honey	Jer 32:22	776
I will plant them in this *l*	Jer 32:41	776
fields shall be bought in this *l*	Jer 32:43	776
witnesses in the *l* of Benjamin	Jer 32:44	776
to return the captivity of the *l*	Jer 33:11	776
in the *l* of Benjamin, and in the	Jer 33:13	776
and righteousness in the *l*	Jer 33:15	776
them forth out of the *l* of Egypt	Jer 34:13	776
and all the people of the *l*	Jer 34:19	776
in the *l* where ye be strangers	Jer 35:7	127
of Babylon came up into the *l*	Jer 35:11	776
ye shall dwell in the *l* which I	Jer 35:15	127
certainly come and destroy this *l*	Jer 36:29	776
made king in the *l* of Judah	Jer 37:1	776
servants, nor the people of the *l*	Jer 37:2	776
return to Egypt into their own *l*	Jer 37:7	776
to go into the *l* of Benjamin	Jer 37:12	776
against you, nor against this *l*	Jer 37:19	776
to Riblah in the *l* of Hamath	Jer 39:5	776
in the *l* of Judah, and gave them	Jer 39:10	776
behold, all the *l* is before thee	Jer 40:4	776
people that were left in the *l*	Jer 40:6	776
son of Ahikam governor in the *l*	Jer 40:7	776
children, and of the poor of the *l*	Jer 40:7	776
dwell in the *l*, and serve the king	Jer 40:9	776
driven, and came to the *l* of Judah	Jer 40:12	776
had made governor over the *l*	Jer 41:2	776
of Babylon made governor in the *l*	Jer 41:18	776
If ye will still abide in this *l*	Jer 42:10	776
cause you to return to your own *l*	Jer 42:12	127
say, We will not dwell in this *l*	Jer 42:13	776
we will go into the *l* of Egypt	Jer 42:14	776
you there in the *l* of Egypt	Jer 42:16	776
LORD, to dwell in the *l* of Judah	Jer 43:4	776
to dwell in the *l* of Judah	Jer 43:5	776
So they came into the *l* of Egypt	Jer 43:7	776
he shall smite the *l* of Egypt	Jer 43:11	776
array himself with the *l* of Egypt	Jer 43:12	776
that is in the *l* of Egypt	Jer 43:13	776
which dwell in the *l* of Egypt	Jer 44:1	776
unto other gods in the *l* of Egypt	Jer 44:8	776
have committed in the *l* of Judah	Jer 44:9	776
the *l* of Egypt to sojourn there	Jer 44:12	776
and fall in the *l* of Egypt	Jer 44:12	776
them that dwell in the *l* of Egypt	Jer 44:13	776
which are gone into the *l* of	Jer 44:14	776
should return into the *l* of Judah	Jer 44:14	776
that dwelt in the *l* of Egypt	Jer 44:15	776
princes, and the people of the *l*	Jer 44:21	776
therefore is your *l* a desolation	Jer 44:22	776
Judah that are in the *l* of Egypt	Jer 44:24	776
that dwell in the *l* of Egypt	Jer 44:26	776
of Judah in all the *l* of Egypt	Jer 44:26	776
men of Judah that are in the *l* of	Jer 44:27	776
l of Egypt into the *l* of Judah	Jer 44:28	776
that are gone into the *l* of Egypt	Jer 44:28	776
will pluck up, even this whole *l*	Jer 45:4	776
and thy cry hath filled the *l*	Jer 46:12	776
come and smite the *l* of Egypt	Jer 46:13	776
to the *l* of our nativity, from	Jer 46:16	776
thy seed from the *l* of their	Jer 46:27	776
flood, and shall overflow the *l*	Jer 47:2	776
inhabitants of the *l* shall howl	Jer 47:2	776
all the cities of the *l* of Moab	Jer 48:24	776
field, and from the *l* of Moab	Jer 48:33	776
against the *l* of the Chaldeans by	Jer 50:1	776
which shall make her *l* desolate	Jer 50:3	776
out of the *l* of the Chaldeans	Jer 50:8	776
shall be a wilderness, a dry *l*	Jer 50:12	
shall flee every one to his own *l*	Jer 50:16	776
the king of Babylon and his *l*	Jer 50:18	776
Go up against the *l* of Merathaim	Jer 50:21	776
A sound of battle is in the *l*	Jer 50:22	776
hosts in the *l* of the Chaldeans	Jer 50:25	776
and escape out of the *l* of Babylon	Jer 50:28	776
that he may give rest to the *l*	Jer 50:34	776
for it is the *l* of graven images,	Jer 50:38	776
against the *l* of the Chaldeans	Jer 50:45	776
fan her, and shall empty her *l*	Jer 51:2	776
fall in the *l* of the Chaldeans	Jer 51:4	776
though their *l* was filled with	Jer 51:5	776
Set ye up a standard in the *l*	Jer 51:27	776
all the *l* of his dominion	Jer 51:28	776
the *l* shall tremble and sorrow	Jer 51:29	776
to make the *l* of Babylon a	Jer 51:29	776
cities are a desolation, a dry *l*	Jer 51:43	776
a *l* wherein no man dwelleth,	Jer 51:43	776
that shall be heard in the *l*	Jer 51:46	776
a rumour, and violence in the *l*	Jer 51:46	776
her whole *l* shall be confounded,	Jer 51:47	776
through all her *l* the wounded	Jer 51:52	776
from the *l* of the Chaldeans	Jer 51:54	776
no bread for the people of the *l*	Jer 52:6	776
to Riblah in the *l* of Hamath	Jer 52:9	776
poor of the *l* for vinedressers	Jer 52:16	776
who mustered the people of the *l*	Jer 52:25	776
men of the people of the *l*	Jer 52:25	776
in Riblah in the *l* of Hamath	Jer 52:27	127
away captive out of his own *l*	Jer 52:27	127
that dwellest in the *l* of Uz	Lam 4:21	776
in the *l* of the Chaldeans by the	Eze 1:3	776
upon them, and make the *l* desolate	Eze 6:14	776
the Lord GOD unto the *l* of Israel	Eze 7:2	127
upon the four corners of the *l*	Eze 7:2	776
O thou that dwellest in the *l*	Eze 7:7	776
for the *l* is full of bloody	Eze 7:23	776
people of the *l* shall be troubled	Eze 7:27	776
have filled the *l* with violence	Eze 8:17	776
the *l* is full of blood, and the	Eze 9:9	776
unto us is this *l* given in	Eze 11:15	776
I will give you the *l* of Israel	Eze 11:17	127
Babylon to the *l* of the Chaldeans	Eze 12:13	776
And say unto the people of the *l*	Eze 12:19	127
Jerusalem, and of the *l* of Israel	Eze 12:19	127
that her *l* may be desolate from	Eze 12:19	776
waste, and the *l* shall be desolate	Eze 12:20	776
that ye have in the *l* of Israel	Eze 12:22	127
they enter into the *l* of Israel	Eze 13:9	127
when the *l* sinneth against me by	Eze 14:13	776
beasts to pass through the *l*	Eze 14:15	776
but the *l* shall be desolate	Eze 14:16	776
Or if I bring a sword upon that *l*	Eze 14:17	776
and say, Sword, go through the *l*	Eze 14:17	776
I send a pestilence into that *l*	Eze 14:19	776
And I will make the *l* desolate	Eze 15:8	776
nativity is of the *l* of Canaan	Eze 16:3	776
in the *l* of Canaan unto Chaldea	Eze 16:29	776
carried it into a *l* of traffick	Eze 17:4	776
He took also of the seed of the *l*	Eze 17:5	776
also taken the mighty of the *l*	Eze 17:13	776
concerning the *l* of Israel	Eze 18:2	127
with chains unto the *l* of Egypt	Eze 19:4	776
the *l* was desolate, and the	Eze 19:7	776
known unto them in the *l* of Egypt	Eze 20:5	776
to bring them forth of the *l* of	Eze 20:6	776
a *l* that I had espied for them	Eze 20:6	776

L

in the midst of the *l* of Egypt	Eze 20:8	776
them forth out of the *l* of Egypt	Eze 20:9	776
to go forth out of the *l* of Egypt	Eze 20:10	776
into the *l* which I had given them	Eze 20:15	776
I had brought them into the *l*	Eze 20:28	776
the wilderness of the *l* of Egypt	Eze 20:36	776
not enter into the *l* of Israel	Eze 20:38	127
of Israel, all of them in the *l*	Eze 20:40	776
bring you into the *l* of Israel	Eze 20:42	127
prophesy against the *l* of Israel	Eze 21:2	127
And say to the *l* of Israel	Eze 21:3	127
shall come forth out of one *l*	Eze 21:19	776
created, in the *l* of thy nativity	Eze 21:30	776
shall be in the midst of the *l*	Eze 21:32	776
Thou art the *l* that is not	Eze 22:24	776
The people of the *l* have used	Eze 22:29	776
in the gap before me for the *l*	Eze 22:30	776
Chaldea, the *l* of their nativity	Eze 23:15	776
the harlot in the *l* of Egypt	Eze 23:19	776
brought from the *l* of Egypt	Eze 23:27	776
lewdness to cease out of the *l*	Eze 23:48	776
and against the *l* of Israel	Eze 25:3	127
despite against the *l* of Israel	Eze 25:6	127
set glory in the *l* of the living	Eze 26:20	776
the *l* of Israel, they were thy	Eze 27:17	776
they shall stand upon the *l*	Eze 27:29	776
then shall they dwell in their *l*	Eze 28:25	127
the *l* of Egypt shall be desolate	Eze 29:9	776
I will make the *l* of Egypt	Eze 29:10	776
I will make the *l* of Egypt	Eze 29:12	776
to return into the *l* of Pathros	Eze 29:14	776
into the *l* of their habitation	Eze 29:14	776
I will give the *l* of Egypt unto	Eze 29:19	776
I have given him the *l* of Egypt	Eze 29:20	776
the men of the *l* that is in	Eze 30:5	776
shall be brought to destroy the *l*	Eze 30:11	776
fill the *l* with the slain	Eze 30:11	776
sell the *l* into the hand of the	Eze 30:12	776
and I will make the *l* waste	Eze 30:12	776
more a prince of the *l* of Egypt	Eze 30:13	776
will put a fear in the *l* of Egypt	Eze 30:13	776
it out upon the *l* of Egypt	Eze 30:25	776
broken by all the rivers of the *l*	Eze 31:12	776
Then will I leave thee upon the *l*	Eze 32:4	776
blood the *l* wherein thou swimmest	Eze 32:6	776
thee, and set darkness upon thy *l*	Eze 32:8	776
make the *l* of Egypt desolate	Eze 32:15	776
terror in the *l* of the living	Eze 32:23	776
terror in the *l* of the living	Eze 32:24	776
was caused in the *l* of the living	Eze 32:25	776
terror in the *l* of the living	Eze 32:26	776
the mighty in the *l* of the living	Eze 32:27	776
my terror in the *l* of the living	Eze 32:32	776
When I bring the sword upon a *l*	Eze 33:2	776
if the people of the *l* take a man	Eze 33:2	776
seeth the sword come upon the *l*	Eze 33:3	776
wastes of the *l* of Israel speak	Eze 33:24	127
was one, and he inherited the *l*	Eze 33:24	776
the *l* is given us for inheritance	Eze 33:24	776
and shall ye possess the *l*	Eze 33:25	776
and shall ye possess the *l*	Eze 33:26	776
I will lay the *l* most desolate	Eze 33:28	776
when I have laid the *l* most	Eze 33:29	776
and will bring them to their own *l*	Eze 34:13	127
evil beasts to cease out of the *l*	Eze 34:25	776
and they shall be safe in their *l*	Eze 34:27	127
the beast of the *l* devour them	Eze 34:28	776
consumed with hunger in the *l*	Eze 34:29	776
which have appointed my *l* into	Eze 36:5	776
concerning the *l* of Israel	Eze 36:6	127
Thou *l* devourest up men, and hast	Eze 36:13	
of Israel dwelt in their own *l*	Eze 36:17	127
that they had shed upon the *l*	Eze 36:18	776
and are gone forth out of his *l*	Eze 36:20	776
and will bring you into your own *l*	Eze 36:24	127
ye shall dwell in the *l* that I	Eze 36:28	776
the desolate *l* shall be tilled,	Eze 36:34	776
This *l* that was desolate is	Eze 36:35	776
and bring you into the *l* of Israel	Eze 37:12	127
I shall place you in your own *l*	Eze 37:14	127
and bring them into their own *l*	Eze 37:21	127
make them one nation in the *l*	Eze 37:22	776
they shall dwell in the *l* that I	Eze 37:25	776
the *l* of Magog, the chief prince	Eze 38:2	776
l that is brought back from the	Eze 38:8	776
be like a cloud to cover the *l*	Eze 38:9	776
I will go up to the *l* of unwalled	Eze 38:11	776
that dwell in the midst of the *l*	Eze 38:12	776
Israel, as a cloud to cover the *l*	Eze 38:16	776
and I will bring thee against my *l*	Eze 38:16	776
come against the *l* of Israel	Eze 38:18	127
great shaking in the *l* of Israel	Eze 38:19	127
them, that they may cleanse the *l*	Eze 39:12	776
people of the *l* shall bury them	Eze 39:13	776
passing through the *l* to bury	Eze 39:14	776
that pass through the *l*, when any	Eze 39:15	776
Thus shall they cleanse the *l*	Eze 39:16	776
when they dwelt safely in their *l*	Eze 39:26	127
gathered them unto their own *l*	Eze 39:28	127
he me into the *l* of Israel	Eze 40:2	776
by lot the *l* for inheritance	Eze 45:1	776
LORD, an holy portion of the *l*	Eze 45:1	776
The holy portion of the *l* shall	Eze 45:4	776
In the *l* shall be his possession	Eze 45:8	776
the rest of the *l* shall they give	Eze 45:8	776
All the people of the *l* shall	Eze 45:16	776
for all the people of the *l* a	Eze 45:22	776
Likewise the people of the *l*	Eze 46:3	776
But when the people of the *l*	Eze 46:9	776
whereby ye shall inherit the *l*	Eze 47:13	776
this *l* shall fall unto you for	Eze 47:14	776
of the *l* toward the north side	Eze 47:15	776
from the *l* of Israel by Jordan,	Eze 47:18	776
So shall ye divide this *l* unto	Eze 47:21	776
this oblation of the *l* that is	Eze 48:12	776
alienate the firstfruits of the *l*	Eze 48:14	776
This is the *l* which ye shall	Eze 48:29	776
which he carried into the *l* of	Dan 1:2	776
east, and toward the pleasant *l*	Dan 8:9	
and to all the people of the *l*	Dan 9:6	776
the *l* of Egypt with a mighty hand	Dan 9:15	776
and shall return into his own *l*	Dan 11:9	127
he shall stand in the glorious *l*	Dan 11:16	776
face toward the fort of his own *l*	Dan 11:19	776
into his *l* with great riches	Dan 11:28	776
exploits, and return to his own *l*	Dan 11:28	776
and shall divide the *l* for gain	Dan 11:39	127
enter also into the glorious *l*	Dan 11:41	776
the *l* of Egypt shall not escape	Dan 11:42	776
for the *l* hath committed great	Hos 1:2	776
they shall come up out of the *l*	Hos 1:11	776
and set her like a dry *l*, and slay	Hos 2:3	776
she came up out of the *l* of Egypt	Hos 2:15	776
with the inhabitants of the *l*	Hos 4:1	776
nor knowledge of God in the *l*	Hos 4:1	776
Therefore shall the *l* mourn	Hos 4:3	776
their derision in the *l* of Egypt	Hos 7:16	776
shall not dwell in the LORD's *l*	Hos 9:3	776
to the goodness of his *l* they	Hos 10:1	776
not return into the *l* of Egypt	Hos 11:5	776
as a dove out of the *l* of Assyria	Hos 11:11	776
am the LORD thy God from the *l* of	Hos 12:9	776
LORD thy God from the *l* of Egypt	Hos 13:4	776
in the *l* of great drought	Hos 13:5	776
ear, all ye inhabitants of the *l*	Joel 1:2	776
For a nation is come up upon my *l*	Joel 1:6	776
field is wasted, the *l* mourneth	Joel 1:10	127
all the inhabitants of the *l* into	Joel 1:14	776
the inhabitants of the *l* tremble	Joel 2:1	776
the *l* is as the garden of Eden	Joel 2:3	776
the LORD be jealous for his *l*	Joel 2:18	776
and will drive him into a *l* barren	Joel 2:20	776
Fear not, O *l*	Joel 2:21	127
among the nations, and parted my *l*	Joel 3:2	776
shed innocent blood in their *l*	Joel 3:19	776
you up from the *l* of Egypt	Amos 2:10	776
to possess the *l* of the Amorite	Amos 2:10	776
I brought up from the *l* of Egypt	Amos 3:1	776
in the palaces in the *l* of Egypt	Amos 3:9	776
shall be even round about the *l*	Amos 3:11	776
she is forsaken upon her *l*	Amos 5:2	127
end of eating the grass of the *l*	Amos 7:2	776
the *l* is not able to bear all his	Amos 7:10	776
away captive out of their own *l*	Amos 7:11	127
thee away into the *l* of Judah	Amos 7:12	776
thy *l* shall be divided by line	Amos 7:17	127
and thou shalt die in a polluted *l*	Amos 7:17	127
go into captivity forth of his *l*	Amos 7:17	127
to make the poor of the *l* to fail	Amos 8:4	776
Shall not the *l* tremble for this,	Amos 8:8	776
I will send a famine in the *l*	Amos 8:11	776
hosts is he that toucheth the *l*	Amos 9:5	776
up Israel out of the *l* of Egypt	Amos 9:7	776
And I will plant them upon their *l*	Amos 9:15	127
their *l* which I have given them	Amos 9:15	127
hath made the sea and the dry *l*	Jonah 1:9	
rowed hard to bring it to the *l*	Jonah 1:13	3004
vomited out Jonah upon the dry *l*	Jonah 2:10	
Assyrian shall come into our *l*	Mic 5:5	776
they shall waste the *l* of Assyria	Mic 5:6	776
the *l* of Nimrod in the entrances	Mic 5:6	776
when he cometh into our *l*	Mic 5:6	776
will cut off the cities of thy *l*	Mic 5:11	776
thee up out of the *l* of Egypt	Mic 6:4	776
Notwithstanding the *l* shall be	Mic 7:13	776
l of Egypt will I shew unto him	Mic 7:15	776
the gates of thy *l* shall be set	Nah 3:13	776
through the breadth of the *l*	Hab 1:6	776
and for the violence of the *l*	Hab 2:8	776
and for the violence of the *l*	Hab 2:17	776
the curtains of the *l* of Midian	Hab 3:7	776
through the *l* in indignation	Hab 3:12	776
consume all things from off the *l*	Zeph 1:2	127
I will cut off man from off the *l*	Zeph 1:3	127
but the whole *l* shall be devoured	Zeph 1:18	776
of all them that dwell in the *l*	Zeph 1:18	776
the *l* of the Philistines, I will	Zeph 2:5	776
fame in every *l* where they have	Zeph 3:19	776
I called for a drought upon the *l*	Hag 1:11	776
be strong, all ye people of the *l*	Hag 2:4	776
earth, and the sea, and the dry *l*	Hag 2:6	
over the *l* of Judah to scatter it	Zec 1:21	776
and flee from the *l* of the north	Zec 2:6	776
Judah his portion in the holy *l*	Zec 2:12	127
the iniquity of that *l* in one day	Zec 3:9	776
it an house in the *l* of Shinar	Zec 5:11	776
unto all the people of the *l*	Zec 7:5	776
Thus the *l* was desolate after	Zec 7:14	776
they laid the pleasant *l* desolate	Zec 7:14	776
of the LORD in the *l* of Hadrach	Zec 9:1	776
lifted up as an ensign upon his *l*	Zec 9:16	127
again also out of the *l* of Egypt	Zec 10:10	776
bring them into the *l* of Gilead	Zec 10:10	776
pity the inhabitants of the *l*	Zec 11:6	776
and they shall smite the *l*	Zec 11:6	776
will raise up a shepherd in the *l*	Zec 11:16	776
the *l* shall mourn, every family	Zec 12:12	776
names of the idols out of the *l*	Zec 13:2	776
spirit to pass out of the *l*	Zec 13:2	776
come to pass, that in all the *l*	Zec 13:8	776
All the *l* shall be turned as a	Zec 14:10	776
for ye shall be a delightsome *l*	Mal 3:12	776
in the *l* of Juda, art not the	Mt 2:6	*1093*
and go into the *l* of Israel	Mt 2:20	*1093*
and came into the *l* of Israel	Mt 2:21	*1093*
The *l* of Zabulon	Mt 4:15	*1093*
the *l* of Nephthalim, by the way	Mt 4:15	*1093*
went abroad into all that *l*	Mt 9:26	*1093*
more tolerable for the *l* of Sodom	Mt 10:15	*1093*
l of Sodom in the day of judgment	Mt 11:24	*1093*
came into the *l* of Gennesaret	Mt 14:34	*1093*
l to make one proselyte, and when	Mt 23:15	*3584*
all the *l* unto the ninth hour	Mt 27:45	*1093*
out unto him all the *l* of Judaea	Mk 1:5	*5561*
multitude was by the sea on the *l*	Mk 4:1	*1093*
of the sea, and he alone on the *l*	Mk 6:47	*1093*
came into the *l* of Gennesaret	Mk 6:53	*1093*
the whole *l* until the ninth hour	Mk 15:33	*1093*
famine was throughout all the *l*	Lk 4:25	*1093*
thrust out a little from the *l*	Lk 5:3	*1093*
they had brought their ships to *l*	Lk 5:11	*1093*
And when he went forth to *l*	Lk 8:27	*1093*
It is neither fit for the *l*	Lk 14:35	*1093*
arose a mighty famine in that *l*	Lk 15:14	*5561*
shall be great distress in the *l*	Lk 21:23	*1093*
disciples into the *l* of Judaea	Jn 3:22	*1093*
was at the *l* whither they went	Jn 6:21	*1093*
(for they were not far from *l*	Jn 21:8	*1093*
soon then as they were come to *l*	Jn 21:9	*1093*
drew the net to *l* full of great	Jn 21:11	*1093*
Having *l*, sold it, and brought the	Acts 4:37	*68*
back part of the price of the *l*	Acts 5:3	*5564*
whether ye sold the *l* for so much	Acts 5:8	*5564*
come into the *l* which I shall	Acts 7:3	*1093*
he out of the *l* of the Chaldaeans	Acts 7:4	*1093*
dead, he removed him into this *l*	Acts 7:4	*1093*
should sojourn in a strange *l*	Acts 7:6	*1093*
a dearth over all the *l* of Egypt	Acts 7:11	*1093*
was a stranger in the *l* of Madian	Acts 7:29	*1093*
and signs in the *l* of Egypt	Acts 7:36	*1093*
brought us out of the *l* of Egypt	Acts 7:40	*1093*
he did both in the *l* of the Jews	Acts 10:39	*5561*
as strangers in the *l* of Egypt	Acts 13:17	*1093*
seven nations in the *l* of Chanaan	Acts 13:19	*1093*
he divided their *l* to them by lot	Acts 13:19	*1093*
it was day, they knew not the *l*	Acts 27:39	*1093*
first into the sea, and get to *l*	Acts 27:43	*1093*
that they escaped all safe to *l*	Acts 27:44	*1093*
lead them out of the *l* of Egypt	Heb 8:9	*1093*
he sojourned in the *l* of promise	Heb 11:9	*1093*
through the Red sea as by dry *l*	Heb 11:29	
the people out of the *l* of Egypt	Jude 5	*1093*

LANDED {2}

And when he had *l* at Caesarea	Acts 18:22	*2718*
sailed into Syria, and *l* at Tyre	Acts 21:3	*2609*

LANDING {1}

l at Syracuse, we tarried there	Acts 28:12	*2609*

LANDMARK {4}

not remove thy neighbour's *l*	Deut 19:14	1366
that removeth his neighbour's *l*	Deut 27:17	1366
Remove not the ancient *l*, which	Prov 22:28	1366
Remove not the old *l*	Prov 23:10	1366

LANDMARKS {1}

Some remove the *l*	Job 24:2	1367

LANDS {46}

the Gentiles divided in their *l*	Gen 10:5	776
after their tongues, in their *l*	Gen 10:31	776
and the dearth was in all *l*	Gen 41:54	776
the famine was so sore in all *l*	Gen 41:57	776
my lord, but our bodies, and our *l*	Gen 47:18	127
wherefore they sold not their *l*	Gen 47:22	127
hearts in the *l* of their enemies	Lev 26:36	776
their iniquity in your enemies' *l*	Lev 26:39	776
restore those *l* again peaceably	Judg 11:13	
of Assyria have done to all *l*	2Kin 19:11	776
destroyed the nations and their *l*	2Kin 19:17	776
fame of David went out into all *l*	1Chr 14:17	776
out of Egypt, and out of all *l*	2Chr 9:28	776
manner of the nations of other *l*	2Chr 13:9	776
the *l* that were round about Judah	2Chr 17:10	776
unto all the people of other *l*	2Chr 32:13	776
gods of the nations of those *l*	2Chr 32:13	776
deliver their *l* out of mine hand	2Chr 32:13	776
gods of the nations of other *l*	2Chr 32:17	776
from the people of the *l*, doing	Ezr 9:1	776
with the people of those *l*	Ezr 9:2	776
the hand of the kings of the *l*	Ezr 9:7	776
filthiness of the people of the *l*	Ezr 9:11	776
said, We have mortgaged our *l*	Neh 5:3	7704
tribute, and that upon our *l*	Neh 5:4	7704
for other men have our *l* and	Neh 5:5	7704
to them, even this day, their *l*	Neh 5:11	7704
the hand of the people of the *l*	Neh 9:30	776
of the *l* unto the law of God	Neh 10:28	776
they call their *l* after their own	Ps 49:11	127
a joyful noise unto God, all ye *l*	Ps 66:1	776
noise unto the LORD, all ye *l*	Ps 100:1	776
gave them the *l* of the heathen	Ps 105:44	776
and to scatter them in the *l*	Ps 106:27	776
And gathered them out of the *l*	Ps 107:3	776

among all the gods of these *l* Is 36:20 776
all *l* by destroying them utterly Is 37:11 776
from all the *l* whither he had Jer 16:15 776
now have I given all these *l* into Jer 27:6 776
which is the glory of all *l* Eze 20:6 776
which is the glory of all *l* Eze 20:15 776
them out of their enemies' *l* Eze 39:27 776
or wife, or children, or *l* Mt 19:29 *68*
or wife, or children, or *l* Mk 10:29 *68*
and mothers, and children, and *l* Mk 10:30 *68*
of *l* or houses sold them, and Acts 4:34 *5564*

LANES {1}
l of the city, and bring in hither Lk 14:21 *4505*

LANGUAGE {27}
And the whole earth was of one *l* Gen 11:1 8193
is one, and they have all one *l* Gen 11:6 8193
down, and there confound their *l* Gen 11:7 8193
confound the *l* of all the earth Gen 11:9 8193
to thy servants in the Syrian *l* 2Kin 18:26
talk not with us in the Jews' *l* 2Kin 18:26
with a loud voice in the Jews' *l* 2Kin 18:28
and could not speak in the Jews' *l* Neh 13:24
according to the *l* of each people Neh 13:24 3956
and to every people after their *l* Est 1:22 3956
to the *l* of every people Est 1:22 3956
and to every people after their *l* Est 3:12 3956
unto every people after their *l* Est 8:9 3956
writing, and according to their *l* Est 8:9 3956
There is no speech nor *l*, where Ps 19:3 1697
where I heard a *l* that I Ps 81:5 8193
Jacob from a people of strange *l* Ps 114:1 3937
of Egypt speak the *l* of Canaan Is 19:18 8193
unto thy servants in the Syrian *l* Is 36:11
and speak not to us in the Jews' *l* Is 36:11
with a loud voice in the Jews' *l* Is 36:13
a nation whose *l* thou knowest not Jer 5:15 3956
a strange speech and of an hard *l* Eze 3:5 3956
a strange speech and of an hard *l* Eze 3:6 3956
That every people, nation, and *l* Dan 3:29 3961
I turn to the people a pure *l* Zeph 3:9 8193
man heard them speak in his own *l* Acts 2:6 *1258*

LANGUAGES {7}
O people, nations, and *l*, Dan 3:4 3961
the people, the nations, and the *l* Dan 3:7 3961
unto all people, nations, and *l* Dan 4:1 3961
him, all people, nations, and *l* Dan 5:19 3961
unto all people, nations, and *l* Dan 6:25 3961
that all people, nations, and *l* Dan 7:14 3961
hold out of all *l* of the nations Zec 8:23 3956

LANGUISH {5}
For the fields of Heshbon *l* Is 16:8 535
nets upon the waters shall *l* Is 19:8 535
haughty people of the earth do *l* Is 24:4 535
mourneth, and the gates thereof *l* Jer 14:2 535
one that dwelleth therein shall *l* Hos 4:3 535

LANGUISHED {1}
they *l* together Lam 2:8 535

LANGUISHETH {8}
and fadeth away, the world *l* Is 24:4 535
The new wine mourneth, the vine *l* Is 24:7 535
The earth mourneth and *l* Is 33:9 535
She that hath borne seven *l* Jer 15:9 535
new wine is dried up, the oil *l* Joel 1:10 535
is dried up, and the fig tree *l* Joel 1:12 535
Bashan *l*, and Carmel Nah 1:4 535
and the flower of Lebanon *l* Nah 1:4 535

LANGUISHING {1}
strengthen him upon the bed of *l* Ps 41:3 1741

LANTERNS {1}
Pharisees, cometh thither with *l* Jn 18:3 *5322*

LAODICEA *(la-od-i-se'-ah)* {6} *Chief city of Phrygia.*
I have for you, and for them at *L* Col 2:1 *2993*
for you, and them that are in *L* Col 4:13 *2993*
the brethren which are in *L* Col 4:15 *2993*
likewise read the epistle from *L* Col 4:16 *2993*
to Timothy was written from *L* 1Ti *s*
and unto Philadelphia, and unto *L* Rev 1:11 *2993*

LAODICEANS *(la-od-i-se'-uns)* {2} *Inhabitants of Laodicea.*
read also in the church of the *L* Col 4:16 *2994*
of the church of the *L* write Rev 3:14 *2994*

LAP {3}
thereof wild gourds his *l* full 2Kin 4:39 899
Also I shook my *l*, and said, So Neh 5:13 2684
The lot is cast into the *l* Prov 16:33 2436

LAPIDOTH *(lap'-i-doth)* {1} *Husband of Deborah.*
a prophetess, the wife of *L* Judg 4:4 3941

LAPPED {2}
And the number of them that *l* Judg 7:6 3952
men that *l* will I save you Judg 7:7 3952

LAPPETH {2}
Every one that *l* of the water Judg 7:5 3952
water with his tongue, as a dog *l* Judg 7:5 3952

LAPPIDOTH See LAPIDOTH.

LAPWING {2}
heron after her kind, and the *l* Lev 11:19 1744
heron after her kind, and the *l* Deut 14:18 1744

LARGE See APPENDIX.

LARGENESS See APPENDIX.

LASCIVIOUSNESS {6}
wickedness, deceit, *l*, an evil Mk 7:22 *766*
l which they have committed 2Cor 12:21 *766*
fornication, uncleanness, *l* Gal 5:19 *766*
have given themselves over unto *l* Eph 4:19 *766*
the Gentiles, when we walked in *l* 1Pet 4:3 *766*
the grace of our God into *l* Jude 4 *766*

LASEA *(la-se'-ah)* {1} *A city on Crete.*
nigh whereunto was the city of *L* Acts 27:8 *2996*

LASHA *(la'-shah)* {1} *A place in southern Canaan.*
and Admah, and Zeboim, even unto *L* Gen 10:19 3962

LASHARON *(lash'-ar-on)* {1} *A Canaanite town.*
the king of *L*, one Josh 12:18 8289

LAST {85}
shall befall you in the *l* days Gen 49:1 319
but he shall overcome at the *l* Gen 49:19 6119
and let my *l* end be like his Num 23:10 319
Why are ye the *l* to bring the 2Sa 19:11 314
ye the *l* to bring back the king 2Sa 19:12 314
Now these be the *l* words of David 2Sa 23:1 314
For by the *l* words of David the 1Chr 23:27 314
of David the king, first and *l* 1Chr 29:29 314
the acts of Solomon, first and *l* 2Chr 9:29 314
the acts of Rehoboam, first and *l* 2Chr 12:15 314
the acts of Asa, first and *l* 2Chr 16:11 314
acts of Jehoshaphat, first and *l* 2Chr 20:34 314
the acts of Amaziah, first and *l* 2Chr 25:26 314
of the acts of Uzziah, first and *l* 2Chr 26:22 314
and of all his ways, first and *l* 2Chr 28:26 314
And his deeds, first and *l*, behold, 2Chr 35:27 314
of the *l* sons of Adonikam, whose Ezr 8:13 314
from the first day unto the *l* day Neh 8:18 314
And thou mourn at the *l*, when thy Prov 5:11 319
At the *l* it biteth like a serpent Prov 23:32 319
shall come to pass in the *l* days Is 2:2 319
LORD, the first, and with the *l* Is 41:4 314
I am the first, and I am the *l* Is 44:6 314
I am the first, I also am the *l* Is 48:12 314
said, He shall not see our *l* end Jer 12:4 319
l this Nebuchadrezzar king of Jer 50:17 314
she remembereth not her *l* end Lam 1:9 319
But at the *l* Daniel came in Dan 4:8 318
other, and the higher came up *l* Dan 8:3 314
in the *l* end of the indignation Dan 8:19 319
I will slay the *l* of them with Amos 9:1 319
But in the *l* days it shall come Mic 4:1 319
the *l* state of that man is worse Mt 12:45 *2078*
many that are first shall be *l* Mt 19:30 *2078*
and the *l* shall be first Mt 19:30 *2078*
from the *l* unto the first Mt 20:8 *2078*
These *l* have wrought but one hour Mt 20:12 *2078*
I will give unto this *l*, even as Mt 20:14 *2078*
So the *l* shall be first Mt 20:16 *2078*
shall be first, and the first *l* Mt 20:16 *2078*
But *l* of all he sent unto them Mt 21:37 *5305*
l of all the woman died also Mt 22:27 *5305*
At the *l* came two false witnesses Mt 26:60 *5305*
so the *l* error shall be worse Mt 27:64 *2078*
first, the same shall be *l* of all Mk 9:35 *2078*
many that are first shall be *l* Mk 10:31 *2078*
and the *l* first Mk 10:31 *2078*
he sent him also *l* unto them Mk 12:6 *2078*
l of all the woman died also Mk 12:22 *2078*
the *l* state of that man is worse Lk 11:26 *2078*
thou hast paid the very *l* mite Lk 12:59 *2078*
there are *l* which shall be first, Lk 13:30 *2078*
there are first which shall be *l* Lk 13:30 *2078*
L of all the woman died also Lk 20:32 *5305*
raise it up again at the *l* day Jn 6:39 *2078*
I will raise him up at the *l* day Jn 6:40 *2078*
I will raise him up at the *l* day Jn 6:44 *2078*
I will raise him up at the *l* day Jn 6:54 *2078*
In the *l* day, that great day of Jn 7:37 *2078*
at the eldest, even unto the *l* Jn 8:9 *2078*
in the resurrection at the *l* day Jn 11:24 *2078*
same shall judge him in the *l* day Jn 12:48 *2078*
shall come to pass in the *l* days Acts 2:17 *2078*
hath set forth us the apostles *l* 1Cor 4:9 *2078*
l of all he was seen of me also, 1Cor 15:8 *2078*
The *l* enemy that shall be 1Cor 15:26 *2078*
the *l* Adam was made a quickening 1Cor 15:45 *2078*
of an eye, at the *l* trump 1Cor 15:52 *2078*
that now at the *l* your care of me Phil 4:10 *4218*
that in the *l* days perilous times 2Ti 3:1 *2078*
Hath in these *l* days spoken unto Heb 1:2 *2078*
treasure together for the *l* days Jas 5:3 *2078*
to be revealed in the *l* time 1Pet 1:5 *2078*
manifest in these *l* times for you 1Pet 1:20 *2078*
shall come in the *l* days scoffers 2Pet 3:3 *2078*
Little children, it is the *l* time 1Jn 2:18 *2078*
we know that it is the *l* time 1Jn 2:18 *2078*
should be mockers in the *l* time Jude 18 *2078*
and Omega, the first and the *l* Rev 1:11 *2078*
I am the first and the *l* Rev 1:17 *2078*
things saith the first and the *l* Rev 2:8 *2078*
the *l* to be more than the first Rev 2:19 *2078*
angels having the seven *l* plagues Rev 15:1 *2078*
vials full of the seven *l* plagues Rev 21:9 *2078*
and the end, the first and the *l* Rev 22:13 *2078*

LASTED {1}
seven days, while their feast *l* Judg 14:17 1961

LASTING {1}
precious things of the *l* hills Deut 33:15 5769

LATCHET {4}
nor the *l* of their shoes be Is 5:27 8288
the *l* of whose shoes I am not Mk 1:7 *2438*
the *l* of whose shoes I am not Lk 3:16 *2438*
whose shoe's *l* I am not worthy to Jn 1:27 *2438*

LATE {3}
you to rise up early, to sit up *l* Ps 127:2 309
Even of *l* my people is risen up Mic 2:8 865
the Jews of *l* sought to stone Jn 11:8 *3568*

LATELY {1}
l come from Italy, with his wife Acts 18:2 *4373*

LATIN *(lat'-in)* {2} *Language spoken by the Romans.*
him in letters of Greek, and *L* Lk 23:38 *4513*
written in Hebrew, and Greek, and *L* Jn 19:20 *4513*

LATTER {42}
believe the voice of the *l* sign Ex 4:8 314
do to thy people in the *l* days Num 24:14 319
but his *l* end shall be that he Num 24:20 319
upon thee, even in the *l* days Deut 4:30 319
to do thee good at thy *l* end Deut 8:16 319
the *l* rain, that thou mayest Deut 11:14 4456
if the *l* husband hate her, and Deut 24:3 314
or if the *l* husband die, which Deut 24:3 314
will befall you in the *l* days Deut 31:29 319
they would consider their *l* end Deut 32:29 319
the *l* end than at the beginning Ruth 3:10 314
will be bitterness in the *l* end 2Sa 2:26 314
yet thy *l* end should greatly Job 8:7 319
stand at the *l* day upon the earth Job 19:25 314
mouth wide as for the *l* rain Job 29:23 4456
So the LORD blessed the *l* end of Job 42:12 319
is as a cloud of the *l* rain Prov 16:15 4456
thou mayest be wise in thy *l* end Prov 19:20 319
them, and know the *l* end of them Is 41:22 319
didst remember the *l* end of it Is 47:7 319
and there hath been no *l* rain Jer 3:3 4456
rain, both the former and the *l* Jer 5:24 4456
in the *l* days ye shall consider Jer 23:20 319
in the *l* days ye shall consider Jer 30:24 319
captivity of Moab in the *l* days Jer 48:47 319
shall come to pass in the *l* days Jer 49:39 319
in the *l* years thou shalt come Eze 38:8 319
it shall be in the *l* days Eze 38:16 319
what shall be in the *l* days Dan 2:28 320
in the *l* time of their kingdom, Dan 8:23 319
befall thy people in the *l* days Dan 10:14 319
not be as the former, or as the *l* Dan 11:29 314
and his goodness in the *l* days Hos 3:5 319
unto us as the rain, as the *l* Hos 6:3 4456
the *l* rain in the first month Joel 2:23 4456
the shooting up of the *l* growth Amos 7:1 3954
it was the *l* growth after the Amos 7:1 3954
The glory of this *l* house shall Hag 2:9 314
rain in the time of the *l* rain Zec 10:1 4456
that in the *l* times some shall 1Ti 4:1 *5305*
he receive the early and *l* rain Jas 5:7 *3797*
the *l* end is worse with them than 2Pet 2:20 *2078*

LATTICE {3}
a window, and cried through the *l* Judg 5:28 822
Ahaziah fell down through a *l* in 2Kin 1:2 7639
shewing himself through the *l* Song 2:9 2762

LAUD {1}
and *l* him, all ye people Rom 15:11 *1867*

LAUGH {18}
Abraham, Wherefore did Sarah *l* Gen 18:13 6711
but thou didst *l* Gen 18:15 6711
Sarah said, God hath made me to *l* Gen 21:6 6712
that all that hear will *l* with me Gen 21:6 6711
and famine thou shalt *l* Job 5:22 7832
he will *l* at the trial of the Job 9:23 3932
the innocent *l* them to scorn Job 22:19 3932
sitteth in the heavens shall *l* Ps 2:4 7832
they that see me *l* me to scorn Ps 22:7 3932
The LORD shall *l* at him Ps 37:13 7832
see, and fear, and shall *l* at him Ps 52:6 7832
But thou, O LORD, shalt *l* at them Ps 59:8 7832
our enemies *l* among themselves Ps 80:6 3932
I also will *l* at your calamity Prov 1:26 7832
foolish man, whether he rage or *l* Prov 29:9 7832
A time to weep, and a time to *l* Eccl 3:4 7832
for ye shall *l* Lk 6:21 *1070*
Woe unto you that *l* now Lk 6:25 *1070*

LAUGHED {13}
Abraham fell upon his face, and *l* Gen 17:17 6711
Therefore Sarah *l* within herself Gen 18:12 6711
Sarah denied, saying, I *l* not Gen 18:15 6711
despised thee, and *l* thee to scorn 2Kin 19:21 3932
but they *l* them to scorn, and 2Chr 30:10 7832
they *l* us to scorn, and despised Neh 2:19 3932
just upright man is *l* to scorn Job 12:4 7832
If I *l* on them, they believed it Job 29:24 7832
despised thee, and *l* thee to scorn Is 37:22 3932
thou shalt be *l* to scorn and had Eze 23:32 6712
And they *l* him to scorn Mt 9:24 *2606*
And they *l* him to scorn Mk 5:40 *2606*
they *l* him to scorn, knowing that Lk 8:53 *2606*

LAUGHETH {1}
he *l* at the shaking of a spear Job 41:29 7832

LAUGHING {1}
Till he fill thy mouth with *l* Job 8:21 7814

LAUGHTER {7}
Then was our mouth filled with *l* Ps 126:2 7814
Even in *l* the heart is sorrowful Prov 14:13 7814
I said of *l*, It is mad Eccl 2:2 7814
Sorrow is better than *l* Eccl 7:3 7814
a pot, so is the *l* of the fool Eccl 7:6 7814
A feast is made for *l*, and wine Eccl 10:19 7814
let your *l* be turned to mourning, Jas 4:9 *1071*

L

LAUNCH {1}

L out into the deep, and let down	Lk 5:4	*1877*

LAUNCHED {4}

And they *l* forth	Lk 8:22	*321*
were gotten from them, and had *l*	Acts 21:1	*321*
into a ship of Adramyttium, we *l*	Acts 27:2	*321*
And when we had *l* from thence	Acts 27:4	*321*

LAVER {15}

Thou shalt also make a *l* of brass	Ex 30:18	3595
with all his vessels, and the *l*	Ex 30:28	3595
with all his furniture, and the *l*	Ex 31:9	3595
staves, and all his vessels, the *l*	Ex 35:16	3595
And he made the *l* of brass	Ex 38:8	3595
staves, and all his vessels, the *l*	Ex 39:39	3595
thou shalt set the *l* between the	Ex 40:7	3595
And thou shalt anoint the *l*	Ex 40:11	3595
he set the *l* between the tent of	Ex 40:30	3595
and all his vessels, both the *l*	Lev 8:11	3595
under the *l* were undersetters	1Kin 7:30	3595
one *l* contained forty baths	1Kin 7:38	3595
and every *l* was four cubits	1Kin 7:38	3595
every one of the ten bases one *l*	1Kin 7:38	3595
removed the *l* from off them	2Kin 16:17	3595

LAVERS {5}

Then made he ten *l* of brass	1Kin 7:38	3595
And Hiram made the *l*, and the	1Kin 7:40	3595
ten bases, and ten *l* on the bases	1Kin 7:43	3595
He made also ten *l*, and put five	2Chr 4:6	3595
and *l* made he upon the bases	2Chr 4:14	3595

LAVISH {1}

They *l* gold out of the bag, and	Is 46:6	2107

LAW {526}

son, and Sarai his daughter in *l*	Gen 11:31	3618
son in *l*, and thy sons, and thy	Gen 19:12	2859
out, and spake unto his sons in *l*	Gen 19:14	2859
that mocked unto his sons in *l*	Gen 19:14	2859
Judah to Tamar his daughter in *l*	Gen 38:11	3618
Behold thy father in *l* goeth up	Gen 38:13	2524
that she was his daughter in *l*	Gen 38:16	3618
Tamar thy daughter in *l* hath	Gen 38:24	3618
she sent to her father in *l*	Gen 38:25	2524
Joseph made it a *l* over the land	Gen 47:26	2706
flock of Jethro his father in *l*	Ex 3:1	2859
to Jethro his father in *l*	Ex 4:18	2859
One *l* shall be to him that is	Ex 12:49	8451
that the LORD's *l* may be in thy	Ex 13:9	8451
whether they will walk in my *l*	Ex 16:4	8451
of Midian, Moses' father in *l*	Ex 18:1	2859
Then Jethro, Moses' father in *l*	Ex 18:2	2859
And Jethro, Moses' father in *l*	Ex 18:5	2859
I thy father in *l* Jethro am come	Ex 18:6	2859
went out to meet his father in *l*	Ex 18:7	2859
Moses told his father in *l* all	Ex 18:8	2859
And Jethro, Moses' father in *l*	Ex 18:12	2859
Moses' father in *l* before God	Ex 18:12	2859
when Moses' father in *l* saw all	Ex 18:14	2859
Moses said unto his father in *l*	Ex 18:15	2859
Moses' father in *l* said unto him	Ex 18:17	2859
to the voice of his father in *l*	Ex 18:24	2859
Moses let his father in *l* depart	Ex 18:27	2859
give thee tables of stone, and a *l*	Ex 24:12	8451
This is the *l* of the burnt	Lev 6:9	8451
this is the *l* of the meat	Lev 6:14	8451
This is the *l* of the sin offering	Lev 6:25	8451
Likewise this is the *l* of the	Lev 7:1	8451
there is one *l* for them	Lev 7:7	8451
this is the *l* of the sacrifice of	Lev 7:11	8451
This is the *l* of the burnt	Lev 7:37	8451
This is the *l* of the beasts, and	Lev 11:46	8451
This is the *l* for her that hath	Lev 12:7	8451
This is the *l* of the plague of	Lev 13:59	8451
This shall be the *l* of the leper	Lev 14:2	8451
This is the *l* of him in whom is	Lev 14:32	8451
This is the *l* for all manner of	Lev 14:54	8451
this is the *l* of leprosy	Lev 14:57	8451
This is the *l* of him that hath an	Lev 15:32	8451
nakedness of thy daughter in *l*	Lev 18:15	3618
a man lie with his daughter in *l*	Lev 20:12	3618
Ye shall have one manner of *l*	Lev 24:22	4941
This is the *l* of jealousies, when	Num 5:29	8451
shall execute upon her all this *l*	Num 5:30	8451
this is the *l* of the Nazarite,	Num 6:13	8451
This is the *l* of the Nazarite who	Num 6:21	8451
do after the *l* of his separation	Num 6:21	8451
the Midianite, Moses' father in *l*	Num 10:29	2859
One *l* and one manner shall be for	Num 15:16	8451
Ye shall have one *l* for him that	Num 15:29	8451
This is the ordinance of the *l*	Num 19:2	8451
This is the *l*, when a man dieth	Num 19:14	8451
This is the ordinance of the *l*	Num 31:21	8451
began Moses to declare this *l*	Deut 1:5	8451
so righteous as all this *l*	Deut 4:8	8451
this is the *l* which Moses set	Deut 4:44	8451
to the sentence of the *l* which	Deut 17:11	8451
l in a book out of that which is	Deut 17:18	8451
to keep all the words of this *l*	Deut 17:19	8451
upon them all the words of this *l*	Deut 27:3	8451
the words of this *l* very plainly	Deut 27:8	8451
that lieth with his mother in *l*	Deut 27:23	2859
the words of this *l* to do them	Deut 27:26	8451
to do all the words of this *l*	Deut 28:58	8451
not written in the book of this *l*	Deut 28:61	8451
are written in this book of the *l*	Deut 29:21	8451
we may do all the words of this *l*	Deut 29:29	8451
are written in this book of the *l*	Deut 30:10	8451
And Moses wrote this *l*, and	Deut 31:9	8451
thou shalt read this *l* before all	Deut 31:11	8451
to do all the words of this *l*	Deut 31:12	8451
the words of this *l* in a book	Deut 31:24	8451
Take this book of the *l*, and put	Deut 31:26	8451
to do, all the words of this *l*	Deut 32:46	8451
hand went a fiery *l* for them	Deut 33:2	1881
Moses commanded us a *l*, even the	Deut 33:4	8451
thy judgments, and Israel thy *l*	Deut 33:10	8451
to do according to all the *l*	Josh 1:7	8451
This book of the *l* shall not	Josh 1:8	8451
in the book of the *l* of Moses	Josh 8:31	8451
stones a copy of the *l* of Moses	Josh 8:32	8451
he read all the words of the *l*	Josh 8:34	8451
is written in the book of the *l*	Josh 8:34	8451
to do the commandment and the *l*	Josh 22:5	8451
in the book of the *l* of Moses	Josh 23:6	8451
words in the book of the *l* of God	Josh 24:26	8451
of the Kenite, Moses' father in *l*	Judg 1:16	2859
of Hobab the father in *l* of Moses	Judg 4:11	2859
the son in *l* of the Timnite,	Judg 15:6	2859
And his father in *l*, the damsel's	Judg 19:4	2859
father said unto his son in *l*	Judg 19:5	2859
depart, his father in *l* urged him	Judg 19:7	2859
and his servant, his father in *l*	Judg 19:9	2859
she arose with her daughters in *l*	Ruth 1:6	3618
her two daughters in *l* with her	Ruth 1:7	3618
said unto her two daughters in *l*	Ruth 1:8	3618
and Orpah kissed her mother in *l*	Ruth 1:14	2545
thy sister in *l* is gone back unto	Ruth 1:15	2994
return thou after thy sister in *l*	Ruth 1:15	2994
the Moabitess, her daughter in *l*	Ruth 1:22	3618
in *l* since the death of thine	Ruth 2:11	2545
her mother in *l* saw what she had	Ruth 2:18	2545
And her mother in *l* said unto her	Ruth 2:19	2545
she shewed her mother in *l* with	Ruth 2:19	2545
Naomi said unto her daughter in *l*	Ruth 2:20	3618
said unto Ruth her daughter in *l*	Ruth 2:22	3618
and dwelt with her mother in *l*	Ruth 2:23	2545
her mother in *l* said unto her	Ruth 3:1	2545
all that her mother in *l* bade her	Ruth 3:6	2545
when she came to her mother in *l*	Ruth 3:16	2545
Go not empty unto thy mother in *l*	Ruth 3:17	2545
for thy daughter in *l*, which	Ruth 4:15	3618
And his daughter in *l*, Phinehas'	1Sa 4:19	3618
taken, and that her father in *l*	1Sa 4:19	2524
and because of her father in *l*	1Sa 4:21	2524
I should be son in *l* to the king	1Sa 18:18	2859
son in *l* in the one of the twain	1Sa 18:21	2860
therefore be the king's son in *l*	1Sa 18:22	2860
thing to be a king's son in *l*	1Sa 18:23	2860
well to be the king's son in *l*	1Sa 18:26	2860
he might be the king's son in *l*	1Sa 18:27	2860
which is the king's son in *l*	1Sa 22:14	2859
it is written in the *l* of Moses	1Kin 2:3	8451
the son in *l* of the house of Ahab	2Kin 8:27	2859
took no heed to walk in the *l* of	2Kin 10:31	8451
in the book of the *l* of Moses	2Kin 14:6	8451
according to all the *l* which I	2Kin 17:13	8451
their ordinances, or after the *l*	2Kin 17:34	8451
and the ordinances, and the *l*	2Kin 17:37	8451
according to all the *l* that my	2Kin 21:8	8451
of the *l* in the house of the LORD	2Kin 22:8	8451
the words of the book of the *l*	2Kin 22:11	8451
l which were written in the book	2Kin 23:24	8451
according to all the *l* of Moses	2Kin 23:25	8451
his daughter in *l* bare him Pharez	1Chr 2:4	3618
the same to Jacob for a *l*	1Chr 16:17	2706
is written in the *l* of the LORD	1Chr 16:40	8451
keep the *l* of the LORD thy God	1Chr 22:12	8451
heed to their way to walk in my *l*	2Chr 6:16	8451
he forsook the *l* of the LORD	2Chr 12:1	8451
of their fathers, and to do the *l*	2Chr 14:4	8451
a teaching priest, and without *l*	2Chr 15:3	8451
had the book of the *l* of the LORD	2Chr 17:9	8451
between blood and blood, between *l*	2Chr 19:10	8451
it is written in the *l* of Moses	2Chr 23:18	8451
in the *l* in the book of Moses	2Chr 25:4	8451
according to the *l* of Moses the	2Chr 30:16	8451
is written in the *l* of the LORD	2Chr 31:3	8451
encouraged in the *l* of the LORD	2Chr 31:4	8451
of the house of God, and in the *l*	2Chr 31:21	8451
them, according to the whole *l*	2Chr 33:8	8451
the *l* of the LORD given by Moses	2Chr 34:14	8451
of the *l* in the house of the LORD	2Chr 34:15	8451
king had heard the words of the *l*	2Chr 34:19	8451
was written in the *l* of the LORD	2Chr 35:26	8451
in the *l* of Moses the man of God	Ezr 3:2	8451
a ready scribe in the *l* of Moses	Ezr 7:6	8451
heart to seek the *l* of the LORD	Ezr 7:10	8451
a scribe of the *l* of the God of	Ezr 7:12	1882
according to the *l* of thy God	Ezr 7:14	1882
the scribe of the *l* of the God of	Ezr 7:21	1882
will not do the *l* of thy God	Ezr 7:26	1882
the *l* of the king, let judgment	Ezr 7:26	1882
let it be done according to the *l*	Ezr 10:3	8451
because he was the son in *l* of	Neh 6:18	2859
bring the book of the *l* of Moses	Neh 8:1	8451
Ezra the priest brought the *l*	Neh 8:2	8451
attentive unto the book of the *l*	Neh 8:3	8451
the people to understand the *l*	Neh 8:7	8451
book in the *l* of God distinctly	Neh 8:8	8451
they heard the words of the *l*	Neh 8:9	8451
to understand the words of the *l*	Neh 8:13	8451
they found written in the *l* which	Neh 8:14	8451
read in the book of the *l* of God	Neh 8:18	8451
read in the book of the *l* of the	Neh 9:3	8451
cast thy *l* behind their backs, and	Neh 9:26	8451
bring them again unto thy *l*	Neh 9:29	8451
nor our fathers, kept thy *l*	Neh 9:34	8451
of the lands unto the *l* of God	Neh 10:28	8451
into an oath, to walk in God's *l*	Neh 10:29	8451
God, as it is written in the *l*	Neh 10:34	8451
cattle, as it is written in the *l*	Neh 10:36	8451
portions of the *l* for the priests	Neh 12:44	8451
pass, when they had heard the *l*	Neh 13:3	8451
was son in *l* to Sanballat the	Neh 13:28	2859
drinking was according to the *l*	Est 1:8	1881
manner toward all that knew *l*	Est 1:13	1881
the queen Vashti according to *l*	Est 1:15	1881
there is one *l* of his to put him	Est 4:11	1881
which is not according to the *l*	Est 4:16	1881
the *l* from his mouth, and lay up	Job 22:22	8451
delight is in the *l* of the LORD	Ps 1:2	8451
in his *l* doth he meditate day and	Ps 1:2	8451
The *l* of the LORD is perfect,	Ps 19:7	8451
The *l* of his God is in his heart	Ps 37:31	8451
yea, thy *l* is within my heart	Ps 40:8	8451
Give ear, O my people, to my *l*	Ps 78:1	8451
Jacob, and appointed a *l* in Israel	Ps 78:5	8451
God, and refused to walk in his *l*	Ps 78:10	8451
and a *l* of the God of Jacob	Ps 81:4	4941
If his children forsake my *l*	Ps 89:30	8451
and teachest him out of thy *l*	Ps 94:12	8451
which frameth mischief by a *l*	Ps 94:20	2706
the same unto Jacob for a *l*	Ps 105:10	2706
who walk in the *l* of the LORD	Ps 119:1	8451
wondrous things out of thy *l*	Ps 119:18	8451
and grant me thy *l* graciously	Ps 119:29	8451
and I shall keep thy *l*	Ps 119:34	8451
So shall I keep thy *l* continually	Ps 119:44	8451
have I not declined from thy *l*	Ps 119:51	8451
of the wicked that forsake thy *l*	Ps 119:53	8451
in the night, and have kept thy *l*	Ps 119:55	8451
but I have not forgotten thy *l*	Ps 119:61	8451
but I delight in thy *l*	Ps 119:70	8451
The *l* of thy mouth is better unto	Ps 119:72	8451
for thy *l* is my delight	Ps 119:77	8451
for me, which are not after thy *l*	Ps 119:85	8451
Unless thy *l* had been my delights	Ps 119:92	8451
O how love I thy *l*	Ps 119:97	8451
yet do I not forget thy *l*	Ps 119:109	8451
but thy *l* do I love	Ps 119:113	8451
for they have made void thy *l*	Ps 119:126	8451
eyes, because they keep not thy *l*	Ps 119:136	8451
and thy *l* is the truth	Ps 119:142	8451
they are far from thy *l*	Ps 119:150	8451
for I do not forget thy *l*	Ps 119:153	8451
but thy *l* do I love	Ps 119:163	8451
peace have they which love thy *l*	Ps 119:165	8451
and thy *l* is my delight	Ps 119:174	8451
forsake not the *l* of thy mother	Prov 1:8	8451
My son, forget not my *l*	Prov 3:1	8451
doctrine, forsake ye not my *l*	Prov 4:2	8451
forsake not the *l* of thy mother	Prov 6:20	8451
and the *l* is light	Prov 6:23	8451
my *l* as the apple of thine eye	Prov 7:2	8451
The *l* of the wise is a fountain	Prov 13:14	8451
forsake the *l* praise the wicked	Prov 28:4	8451
as keep the *l* contend with them	Prov 28:4	8451
Whoso keepeth the *l* is a wise son	Prov 28:7	8451
away his ear from hearing the *l*	Prov 28:9	8451
but he that keepeth the *l*	Prov 29:18	8451
Lest they drink, and forget the *l*	Prov 31:5	2710
her tongue is the *l* of kindness	Prov 31:26	8451
give ear unto the *l* of our God	Is 1:10	8451
out of Zion shall go forth the *l*	Is 2:3	8451
away the *l* of the LORD of hosts	Is 5:24	8451
seal the *l* among my disciples	Is 8:16	8451
To the *l* and to the testimony	Is 8:20	8451
will not hear the *l* of the LORD	Is 30:9	8451
and the isles shall wait for his *l*	Is 42:4	8451
he will magnify the *l*, and make it	Is 42:21	8451
were they obedient unto his *l*	Is 42:24	8451
for a *l* shall proceed from me, and	Is 51:4	8451
the people in whose heart is my *l*	Is 51:7	8451
that handle the *l* knew me not	Jer 2:8	8451
unto my words, nor to my *l*	Jer 6:19	8451
the *l* of the LORD is with us	Jer 8:8	8451
my *l* which I set before them	Jer 9:13	8451
me, and have not kept my *l*	Jer 16:11	8451
for the *l* shall not perish from	Jer 18:18	8451
hearken to me, to walk in my *l*	Jer 26:4	8451
I will put my *l* in their inward	Jer 31:33	8451
was sealed according to the *l*	Jer 32:11	4687
voice, neither walked in thy *l*	Jer 32:23	8451
they feared, nor walked in my *l*	Jer 44:10	8451
of the LORD, nor walked in his *l*	Jer 44:23	8451
the *l* is no more	Lam 2:9	8451
but the *l* shall perish from the	Eze 7:26	8451
lewdly defiled his daughter in *l*	Eze 22:11	3618
Her priests have violated my *l*	Eze 22:26	8451
This is the *l* of the house	Eze 43:12	8451
this is the *l* of the house	Eze 43:12	8451
him concerning the *l* of his God	Dan 6:5	1882
according to the *l* of the Medes	Dan 6:8	1882
according to the *l* of the Medes	Dan 6:12	1882
that the *l* of the Medes and	Dan 6:15	1882
Israel have transgressed thy *l*	Dan 9:11	8451
the *l* of Moses the servant of God	Dan 9:11	8451
it is written in the *l* of Moses	Dan 9:13	8451
hast forgotten the *l* of thy God	Hos 4:6	8451
and trespassed against my *l*	Hos 8:1	8451
to him the great things of my *l*	Hos 8:12	8451
have despised the *l* of the LORD	Amos 2:4	8451
for the *l* shall go forth of Zion,	Mic 4:2	8451
the daughter in *l* against her	Mic 7:6	3618

against her mother in l ... Mic 7:6 2545
Therefore the l is slacked ... Hab 1:4 8451
they have done violence to the l ... Zeph 3:4 8451
now the priests concerning the l ... Hag 2:11 8451
lest they should hear the l ... Zec 7:12 8451
The l of truth was in his mouth, ... Mal 2:6 8451
should seek the l at his mouth ... Mal 2:7 8451
caused many to stumble at the l ... Mal 2:8 8451
but have been partial in the l ... Mal 2:9 8451
Remember ye the l of Moses my ... Mal 4:4 8451
that I am come to destroy the l ... Mt 5:17 3551
shall in no wise pass from the l ... Mt 5:18 3551
if any man will sue thee at the l ... Mt 5:40
for this is the l and the prophets ... Mt 7:12 3551
the daughter in l against her ... Mt 10:35 3565
against her mother in l ... Mt 10:35 3994
the l prophesied until John ... Mt 11:13 3551
Or have ye not read in the l ... Mt 12:5 3551
is the great commandment in the l ... Mt 22:36 3551
two commandments hang all the l ... Mt 22:40 3551
the weightier matters of the l ... Mt 23:23 3551
the l of Moses were accomplished ... Lk 2:22 3551
is written in the l of the Lord ... Lk 2:23 3551
is said in the l of the Lord ... Lk 2:24 3551
for him after the custom of the l ... Lk 2:27 3551
according to the l of the Lord ... Lk 2:39 3551
and doctors of the l sitting by ... Lk 5:17 3547
him, What is written in the l ... Lk 10:26 3551
the mother in l against her ... Lk 12:53 3994
against her daughter in l ... Lk 12:53 3565
the daughter in l against her ... Lk 12:53 3565
against her mother in l ... Lk 12:53 3994
The l and the prophets were until ... Lk 16:16 3551
than one tittle of the l to fail ... Lk 16:17 3551
were written in the l of Moses ... Lk 24:44 3551
For the l was given by Moses, but ... Jn 1:17 3551
found him, of whom Moses in the l ... Jn 1:45 3551
Did not Moses give you the l ... Jn 7:19 3551
and yet none of you keepeth the l ... Jn 7:19 3551
that the l of Moses should not be ... Jn 7:23 3551
who knoweth not the l are cursed ... Jn 7:49 3551
Doth our l judge any man, before ... Jn 7:51 3551
Now Moses in the l commanded us ... Jn 8:5 3551
It is also written in your l ... Jn 8:17 3551
them, Is it not written in your l ... Jn 10:34 3551
We have heard out of the l that ... Jn 12:34 3551
that is written in their l ... Jn 15:25 3551
he was father in l to Caiaphas ... Jn 18:13 3995
and judge him according to your l ... Jn 18:31 3551
Jews answered him, We have a l ... Jn 19:7 3551
by our l he ought to die, because ... Jn 19:7 3551
named Gamaliel, a doctor of the l ... Acts 5:34 3547
against this holy place, and the l ... Acts 6:13 3551
Who have received the l by the ... Acts 7:53 3551
And after the reading of the l ... Acts 13:15 3551
be justified by the l of Moses ... Acts 13:39 3551
them to keep the l of Moses ... Acts 15:5 3551
be circumcised, and keep the l ... Acts 15:24 3551
to worship God contrary to the l ... Acts 18:13 3551
of words and names, and of your l ... Acts 18:15 3551
the l is open, and there are ... Acts 19:38 60
and they are all zealous of the l ... Acts 21:20 3551
walkest orderly, and keepest the l ... Acts 21:24 3551
against the people, and the l ... Acts 21:28 3551
manner of the l of the fathers ... Acts 22:3 3551
a devout man according to the l ... Acts 22:12 3551
thou to judge me after the l ... Acts 23:3 3551
to be smitten contrary to the l ... Acts 23:3 3891
accused of questions of their l ... Acts 23:29 3551
have judged according to our l ... Acts 24:6 3551
things which are written in the l ... Acts 24:14 3551
Neither against the l of the Jews ... Acts 25:8 3551
Jesus, both out of the l of Moses ... Acts 28:23 3551
l shall also perish without l ... Rom 2:12 460
the l shall be judged by the l ... Rom 2:12 3551
of the l are just before God ... Rom 2:13 3551
doers of the l shall be justified ... Rom 2:13 3551
Gentiles, which have not the l ... Rom 2:14 3551
the things contained in the l ... Rom 2:14 3551
these, having not the l ... Rom 2:14 3551
the l, are a l unto themselves ... Rom 2:14 3551
of the l written in their hearts ... Rom 2:15 3551
called a Jew, and restest in the l ... Rom 2:17 3551
being instructed out of the l ... Rom 2:18 3551
and of the truth in the l ... Rom 2:20 3551
that makest thy boast of the l ... Rom 2:23 3551
through breaking the l ... Rom 2:23 3551
profiteth, if thou keep the l ... Rom 2:25 3551
but if thou be a breaker of the l ... Rom 2:25 3551
keep the righteousness of the l ... Rom 2:26 3551
is by nature, if it fulfil the l ... Rom 2:27 3551
dost transgress the l ... Rom 2:27 3551
what things soever the l saith ... Rom 3:19 3551
saith to them who are under the l ... Rom 3:19 3551
of the l there shall no flesh be ... Rom 3:20 3551
for by the l is the knowledge of ... Rom 3:20 3551
God without the l is manifested ... Rom 3:21 3551
being witnessed by the l ... Rom 3:21 3551
By what l? ... Rom 3:27 3551
but by the l of faith ... Rom 3:27 3551
faith without the deeds of the l ... Rom 3:28 3551
make void the l through faith ... Rom 3:31 3551
yea, we establish the l ... Rom 3:31 3551
or to his seed, through the l ... Rom 4:13 3551
they which are of the l be heirs ... Rom 4:14 3551
Because the l worketh wrath ... Rom 4:15 3551
for where no l is, there is no ... Rom 4:15 3551
to that only which is of the l ... Rom 4:16 3551
(For until the l sin was in the ... Rom 5:13 3551
is not imputed when there is no l ... Rom 5:13 3551
Moreover the l entered, that the ... Rom 5:20 3551
for ye are not under the l ... Rom 6:14 3551
because we are not under the l ... Rom 6:15 3551
I speak to them that know the l ... Rom 7:1 3551
how that the l hath dominion ... Rom 7:1 3551
l to her husband so long as he ... Rom 7:2 3551
loosed from the l of her husband ... Rom 7:2 3551
be dead, she is free from that l ... Rom 7:3 3551
to the l by the body of Christ ... Rom 7:4 3551
of sins, which were by the l ... Rom 7:5 3551
now we are delivered from the l ... Rom 7:6 3551
Is the l sin ... Rom 7:7 3551
I had not known sin, but by the l ... Rom 7:7 3551
known lust, except the l had said ... Rom 7:7 3551
For without the l sin was dead ... Rom 7:8 3551
I was alive without the l once ... Rom 7:9 3551
Wherefore the l is holy, and the ... Rom 7:12 3551
we know that the l is spiritual ... Rom 7:14 3551
unto the l that it is good ... Rom 7:16 3551
I find then a l, that, when I ... Rom 7:21 3551
For I delight in the l of God ... Rom 7:22 3551
But I see another l in my members ... Rom 7:23 3551
warring against the l of my mind ... Rom 7:23 3551
me into captivity to the l of sin ... Rom 7:23 3551
mind I myself serve the l of God ... Rom 7:25 3551
but with the flesh the l of sin ... Rom 7:25 3551
For the l of the Spirit of ... Rom 8:2 3551
made me free from the l of sin ... Rom 8:2 3551
For what the l could not do ... Rom 8:3 3551
of the l might be fulfilled in us ... Rom 8:4 3551
it is not subject to the l of God ... Rom 8:7 3551
covenants, and the giving of the l ... Rom 9:4 3548
after the l of righteousness ... Rom 9:31 3551
to the l of righteousness ... Rom 9:31 3551
as it were by the works of the l ... Rom 9:32 3551
For Christ is the end of the l ... Rom 10:4 3551
righteousness which is of the l ... Rom 10:5 3551
another hath fulfilled the l ... Rom 13:8 3551
love is the fulfilling of the l ... Rom 13:10 3551
go to l before the unjust, and not ... 1Cor 6:1 2919
brother goeth to l with brother ... 1Cor 6:6 2919
ye go to l one with another ... 1Cor 6:7 2917
The wife is bound by the l as ... 1Cor 7:39 3551
or saith not the l the same also ... 1Cor 9:8 3551
it is written in the l of Moses ... 1Cor 9:9 3551
are under the l, as under the l ... 1Cor 9:20 3551
gain them that are under the l ... 1Cor 9:20 3551
are without l, as without l ... 1Cor 9:21 459
l, (being not without l to God ... 1Cor 9:21 459
but under the l to Christ ... 1Cor 9:21 1772
gain them that are without l ... 1Cor 9:21 459
In the l it is written, With men ... 1Cor 14:21 3551
obedience, as also saith the l ... 1Cor 14:34 3551
and the strength of sin is the l ... 1Cor 15:56 3551
justified by the works of the l ... Gal 2:16 3551
and not by the works of the l ... Gal 2:16 3551
for by the works of the l shall ... Gal 2:16 3551
For I through the l am dead to ... Gal 2:19 3551
through the l am dead to the l ... Gal 2:19 3551
if righteousness come by the l ... Gal 2:21 3551
the Spirit by the works of the l ... Gal 3:2 3551
doeth he it by the works of the l ... Gal 3:5 3551
of the l are under the curse ... Gal 3:10 3551
in the book of the l to do them ... Gal 3:10 3551
by the l in the sight of God ... Gal 3:11 3551
And the l is not of faith ... Gal 3:12 3551
us from the curse of the l ... Gal 3:13 3551
before of God in Christ, the l ... Gal 3:17 3551
if the inheritance be of the l ... Gal 3:18 3551
Wherefore then serveth the l ... Gal 3:19 3551
Is the l then against the ... Gal 3:21 3551
for if there had been a l given ... Gal 3:21 3551
should have been by the l ... Gal 3:21 3551
came, we were kept under the l ... Gal 3:23 3551
Wherefore the l was our ... Gal 3:24 3551
made of a woman, made under the l ... Gal 4:4 3551
redeem them that were under the l ... Gal 4:5 3551
ye that desire to be under the l ... Gal 4:21 3551
do ye not hear the l ... Gal 4:21 3551
he is a debtor to do the whole l ... Gal 5:3 3551
of you are justified by the l ... Gal 5:4 3551
For all the l is fulfilled in one ... Gal 5:14 3551
Spirit, ye are not under the l ... Gal 5:18 3551
against such there is no l ... Gal 5:23 3551
and so fulfil the l of Christ ... Gal 6:2 3551
who are circumcised keep the l ... Gal 6:13 3551
even the l of commandments ... Eph 2:15 3551
as touching the l, a Pharisee ... Phil 3:5 3551
righteousness which is in the l ... Phil 3:6 3551
righteousness, which is of the l ... Phil 3:9 3551
Desiring to be teachers of the l ... 1Ti 1:7 3547
But we know that the l is good ... 1Ti 1:8 3551
that the l is not made for a ... 1Ti 1:9 3551
and strivings about the l ... Titus 3:9 3544
of the people according to the l ... Heb 7:5 3551
it the people received the l ... Heb 7:11 3549
necessity a change also of the l ... Heb 7:12 3551
not after the l of a carnal ... Heb 7:16 3551
For the l made nothing perfect, ... Heb 7:19 3551
For the l maketh men high priests ... Heb 7:28 3551
the oath, which was since the l ... Heb 7:28 3551
offer gifts according to the l ... Heb 8:4 3551
all the people according to the l ... Heb 9:19 3551
are by the l purged with blood ... Heb 9:22 3551
For the l having a shadow of good ... Heb 10:1 3551
which are offered by the l ... Heb 10:8 3551
He that despised Moses' l died ... Heb 10:28 3551
into the perfect l of liberty ... Jas 1:25 3551
If ye fulfil the royal l ... Jas 2:8 3551
of the l as transgressors ... Jas 2:9 3551
whosoever shall keep the whole l ... Jas 2:10 3551
become a transgressor of the l ... Jas 2:11 3551
be judged by the l of liberty ... Jas 2:12 3551
evil of the l, and judgeth the l ... Jas 4:11 3551
but if thou judge the l ... Jas 4:11 3551
thou art not a doer of the l ... Jas 4:11 3551
sin transgresseth also the l ... 1Jn 3:4 4160,458
sin is the transgression of the l ... 1Jn 3:4 458

LAWFUL {39}

it shall not be l to impose toll ... Ezr 7:24 7990
or the l captive delivered ... Is 49:24 6662
be just, and do that which is l ... Eze 18:5 4941
the son hath done that which is l ... Eze 18:19 4941
statutes, and do that which is l ... Eze 18:21 4941
and doeth that which is l ... Eze 18:27 4941
his sin, and do that which is l ... Eze 33:14 4941
he hath done that which is l ... Eze 33:16 4941
wickedness, and do that which is l ... Eze 33:19 4941
not l to do upon the sabbath day ... Mt 12:2 1832
which was not l for him to eat, ... Mt 12:4 1832
Is it l to heal on the sabbath ... Mt 12:10 1832
Wherefore it is l to do well on ... Mt 12:12 1832
It is not l for thee to have her ... Mt 14:4 1832
Is it l for a man to put away his ... Mt 19:3 1832
Is it not l for me to do what I ... Mt 20:15 1833
Is it l to give tribute unto ... Mt 22:17 1833
It is not l for to put them into ... Mt 27:6 1833
sabbath day that which is not l ... Mk 2:24 1833
which is not l to eat but for the ... Mk 2:26 1833
Is it l to do good on the sabbath ... Mk 3:4 1833
It is not l for thee to have thy ... Mk 6:18 1833
Is it l for a man to put away his ... Mk 10:2 1833
Is it l to give tribute to Caesar ... Mk 12:14 1833
not l to do on the sabbath days ... Lk 6:2 1833
which it is not l to eat but for ... Lk 6:4 1833
Is it l on the sabbath days to do ... Lk 6:9 1833
Is it l to heal on the sabbath ... Lk 14:3 1833
Is it l for us to give tribute ... Lk 20:22 1833
it is not l for thee to carry thy ... Jn 5:10 1833
It is not l for us to put any man ... Jn 18:31 1833
which are not l for us to receive ... Acts 16:21 1833
be determined in a l assembly ... Acts 19:39 1772
Is it l for you to scourge a man ... Acts 22:25 1832
All things are l unto me, but all ... 1Cor 6:12 1832
all things are l for me, but I ... 1Cor 6:12 1832
All things are l for me, but all ... 1Cor 10:23 1832
all things are l for me, but all ... 1Cor 10:23 1832
which it is not l for a man to ... 2Cor 12:4 1832

LAWFULLY {2}

law is good, if a man use it l ... 1Ti 1:8 3545
not crowned, except he strive l ... 2Ti 2:5 3545

LAWGIVER {7}

nor a l from between his feet, ... Gen 49:10 2710
it, by the direction of the l ... Num 21:18 2710
there, in a portion of the l ... Deut 33:21 2710
Judah is my l ... Ps 60:7 2710
Judah is my l ... Ps 108:8 2710
is our judge, the LORD is our l ... Is 33:22 2710
There is one l, who is able to ... Jas 4:12 3550

LAWLESS {1}

a righteous man, but for the l ... 1Ti 1:9 459

LAWS {20}

my statutes, and my l ... Gen 26:5 8451
to keep my commandments and my l ... Ex 16:28 8451
the statutes of God, and his l ... Ex 18:16 8451
shalt teach them ordinances and l ... Ex 18:20 8451
the statutes and judgments and l ... Lev 26:46 8451
all such as know the l of thy God ... Ezr 7:25 1882
them right judgments, and true l ... Neh 9:13 8451
them precepts, statutes, and l ... Neh 9:14 8451
among the l of the Persians ... Est 1:19 1881
their l are diverse from all ... Est 3:8 1881
neither keep they the king's l ... Est 3:8 1881
his statutes, and keep his l ... Ps 105:45 8541
they have transgressed the l ... Is 24:5 8451
thereof, and all the l thereof ... Eze 43:11 8451
of the LORD, and all the l thereof ... Eze 44:5 8451
and they shall keep my l and my ... Eze 44:24 8451
and think to change times and l ... Dan 7:25 1882
LORD our God, to walk in his l ... Dan 9:10 8451
I will put my l into their mind, ... Heb 8:10 3551
I will put my l into their hearts ... Heb 10:16 3551

LAWYER {3}

Then one of them, which was a l ... Mt 22:35 3544
And, behold, a certain l stood up ... Lk 10:25 3544
Bring Zenas the l and Apollos on ... Titus 3:13 3544

LAWYERS {5}

l rejected the counsel of God ... Lk 7:30 3544
Then answered one of the l ... Lk 11:45 3544
he said, Woe unto you also, ye l ... Lk 11:46 3544
Woe unto you, l ... Lk 11:52 3544
Jesus answering spake unto the l ... Lk 14:3 3544

LAY {241}

But before they l down, the men ... Gen 19:4 7901
went in, and l with her father ... Gen 19:33 7901
he perceived not when she l down ... Gen 19:33 7901
I l yesternight with my father ... Gen 19:34 7901
the younger arose, and l with him ... Gen 19:35 7901
he perceived not when she l down ... Gen 19:35 7901
L not thine hand upon the lad, ... Gen 22:12 7971
l down in that place to sleep ... Gen 28:11 7901

And he *l* with her that night	Gen 30:16	7901
l with her, and defiled her	Gen 34:2	7901
l with Bilhah his father's	Gen 35:22	7901
wilderness, and *l* no hand upon him	Gen 37:22	7971
l up corn under the hand of	Gen 41:35	6651
heretofore, ye shall *l* upon them	Ex 5:8	7760
that I may *l* my hand upon Egypt,	Ex 7:4	5414
the dew *l* round about the host	Ex 16:13	7902
when the dew that *l* was gone up	Ex 16:14	7902
there *l* a small round thing	Ex 16:14	
that which remaineth over *l* up	Ex 16:23	3241
l it up before the LORD, to be	Ex 16:33	3241
woman's husband will *l* upon him	Ex 21:22	7896
shalt thou *l* upon him usury	Ex 22:25	7760
l the wood in order upon the fire	Lev 1:7	
shall *l* the parts, the head, and	Lev 1:8	
the priest shall *l* them in order	Lev 1:12	
it, and *l* frankincense thereon	Lev 2:15	7760
he shall *l* his hand upon the head	Lev 3:2	5564
he shall *l* his hand upon the head	Lev 3:8	5564
he shall *l* his hand upon the head	Lev 3:13	5564
shall *l* his hand upon the	Lev 4:4	5564
of the congregation shall *l* their	Lev 4:15	5564
he shall *l* his hand upon the head	Lev 4:24	5564
he shall *l* his hand upon the head	Lev 4:29	5564
he shall *l* his hand upon the head	Lev 4:33	5564
l the burnt offering in order	Lev 6:12	
Aaron shall *l* both his hands upon	Lev 16:21	5564
let all that heard him *l* their	Lev 24:14	5564
the Levites shall *l* their hands	Num 8:12	5564
l not the sin upon us, wherein we	Num 12:11	7896
thou shalt *l* them up in the	Num 17:4	3241
l them up without the camp in a	Num 19:9	3241
he *l* down as a lion, and as a	Num 24:9	7901
spirit, and *l* thine hand upon him	Num 27:18	5564
but will *l* them upon all them	Deut 7:15	5414
Therefore shall ye *l* up these my	Deut 11:18	7760
your God shall *l* the fear of you	Deut 11:25	5414
shalt *l* it up within thy gates	Deut 14:28	3241
l not innocent blood unto thy	Deut 21:8	5414
his mother *l* hold on him, and	Deut 21:19	
the man that *l* with the woman	Deut 22:22	7901
only that *l* with her shall die	Deut 22:25	7901
l hold on her, and lie with her,	Deut 22:28	
Then the man that *l* with her	Deut 22:29	7901
he shall *l* the foundation thereof	Josh 6:26	
l thee an ambush for the city	Josh 8:2	7760
all that *l* near Ashdod, with	Josh 15:46	
her tent, behold, Sisera *l* dead	Judg 4:22	5307
feet he bowed, he fell, he *l* down	Judg 5:27	7901
l them upon this rock, and pour	Judg 6:20	3241
east *l* along in the valley like	Judg 7:12	5307
it, that the tent *l* along	Judg 7:13	5307
because she *l* sore upon him	Judg 14:17	
Samson *l* till midnight, and arose	Judg 16:3	7901
l thine hand upon thy mouth, and	Judg 18:19	7760
uncover his feet, and *l* thee down	Ruth 3:4	7901
and, behold, a woman *l* at his feet	Ruth 3:8	7901
she *l* at his feet until the	Ruth 3:14	7901
how they *l* with the women that	1Sa 2:22	7901
And he went and *l* down	1Sa 3:5	7901
went and *l* down in his place	1Sa 3:9	7901
Samuel *l* until the morning, and	1Sa 3:15	7901
the LORD, and *l* it upon the cart	1Sa 6:8	5414
l it for a reproach upon all	1Sa 11:2	7760
l down naked all that day and all	1Sa 19:24	5307
beheld the place where Saul *l*	1Sa 26:5	7901
Saul *l* in the trench, and the	1Sa 26:5	7901
Saul *l* sleeping within the trench	1Sa 26:7	7901
the people *l* round about him	1Sa 26:7	7901
l thee hold on one of the young	2Sa 2:21	
who *l* on a bed at noon	2Sa 4:5	7901
he *l* on his bed in his bedchamber	2Sa 4:7	7901
in unto him, and he *l* with her	2Sa 11:4	7901
l in his bosom, and was unto him	2Sa 12:3	7901
l all night upon the earth	2Sa 12:16	7901
went in unto her, and *l* with her	2Sa 12:24	7901
L thee down on thy bed, and make	2Sa 13:5	7901
So Amnon *l* down, and made himself	2Sa 13:6	7901
she, forced her, and *l* with her	2Sa 13:14	7901
his garments, and *l* on the earth	2Sa 13:31	7901
sustenance while he *l* at Mahanaim	2Sa 19:32	7871
to *l* the foundation of the house	1Kin 5:17	
that *l* on forty-five pillars,	1Kin 7:3	
the altar, saying, *L* hold on him	1Kin 13:4	
l my bones beside his bones	1Kin 13:31	3241
l it on wood, and put no fire	1Kin 18:23	7760
l it on wood, and put no fire	1Kin 18:23	7760
And as he *l* and slept under a	1Kin 19:5	7901
l in sackcloth, and went softly	1Kin 21:27	7901
into the chamber, and *l* there	2Kin 4:11	7901
l my staff upon the face of the	2Kin 4:29	7760
l upon the child, and put his	2Kin 4:34	7901
for Joram *l* there	2Kin 9:16	7901
L ye them in two heaps at the	2Kin 10:8	7760
be to *l* waste fenced cities into	2Kin 19:25	
to *l* the foundation of the heaps	2Chr 31:7	
for as long as she *l* desolate she	2Chr 36:21	
of such as *l* in wait by the way	Ezr 8:31	
so again, I will *l* hands on you	Neh 13:21	7971
sought to *l* hand on the king	Est 2:21	7971
he thought scorn to *l* hands on	Est 3:6	7971
many *l* in sackcloth and ashes	Est 4:3	3331
who sought to *l* hand on the king	Est 6:2	7971
to *l* hand on such as sought their	Est 9:2	7971
that might *l* his hand upon us	Job 9:33	7896
L down now, put me in a surety	Job 17:3	7760
l your hand upon your mouth	Job 21:5	7760
l up his words in thine heart	Job 22:22	7760
Then shalt thou *l* up gold as dust	Job 22:24	7896
the dew *l* all night upon my	Job 29:19	3885
For he will not *l* upon man more	Job 34:23	7760
I will *l* mine hand upon my mouth	Job 40:4	7760
L thine hand upon him, remember	Job 41:8	7760
I will both *l* me down in peace,	Ps 4:8	7901
l mine honour in the dust	Ps 7:5	7931
after my life *l* snares for me	Ps 38:12	
they that *l* wait for my soul take	Ps 71:10	
where she may *l* her young	Ps 84:3	7896
l them down in their dens	Ps 104:22	7257
let us *l* wait for blood, let us	Prov 1:11	
they *l* wait for their own blood	Prov 1:18	
life to them that *l* hold upon her	Prov 3:18	
l up my commandments with thee	Prov 7:1	6845
Wise men *l* up knowledge	Prov 10:14	6845
L not wait, O wicked man, against	Prov 24:15	
l thine hand upon thy mouth	Prov 30:32	
to *l* hold on folly, till I might	Eccl 2:3	
the living will *l* it to his heart	Eccl 7:2	5414
And I will *l* it waste	Is 5:6	
that *l* field to field, till there	Is 5:8	7126
l hold of the prey, and shall	Is 5:29	
they shall *l* their hand upon Edom	Is 11:14	7971
anger, to *l* the land desolate	Is 13:9	
will *l* low the haughtiness of the	Is 13:11	
David will I *l* upon his shoulder	Is 22:22	5414
l low, and bring to the ground,	Is 25:12	
I *l* in Zion for a foundation a	Is 28:16	
also will I *l* to the line	Is 28:17	7760
will *l* siege against thee with a	Is 29:3	
l a snare for him that reproveth	Is 29:21	
which the LORD shall *l* upon him	Is 30:32	5117
the great owl make her nest, and *l*	Is 34:15	4422
of dragons, where each *l*, shall	Is 35:7	7258
that thou shouldest be to *l* waste	Is 37:26	
l it for a plaister upon the boil	Is 38:21	
so that thou didst not *l* these	Is 47:7	7760
l the foundations of the earth,	Is 51:16	
I will *l* thy stones with fair	Is 54:11	7257
l thy foundations with sapphires	Is 54:11	
they *l* wait, as he that setteth	Jer 5:26	
I will *l* stumblingblocks before	Jer 6:21	5414
They shall *l* hold on bow and spear	Jer 6:23	
I *l* a stumblingblock before him,	Eze 3:20	5414
l it before thee, and pourtray	Eze 4:1	5414
l siege against it, and build a	Eze 4:2	5414
thou shalt *l* siege against it	Eze 4:3	
l the iniquity of the house of	Eze 4:4	7760
I will *l* bands upon thee, and thou	Eze 4:8	
I will *l* the dead carcases of the	Eze 6:5	5414
she *l* down among lions, she	Eze 19:2	7257
for in her youth they *l* with her	Eze 23:8	7901
I will *l* my vengeance upon Edom	Eze 25:14	5414
when I shall *l* my vengeance upon	Eze 25:17	5414
and they shall *l* thy stones	Eze 26:12	7760
l away their robes, and put off	Eze 26:16	5493
I will *l* thee before kings, that	Eze 28:17	5414
I will *l* thy flesh upon the	Eze 32:5	5414
For I will *l* the land most	Eze 33:28	5414
I will *l* thy cities waste, and	Eze 35:4	7760
it, and *l* no famine upon you	Eze 36:29	5414
whereas it *l* desolate in the	Eze 36:34	
I will *l* sinews upon you, and will	Eze 37:6	5414
there shall they *l* the most holy	Eze 42:13	3241
but there they shall *l* their	Eze 42:14	3241
l them in the holy chambers, and	Eze 44:19	3241
they *l* themselves down upon	Amos 2:8	5186
and he *l*, and was fast asleep	Jonah 1:5	7901
l not upon us innocent blood	Jonah 1:14	5414
idols thereof will I *l* desolate	Mic 1:7	7760
they shall *l* their hand upon	Mic 7:16	7760
they shall *l* hold every one on	Zec 14:13	
and if ye will not *l* it to heart	Mal 2:2	7760
because ye do not *l* it to heart	Mal 2:2	7760
L not up for yourselves treasures	Mt 6:19	
But *l* up for yourselves treasures	Mt 6:20	
man hath not where to *l* his head	Mt 8:20	*2827*
l thy hand upon her, and she shall	Mt 9:18	*2007*
day, will he not *l* hold on it	Mt 12:11	
they sought to *l* hands on him	Mt 21:46	
l them on men's shoulders	Mt 23:4	*2007*
see the place where the Lord *l*	Mt 28:6	*2749*
wife's mother *l* sick of a fever	Mk 1:30	*2621*
wherein the sick of the palsy *l*	Mk 2:4	*2621*
they went out to *l* hold on him	Mk 3:21	
l thy hands on her, that she may	Mk 5:23	*2007*
And they sought to *l* hold on him	Mk 12:12	
which *l* bound with them that had	Mk 15:7	
they shall *l* hands on the sick,	Mk 16:18	*2007*
him in, and to *l* him before him	Lk 5:18	*5087*
and took up that whereon he *l*	Lk 5:25	*2621*
years of age, and she *l* a dying	Lk 8:42	
man hath not where to *l* his head	Lk 9:58	*2827*
shall *l* thee even with the ground	Lk 19:44	*1474*
hour sought to *l* hands on him	Lk 20:19	*1911*
they shall *l* their hands on you,	Lk 21:12	*1911*
In these *l* a great multitude of	Jn 5:3	*2621*
I *l* down my life for the sheep	Jn 10:15	*5087*
because I *l* down my life, that I	Jn 10:17	*5087*
but I *l* it down of myself	Jn 10:18	*5087*
I have power to *l* it down	Jn 10:18	*5087*
was a cave, and a stone *l* upon it	Jn 11:38	*1945*
I will *l* down my life for thy	Jn 13:37	*5087*
Wilt thou *l* down thy life for my	Jn 13:38	*5087*
that a man *l* down his life for	Jn 15:13	*5087*
l not this sin to their charge	Acts 7:60	*2476*
that on whomsoever I *l* hands	Acts 8:19	*2007*
to *l* upon you no greater burden	Acts 15:28	*2007*
and no small tempest *l* on us	Acts 27:20	*1945*
of Publius *l* sick of a fever	Acts 28:8	*2621*
Who shall *l* any thing to the	Rom 8:33	*1458*
I *l* in Sion a stumblingstone and	Rom 9:33	*5087*
can no man *l* than that is laid	1Cor 3:11	*5087*
one of you *l* by him in store	1Cor 16:2	*5087*
ought not to *l* up for the parents	2Cor 12:14	*2343*
L hands suddenly on no man,	1Ti 5:22	*2007*
l hold on eternal life, whereunto	1Ti 6:12	*1949*
that they may *l* hold on eternal	1Ti 6:19	*1949*
who have fled for refuge to *l*	Heb 6:18	
let us *l* aside every weight, and	Heb 12:1	*659*
Wherefore *l* apart all filthiness	Jas 1:21	*659*
I *l* in Sion a chief corner stone,	1Pet 2:6	*5087*
we ought to *l* down our lives for	1Jn 3:16	*5087*

LAYEDST {1}

takest up that thou *l* not down	Lk 19:21	*5087*

LAYEST {2}

that thou *l* the burden of all	Num 11:11	7760
wherefore then *l* thou a snare for	1Sa 28:9	

LAYETH {18}

God *l* up his iniquity for his	Job 21:19	6845
yet God *l* not folly to them	Job 24:12	7760
of him that *l* at him cannot hold	Job 41:26	5381
he *l* up the depth in storehouses	Ps 33:7	5414
Who *l* the beams of his chambers	Ps 104:3	7760
He *l* up sound wisdom for the	Prov 2:7	6845
but a fool *l* open his folly	Prov 13:16	
lips, and *l* up deceit within him	Prov 26:24	7896
She *l* her hands to the spindle,	Prov 31:19	7971
the lofty city, he *l* it low	Is 26:5	
he *l* it low, even to the ground	Is 26:5	
the son of man that *l* hold on it	Is 56:2	
and no man *l* it to heart	Is 57:1	7760
mouth, but in heart he *l* his wait	Jer 9:8	7760
because no man *l* it to heart	Jer 12:11	7760
l the foundation of the earth, and	Zec 12:1	
So is he that *l* up treasure for	Lk 12:21	
he *l* it on his shoulders,	Lk 15:5	*2007*

LAYING {13}

or hurl at him by *l* of wait	Num 35:20	
him any thing without *l* of wait	Num 35:22	
they commune of *l* snares privily	Ps 64:5	2934
For *l* aside the commandment of	Mk 7:8	*863*
L wait for him, and seeking to	Lk 11:54	*1748*
when Simon saw that through *l* on	Acts 8:18	*1936*
But their *l* await was known of	Acts 9:24	*1917*
l wait in the way to kill him	Acts 25:3	*4160*
with the *l* on of the hands of the	1Ti 4:14	*1936*
L up in store for themselves a	1Ti 6:19	*597*
not *l* again the foundation of	Heb 6:1	*2598*
and of *l* on of hands, and of	Heb 6:2	*1936*
Wherefore *l* aside all malice, and	1Pet 2:1	*659*

LAZARUS *(laz'-a-rus)* {15}

1. Name for a beggar in a parable of Jesus.

was a certain beggar named *L*	Lk 16:20	*2976*
afar off, and *L* in his bosom	Lk 16:23	*2976*
have mercy on me, and send *L*	Lk 16:24	*2976*
things, and likewise *L* evil things	Lk 16:25	*2976*

2. Man raised from the dead by Jesus.

a certain man was sick, named *L*	Jn 11:1	*2976*
hair, whose brother *L* was sick	Jn 11:2	*2976*
loved Martha, and her sister, and *L*	Jn 11:5	*2976*
unto them, Our friend *L* sleepeth	Jn 11:11	*2976*
unto them plainly, *L* is dead	Jn 11:14	*2976*
he cried with a loud voice, *L*	Jn 11:43	*2976*
where *L* was which had been dead,	Jn 12:1	*2976*
but *L* was one of them that sat at	Jn 12:2	*2976*
but that they might see *L* also	Jn 12:9	*2976*
they might put *L* also to death	Jn 12:10	*2976*
when he called *L* out of his grave	Jn 12:17	*2976*

LEAD {60}

I will *l* on softly, according as	Gen 33:14	5095
of a cloud, to *l* them the way	Ex 13:21	5148
they sank as *l* in the mighty	Ex 15:10	5777
l the people unto the place of	Ex 32:34	5148
them, and which may *l* them out	Num 27:17	3318
the iron, the tin, and the *l*	Num 31:22	5777
whither the LORD shall *l* you	Deut 4:27	5090
of the armies to *l* the people	Deut 20:9	7218
whither the LORD shall *l* thee	Deut 28:37	5090
So the LORD alone did *l* him	Deut 32:12	5148
l thy captivity captive, thou son	Judg 5:12	
that they may *l* them away	1Sa 30:22	5090
before them that *l* them captive	2Chr 30:9	
them by day, to *l* them in the way	Neh 9:19	5148
pen and *l* in the rock for ever	Job 19:24	5777
L me, O LORD, in thy	Ps 5:8	5148
L me in thy truth, and teach me	Ps 25:5	1869
l me in a plain path, because of	Ps 27:11	5148
for thy name's sake *l* me, and	Ps 31:3	5148
let them *l* me	Ps 43:3	5148
who will *l* me into Edom	Ps 60:9	5148
l me to the rock that is higher	Ps 61:2	5148
who will *l* me into Edom	Ps 108:10	5148
the LORD shall *l* them forth with	Ps 125:5	3212
Even there shall thy hand *l* me	Ps 139:10	5148
l me in the way everlasting	Ps 139:24	5148
l me into the land of uprightness	Ps 143:10	5148
When thou goest, it shall *l* thee	Prov 6:22	5148
I *l* in the way of righteousness,	Prov 8:20	1980
I would *l* thee, and bring thee	Song 8:2	5090
they which *l* thee cause thee to	Is 3:12	833
and a little child shall *l* them	Is 11:6	5090

l away the Egyptians prisoners Is 20:4 5090
shall gently *l* those that are Is 40:11 5095
I will *l* them in paths that they Is 42:16 1869
hath mercy on them shall *l* them Is 49:10 5090
I will *l* him also, and restore Is 57:18 5148
so didst thou *l* thy people Is 63:14 5090
the *l* is consumed of the fire Jer 6:29 5777
with supplications will I *l* them Jer 31:9 2986
he shall *l* Zedekiah to Babylon Jer 32:5 3212
are brass, and tin, and iron, and *l* Eze 22:18 5777
silver, and brass, and iron, and *l* Eze 22:20 5777
with silver, iron, tin, and *l* Eze 27:12 5777
her maids shall *l* her as with the Nah 2:7 5090
there was lifted up a talent of *l* Zec 5:7 5777
he cast the weight of *l* upon the Zec 5:8 5777
l us not into temptation, but Mt 6:13 *1533*
And if the blind *l* the blind Mt 15:14 *3594*
But when they shall *l* you Mk 13:11 *71*
take him, and *l* him away safely Mk 14:44 *520*
them, Can the blind *l* the blind Lk 6:39 *3594*
And *l* us not into temptation Lk 11:4 *1533*
stall, and *l* him away to watering Lk 13:15 *520*
seeking some to *l* him by the hand Acts 13:11 *5497*
we not power to *l* about a sister 1Cor 9:5 *4013*
that we may *l* a quiet and 1Ti 2:2 *1236*
l captive silly women laden with 2Ti 3:6 *162*
l them out of the land of Egypt Heb 8:9 *1806*
them, and shall *l* them unto living Rev 7:17 *3594*

LEADER {3}
was the *l* of the Aaronites 1Chr 12:27 5057
and hundreds, and with every *l* 1Chr 13:1 5057
for a witness to the people, a *l* Is 55:4 5057

LEADERS {3}
mighty men of valour, and the *l* 2Chr 32:21 5057
For the *l* of this people cause Is 9:16 833
they be blind *l* of the blind Mt 15:14 *3595*

LEADEST {1}
thou that *l* Joseph like a flock Ps 80:1 5090

LEADETH {14}
unto the way that *l* to Ophrah 1Sa 13:17
He *l* counsellors away spoiled, and Job 12:17 3212
He *l* princes away spoiled, and Job 12:19 3212
he *l* me beside the still waters Ps 23:2 5095
he *l* me in the paths of Ps 23:3 5090
l him into the way that is not Prov 16:29 3212
which *l* thee by the way that thou Is 48:17 1869
that *l* to destruction, and many Mt 7:13 *520*
which *l* unto life, and few there Mt 7:14 *520*
l them up into an high mountain Mk 9:2 *399*
own sheep by name, and *l* them out Jn 10:3 *1806*
iron gate that *l* unto the city Acts 12:10 *5342*
of God *l* thee to repentance Rom 2:4 *71*
He that *l* into captivity shall go Rev 13:10 *4863*

LEAF {11}
mouth was an olive *l* pluckt off Gen 8:11 5929
of a shaken *l* shall chase them Lev 26:36 5929
Wilt thou break a *l* driven to Job 13:25 5929
his *l* also shall not wither Ps 1:3 5929
shall be as an oak whose *l* fadeth Is 1:30 5929
as the *l* falleth off from the Is 34:4 5929
and we all do fade as a *l* Is 64:6 5929
the fig tree, and the *l* shall fade Jer 8:13 5929
cometh, but her *l* shall be green Jer 17:8 5929
whose *l* shall not fade, neither Eze 47:12 5929
the *l* thereof for medicine Eze 47:12 5929

LEAGUE {19}
now therefore make ye a *l* with us Josh 9:6 1285
and how shall we make a *l* with you Josh 9:7 1285
therefore now make ye a *l* with us Josh 9:11 1285
made a *l* with them, to let them Josh 9:15 1285
after they had made a *l* with them Josh 9:16 1285
ye shall make no *l* with the Judg 2:2 1285
made a *l* with the son of Jesse 1Sa 22:8 3772
saying also, Make thy *l* with me 2Sa 3:12 1285
I will make a *l* with thee 2Sa 3:13 1285
that they may make a *l* with thee 2Sa 3:21 1285
king David made a *l* with them in 2Sa 5:3 1285
and they two made a *l* together 1Kin 5:12 1285
There is a *l* between me and thee, 1Kin 15:19 1285
break thy *l* with Baasha king of 1Kin 15:19 1285
There is a *l* between me and thee, 2Chr 16:3 1285
break thy *l* with Baasha king of 2Chr 16:3 1285
For thou shalt be in *l* with the Job 5:23 1285
the men of the land that is in *l* Eze 30:5 1285
after the *l* made with him he Dan 11:23 2266

LEAH *(le'-ah)* {29} See LEAH'S. *Wife of Jacob.*
the name of the elder was *L* Gen 29:16 3812
L was tender eyed Gen 29:17 3812
that he took *L* his daughter Gen 29:23 3812
Laban gave unto his daughter *L* Gen 29:24 3812
in the morning, behold, it was *L* Gen 29:25 3812
he loved also Rachel more than *L* Gen 29:30 3812
the LORD saw that *L* was hated Gen 29:31 3812
L conceived, and bare a son, and Gen 29:32 3812
When *L* saw that she had left Gen 30:9 3812
And *L* said, A troop cometh Gen 30:11 3812
L said, Happy am I, for the Gen 30:13 3812
and brought them unto his mother *L* Gen 30:14 3812
Then Rachel said to *L*, Give me, I Gen 30:14 3812
L went out to meet him, and said, Gen 30:16 3812
And God hearkened unto *L*, and she Gen 30:17 3812
L said, God hath given me my hire Gen 30:18 3812
L conceived again, and bare Jacob Gen 30:19 3812
L said, God hath endued me with a Gen 30:20 3812
L to the field unto his flock, Gen 31:4 3812
L answered and said unto him, Is Gen 31:14 3812
And he divided the children unto *L* Gen 33:1 3812
and their children foremost, and *L* Gen 33:2 3812
L also with her children came Gen 33:7 3812
And Dinah the daughter of *L* Gen 34:1 3812
The sons of *L*; Reuben Gen 35:23 3812
These be the sons of *L*, which she Gen 46:15 3812
whom Laban gave to *L* his daughter Gen 46:18 3812
and there I buried *L* Gen 49:31 3812
thine house like Rachel and like *L* Ruth 4:11 3812

LEAH'S *(le'-ahs)* {5}
Zilpah *L* maid bare Jacob a son Gen 30:10 3812
Zilpah *L* maid bare Jacob a second Gen 30:12 3812
into Jacob's tent, and into *L* tent Gen 31:33 3812
Then went he out of *L* tent Gen 31:33 3812
And the sons of Zilpah, *L* handmaid Gen 35:26 3812

LEAN {11}
And the *l* and the ill favoured kine Gen 41:20 7534
land is, whether it be fat or *l* Num 13:20 7330
standeth, that I may *l* upon them Judg 16:26 8172
the king's son, *l* from day to day 2Sa 13:4 1800
upon Egypt, on which if a man *l* 2Kin 18:21 5564
He shall *l* upon his house, but it Job 8:15 8172
and *l* not unto thine own Prov 3:5 8172
fatness of his flesh shall wax *l* Is 17:4 7329
whereon if a man *l*, it will go Is 36:6 5564
cattle and between the *l* cattle Eze 34:20 7330
yet will they *l* upon the LORD Mic 3:11 8172

LEANED {6}
behold, Saul *l* upon his spear 2Sa 1:6 8172
king *l* answered the man of God 2Kin 7:2 8172
the lord on whose hand he *l* to 2Kin 7:17 8172
and when they *l* upon thee, thou Eze 29:7 8172
l his hand on the wall, and a Amos 5:19 5564
which also *l* on his breast at Jn 21:20 *377*

LEANETH {2}
or that *l* on a staff, or that 2Sa 3:29 2388
he *l* on my hand, and I bow myself 2Kin 5:18 8127

LEANFLESHED {3}
of the river, ill favoured and *l* Gen 41:3 1851,1320
l kine did eat up the seven well Gen 41:4 1851,1320
poor and very ill favoured and *l* Gen 41:19 7534

LEANING {3}
wilderness, *l* upon her beloved Song 8:5 7514
Now there was *l* on Jesus' bosom Jn 13:23 *345*
l upon the top of his staff Heb 11:21

LEANNESS {5}
my *l* rising up in me beareth Job 16:8 3585
but sent *l* into their soul Ps 106:15 7332
hosts, send among his fat ones *l* Is 10:16 7332
But I said, My *l*, my *l*, Is 24:16 7334

LEANNOTH *(le-an'-noth)* {1} *A musical choir.*
chief Musician upon Mahalath *L* Ps 88:*t* 6030

LEAP {9}
all the rams which *l* upon the Gen 31:12 5927
to *l* withal upon the earth Lev 11:21 5425
he shall *l* from Bashan Deut 33:22 2178
lamps, and sparks of fire *l* out Job 41:19 4422
Why *l* ye, ye high hills Ps 68:16 7520
shall the lame man *l* as an hart Is 35:6 1801
tops of mountains shall they *l* Joel 2:5 7540
all those that *l* on the threshold Zeph 1:9 1801
ye in that day, and *l* for joy Lk 6:23 *4640*

LEAPED {8}
the rams which *l* upon the cattle Gen 31:10 5927
by my God have I *l* over a wall 2Sa 22:30 1801
they *l* upon the altar which was 1Kin 18:26 6452
and by my God have I *l* over a wall Ps 18:29 1801
of Mary, the babe *l* in her womb Lk 1:41 *4640*
the babe *l* in my womb for joy Lk 1:44 *4640*
And he *l* and walked Acts 14:10 *242*
the evil spirit was *l* on them Acts 19:16 *2177*

LEAPING {4}
a window, and saw king David *l* 2Sa 6:16 6339
he cometh *l* upon the mountains, Song 2:8 1801
he *l* up stood, and walked, and Acts 3:8 *1814*
into the temple, walking, and *l* Acts 3:8 *242*

LEARN {32}
that they may *l* to fear me all Deut 4:10 3925
ears this day, that ye may *l* them Deut 5:1 3925
that thou mayest *l* to fear the Deut 14:23 3925
that he may *l* to fear the LORD Deut 17:19 3925
thou shalt not *l* to do after the Deut 18:9 3925
they may hear, and that they may *l* Deut 31:12 3925
l to fear the LORD your God, as Deut 31:13 3925
that I might *l* thy statutes Ps 119:71 3925
that I may *l* thy commandments Ps 119:73 3925
Lest thou *l* his ways, and get a Prov 22:25 502
L to do well Is 1:17 3925
neither shall they *l* war any more Is 2:4 3925
of the world will *l* righteousness Is 26:9 3925
yet will he not *l* righteousness Is 26:10 3925
that murmured shall *l* doctrine Is 29:24 3925
L not the way of the heathen, and Jer 10:2 3925
l the ways of my people, to swear Jer 12:16 3925
neither shall they *l* war any more Mic 4:3 3925
l what that meaneth, I will have Mt 9:13 *3129*
Take my yoke upon you, and *l* of me Mt 11:29 *3129*
Now *l* a parable of the fig tree Mt 24:32 *3129*
Now *l* a parable of the fig tree Mk 13:28 *3129*
that ye might *l* in us not to 1Cor 4:6 *3129*
one by one, that all may *l* 1Cor 14:31 *3129*
And if they will *l* any thing 1Cor 14:35 *3129*
This only would I *l* of you Gal 3:2 *3129*
that they may *l* not to blaspheme 1Ti 1:20 *3811*
Let the woman *l* in silence with 1Ti 2:11 *3129*
let them *l* first to shew piety at 1Ti 5:4 *3129*
And withal they *l* to be idle 1Ti 5:13 *3129*
let ours also *l* to maintain good Titus 3:14 *3129*
no man could *l* that song but the Rev 14:3 *3129*

LEARNED {22}
for I have *l* by experience that Gen 30:27 5172
the heathen, and *l* their works Ps 106:35 3925
when I shall have *l* thy righteous Ps 119:7 3925
I neither *l* wisdom, nor have the Prov 30:3 3925
men deliver to one that is *l* Is 29:11 3045,5612
is delivered to him that is not *l* Is 29:12 3045,5612
and he saith, I am not *l* Is 29:12 3045,5612
hath given me the tongue of the *l* Is 50:4 3928
mine ear to hear as the *l* Is 50:4 3928
lion, and it *l* to catch the prey Eze 19:3 3925
l to catch the prey, and devoured Eze 19:6 3925
hath *l* of the Father, cometh unto Jn 6:45 *3129*
this man letters, having never *l* Jn 7:15 *3129*
Moses was *l* in all the wisdom of Acts 7:22 *3811*
to the doctrine which ye have *l* Rom 16:17 *3129*
But ye have not so *l* Christ Eph 4:20 *3129*
things, which ye have both *l* Phil 4:9 *3129*
for I have *l*, in whatsoever state Phil 4:11 *3129*
As ye also *l* of Epaphras our dear Col 1:7 *3129*
in the things which thou hast *l* 2Ti 3:14 *3129*
knowing of whom thou hast *l* them 2Ti 3:14 *3129*
yet *l* he obedience by the things Heb 5:8 *3129*

LEARNING {9}
man will hear, and will increase *l* Prov 1:5 3948
man, and he will increase in *l* Prov 9:9 3948
of the lips increaseth *l* Prov 16:21 3948
mouth, and addeth *l* to his lips Prov 16:23 3948
and whom they might teach the *l* Dan 1:4 5612
them knowledge and skill in all *l* Dan 1:17 5612
much *l* doth make thee mad Acts 26:24 *1121*
aforetime were written for our *l* Rom 15:4 *1319*
Ever *l*, and never able to come to 2Ti 3:7 *3129*

LEASING {2}
ye love vanity, and seek after *l* Ps 4:2 3577
shalt destroy them that speak *l* Ps 5:6 3577

LEAST See APPENDIX.

LEATHER {1}
a girdle of *l* about his loins 2Kin 1:8 5785

LEATHERN {1}
a *l* girdle about his loins Mt 3:4 *1193*

LEAVE {115}
shall a man *l* his father and his Gen 2:24 5800
for I will not *l* thee, until I Gen 28:15 5800
Let me now *l* with thee some of Gen 33:15 3322
l one of your brethren here with Gen 42:33 3241
lord, The lad cannot *l* his father Gen 44:22 5800
for if he should *l* his father Gen 44:22 5800
Let no man *l* of it till the Ex 16:19 3498
what they *l* the beasts of the Ex 23:11 3499
he shall not *l* any of it until Lev 7:15 3241
holy place, and shall *l* them there Lev 16:23 3241
thou shalt *l* them for the poor and Lev 19:10 5800
ye shall *l* none of it until the Lev 22:30 3498
thou shalt *l* them unto the poor, Lev 23:22 5800
They shall *l* none of it unto the Num 9:12 7604
And he said, *L* us not, I pray thee Num 10:31 5800
to give me *l* to go with you Num 22:13 5414
he will yet again *l* them in the Num 32:15 3241
also shall not *l* thee either corn Deut 28:51 7604
of his children which he shall *l* Deut 28:54 3498
l them in the lodging place, Josh 4:3 3241
Should I *l* my fatness, wherewith Judg 9:9 2308
unto them, Should I *l* my wine Judg 9:13 2308
said, Intreat me not to *l* thee Ruth 1:16 5800
l them, that she may glean them, Ruth 2:16 5800
lest my father *l* caring for the 1Sa 9:5 2308
let us not *l* a man of them 1Sa 14:36 7604
David earnestly asked *l* of me 1Sa 20:6
David earnestly asked *l* of me to 1Sa 20:28
if I *l* of all that pertain to him 1Sa 25:22 7604
shall not *l* to my husband neither 2Sa 14:7 7604
let him not *l* us, nor forsake us 1Kin 8:57 5800
soul liveth, I will not *l* thee 2Kin 2:2 5800
soul liveth, I will not *l* thee 2Kin 2:4 5800
soul liveth, I will not *l* thee 2Kin 2:6 5800
soul liveth, I will not *l* thee 2Kin 4:30 5800
shall eat, and shall *l* thereof 2Kin 4:43 3498
Neither did he *l* of the people to 2Kin 13:7 7604
l it for an inheritance for your 1Chr 28:8 5157
to *l* us a remnant to escape, and Ezr 9:8 7604
l it for an inheritance to your Ezr 9:12
pray you, let us *l* off this usury Neh 5:10 5800
the work cease, whilst I *l* it Neh 6:3 7503
that we would *l* the seventh year, Neh 10:31 5203
days obtained I *l* of the king Neh 13:6 7592
I will *l* off my heaviness, and Job 9:27 5800
I will *l* my complaint upon myself Job 10:1 5800
or wilt thou *l* thy labour to him Job 39:11 5800
thou wilt not *l* my soul in hell Ps 16:10 5800
l the rest of their substance to Ps 17:14 3241
l me not, neither forsake me, O Ps 27:9 5203
LORD will not *l* him in his hand Ps 37:33 5800
and *l* their wealth to others Ps 49:10 5800
l me not to mine oppressors Ps 119:121 3241
l not my soul destitute Ps 141:8 6168
Who *l* the paths of uprightness, Prov 2:13 5800
therefore *l* off contention, Prov 17:14 5203
because I should *l* it unto the Eccl 2:18 3241

L

shall he *l* it for his portion ... Eccl 2:21 5414
up against thee, *l* not thy place ... Eccl 10:4 3241
and where will ye *l* your glory ... Is 10:3 5800
ye shall *l* your name for a curse ... Is 65:15 3241
that I might *l* my people, and go ... Jer 9:2 5800
l us not ... Jer 14:9 3241
shall *l* them in the midst of his ... Jer 17:11 5800
Will a man *l* the snow of Lebanon ... Jer 18:14 5800
will not *l* thee altogether ... Jer 30:11
of Judah, to *l* you none to remain ... Jer 44:7 3498
yet will I not *l* thee wholly ... Jer 46:28
l the cities, and dwell in the ... Jer 48:28 5800
would they not *l* some gleaning ... Jer 49:9 7604
L thy fatherless children, I will ... Jer 49:11 5800
Yet will I *l* a remnant, that ye ... Eze 6:8 3498
But I will *l* a few men of them ... Eze 12:16 3498
jewels, and *l* thee naked and bare ... Eze 16:39 3241
I will *l* you there, and melt you ... Eze 22:20 3241
shall *l* thee naked and bare ... Eze 23:29 5800
I will *l* thee thrown into the ... Eze 29:5 5203
Then will I *l* thee upon the land, ... Eze 32:4 5203
l but the sixth part of thee, and ... Eze 39:2 8338
Nevertheless *l* the stump of his ... Dan 4:15 7662
yet *l* the stump of the roots ... Dan 4:23 7662
whereas they commanded to *l* the ... Dan 4:26 7662
shall he *l* his blood upon him ... Hos 12:14 5203
and *l* a blessing behind him ... Joel 2:14 7604
by a thousand shall *l* an hundred ... Amos 5:3 7604
forth by an hundred shall *l* ten ... Amos 5:3 7604
l off righteousness in the earth, ... Amos 5:7 3241
would they not *l* some grapes ... Obad 5 7604
I will also *l* in the midst of ... Zeph 3:12 7604
that it shall *l* them neither root ... Mal 4:1 5800
L there thy gift before the altar ... Mt 5:24 *863*
astray, doth he not *l* the ninety ... Mt 18:12 *863*
this cause shall a man *l* father ... Mt 19:5 *2641*
not to *l* the other undone ... Mt 23:23 *863*
And forthwith Jesus gave them *l* ... Mk 5:13 *2010*
cause shall a man *l* his father ... Mk 10:7 *2641*
l his wife behind him ... Mk 12:19 *2641*
l no children, that his brother ... Mk 12:19 *863*
not to *l* the other undone ... Lk 11:42 *863*
doth not *l* the ninety and nine in ... Lk 15:4 *2641*
they shall not *l* in thee one ... Lk 19:44 *863*
I will not *l* you comfortless ... Jn 14:18 *863*
Peace I *l* with you, my peace I ... Jn 14:27 *863*
I *l* the world, and go to the ... Jn 16:28 *863*
to his own, and shall *l* me alone ... Jn 16:32 *863*
and Pilate gave him *l* ... Jn 19:38 *2010*
thou wilt not *l* my soul in hell ... Acts 2:27 *1459*
that we should *l* the word of God ... Acts 6:2 *2641*
then took his *l* of the brethren, ... Acts 18:18 *657*
we had taken our *l* one of another ... Acts 21:6 *782*
dwell with her, let her not *l* him ... 1Cor 7:13 *863*
but taking my *l* of them, I went ... 2Cor 2:13 *657*
cause shall a man *l* his father ... Eph 5:31 *2641*
he hath said, I will never *l* thee ... Heb 13:5 *447*
which is without the temple *l* out ... Rev 11:2 *1544*

LEAVED {1}
open before him the two *l* gates ... Is 45:1 1817

LEAVEN {23}
put away *l* out of your houses ... Ex 12:15 7603
be no *l* found in your houses ... Ex 12:19 7603
neither shall there be *l* seen ... Ex 13:7 7603
the blood of my sacrifice with *l* ... Ex 34:25 2557
the LORD, shall be made with *l* ... Lev 2:11 2557
for ye shall burn no *l*, nor any ... Lev 2:11 7603
It shall not be baken with *l* ... Lev 6:17 2557
eat it without *l* beside the altar ... Lev 10:12 4682
they shall be baken with *l* ... Lev 23:17 2557
sacrifice of thanksgiving with *l* ... Amos 4:5 2557
kingdom of heaven is like unto *l* ... Mt 13:33 *2219*
beware of the *l* of the Pharisees ... Mt 16:6 *2219*
beware of the *l* of the Pharisees ... Mt 16:11 *2219*
them not beware of the *l* of bread ... Mt 16:12 *2219*
beware of the *l* of the Pharisees, ... Mk 8:15 *2219*
and of the *l* of Herod ... Mk 8:15 *2219*
ye of the *l* of the Pharisees ... Lk 12:1 *2219*
It is like *l*, which a woman took ... Lk 13:21 *2219*
little *l* leaveneth the whole lump ... 1Cor 5:6 *2219*
Purge out therefore the old *l* ... 1Cor 5:7 *2219*
us keep the feast, not with old *l* ... 1Cor 5:8 *2219*
neither with the *l* of malice ... 1Cor 5:8 *2219*
A little *l* leaveneth the whole ... Gal 5:9 *2219*

LEAVENED {14}
for whosoever eateth *l* bread from ... Ex 12:15 2557
whosoever eateth that which is *l* ... Ex 12:19 2557
Ye shall eat nothing *l* ... Ex 12:20 2557
took their dough before it was *l* ... Ex 12:34 2557
out of Egypt, for it was not *l* ... Ex 12:39 2557
there shall no *l* bread be eaten ... Ex 13:3 2557
there shall no *l* bread be seen ... Ex 13:7 2557
of my sacrifice with *l* bread ... Ex 23:18 2557
l bread with the sacrifice of ... Lev 7:13 2557
Thou shalt eat no *l* bread with it ... Deut 16:3 2557
there shall be no *l* bread seen ... Deut 16:4 7603
kneaded the dough, until it be *l* ... Hos 7:4 2557
of meal, till the whole was *l* ... Mt 13:33 *2220*
of meal, till the whole was *l* ... Lk 13:21 *2220*

LEAVENETH {2}
a little leaven *l* the whole lump ... 1Cor 5:6 *2220*
A little leaven *l* the whole lump ... Gal 5:9 *2220*

LEAVES {19}
and they sewed fig *l* together ... Gen 3:7 2529
the two *l* of the one door were ... 1Kin 6:34 6763
the two *l* of the other door were ... 1Kin 6:34 7050
in them, when they cast their *l* ... Is 6:13
Jehudi had read three or four *l* ... Jer 36:23 1817
wither in all the *l* of her spring ... Eze 17:9 2964
two *l* apiece, two turning *l* ... Eze 41:24 1817
two *l* for the one door ... Eze 41:24
and two *l* for the other door ... Eze 41:24 1817
The *l* thereof were fair, and the ... Dan 4:12 6074
off his branches, shake off his *l* ... Dan 4:14 6074
Whose *l* were fair, and the fruit ... Dan 4:21 6074
but *l* only, and said unto it, Let ... Mt 21:19 *5444*
is yet tender, and putteth forth *l* ... Mt 24:32 *5444*
a fig tree afar off having *l* ... Mk 11:13 *5444*
to it, he found nothing but *l* ... Mk 11:13 *5444*
is yet tender, and putteth forth *l* ... Mk 13:28 *5444*
the *l* of the tree were for the ... Rev 22:2 *5444*

LEAVETH {6}
Which *l* her eggs in the earth, and ... Job 39:14 5800
A good man *l* an inheritance to ... Prov 13:22
a sweeping rain which *l* no food ... Prov 28:3
idol shepherd that *l* the flock ... Zec 11:17 5800
Then the devil *l* him, and, behold, ... Mt 4:11 *863*
coming, and *l* the sheep, and fleeth ... Jn 10:12 *863*

LEAVING {5}
l Nazareth, he came and dwelt in ... Mt 4:13 *2641*
him, and departed, *l* him half dead ... Lk 10:30 *863*
l the natural use of the woman, ... Rom 1:27 *863*
Therefore *l* the principles of the ... Heb 6:1 *863*
l us an example, that ye should ... 1Pet 2:21 *5277*

LEBANA *(leb'-a-nah)* {1} See LEBANAH. *A family of exiles.*
The children of *L*, the children ... Neh 7:48 3848

LEBANAH *(leb'-a-nah)* {1} *Same as Lebana.*
The children of *L*, the children ... Ezr 2:45 3848

LEBANON *(leb'-a-non)* {71} *Chief mountain range in Syria.*
land of the Canaanites, and unto *L* ... Deut 1:7 3844
that goodly mountain, and *L* ... Deut 3:25 3844
from the wilderness and *L*, from ... Deut 11:24 3844
this *L* even unto the great river, ... Josh 1:4 3844
of the great sea over against *L* ... Josh 9:1 3844
valley of *L* under mount Hermon ... Josh 11:17 3844
of *L* even unto the mount Halak ... Josh 12:7 3844
land of the Giblites, and all *L* ... Josh 13:5 3844
from *L* unto Misrephoth-maim ... Josh 13:6 3844
the Hivites that dwelt in mount *L* ... Judg 3:3 3844
and devour the cedars of *L* ... Judg 9:15 3844
is in *L* even unto the hyssop that ... 1Kin 4:33 3844
they hew me cedar trees out of *L* ... 1Kin 5:6 3844
them down from *L* unto the sea ... 1Kin 5:9 3844
And he sent them to *L*, ten ... 1Kin 5:14 3844
a month they were in *L*, and two ... 1Kin 5:14 3844
also the house of the forest of *L* ... 1Kin 7:2 3844
to build in Jerusalem, and in *L* ... 1Kin 9:19 3844
in the house of the forest of *L* ... 1Kin 10:17 3844
the forest of *L* were of pure gold ... 1Kin 10:21 3844
The thistle that was in *L* sent to ... 2Kin 14:9 3844
sent to the cedar that was in *L* ... 2Kin 14:9 3844
by a wild beast that was in *L* ... 2Kin 14:9 3844
the mountains, to the sides of *L* ... 2Kin 19:23 3844
trees, and algum trees, out of *L* ... 2Chr 2:8 3844
can skill to cut timber in *L* ... 2Chr 2:8 3844
And we will cut wood out of *L* ... 2Chr 2:16 3844
to build in Jerusalem, and in *L* ... 2Chr 8:6 3844
in the house of the forest of *L* ... 2Chr 9:16 3844
the forest of *L* were of pure gold ... 2Chr 9:20 3844
The thistle that was in *L* sent to ... 2Chr 25:18 3844
sent to the cedar that was in *L* ... 2Chr 25:18 3844
by a wild beast that was in *L* ... 2Chr 25:18 3844
trees from *L* to the sea of Joppa ... Ezr 3:7 3844
the LORD breaketh the cedars of *L* ... Ps 29:5 3844
L and Sirion like a young unicorn ... Ps 29:6 3844
fruit thereof shall shake like *L* ... Ps 72:16 3844
he shall grow like a cedar in *L* ... Ps 92:12 3844
the cedars of *L*, which he hath ... Ps 104:16 3844
a chariot of the wood of *L* ... Song 3:9 3844
Come with me from *L*, my spouse, ... Song 4:8 3844
with me from *L* ... Song 4:8 3844
garments is like the smell of *L* ... Song 4:11 3844
living waters, and streams from *L* ... Song 4:15 3844
his countenance is as *L*, ... Song 5:15 3844
thy nose is as the tower of *L* ... Song 7:4 3844
And upon all the cedars of *L* ... Is 2:13 3844
L shall fall by a mighty one ... Is 10:34 3844
at thee, and the cedars of *L* ... Is 14:8 3844
L shall be turned into a fruitful ... Is 29:17 3844
L is ashamed and hewn down ... Is 33:9 3844
the glory of *L* shall be given ... Is 35:2 3844
the mountains, to the sides of *L* ... Is 37:24 3844
L is not sufficient to burn, nor ... Is 40:16 3844
The glory of *L* shall come unto ... Is 60:13 3844
Will a man leave the snow of *L* ... Jer 18:14 3844
Gilead unto me, and the head of *L* ... Jer 22:6 3844
Go up to *L*, and cry ... Jer 22:20 3844
O inhabitant of *L*, that makest ... Jer 22:23 3844
had divers colours, came unto *L* ... Eze 17:3 3844
from *L* to make masts for thee ... Eze 27:5 3844
a cedar in *L* with fair branches ... Eze 31:3 3844
I caused *L* to mourn for him, and ... Eze 31:15 3844
of Eden, the choice and best of *L* ... Eze 31:16 3844
and cast forth his roots as *L* ... Hos 14:5 3844
the olive tree, and his smell as *L* ... Hos 14:6 3844
thereof shall be as the wine of *L* ... Hos 14:7 3844
and the flower of *L* languisheth ... Nah 1:4 3844
violence of *L* shall cover thee ... Hab 2:17 3844
them into the land of Gilead and *L* ... Zec 10:10 3844
Open thy doors, O *L*, that the ... Zec 11:1 3844

LEBAOTH *(leb'-a-oth)* {1} See BETH-LEBAOTH. *A city in Judah.*
And *L*, and Shilhim, and Ain, and ... Josh 15:32 3822

LEBBAEUS *(leb-be'-us)* {1} See JUDAS, THADDAEUS. *Same as Thaddaeus.*
James the son of Alphaeus, and *L* ... Mt 10:3 *3002*

LEB-KAMAI See MIDST.

LEBONAH *(le-bo'-nah)* {1} *A city in Ephraim.*
to Shechem, and on the south of *L* ... Judg 21:19 3829

LECAH *(le'-cah)* {1} *Son of Er.*
of Judah were, Er the father of *L* ... 1Chr 4:21 3922

LED {68}
the LORD *l* me to the house of my ... Gen 24:27 5148
which had *l* me in the right way ... Gen 24:48 5148
he *l* the flock to the backside of ... Ex 3:1 5090
that God *l* them not through the ... Ex 13:17 5148
But God *l* the people about, ... Ex 13:18 5437
Thou in thy mercy hast *l* forth ... Ex 15:13 5148
l thee these forty years in the ... Deut 8:2 3212
Who *l* thee through that great and ... Deut 8:15 3212
I have *l* you forty years in the ... Deut 29:5 3212
he *l* him about, he instructed him ... Deut 32:10 5437
l him throughout all the land of ... Josh 24:3 3212
which *l* them away captive, and ... 1Kin 8:48
But he *l* them to Samaria ... 2Kin 6:19 3212
Joab *l* forth the power of the ... 1Chr 20:1 5090
l forth his people, and went to ... 2Chr 25:11 5090
thou hast *l* captivity captive ... Ps 68:18
also he *l* them with a cloud ... Ps 78:14 5148
he *l* them on safely, so that they ... Ps 78:53 5148
so he *l* them through the depths, ... Ps 106:9 3212
he *l* them forth by the right way, ... Ps 107:7 1869
To him which *l* his people through ... Ps 136:16 3212
I have *l* thee in right paths ... Prov 4:11 1869
they that are *l* of them are ... Is 9:16 833
he *l* them through the deserts ... Is 48:21 3212
joy, and be *l* forth with peace ... Is 55:12 2986
That *l* them by the right hand of ... Is 63:12 3212
That *l* them through the deep, as ... Is 63:13 3212
that *l* us through the wilderness, ... Jer 2:6 3212
when he *l* thee by the way ... Jer 2:17 3212
whither they have *l* him captive ... Jer 22:12
which *l* the seed of the house of ... Jer 23:8 935
He hath *l* me, and brought me into ... Lam 3:2 5090
l them with him to Babylon ... Eze 17:12 935
which caused them to be *l* into ... Eze 39:28
l me about the way without unto ... Eze 47:2 5437
l you forty years through the ... Amos 2:10 3212
Israel shall surely be *l* away ... Amos 7:11
And Huzzab shall be *l* away captive ... Nah 2:7
Then was Jesus *l* up of the spirit ... Mt 4:1 *321*
that had laid hold on Jesus *l* him ... Mt 26:57 *520*
they *l* him away, and delivered him ... Mt 27:2 *520*
l him away to crucify him ... Mt 27:31 *520*
hand, and *l* him out of the town ... Mk 8:23 *1806*
they *l* Jesus away to the high ... Mk 14:53 *520*
the soldiers *l* him away into the ... Mk 15:16 *520*
him, and *l* him out to crucify him ... Mk 15:20 *1806*
was *l* by the Spirit into the ... Lk 4:1 *71*
l him unto the brow of the hill ... Lk 4:29 *71*
shall be *l* away captive into all ... Lk 21:24 *163*
l him, and brought him into the ... Lk 22:54 *71*
l him into their council, saying, ... Lk 22:66 *321*
them arose, and *l* him unto Pilate ... Lk 23:1 *71*
as they *l* him away, they laid ... Lk 23:26 *520*
l with him to be put to death ... Lk 23:32 *71*
he *l* them out as far as to ... Lk 24:50 *1806*
l him away to Annas first ... Jn 18:13 *520*
Then *l* they Jesus from Caiaphas ... Jn 18:28 *71*
And they took Jesus, and *l* him away ... Jn 19:16 *520*
He was *l* as a sheep to the ... Acts 8:32 *71*
but they *l* him by the hand, and ... Acts 9:8 *5496*
Paul was to be *l* into the castle ... Acts 21:37 *1521*
being *l* by the hand of them that ... Acts 22:11 *5496*
For as many as are *l* by the ... Rom 8:14 *71*
dumb idols, even as ye were *l* ... 1Cor 12:2 *71*
But if ye be *l* of the Spirit, ye ... Gal 5:18 *71*
he *l* captivity captive, and gave ... Eph 4:8 *162*
l away with divers lusts, ... 2Ti 3:6 *71*
being *l* away with the error of ... 2Pet 3:17 *4879*

LEDDEST {5}
over us, thou wast he that *l* out ... 2Sa 5:2 3318
was king, thou wast he that *l* out ... 1Chr 11:2 3318
Moreover thou *l* them in the day ... Neh 9:12 5148
Thou *l* thy people like a flock by ... Ps 77:20 5148
l out into the wilderness four ... Acts 21:38 *1806*

LEDGES {5}
and the borders were between the *l* ... 1Kin 7:28 7948
were between the *l* were lions ... 1Kin 7:29 7948
upon the *l* there was a base above ... 1Kin 7:29 7948
the top of the base the *l* thereof ... 1Kin 7:35 3027
on the plates of the *l* thereof ... 1Kin 7:36 3027

LEEKS {1}
and the melons, and the *l*, and the ... Num 11:5 2682

LEES {4}
things, a feast of wines on the *l* ... Is 25:6 8105
of wines on the *l* well refined ... Is 25:6 8105
and he hath settled on his *l* ... Jer 48:11 8105
men that are settled on their *l* ... Zeph 1:12 8105

LEFT {350}
they *l* off to build the city ... Gen 11:8 2308
if thou wilt take the *l* hand ... Gen 13:9 8040
hand, then I will go to the *l* ... Gen 13:9 8041
which is on the *l* hand of ... Gen 14:15 8040

he *l* off talking with him, and God	Gen 17:22	3615
as soon as he had *l* communing	Gen 18:33	3615
who hath not *l* destitute my	Gen 24:27	5800
to the right hand, or to the *l*	Gen 24:49	8040
and *l* bearing	Gen 29:35	5975
Leah saw that she had *l* bearing	Gen 30:9	5975
company which is *l* shall escape	Gen 32:8	7604
And Jacob was *l* alone	Gen 32:24	3498
he *l* all that he had in Joseph's	Gen 39:6	5800
he *l* his garment in her hand, and	Gen 39:12	5800
he had *l* his garment in her hand	Gen 39:13	5800
that he *l* his garment with me, and	Gen 39:15	5800
that he *l* his garment with me, and	Gen 39:18	5800
very much, until he *l* numbering	Gen 41:49	2308
brother is dead, and he is *l* alone	Gen 42:38	7604
the eldest, and *l* at the youngest	Gen 44:12	3615
he alone is *l* of his mother, and	Gen 44:20	3498
there is not ought *l* in the sight	Gen 47:18	7604
right hand toward Israel's *l* hand	Gen 48:13	8040
Manasseh in his *l* hand toward	Gen 48:13	8040
his *l* hand upon Manasseh's head,	Gen 48:14	8040
they *l* in the land of Goshen	Gen 50:8	5800
why is it that ye have *l* the man	Ex 2:20	5800
word of the LORD *l* his servants	Ex 9:21	5800
even all that the hail hath *l*	Ex 10:12	7604
of the trees which the hail had *l*	Ex 10:15	3498
shall not an hoof be *l* behind	Ex 10:26	7604
their right hand, and on their *l*	Ex 14:22	8040
their right hand, and on their *l*	Ex 14:29	8040
but some of them *l* of it until	Ex 16:20	3498
passover be *l* unto the morning	Ex 34:25	3885
that which is *l* of the meat	Lev 2:10	3498
Ithamar, his sons that were *l*	Lev 10:12	3498
sons of Aaron which were *l* alive	Lev 10:16	3498
into the palm of his own *l* hand	Lev 14:15	8042
in the oil that is in his *l* hand	Lev 14:16	8042
into the palm of his own *l* hand	Lev 14:26	8042
his *l* hand seven times before the	Lev 14:27	8042
upon them that are *l* alive of you	Lev 26:36	7604
they that are *l* of you shall pine	Lev 26:39	7604
The land also shall be *l* of them	Lev 26:43	5800
to the right hand nor to the *l*	Num 20:17	8040
until there was none *l* him alive	Num 21:35	7604
to the right hand or to the *l*	Num 22:26	8040
And there was not *l* a man of them	Num 26:65	3498
unto the right hand nor to the *l*	Deut 2:27	8040
every city, we *l* none to remain	Deut 2:34	7604
until none was *l* to him remaining	Deut 3:3	7604
ye shall be *l* few in number among	Deut 4:27	7604
to the right hand or to the *l*	Deut 5:32	8040
among them, until they that are *l*	Deut 7:20	7604
to the right hand, nor to the *l*	Deut 17:11	8040
to the right hand, or to the *l*	Deut 17:20	8040
to the right hand, or to the *l*	Deut 28:14	8040
hath nothing *l* him in the siege	Deut 28:55	7604
ye shall be *l* few in number,	Deut 28:62	7604
and there is none shut up, or *l*	Deut 32:36	5800
it to the right hand or to the *l*	Josh 1:7	8040
l them without the camp of Israel	Josh 6:23	3241
was not a man *l* in Ai or Beth-el	Josh 8:17	7604
they *l* the city open, and pursued	Josh 8:17	5800
until he had *l* him none remaining	Josh 10:33	7604
he *l* none remaining, according to	Josh 10:37	7604
he *l* none remaining	Josh 10:39	7604
he *l* none remaining, but utterly	Josh 10:40	7604
until they *l* them none remaining	Josh 11:8	7604
there was not any *l* to breathe	Josh 11:11	3498
neither *l* they any to breathe	Josh 11:14	7604
he *l* nothing undone of all that	Josh 11:15	5493
There was none of the Anakims *l*	Josh 11:22	3498
goeth out to Cabul on the *l* hand	Josh 19:27	8040
Ye have not *l* your brethren these	Josh 22:3	5800
to the right hand or to the *l*	Josh 23:6	8040
which Joshua *l* when he died	Judg 2:21	5800
the LORD *l* those nations, without	Judg 2:23	3241
are the nations which the LORD *l*	Judg 3:1	3241
And Ehud put forth his *l* hand	Judg 3:21	8040
and there was not a man *l*	Judg 4:16	7604
l no sustenance for Israel,	Judg 6:4	7604
held the lamps in their *l* hands	Judg 7:20	8040
all that were *l* of all the hosts	Judg 8:10	3498
youngest son of Jerubbaal was *l*	Judg 9:5	3498
hand, and of the other with his *l*	Judg 16:29	8040
and she was *l*, and her two sons	Ruth 1:3	7604
the woman was *l* of her two sons	Ruth 1:5	7604
then she *l* speaking unto her	Ruth 1:18	2308
and how thou hast *l* thy father	Ruth 2:11	5800
did eat, and was sufficed, and *l*	Ruth 2:14	3498
who hath not *l* off his kindness	Ruth 2:20	5800
which hath not *l* thee this day	Ruth 4:14	7673
that every one that is *l* in thine	1Sa 2:36	3498
the stump of Dagon was *l* to him	1Sa 5:4	7604
to the right hand or to the *l*	1Sa 6:12	8040
said, Behold that which is *l*	1Sa 9:24	7604
thy father hath *l* the care of the	1Sa 10:2	5203
two of them were not *l* together	1Sa 11:11	7604
l the sheep with a keeper, and	1Sa 17:20	5203
David *l* his carriage in the hand	1Sa 17:22	5203
with whom hast thou *l* those few	1Sa 17:28	5203
surely there had not been *l* unto	1Sa 25:34	3498
l neither man nor woman alive, and	1Sa 27:9	
those that were *l* behind stayed	1Sa 30:9	3498
and my master *l* me, because three	1Sa 30:13	5800
nor to the *l* from following Abner	2Sa 2:19	8040
to thy right hand or to thy *l*	2Sa 2:21	8040
there they *l* their images, and	2Sa 5:21	5800
that is *l* of the house of Saul	2Sa 9:1	3498
and there is not one of them *l*	2Sa 13:30	3498
shall quench my coal which is *l*	2Sa 14:7	7604
the *l* from ought that my lord the	2Sa 14:19	8041
the king *l* ten women, which were	2Sa 15:16	5800
on his right hand and on his *l*	2Sa 16:6	8040
which he hath *l* to keep the house	2Sa 16:21	3240
shall not be *l* so much as one	2Sa 17:12	3498
whom he had *l* to keep the house,	2Sa 20:3	3240
and he set up the *l* pillar	1Kin 7:21	8042
five on the *l* side of the house	1Kin 7:39	8040
Solomon *l* all the vessels	1Kin 7:47	3240
the right side, and five on the *l*	1Kin 7:49	8040
that were *l* of the Amorites	1Kin 9:20	3498
were *l* after them in the land	1Kin 9:21	3498
l in Israel, and will take away	1Kin 14:10	5800
the gold that were *l* in the	1Kin 15:18	3498
that he *l* off building of Ramah,	1Kin 15:21	2308
he *l* not to Jeroboam any that	1Kin 15:29	7604
he *l* him not one that pisseth	1Kin 16:11	7604
that there was no breath *l* in him	1Kin 17:17	3498
to Judah, and *l* his servant there	1Kin 19:3	3240
and I, even I only, am *l*	1Kin 19:10	3498
and I, even I only, am *l*	1Kin 19:14	3498
Yet I have *l* me seven thousand in	1Kin 19:18	7604
he *l* the oxen, and ran after	1Kin 19:20	5800
thousand of the men that were *l*	1Kin 20:30	3498
that is shut up and *l* in Israel,	1Kin 21:21	5800
him on his right hand and on his *l*	1Kin 22:19	8040
only in Kir-haraseth *l* they the	2Kin 3:25	7604
l thereof, according to the word	2Kin 4:44	3498
l their tents, and their horses,	2Kin 7:7	5800
which are *l* in the city, (behold,	2Kin 7:13	7604
of Israel that are *l* in it	2Kin 7:13	7604
since the day that she *l* the land	2Kin 8:6	5800
that is shut up and *l* in Israel	2Kin 9:8	
until he *l* him none remaining	2Kin 10:11	7604
neither *l* he any of them	2Kin 10:14	7604
was not a man *l* that came not	2Kin 10:21	7604
to the *l* corner of the temple	2Kin 11:11	8042
was not any shut up, nor any *l*	2Kin 14:26	5800
they *l* all the commandments of	2Kin 17:16	5800
there was none *l* but the tribe of	2Kin 17:18	7604
prayer for the remnant that are *l*	2Kin 19:4	4672
nothing shall be *l*, saith the	2Kin 20:17	3498
to the right hand or to the *l*	2Kin 22:2	8040
which were on a man's *l* hand at	2Kin 23:8	8040
people that were *l* in the city	2Kin 25:11	7604
But the captain of the guard *l* of	2Kin 25:12	7604
king of Babylon had *l*, even over	2Kin 25:22	7604
of Merari stood on the *l* hand	1Chr 6:44	8040
which were *l* of the family of	1Chr 6:61	3498
the *l* in hurling stones and	1Chr 12:2	8040
that are *l* in all the land of	1Chr 13:2	7604
when they had *l* their gods there,	1Chr 14:12	5800
So he *l* there before the ark of	1Chr 16:37	5800
right hand, and the other on the *l*	2Chr 3:17	8040
and the name of that on the *l* Boaz	2Chr 3:17	8042
the right hand, and five on the *l*	2Chr 4:6	8040
the right hand, and five on the *l*	2Chr 4:7	8040
the right side, and five on the *l*	2Chr 4:8	8040
that were *l* of the Hittites	2Chr 8:7	3498
who were *l* after them in the land	2Chr 8:8	3498
For the Levites *l* their suburbs	2Chr 11:14	5800
therefore have I also *l* you in	2Chr 12:5	5800
that he *l* off building of Ramah,	2Chr 16:5	2308
on his right hand and on his *l*	2Chr 18:18	8040
so that there was never a son *l* him	2Chr 21:17	7604
to the *l* side of the temple	2Chr 23:10	8042
they *l* the house of the LORD God	2Chr 24:18	5800
(for they *l* him in great diseases	2Chr 24:25	5800
other ten thousand *l* alive did	2Chr 25:12	
So the armed men *l* the captives	2Chr 28:14	5800
enough to eat, and have *l* plenty	2Chr 31:10	3498
that which is *l* is this great	2Chr 31:10	3498
was done in the land, God *l* him	2Chr 32:31	5800
to the right hand, nor to the *l*	2Chr 34:2	8040
and for them that are *l* in Israel	2Chr 34:21	7604
which were *l* of the captivity, and	Neh 1:2	7604
The remnant that are *l* of the	Neh 1:3	7604
there was no breach *l* therein	Neh 6:1	3498
and on his *l* hand, Pedaiah, and	Neh 8:4	8040
There shall none of his meat be *l*	Job 20:21	8300
him that is *l* in his tabernacle	Job 20:26	8300
On the *l* hand, where he doth work	Job 23:9	8040
they *l* off speaking	Job 32:15	6275
he hath *l* off to be wise, and to	Ps 36:3	2308
there was not one of them *l*	Ps 106:11	3498
in her *l* hand riches and honour	Prov 3:16	8040
to the right hand nor to the *l*	Prov 4:27	8040
but a child *l* to himself bringeth	Prov 29:15	7971
but a fool's heart at his *l*	Eccl 10:2	8040
His *l* hand is under my head, and	Song 2:6	8040
His *l* hand should be under my	Song 8:3	8040
the daughter of Zion is *l* as a	Is 1:8	3498
l unto us a very small remnant	Is 1:9	3498
pass, that he that is *l* in Zion	Is 4:3	7604
one eat that is *l* in the land	Is 7:22	3498
and he shall eat on the *l* hand	Is 9:20	8040
as one gathereth eggs that are *l*	Is 10:14	5800
of his people, which shall be *l*	Is 11:11	7604
of his people, which shall be *l*	Is 11:16	7604
gleaning grapes shall be *l* in it	Is 17:6	7604
which they *l* because of the	Is 17:9	5800
They shall be *l* together unto the	Is 18:6	5800
earth are burned, and few men *l*	Is 24:6	7604
In the city is *l* desolation	Is 24:12	7604
forsaken, and *l* like a wilderness	Is 27:10	5800
till ye be *l* as a beacon upon the	Is 30:17	3498
hand, and when ye turn to the *l*	Is 30:21	8041
multitude of the city shall be *l*	Is 32:14	5800
prayer for the remnant that is *l*	Is 37:4	4672
nothing shall be *l*, saith the	Is 39:6	3498
Behold, I was *l* alone	Is 49:21	7604
on the right hand and on the *l*	Is 54:3	8040
house, I have *l* mine heritage	Jer 12:7	5203
such as are *l* in this city from	Jer 21:7	7604
are *l* in the house of the LORD	Jer 27:18	3498
The people which were *l* of the	Jer 31:2	8300
the cities of Judah that were *l*	Jer 34:7	3498
all the women that are *l* in the	Jer 38:22	7604
So they *l* off speaking with him	Jer 38:27	2790
the captain of the guard *l* of the	Jer 39:10	7604
people that were *l* in the land	Jer 40:6	7604
Babylon had *l* a remnant of Judah	Jer 40:11	5414
(for we are *l* but a few of many,	Jer 42:2	7604
the captain of the guard had *l*	Jer 43:6	3240
But since we *l* off to burn	Jer 44:18	2308
How is the city of praise not *l*	Jer 49:25	5800
let nothing of her be *l*	Jer 50:26	7611
the captain of the guard *l*	Jer 52:16	7604
the face of an ox on the *l* side	Eze 1:10	8040
Lie thou also upon thy *l* side	Eze 4:4	8042
were slaying them, and I was *l*	Eze 9:8	7604
therein shall be *l* a remnant that	Eze 14:22	3498
that dwell at thy *l* hand	Eze 16:46	8040
on the right hand, or on the *l*	Eze 21:16	8041
Neither *l* she her whoredoms	Eze 23:8	5800
ye have *l* shall fall by the sword	Eze 24:21	5800
have cut him off, and have *l* him	Eze 31:12	5203
from his shadow, and have *l* him	Eze 31:12	5203
Then the heathen that are *l* round	Eze 36:36	7604
smite thy bow out of thy *l* hand	Eze 39:3	8040
have *l* none of them any more	Eze 39:28	3498
that which was *l* was the place of	Eze 41:9	3240
were toward the place that was *l*	Eze 41:11	3240
was *l* was five cubits round about	Eze 41:11	3240
that are *l* in the breadth over	Eze 48:15	3498
shall not be *l* to other people	Dan 2:44	7662
Therefore I was *l* alone, and saw	Dan 10:8	7604
neither is there breath *l* in me	Dan 10:17	7604
his *l* hand unto heaven, and sware	Dan 12:7	8040
because they have *l* off to take	Hos 4:10	5800
that there shall not be a man *l*	Hos 9:12	
hath *l* hath the locust eaten	Joel 1:4	3499
hath *l* hath the cankerworm eaten	Joel 1:4	3499
hath *l* hath the caterpiller eaten	Joel 1:4	3499
their right hand and their *l* hand	Jonah 4:11	8040
Who is *l* among you that saw this	Hag 2:3	7604
the other upon the *l* side thereof	Zec 4:3	8040
and upon the *l* side thereof	Zec 4:11	8040
on the right hand and on the *l*	Zec 12:6	8040
but the third shall be *l* therein	Zec 13:8	3498
that every one that is *l* of all	Zec 14:16	3498
And they straightway *l* their nets	Mt 4:20	*863*
And they immediately *l* the ship	Mt 4:22	*863*
let not thy *l* hand know what thy	Mt 6:3	*710*
her hand, and the fever *l* her	Mt 8:15	*863*
that was *l* seven baskets full	Mt 15:37	*4052*
And he *l* them, and departed	Mt 16:4	*2641*
right hand, and the other on the *l*	Mt 20:21	*2176*
sit on my right hand, and on my *l*	Mt 20:23	*2176*
he *l* them, and went out of the	Mt 21:17	*2641*
and *l* him, and went their way	Mt 22:22	*863*
l his wife unto his brother	Mt 22:25	*863*
your house is *l* unto you desolate	Mt 23:38	*863*
There shall not be *l* here one	Mt 24:2	*863*
shall be taken, and the other *l*	Mt 24:40	*863*
shall be taken, and the other *l*	Mt 24:41	*863*
hand, but the goats on the *l*	Mt 25:33	*2176*
say also unto them on the *l* hand	Mt 25:41	*2176*
he *l* them, and went away again, and	Mt 26:44	*863*
right hand, and another on the *l*	Mt 27:38	*2176*
they *l* their father Zebedee in	Mk 1:20	*863*
and immediately the fever *l* her	Mk 1:31	*863*
meat that was *l* seven baskets	Mk 8:8	*4051*
he *l* them, and entering into the	Mk 8:13	*863*
say unto him, Lo, we have *l* all	Mk 10:28	*863*
There is no man that hath *l* house	Mk 10:29	*863*
hand, and the other on thy *l* hand	Mk 10:37	*2176*
on my *l* hand is not mine to give	Mk 10:40	*2176*
and they *l* him, and went their way	Mk 12:12	*863*
took a wife, and dying *l* no seed	Mk 12:20	*863*
and died, neither *l* he any seed	Mk 12:21	*863*
the seven had her, and *l* no seed	Mk 12:22	*863*
there shall not be *l* one stone	Mk 13:2	*863*
journey, who *l* his house, and gave	Mk 13:34	*863*
he *l* the linen cloth, and fled	Mk 14:52	*2641*
right hand, and the other on his *l*	Mk 15:27	*2176*
and it *l* her	Lk 4:39	*863*
Now when he had *l* speaking	Lk 5:4	*3973*
he *l* all, rose up, and followed	Lk 5:28	*2641*
sister hath *l* me to serve alone	Lk 10:40	*2641*
your house is *l* unto you desolate	Lk 13:35	*863*
be taken, and the other shall be *l*	Lk 17:34	*863*
shall be taken, and the other *l*	Lk 17:35	*863*
shall be taken, and the other *l*	Lk 17:36	*863*
Peter said, Lo, we have *l* all	Lk 18:28	*863*
There is no man that hath *l* house	Lk 18:29	*863*
they *l* no children, and died	Lk 20:31	*2641*
not be *l* one stone upon another	Lk 21:6	*863*
right hand, and the other on the *l*	Lk 23:33	*710*
He *l* Judaea, and departed again	Jn 4:3	*863*
The woman then *l* her waterpot	Jn 4:28	*863*
the seventh hour the fever *l* him	Jn 4:52	*863*
and Jesus was *l* alone, and the	Jn 8:9	*2641*
the Father hath not *l* me alone	Jn 8:29	*863*
that his soul was not *l* in hell	Acts 2:31	*2641*

L

Nevertheless he *l* not himself Acts 14:17 *863*
came to Ephesus, and *l* them there Acts 18:19 *2641*
we *l* it on the *l* hand, and Acts 21:3 *2641*
Cyprus, we *l* it on the *l* hand Acts 21:3 *2176*
soldiers, they *l* beating of Paul Acts 21:32 *3973*
On the morrow they *l* the horsemen Acts 23:32 *1439*
the Jews a pleasure, *l* Paul bound Acts 24:27 *2641*
a certain man *l* in bonds by Felix Acts 25:14 *2641*
Lord of Sabaoth had *l* us a seed Rom 9:29 *1459*
I am *l* alone, and they seek my Rom 11:3 *5275*
on the right hand and on the *l* 2Cor 6:7 *710*
it good to be *l* at Athens alone 1Th 3:1 *2641*
The cloke that I *l* at Troas with 2Ti 4:13 *620*
have I *l* at Miletum sick 2Ti 4:20 *620*
For this cause *l* I thee in Crete, Titus 1:5 *2641*
he *l* nothing that is not put Heb 2:8 *863*
a promise being *l* us of entering Heb 4:1 *2641*
but *l* their own habitation, he Jude 6 *620*
thou hast *l* thy first love Rev 2:4 *863*
sea, and his *l* foot on the earth, Rev 10:2 *2176*

LEFTEST {1}
therefore *l* thou them in the hand Neh 9:28 5800

LEFTHANDED {2}
of Gera, a Benjamite, a man *l* Judg 3:15 334,3027,3225
seven hundred chosen men *l* Judg 20:16 334,3027,3225

LEG {1}
thy locks, make bare the *l* Is 47:2 7640

LEGION {3}
he answered, saying, My name is *L* Mk 5:9 *3003*
with the devil, and had the *l* Mk 5:15 *3003*
And he said, *L* Lk 8:30 *3003*

LEGIONS {1}
me more than twelve *l* of angels Mt 26:53 *3003*

LEGS {19}
his head with his *l*, and with the Ex 12:9 3767
wash the inwards of him, and his *l* Ex 29:17 3767
his *l* shall he wash in water Lev 1:9 3767
the inwards and the *l* with water Lev 1:13 3767
with his head, and with his *l* Lev 4:11 3767
the inwards and the *l* in water Lev 8:21 3767
he did wash the inwards and the *l* Lev 9:14 3767
which have *l* above their feet, to Lev 11:21 3767
thee in the knees, and in the *l* Deut 28:35 7785
had greaves of brass upon his *l* 1Sa 17:6 7272
not pleasure in the *l* of a man Ps 147:10 7785
The *l* of the lame are not equal Prov 26:7 7785
His *l* are as pillars of marble, Song 5:15 7785
and the ornaments of the *l* Is 3:20 6807
His *l* of iron, his feet part of Dan 2:33 8243
of the mouth of the lion two *l* Amos 3:12 3767
that their *l* might be broken Jn 19:31 *4628*
brake the *l* of the first, and of Jn 19:32 *4628*
already, they brake not his *l* Jn 19:33 *4628*

LEHAB See LEHABIM.

LEHABIM *(le'-ha-bim)* {2} *A son of Mizraim.*
begat Ludim, and Anamim, and *L* Gen 10:13 3853
begat Ludim, and Anamim, and *L* 1Chr 1:11 3853

LEHABITES See LEHABIM.

LEHI *(le'-hi)* {3} See RAMATH-LEHI. *A district near Jerusalem.*
Judah, and spread themselves in *L* Judg 15:9 3896
And when he came unto *L*, the Judg 15:14 3896
which is in *L* unto this day Judg 15:19 3896

LEISURE {1}
they had no *l* so much as to eat Mk 6:31 *2119*

LEMUEL *(lem'-u-el)* {2} *A king mentioned in Proverbs.*
The words of king *L*, the prophecy Prov 31:1 3927
It is not for kings, O *L*, it is Prov 31:4 3927

LEND {16}
If thou *l* money to any of my Ex 22:25 3867
nor *l* him thy victuals for Lev 25:37 5414
thou shalt *l* unto many nations, Deut 15:6 5670
shalt surely *l* him sufficient for Deut 15:8 5670
Thou shalt not *l* upon usury to Deut 23:19 5391
stranger thou mayest *l* upon usury Deut 23:20 5391
thou shalt not *l* upon usury Deut 23:20 5391
When thou dost *l* thy brother any Deut 24:10 5383
the man to whom thou dost *l* shall Deut 24:11 5383
thou shalt *l* unto many nations, Deut 28:12 3867
He shall *l* to thee, and thou shalt Deut 28:44 3867
and thou shalt not *l* to him Deut 28:44 3867
if ye *l* to them of whom ye hope Lk 6:34 *1155*
for sinners also *l* to sinners Lk 6:34 *1155*
ye your enemies, and do good, and *l* Lk 6:35 *1155*
him, Friend, *l* me three loaves Lk 11:5 *5531*

LENDER {2}
the borrower is servant to the *l* Prov 22:7 3867
as with the *l*, so with the Is 24:2 3867

LENDETH {4}
Every creditor that *l* ought unto Deut 15:2 5383
He is ever merciful, and *l* Ps 37:26 3867
A good man sheweth favour, and *l* Ps 112:5 3867
upon the poor *l* unto the LORD Prov 19:17 3867

LENGTH {77}
The *l* of the ark shall be three Gen 6:15 753
through the land in the *l* of it Gen 13:17 753
and a half shall be the *l* thereof Ex 25:10 753
and a half shall be the *l* thereof Ex 25:17 753
two cubits shall be the *l* thereof Ex 25:23 753
The *l* of one curtain shall be Ex 26:2 753
The *l* of one curtain shall be Ex 26:8 753
the *l* of the curtains of the tent Ex 26:13 753
cubits shall be the *l* of a board Ex 26:16 753
l there shall be hangings of an Ex 27:11 753
The *l* of the court shall be an Ex 27:18 753
a span shall be the *l* thereof Ex 28:16 753
A cubit shall be the *l* thereof Ex 30:2 753
The *l* of one curtain was twenty Ex 36:9 753
The *l* of one curtain was thirty Ex 36:15 753
The *l* of a board was ten cubits, Ex 36:21 753
cubits and a half was the *l* of it Ex 37:1 753
and a half was the *l* thereof Ex 37:6 753
two cubits was the *l* thereof Ex 37:10 753
the *l* of it was a cubit, and the Ex 37:25 753
five cubits was the *l* thereof Ex 38:1 753
and twenty cubits was the *l* Ex 38:18 753
a span was the *l* thereof, and a Ex 39:9 753
nine cubits was the *l* thereof Deut 3:11 753
is thy life, and the *l* of thy days Deut 30:20 753
which had two edges, of a cubit *l* Judg 3:16 753
the *l* thereof was threescore 1Kin 6:2 753
twenty cubits was the *l* thereof 1Kin 6:3 753
forepart was twenty cubits in *l* 1Kin 6:20 753
the *l* thereof was an hundred 1Kin 7:2 753
the *l* thereof was fifty cubits, 1Kin 7:6 753
four cubits was the *l* of one base 1Kin 7:27 753
The *l* by cubits after the first 2Chr 3:3 753
the *l* of it was according to the 2Chr 3:4 753
the *l* whereof was according to 2Chr 3:8 753
twenty cubits the *l* thereof 2Chr 4:1 753
in *l* of days understanding Job 12:12 753
even *l* of days for ever and ever Ps 21:4 753
For *l* of days, and long life, and Prov 3:2 753
L of days is in her right hand Prov 3:16 753
have him become his son at the *l* Prov 29:21 319
in the *l* of his branches Eze 31:7 753
the *l* of the gate, thirteen Eze 40:11 753
the *l* of the gates was the lower Eze 40:18 753
north, he measured the *l* thereof Eze 40:20 753
the *l* thereof was fifty cubits, Eze 40:21 753
the *l* was fifty cubits, and the Eze 40:25 753
the *l* was fifty cubits, and the Eze 40:36 753
The *l* of the porch was twenty Eze 40:49 753
and he measured the *l* thereof Eze 41:2 753
So he measured the *l* thereof Eze 41:4 753
the *l* thereof ninety cubits Eze 41:12 753
he measured the *l* of the building Eze 41:15 753
high, and the *l* thereof two cubits Eze 41:22 753
the *l* thereof, and the walls Eze 41:22 753
Before the *l* of an hundred cubits Eze 42:2 753
the *l* thereof was fifty cubits Eze 42:7 753
For the *l* of the chambers that Eze 42:8 753
the *l* shall be the *l* of five Eze 45:1 753
the sanctuary five hundred in *l* Eze 45:2
shalt thou measure the *l* of five Eze 45:3 753
the five and twenty thousand of *l* Eze 45:5 753
the *l* shall be over against one Eze 45:7 753
in *l* as one of the other parts, Eze 48:8 753
of five and twenty thousand in *l* Eze 48:9 753
five and twenty thousand in *l* Eze 48:10 753
five and twenty thousand in *l* Eze 48:10 753
have five and twenty thousand in *l* Eze 48:13 753
all the *l* shall be five and twenty Eze 48:13 753
the residue in *l* over against the Eze 48:18 753
thereof, and what is the *l* thereof Zec 2:2 753
the *l* thereof is twenty cubits, Zec 5:2 753
if by any means now at *l* I might Rom 1:10 *4218*
saints what is the breadth, and *l* Eph 3:18 *3372*
the *l* is as large as the breadth Rev 21:16 *3372*
The *l* and the breadth and the Rev 21:16 *3372*

LENGTHEN {2}
did walk, then I will *l* thy days 1Kin 3:14 748
l thy cords, and strengthen thy Is 54:2 748

LENGTHENED {1}
that thy days may be *l* in the Deut 25:15 748

LENGTHENING {1}
if it may be a *l* of thy Dan 4:27 754

LENT {7}
so that they *l* unto them such Ex 12:36 7592
of any thing that is *l* upon usury Deut 23:19 5391
also I have *l* him to the LORD 1Sa 1:28 7592
liveth he shall be *l* to the LORD 1Sa 1:28 7592
the loan which is *l* to the LORD 1Sa 2:20 7592
I have neither *l* on usury Jer 15:10 5383
nor men have *l* to me on usury Jer 15:10 5383

LENTILES {4}
gave Esau bread and pottage of *l* Gen 25:34 5742
and parched corn, and beans, and *l* 2Sa 17:28 5742
was a piece of ground full of *l* 2Sa 23:11 5742
wheat, and barley, and beans, and *l* Eze 4:9 5742

LEOPARD {6}
the *l* shall lie down with the kid Is 11:6 5246
a *l* shall watch over their cities Jer 5:6 5246
his skin, or the *l* his spots Jer 13:23 5246
I beheld, and lo another, like a *l* Dan 7:6 5245
as a *l* by the way will I observe Hos 13:7 5246
which I saw was like unto a *l* Rev 13:2 *3917*

LEOPARDS {2}
dens, from the mountains of the *l* Song 4:8 5246
also are swifter than the *l* Hab 1:8 5246

LEPER {17}
the *l* in whom the plague is, his Lev 13:45 6879
the *l* in the day of his cleansing Lev 14:2 6879
of leprosy be healed in the *l* Lev 14:3 6879
of the seed of Aaron is a *l* Lev 22:4 6879
they put out of the camp every *l* Num 5:2 6879
hath an issue, or that is a *l* 2Sa 3:29 6879
man in valour, but he was a *l* 2Kin 5:1 6879
over the place, and recover the *l* 2Kin 5:11 6879
his presence a *l* as white as snow 2Kin 5:27 6879
so that he was a *l* unto the day 2Kin 15:5 6879
Uzziah the king was a *l* unto the 2Chr 26:21 6879
in a several house, being a *l* 2Chr 26:21 6879
for they said, He is a *l* 2Chr 26:23 6879
And, behold, there came a *l* Mt 8:2 *3015*
in the house of Simon the *l* Mt 26:6 *3015*
And there came a *l* to him, Mk 1:40 *3015*
in the house of Simon the *l* Mk 14:3 *3015*

LEPERS {6}
And when these *l* came to the 2Kin 7:8 6879
Heal the sick, cleanse the *l* Mt 10:8 *3015*
the *l* are cleansed, and the deaf Mt 11:5 *3015*
many *l* were in Israel in the time Lk 4:27 *3015*
the *l* are cleansed, the deaf hear Lk 7:22 *3015*
there met him ten men that were *l* Lk 17:12 *3015*

LEPROSY {39}
of his flesh like the plague of *l* Lev 13:2 6883
of his flesh, it is a plague of *l* Lev 13:3 6883
it is a *l* Lev 13:8 6883
When the plague of *l* is in a man Lev 13:9 6883
It is an old *l* in the skin of his Lev 13:11 6883
if a *l* break out abroad in the Lev 13:12 6883
the *l* cover all the skin of him Lev 13:12 6883
if the *l* have covered all his Lev 13:13 6883
it is a *l* Lev 13:15 6883
it is a plague of *l* broken out of Lev 13:20 6883
it is a *l* broken out of the Lev 13:25 6883
it is the plague of *l* Lev 13:25 6883
it is the plague of *l* Lev 13:27 6883
even a *l* upon the head or beard Lev 13:30 6883
it is a *l* sprung up in his bald Lev 13:42 6883
as the *l* appeareth in the skin of Lev 13:43 6883
also that the plague of *l* is in Lev 13:47 6883
it is a plague of *l*, and shall be Lev 13:49 6883
the plague is a fretting *l* Lev 13:51 6883
for it is a fretting *l* Lev 13:52 6883
of *l* in a garment of woollen or Lev 13:59 6883
if the plague of *l* be healed in Lev 14:3 6883
cleansed from the *l* seven times Lev 14:7 6883
of him in whom is the plague of *l* Lev 14:32 6883
I put the plague of *l* in a house Lev 14:34 6883
it is a fretting *l* in the house Lev 14:44 6883
law for all manner of plague of *l* Lev 14:54 6883
for the *l* of a garment, and of a Lev 14:55 6883
this is the law of *l* Lev 14:57 6883
Take heed in the plague of *l* Deut 24:8 6883
for he would recover him of his *l* 2Kin 5:3 6883
thou mayest recover him of his *l* 2Kin 5:6 6883
unto me to recover a man of his *l* 2Kin 5:7 6883
The *l* therefore of Naaman shall 2Kin 5:27 6883
the *l* even rose up in his 2Chr 26:19 6883
And immediately his *l* was cleansed Mt 8:3 *3014*
immediately the *l* departed from Mk 1:42 *3014*
city, behold a man full of *l* Lk 5:12 *3014*
immediately the *l* departed from Lk 5:13 *3014*

LEPROUS {6}
behold, his hand was *l* as snow Ex 4:6 6879
He is a *l* man, he is unclean Lev 13:44 6879
and, behold, Miriam became *l* Num 12:10 6879
Miriam, and, behold, she was *l* Num 12:10 6879
there were four *l* men at the 2Kin 7:3 6879
he was *l* in his forehead, and they 2Chr 26:20 6879

LESHEM *(le'-shem)* {2} See LAISH. *Same as Laish.*
of Dan went up to fight against *L* Josh 19:47 3959
it, and dwelt therein, and called *L* Josh 19:47 3959

LESS See APPENDIX.

LESSER See APPENDIX.

LEST See APPENDIX.

LET See APPENDIX.

LETHEK See HOMER.

LETTER {37}
that David wrote a *l* to Joab 2Sa 11:14 5612
And he wrote in the *l*, saying, Set 2Sa 11:15 5612
I will send a *l* unto the king of 2Kin 5:5 5612
he brought the *l* to the king of 2Kin 5:6 5612
Now when this *l* is come unto thee 2Kin 5:6 5612
the king of Israel had read the *l* 2Kin 5:7 5612
as soon as this *l* cometh to you 2Kin 10:2 5612
Then he wrote a *l* the second time 2Kin 10:6 5612
when the *l* came to them, that 2Kin 10:7 5612
Hezekiah received the *l* of the 2Kin 19:14 5612
the writing of the *l* was written Ezr 4:7 5406
Shimshai the scribe wrote a *l* Ezr 4:8 104
of the *l* that they sent unto him Ezr 4:11 104
The *l* which ye sent unto us hath Ezr 4:18 5407
l was read before Rehum, and Ezr 4:23 5407
by *l* concerning this matter Ezr 5:5 5407
The copy of the *l* that Tatnai Ezr 5:6 104
They sent a *l* unto him, wherein Ezr 5:7 6600
Now this is the copy of the *l* Ezr 7:11 5406
a *l* unto Asaph the keeper of the Neh 2:8 107
time with an open *l* in his hand Neh 6:5 107
for all the words of this *l* Est 9:26 107
to confirm this second *l* of Purim Est 9:29 107
Hezekiah received the *l* from the Is 37:14 5612
l that Jeremiah the prophet sent Jer 29:1 5612
l in the ears of Jeremiah the Jer 29:29 5612
he wrote a *l* after this manner Acts 23:25 *1992*
when the governor had read the *l* Acts 23:34
the law, judge thee, who by the *l* Rom 2:27 *1121*
in the spirit, and not in the *l* Rom 2:29 *1121*
and not in the oldness of the *l* Rom 7:6 *1121*

not of the *l*, but of the spirit 2Cor 3:6 *1121*
for the *l* killeth, but the spirit 2Cor 3:6 *1121*
though I made you sorry with a *l* 2Cor 7:8 *1992*
Ye see how large a *l* I have Gal 6:11 *1121*
nor by *l* as from us, as that the 2Th 2:2 *1992*
for I have written a *l* unto you Heb 13:22 *1989*

LETTERS {34}
So she wrote *l* in Ahab's name, and 1Kin 21:8 5612
sent the *l* unto the elders and to 1Kin 21:8 5612
And she wrote in the *l*, saying, 1Kin 21:9 5612
as it was written in the *l* which 1Kin 21:11 5612
And Jehu wrote *l*, and sent to 2Kin 10:1 5612
Baladan, king of Babylon, sent *l* 2Kin 20:12 5612
wrote *l* also to Ephraim and 2Chr 30:1 107
went with the *l* from the king 2Chr 30:6 107
He wrote also *l* to rail on the 2Chr 32:17 5612
king, let *l* be given me to the Neh 2:7 107
river, and gave them the king's *l* Neh 2:9 107
of Judah sent many *l* unto Tobiah Neh 6:17 107
the *l* of Tobiah came unto them Neh 6:17
Tobiah sent *l* to put me in fear Neh 6:19 107
For he sent *l* into all the king's Est 1:22 5612
the *l* were sent by posts into all Est 3:13 5612
the *l* devised by Haman the son of Est 8:5 5612
sent *l* by posts on horseback, and Est 8:10 5612
sent *l* unto all the Jews that Est 9:20 5612
he commanded by *l* that his wicked Est 9:25 5612
he sent the *l* unto all the Jews, Est 9:30 5612
Baladan, king of Babylon, sent *l* Is 39:1 5612
Because thou hast sent *l* in thy Jer 29:25 5612
written over him in *l* of Greek Lk 23:38 *1121*
saying, How knoweth this man *l* Jn 7:15 *1121*
desired of him *l* to Damascus to Acts 9:2 *1992*
they wrote *l* by them after this Acts 15:23
I received *l* unto the brethren Acts 22:5 *1992*
We neither received *l* out of Acts 28:21 *1121*
ye shall approve by your *l* 1Cor 16:3 *1992*
or *l* of commendation from you 2Cor 3:1
as if I would terrify you by *l* 2Cor 10:9 *1992*
For his *l*, say they, are weighty 2Cor 10:10 *1992*
in word by *l* when we are absent 2Cor 10:11 *1992*

LETTEST {3}
l such words go out of thy mouth Job 15:13
with a cord which thou *l* down Job 41:1 8257
now *l* thou thy servant depart in Lk 2:29 *630*

LETTETH {3}
hands escape, he that *l* him go 2Kin 10:24
strife is as when one *l* out water Prov 17:14 6362
only he who now *l* will let 2Th 2:7 *2722*

LETTING See APPENDIX.

LETUSHIM *(le-tu'-shim)* {1} *A son of Dedan.*
sons of Dedan were Asshurim, and *L* Gen 25:3 3912

LETUSHITES See LETUSHIM.

LEUMMIM *(le-um'-mim)* {1} *A son of Dedan.*
were Asshurim, and Letushim, and *L* Gen 25:3 3817

LEVI *(le'-vi)* {72} See LEVITE, LEVITICAL, MATTHEW.
1. A son of Jacob.
therefore was his name called *L* Gen 29:34 3878
of the sons of Jacob, Simeon and *L* Gen 34:25 3878
And Jacob said to Simeon and *L* Gen 34:30 3878
firstborn, and Simeon, and *L* Gen 35:23 3878
Simeon and *L* are brethren Gen 49:5 3878
Reuben, Simeon, *L*, and Judah, Ex 1:2 3878
are the names of the sons of *L* Ex 6:16 3878
life of *L* were an hundred thirty Ex 6:16 3878
were the sons of *L* by their names Num 3:17 3878
the son of Kohath, the son of *L* Num 16:1 3878
was Jochebed, the daughter of *L* Num 26:59 3878
her mother bare to *L* in Egypt Num 26:59 3878
the son of Kohath, the son of *L* 1Chr 6:38 3878
the son of Gershom, the son of *L* 1Chr 6:43 3878
the son of Merari, the son of *L* 1Chr 6:47 3878
the sons of Mahli, the son of *L* Ezr 8:18 3878
2. The tribe.
And the sons of *L* Gen 46:11 3878
went a man of the house of *L* Ex 2:1 3878
and took to wife a daughter of *L* Ex 2:1 3878
these are the families of *L* Ex 6:19 3878
all the sons of *L* gathered Ex 32:26 3878
the children of *L* did according Ex 32:28 3878
shalt not number the tribe of *L* Num 1:49 3878
Bring the tribe of *L* near Num 3:6 3878
Number the children of *L* after Num 3:15 3878
Kohath from among the sons of *L* Num 4:2 3878
too much upon you, ye sons of *L* Num 16:7 3878
Hear, I pray you, ye sons of *L* Num 16:8 3878
brethren the sons of *L* with thee Num 16:10 3878
Aaron's name upon the rod of *L* Num 17:3 3878
for the house of *L* was budded Num 17:8 3878
brethren also of the tribe of *L* Num 18:2 3878
I have given the children of *L* Num 18:21 3878
the LORD separated the tribe of *L* Deut 10:8 3878
Wherefore *L* hath no part nor Deut 10:9 3878
Levites, and all the tribe of *L* Deut 18:1 3878
the sons of *L* shall come near Deut 21:5 3878
Simeon, and *L*, and Judah, and Deut 27:12 3878
it unto the priests the sons of *L* Deut 31:9 3878
of *L* he said, Let thy Thummim and Deut 33:8 3878
Only unto the tribe of *L* he gave Josh 13:14 3878
But unto the tribe of *L* Moses Josh 13:33 3878
who were of the children of *L* Josh 21:10 3878
which were not of the sons of *L* 1Kin 12:31 3878
Reuben, Simeon, *L*, and Judah, 1Chr 2:1 3878
The sons of *L*; Gershon 1Chr 6:1 3878
The sons of *L*; Gershom 1Chr 6:16 3878
companies of the children of *L* 1Chr 9:18 3878
the children of *L* four thousand 1Chr 12:26 3878
But *L* and Benjamin counted he not 1Chr 21:6 3878
into courses among the sons of *L* 1Chr 23:6 3878
sons were named of the tribe of *L* 1Chr 23:14 3878
These were the sons of *L* after 1Chr 23:24 3878
rest of the sons of *L* were these 1Chr 24:20 3878
found there none of the sons of *L* Ezr 8:15 3878
the children of *L* shall bring the Neh 10:39 3878
The sons of *L*, the chief of the Neh 12:23 3878
Bless the LORD, O house of *L* Ps 135:20 3878
sons of Zadok among the sons of *L* Eze 40:46 3878
one gate of Judah, one gate of *L* Eze 48:31 3878
family of the house of *L* apart Zec 12:13 3878
that my covenant might be with *L* Mal 2:4 3878
have corrupted the covenant of *L* Mal 2:8 3878
and he shall purify the sons of *L* Mal 3:3 3878
they that are of the sons of *L* Heb 7:5 *3017*
L also, who receiveth tithes, Heb 7:9 *3017*
Of the tribe of *L* were sealed Rev 7:7 *3017*
3. Same as Matthew the apostle.
he saw *L* the son of Alphaeus Mk 2:14 *3018*
forth, and saw a publican, named *L* Lk 5:27 *3018*
L made him a great feast in his Lk 5:29 *3018*
4. Father of Matthat; ancestor of Jesus.
Matthat, which was the son of *L* Lk 3:24 *3017*
5. Father of another Matthat; ancestor of Jesus.
Matthat, which was the son of *L* Lk 3:29 *3017*

LEVIATHAN {5}
thou draw out *l* with an hook Job 41:1 3882
brakest the heads of *l* in pieces Ps 74:14 3882
there is that *l*, whom thou hast Ps 104:26 3882
punish *l* the piercing serpent Is 27:1 3882
even *l* that crooked serpent Is 27:1 3882

LEVITE *(le'-vite)* {28} See LEVITES, LEVITICAL. *A descendant of Levi.*
Is not Aaron the *L* thy brother Ex 4:14 3881
the *L* that is within your gates Deut 12:12 3881
the *L* that is within thy gates Deut 12:18 3881
that thou forsake not the *L* as Deut 12:19 3881
the *L* that is within thy gates Deut 14:27 3881
And the *L*, (because he hath no Deut 14:29 3881
the *L* that is within thy gates, Deut 16:11 3881
and thy maidservant, and the *L* Deut 16:14 3881
if a *L* come from any of thy gates Deut 18:6 3881
unto thine house, thou, and the *L* Deut 26:11 3881
and hast given it unto the *L* Deut 26:12 3881
also have given them unto the *L* Deut 26:13 3881
the family of Judah, who was a *L* Judg 17:7 3881
I am a *L* of Beth-lehem-judah, and Judg 17:9 3881
So the *L* went in Judg 17:10 3881
the *L* was content to dwell with Judg 17:11 3881
And Micah consecrated the *L* Judg 17:12 3881
seeing I have a *L* to my priest Judg 17:13 3881
the voice of the young man the *L* Judg 18:3 3881
the house of the young man the *L* Judg 18:15 3881
that there was a certain *L* Judg 19:1 3881
And the *L*, the husband of the Judg 20:4 3881
a *L* of the sons of Asaph, came 2Chr 20:14 3881
which Cononiah the *L* was ruler 2Chr 31:12 3881
And Kore the son of Imnah the *L* 2Chr 31:14 3881
and Shabbethai the *L* helped them Ezr 10:15 3881
And likewise a *L*, when he was at Lk 10:32 *3019*
The son of consolation,) a *L* Acts 4:36 *3019*

LEVITES {265}
the *L* according to their families Ex 6:25 3881
Moses, for the service of the *L* Ex 38:21 3881
the cities of the *L*, and the Lev 25:32 3881
may the *L* redeem at any time Lev 25:32 3881
And if a man purchase of the *L* Lev 25:33 3881
L are their possession among the Lev 25:33 3881
But the *L* after the tribe of Num 1:47 3881
the *L* over the tabernacle of Num 1:50 3881
forward, the *L* shall take it down Num 1:51 3881
be pitched, the *L* shall set it up Num 1:51 3881
But the *L* shall pitch round about Num 1:53 3881
the *L* shall keep the charge of Num 1:53 3881
of the *L* in the midst of the camp Num 2:17 3881
But the *L* were not numbered among Num 2:33 3881
thou shalt give the *L* unto Aaron Num 3:9 3881
I have taken the *L* from among the Num 3:12 3881
therefore the *L* shall be mine Num 3:12 3881
These are the families of the *L* Num 3:20 3881
be chief over the chief of the *L* Num 3:32 3881
All that were numbered of the *L* Num 3:39 3881
thou shalt take the *L* for me (I Num 3:41 3881
the cattle of the *L* instead of Num 3:41 3881
Take the *L* instead of all the Num 3:45 3881
the cattle of the *L* instead of Num 3:45 3881
and the *L* shall be mine Num 3:45 3881
Israel, which are more than the *L* Num 3:46 3881
them that were redeemed by the *L* Num 3:49 3881
the Kohathites from among the *L* Num 4:18 3881
those that were numbered of the *L* Num 4:46 3881
thou shalt give them unto the *L* Num 7:5 3881
the oxen, and gave them unto the *L* Num 7:6 3881
Take the *L* from among the Num 8:6 3881
thou shalt bring the *L* before the Num 8:9 3881
shalt bring the *L* before the LORD Num 8:10 3881
shall put their hands upon the *L* Num 8:10 3881
Aaron shall offer the *L* before Num 8:11 3881
the *L* shall lay their hands upon Num 8:12 3881
to make an atonement for the *L* Num 8:12 3881
thou shalt set the *L* before Aaron Num 8:13 3881
the *L* from among the children of Num 8:14 3881
and the *L* shall be mine Num 8:14 3881
after that shall the *L* go in to Num 8:15 3881
I have taken the *L* for all the Num 8:18 3881
I have given the *L* as a gift to Num 8:19 3881
did to the *L* according unto all Num 8:20 3881
commanded Moses concerning the *L* Num 8:20 3881
the *L* were purified, and they Num 8:21 3881
after that went the *L* in to do Num 8:22 3881
commanded Moses concerning the *L* Num 8:22 3881
is it that belongeth unto the *L* Num 8:24 3881
unto the *L* touching their charge Num 8:26 3881
the *L* from among the children of Num 18:6 3881
But the *L* shall do the service of Num 18:23 3881
I have given to the *L* to inherit Num 18:24 3881
Thus speak unto the *L*, and say Num 18:26 3881
unto the *L* as the increase of the Num 18:30 3881
of the *L* after their families Num 26:57 3881
These are the families of the *L* Num 26:58 3881
beasts, and gave them unto the *L* Num 31:30 3881
of beast, and gave them unto the *L* Num 31:47 3881
that they give unto the *L* of the Num 35:2 3881
ye shall give also unto the *L* Num 35:2 3881
which ye shall give unto the *L* Num 35:4 3881
which ye shall give unto the *L* Num 35:6 3881
give to the *L* shall be forty Num 35:7 3881
give of his cities unto the *L* Num 35:8 3881
shalt come unto the priests the *L* Deut 17:9 3881
which is before the priests the *L* Deut 17:18 3881
The priests the *L*, and all the Deut 18:1 3881
God, as all his brethren the *L* do Deut 18:7 3881
the priests the *L* shall teach you Deut 24:8 3881
the priests the *L* spake unto all Deut 27:9 3881
the *L* shall speak, and say unto Deut 27:14 3881
That Moses commanded the *L* Deut 31:25 3881
and the priests the *L* bearing it Josh 3:3 3881
side before the priests the *L* Josh 8:33 3881
but unto the *L* he gave none Josh 14:3 3881
no part unto the *L* in the land Josh 14:4 3881
But the *L* have no part among you Josh 18:7 3881
of the *L* unto Eleazar the priest Josh 21:1 3881
of Israel gave unto the *L* out of Josh 21:3 3881
the priest, which were of the *L* Josh 21:4 3881
of Israel gave by lot unto the *L* Josh 21:8 3881
the *L* which remained of the Josh 21:20 3881
Gershon, of the families of the *L* Josh 21:27 3881
of Merari, the rest of the *L* Josh 21:34 3881
of the families of the *L*, were by Josh 21:40 3881
All the cities of the *L* within Josh 21:41 3881
the *L* took down the ark of the 1Sa 6:15 3881
all the *L* were with him, bearing 2Sa 15:24 3881
did the priests and the *L* bring up 1Kin 8:4 3881
the *L* according to their fathers 1Chr 6:19 3881
Their brethren also the *L* were 1Chr 6:48 3881
children of Israel gave to the *L* 1Chr 6:64 3881
the Israelites, the priests, *L* 1Chr 9:2 3881
And of the *L* 1Chr 9:14 3881
For these *L*, the four chief 1Chr 9:26 3881
And Mattithiah, one of the *L* 1Chr 9:31 3881
chief of the fathers of the *L* 1Chr 9:33 3881
These chief fathers of the *L* were 1Chr 9:34 3881
L which are in their cities and 1Chr 13:2 3881
to carry the ark of God but the *L* 1Chr 15:2 3881
the children of Aaron, and the *L* 1Chr 15:4 3881
the priests, and for the *L* 1Chr 15:11 3881
the chief of the fathers of the *L* 1Chr 15:12 3881
the *L* sanctified themselves to 1Chr 15:14 3881
the children of the *L* bare the 1Chr 15:15 3881
L to appoint their brethren to be 1Chr 15:16 3881
So the *L* appointed Heman the son 1Chr 15:17 3881
And Chenaniah, chief of the *L* 1Chr 15:22 3881
when God helped the *L* that bare 1Chr 15:26 3881
all the *L* that bare the ark, and 1Chr 15:27 3881
he appointed certain of the *L* to 1Chr 16:4 3881
Israel, with the priests and the *L* 1Chr 23:2 3881
Now the *L* were numbered from the 1Chr 23:3 3881
And also unto the *L* 1Chr 23:26 3881
by the last words of David the *L* 1Chr 23:27 3881
the scribe, one of the *L*, wrote 1Chr 24:6 3878
the fathers of the priests and *L* 1Chr 24:6 3881
of the *L* after the house of their 1Chr 24:30 3881
the fathers of the priests and *L* 1Chr 24:31 3881
Eastward were six *L*, northward 1Chr 26:17 3881
And of the *L*, Ahijah was over the 1Chr 26:20 3881
Of the *L*, Hashabiah the son of 1Chr 27:17 3881
courses of the priests and the *L* 1Chr 28:13 3881
courses of the priests and the *L* 1Chr 28:21 3881
and the *L* took up the ark 2Chr 5:4 3881
did the priests and the *L* bring up 2Chr 5:5 3881
Also the *L* which were the singers 2Chr 5:12 3881
the *L* also with instruments of 2Chr 7:6 3881
the *L* to their charges, to praise 2Chr 8:14 3881
L concerning any matter, or 2Chr 8:15 3881
the *L* that were in all Israel 2Chr 11:13 3881
For the *L* left their suburbs and 2Chr 11:14 3881
LORD, the sons of Aaron, and the *L* 2Chr 13:9 3881
the *L* wait upon their business 2Chr 13:10 3881
And with them he sent *L*, even 2Chr 17:8 3881
and Tobijah, and Tob-adonijah, *L* 2Chr 17:8 3881
did Jehoshaphat set of the *L* 2Chr 19:8 3881
also the *L* shall be officers 2Chr 19:11 3881
And the *L*, of the children of the 2Chr 20:19 3881
gathered the *L* out of all the 2Chr 23:2 3881
of the priests and of the *L* 2Chr 23:4 3881
and they that minister of the *L* 2Chr 23:6 3881
the *L* shall compass the king 2Chr 23:7 3881
So the *L* and all Judah did 2Chr 23:8 3881
by the hand of the priests the *L* 2Chr 23:18 3881
together the priests and the *L* 2Chr 24:5 3881
Howbeit the *L* hastened it not 2Chr 24:5 3881
of the *L* to bring in out of Judah 2Chr 24:6 3881

office by the hand of the L ... 2Chr 24:11 3881
brought in the priests and the L ... 2Chr 29:4 3881
And said unto them, Hear me, ye L ... 2Chr 29:5 3881
Then the L arose, Mahath the son ... 2Chr 29:12 3881
the L took it, to carry it out ... 2Chr 29:16 3881
he set the L in the house of the ... 2Chr 29:25 3881
the L stood with the instruments ... 2Chr 29:26 3881
the princes commanded the L to ... 2Chr 29:30 3881
brethren the L did help them ... 2Chr 29:34 3881
for the L were more upright in ... 2Chr 29:34 3881
the L were ashamed, and sanctified ... 2Chr 30:15 3881
received of the hand of the L ... 2Chr 30:16 3881
therefore the L had the charge of ... 2Chr 30:17 3881
and the L and the priests praised ... 2Chr 30:21 3881
L that taught the good knowledge ... 2Chr 30:22 3881
Judah, with the priests and the L ... 2Chr 30:25 3881
Then the priests the L arose ... 2Chr 30:27 3881
the L after their courses, every ... 2Chr 31:2 3881
L for burnt offerings and for ... 2Chr 31:2 3881
portion of the priests and the L ... 2Chr 31:4 3881
the L concerning the heaps ... 2Chr 31:9 3881
the L from twenty years old and ... 2Chr 31:17 3881
by genealogies among the L ... 2Chr 31:19 3881
which the L that kept the doors ... 2Chr 34:9 3881
were Jahath and Obadiah, the L ... 2Chr 34:12 3881
and other of the L, all that could ... 2Chr 34:12 3881
of the L there were scribes, and ... 2Chr 34:13 3881
and the priests, and the L ... 2Chr 34:30 3881
said unto the L that taught all ... 2Chr 35:3 3881
division of the families of the L ... 2Chr 35:5 3881
to the priests, and to the L ... 2Chr 35:8 3881
Jeiel and Jozabad, chief of the L ... 2Chr 35:9 3881
gave unto the L for passover ... 2Chr 35:9 3881
the L in their courses, according ... 2Chr 35:10 3881
their hands, and the L flayed them ... 2Chr 35:11 3881
therefore the L prepared for ... 2Chr 35:14 3881
brethren the L prepared for them ... 2Chr 35:15 3881
kept, and the priests, and the L ... 2Chr 35:18 3881
and the priests, and the L ... Ezr 1:5 3881
The L: the children ... Ezr 2:40 3881
So the priests, and the L, and some ... Ezr 2:70 3881
brethren the priests and the L ... Ezr 3:8 3881
and appointed the L, from twenty ... Ezr 3:8 3881
sons and their brethren the L ... Ezr 3:9 3881
the L the sons of Asaph with ... Ezr 3:10 3881
But many of the priests and L ... Ezr 3:12 3881
of Israel, the priests, and the L ... Ezr 6:16 3879
the L in their courses, for the ... Ezr 6:18 3879
the L were purified together, all ... Ezr 6:20 3881
and of the priests, and the L ... Ezr 7:7 3881
of Israel, and of his priests and L ... Ezr 7:13 3879
touching any of the priests and L ... Ezr 7:24 3879
for the service of the L, two ... Ezr 8:20 3881
the chief of the priests and the L ... Ezr 8:29 3881
the L the weight of the silver ... Ezr 8:30 3881
and Noadiah the son of Binnui, L ... Ezr 8:33 3881
Israel, and the priests, and the L ... Ezr 9:1 3881
and made the chief priests, the L ... Ezr 10:5 3881
Also of the L ... Ezr 10:23 3881
After him repaired the L, Rehum ... Neh 3:17 3881
singers and the L were appointed, ... Neh 7:1 3881
The L: the children ... Neh 7:43 3881
So the priests, and the L, and the ... Neh 7:73 3881
Jozabad, Hanan, Pelaiah, and the L ... Neh 8:7 3881
the L that taught the people, ... Neh 8:9 3881
So the L stilled all the people, ... Neh 8:11 3881
the people, the priests, and the L ... Neh 8:13 3881
up upon the stairs, of the L ... Neh 9:4 3881
Then the L, Jeshua, and Kadmiel, ... Neh 9:5 3881
and our princes, L, and priests, ... Neh 9:38 3881
And the L: both Jeshua ... Neh 10:9 3881
of the people, the priests, the L ... Neh 10:28 3881
the lots among the priests, the L ... Neh 10:34 3881
tithes of our ground unto the L ... Neh 10:37 3881
that the same L might have the ... Neh 10:37 3881
son of Aaron shall be with the L ... Neh 10:38 3881
when the L take tithes ... Neh 10:38 3881
the L shall bring up the tithe of ... Neh 10:38 3881
Israel, the priests, and the L ... Neh 11:3 3881
Also of the L ... Neh 11:15 3881
and Jozabad, of the chief of the L ... Neh 11:16 3881
All the L in the holy city were ... Neh 11:18 3881
Israel, of the priests, and the L ... Neh 11:20 3881
The overseer also of the L at ... Neh 11:22 3881
of the L were divisions in Judah, ... Neh 11:36 3881
and the L that went up with ... Neh 12:1 3881
Moreover the L: Jeshua, ... Neh 12:8 3881
The L in the days of Eliashib, ... Neh 12:22 3881
And the chief of the L ... Neh 12:24 3881
the L out of all their places ... Neh 12:27 3881
the L purified themselves, and ... Neh 12:30 3881
of the law for the priests and L ... Neh 12:44 3881
priests and for the L that waited ... Neh 12:44 3881
sanctified holy things unto the L ... Neh 12:47 3881
the L sanctified them unto the ... Neh 12:47 3881
commanded to be given to the L ... Neh 13:5 3881
of the L had not been given them ... Neh 13:10 3881
for the L and the singers, that ... Neh 13:10 3881
and Zadok the scribe, and of the L ... Neh 13:13 3881
I commanded the L that they ... Neh 13:22 3881
of the priesthood, and of the L ... Neh 13:29 3881
the wards of the priests and the L ... Neh 13:30 3881
take of them for priests and for L ... Is 66:21 3881
L want a man before me to offer ... Jer 33:18 3881
with the L the priests, my ... Jer 33:21 3881
the L that minister unto me ... Jer 33:22 3881
L that be of the seed of Zadok ... Eze 43:19 3881
the L that are gone away far from ... Eze 44:10 3881
But the priests the L, the sons ... Eze 44:15 3881
of breadth, shall also the L ... Eze 45:5 3881
went astray, as the L went astray ... Eze 48:11 3881
most holy by the border of the L ... Eze 48:12 3881
the priests the L shall have five ... Eze 48:13 3881
from the possession of the L ... Eze 48:22 3881
L from Jerusalem to ask him, Who ... Jn 1:19 *3019*

LEVITICAL *(le-vit'-i-cal)* {1} *Belonging to the Levites.*
were by the L priesthood, (for ... Heb 7:11 *3020*

LEVY {6}
l a tribute unto the LORD of the ... Num 31:28 7311
raised a l out of all Israel ... 1Kin 5:13 4522
the l was thirty thousand men ... 1Kin 5:13 4522
and Adoniram was over the l ... 1Kin 5:14 4522
the l which king Solomon raised ... 1Kin 9:15 4522
upon those did Solomon l a ... 1Kin 9:21 5927

LEWD {3}
which are ashamed of thy l way ... Eze 16:27 2154
and unto Aholibah, the l women ... Eze 23:44 2154
took unto them certain l fellows ... Acts 17:5 *4190*

LEWDLY {1}
another hath l defiled his ... Eze 22:11 2154

LEWDNESS {17}
for they have committed l ... Judg 20:6 2154
she hath wrought l with many ... Jer 11:15 4209
the l of thy whoredom, and thine ... Jer 13:27 2154
thou shalt not commit this l ... Eze 16:43 2154
Thou hast borne thy l and thine ... Eze 16:58 2154
the midst of thee they commit l ... Eze 22:9 2154
to remembrance the l of thy youth ... Eze 23:21 2154
I make thy l to cease from thee ... Eze 23:27 2154
shall be discovered, both thy l ... Eze 23:29 2154
therefore bear thou also thy l ... Eze 23:35 2154
Thus will I cause l to cease out ... Eze 23:48 2154
be taught not to do after your l ... Eze 23:48 2154
shall recompense your l upon you ... Eze 23:49 2154
In thy filthiness is l ... Eze 24:13 2154
now will I discover her l in the ... Hos 2:10 5040
for they commit l ... Hos 6:9 2154
a matter of wrong or wicked l ... Acts 18:14 *4467*

LIAR {13}
not so now, who will make me a l ... Job 24:25 3576
a l giveth ear to a naughty ... Prov 17:4 8267
a poor man is better than a l ... Prov 19:22 376,3576
thee, and thou be found a l ... Prov 30:6 3576
thou be altogether unto me as a l ... Jer 15:18 391
for he is a l, and the father of ... Jn 8:44 *5583*
I shall be a l like unto you ... Jn 8:55 *5583*
God be true, but every man a l ... Rom 3:4 *5583*
have not sinned, we make him a l ... 1Jn 1:10 *5583*
not his commandments, is a l ... 1Jn 2:4 *5583*
Who is a l but he that denieth ... 1Jn 2:22 *5583*
and hateth his brother, he is a l ... 1Jn 4:20 *5583*
not God hath made him a l ... 1Jn 5:10 *5583*

LIARS {8}
shall be found l unto thee ... Deut 33:29 3584
I said in my haste, All men are l ... Ps 116:11 3576
frustrateth the tokens of the l ... Is 44:25 907
A sword is upon the l ... Jer 50:36 907
mankind, for menstealers, for l ... 1Ti 1:10 *5583*
said, The Cretians are alway l ... Titus 1:12 *5583*
and are not, and hast found them l ... Rev 2:2 *5571*
sorcerers, and idolaters, and all l ... Rev 21:8 *5571*

LIBERAL {6}
The l soul shall be made fat ... Prov 11:25 1293
person shall be no more called l ... Is 32:5 5081
But the l deviseth l things ... Is 32:8 5081
by l things shall he stand ... Is 32:8 5081
for your l distribution unto them ... 2Cor 9:13 *572*

LIBERALITY {2}
to bring your l unto Jerusalem ... 1Cor 16:3 *5485*
unto the riches of their l ... 2Cor 8:2 *572*

LIBERALLY {2}
furnish him l out of thy flock ... Deut 15:14 6059
of God, that giveth to all men l ... Jas 1:5 *574*

LIBERTINES *(lib'-ur-tins)* {1} *Former Jewish slaves.*
is called the synagogue of the L ... Acts 6:9 *3032*

LIBERTY {27}
proclaim l throughout all the ... Lev 25:10 1865
And I will walk at l ... Ps 119:45 7342
to proclaim l to the captives, and ... Is 61:1 1865
to proclaim l unto them ... Jer 34:8 1865
in proclaiming l every man to his ... Jer 34:15 1865
he had set at l at their pleasure ... Jer 34:16 2670
unto me, in proclaiming l ... Jer 34:17 1865
behold, I proclaim a l for you ... Jer 34:17 1865
it shall be his to the year of l ... Eze 46:17 1865
to set at l them that are bruised ... Lk 4:18 *859*
keep Paul, and to let him have l ... Acts 24:23 *425*
This man might have been set at l ... Acts 26:32 *630*
gave him l to go unto his friends ... Acts 27:3 *2010*
glorious l of the children of God ... Rom 8:21 *1657*
she is at l to be married to whom ... 1Cor 7:39 *1658*
means this l of yours become a ... 1Cor 8:9 *1849*
for why is my l judged of another ... 1Cor 10:29 *1657*
Spirit of the Lord is, there is l ... 2Cor 3:17 *1657*
l which we have in Christ Jesus ... Gal 2:4 *1657*
Stand fast therefore in the l ... Gal 5:1 *1657*
ye have been called unto l ... Gal 5:13 *1657*
only use not l for an occasion to ... Gal 5:13 *1657*
our brother Timothy is set at l ... Heb 13:23 *630*
looketh into the perfect law of l ... Jas 1:25 *1657*
shall be judged by the law of l ... Jas 2:12 *1657*
not using your l for a cloke of ... 1Pet 2:16 *1657*
While they promise them l ... 2Pet 2:19 *1657*

LIBNAH *(lib'-nah)* {18} See LABAN.
1. A Hebrew encampment in the wilderness.
Rimmon-parez, and pitched in L ... Num 33:20 3841
And they removed from L, and ... Num 33:21 3841
2. A Levitical city in Judah.
and all Israel with him, unto L ... Josh 10:29 3841
unto Libnah, and fought against L ... Josh 10:29 3841
And Joshua passed from L, and all ... Josh 10:31 3841
to all that he had done to L ... Josh 10:32 3841
as he had done also to L, and to ... Josh 10:39 3841
The king of L, one ... Josh 12:15 3841
L, and Ether, and Ashan, ... Josh 15:42 3841
and L with her suburbs, ... Josh 21:13 3841
Then L revolted at the same time ... 2Kin 8:22 3841
king of Assyria warring against L ... 2Kin 19:8 3841
the daughter of Jeremiah of L ... 2Kin 23:31 3841
the daughter of Jeremiah of L ... 2Kin 24:18 3841
L with her suburbs, and Jattir, and ... 1Chr 6:57 3841
The same time also did L revolt ... 2Chr 21:10 3841
king of Assyria warring against L ... Is 37:8 3841
the daughter of Jeremiah of L ... Jer 52:1 3841

LIBNI *(lib'-ni)* {5} See LAADAN, LIBNITES.
1. Son of Gershon.
L, and Shimi, according to their ... Ex 6:17 3845
their families; L, and Shimei ... Num 3:18 3845
of Gershom; L, and Shimei ... 1Chr 6:17 3845
L his son, Jahath his son, Zimmah ... 1Chr 6:20 3845
2. Grandson of Merari.
L his son, Shimei his son, Uzza ... 1Chr 6:29 3845

LIBNITES *(lib'-nites)* {2} *Descendants of Libni 1.*
Gershon was the family of the L ... Num 3:21 3864
the family of the L, the family ... Num 26:58 3864

LIBYA *(lib'-e-ah)* {3} See LIBYANS. *A land in north Africa.*
Ethiopia, and L, and Lydia, and all ... Eze 30:5 6316
Persia, Ethiopia, and L with them ... Eze 38:5 6316
and in the parts of L about Cyrene ... Acts 2:10 *3033*

LIBYANS *(lib'-e-uns)* {2} See LEHABIM. *Inhabitants of Libya.*
the Ethiopians and the L, that ... Jer 46:9 6316
and the L and the Ethiopians shall ... Dan 11:43 3864

LICE {6}
that it may become l throughout ... Ex 8:16 3654
the earth, and it became l in man ... Ex 8:17 3654
l throughout all the land of ... Ex 8:17 3654
enchantments to bring forth l ... Ex 8:18 3654
so there were l upon man, and upon ... Ex 8:18 3654
flies, and l in all their coasts ... Ps 105:31 3654

LICENCE {2}
And when he had given him l ... Acts 21:40 *2010*
have l to answer for himself ... Acts 25:16 *5117*

LICK {5}
Now shall this company l up all ... Num 22:4 3897
of Naboth shall dogs l thy blood ... 1Kin 21:19 3952
and his enemies shall l the dust ... Ps 72:9 3897
l up the dust of thy feet ... Is 49:23 3897
They shall l the dust like a ... Mic 7:17 3897

LICKED {4}
l up the water that was in the ... 1Kin 18:38 3897
In the place where dogs l the ... 1Kin 21:19 3952
and the dogs l up his blood ... 1Kin 22:38 3952
the dogs came and l his sores ... Lk 16:21 *621*

LICKETH {1}
as the ox l up the grass of the ... Num 22:4 3897

LID {1}
and bored a hole in the l of it ... 2Kin 12:9 1817

LIE {155}
we will l with him, that we may ... Gen 19:32 7901
l with him, that we may preserve ... Gen 19:34 7901
Therefore he shall l with thee to ... Gen 30:15 7901
and she said, L with me ... Gen 39:7 7901
to l by her, or to be with her ... Gen 39:10 7901
by his garment, saying, L with me ... Gen 39:12 7901
he came in unto me to l with me ... Gen 39:14 7901
But I will l with my fathers, and ... Gen 47:30 7901
if a man l not in wait, but God ... Ex 21:13 6658
l with her, he shall surely endow ... Ex 22:16 7901
thou shalt let it rest and l still ... Ex 23:11 5203
l unto his neighbour in that ... Lev 6:2 3584
shall l with seed of copulation ... Lev 15:18 7901
if any man l with her at all, and ... Lev 15:24 7901
Moreover thou shalt not l ... Lev 18:20 5414,7903
Thou shalt not l with mankind ... Lev 18:22 7901
Neither shalt thou l with any ... Lev 18:23 5414,7903
before a beast to l down thereto ... Lev 18:23 7250
falsely, neither l one to another ... Lev 19:11 8266
if a man l with his daughter in ... Lev 20:12 7901
If a man also l with mankind ... Lev 20:13 7901
if a man l with a beast, he shall ... Lev 20:15 5414,7903
l down thereto, thou shalt kill ... Lev 20:16 7250
if a man shall l with a woman ... Lev 20:18 7901
if a man shall l with his uncle's ... Lev 20:20 7901
in the land, and ye shall l down ... Lev 26:6 7901
a man l with her carnally, and it ... Num 5:13 7901
then the camps that l on the east ... Num 10:5 2583
then the camps that l on the ... Num 10:6 2583
is not a man, that he should l ... Num 23:19 3576
he shall not l down until he eat ... Num 23:24 7901
l in wait for him, and rise up ... Deut 19:11 693
her in the city, and l with her ... Deut 22:23 7901
the man force her, and l with her ... Deut 22:25 7901
l with her, and they be found ... Deut 22:28 7901

judge shall cause him to l down ... Deut 25:2 5307
and another man shall l with her ... Deut 28:30 7693
in this book shall l upon him ... Deut 29:20 7257
ye shall l in wait against the ... Josh 8:4 693
and they went to l in ambush ... Josh 8:9
set them to l in ambush between ... Josh 8:12
thee, and l in wait in the field ... Judg 9:32
let all thy wants l upon me ... Judg 19:20
l in wait in the vineyards ... Judg 21:20
mark the place where he shall l ... Ruth 3:4 7901
he went to l down at the end of ... Ruth 3:7 7901
l down until the morning ... Ruth 3:13 7901
l down again ... 1Sa 3:5 7901
l down again ... 1Sa 3:6 7901
Eli said unto Samuel, Go, l down ... 1Sa 3:9 7901
of Israel will not l nor repent ... 1Sa 15:29 8266
to l in wait, as at this day ... 1Sa 22:8 8266
to l in wait, as at this day ... 1Sa 22:13 8266
and to drink, and to l with my wife ... 2Sa 11:11 7901
at even he went out to l on his ... 2Sa 11:13 7901
he shall l with thy wives in the ... 2Sa 12:11 7901
Come l with me, my sister ... 2Sa 13:11 7901
let her l in thy bosom, that my ... 1Kin 1:2 7901
do not l unto thine handmaid ... 2Kin 4:16 3576
for it is evident unto you if I l ... Job 6:28 3576
When I l down, I say, When shall ... Job 7:4 7901
Also thou shalt l down, and none ... Job 11:19 7257
which shall l down with him in ... Job 20:11 7901
They shall l down alike in the ... Job 21:26 7901
The rich man shall l down ... Job 27:19 7901
Should I l against my right ... Job 34:6 3576
abide in the covert to l in wait ... Job 38:40
He maketh me to l down in green ... Ps 23:2 7257
I l even among them that are set ... Ps 57:4 7901
they l in wait for my soul ... Ps 59:3
and men of high degree are a l ... Ps 62:9 3576
the slain that l in the grave ... Ps 88:5 7901
that I will not l unto David ... Ps 89:35 3576
proud have forged a l against me ... Ps 119:69 3576
yea, thou shalt l down, and thy ... Prov 3:24 7901
wicked are to l in wait for blood ... Prov 12:6
A faithful witness will not l ... Prov 14:5 3576
if two l together, then they have ... Eccl 4:11 7901
he shall l all night betwixt my ... Song 1:13 3885
leopard shall l down with the kid ... Is 11:6 7257
young ones shall l down together ... Is 11:7 7257
of the desert shall l there ... Is 13:21 7257
l in glory, every one in his own ... Is 14:18 7901
the needy shall l down in safety ... Is 14:30 7257
be for flocks, which shall l down ... Is 17:2 7257
feed, and there shall he l down ... Is 27:10 7257
The highways l waste, the ... Is 33:8
to generation it shall l waste ... Is 34:10
they shall l down together, they ... Is 43:17 7901
Is there not a l in my right hand ... Is 44:20 3576
ye shall l down in sorrow ... Is 50:11 7901
they l at the head of all the ... Is 51:20 7901
people, children that will not l ... Is 63:8 8266
place for the herds to l down in ... Is 65:10 7258
We l down in our shame, and our ... Jer 3:25 7901
For they prophesy a l unto you ... Jer 27:10 8267
for they prophesy a l unto you ... Jer 27:14 8267
yet they prophesy a l in my name ... Jer 27:15 8267
for they prophesy a l unto you ... Jer 27:16 8267
this people to trust in a l ... Jer 28:15 8267
which prophesy a l unto you in my ... Jer 29:21 8267
and he caused you to trust in a l ... Jer 29:31 8267
causing their flocks to l down ... Jer 33:12 7257
the old l on the ground in the ... Lam 2:21 7901
L thou also upon thy left side, ... Eze 4:4 7901
of the days that thou shalt l ... Eze 4:4 7901
l again on thy right side, and ... Eze 4:6 7901
that thou shalt l upon thy side ... Eze 4:9 7901
whiles they divine a l unto thee ... Eze 21:29 3576
thou shalt l in the midst of the ... Eze 31:18 7901
they l uncircumcised, slain by ... Eze 32:21 7901
they shall not l with the mighty ... Eze 32:27 7901
shalt l with them that are slain ... Eze 32:28 7901
they shall l with the ... Eze 32:29 7901
they l uncircumcised with them ... Eze 32:30 7901
there shall they l in a good fold ... Eze 34:14 7257
and I will cause them to l down ... Eze 34:15 7257
will make them to l down safely ... Hos 2:18 7901
an oven, whiles they l in wait ... Hos 7:6
l all night in sackcloth, ye ... Joel 1:13 3885
That l upon beds of ivory, and ... Amos 6:4 7901
be a l to the kings of Israel ... Mic 1:14 391
in the spirit and falsehood do l ... Mic 2:11 3576
they all l in wait for blood ... Mic 7:2
the end it shall speak, and not l ... Hab 2:3 3576
shall they l down in the evening ... Zeph 2:7 7257
flocks shall l down in the midst ... Zeph 2:14 7257
a place for beasts to l down in ... Zeph 2:15 4769
l down, and none shall make them ... Zeph 3:13 7257
houses, and this house l waste ... Hag 1:4
and the diviners have seen a l ... Zec 10:2 8267
When Jesus saw him l, and knew ... Jn 5:6 2621
When he speaketh a l, he speaketh ... Jn 8:44 5579
and seeth the linen clothes l ... Jn 20:6 2749
heart to l to the Holy Ghost ... Acts 5:3 5574
for there l in wait for him of ... Acts 23:21
changed the truth of God into a l ... Rom 1:25 5579
through my l unto his glory ... Rom 3:7 5582
I l not, my conscience also ... Rom 9:1 5574
evermore, knoweth that I l not ... 2Cor 11:31 5574
you, behold, before God, I l not ... Gal 1:20 5574
whereby they l in wait to deceive ... Eph 4:14 3180
L not one to another, seeing that ... Col 3:9 5574
that they should believe a l ... 2Th 2:11 5579
the truth in Christ, and l not ... 1Ti 2:7 5574
life, which God, that cannot l ... Titus 1:2 893
it was impossible for God to l ... Heb 6:18 5574
not, and l not against the truth ... Jas 3:14 5574
him, and walk in darkness, we l ... 1Jn 1:6 5574
that no l is of the truth ... 1Jn 2:21 5579
things, and is truth, and is no l ... 1Jn 2:27 5579
are Jews, and are not, but do l ... Rev 3:9 5574
their dead bodies shall l in the ... Rev 11:8 5574
abomination, or maketh a l ... Rev 21:27 5579
and whosoever loveth and maketh a l ... Rev 22:15 5579

LIED {4}
But he l unto him ... 1Kin 13:18 3584
they l unto him with their ... Ps 78:36 3576
or feared, that thou hast l ... Is 57:11 3576
thou hast not l unto men, but ... Acts 5:4 5574

LIEN {3}
lightly have l with thy wife ... Gen 26:10 7901
Though ye have l among the pots ... Ps 68:13 7901
where thou hast not been l with ... Jer 3:2 7693

LIERS {10}
their l in wait on the west of ... Josh 8:13
l in ambush against him behind ... Josh 8:14
the men of Shechem set l in wait ... Judg 9:25
there were l in wait abiding in ... Judg 16:12
Israel set l in wait round about ... Judg 20:29
the l in wait of Israel came ... Judg 20:33
the l in wait which they had set ... Judg 20:36
the l in wait hasted, and rushed ... Judg 20:37
the l in wait drew themselves ... Judg 20:37
the l in wait, that they should ... Judg 20:38

LIES {51}
thou hast mocked me, and told me l ... Judg 16:10 3576
thou hast mocked me, and told me l ... Judg 16:13 3576
Should thy l make men hold their ... Job 11:3 907
But ye are forgers of l, ye are ... Job 13:4 8267
nor such as turn aside to l ... Ps 40:4 3576
soon as they be born, speaking l ... Ps 58:3 3576
they delight in l ... Ps 62:4 3576
that speak l shall be stopped ... Ps 63:11 8267
he that telleth l shall not tarry ... Ps 101:7 8267
A false witness that speaketh l ... Prov 6:19 3576
but a false witness will utter l ... Prov 14:5 3576
a deceitful witness speaketh l ... Prov 14:25 3576
that speaketh l shall not escape ... Prov 19:5 3576
he that speaketh l shall perish ... Prov 19:9 3576
If a ruler hearken to l, all his ... Prov 29:12 1697,8267
Remove far from me vanity and l ... Prov 30:8 1697,3576
and the prophet that teacheth l ... Is 9:15 8267
but his l shall not be so ... Is 16:6 907
for we have made l our refuge ... Is 28:15 3576
shall sweep away the refuge of l ... Is 28:17 3576
your lips have spoken l, your ... Is 59:3 8267
they trust in vanity, and speak l ... Is 59:4 7723
tongues like their bow for l ... Jer 9:3 8267
taught their tongue to speak l ... Jer 9:5 8267
prophets prophesy l in my name ... Jer 14:14 8267
our fathers have inherited l ... Jer 16:19 8267
to whom thou hast prophesied l ... Jer 20:6 8267
commit adultery, and walk in l ... Jer 23:14 8267
said, that prophesy l in my name ... Jer 23:25 8267
of the prophets that prophesy l ... Jer 23:26 8267
cause my people to err by their l ... Jer 23:32 8267
his l shall not so effect it ... Jer 48:30 907
ye have spoken vanity, and seen l ... Eze 13:8 3576
that see vanity, and that divine l ... Eze 13:9 3576
to my people that hear your l ... Eze 13:19 3576
Because with l ye have made the ... Eze 13:22 3576
divining l unto them, saying, ... Eze 22:28 3576
She hath wearied herself with l ... Eze 24:12 8383
they shall speak l at one table ... Dan 11:27 3576
and the princes with their l ... Hos 7:3 3585
yet they have spoken l against me ... Hos 7:13 3576
ye have eaten the fruit of l ... Hos 10:13 3585
compasseth me about with l ... Hos 11:12 3585
he daily increaseth l and ... Hos 12:1 3576
their l caused them to err, after ... Amos 2:4 3576
inhabitants thereof have spoken l ... Mic 6:12 8267
it is all full of l and robbery ... Nah 3:1 3585
molten image, and a teacher of l ... Hab 2:18 8267
not do iniquity, nor speak l ... Zeph 3:13 3576
for thou speakest l in the name ... Zec 13:3 8267
Speaking l in hypocrisy ... 1Ti 4:2 5573

LIEST {5}
the land whereon thou l, to thee ... Gen 28:13 7901
by the way, and when thou l down ... Deut 6:7 7901
by the way, when thou l down ... Deut 11:19 7901
wherefore l thou thus upon thy ... Josh 7:10 5307
When thou l down, thou shalt not ... Prov 3:24 7901

LIETH {59}
doest not well, sin l at the door ... Gen 4:7 7257
of the deep that l under, ... Gen 49:25 7257
Whosoever l with a beast shall ... Ex 22:19 7901
l concerning it, and sweareth ... Lev 6:3 3584
he that l in the house shall wash ... Lev 14:47 7901
whereon he l that hath the issue, ... Lev 15:4 7901
every thing that she l upon in ... Lev 15:20 7901
bed whereon he l shall be unclean ... Lev 15:24 7901
Every bed whereon she l all the ... Lev 15:26 7901
of him that l with her that is ... Lev 15:33 7901
whosoever l carnally with a woman ... Lev 19:20 7901
the man that l with his father's ... Lev 20:11 7901
as he l with a woman, both of ... Lev 20:13 4904
as long as it l desolate ... Lev 26:34
As long as it l desolate it shall ... Lev 26:35
while she l desolate without them ... Lev 26:43
l upon the border of Moab ... Num 21:15 8172
Cursed be he that l with his ... Deut 27:20 7901
Cursed be he that l with any ... Deut 27:21 7901
be he that l with his sister ... Deut 27:22 7901
Cursed be he that l with his ... Deut 27:23 7901
l before the valley of Hinnom ... Josh 15:8
Michmethah, that l before Shechem ... Josh 17:7
near the hill that l on the south ... Josh 18:13
from the hill that l before ... Josh 18:14
l before the valley of the son of ... Josh 18:16
which l in the south of Arad ... Judg 1:16
see wherein his great strength l ... Judg 16:5
wherein thy great strength l ... Judg 16:6
me wherein thy great strength l ... Judg 16:15
the valley that l by Beth-rehob ... Judg 18:28
And it shall be, when he l down ... Ruth 3:4 7901
that l before Giah by the way of ... 2Sa 2:24
l in the midst of the river of ... 2Sa 24:5
l waste, and the gates thereof are ... Neh 2:3
we are in, how Jerusalem l waste ... Neh 2:17
the tower which l out from the ... Neh 3:25 3318
the east, and the tower that l out ... Neh 3:26 3318
the great tower that l out ... Neh 3:27 3318
So man l down, and riseth not ... Job 14:12 7901
He l under the shady trees, in ... Job 40:21 7901
He l in wait secretly as a lion ... Ps 10:9
he l in wait to catch the poor ... Ps 10:9
now that he l he shall rise up no ... Ps 41:8 7901
Thy wrath l hard upon me, and thou ... Ps 88:7 5564
l in wait at every corner ... Prov 7:12
She also l in wait as for a prey, ... Prov 23:28
thou shalt be as he that l down ... Prov 23:34 7901
or as he that l upon the top of a ... Prov 23:34 7901
which l toward the north, and ... Eze 9:2
the great dragon that l in the ... Eze 29:3 6437
from her that l in thy bosom ... Mic 7:5 7901
my servant l at home sick of the ... Mt 8:6 906
My little daughter l at the point ... Mk 5:23 2192
the region that l round about ... Acts 14:6
l toward the south west and north ... Acts 27:12 991
be possible, as much as l in you ... Rom 12:18
the whole world l in wickedness ... 1Jn 5:19 2749
the city l foursquare, and the ... Rev 21:16 2749

LIEUTENANTS {4}
commissions unto the king's l ... Ezr 8:36 323
had commanded unto the king's l ... Est 3:12 323
unto the Jews, and to the l ... Est 8:9 323
rulers of the provinces, and the l ... Est 9:3 323

LIFE {451}
the moving creature that hath l ... Gen 1:20 2416
the earth, wherein there is l ... Gen 1:30 2416
into his nostrils the breath of l ... Gen 2:7 2416
the tree of l also in the midst ... Gen 2:9 2416
thou eat all the days of thy l ... Gen 3:14 2416
eat of it all the days of thy l ... Gen 3:17 2416
and take also of the tree of l ... Gen 3:22 2416
to keep the way of the tree of l ... Gen 3:24 2416
flesh, wherein is the breath of l ... Gen 6:17 2416
six hundredth year of Noah's l ... Gen 7:11 2416
flesh, wherein is the breath of l ... Gen 7:15 2416
nostrils was the breath of l ... Gen 7:22 2416
But flesh with the l thereof ... Gen 9:4 5315
will I require the l of man ... Gen 9:5 5315
thee according to the time of l ... Gen 18:10 2416
thee, according to the time of l ... Gen 18:14 2416
that he said, Escape for thy l ... Gen 19:17 5315
shewed unto me in saving my l ... Gen 19:19 5315
were the years of the l of Sarah ... Gen 23:1 2416
of Abraham's l which he lived ... Gen 25:7 2416
are the years of the l of Ishmael ... Gen 25:17 2416
I am weary of my l because of the ... Gen 27:46 2416
land, what good shall my l do me ... Gen 27:46 2416
to face, and my l is preserved ... Gen 32:30 5315
By the l of Pharaoh ye shall not ... Gen 42:15 2416
or else by the l of Pharaoh ... Gen 42:16 2416
seeing that his l is bound up in ... Gen 44:30 5315
is bound up in the lad's l ... Gen 44:30
send me before you to preserve l ... Gen 45:5
days of the years of my l been ... Gen 47:9 2416
l of my fathers in the days of ... Gen 47:9 2416
me all my l long unto this day ... Gen 48:15
men are dead which sought thy l ... Ex 4:19 5315
the years of the l of Levi were ... Ex 6:16 2416
the years of the l of Kohath were ... Ex 6:18 2416
the years of the l of Amram were ... Ex 6:20 2416
then thou shalt give l for l ... Ex 21:23 5315
give for the ransom of his l ... Ex 21:30 5315
For the l of the flesh is in the ... Lev 17:11 5315
For it is the l of all flesh ... Lev 17:14 5315
blood of it is for the l thereof ... Lev 17:14 5315
for the l of all flesh is the ... Lev 17:14 5315
beside the other in her l time ... Lev 18:18 2416
for the l of a murderer, which is ... Num 35:31 5315
thy heart all the days of thy l ... Deut 4:9 2416
son's son, all the days of thy l ... Deut 6:2 2416
for the blood is the l ... Deut 12:23 5315
not eat the l with the flesh ... Deut 12:23 5315
of Egypt all the days of thy l ... Deut 16:3 2416
therein all the days of his l ... Deut 17:19 2416
but l shall go for l, eye for ... Deut 19:21 5315
l) to employ them in the siege ... Deut 20:19
for he taketh a man's l to pledge ... Deut 24:6 5315
thy l shall hang in doubt before ... Deut 28:66 2416
have none assurance of thy l ... Deut 28:66 2416
I have set before thee this day l ... Deut 30:15 2416
you, that I have set before you l ... Deut 30:19 2416

therefore choose *l*, that both ... Deut 30:19 2416
for he is thy *l*, and the length of ... Deut 30:20 2416
because it is your *l* ... Deut 32:47 2416
before thee all the days of thy *l* ... Josh 1:5 2416
Our *l* for yours, if ye utter not ... Josh 2:14 5315
Moses, all the days of his *l* ... Josh 4:14 2416
for you, and adventured his *l* far ... Judg 9:17 5315
I put my *l* in my hands, and passed ... Judg 12:3 5315
than they which he slew in his *l* ... Judg 16:30 2416
run upon thee, and thou lose thy *l* ... Judg 18:25 5315
be unto thee a restorer of thy *l* ... Ruth 4:15 5315
the LORD all the days of his *l* ... 1Sa 1:11 2416
Israel all the days of his *l* ... 1Sa 7:15 2416
and what is my *l*, or my father's ... 1Sa 18:18 2416
For he did put his *l* in his hand ... 1Sa 19:5 5315
thy father, that he seeketh my *l* ... 1Sa 20:1 5315
seeketh my *l* seeketh thy *l* ... 1Sa 22:23 5315
Saul was come out to seek his *l* ... 1Sa 23:15 5315
bundle of *l* with the LORD thy God ... 1Sa 25:29 2416
as thy *l* was much set by this day ... 1Sa 26:24 5315
so let my *l* be much set by in the ... 1Sa 26:24 5315
then layest thou a snare for my *l* ... 1Sa 28:9 5315
and I have put my *l* in my hand ... 1Sa 28:21 5315
because my *l* is yet whole in me ... 2Sa 1:9 5315
thine enemy, which sought thy *l* ... 2Sa 4:8 5315
for the *l* of his brother whom he ... 2Sa 14:7 5315
shall be, whether in death or *l* ... 2Sa 15:21 2416
forth of my bowels, seeketh my *l* ... 2Sa 16:11 5315
falsehood against mine own *l* ... 2Sa 18:13 5315
which this day have saved thy *l* ... 2Sa 19:5 5315
that thou mayest save thine own *l* ... 1Kin 1:12 5315
and the *l* of thy son Solomon ... 1Kin 1:12 5315
this word against his own *l* ... 1Kin 2:23 5315
hast not asked for thyself long *l* ... 1Kin 3:11 3117
hast asked the *l* of thine enemies ... 1Kin 3:11 5315
Solomon all the days of his *l* ... 1Kin 4:21 2416
his *l* for David my servant's sake ... 1Kin 11:34 2416
him all the days of his *l* ... 1Kin 15:5 2416
and Jeroboam all the days of his *l* ... 1Kin 15:6 2416
if I make not thy *l* as the *l* ... 1Kin 19:2 5315
that, he arose, and went for his *l* ... 1Kin 19:3 5315
now, O LORD, take away my *l* ... 1Kin 19:4 5315
and they seek my *l*, to take it ... 1Kin 19:10 5315
and they seek my *l*, to take it ... 1Kin 19:14 5315
peradventure he will save thy *l* ... 1Kin 20:31 5315
then shall thy *l* be for his *l*, ... 1Kin 20:39 5315
thy *l* shall go for his *l* ... 1Kin 20:42 5315
man of God, I pray thee, let my *l* ... 2Kin 1:13 5315
the *l* of these fifty thy servants ... 2Kin 1:13
therefore let my *l* now be ... 2Kin 1:14 5315
according to the time of *l* ... 2Kin 4:16 2416
her, according to the time of *l* ... 2Kin 4:17 2416
as it was, and fled for their *l* ... 2Kin 7:7 5315
whose son he had restored to *l* ... 2Kin 8:1 2421
he had restored a dead body to *l* ... 2Kin 8:5 2421
whose son he had restored to *l* ... 2Kin 8:5 2421
son, whom Elisha restored to *l* ... 2Kin 8:5 2421
his *l* shall be for the *l* of ... 2Kin 10:24 2421
l shall be for the *l* of him ... 2Kin 10:24 5315
before him all the days of his *l* ... 2Kin 25:29 2416
every day, all the days of his *l* ... 2Kin 25:30 2416
nor the *l* of thine enemies, ... 2Chr 1:11 5315
neither yet hast asked long *l* ... 2Chr 1:11 3117
and pray for the *l* of the king ... Ezr 6:10 2417
go into the temple to save his *l* ... Neh 6:11 2425
let my *l* be given me at my ... Est 7:3 5315
for his *l* to Esther the queen ... Est 7:7 5315
together, and to stand for their *l* ... Est 8:11 5315
a man hath will he give for his *l* ... Job 2:4 5315
but save his *l* ... Job 2:6 5315
l unto the bitter in soul ... Job 3:20 2416
end, that I should prolong my *l* ... Job 6:11 5315
O remember that my *l* is wind ... Job 7:7 2416
and death rather than my *l* ... Job 7:15 6106
I would despise my *l* ... Job 9:21 2416
My soul is weary of my *l* ... Job 10:1 2416
Thou hast granted me *l* and favour, ... Job 10:12 2416
teeth, and put my *l* in mine hand ... Job 13:14 5315
riseth up, and no man is sure of *l* ... Job 24:22 2416
owners thereof to lose their *l* ... Job 31:39 5315
of the Almighty hath given me *l* ... Job 33:4 2421
his *l* from perishing by the sword ... Job 33:18 2416
So that his *l* abhorreth bread, and ... Job 33:20 2416
grave, and his *l* to the destroyers ... Job 33:22 2416
his *l* shall see the light ... Job 33:28 2416
not the *l* of the wicked ... Job 36:6 2421
their *l* is among the unclean ... Job 36:14 2416
tread down my *l* upon the earth ... Ps 7:5 2416
Thou wilt shew me the path of *l* ... Ps 16:11 2416
have their portion in this *l* ... Ps 17:14 2416
He asked *l* of thee, and thou ... Ps 21:4 2416
follow me all the days of my *l* ... Ps 23:6 2416
sinners, nor my *l* with bloody men ... Ps 26:9 2416
the LORD is the strength of my *l* ... Ps 27:1 2416
of the LORD all the days of my *l* ... Ps 27:4 2416
in his favour is *l* ... Ps 30:5 2416
For my *l* is spent with grief, and ... Ps 31:10 2416
they devised to take away my *l* ... Ps 31:13 5315
What man is he that desireth *l* ... Ps 34:12 2416
with thee is the fountain of *l* ... Ps 36:9 2416
seek after my *l* lay snares for me ... Ps 38:12 5315
and my prayer unto the God of my *l* ... Ps 42:8 2416
Thou wilt prolong the king's *l* ... Ps 61:6 3117,5921
lovingkindness is better than *l* ... Ps 63:3 2416
preserve my *l* from fear of the ... Ps 64:1 2416
Which holdeth our soul in *l* ... Ps 66:9 2416
but gave their *l* over to the ... Ps 78:50 2416
my *l* draweth nigh unto the grave ... Ps 88:3 2416

With long *l* will I satisfy him, ... Ps 91:16 3117
redeemeth thy *l* from destruction ... Ps 103:4 2416
Jerusalem all the days of thy *l* ... Ps 128:5 2416
the blessing, even *l* for evermore ... Ps 133:3 2416
smitten my *l* down to the ground ... Ps 143:3 2416
away the *l* of the owners thereof ... Prov 1:19 5315
take they hold of the paths of *l* ... Prov 2:19 2416
For length of days, and long *l* ... Prov 3:2 2416
She is a tree of *l* to them that ... Prov 3:18 2416
So shall they be *l* unto thy soul ... Prov 3:22 2416
the years of thy *l* shall be many ... Prov 4:10 2416
for she is thy *l* ... Prov 4:13 2416
For they are *l* unto those that ... Prov 4:22 2416
for out of it are the issues of *l* ... Prov 4:23 2416
shouldest ponder the path of *l* ... Prov 5:6 2416
of instruction are the way of *l* ... Prov 6:23 2416
will hunt for the precious *l* ... Prov 6:26 5315
knoweth not that it is for his *l* ... Prov 7:23 5315
For whoso findeth me findeth *l* ... Prov 8:35 2416
the years of thy *l* shall be ... Prov 9:11 2416
of a righteous man is a well of *l* ... Prov 10:11 2416
of the righteous tendeth to *l* ... Prov 10:16 2416
He is in the way of *l* that ... Prov 10:17 2416
As righteousness tendeth to *l* ... Prov 11:19 2416
of the righteous is a tree of *l* ... Prov 11:30 2416
man regardeth the *l* of his beast ... Prov 12:10 5315
In the way of righteousness is *l* ... Prov 12:28 2416
keepeth his mouth keepeth his *l* ... Prov 13:3 5315
of a man's *l* are his riches ... Prov 13:8 5315
desire cometh, it is a tree of *l* ... Prov 13:12 2416
of the wise is a fountain of *l* ... Prov 13:14 2416
of the LORD is a fountain of *l* ... Prov 14:27 2416
sound heart is the *l* of the flesh ... Prov 14:30 2416
A wholesome tongue is a tree of *l* ... Prov 15:4 2416
The way of *l* is above to the wise ... Prov 15:24 2416
of *l* abideth among the wise ... Prov 15:31 2416
of the king's countenance is *l* ... Prov 16:15 2416
is a wellspring of *l* unto him ... Prov 16:22 2416
l are in the power of the tongue ... Prov 18:21 2416
The fear of the LORD tendeth to *l* ... Prov 19:23 2416
righteousness and mercy findeth *l* ... Prov 21:21 2416
LORD are riches, and honour, and *l* ... Prov 22:4 2416
and not evil all the days of her *l* ... Prov 31:12 2416
heaven all the days of their *l* ... Eccl 2:3 2416
Therefore I hated *l* ... Eccl 2:17 2416
rejoice, and to do good in his *l* ... Eccl 3:12 2416
the sun all the days of his *l* ... Eccl 5:18 2416
much remember the days of his *l* ... Eccl 5:20 2416
what is good for man in this *l* ... Eccl 6:12 2416
all the days of his vain *l* which ... Eccl 6:12 2416
that wisdom giveth *l* to them that ... Eccl 7:12 2421
his *l* in his wickedness ... Eccl 7:15
of his labour the days of his *l* ... Eccl 8:15 2416
the days of the *l* of thy vanity ... Eccl 9:9 2416
for that is thy portion in this *l* ... Eccl 9:9 2416
his *l* shall be grievous unto him ... Is 15:4 5315
I have cut off like a weaver my *l* ... Is 38:12 2416
things is the *l* of my spirit ... Is 38:16 2416
of our *l* in the house of the LORD ... Is 38:20 2416
men for thee, and people for thy *l* ... Is 43:4 5315
hast found the *l* of thine hand ... Is 57:10 2416
thee, they will seek thy *l* ... Jer 4:30 5315
shall be chosen rather than *l* by ... Jer 8:3 2416
men of Anathoth, that seek thy *l* ... Jer 11:21 5315
hand of those that seek their *l* ... Jer 21:7 5315
I set before you the way of *l* ... Jer 21:8 2416
his *l* shall be unto him for a ... Jer 21:9 5315
the hand of them that seek thy *l* ... Jer 22:25 5315
hand of them that seek their *l* ... Jer 34:20 5315
hand of them that seek their *l* ... Jer 34:21 5315
he shall have his *l* for a prey ... Jer 38:2 5315
hand of these men that seek thy *l* ... Jer 38:16 5315
but thy *l* shall be for a prey ... Jer 39:18 5315
the hand of them that seek his *l* ... Jer 44:30 5315
his enemy, and that sought his *l* ... Jer 44:30 5315
but thy *l* will I give unto thee ... Jer 45:5 5315
and before them that seek their *l* ... Jer 49:37 5315
before him all the days of his *l* ... Jer 52:33 2416
his death, all the days of his *l* ... Jer 52:34 2416
for the *l* of thy young children ... Lam 2:19 5315
have cut off my *l* in the dungeon ... Lam 3:53 2416
thou hast redeemed my *l* ... Lam 3:58
his wicked way, to save his *l* ... Eze 3:18 2421
himself in the iniquity of his *l* ... Eze 7:13 2416
wicked way, by promising him *l* ... Eze 13:22 2421
moment, every man for his own *l* ... Eze 32:10 5315
robbed, walk in the statutes of *l* ... Eze 33:15 2416
awake, some to everlasting *l* ... Dan 12:2 2416
us not perish for this man's *l* ... Jonah 1:14 5315
brought up my *l* from corruption ... Jonah 2:6 2416
I beseech thee, my *l* from me ... Jonah 4:3 5315
My covenant was with him of *l* ... Mal 2:5 2416
which sought the young child's *l* ... Mt 2:20 *5590*
you, Take no thought for your *l* ... Mt 6:25 *5590*
Is not the *l* more than meat, and ... Mt 6:25 *5590*
is the way, which leadeth unto *l* ... Mt 7:14 *2222*
that findeth his *l* shall lose it ... Mt 10:39 *5590*
he that loseth his *l* for my sake ... Mt 10:39 *5590*
will save his *l* shall lose it ... Mt 16:25 *5590*
whosoever will lose his *l* for my ... Mt 16:25 *5590*
to enter into *l* halt or maimed ... Mt 18:8 *2222*
thee to enter into *l* with one eye ... Mt 18:9 *2222*
I do, that I may have eternal *l* ... Mt 19:16 *2222*
but if thou wilt enter into *l* ... Mt 19:17 *2222*
and shall inherit everlasting *l* ... Mt 19:29 *2222*
to give his *l* a ransom for many ... Mt 20:28 *5590*
but the righteous into *l* eternal ... Mt 25:46 *2222*
to save *l*, or to kill ... Mk 3:4 *5590*

will save his *l* shall lose it ... Mk 8:35 *5590*
shall lose his *l* for my sake ... Mk 8:35 *5590*
for thee to enter into *l* maimed ... Mk 9:43 *2222*
for thee to enter halt into *l* ... Mk 9:45 *2222*
I do that I may inherit eternal *l* ... Mk 10:17 *2222*
and in the world to come eternal *l* ... Mk 10:30 *2222*
to give his *l* a ransom for many ... Mk 10:45 *5590*
before him, all the days of our *l* ... Lk 1:75 *2222*
to save *l*, or to destroy it ... Lk 6:9 *5590*
and riches and pleasures of this *l* ... Lk 8:14 *979*
will save his *l* shall lose it ... Lk 9:24 *5590*
will lose his *l* for my sake ... Lk 9:24 *5590*
shall I do to inherit eternal *l* ... Lk 10:25 *2222*
for a man's *l* consisteth not in ... Lk 12:15 *2222*
you, Take no thought for your *l* ... Lk 12:22 *5590*
The *l* is more than meat, and the ... Lk 12:23 *5590*
sisters, yea, and his own *l* also ... Lk 14:26 *5590*
seek to save his *l* shall lose it ... Lk 17:33 *5590*
lose his *l* shall preserve it ... Lk 17:33 *5590*
shall I do to inherit eternal *l* ... Lk 18:18 *2222*
the world to come *l* everlasting ... Lk 18:30 *2222*
drunkenness, and cares of this *l* ... Lk 21:34 *982*
In him was *l* ... Jn 1:4 *2222*
the *l* was the light of men ... Jn 1:4 *2222*
not perish, but have eternal *l* ... Jn 3:15 *2222*
perish, but have everlasting *l* ... Jn 3:16 *2222*
on the Son hath everlasting *l* ... Jn 3:36 *2222*
not the Son shall not see *l* ... Jn 3:36 *2222*
springing up into everlasting *l* ... Jn 4:14 *2222*
and gathereth fruit unto *l* eternal ... Jn 4:36 *2222*
that sent me, hath everlasting *l* ... Jn 5:24 *2222*
but is passed from death unto *l* ... Jn 5:24 *2222*
as the Father hath *l* in himself ... Jn 5:26 *2222*
to the Son to have *l* in himself ... Jn 5:26 *2222*
good, unto the resurrection of *l* ... Jn 5:29 *2222*
them ye think ye have eternal *l* ... Jn 5:39 *2222*
come to me, that ye might have *l* ... Jn 5:40 *2222*
which endureth unto everlasting *l* ... Jn 6:27 *2222*
and giveth *l* unto the world ... Jn 6:33 *2222*
unto them, I am the bread of *l* ... Jn 6:35 *2222*
on him, may have everlasting *l* ... Jn 6:40 *2222*
on me hath everlasting *l* ... Jn 6:47 *2222*
I am that bread of *l* ... Jn 6:48 *2222*
will give for the *l* of the world ... Jn 6:51 *2222*
his blood, ye have no *l* in you ... Jn 6:53 *2222*
drinketh my blood, hath eternal *l* ... Jn 6:54 *2222*
they are spirit, and they are *l* ... Jn 6:63 *2222*
thou hast the words of eternal *l* ... Jn 6:68 *2222*
but shall have the light of *l* ... Jn 8:12 *2222*
I am come that they might have *l* ... Jn 10:10 *2222*
giveth his *l* for the sheep ... Jn 10:11 *5590*
and I lay down my *l* for the sheep ... Jn 10:15 *5590*
love me, because I lay down my *l* ... Jn 10:17 *5590*
And I give unto them eternal *l* ... Jn 10:28 *2222*
I am the resurrection, and the *l* ... Jn 11:25 *2222*
that loveth his *l* shall lose it ... Jn 12:25 *5590*
he that hateth his *l* in this ... Jn 12:25 *5590*
shall keep it unto *l* eternal ... Jn 12:25 *2222*
his commandment is *l* everlasting ... Jn 12:50 *2222*
I will lay down my *l* for thy sake ... Jn 13:37 *5590*
thou lay down thy *l* for my sake ... Jn 13:38 *5590*
I am the way, the truth, and the *l* ... Jn 14:6 *2222*
lay down his *l* for his friends ... Jn 15:13 *5590*
that he should give eternal *l* to ... Jn 17:2 *2222*
And this is *l* eternal, that they ... Jn 17:3 *2222*
ye might have *l* through his name ... Jn 20:31 *2222*
made known to me the ways of *l* ... Acts 2:28 *2222*
And killed the Prince of *l* ... Acts 3:15 *2222*
people all the words of this *l* ... Acts 5:20 *2222*
for his *l* is taken from the earth ... Acts 8:33 *2222*
granted repentance unto *l* ... Acts 11:18 *2222*
unworthy of everlasting *l* ... Acts 13:46 *2222*
ordained to eternal *l* believed ... Acts 13:48 *2222*
thing, seeing he giveth to all *l* ... Acts 17:25 *2222*
for his *l* is in him ... Acts 20:10 *5590*
count I my *l* dear unto myself ... Acts 20:24 *5590*
My manner of *l* from my youth, ... Acts 26:4 *981*
no loss of any man's *l* among you ... Acts 27:22 *5590*
honour and immortality, eternal *l* ... Rom 2:7 *2222*
we shall be saved by his *l* ... Rom 5:10 *2222*
shall reign in *l* by one, Jesus ... Rom 5:17 *2222*
all men unto justification of *l* ... Rom 5:18 *2222*
l by Jesus Christ our Lord ... Rom 5:21 *2222*
also should walk in newness of *l* ... Rom 6:4 *2222*
and the end everlasting *l* ... Rom 6:22 *2222*
l through Jesus Christ our Lord ... Rom 6:23 *2222*
which was ordained to *l*, I found ... Rom 7:10 *2222*
of *l* in Christ Jesus hath made me ... Rom 8:2 *2222*
but to be spiritually minded is *l* ... Rom 8:6 *2222*
but the Spirit is *l* because of ... Rom 8:10 *2222*
that neither death, nor *l* ... Rom 8:38 *2222*
am left alone, and they seek my *l* ... Rom 11:3 *5590*
of them be, but *l* from the dead ... Rom 11:15 *2222*
Who have for my *l* laid down their ... Rom 16:4 *5590*
or Cephas, or the world, or *l* ... 1Cor 3:22 *2222*
things that pertain to this *l* ... 1Cor 6:3 *982*
of things pertaining to this *l* ... 1Cor 6:4 *982*
things without *l* giving sound ... 1Cor 14:7 *895*
If in this *l* only we have hope in ... 1Cor 15:19 *2222*
that we despaired even of *l* ... 2Cor 1:8 *2198*
other the savour of *l* unto *l* ... 2Cor 2:16 *2222*
killeth, but the spirit giveth *l* ... 2Cor 3:6 *2227*
that the *l* also of Jesus might be ... 2Cor 4:10 *2222*
that the *l* also of Jesus might be ... 2Cor 4:11 *2222*
death worketh in us, but *l* in you ... 2Cor 4:12 *2222*
might be swallowed up of *l* ... 2Cor 5:4 *2222*
the *l* which I now live in the ... Gal 2:20
given which could have given *l* ... Gal 3:21 *2227*

of the Spirit reap *l* everlasting	Gal 6:8	*2222*
being alienated from the *l* of God	Eph 4:18	*2222*
in my body, whether it be by *l*	Phil 1:20	*2222*
Holding forth the word of *l*	Phil 2:16	*2222*
unto death, not regarding his *l*	Phil 2:30	*5590*
whose names are in the book of *l*	Phil 4:3	*2222*
your *l* is hid with Christ in God	Col 3:3	*2222*
When Christ, who is our *l*	Col 3:4	*2222*
believe on him to *l* everlasting	1Ti 1:16	*2222*
peaceable *l* in all godliness and	1Ti 2:2	*979*
promise of the *l* that now is	1Ti 4:8	*2222*
of faith, lay hold on eternal *l*	1Ti 6:12	*2222*
they may lay hold on eternal *l*	1Ti 6:19	*2222*
of *l* which is in Christ Jesus	2Ti 1:1	*2222*
death, and hath brought *l* and	2Ti 1:10	*2222*
with the affairs of this *l*	2Ti 2:4	*979*
known my doctrine, manner of *l*	2Ti 3:10	*72*
In hope of eternal *l*, which God,	Titus 1:2	*2222*
to the hope of eternal *l*	Titus 3:7	*2222*
beginning of days, nor end of *l*	Heb 7:3	*2222*
after the power of an endless *l*	Heb 7:16	*2222*
their dead raised to *l* again	Heb 11:35	
he shall receive the crown of *l*	Jas 1:12	*2222*
For what is your *l*	Jas 4:14	*2222*
heirs together of the grace of *l*	1Pet 3:7	*2222*
For he that will love *l*, and see	1Pet 3:10	*2222*
For the time past of our *l* may	1Pet 4:3	*979*
us all things that pertain unto *l*	2Pet 1:3	*2222*
have handled, of the Word of *l*	1Jn 1:1	*2222*
(For the *l* was manifested, and we	1Jn 1:2	*2222*
and shew unto you that eternal *l*	1Jn 1:2	*2222*
of the eyes, and the pride of *l*	1Jn 2:16	*979*
hath promised us, even eternal *l*	1Jn 2:25	*2222*
we have passed from death unto *l*	1Jn 3:14	*2222*
hath eternal *l* abiding in him	1Jn 3:15	*2222*
because he laid down his *l* for us	1Jn 3:16	*5590*
God hath given to us eternal *l*	1Jn 5:11	*2222*
and this *l* is in his Son	1Jn 5:11	*2222*
He that hath the Son hath *l*	1Jn 5:12	*2222*
not the Son of God hath not *l*	1Jn 5:12	*2222*
may know that ye have eternal *l*	1Jn 5:13	*2222*
he shall give him *l* for them that	1Jn 5:16	*2222*
is the true God, and eternal *l*	1Jn 5:20	*2222*
Lord Jesus Christ unto eternal *l*	Jude 21	*2222*
I give to eat of the tree of *l*	Rev 2:7	*2222*
and I will give thee a crown of *l*	Rev 2:10	*2222*
out his name out of the book of *l*	Rev 3:5	*2222*
which were in the sea, and had *l*	Rev 8:9	*5590*
an half the Spirit of *l* from God	Rev 11:11	*2222*
of *l* of the Lamb slain from the	Rev 13:8	*2222*
he had power to give *l* unto the	Rev 13:15	*4151*
of *l* from the foundation of the	Rev 17:8	*2222*
opened, which is the book of *l*	Rev 20:12	*2222*
found written in the book of *l*	Rev 20:15	*2222*
fountain of the water of *l* freely	Rev 21:6	*2222*
written in the Lamb's book of *l*	Rev 21:27	*2222*
me a pure river of water of *l*	Rev 22:1	*2222*
river, was there the tree of *l*	Rev 22:2	*2222*
may have right to the tree of *l*	Rev 22:14	*2222*
him take the water of *l* freely	Rev 22:17	*2222*
his part out of the book of *l*	Rev 22:19	*2222*

LIFETIME {3}

Now Absalom in his *l* had taken	2Sa 18:18	2416
remember that thou in thy *l*	Lk 16:25	*2222*
all their *l* subject to bondage	Heb 2:15	*2198*

LIFT {103}

it was *l* up above the earth	Gen 7:17	7311
L up now thine eyes, and look from	Gen 13:14	5375
I have *l* up mine hand unto the	Gen 14:22	7311
he *l* up his eyes and looked, and,	Gen 18:2	5375
him, and *l* up her voice, and wept	Gen 21:16	5375
l up the lad, and hold him in	Gen 21:18	5375
L up now thine eyes, and see, all	Gen 31:12	5375
shall Pharaoh *l* up thine head	Gen 40:13	5375
l up thy head from off thee	Gen 40:19	5375
without thee shall no man *l* up	Gen 41:44	7311
But *l* thou up thy rod, and stretch	Ex 14:16	7311
for if thou *l* up thy tool upon it	Ex 20:25	5130
The LORD *l* up his countenance	Num 6:26	5375
wherefore then *l* ye up yourselves	Num 16:3	5375
l up himself as a young lion	Num 23:24	5375
l up thine eyes westward, and	Deut 3:27	5375
lest thou *l* up thine eyes unto	Deut 4:19	5375
help him to *l* them up again	Deut 22:4	6965
thou shalt not *l* up any iron tool	Deut 27:5	5130
For I *l* up my hand to heaven, and	Deut 32:40	5375
which no man hath *l* up any iron	Josh 8:31	5130
he *l* up his spear against eight	2Sa 23:8	
wherefore *l* up thy prayer for the	2Kin 19:4	5375
l up the head of Jehoiachin king	2Kin 25:27	5375
words of God, to *l* up the horn	1Chr 25:5	7311
blush to *l* up my face to thee, my	Ezr 9:6	7311
yet will I not *l* up my head	Job 10:15	5375
For then shalt thou *l* up thy face	Job 11:15	5375
shalt *l* up thy face unto God	Job 22:26	5375
Canst thou *l* up thy voice to the	Job 38:34	7311
l thou up the light of thy	Ps 4:6	5375
l up thyself because of the rage	Ps 7:6	5375
O God, *l* up thine hand	Ps 10:12	5375
L up your heads, O ye gates	Ps 24:7	5375
L up your heads, O ye gates	Ps 24:9	5375
even *l* them up, ye everlasting	Ps 24:9	5375
thee, O LORD, do I *l* up my soul	Ps 25:1	5375
when I *l* up my hands toward thy	Ps 28:2	5375
them also, and *l* them up for ever	Ps 28:9	5375
I will *l* up my hands in thy name	Ps 63:4	5375
L up thy feet unto the perpetual	Ps 74:3	7311
to the wicked, *L* not up the horn	Ps 75:4	7311
L not up your horn on high	Ps 75:5	7311
thee, O Lord, do I *l* up my soul	Ps 86:4	5375
the floods *l* up their waves	Ps 93:3	5375
L up thyself, thou judge of the	Ps 94:2	5375
therefore shall he *l* up the head	Ps 110:7	7311
My hands also will I *l* up unto	Ps 119:48	5375
I will *l* up mine eyes unto the	Ps 121:1	5375
Unto thee *l* I up mine eyes, O	Ps 123:1	5375
L up your hands in the sanctuary,	Ps 134:2	5375
for I *l* up my soul unto thee	Ps 143:8	5375
the one will *l* up his fellow	Eccl 4:10	6965
nation shall not *l* up sword	Is 2:4	5375
he will *l* up an ensign to the	Is 5:26	5375
itself against them that *l* it up	Is 10:15	7311
if the staff should *l* up itself	Is 10:15	7311
shall *l* up his staff against thee	Is 10:24	5375
so shall he *l* it up after the	Is 10:26	5375
L up thy voice, O daughter of	Is 10:30	6670
L ye up a banner upon the high	Is 13:2	5375
They shall *l* up their voice, they	Is 24:14	5375
now will I *l* up myself	Is 33:10	5375
wherefore *l* up thy prayer for the	Is 37:4	5375
l up thy voice with strength	Is 40:9	7311
l it up, be not afraid	Is 40:9	7311
L up your eyes on high, and behold	Is 40:26	5375
He shall not cry, nor *l* up	Is 42:2	5375
cities thereof *l* up their voice	Is 42:11	5375
L up thine eyes round about, and	Is 49:18	5375
I will *l* up mine hand to the	Is 49:22	5375
L up your eyes to the heavens, and	Is 51:6	5375
Thy watchmen shall *l* up the voice	Is 52:8	5375
l up thy voice like a trumpet, and	Is 58:1	7311
shall *l* up a standard against him	Is 59:19	5127
L up thine eyes round about, and	Is 60:4	5375
l up a standard for the people	Is 62:10	7311
L up thine eyes unto the high	Jer 3:2	5375
neither *l* up cry nor prayer for	Jer 7:16	5375
neither *l* up a cry or prayer for	Jer 11:14	5375
L up your eyes, and behold them	Jer 13:20	5375
l up thy voice in Bashan, and cry	Jer 22:20	5414
they shall *l* up a shout against	Jer 51:14	6030
l up thy hands toward him for the	Lam 2:19	5375
Let us *l* up our heart with our	Lam 3:41	5375
l up thine eyes now the way	Eze 8:5	5375
the cherubims *l* up their wings	Eze 11:22	5375
that it might not *l* itself up	Eze 17:14	5375
to *l* up the voice with shouting,	Eze 21:22	7311
so that thou shalt not *l* up thine	Eze 23:27	5375
l up the buckler against thee	Eze 26:8	6965
l up your eyes toward your idols,	Eze 33:25	5375
nation shall not *l* up a sword	Mic 4:3	5375
so that no man did *l* up his head	Zec 1:21	5375
L up now thine eyes, and see what	Zec 5:5	5375
not lay hold on it, and *l* it out	Mt 12:11	*1458*
and could in no wise *l* up herself	Lk 13:11	*352*
in hell he *l* up his eyes, being	Lk 16:23	*1869*
would not *l* up so much as his	Lk 18:13	*1869*
then look up, and *l* up your heads	Lk 21:28	*1869*
L up your eyes, and look on the	Jn 4:35	*1869*
Wherefore *l* up the hands which	Heb 12:12	*461*
of the Lord, and he shall *l* you up	Jas 4:10	*5312*

LIFTED {159}

Lot *l* up his eyes, and beheld all	Gen 13:10	5375
third day Abraham *l* up his eyes	Gen 22:4	5375
Abraham *l* up his eyes, and looked,	Gen 22:13	5375
he *l* up his eyes, and saw, and,	Gen 24:63	5375
Rebekah *l* up her eyes, and when	Gen 24:64	5375
Esau *l* up his voice, and wept	Gen 27:38	5375
and *l* up his voice, and wept	Gen 29:11	5375
that I *l* up mine eyes, and saw in	Gen 31:10	5375
Jacob *l* up his eyes, and looked,	Gen 33:1	5375
he *l* up his eyes, and saw the	Gen 33:5	5375
they *l* up their eyes and looked,	Gen 37:25	5375
l up Joseph out of the pit, and	Gen 37:28	5927
he heard that I *l* up my voice	Gen 39:15	7311
as I *l* up my voice and cried, that	Gen 39:18	7311
he *l* up the head of the chief	Gen 40:20	5375
he *l* up his eyes, and saw his	Gen 43:29	5375
he *l* up the rod, and smote the	Ex 7:20	7311
of Israel *l* up their eyes	Ex 14:10	5375
Aaron *l* up his hand toward the	Lev 9:22	5375
the congregation *l* up their voice	Num 14:1	5375
Moses *l* up his hand, and with his	Num 20:11	7311
Balaam *l* up his eyes, and he saw	Num 24:2	5375
Then thine heart be *l* up, and thou	Deut 8:14	7311
be not *l* up above his brethren	Deut 17:20	7311
feet were *l* up unto the dry land	Josh 4:18	5423
that he *l* up his eyes and looked,	Josh 5:13	5375
that the people *l* up their voice	Judg 2:4	5375
so that they *l* up their heads no	Judg 8:28	5375
l up his voice, and cried, and said	Judg 9:7	5375
And when he had *l* up his eyes	Judg 19:17	5375
l up their voices, and wept sore	Judg 21:2	5375
they *l* up their voice, and wept	Ruth 1:9	5375
they *l* up their voice, and wept	Ruth 1:14	5375
they *l* up their eyes, and saw the	1Sa 6:13	5375
all the people *l* up their voices,	1Sa 11:4	5375
Saul *l* up his voice, and wept	1Sa 24:16	5375
were with him *l* up their voice	1Sa 30:4	5375
the king *l* up his voice, and wept	2Sa 3:32	5375
that kept the watch *l* up his eyes	2Sa 13:34	5375
came, and *l* up their voice and wept	2Sa 13:36	5375
l up his eyes, and looked, and	2Sa 18:24	5375
l up their hand against my lord	2Sa 18:28	5375
hath *l* up his hand against the	2Sa 20:21	5375
thou also hast *l* me up on high	2Sa 22:49	7311
he *l* up his spear against three	2Sa 23:18	5782
even he *l* up his hand against the	1Kin 11:26	7311
this was the cause that he *l* up	1Kin 11:27	7311
he *l* up his face to the window,	2Kin 9:32	5375
and thine heart hath *l* thee up	2Kin 14:10	5375
voice, and *l* up thine eyes on high	2Kin 19:22	5375
he *l* up his spear against three	1Chr 11:11	5782
for his kingdom was *l* up on high	1Chr 14:2	5375
David *l* up his eyes, and saw the	1Chr 21:16	5375
when they *l* up their voice with	2Chr 5:13	7311
his heart was *l* up in the ways of	2Chr 17:6	1361
his heart was *l* up to his	2Chr 26:16	1361
for his heart was *l* up	2Chr 32:25	1361
when they *l* up their eyes afar	Job 2:12	5375
they *l* up their voice, and wept	Job 2:12	5375
If I have *l* up my hand against	Job 31:21	5130
or *l* up myself when evil found	Job 31:29	5782
who hath not *l* up his soul unto	Ps 24:4	5375
and be ye *l* up, ye everlasting	Ps 24:7	5375
now shall mine head be *l* up above	Ps 27:6	7311
for thou hast *l* me up, and hast	Ps 30:1	1802
hath *l* up his heel against me	Ps 41:9	1431
l up axes upon the thick trees	Ps 74:5	935
that hate thee have *l* up the head	Ps 83:2	5375
The floods have *l* up, O LORD, the	Ps 93:3	5375
the floods have *l* up their voice	Ps 93:3	5375
for thou hast *l* me up, and cast me	Ps 102:10	5375
Therefore he *l* up his hand	Ps 106:26	5375
and their eyelids are *l* up	Prov 30:13	5375
and upon every one that is *l* up	Is 2:12	5375
l up, and upon all the oaks of	Is 2:13	5375
upon all the hills that are *l* up	Is 2:14	5375
l up, and his train filled the	Is 6:1	5375
LORD, when thy hand is *l* up	Is 26:11	5375
voice, and *l* up thine eyes on high	Is 37:23	5375
is *l* up even to the skies	Jer 51:9	5375
l up the head of Jehoiachin king	Jer 52:31	5375
were *l* up from the earth, the	Eze 1:19	5375
the earth, the wheels were *l* up	Eze 1:19	5375
the wheels were *l* up over against	Eze 1:20	5375
when those were *l* up from the	Eze 1:21	5375
the wheels were *l* up over against	Eze 1:21	5375
So the spirit *l* me up, and took me	Eze 3:14	5375
the spirit *l* me up between the	Eze 8:3	5375
So I *l* up mine eyes the way	Eze 8:5	5375
And the cherubims were *l* up	Eze 10:15	7426
when the cherubims *l* up their	Eze 10:16	5375
and when they were *l* up	Eze 10:17	7311
these *l* up themselves also	Eze 10:17	7426
the cherubims *l* up their wings,	Eze 10:19	5375
Moreover the spirit *l* me up	Eze 11:1	5375
neither hath *l* up his eyes to the	Eze 18:6	5375
hath *l* up his eyes to the idols,	Eze 18:12	5375
neither hath *l* up his eyes to the	Eze 18:15	5375
l up mine hand unto the seed of	Eze 20:5	5375
when I *l* up mine hand unto them,	Eze 20:5	5375
In the day that I *l* up mine hand	Eze 20:6	5375
Yet also I *l* up my hand unto them	Eze 20:15	5375
I *l* up mine hand unto them also	Eze 20:23	5375
for the which I *l* up mine hand to	Eze 20:28	5375
the country for the which I *l* up	Eze 20:42	5375
Because thine heart is *l* up	Eze 28:2	1361
thine heart is *l* up because of	Eze 28:5	1361
Thine heart was *l* up because of	Eze 28:17	1361
Because thou hast *l* up thyself in	Eze 31:10	1361
his heart is *l* up in his height	Eze 31:10	7311
I have *l* up mine hand, Surely the	Eze 36:7	5375
therefore have I *l* up mine hand	Eze 44:12	5375
concerning the which I *l* up mine	Eze 47:14	5375
l up mine eyes unto heaven	Dan 4:34	5191
But when his heart was *l* up	Dan 5:20	7313
But hast *l* up thyself against the	Dan 5:23	7313
it was *l* up from the earth, and	Dan 7:4	5191
Then I *l* up mine eyes, and saw, and	Dan 8:3	5375
Then I *l* up mine eyes, and looked,	Dan 10:5	5375
his heart shall be *l* up	Dan 11:12	7311
Thine hand shall be *l* up upon	Mic 5:9	7311
his soul which is *l* up is not	Hab 2:4	6075
voice, and *l* up his hands on high	Hab 3:10	5375
Then *l* I up mine eyes, and saw, and	Zec 1:18	5375
which *l* up their horn over the	Zec 1:21	5375
I *l* up mine eyes again, and looked	Zec 2:1	5375
l up mine eyes, and looked, and	Zec 5:1	5375
there was *l* up a talent of lead	Zec 5:7	5375
Then *l* I up mine eyes, and looked,	Zec 5:9	5375
they *l* up the ephah between the	Zec 5:9	5375
l up mine eyes, and looked, and,	Zec 6:1	5375
l up as an ensign upon his land	Zec 9:16	5264
and it shall be *l* up, and inhabited	Zec 14:10	7213
And when they had *l* up their eyes	Mt 17:8	*1869*
took her by the hand, and *l* her up	Mk 1:31	*1453*
took him by the hand, and *l* him up	Mk 9:27	*1453*
he *l* up his eyes on his disciples	Lk 6:20	*1869*
of the company *l* up her voice	Lk 11:27	*1869*
they *l* up their voices, and said,	Lk 17:13	*142*
he *l* up his hands, and blessed	Lk 24:50	*1869*
as Moses *l* up the serpent in the	Jn 3:14	*5312*
so must the Son of man be *l* up	Jn 3:14	*5312*
When Jesus then *l* up his eyes	Jn 6:5	*1869*
he *l* up himself, and said unto	Jn 8:7	*352*
When Jesus had *l* up himself	Jn 8:10	*352*
When ye have *l* up the Son of man,	Jn 8:28	*5312*
Jesus *l* up his eyes, and said,	Jn 11:41	*142*
if I be *l* up from the earth, will	Jn 12:32	*5312*
thou, The Son of man must be *l* up	Jn 12:34	*5312*
me hath *l* up his heel against me	Jn 13:18	*1869*
l up his eyes to heaven, and said,	Jn 17:1	*1869*
l up his voice, and said unto them	Acts 2:14	*1869*

by the right hand, and *l* him up ... Acts 3:7 *1453*
they *l* up their voice to God with ... Acts 4:24 *142*
l her up, and when he had called ... Acts 9:41 *450*
they *l* up their voices, saying in ... Acts 14:11 *1869*
then *l* up their voices, and said, ... Acts 22:22 *1869*
lest being *l* up with pride he ... 1Ti 3:6 *5188*
upon the earth *l* up his hand to ... Rev 10:5 *142*

LIFTER {1}
glory, and the *l* up of mine head ... Ps 3:3 7311

LIFTEST {4}
Thou *l* me up to the wind ... Job 30:22 5375
thou that *l* me up from the gates ... Ps 9:13 7311
thou *l* me up above those that ... Ps 18:48 7311
l up thy voice for understanding ... Prov 2:3 5414

LIFTETH {10}
he bringeth low, and *l* up ... 1Sa 2:7 7311
l up the beggar from the dunghill ... 1Sa 2:8 7311
thine heart *l* thee up to boast ... 2Chr 25:19 5375
What time she *l* up herself on ... Job 39:18 4754
which *l* up the waves thereof ... Ps 107:25 7311
l the needy out of the dunghill ... Ps 113:7 7311
The LORD *l* up the meek ... Ps 147:6 5749
when he *l* up an ensign on the ... Is 18:3 5375
against him that *l* himself up in ... Jer 51:3 5927
The horseman *l* up both the bright ... Nah 3:3 5927

LIFTING {9}
for *l* up his spear against three ... 1Chr 11:20 5782
by *l* up the voice with joy ... 1Chr 15:16 7311
Amen, Amen, with *l* up their hands ... Neh 8:6 4607
thou shalt say, There is *l* up ... Job 22:29 1466
the *l* up of my hands as the ... Ps 141:2 4864
done foolishly in *l* up thyself ... Prov 30:32 5375
mount up like the *l* up of smoke ... Is 9:18 1348
at the *l* up of thyself the ... Is 33:3 7427
l up holy hands, without wrath and ... 1Ti 2:8 *1869*

LIGHT {275}
And God said, Let there be *l* ... Gen 1:3 216
and there was *l* ... Gen 1:3 216
And God saw the *l*, that it was ... Gen 1:4 216
God divided the *l* from the ... Gen 1:4 216
And God called the *l* Day, and the ... Gen 1:5 216
heaven to give *l* upon the earth ... Gen 1:15 216
the greater *l* to rule the day, and ... Gen 1:16 3974
the lesser *l* to rule the night ... Gen 1:16 3974
heaven to give *l* upon the earth ... Gen 1:17 216
to divide the *l* from the darkness ... Gen 1:18 216
As soon as the morning was *l* ... Gen 44:3 216
Israel had *l* in their dwellings ... Ex 10:23 216
a pillar of fire, to give them *l* ... Ex 13:21 216
but it gave *l* by night to these ... Ex 14:20 216
Oil for the *l*, spices for ... Ex 25:6 3974
they shall *l* the lamps thereof, ... Ex 25:37 5927
they may give *l* over against it ... Ex 25:37 216
pure oil olive beaten for the *l* ... Ex 27:20 3974
And oil for the *l*, and spices for ... Ex 35:8 3974
The candlestick also for the *l* ... Ex 35:14 3974
his lamps, with the oil for the *l* ... Ex 35:14 3974
And spice, and oil for the *l* ... Ex 35:28 3974
vessels thereof, and the oil for *l* ... Ex 39:37 3974
and *l* the lamps thereof ... Ex 40:4 5927
pure oil olive beaten for the *l* ... Lev 24:2 3974
and cover the candlestick of the *l* ... Num 4:9 3974
pertaineth the oil for the *l* ... Num 4:16 3974
the seven lamps shall give *l* over ... Num 8:2 216
and our soul loatheth this *l* bread ... Num 21:5 7052
Cursed be he that setteth *l* by ... Deut 27:16 7034
l persons, which followed him ... Judg 9:4 6348
where her lord was, till it was *l* ... Judg 19:26 216
her hap was to *l* on a part of the ... Ruth 2:3 7136
and spoil them until the morning *l* ... 1Sa 14:36 216
Seemeth it to you a *l* thing to be ... 1Sa 18:23 7043
l any that pisseth against the ... 1Sa 25:22 216
l any that pisseth against the ... 1Sa 25:34 216
less or more, until the morning *l* ... 1Sa 25:36 216
early in the morning, and have *l* ... 1Sa 29:10 216
Asahel was as *l* of foot as a wild ... 2Sa 2:18 7031
we will *l* upon him as the dew ... 2Sa 17:12 5117
by the morning *l* there lacked not ... 2Sa 17:22 216
thou quench not the *l* of Israel ... 2Sa 21:17 5216
shall be as the *l* of the morning ... 2Sa 23:4 216
l was against *l* in three ... 1Kin 7:4 4237
l was against *l* in three ... 1Kin 7:5 4237
was against *l* in three ranks ... 1Kin 7:5 216
David my servant may have a *l* ... 1Kin 11:36 5216
as if it had been a *l* thing for ... 1Kin 16:31 7043
this is but a *l* thing in the ... 2Kin 3:18 7043
if we tarry till the morning *l* ... 2Kin 7:9 216
him to give him alway a *l* ... 2Kin 8:19 5216
It is a *l* thing for the shadow to ... 2Kin 20:10 7043
as he promised to give a *l* to him ... 2Chr 21:7 5216
to give them *l* in the way wherein ... Neh 9:12 216
of fire by night, to shew them *l* ... Neh 9:19 216
The Jews had *l*, and gladness, and ... Est 8:16 219
neither let the *l* shine upon it ... Job 3:4 5105
let it look for *l*, but have none ... Job 3:9 216
as infants which never saw *l* ... Job 3:16 216
Wherefore is *l* given to him that ... Job 3:20 216
Why is *l* given to a man whose way ... Job 3:23
where the *l* is as darkness ... Job 10:22 3313
bringeth out to *l* the shadow of ... Job 12:22 216
They grope in the dark without *l* ... Job 12:25 216
the *l* is short because of ... Job 17:12 216
the *l* of the wicked shall be put ... Job 18:5 216
The *l* shall be dark in his ... Job 18:6 216
be driven from *l* into darkness ... Job 18:18 216
the *l* shall shine upon thy ways ... Job 22:28 216
of those that rebel against the *l* ... Job 24:13 216
with the *l* killeth the poor ... Job 24:14 216
they know not the *l* ... Job 24:16 216
and upon whom doth not his *l* arise ... Job 25:3 216
is hid bringeth he forth to *l* ... Job 28:11 216
when by his *l* I walked through ... Job 29:3 216
the *l* of my countenance they cast ... Job 29:24 216
and when I waited for *l*, there ... Job 30:26 216
pit, and his life shall see the *l* ... Job 33:28 216
with the *l* of the living ... Job 33:30 216
he spreadeth his *l* upon it ... Job 36:30 216
With clouds he covereth the *l* ... Job 36:32 216
caused the *l* of his cloud to ... Job 37:15 216
bright *l* which is in the clouds ... Job 37:21 216
the wicked their *l* is withholden ... Job 38:15 216
Where is the way where *l* dwelleth ... Job 38:19 216
By what way is the *l* parted ... Job 38:24 216
By his neesings a *l* doth shine ... Job 41:18 216
lift thou up the *l* of thy ... Ps 4:6 216
For thou wilt *l* my candle ... Ps 18:28 215
The LORD is my *l* and my salvation ... Ps 27:1 216
in thy *l* shall we see *l* ... Ps 36:9 216
in thy *l* shall we see *l* ... Ps 36:9 216
forth thy righteousness as the *l* ... Ps 37:6 216
as for the *l* of mine eyes, it ... Ps 38:10 216
O send out thy *l* and thy truth ... Ps 43:3 216
the *l* of thy countenance, because ... Ps 44:3 216
they shall never see *l* ... Ps 49:19 216
before God in the *l* of the living ... Ps 56:13 216
thou hast prepared the *l* and the ... Ps 74:16 3974
and all the night with a *l* of fire ... Ps 78:14 216
in the *l* of thy countenance ... Ps 89:15 216
sins in the *l* of thy countenance ... Ps 90:8 3974
L is sown for the righteous, and ... Ps 97:11 216
thyself with *l* as with a garment ... Ps 104:2 216
and fire to give *l* in the night ... Ps 105:39 216
there ariseth *l* in the darkness ... Ps 112:4 216
the LORD, which hath shewed us *l* ... Ps 118:27 216
unto my feet, and a *l* unto my path ... Ps 119:105 216
entrance of thy words giveth *l* ... Ps 119:130 216
the night shall be *l* about me ... Ps 139:11 216
the *l* are both alike to thee ... Ps 139:12 219
praise him, all ye stars of *l* ... Ps 148:3 216
of the just is as the shining *l* ... Prov 4:18 216
and the law is *l* ... Prov 6:23 216
The *l* of the righteous rejoiceth ... Prov 13:9 216
The *l* of the eyes rejoiceth the ... Prov 15:30 3974
In the *l* of the king's ... Prov 16:15 216
as far as *l* excelleth darkness ... Eccl 2:13 216
Truly the *l* is sweet, and a ... Eccl 11:7 216
While the sun, or the *l*, or the ... Eccl 12:2 216
let us walk in the *l* of the LORD ... Is 2:5 216
for *l*, and *l* for darkness ... Is 5:20 216
the *l* is darkened in the heavens ... Is 5:30 216
is because there is no *l* in them ... Is 8:20 7837
in darkness have seen a great *l* ... Is 9:2 216
upon them hath the *l* shined ... Is 9:2 216
the *l* of Israel shall be for a ... Is 10:17 216
thereof shall not give their *l* ... Is 13:10 216
shall not cause her *l* to shine ... Is 13:10 216
Moreover the *l* of the moon shall ... Is 30:26 216
moon shall be as the *l* of the sun ... Is 30:26 216
the *l* of the sun shall be ... Is 30:26 216
as the *l* of seven days, in the ... Is 30:26 216
people, for a *l* of the Gentiles ... Is 42:6 216
will make darkness *l* before them ... Is 42:16 216
I form the *l*, and create darkness ... Is 45:7 216
It is a *l* thing that thou ... Is 49:6 7043
give thee for a *l* to the Gentiles ... Is 49:6 216
walketh in darkness, and hath no *l* ... Is 50:10 5051
walk in the *l* of your fire, and in ... Is 50:11 217
to rest for a *l* of the people ... Is 51:4 216
Then shall thy *l* break forth as ... Is 58:8 216
then shall thy *l* rise in ... Is 58:10 216
we wait for *l*, but behold ... Is 59:9 216
for thy *l* is come, and the glory ... Is 60:1 216
the Gentiles shall come to thy *l* ... Is 60:3 216
sun shall be no more thy *l* by day ... Is 60:19 216
shall the moon give *l* unto thee ... Is 60:19 216
be unto thee an everlasting *l* ... Is 60:19 216
LORD shall be thine everlasting *l* ... Is 60:20 216
and the heavens, and they had no *l* ... Jer 4:23 216
and, while ye look for *l*, he turn ... Jer 13:16 216
and the *l* of the candle ... Jer 25:10 216
giveth the sun for a *l* by day ... Jer 31:35 216
and of the stars for a *l* by night ... Jer 31:35 216
me into darkness, but not into *l* ... Lam 3:2 216
Is it a *l* thing to the house of ... Eze 8:17 7043
In thee have they set *l* by father ... Eze 22:7 7043
and the moon shall not give her *l* ... Eze 32:7 216
and the *l* dwelleth with him ... Dan 2:22 5094
and in the days of thy father *l* ... Dan 5:11 5094
of the gods is in thee, and that *l* ... Dan 5:14 5094
are as the *l* that goeth forth ... Hos 6:5 216
of the LORD is darkness, and not *l* ... Amos 5:18 216
of the LORD be darkness, and not *l* ... Amos 5:20 216
when the morning is *l*, they ... Mic 2:1 216
the LORD shall be a *l* unto me ... Mic 7:8 216
he will bring me forth to the *l* ... Mic 7:9 216
And his brightness was as the *l* ... Hab 3:4 216
at the *l* of thine arrows they ... Hab 3:11 216
Her prophets are *l* and treacherous ... Zeph 3:4 6348
doth he bring his judgment to *l* ... Zeph 3:5 216
that the *l* shall not be clear, ... Zec 14:6 216
at evening time it shall be *l* ... Zec 14:7 216
which sat in darkness saw great *l* ... Mt 4:16 *5457*
and shadow of death *l* is sprung up ... Mt 4:16 *5457*
Ye are the *l* of the world ... Mt 5:14 *5457*
Neither do men *l* a candle ... Mt 5:15 *2545*
it giveth *l* unto all that are in ... Mt 5:15 *2989*
Let your *l* so shine before men, ... Mt 5:16 *5457*
The *l* of the body is the eye ... Mt 6:22 *5460*
thy whole body shall be full of *l* ... Mt 6:22 *3088*
If therefore the *l* that is in ... Mt 6:23 *5457*
in darkness, that speak ye in *l* ... Mt 10:27 *5457*
yoke is easy, and my burden is *l* ... Mt 11:30 *1645*
and his raiment was white as the *l* ... Mt 17:2 *5457*
But they made *l* of it, and went ... Mt 22:5 *272*
and the moon shall not give her *l* ... Mt 24:29 *5338*
and the moon shall not give her *l* ... Mk 13:24 *5338*
To give *l* to them that sit in ... Lk 1:79 *2014*
A *l* to lighten the Gentiles, and ... Lk 2:32 *5457*
they which enter in may see the *l* ... Lk 8:16 *5457*
they which come in may see the *l* ... Lk 11:33 *5338*
The *l* of the body is the eye ... Lk 11:34 *3088*
thy whole body also is full of *l* ... Lk 11:34 *5460*
the *l* which is in thee be not ... Lk 11:35 *5457*
whole body therefore be full of *l* ... Lk 11:36 *5460*
the whole shall be full of *l* ... Lk 11:36 *5460*
of a candle doth give thee *l* ... Lk 11:36 *5461*
darkness shall be heard in the *l* ... Lk 12:3 *5457*
one piece, doth not *l* a candle ... Lk 15:8 *681*
wiser than the children of *l* ... Lk 16:8 *5457*
and the life was the *l* of men ... Jn 1:4 *5457*
the *l* shineth in darkness ... Jn 1:5 *5457*
witness, to bear witness of the *L* ... Jn 1:7 *5457*
He was not that *L*, but was sent ... Jn 1:8 *5457*
sent to bear witness of that *L* ... Jn 1:8 *5457*
That was the true *L*, which ... Jn 1:9 *5457*
that *l* is come into the world, and ... Jn 3:19 *5457*
men loved darkness rather than *l* ... Jn 3:19 *5457*
one that doeth evil hateth the *l* ... Jn 3:20 *5457*
neither cometh to the *l* ... Jn 3:20 *5457*
that doeth truth cometh to the *l* ... Jn 3:21 *5457*
He was a burning and a shining *l* ... Jn 5:35 *3088*
for a season to rejoice in his *l* ... Jn 5:35 *5457*
saying, I am the *l* of the world ... Jn 8:12 *5457*
but shall have the *l* of life ... Jn 8:12 *5457*
world, I am the *l* of the world ... Jn 9:5 *5457*
he seeth the *l* of this world ... Jn 11:9 *5457*
because there is no *l* in him ... Jn 11:10 *5457*
a little while is the *l* with you ... Jn 12:35 *5457*
Walk while ye have the *l*, lest ... Jn 12:35 *5457*
ye have *l*, believe in the *l* ... Jn 12:36 *5457*
that ye may be the children of *l* ... Jn 12:36 *5457*
I am come a *l* into the world, ... Jn 12:46 *5457*
round about him a *l* from heaven ... Acts 9:3 *5457*
him, and a *l* shined in the prison ... Acts 12:7 *5457*
thee to be a *l* of the Gentiles ... Acts 13:47 *5457*
Then he called for a *l*, and sprang ... Acts 16:29 *5457*
heaven a great *l* round about me ... Acts 22:6 *5457*
were with me saw indeed the *l* ... Acts 22:9 *5457*
not see for the glory of that *l* ... Acts 22:11 *5457*
I saw in the way a *l* from heaven ... Acts 26:13 *5457*
to turn them from darkness to *l* ... Acts 26:18 *5457*
should shew *l* unto the people, and ... Acts 26:23 *5457*
a *l* of them which are in darkness ... Rom 2:19 *5457*
and let us put on the armour of *l* ... Rom 13:12 *5457*
who both will bring to *l* the ... 1Cor 4:5 *5461*
lest the *l* of the glorious gospel ... 2Cor 4:4 *5462*
who commanded the *l* to shine out ... 2Cor 4:6 *5457*
to give the *l* of the knowledge of ... 2Cor 4:6 *5462*
For our *l* affliction, which is ... 2Cor 4:17 *1645*
communion hath *l* with darkness ... 2Cor 6:14 *5457*
is transformed into an angel of *l* ... 2Cor 11:14 *5457*
but now are ye *l* in the Lord ... Eph 5:8 *5457*
walk as children of *l* ... Eph 5:8 *5457*
are made manifest by the *l* ... Eph 5:13 *5457*
doth make manifest is *l* ... Eph 5:13 *5457*
dead, and Christ shall give thee *l* ... Eph 5:14 *2017*
inheritance of the saints in *l* ... Col 1:12 *5457*
Ye are all the children of *l* ... 1Th 5:5 *5457*
dwelling in the *l* which no man ... 1Ti 6:16 *5457*
immortality to *l* through the ... 2Ti 1:10 *5461*
of darkness into his marvellous *l* ... 1Pet 2:9 *5457*
as unto a *l* that shineth in a ... 2Pet 1:19 *3088*
declare unto you, that God is *l* ... 1Jn 1:5 *5457*
in the *l*, as he is in the *l* ... 1Jn 1:7 *5457*
past, and the true *l* now shineth ... 1Jn 2:8 *5457*
He that saith he is in the *l* ... 1Jn 2:9 *5457*
his brother abideth in the *l* ... 1Jn 2:10 *5457*
neither shall the sun *l* on them ... Rev 7:16 *4098*
the *l* of a candle shall shine no ... Rev 18:23 *5457*
her *l* was like unto a stone most ... Rev 21:11 *5458*
it, and the Lamb is the *l* thereof ... Rev 21:23 *3088*
saved shall walk in the *l* of it ... Rev 21:24 *5457*
no candle, neither *l* of the sun ... Rev 22:5 *5457*
for the Lord God giveth them *l* ... Rev 22:5 *5461*

LIGHTED {13}
saw Isaac, she *l* off the camel ... Gen 24:64 5307
he *l* upon a certain place, and ... Gen 28:11 6293
he *l* the lamps before the LORD ... Ex 40:25 5927
he *l* the lamps thereof over ... Num 8:3 5927
and she *l* off her ass ... Josh 15:18 6795
and she *l* from off her ass ... Judg 1:14 6795
so that Sisera *l* down off his ... Judg 4:15 3381
l off the ass, and fell before ... 1Sa 25:23 3381
he *l* down from the chariot to ... 2Kin 5:21 5307
he *l* on Jehonadab the son of ... 2Kin 10:15 4672
Jacob, and it hath *l* upon Israel ... Is 9:8 5307
No man, when he hath *l* a candle ... Lk 8:16 *681*
No man, when he hath *l* a candle ... Lk 11:33 *681*

LIGHTEN {7}
peradventure he will *l* his hand ... 1Sa 6:5 7043
and the LORD will *l* my darkness ... 2Sa 22:29 5050

that our God may *l* our eyes ... Ezr 9:8 215
l mine eyes, lest I sleep the ... Ps 13:3 215
into the sea, to *l* it of them ... Jonah 1:5 7043
A light to *l* the Gentiles, and the ... Lk 2:32 *602*
for the glory of God did *l* it ... Rev 21:23 *5461*

LIGHTENED {5}
They looked unto him, and were *l* ... Ps 34:5 5102
the lightnings *l* the world ... Ps 77:18 215
the next day they *l* the ship ... Acts 27:18 *1546,4160*
they *l* the ship, and cast out the ... Acts 27:38 *2893*
the earth was *l* with his glory ... Rev 18:1 *5461*

LIGHTENETH {2}
the LORD *l* both their eyes ... Prov 29:13 215
that *l* out of the one part under ... Lk 17:24 *797*

LIGHTER {5}
yoke which he put upon us, *l* ... 1Kin 12:4 7043
thy father did put upon us *l* ... 1Kin 12:9 7043
heavy, but make thou it *l* unto us ... 1Kin 12:10 7043
make thou it somewhat *l* for us ... 2Chr 10:10 7043
they are altogether *l* than vanity ... Ps 62:9

LIGHTEST {1}
unto him, When thou *l* the lamps ... Num 8:2 5927

LIGHTETH {3}
when Aaron *l* the lamps at even, ... Ex 30:8 5927
l upon his neighbour, that he die ... Deut 19:5 4672
which *l* every man that cometh ... Jn 1:9 *5461*

LIGHTING {2}
shall shew the *l* down of his arm, ... Is 30:30 5183
like a dove, and *l* upon him ... Mt 3:16 *2064*

LIGHTLY {7}
might *l* have lien with thy wife ... Gen 26:10 4592
l esteemed the Rock of his ... Deut 32:15 5034
despise me shall be *l* esteemed ... 1Sa 2:30 7043
I am a poor man, and *l* esteemed ... 1Sa 18:23 7034
when at the first he *l* afflicted ... Is 9:1 7043
and all the hills moved *l* ... Jer 4:24 7043
that can *l* speak evil of me ... Mk 9:39 *5035*

LIGHTNESS {3}
through the *l* of her whoredom ... Jer 3:9 6963
err by their lies, and by their *l* ... Jer 23:32 6350
was thus minded, did I use *l* ... 2Cor 1:17 *1644*

LIGHTNING {13}
l, and discomfited them ... 2Sa 22:15 1300
a way for the *l* of the thunder ... Job 28:26 2385
his *l* unto the ends of the earth ... Job 37:3 216
or a way for the *l* of thunder ... Job 38:25 2385
Cast forth *l*, and scatter them ... Ps 144:6 1300
and out of the fire went forth *l* ... Eze 1:13 1300
as the appearance of a flash of *l* ... Eze 1:14 965
his face as the appearance of *l* ... Dan 10:6 1300
his arrow shall go forth as the *l* ... Zec 9:14 1300
For as the *l* cometh out of the ... Mt 24:27 *796*
His countenance was like *l* ... Mt 28:3 *796*
Satan as *l* fall from heaven ... Lk 10:18 *796*
For as the *l*, that lighteneth out ... Lk 17:24 *796*

LIGHTNINGS {14}
that there were thunders and *l* ... Ex 19:16 1300
saw the thunderings, and the *l* ... Ex 20:18 3940
Canst thou send *l*, that they may ... Job 38:35 1300
and he shot out *l*, and discomfited ... Ps 18:14 1300
the *l* lightened the world ... Ps 77:18 1300
His *l* enlightened the world ... Ps 97:4 1300
he maketh *l* for the rain ... Ps 135:7 1300
he maketh *l* with rain, and ... Jer 10:13 1300
he maketh *l* with rain, and ... Jer 51:16 1300
they shall run like the *l* ... Nah 2:4 1300
And out of the throne proceeded *l* ... Rev 4:5 *796*
were voices, and thunderings, and *l* ... Rev 8:5 *796*
and there were *l*, and voices, and ... Rev 11:19 *796*
were voices, and thunders, and *l* ... Rev 16:18 *796*

LIGHTS {10}
Let there be *l* in the firmament ... Gen 1:14 3974
And let them be for *l* in the ... Gen 1:15 3974
And God made two great *l* ... Gen 1:16 3974
house he made windows of narrow *l* ... 1Kin 6:4 8261
To him that made great *l* ... Ps 136:7 216
All the bright *l* of heaven will I ... Eze 32:8 3974
girded about, and your *l* burning ... Lk 12:35 *3088*
there were many *l* in the upper ... Acts 20:8 *2985*
whom ye shine as *l* in the world ... Phil 2:15 *5458*
cometh down from the Father of *l* ... Jas 1:17 *5457*

LIGN {1}
as the trees of *l* aloes which the ... Num 24:6

LIGURE {2}
And the third row a *l*, an agate, ... Ex 28:19 3958
And the third row, a *l*, an agate, ... Ex 39:12 3958

LIKE See APPENDIX.

LIKED {1}
he *l* me to make me king over all ... 1Chr 28:4 7521

LIKEMINDED {3}
grant you to be *l* one ... Rom 15:5 *3588,846,5426*
Fulfil ye my joy, that ye be *l* ... Phil 2:2 *3588,846,5426*
For I have no man *l*, who will ... Phil 2:20 *2473*

LIKEN {9}
To whom then will ye *l* God ... Is 40:18 1819
To whom then will ye *l* me ... Is 40:25 1819
To whom will ye *l* me, and make me ... Is 46:5 1819
what thing shall I *l* to thee ... Lam 2:13 1819
I will *l* him unto a wise man, ... Mt 7:24 *3666*
shall I *l* this generation ... Mt 11:16 *3666*
shall we *l* the kingdom of God ... Mk 4:30 *3666*
Whereunto then shall I *l* the men ... Lk 7:31 *3666*
Whereunto shall I *l* the kingdom ... Lk 13:20 *3666*

LIKENED {6}
the mighty can be *l* unto the LORD ... Ps 89:6 1819
I have *l* the daughter of Zion to ... Jer 6:2 1819
shall be *l* unto a foolish man, ... Mt 7:26 *3666*
The kingdom of heaven is *l* unto a ... Mt 13:24 *3666*
of heaven *l* unto a certain king ... Mt 18:23 *3666*
of heaven be *l* unto ten virgins ... Mt 25:1 *3666*

LIKENESS {34}
man in our image, after our *l* ... Gen 1:26 1823
in the *l* of God made he him ... Gen 5:1 1823
and begat a son in his own *l* ... Gen 5:3 1823
or any *l* of any thing that is in ... Ex 20:4 8544
figure, the *l* of male or female, ... Deut 4:16 8403
The *l* of any beast that is on the ... Deut 4:17 8403
the *l* of any winged fowl that ... Deut 4:17 8403
The *l* of any thing that creepeth ... Deut 4:18 8403
the *l* of any fish that is in the ... Deut 4:18 8403
or the *l* of any thing, which the ... Deut 4:23 8544
or the *l* of any thing, and shall ... Deut 4:25 8544
or any *l* of any thing that is in ... Deut 5:8 8544
when I awake, with thy *l* ... Ps 17:15 8544
or what *l* will ye compare unto ... Is 40:18 1823
the *l* of four living creatures ... Eze 1:5 1823
they had the *l* of a man ... Eze 1:5 1823
As for the *l* of their faces, they ... Eze 1:10 1823
As for the *l* of the living ... Eze 1:13 1823
and they four had one *l* ... Eze 1:16 1823
the *l* of the firmament upon the ... Eze 1:22 1823
their heads was the *l* of a throne ... Eze 1:26 1823
upon the *l* of the throne was the ... Eze 1:26 1823
the *l* as the appearance of a man ... Eze 1:26 1823
of the *l* of the glory of the LORD ... Eze 1:28 1823
lo a *l* as the appearance of fire ... Eze 8:2 1823
appearance of the *l* of a throne ... Eze 10:1 1823
appearances, they four had one *l* ... Eze 10:10 1823
the *l* of the hands of a man was ... Eze 10:21 1823
the *l* of their faces was the same ... Eze 10:22 1823
come down to us in the *l* of men ... Acts 14:11 *3666*
together in the *l* of his death ... Rom 6:5 *3667*
also in the *l* of his resurrection ... Rom 6:5
own Son in the *l* of sinful flesh ... Rom 8:3 *3667*
and was made in the *l* of men ... Phil 2:7 *3667*

LIKETH {3}
of thy gates, where it *l* him best ... Deut 23:16 2896
ye also for the Jews, as it *l* you ... Est 8:8 2896
for this *l* you, O ye children of ... Amos 4:5 157

LIKEWISE See APPENDIX.

LIKHI *(lik'-hi)* {1} *Son of Shemidah.*
were, Ahian, and Shechem, and *L* ... 1Chr 7:19 3949

LIKING {2}
Their young ones are in good *l* ... Job 39:4 2492
l than the children which are of ... Dan 1:10

LILIES {10}
brim of a cup, with flowers of *l* ... 1Kin 7:26 7799
brim of a cup, with flowers of *l* ... 2Chr 4:5 7799
he feedeth among the *l* ... Song 2:16 7799
are twins, which feed among the *l* ... Song 4:5 7799
his lips like *l*, dropping sweet ... Song 5:13 7799
in the gardens, and to gather *l* ... Song 6:2 7799
he feedeth among the *l* ... Song 6:3 7799
an heap of wheat set about with *l* ... Song 7:2 7799
Consider the *l* of the field ... Mt 6:28 *2918*
Consider the *l* how they grow ... Lk 12:27 *2918*

LILY {5}
were of *l* work in the porch ... 1Kin 7:19 7799
the top of the pillars was *l* work ... 1Kin 7:22 7799
Sharon, and the *l* of the valleys ... Song 2:1 7799
As the *l* among thorns, so is my ... Song 2:2 7799
he shall grow as the *l*, and cast ... Hos 14:5 7799

LIME {2}
shall be as the burnings of *l* ... Is 33:12 7875
bones of the king of Edom into *l* ... Amos 2:1 7875

LIMIT {1}
l thereof round about shall be ... Eze 43:12 1366

LIMITED {1}
God, and *l* the Holy One of Israel ... Ps 78:41 8428

LIMITETH {1}
he *l* a certain day, saying in ... Heb 4:7 *3724*

LINE {31}
thou shalt bind this *l* of scarlet ... Josh 2:18 8615
bound the scarlet *l* in the window ... Josh 2:21 8615
Moab, and measured them with a *l* ... 2Sa 8:2 2256
and with one full *l* to keep alive ... 2Sa 8:2 2256
a *l* of twelve cubits did compass ... 1Kin 7:15 2339
a *l* of thirty cubits did compass ... 1Kin 7:23 6957
over Jerusalem the *l* of Samaria ... 2Kin 21:13 6957
a *l* of thirty cubits did compass ... 2Chr 4:2 6957
who hath stretched the *l* upon it ... Job 38:5 6957
Their *l* is gone out through all ... Ps 19:4 6957
divided them an inheritance by *l* ... Ps 78:55 2256
l upon *l*, *l* upon *l* ... Is 28:10 6957
l upon *l*, *l* upon *l* ... Is 28:13 6957
Judgment also will I lay to the *l* ... Is 28:17 6957
out upon it the *l* of confusion ... Is 34:11 6957
hath divided it unto them by *l* ... Is 34:17 6957
he marketh it out with a *l* ... Is 44:13 8279
the measuring *l* shall yet go ... Jer 31:39 6957
he hath stretched out a *l* ... Lam 2:8 6957
with a *l* of flax in his hand, and ... Eze 40:3 6616
when the man that had the *l* in ... Eze 47:3 6957
and thy land shall be divided by *l* ... Amos 7:17 2256
a *l* shall be stretched forth upon ... Zec 1:16 6957
with a measuring *l* in his hand ... Zec 2:1 2256
l of things made ready to our ... 2Cor 10:16 *2583*

LINEAGE {1}
he was of the house and *l* of David ... Lk 2:4 *3965*

LINEN {106}
arrayed him in vestures of fine *l* ... Gen 41:42 8336
and purple, and scarlet, and fine *l* ... Ex 25:4 8336
ten curtains of fine twined *l* ... Ex 26:1 8336
fine twined *l* of cunning work ... Ex 26:31 8336
and scarlet, and fine twined *l* ... Ex 26:36 8336
for the court of fine twined *l* of ... Ex 27:9 8336
and scarlet, and fine twined *l* ... Ex 27:16 8336
five cubits of fine twined *l* ... Ex 27:18 8336
and purple, and scarlet, and fine *l* ... Ex 28:5 8336
of scarlet, and fine twined *l* ... Ex 28:6 8336
and scarlet, and fine twined *l* ... Ex 28:8 8336
of scarlet, and of fine twined *l* ... Ex 28:15 8336
embroider the coat of fine *l* ... Ex 28:39 8336
shalt make the mitre of fine *l* ... Ex 28:39 8336
thou shalt make them *l* breeches ... Ex 28:42 906
and purple, and scarlet, and fine *l* ... Ex 35:6 8336
and purple, and scarlet, and fine *l* ... Ex 35:23 8336
and of scarlet, and of fine *l* ... Ex 35:25 8336
purple, in scarlet, and in fine *l* ... Ex 35:35 8336
ten curtains of fine twined *l* ... Ex 36:8 8336
and scarlet, and fine twined *l* ... Ex 36:35 8336
and scarlet, and fine twined *l* ... Ex 36:37 8336
the court were of fine twined *l* ... Ex 38:9 8336
round about were of fine twined *l* ... Ex 38:16 8336
and scarlet, and fine twined *l* ... Ex 38:18 8336
purple, and in scarlet, and fine *l* ... Ex 38:23 8336
and scarlet, and fine twined *l* ... Ex 39:2 8336
in the scarlet, and in the fine *l* ... Ex 39:3 8336
and scarlet, and fine twined *l* ... Ex 39:5 8336
and scarlet, and fine twined *l* ... Ex 39:8 8336
purple, and scarlet, and twined *l* ... Ex 39:24
of fine *l* of woven work for Aaron ... Ex 39:27 8336
And a mitre of fine *l* ... Ex 39:28 8336
and goodly bonnets of fine *l* ... Ex 39:28 8336
l breeches of fine twined *l*, ... Ex 39:28 906
l breeches of fine twined *l* ... Ex 39:28 8336
And a girdle of fine twined *l* ... Ex 39:29 8336
priest shall put on his *l* garment ... Lev 6:10 906
his *l* breeches shall he put upon ... Lev 6:10 906
a woollen garment, or a *l* garment ... Lev 13:47 6593
of *l*, or of woollen ... Lev 13:48 6593
warp or woof, in woollen or in *l* ... Lev 13:52 6593
in a garment of woollen or *l* ... Lev 13:59 6593
He shall put on the holy *l* coat ... Lev 16:4 906
he shall have the *l* breeches upon ... Lev 16:4 906
shall be girded with a *l* girdle ... Lev 16:4 906
with the *l* mitre shall he be ... Lev 16:4 906
and shall put off the *l* garments ... Lev 16:23 906
and shall put on the *l* clothes ... Lev 16:32 906
shall a garment mingled of *l* ... Lev 19:19 8162
as of woollen and *l* together ... Deut 22:11 6593
a child, girded with a *l* ephod ... 1Sa 2:18 906
persons that did wear a *l* ephod ... 1Sa 22:18 906
David was girded with a *l* ephod ... 2Sa 6:14 906
brought out of Egypt, and *l* yarn ... 1Kin 10:28 4723
received the *l* yarn at a price ... 1Kin 10:28 4723
house of them that wrought fine *l* ... 1Chr 4:21 948
was clothed with a robe of fine *l* ... 1Chr 15:27 948
also had upon him an ephod of *l* ... 1Chr 15:27 906
brought out of Egypt, and *l* yarn ... 2Chr 1:16 4723
received the *l* yarn at a price ... 2Chr 1:16 4723
in purple, in blue, and in fine *l* ... 2Chr 2:14 948
and purple, and crimson, and fine *l* ... 2Chr 3:14 948
being arrayed in white *l* ... 2Chr 5:12 948
fastened with cords of fine *l* ... Est 1:6 948
gold, and with a garment of fine *l* ... Est 8:15 948
works, with fine *l* of Egypt ... Prov 7:16 948
She maketh fine *l*, and selleth it ... Prov 31:24 5466
The glasses, and the fine *l* ... Is 3:23 5466
me, Go and get thee a *l* girdle ... Jer 13:1 6593
man among them was clothed with *l* ... Eze 9:2 906
called to the man clothed with *l* ... Eze 9:3 906
behold, the man clothed with *l* ... Eze 9:11 906
spake unto the man clothed with *l* ... Eze 10:2 906
commanded the man clothed with *l* ... Eze 10:6 906
of him that was clothed with *l* ... Eze 10:7 906
I girded thee about with fine *l* ... Eze 16:10 8336
and thy raiment was of fine *l* ... Eze 16:13 8336
Fine *l* with broidered work from ... Eze 27:7 8336
and broidered work, and fine *l* ... Eze 27:16 948
shall be clothed with *l* garments ... Eze 44:17 6593
They shall have *l* bonnets upon ... Eze 44:18 6593
shall have *l* breeches upon their ... Eze 44:18 6593
behold a certain man clothed in *l* ... Dan 10:5 906
one said to the man clothed in *l* ... Dan 12:6 906
And I heard the man clothed in *l* ... Dan 12:7 906
he wrapped it in a clean *l* cloth ... Mt 27:59 *4616*
having a *l* cloth cast about his ... Mk 14:51 *4616*
And he left the *l* cloth, and fled ... Mk 14:52 *4616*
And he bought fine *l*, and took him ... Mk 15:46 *4616*
him down, and wrapped him in the *l* ... Mk 15:46 *4616*
was clothed in purple and fine *l* ... Lk 16:19 *1040*
took it down, and wrapped it in *l* ... Lk 23:53 *4616*
he beheld the *l* clothes laid by ... Lk 24:12 *3608*
wound it in *l* clothes with the ... Jn 19:40 *3608*
in, saw the *l* clothes lying ... Jn 20:5 *3608*
and seeth the *l* clothes lie, ... Jn 20:6 *3608*
not lying with the *l* clothes ... Jn 20:7 *3608*
clothed in pure and white *l* ... Rev 15:6 *3043*
stones, and of pearls, and fine *l* ... Rev 18:12 *1040*
city, that was clothed in fine *l* ... Rev 18:16 *1039*
she should be arrayed in fine *l* ... Rev 19:8 *1039*

for the fine *l* is the ... Rev 19:8 *1039*
white horses, clothed in fine *l* ... Rev 19:14 *1039*

LINES {2}
even with two *l* measured he to ... 2Sa 8:2 2256
The *l* are fallen unto me in ... Ps 16:6 2256

LINGERED {2}
And while he *l*, the men laid hold ... Gen 19:16 4102
For except we had *l*, surely now ... Gen 43:10 4102

LINGERETH {1}
judgment now of a long time *l* not ... 2Pet 2:3 *691*

LINTEL {4}
is in the bason, and strike the *l* ... Ex 12:22 4947
he seeth the blood upon the *l* ... Ex 12:23 4947
the *l* and side posts were a fifth ... 1Kin 6:31 352
Smite the *l* of the door, that the ... Amos 9:1 3730

LINTELS {1}
shall lodge in the upper *l* of it ... Zeph 2:14 3730

LINUS *(li'-nus)* {1} *A Christian at Rome.*
greeteth thee, and Pudens, and *L* ... 2Ti 4:21 *3044*

LION {98}
stooped down, he couched as a *l* ... Gen 49:9 738
and as an old *l* ... Gen 49:9 3833
people shall rise up as a great *l* ... Num 23:24 3833
and lift up himself as a young *l* ... Num 23:24 738
He couched, he lay down as a *l* ... Num 24:9 738
and as a great *l* ... Num 24:9 3833
he dwelleth as a *l*, and teareth ... Deut 33:20 3833
a young *l* roared against him ... Judg 14:5 738
aside to see the carcase of the *l* ... Judg 14:8 738
and honey in the carcase of the *l* ... Judg 14:8 738
honey out of the carcase of the *l* ... Judg 14:9 738
And what is stronger than a *l* ... Judg 14:18 738
father's sheep, and there came a *l* ... 1Sa 17:34 738
Thy servant slew both the *l* ... 1Sa 17:36 738
me out of the paw of the *l* ... 1Sa 17:37 738
heart is as the heart of a *l* ... 2Sa 17:10 738
slew a *l* in the midst of a pit in ... 2Sa 23:20 738
a *l* met him by the way, and slew ... 1Kin 13:24 738
the *l* also stood by the carcase ... 1Kin 13:24 738
the *l* standing by the carcase ... 1Kin 13:25 738
hath delivered him unto the *l* ... 1Kin 13:26 738
the *l* standing by the carcase ... 1Kin 13:28 738
the *l* had not eaten the carcase, ... 1Kin 13:28 738
from me, a *l* shall slay thee ... 1Kin 20:36 738
a *l* found him, and slew him ... 1Kin 20:36 738
slew a *l* in a pit in a snowy day ... 1Chr 11:22 738
The roaring of the *l* ... Job 4:10 738
and the voice of the fierce *l* ... Job 4:10 7826
The old *l* perisheth for lack of ... Job 4:11 3918
Thou huntest me as a fierce *l* ... Job 10:16 7826
it, nor the fierce *l* passed by it ... Job 28:8 7826
Wilt thou hunt the prey for the *l* ... Job 38:39 3833
Lest he tear my soul like a *l* ... Ps 7:2 738
wait secretly as a *l* in his den ... Ps 10:9 738
Like as a *l* that is greedy of his ... Ps 17:12 738
as it were a young *l* lurking in ... Ps 17:12 3715
as a ravening and a roaring *l* ... Ps 22:13 738
Thou shalt tread upon the *l* ... Ps 91:13 7826
the young *l* and the dragon shalt ... Ps 91:13 3715
wrath is as the roaring of a *l* ... Prov 19:12 3715
a king is as the roaring of a *l* ... Prov 20:2 3715
man saith, There is a *l* without ... Prov 22:13 738
saith, There is a *l* in the way ... Prov 26:13 738
a *l* is in the streets ... Prov 26:13 738
but the righteous are bold as a *l* ... Prov 28:1 3715
As a roaring *l*, and a ranging bear ... Prov 28:15 739
A *l* which is strongest among ... Prov 30:30 3918
dog is better than a dead *l* ... Eccl 9:4 738
Their roaring shall be like a *l* ... Is 5:29 3833
and the calf and the young *l* ... Is 11:6 3715
the *l* shall eat straw like the ox ... Is 11:7 738
And he cried, A *l* ... Is 21:8 738
whence come the young and old *l* ... Is 30:6 3918
spoken unto me, Like as the *l* ... Is 31:4 738
the young *l* roaring on his prey, ... Is 31:4 3715
No *l* shall be there, nor any ... Is 35:9 738
till morning, that, as a *l* ... Is 38:13 738
the *l* shall eat straw like the ... Is 65:25 738
prophets, like a destroying *l* ... Jer 2:30 738
The *l* is come up from his thicket ... Jer 4:7 738
Wherefore a *l* out of the forest ... Jer 5:6 738
is unto me as a *l* in the forest ... Jer 12:8 738
forsaken his covert, as the *l* ... Jer 25:38 3715
he shall come up like a *l* from ... Jer 49:19 738
he shall come up like a *l* from ... Jer 50:44 738
wait, and as a *l* in secret places ... Lam 3:10 738
face of a man, and the face of a *l* ... Eze 1:10 738
man, and the third the face of a *l* ... Eze 10:14 738
it became a young *l*, and it ... Eze 19:3 3715
her whelps, and made him a young *l* ... Eze 19:5 3715
the lions, he became a young *l* ... Eze 19:6 3715
like a roaring *l* ravening the ... Eze 22:25 738
art like a young *l* of the nations ... Eze 32:2 3715
the face of a young *l* toward the ... Eze 41:19 3715
The first was like a *l*, and had ... Dan 7:4 738
For I will be unto Ephraim as a *l* ... Hos 5:14 7826
as a young *l* to the house of ... Hos 5:14 3715
he shall roar like a *l* ... Hos 11:10 738
I will be unto them as a *l* ... Hos 13:7 7826
there will I devour them like a *l* ... Hos 13:8 3833
whose teeth are the teeth of a *l* ... Joel 1:6 738
hath the cheek teeth of a great *l* ... Joel 1:6 3833
Will a *l* roar in the forest, when ... Amos 3:4 738
will a young *l* cry out of his den ... Amos 3:4 3715
The *l* hath roared, who will not ... Amos 3:8 738
of the mouth of the *l* two legs ... Amos 3:12 738
As if a man did flee from a *l* ... Amos 5:19 738
the midst of many people as a *l* ... Mic 5:8 738
as a young *l* among the flocks of ... Mic 5:8 3715
of the young lions, where the *l* ... Nah 2:11 739
even the old *l* ... Nah 2:11 3833
The *l* did tear in pieces enough ... Nah 2:12 738
out of the mouth of the *l* ... 2Ti 4:17 *3023*
the devil, as a roaring *l* ... 1Pet 5:8 *3023*
And the first beast was like a *l* ... Rev 4:7 *3023*
the *L* of the tribe of Juda, the ... Rev 5:5 *3023*
a loud voice, as when a *l* roareth ... Rev 10:3 *3023*
and his mouth as the mouth of a *l* ... Rev 13:2 *3023*

LIONESS {1}
A *l*: she lay down ... Eze 19:2 3833

LIONESSES {1}
whelps, and strangled for his *l* ... Nah 2:12 3833

LIONLIKE {2}
acts, he slew two *l* men of Moab ... 2Sa 23:20 739
he slew two *l* men of Moab ... 1Chr 11:22 739

LION'S {6}
Judah is a *l* whelp ... Gen 49:9 738
of Dan he said, Dan is a *l* whelp ... Deut 33:22 738
the stout *l* whelps are scattered ... Job 4:11 3833
The *l* whelps have not trodden it, ... Job 28:8 7830
Save me from the *l* mouth ... Ps 22:21 738
the *l* whelp, and none made them ... Nah 2:11 738

LIONS {43}
eagles, they were stronger than *l* ... 2Sa 1:23 738
were between the ledges were *l* ... 1Kin 7:29 738
and beneath the *l* and oxen were ... 1Kin 7:29 738
thereof, he graved cherubims, *l* ... 1Kin 7:36 738
two *l* stood beside the stays ... 1Kin 10:19 738
twelve *l* stood there on the one ... 1Kin 10:20 738
the LORD sent *l* among them ... 2Kin 17:25 738
he hath sent *l* among them ... 2Kin 17:26 738
faces were like the faces of *l* ... 1Chr 12:8 738
two *l* standing by the stays ... 2Chr 9:18 738
twelve *l* stood there on the one ... 2Chr 9:19 738
lion, and the teeth of the young *l* ... Job 4:10 3715
fill the appetite of the young *l* ... Job 38:39 3715
The young *l* do lack, and suffer ... Ps 34:10 3715
my darling from the *l* ... Ps 35:17 3715
My soul is among *l* ... Ps 57:4 3833
the great teeth of the young *l* ... Ps 58:6 3715
The young *l* roar after their prey ... Ps 104:21 3715
they shall roar like young *l* ... Is 5:29 3715
l upon him that escapeth of Moab, ... Is 15:9 738
The young *l* roared upon him, and ... Jer 2:15 3715
the *l* have driven him away ... Jer 50:17 738
They shall roar together like *l* ... Jer 51:38 3715
she lay down among *l*, she ... Eze 19:2 738
her whelps among young *l* ... Eze 19:2 3715
And he went up and down among the *l* .. Eze 19:6 738
with all the young *l* thereof ... Eze 38:13 3715
shall be cast into the den of *l* ... Dan 6:7 744
shall be cast into the den of *l* ... Dan 6:12 744
and cast him into the den of *l* ... Dan 6:16 744
went in haste unto the den of *l* ... Dan 6:19 744
able to deliver thee from the *l* ... Dan 6:20 744
they cast them into the den of *l* ... Dan 6:24 744
the *l* had the mastery of them, and ... Dan 6:24 744
Daniel from the power of the *l* ... Dan 6:27 744
Where is the dwelling of the *l* ... Nah 2:11 738
the feeding place of the young *l* ... Nah 2:11 3715
sword shall devour thy young *l* ... Nah 2:13 3715
princes within her are roaring *l* ... Zeph 3:3 738
a voice of the roaring of young *l* ... Zec 11:3 3715
promises, stopped the mouths of *l* ... Heb 11:33 *3023*
teeth were as the teeth of *l* ... Rev 9:8 *3023*
the horses were as the heads of *l* ... Rev 9:17 *3023*

LIONS' {3}
Shenir and Hermon, from the *l* dens ... Song 4:8 738
they shall yell as *l* whelps ... Jer 51:38 738
angel, and hath shut the *l* mouths ... Dan 6:22 744

LIP {3}
put a covering upon his upper *l* ... Lev 13:45 822
they shoot out the *l*, they shake ... Ps 22:7 8193
The *l* of truth shall be ... Prov 12:19 8193

LIPS {119}
me, who am of uncircumcised *l* ... Ex 6:12 8193
Behold, I am of uncircumcised *l* ... Ex 6:30 8193
pronouncing with his *l* to do evil ... Lev 5:4 8193
or uttered ought out of her *l* ... Num 30:6 8193
that which she uttered with her *l* ... Num 30:8 8193
out of her *l* concerning her vows ... Num 30:12 8193
gone out of thy *l* thou shalt keep ... Deut 23:23 8193
only her *l* moved, but her voice ... 1Sa 1:13 8193
thy nose, and my bridle in thy *l* ... 2Kin 19:28 8193
this did not Job sin with his *l* ... Job 2:10 8193
laughing, and thy *l* with rejoicing ... Job 8:21 8193
speak, and open his *l* against thee ... Job 11:5 8193
hearken to the pleadings of my *l* ... Job 13:6 8193
thine own *l* testify against thee ... Job 15:6 8193
the moving of my *l* should asswage ... Job 16:5 8193
from the commandment of his *l* ... Job 23:12 8193
My *l* shall not speak wickedness, ... Job 27:4 8193
I will open my *l* and answer ... Job 32:20 8193
my *l* shall utter knowledge ... Job 33:3 8193
with flattering *l* and with a ... Ps 12:2 8193
shall cut off all flattering *l* ... Ps 12:3 8193
our *l* are our own ... Ps 12:4 8193
nor take up their names into my *l* ... Ps 16:4 8193
that goeth not out of feigned *l* ... Ps 17:1 8193
by the word of thy *l* I have kept ... Ps 17:4 8193
withholden the request of his *l* ... Ps 21:2 8193
Let the lying *l* be put to silence ... Ps 31:18 8193
thy *l* from speaking guile ... Ps 34:13 8193
lo, I have not refrained my *l* ... Ps 40:9 8193
grace is poured into thy *l* ... Ps 45:2 8193
O Lord, open thou my *l* ... Ps 51:15 8193
swords are in their *l* ... Ps 59:7 8193
the words of their *l* let them ... Ps 59:12 8193
than life, my *l* shall praise thee ... Ps 63:3 8193
shall praise thee with joyful *l* ... Ps 63:5 8193
Which my *l* have uttered, and my ... Ps 66:14 8193
My *l* shall greatly rejoice when I ... Ps 71:23 8193
thing that is gone out of my *l* ... Ps 89:34 8193
he spake unadvisedly with his *l* ... Ps 106:33 8193
With my *l* have I declared all the ... Ps 119:13 8193
My *l* shall utter praise, when ... Ps 119:171 8193
my soul, O LORD, from lying *l* ... Ps 120:2 8193
adders' poison is under their *l* ... Ps 140:3 8193
of their own *l* cover them ... Ps 140:9 8193
Keep the door of my *l* ... Ps 141:3 8193
perverse *l* put far from thee ... Prov 4:24 8193
that thy *l* may keep knowledge ... Prov 5:2 8193
For the *l* of a strange woman drop ... Prov 5:3 8193
of her *l* she forced him ... Prov 7:21 8193
the opening of my *l* shall be ... Prov 8:6 8193
is an abomination to my *l* ... Prov 8:7 8193
In the *l* of him that hath ... Prov 10:13 2193
that hideth hatred with lying *l* ... Prov 10:18 8193
he that refraineth his *l* is wise ... Prov 10:19 8193
The *l* of the righteous feed many ... Prov 10:21 8193
The *l* of the righteous know what ... Prov 10:32 8193
by the transgression of his *l* ... Prov 12:13 8193
Lying *l* are abomination to the ... Prov 12:22 8193
wide his *l* shall have destruction ... Prov 13:3 8193
but the *l* of the wise shall ... Prov 14:3 8193
not in him the *l* of knowledge ... Prov 14:7 8193
but the talk of the *l* tendeth ... Prov 14:23 8193
The *l* of the wise disperse ... Prov 15:7 8193
sentence is in the *l* of the king ... Prov 16:10 8193
Righteous *l* are the delight of ... Prov 16:13 8193
of the *l* increaseth learning ... Prov 16:21 8193
and addeth learning to his *l* ... Prov 16:23 8193
in his *l* there is as a burning ... Prov 16:27 8193
moving his *l* he bringeth evil to ... Prov 16:30 8193
doer giveth heed to false *l* ... Prov 17:4 8193
much less do lying *l* a prince ... Prov 17:7 8193
his *l* is esteemed a man of ... Prov 17:28 8193
A fool's *l* enter into contention, ... Prov 18:6 8193
his *l* are the snare of his soul ... Prov 18:7 8193
of his *l* shall he be filled ... Prov 18:20 8193
than he that is perverse in his *l* ... Prov 19:1 8193
but the *l* of knowledge are a ... Prov 20:15 8193
him that flattereth with his *l* ... Prov 20:19 8193
for the grace of his *l* the king ... Prov 22:11 8193
shall withal be fitted in thy *l* ... Prov 22:18 8193
when thy *l* speak right things ... Prov 23:16 8193
and their *l* talk of mischief ... Prov 24:2 8193
Every man shall kiss his *l* that ... Prov 24:26 8193
and deceive not with thy *l* ... Prov 24:28 8193
Burning *l* and a wicked heart are ... Prov 26:23 8193
hateth dissembleth with his *l* ... Prov 26:24 8193
a stranger, and not thine own *l* ... Prov 27:2 8193
but the *l* of a fool will swallow ... Eccl 10:12 8193
Thy *l* are like a thread of ... Song 4:3 8193
Thy *l*, O my spouse, drop as the ... Song 4:11 8193
his *l* like lilies, dropping sweet ... Song 5:13 8193
causing the *l* of those that are ... Song 7:9 8193
because I am a man of unclean *l* ... Is 6:5 8193
midst of a people of unclean *l* ... Is 6:5 8193
said, Lo, this hath touched thy *l* ... Is 6:7 8193
with the breath of his *l* shall he ... Is 11:4 8193
For with stammering *l* and another ... Is 28:11 8193
with their *l* do honour me, but ... Is 29:13 8193
his *l* are full of indignation, and ... Is 30:27 8193
thy nose, and my bridle in thy *l* ... Is 37:29 8193
I create the fruit of the *l* ... Is 57:19 8193
your *l* have spoken lies, your ... Is 59:3 8193
out of my *l* was right before thee ... Jer 17:16 8193
The *l* of those that rose up ... Lam 3:62 8193
upon thy feet, and cover not thy *l* ... Eze 24:17 8222
ye shall not cover your *l* ... Eze 24:22 8222
are taken up in the *l* of talkers ... Eze 36:3 8193
of the sons of men touched my *l* ... Dan 10:16 8193
we render the calves of our *l* ... Hos 14:2 8193
yea, they shall all cover their *l* ... Mic 3:7 8222
my *l* quivered at the voice ... Hab 3:16 8193
iniquity was not found in his *l* ... Mal 2:6 8193
For the priest's *l* should keep ... Mal 2:7 8193
and honoureth me with their *l* ... Mt 15:8 *5491*
people honoureth me with their *l* ... Mk 7:6 *5491*
poison of asps is under their *l* ... Rom 3:13 *5491*
other *l* will I speak unto this ... 1Cor 14:21 *5491*
the fruit of our *l* giving thanks ... Heb 13:15 *5491*
his *l* that they speak no guile ... 1Pet 3:10 *5491*

LIQUOR {2}
shall he drink any *l* of grapes ... Num 6:3 4952
round goblet, which wanteth not *l* ... Song 7:2 4197

LIQUORS {1}
of thy ripe fruits, and of thy *l* ... Ex 22:29 1831

LISTED {2}
done unto him whatsoever they *l* ... Mt 17:12 *2309*
done unto him whatsoever they *l* ... Mk 9:13 *2309*

LISTEN {1}
L, O isles, unto me ... Is 49:1 8085

LISTETH {2}
The wind bloweth where it *l* Jn 3:8 *2309*
whithersoever the governor *l* Jas 3:4 *3730,1014*

LITTERS {1}
horses, and in chariots, and in *l* Is 66:20 6632

LITTLE {242}
Let a *l* water, I pray you, be Gen 18:4 4592
to flee unto, and it is a *l* one Gen 19:20 4705
thither, (is it not a *l* one Gen 19:20 4705
drink a *l* water of thy pitcher Gen 24:17 4592
a *l* water of thy pitcher to drink Gen 24:43 4592
For it was *l* which thou hadst Gen 30:30 4592
their wealth, and all their *l* ones Gen 34:29 2945
there was but a *l* way to come to Gen 35:16 3530
them, Go again, buy us a *l* food Gen 43:2 4592
we, and thou, and also our *l* ones Gen 43:8 2945
a *l* balm, and a *l* honey, Gen 43:11 4592
a child of his old age, a *l* one Gen 44:20 6966
Go again, and buy us a *l* food Gen 44:25 4592
the land of Egypt for your *l* ones Gen 45:19 2945
their father, and their *l* ones Gen 46:5 2945
and for food for your *l* ones Gen 47:24 2945
but a *l* way to come unto Ephrath Gen 48:7 3530
only their *l* ones, and their Gen 50:8 2945
will nourish you, and your *l* ones Gen 50:21 2945
I will let you go, and your *l* ones Ex 10:10 2945
let your *l* ones also go with you Ex 10:24 2945
household be too *l* for the lamb Ex 12:4 4591
and he that gathered *l* had no lack Ex 16:18 4591
By *l* and *l* I will drive them Ex 23:30 4592
And the *l* owl, and the cormorant, Lev 11:17 3563
But your *l* ones, which ye said Num 14:31 2945
their sons, and their *l* children Num 16:27 2945
Midian captives, and their *l* ones Num 31:9 2945
kill every male among the *l* ones Num 31:17 2945
cattle, and cities for our *l* ones Num 32:16 2945
our *l* ones shall dwell in the Num 32:17 2945
Build you cities for your *l* ones Num 32:24 2945
Our *l* ones, our wives, our flocks Num 32:26 2945
Moreover your *l* ones, which ye Deut 1:39 2945
the *l* ones, of every city, we Deut 2:34 2945
But your wives, and your *l* ones Deut 3:19 2945
before thee by *l* and *l* Deut 7:22 4592
The *l* owl, and the great owl, and Deut 14:16 3563
the *l* ones, and the cattle, and all Deut 20:14 2945
field, and shalt gather but *l* in Deut 28:38 4592
Your *l* ones, your wives, and thy Deut 29:11 2945
Your wives, your *l* ones, and your Josh 1:14 2945
the *l* ones, and the strangers that Josh 8:35 2945
of Dan went out too *l* for them Josh 19:47
the iniquity of Peor too *l* for us Josh 22:17 4592
I pray thee, a *l* water to drink Judg 4:19 4592
and departed, and put the *l* ones Judg 18:21 2945
that she tarried a *l* in the house Ruth 2:7 4592
his mother made him a *l* coat 1Sa 2:19 6996
I tasted a *l* of this honey 1Sa 14:29 4592
I did but taste a *l* honey with 1Sa 14:43 4592
When thou wast *l* in thine own 1Sa 15:17 6996
with David, and a *l* lad with him 1Sa 20:35 6996
had nothing, save one *l* ewe lamb 2Sa 12:3 6996
and if that had been too *l* 2Sa 12:8 4592
all the *l* ones that were with him 2Sa 15:22 2945
when David was a *l* past the top 2Sa 16:1 4592
Thy servant will go a *l* way over 2Sa 19:36 4592
and I am but a *l* child 1Kin 3:7 6996
was before the LORD was too *l* to 1Kin 8:64 6996
Hadad being yet a *l* child 1Kin 11:17 6996
My *l* finger shall be thicker than 1Kin 12:10 6996
a *l* water in a vessel, that I may 1Kin 17:10 4592
a barrel, and a *l* oil in a cruse 1Kin 17:12 4592
make me thereof a *l* cake first 1Kin 17:13 6996
there ariseth a *l* cloud out of 1Kin 18:44 6996
them like two *l* flocks of kids 1Kin 20:27 2835
there came forth *l* children out 2Kin 2:23 6996
Let us make a *l* chamber, I pray 2Kin 4:10 6996
of the land of Israel a *l* maid 2Kin 5:2 6996
like unto the flesh of a *l* child 2Kin 5:14 6995
So he departed from him a *l* way 2Kin 5:19 3530
unto them, Ahab served Baal a *l* 2Kin 10:18 4592
My *l* finger shall be thicker than 2Chr 10:10 6996
the LORD, with their *l* ones 2Chr 20:13 2945
the genealogy of all their *l* ones 2Chr 31:18 2945
way for us, and for our *l* ones Ezr 8:21 2945
now for a *l* space grace hath been Ezr 9:8 4592
give us a *l* reviving in our Ezr 9:8 4592
the trouble seem *l* before thee Neh 9:32 4591
l children and women, in one day, Est 3:13 2945
would assault them, both *l* ones Est 8:11 2945
and mine ear received a *l* thereof Job 4:12 8102
that I may take comfort a *l* Job 10:20 4592
forth their *l* ones like a flock Job 21:11 5759
They are exalted for a *l* while Job 24:24 4592
but how *l* a portion is heard of Job 26:14 8102
Suffer me a *l*, and I will shew Job 36:2 2191
when his wrath is kindled but a *l* Ps 2:12 4592
him a *l* lower than the angels Ps 8:5 4592
For yet a *l* while, and the wicked Ps 37:10 4592
A *l* that a righteous man hath is Ps 37:16 4592
the *l* hills rejoice on every side Ps 65:12
There is *l* Benjamin with their Ps 68:27 6810
the *l* hills, by righteousness Ps 72:3
rams, and the *l* hills like lambs Ps 114:4
and ye *l* hills, like lambs Ps 114:6
dasheth thy *l* ones against the Ps 137:9 5768
Yet a *l* sleep, a *l* slumber, Prov 6:10 4592
a *l* folding of the hands to sleep Prov 6:10 4592
heart of the wicked is *l* worth Prov 10:20 4592
Better is *l* with the fear of the Prov 15:16 4592
Better is a *l* with righteousness Prov 16:8 4592
Yet a *l* sleep, a *l* slumber, Prov 24:33 4592
a *l* folding of the hands to sleep Prov 24:33 4592
things which are *l* upon the earth Prov 30:24 6996
sweet, whether he eat *l* or much Eccl 5:12 4592
There was a *l* city, and few men Eccl 9:14 6996
so doth a *l* folly him that is in Eccl 10:1 4592
the *l* foxes, that spoil the vines Song 2:15 6996
It was but a *l* that I passed from Song 3:4 4592
We have a *l* sister, and she hath Song 8:8 6996
For yet a very *l* while, and the Is 10:25 4592
a *l* child shall lead them Is 11:6 6995
thyself as it were for a *l* moment Is 26:20 4592
here a *l*, and there a *l* Is 28:10 2191
here a *l*, and there a *l* Is 28:13 2191
Is it not yet a very *l* while Is 29:17 4592
up the isles as a very *l* thing Is 40:15 1851
In a *l* wrath I hid my face from Is 54:8 8241
A *l* one shall become a thousand, Is 60:22 6996
have possessed it but a *l* while Is 63:18 4705
sent their *l* ones to the waters Jer 14:3 6810
her *l* ones have caused a cry to Jer 48:4 6810
yet a *l* while, and the time of her Jer 51:33 4592
maids, and *l* children, and women Eze 9:6 2945
as a *l* sanctuary in the countries Eze 11:16 4592
as if that were a very *l* thing Eze 16:47 4592
sent out her *l* rivers unto all Eze 31:4 8585
every *l* chamber was one reed long Eze 40:7
between the *l* chambers were five Eze 40:7
the *l* chambers of the gate Eze 40:10
The space also before the *l* Eze 40:12
the *l* chambers were six cubits on Eze 40:12
the gate from the roof of one *l* Eze 40:13
narrow windows to the *l* chambers Eze 40:16
the *l* chambers thereof were three Eze 40:21
the *l* chambers thereof, and the Eze 40:29
the *l* chambers thereof, and the Eze 40:33
The *l* chambers thereof, the posts Eze 40:36
came up among them another *l* horn Dan 7:8 2192
one of them came forth a *l* horn Dan 8:9 4704
shall be holpen with a *l* help Dan 11:34 4592
for yet a *l* while, and I will Hos 1:4 4592
they shall sorrow a *l* for the Hos 8:10 4592
and the *l* house with clefts Amos 6:11 6996
though thou be *l* among the Mic 5:2 6810
Ye have sown much, and bring in *l* Hag 1:6 4592
for much, and, lo, it came to *l* Hag 1:9 4592
Yet once, it is a *l* while Hag 2:6 4592
for I was but a *l* displeased Zec 1:15 4592
turn mine hand upon the *l* ones Zec 13:7 6819
more clothe you, O ye of *l* faith Mt 6:30 *3640*
are ye fearful, O ye of *l* faith Mt 8:26 *3640*
l ones a cup of cold water only Mt 10:42 *3398*
said unto him, O thou of *l* faith Mt 14:31 *3640*
said, Seven, and a few *l* fishes Mt 15:34 *2485*
said unto them, O ye of *l* faith Mt 16:8 *3640*
Jesus called a *l* child unto him Mt 18:2 *3813*
and become as *l* children, ye Mt 18:3 *3813*
humble himself as this *l* child Mt 18:4 *3813*
whoso shall receive one such *l* Mt 18:5 *3813*
these *l* ones which believe in me Mt 18:6 *3398*
despise not one of these *l* ones Mt 18:10 *3398*
that one of these *l* ones should Mt 18:14 *3398*
there brought unto him *l* children Mt 19:13 *3813*
Suffer *l* children, and forbid them Mt 19:14 *3813*
And he went a *l* farther, and fell Mt 26:39 *3397*
he had gone a *l* farther thence Mk 1:19 *3641*
were also with him other *l* ships Mk 4:36 *4142*
My *l* daughter lieth at the point Mk 5:23 *2365*
these *l* ones that believe in me Mk 9:42 *3398*
Suffer the *l* children to come Mk 10:14 *3813*
the kingdom of God as a *l* child Mk 10:15 *3813*
And he went forward a *l*, and fell Mk 14:35 *3397*
a *l* after, they that stood by Mk 14:70 *3397*
thrust out a *l* from the land Lk 5:3 *3641*
but to whom *l* is forgiven Lk 7:47 *3641*
is forgiven, the same loveth *l* Lk 7:47 *3641*
he clothe you, O ye of *l* faith Lk 12:28 *3640*
Fear not, *l* flock Lk 12:32 *3398*
should offend one of these *l* ones Lk 17:2 *3398*
Suffer *l* children to come unto me Lk 18:16 *3813*
a *l* child shall in no wise enter Lk 18:17 *3813*
because he was *l* of stature Lk 19:3 *3398*
hast been faithful in a very *l* Lk 19:17 *1646*
after a *l* while another saw him, Lk 22:58 *1024*
every one of them may take a *l* Jn 6:7 *1024*
Yet a *l* while am I with you, and Jn 7:33 *3398*
Yet a *l* while is the light with Jn 12:35 *3398*
L children, yet a *l* while I Jn 13:33 *5040*
Yet a *l* while, and the world seeth Jn 14:19 *3397*
A *l* while, and ye shall not see me Jn 16:16 *3397*
a *l* while, and ye shall see me, Jn 16:16 *3397*
A *l* while, and ye shall not see me Jn 16:17 *3397*
a *l* while, and ye shall see me Jn 16:17 *3397*
is this that he saith, A *l* while Jn 16:18 *3397*
A *l* while, and ye shall not see me Jn 16:19 *3397*
a *l* while, and ye shall see me Jn 16:19 *3397*
other disciples came in a *l* ship Jn 21:8 *4142*
put the apostles forth a *l* space Acts 5:34 *1024*
alive, and were not a *l* comforted Acts 20:12 *3357*
and when they had gone a *l* further Acts 27:28 *1024*
people shewed us no *l* kindness Acts 28:2 *5177*
Know ye not that a *l* leaven 1Cor 5:6 *3398*
that had gathered *l* had no lack 2Cor 8:15 *3641*
bear with me a *l* in my folly 2Cor 11:1 *3397*
me, that I may boast myself a *l* 2Cor 11:16 *3397*
My *l* children, of whom I travail Gal 4:19 *5040*
A *l* leaven leaveneth the whole Gal 5:9 *3398*
For bodily exercise profiteth *l* 1Ti 4:8 *3641*
water, but use a *l* wine for thy 1Ti 5:23 *3641*
Thou madest him a *l* lower than Heb 2:7 *1024*
who was made a *l* lower than the Heb 2:9 *1024*
For yet a *l* while, and he that Heb 10:37 *3397*
Even so the tongue is a *l* member Jas 3:5 *3398*
great a matter a *l* fire kindleth Jas 3:5 *3641*
that appeareth for a *l* time Jas 4:14 *3641*
My *l* children, these things write 1Jn 2:1 *5040*
l children, because your sins are 1Jn 2:12 *5040*
l children, because ye have known 1Jn 2:13 *3813*
L children, it is the last time 1Jn 2:18 *3813*
And now, *l* children, abide in him 1Jn 2:28 *5040*
L children, let no man deceive 1Jn 3:7 *5040*
My *l* children, let us not love in 1Jn 3:18 *5040*
l children, and have overcome them 1Jn 4:4 *5040*
L children, keep yourselves from 1Jn 5:21 *5040*
for thou hast a *l* strength Rev 3:8 *3398*
should rest yet for a *l* season Rev 6:11 *3398*
he had in his hand a *l* book open Rev 10:2 *974*
take the *l* book which is open in Rev 10:8 *974*
said unto him, Give me the *l* book Rev 10:9 *974*
I took the *l* book out of the Rev 10:10 *974*
that he must be loosed a *l* season Rev 20:3 *3398*

LIVE {247}
of life, and eat, and *l* for ever Gen 3:22 2425
my soul shall *l* because of thee Gen 12:13 2421
that Ishmael might *l* before thee Gen 17:18 2421
and my soul shall *l* Gen 19:20 2421
pray for thee, and thou shalt *l* Gen 20:7 2421
And by thy sword shalt thou *l* Gen 27:40 2421
findest thy gods, let him not *l* Gen 31:32 2421
that we may *l*, and not die Gen 42:2 2421
them the third day, This do, and *l* Gen 42:18 2421
that we may *l*, and not die, both Gen 43:8 2421
doth my father yet *l* Gen 45:3 2416
and give us seed, that we may *l* Gen 47:19 2421
be a daughter, then she shall *l* Ex 1:16 2425
be beast or man, it shall not *l* Ex 19:13 2421
then they shall sell the *l* ox Ex 21:35 2416
shalt not suffer a witch to *l* Ex 22:18 2421
there shall no man see me, and *l* Ex 33:20 2425
altar, he shall bring the *l* goat Lev 16:20 2416
hands upon the head of the *l* goat Lev 16:21 2416
if a man do, he shall *l* in them Lev 18:5 2425
that he may *l* with thee Lev 25:35 2416
that thy brother may *l* with thee Lev 25:36 2416
do unto them, that they may *l* Num 4:19 2421
But as truly as I *l*, all the Num 14:21 2416
Say unto them, As truly as I *l* Num 14:28 2416
when he looketh upon it, shall *l* Num 21:8 2425
who shall *l* when God doeth this Num 24:23 2421
for to do them, that ye may *l* Deut 4:1 2421
that they shall *l* upon the earth Deut 4:10 2416
fire, as thou hast heard, and *l* Deut 4:33 2421
one of these cities he might *l* Deut 4:42 2425
hath commanded you, that ye may *l* Deut 5:33 2421
ye observe to do, that ye may *l* Deut 8:1 2421
that man doth not *l* by bread only Deut 8:3 2421
the mouth of the LORD doth man *l* Deut 8:3 2421
the days that ye *l* upon the earth Deut 12:1 2416
thou follow, that thou mayest *l* Deut 16:20 2421
shall flee thither, that he may *l* Deut 19:4 2425
unto one of those cities, and *l* Deut 19:5 2425
all thy soul, that thou mayest *l* Deut 30:6 2416
his judgments, that thou mayest *l* Deut 30:16 2421
that both thou and thy seed may *l* Deut 30:19 2421
as long as ye *l* in the land Deut 31:13 2416
to heaven, and say, I *l* for ever Deut 32:40 2416
Let Reuben *l*, and not die Deut 33:6 2421
only Rahab the harlot shall *l* Josh 6:17 2421
a league with them, to let them *l* Josh 9:15 2421
we will even let them *l*, lest Josh 9:20 2421
said unto them, Let them *l* Josh 9:21 2421
I *l* shew me the kindness of the 1Sa 20:14 2416
not *l* after that he was fallen 2Sa 1:10 2421
to me, that the child may *l* 2Sa 12:22 2416
the king, How long have I to *l* 2Sa 19:34 2416
Let my lord king David *l* for ever 1Kin 1:31 2421
thee all the days that they *l* in 1Kin 8:40 2416
saith, I pray thee, let me *l* 1Kin 20:32 2421
l thou and thy children of the 2Kin 4:7 2421
if they save us alive, we shall *l* 2Kin 7:4 2421
shall be wanting, he shall not *l* 2Kin 10:19 2421
olive and of honey, that ye may *l* 2Kin 18:32 2421
for thou shalt die, and not *l* 2Kin 20:1 2421
so long as they *l* in the land 2Chr 6:31 2416
the king, Let the king *l* for ever Neh 2:3 2421
for them, that we may eat, and *l* Neh 5:2 2421
if a man do, he shall *l* in them Neh 9:29 2421
the golden sceptre, that he may *l* Est 4:11 2421
I would not *l* alway Job 7:16 2421
If a man die, shall he *l* again Job 14:14 2421
Wherefore do the wicked *l* Job 21:7 2421
not reproach me so long as I *l* Job 27:6 3117
your heart shall *l* for ever Ps 22:26 2421
That he should still *l* for ever Ps 49:9 2421
shall not *l* out half their days Ps 55:23
Thus will I bless thee while I *l* Ps 63:4 2416
your heart shall *l* that seek God Ps 69:32 2421
And he shall *l*, and to him shall be Ps 72:15 2421
sing unto the LORD as long as I *l* Ps 104:33 2416
I call upon him as long as I *l* Ps 116:2 3117
I shall not die, but *l*, and Ps 118:17 2421
with thy servant, that I may *l* Ps 119:17 2421
come unto me, that I may *l* Ps 119:77 2421

L

unto thy word, that I may *l* ... Ps 119:116 2421
me understanding, and I shall *l* ... Ps 119:144 2421
Let my soul *l*, and it shall praise ... Ps 119:175 2421
While I *l* will I praise the LORD ... Ps 146:2 2416
keep my commandments, and *l* ... Prov 4:4 2421
Keep my commandments, and *l* ... Prov 7:2 2421
Forsake the foolish, and *l* ... Prov 9:6 2421
but he that hateth gifts shall *l* ... Prov 15:27 2421
l many years, so that the days of ... Eccl 6:3 2421
though he *l* a thousand years ... Eccl 6:6 2421
is in their heart while they *l* ... Eccl 9:3 2416
L joyfully with the wife whom ... Eccl 9:9 2416
But if a man *l* many years ... Eccl 11:8 2421
having a *l* coal in his hand, ... Is 6:6 7531
They are dead, they shall not *l* ... Is 26:14 2421
Thy dead men shall *l*, together ... Is 26:19 2421
for thou shalt die, and not *l* ... Is 38:1 2421
O Lord, by these things men *l* ... Is 38:16 2421
thou recover me, and make me to *l* ... Is 38:16 2421
As I *l*, saith the LORD, thou ... Is 49:18 2416
hear, and your soul shall *l* ... Is 55:3 2421
that besiege you, he shall *l* ... Jer 21:9 2421
As I *l*, saith the LORD, though ... Jer 22:24 2416
and serve him and his people, and *l* ... Jer 27:12 2421
serve the king of Babylon, and *l* ... Jer 27:17 2421
that ye may *l* many days in the ... Jer 35:7 2421
forth to the Chaldeans shall *l* ... Jer 38:2 2421
his life for a prey, and shall *l* ... Jer 38:2 2425
princes, then thy soul shall *l* ... Jer 38:17 2421
and thou shalt *l*, and thine house ... Jer 38:17 2421
unto thee, and thy soul shall *l* ... Jer 38:20 2421
As I *l*, saith the King, whose ... Jer 46:18 2416
we shall *l* among the heathen ... Lam 4:20 2421
doth not sin, he shall surely *l* ... Eze 3:21 2421
Wherefore, as I *l*, saith the Lord ... Eze 5:11 2416
the souls alive that should not *l* ... Eze 13:19 2421
three men were in it, as I *l* ... Eze 14:16 2416
three men were in it, as I *l* ... Eze 14:18 2416
and Job, were in it, as I *l* ... Eze 14:20 2416
when thou wast in thy blood, *L* ... Eze 16:6 2421
when thou wast in thy blood, *L* ... Eze 16:6 2421
As I *l*, saith the Lord GOD, Sodom ... Eze 16:48 2416
As I *l*, saith the Lord GOD, ... Eze 17:16 2416
As I *l*, surely mine oath that he ... Eze 17:19 2416
As I *l*, saith the Lord GOD, ye ... Eze 18:3 2416
he is just, he shall surely *l* ... Eze 18:9 2421
shall he then *l* ... Eze 18:13 2425
he shall not *l* ... Eze 18:13 2421
of his father, he shall surely *l* ... Eze 18:17 2421
hath done them, he shall surely *l* ... Eze 18:19 2421
and right, he shall surely *l* ... Eze 18:21 2421
that he hath done he shall *l* ... Eze 18:22 2421
should return from his ways, and *l* ... Eze 18:23 2421
the wicked man doeth, shall he *l* ... Eze 18:24 2425
hath committed, he shall surely *l* ... Eze 18:28 2421
turn yourselves, and *l* ye ... Eze 18:32 2421
As I *l*, saith the Lord GOD, I ... Eze 20:3 2416
a man do, he shall even *l* in them ... Eze 20:11 2425
a man do, he shall even *l* in them ... Eze 20:13 2425
a man do, he shall even *l* in them ... Eze 20:21 2425
whereby they should not *l* ... Eze 20:25 2421
As I *l*, saith the Lord GOD, I ... Eze 20:31 2416
As I *l*, saith the Lord GOD, ... Eze 20:33
in them, how should we then *l* ... Eze 33:10 2421
Say unto them, As I *l*, saith the ... Eze 33:11 2416
the wicked turn from his way and *l* ... Eze 33:11 2421
to *l* for his righteousness in the ... Eze 33:12 2421
righteous, that he shall surely *l* ... Eze 33:13 2421
he shall surely *l*, he shall not ... Eze 33:15 2421
he shall surely *l* ... Eze 33:16 2421
and right, he shall *l* thereby ... Eze 33:19 2421
As I *l*, surely they that are in ... Eze 33:27 2416
As I *l* saith the Lord GOD, surely ... Eze 34:8 2416
Therefore, as I *l*, saith the Lord ... Eze 35:6 2416
Therefore, as I *l*, saith the Lord ... Eze 35:11 2416
me, Son of man, can these bones *l* ... Eze 37:3 2421
to enter into you, and ye shall *l* ... Eze 37:5 2421
put breath in you, and ye shall *l* ... Eze 37:6 2421
upon these slain, that they may *l* ... Eze 37:9 2421
my spirit in you, and ye shall *l* ... Eze 37:14 2421
the rivers shall come, shall *l* ... Eze 47:9 2421
every thing shall *l* whither the ... Eze 47:9 2425
in Syriack, O king, *l* for ever ... Dan 2:4 2418
O king, *l* for ever ... Dan 3:9 2418
spake and said, O king, *l* for ever ... Dan 5:10 2414
unto him, King Darius, *l* for ever ... Dan 6:6 2414
unto the king, O king, *l* for ever ... Dan 6:21 2414
us up, and we shall *l* in his sight ... Hos 6:2 2421
Israel, Seek ye me, and ye shall *l* ... Amos 5:4 2421
Seek the LORD, and ye shall *l* ... Amos 5:6 2421
good, and not evil, that ye may *l* ... Amos 5:14 2421
is better for me to die than to *l* ... Jonah 4:3 2416
is better for me to die than to *l* ... Jonah 4:8 2416
but the just shall *l* by his faith ... Hab 2:4 2421
Therefore as I *l*, saith the LORD ... Zeph 2:9 2416
the prophets, do they *l* for ever ... Zec 1:5 2421
they shall *l* with their children, ... Zec 10:9 2421
say unto him, Thou shalt not *l* ... Zec 13:3 2421
Man shall not *l* by bread alone, ... Mt 4:4 *2198*
thy hand upon her, and she shall *l* ... Mt 9:18 *2198*
and she shall *l* ... Mk 5:23 *2198*
man shall not *l* by bread alone ... Lk 4:4 *2198*
l delicately, are in kings' ... Lk 7:25 *5225*
this do, and thou shalt *l* ... Lk 10:28 *2198*
for all *l* unto him ... Lk 20:38 *2198*
and they that hear shall *l* ... Jn 5:25 *2198*
this bread, he shall *l* for ever ... Jn 6:51 *2198*
sent me, and I *l* by the Father ... Jn 6:57 *2198*
eateth me, even he shall *l* by me ... Jn 6:57 *2198*
of this bread shall *l* for ever ... Jn 6:58 *2198*
he were dead, yet shall he *l* ... Jn 11:25 *2198*
because I *l*, ye shall *l* also ... Jn 14:19 *2198*
to the end they might not *l* ... Acts 7:19 *2225*
For in him we *l*, and move, and have ... Acts 17:28 *2198*
it is not fit that he should *l* ... Acts 22:22 *2198*
that he ought not to *l* any longer ... Acts 25:24 *2198*
yet vengeance suffereth not to *l* ... Acts 28:4 *2198*
The just shall *l* by faith ... Rom 1:17 *2198*
dead to sin, *l* any longer therein ... Rom 6:2 *2198*
that we shall also *l* with him ... Rom 6:8 *4800*
the flesh, to *l* after the flesh ... Rom 8:12 *2198*
For if ye *l* after the flesh, ye ... Rom 8:13 *2198*
the deeds of the body, ye shall *l* ... Rom 8:13 *2198*
those things shall *l* by them ... Rom 10:5 *2198*
in you, *l* peaceably with all men ... Rom 12:18 *1514*
we *l*, we *l* unto the Lord ... Rom 14:8 *2198*
whether we *l* therefore, or die, ... Rom 14:8 *2198*
For it is written, As I *l* ... Rom 14:11 *2198*
minister about holy things *l* of ... 1Cor 9:13 *2068*
the gospel should *l* of the gospel ... 1Cor 9:14 *2198*
For we which *l* are alway ... 2Cor 4:11 *2198*
that they which *l* should not ... 2Cor 5:15 *2198*
not henceforth *l* unto themselves ... 2Cor 5:15 *2198*
as dying, and, behold, we *l* ... 2Cor 6:9 *2198*
our hearts to die and *l* with you ... 2Cor 7:3 *4800*
but we shall *l* with him by the ... 2Cor 13:4 *2198*
be of one mind, *l* in peace ... 2Cor 13:11 *1514*
the Gentiles to *l* as do the Jews ... Gal 2:14 *2198*
the law, that I might *l* unto God ... Gal 2:19 *2198*
nevertheless I *l* ... Gal 2:20 *2198*
the life which I now *l* in the ... Gal 2:20 *2198*
l by the faith of the Son of God ... Gal 2:20 *2198*
for, The just shall *l* by faith ... Gal 3:11 *2198*
that doeth them shall *l* in them ... Gal 3:12 *2198*
If we *l* in the Spirit, let us ... Gal 5:25 *2198*
thou mayest *l* long on the earth ... Eph 6:3 *2071,3118*
For to me to *l* is Christ, and to ... Phil 1:21 *2198*
But if I *l* in the flesh, this is ... Phil 1:22 *2198*
For now we *l*, if ye stand fast in ... 1Th 3:8 *2198*
we should *l* together with him ... 1Th 5:10 *2198*
him, we shall also *l* with him ... 2Ti 2:11 *4800*
all that will *l* godly in Christ ... 2Ti 3:12 *2198*
lusts, we should *l* soberly ... Titus 2:12 *2198*
Now the just shall *l* by faith ... Heb 10:38 *2198*
unto the Father of spirits, and *l* ... Heb 12:9 *2198*
all things willing to *l* honestly ... Heb 13:18 *390*
say, If the Lord will, we shall *l* ... Jas 4:15 *2198*
should *l* unto righteousness ... 1Pet 2:24 *2198*
That he no longer should *l* the ... 1Pet 4:2 *980*
but *l* according to God in the ... 1Pet 4:6 *2198*
those that after should *l* ungodly ... 2Pet 2:6
escaped from them who *l* in error ... 2Pet 2:18 *390*
that we might *l* through him ... 1Jn 4:9 *2198*
the wound by a sword, and did *l* ... Rev 13:14 *2198*

LIVED {58}

Adam *l* an hundred and thirty years ... Gen 5:3 2421
that Adam *l* were nine hundred ... Gen 5:5 2425
Seth *l* an hundred and five years, ... Gen 5:6 2421
Seth *l* after he begat Enos eight ... Gen 5:7 2421
Enos *l* ninety years, and begat ... Gen 5:9 2421
Enos *l* after he begat Cainan ... Gen 5:10 2421
Cainan *l* seventy years, and begat ... Gen 5:12 2421
And Cainan *l* after he begat ... Gen 5:13 2421
And Mahalaleel *l* sixty and five ... Gen 5:15 2421
Mahalaleel *l* after he begat Jared ... Gen 5:16 2421
Jared *l* an hundred sixty and two ... Gen 5:18 2421
Jared *l* after he begat Enoch ... Gen 5:19 2421
And Enoch *l* sixty and five years, ... Gen 5:21 2421
Methuselah *l* an hundred eighty and ... Gen 5:25 2421
Methuselah *l* after he begat ... Gen 5:26 2421
Lamech *l* an hundred eighty and two ... Gen 5:28 2421
Lamech *l* after he begat Noah five ... Gen 5:30 2421
Noah *l* after the flood three ... Gen 9:28 2421
Shem *l* after he begat Arphaxad ... Gen 11:11 2421
And Arphaxad *l* five and thirty ... Gen 11:12 2425
Arphaxad *l* after he begat Salah ... Gen 11:13 2421
Salah *l* thirty years, and begat ... Gen 11:14 2425
Salah *l* after he begat Eber four ... Gen 11:15 2421
And Eber *l* four and thirty years, ... Gen 11:16 2421
Eber *l* after he begat Peleg four ... Gen 11:17 2421
Peleg *l* thirty years, and begat ... Gen 11:18 2421
Peleg *l* after he begat Reu two ... Gen 11:19 2421
And Reu *l* two and thirty years, and ... Gen 11:20 2421
Reu *l* after he begat Serug two ... Gen 11:21 2421
Serug *l* thirty years, and begat ... Gen 11:22 2421
Serug *l* after he begat Nahor two ... Gen 11:23 2421
And Nahor *l* nine and twenty years, ... Gen 11:24 2421
Nahor *l* after he begat Terah an ... Gen 11:25 2421
Terah *l* seventy years, and begat ... Gen 11:26 2421
Isaac his son, while he yet *l* ... Gen 25:6 2416
of Abraham's life which he *l* ... Gen 25:7 2425
Jacob *l* in the land of Egypt ... Gen 47:28 2421
Joseph *l* an hundred and ten years ... Gen 50:22 2421
went to search the land, *l* still ... Num 14:38 2421
beheld the serpent of brass, he *l* ... Num 21:9 2425
of the fire, as we have, and *l* ... Deut 5:26 2421
I perceive, that if Absalom had *l* ... 2Sa 19:6 2416
Solomon his father while he yet *l* ... 1Kin 12:6 2416
l after the death of Jehoash son ... 2Kin 14:17 2421
Solomon his father while he yet *l* ... 2Chr 10:6 2416
the son of Joash king of Judah *l* ... 2Chr 25:25 2421
After this *l* Job an hundred and ... Job 42:16 2421
Though while he *l* he blessed his ... Ps 49:18 2416
breath came into them, and they *l* ... Eze 37:10 2421
had *l* with an husband seven years ... Lk 2:36 *2198*
I have *l* in all good conscience ... Acts 23:1 *4176*
of our religion I *l* a Pharisee ... Acts 26:5 *2198*
some time, when ye *l* in them ... Col 3:7 *2198*
Ye have *l* in pleasure on the ... Jas 5:5 *5171*
l deliciously, so much torment and ... Rev 18:7
l deliciously with her, shall ... Rev 18:9
and they *l* and reigned with Christ ... Rev 20:4 *2198*
But the rest of the dead *l* not ... Rev 20:5 *326*

LIVELY {5}

for they are *l*, and are delivered ... Ex 1:19 2422
But mine enemies are *l*, and they ... Ps 38:19 2416
who received the *l* oracles to ... Acts 7:38 *2198*
a *l* hope by the resurrection of ... 1Pet 1:3 *2198*
as *l* stones, are built up a ... 1Pet 2:5 *2198*

LIVER {14}

and the caul that is above the *l* ... Ex 29:13 3516
inwards, and the caul above the *l* ... Ex 29:22 3516
flanks, and the caul above the *l* ... Lev 3:4 3516
flanks, and the caul above the *l* ... Lev 3:10 3516
flanks, and the caul above the *l* ... Lev 3:15 3516
flanks, and the caul above the *l* ... Lev 4:9 3516
and the caul that is above the *l* ... Lev 7:4 3516
inwards, and the caul above the *l* ... Lev 8:16 3516
inwards, and the caul above the *l* ... Lev 8:25 3516
the caul above the *l* of the sin ... Lev 9:10 3516
kidneys, and the caul above the *l* ... Lev 9:19 3516
Till a dart strike through his *l* ... Prov 7:23 3516
my *l* is poured upon the earth, ... Lam 2:11 3516
with images, he looked in the *l* ... Eze 21:21 3516

LIVES {28}

blood of your *l* will I require ... Gen 9:5 5315
to save your *l* by a great ... Gen 45:7 2421
they said, Thou hast saved our *l* ... Gen 47:25 2421
they made their *l* bitter with ... Ex 1:14 2416
have, and deliver our *l* from death ... Josh 2:13 5315
afraid of our *l* because of you ... Josh 9:24 5315
l unto the death in the high ... Judg 5:18 5315
with the *l* of thy household ... Judg 18:25 5315
lovely and pleasant in their *l* ... 2Sa 1:23 2416
the *l* of thy sons and of thy ... 2Sa 19:5 5315
the *l* of thy wives ... 2Sa 19:5 5315
and the *l* of thy concubines ... 2Sa 19:5 5315
that went in jeopardy of their *l* ... 2Sa 23:17 5315
that have put their *l* in jeopardy ... 1Chr 11:19 5315
of their *l* they brought it ... 1Chr 11:19 5315
together, and stood for their *l* ... Est 9:16 5315
they lurk privily for their own *l* ... Prov 1:18 5315
hands of them that seek their *l* ... Jer 19:7 5315
and they that seek their *l* ... Jer 19:9 5315
hand of those that seek their *l* ... Jer 46:26 5315
Flee, save your *l*, and be like the ... Jer 48:6 5315
our *l* because of the sword of the ... Lam 5:9 5315
yet their *l* were prolonged for a ... Dan 7:12 2417
is not come to destroy men's *l* ... Lk 9:56 *5590*
Men that have hazarded their *l* ... Acts 15:26 *5590*
lading and ship, but also of our *l* ... Acts 27:10 *5590*
lay down our *l* for the brethren ... 1Jn 3:16 *5590*
loved not their *l* unto the death ... Rev 12:11 *5590*

LIVEST {4}

as long as thou *l* upon the earth ... Deut 12:19 3117
as thou *l*, and as thy soul liveth, ... 2Sa 11:11 2416
l after the manner of Gentiles, ... Gal 2:14 *2198*
that thou hast a name that thou *l* ... Rev 3:1 *2198*

LIVETH {96}

that *l* shall be meat for you ... Gen 9:3 2416
God doth talk with man, and he *l* ... Deut 5:24 2425
as the LORD *l*, if ye had saved ... Judg 8:19 2416
a kinsman to thee, as the LORD *l* ... Ruth 3:13 2416
said, Oh my lord, as thy soul *l* ... 1Sa 1:26 2416
as long as he *l* he shall be lent ... 1Sa 1:28 3117
For, as the LORD *l*, which saveth ... 1Sa 14:39 2416
as the LORD *l*, there shall not ... 1Sa 14:45 2416
And Abner said, As thy soul *l* ... 1Sa 17:55 2416
and Saul sware, As the LORD *l* ... 1Sa 19:6 2416
the LORD *l*, and as thy soul *l* ... 1Sa 20:3 2416
as the LORD *l* ... 1Sa 20:21 2416
son of Jesse *l* upon the ground ... 1Sa 20:31 2425
say to him that *l* in prosperity ... 1Sa 25:6 2416
the LORD *l*, and as thy soul *l* ... 1Sa 25:26 2416
deed, as the LORD God of Israel *l* ... 1Sa 25:34 2416
said furthermore, As the LORD *l* ... 1Sa 26:10 2416
As the LORD *l*, ye are worthy to ... 1Sa 26:16 2416
the LORD, saying, As the LORD *l* ... 1Sa 28:10 2416
unto him, Surely, as the LORD *l* ... 1Sa 29:6 2416
And Joab said, As God *l*, unless ... 2Sa 2:27 2416
and said unto them, As the LORD *l* ... 2Sa 4:9 2416
as thou livest, and as thy soul *l* ... 2Sa 11:11 2416
he said to Nathan, As the LORD *l* ... 2Sa 12:5 2416
And he said, As the LORD *l* ... 2Sa 14:11 2416
answered and said, As thy soul *l* ... 2Sa 14:19 2416
the king, and said, As the LORD *l* ... 2Sa 15:21 2416
and as my lord the king *l* ... 2Sa 15:21 2416
The LORD *l* ... 2Sa 22:47 2416
sware, and said, As the LORD *l* ... 1Kin 1:29 2416
Now therefore, as the LORD *l* ... 1Kin 2:24 2416
one saith, This is my son that *l* ... 1Kin 3:23 2416
Ahab, As the LORD God of Israel *l* ... 1Kin 17:1 2416
she said, As the LORD thy God *l* ... 1Kin 17:12 2416
and Elijah said, See, thy son *l* ... 1Kin 17:23 2416
As the LORD thy God *l*, there is ... 1Kin 18:10 2416
said, As the LORD of hosts *l* ... 1Kin 18:15 2416
And Micaiah said, As the LORD *l* ... 1Kin 22:14 2416
the LORD *l*, and as thy soul *l* ... 2Kin 2:2 2416
the LORD *l*, and as thy soul *l* ... 2Kin 2:4 2416
the LORD *l*, and as thy soul *l* ... 2Kin 2:6 2416
said, As the LORD of hosts *l* ... 2Kin 3:14 2416

the LORD *l*, and as thy soul *l* 2Kin 4:30 2416
But he said, As the LORD *l* 2Kin 5:16 2416
but, as the LORD *l*, I will run 2Kin 5:20 2416
And Micaiah said, As the LORD *l* 2Chr 18:13 2416
For I know that my redeemer *l* Job 19:25 2416
As God *l*, who hath taken away my Job 27:2 2416
The LORD *l* Ps 18:46 2416
What man is he that *l*, and shall Ps 89:48 2421
And thou shalt swear, The LORD *l* Jer 4:2 2416
And though they say, The LORD *l* Jer 5:2 2416
to swear by my name, The LORD *l* Jer 12:16 2416
shall no more be said, The LORD *l* Jer 16:14 2416
But, The LORD *l*, that brought up Jer 16:15 2416
shall no more say, The LORD *l* Jer 23:7 2416
But, The LORD *l*, which brought up Jer 23:8 2416
Jeremiah, saying, As the LORD *l* Jer 38:16 2416
of Egypt, saying, The Lord GOD *l* Jer 44:26 2416
to pass, that every thing that *l* Eze 47:9 2416
and honoured him that *l* for ever Dan 4:34 2416
sware by him that *l* for ever that Dan 12:7 2416
Beth-aven, nor swear, The LORD *l* Hos 4:15 2416
and say, Thy god, O Dan, *l* Amos 8:14 2416
and, The manner of Beer-sheba *l* Amos 8:14 2416
thy son *l* Jn 4:50 *2198*
and told him, saying, Thy son *l* Jn 4:51 *2198*
Jesus said unto him, Thy son *l* Jn 4:53 *2198*
And whosoever *l* and believeth in me Jn 11:26 *2198*
in that he *l*, he *l* unto God Rom 6:10 *2198*
over a man as long as he *l* Rom 7:1 *2198*
to her husband so long as he *l* Rom 7:2 *2198*
So then if, while her husband *l* Rom 7:3 *2198*
For none of us *l* to himself Rom 14:7 *2198*
the law as long as her husband *l* 1Cor 7:39 *2198*
yet he *l* by the power of God 2Cor 13:4 *2198*
yet not I, but Christ *l* in me Gal 2:20 *2198*
But she that *l* in pleasure is 1Ti 5:6 *2198*
in pleasure is dead while she *l* 1Ti 5:6 *2198*
of whom it is witnessed that he *l* Heb 7:8 *2198*
by him, seeing he ever *l* to make Heb 7:25 *2198*
at all while the testator *l* Heb 9:17 *2198*
by the word of God, which *l* 1Pet 1:23 *2198*
I am he that *l*, and was dead Rev 1:18 *2198*
throne, who *l* for ever and ever, Rev 4:9 *2198*
and worship him that *l* for ever Rev 4:10 *2198*
and worshipped him that *l* for ever Rev 5:14 *2198*
And sware by him that *l* for ever Rev 10:6 *2198*
of God, who *l* for ever and ever Rev 15:7 *2198*

LIVING {147}

every *l* creature that moveth, Gen 1:21 2416
the *l* creature after his kind Gen 1:24 2416
over every *l* thing that moveth Gen 1:28 2416
and man became a *l* soul Gen 2:7 2416
Adam called every *l* creature Gen 2:19 2416
she was the mother of all *l* Gen 3:20 2416
of every *l* thing of all flesh, Gen 6:19 2416
every *l* substance that I have Gen 7:4
every *l* substance was destroyed Gen 7:23
remembered Noah, and every *l* thing Gen 8:1 2416
every *l* thing that is with thee Gen 8:17 2416
smite any more every thing *l* Gen 8:21 2416
with every *l* creature that is Gen 9:10 2416
every *l* creature that is with you Gen 9:12 2416
every *l* creature of all flesh Gen 9:15 2416
every *l* creature of all flesh Gen 9:16 2416
of any *l* thing which is in the Lev 11:10 2416
of every *l* creature that moveth Lev 11:46 2416
As for the *l* bird, he shall take Lev 14:6 2416
the *l* bird in the blood of the Lev 14:6 2416
shall let the *l* bird loose into Lev 14:7 2416
the *l* bird, and dip them in the Lev 14:51 2416
running water, and with the *l* bird Lev 14:52 2416
But he shall let go the *l* bird Lev 14:53 2416
or by any manner of *l* thing that Lev 20:25
stood between the dead and the *l* Num 16:48 2416
hath heard the voice of the *l* God Deut 5:26 2416
know that the *l* God is among you Josh 3:10 2416
left off his kindness to the *l* Ruth 2:20 2416
defy the armies of the *l* God 1Sa 17:26 2416
defied the armies of the *l* God 1Sa 17:36 2416
of their death, *l* in widowhood 2Sa 20:3 2424
but the *l* is my son, and the dead 1Kin 3:22 2416
is thy son, and the *l* is my son 1Kin 3:22 2416
is the dead, and my son is the *l* 1Kin 3:23 2416
Divide the *l* child in two, and 1Kin 3:25 2416
the *l* child was unto the king 1Kin 3:26 2416
O my lord, give her the *l* child 1Kin 3:26 2416
and said, Give her the *l* child 1Kin 3:27 2416
hath sent to reproach the *l* God 2Kin 19:4 2416
sent him to reproach the *l* God 2Kin 19:16 2416
hand is the soul of every *l* thing Job 12:10 2416
is it found in the land of the *l* Job 28:13 2416
it is hid from the eyes of all *l* Job 28:21 2416
to the house appointed for all *l* Job 30:23 2416
with the light of the *l* Job 33:30 2416
of the LORD in the land of the *l* Ps 27:13 2416
thirsteth for God, for the *l* God Ps 42:2 2416
thee out of the land of the *l* Ps 52:5 2416
before God in the light of the *l* Ps 56:13 2416
away as with a whirlwind, both *l* Ps 58:9 2416
blotted out of the book of the *l* Ps 69:28 2416
my flesh crieth out for the *l* God Ps 84:2 2416
the LORD in the land of the *l* Ps 116:9 2416
my portion in the land of the *l* Ps 142:5 2416
sight shall no man *l* be justified Ps 143:2 2416
the desire of every *l* thing Ps 145:16 2416
than the *l* which are yet alive Eccl 4:2 2416
I considered all the *l* which walk Eccl 4:15 2416
that knoweth to walk before the *l* Eccl 6:8 2416
the *l* will lay it to his heart Eccl 7:2 2416
joined to all the *l* there is hope Eccl 9:4 2416
for a *l* dog is better than a dead Eccl 9:4 2416
For the *l* know that they shall Eccl 9:5 2416
of gardens, a well of *l* waters Song 4:15 2416
written among the *l* in Jerusalem Is 4:3 2416
for the *l* to the dead Is 8:19 2416
hath sent to reproach the *l* God Is 37:4 2416
hath sent to reproach the *l* God Is 37:17 2416
the LORD, in the land of the *l* Is 38:11 2416
The *l*, the *l*, he shall Is 38:19 2416
cut off out of the land of the *l* Is 53:8 2416
me the fountain of *l* waters Jer 2:13 2416
is the true God, he is the *l* God Jer 10:10 2416
him off from the land of the *l* Jer 11:19 2416
LORD, the fountain of *l* waters Jer 17:13 2416
perverted the words of the *l* God Jer 23:36 2416
Wherefore doth a *l* man complain Lam 3:39 2416
the likeness of four *l* creatures Eze 1:5 2416
the likeness of the *l* creatures Eze 1:13 2416
up and down among the *l* creatures Eze 1:13 2416
the *l* creatures ran and returned Eze 1:14 2416
Now as I beheld the *l* creatures Eze 1:15 2416
upon the earth by the *l* creatures Eze 1:15 2416
when the *l* creatures went, the Eze 1:19 2416
when the *l* creatures were lifted Eze 1:19 2416
for the spirit of the *l* creature Eze 1:20 2416
for the spirit of the *l* creature Eze 1:21 2416
l creature was as the colour of Eze 1:22 2416
the *l* creatures that touched one Eze 3:13 2416
This is the *l* creature that I saw Eze 10:15 2416
of the *l* creature was in them Eze 10:17 2416
This is the *l* creature that I saw Eze 10:20 2416
set glory in the land of the *l* Eze 26:20 2416
terror in the land of the *l* Eze 32:23 2416
their terror in the land of the *l* Eze 32:24 2416
was caused in the land of the *l* Eze 32:25 2416
their terror in the land of the *l* Eze 32:26 2416
the mighty in the land of the *l* Eze 32:27 2416
my terror in the land of the *l* Eze 32:32 2416
that I have more than any *l* Dan 2:30 2417
to the intent that the *l* may know Dan 4:17 2417
O Daniel, servant of the *l* God Dan 6:20 2417
for he is the *l* God, and stedfast Dan 6:26 2417
Ye are the sons of the *l* God Hos 1:10 2416
that *l* waters shall go out from Zec 14:8 2416
the Christ, the Son of the *l* God Mt 16:16 *2198*
the God of the dead, but of the *l* Mt 22:32 *2198*
him, I adjure thee by the *l* God Mt 26:63 *2198*
of the dead, but the God of the *l* Mk 12:27 *2198*
all that she had, even all her *l* Mk 12:44 *979*
spent all her *l* upon physicians Lk 8:43 *979*
And he divided unto them his *l* Lk 15:12 *979*
his substance with riotous *l* Lk 15:13 *2198*
hath devoured thy *l* with harlots Lk 15:30 *979*
a God of the dead, but of the *l* Lk 20:38 *2198*
cast in all the *l* that she had Lk 21:4 *979*
Why seek ye the *l* among the dead Lk 24:5 *2198*
he would have given thee *l* water Jn 4:10 *2198*
then hast thou that *l* water Jn 4:11 *2198*
I am the *l* bread which came down Jn 6:51 *2198*
As the *l* Father hath sent me, and Jn 6:57 *2198*
that Christ, the Son of the *l* God Jn 6:69 *2198*
shall flow rivers of *l* water Jn 7:38 *2198*
these vanities unto the *l* God Acts 14:15 *2198*
called the children of the *l* God Rom 9:26 *2198*
present your bodies a *l* sacrifice Rom 12:1 *2198*
be Lord both of the dead and *l* Rom 14:9 *2198*
first man Adam was made a *l* soul 1Cor 15:45 *2198*
but with the Spirit of the *l* God 2Cor 3:3 *2198*
ye are the temple of the *l* God 2Cor 6:16 *2198*
as though *l* in the world, are ye Col 2:20 *2198*
to God from idols to serve the *l* 1Th 1:9 *2198*
which is the church of the *l* God 1Ti 3:15 *2198*
because we trust in the *l* God 1Ti 4:10 *2198*
riches, but in the *l* God, who 1Ti 6:17 *2198*
l in malice and envy, hateful, and Titus 3:3 *1236*
in departing from the *l* God Heb 3:12 *2198*
dead works to serve the *l* God Heb 9:14 *2198*
l way, which he hath consecrated Heb 10:20 *2198*
fall into the hands of the *l* God Heb 10:31 *2198*
and unto the city of the *l* God Heb 12:22 *2198*
To whom coming, as unto a *l* stone 1Pet 2:4 *2198*
having the seal of the *l* God Rev 7:2 *2198*
them unto *l* fountains of waters Rev 7:17 *2198*
every *l* soul died in the sea Rev 16:3 *2198*

LIZARD {1}

and the chameleon, and the *l* Lev 11:30 3911

LO {159}

and, *l*, in her mouth was an olive Gen 8:11 2009
and, *l*, one born in my house is Gen 15:3 2009
and, *l*, an horror of great Gen 15:12 2009
lift up his eyes and looked, and, *l* Gen 18:2 2009
and, *l*, Sarah thy wife shall have Gen 18:10 2009
of the plain, and beheld, and, *l* Gen 19:28 2009
behold a well in the field, and, *l* Gen 29:2 2009
And he said, *L*, it is yet high day Gen 29:7 2005
sheaves in the field, and, *l* Gen 37:7 2009
and, *l*, it is even in my sack Gen 42:28 2009
l, here is seed for you, and ye Gen 47:23 1883
and, *l*, God hath shewed me also Gen 48:11 2009
father made me swear, saying, *L* Gen 50:5 2009
l, he goeth out unto the water Ex 7:15 2009
l, he cometh forth to the water Ex 8:20 2009
l, shall we sacrifice the Ex 8:26 2005
And the LORD said unto Moses, *L* Ex 19:9 2009
top of the mountain, saying, *L* Num 14:40 2009
And Balaam said unto Balak, *L* Num 22:38 2009
And he returned unto him and, *l* Num 23:6 2009
l, the people shall dwell alone, Num 23:9 2005
but, *l*, the LORD hath kept thee Num 24:11 2009
And, *l*, he hath given occasions of Deut 22:17 2009
and now, *l*, I am this day Josh 14:10 2009
Behold, I dreamed a dream, and, *l* Judg 7:13 2009
For, *l*, thou shalt conceive, and Judg 13:5 2009
And when he came, *l*, Eli sat upon 1Sa 4:13 2009
and, *l*, thy father hath left the 1Sa 10:2 2009
rod that was in mine hand, and, *l* 1Sa 14:43 2114
said Achish unto his servants, *L* 1Sa 21:14 2009
and, *l*, the chariots and horsemen 2Sa 1:6 2009
l Zadok also, and all the Levites 2Sa 15:24 2009
that smote the people, and said, *L* 2Sa 24:17 2009
And, *l*, while she yet talked with 1Kin 1:22 2009
for, *l*, he hath caught hold on 1Kin 1:51 2009
l, I have given thee a wise and an 1Kin 3:12 2009
and they said one to another, *L* 2Kin 7:6 2009
and, *l*, all the way was full of 2Kin 7:15 2009
said to Nathan the prophet, *L* 1Chr 17:1 2009
l, I give thee the oxen also for 1Chr 21:23 7200
the acts of Asa, first and last, *l* 2Chr 16:11 2009
Thou sayest, *L*, thou hast smitten 2Chr 25:19 2009
and all his wars, and his ways, *l* 2Chr 27:7 2005
For, *l*, our fathers have fallen 2Chr 29:9 2009
and, *l*, we bring into bondage our Neh 5:5 2009
And, *l*, I perceived that God had Neh 6:12 2009
L, let that night be solitary Job 3:7 2009
L this, we have searched it, so Job 5:27 2009
L, he goeth by me, and I see him Job 9:11 2005
If I speak of strength, *l* Job 9:19 2009
L, mine eye hath seen all this, Job 13:1 2005
L, their good is not in their Job 21:16 2005
L, these are parts of his ways Job 26:14 2005
L, all these things worketh God Job 33:29 2005
L now, his strength is in his Job 40:16 2009
For, *l*, the wicked bend their bow Ps 11:2 2009
Yet he passed away, and, *l* Ps 37:36 2009
Then said I, *L*, I come Ps 40:7 2009
l, I have not refrained my lips, Ps 40:9 2009
For, *l*, the kings were assembled, Ps 48:4 2009
L, this is the man that made not Ps 52:7 2009
L, then would I wander far off, Ps 55:7 2009
For, *l*, they lie in wait for my Ps 59:3 2009
l, he doth send out his voice, and Ps 68:33 2005
For, *l*, they that are far from Ps 73:27 2005
For, *l*, thine enemies make a Ps 83:2 2009
l, thine enemies, O LORD, for, *l* Ps 92:9 2009
L, children are an heritage of Ps 127:3 2009
L, we heard of it at Ephratah Ps 132:6 2009
not a word in my tongue, but, *l* Ps 139:4 2005
And, *l*, it was all grown over with Prov 24:31 2009
with mine own heart, saying, *L* Eccl 1:16 2009
L, this only have I found, that Eccl 7:29 7200
For, *l*, the winter is past, the Song 2:11 2009
laid it upon my mouth, and said, *L* Is 6:7 2009
it shall be said in that day, *L* Is 25:9 2009
L, thou trustest in the staff of Is 36:6 2009
and, *l*, these from the north and Is 49:12 2009
l, they all shall wax old as a Is 50:9 2005
For, *l*, I will call all the Jer 1:15 2009
I beheld the earth, and, *l* Jer 4:23 2009
I beheld the mountains, and, *l* Jer 4:24 2009
I beheld, and, *l*, there was no man Jer 4:25 2009
I beheld, and, *l*, the fruitful Jer 4:26 2009
L, I will bring a nation upon you Jer 5:15 2009
L, certainly in vain made he it Jer 8:8 2009
l, they have rejected the word of Jer 8:9 2009
For, *l*, I begin to bring evil on Jer 25:29 2009
For, *l*, the days come, saith the Jer 30:3 2009
for, *l*, I will save thee from Jer 30:10 2009
and, *l*, all the princes sat there, Jer 36:12 2009
For, *l*, I will make thee small Jer 49:15 2009
For, *l*, I will raise and cause to Jer 50:9 2009
and, *l*, a roll of a book was Eze 2:9 2009
Then he said unto me, *L*, I have Eze 4:15 7200
l a likeness as the appearance of Eze 8:2 2009
and, *l*, they put the branch to Eze 8:17 2009
and one built up a wall, and, *l* Eze 13:10 2009
L, when the wall is fallen, shall Eze 13:12 2009
by breaking the covenant, when, *l* Eze 17:18 2009
Now, *l*, if he beget a son, that Eze 18:14 2009
is not good among his people, *l* Eze 18:18 2009
and, *l*, thus have they done in the Eze 23:39 2009
and, *l*, they came Eze 23:40 2009
for, *l*, it cometh Eze 30:9 2009
and, *l*, it shall not be bound up Eze 30:21 2009
And, *l*, thou art unto them as a Eze 33:32 2009
And when this cometh to pass, (*l* Eze 33:33 2009
and, *l*, they were very dry Eze 37:2 2009
And when I beheld, *l*, the sinews Eze 37:8 2009
me into the outward court, and, *l* Eze 40:17 2009
and, *l*, before the temple were an Eze 42:8 2009
He answered and said, *L*, I see Dan 3:25 1888
l another, like a leopard, which Dan 7:6 718
but, *l*, Michael, one of the chief Dan 10:13 2009
and when I am gone forth, *l* Dan 10:20 2009
For, *l*, they are gone because of Hos 9:6 2009
sworn by his holiness, that, *l* Amos 4:2 2009
For, *l*, he that formeth the Amos 4:13 2009
and, *l*, it was the latter growth Amos 7:1 2009
For, *l*, I will command, and I will Amos 9:9 2009
For, *l*, I raise up the Chaldeans, Hab 1:6 2009
Ye looked for much, and, *l* Hag 1:9 2009
for, *l*, I come, and I will dwell Zec 2:10
but, *l*, I will deliver the men Zec 11:6

For, *l*, I will raise up a ... Zec 11:16
and, *l*, the star, which they saw ... Mt 2:9 *2400*
and, *l*, the heavens were opened ... Mt 3:16 *2400*
l a voice from heaven, saying, ... Mt 3:17 *2400*
if any man shall say unto you, *L* ... Mt 24:23 *2400*
l, there thou hast that is thine ... Mt 25:25 *2395*
And while he yet spake, *l*, Judas, ... Mt 26:47 *2400*
l, I have told you ... Mt 28:7 *2400*
and, *l*, I am with you alway, even ... Mt 28:20 *2400*
Peter began to say unto him, *L* ... Mk 10:28 *2400*
if any man shall say to you, *L* ... Mk 13:21 *2400*
or, *l*, he is there ... Mk 13:21 *2400*
l, he that betrayeth me is at ... Mk 14:42 *2400*
For, *l*, as soon as the voice of ... Lk 1:44 *2400*
And, *l*, the angel of the Lord came ... Lk 2:9 *2400*
And, *l*, a spirit taketh him, and he ... Lk 9:39 *2400*
Abraham, whom Satan hath bound, *l* ... Lk 13:16 *2400*
answering said to his father, *L* ... Lk 15:29 *2400*
Neither shall they say, *L* here ... Lk 17:21 *2400*
or, *l* there ... Lk 17:21 *2400*
Then Peter said, *L*, we have left ... Lk 18:28 *2400*
and, *l*, nothing worthy of death is ... Lk 23:15 *2400*
But, *l*, he speaketh boldly, and ... Jn 7:26 *2396*
His disciples said unto him, *L* ... Jn 16:29 *2396*
unworthy of everlasting life, *l* ... Acts 13:46 *2400*
and, *l*, God hath given thee all ... Acts 27:24 *2400*
Then said I, *L*, I come (in the ... Heb 10:7 *2400*
Then said he, *L*, I come to do thy ... Heb 10:9 *2400*
And I beheld, and, *l*, in the midst ... Rev 5:6 *2400*
And I beheld, and *l* a black horse ... Rev 6:5 *2400*
had opened the sixth seal, and, *l* ... Rev 6:12 *2400*
After this I beheld, and, *l* ... Rev 7:9 *2400*
And I looked, and, *l*, a Lamb stood ... Rev 14:1 *2400*

LOADEN {1}
your carriages were heavy *l* ... Is 46:1 6006

LOADETH {1}
who daily *l* us with benefits, ... Ps 68:19 6006

LOAF {3}
one *l* of bread, and one cake of ... Ex 29:23 3603
woman, to every one a *l* of bread ... 1Chr 16:3 3603
ship with them more than one *l* ... Mk 8:14 *740*

LO-AMMI *(lo-am'-mi)* {1} *Symbolic name meaning "Not My People."*
Then said God, Call his name *L* ... Hos 1:9 3818

LOAN {1}
the *l* which is lent to the LORD ... 1Sa 2:20 7596

LOATHE {1}
I *l* it ... Job 7:16 3988

LOATHETH {2}
our soul *l* this light bread ... Num 21:5 6973
The full soul *l* an honeycomb ... Prov 27:7 947

LOATHSOME {4}
nostrils, and it be *l* unto you ... Num 11:20 2214
my skin is broken, and become *l* ... Job 7:5 3988
loins are filled with a *l* disease ... Ps 38:7 7033
but a wicked man is *l*, and cometh ... Prov 13:5 887

LOAVES {32}
two wave *l* of two tenth deals ... Lev 23:17 3899
l of bread unto the people that ... Judg 8:5 3603
another carrying three *l* of bread ... 1Sa 10:3 3603
thee, and give thee two *l* of bread ... 1Sa 10:4
this parched corn, and these ten *l* ... 1Sa 17:17 3899
give me five *l* of bread in mine ... 1Sa 21:3
made haste, and took two hundred *l* ... 1Sa 25:18 3899
upon them two hundred *l* of bread ... 2Sa 16:1
And take with thee ten *l*, and ... 1Kin 14:3 3899
twenty *l* of barley, and full ears ... 2Kin 4:42 3899
unto him, We have here but five *l* ... Mt 14:17 *740*
on the grass, and took the five *l* ... Mt 14:19 *740*
gave the *l* to his disciples, and ... Mt 14:19 *740*
unto them, How many *l* have ye ... Mt 15:34 *740*
And he took the seven *l* and the ... Mt 15:36 *740*
the five *l* of the five thousand ... Mt 16:9 *740*
Neither the seven *l* of the four ... Mt 16:10 *740*
unto them, How many *l* have ye ... Mk 6:38 *740*
And when he had taken the five *l* ... Mk 6:41 *740*
and blessed, and brake the *l* ... Mk 6:41 *740*
they that did eat of the *l* were ... Mk 6:44 *740*
not the miracle of the *l* ... Mk 6:52 *740*
he asked them, How many *l* have ye ... Mk 8:5 *740*
and he took the seven *l*, and gave ... Mk 8:6 *740*
the five *l* among five thousand ... Mk 8:19 *740*
said, We have no more but five *l* ... Lk 9:13 *740*
Then he took the five *l* and the ... Lk 9:16 *740*
unto him, Friend, lend me three *l* ... Lk 11:5 *740*
here, which hath five barley *l* ... Jn 6:9 *740*
And Jesus took the *l* ... Jn 6:11 *740*
fragments of the five barley *l* ... Jn 6:13 *740*
but because ye did eat of the *l* ... Jn 6:26 *740*

LOCK {2}
myrrh, upon the handles of the *l* ... Song 5:5 4514
and took me by a *l* of mine head ... Eze 8:3 6734

LOCKED {2}
the parlour upon him, and *l* them ... Judg 3:23 5274
the doors of the parlour were *l* ... Judg 3:24 5274

LOCKS {15}
shall let the *l* of the hair of ... Num 6:5 6545
seven *l* of my head with the web ... Judg 16:13 4253
shave off the seven *l* of his head ... Judg 16:19 4253
the *l* thereof, and the bars ... Neh 3:3 4514
the *l* thereof, and the bars ... Neh 3:6 4514
the *l* thereof, and the bars ... Neh 3:13 4514
the *l* thereof, and the bars ... Neh 3:14 4514
the *l* thereof, and the bars ... Neh 3:15 4514
hast doves' eyes within thy *l* ... Song 4:1 6777
of a pomegranate within thy *l* ... Song 4:3 6777
my *l* with the drops of the night ... Song 5:2 6977
his *l* are bushy, and black as a ... Song 5:11 6977
are thy temples within thy *l* ... Song 6:7 6777
uncover thy *l*, make bare the leg, ... Is 47:2 6777
nor suffer their *l* to grow long ... Eze 44:20 6545

LOCUST {11}
there remained not one *l* in all ... Ex 10:19 697
the *l* after his kind, and the bald ... Lev 11:22 697
the bald *l* after his kind, and the ... Lev 11:22 5556
for the *l* shall consume it ... Deut 28:38 697
of thy land shall the *l* consume ... Deut 28:42 6767
pestilence, blasting, mildew, *l* ... 1Kin 8:37 697
and their labour unto the *l* ... Ps 78:46 697
I am tossed up and down as the *l* ... Ps 109:23 697
hath left hath the *l* eaten ... Joel 1:4 697
that which the *l* hath left hath ... Joel 1:4 697
the years that the *l* hath eaten ... Joel 2:25 697

LOCUSTS {17}
will I bring the *l* into thy coast ... Ex 10:4 697
over the land of Egypt for the *l* ... Ex 10:12 697
the east wind brought the *l* ... Ex 10:13 697
the *l* went up over all the land ... Ex 10:14 697
them there were no such *l* as they ... Ex 10:14 697
west wind, which took away the *l* ... Ex 10:19 697
there be blasting, or mildew, *l* ... 2Chr 6:28 697
command the *l* to devour the land ... 2Chr 7:13 2284
the *l* came, and caterpillers, and ... Ps 105:34 697
The *l* have no king, yet go they ... Prov 30:27 697
fro of *l* shall he run upon them ... Is 33:4 1357
make thyself many as the *l* ... Nah 3:15 697
Thy crowned are as the *l*, and thy ... Nah 3:17 697
and his meat was *l* and wild honey ... Mt 3:4 *200*
and he did eat *l* and wild honey ... Mk 1:6 *200*
out of the smoke *l* upon the earth ... Rev 9:3 *200*
the shapes of the *l* were like ... Rev 9:7 *200*

LOD {4} *A city in Benjamin.*
and Shamed, who built Ono, and *L* ... 1Chr 8:12 3850
The children of *L*, Hadid, and Ono, ... Ezr 2:33 3850
The children of *L*, Hadid, and Ono, ... Neh 7:37 3850
L, and Ono, the valley of ... Neh 11:35 3850

LO-DEBAR *(lo-de'-bar)* {3} *A city in Manasseh.*
Machir, the son of Ammiel, in *L* ... 2Sa 9:4 3810
Machir, the son of Ammiel, from *L* ... 2Sa 9:5 3810
and Machir the son of Ammiel of *L* ... 2Sa 17:27 3810

LODGE {27}
thy father's house for us to *l* in ... Gen 24:23 3885
provender enough, and room to *l* in ... Gen 24:25 3885
L here this night, and I will ... Num 22:8 3885
where ye shall *l* this night ... Josh 4:3 3885
l here, that thine heart may be ... Judg 19:9 3885
city of the Jebusites, and *l* in it ... Judg 19:11 3885
of these places to *l* all night ... Judg 19:13 3885
to go in and to *l* in Gibeah ... Judg 19:15 3885
only *l* not in the street ... Judg 19:20 3885
Benjamin, I and my concubine, to *l* ... Judg 20:4 3885
and where thou lodgest, I will *l* ... Ruth 1:16 3885
will not *l* with the people ... 2Sa 17:8 3885
L not this night in the plains of ... 2Sa 17:16 3885
his servant *l* within Jerusalem ... Neh 4:22 3885
them, Why *l* ye about the wall ... Neh 13:21 3885
the naked to *l* without clothing ... Job 24:7 3885
stranger did not *l* in the street ... Job 31:32 3885
let us *l* in the villages ... Song 7:11 3885
as a *l* in a garden of cucumbers, ... Is 1:8 4412
the forest in Arabia shall ye *l* ... Is 21:13 3885
l in the monuments, which eat ... Is 65:4 3885
thy vain thoughts *l* within thee ... Jer 4:14 3885
the bittern shall *l* in the upper ... Zeph 2:14 3885
l in the branches thereof ... Mt 13:32 *2681*
air may *l* under the shadow of it ... Mk 4:32 *2681*
and country round about, and *l* ... Lk 9:12 *2647*
disciple, with whom we should *l* ... Acts 21:16 *3579*

LODGED {21}
he *l* there that same night ... Gen 32:13 3885
himself *l* that night in the ... Gen 32:21 3885
house, named Rahab, and *l* there ... Josh 2:1 7901
l there before they passed over ... Josh 3:1 3885
them unto the place where they *l* ... Josh 4:8 4411
into the camp, and *l* in the camp ... Josh 6:11 3885
but Joshua *l* that night among the ... Josh 8:9 3885
the house of Micah, they *l* there ... Judg 18:2 3885
they did eat and drink, and *l* there ... Judg 19:4 3885
therefore he *l* there again ... Judg 19:7 3885
thither unto a cave, and *l* there ... 1Kin 19:9 3885
they *l* round about the house of ... 1Chr 9:27 3885
sellers of all kind of ware *l* ... Neh 13:20 3885
righteousness *l* in it ... Is 1:21 3885
and he *l* there ... Mt 21:17 *835*
the fowls of the air *l* in the ... Lk 13:19 *2681*
was surnamed Peter, were *l* there ... Acts 10:18 *3579*
Then called he them in, and *l* them ... Acts 10:23 *3579*
he is *l* in the house of one Simon ... Acts 10:32 *3579*
l us three days courteously ... Acts 28:7 *3579*
children, if she have *l* strangers ... 1Ti 5:10 *3580*

LODGEST {1}
and where thou *l*, I will lodge ... Ruth 1:16 3885

LODGETH {1}
He *l* with one Simon a tanner, ... Acts 10:6 *3579*

LODGING {6}
you, and leave them in the *l* place ... Josh 4:3 4411
took them into his house to *l* ... Judg 19:15 3885
have taken up their *l* at Geba ... Is 10:29 4411
a *l* place of wayfaring men ... Jer 9:2 4411
there came many to him into his *l* ... Acts 28:23 *3578*
But withal prepare me also a *l* ... Philem 22 *3578*

LODGINGS {1}
enter into the *l* of his borders ... 2Kin 19:23 4411

LOFT {2}
bosom, and carried him up into a *l* ... 1Kin 17:19 5944
and fell down from the third *l* ... Acts 20:9

LOFTILY {1}
they speak *l* ... Ps 73:8 4791

LOFTINESS {2}
the *l* of man shall be bowed down, ... Is 2:17 1365
(he is exceeding proud) his *l* ... Jer 48:29 1363

LOFTY {8}
is not haughty, nor mine eyes *l* ... Ps 131:1 7311
O how *l* are their eyes ... Prov 30:13 7311
The *l* looks of man shall be ... Is 2:11 1365
upon every one that is proud and *l* ... Is 2:12 7311
the eyes of the *l* shall be ... Is 5:15 1364
the *l* city, he layeth it low ... Is 26:5 7682
Upon a *l* and high mountain hast ... Is 57:7 1364
l One that inhabiteth eternity, ... Is 57:15 5375

LOG {5}
mingled with oil, and one *l* of oil ... Lev 14:10 3849
the *l* of oil, and wave them for a ... Lev 14:12 3849
shall take some of the *l* of oil ... Lev 14:15 3849
a meat offering, and a *l* of oil ... Lev 14:21 3849
the *l* of oil, and the priest shall ... Lev 14:24 3849

LOINS {62}
and kings shall come out of thy *l* ... Gen 35:11 2504
and put sackcloth upon his *l* ... Gen 37:34 4975
Egypt, which came out of his *l* ... Gen 46:26 3409
the *l* of Jacob were seventy souls ... Ex 1:5 3409
with your *l* girded, your shoes on ... Ex 12:11 4975
from the *l* even unto the thighs ... Ex 28:42 4975
smite through the *l* of them that ... Deut 33:11 4975
upon his *l* in the sheath thereof ... 2Sa 20:8 4975
his girdle that was about his *l* ... 1Kin 2:5 4975
shall come forth out of thy *l* ... 1Kin 8:19 2504
be thicker than my father's *l* ... 1Kin 12:10 4975
and he girded up his *l*, and ran ... 1Kin 18:46 4975
pray thee, put sackcloth on our *l* ... 1Kin 20:31 4975
they girded sackcloth on their *l* ... 1Kin 20:32 4975
a girdle of leather about his *l* ... 2Kin 1:8 4975
he said to Gehazi, Gird up thy *l* ... 2Kin 4:29 4975
and said unto him, Gird up thy *l* ... 2Kin 9:1 4975
shall come forth out of thy *l* ... 2Chr 6:9 2504
be thicker than my father's *l* ... 2Chr 10:10 4975
and girdeth their *l* with a girdle ... Job 12:18 4975
If his *l* have not blessed me, and ... Job 31:20 2504
Gird up now thy *l* like a man ... Job 38:3 2504
Gird up thy *l* now like a man ... Job 40:7 2504
Lo now, his strength is in his *l* ... Job 40:16 4975
For my *l* are filled with a ... Ps 38:7 3689
thou laidst affliction upon our *l* ... Ps 66:11 4975
make their *l* continually to shake ... Ps 69:23 4975
She girdeth her *l* with strength ... Prov 31:17 4975
the girdle of their *l* be loosed ... Is 5:27 2504
shall be the girdle of his *l* ... Is 11:5 4975
the sackcloth from off thy *l* ... Is 20:2 4975
are my *l* filled with pain ... Is 21:3 4975
and gird sackcloth upon your *l* ... Is 32:11 2504
and I will loose the *l* of kings ... Is 45:1 4975
Thou therefore gird up thy *l* ... Jer 1:17 4975
girdle, and put it upon thy *l* ... Jer 13:1 4975
of the LORD, and put it on my *l* ... Jer 13:2 4975
hast got, which is upon thy *l* ... Jer 13:4 4975
girdle cleaveth to the *l* of a man ... Jer 13:11 4975
every man with his hands on his *l* ... Jer 30:6 2504
cuttings, and upon the *l* sackcloth ... Jer 48:37 4975
appearance of his *l* even upward ... Eze 1:27 4975
appearance of his *l* even downward ... Eze 1:27 4975
appearance of his *l* even downward ... Eze 8:2 4975
from his *l* even upward, as the ... Eze 8:2 4975
man, with the breaking of thy *l* ... Eze 21:6 4975
Girded with girdles upon their *l* ... Eze 23:15 4975
all their *l* to be at a stand ... Eze 29:7 4975
have linen breeches upon their *l* ... Eze 44:18 4975
the waters were to the *l* ... Eze 47:4 4975
the joints of his *l* were loosed ... Dan 5:6 2788
whose *l* were girded with fine ... Dan 10:5 4975
bring up sackcloth upon all *l* ... Amos 8:10 4975
watch the way, make thy *l* strong ... Nah 2:1 4975
and much pain is in all *l* ... Nah 2:10 4975
and a leathern girdle about his *l* ... Mt 3:4 *3751*
a girdle of a skin about his *l* ... Mk 1:6 *3751*
Let your *l* be girded about, and ... Lk 12:35 *3751*
him, that of the fruit of his *l* ... Acts 2:30 *3751*
having your *l* girt about with ... Eph 6:14 *3751*
they come out of the *l* of Abraham ... Heb 7:5 *3751*
he was yet in the *l* of his father ... Heb 7:10 *3751*
gird up the *l* of your mind ... 1Pet 1:13 *3751*

LOIS *(lo'-is)* {1} *Grandmother of Timothy.*
dwelt first in thy grandmother *L* ... 2Ti 1:5 *3090*

LONG {211}
when he had been there a *l* time ... Gen 26:8 748
me all my life *l* unto this day ... Gen 48:15 5750
How *l* wilt thou refuse to humble ... Ex 10:3 4970
How *l* shall this man be a snare ... Ex 10:7 5704
How *l* refuse ye to keep my ... Ex 16:28 5704
when the trumpet soundeth *l* ... Ex 19:13 4900
voice of the trumpet sounded *l* ... Ex 19:19
that thy days may be *l* upon the ... Ex 20:12 748
of shittim wood, five cubits *l* ... Ex 27:1 753
an hundred cubits *l* for one side ... Ex 27:9 753
hangings of an hundred cubits *l* ... Ex 27:11 753

as *l* as she is put apart for her ..... Lev 18:19
as *l* as it lieth desolate, and ye ..... Lev 26:34 3117
As *l* as it lieth desolate it ..... Lev 26:35 3117
as *l* as the cloud abode upon the ..... Num 9:18 3117
when the cloud tarried *l* upon the ..... Num 9:19
How *l* will this people provoke me ..... Num 14:11 5704
how *l* will it be ere they believe ..... Num 14:11 5704
How *l* shall I bear with this evil ..... Num 14:27 5704
we have dwelt in Egypt a *l* time ..... Num 20:15 7227
Ye have dwelt *l* enough in this ..... Deut 1:6 7227
compassed this mountain *l* enough ..... Deut 2:3 7227
shall have remained *l* in the land ..... Deut 4:25
l as thou livest upon the earth ..... Deut 12:19 3117
And if the way be too *l* for thee ..... Deut 14:24 7235
him, because the way is *l* ..... Deut 19:6 7235
shalt besiege a city a *l* time ..... Deut 20:19 7227
longing for them all the day *l* ..... Deut 28:32
of *l* continuance, and sore ..... Deut 28:59
sicknesses, and of *l* continuance ..... Deut 28:59
as *l* as ye live in the land ..... Deut 31:13 3117
shall cover him all the day *l* ..... Deut 33:12
that when they make a *l* blast ..... Josh 6:5 4900
by reason of the very *l* journey ..... Josh 9:13 7230
Joshua made war a *l* time with all ..... Josh 11:18 7227
How *l* are ye slack to go to ..... Josh 18:3 5704
it came to pass a *l* time after ..... Josh 23:1 7227
in the wilderness a *l* season ..... Josh 24:7 7227
Why is his chariot so *l* in coming ..... Judg 5:28 954
How *l* wilt thou be drunken 1Sa 1:14 3117
as *l* as he liveth he shall be 1Sa 1:28 3117
that the time was *l* 1Sa 7:2 7235
How *l* wilt thou mourn for Saul, ... 1Sa 16:1 5704
For as *l* as the son of Jesse 1Sa 20:31 3117
as *l* as we were conversant with 1Sa 25:15 3117
thou found in thy servant so *l* as 1Sa 29:8 3117
how *l* shall it be then, ere thou 2Sa 2:26 5704
Now there was *l* war between the 2Sa 3:1 752
had a *l* time mourned for the dead 2Sa 14:2 7227
How *l* have I to live, that I 2Sa 19:34 3117
hast not asked for thyself *l* life 1Kin 3:11 7221
before it, was forty cubits *l* 1Kin 6:17
How *l* halt ye between two 1Kin 18:21 5704
so *l* as the whoredoms of thy 2Kin 9:22 5704
Hast thou not heard *l* ago how I 2Kin 19:25 7350
neither yet hast asked *l* life 2Chr 1:11 7227
cherubims were twenty cubits *l* 2Chr 3:11 753
brasen scaffold, of five cubits *l* 2Chr 6:13 753
so *l* as they live in the land 2Chr 6:31 3117
Now for a *l* season Israel hath 2Chr 15:3 7227
as *l* as he sought the LORD, God 2Chr 26:5 3117
a *l* time in such sort as it was 2Chr 30:5 7230
for as *l* as she lay desolate she 2Chr 36:21 3117
For how *l* shall thy journey be ..... Neh 2:6 5704
so *l* as I see Mordecai the Jew ..... Est 5:13 6256
Which *l* for death, but it cometh ..... Job 3:21 2442
grant me the thing that I *l* for ..... Job 6:8 8615
How *l* wilt thou not depart from ..... Job 7:19 4101
How *l* wilt thou speak these ..... Job 8:2 5704
how *l* shall the words of thy ..... Job 8:2
How *l* will it be ere ye make an ..... Job 18:2 5704
How *l* will ye vex my soul, and ..... Job 19:2 5704
not reproach me so *l* as I live ..... Job 27:6 3117
how *l* will ye turn my glory into ..... Ps 4:2 5704
how *l* will ye love vanity, and ..... Ps 4:2
but thou, O LORD, how *l* ..... Ps 6:3 5704
How *l* wilt thou forget me, O LORD ..... Ps 13:1 5704
how *l* wilt thou hide thy face ..... Ps 13:1 5704
How *l* shall I take counsel in my ..... Ps 13:2 5704
how *l* shall mine enemy be exalted ..... Ps 13:2 5704
through my roaring all the day *l* ..... Ps 32:3
LORD, how *l* wilt thou look on ..... Ps 35:17 5704
and of thy praise all the day *l* ..... Ps 35:28
I go mourning all the day *l* ..... Ps 38:6
and imagine deceits all the day *l* ..... Ps 38:12
In God we boast all the day *l* ..... Ps 44:8
sake are we killed all the day *l* ..... Ps 44:22
How *l* will ye imagine mischief ..... Ps 62:3 5704
thy righteousness all the day *l* ..... Ps 71:24
shall fear thee as *l* as the sun ..... Ps 72:5 5973
peace so *l* as the moon endureth ..... Ps 72:7 5704
be continued as *l* as the sun ..... Ps 72:17 6440
For all the day *l* have I been ..... Ps 73:14
among us any that knoweth how *l* ..... Ps 74:9 5704
how *l* shall the adversary ..... Ps 74:10 5704
How *l*, LORD ..... Ps 79:5 5704
how *l* wilt thou be angry against ..... Ps 80:4 5704
How *l* will ye judge unjustly, and ..... Ps 82:2 5704
How *l*, LORD? ..... Ps 89:46 5704
Return, O LORD, how *l* ..... Ps 90:13 5704
With *l* life will I satisfy him, ... Ps 91:16 753
how *l* shall the wicked ..... Ps 94:3 5704
how *l* shall the wicked triumph ..... Ps 94:3 5704
How *l* shall they utter and speak ..... Ps 94:4 5704
Forty years *l* was I grieved with ..... Ps 95:10
sing unto the LORD as *l* as I live ..... Ps 104:33 5704
I call upon him as *l* as I live ..... Ps 116:2 3117
My soul hath *l* dwelt with him ..... Ps 120:6 7227
they made *l* their furrows ..... Ps 129:3 748
as those that have been *l* dead ..... Ps 143:3 5769
How *l*, ye simple ones, will ye ..... Prov 1:22 5704
l life, and peace, shall they add ..... Prov 3:2 753
How *l* wilt thou sleep, O sluggard ..... Prov 6:9 5704
at home, he is gone a *l* journey ..... Prov 7:19 7350
coveteth greedily all the day *l* ..... Prov 21:26
fear of the LORD all the day *l* ..... Prov 23:17
They that tarry *l* at the wine ..... Prov 23:30
By *l* forbearing is a prince ..... Prov 25:15 753
because man goeth to his *l* home ..... Eccl 12:5 5769
Then said I, Lord, how *l* ..... Is 6:11 5704
unto him that fashioned it *l* ago ..... Is 22:11 7350
Hast thou not heard *l* ago ..... Is 37:26 5704
I have *l* time holden my peace ..... Is 42:14 5769
mine elect shall *l* enjoy the work ..... Is 65:22
How *l* shall thy vain thoughts ..... Jer 4:14 5704
How *l* shall I see the standard, ... Jer 4:21 5704
How *l* shall the land mourn, and ..... Jer 12:4 5704
How *l* shall this be in the heart ..... Jer 23:26 5704
saying, This captivity is *l* ..... Jer 29:28 752
How *l* wilt thou go about, O thou ..... Jer 31:22 5704
how *l* wilt thou cut thyself ..... Jer 47:5 5704
how *l* will it be ere thou be ..... Jer 47:6 5704
fruit, and children of a span *l* ..... Lam 2:20
for ever, and forsake us so *l* time ..... Lam 5:20 753
his branches became *l* because of ..... Eze 31:5 748
reed of six cubits *l* by the cubit ..... Eze 40:5
little chamber was one reed *l* ..... Eze 40:7 753
it was fifty cubits *l*, and five and ..... Eze 40:29 753
were five and twenty cubits *l* ..... Eze 40:30 753
it was fifty cubits *l*, and five and ..... Eze 40:33 753
offering, of a cubit and an half *l* ..... Eze 40:42 753
the court, an hundred cubits *l* ..... Eze 40:47 753
the house, an hundred cubits *l* ..... Eze 41:13 753
thereof, an hundred cubits *l* ..... Eze 41:13 753
as *l* as they, and as broad as they ..... Eze 42:11 753
round about, five hundred reeds *l* ..... Eze 42:20 753
altar shall be twelve cubits *l* ..... Eze 43:16 753
settle shall be fourteen cubits *l* ..... Eze 43:17 753
nor suffer their locks to grow *l* ..... Eze 44:20
and five and twenty thousand *l* ..... Eze 45:6 753
courts joined of forty cubits *l* ..... Eze 46:22 753
How *l* shall be the vision ..... Dan 8:13 5704
but the time appointed was *l* ..... Dan 10:1 1419
How *l* shall it be to the end of ..... Dan 12:6 5704
how *l* will it be ere they attain ..... Hos 8:5 5704
for he should not stay *l* in the ..... Hos 13:13
how *l* shall I cry, and thou wilt ..... Hab 1:2 5704
which is not his! how *l*? ..... Hab 2:6 5704
how *l* wilt thou not have mercy on ..... Zec 1:12 5704
as *l* as the bridegroom is with ..... Mt 9:15 *1909*
have repented *l* ago in sackcloth ..... Mt 11:21 *3819*
how *l* shall I be with you ..... Mt 17:17 *2193*
how *l* shall I suffer you ..... Mt 17:17 *2193*
and for a pretence make *l* prayer ..... Mt 23:14 *3117*
After a *l* time the lord of those ..... Mt 25:19 *4183*
as *l* as they have the bridegroom ..... Mk 2:19 *5550*
how *l* shall I be with you ..... Mk 9:19 *2193*
how *l* shall I suffer you ..... Mk 9:19 *2193*
How *l* is it ago since this came ..... Mk 9:21 *4214*
which love to go in *l* clothing ..... Mk 12:38
and for a pretence make *l* prayers ..... Mk 12:40 *3117*
clothed in a *l* white garment ..... Mk 16:5
he tarried so *l* in the temple ..... Lk 1:21
man, which had devils *l* time ..... Lk 8:27 *2425*
how *l* shall I be with you, and ..... Lk 9:41 *2193*
him, though he bear *l* with them ..... Lk 18:7 *3114*
into a far country for a *l* time ..... Lk 20:9 *2425*
which desire to walk in *l* robes ..... Lk 20:46
and for a shew make *l* prayers ..... Lk 20:47 *3117*
desirous to see him of a *l* season ..... Lk 23:8 *2425*
been now a *l* time in that case ..... Jn 5:6 *4183*
As *l* as I am in the world, I am ..... Jn 9:5 *3752*
How *l* dost thou make us to doubt ..... Jn 10:24 *2193*
Have I been so *l* time with you ..... Jn 14:9 *5118*
because that of *l* time he had ..... Acts 8:11 *2425*
L time therefore abode they ..... Acts 14:3 *2425*
there they abode *l* time with the ..... Acts 14:28 *3756,3641*
and as Paul was *l* preaching ..... Acts 20:9 *1909,4119*
and eaten, and talked a *l* while ..... Acts 20:11 *2425*
But not *l* after there arose ..... Acts 27:14 *4183*
But after *l* abstinence Paul stood ..... Acts 27:21 *4183*
For I *l* to see you, that I may ..... Rom 1:11 *1971*
over a man as *l* as he liveth ..... Rom 7:1 *5550*
to her husband so *l* as he liveth ..... Rom 7:2
sake we are killed all the day *l* ..... Rom 8:36
All day *l* I have stretched forth ..... Rom 10:21
law as *l* as her husband liveth 1Cor 7:39 *5550*
you, that, if a man have *l* hair 1Cor 11:14 *2863*
But if a woman have *l* hair 1Cor 11:15 *2863*
Charity suffereth *l*, and is kind 1Cor 13:4 *3114*
which *l* after you for the 2Cor 9:14 *1971*
as *l* as he is a child, differeth ..... Gal 4:1 *5550*
thou mayest live *l* on the earth ..... Eph 6:3 *2118*
how greatly I *l* after you all in ..... Phil 1:8 *1971*
But if I tarry *l*, that thou 1Ti 3:15
David, To day, after so *l* a time ..... Heb 4:7 *5118*
hath *l* patience for it, until he ..... Jas 5:7 *3114*
as *l* as ye do well, and are not 1Pet 3:6
as *l* as I am in this tabernacle, ... 2Pet 1:13
now of a *l* time lingereth not 2Pet 2:3
with a loud voice, saying, How *l* ..... Rev 6:10 *2193*

LONGED {8}
the soul of king David *l* to go 2Sa 13:39 3615
And David *l*, and said, Oh that one 2Sa 23:15 183
And David *l*, and said, Oh that one 1Chr 11:17 183
I have *l* after thy precepts ..... Ps 119:40 8373
for I *l* for thy commandments ..... Ps 119:131 2968
I have *l* for thy salvation, O ..... Ps 119:174 8373
For he *l* after you all, and was ..... Phil 2:26 *1971*
l for, my joy and crown, so stand ..... Phil 4:1 *1973*

LONGEDST {1}
because thou sore *l* after thy ..... Gen 31:30 3700

LONGER {17}
And when she could not *l* hide him ..... Ex 2:3 5750
let you go, and ye shall stay no *l* ..... Ex 9:28 3254
any *l* stand before their enemies ..... Judg 2:14 5750
but he tarried *l* than the set 2Sa 20:5
should I wait for the LORD any *l* 2Kin 6:33 5750
thereof is *l* than the earth ..... Job 11:9 752
So that the LORD could no *l* bear ..... Jer 44:22 5750
for thou mayest be no *l* steward ..... Lk 16:2 *2089*
him to tarry *l* time with them ..... Acts 18:20 *4119*
that he ought not to live any *l* ..... Acts 25:24 *3370*
dead to sin, live any *l* therein ..... Rom 6:2 *2089*
we are no *l* under a schoolmaster ..... Gal 3:25 *2089*
when we could no *l* forbear 1Th 3:1 *3370*
cause, when I could no *l* forbear 1Th 3:5 *3370*
Drink no *l* water, but use a 1Ti 5:23 *3370*
That he no *l* should live the rest 1Pet 4:2 *3370*
that there should be time no *l* ..... Rev 10:6 *2089*

LONGETH {4}
son Shechem *l* for your daughter ..... Gen 34:8 2836
because thy soul *l* to eat flesh ..... Deut 12:20 183
my flesh *l* for thee in a dry and ..... Ps 63:1 3642
My soul *l*, yea, even fainteth for ..... Ps 84:2 3700

LONGING {3}
fail with *l* for them all the day ..... Deut 28:32
For he satisfieth the *l* soul ..... Ps 107:9 0204
My soul breaketh for the *l* that ..... Ps 119:20 8375

LONGSUFFERING {17}
God, merciful and gracious, *l* ..... Ex 34:6 750,639
The LORD is *l*, and of great mercy, . Num 14:18 750,639
of compassion, and gracious, *l* ..... Ps 86:15 750,639
take me not away in thy *l* ..... Jer 15:15 750,639
his goodness and forbearance and *l* ..... Rom 2:4 *3115*
endured with much *l* the vessels ..... Rom 9:22 *3115*
By pureness, by knowledge, by *l* 2Cor 6:6 *3115*
the Spirit is love, joy, peace, *l* ..... Gal 5:22 *3115*
all lowliness and meekness, with *l* ..... Eph 4:2 *3115*
all patience and *l* with joyfulness ..... Col 1:11 *3115*
humbleness of mind, meekness, *l* ..... Col 3:12 *3115*
Christ might shew forth all *l* 1Ti 1:16 *3115*
manner of life, purpose, faith, *l* 2Ti 3:10 *3115*
rebuke, exhort with all *l* 2Ti 4:2 *3115*
when once the *l* of God waited in 1Pet 3:20 *3115*
but is *l* to us-ward, not willing 2Pet 3:9 *3114*
account that the *l* of our Lord is 2Pet 3:15 *3115*

LONGWINGED {1}
A great eagle with great wings, *l* .... Eze 17:3 750,83

LOOK {155}
I will *l* upon it, that I may ..... Gen 9:16 7200
thou art a fair woman to *l* upon ..... Gen 12:11 4758
l from the place where thou art ..... Gen 13:14 7200
L now toward heaven, and tell the ..... Gen 15:5 5027
l not behind thee, neither stay ..... Gen 19:17 5027
damsel was very fair to *l* upon ..... Gen 24:16 4758
because she was fair to *l* upon ..... Gen 26:7 4758
Wherefore *l* ye so sadly to day ..... Gen 40:7 6440
let Pharaoh *l* out a man discreet ..... Gen 41:33 7200
Why do ye *l* one upon another ..... Gen 42:1 7200
for he was afraid to *l* upon God ..... Ex 3:6 5027
unto them, The LORD *l* upon you ..... Ex 5:21 7200
l to it ..... Ex 10:10 7200
faces shall *l* one to another ..... Ex 25:20
l that thou make them after their ..... Ex 25:40 7200
Moses did *l* upon all the work, and ..... Ex 39:43 7200
the priest shall *l* on the plague ..... Lev 13:3 7200
and the priest shall *l* on him ..... Lev 13:3 7200
the priest shall *l* on him the ..... Lev 13:5 7200
the priest shall *l* on him again ..... Lev 13:6 7200
But if the priest *l* on it ..... Lev 13:21 7200
Then the priest shall *l* upon it ..... Lev 13:25 7200
But if the priest *l* on it ..... Lev 13:26 7200
the priest shall *l* upon him the ..... Lev 13:27 7200
if the priest *l* on the plague of ..... Lev 13:31 7200
the priest shall *l* on the plague ..... Lev 13:32 7200
the priest shall *l* on the scall ..... Lev 13:34 7200
Then the priest shall *l* on him ..... Lev 13:36 7200
Then the priest shall *l* ..... Lev 13:39 7200
Then the priest shall *l* upon it ..... Lev 13:43 7200
priest shall *l* upon the plague ..... Lev 13:50 7200
he shall *l* on the plague on the ..... Lev 13:51 7200
And if the priest shall *l*, and, ... Lev 13:53 7200
the priest shall *l* on the plague ..... Lev 13:55 7200
And if the priest *l*, and, behold, ... Lev 13:56 7200
and the priest shall *l*, and, behold ..... Lev 14:3 7200
he shall *l* on the plague, and, ... Lev 14:37 7200
again the seventh day, and shall *l* ..... Lev 14:39 7200
Then the priest shall come and *l* ..... Lev 14:44 7200
l upon it, and, behold, the plague ..... Lev 14:48 7200
a fringe, that ye may *l* upon it ..... Num 15:39 7200
l not unto the stubbornness of ..... Deut 9:27 6437
L down from thy holy habitation, ... Deut 26:15 8259
people, and thine eyes shall *l* ..... Deut 28:32 7200
them, *L* on me, and do likewise ..... Judg 7:17 7200
if thou wilt indeed *l* on the 1Sa 1:11 7200
L not on his countenance, or on 1Sa 16:7 5027
countenance, and goodly to *l* to 1Sa 16:12 7210
l how thy brethren fare, and take 1Sa 17:18 6485
that thou shouldest *l* upon such a 2Sa 9:8 6437
was very beautiful to *l* upon 2Sa 11:2 4758
LORD will *l* on mine affliction 2Sa 16:12 7200
Go up now, *l* toward the sea 1Kin 18:43 5027
Judah, I would not *l* toward thee 2Kin 3:14 5027
l, when the messenger cometh 2Kin 6:32 7200
l out there Jehu the son of 2Kin 9:2 7200
L even out the best and meetest of 2Kin 10:3 7200
l that there be here with you 2Kin 10:23 7200
let us *l* one another in the face 2Kin 14:8 7200
the God of our fathers *l* thereon 1Chr 12:17 7200
died, he said, The LORD *l* upon it 2Chr 24:22 7200
for she was fair to *l* on ..... Est 1:11 4758

L

let it *l* for light, but have none ... Job 3:9 6960
therefore be content, *l* upon me ... Job 6:28 6437
shall no man *l* for his goods ... Job 20:21 2342
L unto the heavens, and see ... Job 35:5 5027
L on every one that is proud, and ... Job 40:12 7200
my prayer unto thee, and will *l* up ... Ps 5:3 6822
they *l* and stare upon me ... Ps 22:17 5027
L upon mine affliction and my pain ... Ps 25:18 7200
LORD, how long wilt thou *l* on ... Ps 35:17 7200
me, so that I am not able to *l* up ... Ps 40:12 7200
l down from heaven, and behold, and ... Ps 80:14 5027
l upon the face of thine anointed ... Ps 84:9 5027
shall *l* down from heaven ... Ps 85:11 8259
him that hath an high *l* and a ... Ps 101:5 5869
L thou upon me, and be merciful ... Ps 119:132 6437
as the eyes of servants *l* unto ... Ps 123:2
Let thine eyes *l* right on ... Prov 4:25 5027
let thine eyelids *l* straight ... Prov 4:25
A proud *l*, a lying tongue, and ... Prov 6:17 5869
An high *l*, and a proud heart, and ... Prov 21:4 5869
L not thou upon the wine when it ... Prov 23:31 7200
flocks, and *l* well to thy herds ... Prov 27:23 7896
those that *l* out of the windows ... Eccl 12:3 7200
L not upon me, because I am black ... Song 1:6 7200
l from the top of Amana, from the ... Song 4:8 7789
return, that we may *l* upon thee ... Song 6:13 2372
if one *l* unto the land, behold ... Is 5:30 5027
of Jacob, and I will *l* for him ... Is 8:17 6960
king and their God, and *l* upward ... Is 8:21 6437
they shall *l* unto the earth ... Is 8:22 5027
thee shall narrowly *l* upon thee ... Is 14:16 7688
day shall a man *l* to his Maker ... Is 17:7 8159
he shall not *l* to the altars, the ... Is 17:8 8159
Therefore said I, *L* away from me ... Is 22:4 8159
thou didst *l* in that day to the ... Is 22:8 5027
but they *l* not unto the Holy One ... Is 31:1 8159
L upon Zion, the city of our ... Is 33:20 2372
and *l*, ye blind, that ye may see ... Is 42:18 5027
L unto me, and be ye saved, all ... Is 45:22 6437
l unto the rock whence ye are ... Is 51:1 5027
L unto Abraham your father, and ... Is 51:2 5027
and *l* upon the earth beneath ... Is 51:6 5027
they all *l* to their own way, ... Is 56:11 6437
we *l* for judgment, but there is ... Is 59:11 6960
L down from heaven, and behold ... Is 63:15 5027
but to this man will I *l*, even to ... Is 66:2 5027
l upon the carcases of the men ... Is 66:24 7200
while ye *l* for light, he turn it ... Jer 13:16 6960
l well to him, and do him no harm ... Jer 39:12 7760
and I will *l* well unto thee ... Jer 40:4 7760
and are fled apace, and *l* not back ... Jer 46:5 6437
the fathers shall not *l* back to ... Jer 47:3 6437
Till the LORD *l* down, and behold ... Lam 3:50 8259
all of them princes to *l* to ... Eze 23:15 4758
when they shall *l* after them ... Eze 29:16 6437
stairs shall *l* toward the east ... Eze 43:17 6437
whose *l* was more stout than his ... Dan 7:20 2376
who *l* to other gods, and love ... Hos 3:1 6437
yet I will *l* again toward thy ... Jonah 2:4 5027
and let our eye *l* upon Zion ... Mic 4:11 2372
Therefore I will *l* unto the LORD ... Mic 7:7 6822
but none shall *l* back ... Nah 2:8 6437
that all they that *l* upon thee ... Nah 3:7 7200
evil, and canst not *l* on iniquity ... Hab 1:13 5027
that thou mayest *l* on their ... Hab 2:15 5027
they shall *l* upon me whom they ... Zec 12:10 5027
come, or do we *l* for another ... Mt 11:3 *4328*
upon his eyes, and made him *l* up ... Mk 8:25 *308*
or *l* we for another ... Lk 7:19 *4328*
or *l* we for another ... Lk 7:20 *4328*
I beseech thee, *l* upon my son ... Lk 9:38 *1914*
begin to come to pass, then *l* up ... Lk 21:28 *352*
up your eyes, and *l* on the fields ... Jn 4:35 *2300*
Search, and *l* ... Jn 7:52 *1492*
They shall *l* on him whom they ... Jn 19:37 *3700*
upon him with John, said, *L* on us ... Acts 3:4 *991*
or why *l* ye so earnestly on us, ... Acts 3:12 *816*
l ye out among you seven men of ... Acts 6:3 *1980*
names, and of your law, *l* ye to it ... Acts 18:15 *3700*
for I *l* for him with the brethren ... 1Cor 16:11 *1551*
l to the end of that which is ... 2Cor 3:13 *816*
While we *l* not at the things ... 2Cor 4:18 *4648*
Do ye *l* on things after the ... 2Cor 10:7 *991*
L not every man on his own things ... Phil 2:4 *4648*
whence also we *l* for the Saviour ... Phil 3:20 *553*
unto them that *l* for him shall he ... Heb 9:28 *553*
the angels desire to *l* into ... 1Pet 1:12 *3879*
l for new heavens and a new earth, ... 2Pet 3:13 *4328*
seeing that ye *l* for such things, ... 2Pet 3:14 *4328*
L to yourselves, that we lose not ... 2Jn 8 *991*
sat was to *l* upon like a jasper ... Rev 4:3 *3706*
the book, neither to *l* thereon ... Rev 5:3 *991*
the book, neither to *l* thereon ... Rev 5:4 *991*

LOOKED {143}

God *l* upon the earth, and, behold, ... Gen 6:12 7200
the covering of the ark, and *l* ... Gen 8:13 7200
Have I also here *l* after him that ... Gen 16:13 7200
And he lift up his eyes and *l* ... Gen 18:2 7200
up from thence, and *l* toward Sodom ... Gen 18:16 8259
But his wife *l* back from behind ... Gen 19:26 5027
he *l* toward Sodom and Gomorrah, ... Gen 19:28 8259
Abraham lifted up his eyes, and *l* ... Gen 22:13 7200
the Philistines *l* out at a window ... Gen 26:8 8259
And he *l*, and behold a well in the ... Gen 29:2 7200
LORD hath *l* upon my affliction ... Gen 29:32 7200
And Jacob lifted up his eyes, and *l* ... Gen 33:1 7200
and they lifted up their eyes and *l* ... Gen 37:25 7200
The keeper of the prison *l* not to ... Gen 39:23 7200
l upon them, and, behold, they ... Gen 40:6 7200
brethren, and *l* on their burdens ... Ex 2:11 7200
he *l* this way and that way, and ... Ex 2:12 6437
God *l* upon the children of Israel ... Ex 2:25 7200
and he *l*, and, behold, the bush ... Ex 3:2 7200
and that he had *l* upon their ... Ex 4:31 7200
in the morning watch the LORD *l* ... Ex 14:24 8259
that they *l* toward the wilderness ... Ex 16:10 6437
l after Moses, until he was gone ... Ex 33:8 5027
Aaron *l* upon Miriam, and, behold, ... Num 12:10 6437
that they *l* toward the tabernacle ... Num 16:42 6437
and they *l*, and took every man his ... Num 17:9 7200
when he *l* on Amalek, he took up ... Num 24:20 7200
he *l* on the Kenites, and took up ... Num 24:21 7200
And I *l*, and, behold, ye had sinned ... Deut 9:16 7200
l on our affliction, and our ... Deut 26:7 7200
that he lifted up his eyes and *l* ... Josh 5:13 7200
when the men of Ai *l* behind them ... Josh 8:20 6437
of Sisera *l* out at a window ... Judg 5:28 8259
And the LORD *l* upon him, and said, ... Judg 6:14 6437
and laid wait in the field, and *l* ... Judg 9:43 7200
and Manoah and his wife *l* on ... Judg 13:19 7200
And Manoah and his wife *l* on it ... Judg 13:20 7200
the Benjamites *l* behind them ... Judg 20:40 6437
because they had *l* into the ark ... 1Sa 6:19 7200
for I have *l* upon my people, ... 1Sa 9:16 7200
of Saul in Gibeah of Benjamin *l* ... 1Sa 14:16 7200
that he *l* on Eliab, and said, ... 1Sa 16:6 7200
And when the Philistine *l* about ... 1Sa 17:42 5027
when Saul *l* behind him, David ... 1Sa 24:8 5027
when he *l* behind him, he saw me, ... 2Sa 1:7 6437
Then Abner *l* behind him, and said, ... 2Sa 2:20 6437
daughter *l* through a window ... 2Sa 6:16 8259
watch lifted up his eyes, and *l* ... 2Sa 13:34 7200
wall, and lifted up his eyes, and *l* ... 2Sa 18:24 7200
They *l*, but there was none to ... 2Sa 22:42 8159
And Araunah *l*, and saw the king and ... 2Sa 24:20 8259
And he went up, and *l*, and said, ... 1Kin 18:43 5027
And he *l*, and, behold, there was a ... 1Kin 19:6 5027
l on them, and cursed them in the ... 2Kin 2:24 7200
by upon the wall, and the people *l* ... 2Kin 6:30 7200
her head, and *l* out at a window ... 2Kin 9:30 8259
there *l* out to him two or three ... 2Kin 9:32 8259
And when she *l*, behold, the king ... 2Kin 11:14 7200
Amaziah king of Judah *l* one ... 2Kin 14:11 7200
as David came to Ornan, Ornan *l* ... 1Chr 21:21 5027
And when Judah *l* back, behold, the ... 2Chr 13:14 6437
they *l* unto the multitude, and, ... 2Chr 20:24 6437
And she *l*, and, behold, the king ... 2Chr 23:13 7200
l upon him, and, behold, he was ... 2Chr 26:20 6437
And I *l*, and rose up, and said unto ... Neh 4:14 7200
sight of all them that *l* upon her ... Est 2:15 6437
The troops of Tema *l*, the ... Job 6:19 5027
When I *l* for good, then evil came ... Job 30:26 6960
The LORD *l* down from heaven upon ... Ps 14:2 8559
They *l* unto him, and were ... Ps 34:5 5027
God *l* down from heaven upon the ... Ps 53:2 8259
I *l* for some to take pity, but ... Ps 69:20 6960
For he hath *l* down from the ... Ps 102:19 8259
when they *l* upon me they shaked ... Ps 109:25 7200
I *l* on my right hand, and beheld, ... Ps 142:4 5027
my house I *l* through my casement ... Prov 7:6 8259
I *l* upon it, and received ... Prov 24:32 7200
Then I *l* on all the works that my ... Eccl 2:11 6437
because the sun hath *l* upon me ... Song 1:6 7805
he *l* that it should bring forth ... Is 5:2 6960
when I *l* that it should bring ... Is 5:4 6960
he *l* for judgment, but behold ... Is 5:7 6970
but ye have not *l* unto the maker ... Is 22:11 5027
And I *l*, and there was none to help ... Is 63:5 5027
things which we *l* not for ... Is 64:3 6960
We *l* for peace, but no good came ... Jer 8:15 6960
we *l* for peace, and there is no ... Jer 14:19 6960
this is the day that we *l* for ... Lam 2:16 6960
And I *l*, and, behold, a whirlwind ... Eze 1:4 7200
And when I *l*, behold, an hand was ... Eze 2:9 7200
and when I *l*, behold a hole in the ... Eze 8:7 7200
Then I *l*, and, behold, in the ... Eze 10:1 7200
And when I *l*, behold the four ... Eze 10:9 7200
the head *l* they followed it ... Eze 10:11 6437
l upon thee, behold, thy time was ... Eze 16:8 7200
with images, he *l* in the liver ... Eze 21:21 7200
court that *l* toward the north ... Eze 40:20 6440
and I *l*, and, behold, the glory of ... Eze 44:4 7200
priests, which *l* toward the north ... Eze 46:19 6437
be *l* upon before thee, and the ... Dan 1:13 7200
Then I lifted up mine eyes, and *l* ... Dan 10:5 7200
Then I Daniel *l*, and, behold, ... Dan 12:5 7200
But thou shouldest not have *l* on ... Obad 12 7200
thou shouldest not have *l* on ... Obad 13 7200
Ye *l* for much, and, lo, it came to ... Hag 1:9 6437
I lifted up mine eyes again, and *l* ... Zec 2:1 7200
And I said, I have *l*, and behold a ... Zec 4:2 7200
and lifted up mine eyes, and *l* ... Zec 5:1 7200
Then lifted I up mine eyes, and *l* ... Zec 5:9 7200
and lifted up mine eyes, and *l* ... Zec 6:1 7200
when he had *l* round about on them ... Mk 3:5 *4017*
he *l* round about on them which ... Mk 3:34 *4017*
he *l* round about to see her that ... Mk 5:32 *4017*
he *l* up to heaven, and blessed, and ... Mk 6:41 *308*
And he *l* up, and said, I see men as ... Mk 8:24 *308*
l on his disciples, he rebuked ... Mk 8:33 *1492*
when they had *l* round about ... Mk 9:8 *4017*
Jesus *l* round about, and saith ... Mk 10:23 *4017*
when he had *l* round about upon ... Mk 11:11 *4017*
she *l* upon him, and said, And thou ... Mk 14:67 *1689*
And when they *l*, they saw that the ... Mk 16:4 *308*
me in the days wherein he *l* on me ... Lk 1:25 *1869*
l for redemption in Jerusalem ... Lk 2:38 *4327*
l on him, and passed by on the ... Lk 10:32 *1492*
Jesus came to the place, he *l* up ... Lk 19:5 *308*
And he *l* up, and saw the rich men ... Lk 21:1 *308*
the fire, and earnestly *l* upon him ... Lk 22:56 *816*
the Lord turned, and *l* upon Peter ... Lk 22:61 *1689*
the disciples *l* one on another ... Jn 13:22 *991*
down, and *l* into the sepulchre, ... Jn 20:11
while they *l* stedfastly toward ... Acts 1:10 *816*
l up stedfastly into heaven, and ... Acts 7:55 *816*
And when he *l* on him, he was ... Acts 10:4 *816*
And the same hour I *l* up upon him ... Acts 22:13 *308*
Howbeit they *l* when he should ... Acts 28:6 *4328*
after they had *l* a great while ... Acts 28:6 *4328*
For he *l* for a city which hath ... Heb 11:10 *1551*
our eyes, which we have *l* upon ... 1Jn 1:1 *2300*
After this I *l*, and, behold, a ... Rev 4:1 *1492*
And I *l*, and behold a pale horse ... Rev 6:8 *1492*
And I *l*, and, lo, a Lamb stood on ... Rev 14:1 *1492*
And I *l*, and behold a white cloud, ... Rev 14:14 *1492*
And after that I *l*, and, behold, ... Rev 15:5 *1492*

LOOKEST {2}

l narrowly unto all my paths ... Job 13:27 8104
wherefore *l* thou upon them that ... Hab 1:13 5027

LOOKETH {33}

foot, wheresoever the priest *l* ... Lev 13:12 4758,5869
that is bitten, when he *l* upon it ... Num 21:8 7200
Pisgah, which *l* toward Jeshimon ... Num 21:20 8259
of Peor, that *l* toward Jeshimon ... Num 23:28 8259
from the bay that *l* southward ... Josh 15:2 6437
to the way of the border that *l* ... 1Sa 13:18 8259
for man *l* on the outward ... 1Sa 16:7 7200
but the LORD *l* on the heart ... 1Sa 16:7 7200
as a hireling *l* for the reward of ... Job 7:2 6960
For he *l* to the ends of the earth ... Job 28:24 5027
He *l* upon men, and if any say, I ... Job 33:27 7789
The LORD *l* from heaven ... Ps 33:13 5027
the place of his habitation he *l* ... Ps 33:14 7688
He *l* on the earth, and it ... Ps 104:32 5027
prudent man *l* well to his going ... Prov 14:15 995
She *l* well to the ways of her ... Prov 31:27 6822
he *l* forth at the windows, ... Song 2:9 7688
Who is she that *l* forth as the ... Song 6:10 8259
Lebanon which *l* toward Damascus ... Song 7:4 6822
when he that *l* upon it seeth ... Is 28:4 7200
gate, that *l* toward the north ... Eze 8:3 6437
LORD's house, which *l* eastward ... Eze 11:1 6437
the gate which *l* toward the east ... Eze 40:6 6440
the gate that *l* toward the east ... Eze 40:22 6440
the gate that *l* toward the east ... Eze 43:1 6437
sanctuary which *l* toward the east ... Eze 44:1 6437
gate of the inner court that *l* ... Eze 46:1 6437
the gate that *l* toward the east ... Eze 46:12 6437
gate by the way that *l* eastward ... Eze 47:2 6437
That whosoever *l* on a woman to ... Mt 5:28 *991*
in a day when he *l* not for him ... Mt 24:50 *4328*
in a day when he *l* not for him ... Lk 12:46 *4328*
But whoso *l* into the perfect law ... Jas 1:25 *3879*

LOOKING {30}

l toward Gilgal, that is before ... Josh 15:7 6437
three *l* toward the north, and ... 1Kin 7:25 6437
three *l* toward the west ... 1Kin 7:25 6437
three *l* toward the south ... 1Kin 7:25 6437
and three *l* toward the east ... 1Kin 7:25 6437
Michal the daughter of Saul *l* out ... 1Chr 15:29 8259
three *l* toward the north, and ... 2Chr 4:4 6437
three *l* toward the west ... 2Chr 4:4 6437
three *l* toward the south ... 2Chr 4:4 6437
and three *l* toward the east ... 2Chr 4:4 6437
is strong, and as a molten *l* glass ... Job 37:18 7209
mine eyes fail with *l* upward ... Is 38:14
l up to heaven, he blessed, and ... Mt 14:19 *308*
l up to heaven, he sighed, and ... Mk 7:34 *308*
Jesus *l* upon them saith, With men ... Mk 10:27 *1689*
were also women *l* on afar off ... Mk 15:40 *2334*
l round about upon them all, he ... Lk 6:10 *4017*
l up to heaven, he blessed them ... Lk 9:16 *308*
l back, is fit for the kingdom of ... Lk 9:62 *991*
for *l* after those things which ... Lk 21:26 *4329*
l upon Jesus as he walked, he ... Jn 1:36 *1689*
l in, saw the linen clothes lying ... Jn 20:5
l stedfastly on him, saw his face ... Acts 6:15 *816*
l for a promise from thee ... Acts 23:21 *4327*
L for that blessed hope, and the ... Titus 2:13 *4327*
certain fearful *l* for of judgment ... Heb 10:27 *1561*
L unto Jesus the author and ... Heb 12:2 *872*
L diligently lest any man fail of ... Heb 12:15 *1983*
L for and hasting unto the coming ... 2Pet 3:12 *4328*
l for the mercy of our Lord Jesus ... Jude 21 *4327*

LOOKINGGLASSES {1}

of the *l* of the women assembling, ... Ex 38:8 4759

LOOKS {5}

but wilt bring down high *l* ... Ps 18:27 5869
The lofty *l* of man shall be ... Is 2:11 5869
and the glory of his high *l* ... Is 10:12 5869
words, nor be dismayed at their *l* ... Eze 2:6 6400
neither be dismayed at their *l* ... Eze 3:9 6400

LOOPS {13}

thou shalt make *l* of blue upon ... Ex 26:4 3924
Fifty *l* shalt thou make in the ... Ex 26:5 3924
fifty *l* shalt thou make in the ... Ex 26:5 3924
that the *l* may take hold one of ... Ex 26:5 3924
thou shalt make fifty *l* on the ... Ex 26:10 3924
fifty *l* in the edge of the ... Ex 26:10 3924
and put the taches into the *l* ... Ex 26:11 3924

he made *l* of blue on the edge of ... Ex 36:11 3924
Fifty *l* made he in one curtain, ... Ex 36:12 3924
fifty *l* made he in the edge of ... Ex 36:12 3924
the *l* held one curtain to another ... Ex 36:12 3924
And he made fifty *l* upon the ... Ex 36:17 3924
fifty *l* made he upon the edge of ... Ex 36:17 3924

LOOSE {29}

Naphtali is a hind let *l* ... Gen 49:21 7971
living bird *l* into the open field ... Lev 14:7 7971
l his shoe from off his foot, and ... Deut 25:9 2502
L thy shoe from off thy foot ... Josh 5:15 5394
that he would let *l* his hand ... Job 6:9 5425
they have also let *l* the bridle ... Job 30:11 7971
Pleiades, or *l* the bands of Orion ... Job 38:31 6605
to *l* those that are appointed to ... Ps 102:20 6605
l the sackcloth from off thy ... Is 20:2 6605
I will *l* the loins of kings, to ... Is 45:1 6605
l thyself from the bands of thy ... Is 52:2 6605
to *l* the bands of wickedness, to ... Is 58:6 6605
I *l* thee this day from the chains ... Jer 40:4 6605
and said, Lo, I see four men *l* ... Dan 3:25 8271
whatsoever thou shalt *l* on earth ... Mt 16:19 *3089*
whatsoever ye shall *l* on earth ... Mt 18:18 *3089*
l them, and bring them unto me ... Mt 21:2 *3089*
l him, and bring him ... Mk 11:2 *3089*
and they *l* him ... Mk 11:4 *3089*
l his ox or his ass from the ... Lk 13:15 *3089*
l him, and bring him hither ... Lk 19:30 *3089*
any man ask you, Why do ye *l* him ... Lk 19:31 *3089*
said unto them, Why *l* ye the colt ... Lk 19:33 *3089*
unto them, *L* him, and let him go ... Jn 11:44 *3089*
of his feet I am not worthy to *l* ... Acts 13:25 *3089*
him of Paul, that he might *l* him ... Acts 24:26 *3089*
book, and to *l* the seals thereof ... Rev 5:2 *3089*
to *l* the seven seals thereof ... Rev 5:5 *3089*
L the four angels which are bound ... Rev 9:14 *3089*

LOOSED {32}

be not *l* from the ephod ... Ex 28:28 2118
might not be *l* from the ephod ... Ex 39:21 2118
house of him that hath his shoe *l* ... Deut 25:10 2502
his bands *l* from off his hands ... Judg 15:14 4549
Because he hath *l* my cord ... Job 30:11 6605
or who hath *l* the bands of the ... Job 39:5 6605
The king sent and *l* him ... Ps 105:20 5425
thou hast *l* my bonds ... Ps 116:16 6605
Or ever the silver cord be *l* ... Eccl 12:6 7368
the girdle of their loins be *l* ... Is 5:27 6605
Thy tacklings are *l* ... Is 33:23 5203
exile hasteneth that he may be *l* ... Is 51:14 6605
the joints of his loins were *l* ... Dan 5:6 8271
on earth shall be *l* in heaven ... Mt 16:19 *3089*
on earth shall be *l* in heaven ... Mt 18:18 *3089*
l him, and forgave him the debt ... Mt 18:27 *630*
and the string of his tongue was *l* ... Mk 7:35 *3089*
immediately, and his tongue *l* ... Lk 1:64
thou art *l* from thine infirmity ... Lk 13:12 *630*
be *l* from this bond on the ... Lk 13:16 *3089*
having *l* the pains of death ... Acts 2:24 *3089*
Paul and his company *l* from Paphos ... Acts 13:13 *321*
and every one's bands were *l* ... Acts 16:26 *447*
he *l* him from his bands, and ... Acts 22:30 *3089*
not have *l* from Crete, and to have ... Acts 27:21 *321*
l the rudder bands, and hoised up ... Acts 27:40 *447*
she is *l* from the law of her ... Rom 7:2 *2673*
seek not to be *l* ... 1Cor 7:27 *3089*
Art thou *l* from a wife ... 1Cor 7:27 *3080*
And the four angels were *l* ... Rev 9:15 *3089*
that he must be *l* a little season ... Rev 20:3 *3089*
Satan shall be *l* out of his ... Rev 20:7 *3089*

LOOSETH {2}

He *l* the bond of kings, and ... Job 12:18 6605
The LORD *l* the prisoners ... Ps 146:7 5425

LOOSING {4}

unto them, What do ye, *l* the colt ... Mk 11:5 *3089*
And as they were *l* the colt ... Lk 19:33 *3089*
Therefore *l* from Troas, we came ... Acts 16:11 *321*
l thence, they sailed close by ... Acts 27:13 *142*

LOP {1}

shall *l* the bough with terror ... Is 10:33 5586

LORD {7838}

1. God.

day that the *L* God made the earth ... Gen 2:4 3068
for the *L* God had not caused it ... Gen 2:5 3068
the *L* God formed man of the dust ... Gen 2:7 3068
the *L* God planted a garden ... Gen 2:8 3068
out of the ground made the *L* God ... Gen 2:9 3068
the *L* God took the man, and put ... Gen 2:15 3068
the *L* God commanded the man, ... Gen 2:16 3068
the *L* God said, It is not good ... Gen 2:18 3068
out of the ground the *L* God ... Gen 2:19 3068
the *L* God caused a deep sleep to ... Gen 2:21 3068
which the *L* God had taken from ... Gen 2:22 3068
field which the *L* God had made ... Gen 3:1 3068
they heard the voice of the *L* God ... Gen 3:8 3068
from the presence of the *L* God ... Gen 3:8 3068
the *L* God called unto Adam, and ... Gen 3:9 3068
the *L* God said unto the woman, ... Gen 3:13 3068
the *L* God said unto the serpent, ... Gen 3:14 3068
to his wife did the *L* God make ... Gen 3:21 3068
the *L* God said, Behold, the man ... Gen 3:22 3068
Therefore the *L* God sent him ... Gen 3:23 3068
I have gotten a man from the *L* ... Gen 4:1 3068
the ground an offering unto the *L* ... Gen 4:3 3068
the *L* had respect unto Abel and to ... Gen 4:4 3068
the *L* said unto Cain, Why art ... Gen 4:6 3068
the *L* said unto Cain, Where is ... Gen 4:9 3068
And Cain said unto the *L*, My ... Gen 4:13 3068
the *L* said unto him, Therefore ... Gen 4:15 3068
the *L* set a mark upon Cain, lest ... Gen 4:15 3068
out from the presence of the *L* ... Gen 4:16 3068
to call upon the name of the *L* ... Gen 4:26 3068
ground which the *L* hath cursed ... Gen 5:29 3068
the *L* said, My spirit shall not ... Gen 6:3 3068
it repented the *L* that he had ... Gen 6:6 3068
the *L* said, I will destroy man ... Gen 6:7 3068
found grace in the eyes of the *L* ... Gen 6:8 3068
the *L* said unto Noah, Come thou ... Gen 7:1 3068
unto all that the *L* commanded him ... Gen 7:5 3068
and the *L* shut him in ... Gen 7:16 3068
Noah builded an altar unto the *L* ... Gen 8:20 3068
the *L* smelled a sweet savour ... Gen 8:21 3068
the *L* said in his heart, I will ... Gen 8:21 3068
Blessed be the *L* God of Shem ... Gen 9:26 3068
was a mighty hunter before the *L* ... Gen 10:9 3068
the mighty hunter before the *L* ... Gen 10:9 3068
the *L* came down to see the city ... Gen 11:5 3068
the *L* said, Behold, the people is ... Gen 11:6 3068
So the *L* scattered them abroad ... Gen 11:8 3068
because the *L* did there confound ... Gen 11:9 3068
from thence did the *L* scatter ... Gen 11:9 3068
Now the *L* had said unto Abram, ... Gen 12:1 3068
as the *L* had spoken unto him ... Gen 12:4 3068
the *L* appeared unto Abram, and ... Gen 12:7 3068
builded he an altar unto the *L* ... Gen 12:7 3068
he builded an altar unto the *L* ... Gen 12:8 3068
and called upon the name of the *L* ... Gen 12:8 3068
the *L* plagued Pharaoh and his ... Gen 12:17 3068
Abram called on the name of the *L* ... Gen 13:4 3068
before the *L* destroyed Sodom and ... Gen 13:10 3068
even as the garden of the *L* ... Gen 13:10 3068
sinners before the *L* exceedingly ... Gen 13:13 3068
the *L* said unto Abram, after that ... Gen 13:14 3068
built there an altar unto the *L* ... Gen 13:18 3068
have lift up mine hand unto the *L* ... Gen 14:22 3068
the *L* came unto Abram in a vision ... Gen 15:1 3068
L GOD, what wilt thou give me, ... Gen 15:2 136
the word of the *L* came unto him ... Gen 15:4 3068
And he believed in the *L* ... Gen 15:6 3068
I am the *L* that brought thee out ... Gen 15:7 3068
L GOD, whereby shall I know that ... Gen 15:8 136
In the same day the *L* made a ... Gen 15:18 3068
the *L* hath restrained me from ... Gen 16:2 3068
the *L* judge between me and thee ... Gen 16:5 3068
the angel of the *L* found her by a ... Gen 16:7 3068
the angel of the *L* said unto her ... Gen 16:9 3068
the angel of the *L* said unto her ... Gen 16:10 3068
the angel of the *L* said unto her ... Gen 16:11 3068
because the *L* hath heard thy ... Gen 16:11 3068
name of the *L* that spake unto her ... Gen 16:13 3068
the *L* appeared to Abram, and said ... Gen 17:1 3068
the *L* appeared unto him in the ... Gen 18:1 3068
And said, My *L*, if now I have ... Gen 18:3 136
And the *L* said unto Abraham, ... Gen 18:13 3068
Is any thing too hard for the *L* ... Gen 18:14 3068
the *L* said, Shall I hide from ... Gen 18:17 3068
they shall keep the way of the *L* ... Gen 18:19 3068
that the *L* may bring upon Abraham ... Gen 18:19 3068
the *L* said, Because the cry of ... Gen 18:20 3068
Abraham stood yet before the *L* ... Gen 18:22 3068
the *L* said, If I find in Sodom ... Gen 18:26 3068
taken upon me to speak unto the *L* ... Gen 18:27 136
him, Oh let not the *L* be angry ... Gen 18:30 136
taken upon me to speak unto the *L* ... Gen 18:31 136
said, Oh let not the *L* be angry ... Gen 18:32 136
the *L* went his way, as soon as he ... Gen 18:33 3068
great before the face of the *L* ... Gen 19:13 3068
the *L* hath sent us to destroy it ... Gen 19:13 3068
for the *L* will destroy this city ... Gen 19:14 3068
the *L* being merciful unto him ... Gen 19:16 3068
Then the *L* rained upon Sodom and ... Gen 19:24 3068
and fire from the *L* out of heaven ... Gen 19:24 3068
place where he stood before the *L* ... Gen 19:27 3068
and he said, *L*, wilt thou slay ... Gen 20:4 136
For the *L* had fast closed up all ... Gen 20:18 3068
the *L* visited Sarah as he had ... Gen 21:1 3068
the *L* did unto Sarah as he had ... Gen 21:1 3068
called there on the name of the *L* ... Gen 21:33 3068
the angel of the *L* called unto ... Gen 22:11 3068
mount of the *L* it shall be seen ... Gen 22:14 3068
the angel of the *L* called unto ... Gen 22:15 3068
myself have I sworn, saith the *L* ... Gen 22:16 3068
the *L* had blessed Abraham in all ... Gen 24:1 3068
I will make thee swear by the *L* ... Gen 24:3 3068
The *L* God of heaven, which took ... Gen 24:7 3068
O *L* God of my master Abraham, I ... Gen 24:12 3068
to wit whether the *L* had made his ... Gen 24:21 3068
his head, and worshipped the *L* ... Gen 24:26 3068
Blessed be the *L* God of my master ... Gen 24:27 3068
the *L* led me to the house of my ... Gen 24:27 3068
Come in, thou blessed of the *L* ... Gen 24:31 3068
the *L* hath blessed my master ... Gen 24:35 3068
And he said unto me, The *L* ... Gen 24:40 3068
O *L* God of my master Abraham, if ... Gen 24:42 3068
the *L* hath appointed out for my ... Gen 24:44 3068
down my head, and worshipped the *L* ... Gen 24:48 3068
blessed the *L* God of my master ... Gen 24:48 3068
The thing proceedeth from the *L* ... Gen 24:50 3068
son's wife, as the *L* hath spoken ... Gen 24:51 3068
their words, he worshipped the *L* ... Gen 24:52 3068
seeing the *L* hath prospered my ... Gen 24:56 3068
intreated the *L* for his wife ... Gen 25:21 3068
the *L* was intreated of him, and ... Gen 25:21 3068
And she went to enquire of the *L* ... Gen 25:22 3068
the *L* said unto her, Two nations ... Gen 25:23 3068
the *L* appeared unto him, and said, ... Gen 26:2 3068
and the *L* blessed him ... Gen 26:12 3068
For now the *L* hath made room for ... Gen 26:22 3068
the *L* appeared unto him the same ... Gen 26:24 3068
and called upon the name of the *L* ... Gen 26:25 3068
that the *L* was with thee ... Gen 26:28 3068
thou art now the blessed of the *L* ... Gen 26:29 3068
thee before the *L* before my death ... Gen 27:7 3068
Because the *L* thy God brought it ... Gen 27:20 3068
a field which the *L* hath blessed ... Gen 27:27 3068
the *L* stood above it, and said ... Gen 28:13 3068
I am the *L* God of Abraham thy ... Gen 28:13 3068
Surely the *L* is in this place ... Gen 28:16 3068
then shall the *L* be my God ... Gen 28:21 3068
when the *L* saw that Leah was ... Gen 29:31 3068
Surely the *L* hath looked upon my ... Gen 29:32 3068
Because the *L* hath heard that I ... Gen 29:33 3068
she said, Now will I praise the *L* ... Gen 29:35 3068
The *L* shall add to me another son ... Gen 30:24 3068
L hath blessed me for thy sake ... Gen 30:27 3068
the *L* hath blessed thee since my ... Gen 30:30 3068
the *L* said unto Jacob, Return ... Gen 31:3 3068
The *L* watch between me and thee, ... Gen 31:49 3068
the *L* which saidst unto me, ... Gen 32:9 3068
was wicked in the sight of the *L* ... Gen 38:7 3068
and the *L* slew him ... Gen 38:7 3068
which he did displeased the *L* ... Gen 38:10 3068
the *L* was with Joseph, and he was ... Gen 39:2 3068
saw that the *L* was with him ... Gen 39:3 3068
that the *L* made all that he did ... Gen 39:3 3068
that the *L* blessed the Egyptian's ... Gen 39:5 3068
the blessing of the *L* was upon ... Gen 39:5 3068
But the *L* was with Joseph, and ... Gen 39:21 3068
because the *L* was with him, and ... Gen 39:23 3068
he did, the *L* made it to prosper ... Gen 39:23 3068
waited for thy salvation, O *L* ... Gen 49:18 3068
the angel of the *L* appeared unto ... Ex 3:2 3068
when the *L* saw that he turned ... Ex 3:4 3068
the *L* said, I have surely seen ... Ex 3:7 3068
The *L* God of your fathers, the ... Ex 3:15 3068
The *L* God of your fathers, the ... Ex 3:16 3068
The *L* God of the Hebrews hath met ... Ex 3:18 3068
we may sacrifice to the *L* our God ... Ex 3:18 3068
The *L* hath not appeared unto thee ... Ex 4:1 3068
the *L* said unto him, What is that ... Ex 4:2 3068
the *L* said unto Moses, Put forth ... Ex 4:4 3068
that the *L* God of their fathers ... Ex 4:5 3068
the *L* said furthermore unto him, ... Ex 4:6 3068
And Moses said unto the *L* ... Ex 4:10 3068
O my *L*, I am not eloquent ... Ex 4:10 136
the *L* said unto him, Who hath ... Ex 4:11 3068
have not I the *L* ... Ex 4:11 3068
And he said, O my *L*, send, I pray ... Ex 4:13 136
the anger of the *L* was kindled ... Ex 4:14 3068
the *L* said unto Moses in Midian, ... Ex 4:19 3068
the *L* said unto Moses, When thou ... Ex 4:21 3068
unto Pharaoh, Thus saith the *L* ... Ex 4:22 3068
in the inn, that the *L* met him ... Ex 4:24 3068
the *L* said to Aaron, Go into the ... Ex 4:27 3068
words of the *L* who had sent him ... Ex 4:28 3068
which the *L* had spoken unto Moses ... Ex 4:30 3068
when they heard that the *L* had ... Ex 4:31 3068
Thus saith the *L* God of Israel ... Ex 5:1 3068
And Pharaoh said, Who is the *L* ... Ex 5:2 3068
I know not the *L*, neither will I ... Ex 5:2 3068
and sacrifice unto the *L* our God ... Ex 5:3 3068
us go and do sacrifice to the *L* ... Ex 5:17 3068
The *L* look upon you, and judge ... Ex 5:21 3068
And Moses returned unto the *L* ... Ex 5:22 3068
and said, *L*, wherefore hast ... Ex 5:22 136
Then the *L* said unto Moses, Now ... Ex 6:1 3068
and said unto him, I am the *L* ... Ex 6:2 3068
children of Israel, I am the *L* ... Ex 6:6 3068
know that I am the *L* your God ... Ex 6:7 3068
I am the *L* ... Ex 6:8 3068
the *L* spake unto Moses, saying, ... Ex 6:10 3068
And Moses spake before the *L* ... Ex 6:12 3068
the *L* spake unto Moses and unto ... Ex 6:13 3068
and Moses, to whom the *L* said ... Ex 6:26 3068
to pass on the day when the *L* ... Ex 6:28 3068
That the *L* spake unto Moses, ... Ex 6:29 3068
unto Moses, saying, I am the *L* ... Ex 6:29 3068
And Moses said before the *L* ... Ex 6:30 3068
the *L* said unto Moses, See, I ... Ex 7:1 3068
shall know that I am the *L* ... Ex 7:5 3068
Aaron did as the *L* commanded them ... Ex 7:6 3068
the *L* spake unto Moses and unto ... Ex 7:8 3068
did so as the *L* had commanded ... Ex 7:10 3068
as the *L* had said ... Ex 7:13 3068
the *L* said unto Moses, Pharaoh's ... Ex 7:14 3068
The *L* God of the Hebrews hath ... Ex 7:16 3068
Thus saith the *L*, In this thou ... Ex 7:17 3068
thou shalt know that I am the *L* ... Ex 7:17 3068
the *L* spake unto Moses, Say unto ... Ex 7:19 3068
Aaron did so, as the *L* commanded ... Ex 7:20 3068
as the *L* had said ... Ex 7:22 3068
after that the *L* had smitten the ... Ex 7:25 3068
the *L* spake unto Moses, Go unto ... Ex 8:1 3068
and say unto him, Thus saith the *L* ... Ex 8:1 3068
the *L* spake unto Moses, Say unto ... Ex 8:5 3068
and Aaron, and said, Intreat the *L* ... Ex 8:8 3068
they may do sacrifice unto the *L* ... Ex 8:8 3068
is none like unto the *L* our God ... Ex 8:10 3068
Moses cried unto the *L* because of ... Ex 8:12 3068
the *L* did according to the word ... Ex 8:13 3068
as the *L* had said ... Ex 8:15 3068
the *L* said unto Moses, Say unto ... Ex 8:16 3068
as the *L* had said ... Ex 8:19 3068

L

the *L* said unto Moses, Rise up ... Ex 8:20 3068
and say unto him, Thus saith the *L* ... Ex 8:20 3068
the *L* in the midst of the earth ... Ex 8:22 3068
And the *L* did so ... Ex 8:24 3068
of the Egyptians to the *L* our God ... Ex 8:26 3068
and sacrifice to the *L* our God ... Ex 8:27 3068
the *L* your God in the wilderness ... Ex 8:28 3068
I will intreat the *L* that the ... Ex 8:29 3068
people go to sacrifice to the *L* ... Ex 8:29 3068
from Pharaoh, and intreated the *L* ... Ex 8:30 3068
the *L* did according to the word ... Ex 8:31 3068
Then the *L* said unto Moses, Go in ... Ex 9:1 3068
Thus saith the *L* God of the ... Ex 9:1 3068
the hand of the *L* is upon thy ... Ex 9:3 3068
the *L* shall sever between the ... Ex 9:4 3068
the *L* appointed a set time, ... Ex 9:5 3068
To morrow the *L* shall do this ... Ex 9:5 3068
the *L* did that thing on the ... Ex 9:6 3068
the *L* said unto Moses and unto ... Ex 9:8 3068
the *L* hardened the heart of ... Ex 9:12 3068
as the *L* had spoken unto Moses ... Ex 9:12 3068
the *L* said unto Moses, Rise up ... Ex 9:13 3068
Thus saith the *L* God of the ... Ex 9:13 3068
L among the servants of Pharaoh ... Ex 9:20 3068
word of the *L* left his servants ... Ex 9:21 3068
the *L* said unto Moses, Stretch ... Ex 9:22 3068
the *L* sent thunder and hail, and ... Ex 9:23 3068
the *L* rained hail upon the land ... Ex 9:23 3068
the *L* is righteous, and I and my ... Ex 9:27 3068
Intreat the *L* (for it is enough) ... Ex 9:28 3068
spread abroad my hands unto the *L* ... Ex 9:29 3068
ye will not yet fear the *L* God ... Ex 9:30 3068
abroad his hands unto the *L* ... Ex 9:33 3068
as the *L* had spoken by Moses ... Ex 9:35 3068
the *L* said unto Moses, Go in unto ... Ex 10:1 3068
ye may know how that I am the *L* ... Ex 10:2 3068
Thus saith the *L* God of the ... Ex 10:3 3068
they may serve the *L* their God ... Ex 10:7 3068
them, Go, serve the *L* your God ... Ex 10:8 3068
we must hold a feast unto the *L* ... Ex 10:9 3068
Let the *L* be so with you, as I ... Ex 10:10 3068
ye that are men, and serve the *L* ... Ex 10:11 3068
the *L* said unto Moses, Stretch ... Ex 10:12 3068
the *L* brought an east wind upon ... Ex 10:13 3068
sinned against the *L* your God ... Ex 10:16 3068
once, and intreat the *L* your God ... Ex 10:17 3068
from Pharaoh, and intreated the *L* ... Ex 10:18 3068
the *L* turned a mighty strong west ... Ex 10:19 3068
But the *L* hardened Pharaoh's ... Ex 10:20 3068
the *L* said unto Moses, Stretch ... Ex 10:21 3068
and said, Go ye, serve the *L* ... Ex 10:24 3068
may sacrifice unto the *L* our God ... Ex 10:25 3068
we take to serve the *L* our God ... Ex 10:26 3068
not with what we must serve the *L* ... Ex 10:26 3068
But the *L* hardened Pharaoh's ... Ex 10:27 3068
the *L* said unto Moses, Yet will I ... Ex 11:1 3068
the *L* gave the people favour in ... Ex 11:3 3068
And Moses said, Thus saith the *L* ... Ex 11:4 3068
L doth put a difference between ... Ex 11:7 3068
the *L* said unto Moses, Pharaoh ... Ex 11:9 3068
the *L* hardened Pharaoh's heart, ... Ex 11:10 3068
the *L* spake unto Moses and Aaron ... Ex 12:1 3068
I am the *L* ... Ex 12:12 3068
the *L* throughout your generations ... Ex 12:14 3068
For the *L* will pass through to ... Ex 12:23 3068
the *L* will pass over the door, and ... Ex 12:23 3068
land which the *L* will give you ... Ex 12:25 3068
did as the *L* had commanded Moses ... Ex 12:28 3068
that at midnight the *L* smote all ... Ex 12:29 3068
and go, serve the *L*, as ye have ... Ex 12:31 3068
the *L* gave the people favour in ... Ex 12:36 3068
that all the hosts of the *L* went ... Ex 12:41 3068
to be much observed unto the *L* ... Ex 12:42 3068
the *L* to be observed of all the ... Ex 12:42 3068
the *L* said unto Moses and Aaron, ... Ex 12:43 3068
will keep the passover to the *L* ... Ex 12:48 3068
the *L* commanded Moses and Aaron ... Ex 12:50 3068
that the *L* did bring the children ... Ex 12:51 3068
the *L* spake unto Moses, saying, ... Ex 13:1 3068
for by strength of hand the *L* ... Ex 13:3 3068
it shall be when the *L* shall ... Ex 13:5 3068
day shall be a feast to the *L* ... Ex 13:6 3068
L did unto me when I came forth ... Ex 13:8 3068
the *L* brought thee out of Egypt ... Ex 13:9 3068
it shall be when the *L* shall ... Ex 13:11 3068
the *L* all that openeth the matrix ... Ex 13:12 3068
By strength of hand the *L* brought ... Ex 13:14 3068
that the *L* slew all the firstborn ... Ex 13:15 3068
the *L* all that openeth the matrix ... Ex 13:15 3068
for by strength of hand the *L* ... Ex 13:16 3068
the *L* went before them by day in ... Ex 13:21 3068
the *L* spake unto Moses, saying, ... Ex 14:1 3068
may know that I am the *L* ... Ex 14:4 3068
the *L* hardened the heart of ... Ex 14:8 3068
of Israel cried out unto the *L* ... Ex 14:10 3068
and see the salvation of the *L* ... Ex 14:13 3068
The *L* shall fight for you, and ye ... Ex 14:14 3068
the *L* said unto Moses, Wherefore ... Ex 14:15 3068
shall know that I am the *L* ... Ex 14:18 3068
the *L* caused the sea to go back ... Ex 14:21 3068
the *L* looked unto the host of the ... Ex 14:24 3068
for the *L* fighteth for them ... Ex 14:25 3068
the *L* said unto Moses, Stretch ... Ex 14:26 3068
the *L* overthrew the Egyptians in ... Ex 14:27 3068
Thus the *L* saved Israel that day ... Ex 14:30 3068
the *L* did upon the Egyptians ... Ex 14:31 3068
and the people feared the *L* ... Ex 14:31 3068
and believed the *L* ... Ex 14:31 3068
of Israel this song unto the *L* ... Ex 15:1 3068
saying, I will sing unto the *L* ... Ex 15:1 3068
The *L* is my strength and song, and ... Ex 15:2 3068
The *L* is a man of war ... Ex 15:3 3068
the *L* is his name ... Ex 15:3 3068
Thy right hand, O *L*, is become ... Ex 15:6 3068
thy right hand, O *L*, hath dashed ... Ex 15:6 3068
Who is like unto thee, O *L* ... Ex 15:11 3068
till thy people pass over, O *L* ... Ex 15:16 3068
inheritance, in the place, O *L* ... Ex 15:17 3068
dwell in, in the Sanctuary, O *L* ... Ex 15:17 3068
The *L* shall reign for ever and ... Ex 15:18 3068
the *L* brought again the waters of ... Ex 15:19 3068
answered them, Sing ye to the *L* ... Ex 15:21 3068
And he cried unto the *L* ... Ex 15:25 3068
the *L* shewed him a tree, which ... Ex 15:25 3068
to the voice of the *L* thy God ... Ex 15:26 3068
for I am the *L* that healeth thee ... Ex 15:26 3068
of the *L* in the land of Egypt ... Ex 16:3 3068
Then said the *L* unto Moses ... Ex 16:4 3068
then ye shall know that the *L* ... Ex 16:6 3068
ye shall see the glory of the *L* ... Ex 16:7 3068
your murmurings against the *L* ... Ex 16:7 3068
when the *L* shall give you in the ... Ex 16:8 3068
for that the *L* heareth your ... Ex 16:8 3068
not against us, but against the *L* ... Ex 16:8 3068
of Israel, Come near before the *L* ... Ex 16:9 3068
the glory of the *L* appeared in ... Ex 16:10 3068
the *L* spake unto Moses, saying, ... Ex 16:11 3068
know that I am the *L* your God ... Ex 16:12 3068
which the *L* hath given you to eat ... Ex 16:15 3068
thing which the *L* hath commanded ... Ex 16:16 3068
is that which the *L* hath said ... Ex 16:23 3068
of the holy sabbath unto the *L* ... Ex 16:23 3068
to day is a sabbath unto the *L* ... Ex 16:25 3068
the *L* said unto Moses, How long ... Ex 16:28 3068
for that the *L* hath given you the ... Ex 16:29 3068
the thing which the *L* commandeth ... Ex 16:32 3068
and lay it up before the *L* ... Ex 16:33 3068
As the *L* commanded Moses, so ... Ex 16:34 3068
to the commandment of the *L* ... Ex 17:1 3068
wherefore do ye tempt the *L* ... Ex 17:2 3068
And Moses cried unto the *L* ... Ex 17:4 3068
the *L* said unto Moses, Go on ... Ex 17:5 3068
and because they tempted the *L* ... Ex 17:7 3068
Is the *L* among us, or not ... Ex 17:7 3068
the *L* said unto Moses, Write this ... Ex 17:14 3068
the *L* hath sworn that the *L* ... Ex 17:16 3068
that the *L* had brought Israel out ... Ex 18:1 3068
that the *L* had done unto Pharaoh ... Ex 18:8 3068
way, and how the *L* delivered them ... Ex 18:8 3068
which the *L* had done to Israel ... Ex 18:9 3068
And Jethro said, Blessed be the *L* ... Ex 18:10 3068
Now I know that the *L* is greater ... Ex 18:11 3068
the *L* called unto him out of the ... Ex 19:3 3068
words which the *L* commanded him ... Ex 19:7 3068
All that the *L* hath spoken we ... Ex 19:8 3068
words of the people unto the *L* ... Ex 19:8 3068
the *L* said unto Moses, Lo, I come ... Ex 19:9 3068
words of the people unto the *L* ... Ex 19:9 3068
the *L* said unto Moses, Go unto ... Ex 19:10 3068
for the third day the *L* will come ... Ex 19:11 3068
because the *L* descended upon it ... Ex 19:18 3068
the *L* came down upon mount Sinai, ... Ex 19:20 3068
the *L* called Moses up to the top ... Ex 19:20 3068
the *L* said unto Moses, Go down, ... Ex 19:21 3068
break through unto the *L* to gaze ... Ex 19:21 3068
also, which come near to the *L* ... Ex 19:22 3068
lest the *L* break forth upon them ... Ex 19:22 3068
And Moses said unto the *L*, The ... Ex 19:23 3068
the *L* said unto him, Away, get ... Ex 19:24 3068
through to come up unto the *L* ... Ex 19:24 3068
I am the *L* thy God, which have ... Ex 20:2 3068
for I the *L* thy God am a jealous ... Ex 20:5 3068
the name of the *L* thy God in vain ... Ex 20:7 3068
for the *L* will not hold him ... Ex 20:7 3068
is the sabbath of the *L* thy God ... Ex 20:10 3068
For in six days the *L* made heaven ... Ex 20:11 3068
wherefore the *L* blessed the ... Ex 20:11 3068
which the *L* thy God giveth thee ... Ex 20:12 3068
the *L* said unto Moses, Thus thou ... Ex 20:22 3068
of the *L* be between them both ... Ex 22:11 3068
any god, save unto the *L* only ... Ex 22:20 3068
shall appear before the *L* GOD ... Ex 23:17 3068
into the house of the *L* thy God ... Ex 23:19 3068
And ye shall serve the *L* your God ... Ex 23:25 3068
unto Moses, Come up unto the *L* ... Ex 24:1 3068
Moses alone shall come near the *L* ... Ex 24:2 3068
the people all the words of the *L* ... Ex 24:3 3068
which the *L* hath said will we do ... Ex 24:3 3068
wrote all the words of the *L* ... Ex 24:4 3068
offerings of oxen unto the *L* ... Ex 24:5 3068
All that the *L* hath said will we ... Ex 24:7 3068
which the *L* hath made with you ... Ex 24:8 3068
the *L* said unto Moses, Come up to ... Ex 24:12 3068
the glory of the *L* abode upon ... Ex 24:16 3068
the sight of the glory of the *L* ... Ex 24:17 3068
the *L* spake unto Moses, saying, ... Ex 25:1 3068
evening to morning before the *L* ... Ex 27:21 3068
bear their names before the *L* ... Ex 28:12 3068
memorial before the *L* continually ... Ex 28:29 3068
when he goeth in before the *L* ... Ex 28:30 3068
heart before the *L* continually ... Ex 28:30 3068
unto the holy place before the *L* ... Ex 28:35 3068
of a signet, HOLINESS TO THE *L* ... Ex 28:36 3068
they may be accepted before the *L* ... Ex 28:38 3068
kill the bullock before the *L* ... Ex 29:11 3068
it is a burnt offering unto the *L* ... Ex 29:18 3068
offering made by fire unto the *L* ... Ex 29:18 3068
bread that is before the *L* ... Ex 29:23 3068
for a wave offering before the *L* ... Ex 29:24 3068
for a sweet savour before the *L* ... Ex 29:25 3068
offering made by fire unto the *L* ... Ex 29:25 3068
for a wave offering before the *L* ... Ex 29:26 3068
their heave offering unto the *L* ... Ex 29:28 3068
offering made by fire unto the *L* ... Ex 29:41 3068
of the congregation before the *L* ... Ex 29:42 3068
know that I am the *L* their God ... Ex 29:46 3068
I am the *L* their God ... Ex 29:46 3068
the *L* throughout your generations ... Ex 30:8 3068
it is most holy unto the *L* ... Ex 30:10 3068
the *L* spake unto Moses, saying, ... Ex 30:11 3068
a ransom for his soul unto the *L* ... Ex 30:12 3068
shall be the offering of the *L* ... Ex 30:13 3068
shall give an offering unto the *L* ... Ex 30:14 3068
they give an offering unto the *L* ... Ex 30:15 3068
children of Israel before the *L* ... Ex 30:16 3068
the *L* spake unto Moses, saying, ... Ex 30:17 3068
offering made by fire unto the *L* ... Ex 30:20 3068
Moreover the *L* spake unto Moses, ... Ex 30:22 3068
the *L* said unto Moses, Take unto ... Ex 30:34 3068
shall be unto thee holy for the *L* ... Ex 30:37 3068
the *L* spake unto Moses, saying, ... Ex 31:1 3068
the *L* spake unto Moses, saying, ... Ex 31:12 3068
I am the *L* that doth sanctify you ... Ex 31:13 3068
sabbath of rest, holy to the *L* ... Ex 31:15 3068
for in six days the *L* made heaven ... Ex 31:17 3068
To morrow is a feast to the *L* ... Ex 32:5 3068
the *L* said unto Moses, Go, get ... Ex 32:7 3068
the *L* said unto Moses, I have ... Ex 32:9 3068
the *L* his God, and said, *L* ... Ex 32:11 3068
the *L* repented of the evil which ... Ex 32:14 3068
Thus saith the *L* God of Israel ... Ex 32:27 3068
yourselves to day to the *L* ... Ex 32:29 3068
and now I will go up unto the *L* ... Ex 32:30 3068
And Moses returned unto the *L* ... Ex 32:31 3068
the *L* said unto Moses, Whosoever ... Ex 32:33 3068
the *L* plagued the people, because ... Ex 32:35 3068
the *L* said unto Moses, Depart, and ... Ex 33:1 3068
For the *L* had said unto Moses, ... Ex 33:5 3068
L went out unto the tabernacle of ... Ex 33:7 3068
and the *L* talked with Moses ... Ex 33:9
the *L* spake unto Moses face to ... Ex 33:11 3068
And Moses said unto the *L*, See, ... Ex 33:12 3068
the *L* said unto Moses, I will do ... Ex 33:17 3068
the name of the *L* before thee ... Ex 33:19 3068
the *L* said, Behold, there is a ... Ex 33:21 3068
the *L* said unto Moses, Hew thee ... Ex 34:1 3068
as the *L* had commanded him, and ... Ex 34:4 3068
the *L* descended in the cloud, and ... Ex 34:5 3068
and proclaimed the name of the *L* ... Ex 34:5 3068
the *L* passed by before him, and ... Ex 34:6 3068
proclaimed, The *L*, The *L* God ... Ex 34:6 3068
in thy sight, O *L*, let my *L* ... Ex 34:9 136
art shall see the work of the *L* ... Ex 34:10 3068
for the *L*, whose name is Jealous, ... Ex 34:14 3068
children appear before the *L* GOD ... Ex 34:23 3068
the *L* thy God thrice in the year ... Ex 34:24 3068
unto the house of the *L* thy God ... Ex 34:26 3068
the *L* said unto Moses, Write thou ... Ex 34:27 3068
was there with the *L* forty days ... Ex 34:28 3068
in commandment all that the *L* had ... Ex 34:32 3068
in before the *L* to speak with him ... Ex 34:34 3068
words which the *L* hath commanded ... Ex 35:1 3068
day, a sabbath of rest to the *L* ... Ex 35:2 3068
the thing which the *L* commanded ... Ex 35:4 3068
among you an offering unto the *L* ... Ex 35:5 3068
bring it, an offering of the *L* ... Ex 35:5 3068
all that the *L* hath commanded ... Ex 35:10 3068
an offering of gold unto the *L* ... Ex 35:22 3068
a willing offering unto the *L* ... Ex 35:29 3068
which the *L* had commanded to be ... Ex 35:29 3068
the *L* hath called by name ... Ex 35:30 3068
man, in whom the *L* put wisdom ... Ex 36:1 3068
to all that the *L* had commanded ... Ex 36:1 3068
whose heart the *L* had put wisdom ... Ex 36:2 3068
which the *L* commanded to make ... Ex 36:5 3068
all that the *L* commanded Moses ... Ex 38:22 3068
as the *L* commanded Moses ... Ex 39:1 3068
as the *L* commanded Moses ... Ex 39:5 3068
as the *L* commanded Moses ... Ex 39:7 3068
as the *L* commanded Moses ... Ex 39:21 3068
as the *L* commanded Moses ... Ex 39:26 3068
as the *L* commanded Moses ... Ex 39:29 3068
of a signet, HOLINESS TO THE *L* ... Ex 39:30 3068
as the *L* commanded Moses ... Ex 39:31 3068
to all that the *L* commanded Moses ... Ex 39:32 3068
to all that the *L* commanded Moses ... Ex 39:42 3068
done it as the *L* had commanded ... Ex 39:43 3068
the *L* spake unto Moses, saying, ... Ex 40:1 3068
to all that the *L* commanded him ... Ex 40:16 3068
as the *L* commanded Moses ... Ex 40:19 3068
as the *L* commanded Moses ... Ex 40:21 3068
in order upon it before the *L* ... Ex 40:23 3068
as the *L* had commanded Moses ... Ex 40:23 3068
he lighted the lamps before the *L* ... Ex 40:25 3068
as the *L* commanded Moses ... Ex 40:25 3068
as the *L* commanded Moses ... Ex 40:27 3068
as the *L* commanded Moses ... Ex 40:29 3068
as the *L* commanded Moses ... Ex 40:32 3068
the glory of the *L* filled the ... Ex 40:34 3068
the glory of the *L* filled the ... Ex 40:35 3068
For the cloud of the *L* was upon ... Ex 40:38 3068
the *L* called unto Moses, and spake ... Lev 1:1 3068
you bring an offering unto the *L* ... Lev 1:2 3068
of the congregation before the *L* ... Lev 1:3 3068

kill the bullock before the *L*	Lev 1:5	3068
of a sweet savour unto the *L*	Lev 1:9	3068
the altar northward before the *L*	Lev 1:11	3068
of a sweet savour unto the *L*	Lev 1:13	3068
his offering to the *L* be of fowls	Lev 1:14	3068
of a sweet savour unto the *L*	Lev 1:17	3068
offer a meat offering unto the *L*	Lev 2:1	3068
of a sweet savour unto the *L*	Lev 2:2	3068
offerings of the *L* made by fire	Lev 2:3	3068
made of these things unto the *L*	Lev 2:8	3068
of a sweet savour unto the *L*	Lev 2:9	3068
offerings of the *L* made by fire	Lev 2:10	3068
which ye shall bring unto the *L*	Lev 2:11	3068
offering of the *L* made by fire	Lev 2:11	3068
ye shall offer them unto the *L*	Lev 2:12	3068
of thy firstfruits unto the *L*	Lev 2:14	3068
offering made by fire unto the *L*	Lev 2:16	3068
it without blemish before the *L*	Lev 3:1	3068
offering made by fire unto the *L*	Lev 3:3	3068
of a sweet savour unto the *L*	Lev 3:5	3068
unto the *L* be of the flock	Lev 3:6	3068
shall he offer it before the *L*	Lev 3:7	3068
offering made by fire unto the *L*	Lev 3:9	3068
offering made by fire unto the *L*	Lev 3:11	3068
he shall offer it before the *L*	Lev 3:12	3068
offering made by fire unto the *L*	Lev 3:14	3068
the *L* spake unto Moses, saying,	Lev 4:1	3068
L concerning things which ought	Lev 4:2	3068
unto the *L* for a sin offering	Lev 4:3	3068
of the congregation before the *L*	Lev 4:4	3068
and kill the bullock before the *L*	Lev 4:4	3068
blood seven times before the *L*	Lev 4:6	3068
of sweet incense before the *L*	Lev 4:7	3068
L concerning things which should	Lev 4:13	3068
head of the bullock before the *L*	Lev 4:15	3068
shall be killed before the *L*	Lev 4:15	3068
it seven times before the *L*	Lev 4:17	3068
the altar which is before the *L*	Lev 4:18	3068
any of the commandments of the *L*	Lev 4:22	3068
the burnt offering before the *L*	Lev 4:24	3068
L concerning things which ought	Lev 4:27	3068
for a sweet savour unto the *L*	Lev 4:31	3068
offerings made by fire unto the *L*	Lev 4:35	3068
the *L* for his sin which he hath	Lev 5:6	3068
or two young pigeons, unto the *L*	Lev 5:7	3068
offerings made by fire unto the *L*	Lev 5:12	3068
the *L* spake unto Moses, saying,	Lev 5:14	3068
in the holy things of the *L*	Lev 5:15	3068
L a ram without blemish out of	Lev 5:15	3068
done by the commandments of the *L*	Lev 5:17	3068
trespassed against the *L*	Lev 5:19	3068
the *L* spake unto Moses, saying,	Lev 6:1	3068
commit a trespass against the *L*	Lev 6:2	3068
his trespass offering unto the *L*	Lev 6:6	3068
an atonement for him before the *L*	Lev 6:7	3068
the *L* spake unto Moses, saying,	Lev 6:8	3068
Aaron shall offer it before the *L*	Lev 6:14	3068
the memorial of it, unto the *L*	Lev 6:15	3068
offerings of the *L* made by fire	Lev 6:18	3068
the *L* spake unto Moses, saying,	Lev 6:19	3068
L in the day when he is anointed	Lev 6:20	3068
for a sweet savour unto the *L*	Lev 6:21	3068
is a statute for ever unto the *L*	Lev 6:22	3068
the *L* spake unto Moses, saying,	Lev 6:24	3068
offering be killed before the *L*	Lev 6:25	3068
offering made by fire unto the *L*	Lev 7:5	3068
which he shall offer unto the *L*	Lev 7:11	3068
for an heave offering unto the *L*	Lev 7:14	3068
that pertain unto the *L*, having	Lev 7:20	3068
which pertain unto the *L*	Lev 7:21	3068
the *L* spake unto Moses, saying,	Lev 7:22	3068
offering made by fire unto the *L*	Lev 7:25	3068
the *L* spake unto Moses, saying,	Lev 7:28	3068
L shall bring his oblation unto	Lev 7:29	3068
bring his oblation unto the *L* of	Lev 7:29	3068
offerings of the *L* made by fire	Lev 7:30	3068
for a wave offering before the *L*	Lev 7:30	3068
offerings of the *L* made by fire	Lev 7:35	3068
unto the *L* in the priest's office	Lev 7:35	3068
Which the *L* commanded to be given	Lev 7:36	3068
Which the *L* commanded Moses in	Lev 7:38	3068
offer their oblations unto the *L*	Lev 7:38	3068
the *L* spake unto Moses, saying,	Lev 8:1	3068
Moses did as the *L* commanded him	Lev 8:4	3068
which the *L* commanded to be done	Lev 8:5	3068
as the *L* commanded Moses	Lev 8:9	3068
as the *L* commanded Moses	Lev 8:13	3068
as the *L* commanded Moses	Lev 8:17	3068
offering made by fire unto the *L*	Lev 8:21	3068
as the *L* commanded Moses	Lev 8:21	3068
bread, that was before the *L*	Lev 8:26	3068
for a wave offering before the *L*	Lev 8:27	3068
offering made by fire unto the *L*	Lev 8:28	3068
for a wave offering before the *L*	Lev 8:29	3068
as the *L* commanded Moses	Lev 8:29	3068
so the *L* hath commanded to do, to	Lev 8:34	3068
days, and keep the charge of the *L*	Lev 8:35	3068
sons did all things which the *L*	Lev 8:36	3068
and offer them before the *L*	Lev 9:2	3068
to sacrifice before the *L*	Lev 9:4	3068
for to day the *L* will appear unto	Lev 9:4	3068
drew near and stood before the *L*	Lev 9:5	3068
the *L* commanded that ye should do	Lev 9:6	3068
the glory of the *L* shall appear	Lev 9:6	3068
as the *L* commanded	Lev 9:7	3068
as the *L* commanded Moses	Lev 9:10	3068
for a wave offering before the *L*	Lev 9:21	3068
the glory of the *L* appeared unto	Lev 9:23	3068
came a fire out from before the *L*	Lev 9:24	3068
offered strange fire before the *L*	Lev 10:1	3068
And there went out fire from the *L*	Lev 10:2	3068
them, and they died before the *L*	Lev 10:2	3068
This is it that the *L* spake	Lev 10:3	3068
burning which the *L* hath kindled	Lev 10:6	3068
oil of the *L* is upon you	Lev 10:7	3068
the *L* spake unto Aaron, saying,	Lev 10:8	3068
all the statutes which the *L* hath	Lev 10:11	3068
offerings of the *L* made by fire	Lev 10:12	3068
sacrifices of the *L* made by fire	Lev 10:13	3068
for a wave offering before the *L*	Lev 10:15	3068
as the *L* hath commanded	Lev 10:15	3068
atonement for them before the *L*	Lev 10:17	3068
their burnt offering before the *L*	Lev 10:19	3068
accepted in the sight of the *L*	Lev 10:19	3068
the *L* spake unto Moses and to	Lev 11:1	3068
For I am the *L* your God	Lev 11:44	3068
For I am the *L* that bringeth you	Lev 11:45	3068
the *L* spake unto Moses, saying,	Lev 12:1	3068
Who shall offer it before the *L*	Lev 12:7	3068
the *L* spake unto Moses and Aaron,	Lev 13:1	3068
the *L* spake unto Moses, saying,	Lev 14:1	3068
and those things, before the *L*	Lev 14:11	3068
for a wave offering before the *L*	Lev 14:12	3068
finger seven times before the *L*	Lev 14:16	3068
an atonement for him before the *L*	Lev 14:18	3068
of the congregation, before the *L*	Lev 14:23	3068
for a wave offering before the *L*	Lev 14:24	3068
hand seven times before the *L*	Lev 14:27	3068
an atonement for him before the *L*	Lev 14:29	3068
is to be cleansed before the *L*	Lev 14:31	3068
the *L* spake unto Moses and unto	Lev 14:33	3068
the *L* spake unto Moses and to	Lev 15:1	3068
come before the *L* unto the door	Lev 15:14	3068
him before the *L* for his issue	Lev 15:15	3068
before the *L* for the issue of her	Lev 15:30	3068
the *L* spake unto Moses after the	Lev 16:1	3068
when they offered before the *L*	Lev 16:1	3068
the *L* said unto Moses, Speak unto	Lev 16:2	3068
present them before the *L* at the	Lev 16:7	3068
one lot for the *L*, and the other	Lev 16:8	3068
be presented alive before the *L*	Lev 16:10	3068
from off the altar before the *L*	Lev 16:12	3068
upon the fire before the *L*	Lev 16:13	3068
the altar that is before the *L*	Lev 16:18	3068
from all your sins before the *L*	Lev 16:30	3068
he did as the *L* commanded Moses	Lev 16:34	3068
the *L* spake unto Moses, saying,	Lev 17:1	3068
thing which the *L* hath commanded	Lev 17:2	3068
L before the tabernacle of the	Lev 17:4	3068
before the tabernacle of the *L*	Lev 17:4	3068
they may bring them unto the *L*	Lev 17:5	3068
for peace offerings unto the *L*	Lev 17:5	3068
L at the door of the tabernacle	Lev 17:6	3068
fat for a sweet savour unto the *L*	Lev 17:6	3068
to offer it unto the *L*	Lev 17:9	3068
the *L* spake unto Moses, saying,	Lev 18:1	3068
unto them, I am the *L* your God	Lev 18:2	3068
I am the *L* your God	Lev 18:4	3068
I am the *L*	Lev 18:5	3068
I am the *L*	Lev 18:6	3068
I am the *L*	Lev 18:21	3068
I am the *L* your God	Lev 18:30	3068
the *L* spake unto Moses, saying,	Lev 19:1	3068
for I the *L* your God am holy	Lev 19:2	3068
I am the *L* your God	Lev 19:3	3068
I am the *L* your God	Lev 19:4	3068
of peace offerings unto the *L*	Lev 19:5	3068
the hallowed thing of the *L*	Lev 19:8	3068
I am the *L* your God	Lev 19:10	3068
I am the *L*	Lev 19:12	3068
I am the *L*	Lev 19:14	3068
I am the *L*	Lev 19:16	3068
I am the *L*	Lev 19:18	3068
his trespass offering unto the *L*	Lev 19:21	3068
trespass offering before the *L*	Lev 19:22	3068
be holy to praise the *L* withal	Lev 19:24	3068
I am the *L* your God	Lev 19:25	3068
I am the *L*	Lev 19:28	3068
I am the *L*	Lev 19:30	3068
I am the *L* your God	Lev 19:31	3068
I am the *L*	Lev 19:32	3068
I am the *L* your God	Lev 19:34	3068
I am the *L* your God, which	Lev 19:36	3068
I am the *L*	Lev 19:37	3068
the *L* spake unto Moses, saying,	Lev 20:1	3068
for I am the *L* your God	Lev 20:7	3068
I am the *L* which sanctify you	Lev 20:8	3068
I am the *L* your God, which have	Lev 20:24	3068
for I the *L* am holy, and have	Lev 20:26	3068
the *L* said unto Moses, Speak unto	Lev 21:1	3068
offerings of the *L* made by fire	Lev 21:6	3068
for I the *L*, which sanctify you,	Lev 21:8	3068
I am the *L*	Lev 21:12	3068
for I the *L* do sanctify him	Lev 21:15	3068
the *L* spake unto Moses, saying,	Lev 21:16	3068
offerings of the *L* made by fire	Lev 21:21	3068
for I the *L* do sanctify them	Lev 21:23	3068
the *L* spake unto Moses, saying,	Lev 22:1	3068
I am the *L*	Lev 22:2	3068
of Israel hallow unto the *L*	Lev 22:3	3068
I am the *L*	Lev 22:3	3068
I am the *L*	Lev 22:8	3068
I the *L* do sanctify them	Lev 22:9	3068
which they offer unto the *L*	Lev 22:15	3068
for I the *L* do sanctify them	Lev 22:16	3068
the *L* spake unto Moses, saying,	Lev 22:17	3068
unto the *L* for a burnt offering	Lev 22:18	3068
unto the *L* to accomplish his vow	Lev 22:21	3068
shall not offer these unto the *L*	Lev 22:22	3068
of them upon the altar unto the *L*	Lev 22:22	3068
unto the *L* that which is bruised	Lev 22:24	3068
the *L* spake unto Moses, saying,	Lev 22:26	3068
offering made by fire unto the *L*	Lev 22:27	3068
of thanksgiving unto the *L*	Lev 22:29	3068
I am the *L*	Lev 22:30	3068
I am the *L*	Lev 22:31	3068
I am the *L* which hallow you,	Lev 22:32	3068
I am the *L*	Lev 22:33	3068
the *L* spake unto Moses, saying,	Lev 23:1	3068
Concerning the feasts of the *L*	Lev 23:2	3068
of the *L* in all your dwellings	Lev 23:3	3068
These are the feasts of the *L*	Lev 23:4	3068
of unleavened bread unto the *L*	Lev 23:6	3068
by fire unto the *L* seven days	Lev 23:8	3068
the *L* spake unto Moses, saying,	Lev 23:9	3068
shall wave the sheaf before the *L*	Lev 23:11	3068
for a burnt offering unto the *L*	Lev 23:12	3068
unto the *L* for a sweet savour	Lev 23:13	3068
a new meat offering unto the *L*	Lev 23:16	3068
are the firstfruits unto the *L*	Lev 23:17	3068
for a burnt offering unto the *L*	Lev 23:18	3068
fire, of sweet savour unto the *L*	Lev 23:18	3068
for a wave offering before the *L*	Lev 23:20	3068
be holy to the *L* for the priest	Lev 23:20	3068
I am the *L* your God	Lev 23:22	3068
the *L* spake unto Moses, saying,	Lev 23:23	3068
offering made by fire unto the *L*	Lev 23:25	3068
the *L* spake unto Moses, saying,	Lev 23:26	3068
offering made by fire unto the *L*	Lev 23:27	3068
for you before the *L* your God	Lev 23:28	3068
the *L* spake unto Moses, saying,	Lev 23:33	3068
for seven days unto the *L*	Lev 23:34	3068
offering made by fire unto the *L*	Lev 23:36	3068
offering made by fire unto the *L*	Lev 23:36	3068
These are the feasts of the *L*	Lev 23:37	3068
offering made by fire unto the *L*	Lev 23:37	3068
Beside the sabbaths of the *L*	Lev 23:38	3068
which ye give unto the *L*	Lev 23:38	3068
a feast unto the *L* seven days	Lev 23:39	3068
before the *L* your God seven days	Lev 23:40	3068
unto the *L* seven days in the year	Lev 23:41	3068
I am the *L* your God	Lev 23:43	3068
of Israel the feasts of the *L*	Lev 23:44	3068
the *L* spake unto Moses, saying,	Lev 24:1	3068
morning before the *L* continually	Lev 24:3	3068
before the *L* continually	Lev 24:4	3068
upon the pure table before the *L*	Lev 24:6	3068
offering made by fire unto the *L*	Lev 24:7	3068
in order before the *L* continually	Lev 24:8	3068
the *L* made by fire by a perpetual	Lev 24:9	3068
son blasphemed the name of the *L*	Lev 24:11	3068
of the *L* might be shewed them	Lev 24:12	3068
the *L* spake unto Moses, saying,	Lev 24:13	3068
blasphemeth the name of the *L*	Lev 24:16	3068
he blasphemeth the name of the *L*	Lev 24:16	3068
for I am the *L* your God	Lev 24:22	3068
did as the *L* commanded Moses	Lev 24:23	3068
the *L* spake unto Moses in mount	Lev 25:1	3068
land keep a sabbath unto the *L*	Lev 25:2	3068
the land, a sabbath for the *L*	Lev 25:4	3068
for I am the *L* your God	Lev 25:17	3068
I am the *L* your God, which	Lev 25:38	3068
I am the *L* your God	Lev 25:55	3068
for I am the *L* your God	Lev 26:1	3068
I am the *L*	Lev 26:2	3068
I am the *L* your God, which	Lev 26:13	3068
for I am the *L* their God	Lev 26:44	3068
I am the *L*	Lev 26:45	3068
which the *L* made between him and	Lev 26:46	3068
the *L* spake unto Moses, saying,	Lev 27:1	3068
be for the *L* by thy estimation	Lev 27:2	3068
men bring an offering unto the *L*	Lev 27:9	3068
of such unto the *L* shall be holy	Lev 27:9	3068
not offer a sacrifice unto the *L*	Lev 27:11	3068
his house to be holy unto the *L*	Lev 27:14	3068
the *L* some part of a field of his	Lev 27:16	3068
jubile, shall be holy unto the *L*	Lev 27:21	3068
if a man sanctify unto the *L* a	Lev 27:22	3068
day, as a holy thing unto the *L*	Lev 27:23	3068
unto the *L* of all that he hath	Lev 27:28	3068
thing is most holy unto the *L*	Lev 27:28	3068
it is holy unto the *L*	Lev 27:30	3068
tenth shall be holy unto the *L*	Lev 27:32	3068
which the *L* commanded Moses for	Lev 27:34	3068
the *L* spake unto Moses in the	Num 1:1	3068
As the *L* commanded Moses, so he	Num 1:19	3068
For the *L* had spoken unto Moses,	Num 1:48	3068
to all that the *L* commanded Moses	Num 1:54	3068
the *L* spake unto Moses and unto	Num 2:1	3068
as the *L* commanded Moses	Num 2:33	3068
to all that the *L* commanded Moses	Num 2:34	3068
Moses in the day that the *L* spake	Num 3:1	3068
Nadab and Abihu died before the *L*	Num 3:4	3068
offered strange fire before the *L*	Num 3:4	3068
the *L* spake unto Moses, saying,	Num 3:5	3068
the *L* spake unto Moses, saying,	Num 3:11	3068
I am the *L*	Num 3:13	3068
the *L* spake unto Moses in the	Num 3:14	3068
according to the word of the *L*	Num 3:16	3068
at the commandment of the *L*	Num 3:39	3068
the *L* said unto Moses, Number all	Num 3:40	3068
the Levites for me (I am the *L*)	Num 3:41	3068
as the *L* commanded him, all the	Num 3:42	3068
the *L* spake unto Moses, saying,	Num 3:44	3068

Context	Reference	Strong's
I am the *L*	Num 3:45	3068
according to the word of the *L*	Num 3:51	3068
as the *L* commanded Moses	Num 3:51	3068
the *L* spake unto Moses and unto	Num 4:1	3068
the *L* spake unto Moses and unto	Num 4:17	3068
the *L* spake unto Moses, saying,	Num 4:21	3068
of the *L* by the hand of Moses	Num 4:37	3068
to the commandment of the *L*	Num 4:41	3068
of the *L* by the hand of Moses	Num 4:45	3068
to the commandment of the *L* they	Num 4:49	3068
of him, as the *L* commanded Moses	Num 4:49	3068
the *L* spake unto Moses, saying,	Num 5:1	3068
as the *L* spake unto Moses, so did	Num 5:4	3068
the *L* spake unto Moses, saying,	Num 5:5	3068
to do a trespass against the *L*	Num 5:6	3068
be recompensed unto the *L*	Num 5:8	3068
the *L* spake unto Moses, saying,	Num 5:11	3068
her near, and set her before the *L*	Num 5:16	3068
shall set the woman before the *L*	Num 5:18	3068
The *L* make thee a curse and an	Num 5:21	3068
when the *L* doth make thy thigh to	Num 5:21	3068
wave the offering before the *L*	Num 5:25	3068
shall set the woman before the *L*	Num 5:30	3068
the *L* spake unto Moses, saying,	Num 6:1	3068
to separate themselves unto the *L*	Num 6:2	3068
he separateth himself unto the *L*	Num 6:5	3068
L he shall come at no dead body	Num 6:6	3068
separation he is holy unto the *L*	Num 6:8	3068
the *L* the days of his separation	Num 6:12	3068
offer his offering unto the *L*	Num 6:14	3068
shall bring them before the *L*	Num 6:16	3068
of peace offerings unto the *L*	Num 6:17	3068
for a wave offering before the *L*	Num 6:20	3068
unto the *L* for his separation	Num 6:21	3068
the *L* spake unto Moses, saying,	Num 6:22	3068
The *L* bless thee, and keep thee	Num 6:24	3068
The *L* make his face shine upon	Num 6:25	3068
The *L* lift up his countenance	Num 6:26	3068
their offering before the *L*	Num 7:3	3068
the *L* spake unto Moses, saying,	Num 7:4	3068
the *L* said unto Moses, They shall	Num 7:11	3068
the *L* spake unto Moses, saying,	Num 8:1	3068
as the *L* commanded Moses	Num 8:3	3068
which the *L* had shewed Moses	Num 8:4	3068
the *L* spake unto Moses, saying,	Num 8:5	3068
bring the Levites before the *L*	Num 8:10	3068
offer the Levites before the *L*	Num 8:11	3068
may execute the service of the *L*	Num 8:11	3068
for a burnt offering, unto the *L*	Num 8:12	3068
them for an offering unto the *L*	Num 8:13	3068
according unto all that the *L*	Num 8:20	3068
them as an offering before the *L*	Num 8:21	3068
as the *L* had commanded Moses	Num 8:22	3068
the *L* spake unto Moses, saying,	Num 8:23	3068
the *L* spake unto Moses in the	Num 9:1	3068
to all that the *L* commanded Moses	Num 9:5	3068
not offer an offering of the *L* in	Num 9:7	3068
I will hear what the *L* will	Num 9:8	3068
the *L* spake unto Moses, saying,	Num 9:9	3068
keep the passover unto the *L*	Num 9:10	3068
of the *L* in his appointed season	Num 9:13	3068
will keep the passover unto the *L*	Num 9:14	3068
of the *L* the children of Israel	Num 9:18	3068
commandment of the *L* they pitched	Num 9:18	3068
Israel kept the charge of the *L*	Num 9:19	3068
the *L* they abode in their tents	Num 9:20	3068
of the *L* they journeyed	Num 9:20	3068
of the *L* they rested in the tents	Num 9:23	3068
of the *L* they journeyed	Num 9:23	3068
they kept the charge of the *L*	Num 9:23	3068
of the *L* by the hand of Moses	Num 9:23	3068
the *L* spake unto Moses, saying,	Num 10:1	3068
remembered before the *L* your God	Num 10:9	3068
I am the *L* your God	Num 10:10	3068
of the *L* by the hand of Moses	Num 10:13	3068
the place of which the *L* said	Num 10:29	3068
for the *L* hath spoken good	Num 10:29	3068
goodness the *L* shall do unto us	Num 10:32	3068
of the *L* three days' journey	Num 10:33	3068
L went before them in the three	Num 10:33	3068
the cloud of the *L* was upon them	Num 10:34	3068
that Moses said, Rise up, *L*	Num 10:35	3068
it rested, he said, Return, O *L*	Num 10:36	3068
complained, it displeased the *L*	Num 11:1	3068
and the *L* heard it	Num 11:1	3068
the fire of the *L* burnt among	Num 11:1	3068
and when Moses prayed unto the *L*	Num 11:2	3068
fire of the *L* burnt among them	Num 11:3	3068
the anger of the *L* was kindled	Num 11:10	3068
And Moses said unto the *L*,	Num 11:11	3068
the *L* said unto Moses, Gather	Num 11:16	3068
ye have wept in the ears of the *L*	Num 11:18	3068
therefore the *L* will give you	Num 11:18	3068
despised the *L* which is among you	Num 11:20	3068
the *L* said unto Moses, Is the	Num 11:23	3068
the people the words of the *L*	Num 11:24	3068
the *L* came down in a cloud, and	Num 11:25	3068
that the *L* would put his spirit	Num 11:29	3068
went forth a wind from the *L*	Num 11:31	3068
the wrath of the *L* was kindled	Num 11:33	3068
the *L* smote the people with a	Num 11:33	3068
Hath the *L* indeed spoken only by	Num 12:2	3068
And the *L* heard it	Num 12:2	3068
the *L* spake suddenly unto Moses,	Num 12:4	3068
the *L* came down in the pillar of	Num 12:5	3068
I the *L* will make myself known	Num 12:6	3068
of the *L* shall he behold	Num 12:8	3068
the anger of the *L* was kindled	Num 12:9	3068
And Moses cried unto the *L*	Num 12:13	3068
the *L* said unto Moses, If her	Num 12:14	3068
the *L* spake unto Moses, saying,	Num 13:1	3068
L sent them from the wilderness	Num 13:3	3068
wherefore hath the *L* brought us	Num 14:3	3068
If the *L* delight in us, then he	Num 14:8	3068
Only rebel not ye against the *L*	Num 14:9	3068
from them, and the *L* is with us	Num 14:9	3068
the glory of the *L* appeared in	Num 14:10	3068
the *L* said unto Moses, How long	Num 14:11	3068
And Moses said unto the *L*, Then	Num 14:13	3068
that thou *L* art among this people	Num 14:14	3068
that thou *L* art seen face to face	Num 14:14	3068
Because the *L* was not able to	Num 14:16	3068
let the power of my *L* be great	Num 14:17	136
The *L* is longsuffering, and of	Num 14:18	3068
the *L* said, I have pardoned	Num 14:20	3068
be filled with the glory of the *L*	Num 14:21	3068
the *L* spake unto Moses and unto	Num 14:26	3068
As truly as I live, saith the *L*	Num 14:28	3068
I the *L* have said, I will surely	Num 14:35	3068
died by the plague before the *L*	Num 14:37	3068
place which the *L* hath promised	Num 14:40	3068
the commandment of the *L*	Num 14:41	3068
for the *L* is not among you	Num 14:42	3068
ye are turned away from the *L*	Num 14:43	3068
therefore the *L* will not be with	Num 14:43	3068
the ark of the covenant of the *L*	Num 14:44	3068
the *L* spake unto Moses, saying,	Num 15:1	3068
an offering by fire unto the *L*	Num 15:3	3068
to make a sweet savour unto the *L*	Num 15:3	3068
the *L* bring a meat offering of a	Num 15:4	3068
for a sweet savour unto the *L*	Num 15:7	3068
or peace offerings unto the *L*	Num 15:8	3068
of a sweet savour unto the *L*	Num 15:10	3068
of a sweet savour unto the *L*	Num 15:13	3068
of a sweet savour unto the *L*	Num 15:14	3068
the stranger be before the *L*	Num 15:15	3068
the *L* spake unto Moses, saying,	Num 15:17	3068
up an heave offering unto the *L*	Num 15:19	3068
the *L* an heave offering in your	Num 15:21	3068
which the *L* hath spoken unto	Num 15:22	3068
Even all that the *L* hath	Num 15:23	3068
day that the *L* commanded Moses	Num 15:23	3068
for a sweet savour unto the *L*	Num 15:24	3068
sacrifice made by fire unto the *L*	Num 15:25	3068
their sin offering before the *L*	Num 15:25	3068
sinneth by ignorance before the *L*	Num 15:28	3068
the same reproacheth the *L*	Num 15:30	3068
hath despised the word of the *L*	Num 15:31	3068
the *L* said unto Moses, The man	Num 15:35	3068
as the *L* commanded Moses	Num 15:36	3068
the *L* spake unto Moses, saying,	Num 15:37	3068
all the commandments of the *L*	Num 15:39	3068
I am the *L* your God, which	Num 15:41	3068
I am the *L* your God	Num 15:41	3068
of them, and the *L* is among them	Num 16:3	3068
above the congregation of the *L*	Num 16:3	3068
Even to morrow the *L* will shew	Num 16:5	3068
in them before the *L* to morrow	Num 16:7	3068
the man whom the *L* doth choose	Num 16:7	3068
of the tabernacle of the *L*	Num 16:9	3068
gathered together against the *L*	Num 16:11	3068
very wroth, and said unto the *L*	Num 16:15	3068
and all thy company before the *L*	Num 16:16	3068
bring ye before the *L* every man	Num 16:17	3068
the glory of the *L* appeared unto	Num 16:19	3068
the *L* spake unto Moses and unto	Num 16:20	3068
the *L* spake unto Moses, saying,	Num 16:23	3068
L hath sent me to do all these	Num 16:28	3068
then the *L* hath not sent me	Num 16:29	3068
But if the *L* make a new thing, and	Num 16:30	3068
these men have provoked the *L*	Num 16:30	3068
there came out a fire from the *L*	Num 16:35	3068
the *L* spake unto Moses, saying,	Num 16:36	3068
they offered them before the *L*	Num 16:38	3068
to offer incense before the *L*	Num 16:40	3068
as the *L* said to him by the hand	Num 16:40	3068
have killed the people of the *L*	Num 16:41	3068
and the glory of the *L* appeared	Num 16:42	3068
the *L* spake unto Moses, saying,	Num 16:44	3068
is wrath gone out from the *L*	Num 16:46	3068
the *L* spake unto Moses, saying,	Num 17:1	3068
laid up the rods before the *L* in	Num 17:7	3068
all the rods from before the *L*	Num 17:9	3068
the *L* said unto Moses, Bring	Num 17:10	3068
as the *L* commanded him, so did he	Num 17:11	3068
the tabernacle of the *L* shall die	Num 17:13	3068
the *L* said unto Aaron, Thou and	Num 18:1	3068
are given as a gift for the *L*	Num 18:6	3068
the *L* spake unto Aaron, Behold, I	Num 18:8	3068
which they shall offer unto the *L*	Num 18:12	3068
which they shall bring unto the *L*	Num 18:13	3068
which they bring unto the *L*	Num 18:15	3068
for a sweet savour unto the *L*	Num 18:17	3068
of Israel offer unto the *L*	Num 18:19	3068
for ever before the *L* unto thee	Num 18:19	3068
the *L* spake unto Aaron, Thou	Num 18:20	3068
as an heave offering unto the *L*	Num 18:24	3068
the *L* spake unto Moses, saying,	Num 18:25	3068
an heave offering of it for the *L*	Num 18:26	3068
unto the *L* of all your tithes	Num 18:28	3068
every heave offering of the *L*	Num 18:29	3068
the *L* spake unto Moses and unto	Num 19:1	3068
law which the *L* hath commanded	Num 19:2	3068
defileth the tabernacle of the *L*	Num 19:13	3068
defiled the sanctuary of the *L*	Num 19:20	3068
our brethren died before the *L*	Num 20:3	3068
of the *L* into this wilderness	Num 20:4	3068
the glory of the *L* appeared unto	Num 20:6	3068
the *L* spake unto Moses, saying,	Num 20:7	3068
took the rod from before the *L*	Num 20:9	3068
the *L* spake unto Moses and Aaron,	Num 20:12	3068
of Israel strove with the *L*	Num 20:13	3068
And when we cried unto the *L*	Num 20:16	3068
the *L* spake unto Moses and Aaron	Num 20:23	3068
And Moses did as the *L* commanded	Num 20:27	3068
And Israel vowed a vow unto the *L*	Num 21:2	3068
the *L* hearkened to the voice of	Num 21:3	3068
the *L* sent fiery serpents among	Num 21:6	3068
for we have spoken against the *L*	Num 21:7	3068
pray unto the *L*, that he take	Num 21:7	3068
the *L* said unto Moses, Make thee	Num 21:8	3068
in the book of the wars of the *L*	Num 21:14	3068
whereof the *L* spake unto Moses	Num 21:16	3068
the *L* said unto Moses, Fear him	Num 21:34	3068
as the *L* shall speak unto me	Num 22:8	3068
for the *L* refuseth to give me	Num 22:13	3068
beyond the word of the *L* my God	Num 22:18	3068
what the *L* will say unto me more	Num 22:19	3068
the angel of the *L* stood in the	Num 22:22	3068
of the *L* standing in the way	Num 22:23	3068
But the angel of the *L* stood in a	Num 22:24	3068
the ass saw the angel of the *L*	Num 22:25	3068
the angel of the *L* went further	Num 22:26	3068
the ass saw the angel of the *L*	Num 22:27	3068
the *L* opened the mouth of the ass	Num 22:28	3068
Then the *L* opened the eyes of	Num 22:31	3068
of the *L* standing in the way	Num 22:31	3068
the angel of the *L* said unto him	Num 22:32	3068
said unto the angel of the *L*	Num 22:34	3068
angel of the *L* said unto Balaam	Num 22:35	3068
peradventure the *L* will come to	Num 23:3	3068
the *L* put a word in Balaam's	Num 23:5	3068
whom the *L* hath not defied	Num 23:8	3068
which the *L* hath put in my mouth	Num 23:12	3068
while I meet the *L* yonder	Num 23:15	
the *L* met Balaam, and put a word	Num 23:16	3068
unto him, What hath the *L* spoken	Num 23:17	3068
the *L* his God is with him, and the	Num 23:21	3068
saying, All that the *L* speaketh	Num 23:26	3068
it pleased the *L* to bless Israel	Num 24:1	3068
aloes which the *L* hath planted	Num 24:6	3068
the *L* hath kept thee back from	Num 24:11	3068
beyond the commandment of the *L*	Num 24:13	3068
but what the *L* saith, that will I	Num 24:13	3068
the anger of the *L* was kindled	Num 25:3	3068
the *L* said unto Moses, Take all	Num 25:4	3068
up before the *L* against the sun	Num 25:4	3068
that the fierce anger of the *L*	Num 25:4	3068
the *L* spake unto Moses, saying,	Num 25:10	3068
the *L* spake unto Moses, saying,	Num 25:16	3068
that the *L* spake unto Moses and	Num 26:1	3068
as the *L* commanded Moses and the	Num 26:4	3068
when they strove against the *L*	Num 26:9	3068
the *L* spake unto Moses, saying,	Num 26:52	3068
offered strange fire before the *L*	Num 26:61	3068
For the *L* had said of them, They	Num 26:65	3068
the *L* in the company of Korah	Num 27:3	3068
brought their cause before the *L*	Num 27:5	3068
the *L* spake unto Moses, saying,	Num 27:6	3068
as the *L* commanded Moses	Num 27:11	3068
the *L* said unto Moses, Get thee	Num 27:12	3068
And Moses spake unto the *L*	Num 27:15	3068
Let the *L*, the God of the spirits	Num 27:16	3068
that the congregation of the *L* be	Num 27:17	3068
the *L* said unto Moses, Take thee	Num 27:18	3068
the judgment of Urim before the *L*	Num 27:21	3068
Moses did as the *L* commanded him	Num 27:22	3068
as the *L* commanded by the hand of	Num 27:23	3068
the *L* spake unto Moses, saying,	Num 28:1	3068
which ye shall offer unto the *L*	Num 28:3	3068
sacrifice made by fire unto the *L*	Num 28:6	3068
unto the *L* for a drink offering	Num 28:7	3068
of a sweet savour unto the *L*	Num 28:8	3068
offer a burnt offering unto the *L*	Num 28:11	3068
sacrifice made by fire unto the *L*	Num 28:13	3068
unto the *L* shall be offered	Num 28:15	3068
month is the passover of the *L*	Num 28:16	3068
for a burnt offering unto the *L*	Num 28:19	3068
of a sweet savour unto the *L*	Num 28:24	3068
a new meat offering unto the *L*	Num 28:26	3068
for a sweet savour unto the *L*	Num 28:27	3068
for a sweet savour unto the *L*	Num 29:2	3068
sacrifice made by fire unto the *L*	Num 29:6	3068
unto the *L* for a sweet savour	Num 29:8	3068
a feast unto the *L* seven days	Num 29:12	3068
of a sweet savour unto the *L*	Num 29:13	3068
of a sweet savour unto the *L*	Num 29:36	3068
do unto the *L* in your set feasts	Num 29:39	3068
to all that the *L* commanded Moses	Num 29:40	3068
thing which the *L* hath commanded	Num 30:1	3068
If a man vow a vow unto the *L*	Num 30:2	3068
a woman also vow a vow unto the *L*	Num 30:3	3068
the *L* shall forgive her, because	Num 30:5	3068
and the *L* shall forgive her	Num 30:8	3068
and the *L* shall forgive her	Num 30:12	3068
which the *L* commanded Moses,	Num 30:16	3068
the *L* spake unto Moses, saying,	Num 31:1	3068
and avenge the *L* of Midian	Num 31:3	3068
as the *L* commanded Moses	Num 31:7	3068
the *L* in the matter of Peor	Num 31:16	3068
among the congregation of the *L*	Num 31:16	3068
law which the *L* commanded Moses	Num 31:21	3068
the *L* spake unto Moses, saying,	Num 31:25	3068
levy a tribute unto the *L* of the	Num 31:28	3068

for an heave offering of the *L*	Num 31:29	3068
charge of the tabernacle of the *L*	Num 31:30	3068
did as the *L* commanded Moses	Num 31:31	3068
priest, as the *L* commanded Moses	Num 31:41	3068
charge of the tabernacle of the *L*	Num 31:47	3068
as the *L* commanded Moses	Num 31:47	3068
brought an oblation for the *L*	Num 31:50	3068
for our souls before the *L*	Num 31:50	3068
that they offered up to the *L*	Num 31:52	3068
children of Israel before the *L*	Num 31:54	3068
Even the country which the *L*	Num 32:4	3068
land which the *L* hath given them	Num 32:7	3068
land which the *L* had given them	Num 32:9	3068
they have wholly followed the *L*	Num 32:12	3068
done evil in the sight of the *L*	Num 32:13	3068
anger of the *L* toward Israel	Num 32:14	3068
will go armed before the *L* to war	Num 32:20	3068
armed over Jordan before the *L*	Num 32:21	3068
the land be subdued before the *L*	Num 32:22	3068
and be guiltless before the *L*	Num 32:22	3068
be your possession before the *L*	Num 32:22	3068
ye have sinned against the *L*	Num 32:23	3068
for war, before the *L* to battle	Num 32:27	3068
man armed to battle, before the *L*	Num 32:29	3068
As the *L* hath said unto thy	Num 32:31	3068
the *L* into the land of Canaan	Num 32:32	3068
by the commandment of the *L*	Num 33:2	3068
which the *L* had smitten among	Num 33:4	3068
also the *L* executed judgments	Num 33:4	3068
Hor at the commandment of the *L*	Num 33:38	3068
the *L* spake unto Moses in the	Num 33:50	3068
the *L* spake unto Moses, saying,	Num 34:1	3068
which the *L* commanded to give	Num 34:13	3068
the *L* spake unto Moses, saying,	Num 34:16	3068
the *L* commanded to divide the	Num 34:29	3068
the *L* spake unto Moses in the	Num 35:1	3068
the *L* spake unto Moses, saying,	Num 35:9	3068
for I the *L* dwell among the	Num 35:34	3068
The *L* commanded my *l* to give	Num 36:2	3068
was commanded by the *L* to give	Num 36:2	3068
according to the word of the *L*	Num 36:5	3068
the *L* doth command concerning the	Num 36:6	3068
Even as the *L* commanded Moses, so	Num 36:10	3068
which the *L* commanded by the hand	Num 36:13	3068
According unto all that the *L* had	Deut 1:3	3068
The *L* our God spake unto us in	Deut 1:6	3068
the *L* sware unto your fathers	Deut 1:8	3068
The *L* your God hath multiplied	Deut 1:10	3068
(The *L* God of your fathers make	Deut 1:11	3068
as the *L* our God commanded us	Deut 1:19	3068
which the *L* our God doth give	Deut 1:20	3068
the *L* thy God hath set the land	Deut 1:21	3068
as the *L* God of thy fathers hath	Deut 1:21	3068
which the *L* our God doth give us	Deut 1:25	3068
the commandment of the *L* your God	Deut 1:26	3068
and said, Because the *L* hated us	Deut 1:27	3068
The *L* your God which goeth before	Deut 1:30	3068
how that the *L* thy God bare thee	Deut 1:31	3068
ye did not believe the *L* your God	Deut 1:32	3068
the *L* heard the voice of your	Deut 1:34	3068
he hath wholly followed the *L*	Deut 1:36	3068
Also the *L* was angry with me for	Deut 1:37	3068
me, We have sinned against the *L*	Deut 1:41	3068
that the *L* our God commanded us	Deut 1:41	3068
the *L* said unto me, Say unto them	Deut 1:42	3068
against the commandment of the *L*	Deut 1:43	3068
ye returned and wept before the *L*	Deut 1:45	3068
but the *L* would not hearken to	Deut 1:45	3068
Red sea, as the *L* spake unto me	Deut 2:1	3068
the *L* spake unto me, saying,	Deut 2:2	3068
For the *L* thy God hath blessed	Deut 2:7	3068
these forty years the *L* thy God	Deut 2:7	3068
the *L* said unto me, Distress not	Deut 2:9	3068
which the *L* gave unto them	Deut 2:12	3068
host, as the *L* sware unto them	Deut 2:14	3068
hand of the *L* was against them	Deut 2:15	3068
That the *L* spake unto me, saying,	Deut 2:17	3068
but the *L* destroyed them before	Deut 2:21	3068
which the *L* our God giveth us	Deut 2:29	3068
for the *L* thy God hardened his	Deut 2:30	3068
the *L* said unto me, Behold, I	Deut 2:31	3068
the *L* our God delivered him	Deut 2:33	3068
the *L* our God delivered all unto	Deut 2:36	3068
the *L* our God forbad us	Deut 2:37	3068
the *L* said unto me, Fear him not	Deut 3:2	3068
So the *L* our God delivered into	Deut 3:3	3068
The *L* your God hath given you	Deut 3:18	3068
Until the *L* have given rest unto	Deut 3:20	3068
L your God hath given them beyond	Deut 3:20	3068
eyes have seen all that the *L*	Deut 3:21	3068
so shall the *L* do unto all the	Deut 3:21	3068
for the *L* your God he shall fight	Deut 3:22	3068
And I besought the *L* at that time	Deut 3:23	3068
O *L* GOD, thou hast begun to shew	Deut 3:24	136
But the *L* was wroth with me for	Deut 3:26	3068
the *L* said unto me, Let it	Deut 3:26	3068
possess the land which the *L* God	Deut 4:1	3068
L your God which I command you	Deut 4:2	3068
the *L* did because of Baal-peor	Deut 4:3	3068
the *L* thy God hath destroyed them	Deut 4:3	3068
L your God are alive every one of	Deut 4:4	3068
even as the *L* my God commanded me	Deut 4:5	3068
as the *L* our God is in all things	Deut 4:7	3068
before the *L* thy God in Horeb	Deut 4:10	3068
when the *L* said unto me, Gather	Deut 4:10	3068
the *L* spake unto you out of the	Deut 4:12	3068
the *L* commanded me at that time	Deut 4:14	3068
L spake unto you in Horeb out of	Deut 4:15	3068
which the *L* thy God hath divided	Deut 4:19	3068
But the *L* hath taken you, and	Deut 4:20	3068
Furthermore the *L* was angry with	Deut 4:21	3068
which the *L* thy God giveth thee	Deut 4:21	3068
the covenant of the *L* your God	Deut 4:23	3068
thing, which the *L* thy God hath	Deut 4:23	3068
For the *L* thy God is a consuming	Deut 4:24	3068
in the sight of the *L* thy God	Deut 4:25	3068
the *L* shall scatter you among the	Deut 4:27	3068
whither the *L* shall lead you	Deut 4:27	3068
thou shalt seek the *L* thy God	Deut 4:29	3068
if thou turn to the *L* thy God	Deut 4:30	3068
(For the *L* thy God is a merciful	Deut 4:31	3068
according to all that the *L* your	Deut 4:34	3068
know that the *L* he is God	Deut 4:35	3068
that the *L* he is God in heaven	Deut 4:39	3068
which the *L* thy God giveth thee,	Deut 4:40	3068
The *L* our God made a covenant	Deut 5:2	3068
The *L* made not this covenant with	Deut 5:3	3068
The *L* talked with you face to	Deut 5:4	3068
(I stood between the *L* and you at	Deut 5:5	3068
to shew you the word of the *L*	Deut 5:5	3068
I am the *L* thy God, which brought	Deut 5:6	3068
for I the *L* thy God am a jealous	Deut 5:9	3068
the name of the *L* thy God in vain	Deut 5:11	3068
for the *L* will not hold him	Deut 5:11	3068
as the *L* thy God hath commanded	Deut 5:12	3068
is the sabbath of the *L* thy God	Deut 5:14	3068
that the *L* thy God brought thee	Deut 5:15	3068
therefore the *L* thy God commanded	Deut 5:15	3068
as the *L* thy God hath commanded	Deut 5:16	3068
which the *L* thy God giveth thee	Deut 5:16	3068
These words the *L* spake unto all	Deut 5:22	3068
the *L* our God hath shewed us his	Deut 5:24	3068
voice of the *L* our God any more	Deut 5:25	3068
all that the *L* our God shall say	Deut 5:27	3068
L our God shall speak unto thee	Deut 5:27	3068
the *L* heard the voice of your	Deut 5:28	3068
the *L* said unto me, I have heard	Deut 5:28	3068
the *L* your God hath commanded you	Deut 5:32	3068
the *L* your God hath commanded you	Deut 5:33	3068
which the *L* your God commanded to	Deut 6:1	3068
thou mightest fear the *L* thy God	Deut 6:2	3068
as the *L* God of thy fathers hath	Deut 6:3	3068
The *L* our God is one *L*	Deut 6:4	3068
thou shalt love the *L* thy God	Deut 6:5	3068
when the *L* thy God shall have	Deut 6:10	3068
beware lest thou forget the *L*	Deut 6:12	3068
Thou shalt fear the *L* thy God	Deut 6:13	3068
(For the *L* thy God is a jealous	Deut 6:15	3068
you) lest the anger of the *L* thy	Deut 6:15	3068
Ye shall not tempt the *L* your God	Deut 6:16	3068
commandments of the *L* your God	Deut 6:17	3068
and good in the sight of the *L*	Deut 6:18	3068
the *L* sware unto thy fathers	Deut 6:18	3068
before thee, as the *L* hath spoken	Deut 6:19	3068
which the *L* our God hath	Deut 6:20	3068
the *L* brought us out of Egypt	Deut 6:21	3068
the *L* shewed signs and wonders,	Deut 6:22	3068
the *L* commanded us to do all	Deut 6:24	3068
statutes, to fear the *L* our God	Deut 6:24	3068
commandments before the *L* our God	Deut 6:25	3068
When the *L* thy God shall bring	Deut 7:1	3068
when the *L* thy God shall deliver	Deut 7:2	3068
of the *L* be kindled against you	Deut 7:4	3068
an holy people unto the *L* thy God	Deut 7:6	3068
the *L* thy God hath chosen thee to	Deut 7:6	3068
The *L* did not set his love upon	Deut 7:7	3068
But because the *L* loved you	Deut 7:8	3068
hath the *L* brought you out with a	Deut 7:8	3068
Know therefore that the *L* thy God	Deut 7:9	3068
that the *L* thy God shall keep	Deut 7:12	3068
the *L* will take away from thee	Deut 7:15	3068
all the people which the *L* thy	Deut 7:16	3068
the *L* thy God did unto Pharaoh	Deut 7:18	3068
whereby the *L* thy God brought	Deut 7:19	3068
so shall the *L* thy God do unto	Deut 7:19	3068
Moreover the *L* thy God will send	Deut 7:20	3068
for the *L* thy God is among you, a	Deut 7:21	3068
the *L* thy God will put out those	Deut 7:22	3068
But the *L* thy God shall deliver	Deut 7:23	3068
an abomination to the *L* thy God	Deut 7:25	3068
the *L* sware unto your fathers	Deut 8:1	3068
L thy God led thee these forty	Deut 8:2	3068
the mouth of the *L* doth man live	Deut 8:3	3068
so the *L* thy God chasteneth thee	Deut 8:5	3068
the commandments of the *L* thy God	Deut 8:6	3068
For the *L* thy God bringeth thee	Deut 8:7	3068
then thou shalt bless the *L* thy	Deut 8:10	3068
thou forget not the *L* thy God	Deut 8:11	3068
up, and thou forget the *L* thy God	Deut 8:14	3068
thou shalt remember the *L* thy God	Deut 8:18	3068
do at all forget the *L* thy God	Deut 8:19	3068
As the nations which the *L*	Deut 8:20	3068
unto the voice of the *L* your God	Deut 8:20	3068
that the *L* thy God is he which	Deut 9:3	3068
as the *L* hath said unto thee	Deut 9:3	3068
after that the *L* thy God hath	Deut 9:4	3068
For my righteousness the *L* hath	Deut 9:4	3068
L doth drive them out from before	Deut 9:4	3068
the *L* thy God doth drive them out	Deut 9:5	3068
the *L* sware unto thy fathers	Deut 9:5	3068
that the *L* thy God giveth thee	Deut 9:6	3068
the *L* thy God to wrath in the	Deut 9:7	3068
been rebellious against the *L*	Deut 9:7	3068
Horeb ye provoked the *L* to wrath	Deut 9:8	3068
so that the *L* was angry with you	Deut 9:8	3068
which the *L* made with you	Deut 9:9	3068
the *L* delivered unto me two	Deut 9:10	3068
which the *L* spake with you in the	Deut 9:10	3068
that the *L* gave me the two tables	Deut 9:11	3068
the *L* said unto me, Arise, get	Deut 9:12	3068
Furthermore the *L* spake unto me	Deut 9:13	3068
had sinned against the *L* your God	Deut 9:16	3068
way which the *L* had commanded you	Deut 9:16	3068
And I fell down before the *L*	Deut 9:18	3068
wickedly in the sight of the *L*	Deut 9:18	3068
wherewith the *L* was wroth against	Deut 9:19	3068
But the *L* hearkened unto me at	Deut 9:19	3068
the *L* was very angry with Aaron	Deut 9:20	3068
ye provoked the *L* to wrath	Deut 9:22	3068
Likewise when the *L* sent you from	Deut 9:23	3068
the commandment of the *L* your God	Deut 9:23	3068
been rebellious against the *L*	Deut 9:24	3068
fell down before the *L* forty days	Deut 9:25	3068
because the *L* had said he would	Deut 9:25	3068
I prayed therefore unto the *L*	Deut 9:26	3068
O *L* GOD, destroy not thy people	Deut 9:26	136
Because the *L* was not able to	Deut 9:28	3068
At that time the *L* said unto me	Deut 10:1	3068
which the *L* spake unto you in the	Deut 10:4	3068
and the *L* gave them unto me	Deut 10:4	3068
they be, as the *L* commanded me	Deut 10:5	3068
At that time the *L* separated the	Deut 10:8	3068
the ark of the covenant of the *L*	Deut 10:8	3068
to stand before the *L* to minister	Deut 10:8	3068
the *L* is his inheritance,	Deut 10:9	3068
according as the *L* thy God	Deut 10:9	3068
the *L* hearkened unto me at that	Deut 10:10	3068
the *L* would not destroy thee	Deut 10:10	3068
the *L* said unto me, Arise, take	Deut 10:11	3068
what doth the *L* thy God require	Deut 10:12	3068
thee, but to fear the *L* thy God	Deut 10:12	3068
to serve the *L* thy God with all	Deut 10:12	3068
To keep the commandments of the *L*	Deut 10:13	3068
Only the *L* had a delight in thy	Deut 10:15	3068
For the *L* your God is God of gods	Deut 10:17	3068
L of lords, a great God, a mighty	Deut 10:17	113
Thou shalt fear the *L* thy God	Deut 10:20	3068
now the *L* thy God hath made thee	Deut 10:22	3068
thou shalt love the *L* thy God	Deut 11:1	3068
chastisement of the *L* your God	Deut 11:2	3068
how the *L* hath destroyed them	Deut 11:4	3068
great acts of the *L* which he did	Deut 11:7	3068
which the *L* sware unto your	Deut 11:9	3068
A land which the *L* thy God careth	Deut 11:12	3068
the eyes of the *L* thy God are	Deut 11:12	3068
this day, to love the *L* your God	Deut 11:13	3068
good land which the *L* giveth you	Deut 11:17	3068
in the land which the *L* sware	Deut 11:21	3068
do them, to love the *L* your God	Deut 11:22	3068
Then will the *L* drive out all	Deut 11:23	3068
for the *L* your God shall lay the	Deut 11:25	3068
commandments of the *L* your God	Deut 11:27	3068
commandments of the *L* your God	Deut 11:28	3068
when the *L* thy God hath brought	Deut 11:29	3068
which the *L* your God giveth you	Deut 11:31	3068
which the *L* God of thy fathers	Deut 12:1	3068
not do so unto the *L* your God	Deut 12:4	3068
L your God shall choose out of	Deut 12:5	3068
shall eat before the *L* your God	Deut 12:7	3068
wherein the *L* thy God hath	Deut 12:7	3068
which the *L* your God giveth you	Deut 12:9	3068
dwell in the land which the *L*	Deut 12:10	3068
shall be a place which the *L* your	Deut 12:11	3068
vows which ye vow unto the *L*	Deut 12:11	3068
rejoice before the *L* your God	Deut 12:12	3068
the *L* shall choose in one of thy	Deut 12:14	3068
to the blessing of the *L* thy God	Deut 12:15	3068
thou must eat them before the *L*	Deut 12:18	3068
which the *L* thy God shall choose	Deut 12:18	3068
the *L* thy God in all that thou	Deut 12:18	3068
When the *L* thy God shall enlarge	Deut 12:20	3068
If the place which the *L* thy God	Deut 12:21	3068
which the *L* hath given thee, as I	Deut 12:21	3068
is right in the sight of the *L*	Deut 12:25	3068
place which the *L* shall choose	Deut 12:26	3068
upon the altar of the *L* thy God	Deut 12:27	3068
upon the altar of the *L* thy God	Deut 12:27	3068
in the sight of the *L* thy God	Deut 12:28	3068
When the *L* thy God shall cut off	Deut 12:29	3068
not do so unto the *L* thy God	Deut 12:31	3068
for every abomination to the *L*	Deut 12:31	3068
for the *L* your God proveth you,	Deut 13:3	3068
to know whether ye love the *L*	Deut 13:3	3068
shall walk after the *L* your God	Deut 13:4	3068
turn you away from the *L* your God	Deut 13:5	3068
thee out of the way which the *L*	Deut 13:5	3068
thee away from the *L* thy God	Deut 13:10	3068
which the *L* thy God hath given	Deut 13:12	3068
every whit, for the *L* thy God	Deut 13:16	3068
that the *L* may turn from the	Deut 13:17	3068
to the voice of the *L* thy God	Deut 13:18	3068
in the eyes of the *L* thy God	Deut 13:18	3068
the children of the *L* your God	Deut 14:1	3068
an holy people unto the *L* thy God	Deut 14:2	3068
the *L* hath chosen thee to be a	Deut 14:2	3068
an holy people unto the *L* thy God	Deut 14:21	3068
shalt eat before the *L* thy God	Deut 14:23	3068
to fear the *L* thy God always	Deut 14:23	3068
which the *L* thy God shall choose	Deut 14:24	3068
when the *L* thy God hath blessed	Deut 14:24	3068
which the *L* thy God shall choose	Deut 14:25	3068
eat there before the *L* thy God	Deut 14:26	3068
that the *L* thy God may bless thee	Deut 14:29	3068
for the *L* shall greatly bless	Deut 15:4	3068

the *L* thy God giveth thee for an	Deut 15:4	3068
unto the voice of the *L* thy God	Deut 15:5	3068
For the *L* thy God blesseth thee,	Deut 15:6	3068
which the *L* thy God giveth thee	Deut 15:7	3068
and he cry unto the *L* against thee	Deut 15:9	3068
L thy God shall bless thee in all	Deut 15:10	3068
of that wherewith the *L* thy God	Deut 15:14	3068
the *L* thy God redeemed thee	Deut 15:15	3068
the *L* thy God shall bless thee in	Deut 15:18	3068
shalt sanctify unto the *L* thy God	Deut 15:19	3068
the *L* thy God year by year in the	Deut 15:20	3068
place which the *L* shall choose	Deut 15:20	3068
sacrifice it unto the *L* thy God	Deut 15:21	3068
the passover unto the *L* thy God	Deut 16:1	3068
for in the month of Abib the *L*	Deut 16:1	3068
the passover unto the *L* thy God	Deut 16:2	3068
in the place which the *L* shall	Deut 16:2	3068
which the *L* thy God giveth thee	Deut 16:5	3068
But at the place which the *L* thy	Deut 16:6	3068
which the *L* thy God shall choose	Deut 16:7	3068
solemn assembly to the *L* thy God	Deut 16:8	3068
the *L* thy God with a tribute of a	Deut 16:10	3068
shalt give unto the *L* thy God	Deut 16:10	
according as the *L* thy God hath	Deut 16:10	3068
rejoice before the *L* thy God	Deut 16:11	3068
in the place which the *L* thy God	Deut 16:11	3068
keep a solemn feast unto the *L*	Deut 16:15	3068
place which the *L* shall choose	Deut 16:15	3068
because the *L* thy God shall bless	Deut 16:15	3068
L thy God in the place which he	Deut 16:16	3068
not appear before the *L* empty	Deut 16:16	3068
to the blessing of the *L* thy God	Deut 16:17	3068
which the *L* thy God giveth thee,	Deut 16:18	3068
which the *L* thy God giveth thee	Deut 16:20	3068
unto the altar of the *L* thy God	Deut 16:21	3068
which the *L* thy God hateth	Deut 16:22	3068
unto the *L* thy God any bullock	Deut 17:1	3068
an abomination unto the *L* thy God	Deut 17:1	3068
which the *L* thy God giveth thee	Deut 17:2	3068
in the sight of the *L* thy God	Deut 17:2	3068
which the *L* thy God shall choose	Deut 17:8	3068
L shall choose shall shew thee	Deut 17:10	3068
there before the *L* thy God	Deut 17:12	3068
which the *L* thy God giveth thee	Deut 17:14	3068
whom the *L* thy God shall choose	Deut 17:15	3068
forasmuch as the *L* hath said unto	Deut 17:16	3068
may learn to fear the *L* his God	Deut 17:19	3068
offerings of the *L* made by fire	Deut 18:1	3068
the *L* is their inheritance, as he	Deut 18:2	3068
For the *L* thy God hath chosen him	Deut 18:5	3068
to minister in the name of the *L*	Deut 18:5	3068
place which the *L* shall choose	Deut 18:6	3068
in the name of the *L* his God	Deut 18:7	3068
which stand there before the *L*	Deut 18:7	3068
which the *L* thy God giveth thee	Deut 18:9	3068
are an abomination unto the *L*	Deut 18:12	3068
of these abominations the *L* thy	Deut 18:12	3068
be perfect with the *L* thy God	Deut 18:13	3068
the *L* thy God hath not suffered	Deut 18:14	3068
The *L* thy God will raise up unto	Deut 18:15	3068
L thy God in Horeb in the day of	Deut 18:16	3068
again the voice of the *L* my God	Deut 18:16	3068
the *L* said unto me, They have	Deut 18:17	3068
word which the *L* hath not spoken	Deut 18:21	3068
speaketh in the name of the *L*	Deut 18:22	3068
thing which the *L* hath not spoken	Deut 18:22	3068
When the *L* thy God hath cut off	Deut 19:1	3068
whose land the *L* thy God giveth	Deut 19:1	3068
which the *L* thy God giveth thee	Deut 19:2	3068
which the *L* thy God giveth thee	Deut 19:3	3068
if the *L* thy God enlarge thy	Deut 19:8	3068
this day, to love the *L* thy God	Deut 19:9	3068
which the *L* thy God giveth thee	Deut 19:10	3068
inherit in the land that the *L*	Deut 19:14	3068
is, shall stand before the *L*	Deut 19:17	3068
for the *L* thy God is with thee,	Deut 20:1	3068
For the *L* your God is he that	Deut 20:4	3068
when the *L* thy God hath delivered	Deut 20:13	3068
which the *L* thy God hath given	Deut 20:14	3068
which the *L* thy God doth give	Deut 20:16	3068
as the *L* thy God hath commanded	Deut 20:17	3068
ye sin against the *L* your God	Deut 20:18	3068
slain in the land which the *L* thy	Deut 21:1	3068
for them the *L* thy God hath	Deut 21:5	3068
and to bless in the name of the *L*	Deut 21:5	3068
Be merciful, O *L*, unto thy people	Deut 21:8	3068
is right in the sight of the *L*	Deut 21:9	3068
the *L* thy God hath delivered them	Deut 21:10	3068
which the *L* thy God giveth thee	Deut 21:23	3068
abomination unto the *L* thy God	Deut 22:5	3068
into the congregation of the *L*	Deut 23:1	3068
into the congregation of the *L*	Deut 23:2	3068
into the congregation of the *L*	Deut 23:2	3068
into the congregation of the *L*	Deut 23:3	3068
congregation of the *L* for ever	Deut 23:3	3068
Nevertheless the *L* thy God would	Deut 23:5	3068
but the *L* thy God turned the	Deut 23:5	3068
because the *L* thy God loved thee	Deut 23:5	3068
the *L* in their third generation	Deut 23:8	3068
For the *L* thy God walketh in the	Deut 23:14	3068
of the *L* thy God for any vow	Deut 23:18	3068
abomination unto the *L* thy God	Deut 23:18	3068
that the *L* thy God may bless thee	Deut 23:20	3068
vow a vow unto the *L* thy God	Deut 23:21	3068
for the *L* thy God will surely	Deut 23:21	3068
hast vowed unto the *L* thy God	Deut 23:23	3068
that is abomination before the *L*	Deut 24:4	3068
which the *L* thy God giveth thee	Deut 24:4	3068
Remember what the *L* thy God did	Deut 24:9	3068
unto thee before the *L* thy God	Deut 24:13	3068
he cry against thee unto the *L*	Deut 24:15	3068
the *L* thy God redeemed thee	Deut 24:18	3068
that the *L* thy God may bless thee	Deut 24:19	3068
which the *L* thy God giveth thee	Deut 25:15	3068
an abomination unto the *L* thy God	Deut 25:16	3068
when the *L* thy God hath given	Deut 25:19	3068
in the land which the *L* thy God	Deut 25:19	3068
the *L* thy God giveth thee for an	Deut 26:1	3068
that the *L* thy God giveth thee	Deut 26:2	3068
go unto the place which the *L* thy	Deut 26:2	3068
this day unto the *L* thy God	Deut 26:3	3068
L sware unto our fathers for to	Deut 26:3	3068
before the altar of the *L* thy God	Deut 26:4	3068
speak and say before the *L* thy God	Deut 26:5	3068
unto the *L* God of our fathers	Deut 26:7	3068
the *L* heard our voice, and looked	Deut 26:7	3068
the *L* brought us forth out of	Deut 26:8	3068
of the land, which thou, O *L*	Deut 26:10	3068
shalt set it before the *L* thy God	Deut 26:10	3068
and worship before the *L* thy God	Deut 26:10	3068
L thy God hath given unto thee	Deut 26:11	3068
shalt say before the *L* thy God	Deut 26:13	3068
to the voice of the *L* my God	Deut 26:14	3068
This day the *L* thy God hath	Deut 26:16	3068
the *L* this day to be thy God	Deut 26:17	3068
the *L* hath avouched thee this day	Deut 26:18	3068
an holy people unto the *L* thy God	Deut 26:19	3068
which the *L* thy God giveth thee	Deut 27:2	3068
which the *L* thy God giveth thee	Deut 27:3	3068
as the *L* God of thy fathers hath	Deut 27:3	3068
build an altar unto the *L* thy God	Deut 27:5	3068
of the *L* thy God of whole stones	Deut 27:6	3068
thereon unto the *L* thy God	Deut 27:6	3068
and rejoice before the *L* thy God	Deut 27:7	3068
the people of the *L* thy God	Deut 27:9	3068
obey the voice of the *L* thy God	Deut 27:10	3068
image, an abomination unto the *L*	Deut 27:15	3068
unto the voice of the *L* thy God	Deut 28:1	3068
that the *L* thy God will set thee	Deut 28:1	3068
unto the voice of the *L* thy God	Deut 28:2	3068
The *L* shall cause thine enemies	Deut 28:7	3068
The *L* shall command the blessing	Deut 28:8	3068
which the *L* thy God giveth thee	Deut 28:8	3068
The *L* shall establish thee an	Deut 28:9	3068
the commandments of the *L* thy God	Deut 28:9	3068
art called by the name of the *L*	Deut 28:10	3068
the *L* shall make thee plenteous	Deut 28:11	3068
in the land which the *L* sware	Deut 28:11	3068
The *L* shall open unto thee his	Deut 28:12	3068
the *L* shall make thee the head,	Deut 28:13	3068
the commandments of the *L* thy God	Deut 28:13	3068
unto the voice of the *L* thy God	Deut 28:15	3068
The *L* shall send upon thee	Deut 28:20	3068
The *L* shall make the pestilence	Deut 28:21	3068
The *L* shall smite thee with a	Deut 28:22	3068
The *L* shall make the rain of thy	Deut 28:24	3068
The *L* shall cause thee to be	Deut 28:25	3068
The *L* will smite thee with the	Deut 28:27	3068
The *L* shall smite thee with	Deut 28:28	3068
The *L* shall smite thee in the	Deut 28:35	3068
The *L* shall bring thee, and thy	Deut 28:36	3068
whither the *L* shall lead thee	Deut 28:37	3068
unto the voice of the *L* thy God	Deut 28:45	3068
not the *L* thy God with joyfulness	Deut 28:47	3068
the *L* shall send against thee	Deut 28:48	3068
The *L* shall bring a nation	Deut 28:49	3068
which the *L* thy God hath given	Deut 28:52	3068
which the *L* thy God hath given	Deut 28:53	3068
and fearful name, THE *L* THY GOD	Deut 28:58	3068
Then the *L* will make thy plagues	Deut 28:59	3068
them will the *L* bring upon thee,	Deut 28:61	3068
obey the voice of the *L* thy God	Deut 28:62	3068
that as the *L* rejoiced over you	Deut 28:63	3068
so the *L* will rejoice over you to	Deut 28:63	3068
the *L* shall scatter thee among	Deut 28:64	3068
but the *L* shall give thee there a	Deut 28:65	3068
the *L* shall bring thee into Egypt	Deut 28:68	3068
which the *L* commanded Moses to	Deut 29:1	3068
Ye have seen all that the *L* did	Deut 29:2	3068
Yet the *L* hath not given you an	Deut 29:4	3068
know that I am the *L* your God	Deut 29:6	3068
all of you before the *L* your God	Deut 29:10	3068
into covenant with the *L* thy God	Deut 29:12	3068
which the *L* thy God maketh with	Deut 29:12	3068
us this day before the *L* our God	Deut 29:15	3068
away this day from the *L* our God	Deut 29:18	3068
The *L* will not spare him	Deut 29:20	3068
but then the anger of the *L*	Deut 29:20	3068
the *L* shall blot out his name	Deut 29:20	3068
the *L* shall separate him unto	Deut 29:21	3068
which the *L* hath laid upon it	Deut 29:22	3068
which the *L* overthrew in his	Deut 29:23	3068
Wherefore hath the *L* done thus	Deut 29:24	3068
of the *L* God of their fathers	Deut 29:25	3068
the anger of the *L* was kindled	Deut 29:27	3068
the *L* rooted them out of their	Deut 29:28	3068
things belong unto the *L* our God	Deut 29:29	3068
whither the *L* thy God hath driven	Deut 30:1	3068
shalt return unto the *L* thy God	Deut 30:2	3068
That then the *L* thy God will turn	Deut 30:3	3068
whither the *L* thy God hath	Deut 30:3	3068
will the *L* thy God gather thee	Deut 30:4	3068
the *L* thy God will bring thee	Deut 30:5	3068
the *L* thy God will circumcise	Deut 30:6	3068
to love the *L* thy God with all	Deut 30:6	3068
the *L* thy God will put all these	Deut 30:7	3068
return and obey the voice of the *L*	Deut 30:8	3068
the *L* thy God will make thee	Deut 30:9	3068
for the *L* will again rejoice over	Deut 30:9	3068
unto the voice of the *L* thy God	Deut 30:10	3068
if thou turn unto the *L* thy God	Deut 30:10	3068
this day to love the *L* thy God	Deut 30:16	3068
the *L* thy God shall bless thee in	Deut 30:16	3068
thou mayest love the *L* thy God	Deut 30:20	3068
the *L* sware unto thy fathers	Deut 30:20	3068
also the *L* hath said unto me,	Deut 31:2	3068
The *L* thy God, he will go over	Deut 31:3	3068
before thee, as the *L* hath said	Deut 31:3	3068
the *L* shall do unto them as he	Deut 31:4	3068
the *L* shall give them up before	Deut 31:5	3068
for the *L* thy God, he it is that	Deut 31:6	3068
L hath sworn unto their fathers	Deut 31:7	3068
And the *L*, he it is that doth go	Deut 31:8	3068
the ark of the covenant of the *L*	Deut 31:9	3068
is come to appear before the *L*	Deut 31:11	3068
may learn, and fear the *L* your God	Deut 31:12	3068
and learn to fear the *L* your God	Deut 31:13	3068
the *L* said unto Moses, Behold,	Deut 31:14	3068
the *L* appeared in the tabernacle	Deut 31:15	3068
the *L* said unto Moses, Behold,	Deut 31:16	3068
the ark of the covenant of the *L*	Deut 31:25	3068
of the covenant of the *L* your God	Deut 31:26	3068
been rebellious against the *L*	Deut 31:27	3068
do evil in the sight of the *L*	Deut 31:29	3068
I will publish the name of the *L*	Deut 32:3	3068
Do ye thus requite the *L*, O	Deut 32:6	3068
So the *L* alone did lead him, and	Deut 32:12	3068
And when the *L* saw it, he abhorred	Deut 32:19	3068
the *L* hath not done all this	Deut 32:27	3068
them, and the *L* had shut them up	Deut 32:30	3068
For the *L* shall judge his people,	Deut 32:36	3068
the *L* spake unto Moses that	Deut 32:48	3068
The *L* came from Sinai, and rose up	Deut 33:2	3068
and he said, Hear, *L*, the voice of	Deut 33:7	3068
Bless, *L*, his substance, and	Deut 33:11	3068
The beloved of the *L* shall dwell	Deut 33:12	3068
the *L* shall cover him all the day	Deut 33:12	
Blessed of the *L* be his land	Deut 33:13	3068
he executed the justice of the *L*	Deut 33:21	3068
full with the blessing of the *L*	Deut 33:23	3068
thee, O people saved by the *L*	Deut 33:29	3068
the *L* shewed him all the land of	Deut 34:1	3068
the *L* said unto him, This is the	Deut 34:4	3068
So Moses the servant of the *L*	Deut 34:5	3068
according to the word of the *L*	Deut 34:5	3068
did as the *L* commanded Moses	Deut 34:9	3068
whom the *L* knew face to face,	Deut 34:10	3068
which the *L* sent him to do in the	Deut 34:11	3068
servant of the *L* it came to pass	Josh 1:1	3068
that the *L* spake unto Joshua the	Josh 1:1	3068
for the *L* thy God is with thee	Josh 1:9	3068
which the *L* your God giveth you	Josh 1:11	3068
servant of the *L* commanded you	Josh 1:13	3068
The *L* your God hath given you	Josh 1:13	3068
Until the *L* have given your	Josh 1:15	3068
which the *L* your God giveth them	Josh 1:15	3068
only the *L* thy God be with thee,	Josh 1:17	3068
I know that the *L* hath given you	Josh 2:9	3068
For we have heard how the *L* dried	Josh 2:10	3068
for the *L* your God, he is God in	Josh 2:11	3068
pray you, swear unto me by the *L*	Josh 2:12	3068
when the *L* hath given us the land	Josh 2:14	3068
Truly the *L* hath delivered into	Josh 2:24	3068
of the covenant of the *L* your God	Josh 3:3	3068
for to morrow the *L* will do	Josh 3:5	3068
the *L* said unto Joshua, This day	Josh 3:7	3068
hear the words of the *L* your God	Josh 3:9	3068
L of all the earth passeth over	Josh 3:11	113
that bear the ark of the *L*	Josh 3:13	3068
the *L* of all the earth, shall	Josh 3:13	113
the ark of the covenant of the *L*	Josh 3:17	3068
that the *L* spake unto Joshua,	Josh 4:1	3068
the *L* your God into the midst of	Josh 4:5	3068
the ark of the covenant of the *L*	Josh 4:7	3068
as the *L* spake unto Joshua,	Josh 4:8	3068
thing was finished that the *L*	Josh 4:10	3068
that the ark of the *L* passed over	Josh 4:11	3068
over before the *L* unto battle	Josh 4:13	3068
On that day the *L* magnified	Josh 4:14	3068
the *L* spake unto Joshua, saying,	Josh 4:15	3068
L were come up out of the midst	Josh 4:18	3068
For the *L* your God dried up the	Josh 4:23	3068
as the *L* your God did to the Red	Josh 4:23	3068
might know the hand of the *L*	Josh 4:24	3068
fear the *L* your God for ever	Josh 4:24	3068
heard that the *L* had dried up the	Josh 5:1	3068
that time the *L* said unto Joshua	Josh 5:2	3068
obeyed not the voice of the *L*	Josh 5:6	3068
unto whom the *L* sware that he	Josh 5:6	3068
which the *L* sware unto their	Josh 5:6	3068
the *L* said unto Joshua, This day	Josh 5:9	3068
the host of the *L* am I now come	Josh 5:14	113
What saith my *l* unto his servant	Josh 5:14	3068
the *L* said unto Joshua, See, I	Josh 6:2	3068
horns before the ark of the *L*	Josh 6:6	3068
pass on before the ark of the *L*	Josh 6:7	3068
horns passed on before the *L*	Josh 6:8	3068
covenant of the *L* followed them	Josh 6:8	3068
So the ark of the *L* compassed the	Josh 6:11	3068
priests took up the ark of the *L*	Josh 6:12	3068
ark of the *L* went on continually	Josh 6:13	3068
came after the ark of the *L*	Josh 6:13	3068
for the *L* hath given you the city	Josh 6:16	3068
and all that are therein, to the *L*	Josh 6:17	3068

iron, are consecrated unto the *L*	Josh 6:19	3068
come into the treasury of the *L*	Josh 6:19	3068
treasury of the house of the *L*	Josh 6:24	3068
Cursed be the man before the *L*	Josh 6:26	3068
So the *L* was with Joshua	Josh 6:27	3068
the anger of the *L* was kindled	Josh 7:1	3068
ark of the *L* until the eventide	Josh 7:6	3068
O *L* GOD, wherefore hast thou at	Josh 7:7	136
O *L*, what shall I say, when	Josh 7:8	136
the *L* said unto Joshua, Get thee	Josh 7:10	3068
thus saith the *L* God of Israel	Josh 7:13	3068
that the tribe which the *L* taketh	Josh 7:14	3068
the family which the *L* shall take	Josh 7:14	3068
the household which the *L* shall	Josh 7:14	3068
the covenant of the *L*, and because	Josh 7:15	3068
glory to the *L* God of Israel, and	Josh 7:19	3068
against the *L* God of Israel	Josh 7:20	3068
and laid them out before the *L*	Josh 7:23	3068
the *L* shall trouble thee this day	Josh 7:25	3068
So the *L* turned from the	Josh 7:26	3068
the *L* said unto Joshua, Fear not	Josh 8:1	3068
for the *L* your God will deliver	Josh 8:7	3068
commandment of the *L* shall ye do	Josh 8:8	3068
the *L* said unto Joshua, Stretch	Josh 8:18	3068
the *L* which he commanded Joshua	Josh 8:27	3068
the *L* God of Israel in mount Ebal	Josh 8:30	3068
the *L* commanded the children of	Josh 8:31	3068
burnt offerings unto the *L*	Josh 8:31	3068
the ark of the covenant of the *L*	Josh 8:33	3068
of the *L* had commanded before	Josh 8:33	3068
of the name of the *L* thy God	Josh 9:9	3068
not counsel at the mouth of the *L*	Josh 9:14	3068
unto them by the *L* God of Israel	Josh 9:18	3068
unto them by the *L* God of Israel	Josh 9:19	3068
how that the *L* thy God commanded	Josh 9:24	3068
and for the altar of the *L*	Josh 9:27	3068
the *L* said unto Joshua, Fear them	Josh 10:8	3068
the *L* discomfited them before	Josh 10:10	3068
that the *L* cast down great stones	Josh 10:11	3068
to the *L* in the day when the *L*	Josh 10:12	3068
that the *L* hearkened unto the	Josh 10:14	3068
for the *L* fought for Israel	Josh 10:14	3068
for the *L* your God hath delivered	Josh 10:19	3068
for thus shall the *L* do to all	Josh 10:25	3068
the *L* delivered it also, and the	Josh 10:30	3068
the *L* delivered Lachish into the	Josh 10:32	3068
as the *L* God of Israel commanded	Josh 10:40	3068
because the *L* God of Israel	Josh 10:42	3068
the *L* said unto Joshua, Be not	Josh 11:6	3068
the *L* delivered them into the	Josh 11:8	3068
did unto them as the *L* bade him	Josh 11:9	3068
the servant of the *L* commanded	Josh 11:12	3068
As the *L* commanded Moses his	Josh 11:15	3068
of all that the *L* commanded Moses	Josh 11:15	3068
For it was of the *L* to harden	Josh 11:20	3068
them, as the *L* commanded Moses	Josh 11:20	3068
to all that the *L* said unto Moses	Josh 11:23	3068
did Moses the servant of the *L*	Josh 12:6	3068
Moses the servant of the *L* gave	Josh 12:6	3068
the *L* said unto him, Thou art old	Josh 13:1	3068
the servant of the *L* gave them	Josh 13:8	3068
the sacrifices of the *L* God of	Josh 13:14	3068
the *L* God of Israel was their	Josh 13:33	3068
as the *L* commanded by the hand of	Josh 14:2	3068
As the *L* commanded Moses, so the	Josh 14:5	3068
L said unto Moses the man of God	Josh 14:6	3068
L sent me from Kadesh-barnea to	Josh 14:7	3068
I wholly followed the *L* my God	Josh 14:8	3068
hast wholly followed the *L* my God	Josh 14:9	3068
the *L* hath kept me alive, as he	Josh 14:10	3068
even since the *L* spake this word	Josh 14:10	3068
whereof the *L* spake in that day	Josh 14:12	3068
if so be the *L* will be with me,	Josh 14:12	3068
to drive them out, as the *L* said	Josh 14:12	3068
followed the *L* God of Israel	Josh 14:14	3068
commandment of the *L* to Joshua	Josh 15:13	3068
The *L* commanded Moses to give us	Josh 17:4	3068
to the commandment of the *L* he	Josh 17:4	3068
forasmuch as the *L* hath blessed	Josh 17:14	3068
which the *L* God of your fathers	Josh 18:3	3068
for you here before the *L* our God	Josh 18:6	3068
of the *L* is their inheritance	Josh 18:7	3068
the servant of the *L* gave them	Josh 18:7	3068
for you before the *L* in Shiloh	Josh 18:8	3068
for them in Shiloh before the *L*	Josh 18:10	3068
According to the word of the *L*	Josh 19:50	3068
by lot in Shiloh before the *L*	Josh 19:51	3068
The *L* also spake unto Joshua,	Josh 20:1	3068
The *L* commanded by the hand of	Josh 21:2	3068
at the commandment of the *L*	Josh 21:3	3068
as the *L* commanded by the hand of	Josh 21:8	3068
the *L* gave unto Israel all the	Josh 21:43	3068
the *L* gave them rest round about,	Josh 21:44	3068
the *L* delivered all their enemies	Josh 21:44	3068
of any good thing which the *L* had	Josh 21:45	3068
servant of the *L* commanded you	Josh 22:2	3068
the commandment of the *L* your God	Josh 22:3	3068
now the *L* your God hath given	Josh 22:4	3068
the *L* gave you on the other side	Josh 22:4	3068
the servant of the *L* charged you	Josh 22:5	3068
you, to love the *L* your God	Josh 22:5	3068
of the *L* by the hand of Moses	Josh 22:9	3068
the whole congregation of the *L*	Josh 22:16	3068
this day from following the *L*	Josh 22:16	3068
rebel this day against the *L*	Josh 22:16	3068
in the congregation of the *L*	Josh 22:17	3068
this day from following the *L*	Josh 22:18	3068
ye rebel to day against the *L*	Josh 22:18	3068
land of the possession of the *L*	Josh 22:19	3068
but rebel not against the *L*	Josh 22:19	3068
beside the altar of the *L* our God	Josh 22:19	3068
The *L* God of gods, the *L* God	Josh 22:22	3068
if in transgression against the *L*	Josh 22:22	3068
to turn from following the *L*	Josh 22:23	3068
let the *L* himself require it	Josh 22:23	3068
ye to do with the *L* God of Israel	Josh 22:24	3068
For the *L* hath made Jordan a	Josh 22:25	3068
ye have no part in the *L*	Josh 22:25	3068
children cease from fearing the *L*	Josh 22:25	3068
the *L* before him with our burnt	Josh 22:27	3068
to come, Ye have no part in the *L*	Josh 22:27	3068
the pattern of the altar of the *L*	Josh 22:28	3068
we should rebel against the *L*	Josh 22:29	3068
this day from following the *L*	Josh 22:29	3068
beside the altar of the *L* our God	Josh 22:29	3068
perceive that the *L* is among us	Josh 22:31	3068
this trespass against the *L*	Josh 22:31	3068
Israel out of the hand of the *L*	Josh 22:31	3068
between us that the *L* is God	Josh 22:34	3068
L had given rest unto Israel from	Josh 23:1	3068
ye have seen all that the *L* your	Josh 23:3	3068
for the *L* your God is he that	Josh 23:3	3068
the *L* your God, he shall expel	Josh 23:5	3068
as the *L* your God hath promised	Josh 23:5	3068
But cleave unto the *L* your God	Josh 23:8	3068
For the *L* hath driven out from	Josh 23:9	3068
for the *L* your God, he it is that	Josh 23:10	3068
that ye love the *L* your God	Josh 23:11	3068
Know for a certainty that the *L*	Josh 23:13	3068
the *L* your God hath given you	Josh 23:13	3068
L your God spake concerning you	Josh 23:14	3068
which the *L* your God promised you	Josh 23:15	3068
so shall the *L* bring upon you all	Josh 23:15	3068
the *L* your God hath given you	Josh 23:15	3068
the covenant of the *L* your God	Josh 23:16	3068
of the *L* be kindled against you	Josh 23:16	3068
Thus saith the *L* God of Israel	Josh 24:2	3068
And when they cried unto the *L*	Josh 24:7	3068
Now therefore fear the *L*, and	Josh 24:14	3068
and serve ye the *L*	Josh 24:14	3068
seem evil unto you to serve the *L*	Josh 24:15	3068
and my house, we will serve the *L*	Josh 24:15	3068
that we should forsake the *L*	Josh 24:16	3068
For the *L* our God, he it is that	Josh 24:17	3068
the *L* drave out from before us	Josh 24:18	3068
will we also serve the *L*	Josh 24:18	3068
the people, Ye cannot serve the *L*	Josh 24:19	3068
If ye forsake the *L*, and serve	Josh 24:20	3068
but we will serve the *L*	Josh 24:21	3068
that ye have chosen you the *L*	Josh 24:22	3068
heart unto the *L* God of Israel	Josh 24:23	3068
The *L* our God will we serve, and	Josh 24:24	3068
was by the sanctuary of the *L*	Josh 24:26	3068
of the *L* which he spake unto us	Josh 24:27	3068
son of Nun, the servant of the *L*	Josh 24:29	3068
Israel served the *L* all the days	Josh 24:31	3068
had known all the works of the *L*	Josh 24:31	3068
children of Israel asked the *L*	Judg 1:1	3068
the *L* said, Judah shall go up	Judg 1:2	3068
the *L* delivered the Canaanites and	Judg 1:4	3068
And the *L* was with Judah	Judg 1:19	3068
and the *L* was with them	Judg 1:22	3068
an angel of the *L* came up from	Judg 2:1	3068
when the angel of the *L* spake	Judg 2:4	3068
they sacrificed there unto the *L*	Judg 2:5	3068
the people served the *L* all the	Judg 2:7	3068
seen all the great works of the *L*	Judg 2:7	3068
son of Nun, the servant of the *L*	Judg 2:8	3068
after them, which knew not the *L*	Judg 2:10	3068
did evil in the sight of the *L*	Judg 2:11	3068
they forsook the *L* God of their	Judg 2:12	3068
them, and provoked the *L* to anger	Judg 2:12	3068
And they forsook the *L*, and served	Judg 2:13	3068
the anger of the *L* was hot	Judg 2:14	3068
the hand of the *L* was against	Judg 2:15	3068
as the *L* had said, and as the *L*	Judg 2:15	3068
the *L* raised up judges, which	Judg 2:16	3068
obeying the commandments of the *L*	Judg 2:17	3068
when the *L* raised them up judges,	Judg 2:18	3068
then the *L* was with the judge, and	Judg 2:18	3068
for it repented the *L* because of	Judg 2:18	3068
the anger of the *L* was hot	Judg 2:20	3068
the way of the *L* to walk therein	Judg 2:22	3068
Therefore the *L* left those	Judg 2:23	3068
are the nations which the *L* left	Judg 3:1	3068
unto the commandments of the *L*	Judg 3:4	3068
did evil in the sight of the *L*	Judg 3:7	3068
and forgat the *L* their God	Judg 3:7	3068
of the *L* was hot against Israel	Judg 3:8	3068
of Israel cried unto the *L*	Judg 3:9	3068
the *L* raised up a deliverer to	Judg 3:9	3068
the spirit of the *L* came upon him	Judg 3:10	3068
and the *L* delivered	Judg 3:10	3068
evil again in the sight of the *L*	Judg 3:12	3068
the *L* strengthened Eglon the king	Judg 3:12	3068
done evil in the sight of the *L*	Judg 3:12	3068
of Israel cried unto the *L*	Judg 3:15	3068
the *L* raised them up a deliverer,	Judg 3:15	3068
for the *L* hath delivered your	Judg 3:28	3068
did evil in the sight of the *L*	Judg 4:1	3068
the *L* sold them into the hand of	Judg 4:2	3068
of Israel cried unto the *L*	Judg 4:3	3068
Hath not the *L* God of Israel	Judg 4:6	3068
for the *L* shall sell Sisera into	Judg 4:9	3068
the *L* hath delivered Sisera into	Judg 4:14	3068
is not the *L* gone out before thee	Judg 4:14	3068
the *L* discomfited Sisera, and all	Judg 4:15	3068
Praise ye the *L* for the avenging	Judg 5:2	3068
I, even I, will sing unto the *L*	Judg 5:3	3068
praise to the *L* God of Israel	Judg 5:3	3068
L, when thou wentest out of Seir,	Judg 5:4	3068
melted from before the *L*, even	Judg 5:5	3068
from before the *L* God of Israel	Judg 5:5	3068
Bless ye the *L*	Judg 5:9	3068
the righteous acts of the *L*	Judg 5:11	3068
of the *L* go down to the gates	Judg 5:11	3068
the *L* made me have dominion over	Judg 5:13	3068
ye Meroz, said the angel of the *L*	Judg 5:23	3068
came not to the help of the *L*	Judg 5:23	3068
help of the *L* against the mighty	Judg 5:23	3068
let all thine enemies perish, O *L*	Judg 5:31	3068
did evil in the sight of the *L*	Judg 6:1	3068
the *L* delivered them into the	Judg 6:1	3068
of Israel cried unto the *L*	Judg 6:6	3068
of Israel cried unto the *L*	Judg 6:7	3068
That the *L* sent a prophet unto	Judg 6:8	3068
Thus saith the *L* God of Israel	Judg 6:8	3068
unto you, I am the *L* your God	Judg 6:10	3068
And there came an angel of the *L*	Judg 6:11	3068
the angel of the *L* appeared unto	Judg 6:12	3068
The *L* is with thee, thou mighty	Judg 6:12	3068
if the *L* be with us, why then is	Judg 6:13	3068
Did not the *L* bring us up from	Judg 6:13	3068
but now the *L* hath forsaken us,	Judg 6:13	3068
the *L* looked upon him, and said,	Judg 6:14	3068
And he said unto him, Oh my *L*	Judg 6:15	136
the *L* said unto him, Surely I	Judg 6:16	3068
Then the angel of the *L* put forth	Judg 6:21	3068
Then the angel of the *L* departed	Judg 6:21	3068
that he was an angel of the *L*	Judg 6:22	3068
Gideon said, Alas, O *L* GOD	Judg 6:22	136
an angel of the *L* face to face	Judg 6:22	3068
the *L* said unto him, Peace be	Judg 6:23	3068
built an altar there unto the *L*	Judg 6:24	3068
that the *L* said unto him, Take	Judg 6:25	3068
build an altar unto the *L* thy God	Judg 6:26	3068
did as the *L* had said unto him	Judg 6:27	3068
Spirit of the *L* came upon Gideon	Judg 6:34	3068
the *L* said unto Gideon, The	Judg 7:2	3068
the *L* said unto Gideon, The	Judg 7:4	3068
the *L* said unto Gideon, Every one	Judg 7:5	3068
the *L* said unto Gideon, By the	Judg 7:7	3068
that the *L* said unto him, Arise,	Judg 7:9	3068
for the *L* hath delivered into	Judg 7:15	3068
camp, and say, The sword of the *L*	Judg 7:18	3068
and they cried, The sword of the *L*	Judg 7:20	3068
the *L* set every man's sword	Judg 7:22	3068
Therefore when the *L* hath	Judg 8:7	3068
as the *L* liveth, if ye had saved	Judg 8:19	3068
the *L* shall rule over you	Judg 8:23	3068
remembered not the *L* their God	Judg 8:34	3068
evil again in the sight of the *L*	Judg 10:6	3068
the Philistines, and forsook the *L*	Judg 10:6	3068
the anger of the *L* was hot	Judg 10:7	3068
of Israel cried unto the *L*	Judg 10:10	3068
the *L* said unto the children of	Judg 10:11	3068
of Israel said unto the *L*	Judg 10:15	3068
from among them, and served the *L*	Judg 10:16	3068
the *L* deliver them before me,	Judg 11:9	3068
The *L* be witness between us, if	Judg 11:10	3068
his words before the *L* in Mizpeh	Judg 11:11	3068
the *L* God of Israel delivered	Judg 11:21	3068
So now the *L* God of Israel hath	Judg 11:23	3068
So whomsoever the *L* our God shall	Judg 11:24	3068
the *L* the Judge be judge this day	Judg 11:27	3068
of the *L* came upon Jephthah	Judg 11:29	3068
Jephthah vowed a vow unto the *L*	Judg 11:30	3068
the *L* delivered them into his	Judg 11:32	3068
I have opened my mouth unto the *L*	Judg 11:35	3068
hast opened thy mouth unto the *L*	Judg 11:36	3068
forasmuch as the *L* hath taken	Judg 11:36	3068
the *L* delivered them into my hand	Judg 12:3	3068
evil again in the sight of the *L*	Judg 13:1	3068
the *L* delivered them into the	Judg 13:1	3068
the angel of the *L* appeared unto	Judg 13:3	3068
the *L*, and said, O my *L*	Judg 13:8	3068
angel of the *L* said unto Manoah	Judg 13:13	3068
said unto the angel of the *L*	Judg 13:15	3068
angel of the *L* said unto Manoah	Judg 13:16	3068
thou must offer it unto the *L*	Judg 13:16	3068
not that he was an angel of the *L*	Judg 13:16	3068
said unto the angel of the *L*	Judg 13:17	3068
the angel of the *L* said unto him	Judg 13:18	3068
offered it upon a rock unto the *L*	Judg 13:19	3068
that the angel of the *L* ascended	Judg 13:20	3068
But the angel of the *L* did no	Judg 13:21	3068
that he was an angel of the *L*	Judg 13:21	3068
If the *L* were pleased to kill us,	Judg 13:23	3068
child grew, and the *L* blessed him	Judg 13:24	3068
the Spirit of the *L* began to move	Judg 13:25	3068
knew not that it was of the *L*	Judg 14:4	3068
the Spirit of the *L* came mightily	Judg 14:6	3068
the Spirit of the *L* came upon him	Judg 14:19	3068
the Spirit of the *L* came mightily	Judg 15:14	3068
sore athirst, and called on the *L*	Judg 15:18	3068
he wist not that the *L* was	Judg 16:20	3068
And Samson called unto the *L*	Judg 16:28	3068
O *L* GOD, remember me, I pray thee	Judg 16:28	136
said, Blessed be thou of the *L*	Judg 17:2	3068
the *L* from my hand for my son	Judg 17:3	3068
know I that the *L* will do me good	Judg 17:13	3068
before the *L* is your way wherein	Judg 18:6	3068
now going to the house of the *L*	Judg 19:18	3068
the man's house where her *l* was	Judg 19:26	113

her *l* rose up in the morning, and ... Judg 19:27 113
of Gilead, unto the *L* in Mizpeh ... Judg 20:1 3068
the *L* said, Judah shall go up ... Judg 20:18 3068
and wept before the *L* until even ... Judg 20:23 3068
and asked counsel of the *L* ... Judg 20:23 3068
the *L* said, Go up against him ... Judg 20:23 3068
wept, and sat there before the *L* ... Judg 20:26 3068
and peace offerings before the *L* ... Judg 20:26 3068
of Israel enquired of the *L* ... Judg 20:27 3068
And the *L* said, Go up ... Judg 20:28 3068
the *L* smote Benjamin before ... Judg 20:35 3068
O *L* God of Israel, why is this ... Judg 21:3 3068
with the congregation unto the *L* ... Judg 21:5 3068
came not up to the *L* to Mizpeh ... Judg 21:5 3068
seeing we have sworn by the *L* ... Judg 21:7 3068
came not up to Mizpeh to the *L* ... Judg 21:8 3068
because that the *L* had made a ... Judg 21:15 3068
there is a feast of the *L* in ... Judg 21:19 3068
the *L* had visited his people in ... Ruth 1:6 3068
the *L* deal kindly with you, as ye ... Ruth 1:8 3068
The *L* grant you that ye may find ... Ruth 1:9 3068
of the *L* is gone out against me ... Ruth 1:13 113
the *L* do so to me, and more also, ... Ruth 1:17 3068
the *L* hath brought me home again ... Ruth 1:21 3068
seeing the *L* hath testified ... Ruth 1:21 3068
the reapers, The *L* be with you ... Ruth 2:4 3068
answered him, The *L* bless thee ... Ruth 2:4 3068
The *L* recompense thy work, and a ... Ruth 2:12 3068
given thee of the *L* God of Israel ... Ruth 2:12 3068
in law, Blessed be he of the *L* ... Ruth 2:20 3068
he said, Blessed be thou of the *L* ... Ruth 3:10 3068
kinsman to thee, as the *L* liveth ... Ruth 3:13 3068
The *L* make the woman that is come ... Ruth 4:11 3068
of the seed which the *L* shall ... Ruth 4:12 3068
the *L* gave her conception, and she ... Ruth 4:13 3068
said unto Naomi, Blessed be the *L* ... Ruth 4:14 3068
unto the *L* of hosts in Shiloh ... 1Sa 1:3 3068
and Phinehas, the priests of the *L* ... 1Sa 1:3 3068
but the *L* had shut up her womb ... 1Sa 1:5 3068
because the *L* had shut up her ... 1Sa 1:6 3068
she went up to the house of the *L* ... 1Sa 1:7 3068
by a post of the temple of the *L* ... 1Sa 1:9 3068
of soul, and prayed unto the *L* ... 1Sa 1:10 3068
O *L* of hosts, if thou wilt indeed ... 1Sa 1:11 3068
the *L* all the days of his life ... 1Sa 1:11 3068
continued praying before the *L* ... 1Sa 1:12 3068
Hannah answered and said, No, my *l* ... 1Sa 1:15 113
poured out my soul before the *L* ... 1Sa 1:15 3068
early, and worshipped before the *L* ... 1Sa 1:19 3068
and the *L* remembered her ... 1Sa 1:19 3068
Because I have asked him of the *L* ... 1Sa 1:20 3068
unto the *L* the yearly sacrifice ... 1Sa 1:21 3068
that he may appear before the *L* ... 1Sa 1:22 3068
only the *L* establish his word ... 1Sa 1:23 3068
unto the house of the *L* in Shiloh ... 1Sa 1:24 3068
And she said, Oh my *l*, as thy soul ... 1Sa 1:26 113
by thee here, praying unto the *L* ... 1Sa 1:26 113
the *L* hath given me my petition ... 1Sa 1:27 3068
also I have lent him to the *L* ... 1Sa 1:28 3068
liveth he shall be lent to the *L* ... 1Sa 1:28 3068
And he worshipped the *L* there ... 1Sa 1:28 3068
said, My heart rejoiceth in the *L* ... 1Sa 2:1 3068
mine horn is exalted in the *L* ... 1Sa 2:1 3068
There is none holy as the *L* ... 1Sa 2:2 3068
for the *L* is a God of knowledge, ... 1Sa 2:3 3068
The *L* killeth, and maketh alive ... 1Sa 2:6 3068
The *L* maketh poor, and maketh rich ... 1Sa 2:7 3068
The adversaries of the *L* shall be ... 1Sa 2:10 3068
the *L* shall judge the ends of the ... 1Sa 2:10 3068
unto the *L* before Eli the priest ... 1Sa 2:11 3068
they knew not the *L* ... 1Sa 2:12 3068
men was very great before the *L* ... 1Sa 2:17 3068
abhorred the offering of the *L* ... 1Sa 2:17 3068
Samuel ministered before the *L* ... 1Sa 2:18 3068
The *L* give thee seed of this ... 1Sa 2:20 3068
the loan which is lent to the *L* ... 1Sa 2:20 3068
the *L* visited Hannah, so that she ... 1Sa 2:21 3068
child Samuel grew before the *L* ... 1Sa 2:21 3068
but if a man sin against the *L* ... 1Sa 2:25 3068
because the *L* would slay them ... 1Sa 2:25 3068
and was in favour both with the *L* ... 1Sa 2:26 3068
said unto him, Thus saith the *L* ... 1Sa 2:27 3068
Wherefore the *L* God of Israel ... 1Sa 2:30 3068
but now the *L* saith, Be it far ... 1Sa 2:30 3068
ministered unto the *L* before Eli ... 1Sa 3:1 3068
the word of the *L* was precious in ... 1Sa 3:1 3068
went out in the temple of the *L* ... 1Sa 3:3 3068
That the *L* called Samuel ... 1Sa 3:4 3068
the *L* called yet again, Samuel ... 1Sa 3:6 3068
Now Samuel did not yet know the *L* ... 1Sa 3:7 3068
of the *L* yet revealed unto him ... 1Sa 3:7 3068
the *L* called Samuel again the ... 1Sa 3:8 3068
that the *L* had called the child ... 1Sa 3:8 3068
that thou shalt say, Speak, *L* ... 1Sa 3:9 3068
the *L* came, and stood, and called ... 1Sa 3:10 3068
the *L* said to Samuel, Behold, I ... 1Sa 3:11 3068
the doors of the house of the *L* ... 1Sa 3:15
that the *L* hath said unto thee ... 1Sa 3:17
And he said, It is the *L* ... 1Sa 3:18 3068
the *L* was with him, and did let ... 1Sa 3:19 3068
to be a prophet of the *L* ... 1Sa 3:20 3068
the *L* appeared again in Shiloh ... 1Sa 3:21 3068
for the *L* revealed himself to ... 1Sa 3:21 3068
in Shiloh by the word of the *L* ... 1Sa 3:21 3068
Wherefore hath the *L* smitten us ... 1Sa 4:3 3068
of the *L* out of Shiloh unto us ... 1Sa 4:3 3068
of the covenant of the *L* of hosts ... 1Sa 4:4 3068
of the *L* came into the camp ... 1Sa 4:5 3068
of the *L* was come into the camp ... 1Sa 4:6 3068
the earth before the ark of the *L* ... 1Sa 5:3 3068
ground before the ark of the *L* ... 1Sa 5:4 3068
But the hand of the *L* was heavy ... 1Sa 5:6 3068
the hand of the *L* was against the ... 1Sa 5:9 3068
the ark of the *L* was in the ... 1Sa 6:1 3068
shall we do to the ark of the *L* ... 1Sa 6:2 3068
And take the ark of the *L*, and lay ... 1Sa 6:8 3068
the ark of the *L* upon the cart ... 1Sa 6:11 3068
kine a burnt offering unto the *L* ... 1Sa 6:14 3068
took down the ark of the *L* ... 1Sa 6:15 3068
the same day unto the *L* ... 1Sa 6:15 3068
a trespass offering unto the *L* ... 1Sa 6:17 3068
they set down the ark of the *L* ... 1Sa 6:18 3068
had looked into the ark of the *L* ... 1Sa 6:19 3068
because the *L* had smitten many of ... 1Sa 6:19 3068
to stand before this holy *L* God ... 1Sa 6:20 3068
brought again the ark of the *L* ... 1Sa 6:21 3068
and brought up the ark of the *L* ... 1Sa 7:1 3068
his son to keep the ark of the *L* ... 1Sa 7:1 3068
of Israel lamented after the *L* ... 1Sa 7:2 3068
unto the *L* with all your hearts ... 1Sa 7:3 3068
and prepare your hearts unto the *L* ... 1Sa 7:3 3068
Ashtaroth, and served the *L* only ... 1Sa 7:4 3068
and I will pray for you unto the *L* ... 1Sa 7:5 3068
and poured it out before the *L* ... 1Sa 7:6 3068
We have sinned against the *L* ... 1Sa 7:6 3068
to cry unto the *L* our God for us ... 1Sa 7:8 3068
burnt offering wholly unto the *L* ... 1Sa 7:9 3068
cried unto the *L* for Israel ... 1Sa 7:9 3068
and the *L* heard him ... 1Sa 7:9 3068
but the *L* thundered with a great ... 1Sa 7:10 3068
Hitherto hath the *L* helped us ... 1Sa 7:12 3068
the hand of the *L* was against the ... 1Sa 7:13 3068
he built an altar unto the *L* ... 1Sa 7:17 3068
And Samuel prayed unto the *L* ... 1Sa 8:6 3068
the *L* said unto Samuel, Hearken ... 1Sa 8:7 3068
told all the words of the *L* unto ... 1Sa 8:10 3068
the *L* will not hear you in that ... 1Sa 8:18 3068
them in the ears of the *L* ... 1Sa 8:21 3068
the *L* said to Samuel, Hearken ... 1Sa 8:22 3068
Now the *L* had told Samuel in his ... 1Sa 9:15 3068
the *L* said unto him, Behold the ... 1Sa 9:17 3068
Is it not because the *L* hath ... 1Sa 10:1 3068
the Spirit of the *L* will come ... 1Sa 10:6 3068
together unto the *L* to Mizpeh ... 1Sa 10:17 3068
Thus saith the *L* God of Israel ... 1Sa 10:18 3068
before the *L* by your tribes ... 1Sa 10:19 3068
they enquired of the *L* further ... 1Sa 10:22 3068
the *L* answered, Behold, he hath ... 1Sa 10:22 3068
See ye him whom the *L* hath chosen ... 1Sa 10:24 3068
book, and laid it up before the *L* ... 1Sa 10:25 3068
the fear of the *L* fell on the ... 1Sa 11:7 3068
for to day the *L* hath wrought ... 1Sa 11:13 3068
Saul king before the *L* in Gilgal ... 1Sa 11:15 3068
of peace offerings before the *L* ... 1Sa 11:15 3068
witness against me before the *L* ... 1Sa 12:3 3068
The *L* is witness against you, and ... 1Sa 12:5 3068
It is the *L* that advanced Moses ... 1Sa 12:6 3068
L of all the righteous acts of ... 1Sa 12:7 3068
all the righteous acts of the *L* ... 1Sa 12:7 3068
and your fathers cried unto the *L* ... 1Sa 12:8 3068
then the *L* sent Moses and Aaron, ... 1Sa 12:8 3068
when they forgat the *L* their God ... 1Sa 12:9 3068
And they cried unto the *L*, and said ... 1Sa 12:10 3068
because we have forsaken the *L* ... 1Sa 12:10 3068
the *L* sent Jerubbaal, and Bedan, ... 1Sa 12:11 3068
when the *L* your God was your king ... 1Sa 12:12 3068
the *L* hath set a king over you ... 1Sa 12:13 3068
If ye will fear the *L*, and serve ... 1Sa 12:14 3068
of the *L* then shall both ye ... 1Sa 12:14 3068
continue following the *L* your God ... 1Sa 12:14 3068
will not obey the voice of the *L* ... 1Sa 12:15 3068
against the commandment of the *L* ... 1Sa 12:15 3068
the hand of the *L* be against you ... 1Sa 12:15 3068
which the *L* will do before your ... 1Sa 12:16 3068
I will call unto the *L*, and he ... 1Sa 12:17 3068
have done in the sight of the *L* ... 1Sa 12:17 3068
So Samuel called unto the *L* ... 1Sa 12:18 3068
the *L* sent thunder and rain that ... 1Sa 12:18 3068
the people greatly feared the *L* ... 1Sa 12:18 3068
thy servants unto the *L* thy God ... 1Sa 12:19 3068
not aside from following the *L* ... 1Sa 12:20 3068
but serve the *L* with all your ... 1Sa 12:20 3068
For the *L* will not forsake his ... 1Sa 12:22 3068
the *L* to make you his people ... 1Sa 12:22 3068
the *L* in ceasing to pray for you ... 1Sa 12:23 3068
Only fear the *L*, and serve him in ... 1Sa 12:24 3068
not made supplication unto the *L* ... 1Sa 13:12 3068
the commandment of the *L* thy God ... 1Sa 13:13 3068
for now would the *L* have ... 1Sa 13:13 3068
the *L* hath sought him a man after ... 1Sa 13:14 3068
the *L* hath commanded him to be ... 1Sa 13:14 3068
that which the *L* commanded thee ... 1Sa 13:14 3068
be that the *L* will work for us ... 1Sa 14:6 3068
the *L* to save by many or by few ... 1Sa 14:6 3068
for the *L* hath delivered them ... 1Sa 14:10 3068
for the *L* hath delivered them ... 1Sa 14:12 3068
So the *L* saved Israel that day ... 1Sa 14:23 3068
the people sin against the *L* ... 1Sa 14:33 3068
sin not against the *L* in eating ... 1Sa 14:34 3068
And Saul built an altar unto the *L* ... 1Sa 14:35 3068
altar that he built unto the *L* ... 1Sa 14:35 3068
For, as the *L* liveth, which ... 1Sa 14:39 3068
said unto the *L* God of Israel ... 1Sa 14:41 3068
as the *L* liveth, there shall not ... 1Sa 14:45 3068
The *L* sent me to anoint thee to ... 1Sa 15:1 3068
the voice of the words of the *L* ... 1Sa 15:1 3068
Thus saith the *L* of hosts ... 1Sa 15:2 3068
the word of the *L* unto Samuel ... 1Sa 15:10 3068
and he cried unto the *L* all night ... 1Sa 15:11 3068
him, Blessed be thou of the *L* ... 1Sa 15:13 3068
the commandment of the *L* ... 1Sa 15:13 3068
to sacrifice unto the *L* thy God ... 1Sa 15:15 3068
I will tell thee what the *L* hath ... 1Sa 15:16 3068
the *L* anointed thee king over ... 1Sa 15:17 3068
the *L* sent thee on a journey, and ... 1Sa 15:18 3068
thou not obey the voice of the *L* ... 1Sa 15:19 3068
didst evil in the sight of the *L* ... 1Sa 15:19 3068
I have obeyed the voice of the *L* ... 1Sa 15:20 3068
gone the way which the *L* sent me ... 1Sa 15:20 3068
unto the *L* thy God in Gilgal ... 1Sa 15:21 3068
Hath the *L* as great delight in ... 1Sa 15:22 3068
as in obeying the voice of the *L* ... 1Sa 15:22 3068
hast rejected the word of the *L* ... 1Sa 15:23 3068
the commandment of the *L*, and thy ... 1Sa 15:24 3068
with me, that I may worship the *L* ... 1Sa 15:25 3068
hast rejected the word of the *L* ... 1Sa 15:26 3068
the *L* hath rejected thee from ... 1Sa 15:26 3068
The *L* hath rent the kingdom of ... 1Sa 15:28 3068
that I may worship the *L* thy God ... 1Sa 15:30 3068
and Saul worshipped the *L* ... 1Sa 15:31 3068
in pieces before the *L* in Gilgal ... 1Sa 15:33 3068
the *L* repented that he had made ... 1Sa 15:35 3068
the *L* said unto Samuel, How long ... 1Sa 16:1 3068
the *L* said, Take an heifer with ... 1Sa 16:2 3068
I am come to sacrifice to the *L* ... 1Sa 16:2 3068
Samuel did that which the *L* spake ... 1Sa 16:4 3068
I am come to sacrifice unto the *L* ... 1Sa 16:5 3068
But the *L* said unto Samuel, Look ... 1Sa 16:7 3068
for the *L* seeth not as man seeth ... 1Sa 16:7 3068
but the *L* looketh on the heart ... 1Sa 16:7 3068
Neither hath the *L* chosen this ... 1Sa 16:8 3068
Neither hath the *L* chosen this ... 1Sa 16:9 3068
The *L* hath not chosen these ... 1Sa 16:10 3068
the *L* said, Arise, anoint him ... 1Sa 16:12 3068
the Spirit of the *L* came upon ... 1Sa 16:13 3068
of the *L* departed from Saul ... 1Sa 16:14 3068
spirit from the *L* troubled him ... 1Sa 16:14 3068
person, and the *L* is with him ... 1Sa 16:18 3068
The *L* that delivered me out of ... 1Sa 17:37 3068
David, Go, and the *L* be with thee ... 1Sa 17:37 3068
in the name of the *L* of hosts ... 1Sa 17:45 3068
This day will the *L* deliver thee ... 1Sa 17:46 3068
that the *L* saveth not with sword ... 1Sa 17:47 3068
because the *L* was with him, and ... 1Sa 18:12 3068
and the *L* was with him ... 1Sa 18:14 3068
knew that the *L* was with David, ... 1Sa 18:28 3068
the *L* wrought a great salvation ... 1Sa 19:5 3068
and Saul sware, As the *L* liveth ... 1Sa 19:6 3068
spirit from the *L* was upon Saul ... 1Sa 19:9 3068
but truly as the *L* liveth ... 1Sa 20:3 3068
a covenant of the *L* with thee ... 1Sa 20:8 3068
O *L* God of Israel, when I have ... 1Sa 20:12 3068
The *L* do so and much more to ... 1Sa 20:13 3068
the *L* be with thee, as he hath ... 1Sa 20:13 3068
shew me the kindness of the *L* ... 1Sa 20:14 3068
not when the *L* hath cut off the ... 1Sa 20:15 3068
Let the *L* even require it at the ... 1Sa 20:16 3068
as the *L* liveth ... 1Sa 20:21 3068
for the *L* hath sent thee away ... 1Sa 20:22 3068
the *L* be between thee and me for ... 1Sa 20:23 3068
both of us in the name of the *L* ... 1Sa 20:42 3068
The *L* be between me and thee, and ... 1Sa 20:42 3068
that was taken from before the *L* ... 1Sa 21:6 3068
that day, detained before the *L* ... 1Sa 21:7 3068
And he enquired of the *L* for him ... 1Sa 22:10 3068
and slay the priests of the *L* ... 1Sa 22:17 3068
to fall upon the priests of the *L* ... 1Sa 22:17 3068
Therefore David enquired of the *L* ... 1Sa 23:2 3068
the *L* said unto David, Go, and ... 1Sa 23:2 3068
David enquired of the *L* yet again ... 1Sa 23:4 3068
the *L* answered him and said, Arise ... 1Sa 23:4 3068
O *L* God of Israel, thy servant ... 1Sa 23:10 3068
O *L* God of Israel, I beseech thee ... 1Sa 23:11 3068
the *L* said, He will come down ... 1Sa 23:11 3068
the *L* said, They will deliver ... 1Sa 23:12 3068
two made a covenant before the *L* ... 1Sa 23:18 3068
Saul said, Blessed be ye of the *L* ... 1Sa 23:21 3068
day of which the *L* said unto thee ... 1Sa 24:4 3068
The *L* forbid that I should do ... 1Sa 24:6 3068
he is the anointed of the *L* ... 1Sa 24:6 3068
eyes have seen how that the *L* had ... 1Sa 24:10 3068
The *L* judge between me and thee, ... 1Sa 24:12 3068
and the *L* avenge me of thee ... 1Sa 24:12 3068
The *L* therefore be judge, and ... 1Sa 24:15 3068
forasmuch as when the *L* had ... 1Sa 24:18 3068
wherefore the *L* reward thee good ... 1Sa 24:19 3068
now therefore unto me by the *L* ... 1Sa 24:21 3068
as the *L* liveth ... 1Sa 25:26 3068
seeing the *L* hath withholden thee ... 1Sa 25:26 3068
for the *L* will certainly make my ... 1Sa 25:28 3068
fighteth the battles of the *L* ... 1Sa 25:28 3068
bundle of life with the *L* thy God ... 1Sa 25:29 3068
when the *L* shall have done to my ... 1Sa 25:30 3068
but when the *L* shall have dealt ... 1Sa 25:31 3068
Blessed be the *L* God of Israel ... 1Sa 25:32 3068
as the *L* God of Israel liveth, ... 1Sa 25:34 3068
that the *L* smote Nabal, that he ... 1Sa 25:38 3068
dead, he said, Blessed be the *L* ... 1Sa 25:39 3068
for the *L* hath returned the ... 1Sa 25:39 3068
said furthermore, As the *L* liveth ... 1Sa 26:10 3068
the *L* shall smite him ... 1Sa 26:10 3068
The *L* forbid that I should ... 1Sa 26:11 3068
from the *L* was fallen upon them ... 1Sa 26:12 113
As the *L* liveth, ye are worthy to ... 1Sa 26:16 3068

If the *L* have stirred thee up 1Sa 26:19 3068
men, cursed be they before the *L* 1Sa 26:19 3068
in the inheritance of the *L* 1Sa 26:19 3068
earth before the face of the *L* 1Sa 26:20 3068
The *L* render to every man his 1Sa 26:23 3068
for the *L* delivered thee into my 1Sa 26:23 3068
much set by in the eyes of the *L* 1Sa 26:24 3068
And when Saul enquired of the *L* 1Sa 28:6 3068
the *L* answered him not, neither 1Sa 28:6 3068
the *L*, saying, As the *L* liveth 1Sa 28:10 3068
seeing the *L* is departed from 1Sa 28:16 3068
the *L* hath done to him, as he 1Sa 28:17 3068
for the *L* hath rent the kingdom 1Sa 28:17 3068
obeyedst not the voice of the *L* 1Sa 28:18 3068
therefore hath the *L* done this 1Sa 28:18 3068
Moreover the *L* will also deliver 1Sa 28:19 3068
the *L* also shall deliver the host 1Sa 28:19 3068
unto him, Surely, as the *L* liveth 1Sa 29:6 3068
himself in the *L* his God 1Sa 30:6 3068
And David enquired at the *L* 1Sa 30:8 3068
that which the *L* hath given us 1Sa 30:23 3068
the spoil of the enemies of the *L* 1Sa 30:26 3068
son, and for the people of the *L* 2Sa 1:12 3068
that David enquired of the *L* 2Sa 2:1 3068
the *L* said unto him, Go up 2Sa 2:1 3068
unto them, Blessed be ye of the *L* 2Sa 2:5 3068
now the *L* shew kindness and truth 2Sa 2:6 3068
as the *L* hath sworn to David, 2Sa 3:9 3068
for the *L* hath spoken of David, 2Sa 3:18 3068
are guiltless before the *L* for 2Sa 3:28 3068
the *L* shall reward the doer of 2Sa 3:39 3068
the *L* hath avenged my 2Sa 4:8 3068
said unto them, As the *L* liveth 2Sa 4:9 3068
the *L* said to thee, Thou shalt 2Sa 5:2 3068
with them in Hebron before the *L* 2Sa 5:3 3068
the *L* God of hosts was with him 2Sa 5:10 3068
David perceived that the *L* had 2Sa 5:12 3068
And David enquired of the *L* 2Sa 5:19 3068
the *L* said unto David, Go up 2Sa 5:19 3068
The *L* hath broken forth upon mine 2Sa 5:20 3068
And when David enquired of the *L* 2Sa 5:23 3068
shall the *L* go out before thee 2Sa 5:24 3068
as the *L* had commanded him 2Sa 5:25 3068
is called by the name of the *L* of 2Sa 6:2 3068
of Israel played before the *L* on 2Sa 6:5 3068
the anger of the *L* was kindled 2Sa 6:7 3068
because the *L* had made a breach 2Sa 6:8 3068
was afraid of the *L* that day 2Sa 6:9 3068
shall the ark of the *L* come to me 2Sa 6:9 3068
L unto him into the city of David 2Sa 6:10 3068
the ark of the *L* continued in the 2Sa 6:11 3068
the *L* blessed Obed-edom, and all 2Sa 6:11 3068
The *L* hath blessed the house of 2Sa 6:12 3068
ark of the *L* had gone six paces 2Sa 6:13 3068
before the *L* with all his might 2Sa 6:14 3068
up the ark of the *L* with shouting 2Sa 6:15 3068
as the ark of the *L* came into the 2Sa 6:16 3068
leaping and dancing before the *L* 2Sa 6:16 3068
they brought in the ark of the *L* 2Sa 6:17 3068
and peace offerings before the *L* 2Sa 6:17 3068
in the name of the *L* of hosts 2Sa 6:18 3068
unto Michal, It was before the *L* 2Sa 6:21 3068
me ruler over the people of the *L* 2Sa 6:21 3068
will I play before the *L* 2Sa 6:21 3068
the *L* had given him rest round 2Sa 7:1 3068
for the *L* is with thee 2Sa 7:3 3068
word of the *L* came unto Nathan 2Sa 7:4 3068
servant David, Thus saith the *L* 2Sa 7:5 3068
David, Thus saith the *L* of hosts 2Sa 7:8 3068
Also the *L* telleth thee that he 2Sa 7:11 3068
David in, and sat before the *L* 2Sa 7:18 3068
and he said, Who am I, O *L* GOD 2Sa 7:18 136
small thing in thy sight, O *L* GOD 2Sa 7:19 136
this the manner of man, O *L* GOD 2Sa 7:19 136
L GOD, knowest thy servant 2Sa 7:20 136
Wherefore thou art great, O *L* God 2Sa 7:22 3068
and thou, *L*, art become their God 2Sa 7:24 3068
O *L* God, the word that thou hast 2Sa 7:25 3068
The *L* of hosts is the God over 2Sa 7:26 3068
O *L* of hosts, God of Israel, hast 2Sa 7:27 3068
O *L* GOD, thou art that God, and 2Sa 7:28 136
for thou, O *L* GOD, hast spoken it 2Sa 7:29 136
And the *L* preserved David 2Sa 8:6 3068
David did dedicate unto the *L* 2Sa 8:11 3068
And the *L* preserved David 2Sa 8:14 3068
the *L* do that which seemeth him 2Sa 10:12 3068
David had done displeased the *L* 2Sa 11:27 3068
the *L* sent Nathan unto David 2Sa 12:1 3068
said to Nathan, As the *L* liveth 2Sa 12:5 3068
Thus saith the *L* God of Israel 2Sa 12:7 3068
despised the commandment of the *L* 2Sa 12:9 3068
Thus saith the *L*, Behold, I will 2Sa 12:11 3068
I have sinned against the *L* 2Sa 12:13 3068
The *L* also hath put away thy sin 2Sa 12:13 3068
the enemies of the *L* to blaspheme 2Sa 12:14 3068
the *L* struck the child that 2Sa 12:15 3068
and came into the house of the *L* 2Sa 12:20 3068
and the *L* loved him 2Sa 12:24 3068
name Jedidiah, because of the *L* 2Sa 12:25 3068
the king remember the *L* thy God 2Sa 14:11 3068
And he said, As the *L* liveth 2Sa 14:11 3068
therefore the *L* thy God will be 2Sa 14:17 3068
which I have vowed unto the *L* 2Sa 15:7 3068
If the *L* shall bring me again 2Sa 15:8 3068
then I will serve the *L* 2Sa 15:8 3068
king, and said, As the *L* liveth 2Sa 15:21 3068
find favour in the eyes of the *L* 2Sa 15:25 3068
And David said, O *L*, I pray thee, 2Sa 15:31 3068

The *L* hath returned upon thee all 2Sa 16:8 3068
the *L* hath delivered the kingdom 2Sa 16:8 3068
because the *L* hath said unto him, 2Sa 16:10 3068
for the *L* hath bidden him 2Sa 16:11 3068
It may be that the *L* will look on 2Sa 16:12 3068
that the *L* will requite me good 2Sa 16:12 3068
but whom the *L*, and this people, 2Sa 16:18 3068
For the *L* had appointed to defeat 2Sa 17:14 3068
to the intent that the *L* might 2Sa 17:14 3068
how that the *L* hath avenged him 2Sa 18:19 3068
and said, Blessed be the *L* thy God 2Sa 18:28 3068
for the *L* hath avenged thee this 2Sa 18:31 3068
for I swear by the *L*, if thou go 2Sa 19:7 3068
up the inheritance of the *L* 2Sa 20:19 3068
and David enquired of the *L* 2Sa 21:1 3068
the *L* answered, It is for Saul, 2Sa 21:1 3068
bless the inheritance of the *L* 2Sa 21:3 3068
up unto the *L* in Gibeah of Saul 2Sa 21:6 3068
of Saul, whom the *L* did choose 2Sa 21:6 3068
them in the hill before the *L* 2Sa 21:9 3068
David spake unto the *L* the words 2Sa 22:1 3068
in the day that the *L* had 2Sa 22:1 3068
The *L* is my rock, and my fortress, 2Sa 22:2 3068
I will call on the *L*, who is 2Sa 22:4 3068
my distress I called upon the *L* 2Sa 22:7 3068
The *L* thundered from heaven, and 2Sa 22:14 3068
at the rebuking of the *L* 2Sa 22:16 3068
but the *L* was my stay 2Sa 22:19 3068
The *L* rewarded me according to my 2Sa 22:21 3068
For I have kept the ways of the *L* 2Sa 22:22 3068
Therefore the *L* hath recompensed 2Sa 22:25 3068
For thou art my lamp, O *L* 2Sa 22:29 3068
the *L* will lighten my darkness 2Sa 22:29 3068
the word of the *L* is tried 2Sa 22:31 3068
For who is God, save the *L* 2Sa 22:32 3068
even unto the *L*, but he answered 2Sa 22:42 3068
The *L* liveth 2Sa 22:47 3068
I will give thanks unto thee, O *L* 2Sa 22:50 3068
The Spirit of the *L* spake by me 2Sa 23:2 3068
the *L* wrought a great victory 2Sa 23:10 3068
the *L* wrought a great victory 2Sa 23:12 3068
but poured it out unto the *L* 2Sa 23:16 3068
he said, Be it far from me, O *L* 2Sa 23:17 3068
again the anger of the *L* was 2Sa 24:1 3068
Now the *L* thy God add unto the 2Sa 24:3 3068
And David said unto the *L*, I have 2Sa 24:10 3068
and now, I beseech thee, O *L* 2Sa 24:10 3068
the word of the *L* came unto the 2Sa 24:11 3068
say unto David, Thus saith the *L* 2Sa 24:12 3068
fall now into the hand of the *L* 2Sa 24:14 3068
So the *L* sent a pestilence upon 2Sa 24:15 3068
the *L* repented him of the evil, 2Sa 24:16 3068
the angel of the *L* was by the 2Sa 24:16 3068
David spake unto the *L* when he 2Sa 24:17 3068
rear an altar unto the *L* in the 2Sa 24:18 3068
Gad, went up as the *L* commanded 2Sa 24:19 3068
to build an altar unto the *L* 2Sa 24:21 3068
The *L* thy God accept thee 2Sa 24:23 3068
L my God of that which doth cost 2Sa 24:24 3068
built there an altar unto the *L* 2Sa 24:25 3068
So the *L* was intreated for the 2Sa 24:25 3068
thou swarest by the *L* thy God 1Kin 1:17 3068
sware, and said, As the *L* liveth 1Kin 1:29 3068
unto thee by the *L* God of Israel 1Kin 1:30 3068
the *L* God of my 1Kin 1:36 3068
As the *L* hath been with my 1Kin 1:37 3068
Blessed be the *L* God of Israel 1Kin 1:48 3068
keep the charge of the *L* thy God 1Kin 2:3 3068
That the *L* may continue his word 1Kin 2:4 3068
and I sware to him by the *L* 1Kin 2:8 3068
for it was his from the *L* 1Kin 2:15 3068
Then king Solomon sware by the *L* 1Kin 2:23 3068
Now therefore, as the *L* liveth 1Kin 2:24 3068
the *L* GOD before David my father 1Kin 2:26 136
from being priest unto the *L* 1Kin 2:27 3068
he might fulfil the word of the *L* 1Kin 2:27 3068
fled unto the tabernacle of the *L* 1Kin 2:28 3068
fled unto the tabernacle of the *L* 1Kin 2:29 3068
came to the tabernacle of the *L* 1Kin 2:30 3068
the *L* shall return his blood upon 1Kin 2:32 3068
be peace for ever from the *L* 1Kin 2:33 3068
I not make thee to swear by the *L* 1Kin 2:42 3068
thou not kept the oath of the *L* 1Kin 2:43 3068
therefore the *L* shall return thy 1Kin 2:44 3068
established before the *L* for ever 1Kin 2:45 3068
own house, and the house of the *L* 1Kin 3:1 3068
built unto the name of the *L* 1Kin 3:2 3068
And Solomon loved the *L*, walking 1Kin 3:3 3068
In Gibeon the *L* appeared to 1Kin 3:5 3068
O *L* my God, thou hast made thy 1Kin 3:7 3068
And the speech pleased the *L* 1Kin 3:10 136
the ark of the covenant of the *L* 1Kin 3:15 3068
an house unto the name of the *L* 1Kin 5:3 3068
until the *L* put them under the 1Kin 5:3 3068
But now the *L* my God hath given 1Kin 5:4 3068
unto the name of the *L* my God 1Kin 5:5 3068
as the *L* spake unto David my 1Kin 5:5 3068
said, Blessed be the *L* this day 1Kin 5:7 3068
the *L* gave Solomon wisdom, as he 1Kin 5:12 3068
began to build the house of the *L* 1Kin 6:1 3068
king Solomon built for the *L* 1Kin 6:2 3068
the word of the *L* came to Solomon 1Kin 6:11 3068
the ark of the covenant of the *L* 1Kin 6:19 3068
of the house of the *L* laid 1Kin 6:37 3068
inner court of the house of the *L* 1Kin 7:12 3068
Solomon for the house of the *L* 1Kin 7:40 3068
Solomon for the house of the *L* 1Kin 7:45 3068
pertained unto the house of the *L* 1Kin 7:48 3068

made for the house of the *L* 1Kin 7:51 3068
treasures of the house of the *L* 1Kin 7:51 3068
of the *L* out of the city of David 1Kin 8:1 3068
they brought up the ark of the *L* 1Kin 8:4 3068
covenant of the *L* unto his place 1Kin 8:6 3068
when the *L* made a covenant with 1Kin 8:9 3068
cloud filled the house of the *L* 1Kin 8:10 3068
for the glory of the *L* had filled 1Kin 8:11 3068
had filled the house of the *L* 1Kin 8:11 3068
The *L* said that he would dwell in 1Kin 8:12 3068
Blessed be the *L* God of Israel 1Kin 8:15 3068
the name of the *L* God of Israel 1Kin 8:17 3068
the *L* said unto David my father, 1Kin 8:18 3068
the *L* hath performed his word 1Kin 8:20 3068
as the *L* promised, and have built 1Kin 8:20 3068
the name of the *L* God of Israel 1Kin 8:20 3068
wherein is the covenant of the *L* 1Kin 8:21 3068
the *L* in the presence of all the 1Kin 8:22 3068
L God of Israel, there is no God 1Kin 8:23 3068
L God of Israel, keep with thy 1Kin 8:25 3068
O *L* my God, to hearken unto the 1Kin 8:28 3068
shall pray unto the *L* toward the 1Kin 8:44 3068
our fathers out of Egypt, O *L* GOD 1Kin 8:53 136
prayer and supplication unto the *L* 1Kin 8:54 3068
from before the altar of the *L* 1Kin 8:54 3068
Blessed be the *L*, that hath given 1Kin 8:56 3068
The *L* our God be with us, as he 1Kin 8:57 3068
made supplication before the *L* 1Kin 8:59 3068
be nigh unto the *L* our God day 1Kin 8:59 3068
earth may know that the *L* is God 1Kin 8:60 3068
be perfect with the *L* our God 1Kin 8:61 3068
offered sacrifice before the *L* 1Kin 8:62 3068
which he offered unto the *L* 1Kin 8:63 3068
dedicated the house of the *L* 1Kin 8:63 3068
was before the house of the *L* 1Kin 8:64 3068
altar that was before the *L* was 1Kin 8:64 3068
of Egypt, before the *L* our God 1Kin 8:65 3068
for all the goodness that the *L* 1Kin 8:66 3068
building of the house of the *L* 1Kin 9:1 3068
That the *L* appeared to Solomon 1Kin 9:2 3068
the *L* said unto him, I have heard 1Kin 9:3 3068
Why hath the *L* done thus unto 1Kin 9:8 3068
they forsook the *L* their God 1Kin 9:9 3068
therefore hath the *L* brought upon 1Kin 9:9 3068
two houses, the house of the *L* 1Kin 9:10 3068
for to build the house of the *L* 1Kin 9:15 3068
altar which he built unto the *L* 1Kin 9:25 3068
the altar that was before the *L* 1Kin 9:25 3068
concerning the name of the *L* 1Kin 10:1 3068
went up unto the house of the *L* 1Kin 10:5 3068
Blessed be the *L* thy God, which 1Kin 10:9 3068
because the *L* loved Israel for 1Kin 10:9 3068
pillars for the house of the *L* 1Kin 10:12 3068
the *L* said unto the children of 1Kin 11:2 3068
not perfect with the *L* his God 1Kin 11:4 3068
did evil in the sight of the *L* 1Kin 11:6 3068
and went not fully after the *L* 1Kin 11:6 3068
the *L* was angry with Solomon, 1Kin 11:9 3068
turned from the *L* God of Israel 1Kin 11:9 3068
not that which the *L* commanded 1Kin 11:10 3068
Wherefore the *L* said unto Solomon 1Kin 11:11 3068
the *L* stirred up an adversary 1Kin 11:14 3068
for thus saith the *L*, the God of 1Kin 11:31 3068
for the cause was from the *L* 1Kin 12:15 3068
which the *L* spake by Ahijah the 1Kin 12:15 3068
Thus saith the *L*, Ye shall not go 1Kin 12:24 3068
therefore to the word of the *L* 1Kin 12:24 3068
according to the word of the *L* 1Kin 12:24 3068
the house of the *L* at Jerusalem 1Kin 12:27 3068
by the word of the *L* unto Beth-el 1Kin 13:1 3068
the altar in the word of the *L* 1Kin 13:2 3068
O altar, altar, thus saith the *L* 1Kin 13:2 3068
the sign which the *L* hath spoken 1Kin 13:3 3068
had given by the word of the *L* 1Kin 13:5 3068
now the face of the *L* thy God 1Kin 13:6 3068
And the man of God besought the *L* 1Kin 13:6 3068
charged me by the word of the *L* 1Kin 13:9 3068
said to me by the word of the *L* 1Kin 13:17 3068
unto me by the word of the *L* 1Kin 13:18 3068
that the word of the *L* came unto 1Kin 13:20 3068
Judah, saying, Thus saith the *L* 1Kin 13:21 3068
hast disobeyed the mouth of the *L* 1Kin 13:21 3068
the *L* thy God commanded thee 1Kin 13:21 3068
the which the *L* did say to thee 1Kin 13:22
unto the word of the *L* 1Kin 13:26 3068
therefore the *L* hath delivered 1Kin 13:26 3068
according to the word of the *L* 1Kin 13:26 3068
he cried by the word of the *L* 1Kin 13:32 3068
the *L* said unto Ahijah, Behold, 1Kin 14:5 3068
Thus saith the *L* God of Israel 1Kin 14:7 3068
for the *L* hath spoken it 1Kin 14:11 3068
some good thing toward the *L* God 1Kin 14:13 3068
Moreover the *L* shall raise him up 1Kin 14:14 3068
For the *L* shall smite Israel, as 1Kin 14:15 3068
groves, provoking the *L* to anger 1Kin 14:15 3068
according to the word of the *L* 1Kin 14:18 3068
the city which the *L* did choose 1Kin 14:21 3068
did evil in the sight of the *L* 1Kin 14:22 3068
of the nations which the *L* cast 1Kin 14:24 3068
treasures of the house of the *L* 1Kin 14:26 3068
king went into the house of the *L* 1Kin 14:28 3068
not perfect with the *L* his God 1Kin 15:3 3068
for David's sake did the *L* his 1Kin 15:4 3068
was right in the eyes of the *L* 1Kin 15:5 3068
was right in the eyes of the *L* 1Kin 15:11 3068
perfect with the *L* all his days 1Kin 15:14 3068
into the house of the *L*, silver, 1Kin 15:15 3068
treasures of the house of the *L* 1Kin 15:18 3068

Context	Reference	Strong's
he did evil in the sight of the *L*	1Kin 15:26	3068
unto the saying of the *L*, which	1Kin 15:29	3068
the *L* God of Israel to anger	1Kin 15:30	3068
he did evil in the sight of the *L*	1Kin 15:34	3068
Then the word of the *L* came to	1Kin 16:1	3068
the word of the *L* against Baasha	1Kin 16:7	3068
that he did in the sight of the *L*	1Kin 16:7	3068
according to the word of the *L*	1Kin 16:12	3068
in provoking the *L* God of Israel	1Kin 16:13	3068
doing evil in the sight of the *L*	1Kin 16:19	3068
wrought evil in the eyes of the *L*	1Kin 16:25	3068
to provoke the *L* God of Israel to	1Kin 16:26	3068
did evil in the sight of the *L*	1Kin 16:30	3068
Ahab did more to provoke the *L*	1Kin 16:33	3068
according to the word of the *L*	1Kin 16:34	3068
As the *L* God of Israel liveth,	1Kin 17:1	3068
the word of the *L* came unto him	1Kin 17:2	3068
according unto the word of the *L*	1Kin 17:5	3068
the word of the *L* came unto him	1Kin 17:8	3068
As the *L* thy God liveth, I have	1Kin 17:12	3068
thus saith the *L* God of Israel	1Kin 17:14	3068
until the day that the *L* sendeth	1Kin 17:14	3068
according to the word of the *L*	1Kin 17:16	3068
And he cried unto the *L*, and said,	1Kin 17:20	3068
O *L* my God, hast thou also	1Kin 17:20	3068
three times, and cried unto the *L*	1Kin 17:21	3068
O *L* my God, I pray thee, let this	1Kin 17:21	3068
the *L* heard the voice of Elijah	1Kin 17:22	3068
that the word of the *L* in thy	1Kin 17:24	3068
that the word of the *L* came to	1Kin 18:1	3068
(Now Obadiah feared the *L* greatly	1Kin 18:3	3068
cut off the prophets of the *L*	1Kin 18:4	3068
As the *L* thy God liveth, there is	1Kin 18:10	3068
that the Spirit of the *L* shall	1Kin 18:12	3068
servant fear the *L* from my youth	1Kin 18:12	3068
slew the prophets of the *L*	1Kin 18:13	3068
As the *L* of hosts liveth, before	1Kin 18:15	3068
the commandments of the *L*	1Kin 18:18	3068
if the *L* be God, follow him	1Kin 18:21	3068
I only, remain a prophet of the *L*	1Kin 18:22	3068
I will call on the name of the *L*	1Kin 18:24	3068
of the *L* that was broken down	1Kin 18:30	3068
unto whom the word of the *L* came	1Kin 18:31	3068
an altar in the name of the *L*	1Kin 18:32	3068
L God of Abraham, Isaac, and of	1Kin 18:36	3068
Hear me, O *L*, hear me, that this	1Kin 18:37	3068
may know that thou art the *L* God	1Kin 18:37	3068
Then the fire of the *L* fell	1Kin 18:38	3068
and they said, The *L*, he is the	1Kin 18:39	3068
the *L*, he is the God	1Kin 18:39	3068
the hand of the *L* was on Elijah	1Kin 18:46	3068
now, O *L*, take away my life	1Kin 19:4	3068
the angel of the *L* came again the	1Kin 19:7	3068
the word of the *L* came to him	1Kin 19:9	3068
jealous for the *L* God of hosts	1Kin 19:10	3068
stand upon the mount before the *L*	1Kin 19:11	3068
the *L* passed by, and a great and	1Kin 19:11	3068
in pieces the rocks before the *L*	1Kin 19:11	3068
but the *L* was not in the wind	1Kin 19:11	3068
but the *L* was not in the	1Kin 19:11	3068
but the *L* was not in the fire	1Kin 19:12	3068
jealous for the *L* God of hosts	1Kin 19:14	3068
the *L* said unto him, Go, return	1Kin 19:15	3068
Israel, saying, Thus saith the *L*	1Kin 20:13	3068
thou shalt know that I am the *L*	1Kin 20:13	3068
And he said, Thus saith the *L*	1Kin 20:14	3068
Israel, and said, Thus saith the *L*	1Kin 20:28	3068
The *L* is God of the hills, but he	1Kin 20:28	3068
and ye shall know that I am the *L*	1Kin 20:28	3068
neighbour in the word of the *L*	1Kin 20:35	3068
not obeyed the voice of the *L*	1Kin 20:36	3068
said unto him, Thus saith the *L*	1Kin 20:42	3068
The *L* forbid it me, that I should	1Kin 21:3	3068
the word of the *L* came to Elijah	1Kin 21:17	3068
him, saying, Thus saith the *L*	1Kin 21:19	3068
him, saying, Thus saith the *L*	1Kin 21:19	3068
work evil in the sight of the *L*	1Kin 21:20	3068
And of Jezebel also spake the *L*	1Kin 21:23	3068
wickedness in the sight of the *L*	1Kin 21:25	3068
whom the *L* cast out before the	1Kin 21:26	3068
the word of the *L* came to Elijah	1Kin 21:28	3068
thee, at the word of the *L* to day	1Kin 22:5	3068
for the *L* shall deliver it into	1Kin 22:6	136
here a prophet of the *L* besides	1Kin 22:7	3068
by whom we may enquire of the *L*	1Kin 22:8	3068
and he said, Thus saith the *L*	1Kin 22:11	3068
for the *L* shall deliver it into	1Kin 22:12	3068
And Micaiah said, As the *L* liveth	1Kin 22:14	3068
what the *L* saith unto me, that	1Kin 22:14	3068
for the *L* shall deliver it into	1Kin 22:15	3068
is true in the name of the *L*	1Kin 22:16	3068
the *L* said, These have no master	1Kin 22:17	3068
thou therefore the word of the *L*	1Kin 22:19	3068
I saw the *L* sitting on his throne	1Kin 22:19	3068
the *L* said, Who shall persuade	1Kin 22:20	3068
a spirit, and stood before the *L*	1Kin 22:21	3068
the *L* said unto him, Wherewith	1Kin 22:22	3068
the *L* hath put a lying spirit in	1Kin 22:23	3068
the *L* hath spoken evil concerning	1Kin 22:23	3068
the *L* from me to speak unto thee	1Kin 22:24	3068
the *L* hath not spoken by me	1Kin 22:28	3068
the word of the *L* which he spake	1Kin 22:38	3068
was right in the eyes of the *L*	1Kin 22:43	3068
he did evil in the sight of the *L*	1Kin 22:52	3068
to anger the *L* God of Israel	1Kin 22:53	3068
But the angel of the *L* said to	2Kin 1:3	3068
Now therefore thus saith the *L*	2Kin 1:4	3068
and say unto him, Thus saith the *L*	2Kin 1:6	3068
angel of the *L* said unto Elijah	2Kin 1:15	3068
said unto him, Thus saith the *L*	2Kin 1:16	3068
of the *L* which Elijah had spoken	2Kin 1:17	3068
when the *L* would take up Elijah	2Kin 2:1	3068
for the *L* hath sent me to Beth-el	2Kin 2:2	3068
said unto him, As the *L* liveth	2Kin 2:2	3068
Knowest thou that the *L* will take	2Kin 2:3	3068
for the *L* hath sent me to Jericho	2Kin 2:4	3068
And he said, As the *L* liveth	2Kin 2:4	3068
Knowest thou that the *L* will take	2Kin 2:5	3068
for the *L* hath sent me to Jordan	2Kin 2:6	3068
And he said, As the *L* liveth	2Kin 2:6	3068
Where is the *L* God of Elijah	2Kin 2:14	3068
Spirit of the *L* hath taken him up	2Kin 2:16	3068
there, and said, Thus saith the *L*	2Kin 2:21	3068
cursed them in the name of the *L*	2Kin 2:24	3068
evil in the sight of the *L*	2Kin 3:2	3068
that the *L* hath called these	2Kin 3:10	3068
there not here a prophet of the *L*	2Kin 3:11	3068
we may enquire of the *L* by him	2Kin 3:11	3068
The word of the *L* is with him	2Kin 3:12	3068
for the *L* hath called these three	2Kin 3:13	3068
As the *L* of hosts liveth, before	2Kin 3:14	3068
the hand of the *L* came upon him	2Kin 3:15	3068
And he said, Thus saith the *L*	2Kin 3:16	3068
For thus saith the *L*, Ye shall	2Kin 3:17	3068
light thing in the sight of the *L*	2Kin 3:18	3068
that thy servant did fear the *L*	2Kin 4:1	3068
the *L* hath hid it from me, and	2Kin 4:27	3068
the child said, As the *L* liveth	2Kin 4:30	3068
them twain, and prayed unto the *L*	2Kin 4:33	3068
for thus saith the *L*, They shall	2Kin 4:43	3068
according to the word of the *L*	2Kin 4:44	3068
because by him the *L* had given	2Kin 5:1	3068
call on the name of the *L* his God	2Kin 5:11	3068
But he said, As the *L* liveth	2Kin 5:16	3068
unto other gods, but unto the *L*	2Kin 5:17	3068
In this thing the *L* pardon thy	2Kin 5:18	3068
the *L* pardon thy servant in this	2Kin 5:18	3068
but, as the *L* liveth, I will run	2Kin 5:20	3068
And Elisha prayed, and said, *L*	2Kin 6:17	3068
the *L* opened the eyes of the	2Kin 6:17	3068
to him, Elisha prayed unto the *L*	2Kin 6:18	3068
into Samaria, that Elisha said, *L*	2Kin 6:20	3068
the *L* opened their eyes, and they	2Kin 6:20	3068
If the *L* do not help thee, whence	2Kin 6:27	3068
Behold, this evil is of the *L*	2Kin 6:33	3068
I wait for the *L* any longer	2Kin 6:33	3068
said, Hear ye the word of the *L*	2Kin 7:1	3068
Thus saith the *L*, To morrow about	2Kin 7:1	3068
if the *L* would make windows in	2Kin 7:2	3068
For the *L* had made the host of	2Kin 7:6	136
according to the word of the *L*	2Kin 7:16	3068
if the *L* should make windows in	2Kin 7:19	3068
for the *L* hath called for a	2Kin 8:1	3068
God, and enquire of the *L* by him	2Kin 8:8	3068
howbeit the *L* hath shewed me that	2Kin 8:10	3068
The *L* hath shewed me that thou	2Kin 8:13	3068
he did evil in the sight of the *L*	2Kin 8:18	3068
Yet the *L* would not destroy Judah	2Kin 8:19	3068
and did evil in the sight of the *L*	2Kin 8:27	3068
head, and say, Thus saith the *L*	2Kin 9:3	3068
Thus saith the *L* God of Israel	2Kin 9:6	3068
king over the people of the *L*	2Kin 9:6	3068
of all the servants of the *L*	2Kin 9:7	3068
to me, saying, Thus saith the *L*	2Kin 9:12	3068
the *L* laid this burden upon him	2Kin 9:25	3068
blood of his sons, saith the *L*	2Kin 9:26	3068
thee in this plat, saith the *L*	2Kin 9:26	3068
according to the word of the *L*	2Kin 9:26	3068
said, This is the word of the *L*	2Kin 9:36	3068
nothing of the word of the *L*	2Kin 10:10	3068
which the *L* spake concerning the	2Kin 10:10	3068
for the *L* hath done that which he	2Kin 10:10	3068
with me, and see my zeal for the *L*	2Kin 10:16	3068
according to the saying of the *L*	2Kin 10:17	3068
you none of the servants of the *L*	2Kin 10:23	3068
the *L* said unto Jehu, Because	2Kin 10:30	3068
the *L* God of Israel with all his	2Kin 10:31	3068
In those days the *L* began to cut	2Kin 10:32	3068
in the house of the *L* six years	2Kin 11:3	3068
to him into the house of the *L*	2Kin 11:4	3068
of them in the house of the *L*	2Kin 11:4	3068
the house of the *L* about the king	2Kin 11:7	3068
that were in the temple of the *L*	2Kin 11:10	3068
people into the temple of the *L*	2Kin 11:13	3068
be slain in the house of the *L*	2Kin 11:15	3068
made a covenant between the *L*	2Kin 11:17	3068
officers over the house of the *L*	2Kin 11:18	3068
the king from the house of the *L*	2Kin 11:19	3068
L all his days wherein Jehoiada	2Kin 12:2	3068
brought into the house of the *L*	2Kin 12:4	3068
to bring into the house of the *L*	2Kin 12:4	3068
cometh into the house of the *L*	2Kin 12:9	3068
brought into the house of the *L*	2Kin 12:9	3068
was found in the house of the *L*	2Kin 12:10	3068
oversight of the house of the *L*	2Kin 12:11	3068
wrought upon the house of the *L*	2Kin 12:11	3068
breaches of the house of the *L*	2Kin 12:12	3068
house of the *L* bowls of silver	2Kin 12:13	3068
brought into the house of the *L*	2Kin 12:13	3068
therewith the house of the *L*	2Kin 12:14	3068
brought into the house of the *L*	2Kin 12:16	3068
treasures of the house of the *L*	2Kin 12:18	3068
was evil in the sight of the *L*	2Kin 13:2	3068
the anger of the *L* was kindled	2Kin 13:3	3068
And Jehoahaz besought the *L*	2Kin 13:4	3068
and the *L* hearkened unto him	2Kin 13:4	3068
the *L* gave Israel a saviour, so	2Kin 13:5	3068
was evil in the sight of the *L*	2Kin 13:11	3068
the *L* was gracious unto them, and	2Kin 13:23	3068
was right in the sight of the *L*	2Kin 14:3	3068
of Moses, wherein the *L* commanded	2Kin 14:6	3068
were found in the house of the *L*	2Kin 14:14	3068
was evil in the sight of the *L*	2Kin 14:24	3068
the word of the *L* God of Israel	2Kin 14:25	3068
For the *L* saw the affliction of	2Kin 14:26	3068
the *L* said not that he would blot	2Kin 14:27	3068
was right in the sight of the *L*	2Kin 15:3	3068
the *L* smote the king, so that he	2Kin 15:5	3068
was evil in the sight of the *L*	2Kin 15:9	3068
of the *L* which he spake unto Jehu	2Kin 15:12	3068
was evil in the sight of the *L*	2Kin 15:18	3068
was evil in the sight of the *L*	2Kin 15:24	3068
was evil in the sight of the *L*	2Kin 15:28	3068
was right in the sight of the *L*	2Kin 15:34	3068
higher gate of the house of the *L*	2Kin 15:35	3068
In those days the *L* began to send	2Kin 15:37	3068
in the sight of the *L* his God	2Kin 16:2	3068
whom the *L* cast out from before	2Kin 16:3	3068
was found in the house of the *L*	2Kin 16:8	3068
altar, which was before the *L*	2Kin 16:14	3068
the altar and the house of the *L*	2Kin 16:14	3068
of the *L* for the king of Assyria	2Kin 16:18	3068
was evil in the sight of the *L*	2Kin 17:2	3068
sinned against the *L* their God	2Kin 17:7	3068
whom the *L* cast out from before	2Kin 17:8	3068
not right against the *L* their God	2Kin 17:9	3068
the *L* carried away before them	2Kin 17:11	3068
things to provoke the *L* to anger	2Kin 17:11	3068
whereof the *L* had said unto them,	2Kin 17:12	3068
Yet the *L* testified against	2Kin 17:13	3068
not believe in the *L* their God	2Kin 17:14	3068
whom the *L* had charged them	2Kin 17:15	3068
commandments of the *L* their God	2Kin 17:16	3068
to do evil in the sight of the *L*	2Kin 17:17	3068
Therefore the *L* was very angry	2Kin 17:18	3068
commandments of the *L* their God	2Kin 17:19	3068
the *L* rejected all the seed of	2Kin 17:20	3068
drave Israel from following the *L*	2Kin 17:21	3068
Until the *L* removed Israel out of	2Kin 17:23	3068
there, that they feared not the *L*	2Kin 17:25	3068
therefore the *L* sent lions among	2Kin 17:25	3068
them how they should fear the *L*	2Kin 17:28	3068
So they feared the *L*, and made	2Kin 17:32	3068
They feared the *L*, and served	2Kin 17:33	3068
they fear not the *L*, neither do	2Kin 17:34	3068
which the *L* commanded	2Kin 17:34	3068
With whom the *L* had made a	2Kin 17:35	3068
But the *L*, who brought you up out	2Kin 17:36	3068
But the *L* your God ye shall fear	2Kin 17:39	3068
So these nations feared the *L*	2Kin 17:41	3068
was right in the sight of the *L*	2Kin 18:3	3068
He trusted in the *L* God of Israel	2Kin 18:5	3068
For he clave to the *L*, and	2Kin 18:6	3068
which the *L* commanded Moses	2Kin 18:6	3068
And the *L* was with him	2Kin 18:7	3068
not the voice of the *L* their God	2Kin 18:12	3068
the servant of the *L* commanded	2Kin 18:12	3068
was found in the house of the *L*	2Kin 18:15	3068
the doors of the temple of the *L*	2Kin 18:16	3068
me, We trust in the *L* our God	2Kin 18:22	3068
Am I now come up without the *L*	2Kin 18:25	3068
The *L* said to me, Go up against	2Kin 18:25	3068
Hezekiah make you trust in the *L*	2Kin 18:30	3068
The *L* will surely deliver us, and	2Kin 18:30	3068
saying, The *L* will deliver us	2Kin 18:32	3068
that the *L* should deliver	2Kin 18:35	3068
and went into the house of the *L*	2Kin 19:1	3068
It may be the *L* thy God will hear	2Kin 19:4	3068
which the *L* thy God hath heard	2Kin 19:4	3068
to your master, Thus saith the *L*	2Kin 19:6	3068
went up into the house of the *L*	2Kin 19:14	3068
and spread it before the *L*	2Kin 19:14	3068
And Hezekiah prayed before the *L*	2Kin 19:15	3068
O *L* God of Israel, which dwellest	2Kin 19:15	3068
L, bow down thine ear, and hear	2Kin 19:16	3068
open, *L*, thine eyes, and see	2Kin 19:16	3068
Of a truth, *L*, the kings of	2Kin 19:17	3068
O *L* our God, I beseech thee, save	2Kin 19:19	3068
may know that thou art the *L* God	2Kin 19:19	3068
Thus saith the *L* God of Israel	2Kin 19:20	3068
This is the word that the *L* hath	2Kin 19:21	3068
thou hast reproached the *L*	2Kin 19:23	3068
the zeal of the *L* of hosts shall	2Kin 19:31	3068
Therefore thus saith the *L*	2Kin 19:32	3068
come into this city, saith the *L*	2Kin 19:33	3068
that the angel of the *L* went out	2Kin 19:35	3068
said unto him, Thus saith the *L*	2Kin 20:1	3068
to the wall, and prayed unto the *L*	2Kin 20:2	3068
I beseech thee, O *L*, remember now	2Kin 20:3	3068
the word of the *L* came to him	2Kin 20:4	3068
of my people, Thus saith the *L*	2Kin 20:5	3068
go up unto the house of the *L*	2Kin 20:5	3068
the sign that the *L* will heal me	2Kin 20:8	3068
the house of the *L* the third day	2Kin 20:8	3068
sign shalt thou have of the *L*	2Kin 20:9	3068
that the *L* will do the thing that	2Kin 20:9	3068
the prophet cried unto the *L*	2Kin 20:11	3068
Hezekiah, Hear the word of the *L*	2Kin 20:16	3068
shall be left, saith the *L*	2Kin 20:17	3068
of the *L* which thou hast spoken	2Kin 20:19	3068
was evil in the sight of the *L*	2Kin 21:2	3068
whom the *L* cast out before the	2Kin 21:2	3068
of the *L*, of which the *L* said	2Kin 21:4	3068
two courts of the house of the *L*	2Kin 21:5	3068

wickedness in the sight of the *L* 2Kin 21:6 3068
of which the *L* said to David, and 2Kin 21:7 3068
L destroyed before the children 2Kin 21:9 3068
the *L* spake by his servants the 2Kin 21:10 3068
thus saith the *L* God of Israel 2Kin 21:12 3068
was evil in the sight of the *L* 2Kin 21:16 3068
was evil in the sight of the *L* 2Kin 21:20 3068
he forsook the *L* God of his 2Kin 21:22 3068
and walked not in the way of the *L* 2Kin 21:22 3068
was right in the sight of the *L* 2Kin 22:2 3068
the scribe, to the house of the *L* 2Kin 22:3 3068
brought into the house of the *L* 2Kin 22:4 3068
oversight of the house of the *L* 2Kin 22:5 3068
which is in the house of the *L* 2Kin 22:5 3068
of the law in the house of the *L* 2Kin 22:8 3068
oversight of the house of the *L* 2Kin 22:9 3068
Go ye, enquire of the *L* for me 2Kin 22:13 3068
the *L* that is kindled against us 2Kin 22:13 3068
Thus saith the *L* God of Israel 2Kin 22:15 3068
Thus saith the *L*, Behold, I will 2Kin 22:16 3068
sent you to enquire of the *L* 2Kin 22:18 3068
Thus saith the *L* God of Israel 2Kin 22:18 3068
hast humbled thyself before the *L* 2Kin 22:19 3068
also have heard thee, saith the *L* 2Kin 22:19 3068
went up into the house of the *L* 2Kin 23:2 3068
was found in the house of the *L* 2Kin 23:2 3068
and made a covenant before the *L* 2Kin 23:3 3068
to walk after the *L* 2Kin 23:3 3068
L all the vessels that were made 2Kin 23:4 3068
the grove from the house of the *L* 2Kin 23:6 3068
that were by the house of the *L* 2Kin 23:7 3068
the altar of the *L* in Jerusalem 2Kin 23:9 3068
entering in of the house of the *L* 2Kin 23:11 3068
two courts of the house of the *L* 2Kin 23:12 3068
according to the word of the *L* 2Kin 23:16 3068
made to provoke the *L* to anger 2Kin 23:19
the passover unto the *L* your God 2Kin 23:21 3068
was holden to the *L* in Jerusalem 2Kin 23:23 3068
found in the house of the *L* 2Kin 23:24 3068
to the *L* with all his heart 2Kin 23:25 3068
Notwithstanding the *L* turned not 2Kin 23:26 3068
the *L* said, I will remove Judah 2Kin 23:27 3068
was evil in the sight of the *L* 2Kin 23:32 3068
was evil in the sight of the *L* 2Kin 23:37 3068
the *L* sent against him bands of 2Kin 24:2 3068
according to the word of the *L* 2Kin 24:2 3068
of the *L* came this upon Judah 2Kin 24:3 3068
which the *L* would not pardon 2Kin 24:4 3068
was evil in the sight of the *L* 2Kin 24:9 3068
treasures of the house of the *L* 2Kin 24:13 3068
had made in the temple of the *L* 2Kin 24:13 3068
as the *L* had said 2Kin 24:13 3068
was evil in the sight of the *L* 2Kin 24:19 3068
L it came to pass in Jerusalem 2Kin 24:20 3068
And he burnt the house of the *L* 2Kin 25:9 3068
that were in the house of the *L* 2Kin 25:13 3068
that was in the house of the *L* 2Kin 25:13 3068
had made for the house of the *L* 2Kin 25:16 3068
was evil in the sight of the *L* 1Chr 2:3 3068
when the *L* carried away Judah and 1Chr 6:15 3068
of song in the house of the *L* 1Chr 6:31 3068
the house of the *L* in Jerusalem 1Chr 6:32 3068
being over the host of the *L* 1Chr 9:19 3068
time past, and the *L* was with him 1Chr 9:20 3068
the gates of the house of the *L* 1Chr 9:23 3068
which he committed against the *L* 1Chr 10:13 3068
even against the word of the *L* 1Chr 10:13 3068
And enquired not of the *L* 1Chr 10:14 3068
the *L* thy God said unto thee, 1Chr 11:2 3068
with them in Hebron before the *L* 1Chr 11:3 3068
to the word of the *L* by Samuel 1Chr 11:3 3068
for the *L* of hosts was with him 1Chr 11:9 3068
word of the *L* concerning Israel 1Chr 11:10 3068
the *L* saved them by a great 1Chr 11:14 3068
of it, but poured it out to the *L* 1Chr 11:18 3068
according to the word of the *L* 1Chr 12:23 3068
and that it be of the *L* our God 1Chr 13:2 3068
up thence the ark of God the *L* 1Chr 13:6 3068
the anger of the *L* was kindled 1Chr 13:10 3068
because the *L* had made a breach 1Chr 13:11 3068
the *L* blessed the house of 1Chr 13:14 3068
David perceived that the *L* had 1Chr 14:2 3068
the *L* said unto him, Go up 1Chr 14:10 3068
the *L* brought the fear of him 1Chr 14:17 3068
for them hath the *L* chosen to 1Chr 15:2 3068
the ark of the *L* unto his place 1Chr 15:3 3068
L God of Israel unto the place 1Chr 15:12 3068
the *L* our God made a breach upon 1Chr 15:13 3068
up the ark of the *L* God of Israel 1Chr 15:14 3068
according to the word of the *L* 1Chr 15:15 3068
L out of the house of Obed-edom 1Chr 15:25 3068
the ark of the covenant of the *L* 1Chr 15:26 3068
covenant of the *L* with shouting 1Chr 15:28 3068
the *L* came to the city of David 1Chr 15:29 3068
the people in the name of the *L* 1Chr 16:2 3068
minister before the ark of the *L* 1Chr 16:4 3068
praise the *L* God of Israel 1Chr 16:4 3068
the *L* into the hand of Asaph 1Chr 16:7 3068
Give thanks unto the *L*, call upon 1Chr 16:8 3068
of them rejoice that seek the *L* 1Chr 16:10 3068
Seek the *L* and his strength, seek 1Chr 16:11 3068
He is the *L* our God 1Chr 16:14 3068
Sing unto the *L*, all the earth 1Chr 16:23 3068
For great is the *L*, and greatly to 1Chr 16:25 3068
but the *L* made the heavens 1Chr 16:26 3068
Give unto the *L*, ye kindreds of 1Chr 16:28 3068
the people, give unto the *L* glory 1Chr 16:28 3068
Give unto the *L* the glory due 1Chr 16:29 3068

worship the *L* in the beauty of 1Chr 16:29 3068
among the nations, The *L* reigneth 1Chr 16:31 3068
sing out at the presence of the *L* 1Chr 16:33 3068
O give thanks unto the *L* 1Chr 16:34 3068
Blessed be the *L* God of Israel 1Chr 16:36 3068
said, Amen, and praised the *L* 1Chr 16:36 3068
of the covenant of the *L* Asaph 1Chr 16:37 3068
before the tabernacle of the *L* in 1Chr 16:39 3068
the *L* upon the altar of the burnt 1Chr 16:40 3068
is written in the law of the *L* 1Chr 16:40 3068
by name, to give thanks to the *L* 1Chr 16:41 3068
of the *L* remaineth under curtains 1Chr 17:1 3068
my servant, Thus saith the *L* 1Chr 17:4 3068
David, Thus saith the *L* of hosts 1Chr 17:7 3068
I tell thee that the *L* will build 1Chr 17:10 3068
the king came and sat before the *L* 1Chr 17:16 3068
O *L* God, and what is mine house, 1Chr 17:16 3068
of a man of high degree, O *L* God 1Chr 17:17 3068
O *L*, for thy servant's sake, and 1Chr 17:19 3068
O *L*, there is none like thee, 1Chr 17:20 3068
and thou, *L*, becamest their God 1Chr 17:22 3068
Therefore now, *L*, let the thing 1Chr 17:23 3068
The *L* of hosts is the God of 1Chr 17:24 3068
And now, *L*, thou art God, and hast 1Chr 17:26 3068
for thou blessest, O *L*, and it 1Chr 17:27 3068
Thus the *L* preserved David 1Chr 18:6 3068
king David dedicated unto the *L* 1Chr 18:11 3068
Thus the *L* preserved David 1Chr 18:13 3068
let the *L* do that which is good 1Chr 19:13 3068
The *L* make his people an hundred 1Chr 21:3 3068
the *L* spake unto Gad, David's 1Chr 21:9 3068
David, saying, Thus saith the *L* 1Chr 21:10 3068
said unto him, Thus saith the *L* 1Chr 21:11 3068
three days the sword of the *L* 1Chr 21:12 3068
the angel of the *L* destroying 1Chr 21:12 3068
fall now into the hand of the *L* 1Chr 21:13 3068
So the *L* sent pestilence upon 1Chr 21:14 3068
the *L* beheld, and he repented him 1Chr 21:15 3068
the angel of the *L* stood by the 1Chr 21:15 3068
saw the angel of the *L* stand 1Chr 21:16 3068
O *L* my God, be on me, and on my 1Chr 21:17 3068
Then the angel of the *L* commanded 1Chr 21:18 3068
set up an altar unto the *L* in the 1Chr 21:18 3068
he spake in the name of the *L* 1Chr 21:19 3068
build an altar therein unto the *L* 1Chr 21:22 3068
that which is thine for the *L* 1Chr 21:24 3068
built there an altar unto the *L* 1Chr 21:26 3068
offerings, and called upon the *L* 1Chr 21:26 3068
the *L* commanded the angel 1Chr 21:27 3068
the *L* had answered him in the 1Chr 21:28 3068
For the tabernacle of the *L* 1Chr 21:29 3068
the sword of the angel of the *L* 1Chr 21:30 3068
This is the house of the *L* God 1Chr 22:1 3068
L must be exceeding magnifical 1Chr 22:5 3068
an house for the *L* God of Israel 1Chr 22:6 3068
unto the name of the *L* my God 1Chr 22:7 3068
But the word of the *L* came to me 1Chr 22:8 3068
Now, my son, the *L* be with thee 1Chr 22:11 3068
build the house of the *L* thy God 1Chr 22:11 3068
Only the *L* give thee wisdom and 1Chr 22:12 3068
keep the law of the *L* thy God 1Chr 22:12 3068
judgments which the *L* charged 1Chr 22:13 3068
prepared for the house of the *L* 1Chr 22:14 3068
be doing, and the *L* be with thee 1Chr 22:16 3068
Is not the *L* your God with you 1Chr 22:18 3068
the land is subdued before the *L* 1Chr 22:18 3068
your soul to seek the *L* your God 1Chr 22:19 3068
ye the sanctuary of the *L* God 1Chr 22:19 3068
the ark of the covenant of the *L* 1Chr 22:19 3068
to be built to the name of the *L* 1Chr 22:19 3068
the work of the house of the *L* 1Chr 23:4 3068
four thousand praised the *L* with 1Chr 23:5 3068
to burn incense before the *L* 1Chr 23:13 3068
the service of the house of the *L* 1Chr 23:24 3068
The *L* God of Israel hath given 1Chr 23:25 3068
the service of the house of the *L* 1Chr 23:28 3068
morning to thank and praise the *L* 1Chr 23:30 3068
unto the *L* in the sabbaths 1Chr 23:31 3068
them, continually before the *L* 1Chr 23:31 3068
the service of the house of the *L* 1Chr 23:32 3068
to come into the house of the *L* 1Chr 24:19 3068
as the *L* God of Israel had 1Chr 24:19 3068
to give thanks and to praise the *L* 1Chr 25:3 3068
for song in the house of the *L* 1Chr 25:6 3068
instructed in the songs of the *L* 1Chr 25:7 3068
to minister in the house of the *L* 1Chr 26:12 3068
treasures of the house of the *L* 1Chr 26:22 3068
to maintain the house of the *L* 1Chr 26:27 3068
in all the business of the *L* 1Chr 26:30 3068
because the *L* had said he would 1Chr 27:23 3068
the ark of the covenant of the *L* 1Chr 28:2 3068
Howbeit the *L* God of Israel chose 1Chr 28:4 3068
(for the *L* hath given me many 1Chr 28:5 3068
the kingdom of the *L* over Israel 1Chr 28:5 3068
Israel the congregation of the *L* 1Chr 28:8 3068
commandments of the *L* your God 1Chr 28:8 3068
for the *L* searcheth all hearts, 1Chr 28:9 3068
for the *L* hath chosen thee to 1Chr 28:10 3068
the courts of the house of the *L* 1Chr 28:12 3068
the service of the house of the *L* 1Chr 28:13 3068
of service in the house of the *L* 1Chr 28:13 3068
the ark of the covenant of the *L* 1Chr 28:18 3068
the *L* made me understand in 1Chr 28:19 3068
for the *L* God, even my God, will 1Chr 28:20 3068
the service of the house of the *L* 1Chr 28:20 3068
is not for man, but for the *L* God 1Chr 29:1 3068
his service this day unto the *L* 1Chr 29:5 3068
treasure of the house of the *L* 1Chr 29:8 3068

they offered willingly to the *L* 1Chr 29:9 3068
the *L* before all the congregation 1Chr 29:10 3068
L God of Israel our father, for 1Chr 29:10 3068
Thine, O *L*, is the greatness, and 1Chr 29:11 3068
thine is the kingdom, O *L* 1Chr 29:11 3068
O *L* our God, all this store that 1Chr 29:16 3068
O *L* God of Abraham, Isaac, and of 1Chr 29:18 3068
Now bless the *L* your God 1Chr 29:20 3068
the *L* God of their fathers 1Chr 29:20 3068
their heads, and worshipped the *L* 1Chr 29:20 3068
sacrificed sacrifices unto the *L* 1Chr 29:21 3068
burnt offerings unto the *L* 1Chr 29:21 3068
drink before the *L* on that day 1Chr 29:22 3068
anointed him unto the *L* to be the 1Chr 29:22 3068
sat on the throne of the *L* as 1Chr 29:23 3068
And the *L* magnified Solomon 1Chr 29:25 3068
the *L* his God was with him, and 2Chr 1:1 3068
the *L* had made in the wilderness 2Chr 1:3 3068
before the tabernacle of the *L* 2Chr 1:5 3068
to the brasen altar before the *L* 2Chr 1:6 3068
O *L* God, let thy promise unto 2Chr 1:9 3068
an house for the name of the *L* 2Chr 2:1 3068
house to the name of the *L* my God 2Chr 2:4 3068
solemn feasts of the *L* our God 2Chr 2:4 3068
Because the *L* hath loved his 2Chr 2:11 3068
Blessed be the *L* God of Israel 2Chr 2:12 3068
might build an house for the *L* 2Chr 2:12 3068
L at Jerusalem in mount Moriah 2Chr 3:1 3068
where the *L* appeared unto David 2Chr 3:1
house of the *L* of bright brass 2Chr 4:16 3068
the house of the *L* was finished 2Chr 5:1 3068
of the *L* out of the city of David 2Chr 5:2 3068
covenant of the *L* unto his place 2Chr 5:7 3068
when the *L* made a covenant with 2Chr 5:10 3068
in praising and thanking the *L* 2Chr 5:13 3068
of musick, and praised the *L* 2Chr 5:13 3068
a cloud, even the house of the *L* 2Chr 5:13 3068
for the glory of the *L* had filled 2Chr 5:14 3068
The *L* hath said that he would 2Chr 6:1 3068
Blessed be the *L* God of Israel 2Chr 6:4 3068
the name of the *L* God of Israel 2Chr 6:7 3068
But the *L* said to David my father 2Chr 6:8 3068
The *L* therefore hath performed 2Chr 6:10 3068
as the *L* promised, and have built 2Chr 6:10 3068
the name of the *L* God of Israel 2Chr 6:10 3068
wherein is the covenant of the *L* 2Chr 6:11 3068
the *L* in the presence of all the 2Chr 6:12 3068
O *L* God of Israel, there is no 2Chr 6:14 3068
O *L* God of Israel, keep with thy 2Chr 6:16 3068
O *L* God of Israel, let thy word 2Chr 6:17 3068
O *L* my God, to hearken unto the 2Chr 6:19 3068
O *L* God, into thy resting place, 2Chr 6:41 3068
priests, O *L* God, be clothed with 2Chr 6:41 3068
O *L* God, turn not away the face 2Chr 6:42 3068
glory of the *L* filled the house 2Chr 7:1 3068
not enter into the house of the *L* 2Chr 7:2 3068
because the glory of the *L* had 2Chr 7:2 3068
the glory of the *L* upon the house 2Chr 7:3 3068
and worshipped, and praised the *L* 2Chr 7:3 3068
offered sacrifices before the *L* 2Chr 7:4 3068
instruments of musick of the *L* 2Chr 7:6 3068
the king had made to praise the *L* 2Chr 7:6 3068
was before the house of the *L* 2Chr 7:7 3068
that the *L* had shewed unto David 2Chr 7:10 3068
finished the house of the *L* 2Chr 7:11 3068
to make in the house of the *L* 2Chr 7:11 3068
the *L* appeared to Solomon by 2Chr 7:12 3068
Why hath the *L* done thus unto 2Chr 7:21 3068
the *L* God of their fathers 2Chr 7:22 3068
had built the house of the *L* 2Chr 8:1 3068
the ark of the *L* hath come 2Chr 8:11 3068
the *L* on the altar of the *L* 2Chr 8:12 3068
foundation of the house of the *L* 2Chr 8:16 3068
the house of the *L* was perfected 2Chr 8:16 3068
went up into the house of the *L* 2Chr 9:4 3068
Blessed be the *L* thy God, which 2Chr 9:8 3068
to be king for the *L* thy God 2Chr 9:8 3068
terraces to the house of the *L* 2Chr 9:11 3068
that the *L* might perform his word 2Chr 10:15 3068
But the word of the *L* came to 2Chr 11:2 3068
Thus saith the *L*, Ye shall not go 2Chr 11:4 3068
And they obeyed the words of the *L* 2Chr 11:4 3068
the priest's office unto the *L* 2Chr 11:14 3068
L God of Israel came to Jerusalem 2Chr 11:16 3068
unto the *L* God of their fathers 2Chr 11:16 3068
he forsook the law of the *L* 2Chr 12:1 3068
had transgressed against the *L* 2Chr 12:2 3068
said unto them, Thus saith the *L* 2Chr 12:5 3068
and they said, The *L* is righteous 2Chr 12:6 3068
when the *L* saw that they humbled 2Chr 12:7 3068
the word of the *L* came to 2Chr 12:7 3068
treasures of the house of the *L* 2Chr 12:9 3068
entered into the house of the *L* 2Chr 12:11 3068
wrath of the *L* turned from him 2Chr 12:12 3068
the city which the *L* had chosen 2Chr 12:13 3068
not his heart to seek the *L* 2Chr 12:14 3068
Ought ye not to know that the *L* 2Chr 13:5 3068
the *L* in the hand of the sons of 2Chr 13:8 3068
not cast out the priests of the *L* 2Chr 13:9 3068
the *L* is our God, and we have not 2Chr 13:10 3068
which minister unto the *L* 2Chr 13:10 3068
burn unto the *L* every morning 2Chr 13:11 3068
keep the charge of the *L* our God 2Chr 13:11 3068
against the *L* God of your fathers 2Chr 13:12 3068
and they cried unto the *L*, and the 2Chr 13:14 3068
upon the *L* God of their fathers 2Chr 13:18 3068
the *L* struck him, and he died 2Chr 13:20 3068
in the eyes of the *L* his God 2Chr 14:2 3068

seek the *L* God of their fathers 2Chr 14:4 3068
because the *L* had given him rest 2Chr 14:6 3068
we have sought the *L* our God 2Chr 14:7 3068
unto the *L* his God, and said, *L* 2Chr 14:11 3068
help us, O *L* our God 2Chr 14:11 3068
O *L*, thou art our God 2Chr 14:11 3068
So the *L* smote the Ethiopians 2Chr 14:12 3068
they were destroyed before the *L* 2Chr 14:13 3068
the fear of the *L* came upon them 2Chr 14:14 3068
The *L* is with you, while ye be 2Chr 15:2 3068
did turn unto the *L* God of Israel 2Chr 15:4 3068
and renewed the altar of the *L* 2Chr 15:8 3068
was before the porch of the *L* 2Chr 15:8 3068
that the *L* his God was with him 2Chr 15:9 3068
offered unto the *L* the same time 2Chr 15:11 3068
into a covenant to seek the *L* God 2Chr 15:12 3068
whosoever would not seek the *L* 2Chr 15:13 3068
unto the *L* with a loud voice 2Chr 15:14 3068
the *L* gave them rest round about 2Chr 15:15 3068
treasures of the house of the *L* 2Chr 16:2 3068
and not relied on the *L* thy God 2Chr 16:7 3068
because thou didst rely on the *L* 2Chr 16:8 3068
For the eyes of the *L* run to 2Chr 16:9 3068
disease he sought not to the *L* 2Chr 16:12 3068
the *L* was with Jehoshaphat, 2Chr 17:3 3068
sought to the *L* God of his father 2Chr 17:4 3068
Therefore the *L* stablished the 2Chr 17:5 3068
lifted up in the ways of the *L* 2Chr 17:6 3068
of the law of the *L* with them 2Chr 17:9 3068
the fear of the *L* fell upon all 2Chr 17:10 3068
offered himself unto the *L* 2Chr 17:16 3068
thee, at the word of the *L* to day 2Chr 18:4 3068
here a prophet of the *L* besides 2Chr 18:6 3068
by whom we may enquire of the *L* 2Chr 18:7 3068
iron, and said, Thus saith the *L* 2Chr 18:10 3068
for the *L* shall deliver it into 2Chr 18:11 3068
And Micaiah said, As the *L* liveth 2Chr 18:13 3068
truth to me in the name of the *L* 2Chr 18:15 3068
the *L* said, These have no master 2Chr 18:16 3068
Therefore hear the word of the *L* 2Chr 18:18 3068
I saw the *L* sitting upon his 2Chr 18:18 3068
the *L* said, Who shall entice Ahab 2Chr 18:19 3068
a spirit, and stood before the *L* 2Chr 18:20 3068
the *L* said unto him, Wherewith 2Chr 18:20 3068
the *L* said, Thou shalt entice him 2Chr 18:21
the *L* hath put a lying spirit in 2Chr 18:22 3068
the *L* hath spoken evil against 2Chr 18:22 3068
the *L* from me to speak unto thee 2Chr 18:23 3068
then hath not the *L* spoken by me 2Chr 18:27 3068
cried out, and the *L* helped him 2Chr 18:31 3068
and love them that hate the *L* 2Chr 19:2 3068
wrath upon thee from before the *L* 2Chr 19:2 3068
unto the *L* God of their fathers 2Chr 19:4 3068
judge not for man, but for the *L* 2Chr 19:6 3068
let the fear of the *L* be upon you 2Chr 19:7 3068
is no iniquity with the *L* our God 2Chr 19:7 3068
Israel, for the judgment of the *L* 2Chr 19:8 3068
shall ye do in the fear of the *L* 2Chr 19:9 3068
they trespass not against the *L* 2Chr 19:10 3068
over you in all matters of the *L* 2Chr 19:11 3068
the *L* shall be with the good 2Chr 19:11 3068
and set himself to seek the *L* 2Chr 20:3 3068
together, to ask help of the *L* 2Chr 20:4 3068
of Judah they came to seek the *L* 2Chr 20:4 3068
Jerusalem, in the house of the *L* 2Chr 20:5 3068
O *L* God of our fathers, art not 2Chr 20:6 3068
And all Judah stood before the *L* 2Chr 20:13 3068
of the *L* in the midst of the 2Chr 20:14 3068
Thus saith the *L* unto you 2Chr 20:15 3068
the salvation of the *L* with you 2Chr 20:17 3068
for the *L* will be with you 2Chr 20:17 3068
the *L*, worshipping the *L* 2Chr 20:18 3068
stood up to praise the *L* God of 2Chr 20:19 3068
Believe in the *L* your God 2Chr 20:20 3068
he appointed singers unto the *L* 2Chr 20:21 3068
the army, and to say, Praise the *L* 2Chr 20:21 3068
the *L* set ambushments against the 2Chr 20:22 3068
for there they blessed the *L* 2Chr 20:26 3068
for the *L* had made them to 2Chr 20:27 3068
trumpets unto the house of the *L* 2Chr 20:28 3068
when they had heard that the *L* 2Chr 20:29 3068
was right in the sight of the *L* 2Chr 20:32 3068
the *L* hath broken thy works 2Chr 20:37 3068
was evil in the eyes of the *L* 2Chr 21:6 3068
Howbeit the *L* would not destroy 2Chr 21:7 3068
forsaken the *L* God of his fathers 2Chr 21:10 3068
Thus saith the *L* God of David thy 2Chr 21:12 3068
will the *L* smite thy people 2Chr 21:14 3068
Moreover the *L* stirred up against 2Chr 21:16 3068
after all this the *L* smote him in 2Chr 21:18 3068
of the *L* like the house of Ahab 2Chr 22:4 3068
whom the *L* had anointed to cut 2Chr 22:7 3068
who sought the *L* with all his 2Chr 22:9 3068
as the *L* hath said of the sons of 2Chr 23:3 3068
the courts of the house of the *L* 2Chr 23:5 3068
none come into the house of the *L* 2Chr 23:6 3068
shall keep the watch of the *L* 2Chr 23:6 3068
people into the house of the *L* 2Chr 23:12 3068
her not in the house of the *L* 2Chr 23:14 3068
L by the hand of the priests the 2Chr 23:18 3068
distributed in the house of the *L* 2Chr 23:18 3068
the burnt offerings of the *L* 2Chr 23:18 3068
the gates of the house of the *L* 2Chr 23:19 3068
the king from the house of the *L* 2Chr 23:20 3068
L all the days of Jehoiada the 2Chr 24:2 3068
to repair the house of the *L* 2Chr 24:4 3068
of Moses the servant of the *L* 2Chr 24:6 3068
things of the house of the *L* did 2Chr 24:7 3068
at the gate of the house of the *L* 2Chr 24:8 3068
to bring in to the *L* the 2Chr 24:9 3068
the service of the house of the *L* 2Chr 24:12 3068
to repair the house of the *L* 2Chr 24:12 3068
brass to mend the house of the *L* 2Chr 24:12 3068
vessels for the house of the *L* 2Chr 24:14 3068
the *L* continually all the days of 2Chr 24:14 3068
of the *L* God of their fathers 2Chr 24:18 3068
to bring them again unto the *L* 2Chr 24:19 3068
ye the commandments of the *L* 2Chr 24:20 3068
because ye have forsaken the *L* 2Chr 24:20 3068
the court of the house of the *L* 2Chr 24:21 3068
The *L* look upon it, and require it 2Chr 24:22 3068
the *L* delivered a very great host 2Chr 24:24 3068
the *L* God of their fathers 2Chr 24:24 3068
was right in the sight of the *L* 2Chr 25:2 3068
of Moses, where the *L* commanded 2Chr 25:4 3068
for the *L* is not with Israel, to 2Chr 25:7 3068
The *L* is able to give thee much 2Chr 25:9 3068
Wherefore the anger of the *L* was 2Chr 25:15 3068
turn away from following the *L* 2Chr 25:27 3068
was right in the sight of the *L* 2Chr 26:4 3068
and as long as he sought the *L* 2Chr 26:5 3068
against the *L* his God 2Chr 26:16 3068
went into the temple of the *L* to 2Chr 26:16 3068
him fourscore priests of the *L* 2Chr 26:17 3068
to burn incense unto the *L* 2Chr 26:18 3068
for thine honour from the *L* God 2Chr 26:18 3068
the priests in the house of the *L* 2Chr 26:19 3068
because the *L* had smitten him 2Chr 26:20 3068
cut off from the house of the *L* 2Chr 26:21 3068
was right in the sight of the *L* 2Chr 27:2 3068
not into the temple of the *L* 2Chr 27:2 3068
high gate of the house of the *L* 2Chr 27:3 3068
his ways before the *L* his God 2Chr 27:6 3068
was right in the sight of the *L* 2Chr 28:1 3068
the *L* had cast out before the 2Chr 28:3 3068
Wherefore the *L* his God delivered 2Chr 28:5 3068
the *L* God of their fathers 2Chr 28:6 3068
But a prophet of the *L* was there 2Chr 28:9 3068
because the *L* God of your fathers 2Chr 28:9 3068
you, sins against the *L* your God 2Chr 28:10 3068
fierce wrath of the *L* is upon you 2Chr 28:11 3068
offended against the *L* already 2Chr 28:13 3068
For the *L* brought Judah low 2Chr 28:19 3068
transgressed sore against the *L* 2Chr 28:19 3068
portion out of the house of the *L* 2Chr 28:21 3068
trespass yet more against the *L* 2Chr 28:22 3068
the doors of the house of the *L* 2Chr 28:24 3068
to anger the *L* God of his fathers 2Chr 28:25 3068
was right in the sight of the *L* 2Chr 29:2 3068
the doors of the house of the *L* 2Chr 29:3 3068
of the *L* God of your fathers 2Chr 29:5 3068
evil in the eyes of the *L* our God 2Chr 29:6 3068
from the habitation of the *L* 2Chr 29:6 3068
the wrath of the *L* was upon Judah 2Chr 29:8 3068
covenant with the *L* God of Israel 2Chr 29:10 3068
for the *L* hath chosen you to 2Chr 29:11 3068
the king, by the words of the *L* 2Chr 29:15 3068
to cleanse the house of the *L* 2Chr 29:15 3068
inner part of the house of the *L* 2Chr 29:16 3068
L into the court of the house of 2Chr 29:16 3068
the court of the house of the *L* 2Chr 29:16 3068
came they to the porch of the *L* 2Chr 29:17 3068
the house of the *L* in eight days 2Chr 29:17 3068
cleansed all the house of the *L* 2Chr 29:18 3068
are before the altar of the *L* 2Chr 29:19 3068
and went up to the house of the *L* 2Chr 29:20 3068
offer them on the altar of the *L* 2Chr 29:21 3068
the house of the *L* with cymbals 2Chr 29:25 3068
of the *L* by his prophets 2Chr 29:25 3068
the song of the *L* began also with 2Chr 29:27 3068
the *L* with the words of David 2Chr 29:30 3068
consecrated yourselves unto the *L* 2Chr 29:31 3068
offerings into the house of the *L* 2Chr 29:31 3068
for a burnt offering to the *L* 2Chr 29:32 3068
house of the *L* was set in order 2Chr 29:35 3068
the house of the *L* at Jerusalem 2Chr 30:1 3068
passover unto the *L* God of Israel 2Chr 30:1 3068
the *L* God of Israel at Jerusalem 2Chr 30:5 3068
again unto the *L* God of Abraham 2Chr 30:6 3068
the *L* God of their fathers 2Chr 30:7 3068
but yield yourselves unto the *L* 2Chr 30:8 3068
and serve the *L* your God, that the 2Chr 30:8 3068
For if ye turn again unto the *L* 2Chr 30:9 3068
for the *L* your God is gracious and 2Chr 30:9 3068
the princes, by the word of the *L* 2Chr 30:12 3068
offerings into the house of the *L* 2Chr 30:15 3068
to sanctify them unto the *L* 2Chr 30:17 3068
The good *L* pardon every one 2Chr 30:18 3068
the *L* God of his fathers, though 2Chr 30:19 3068
the *L* hearkened to Hezekiah, and 2Chr 30:20 3068
priests praised the *L* day by day 2Chr 30:21 3068
with loud instruments unto the *L* 2Chr 30:21 3068
the good knowledge of the *L* 2Chr 30:22 3068
to the *L* God of their fathers 2Chr 30:22 3068
the gates of the tents of the *L* 2Chr 31:2 3068
it is written in the law of the *L* 2Chr 31:3 3068
be encouraged in the law of the *L* 2Chr 31:4 3068
consecrated unto the *L* their God 2Chr 31:6 3068
saw the heaps, they blessed the *L* 2Chr 31:8 3068
offerings into the house of the *L* 2Chr 31:10 3068
for the *L* hath blessed his people 2Chr 31:10 3068
chambers in the house of the *L* 2Chr 31:11 3068
distribute the oblations of the *L* 2Chr 31:14 3068
entereth into the house of the *L* 2Chr 31:16 3068
and truth before the *L* his God 2Chr 31:20 3068
us is the *L* our God to help us 2Chr 32:8 3068
The *L* our God shall deliver us 2Chr 32:11 3068
spake yet more against the *L* God 2Chr 32:16 3068
to rail on the *L* God of Israel 2Chr 32:17 3068
the *L* sent an angel, which cut 2Chr 32:21 3068
Thus the *L* saved Hezekiah and the 2Chr 32:22 3068
gifts unto the *L* to Jerusalem 2Chr 32:23 3068
the death, and prayed unto the *L* 2Chr 32:24 3068
so that the wrath of the *L* came 2Chr 32:26 3068
was evil in the sight of the *L* 2Chr 33:2 3068
whom the *L* had cast out before 2Chr 33:2 3068
altars in the house of the *L* 2Chr 33:4 3068
whereof the *L* had said 2Chr 33:4 3068
two courts of the house of the *L* 2Chr 33:5 3068
much evil in the sight of the *L* 2Chr 33:6 3068
whom the *L* had destroyed before 2Chr 33:9 3068
the *L* spake to Manasseh, and to 2Chr 33:10 3068
Wherefore the *L* brought upon them 2Chr 33:11 3068
he besought the *L* his God 2Chr 33:12 3068
knew that the *L* he was God 2Chr 33:13 3068
idol out of the house of the *L* 2Chr 33:15 3068
the mount of the house of the *L* 2Chr 33:15 3068
And he repaired the altar of the *L* 2Chr 33:16 3068
to serve the *L* God of Israel 2Chr 33:16 3068
yet unto the *L* their God only 2Chr 33:17 3068
the name of the *L* God of Israel 2Chr 33:18 3068
was evil in the sight of the *L* 2Chr 33:22 3068
humbled not himself before the *L* 2Chr 33:23 3068
was right in the sight of the *L* 2Chr 34:2 3068
repair the house of the *L* his God 2Chr 34:8 3068
oversight of the house of the *L* 2Chr 34:10 3068
wrought in the house of the *L* 2Chr 34:10 3068
brought into the house of the *L* 2Chr 34:14 3068
the law of the *L* given by Moses 2Chr 34:14 3068
of the law in the house of the *L* 2Chr 34:15 3068
was found in the house of the *L* 2Chr 34:17 3068
Go, enquire of the *L* for me 2Chr 34:21 3068
the *L* that is poured out upon us 2Chr 34:21 3068
have not kept the word of the *L* 2Chr 34:21 3068
Thus saith the *L* God of Israel 2Chr 34:23 3068
Thus saith the *L*, Behold, I will 2Chr 34:24 3068
who sent you to enquire of the *L* 2Chr 34:26 3068
Thus saith the *L* God of Israel 2Chr 34:26 3068
even heard thee also, saith the *L* 2Chr 34:27 3068
went up into the house of the *L* 2Chr 34:30 3068
was found in the house of the *L* 2Chr 34:30 3068
and made a covenant before the *L* 2Chr 34:31 3068
to walk after the *L* 2Chr 34:31 3068
even to serve the *L* their God 2Chr 34:33 3068
departed not from following the *L* 2Chr 34:33 3068
passover unto the *L* in Jerusalem 2Chr 35:1 3068
the service of the house of the *L* 2Chr 35:2 3068
which were holy unto the *L* 2Chr 35:3 3068
serve now the *L* your God, and his 2Chr 35:3 3068
of the *L* by the hand of Moses 2Chr 35:6 3068
the people, to offer unto the *L* 2Chr 35:12 3068
the *L* was prepared the same day 2Chr 35:16 3068
offerings upon the altar of the *L* 2Chr 35:16 3068
was written in the law of the *L* 2Chr 35:26 3068
in the sight of the *L* his God 2Chr 36:5 3068
of the house of the *L* to Babylon 2Chr 36:7 3068
was evil in the sight of the *L* 2Chr 36:9 3068
vessels of the house of the *L* 2Chr 36:10 3068
in the sight of the *L* his God 2Chr 36:12 3068
speaking from the mouth of the *L* 2Chr 36:12 3068
turning unto the *L* God of Israel 2Chr 36:13 3068
of the *L* which he had hallowed in 2Chr 36:14 3068
the *L* God of their fathers sent 2Chr 36:15 3068
until the wrath of the *L* arose 2Chr 36:16 3068
treasures of the house of the *L* 2Chr 36:18 3068
of the *L* by the mouth of Jeremiah 2Chr 36:21 3068
that the word of the *L* spoken by 2Chr 36:22 3068
the *L* stirred up the spirit of 2Chr 36:22 3068
hath the *L* God of heaven given me 2Chr 36:23 3068
The *L* his God be with him, and let 2Chr 36:23 3068
that the word of the *L* by the Ezr 1:1 3068
the *L* stirred up the spirit of Ezr 1:1 3068
The *L* God of heaven hath given me Ezr 1:2 3068
the house of the *L* God of Israel Ezr 1:3 3068
of the *L* which is in Jerusalem Ezr 1:5 3068
the vessels of the house of the *L* Ezr 1:7 3068
of the *L* which is at Jerusalem Ezr 2:68 3068
offerings thereon unto the *L* Ezr 3:3 3068
of the *L* that were consecrated Ezr 3:5 3068
a freewill offering unto the *L* Ezr 3:5 3068
offer burnt offerings unto the *L* Ezr 3:6 3068
temple of the *L* was not yet laid Ezr 3:6 3068
the work of the house of the *L* Ezr 3:8 3068
foundation of the temple of the *L* Ezr 3:10 3068
with cymbals, to praise the *L* Ezr 3:10 3068
and giving thanks unto the *L* Ezr 3:11 3068
shout, when they praised the *L* Ezr 3:11 3068
of the house of the *L* was laid Ezr 3:11 3068
temple unto the *L* God of Israel Ezr 4:1 3068
build unto the *L* God of Israel Ezr 4:3 3068
to seek the *L* God of Israel, did Ezr 6:21 3068
for the *L* had made them joyful, Ezr 6:22 3068
which the *L* God of Israel had Ezr 7:6 3068
hand of the *L* his God upon him Ezr 7:6 3068
heart to seek the law of the *L* Ezr 7:10 3068
of the commandments of the *L* Ezr 7:11 3068
Blessed be the *L* God of our Ezr 7:27 3068
of the *L* which is in Jerusalem Ezr 7:27 3068
hand of the *L* my God was upon me Ezr 7:28 3068
unto them, Ye are holy unto the *L* Ezr 8:28 3068
unto the *L* God of your fathers Ezr 8:28 3068
chambers of the house of the *L* Ezr 8:29 3068
was a burnt offering unto the *L* Ezr 8:35 3068
out my hands unto the *L* my God Ezr 9:5 3068

been shewed from the *L* our God	Ezr 9:8	3068
O *L* God of Israel, thou art	Ezr 9:15	3068
unto the *L* God of your fathers	Ezr 10:11	3068
O *L* God of heaven, the great and	Neh 1:5	3068
O *L*, I beseech thee, let now	Neh 1:11	136
necks to the work of their *L*	Neh 3:5	113
remember the *L*, which is great and	Neh 4:14	136
said, Amen, and praised the *L*	Neh 5:13	3068
which the *L* had commanded to	Neh 8:1	3068
And Ezra blessed the *L*, the great	Neh 8:6	3068
worshipped the *L* with their faces	Neh 8:6	3068
day is holy unto the *L* your God	Neh 8:9	3068
for this day is holy unto our *L*	Neh 8:10	113
the joy of the *L* is your strength	Neh 8:10	3068
the *L* had commanded by Moses	Neh 8:14	3068
L their God one fourth part of	Neh 9:3	3068
and worshipped the *L* their God	Neh 9:3	3068
a loud voice unto the *L* their God	Neh 9:4	3068
bless the *L* your God for ever and	Neh 9:5	3068
Thou, even thou, art *L* alone	Neh 9:6	3068
Thou art the *L* the God, who didst	Neh 9:7	3068
commandments of the *L* our *L*	Neh 10:29	3068
commandments of the *L* our *L*	Neh 10:29	113
upon the altar of the *L* our God	Neh 10:34	3068
by year, unto the house of the *L*	Neh 10:35	3068
present themselves before the *L*	Job 1:6	3068
the *L* said unto Satan, Whence	Job 1:7	3068
Then Satan answered the *L*	Job 1:7	3068
the *L* said unto Satan, Hast thou	Job 1:8	3068
Then Satan answered the *L*	Job 1:9	3068
the *L* said unto Satan, Behold,	Job 1:12	3068
forth from the presence of the *L*	Job 1:12	3068
the *L* gave, and the *L* hath	Job 1:21	3068
blessed be the name of the *L*	Job 1:21	3068
present themselves before the *L*	Job 2:1	3068
to present himself before the *L*	Job 2:1	3068
the *L* said unto Satan, From	Job 2:2	3068
And Satan answered the *L*, and said,	Job 2:2	3068
the *L* said unto Satan, Hast thou	Job 2:3	3068
And Satan answered the *L*, and said,	Job 2:4	3068
the *L* said unto Satan, Behold, he	Job 2:6	3068
forth from the presence of the *L*	Job 2:7	3068
hand of the *L* hath wrought this	Job 12:9	3068
said, Behold, the fear of the *L*	Job 28:28	136
Then the *L* answered Job out of	Job 38:1	3068
Moreover the *L* answered Job	Job 40:1	3068
Then Job answered the *L*, and said,	Job 40:3	3068
Then answered the *L* unto Job out	Job 40:6	3068
Then Job answered the *L*, and said,	Job 42:1	3068
that after the *L* had spoken these	Job 42:7	3068
the *L* said to Eliphaz the	Job 42:7	3068
according as the *L* commanded them	Job 42:9	3068
the *L* also accepted Job	Job 42:9	3068
the *L* turned the captivity of Job	Job 42:10	3068
also the *L* gave Job twice as much	Job 42:10	3068
that the *L* had brought upon him	Job 42:11	3068
So the *L* blessed the latter end	Job 42:12	3068
delight is in the law of the *L*	Ps 1:2	3068
For the *L* knoweth the way of the	Ps 1:6	3068
counsel together, against the *L*	Ps 2:2	3068
the *L* shall have them in derision	Ps 2:4	136
The *L* hath said unto me, Thou art	Ps 2:7	3068
Serve the *L* with fear, and rejoice	Ps 2:11	3068
L, how are they increased that	Ps 3:1	3068
But thou, O *L*, art a shield for	Ps 3:3	3068
I cried unto the *L* with my voice	Ps 3:4	3068
for the *L* sustained me	Ps 3:5	3068
Arise, O *L*	Ps 3:7	3068
Salvation belongeth unto the *L*	Ps 3:8	3068
But know that the *L* hath set	Ps 4:3	3068
the *L* will hear when I call unto	Ps 4:3	3068
and put your trust in the *L*	Ps 4:5	3068
L, lift thou up the light of thy	Ps 4:6	3068
for thou, *L*, only makest me dwell	Ps 4:8	3068
Give ear to my words, O *L*	Ps 5:1	3068
thou hear in the morning, O *L*	Ps 5:3	3068
the *L* will abhor the bloody and	Ps 5:6	3068
Lead me, O *L*, in thy	Ps 5:8	3068
For thou, *L*, wilt bless the	Ps 5:12	3068
O *L*, rebuke me not in thine anger	Ps 6:1	3068
Have mercy upon me, O *L*	Ps 6:2	3068
O *L*, heal me	Ps 6:2	3068
but thou, O *L*, how long	Ps 6:3	3068
Return, O *L*, deliver my soul	Ps 6:4	3068
for the *L* hath heard the voice of	Ps 6:8	3068
The *L* hath heard my supplication	Ps 6:9	3068
the *L* will receive my prayer	Ps 6:9	3068
David, which he sang unto the *L*	Ps 7:*t*	3068
O *L* my God, in thee do I put my	Ps 7:1	3068
O *L* my God, if I have done this	Ps 7:3	3068
Arise, O *L*, in thine anger, lift	Ps 7:6	3068
The *L* shall judge the people	Ps 7:8	3068
judge me, O *L*, according to my	Ps 7:8	3068
I will praise the *L* according to	Ps 7:17	3068
to the name of the *L* most high	Ps 7:17	3068
O *L*	Ps 8:1	3068
our *L*, how excellent is	Ps 8:1	113
O *L*	Ps 8:9	3068
our *L*, how excellent is	Ps 8:9	113
I will praise thee, O *L*, with my	Ps 9:1	3068
But the *L* shall endure for ever	Ps 9:7	3068
The *L* also will be a refuge for	Ps 9:9	3068
for thou, *L*, hast not forsaken	Ps 9:10	3068
Sing praises to the *L*, which	Ps 9:11	3068
Have mercy upon me, O *L*	Ps 9:13	3068
The *L* is known by the judgment	Ps 9:16	3068
Arise, O *L*	Ps 9:19	3068
Put them in fear, O *L*	Ps 9:20	3068
Why standest thou afar off, O *L*	Ps 10:1	3068
covetous, whom the *L* abhorreth	Ps 10:3	3068
Arise, O *L*	Ps 10:12	3068
The *L* is King for ever and ever	Ps 10:16	3068
L, thou hast heard the desire of	Ps 10:17	3068
In the *L* put I my trust	Ps 11:1	3068
The *L* is in his holy temple, the	Ps 11:4	3068
The *L* trieth the righteous	Ps 11:5	3068
For the righteous *L* loveth	Ps 11:7	3068
Help, *L*; for the	Ps 12:1	3068
The *L* shall cut off all	Ps 12:3	3068
now will I arise, saith the *L*	Ps 12:5	3068
The words of the *L* are pure words	Ps 12:6	3068
Thou shalt keep them, O *L*	Ps 12:7	3068
How long wilt thou forget me, O *L*	Ps 13:1	3068
Consider and hear me, O *L* my God	Ps 13:3	3068
I will sing unto the *L*, because	Ps 13:6	3068
The *L* looked down from heaven	Ps 14:2	3068
eat bread, and call not upon the *L*	Ps 14:4	3068
because the *L* is his refuge	Ps 14:6	3068
when the *L* bringeth back the	Ps 14:7	3068
L, who shall abide in thy	Ps 15:1	3068
he honoureth them that fear the *L*	Ps 15:4	3068
soul, thou hast said unto the *L*	Ps 16:2	3068
Thou art my *L*	Ps 16:2	136
The *L* is the portion of mine	Ps 16:5	3068
I will bless the *L*, who hath	Ps 16:7	3068
I have set the *L* always before me	Ps 16:8	3068
Hear the right, O *L*, attend unto	Ps 17:1	3068
Arise, O *L*, disappoint him, cast	Ps 17:13	3068
From men which are thy hand, O *L*	Ps 17:14	3068
of David, the servant of the *L*	Ps 18:*t*	3068
who spake unto the *L* the words of	Ps 18:*t*	3068
this song in the day that the *L*	Ps 18:*t*	3068
I will love thee, O *L*, my	Ps 18:1	3068
The *L* is my rock, and my fortress,	Ps 18:2	3068
I will call upon the *L*, who is	Ps 18:3	3068
my distress I called upon the *L*	Ps 18:6	3068
The *L* also thundered in the	Ps 18:13	3068
discovered at thy rebuke, O *L*	Ps 18:15	3068
but the *L* was my stay	Ps 18:18	3068
The *L* rewarded me according to my	Ps 18:20	3068
For I have kept the ways of the *L*	Ps 18:21	3068
Therefore hath the *L* recompensed	Ps 18:24	3068
the *L* my God will enlighten my	Ps 18:28	3068
the word of the *L* is tried	Ps 18:30	3068
For who is God save the *L*	Ps 18:31	3068
even unto the *L*, but he answered	Ps 18:41	3068
The *L* liveth	Ps 18:46	3068
will I give thanks unto thee, O *L*	Ps 18:49	3068
The law of the *L* is perfect	Ps 19:7	3068
the testimony of the *L* is sure	Ps 19:7	3068
The statutes of the *L* are right	Ps 19:8	3068
the commandment of the *L* is pure	Ps 19:8	3068
The fear of the *L* is clean	Ps 19:9	3068
the judgments of the *L* are true	Ps 19:9	3068
be acceptable in thy sight, O *L*	Ps 19:14	3068
The *L* hear thee in the day of	Ps 20:1	3068
the *L* fulfil all thy petitions	Ps 20:5	3068
I that the *L* saveth his anointed	Ps 20:6	3068
the name of the *L* our God	Ps 20:7	3068
Save, *L*	Ps 20:9	3068
shall joy in thy strength, O *L*	Ps 21:1	3068
For the king trusteth in the *L*	Ps 21:7	3068
the *L* shall swallow them up in	Ps 21:9	3068
Be thou exalted, *L*, in thine own	Ps 21:13	3068
He trusted on the *L* that he would	Ps 22:8	3068
But be not thou far from me, O *L*	Ps 22:19	3068
Ye that fear the *L*, praise him	Ps 22:23	3068
shall praise the *L* that seek him	Ps 22:26	3068
shall remember and turn unto the *L*	Ps 22:27	3068
to the *L* for a generation	Ps 22:30	136
The *L* is my shepherd	Ps 23:1	3068
in the house of the *L* for ever	Ps 23:6	3068
ascend into the hill of the *L*	Ps 24:3	3068
receive the blessing from the *L*	Ps 24:5	3068
The *L* strong and mighty, the *L*	Ps 24:8	3068
The *L* of hosts, he is the King of	Ps 24:10	3068
Unto thee, O *L*, do I lift up my	Ps 25:1	3068
Shew me thy ways, O *L*	Ps 25:4	3068
Remember, O *L*, thy tender mercies	Ps 25:6	3068
me for thy goodness' sake, O *L*	Ps 25:7	3068
Good and upright is the *L*	Ps 25:8	3068
All the paths of the *L* are mercy	Ps 25:10	3068
For thy name's sake, O *L*, pardon	Ps 25:11	3068
What man is he that feareth the *L*	Ps 25:12	3068
The secret of the *L* is with them	Ps 25:14	3068
Mine eyes are ever toward the *L*	Ps 25:15	3068
Judge me, O *L*	Ps 26:1	3068
I have trusted also in the *L*	Ps 26:1	3068
Examine me, O *L*, and prove me	Ps 26:2	3068
will I compass thine altar, O *L*	Ps 26:6	3068
L, I have loved the habitation of	Ps 26:8	3068
congregations will I bless the *L*	Ps 26:12	3068
The *L* is my light and my salvation	Ps 27:1	3068
the *L* is the strength of my life	Ps 27:1	3068
One thing have I desired of the *L*	Ps 27:4	3068
of the *L* all the days of my life	Ps 27:4	3068
to behold the beauty of the *L*	Ps 27:4	3068
I will sing praises unto the *L*	Ps 27:6	3068
Hear, O *L*, when I cry with my	Ps 27:7	3068
heart said unto thee, Thy face, *L*	Ps 27:8	3068
then the *L* will take me up	Ps 27:10	3068
Teach me thy way, O *L*, and lead me	Ps 27:11	3068
the *L* in the land of the living	Ps 27:13	3068
Wait on the *L*	Ps 27:14	3068
wait, I say, on the *L*	Ps 27:14	3068
Unto thee will I cry, O *L* my rock	Ps 28:1	3068
regard not the works of the *L*	Ps 28:5	3068
Blessed be the *L*, because he hath	Ps 28:6	3068
The *L* is my strength and my shield	Ps 28:7	3068
The *L* is their strength, and he is	Ps 28:8	3068
Give unto the *L*, O ye mighty,	Ps 29:1	3068
give unto the *L* glory	Ps 29:1	3068
Give unto the *L* the glory due	Ps 29:2	3068
worship the *L* in the beauty of	Ps 29:2	3068
The voice of the *L* is upon the	Ps 29:3	3068
the *L* is upon many waters	Ps 29:3	3068
The voice of the *L* is powerful	Ps 29:4	3068
the voice of the *L* is full of	Ps 29:4	3068
The voice of the *L* breaketh the	Ps 29:5	3068
the *L* breaketh the cedars of	Ps 29:5	3068
The voice of the *L* divideth the	Ps 29:7	3068
The voice of the *L* shaketh the	Ps 29:8	3068
the *L* shaketh the wilderness of	Ps 29:8	3068
The voice of the *L* maketh the	Ps 29:9	3068
The *L* sitteth upon the flood	Ps 29:10	3068
the *L* sitteth King for ever	Ps 29:10	3068
The *L* will give strength unto his	Ps 29:11	3068
the *L* will bless his people with	Ps 29:11	3068
I will extol thee, O *L*	Ps 30:1	3068
O *L* my God, I cried unto thee, and	Ps 30:2	3068
O *L*, thou hast brought up my soul	Ps 30:3	3068
Sing unto the *L*, O ye saints of	Ps 30:4	3068
L, by thy favour thou hast made	Ps 30:7	3068
I cried to thee, O *L*	Ps 30:8	3068
unto the *L* I made supplication	Ps 30:8	3068
Hear, O *L*, and have mercy upon me	Ps 30:10	3068
L, be thou my helper	Ps 30:10	3068
O *L* my God, I will give thanks	Ps 30:12	3068
IN thee, O *L*, do I put my trust	Ps 31:1	3068
redeemed me, O *L* God of truth	Ps 31:5	3068
but I trust in the *L*	Ps 31:6	3068
Have mercy upon me, O *L*, for I am	Ps 31:9	3068
But I trusted in thee, O *L*	Ps 31:14	3068
Let me not be ashamed, O *L*	Ps 31:17	3068
Blessed be the *L*	Ps 31:21	3068
O love the *L*, all ye his saints	Ps 31:23	3068
for the *L* preserveth the faithful	Ps 31:23	3068
heart, all ye that hope in the *L*	Ps 31:24	3068
whom the *L* imputeth not iniquity	Ps 32:2	3068
my transgressions unto the *L*	Ps 32:5	3068
but he that trusteth in the *L*	Ps 32:10	3068
Be glad in the *L*, and rejoice, ye	Ps 32:11	3068
Rejoice in the *L*, O ye righteous	Ps 33:1	3068
Praise the *L* with harp	Ps 33:2	3068
For the word of the *L* is right	Ps 33:4	3068
is full of the goodness of the *L*	Ps 33:5	3068
By the word of the *L* were the	Ps 33:6	3068
Let all the earth fear the *L*	Ps 33:8	3068
The *L* bringeth the counsel of the	Ps 33:10	3068
of the *L* standeth for ever	Ps 33:11	3068
is the nation whose God is the *L*	Ps 33:12	3068
The *L* looketh from heaven	Ps 33:13	3068
the eye of the *L* is upon them	Ps 33:18	3068
Our soul waiteth for the *L*	Ps 33:20	3068
Let thy mercy, O *L*, be upon us,	Ps 33:22	3068
I will bless the *L* at all times	Ps 34:1	3068
shall make her boast in the *L*	Ps 34:2	3068
O magnify the *L* with me, and let	Ps 34:3	3068
I sought the *L*, and he heard me,	Ps 34:4	3068
the *L* heard him, and saved him out	Ps 34:6	3068
The angel of the *L* encampeth	Ps 34:7	3068
O taste and see that the *L* is good	Ps 34:8	3068
O fear the *L*, ye his saints	Ps 34:9	3068
but they that seek the *L* shall	Ps 34:10	3068
will teach you the fear of the *L*	Ps 34:11	3068
The eyes of the *L* are upon the	Ps 34:15	3068
The face of the *L* is against them	Ps 34:16	3068
the *L* heareth, and delivereth them	Ps 34:17	3068
The *L* is nigh unto them that are	Ps 34:18	3068
but the *L* delivereth him out of	Ps 34:19	3068
The *L* redeemeth the soul of his	Ps 34:22	3068
Plead my cause, O *L*, with them	Ps 35:1	3068
let the angel of the *L* chase them	Ps 35:5	3068
the angel of the *L* persecute them	Ps 35:6	3068
my soul shall be joyful in the *L*	Ps 35:9	3068
All my bones shall say, *L*	Ps 35:10	3068
L, how long wilt thou look on	Ps 35:17	136
This thou hast seen, O *L*	Ps 35:22	3068
O *L*, be not far from me	Ps 35:22	3068
unto my cause, my God and my *L*	Ps 35:23	136
O *L* my God, according to thy	Ps 35:24	3068
Let the *L* be magnified, which	Ps 35:27	3068
of David, the servant of the *L*	Ps 36:*t*	3068
Thy mercy, O *L*, is in the heavens	Ps 36:5	3068
O *L*, thou preservest man and beast	Ps 36:6	3068
Trust in the *L*, and do good	Ps 37:3	3068
Delight thyself also in the *L*	Ps 37:4	3068
Commit thy way unto the *L*	Ps 37:5	3068
Rest in the *L*, and wait patiently	Ps 37:7	3068
but those that wait upon the *L*	Ps 37:9	3068
The *L* shall laugh at him	Ps 37:13	136
but the *L* upholdeth the righteous	Ps 37:17	3068
The *L* knoweth the days of the	Ps 37:18	3068
the enemies of the *L* shall be as	Ps 37:20	3068
a good man are ordered by the *L*	Ps 37:23	3068
for the *L* upholdeth him with his	Ps 37:24	3068
For the *L* loveth judgment, and	Ps 37:28	3068
The *L* will not leave him in his	Ps 37:33	3068
Wait on the *L*, and keep his way,	Ps 37:34	3068
of the righteous is of the *L*	Ps 37:39	3068
the *L* shall help them, and deliver	Ps 37:40	3068
O *L*, rebuke me not in thy wrath	Ps 38:1	3068
L, all my desire is before thee	Ps 38:9	136
For in thee, O *L*, do I hope	Ps 38:15	3068

thou wilt hear, O *L* my God	Ps 38:15	136
Forsake me not, O *L*	Ps 38:21	3068
to help me, O *L* my salvation	Ps 38:22	136
L, make me to know mine end, and	Ps 39:4	3068
And now, *L*, what wait I for	Ps 39:7	136
Hear my prayer, O *L*, and give ear	Ps 39:12	3068
I waited patiently for the *L*	Ps 40:1	3068
and fear, and shall trust in the *L*	Ps 40:3	3068
man that maketh the *L* his trust	Ps 40:4	3068
O *L* my God, are thy wonderful	Ps 40:5	3068
I have not refrained my lips, O *L*	Ps 40:9	3068
thy tender mercies from me, O *L*	Ps 40:11	3068
Be pleased, O *L*, to deliver me	Ps 40:13	3068
O *L*, make haste to help me	Ps 40:13	3068
continually, The *L* be magnified	Ps 40:16	3068
yet the *L* thinketh upon me	Ps 40:17	136
the *L* will deliver him in time of	Ps 41:1	3068
The *L* will preserve him, and keep	Ps 41:2	3068
The *L* will strengthen him upon	Ps 41:3	3068
I said, *L*, be merciful unto me	Ps 41:4	3068
But thou, O *L*, be merciful unto	Ps 41:10	3068
Blessed be the *L* God of Israel	Ps 41:13	3068
Yet the *L* will command his	Ps 42:8	3068
Awake, why sleepest thou, O *L*	Ps 44:23	136
for he is thy *L*	Ps 45:11	113
The *L* of hosts is with us	Ps 46:7	3068
Come, behold the works of the *L*	Ps 46:8	3068
The *L* of hosts is with us	Ps 46:11	3068
For the *L* most high is terrible	Ps 47:2	3068
the *L* with the sound of a trumpet	Ps 47:5	3068
Great is the *L*, and greatly to be	Ps 48:1	3068
in the city of the *L* of hosts	Ps 48:8	3068
The mighty God, even the *L*	Ps 50:1	3068
O *L*, open thou my lips	Ps 51:15	136
the *L* is with them that uphold my	Ps 54:4	136
I will praise thy name, O *L*	Ps 54:6	3068
Destroy, O *L*, and divide their	Ps 55:9	136
and the *L* shall save me	Ps 55:16	3068
Cast thy burden upon the *L*	Ps 55:22	3068
in the *L* will I praise his word	Ps 56:10	3068
I will praise thee, O *L*, among	Ps 57:9	136
teeth of the young lions, O *L*	Ps 58:6	3068
nor for my sin, O *L*	Ps 59:3	3068
O *L* God of hosts, the God of	Ps 59:5	3068
But thou, O *L*, shalt laugh at	Ps 59:8	3068
bring them down, O *L* our shield	Ps 59:11	136
Also unto thee, O *L*, belongeth	Ps 62:12	136
righteous shall be glad in the *L*	Ps 64:10	3068
my heart, the *L* will not hear me	Ps 66:18	136
The *L* gave the word	Ps 68:11	136
the *L* will dwell in it for ever	Ps 68:16	3068
the *L* is among them, as in Sinai,	Ps 68:17	136
that the *L* God might dwell among	Ps 68:18	136
Blessed be the *L*, who daily	Ps 68:19	136
unto GOD the *L* belong the issues	Ps 68:20	136
The *L* said, I will bring again	Ps 68:22	136
in the congregations, even the *L*	Ps 68:26	136
O sing praises unto the *L*	Ps 68:32	136
O *L* GOD of hosts, be ashamed for	Ps 69:6	136
me, my prayer is unto thee, O *L*	Ps 69:13	3068
Hear me, O *L*	Ps 69:16	3068
This also shall please the *L*	Ps 69:31	3068
For the *L* heareth the poor, and	Ps 69:33	3068
make haste to help me, O *L*	Ps 70:1	3068
O *L*, make no tarrying	Ps 70:5	3068
In thee, O *L*, do I put my trust	Ps 71:1	3068
For thou art my hope, O *L* GOD	Ps 71:5	136
go in the strength of the *L* GOD	Ps 71:16	136
Blessed be the *L* God, the God of	Ps 72:18	3068
so, O *L*, when thou awakest, thou	Ps 73:20	136
I have put my trust in the *L* GOD	Ps 73:28	136
the enemy hath reproached, O *L*	Ps 74:18	3068
the hand of the *L* there is a cup	Ps 75:8	3068
Vow, and pay unto the *L* your God	Ps 76:11	3068
day of my trouble I sought the *L*	Ps 77:2	136
Will the *L* cast off for ever	Ps 77:7	136
will remember the works of the *L*	Ps 77:11	3050
to come the praises of the *L*	Ps 78:4	3068
Therefore the *L* heard this	Ps 78:21	3068
Then the *L* awaked as one out of	Ps 78:65	136
How long, *L*?	Ps 79:5	3068
they have reproached thee, O *L*	Ps 79:12	136
O *L* God of hosts, how long wilt	Ps 80:4	3068
O *L* God of hosts, cause thy face	Ps 80:19	3068
I am the *L* thy God, which brought	Ps 81:10	3068
The haters of the *L* should have	Ps 81:15	3068
that they may seek thy name, O *L*	Ps 83:16	3068
are thy tabernacles, O *L* of hosts	Ps 84:1	3068
fainteth for the courts of the *L*	Ps 84:2	3068
O *L* of hosts, my King, and my God	Ps 84:3	3068
O *L* God of hosts, hear my prayer	Ps 84:8	3068
For the *L* God is a sun and shield	Ps 84:11	3068
the *L* will give grace and glory	Ps 84:11	3068
O *L* of hosts, blessed is the man	Ps 84:12	3068
L, thou hast been favourable unto	Ps 85:1	3068
Shew us thy mercy, O *L*, and grant	Ps 85:7	3068
hear what God the *L* will speak	Ps 85:8	3068
the *L* shall give that which is	Ps 85:12	3068
Bow down thine ear, O *L*, hear me	Ps 86:1	3068
Be merciful unto me, O *L*	Ps 86:3	136
for unto thee, O *L*, do I lift up	Ps 86:4	136
For thou, *L*, art good, and ready	Ps 86:5	136
Give ear, O *L*, unto my prayer	Ps 86:6	3068
there is none like unto thee, O *L*	Ps 86:8	136
come and worship before thee, O *L*	Ps 86:9	136
Teach me thy way, O *L*	Ps 86:11	3068
O *L* my God, with all my heart	Ps 86:12	136
But thou, O *L*, art a God full of	Ps 86:15	136
because thou, *L*, hast holpen me,	Ps 86:17	3068
The *L* loveth the gates of Zion	Ps 87:2	3068
The *L* shall count, when he	Ps 87:6	3068
O *L* God of my salvation, I have	Ps 88:1	3068
L, I have called daily upon thee,	Ps 88:9	3068
But unto thee have I cried, O *L*	Ps 88:13	3068
L, why castest thou off my soul	Ps 88:14	3068
of the mercies of the *L* for ever	Ps 89:1	3068
shall praise thy wonders, O *L*	Ps 89:5	3068
heaven can be compared unto the *L*	Ps 89:6	3068
mighty can be likened unto the *L*	Ps 89:6	3068
O *L* God of hosts, who is a strong	Ps 89:8	3050
who is a strong *L* like unto thee	Ps 89:8	3050
they shall walk, O *L*, in the	Ps 89:15	3068
For the *L* is our defence	Ps 89:18	3068
How long, *L*?	Ps 89:46	3068
L, where are thy former	Ps 89:49	136
Remember, *L*, the reproach of thy	Ps 89:50	136
enemies have reproached, O *L*	Ps 89:51	3068
Blessed be the *L* for evermore	Ps 89:52	3068
L, thou hast been our dwelling	Ps 90:1	136
Return, O *L*, how long	Ps 90:13	3068
of the *L* our God be upon us	Ps 90:17	136
I will say of the *L*, He is my	Ps 91:2	3068
Because thou hast made the *L*	Ps 91:9	3068
thing to give thanks unto the *L*	Ps 92:1	3068
For thou, *L*, hast made me glad	Ps 92:4	3068
O *L*, how great are thy works	Ps 92:5	3068
But thou, *L*, art most high for	Ps 92:8	3068
For, lo, thine enemies, O *L*	Ps 92:9	3068
be planted in the house of the *L*	Ps 92:13	3068
To shew that the *L* is upright	Ps 92:15	3068
The *L* reigneth, he is clothed	Ps 93:1	3068
the *L* is clothed with strength,	Ps 93:1	3068
The floods have lifted up, O *L*	Ps 93:3	3068
The *L* on high is mightier than	Ps 93:4	3068
becometh thine house, O *L*	Ps 93:5	3068
O *L* God, to whom vengeance	Ps 94:1	3068
L, how long shall the wicked, how	Ps 94:3	3068
break in pieces thy people, O *L*	Ps 94:5	3068
The *L* shall not see, neither	Ps 94:7	3050
The *L* knoweth the thoughts of man	Ps 94:11	3068
the man whom thou chastenest, O *L*	Ps 94:12	3050
For the *L* will not cast off his	Ps 94:14	3068
Unless the *L* had been my help, my	Ps 94:17	3068
thy mercy, O *L*, held me up	Ps 94:18	3068
But the *L* is my defence	Ps 94:22	3068
the *L* our God shall cut them off	Ps 94:23	3068
O come, let us sing unto the *L*	Ps 95:1	3068
For the *L* is a great God, and a	Ps 95:3	3068
us kneel before the *L* our maker	Ps 95:6	3068
O sing unto the *L* a new song	Ps 96:1	3068
sing unto the *L*, all the earth	Ps 96:1	3068
Sing unto the *L*, bless his name	Ps 96:2	3068
For the *L* is great, and greatly to	Ps 96:4	3068
but the *L* made the heavens	Ps 96:5	3068
Give unto the *L*, O ye kindreds of	Ps 96:7	3068
the people, give unto the *L* glory	Ps 96:7	3068
Give unto the *L* the glory due	Ps 96:8	3068
O worship the *L* in the beauty of	Ps 96:9	3068
the heathen that the *L* reigneth	Ps 96:10	3068
Before the *L*: for he cometh	Ps 96:13	3068
The *L* reigneth	Ps 97:1	3068
like wax at the presence of the *L*	Ps 97:5	113
of the *L* of the whole earth	Ps 97:5	3068
because of thy judgments, O *L*	Ps 97:8	3068
For thou, *L*, art high above all	Ps 97:9	3068
Ye that love the *L*, hate evil	Ps 97:10	3068
Rejoice in the *L*, ye righteous	Ps 97:12	3068
O sing unto the *L* a new song	Ps 98:1	3068
The *L* hath made known his	Ps 98:2	3068
Make a joyful noise unto the *L*	Ps 98:4	3068
Sing unto the *L* with the harp	Ps 98:5	3068
make a joyful noise before the *L*	Ps 98:6	3068
Before the *L*; for he cometh	Ps 98:9	3068
The *L* reigneth	Ps 99:1	3068
The *L* is great in Zion	Ps 99:2	3068
Exalt ye the *L* our God, and	Ps 99:5	3068
they called upon the *L*, and he	Ps 99:6	3068
Thou answeredst them, O *L* our God	Ps 99:8	3068
Exalt the *L* our God, and worship	Ps 99:9	3068
for the *L* our God is holy	Ps 99:9	3068
Make a joyful noise unto the *L*	Ps 100:1	3068
Serve the *L* with gladness	Ps 100:2	3068
Know ye that the *L* he is God	Ps 100:3	3068
For the *L* is good	Ps 100:5	3068
unto thee, O *L*, will I sing	Ps 101:1	3068
doers from the city of the *L*	Ps 101:8	3068
out his complaint before the *L*	Ps 102:*t*	3068
Hear my prayer, O *L*, and let my	Ps 102:1	3068
But thou, O *L*, shalt endure for	Ps 102:12	3068
shall fear the name of the *L*	Ps 102:15	3068
When the *L* shall build up Zion,	Ps 102:16	3068
be created shall praise the *L*	Ps 102:18	3050
heaven did the *L* behold the earth	Ps 102:19	3068
declare the name of the *L* in Zion	Ps 102:21	3068
and the kingdoms, to serve the *L*	Ps 102:22	3068
Bless the *L*, O my soul	Ps 103:1	3068
Bless the *L*, O my soul, and forget	Ps 103:2	3068
The *L* executeth righteousness and	Ps 103:6	3068
The *L* is merciful and gracious,	Ps 103:8	3068
so the *L* pitieth them that fear	Ps 103:13	3068
But the mercy of the *L* is from	Ps 103:17	3068
The *L* hath prepared his throne in	Ps 103:19	3068
Bless the *L*, ye his angels, that	Ps 103:20	3068
Bless ye the *L*, all ye his hosts	Ps 103:21	3068
Bless the *L*, all his works in all	Ps 103:22	3068
bless the *L*, O my soul	Ps 103:22	3068
Bless the *L*, O my soul	Ps 104:1	3068
O *L* my God, thou art very great	Ps 104:1	3068
trees of the *L* are full of sap	Ps 104:16	3068
O *L*, how manifold are thy works	Ps 104:24	3068
The glory of the *L* shall endure	Ps 104:31	3068
the *L* shall rejoice in his works	Ps 104:31	3068
sing unto the *L* as long as I live	Ps 104:33	3068
I will be glad in the *L*	Ps 104:34	3068
Bless thou the *L*, O my soul	Ps 104:35	3050
Praise ye the *L*	Ps 104:35	3050
O give thanks unto the *L*	Ps 105:1	3050
of them rejoice that seek the *L*	Ps 105:3	3050
Seek the *L*, and his strength	Ps 105:4	3050
He is the *L* our God	Ps 105:7	3050
the word of the *L* tried him	Ps 105:19	3050
Praise ye the *L*	Ps 105:45	3050
Praise ye the *L*	Ps 106:1	3050
O give thanks unto the *L*	Ps 106:1	3068
utter the mighty acts of the *L*	Ps 106:2	3068
Remember me, O *L*, with the favour	Ps 106:4	3068
camp, and Aaron the saint of the *L*	Ps 106:16	3068
not unto the voice of the *L*	Ps 106:25	3068
whom the *L* commanded them	Ps 106:34	3068
the *L* kindled against his people	Ps 106:40	3068
O *L* our God, and gather us from	Ps 106:47	3068
Blessed be the *L* God of Israel	Ps 106:48	3068
Praise ye the *L*	Ps 106:48	3050
O give thanks unto the *L*, for he	Ps 107:1	3068
Let the redeemed of the *L* say so	Ps 107:2	3068
cried unto the *L* in their trouble	Ps 107:6	3068
praise the *L* for his goodness	Ps 107:8	3068
cried unto the *L* in their trouble	Ps 107:13	3068
praise the *L* for his goodness	Ps 107:15	3068
cry unto the *L* in their trouble	Ps 107:19	3068
praise the *L* for his goodness	Ps 107:21	3068
These see the works of the *L*	Ps 107:24	3068
cry unto the *L* in their trouble	Ps 107:28	3068
praise the *L* for his goodness	Ps 107:31	3068
the lovingkindness of the *L*	Ps 107:43	3068
I will praise thee, O *L*, among	Ps 108:3	3068
fathers be remembered with the *L*	Ps 109:14	3068
them be before the *L* continually	Ps 109:15	3068
of mine adversaries from the *L*	Ps 109:20	3068
But do thou for me, O GOD the *L*	Ps 109:21	136
Help me, O *L* my God	Ps 109:26	3068
that thou, *L*, hast done it	Ps 109:27	3068
praise the *L* with my mouth	Ps 109:30	3068
The *L* said unto my	Ps 110:1	3068
said unto my *L*, Sit thou	Ps 110:1	113
The *L* shall send the rod of thy	Ps 110:2	3068
The *L* hath sworn, and will not	Ps 110:4	3068
The *L* at thy right hand shall	Ps 110:5	136
Praise ye the *L*	Ps 111:1	3050
I will praise the *L* with my whole	Ps 111:1	3068
The works of the *L* are great	Ps 111:2	3068
the *L* is gracious and full of	Ps 111:4	3068
The fear of the *L* is the	Ps 111:10	3068
Praise ye the *L*	Ps 112:1	3050
is the man that feareth the *L*	Ps 112:1	3068
heart is fixed, trusting in the *L*	Ps 112:7	3068
Praise ye the *L*	Ps 113:1	3050
Praise, O ye servants of the *L*	Ps 113:1	3068
praise the name of the *L*	Ps 113:1	3068
of the *L* from this time forth	Ps 113:2	3068
The *L* is high above all nations,	Ps 113:4	3068
Who is like unto the *L* our God	Ps 113:5	3068
Praise ye the *L*	Ps 113:9	3050
earth, at the presence of the *L*	Ps 114:7	113
Not unto us, O *L*, not unto us,	Ps 115:1	3068
O Israel, trust thou in the *L*	Ps 115:9	3068
O house of Aaron, trust in the *L*	Ps 115:10	3068
fear the *L*, trust in the *L*	Ps 115:11	3068
The *L* hath been mindful of us	Ps 115:12	3068
will bless them that fear the *L*	Ps 115:13	3068
The *L* shall increase you more and	Ps 115:14	3068
of the *L* which made heaven	Ps 115:15	3068
The dead praise not the *L*	Ps 115:17	3050
bless the *L* from this time forth	Ps 115:18	3050
Praise the *L*	Ps 115:18	3050
I love the *L*, because he hath	Ps 116:1	3068
called I upon the name of the *L*	Ps 116:4	3068
O *L*, I beseech thee, deliver my	Ps 116:4	3068
Gracious is the *L*, and righteous	Ps 116:5	3068
The *L* preserveth the simple	Ps 116:6	3068
for the *L* hath dealt bountifully	Ps 116:7	3068
I will walk before the *L* in the	Ps 116:9	3068
What shall I render unto the *L*	Ps 116:12	3068
and call upon the name of the *L*	Ps 116:13	3068
I will pay my vows unto the *L* now	Ps 116:14	3068
the *L* is the death of his saints	Ps 116:15	3068
O *L*, truly I am thy servant	Ps 116:16	3068
will call upon the name of the *L*	Ps 116:17	3068
I will pay my vows unto the *L* now	Ps 116:18	3068
Praise ye the *L*	Ps 116:19	3050
O praise the *L*, all ye nations	Ps 117:1	3068
the truth of the *L* endureth for	Ps 117:2	3068
Praise ye the *L*	Ps 117:2	3050
O give thanks unto the *L*	Ps 118:1	3068
Let them now that fear the *L* say	Ps 118:4	3068
I called upon the *L* in distress	Ps 118:5	3050
the *L* answered me, and set me in a	Ps 118:5	3050
The *L* is on my side	Ps 118:6	3068
The *L* taketh my part with them	Ps 118:7	3068
It is better to trust in the *L*	Ps 118:8	3068
the *L* than to put confidence in	Ps 118:9	3068
name of the *L* will I destroy them	Ps 118:10	3068
name of the *L* I will destroy them	Ps 118:11	3068
name of the *L* I will destroy them	Ps 118:12	3068

but the *L* helped me ... Ps 118:13 3068
The *L* is my strength and song, and ... Ps 118:14 3050
hand of the *L* doeth valiantly ... Ps 118:15 3068
right hand of the *L* is exalted ... Ps 118:16 3068
hand of the *L* doeth valiantly ... Ps 118:16 3068
and declare the works of the *L* ... Ps 118:17 3050
The *L* hath chastened me sore ... Ps 118:18 3050
into them, and I will praise the *L* ... Ps 118:19 3050
This gate of the *L*, into which ... Ps 118:20 3068
is the day which the *L* hath made ... Ps 118:24 3068
Save now, I beseech thee, O *L* ... Ps 118:25 3068
O *L*, I beseech thee, send now ... Ps 118:25 3068
that cometh in the name of the *L* ... Ps 118:26 3068
you out of the house of the *L* ... Ps 118:26 3068
God is the *L*, which hath shewed ... Ps 118:27 3068
O give thanks unto the *L* ... Ps 118:29 3068
way, who walk in the law of the *L* ... Ps 119:1 3068
Blessed art thou, O *L* ... Ps 119:12 3068
O *L*, put me not to shame ... Ps 119:31 3068
Teach me, O *L*, the way of thy ... Ps 119:33 3068
mercies come also unto me, O *L* ... Ps 119:41 3068
thy judgments of old, O *L* ... Ps 119:52 3068
I have remembered thy name, O *L* ... Ps 119:55 3068
Thou art my portion, O *L* ... Ps 119:57 3068
The earth, O *L*, is full of thy ... Ps 119:64 3068
dealt well with thy servant, O *L* ... Ps 119:65 3068
I know, O *L*, that thy judgments ... Ps 119:75 3068
For ever, O *L*, thy word is ... Ps 119:89 3068
quicken me, O *L*, according unto ... Ps 119:107 3068
offerings of my mouth, O *L* ... Ps 119:108 3068
It is time for thee, *L*, to work ... Ps 119:126 3068
Righteous art thou, O *L*, and ... Ps 119:137 3068
hear me, O *L* ... Ps 119:145 3068
O *L*, quicken me according to thy ... Ps 119:149 3068
Thou art near, O *L* ... Ps 119:151 3068
Great are thy tender mercies, O *L* ... Ps 119:156 3068
quicken me, O *L*, according to thy ... Ps 119:159 3068
L, I have hoped for thy salvation ... Ps 119:166 3068
my cry come near before thee, O *L* ... Ps 119:169 3068
longed for thy salvation, O *L* ... Ps 119:174 3068
In my distress I cried unto the *L* ... Ps 120:1 3068
Deliver my soul, O *L*, from lying ... Ps 120:2 3068
My help cometh from the *L* ... Ps 121:2 3068
The *L* is thy keeper ... Ps 121:5 3068
the *L* is thy shade upon thy right ... Ps 121:5 3068
The *L* shall preserve thee from ... Ps 121:7 3068
The *L* shall preserve thy going ... Ps 121:8 3068
Let us go into the house of the *L* ... Ps 122:1 3068
tribes go up, the tribes of the *L* ... Ps 122:4 3050
thanks unto the name of the *L* ... Ps 122:4 3068
Because of the house of the *L* our ... Ps 122:9 3068
our eyes wait upon the *L* our God ... Ps 123:2 3068
Have mercy upon us, O *L*, have ... Ps 123:3 3068
been the *L* who was on our side ... Ps 124:1 3068
been the *L* who was on our side ... Ps 124:2 3068
Blessed be the *L*, who hath not ... Ps 124:6 3068
Our help is in the name of the *L* ... Ps 124:8 3068
in the *L* shall be as mount Zion ... Ps 125:1 3068
so the *L* is round about his ... Ps 125:2 3068
Do good, O *L*, unto those that be ... Ps 125:4 3068
the *L* shall lead them forth with ... Ps 125:5 3068
When the *L* turned again the ... Ps 126:1 3068
The *L* hath done great things for ... Ps 126:2 3068
The *L* hath done great things for ... Ps 126:3 3068
Turn again our captivity, O *L* ... Ps 126:4 3068
Except the *L* build the house, ... Ps 127:1 3068
except the *L* keep the city, the ... Ps 127:1 3068
children are an heritage of the *L* ... Ps 127:3 3068
is every one that feareth the *L* ... Ps 128:1 3068
man be blessed that feareth the *L* ... Ps 128:4 3068
The *L* shall bless thee out of ... Ps 128:5 3068
The *L* is righteous ... Ps 129:4 3068
The blessing of the *L* be upon you ... Ps 129:8 3068
we bless you in the name of the *L* ... Ps 129:8 3068
have I cried unto thee, O *L* ... Ps 130:1 3068
L, hear my voice ... Ps 130:2 136
If thou, *L*, shouldest mark ... Ps 130:3 3050
shouldest mark iniquities, O *L* ... Ps 130:3 136
I wait for the *L*, my soul doth ... Ps 130:5 3068
My soul waiteth for the *L* more ... Ps 130:6 136
Let Israel hope in the *L* ... Ps 130:7 3068
for with the *L* there is mercy, and ... Ps 130:7 3068
L, my heart is not haughty, nor ... Ps 131:1 3068
hope in the *L* from henceforth ... Ps 131:3 3068
L, remember David, and all his ... Ps 132:1 3068
How he sware unto the *L*, and vowed ... Ps 132:2 3068
I find out a place for the *L* ... Ps 132:5 3068
Arise, O *L*, into thy rest ... Ps 132:8 3068
The *L* hath sworn in truth unto ... Ps 132:11 3068
For the *L* hath chosen Zion ... Ps 132:13 3068
for there the *L* commanded the ... Ps 133:3 3068
Behold, bless ye the *L* ... Ps 134:1 3068
all ye servants of the *L* ... Ps 134:1 3068
night stand in the house of the *L* ... Ps 134:1 3068
in the sanctuary, and bless the *L* ... Ps 134:2 3068
The *L* that made heaven and earth ... Ps 134:3 3068
Praise ye the *L* ... Ps 135:1 3050
Praise ye the name of the *L* ... Ps 135:1 3068
him, O ye servants of the *L* ... Ps 135:1 3068
that stand in the house of the *L* ... Ps 135:2 3068
Praise the *L* ... Ps 135:3 3050
for the *L* is good ... Ps 135:3 3068
For the *L* hath chosen Jacob unto ... Ps 135:4 3050
For I know that the *L* is great ... Ps 135:5 3068
that our *L* is above all gods ... Ps 135:5 113
Whatsoever the *L* pleased, that ... Ps 135:6 3068
Thy name, O *L*, endureth for ever ... Ps 135:13 3068
and thy memorial, O *L*, throughout ... Ps 135:13 3068
For the *L* will judge his people, ... Ps 135:14 3068
Bless the *L*, O house of Israel ... Ps 135:19 3068
bless the *L*, O house of Aaron ... Ps 135:19 3068
Bless the *L*, O house of Levi ... Ps 135:20 3068
that fear the *L*, bless the *L* ... Ps 135:20 3068
Blessed be the *L* out of Zion ... Ps 135:21 3068
Praise ye the *L* ... Ps 135:21 3050
O Give thanks unto the *L* ... Ps 136:1 3068
O give thanks to the *L* of lords ... Ps 136:3 113
Remember, O *L*, the children of ... Ps 137:7 3068
the earth shall praise thee, O *L* ... Ps 138:4 3068
shall sing in the ways of the *L* ... Ps 138:5 3068
for great is the glory of the *L* ... Ps 138:5 3068
Though the *L* be high, yet hath he ... Ps 138:6 3068
The *L* will perfect that which ... Ps 138:8 3068
thy mercy, O *L*, endureth for ever ... Ps 138:8 3068
O *L*, thou hast searched me, and ... Ps 139:1 3068
a word in my tongue, but, lo, O *L* ... Ps 139:4 3068
Do not I hate them, O *L*, that ... Ps 139:21 3068
Deliver me, O *L*, from the evil ... Ps 140:1 3068
Keep me, O *L*, from the hands of ... Ps 140:4 3068
I said unto the *L*, Thou art my ... Ps 140:6 3068
voice of my supplications, O *L* ... Ps 140:6 3068
O God the *L*, the strength of my ... Ps 140:7 136
Grant not, O *L*, the desires of ... Ps 140:8 3068
I know that the *L* will maintain ... Ps 140:12 3068
L, I cry unto thee ... Ps 141:1 3068
Set a watch, O *L*, before my mouth ... Ps 141:3 3068
eyes are unto thee, O GOD the *L* ... Ps 141:8 136
I cried unto the *L* with my voice ... Ps 142:1 3068
with my voice unto the *L* did I ... Ps 142:1 3068
I cried unto thee, O *L* ... Ps 142:5 3068
Hear my prayer, O *L*, give ear to ... Ps 143:1 3068
Hear me speedily, O *L* ... Ps 143:7 3068
Deliver me, O *L*, from mine ... Ps 143:9 3068
Quicken me, O *L*, for thy name's ... Ps 143:11 3068
Blessed be the *L* my strength ... Ps 144:1 3068
L, what is man, that thou takest ... Ps 144:3 3068
Bow thy heavens, O *L*, and come ... Ps 144:5 3068
that people, whose God is the *L* ... Ps 144:15 3068
Great is the *L*, and greatly to be ... Ps 145:3 3068
The *L* is gracious, and full of ... Ps 145:8 3068
The *L* is good to all ... Ps 145:9 3068
thy works shall praise thee, O *L* ... Ps 145:10 3068
The *L* upholdeth all that fall, and ... Ps 145:14 3068
The *L* is righteous in all his ... Ps 145:17 3068
The *L* is nigh unto all them that ... Ps 145:18 3068
The *L* preserveth all them that ... Ps 145:20 3068
shall speak the praise of the *L* ... Ps 145:21 3068
Praise ye the *L* ... Ps 146:1 3050
Praise the *L*, O my soul ... Ps 146:1 3068
While I live will I praise the *L* ... Ps 146:2 3068
whose hope is in the *L* his God ... Ps 146:5 3068
The *L* looseth the prisoners ... Ps 146:7 3068
The *L* openeth the eyes of the ... Ps 146:8 3068
the *L* raiseth them that are bowed ... Ps 146:8 3068
the *L* loveth the righteous ... Ps 146:8 3068
The *L* preserveth the strangers ... Ps 146:9 3068
The *L* shall reign for ever, even ... Ps 146:10 3068
Praise ye the *L* ... Ps 146:10 3050
Praise ye the *L* ... Ps 147:1 3050
The *L* doth build up Jerusalem ... Ps 147:2 3068
Great is our *L*, and of great power ... Ps 147:5 113
The *L* lifteth up the meek ... Ps 147:6 3068
Sing unto the *L* with thanksgiving ... Ps 147:7 3068
The *L* taketh pleasure in them ... Ps 147:11 3068
Praise the *L*, O Jerusalem ... Ps 147:12 3068
Praise ye the *L* ... Ps 147:20 3050
Praise ye the *L* ... Ps 148:1 3050
Praise ye the *L* from the heavens ... Ps 148:1 3068
Let them praise the name of the *L* ... Ps 148:5 3068
Praise the *L* from the earth, ye ... Ps 148:7 3068
Let them praise the name of the *L* ... Ps 148:13 3068
Praise ye the *L* ... Ps 148:14 3050
Praise ye the *L* ... Ps 149:1 3050
Sing unto the *L* a new song ... Ps 149:1 3068
For the *L* taketh pleasure in his ... Ps 149:4 3068
Praise ye the *L* ... Ps 149:9 3050
Praise ye the *L* ... Ps 150:1 3050
that hath breath praise the *L* ... Ps 150:6 3050
Praise ye the *L* ... Ps 150:6 3050
The fear of the *L* is the ... Prov 1:7 3068
did not choose the fear of the *L* ... Prov 1:29 3068
thou understand the fear of the *L* ... Prov 2:5 3068
For the *L* giveth wisdom ... Prov 2:6 3068
Trust in the *L* with all thine ... Prov 3:5 3068
fear the *L*, and depart from evil ... Prov 3:7 3068
Honour the *L* with thy substance, ... Prov 3:9 3068
not the chastening of the *L* ... Prov 3:11 3068
For whom the *L* loveth he ... Prov 3:12 3068
The *L* by wisdom hath founded the ... Prov 3:19 3068
For the *L* shall be thy confidence ... Prov 3:26 3068
froward is abomination to the *L* ... Prov 3:32 3068
The curse of the *L* is in the ... Prov 3:33 3068
man are before the eyes of the *L* ... Prov 5:21 3068
These six things doth the *L* hate ... Prov 6:16 3068
The fear of the *L* is to hate evil ... Prov 8:13 3068
The *L* possessed me in the ... Prov 8:22 3068
and shall obtain favour of the *L* ... Prov 8:35 3068
The fear of the *L* is the ... Prov 9:10 3068
The *L* will not suffer the soul of ... Prov 10:3 3068
The blessing of the *L*, it maketh ... Prov 10:22 3068
The fear of the *L* prolongeth days ... Prov 10:27 3068
The way of the *L* is strength to ... Prov 10:29 3068
balance is abomination to the *L* ... Prov 11:1 3068
heart are abomination to the *L* ... Prov 11:20 3068
man obtaineth favour of the *L* ... Prov 12:2 3068
lips are abomination to the *L* ... Prov 12:22 3068
in his uprightness feareth the *L* ... Prov 14:2 3068
In the fear of the *L* is strong ... Prov 14:26 3068
The fear of the *L* is a fountain ... Prov 14:27 3068
The eyes of the *L* are in every ... Prov 15:3 3068
wicked is an abomination to the *L* ... Prov 15:8 3068
is an abomination unto the *L* ... Prov 15:9 3068
and destruction are before the *L* ... Prov 15:11 3068
fear of the *L* than great treasure ... Prov 15:16 3068
The *L* will destroy the house of ... Prov 15:25 3068
are an abomination to the *L* ... Prov 15:26 3068
The *L* is far from the wicked ... Prov 15:29 3068
The fear of the *L* is the ... Prov 15:33 3068
of the tongue, is from the *L* ... Prov 16:1 3068
but the *L* weigheth the spirits ... Prov 16:2 3068
Commit thy works unto the *L* ... Prov 16:3 3068
The *L* hath made all things for ... Prov 16:4 3068
heart is an abomination to the *L* ... Prov 16:5 3068
by the fear of the *L* men depart ... Prov 16:6 3068
When a man's ways please the *L* ... Prov 16:7 3068
but the *L* directeth his steps ... Prov 16:9 3068
and whoso trusteth in the *L* ... Prov 16:20 3068
disposing thereof is of the *L* ... Prov 16:33 3068
but the *L* trieth the hearts ... Prov 17:3 3068
both are abomination to the *L* ... Prov 17:15 3068
The name of the *L* is a strong ... Prov 18:10 3068
and obtaineth favour of the *L* ... Prov 18:22 3068
his heart fretteth against the *L* ... Prov 19:3 3068
and a prudent wife is from the *L* ... Prov 19:14 3068
upon the poor lendeth unto the *L* ... Prov 19:17 3068
nevertheless the counsel of the *L* ... Prov 19:21 3068
The fear of the *L* tendeth to life ... Prov 19:23 3068
are alike abomination to the *L* ... Prov 20:10 3068
the *L* hath made even both of them ... Prov 20:12 3068
but wait on the *L*, and he shall ... Prov 20:22 3068
are an abomination unto the *L* ... Prov 20:23 3068
Man's goings are of the *L* ... Prov 20:24 3068
of man is the candle of the *L* ... Prov 20:27 3068
heart is in the hand of the *L* ... Prov 21:1 3068
but the *L* pondereth the hearts ... Prov 21:2 3068
to the *L* than sacrifice ... Prov 21:3 3068
nor counsel against the *L* ... Prov 21:30 3068
but safety is of the *L* ... Prov 21:31 3068
the *L* is the maker of them all ... Prov 22:2 3068
and the fear of the *L* are riches ... Prov 22:4 3068
The eyes of the *L* preserve ... Prov 22:12 3068
of the *L* shall fall therein ... Prov 22:14 3068
That thy trust may be in the *L* ... Prov 22:19 3068
For the *L* will plead their cause, ... Prov 22:23 3068
fear of the *L* all the day long ... Prov 23:17 3068
Lest the *L* see it, and it ... Prov 24:18 3068
My son, fear thou the *L* and the ... Prov 24:21 3068
head, and the *L* shall reward thee ... Prov 25:22 3068
seek the *L* understand all things ... Prov 28:5 3068
trust in the *L* shall be made fat ... Prov 28:25 3068
the *L* lighteneth both their eyes ... Prov 29:13 3068
his trust in the *L* shall be safe ... Prov 29:25 3068
man's judgment cometh from the *L* ... Prov 29:26 3068
deny thee, and say, Who is the *L* ... Prov 30:9 3068
but a woman that feareth the *L* ... Prov 31:30 3068
for the *L* hath spoken, I have ... Is 1:2 3068
they have forsaken the *L*, they ... Is 1:4 3068
Except the *L* of hosts had left ... Is 1:9 3068
Hear the word of the *L*, ye rulers ... Is 1:10 3068
saith the *L* ... Is 1:11 3068
us reason together, saith the *L* ... Is 1:18 3068
the mouth of the *L* hath spoken it ... Is 1:20 3068
Therefore saith the *L*, the *L* ... Is 1:24 113
the *L* of hosts, the mighty One of ... Is 1:24 3068
forsake the *L* shall be consumed ... Is 1:28 3068
us go up to the mountain of the *L* ... Is 2:3 3068
the word of the *L* from Jerusalem ... Is 2:3 3068
let us walk in the light of the *L* ... Is 2:5 3068
in the dust, for fear of the *L* ... Is 2:10 3068
the *L* alone shall be exalted in ... Is 2:11 3068
For the day of the *L* of hosts ... Is 2:12 3068
the *L* alone shall be exalted in ... Is 2:17 3068
of the earth, for fear of the *L* ... Is 2:19 3068
ragged rocks, for fear of the *L* ... Is 2:21 3068
For, behold, the *L*, the *L* of ... Is 3:1 113
the *L* of hosts, doth take away ... Is 3:1 3068
and their doings are against the *L* ... Is 3:8 3068
The *L* standeth up to plead, and ... Is 3:13 3068
The *L* will enter into judgment ... Is 3:14 3068
saith the *L* GOD of hosts ... Is 3:15 136
Moreover the *L* saith, Because the ... Is 3:16 3068
Therefore the *L* will smite with a ... Is 3:17 136
the *L* will discover their secret ... Is 3:17 3068
In that day the *L* will take away ... Is 3:18 136
the branch of the *L* be beautiful ... Is 4:2 3068
When the *L* shall have washed away ... Is 4:4 136
the *L* will create upon every ... Is 4:5 3068
For the vineyard of the *L* of ... Is 5:7 3068
In mine ears said the *L* of hosts ... Is 5:9 3068
they regard not the work of the *L* ... Is 5:12 3068
But the *L* of hosts shall be ... Is 5:16 3068
away the law of the *L* of hosts ... Is 5:24 3068
the *L* kindled against his people ... Is 5:25 3068
also the *L* sitting upon a throne ... Is 6:1 136
holy, holy, is the *L* of hosts ... Is 6:3 3068
seen the King, the *L* of hosts ... Is 6:5 3068
Also I heard the voice of the *L* ... Is 6:8 136
Then said I, *L*, how long ... Is 6:11 136
the *L* have removed men far away, ... Is 6:12 3068
Then said the *L* unto Isaiah ... Is 7:3 3068
Thus saith the *L* GOD, It shall ... Is 7:7 136
Moreover the *L* spake again unto ... Is 7:10 3068
Ask thee a sign of the *L* thy God ... Is 7:11 3068
ask, neither will I tempt the *L* ... Is 7:12 3068

L

Therefore the *L* himself shall	Is 7:14	136
The *L* shall bring upon thee, and	Is 7:17	3068
that the *L* shall hiss for the fly	Is 7:18	3068
In the same day shall the *L* shave	Is 7:20	136
Moreover the *L* said unto me	Is 8:1	3068
Then said the *L* to me, Call his	Is 8:3	3068
The *L* spake also unto me again,	Is 8:5	3068
the *L* bringeth up upon them the	Is 8:7	136
For the *L* spake thus to me with a	Is 8:11	3068
Sanctify the *L* of hosts himself	Is 8:13	3068
And I will wait upon the *L*	Is 8:17	3068
the children whom the *L* hath	Is 8:18	3068
in Israel from the *L* of hosts	Is 8:18	3068
The zeal of the *L* of hosts will	Is 9:7	3068
The *L* sent a word into Jacob, and	Is 9:8	136
Therefore the *L* shall set up the	Is 9:11	3068
do they seek the *L* of hosts	Is 9:13	3068
Therefore the *L* will cut off from	Is 9:14	3068
Therefore the *L* shall have no joy	Is 9:17	136
Through the wrath of the *L* of	Is 9:19	3068
that when the *L* hath performed	Is 10:12	136
Therefore shall the *L*	Is 10:16	113
the *L* of hosts, send among his	Is 10:16	136
but shall stay upon the *L*	Is 10:20	3068
For the *L* GOD of hosts shall make	Is 10:23	136
thus saith the *L* GOD of hosts	Is 10:24	136
the *L* of hosts shall stir up a	Is 10:26	3068
Behold, the *L*	Is 10:33	113
the *L* of hosts, shall lop the	Is 10:33	3068
the spirit of the *L* shall rest	Is 11:2	3068
knowledge and of the fear of the *L*	Is 11:2	3068
in the fear of the *L*	Is 11:3	3068
be full of the knowledge of the *L*	Is 11:9	3068
that the *L* shall set his hand	Is 11:11	136
the *L* shall utterly destroy the	Is 11:15	3068
in that day thou shalt say, O *L*	Is 12:1	3068
for the *L* JEHOVAH is my strength	Is 12:2	3050
day shall ye say, Praise the *L*	Is 12:4	3068
Sing unto the *L*	Is 12:5	3068
the *L* of hosts mustereth the host	Is 13:4	3068
the end of heaven, even the *L*	Is 13:5	3068
for the day of the *L* is at hand	Is 13:6	3068
Behold, the day of the *L* cometh	Is 13:9	3068
in the wrath of the *L* of hosts	Is 13:13	3068
For the *L* will have mercy on	Is 14:1	3068
in the land of the *L* for servants	Is 14:2	3068
to pass in the day that the *L*	Is 14:3	3068
The *L* hath broken the staff of	Is 14:5	3068
them, saith the *L* of hosts	Is 14:22	3068
and son, and nephew, saith the *L*	Is 14:22	3068
destruction, saith the *L* of hosts	Is 14:23	3068
The *L* of hosts hath sworn, saying	Is 14:24	3068
For the *L* of hosts hath purposed,	Is 14:27	3068
That the *L* hath founded Zion, and	Is 14:32	3068
This is the word that the *L* hath	Is 16:13	3068
But now the *L* hath spoken	Is 16:14	3068
of Israel, saith the *L* of hosts	Is 17:3	3068
saith the *L* God of Israel	Is 17:6	3068
For so the *L* said unto me, I will	Is 18:4	3068
L of hosts of a people scattered	Is 18:7	3068
of the name of the *L* of hosts	Is 18:7	3068
the *L* rideth upon a swift cloud,	Is 19:1	3068
shall rule over them, saith the *L*	Is 19:4	113
the *L* of hosts	Is 19:4	3068
let them know what the *L* of hosts	Is 19:12	3068
The *L* hath mingled a perverse	Is 19:14	3068
of the hand of the *L* of hosts	Is 19:16	3068
of the counsel of the *L* of hosts	Is 19:17	3068
and swear to the *L* of hosts	Is 19:18	3068
the *L* in the midst of the land of	Is 19:19	3068
at the border thereof to the *L*	Is 19:19	3068
for a witness unto the *L* of hosts	Is 19:20	3068
the *L* because of the oppressors	Is 19:20	3068
the *L* shall be known to Egypt, and	Is 19:21	3068
shall know the *L* in that day	Is 19:21	3068
they shall vow a vow unto the *L*	Is 19:21	3068
And the *L* shall smite Egypt	Is 19:22	3068
they shall return even to the *L*	Is 19:22	3068
Whom the *L* of hosts shall bless,	Is 19:25	3068
the *L* by Isaiah the son of Amoz	Is 20:2	3068
the *L* said, Like as my servant	Is 20:3	3068
For thus hath the *L* said unto me	Is 21:6	136
I have heard of the *L* of hosts	Is 21:10	3068
For thus hath the *L* said unto me	Is 21:16	136
for the *L* God of Israel hath	Is 21:17	3068
of perplexity by the *L* GOD of	Is 22:5	136
in that day did the *L* GOD of	Is 22:12	136
in mine ears by the *L* of hosts	Is 22:14	3068
ye die, saith the *L* GOD of hosts	Is 22:14	136
Thus saith the *L* GOD of hosts	Is 22:15	136
the *L* will carry thee away with a	Is 22:17	3068
In that day, saith the *L* of hosts	Is 22:25	3068
for the *L* hath spoken it	Is 22:25	3068
The *L* of hosts hath purposed it,	Is 23:9	3068
the *L* hath given a commandment	Is 23:11	3068
that the *L* will visit Tyre, and	Is 23:17	3068
hire shall be holiness to the *L*	Is 23:18	3068
for them that dwell before the *L*	Is 23:18	3068
the *L* maketh the earth empty, and	Is 24:1	3068
for the *L* hath spoken this word	Is 24:3	3068
sing for the majesty of the *L*	Is 24:14	3068
glorify ye the *L* in the fires	Is 24:15	3068
even the name of the *L* God of	Is 24:15	3068
that the *L* shall punish the host	Is 24:21	3068
when the *L* of hosts shall reign	Is 24:23	3068
O *L*, thou art my God	Is 25:1	3068
in this mountain shall the *L* of	Is 25:6	3068
the *L* GOD will wipe away tears	Is 25:8	136
for the *L* hath spoken it	Is 25:8	3068
this is the *L*	Is 25:9	3068
shall the hand of the *L* rest	Is 25:10	3068
Trust ye in the *L* for ever	Is 26:4	3068
for in the *L* JEHOVAH is	Is 26:4	3050
in the way of thy judgments, O *L*	Is 26:8	3068
not behold the majesty of the *L*	Is 26:10	3068
L, when thy hand is lifted up,	Is 26:11	3068
L, thou wilt ordain peace for us	Is 26:12	3068
O *L* our God, other lords besides	Is 26:13	3068
hast increased the nation, O *L*	Is 26:15	3068
L, in trouble have they visited	Is 26:16	3068
so have we been in thy sight, O *L*	Is 26:17	3068
the *L* cometh out of his place to	Is 26:21	3068
In that day the *L* with his sore	Is 27:1	3068
I the *L* do keep it	Is 27:3	3068
that the *L* shall beat off from	Is 27:12	3068
shall worship the *L* in the holy	Is 27:13	3068
the *L* hath a mighty and strong one	Is 28:2	136
In that day shall the *L* of hosts	Is 28:5	3068
But the word of the *L* was unto	Is 28:13	3068
Wherefore hear the word of the *L*	Is 28:14	3068
Therefore thus saith the *L* GOD	Is 28:16	136
For the *L* shall rise up as in	Is 28:21	3068
for I have heard from the *L* GOD	Is 28:22	136
cometh forth from the *L* of hosts	Is 28:29	3068
of the *L* of hosts with thunder	Is 29:6	3068
For the *L* hath poured out upon	Is 29:10	3068
Wherefore the *L* said, Forasmuch	Is 29:13	136
to hide their counsel from the *L*	Is 29:15	3068
shall increase their joy in the *L*	Is 29:19	3068
Therefore thus saith the *L*	Is 29:22	3068
rebellious children, saith the *L*	Is 30:1	3068
will not hear the law of the *L*	Is 30:9	3068
For thus saith the *L* GOD, the	Is 30:15	136
And therefore will the *L* wait	Is 30:18	3068
for the *L* is a God of judgment	Is 30:18	3068
though the *L* give you the bread	Is 30:20	136
in the day that the *L* bindeth up	Is 30:26	3068
the name of the *L* cometh from far	Is 30:27	3068
come into the mountain of the *L*	Is 30:29	3068
the *L* shall cause his glorious	Is 30:30	3068
L shall the Assyrian be beaten	Is 30:31	3068
which the *L* shall lay upon him,	Is 30:32	3068
the breath of the *L*, like a	Is 30:33	3068
One of Israel, neither seek the *L*	Is 31:1	3068
When the *L* shall stretch out his	Is 31:3	3068
thus hath the *L* spoken unto me	Is 31:4	3068
so shall the *L* of hosts come down	Is 31:4	3068
so will the *L* of hosts defend	Is 31:5	3068
afraid of the ensign, saith the *L*	Is 31:9	3068
and to utter error against the *L*	Is 32:6	3068
O *L*, be gracious unto us	Is 33:2	3068
The *L* is exalted	Is 33:5	3068
the fear of the *L* is his treasure	Is 33:6	3068
Now will I rise, saith the *L*	Is 33:10	3068
But there the glorious *L* will be	Is 33:21	3068
For the *L* is our judge	Is 33:22	3068
the *L* is our lawgiver	Is 33:22	3068
the *L* is our king	Is 33:22	3068
of the *L* is upon all nations	Is 34:2	3068
The sword of the *L* is filled with	Is 34:6	3068
for the *L* hath a sacrifice in	Is 34:6	3068
Seek ye out of the book of the *L*	Is 34:16	3068
they shall see the glory of the *L*	Is 35:2	3068
ransomed of the *L* shall return	Is 35:10	3068
to me, We trust in the *L* our God	Is 36:7	3068
am I now come up without the *L*	Is 36:10	3068
the *L* said unto me, Go up against	Is 36:10	3068
Hezekiah make you trust in the *L*	Is 36:15	3068
The *L* will surely deliver us	Is 36:15	3068
saying, The *L* will deliver us	Is 36:18	3068
that the *L* should deliver	Is 36:20	3068
and went into the house of the *L*	Is 37:1	3068
It may be the *L* thy God will hear	Is 37:4	3068
which the *L* thy God hath heard	Is 37:4	3068
your master, Thus saith the *L*	Is 37:6	3068
went up unto the house of the *L*	Is 37:14	3068
and spread it before the *L*	Is 37:14	3068
And Hezekiah prayed unto the *L*	Is 37:15	3068
O *L* of hosts, God of Israel, that	Is 37:16	3068
Incline thine ear, O *L*, and hear	Is 37:17	3068
open thine eyes, O *L*, and see	Is 37:17	3068
Of a truth, *L*, the kings of	Is 37:18	3068
O *L* our God, save us from his	Is 37:20	3068
may know that thou art the *L*	Is 37:20	3068
Thus saith the *L* God of Israel	Is 37:21	3068
the *L* hath spoken concerning him	Is 37:22	3068
hast thou reproached the *L*	Is 37:24	136
the zeal of the *L* of hosts shall	Is 37:32	3068
Therefore thus saith the *L*	Is 37:33	3068
come into this city, saith the *L*	Is 37:34	3068
the angel of the *L* went forth	Is 37:36	3068
said unto him, Thus saith the *L*	Is 38:1	3068
the wall, and prayed unto the *L*	Is 38:2	3068
And said, Remember now, O *L*	Is 38:3	3068
came the word of the *L* to Isaiah	Is 38:4	3068
say to Hezekiah, Thus saith the *L*	Is 38:5	3068
be a sign unto thee from the *L*	Is 38:7	3068
that the *L* will do this thing	Is 38:7	3068
not see the *L*, even the *L*	Is 38:11	3050
O *L*, I am oppressed	Is 38:14	3068
O *L*, by these things men live, and	Is 38:16	136
The *L* was ready to save me	Is 38:20	3068
of our life in the house of the *L*	Is 38:20	3068
shall go up to the house of the *L*	Is 38:22	3068
Hear the word of the *L* of hosts	Is 39:5	3068
shall be left, saith the *L*	Is 39:6	3068
of the *L* which thou hast spoken	Is 39:8	3068
Prepare ye the way of the *L*	Is 40:3	3068
the glory of the *L* shall be	Is 40:5	3068
the mouth of the *L* hath spoken it	Is 40:5	3068
spirit of the *L* bloweth upon it	Is 40:7	3068
the *L* GOD will come with strong	Is 40:10	136
hath directed the Spirit of the *L*	Is 40:13	3068
Israel, My way is hid from the *L*	Is 40:27	3068
that the everlasting God, the *L*	Is 40:28	3068
the *L* shall renew their strength	Is 40:31	3068
I the *L*, the first, and with the	Is 41:4	3068
For I the *L* thy God will hold thy	Is 41:13	3068
I will help thee, saith the *L*	Is 41:14	3068
and thou shalt rejoice in the *L*	Is 41:16	3068
I the *L* will hear them, I the God	Is 41:17	3068
the hand of the *L* hath done this	Is 41:20	3068
Produce your cause, saith the *L*	Is 41:21	3068
Thus saith God the *L*, he that	Is 42:5	3068
I the *L* have called thee in	Is 42:6	3068
I am the *L*	Is 42:8	3068
Sing unto the *L* a new song	Is 42:10	3068
Let them give glory unto the *L*	Is 42:12	3068
The *L* shall go forth as a mighty	Is 42:13	3068
The *L* is well pleased for his	Is 42:21	3068
did not the *L*, he against whom we	Is 42:24	3068
saith the *L* that created thee	Is 43:1	3068
For I am the *L* thy God, the Holy	Is 43:3	3068
Ye are my witnesses, saith the *L*	Is 43:10	3068
I, even I, am the *L*	Is 43:11	3068
ye are my witnesses, saith the *L*	Is 43:12	3068
Thus saith the *L*, your redeemer,	Is 43:14	3068
I am the *L*, your Holy One, the	Is 43:15	3068
Thus saith the *L*, which maketh a	Is 43:16	3068
Thus saith the *L* that made thee	Is 44:2	3068
with his hand unto the *L*, and	Is 44:5	3068
Thus saith the *L* the King of	Is 44:6	3068
and his redeemer the *L* of hosts	Is 44:6	3068
for the *L* hath done it	Is 44:23	3068
for the *L* hath redeemed Jacob, and	Is 44:23	3068
Thus saith the *L*, thy redeemer,	Is 44:24	3068
I am the *L* that maketh all things	Is 44:24	3068
Thus saith the *L* to his anointed,	Is 45:1	3068
thou mayest know that I, the *L*	Is 45:3	3068
I am the *L*, and there is none else	Is 45:5	3068
I am the *L*, and there is none else	Is 45:6	3068
I the *L* do all these things	Is 45:7	3068
I the *L* have created it	Is 45:8	3068
Thus saith the *L*, the Holy One of	Is 45:11	3068
nor reward, saith the *L* of hosts	Is 45:13	3068
Thus saith the *L*, The labour of	Is 45:14	3068
Israel shall be saved in the *L*	Is 45:17	3068
For thus saith the *L* that created	Is 45:18	3068
I am the *L*	Is 45:18	3068
I the *L* speak righteousness, I	Is 45:19	3068
have not I the *L*	Is 45:21	3068
in the *L* have I righteousness and	Is 45:24	3068
In the *L* shall all the seed of	Is 45:25	3068
the *L* of hosts is his name, the	Is 47:4	3068
which swear by the name of the *L*	Is 48:1	3068
The *L* of hosts is his name	Is 48:2	3068
The *L* hath loved him	Is 48:14	3068
and now the *L* GOD, and his Spirit,	Is 48:16	136
Thus saith the *L*, thy Redeemer,	Is 48:17	3068
I am the *L* thy God which teacheth	Is 48:17	3068
The *L* hath redeemed his servant	Is 48:20	3068
There is no peace, saith the *L*	Is 48:22	3068
The *L* hath called me from the	Is 49:1	3068
surely my judgment is with the *L*	Is 49:4	3068
saith the *L* that formed me from	Is 49:5	3068
be glorious in the eyes of the *L*	Is 49:5	3068
Thus saith the *L*, the Redeemer of	Is 49:7	3068
because of the *L* that is faithful	Is 49:7	3068
Thus saith the *L*, In an	Is 49:8	3068
for the *L* hath comforted his	Is 49:13	3068
The *L* hath forsaken me	Is 49:14	3068
and my *L* hath forgotten me	Is 49:14	136
As I live, saith the *L*, thou	Is 49:18	3068
Thus saith the *L* GOD, Behold, I	Is 49:22	136
thou shalt know that I am the *L*	Is 49:23	3068
But thus saith the *L*, Even the	Is 49:25	3068
know that I the *L* am thy Saviour	Is 49:26	3068
Thus saith the *L*, Where is the	Is 50:1	3068
The *L* GOD hath given me the	Is 50:4	136
The *L* GOD hath opened mine ear,	Is 50:5	136
For the *L* GOD will help me	Is 50:7	136
Behold, the *L* GOD will help me	Is 50:9	136
is among you that feareth the *L*	Is 50:10	3068
him trust in the name of the *L*	Is 50:10	3068
righteousness, ye that seek the *L*	Is 51:1	3068
For the *L* shall comfort Zion	Is 51:3	3068
desert like the garden of the *L*	Is 51:3	3068
put on strength, O arm of the *L*	Is 51:9	3068
redeemed of the *L* shall return	Is 51:11	3068
And forgettest the *L* thy maker	Is 51:13	3068
But I am the *L* thy God, that	Is 51:15	3068
The *L* of hosts is his name	Is 51:15	3068
hand of the *L* the cup of his fury	Is 51:17	3068
are full of the fury of the *L*	Is 51:20	3068
Thus saith thy *L*	Is 51:22	113
the *L*, and thy God	Is 51:22	3068
For thus saith the *L*, Ye have	Is 52:3	3068
For thus saith the *L* GOD, My	Is 52:4	136
what have I here, saith the *L*	Is 52:5	3068
make them to howl, saith the *L*	Is 52:5	3068
when the *L* shall bring again Zion	Is 52:8	3068
for the *L* hath comforted his	Is 52:9	3068
The *L* hath made bare his holy arm	Is 52:10	3068
that bear the vessels of the *L*	Is 52:11	3068

for the *L* will go before you	Is 52:12	3068
whom is the arm of the *L* revealed	Is 53:1	3068
the *L* hath laid on him the	Is 53:6	3068
it pleased the *L* to bruise him	Is 53:10	3068
the pleasure of the *L* shall	Is 53:10	3068
of the married wife, saith the *L*	Is 54:1	3068
the *L* of hosts is his name	Is 54:5	3068
For the *L* hath called thee as a	Is 54:6	3068
on thee, saith the *L* thy Redeemer	Is 54:8	3068
saith the *L* that hath mercy on	Is 54:10	3068
children shall be taught of the *L*	Is 54:13	3068
heritage of the servants of the *L*	Is 54:17	3068
is of me, saith the *L*	Is 54:17	3068
thee because of the *L* thy God	Is 55:5	3068
Seek ye the *L* while he may be	Is 55:6	3068
and let him return unto the *L*	Is 55:7	3068
your ways my ways, saith the *L*	Is 55:8	3068
it shall be to the *L* for a name	Is 55:13	3068
Thus saith the *L*, Keep ye	Is 56:1	3068
that hath joined himself to the *L*	Is 56:3	3068
The *L* hath utterly separated me	Is 56:3	3068
For thus saith the *L* unto the	Is 56:4	3068
that join themselves to the *L*	Is 56:6	3068
him, and to love the name of the *L*	Is 56:6	3068
The *L* GOD which gathereth the	Is 56:8	136
to him that is near, saith the *L*	Is 57:19	3068
and an acceptable day to the *L*	Is 58:5	3068
the glory of the *L* shall be thy	Is 58:8	3068
thou call, and the *L* shall answer	Is 58:9	3068
And the *L* shall guide thee	Is 58:11	3068
a delight, the holy of the *L*	Is 58:13	3068
thou delight thyself in the *L*	Is 58:14	3068
the mouth of the *L* hath spoken it	Is 58:14	3068
and lying against the *L*, and	Is 59:13	3068
the *L* saw it, and it displeased	Is 59:15	3068
the name of the *L* from the west	Is 59:19	3068
the Spirit of the *L* shall lift up	Is 59:19	3068
in Jacob, saith the *L*	Is 59:20	3068
covenant with them, saith the *L*	Is 59:21	3068
of thy seed's seed, saith the *L*	Is 59:21	3068
the glory of the *L* is risen upon	Is 60:1	3068
but the *L* shall arise upon thee,	Is 60:2	3068
shew forth the praises of the *L*	Is 60:6	3068
unto the name of the *L* thy God	Is 60:9	3068
call thee, The city of the *L*	Is 60:14	3068
know that I the *L* am thy Saviour	Is 60:16	3068
but the *L* shall be unto thee an	Is 60:19	3068
for the *L* shall be thine	Is 60:20	3068
I the *L* will hasten it in his	Is 60:22	3068
Spirit of the *L* GOD is upon me	Is 61:1	136
because the *L* hath anointed me to	Is 61:1	3068
the acceptable year of the *L*	Is 61:2	3068
the planting of the *L*, that he	Is 61:3	3068
be named the Priests of the *L*	Is 61:6	3068
For I the *L* love judgment, I hate	Is 61:8	3068
the seed which the *L* hath blessed	Is 61:9	3068
I will greatly rejoice in the *L*	Is 61:10	3068
so the *L* GOD will cause	Is 61:11	136
the mouth of the *L* shall name	Is 62:2	3068
of glory in the hand of the *L*	Is 62:3	3068
for the *L* delighteth in thee, and	Is 62:4	3068
ye that make mention of the *L*	Is 62:6	3068
The *L* hath sworn by his right	Is 62:8	3068
it shall eat it, and praise the *L*	Is 62:9	3068
the *L* hath proclaimed unto the	Is 62:11	3068
people, The redeemed of the *L*	Is 62:12	3068
the lovingkindnesses of the *L*	Is 63:7	3068
and the praises of the *L*	Is 63:7	3068
that the *L* hath bestowed on us	Is 63:7	3068
the Spirit of the *L* caused him to	Is 63:14	3068
thou, O *L*, art our father, our	Is 63:16	3068
O *L*, why hast thou made us to err	Is 63:17	3068
But now, O *L*, thou art our father	Is 64:8	3068
Be not wroth very sore, O *L*	Is 64:9	3068
thyself for these things, O *L*	Is 64:12	3068
fathers together, saith the *L*	Is 65:7	3068
Thus saith the *L*, As the new wine	Is 65:8	3068
ye are they that forsake the *L*	Is 65:11	3068
Therefore thus saith the *L* GOD	Is 65:13	136
for the *L* GOD shall slay thee, and	Is 65:15	136
the seed of the blessed of the *L*	Is 65:23	3068
all my holy mountain, saith the *L*	Is 65:25	3068
Thus saith the *L*, The heaven is	Is 66:1	3068
things have been, saith the *L*	Is 66:2	3068
Hear the word of the *L*, ye that	Is 66:5	3068
said, Let the *L* be glorified	Is 66:5	3068
a voice of the *L* that rendereth	Is 66:6	3068
saith the *L*	Is 66:9	3068
For thus saith the *L*, Behold, I	Is 66:12	3068
the hand of the *L* shall be known	Is 66:14	3068
the *L* will come with fire, and	Is 66:15	3068
will the *L* plead with all flesh	Is 66:16	3068
the slain of the *L* shall be many	Is 66:16	3068
be consumed together, saith the *L*	Is 66:17	3068
for an offering unto the *L* out of	Is 66:20	3068
mountain Jerusalem, saith the *L*	Is 66:20	3068
vessel into the house of the *L*	Is 66:20	3068
and for Levites, saith the *L*	Is 66:21	3068
remain before me, saith the *L*	Is 66:22	3068
to worship before me, saith the *L*	Is 66:23	3068
To whom the word of the *L* came in	Jer 1:2	3068
the word of the *L* came unto me	Jer 1:4	3068
Then said I, Ah, *L* GOD	Jer 1:6	136
But the *L* said unto me, Say not,	Jer 1:7	3068
thee to deliver thee, saith the *L*	Jer 1:8	3068
Then the *L* put forth his hand, and	Jer 1:9	3068
the *L* said unto me, Behold, I	Jer 1:9	3068
the word of the *L* came unto me	Jer 1:11	3068
Then said the *L* unto me, Thou	Jer 1:12	3068
the word of the *L* came unto me	Jer 1:13	3068
Then the *L* said unto me, Out of	Jer 1:14	3068
of the north, saith the *L*	Jer 1:15	3068
for I am with thee, saith the *L*	Jer 1:19	3068
the word of the *L* came to me	Jer 2:1	3068
saying, Thus saith the *L*	Jer 2:2	3068
Israel was holiness unto the *L*	Jer 2:3	3068
shall come upon them, saith the *L*	Jer 2:3	3068
Hear ye the word of the *L*	Jer 2:4	3068
Thus saith the *L*, What iniquity	Jer 2:5	3068
Where is the *L* that brought us up	Jer 2:6	3068
priests said not, Where is the *L*	Jer 2:8	3068
yet plead with you, saith the *L*	Jer 2:9	3068
be ye very desolate, saith the *L*	Jer 2:12	3068
thou hast forsaken the *L* thy God	Jer 2:17	3068
thou hast forsaken the *L* thy God	Jer 2:19	3068
in thee, saith the *L* GOD of hosts	Jer 2:19	136
marked before me, saith the *L* GOD	Jer 2:22	136
against me, saith the *L*	Jer 2:29	3068
see ye the word of the *L*	Jer 2:31	3068
for the *L* hath rejected thy	Jer 2:37	3068
return again to me, saith the *L*	Jer 3:1	3068
The *L* said also unto me in the	Jer 3:6	3068
heart, but feignedly, saith the *L*	Jer 3:10	3068
And the *L* said unto me, The	Jer 3:11	3068
backsliding Israel, saith the *L*	Jer 3:12	3068
for I am merciful, saith the *L*	Jer 3:12	3068
against the *L* thy God, and hast	Jer 3:13	3068
not obeyed my voice, saith the *L*	Jer 3:13	3068
backsliding children, saith the *L*	Jer 3:14	3068
land, in those days, saith the *L*	Jer 3:16	3068
The ark of the covenant of the *L*	Jer 3:16	3068
Jerusalem the throne of the *L*	Jer 3:17	3068
unto it, to the name of the *L*	Jer 3:17	3068
O house of Israel, saith the *L*	Jer 3:20	3068
have forgotten the *L* their God	Jer 3:21	3068
for thou art the *L* our God	Jer 3:22	3068
truly in the *L* our God is the	Jer 3:23	3068
have sinned against the *L* our God	Jer 3:25	3068
obeyed the voice of the *L* our God	Jer 3:25	3068
return, O Israel, saith the *L*	Jer 4:1	3068
The *L* liveth, in truth, in	Jer 4:2	3068
For thus saith the *L* to the men	Jer 4:3	3068
Circumcise yourselves to the *L*	Jer 4:4	3068
the *L* is not turned back from us	Jer 4:8	3068
to pass at that day, saith the *L*	Jer 4:9	3068
Then said I, Ah, *L* GOD	Jer 4:10	136
against me, saith the *L*	Jer 4:17	3068
down at the presence of the *L*	Jer 4:26	3068
For thus hath the *L* said, The	Jer 4:27	3068
And though they say, The *L* liveth	Jer 5:2	3068
O *L*, are not thine eyes upon the	Jer 5:3	3068
they know not the way of the *L*	Jer 5:4	3068
they have known the way of the *L*	Jer 5:5	3068
for these things? saith the *L*	Jer 5:9	3068
against me, saith the *L*	Jer 5:11	3068
They have belied the *L*, and said,	Jer 5:12	3068
thus saith the *L* God of hosts	Jer 5:14	3068
O house of Israel, saith the *L*	Jer 5:15	3068
in those days, saith the *L*	Jer 5:18	3068
Wherefore doeth the *L* our God all	Jer 5:19	3068
Fear ye not me? saith the *L*	Jer 5:22	3068
Let us now fear the *L* our God	Jer 5:24	3068
these things? saith the *L*	Jer 5:29	3068
For thus hath the *L* of hosts said	Jer 6:6	3068
Thus saith the *L* of hosts	Jer 6:9	3068
the word of the *L* is unto them a	Jer 6:10	3068
I am full of the fury of the *L*	Jer 6:11	3068
of the land, saith the *L*	Jer 6:12	3068
shall be cast down, saith the *L*	Jer 6:15	3068
Thus saith the *L*, Stand ye in the	Jer 6:16	3068
Therefore thus saith the *L*	Jer 6:21	3068
Thus saith the *L*, Behold, a	Jer 6:22	3068
because the *L* hath rejected them	Jer 6:30	3068
that came to Jeremiah from the *L*	Jer 7:1	3068
and say, Hear the word of the *L*	Jer 7:2	3068
at these gates to worship the *L*	Jer 7:2	3068
Thus saith the *L* of hosts	Jer 7:3	3068
saying, The temple of the *L*	Jer 7:4	3068
of the *L*, The temple of the *L*	Jer 7:4	3068
even I have seen it, saith the *L*	Jer 7:11	3068
done all these works, saith the *L*	Jer 7:13	3068
to anger? saith the *L*	Jer 7:19	3068
Therefore thus saith the *L* GOD	Jer 7:20	136
Thus saith the *L* of hosts	Jer 7:21	3068
not the voice of the *L* their God	Jer 7:28	3068
for the *L* hath rejected and	Jer 7:29	3068
evil in my sight, saith the *L*	Jer 7:30	3068
the days come, saith the *L*	Jer 7:32	3068
At that time, saith the *L*	Jer 8:1	3068
driven them, saith the *L* of hosts	Jer 8:3	3068
say unto them, Thus saith the *L*	Jer 8:4	3068
know not the judgment of the *L*	Jer 8:7	3068
and the law of the *L* is with us	Jer 8:8	3068
have rejected the word of the *L*	Jer 8:9	3068
shall be cast down, saith the *L*	Jer 8:12	3068
surely consume them, saith the *L*	Jer 8:13	3068
for the *L* our God hath put us to	Jer 8:14	3068
we have sinned against the *L*	Jer 8:14	3068
they shall bite you, saith the *L*	Jer 8:17	3068
Is not the *L* in Zion	Jer 8:19	3068
and they know not me, saith the *L*	Jer 9:3	3068
refuse to know me, saith the *L*	Jer 9:6	3068
thus saith the *L* of hosts	Jer 9:7	3068
these things? saith the *L*	Jer 9:9	3068
the mouth of the *L* hath spoken	Jer 9:12	3068
the *L* saith, Because they have	Jer 9:13	3068
thus saith the *L* of hosts	Jer 9:15	3068
Thus saith the *L* of hosts	Jer 9:17	3068
Yet hear the word of the *L*	Jer 9:20	3068
Speak, Thus saith the *L*, Even the	Jer 9:22	3068
Thus saith the *L*, Let not the	Jer 9:23	3068
that I am the *L* which exercise	Jer 9:24	3068
things I delight, saith the *L*	Jer 9:24	3068
the days come, saith the *L*	Jer 9:25	3068
which the *L* speaketh unto you	Jer 10:1	3068
Thus saith the *L*, Learn not the	Jer 10:2	3068
there is none like unto thee, O *L*	Jer 10:6	3068
But the *L* is the true God, he is	Jer 10:10	3068
The *L* of hosts is his name	Jer 10:16	3068
For thus saith the *L*, Behold, I	Jer 10:18	3068
brutish, and have not sought the *L*	Jer 10:21	3068
O *L*, I know that the way of man	Jer 10:23	3068
O *L*, correct me, but with	Jer 10:24	3068
that came to Jeremiah from the *L*	Jer 11:1	3068
Thus saith the *L* God of Israel	Jer 11:3	3068
I, and said, So be it, O *L*	Jer 11:5	3068
Then the *L* said unto me, Proclaim	Jer 11:6	3068
the *L* said unto me, A conspiracy	Jer 11:9	3068
Therefore thus saith the *L*	Jer 11:11	3068
The *L* called thy name, A green	Jer 11:16	3068
For the *L* of hosts, that planted	Jer 11:17	3068
the *L* hath given me knowledge of	Jer 11:18	3068
O *L* of hosts, that judgest	Jer 11:20	3068
the *L* of the men of Anathoth	Jer 11:21	3068
Prophesy not in the name of the *L*	Jer 11:21	3068
thus saith the *L* of hosts	Jer 11:22	3068
Righteous art thou, O *L*, when I	Jer 12:1	3068
But thou, O *L*, knowest me	Jer 12:3	3068
for the sword of the *L* shall	Jer 12:12	3068
of the fierce anger of the *L*	Jer 12:13	3068
Thus saith the *L* against all mine	Jer 12:14	3068
to swear by my name, The *L* liveth	Jer 12:16	3068
destroy that nation, saith the *L*	Jer 12:17	3068
Thus saith the *L* unto me, Go and	Jer 13:1	3068
according to the word of the *L*	Jer 13:2	3068
the word of the *L* came unto me	Jer 13:3	3068
Euphrates, as the *L* commanded me	Jer 13:5	3068
that the *L* said unto me, Arise,	Jer 13:6	3068
the word of the *L* came unto me	Jer 13:8	3068
Thus saith the *L*, After this	Jer 13:9	3068
whole house of Judah, saith the *L*	Jer 13:11	3068
Thus saith the *L* God of Israel	Jer 13:12	3068
say unto them, Thus saith the *L*	Jer 13:13	3068
and the sons together, saith the *L*	Jer 13:14	3068
for the *L* hath spoken	Jer 13:15	3068
Give glory to the *L* your God	Jer 13:16	3068
thy measures from me, saith the *L*	Jer 13:25	3068
The word of the *L* that came to	Jer 14:1	3068
O *L*, though our iniquities	Jer 14:7	3068
yet thou, O *L*, art in the midst	Jer 14:9	3068
Thus saith the *L* unto this people	Jer 14:10	3068
therefore the *L* doth not accept	Jer 14:10	3068
Then said the *L* unto me, Pray not	Jer 14:11	3068
Then said I, Ah, *L* GOD	Jer 14:13	136
Then the *L* said unto me, The	Jer 14:14	3068
Therefore thus saith the *L*	Jer 14:15	3068
We acknowledge, O *L*, our	Jer 14:20	3068
art not thou he, O *L* our God	Jer 14:22	3068
Then said the *L* unto me, Though	Jer 15:1	3068
shalt tell them, Thus saith the *L*	Jer 15:2	3068
over them four kinds, saith the *L*	Jer 15:3	3068
hast forsaken me, saith the *L*	Jer 15:6	3068
before their enemies, saith the *L*	Jer 15:9	3068
The *L* said, Verily it shall be	Jer 15:11	3068
O *L*, thou knowest	Jer 15:15	3068
by thy name, O *L* God of hosts	Jer 15:16	3068
Therefore thus saith the *L*	Jer 15:19	3068
and to deliver thee, saith the *L*	Jer 15:20	3068
The word of the *L* came also unto	Jer 16:1	3068
For thus saith the *L* concerning	Jer 16:3	3068
For thus saith the *L*, Enter not	Jer 16:5	3068
from this people, saith the *L*	Jer 16:5	3068
For thus saith the *L* of hosts	Jer 16:9	3068
Wherefore hath the *L* pronounced	Jer 16:10	3068
committed against the *L* our God	Jer 16:10	3068
have forsaken me, saith the *L*	Jer 16:11	3068
the days come, saith the *L*	Jer 16:14	3068
The *L* liveth, that brought up the	Jer 16:14	3068
The *L* liveth, that brought up the	Jer 16:15	3068
for many fishers, saith the *L*	Jer 16:16	3068
O *L*, my strength, and my fortress	Jer 16:19	3068
shall know that my name is The *L*	Jer 16:21	3068
Thus saith the *L*	Jer 17:5	3068
whose heart departeth from the *L*	Jer 17:5	3068
is the man that trusteth in the *L*	Jer 17:7	3068
and whose hope the *L* is	Jer 17:7	3068
I the *L* search the heart, I try	Jer 17:10	3068
O *L*, the hope of Israel, all that	Jer 17:13	3068
because they have forsaken the *L*	Jer 17:13	3068
Heal me, O *L*, and I shall be	Jer 17:14	3068
me, Where is the word of the *L*	Jer 17:15	3068
Thus said the *L* unto me	Jer 17:19	3068
them, Hear ye the word of the *L*	Jer 17:20	3068
Thus saith the *L*	Jer 17:21	3068
hearken unto me, saith the *L*	Jer 17:24	3068
praise, unto the house of the *L*	Jer 17:26	3068
which came to Jeremiah from the *L*	Jer 18:1	3068
Then the word of the *L* came to me	Jer 18:5	3068
this potter? saith the *L*	Jer 18:6	3068
saying, Thus saith the *L*	Jer 18:11	3068
Therefore thus saith the *L*	Jer 18:13	3068
Give heed to me, O *L*, and hearken	Jer 18:19	3068
Yet, *L*, thou knowest all their	Jer 18:23	3068
Thus saith the *L*, Go and get a	Jer 19:1	3068

And say, Hear ye the word of the *L*	Jer 19:3	3068
Thus saith the *L* of hosts	Jer 19:3	3068
the days come, saith the *L*	Jer 19:6	3068
them, Thus saith the *L* of hosts	Jer 19:11	3068
I do unto this place, saith the *L*	Jer 19:12	3068
whither the *L* had sent him to	Jer 19:14	3068
Thus saith the *L* of hosts	Jer 19:15	3068
governor in the house of the *L*	Jer 20:1	3068
which was by the house of the *L*	Jer 20:2	3068
The *L* hath not called thy name	Jer 20:3	3068
For thus saith the *L*, Behold, I	Jer 20:4	3068
O *L*, thou hast deceived me, and I	Jer 20:7	3068
because the word of the *L* was	Jer 20:8	3068
But the *L* is with me as a mighty	Jer 20:11	3068
O *L* of hosts, that triest the	Jer 20:12	3068
unto the *L*, praise ye the *L*	Jer 20:13	3068
the cities which the *L* overthrew	Jer 20:16	3068
came unto Jeremiah from the *L*	Jer 21:1	3068
I pray thee, of the *L* for us	Jer 21:2	3068
if so be that the *L* will deal	Jer 21:2	3068
Thus saith the *L* God of Israel	Jer 21:4	3068
And afterward, saith the *L*	Jer 21:7	3068
thou shalt say, Thus saith the *L*	Jer 21:8	3068
and not for good, saith the *L*	Jer 21:10	3068
say, Hear ye the word of the *L*	Jer 21:11	3068
house of David, thus saith the *L*	Jer 21:12	3068
and rock of the plain, saith the *L*	Jer 21:13	3068
fruit of your doings, saith the *L*	Jer 21:14	3068
Thus saith the *L*	Jer 22:1	3068
And say, Hear the word of the *L*	Jer 22:2	3068
Thus saith the *L*	Jer 22:3	3068
I swear by myself, saith the *L*	Jer 22:5	3068
For thus saith the *L* unto the	Jer 22:6	3068
Wherefore hath the *L* done thus	Jer 22:8	3068
the covenant of the *L* their God	Jer 22:9	3068
For thus saith the *L* touching	Jer 22:11	3068
know me? saith the *L*	Jer 22:16	3068
Therefore thus saith the *L*	Jer 22:18	3068
As I live, saith the *L*, though	Jer 22:24	3068
earth, hear the word of the *L*	Jer 22:29	3068
Thus saith the *L*, Write ye this	Jer 22:30	3068
my pasture! saith the *L*	Jer 23:1	3068
Therefore thus saith the *L* God of	Jer 23:2	3068
evil of your doings, saith the *L*	Jer 23:2	3068
they be lacking, saith the *L*	Jer 23:4	3068
the days come, saith the *L*	Jer 23:5	3068
called, THE *L* OUR RIGHTEOUSNESS	Jer 23:6	3068
the days come, saith the *L*	Jer 23:7	3068
The *L* liveth, which brought up	Jer 23:7	3068
The *L* liveth, which brought up and	Jer 23:8	3068
hath overcome, because of the *L*	Jer 23:9	3068
their wickedness, saith the *L*	Jer 23:11	3068
of their visitation, saith the *L*	Jer 23:12	3068
the *L* of hosts concerning the	Jer 23:15	3068
Thus saith the *L* of hosts	Jer 23:16	3068
and not out of the mouth of the *L*	Jer 23:16	3068
The *L* hath said, Ye shall have	Jer 23:17	3068
stood in the counsel of the *L*	Jer 23:18	3068
a whirlwind of the *L* is gone	Jer 23:19	3068
anger of the *L* shall not return	Jer 23:20	3068
Am I a God at hand, saith the *L*	Jer 23:23	3068
see him? saith the *L*	Jer 23:24	3068
and earth? saith the *L*	Jer 23:24	3068
the wheat? saith the *L*	Jer 23:28	3068
a fire? saith the *L*	Jer 23:29	3068
against the prophets, saith the *L*	Jer 23:30	3068
against the prophets, saith the *L*	Jer 23:31	3068
false dreams, saith the *L*	Jer 23:32	3068
this people at all, saith the *L*	Jer 23:32	3068
What is the burden of the *L*	Jer 23:33	3068
even forsake you, saith the *L*	Jer 23:33	3068
shall say, The burden of the *L*	Jer 23:34	3068
brother, What hath the *L* answered	Jer 23:35	3068
and, What hath the *L* spoken	Jer 23:35	3068
the burden of the *L* shall ye	Jer 23:36	3068
of the *L* of hosts our God	Jer 23:36	3068
What hath the *L* answered thee	Jer 23:37	3068
and, What hath the *L* spoken	Jer 23:37	3068
since ye say, The burden of the *L*	Jer 23:38	3068
therefore thus saith the *L*	Jer 23:38	3068
this word, The burden of the *L*	Jer 23:38	3068
not say, The burden of the *L*	Jer 23:38	3068
The *L* shewed me, and, behold, two	Jer 24:1	3068
set before the temple of the *L*	Jer 24:1	3068
Then said the *L* unto me, What	Jer 24:3	3068
the word of the *L* came unto me	Jer 24:4	3068
Thus saith the *L*, the God of	Jer 24:5	3068
heart to know me, that I am the *L*	Jer 24:7	3068
surely thus saith the *L*, So will	Jer 24:8	3068
the word of the *L* hath come unto	Jer 25:3	3068
the *L* hath sent unto you all his	Jer 25:4	3068
that the *L* hath given unto you	Jer 25:5	3068
hearkened unto me, saith the *L*	Jer 25:7	3068
thus saith the *L* of hosts	Jer 25:8	3068
of the north, saith the *L*	Jer 25:9	3068
and that nation, saith the *L*	Jer 25:12	3068
For thus saith the *L* God of	Jer 25:15	3068
unto whom the *L* had sent me	Jer 25:17	3068
them, Thus saith the *L* of hosts	Jer 25:27	3068
them, Thus saith the *L* of hosts	Jer 25:28	3068
the earth, saith the *L* of hosts	Jer 25:29	3068
The *L* shall roar from on high, and	Jer 25:30	3068
for the *L* hath a controversy with	Jer 25:31	3068
wicked to the sword, saith the *L*	Jer 25:31	3068
Thus saith the *L* of hosts	Jer 25:32	3068
the slain of the *L* shall be at	Jer 25:33	3068
for the *L* hath spoiled their	Jer 25:36	3068
of the fierce anger of the *L*	Jer 25:37	3068
Judah came this word from the *L*	Jer 26:1	3068
Thus saith the *L*	Jer 26:2	3068
say unto them, Thus saith the *L*	Jer 26:4	3068
these words in the house of the *L*	Jer 26:7	3068
L had commanded him to speak unto	Jer 26:8	3068
prophesied in the name of the *L*	Jer 26:9	3068
Jeremiah in the house of the *L*	Jer 26:9	3068
house unto the house of the *L*	Jer 26:10	3068
The *L* sent me to prophesy against	Jer 26:12	3068
obey the voice of the *L* your God	Jer 26:13	3068
the *L* will repent him of the evil	Jer 26:13	3068
for of a truth the *L* hath sent me	Jer 26:15	3068
us in the name of the *L* our God	Jer 26:16	3068
saying, Thus saith the *L* of hosts	Jer 26:18	3068
did he not fear the *L*, and	Jer 26:19	3068
fear the *L*, and besought the *L*	Jer 26:19	3068
prophesied in the name of the *L*	Jer 26:20	3068
word unto Jeremiah from the *L*	Jer 27:1	3068
Thus saith the *L* to me	Jer 27:2	3068
Thus saith the *L* of hosts	Jer 27:4	3068
nation will I punish, saith the *L*	Jer 27:8	3068
in their own land, saith the *L*	Jer 27:11	3068
as the *L* hath spoken against the	Jer 27:13	3068
I have not sent them, saith the *L*	Jer 27:15	3068
people, saying, Thus saith the *L*	Jer 27:16	3068
if the word of the *L* be with them	Jer 27:18	3068
intercession to the *L* of hosts	Jer 27:18	3068
are left in the house of the *L*	Jer 27:18	3068
For thus saith the *L* of hosts	Jer 27:19	3068
Yea, thus saith the *L* of hosts	Jer 27:21	3068
that remain in the house of the *L*	Jer 27:21	3068
that I visit them, saith the *L*	Jer 27:22	3068
unto me in the house of the *L*	Jer 28:1	3068
Thus speaketh the *L* of hosts	Jer 28:2	3068
went into Babylon, saith the *L*	Jer 28:4	3068
that stood in the house of the *L*	Jer 28:5	3068
the *L* do so	Jer 28:6	3068
the *L* perform thy words which	Jer 28:6	3068
that the *L* hath truly sent him	Jer 28:9	3068
people, saying, Thus saith the *L*	Jer 28:11	3068
Then the word of the *L* came unto	Jer 28:12	3068
saying, Thus saith the *L*	Jer 28:13	3068
For thus saith the *L* of hosts	Jer 28:14	3068
The *L* hath not sent thee	Jer 28:15	3068
Therefore thus saith the *L*	Jer 28:16	3068
taught rebellion against the *L*	Jer 28:16	3068
Thus saith the *L* of hosts	Jer 29:4	3068
and pray unto the *L* for it	Jer 29:7	3068
For thus saith the *L* of hosts	Jer 29:8	3068
I have not sent them, saith the *L*	Jer 29:9	3068
For thus saith the *L*, That after	Jer 29:10	3068
I think toward you, saith the *L*	Jer 29:11	3068
will be found of you, saith the *L*	Jer 29:14	3068
I have driven you, saith the *L*	Jer 29:14	3068
The *L* hath raised us up prophets	Jer 29:15	3068
Know that thus saith the *L* of the	Jer 29:16	3068
Thus saith the *L* of hosts	Jer 29:17	3068
to my words, saith the *L*, which I	Jer 29:19	3068
ye would not hear, saith the *L*	Jer 29:19	3068
ye therefore the word of the *L*	Jer 29:20	3068
Thus saith the *L* of hosts	Jer 29:21	3068
The *L* make thee like Zedekiah and	Jer 29:22	3068
and am a witness, saith the *L*	Jer 29:23	3068
Thus speaketh the *L* of hosts	Jer 29:25	3068
The *L* hath made thee priest in	Jer 29:26	3068
be officers in the house of the *L*	Jer 29:26	3068
the word of the *L* unto Jeremiah	Jer 29:30	3068
Thus saith the *L* concerning	Jer 29:31	3068
Therefore thus saith the *L*	Jer 29:32	3068
do for my people, saith the *L*	Jer 29:32	3068
taught rebellion against the *L*	Jer 29:32	3068
that came to Jeremiah from the *L*	Jer 30:1	3068
Thus speaketh the *L* God of Israel	Jer 30:2	3068
lo, the days come, saith the *L*	Jer 30:3	3068
Israel and Judah, saith the *L*	Jer 30:3	3068
the *L* spake concerning Israel	Jer 30:4	3068
For thus saith the *L*	Jer 30:5	3068
in that day, saith the *L* of hosts	Jer 30:8	3068
they shall serve the *L* their God	Jer 30:9	3068
O my servant Jacob, saith the *L*	Jer 30:10	3068
For I am with thee, saith the *L*	Jer 30:11	3068
For thus saith the *L*, Thy bruise	Jer 30:12	3068
thee of thy wounds, saith the *L*	Jer 30:17	3068
Thus saith the *L*	Jer 30:18	3068
unto me? saith the *L*	Jer 30:21	3068
the whirlwind of the *L* goeth	Jer 30:23	3068
anger of the *L* shall not return	Jer 30:24	3068
At the same time, saith the *L*	Jer 31:1	3068
Thus saith the *L*, The people	Jer 31:2	3068
The *L* hath appeared of old unto	Jer 31:3	3068
go up to Zion unto the *L* our God	Jer 31:6	3068
For thus saith the *L*	Jer 31:7	3068
ye, praise ye, and say, O *L*	Jer 31:7	3068
Hear the word of the *L*, O ye	Jer 31:10	3068
For the *L* hath redeemed Jacob, and	Jer 31:11	3068
together to the goodness of the *L*	Jer 31:12	3068
with my goodness, saith the *L*	Jer 31:14	3068
Thus saith the *L*	Jer 31:15	3068
Thus saith the *L*	Jer 31:16	3068
shall be rewarded, saith the *L*	Jer 31:16	3068
is hope in thine end, saith the *L*	Jer 31:17	3068
for thou art the *L* my God	Jer 31:18	3068
have mercy upon him, saith the *L*	Jer 31:20	3068
for the *L* hath created a new	Jer 31:22	3068
Thus saith the *L* of hosts	Jer 31:23	3068
The *L* bless thee, O habitation of	Jer 31:23	3068
the days come, saith the *L*	Jer 31:27	3068
build, and to plant, saith the *L*	Jer 31:28	3068
the days come, saith the *L*	Jer 31:31	3068
an husband unto them, saith the *L*	Jer 31:32	3068
After those days, saith the *L*	Jer 31:33	3068
his brother, saying, Know the *L*	Jer 31:34	3068
the greatest of them, saith the *L*	Jer 31:34	3068
Thus saith the *L*, which giveth	Jer 31:35	3068
The *L* of hosts is his name	Jer 31:35	3068
from before me, saith the *L*	Jer 31:36	3068
Thus saith the *L*	Jer 31:37	3068
that they have done, saith the *L*	Jer 31:37	3068
the days come, saith the *L*	Jer 31:38	3068
the city shall be built to the *L*	Jer 31:38	3068
east, shall be holy unto the *L*	Jer 31:40	3068
L in the tenth year of Zedekiah	Jer 32:1	3068
and say, Thus saith the *L*	Jer 32:3	3068
be until I visit him, saith the *L*	Jer 32:5	3068
The word of the *L* came unto me	Jer 32:6	3068
according to the word of the *L*	Jer 32:8	3068
that this was the word of the *L*	Jer 32:8	3068
Thus saith the *L* of hosts	Jer 32:14	3068
For thus saith the *L* of hosts	Jer 32:15	3068
of Neriah, I prayed unto the *L*	Jer 32:16	3068
Ah *L* GOD	Jer 32:17	136
the *L* of hosts, is his name	Jer 32:18	3068
O *L* GOD, Buy thee the field for	Jer 32:25	136
the word of the *L* unto Jeremiah	Jer 32:26	3068
Behold, I am the *L*, the God of	Jer 32:27	3068
Therefore thus saith the *L*	Jer 32:28	3068
work of their hands, saith the *L*	Jer 32:30	3068
And now therefore thus saith the *L*	Jer 32:36	3068
For thus saith the *L*	Jer 32:42	3068
captivity to return, saith the *L*	Jer 32:44	3068
Moreover the word of the *L* came	Jer 33:1	3068
Thus saith the *L* the maker	Jer 33:2	3068
thereof, the *L* that formed it, to	Jer 33:2	3068
the *L* is his name	Jer 33:2	3068
For thus saith the *L*, the God of	Jer 33:4	3068
Thus saith the *L*	Jer 33:10	3068
shall say, Praise the *L* of hosts	Jer 33:11	3068
for the *L* is good	Jer 33:11	3068
of praise into the house of the *L*	Jer 33:11	3068
as at the first, saith the *L*	Jer 33:11	3068
Thus saith the *L* of hosts	Jer 33:12	3068
that telleth them, saith the *L*	Jer 33:13	3068
the days come, saith the *L*	Jer 33:14	3068
called, The *L* our righteousness	Jer 33:16	3068
For thus saith the *L*	Jer 33:17	3068
the word of the *L* came unto	Jer 33:19	3068
Thus saith the *L*	Jer 33:20	3068
word of the *L* came to Jeremiah	Jer 33:23	3068
families which the *L* hath chosen	Jer 33:24	3068
Thus saith the *L*	Jer 33:25	3068
came unto Jeremiah from the *L*	Jer 34:1	3068
Thus saith the *L*, the God of	Jer 34:2	3068
and tell him, Thus saith the *L*	Jer 34:2	3068
Yet hear the word of the *L*	Jer 34:4	3068
Thus saith the *L* of thee, Thou	Jer 34:4	3068
pronounced the word, saith the *L*	Jer 34:5	3068
came unto Jeremiah from the *L*	Jer 34:8	3068
Therefore the word of the *L* came	Jer 34:12	3068
came to Jeremiah from the *L*	Jer 34:12	3068
Thus saith the *L*, the God of	Jer 34:13	3068
Therefore thus saith the *L*	Jer 34:17	3068
a liberty for you, saith the *L*	Jer 34:17	3068
I will command, saith the *L*	Jer 34:22	3068
came unto Jeremiah from the *L* in	Jer 35:1	3068
them into the house of the *L*	Jer 35:2	3068
them into the house of the *L*	Jer 35:4	3068
the word of the *L* unto Jeremiah	Jer 35:12	3068
Thus saith the *L* of hosts	Jer 35:13	3068
my words? saith the *L*	Jer 35:13	3068
thus saith the *L* God of hosts	Jer 35:17	3068
Thus saith the *L* of hosts	Jer 35:18	3068
thus saith the *L* of hosts	Jer 35:19	3068
came unto Jeremiah from the *L*	Jer 36:1	3068
Jeremiah all the words of the *L*	Jer 36:4	3068
cannot go into the house of the *L*	Jer 36:5	3068
the words of the *L* in the ears of	Jer 36:6	3068
their supplication before the *L*	Jer 36:7	3068
anger and the fury that the *L* hath	Jer 36:7	3068
of the *L* in the LORD's house	Jer 36:8	3068
proclaimed a fast before the *L* to	Jer 36:9	3068
of Jeremiah in the house of the *L*	Jer 36:10	3068
the book all the words of the *L*	Jer 36:11	3068
but the *L* hid them	Jer 36:26	3068
word of the *L* came to Jeremiah	Jer 36:27	3068
king of Judah, Thus saith the *L*	Jer 36:29	3068
Therefore thus saith the *L* of	Jer 36:30	3068
hearken unto the words of the *L*	Jer 37:2	3068
now unto the *L* our God for us	Jer 37:3	3068
the *L* unto the prophet Jeremiah	Jer 37:6	3068
Thus saith the *L*, the God of	Jer 37:7	3068
Thus saith the *L*	Jer 37:9	3068
Is there any word from the *L*	Jer 37:17	3068
Thus saith the *L*, He that	Jer 38:2	3068
Thus saith the *L*, This city shall	Jer 38:3	3068
that is in the house of the *L*	Jer 38:14	3068
Jeremiah, saying, As the *L* liveth	Jer 38:16	3068
unto Zedekiah, Thus saith the *L*	Jer 38:17	3068
beseech thee, the voice of the *L*	Jer 38:20	3068
word that the *L* hath shewed me	Jer 38:21	3068
word of the *L* came unto Jeremiah	Jer 39:15	3068
saying, Thus saith the *L* of hosts	Jer 39:16	3068
thee in that day, saith the *L*	Jer 39:17	3068
put thy trust in me, saith the *L*	Jer 39:18	3068
that came to Jeremiah from the *L*	Jer 40:1	3068
The *L* thy God hath pronounced	Jer 40:2	3068
Now the *L* hath brought it, and	Jer 40:3	3068

ye have sinned against the *L*	Jer 40:3	3068
bring them to the house of the *L*	Jer 41:5	3068
and pray for us unto the *L* thy God	Jer 42:2	3068
That the *L* thy God may shew us	Jer 42:3	3068
I will pray unto the *L* your God	Jer 42:4	3068
thing the *L* shall answer you	Jer 42:4	3068
The *L* be a true and faithful	Jer 42:5	3068
L thy God shall send thee to us	Jer 42:5	3068
obey the voice of the *L* our God	Jer 42:6	3068
obey the voice of the *L* our God	Jer 42:6	3068
word of the *L* came unto Jeremiah	Jer 42:7	3068
said unto them, Thus saith the *L*	Jer 42:9	3068
be not afraid of him, saith the *L*	Jer 42:11	3068
obey the voice of the *L* your God	Jer 42:13	3068
therefore hear the word of the *L*	Jer 42:15	3068
Thus saith the *L* of hosts	Jer 42:15	3068
For thus saith the *L* of hosts	Jer 42:18	3068
The *L* hath said concerning you, O	Jer 42:19	3068
ye sent me unto the *L* your God	Jer 42:20	3068
Pray for us unto the *L* our God	Jer 42:20	3068
all that the *L* our God shall say	Jer 42:20	3068
the voice of the *L* your God	Jer 42:21	3068
all the words of the *L* their God	Jer 43:1	3068
for which the *L* their God had	Jer 43:1	3068
the *L* our God hath not sent thee	Jer 43:2	3068
obeyed not the voice of the *L*	Jer 43:4	3068
obeyed not the voice of the *L*	Jer 43:7	3068
Then came the word of the *L* unto	Jer 43:8	3068
them, Thus saith the *L* of hosts	Jer 43:10	3068
Thus saith the *L* of hosts	Jer 44:2	3068
Therefore now thus saith the *L*	Jer 44:7	3068
thus saith the *L* of hosts	Jer 44:11	3068
unto us in the name of the *L*	Jer 44:16	3068
did not the *L* remember them, and	Jer 44:21	3068
So that the *L* could no longer	Jer 44:22	3068
ye have sinned against the *L*	Jer 44:23	3068
not obeyed the voice of the *L*	Jer 44:23	3068
the women, Hear the word of the *L*	Jer 44:24	3068
Thus saith the *L* of hosts	Jer 44:25	3068
hear ye the word of the *L*	Jer 44:26	3068
by my great name, saith the *L*	Jer 44:26	3068
Egypt, saying, The *L* GOD liveth	Jer 44:26	136
be a sign unto you, saith the *L*	Jer 44:29	3068
Thus saith the *L*	Jer 44:30	3068
Thus saith the *L*, the God of	Jer 45:2	3068
for the *L* hath added grief to my	Jer 45:3	3068
say unto him, The *L* saith thus	Jer 45:4	3068
evil upon all flesh, saith the *L*	Jer 45:5	3068
The word of the *L* which came to	Jer 46:1	3068
fear was round about, saith the *L*	Jer 46:5	3068
is the day of the *L* GOD of hosts	Jer 46:10	136
for the *L* GOD of hosts hath a	Jer 46:10	136
The word that the *L* spake to	Jer 46:13	3068
because the *L* did drive them	Jer 46:15	3068
whose name is the *L* of hosts	Jer 46:18	3068
cut down her forest, saith the *L*	Jer 46:23	3068
The *L* of hosts, the God of Israel	Jer 46:25	3068
in the days of old, saith the *L*	Jer 46:26	3068
O Jacob my servant, saith the *L*	Jer 46:28	3068
The word of the *L* that came to	Jer 47:1	3068
Thus saith the *L*	Jer 47:2	3068
for the *L* will spoil the	Jer 47:4	3068
O thou sword of the *L*, how long	Jer 47:6	3068
seeing the *L* hath given it a	Jer 47:7	3068
Moab thus saith the *L* of hosts	Jer 48:1	3068
destroyed, as the *L* hath spoken	Jer 48:8	3068
the work of the *L* deceitfully	Jer 48:10	3068
the days come, saith the *L*	Jer 48:12	3068
whose name is the *L* of hosts	Jer 48:15	3068
and his arm is broken, saith the *L*	Jer 48:25	3068
magnified himself against the *L*	Jer 48:26	3068
I know his wrath, saith the *L*	Jer 48:30	3068
to cease in Moab, saith the *L*	Jer 48:35	3068
is no pleasure, saith the *L*	Jer 48:38	3068
For thus saith the *L*	Jer 48:40	3068
magnified himself against the *L*	Jer 48:42	3068
O inhabitant of Moab, saith the *L*	Jer 48:43	3068
of their visitation, saith the *L*	Jer 48:44	3068
in the latter days, saith the *L*	Jer 48:47	3068
The Ammonites, thus saith the *L*	Jer 49:1	3068
the days come, saith the *L*	Jer 49:2	3068
that were his heirs, saith the *L*	Jer 49:2	3068
saith the *L* GOD of hosts, from	Jer 49:5	136
children of Ammon, saith the *L*	Jer 49:6	3068
Edom, thus saith the *L* of hosts	Jer 49:7	3068
For thus saith the *L*	Jer 49:12	3068
have sworn by myself, saith the *L*	Jer 49:13	3068
I have heard a rumour from the *L*	Jer 49:14	3068
down from thence, saith the *L*	Jer 49:16	3068
cities thereof, saith the *L*	Jer 49:18	3068
hear the counsel of the *L*	Jer 49:20	3068
in that day, saith the *L* of hosts	Jer 49:26	3068
shall smite, thus saith the *L*	Jer 49:28	3068
inhabitants of Hazor, saith the *L*	Jer 49:30	3068
without care, saith the *L*	Jer 49:31	3068
all sides thereof, saith the *L*	Jer 49:32	3068
The word of the *L* that came to	Jer 49:34	3068
Thus saith the *L* of hosts	Jer 49:35	3068
even my fierce anger, saith the *L*	Jer 49:37	3068
king and the princes, saith the *L*	Jer 49:38	3068
captivity of Elam, saith the *L*	Jer 49:39	3068
The word that the *L* spake against	Jer 50:1	3068
and in that time, saith the *L*	Jer 50:4	3068
shall go, and seek the *L* their God	Jer 50:4	3068
L in a perpetual covenant that	Jer 50:5	3068
they have sinned against the *L*	Jer 50:7	3068
habitation of justice, even the *L*	Jer 50:7	3068
shall be satisfied, saith the *L*	Jer 50:10	3068
the *L* it shall not be inhabited	Jer 50:13	3068
for she hath sinned against the *L*	Jer 50:14	3068
for it is the vengeance of the *L*	Jer 50:15	3068
thus saith the *L* of hosts	Jer 50:18	3068
and in that time, saith the *L*	Jer 50:20	3068
destroy after them, saith the *L*	Jer 50:21	3068
thou hast striven against the *L*	Jer 50:24	3068
The *L* hath opened his armoury, and	Jer 50:25	3068
for this is the work of the *L* GOD	Jer 50:25	136
the vengeance of the *L* our God	Jer 50:28	3068
she hath been proud against the *L*	Jer 50:29	3068
cut off in that day, saith the *L*	Jer 50:30	3068
proud, saith the *L* GOD of hosts	Jer 50:31	136
Thus saith the *L* of hosts	Jer 50:33	3068
the *L* of hosts is his name	Jer 50:34	3068
upon the Chaldeans, saith the *L*	Jer 50:35	3068
cities thereof, saith the *L*	Jer 50:40	3068
hear ye the counsel of the *L*	Jer 50:45	3068
Thus saith the *L*	Jer 51:1	3068
of his God, of the *L* of hosts	Jer 51:5	3068
The *L* hath brought forth our	Jer 51:10	3068
in Zion the work of the *L* our God	Jer 51:10	3068
the *L* hath raised up the spirit	Jer 51:11	3068
it is the vengeance of the *L*	Jer 51:11	3068
for the *L* hath both devised and	Jer 51:12	3068
The *L* of hosts hath sworn by	Jer 51:14	3068
the *L* of hosts is his name	Jer 51:19	3068
Zion in your sight, saith the *L*	Jer 51:24	3068
destroying mountain, saith the *L*	Jer 51:25	3068
be desolate for ever, saith the *L*	Jer 51:26	3068
for every purpose of the *L* shall	Jer 51:29	3068
For thus saith the *L* of hosts	Jer 51:33	3068
Therefore thus saith the *L*	Jer 51:36	3068
sleep, and not wake, saith the *L*	Jer 51:39	3068
from the fierce anger of the *L*	Jer 51:45	3068
her from the north, saith the *L*	Jer 51:48	3068
remember the *L* afar off, and let	Jer 51:50	3068
the days come, saith the *L*	Jer 51:52	3068
come unto her, saith the *L*	Jer 51:53	3068
Because the *L* hath spoiled	Jer 51:55	3068
for the *L* God of recompences	Jer 51:56	3068
whose name is the *L* of hosts	Jer 51:57	3068
Thus saith the *L* of hosts	Jer 51:58	3068
Then shalt thou say, O *L*, thou	Jer 51:62	3068
was evil in the eyes of the *L*	Jer 52:2	3068
L it came to pass in Jerusalem	Jer 52:3	3068
And burned the house of the *L*	Jer 52:13	3068
that were in the house of the *L*	Jer 52:17	3068
that was in the house of the *L*	Jer 52:17	3068
had made in the house of the *L*	Jer 52:20	3068
for the *L* hath afflicted her for	Lam 1:5	3068
O *L*, behold my affliction	Lam 1:9	3068
see, O *L*, and consider	Lam 1:11	3068
wherewith the *L* hath afflicted me	Lam 1:12	3068
the *L* hath delivered me into	Lam 1:14	136
The *L* hath trodden under foot all	Lam 1:15	136
the *L* hath trodden the virgin,	Lam 1:15	136
the *L* hath commanded concerning	Lam 1:17	3068
The *L* is righteous	Lam 1:18	3068
Behold, O *L*	Lam 1:20	3068
How hath the *L* covered the	Lam 2:1	136
The *L* hath swallowed up all the	Lam 2:2	136
The *L* was as an enemy	Lam 2:5	136
the *L* hath caused the solemn	Lam 2:6	3068
The *L* hath cast off his altar, he	Lam 2:7	136
a noise in the house of the *L*	Lam 2:7	3068
The *L* hath purposed to destroy	Lam 2:8	3068
also find no vision from the *L*	Lam 2:9	3068
The *L* hath done that which he had	Lam 2:17	3068
Their heart cried unto the *L*	Lam 2:18	136
water before the face of the *L*	Lam 2:19	136
Behold, O *L*, and consider to whom	Lam 2:20	3068
slain in the sanctuary of the *L*	Lam 2:20	136
and my hope is perished from the *L*	Lam 3:18	3068
The *L* is my portion, saith my	Lam 3:24	3068
The *L* is good unto them that wait	Lam 3:25	3068
wait for the salvation of the *L*	Lam 3:26	3068
For the *L* will not cast off for	Lam 3:31	136
in his cause, the *L* approveth not	Lam 3:36	136
when the *L* commandeth it not	Lam 3:37	136
our ways, and turn again to the *L*	Lam 3:40	3068
Till the *L* look down, and behold	Lam 3:50	3068
I called upon thy name, O *L*	Lam 3:55	3068
O *L*, thou hast pleaded the causes	Lam 3:58	136
O *L*, thou hast seen my wrong	Lam 3:59	3068
hast heard their reproach, O *L*	Lam 3:61	3068
unto them a recompence, O *L*	Lam 3:64	3068
from under the heavens of the *L*	Lam 3:66	3068
The *L* hath accomplished his fury	Lam 4:11	3068
The anger of the *L* hath divided	Lam 4:16	3068
nostrils, the anointed of the *L*	Lam 4:20	3068
Remember, O *L*, what is come upon	Lam 5:1	3068
Thou, O *L*, remainest for ever	Lam 5:19	3068
Turn thou us unto thee, O *L*	Lam 5:21	3068
The word of the *L* came expressly	Eze 1:3	3068
the hand of the *L* was there upon	Eze 1:3	3068
likeness of the glory of the *L*	Eze 1:28	3068
unto them, Thus saith the *L* GOD	Eze 2:4	136
tell them, Thus saith the *L* GOD	Eze 3:11	136
the glory of the *L* from his place	Eze 3:12	3068
hand of the *L* was strong upon me	Eze 3:14	3068
the word of the *L* came unto me	Eze 3:16	3068
the hand of the *L* was there upon	Eze 3:22	3068
the glory of the *L* stood there	Eze 3:23	3068
unto them, Thus saith the *L* GOD	Eze 3:27	136
the *L* said, Even thus shall the	Eze 4:13	3068
Then said I, Ah *L* GOD	Eze 4:14	136
Thus saith the *L* GOD	Eze 5:5	136
Therefore thus saith the *L* GOD	Eze 5:7	136
Therefore thus saith the *L* GOD	Eze 5:8	136
as I live, saith the *L* GOD	Eze 5:11	136
I the *L* have spoken it in my zeal	Eze 5:13	3068
I the *L* have spoken it	Eze 5:15	3068
I the *L* have spoken it	Eze 5:17	3068
And the word of the *L* came unto me	Eze 6:1	3068
hear the word of the *L* GOD	Eze 6:3	136
Thus saith the *L* GOD to the	Eze 6:3	136
and ye shall know that I am the *L*	Eze 6:7	3068
they shall know that I am the *L*	Eze 6:10	3068
Thus saith the *L* GOD	Eze 6:11	136
shall ye know that I am the *L*	Eze 6:13	3068
they shall know that I am the *L*	Eze 6:14	3068
the word of the *L* came unto me	Eze 7:1	3068
thus saith the *L* GOD unto the	Eze 7:2	136
and ye shall know that I am the *L*	Eze 7:4	3068
Thus saith the *L* GOD	Eze 7:5	136
know that I am the *L* that smiteth	Eze 7:9	3068
in the day of the wrath of the *L*	Eze 7:19	3068
they shall know that I am the *L*	Eze 7:27	3068
that the hand of the *L* GOD fell	Eze 8:1	136
for they say, The *L* seeth us not	Eze 8:12	3068
the *L* hath forsaken the earth	Eze 8:12	3068
the door of the temple of the *L*	Eze 8:16	3068
backs toward the temple of the *L*	Eze 8:16	3068
the *L* said unto him, Go through	Eze 9:4	3068
face, and cried, and said, Ah *L* GOD	Eze 9:8	136
The *L* hath forsaken the earth	Eze 9:9	3068
and the *L* seeth not	Eze 9:9	3068
Then the glory of the *L* went up	Eze 10:4	3068
Then the glory of the *L* departed	Eze 10:18	3068
the Spirit of the *L* fell upon me	Eze 11:5	3068
Thus saith the *L*	Eze 11:5	3068
Therefore thus saith the *L* GOD	Eze 11:7	136
a sword upon you, saith the *L* GOD	Eze 11:8	136
and ye shall know that I am the *L*	Eze 11:10	3068
And ye shall know that I am the *L*	Eze 11:12	3068
a loud voice, and said, Ah *L* GOD	Eze 11:13	136
the word of the *L* came unto me	Eze 11:14	3068
have said, Get you far from the *L*	Eze 11:15	3068
say, Thus saith the *L* GOD	Eze 11:16	136
say, Thus saith the *L* GOD	Eze 11:17	136
their own heads, saith the *L* GOD	Eze 11:21	136
the glory of the *L* went up from	Eze 11:23	3068
things that the *L* had shewed me	Eze 11:25	3068
The word of the *L* also came unto	Eze 12:1	3068
came the word of the *L* unto me	Eze 12:8	3068
unto them, Thus saith the *L* GOD	Eze 12:10	136
they shall know that I am the *L*	Eze 12:15	3068
they shall know that I am the *L*	Eze 12:16	3068
the word of the *L* came to me	Eze 12:17	3068
Thus saith the *L* GOD of the	Eze 12:19	136
and ye shall know that I am the *L*	Eze 12:20	3068
And the word of the *L* came unto me	Eze 12:21	3068
therefore, Thus saith the *L* GOD	Eze 12:23	136
For I am the *L*	Eze 12:25	3068
will perform it, saith the *L* GOD	Eze 12:25	136
the word of the *L* came to me	Eze 12:26	3068
unto them, Thus saith the *L* GOD	Eze 12:28	136
shall be done, saith the *L* GOD	Eze 12:28	136
And the word of the *L* came unto me	Eze 13:1	3068
hearts, Hear ye the word of the *L*	Eze 13:2	3068
Thus saith the *L* GOD	Eze 13:3	136
in the battle in the day of the *L*	Eze 13:5	3068
divination, saying, The *L* saith	Eze 13:6	3068
and the *L* hath not sent them	Eze 13:6	3068
whereas ye say, The *L* saith it	Eze 13:7	3068
Therefore thus saith the *L* GOD	Eze 13:8	136
I am against you, saith the *L* GOD	Eze 13:8	136
ye shall know that I am the *L* GOD	Eze 13:9	136
Therefore thus saith the *L* GOD	Eze 13:13	136
and ye shall know that I am the *L*	Eze 13:14	3068
is no peace, saith the *L* GOD	Eze 13:16	136
And say, Thus saith the *L* GOD	Eze 13:18	136
Wherefore thus saith the *L* GOD	Eze 13:20	136
and ye shall know that I am the *L*	Eze 13:21	3068
and ye shall know that I am the *L*	Eze 13:23	3068
And the word of the *L* came unto me	Eze 14:2	3068
unto them, Thus saith the *L* GOD	Eze 14:4	136
I the *L* will answer him that	Eze 14:4	3068
of Israel, Thus saith the *L* GOD	Eze 14:6	136
I the *L* will answer him by myself	Eze 14:7	3068
and ye shall know that I am the *L*	Eze 14:8	3068
I the *L* have deceived that	Eze 14:9	3068
may be their God, saith the *L* GOD	Eze 14:11	136
The word of the *L* came again to	Eze 14:12	3068
righteousness, saith the *L* GOD	Eze 14:14	136
in it, as I live, saith the *L* GOD	Eze 14:16	136
in it, as I live, saith the *L* GOD	Eze 14:18	136
in it, as I live, saith the *L* GOD	Eze 14:20	136
For thus saith the *L* GOD	Eze 14:21	136
have done in it, saith the *L* GOD	Eze 14:23	136
And the word of the *L* came unto me	Eze 15:1	3068
Therefore thus saith the *L* GOD	Eze 15:6	136
and ye shall know that I am the *L*	Eze 15:7	3068
a trespass, saith the *L* GOD	Eze 15:8	136
the word of the *L* came unto me	Eze 16:1	3068
Thus saith the *L* GOD unto	Eze 16:3	136
with thee, saith the *L* GOD	Eze 16:8	136
put upon thee, saith the *L* GOD	Eze 16:14	136
and thus it was, saith the *L* GOD	Eze 16:19	136
saith the *L* GOD	Eze 16:23	136
is thine heart, saith the *L* GOD	Eze 16:30	136
O harlot, hear the word of the *L*	Eze 16:35	3068
Thus saith the *L* GOD	Eze 16:36	136
upon thine head, saith the *L* GOD	Eze 16:43	136
As I live, saith the *L* GOD	Eze 16:48	136

L

thine abominations, saith the *L*	Eze 16:58	3068
For thus saith the *L* GOD	Eze 16:59	136
thou shalt know that I am the *L*	Eze 16:62	3068
thou hast done, saith the *L* GOD	Eze 16:63	136
And the word of the *L* came unto me	Eze 17:1	3068
And say, Thus saith the *L* GOD	Eze 17:3	136
Say thou, Thus saith the *L* GOD	Eze 17:9	136
the word of the *L* came unto me	Eze 17:11	3068
As I live, saith the *L* GOD	Eze 17:16	136
Therefore thus saith the *L* GOD	Eze 17:19	136
know that I the *L* have spoken it	Eze 17:21	3068
Thus saith the *L* GOD	Eze 17:22	136
L have brought down the high tree	Eze 17:24	3068
I the *L* have spoken and have done	Eze 17:24	3068
The word of the *L* came unto me	Eze 18:1	3068
As I live, saith the *L* GOD	Eze 18:3	136
surely live, saith the *L* GOD	Eze 18:9	136
saith the *L* GOD	Eze 18:23	136
The way of the *L* is not equal	Eze 18:25	136
The way of the *L* is not equal	Eze 18:29	136
to his ways, saith the *L* GOD	Eze 18:30	136
him that dieth, saith the *L* GOD	Eze 18:32	136
Israel came to enquire of the *L*	Eze 20:1	3068
came the word of the *L* unto me	Eze 20:2	3068
unto them, Thus saith the *L* GOD	Eze 20:3	136
As I live, saith the *L* GOD	Eze 20:3	136
unto them, Thus saith the *L* GOD	Eze 20:5	136
them, saying, I am the *L* your God	Eze 20:5	3068
I am the *L* your God	Eze 20:7	3068
I am the *L* that sanctify them	Eze 20:12	3068
I am the *L* your God	Eze 20:19	3068
may know that I am the *L* your God	Eze 20:20	3068
they might know that I am the *L*	Eze 20:26	3068
unto them, Thus saith the *L* GOD	Eze 20:27	136
of Israel, Thus saith the *L* GOD	Eze 20:30	136
As I live, saith the *L* GOD	Eze 20:31	136
As I live, saith the *L* GOD	Eze 20:33	136
I plead with you, saith the *L* GOD	Eze 20:36	136
and ye shall know that I am the *L*	Eze 20:38	3068
of Israel, thus saith the *L* GOD	Eze 20:39	136
height of Israel, saith the *L* GOD	Eze 20:40	136
And ye shall know that I am the *L*	Eze 20:42	3068
And ye shall know that I am the *L*	Eze 20:44	3068
house of Israel, saith the *L* GOD	Eze 20:44	136
the word of the *L* came unto me	Eze 20:45	3068
the south, Hear the word of the *L*	Eze 20:47	3068
Thus saith the *L* GOD	Eze 20:47	136
see that I the *L* have kindled it	Eze 20:48	3068
Then said I, Ah *L* GOD	Eze 20:49	136
And the word of the *L* came unto me	Eze 21:1	3068
land of Israel, Thus saith the *L*	Eze 21:3	3068
L have drawn forth my sword out	Eze 21:5	3068
brought to pass, saith the *L* GOD	Eze 21:7	136
the word of the *L* came unto me	Eze 21:8	3068
and say, Thus saith the *L*	Eze 21:9	3068
shall be no more, saith the *L* GOD	Eze 21:13	136
I the *L* have said it	Eze 21:17	3068
The word of the *L* came unto me	Eze 21:18	3068
Therefore thus saith the *L* GOD	Eze 21:24	136
Thus saith the *L* GOD	Eze 21:26	136
Thus saith the *L* GOD concerning	Eze 21:28	136
for I the *L* have spoken it	Eze 21:32	3068
the word of the *L* came unto me	Eze 22:1	3068
say thou, Thus saith the *L* GOD	Eze 22:3	136
forgotten me, saith the *L* GOD	Eze 22:12	136
I the *L* have spoken it, and will	Eze 22:14	3068
thou shalt know that I am the *L*	Eze 22:16	3068
And the word of the *L* came unto me	Eze 22:17	3068
Therefore thus saith the *L* GOD	Eze 22:19	136
ye shall know that I the *L* have	Eze 22:22	3068
And the word of the *L* came unto me	Eze 22:23	3068
saying, Thus saith the *L* GOD	Eze 22:28	136
when the *L* hath not spoken	Eze 22:28	3068
upon their heads, saith the *L* GOD	Eze 22:31	136
The word of the *L* came again unto	Eze 23:1	3068
O Aholibah, thus saith the *L* GOD	Eze 23:22	136
For thus saith the *L* GOD	Eze 23:28	136
Thus saith the *L* GOD	Eze 23:32	136
I have spoken it, saith the *L* GOD	Eze 23:34	136
Therefore thus saith the *L* GOD	Eze 23:35	136
The *L* said moreover unto me	Eze 23:36	3068
For thus saith the *L* GOD	Eze 23:46	136
ye shall know that I am the *L* GOD	Eze 23:49	136
the word of the *L* came unto me	Eze 24:1	3068
unto them, Thus saith the *L* GOD	Eze 24:3	136
Wherefore thus saith the *L* GOD	Eze 24:6	136
Therefore thus saith the *L* GOD	Eze 24:9	136
I the *L* have spoken it	Eze 24:14	3068
they judge thee, saith the *L* GOD	Eze 24:14	136
the word of the *L* came unto me	Eze 24:15	3068
The word of the *L* came unto me	Eze 24:20	3068
of Israel, Thus saith the *L* GOD	Eze 24:21	136
ye shall know that I am the *L* GOD	Eze 24:24	136
they shall know that I am the *L*	Eze 24:27	3068
The word of the *L* came again unto	Eze 25:1	3068
Hear the word of the *L* GOD	Eze 25:3	136
Thus saith the *L* GOD	Eze 25:3	136
and ye shall know that I am the *L*	Eze 25:5	3068
For thus saith the *L* GOD	Eze 25:6	136
thou shalt know that I am the *L*	Eze 25:7	3068
Thus saith the *L* GOD	Eze 25:8	136
they shall know that I am the *L*	Eze 25:11	3068
Thus saith the *L* GOD	Eze 25:12	136
Therefore thus saith the *L* GOD	Eze 25:13	136
my vengeance, saith the *L* GOD	Eze 25:14	136
Thus saith the *L* GOD	Eze 25:15	136
Therefore thus saith the *L* GOD	Eze 25:16	136
they shall know that I am the *L*	Eze 25:17	3068
the word of the *L* came unto me	Eze 26:1	3068
Therefore thus saith the *L* GOD	Eze 26:3	136
I have spoken it, saith the *L* GOD	Eze 26:5	136
they shall know that I am the *L*	Eze 26:6	3068
For thus saith the *L* GOD	Eze 26:7	136
for I the *L* have spoken it	Eze 26:14	3068
have spoken it, saith the *L* GOD	Eze 26:14	136
Thus saith the *L* GOD to Tyrus	Eze 26:15	136
For thus saith the *L* GOD	Eze 26:19	136
be found again, saith the *L* GOD	Eze 26:21	136
The word of the *L* came again unto	Eze 27:1	3068
many isles, Thus saith the *L* GOD	Eze 27:3	136
The word of the *L* came again unto	Eze 28:1	3068
of Tyrus, Thus saith the *L* GOD	Eze 28:2	136
Therefore thus saith the *L* GOD	Eze 28:6	136
I have spoken it, saith the *L* GOD	Eze 28:10	136
the word of the *L* came unto me	Eze 28:11	3068
unto him, Thus saith the *L* GOD	Eze 28:12	136
the word of the *L* came unto me	Eze 28:20	3068
And say, Thus saith the *L* GOD	Eze 28:22	136
they shall know that I am the *L*	Eze 28:22	3068
they shall know that I am the *L*	Eze 28:23	3068
shall know that I am the *L* GOD	Eze 28:24	136
Thus saith the *L* GOD	Eze 28:25	136
know that I am the *L* their God	Eze 28:26	3068
the word of the *L* came unto me	Eze 29:1	3068
and say, Thus saith the *L* GOD	Eze 29:3	136
Egypt shall know that I am the *L*	Eze 29:6	3068
Therefore thus saith the *L* GOD	Eze 29:8	136
they shall know that I am the *L*	Eze 29:9	3068
Yet thus saith the *L* GOD	Eze 29:13	136
shall know that I am the *L* GOD	Eze 29:16	136
the word of the *L* came unto me	Eze 29:17	3068
Therefore thus saith the *L* GOD	Eze 29:19	136
wrought for me, saith the *L* GOD	Eze 29:20	136
they shall know that I am the *L*	Eze 29:21	3068
The word of the *L* came again unto	Eze 30:1	3068
and say, Thus saith the *L* GOD	Eze 30:2	136
even the day of the *L* is near	Eze 30:3	3068
Thus saith the *L*	Eze 30:6	3068
it by the sword, saith the *L* GOD	Eze 30:6	136
they shall know that I am the *L*	Eze 30:8	3068
Thus saith the *L* GOD	Eze 30:10	136
I the *L* have spoken it	Eze 30:12	3068
Thus saith the *L* GOD	Eze 30:13	136
they shall know that I am the *L*	Eze 30:19	3068
the word of the *L* came unto me	Eze 30:20	3068
Therefore thus saith the *L* GOD	Eze 30:22	136
they shall know that I am the *L*	Eze 30:25	3068
they shall know that I am the *L*	Eze 30:26	3068
the word of the *L* came unto me	Eze 31:1	3068
Therefore thus saith the *L* GOD	Eze 31:10	136
Thus saith the *L* GOD	Eze 31:15	136
his multitude, saith the *L* GOD	Eze 31:18	136
the word of the *L* came unto me	Eze 32:1	3068
Thus saith the *L* GOD	Eze 32:3	136
upon thy land, saith the *L* GOD	Eze 32:8	136
For thus saith the *L* GOD	Eze 32:11	136
to run like oil, saith the *L* GOD	Eze 32:14	136
shall they know that I am the *L*	Eze 32:15	3068
her multitude, saith the *L* GOD	Eze 32:16	136
the word of the *L* came unto me	Eze 32:17	3068
by the sword, saith the *L* GOD	Eze 32:31	136
his multitude, saith the *L* GOD	Eze 32:32	136
the word of the *L* came unto me	Eze 33:1	3068
them, As I live, saith the *L* GOD	Eze 33:11	136
The way of the *L* is not equal	Eze 33:17	136
The way of the *L* is not equal	Eze 33:20	136
Now the hand of the *L* was upon me	Eze 33:22	3068
the word of the *L* came unto me	Eze 33:23	3068
unto them, Thus saith the *L* GOD	Eze 33:25	136
unto them, Thus saith the *L* GOD	Eze 33:27	136
shall they know that I am the *L*	Eze 33:29	3068
word that cometh forth from the *L*	Eze 33:30	3068
And the word of the *L* came unto me	Eze 34:1	3068
Thus saith the *L* GOD unto the	Eze 34:2	136
shepherds, hear the word of the *L*	Eze 34:7	3068
As I live saith the *L* GOD	Eze 34:8	136
shepherds, hear the word of the *L*	Eze 34:9	3068
Thus saith the *L* GOD	Eze 34:10	136
For thus saith the *L* GOD	Eze 34:11	136
them to lie down, saith the *L* GOD	Eze 34:15	136
O my flock, thus saith the *L* GOD	Eze 34:17	136
thus saith the *L* GOD unto them	Eze 34:20	136
I the *L* will be their God, and my	Eze 34:24	3068
I the *L* have spoken it	Eze 34:24	3068
and shall know that I am the *L*	Eze 34:27	3068
I the *L* their God am with them	Eze 34:30	3068
are my people, saith the *L* GOD	Eze 34:30	136
and I am your God, saith the *L* GOD	Eze 34:31	136
the word of the *L* came unto me	Eze 35:1	3068
say unto it, Thus saith the *L* GOD	Eze 35:3	136
thou shalt know that I am the *L*	Eze 35:4	3068
as I live, saith the *L* GOD	Eze 35:6	136
and ye shall know that I am the *L*	Eze 35:9	3068
whereas the *L* was there	Eze 35:10	3068
as I live, saith the *L* GOD	Eze 35:11	136
thou shalt know that I am the *L*	Eze 35:12	3068
Thus saith the *L* GOD	Eze 35:14	136
they shall know that I am the *L*	Eze 35:15	3068
of Israel, hear the word of the *L*	Eze 36:1	3068
Thus saith the *L* GOD	Eze 36:2	136
and say, Thus saith the *L* GOD	Eze 36:3	136
hear the word of the *L* GOD	Eze 36:4	136
Thus saith the *L* GOD to the	Eze 36:4	136
Therefore thus saith the *L* GOD	Eze 36:5	136
the valleys, Thus saith the *L* GOD	Eze 36:6	136
Therefore thus saith the *L* GOD	Eze 36:7	136
and ye shall know that I am the *L*	Eze 36:11	3068
Thus saith the *L* GOD	Eze 36:13	136
nations any more, saith the *L* GOD	Eze 36:14	136
to fall any more, saith the *L* GOD	Eze 36:15	136
the word of the *L* came unto me	Eze 36:16	3068
These are the people of the *L*	Eze 36:20	3068
of Israel, Thus saith the *L* GOD	Eze 36:22	136
shall know that I am the *L*	Eze 36:23	3068
saith the *L* GOD	Eze 36:23	136
sakes do I this, saith the *L* GOD	Eze 36:32	136
Thus saith the *L* GOD	Eze 36:33	136
I the *L* build the ruined places	Eze 36:36	3068
I the *L* have spoken it, and I will	Eze 36:36	3068
Thus saith the *L* GOD	Eze 36:37	136
they shall know that I am the *L*	Eze 36:38	3068
The hand of the *L* was upon me	Eze 37:1	3068
me out in the spirit of the *L*	Eze 37:1	3068
I answered, O *L* GOD, thou knowest	Eze 37:3	136
dry bones, hear the word of the *L*	Eze 37:4	3068
Thus saith the *L* GOD unto these	Eze 37:5	136
and ye shall know that I am the *L*	Eze 37:6	3068
to the wind, Thus saith the *L* GOD	Eze 37:9	136
unto them, Thus saith the *L* GOD	Eze 37:12	136
And ye shall know that I am the *L*	Eze 37:13	3068
know that I the *L* have spoken it	Eze 37:14	3068
and performed it, saith the *L*	Eze 37:14	136
The word of the *L* came again unto	Eze 37:15	3068
unto them, Thus saith the *L* GOD	Eze 37:19	136
unto them, Thus saith the *L* GOD	Eze 37:21	136
that I the *L* do sanctify Israel	Eze 37:28	3068
And the word of the *L* came unto me	Eze 38:1	3068
And say, Thus saith the *L* GOD	Eze 38:3	136
Thus saith the *L* GOD	Eze 38:10	136
unto Gog, Thus saith the *L* GOD	Eze 38:14	136
Thus saith the *L* GOD	Eze 38:17	136
land of Israel, saith the *L* GOD	Eze 38:18	136
all my mountains, saith the *L* GOD	Eze 38:21	136
they shall know that I am the *L*	Eze 38:23	3068
Gog, and say, Thus saith the *L* GOD	Eze 39:1	136
I have spoken it, saith the *L* GOD	Eze 39:5	136
they shall know that I am the *L*	Eze 39:6	3068
shall know that I am the *L*	Eze 39:7	3068
and it is done, saith the *L* GOD	Eze 39:8	136
that robbed them, saith the *L* GOD	Eze 39:10	136
be glorified, saith the *L* GOD	Eze 39:13	136
son of man, thus saith the *L* GOD	Eze 39:17	136
all men of war, saith the *L* GOD	Eze 39:20	136
am the *L* their God from that day	Eze 39:22	3068
Therefore thus saith the *L* GOD	Eze 39:25	136
know that I am the *L* their God	Eze 39:28	3068
house of Israel, saith the *L* GOD	Eze 39:29	136
day the hand of the *L* was upon me	Eze 40:1	3068
to the *L* to minister unto him	Eze 40:46	3068
is the table that is before the *L*	Eze 41:22	3068
L shall eat the most holy things	Eze 42:13	3068
the glory of the *L* came into the	Eze 43:4	3068
glory of the *L* filled the house	Eze 43:5	3068
Son of man, thus saith the *L* GOD	Eze 43:18	136
minister unto me, saith the *L* GOD	Eze 43:19	136
shalt offer them before the *L*	Eze 43:24	3068
for a burnt offering unto the *L*	Eze 43:24	3068
will accept you, saith the *L* GOD	Eze 43:27	136
Then said the *L* unto me	Eze 44:2	3068
because the *L*, the God of Israel,	Eze 44:2	3068
in it to eat bread before the *L*	Eze 44:3	3068
L filled the house of the *L*	Eze 44:4	3068
the *L* said unto me, Son of man,	Eze 44:5	3068
ordinances of the house of the *L*	Eze 44:5	3068
of Israel, Thus saith the *L* GOD	Eze 44:6	136
Thus saith the *L* GOD	Eze 44:9	136
against them, saith the *L* GOD	Eze 44:12	136
fat and the blood, saith the *L* GOD	Eze 44:15	136
his sin offering, saith the *L* GOD	Eze 44:27	136
offer an oblation unto the *L*	Eze 45:1	3068
come near to minister unto the *L*	Eze 45:4	3068
Thus saith the *L* GOD	Eze 45:9	136
from my people, saith the *L* GOD	Eze 45:9	136
for them, saith the *L* GOD	Eze 45:15	136
Thus saith the *L* GOD	Eze 45:18	136
prepare a burnt offering to the *L*	Eze 45:23	3068
Thus saith the *L* GOD	Eze 46:1	136
gate before the *L* in the sabbaths	Eze 46:3	3068
L in the sabbath day shall be six	Eze 46:4	3068
before the *L* in the solemn feasts	Eze 46:9	3068
offerings voluntarily unto the *L*	Eze 46:12	3068
a burnt offering unto the *L* of a	Eze 46:13	3068
a perpetual ordinance unto the *L*	Eze 46:14	3068
Thus saith the *L* GOD	Eze 46:16	136
Thus saith the *L* GOD	Eze 47:13	136
his inheritance, saith the *L* GOD	Eze 47:23	136
offer unto the *L* shall be of five	Eze 48:9	3068
the sanctuary of the *L* shall be	Eze 48:10	3068
for it is holy unto the *L*	Eze 48:14	3068
their portions, saith the *L* GOD	Eze 48:29	136
that day shall be, The *L* is there	Eze 48:35	3068
the *L* gave Jehoiakim king of	Dan 1:2	136
a *L* of kings, and a revealer of	Dan 2:47	4756
thyself against the *L* of heaven	Dan 5:23	4756
whereof the word of the *L* came to	Dan 9:2	3068
And I set my face unto the *L* God	Dan 9:3	136
And I prayed unto the *L* my God	Dan 9:4	3068
made my confession, and said, O *L*	Dan 9:4	136
O *L*, righteousness belongeth unto	Dan 9:7	136
O *L*, to us belongeth confusion of	Dan 9:8	136
To the *L* our God belong mercies	Dan 9:9	136
obeyed the voice of the *L* our God	Dan 9:10	3068
our prayer before the *L* our God	Dan 9:13	3068
Therefore hath the *L* watched upon	Dan 9:14	3068

for the *L* our God is righteous in Dan 9:14 3068
O *L* our God, that hast brought Dan 9:15 136
O *L*, according to all thy Dan 9:16 136
O *L*, hear Dan 9:19 136
O *L*, forgive Dan 9:19 136
O *L*, hearken and do Dan 9:19 136
my supplication before the *L* my Dan 9:20 3068
then said I, O my *L*, what shall Dan 12:8 113
The word of the *L* that came unto Hos 1:1 3068
of the word of the *L* by Hosea Hos 1:2 3068
the *L* said to Hosea, Go, take Hos 1:2 3068
whoredom, departing from the *L* Hos 1:2 3068
the *L* said unto him, Call his Hos 1:4 3068
will save them by the *L* their God Hos 1:7 3068
lovers, and forgat me, saith the *L* Hos 2:13 3068
shall be at that day, saith the *L* Hos 2:16 3068
and thou shalt know the *L* Hos 2:20 3068
day, I will hear, saith the *L* Hos 2:21 3068
Then said the *L* unto me, Go yet, Hos 3:1 3068
according to the love of the *L* Hos 3:1 3068
seek the *L* their God, and David Hos 3:5 3068
and shall fear the *L* and his Hos 3:5 3068
Hear the word of the *L*, ye Hos 4:1 3068
for the *L* hath a controversy with Hos 4:1 3068
left off to take heed to the *L* Hos 4:10 3068
nor swear, The *L* liveth Hos 4:15 3068
now the *L* will feed them as a Hos 4:16 3068
and they have not known the *L* Hos 5:4 3068
and with their herds to seek the *L* Hos 5:6 3068
dealt treacherously against the *L* Hos 5:7 3068
Come, and let us return unto the *L* Hos 6:1 3068
if we follow on to know the *L* Hos 6:3 3068
do not return to the *L* their God Hos 7:10 3068
eagle against the house of the *L* Hos 8:1 3068
but the *L* accepteth them not Hos 8:13 3068
not offer wine offerings to the *L* Hos 9:4 3068
not come into the house of the *L* Hos 9:4 3068
in the day of the feast of the *L* Hos 9:5 3068
Give them, O *L* Hos 9:14 3068
king, because we feared not the *L* Hos 10:3 3068
for it is time to seek the *L* Hos 10:12 3068
They shall walk after the *L* Hos 11:10 3068
them in their houses, saith the *L* Hos 11:11 3068
The *L* hath also a controversy Hos 12:2 3068
Even the *L* God of hosts Hos 12:5 3068
the *L* is his memorial Hos 12:5 3068
I that am the *L* thy God from the Hos 12:9 3068
by a prophet the *L* brought Israel Hos 12:13 3068
shall his *L* return unto him Hos 12:14 113
Yet I am the *L* thy God from the Hos 13:4 3068
the wind of the *L* shall come up Hos 13:15 3068
Israel, return unto the *L* thy God Hos 14:1 3068
with you words, and turn to the *L* Hos 14:2 3068
for the ways of the *L* are right Hos 14:9 3068
The word of the *L* that came to Joel 1:1 3068
cut off from the house of the *L* Joel 1:9 3068
into the house of the *L* your God Joel 1:14 3068
and cry unto the *L* Joel 1:14 3068
for the day of the *L* is at hand Joel 1:15 3068
O *L*, to thee will I cry Joel 1:19 3068
for the day of the *L* cometh Joel 2:1 3068
the *L* shall utter his voice Joel 2:11 3068
for the day of the *L* is great Joel 2:11 3068
Therefore also now, saith the *L* Joel 2:12 3068
and turn unto the *L* your God Joel 2:13 3068
offering unto the *L* your God Joel 2:14 3068
priests, the ministers of the *L* Joel 2:17 3068
them say, Spare thy people, O *L* Joel 2:17 3068
Then will the *L* be jealous for Joel 2:18 3068
the *L* will answer and say unto his Joel 2:19 3068
for the *L* will do great things Joel 2:21 3068
and rejoice in the *L* your God Joel 2:23 3068
praise the name of the *L* your God Joel 2:26 3068
and that I am the *L* your God Joel 2:27 3068
and the terrible day of the *L* come Joel 2:31 3068
name of the *L* shall be delivered Joel 2:32 3068
as the *L* hath said, and in the Joel 2:32 3068
the remnant whom the *L* shall call Joel 2:32 3068
for the *L* hath spoken it Joel 3:8 3068
thy mighty ones to come down, O *L* Joel 3:11 3068
for the day of the *L* is near in Joel 3:14 3068
The *L* also shall roar out of Zion Joel 3:16 3068
but the *L* will be the hope of his Joel 3:16 3068
the *L* your God dwelling in Zion Joel 3:17 3068
come forth of the house of the *L* Joel 3:18 3068
for the *L* dwelleth in Zion Joel 3:21 3068
The *L* will roar from Zion, and Amos 1:2 3068
Thus saith the *L* Amos 1:3 3068
captivity unto Kir, saith the *L* Amos 1:5 3068
Thus saith the *L* Amos 1:6 3068
shall perish, saith the *L* GOD Amos 1:8 136
Thus saith the *L* Amos 1:9 3068
Thus saith the *L* Amos 1:11 3068
Thus saith the *L* Amos 1:13 3068
his princes together, saith the *L* Amos 1:15 3068
Thus saith the *L* Amos 2:1 3068
thereof with him, saith the *L* Amos 2:3 3068
Thus saith the *L* Amos 2:4 3068
have despised the law of the *L* Amos 2:4 3068
Thus saith the *L* Amos 2:6 3068
saith the *L* Amos 2:11 3068
naked in that day, saith the *L* Amos 2:16 3068
the *L* hath spoken against you Amos 3:1 3068
a city, and the *L* hath not done it Amos 3:6 3068
Surely the *L* GOD will do nothing, Amos 3:7 136
the *L* GOD hath spoken, who can Amos 3:8 136
know not to do right, saith the *L* Amos 3:10 3068
Therefore thus saith the *L* GOD Amos 3:11 136

Thus saith the *L* Amos 3:12 3068
house of Jacob, saith the *L* GOD Amos 3:13 136
shall have an end, saith the *L* Amos 3:15 3068
The *L* GOD hath sworn by his Amos 4:2 136
them into the palace, saith the *L* Amos 4:3 3068
of Israel, saith the *L* GOD Amos 4:5 136
not returned unto me, saith the *L* Amos 4:6 3068
not returned unto me, saith the *L* Amos 4:8 3068
not returned unto me, saith the *L* Amos 4:9 3068
not returned unto me, saith the *L* Amos 4:10 3068
not returned unto me, saith the *L* Amos 4:11 3068
high places of the earth, The *L* Amos 4:13 3068
For thus saith the *L* GOD Amos 5:3 136
For thus saith the *L* unto the Amos 5:4 3068
Seek the *L*, and ye shall live Amos 5:6 3068
The *L* is his name Amos 5:8 3068
and so the *L*, the God of hosts, Amos 5:14 3068
it may be that the *L* God of hosts Amos 5:15 3068
Therefore the *L*, the God of hosts Amos 5:16 3068
the God of hosts, the *L* Amos 5:16 136
pass through thee, saith the *L* Amos 5:17 3068
you that desire the day of the *L* Amos 5:18 3068
the day of the *L* is darkness Amos 5:18 3068
not the day of the *L* be darkness Amos 5:20 3068
beyond Damascus, saith the *L* Amos 5:27 3068
The *L* GOD hath sworn by himself, Amos 6:8 136
saith the *L* the God of hosts, I Amos 6:8 3068
make mention of the name of the *L* Amos 6:10 3068
the *L* commandeth, and he will Amos 6:11 3068
saith the *L* the God of hosts Amos 6:14 3068
Thus hath the *L* GOD shewed unto Amos 7:1 136
O *L* GOD, forgive, I beseech thee Amos 7:2 136
The *L* repented for this Amos 7:3 3068
It shall not be, saith the *L* Amos 7:3 3068
Thus hath the *L* GOD shewed unto Amos 7:4 136
the *L* GOD called to contend by Amos 7:4 136
O *L* GOD, cease, I beseech thee Amos 7:5 136
The *L* repented for this Amos 7:6 3068
shall not be, saith the *L* GOD Amos 7:6 136
the *L* stood upon a wall made by a Amos 7:7 136
the *L* said unto me, Amos, what Amos 7:8 3068
Then said the *L*, Behold, I will Amos 7:8 136
the *L* took me as I followed the Amos 7:15 3068
the *L* said unto me, Go, prophesy Amos 7:15 3068
hear thou the word of the *L* Amos 7:16 3068
Therefore thus saith the *L* Amos 7:17 3068
Thus hath the *L* GOD shewed unto Amos 8:1 136
Then said the *L* unto me, The end Amos 8:2 3068
in that day, saith the *L* GOD Amos 8:3 136
The *L* hath sworn by the Amos 8:7 3068
pass in that day, saith the *L* GOD Amos 8:9 136
the days come, saith the *L* GOD Amos 8:11 136
but of hearing the words of the *L* Amos 8:11 3068
and fro to seek the word of the *L* Amos 8:12 3068
I saw the *L* standing upon the Amos 9:1 136
the *L* GOD of hosts is he that Amos 9:5 136
The *L* is his name Amos 9:6 3068
of Israel? saith the *L* Amos 9:7 3068
the eyes of the *L* GOD are upon Amos 9:8 136
the house of Jacob, saith the *L* Amos 9:8 3068
saith the *L* that doeth this Amos 9:12 3068
the days come, saith the *L* Amos 9:13 3068
given them, saith the *L* thy God Amos 9:15 3068
Thus saith the *L* GOD concerning Obad 1 136
We have heard a rumour from the *L* Obad 1 3068
I bring thee down, saith the *L* Obad 4 3068
I not in that day, saith the *L* Obad 8 3068
For the day of the *L* is near upon Obad 15 3068
for the *L* hath spoken it Obad 18 3068
Now the word of the *L* came unto Jonah 1:1 3068
from the presence of the *L* Jonah 1:3 3068
from the presence of the *L* Jonah 1:3 3068
But the *L* sent out a great wind Jonah 1:4 3068
and I fear the *L*, the God of Jonah 1:9 3068
fled from the presence of the *L* Jonah 1:10 3068
Wherefore they cried unto the *L* Jonah 1:14 3068
and said, We beseech thee, O *L* Jonah 1:14 3068
for thou, O *L*, hast done as it Jonah 1:14 3068
the men feared the *L* exceedingly Jonah 1:16 3068
and offered a sacrifice unto the *L* Jonah 1:16 3068
Now the *L* had prepared a great Jonah 1:17 3068
Then Jonah prayed unto the *L* his Jonah 2:1 3068
of mine affliction unto the *L* Jonah 2:2 3068
life from corruption, O *L* my God Jonah 2:6 3068
within me I remembered the *L* Jonah 2:7 3068
Salvation is of the *L* Jonah 2:9 3068
the *L* spake unto the fish, and it Jonah 2:10 3068
the word of the *L* came unto Jonah Jonah 3:1 3068
according to the word of the *L* Jonah 3:3 3068
And he prayed unto the *L* Jonah 4:2 3068
and said, I pray thee, O *L* Jonah 4:2 3068
Therefore now, O *L*, take, I Jonah 4:3 3068
Then said the *L*, Doest thou well Jonah 4:4 3068
the *L* God prepared a gourd, and Jonah 4:6 3068
Then said the *L*, Thou hast had Jonah 4:10 3068
The word of the *L* that came to Mic 1:1 3068
let the *L* GOD be witness against Mic 1:2 136
the *L* from his holy temple Mic 1:2 136
the *L* cometh forth out of his Mic 1:3 3068
the *L* unto the gate of Jerusalem Mic 1:12 3068
Therefore thus saith the *L* Mic 2:3 3068
lot in the congregation of the *L* Mic 2:5 3068
is the spirit of the *L* straitened Mic 2:7 3068
the *L* on the head of them Mic 2:13 3068
Then shall they cry unto the *L* Mic 3:4 3068
Thus saith the *L* concerning the Mic 3:5 3068
of power by the spirit of the *L* Mic 3:8 3068
yet will they lean upon the *L* Mic 3:11 3068

and say, Is not the *L* among us Mic 3:11 3068
mountain of the house of the *L* Mic 4:1 3068
us go up to the mountain of the *L* Mic 4:2 3068
the word of the *L* from Jerusalem Mic 4:2 3068
for the mouth of the *L* of hosts Mic 4:4 3068
name of the *L* our God for ever Mic 4:5 3068
In that day, saith the *L*, will I Mic 4:6 3068
the *L* shall reign over them in Mic 4:7 3068
there the *L* shall redeem thee Mic 4:10 3068
know not the thoughts of the *L* Mic 4:12 3068
consecrate their gain unto the *L* Mic 4:13 3068
unto the *L* of the whole earth Mic 4:13 113
and feed in the strength of the *L* Mic 5:4 3068
of the name of the *L* his God Mic 5:4 3068
many people as a dew from the *L* Mic 5:7 3068
to pass in that day, saith the *L* Mic 5:10 3068
Hear ye now what the *L* saith Mic 6:1 3068
for the *L* hath a controversy with Mic 6:2 3068
know the righteousness of the *L* Mic 6:5 3068
shall I come before the *L* Mic 6:6 3068
Will the *L* be pleased with Mic 6:7 3068
what doth the *L* require of thee, Mic 6:8 3068
Therefore I will look unto the *L* Mic 7:7 3068
the *L* shall be a light unto me Mic 7:8 3068
bear the indignation of the *L* Mic 7:9 3068
unto me, Where is the *L* thy God Mic 7:10 3068
shall be afraid of the *L* our God Mic 7:17 3068
is jealous, and the *L* revengeth Nah 1:2 3068
the *L* revengeth, and is furious Nah 1:2 3068
the *L* will take vengeance on his Nah 1:2 3068
The *L* is slow to anger, and great Nah 1:3 3068
the *L* hath his way in the Nah 1:3 3068
The *L* is good, a strong hold in Nah 1:7 3068
What do ye imagine against the *L* Nah 1:9 3068
that imagineth evil against the *L* Nah 1:11 3068
Thus saith the *L* Nah 1:12 3068
the *L* hath given a commandment Nah 1:14 3068
For the *L* hath turned away the Nah 2:2 3068
thee, saith the *L* of hosts Nah 2:13 3068
thee, saith the *L* of hosts Nah 3:5 3068
O *L*, how long shall I cry, and Hab 1:2 3068
O *L* my God, mine Holy One Hab 1:12 3068
O *L*, thou hast ordained them for Hab 1:12 3068
the *L* answered me, and said, Write Hab 2:2 3068
is it not of the *L* of hosts that Hab 2:13 3068
knowledge of the glory of the *L* Hab 2:14 3068
But the *L* is in his holy temple Hab 2:20 3068
O *L*, I have heard thy speech, and Hab 3:2 3068
O *L*, revive thy work in the midst Hab 3:2 3068
Was the *L* displeased against the Hab 3:8 3068
Yet I will rejoice in the *L* Hab 3:18 3068
The *L* God is my strength, and he Hab 3:19 3068
The word of the *L* which came unto Zeph 1:1 3068
from off the land, saith the *L* Zeph 1:2 3068
from off the land, saith the *L* Zeph 1:3 3068
worship and that swear by the *L* Zeph 1:5 3068
that are turned back from the *L* Zeph 1:6 3068
those that have not sought the *L* Zeph 1:6 3068
at the presence of the *L* GOD Zeph 1:7 136
for the day of the *L* is at hand Zeph 1:7 3068
for the *L* hath prepared a Zeph 1:7 3068
to pass in that day, saith the *L* Zeph 1:10 3068
The *L* will not do good, neither Zeph 1:12 3068
The great day of the *L* is near Zeph 1:14 3068
the voice of the day of the *L* Zeph 1:14 3068
they have sinned against the *L* Zeph 1:17 3068
anger of the *L* come upon you Zeph 2:2 3068
Seek ye the *L*, all ye meek of the Zeph 2:3 3068
the word of the *L* is against you Zeph 2:5 3068
for the *L* their God shall visit Zeph 2:7 3068
as I live, saith the *L* of hosts Zeph 2:9 3068
the people of the *L* of hosts Zeph 2:10 3068
The *L* will be terrible unto them Zeph 2:11 3068
she trusted not in the *L* Zeph 3:2 3068
The just *L* is in the midst Zeph 3:5 3068
wait ye upon me, saith the *L* Zeph 3:8 3068
all call upon the name of the *L* Zeph 3:9 3068
shall trust in the name of the *L* Zeph 3:12 3068
The *L* hath taken away thy Zeph 3:15 3068
the king of Israel, even the *L* Zeph 3:15 3068
The *L* thy God in the midst of Zeph 3:17 3068
before your eyes, saith the *L* Zeph 3:20 3068
came the word of the *L* by Haggai Hag 1:1 3068
Thus speaketh the *L* of hosts Hag 1:2 3068
of the *L* by Haggai the prophet Hag 1:3 3068
thus saith the *L* of hosts Hag 1:5 3068
Thus saith the *L* of hosts Hag 1:7 3068
I will be glorified, saith the *L* Hag 1:8 3068
saith the *L* of hosts Hag 1:9 3068
the voice of the *L* their God Hag 1:12 3068
as the *L* their God had sent him, Hag 1:12 3068
the people did fear before the *L* Hag 1:12 3068
I am with you, saith the *L* Hag 1:13 3068
the *L* stirred up the spirit of Hag 1:14 3068
in the house of the *L* of hosts Hag 1:14 3068
came the word of the *L* by the Hag 2:1 3068
strong, O Zerubbabel, saith the *L* Hag 2:4 3068
people of the land, saith the *L* Hag 2:4 3068
am with you, saith the *L* of hosts Hag 2:4 3068
For thus saith the *L* of hosts Hag 2:6 3068
with glory, saith the *L* of hosts Hag 2:7 3068
is mine, saith the *L* of hosts Hag 2:8 3068
the former, saith the *L* of hosts Hag 2:9 3068
give peace, saith the *L* of hosts Hag 2:9 3068
came the word of the *L* by Haggai Hag 2:10 3068
Thus saith the *L* of hosts Hag 2:11 3068
nation before me, saith the *L* Hag 2:14 3068
a stone in the temple of the *L* Hag 2:15 3068

L

ye turned not to me, saith the *L*	Hag 2:17	3068
again the word of the *L* came unto	Hag 2:20	3068
In that day, saith the *L* of hosts	Hag 2:23	3068
the son of Shealtiel, saith the *L*	Hag 2:23	3068
chosen thee, saith the *L* of hosts	Hag 2:23	3068
the word of the *L* unto Zechariah	Zec 1:1	3068
The *L* hath been sore displeased	Zec 1:2	3068
them, Thus saith the *L* of hosts	Zec 1:3	3068
ye unto me, saith the *L* of hosts	Zec 1:3	3068
unto you, saith the *L* of hosts	Zec 1:3	3068
saying, Thus saith the *L* of hosts	Zec 1:4	3068
nor hearken unto me, saith the *L*	Zec 1:4	3068
Like as the *L* of hosts thought to	Zec 1:6	3068
the word of the *L* unto Zechariah	Zec 1:7	3068
whom the *L* hath sent to walk to	Zec 1:10	3068
the *L* that stood among the myrtle	Zec 1:11	3068
Then the angel of the *L* answered	Zec 1:12	3068
O *L* of hosts, how long wilt thou	Zec 1:12	3068
the *L* answered the angel that	Zec 1:13	3068
saying, Thus saith the *L* of hosts	Zec 1:14	3068
Therefore thus saith the *L*	Zec 1:16	3068
built in it, saith the *L* of hosts	Zec 1:16	3068
saying, Thus saith the *L* of hosts	Zec 1:17	3068
the *L* shall yet comfort Zion, and	Zec 1:17	3068
the *L* shewed me four carpenters	Zec 1:20	3068
For I, saith the *L*, will be unto	Zec 2:5	3068
land of the north, saith the *L*	Zec 2:6	3068
winds of the heaven, saith the *L*	Zec 2:6	3068
For thus saith the *L* of hosts	Zec 2:8	3068
that the *L* of hosts hath sent me	Zec 2:9	3068
in the midst of thee, saith the *L*	Zec 2:10	3068
be joined to the *L* in that day	Zec 2:11	3068
thou shalt know that the *L* of	Zec 2:11	3068
the *L* shall inherit Judah his	Zec 2:12	3068
silent, O all flesh, before the *L*	Zec 2:13	3068
before the angel of the *L*	Zec 3:1	3068
the *L* said unto Satan	Zec 3:2	3068
The *L* rebuke thee, O Satan	Zec 3:2	3068
even the *L* that hath chosen	Zec 3:2	3068
And the angel of the *L* stood by	Zec 3:5	3068
the angel of the *L* protested unto	Zec 3:6	3068
Thus saith the *L* of hosts	Zec 3:7	3068
thereof, saith the *L* of hosts	Zec 3:9	3068
In that day, saith the *L* of hosts	Zec 3:10	3068
the word of the *L* unto Zerubbabel	Zec 4:6	3068
my spirit, saith the *L* of hosts	Zec 4:6	3068
the word of the *L* came unto me	Zec 4:8	3068
thou shalt know that the *L* of	Zec 4:9	3068
they are the eyes of the *L*	Zec 4:10	3068
that stand by the *L* of the whole	Zec 4:14	113
it forth, saith the *L* of hosts	Zec 5:4	3068
before the *L* of all the earth	Zec 6:5	113
And the word of the *L* came unto me	Zec 6:9	3068
Thus speaketh the *L* of hosts	Zec 6:12	3068
shall build the temple of the *L*	Zec 6:12	3068
shall build the temple of the *L*	Zec 6:13	3068
a memorial in the temple of the *L*	Zec 6:14	3068
and build in the temple of the *L*	Zec 6:15	3068
ye shall know that the *L* of hosts	Zec 6:15	3068
obey the voice of the *L* your God	Zec 6:15	3068
that the word of the *L* came unto	Zec 7:1	3068
their men, to pray before the *L*	Zec 7:2	3068
in the house of the *L* of hosts	Zec 7:3	3068
word of the *L* of hosts unto me	Zec 7:4	3068
the *L* hath cried by the former	Zec 7:7	3068
the word of the *L* came unto	Zec 7:8	3068
Thus speaketh the *L* of hosts	Zec 7:9	3068
the words which the *L* of hosts	Zec 7:12	3068
a great wrath from the *L* of hosts	Zec 7:12	3068
not hear, saith the *L* of hosts	Zec 7:13	3068
word of the *L* of hosts came to me	Zec 8:1	3068
Thus saith the *L* of hosts	Zec 8:2	3068
Thus saith the *L*	Zec 8:3	3068
the mountain of the *L* of hosts	Zec 8:3	3068
Thus saith the *L* of hosts	Zec 8:4	3068
Thus saith the *L* of hosts	Zec 8:6	3068
saith the *L* of hosts	Zec 8:6	3068
Thus saith the *L* of hosts	Zec 8:7	3068
Thus saith the *L* of hosts	Zec 8:9	3068
house of the *L* of hosts was laid	Zec 8:9	3068
former days, saith the *L* of hosts	Zec 8:11	3068
For thus saith the *L* of hosts	Zec 8:14	3068
me to wrath, saith the *L* of hosts	Zec 8:14	3068
things that I hate, saith the *L*	Zec 8:17	3068
the word of the *L* of hosts came	Zec 8:18	3068
Thus saith the *L* of hosts	Zec 8:19	3068
Thus saith the *L* of hosts	Zec 8:20	3068
go speedily to pray before the *L*	Zec 8:21	3068
and to seek the *L* of hosts	Zec 8:21	3068
seek the *L* of hosts in Jerusalem	Zec 8:22	3068
and to pray before the *L*	Zec 8:22	3068
Thus saith the *L* of hosts	Zec 8:23	3068
of the *L* in the land of Hadrach	Zec 9:1	3068
of Israel, shall be toward the *L*	Zec 9:1	3068
the *L* will cast her out, and he	Zec 9:4	136
the *L* shall be seen over them, and	Zec 9:14	3068
the *L* GOD shall blow the trumpet,	Zec 9:14	136
The *L* of hosts shall defend them	Zec 9:15	3068
the *L* their God shall save them	Zec 9:16	3068
Ask ye of the *L* rain in the time	Zec 10:1	3068
so the *L* shall make bright clouds	Zec 10:1	3068
for the *L* of hosts hath visited	Zec 10:3	3068
because the *L* is with them, and	Zec 10:5	3068
for I am the *L* their God, and will	Zec 10:6	3068
heart shall rejoice in the *L*	Zec 10:7	3068
I will strengthen them in the *L*	Zec 10:12	3068
and down in his name, saith the *L*	Zec 10:12	3068
Thus saith the *L* my God	Zec 11:4	3068
sell them say, Blessed be the *L*	Zec 11:5	3068
of the land, saith the *L*	Zec 11:6	3068
that it was the word of the *L*	Zec 11:11	3068
the *L* said unto me, Cast it unto	Zec 11:13	3068
the potter in the house of the *L*	Zec 11:13	3068
the *L* said unto me, Take unto	Zec 11:15	3068
of the word of the *L* for Israel	Zec 12:1	3068
for Israel, saith the *L*	Zec 12:1	3068
In that day, saith the *L*, I will	Zec 12:4	3068
in the *L* of hosts their God	Zec 12:5	3068
The *L* also shall save the tents	Zec 12:7	3068
In that day shall the *L* defend	Zec 12:8	3068
as the angel of the *L* before them	Zec 12:8	3068
in that day, saith the *L* of hosts	Zec 13:2	3068
lies in the name of the *L*	Zec 13:3	3068
my fellow, saith the *L* of hosts	Zec 13:7	3068
that in all the land, saith the *L*	Zec 13:8	3068
they shall say, The *L* is my God	Zec 13:9	3068
Behold, the day of the *L* cometh	Zec 14:1	3068
Then shall the *L* go forth	Zec 14:3	3068
the *L* my God shall come, and all	Zec 14:5	3068
day which shall be known to the *L*	Zec 14:7	3068
the *L* shall be king over all the	Zec 14:9	3068
in that day shall there be one *L*	Zec 14:9	3068
be the plague wherewith the *L*	Zec 14:12	3068
from the *L* shall be among them	Zec 14:13	3068
the *L* of hosts, and to keep the	Zec 14:16	3068
the *L* of hosts, even upon them	Zec 14:17	3068
wherewith the *L* will smite the	Zec 14:18	3068
the horses, HOLINESS UNTO THE *L*	Zec 14:20	3068
be holiness unto the *L* of hosts	Zec 14:21	3068
in the house of the *L* of hosts	Zec 14:21	3068
of the *L* to Israel by Malachi	Mal 1:1	3068
I have loved you, saith the *L*	Mal 1:2	3068
Jacob's brother? saith the *L*	Mal 1:2	3068
thus saith the *L* of hosts	Mal 1:4	3068
the *L* hath indignation for ever	Mal 1:4	3068
The *L* will be magnified from the	Mal 1:5	3068
saith the *L* of hosts unto you, O	Mal 1:6	3068
table of the *L* is contemptible	Mal 1:7	3068
saith the *L* of hosts	Mal 1:8	3068
saith the *L* of hosts	Mal 1:9	3068
in you, saith the *L* of hosts	Mal 1:10	3068
the heathen, saith the *L* of hosts	Mal 1:11	3068
The table of the *L* is polluted	Mal 1:12	3068
at it, saith the *L* of hosts	Mal 1:13	3068
your hand? saith the *L*	Mal 1:13	3068
unto the *L* a corrupt thing	Mal 1:14	136
great King, saith the *L* of hosts	Mal 1:14	3068
my name, saith the *L* of hosts	Mal 2:2	3068
with Levi, saith the *L* of hosts	Mal 2:4	3068
the messenger of the *L* of hosts	Mal 2:7	3068
of Levi, saith the *L* of hosts	Mal 2:8	3068
holiness of the *L* which he loved	Mal 2:11	3068
The *L* will cut off the man that	Mal 2:12	3068
an offering unto the *L* of hosts	Mal 2:12	3068
the altar of the *L* with tears	Mal 2:13	3068
Because the *L* hath been witness	Mal 2:14	3068
For the *L*, the God of Israel,	Mal 2:16	3068
his garment, saith the *L* of hosts	Mal 2:16	3068
wearied the *L* with your words	Mal 2:17	3068
is good in the sight of the *L*	Mal 2:17	3068
and the *L*, whom ye seek, shall	Mal 3:1	113
shall come, saith the *L* of hosts	Mal 3:1	3068
L an offering in righteousness	Mal 3:3	3068
Jerusalem be pleasant unto the *L*	Mal 3:4	3068
fear not me, saith the *L* of hosts	Mal 3:5	3068
For I am the *L*, I change not	Mal 3:6	3068
unto you, saith the *L* of hosts	Mal 3:7	3068
herewith, saith the *L* of hosts	Mal 3:10	3068
the field, saith the *L* of hosts	Mal 3:11	3068
land, saith the *L* of hosts	Mal 3:12	3068
stout against me, saith the *L*	Mal 3:13	3068
mournfully before the *L* of hosts	Mal 3:14	3068
Then they that feared the *L* spake	Mal 3:16	3068
the *L* hearkened, and heard it, and	Mal 3:16	3068
him for them that feared the *L*	Mal 3:16	3068
be mine, saith the *L* of hosts	Mal 3:17	3068
them up, saith the *L* of hosts	Mal 4:1	3068
do this, saith the *L* of hosts	Mal 4:3	3068
great and dreadful day of the *L*	Mal 4:5	3068
the angel of the *L* appeared unto	Mt 1:20	*2962*
spoken of the *L* by the prophet	Mt 1:22	*2962*
the angel of the *L* had bidden him	Mt 1:24	*2962*
the angel of the *L* appeareth to	Mt 2:13	*2962*
spoken of the *L* by the prophet	Mt 2:15	*2962*
an angel of the *L* appeareth in a	Mt 2:19	*2962*
Prepare ye the way of the *L*	Mt 3:3	*2962*
shalt not tempt the *L* thy God	Mt 4:7	*2962*
Thou shalt worship the *L* thy God	Mt 4:10	*2962*
perform unto the *L* thine oaths	Mt 5:33	*2962*
one that saith unto me, *L*, *L*	Mt 7:21	*2962*
say to me in that day, *L*, *L*	Mt 7:22	*2962*
and worshipped him, saying, *L*	Mt 8:2	*2962*
And saying, *L*, my servant lieth at	Mt 8:6	*2962*
The centurion answered and said, *L*	Mt 8:8	*2962*
of his disciples said unto him, *L*	Mt 8:21	*2962*
to him, and awoke him, saying, *L*	Mt 8:25	*2962*
They said unto him, Yea, *L*	Mt 9:28	*2962*
ye therefore the *L* of the harvest	Mt 9:38	*2962*
L of heaven and earth, because	Mt 11:25	*2962*
For the Son of man is *L* even of	Mt 12:8	*2962*
They say unto him, Yea, *L*	Mt 13:51	*2962*
And Peter answered him and said, *L*	Mt 14:28	*2962*
to sink, he cried, saying, *L*	Mt 14:30	*2962*
saying, Have mercy on me, O *L*	Mt 15:22	*2962*
she and worshipped him, saying, *L*	Mt 15:25	*2962*
And she said, Truth, *L*	Mt 15:27	*2962*
saying, Be it far from thee, *L*	Mt 16:22	*2962*
Peter, and said unto Jesus, *L*	Mt 17:4	*2962*
L, have mercy on my son	Mt 17:15	*2962*
came Peter to him, and said, *L*	Mt 18:21	*2962*
and worshipped him, saying, *L*	Mt 18:26	*2962*
saying, Have mercy on us, O *L*	Mt 20:30	*2962*
saying, Have mercy on us, O *L*	Mt 20:31	*2962*
They say unto him, *L*, that our	Mt 20:33	*2962*
say, The *L* hath need of them	Mt 21:3	*2962*
that cometh in the name of the *L*	Mt 21:9	*2962*
When the *l* therefore of the	Mt 21:40	*2962*
Thou shalt love the *L* thy God	Mt 22:37	*2962*
doth David in spirit call him *L*	Mt 22:43	*2962*
The *L* said unto my *L*, Sit thou	Mt 22:44	*2962*
If David then call him *L*	Mt 22:45	*2962*
that cometh in the name of the *L*	Mt 23:39	*2962*
not what hour your *L* doth come	Mt 24:42	*2962*
other virgins, saying, *L*, *L*	Mt 25:11	*2962*
righteous answer him, saying, *L*	Mt 25:37	*2962*
they also answer him, saying, *L*	Mt 25:44	*2962*
one of them to say unto him, *L*	Mt 26:22	*2962*
field, as the *L* appointed me	Mt 27:10	*2962*
for the angel of the *L* descended	Mt 28:2	*2962*
see the place where the *L* lay	Mt 28:6	*2962*
Prepare ye the way of the *L*	Mk 1:3	*2962*
of man is *L* also of the sabbath	Mk 2:28	*2962*
things the *L* hath done for thee	Mk 5:19	*2962*
answered and said unto him, Yes, *L*	Mk 7:28	*2962*
cried out, and said with tears, *L*	Mk 9:24	*2962*
The blind man said unto him, *L*	Mk 10:51	*4462*
say ye that the *L* hath need of	Mk 11:3	*2962*
that cometh in the name of the *L*	Mk 11:9	*2962*
that cometh in the name of the *L*	Mk 11:10	*2962*
The *L* our God is one *L*	Mk 12:29	*2962*
thou shalt love the *L* thy God	Mk 12:30	*2962*
The *L* said to my *L*, Sit thou	Mk 12:36	*2962*
therefore himself calleth him *L*	Mk 12:37	*2962*
except that the *L* had shortened	Mk 13:20	*2962*
So then after the *L* had spoken	Mk 16:19	*2962*
the *L* working with them, and	Mk 16:20	*2962*
and ordinances of the *L* blameless	Lk 1:6	*2962*
he went into the temple of the *L*	Lk 1:9	*2962*
unto him an angel of the *L*	Lk 1:11	*2962*
be great in the sight of the *L*	Lk 1:15	*2962*
shall he turn to the *L* their God	Lk 1:16	*2962*
ready a people prepared for the *L*	Lk 1:17	*2962*
Thus hath the *L* dealt with me in	Lk 1:25	*2962*
favoured, the *L* is with thee	Lk 1:28	*2962*
the *L* God shall give unto him the	Lk 1:32	*2962*
Behold the handmaid of the *L*	Lk 1:38	*2962*
mother of my *L* should come to me	Lk 1:43	*2962*
which were told her from the *L*	Lk 1:45	*2962*
said, My soul doth magnify the *L*	Lk 1:46	*2962*
her cousins heard how the *L* had	Lk 1:58	*2962*
And the hand of the *L* was with him	Lk 1:66	*2962*
Blessed be the *L* God of Israel	Lk 1:68	*2962*
face of the *L* to prepare his ways	Lk 1:76	*2962*
the angel of the *L* came upon them	Lk 2:9	*2962*
the glory of the *L* shone round	Lk 2:9	*2962*
a Saviour, which is Christ the *L*	Lk 2:11	*2962*
which the *L* hath made known unto	Lk 2:15	*2962*
to present him to the *L*	Lk 2:22	*2962*
it is written in the law of the *L*	Lk 2:23	*2962*
shall be called holy to the *L*	Lk 2:23	*2962*
which is said in the law of the *L*	Lk 2:24	*2962*
L, now lettest thou thy servant	Lk 2:29	*1203*
gave thanks likewise unto the *L*	Lk 2:38	*2962*
according to the law of the *L*	Lk 2:39	*2962*
Prepare ye the way of the *L*	Lk 3:4	*2962*
Thou shalt worship the *L* thy God	Lk 4:8	*2962*
shalt not tempt the *L* thy God	Lk 4:12	*2962*
The Spirit of the *L* is upon me	Lk 4:18	*2962*
the acceptable year of the *L*	Lk 4:19	*2962*
for I am a sinful man, O *L*	Lk 5:8	*2962*
face, and besought him, saying, *L*	Lk 5:12	*2962*
the power of the *L* was present to	Lk 5:17	*2962*
of man is *L* also of the sabbath	Lk 6:5	*2962*
And why call ye me, *L*, *L*	Lk 6:46	*2962*
to him, saying unto him, *L*	Lk 7:6	*2962*
And when the *L* saw her, he had	Lk 7:13	*2962*
the *L* said, Whereunto then shall	Lk 7:31	*2962*
and John saw this, they said, *L*	Lk 9:54	*2962*
a certain man said unto him, *L*	Lk 9:57	*2962*
But he said, *L*, suffer me first	Lk 9:59	*2962*
And another also said, *L*, I will	Lk 9:61	*2962*
After these things the *L*	Lk 10:1	*2962*
ye therefore the *L* of the harvest	Lk 10:2	*2962*
again with joy, saying, *L*	Lk 10:17	*2962*
L of heaven and earth, that thou	Lk 10:21	*2962*
Thou shalt love the *L* thy God	Lk 10:27	*2962*
and came to him, and said, *L*	Lk 10:40	*2962*
of his disciples said unto him, *L*	Lk 11:1	*2962*
the *L* said unto him, Now do ye	Lk 11:39	*2962*
Then Peter said unto him, *L*	Lk 12:41	*2962*
the *L* said, Who then is that	Lk 12:42	*2962*
And he answering said unto him, *L*	Lk 13:8	*2962*
The *L* then answered him, and said,	Lk 13:15	*2962*
Then said one unto him, *L*	Lk 13:23	*2962*
at the door, saying, *L*, *L*	Lk 13:25	*2962*
that cometh in the name of the *L*	Lk 13:35	*2962*
And the apostles said unto the *L*	Lk 17:5	*2962*
the *L* said, If ye had faith as a	Lk 17:6	*2962*
and said unto him, Where, *L*	Lk 17:37	*2962*
the *L* said, Hear what the unjust	Lk 18:6	*2962*
And he said, *L*, that I may receive	Lk 18:41	*2962*
stood, and said unto the *L*	Lk 19:8	*2962*
Behold, *L*, the half of my goods I	Lk 19:8	*2962*
Then came the first, saying, *L*	Lk 19:16	*2962*

And the second came, saying, *L* ... Lk 19:18 *2962*
And another came, saying, *L* ... Lk 19:20 *2962*
(And they said unto him, *L* ... Lk 19:25 *2962*
Because the *L* hath need of him ... Lk 19:31 *2962*
they said, The *L* hath need of him ... Lk 19:34 *2962*
that cometh in the name of the *L* ... Lk 19:38 *2962*
calleth the *L* the God of Abraham ... Lk 20:37 *2962*
The *L* said unto my *L*, Sit thou ... Lk 20:42 *2962*
David therefore calleth him *L* ... Lk 20:44 *2962*
the *L* said, Simon, Simon, behold, ... Lk 22:31 *2962*
And he said unto him, *L*, I am ... Lk 22:33 *2962*
And they said, *L*, behold, here are ... Lk 22:38 *2962*
follow, they said unto him, *L* ... Lk 22:49 *2962*
the *L* turned, and looked upon ... Lk 22:61 *2962*
remembered the word of the *L* ... Lk 22:61 *2962*
And he said unto Jesus, *L*, ... Lk 23:42 *2962*
found not the body of the *L* Jesus ... Lk 24:3 *2962*
The *L* is risen indeed, and hath ... Lk 24:34 *2962*
Make straight the way of the *L* ... Jn 1:23 *2962*
When therefore the *L* knew how the ... Jn 4:1 *2962*
after that the *L* had given thanks ... Jn 6:23 *2962*
Then said they unto him, *L* ... Jn 6:34 *2962*
Then Simon Peter answered him, *L* ... Jn 6:68 *2962*
She said, No man, *L* ... Jn 8:11 *2962*
He answered and said, Who is he, *L* ... Jn 9:36 *2962*
And he said, *L*, I believe ... Jn 9:38 *2962*
anointed the *L* with ointment ... Jn 11:2 *2962*
sisters sent unto him, saying, *L* ... Jn 11:3 *2962*
Then said his disciples, *L* ... Jn 11:12 *2962*
Then said Martha unto Jesus, *L* ... Jn 11:21 *2962*
She saith unto him, Yea, *L* ... Jn 11:27 *2962*
at his feet, saying unto him, *L* ... Jn 11:32 *2962*
They said unto him, *L*, come and ... Jn 11:34 *2962*
that was dead, saith unto him, *L* ... Jn 11:39 *2962*
that cometh in the name of the *L* ... Jn 12:13 *2962*
be fulfilled, which he spake, *L* ... Jn 12:38 *2962*
the arm of the *L* been revealed ... Jn 12:38 *2962*
and Peter saith unto him, *L* ... Jn 13:6 *2962*
Simon Peter saith unto him, *L* ... Jn 13:9 *2962*
Ye call me Master and *L* ... Jn 13:13 *2962*
If I then, your *L* and Master, have ... Jn 13:14 *2962*
Jesus' breast saith unto him, *L* ... Jn 13:25 *2962*
Simon Peter said unto him, *L* ... Jn 13:36 *2962*
Peter said unto him, *L*, why ... Jn 13:37 *2962*
Thomas saith unto him, *L*, we know ... Jn 14:5 *2962*
Philip saith unto him, *L*, shew us ... Jn 14:8 *2962*
saith unto him, not Iscariot, *L* ... Jn 14:22 *2962*
away the *L* out of the sepulchre ... Jn 20:2 *2962*
Because they have taken away my *L* ... Jn 20:13 *2962*
disciples that she had seen the *L* ... Jn 20:18 *2962*
glad, when they saw the *L* ... Jn 20:20 *2962*
said unto him, We have seen the *L* ... Jn 20:25 *2962*
answered and said unto him, My *L* ... Jn 20:28 *2962*
saith unto Peter, It is the *L* ... Jn 21:7 *2962*
Peter heard that it was the *L* ... Jn 21:7 *2962*
knowing that it was the *L* ... Jn 21:12 *2962*
He saith unto him, Yea, *L* ... Jn 21:15 *2962*
He saith unto him, Yea, *L* ... Jn 21:16 *2962*
And he said unto him, *L*, thou ... Jn 21:17 *2962*
his breast at supper, and said, *L* ... Jn 21:20 *2962*
seeing him saith to Jesus, *L* ... Jn 21:21 *2962*
they asked of him, saying, *L* ... Acts 1:6 *2962*
the time that the *L* Jesus went in ... Acts 1:21 *2962*
And they prayed, and said, Thou, *L* ... Acts 1:24 *2962*
and notable day of the *L* come ... Acts 2:20 *2962*
the name of the *L* shall be saved ... Acts 2:21 *2962*
I foresaw the *L* always before my ... Acts 2:25 *2962*
The *L* said unto my *L*, Sit thou ... Acts 2:34 *2962*
whom ye have crucified, both *L* ... Acts 2:36 *2962*
many as the *L* our God shall call ... Acts 2:39 *2962*
the *L* added to the church daily ... Acts 2:47 *2962*
come from the presence of the *L* ... Acts 3:19 *2962*
A prophet shall the *L* your God ... Acts 3:22 *2962*
God with one accord, and said, *L* ... Acts 4:24 *1203*
gathered together against the *L* ... Acts 4:26 *2962*
And now, *L*, behold their ... Acts 4:29 *2962*
the resurrection of the *L* Jesus ... Acts 4:33 *2962*
to tempt the Spirit of the *L* ... Acts 5:9 *2962*
were the more added to the *L* ... Acts 5:14 *2962*
But the angel of the *L* by night ... Acts 5:19 *2962*
L in a flame of fire in a bush ... Acts 7:30 *2962*
the voice of the *L* came unto him ... Acts 7:31 *2962*
Then said the *L* to him, Put off ... Acts 7:33 *2962*
A prophet shall the *L* your God ... Acts 7:37 *2962*
build me? saith the *L* ... Acts 7:49 *2962*
L Jesus, receive my spirit ... Acts 7:59 *2962*
and cried with a loud voice, *L* ... Acts 7:60 *2962*
in the name of the *L* Jesus ... Acts 8:16 *2962*
and said, Pray ye to the *L* for me ... Acts 8:24 *2962*
and preached the word of the *L* ... Acts 8:25 *2962*
the angel of the *L* spake unto ... Acts 8:26 *2962*
the Spirit of the *L* caught away ... Acts 8:39 *2962*
against the disciples of the *L* ... Acts 9:1 *2962*
And he said, Who art thou, *L* ... Acts 9:5 *2962*
the *L* said, I am Jesus whom thou ... Acts 9:5 *2962*
trembling and astonished said, *L* ... Acts 9:6 *2962*
the *L* said unto him, Arise, and go ... Acts 9:6 *2962*
and to him said the *L* in a vision ... Acts 9:10 *2962*
And he said, Behold, I am here, *L* ... Acts 9:10 *2962*
the *L* said unto him, Arise, and go ... Acts 9:11 *2962*
Then Ananias answered, *L*, I have ... Acts 9:13 *2962*
But the *L* said unto him, Go thy ... Acts 9:15 *2962*
on him said, Brother Saul, the *L* ... Acts 9:17 *2962*
how he had seen the *L* in the way ... Acts 9:27 *2962*
boldly in the name of the *L* Jesus ... Acts 9:29 *2962*
and walking in the fear of the *L* ... Acts 9:31 *2962*
Saron saw him, and turned to the *L* ... Acts 9:35 *2962*
and many believed in the *L* ... Acts 9:42 *2962*
afraid, and said, What is it, *L* ... Acts 10:4 *2962*
But Peter said, Not so, *L* ... Acts 10:14 *2962*
(he is *L* of all ... Acts 10:36 *2962*
be baptized in the name of the *L* ... Acts 10:48 *2962*
But I said, Not so, *L* ... Acts 11:8 *2962*
remembered I the word of the *L* ... Acts 11:16 *2962*
believed on the *L* Jesus Christ ... Acts 11:17 *2962*
Grecians, preaching the *L* Jesus ... Acts 11:20 *2962*
the hand of the *L* was with them ... Acts 11:21 *2962*
believed, and turned unto the *L* ... Acts 11:21 *2962*
they would cleave unto the *L* ... Acts 11:23 *2962*
much people was added unto the *L* ... Acts 11:24 *2962*
the angel of the *L* came upon him ... Acts 12:7 *2962*
that the *L* hath sent his angel, ... Acts 12:11 *2962*
the *L* had brought him out of the ... Acts 12:17 *2962*
the angel of the *L* smote him ... Acts 12:23 *2962*
As they ministered to the *L* ... Acts 13:2 *2962*
pervert the right ways of the *L* ... Acts 13:10 *2962*
the hand of the *L* is upon thee ... Acts 13:11 *2962*
at the doctrine of the *L* ... Acts 13:12 *2962*
For so hath the *L* commanded us ... Acts 13:47 *2962*
and glorified the word of the *L* ... Acts 13:48 *2962*
the word of the *L* was published ... Acts 13:49 *2962*
they speaking boldly in the *L* ... Acts 14:3 *2962*
they commended them to the *L* ... Acts 14:23 *2962*
that through the grace of the *L* ... Acts 15:11 *2962*
of men might seek after the *L* ... Acts 15:17 *2962*
my name is called, saith the *L* ... Acts 15:17 *2962*
the name of our *L* Jesus Christ ... Acts 15:26 *2962*
and preaching the word of the *L* ... Acts 15:35 *2962*
have preached the word of the *L* ... Acts 15:36 *2962*
assuredly gathering that the *L* ... Acts 16:10 *2962*
whose heart the *L* opened, that ... Acts 16:14 *2962*
judged me to be faithful to the *L* ... Acts 16:15 *2962*
Believe on the *L* Jesus Christ ... Acts 16:31 *2962*
spake unto him the word of the *L* ... Acts 16:32 *2962*
seeing that he is *L* of heaven ... Acts 17:24 *2962*
That they should seek the *L* ... Acts 17:27 *2962*
believed on the *L* with all his ... Acts 18:8 *2962*
Then spake the *L* to Paul in the ... Acts 18:9 *2962*
instructed in the way of the *L* ... Acts 18:25 *2962*
diligently the things of the *L* ... Acts 18:25 *2962*
in the name of the *L* Jesus ... Acts 19:5 *2962*
heard the word of the *L* Jesus ... Acts 19:10 *2962*
spirits the name of the *L* Jesus ... Acts 19:13 *2962*
the name of the *L* Jesus was ... Acts 19:17 *2962*
Serving the *L* with all humility ... Acts 20:19 *2962*
faith toward our *L* Jesus Christ ... Acts 20:21 *2962*
I have received of the *L* Jesus ... Acts 20:24 *2962*
remember the words of the *L* Jesus ... Acts 20:35 *2962*
for the name of the *L* Jesus ... Acts 21:13 *2962*
saying, The will of the *L* be done ... Acts 21:14 *2962*
heard it, they glorified the *L* ... Acts 21:20 *2962*
And I answered, Who art thou, *L* ... Acts 22:8 *2962*
And I said, What shall I do, *L* ... Acts 22:10 *2962*
the *L* said unto me, Arise, and go ... Acts 22:10 *2962*
calling on the name of the *L* ... Acts 22:16 *2962*
And I said, *L*, they know that I ... Acts 22:19 *2962*
following the *L* stood by him ... Acts 23:11 *2962*
And I said, Who art thou, *L* ... Acts 26:15 *2962*
which concern the *L* Jesus Christ ... Acts 28:31 *2962*
his Son Jesus Christ our *L* ... Rom 1:3 *2962*
our Father, and the *L* Jesus Christ ... Rom 1:7 *2962*
to whom the *L* will not impute sin ... Rom 4:8 *2962*
up Jesus our *L* from the dead ... Rom 4:24 *2962*
God through our *L* Jesus Christ ... Rom 5:1 *2962*
in God through our *L* Jesus Christ ... Rom 5:11 *2962*
life by Jesus Christ our *L* ... Rom 5:21 *2962*
God through Jesus Christ our *L* ... Rom 6:11 *2962*
life through Jesus Christ our *L* ... Rom 6:23 *2962*
God through Jesus Christ our *L* ... Rom 7:25 *2962*
which is in Christ Jesus our *L* ... Rom 8:39 *2962*
will the *L* make upon the earth ... Rom 9:28 *2962*
Except the *L* of Sabaoth had left ... Rom 9:29 *2962*
with thy mouth the *L* Jesus ... Rom 10:9 *2962*
for the same *L* over all is rich ... Rom 10:12 *2962*
the name of the *L* shall be saved ... Rom 10:13 *2962*
For Esaias saith, *L*, who hath ... Rom 10:16 *2962*
L, they have killed thy prophets, ... Rom 11:3 *2962*
who hath known the mind of the *L* ... Rom 11:34 *2962*
fervent in spirit; serving the *L* ... Rom 12:11 *2962*
I will repay, saith the *L* ... Rom 12:19 *2962*
But put ye on the *L* Jesus Christ ... Rom 13:14 *2962*
the day, regardeth it unto the *L* ... Rom 14:6 *2962*
to the *L* he doth not regard it ... Rom 14:6 *2962*
He that eateth, eateth to the *L* ... Rom 14:6 *2962*
to the *L* he eateth not, and giveth ... Rom 14:6 *2962*
we live, we live unto the *L* ... Rom 14:8 *2962*
whether we die, we die unto the *L* ... Rom 14:8 *2962*
he might be *L* both of the dead ... Rom 14:9 *2961*
written, As I live, saith the *L* ... Rom 14:11 *2962*
and am persuaded by the *L* Jesus ... Rom 14:14 *2962*
the Father of our *L* Jesus Christ ... Rom 15:6 *2962*
And again, Praise the *L*, all ye ... Rom 15:11 *2962*
for the *L* Jesus Christ's sake, and ... Rom 15:30 *2962*
That ye receive her in the *L* ... Rom 16:2 *2962*
Greet Amplias my beloved in the *L* ... Rom 16:8 *2962*
of Narcissus, which are in the *L* ... Rom 16:11 *2962*
and Tryphosa, who labour in the *L* ... Rom 16:12 *2962*
which laboured much in the *L* ... Rom 16:12 *2962*
Salute Rufus chosen in the *L* ... Rom 16:13 *2962*
such serve not our *L* Jesus Christ ... Rom 16:18 *2962*
The grace of our *L* Jesus Christ ... Rom 16:20 *2962*
this epistle, salute you in the *L* ... Rom 16:22 *2962*
The grace of our *L* Jesus Christ ... Rom 16:24 *2962*
the name of Jesus Christ our *L* ... 1Cor 1:2 *2962*
and from the *L* Jesus Christ ... 1Cor 1:3 *2962*
the coming of our *L* Jesus Christ ... 1Cor 1:7 *2962*
in the day of our *L* Jesus Christ ... 1Cor 1:8 *2962*
of his Son Jesus Christ our *L* ... 1Cor 1:9 *2962*
by the name of our *L* Jesus Christ ... 1Cor 1:10 *2962*
glorieth, let him glory in the *L* ... 1Cor 1:31 *2962*
not have crucified the *L* of glory ... 1Cor 2:8 *2962*
who hath known the mind of the *L* ... 1Cor 2:16 *2962*
even as the *L* gave to every man ... 1Cor 3:5 *2962*
The *L* knoweth the thoughts of the ... 1Cor 3:20 *2962*
but he that judgeth me is the *L* ... 1Cor 4:4 *2962*
before the time, until the *L* come ... 1Cor 4:5 *2962*
beloved son, and faithful in the *L* ... 1Cor 4:17 *2962*
to you shortly, if the *L* will ... 1Cor 4:19 *2962*
In the name of our *L* Jesus Christ ... 1Cor 5:4 *2962*
the power of our *L* Jesus Christ ... 1Cor 5:4 *2962*
saved in the day of the *L* Jesus ... 1Cor 5:5 *2962*
in the name of the *L* Jesus ... 1Cor 6:11 *2962*
for fornication, but for the *L* ... 1Cor 6:13 *2962*
and the *L* for the body ... 1Cor 6:13 *2962*
And God hath both raised up the *L* ... 1Cor 6:14 *2962*
joined unto the *L* is one spirit ... 1Cor 6:17 *2962*
I command, yet not I, but the *L* ... 1Cor 7:10 *2962*
to the rest speak I, not the *L* ... 1Cor 7:12 *2962*
as the *L* hath called every one, ... 1Cor 7:17 *2962*
For he that is called in the *L* ... 1Cor 7:22 *2962*
I have no commandment of the *L* ... 1Cor 7:25 *2962*
mercy of the *L* to be faithful ... 1Cor 7:25 *2962*
the things that belong to the *L* ... 1Cor 7:32 *2962*
how he may please the *L* ... 1Cor 7:32 *2962*
careth for the things of the *L* ... 1Cor 7:34 *2962*
upon the *L* without distraction ... 1Cor 7:35 *2962*
whom she will; only in the *L* ... 1Cor 7:39 *2962*
one *L* Jesus Christ, by whom are ... 1Cor 8:6 *2962*
I not seen Jesus Christ our *L* ... 1Cor 9:1 *2962*
are not ye my work in the *L* ... 1Cor 9:1 *2962*
mine apostleship are ye in the *L* ... 1Cor 9:2 *2962*
and as the brethren of the *L* ... 1Cor 9:5 *2962*
Even so hath the *L* ordained that ... 1Cor 9:14 *2962*
Ye cannot drink the cup of the *L* ... 1Cor 10:21 *2962*
Do we provoke the *L* to jealousy ... 1Cor 10:22 *2962*
woman without the man, in the *L* ... 1Cor 11:11 *2962*
For I have received of the *L* that ... 1Cor 11:23 *2962*
That the *L* Jesus the same night ... 1Cor 11:23 *2962*
bread, and drink this cup of the *L* ... 1Cor 11:27 *2962*
of the body and blood of the *L* ... 1Cor 11:27 *2962*
judged, we are chastened of the *L* ... 1Cor 11:32 *2962*
man can say that Jesus is the *L* ... 1Cor 12:3 *2962*
administrations, but the same *L* ... 1Cor 12:5 *2962*
they not hear me, saith the *L* ... 1Cor 14:21 *2962*
you are the commandments of the *L* ... 1Cor 14:37 *2962*
I have in Christ Jesus our *L* ... 1Cor 15:31 *2962*
second man is the *L* from heaven ... 1Cor 15:47 *2962*
through our *L* Jesus Christ ... 1Cor 15:57 *2962*
abounding in the work of the *L* ... 1Cor 15:58 *2962*
labour is not in vain in the *L* ... 1Cor 15:58 *2962*
a while with you, if the *L* permit ... 1Cor 16:7 *2962*
for he worketh the work of the *L* ... 1Cor 16:10 *2962*
salute you much in the *L*, with ... 1Cor 16:19 *2962*
man love not the *L* Jesus Christ ... 1Cor 16:22 *2962*
The grace of our *L* Jesus Christ ... 1Cor 16:23 *2962*
and from the *L* Jesus Christ ... 2Cor 1:2 *2962*
the Father of our *L* Jesus Christ ... 2Cor 1:3 *2962*
ours in the day of the *L* Jesus ... 2Cor 1:14 *2962*
door was opened unto me of the *L* ... 2Cor 2:12 *2962*
when it shall turn to the *L* ... 2Cor 3:16 *2962*
Now the *L* is that Spirit ... 2Cor 3:17 *2962*
and where the Spirit of the *L* is ... 2Cor 3:17 *2962*
as in a glass the glory of the *L* ... 2Cor 3:18 *2962*
even as by the Spirit of the *L* ... 2Cor 3:18 *2962*
ourselves, but Christ Jesus the *L* ... 2Cor 4:5 *2962*
the body the dying of the *L* Jesus ... 2Cor 4:10 *2962*
that he which raised up the *L* ... 2Cor 4:14 *2962*
body, we are absent from the *L* ... 2Cor 5:6 *2962*
body, and to be present with the *L* ... 2Cor 5:8 *2962*
therefore the terror of the *L* ... 2Cor 5:11 *2962*
and be ye separate, saith the *L* ... 2Cor 6:17 *2962*
daughters, saith the *L* Almighty ... 2Cor 6:18 *2962*
gave their own selves to the *L* ... 2Cor 8:5 *2962*
the grace of our *L* Jesus Christ ... 2Cor 8:9 *2962*
by us to the glory of the same *L* ... 2Cor 8:19 *2962*
not only in the sight of the *L* ... 2Cor 8:21 *2962*
which the *L* hath given us for ... 2Cor 10:8 *2962*
glorieth, let him glory in the *L* ... 2Cor 10:17 *2962*
but whom the *L* commendeth ... 2Cor 10:18 *2962*
speak, I speak it not after the *L* ... 2Cor 11:17 *2962*
and Father of our *L* Jesus Christ ... 2Cor 11:31 *2962*
visions and revelations of the *L* ... 2Cor 12:1 *2962*
thing I besought the *L* thrice ... 2Cor 12:8 *2962*
to the power which the *L* hath ... 2Cor 13:10 *2962*
The grace of the *L* Jesus Christ ... 2Cor 13:14 *2962*
and from our *L* Jesus Christ, ... Gal 1:3 *2962*
confidence in you through the *L* ... Gal 5:10 *2962*
the cross of our *L* Jesus Christ ... Gal 6:14 *2962*
my body the marks of the *L* Jesus ... Gal 6:17 *2962*
the grace of our *L* Jesus Christ ... Gal 6:18 *2962*
and from the *L* Jesus Christ ... Eph 1:2 *2962*
and Father of our *L* Jesus Christ ... Eph 1:3 *2962*
of your faith in the *L* Jesus ... Eph 1:15 *2962*
the God of our *L* Jesus Christ ... Eph 1:17 *2962*
unto an holy temple in the *L* ... Eph 2:21 *2962*
he purposed in Christ Jesus our *L* ... Eph 3:11 *2962*
the Father of our *L* Jesus Christ ... Eph 3:14 *2962*
therefore, the prisoner of the *L* ... Eph 4:1 *2962*
One *L*, one faith, one baptism, ... Eph 4:5 *2962*
therefore, and testify in the *L* ... Eph 4:17 *2962*
but now are ye light in the *L* ... Eph 5:8 *2962*
what is acceptable unto the *L* ... Eph 5:10 *2962*
what the will of the *L* is ... Eph 5:17 *2962*
melody in your heart to the *L* ... Eph 5:19 *2962*

in the name of our *L* Jesus Christ	Eph 5:20	*2962*
your own husbands, as unto the *L*	Eph 5:22	*2962*
it, even as the *L* the church	Eph 5:29	*2962*
obey your parents in the *L*	Eph 6:1	*2962*
nurture and admonition of the *L*	Eph 6:4	*2962*
will doing service, as to the *L*	Eph 6:7	*2962*
same shall he receive of the *L*	Eph 6:8	*2962*
my brethren, be strong in the *L*	Eph 6:10	*2962*
and faithful minister in the *L*	Eph 6:21	*2962*
the Father and the *L* Jesus Christ	Eph 6:23	*2962*
our *L* Jesus Christ in sincerity	Eph 6:24	*2962*
and from the *L* Jesus Christ	Phil 1:2	*2962*
And many of the brethren in the *L*	Phil 1:14	*2962*
confess that Jesus Christ is *L*	Phil 2:11	*2962*
But I trust in the *L* Jesus to	Phil 2:19	*2962*
But I trust in the *L* that I also	Phil 2:24	*2962*
in the *L* with all gladness	Phil 2:29	*2962*
my brethren, rejoice in the *L*	Phil 3:1	*2962*
knowledge of Christ Jesus my *L*	Phil 3:8	*2962*
the Saviour, the *L* Jesus Christ	Phil 3:20	*2962*
and crown, so stand fast in the *L*	Phil 4:1	*2962*
they be of the same mind in the *L*	Phil 4:2	*2962*
Rejoice in the *L* alway	Phil 4:4	*2962*
The *L* is at hand	Phil 4:5	*2962*
But I rejoiced in the *L* greatly	Phil 4:10	*2962*
The grace of our *L* Jesus Christ	Phil 4:23	*2962*
our Father and the *L* Jesus Christ	Col 1:2	*2962*
the Father of our *L* Jesus Christ	Col 1:3	*2962*
worthy of the *L* unto all pleasing	Col 1:10	*2962*
received Christ Jesus the *L*	Col 2:6	*2962*
grace in your hearts to the *L*	Col 3:16	*2962*
do all in the name of the *L* Jesus	Col 3:17	*2962*
husbands, as it is fit in the *L*	Col 3:18	*2962*
this is well pleasing unto the *L*	Col 3:20	*2962*
do, do it heartily, as to the *L*	Col 3:23	*2962*
Knowing that of the *L* ye shall	Col 3:24	*2962*
for ye serve the *L* Christ	Col 3:24	*2962*
and fellowservant in the *L*	Col 4:7	*2962*
which thou hast received in the *L*	Col 4:17	*2962*
Father and in the *L* Jesus Christ	1Th 1:1	*2962*
our Father, and the *L* Jesus Christ	1Th 1:1	*2962*
of hope in our *L* Jesus Christ	1Th 1:3	*2962*
followers of us, and of the *L*	1Th 1:6	*2962*
of the *L* not only in Macedonia	1Th 1:8	*2962*
Who both killed the *L* Jesus	1Th 2:15	*2962*
our *L* Jesus Christ at his coming	1Th 2:19	*2962*
live, if ye stand fast in the *L*	1Th 3:8	*2962*
our *L* Jesus Christ, direct our	1Th 3:11	*2962*
the *L* make you to increase and	1Th 3:12	*2962*
at the coming of our *L* Jesus	1Th 3:13	*2962*
and exhort you by the *L* Jesus	1Th 4:1	*2962*
we gave you by the *L* Jesus	1Th 4:2	*2962*
because that the *L* is the avenger	1Th 4:6	*2962*
say unto you by the word of the *L*	1Th 4:15	*2962*
L shall not prevent them which	1Th 4:15	*2962*
For the *L* himself shall descend	1Th 4:16	*2962*
clouds, to meet the *L* in the air	1Th 4:17	*2962*
and so shall we ever be with the *L*	1Th 4:17	*2962*
the *L* so cometh as a thief in the	1Th 5:2	*2962*
salvation by our *L* Jesus Christ	1Th 5:9	*2962*
you, and are over you in the *L*	1Th 5:12	*2962*
the coming of our *L* Jesus Christ	1Th 5:23	*2962*
I charge you by the *L* that this	1Th 5:27	*2962*
The grace of our *L* Jesus Christ	1Th 5:28	*2962*
our Father and the *L* Jesus Christ	2Th 1:1	*2962*
our Father and the *L* Jesus Christ	2Th 1:2	*2962*
when the *L* Jesus shall be	2Th 1:7	*2962*
the gospel of our *L* Jesus Christ	2Th 1:8	*2962*
from the presence of the *L*	2Th 1:9	*2962*
That the name of our *L* Jesus	2Th 1:12	*2962*
of our God and the *L* Jesus Christ	2Th 1:12	*2962*
the coming of our *L* Jesus Christ	2Th 2:1	*2962*
whom the *L* shall consume with the	2Th 2:8	*2962*
you, brethren beloved of the *L*	2Th 2:13	*2962*
the glory of our *L* Jesus Christ	2Th 2:14	*2962*
Now our *L* Jesus Christ himself,	2Th 2:16	*2962*
of the *L* may have free course	2Th 3:1	*2962*
But the *L* is faithful, who shall	2Th 3:3	*2962*
confidence in the *L* touching you	2Th 3:4	*2962*
the *L* direct your hearts into the	2Th 3:5	*2962*
in the name of our *L* Jesus Christ	2Th 3:6	*2962*
and exhort by our *L* Jesus Christ	2Th 3:12	*2962*
Now the *L* of peace himself give	2Th 3:16	*2962*
The *L* be with you all	2Th 3:16	*2962*
The grace of our *L* Jesus Christ	2Th 3:18	*2962*
L Jesus Christ, which is our hope	1Ti 1:1	*2962*
our Father and Jesus Christ our *L*	1Ti 1:2	*2962*
And I thank Christ Jesus our *L*	1Ti 1:12	*2962*
the grace of our *L* was exceeding	1Ti 1:14	*2962*
the *L* Jesus Christ, and the elect	1Ti 5:21	*2962*
the words of our *L* Jesus Christ	1Ti 6:3	*2962*
appearing of our *L* Jesus Christ	1Ti 6:14	*2962*
the King of kings, and *L* of lords	1Ti 6:15	*2962*
the Father and Christ Jesus our *L*	2Ti 1:2	*2962*
ashamed of the testimony of our *L*	2Ti 1:8	*2962*
The *L* give mercy unto the house	2Ti 1:16	*2962*
The *L* grant unto him that he may	2Ti 1:18	*2962*
find mercy of the *L* in that day	2Ti 1:18	*2962*
the *L* give thee understanding in	2Ti 2:7	*2962*
charging them before the *L* that	2Ti 2:14	*2962*
The *L* knoweth them that are his	2Ti 2:19	*2962*
call on the *L* out of a pure heart	2Ti 2:22	*2962*
servant of the *L* must not strive	2Ti 2:24	*2962*
of them all the *L* delivered me	2Ti 3:11	*2962*
the *L* Jesus Christ, who shall	2Ti 4:1	*2962*
of righteousness, which the *L*	2Ti 4:8	*2962*
the *L* reward him according to his	2Ti 4:14	*2962*
the *L* stood with me, and	2Ti 4:17	*2962*
the *L* shall deliver me from every	2Ti 4:18	*2962*
The *L* Jesus Christ be with thy	2Ti 4:22	*2962*
the *L* Jesus Christ our Saviour	Titus 1:4	*2962*
our Father and the *L* Jesus Christ	Philem 3	*2962*
thou hast toward the *L* Jesus	Philem 5	*2962*
both in the flesh, and in the *L*	Philem 16	*2962*
let me have joy of thee in the *L*	Philem 20	*2962*
refresh my bowels in the *L*	Philem 20	*2962*
The grace of our *L* Jesus Christ	Philem 25	*2962*
And, Thou, *L*, in the beginning	Heb 1:10	*2962*
first began to be spoken by the *L*	Heb 2:3	*2962*
that our *L* sprang out of Juda	Heb 7:14	*2962*
The *L* sware and will not repent,	Heb 7:21	*2962*
tabernacle, which the *L* pitched	Heb 8:2	*2962*
the days come, saith the *L*	Heb 8:8	*2962*
I regarded them not, saith the *L*	Heb 8:9	*2962*
after those days, saith the *L*	Heb 8:10	*2962*
his brother, saying, Know the *L*	Heb 8:11	*2962*
after those days, saith the *L*	Heb 10:16	*2962*
I will recompense, saith the *L*	Heb 10:30	*2962*
The *L* shall judge his people	Heb 10:30	*2962*
not thou the chastening of the *L*	Heb 12:5	*2962*
For whom the *L* loveth he	Heb 12:6	*2962*
which no man shall see the *L*	Heb 12:14	*2962*
The *L* is my helper, and I will not	Heb 13:6	*2962*
again from the dead our *L* Jesus	Heb 13:20	*2962*
of the *L* Jesus Christ, to the	Jas 1:1	*2962*
shall receive any thing of the *L*	Jas 1:7	*2962*
which the *L* hath promised to them	Jas 1:12	*2962*
the faith of our *L* Jesus Christ	Jas 2:1	*2962*
the *L* of glory, with respect of	Jas 2:1	
yourselves in the sight of the *L*	Jas 4:10	*2962*
ye ought to say, If the *L* will	Jas 4:15	*2962*
into the ears of the *L* of Sabaoth	Jas 5:4	*2962*
unto the coming of the *L*	Jas 5:7	*2962*
the coming of the *L* draweth nigh	Jas 5:8	*2962*
have spoken in the name of the *L*	Jas 5:10	*2962*
and have seen the end of the *L*	Jas 5:11	*2962*
that the *L* is very pitiful, and of	Jas 5:11	*2962*
him with oil in the name of the *L*	Jas 5:14	*2962*
sick, and the *L* shall raise him up	Jas 5:15	*2962*
and Father of our *L* Jesus Christ	1Pet 1:3	*2962*
word of the *L* endureth for ever	1Pet 1:25	*2962*
tasted that the *L* is gracious	1Pet 2:3	*2962*
For the eyes of the *L* are over	1Pet 3:12	*2962*
but the face of the *L* is against	1Pet 3:12	*2962*
But sanctify the *L* God in your	1Pet 3:15	*2962*
of God, and of Jesus our *L*	2Pet 1:2	*2962*
knowledge of our *L* Jesus Christ	2Pet 1:8	*2962*
the everlasting kingdom of our *L*	2Pet 1:11	*2962*
even as our *L* Jesus Christ hath	2Pet 1:14	*2962*
and coming of our *L* Jesus Christ	2Pet 1:16	*2962*
denying the *L* that bought them	2Pet 2:1	*1203*
The *L* knoweth how to deliver the	2Pet 2:9	*2962*
against them before the *L*	2Pet 2:11	*2962*
through the knowledge of the *L*	2Pet 2:20	*2962*
of us the apostles of the *L*	2Pet 3:2	*2962*
is with the *L* as a thousand years	2Pet 3:8	*2962*
The *L* is not slack concerning his	2Pet 3:9	*2962*
But the day of the *L* will come as	2Pet 3:10	*2962*
of our *L* is salvation	2Pet 3:15	*2962*
and in the knowledge of our *L*	2Pet 3:18	*2962*
from the *L* Jesus Christ, the Son	2Jn 3	*2962*
and denying the only *L* God	Jude 4	*2962*
and our *L* Jesus Christ	Jude 4	*2962*
ye once knew this, how that the *L*	Jude 5	*2962*
but said, The *L* rebuke thee	Jude 9	*2962*
the *L* cometh with ten thousands	Jude 14	*2962*
apostles of our *L* Jesus Christ	Jude 17	*2962*
looking for the mercy of our *L*	Jude 21	*2962*
and the ending, saith the *L*	Rev 1:8	*2962*
L God Almighty, which was, and is,	Rev 4:8	*2962*
Thou art worthy, O *L*, to receive	Rev 4:11	*2962*
loud voice, saying, How long, O *L*	Rev 6:10	*1203*
where also our *L* was crucified	Rev 11:8	*2962*
are become the kingdoms of our *L*	Rev 11:15	*2962*
O *L* God Almighty, which art, and	Rev 11:17	*2962*
die in the *L* from henceforth	Rev 14:13	*2962*
are thy works, *L* God Almighty	Rev 15:3	*2962*
Who shall not fear thee, O *L*	Rev 15:4	*2962*
say, Thou art righteous, O *L*	Rev 16:5	*2962*
L God Almighty, true and righteous	Rev 16:7	*2962*
for he is *L* of lords, and King of	Rev 17:14	*2962*
for strong is the *L* God who	Rev 18:8	*2962*
and power, unto the *L* our God	Rev 19:1	*2962*
for the *L* God omnipotent reigneth	Rev 19:6	*2962*
KING OF KINGS, AND *L* OF LORDS	Rev 19:16	*2962*
for the *L* God Almighty and the	Rev 21:22	*2962*
for the *L* God giveth them light	Rev 22:5	*2962*
the *L* God of the holy prophets	Rev 22:6	*2962*
Even so, come, *L* Jesus	Rev 22:20	*2962*
The grace of our *L* Jesus Christ	Rev 22:21	*2962*

2. A human title of honor.

pleasure, my *l* being old also	Gen 18:12	113
said unto them, Oh, not so, my *l*	Gen 19:18	113
Hear us, my *l*	Gen 23:6	113
Nay, my *l*, hear me	Gen 23:11	113
My *l*, hearken unto me	Gen 23:15	113
And she said, Drink, my *l*	Gen 24:18	113
be *l* over thy brethren, and let	Gen 27:29	1376
Behold, I have made him thy *l*	Gen 27:37	1376
Let it not displease my *l* that I	Gen 31:35	113
shall ye speak unto my *l* Esau	Gen 32:4	113
and I have sent to tell my *l*	Gen 32:5	113
is a present sent unto my *l* Esau	Gen 32:18	113
find grace in the sight of my *l*	Gen 33:8	113
My *l* knoweth that the children	Gen 33:13	113
Let my *l*, I pray thee, pass over	Gen 33:14	113
until I come unto my *l* unto Seir	Gen 33:14	113
find grace in the sight of my *l*	Gen 33:15	113
by her, until his *l* came home	Gen 39:16	113
their *l* the king of Egypt	Gen 40:1	113
And they said unto him, Nay, my *l*	Gen 42:10	113
who is the *l* of the land, spake	Gen 42:30	113
the *l* of the country, said unto	Gen 42:33	113
this it in which my *l* drinketh	Gen 44:5	113
Wherefore saith my *l* these words	Gen 44:7	113
said, What shall we say unto my *l*	Gen 44:16	113
near unto him, and said, Oh my *l*	Gen 44:18	113
My *l* asked his servants, saying,	Gen 44:19	113
And we said unto my *l*, We have a	Gen 44:20	113
And we said unto my *l*, The lad	Gen 44:22	113
we told him the words of my *l*	Gen 44:24	113
of the lad a bondman to my *l*	Gen 44:33	113
l of all his house, and a ruler	Gen 45:8	113
God hath made me *l* of all Egypt	Gen 45:9	113
We will not hide it from my *l*	Gen 47:18	113
my *l* also hath our herds of	Gen 47:18	113
ought left in the sight of my *l*	Gen 47:18	113
find grace in the sight of my *l*	Gen 47:25	113
Let not the anger of my *l* wax hot	Ex 32:22	113
and said, My *l* Moses, forbid them	Num 11:28	113
Aaron said unto Moses, Alas, my *l*	Num 12:11	113
will do as my *l* commandeth	Num 32:25	113
to battle, as my *l* saith	Num 32:27	113
their *l* was fallen down dead on	Judg 3:25	113
and said unto him, Turn in, my *l*	Judg 4:18	3068
And Gideon said unto him, Oh my *l*	Judg 6:13	113
me find favour in thy sight, my *l*	Ruth 2:13	3068
my *l*, as thy soul liveth, my *l*	1Sa 1:26	113
Let our *l* now command thy	1Sa 16:16	113
And he answered, Here I am, my *l*	1Sa 22:12	113
after Saul, saying, My *l* the king	1Sa 24:8	113
put forth mine hand against my *l*	1Sa 24:10	113
his feet, and said, Upon me, my *l*	1Sa 25:24	113
Let not my *l*, I pray thee, regard	1Sa 25:25	113
saw not the young men of my *l*	1Sa 25:25	113
and they that seek evil to my *l*	1Sa 25:26	113
handmaid hath brought unto my *l*	1Sa 25:27	113
the young men that follow my *l*	1Sa 25:27	113
certainly make my *l* a sure house	1Sa 25:28	113
because my *l* fighteth the battles	1Sa 25:28	113
but the soul of my *l* shall be	1Sa 25:29	113
l according to all the good that	1Sa 25:30	113
nor offence of heart unto my *l*	1Sa 25:31	136
or that my *l* hath avenged himself	1Sa 25:31	136
shall have dealt well with my *l*	1Sa 25:31	113
the feet of the servants of my *l*	1Sa 25:41	113
hast thou not kept thy *l* the king	1Sa 26:15	113
in to destroy the king thy *l*	1Sa 26:15	3068
David said, It is my voice, my *l*	1Sa 26:17	113
Wherefore doth my *l* thus pursue	1Sa 26:18	113
let my *l* the king hear the words	1Sa 26:19	113
the enemies of my *l* the king	1Sa 29:8	113
brought them hither unto my *l*	2Sa 1:10	113
shewed this kindness unto your *l*	2Sa 2:5	113
all Israel unto my *l* the king	2Sa 3:21	113
According to all that my *l* the	2Sa 9:11	113
of Ammon said unto Hanun their *l*	2Sa 10:3	113
with all the servants of his *l*	2Sa 11:9	113
my *l* Joab, and the servants of my	2Sa 11:11	113
Joab, and the servants of my *l*	2Sa 11:11	113
bed with the servants of his *l*	2Sa 11:13	113
Let not my *l* suppose that they	2Sa 13:32	113
Now therefore let not my *l* the	2Sa 13:33	113
Tekoah said unto the king, My *l*	2Sa 14:9	113
speak one word unto my *l* the king	2Sa 14:12	113
of this thing unto my *l* the king	2Sa 14:15	113
The word of my *l* the king shall	2Sa 14:17	113
so is my *l* the king to discern	2Sa 14:17	113
Let my *l* the king now speak	2Sa 14:18	113
my *l* the king, none can turn to	2Sa 14:19	113
that my *l* the king hath spoken	2Sa 14:19	113
my *l* is wise, according to the	2Sa 14:20	113
found grace in thy sight, my *l*	2Sa 14:22	113
my *l* the king shall appoint	2Sa 15:15	113
as my *l* the king liveth, surely	2Sa 15:21	113
what place my *l* the king shall be	2Sa 15:21	113
may find grace in thy sight, my *l*	2Sa 16:4	113
this dead dog curse my *l* the king	2Sa 16:9	113
their hand against my *l* the king	2Sa 18:28	113
said, Tidings, my *l* the king	2Sa 18:31	113
The enemies of my *l* the king	2Sa 18:32	113
Let not my *l* impute iniquity unto	2Sa 19:19	113
l the king went out of Jerusalem	2Sa 19:19	113
to go down to meet my *l* the king	2Sa 19:20	113
And he answered, My *l*, O king, my	2Sa 19:26	113
thy servant unto my *l* the king	2Sa 19:27	113
but my *l* the king is as an angel	2Sa 19:27	113
but dead men before my *l* the king	2Sa 19:28	113
forasmuch as my *l* the king is	2Sa 19:30	113
yet a burden unto my *l* the king	2Sa 19:35	113
him go over with my *l* the king	2Sa 19:37	3068
eyes of my *l* the king may see it	2Sa 24:3	113
but why doth my *l* the king	2Sa 24:3	113
Wherefore is my *l* the king come	2Sa 24:21	113
Let my *l* the king take and offer	2Sa 24:22	113
for my *l* the king a young virgin	1Kin 1:2	113
that my *l* the king may get heat	1Kin 1:2	113
David our *l* knoweth it not	1Kin 1:11	113
unto him, Didst not thou, my *l*	1Kin 1:13	113
And she said unto him, My *l*	1Kin 1:17	113
my *l* the king, thou knowest it	1Kin 1:18	113
And thou, my *l*, O king, the eyes	1Kin 1:20	113
throne of my *l* the king after him	1Kin 1:20	113
when my *l* the king shall sleep	1Kin 1:21	113

And Nathan said, My *l*, O king, ... 1Kin 1:24 113
this thing done by my *l* the king ... 1Kin 1:27 113
throne of my *l* the king after him ... 1Kin 1:27 113
Let my *l* king David live for ever ... 1Kin 1:31 113
with you the servants of your *l* ... 1Kin 1:33 113
the throne of my *l* king David ... 1Kin 1:37 113
Verily our *l* king David hath made ... 1Kin 1:43 113
came to bless our *l* king David ... 1Kin 1:47 113
as my *l* the king hath said, so ... 1Kin 2:38 113
And the one woman said, O my *l* ... 1Kin 3:17 113
upon her son, and she said, O my *l* ... 1Kin 3:26 113
which fled from his *l* Hadadezer ... 1Kin 11:23 113
people turn again unto their *l* ... 1Kin 12:27 3068
said, Art thou that my *l* Elijah ... 1Kin 18:7 113
go, tell thy *l*, Behold, Elijah is ... 1Kin 18:8 113
whither my *l* hath not sent to ... 1Kin 18:10 113
now thou sayest, Go, tell thy *l* ... 1Kin 18:11 3068
Was it not told my *l* what I did ... 1Kin 18:13 113
now thou sayest, Go, tell thy *l* ... 1Kin 18:14 113
of Israel answered and said, My *l* ... 1Kin 20:4 113
Tell my *l* the king, All that thou ... 1Kin 20:9 113
city is pleasant, as my *l* seeth ... 2Kin 2:19 113
And she said, Nay, my *l*, thou man ... 2Kin 4:16 113
said, Did I desire a son of my *l* ... 2Kin 4:28 113
Would God my *l* were with the ... 2Kin 5:3 113
And one went in, and told his *l* ... 2Kin 5:4 113
of his servants said, None, my *l* ... 2Kin 6:12 113
unto him, saying, Help, my *l* ... 2Kin 6:26 113
Then a *l* on whose hand the king ... 2Kin 7:2 7991
the king appointed the *l* on whose ... 2Kin 7:17 7991
that *l* answered the man of God, ... 2Kin 7:19 7991
And Gehazi said, My *l*, O king, ... 2Kin 8:5 113
And Hazael said, Why weepeth my *l* ... 2Kin 8:12 113
forth to the servants of his *l* ... 2Kin 9:11 113
give pledges to my *l* the king of ... 2Kin 18:23 113
my *l* the king, are they not all ... 1Chr 21:3 113
why then doth my *l* require this ... 1Chr 21:3 113
let my *l* the king do that which ... 1Chr 21:23 113
men of my *l* David thy father ... 2Chr 2:14 113
which my *l* hath spoken of, let ... 2Chr 2:15 113
and hath rebelled against his *l* ... 2Chr 13:6 113
according to the counsel of my *l* ... Ezr 10:3 136
who is *l* over us ... Ps 12:4 113
He made him *l* of his house, and ... Ps 105:21 3050
over into the hand of a cruel *l* ... Is 19:4 113
My *l*, I stand continually upon ... Is 21:8 136
not lament for him, saying, Ah *l* ... Jer 22:18 113
will lament thee, saying, Ah *l* ... Jer 34:5 113
now, I pray thee, O my *l* the king ... Jer 37:20 113
My *l* the king, these men have ... Jer 38:9 113
unto Daniel, I fear my *l* the king ... Dan 1:10 113
therefore there is no king, *l* ... Dan 2:10 7229
answered and said, My *l*, the dream ... Dan 4:19 4756
which is come upon my *l* the king ... Dan 4:24 4756
him that stood before me, O my *l* ... Dan 10:16 113
this my *l* talk with this my lord ... Dan 10:17 113
and said, Let my *l* speak ... Dan 10:19 113
Then said I, O my *l*, what are ... Zec 1:9 113
me, saying, What are these, my *l* ... Zec 4:4 113
And I said, No, my *l* ... Zec 4:5 113
And I said, No, my *l* ... Zec 4:13 113
with me, What are these, my *l* ... Zec 6:4 113
nor the servant above his *l* ... Mt 10:24 *2962*
master, and the servant as his *l* ... Mt 10:25 *2962*
his *l* commanded him to be sold, ... Mt 18:25 *2962*
Then the *l* of that servant was ... Mt 18:27 *2962*
told unto their *l* all that was ... Mt 18:31 *2962*
Then his *l*, after that he had ... Mt 18:32 *2962*
his *l* was wroth, and delivered him ... Mt 18:34 *2962*
the *l* of the vineyard saith unto ... Mt 20:8 *2962*
whom his *l* hath made ruler over ... Mt 24:45 *2962*
whom his *l* when he cometh shall ... Mt 24:46 *2962*
heart, My *l* delayeth his coming ... Mt 24:48 *2962*
The *l* of that servant shall come ... Mt 24:50 *2962*
After a long time the *l* of those ... Mt 25:19 *2962*
other five talents, saying, *L* ... Mt 25:20 *2962*
His *l* said unto him, Well done, ... Mt 25:21 *2962*
enter thou into the joy of thy *l* ... Mt 25:21 *2962*
two talents came and said, *L* ... Mt 25:22 *2962*
His *l* said unto him, Well done, ... Mt 25:23 *2962*
enter thou into the joy of thy *l* ... Mt 25:23 *2962*
the one talent came and said, *L* ... Mt 25:24 *2962*
His *l* answered and said unto him, ... Mt 25:26 *2962*
the *l* of the vineyard do ... Mk 12:9 *2962*
unto men that wait for their *l* ... Lk 12:36 *2962*
whom the *l* when he cometh shall ... Lk 12:37 *2962*
whom his *l* shall make ruler over ... Lk 12:42 *2962*
whom his *l* when he cometh shall ... Lk 12:43 *2962*
heart, My *l* delayeth his coming ... Lk 12:45 *2962*
The *l* of that servant will come ... Lk 12:46 *2962*
shewed his *l* these things ... Lk 14:21 *2962*
And the servant said, *L*, it is ... Lk 14:22 *2962*
the *l* said unto the servant, Go ... Lk 14:23 *2962*
for my *l* taketh away from me the ... Lk 16:3 *2962*
How much owest thou unto my *l* ... Lk 16:5 *2962*
the *l* commended the unjust ... Lk 16:8 *2962*
Then said the *l* of the vineyard, ... Lk 20:13 *2962*
What therefore shall the *l* of the ... Lk 20:15 *2962*
servant is not greater than his *l* ... Jn 13:16 *2962*
knoweth not what his *l* doeth ... Jn 15:15 *2962*
servant is not greater than his *l* ... Jn 15:20 *2962*
certain thing to write unto my *l* ... Acts 25:26 *2962*
a servant, though he be *l* of all ... Gal 4:1 *2962*
obeyed Abraham, calling him *l* ... 1Pet 3:6 *2962*

LORDLY {1}
brought forth butter in a *l* dish ... Judg 5:25 117

LORD'S {123}
1. Refers to Lord 1.
know how that the earth is the *L* ... Ex 9:29 3068
it is the *L* passover ... Ex 12:11 3068
the sacrifice of the *L* passover ... Ex 12:27 3068
that the *L* law may be in thy ... Ex 13:9 3068
the males shall be the *L* ... Ex 13:12 3068
and said, Who is on the *L* side ... Ex 32:26 3068
they brought the *L* offering to ... Ex 35:21 3068
and brass brought the *L* offering ... Ex 35:24 3068
all the fat is the *L* ... Lev 3:16 3068
goat upon which the *L* lot fell ... Lev 16:9 3068
month at even is the *L* passover ... Lev 23:5 3068
which should be the *L* firstling ... Lev 27:26 3068
it is the *L* ... Lev 27:26 3068
the fruit of the tree, is the *L* ... Lev 27:30 3068
Is the *L* hand waxed short ... Num 11:23 3068
all the *L* people were prophets ... Num 11:29 3068
ye shall give thereof the *L* heave ... Num 18:28 3068
the *L* tribute of the sheep was ... Num 31:37 3068
of which the *L* tribute was ... Num 31:38 3068
of which the *L* tribute was ... Num 31:39 3068
of which the *L* tribute was thirty ... Num 31:40 3068
which was the *L* heave offering, ... Num 31:41 3068
the *L* anger was kindled the same ... Num 32:10 3068
the *L* anger was kindled against ... Num 32:13 3068
of heavens is the *L* thy God ... Deut 10:14 3068
then the *L* wrath be kindled ... Deut 11:17 3068
it is called the *L* release ... Deut 15:2 3068
For the *L* portion is his people ... Deut 32:9 3068
which Moses the *L* servant gave ... Josh 1:15 3068
the captain of the *L* host said ... Josh 5:15 3068
wherein the *L* tabernacle dwelleth ... Josh 22:19 3068
of Ammon, shall surely be the *L* ... Judg 11:31 3068
pillars of the earth are the *L* ... 1Sa 2:8 3068
ye make the *L* people to ... 1Sa 2:24 3068
the *L* priest in Shiloh, wearing ... 1Sa 14:3 3068
Surely the *L* anointed is before ... 1Sa 16:6 3068
for the battle is the *L*, and he ... 1Sa 17:47 3068
for me, and fight the *L* battles ... 1Sa 18:17 3068
that Saul had slain the *L* priests ... 1Sa 22:21 3068
the *L* anointed, to stretch forth ... 1Sa 24:6 3068
for he is the *L* anointed ... 1Sa 24:10 3068
his hand against the *L* anointed ... 1Sa 26:9 3068
mine hand against the *L* anointed ... 1Sa 26:11 3068
kept your master, the *L* anointed ... 1Sa 26:16 3068
mine hand against the *L* anointed ... 1Sa 26:23 3068
hand to destroy the *L* anointed ... 2Sa 1:14 3068
I have slain the *L* anointed ... 2Sa 1:16 3068
because he cursed the *L* anointed ... 2Sa 19:21 3068
because of the *L* oath that was ... 2Sa 21:7 3068
the *L* prophets by fifty in a cave ... 1Kin 18:13 3068
that they should be the *L* people ... 2Kin 11:17 3068
The arrow of the *L* deliverance ... 2Kin 13:17 3068
the LORD had filled the *L* house ... 2Chr 7:2 3068
that they should be the *L* people ... 2Chr 23:16 3068
the *L* throne is in heaven ... Ps 11:4 3068
For the kingdom is the *L* ... Ps 22:28 3068
The earth is the *L*, and the ... Ps 24:1 3068
same the *L* name is to be praised ... Ps 113:3 3068
even the heavens, are the *L* ... Ps 115:16 3068
In the courts of the *L* house ... Ps 116:19 3068
This is the *L* doing ... Ps 118:23 3068
How shall we sing the *L* song in a ... Ps 137:4 3068
just weight and balance are the *L* ... Prov 16:11 3068
that the mountain of the *L* house ... Is 2:2 3068
it is the day of the *L* vengeance ... Is 34:8 3068
L hand double for all her sins ... Is 40:2 3068
and blind as the *L* servant ... Is 42:19 3068
One shall say, I am the *L* ... Is 44:5 3068
the *L* hand is not shortened, that ... Is 59:1 3068
for they are not the *L* ... Jer 5:10 3068
Stand in the gate of the *L* house ... Jer 7:2 3068
because the *L* flock is carried ... Jer 13:17 3068
stood in the court of the *L* house ... Jer 19:14 3068
Then took I the cup at the *L* hand ... Jer 25:17 3068
Stand in the court of the *L* house ... Jer 26:2 3068
come to worship in the *L* house ... Jer 26:2 3068
of the new gate of the *L* house ... Jer 26:10 3068
the vessels of the *L* house shall ... Jer 27:16 3068
all the vessels of the *L* house ... Jer 28:3 3068
again the vessels of the *L* house ... Jer 28:6 3068
the *L* house upon the fasting day ... Jer 36:6 3068
words of the LORD in the *L* house ... Jer 36:8 3068
of the new gate of the *L* house ... Jer 36:10 3068
is the time of the *L* vengeance ... Jer 51:6 3068
been a golden cup in the *L* hand ... Jer 51:7 3068
the sanctuaries of the *L* house ... Jer 51:51 3068
so that in the day of the *L* anger ... Lam 2:22 3068
It is of the *L* mercies that we ... Lam 3:22 3068
the *L* house which was toward the ... Eze 8:14 3068
the inner court of the *L* house ... Eze 8:16 3068
of the brightness of the *L* glory ... Eze 10:4 3068
of the east gate of the *L* house ... Eze 10:19 3068
unto the east gate of the *L* house ... Eze 11:1 3068
that is desolate, for the *L* sake ... Dan 9:17 136
shall not dwell in the *L* land ... Hos 9:3 3068
priests, the *L* ministers, mourn ... Joel 1:9 3068
and the kingdom shall be the *L* ... Obad 21 3068
the *L* controversy, and ye strong ... Mic 6:2 3068
The *L* voice crieth unto the city, ... Mic 6:9 3068
the cup of the *L* right hand shall ... Hab 2:16 3068
in the day of the *L* sacrifice ... Zeph 1:8 3068
them in the day of the *L* wrath ... Zeph 1:18 3068
day of the *L* anger come upon you ... Zeph 2:2 3068
be hid in the day of the *L* anger ... Zeph 2:3 3068
the time that the *L* house should ... Hag 1:2 3068
Then spake Haggai the *L* messenger ... Hag 1:13 3068
in the *L* message unto the people ... Hag 1:13 3068
of the *L* temple was laid, ... Hag 2:18 3068
the pots in the *L* house shall be ... Zec 14:20 3068
this is the *L* doing, and it is ... Mt 21:42 *2962*
This was the *L* doing, and it is ... Mk 12:11 *2962*
before he had seen the *L* Christ ... Lk 2:26 *2962*
therefore, or die, we are the *L* ... Rom 14:8 *2962*
being a servant, is the *L* freeman ... 1Cor 7:22 *2962*
be partakers of the *L* table ... 1Cor 10:21 *2962*
For the earth is the *L*, and the ... 1Cor 10:26 *2962*
for the earth is the *L*, and the ... 1Cor 10:28 *2962*
this is not to eat the *L* supper ... 1Cor 11:20 *2960*
ye do shew the *L* death till he ... 1Cor 11:26 *2962*
not discerning the *L* body ... 1Cor 11:29 *2962*
I none, save James the *L* brother ... Gal 1:19 *2962*
ordinance of man for the *L* sake ... 1Pet 2:13 *2962*
I was in the Spirit on the *L* day ... Rev 1:10 *2960*
2. Refers to Lord 2.
him in the ward of his *l* house ... Gen 40:7 113
out of thy *l* house silver or gold ... Gen 44:8 113
and we also will be my *l* bondmen ... Gen 44:9 113
behold, we are my *l* servants ... Gen 44:16 113
thee, speak a word in my *l* ears ... Gen 44:18 113
take thou thy *l* servants, and ... 2Sa 20:6 113
are they not all my *l* servants ... 1Chr 21:3 113
shall be the shame of thy *l* house ... Is 22:18 113
in the earth, and hid his *l* money ... Mt 25:18 *2962*
servant, which knew his *l* will ... Lk 12:47 *2962*
one of his *l* debtors unto him ... Lk 16:5 *2962*

LORDS {42}
And he said, Behold now, my *l* ... Gen 19:2 113
the *l* of the high places of Arnon ... Num 21:28 1167
God is God of gods, and Lord of *l* ... Deut 10:17 113
five *l* of the Philistines ... Josh 13:3 5633
five *l* of the Philistines, and all ... Judg 3:3 5633
the *l* of the Philistines came up ... Judg 16:5 5633
Then the *l* of the Philistines ... Judg 16:8 5633
sent and called for the *l* of the ... Judg 16:18 5633
Then the *l* of the Philistines ... Judg 16:18 5633
Then the *l* of the Philistines ... Judg 16:23 5633
all the *l* of the Philistines were ... Judg 16:27 5633
and the house fell upon the *l* ... Judg 16:30 5633
gathered all the *l* of the ... 1Sa 5:8 5633
all the *l* of the Philistines ... 1Sa 5:11 5633
of the *l* of the Philistines ... 1Sa 6:4 5633
was on you all, and on your *l* ... 1Sa 6:4 5633
the *l* of the Philistines went ... 1Sa 6:12 5633
And when the five *l* of the ... 1Sa 6:16 5633
belonging to the five *l*, both of ... 1Sa 6:18 5633
the *l* of the Philistines went up ... 1Sa 7:7 5633
the *l* of the Philistines passed ... 1Sa 29:2 5633
the *l* favour thee not ... 1Sa 29:6 5633
not the *l* of the Philistines ... 1Sa 29:7 5633
for the *l* of the Philistines upon ... 1Chr 12:19 5633
and his counsellors, and his *l* ... Ezr 8:25 8269
O give thanks to the Lord of *l* ... Ps 136:3 113
the *l* of the heathen have broken ... Is 16:8 1167
other *l* besides thee have had ... Is 26:13 113
wherefore say my people, We are *l* ... Jer 2:31 7300
men, captains and rulers, great *l* ... Eze 23:23 7991
and my *l* sought unto me ... Dan 4:36 7261
feast to a thousand of his *l* ... Dan 5:1 7261
in him, and his *l* were astonied ... Dan 5:9 7261
of the words of the king and his *l* ... Dan 5:10 7261
before thee, and thou, and thy *l* ... Dan 5:23 7261
and with the signet of his *l* ... Dan 6:17 7261
birthday made a supper to his *l* ... Mk 6:21 *3175*
there be gods many, and *l* many,) ... 1Cor 8:5 *2962*
the King of kings, and Lord of *l* ... 1Ti 6:15 *2961*
Neither as being *l* over God's ... 1Pet 5:3 *2634*
for he is Lord of *l*, and King of ... Rev 17:14 *2962*
KING OF KINGS, AND LORD OF *L* ... Rev 19:16 *2962*

LORDSHIP {2}
the Gentiles exercise *l* over them ... Mk 10:42 *2634*
the Gentiles exercise *l* over them ... Lk 22:25 *2961*

LO-RUHAMAH *(lo-ru-ha'-mah)* {2} *Symbolic name meaning "Not pitied."*
said unto him, Call her name *L* ... Hos 1:6 3819
Now when she had weaned *L* ... Hos 1:8 3819

LOSE {24}
thou *l* thy life, with the lives ... Judg 18:25 622
that we *l* not all the beasts ... 1Kin 18:5 3772
owners thereof to *l* their life ... Job 31:39 5307
vomit up, and *l* thy sweet words ... Prov 23:8 7843
A time to get, and a time to *l* ... Eccl 3:6 6
that findeth his life shall *l* it ... Mt 10:39 *622*
he shall in no wise *l* his reward ... Mt 10:42 *622*
will save his life shall *l* it ... Mt 16:25 *622*
whosoever will *l* his life for my ... Mt 16:25 *622*
whole world, and *l* his own soul ... Mt 16:26 *2210*
will save his life shall *l* it ... Mk 8:35 *622*
but whosoever shall *l* his life ... Mk 8:35 *622*
whole world, and *l* his own soul ... Mk 8:36 *2210*
you, he shall not *l* his reward ... Mk 9:41 *622*
will save his life shall *l* it ... Lk 9:24 *622*
but whosoever will *l* his life for ... Lk 9:24 *622*
l himself, or be cast away ... Lk 9:25 *622*
if he *l* one of them, doth not ... Lk 15:4 *622*
if she *l* one piece, doth not ... Lk 15:8 *622*
seek to save his life shall *l* it ... Lk 17:33 *622*
whosoever shall *l* his life shall ... Lk 17:33 *622*
hath given me I should *l* nothing ... Jn 6:39 *622*
that loveth his life shall *l* it ... Jn 12:25 *622*
that we *l* not those things which ... 2Jn 8 *622*

LOSETH {1}
he that *l* his life for my sake ... Mt 10:39 *622*

LOSS {10}
I bare the *l* of it ... Gen 31:39 2398
shall pay for the *l* of his time ... Ex 21:19 7674
shall I know the *l* of children ... Is 47:8 7921
the *l* of children, and widowhood ... Is 47:9 7921
and to have gained this harm and *l* ... Acts 27:21 *2209*
for there shall be no *l* of any ... Acts 27:22 *580*
be burned, he shall suffer *l*. ... 1Cor 3:15 *2210*
me, those I counted *l* for Christ ... Phil 3:7 *2209*
I count all things but *l* for the ... Phil 3:8 *2209*
have suffered the *l* of all things ... Phil 3:8 *2210*

LOST {33}
or for any manner of *l* thing ... Ex 22:9 9
Or have found that which was *l* ... Lev 6:3 9
or the *l* thing which he found, ... Lev 6:4 9
days that were before shall be *l* ... Num 6:12 5307
and with all *l* things of thy ... Deut 22:3 9
of thy brother's, which he hath *l* ... Deut 22:3 6
of Kish Saul's father were *l*. ... 1Sa 9:3 6
asses that were *l* three days ago ... 1Sa 9:20 6
like the army that thou hast *l* ... 1Kin 20:25 5307
I have gone astray like a *l* sheep ... Ps 119:176 6
have, after thou hast *l* the other ... Is 49:20 7923
seeing I have *l* my children ... Is 49:21 7908
My people hath been *l* sheep ... Jer 50:6 6
she had waited, and her hope was *l* ... Eze 19:5 6
have ye sought that which was *l* ... Eze 34:4 6
I will seek that which was *l* ... Eze 34:16 6
bones are dried, and our hope is *l* ... Eze 37:11 6
but if the salt have *l* his savour ... Mt 5:13 *3471*
But go rather to the *l* sheep of ... Mt 10:6 *622*
I am not sent but unto the *l* ... Mt 15:24 *622*
is come to save that which was *l* ... Mt 18:11 *622*
if the salt have *l* his saltness ... Mk 9:50 *358,1096*
but if the salt have *l* his savour ... Lk 14:34 *3471*
and go after that which is *l*, ... Lk 15:4 *622*
I have found my sheep which was *l* ... Lk 15:6 *622*
found the piece which I had *l*. ... Lk 15:9 *622*
he was *l*, and is found ... Lk 15:24 *622*
and was *l*, and is found ... Lk 15:32 *622*
seek and to save that which was *l* ... Lk 19:10 *622*
that remain, that nothing be *l* ... Jn 6:12 *622*
I have kept, and none of them is *l* ... Jn 17:12 *622*
thou gavest me have I *l* none ... Jn 18:9 *622*
hid, it is hid to them that are *l* ... 2Cor 4:3 *622*

LOT *(lot)* {111} See LOT'S.
1. *Abraham's nephew.*
and Haran begat *L* ... Gen 11:27 3876
L the son of Haran his son's son, ... Gen 11:31 3876
and *L* went with him ... Gen 12:4 3876
L his brother's son, and all their ... Gen 12:5 3876
L with him, into the south ... Gen 13:1 3876
L also, which went with Abram, ... Gen 13:5 3876
And Abram said unto *L*, Let there ... Gen 13:8 3876
L lifted up his eyes, and beheld ... Gen 13:10 3876
Then *L* chose him all the plain of ... Gen 13:11 3876
and *L* journeyed east ... Gen 13:11 3876
L dwelled in the cities of the ... Gen 13:12 3876
after that *L* was separated from ... Gen 13:14 3876
And they took *L*, Abram's brother's ... Gen 14:12 3876
also brought again his brother *L* ... Gen 14:16 3876
L sat in the gate of Sodom ... Gen 19:1 3876
L seeing them rose up to meet ... Gen 19:1 3876
And they called unto *L*, and said ... Gen 19:5 3876
L went out at the door unto them, ... Gen 19:6 3876
pressed sore upon the man, even *L* ... Gen 19:9 3876
pulled *L* into the house to them, ... Gen 19:10 3876
And the men said unto *L*, Hast thou ... Gen 19:12 3876
L went out, and spake unto his ... Gen 19:14 3876
arose, then the angels hastened *L* ... Gen 19:15 3876
L said unto them, Oh, not so, my ... Gen 19:18 3876
earth when *L* entered into Zoar ... Gen 19:23 3876
sent *L* out of the midst of the ... Gen 19:29 3876
the cities in the which *L* dwelt ... Gen 19:29 3876
L went up out of Zoar, and dwelt ... Gen 19:30 3876
of *L* with child by their father ... Gen 19:36 3876
children of *L* for a possession ... Deut 2:9 3876
children of *L* for a possession ... Deut 2:19 3876
have holpen the children of *L* ... Ps 83:8 3876
also as it was in the days of *L* ... Lk 17:28 *3091*
But the same day that *L* went out ... Lk 17:29 *3091*
And delivered just *L*, vexed with ... 2Pet 2:7 *3091*
2. *A die.*
one *l* for the LORD, and the other *l* ... Lev 16:8 1486
goat upon which the LORD's *l* fell ... Lev 16:9 1486
on which the *l* fell to be the ... Lev 16:10 1486
the land shall be divided by *l* ... Num 26:55 1486
According to the *l* shall the ... Num 26:56 1486
ye shall divide the land by *l* for ... Num 33:54 1486
in the place where his *l* falleth ... Num 33:54 1486
land which ye shall inherit by *l* ... Num 34:13 1486
by *l* to the children of Israel ... Num 36:2 1486
from the *l* of our inheritance ... Num 36:3 1486
Jacob is the *l* of his inheritance ... Deut 32:9 2256
only divide thou it by *l* unto the ... Josh 13:6
By *l* was their inheritance, as ... Josh 14:2 1486
This then was the *l* of the tribe ... Josh 15:1 1486
the *l* of the children of Joseph ... Josh 16:1 1486
There was also a *l* for the tribe ... Josh 17:1 1486
There was also a *l* for the rest ... Josh 17:2
Why hast thou given me but one *l* ... Josh 17:14 1486
thou shalt not have one *l* only ... Josh 17:17 1486
the *l* of the tribe of the ... Josh 18:11 1486
the coast of their *l* came forth ... Josh 18:11 1486
the second *l* came forth to Simeon ... Josh 19:1 1486
the third *l* came up for the ... Josh 19:10 1486
the fourth *l* came out to Issachar ... Josh 19:17 1486
the fifth *l* came out for the ... Josh 19:24 1486
The sixth *l* came out to the ... Josh 19:32 1486
the seventh *l* came out for the ... Josh 19:40 1486
by *l* in Shiloh before the LORD ... Josh 19:51 1486
the *l* came out for the families ... Josh 21:4 1486
had by *l* out of the tribe of ... Josh 21:4 1486
by *l* out of the families of the ... Josh 21:5 1486
by *l* out of the families of the ... Josh 21:6 1486
l unto the Levites these cities ... Josh 21:8 1486
for theirs was the first *l* ... Josh 21:10 1486
l out of the tribe of Ephraim ... Josh 21:20 1486
were by their *l* twelve cities ... Josh 21:40 1486
by *l* these nations that remain ... Josh 23:4
Come up with me into my *l* ... Judg 1:3 1486
will go with thee into thy *l* ... Judg 1:3 1486
we will go up by *l* against it ... Judg 20:9 1486
God of Israel, Give a perfect *l* ... 1Sa 14:41
for theirs was the *l* ... 1Chr 6:54 1486
the half tribe of Manasseh, by *l* ... 1Chr 6:61 1486
sons of Merari were given by *l* ... 1Chr 6:63 1486
they gave by *l* out of the tribe ... 1Chr 6:65 1486
the *l* of your inheritance ... 1Chr 16:18 2256
Thus were they divided by *l* ... 1Chr 24:5 1486
Now the first *l* came forth to ... 1Chr 24:7 1486
Now the first *l* came forth for ... 1Chr 25:9 1486
the *l* eastward fell to Shelemiah ... 1Chr 26:14 1486
and his *l* came out northward ... 1Chr 26:14 1486
Hosah the *l* came forth westward, ... 1Chr 26:16
they cast Pur, that is, the *l* ... Est 3:7 1486
and had cast Pur, that is, the *l* ... Est 9:24 1486
thou maintainest my *l* ... Ps 16:5 1486
the *l* of your inheritance ... Ps 105:11 2256
rest upon the *l* of the righteous ... Ps 125:3 1486
Cast in thy *l* among us ... Prov 1:14 1486
The *l* is cast into the lap ... Prov 16:33 1486
The *l* causeth contentions to ... Prov 18:18 1486
the *l* of them that rob us ... Is 17:14 1486
And he hath cast the *l* for them ... Is 34:17 1486
they, they are thy *l* ... Is 57:6 1486
This is thy *l*, the portion of thy ... Jer 13:25 1486
let no *l* fall upon it ... Eze 24:6 1486
when ye shall divide by *l* the ... Eze 45:1
that ye shall divide it by *l* for ... Eze 47:22
l unto the tribes of Israel for ... Eze 48:29
stand in thy *l* at the end of the ... Dan 12:13 1486
lots, and the *l* fell upon Jonah ... Jonah 1:7 1486
none that shall cast a cord by *l* ... Mic 2:5 1486
his *l* was to burn incense when he ... Lk 1:9 *2975*
and the *l* fell upon Matthias ... Acts 1:26 *2819*
neither part nor *l* in this matter ... Acts 8:21 *2819*
divided their land to them by *l* ... Acts 13:19 *2624*

LOTAN *(lo'-tan)* {5} See LOTAN'S. *Son of Seir.*
L, and Shobal, and Zibeon, and Anah, ... Gen 36:20 3877
And the children of *L* were Hori ... Gen 36:22 3877
duke *L*, duke Shobal, duke Zibeon, ... Gen 36:29 3877
L, and Shobal, and Zibeon, and Anah, ... 1Chr 1:38 3877
And the sons of *L* ... 1Chr 1:39 3877

LOTAN'S *(lo'-tans)* {2}
and *L* sister was Timna ... Gen 36:22 3877
and Timna was *L* sister ... 1Chr 1:39 3877

LOTHE {4}
the Egyptians shall *l* to drink of ... Ex 7:18 3811
they shall *l* themselves for the ... Eze 6:9 6962
ye shall *l* yourselves in your own ... Eze 20:43 6962
shall *l* yourselves in your own ... Eze 36:31 6962

LOTHED {3}
hath thy soul *l* Zion ... Jer 14:19 1602
which *l* their husbands and their ... Eze 16:45 1602
and my soul *l* them, and their soul ... Zec 11:8 7114

LOTHETH {1}
that *l* her husband and her ... Eze 16:45 1602

LOTHING {1}
to the *l* of thy person, in the ... Eze 16:5 1604

LOT'S *(lots)* {2}
cattle and the herdmen of *L* cattle ... Gen 13:7 3876
Remember *L* wife ... Lk 17:32

LOTS {24}
Aaron shall cast *l* upon the two ... Lev 16:8 1486
that I may cast *l* for you here ... Josh 18:6 1486
that I may here cast *l* for you ... Josh 18:8 1486
Joshua cast *l* for them in Shiloh ... Josh 18:10 1486
Cast *l* between me and Jonathan my ... 1Sa 14:42
These likewise cast *l* over ... 1Chr 24:31 1486
And they cast *l*, ward against ward ... 1Chr 25:8 1486
And they cast *l*, as well the small ... 1Chr 26:13 1486
a wise counsellor, they cast *l* ... 1Chr 26:14 1486
we cast the *l* among the priests, ... Neh 10:34 1486
rest of the people also cast *l* ... Neh 11:1 1486
them, and cast *l* upon my vesture ... Ps 22:18 1486
And they have cast *l* for my people ... Joel 3:3 1486
cast *l* upon Jerusalem, even thou ... Obad 11 1486
fellow, Come, and let us cast *l* ... Jonah 1:7 1486
So they cast *l*, and the lot fell ... Jonah 1:7 1486
they cast *l* for her honourable ... Nah 3:10 1486
and parted his garments, casting *l* ... Mt 27:35 *2819*
upon my vesture did they cast *l* ... Mt 27:35 *2819*
casting *l* upon them, what every ... Mk 15:24 *2819*
parted his raiment, and cast *l* ... Lk 23:34 *2819*
us not rend it, but cast *l* for it ... Jn 19:24 *2819*
and for my vesture they did cast *l* ... Jn 19:24 *2975*
And they gave forth their *l* ... Acts 1:26 *2819*

LOUD {60}
me, and I cried with a *l* voice ... Gen 39:14 1419
voice of the trumpet exceeding *l* ... Ex 19:16 2389
the men of Israel with a *l* voice ... Deut 27:14 7311
Samuel, she cried with a *l* voice ... 1Sa 28:12 1419
the country wept with a *l* voice ... 2Sa 15:23 1419
and the king cried with a *l* voice ... 2Sa 19:4 1419
of Israel with a *l* voice, saying, ... 1Kin 8:55 1419
cried with a *l* voice in the Jews' ... 2Kin 18:28 1419
unto the LORD with a *l* voice ... 2Chr 15:14 1419
of Israel with a *l* voice on high ... 2Chr 20:19 1419
singing with *l* instruments unto ... 2Chr 30:21 5797
Then they cried with a *l* voice in ... 2Chr 32:18 1419
their eyes, wept with a *l* voice ... Ezr 3:12 1419
the people shouted with a *l* shout ... Ezr 3:13 1419
answered and said with a *l* voice ... Ezr 10:12 1419
cried with a *l* voice unto the ... Neh 9:4 1419
And the singers sang *l*, with ... Neh 12:42 8085
of the city, and cried with a *l* ... Est 4:1 1419
play skilfully with a *l* noise ... Ps 33:3
make a *l* noise, and rejoice, and ... Ps 98:4
Praise him upon the *l* cymbals ... Ps 150:5 8085
(She is *l* and stubborn ... Prov 7:11 1993
his friend with a *l* voice ... Prov 27:14 1419
cried with a *l* voice in the Jews' ... Is 36:13 1419
cry in mine ears with a *l* voice ... Eze 8:18 1419
also in mine ears with a *l* voice ... Eze 9:1 1419
my face, and cried with a *l* voice ... Eze 11:13 1419
hour Jesus cried with a *l* voice ... Mt 27:46 *3173*
he had cried again with a *l* voice ... Mt 27:50 *3173*
torn him, and cried with a *l* voice ... Mk 1:26 *3173*
And cried with a *l* voice, and said, ... Mk 5:7 *3173*
hour Jesus cried with a *l* voice ... Mk 15:34 *3173*
And Jesus cried with a *l* voice ... Mk 15:37 *3173*
And she spake out with a *l* voice ... Lk 1:42 *3173*
and cried out with a *l* voice ... Lk 4:33 *3173*
with a *l* voice said, What have I ... Lk 8:28 *3173*
with a *l* voice glorified God, ... Lk 17:15 *3173*
praise God with a *l* voice for all ... Lk 19:37 *3173*
they were instant with *l* voices ... Lk 23:23 *3173*
Jesus had cried with a *l* voice ... Lk 23:46 *3173*
spoken, he cried with a *l* voice ... Jn 11:43 *3173*
they cried out with a *l* voice ... Acts 7:57 *3173*
down, and cried with a *l* voice ... Acts 7:60 *3173*
spirits, crying with *l* voice ... Acts 8:7 *3173*
Said with a *l* voice, Stand ... Acts 14:10 *3173*
But Paul cried with a *l* voice ... Acts 16:28 *3173*
Festus said with a *l* voice ... Acts 26:24 *3173*
angel proclaiming with a *l* voice ... Rev 5:2 *3173*
Saying with a *l* voice, Worthy is ... Rev 5:12 *3173*
And they cried with a *l* voice ... Rev 6:10 *3173*
he cried with a *l* voice to the ... Rev 7:2 *3173*
And cried with a *l* voice, saying, ... Rev 7:10 *3173*
of heaven, saying with a *l* voice ... Rev 8:13 *3173*
And cried with a *l* voice, as when ... Rev 10:3 *3173*
I heard a *l* voice saying in ... Rev 12:10 *3173*
Saying with a *l* voice, Fear God, ... Rev 14:7 *3173*
them, saying with a *l* voice ... Rev 14:9 *3173*
crying with a *l* voice to him that ... Rev 14:15 *3173*
cried with a *l* cry to him that ... Rev 14:18 *3173*
and he cried with a *l* voice ... Rev 19:17 *3173*

LOUDER {2}
long, and waxed *l* and *l* ... Ex 19:19 3966

LOVE {310}
make me savoury meat, such as I *l* ... Gen 27:4 157
few days, for the *l* he had to her ... Gen 29:20 160
therefore my husband will *l* me ... Gen 29:32 157
unto thousands of them that *l* me ... Ex 20:6 157
I *l* my master, my wife, and my ... Ex 21:5 157
but thou shalt *l* thy neighbour as ... Lev 19:18 157
thou shalt *l* him as thyself ... Lev 19:34 157
unto thousands of them that *l* me ... Deut 5:10 157
thou shalt *l* the LORD thy God ... Deut 6:5 157
LORD did not set his *l* upon you ... Deut 7:7 2836
and mercy with them that *l* him ... Deut 7:9 157
And he will *l* thee, and bless thee, ... Deut 7:13 157
to *l* him, and to serve the LORD ... Deut 10:12 157
delight in thy fathers to *l* them ... Deut 10:15 157
L ye therefore the stranger ... Deut 10:19 157
thou shalt *l* the LORD thy God ... Deut 11:1 157
to *l* the LORD your God, and to ... Deut 11:13 157
to *l* the LORD your God, to walk ... Deut 11:22 157
to know whether ye *l* the LORD ... Deut 13:3 157
to *l* the LORD thy God, and to walk ... Deut 19:9 157
to *l* the LORD thy God with all ... Deut 30:6 157
this day to *l* the LORD thy God ... Deut 30:16 157
thou mayest *l* the LORD thy God ... Deut 30:20 157
to *l* the LORD your God, and to ... Josh 22:5 157
that ye *l* the LORD your God ... Josh 23:11 157
but let them that *l* him be as the ... Judg 5:31 157
I *l* thee, when thine heart is not ... Judg 16:15 157
thee, and all his servants *l* thee ... 1Sa 18:22 157
thy *l* to me was wonderful, ... 2Sa 1:26 160
passing the *l* of women ... 2Sa 1:26 160
I *l* Tamar, my brother Absalom's ... 2Sa 13:4 157
the *l* wherewith he had loved her ... 2Sa 13:15 160
Solomon clave unto these in *l* ... 1Kin 11:2 160
l them that hate the LORD ... 2Chr 19:2 157
and mercy for them that *l* him ... Neh 1:5 157
how long will ye *l* vanity ... Ps 4:2 157
let them also that *l* thy name be ... Ps 5:11 157
I will *l* thee, O LORD, my ... Ps 18:1 7355
O *l* the LORD, all ye his saints ... Ps 31:23 157
let such as *l* thy salvation say ... Ps 40:16 157
they that *l* his name shall dwell ... Ps 69:36 157
let such as *l* thy salvation say ... Ps 70:4 157
Because he hath set his *l* upon me ... Ps 91:14 2836

Ye that *l* the LORD, hate evil Ps 97:10 157
For my *l* they are my adversaries Ps 109:4 160
evil for good, and hatred for my *l* Ps 109:5 160
I *l* the LORD, because he hath Ps 116:1 157
O how *l* I thy law Ps 119:97 157
but thy law do I *l* Ps 119:113 157
therefore I *l* thy testimonies Ps 119:119 157
Therefore I *l* thy commandments Ps 119:127 157
to do unto those that *l* thy name Ps 119:132 157
Consider how I *l* thy precepts Ps 119:159 157
but thy law do I *l* Ps 119:163 157
peace have they which *l* thy law Ps 119:165 157
and I *l* them exceedingly Ps 119:167 157
they shall prosper that *l* thee Ps 122:6 157
preserveth all them that *l* him Ps 145:20 157
simple ones, will ye *l* simplicity Prov 1:22 157
l her, and she shall keep thee Prov 4:6 157
thou ravished always with her *l* Prov 5:19 160
our fill of *l* until the morning Prov 7:18 1730
I *l* them that *l* me Prov 8:17 157
that *l* me to inherit substance Prov 8:21 157
all they that hate me *l* death Prov 8:36 157
a wise man, and he will *l* thee Prov 9:8 157
but *l* covereth all sins Prov 10:12 160
is a dinner of herbs where *l* is Prov 15:17 160
they *l* him that speaketh right Prov 16:13 157
a transgression seeketh *l* Prov 17:9 160
they that *l* it shall eat the Prov 18:21 157
L not sleep, lest thou come to Prov 20:13 157
rebuke is better than secret *l* Prov 27:5 160
A time to *l*, and a time to hate Eccl 3:8 157
no man knoweth either *l* or hatred Eccl 9:1 160
Also their *l*, and their hatred, and Eccl 9:6 160
for thy *l* is better than wine Song 1:2 1730
therefore do the virgins *l* thee Song 1:3 157
remember thy *l* more than wine Song 1:4 1730
the upright *l* thee Song 1:4 157
I have compared thee, O my *l* Song 1:9 7474
Behold, thou art fair, my *l* Song 1:15 7474
so is my *l* among the daughters Song 2:2 7474
and his banner over me was *l* Song 2:4 160
for I am sick of *l* Song 2:5 160
ye stir not up, nor awake my *l* Song 2:7 160
and said unto me, Rise up, my *l* Song 2:10 7474
Arise, my *l*, my fair one, and come Song 2:13 7474
ye stir not up, nor awake my *l* Song 3:5 160
midst thereof being paved with *l* Song 3:10 160
Behold, thou art fair, my *l* Song 4:1 7474
Thou art all fair, my *l* Song 4:7 7474
How fair is thy *l*, my sister, my Song 4:10 1730
much better is thy *l* than wine Song 4:10 1730
Open to me, my sister, my *l* Song 5:2 7474
ye tell him, that I am sick of *l* Song 5:8 160
Thou art beautiful, O my *l* Song 6:4 7474
and how pleasant art thou, O *l* Song 7:6 160
ye stir not up, nor awake my *l* Song 8:4 160
for *l* is strong as death Song 8:6 160
Many waters cannot quench *l* Song 8:7 160
the substance of his house for *l* Song 8:7 160
but thou hast in *l* to my soul Is 38:17 2836
to *l* the name of the LORD, to be Is 56:6 157
For I the LORD *l* judgment Is 61:8 157
in his *l* and in his pity he Is 63:9 160
glad with her, all ye that *l* her Is 66:10 157
the *l* of thine espousals, when Jer 2:2 160
trimmest thou thy way to seek *l* Jer 2:33 160
my people *l* to have it so Jer 5:31 157
loved thee with an everlasting *l* Jer 31:3 160
thy time was the time of *l* Eze 16:8 1730
in her inordinate *l* than she Eze 23:11 5691
came to her into the bed of *l* Eze 23:17 1730
with their mouth they shew much *l* Eze 33:31 5690
tender *l* with the prince of the Dan 1:9
and mercy to them that *l* him Dan 9:4 157
l a woman beloved of her friend, Hos 3:1 157
according to the *l* of the LORD Hos 3:1 160
other gods, and *l* flagons of wine Hos 3:1 157
her rulers with shame do *l* Hos 4:18 157
mine house, I will *l* them no more Hos 9:15 160
cords of a man, with bands of *l* Hos 11:4 160
backsliding, I will *l* them freely Hos 14:4 157
l the good, and establish judgment Amos 5:15 157
Who hate the good, and *l* the evil Mic 3:2 157
to *l* mercy, and to walk humbly Mic 6:8 160
he will rest in his *l*, he will Zeph 3:17 160
and *l* no false oath Zec 8:17 157
therefore *l* the truth and peace Zec 8:19 157
Thou shalt *l* thy neighbour, and Mt 5:43 *25*
L your enemies, bless them that Mt 5:44 *25*
For if ye *l* them which *l* you, Mt 5:46 *25*
for they *l* to pray standing in Mt 6:5 *5368*
will hate the one, and *l* the other Mt 6:24 *25*
Thou shalt *l* thy neighbour as Mt 19:19 *25*
Thou shalt *l* the Lord thy God Mt 22:37 *25*
Thou shalt *l* thy neighbour as Mt 22:39 *25*
l the uppermost rooms at feasts, Mt 23:6 *5368*
the *l* of many shall wax cold Mt 24:12 *26*
thou shalt *l* the Lord thy God Mk 12:30 *25*
Thou shalt *l* thy neighbour as Mk 12:31 *25*
to *l* him with all the heart, and Mk 12:33 *25*
to *l* his neighbour as himself, is Mk 12:33 *25*
which *l* to go in long clothing, Mk 12:38 *2309*
l salutations in the marketplaces Mk 12:38
L your enemies, do good to them Lk 6:27 *25*
For if ye *l* them which *l* you Lk 6:32 *25*
also *l* those that *l* them Lk 6:32 *25*
But *l* ye your enemies, and do good Lk 6:35 *25*
which of them will *l* him most Lk 7:42 *25*
Thou shalt *l* the Lord thy God Lk 10:27 *25*
over judgment and the *l* of God Lk 11:42 *26*
for ye *l* the uppermost seats in Lk 11:43 *25*
will hate the one, and *l* the other Lk 16:13 *25*
l greetings in the markets, and Lk 20:46 *5368*
ye have not the *l* of God in you Jn 5:42 *26*
were your Father, ye would *l* me Jn 8:42 *25*
Therefore doth my Father *l* me Jn 10:17 *25*
unto you, That ye *l* one another Jn 13:34 *25*
you, that ye also *l* one another Jn 13:34 *25*
if ye have *l* one to another Jn 13:35 *26*
If ye *l* me, keep my commandments Jn 14:15 *25*
of my Father, and I will *l* him Jn 14:21 *25*
and said unto him, If a man *l* me Jn 14:23 *25*
and my Father will *l* him, and we Jn 14:23 *25*
may know that I *l* the Father Jn 14:31 *25*
continue ye in my *l* Jn 15:9 *26*
ye shall abide in my *l* Jn 15:10 *26*
commandments, and abide in his *l* Jn 15:10 *26*
That ye *l* one another, as I have Jn 15:12 *25*
Greater *l* hath no man than this, Jn 15:13 *26*
you, that ye *l* one another Jn 15:17 *25*
world, the world would *l* his own Jn 15:19 *5368*
that the *l* wherewith thou hast Jn 17:26 *26*
thou knowest that I *l* thee Jn 21:15 *5368*
thou knowest that I *l* thee Jn 21:16 *5368*
thou knowest that I *l* thee Jn 21:17 *5368*
because the *l* of God is shed Rom 5:5 *26*
God commendeth his *l* toward us Rom 5:8 *26*
for good to them that *l* God Rom 8:28 *25*
separate us from the *l* of Christ Rom 8:35 *26*
to separate us from the *l* of God Rom 8:39 *26*
Let *l* be without dissimulation Rom 12:9 *26*
one to another with brotherly *l* Rom 12:10 *5360*
any thing, but to *l* one another Rom 13:8 *25*
Thou shalt *l* thy neighbour as Rom 13:9 *25*
L worketh no ill to his neighbour Rom 13:10 *26*
therefore *l* is the fulfilling of Rom 13:10 *26*
for the *l* of the Spirit, that ye Rom 15:30 *26*
hath prepared for them that *l* him 1Cor 2:9 *25*
come unto you with a rod, or in *l* 1Cor 4:21 *26*
But if any man *l* God, the same is 1Cor 8:3 *25*
If any man *l* not the Lord Jesus 1Cor 16:22 *5368*
My *l* be with you all in Christ 1Cor 16:24 *26*
but that ye might know the *l* 2Cor 2:4 *26*
would confirm your *l* toward him 2Cor 2:8 *26*
For the *l* of Christ constraineth 2Cor 5:14 *26*
the Holy Ghost, by *l* unfeigned, 2Cor 6:6 *26*
all diligence, and in your *l* to us 2Cor 8:7 *26*
to prove the sincerity of your *l* 2Cor 8:8 *26*
the churches, the proof of your *l* 2Cor 8:24 *26*
because I *l* you not 2Cor 11:11 *25*
the more abundantly I *l* you 2Cor 12:15 *25*
and the God of *l* and peace shall be 2Cor 13:11 *26*
the *l* of God, and the communion of 2Cor 13:14 *26*
but faith which worketh by *l* Gal 5:6 *26*
but by *l* serve one another Gal 5:13 *26*
Thou shalt *l* thy neighbour as Gal 5:14 *25*
But the fruit of the Spirit is *l* Gal 5:22 *26*
and without blame before him in *l* Eph 1:4 *26*
Jesus, and *l* unto all the saints, Eph 1:15 *26*
for his great *l* wherewith he Eph 2:4 *26*
ye, being rooted and grounded in *l* Eph 3:17 *26*
And to know the *l* of Christ Eph 3:19 *26*
forbearing one another in *l* Eph 4:2 *26*
But speaking the truth in *l* Eph 4:15 *26*
unto the edifying of itself in *l* Eph 4:16 *26*
And walk in *l*, as Christ also hath Eph 5:2 *26*
l your wives, even as Christ also Eph 5:25 *25*
So ought men to *l* their wives as Eph 5:28 *25*
so *l* his wife even as himself Eph 5:33 *25*
l with faith, from God the Father Eph 6:23 *26*
that *l* our Lord Jesus Christ in Eph 6:24 *25*
that your *l* may abound yet more Phil 1:9 *26*
But the other of *l*, knowing that Phil 1:17 *26*
in Christ, if any comfort of *l* Phil 2:1 *26*
be likeminded, having the same *l* Phil 2:2 *26*
of the *l* which ye have to all the Col 1:4 *26*
unto us your *l* in the Spirit Col 1:8 *26*
being knit together in *l* Col 2:2 *26*
l your wives, and be not bitter Col 3:19 *25*
work of faith, and labour of *l* 1Th 1:3 *26*
abound in *l* one toward another, 1Th 3:12 *26*
But as touching brotherly *l* ye 1Th 4:9 *5360*
taught of God to *l* one another 1Th 4:9 *25*
on the breastplate of faith and *l* 1Th 5:8 *26*
highly in *l* for their work's sake 1Th 5:13 *26*
received not the *l* of the truth 2Th 2:10 *26*
your hearts into the *l* of God 2Th 3:5 *26*
l which is in Christ Jesus 1Ti 1:14 *26*
For the *l* of money is the root of 1Ti 6:10 *5365*
godliness, faith, *l*, patience, 1Ti 6:11 *26*
but of power, and of *l*, and of a 2Ti 1:7 *26*
l which is in Christ Jesus 2Ti 1:13 *26*
them also that *l* his appearing 2Ti 4:8 *25*
be sober, to *l* their husbands Titus 2:4 *5362*
to *l* their children Titus 2:4 *5388*
l of God our Saviour toward man Titus 3:4 *5363*
Greet them that *l* us in the faith Titus 3:15 *5368*
Hearing of thy *l* and faith, which Philem 5 *26*
great joy and consolation in thy *l* Philem 7 *26*
forget your work and labour of *l* Heb 6:10 *26*
one another to provoke unto *l* Heb 10:24 *26*
Let brotherly *l* continue Heb 13:1 *5360*
hath promised to them that *l* him Jas 1:12 *25*
hath promised to them that *l* him Jas 2:5 *25*
Thou shalt *l* thy neighbour as Jas 2:8 *25*
Whom having not seen, ye *l* 1Pet 1:8 *25*
unto unfeigned *l* of the brethren 1Pet 1:22 *5360*
see that ye *l* one another with a 1Pet 1:22 *25*
L the brotherhood 1Pet 2:17 *25*
l as brethren, be pitiful, be 1Pet 3:8 *5361*
For he that will *l* life, and see 1Pet 3:10 *25*
verily is the *l* of God perfected 1Jn 2:5 *26*
L not the world, neither the 1Jn 2:15 *25*
If any man *l* the world 1Jn 2:15 *25*
the *l* of the Father is not in him 1Jn 2:15 *26*
what manner of *l* the Father hath 1Jn 3:1 *26*
that we should *l* one another 1Jn 3:11 *25*
because we *l* the brethren 1Jn 3:14 *25*
Hereby perceive we the *l* of God 1Jn 3:16 *26*
how dwelleth the *l* of God in him 1Jn 3:17 *26*
children, let us not *l* in word 1Jn 3:18 *25*
l one another, as he gave us 1Jn 3:23 *25*
Beloved, let us *l* one another 1Jn 4:7 *25*
for *l* is of God 1Jn 4:7 *26*
for God is *l* 1Jn 4:8 *26*
manifested the *l* of God toward us 1Jn 4:9 *26*
Herein is *l*, not that we loved 1Jn 4:10 *26*
we ought also to *l* one another 1Jn 4:11 *25*
If we *l* one another, God dwelleth 1Jn 4:12 *26*
us, and his *l* is perfected in us 1Jn 4:12 *25*
believed the *l* that God hath to 1Jn 4:16 *26*
God is *l* 1Jn 4:16 *26*
dwelleth in *l* dwelleth in God 1Jn 4:16 *26*
Herein is our *l* made perfect 1Jn 4:17 *26*
There is no fear in *l* 1Jn 4:18 *26*
but perfect *l* casteth out fear 1Jn 4:18 *26*
feareth is not made perfect in *l* 1Jn 4:18 *26*
We *l* him, because he first loved 1Jn 4:19 *25*
I *l* God, and hateth his brother, 1Jn 4:20 *25*
how can he *l* God whom he hath not 1Jn 4:20 *25*
who loveth God *l* his brother also 1Jn 4:21 *25*
that we *l* the children of God 1Jn 5:2 *25*
children of God, when we *l* God 1Jn 5:2 *25*
For this is the *l* of God, that we 1Jn 5:3 *26*
children, whom I *l* in the truth 2Jn 1 *25*
Son of the Father, in truth and *l* 2Jn 3 *26*
beginning, that we *l* one another 2Jn 5 *25*
And this is *l*, that we walk after 2Jn 6 *26*
Gaius, whom I *l* in the truth 3Jn 1 *25*
Mercy unto you, and peace, and *l* Jude 2 *26*
Keep yourselves in the *l* of God Jude 21 *26*
thou hast left thy first *l* Rev 2:4 *26*
As many as I *l*, I rebuke and Rev 3:19 *5368*

LOVED {98}

his wife; and he *l* her Gen 24:67 157
And Isaac *l* Esau, because he did Gen 25:28 157
but Rebekah *l* Jacob Gen 25:28 157
meat, such as his father *l* Gen 27:14 157
And Jacob *l* Rachel Gen 29:18 157
he *l* also Rachel more than Leah, Gen 29:30 157
he *l* the damsel, and spake kindly Gen 34:3 157
Now Israel *l* Joseph more than all Gen 37:3 157
l him more than all his brethren Gen 37:4 157
because he *l* thy fathers, Deut 4:37 157
But because the LORD *l* you Deut 7:8 160
because the LORD thy God *l* thee Deut 23:5 157
Yea, he *l* the people Deut 33:3 2245
that he *l* a woman in the valley Judg 16:4 157
for he *l* Hannah 1Sa 1:5 157
and he *l* him greatly 1Sa 16:21 157
Jonathan *l* him as his own soul 1Sa 18:1 157
because he *l* him as his own soul 1Sa 18:3 160
But all Israel and Judah *l* David 1Sa 18:16 157
And Michal Saul's daughter *l* David 1Sa 18:20 157
that Michal Saul's daughter *l* him 1Sa 18:28 157
to swear again, because he *l* him 1Sa 20:17 160
for he *l* him as he 1Sa 20:17 157
him as he *l* his own soul 1Sa 20:17 160
and the LORD *l* him 2Sa 12:24 157
and Amnon the son of David *l* her 2Sa 13:1 157
the love wherewith he had *l* her 2Sa 13:15 157
Solomon *l* the LORD, walking in 1Kin 3:3 157
the LORD *l* Israel for ever 1Kin 10:9 160
But king Solomon *l* many strange 1Kin 11:1 157
the LORD hath *l* his people 2Chr 2:11 160
because thy God *l* Israel, to 2Chr 9:8 160
Rehoboam *l* Maachah the daughter 2Chr 11:21 157
for he *l* husbandry 2Chr 26:10 157
the king *l* Esther above all the Est 2:17 157
they whom I *l* are turned against Job 19:19 157
I have *l* the habitation of thy Ps 26:8 157
the excellency of Jacob whom he *l* Ps 47:4 157
Judah, the mount Zion which he *l* Ps 78:68 157
As he *l* cursing, so let it come Ps 109:17 157
thy commandments, which I have *l* Ps 119:47 157
thy commandments, which I have *l* Ps 119:48 157
been honourable, and I have *l* thee Is 43:4 157
The LORD hath *l* him Is 48:14 157
for I have *l* strangers, and after Jer 2:25 157
host of heaven, whom they have *l* Jer 8:2 157
Thus have they *l* to wander Jer 14:10 157
I have *l* thee with an everlasting Jer 31:3 157
and all them that thou hast *l* Eze 16:37 157
thou hast *l* a reward upon every Hos 9:1 157
were according as they *l* Hos 9:10 157
Israel was a child, then I *l* him Hos 11:1 157
I have *l* you, saith the LORD Mal 1:2 157
ye say, Wherein hast thou *l* us Mal 1:2 157
yet I *l* Jacob, Mal 1:2 157
holiness of the LORD which he *l* Mal 2:11 157
Then Jesus beholding him *l* him Mk 10:21 *25*
for she *l* much Lk 7:47 *25*
For God so *l* the world, that he Jn 3:16 *25*

L

men *l* darkness rather than light Jn 3:19 *25*
Now Jesus *l* Martha, and her sister Jn 11:5 *25*
the Jews, Behold how he *l* him Jn 11:36 *5368*
For they *l* the praise of men more Jn 12:43 *25*
having *l* his own which were in Jn 13:1 *25*
the world, he *l* them unto the end Jn 13:1 *25*
of his disciples, whom Jesus *l* Jn 13:23 *25*
as I have *l* you, that ye also Jn 13:34 *25*
loveth me shall be *l* of my Father Jn 14:21 *25*
If ye *l* me, ye would rejoice, Jn 14:28 *25*
hath *l* me, so have I *l* you Jn 15:9 *25*
love one another, as I have *l* you Jn 15:12 *25*
loveth you, because ye have *l* me Jn 16:27 *5368*
thou hast sent me, and hast *l* them Jn 17:23 *25*
as thou hast *l* me Jn 17:23 *25*
thou hast *l* me may be in them Jn 17:26 *25*
disciple standing by, whom he *l* Jn 19:26 *25*
the other disciple, whom Jesus *l* Jn 20:2 *5368*
whom Jesus *l* saith unto Peter Jn 21:7 *25*
disciple whom Jesus *l* following Jn 21:20 *25*
conquerors through him that *l* us Rom 8:37 *25*
As it is written, Jacob have I *l* Rom 9:13 *25*
I love you, the less I be *l* 2Cor 12:15 *25*
faith of the Son of God, who *l* me Gal 2:20 *25*
his great love wherewith he *l* us Eph 2:4 *25*
in love, as Christ also hath *l* us Eph 5:2 *26*
even as Christ also *l* the church Eph 5:25 *25*
even our Father, which hath *l* us 2Th 2:16 *25*
having *l* this present world, and 2Ti 4:10 *25*
Thou hast *l* righteousness, and Heb 1:9 *25*
son of Bosor, who *l* the wages of 2Pet 2:15 *25*
Herein is love, not that we *l* God 1Jn 4:10 *25*
but that he *l* us 1Jn 4:10 *25*
Beloved, if God so *l* us, we ought 1Jn 4:11 *25*
love him, because he first *l* us 1Jn 4:19 *25*
Unto him that *l* us, and washed us Rev 1:5 *25*
and to know that I have *l* thee Rev 3:9 *25*
they *l* not their lives unto the Rev 12:11 *25*

LOVEDST {2}
thou *l* their bed where thou Is 57:8 157
for thou *l* me before the Jn 17:24 *25*

LOVELY {4}
Saul and Jonathan were *l* and 2Sa 1:23 157
yea, he is altogether *l* Song 5:16 4261
a very *l* song of one that hath a Eze 33:32 5690
are pure, whatsoever things are *l* Phil 4:8 *4375*

LOVER {4}
for Hiram was ever a *l* of David 1Kin 5:1 157
L and friend hast thou put far Ps 88:18 157
But a *l* of hospitality Titus 1:8 *5382*
a *l* of good men, sober, just, Titus 1:8 *5358*

LOVERS {23}
My *l* and my friends stand aloof Ps 38:11 157
played the harlot with many *l* Jer 3:1 7453
thy *l* will despise thee, they Jer 4:30 5689
for all thy *l* are destroyed Jer 22:20 157
thy *l* shall go into captivity Jer 22:22 157
All thy *l* have forgotten thee Jer 30:14 157
among all her *l* she hath none to Lam 1:2 157
I called for my *l*, but they Lam 1:19 157
givest thy gifts to all thy *l* Eze 16:33 157
through thy whoredoms with thy *l* Eze 16:36 157
therefore I will gather all thy *l* Eze 16:37 157
and she doted on her *l*, on the Eze 23:5 157
her into the hand of her *l* Eze 23:9 157
will raise up thy *l* against thee Eze 23:22 157
she said, I will go after my *l* Hos 2:5 157
And she shall follow after her *l* Hos 2:7 157
lewdness in the sight of her *l* Hos 2:10 157
rewards that my *l* have given me Hos 2:12 157
jewels, and she went after her *l* Hos 2:13 157
Ephraim hath hired *l* Hos 8:9 158
For men shall be *l* of their own 2Ti 3:2 *5367*
l of pleasures more than 2Ti 3:4 *5369*
of pleasures more than *l* of God 2Ti 3:4 *5377*

LOVE'S {1}
Yet for *l* sake I rather beseech Philem 9 *26*

LOVES {3}
of Korah, A Maschil, A Song of *l* Ps 45:*t* 3039
let us solace ourselves with *l* Prov 7:18 159
there will I give thee my *l* Song 7:12 1730

LOVEST {12}
thine only son Isaac, whom thou *l* Gen 22:2 157
dost but hate me, and *l* me not Judg 14:16 157
In that thou *l* thine enemies, and 2Sa 19:6 157
Thou *l* righteousness, and hatest Ps 45:7 157
Thou *l* evil more than good Ps 52:3 157
Thou *l* all devouring words, O Ps 52:4 157
with the wife whom thou *l* all the Eccl 9:9 157
behold, he whom thou *l* is sick Jn 11:3 *5368*
l thou me more than these Jn 21:15 *25*
Simon, son of Jonas, *l* thou me Jn 21:16 *25*
Simon, son of Jonas, *l* thou me Jn 21:17 *5368*
him the third time, *L* thou me Jn 21:17 *5368*

LOVETH {65}
meat for thy father, such as he *l* Gen 27:9 157
his mother, and his father *l* him Gen 44:20 157
l the stranger, in giving him Deut 10:18 157
because he *l* thee and thine house, Deut 15:16 157
thy daughter in law, which *l* thee Ruth 4:15 157
him that *l* violence his soul Ps 11:5 157
righteous LORD *l* righteousness Ps 11:7 157
He *l* righteousness and judgment Ps 33:5 157
l many days, that he may see good Ps 34:12 157
For the LORD *l* judgment, and Ps 37:28 157
The LORD *l* the gates of Zion more Ps 87:2 157
king's strength also *l* judgment Ps 99:4 157
therefore thy servant *l* it Ps 119:140 157
the LORD *l* the righteous Ps 146:8 157
For whom the LORD *l* he correcteth Prov 3:12 157
l instruction *l* knowledge Prov 12:1 157
but he that *l* him chasteneth him Prov 13:24 157
but he *l* him that followeth after Prov 15:9 157
A scorner *l* not one that Prov 15:12 157
A friend *l* at all times, and a Prov 17:17 157
He *l* transgression that Prov 17:19 157
transgression that *l* strife Prov 17:19 157
getteth wisdom *l* his own soul Prov 19:8 157
He that *l* pleasure shall be a Prov 21:17 157
he that *l* wine and oil shall not Prov 21:17 157
He that *l* pureness of heart, for Prov 22:11 157
Whoso *l* wisdom rejoiceth his Prov 29:3 157
He that *l* silver shall not be Eccl 5:10 157
nor he that *l* abundance with Eccl 5:10 157
Tell me, O thou whom my soul *l* Song 1:7 157
bed I sought him whom my soul *l* Song 3:1 157
I will seek him whom my soul *l* Song 3:2 157
I said, Saw ye him whom my soul *l* Song 3:3 157
but I found him whom my soul *l* Song 3:4 157
every one *l* gifts, and followeth Is 1:23 157
and *l* to tread out the corn Hos 10:11 157
he *l* to oppress Hos 12:7 157
He that *l* father or mother more Mt 10:37 *5368*
he that *l* son or daughter more Mt 10:37 *5368*
For he *l* our nation, and he hath Lk 7:5 *25*
is forgiven, the same *l* little Lk 7:47 *25*
The Father *l* the Son, and hath Jn 3:35 *25*
For the Father *l* the Son, and Jn 5:20 *5368*
He that *l* his life shall lose it Jn 12:25 *5368*
keepeth them, he it is that *l* me Jn 14:21 *25*
he that *l* me shall be loved of my Jn 14:21 *25*
He that *l* me not keepeth not my Jn 14:24 *25*
For the Father himself *l* you Jn 16:27 *5368*
for he that *l* another hath Rom 13:8 *25*
for God *l* a cheerful giver 2Cor 9:7 *25*
He that *l* his wife *l* himself Eph 5:28 *25*
For whom the Lord *l* he chasteneth Heb 12:6 *25*
He that *l* his brother abideth in 1Jn 2:10 *25*
neither he that *l* not his brother 1Jn 3:10 *25*
He that *l* not his brother abideth 1Jn 3:14 *25*
every one that *l* is born of God 1Jn 4:7 *25*
He that *l* not knoweth not God 1Jn 4:8 *25*
for he that *l* not his brother 1Jn 4:20 *25*
That he who *l* God love his 1Jn 4:21 *25*
every one that *l* him that begat 1Jn 5:1 *25*
l him also that is begotten of 1Jn 5:1 *25*
who *l* to have the preeminence 3Jn 9 *5383*
and idolaters, and whosoever *l* Rev 22:15 *5368*

LOVING {3}
Let her be as the *l* hind and Prov 5:19 158
l favour rather than silver and Prov 22:1 2896
lying down, *l* to slumber Is 56:10 157

LOVINGKINDNESS {26}
Shew thy marvellous *l*, O thou Ps 17:7 2617
For thy *l* is before mine eyes Ps 26:3 2617
How excellent is thy *l*, O God Ps 36:7 2617
O continue thy *l* unto them that Ps 36:10 2617
I have not concealed thy *l* Ps 40:10 2617
let thy *l* and thy truth Ps 40:11 2617
will command his *l* in the daytime Ps 42:8 2617
We have thought of thy *l*, O God, Ps 48:9 2617
me, O God, according to thy *l* Ps 51:1 2617
Because thy *l* is better than life Ps 63:3 2617
for thy *l* is good Ps 69:16 2617
Shall thy *l* be declared in the Ps 88:11 2617
Nevertheless my *l* will I not Ps 89:33 2617
shew forth thy *l* in the morning Ps 92:2 2617
who crowneth thee with *l* and Ps 103:4 2617
understand the *l* of the LORD Ps 107:43 2617
Quicken me after thy *l* Ps 119:88 2617
my voice according unto thy *l* Ps 119:149 2617
me, O LORD, according to thy *l* Ps 119:159 2617
and praise thy name for thy *l* Ps 138:2 2617
me to hear thy *l* in the morning Ps 143:8 2617
I am the LORD which exercise *l* Jer 9:24 2617
people, saith the LORD, even *l* Jer 16:5 2617
therefore with *l* have I drawn Jer 31:3 2617
Thou shewest *l* unto thousands, and Jer 32:18 2617
and in judgment, and in *l*, and in Hos 2:19 2617

LOVINGKINDNESSES {4}
LORD, thy tender mercies and thy *l* Ps 25:6 2617
Lord, where are thy former *l* Ps 89:49 2617
I will mention the *l* of the LORD Is 63:7 2617
to the multitude of his *l* Is 63:7 2617

LOW See APPENDIX.

LOWER See APPENDIX.

LOWEST See APPENDIX.

LOWETH {1}
or *l* the ox over his fodder Job 6:5 1600

LOWING {2}
l as they went, and turned not 1Sa 6:12 1600
the *l* of the oxen which I hear 1Sa 15:14 6963

LOWLINESS {1}
With all *l* and meekness, with Eph 4:2 *5012*
but in *l* of mind let each esteem Phil 2:3 *5012*

LOWLY {6}
yet hath he respect unto the *l* Ps 138:6 8217
but he giveth grace unto the *l* Prov 3:34 6041
but with the *l* is wisdom Prov 11:2 6800
be of an humble spirit with the *l* Prov 16:19 6041
l, and riding upon an ass, and upon Zec 9:9 6041
for I am meek and *l* in heart Mt 11:29 *5011*

LOWRING {1}
for the sky is red and *l* Mt 16:3 *4768*

LUBIM *(lu'-bim)* {2} See LUBIMS. *An African race.*
the *L*, the Sukkiims, and the 2Chr 12:3 3864
Put and *L* were thy helpers Nah 3:9 3864

LUBIMS *(lu'-bims)* {1} See LEHABIM, LUBIM. *Same as Lubim.*
the *L* a huge host, with very many 2Chr 16:8 3864

LUCAS *(lu'-cas)* {2} See LUKE. *Same as Luke.*
city of Macedonia, by Titus and *L* 2Cor *s* *3065*
Marcus, Aristarchus, Demas, *L* Philem 24 *3065*

LUCIFER *(lu'-sif-ur)* {1} *Title applied to king of Babylon.*
art thou fallen from heaven, O *L* Is 14:12 1966

LUCIUS *(lu'-she-us)* {2}
1. A Christian from Cyrene.
L of Cyrene, and Manaen, which had Acts 13:1 *3066*
2. A relative of Paul.
Timotheus my workfellow, and *L* Rom 16:21 *3066*

LUCRE {5}
ways, but turned aside after *l* 1Sa 8:3 1215
striker, not greedy of filthy *l* 1Ti 3:3 *866*
much wine, not greedy of filthy *l* 1Ti 3:8 *146*
no striker, not given to filthy *l* Titus 1:7 *146*
not for filthy *l*, but of a ready 1Pet 5:2 *147*

LUCRE'S {1}
they ought not, for filthy *l* sake Titus 1:11 *2771*

LUD *(lud)* {4} See LUDIM, LYDIA.
1. Son of Shem.
and Asshur, and Arphaxad, and *L* Gen 10:22 3865
and Asshur, and Arphaxad, and *L* 1Chr 1:17 3865
2. Descendants of Lud 1.
nations, to Tarshish, Pul, and *L* Is 66:19 3865
They of Persia and of *L* and of Phut Eze 27:10 3865

LUDIM *(lu'-dim)* {2} See LUD. *Son of Mizraim.*
Mizraim begat *L*, and Anamim, and Gen 10:13 3866
And Mizraim begat *L*, and Anamim 1Chr 1:11 3866

LUHITH *(lu'-hith)* {2} *A Moabite city.*
for by the mounting up of *L* with Is 15:5 3872
For in the going up of *L* Jer 48:5 3872

LUKE *(luke)* {2} See LUCAS. *A companion of Paul.*
L, the beloved physician, and Col 4:14 *3065*
Only *L* is with me 2Ti 4:11 *3065*

LUKEWARM {1}
So then because thou art *l* Rev 3:16 *5513*

LUMP {7}
And Isaiah said, Take a *l* of figs 2Kin 20:7 1690
said, Let them take a *l* of figs Is 38:21 1690
of the same *l* to make one vessel Rom 9:21 *5445*
be holy, the *l* is also holy Rom 11:16 *5445*
leaven leaveneth the whole *l* 1Cor 5:6 *5445*
leaven, that ye may be a new *l* 1Cor 5:7 *5445*
leaven leaveneth the whole *l* Gal 5:9 *5445*

LUNATICK {2}
devils, and those which were *l* Mt 4:24 *4583*
for he is *l*, and sore vexed Mt 17:15 *4583*

LURK {2}
let us *l* privily for the innocent Prov 1:11 6845
they *l* privily for their own Prov 1:18 6845

LURKING {3}
take knowledge of all the *l* 1Sa 23:23 4224
He sitteth in the *l* places of the Ps 10:8 3993
a young lion *l* in secret places Ps 17:12 3427

LUST {19}
my *l* shall be satisfied upon them Ex 15:9 5315
heart by asking meat for their *l* Ps 78:18 5315
were not estranged from their *l* Ps 78:30 8378
them up unto their own hearts' *l* Ps 81:12 8307
L not after her beauty in thine Prov 6:25 2530
to *l* after her hath committed Mt 5:28 *1937*
burned in their *l* one toward Rom 1:27 *3715*
for I had not known *l*, except the Rom 7:7 *1939*
we should not *l* after evil things 1Cor 10:6 *1511,1938*
not fulfil the *l* of the flesh Gal 5:16 *1939*
Not in the *l* of concupiscence, 1Th 4:5 *3806*
he is drawn away of his own *l* Jas 1:14 *1939*
Then when *l* hath conceived, it Jas 1:15 *1939*
Ye *l*, and have not Jas 4:2 *1937*
that is in the world through *l* 2Pet 1:4 *1939*
the flesh in the *l* of uncleanness 2Pet 2:10 *1939*
the *l* of the flesh 1Jn 2:16 *1939*
the *l* of the eyes, and the pride 1Jn 2:16 *1939*
passeth away, and the *l* thereof 1Jn 2:17 *1939*

LUSTED {4}
they buried the people that *l* Num 11:34 183
But *l* exceedingly in the Ps 106:14 183
after evil things, as they also *l* 1Cor 10:6 *1937*
the fruits that thy soul *l* after Rev 18:14 *1937*

LUSTETH {6}
whatsoever thy soul *l* after Deut 12:15 183
whatsoever thy soul *l* after Deut 12:20 183
gates whatsoever thy soul *l* after Deut 12:21 183
for whatsoever thy soul *l* after Deut 14:26 183
For the flesh *l* against the Gal 5:17 *1937*
that dwelleth in us *l* to envy Jas 4:5 *1971*

LUSTING {1}
that was among them fell a *l* Num 11:4 8378

LUSTS {24}
the l of other things entering in ... Mk 4:19 1939
the l of your father ye will do ... Jn 8:44 1939
through the l of their own hearts ... Rom 1:24 1939
should obey it in the l thereof ... Rom 6:12 1939
flesh, to fulfil the l thereof ... Rom 13:14 1939
flesh with the affections and l ... Gal 5:24 1939
times past in the l of our flesh ... Eph 2:3 1939
according to the deceitful l ... Eph 4:22 1939
and into many foolish and hurtful l ... 1Ti 6:9 1939
Flee also youthful l ... 2Ti 2:22 1939
with sins, led away with divers l ... 2Ti 3:6 1939
but after their own l shall they ... 2Ti 4:3 1939
denying ungodliness and worldly l ... Titus 2:12 1939
deceived, serving divers l ... Titus 3:3 1939
even of your l that war in your ... Jas 4:1 2237
ye may consume it upon your l ... Jas 4:3 2237
to the former l in your ignorance ... 1Pet 1:14 1939
pilgrims, abstain from fleshly l ... 1Pet 2:11 1939
time in the flesh to the l of men ... 1Pet 4:2 1939
we walked in lasciviousness, l ... 1Pet 4:3 1939
allure through the l of the flesh ... 2Pet 2:18 1939
walking after their own l ... 2Pet 3:3 1939
walking after their own l ... Jude 16 1939
walk after their own ungodly l ... Jude 18 1939

LUSTY {1}
about ten thousand men, all l ... Judg 3:29 8082

LUZ *(luz)* {8} See BETH-EL.
1. A Canaanite city.
city was called L at the first ... Gen 28:19 3870
So Jacob came to L, which is in ... Gen 35:6 3870
me at L in the land of Canaan ... Gen 48:3 3870
And goeth out from Beth-el to L ... Josh 16:2 3870
toward L, to the side of L ... Josh 18:13 3870
the name of the city before was L ... Judg 1:23 3870
2. A Hittite city.
and called the name thereof L ... Judg 1:26 3870

LYCAONIA *(li-ca-o'-ne-ah)* {2} *A Roman province in Asia Minor.*
unto Lystra and Derbe, cities of L ... Acts 14:6 3071
voices, saying in the speech of L ... Acts 14:11 3071

LYCAONIAN See LYCAONIA.

LYCIA *(lish'-e-ah)* {1} *A Roman province in Asia Minor.*
we came to Myra, a city of L ... Acts 27:5 3073

LYDDA *(lid'-dah)* {3} See LOD. *A city in Judea.*
to the saints which dwelt at L ... Acts 9:32 3069
And all that dwelt at L and Saron ... Acts 9:35 3069
forasmuch as L was nigh to Joppa, ... Acts 9:38 3069

LYDIA *(lid'-e-ah)* {3} See LUDIM, LYDIANS.
1. A people in North Africa.
Ethiopia, and Libya, and L, and all ... Eze 30:5 3865
2. A Christian woman.
And a certain woman named L ... Acts 16:14 3070
and entered into the house of L ... Acts 16:40 3070

LYDIANS *(lid'-e-uns)* {1} *Same as Lydia 1.*
and the L, that handle and bend the ... Jer 46:9 3866

LYING {57}
three flocks of sheep l by it ... Gen 29:2 7257
Israel in l with Jacob's daughter ... Gen 34:7 7901
hateth thee l under his burden ... Ex 23:5 7257
that hath known man by l with him ... Num 31:17 4904
not known a man by l with him ... Num 31:18 4904
had not known man by l with him ... Num 31:35 4904
l in the field, and it be not ... Deut 21:1 5307
If a man be found l with a woman ... Deut 22:22 7901
were with him, from l in wait ... Judg 9:35
Now there were men l in wait ... Judg 16:9
known no man by l with any male ... Judg 21:12 4904
I will be a l spirit in the mouth ... 1Kin 22:22 8267
the LORD hath put a l spirit in ... 1Kin 22:23 8267
be a l spirit in the mouth of all ... 2Chr 18:21 8267
the LORD hath put a l spirit in ... 2Chr 18:22 8267
hated them that regard l vanities ... Ps 31:6 7723
Let the l lips be put to silence ... Ps 31:18 8267
and l rather than to speak ... Ps 52:3 8267
for cursing and l which they speak ... Ps 59:12 3585
spoken against me with a l tongue ... Ps 109:2 8267
Remove from me the way of l ... Ps 119:29 8267
I hate and abhor l ... Ps 119:163 8267
my soul, O LORD, from l lips ... Ps 120:2 8267
my l down, and art acquainted with ... Ps 139:3 7252
a l tongue, and hands that shed ... Prov 6:17 8267
He that hideth hatred with l lips ... Prov 10:18 8267
but a l tongue is but for a ... Prov 12:19 8267
L lips are abomination to the ... Prov 12:22 8267
A righteous man hateth l ... Prov 13:5
much less do l lips a prince ... Prov 17:7 8267
a l tongue is a vanity tossed to ... Prov 21:6 8267
A l tongue hateth those that are ... Prov 26:28 8267
l children, children that will ... Is 30:9 3586
to destroy the poor with l words ... Is 32:7 8267
l down, loving to slumber ... Is 56:10 7901
l against the LORD, and departing ... Is 59:13 3584
Trust ye not in l words, saying, ... Jer 7:4 8267
Behold, ye trust in l words ... Jer 7:8 8267
have spoken l words in my name, ... Jer 29:23 8267
was unto me as a bear l in wait ... Lam 3:10
l divination, saying, The LORD ... Eze 13:6 3577
have ye not spoken a l divination ... Eze 13:7 3577
by your l to my people that hear ... Eze 13:19 3576
for ye have prepared l and corrupt ... Dan 2:9 3538
By swearing, and l, and killing, and ... Hos 4:2 3584
They that observe l vanities ... Jonah 2:8 7723
man sick of the palsy, l on a bed ... Mt 9:2 906
in where the damsel was l ... Mk 5:40 345
swaddling clothes, l in a manger ... Lk 2:12 2749
Joseph, and the babe l in a manger ... Lk 2:16 2749
He then l on Jesus' breast saith ... Jn 13:25 1968
in, saw the linen clothes l ... Jn 20:5 2749
not l with the linen clothes, but ... Jn 20:7 2749
me by the l in wait of the Jews ... Acts 20:19
son heard of their l in wait ... Acts 23:16
Wherefore putting away l, speak ... Eph 4:25 5579
all power and signs and l wonders, ... 2Th 2:9 5579

LYSANIAS *(li-sa'-ne-as)* {1} *Governor of Abilene.*
L the tetrarch of Abilene, ... Lk 3:1 3078

LYSIAS *(lis'-e-as)* {3} *A Roman commander.*
Claudius L unto the most ... Acts 23:26 3079
the chief captain L came upon us ... Acts 24:7 3079
When L the chief captain shall ... Acts 24:22 3079

LYSTRA *(lis'-trah)* {6} *A city in Lycaonia.*
were ware of it, and fled unto L ... Acts 14:6 3082
And there sat a certain man at L ... Acts 14:8 3082
many, they returned again to L ... Acts 14:21 3082
Then came he to Derbe and L ... Acts 16:1 3082
of by the brethren that were at L ... Acts 16:2 3082
me at Antioch, at Iconium, at L ... 2Ti 3:11 3082

M

MAACAH *(ma'-a-kah)* {3} See MAACHAH.
1. A wife of David.
Absalom the son of M the daughter ... 2Sa 3:3 4601
2. A king of Maacah 3.
of king M a thousand men, and of ... 2Sa 10:6 4601
3. A district of Syria.
and of Rehob, and Ish-tob, and M ... 2Sa 10:8 4601

MAACATH See MAACHATHITE.

MAACATHITE See MAACHATHITE.

MAACHAH *(ma'-a-kah)* {18} See BETH-MAACHAH, MACAH, MAACHATHITE, SYRIA-MAACHAH.
1. A son of Nahor.
and Gaham, and Thahash, and M ... Gen 22:24 4601
2. Father of Achish.
unto Achish son of M king of Gath ... 1Kin 2:39 4601
3. Wife of King Rehoboam.
And his mother's name was M ... 1Kin 15:2 4601
And his mother's name was M ... 1Kin 15:10 4601
after her he took M the daughter ... 2Chr 11:20 4601
Rehoboam loved M the daughter of ... 2Chr 11:21 4601
Abijah the son of M the chief ... 2Chr 11:22 4601
4. Mother of King Asa.
also M his mother, even her he ... 1Kin 15:13 4601
also concerning M the mother of ... 2Chr 15:16 4601
5. Concubine of Caleb.
M, Caleb's concubine, bare Sheber ... 1Chr 2:48 4601
6. A wife of David.
Absalom the son of M the daughter ... 1Chr 3:2 4601
7. A wife of Machir.
whose sister's name was M ... 1Chr 7:15 4601
M the wife of Machir bare a son, ... 1Chr 7:16 4601
8. Wife of Jehiel.
whose wife's name was M ... 1Chr 8:29 4601
Jehiel, whose wife's name was M ... 1Chr 9:35 4601
9. Father of Hanan.
Hanan the son of M, and Joshaphat ... 1Chr 11:43 4601
10. A district of Syria.
chariots, and the king of M ... 1Chr 19:7 4601
11. Father of Shephatiah.
Shephatiah the son of M ... 1Chr 27:16 4601

MAACHATHI *(ma-ak'-a-thi)* {1} See MAACHATHITE. *Inhabitants of Maachah 10.*
unto the coasts of Geshuri and M ... Deut 3:14 4602

MAACHATHITE *(ma-ak'-a-thite)* {4} See MAACHATHI, MAACHATHITES. *Same as Maachathi.*
son of Ahasbai, the son of the M ... 2Sa 23:34 4602
and Jaazaniah the son of a M ... 2Kin 25:23 4602
the Garmite, and Eshtemoa the M ... 1Chr 4:19 4602
and Jezaniah the son of a M ... Jer 40:8 4602

MAACHATHITES {4}
border of the Geshurites and the M ... Josh 12:5 4602
the border of the Geshurites and M ... Josh 13:11 4602
not the Geshurites, nor the M ... Josh 13:13 4602
the M dwell among the Israelites ... Josh 13:13 4602

MAADAI *(ma'-a-dahee)* {1} *Married a foreigner in exile.*
M, Amram, and Uel, ... Ezr 10:34 4572

MAADIAH *(ma-a-di'-ah)* {1} See MOADIAH. *A priest with Zerubbabel.*
Miamin, M, Bilgah, ... Neh 12:5 4573

MAAI *(ma'-ahee)* {1} *A priest.*
and Azarael, Milalai, Gilalai, M ... Neh 12:36 4597

MAALEH-ACRABBIM *(ma'-a-leh-ac-rab'-bim)* {1} See AKRABBIM. *A pass on Judah's southern border.*
went out to the south side to M ... Josh 15:3 4610

MAARATH *(ma'-a-rath)* {1} *A city in Judah.*
And M, and Beth-anoth, and Eltekon ... Josh 15:59 4638

MAAREH-GEBA See GIBEAH.

MAASAI See MAASIAI.

MAASEIAH *(ma-a-si'-ah)* {25}
1. A priest who relocated the Ark.
and Unni, Eliab, and Benaiah, and M ... 1Chr 15:18 4641
Jehiel, and Unni, and Eliab, and M ... 1Chr 15:20 4641
2. Son of Adaiah.
Obed, and M the son of Adaiah, and ... 2Chr 23:1 4641
3. An officer of King Uzziah.
M the ruler, under the hand of ... 2Chr 26:11 4641
4. A son of King Ahaz.
slew M the king's son, and Azrikam ... 2Chr 28:7 4641
5. A governor of Jerusalem.
M the governor of the city, and ... 2Chr 34:8 4641
6. A priest who married a foreigner.
M, and Eliezer, and Jarib, and ... Ezr 10:18 4641
7. A priest of the Harim family.
M, and Elijah, and Shemaiah, and ... Ezr 10:21 4641
8. A priest of the Pashur family.
Elioenai, M, Ishmael, Nethaneel, ... Ezr 10:22 4641
9. A priest of the Pahath-moab family.
Adna, and Chelal, Benaiah, M ... Ezr 10:30 4641
10. Father of Azariah.
M the son of Ananiah by his house ... Neh 3:23 4641
11. A priest with Ezra.
and Urijah, and Hilkiah, and M ... Neh 8:4 4641
12. Another priest with Ezra.
Akkub, Shabbethai, Hodijah, M ... Neh 8:7 4641
13. An Israelite who renewed the covenant.
Rehum, Hashabnah, M, ... Neh 10:25 4641
14. A family of exiles.
M the son of Baruch, the son of ... Neh 11:5 4641
15. A descendant of Benjamin.
the son of Kolaiah, the son of M ... Neh 11:7 4641
16. A priest who dedicated the wall.
Eliakim, M, Miniamin, Michaiah, ... Neh 12:41 4641
17. Another priest who dedicated the wall.
And M, and Shemaiah, and Eleazar ... Neh 12:42 4641
18. Father of Zephaniah.
Zephaniah the son of M the priest ... Jer 21:1 4641
Zephaniah the son of M the priest ... Jer 29:25 4641
Zephaniah the son of M the priest ... Jer 37:3 4641
19. Father of Zedekiah.
and of Zedekiah the son of M ... Jer 29:21 4641
20. A Temple officer.
chamber of M the son of Shallum ... Jer 35:4 4641
21. Grandfather of Baruch.
the son of Neriah, the son of M ... Jer 32:12 4271
the son of Neriah, the son of M ... Jer 51:59 4271

MAASIAI *(ma-a'-see-ahee)* {1} *A family of exiles.*
M the son of Adiel, the son of ... 1Chr 9:12 4640

MAATH *(ma'-ath)* {1} *Father of Nagge; ancestor of Jesus.*
Which was the son of M, which was ... Lk 3:26 3092

MAAZ *(ma'-az)* {1} *A son of Ram.*
firstborn of Jerahmeel were, M ... 1Chr 2:27 4619

MAAZIAH *(ma-a-zi'-ah)* {2}
1. A sanctuary servant.
the four and twentieth to M ... 1Chr 24:18 4590
2. A priest who renewed the covenant.
M, Bilgai, Shemaiah ... Neh 10:8 4590

MACBENNAH See MACHBENAH.

MACEDONIA *(mas-e-do'-nee-ah)* {28} See MACEDONIAN. *A Roman province north of Greece.*
There stood a man of M, and prayed ... Acts 16:9 3110
him, saying, Come over into M ... Acts 16:9 3109
we endeavoured to go into M ... Acts 16:10 3109
the chief city of that part of M ... Acts 16:12 3109
and Timotheus were come from M ... Acts 18:5 3109
when he had passed through M ... Acts 19:21 3109
So he sent into M two of them ... Acts 19:22 3109
Gaius and Aristarchus, men of M ... Acts 19:29 3110
and departed for to go into M ... Acts 20:1 3109
he purposed to return through M ... Acts 20:3 3109
For it hath pleased them of M ... Rom 15:26 3109
you, when I shall pass through M ... 1Cor 16:5 3109
for I do pass through M ... 1Cor 16:5 3109
And to pass by you into M ... 2Cor 1:16 3109
to come again out of M unto you ... 2Cor 1:16 3109
them, I went from thence into M ... 2Cor 2:13 3109
For, when we were come into M ... 2Cor 7:5 3109
God bestowed on the churches of M ... 2Cor 8:1 3109
which I boast of you to them of M ... 2Cor 9:2 3110
haply if they of M come with me ... 2Cor 9:4 3110
which came from M supplied ... 2Cor 11:9 3109
from Philippi, a city of M ... 2Cor s 3109
gospel, when I departed from M ... Phil 4:15 3109
to all that believe in M and ... 1Th 1:7 3109
word of the Lord not only in M ... 1Th 1:8 3109
the brethren which are in all M ... 1Th 4:10 3109
at Ephesus, when I went into M ... 1Ti 1:3 3109
the Cretians, from Nicopolis of M ... Titus s 3109

MACEDONIAN *(mas-e-do'-nee-an)* {} *An inhabitant of Macedonia.*
a M of Thessalonica, being with ... Acts 27:2 3110

M

MACHBANAI *(mak'-ba-nahee)* {1} *A warrior in David's army.*
the tenth, *M* the eleventh ... 1Chr 12:13 4344

MACHBANNAI See MACEBANAI.

MACHBENA See MACHBENAH.

MACHBENAH *(mak'-be-nah)* {1} *A descendant of Caleb.*
Madmannah, Sheva the father of *M* ... 1Chr 2:49 4343

MACHI *(ma'-ki)* {1} *Father of Geuel.*
tribe of Gad, Geuel the son of *M* ... Num 13:15 4352

MACHIR *(ma'-kur)* {22} See MACHIRITE.
1. Son of Manasseh.
the children also of *M* the son of ... Gen 50:23 4353
of *M*, the family of the ... Num 26:29 4353
and *M* begat Gilead ... Num 26:29 4353
the son of Gilead, the son of *M* ... Num 27:1 4353
the children of *M* the son of ... Num 32:39 4353
Gilead unto *M* the son of Manasseh ... Num 32:40 4353
children of Gilead, the son of *M* ... Num 36:1 4353
And I gave Gilead unto *M* ... Deut 3:15 4353
children of *M* the son of Manasseh ... Josh 13:31 4353
children of *M* by their families ... Josh 13:31 4353
for *M* the firstborn of Manasseh, ... Josh 17:1 4353
the son of Gilead, the son of *M* ... Josh 17:3 4353
out of *M* came down governors, and ... Judg 5:14 4353
of *M* the father of Gilead ... 1Chr 2:21 4353
sons of *M* the father of Gilead ... 1Chr 2:23 4353
bare *M* the father of Gilead ... 1Chr 7:14 4353
M took to wife the sister of ... 1Chr 7:15 4353
Maachah the wife of *M* bare a son ... 1Chr 7:16 4353
the sons of Gilead, the son of *M* ... 1Chr 7:17 4353
2. Son of Ammiel.
Behold, he is in the house of *M* ... 2Sa 9:4 4353
fetched him out of the house of *M* ... 2Sa 9:5 4353
M the son of Ammiel of Lo-debar, ... 2Sa 17:27 4353

MACHIRITES *(ma'-kur-ites)* {1} *Descendants of Machir 1.*
of Machir, the family of the *M* ... Num 26:29 4354

MACHNADEBAI *(mak-nad'-e-bahee)* {1} *Married a foreigner in exile.*
M, Shashai, Sharai, ... Ezr 10:40 4367

MACHPELAH *(mak-pe'-lah)* {6} *Burial place of Abraham.*
That he may give me the cave of *M* ... Gen 23:9 4375
field of Ephron, which was in *M* ... Gen 23:17 4375
of the field of *M* before Mamre ... Gen 23:19 4375
buried him in the cave of *M* ... Gen 25:9 4375
cave that is in the field of *M* ... Gen 49:30 4375
him in the cave of the field of *M* ... Gen 50:13 4375

MAD {22}
So that thou shalt be *m* for the ... Deut 28:34 7696
feigned himself *m* in their hands ... 1Sa 21:13 1984
servants, Lo, ye see the man is *m* ... 1Sa 21:14 7696
Have I need of *m* men, that ye ... 1Sa 21:15 7696
to play the *m* man in my presence ... 1Sa 21:15 7696
came this *m* fellow to thee ... 2Kin 9:11 7696
they that are *m* against me are ... Ps 102:8 1984
As a *m* man who casteth firebrands ... Prov 26:18 3856
I said of laughter, It is *m* ... Eccl 2:2 1984
oppression maketh a wise man *m* ... Eccl 7:7 1984
the liars, and maketh diviners *m* ... Is 44:25 1984
shall drink, and be moved, and be *m* ... Jer 25:16 1984
the LORD, for every man that is *m* ... Jer 29:26 7696
they are *m* upon their idols ... Jer 50:38 1984
therefore the nations are *m* ... Jer 51:7 1984
is a fool, the spiritual man is *m* ... Hos 9:7 7696
said, He hath a devil, and is *m* ... Jn 10:20 *3105*
And they said unto her, Thou art *m* ... Acts 12:15 *3105*
being exceedingly *m* against them ... Acts 26:11 *1693*
much learning doth make thee *m* ... Acts 26:24 *1519,3130*
But he said, I am not *m*, most ... Acts 26:25 *3105*
will they not say that ye are *m* ... 1Cor 14:23 *3105*

MADAI *(ma'-dahee)* {} See MEDE, MEDIA. *Son of Japheth.*
Gomer, and Magog, and *M*, and Javan, ... Gen 10:2 4074
Gomer, and Magog, and *M*, and Javan, ... 1Chr 1:5 4074

MADE {1406}
God *m* the firmament, and divided ... Gen 1:7 6213
And God *m* two great lights ... Gen 1:16 6213
he *m* the stars also ... Gen 1:16
God *m* the beast of the earth ... Gen 1:25 6213
God saw every thing that he had *m* ... Gen 1:31 6213
God ended his work which he had *m* ... Gen 2:2 6213
from all his work which he had *m* ... Gen 2:2 6213
his work which God created and *m* ... Gen 2:3 6213
day that the LORD God *m* the earth ... Gen 2:4 6213
out of the ground *m* the LORD God ... Gen 2:9
m he a woman, and brought her unto ... Gen 2:22 1129
field which the LORD God had *m* ... Gen 3:1 6213
together, and *m* themselves aprons ... Gen 3:7 6213
in the likeness of God *m* he him ... Gen 5:1 6213
that he had *m* man on the earth ... Gen 6:6 6213
repenteth me that I have *m* them ... Gen 6:7 6213
m will I destroy from off the ... Gen 7:4 6213
God *m* a wind to pass over the ... Gen 8:1
window of the ark which he had *m* ... Gen 8:6 6213
for in the image of God *m* he man ... Gen 9:6 6213
which he had *m* there at the first ... Gen 13:4 6213
That these *m* war with Bera king ... Gen 14:2 6213
say, I have *m* Abram rich ... Gen 14:23 6213
the LORD *m* a covenant with Abram ... Gen 15:18 3772
of many nations have I *m* thee ... Gen 17:5 5414
he *m* them a feast, and did bake ... Gen 19:3 6213
they *m* their father drink wine ... Gen 19:33
they *m* their father drink wine ... Gen 19:35
God hath *m* me to laugh, so that ... Gen 21:6 6213
Abraham *m* a great feast the same ... Gen 21:8 6213
and both of them *m* a covenant ... Gen 21:27 3772
Thus they *m* a covenant at ... Gen 21:32 3772
borders round about, were *m* sure ... Gen 23:17
were *m* sure unto Abraham for a ... Gen 23:20
he *m* his camels to kneel down ... Gen 24:11
to wit whether the LORD had *m* his ... Gen 24:21 6743
And my master *m* me swear, saying, ... Gen 24:37
she *m* haste, and let down her ... Gen 24:46
she *m* the camels drink also ... Gen 24:46
now the LORD hath *m* room for us ... Gen 26:22
he *m* them a feast, and they did ... Gen 26:30 6213
his mother *m* savoury meat, such ... Gen 27:14 6213
as soon as Isaac had *m* an end of ... Gen 27:30
he also had *m* savoury meat, and ... Gen 27:31 6213
I have *m* him thy lord, and all his ... Gen 27:37 7760
men of the place, and *m* a feast ... Gen 29:22 6213
m the white appear which was in ... Gen 30:37
and they took stones, and *m* an heap ... Gen 31:46 6213
house, and *m* booths for his cattle ... Gen 33:17 6213
he *m* him a coat of many colours ... Gen 37:3 6213
about, and *m* obeisance to my sheaf ... Gen 37:7
eleven stars *m* obeisance to me ... Gen 37:9
that the LORD *m* all that he did ... Gen 39:3
he *m* him overseer over his house, ... Gen 39:4
had *m* him overseer in his house ... Gen 39:5
he did, the LORD *m* it to prosper ... Gen 39:23
that he *m* a feast unto all his ... Gen 40:20 6213
he *m* him to ride in the second ... Gen 41:43
he *m* him ruler over all the land ... Gen 41:43 5414
hath *m* me forget all my toil, and ... Gen 41:51
but *m* himself strange unto them, ... Gen 42:7
they *m* ready the present against ... Gen 43:25
down their heads, and *m* obeisance ... Gen 43:28
And Joseph *m* haste ... Gen 43:30
while Joseph *m* himself known unto ... Gen 45:1
he hath *m* me a father to Pharaoh, ... Gen 45:8 7760
God hath *m* me lord of all Egypt ... Gen 45:9 7760
Joseph *m* ready his chariot, and ... Gen 46:29
Joseph *m* it a law over the land ... Gen 47:26 7760
were *m* strong by the hands of the ... Gen 49:24
when Jacob had *m* an end of ... Gen 49:33
My father *m* me swear, saying, Lo, ... Gen 50:5
according as he *m* thee swear ... Gen 50:6
he *m* a mourning for his father ... Gen 50:10 6213
the Egyptians *m* the children of ... Ex 1:13
they *m* their lives bitter with ... Ex 1:14
wherein they *m* them serve ... Ex 1:14
feared God, that he *m* them houses ... Ex 1:21 6213
Who *m* thee a prince and a judge ... Ex 2:14 7760
unto him, Who hath *m* man's mouth ... Ex 4:11 7760
because ye have *m* our savour to ... Ex 5:21
I have *m* thee a god to Pharaoh ... Ex 7:1 5414
of Pharaoh *m* his servants ... Ex 9:20
he *m* ready his chariot, and took ... Ex 14:6
m the sea dry land, and the waters ... Ex 14:21 7760
which thou hast *m* for thee to ... Ex 15:17 6466
waters, the waters were *m* sweet ... Ex 15:25
there he *m* for them a statute and ... Ex 15:25 7760
it was like wafers *m* with honey ... Ex 16:31
m them heads over the people, ... Ex 18:25 5414
For in six days the LORD *m* heaven ... Ex 20:11 6213
which the LORD hath *m* with you ... Ex 24:8 3772
work shall the candlestick be *m* ... Ex 25:31 6213
Three bowls *m* like unto almonds, ... Ex 25:33
three bowls *m* like almonds in the ... Ex 25:33
be four bowls *m* like unto almonds ... Ex 25:34
with cherubims shall it be *m* ... Ex 26:31 6213
an offering *m* by fire unto the ... Ex 29:18
it is an offering *m* by fire unto ... Ex 29:25
wherewith the atonement was *m* ... Ex 29:33
when thou hast *m* an atonement for ... Ex 29:36
an offering *m* by fire unto the ... Ex 29:41
to burn offering *m* by fire unto ... Ex 30:20
for in six days the LORD *m* heaven ... Ex 31:17 6213
when he had *m* an end of communing ... Ex 31:18
after he had *m* it a molten calf ... Ex 32:4 6213
Aaron *m* proclamation, and said, To ... Ex 32:5 7121
they have *m* them a molten calf, ... Ex 32:8 6213
he took the calf which they had *m* ... Ex 32:20 6213
m the children of Israel drink of ... Ex 32:20
(for Aaron had *m* them naked unto ... Ex 32:25
sin, and have *m* them gods of gold ... Ex 32:31 6213
they *m* the calf, which Aaron *m* ... Ex 32:35 6213
And Moses *m* haste, and bowed his ... Ex 34:8
I have *m* a covenant with thee ... Ex 34:27 3772
one whom his spirit *m* willing ... Ex 35:21 5068
whose heart *m* them willing to ... Ex 35:29 5068
to be *m* by the hand of Moses ... Ex 35:29 6213
man from his work which they *m* ... Ex 36:4 6213
the work of the tabernacle *m* ten ... Ex 36:8 6213
of cunning work *m* he them ... Ex 36:8 6213
he *m* loops of blue on the edge of ... Ex 36:11 6213
likewise he *m* in the uttermost ... Ex 36:11 6213
Fifty loops *m* he in one curtain, ... Ex 36:12 6213
fifty loops *m* he in the edge of ... Ex 36:12 6213
he *m* fifty taches of gold, and ... Ex 36:13 6213
he *m* curtains of goats' hair for ... Ex 36:14 6213
eleven curtains he *m* them ... Ex 36:14 6213
he *m* fifty loops upon the ... Ex 36:17 6213
fifty loops *m* he upon the edge of ... Ex 36:17 6213
he *m* fifty taches of brass to ... Ex 36:18 6213
he *m* a covering for the tent of ... Ex 36:19 6213
he *m* boards for the tabernacle of ... Ex 36:20 6213
he *m* boards for the tabernacle ... Ex 36:23 6213
he *m* under the twenty boards ... Ex 36:24 6213
north corner, he *m* twenty boards, ... Ex 36:25 6213
westward he *m* six boards ... Ex 36:27 6213
two boards *m* he for the corners ... Ex 36:28 6213
he *m* bars of shittim wood ... Ex 36:31 6213
he *m* the middle bar to shoot ... Ex 36:33 6213
m their rings of gold to be ... Ex 36:34 6213
he *m* a vail of blue, and purple, ... Ex 36:35 6213
with cherubims *m* he it of cunning ... Ex 36:35 6213
he *m* thereunto four pillars of ... Ex 36:36 6213
And he *m* an hanging for the ... Ex 36:37 6213
Bezaleel *m* the ark of shittim ... Ex 37:1 6213
m a crown of gold to it round ... Ex 37:2 6213
he *m* staves of shittim wood, and ... Ex 37:4 6213
he *m* the mercy seat of pure gold ... Ex 37:6 6213
he *m* two cherubims of gold, ... Ex 37:7 6213
beaten out of one piece *m* he them ... Ex 37:7 6213
out of the mercy seat *m* he the ... Ex 37:8 6213
he *m* the table of shittim wood ... Ex 37:10 6213
m thereunto a crown of gold round ... Ex 37:11 6213
Also he *m* thereunto a border of ... Ex 37:12 6213
m a crown of gold for the border ... Ex 37:12 6213
he *m* the staves of shittim wood, ... Ex 37:15 6213
he *m* the vessels which were upon ... Ex 37:16 6213
he *m* the candlestick of pure gold ... Ex 37:17 6213
of beaten work *m* he the ... Ex 37:17 6213
Three bowls *m* after the fashion ... Ex 37:19
three bowls *m* like almonds in ... Ex 37:19
were four bowls *m* like almonds ... Ex 37:20
he *m* his seven lamps, and his ... Ex 37:23 6213
Of a talent of pure gold *m* he it ... Ex 37:24 6213
he *m* the incense altar of shittim ... Ex 37:25 6213
also he *m* unto it a crown of gold ... Ex 37:26 6213
he *m* two rings of gold for it ... Ex 37:27 6213
he *m* the staves of shittim wood, ... Ex 37:28 6213
he *m* the holy anointing oil, and ... Ex 37:29 6213
he *m* the altar of burnt offering ... Ex 38:1 6213
he *m* the horns thereof on the ... Ex 38:2 6213
he *m* all the vessels of the altar ... Ex 38:3 6213
the vessels thereof *m* he of brass ... Ex 38:3 6213
he *m* for the altar a brasen grate ... Ex 38:4 6213
he *m* the staves of shittim wood, ... Ex 38:6 6213
he *m* the altar hollow with boards ... Ex 38:7 6213
he *m* the laver of brass, and the ... Ex 38:8 6213
And he *m* the court ... Ex 38:9 6213
m all that the LORD commanded ... Ex 38:22 6213
five shekels he *m* hooks for the ... Ex 38:28 6213
therewith he *m* the sockets to the ... Ex 38:30 6213
they *m* cloths of service, to do ... Ex 39:1 6213
m the holy garments for Aaron ... Ex 39:1 6213
he *m* the ephod of gold, blue, and ... Ex 39:2 6213
They *m* shoulderpieces for it, to ... Ex 39:4 6213
he *m* the breastplate of cunning ... Ex 39:8 6213
they *m* the breastplate double ... Ex 39:9 6213
they *m* upon the breastplate ... Ex 39:15 6213
they *m* two ouches of gold, and two ... Ex 39:16 6213
they *m* two rings of gold, and put ... Ex 39:19 6213
they *m* two other golden rings, and ... Ex 39:20 6213
he *m* the robe of the ephod of ... Ex 39:22 6213
they *m* upon the hems of the robe ... Ex 39:24 6213
they *m* bells of pure gold, and put ... Ex 39:25 6213
they *m* coats of fine linen of ... Ex 39:27 6213
they *m* the plate of the holy ... Ex 39:30 6213
children of Israel *m* all the work ... Ex 39:42 6213
sacrifice, an offering *m* by fire ... Lev 1:9
sacrifice, an offering *m* by fire ... Lev 1:13
sacrifice, an offering *m* by fire ... Lev 1:17
to be an offering *m* by fire ... Lev 2:2
offerings of the LORD *m* by fire ... Lev 2:3
it shall be *m* of fine flour with ... Lev 2:7 6213
m of these things unto the LORD ... Lev 2:8 6213
it is an offering *m* by fire ... Lev 2:9
offerings of the LORD *m* by fire ... Lev 2:10
the LORD, shall be *m* with leaven ... Lev 2:11 6213
offering of the LORD *m* by fire ... Lev 2:11
it is an offering *m* by fire unto ... Lev 2:16
offering *m* by fire unto the LORD ... Lev 3:3
it is an offering *m* by fire ... Lev 3:5
offering *m* by fire unto the LORD ... Lev 3:9
offering *m* by fire unto the LORD ... Lev 3:11
even an offering *m* by fire unto ... Lev 3:14
m by fire for a sweet savour ... Lev 3:16
offerings *m* by fire unto the LORD ... Lev 4:35
offerings *m* by fire unto the LORD ... Lev 5:12
portion of my offerings *m* by fire ... Lev 6:17
offerings of the LORD *m* by fire ... Lev 6:18
In a pan it shall be *m* with oil ... Lev 6:21 6213
offering *m* by fire unto the LORD ... Lev 7:5
offering *m* by fire unto the LORD ... Lev 7:25
offerings of the LORD *m* by fire ... Lev 7:30
offerings of the LORD *m* by fire ... Lev 7:35
an offering *m* by fire unto the ... Lev 8:21
it is an offering *m* by fire unto ... Lev 8:28
offerings of the LORD *m* by fire ... Lev 10:12
sacrifices of the LORD *m* by fire ... Lev 10:13
offerings *m* by fire of the fat ... Lev 10:15
a skin, or in any thing *m* of skin ... Lev 13:48 4399
or in any work that is *m* of skin ... Lev 13:51 6213
the man that is to be *m* clean ... Lev 14:11
is in the house be not *m* unclean ... Lev 14:36
have *m* an atonement for himself, ... Lev 16:17
And when he hath *m* an end of ... Lev 16:20
offerings of the LORD *m* by fire ... Lev 21:6
offerings of the LORD *m* by fire ... Lev 21:21
whereby he may be *m* unclean ... Lev 22:5
offering *m* by fire unto the LORD ... Lev 22:27
m by fire unto the LORD seven ... Lev 23:8
an offering *m* by fire unto the ... Lev 23:13
even an offering *m* by fire ... Lev 23:18

offering *m* by fire unto the LORD ... Lev 23:25
offer an offering *m* by fire unto ... Lev 23:27
offering *m* by fire unto the LORD ... Lev 23:36
offering *m* by fire unto the LORD ... Lev 23:36
to offer an offering *m* by fire ... Lev 23:37
generations may know that I *m* the ... Lev 23:43
even an offering *m* by fire unto ... Lev 24:7
of the offerings of the LORD *m* by ... Lev 24:9
of your yoke, and *m* you go upright ... Lev 26:13
which the LORD *m* between him ... Lev 26:46 5414
his sons have *m* an end of ... Num 4:15
and all that is *m* for them ... Num 4:26 6213
an atonement shall be *m* for him ... Num 5:8
when he hath *m* her to drink the ... Num 5:27
that is *m* of the vine tree ... Num 6:4 6213
Moses, so he *m* the candlestick ... Num 8:4 6213
Aaron *m* an atonement for them to ... Num 8:21
it in pans, and *m* cakes of it ... Num 11:8 6213
m all the congregation to murmur ... Num 14:36
wine, for an offering *m* by fire ... Num 15:10
in offering an offering *m* by fire ... Num 15:13
will offer an offering *m* by fire ... Num 15:14
a sacrifice *m* by fire unto the ... Num 15:25
as he had *m* an end of speaking ... Num 16:31
they were *m* broad plates for a ... Num 16:39
m an atonement for the people ... Num 16:47
fat for an offering *m* by fire ... Num 18:17
wherefore have ye *m* us to come up ... Num 20:5
Moses *m* a serpent of brass, and ... Num 21:9 6213
m an atonement for the children ... Num 25:13
bread for my sacrifices *m* by fire ... Num 28:2
This is the offering *m* by fire ... Num 28:3
a sacrifice *m* by fire unto the ... Num 28:6
offer it, a sacrifice *m* by fire ... Num 28:8
a sacrifice *m* by fire unto the ... Num 28:13
m by fire for a burnt offering ... Num 28:19
meat of the sacrifice *m* by fire ... Num 28:24
a sacrifice *m* by fire unto the ... Num 29:6
offering, a sacrifice *m* by fire ... Num 29:13
offering, a sacrifice *m* by fire ... Num 29:36
m them void on the day he heard ... Num 30:12
her husband hath *m* them void ... Num 30:12
and all that is *m* of skins ... Num 31:20 3627
hair, and all things *m* of wood ... Num 31:20
and he *m* them wander in the ... Num 32:13
m them heads over you, captains ... Deut 1:15 5414
m his heart obstinate, that he ... Deut 2:30
your God, which he *m* with you ... Deut 4:23 3772
Out of heaven he *m* thee to hear ... Deut 4:36
The LORD our God *m* a covenant ... Deut 5:2 3772
The LORD *m* not this covenant with ... Deut 5:3 3772
which the LORD *m* with you ... Deut 9:9 3772
they have *m* them a molten image ... Deut 9:12 6213
God, and had *m* you a molten calf ... Deut 9:16 6213
your sin, the calf which ye had *m* ... Deut 9:21 6213
I *m* an ark of shittim wood, and ... Deut 10:3 6213
tables in the ark which I had *m* ... Deut 10:5 6213
now the LORD thy God hath *m* thee ... Deut 10:22 7760
how he *m* the water of the Red sea ... Deut 11:4
offerings of the LORD *m* by fire ... Deut 18:1
when the officers have *m* an end ... Deut 20:9
When thou hast *m* an end of ... Deut 26:12
above all nations which he hath *m* ... Deut 26:19 6213
which he *m* with them in Horeb ... Deut 29:1 3772
which he *m* with them when he ... Deut 29:25 3772
covenant which I have *m* with them ... Deut 31:16 3772
when Moses had *m* an end of ... Deut 31:24
Hath he not *m* thee, and ... Deut 32:6 6213
He *m* him ride on the high places ... Deut 32:13
he *m* him to suck honey out of the ... Deut 32:13
then he forsook God which *m* him ... Deut 32:15 6213
Moses *m* an end of speaking all ... Deut 32:45
oath which thou hast *m* us swear ... Josh 2:17
which thou hast *m* us to swear ... Josh 2:20
Joshua *m* him sharp knives, and ... Josh 5:3 6213
all Israel *m* as if they were ... Josh 8:15
when Israel had *m* an end of ... Josh 8:24
m it an heap for ever, even a ... Josh 8:28 7760
m as if they had been ambassadors ... Josh 9:4
Joshua *m* peace with them ... Josh 9:15 6213
m a league with them, to let them ... Josh 9:15 6213
they had *m* a league with them ... Josh 9:16 3772
Joshua *m* them that day hewers of ... Josh 9:27 5414
of Gibeon had *m* peace with Israel ... Josh 10:1
for it hath *m* peace with Joshua ... Josh 10:4
Gibeon, and *m* war against it ... Josh 10:5
the children of Israel had *m* an ... Josh 10:20
Joshua *m* war a long time with all ... Josh 11:18 6213
There was not a city that *m* peace ... Josh 11:19
of the LORD God of Israel *m* by ... Josh 13:14
me *m* the heart of the people melt ... Josh 14:8
When they had *m* an end of ... Josh 19:49
So they *m* an end of dividing the ... Josh 19:51
For the LORD hath *m* Jordan a ... Josh 22:25 5414
of the LORD, which our fathers *m* ... Josh 22:28 6213
So Joshua *m* a covenant with the ... Josh 24:25 3772
I *m* you to go up out of Egypt, and ... Judg 2:1
But Ehud *m* him a dagger which had ... Judg 3:16 6213
when he had *m* an end to offer the ... Judg 3:18
Then he *m* him that remaineth have ... Judg 5:13
the LORD *m* me have dominion over ... Judg 5:13
the children of Israel *m* them the ... Judg 6:2 6213
m ready a kid, and unleavened ... Judg 6:19 6213
Gideon *m* an ephod thereof, and put ... Judg 8:27 6213
and *m* Baal-berith their god ... Judg 8:33 7760
m Abimelech king, by the plain of ... Judg 9:6
in that ye have *m* Abimelech king ... Judg 9:16
have *m* Abimelech, the son of his ... Judg 9:18
m merry, and went into the house ... Judg 9:27 6213
of Ammon *m* war against Israel ... Judg 11:4
of Ammon *m* war against Israel ... Judg 11:5
Gilead, and the people *m* him head ... Judg 11:11 7760
And the woman *m* haste, and ran, and ... Judg 13:10
until we shall have *m* ready a kid ... Judg 13:15 6213
and Samson *m* there a feast ... Judg 14:10 6213
when he had *m* an end of speaking, ... Judg 15:17
she *m* him sleep upon her knees ... Judg 16:19
and he *m* them sport ... Judg 16:25
that beheld while Samson *m* sport ... Judg 16:27
who *m* thereof a graven image and a ... Judg 17:4 6213
m an ephod, and teraphim, and ... Judg 17:5 6213
have taken away my gods which I *m* ... Judg 18:24 6213
took the things which Micah had *m* ... Judg 18:27 6213
Micah's graven image, which he *m* ... Judg 18:31 6213
For they had *m* a great oath ... Judg 21:5
had *m* a breach in the tribes of ... Judg 21:15 6213
his mother *m* him a little coat ... 1Sa 2:19 6213
m by fire of the children of ... 1Sa 2:28
his sons *m* themselves vile ... 1Sa 3:13
when he *m* mention of the ark of ... 1Sa 4:18
that he *m* his sons judges over ... 1Sa 8:1 7760
m them sit in the chiefest place ... 1Sa 9:22 5414
And when he had *m* an end of ... 1Sa 10:13
there they *m* Saul king before the ... 1Sa 11:15
me, and have *m* a king over you ... 1Sa 12:1
m them dwell in this place ... 1Sa 12:8
that as soon as he had *m* an end ... 1Sa 13:10
I have not *m* supplication unto ... 1Sa 13:12
Jonathan and his armourbearer *m* ... 1Sa 14:14 5221
wast thou not *m* the head of the ... 1Sa 15:17
thy sword hath *m* women childless ... 1Sa 15:33
he had *m* Saul king over Israel ... 1Sa 15:35
and *m* him pass before Samuel ... 1Sa 16:8
Then Jesse *m* Shammah to pass by ... 1Sa 16:9
Jesse *m* seven of his sons to pass ... 1Sa 16:10
when he had *m* an end of speaking ... 1Sa 18:1
David *m* a covenant, because he ... 1Sa 18:3 3772
m him his captain over a thousand ... 1Sa 18:13 7760
So Jonathan *m* a covenant with the ... 1Sa 20:16 3772
sheweth me that my son hath *m* a ... 1Sa 22:8 3772
they two *m* a covenant before the ... 1Sa 23:18 3772
David *m* haste to get away for ... 1Sa 23:26
when David had *m* an end of ... 1Sa 24:16
Then Abigail *m* haste, and took two ... 1Sa 25:18
Whither have ye *m* a road to day ... 1Sa 27:10 6584
He hath *m* his people Israel ... 1Sa 27:12
and they *m* him drink water ... 1Sa 30:11
We *m* an invasion upon the south ... 1Sa 30:14 6584
whom they had *m* also to abide at ... 1Sa 30:21
that he *m* it a statute and an ... 1Sa 30:25 7760
m him king over Gilead, and over ... 2Sa 2:9
that Abner *m* himself strong for ... 2Sa 3:6
And David *m* Abner and the men that ... 2Sa 3:20 6213
as she *m* haste to flee, that he ... 2Sa 4:4
king David *m* a league with them ... 2Sa 5:3 3772
of instruments *m* of fir wood ... 2Sa 6:5
LORD had *m* a breach upon Uzzah ... 2Sa 6:8 6555
as soon as David had *m* an end of ... 2Sa 6:18
have *m* thee a great name, like ... 2Sa 7:9 6213
they *m* peace with Israel, and ... 2Sa 10:19
and he *m* him drunk ... 2Sa 11:13
When thou hast *m* an end of ... 2Sa 11:19
m them pass through the brickkiln ... 2Sa 12:31
Amnon lay down, and *m* himself sick ... 2Sa 13:6
m cakes in his sight, and did bake ... 2Sa 13:8 3835
took the cakes which she had *m* ... 2Sa 13:10 6213
as soon as he had *m* an end of ... 2Sa 13:36
the people have *m* me afraid ... 2Sa 14:15
Oh that I were *m* judge in the ... 2Sa 15:4 7760
Absalom *m* Amasa captain of the ... 2Sa 17:25 7760
floods of ungodly men *m* me afraid ... 2Sa 22:5 7760
he *m* darkness pavilions round ... 2Sa 22:12 7896
and thy gentleness hath *m* me great ... 2Sa 22:36
yet he hath *m* with me an ... 2Sa 23:5 7760
it as they had *m* an end of eating ... 1Kin 1:41
king David hath *m* Solomon king ... 1Kin 1:43
who hath *m* me an house, as he ... 1Kin 2:24 6213
Solomon *m* affinity with Pharaoh ... 1Kin 3:1
until he had *m* an end of building ... 1Kin 3:1
thou hast *m* thy servant king ... 1Kin 3:7
m a feast to all his servants ... 1Kin 3:15 6213
his month in a year *m* provision ... 1Kin 4:7
they two *m* a league together ... 1Kin 5:12 3772
for the house he *m* windows of ... 1Kin 6:4 6213
he *m* chambers round about ... 1Kin 6:5 6213
he *m* narrowed rests round about ... 1Kin 6:6 5414
was built of stone *m* ready before ... 1Kin 6:7
he *m* a partition by the chains of ... 1Kin 6:21
within the oracle he *m* two ... 1Kin 6:23 6213
oracle he *m* doors of olive tree ... 1Kin 6:31 6213
So also *m* he for the door of the ... 1Kin 6:33 6213
And he *m* a porch of pillars ... 1Kin 7:6 6213
Then he *m* a porch for the throne ... 1Kin 7:7 6213
Solomon *m* also an house for ... 1Kin 7:8 6213
he *m* two chapiters of molten ... 1Kin 7:16 6213
he *m* the pillars, and two rows ... 1Kin 7:18 6213
he *m* a molten sea, ten cubits ... 1Kin 7:23 6213
And he *m* ten bases of brass ... 1Kin 7:27 6213
certain additions *m* of thin work ... 1Kin 7:29 6213
this manner he *m* the ten bases ... 1Kin 7:37 6213
Then *m* he ten lavers of brass ... 1Kin 7:38 6213
Hiram *m* the lavers, and the ... 1Kin 7:40 6213
So Hiram *m* an end of doing all ... 1Kin 7:40 6213
m king Solomon for the house of ... 1Kin 7:40 6213
which Hiram *m* to king Solomon for ... 1Kin 7:45 6213
Solomon *m* all the vessels that ... 1Kin 7:48 6213
m for the house of the LORD ... 1Kin 7:51 6213
when the LORD *m* a covenant with ... 1Kin 8:9 3772
which he *m* with our fathers, when ... 1Kin 8:21 3772
soever be *m* by any man, or by all ... 1Kin 8:38
that when Solomon had *m* an end of ... 1Kin 8:54
wherewith I have *m* supplication ... 1Kin 8:59
that thou hast *m* before me ... 1Kin 9:3 2589
king Solomon *m* a navy of ships in ... 1Kin 9:26 6213
therefore *m* he thee king, to do ... 1Kin 10:9 7760
the king *m* of the almug trees ... 1Kin 10:12 6213
king Solomon *m* two hundred ... 1Kin 10:16 6213
he *m* three hundred shields of ... 1Kin 10:17
Moreover the king *m* a great ... 1Kin 10:18 6213
was not the like *m* in any kingdom ... 1Kin 10:20 6213
the king *m* silver to be in ... 1Kin 10:27 5414
cedars *m* he to be as the sycomore ... 1Kin 10:27 5414
he *m* him ruler over all the ... 1Kin 11:28
Thy father *m* our yoke grievous ... 1Kin 12:4
Thy father *m* our yoke heavy, but ... 1Kin 12:10
My father *m* your yoke heavy, and I ... 1Kin 12:14
Therefore king Rehoboam *m* speed ... 1Kin 12:18
m him king over all Israel ... 1Kin 12:20
m two calves of gold, and said ... 1Kin 12:28 6213
he *m* an house of high places, and ... 1Kin 12:31 6213
m priests of the lowest of the ... 1Kin 12:31 6213
unto the calves that he had *m* ... 1Kin 12:32 6213
of the high places which he had *m* ... 1Kin 12:32 6213
upon the altar which he had *m* in ... 1Kin 12:33 6213
but *m* again of the lowest of the ... 1Kin 13:33 6213
m thee prince over my people ... 1Kin 14:7 5414
m thee other gods, and molten ... 1Kin 14:9 6213
because they have *m* their groves ... 1Kin 14:15 6213
did sin, and who *m* Israel to sin ... 1Kin 14:16
of gold which Solomon had *m* ... 1Kin 14:26 6213
king Rehoboam *m* in their stead ... 1Kin 14:27 6213
the idols that his fathers had *m* ... 1Kin 15:12 6213
because she had *m* an idol in a ... 1Kin 15:13 6213
Then king Asa *m* a proclamation ... 1Kin 15:22 6213
sin wherewith he *m* Israel to sin ... 1Kin 15:26
which he *m* Israel sin, by his ... 1Kin 15:30
sin wherewith he *m* Israel to sin ... 1Kin 15:34
m thee prince over my people ... 1Kin 16:2 5414
hast *m* my people Israel to sin, ... 1Kin 16:2
and by which they *m* Israel to sin ... 1Kin 16:13
wherefore all Israel *m* Omri ... 1Kin 16:16
sin wherewith he *m* Israel to sin ... 1Kin 16:26
And Ahab *m* a grove ... 1Kin 16:33 6213
leaped upon the altar which was *m* ... 1Kin 18:26 6213
he *m* a trench about the altar, as ... 1Kin 18:32 6213
as my father *m* in Samaria ... 1Kin 20:34 7760
So he *m* a covenant with him, and ... 1Kin 20:34 3772
me to anger, and *m* Israel to sin ... 1Kin 21:22
of Chenaanah *m* him horns of iron ... 1Kin 22:11 6213
and the ivory house which he *m* ... 1Kin 22:39 1129
Jehoshaphat *m* peace with the king ... 1Kin 22:44
Jehoshaphat *m* ships of Tharshish ... 1Kin 22:48 6235
son of Nebat, who *m* Israel to sin ... 1Kin 22:52
of Baal that his father had *m* ... 2Kin 3:2 6213
of Nebat, which *m* Israel to sin ... 2Kin 3:3
For the LORD had *m* the host of ... 2Kin 7:6
and *m* a king over themselves ... 2Kin 8:20
And his chariot was *m* ready ... 2Kin 9:21 631
So they *m* him ride in his chariot ... 2Kin 10:16
as soon as he had *m* an end of ... 2Kin 10:25
m it a draught house unto this ... 2Kin 10:27 7760
who *m* Israel to sin, Jehu ... 2Kin 10:29
Jeroboam, which *m* Israel to sin ... 2Kin 10:31
m a covenant with them, and took ... 2Kin 11:4 3772
they *m* him king, and anointed him ... 2Kin 11:12
Jehoiada *m* a covenant between the ... 2Kin 11:17 3772
Howbeit there were not *m* for the ... 2Kin 12:13 6213
m a conspiracy, and slew Joash in ... 2Kin 12:20
of Nebat, which *m* Israel to sin ... 2Kin 13:2
who *m* Israel sin, but walked ... 2Kin 13:6
had *m* them like the dust by ... 2Kin 13:7 7760
son of Nebat, who *m* Israel sin ... 2Kin 13:11
Now they *m* a conspiracy against ... 2Kin 14:19
m him king instead of his father ... 2Kin 14:21
son of Nebat, who *m* Israel to sin ... 2Kin 14:24
son of Nebat, who *m* Israel to sin ... 2Kin 15:9
and his conspiracy which he *m* ... 2Kin 15:15 7194
son of Nebat, who *m* Israel to sin ... 2Kin 15:18
son of Nebat, who *m* Israel to sin ... 2Kin 15:24
son of Nebat, who *m* Israel to sin ... 2Kin 15:28
Hoshea the son of Elah *m* a ... 2Kin 15:30 7194
m his son to pass through the ... 2Kin 16:3
so Urijah the priest *m* it against ... 2Kin 16:11 6213
kings of Israel, which they had *m* ... 2Kin 17:8 6213
that he *m* with their fathers ... 2Kin 17:15 3772
m them molten images, even two ... 2Kin 17:16 6213
m a grove, and worshipped all the ... 2Kin 17:16 6213
statutes of Israel which they *m* ... 2Kin 17:19 6213
they *m* Jeroboam the son of Nebat ... 2Kin 17:21
LORD, and *m* them sin a great sin ... 2Kin 17:21
every nation *m* gods of their own ... 2Kin 17:29 6213
places which the Samaritans had *m* ... 2Kin 17:29 6213
men of Babylon *m* Succoth-benoth ... 2Kin 17:30 6213
and the men of Cuth *m* Nergal ... 2Kin 17:30 6213
and the men of Hamath *m* Ashima ... 2Kin 17:30 6213
And the Avites *m* Nibhaz and Tartak ... 2Kin 17:31 6213
m unto themselves of the lowest ... 2Kin 17:32 6213
whom the LORD had *m* a covenant ... 2Kin 17:35 3772
the covenant that I have *m* with ... 2Kin 17:38 3772
brasen serpent that Moses had *m* ... 2Kin 18:4 6213
thou hast *m* heaven and earth ... 2Kin 19:15 6213
all his might, and how he *m* a pool ... 2Kin 20:20 6213
m a grove, as did Ahab king of ... 2Kin 21:3 6213
he *m* his son pass through the ... 2Kin 21:6

grove that he had *m* in the house 2Kin 21:7 6213
hath *m* Judah also to sin with his 2Kin 21:11
sin wherewith he *m* Judah to sin 2Kin 21:16
the people of the land *m* Josiah 2Kin 21:24
Howbeit there was no reckoning *m* 2Kin 22:7
m a covenant before the LORD, to 2Kin 23:3 3772
the vessels that were *m* for Baal 2Kin 23:4 6213
which the kings of Judah had *m* 2Kin 23:12 6213
the altars which Manasseh had *m* 2Kin 23:12 6213
who *m* Israel to sin 2Kin 23:15
had *m*, both that altar 2Kin 23:15 6213
m to provoke the LORD to anger 2Kin 23:19 6213
m him king in his father's stead 2Kin 23:30
Pharaoh-nechoh *m* Eliakim the son 2Kin 23:34
had *m* in the temple of the LORD 2Kin 24:13 6213
the king of Babylon *m* Mattaniah 2Kin 24:17
had *m* for the house of the LORD 2Kin 25:16 6213
even over them he *m* Gedaliah the 2Kin 25:22
Babylon had *m* Gedaliah governor 2Kin 25:23
they *m* war with the Hagarites 1Chr 5:10 6213
they *m* war with the Hagarites, 1Chr 5:19 6213
m the ointment of the spices 1Chr 9:30 7543
things that were *m* in the pans 1Chr 9:31 4639
David *m* a covenant with them in 1Chr 11:3 3772
m them captains of the band 1Chr 12:18 5414
the LORD had *m* a breach upon Uzza 1Chr 13:11 6555
David *m* him houses in the city of 1Chr 15:1 6213
LORD our God *m* a breach upon us 1Chr 15:13 6555
when David had *m* an end of 1Chr 16:2
but Asaph *m* a sound with cymbals 1Chr 16:5
covenant which he *m* with Abraham 1Chr 16:16 3772
but the LORD *m* the heavens 1Chr 16:26 6213
have *m* thee a name like the name 1Chr 17:8 6213
Solomon *m* the brasen sea, and the 1Chr 18:8 6213
had *m* themselves odious to David 1Chr 19:6
they *m* peace with David, and 1Chr 19:19
which Moses *m* in the wilderness, 1Chr 21:29 6213
abundantly, and hast *m* great wars 1Chr 22:8 6213
he *m* Solomon his son king over 1Chr 23:1
with the instruments which I *m* 1Chr 23:5 6213
yet his father *m* him the chief 1Chr 26:10 7760
whom king David *m* rulers over the 1Chr 26:32
had *m* ready for the building 1Chr 28:2 6213
the LORD *m* me understand in 1Chr 28:19
gold for things to be *m* of gold 1Chr 29:2
be *m* by the hands of artificers 1Chr 29:5
for the which I have *m* provision 1Chr 29:19
they *m* Solomon the son of David 1Chr 29:22
the LORD had *m* in the wilderness 2Chr 1:3 6213
son of Uri, the son of Hur, had *m* 2Chr 1:5 6213
hast *m* me to reign in his stead 2Chr 1:8
for thou hast *m* me king over a 2Chr 1:9
over whom I have *m* thee king 2Chr 1:11
And the king *m* silver and gold at 2Chr 1:15 5414
cedar trees *m* he as the sycomore 2Chr 1:15 5414
he hath *m* thee king over them 2Chr 2:11 5414
that *m* heaven and earth, who hath 2Chr 2:12 6213
he *m* the most holy house, the 2Chr 3:8 6213
in the most holy house he *m* two 2Chr 3:10 6213
he *m* the vail of blue, and purple, 2Chr 3:14 6213
Also he *m* before the house two 2Chr 3:15 6213
he *m* chains, as in the oracle, and 2Chr 3:16 6213
m an hundred pomegranates, and put 2Chr 3:16 6213
Moreover he *m* an altar of brass, 2Chr 4:1 6213
Also he *m* a molten sea of ten 2Chr 4:2 6213
He *m* also ten lavers, and put five 2Chr 4:6 6213
he *m* ten candlesticks of gold 2Chr 4:7 6213
He *m* also ten tables, and placed 2Chr 4:8 6213
he *m* an hundred basons of gold 2Chr 4:8 6213
Furthermore he *m* the court of the 2Chr 4:9 6213
Huram *m* the pots, and the shovels, 2Chr 4:11 6213
He *m* also bases, and lavers *m* 2Chr 4:14 6213
Thus Solomon *m* all these vessels 2Chr 4:18 6213
Solomon *m* all the vessels that 2Chr 4:19 6213
m he of gold, and that perfect 2Chr 4:21
m for the house of the LORD was 2Chr 5:1 6213
when the LORD *m* a covenant with 2Chr 5:10 3772
that he *m* with the children of 2Chr 6:11 3772
For Solomon had *m* a brasen 2Chr 6:13 6213
soever shall be *m* of any man 2Chr 6:29
prayer that is *m* in this place 2Chr 6:40
Solomon had *m* an end of praying 2Chr 7:1
the king had *m* to praise the LORD 2Chr 7:6 6213
had *m* was not able to receive the 2Chr 7:7 6213
day they *m* a solemn assembly 2Chr 7:9 6213
prayer that is *m* in this place 2Chr 7:15
therefore *m* he thee king over 2Chr 9:8 5414
the king *m* of the algum trees 2Chr 9:11 6213
king Solomon *m* two hundred 2Chr 9:15 6213
shields *m* he of beaten gold 2Chr 9:16
Moreover the king *m* a great 2Chr 9:17 6213
was not the like *m* in any kingdom 2Chr 9:19 6213
the king *m* silver in Jerusalem as 2Chr 9:27 5414
cedar trees *m* he as the sycomore 2Chr 9:27 5414
Thy father *m* our yoke grievous 2Chr 10:4
Thy father *m* our yoke heavy, but 2Chr 10:10
My father *m* your yoke heavy, but 2Chr 10:14
But king Rehoboam *m* speed to get 2Chr 10:18
m them exceeding strong, having 2Chr 11:12
and for the calves which he had *m* 2Chr 11:15 6213
m Rehoboam the son of Solomon 2Chr 11:17
Rehoboam *m* Abijah the son of 2Chr 11:22
of gold which Solomon had *m* 2Chr 12:9 6213
king Rehoboam *m* shields of brass 2Chr 12:10 6213
which Jeroboam *m* you for gods 2Chr 13:8 6213
have *m* you priests after the 2Chr 13:9 6213
because she had *m* an idol in a 2Chr 15:16 6213
which he had *m* for himself in the 2Chr 16:14 3738

they *m* a very great burning for 2Chr 16:14 8313
so that they *m* no war against 2Chr 17:10
Chenaanah had *m* him horns of iron 2Chr 18:10 6213
when they had *m* an end of the 2Chr 20:23
for the LORD had *m* them to 2Chr 20:27
they *m* the ships in Ezion-gaber 2Chr 20:36 6213
covenant that he had *m* with David 2Chr 21:7 3772
of Judah, and *m* themselves a king 2Chr 21:8
Moreover he *m* high places in the 2Chr 21:11 6213
hast *m* Judah and the inhabitants 2Chr 21:13
his people *m* no burning for him, 2Chr 21:19 6213
the inhabitants of Jerusalem *m* 2Chr 22:1
all the congregation *m* a covenant 2Chr 23:3 3772
him the testimony, and *m* him king 2Chr 23:11
Jehoiada *m* a covenant between him 2Chr 23:16 3772
king's commandment they *m* a chest 2Chr 24:8 6213
they *m* a proclamation through 2Chr 24:9 5414
chest, until they had *m* an end 2Chr 24:10
whereof were *m* vessels for the 2Chr 24:14 6213
Judah, and *m* obeisance to the king 2Chr 24:17
m them captains over thousands, 2Chr 25:5 5975
Art thou *m* of the king's counsel 2Chr 25:16 5414
m a conspiracy against him in 2Chr 25:27 7194
m him king in the room of his 2Chr 26:1
the LORD, God *m* him to prosper 2Chr 26:5
that *m* war with mighty power, to 2Chr 26:13 6213
he *m* in Jerusalem engines, 2Chr 26:15 6213
m also molten images for Baalim 2Chr 28:2 6213
for he *m* Judah naked, and 2Chr 28:19
he *m* him altars in every corner 2Chr 28:24 6213
he *m* high places to burn incense 2Chr 28:25 6213
of the first month they *m* an end 2Chr 29:17
they *m* reconciliation with their 2Chr 29:24
should be *m* for all Israel 2Chr 29:24
when they had *m* an end of 2Chr 29:29
m darts and shields in abundance 2Chr 32:5 6213
he *m* himself treasuries for 2Chr 32:27 6213
m groves, and worshipped all the 2Chr 33:3 6213
image, the idol which he had *m* 2Chr 33:7 6213
So Manasseh *m* Judah and the 2Chr 33:9
which Manasseh his father had *m* 2Chr 33:22 6213
the people of the land *m* Josiah 2Chr 33:25
m dust of them, and strowed it 2Chr 34:4 1854
m a covenant before the LORD, to 2Chr 34:31 3772
m all that were present in Israel 2Chr 34:33
afterward they *m* ready for 2Chr 35:14
m them an ordinance in Israel 2Chr 35:25 5414
m him king in his father's stead 2Chr 36:1
the king of Egypt *m* Eliakim his 2Chr 36:4
m Zedekiah his brother king over 2Chr 36:10
who had *m* him swear by God 2Chr 36:13
Persia, that he *m* a proclamation 2Chr 36:22 5674
Persia, that he *m* a proclamation Ezr 1:1 5674
That search may be *m* in the book Ezr 4:15
commanded, and search hath been *m* Ezr 4:19
hath *m* insurrection against kings Ezr 4:19 5648
and sedition have been *m* therein Ezr 4:19 5648
m them to cease by force and power Ezr 4:23
of Babylon the same king Cyrus *m* Ezr 5:13 7761
whom he had *m* governor Ezr 5:14 7761
let there be search *m* in the Ezr 5:17
that a decree was *m* of Cyrus the Ezr 5:17 7761
Then Darius the king *m* a decree Ezr 6:1 7761
search was *m* in the house of the Ezr 6:1
king the same Cyrus the king *m* a Ezr 6:3 7761
Also I have *m* a decree, that Ezr 6:11 7761
let his house be *m* a dunghill for Ezr 6:11 5648
I Darius have *m* a decree Ezr 6:12 7761
for the LORD had *m* them joyful Ezr 6:22
m the chief priests, the Levites, Ezr 10:5
they *m* proclamation throughout Ezr 10:7 5674
they *m* an end with all the men Ezr 10:17
David, and to the pool that was *m* Neh 3:16 6213
the walls of Jerusalem were *m* up Neh 4:7 5927
Nevertheless we *m* our prayer unto Neh 4:9
For they all *m* us afraid, saying, Neh 6:9
which they had *m* for the purpose Neh 8:4 6213
m themselves booths, every one Neh 8:16 6213
out of the captivity *m* booths Neh 8:17 6213
thou hast *m* heaven, the heaven of Neh 9:6 6213
when they had *m* them a molten Neh 9:18 6213
Also we *m* ordinances for us, to Neh 10:32 5975
for God had *m* them rejoice with Neh 12:43
And I *m* treasurers over the Neh 13:13
m them swear by God, saying, Ye Neh 13:25
God *m* him king over all Israel Neh 13:26 5414
he *m* a feast unto all his princes Est 1:3 6213
the king *m* a feast unto all the Est 1:5 6213
Also Vashti the queen *m* a feast Est 1:9 6213
m her queen instead of Vashti Est 2:17
Then the king *m* a great feast Est 2:18 6213
he *m* a release to the provinces, Est 2:18 6213
inquisition was *m* of the matter Est 2:23
Let a gallows be *m* of fifty Est 5:14 6213
and he caused the gallows to be *m* Est 5:14 6213
which Haman had *m* for Mordecai Est 7:9 6213
m it a day of feasting and Est 9:17 6213
m it a day of feasting and Est 9:18 6213
m the fourteenth day of the month Est 9:19 6213
Hast not thou *m* an hedge about Job 1:10 7753
The Chaldeans *m* out three bands, Job 1:17 7760
for they had *m* an appointment Job 2:11
which *m* all my bones to shake Job 4:14
So am I *m* to possess months of Job 7:3
Thine hands have *m* me and Job 10:8 6087
that thou hast *m* me as the clay Job 10:9 6213
or wast thou *m* before the hills Job 15:7 2342
But now he hath *m* me weary Job 16:7

thou hast *m* desolate all my Job 16:7
He hath *m* me also a byword of the Job 17:6 3322
I have *m* my bed in the darkness Job 17:13 7502
No mention shall be *m* of coral Job 28:18
When he *m* a decree for the rain, Job 28:26 6213
I *m* a covenant with mine eyes Job 31:1 3772
Did not he that *m* me in the womb Job 31:15 6213
If I have *m* gold my hope, or have Job 31:24 7760
The spirit of God hath *m* me Job 33:4 6213
When I *m* the cloud the garment Job 38:9 7760
house I have *m* the wilderness Job 39:6 7760
now behemoth, which I *m* with thee Job 40:15 6213
he that *m* him can make his sword Job 40:19 6213
his like, who is *m* without fear Job 41:33 6213
hath bent his bow, and *m* it ready Ps 7:12
He *m* a pit, and digged it, and is Ps 7:15 3738
fallen into the ditch which he *m* Ps 7:15 6466
For thou hast *m* him a little Ps 8:5
sunk down in the pit that they *m* Ps 9:15 6213
floods of ungodly men *m* me afraid Ps 18:4
He *m* darkness his secret place Ps 18:11 7896
and thy gentleness hath *m* me great Ps 18:35
thou hast *m* me the head of the Ps 18:43 7760
For thou hast *m* him most blessed Ps 21:6 7896
thou hast *m* him exceeding glad Ps 21:6
hast not *m* my foes to rejoice Ps 30:1
by thy favour thou hast *m* my Ps 30:7
and unto the LORD I *m* supplication Ps 30:8
of the LORD were the heavens *m* Ps 33:6 6213
thou hast *m* my days as an Ps 39:5 5414
which I have *m* touching the king Ps 45:1 4639
whereby they have *m* thee glad Ps 45:8
he hath *m* in the earth Ps 46:8 7760
thou afraid when one is *m* rich Ps 49:16
those that have *m* a covenant with Ps 50:5 3772
man that *m* not God his strength Ps 52:7 7760
Thou hast *m* the earth to tremble Ps 60:2
thou hast *m* us to drink the wine Ps 60:3
I *m* sackcloth also my garment Ps 69:11 5414
shall be *m* for him continually Ps 72:15
thou hast *m* summer and winter Ps 74:17 3335
my spirit *m* diligent search Ps 77:6
he *m* the waters to stand as an Ps 78:13
He *m* a way to his anger Ps 78:50 6424
But *m* his own people to go forth Ps 78:52
m the tribes of Israel to dwell Ps 78:55
their widows *m* no lamentation Ps 78:64
whom thou hast *m* shall come Ps 86:9 6213
thou hast *m* me an abomination Ps 88:8 7896
I have *m* a covenant with my Ps 89:3 3772
Thou hast *m* void the covenant of Ps 89:39
thou hast *m* all his enemies to Ps 89:42
hast not *m* him to stand in the Ps 89:43
Thou hast *m* his glory to cease, Ps 89:44
hast thou *m* all men in vain Ps 89:47 1254
Because thou hast *m* the LORD Ps 91:9 7760
hast *m* me glad through thy work Ps 92:4
The sea is his, and he *m* it Ps 95:5 6213
but the LORD *m* the heavens Ps 96:5 6213
The LORD hath *m* known his Ps 98:2
it is he that hath *m* us, and not Ps 100:3 6213
He *m* known his ways unto Moses, Ps 103:7
In wisdom hast thou *m* them all Ps 104:24 6213
whom thou hast *m* to play therein Ps 104:26 3335
Which covenant he *m* with Abraham Ps 105:9 3772
He *m* him lord of his house, and Ps 105:21 7760
m them stronger than their Ps 105:24
He sent darkness, and *m* it dark Ps 105:28
They *m* a calf in Horeb, and Ps 106:19 6213
He *m* them also to be pitied of Ps 106:46 5414
He hath *m* his wonderful works to Ps 111:4 6213
of the LORD which *m* heaven Ps 115:15 6213
is the day which the LORD hath *m* Ps 118:24 6213
I *m* haste, and delayed not to keep Ps 119:60 2363
Thy hands have *m* me and fashioned Ps 119:73 6213
hast *m* me wiser than mine enemies Ps 119:98
for they have *m* void thy law Ps 119:126
the LORD, which *m* heaven and earth Ps 121:2 6213
the LORD, who *m* heaven and earth Ps 124:8 6213
they *m* long their furrows Ps 129:3
The LORD that *m* heaven and earth Ps 134:3 6213
him that by wisdom *m* the heavens Ps 136:5 6213
To him that *m* great lights Ps 136:7 6213
m Israel to pass through the Ps 136:14
I am fearfully and wonderfully *m* Ps 139:14
from thee, when I was *m* in secret Ps 139:15 6213
he hath *m* me to dwell in darkness Ps 143:3
Which *m* heaven, and earth, the sea Ps 146:6 6213
he hath *m* a decree which shall Ps 148:6 5414
Israel rejoice in him that *m* him Ps 149:2 6213
as yet he had not *m* the earth Prov 8:26 6213
The liberal soul shall be *m* fat Prov 11:25
of the diligent shall be *m* fat Prov 13:4
in the midst of fools is *m* known Prov 14:33
way of the righteous is *m* plain Prov 15:19
The LORD hath *m* all things for Prov 16:4 6466
I have *m* my heart clean, I am Prov 20:9
the LORD hath *m* even both of them Prov 20:12 6213
is punished, the simple is *m* wise Prov 21:11
I have *m* known to thee this day, Prov 22:19
trust in the LORD shall be *m* fat Prov 28:25
is crooked cannot be *m* straight Eccl 1:15
I *m* me great works Eccl 2:4
I *m* me gardens and orchards, and I Eccl 2:5 6213
I *m* me pools of water, to water Eccl 2:6 6213
He hath *m* every thing beautiful Eccl 3:11 6213
countenance the heart is *m* better Eccl 7:3
straight, which he hath *m* crooked Eccl 7:13

that God hath *m* man upright Eccl 7:29 6213
A feast is *m* for laughter, and Eccl 10:19 6213
they *m* me the keeper of the Song 1:6 7760
King Solomon *m* himself a chariot Song 3:9 6213
He *m* the pillars thereof of Song 3:10 6213
my soul *m* me like the chariots of Song 6:12 7760
which their own fingers have *m* Is 2:8 6213
haughtiness of men shall be *m* low Is 2:17 8213
which they *m* each one for himself Is 2:20 6213
also *m* a winepress therein Is 5:2 2672
wherein thou wast *m* to serve Is 14:3
man that *m* the earth to tremble Is 14:16
That *m* the world as a wilderness, Is 14:17 7760
I have *m* their vintage shouting Is 16:10
glory of Jacob shall be *m* thin Is 17:4
that which his fingers have *m* Is 17:8 6213
sighing thereof have I *m* to cease Is 21:2
Ye *m* also a ditch between the two Is 22:11 6213
For thou hast *m* of a city an heap Is 25:2 7760
m all their memory to perish Is 26:14
therefore he that *m* them will not Is 27:11 6213
We have *m* a covenant with death, Is 28:15 3772
for we have *m* lies our refuge, and Is 28:15 7760
lest your bands be *m* strong Is 28:22
When he hath *m* plain the face Is 28:25
of him that *m* it, He *m* me not Is 29:16 6213
he hath *m* it deep and large Is 30:33
hands have *m* unto you for a sin Is 31:7 6213
it is *m* fat with fatness, and with Is 34:6
their dust *m* fat with fatness Is 34:7
thou hast *m* heaven and earth Is 37:16 6213
mountain and hill shall be *m* low Is 40:4
the crooked shall be *m* straight Is 40:4
him, and *m* him rule over kings Is 41:2
yea, I have *m* him Is 43:7 6213
but thou hast *m* me to serve with Is 43:24
Thus saith the LORD that *m* thee Is 44:2 6213
I have *m* the earth, and created Is 45:12 6213
that formed the earth and *m* it Is 45:18 6213
I have *m*, and I will bear Is 46:4 6213
hath he *m* mention of my name Is 49:1
he hath *m* my mouth like a sharp Is 49:2 7760
hid me, and *m* me a polished shaft Is 49:2 7760
they that *m* thee waste shall go Is 49:17
that hath *m* the depths of the sea Is 51:10 7760
of man which shall be *m* as grass Is 51:12 5414
The LORD hath *m* bare his holy arm Is 52:10
he *m* his grave with the wicked, Is 53:9 5414
many, and *m* intercession for the Is 53:12
m thee a covenant with them Is 57:8 3772
me, and the souls which I have *m* Is 57:16 6213
they have *m* them crooked paths Is 59:8
why hast thou *m* us to err from Is 63:17
all those things hath mine hand *m* Is 66:2 6213
Shall the earth be *m* to bring Is 66:8
I have *m* thee this day a defenced Jer 1:18 5414
m mine heritage an abomination Jer 2:7 7760
yelled, and they *m* his land waste Jer 2:15 7896
thy gods that thou hast *m* thee Jer 2:28 6213
they have *m* their faces harder Jer 5:3
Lo, certainly in vain *m* he it Jer 8:8 6213
gods that have not *m* the heavens Jer 10:11 5648
He hath *m* the earth by his power, Jer 10:12 6213
have *m* his habitation desolate Jer 10:25
which I *m* with their fathers Jer 11:10 3772
they have *m* my pleasant portion a Jer 12:10 5414
They have *m* it desolate, and being Jer 12:11 7760
the whole land is *m* desolate Jer 12:11
discovered, and thy heels *m* bare Jer 13:22
wilt thou not be *m* clean Jer 13:27
for thou hast *m* all these things Jer 14:22 6213
but *m* their neck stiff, that they Jer 17:23
the vessel that he *m* of clay was Jer 18:4 6213
so he *m* it again another vessel, Jer 18:4 6213
that cannot be *m* whole again Jer 19:11 7495
the LORD was *m* a reproach unto me Jer 20:8 1961
m all the nations to drink, unto Jer 25:17
when Jeremiah had *m* an end of Jer 26:8
I have *m* the earth, the man and Jer 27:5 6213
The LORD hath *m* thee priest in Jer 29:26 5414
to the covenant that I *m* with Jer 31:32 3772
thou hast *m* the heaven and the Jer 32:17 6213
hast *m* thee a name, as at this Jer 32:20 6213
that the king Zedekiah had *m* a Jer 34:8 3772
I *m* a covenant with your fathers Jer 34:13 3772
ye had *m* a covenant before me in Jer 34:15 3772
which they had *m* before me Jer 34:18 3772
Gemariah had *m* intercession to Jer 36:25
m king in the land of Judah Jer 37:1
for they had *m* that the prison Jer 37:15 6213
that *m* us this soul, I will not Jer 38:16 6213
m governor over the cities of Jer 40:5
had *m* Gedaliah the son of Ahikam Jer 40:7
had *m* governor over the land Jer 41:2
had *m* for fear of Baasha king of Jer 41:9 6213
of Babylon *m* governor in the land Jer 41:18
that when Jeremiah had *m* an end Jer 43:1
and *m* drunk with their blood Jer 46:10
He *m* many to fall, yea, one fell Jer 46:16
But I have *m* Esau bare, I have Jer 49:10
that *m* all the earth drunken Jer 51:7
He hath *m* the earth by his power, Jer 51:15 6213
he hath *m* me an empty vessel, he Jer 51:34 3322
when thou hast *m* an end of Jer 51:63
which king Solomon had *m* in the Jer 52:20 6213
he hath *m* me desolate and faint Lam 1:13 5414
he hath *m* my strength to fall, Lam 1:14
they have *m* a noise in the house Lam 2:7 5414

therefore he *m* the rampart Lam 2:8
My flesh and my skin hath he *m* old Lam 3:4
he hath *m* my chain heavy Lam 3:7
he hath *m* my paths crooked Lam 3:9
he hath *m* me desolate Lam 3:11 7760
he hath *m* me drunken with Lam 3:15
Thou hast *m* us as the offscouring Lam 3:45 7760
I have *m* thy face strong against Eze 3:8 5414
than flint have I *m* thy forehead Eze 3:9 5414
I have *m* thee a watchman unto the Eze 3:17 5414
m desolate, and your idols may be Eze 6:6
but they *m* the images of their Eze 7:20 6213
neither *m* up the hedge for the Eze 13:5 1443
they have *m* others to hope that Eze 13:6
Because with lies ye have *m* the Eze 13:22
sad, whom I have not *m* sad Eze 13:22
hast *m* thee an high place in Eze 16:24 6213
hast *m* thy beauty to be abhorred, Eze 16:25
m a covenant with him, and hath Eze 17:13 3772
the king dwelleth that *m* him king Eze 17:16
have *m* the dry tree to flourish Eze 17:24
her whelps, and *m* him a young lion Eze 19:5 7760
m myself known unto them in the Eze 20:5
in whose sight I *m* myself known Eze 20:9
there also they *m* their sweet Eze 20:28 7760
it is *m* bright, it is wrapped up Eze 21:15 6213
he *m* his arrows bright, he Eze 21:21
Because ye have *m* your iniquity Eze 21:24
in thine idols which thou hast *m* Eze 22:4 6213
therefore have I *m* thee a Eze 22:4 5414
dishonest gain which thou hast *m* Eze 22:13 6213
they have *m* her many widows in Eze 22:25
into a city wherein is *m* a breach Eze 26:10
is *m* in the midst of thee Eze 26:15 2026
They have *m* all thy ship boards Eze 27:5 1129
of Bashan have they *m* thine oars Eze 27:6 6213
have *m* thy benches of ivory Eze 27:6 6213
they have *m* thy beauty perfect Eze 27:11 6213
m of cedar, among thy merchandise Eze 27:24
m very glorious in the midst of Eze 27:25
own, and I have *m* it for myself Eze 29:3 6213
The river is mine, and I have *m* it Eze 29:9 6213
every head was *m* bald, and every Eze 29:18
The waters *m* him great, the deep Eze 31:4
All the fowls of heaven *m* their Eze 31:6
I have *m* him fair by the Eze 31:9 6213
I *m* the nations to shake at the Eze 31:16
Because they have *m* you desolate Eze 36:3
their land, and none *m* them afraid Eze 39:26
He *m* also posts of threescore Eze 40:14 6213
a pavement *m* for the court round Eze 40:17 6213
it was *m* with cherubims and palm Eze 41:18 6213
it was *m* through all the house Eze 41:19 6213
were cherubims and palm trees *m* Eze 41:20 6213
And there were *m* on them, on the Eze 41:25 6213
like as were *m* upon the walls Eze 41:25 6213
Now when he had *m* an end of Eze 42:15
When thou hast *m* an end of Eze 43:23
it was *m* with boiling places Eze 46:23 6213
your houses shall be *m* a dunghill Dan 2:5 7761
Then Arioch *m* the thing known to Dan 2:15
m the thing known to Hananiah, Dan 2:17
hast *m* known unto me now what we Dan 2:23
for thou hast now *m* known unto us Dan 2:23
hath *m* thee ruler over them all Dan 2:38
the great God hath *m* known to the Dan 2:45
Then the king *m* Daniel a great Dan 2:48 7236
m him ruler over the whole Dan 2:48
the king *m* an image of gold Dan 3:1 5648
hast *m* a decree, that every man Dan 3:10 7761
worship the image which I have *m* Dan 3:15 5648
houses shall be *m* a dunghill Dan 3:29 7739
I saw a dream which *m* me afraid Dan 4:5
Therefore *m* I a decree to bring Dan 4:6 7761
Belshazzar the king *m* a great Dan 5:1 5648
m master of the magicians, Dan 5:11 6966
his heart was *m* like the beasts, Dan 5:21 7737
m a proclamation concerning him, Dan 5:29
m stand upon the feet as a man, Dan 7:4
m me know the interpretation of Dan 7:16
the same horn *m* war with the Dan 7:21 5648
which was *m* king over the realm Dan 9:1
m my confession, and said, O Lord, Dan 9:4
yet *m* we not our prayer before Dan 9:13
after the league *m* with him he Dan 11:23
be purified, and *m* white, and tried Dan 12:10
the tribes of Israel have I *m* Hos 5:9
of our king the princes have *m* Hos 7:5
For they have *m* ready their heart Hos 7:6
they have *m* princes, and I knew it Hos 8:4
their gold have they *m* them idols Hos 8:4 6213
the workman *m* it Hos 8:6 6213
Ephraim hath *m* many altars to sin Hos 8:11
land they have *m* goodly images Hos 10:1
wept, and *m* supplication unto him Hos 12:4
have *m* them molten images of Hos 13:2 6213
he hath *m* it clean bare, and cast Joel 1:7
the branches thereof are *m* white Joel 1:7
flocks of sheep are *m* desolate Joel 1:18
I have *m* the stink of your camps Amos 4:10
god, which ye *m* to yourselves Amos 5:26 6213
that when they had *m* an end of Amos 7:2
upon a wall *m* by a plumbline Amos 7:7
I have *m* thee small among the Obad 2 5414
of heaven, which hath *m* the sea Jonah 1:9 6213
unto the LORD, and *m* vows Jonah 1:16 5087
there *m* him a booth, and sat under Jonah 4:5 6213
m it to come up over Jonah, that Jonah 4:6

shield of his mighty men is *m* red Nah 2:3
whelp, and none *m* them afraid Nah 2:11
which *m* them afraid, because of Hab 2:17
Thy bow was *m* quite naked Hab 3:9
I *m* their streets waste, that Zeph 3:6
they *m* their hearts as an adamant Zec 7:12 7760
m thee as the sword of a mighty Zec 9:13 7760
hath *m* them as his goodly horse Zec 10:3 7760
which I had *m* with all the people Zec 11:10 3772
have I also *m* you contemptible Mal 2:9 5414
that these stones be *m* bread Mt 4:3 *1096*
garment, and the rent is *m* worse Mt 9:16 *1096*
thy faith hath *m* thee whole Mt 9:22 *4982*
the woman was *m* whole from that Mt 9:22 *4982*
when Jesus had *m* an end of Mt 11:1 *5055*
as touched were *m* perfectly whole Mt 14:36 *1295*
Thus have ye *m* the commandment of Mt 15:6 *208*
her daughter was *m* whole from Mt 15:28 *2390*
that he had, and payment to be *m* Mt 18:25 *591*
that he which *m* them at the Mt 19:4 *4160*
them at the beginning *m* them male Mt 19:4 *4160*
which were *m* eunuchs of men Mt 19:12 *2134*
which have *m* themselves eunuchs Mt 19:12 *2134*
thou hast *m* them equal unto us, Mt 20:12 *4160*
but ye have *m* it a den of thieves Mt 21:13 *4160*
which *m* a marriage for his son, Mt 22:2 *4160*
But they *m* light of it, and went Mt 22:5 *272*
one proselyte, and when he is *m* Mt 23:15 *1096*
whom his lord hath *m* ruler over Mt 24:45 *2525*
And at midnight there was a cry *m* Mt 25:6 *1096*
m them other five talents Mt 25:16 *4160*
they *m* ready the passover Mt 26:19 *2090*
but that rather a tumult was *m* Mt 27:24 *1096*
be *m* sure until the third day Mt 27:64 *805*
m the sepulchre sure, sealing the Mt 27:66 *805*
the old, and the rent is *m* worse Mk 2:21 *1096*
them, The sabbath was *m* for man Mk 2:27 *1096*
thy faith hath *m* thee whole Mk 5:34 *4982*
birthday *m* a supper to his lords Mk 6:21 *4160*
many as touched him were *m* whole Mk 6:56 *4982*
upon his eyes, and *m* him look up Mk 8:25 *4160*
of the creation God *m* them male Mk 10:6 *4160*
thy faith hath *m* thee whole Mk 10:52 *4982*
but ye have *m* it a den of thieves Mk 11:17 *4160*
was this waste of the ointment *m* Mk 14:4 *1096*
they *m* ready the passover Mk 14:16 *2090*
this temple that is *m* with hands Mk 14:58 *5499*
build another *m* without hands Mk 14:58 *886*
that had *m* insurrection with him Mk 15:7 *4955*
they *m* signs to his father, how Lk 1:62 *1770*
this taxing was first *m* when Lk 2:2 *1096*
the Lord hath *m* known unto us Lk 2:15 *1107*
they *m* known abroad the saying Lk 2:17 *1232*
the crooked shall be *m* straight Lk 3:5 *1519*
the rough ways shall be *m* smooth Lk 3:5 *1519*
this stone that it be *m* bread Lk 4:3 *1096*
Levi *m* him a great feast in his Lk 5:29 *4160*
that shall not be *m* manifest Lk 8:17 *1096*
thy faith hath *m* thee whole Lk 8:48 *4982*
only, and she shall be *m* whole Lk 8:50 *4982*
did so, and *m* them all sit down Lk 9:15 *347*
did not he that *m* that which is Lk 11:40 *4160*
who *m* me a judge or a divider Lk 12:14 *2525*
and immediately she was *m* straight Lk 13:13 *461*
again, and a recompence be *m* thee Lk 14:12 *1096*
A certain man *m* a great supper, Lk 14:16 *4160*
thy faith hath *m* thee whole Lk 17:19 *4982*
he *m* haste, and came down, and Lk 19:6 *4692*
but ye have *m* it a den of thieves Lk 19:46 *4160*
they *m* ready the passover Lk 22:13 *2090*
Herod were *m* friends together Lk 23:12 *1096*
a certain sedition *m* in the city Lk 23:19 *1096*
of our company *m* us astonished Lk 24:22 *1839*
he *m* as though he would have gone Lk 24:28 *4364*
All things were *m* by him Jn 1:3 *1096*
was not any thing *m* that was *m* Jn 1:3 *1096*
world, and the world was *m* by him Jn 1:10 *1096*
And the Word was *m* flesh, and dwelt Jn 1:14 *1096*
he should be *m* manifest to Israel Jn 1:31 *1096*
tasted the water that was *m* wine Jn 2:9 *1096*
when he had *m* a scourge of small Jn 2:15 *4160*
that his deeds may be *m* manifest Jn 3:21 *5319*
Pharisees had heard that Jesus *m* Jn 4:1 *4160*
where he *m* the water wine Jn 4:46 *4160*
of the water stepped in was *m* Jn 5:4 *1096*
unto him, Wilt thou be *m* whole Jn 5:6 *1096*
immediately the man was *m* whole Jn 5:9 *1096*
He that *m* me whole, the same said Jn 5:11 *4160*
him, Behold, thou art *m* whole Jn 5:14 *1096*
was Jesus, which had *m* him whole Jn 5:15 *4160*
because I have *m* a man every whit Jn 7:23 *4160*
sayest thou, Ye shall be *m* free Jn 8:33 *1096*
God should be *m* manifest in him Jn 9:3
m clay of the spittle, and he Jn 9:6 *4160*
A man that is called Jesus *m* clay Jn 9:11 *4160*
sabbath day when Jesus *m* the clay Jn 9:14 *4160*
they which see might be *m* blind Jn 9:39 *1096*
There they *m* him a supper Jn 12:2 *4160*
my Father I have *m* known unto you Jn 15:15 *1107*
that they may be *m* perfect in one Jn 17:23 *5048*
who had *m* a fire of coals Jn 18:18 *4160*
because he *m* himself the Son of Jn 19:7 *4160*
m four parts, to every soldier a Jn 19:23 *4160*
The former treatise have I *m* Acts 1:1 *4160*
Thou hast *m* known to me the ways Acts 2:28 *1107*
that God hath *m* that same Jesus, Acts 2:36 *4160*
we had *m* this man to walk Acts 3:12 *4160*
his name hath *m* this man strong Acts 3:16 *4732*

which God *m* with our fathers ... Acts 3:25 1303
man, by what means he is *m* whole ... Acts 4:9 4982
thou art God, which hast *m* heaven ... Acts 4:24 4160
distribution was *m* unto every man ... Acts 4:35 1239
he *m* him governor over Egypt and ... Acts 7:10 2525
was *m* known to his brethren ... Acts 7:13 319
kindred was *m* known unto Pharaoh ... Acts 7:13 1096
Who *m* thee a ruler and a judge ... Acts 7:27 2525
Who *m* thee a ruler and a judge ... Acts 7:35 2525
they *m* a calf in those days, and ... Acts 7:41 3447
which ye *m* to worship them ... Acts 7:43 4160
not in temples *m* with hands ... Acts 7:48 5499
not my hand *m* all these things ... Acts 7:50 4160
m great lamentation over him ... Acts 8:2 4160
he *m* havock of the church, ... Acts 8:3 1096
coats and garments which Dorcas *m* ... Acts 9:39 4160
but while they *m* ready, he fell ... Acts 10:10 3903
had *m* enquiry for Simon's house ... Acts 10:17 1239
but prayer was *m* without ceasing ... Acts 12:5 1096
having *m* Blastus the king's ... Acts 12:20 3982
throne, and *m* an oration unto them ... Acts 12:21 1215
which was *m* unto the fathers ... Acts 13:32 1096
m their minds evil affected ... Acts 14:2 2559
an assault *m* both of the Gentiles ... Acts 14:5 1096
which *m* heaven, and earth, and the ... Acts 14:15 4160
while ago God *m* choice among us ... Acts 15:7 1586
where prayer was wont to be *m* ... Acts 16:13 1511
m their feet fast in the stocks ... Acts 16:24 805
God that *m* the world and all ... Acts 17:24 4160
not in temples *m* with hands ... Acts 17:24 5499
hath *m* of one blood all nations ... Acts 17:26 4160
the Jews *m* insurrection with one ... Acts 18:12 2721
which *m* silver shrines for Diana, ... Acts 19:24 4160
no gods, which are *m* with hands ... Acts 19:26 1096
would have *m* his defence unto the ... Acts 19:33 626
Holy Ghost hath *m* you overseers ... Acts 20:28 5087
when there was *m* a great silence, ... Acts 21:40 1096
as I *m* my journey, and was come ... Acts 22:6 4198
forty which had *m* this conspiracy ... Acts 23:13 4160
promise *m* of God unto our fathers ... Acts 26:6 1096
to the wind, and *m* toward shore ... Acts 27:40 2722
which was *m* of the seed of David ... Rom 1:3 1096
by the things that are *m*, even ... Rom 1:20 4161
image *m* like to corruptible man ... Rom 1:23
circumcision is *m* uncircumcision ... Rom 2:25 1096
the law be heirs, faith is *m* void ... Rom 4:14 2758
the promise *m* of none effect ... Rom 4:14 2673
I have *m* thee a father of many ... Rom 4:17 5087
disobedience many were *m* sinners ... Rom 5:19 2525
of one shall many be *m* righteous ... Rom 5:19 2525
Being then *m* free from sin, ye ... Rom 6:18 1659
But now being *m* free from sin ... Rom 6:22 1659
which is good *m* death unto me ... Rom 7:13 1096
m me free from the law of sin ... Rom 8:2 1659
creature was *m* subject to vanity ... Rom 8:20 5293
it, Why hast thou *m* me thus ... Rom 9:20 4160
been *m* like unto Gomorrha ... Rom 9:29 3666
confession is *m* unto salvation ... Rom 10:10 3670
I was *m* manifest unto them that ... Rom 10:20 1096
Let their table be *m* a snare ... Rom 11:9 1096
or is offended, or is *m* weak ... Rom 14:21 770
the promises *m* unto the fathers ... Rom 15:8
m partakers of their spiritual ... Rom 15:27 2841
But now is *m* manifest, and by the ... Rom 16:26 5319
m known to all nations for the ... Rom 16:26 1107
Christ should be *m* of none effect ... 1Cor 1:17 2758
hath not God *m* foolish the wisdom ... 1Cor 1:20 3471
who of God is *m* unto us wisdom, ... 1Cor 1:30 1096
man's work shall be *m* manifest ... 1Cor 3:13 1096
for we are *m* a spectacle unto the ... 1Cor 4:9 1096
we are *m* as the filth of the ... 1Cor 4:13 1096
but if thou mayest be *m* free ... 1Cor 7:21 1096
yet have I *m* myself servant unto ... 1Cor 9:19 1402
I am *m* all things to all men, ... 1Cor 9:22 1096
may be *m* manifest among you ... 1Cor 11:19 1096
have been all *m* to drink into one ... 1Cor 12:13 4222
secrets of his heart *m* manifest ... 1Cor 14:25 1096
so in Christ shall all be *m* alive ... 1Cor 15:22 2227
man Adam was *m* a living soul ... 1Cor 15:45 1096
the last Adam was *m* a quickening ... 1Cor 15:45
the same which is *m* sorry by me ... 2Cor 2:2 3076
Who also hath *m* us able ministers ... 2Cor 3:6 2427
For even that which was *m* ... 2Cor 3:10 1392
might be *m* manifest in our body ... 2Cor 4:10 5319
be *m* manifest in our mortal flesh ... 2Cor 4:11 5319
of God, an house not *m* with hands ... 2Cor 5:1 886
but we are *m* manifest unto God ... 2Cor 5:11 5319
I trust also are *m* manifest in ... 2Cor 5:11 5319
For he hath *m* him to be sin for ... 2Cor 5:21 4160
that we might be *m* the ... 2Cor 5:21 1096
For though I *m* you sorry with a ... 2Cor 7:8 3076
the same epistle hath *m* you sorry ... 2Cor 7:8 3076
rejoice, not that ye were *m* sorry ... 2Cor 7:9 3076
for ye were *m* sorry after a godly ... 2Cor 7:9 3076
which I *m* before Titus, is found ... 2Cor 7:14
of things *m* ready to our hand ... 2Cor 10:16 2092
m manifest among you in all ... 2Cor 11:6 5319
for my strength is *m* perfect in ... 2Cor 12:9 5048
are ye now *m* perfect by the flesh ... Gal 3:3 2005
the law, being *m* a curse for us ... Gal 3:13 1096
and his seed were the promises *m* ... Gal 3:16 4483
come to whom the promise was *m* ... Gal 3:19 1861
m of a woman, *m* under the law, ... Gal 4:4 1096
wherewith Christ hath *m* us free ... Gal 5:1 1659
wherein he hath *m* us accepted in ... Eph 1:6 5487
Having *m* known unto us the ... Eph 1:9 1107
m us sit together in heavenly ... Eph 2:6 4776
in the flesh *m* by hands ... Eph 2:11 5499
are *m* nigh by the blood of Christ ... Eph 2:13 1096
is our peace, who hath *m* both one ... Eph 2:14 4160
he *m* known unto me the mystery ... Eph 3:3 1107
not *m* known unto the sons of men ... Eph 3:5 1107
Whereof I was *m* a minister ... Eph 3:7 1096
are *m* manifest by the light ... Eph 5:13 5319
But *m* himself of no reputation, ... Phil 2:7 1096
was *m* in the likeness of men ... Phil 2:7 1096
being *m* conformable unto his ... Phil 3:10 4832
your requests be *m* known unto God ... Phil 4:6 1107
which hath *m* us meet to be ... Col 1:12 2427
having *m* peace through the blood ... Col 1:20 1517
whereof I Paul am *m* a minister ... Col 1:23 1096
Whereof I am *m* a minister ... Col 1:25 1096
but now is *m* manifest to his ... Col 1:26 5319
the circumcision *m* without hands ... Col 2:11 1096
he *m* a shew of them openly, ... Col 2:15 1165
law is not *m* for a righteous man ... 1Ti 1:9 2749
concerning faith have *m* shipwreck ... 1Ti 1:19 3489
of thanks, be *m* for all men ... 1Ti 2:1 4160
But is now *m* manifest by the ... 2Ti 1:10 5319
we should be *m* heirs according to ... Titus 3:7 1096
by whom also he *m* the worlds ... Heb 1:2 4160
Being *m* so much better than the ... Heb 1:4 1096
who was *m* a little lower than the ... Heb 2:9 1642
to be *m* like unto his brethren ... Heb 2:17 3666
For we are *m* partakers of Christ, ... Heb 3:14 1096
himself to be *m* an high priest ... Heb 5:5 1096
being *m* perfect, he became the ... Heb 5:9 5048
were *m* partakers of the Holy ... Heb 6:4 1096
For when God *m* promise to Abraham ... Heb 6:13 1861
m an high priest for ever after ... Heb 6:20 1096
but *m* like unto the Son of God ... Heb 7:3 871
there is *m* of necessity a change ... Heb 7:12 1096
Who is *m*, not after the law of a ... Heb 7:16 1096
For the law *m* nothing perfect, ... Heb 7:19 5048
without an oath he was *m* priest ... Heb 7:20
priests were *m* without an oath ... Heb 7:21 1096
By so much was Jesus *m* a surety ... Heb 7:22 1096
m higher than the heavens ... Heb 7:26 1096
that I *m* with their fathers ... Heb 8:9 4160
covenant, he hath *m* the first old ... Heb 8:13 3822
For there was a tabernacle *m* ... Heb 9:2 2680
of all was not yet *m* manifest ... Heb 9:8 5319
not *m* with hands, that is to say, ... Heb 9:11 5499
into the holy places *m* with hands ... Heb 9:24 5499
again *m* of sins every year ... Heb 10:3
his enemies be *m* his footstool ... Heb 10:13 5087
whilst ye were *m* a gazingstock ... Heb 10:33 2301
not *m* of things which do appear ... Heb 11:3 1096
m mention of the departing of the ... Heb 11:22 3421
out of weakness were *m* strong ... Heb 11:34 1743
us should not be *m* perfect ... Heb 11:40 5048
the spirits of just men *m* perfect ... Heb 12:23 5048
shaken, as of things that are *m* ... Heb 12:27 4160
But the rich, in that he is *m* low ... Jas 1:10 5014
and by works was faith *m* perfect ... Jas 2:22 5048
which are *m* after the similitude ... Jas 3:9 1096
the same is *m* the head of the ... 1Pet 2:7 1096
powers being *m* subject unto him ... 1Pet 3:22 5293
when we *m* known unto you the ... 2Pet 1:16 1107
m to be taken and destroyed, speak ... 2Pet 2:12 1080
that they might be *m* manifest ... 1Jn 2:19 5319
Herein is our love *m* perfect ... 1Jn 4:17 5048
feareth is not *m* perfect in love ... 1Jn 4:18 5048
not God hath *m* him a liar ... 1Jn 5:10 4160
hath *m* us kings and priests unto ... Rev 1:6 4160
hast *m* us unto our God kings and ... Rev 5:10 4160
m them white in the blood of the ... Rev 7:14 3021
because they were *m* bitter ... Rev 8:11 4087
and worship him that *m* heaven ... Rev 14:7 4160
because she *m* all nations drink ... Rev 14:8 4222
for thy judgments are *m* manifest ... Rev 15:4 5319
of the earth have been *m* drunk ... Rev 17:2 3182
which were *m* rich by her, shall ... Rev 18:15 4147
wherein were *m* rich all that had ... Rev 18:19 4147
for in one hour is she *m* desolate ... Rev 18:19 2049
and his wife hath *m* herself ready ... Rev 19:7 2090

MADEST {10}
m a covenant with him to give the ... Neh 9:8 3772
m known unto them thy holy ... Neh 9:14 3045
Thou *m* him to have dominion over ... Ps 8:6
that thou *m* strong for thyself ... Ps 80:15
whom thou *m* strong for thyself ... Ps 80:17
m to thyself images of men, and ... Eze 16:17 6213
m all their loins to be at a ... Eze 29:7
not laboured, neither *m* it grow ... Jonah 4:10
before these days *m* an uproar ... Acts 21:38 387
Thou *m* him a little lower than ... Heb 2:7 1642

MADIAN *(ma'-de-an)* {1} See MIDIAN. *Same as Midian 2.*
was a stranger in the land of *M* ... Acts 7:29 3099

MADMANNAH *(mad-man'-nah)* {2}
1. A city in Judah.
And Ziklag, and *M*, and Sansannah, ... Josh 15:31 4089
2. Grandson of Caleb.
bare also Shaaph the father of *M* ... 1Chr 2:49 4089

MADMEN *(mad'-men)* {1} See MADMENAH. *A Moabite city.*
Also thou shalt be cut down, O *M* ... Jer 48:2 4086

MADMENAH *(mad-me'-nah)* {1} See MADMEN. *A city in Benjamin.*
M is removed ... Is 10:31 4088

MADNESS {9}
The LORD shall smite thee with *m* ... Deut 28:28 7697
to know wisdom, and to know *m* ... Eccl 1:17 1947
myself to behold wisdom, and *m* ... Eccl 2:12 1947
folly, even of foolishness and *m* ... Eccl 7:25 1947
m is in their heart while they ... Eccl 9:3 1947
end of his talk is mischievous *m* ... Eccl 10:13 1948
astonishment, and his rider with *m* ... Zec 12:4 7697
And they were filled with *m* ... Lk 6:11 454
voice forbad the *m* of the prophet ... 2Pet 2:16 3913

MADON *(ma'-don)* {2} *A Canaanite city.*
that he sent to Jobab king of *M* ... Josh 11:1 4068
The king of *M*, one ... Josh 12:19 4068

MAGADAN See MAGDALA.

MAGBISH *(mag'-bish)* {1} *A family of exiles.*
The children of *M*, an hundred ... Ezr 2:30 4019

MAGDALA *(mag'-da-lah)* {1} See MAGDALENE. *A city in Galilee.*
and came into the coasts of *M* ... Mt 15:39 3093

MAGDALENE *(mag'-da-leen)* {12} *A woman acquaintance of Jesus.*
Among which was Mary *M*, and Mary ... Mt 27:56 3094
And there was Mary *M*, and the other ... Mt 27:61 3094
day of the week, came Mary *M* ... Mt 28:1 3094
among whom was Mary *M*, and Mary ... Mk 15:40 3094
And Mary *M* and Mary the mother of ... Mk 15:47 3094
when the sabbath was past, Mary *M* ... Mk 16:1 3094
week, he appeared first to Mary *M* ... Mk 16:9 3094
and infirmities, Mary called *M* ... Lk 8:2 3094
It was Mary *M*, and Joanna, and Mary ... Lk 24:10 3094
the wife of Cleophas, and Mary *M* ... Jn 19:25 3094
of the week cometh Mary *M* early ... Jn 20:1 3094
Mary *M* came and told the disciples ... Jn 20:18 3094

MAGDIEL *(mag'-de-el)* {2} *A duke of Edom.*
Duke *M*, duke Iram ... Gen 36:43 4025
Duke *M*, duke Iram ... 1Chr 1:54 4025

MAGICIAN {1}
that asked such things at any *m* ... Dan 2:10 2749

MAGICIANS {15}
and called for all the *m* of Egypt ... Gen 41:8 2748
and I told this unto the *m* ... Gen 41:24 2748
now the *m* of Egypt, they also did ... Ex 7:11 2748
the *m* of Egypt did so with their ... Ex 7:22 2748
And the *m* did so with their ... Ex 8:7 2748
And the *m* did so with their ... Ex 8:18 2748
Then the *m* said unto Pharaoh, ... Ex 8:19 2748
the *m* could not stand before ... Ex 9:11 2748
for the boil was upon the *m* ... Ex 9:11 2748
ten times better than all the *m* ... Dan 1:20 2748
the king commanded to call the *m* ... Dan 2:2 2748
wise men, the astrologers, the *m* ... Dan 2:27 2749
Then came in the *m*, the ... Dan 4:7 2749
O Belteshazzar, master of the *m* ... Dan 4:9 2749
thy father, made master of the *m* ... Dan 5:11 2749

MAGISTRATE {2}
and there was no *m* in the land ... Judg 18:7 3423,6114
with thine adversary to the *m* ... Lk 12:58 758

MAGISTRATES {8}
God, that is in thine hand, set *m* ... Ezr 7:25 8200
unto the synagogues, and unto *m*, ... Lk 12:11 746
And brought them to the *m*, saying, ... Acts 16:20 4755
the *m* rent off their clothes, and ... Acts 16:22 4755
the *m* sent the serjeants, saying, ... Acts 16:35 4755
The *m* have sent to let you go ... Acts 16:36 4755
told these words unto the *m* ... Acts 16:38 4755
and powers, to obey *m*, to be ready ... Titus 3:1 3980

MAGNIFICAL {1}
for the LORD must be exceeding *m* ... 1Chr 22:5 1431

MAGNIFICENCE {1}
her *m* should be destroyed, whom ... Acts 19:27 3168

MAGNIFIED {21}
sight, and thou hast *m* thy mercy ... Gen 19:19 1431
On that day the LORD *m* Joshua in ... Josh 4:14 1431
And let thy name be *m* for ever ... 2Sa 7:26 1431
that thy name may be *m* for ever ... 1Chr 17:24 1431
the LORD *m* Solomon exceedingly in ... 1Chr 29:25 1431
with him, and *m* him exceedingly ... 2Chr 1:1 1431
so that he was *m* in the sight of ... 2Chr 32:23 5375
continually, Let the LORD be *m* ... Ps 35:27 1431
say continually, The LORD be *m* ... Ps 40:16 1431
say continually, Let God be *m* ... Ps 70:4 1431
for thou hast *m* thy word above ... Ps 138:2 1431
for he *m* himself against the LORD ... Jer 48:26 1431
because he hath *m* himself against ... Jer 48:42 1431
for the enemy hath *m* himself ... Lam 1:9 1431
he *m* himself even to the prince ... Dan 8:11 1431
m themselves against their border ... Zeph 2:8 1431
m themselves against the people ... Zeph 2:10 1431
The LORD will be *m* from the ... Mal 1:5 1431
but the people *m* them ... Acts 5:13 3170
the name of the Lord Jesus was *m* ... Acts 19:17 3170
also Christ shall be *m* in my body ... Phil 1:20 3170

MAGNIFY {19}
This day will I begin to *m* thee ... Josh 3:7 1431
is man, that thou shouldest *m* him ... Job 7:17 1431
If indeed ye will *m* yourselves ... Job 19:5 1431
Remember that thou *m* his work ... Job 36:24 7679
O *m* the LORD with me, and let us ... Ps 34:3 1431
dishonour that *m* themselves ... Ps 35:26 1431
they *m* themselves against me ... Ps 38:16 1431
me that did *m* himself against me ... Ps 55:12 1431
will *m* him with thanksgiving ... Ps 69:30 1431
or shall the saw *m* itself against ... Is 10:15 1431
he will *m* the law, and make it ... Is 42:21 1431
Thus will I *m* myself, and sanctify ... Eze 38:23 1431
he shall *m* himself in his heart, ... Dan 8:25 1431
m himself above every god, and ... Dan 11:36 1431

for he shall *m* himself above all ... Dan 11:37 1431
do not *m* themselves against Judah ... Zec 12:7 1431
said, My soul doth *m* the Lord ... Lk 1:46 *3170*
them speak with tongues, and *m* God ... Acts 10:46 *3170*
of the Gentiles, I *m* mine office ... Rom 11:13 *1392*

MAGOG *(ma'-gog)* {5}
1. A son of Japheth.
Gomer, and *M*, and Madai, and Javan, ... Gen 10:2 4031
Gomer, and *M*, and Madai, and Javan, ... 1Chr 1:5 4031
2. Descendants of Magog.
face against Gog, the land of *M* ... Eze 38:2 4031
And I will send a fire on *M* ... Eze 39:6 4031
quarters of the earth, Gog and *M* ... Rev 20:8 *3098*

MAGOR-MISSABIB *(ma'-gor-mis'-sa-bib)* {1} *A symbolic name of Pashur.*
not called thy name Pashur, but *M* ... Jer 20:3 4036

MAGPIASH *(mag'-pe-ash)* {1} *A chief Israelite who renewed the covenant.*
M, Meshullam, Hezir, ... Neh 10:20 4047

MAHALAH *(ma'-ha-lah)* {1} See MAHLAH. *Great-grandson of Manasseh.*
bare Ishod, and Abiezer, and *M* ... 1Chr 7:18 4244

MAHALALEEL *(ma-hal'-a-le-el)* {7} See MALELEEL.
1. Son of Cainan.
lived seventy years, and begat *M* ... Gen 5:12 4111
after he begat *M* eight hundred ... Gen 5:13 4111
M lived sixty and five years, and ... Gen 5:15 4111
M lived after he begat Jared ... Gen 5:16 4111
all the days of *M* were eight ... Gen 5:17 4111
Kenan, *M*, Jered, ... 1Chr 1:2 4111
2. A family of exiles.
son of Shephatiah, the son of *M* ... Neh 11:4 4111

MAHALALEL See MAHALEEL.

MAHALATH *(ma'-ha-lath)* {4} See BASHEMATH.
1. A daughter of Ishmael.
he had *M* the daughter of Ishmael ... Gen 28:9 4258
2. A granddaughter of David.
Rehoboam took him *M* the daughter ... 2Chr 11:18 4258
3. A musical choir.
To the chief Musician upon *M* ... Ps 53:*t* 4257
chief Musician upon *M* Leannoth ... Ps 88:*t* 4257

MAHALI *(ma'-ha-li)* {1} See MAHLI. *Same as Mahli 1.*
sons of Merari; *M* and Mushi ... Ex 6:19 4249

MAHANAIM *(ma-ha-na'-im)* {13} *A town east of the Jordan.*
called the name of that place *M* ... Gen 32:2 4266
from *M* unto the border of Debir ... Josh 13:26 4266
And their coast was from *M* ... Josh 13:30 4266
and *M* with her suburbs, ... Josh 21:38 4266
of Saul, and brought him over to *M* ... 2Sa 2:8 4266
Saul, went out from *M* to Gibeon ... 2Sa 2:12 4266
all Bithron, and they came to *M* ... 2Sa 2:29 4266
Then David came to *M* ... 2Sa 17:24 4266
to pass, when David was come to *M* ... 2Sa 17:27 4266
of sustenance while he lay at *M* ... 2Sa 19:32 4266
curse in the day when I went to *M* ... 1Kin 2:8 4266
Ahinadab the son of Iddo had *M* ... 1Kin 4:14 4266
suburbs, and *M* with her suburbs, ... 1Chr 6:80 4266

MAHANEH-DAN *(ma'-ha-neh-dan)* {1} *A place in Judah.*
called that place *M* unto this day ... Judg 18:12 4265

MAHARAI *(ma'-ha-rahee)* {3} *A warrior of David.*
the Ahohite, *M* the Netophathite, ... 2Sa 23:28 4121
M the Netophathite, Heled the son ... 1Chr 11:30 4121
month was *M* the Netophathite ... 1Chr 27:13 4121

MAHATH *(ma'-hath)* {3}
1. A descendant of Kohath.
the son of Elkanah, the son of *M* ... 1Chr 6:35 4287
M the son of Amasai, and Joel the ... 2Chr 29:12 4287
2. A Temple servant.
and Eliel, and Ismachiah, and *M* ... 2Chr 31:13 4287

MAHAVITE *(ma'-ha-vite)* {1} *Family name of Eliel.*
Eliel the *M*, and Jeribai, and ... 1Chr 11:46 4233

MAHAZIOTH *(ma-ha'-ze-oth)* {2} *A sanctuary servant.*
Mallothi, Hothir, and *M* ... 1Chr 25:4 4238
The three and twentieth to *M* ... 1Chr 25:30 4238

MAHER-SHALAL-HASH-BAZ *(ma'-her-sha'-lal-hash'-baz)* {2} *A son of Isaiah.*
it with a man's pen concerning *M* ... Is 8:1 4122
the LORD to me, Call his name *M* ... Is 8:3 4122

MAHLAH *(mah'-lah)* {4} *A daughter of Zelophehad.*
daughters of Zelophehad were *M* ... Num 26:33 4244
M, Noah, and Hoglah, and Milcah ... Num 27:1 4244
For *M*, Tirzah, and Hoglah, and ... Num 36:11 4244
are the names of his daughters, *M* ... Josh 17:3 4244

MAHLI *(mah'-li)* {11} See MAHALI, MAHLITES.
1. Son of Merari.
their families; *M*, and Mushi ... Num 3:20 4249
of Merari; *M*, and Mushi ... 1Chr 6:19 4249
M, Libni his son, Shimei his son, ... 1Chr 6:29 4249
M, and Mushi. The sons of *M* ... 1Chr 23:21 4249
The sons of Merari were *M* ... 1Chr 24:26 4249
Of *M* came Eleazar, who had no ... 1Chr 24:28 4249
understanding, of the sons of *M* ... Ezr 8:18 4249
2. Son of Mushi.
The son of *M*, the son of Mushi, ... 1Chr 6:47 4249
M, and Eder, and Jeremoth, three ... 1Chr 23:23 4249
M, and Eder, and Jerimoth ... 1Chr 24:30 4249

MAHLITES *(mah'-lites)* {2} *Descendants of Mahli 1.*
Of Merari was the family of the *M* ... Num 3:33 4250
Hebronites, the family of the *M* ... Num 26:58 4250

MAHLON *(mah'-lon)* {3} See MAHLON'S. *A son of Naomi.*
and the name of his two sons *M* ... Ruth 1:2 4248
And *M* and Chilion died also both of ... Ruth 1:5 4248
Ruth the Moabitess, the wife of *M* ... Ruth 4:10 4248

MAHLON'S *(mah'-lons)* {1}
and all that was Chilion's and *M* ... Ruth 4:9 4248

MAHOL *(ma'-hol)* {1} *Father of some wise men.*
Chalcol, and Darda, the sons of *M* ... 1Kin 4:31 4235

MAHSEIAH See MASEIAH.

MAID {36}
I pray thee, go in unto my *m* ... Gen 16:2 8198
took Hagar her *m* the Egyptian ... Gen 16:3 8198
I have given my *m* into thy bosom ... Gen 16:5 8198
Behold, thy *m* is in thy hand ... Gen 16:6 8198
And he said, Hagar, Sarai's *m* ... Gen 16:8 8198
Leah Zilpah his *m* for an handmaid ... Gen 29:24 8198
Bilhah his handmaid to be her *m* ... Gen 29:29 8198
And she said, Behold my *m* Bilhah ... Gen 30:3 519
Bilhah Rachel's *m* conceived again ... Gen 30:7 8198
bearing, she took Zilpah her *m* ... Gen 30:9 8198
Zilpah Leah's *m* bare Jacob a son ... Gen 30:10 8198
Zilpah Leah's *m* bare Jacob a ... Gen 30:12 8198
flags, she sent her *m* to fetch it ... Ex 2:5 519
the *m* went and called the child's ... Ex 2:8 5959
a man smite his servant, or his *m* ... Ex 21:20 519
his servant, or the eye of his *m* ... Ex 21:26 519
if a man entice a *m* that is not ... Ex 22:16 1330
But if she bear a *m* child ... Lev 12:5 5347
and for thy servant, and for thy *m* ... Lev 25:6 519
came to her, I found her not a *m* ... Deut 22:14 1331
I found not thy daughter a *m* ... Deut 22:17 1331
of the land of Israel a little *m* ... 2Kin 5:2 5291
thus said the *m* that is of the ... 2Kin 5:4 5291
the *m* was fair and beautiful ... Est 2:7 5291
why then should I think upon a *m* ... Job 31:1 1330
and the way of a man with a *m* ... Prov 30:19 5959
as with the *m*, so with her ... Is 24:2 8198
Can a *m* forget her ornaments, or ... Jer 2:32 1330
in pieces the young man and the *m* ... Jer 51:22 1330
father will go in unto the same *m* ... Amos 2:7 5291
for the *m* is not dead, but ... Mt 9:24 *2877*
her by the hand, and the *m* arose ... Mt 9:25 *2877*
into the porch, another *m* saw him ... Mt 26:71
a *m* saw him again, and began to ... Mk 14:69 *3814*
by the hand, and called, saying, *M* ... Lk 8:54 *3816*
But a certain *m* beheld him as he ... Lk 22:56 *3814*

MAIDEN {8}
I have given my *m* to my husband ... Gen 30:18 8198
Behold, here is my daughter a *m* ... Judg 19:24 1330
no compassion upon young man or *m* ... 2Chr 36:17 1330
let the *m* which pleaseth the king ... Est 2:4 5291
the *m* pleased him, and she ... Est 2:9 5291
thus came every *m* unto the king ... Est 2:13 5291
as the eyes of a *m* unto the hand ... Ps 123:2 8198
the father and the mother of the *m* ... Lk 8:51 *3816*

MAIDENS {18}
her *m* walked along by the river's ... Ex 2:5 5291
but abide here fast by my *m* ... Ruth 2:8 5291
that thou go out with his *m* ... Ruth 2:22 5291
So she kept fast by the *m* of Boaz ... Ruth 2:23 5291
kindred, with whose *m* thou wast ... Ruth 3:2 5291
they found young *m* going out to ... 1Sa 9:11 5291
when many *m* were gathered ... Est 2:8 5291
as belonged to her, and seven *m* ... Est 2:9 5291
I also and my *m* will fast likewise ... Est 4:16 5291
or wilt thou bind him for thy *m* ... Job 41:5 5291
their *m* were not given to ... Ps 78:63 1330
Both young men, and *m* ... Ps 148:12 1330
She hath sent forth her *m* ... Prov 9:3 5291
and for the maintenance for thy *m* ... Prov 27:27 5291
household, and a portion to her *m* ... Prov 31:15 5291
I got me servants and *m*, and had ... Eccl 2:7 8198
but they shall take *m* of the seed ... Eze 44:22 1330
to beat the menservants and *m* ... Lk 12:45 *3814*

MAID'S {1}
Now when every *m* turn was come to ... Est 2:12 5291

MAIDS {9}
Beside their servants and their *m* ... Ezr 2:65 519
her *m* unto the best place of the ... Est 2:9 5291
So Esther's *m* and her chamberlains ... Est 4:4 5291
that dwell in mine house, and my *m* ... Job 19:15 519
the *m* in the cities of Judah ... Lam 5:11 1330
Slay utterly old and young, both *m* ... Eze 9:6 1330
her *m* shall lead her as with the ... Nah 2:7 519
men cheerful, and new wine the *m* ... Zec 9:17 1330
one of the *m* of the high priest ... Mk 14:66 *3814*

MAIDSERVANT {16}
of the *m* that is behind the mill ... Ex 11:5 8198
thy manservant, nor thy *m* ... Ex 20:10 519
nor his manservant, nor his *m* ... Ex 20:17 519
a man sell his daughter to be a *m* ... Ex 21:7 519
ox shall push a manservant or a *m* ... Ex 21:32 519
nor thy manservant, nor thy *m* ... Deut 5:14 519
thy *m* may rest as well as thou ... Deut 5:14 519
or his manservant, or his *m* ... Deut 5:21 519
and thy manservant, and thy *m* ... Deut 12:18 519
also unto thy *m* thou shalt do ... Deut 15:17 519
and thy manservant, and thy *m* ... Deut 16:11 519
and thy manservant, and thy *m* ... Deut 16:14 519
made Abimelech, the son of his *m* ... Judg 9:18 519
cause of my manservant or of my *m* ... Job 31:13 519
manservant, and every man his *m* ... Jer 34:9 8198
manservant, and every one his *m* ... Jer 34:10 8198

MAIDSERVANT'S {1}
tooth, or his *m* tooth ... Ex 21:27 519

MAIDSERVANTS {9}
and he asses, and menservants, and *m* ... Gen 12:16 8198
Abimelech, and his wife, and his *m* ... Gen 20:17 519
and gold, and menservants, and *m* ... Gen 24:35 8198
and had much cattle, and *m* ... Gen 30:43 8198
and your menservants, and your *m* ... Deut 12:12 519
take your menservants, and your *m* ... 1Sa 8:16 8198
of the *m* which thou hast spoken ... 2Sa 6:22 519
and oxen, and menservants, and *m* ... 2Kin 5:26 8198
their manservants and their *m* ... Neh 7:67 519

MAIDSERVANTS' {1}
tent, and into the two *m* tents ... Gen 31:33 519

MAIL {2}
and he was armed with a coat of *m* ... 1Sa 17:5 7193
he armed him with a coat of *m* ... 1Sa 17:38 7193

MAIMED {7}
Blind, or broken, or *m*, or having ... Lev 22:22 2782
that were lame, blind, dumb, *m* ... Mt 15:30 *2948*
the *m* to be whole, the lame to ... Mt 15:31 *2948*
thee to enter into life halt or *m* ... Mt 18:8 *2948*
for thee to enter into life *m* ... Mk 9:43 *2948*
a feast, call the poor, the *m* ... Lk 14:13 *376*
in hither the poor, and the *m* ... Lk 14:21 *376*

MAINSAIL {1}
and hoised up the *m* to the wind ... Acts 27:40 *736*

MAINTAIN {10}
supplication, and *m* their cause ... 1Kin 8:45 6213
dwelling place, and *m* their cause, ... 1Kin 8:49 6213
that he *m* the cause of his ... 1Kin 8:59 6213
to *m* the house of the LORD ... 1Chr 26:27 2388
supplication, and *m* their cause ... 2Chr 6:35 6213
m their cause, and forgive thy ... 2Chr 6:39 6213
but I will *m* mine own ways before ... Job 13:15 3198
I know that the LORD will *m* the ... Ps 140:12 6213
might be careful to *m* good works ... Titus 3:8 *4291*
let ours also learn to *m* good ... Titus 3:14 *4291*

MAINTAINED {1}
For thou hast *m* my right and my ... Ps 9:4 6213

MAINTAINEST {1}
thou *m* my lot ... Ps 16:5 8551

MAINTENANCE {2}
Now because we have *m* from the ... Ezr 4:14 4415
for the *m* for thy maidens ... Prov 27:27 2416

MAJESTY {29}
glory, and the victory, and the *m* ... 1Chr 29:11 1935
m as had not been on any king ... 1Chr 29:25 1935
of his excellent *m* many days ... Est 1:4 1420
with God is terrible *m* ... Job 37:22 1935
Deck thyself now with *m* and ... Job 40:10 1347
m hast thou laid upon him ... Ps 21:5 1926
voice of the LORD is full of *m* ... Ps 29:4 1926
mighty, with thy glory and thy *m* ... Ps 45:3 1926
in thy *m* ride prosperously ... Ps 45:4 1926
reigneth, he is clothed with *m* ... Ps 93:1 1348
Honour and *m* are before him ... Ps 96:6 1926
thou art clothed with honour and *m* ... Ps 104:1 1926
of the glorious honour of thy *m* ... Ps 145:5 1935
the glorious *m* of his kingdom ... Ps 145:12 1926
LORD, and for the glory of his *m* ... Is 2:10 1347
LORD, and for the glory of his *m* ... Is 2:19 1347
LORD, and for the glory of his *m* ... Is 2:21 1347
shall sing for the *m* of the LORD ... Is 24:14 1347
will not behold the *m* of the LORD ... Is 26:10 1348
of his ornament, he set it in *m* ... Eze 7:20 1347
power, and for the honour of my *m* ... Dan 4:30 1923
excellent *m* was added unto me ... Dan 4:36 7238
thy father a kingdom and *m* ... Dan 5:18 7238
for the *m* that he gave him, all ... Dan 5:19 7238
in the *m* of the name of the LORD ... Mic 5:4 1347
the right hand of the *M* on high ... Heb 1:3 *3172*
throne of the *M* in the heavens ... Heb 8:1 *3172*
but were eyewitnesses of his *m* ... 2Pet 1:16 *3168*
God our Saviour, be glory and *m* ... Jude 25 *3172*

MAKAZ *(ma'-kaz)* {1} *A town in Judah.*
The son of Dekar, in *M*, and in ... 1Kin 4:9 4739

MAKE {1054}
Let us *m* man in our image, after ... Gen 1:26 6213
I will *m* him an help meet for him ... Gen 2:18 6213
tree to be desired to *m* one wise ... Gen 3:6
did the LORD God *m* coats of skins ... Gen 3:21 6213
M thee an ark of gopher wood ... Gen 6:14 6213
rooms shalt thou *m* in the ark ... Gen 6:14 6213
fashion which thou shalt *m* it of ... Gen 6:15 6213
A window shalt thou *m* to the ark ... Gen 6:16 6213
and third stories shalt thou *m* it ... Gen 6:16 6213
the covenant which I *m* between me ... Gen 9:12 5414
to another, Go to, let us *m* brick ... Gen 11:3 3835
let us *m* us a name, lest we be ... Gen 11:4 6213
I will *m* of thee a great nation, ... Gen 12:2 6213
bless thee, and *m* thy name great ... Gen 12:2
I will *m* thy seed as the dust of ... Gen 13:16 7760
I will *m* my covenant between me ... Gen 17:2 5414
I will *m* thee exceeding fruitful, ... Gen 17:6
I will *m* nations of thee, and ... Gen 17:6 5414
will *m* him fruitful, and will ... Gen 17:20
I will *m* him a great nation ... Gen 17:20 5414
M ready quickly three measures of ... Gen 18:6
it, and *m* cakes upon the hearth ... Gen 18:6 6213
let us *m* our father drink wine, ... Gen 19:32
let us *m* him drink wine this ... Gen 19:34
the bondwoman will I *m* a nation ... Gen 21:13 7760
for I will *m* him a great nation ... Gen 21:18 7760

M

Context	Reference	Strong's
I will *m* thee swear by the LORD,	Gen 24:3	
I will *m* thy seed to multiply as	Gen 26:4	
let us *m* a covenant with thee	Gen 26:28	3772
m me savoury meat, such as I love	Gen 27:4	6213
m me savoury meat, that I may eat	Gen 27:7	6213
I will *m* them savoury meat for	Gen 27:9	6213
m thee fruitful, and multiply thee	Gen 28:3	
let us *m* a covenant, I and thou	Gen 31:44	3772
m thy seed as the sand of the sea	Gen 32:12	7760
m ye marriages with us, and give	Gen 34:9	
me to *m* me to stink among the	Gen 34:30	
m there an altar unto God, that	Gen 35:1	6213
I will *m* there an altar unto God,	Gen 35:3	6213
m mention of me unto Pharaoh, and	Gen 40:14	
men home, and slay, and *m* ready	Gen 43:16	
for I will there *m* of thee a	Gen 46:3	6213
the best of the land *m* thy father	Gen 47:6	
then *m* them rulers over my cattle	Gen 47:6	7760
I will *m* thee fruitful, and	Gen 48:4	
I will *m* of thee a multitude of	Gen 48:4	5414
God *m* thee as Ephraim and as	Gen 48:20	6213
ye *m* them rest from their burdens	Ex 5:5	
give the people straw to *m* brick	Ex 5:7	3835
which they did *m* heretofore	Ex 5:8	6213
and they say to us, *M* brick	Ex 5:16	6213
shall *m* your count for the lamb	Ex 12:4	
I do *m* them know the statutes of	Ex 18:16	5414
Thou shalt not *m* unto thee any	Ex 20:4	6213
Ye shall not *m* with me gods of	Ex 20:23	6213
neither shall ye *m* unto you gods	Ex 20:23	6213
of earth thou shalt *m* unto me	Ex 20:24	6213
if thou wilt *m* me an altar of	Ex 20:25	6213
owner of the pit shall *m* it good	Ex 21:34	7999
for he should *m* full restitution	Ex 22:3	7999
vineyard, shall he *m* restitution	Ex 22:5	7999
fire shall surely *m* restitution	Ex 22:6	7999
and he shall not *m* it good	Ex 22:11	7999
he shall *m* restitution unto the	Ex 22:12	7999
he shall not *m* good that which	Ex 22:13	7999
it, he shall surely *m* it good	Ex 22:14	7999
with it, he shall not *m* it good	Ex 22:15	7999
m no mention of the name of other	Ex 23:13	
I will *m* all thine enemies turn	Ex 23:27	5414
Thou shalt *m* no covenant with	Ex 23:32	3772
lest they *m* thee sin against me	Ex 23:33	
let them *m* me a sanctuary	Ex 25:8	6213
thereof, even so shall ye *m* it	Ex 25:9	6213
they shall *m* an ark of shittim	Ex 25:10	6213
shalt *m* upon it a crown of gold	Ex 25:11	6213
thou shalt *m* staves of shittim	Ex 25:13	6213
thou shalt *m* a mercy seat of pure	Ex 25:17	6213
thou shalt *m* two cherubims of	Ex 25:18	6213
of beaten work shalt thou *m* them	Ex 25:18	6213
m one cherub on the one end, and	Ex 25:19	6213
m the cherubims on the two ends	Ex 25:19	6213
Thou shalt also *m* a table of	Ex 25:23	6213
m thereto a crown of gold round	Ex 25:24	6213
thou shalt *m* unto it a border of	Ex 25:25	6213
thou shalt *m* a golden crown to	Ex 25:25	6213
thou shalt *m* for it four rings of	Ex 25:26	6213
thou shalt *m* the staves of	Ex 25:28	6213
thou shalt *m* the dishes thereof,	Ex 25:29	6213
of pure gold shalt thou *m* them	Ex 25:29	6213
thou shalt *m* a candlestick of	Ex 25:31	6213
thou shalt *m* the seven lamps	Ex 25:37	6213
talent of pure gold shall he *m* it	Ex 25:39	6213
look that thou *m* them after their	Ex 25:40	6213
Moreover thou shalt *m* the	Ex 26:1	6213
of cunning work shalt thou *m* them	Ex 26:1	6213
thou shalt *m* loops of blue upon	Ex 26:4	6213
likewise shalt thou *m* in the	Ex 26:4	6213
shalt thou *m* in the one curtain	Ex 26:5	6213
fifty loops shalt thou *m* in the	Ex 26:5	6213
thou shalt *m* fifty taches of gold	Ex 26:6	6213
thou shalt *m* curtains of goats'	Ex 26:7	6213
eleven curtains shalt thou *m*	Ex 26:7	6213
thou shalt *m* fifty loops on the	Ex 26:10	6213
thou shalt *m* fifty taches of	Ex 26:11	6213
thou shalt *m* a covering for the	Ex 26:14	6213
thou shalt *m* boards for the	Ex 26:15	6213
thus shalt thou *m* for all the	Ex 26:17	6213
thou shalt *m* the boards for the	Ex 26:18	6213
thou shalt *m* forty sockets of	Ex 26:19	6213
westward thou shalt *m* six boards	Ex 26:22	6213
two boards shalt thou *m* for the	Ex 26:23	6213
thou shalt *m* bars of shittim wood	Ex 26:26	6213
m their rings of gold for places	Ex 26:29	6213
thou shalt *m* a vail of blue, and	Ex 26:31	6213
thou shalt *m* an hanging for the	Ex 26:36	6213
thou shalt *m* for the hanging five	Ex 26:37	6213
thou shalt *m* an altar of shittim	Ex 27:1	6213
thou shalt *m* the horns of it upon	Ex 27:2	6213
thou shalt *m* his pans to receive	Ex 27:3	6213
thereof thou shalt *m* of brass	Ex 27:3	6213
thou shalt *m* for it a grate of	Ex 27:4	6213
upon the net shalt thou *m* four	Ex 27:4	6213
thou shalt *m* staves for the altar	Ex 27:6	6213
with boards shalt thou *m* it	Ex 27:8	6213
in the mount, so shall they *m* it	Ex 27:8	6213
thou shalt *m* the court of the	Ex 27:9	6213
thou shalt *m* holy garments for	Ex 28:2	6213
that they may *m* Aaron's garments	Ex 28:3	6213
the garments which they shall *m*	Ex 28:4	6213
they shall *m* holy garments for	Ex 28:4	6213
they shall *m* the ephod of gold,	Ex 28:6	6213
thou shalt *m* them to be set in	Ex 28:11	6213
thou shalt *m* ouches of gold	Ex 28:13	6213
wreathen work shalt thou *m* them	Ex 28:14	6213
thou shalt *m* the breastplate of	Ex 28:15	6213
work of the ephod thou shalt *m* it	Ex 28:15	6213
twined linen, shalt thou *m* it	Ex 28:15	6213
thou shalt *m* upon the breastplate	Ex 28:22	6213
thou shalt *m* upon the breastplate	Ex 28:23	6213
thou shalt *m* two rings of gold,	Ex 28:26	6213
other rings of gold thou shalt *m*	Ex 28:27	6213
thou shalt *m* the robe of the	Ex 28:31	6213
thou shalt *m* pomegranates of blue	Ex 28:33	6213
thou shalt *m* a plate of pure gold	Ex 28:36	6213
thou shalt *m* the mitre of fine	Ex 28:39	6213
thou shalt *m* the girdle of	Ex 28:39	6213
Aaron's sons thou shalt *m* coats	Ex 28:40	6213
thou shalt *m* for them girdles, and	Ex 28:40	6213
and bonnets shalt thou *m* for them	Ex 28:40	6213
thou shalt *m* them linen breeches	Ex 28:42	6213
wheaten flour shalt thou *m* them	Ex 29:2	6213
Seven days thou shalt *m* an	Ex 29:37	
thou shalt *m* an altar to burn	Ex 30:1	6213
of shittim wood shalt thou *m* it	Ex 30:1	6213
thou shalt *m* unto it a crown of	Ex 30:3	6213
m to it under the crown of it	Ex 30:4	6213
two sides of it shalt thou *m* it	Ex 30:4	6213
thou shalt *m* the staves of	Ex 30:5	6213
Aaron shall *m* an atonement upon	Ex 30:10	
once in the year shall he *m*	Ex 30:10	
to *m* an atonement for your souls	Ex 30:15	
to *m* an atonement for your souls	Ex 30:16	
Thou shalt also *m* a laver of	Ex 30:18	6213
thou shalt *m* it an oil of holy	Ex 30:25	6213
neither shall ye *m* any other like	Ex 30:32	6213
thou shalt *m* it a perfume, a	Ex 30:35	6213
the perfume which thou shalt *m*	Ex 30:37	6213
ye shall not *m* to yourselves	Ex 30:37	6213
Whosoever shall *m* like unto that	Ex 30:38	6213
that they may *m* all that I have	Ex 31:6	6213
m us gods, which shall go before	Ex 32:1	6213
I will *m* of thee a great nation	Ex 32:10	6213
M us gods, which shall go before	Ex 32:23	6213
peradventure I shall *m* an	Ex 32:30	
I will *m* all my goodness pass	Ex 33:19	
he said, Behold, I *m* a covenant	Ex 34:10	3772
lest thou *m* a covenant with the	Ex 34:12	3772
Lest thou *m* a covenant with the	Ex 34:15	3772
m thy sons go a whoring after	Ex 34:16	
Thou shalt *m* thee no molten gods	Ex 34:17	6213
come, and *m* all that the LORD hath	Ex 35:10	6213
to *m* any manner of cunning work	Ex 35:33	6213
of the sanctuary, to *m* it withal	Ex 36:3	6213
which the LORD commanded to *m*	Ex 36:5	6213
Let neither man nor woman *m* any	Ex 36:6	6213
for all the work to *m* it, and too	Ex 36:7	6213
thus did he *m* for all the boards	Ex 36:22	6213
for him to *m* atonement for him	Lev 1:4	
the priest shall *m* an atonement	Lev 4:20	
the priest shall *m* an atonement	Lev 4:26	
the priest shall *m* an atonement	Lev 4:31	
the priest shall *m* an atonement	Lev 4:35	
the priest shall *m* an atonement	Lev 5:6	
the priest shall *m* an atonement	Lev 5:10	
the priest shall *m* an atonement	Lev 5:13	
he shall *m* amends for the harm	Lev 5:16	7999
the priest shall *m* an atonement	Lev 5:16	
the priest shall *m* an atonement	Lev 5:18	
the priest shall *m* an atonement	Lev 6:7	
to *m* reconciliation upon it	Lev 8:15	
to *m* an atonement for you	Lev 8:34	
m an atonement for thyself, and	Lev 9:7	
and *m* an atonement for them	Lev 9:7	
to *m* atonement for them before	Lev 10:17	
Ye shall not *m* yourselves	Lev 11:43	
neither shall ye *m* yourselves	Lev 11:43	
To *m* a difference between the	Lev 11:47	
LORD, and *m* an atonement for her	Lev 12:7	
the priest shall *m* an atonement	Lev 12:8	
the priest shall *m* an atonement	Lev 14:18	
m an atonement for him that is to	Lev 14:19	
the priest shall *m* an atonement	Lev 14:20	
to *m* an atonement for him, and one	Lev 14:21	
to *m* an atonement for him before	Lev 14:29	
the priest shall *m* an atonement	Lev 14:31	
m an atonement for the house	Lev 14:53	
the priest shall *m* an atonement	Lev 15:15	
the priest shall *m* an atonement	Lev 15:30	
m an atonement for himself, and	Lev 16:6	
to *m* an atonement with him, and to	Lev 16:10	
shall *m* an atonement for himself,	Lev 16:11	
he shall *m* an atonement for the	Lev 16:16	
when he goeth in to *m* an	Lev 16:17	
LORD, and *m* an atonement for it	Lev 16:18	
m an atonement for himself, and	Lev 16:24	
to *m* atonement in the holy place	Lev 16:27	
the priest *m* an atonement for you	Lev 16:30	
shall *m* the atonement, and shall	Lev 16:32	
he shall *m* an atonement for the	Lev 16:33	
he shall *m* an atonement for the	Lev 16:33	
he shall *m* an atonement for the	Lev 16:33	
to *m* an atonement for the	Lev 16:34	
to *m* an atonement for your souls	Lev 17:11	
nor *m* to yourselves molten gods	Lev 19:4	6213
the priest shall *m* an atonement	Lev 19:22	
Ye shall not *m* any cuttings in	Lev 19:28	5414
ye shall not *m* your souls	Lev 20:25	
They shall not *m* baldness upon	Lev 21:5	7139
nor *m* any cuttings in their flesh	Lev 21:5	8295
nor *m* an offering by fire of them	Lev 22:22	5414
neither shall ye *m* any offering	Lev 22:24	6213
thou shalt not *m* clean riddance	Lev 23:22	
to *m* an atonement for you before	Lev 23:28	
killeth a beast shall *m* it good	Lev 24:18	7999
ye *m* the trumpet sound throughout	Lev 25:9	
Ye shall *m* you no idols nor	Lev 26:1	6213
down, and none shall *m* you afraid	Lev 26:6	
m you fruitful, and multiply you,	Lev 26:9	
I will *m* your heaven as iron, and	Lev 26:19	5414
cattle, and *m* you few in number	Lev 26:22	
I will *m* your cities waste, and	Lev 26:31	5414
When a man shall *m* a singular vow	Lev 27:2	
The LORD *m* thee a curse and an	Num 5:21	5414
the LORD doth *m* thy thigh to rot	Num 5:21	5414
to *m* thy belly to swell, and thy	Num 5:22	
He shall not *m* himself unclean	Num 6:7	
m an atonement for him, for that	Num 6:11	
The LORD *m* his face shine upon	Num 6:25	
clothes, and so *m* themselves clean	Num 8:7	
to *m* an atonement for the Levites	Num 8:12	
to *m* an atonement for the	Num 8:19	
M thee two trumpets of silver	Num 10:2	6213
a whole piece shalt thou *m* them	Num 10:2	6213
I the LORD will *m* myself known	Num 12:6	
Let us *m* a captain, and let us	Num 14:4	5414
will *m* of thee a greater nation	Num 14:12	6213
I sware to *m* you dwell therein	Num 14:30	
will *m* an offering by fire unto	Num 15:3	6213
to *m* a sweet savour unto the LORD	Num 15:3	6213
the priest shall *m* an atonement	Num 15:25	
the priest shall *m* an atonement	Num 15:28	
to *m* an atonement for him	Num 15:28	
bid them that they *m* them fringes	Num 15:38	6213
except thou *m* thyself altogether	Num 16:13	
But if the LORD *m* a new thing	Num 16:30	1254
let them *m* them broad plates for	Num 16:38	6213
and *m* an atonement for them	Num 16:46	
I will *m* to cease from me the	Num 17:5	
M thee a fiery serpent, and set it	Num 21:8	6213
to *m* an atonement for you	Num 28:22	
to *m* an atonement for you	Num 28:30	
to *m* an atonement for you	Num 29:5	
then he shall *m* her vow which she	Num 30:8	
it, or her husband may *m* it void	Num 30:13	
But if he shall any ways *m* them	Num 30:15	
ye shall *m* it go through the fire	Num 31:23	5674
ye shall *m* go through the water	Num 31:23	5674
to *m* an atonement for our souls	Num 31:50	
m you a thousand times so many	Deut 1:11	3254
I will *m* them rulers over you	Deut 1:13	7760
I will *m* them hear my words, that	Deut 4:10	
m you a graven image, the	Deut 4:16	6213
m you a graven image, or the	Deut 4:23	6213
m a graven image, or the likeness	Deut 4:25	6213
Thou shalt not *m* thee any graven	Deut 5:8	6213
thou shalt *m* no covenant with	Deut 7:2	3772
Neither shalt thou *m* marriages	Deut 7:3	
that he might *m* thee know that	Deut 8:3	
I will *m* of thee a nation	Deut 9:14	6213
mount, and *m* thee an ark of wood	Deut 10:1	6213
m search, and ask diligently	Deut 13:14	
nor *m* any baldness between your	Deut 14:1	7760
years thou shalt *m* a release	Deut 15:1	6213
officers shalt thou *m* thee in all	Deut 16:18	5414
thy God, which thou shalt *m* thee	Deut 16:21	6213
the judges shall *m* diligent	Deut 19:18	
that they shall *m* captains of the	Deut 20:9	6485
if it *m* thee answer of peace, and	Deut 20:11	
if it will *m* no peace with thee,	Deut 20:12	
but will *m* war against thee, then	Deut 20:12	6213
thou shalt not *m* merchandise of	Deut 21:14	6014
that he may not *m* the son of the	Deut 21:16	
then thou shalt *m* a battlement	Deut 22:8	6213
Thou shalt *m* thee fringes upon	Deut 22:12	6213
to *m* thee high above all nations	Deut 26:19	6213
the LORD shall *m* thee plenteous	Deut 28:11	
And the LORD shall *m* thee the head	Deut 28:13	5414
The LORD shall *m* the pestilence	Deut 28:21	
The LORD shall *m* the rain of thy	Deut 28:24	5414
Then the LORD will *m* thy plagues	Deut 28:59	6381
the LORD commanded Moses to *m*	Deut 29:1	3772
you only do I *m* this covenant	Deut 29:14	3772
the LORD thy God will *m* thee	Deut 30:9	
I would *m* the remembrance of them	Deut 32:26	
that shall come upon them *m* haste	Deut 32:35	2363
I kill, and I *m* alive	Deut 32:39	
I will *m* mine arrows drunk with	Deut 32:42	
thou shalt *m* thy way prosperous	Josh 1:8	
Joshua, *M* thee sharp knives, and	Josh 5:2	6213
that when they *m* a long blast	Josh 6:5	4900
nor *m* any noise with your voice,	Josh 6:10	
lest ye *m* yourselves accursed,	Josh 6:18	
m the camp of Israel a curse, and	Josh 6:18	7760
m not all the people to labour	Josh 7:3	
Israel, and *m* confession unto him	Josh 7:19	5414
now therefore *m* ye a league with	Josh 9:6	3772
how shall we *m* a league with you	Josh 9:7	3772
therefore now *m* ye a league with	Josh 9:11	3772
so shall your children *m* our	Josh 22:25	
neither *m* mention of the names of	Josh 23:7	
shall *m* marriages with them, and	Josh 23:12	
ye shall *m* no league with the	Judg 2:2	3772
m haste, and do as I have done	Judg 9:48	4116
Samson, that he may *m* us sport	Judg 16:25	
to *m* a graven image and a molten	Judg 17:3	6213
that they should *m* a great flame	Judg 20:38	
m not thyself known unto the	Ruth 3:3	
The LORD *m* the woman that is come	Ruth 4:11	5414
for to *m* her fret, because the	1Sa 1:6	
to *m* them inherit the throne of	1Sa 2:8	

ye *m* the LORD's people to	1Sa 2:24	
to *m* yourselves fat with the	1Sa 2:29	
I begin, I will also *m* an end	1Sa 3:12	
Wherefore ye shall *m* images of	1Sa 6:5	6213
Now therefore *m* a new cart	1Sa 6:7	6213
now *m* us a king to judge us like	1Sa 8:5	7760
to *m* his instruments of war, and	1Sa 8:12	6213
their voice, and *m* them a king	1Sa 8:22	
m haste now, for he came to day	1Sa 9:12	4116
M a covenant with us, and we will	1Sa 11:1	3772
will I *m* a covenant with you	1Sa 11:2	3772
the LORD to *m* you his people	1Sa 12:22	6213
Lest the Hebrews *m* them swords or	1Sa 13:19	6213
m his father's house free in	1Sa 17:25	6213
But Saul thought to *m* David fall	1Sa 18:25	
the lad, *M* speed, haste, stay not	1Sa 20:38	
m you all captains of thousands,	1Sa 22:7	7760
certainly *m* my lord a sure house	1Sa 25:28	6213
Therefore will I *m* thee keeper of	1Sa 28:2	7760
the Philistines *m* war against me	1Sa 28:15	3898
that thou mayest *m* known unto me	1Sa 28:15	
M this fellow return, that he may	1Sa 29:4	
M thy league with me, and, behold,	2Sa 3:12	3772
I will *m* a league with thee	2Sa 3:13	3772
that they may *m* a league with	2Sa 3:21	3772
thee that he will *m* thee an house	2Sa 7:11	6213
to *m* thy servant know them	2Sa 7:21	
to *m* him a name, and to do for you	2Sa 7:23	7760
m thy battle more strong against	2Sa 11:25	
on thy bed, and *m* thyself sick	2Sa 13:5	
m me a couple of cakes in my	2Sa 13:6	3823
m speed to depart, lest he	2Sa 15:14	4116
should I this day *m* thee go up	2Sa 15:20	
weak handed, and will *m* him afraid	2Sa 17:2	
wherewith shall I *m* the atonement	2Sa 21:3	
although he *m* it not to grow	2Sa 23:5	
m his throne greater than the	1Kin 1:37	
God *m* the name of Solomon better	1Kin 1:47	
m his throne greater than thy	1Kin 1:47	
Did I not *m* thee to swear by the	1Kin 2:42	
servant shall *m* toward this place	1Kin 8:29	6419
m supplication unto thee in this	1Kin 8:33	
m supplication unto thee in the	1Kin 8:47	
Israel did Solomon *m* no bondmen	1Kin 9:22	5414
but I will *m* him prince all the	1Kin 11:34	7896
come to Shechem to *m* him king	1Kin 12:1	
now therefore *m* thou the grievous	1Kin 12:4	
M the yoke which thy father did	1Kin 12:9	
but *m* thou it lighter unto us	1Kin 12:10	
will *m* thy house like the house	1Kin 16:3	5414
which he did, to *m* Israel to sin	1Kin 16:19	
the son of Ginath, to *m* him king	1Kin 16:21	
but *m* me thereof a little cake	1Kin 17:13	6213
after *m* for thee and for thy son	1Kin 17:13	6213
if I *m* not thy life as the life	1Kin 19:2	7760
thou shalt *m* streets for thee in	1Kin 20:34	7760
will *m* thine house like the house	1Kin 21:22	5414
M this valley full of ditches	2Kin 3:16	6213
Let us *m* a little chamber, I pray	2Kin 4:10	6213
to *m* alive, that this man doth	2Kin 5:7	
let us *m* us a place there, where	2Kin 6:2	6213
LORD would *m* windows in heaven	2Kin 7:2	6213
LORD should *m* windows in heaven	2Kin 7:19	6213
m him arise up from among his	2Kin 9:2	
I will *m* the house of Ahab like	2Kin 9:9	5414
And Joram said, *M* ready	2Kin 9:21	631
we will not *m* any king	2Kin 10:5	
Neither let Hezekiah *m* you trust	2Kin 18:30	
M an agreement with me by a	2Kin 18:31	6213
Neither will I *m* the feet of	2Kin 21:8	
that no man might *m* his son or	2Kin 23:10	
to *m* an atonement for Israel,	1Chr 6:49	
to *m* him king, according to the	1Chr 11:10	
by name, to come and *m* David king	1Chr 12:31	
to *m* David king over all Israel	1Chr 12:38	
were of one heart to *m* David king	1Chr 12:38	
m known his deeds among the	1Chr 16:8	
for those that should *m* a sound	1Chr 16:42	
to *m* thee a name of greatness and	1Chr 17:21	7760
thou *m* thine own people for ever	1Chr 17:22	5414
The LORD *m* his people an hundred	1Chr 21:3	3254
now *m* preparation for it	1Chr 22:5	
me to *m* me king over all Israel	1Chr 28:4	
and in thine hand it is to *m* great	1Chr 29:12	
the work that he was to *m* for	2Chr 4:11	6213
did Huram his father *m* to king	2Chr 4:16	6213
to *m* one sound to be heard in	2Chr 5:13	
which they shall *m* toward this	2Chr 6:21	6419
be laid upon him to *m* him swear	2Chr 6:22	
m supplication before thee in	2Chr 6:24	
to *m* in the house of the LORD	2Chr 7:11	6213
will *m* it to be a proverb and a	2Chr 7:20	5414
them did Solomon *m* to pay tribute	2Chr 8:8	
m no servants for his work	2Chr 8:9	5414
all Israel come to *m* him king	2Chr 10:1	
but *m* thou it somewhat lighter	2Chr 10:10	
for he thought to *m* him king	2Chr 11:22	
m about them walls, and towers,	2Chr 14:7	
him to *m* ships to go to Tarshish	2Chr 20:36	6213
God shall *m* thee fall before the	2Chr 25:8	
Now it is in mine heart to *m* a	2Chr 29:10	3772
to *m* an atonement for all Israel	2Chr 29:24	
to *m* proclamation throughout all	2Chr 30:5	
for God commanded me to *m* haste	2Chr 35:21	
this house, and to *m* up this wall	Ezr 5:3	3635
of the men that *m* this building	Ezr 5:4	1124
house, and to *m* up these walls	Ezr 5:9	3635
Moreover I *m* a decree what ye	Ezr 6:8	7761
I *m* a decree, that all they of	Ezr 7:13	7761
king, do *m* a decree to all the	Ezr 7:21	7761
Now therefore let us *m* a covenant	Ezr 10:3	3772
Now therefore *m* confession unto	Ezr 10:11	5414
me, For what dost thou *m* request	Neh 2:4	
to *m* beams for the gates of the	Neh 2:8	
will they *m* an end in a day	Neh 4:2	
to *m* great mirth, because they	Neh 8:12	6213
to *m* booths, as it is written	Neh 8:15	6213
of all this we *m* a sure covenant	Neh 9:38	3772
to *m* an atonement for Israel	Neh 10:33	
king's decree which he shall *m*	Est 1:20	6213
to *m* supplication unto him, and to	Est 4:8	
to *m* request before him for her	Est 4:8	
king said, Cause Haman to *m* haste	Est 5:5	
M haste, and take the apparel and	Est 6:10	4116
Haman stood up to *m* request for	Est 7:7	
that they should *m* them days of	Est 9:22	6213
he woundeth, and his hands *m* whole	Job 5:18	
m thy supplication to the	Job 8:5	
thee, and *m* the habitation of thy	Job 8:6	
but I would *m* supplication to my	Job 9:15	
m my hands never so clean	Job 9:30	
Should thy lies *m* men hold their	Job 11:3	
shall no man *m* thee ashamed	Job 11:3	
down, and none shall *m* thee afraid	Job 11:19	
many shall *m* suit unto thee	Job 11:19	
not his excellency *m* you afraid	Job 13:11	
and let not thy dread *m* me afraid	Job 13:21	
m me to know my transgression and	Job 13:23	
and anguish shall *m* him afraid	Job 15:24	
it be ere ye *m* an end of words	Job 18:2	7760
Terrors shall *m* him afraid on	Job 18:11	
ye *m* yourselves strange to me	Job 19:3	
to answer, and for this I *m* haste	Job 20:2	2363
Thou shalt *m* thy prayer unto him,	Job 22:27	
Which *m* oil within their walls,	Job 24:11	
who will *m* me a liar	Job 24:25	7760
m my speech nothing worth	Job 24:25	7760
To *m* the weight for the winds	Job 28:25	6213
he that made me in the womb *m* him	Job 31:15	6213
my terror shall not *m* thee afraid	Job 33:7	
quietness, who then can *m* trouble	Job 34:29	
they *m* the oppressed to cry	Job 35:9	
Canst thou *m* him afraid as a	Job 39:20	
command, and *m* her nest on high	Job 39:27	
he that made him can *m* his sword	Job 40:19	
Will he *m* many supplications unto	Job 41:3	
Will he *m* a covenant with thee	Job 41:4	3772
the companions *m* a banquet of him	Job 41:6	3739
The arrow cannot *m* him flee	Job 41:28	
m thy way straight before my face	Ps 5:8	
all the night *m* I my bed to swim	Ps 6:6	
they *m* ready their arrow upon the	Ps 11:2	
Thou shalt *m* them as a fiery oven	Ps 21:9	7896
shalt thou *m* them turn their back	Ps 21:12	
when thou shalt *m* ready thine	Ps 21:12	
thou didst *m* me hope when I was	Ps 22:9	
M thy face to shine upon thy	Ps 31:16	
My soul shall *m* her boast in the	Ps 34:2	
thou shalt *m* them drink of the	Ps 36:8	
M haste to help me, O Lord my	Ps 38:22	2363
m me to know mine end, and the	Ps 39:4	
m me not the reproach of the	Ps 39:8	7760
O LORD, *m* haste to help me	Ps 40:13	2363
m no tarrying, O my God	Ps 40:17	
thou wilt *m* all his bed in his	Ps 41:3	2015
whom thou mayest *m* princes in all	Ps 45:16	7596
I will *m* thy name to be	Ps 45:17	
shall *m* glad the city of God	Ps 46:4	
thou shalt *m* me to know wisdom	Ps 51:6	
M me to hear joy and gladness	Ps 51:8	
in my complaint, and *m* a noise	Ps 55:2	
of thy wings will I *m* my refuge	Ps 57:1	2620
they *m* a noise like a dog, and go	Ps 59:6	1993
let them *m* a noise like a dog, and	Ps 59:14	1993
So they shall *m* their own tongue	Ps 64:8	
M a joyful noise unto God, all ye	Ps 66:1	
m his praise glorious	Ps 66:2	7760
m the voice of his praise to be	Ps 66:8	
m their loins continually to	Ps 69:23	
M haste, O God, to deliver me	Ps 70:1	
m haste to help me, O LORD	Ps 70:1	2363
m haste unto me, O God	Ps 70:5	2363
O LORD, *m* no tarrying	Ps 70:5	
O my God, *m* haste for my help	Ps 71:12	2439
I will *m* mention of thy	Ps 71:16	
that they should *m* them known to	Ps 78:5	
m a joyful noise unto the God of	Ps 81:1	
For, lo, thine enemies *m* a tumult	Ps 83:2	1993
M their nobles like Oreb, and like	Ps 83:11	7896
O my God, *m* them like a wheel	Ps 83:13	7896
m them afraid with thy storm	Ps 83:15	
the valley of Baca *m* it a well	Ps 84:6	6213
I will *m* mention of Rahab and	Ps 87:4	
with my mouth will I *m* known thy	Ps 89:1	
Also I will *m* him my firstborn,	Ps 89:27	5414
also will I *m* to endure for ever	Ps 89:29	7760
M us glad according to the days	Ps 90:15	
let us *m* a joyful noise to the	Ps 95:1	
m a joyful noise unto him with	Ps 95:2	
M a joyful noise unto the LORD,	Ps 98:4	
m a loud noise, and rejoice, and	Ps 98:4	
sound of cornet *m* a joyful noise	Ps 98:6	
M a joyful noise unto the LORD,	Ps 100:1	
oil to *m* his face to shine, and	Ps 104:15	
Where the birds *m* their nests	Ps 104:17	
m known his deeds among the	Ps 105:1	
that he might *m* his mighty power	Ps 106:8	
until I *m* thine enemies thy	Ps 110:1	7896
They that *m* them are like unto	Ps 115:8	6213
M me to understand the way of thy	Ps 119:27	
M me to go in the path of thy	Ps 119:35	
M thy face to shine upon thy	Ps 119:135	
There will I *m* the horn of David	Ps 132:17	6213
They that *m* them are like unto	Ps 135:18	6213
if I *m* my bed in hell, behold,	Ps 139:8	3331
m haste unto me	Ps 141:1	2363
the LORD did I *m* my supplication	Ps 142:1	
To *m* known to the sons of men his	Ps 145:12	
to evil, and *m* haste to shed blood	Prov 1:16	4116
I will *m* known my words unto you	Prov 1:23	
thyself, and *m* sure thy friend	Prov 6:3	7292
Fools *m* a mock at sin	Prov 14:9	
and with good advice *m* war	Prov 20:18	6213
holy, and after vows to *m* enquiry	Prov 20:25	
That I might *m* thee know the	Prov 22:21	
M no friendship with an angry man	Prov 22:24	
certainly *m* themselves wings	Prov 23:5	6213
wise counsel thou shalt *m* thy war	Prov 24:6	6213
m it fit for thyself in the field	Prov 24:27	6257
m my heart glad, that I may	Prov 27:11	
yet *m* they their houses in the	Prov 30:26	7760
that he should *m* his soul enjoy	Eccl 2:24	
for who can *m* that straight,	Eccl 7:13	
neither *m* thyself over wise	Eccl 7:16	
We will *m* thee borders of gold	Song 1:11	6213
M haste, my beloved, and be thou	Song 8:14	1272
when ye *m* many prayers, I will	Is 1:15	
Wash you, *m* you clean	Is 1:16	
m me not a ruler of the people	Is 3:7	7760
That say, Let him *m* speed	Is 5:19	4116
M the heart of this people fat,	Is 6:10	
m their ears heavy, and shut their	Is 6:10	
let us *m* a breach therein for us,	Is 7:6	
of hosts shall *m* a consumption	Is 10:23	6213
And shall *m* him of quick	Is 11:3	
streams, and *m* men go over dryshod	Is 11:15	
m mention that his name is	Is 12:4	
I will *m* a man more precious than	Is 13:12	
the shepherds *m* their fold there	Is 13:20	
I will also *m* it a possession for	Is 14:23	7760
m thy shadow as the night in the	Is 16:3	7896
down, and none shall *m* them afraid	Is 17:2	
shalt thou *m* thy plant to grow	Is 17:11	
shalt thou *m* thy seed to flourish	Is 17:11	
which *m* a noise like the noise of	Is 17:12	1993
that *m* a rushing like the rushing	Is 17:12	
thereof, all that *m* sluices	Is 19:10	6213
m sweet melody, sing many songs,	Is 23:16	
shall the LORD of hosts *m* unto	Is 25:6	6213
will we *m* mention of thy name	Is 26:13	
that he may *m* peace with me	Is 27:5	6213
and he shall *m* peace with me	Is 27:5	6213
whom shall he *m* to understand	Is 28:9	
that believeth shall not *m* haste	Is 28:16	2363
That *m* a man an offender for a	Is 29:21	
to *m* empty the soul of the hungry	Is 32:6	
m you bare, and gird sackcloth	Is 32:11	
when thou shalt *m* an end to deal	Is 33:1	
shall the great owl *m* her nest	Is 34:15	
Neither let Hezekiah *m* you trust	Is 36:15	
M an agreement with me by a	Is 36:16	6213
is come forth to *m* war with thee	Is 37:9	
to night wilt thou *m* an end of me	Is 38:12	
to night wilt thou *m* an end of me	Is 38:13	
thou recover me, and *m* me to live	Is 38:16	
children shall *m* known thy truth	Is 38:19	
m straight in the desert a	Is 40:3	
I will *m* thee a new sharp	Is 41:15	7760
shalt *m* the hills as chaff	Is 41:15	7760
I will *m* the wilderness a pool of	Is 41:18	7760
I will *m* waste mountains and hills	Is 42:15	7760
I will *m* the rivers islands, and I	Is 42:15	7760
I will *m* darkness light before	Is 42:16	7760
the law, and *m* it honourable	Is 42:21	
I will even *m* a way in the	Is 43:19	7760
They that *m* a graven image are	Is 44:9	3335
shall I *m* the residue thereof an	Is 44:19	6213
m the crooked places straight	Is 45:2	
I *m* peace, and create evil	Is 45:7	6213
they shall *m* supplication unto	Is 45:14	
m me equal, and compare me, that	Is 46:5	
m bare the leg, uncover the thigh	Is 47:2	
m mention of the God of Israel,	Is 48:1	
he shall *m* his way prosperous	Is 48:15	
I will *m* all my mountains a way,	Is 49:11	7760
Thy children shall *m* haste	Is 49:17	4116
I *m* the rivers a wilderness	Is 50:2	7760
I *m* sackcloth their covering	Is 50:3	7760
he will *m* her wilderness like	Is 51:3	7760
I will *m* my judgment to rest for	Is 51:4	
rule over them *m* them to howl	Is 52:5	
when thou shalt *m* his soul an	Is 53:10	7760
m the desolate cities to be	Is 54:3	
I will *m* thy windows of agates,	Is 54:12	7760
I will *m* an everlasting covenant	Is 55:3	3772
m them joyful in my house of	Is 56:7	
against whom *m* ye a wide mouth,	Is 57:4	
to *m* your voice to be heard on	Is 58:4	
in drought, and *m* fat thy bones	Is 58:11	
they *m* haste to shed innocent	Is 59:7	4116
I will *m* the place of my feet	Is 60:13	7760
thee, I will *m* thee an eternal	Is 60:15	7760
I will also *m* thy officers peace,	Is 60:17	7760
I will *m* an everlasting covenant	Is 61:8	3772

M

ye that *m* mention of the LORD, ... Is 62:6
till he *m* Jerusalem a praise in ... Is 62:7 7760
m them drunk in my fury, and I ... Is 63:6
to *m* himself an everlasting name ... Is 63:12 6213
to *m* thyself a glorious name ... Is 63:14 6213
to *m* thy name known to thine ... Is 64:2
and the new earth, which I will *m* ... Is 66:22 6213
his place to *m* thy land desolate ... Jer 4:7 7760
M ye mention to the nations ... Jer 4:16
yet will I not *m* a full end ... Jer 4:27 6213
in vain shalt thou *m* thyself fair ... Jer 4:30
but *m* not a full end ... Jer 5:10 6213
I will *m* my words in thy mouth ... Jer 5:14 5414
I will not *m* a full end with you ... Jer 5:18 6213
lest I *m* thee desolate, a land ... Jer 6:8 7760
m thee mourning, as for an only ... Jer 6:26 6213
neither *m* intercession to me ... Jer 7:16
to *m* cakes to the queen of heaven ... Jer 7:18 6213
I will *m* Jerusalem heaps, and a ... Jer 9:11 5414
I will *m* the cities of Judah ... Jer 9:11 5414
And let them *m* haste, and take up a ... Jer 9:18 4116
to *m* the cities of Judah desolate ... Jer 10:22 7760
of death, and *m* it gross darkness ... Jer 13:16 7896
I will *m* thee to pass with thine ... Jer 15:14
I will *m* thee unto this people a ... Jer 15:20 5414
nor *m* themselves bald for them ... Jer 16:6
Shall a man *m* gods unto himself, ... Jer 16:20 6213
seemed good to the potter to *m* it ... Jer 18:4 6213
m your ways and your doings good ... Jer 18:11
To *m* their land desolate, and a ... Jer 18:16 7760
I will *m* void the counsel of ... Jer 19:7
I will *m* this city desolate, and ... Jer 19:8 7760
even *m* this city as Tophet ... Jer 19:12 5414
I will *m* thee a terror to thyself ... Jer 20:4 5414
I will not *m* mention of him, nor ... Jer 20:9
surely I will *m* thee a wilderness ... Jer 22:6 7896
m them drink the water of gall ... Jer 23:15
they *m* you vain ... Jer 23:16
m them an astonishment, and an ... Jer 25:9 7760
will *m* it perpetual desolations ... Jer 25:12 7760
to *m* them a desolation, an ... Jer 25:18 5414
Then will I *m* this house like ... Jer 26:6 5414
will *m* this city a curse to all ... Jer 26:6 5414
M thee bonds and yokes, and put ... Jer 27:2 6213
let them now *m* intercession to ... Jer 27:18
but thou shalt *m* for them yokes ... Jer 28:13 6213
will *m* them like vile figs, that ... Jer 29:17 5414
The LORD *m* thee like Zedekiah and ... Jer 29:22 7760
quiet, and none shall *m* him afraid ... Jer 30:10
though I *m* a full end of all ... Jer 30:11 6213
yet will I not *m* a full end of ... Jer 30:11 6213
and the voice of them that *m* merry ... Jer 30:19
the dances of them that *m* merry ... Jer 31:4
m them rejoice from their sorrow ... Jer 31:13
up waymarks, *m* thee high heaps ... Jer 31:21 7760
that I will *m* a new covenant with ... Jer 31:31 3772
I will *m* with the house of Israel ... Jer 31:33 3772
I will *m* an everlasting covenant ... Jer 32:40 3772
I will *m* you to be removed into ... Jer 34:17 5414
I will *m* the cities of Judah a ... Jer 34:22 5414
did we *m* her cakes to worship her ... Jer 44:19 6213
ease, and none shall *m* him afraid ... Jer 46:27
for I will *m* a full end of all ... Jer 46:28 6213
but I will not *m* a full end of ... Jer 46:28 6213
M ye him drunken ... Jer 48:26
I will *m* thee small among the ... Jer 49:15 5414
though thou shouldest *m* thy nest ... Jer 49:16
but I will suddenly *m* him run ... Jer 49:19
surely he shall *m* their ... Jer 49:20
which shall *m* her land desolate, ... Jer 50:3 7896
but I will *m* them suddenly run ... Jer 50:44
surely he shall *m* their ... Jer 50:45
M bright the arrows ... Jer 51:11
m the watch strong, set up the ... Jer 51:12
will *m* thee a burnt mountain ... Jer 51:25 5414
to *m* the land of Babylon a ... Jer 51:29 7760
up her sea, and *m* her springs dry ... Jer 51:36
their heat I will *m* their feasts ... Jer 51:39 7896
I will *m* them drunken, that they ... Jer 51:39
I will *m* drunk her princes, and ... Jer 51:57
drunken, and shalt *m* thyself naked ... Lam 4:21
I will *m* thy tongue cleave to the ... Eze 3:26
m thee bread thereof, according ... Eze 4:9 6213
Moreover I will *m* thee waste ... Eze 5:14 5414
m the land desolate, yea, more ... Eze 6:14 5414
the trumpet, even to *m* all ready ... Eze 7:14
M a chain: for the land ... Eze 7:23 6213
I will also *m* the pomp of the ... Eze 7:24
wilt thou *m* a full end of the ... Eze 11:13 6213
I will *m* this proverb to cease, ... Eze 12:23
m kerchiefs upon the head of ... Eze 13:18 6213
hunt the souls to *m* them fly ... Eze 13:20
souls that ye hunt to *m* them fly ... Eze 13:20
will *m* him a sign and a proverb, ... Eze 14:8 8074
I will *m* the land desolate, ... Eze 15:8 5414
So will I *m* my fury toward thee ... Eze 16:42
great company *m* for him in the ... Eze 17:17 6213
m you a new heart and a new spirit ... Eze 18:31 6213
neither did I *m* an end of them in ... Eze 20:17 6213
that I might *m* them desolate, to ... Eze 20:26
when ye *m* your sons to pass ... Eze 20:31
sharpened to *m* a sore slaughter ... Eze 21:10
should we then *m* mirth ... Eze 21:10 2874
that should *m* up the hedge, and ... Eze 22:30 1443
Thus will I *m* thy lewdness to ... Eze 23:27
m it boil well, and let them ... Eze 24:5
I will even *m* the pile for fire ... Eze 24:9
m no mourning for the dead, bind ... Eze 24:17 6213

m their dwellings in thee ... Eze 25:4 5414
I will *m* Rabbah a stable for ... Eze 25:5 5414
I will *m* it desolate from Teman ... Eze 25:13 5414
m her like the top of a rock ... Eze 26:4 5414
he shall *m* a fort against thee, ... Eze 26:8 5414
they shall *m* a spoil of thy ... Eze 26:12
m a prey of thy merchandise ... Eze 26:12
I will *m* thee like the top of a ... Eze 26:14 5414
When I shall *m* thee a desolate ... Eze 26:19 5414
I will *m* thee a terror, and thou ... Eze 26:21 5414
from Lebanon to *m* masts for thee ... Eze 27:5 6213
they shall *m* themselves utterly ... Eze 27:31
I will *m* the land of Egypt ... Eze 29:10 5414
I will *m* the land of Egypt ... Eze 29:12 5414
go forth from me in ships to *m* ... Eze 30:9
I will also *m* the multitude of ... Eze 30:10
I will *m* the rivers dry, and sell ... Eze 30:12 5414
I will *m* the land waste, and all ... Eze 30:12
I will *m* Pathros desolate, and ... Eze 30:14
to *m* it strong to hold the sword ... Eze 30:21
and *m* the stars thereof dark ... Eze 32:7
of heaven will I *m* dark over thee ... Eze 32:8
I will *m* many people amazed at ... Eze 32:10
Then will I *m* their waters deep, ... Eze 32:14
When I shall *m* the land of Egypt ... Eze 32:15 5414
I will *m* with them a covenant of ... Eze 34:25 3772
And I will *m* them and the places ... Eze 34:26 5414
and none shall *m* them afraid ... Eze 34:28
I will *m* thee most desolate ... Eze 35:3 5414
Thus will I *m* mount Seir most ... Eze 35:7 5414
I will *m* thee perpetual ... Eze 35:9 5414
I will *m* myself known among them, ... Eze 35:11 6213
rejoiceth, I will *m* thee desolate ... Eze 35:14 6213
m them one stick, and they shall ... Eze 37:19 6213
I will *m* them one nation in the ... Eze 37:22 6213
Moreover I will *m* a covenant of ... Eze 37:26 3772
So will I *m* my holy name known in ... Eze 39:7
to *m* a separation between the ... Eze 42:20
in the day when they shall *m* it ... Eze 43:18 6213
the priests shall *m* your burnt ... Eze 43:27 6213
But I will *m* them keepers of the ... Eze 44:14 5414
to *m* reconciliation for them, ... Eze 45:15
to *m* reconciliation for the house ... Eze 45:17
then shall ye *m* me endanger my ... Dan 1:10
if ye will not *m* known unto me ... Dan 2:5
But if ye will not *m* known unto ... Dan 2:9
that will *m* known unto the king ... Dan 2:25
Art thou able to *m* known unto me ... Dan 2:26
but for their sakes that shall *m* ... Dan 2:30
Therefore I *m* a decree, That ... Dan 3:29 7761
that they might *m* known unto me ... Dan 4:6
but they did not *m* known unto me ... Dan 4:7
not able to *m* known unto me the ... Dan 4:18
they shall *m* thee to eat grass as ... Dan 4:25
they shall *m* thee to eat grass as ... Dan 4:32
nor *m* known to the king the ... Dan 5:8
writing, and *m* known unto me the ... Dan 5:15
that thou canst *m* interpretations ... Dan 5:16 6590
m known to me the interpretation ... Dan 5:16
m known to him the interpretation ... Dan 5:17
and to *m* a firm decree, that ... Dan 6:7
I *m* a decree, That in every ... Dan 6:26 7761
m this man to understand the ... Dan 8:16
I will *m* thee know what shall be ... Dan 8:19
to *m* an end of sins ... Dan 9:24
to *m* reconciliation for iniquity, ... Dan 9:24
he shall *m* it desolate, even ... Dan 9:27
Now I am come to *m* thee ... Dan 10:14
of the north to *m* an agreement ... Dan 11:6 6213
to *m* them white, even to the time ... Dan 11:35
and utterly to *m* away many ... Dan 11:44
m her as a wilderness, and set her ... Hos 2:3 7760
m a wall, that she shall not find ... Hos 2:6 1443
I will *m* them a forest, and the ... Hos 2:12 7760
in that day will I *m* a covenant ... Hos 2:18 3772
will *m* them to lie down safely ... Hos 2:18
are profound to *m* slaughter ... Hos 5:2
They *m* the king glad with their ... Hos 7:3
I will *m* Ephraim to ride ... Hos 10:11
how shall I *m* thee as Admah ... Hos 11:8 5414
they do *m* a covenant with the ... Hos 12:1 3772
m thee to dwell in tabernacles ... Hos 12:9
I will no more *m* you a reproach ... Joel 2:19 5414
for we may not *m* mention of the ... Amos 6:10
even to *m* the poor of the land to ... Amos 8:4
I will *m* it as the mourning of an ... Amos 8:10 7760
they shall also *m* gardens ... Amos 9:14 6213
Therefore I will *m* Samaria as an ... Mic 1:6 7760
I will *m* a wailing like the ... Mic 1:8 6213
M thee bald, and poll thee for thy ... Mic 1:16 7139
they shall *m* great noise by ... Mic 2:12
the prophets that *m* my people err ... Mic 3:5
and none shall *m* them afraid ... Mic 4:4
I will *m* her that halted a ... Mic 4:7 7760
for I will *m* thine horn iron ... Mic 4:13 7760
and I will *m* thy hoofs brass ... Mic 4:13 7760
Therefore also will I *m* thee sick ... Mic 6:13
that I should *m* thee a desolation ... Mic 6:16 5414
will *m* an utter end of the place ... Nah 1:8 6213
he will *m* an utter end ... Nah 1:9 6213
I will *m* thy grave ... Nah 1:14 7760
m thy loins strong, fortify thy ... Nah 2:1
they shall *m* haste to the wall ... Nah 2:5 4116
m thee vile, and will set thee as ... Nah 3:6
morter, *m* strong the brickkiln ... Nah 3:14
m thyself many as the cankerworm, ... Nah 3:15
m thyself many as the locusts ... Nah 3:15
m it plain upon tables, that he ... Hab 2:2

trusteth therein, to *m* dumb idols ... Hab 2:18 6213
in the midst of the years *m* known ... Hab 3:2
he will *m* my feet like hinds' ... Hab 3:19 7760
he will *m* me to walk upon mine ... Hab 3:19
for he shall *m* even a speedy ... Zeph 1:18 6213
will *m* Nineveh a desolation, and ... Zeph 2:13 7760
down, and none shall *m* them afraid ... Zeph 3:13
for I will *m* you a name and a ... Zeph 3:20 5414
LORD, and will *m* thee as a signet ... Hag 2:23 7760
m crowns, and set them upon the ... Zec 6:11 6213
m a noise as through wine ... Zec 9:15
corn shall *m* the young men ... Zec 9:17
so the LORD shall *m* bright clouds ... Zec 10:1 6213
I will *m* Jerusalem a cup of ... Zec 12:2 7760
in that day will I *m* Jerusalem a ... Zec 12:3 7760
In that day will I *m* the ... Zec 12:6 7760
And did not he *m* one ... Mal 2:15 6213
in that day when I *m* up my jewels ... Mal 3:17 6213
not willing to *m* her a publick ... Mt 1:19 *3856*
of the Lord, *m* his paths straight ... Mt 3:3 *4160*
I will *m* you fishers of men ... Mt 4:19 *4160*
because thou canst not *m* one hair ... Mt 5:36 *4160*
thou wilt, thou canst *m* me clean ... Mt 8:2 *2511*
that they should not *m* him known ... Mt 12:16 *4160*
Either *m* the tree good, and his ... Mt 12:33 *4160*
or else *m* the tree corrupt, and ... Mt 12:33 *4160*
let us *m* here three tabernacles ... Mt 17:4 *4160*
till I *m* thine enemies thy ... Mt 22:44 *5087*
they *m* broad their phylacteries, ... Mt 23:5 *4115*
and for a pretence *m* long prayer ... Mt 23:14 *4336*
land to *m* one proselyte, and when ... Mt 23:15 *4160*
ye *m* him twofold more the child ... Mt 23:15 *4160*
for ye *m* clean the outside of the ... Mt 23:25 *2511*
That he shall *m* him ruler over ... Mt 24:47 *2525*
I will *m* thee ruler over many ... Mt 25:21 *2525*
I will *m* thee ruler over many ... Mt 25:23 *2525*
your way, *m* it as sure as ye can ... Mt 27:65 *805*
of the Lord, *m* his paths straight ... Mk 1:3 *4160*
I will *m* you to become fishers of ... Mk 1:17 *4160*
thou wilt, thou canst *m* me clean ... Mk 1:40 *2511*
that they should not *m* him known ... Mk 3:12 *4160*
Why *m* ye this ado, and weep ... Mk 5:39 *2350*
he commanded them to *m* all sit ... Mk 6:39 *347*
let us *m* three tabernacles ... Mk 9:5 *4160*
till I *m* thine enemies thy ... Mk 12:36 *5087*
and for a pretence *m* long prayers ... Mk 12:40 *4336*
in two mites, which *m* a farthing ... Mk 12:42 *1510*
there *m* ready for us ... Mk 14:15 *2090*
to *m* ready a people prepared for ... Lk 1:17 *2090*
of the Lord, *m* his paths straight ... Lk 3:4 *4160*
thou wilt, thou canst *m* me clean ... Lk 5:12 *2511*
m prayers, and likewise the ... Lk 5:33 *4160*
Can ye *m* the children of the ... Lk 5:34 *4160*
M them sit down by fifties in a ... *Lk 9:14* *2625*
let us *m* three tabernacles ... *Lk 9:33* *4160*
Samaritans, to *m* ready for him ... *Lk 9:52* *2090*
Now do ye Pharisees *m* clean the ... Lk 11:39 *2511*
m that which is within also ... Lk 11:40 *4160*
m them to sit down to meat, and ... Lk 12:37 *347*
whom his lord shall *m* ruler over ... Lk 12:42 *2525*
that he will *m* him ruler over all ... Lk 12:44 *2525*
one consent began to *m* excuse ... Lk 14:18 *3868*
going to *m* war against another ... Lk 14:31 *4820*
m me as one of thy hired servants ... Lk 15:19 *4160*
that I might *m* merry with my ... Lk 15:29 *2165*
was meet that we should *m* merry ... Lk 15:32 *2165*
M to yourselves friends of the ... Lk 16:9 *4160*
M ready wherewith I may sup, and ... Lk 17:8 *2090*
Zacchaeus, *m* haste, and come down ... Lk 19:5 *4692*
Till I *m* thine enemies thy ... Lk 20:43 *5087*
for a shew *m* long prayers ... Lk 20:47 *4336*
there *m* ready ... Lk 22:12 *2090*
M straight the way of the Lord, ... Jn 1:23 *2116*
m not my Father's house an house ... Jn 2:16 *4160*
And Jesus said, *M* the men sit down ... Jn 6:10 *4160*
to *m* him a king, he departed ... Jn 6:15 *4160*
and the truth shall *m* you free ... Jn 8:32 *1659*
Son therefore shall *m* you free ... Jn 8:36 *1659*
How long dost thou *m* us to doubt ... Jn 10:24 *142*
unto him, and *m* our abode with him ... Jn 14:23 *4160*
thou shalt *m* me full of joy with ... Acts 2:28 *4137*
Until I *m* thy foes thy footstool ... Acts 2:35 *5087*
M us gods to go before us ... Acts 7:40 *4160*
that he should *m* it according to ... Acts 7:44 *4160*
arise, and *m* thy bed ... Acts 9:34 *4766*
my defence which I *m* now unto you ... Acts 22:1
M haste, and get thee quickly out ... Acts 22:18 *4692*
M ready two hundred soldiers to ... Acts 23:23 *2090*
to *m* thee a minister and a witness ... Acts 26:16 *4400*
much learning doth *m* thee mad ... Acts 26:24 *4062*
that without ceasing I *m* mention ... Rom 1:9 *4160*
shall their unbelief *m* the faith ... Rom 3:3 *2673*
Do we then *m* void the law through ... Rom 3:31 *2673*
of the same lump to *m* one vessel ... Rom 9:21 *4160*
to *m* his power known, endured ... Rom 9:22 *1107*
that he might *m* known the riches ... Rom 9:23 *1107*
will the Lord *m* upon the earth ... Rom 9:28 *4160*
m not provision for the flesh, to ... Rom 13:14 *4160*
for God is able to *m* him stand ... Rom 14:4 *2476*
the things which *m* for peace ... Rom 14:19 *3753*
to *m* the Gentiles obedient, by ... Rom 15:18 *1519*
and Achaia to *m* a certain ... Rom 15:26 *4160*
will *m* manifest the counsels of ... 1Cor 4:5 *5319*
m them the members of an harlot ... 1Cor 6:15 *4160*
if meat *m* my brother to offend, I ... 1Cor 8:13 *4624*
lest I *m* my brother to offend ... 1Cor 8:13 *4624*
any man should *m* my glorying void ... 1Cor 9:15 *2758*
I may *m* the gospel of Christ ... 1Cor 9:18 *5087*

temptation also *m* a way to escape 1Cor 10:13 *4160*
For if I *m* you sorry, who is he 2Cor 2:2 *3076*
m up beforehand your bounty, ... 2Cor 9:5 *4294*
God is able to *m* all grace abound 2Cor 9:8 *4052*
For we dare not *m* ourselves of 2Cor 10:12
Did I *m* a gain of you by any of 2Cor 12:17 *4122*
Did Titus *m* a gain of you 2Cor 12:18 *4122*
I *m* myself a transgressor .... Gal 2:18 *4921*
that it should *m* the promise of .... Gal 3:17 *2673*
As many as desire to *m* a fair .... Gal 6:12 *2146*
for to *m* in himself of twain one .... Eph 2:15 *2936*
to *m* all men see what is the .... Eph 3:9 *5461*
doth *m* manifest is light .... Eph 5:13 *4160*
to *m* known the mystery of the .... Eph 6:19 *1107*
shall *m* known to you all things .... Eph 6:21 *1107*
To whom God would *m* known what is .... Col 1:27 *1107*
That I may *m* it manifest, as I .... Col 4:4 *5319*
They shall *m* known unto you all .... Col 4:9 *1107*
the Lord *m* you to increase and 1Th 3:12 *4121*
but to *m* ourselves an ensample 2Th 3:9 *1325*
which are able to *m* thee wise 2Ti 3:15 *4679*
m full proof of thy ministry 2Ti 4:5 *4135*
until I *m* thine enemies thy .... Heb 1:13 *5087*
to *m* the captain of their .... Heb 2:10 *5055*
to *m* reconciliation for the sins .... Heb 2:17 *2433*
liveth to *m* intercession for them .... Heb 7:25 *1793*
he was about to *m* the tabernacle .... Heb 8:5 *2005*
that thou *m* all things according .... Heb 8:5 *4160*
when I will *m* a new covenant with .... Heb 8:8 *4931*
is the covenant that I will *m* .... Heb 8:10 *1303*
that could not *m* him that did the .... Heb 9:9 *5055*
year by year continually *m* the .... Heb 10:1 *5055*
will *m* with them after those days .... Heb 10:16 *1303*
m straight paths for your feet, ... Heb 12:13 *4160*
M you perfect in every good work .... Heb 13:21 *2675*
in peace of them that *m* peace .... Jas 3:18 *4160*
a while, *m* you perfect, stablish, ... 1Pet 5:10 *2675*
they *m* you that ye shall neither 2Pet 1:8 *2525*
give diligence to *m* your calling 2Pet 1:10 *4160*
words *m* merchandise of you 2Pet 2:3 *1710*
we *m* him a liar, and his word is 1Jn 1:10 *4160*
I will *m* them of the synagogue of .... Rev 3:9 *1325*
I will *m* them to come and worship .... Rev 3:9 *4160*
Him that overcometh will I *m* a .... Rev 3:12 *4160*
it shall *m* thy belly bitter, but .... Rev 10:9 *4087*
pit shall *m* war against them .... Rev 11:7 *4160*
m merry, and shall send gifts one .... Rev 11:10 *2165*
went to *m* war with the remnant of .... Rev 12:17 *4160*
who is able to *m* war with him .... Rev 13:4 *4170*
unto him to *m* war with the saints .... Rev 13:7 *4160*
that they should *m* an image to .... Rev 13:14 *4160*
These shall *m* war with the Lamb, ... Rev 17:14 *4170*
shall *m* her desolate and naked, and .... Rev 17:16 *4160*
he doth judge and *m* war .... Rev 19:11 *4170*
gathered together to *m* war .... Rev 19:19 *4160*
said, Behold, I *m* all things new .... Rev 21:5 *4160*

MAKER {20}
a man be more pure than his *m* .... Job 4:17 6213
in so doing my *m* would soon take .... Job 32:22 6213
But none saith, Where is God my *m* .... Job 35:10 6213
ascribe righteousness to my *M* .... Job 36:3 6466
us kneel before the LORD our *m* .... Ps 95:6 6213
the poor reproacheth his *M* .... Prov 14:31 6213
the poor reproacheth his *M* .... Prov 17:5 6213
the LORD is the *m* of them all .... Prov 22:2 6213
the *m* of it as a spark, and they .... Is 1:31 6467
day shall a man look to his *M* .... Is 17:7 6213
not looked unto the *m* thereof .... Is 22:11 6213
unto him that striveth with his *M* .... Is 45:9 3335
the Holy One of Israel, and his *M* .... Is 45:11 3335
And forgettest the LORD thy *m* .... Is 51:13 6213
For thy *M* is thine husband .... Is 54:5 6213
Thus saith the LORD the *m* thereof .... Jer 33:2 6213
For Israel hath forgotten his *M* .... Hos 8:14 6213
that the *m* thereof hath graven it .... Hab 2:18 3335
that the *m* of his work trusteth .... Hab 2:18 3335
whose builder and *m* is God .... Heb 11:10 *1217*

MAKERS {1}
together that are *m* of idols .... Is 45:16 2796

MAKEST {26}
what *m* thou in this place .... Judg 18:3 6213
m me to possess the iniquities of .... Job 13:26
that thou *m* thy ways perfect .... Job 22:3
only *m* me dwell in safety .... Ps 4:8
thou *m* his beauty to consume away .... Ps 39:11
Thou *m* us to turn back from the .... Ps 44:10
Thou *m* us a reproach to our .... Ps 44:13 6213
Thou *m* us a byword among the .... Ps 44:14 6213
thou *m* the outgoings of the .... Ps 65:8
thou *m* it soft with showers .... Ps 65:10
Thou *m* us a strife unto our .... Ps 80:6 7760
Thou *m* darkness, and it is night .... Ps 104:20 7896
that thou *m* account of him .... Ps 144:3
where thou *m* thy flock to rest at .... Song 1:7
that fashioneth it, What *m* thou .... Is 45:9 6213
that *m* thy nest in the cedars, ... Jer 22:23
but thou *m* this people to trust .... Jer 28:15
m thine high place in every .... Eze 16:31 6213
m men as the fishes of the sea, ... Hab 1:14 6213
m him drunken also, that thou .... Hab 2:15
When thou *m* a dinner or a supper, ... Lk 14:12 *4160*
But when thou *m* a feast, call the .... Lk 14:13 *4160*
whom *m* thou thyself .... Jn 8:53 *4160*
thou, being a man, *m* thyself God .... Jn 10:33 *4160*
the law, and *m* thy boast of God, ... Rom 2:17 *2744*
Thou that *m* thy boast of the law, ... Rom 2:23 *2744*

MAKETH {126}
or who *m* the dumb, or deaf, or .... Ex 4:11 7760
the priest that *m* atonement .... Lev 7:7
the priest that *m* him clean shall .... Lev 14:11
for it is the blood that *m* an .... Lev 17:11
m his son or his daughter to pass .... Deut 18:10
the city that *m* war with thee .... Deut 20:20 6213
when he *m* his sons to inherit .... Deut 21:16
m merchandise of him, or selleth .... Deut 24:7
Cursed be the man that *m* any .... Deut 27:15 6213
Cursed be he that *m* the blind to .... Deut 27:18
LORD thy God *m* with thee this day .... Deut 29:12 3772
The LORD killeth, and *m* alive 1Sa 2:6
The LORD *m* poor, and *m* rich 1Sa 2:7
and he *m* my way perfect 2Sa 22:33
He *m* my feet like hinds' feet 2Sa 22:34 7737
For he *m* sore, and bindeth up .... Job 5:18
Which *m* Arcturus, Orion, and .... Job 9:9 6213
spoiled, and *m* the judges fools .... Job 12:17
he *m* them to stagger like a .... Job 12:25
m collops of fat on his flanks .... Job 15:27 6213
For God *m* my heart soft, and the .... Job 23:16
he *m* peace in his high places .... Job 25:2 6213
and as a booth that the keeper *m* .... Job 27:18 6213
m us wiser than the fowls of .... Job 35:11
For he *m* small the drops of water .... Job 36:27
He *m* the deep to boil like a pot .... Job 41:31
he *m* the sea like a pot of .... Job 41:31 7760
He *m* a path to shine after him .... Job 41:32
When he *m* inquisition for blood, ... Ps 9:12 1875
strength, and *m* my way perfect .... Ps 18:32 5414
He *m* my feet like hinds' feet, and .... Ps 18:33 7737
He *m* me to lie down in green .... Ps 23:2
He *m* them also to skip like a .... Ps 29:6
of the LORD *m* the hinds to calve .... Ps 29:9
he *m* the devices of the people of .... Ps 33:10
man that *m* the LORD his trust .... Ps 40:4 7760
He *m* wars to cease unto the end .... Ps 46:9
who *m* the clouds his chariot .... Ps 104:3 7706
Who *m* his angels spirits .... Ps 104:4 6213
wine that *m* glad the heart of man .... Ps 104:15
He *m* the storm a calm, so that .... Ps 107:29 6965
there he *m* the hungry to dwell, ... Ps 107:36
m him families like a flock .... Ps 107:41 7760
He *m* the barren woman to keep .... Ps 113:9
he *m* lightnings for the rain .... Ps 135:7 6213
who *m* grass to grow upon the .... Ps 147:8
He *m* peace in thy borders, and .... Ps 147:14 7760
A wise son *m* a glad father .... Prov 10:1
the hand of the diligent *m* rich .... Prov 10:4
it *m* rich, and he addeth no sorrow .... Prov 10:22
but she that *m* ashamed is as .... Prov 12:4
in the heart of man *m* it stoop .... Prov 12:25
but a good word *m* it glad .... Prov 12:25
There is that *m* himself rich .... Prov 13:7
there is that *m* himself poor .... Prov 13:7
Hope deferred *m* the heart sick, ... Prov 13:12
A merry heart *m* a cheerful .... Prov 15:13
A wise son *m* a glad father .... Prov 15:20
and a good report *m* the bones fat .... Prov 15:30
he *m* even his enemies to be at .... Prov 16:7
A man's gift *m* room for him .... Prov 18:16
Wealth *m* many friends .... Prov 19:4 3254
but he that *m* haste to be rich .... Prov 28:20 213
She *m* herself coverings of .... Prov 31:22 6213
She *m* fine linen, and selleth it .... Prov 31:24 6213
m from the beginning to the end .... Eccl 3:11 6213
oppression *m* a wise man mad .... Eccl 7:7
a man's wisdom *m* his face to .... Eccl 8:1
for laughter, and wine *m* merry .... Eccl 10:19
not the works of God who *m* all .... Eccl 11:5 6213
every one that *m* mention thereof .... Is 19:17
the LORD *m* the earth empty, and .... Is 24:1
m it waste, and turneth it upside .... Is 24:1
when he *m* all the stones of the .... Is 27:9 7760
he *m* the judges of the earth as .... Is 40:23 6213
which *m* a way in the sea, and a .... Is 43:16 5414
m it after the figure of a man, ... Is 44:13 6213
he *m* a god, and worshippeth it .... Is 44:15 6466
he *m* it a graven image, and .... Is 44:15 6213
And the residue thereof he *m* a god .... Is 44:17 6213
I am the LORD that *m* all things .... Is 44:24 6213
of the liars, and *m* diviners mad .... Is 44:25
m their knowledge foolish .... Is 44:25
and he *m* it a god .... Is 46:6 6213
m it bring forth and bud, that it .... Is 55:10
from evil *m* himself a prey .... Is 59:15
my heart *m* a noise in me .... Jer 4:19
he *m* lightnings with rain, and .... Jer 10:13 6213
m flesh his arm, and whose heart .... Jer 17:5 7760
king of Babylon *m* war against us .... Jer 21:2
m himself a prophet, that thou .... Jer 29:26
which *m* himself a prophet to you .... Jer 29:27
be like the dove that *m* her nest .... Jer 48:28
he *m* lightnings with rain, and .... Jer 51:16 6213
m idols against herself to defile .... Eze 22:3 6213
secrets, and *m* known to the king .... Dan 2:28
he that revealeth secrets *m* known .... Dan 2:29
but *m* his petition three times a .... Dan 6:13
the abomination that *m* desolate .... Dan 11:31
that *m* desolate set up, there .... Dan 12:11
that *m* the morning darkness, and .... Amos 4:13 6213
Seek him that *m* the seven stars .... Amos 5:8 6213
m the day dark with night .... Amos 5:8
m it dry, and drieth up all the .... Nah 1:4
for he *m* his sun to rise on the .... Mt 5:45 *393*
he *m* both the deaf to hear, and .... Mk 7:37 *4160*
then both the new *m* a rent .... Lk 5:36 *4977*

whosoever *m* himself a king .... Jn 19:12 *4160*
Aeneas, Jesus Christ *m* thee whole .... Acts 9:34 *2390*
And hope *m* not ashamed .... Rom 5:5 *2617*
but the Spirit itself *m* .... Rom 8:26 *5241*
because he *m* intercession for the .... Rom 8:27 *1793*
who also *m* intercession for us .... Rom 8:34 *1793*
how he *m* intercession to God .... Rom 11:2 *1793*
For who *m* thee to differ from 1Cor 4:7 *1252*
who is he then that *m* me glad 2Cor 2:2 *2165*
m manifest the savour of his 2Cor 2:14 *5319*
they were, it *m* no matter to me .... Gal 2:6 *1308*
m increase of the body unto the .... Eph 4:16 *4160*
Who *m* his angels spirits, and his .... Heb 1:7 *4160*
For the law *m* men high priests .... Heb 7:28 *2525*
m the Son, who is consecrated for .... Heb 7:28
so that he *m* fire come down from .... Rev 13:13 *4160*
worketh abomination, or *m* a lie .... Rev 21:27
and whosoever loveth and *m* a lie .... Rev 22:15 *4160*

MAKHELOTH *(mak'-he-loth)* {2} *An Israelite encampment in the wilderness.*
from Haradah, and pitched in *M* .... Num 33:25 4721
And they removed from *M*, and .... Num 33:26 4721

MAKI See MACHI.

MAKING {30}
task in *m* brick both yesterday .... Ex 5:14
in *m* war against it to take it, ... Deut 20:19
Now as they were *m* their hearts .... Judg 19:22
eating and drinking, and *m* merry 1Kin 4:20
m a noise with psalteries and 1Chr 15:28
in *m* known all these great things 1Chr 17:19
m confession to the LORD God of 2Chr 30:22
LORD is sure, *m* wise the simple .... Ps 19:7
of *m* many books there is no end .... Eccl 12:12 6213
m a tinkling with their feet .... Is 3:16
m him very glad .... Jer 20:15
multitude of the wares of thy *m* .... Eze 27:16 4639
multitude of the wares of thy *m* .... Eze 27:18 4639
m supplication before his God .... Dan 6:11
swearing falsely in *m* a covenant .... Hos 10:4 3772
m the ephah small, and the shekel .... Amos 8:5
in *m* thee desolate because of thy .... Mic 6:13
minstrels and the people *m* a noise .... Mt 9:23 *2350*
M the word of God of none effect .... Mk 7:13 *208*
Father, *m* himself equal with God .... Jn 5:18 *4160*
M request, if by any means now at .... Rom 1:10 *1189*
as poor, yet *m* many rich 2Cor 6:10 *4148*
m mention of you in my prayers .... Eph 1:16 *4160*
of twain one new man, so *m* peace .... Eph 2:15 *4160*
m melody in your heart to the .... Eph 5:19 *5567*
for you all *m* request with joy .... Phil 1:4 *4160*
m mention of you in our prayers 1Th 1:2 *4160*
m mention of thee always in my .... Philem 4 *4160*
m them an ensample unto those 2Pet 2:6 *4160*
have compassion, *m* a difference .... Jude 22 *1252*

MAKIR See MACHIR.

MAKIRITE See MACHIRITES.

MAKKEDAH *(mak'-ke-dah)* {9} *A city in Judah.*
smote them to Azekah, and unto *M* .... Josh 10:10 4719
and hid themselves in a cave at *M* .... Josh 10:16 4719
are found hid in a cave at *M* .... Josh 10:17 4719
the camp to Joshua at *M* in peace .... Josh 10:21 4719
And that day Joshua took *M* .... Josh 10:28 4719
he did to the king of *M* as he did .... Josh 10:28 4719
Then Joshua passed from *M* .... Josh 10:29 4719
The king of *M*, one .... Josh 12:16 4719
Beth-dagon, and Naamah, and *M* .... Josh 15:41 4719

MAKTESH *(mak'-tesh)* {1} *A district near Jerusalem.*
Howl, ye inhabitants of *M* .... Zeph 1:11 4389

MALACHI *(mal'-a-ki)* {1} *A prophet.*
word of the LORD to Israel by *M* .... Mal 1:1 4401

MALCAM See MALCHAM.

MALCHAM *(mal'-kam)* {2} See MILCOM.
1. Son of Shaharaim.
Jobab, and Zibia, and Mesha, and *M* 1Chr 8:9 4445
2. An Ammonite idol.
by the LORD, and that swear by *M* .... Zeph 1:5 4445

MALCHIAH *(mal-ki'-ah)* {9} See MALCHIJAH, MELCHIAH.
1. Father of Baaseiah.
the son of Baaseiah, the son of *M* 1Chr 6:40 4441
2. A descendant of Parosh.
Ramiah, and Jeziah, and *M*, and .... Ezr 10:25 4441
the son of Pashur, the son of *M* .... Neh 11:12 4441
3. Another descendant of Parosh.
Eliezer, Ishijah, *M*, Shemaiah, ... Ezr 10:31 4441
4. A repairer of Jerusalem's wall.
gate repaired *M* the son of Rechab .... Neh 3:14 4441
5. Another repairer of Jerusalem's wall.
After him repaired *M* the .... Neh 3:31 4441
6. A priest who aided Ezra.
hand, Pedaiah, and Mishael, and *M* .... Neh 8:4 4441
7. A priest who dedicated the wall.
Shelemiah, and Pashur the son of *M* .... Jer 38:1 4441
dungeon of *M* the son of Hammelech .... Jer 38:6 4441

MALCHIEL *(mal'-ke-el)* {3} See MALCHIELITES. *A son of Beriah.*
Heber, and *M* .... Gen 46:17 4439
of *M*, the family of the .... Num 26:45 4439
Heber, and *M*, who is the father of 1Chr 7:31 4439

MALCHIELITES *(mal'-ke-el-ites)* {1} *Descendants of Malchiel.*
of Malchiel, the family of the *M* .... Num 26:45 4440

MALCHIJAH *(mal-ki'-jah)* {6} See MALCHIAH.
1. A family of exiles.
the son of Pashur, the son of *M* 1Chr 9:12 4441
2. A sanctuary servant.
The fifth to *M*, the sixth to 1Chr 24:9 4441
3. Married a foreigner in exile.
and Miamin, and Eleazar, and *M* Ezr 10:25 4441
4. A rebuilder of Jerusalem's wall.
M the son of Harim, and Hashub the Neh 3:11 4441
5. A priest who dedicated the wall.
Pashur, Amariah, *M*, Neh 10:3 4441
and Uzzi, and Jehohanan, and *M* Neh 12:42 4441

MALCHIRAM *(mal'-ki-ram)* {1} *A descendant of King Jehoiakim.*
M also, and Pedaiah, and Shenazar, 1Chr 3:18 4443

MALCHI-SHUA *(mal'-ki-shu'-ah)* {3} See MELCHISHUA. *A son of King Saul.*
and Saul begat Jonathan, and *M* 1Chr 8:33 4444
and Saul begat Jonathan, and *M* 1Chr 9:39 4444
slew Jonathan, and Abinadab, and *M* 1Chr 10:2 4444

MALCHUS *(mal'-kus)* {1} *A servant wounded by Simon Peter.*
The servant's name was *M* Jn 18:10 *3124*

MALE {46}
m and female created he them Gen 1:27 2145
M and female created he them Gen 5:2 2145
they shall be *m* and female Gen 6:19 2145
take to thee by sevens, the *m* Gen 7:2 376
that are not clean by two, the *m* Gen 7:2 376
also of the air by sevens, the *m* Gen 7:3 2145
two unto Noah into the ark, the *m* Gen 7:9 2145
And they that went in, went in *m* Gen 7:16 2145
money, every *m* among the men of Gen 17:23 2145
as we be, that every *m* of you be Gen 34:15 2145
people, if every *m* among us be Gen 34:22 2145
every *m* was circumcised, all that Gen 34:24 2145
blemish, a *m* of the first year Ex 12:5 2145
whether ox or sheep, that is *m* Ex 34:19 2142
let him offer a *m* without blemish Lev 1:3 2145
bring it a *m* without blemish Lev 1:10 2145
whether it be a *m* or female Lev 3:1 2145
m or female, he shall offer it Lev 3:6 2145
of the goats, a *m* without blemish Lev 4:23 2145
Every *m* among the priests shall Lev 7:6 2145
that hath born a *m* or a female Lev 12:7 2145
your own will a *m* without blemish Lev 22:19 2145
thy estimation shall be of the *m* Lev 27:3 2145
shall be of the *m* twenty shekels Lev 27:5 2145
of the *m* five shekels of silver Lev 27:6 2145
if it be a *m*, then thy estimation Lev 27:7 2145
names, every *m* by their polls Num 1:2 2145
every *m* from twenty years old and Num 1:20 2145
every *m* from twenty years old and Num 1:22 2145
every *m* from a month old and Num 3:15 2145
Both *m* and female shall ye put out Num 5:3 2145
every *m* shall eat it Num 18:10 2145
every *m* among the little ones Num 31:17 2145
the likeness of *m* or female Deut 4:16 2145
there shall not be *m* or female Deut 7:14
thou shalt smite every *m* thereof Deut 20:13 2138
these were the *m* children of Josh 17:2 2145
Ye shall utterly destroy every *m* Judg 21:11 2145
known no man by lying with any *m* Judg 21:12 2145
he had smitten every *m* in Edom 1Kin 11:15 2145
he had cut off every *m* in Edom 1Kin 11:16 2145
which hath in his flock a *m* Mal 1:14 2145
them at the beginning made them *m* Mt 19:4 *730*
of the creation God made them *m* Mk 10:6 *730*
Every *m* that openeth the womb Lk 2:23 *730*
there is neither *m* nor female Gal 3:28 *730*

MALEFACTOR {1}
said unto him, If he were not a *m* Jn 18:30 *2555*

MALEFACTORS {3}
And there were also two others, *m* Lk 23:32 *2557*
they crucified him, and the *m* Lk 23:33 *2557*
one of the *m* which were hanged Lk 23:39 *2557*

MALELEEL *(mal'-e-le-el)* {1} See MAHALALEEL. *Son of Cainan; ancestor of Jesus.*
of Jared, which was the son of *M* Lk 3:37 *3121*

MALES {32}
city boldly, and slew all the *m* Gen 34:25 2145
let all his *m* be circumcised, and Ex 12:48 2145
the *m* shall be the LORD's Ex 13:12 2145
that openeth the matrix, being *m* Ex 13:15 2145
m shall appear before the Lord Ex 23:17 2138
All the *m* among the children of Lev 6:18 2145
All the *m* among the priests shall Lev 6:29 2145
to the number of all the *m* Num 3:22 2145
In the number of all the *m* Num 3:28 2145
to the number of all the *m* Num 3:34 2145
all the *m* from a month old and Num 3:39 2145
m of the children of Israel from Num 3:40 2145
all the firstborn *m* by the number Num 3:43 2145
all *m* from a month old and upward Num 26:62 2145
and they slew all the *m* Num 31:7 2145
All the firstling *m* that come of Deut 15:19 2145
times in a year shall all thy *m* Deut 16:16 2138
came out of Egypt, that were *m* Josh 5:4 2145
Beside their genealogy of *m* 2Chr 31:16 2145
to all the *m* among the priests 2Chr 31:19 2145
by genealogy of the *m* an hundred Ezr 8:3 2145
and with him two hundred *m* Ezr 8:4 2145
and with him three hundred *m* Ezr 8:5 2145
of Jonathan, and with him fifty *m* Ezr 8:6 2145
Athaliah, and with him seventy *m* Ezr 8:7 2145
Michael, and with him fourscore *m* Ezr 8:8 2145
him two hundred and eighteen *m* Ezr 8:9 2145
him an hundred and threescore *m* Ezr 8:10 2145
and with him twenty and eight *m* Ezr 8:11 2145
and with him an hundred and ten *m* Ezr 8:12 2145
and with them threescore *m* Ezr 8:13 2145
Zabbud, and with them seventy *m* Ezr 8:14 2145

MALICE {6}
neither with the leaven of *m* 1Cor 5:8 *2549*
howbeit in *m* be ye children, but 1Cor 14:20 *2549*
be put away from you, with all *m* Eph 4:31 *2549*
anger, wrath, *m*, blasphemy, Col 3:8 *2549*
lusts and pleasures, living in *m* Titus 3:3 *2549*
Wherefore laying aside all *m* 1Pet 2:1 *2549*

MALICIOUS {1}
prating against us with *m* words 3Jn 10 *4190*

MALICIOUSNESS {2}
wickedness, covetousness, *m* Rom 1:29 *2549*
your liberty for a cloke of *m* 1Pet 2:16 *2549*

MALIGNITY {1}
envy, murder, debate, deceit, *m* Rom 1:29 *2550*

MALLOTHI *(mal'-lo-thi)* {2} *A son of Heman.*
and Romamti-ezer, Joshbekashah, *M* 1Chr 25:4 4413
The nineteenth to *M*, he, his sons 1Chr 25:26 4413

MALLOWS {1}
Who cut up *m* by the bushes, and Job 30:4 4408

MALLUCH *(mal'-luk)* {6} See MELICU.
1. Ancestor of Ethan.
the son of Abdi, the son of *M* 1Chr 6:44 4409
2. A son of Bani.
Meshullam, *M*, and Adaiah, Jashub, Ezr 10:29 4409
3. A descendant of Harim.
Benjamin, *M*, and Shemariah Ezr 10:32 4409
4. A priest who renewed the covenant.
Hattush, Shebaniah, *M*, Neh 10:4 4409
Amariah, *M*, Hattush, Neh 12:2 4409
5. A clan leader who renewed the covenant.
M, Harim, Baanah Neh 10:27 4409

MALLUCHI See MELICU.

MALTA See MELITA.

MAMMON {4}
Ye cannot serve God and *m* Mt 6:24 *3126*
of the *m* of unrighteousness Lk 16:9 *3126*
faithful in the unrighteous *m* Lk 16:11 *3126*
Ye cannot serve God and *m* Lk 16:13 *3126*

MAMRE *(mam'-re)* {10}
1. A place near Hebron.
came and dwelt in the plain of *M* Gen 13:18 4471
unto him in the plains of *M* Gen 18:1 4471
in Machpelah, which was before *M* Gen 23:17 4471
the field of Machpelah before *M* Gen 23:19 4471
the Hittite, which is before *M* Gen 25:9 4471
came unto Isaac his father unto *M* Gen 35:27 4471
of Machpelah, which is before *M* Gen 49:30 4471
of Ephron the Hittite, before *M* Gen 50:13 4471
2. An Amorite ally of Abraham.
in the plain of *M* the Amorite Gen 14:13 4471
went with me, Aner, Eshcol, and *M* Gen 14:24 4471

MAN {2617}
Let us make *m* in our image, after Gen 1:26 120
So God created *m* in his own image Gen 1:27 120
there was not a *m* to till the Gen 2:5 120
the LORD God formed *m* of the dust Gen 2:7 120
and *m* became a living soul Gen 2:7 120
there he put the *m* whom he had Gen 2:8 120
And the LORD God took the *m* Gen 2:15 120
And the LORD God commanded the *m* Gen 2:16 120
good that the *m* should be alone Gen 2:18 120
the LORD God had taken from *m* Gen 2:22 120
woman, and brought her unto the *m* Gen 2:22 120
because she was taken out of *M* Gen 2:23 376
shall a *m* leave his father Gen 2:24 376
And they were both naked, the *m* Gen 2:25 120
the *m* said, The woman whom thou Gen 3:12 120
the *m* is become as one of us, to Gen 3:22 120
So he drove out the *m* Gen 3:24 120
I have gotten a *m* from the LORD Gen 4:1 376
I have slain a *m* to my wounding Gen 4:23 376
and a young *m* to my hurt Gen 4:23
In the day that God created *m* Gen 5:1 120
shall not always strive with *m* Gen 6:3 120
of *m* was great in the earth Gen 6:5 120
that he had made *m* on the earth Gen 6:6 120
I will destroy *m* whom I have Gen 6:7 120
both *m*, and beast, and the creeping Gen 6:7 120
Noah was a just *m* and perfect in Gen 6:9 376
upon the earth, and every *m* Gen 7:21 120
the face of the ground, both *m* Gen 7:23 120
I require it, and at the hand of *m* Gen 9:5 120
will I require the life of *m* Gen 9:5 120
by *m* shall his blood be shed Gen 9:6 120
for in the image of God made he *m* Gen 9:6 120
so that if a *m* can number the Gen 13:16 376
And he will be a wild *m* Gen 16:12 120
his hand will be against every *m* Gen 16:12
Every *m* child among you shall be Gen 17:10 2145
every *m* child in your generations Gen 17:12 2145
the uncircumcised *m* child whose Gen 17:14 2145
good, and gave it unto a young *m* Gen 18:7
daughters which have not known *m* Gen 19:8 376
And they pressed sore upon the *m* Gen 19:9 376
there is not a *m* in the earth to Gen 19:31 376
Behold, thou art but a dead *m* Gen 20:3 376
therefore restore the *m* his wife Gen 20:7 376
neither had any *m* known her Gen 24:16 376
the *m* wondering at her held his Gen 24:21 376
that the *m* took a golden earring Gen 24:22 376
the *m* bowed down his head, and Gen 24:26 376
and Laban ran out unto the *m* Gen 24:29 376
saying, Thus spake the *m* unto me Gen 24:30 376
that he came unto the *m* Gen 24:30 376
the *m* came into the house Gen 24:32 376
her, Wilt thou go with this *m* Gen 24:58 376
the camels, and followed the *m* Gen 24:61 376
What *m* is this that walketh in Gen 24:65 376
died in a good old age, an old *m* Gen 25:8
cunning hunter, a *m* of the field Gen 25:27 376
and Jacob was a plain *m*, dwelling Gen 25:27 376
He that toucheth this *m* or his Gen 26:11 376
the *m* waxed great, and went Gen 26:13 376
Esau my brother is a hairy *m* Gen 27:11 376
and I am a smooth *m* Gen 27:11 376
I should give her to another *m* Gen 29:19 376
the *m* increased exceedingly, and Gen 30:43 376
my daughters, no *m* is with us Gen 31:50 376
there wrestled a *m* with him until Gen 32:24 376
the young *m* deferred not to do Gen 34:19
brethren, took each *m* his sword Gen 34:25 376
And a certain *m* found him, and, Gen 37:15 376
the *m* asked him, saying, What Gen 37:15 376
the *m* said, They are departed Gen 37:17 376
father in law, saying, By the *m* Gen 38:25 376
Joseph, and he was a prosperous *m* Gen 39:2 376
each *m* his dream in one night, Gen 40:5 376
each *m* according to the Gen 40:5 376
we dreamed each *m* according to Gen 41:11 376
there was there with us a young *m* Gen 41:12 376
to each *m* according to his dream Gen 41:12 376
let Pharaoh look out a *m* discreet Gen 41:33 376
a *m* in whom the Spirit of God is Gen 41:38 376
without thee shall no *m* lift up Gen 41:44 376
the sons of one *m* in the land of Gen 42:13 376
The *m*, who is the lord of the Gen 42:30 376
And the *m*, the lord of the country Gen 42:33 376
The *m* did solemnly protest unto Gen 43:3 376
for the *m* said unto us, Ye shall Gen 43:5 376
as to tell the *m* whether ye had Gen 43:6 376
The *m* asked us straitly of our Gen 43:7 376
and carry down the *m* a present Gen 43:11 376
and arise, go again unto the *m* Gen 43:13 376
give you mercy before the *m* Gen 43:14 376
And the *m* did as Joseph bade Gen 43:17 376
the *m* brought the men into Gen 43:17 376
the *m* brought the men into Gen 43:24 376
the old *m* of whom ye spake Gen 43:27
every *m* his sack to the ground Gen 44:11 376
and opened every *m* his sack Gen 44:11 376
clothes, and laded every *m* his ass Gen 44:13 376
wot ye not that such a *m* as I can Gen 44:15 376
but the *m* in whose hand the cup Gen 44:17 376
lord, We have a father, an old *m* Gen 44:20 376
Cause every *m* to go out from me Gen 45:1 376
And there stood no *m* with him Gen 45:1 376
he gave each *m* changes of raiment Gen 45:22 376
Egyptians sold every *m* his field Gen 47:20 376
for in their anger they slew a *m* Gen 49:6 376
every *m* and his household came Ex 1:1 376
there went a *m* of the house of Ex 2:1 376
when he saw that there was no *m* Ex 2:12 376
why is it that ye have left the *m* Ex 2:20 376
was content to dwell with the *m* Ex 2:21 376
they cast down every *m* his rod Ex 7:12 376
the earth, and it became lice in *m* Ex 8:17 120
so there were lice upon *m* Ex 8:18 120
breaking forth with blains upon *m* Ex 9:9 120
breaking forth with blains upon *m* Ex 9:10 120
for upon every *m* and beast which Ex 9:19 120
in all the land of Egypt, upon *m* Ex 9:22 120
all that was in the field, both *m* Ex 9:25 120
shall this *m* be a snare unto us Ex 10:7
let every *m* borrow of his Ex 11:2 376
Moreover the *m* Moses was very Ex 11:3 376
his tongue, against *m* or beast Ex 11:7 376
shall take to them every *m* a lamb Ex 12:3 376
every *m* according to his eating Ex 12:4 376
in the land of Egypt, both *m* Ex 12:12 120
save that which every *m* must eat Ex 12:16 5315
the children of Israel, both of *m* Ex 13:2 120
all the firstborn of *m* among thy Ex 13:13 120
of Egypt, both the firstborn of *m* Ex 13:15 120
The LORD is a *m* of war Ex 15:3 376
Gather of it every *m* according to Ex 16:16 376
his eating, an omer for every *m* Ex 16:16 1538
take ye every *m* for them which Ex 16:16 376
they gathered every *m* according Ex 16:18 376
Let no *m* leave of it till the Ex 16:19 376
every *m* according to his eating Ex 16:21 376
much bread, two omers for one *m* Ex 16:22
abide ye every *m* in his place Ex 16:29 376
let no *m* go out of his place on Ex 16:29 376
whether it be beast or *m*, it Ex 19:13 376
if a *m* sell his daughter to be a Ex 21:7 376
He that smiteth a *m*, so that he Ex 21:12 376
if a *m* lie not in wait, but God Ex 21:13
But if a *m* come presumptuously Ex 21:14 376
And he that stealeth a *m*, and Ex 21:16 376
if a *m* smite his servant, or his Ex 21:20 376
if a *m* smite the eye of his Ex 21:26 376
If an ox gore a *m* or a woman Ex 21:28 376
he hath killed a *m* or a woman Ex 21:29 376
if a *m* shall open a pit Ex 21:33 376
or if a *m* shall dig a pit, and not Ex 21:33 376

If a *m* shall steal an ox, or a ... Ex 22:1 376
If a *m* shall cause a field or ... Ex 22:5 376
If a *m* shall deliver unto his ... Ex 22:7 376
If a *m* deliver unto his neighbour ... Ex 22:10 376
or driven away, no *m* seeing it ... Ex 22:10
if a *m* borrow ought of his ... Ex 22:14 376
if a *m* entice a maid that is not ... Ex 22:16 376
countenance a poor *m* in his cause ... Ex 23:3
if any *m* have any matters to do, ... Ex 24:14 1167
of every *m* that giveth it ... Ex 25:2 376
then shall they give every *m* a ... Ex 30:12 376
the *m* that brought us up out of ... Ex 32:1 376
the *m* that brought us up out of ... Ex 32:23 376
Put every *m* his sword by his side ... Ex 32:27 376
slay every *m* his brother, and ... Ex 32:27 376
every *m* his companion ... Ex 32:27 376
and every *m* his neighbour ... Ex 32:27 376
even every *m* upon his son, and ... Ex 32:29 376
no *m* did put on him his ornaments ... Ex 33:4 376
stood every *m* at his tent door, ... Ex 33:8 376
every *m* in his tent door ... Ex 33:10 376
as a *m* speaketh unto his friend ... Ex 33:11 376
Joshua, the son of Nun, a young *m* ... Ex 33:11
for there shall no *m* see me ... Ex 33:20 120
no *m* shall come up with thee, ... Ex 34:3 376
neither let any *m* be seen ... Ex 34:3 376
shall any *m* desire thy land ... Ex 34:24 376
every *m* that offered offered an ... Ex 35:22 376
And every *m*, with whom was found ... Ex 35:23 376
and every *m*, with whom was found ... Ex 35:24 376
offering unto the LORD, every *m* ... Ex 35:29 376
Aholiab, and every wise hearted *m* ... Ex 36:1 376
Aholiab, and every wise hearted *m* ... Ex 36:2 376
came every *m* from his work which ... Ex 36:4 376
Let neither *m* nor woman make any ... Ex 36:6 376
every wise hearted *m* among them ... Ex 36:8 376
A bekah for every *m*, that is, ... Ex 38:26 1538
If any *m* of you bring an offering ... Lev 1:2 120
if he touch the uncleanness of *m* ... Lev 5:3 120
that a *m* shall be defiled withal ... Lev 5:3 120
whatsoever it be that a *m* shall ... Lev 5:4 120
any of all these that a *m* doeth ... Lev 6:3 120
thing, as the uncleanness of *m* ... Lev 7:21 120
conceived seed, and born a *m* child ... Lev 12:2 2145
When a *m* shall have in the skin ... Lev 13:2 120
the plague of leprosy is in a *m* ... Lev 13:9 120
If a *m* or woman have a plague ... Lev 13:29 376
If a *m* also or a woman have in ... Lev 13:38 376
the *m* whose hair is fallen off ... Lev 13:40 376
He is a leprous *m*, he is unclean ... Lev 13:44 376
the *m* that is to be made clean ... Lev 14:11 376
When any *m* hath a running issue ... Lev 15:2 376
whom *m* shall lie with seed of ... Lev 15:18 376
if any *m* lie with her at all, and ... Lev 15:24 376
him that hath an issue, of the *m* ... Lev 15:33 2145
there shall be no *m* in the ... Lev 16:17 120
of a fit *m* into the wilderness ... Lev 16:21 376
What *m* soever there be of the ... Lev 17:3 376
shall be imputed unto that *m* ... Lev 17:4 376
that *m* shall be cut off from ... Lev 17:4 376
Whatsoever *m* there be of the ... Lev 17:8 376
even that *m* shall be cut off from ... Lev 17:9 376
whatsoever *m* there be of the ... Lev 17:10 376
whatsoever *m* there be of the ... Lev 17:13 376
which if a *m* do, he shall live in ... Lev 18:5 120
Ye shall fear every *m* his mother ... Lev 19:3 376
and honour the face of the old *m* ... Lev 19:32
I will set my face against that *m* ... Lev 20:3 376
ways hide their eyes from the *m* ... Lev 20:4 376
I will set my face against that *m* ... Lev 20:5 376
the *m* that committeth adultery ... Lev 20:10 376
the *m* that lieth with his ... Lev 20:11 376
if a *m* lie with his daughter in ... Lev 20:12 376
If a *m* also lie with mankind, as ... Lev 20:13 376
if a *m* take a wife and her mother, ... Lev 20:14 376
if a *m* lie with a beast, he shall ... Lev 20:15 376
if a *m* shall take his sister, his ... Lev 20:17 376
if a *m* shall lie with a woman ... Lev 20:18 376
if a *m* shall lie with his uncle's ... Lev 20:20 376
if a *m* shall take his brother's ... Lev 20:21 376
A *m* also or woman that hath a ... Lev 20:27 376
being a chief *m* among his people, ... Lev 21:4 1167
For whatsoever *m* he be that hath ... Lev 21:18 376
a blind *m*, or a lame, or he that ... Lev 21:18 376
Or a *m* that is brokenfooted, or ... Lev 21:19 376
No *m* that hath a blemish of the ... Lev 21:21 376
What *m* soever of the seed of ... Lev 22:4 376
or a *m* whose seed goeth from him ... Lev 22:4 376
or a *m* of whom he may take ... Lev 22:5 120
if a *m* eat of the holy thing ... Lev 22:14 376
a *m* of Israel strove together in ... Lev 24:10 376
he that killeth any *m* shall ... Lev 24:17 120
if a *m* cause a blemish in his ... Lev 24:19 376
he hath caused a blemish in a *m* ... Lev 24:20 120
and he that killeth a *m*, he shall ... Lev 24:21 120
every *m* unto his possession ... Lev 25:10 376
return every *m* unto his family ... Lev 25:10 376
every *m* unto his possession ... Lev 25:13 376
if the *m* have none to redeem it, ... Lev 25:26 376
unto the *m* to whom he sold it ... Lev 25:27 376
if a *m* sell a dwelling house in a ... Lev 25:29 376
if a *m* purchase of the Levites, ... Lev 25:33
When a *m* shall make a singular ... Lev 27:2 376
all that any *m* giveth of such ... Lev 27:9
when a *m* shall sanctify his house ... Lev 27:14 376
if a *m* shall sanctify unto the ... Lev 27:16 376
have sold the field to another *m* ... Lev 27:20 376
if a *m* sanctify unto the LORD a ... Lev 27:22

firstling, no *m* shall sanctify it ... Lev 27:26 376
that a *m* shall devote unto the ... Lev 27:28 376
of all that he hath, both of *m* ... Lev 27:28 120
if a *m* will at all redeem ought ... Lev 27:31 376
there shall be a *m* of every tribe ... Num 1:4 376
every *m* by his own camp, and every ... Num 1:52 376
every *m* by his own standard, ... Num 1:52 376
Every *m* of the children of Israel ... Num 2:2 376
every *m* in his place by their ... Num 2:17 376
the firstborn in Israel, both *m* ... Num 3:13 120
When a *m* or woman shall commit ... Num 5:6 376
But if the *m* have no kinsman to ... Num 5:8 376
whatsoever any *m* giveth the ... Num 5:10 376
a *m* lie with her carnally, and it ... Num 5:13 376
Then shall the *m* bring his wife ... Num 5:15 376
If no *m* have lain with thee, and ... Num 5:19 376
some *m* have lain with thee beside ... Num 5:20 376
Then shall the *m* be guiltless ... Num 5:31 376
When either *m* or woman shall ... Num 6:2 376
if any *m* die very suddenly by him ... Num 6:9 376
to every *m* according to his ... Num 7:5 376
of Israel are mine, both *m* ... Num 8:17 120
defiled by the dead body of a *m* ... Num 9:6 120
defiled by the dead body of a *m* ... Num 9:7 120
If any *m* of you or of your ... Num 9:10 376
But the *m* that is clean, and is ... Num 9:13 376
that *m* shall bear his sin ... Num 9:13 376
every *m* in the door of his tent ... Num 11:10 376
And there ran a young *m*, and told ... Num 11:27
(Now the *m* Moses was very meek, ... Num 12:3 376
their fathers shall ye send a *m* ... Num 13:2 376
kill all this people as one *m* ... Num 14:15 376
they found a *m* that gathered ... Num 15:32 376
The *m* shall be surely put to ... Num 15:35 376
it shall be that the *m* whom the ... Num 16:7 376
And take every *m* his censer ... Num 16:17 376
the LORD every *m* his censer ... Num 16:17 376
And they took every *m* his censer ... Num 16:18 376
of all flesh, shall one *m* sin ... Num 16:22 376
looked, and took every *m* his rod ... Num 17:9 376
of *m* shalt thou surely redeem ... Num 18:15 120
a *m* that is clean shall gather up ... Num 19:9 376
any *m* shall be unclean seven days ... Num 19:11 120
dead body of any *m* that is dead ... Num 19:13 120
the law, when a *m* dieth in a tent ... Num 19:14 120
or a dead body, or a bone of a *m* ... Num 19:16 120
But the *m* that shall be unclean, ... Num 19:20 376
if a serpent had bitten any *m* ... Num 21:9 376
God is not a *m*, that he should ... Num 23:19 376
neither the son of *m*, that he ... Num 23:19 120
the *m* whose eyes are open hath ... Num 24:3 1397
the *m* whose eyes are open hath ... Num 24:15 1397
he went after the *m* of Israel ... Num 25:8 376
the *m* of Israel, and the woman ... Num 25:8 376
was not a *m* of them whom Moses ... Num 26:64 376
And there was not left a *m* of them ... Num 26:65 376
of Israel, saying, If a *m* die ... Num 27:8 376
set a *m* over the congregation, ... Num 27:16 376
a *m* in whom is the spirit, and lay ... Num 27:18 376
If a *m* vow a vow unto the LORD, ... Num 30:2 376
commanded Moses, between a *m* ... Num 30:16 376
hath known *m* by lying with him ... Num 31:17 376,2145
not known a *m* by lying with him ... Num 31:18 2145
prey that was taken, both of *m* ... Num 31:26 120
had not known *m* by lying with him ... Num 31:35 2145
one portion of fifty, both of *m* ... Num 31:47 120
and there lacketh not one *m* of us ... Num 31:49 376
what every *m* hath gotten, of ... Num 31:50 376
taken spoil, every *m* for himself ... Num 31:53 376
inherited every *m* his inheritance ... Num 32:18 376
every *m* armed for war, before the ... Num 32:27
every *m* armed to battle, before ... Num 32:29
any stone, wherewith a *m* may die ... Num 35:23
of Israel may enjoy every *m* the ... Num 36:8 376
judge righteously between every *m* ... Deut 1:16 376
not be afraid of the face of *m* ... Deut 1:17 376
as a *m* doth bear his son, in all ... Deut 1:31 376
on every *m* his weapons of war ... Deut 1:41 376
of it, after the cubit of a *m* ... Deut 3:11 376
every *m* unto his possession ... Deut 3:20 376
that God created *m* upon the earth ... Deut 4:32 120
day that God doth talk with *m* ... Deut 5:24 120
there shall no *m* be able to stand ... Deut 7:24 375
m doth not live by bread only ... Deut 8:3 120
the mouth of the LORD doth *m* live ... Deut 8:3 120
as a *m* chasteneth his son, so the ... Deut 8:5 376
There shall no *m* be able to stand ... Deut 11:25 376
every *m* whatsoever is right in ... Deut 12:8 376
If there be among you a poor *m* of ... Deut 15:7
And if thy brother, an Hebrew *m* ... Deut 15:12
Every *m* shall give as he is able, ... Deut 16:17 376
m or woman, that hath wrought ... Deut 17:2 376
bring forth that *m* or that woman ... Deut 17:5 376
even that *m* or that woman, and ... Deut 17:5 376
the *m* that will do presumptuously ... Deut 17:12 376
the judge, even that *m* shall die ... Deut 17:12 376
As when a *m* goeth into the wood ... Deut 19:5
But if any *m* hate his neighbour, ... Deut 19:11 376
up against a *m* for any iniquity ... Deut 19:15 376
any *m* to testify against him that ... Deut 19:16 376
What *m* is there that hath built a ... Deut 20:5 376
battle, and another *m* dedicate it ... Deut 20:5 376
what *m* is he that hath planted a ... Deut 20:6 376
battle, and another *m* eat of it ... Deut 20:6 376
what *m* is there that hath ... Deut 20:7 376
the battle, and another *m* take her ... Deut 20:7 376
What *m* is there that is fearful ... Deut 20:8 376
which is next unto the slain *m* ... Deut 21:3 376

that are next unto the slain *m* ... Deut 21:6
If a *m* have two wives, one ... Deut 21:15 376
If a *m* have a stubborn and ... Deut 21:18 376
if a *m* have committed a sin ... Deut 21:22 376
that which pertaineth unto a *m* ... Deut 22:5 1397
neither shall a *m* put on a ... Deut 22:5 1397
if any *m* fall from thence ... Deut 22:8
If any *m* take a wife, and go in ... Deut 22:13 376
my daughter unto this *m* to wife ... Deut 22:16 376
of that city shall take that *m* ... Deut 22:18 376
If a *m* be found lying with a ... Deut 22:22 376
both the *m* that lay with the ... Deut 22:22 376
a *m* find her in the city, and lie ... Deut 22:23 376
and the *m*, because he hath humbled ... Deut 22:24 376
But if a *m* find a betrothed ... Deut 22:25 376
the *m* force her, and lie with her ... Deut 22:25 376
then the *m* only that lay with her ... Deut 22:25 376
for as when a *m* riseth against ... Deut 22:26 376
If a *m* find a damsel that is a ... Deut 22:28 376
Then the *m* that lay with her ... Deut 22:29 376
A *m* shall not take his father's ... Deut 22:30 376
If there be among you any *m* ... Deut 23:10 376
When a *m* hath taken a wife, and ... Deut 24:1 376
When a *m* hath taken a new wife, ... Deut 24:5 376
No *m* shall take the nether or the ... Deut 24:6
If a *m* be found stealing any of ... Deut 24:7 376
the *m* to whom thou dost lend ... Deut 24:11 376
if the *m* be poor, thou shalt not ... Deut 24:12 376
every *m* shall be put to death for ... Deut 24:16 376
if the wicked *m* be worthy to be ... Deut 25:2
if the *m* like not to take his ... Deut 25:7 376
that *m* that will not build up his ... Deut 25:9 376
Cursed be the *m* that maketh any ... Deut 27:15 376
no *m* shall fray them away ... Deut 28:26
evermore, and no *m* shall save thee ... Deut 28:29
another *m* shall lie with her ... Deut 28:30 376
So that the *m* that is tender ... Deut 28:54 376
bondwomen, and no *m* shall buy you ... Deut 28:68
Lest there should be among you *m* ... Deut 29:18 376
shall smoke against that *m* ... Deut 29:20 376
shall destroy both the young *m* ... Deut 32:25
also with the *m* of gray hairs ... Deut 32:25 376
wherewith Moses the *m* of God ... Deut 33:1 376
but no *m* knoweth of his sepulchre ... Deut 34:6 376
There shall not any *m* be able to ... Josh 1:5 376
remain any more courage in any *m* ... Josh 2:11 376
of Israel, out of every tribe a *m* ... Josh 3:12 376
people, out of every tribe a *m* ... Josh 4:2 376
of Israel, out of every tribe a *m* ... Josh 4:4 376
take you up every *m* of you a ... Josh 4:5 376
there stood a *m* over against him ... Josh 5:13 376
up every *m* straight before him ... Josh 6:5 376
every *m* straight before him, and ... Josh 6:20 376
all that was in the city, both *m* ... Josh 6:21 376
Cursed be the *m* before the LORD, ... Josh 6:26 376
shall take shall come *m* by *m* ... Josh 7:14 1397
family of the Zarhites *m* by *m* ... Josh 7:17 1397
he brought his household *m* by *m* ... Josh 7:18 1397
there was not a *m* left in Ai or ... Josh 8:17 376
over which no *m* hath lift up any ... Josh 8:31
there shall not a *m* of them stand ... Josh 10:8 376
hearkened unto the voice of a *m* ... Josh 10:14 376
but every *m* they smote with the ... Josh 11:14 120
Moses the *m* of God concerning me ... Josh 14:6 376
was a great *m* among the Anakims ... Josh 14:15 120
because he was a *m* of war ... Josh 17:1 376
there stood not a *m* of all their ... Josh 21:44 376
that *m* perished not alone in his ... Josh 22:20 376
no *m* hath been able to stand ... Josh 23:9 376
One *m* of you shall chase a ... Josh 23:10 376
every *m* unto his inheritance ... Josh 24:28 376
the spies saw a *m* come forth out ... Judg 1:24 376
but they let go the *m* and all his ... Judg 1:25 376
the *m* went into the land of the ... Judg 1:26 376
children of Israel went every *m* ... Judg 2:6 376
Gera, a Benjamite, a *m* lefthanded ... Judg 3:15 376
and Eglon was a very fat *m* ... Judg 3:17 376
and suffered not a *m* to pass over ... Judg 3:28 376
and there escaped not a *m* ... Judg 3:29 376
and there was not a *m* left ... Judg 4:16
when any *m* doth come and enquire ... Judg 4:20 376
thee, and say, Is there any *m* here ... Judg 4:20 376
shew thee the *m* whom thou seekest ... Judg 4:22 376
to every *m* a damsel or two ... Judg 5:30 1397
thee, thou mighty *m* of valour ... Judg 6:12
smite the Midianites as one *m* ... Judg 6:16 376
people go every *m* unto his place ... Judg 7:7 376
of Israel every *m* unto his tent ... Judg 7:8 376
there was a *m* that told a dream ... Judg 7:13 376
the son of Joash, a *m* of Israel ... Judg 7:14 376
they stood every *m* in his place ... Judg 7:21 376
caught a young *m* of the men of ... Judg 8:14
for as the *m* is, so is his ... Judg 8:21 376
every *m* the earrings of his prey ... Judg 8:24 376
did cast therein every *m* the ... Judg 8:25 376
by me they honour God and *m* ... Judg 9:9 376
my wine, which cheereth God and *m* ... Judg 9:13 376
cut down every *m* his bough ... Judg 9:49 376
unto the young *m* his armourbearer ... Judg 9:54
his young *m* thrust him through, ... Judg 9:54
departed every *m* unto his place ... Judg 9:55 376
the son of Dodo, a *m* of Issachar ... Judg 10:1 376
What *m* is he that will begin to ... Judg 10:18 376
was a mighty *m* of valour, and he ... Judg 11:1 376
and she knew no *m* ... Judg 11:39 376
And there was a certain *m* of Zorah ... Judg 13:2 376
A *m* of God came unto me, and his ... Judg 13:6 376
let the *m* of God which thou didst ... Judg 13:8 376

M

the *m* hath appeared unto me, that	Judg 13:10	376
after his wife, and came to the *m*	Judg 13:11	376
Art thou the *m* that spakest unto	Judg 13:11	376
I be weak, and be as another *m*	Judg 16:7	120
I be weak, and be as another *m*	Judg 16:11	120
weak, and be like any other *m*	Judg 16:17	120
and she called for a *m*, and she	Judg 16:19	376
there was a *m* of mount Ephraim,	Judg 17:1	376
the *m* Micah had an house of gods,	Judg 17:5	376
but every *m* did that which was	Judg 17:6	376
there was a young *m* out of	Judg 17:7	
the *m* departed out of the city	Judg 17:8	376
was content to dwell with the *m*	Judg 17:11	376
the young *m* was unto him as one	Judg 17:11	
the young *m* became his priest, and	Judg 17:12	
voice of the young *m* the Levite	Judg 18:3	
and had no business with any *m*	Judg 18:7	120
house of the young *m* the Levite	Judg 18:15	
a priest unto the house of one *m*	Judg 18:19	376
they had no business with any *m*	Judg 18:28	120
father had said unto the *m*	Judg 19:6	376
when the *m* rose up to depart, his	Judg 19:7	376
when the *m* rose up to depart, he,	Judg 19:9	376
But the *m* would not tarry that	Judg 19:10	376
for there was no *m* that took them	Judg 19:15	376
there came an old *m* from his work	Judg 19:16	376
he saw a wayfaring *m* in the	Judg 19:17	376
and the old *m* said, Whither goest	Judg 19:17	376
there is no *m* that receiveth me	Judg 19:18	376
for the young *m* which is with thy	Judg 19:19	
And the old *m* said, Peace be with	Judg 19:20	376
master of the house, the old *m*	Judg 19:22	376
Bring forth the *m* that came into	Judg 19:22	376
And the *m*, the master of the house	Judg 19:23	376
seeing that this *m* is come into	Judg 19:23	376
but unto this *m* do not so vile a	Judg 19:24	376
so the *m* took his concubine, and	Judg 19:25	376
Then the *m* took her up upon an	Judg 19:28	376
the *m* rose up, and gat him unto	Judg 19:28	376
was gathered together as one *m*	Judg 20:1	376
And all the people arose as one *m*	Judg 20:8	376
the city, knit together as one *m*	Judg 20:11	376
every woman that hath lain by *m*	Judg 21:11	2145
that had known no *m* by lying with	Judg 21:12	376
catch you every *m* his wife of the	Judg 21:21	376
not to each *m* his wife in the war	Judg 21:22	376
every *m* to his tribe and to his	Judg 21:24	376
thence every *m* to his inheritance	Judg 21:24	376
every *m* did that which was right	Judg 21:25	376
a certain *m* of Beth-lehem-judah	Ruth 1:1	376
the name of the *m* was Elimelech	Ruth 1:2	376
a mighty *m* of wealth, of the	Ruth 2:1	376
The *m* is near of kin unto us, one	Ruth 2:20	376
make not thyself known unto the *m*	Ruth 3:3	376
that the *m* was afraid, and turned	Ruth 3:8	376
all that the *m* had done to her	Ruth 3:16	376
for the *m* will not be in rest,	Ruth 3:18	376
a *m* plucked off his shoe, and gave	Ruth 4:7	376
a certain *m* of Ramathaim-zophim	1Sa 1:1	376
this *m* went up out of his city	1Sa 1:3	376
unto thine handmaid a *m* child	1Sa 1:11	582
the *m* Elkanah, and all his house,	1Sa 1:21	376
by strength shall no *m* prevail	1Sa 2:9	376
when any *m* offered sacrifice, the	1Sa 2:13	376
said to the *m* that sacrificed,	1Sa 2:15	376
if any *m* said unto him, Let them	1Sa 2:16	376
If one *m* sin against another, the	1Sa 2:25	376
but if a *m* sin against the LORD,	1Sa 2:25	376
there came a *m* of God unto Eli,	1Sa 2:27	376
not be an old *m* in thine house	1Sa 2:31	
an old *m* in thine house for ever	1Sa 2:32	
the *m* of thine, whom I shall not	1Sa 2:33	376
they fled every *m* into his tent	1Sa 4:10	376
there ran a *m* of Benjamin out of	1Sa 4:12	376
when the *m* came into the city, and	1Sa 4:13	376
the *m* came in hastily, and told	1Sa 4:14	376
the *m* said unto Eli, I am he that	1Sa 4:16	376
for he was an old *m*, and heavy	1Sa 4:18	376
Go ye every *m* unto his city	1Sa 8:22	376
Now there was a *m* of Benjamin	1Sa 9:1	376
a Benjamite, a mighty *m* of power	1Sa 9:1	376
name was Saul, a choice young *m*	1Sa 9:2	
there is in this city a *m* of God	1Sa 9:6	376
and he is an honourable *m*	1Sa 9:6	376
we go, what shall we bring the *m*	1Sa 9:7	376
present to bring to the *m* of God	1Sa 9:7	376
that will I give to the *m* of God	1Sa 9:8	376
when a *m* went to enquire of God,	1Sa 9:9	376
the city where the *m* of God was	1Sa 9:10	376
a *m* out of the land of Benjamin	1Sa 9:16	376
Behold the *m* whom I spake to thee	1Sa 9:17	376
and shalt be turned into another *m*	1Sa 10:6	376
if the *m* should yet come thither	1Sa 10:22	376
people away, every *m* to his house	1Sa 10:25	376
said, How shall this *m* save us	1Sa 10:27	
then, if there be no *m* to save us	1Sa 11:3	
There shall not a *m* be put to	1Sa 11:13	376
he sent every *m* to his tent	1Sa 13:2	376
him a *m* after his own heart	1Sa 13:14	376
to sharpen every *m* his share	1Sa 13:20	376
the young *m* that bare his armour	1Sa 14:1	
the young *m* that bare his armour	1Sa 14:6	
Cursed be the *m* that eateth any	1Sa 14:24	376
but no *m* put his hand to his	1Sa 14:26	
Cursed be the *m* that eateth any	1Sa 14:28	376
Bring me hither every *m* his ox	1Sa 14:34	376
every *m* his sheep, and slay them	1Sa 14:34	376
m his ox with him that night	1Sa 14:34	376
and let us not leave a *m* of them	1Sa 14:36	376
But there was not a *m* among all	1Sa 14:39	
and when Saul saw any strong *m*	1Sa 14:52	376
or any valiant *m*	1Sa 14:52	1121
but slay both *m* and woman, infant	1Sa 15:3	376
for he is not a *m*, that he should	1Sa 15:29	120
for the LORD seeth not as *m* seeth	1Sa 16:7	120
for *m* looketh on the outward	1Sa 16:7	120
are before thee, to seek out a *m*	1Sa 16:16	376
Provide me now a *m* that can play	1Sa 16:17	376
in playing, and a mighty valiant *m*	1Sa 16:18	
a *m* of war, and prudent in matters	1Sa 16:18	376
choose you a *m* for you, and let	1Sa 17:8	376
give me a *m*, that we may fight	1Sa 17:10	376
the *m* went among men for an old	1Sa 17:12	376
for an old *m* in the days of Saul	1Sa 17:12	
of Israel, when they saw the *m*	1Sa 17:24	376
ye seen this *m* that is come up	1Sa 17:25	376
that the *m* who killeth him, the	1Sa 17:25	376
What shall be done to the *m* that	1Sa 17:26	376
be done to the *m* that killeth him	1Sa 17:27	376
he a *m* of war from his youth	1Sa 17:33	376
the *m* that bare the shield went	1Sa 17:41	376
Whose son art thou, thou young *m*	1Sa 17:58	
in law, seeing that I am a poor *m*	1Sa 18:23	376
if I say thus unto the young *m*	1Sa 20:22	5958
art thou alone, and no *m* with thee	1Sa 21:1	376
Let no *m* know any thing of the	1Sa 21:2	376
Now a certain *m* of the servants	1Sa 21:7	376
servants, Lo, ye see the *m* is mad	1Sa 21:14	376
to play the mad *m* in my presence	1Sa 21:15	
For if a *m* find his enemy, will	1Sa 24:19	376
And there was a *m* in Maon, whose	1Sa 25:2	376
the *m* was very great, and he had	1Sa 25:2	376
Now the name of the *m* was Nabal	1Sa 25:3	376
but the *m* was churlish and evil in	1Sa 25:3	376
away every *m* from his master	1Sa 25:10	376
men, Gird ye on every *m* his sword	1Sa 25:13	376
they girded on every *m* his sword	1Sa 25:13	376
that a *m* cannot speak to him	1Sa 25:17	
thee, regard this *m* of Belial	1Sa 25:25	376
Yet a *m* is risen to pursue thee,	1Sa 25:29	120
no *m* saw it, nor knew it, neither	1Sa 26:12	
Abner, Art not thou a valiant *m*	1Sa 26:15	376
to every *m* his righteousness	1Sa 26:23	376
every *m* with his household, even	1Sa 27:3	376
left neither *m* nor woman alive,	1Sa 27:9	376
saved neither *m* nor woman alive,	1Sa 27:11	376
And she said, An old *m* cometh up	1Sa 28:14	376
every *m* for his sons and for his	1Sa 30:6	376
he said, I am a young *m* of Egypt	1Sa 30:13	
and there escaped not a *m* of them	1Sa 30:17	376
save to every *m* his wife	1Sa 30:22	376
a *m* came out of the camp from	2Sa 1:2	376
unto the young *m* that told him	2Sa 1:5	
the young *m* that told him said,	2Sa 1:6	
unto the young *m* that told him	2Sa 1:13	
every *m* with his household	2Sa 2:3	376
as a *m* falleth before wicked men,	2Sa 3:34	1121
a great *m* fallen this day in	2Sa 3:38	
And is this the manner of *m*	2Sa 7:19	120
The rich *m* had exceeding many	2Sa 12:2	
But the poor *m* had nothing	2Sa 12:3	
came a traveller unto the rich *m*	2Sa 12:4	376
m that was come unto him	2Sa 12:4	
dressed it for the *m* that was	2Sa 12:4	376
was greatly kindled against the *m*	2Sa 12:5	376
the *m* that hath done this thing	2Sa 12:5	376
said to David, Thou art the *m*	2Sa 12:7	376
and Jonadab was a very subtil *m*	2Sa 13:3	376
And they went out every *m* from him	2Sa 13:9	376
every *m* gat him up upon his mule,	2Sa 13:29	376
the young *m* that kept the watch	2Sa 13:34	
of the *m* that would destroy me	2Sa 14:16	376
bring the young *m* Absalom again	2Sa 14:21	
that when any *m* that had a	2Sa 15:2	376
but there is no *m* deputed of the	2Sa 15:3	
that every *m* which hath any suit	2Sa 15:4	376
that when any *m* came nigh to him	2Sa 15:5	376
with him covered every *m* his head	2Sa 15:30	376
thence came out a *m* of the family	2Sa 16:5	376
bloody *m*, and thou *m* of Belial	2Sa 16:7	376
because thou art a bloody *m*	2Sa 16:8	376
was as if a *m* had enquired at the	2Sa 16:23	376
the *m* whom thou seekest is as if	2Sa 17:3	376
and thy father is a *m* of war	2Sa 17:8	376
that thy father is a mighty *m*	2Sa 17:10	
for my sake with the young *m*	2Sa 18:5	
And a certain *m* saw it, and told	2Sa 18:10	376
said unto the *m* that told him	2Sa 18:11	376
the *m* said unto Joab, Though I	2Sa 18:12	376
none touch the young *m* Absalom	2Sa 18:12	
and behold a *m* running alone	2Sa 18:24	376
watchman saw another *m* running	2Sa 18:26	376
Behold another *m* running alone	2Sa 18:26	376
And the king said, He is a good *m*	2Sa 18:27	376
said, Is the young *m* Absalom safe	2Sa 18:29	
Is the young *m* Absalom safe	2Sa 18:32	
thee hurt, be as that young *m* is	2Sa 18:32	
had fled every *m* to his tent	2Sa 19:8	376
Judah, even as the heart of one *m*	2Sa 19:14	376
shall there any *m* be put to death	2Sa 19:22	376
Now Barzillai was a very aged *m*	2Sa 19:32	
for he was a very great *m*	2Sa 19:32	376
to be there a *m* of Belial	2Sa 20:1	376
every *m* to his tents, O Israel	2Sa 20:1	376
So every *m* of Israel went up from	2Sa 20:2	376
when the *m* saw that all the	2Sa 20:12	376
but a *m* of mount Ephraim, Sheba	2Sa 20:21	376
the city, every *m* to his tent	2Sa 20:22	376
shalt thou kill any *m* in Israel	2Sa 21:4	376
The *m* that consumed us, and that	2Sa 21:5	376
where was a *m* of great stature,	2Sa 21:20	376
with the upright *m* thou wilt shew	2Sa 22:26	
delivered me from the violent *m*	2Sa 22:49	376
the *m* who was raised up on high,	2Sa 23:1	1397
But the *m* that shall touch them	2Sa 23:7	376
Jehoiada, the son of a valiant *m*	2Sa 23:20	376
he slew an Egyptian, a goodly *m*	2Sa 23:21	376
me not fall into the hand of *m*	2Sa 24:14	120
and he also was a very goodly *m*	1Kin 1:6	
for thou art a valiant *m*, and	1Kin 1:42	376
rose up, and went every *m* his way	1Kin 1:49	376
he will shew himself a worthy *m*	1Kin 1:52	1121
therefore, and shew thyself a *m*	1Kin 2:2	376
he) a *m* on the throne of Israel	1Kin 2:4	376
for thou art a wise *m*, and knowest	1Kin 2:9	376
each *m* his month in a year made	1Kin 4:7	
every *m* under his vine and under	1Kin 4:25	376
table, every *m* in his month	1Kin 4:27	376
every *m* according to his charge	1Kin 4:28	376
and his father was a *m* of Tyre	1Kin 7:14	376
a *m* in my sight to sit on the	1Kin 8:25	376
If any *m* trespass against his	1Kin 8:31	376
soever be made by any *m*, or by	1Kin 8:38	120
which shall know every *m* the	1Kin 8:38	376
give to every *m* according to his	1Kin 8:39	376
there is no *m* that sinneth not	1Kin 8:46	120
a *m* upon the throne of Israel	1Kin 9:5	376
they brought every *m* his present	1Kin 10:25	376
the *m* Jeroboam was a mighty	1Kin 11:28	376
Jeroboam was a mighty *m* of valour	1Kin 11:28	
young *m* that he was industrious	1Kin 11:28	
came unto Shemaiah the *m* of God	1Kin 12:22	376
return every *m* to his house	1Kin 12:24	376
there came a *m* of God out of	1Kin 13:1	376
heard the saying of the *m* of God	1Kin 13:4	376
m of God had given by the word of	1Kin 13:5	376
and said unto the *m* of God	1Kin 13:6	376
the *m* of God besought the LORD,	1Kin 13:6	376
the king said unto the *m* of God	1Kin 13:7	376
the *m* of God said unto the king,	1Kin 13:8	376
the *m* of God had done that day in	1Kin 13:11	376
seen what way the *m* of God went	1Kin 13:12	376
And went after the *m* of God	1Kin 13:14	376
Art thou the *m* of God that camest	1Kin 13:14	376
he cried unto the *m* of God that	1Kin 13:21	376
he said, It is the *m* of God	1Kin 13:26	376
up the carcase of the *m* of God	1Kin 13:29	376
wherein the *m* of God is buried	1Kin 13:31	376
as a *m* taketh away dung, till it	1Kin 14:10	
to do with thee, O thou *m* of God	1Kin 17:18	376
I know that thou art a *m* of God	1Kin 17:24	376
see how this *m* seeketh mischief	1Kin 20:7	
And they slew every one his *m*	1Kin 20:20	376
every *m* out of his place, and put	1Kin 20:24	376
And there came a *m* of God, and	1Kin 20:28	376
a certain *m* of the sons of the	1Kin 20:35	376
the *m* refused to smite him	1Kin 20:35	376
Then he found another *m*, and said,	1Kin 20:37	376
the *m* smote him, so that in	1Kin 20:37	376
a *m* turned aside, and brought a	1Kin 20:39	376
m unto me, and said, Keep this *m*	1Kin 20:39	376
a *m* whom I appointed to utter	1Kin 20:42	376
Jehoshaphat, There is yet one *m*	1Kin 22:8	376
every *m* to his house in peace	1Kin 22:17	376
a certain *m* drew a bow at a	1Kin 22:34	376
Every *m* to his city	1Kin 22:36	376
every *m* to his own country	1Kin 22:36	376
There came a *m* up to meet us, and	2Kin 1:6	376
What manner of *m* was he which	2Kin 1:7	376
answered him, He was an hairy *m*	2Kin 1:8	376
Thou *m* of God, the king hath said	2Kin 1:9	376
of fifty, If I be a *m* of God	2Kin 1:10	376
O *m* of God, thus hath the king	2Kin 1:11	376
unto them, If I be a *m* of God	2Kin 1:12	376
O *m* of God, I pray thee, let my	2Kin 1:13	376
of land cast every *m* his stone	2Kin 3:25	376
she came and told the *m* of God	2Kin 4:7	376
that this is an holy *m* of God	2Kin 4:9	376
thou *m* of God, do not lie unto	2Kin 4:16	376
him on the bed of the *m* of God	2Kin 4:21	376
that I may run to the *m* of God	2Kin 4:22	376
came unto the *m* of God to mount	2Kin 4:25	376
when the *m* of God saw her afar	2Kin 4:25	376
came to the *m* of God to the hill	2Kin 4:27	376
the *m* of God said, Let her alone	2Kin 4:27	376
if thou meet any *m*, salute him	2Kin 4:29	376
out, and said, O thou *m* of God	2Kin 4:40	376
there came a *m* from Baal-shalisha	2Kin 4:42	376
brought the *m* of God bread of the	2Kin 4:42	376
was a great *m* with his master, and	2Kin 5:1	376
he was also a mighty *m* in valour	2Kin 5:1	376
that this *m* doth send unto me to	2Kin 5:7	
me to recover a *m* of his leprosy	2Kin 5:7	376
when Elisha the *m* of God had	2Kin 5:8	376
to the saying of the *m* of God	2Kin 5:14	376
And he returned to the *m* of God	2Kin 5:15	376
servant of Elisha the *m* of God	2Kin 5:20	376
when the *m* turned again from his	2Kin 5:26	376
and take thence every *m* a beam	2Kin 6:2	376
the *m* of God said, Where fell it	2Kin 6:6	376
the *m* of God sent unto the king	2Kin 6:9	376
place which the *m* of God told him	2Kin 6:10	376
of the *m* of God was risen early	2Kin 6:15	376
opened the eyes of the young *m*	2Kin 6:17	

bring you to the *m* whom ye seek 2Kin 6:19 376
the king sent a *m* from before him.......... 2Kin 6:32 376
king leaned answered the *m* of God.......... 2Kin 7:2 376
behold, there was no *m* there 2Kin 7:5 376
and, behold, there was no *m* there 2Kin 7:10 376
neither voice of *m*.......... 2Kin 7:10 120
as the *m* of God had said, who.......... 2Kin 7:17 376
it came to pass as the *m* of God.......... 2Kin 7:18 376
that lord answered the *m* of God 2Kin 7:19 376
after the saying of the *m* of God 2Kin 8:2 376
the servant of the *m* of God 2Kin 8:4 376
The *m* of God is come hither.......... 2Kin 8:7 376
hand, and go, meet the *m* of God.......... 2Kin 8:8 376
and the *m* of God wept.......... 2Kin 8:11 376
So the young *m*, even the young.......... 2Kin 9:4
even the young *m* the prophet.......... 2Kin 9:4 376
he said unto them, Ye know the *m* 2Kin 9:11 376
took every *m* his garment, and put 2Kin 9:13 376
was not a *m* left that came not.......... 2Kin 10:21 376
every *m* with his weapons in his 2Kin 11:8 376
they took every *m* his men that.......... 2Kin 11:9 376
every *m* with his weapons in his 2Kin 11:11 376
the money that every *m* is set at 2Kin 12:4 5315
every *m* of his acquaintance.......... 2Kin 12:5 376
the *m* of God was wroth with him, ... 2Kin 13:19 376
to pass, as they were burying a *m*.......... 2Kin 13:21 376
and they cast the *m* into the.......... 2Kin 13:21 376
when the *m* was let down, and.......... 2Kin 13:21 376
but every *m* shall be put to death 2Kin 14:6 376
they fled every *m* to their tents.......... 2Kin 14:12 376
of each *m* fifty shekels of silver 2Kin 15:20 376
upon Egypt, on which if a *m* lean 2Kin 18:21 376
eat ye every *m* of his own vine 2Kin 18:31 376
Jerusalem as a *m* wipeth a dish 2Kin 21:13
Tell the *m* that sent you to me,.......... 2Kin 22:15 376
that no *m* might make his son or 2Kin 23:10 376
which the *m* of God proclaimed.......... 2Kin 23:16 376
is the sepulchre of the *m* of God 2Kin 23:17 376
let no *m* move his bones.......... 2Kin 23:18 376
the son of a valiant *m* of Kabzeel 1Chr 11:22 376
a *m* of great stature, five cubits 1Chr 11:23 376
a mighty *m* among the thirty, and.......... 1Chr 12:4
a young *m* mighty of valour, and of 1Chr 12:28
to every one of Israel, both *m*.......... 1Chr 16:3 376
He suffered no *m* to do them wrong.......... 1Chr 16:21 376
departed every *m* to his house.......... 1Chr 16:43 376
the estate of a *m* of high degree.......... 1Chr 17:17 120
where was a *m* of great stature, ... 1Chr 20:6 376
me not fall into the hand of *m* 1Chr 21:13 120
to thee, who shall be a *m* of rest 1Chr 22:9 376
m by *m*, was thirty and eight 1Chr 23:3 1397
number by their polls, *m* by *m* 1Chr 23:3 1397
Now concerning Moses the *m* of God.......... 1Chr 23:14 376
uncle was a counsellor, a wise *m*.......... 1Chr 27:32 376
because thou hast been a *m* of war.......... 1Chr 28:3 376
every willing skilful *m*, for any 1Chr 28:21
for the palace is not for *m*.......... 1Chr 29:1 120
a *m* cunning to work in gold.......... 2Chr 2:7 376
And now I have sent a cunning *m*.......... 2Chr 2:13 376
and his father was a *m* of Tyre.......... 2Chr 2:14 376
neither chose I any *m* to be a 2Chr 6:5 376
a *m* in my sight to sit upon the 2Chr 6:16 376
If a *m* sin against his neighbour,.......... 2Chr 6:22 376
soever shall be made of any *m* 2Chr 6:29 120
render unto every *m* according.......... 2Chr 6:30 120
(for there is no *m* which sinneth 2Chr 6:36 120
thee a *m* to be ruler in Israel.......... 2Chr 7:18 376
had David the *m* of God commanded 2Chr 8:14 376
they brought every *m* his present.......... 2Chr 9:24 376
every *m* to your tents, O Israel,.......... 2Chr 10:16 376
came to Shemaiah the *m* of God.......... 2Chr 11:2 376
return every *m* to his house.......... 2Chr 11:4 376
let not *m* prevail against thee.......... 2Chr 14:11 582
or great, whether *m* or woman.......... 2Chr 15:13 376
Eliada a mighty *m* of valour 2Chr 17:17
Jehoshaphat, There is yet one *m* 2Chr 18:7 376
every *m* to his house in peace.......... 2Chr 18:16 376
a certain *m* drew a bow at a.......... 2Chr 18:33
he said to his chariot *m*, Turn 2Chr 18:33 376
for ye judge not for *m*, but for 2Chr 19:6 120
every *m* of Judah and Jerusalem, and 2Chr 20:27 376
every *m* with his weapons in his 2Chr 23:7 376
took every *m* his men that were to.......... 2Chr 23:8 376
every *m* having his weapon in his 2Chr 23:10 376
but every *m* shall die for his own.......... 2Chr 25:4 376
But there came a *m* of God to him.......... 2Chr 25:7 376
And Amaziah said to the *m* of God.......... 2Chr 25:9 376
the *m* of God answered, The LORD.......... 2Chr 25:9 376
and they fled every *m* to his tent 2Chr 25:22 376
a mighty *m* of Ephraim, slew 2Chr 28:7
to the law of Moses the *m* of God 2Chr 30:16 376
every *m* to his possession, into.......... 2Chr 31:1 376
every *m* according to his service,.......... 2Chr 31:2 376
were the work of the hands of *m* 2Chr 32:19 120
Tell ye the *m* that sent you to me.......... 2Chr 34:23 376
upon young *m* or maiden, old *m* 2Chr 36:17
together as one *m* to Jerusalem.......... Ezr 3:1 376
in the law of Moses the *m* of God .... Ezr 3:2 376
brought us a *m* of understanding.......... Ezr 8:18 376
him mercy in the sight of this *m* .... Neh 1:11 376
that there was come a *m* to seek .... Neh 2:10 120
neither told I any *m* what my God.......... Neh 2:12 120
shake out every *m* from his house.......... Neh 5:13 376
I said, Should such a *m* as I flee .... Neh 6:11 376
for he was a faithful *m*, and.......... Neh 7:2 376
themselves together as one *m* into .... Neh 8:1 376
thy judgments, (which if a *m* do.......... Neh 9:29 120
commandment of David the *m* of God.......... Neh 12:24 376

instruments of David the *m* of God .... Neh 12:36 376
that every *m* should bear rule in.......... Est 1:22 376
whether *m* or woman, shall come .... Est 4:11 376
Esther the queen did let no *m*.......... Est 5:12
the *m* whom the king delighteth to.......... Est 6:6 376
the king, For the *m* whom the king.......... Est 6:7 376
that they may array the *m* withal .... Est 6:9 376
the *m* whom the king delighteth to.......... Est 6:9 376
the *m* whom the king delighteth to.......... Est 6:11 376
the king's ring, may no *m* reverse.......... Est 8:8
no *m* could withstand them.......... Est 9:2 376
for this *m* Mordecai waxed greater .... Est 9:4 376
There was a *m* in the land of Uz,.......... Job 1:1 376
that *m* was perfect and upright, and .... Job 1:1 376
so that this *m* was the greatest.......... Job 1:3 376
earth, a perfect and an upright *m*.......... Job 1:8 376
earth, a perfect and an upright *m*.......... Job 2:3 376
all that a *m* hath will he give.......... Job 2:4 376
There is a *m* child conceived .... Job 3:3 1397
given to a *m* whose way is hid.......... Job 3:23 1397
Shall mortal *m* be more just than .... Job 4:17 582
shall a *m* be more pure than his.......... Job 4:17 1396
For wrath killeth the foolish *m* .... Job 5:2
Yet *m* is born unto trouble, as.......... Job 5:7 120
Behold, happy is the *m* whom God .... Job 5:17 582
an appointed time to *m* upon earth.......... Job 7:1 582
What is *m*, that thou shouldest .... Job 7:17 582
will not cast away a perfect *m* .... Job 8:20
but how should *m* be just with God.......... Job 9:2 582
For he is not a *m*, as I am, that .... Job 9:32 376
or seest thou as *m* seeth .... Job 10:4 582
Are thy days as the days of *m* .... Job 10:5 582
should a *m* full of talk be.......... Job 11:2 376
shall no *m* make thee ashamed .... Job 11:3
For vain *m* would be wise, though .... Job 11:12 376
though *m* be born like a wild.......... Job 11:12 120
the just upright *m* is laughed to.......... Job 12:4
he shutteth up a *m*, and there can .... Job 12:14 376
them to stagger like a drunken *m* .... Job 12:25
or as one *m* mocketh another, do .... Job 13:9 582
M that is born of a woman is of.......... Job 14:1 120
But *m* dieth, and wasteth away.......... Job 14:10 1397
m giveth up the ghost, and where .... Job 14:10 120
So *m* lieth down, and riseth not.......... Job 14:12 376
If a *m* die, shall he live again.......... Job 14:14 1397
and thou destroyest the hope of *m*.......... Job 14:19 582
Should a wise *m* utter vain .... Job 15:2
thou the first *m* that was born .... Job 15:7 120
What is *m*, that he should be .... Job 15:14 582
more abominable and filthy is *m* .... Job 15:16 376
The wicked *m* travaileth with pain.......... Job 15:20
in houses which no *m* inhabiteth .... Job 15:28
one might plead for a *m* with God.......... Job 16:21 1397
as a *m* pleadeth for his neighbour.......... Job 16:21 120
cannot find one wise *m* among you.......... Job 17:10
since *m* was placed upon earth, ... Job 20:4 120
shall no *m* look for his goods .... Job 20:21
portion of a wicked *m* from God.......... Job 20:29 120
As for me, is my complaint to *m* .... Job 21:4 120
every *m* shall draw after him, as.......... Job 21:33 120
Can a *m* be profitable unto God, ... Job 22:2 1397
But as for the mighty *m*, he had .... Job 22:8 376
and the honourable *m* dwelt in it.......... Job 22:8
up, and no *m* is sure of life.......... Job 24:22
How then can *m* be justified with.......... Job 25:4 582
How much less *m*, that is a worm .... Job 25:6 582
and the son of *m*, which is a worm .... Job 25:6 120
portion of a wicked *m* with God.......... Job 27:13 120
The rich *m* shall lie down, but he .... Job 27:19
M knoweth not the price thereof.......... Job 28:13 582
unto *m* he said, Behold, the fear .... Job 28:28 120
But there is a spirit in *m*.......... Job 32:8 582
God thrusteth him down, not *m*.......... Job 32:13 376
me give flattering titles unto *m*.......... Job 32:21 120
thee, that God is greater than *m*.......... Job 33:12 582
twice, yet *m* perceiveth it not.......... Job 33:14
may withdraw *m* from his purpose .... Job 33:17 120
his purpose, and hide pride from *m*.......... Job 33:17 1397
to shew unto *m* his uprightness .... Job 33:23 120
render unto *m* his righteousness .... Job 33:26 582
worketh God oftentimes with *m* .... Job 33:29 1397
What *m* is like Job, who drinketh .... Job 34:7 1397
It profiteth a *m* nothing that he.......... Job 34:9 1397
For the work of a *m* shall he .... Job 34:11 120
cause every *m* to find according.......... Job 34:11 376
If he set his heart upon *m* .... Job 34:14
m shall turn again unto dust.......... Job 34:15 120
his eyes are upon the ways of *m*.......... Job 34:21 376
not lay upon *m* more than right.......... Job 34:23 376
a nation, or against a *m* only.......... Job 34:29 120
let a wise *m* hearken unto me .... Job 34:34 1397
may hurt a *m* as thou art.......... Job 35:8 376
may profit the son of *m*.......... Job 35:8 120
Every *m* may see it .... Job 36:25 120
m may behold it afar off.......... Job 36:25 582
drop and distil upon *m* abundantly .... Job 36:28 120
He sealeth up the hand of every *m*.......... Job 37:7 120
If a *m* speak, surely he shall be.......... Job 37:20 376
Gird up now thy loins like a *m* .... Job 38:3 1397
rain on the earth, where no *m* is .... Job 38:26 376
wilderness, wherein there is no *m*.......... Job 38:26 120
Gird up thy loins now like a *m* .... Job 40:7 1397
every *m* also gave him a piece of.......... Job 42:11 376
Blessed is the *m* that walketh not.......... Ps 1:1 376
abhor the bloody and deceitful *m* .... Ps 5:6 376
What is *m*, that thou art mindful.......... Ps 8:4 582
and the son of *m*, that thou.......... Ps 8:4 120
let not *m* prevail .... Ps 9:19 582

arm of the wicked and the evil *m* .... Ps 10:15
that the *m* of the earth may no .... Ps 10:18 582
for the godly *m* ceaseth .... Ps 12:1 376
with an upright *m* thou wilt shew .... Ps 18:25 1397
delivered me from the violent *m* .... Ps 18:48 376
as a strong *m* to run a race.......... Ps 19:5
But I am a worm, and no *m* .... Ps 22:6 376
What *m* is he that feareth the .... Ps 25:12 376
forgotten as a dead *m* out of mind.......... Ps 31:12
thy presence from the pride of *m*.......... Ps 31:20 376
Blessed is the *m* unto whom the.......... Ps 32:2 120
a mighty *m* is not delivered by.......... Ps 33:16
This poor *m* cried, and the LORD .... Ps 34:6
blessed is the *m* that trusteth in.......... Ps 34:8 1397
What *m* is he that desireth life,.......... Ps 34:12 376
O LORD, thou preservest *m*.......... Ps 36:6 120
because of the *m* who bringeth .... Ps 37:7 376
A little that a righteous *m* hath .... Ps 37:16
The steps of a good *m* are ordered .... Ps 37:23 1397
Mark the perfect *m*, and behold the.......... Ps 37:37
for the end of that *m* is peace .... Ps 37:37 376
But I, as a deaf *m*, heard not.......... Ps 38:13
I was as a dumb *m* that openeth .... Ps 38:13
Thus I was as a *m* that heareth .... Ps 38:14 376
verily every *m* at his best state.......... Ps 39:5 120
Surely every *m* walketh in a vain.......... Ps 39:6 376
dost correct *m* for iniquity .... Ps 39:11 376
surely every *m* is vanity.......... Ps 39:11 120
Blessed is that *m* that maketh the.......... Ps 40:4 1397
me from the deceitful and unjust *m*.......... Ps 43:1 376
Nevertheless *m* being in honour.......... Ps 49:12 120
M that is in honour, and.......... Ps 49:20 120
thyself in mischief, O mighty *m* .... Ps 52:1
this is the *m* that made not God .... Ps 52:7 1397
a *m* mine equal, my guide, and mine .... Ps 55:13 582
for *m* would swallow me up .... Ps 56:1 582
be afraid what *m* can do unto me.......... Ps 56:11 120
So that a *m* shall say, Verily .... Ps 58:11 120
for vain is the help of *m*.......... Ps 60:11 120
ye imagine mischief against a *m* .... Ps 62:3 376
to every *m* according to his work.......... Ps 62:12 376
Blessed is the *m* whom thou.......... Ps 65:4
of the unrighteous and cruel *m* .... Ps 71:4
A *m* was famous according as he .... Ps 74:5
foolish *m* reproacheth thee daily.......... Ps 74:22
the wrath of *m* shall praise thee .... Ps 76:10 120
M did eat angels' food .... Ps 78:25 376
like a mighty *m* that shouteth by.......... Ps 78:65
be upon the *m* of thy right hand.......... Ps 80:17 376
upon the son of *m* whom thou.......... Ps 80:17 120
Blessed is the *m* whose strength.......... Ps 84:5 120
blessed is the *m* that trusteth in.......... Ps 84:12 120
this *m* was born there.......... Ps 87:4
This and that *m* was born in her.......... Ps 87:5 376
that this *m* was born there .... Ps 87:6
I am as a *m* that hath no strength.......... Ps 88:4 1397
What *m* is he that liveth, and.......... Ps 89:48 1397
A Prayer of Moses, the *m* of God .... Ps 90:*t* 376
Thou turnest *m* to destruction .... Ps 90:3 582
A brutish *m* knoweth not .... Ps 92:6 376
he that teacheth *m* knowledge .... Ps 94:10 120
LORD knoweth the thoughts of *m*.......... Ps 94:11 120
Blessed is the *m* whom thou.......... Ps 94:12 1397
As for *m*, his days are as grass .... Ps 103:15 582
and herb for the service of *m* .... Ps 104:14 120
that maketh glad the heart of *m* .... Ps 104:15 582
M goeth forth unto his work and to.......... Ps 104:23 120
He suffered no *m* to do them wrong.......... Ps 105:14 120
He sent a *m* before them, even .... Ps 105:17 376
fro, and stagger like a drunken *m*.......... Ps 107:27
for vain is the help of *m* .... Ps 108:12 120
Set thou a wicked *m* over him.......... Ps 109:6
persecuted the poor and needy *m*.......... Ps 109:16 376
Blessed is the *m* that feareth the.......... Ps 112:1 376
A good *m* sheweth favour, and .... Ps 112:5 376
what can *m* do unto me.......... Ps 118:6 120
LORD than to put confidence in *m* .... Ps 118:8 120
shall a young *m* cleanse his way .... Ps 119:9
me from the oppression of *m*.......... Ps 119:134 120
are in the hand of a mighty *m*.......... Ps 127:4
Happy is the *m* that hath his.......... Ps 127:5 1397
that thus shall the *m* be blessed.......... Ps 128:4 1397
the firstborn of Egypt, both of *m*.......... Ps 135:8 120
me, O LORD, from the evil *m* .... Ps 140:1 120
preserve me from the violent *m*.......... Ps 140:1 376
preserve me from the violent *m*.......... Ps 140:4 376
the violent *m* to overthrow him.......... Ps 140:11 376
but there was no *m* that would .... Ps 142:4
no *m* cared for my soul.......... Ps 142:4
shall no *m* living be justified.......... Ps 143:2
LORD, what is *m*, that thou takest.......... Ps 144:3 120
or the son of *m*, that thou makest.......... Ps 144:3 582
M is like to vanity.......... Ps 144:4 120
in princes, nor in the son of *m* .... Ps 146:3 120
not pleasure in the legs of a *m*.......... Ps 147:10 376
simple, to the young *m* knowledge.......... Prov 1:4
A wise *m* will hear, and will.......... Prov 1:5
a *m* of understanding shall attain.......... Prov 1:5
out my hand, and no *m* regarded .... Prov 1:24
thee from the way of the evil *m* .... Prov 2:12
from the *m* that speaketh froward .... Prov 2:12 376
in the sight of God and *m* .... Prov 3:4 120
Happy is the *m* that findeth.......... Prov 3:13 120
the *m* that getteth understanding .... Prov 3:13 120
Strive not with a *m* without cause.......... Prov 3:30 120
For the ways of *m* are before the.......... Prov 5:21 376
and thy want as an armed *m*.......... Prov 6:11 376
A naughty person, a wicked *m*.......... Prov 6:12 376

M

by means of a whorish woman a *m* ... Prov 6:26
Can a *m* take fire in his bosom, ... Prov 6:27 376
For jealousy is the rage of a *m* ... Prov 6:34 1397
a young *m* void of understanding, ... Prov 7:7
and my voice is to the sons of *m* ... Prov 8:4 120
Blessed is the *m* that heareth me, ... Prov 8:34 120
a wicked *m* getteth himself a blot ... Prov 9:7
rebuke a wise *m*, and he will love ... Prov 9:8
Give instruction to a wise *m* ... Prov 9:9
teach a just *m*, and he will ... Prov 9:9
a righteous *m* is a well of life ... Prov 10:11
but a *m* of understanding hath ... Prov 10:23 376
When a wicked *m* dieth, his ... Prov 11:7 120
but a *m* of understanding holdeth ... Prov 11:12 376
The merciful *m* doeth good to his ... Prov 11:17 376
A good *m* obtaineth favour of the ... Prov 12:2
but a *m* of wicked devices will he ... Prov 12:2 376
A *m* shall not be established by ... Prov 12:3 120
A *m* shall be commended according ... Prov 12:8 376
A righteous *m* regardeth the life ... Prov 12:10
A *m* shall be satisfied with good ... Prov 12:14 376
but a prudent *m* covereth shame ... Prov 12:16
A prudent *m* concealeth knowledge ... Prov 12:23 120
in the heart of *m* maketh it stoop ... Prov 12:25 376
The slothful *m* roasteth not that ... Prov 12:27
of a diligent *m* is precious ... Prov 12:27 120
A *m* shall eat good by the fruit ... Prov 13:2 376
A righteous *m* hateth lying ... Prov 13:5
but a wicked *m* is loathsome ... Prov 13:5
Every prudent *m* dealeth with ... Prov 13:16
A good *m* leaveth an inheritance ... Prov 13:22
from the presence of a foolish *m* ... Prov 14:7 376
way which seemeth right unto a *m* ... Prov 14:12 376
a good *m* shall be satisfied from ... Prov 14:14 376
but the prudent *m* looketh well to ... Prov 14:15
A wise *m* feareth, and departeth ... Prov 14:16
a *m* of wicked devices is hated ... Prov 14:17 376
A wrathful *m* stirreth up strife ... Prov 15:18 376
The way of the slothful *m* is as ... Prov 15:19
but a foolish *m* despiseth his ... Prov 15:20 120
but a *m* of understanding walketh ... Prov 15:21 376
A *m* hath joy by the answer of his ... Prov 15:23 376
preparations of the heart in *m* ... Prov 16:1 120
All the ways of a *m* are clean in ... Prov 16:2 376
but a wise *m* will pacify it ... Prov 16:14 376
a way that seemeth right unto a *m* ... Prov 16:25 376
An ungodly *m* diggeth up evil ... Prov 16:27 376
A froward *m* soweth strife ... Prov 16:28 376
A violent *m* enticeth his ... Prov 16:29 376
entereth more into a wise *m* than ... Prov 17:10
An evil *m* seeketh only rebellion ... Prov 17:11
robbed of her whelps meet a *m* ... Prov 17:12 376
A *m* void of understanding ... Prov 17:18 120
A wicked *m* taketh a gift out of ... Prov 17:23
a *m* of understanding is of an ... Prov 17:27 376
is esteemed a *m* of understanding ... Prov 17:28
Through desire a *m*, having ... Prov 18:1
the heart of *m* is haughty ... Prov 18:12 376
The spirit of a *m* will sustain ... Prov 18:14 376
A *m* that hath friends must shew ... Prov 18:24 376
of *m* perverteth his way ... Prov 19:3 120
every *m* is a friend to him that ... Prov 19:6
of a *m* deferreth his anger ... Prov 19:11 120
A *m* of great wrath shall suffer ... Prov 19:19
The desire of a *m* is his kindness ... Prov 19:22 120
a poor *m* is better than a liar ... Prov 19:22
A slothful *m* hideth his hand in ... Prov 19:24
for a *m* to cease from strife ... Prov 20:3 376
the heart of *m* is like deep water ... Prov 20:5 376
but a *m* of understanding will ... Prov 20:5 376
but a faithful *m* who can find ... Prov 20:6 376
The just *m* walketh in his ... Prov 20:7
Bread of deceit is sweet to a *m* ... Prov 20:17 376
how can a *m* then understand his ... Prov 20:24 120
It is a snare to the *m* who ... Prov 20:25 120
The spirit of *m* is the candle of ... Prov 20:27 120
Every way of a *m* is right in his ... Prov 21:2 376
The way of *m* is froward and ... Prov 21:8 376
The righteous *m* wisely ... Prov 21:12
The *m* that wandereth out of the ... Prov 21:16 120
loveth pleasure shall be a poor *m* ... Prov 21:17 376
but a foolish *m* spendeth it up ... Prov 21:20 120
A wise *m* scaleth the city of the ... Prov 21:22
but the *m* that heareth speaketh ... Prov 21:28 376
A wicked *m* hardeneth his face ... Prov 21:29 376
A prudent *m* foreseeth the evil, ... Prov 22:3
The slothful *m* saith, There is a ... Prov 22:13
no friendship with an angry *m* ... Prov 22:24 1167
with a furious *m* thou shalt not ... Prov 22:24 376
Seest thou a *m* diligent in his ... Prov 22:29 376
if thou be a *m* given to appetite ... Prov 23:2 1167
shall clothe a *m* with rags ... Prov 23:21
A wise *m* is strong ... Prov 24:5 1397
a *m* of knowledge increaseth ... Prov 24:5 376
to every *m* according to his works ... Prov 24:12 120
Lay not wait, O wicked *m*, against ... Prov 24:15 376
For a just *m* falleth seven times, ... Prov 24:16
shall be no reward to the evil *m* ... Prov 24:20
Every *m* shall kiss his lips that ... Prov 24:26
I will render to the *m* according ... Prov 24:29 376
of the *m* void of understanding ... Prov 24:30 120
and thy want as an armed *m* ... Prov 24:34 376
A *m* that beareth false witness ... Prov 25:18 376
Confidence in an unfaithful *m* in ... Prov 25:19
A righteous *m* falling down before ... Prov 25:26
Seest thou a *m* wise in his own ... Prov 26:12 376
The slothful *m* saith, There is a ... Prov 26:13
As a mad *m* who casteth firebrands ... Prov 26:18
So is the *m* that deceiveth his ... Prov 26:19 376
a contentious *m* to kindle strife ... Prov 26:21 376
Let another *m* praise thee ... Prov 27:2
so is a *m* that wandereth from his ... Prov 27:8 376
A prudent *m* foreseeth the evil, ... Prov 27:12
so a *m* sharpeneth the countenance ... Prov 27:17 376
to face, so the heart of *m* to *m* ... Prov 27:19 120
so the eyes of *m* are never ... Prov 27:20 120
so is a *m* to his praise ... Prov 27:21 376
wicked flee when no *m* pursueth ... Prov 28:1
but by a *m* of understanding and ... Prov 28:2 120
A poor *m* that oppresseth the poor ... Prov 28:3 1397
The rich *m* is wise in his own ... Prov 28:11 376
the wicked rise, a *m* is hidden ... Prov 28:12 120
Happy is the *m* that feareth alway ... Prov 28:14 120
A *m* that doeth violence to the ... Prov 28:17 120
let no *m* stay him ... Prov 28:17 376
A faithful *m* shall abound with ... Prov 28:20 376
of bread that *m* will transgress ... Prov 28:21 1397
He that rebuketh a *m* afterwards ... Prov 28:23 120
A *m* that flattereth his neighbour ... Prov 29:5 1397
of an evil *m* there is a snare ... Prov 29:6 376
m contendeth with a foolish *m* ... Prov 29:9 376
but a wise *m* keepeth it in till ... Prov 29:11
and the deceitful *m* meet together ... Prov 29:13 376
Seest thou a *m* that is hasty in ... Prov 29:20 376
An angry *m* stirreth up strife ... Prov 29:22 376
and a furious *m* aboundeth in ... Prov 29:22 1167
The fear of *m* bringeth a snare ... Prov 29:25 120
An unjust *m* is an abomination to ... Prov 29:27 376
the *m* spake unto Ithiel, even ... Prov 30:1 1397
I am more brutish than any *m* ... Prov 30:2 376
have not the understanding of a *m* ... Prov 30:2 120
and the way of a *m* with a maid ... Prov 30:19 1397
What profit hath a *m* of all his ... Eccl 1:3 120
m cannot utter it ... Eccl 1:8 376
of *m* to be exercised therewith ... Eccl 1:13 120
for what can the *m* do that cometh ... Eccl 2:12 120
And how dieth the wise *m* ... Eccl 2:16
unto the *m* that shall be after me ... Eccl 2:18 120
he shall be a wise *m* or a fool ... Eccl 2:19
For there is a *m* whose labour is ... Eccl 2:21 120
yet to a *m* that hath not laboured ... Eccl 2:21 120
For what hath *m* of all his labour ... Eccl 2:22 120
There is nothing better for a *m* ... Eccl 2:24 120
For God giveth to a *m* that is ... Eccl 2:26 120
so that no *m* can find out the ... Eccl 3:11 120
but for a *m* to rejoice, and to do ... Eccl 3:12
And also that every *m* should eat ... Eccl 3:13 120
so that a *m* hath no preeminence ... Eccl 3:19 120
the spirit of *m* that goeth upward ... Eccl 3:21 1121,120
than that a *m* should rejoice in ... Eccl 3:22 120
that for this a *m* is envied of ... Eccl 4:4 376
sleep of a labouring *m* is sweet ... Eccl 5:12
Every *m* also to whom God hath ... Eccl 5:19 120
A *m* to whom God hath given riches ... Eccl 6:2 376
If a *m* beget an hundred children, ... Eccl 6:3 376
the labour of *m* is for his mouth ... Eccl 6:7 120
and it is known that it is *m* ... Eccl 6:10 120
vanity, what is *m* the better ... Eccl 6:11 120
what is good for *m* in this life ... Eccl 6:12 120
for who can tell a *m* what shall ... Eccl 6:12 120
than for a *m* to hear the song of ... Eccl 7:5 376
oppression maketh a wise *m* mad ... Eccl 7:7
to the end that *m* should find ... Eccl 7:14 120
there is a just *m* that perisheth ... Eccl 7:15
and there is a wicked *m* that ... Eccl 7:15
there is not a just *m* upon earth ... Eccl 7:20 120
one *m* among a thousand have I ... Eccl 7:28 120
that God hath made *m* upright ... Eccl 7:29 120
Who is as the wise *m* ... Eccl 8:1 376
the misery of *m* is great upon him ... Eccl 8:6 120
There is no *m* that hath power ... Eccl 8:8 120
there is a time wherein one *m* ... Eccl 8:9 120
because a *m* hath no better thing ... Eccl 8:15 120
that a *m* cannot find out the work ... Eccl 8:17 120
because though a *m* labour to seek ... Eccl 8:17 120
though a wise *m* think to know it, ... Eccl 8:17
no *m* knoweth either love or ... Eccl 9:1 120
For *m* also knoweth not his time ... Eccl 9:12 120
was found in it a poor wise *m* ... Eccl 9:15 376
m remembered that same poor *m* ... Eccl 9:15 376
a *m* cannot tell what shall be ... Eccl 10:14 120
But if a *m* live many years, and ... Eccl 11:8 120
Rejoice, O young *m*, in thy youth ... Eccl 11:9
because *m* goeth to his long home, ... Eccl 12:5 120
for this is the whole duty of *m* ... Eccl 12:13 120
every *m* hath his sword upon his ... Song 3:8 376
if a *m* would give all the ... Song 8:7 376
the mean *m* boweth down, and the ... Is 2:9 1201
the great *m* humbleth himself ... Is 2:9 376
lofty looks of *m* shall be humbled ... Is 2:11 120
the loftiness of *m* shall be bowed ... Is 2:17 120
In that day a *m* shall cast his ... Is 2:20 120
Cease ye from *m*, whose breath is ... Is 2:22 120
The mighty *m*, and the ... Is 3:2
the *m* of war, the judge, and the ... Is 3:2 376
of fifty, and the honourable *m* ... Is 3:3
When a *m* shall take hold of his ... Is 3:6 376
women shall take hold of one *m* ... Is 4:1 376
the mean *m* shall be brought down, ... Is 5:15 120
the mighty *m* shall be humbled, and ... Is 5:15 376
because I am a *m* of unclean lips, ... Is 6:5 376
and the houses without *m*, and the ... Is 6:11 120
that a *m* shall nourish a young ... Is 7:21 376
no *m* shall spare his brother ... Is 9:19 376
they shall eat every *m* the flesh ... Is 9:20 376
the inhabitants like a valiant *m* ... Is 10:13
I will make a *m* more precious ... Is 13:12 582
even a *m* than the golden wedge of ... Is 13:12 120
and as a sheep that no *m* taketh up ... Is 13:14
they shall every *m* turn to his ... Is 13:14 376
Is this the *m* that made the earth ... Is 14:16 376
day shall a *m* look to his Maker ... Is 17:7 120
as a drunken *m* staggereth in his ... Is 19:14
is shut up, that no *m* may come in ... Is 24:10 935
a *m* can stretch himself on it ... Is 28:20 376
be as when an hungry *m* dreameth ... Is 29:8
or as when a thirsty *m* dreameth ... Is 29:8
That make a *m* an offender for a ... Is 29:21 120
For in that day every *m* shall ... Is 31:7 376
with the sword, not of a mighty *m* ... Is 31:8 376
and the sword, not of a mean *m* ... Is 31:8 120
a *m* shall be as an hiding place ... Is 32:2 376
waste, the wayfaring *m* ceaseth ... Is 33:8
the cities, he regardeth no *m* ... Is 33:8 582
shall the lame *m* leap as an hart ... Is 35:6
whereon if a *m* lean, it will go ... Is 36:6 376
I shall behold *m* no more with the ... Is 38:11 120
up the righteous *m* from the east ... Is 41:2
For I beheld, and there was no *m* ... Is 41:28 376
LORD shall go forth as a mighty *m* ... Is 42:13 376
stir up jealousy like a *m* of war ... Is 42:13 376
maketh it after the figure of a *m* ... Is 44:13 376
according to the beauty of a *m* ... Is 44:13 120
Then shall it be for a *m* to burn ... Is 44:15 120
the earth, and created *m* upon it ... Is 45:12 120
the *m* that executeth my counsel ... Is 46:11 376
and I will not meet thee as a *m* ... Is 47:3 120
Holy One, to him whom *m* despiseth ... Is 49:7 5315
when I came, was there no *m* ... Is 50:2 376
be afraid of a *m* that shall die ... Is 51:12 582
of the son of *m* which shall be ... Is 51:12 120
was so marred more than any *m* ... Is 52:14 376
a *m* of sorrows, and acquainted ... Is 53:3 376
and the unrighteous *m* his thoughts ... Is 55:7 376
Blessed is the *m* that doeth this, ... Is 56:2 582
the son of *m* that layeth hold on ... Is 56:2 120
and no *m* layeth it to heart ... Is 57:1 376
a day for a *m* to afflict his soul ... Is 58:5 120
And he saw that there was no *m* ... Is 59:16 376
so that no *m* went through thee, I ... Is 60:15
For as a young *m* marrieth a ... Is 62:5
nor an old *m* that hath not filled ... Is 65:20
but to this *m* will I look ... Is 66:2
an ox is as if he slew a *m* ... Is 66:3 376
she was delivered of a *m* child ... Is 66:7 2145
a land that no *m* passed through ... Jer 2:6 376
and where no *m* dwelt ... Jer 2:6 120
If a *m* put away his wife, and she ... Jer 3:1 376
I beheld, and, lo, there was no *m* ... Jer 4:25 120
and not a *m* dwell therein ... Jer 4:29 376
thereof, if ye can find a *m* ... Jer 5:1 376
execute judgment between a *m* ... Jer 7:5 376
out upon this place, upon *m* ... Jer 7:20 120
no *m* repented him of his ... Jer 8:6 376
Who is the wise *m*, that may ... Jer 9:12 376
Let not the wise *m* glory in his ... Jer 9:23
the mighty *m* glory in his might ... Jer 9:23
let not the rich *m* glory in his ... Jer 9:23
Every *m* is brutish in his ... Jer 10:14 120
the way of *m* is not in himself ... Jer 10:23 120
it is not in *m* that walketh to ... Jer 10:23
Cursed be the *m* that obeyeth not ... Jer 11:3 376
because no *m* layeth it to heart ... Jer 12:11 376
every *m* to his heritage ... Jer 12:15 376
and every *m* to his land ... Jer 12:15 376
cleaveth to the loins of a *m* ... Jer 13:11 376
as a wayfaring *m* that turneth ... Jer 14:8
shouldest thou be as a *m* astonied ... Jer 14:9 376
as a mighty *m* that cannot save ... Jer 14:9 376
thou hast borne me a *m* of strife ... Jer 15:10 376
a *m* of contention to the whole ... Jer 15:10 376
Shall a *m* make gods unto himself, ... Jer 16:20 120
Cursed be the *m* that trusteth in ... Jer 17:5 1397
that trusteth in *m* ... Jer 17:5 120
Blessed is the *m* that trusteth in ... Jer 17:7 1397
even to give every *m* according to ... Jer 17:10 376
Will a *m* leave the snow of ... Jer 18:14
Cursed be the *m* who brought ... Jer 20:15 376
A *m* child is born unto thee ... Jer 20:15 2145
let that *m* be as the cities which ... Jer 20:16 376
inhabitants of this city, both *m* ... Jer 21:6 120
say every *m* to his neighbour ... Jer 22:8 376
Is this *m* Coniah a despised ... Jer 22:28 376
LORD, Write ye this *m* childless ... Jer 22:30 376
a *m* that shall not prosper in his ... Jer 22:30 1397
for no *m* of his seed shall ... Jer 22:30 376
I am like a drunken *m*, and like a ... Jer 23:9 376
like a *m* whom wine hath overcome, ... Jer 23:9 1397
tell every *m* to his neighbour ... Jer 23:27 376
LORD, I will even punish that *m* ... Jer 23:34 376
turn every *m* from his evil way, ... Jer 26:3 376
saying, This *m* is worthy to die ... Jer 26:11 376
This *m* is not worthy to die ... Jer 26:16 376
And there was also a *m* that ... Jer 26:20 376
I have made the earth, the *m* ... Jer 27:5 120
for every *m* that is mad, and ... Jer 29:26 376
he shall not have a *m* to dwell ... Jer 29:32 376
see whether a *m* doth travail with ... Jer 30:6 2145
wherefore do I see every *m* with ... Jer 30:6 1397
is Zion, whom no *m* seeketh after ... Jer 30:17
earth, A woman shall compass a *m* ... Jer 31:22 1397
house of Judah with the seed of *m* ... Jer 31:27 120
every *m* that eateth the sour ... Jer 31:30 120
no more every *m* his neighbour ... Jer 31:34 376

every *m* his brother, saying, Know	Jer 31:34	376
It is desolate without *m* or beast	Jer 32:43	120
say shall be desolate without *m*	Jer 33:10	120
that are desolate, without *m*	Jer 33:10	120
which is desolate without *m*	Jer 33:12	120
David shall never want a *m* to sit	Jer 33:17	376
want a *m* before me to offer burnt	Jer 33:18	376
That every *m* should let his	Jer 34:9	376
every *m* his maidservant, being an	Jer 34:9	376
go every *m* his brother an Hebrew	Jer 34:14	376
liberty every *m* to his neighbour	Jer 34:15	376
and caused every *m* his servant	Jer 34:16	376
every *m* his handmaid, whom he had	Jer 34:16	376
and every *m* to his neighbour	Jer 34:17	376
a *m* of God, which was by the	Jer 35:4	376
ye now every *m* from his evil way	Jer 35:15	376
a *m* to stand before me for ever	Jer 35:19	376
return every *m* from his evil way	Jer 36:3	376
let no *m* know where ye be	Jer 36:19	376
cause to cease from thence *m*	Jer 36:29	120
they rise up every *m* in his tent	Jer 37:10	376
let this *m* be put to death	Jer 38:4	376
for this *m* seeketh not the	Jer 38:4	376
Let no *m* know of these words, and	Jer 38:24	376
Nethaniah, and no *m* shall know it	Jer 40:15	376
slain Gedaliah, and no *m* knew it,	Jer 41:4	376
and no *m* dwelleth therein,	Jer 44:2	
your souls, to cut off from you *m*	Jer 44:7	376
any *m* of Judah in all the land of	Jer 44:26	376
away, nor the mighty *m* escape	Jer 46:6	
for the mighty *m* hath stumbled	Jer 46:12	
be driven out every *m* right forth	Jer 49:5	376
no *m* shall abide there, neither	Jer 49:18	376
shall a son of *m* dwell in it	Jer 49:18	120
and who is a chosen *m*, that I may	Jer 49:19	
there shall no *m* abide there	Jer 49:33	376
nor any son of *m* dwell in it	Jer 49:33	120
remove, they shall depart, both *m*	Jer 50:3	120
shall be as of a mighty expert *m*	Jer 50:9	
so shall no *m* abide there	Jer 50:40	376
shall any son of *m* dwell therein	Jer 50:40	120
like a *m* to the battle, against	Jer 50:42	376
and who is a chosen *m*, that I may	Jer 50:44	
and deliver every *m* his soul	Jer 51:6	376
Every *m* is brutish by his	Jer 51:17	120
also will I break in pieces *m*	Jer 51:22	376
I break in pieces the young *m*	Jer 51:22	
a land wherein no *m* dwelleth	Jer 51:43	376
doth any son of *m* pass thereby	Jer 51:43	120
deliver ye every *m* his soul from	Jer 51:45	376
neither *m* nor beast, but that it	Jer 51:62	120
I am the *m* that hath seen	Lam 3:1	1397
is good that a *m* should both hope	Lam 3:26	120
It is good for a *m* that he bear	Lam 3:27	1397
a *m* before the face of the most	Lam 3:35	1397
To subvert a *m* in his cause	Lam 3:36	120
doth a living *m* complain	Lam 3:39	120
a *m* for the punishment of his	Lam 3:39	1397
no *m* breaketh it unto them	Lam 4:4	
they had the likeness of a *m*	Eze 1:5	120
they had the hands of a *m* under	Eze 1:8	120
they four had the face of a *m*	Eze 1:10	120
appearance of a *m* above upon it	Eze 1:26	120
And he said unto me, Son of *m*	Eze 2:1	120
And he said unto me, Son of *m*	Eze 2:3	120
And thou, son of *m*, be not afraid	Eze 2:6	120
But thou, son of *m*, hear what I	Eze 2:8	120
he said unto me, Son of *m*	Eze 3:1	120
And he said unto me, Son of *m*	Eze 3:3	120
And he said unto me, Son of *m*	Eze 3:4	120
he said unto me, Son of *m*	Eze 3:10	120
Son of *m*, I have made thee a	Eze 3:17	120
the same wicked *m* shall die in	Eze 3:18	
When a righteous *m* doth turn from	Eze 3:20	
if thou warn the righteous *m*	Eze 3:21	
But thou, O son of *m*, behold,	Eze 3:25	120
Thou also, son of *m*, take thee a	Eze 4:1	120
it with dung that cometh out of *m*	Eze 4:12	120
he said unto me, Son of *m*	Eze 4:16	120
And thou, son of *m*, take thee a	Eze 5:1	120
Son of *m*, set thy face toward the	Eze 6:2	120
Also, thou son of *m*, thus saith	Eze 7:2	120
Then said he unto me, Son of *m*	Eze 8:5	120
furthermore unto me, Son of *m*	Eze 8:6	120
Then said he unto me, Son of *m*	Eze 8:8	120
with every *m* his censer in his	Eze 8:11	376
Then said he unto me, Son of *m*	Eze 8:12	120
every *m* in the chambers of his	Eze 8:12	376
Hast thou seen this, O son of *m*	Eze 8:15	120
Hast thou seen this, O son of *m*	Eze 8:17	120
even every *m* with his destroying	Eze 9:1	376
every *m* a slaughter weapon in his	Eze 9:2	376
one *m* among them was clothed with	Eze 9:2	376
he called to the *m* clothed with	Eze 9:3	376
near any *m* upon whom is the mark	Eze 9:6	376
the *m* clothed with linen, which	Eze 9:11	376
he spake unto the *m* clothed with	Eze 10:2	376
of the house, when the *m* went in	Eze 10:3	376
the *m* clothed with linen, saying,	Eze 10:6	376
second face was the face of a *m*	Eze 10:14	120
of a *m* was under their wings	Eze 10:21	120
Then said he unto me, Son of *m*	Eze 11:2	120
them, prophesy, O son of *m*	Eze 11:4	120
Son of *m*, thy brethren, even thy	Eze 11:15	120
Son of *m*, thou dwellest in the	Eze 12:2	120
Therefore, thou son of *m*, prepare	Eze 12:3	120
Son of *m*, hath not the house of	Eze 12:9	120
Son of *m*, eat thy bread with	Eze 12:18	120
Son of *m*, what is that proverb	Eze 12:22	120
Son of *m*, behold, they of the	Eze 12:27	120
Son of *m*, prophesy against the	Eze 13:2	120
Likewise, thou son of *m*, set thy	Eze 13:17	120
Son of *m*, these men have set up	Eze 14:3	120
Every *m* of the house of Israel	Eze 14:4	376
I will set my face against that *m*	Eze 14:8	376
Son of *m*, when the land sinneth	Eze 14:13	120
famine upon it, and will cut off *m*	Eze 14:13	120
that no *m* may pass through	Eze 14:15	
so that I cut off *m* and beast from	Eze 14:17	120
it in blood, to cut off from it *m*	Eze 14:19	120
pestilence, to cut off from it *m*	Eze 14:21	120
Son of *m*, What is the vine tree	Eze 15:2	120
Son of *m*, cause Jerusalem to know	Eze 16:2	120
Son of *m*, put forth a riddle, and	Eze 17:2	120
But if a *m* be just, and do that	Eze 18:5	376
true judgment between *m* and *m*	Eze 18:8	376
that the wicked *m* doeth, shall he	Eze 18:24	
When a righteous *m* turneth away	Eze 18:26	
when the wicked *m* turneth away	Eze 18:27	
Son of *m*, speak unto the elders	Eze 20:3	120
Wilt thou judge them, son of *m*	Eze 20:4	120
them, Cast ye away every *m* the	Eze 20:7	376
they did not every *m* cast away	Eze 20:8	376
my judgments, which if a *m* do	Eze 20:11	120
my judgments, which if a *m* do	Eze 20:13	120
to do them, which if a *m* do	Eze 20:21	120
Therefore, son of *m*, speak unto	Eze 20:27	120
Son of *m*, set thy face toward the	Eze 20:46	120
Son of *m*, set thy face toward	Eze 21:2	120
Sigh therefore, thou son of *m*	Eze 21:6	120
Son of *m*, prophesy, and say, Thus	Eze 21:9	120
Cry and howl, son of *m*	Eze 21:12	120
Thou therefore, son of *m*,	Eze 21:14	120
Also, thou son of *m*, appoint thee	Eze 21:19	120
And thou, son of *m*, prophesy and	Eze 21:28	120
Now, thou son of *m*, wilt thou	Eze 22:2	120
Son of *m*, the house of Israel is	Eze 22:18	120
Son of *m*, say unto her, Thou art	Eze 22:24	120
And I sought for a *m* among them	Eze 22:30	376
Son of *m*, there were two women,	Eze 23:2	120
Son of *m*, wilt thou judge Aholah	Eze 23:36	120
Son of *m*, write thee the name of	Eze 24:2	120
Son of *m*, behold, I take away	Eze 24:16	120
Also, thou son of *m*, shall it not	Eze 24:25	120
Son of *m*, set thy face against	Eze 25:2	120
hand upon Edom, and will cut off *m*	Eze 25:13	120
Son of *m*, because that Tyrus hath	Eze 26:2	120
Now, thou son of *m*, take up a	Eze 27:2	120
Son of *m*, say unto the prince of	Eze 28:2	120
yet thou art a *m*, and not God,	Eze 28:2	120
but thou shalt be a *m*, and no God,	Eze 28:9	120
Son of *m*, take up a lamentation	Eze 28:12	120
Son of *m*, set thy face against	Eze 28:21	120
Son of *m*, set thy face against	Eze 29:2	120
a sword upon thee, and cut off *m*	Eze 29:8	120
No foot of *m* shall pass through	Eze 29:11	120
Son of *m*, Nebuchadrezzar king of	Eze 29:18	120
Son of *m*, prophesy and say, Thus	Eze 30:2	120
Son of *m*, I have broken the arm	Eze 30:21	120
groanings of a deadly wounded *m*	Eze 30:24	
Son of *m*, speak unto Pharaoh king	Eze 31:2	120
Son of *m*, take up a lamentation	Eze 32:2	120
every *m* for his own life, in the	Eze 32:10	376
foot of *m* trouble them any more	Eze 32:13	120
Son of *m*, wail for the multitude	Eze 32:18	120
Son of *m*, speak to the children	Eze 33:2	120
the land take a *m* of their coasts	Eze 33:2	376
So thou, O son of *m*, I have set	Eze 33:7	120
I say unto the wicked, O wicked *m*	Eze 33:8	
that wicked *m* shall die in his	Eze 33:8	
Therefore, O thou son of *m*	Eze 33:10	120
Therefore, thou son of *m*, say	Eze 33:12	120
Son of *m*, they that inhabit those	Eze 33:24	120
Also, thou son of *m*, the children	Eze 33:30	120
Son of *m*, prophesy against the	Eze 34:2	120
Son of *m*, set thy face against	Eze 35:2	120
Also, thou son of *m*, prophesy	Eze 36:1	120
And I will multiply upon you *m*	Eze 36:11	120
Son of *m*, when the house of	Eze 36:17	120
And he said unto me, Son of *m*	Eze 37:3	120
unto the wind, prophesy, son of *m*	Eze 37:9	120
Then he said unto me, Son of *m*	Eze 37:11	120
Moreover, thou son of *m*, take	Eze 37:16	120
Son of *m*, set thy face against	Eze 38:2	120
Therefore, son of *m*, prophesy and	Eze 38:14	120
Therefore, thou son of *m*,	Eze 39:1	120
And, thou son of *m*, thus saith the	Eze 39:17	120
and, behold, there was a *m*	Eze 40:3	376
And the *m* said unto me	Eze 40:4	376
said unto me, Son of *m*	Eze 40:4	120
So that the face of a *m* was	Eze 41:19	120
and the *m* stood by me	Eze 43:6	376
And he said unto me, Son of *m*	Eze 43:7	120
Thou son of *m*, shew the house to	Eze 43:10	120
And he said unto me, Son of *m*	Eze 43:18	120
no *m* shall enter in by it	Eze 44:2	376
the LORD said unto me, Son of *m*	Eze 44:5	120
every *m* from his possession	Eze 46:18	376
when the *m* that had the line in	Eze 47:3	376
And he said unto me, Son of *m*	Eze 47:6	120
till a *m* come over against Hamath	Eze 47:20	
There is not a *m* upon the earth	Dan 2:10	606
I have found a *m* of the captives	Dan 2:25	1400
the king made Daniel a great *m*	Dan 2:48	
that every *m* that shall hear the	Dan 3:10	606
There is a *m* in thy kingdom, in	Dan 5:11	1400
of any God or *m* for thirty days	Dan 6:7	606
that every *m* that shall ask a	Dan 6:12	606
any God or *m* within thirty days	Dan 6:12	606
made stand upon the feet as a *m*	Dan 7:4	606
horn were eyes like the eyes of *m*	Dan 7:8	606
one like the Son of *m* came with	Dan 7:13	606
me as the appearance of a *m*	Dan 8:15	1397
make this *m* to understand the	Dan 8:16	
unto me, Understand, O son of *m*	Dan 8:17	120
in prayer, even the *m* Gabriel	Dan 9:21	376
a certain *m* clothed in linen	Dan 10:5	376
a *m* greatly beloved, understand	Dan 10:11	376
me one like the appearance of a *m*	Dan 10:18	120
O *m* greatly beloved, fear not	Dan 10:19	376
one said to the *m* clothed in	Dan 12:6	376
I heard the *m* clothed in linen,	Dan 12:7	376
thou shalt not be for another *m*	Hos 3:3	376
Yet let no *m* strive, nor reprove	Hos 4:4	376
as troops of robbers wait for a *m*	Hos 6:9	376
is a fool, the spiritual *m* is mad	Hos 9:7	376
that there shall not be a *m* left	Hos 9:12	120
I drew them with cords of a *m*	Hos 11:4	120
for I am God, and not *m*	Hos 11:9	376
and a *m* and his father will go in	Amos 2:7	376
declareth unto *m* what is his	Amos 4:13	120
As if a *m* did flee from a lion,	Amos 5:19	376
cried every *m* unto his god, and	Jonah 1:5	
saying, Let neither *m* nor beast	Jonah 3:7	120
But let *m* and beast be covered	Jonah 3:8	120
so they oppress a *m* and his house,	Mic 2:2	1397
and his house, even a *m*	Mic 2:2	376
If a *m* walking in the spirit and	Mic 2:11	376
shall sit every *m* under his vine	Mic 4:4	376
this *m* shall be the peace, when	Mic 5:5	
grass, that tarrieth not for *m*	Mic 5:7	376
He hath shewed thee, O *m*, what is	Mic 6:8	120
the *m* of wisdom shall see thy	Mic 6:9	
The good *m* is perished out of the	Mic 7:2	
they hunt every *m* his brother	Mic 7:2	376
and the great *m*, he uttereth his	Mic 7:3	
mountains, and no *m* gathereth them	Nah 3:18	
when the wicked devoureth the *m*	Hab 1:13	
by wine, he is a proud *m*, neither	Hab 2:5	1397
I will consume *m* and beast	Zeph 1:3	120
I will cut off *m* from off the	Zeph 1:3	120
the mighty *m* shall cry there	Zeph 1:14	
destroyed, so that there is no *m*	Zeph 3:6	376
ye run every *m* unto his own house	Hag 1:9	376
behold a *m* riding upon a red	Zec 1:8	376
the *m* that stood among the myrtle	Zec 1:10	376
so that no *m* did lift up his head	Zec 1:21	376
behold a *m* with a measuring line	Zec 2:1	376
him, Run, speak to this young *m*	Zec 2:4	
shall ye call every *m* his	Zec 3:10	
as a *m* that is wakened out of his	Zec 4:1	376
Behold the *m* whose name is The	Zec 6:12	376
every *m* to his brother	Zec 7:9	376
that no *m* passed through nor	Zec 7:14	
every *m* with his staff in his	Zec 8:4	376
days there was no hire for *m*	Zec 8:10	120
Speak ye every *m* the truth to his	Zec 8:16	376
when the eyes of *m*, as of all the	Zec 9:1	120
thee as the sword of a mighty *m*	Zec 9:13	
Ephraim shall be like a mighty *m*	Zec 10:7	
the spirit of *m* within him	Zec 12:1	120
for *m* taught me to keep cattle	Zec 13:5	120
against the *m* that is my fellow,	Zec 13:7	1397
every *m* against his brother	Mal 2:10	376
cut off the *m* that doeth this	Mal 2:12	376
Will a *m* rob God	Mal 3:8	120
as a *m* spareth his own son that	Mal 3:17	376
her husband, being a just *m*	Mt 1:19	
M shall not live by bread alone,	Mt 4:4	*444*
if any *m* will sue thee at the law	Mt 5:40	
No *m* can serve two masters	Mt 6:24	*3762*
Or what *m* is there of you, whom	Mt 7:9	*444*
I will liken him unto a wise *m*	Mt 7:24	*435*
shall be likened unto a foolish *m*	Mt 7:26	*435*
unto him, See thou tell no *m*	Mt 8:4	*3367*
For I am a *m* under authority,	Mt 8:9	*444*
and I say to this *m*, Go, and he	Mt 8:9	
but the Son of *m* hath not where	Mt 8:20	*444*
saying, What manner of *m* is this	Mt 8:27	
so that no *m* might pass by that	Mt 8:28	*5100*
to him a *m* sick of the palsy	Mt 9:2	
themselves, This *m* blasphemeth	Mt 9:3	
ye may know that the Son of *m*	Mt 9:6	*444*
forth from thence, he saw a *m*	Mt 9:9	*444*
No *m* putteth a piece of new cloth	Mt 9:16	*3762*
saying, See that no *m* know it	Mt 9:30	*3367*
a dumb *m* possessed with a devil	Mt 9:32	*444*
Israel, till the Son of *m* be come	Mt 10:23	*444*
For I am come to set a *m* at	Mt 10:35	*444*
he that receiveth a righteous *m*	Mt 10:41	
in the name of a righteous *m*	Mt 10:41	
A *m* clothed in soft raiment	Mt 11:8	*444*
The Son of *m* came eating and	Mt 11:19	*444*
Behold a *m* gluttonous, and a	Mt 11:19	*444*
no *m* knoweth the Son, but the	Mt 11:27	*3762*
neither knoweth any *m* the Father	Mt 11:27	
For the Son of *m* is Lord even of	Mt 12:8	*444*
there was a *m* which had his hand	Mt 12:10	*444*
What *m* shall there be among you,	Mt 12:11	*444*
How much then is a *m* better than	Mt 12:12	*444*
Then saith he to the *m*, Stretch	Mt 12:13	*444*
neither shall any *m* hear his	Mt 12:19	
except he first bind the strong *m*	Mt 12:29	
a word against the Son of *m*	Mt 12:32	*444*

A good *m* out of the good treasure	Mt 12:35	*444*
an evil *m* out of the evil	Mt 12:35	*444*
shall the Son of *m* be three days	Mt 12:40	*444*
unclean spirit is gone out of a *m*	Mt 12:43	*444*
the last state of that *m* is worse	Mt 12:45	*444*
of heaven is likened unto a *m*	Mt 13:24	*444*
of mustard seed, which a *m* took	Mt 13:31	*444*
the good seed is the Son of *m*	Mt 13:37	*444*
The Son of *m* shall send forth his	Mt 13:41	*444*
the which when a *m* hath found	Mt 13:44	*444*
heaven is like unto a merchant *m*	Mt 13:45	*444*
unto a *m* that is an householder	Mt 13:52	*444*
Whence hath this *m* this wisdom	Mt 13:54	
then hath this *m* all these things	Mt 13:56	
goeth into the mouth defileth a *m*	Mt 15:11	*444*
of the mouth, this defileth a *m*	Mt 15:11	*444*
and they defile the *m*	Mt 15:18	*444*
are the things which defile a *m*	Mt 15:20	*444*
unwashen hands defileth not a *m*	Mt 15:20	*444*
do men say that I the Son of *m* am	Mt 16:13	*444*
that they should tell no *m* that	Mt 16:20	*3367*
If any *m* will come after me, let	Mt 16:24	
For what is a *m* profited, if he	Mt 16:26	*444*
or what shall a *m* give in	Mt 16:26	*444*
For the Son of *m* shall come in	Mt 16:27	*444*
every *m* according to his works	Mt 16:27	
Son of *m* coming in his kingdom	Mt 16:28	*444*
up their eyes, they saw no *m*	Mt 17:8	*3762*
saying, Tell the vision to no *m*	Mt 17:9	*3367*
until the Son of *m* be risen again	Mt 17:9	*444*
also the Son of *m* suffer of them	Mt 17:12	*444*
there came to him a certain *m*	Mt 17:14	*444*
The Son of *m* shall be betrayed	Mt 17:22	*444*
but woe to that *m* by whom the	Mt 18:7	*444*
For the Son of *m* is come to save	Mt 18:11	*444*
if a *m* have an hundred sheep, and	Mt 18:12	*444*
him be unto thee as an heathen *m*	Mt 18:17	
Is it lawful for a *m* to put away	Mt 19:3	*444*
this cause shall a *m* leave father	Mt 19:5	*444*
together, let not *m* put asunder	Mt 19:6	*444*
If the case of the *m* be so with	Mt 19:10	*444*
The young *m* saith unto him, All	Mt 19:20	*3495*
the young *m* heard that saying	Mt 19:22	*3495*
That a rich *m* shall hardly enter	Mt 19:23	
than for a rich *m* to enter into	Mt 19:24	
regeneration when the Son of *m*	Mt 19:28	*444*
unto a *m* that is an householder	Mt 20:1	*444*
Because no *m* hath hired us	Mt 20:7	*3762*
they received every *m* a penny	Mt 20:9	
likewise received every *m* a penny	Mt 20:10	
the Son of *m* shall be betrayed	Mt 20:18	*444*
Even as the Son of *m* came not to	Mt 20:28	*444*
if any *m* say ought unto you, ye	Mt 21:3	
A certain *m* had two sons	Mt 21:28	*444*
he saw there a *m* which had not on	Mt 22:11	*444*
neither carest thou for any *m*	Mt 22:16	*3762*
Master, Moses said, If a *m* die	Mt 22:24	*5100*
no *m* was able to answer him a	Mt 22:46	*3762*
neither durst any *m* from that day	Mt 22:46	
call no *m* your father upon the	Mt 23:9	
Take heed that no *m* deceive you	Mt 24:4	*5100*
Then if any *m* shall say unto you	Mt 24:23	
the coming of the Son of *m* be	Mt 24:27	*444*
sign of the Son of *m* in heaven	Mt 24:30	*444*
they shall see the Son of *m*	Mt 24:30	*444*
of that day and hour knoweth no *m*	Mt 24:36	*3762*
the coming of the Son of *m* be	Mt 24:37	*444*
the coming of the Son of *m* be	Mt 24:39	*444*
ye think not the Son of *m* cometh	Mt 24:44	*444*
hour wherein the Son of *m* cometh	Mt 25:13	*444*
a *m* travelling into a far country	Mt 25:14	*444*
to every *m* according to his	Mt 25:15	
knew thee that thou art an hard *m*	Mt 25:24	*444*
When the Son of *m* shall come in	Mt 25:31	*444*
the Son of *m* is betrayed to be	Mt 26:2	*444*
Go into the city to such a *m*	Mt 26:18	
The Son of *m* goeth as it is	Mt 26:24	*444*
but woe unto that *m* by whom the	Mt 26:24	*444*
by whom the Son of *m* is betrayed	Mt 26:24	*444*
that *m* if he had not been born	Mt 26:24	*444*
the Son of *m* is betrayed into the	Mt 26:45	*444*
shall ye see the Son of *m* sitting	Mt 26:64	*444*
with an oath, I do not know the *m*	Mt 26:72	*444*
swear, saying, I know not the *m*	Mt 26:74	*444*
nothing to do with that just *m*	Mt 27:19	
out, they found a *m* of Cyrene	Mt 27:32	*444*
said, This *m* calleth for Elias	Mt 27:47	
there came a rich *m* of Arimathaea	Mt 27:57	*444*
a *m* with an unclean spirit	Mk 1:23	*444*
See thou say nothing to any *m*	Mk 1:44	*3367*
Why doth this *m* thus speak	Mk 2:7	
ye may know that the Son of *m*	Mk 2:10	*444*
No *m* also seweth a piece of new	Mk 2:21	*3762*
no *m* putteth new wine into old	Mk 2:22	*3762*
them, The sabbath was made for *m*	Mk 2:27	*444*
and not *m* for the sabbath	Mk 2:27	*444*
Therefore the Son of *m* is Lord	Mk 2:28	*444*
there was a *m* there which had a	Mk 3:1	*444*
he saith unto the *m* which had the	Mk 3:3	*444*
their hearts, he saith unto the *m*	Mk 3:5	*444*
No *m* can enter into a strong	Mk 3:27	*3762*
he will first bind the strong *m*	Mk 3:27	*2478*
If any *m* have ears to hear, let	Mk 4:23	
as if a *m* should cast seed into	Mk 4:26	*444*
another, What manner of *m* is this	Mk 4:41	
tombs a *m* with an unclean spirit	Mk 5:2	*444*
no *m* could bind him, no, not with	Mk 5:3	*3762*
neither could any *m* tame him	Mk 5:4	
said unto him, Come out of the *m*	Mk 5:8	*444*
And he suffered no *m* to follow him	Mk 5:37	*3762*
straitly that no *m* should know it	Mk 5:43	*3367*
whence hath this *m* these things	Mk 6:2	
knowing that he was a just *m*	Mk 6:20	*435*
If a *m* shall say to his father or	Mk 7:11	*444*
There is nothing from without a *m*	Mk 7:15	*444*
those are they that defile the *m*	Mk 7:15	*444*
If any *m* have ears to hear, let	Mk 7:16	
from without entereth into the *m*	Mk 7:18	*444*
of the *m*, that defileth the *m*	Mk 7:20	*444*
come from within, and defile the *m*	Mk 7:23	*444*
house, and would have no *m* know it	Mk 7:24	*3762*
them that they should tell no *m*	Mk 7:36	*3367*
From whence can a *m* satisfy these	Mk 8:4	*5100*
and they bring a blind *m* unto him	Mk 8:22	
he took the blind *m* by the hand	Mk 8:23	
restored, and saw every *m* clearly	Mk 8:25	
that they should tell no *m* of him	Mk 8:30	*3367*
that the Son of *m* must suffer	Mk 8:31	*444*
For what shall it profit a *m*	Mk 8:36	*444*
Or what shall a *m* give in	Mk 8:37	*444*
shall the Son of *m* be ashamed	Mk 8:38	*444*
about, they saw no *m* any more	Mk 9:8	*3762*
no *m* what things they had seen	Mk 9:9	*3367*
till the Son of *m* were risen from	Mk 9:9	*444*
how it is written of the Son of *m*	Mk 9:12	*444*
not that any *m* should know it	Mk 9:30	
The Son of *m* is delivered into	Mk 9:31	*444*
If any *m* desire to be first, the	Mk 9:35	
for there is no *m* which shall do	Mk 9:39	*3762*
Is it lawful for a *m* to put away	Mk 10:2	*435*
cause shall a *m* leave his father	Mk 10:7	*444*
together, let not *m* put asunder	Mk 10:9	*444*
than for a rich *m* to enter into	Mk 10:25	
There is no *m* that hath left	Mk 10:29	*3762*
the Son of *m* shall be delivered	Mk 10:33	*444*
For even the Son of *m* came not to	Mk 10:45	*444*
And they call the blind *m*, saying	Mk 10:49	
The blind *m* said unto him, Lord	Mk 10:51	
a colt tied, whereon never *m* sat	Mk 11:2	*444*
if any *m* say unto you, Why do ye	Mk 11:3	
No *m* eat fruit of thee hereafter	Mk 11:14	*3367*
would not suffer that any *m*	Mk 11:16	
A certain *m* planted a vineyard	Mk 12:1	*444*
thou art true, and carest for no *m*	Mk 12:14	*444*
no *m* after that durst ask him any	Mk 12:34	*3762*
Take heed lest any *m* deceive you	Mk 13:5	
then if any *m* shall say to you	Mk 13:21	
then shall they see the Son of *m*	Mk 13:26	*444*
day and that hour knoweth no *m*	Mk 13:32	*3762*
For the Son of *m* is as a	Mk 13:34	
is as a *m* taking a far journey	Mk 13:34	*444*
servants, and to every *m* his work	Mk 13:34	
there shall meet you a *m* bearing	Mk 14:13	*444*
The Son of *m* indeed goeth, as it	Mk 14:21	*444*
but woe to that *m* by whom the Son	Mk 14:21	*444*
by whom the Son of *m* is betrayed	Mk 14:21	*444*
good were it for that *m* if he had	Mk 14:21	*444*
the Son of *m* is betrayed into the	Mk 14:41	*444*
followed him a certain young *m*	Mk 14:51	*3495*
ye shall see the Son of *m* sitting	Mk 14:62	*444*
I know not this *m* of whom ye	Mk 14:71	*444*
them, what every *m* should take	Mk 15:24	
Truly this *m* was the Son of God	Mk 15:39	*444*
they saw a young *m* sitting on the	Mk 16:5	*3495*
to any *m* for they were afraid	Mk 16:8	*3762*
for I am an old *m*, and my wife	Lk 1:18	
to a *m* whose name was Joseph	Lk 1:27	*435*
this be, seeing I know not a *m*	Lk 1:34	*435*
there was a *m* in Jerusalem, whose	Lk 2:25	*444*
and the same *m* was just and devout	Lk 2:25	*444*
and in favour with God and *m*	Lk 2:52	*444*
unto them, Do violence to no *m*	Lk 3:14	*3367*
That *m* shall not live by bread	Lk 4:4	*444*
And in the synagogue there was a *m*	Lk 4:33	*444*
for I am a sinful *m*, O Lord	Lk 5:8	*435*
behold a *m* full of leprosy	Lk 5:12	*435*
And he charged him to tell no *m*	Lk 5:14	*3367*
men brought in a bed a *m* which	Lk 5:18	*444*
their faith, he said unto him, *M*	Lk 5:20	*444*
Son of *m* hath power upon earth to	Lk 5:24	*444*
No *m* putteth a piece of a new	Lk 5:36	*3762*
no *m* putteth new wine into old	Lk 5:37	*3762*
No *m* also having drunk old wine	Lk 5:39	*3762*
That the Son of *m* is Lord also of	Lk 6:5	*444*
there was a *m* whose right hand	Lk 6:6	*444*
said to the *m* which had the	Lk 6:8	*444*
upon them all, he said unto the *m*	Lk 6:10	*444*
Give to every *m* that asketh of	Lk 6:30	
A good *m* out of the good treasure	Lk 6:45	*444*
an evil *m* out of the evil	Lk 6:45	*444*
He is like a *m* which built an	Lk 6:48	*444*
is like a *m* that without a	Lk 6:49	*444*
For I also am a *m* set under	Lk 7:8	*444*
there was a dead *m* carried out	Lk 7:12	
And he said, Young *m*, I say unto	Lk 7:14	*3495*
A *m* clothed in soft raiment	Lk 7:25	*444*
The Son of *m* is come eating and	Lk 7:34	*444*
and ye say, Behold a gluttonous *m*	Lk 7:34	*444*
within himself, saying, This *m*	Lk 7:39	
No *m*, when he hath lighted a	Lk 8:16	*3762*
another, What manner of *m* is this	Lk 8:25	
him out of the city a certain *m*	Lk 8:27	*435*
spirit to come out of the *m*	Lk 8:29	*444*
Then went the devils out of the *m*	Lk 8:33	*444*
and came to Jesus, and found the *m*	Lk 8:35	*444*
Now the *m* out of whom the devils	Lk 8:38	*435*
there came a *m* named Jairus	Lk 8:41	*435*
house, he suffered no *m* to go in	Lk 8:51	*3762*
should tell no *m* what was done	Lk 8:56	*3367*
them to tell no *m* that thing	Lk 9:21	*3367*
The Son of *m* must suffer many	Lk 9:22	*444*
If any *m* will come after me, let	Lk 9:23	
For what is a *m* advantaged	Lk 9:25	*444*
him shall the Son of *m* be ashamed	Lk 9:26	*444*
told no *m* in those days any of	Lk 9:36	*3762*
a *m* of the company cried out	Lk 9:38	*435*
for the Son of *m* shall be	Lk 9:44	*444*
For the Son of *m* is not come to	Lk 9:56	*444*
a certain *m* said unto him, Lord	Lk 9:57	
but the Son of *m* hath not where	Lk 9:58	*444*
And Jesus said unto him, No *m*	Lk 9:62	*3762*
and salute no *m* by the way	Lk 10:4	*3367*
no *m* knoweth who the Son is, but	Lk 10:22	*3762*
A certain *m* went down from	Lk 10:30	*444*
When a strong *m* armed keepeth his	Lk 11:21	
unclean spirit is gone out of a *m*	Lk 11:24	*444*
the last state of that *m* is worse	Lk 11:26	*444*
Son of *m* be to this generation	Lk 11:30	*444*
No *m*, when he hath lighted a	Lk 11:33	*3762*
him shall the Son of *m* also	Lk 12:8	*444*
speak a word against the Son of *m*	Lk 12:10	*444*
And he said unto him, *M*, who made	Lk 12:14	*444*
rich *m* brought forth plentifully	Lk 12:16	*444*
for the Son of *m* cometh at an	Lk 12:40	*444*
A certain *m* had a fig tree	Lk 13:6	
of mustard seed, which a *m* took	Lk 13:19	*444*
there was a certain *m* before him	Lk 14:2	*444*
art bidden of any *m* to a wedding	Lk 14:8	
lest a more honourable *m* than	Lk 14:8	
and say to thee, Give this *m* place	Lk 14:9	
A certain *m* made a great supper	Lk 14:16	*444*
If any *m* come to me, and hate not	Lk 14:26	
This *m* began to build, and was not	Lk 14:30	*444*
This *m* receiveth sinners, and	Lk 15:2	
What *m* of you, having an hundred	Lk 15:4	*444*
he said, A certain *m* had two sons	Lk 15:11	*444*
and no *m* gave unto him	Lk 15:16	*3762*
There was a certain rich *m*	Lk 16:1	*444*
and every *m* presseth into it	Lk 16:16	
There was a certain rich *m*	Lk 16:19	*444*
the rich *m* also died, and was	Lk 16:22	
one of the days of the Son of *m*	Lk 17:22	*444*
also the Son of *m* be in his day	Lk 17:24	*444*
also in the days of the Son of *m*	Lk 17:26	*444*
day when the Son of *m* is revealed	Lk 17:30	*444*
not God, neither regarded *m*	Lk 18:2	*444*
I fear not God, nor regard *m*	Lk 18:4	*444*
when the Son of *m* cometh, shall	Lk 18:8	*444*
this *m* went down to his house	Lk 18:14	
than for a rich *m* to enter into	Lk 18:25	
There is no *m* that hath left	Lk 18:29	*3762*
Son of *m* shall be accomplished	Lk 18:31	*444*
a certain blind *m* sat by the way	Lk 18:35	
there was a *m* named Zacchaeus	Lk 19:2	*435*
guest with a *m* that is a sinner	Lk 19:7	*435*
from any *m* by false accusation	Lk 19:8	
For the Son of *m* is come to seek	Lk 19:10	*444*
not have this *m* to reign over us	Lk 19:14	
every *m* had gained by trading	Lk 19:15	
because thou art an austere *m*	Lk 19:21	*444*
knewest that I was an austere *m*	Lk 19:22	*444*
tied, whereon yet never *m* sat	Lk 19:30	*444*
if any *m* ask you, Why do ye loose	Lk 19:31	
A certain *m* planted a vineyard	Lk 20:9	*444*
of *m* coming in a cloud with power	Lk 21:27	*444*
and to stand before the Son of *m*	Lk 21:36	*444*
city, there shall a *m* meet you	Lk 22:10	*444*
And truly the Son of *m* goeth	Lk 22:22	*444*
but woe unto that *m* by whom he is	Lk 22:22	*444*
thou the Son of *m* with a kiss	Lk 22:48	*444*
and said, This *m* was also with him	Lk 22:56	
And Peter said, *M*, I am not	Lk 22:58	*444*
And Peter said, *M*, I know not what	Lk 22:60	*444*
Hereafter shall the Son of *m* sit	Lk 22:69	*444*
people, I find no fault in this *m*	Lk 23:4	*444*
whether the *m* were a Galilaean	Lk 23:6	*444*
Ye have brought this *m* unto me	Lk 23:14	*444*
have found no fault in this *m*	Lk 23:14	*444*
at once, saying, Away with this *m*	Lk 23:18	
but this *m* hath done nothing	Lk 23:41	
Certainly this was a righteous *m*	Lk 23:47	*444*
there was a *m* named Joseph, a	Lk 23:50	*435*
and he was a good *m*, and a just	Lk 23:50	*435*
This *m* went unto Pilate, and	Lk 23:52	
wherein never *m* before was laid	Lk 23:53	*3762*
The Son of *m* must be delivered	Lk 24:7	*444*
There was a *m* sent from God	Jn 1:6	*444*
which lighteth every *m* that	Jn 1:9	*444*
the flesh, nor of the will of *m*	Jn 1:13	*435*
No *m* hath seen God at any time	Jn 1:18	*3762*
After me cometh a *m* which is	Jn 1:30	*435*
and descending upon the Son of *m*	Jn 1:51	*444*
Every *m* at the beginning doth set	Jn 2:10	*444*
not that any should testify of *m*	Jn 2:25	*444*
for he knew what was in *m*	Jn 2:25	*444*
There was a *m* of the Pharisees	Jn 3:1	*444*
for no *m* can do these miracles	Jn 3:2	*3762*
Except a *m* be born again, he	Jn 3:3	*5100*
How can a *m* be born when he is	Jn 3:4	*444*
Except a *m* be born of water and of	Jn 3:5	*5100*
no *m* hath ascended up to heaven	Jn 3:13	*3762*
even the Son of *m* which is in	Jn 3:13	*444*
so must the Son of *m* be lifted up	Jn 3:14	*444*
A *m* can receive nothing, except	Jn 3:27	*444*

no *m* receiveth his testimony Jn 3:32 *3762*
yet no *m* said, What seekest thou Jn 4:27 *3762*
Come, see a *m*, which told me all Jn 4:29 *444*
Hath any *m* brought him ought to Jn 4:33
the *m* believed the word that Jn 4:50 *444*
And a certain *m* was there, which Jn 5:5 *444*
The impotent *m* answered him Jn 5:7
answered him, Sir, I have no *m* Jn 5:7 *444*
immediately the *m* was made whole Jn 5:9 *444*
What *m* is that which said unto Jn 5:12 *444*
The *m* departed, and told the Jews Jn 5:15 *444*
For the Father judgeth no *m* Jn 5:22 *3762*
also, because he is the Son of *m* Jn 5:27 *444*
I receive not testimony from *m* Jn 5:34 *444*
which the Son of *m* shall give Jn 6:27 *444*
No *m* can come to me, except the Jn 6:44 *3762*
Every *m* therefore that hath heard Jn 6:45
Not that any *m* hath seen the Jn 6:46
that a *m* may eat thereof, and not Jn 6:50 *5100*
if any *m* eat of this bread, he Jn 6:51
How can this *m* give us his flesh Jn 6:52
ye eat the flesh of the Son of *m* Jn 6:53 *444*
if ye shall see the Son of *m* Jn 6:62 *444*
that no *m* can come unto me, Jn 6:65 *3762*
For there is no *m* that doeth any Jn 7:4 *3762*
for some said, He is a good *m* Jn 7:12
Howbeit no *m* spake openly of him Jn 7:13 *3762*
How knoweth this *m* letters Jn 7:15
If any *m* will do his will, he Jn 7:17
on the sabbath day circumcise a *m* Jn 7:22 *444*
If a *m* on the sabbath day receive Jn 7:23 *444*
because I have made a *m* every Jn 7:23 *444*
we know this *m* whence he is Jn 7:27
no *m* knoweth whence he is Jn 7:27 *3762*
but no *m* laid hands on him, Jn 7:30 *3762*
than these which this *m* hath done Jn 7:31
and cried, saying, If any *m* thirst Jn 7:37
but no *m* laid hands on him Jn 7:44 *3762*
Never *m* spake like this *m*, Jn 7:46 *444*
Doth our law judge any *m*, before Jn 7:51 *444*
every *m* went unto his own house Jn 7:53
hath no *m* condemned thee Jn 8:10 *3762*
She said, No *m*, Lord Jn 8:11 *3762*
I judge no *m* Jn 8:15 *3762*
and no *m* laid hands on him Jn 8:20 *3762*
ye have lifted up the Son of *m* Jn 8:28 *444*
and were never in bondage to any *m* Jn 8:33
a *m* that hath told you the truth, Jn 8:40 *444*
If a *m* keep my saying, he shall Jn 8:51 *5100*
If a *m* keep my saying, he shall Jn 8:52 *5100*
he saw a *m* which was blind from Jn 9:1 *444*
Master, who did sin, this *m* Jn 9:2
Neither hath this *m* sinned Jn 9:3
night cometh, when no *m* can work Jn 9:4 *3762*
eyes of the blind *m* with the clay Jn 9:6
A *m* that is called Jesus made Jn 9:11 *444*
This *m* is not of God, because he Jn 9:16 *444*
How can a *m* that is a sinner do Jn 9:16 *444*
They say unto the blind *m* again Jn 9:17
that if any *m* did confess that he Jn 9:22
called they the *m* that was blind Jn 9:24 *444*
we know that this *m* is a sinner Jn 9:24 *444*
The *m* answered and said unto them, Jn 9:30 *444*
but if any *m* be a worshipper of Jn 9:31
m opened the eyes of one that was Jn 9:32
If this *m* were not of God, he Jn 9:33
by me if any *m* enter in, he shall Jn 10:9
No *m* taketh it from me, but I lay Jn 10:18 *3762*
neither shall any *m* pluck them Jn 10:28
no *m* is able to pluck them out of Jn 10:29 *3762*
and because that thou, being a *m* Jn 10:33 *444*
John spake of this *m* were true Jn 10:41
Now a certain *m* was sick, named Jn 11:1
If any *m* walk in the day, he Jn 11:9
But if a *m* walk in the night, he Jn 11:10 *5100*
of them said, Could not this *m* Jn 11:37
even this *m* should not have died Jn 11:37
for this *m* doeth many miracles Jn 11:47 *444*
that one *m* should die for the Jn 11:50 *444*
if any *m* knew where he were, he Jn 11:57
that the Son of *m* should be Jn 12:23 *444*
If any *m* serve me, let him follow Jn 12:26
if any *m* serve me, him will my Jn 12:26
The Son of *m* must be lifted up Jn 12:34 *444*
who is this Son of *m* Jn 12:34 *444*
if any *m* hear my words, and Jn 12:47
Now no *m* at the table knew for Jn 13:28 *3762*
Now is the Son of *m* glorified Jn 13:31 *444*
no *m* cometh unto the Father, but Jn 14:6 *3762*
If a *m* love me, he will keep my Jn 14:23 *5100*
If a *m* abide not in me, he is Jn 15:6 *5100*
Greater love hath no *m* than this Jn 15:13 *3762*
that a *m* lay down his life for Jn 15:13 *5100*
the works which none other *m* did Jn 15:24
for joy that a *m* is born into the Jn 16:21 *444*
your joy no *m* taketh from you Jn 16:22 *3762*
not that any *m* should ask thee Jn 16:30
every *m* to his own, and shall Jn 16:32
one *m* should die for the people Jn 18:14 *444*
bring ye against this *m* Jn 18:29 *444*
for us to put any *m* to death Jn 18:31 *3762*
all again, saying, Not this *m* Jn 18:40 *444*
saith unto them, Behold the *m* Jn 19:5 *444*
saying, If thou let this *m* go Jn 19:12 *444*
wherein was never *m* yet laid Jn 19:41 *3762*
Lord, and what shall this *m* do Jn 21:21
Now this *m* purchased a field with Acts 1:18
and let no *m* dwell therein Acts 1:20

because that every *m* heard them Acts 2:6 *1520*
hear we every *m* in our own tongue Acts 2:8 *1520*
a *m* approved of God among you by Acts 2:22 *435*
to all men, as every *m* had need Acts 2:45
a certain *m* lame from his Acts 3:2 *435*
as the lame *m* which was healed Acts 3:11
we had made this *m* to walk Acts 3:12
his name hath made this *m* strong Acts 3:16
good deed done to the impotent *m* Acts 4:9 *444*
even by him doth this *m* stand Acts 4:10
beholding the *m* which was healed Acts 4:14 *444*
henceforth to no *m* in this name Acts 4:17 *444*
For the *m* was above forty years Acts 4:22 *444*
was made unto every *m* according Acts 4:35
But a certain *m* named Ananias Acts 5:1 *435*
durst no *m* join himself to them Acts 5:13 *3762*
had opened, we found no *m* within Acts 5:23 *3762*
After this *m* rose up Judas of Acts 5:37
a *m* full of faith and of the Holy Acts 6:5 *435*
This *m* ceaseth not to speak Acts 6:13 *444*
the Son of *m* standing on the Acts 7:56 *444*
But there was a certain *m* Acts 8:9 *435*
This *m* is the great power of God Acts 8:10
a *m* of Ethiopia, an eunuch of Acts 8:27 *435*
except some *m* should guide me Acts 8:31
of himself, or of some other *m* Acts 8:34
hearing a voice, but seeing no *m* Acts 9:7 *3367*
his eyes were opened, he saw no *m* Acts 9:8 *3762*
a *m* named Ananias coming in Acts 9:12 *435*
I have heard by many of this *m* Acts 9:13 *435*
he found a certain *m* named Aeneas Acts 9:33 *444*
There was a certain *m* in Caesarea Acts 10:1 *435*
A devout *m*, and one that feared Acts 10:2
Cornelius the centurion, a just *m* Acts 10:22 *435*
I myself also am a *m* Acts 10:26 *444*
a *m* that is a Jew to keep company Acts 10:28 *435*
not call any *m* common or unclean Acts 10:28 *444*
a *m* stood before me in bright Acts 10:30 *435*
Can any *m* forbid water, that Acts 10:47 *5100*
For he was a good *m*, and full of Acts 11:24 *435*
every *m* according to his ability, Acts 11:29 *1538*
the voice of a god, and not of a *m* Acts 12:22 *444*
Sergius Paulus, a prudent *m* Acts 13:7 *435*
a *m* of the tribe of Benjamin, by Acts 13:21 *435*
a *m* after mine own heart, which Acts 13:22 *435*
that through this *m* is preached Acts 13:38
though a *m* declare it unto you Acts 13:41 *5100*
there sat a certain *m* at Lystra Acts 14:8 *435*
There stood a *m* of Macedonia Acts 16:9 *435*
by that *m* whom he hath ordained Acts 17:31 *435*
no *m* shall set on thee to hurt Acts 18:10 *3762*
born at Alexandria, an eloquent *m* Acts 18:24 *435*
This *m* was instructed in the way Acts 18:25
the *m* in whom the evil spirit was Acts 19:16 *444*
For a certain *m* named Demetrius, Acts 19:24
what *m* is there that knoweth not Acts 19:35 *444*
him, have a matter against any *m* Acts 19:38
a certain young *m* named Eutychus Acts 20:9 *3494*
And they brought the young *m* alive Acts 20:12
the same *m* had four daughters, Acts 21:9
the *m* that owneth this girdle Acts 21:11 *435*
This is the *m*, that teacheth all Acts 21:28 *444*
I am a *m* which am a Jew of Tarsus Acts 21:39 *444*
I am verily a *m* which am a Jew, Acts 22:3 *435*
a devout *m* according to the law, Acts 22:12 *435*
to scourge a *m* that is a Roman Acts 22:25 *444*
for this *m* is a Roman Acts 22:26 *444*
saying, We find no evil in this *m* Acts 23:9 *444*
Bring this young *m* unto the chief Acts 23:17 *3494*
to bring this young *m* unto thee Acts 23:18 *3494*
then let the young *m* depart Acts 23:22 *3494*
See thou tell no *m* that thou hast Acts 23:22 *3367*
This *m* was taken of the Jews, and Acts 23:27 *435*
that the Jews laid wait for the *m* Acts 23:30 *435*
found this *m* a pestilent fellow Acts 24:5 *435*
the temple disputing with any *m* Acts 24:12
go down with me, and accuse this *m* Acts 25:5 *435*
no *m* may deliver me unto them Acts 25:11 *3762*
There is a certain *m* left in Acts 25:14 *435*
Romans to deliver any *m* to die Acts 25:16 *444*
commanded the *m* to be brought Acts 25:17 *435*
I would also hear the *m* myself Acts 25:22 *444*
present with us, ye see this *m* Acts 25:24
This *m* doeth nothing worthy of Acts 26:31 *444*
This *m* might have been set at Acts 26:32 *444*
No doubt this *m* is a murderer Acts 28:4 *444*
of the chief *m* of the island Acts 28:7
confidence, no *m* forbidding him Acts 28:31
image made like to corruptible *m* Rom 1:23 *444*
thou art inexcusable, O *m* Rom 2:1 *444*
And thinkest thou this, O *m* Rom 2:3 *444*
to every *m* according to his deeds Rom 2:6
every soul of *m* that doeth evil Rom 2:9 *444*
to every *m* that worketh good, to Rom 2:10 *3956*
preachest a *m* should not steal Rom 2:21
Thou that sayest a *m* should not Rom 2:22
God be true, but every *m* a liar Rom 3:4 *444*
(I speak as a *m*) Rom 3:5 *444*
Therefore we conclude that a *m* is Rom 3:28 *444*
the blessedness of the *m*, unto Rom 4:6 *444*
Blessed is the *m* to whom the Lord Rom 4:8 *435*
for a righteous *m* will one die Rom 5:7
m some would even dare to die Rom 5:7
as by one *m* sin entered into the Rom 5:12 *444*
gift by grace, which is by one *m* Rom 5:15 *444*
that our old *m* is crucified with Rom 6:6 *444*
over a *m* as long as he liveth Rom 7:1 *444*
she be married to another *m* Rom 7:3 *435*

she be married to another *m* Rom 7:3 *435*
the law of God after the inward *m* Rom 7:22 *444*
O wretched *m* that I am Rom 7:24 *444*
Now if any *m* have not the Spirit Rom 8:9
for what a *m* seeth, why doth he Rom 8:24 *5100*
Nay but, O *m*, who art thou that Rom 9:20 *444*
That the *m* which doeth those Rom 10:5 *444*
For with the heart *m* believeth Rom 10:10
to every *m* that is among you, not Rom 12:3
to every *m* the measure of faith Rom 12:3
Recompense to no *m* evil for evil Rom 12:17 *3367*
Owe no *m* any thing, but to love Rom 13:8 *3367*
One *m* esteemeth one day above Rom 14:5
Let every *m* be fully persuaded in Rom 14:5
himself, and no *m* dieth to himself Rom 14:7 *3762*
that no *m* put a stumblingblock or Rom 14:13
that *m* who eateth with offence Rom 14:20 *444*
have entered into the heart of *m* 1Cor 2:9 *444*
For what *m* knoweth the things of 1Cor 2:11 *444*
knoweth the things of a *m* 1Cor 2:11 *444*
the spirit of *m* which is in him 1Cor 2:11 *444*
so the things of God knoweth no *m* 1Cor 2:11 *3762*
But the natural *m* receiveth not 1Cor 2:14 *444*
yet he himself is judged of no *m* 1Cor 2:15 *3762*
even as the Lord gave to every *m* 1Cor 3:5
every *m* shall receive his own 1Cor 3:8
But let every *m* take heed how he 1Cor 3:10
can no *m* lay than that is laid 1Cor 3:11 *3762*
Now if any *m* build upon this 1Cor 3:12
If any *m* defile the temple of God 1Cor 3:17
Let no *m* deceive himself 1Cor 3:18 *3367*
If any *m* among you seemeth to be 1Cor 3:18
Therefore let no *m* glory in men 1Cor 3:21 *3367*
Let a *m* so account of us, as of 1Cor 4:1 *444*
that a *m* be found faithful 1Cor 4:2 *5100*
then shall every *m* have praise of 1Cor 4:5
if any *m* that is called a brother 1Cor 5:11
there is not a wise *m* among you 1Cor 6:5
Every sin that a *m* doeth is 1Cor 6:18 *444*
It is good for a *m* not to touch a 1Cor 7:1 *444*
let every *m* have his own wife, and 1Cor 7:2
But every *m* hath his proper gift 1Cor 7:7
or how knowest thou, O *m*, whether 1Cor 7:16 *435*
God hath distributed to every *m* 1Cor 7:17
Is any *m* called being circumcised 1Cor 7:18
Let every *m* abide in the same 1Cor 7:20
Brethren, let every *m*, wherein he 1Cor 7:24
that it is good for a *m* so to be 1Cor 7:26 *444*
But if any *m* think that he 1Cor 7:36
if any *m* think that he knoweth 1Cor 8:2
But if any *m* love God, the same 1Cor 8:3
is not in every *m* that knowledge 1Cor 8:7 *3956*
For if any *m* see thee which hast 1Cor 8:10
Say I these things as a *m* 1Cor 9:8 *444*
than that any *m* should make my 1Cor 9:15
every *m* that striveth for the 1Cor 9:25
you but such as is common to *m* 1Cor 10:13 *442*
Let no *m* seek his own 1Cor 10:24 *3367*
but every *m* another's wealth 1Cor 10:24
But if any *m* say unto you, This 1Cor 10:28
the head of every *m* is Christ 1Cor 11:3 *435*
and the head of the woman is the *m* 1Cor 11:3 *435*
Every *m* praying or prophesying, 1Cor 11:4 *435*
For a *m* indeed ought not to cover 1Cor 11:7 *435*
the woman is the glory of the *m* 1Cor 11:7 *435*
For the *m* is not of the woman 1Cor 11:8 *435*
but the woman of the *m* 1Cor 11:8 *435*
Neither was the *m* created for the 1Cor 11:9 *435*
but the woman for the *m* 1Cor 11:9 *435*
is the *m* without the woman 1Cor 11:11 *435*
neither the woman without the *m* 1Cor 11:11 *435*
For as the woman is of the *m* 1Cor 11:12 *435*
even so is the *m* also by the 1Cor 11:12 *435*
if a *m* have long hair, it is a 1Cor 11:14 *435*
But if any *m* seem to be 1Cor 11:16
But let a *m* examine himself, and 1Cor 11:28 *444*
And if any *m* hunger, let him eat 1Cor 11:34
that no *m* speaking by the Spirit 1Cor 12:3 *3762*
that no *m* can say that Jesus is 1Cor 12:3 *3762*
given to every *m* to profit withal 1Cor 12:7 *1538*
dividing to every *m* severally as 1Cor 12:11 *1538*
but when I became a *m*, I put away 1Cor 13:11 *435*
for no *m* understandeth him 1Cor 14:2 *3762*
If any *m* speak in an unknown 1Cor 14:27
If any *m* think himself to be a 1Cor 14:37
But if any *m* be ignorant, let him 1Cor 14:38
For since by *m* came death 1Cor 15:21 *444*
by *m* came also the resurrection 1Cor 15:21 *444*
But every *m* in his own order 1Cor 15:23
But some *m* will say, How are the 1Cor 15:35
The first *m* Adam was made a 1Cor 15:45 *444*
The first *m* is of the earth, 1Cor 15:47 *444*
the second *m* is the Lord from 1Cor 15:47 *444*
Let no *m* therefore despise him 1Cor 16:11 *5100*
If any *m* love not the Lord Jesus 1Cor 16:22
to such a *m* is this punishment 2Cor 2:6
but though our outward *m* perish 2Cor 4:16 *444*
yet the inward *m* is renewed day 2Cor 4:16
know we no *m* after the flesh 2Cor 5:16 *3762*
Therefore if any *m* be in Christ 2Cor 5:17
we have wronged no *m* 2Cor 7:2 *3762*
we have corrupted no *m* 2Cor 7:2 *3762*
we have defrauded no *m* 2Cor 7:2 *3762*
according to that a *m* hath 2Cor 8:12 *5100*
that no *m* should blame us in this 2Cor 8:20 *5100*
Every *m* according as he purposeth 2Cor 9:7
If any *m* trust to himself that he 2Cor 10:7
wanted, I was chargeable to no *m* 2Cor 11:9 *3762*

no *m* shall stop me of this 2Cor 11:10
again, Let no *m* think me a fool 2Cor 11:16 *5100*
if a *m* bring you into bondage 2Cor 11:20 *5100*
if a *m* devour you 2Cor 11:20 *5100*
if a *m* take of you 2Cor 11:20 *5100*
if a *m* exalt himself 2Cor 11:20 *5100*
if a *m* smite you on the face 2Cor 11:20 *5100*
I knew a *m* in Christ above 2Cor 12:2 *444*
And I knew such a *m*, (whether in 2Cor 12:3 *444*
it is not lawful for a *m* to utter 2Cor 12:4 *444*
lest any *m* should think of me 2Cor 12:6
(not of men, neither by *m* Gal 1:1 *444*
If any *m* preach any other gospel Gal 1:9
was preached of me is not after *m* Gal 1:11 *444*
For I neither received it of *m* Gal 1:12 *444*
Knowing that a *m* is not justified Gal 2:16 *444*
But that no *m* is justified by the Gal 3:11 *3762*
The *m* that doeth them shall live Gal 3:12 *444*
no *m* disannulleth, or addeth Gal 3:15 *3762*
to every *m* that is circumcised Gal 5:3 *444*
if a *m* be overtaken in a fault, Gal 6:1 *444*
For if a *m* think himself to be Gal 6:3 *5100*
But let every *m* prove his own Gal 6:4
For every *m* shall bear his own Gal 6:5
for whatsoever a *m* soweth Gal 6:7 *444*
henceforth let no *m* trouble me Gal 6:17 *3367*
of works, lest any *m* should boast Eph 2:9
in himself of twain one new *m* Eph 2:15 *444*
by his Spirit in the inner *m* Eph 3:16 *444*
the Son of God, unto a perfect *m* Eph 4:13 *435*
the former conversation the old *m* Eph 4:22 *444*
And that ye put on the new *m* Eph 4:24 *444*
speak every *m* truth with his Eph 4:25
unclean person, nor covetous *m* Eph 5:5 *444*
Let no *m* deceive you with vain Eph 5:6 *3367*
For no *m* ever yet hated his own Eph 5:29 *3762*
cause shall a *m* leave his father Eph 5:31 *444*
whatsoever good thing any *m* doeth Eph 6:8
Look not every *m* on his own Phil 2:4
but every *m* also on the things of Phil 2:4
And being found in fashion as a *m* Phil 2:8 *444*
For I have no *m* likeminded Phil 2:20 *3762*
If any other *m* thinketh that he Phil 3:4
Whom we preach, warning every *m* Col 1:28 *444*
and teaching every *m* in all wisdom Col 1:28 *444*
every *m* perfect in Christ Jesus Col 1:28 *444*
lest any *m* should beguile you Col 2:4
Beware lest any *m* spoil you Col 2:8
Let no *m* therefore judge you in Col 2:16 *5100*
Let no *m* beguile you of your Col 2:18 *3367*
put off the old *m* with his deeds Col 3:9 *444*
And have put on the new *m*, which Col 3:10
if any *m* have a quarrel against Col 3:13
how ye ought to answer every *m* Col 4:6 *1520*
That no *m* should be moved by 1Th 3:3 *3367*
That no *m* go beyond and defraud 1Th 4:6
that despiseth, despiseth not *m* 1Th 4:8 *444*
render evil for evil unto any *m* 1Th 5:15
Let no *m* deceive you by any means 2Th 2:3 *5100*
that *m* of sin be revealed, the 2Th 2:3 *444*
if any *m* obey not our word by 2Th 3:14
word by this epistle, note that *m* 2Th 3:14
is good, if a *m* use it lawfully 1Ti 1:8 *5100*
law is not made for a righteous *m* 1Ti 1:9
God and men, the *m* Christ Jesus 1Ti 2:5 *444*
nor to usurp authority over the *m* 1Ti 2:12 *435*
If a *m* desire the office of a 1Ti 3:1 *5100*
(For if a *m* know not how to rule 1Ti 3:5 *5100*
Let no *m* despise thy youth 1Ti 4:12 *3367*
having been the wife of one *m* 1Ti 5:9 *435*
If any *m* or woman that believeth 1Ti 5:16
Lay hands suddenly on no *m* 1Ti 5:22 *3367*
If any *m* teach otherwise, and 1Ti 6:3
O *m* of God, flee these things 1Ti 6:11 *444*
which no *m* can approach unto 1Ti 6:16
whom no *m* hath seen, nor can see 1Ti 6:16 *444*
No *m* that warreth entangleth 2Ti 2:4 *3762*
if a *m* also strive for masteries, 2Ti 2:5 *5100*
If a *m* therefore purge himself 2Ti 2:21 *5100*
That the *m* of God may be perfect, 2Ti 3:17 *444*
first answer no *m* stood with me 2Ti 4:16 *3762*
Let no *m* despise thee Titus 2:15 *3367*
To speak evil of no *m*, to be no Titus 3:2 *3367*
God our Saviour toward *m* appeared Titus 3:4
A *m* that is an heretick after the Titus 3:10 *444*
testified, saying, What is *m* Heb 2:6 *444*
or the son of *m*, that thou Heb 2:6 *444*
should taste death for every *m* Heb 2:9
For this *m* was counted worthy of Heb 3:3
every house is builded by some *m* Heb 3:4
lest any *m* fall after the same Heb 4:11
no *m* taketh this honour unto Heb 5:4 *5100*
Now consider how great this *m* was Heb 7:4
of which no *m* gave attendance at Heb 7:13 *3762*
But this *m*, because he continueth Heb 7:24
which the Lord pitched, and not *m* Heb 8:2 *444*
m have somewhat also to offer Heb 8:3
not teach every *m* his neighbour Heb 8:11
every *m* his brother, saying, Know Heb 8:11
But this *m*, after he had offered Heb 10:12
but if any *m* draw back, my soul Heb 10:38
without which no *m* shall see the Heb 12:14 *3762*
any *m* fail of the grace of God Heb 12:15
not fear what *m* shall do unto me Heb 13:6 *444*
For let not that *m* think that he Jas 1:7 *444*
A double minded *m* is unstable in Jas 1:8 *435*
the rich *m* fade away in his ways Jas 1:11
Blessed is the *m* that endureth Jas 1:12 *435*
Let no *m* say when he is tempted, Jas 1:13 *3367*
evil, neither tempteth he any *m* Jas 1:13 *3762*
But every *m* is tempted, when he Jas 1:14
let every *m* be swift to hear, Jas 1:19 *444*
For the wrath of *m* worketh not Jas 1:20 *435*
he is like unto a *m* beholding his Jas 1:23 *435*
what manner of *m* he was Jas 1:24
this *m* shall be blessed in his Jas 1:25
If any *m* among you seem to be Jas 1:26
assembly a *m* with a gold ring Jas 2:2 *435*
in also a poor *m* in vile raiment Jas 2:2
though a *m* say he hath faith, and Jas 2:14 *5100*
a *m* may say, Thou hast faith, and Jas 2:18 *5100*
But wilt thou know, O vain *m* Jas 2:20 *444*
that by works a *m* is justified Jas 2:24 *444*
If any *m* offend not in word Jas 3:2
the same is a perfect *m* Jas 3:2 *435*
But the tongue can no *m* tame Jas 3:8 *444*
Who is a wise *m* and endued with Jas 3:13
of a righteous *m* availeth much Jas 5:16
Elias was a *m* subject to like Jas 5:17 *444*
all the glory of *m* as the flower 1Pet 1:24 *444*
of *m* for the Lord's sake 1Pet 2:13 *442*
if a *m* for conscience toward God 1Pet 2:19 *5100*
it be the hidden *m* of the heart 1Pet 3:4 *444*
to give an answer to every *m* that 1Pet 3:15
As every *m* hath received the gift 1Pet 4:10
If any *m* speak, let him speak as 1Pet 4:11
if any *m* minister, let him do it 1Pet 4:11
Yet if any *m* suffer as a 1Pet 4:16
not in old time by the will of *m* 2Pet 1:21 *444*
righteous *m* dwelling among them 2Pet 2:8
for of whom a *m* is overcome 2Pet 2:19 *5100*
And if any *m* sin, we have an 1Jn 2:1
If any *m* love the world, the love 1Jn 2:15
ye need not that any *m* teach you 1Jn 2:27
every *m* that hath this hope in 1Jn 3:3
children, let no *m* deceive you 1Jn 3:7 *3367*
No *m* hath seen God at any time 1Jn 4:12 *3762*
If a *m* say, I love God, and hateth 1Jn 4:20
If any *m* see his brother sin a 1Jn 5:16
one like unto the Son of *m* Rev 1:13 *444*
which no *m* knoweth saving he that Rev 2:17 *3762*
he that openeth, and no *m* shutteth Rev 3:7 *3762*
and shutteth, and no *m* openeth Rev 3:7 *3762*
an open door, and no *m* can shut it Rev 3:8 *3762*
hast, that no *m* take thy crown Rev 3:11 *3367*
if any *m* hear my voice, and open Rev 3:20
the third beast had a face as a *m* Rev 4:7 *444*
no *m* in heaven, nor in earth, Rev 5:3 *3762*
because no *m* was found worthy to Rev 5:4 *3762*
and every bondman, and every free *m* Rev 6:15
which no *m* could number, of all Rev 7:9 *3762*
a scorpion, when he striketh a *m* Rev 9:5 *444*
if any *m* will hurt them, fire Rev 11:5
if any *m* will hurt them, he must Rev 11:5
And she brought forth a *m* child Rev 12:5 *730*
which brought forth the *m* child Rev 12:13 *730*
If any *m* have an ear, let him Rev 13:9
that no *m* might buy or sell, save Rev 13:17 *5100*
for it is the number of a *m* Rev 13:18 *444*
no *m* could learn that song but Rev 14:3 *3762*
If any *m* worship the beast and his Rev 14:9
one sat like unto the Son of *m* Rev 14:14 *444*
no *m* was able to enter into the Rev 15:8 *3762*
became as the blood of a dead *m* Rev 16:3
for no *m* buyeth their merchandise Rev 18:11 *3762*
a name written, that no *m* knew Rev 19:12 *3762*
and they were judged every *m* Rev 20:13
according to the measure of a *m* Rev 21:17 *444*
to give every *m* according as his Rev 22:12
For I testify unto every *m* that Rev 22:18 *3956*
If any *m* shall add unto these Rev 22:18
if any *m* shall take away from the Rev 22:19

MANAEN *(man'-a-en)* {1} *A Christian teacher at Antioch.*
Niger, and Lucius of Cyrene, and *M* Acts 13:1 *3127*

MANAHATH *(man'-a-hath)* {3}
1. A son of Shobal.
Alvan, and *M*, and Ebal, Shepho, and Gen 36:23 4506
Alian, and *M*, and Ebal, Shephi, and 1Chr 1:40 4506
2. A city in Benjamin.
Geba, and they removed them to *M* 1Chr 8:6 4506

MANAHETHITES *(man'-a-heth-ites)* {2} *Descendants of Shobal.*
Haroeh, and half of the *M* 1Chr 2:52 2679
house of Joab, and half of the *M* 1Chr 2:54 2680

MANASSEH *(ma-nas'-seh)* {142} See MANASSEH'S, MANASSES, MANASSITES.
1. A son of Joseph.
the name of the firstborn *M* Gen 41:51 4519
in the land of Egypt were born *M* Gen 46:20 4519
he took with him his two sons, *M* Gen 48:1 4519
And now thy two sons, Ephraim and *M* Gen 48:5 4519
M in his left hand toward Gen 48:13 4519
for *M* was the firstborn Gen 48:14 4519
God make thee as Ephraim and as *M* Gen 48:20 4519
and he set Ephraim before *M* Gen 48:20 4519
also of Machir the son of *M* were Gen 50:23 4519
after their families were *M* Num 26:28 4519
Of the sons of *M* Num 26:29 4519
the son of Machir, the son of *M* Num 27:1 4519
families of *M* the son of Joseph Num 27:1 4519
the son of *M* went to Gilead Num 32:39 4519
Gilead unto Machir the son of *M* Num 32:40 4519
And Jair the son of *M* went Num 32:41 4519
the son of Machir, the son of *M* Num 36:1 4519
Jair the son of *M* took all the Deut 3:14 4519
children of Machir the son of *M* Josh 13:31 4519
for Machir the firstborn of *M* Josh 17:1 4519
of *M* the son of Joseph by their Josh 17:2 4519
the son of Machir, the son of *M* Josh 17:3 4519
the towns of Jair the son of *M* 1Kin 4:13 4519
The sons of *M* 1Chr 7:14 4519
the son of Machir, the son of *M* 1Chr 7:17 4519
2. Descendants and land of Manasseh 1.
of *M*; Gamaliel the son Num 1:10 4519
Of the children of *M*, by their Num 1:34 4519
of them, even of the tribe of *M* Num 1:35 4519
And by him shall be the tribe of *M* Num 2:20 4519
of *M* shall be Gamaliel the son of Num 2:20 4519
prince of the children of *M* Num 7:54 4519
of *M* was Gamaliel the son of Num 10:23 4519
Joseph, namely, of the tribe of *M* Num 13:11 4519
These are the families of *M* Num 26:34 4519
the tribe of *M* the son of Joseph Num 32:33 4519
half the tribe of *M* have received Num 34:14 4519
the tribe of the children of *M* Num 34:23 4519
the sons of *M* the son of Joseph Num 36:12 4519
gave I unto the half tribe of *M* Deut 3:13 4519
and to the half tribe of *M* Deut 29:8 4520
and they are the thousands of *M* Deut 33:17 4519
and the land of Ephraim, and *M* Deut 34:2 4519
and to half the tribe of *M* Josh 1:12 4519
of Gad, and half the tribe of *M* Josh 4:12 4519
Gadites, and the half tribe of *M* Josh 12:6 4519
tribes, and the half tribe of *M* Josh 13:7 4519
unto the half tribe of *M* Josh 13:29 4519
children of *M* by their families Josh 13:29 4519
of Joseph were two tribes, *M* Josh 14:4 4519
So the children of Joseph, *M* Josh 16:4 4519
inheritance of the children of *M* Josh 16:9 4519
was also a lot for the tribe of *M* Josh 17:1 4519
children of *M* by their families Josh 17:2 4519
And there fell ten portions to *M* Josh 17:5 4519
Because the daughters of *M* had an Josh 17:6 4519
the coast of *M* was from Asher to Josh 17:7 4519
Now *M* had the land of Tappuah Josh 17:8 4519
of *M* belonged to the children of Josh 17:8 4519
Ephraim are among the cities of *M* Josh 17:9 4519
the coast of *M* also was on the Josh 17:9 4519
M had in Issachar and in Asher Josh 17:11 4519
Yet the children of *M* could not Josh 17:12 4519
Joseph, even to Ephraim and to *M* Josh 17:17 4519
and Reuben, and half the tribe of *M* Josh 18:7 4519
in Bashan out of the tribe of *M* Josh 20:8 4519
and out of the half tribe of *M* Josh 21:5 4519
of the half tribe of *M* in Bashan Josh 21:6 4519
And out of the half tribe of *M* Josh 21:25 4519
M they gave Golan in Bashan with Josh 21:27 4519
Gadites, and the half tribe of *M* Josh 22:1 4519
M Moses had given possession in Josh 22:7 4519
and the half tribe of *M* returned Josh 22:9 4519
the half tribe of *M* built there Josh 22:10 4519
the half tribe of *M* have built an Josh 22:11 4519
of Gad, and to the half tribe of *M* Josh 22:13 4519
of Gad, and to the half tribe of *M* Josh 22:15 4519
and the half tribe of *M* answered Josh 22:21 4519
of Gad and the children of *M* spake Josh 22:30 4519
of Gad, and to the children of *M* Josh 22:31 4519
Neither did *M* drive out the Judg 1:27 4519
behold, my family is poor in *M* Judg 6:15 4519
sent messengers throughout all *M* Judg 6:35 4519
and out of Asher, and out of all *M* Judg 7:23 4519
and he passed over Gilead, and *M* Judg 11:29 4519
Gadites, and half the tribe of *M* 1Chr 5:18 4519
half tribe of *M* dwelt in the land 1Chr 5:23 4519
Gadites, and the half tribe of *M* 1Chr 5:26 4519
out of the half tribe of *M* 1Chr 6:61 4519
out of the tribe of *M* in Bashan 1Chr 6:62 4519
And out of the half tribe of *M* 1Chr 6:70 4519
the family of the half tribe of *M* 1Chr 6:71 4519
the borders of the children of *M* 1Chr 7:29 4519
of the children of Ephraim, and *M* 1Chr 9:3 4519
And there fell some of *M* to David 1Chr 12:19 4519
to Ziklag, there fell to him of *M* 1Chr 12:20 4519
of the thousands that were of *M* 1Chr 12:20 4519
half tribe of *M* eighteen thousand 1Chr 12:31 4519
and of the half tribe of *M* 1Chr 12:37 4519
Gadites, and the half tribe of *M* 1Chr 26:32 4520
of the half tribe of *M*, Joel the 1Chr 27:20 4519
Of the half tribe of *M* in Gilead 1Chr 27:21 4519
with them out of Ephraim and *M* 2Chr 15:9 4519
letters also to Ephraim and *M* 2Chr 30:1 4519
of Ephraim and *M* even unto Zebulun 2Chr 30:10 4519
Nevertheless divers of Asher and *M* 2Chr 30:11 4519
even many of Ephraim, and *M* 2Chr 30:18 4519
and Benjamin, in Ephraim also and *M* 2Chr 31:1 4519
And so did he in the cities of *M* 2Chr 34:6 4519
had gathered of the hand of *M* 2Chr 34:9 4519
Gilead is mine, and *M* is mine Ps 60:7 4519
M stir up thy strength, and come Ps 80:2 4519
M is mine Ps 108:8 4519
M, Ephraim; and Ephraim Is 9:21 4519
and Ephraim, *M* Is 9:21 4519
the west side, a portion for *M* Eze 48:4 4519
And by the border of *M*, from the Eze 48:5 4519
3. Grandfather of Jonathan.
the son of Gershom, the son of *M* Judg 18:30 4519
4. Son of King Hezekiah.
M his son reigned in his stead 2Kin 20:21 4519
M was twelve years old when he 2Kin 21:1 4519
M seduced them to do more evil 2Kin 21:9 4519
Because *M* king of Judah hath done 2Kin 21:11 4519

Moreover *M* shed innocent blood 2Kin 21:16 4519
Now the rest of the acts of *M* 2Kin 21:17 4519
M slept with his fathers, and was 2Kin 21:18 4519
of the LORD, as his father *M* did 2Kin 21:20 4519
the altars which *M* had made in 2Kin 23:12 4519
that *M* had provoked him withal 2Kin 23:26 4519
of his sight, for the sins of *M* 2Kin 24:3 4519
son, Hezekiah his son, *M* his son, 1Chr 3:13 4519
M his son reigned in his stead 2Chr 32:33 4519
M was twelve years old when he 2Chr 33:1 4519
So *M* made Judah and the 2Chr 33:9 4519
And the LORD spake to *M*, and to his 2Chr 33:10 4519
which took *M* among the thorns, and 2Chr 33:11 4519
Then *M* knew that the LORD he was 2Chr 33:13 4519
Now the rest of the acts of *M* 2Chr 33:18 4519
So *M* slept with his fathers, and 2Chr 33:20 4519
of the LORD, as did *M* his father 2Chr 33:22 4519
which *M* his father had made 2Chr 33:22 4519
as *M* his father had humbled 2Chr 33:23 4519
because of *M* the son of Hezekiah Jer 15:4 4519
5. Married a foreigner in exile.
Bezaleel, and Binnui, and *M* Ezr 10:30 4519
6. A descendant of Hashum.
Zabad, Eliphelet, Jeremai, *M* Ezr 10:33 4519

MANASSEH'S *(ma-nas'-sez)* {4}
1. Refers to Manasseh 1.
and his left hand upon *M* head Gen 48:14 4519
from Ephraim's head unto *M* head Gen 48:17 4519
the rest of *M* sons had the land Josh 17:6 4519
2. Refers to Manasseh 2.
Ephraim's, and northward it was *M* Josh 17:10 4519

MANASSES *(ma-nas'-seez)* {3} See MANASSEH.
1. Greek form of Manasseh; ancestor of Jesus.
And Ezekias begat *M* Mt 1:10 *3128*
and *M* begat Amon Mt 1:10 *3128*
2. Greek form of Manasseh 2.
Of the tribe of *M* were sealed Rev 7:6 *3128*

MANASSITES *(ma-nas'-sites)* {3} *Same as Manasseh 2.*
and Golan in Bashan, of the *M* Deut 4:43 4520
the Ephraimites, and among the *M* Judg 12:4 4519
and the Reubenites, and the *M* 2Kin 10:33 4520

MANDRAKES {6}
found *m* in the field, and brought Gen 30:14 1736
me, I pray thee, of thy son's *m* Gen 30:14 1736
thou take away my son's *m* also Gen 30:15 1736
thee to night for thy son's *m* Gen 30:15 1736
I have hired thee with my son's *m* Gen 30:16 1736
The *m* give a smell, and at our Song 7:13 1736

MANEH {1}
fifteen shekels, shall be your *m* Eze 45:12 4488

MANGER {3}
clothes, and laid him in a *m* Lk 2:7 *5336*
swaddling clothes, lying in a *m* Lk 2:12 *5336*
Joseph, and the babe lying in a *m* Lk 2:16 *5336*

MANIFEST {39}
of men, that God might *m* them Eccl 3:18 1305
secret, that shall not be made *m* Lk 8:17 *5318*
he should be made *m* to Israel Jn 1:31 *5319*
that his deeds may be made *m* Jn 3:21 *5319*
of God should be made *m* in him Jn 9:3 *5319*
love him, and will *m* myself to him Jn 14:21 *1718*
that thou wilt *m* thyself unto us Jn 14:22 *1718*
is *m* to all them that dwell in Acts 4:16 *5319*
may be known of God is *m* in them Rom 1:19 *5319*
I was made *m* unto them that asked Rom 10:20 *1717*
But now is made *m*, and by the Rom 16:26 *5319*
Every man's work shall be made *m* 1Cor 3:13 *5318*
will make *m* the counsels of the 1Cor 4:5 *5319*
approved may be made *m* among you 1Cor 11:19 *5318*
the secrets of his heart made *m* 1Cor 14:25 *5318*
it is *m* that he is excepted, 1Cor 15:27 *1212*
maketh *m* the savour of his 2Cor 2:14 *5319*
Jesus might be made *m* in our body 2Cor 4:10 *5319*
be made *m* in our mortal flesh 2Cor 4:11 *5319*
but we are made *m* unto God 2Cor 5:11 *5319*
are made *m* in your consciences 2Cor 5:11 *5319*
made *m* among you in all things 2Cor 11:6 *5319*
Now the works of the flesh are *m* Gal 5:19 *5318*
reproved are made *m* by the light Eph 5:13 *5319*
whatsoever doth make *m* is light Eph 5:13 *5319*
in Christ are *m* in all the palace Phil 1:13 *5318*
but now is made *m* to his saints Col 1:26 *5319*
That I may make it *m*, as I ought Col 4:4 *5319*
Which is a *m* token of the 2Th 1:5
God was *m* in the flesh, justified 1Ti 3:16 *5319*
works of some are *m* beforehand 1Ti 5:25 *4271*
But is now made *m* by the 2Ti 1:10 *5319*
folly shall be *m* unto all men 2Ti 3:9 *1552*
that is not *m* in his sight Heb 4:13 *852*
holiest of all was not yet made *m* Heb 9:8 *5319*
but was *m* in these last times for 1Pet 1:20 *5319*
that they might be made *m* that 1Jn 2:19 *5319*
In this the children of God are *m* 1Jn 3:10 *5318*
for thy judgments are made *m* Rev 15:4 *5319*

MANIFESTATION {3}
for the *m* of the sons of God Rom 8:19 *602*
But the *m* of the Spirit is given 1Cor 12:7 *5321*
but by *m* of the truth commending 2Cor 4:2 *5321*

MANIFESTED {10}
nothing hid, which shall not be *m* Mk 4:22 *5319*
of Galilee, and *m* forth his glory Jn 2:11 *5319*
I have *m* thy name unto the men Jn 17:6 *5319*
of God without the law is *m* Rom 3:21 *5319*
But hath in due times *m* his word Titus 1:3 *5319*
(For the life was *m*, and we have 1Jn 1:2 *5319*
with the Father, and was *m* unto us 1Jn 1:2 *5319*
ye know that he was *m* to take 1Jn 3:5 *5319*
this purpose the Son of God was *m* 1Jn 3:8 *5319*
In this was *m* the love of God 1Jn 4:9 *5319*

MANIFESTLY {1}
Forasmuch as ye are *m* declared to 2Cor 3:3 *5319*

MANIFOLD {8}
Yet thou in thy *m* mercies Neh 9:19 7227
according to thy *m* mercies thou Neh 9:27 7227
O LORD, how *m* are thy works Ps 104:24 7231
For I know your *m* transgressions Amos 5:12 7227
Who shall not receive *m* more in Lk 18:30 *4179*
by the church the *m* wisdom of God Eph 3:10 *4182*
heaviness through *m* temptations 1Pet 1:6 *4164*
stewards of the *m* grace of God 1Pet 4:10 *4164*

MANKIND {6}
Thou shalt not lie with *m* Lev 18:22 2145
If a man also lie with *m*, as he Lev 20:13 2145
thing, and the breath of all *m* Job 12:10 1320,376
nor abusers of themselves with *m* 1Cor 6:9 *733*
that defile themselves with *m* 1Ti 1:10 *733*
and hath been tamed of *m* Jas 3:7 *5449,442*

MANNA {19}
they said one to another, It is *m* Ex 16:15 4478
Israel called the name thereof *M* Ex 16:31 4478
and put an omer full of *m* therein Ex 16:33 4478
of Israel did eat *m* forty years Ex 16:35 4478
they did eat *m*, until they came Ex 16:35 4478
is nothing at all, beside this *m* Num 11:6 4478
the *m* was as coriander seed, and Num 11:7 4478
in the night, the *m* fell upon it Num 11:9 4478
to hunger, and fed thee with *m* Deut 8:3 4478
fed thee in the wilderness with *m* Deut 8:16 4478
the *m* ceased on the morrow after Josh 5:12 4478
the children of Israel *m* any more Josh 5:12 4478
not thy *m* from their mouth Neh 9:20 4478
had rained down *m* upon them to Ps 78:24 4478
fathers did eat *m* in the desert Jn 6:31 *3131*
did eat *m* in the wilderness Jn 6:49 *3131*
not as your fathers did eat *m* Jn 6:58 *3131*
was the golden pot that had *m* Heb 9:4 *3131*
I give to eat of the hidden *m* Rev 2:17 *3131*

MANNER {196}
with Sarah after the *m* of women Gen 18:11 734
far from thee to do after this *m* Gen 18:25 1697
us after the *m* of all the earth Gen 19:31 1870
womb, and two *m* of people shall be Gen 25:23
On this *m* shall ye speak unto Gen 32:19 1697
After this *m* did thy servant to Gen 39:19 1697
after the former *m* when thou wast Gen 40:13 4941
basket there was of all *m* of Gen 40:17
his father he sent after this *m* Gen 45:23
in all *m* of service in the field Ex 1:14
they also did in like *m* with Ex 7:11 3651
no *m* of work shall be done in Ex 12:16
with her after the *m* of daughters Ex 21:9 4941
For all *m* of trespass, whether it Ex 22:9 1697
or for any *m* of lost thing, which Ex 22:9
In like *m* thou shalt deal with Ex 23:11 3651
and in all *m* of workmanship, Ex 31:3
to work in all *m* of workmanship Ex 31:5
to bring for all *m* of work Ex 35:29
and in all *m* of workmanship Ex 35:31
to make any *m* of cunning work Ex 35:33
of heart, to work all *m* of work Ex 35:35 3605
to know how to work all *m* of work Ex 36:1
offering, according to the *m* Lev 5:10 4941
saying, Ye shall eat no *m* of fat Lev 7:23
ye shall eat no *m* of blood Lev 7:26
it be that eateth any *m* of blood Lev 7:27
and offered it according to the *m* Lev 9:16 4941
among all *m* of beasts that go on Lev 11:27
ye defile yourselves with any *m* Lev 11:44
for all *m* of plague of leprosy Lev 14:54
you, that eateth any *m* of blood Lev 17:10
eat the blood of no *m* of flesh Lev 17:14
planted all *m* of trees for food Lev 19:23
or by any *m* of living thing that Lev 20:25
Ye shall do no *m* of work Lev 23:31
Ye shall have one *m* of law Lev 24:22 4941
neither she be taken with the *m* Num 5:13
and according to the *m* thereof Num 9:14 4941
do these things after this *m* Num 15:13 3541
one *m* shall be for you, and for Num 15:16 4941
offering, according to the *m* Num 15:24 4941
ye shall do no *m* of servile work Num 28:18
After this *m* ye shall offer daily Num 28:24
offerings, according unto their *m* Num 29:6 4941
to their number, after the *m* Num 29:18 4941
to their number, after the *m* Num 29:21 4941
to their number, after the *m* Num 29:24 4941
to their number, after the *m* Num 29:27 4941
to their number, after the *m* Num 29:30 4941
to their number, after the *m* Num 29:33 4941
to their number, after the *m* Num 29:37 4941
of all *m* of beasts, and give them Num 31:30
for ye saw no *m* of similitude on Deut 4:15
this is the *m* of the release Deut 15:2 1697
In like *m* shalt thou do with his Deut 22:3 3651
he that lieth with any *m* of beast Deut 27:21
city after the same *m* seven times Josh 6:15 4941
What *m* of men were they whom ye Judg 8:18
in like *m* they sent unto the king Judg 11:17
after the *m* of the Zidonians, Judg 18:7 4941
Now this was the *m* in former time Ruth 4:7
shew them the *m* of the king that 1Sa 8:9 4941
This will be the *m* of the king 1Sa 8:11 4941
the people the *m* of the kingdom 1Sa 10:25 4941
people answered him after this *m* 1Sa 17:27 1697
and spake after the same *m* 1Sa 17:30 1697
him again after the former *m* 1Sa 17:30 1697
saying, On this *m* spake David 1Sa 18:24 1697
before Samuel in like *m*, and lay 1Sa 19:24 1571
and the bread is in a *m* common 1Sa 21:5 1870
so will be his *m* all the while he 1Sa 27:11 3541
played before the LORD on all *m* 2Sa 6:5
And is this the *m* of man, O Lord 2Sa 7:19 8452
king, and speak on this *m* unto him 2Sa 14:3 1697
on this *m* did Absalom to all 2Sa 15:6 1697
hath spoken after this *m* 2Sa 17:6 1697
work of the bases was on this *m* 1Kin 7:28
After this *m* he made the ten 1Kin 7:37
after their *m* with knives 1Kin 18:28 4941
And one said on this *m* 1Kin 22:20 3541
and another said on that *m* 1Kin 22:20 3541
What *m* of man was he which came 2Kin 1:7 4941
stood by a pillar, as the *m* was 2Kin 11:14 4941
know not the *m* of the God of the 2Kin 17:26 4941
not the *m* of the God of the land 2Kin 17:26 4941
them the *m* of the God of the land 2Kin 17:27 4941
after the *m* of the nations whom 2Kin 17:33 4941
but they did after their former *m* 2Kin 17:40 4941
m of service of the tabernacle of 1Chr 6:48
with all *m* of instruments of war 1Chr 12:37
with him all *m* of vessels of gold 1Chr 18:10
all *m* of cunning men for every 1Chr 22:15
cunning men for every *m* of work 1Chr 22:15
for all *m* of measure and size 1Chr 23:29
of the LORD, according to their *m* 1Chr 24:19 4941
instruments of all *m* of service 1Chr 28:14
shall be with thee for all *m* of 1Chr 28:21
skilful man, for any *m* of service 1Chr 28:21
all *m* of precious stones, and 1Chr 29:2
for all *m* of work to be made by 1Chr 29:5
also to grave any *m* of graving 2Chr 2:14
after the *m* before the oracle 2Chr 4:20 4941
m of the nations of other lands 2Chr 13:9
And one spake saying after this *m* 2Chr 18:19 3541
and another saying after that *m* 2Chr 18:19
in their place after their *m* 2Chr 30:16 4941
you, nor persuade you on this *m* 2Chr 32:15
for all *m* of pleasant jewels 2Chr 32:27
and stalls for all *m* of beasts 2Chr 32:28
the work in any *m* of service 2Chr 34:13
said we unto them after this *m* Ezr 5:4
I answered them after the same *m* Neh 6:4 1697
m the fifth time with an open Neh 6:5 1697
assembly, according unto the *m* Neh 8:18 4941
and the fruit of all *m* of trees Neh 10:37
all *m* of burdens, which they Neh 13:15
all *m* of ware, and sold on the Neh 13:16
(for so was the king's *m* toward Est 1:13 1697
according to the *m* of the women Est 2:12 1881
soul abhorreth all *m* of meat Ps 107:18
be full, affording all *m* of store Ps 144:13 2177
are all *m* of pleasant fruits Song 7:13
the lambs feed after their *m* Is 5:17 1699
thee, after the *m* of Egypt Is 10:24 1870
lift it up after the *m* of Egypt Is 10:26 1870
dwell therein shall die in like *m* Is 51:6 3654
After this *m* will I mar the pride Jer 13:9 3541
hath been thy *m* from thy youth Jer 22:21 1870
shall remain after the *m* thereof Jer 30:18 4941
after the *m* of your fathers Eze 20:30 1870
after the *m* of the Babylonians of Eze 23:15 1823
them after the *m* of adulteresses Eze 23:45 4941
after the *m* of women that shed Eze 23:45 4941
no *m* of hurt was found upon him, Dan 6:23
pestilence after the *m* of Egypt Amos 4:10 1870
The *m* of Beer-sheba liveth Amos 8:14 1870
and healing all *m* of sickness Mt 4:23
all *m* of disease among the people Mt 4:23
shall say all *m* of evil against Mt 5:11
After this *m* therefore pray ye Mt 6:9 *3779*
What *m* of man is this, that even Mt 8:27 *4217*
out, and to heal all *m* of sickness Mt 10:1
of sickness and all *m* of disease Mt 10:1
All *m* of sin and blasphemy shall Mt 12:31
What *m* of man is this, that even Mk 4:41 *686*
see what *m* of stones and what Mk 13:1 *4217*
So ye in like *m*, when ye shall Mk 13:29 *3779*
cast in her mind what *m* of Lk 1:29 *4217*
What *m* of child shall this be Lk 1:66 *686*
for in the like *m* did their Lk 6:23
what *m* of woman this is that Lk 7:39 *4217*
to another, What *m* of man is this Lk 8:25 *686*
Ye know not what *m* of spirit ye Lk 9:55 *3634*
all *m* of herbs, and pass over Lk 11:42
and in like *m* the seven also Lk 20:31 *5615*
What *m* of communications are Lk 24:17
after the *m* of the purifying of Jn 2:6
What *m* of saying is this that he Jn 7:36
as the *m* of the Jews is to bury Jn 19:40 *1485*
shall so come in like *m* as ye Acts 1:11 *5158*
Wherein were all *m* of fourfooted Acts 10:12 *1485*
circumcised after the *m* of Moses Acts 15:1 *1485*
letters by them after this *m* Acts 15:23 *3592*
And Paul, as his *m* was, went in Acts 17:2 *1486*
after what *m* I have been with you Acts 20:18 *4458*
m of the law of the fathers Acts 22:3 *195*
And he wrote a letter after this *m* Acts 23:25 *5179*
It is not the *m* of the Romans to Acts 25:16 *1485*
I doubted of such *m* of questions Acts 25:20 *4012*
My *m* of life from my youth, which Acts 26:4 *981*

M

I speak after the *m* of men ... Rom 6:19 *442*
in me all *m* of concupiscence ... Rom 7:8
gift of God, one after this *m* ... 1Cor 7:7 *3779*
After the same *m* also he took the ... 1Cor 11:25 *5615*
If after the *m* of men I have ... 1Cor 15:32
were made sorry after a godly *m* ... 2Cor 7:9
livest after the *m* of Gentiles ... Gal 2:14 *1483*
I speak after the *m* of men ... Gal 3:15
as ye know what *m* of men we were ... 1Th 1:5 *3634*
m of entering in we had unto you ... 1Th 1:9 *3697*
In like *m* also, that women adorn ... 1Ti 2:9
m of life, purpose, faith, ... 2Ti 3:10 *72*
together, as the *m* of some is ... Heb 10:25 *1485*
forgetteth what *m* of man he was ... Jas 1:24 *3697*
or what *m* of time the Spirit of ... 1Pet 1:11 *4169*
ye holy in all *m* of conversation ... 1Pet 1:15
For after this *m* in the old time ... 1Pet 3:5 *3779*
what *m* of persons ought ye to be ... 2Pet 3:11 *4217*
what *m* of love the Father hath ... 1Jn 3:1 *4217*
the cities about them in like *m* ... Jude 7 *5158*
them, he must in this *m* be killed ... Rev 11:5 *3779*
all *m* vessels of ivory ... Rev 18:12
all *m* vessels of most precious ... Rev 18:12
with all *m* of precious stones ... Rev 21:19
which bare twelve *m* of fruits ... Rev 22:2

MANNERS {6}
not walk in the *m* of the nation ... Lev 20:23 2708
day they do after the former *m* ... 2Kin 17:34 4941
but have done after the *m* of the ... Eze 11:12 4941
he their *m* in the wilderness ... Acts 13:18 *5159*
communications corrupt good *m* ... 1Cor 15:33 *2239*
in divers *m* spake in time past ... Heb 1:1 *4187*

MANOAH *(ma-no'-ah)* {18} *Father of Samson.*
of the Danites, whose name was *M* ... Judg 13:2 4495
Then *M* intreated the LORD, and ... Judg 13:8 4495
God hearkened to the voice of *M* ... Judg 13:9 4495
but *M* her husband was not with ... Judg 13:9 4495
M arose, and went after his wife, ... Judg 13:11 4495
M said, Now let thy words come to ... Judg 13:12 4495
the angel of the LORD said unto *M* ... Judg 13:13 4495
M said unto the angel of the LORD ... Judg 13:15 4495
the angel of the LORD said unto *M* ... Judg 13:16 4495
For *M* knew not that he was an ... Judg 13:16 4495
M said unto the angel of the LORD ... Judg 13:17 4495
So *M* took a kid with a meat ... Judg 13:19 4495
and *M* and his wife looked on ... Judg 13:19 4495
And *M* and his wife looked on it, and ... Judg 13:20 4495
the LORD did no more appear to *M* ... Judg 13:21 4495
Then *M* knew that he was an angel ... Judg 13:21 4495
M said unto his wife, We shall ... Judg 13:22 4495
the buryingplace of *M* his father ... Judg 16:31 4495

MAN'S See APPENDIX.

MANSERVANT {12}
thy son, nor thy daughter, thy *m* ... Ex 20:10 5650
thy neighbour's wife, nor his *m* ... Ex 20:17 5650
shall push a *m* or a maidservant ... Ex 21:32 5650
son, nor thy daughter, nor thy *m* ... Deut 5:14 5650
that thy *m* and thy maidservant may ... Deut 5:14 5650
house, his field, or his *m* ... Deut 5:21 5650
son, and thy daughter, and thy *m* ... Deut 12:18 5650
son, and thy daughter, and thy *m* ... Deut 16:11 5650
son, and thy daughter, and thy *m* ... Deut 16:14 5650
of my *m* or of my maidservant ... Job 31:13 5650
That every man should let his *m* ... Jer 34:9 5650
that every one should let his *m* ... Jer 34:10 5650

MANSERVANT'S {1}
And if he smite out his *m* tooth ... Ex 21:27 5650

MANSERVANTS {1}
Beside their *m* and their ... Neh 7:67 5650

MANSIONS {1}
In my Father's house are many *m* ... Jn 14:2 *3438*

MANSLAYER {2}
which ye shall appoint for the *m* ... Num 35:6 7523
that the *m* die not, until he ... Num 35:12 7523

MANSLAYERS {1}
and murderers of mothers, for *m* ... 1Ti 1:9 *409*

MANTLE {13}
tent, she covered him with a *m* ... Judg 4:18 8063
laid hold upon the skirt of his *m* ... 1Sa 15:27 4598
and he is covered with a *m* ... 1Sa 28:14 4598
that he wrapped his face in his *m* ... 1Kin 19:13 155
by him, and cast his *m* upon him ... 1Kin 19:19 155
And Elijah took his *m*, and wrapped ... 2Kin 2:8 155
He took up also the *m* of Elijah ... 2Kin 2:13 155
he took the *m* of Elijah that fell ... 2Kin 2:14 155
thing, I rent my garment and my *m* ... Ezr 9:3 4598
having rent my garment and my *m* ... Ezr 9:5 4598
Then Job arose, and rent his *m* ... Job 1:20 4598
and they rent every one his *m* ... Job 2:12 4598
their own confusion, as with a *m* ... Ps 109:29 4598

MANTLES {1}
suits of apparel, and the *m* ... Is 3:22 4595

MANY See APPENDIX.

MAOCH *(ma'-ok)* {1} *Father of Achish.*
him unto Achish, the son of *M* ... 1Sa 27:2 4582

MAON *(ma'-on)* {7} See MAONITES.
1. A city in Judah.
M, Carmel, and Ziph, and Juttah, ... Josh 15:55 4584
And there was a man in *M*, whose ... 1Sa 25:2 4584
2. A descendant of Caleb.
And the son of Shammai was *M* ... 1Chr 2:45 4584
M was the father of Beth-zur ... 1Chr 2:45 4584
3. A wilderness in Judah.
men were in the wilderness of *M* ... 1Sa 23:24 4584
and abode in the wilderness of *M* ... 1Sa 23:25 4584
David in the wilderness of *M* ... 1Sa 23:25 4584

MAONITES *(ma'-on-ites)* {1} See MEHUNIM. *An enemy tribe of Israel.*
also, and the Amalekites, and the *M* ... Judg 10:12 4584

MAR {6}
neither shalt thou *m* the corners ... Lev 19:27 7843
lest I *m* mine own inheritance ... Ruth 4:6 7843
of your mice that *m* the land ... 1Sa 6:5 7843
m every good piece of land with ... 2Kin 3:19 3510
They *m* my path, they set forward ... Job 30:13 5420
will I *m* the pride of Judah ... Jer 13:9 7843

MARA *(ma'-rah)* {1} *Another name for Naomi.*
Call me not Naomi, call me *M* ... Ruth 1:20 4755

MARAH *(ma'-rah)* {5} *An Israelite encampment in the wilderness.*
And when they came to *M*, they ... Ex 15:23 4785
not drink of the waters of *M* ... Ex 15:23 4785
the name of it was called *M* ... Ex 15:23 4785
of Etham, and pitched in *M* ... Num 33:8 4785
And they removed from *M*, and came ... Num 33:9 4785

MARALAH *(mar'-a-lah)* {1} *A city in Zebulun.*
went up toward the sea, and *M* ... Josh 19:11 4831

MARANATHA {1}
Christ, let him be Anathema *M* ... 1Cor 16:22 *3134*

MARBLE {5}
stones, and *m* stones in abundance ... 1Chr 29:2 7898
to silver rings and pillars of *m* ... Est 1:6 8338
and blue, and white, and black, *m* ... Est 1:6 8336
His legs are as pillars of *m* ... Song 5:15 8336
wood, and of brass, and iron, and *m* ... Rev 18:12 *3139*

MARCH {5}
when thou didst *m* through the ... Ps 68:7 6805
for they shall *m* with an army ... Jer 46:22 3212
they shall *m* every one on his ... Joel 2:7 3212
which shall *m* through the breadth ... Hab 1:6 1980
Thou didst *m* through the land in ... Hab 3:12 6805

MARCHED {1}
the Egyptians *m* after them ... Ex 14:10 5265

MARCHEDST {1}
when thou *m* out of the field of ... Judg 5:4 6805

MARCUS *(mar'-cus)* {3} See MARK. *Latin form of Mark.*
fellowprisoner saluteth you, and *M* ... Col 4:10 *3138*
M, Aristarchus, Demas, Lucas, my ... Philem 24 *3138*
and so doth *M* my son ... 1Pet 5:13 *3138*

MARDUK See MERODACH.

MAREAL See MARALAH.

MARESHAH {8}
1. A city in Judah.
And Keilah, and Achzib, and *M* ... Josh 15:44 4762
And Gath, and *M*, and Ziph, ... 2Chr 11:8 4762
and came unto *M* ... 2Chr 14:9 4762
in the valley of Zephathah at *M* ... 2Chr 14:10 4762
Eliezer the son of Dodavah of *M* ... 2Chr 20:37 4762
heir unto thee, O inhabitant of *M* ... Mic 1:15 4762
2. Father of Hebron.
the sons of *M* the father of ... 1Chr 2:42 4762
3. A descendant of Shelah.
Lecah, and Laadah the father of *M* ... 1Chr 4:21 4762

MARINERS {5}
of Zidon and Arvad were thy *m* ... Eze 27:8 7751
m were in thee to occupy thy ... Eze 27:9 4419
thy fairs, thy merchandise, thy *m* ... Eze 27:27 4419
And all that handle the oar, the *m* ... Eze 27:29 4419
Then the *m* were afraid, and cried ... Jonah 1:5 4419

MARISHES {1}
the *m* thereof shall not be healed ... Eze 47:11 1360

MARK See MARCUS.
And the LORD set a *m* upon Cain ... Gen 4:15 226
that thou shalt *m* the place where ... Ruth 3:4 3045
thereof, as though I shot at a *m* ... 1Sa 20:20 4307
M ye now when Amnon's heart is ... 2Sa 13:28 7200
elders of the land, and said, *M* ... 1Kin 20:7 3045
him, Go, strengthen thyself, and *m* ... 1Kin 20:22 3045
thou set me as a *m* against thee ... Job 7:20 4645
to pieces, and set me up for his *m* ... Job 16:12 4307
m, and afterwards we will speak ... Job 18:2 995
M me, and be astonished, and lay ... Job 21:5 6437
M well, O Job, hearken unto me ... Job 33:31 7181
or canst thou *m* when the hinds do ... Job 39:1 8104
M the perfect man, and behold the ... Ps 37:37 8104
M ye well her bulwarks, consider ... Ps 48:13 7896
they *m* my steps, when they wait ... Ps 56:6 8104
shouldest *m* iniquities, O Lord, ... Ps 130:3 8104
set me as a *m* for the arrow ... Lam 3:12 4307
set a *m* upon the foreheads of the ... Eze 9:4 8420
near any man upon whom is the *m* ... Eze 9:6 8420
m well, and behold with thine eyes ... Eze 44:5 7760
m well the entering in of the ... Eze 44:5 7760
m them which cause divisions and ... Rom 16:17 *4648*
I press toward the *m* for the ... Phil 3:14 *4649*
m them which walk so as ye have ... Phil 3:17 *4648*
to receive a *m* in their right ... Rev 13:16 *5480*
or sell, save he that had the *m* ... Rev 13:17 *5480*
receive his *m* in his forehead, or ... Rev 14:9 *5480*
receiveth the *m* of his name ... Rev 14:11 *5480*
and over his image, and over his *m* ... Rev 15:2 *5480*
men which had the *m* of the beast ... Rev 16:2 *5480*
had received the *m* of the beast ... Rev 19:20 *5480*
his *m* upon their foreheads ... Rev 20:4 *5480*
Companion of Paul..
of John, whose surname was *M* ... Acts 12:12 *3138*
them John, whose surname was *M* ... Acts 12:25 *3138*
them John, whose surname was *M* ... Acts 15:37 *3138*
and so Barnabas took *M*, and sailed ... Acts 15:39 *3138*
Take *M*, and bring him with thee ... 2Ti 4:11 *3138*

MARKED {6}
the LORD, that Eli *m* her mouth ... 1Sa 1:12 8104
Hast thou *m* the old way which ... Job 22:15 8104
which they had *m* for themselves ... Job 24:16 2856
yet thine iniquity is *m* before me ... Jer 2:22 3799
who hath *m* his word, and heard it ... Jer 23:18 7181
when he *m* how they chose out the ... Lk 14:7 *1907*

MARKEST {1}
If I sin, then thou *m* me, and thou ... Job 10:14 8104

MARKET {7}
men and vessels of brass in thy *m* ... Eze 27:13 4627
traded in thy *m* wheat of Minnith ... Eze 27:17 4627
cassia, and calamus, were in thy *m* ... Eze 27:19 4627
did sing of thee in thy *m* ... Eze 27:25 4627
And when they come from the *m* ... Mk 7:4 *58*
Jerusalem by the sheep *m* a pool ... Jn 5:2
in the *m* daily with them that met ... Acts 17:17 *58*

MARKETH {3}
in the stocks, he *m* all my paths ... Job 33:11 8104
he *m* it out with a line ... Is 44:13 8388
he *m* it out with the compass, and ... Is 44:13 8388

MARKETPLACE {3}
saw others standing idle in the *m* ... Mt 20:3 *58*
unto children sitting in the *m* ... Lk 7:32 *58*
them into the *m* unto the rulers ... Acts 16:19 *58*

MARKETPLACES {1}
and love salutations in the *m* ... Mk 12:38 *58*

MARKETS {4}
unto children sitting in the *m* ... Mt 11:16 *58*
And greetings in the *m*, and to be ... Mt 23:7 *58*
synagogues, and greetings in the *m* ... Lk 11:43 *58*
robes, and love greetings in the *m* ... Lk 20:46 *58*

MARKS {2}
dead, nor print any *m* upon you ... Lev 19:28 7085
my body the *m* of the Lord Jesus ... Gal 6:17 *4742*

MAROTH *(ma'-roth)* {1} *A city in Judah.*
For the inhabitant of *M* waited ... Mic 1:12 4796

MARRED {5}
visage was so *m* more than any man ... Is 52:14 4893
and, behold, the girdle was *m* ... Jer 13:7 7843
was *m* in the hand of the potter ... Jer 18:4 7843
out, and *m* their vine branches ... Nah 2:2 7843
spilled, and the bottles will be *m* ... Mk 2:22 *622*

MARRIAGE {19}
her raiment, and her duty of *m* ... Ex 21:10 5772
their maidens were not given to *m* ... Ps 78:63 1984
king, which made a *m* for his son ... Mt 22:2 *1062*
are ready: come unto the *m* ... Mt 22:4 *1062*
as ye shall find, bid to the *m* ... Mt 22:9 *1062*
neither marry, nor are given in *m* ... Mt 22:30 *1548*
drinking, marrying and giving in *m* ... Mt 24:38 *1547*
ready went in with him to the *m* ... Mt 25:10 *1062*
neither marry, nor are given in *m* ... Mk 12:25 *1061*
wives, they were given in *m* ... Lk 17:27 *1548*
world marry, and are given in *m* ... Lk 20:34 *1548*
neither marry, nor are given in *m* ... Lk 20:35 *1548*
there was a *m* in Cana of Galilee ... Jn 2:1 *1062*
and his disciples, to the *m* ... Jn 2:2 *1062*
that giveth her in *m* doeth well ... 1Cor 7:38 *1547*
giveth her not in *m* doeth better ... 1Cor 7:38 *1547*
M is honourable in all, and the ... Heb 13:4 *1062*
for the *m* of the Lamb is come, and ... Rev 19:7 *1062*
unto the *m* supper of the Lamb ... Rev 19:9 *1062*

MARRIAGES {3}
And make ye *m* with us, and give ... Gen 34:9 2859
shalt thou make *m* with them ... Deut 7:3 2859
you, and shall make *m* with them ... Josh 23:12 2859

MARRIED {30}
which *m* his daughters, and said, ... Gen 19:14 3947
if he were *m*, then his wife shall ... Ex 21:3 1166,802
also be *m* unto a stranger ... Lev 22:12
the Ethiopian woman whom he had *m* ... Num 12:1 3947
for he had *m* an Ethiopian woman ... Num 12:1 3947
if they be *m* to any of the sons ... Num 36:3 802
were *m* unto their father's ... Num 36:11 802
they were *m* into the families of ... Num 36:12 802
with a woman *m* to an husband ... Deut 22:22 1166
m her, and it come to pass that ... Deut 24:1 1166
whom he *m* when he was threescore ... 1Chr 2:21 3947
m fourteen wives, and begat twenty ... 2Chr 13:21 5375
I Jews that had *m* wives of Ashdod ... Neh 13:23 3427
For an odious woman when she is *m* ... Prov 30:23 1166
than the children of the *m* wife ... Is 54:1 1166
in thee, and thy land shall be *m* ... Is 62:4 1166
for I am *m* unto you ... Jer 3:14 1166
hath *m* the daughter of a strange ... Mal 2:11 1166
the first, when he had *m* a wife ... Mt 22:25 *1060*
for he had *m* her ... Mk 6:17 *1060*
be *m* to another, she committeth ... Mk 10:12 *1060*
And another said, I have *m* a wife ... Lk 14:20 *1060*
they *m* wives, they were given in ... Lk 17:27 *1060*
she be *m* to another man, she ... Rom 7:3 *1096*
though she be *m* to another man ... Rom 7:3 *1096*
that ye should be *m* to another ... Rom 7:4 *1096*
unto the *m* I command, yet not I, ... 1Cor 7:10 *1060*
But he that is *m* careth for the ... 1Cor 7:33 *1060*
but she that is *m* careth for the ... 1Cor 7:34 *1060*
liberty to be *m* to whom she will ... 1Cor 7:39 *1060*

MARRIETH {4}
For as a young man *m* a virgin ... Is 62:5 ... 1166
whoso *m* her which is put away ... Mt 19:9 ... *1060*
m another, committeth adultery ... Lk 16:18 ... *1060*
whosoever *m* her that is put away ... Lk 16:18 ... *1060*

MARROW {5}
and his bones are moistened with *m* ... Job 21:24 ... 4221
soul shall be satisfied as with *m* ... Ps 63:5 ... 2459
to thy navel, and *m* to thy bones ... Prov 3:8 ... 8250
the lees, of fat things full of *m* ... Is 25:6 ... 4229
and spirit, and of the joints and *m* ... Heb 4:12 ... *3452*

MARRY {22}
m her, and raise up seed to thy ... Gen 38:8 ... 2992
Let them *m* to whom they think ... Num 36:6 ... 802
of their father shall they *m* ... Num 36:6 ... 802
not *m* without unto a stranger ... Deut 25:5 ... 1961,376
virgin, so shall thy sons *m* thee ... Is 62:5 ... 1166
whosoever shall *m* her that is ... Mt 5:32 ... *1060*
shall *m* another, committeth ... Mt 19:9 ... *1060*
his wife, it is not good to *m* ... Mt 19:10 ... *1060*
his brother shall *m* his wife ... Mt 22:24 ... *1918*
the resurrection they neither *m* ... Mt 22:30 ... *1060*
m another, committeth adultery ... Mk 10:11 ... *1060*
from the dead, they neither *m* ... Mk 12:25 ... *1060*
The children of this world *m* ... Lk 20:34 ... *1060*
from the dead, neither *m*, nor are ... Lk 20:35 ... *1060*
they cannot contain, let them *m* ... 1Cor 7:9 ... *1060*
it is better to *m* than to burn ... 1Cor 7:9 ... *1060*
But and if thou *m*, thou hast not ... 1Cor 7:28 ... *1060*
and if a virgin *m*, she hath not ... 1Cor 7:28 ... *1060*
he sinneth not: let them *m* ... 1Cor 7:36 ... *1060*
Forbidding to *m*, and commanding to ... 1Ti 4:3 ... *1060*
against Christ, they will *m* ... 1Ti 5:11 ... *1060*
that the younger women *m*, bear ... 1Ti 5:14 ... *1060*

MARRYING {2}
our God in *m* strange wives ... Neh 13:27 ... 3427
they were eating and drinking, *m* ... Mt 24:38 ... *1060*

MARS' *(marz)* {1} *Refers to a landmark in Athens.*
Paul stood in the midst of *M* hill ... Acts 17:22 ... *697*

MARSENA *(mar'-se-nah)* {1} *A prince of Media and Persia.*
Admatha, Tarshish, Meres, *M* ... Est 1:14 ... 4826

MART {1}
and she is a *m* of nations ... Is 23:3 ... 5505

MARTHA *(mar'-thah)* {13} *Sister of Lazarus.*
a certain woman named *M* received ... Lk 10:38 ... *3136*
But *M* was cumbered about much ... Lk 10:40 ... *3136*
and said unto her, *M*, *M* ... Lk 10:41 ... *3136*
the town of Mary and her sister *M* ... Jn 11:1 ... *3136*
Now Jesus loved *M*, and her sister ... Jn 11:5 ... *3136*
And many of the Jews came to *M* ... Jn 11:19 ... *3136*
Then *M*, as soon as she heard that ... Jn 11:20 ... *3136*
Then said *M* unto Jesus, Lord, if ... Jn 11:21 ... *3136*
M saith unto him, I know that he ... Jn 11:24 ... *3136*
was in that place where *M* met him ... Jn 11:30 ... *3136*
M, the sister of him that was ... Jn 11:39 ... *3136*
a supper; and *M* served ... Jn 12:2 ... *3136*

MARTYR {2}
blood of thy *m* Stephen was shed ... Acts 22:20 ... *3144*
wherein Antipas was my faithful *m* ... Rev 2:13 ... *3144*

MARTYRS {1}
with the blood of the *m* of Jesus ... Rev 17:6 ... *3144*

MARVEL {11}
a province, *m* not at the matter ... Eccl 5:8 ... 8539
and all men did *m* ... Mk 5:20 ... *2296*
M not that I said unto thee, Ye ... Jn 3:7 ... *2296*
works than these, that ye may *m* ... Jn 5:20 ... *2296*
M not at this ... Jn 5:28 ... *2296*
I have done one work, and ye all *m* ... Jn 7:21 ... *2296*
men of Israel, why *m* ye at this ... Acts 3:12 ... *2296*
And no *m*; for Satan himself ... 2Cor 11:14 ... *2298*
I *m* that ye are so soon removed ... Gal 1:6 ... *2296*
M not, my brethren, if the world ... 1Jn 3:13 ... *2296*
unto me, Wherefore didst thou *m* ... Rev 17:7 ... *2296*

MARVELLED {23}
and the men *m* one at another ... Gen 43:33 ... 8539
They saw it, and so they *m* ... Ps 48:5 ... 8539
When Jesus heard it, he *m* ... Mt 8:10 ... *2296*
But the men *m*, saying, What ... Mt 8:27 ... *2296*
the multitudes saw it, they *m* ... Mt 9:8 ... *2296*
and the multitudes *m*, saying, It ... Mt 9:33 ... *2296*
when the disciples saw it, they *m* ... Mt 21:20 ... *2296*
had heard these words, they *m* ... Mt 22:22 ... *2296*
that the governor *m* greatly ... Mt 27:14 ... *2296*
he *m* because of their unbelief ... Mk 6:6 ... *2296*
And they *m* at him ... Mk 12:17 ... *2296*
so that Pilate *m* ... Mk 15:5 ... *2296*
Pilate *m* if he were already dead ... Mk 15:44 ... *2296*
m that he tarried so long in the ... Lk 1:21 ... *2296*
And they *m* all ... Lk 1:63 ... *2296*
his mother *m* at those things ... Lk 2:33 ... *2296*
he *m* at him, and turned him about ... Lk 7:9 ... *2296*
he *m* that he had not first washed ... Lk 11:38 ... *2296*
they *m* at his answer, and held ... Lk 20:26 ... *2296*
m that he talked with the woman ... Jn 4:27 ... *2296*
And the Jews *m*, saying, How ... Jn 7:15 ... *2296*
And they were all amazed and *m* ... Acts 2:7 ... *2296*
unlearned and ignorant men, they *m* ... Acts 4:13 ... *2296*

MARVELLOUS {24}
Remember his *m* works that he hath ... 1Chr 16:12 ... 6381
his *m* works among all nations ... 1Chr 16:24 ... 6381
m things without number ... Job 5:9 ... 6381
thou shewest thyself *m* upon me ... Job 10:16 ... 6381
I will shew forth all thy *m* works ... Ps 9:1 ... 6381
Shew thy *m* lovingkindness, O thou ... Ps 17:7 ... 6395
his *m* kindness in a strong city ... Ps 31:21 ... 6381
M things did he in the sight of ... Ps 78:12 ... 6382
for he hath done *m* things ... Ps 98:1 ... 6381
Remember his *m* works that he hath ... Ps 105:5 ... 6381
it is *m* in our eyes ... Ps 118:23 ... 6381
m are thy works ... Ps 139:14 ... 6381
to do a *m* work among this people ... Is 29:14 ... 6381
among this people, even a *m* work ... Is 29:14 ... 6381
shall speak *m* things against the ... Dan 11:36 ... 6381
will I shew unto him *m* things ... Mic 7:15 ... 6381
If it be *m* in the eyes of the ... Zec 8:6 ... 6381
should it also be *m* in mine eyes ... Zec 8:6 ... 6381
doing, and it is *m* in our eyes ... Mt 21:42 ... *2298*
doing, and it is *m* in our eyes ... Mk 12:11 ... *2298*
them, Why herein is a *m* thing ... Jn 9:30 ... *2298*
out of darkness into his *m* light ... 1Pet 2:9 ... *2298*
sign in heaven, great and *m* ... Rev 15:1 ... *2298*
m are thy works, Lord God ... Rev 15:3 ... *2298*

MARVELLOUSLY {3}
for he was *m* helped, till he was ... 2Chr 26:15 ... 6381
God thundereth *m* with his voice ... Job 37:5 ... 6381
heathen, and regard, and wonder *m* ... Hab 1:5 ... 8539

MARVELS {1}
before all thy people I will do *m* ... Ex 34:10 ... 6381

MARY *(ma'-ry)* {54}
1. Mother of Jesus.
begat Joseph the husband of *M* ... Mt 1:16 ... *3137*
When as his mother *M* was espoused ... Mt 1:18 ... *3137*
not to take unto thee *M* thy wife ... Mt 1:20 ... *3137*
the young child with *M* his mother ... Mt 2:11 ... *3137*
is not his mother called *M* ... Mt 13:55 ... *3137*
this the carpenter, the son of *M* ... Mk 6:3 ... *3137*
and the virgin's name was *M* ... Lk 1:27 ... *3137*
angel said unto her, Fear not, *M* ... Lk 1:30 ... *3137*
Then said *M* unto the angel, How ... Lk 1:34 ... *3137*
M said, Behold the handmaid of ... Lk 1:38 ... *3137*
M arose in those days, and went ... Lk 1:39 ... *3137*
heard the salutation of *M* ... Lk 1:41 ... *3137*
M said, My soul doth magnify the ... Lk 1:46 ... *3137*
M abode with her about three ... Lk 1:56 ... *3137*
To be taxed with *M* his espoused ... Lk 2:5 ... *3137*
they came with haste, and found *M* ... Lk 2:16 ... *3137*
But *M* kept all these things, and ... Lk 2:19 ... *3137*
said unto *M* his mother, Behold ... Lk 2:34 ... *3137*
M the mother of Jesus, and with ... Acts 1:14 ... *3137*
2. A woman of Magdala.
Among which was *M* Magdalene ... Mt 27:56 ... *3137*
And there was *M* Magdalene, and the ... Mt 27:61 ... *3137*
came *M* Magdalene and the other ... Mt 28:1 ... *3137*
among whom was *M* Magdalene ... Mk 15:40 ... *3137*
M Magdalene and Mary the mother of ... Mk 15:47 ... *3137*
he appeared first to *M* Magdalene ... Mk 16:9 ... *3137*
M called Magdalene, out of whom ... Lk 8:2 ... *3137*
It was *M* Magdalene, and Joanna, and ... Lk 24:10 ... *3137*
wife of Cleophas, and *M* Magdalene ... Jn 19:25 ... *3137*
the week cometh *M* Magdalene early ... Jn 20:1 ... *3137*
But *M* stood without at the ... Jn 20:11 ... *3137*
Jesus saith unto her, *M* ... Jn 20:16 ... *3137*
M Magdalene came and told the ... Jn 20:18 ... *3137*
3. Mother of James and Joses.
M the mother of James and Joses ... Mt 27:56 ... *3137*
Mary Magdalene, and the other *M* ... Mt 27:61 ... *3137*
the other *M* to see the sepulchre ... Mt 28:1 ... *3137*
M the mother of James the less and ... Mk 15:40 ... *3137*
M the mother of Joses beheld ... Mk 15:47 ... *3137*
M Magdalene, and Mary the mother ... Mk 16:1 ... *3137*
M the mother of James, and Salome ... Mk 16:1 ... *3137*
M the mother of James, and other ... Lk 24:10 ... *3137*
4. Wife of Cleophas.
M the wife of Cleophas, and Mary ... Jn 19:25 ... *3137*
5. Sister of Lazarus.
And she had a sister called *M* ... Lk 10:39 ... *3137*
M hath chosen that good part ... Lk 10:42 ... *3137*
of Bethany, the town of *M* ... Jn 11:1 ... *3137*
(It was that *M* which anointed the ... Jn 11:2 ... *3137*
of the Jews came to Martha and *M* ... Jn 11:19 ... *3137*
but *M* sat still in the house ... Jn 11:20 ... *3137*
called *M* her sister secretly ... Jn 11:28 ... *3137*
and comforted her, when they saw *M* ... Jn 11:31 ... *3137*
Then when *M* was come where Jesus ... Jn 11:32 ... *3137*
many of the Jews which came to *M* ... Jn 11:45 ... *3137*
Then took *M* a pound of ointment ... Jn 12:3 ... *3137*
6. Mother of John Mark.
the house of *M* the mother of John ... Acts 12:12 ... *3137*
7. A Christian in Rome.
Greet *M*, who bestowed much labour ... Rom 16:6 ... *3137*

MASCHIL *(mas'-kil)* {13} *A didactic poem.*
A Psalm of David, A *M* ... Ps 32:*t* ... 4905
To the chief Musician, *M*, for the ... Ps 42:*t* ... 4905
Musician for the sons of Korah, *M* ... Ps 44:*t* ... 4905
for the sons of Korah, A *M* ... Ps 45:*t* ... 4905
To the chief Musician, *M*, A Psalm ... Ps 52:*t* ... 4905
chief Musician upon Mahalath, *M* ... Ps 53:*t* ... 4905
the chief Musician on Neginoth, *M* ... Ps 54:*t* ... 4905
the chief Musician on Neginoth, *M* ... Ps 55:*t* ... 4905
M of Asaph ... Ps 74:*t* ... 4905
M of Asaph ... Ps 78:*t* ... 4905
Leannoth, *M* of Heman the Ezrahite ... Ps 88:*t* ... 4905
M of Ethan the Ezrahite ... Ps 89:*t* ... 4905
M of David ... Ps 142:*t* ... 4905

MASH *(mash)* {1} *A son of Aram.*
Uz, and Hul, and Gether, and *M* ... Gen 10:23 ... 4851

MASHAL *(ma'-shal)* {1} *A Levitical city in Asher.*
M with her suburbs, and Abdon with ... 1Chr 6:74 ... 4913

MASONS {7}
cedar trees, and carpenters, and *m* ... 2Sa 5:11
And to *m*, and hewers of stone, and ... 2Kin 12:12 ... 1443
carpenters, and builders, and *m* ... 2Kin 22:6 ... 1443
and timber of cedars, with *m* ... 1Chr 14:1
he set *m* to hew wrought stones to ... 1Chr 22:2 ... 2672
the house of the LORD, and hired *m* ... 2Chr 24:12 ... 2672
They gave money also unto the *m* ... Ezr 3:7 ... 2672

MASREKAH *(mas'-re-kah)* {2} *A place in Edom.*
Samlah of *M* reigned in his stead ... Gen 36:36 ... 4957
Samlah of *M* reigned in his stead ... 1Chr 1:47 ... 4957

MASSA *(mas'-sah)* {2} *A son of Ishmael.*
And Mishma, and Dumah, and *M* ... Gen 25:14 ... 4854
Mishma, and Dumah, *M*, Hadad, and ... 1Chr 1:30 ... 4854

MASSAH *(mas'-sah)* {4} See MERIBAH. *A place in the wilderness where the Israelites murmured.*
he called the name of the place *M* ... Ex 17:7 ... 4532
your God, as ye tempted him in *M* ... Deut 6:16 ... 4532
And at Taberah, and at *M*, and at ... Deut 9:22 ... 4532
one, whom thou didst prove at *M* ... Deut 33:8 ... 4532

MAST {2}
he that lieth upon the top of a *m* ... Prov 23:34 ... 2260
could not well strengthen their *m* ... Is 33:23 ... 8650

MASTER {157}
under the thigh of Abraham his *m* ... Gen 24:9 ... 113
ten camels of the camels of his *m* ... Gen 24:10 ... 113
goods of his *m* were in his hand ... Gen 24:10 ... 113
said, O LORD God of my *m* Abraham ... Gen 24:12 ... 113
shew kindness unto my *m* Abraham ... Gen 24:12 ... 113
hast shewed kindness unto my *m* ... Gen 24:14 ... 113
be the LORD God of my *m* Abraham ... Gen 24:27 ... 113
left destitute my *m* of his mercy ... Gen 24:27 ... 113
LORD hath blessed my *m* greatly ... Gen 24:35 ... 113
a son to my *m* when she was old ... Gen 24:36 ... 113
my *m* made me swear, saying, Thou ... Gen 24:37 ... 113
And I said unto my *m*, Peradventure ... Gen 24:39 ... 113
said, O LORD God of my *m* Abraham ... Gen 24:42 ... 113
the LORD God of my *m* Abraham ... Gen 24:48 ... 113
deal kindly and truly with my *m* ... Gen 24:49 ... 113
he said, Send me away unto my *m* ... Gen 24:54 ... 113
me away that I may go to my *m* ... Gen 24:56 ... 113
the servant had said, It is my *m* ... Gen 24:65 ... 113
the house of his *m* the Egyptian ... Gen 39:2 ... 113
his *m* saw that the LORD was with ... Gen 39:3 ... 113
my *m* wotteth not what is with me ... Gen 39:8 ... 113
when his *m* heard the words of his ... Gen 39:19 ... 113
And Joseph's *m* took him, and put ... Gen 39:20 ... 113
If his *m* have given him a wife ... Ex 21:4 ... 113
shall plainly say, I love my *m* ... Ex 21:5 ... 113
Then his *m* shall bring him unto ... Ex 21:6 ... 113
his *m* shall bore his ear through ... Ex 21:6 ... 113
If she please not her *m*, who hath ... Ex 21:8 ... 113
their *m* thirty shekels of silver ... Ex 21:32 ... 113
then the *m* of the house shall be ... Ex 22:8 ... 1167
m the servant which is escaped ... Deut 23:15 ... 113
is escaped from his *m* unto thee ... Deut 23:15 ... 113
and the servant said unto his *m* ... Judg 19:11 ... 113
his *m* said unto him, We will not ... Judg 19:12 ... 113
and spake to the *m* of the house ... Judg 19:22 ... 1167
the *m* of the house, went out unto ... Judg 19:23 ... 1167
up the arrows, and came to his *m* ... 1Sa 20:38 ... 113
I should do this thing unto my *m* ... 1Sa 24:6 ... 113
break away every man from his *m* ... 1Sa 25:10 ... 113
of the wilderness to salute our *m* ... 1Sa 25:14 ... 113
evil is determined against our *m* ... 1Sa 25:17 ... 113
because ye have not kept your *m* ... 1Sa 26:16 ... 113
he reconcile himself unto his *m* ... 1Sa 29:4 ... 113
my *m* left me, because three days ... 1Sa 30:13 ... 113
deliver me into the hands of my *m* ... 1Sa 30:15 ... 113
for your *m* Saul is dead, and also ... 2Sa 2:7 ... 113
and the LORD said, These have no *m* ... 1Kin 22:17 ... 113
away thy *m* from thy head to day ... 2Kin 2:3 ... 113
away thy *m* from thy head to day ... 2Kin 2:5 ... 113
go, we pray thee, and seek thy *m* ... 2Kin 2:16 ... 113
Syria, was a great man with his *m* ... 2Kin 5:1 ... 113
that when my *m* goeth into the ... 2Kin 5:18 ... 113
my *m* hath spared Naaman this ... 2Kin 5:20 ... 113
My *m* hath sent me, saying, Behold ... 2Kin 5:22 ... 113
he went in, and stood before his *m* ... 2Kin 5:25 ... 113
and he cried, and said, Alas, *m* ... 2Kin 6:5 ... 113
servant said unto him, Alas, my *m* ... 2Kin 6:15 ... 113
eat and drink, and go to their *m* ... 2Kin 6:22 ... 113
away, and they went to their *m* ... 2Kin 6:23 ... 113
from Elisha, and came to his *m* ... 2Kin 8:14 ... 113
smite the house of Ahab thy *m* ... 2Kin 9:7 ... 113
Had Zimri peace, who slew his *m* ... 2Kin 9:31 ... 113
behold, I conspired against my *m* ... 2Kin 10:9 ... 113
Hath my *m* sent me to thy *m* ... 2Kin 18:27 ... 113
his *m* hath sent to reproach the ... 2Kin 19:4 ... 113
them, Thus shall ye say to your *m* ... 2Kin 19:6 ... 113
He will fall to his *m* Saul to the ... 1Chr 12:19 ... 113
Chenaniah the *m* of the song with ... 1Chr 15:27 ... 8269
and the LORD said, These have no *m* ... 2Chr 18:16 ... 113
and the servant is free from his *m* ... Job 3:19 ... 113
on his *m* shall be honoured ... Prov 27:18 ... 113
Accuse not a servant unto his *m* ... Prov 30:10 ... 113
with the servant, so with his *m* ... Is 24:2 ... 113
to my *m* the king of Assyria, and I ... Is 36:8 ... 113
Hath my *m* sent me to thy *m* ... Is 36:12 ... 113
his *m* hath sent to reproach the ... Is 37:4 ... 113
Thus shall ye say unto your *m* ... Is 37:6 ... 113
Ashpenaz the *m* of his eunuchs ... Dan 1:3 ... 7227
m of the magicians, because I ... Dan 4:9 ... 729
father, made *m* of the magicians ... Dan 5:11 ... 729
his father, and a servant his *m* ... Mal 1:6 ... 113
and if I be a *m*, where is my fear ... Mal 1:6 ... 113

the man that doeth this, the *m* Mal 2:12 5782
scribe came, and said unto him, *M* Mt 8:19 *1320*
Why eateth your *M* with publicans Mt 9:11 *1320*
The disciple is not above his *m* Mt 10:24 *1320*
the disciple that he be as his *m* Mt 10:25 *1320*
the *m* of the house Beelzebub Mt 10:25 *1320*
the Pharisees answered, saying, *M* Mt 12:38 *1320*
said, Doth not your *m* pay tribute Mt 17:24 *1320*
one came and said unto him, Good *M* Mt 19:16 *1320*
with the Herodians, saying, *M* Mt 22:16 *1320*
Saying, *M*, Moses said, If a man Mt 22:24 *1320*
M, which is the great commandment Mt 22:36 *1320*
for one is your *M*, even Christ Mt 23:8 *2519*
for one is your *M*, even Christ Mt 23:10 *2519*
The *M* saith, My time is at hand Mt 26:18 *1320*
betrayed him, answered and said, *M* Mt 26:25 *4461*
came to Jesus, and said, Hail, *m* Mt 26:49 *4461*
awake him, and say unto him, *M* Mk 4:38 *1320*
troublest thou the *M* any further Mk 5:35 *1320*
answered and said to Jesus, *M* Mk 9:5 *4461*
the multitude answered and said, *M* Mk 9:17 *1320*
And John answered him, saying, *M* Mk 9:38 *1320*
to him, and asked him, Good *M* Mk 10:17 *1320*
he answered and said unto him, *M* Mk 10:20 *1320*
Zebedee, come unto him, saying, *M* Mk 10:35 *1320*
to remembrance saith unto him, *M* Mk 11:21 *4461*
were come, they say unto him, *M* Mk 12:14 *1320*
M, Moses wrote unto us, If a Mk 12:19 *1320*
the scribe said unto him, Well, *M* Mk 12:32 *1320*
his disciples saith unto him, *M* Mk 13:1 *1320*
when the *m* of the house cometh Mk 13:35 *2962*
The *M* saith, Where is the Mk 14:14 *1320*
to him, and saith, *M*, *m* Mk 14:45 *4461*
be baptized, and said unto him, *M* Lk 3:12 *1320*
Simon answering said unto him, *M* Lk 5:5 *1988*
The disciple is not above his *m* Lk 6:40 *1320*
that is perfect shall be as his *m* Lk 6:40 *1320*
And he saith, *M*, say on Lk 7:40 *1320*
and awoke him, saying, *M*, *m* Lk 8:24 *1988*
they that were with him said, *M* Lk 8:45 *1988*
trouble not the *M* Lk 8:49 *1320*
him, Peter said unto Jesus, *M* Lk 9:33 *1988*
the company cried out, saying, *M* Lk 9:38 *1320*
And John answered and said, *M* Lk 9:49 *1988*
up, and tempted him, saying, *M* Lk 10:25 *1320*
the lawyers, and said unto him, *M* Lk 11:45 *1320*
of the company said unto him, *M* Lk 12:13 *1320*
When once the *m* of the house is Lk 13:25 *3617*
Then the *m* of the house being Lk 14:21 *3617*
their voices, and said, Jesus, *M* Lk 17:13 *1988*
ruler asked him, saying, Good *M* Lk 18:18 *1320*
the multitude said unto him, *M* Lk 19:39 *1320*
And they asked him, saying, *M* Lk 20:21 *1320*
Saying, *M*, Moses wrote unto us Lk 20:28 *1320*
of the scribes answering said, *M* Lk 20:39 *1320*
And they asked him, saying, *M* Lk 21:7 *1320*
The *M* saith unto thee, Where is Lk 22:11 *1320*
is to say, being interpreted, *M* Jn 1:38 *1320*
unto him, Art thou a *m* of Israel Jn 3:10 *1320*
disciples prayed him, saying, *M* Jn 4:31 *4461*
They say unto him, *M*, this woman Jn 8:4 *1320*
disciples asked him, saying, *M* Jn 9:2 *4461*
His disciples say unto him, *M* Jn 11:8 *4461*
The *M* is come, and calleth for Jn 11:28 *1320*
Ye call me *M* and Lord Jn 13:13 *1320*
If I then, your Lord and *M* Jn 13:14 *1320*
which is to say, *M* Jn 20:16 *1320*
the centurion believed the *m* Acts 27:11 *2942*
to his own *m* he standeth or Rom 14:4 *2962*
that your *M* also is in heaven Eph 6:9 *2962*
that ye also have a *M* in heaven Col 4:1 *2962*

MASTERBUILDER {1}
is given unto me, as a wise *m* 1Cor 3:10 *753*

MASTERIES {1}
And if a man also strive for *m* 2Ti 2:5

MASTER'S {24}
me to the house of my *m* brethren Gen 24:27 113
Sarah my *m* wife bare a son to my Gen 24:36 113
hath appointed out for my *m* son Gen 24:44 113
me in the right way to take my *m* Gen 24:48 113
and let her be thy *m* son's wife Gen 24:51 113
that his *m* wife cast her eyes Gen 39:7 113
refused, and said unto his *m* wife Gen 39:8 113
and her children shall be her *m* Ex 21:4 113
thy *m* servants that are come with 1Sa 29:10 113
I have given unto thy *m* son all 2Sa 9:9 113
that thy *m* son may have food to 2Sa 9:10 113
but Mephibosheth thy *m* son shall 2Sa 9:10 113
And I gave thee thy *m* house 2Sa 12:8 113
thy *m* wives into thy bosom, and 2Sa 12:8 113
king said, And where is thy *m* son 2Sa 16:3 113
sound of his *m* feet behind him 2Kin 6:32 113
seeing your *m* sons are with you, 2Kin 10:2 113
best and meetest of your *m* sons 2Kin 10:3 113
throne, and fight for your *m* house 2Kin 10:3 113
the heads of the men your *m* sons 2Kin 10:6 113
of the least of my *m* servants 2Kin 18:24 113
his owner, and the ass his *m* crib Is 1:3 1167
of the least of my *m* servants Is 36:9 113
sanctified, and meet for the *m* use 2Ti 2:21 *1203*

MASTERS {20}
look unto the hand of their *m* Ps 123:2 113
he refresheth the soul of his *m* Prov 25:13 113
fastened by the *m* of assemblies Eccl 12:11 1167
command them to say unto their *m* Jer 27:4 113
Thus shall ye say unto your *m* Jer 27:4 113
the needy, which say to their *m* Amos 4:1 113
No man can serve two *m* Mt 6:24 *2962*
Neither be ye called *m* Mt 23:10 *2519*
No servant can serve two *m* Lk 16:13 *2962*
which brought her *m* much gain by Acts 16:16 *2962*
when her *m* saw that the hope of Acts 16:19 *2962*
are your *m* according to the flesh Eph 6:5 *2962*
And, ye *m*, do the same things unto Eph 6:9 *2962*
your *m* according to the flesh Col 3:22 *2962*
M, give unto your servants that Col 4:1 *2962*
their own *m* worthy of all honour 1Ti 6:1 *1203*
And they that have believing *m* 1Ti 6:2 *1203*
to be obedient unto their own *m* Titus 2:9 *1203*
My brethren, be not many *m* Jas 3:1 *1320*
subject to your *m* with all fear 1Pet 2:18 *1203*

MASTERS' {2}
which fill their *m* houses with Zeph 1:9 113
which fall from their *m* table Mt 15:27 *2962*

MASTERY {3}
voice of them that shout for *m* Ex 32:18 1369
and the lions had the *m* of them Dan 6:24 6981
the *m* is temperate in all things 1Cor 9:25

MASTS {1}
from Lebanon to make *m* for thee Eze 27:5 8650

MATE {2}
be gathered, every one with her *m* Is 34:15 7468
shall fail, none shall want her *m* Is 34:16 7468

MATHUSALA *(ma-thu'-sa-lah)* {1} See METHUSALAH. *Son of Enoch; ancestor of Jesus.*
Which was the son of *M*, which was Lk 3:37 *3103*

MATRED *(ma'-tred)* {2} *Mother of Mehetabel.*
was Mehetabel, the daughter of *M* Gen 36:39 4308
was Mehetabel, the daughter of *M* 1Chr 1:50 4308

MATRI *(ma'-tri)* {1} *An ancestoral family of King Saul.*
the family of *M* was taken 1Sa 10:21 4309

MATRITE See MATRI.

MATRIX {5}
the LORD all that openeth the *m* Ex 13:12 7358
the LORD all that openeth the *m* Ex 13:15 7358
All that openeth the *m* is mine Ex 34:19 7358
m among the children of Israel Num 3:12 7358
that openeth the *m* in all flesh Num 18:15 7358

MATTAN *(mat'-tan)* {3}
1. A priest of Baal.
slew *M* the priest of Baal before 2Kin 11:18 4977
slew *M* the priest of Baal before 2Chr 23:17 4977
2. Father of Shephatiah.
Then Shephatiah the son of *M* Jer 38:1 4977

MATTANAH *(mat'-ta-nah)* {2} *An encampment of Israel in the wilderness.*
the wilderness they went to *M* Num 21:18 4980
And from *M* to Nahaliel Num 21:19 4980

MATTANIAH *(mat-ta-ni'-ah)* {16} See ZEDEKIAH.
1. Same as Zedekiah, king of Judah.
the king of Babylon made *M* his 2Kin 24:17 4983
2. A family of exiles.
M the son of Micah, the son of 1Chr 9:15 4983
the son of Jeiel, the son of *M* 2Chr 20:14 4983
M the son of Micha, the son of Neh 11:17 4983
son of Hashabiah, the son of *M* Neh 11:22 4983
Kadmiel, Sherebiah, Judah, and *M* Neh 12:8 4983
M, and Bakbukiah, Obadiah, Neh 12:25 4983
the son of Shemaiah, the son of *M* Neh 12:35 4983
3. A sanctuary servant.
Bukkiah, *M*, Uzziel, Shebuel, and 1Chr 25:4 4983
The ninth to *M*, he, his sons, and 1Chr 25:16 4983
4. A descendant of Asaph.
Zechariah, and *M* 2Chr 29:13 4983
5. A descendant of Elam.
M, Zechariah, and Jehiel, and Abdi, Ezr 10:26 4983
6. A descendant of Zattu.
Elioenai, Eliashib, *M*, and Ezr 10:27 4983
7. A descendant of Pahath-Moab.
and Chelal, Benaiah, Maaseiah, *M* Ezr 10:30 4983
8. A descendant of Bani.
M, Mattenai, and Jaasau, Ezr 10:37 4983
9. Father of Zaccur.
the son of Zaccur, the son of *M* Neh 13:13 4983

MATTATHA *(mat'-ta-thah)* {1} See MATTATHAH. *A son of Nathan; ancestor of Jesus.*
of Menan, which was the son of *M* Lk 3:31 *3160*

MATTATHAH *(mat'-ta-thah)* {1} See MATTATHA. *Married a foreigner in exile.*
Mattenai, *M*, Zabad, Eliphelet, Ezr 10:33 4992

MATTATHIAH See MATTATHIAS.

MATTATHIAS *(mat-ta-thi'-as)* {2} See MATTITHIAH.
1. A son of Amos; ancestor of Jesus.
Which was the son of *M*, which was Lk 3:25 *3161*
2. A son of Semei; ancestor of Jesus.
of Maath, which was the son of *M* Lk 3:26 *3161*

MATTATTAH See MATTATHAH.

MATTENAI *(mat'-te-nahee)* {3}
1. A descendant of Hashum.
M, Mattathah, Zabad, Eliphelet, Ezr 10:33 4982
2. A descendant of Bani.
Mattaniah, *M*, and Jaasau, Ezr 10:37 4982
3. A priest.
And of Joiarib, *M* Neh 12:19 4982

MATTER See APPENDIX.

MATTERS See APPENDIX.

MATTHAN *(mat'-than)* {2} *Son of Eleazar; ancestor of Jesus.*
and Eleazar begat *M* Mt 1:15 *3157*
and *M* begat Jacob Mt 1:15 *3157*

MATTHAT *(mat'-that)* {2}
1. Son of Levi; an ancestor of Jesus.
Which was the son of *M*, which was Lk 3:24 *3158*
2. Father of Jorim; an ancestor of Jesus.
of Jorim, which was the son of *M* Lk 3:29 *3158*

MATTHEW *(math'-ew)* {5} See LEVI. *A disciple of Jesus.*
thence, he saw a man, named *M* Mt 9:9 *3156*
Thomas, and *M* the publican Mt 10:3 *3156*
and Philip, and Bartholomew, and *M* Mk 3:18 *3156*
M and Thomas, James the son of Lk 6:15 *3156*
and Thomas, Bartholomew, and *M* Acts 1:13 *3156*

MATTHIAS *(mat'-thias)* {2} *Successor to Judas Iscariot as apostle.*
who was surnamed Justus, and *M* Acts 1:23 *3159*
and the lot fell upon *M* Acts 1:26 *3159*

MATTITHIAH *(mat-tith-i'-ah)* {8} See MATTATHIAS.
1. A son of Shallum.
And *M*, one of the Levites, who was 1Chr 9:31 4993
2. A Levite gatekeeper.
and Benaiah, and Maaseiah, and *M* 1Chr 15:18 4993
And *M*, and Elipheleh, and Mikneiah, 1Chr 15:21 4993
and Shemiramoth, and Jehiel, and *M* 1Chr 16:5 4993
3. Son of Jeduthun.
and Jeshaiah, Hashabiah, and *M* 1Chr 25:3 4993
The fourteenth to *M*, he, his sons 1Chr 25:21 4993
4. Married a foreigner in exile.
Jeiel, *M*, Zabad, Zebina, Jadau, Ezr 10:43 4993
5. A priest who aided Ezra.
and beside him stood *M*, and Shema, Neh 8:4 4993

MATTOCK {2}
his coulter, and his ax, and his *m* 1Sa 13:20 4281
that shall be digged with the *m* Is 7:25 4576

MATTOCKS {2}
Yet they had a file for the *m* 1Sa 13:21 4281
with their *m* round about 2Chr 34:6 2719

MAUL {1}
against his neighbour is a *m* Prov 25:18 4650

MAW {1}
and the two cheeks, and the *m* Deut 18:3 6896

MAY {1027}
fowl that *m* fly above the earth Gen 1:20
We *m* eat of the fruit of the Gen 3:2
that they *m* breed abundantly in Gen 8:17
that I *m* remember the everlasting Gen 9:16
whose top *m* reach unto heaven Gen 11:4
that they *m* not understand one Gen 11:7
that it *m* be well with me for thy Gen 12:13
unto my maid; it *m* Gen 16:2 194
that I *m* obtain children Gen 16:2
that the LORD *m* bring upon Gen 18:19
out unto us, that we *m* know them Gen 19:5
that we *m* preserve seed of our Gen 19:32
that we *m* preserve seed of our Gen 19:34
that they *m* be a witness unto me, Gen 21:30 1961
that I *m* bury my dead out of my Gen 23:4
That he *m* give me the cave of Gen 23:9
I pray thee, that I *m* drink Gen 24:14
that I *m* turn to the right hand, Gen 24:49
me away that I *m* go to my master Gen 24:56
and bring it to me, that I *m* eat Gen 27:4
that my soul *m* bless thee before Gen 27:4
me savoury meat, that I *m* eat Gen 27:7
it to thy father, that he *m* eat Gen 27:10
that he *m* bless thee before his Gen 27:10
venison, that thy soul *m* bless me Gen 27:19
that I *m* feel thee, my son, Gen 27:21
that my soul *m* bless thee Gen 27:25
venison, that thy soul *m* bless me Gen 27:31
that I *m* go in unto her Gen 29:21
that I *m* also have children by Gen 30:3
that I *m* go unto mine own place, Gen 30:25
that they *m* judge betwixt us both Gen 31:37
that I *m* find grace in thy sight Gen 32:5
that we *m* live, and not die Gen 42:2
that your words *m* be proved Gen 42:16
that we *m* live, and not die, both Gen 43:8
that he *m* send away your other Gen 43:14
that he *m* seek occasion against Gen 43:18
that I *m* set mine eyes upon him Gen 44:21
for we *m* not see the man's face, Gen 44:26 3201
that ye *m* dwell in the land of Gen 46:34
and give us seed, that we *m* live Gen 47:19
that I *m* tell you that which Gen 49:1
that she *m* nurse the child for Ex 2:7
call him, that he *m* eat bread Ex 2:20
that we *m* sacrifice to the LORD Ex 3:18
That they *m* believe that the LORD Ex 4:5
Let my son go, that he *m* serve me Ex 4:23
that they *m* hold a feast unto me Ex 5:1
that they *m* labour therein Ex 5:9
that I *m* lay my hand upon Egypt, Ex 7:4
that they *m* serve me in the Ex 7:16
water, that they *m* become blood Ex 7:19 1961
that there *m* be blood throughout Ex 7:19 1961
people go, that they *m* serve me Ex 8:1
that he *m* take away the frogs Ex 8:8
that they *m* do sacrifice unto the Ex 8:8
that they *m* remain in the river Ex 8:9
that it *m* become lice throughout Ex 8:16 1961
people go, that they *m* serve me Ex 8:20
that ye *m* sacrifice to the LORD Ex 8:28

of flies *m* depart from Pharaoh ... Ex 8:29
people go, that they *m* serve me ... Ex 9:1
people go, that they *m* serve me ... Ex 9:13
that I *m* smite thee and thy people ... Ex 9:15
that my name *m* be declared ... Ex 9:16
that there *m* be hail in all the ... Ex 9:22
that ye *m* know how that I am the ... Ex 10:2
people go, that they *m* serve me ... Ex 10:3
that they *m* serve the LORD their ... Ex 10:7
that they *m* come up upon the land ... Ex 10:12
that he *m* take away from me this ... Ex 10:17
that there *m* be darkness over the ... Ex 10:21 1961
even darkness which *m* be felt ... Ex 10:21
that we *m* sacrifice unto the LORD ... Ex 10:25
that ye *m* know how that the LORD ... Ex 11:7
that my wonders *m* be multiplied ... Ex 11:9
that only *m* be done of you ... Ex 12:16
the LORD's law *m* be in thy mouth ... Ex 13:9 1961
that the Egyptians *m* know that I ... Ex 14:4
that we *m* serve the Egyptians ... Ex 14:12
that the waters *m* come again upon ... Ex 14:26
that I *m* prove them, whether they ... Ex 16:4
that they *m* see the bread ... Ex 16:32
Give us water that we *m* drink ... Ex 17:2
of it, that the people *m* drink ... Ex 17:6
that the people *m* hear when I ... Ex 19:9
that thy days *m* be long upon the ... Ex 20:12
that his fear *m* be before your ... Ex 20:20 1961
from mine altar, that he *m* die ... Ex 21:14
that the poor of thy people *m* eat ... Ex 23:11
that thine ox and thine ass *m* rest ... Ex 23:12
and the stranger, *m* be refreshed ... Ex 23:12
that I *m* dwell among them ... Ex 25:8
that the ark *m* be borne with them ... Ex 25:14
that the table *m* be borne with ... Ex 25:28
that they *m* give light over ... Ex 25:37
that the loops *m* take hold one of ... Ex 26:5
tent together, that it *m* be one ... Ex 26:11 1961
that the net *m* be even to the ... Ex 27:5 1961
that he *m* minister unto me in the ... Ex 28:1
that they *m* make Aaron's garments ... Ex 28:3
that he *m* minister unto me in the ... Ex 28:3
that he *m* minister unto me in the ... Ex 28:4
that it *m* be above the curious ... Ex 28:28 1961
that it *m* be upon the mitre ... Ex 28:37 1961
that Aaron *m* bear the iniquity of ... Ex 28:38
that they *m* be accepted before ... Ex 28:38
that they *m* minister unto me in ... Ex 28:41
that I *m* dwell among them ... Ex 29:46
that it *m* be a memorial unto the ... Ex 30:16 1961
them, that they *m* be most holy ... Ex 30:29 1961
that they *m* minister unto me in ... Ex 30:30
that they *m* make all that I have ... Ex 31:6
that ye *m* know that I am the LORD ... Ex 31:13
Six days *m* work be done ... Ex 31:15
that my wrath *m* wax hot against ... Ex 32:10
them, and that I *m* consume them ... Ex 32:10
that he *m* bestow upon you a ... Ex 32:29
that I *m* know what to do unto ... Ex 33:5
that I *m* know thee, that I *m* ... Ex 33:13
put in his heart that he *m* teach ... Ex 35:34
that he *m* minister unto me in the ... Ex 40:13
that they *m* minister unto me in ... Ex 40:15
m be used in any other use ... Lev 7:24
that the breast *m* be waved for a ... Lev 7:30
that ye *m* put difference between ... Lev 10:10
that ye *m* teach the children of ... Lev 10:11
Yet these *m* ye eat of every ... Lev 11:21
Even these of them ye *m* eat ... Lev 11:22
Of all meat which *m* be eaten ... Lev 11:34
all drink that *m* be drunk in ... Lev 11:34
if any beast, of which ye *m* eat ... Lev 11:39
between the beast that *m* be eaten ... Lev 11:47
and the beast that *m* not be eaten ... Lev 11:47
in water, that he *m* be clean ... Lev 14:8
m cover the mercy seat that is ... Lev 16:13
that ye *m* be clean from all your ... Lev 16:30
Israel *m* bring their sacrifices ... Lev 17:5
even that they *m* bring them unto ... Lev 17:5
any beast or fowl that *m* be eaten ... Lev 17:13
that it *m* yield unto you the ... Lev 19:25
for her *m* he be defiled ... Lev 21:3
whereby he *m* be made unclean, or ... Lev 22:5
man of whom he *m* take uncleanness ... Lev 22:5
she *m* not eat of an offering of ... Lev 22:12
that it *m* be an holy convocation ... Lev 23:21 1961
That your generations *m* know that ... Lev 23:43
that it *m* be on the bread for a ... Lev 24:7 1961
that he *m* return unto his ... Lev 25:27
then he *m* redeem it within a ... Lev 25:29
within a full year *m* he redeem it ... Lev 25:29
they *m* be redeemed, and they shall ... Lev 25:31
m the Levites redeem at any time ... Lev 25:32
of their cities *m* not be sold ... Lev 25:34
that he *m* live with thee ... Lev 25:35
that thy brother *m* live with thee ... Lev 25:36
he is sold he *m* be redeemed again ... Lev 25:48
one of his brethren *m* redeem him ... Lev 25:48
m redeem him, or any that is nigh ... Lev 25:49
him of his family *m* redeem him ... Lev 25:49
he be able, he *m* redeem himself ... Lev 25:49
that they *m* minister unto him ... Num 3:6
do unto them, that they *m* live ... Num 4:19
that the Nazarite *m* drink wine ... Num 6:20
that they *m* be to do the service ... Num 7:5 1961
that they *m* execute the service ... Num 8:11
that we *m* not offer an offering ... Num 9:7
that they *m* be to you for a ... Num 10:10 1961

Give us flesh, that we *m* eat ... Num 11:13
that they *m* stand there with thee ... Num 11:16
that they *m* eat a whole month ... Num 11:21
that they *m* search the land of ... Num 13:2
that ye *m* look upon it, and ... Num 15:39
That ye *m* remember, and do all my ... Num 15:40
that I *m* consume them in a moment ... Num 16:21
that I *m* consume them as in a ... Num 16:45
that they *m* be joined unto thee ... Num 18:2
that he *m* bring her forth without ... Num 19:3
that we *m* smite them, and that I ... Num 22:6
that I *m* drive them out of the ... Num 22:6
that I *m* know what the LORD will ... Num 22:19
LORD *m* be turned away from Israel ... Num 25:4
Which *m* go out before them, and ... Num 27:17
which *m* go in before them, and ... Num 27:17
which *m* lead them out ... Num 27:17
and which *m* bring them in ... Num 27:17
children of Israel *m* be obedient ... Num 27:20
her husband *m* establish it ... Num 30:13
or her husband *m* make it void ... Num 30:13
Every thing that *m* abide the fire ... Num 31:23
on this side Jordan *m* be ours ... Num 32:32
manslayer, that he *m* flee thither ... Num 35:6
that the slayer *m* flee thither ... Num 35:11
person unawares *m* flee thither ... Num 35:15
a stone, wherewith he *m* die ... Num 35:17
of wood, wherewith he *m* die ... Num 35:18
any stone, wherewith a man *m* die ... Num 35:23
that the children of Israel *m* ... Num 36:8
of them for money, that ye *m* eat ... Deut 2:6
them for money, that ye *m* drink ... Deut 2:6
me meat for money, that I *m* eat ... Deut 2:28
water for money, that I *m* drink ... Deut 2:28
for to do them, that ye *m* live ... Deut 4:1
that ye *m* keep the commandments ... Deut 4:2
that they *m* learn to fear me all ... Deut 4:10
that they *m* teach their children ... Deut 4:10
that it *m* go well with thee, and ... Deut 4:40
that ye *m* learn them, and keep, and ... Deut 5:1
thy maidservant *m* rest as well as ... Deut 5:14
that thy days *m* be prolonged ... Deut 5:16
that it *m* go well with thee, in ... Deut 5:16
that they *m* do them in the land ... Deut 5:31
commanded you, that ye *m* live ... Deut 5:33
that it *m* be well with you, and ... Deut 5:33
that ye *m* prolong your days in ... Deut 5:33
and that thy days *m* be prolonged ... Deut 6:2
that it *m* be well with thee, and ... Deut 6:3
that ye *m* increase mightily, as ... Deut 6:3
that it *m* be well with thee, and ... Deut 6:18
that they *m* serve other gods ... Deut 7:4
ye observe to do, that ye *m* live ... Deut 8:1
that he *m* establish his covenant ... Deut 8:18
that he *m* perform the word which ... Deut 9:5
that I *m* destroy them, and blot ... Deut 9:14
the people, that they *m* go in ... Deut 10:11
that ye *m* be strong, and go in and ... Deut 11:8
that ye *m* prolong your days in ... Deut 11:9
that they *m* be as frontlets ... Deut 11:18 1961
That your days *m* be multiplied ... Deut 11:21
the clean *m* eat thereof, as of ... Deut 12:15
that it *m* go well with thee, and ... Deut 12:25
that it *m* go well with thee, and ... Deut 12:28
that the LORD *m* turn from the ... Deut 13:17
not fins and scales ye *m* not eat ... Deut 14:10
But of all clean fowls ye *m* eat ... Deut 14:20
is in thy gates, that he *m* eat it ... Deut 14:21
that the LORD thy God *m* bless ... Deut 14:29
that he *m* learn to fear the LORD ... Deut 17:19
to the end that he *m* prolong his ... Deut 17:20
that every slayer *m* flee thither ... Deut 19:3
flee thither, that he *m* live ... Deut 19:4
avenger of blood, that he *m* die ... Deut 19:12
that it *m* go well with thee ... Deut 19:13
that he *m* not make the son of the ... Deut 21:16 3201
that it *m* be well with thee, and ... Deut 22:7
he *m* not put her away all his ... Deut 22:19 3201
he *m* not put her away all his ... Deut 22:29 3201
that the LORD thy God *m* bless ... Deut 23:20
out of his house, she *m* go ... Deut 24:2
m not take her again to be his ... Deut 24:4 3201
that he *m* sleep in his own ... Deut 24:13
that the LORD thy God *m* bless ... Deut 24:19
that the judges *m* judge them ... Deut 25:1
Forty stripes he *m* give him ... Deut 25:3
that thy days *m* be lengthened in ... Deut 25:15
that they *m* eat within thy gates ... Deut 26:12
that ye *m* prosper in all that ye ... Deut 29:9
That he *m* establish thee to day ... Deut 29:13
that he *m* be unto thee a God, as ... Deut 29:13
that we *m* do all the words of ... Deut 29:29
it unto us, that we *m* hear it ... Deut 30:12
it unto us, that we *m* hear it ... Deut 30:13
that both thou and thy seed *m* live ... Deut 30:19
that ye *m* do unto them according ... Deut 31:5
m hear, and that they *m* learn ... Deut 31:12
m hear, and learn to fear the LORD ... Deut 31:13
that I *m* give him a charge ... Deut 31:14
that this song *m* be a witness for ... Deut 31:19 1961
that it *m* be there for a witness ... Deut 31:26 1961
that I *m* speak these words in ... Deut 31:28
afterward *m* ye go your way ... Josh 2:16
that ye *m* know the way by which ... Josh 3:4
all Israel, that they *m* know that ... Josh 3:7
That this *m* be a sign among you ... Josh 4:6 1961
now therefore we *m* not touch them ... Josh 9:19 3201
help me, that we *m* smite Gibeon ... Josh 10:4

that I *m* cast lots for you here ... Josh 18:6
that I *m* here cast lots for you ... Josh 18:8
unwittingly *m* flee thither ... Josh 20:3
that he *m* dwell among them ... Josh 20:4
But that it *m* be a witness ... Josh 22:27
that your children *m* not say to ... Josh 22:27
that we *m* say again, Behold the ... Josh 22:28
that we *m* fight against the ... Judg 1:3
through them I *m* prove Israel ... Judg 2:22
Bring out thy son, that he *m* die ... Judg 6:30
that God *m* hearken unto you ... Judg 9:7
that we *m* fight with the children ... Judg 11:6
alone two months, that I *m* go up ... Judg 11:37
She *m* not eat of any thing that ... Judg 13:14
come to pass we *m* do thee honour ... Judg 13:17
thy riddle, that we *m* hear it ... Judg 14:13
that he *m* declare unto us the ... Judg 14:15
that we *m* deliver thee into the ... Judg 15:12
by what means we *m* prevail ... Judg 16:5
that we *m* bind him to afflict him ... Judg 16:5
Samson, that he *m* make us sport ... Judg 16:25
Suffer me that I *m* feel the ... Judg 16:26
standeth, that I *m* lean upon them ... Judg 16:26
that I *m* be at once avenged of ... Judg 16:28
to sojourn where I *m* find a place ... Judg 17:9
that we *m* know whether our way ... Judg 18:5
that we *m* go up against them ... Judg 18:9
here, that thine heart *m* be merry ... Judg 19:9
thine house, that we *m* know him ... Judg 19:22
for the people, that they *m* do ... Judg 20:10
that we *m* put them to death, and ... Judg 20:13
Howbeit we *m* not give them wives ... Judg 21:18 3201
grant you that ye *m* find rest ... Ruth 1:9
that they *m* be your husbands ... Ruth 1:11
that she *m* glean them, and rebuke ... Ruth 2:16
that it *m* be well with thee ... Ruth 3:1
it, then tell me, that I *m* know ... Ruth 4:4
that his name *m* be famous in ... Ruth 4:14
that he *m* appear before the LORD ... 1Sa 1:22
that I *m* eat a piece of bread ... 1Sa 2:36
it *m* save us out of the hand of ... 1Sa 4:3
and send it away, that it *m* go ... 1Sa 6:8
That we also *m* be like all the ... 1Sa 8:20 1961
and that our king *m* judge us ... 1Sa 8:20
that he *m* save my people out of ... 1Sa 9:16
Up, that I *m* send thee away ... 1Sa 9:26
that I *m* shew thee the word of ... 1Sa 9:27
that I *m* thrust out all your ... 1Sa 11:2
that we *m* send messengers unto ... 1Sa 11:3
that we *m* put them to death ... 1Sa 11:12
that I *m* reason with you before ... 1Sa 12:7
that ye *m* perceive and see that ... 1Sa 12:17
it *m* be that the LORD will work ... 1Sa 14:6 194
that I *m* be avenged on mine ... 1Sa 14:24
that I *m* worship the LORD ... 1Sa 15:25
that I *m* worship the LORD thy God ... 1Sa 15:30
a man, that we *m* fight together ... 1Sa 17:10
that all the earth *m* know that ... 1Sa 17:46
that she *m* be a snare to him, and ... 1Sa 18:21 1961
the Philistines *m* be against him ... 1Sa 18:21 1961
me in the bed, that I *m* slay him ... 1Sa 19:15
that I *m* hide myself in the field ... 1Sa 20:5
the country, that I *m* dwell there ... 1Sa 27:5
that I *m* go to her, and enquire of ... 1Sa 28:7
that he *m* go again to his place ... 1Sa 29:4
that I *m* not go fight against the ... 1Sa 29:8
that they *m* lead them away, and ... 1Sa 30:22
that they *m* make a league with ... 2Sa 3:21
that they *m* dwell in a place of ... 2Sa 7:10
that it *m* continue for ever ... 2Sa 7:29
that I *m* shew him kindness for ... 2Sa 9:1
that I *m* shew the kindness of God ... 2Sa 9:3
master's son *m* have food to eat ... 2Sa 9:10
that he *m* be smitten, and die ... 2Sa 11:15
to me, that the child *m* live ... 2Sa 12:22
meat in my sight, that I *m* see it ... 2Sa 13:5
sight, that I *m* eat at her hand ... 2Sa 13:6
that I *m* eat of thine hand ... 2Sa 13:10
that we *m* kill him, for the life ... 2Sa 14:7
it *m* be that the king will ... 2Sa 14:15 194
that I *m* send thee to the king ... 2Sa 14:32
seeing I go whither I *m*, return ... 2Sa 15:20
faint in the wilderness *m* drink ... 2Sa 16:2
that I *m* find grace in thy sight ... 2Sa 16:4
how much more now *m* this ... 2Sa 16:11
It *m* be that the LORD will look ... 2Sa 16:12 194
I *m* not tarry thus with thee ... 2Sa 18:14
that I *m* ride thereon, and go to ... 2Sa 19:26
that I *m* die in mine own city, and ... 2Sa 19:37
hither, that I *m* speak with thee ... 2Sa 20:16
that ye *m* bless the inheritance ... 2Sa 21:3
that I *m* know the number of the ... 2Sa 24:2
eyes of my lord the king *m* see it ... 2Sa 24:3
of them, that I *m* do it unto thee ... 2Sa 24:12
that the plague *m* be stayed from ... 2Sa 24:21
that my lord the king *m* get heat ... 1Kin 1:2
come up after him, that he *m* come ... 1Kin 1:35
That the LORD *m* continue his word ... 1Kin 2:4
that I *m* discern between good and ... 1Kin 3:9
That thine eyes *m* be open toward ... 1Kin 8:29
That they *m* fear thee all the ... 1Kin 8:40
of the earth *m* know thy name ... 1Kin 8:43
that they *m* know that this house ... 1Kin 8:43
that they *m* have compassion on ... 1Kin 8:50
That thine eyes *m* be open unto ... 1Kin 8:52
That he *m* incline our hearts unto ... 1Kin 8:58
earth *m* know that the LORD is God ... 1Kin 8:60
that I *m* go to mine own country ... 1Kin 11:21

M

that David my servant *m* have a	1Kin 11:36	1961
that I *m* answer this people	1Kin 12:6	
ye that we *m* answer this people	1Kin 12:9	
that my hand *m* be restored me	1Kin 13:6	
I *m* not return with thee, nor go	1Kin 13:16	3201
that he *m* eat bread and drink	1Kin 13:18	
Israel, that he *m* depart from me	1Kin 15:19	
water in a vessel, that I *m* drink	1Kin 17:10	
two sticks, that I *m* go in	1Kin 17:12	
me and my son, that we *m* eat it	1Kin 17:12	
peradventure we *m* find grass to	1Kin 18:5	
that this people *m* know that thou	1Kin 18:37	
but this thing I *m* not do	1Kin 20:9	3201
that I *m* have it for a garden of	1Kin 21:2	1961
out, and stone him, that he *m* die	1Kin 21:10	
by whom we *m* enquire of the LORD	1Kin 22:8	
persuade Ahab, that he *m* go up	1Kin 22:20	
that we *m* enquire of the LORD by	2Kin 3:11	
with water, that ye *m* drink	2Kin 3:17	
that I *m* run to the man of God,	2Kin 4:22	
for the people, that they *m* eat	2Kin 4:41	
unto the people, that they *m* eat	2Kin 4:42	
Give the people, that they *m* eat	2Kin 4:43	
m I not wash in them, and be clean	2Kin 5:12	
a place there, where we *m* dwell	2Kin 6:2	
and spy where he is, that I *m* send	2Kin 6:13	
open his eyes, that he *m* see	2Kin 6:17	
of these men, that they *m* see	2Kin 6:20	
before them, that they *m* eat	2Kin 6:22	
that we *m* eat him to day, and we	2Kin 6:28	
Give thy son, that we *m* eat him	2Kin 6:29	
now therefore come, that we *m* go	2Kin 7:9	
that I *m* avenge the blood of my	2Kin 9:7	
that they *m* eat their own dung,	2Kin 18:27	
olive and of honey, that ye *m* live	2Kin 18:32	
It *m* be the LORD thy God will	2Kin 19:4	194
all the kingdoms of the earth *m*	2Kin 19:19	
that he *m* sum the silver which is	2Kin 22:4	
evil, that it *m* not grieve me	1Chr 4:10	
that they *m* gather themselves	1Chr 13:2	
that ye *m* bring up the ark of the	1Chr 15:12	
that we *m* give thanks to thy holy	1Chr 16:35	
that thy name *m* be magnified for	1Chr 17:24	
that it *m* be before thee for ever	1Chr 17:27	1961
of them to me, that I *m* know it	1Chr 21:2	
of them, that I *m* do it unto thee	1Chr 21:10	
that I *m* build an altar therein	1Chr 21:22	
that the plague *m* be stayed from	1Chr 21:22	
that they *m* dwell in Jerusalem	1Chr 23:25	
that ye *m* possess this good land,	1Chr 28:8	
and knowledge, that I *m* go out	2Chr 1:10	
That thine eyes *m* be open upon	2Chr 6:20	
That they *m* fear thee, to walk in	2Chr 6:31	
of the earth *m* know thy name	2Chr 6:33	
m know that this house which I	2Chr 6:33	
that my name *m* be there for ever	2Chr 7:16	1961
What advice give ye that we *m*	2Chr 10:9	
that they *m* know my service, and	2Chr 12:8	
the same *m* be a priest of them	2Chr 13:9	1961
Israel, that he *m* depart from me	2Chr 16:3	
by whom we *m* enquire of the LORD	2Chr 18:7	
king of Israel, that he *m* go up	2Chr 18:19	
to them, that they *m* help me	2Chr 28:23	
fierce wrath *m* turn away from us	2Chr 29:10	
of his wrath *m* turn away from you	2Chr 30:8	
That they *m* do according to the	2Chr 35:6	
That search *m* be made in the book	Ezr 4:15	
That they *m* offer sacrifices of	Ezr 6:10	
which *m* judge all the people that	Ezr 7:25	
that our God *m* lighten our eyes,	Ezr 9:8	
that ye *m* be strong, and eat the	Ezr 9:12	
sepulchres, that I *m* build it	Neh 2:5	
that they *m* convey me over till I	Neh 2:7	
that he *m* give me timber to make	Neh 2:8	
the night they *m* be a guard to us	Neh 4:22	1961
up corn for them, that we *m* eat	Neh 5:2	
that they *m* gather together all	Est 2:3	
written that they *m* be destroyed	Est 3:9	
golden sceptre, that he *m* live	Est 4:11	
that he *m* do as Esther hath said	Est 5:5	
that Mordecai *m* be hanged thereon	Est 5:14	
that they *m* array the man withal	Est 6:9	
the king's ring, *m* no man reverse	Est 8:8	
It *m* be that my sons have sinned,	Job 1:5	194
mourn *m* be exalted to safety	Job 5:11	
that I *m* take comfort a little,	Job 10:20	
let me alone, that I *m* speak	Job 13:13	
Turn from him, that he *m* rest	Job 14:6	
that ye *m* know there is a	Job 19:29	
Suffer me that I *m* speak	Job 21:3	
unto God, as he that is wise *m* be	Job 22:2	
He *m* prepare it, but the just	Job 27:17	
that God *m* know mine integrity	Job 31:6	
will speak, that I *m* be refreshed	Job 32:20	
That he *m* withdraw man from his	Job 33:17	
of iniquity *m* hide themselves	Job 34:22	
that Job *m* be tried unto the end	Job 34:36	
Thy wickedness *m* hurt a man as	Job 35:8	
thy righteousness *m* profit the	Job 35:8	
Every man *m* see it	Job 36:25	
man *m* behold it afar off	Job 36:25	
that all men *m* know his work	Job 37:7	
that they *m* do whatsoever he	Job 37:12	
abundance of waters *m* cover thee	Job 38:34	
send lightnings, that they *m* go	Job 38:35	
that the foot *m* crush them	Job 39:15	
that the wild beast *m* break them	Job 39:15	
That I *m* shew forth all thy	Ps 9:14	
that the nations *m* know	Ps 9:20	
that the poor *m* fall by his	Ps 10:10	
of the earth *m* no more oppress	Ps 10:18	
that they *m* privily shoot at the	Ps 11:2	
I *m* tell all my bones	Ps 22:17	
That I *m* publish with the voice	Ps 26:7	
that I *m* dwell in the house of	Ps 27:4	
weeping *m* endure for a night, but	Ps 30:5	
my glory *m* sing praise to thee	Ps 30:12	
many days, that he *m* see good	Ps 34:12	
that I *m* know how frail I am	Ps 39:4	
that I *m* recover strength, before	Ps 39:13	
me up, that I *m* requite them	Ps 41:10	
that ye *m* tell it to the	Ps 48:13	
that he *m* judge his people	Ps 50:4	
which thou hast broken *m* rejoice	Ps 51:8	
that I *m* walk before God in the	Ps 56:13	
that they *m* not see the sun	Ps 58:8	
consume them, that they *m* not be	Ps 59:13	
that it *m* be displayed because of	Ps 60:4	
That thy beloved *m* be delivered	Ps 60:5	
and truth, which *m* preserve him	Ps 61:7	
that I *m* daily perform my vows	Ps 61:8	
That they *m* shoot in secret at	Ps 64:4	
that he *m* dwell in thy courts	Ps 65:4	
That thy way *m* be known upon	Ps 67:2	
That thy foot *m* be dipped in the	Ps 68:23	
that they *m* dwell there, and have	Ps 69:35	
whereunto I *m* continually resort	Ps 71:3	
that I *m* declare all thy works	Ps 73:28	
who *m* stand in thy sight when	Ps 76:7	
that the name of Israel *m* be no	Ps 83:4	
that they *m* seek thy name, O LORD	Ps 83:16	
That men *m* know that thou, whose	Ps 83:18	
where she *m* lay her young, even	Ps 84:3	
that thy people *m* rejoice in thee	Ps 85:6	
that glory *m* dwell in our land	Ps 85:9	
that they which hate me *m* see it	Ps 86:17	
that we *m* apply our hearts unto	Ps 90:12	
that we *m* rejoice and be glad all	Ps 90:14	
that they *m* dwell with me	Ps 101:6	
that I *m* cut off all wicked doers	Ps 101:8	
a bound that they *m* not pass over	Ps 104:9	
that he *m* bring forth food out of	Ps 104:14	
That I *m* see the good of thy	Ps 106:5	
that I *m* rejoice in the gladness	Ps 106:5	
that I *m* glory with thine	Ps 106:5	
that they *m* prepare a city for	Ps 107:36	
which *m* yield fruits of increase	Ps 107:37	
That thy beloved *m* be delivered	Ps 108:6	
that he *m* cut off the memory of	Ps 109:15	
That they *m* know that this is thy	Ps 109:27	
that he *m* give them the heritage	Ps 111:6	
That he *m* set him with princes,	Ps 113:8	
with thy servant, that I *m* live	Ps 119:17	
that I *m* behold wondrous things	Ps 119:18	
that I *m* learn thy commandments	Ps 119:73	
come unto me, that I *m* live	Ps 119:77	
unto thy word, that I *m* live	Ps 119:116	
that I *m* know thy testimonies	Ps 119:125	
was on our side, now *m* Israel say	Ps 124:1	
from my youth, *m* Israel now say	Ps 129:1	
prison, that I *m* praise thy name	Ps 142:7	
That our sons *m* be as plants	Ps 144:12	
that our daughters *m* be as corner	Ps 144:12	
That our garners *m* be full	Ps 144:13	
that our sheep *m* bring forth	Ps 144:13	
That our oxen *m* be strong to	Ps 144:14	
that thy lips *m* keep knowledge	Prov 5:2	
That they *m* keep thee from the	Prov 7:5	
all the things that *m* be desired	Prov 8:11	
That I *m* cause those that love me	Prov 8:21	
that he *m* depart from hell	Prov 15:24	
that his heart *m* discover itself	Prov 18:2	
An inheritance *m* be gotten	Prov 20:21	
That thy trust *m* be in the LORD	Prov 22:19	1961
not what a day *m* bring forth	Prov 27:1	
glad, that I *m* answer him that	Prov 27:11	
any thing whereof it *m* be said	Eccl 1:10	
that he *m* give to him that is	Eccl 2:26	
which he *m* carry away in his hand	Eccl 5:15	
neither *m* he contend with him	Eccl 6:10	3201
who *m* say unto him, What doest	Eccl 8:4	
the spices thereof *m* flow out	Song 4:16	
that we *m* seek him with thee	Song 6:1	
return, that we *m* look upon thee	Song 6:13	
that they *m* be placed alone in	Is 5:8	
that they *m* follow strong drink	Is 5:11	
hasten his work, that we *m* see it	Is 5:19	
nigh and come, that we *m* know it	Is 5:19	
that he *m* know to refuse the evil	Is 7:15	
that widows *m* be their prey, and	Is 10:2	1961
that they *m* rob the fatherless	Is 10:2	
be few, that a child *m* write them	Is 10:19	
that they *m* go into the gates of	Is 13:2	
or tail, branch or rush, *m* do	Is 19:15	
is shut up, that no man *m* come in	Is 24:10	
keepeth the truth *m* enter in	Is 26:2	
that he *m* make peace with me	Is 27:5	
ye *m* cause the weary to rest	Is 28:12	
that he *m* do his work, his	Is 28:21	
that they *m* add sin to sin	Is 30:1	
that it *m* be for the time to come	Is 30:8	1961
that he *m* be gracious unto you,	Is 30:18	
that he *m* have mercy upon you	Is 30:18	
that they *m* eat their own dung,	Is 36:12	
It *m* be the LORD thy God will	Is 37:4	194
m know that thou art the LORD	Is 37:20	
That they *m* see, and know, and	Is 41:20	
that we *m* consider them, and know	Is 41:22	
that we *m* know that ye are gods	Is 41:23	
that we *m* be dismayed, and behold	Is 41:23	
the beginning, that we *m* know	Is 41:26	
and beforetime, that we *m* say	Is 41:26	
and look, ye blind, that ye *m* see	Is 42:18	
that they *m* be justified	Is 43:9	
that ye *m* know and believe me, and	Is 43:10	
that they *m* be ashamed	Is 44:9	
that it *m* remain in the house	Is 44:13	
That they *m* know from the rising	Is 45:6	
and compare me, that we *m* be like	Is 46:5	
they *m* forget, yet will I not	Is 49:15	
give place to me that I *m* dwell	Is 49:20	
hasteneth that he *m* be loosed	Is 51:14	
that I *m* plant the heavens, and	Is 51:16	
soul, Bow down, that we *m* go over	Is 51:23	
ye the LORD while he *m* be found	Is 55:6	
that it *m* give seed to the sower,	Is 55:10	
that men *m* bring unto thee the	Is 60:11	
and that their kings *m* be brought	Is 60:11	
my hands, that I *m* be glorified	Is 60:21	
that the nations *m* tremble at thy	Is 64:2	
that I *m* not destroy them all	Is 65:8	
That ye *m* suck, and be satisfied	Is 66:11	
that ye *m* milk out, and be	Is 66:11	
and give warning, that they *m* hear	Jer 6:10	
that they *m* provoke me to anger	Jer 7:18	
that it *m* be well unto you	Jer 7:23	
wise man, that *m* understand this	Jer 9:12	
that he *m* declare it, for what	Jer 9:12	
mourning women, that they *m* come	Jer 9:17	
cunning women, that they *m* come	Jer 9:17	
that our eyes *m* run down with	Jer 9:18	
them, that they *m* find it so	Jer 10:18	
That I *m* perform the oath which I	Jer 11:5	
that his name *m* be no more	Jer 11:19	
then *m* ye also do good, that are	Jer 13:23	3201
thy face, that thy shame *m* appear	Jer 13:26	
that they *m* not hearken unto me	Jer 16:12	
works, that he *m* go up from us	Jer 21:2	
that I *m* repent me of the evil,	Jer 26:3	
that they *m* serve Nebuchadnezzar	Jer 28:14	
husbands, that they *m* bear sons	Jer 29:6	
that ye *m* be increased there, and	Jer 29:6	
that they *m* continue many days	Jer 32:14	
that they *m* fear me for ever, for	Jer 32:39	
Then *m* also my covenant be broken	Jer 33:21	
that ye *m* live many days in the	Jer 35:7	
It *m* be that the house of Judah	Jer 36:3	194
that they *m* return every man from	Jer 36:3	
that I *m* forgive their iniquity	Jer 36:3	
It *m* be they will present their	Jer 36:7	194
That the LORD thy God *m* shew us	Jer 42:3	
shew us the way wherein we *m* walk	Jer 42:3	
and the thing that we *m* do	Jer 42:3	
that it *m* be well with us, when	Jer 42:6	
that he *m* have mercy upon you, and	Jer 42:12	
that ye *m* know that my words	Jer 44:29	
that he *m* avenge him of his	Jer 46:10	
wings unto Moab, that it *m* flee	Jer 48:9	
that I *m* appoint over her	Jer 49:19	
that he *m* give rest to the land,	Jer 50:34	
that I *m* appoint over her	Jer 50:44	
pain, if so be she *m* be healed	Jer 51:8	
them drunken, that they *m* rejoice	Jer 51:39	
that I *m* comfort thee, O virgin	Lam 2:13	
if so be there *m* be hope	Lam 3:29	
That they *m* want bread and water,	Eze 4:17	
that your altars *m* be laid waste	Eze 6:6	
and your idols *m* be broken	Eze 6:6	
and your images *m* be cut down	Eze 6:6	
your works *m* be abolished	Eze 6:6	
that ye *m* have some that shall	Eze 6:8	1961
That they *m* walk in my statutes,	Eze 11:20	
it *m* be they will consider,	Eze 12:3	194
that they *m* declare all their	Eze 12:16	
that her land *m* be desolate from	Eze 12:19	
That I *m* take the house of Israel	Eze 14:5	
That the house of Israel *m* go no	Eze 14:11	
but that they *m* be my people	Eze 14:11	1961
I *m* be their God, saith the Lord	Eze 14:11	1961
that no man *m* pass through	Eze 14:15	
that they *m* come unto thee on	Eze 16:33	
that they *m* see all thy nakedness	Eze 16:37	
that ye *m* know that I am the LORD	Eze 20:20	
That all flesh *m* know that I the	Eze 21:5	
it is furbished that it *m* glitter	Eze 21:10	
furbished, that it *m* be handled	Eze 21:11	
gates, that their heart *m* faint	Eze 21:15	
of the king of Babylon *m* come	Eze 21:19	
that the sword *m* come to Rabbath	Eze 21:20	
iniquity, that they *m* be taken	Eze 21:23	
midst of it, that her time *m* come	Eze 22:3	
that all women *m* be taught not to	Eze 23:48	
that the brass of it *m* be hot	Eze 24:11	
m burn, and that the filthiness of	Eze 24:11	
of it *m* be molten in it	Eze 24:11	
that the scum of it *m* be consumed	Eze 24:11	
that the Ammonites *m* not be	Eze 25:10	
kings, that they *m* behold thee	Eze 28:17	
that they *m* not be meat for them	Eze 34:10	1961
these slain, that they *m* live	Eze 37:9	
land, that the heathen *m* know me	Eze 38:16	
that they *m* cleanse the land	Eze 39:12	
that ye *m* eat flesh, and drink	Eze 39:17	
that they *m* be ashamed of their	Eze 43:10	

that they *m* keep the whole form ... Eze 43:11
husband, they *m* defile themselves ... Eze 44:25
that he *m* cause the blessing to ... Eze 44:30
that the bath *m* contain the tenth ... Eze 45:11
to the intent that the living *m* ... Dan 4:17
if it *m* be a lengthening of thy ... Dan 4:27
king establisheth *m* be changed ... Dan 6:15
idols, that they *m* be cut off ... Hos 8:4
where is any other that *m* save ... Hos 13:10
good, and not evil, that ye *m* live ... Amos 5:14
it *m* be that the LORD God of ... Amos 5:15 194
for we *m* not make mention of the ... Amos 6:10
moon be gone, that we *m* sell corn ... Amos 8:5
that we *m* set forth wheat, making ... Amos 8:5
That we *m* buy the poor for silver ... Amos 8:6
the door, that the posts *m* shake ... Amos 9:1
That they *m* possess the remnant ... Amos 9:12
of Esau *m* be cut off by slaughter ... Obad 9
that we *m* know for whose cause ... Jonah 1:7
that the sea *m* be calm unto us ... Jonah 1:11
that ye *m* know the righteousness ... Mic 6:5
That they *m* do evil with both ... Mic 7:3
that he *m* run that readeth it ... Hab 2:2
that he *m* set his nest on high, ... Hab 2:9
that he *m* be delivered from the ... Hab 2:9
it *m* be ye shall be hid in the ... Zeph 2:3 194
that I *m* assemble the kingdoms, ... Zeph 3:8
that they *m* all call upon the ... Zeph 3:9
that the fire *m* devour thy cedars ... Zec 11:1
But who *m* abide the day of his ... Mal 3:2
that they *m* offer unto the LORD ... Mal 3:3
that there *m* be meat in mine ... Mal 3:10 1961
me word again, that I *m* come ... Mt 2:8
that they *m* see your good works, ... Mt 5:16
That ye *m* be the children of your ... Mt 5:45 *1096*
that they *m* have glory of men ... Mt 6:2
That thine alms *m* be in secret ... Mt 6:4 *1410*
that they *m* be seen of men ... Mt 6:5
that they *m* appear unto men to ... Mt 6:16
But that ye *m* know that the Son ... Mt 9:6
If I *m* but touch his garment, I ... Mt 9:21
that they *m* go into the villages, ... Mt 14:15
every word *m* be established ... Mt 18:16
that I *m* have eternal life ... Mt 19:16
that these my two sons *m* sit ... Mt 20:21
Lord, that our eyes *m* be opened ... Mt 20:33
outside of them *m* be clean also ... Mt 23:26
That upon you *m* come all the ... Mt 23:35
if this cup *m* not pass away from ... Mt 26:42 *1410*
that I *m* preach there also ... Mk 1:38
But that ye *m* know that the Son ... Mk 2:10
That seeing they *m* see, and not ... Mk 4:12
and hearing they *m* hear, and not ... Mk 4:12
m lodge under the shadow of it ... Mk 4:32 *1410*
that we *m* enter into them ... Mk 5:12
on her, that she *m* be healed ... Mk 5:23
If I *m* touch but his clothes, I ... Mk 5:28
that they *m* go into the country ... Mk 6:36
that ye *m* keep your own tradition ... Mk 7:9
do that I *m* inherit eternal life ... Mk 10:17
him, Grant unto us that we *m* sit ... Mk 10:37
m forgive you your trespasses ... Mk 11:25
bring me a penny, that I *m* see it ... Mk 12:15
ye will ye *m* do them good ... Mk 14:7 *1410*
now from the cross, that we *m* see ... Mk 15:32
of many hearts *m* be revealed ... Lk 2:35
But that ye *m* know that the Son ... Lk 5:24
which enter in *m* see the light ... Lk 8:16
that they *m* go into the towns and ... Lk 9:12
which come in *m* see the light ... Lk 11:33
m be required of this generation ... Lk 11:50
they *m* open unto him immediately ... Lk 12:36
he *m* say unto thee, Friend, go up ... Lk 14:10
in, that my house *m* be filled ... Lk 14:23
they *m* receive me into their ... Lk 16:4
ye fail, they *m* receive you into ... Lk 16:9
that he *m* dip the tip of his ... Lk 16:24
that he *m* testify unto them, lest ... Lk 16:28
him, Make ready wherewith I *m* sup ... Lk 17:8
that I *m* receive my sight ... Lk 18:41
it *m* be they will reverence him ... Lk 20:13 *2481*
that the inheritance *m* be ours ... Lk 20:14 *1096*
which are written *m* be fulfilled ... Lk 21:22
that ye *m* be accounted worthy to ... Lk 21:36
us the passover, that we *m* eat ... Lk 22:8
That ye *m* eat and drink at my ... Lk 22:30
that he *m* sift you as wheat ... Lk 22:31
that we *m* give an answer to them ... Jn 1:22
that his deeds *m* be made manifest ... Jn 3:21
he that reapeth *m* rejoice ... Jn 4:36
than these, that ye *m* marvel ... Jn 5:20
we buy bread, that these *m* eat ... Jn 6:5
every one of them *m* take a little ... Jn 6:7
shewest thou then, that we *m* see ... Jn 6:30
on him, *m* have everlasting life ... Jn 6:40
that a man *m* eat thereof, and not ... Jn 6:50
that thy disciples also *m* see the ... Jn 7:3
that ye *m* know, and believe, that ... Jn 10:38
that I *m* awake him out of sleep ... Jn 11:11
there, to the intent ye *m* believe ... Jn 11:15
also go, that we *m* die with him ... Jn 11:16
that they *m* believe that thou ... Jn 11:42
that ye *m* be the children of ... Jn 12:36 *1096*
that the scripture *m* be fulfilled ... Jn 13:18
ye *m* believe that I am he ... Jn 13:19
where I am, there ye *m* be also ... Jn 14:3 *5600*
that the Father *m* be glorified in ... Jn 14:13
that he *m* abide with you for ever ... Jn 14:16
But that the world *m* know that I ... Jn 14:31
that it *m* bring forth more fruit ... Jn 15:2
in my name, he *m* give it you ... Jn 15:16
ye *m* remember that I told you of ... Jn 16:4
receive, that your joy *m* be full ... Jn 16:24
that thy Son also *m* glorify thee ... Jn 17:1
hast given me, that they *m* be one ... Jn 17:11 *5600*
That they all *m* be one ... Jn 17:21 *5600*
that they also *m* be one in us ... Jn 17:21 *5600*
that the world *m* believe that ... Jn 17:21
that they *m* be one, even as we ... Jn 17:22 *5600*
that they *m* be made perfect in ... Jn 17:23 *5600*
that the world *m* know that thou ... Jn 17:23
that they *m* behold my glory ... Jn 17:24
thou hast loved me *m* be in them ... Jn 17:26 *5600*
that ye *m* know that I find no ... Jn 19:4
That he *m* take part of this ... Acts 1:25
that your sins *m* be blotted out ... Acts 3:19
boldness they *m* speak thy word ... Acts 4:29
wonders *m* be done by the name of ... Acts 4:30
whom we *m* appoint over this ... Acts 6:3
he *m* receive the Holy Ghost ... Acts 8:19
of God *m* be purchased with money ... Acts 8:20
of thine heart *m* be forgiven thee ... Acts 8:22
M we know what this new doctrine, ... Acts 17:19 *1410*
we *m* give an account of this ... Acts 19:40 *1410*
that they *m* shave their heads ... Acts 21:24
all *m* know that those things ... Acts 21:24
captain, *M* I speak unto thee ... Acts 21:37 *1832*
that they *m* set Paul on, and bring ... Acts 23:24
no man *m* deliver me unto them ... Acts 25:11 *1410*
that they *m* receive forgiveness ... Acts 26:18
that I *m* impart unto you some ... Rom 1:11
to the end ye *m* be established ... Rom 1:11
that I *m* be comforted together ... Rom 1:12
Because that which *m* be known of ... Rom 1:19
Let us do evil, that good *m* come ... Rom 3:8
that every mouth *m* be stopped ... Rom 3:19
all the world *m* become guilty ... Rom 3:19
in sin, that grace *m* abound ... Rom 6:1
that we *m* be also glorified ... Rom 8:17
be darkened, that they *m* not see ... Rom 11:10
If by any means I *m* provoke to ... Rom 11:14
mercy they also *m* obtain mercy ... Rom 11:31
that ye *m* prove what is that good ... Rom 12:2
that he *m* eat all things ... Rom 14:2
wherewith one *m* edify another ... Rom 14:19
That ye *m* with one mind and one ... Rom 15:6
that ye *m* abound in hope, through ... Rom 15:13
I have therefore whereof I *m* ... Rom 15:17
That I *m* be delivered from them ... Rom 15:31
m be accepted of the saints ... Rom 15:31
That I *m* come unto you with joy ... Rom 15:32
God, and *m* with you be refreshed ... Rom 15:32
that ye *m* be blameless in the day ... 1Cor 1:8
the Lord, that he *m* instruct him ... 1Cor 2:16
become a fool, that he *m* be wise ... 1Cor 3:18
that the spirit *m* be saved in the ... 1Cor 5:5
that ye *m* be a new lump, as ye ... 1Cor 5:7 *5600*
that ye *m* give yourselves to ... 1Cor 7:5
Lord, how he *m* please the Lord ... 1Cor 7:32
world, how he *m* please his wife ... 1Cor 7:33
that she *m* be holy both in body ... 1Cor 7:34 *5600*
how she *m* please her husband ... 1Cor 7:34
not that I *m* cast a snare upon ... 1Cor 7:35
that ye *m* attend upon the Lord ... 1Cor 7:35
I *m* make the gospel of Christ ... 1Cor 9:18
So run, that ye *m* obtain ... 1Cor 9:24
that ye *m* be able to bear it ... 1Cor 10:13
of many, that they *m* be saved ... 1Cor 10:33
m be made manifest among you ... 1Cor 11:19
but rather that ye *m* prophesy ... 1Cor 14:1
that the church *m* receive ... 1Cor 14:5
There are, it *m* be, so many kinds ... 1Cor 14:10 *5177*
seek that ye *m* excel to the ... 1Cor 14:12
tongue pray that he *m* interpret ... 1Cor 14:13
For ye *m* all prophesy one by one, ... 1Cor 14:31 *1410*
m learn, and all *m* be comforted ... 1Cor 14:31
him, that God *m* be all in all ... 1Cor 15:28 *5600*
it *m* chance of wheat, or of some ... 1Cor 15:37 *5177*
it *m* be that I will abide, yea, ... 1Cor 16:6 *5177*
that ye *m* bring me on my journey ... 1Cor 16:6
see that he *m* be with you without ... 1Cor 16:10 *1096*
in peace, that he *m* come unto me ... 1Cor 16:11
that we *m* be able to comfort them ... 2Cor 1:4
means of many persons thanks *m* be ... 2Cor 1:11
that I *m* not overcharge you all ... 2Cor 2:5
of the power *m* be of God, and not ... 2Cor 4:7 *5600*
absent, we *m* be accepted of him ... 2Cor 5:9
that every one *m* receive the ... 2Cor 5:10
that ye *m* have somewhat to answer ... 2Cor 5:12
so there *m* be a performance also ... 2Cor 8:11
m be a supply for their want ... 2Cor 8:14
also *m* be a supply for your want ... 2Cor 8:14 *1096*
that there *m* be equality ... 2Cor 8:14 *1096*
that, as I said, ye *m* be ready ... 2Cor 9:3
m abound to every good work ... 2Cor 9:8
that I *m* not be bold when I am ... 2Cor 10:2
That I *m* not seem as if I would ... 2Cor 10:9
that I *m* present you as a chaste ... 2Cor 11:2
that I *m* cut off occasion from ... 2Cor 11:12
they *m* be found even as we ... 2Cor 11:12
that I *m* boast myself a little ... 2Cor 11:16
power of Christ *m* rest upon me ... 2Cor 12:9
that they *m* glory in your flesh ... Gal 6:13
m give unto you the spirit of ... Eph 1:17
that ye *m* know what is the hope ... Eph 1:18
ye *m* understand my knowledge in ... Eph 3:4 *1410*
That Christ *m* dwell in your ... Eph 3:17
M be able to comprehend with all ... Eph 3:18
m grow up into him in all things, ... Eph 4:15
that he *m* have to give to him ... Eph 4:28
that it *m* minister grace unto the ... Eph 4:29
That it *m* be well with thee, and ... Eph 6:3
that ye *m* be able to stand ... Eph 6:11
that ye *m* be able to withstand in ... Eph 6:13
that utterance *m* be given unto me ... Eph 6:19
that I *m* open my mouth boldly, to ... Eph 6:19
that therein I *m* speak boldly ... Eph 6:20
that ye also *m* know my affairs ... Eph 6:21
that your love *m* abound yet more ... Phil 1:9
That ye *m* approve things that are ... Phil 1:10
that ye *m* be sincere and without ... Phil 1:10
That your rejoicing *m* be more ... Phil 1:26
I *m* hear of your affairs, that ye ... Phil 1:27
That ye *m* be blameless and ... Phil 2:15
that I *m* rejoice in the day of ... Phil 2:16
that I also *m* be of good comfort, ... Phil 2:19
ye *m* rejoice, and that I *m* be ... Phil 2:28
but dung, that I *m* win Christ, ... Phil 3:8
That I *m* know him, and the power ... Phil 3:10
if that I *m* apprehend that for ... Phil 3:12
that it *m* be fashioned like unto ... Phil 3:21
that *m* abound to your account ... Phil 4:17
that we *m* present every man ... Col 1:28
That I *m* make it manifest, as I ... Col 4:4
that ye *m* know how ye ought to ... Col 4:6
that ye *m* stand perfect and ... Col 4:12
To the end he *m* stablish your ... 1Th 3:13
That ye *m* walk honestly toward ... 1Th 4:12
that ye *m* have lack of nothing ... 1Th 4:12
that ye *m* be counted worthy of ... 2Th 1:5
Christ *m* be glorified in you ... 2Th 1:12
of the Lord *m* have free course ... 2Th 3:1
that we *m* be delivered from ... 2Th 3:2
with him, that he *m* be ashamed ... 2Th 3:14
Satan, that they *m* learn not to ... 1Ti 1:20
that we *m* lead a quiet and ... 1Ti 2:2
thy profiting *m* appear to all ... 1Ti 4:15
charge, that they *m* be blameless ... 1Ti 5:7
that it *m* relieve them that are ... 1Ti 5:16
all, that others also *m* fear ... 1Ti 5:20
that they *m* lay hold on eternal ... 1Ti 6:19
that I *m* be filled with joy ... 2Ti 1:4
m find mercy of the Lord in that ... 2Ti 1:18
that he *m* please him who hath ... 2Ti 2:4
that they *m* also obtain the ... 2Ti 2:10
that they *m* recover themselves ... 2Ti 2:26
That the man of God *m* be perfect ... 2Ti 3:17
I pray God that it *m* not be laid ... 2Ti 4:16
that he *m* be able by sound ... Titus 1:9
that they *m* be sound in the faith ... Titus 1:13
That they *m* teach the young women ... Titus 2:4
of the contrary part *m* be ashamed ... Titus 2:8
that they *m* adorn the doctrine of ... Titus 2:10
faith *m* become effectual by the ... Philem 6
that we *m* obtain mercy, and find ... Heb 4:16
that he *m* offer both gifts and ... Heb 5:1
as I *m* so say, Levi also, who ... Heb 7:9
that he *m* establish the second ... Heb 10:9
which cannot be shaken *m* remain ... Heb 12:27
whereby we *m* serve God acceptably ... Heb 12:28
So that we *m* boldly say, The Lord ... Heb 13:6
that they *m* do it with joy, and ... Heb 13:17
that I *m* be restored to you the ... Heb 13:19
that ye *m* be perfect and entire, ... Jas 1:4
Yea, a man *m* say, Thou hast faith ... Jas 2:18
mouths, that they *m* obey us ... Jas 3:3
that ye *m* consume it upon your ... Jas 4:3
for another, that ye *m* be healed ... Jas 5:16
the word, that ye *m* grow thereby ... 1Pet 2:2
they *m* by your good works, which ... 1Pet 2:12
that with well doing ye *m* put to ... 1Pet 2:15
they also *m* without the word be ... 1Pet 3:1
they *m* be ashamed that falsely ... 1Pet 3:16
For the time past of our life *m* ... 1Pet 4:3
that God in all things *m* be ... 1Pet 4:11
ye *m* be glad also with exceeding ... 1Pet 4:13
that he *m* exalt you in due time ... 1Pet 5:6
about, seeking whom he *m* devour ... 1Pet 5:8
I will endeavour that ye *m* be ... 2Pet 1:15
That ye *m* be mindful of the words ... 2Pet 3:2
be diligent that ye *m* be found of ... 2Pet 3:14
that ye also *m* have fellowship ... 1Jn 1:3
unto you, that your joy *m* be full ... 1Jn 1:4
we *m* have confidence, and not be ... 1Jn 2:28
that we *m* have boldness in the ... 1Jn 4:17
that ye *m* know that ye have ... 1Jn 5:13
that ye *m* believe on the name of ... 1Jn 5:13
that we *m* know him that is true, ... 1Jn 5:20
to face, that our joy *m* be full ... 2Jn 12
into prison, that ye *m* be tried ... Rev 2:10
that they *m* rest from their ... Rev 14:13
That ye *m* eat the flesh of kings, ... Rev 19:18
that they *m* have right to the ... Rev 22:14
m enter in through the gates into ... Rev 22:14

MAYEST {114}

of the garden thou *m* freely eat ... Gen 2:16
but that thou *m* bury thy dead ... Gen 23:6
that thou *m* be a multitude of ... Gen 28:3 1961
that thou *m* inherit the land ... Gen 28:4
that thou *m* come in unto me ... Gen 38:16
that thou *m* bring forth my people ... Ex 3:10
that thou *m* know that there is ... Ex 8:10
to the end thou *m* know that I am ... Ex 8:22

that thou *m* know that there is ... Ex 9:14
that thou *m* know how that the ... Ex 9:29
that thou *m* tell in the ears of ... Ex 10:2
that thou *m* bring the causes unto ... Ex 18:19
that thou *m* teach them ... Ex 24:12
that *m* bring in thither ... Ex 26:33
that *m* thou offer for a freewill ... Lev 22:23
that thou *m* use them for the ... Num 10:2
thou *m* be to us instead of eyes ... Num 10:31 1961
from whence thou *m* see them ... Num 23:13
thou *m* curse me them from thence ... Num 23:27
that thou *m* inherit his land ... Deut 2:31
that thou *m* prolong thy days upon ... Deut 4:40
with thee, and that thou *m* go in ... Deut 6:18
thou *m* not consume them at once, ... Deut 7:22 3201
of whose hills thou *m* dig brass ... Deut 8:9
that thou *m* gather in thy corn, ... Deut 11:14
for thy cattle, that thou *m* eat ... Deut 11:15
Notwithstanding thou *m* kill ... Deut 12:15
Thou *m* not eat within thy gates ... Deut 12:17 3201
thou *m* eat flesh, whatsoever thy ... Deut 12:20
thou *m* not eat the life with the ... Deut 12:23
or thou *m* sell it unto an alien ... Deut 14:21
that thou *m* learn to fear the ... Deut 14:23
a foreigner thou *m* exact it again ... Deut 15:3
that thou *m* remember the day when ... Deut 16:3
Thou *m* not sacrifice the passover ... Deut 16:5 3201
thou follow, that thou *m* live ... Deut 16:20
thou *m* not set a stranger over ... Deut 17:15 3201
for thou *m* eat of them, and thou ... Deut 20:19 1961
thou *m* not hide thyself ... Deut 22:3 3201
that thou *m* prolong thy days ... Deut 22:7
a stranger thou *m* lend upon usury ... Deut 23:20
then thou *m* eat grapes thy fill ... Deut 23:24
then thou *m* pluck the ears with ... Deut 23:25
that thou *m* be an holy people ... Deut 26:19 1961
that thou *m* go in unto the land ... Deut 27:3
that thou *m* fear this glorious and ... Deut 28:58
all thy soul, that thou *m* live ... Deut 30:6
in thy heart, that thou *m* do it ... Deut 30:14
his judgments, that thou *m* live ... Deut 30:16
That thou *m* love the LORD thy God ... Deut 30:20
that thou *m* obey his voice, and ... Deut 30:20
that thou *m* cleave unto him ... Deut 30:20
that thou *m* dwell in the land ... Deut 30:20
that thou *m* observe to do ... Josh 1:7
that thou *m* prosper whithersoever ... Josh 1:7
that thou *m* observe to do ... Josh 1:8
then *m* thou do to them as thou ... Judg 9:33
that thou *m* go with us, and fight ... Judg 11:8
on your way, that thou *m* go home ... Judg 19:9
away, that thou *m* go in peace ... 1Sa 20:13
that thou *m* do to him as it shall ... 1Sa 24:4
that thou *m* make known unto me ... 1Sa 28:15
that thou *m* have strength, when ... 1Sa 28:22
that thou *m* reign over all that ... 2Sa 3:21
then *m* thou for me defeat the ... 2Sa 15:34
that thou *m* bring them down ... 2Sa 22:28
that thou *m* save thine own life, ... 1Kin 1:12
that thou *m* prosper in all that ... 1Kin 2:3
that thou *m* take away the ... 1Kin 2:31
that thou *m* hearken unto the ... 1Kin 8:29
that thou *m* recover him of his ... 2Kin 5:6
him, Thou *m* certainly recover ... 2Kin 8:10
that thou *m* keep the law of the ... 1Chr 22:12
and thou *m* add thereto ... 1Chr 22:14
that thou *m* judge my people, over ... 2Chr 1:11
that thou *m* carry me out of the ... 2Chr 18:33
That thou *m* buy speedily with ... Ezr 7:17
that thou *m* hear the prayer of ... Neh 1:6
that thou *m* be their king, ... Neh 6:6 1933
me, that thou *m* be righteous ... Job 40:8
in a time when thou *m* be found ... Ps 32:6
whom thou *m* make princes in all ... Ps 45:16
That thou *m* give him rest from ... Ps 94:13
that thou *m* give them their meat ... Ps 104:27
with thee, that thou *m* be feared ... Ps 130:4
That thou *m* walk in the way of ... Prov 2:20
That thou *m* regard discretion, and ... Prov 5:2
that thou *m* be wise in thy latter ... Prov 19:20
that thou *m* be remembered ... Is 23:16
thou, that thou *m* be justified ... Is 43:26
that thou *m* know that I, the LORD ... Is 45:3
profit, if so be thou *m* prevail ... Is 47:12
that thou *m* be my salvation unto ... Is 49:6 1961
That thou *m* say to the prisoners, ... Is 49:9
wickedness, that thou *m* be saved ... Jer 4:14
among my people, that thou *m* know ... Jer 6:27
cause, that thou *m* be bound up ... Jer 30:13
That thou *m* bear thine own shame, ... Eze 16:54
m be confounded in all that thou ... Eze 16:54
That thou *m* remember, and be ... Eze 16:63
that thou *m* look on their ... Hab 2:15
that thou *m* eat the passover ... Mk 14:12
that thou *m* be delivered from him ... Lk 12:58
for thou *m* be no longer steward ... Lk 16:2 *1410*
with all thine heart, thou *m* ... Acts 8:37 *1832*
m take knowledge of all these ... Acts 24:8
Because that thou *m* understand ... Acts 24:11
but if thou *m* be made free, use ... 1Cor 7:21 *1410*
thou *m* live long on the earth ... Eph 6:3
that thou *m* know how thou ... 1Ti 3:15
all things that thou *m* prosper ... 3Jn 2
in the fire, that thou *m* be rich ... Rev 3:18
that thou *m* be clothed, and that ... Rev 3:18
with eyesalve, that thou *m* see ... Rev 3:18

MAZZAROTH *(maz'-za-roth)* {1} *The twelve signs of the Zodiac.*
thou bring forth *M* in his season ... Job 38:32 4216

ME See APPENDIX.

MEADOW {2}
and they fed in a *m* ... Gen 41:2 260
and they fed in a *m* ... Gen 41:18 260

MEADOWS {1}
even out of the *m* of Gibeah ... Judg 20:33 4629

MEAH *(me'-ah)* {2} *A tower on Jerusalem's wall.*
the tower of *M* they sanctified it ... Neh 3:1 3968
of Hananeel, and the tower of *M* ... Neh 12:39 3968

MEAL {12}
three measures of fine *m* ... Gen 18:6 7058,5560
part of an ephah of barley *m* ... Num 5:15 7058
and threescore measures of *m* ... 1Kin 4:22 7058
but an handful of *m* in a barrel ... 1Kin 17:12 7058
The barrel of *m* shall not waste, ... 1Kin 17:14 7058
And the barrel of *m* wasted not ... 1Kin 17:16 7058
But he said, Then bring *m* ... 2Kin 4:41 7058
on mules, and on oxen, and meat, *m* ... 1Chr 12:40 7058
Take the millstones, and grind *m* ... Is 47:2 7058
the bud shall yield no *m* ... Hos 8:7 7058
and hid in three measures of *m* ... Mt 13:33 *224*
and hid in three measures of *m* ... Lk 13:21 *224*

MEALTIME {1}
m come thou hither, and eat of ... Ruth 2:14 6256,400

MEAN {22}
What *m* these seven ewe lambs ... Gen 21:29
What *m* ye by this service ... Ex 12:26
What *m* the testimonies, and the ... Deut 6:20
What *m* ye by these stones ... Josh 4:6
come, saying, What *m* these stones ... Josh 4:21
came to pass in the *m* while ... 1Kin 18:45 5704,3541
he shall not stand before *m* men ... Prov 22:29 2823
the *m* man boweth down, and the ... Is 2:9 120
What *m* ye that ye beat my people ... Is 3:15
the *m* man shall be brought down, ... Is 5:15 120
and the sword, not of a *m* man ... Is 31:8 120
Know ye not what these things *m* ... Eze 17:12
What *m* ye, that ye use this ... Eze 18:2
the rising from the dead should *m* ... Mk 9:10 *2076*
In the *m* time, when there were ... Lk 12:1
In the *m* while his disciples ... Jn 4:31 *3342*
vision which he had seen should *m* ... Acts 10:17 *1498*
what these things *m* ... Acts 17:20 *2309,1511*
What *m* ye to weep and to break ... Acts 21:13 *4160*
Cilicia, a citizen of no *m* city ... Acts 21:39 *767*
their thoughts the *m* while ... Rom 2:15 *3342*
For I *m* not that other men be ... 2Cor 8:13

MEANEST {4}
What *m* thou by all this drove ... Gen 33:8
unto Ziba, What *m* thou by these ... 2Sa 16:2
not shew us what thou *m* by these ... Eze 37:18
and said unto him, What *m* thou ... Jonah 1:6

MEANETH {8}
what *m* the heat of this great ... Deut 29:24
What *m* the noise of this great ... 1Sa 4:6
What *m* the noise of this tumult ... 1Sa 4:14
What *m* then this bleating of the ... 1Sa 15:14
Howbeit he *m* not so, neither doth ... Is 10:7 1819
But go ye and learn what that *m* ... Mt 9:13 *2076*
But if ye had known what this *m* ... Mt 12:7 *2076*
one to another, What *m* this ... Acts 2:12 *2309,1511*

MEANING {3}
the vision, and sought for the *m* ... Dan 8:15 998
m to sail by the coasts of Asia ... Acts 27:2 *3195*
if I know not the *m* of the voice ... 1Cor 14:11 *1411*

MEANS {35}
that will by no *m* clear the ... Ex 34:7
by no *m* clearing the guilty, ... Num 14:18
broken by the *m* of the pransings ... Judg 5:22
by what *m* we may prevail against ... Judg 16:5
yet doth he devise *m*, that his ... 2Sa 14:14 4284
they bring them out by their *m* ... 1Kin 10:29 3027
if by any *m* he be missing, then ... 1Kin 20:39
the kings of Syria, by their *m* ... 2Chr 1:17 3027
by this *m* thou shalt have no ... Ezr 4:16 6903
can by any *m* redeem his brother ... Ps 49:7
For by *m* of a whorish woman a man ... Prov 6:26 1157
the priests bear rule by their *m* ... Jer 5:31 3027
this hath been by your *m* ... Mal 1:9 3027
shalt by no *m* come out thence ... Mt 5:26 *3361*
they sought *m* to bring him in, and ... Lk 5:18
m he that was possessed of the ... Lk 8:36 *4459*
nothing shall by any *m* hurt you ... Lk 10:19 *3364*
But by what *m* he now seeth, we ... Jn 9:21 *4459*
by what *m* he is made whole ... Acts 4:9
I must by all *m* keep this feast ... Acts 18:21 *3843*
if by any *m* they might attain to ... Acts 27:12 *4458*
if by any *m* now at length I might ... Rom 1:10 *4458*
If by any *m* I may provoke to ... Rom 11:14 *4458*
But take heed lest by any *m* this ... 1Cor 8:9 *4458*
that I might by all *m* save some ... 1Cor 9:22 *3843*
lest that by any *m*, when I have ... 1Cor 9:27 *4458*
gift bestowed upon us by the *m* of ... 2Cor 1:11
But I fear, lest by any *m* ... 2Cor 11:3 *4458*
lest by any *m* I should run, or ... Gal 2:2 *4458*
If by any *m* I might attain unto ... Phil 3:11 *4458*
lest by some *m* the tempter have ... 1Th 3:5 *4458*
Let no man deceive you by any *m* ... 2Th 2:3 *5158*
give you peace always by all *m* ... 2Th 3:16 *5158*
that by *m* of death, for the ... Heb 9:15 *1096*
m of those miracles which he had ... Rev 13:14

MEANT {3}
but God *m* it unto good, to bring ... Gen 50:20 2803
and asked what these things *m* ... Lk 15:26 *1498*
pass by, he asked what it *m* ... Lk 18:36 *1498*

MEARAH *(me'-a-rah)* {1} *A place near Sidon.*
M that is beside the Sidonians, ... Josh 13:4 4632

MEASURE {69}
of the curtains shall have one *m* ... Ex 26:2 4060
curtains shall be all of one *m* ... Ex 26:8 4060
in meteyard, in weight, or in *m* ... Lev 19:35 4884
ye shall *m* from without the city ... Num 35:5 4058
they shall *m* unto the cities ... Deut 21:2 4058
perfect and just *m* shalt thou have ... Deut 25:15 374
about two thousand cubits by *m* ... Josh 3:4 4060
both the cherubims were of one *m* ... 1Kin 6:25 4060
of them had one casting, one *m* ... 1Kin 7:37 4060
a *m* of fine flour be sold for a ... 2Kin 7:1 5429
So a *m* of fine flour was sold for ... 2Kin 7:16 5429
a *m* of fine flour for a shekel, ... 2Kin 7:18 5429
is fried, and for all manner of *m* ... 1Chr 23:29 4884
the first *m* was threescore cubits ... 2Chr 3:3 4060
The *m* thereof is longer than the ... Job 11:9 4055
and he weigheth the waters by *m* ... Job 28:25 4060
the *m* of my days, what it is ... Ps 39:4 4060
them tears to drink in great *m* ... Ps 80:5 7991
and opened her mouth without *m* ... Is 5:14 2706
In *m*, when it shooteth forth, ... Is 27:8 5432
the dust of the earth in a *m* ... Is 40:12 7991
therefore will I *m* their former ... Is 65:7 4058
but I will correct thee in *m* ... Jer 30:11 4941
of thee, but correct thee in *m* ... Jer 46:28 4941
the *m* of thy covetousness ... Jer 51:13 520
Thou shalt drink also water by *m* ... Eze 4:11 4884
and they shall drink water by *m* ... Eze 4:16 4884
they three were of one *m* ... Eze 40:10 4060
the posts had one *m* on this side ... Eze 40:10 4060
after the *m* of the first gate ... Eze 40:21 4060
were after the *m* of the gate that ... Eze 40:22 4060
about within and without, by *m* ... Eze 41:17 4060
and let them *m* the pattern ... Eze 43:10 4058
of this *m* shalt thou ... Eze 45:3 4060
shalt thou *m* the length of five ... Eze 45:3 4058
and the bath shall be of one *m* ... Eze 45:11 8506
the *m* thereof shall be after the ... Eze 45:11 4971
these four corners were of one *m* ... Eze 46:22 4060
east side ye shall *m* from Hauran ... Eze 47:18 4058
the scant *m* that is abominable ... Mic 6:10 374
To *m* Jerusalem, to see what is ... Zec 2:2 4058
and with what *m* ye mete, it shall ... Mt 7:2 *3358*
ye up then the *m* of your fathers ... Mt 23:32 *3358*
with what *m* ye mete, it shall be ... Mk 4:24 *3358*
amazed in themselves beyond *m* ... Mk 6:51 *4053*
And were beyond *m* astonished ... Mk 7:37 *5249*
And they were astonished out of *m* ... Mk 10:26 *4057*
good *m*, pressed down, and shaken ... Lk 6:38 *3358*
For with the same *m* that ye mete ... Lk 6:38 *3358*
not the Spirit by *m* unto him ... Jn 3:34 *3358*
dealt to every man the *m* of faith ... Rom 12:3 *3358*
that we were pressed out of *m* ... 2Cor 1:8 *5236*
not boast of things without our *m* ... 2Cor 10:13 *280*
but according to the *m* of the ... 2Cor 10:13 *3358*
a *m* to reach even unto you ... 2Cor 10:13 *3358*
not ourselves beyond our *m* ... 2Cor 10:14
boasting of things without our *m* ... 2Cor 10:15 *280*
more abundant, in stripes above *m* ... 2Cor 11:23 *5234*
m through the abundance of the ... 2Cor 12:7
lest I should be exalted above *m* ... 2Cor 12:7
how that beyond *m* I persecuted ... Gal 1:13 *5236*
to the *m* of the gift of Christ ... Eph 4:7 *3358*
unto the *m* of the stature of the ... Eph 4:13 *3358*
working in the *m* of every part ... Eph 4:16 *3358*
A *m* of wheat for a penny, and ... Rev 6:6 *5518*
m the temple of God, and the altar ... Rev 11:1 *3354*
the temple leave out, and *m* it not ... Rev 11:2 *3354*
had a golden reed to *m* the city ... Rev 21:15 *3354*
according to the *m* of a man ... Rev 21:17 *3358*

MEASURED {46}
he *m* six measures of barley, and ... Ruth 3:15 4058
m them with a line, casting them ... 2Sa 8:2 4058
two lines *m* he to put to death ... 2Sa 8:2 4058
Who hath *m* the waters in the ... Is 40:12 4058
If heaven above can be *m*, and the ... Jer 31:37 4058
neither the sand of the sea *m* ... Jer 33:22 4058
so he *m* the breadth of the ... Eze 40:5 4058
m the threshold of the gate, ... Eze 40:6 4058
He *m* also the porch of the gate ... Eze 40:8 4058
Then *m* he the porch of the gate, ... Eze 40:9 4058
he *m* the breadth of the entry of ... Eze 40:11 4058
He *m* then the gate from the roof ... Eze 40:13 4058
Then he *m* the breadth from the ... Eze 40:19 4058
he *m* the length thereof, and the ... Eze 40:20 4058
he *m* from gate to gate an hundred ... Eze 40:23 4058
he *m* the posts thereof and the ... Eze 40:24 4058
he *m* from gate to gate toward the ... Eze 40:27 4058
he *m* the south gate according to ... Eze 40:28 4058
he *m* the gate according to these ... Eze 40:32 4058
m it according to these measures ... Eze 40:35 4058
So he *m* the court, an hundred ... Eze 40:47 4058
m each post of the porch, five ... Eze 40:48 4058
m the posts, six cubits broad on ... Eze 41:1 4058
he *m* the length thereof, forty ... Eze 41:2 4058
m the post of the door, two ... Eze 41:3 4058
So he *m* the length thereof, ... Eze 41:4 4058
After he *m* the wall of the house, ... Eze 41:5 4058
So he *m* the house, an hundred ... Eze 41:13 4058
he *m* the length of the building ... Eze 41:15 4058
the east, and *m* it round about ... Eze 42:15 4058

He *m* the east side with the ... Eze 42:16 4058
He *m* the north side, five hundred ... Eze 42:17 4058
He *m* the south side, five hundred ... Eze 42:18 4058
m five hundred reeds with the ... Eze 42:19 4058
He *m* it by the four sides ... Eze 42:20 4058
he *m* a thousand cubits, and he ... Eze 47:3 4058
Again he *m* a thousand, and brought ... Eze 47:4 4058
Again he *m* a thousand, and brought ... Eze 47:4 4058
Afterward he *m* a thousand ... Eze 47:5 4058
which cannot be *m* nor numbered ... Hos 1:10 4058
He stood, and *m* the earth ... Hab 3:6 4128
it shall be *m* to you again ... Mt 7:2 *488*
ye mete, it shall be *m* to you ... Mk 4:24 *3354*
withal it shall be *m* to you again ... Lk 6:38 *488*
he *m* the city with the reed, ... Rev 21:16 *3354*
he *m* the wall thereof, an hundred ... Rev 21:17 *3354*

MEASURES {39}

quickly three *m* of fine meal ... Gen 18:6 5429
not have in thine house divers *m* ... Deut 25:14 374
it, he measured six *m* of barley ... Ruth 3:15
These six *m* of barley gave he me ... Ruth 3:17
five *m* of parched corn, and an ... 1Sa 25:18 5429
day was thirty *m* of fine flour ... 1Kin 4:22 3734
and threescore *m* of meal ... 1Kin 4:22 3734
m of wheat for food to his ... 1Kin 5:11 3734
and twenty *m* of pure oil ... 1Kin 5:11 3734
to the *m* of hewed stones, sawed ... 1Kin 7:9 4060
after the *m* of hewed stones, and ... 1Kin 7:11 4060
as would contain two *m* of seed ... 1Kin 18:32 5429
two *m* of barley for a shekel, in ... 2Kin 7:1 5429
two *m* of barley for a shekel, ... 2Kin 7:16 5429
Two *m* of barley for a shekel, and ... 2Kin 7:18 5429
twenty thousand *m* of beaten wheat ... 2Chr 2:10 3734
and twenty thousand *m* of barley ... 2Chr 2:10 3734
and ten thousand *m* of wheat ... 2Chr 27:5 3734
and to an hundred *m* of wheat ... Ezr 7:22 3734
Who hath laid the *m* thereof ... Job 38:5 4461
Divers weights, and divers *m* ... Prov 20:10 374
lot, the portion of thy *m* from me ... Jer 13:25 4055
thereof according to these *m* ... Eze 40:24 4060
south gate according to these *m* ... Eze 40:28 4060
thereof, according to these *m* ... Eze 40:29 4060
the gate according to these *m* ... Eze 40:32 4060
were according to these *m* ... Eze 40:33 4060
measured it according to these *m* ... Eze 40:35 4060
these are the *m* of the altar ... Eze 43:13 4060
And these shall be the *m* thereof ... Eze 48:16 4060
four thousand and five hundred *m* ... Eze 48:30 4060
four thousand and five hundred *m* ... Eze 48:33 4060
round about eighteen thousand *m* ... Eze 48:35
one came to an heap of twenty *m* ... Hag 2:16
took, and hid in three *m* of meal ... Mt 13:33 *4568*
took and hid in three *m* of meal ... Lk 13:21 *4568*
And he said, An hundred *m* of oil ... Lk 16:6 *943*
And he said, An hundred *m* of wheat ... Lk 16:7 *2884*
three *m* of barley for a penny ... Rev 6:6 *5518*

MEASURING {11}

the *m* line shall yet go forth ... Jer 31:39 4060
of flax in his hand, and a *m* reed ... Eze 40:3 4060
in the man's hand a *m* reed of six ... Eze 40:5 4060
made an end of *m* the inner house ... Eze 42:15 4060
the east side with the *m* reed ... Eze 42:16 4060
with the *m* reed round about ... Eze 42:16 4060
with the *m* reed round about ... Eze 42:17 4060
hundred reeds, with the *m* reed ... Eze 42:18 4060
hundred reeds with the *m* reed ... Eze 42:19 4060
a man with a *m* line in his hand ... Zec 2:1 4060
but they *m* themselves by ... 2Cor 10:12 *3354*

MEAT {290}

to you it shall be for *m* ... Gen 1:29 402
have given every green herb for *m* ... Gen 1:30 402
that liveth shall be *m* for you ... Gen 9:3 402
there was set *m* before him to eat ... Gen 24:33
And make me savoury *m*, such as I ... Gen 27:4
me venison, and make me savoury *m* ... Gen 27:7
them savoury *m* for thy father ... Gen 27:9
and his mother made savoury *m* ... Gen 27:14
And she gave the savoury *m* ... Gen 27:17
And he also had made savoury *m* ... Gen 27:31
m for his father by the way ... Gen 45:23 4202
to the *m* offering of the morning ... Ex 29:41
burnt sacrifice, nor *m* offering ... Ex 30:9
burnt offering and the *m* offering ... Ex 40:29
when any will offer a *m* offering ... Lev 2:1
the remnant of the *m* offerings ... Lev 2:3
of a *m* offering baken in the oven ... Lev 2:4
if thy oblation be a *m* offering ... Lev 2:5
it is a *m* offering ... Lev 2:6
if thy oblation be a *m* offering ... Lev 2:7
thou shalt bring the *m* offering ... Lev 2:8
the *m* offering a memorial thereof ... Lev 2:9
the *m* offering shall be Aaron's ... Lev 2:10
No *m* offering, which ye shall ... Lev 2:11
every oblation of thy *m* offering ... Lev 2:13
to be lacking from thy *m* offering ... Lev 2:13
if thou offer a *m* offering of thy ... Lev 2:14
thou shalt offer for the *m* ... Lev 2:14
it is a *m* offering ... Lev 2:15
be the priest's, as a *m* offering ... Lev 5:13
this is the law of the *m* offering ... Lev 6:14
of the flour of the *m* offering ... Lev 6:15
which is upon the *m* offering ... Lev 6:15
flour for a *m* offering perpetual ... Lev 6:20
the baken pieces of the *m* ... Lev 6:21
For every *m* offering for the ... Lev 6:23
all the *m* offering that is baken ... Lev 7:9
every *m* offering, mingled with ... Lev 7:10
of the *m* offering, and of the sin ... Lev 7:37
a *m* offering mingled with oil ... Lev 9:4
And he brought the *m* offering ... Lev 9:17
left, Take the *m* offering that ... Lev 10:12
Of all *m* which may be eaten, that ... Lev 11:34 400
of fine flour for a *m* offering ... Lev 14:10
the *m* offering upon the altar ... Lev 14:20
mingled with oil for a *m* offering ... Lev 14:21
offering, with the *m* offering ... Lev 14:31
they shall eat of his *m* ... Lev 22:11 3899
she shall eat of her father's *m* ... Lev 22:13 3899
the *m* offering thereof shall be ... Lev 23:13
ye shall offer a new *m* offering ... Lev 23:16
the LORD, with their *m* offering ... Lev 23:18
a *m* offering, a sacrifice, and ... Lev 23:37
of the land shall be *m* for you ... Lev 25:6 402
all the increase thereof be *m* ... Lev 25:7 398
incense, and the daily *m* offering ... Num 4:16
their *m* offering, and their drink ... Num 6:15
shall offer also his *m* offering ... Num 6:17
mingled with oil for a *m* offering ... Num 7:13
mingled with oil for a *m* offering ... Num 7:19
mingled with oil for a *m* offering ... Num 7:25
mingled with oil for a *m* offering ... Num 7:31
mingled with oil for a *m* offering ... Num 7:37
mingled with oil for a *m* offering ... Num 7:43
mingled with oil for a *m* offering ... Num 7:49
mingled with oil for a *m* offering ... Num 7:55
mingled with oil for a *m* offering ... Num 7:61
mingled with oil for a *m* offering ... Num 7:67
mingled with oil for a *m* offering ... Num 7:73
mingled with oil for a *m* offering ... Num 7:79
twelve, with their *m* offering ... Num 7:87
young bullock with his *m* offering ... Num 8:8
a *m* offering of a tenth deal of ... Num 15:4
thou shalt prepare for a *m* ... Num 15:6
a *m* offering of three tenth deals ... Num 15:9
the LORD, with his *m* offering ... Num 15:24
every *m* offering of theirs, and ... Num 18:9
ephah of flour for a *m* offering ... Num 28:5
as the *m* offering of the morning, ... Num 28:8
deals of flour for a *m* offering ... Num 28:9
deals of flour for a *m* offering ... Num 28:12
deals of flour for a *m* offering ... Num 28:12
for a *m* offering unto one lamb ... Num 28:13
their *m* offering shall be of ... Num 28:20
the *m* of the sacrifice made by ... Num 28:24 3899
when ye bring a new *m* offering ... Num 28:26
their *m* offering of flour mingled ... Num 28:28
his *m* offering, (they shall be ... Num 28:31
their *m* offering shall be of ... Num 29:3
his *m* offering, and the daily ... Num 29:6
his *m* offering, and their drink ... Num 29:6
their *m* offering shall be of ... Num 29:9
the *m* offering of it, and their ... Num 29:11
their *m* offering shall be of ... Num 29:14
his *m* offering, and his drink ... Num 29:16
their *m* offering and their drink ... Num 29:18
the *m* offering thereof, and their ... Num 29:19
their *m* offering and their drink ... Num 29:21
his *m* offering, and his drink ... Num 29:22
Their *m* offering and their drink ... Num 29:24
his *m* offering, and his drink ... Num 29:25
their *m* offering and their drink ... Num 29:27
his *m* offering, and his drink ... Num 29:28
their *m* offering and their drink ... Num 29:30
his *m* offering, and his drink ... Num 29:31
their *m* offering and their drink ... Num 29:33
his *m* offering, and his drink ... Num 29:34
Their *m* offering and their drink ... Num 29:37
his *m* offering, and his drink ... Num 29:38
for your *m* offerings, and for your ... Num 29:39
Ye shall buy *m* of them for money, ... Deut 2:6 400
Thou shalt sell me *m* for money ... Deut 2:28 400
that they be not trees for *m* ... Deut 20:20 3978
thy carcase shall be *m* unto all ... Deut 28:26 3978
burnt offering or *m* offering ... Josh 22:23
for *m* offerings, or for ... Josh 22:29
gathered their *m* under my table ... Judg 1:7
took a kid with a *m* offering ... Judg 13:19
a *m* offering at our hands, ... Judg 13:23
Out of the eater came forth *m* ... Judg 14:14 3978
fail to sit with the king at *m* ... 1Sa 20:5 398
the king sat him down to eat *m* ... 1Sa 20:24 3899
cometh not the son of Jesse to *m* ... 1Sa 20:27 3899
did eat no *m* the second day of ... 1Sa 20:34 3899
to eat *m* while it was yet day ... 2Sa 3:35 3899
him a mess of *m* from the king ... 2Sa 11:8
it did eat of his own *m*, and drank ... 2Sa 12:3 6595
sister Tamar come, and give me *m* ... 2Sa 13:5 3899
dress the *m* in my sight, that I ... 2Sa 13:5 1279
Amnon's house, and dress him *m* ... 2Sa 13:7 1279
Bring the *m* into the chamber, ... 2Sa 13:10 1279
m offerings, and the fat of the ... 1Kin 8:64
m offerings, and the fat of the ... 1Kin 8:64
the *m* of his table, and the ... 1Kin 10:5 3978
the strength of that *m* forty days ... 1Kin 19:8 396
when the *m* offering was offered, ... 2Kin 3:20
his *m* offering, and poured his ... 2Kin 16:13
and the evening *m* offering ... 2Kin 16:15
his *m* offering, with the burnt ... 2Kin 16:15
their *m* offering, and their drink ... 2Kin 16:15
and on mules, and on oxen, and *m* ... 1Chr 12:40 3978
and the wheat for the *m* offering ... 1Chr 21:23
for the fine flour for *m* offering ... 1Chr 23:29
the *m* offerings, and the fat ... 2Chr 7:7
the *m* of his table, and the ... 2Chr 9:4 3978
and *m*, and drink, and oil, unto them ... Ezr 3:7 3978
lambs, with their *m* offerings ... Ezr 7:17
and for the continual *m* offering ... Neh 10:33
they laid the *m* offerings ... Neh 13:5
house of God, with the *m* offering ... Neh 13:9
to touch are as my sorrowful *m* ... Job 6:7 3899
and the mouth taste his *m* ... Job 12:11 400
Yet his *m* in his bowels is turned ... Job 20:14 3899
There shall none of his *m* be left ... Job 20:21 400
and juniper roots for their *m* ... Job 30:4 3899
bread, and his soul dainty *m* ... Job 33:20 3978
words, as the mouth tasteth *m* ... Job 34:3 398
he giveth *m* in abundance ... Job 36:31 400
God, they wander for lack of *m* ... Job 38:41 400
My tears have been my *m* day ... Ps 42:3 3899
us like sheep appointed for *m* ... Ps 44:11 3978
Let them wander up and down for *m* ... Ps 59:15 398
They gave me also gall for my *m* ... Ps 69:21 1267
gavest him to be *m* to the people ... Ps 74:14 3978
heart by asking *m* for their lust ... Ps 78:18 400
he sent them *m* to the full ... Ps 78:25 6720
but while their *m* was yet in ... Ps 78:30 400
be *m* unto the fowls of the heaven ... Ps 79:2 3978
prey, and seek their *m* from God ... Ps 104:21 400
give them their *m* in due season ... Ps 104:27 400
soul abhorreth all manner of *m* ... Ps 107:18 400
He hath given *m* unto them that ... Ps 111:5 2964
givest them their *m* in due season ... Ps 145:15 400
Provideth her *m* in the summer ... Prov 6:8 3899
for they are deceitful *m* ... Prov 23:3 3899
a fool when he is filled with *m* ... Prov 30:22 3899
prepare their *m* in the summer ... Prov 30:25 3899
giveth *m* to her household, and a ... Prov 31:15 2964
thou hast offered a *m* offering ... Is 57:6
corn to be *m* for thine enemies ... Is 62:8 3978
and dust shall be the serpent's *m* ... Is 65:25 3899
of this people shall be *m* for the ... Jer 7:33 3978
be *m* for the fowls of heaven ... Jer 16:4 3978
m offerings, and incense, and ... Jer 17:26
carcases will I give to be *m* for ... Jer 19:7 3978
and to kindle *m* offerings ... Jer 33:18
m unto the fowls of the heaven ... Jer 34:20 3978
things for *m* to relieve the soul ... Lam 1:11 400
their *m* to relieve their souls ... Lam 1:19 400
they were their *m* in the ... Lam 4:10 1262
thy *m* which thou shalt eat shall ... Eze 4:10 3978
My *m* also which I gave thee, fine ... Eze 16:19 3899
I have given thee for *m* to the ... Eze 29:5 402
they became *m* to all the beasts ... Eze 34:5 402
my flock became *m* to every beast ... Eze 34:8 402
that they may not be *m* for them ... Eze 34:10 402
the *m* offering, and the sin ... Eze 42:13
They shall eat the *m* offering ... Eze 44:29
for a *m* offering, and for a burnt ... Eze 45:15
m offerings, and drink offerings, ... Eze 45:17
the *m* offering, and the burnt ... Eze 45:17
he shall prepare a *m* offering of ... Eze 45:24
and according to the *m* offering ... Eze 45:25
the *m* offering shall be an ephah ... Eze 46:5
the *m* offering for the lambs as ... Eze 46:5
And he shall prepare a *m* offering ... Eze 46:7
in the solemnities the *m* offering ... Eze 46:11
thou shalt prepare a *m* offering ... Eze 46:14
a *m* offering continually by a ... Eze 46:14
the *m* offering, and the oil, every ... Eze 46:15
they shall bake the *m* offering ... Eze 46:20
side, shall grow all trees for *m* ... Eze 47:12 3978
the fruit thereof shall be for *m* ... Eze 47:12 3978
a daily provision of the king's *m* ... Dan 1:5 6598
with the portion of the king's *m* ... Dan 1:8 6598
king, who hath appointed your *m* ... Dan 1:10 3978
of the portion of the king's *m* ... Dan 1:13 6598
eat the portion of the king's *m* ... Dan 1:15 6598
took away the portion of their *m* ... Dan 1:16 6598
much, and in it was *m* for all ... Dan 4:12 4203
much, and in it was *m* for all ... Dan 4:21 4203
of his *m* shall destroy him ... Dan 11:26 6598
their jaws, and I laid *m* unto them ... Hos 11:4 398
The *m* offering and the drink ... Joel 1:9
for the *m* offering and the drink ... Joel 1:13
Is not the *m* cut off before our ... Joel 1:16 400
even a *m* offering and a drink ... Joel 2:14
your *m* offerings, I will not ... Amos 5:22
is fat, and their *m* plenteous ... Hab 1:16 3978
and the fields shall yield no *m* ... Hab 3:17 400
or wine, or oil, or any *m* ... Hag 2:12 3978
and the fruit thereof, even his *m* ... Mal 1:12 400
that there may be *m* in mine house ... Mal 3:10 2964
his *m* was locusts and wild honey ... Mt 3:4 *5160*
Is not the life more than *m* ... Mt 6:25 *5160*
as Jesus sat at *m* in the house ... Mt 9:10
the workman is worthy of his *m* ... Mt 10:10 *5160*
and them which sat with him at *m* ... Mt 14:9
they took up of the broken *m* that ... Mt 15:37
to give them *m* in due season ... Mt 24:45 *5160*
I was an hungred, and ye gave me *m* ... Mt 25:35 *5315*
an hungred, and ye gave me no *m* ... Mt 25:42 *5315*
it on his head, as he sat at *m* ... Mt 26:7
as Jesus sat at *m* in his house ... Mk 2:15
they took up of the broken *m* that ... Mk 8:8
Simon the leper, as he sat at *m* ... Mk 14:3
unto the eleven as they sat at *m* ... Mk 16:14
and he that hath *m*, let him do ... Lk 3:11 *1033*
house, and sat down to *m* ... Lk 7:36
sat at *m* in the Pharisee's house ... Lk 7:37
they that sat at *m* with him began ... Lk 7:49
and he commanded to give her *m* ... Lk 8:55 *5315*
buy *m* for all this people ... Lk 9:13 *1033*
and he went in, and sat down to *m* ... Lk 11:37

M

The life is more than *m*, and the... Lk 12:23 *5160*
and make them to sit down to *m*... Lk 12:37
their portion of *m* in due season... Lk 12:42 *4620*
of them that sit at *m* with thee... Lk 14:10
at *m* with him heard these things... Lk 14:15
the field, Go and sit down to *m*... Lk 17:7
is greater, he that sitteth at *m*... Lk 22:27
is not he that sitteth at *m*... Lk 22:27
to pass, as he sat at *m* with them... Lk 24:30
unto them, Have ye here any *m*... Lk 24:41 *1034*
gone away unto the city to buy *m*... Jn 4:8 *5160*
I have *m* to eat that ye know not... Jn 4:32 *1035*
My *m* is to do the will of him... Jn 4:34 *1033*
not for the *m* which perisheth... Jn 6:27 *1035*
but for that *m* which endureth... Jn 6:27 *1035*
For my flesh is *m* indeed, and my... Jn 6:55 *1035*
them, Children, have ye any *m*... Jn 21:5 *4371*
did eat their *m* with gladness... Acts 2:46 *5160*
And when he had received *m*... Acts 9:19 *5160*
he set *m* before them, and rejoiced... Acts 16:34 *5132*
Paul besought them all to take *m*... Acts 27:33 *5160*
I pray you to take some *m*... Acts 27:34 *5160*
cheer, and they also took some *m*... Acts 27:36 *5160*
thy brother be grieved with thy *m*... Rom 14:15 *1033*
Destroy not him with thy *m*... Rom 14:15 *1033*
For the kingdom of God is not *m*... Rom 14:17 *1035*
For *m* destroy not the work of God... Rom 14:20 *1033*
fed you with milk, and not with *m*... 1Cor 3:2 *1033*
But *m* commendeth us not to God... 1Cor 8:8 *1033*
sit at *m* in the idol's temple... 1Cor 8:10
if *m* make my brother to offend, I... 1Cor 8:13 *1033*
did all eat the same spiritual *m*... 1Cor 10:3 *1033*
no man therefore judge you in *m*... Col 2:16 *1035*
need of milk, and not of strong *m*... Heb 5:12 *5160*
But strong *m* belongeth to them... Heb 5:14 *5160*
morsel of *m* sold his birthright... Heb 12:16 *1035*

MEATS {8}
neither desire thou his dainty *m*... Prov 23:6
into the draught, purging all *m*... Mk 7:19 *1033*
abstain from *m* offered to idols... Acts 15:29
M for the belly, and the belly for... 1Cor 6:13 *1033*
for the belly, and the belly for *m*... 1Cor 6:13 *1033*
and commanding to abstain from *m*... 1Ti 4:3 *1033*
Which stood only in *m* and drinks,... Heb 9:10 *1033*
not with *m*, which have not... Heb 13:9 *1033*

MEBUNNAI *(me-bun'-nahee)* {1} See SIBBECHAI. *A "mighty man" of David.*
Anethothite, *M* the Hushathite,... 2Sa 23:27 4012

MECHERATHITE *(me-ker'-ath-ite)* {1} *A family name of a "mighty man" of David.*
Hepher the *M*, Ahijah the Pelonite... 1Chr 11:36 4382

MECONAH See MEKONAH.

MEDAD *(me'-dad)* {2} *An elder of Israel.*
Eldad, and the name of the other *M*... Num 11:26 4312
M do prophesy in the camp... Num 11:27 4312

MEDAN *(me'-dan)* {2} *A son of Abraham.*
bare him Zimran, and Jokshan, and *M*... Gen 25:2 4091
she bare Zimran, and Jokshan, and *M*... 1Chr 1:32 4091

MEDDLE {6}
M not with them... Deut 2:5 1624
them not, nor *m* with them... Deut 2:19 1624
why shouldest thou *m* to thy hurt... 2Kin 14:10 1624
shouldest thou *m* to thine hurt... 2Chr 25:19 1624
therefore *m* not with him that... Prov 20:19 6148
m not with them that are given to... Prov 24:21 6148

MEDDLED {1}
contention, before it be *m* with... Prov 17:14 1566

MEDDLETH {1}
m with strife belonging not to... Prov 26:17 5674

MEDDLING {2}
forbear thee from *m* with God... 2Chr 35:21
but every fool will be *m*... Prov 20:3 1566

MEDE *(meed)* {1} See MEDES, MEDIAN. *An inhabitant of Media.*
in the first year of Darius the *M*... Dan 11:1 4075

MEDEBA *(med'-e-bah)* {5} *A city in Reuben.*
Nophah, which reacheth unto *M*... Num 21:30 4311
and all the plain of *M* unto Dibon... Josh 13:9 4311
the river, and all the plain by *M*... Josh 13:16 4311
who came and pitched before *M*... 1Chr 19:7 4311
shall howl over Nebo, and over *M*... Is 15:2 4311

MEDES *(meeds)* {14}
Gozan, and in the cities of the *M*... 2Kin 17:6 4074
Gozan, and in the cities of the *M*... 2Kin 18:11 4074
that is in the province of the *M*... Ezr 6:2 4074
the laws of the Persians and the *M*... Est 1:19 4074
I will stir up the *M* against them... Is 13:17 4074
Elam, and all the kings of the *M*... Jer 25:25 4074
the spirit of the kings of the *M*... Jer 51:11 4074
nations with the kings of the *M*... Jer 51:28 4074
is divided, and given to the *M*... Dan 5:28 4076
according to the law of the *M*... Dan 6:8 4076
according to the law of the *M*... Dan 6:12 4076
O king, that the law of the *M*... Dan 6:15 4076
Ahasuerus, of the seed of the *M*... Dan 9:1 4074
Parthians, and *M*, and Elamites, and... Acts 2:9 *3370*

MEDIA *(me'-de-ah)* {6} See MADAI, MEDE, MEDIAN. *A country north of Persia.*
the power of Persia and *M*, the... Est 1:3 4074
the seven princes of Persia and *M*... Est 1:14 4074
M say this day unto all the... Est 1:18 4074
the chronicles of the kings of *M*... Est 10:2 4074
besiege, O *M*... Is 21:2 4074
two horns are the kings of *M*... Dan 8:20 4074

MEDIAN *(me'-de-an)* {1} See MEDE. *A native of Media.*
Darius the *M* took the kingdom,... Dan 5:31 4077

MEDIATOR {17}
by angels in the hand of a *m*... Gal 3:19 *3316*
Now a *m* is not a... Gal 3:20 *3316*
is not a *m* of one... Gal 3:20
one *m* between God and men, the man... 1Ti 2:5 *3316*
he is the *m* of a better covenant... Heb 8:6 *3316*
he is the *m* of the new testament... Heb 9:15 *3316*
to Jesus the *m* of the new... Heb 12:24 *3316*

MEDICINE {2}
A merry heart doeth good like a *m*... Prov 17:22 1456
meat, and the leaf thereof for *m*... Eze 47:12 8644

MEDICINES {2}
thou hast no healing *m*... Jer 30:13 7499
in vain shalt thou use many *m*... Jer 46:11 7499

MEDITATE {14}
Isaac went out to *m* in the field... Gen 24:63 7742
but thou shalt *m* therein day... Josh 1:8 1897
and in his law doth he *m* day... Ps 1:2 1897
m on thee in the night watches... Ps 63:6 1897
I will *m* also of all thy work, and... Ps 77:12 1897
I will *m* in thy precepts, and have... Ps 119:15 7878
thy servant did *m* in thy statutes... Ps 119:23 7878
and I will *m* in thy statutes... Ps 119:48 7878
but I will *m* in thy precepts... Ps 119:78 7878
that I might *m* in thy word... Ps 119:148 7878
I *m* on all thy works... Ps 143:5 1897
Thine heart shall *m* terror... Is 33:18 1897
not to *m* before what ye shall... Lk 21:14 *4304*
M upon these things... 1Ti 4:15 *3191*

MEDITATION {6}
consider my *m*... Ps 5:1 1901
the *m* of my heart, be acceptable... Ps 19:14 1902
the *m* of my heart shall be of... Ps 49:3 1900
My *m* of him shall be sweet... Ps 104:34 7879
it is my *m* all the day... Ps 119:97 7881
for thy testimonies are my *m*... Ps 119:99 7881

MEEK {17}
(Now the man Moses was very *m*... Num 12:3 6035
The *m* shall eat and be satisfied... Ps 22:26 6035
The *m* will he guide in judgment... Ps 25:9 6035
the *m* will he teach his way... Ps 25:9 6035
But the *m* shall inherit the earth... Ps 37:11 6035
to save all the *m* of the earth... Ps 76:9 6035
The LORD lifteth up the *m*... Ps 147:6 6035
beautify the *m* with salvation... Ps 149:4 6035
equity for the *m* of the earth... Is 11:4 6035
The *m* also shall increase their... Is 29:19 6035
to preach good tidings unto the *m*... Is 61:1 6035
and turn aside the way of the *m*... Amos 2:7 6035
all ye *m* of the earth, which have... Zeph 2:3 6035
Blessed are the *m*... Mt 5:5 *4239*
for I am *m* and lowly in heart... Mt 11:29 *4235*
thy King cometh unto thee, *m*... Mt 21:5 *4239*
even the ornament of a *m*... 1Pet 3:4 *4239*

MEEKNESS {14}
because of truth and *m* and... Ps 45:4 6037
seek righteousness, seek *m*... Zeph 2:3 6038
or in love, and in the spirit of *m*... 1Cor 4:21 *4236*
Paul myself beseech you by the *m*... 2Cor 10:1 *4236*
M, temperance... Gal 5:23 *4236*
such an one in the spirit of *m*... Gal 6:1 *4236*
With all lowliness and *m*, with... Eph 4:2 *4236*
kindness, humbleness of mind, *m*... Col 3:12 *4236*
faith, love, patience, *m*... 1Ti 6:11 *4236*
In *m* instructing those that... 2Ti 2:25 *4236*
shewing all *m* unto all men... Titus 3:2 *4236*
receive with *m* the engrafted word... Jas 1:21 *4240*
his works with *m* of wisdom... Jas 3:13 *4240*
of the hope that is in you with *m*... 1Pet 3:15 *4240*

MEET {132}
I will make him an help *m* for him... Gen 2:18 5828
was not found an help *m* for him... Gen 2:20 5828
m him after his return from the... Gen 14:17 7125
he ran to *m* them from the tent... Gen 18:2 7125
Lot seeing them rose up to *m* them... Gen 19:1 7125
And the servant ran to *m* her... Gen 24:17 7125
that walketh in the field to *m* us... Gen 24:65 7125
son, that he ran to *m* him... Gen 29:13 7125
and Leah went out to *m* him... Gen 30:16 7125
Esau, and also he cometh to *m* thee... Gen 32:6 7125
Esau ran to *m* him, and embraced... Gen 33:4 7125
went up to *m* Israel his father,... Gen 46:29 7125
behold, he cometh forth to *m* thee... Ex 4:14 7125
Go into the wilderness to *m* Moses... Ex 4:27 7125
Moses said, It is not *m* so to do... Ex 8:26 3559
went out to *m* his father in law... Ex 18:7 7125
out of the camp to *m* with God... Ex 19:17 7125
If thou *m* thine enemy's ox or his... Ex 23:4 6293
And there I will *m* with thee... Ex 25:22 3259
where I will *m* you, to speak... Ex 29:42 3259
there I will *m* with the children... Ex 29:43 3259
where I will *m* with thee... Ex 30:6 3259
where I will *m* with thee... Ex 30:36 3259
where I will *m* with you... Num 17:4 3259
he went out to *m* him unto a city... Num 22:36 7125
the LORD will come to *m* me... Num 23:3 7125
while I *m* the LORD yonder... Num 23:15 7136
went forth to *m* them without the... Num 31:13 7125
all that are *m* for the war... Deut 3:18 1121
mountain, lest the pursuers *m* you... Josh 2:16 6293
for the journey, and go to *m* them... Josh 9:11 7125
And Jael went out to *m* Sisera... Judg 4:18 7125
Sisera, Jael came out to *m* him... Judg 4:22 7125
m for the necks of them that take... Judg 5:30
and they came up to *m* them... Judg 6:35 7125
of the doors of my house to *m* me... Judg 11:31 7125
came out to *m* him with timbrels... Judg 11:34 7125
saw him, he rejoiced to *m* him... Judg 19:3 7125
that they *m* thee not in any other... Ruth 2:22 6293
there shall *m* thee three men... 1Sa 10:3 4672
that thou shalt *m* a company of... 1Sa 10:5 6293
and Saul went out to *m* him... 1Sa 13:10 7125
early to *m* Saul in the morning... 1Sa 15:12 7125
and came and drew nigh to *m* David... 1Sa 17:48 7125
the army to *m* the Philistine... 1Sa 17:48 7125
to *m* king Saul, with tabrets,... 1Sa 18:6 7125
which sent thee this day to *m* me... 1Sa 25:32 7125
thou hadst hasted and come to *m* me... 1Sa 25:34 7125
and they went forth to *m* David... 1Sa 30:21 7125
to *m* the people that were with... 1Sa 30:21 7125
of Saul came out to *m* David... 2Sa 6:20 7125
it unto David, he sent to *m* them... 2Sa 10:5 7125
came to *m* him with his coat rent... 2Sa 15:32 7125
to Gilgal, to go to *m* the king... 2Sa 19:15 7125
the men of Judah to *m* king David... 2Sa 19:16 7125
to go down to *m* my lord the king... 2Sa 19:20 7125
of Saul came down to *m* the king... 2Sa 19:24 7125
come to Jerusalem to *m* the king... 2Sa 19:25 7125
he came down to *m* me at Jordan... 1Kin 2:8 7125
And the king rose up to *m* her... 1Kin 2:19 7125
So Obadiah went to *m* Ahab... 1Kin 18:16 7125
and Ahab went to *m* Elijah... 1Kin 18:16 7125
go down to *m* Ahab king of Israel,... 1Kin 21:18 7125
go up to *m* the messengers of the... 2Kin 1:3 7125
him, There came a man up to *m* us... 2Kin 1:6 7125
man was he which came up to *m* you... 2Kin 1:7 7125
And they came to *m* him, and bowed... 2Kin 2:15 7125
to *m* her, and say unto her, Is it... 2Kin 4:26 7125
if thou *m* any man, salute him not... 2Kin 4:29 4672
Wherefore he went again to *m* him... 2Kin 4:31 7125
down from the chariot to *m* him... 2Kin 5:21 7125
again from his chariot to *m* thee... 2Kin 5:26 7125
m the man of God, and enquire of... 2Kin 8:8 7125
So Hazael went to *m* him, and took... 2Kin 8:9 7125
an horseman, and send to *m* them... 2Kin 9:17 7125
went one on horseback to *m* him... 2Kin 9:18 7125
the son of Rechab coming to *m* him... 2Kin 10:15 7125
king Ahaz went to Damascus to *m*... 2Kin 16:10 7125
And David went out to *m* them... 1Chr 12:17 6440
And he sent to *m* them... 1Chr 19:5 7125
And he went out to *m* Asa, and said... 2Chr 15:2 6440
Hanani the seer went out to *m* him... 2Chr 19:2 6440
it was not *m* for us to see the... Ezr 4:14 749
let us *m* together in some one of... Neh 6:2 3259
Let us *m* together in the house of... Neh 6:10 3259
which were *m* to be given her, out... Est 2:9 7200
They *m* with darkness in the... Job 5:14 6298
Surely it is *m* to be said unto... Job 34:31
he goeth on to *m* the armed men... Job 39:21 7125
Therefore came I forth to *m* thee... Prov 7:15 7125
that withholdeth more than is *m*... Prov 11:24 3476
bear robbed of her whelps *m* a man... Prov 17:12 6298
The rich and poor *m* together... Prov 22:2 6298
and the deceitful man *m* together... Prov 29:13 6298
Isaiah, Go forth now to *m* Ahaz... Is 7:3 7125
for thee to *m* thee at thy coming... Is 14:9 7125
m with the wild beasts of the... Is 34:14 6298
I will not *m* thee as a man... Is 47:3 6293
me as seemeth good and *m* unto you... Jer 26:14 3477
it unto whom it seemed *m* unto me... Jer 27:5 3474
went forth from Mizpah to *m* them... Jer 41:6 7125
One post shall run to *m* another... Jer 51:31 7125
and one messenger to *m* another... Jer 51:31 7125
Is it *m* for any work... Eze 15:4 6743
was whole, it was *m* for no work... Eze 15:5 6213
shall it be *m* yet for any work... Eze 15:5 6213
I will *m* them as a bear that is... Hos 13:8 6298
unto thee, prepare to *m* thy God... Amos 4:12 7125
another angel went out to *m* him... Zec 2:3 7125
therefore fruits *m* for repentance... Mt 3:8 *514*
whole city came out to *m* Jesus... Mt 8:34 *4877*
and said, It is not *m* to take the... Mt 15:26 *2570*
went forth to *m* the bridegroom... Mt 25:1 *529*
go ye out to *m* him... Mt 25:6 *529*
for it is not *m* to take the... Mk 7:27 *2570*
there shall *m* you a man bearing a... Mk 14:13 *528*
to *m* him that cometh against him... Lk 14:31 *528*
It was *m* that we should make... Lk 15:32 *1163*
the city, there shall a man *m* you... Lk 22:10 *4876*
trees, and went forth to *m* him... Jn 12:13 *5222*
do works *m* for repentance... Acts 26:20 *514*
they came to *m* us as far as Appii... Acts 28:15 *529*
of their error which was *m*... Rom 1:27 *1163*
that am not *m* to be called an... 1Cor 15:9 *2425*
if it be *m* that I go also, they... 1Cor 16:4 *514*
Even as it is *m* for me to think... Phil 1:7 *1342*
which hath made us *m* to be... Col 1:12 *2427*
clouds, to *m* the Lord in the air... 1Th 4:17 *529*
for you, brethren, as it is *m*... 2Th 1:3 *514*
m for the master's use, and... 2Ti 2:21 *2173*
bringeth forth herbs *m* for them... Heb 6:7 *2111*
Yea, I think it *m*, as long as I... 2Pet 1:13 *1342*

MEETEST {2}
m of your master's sons, and set... 2Kin 10:3 3477
Thou *m* him that rejoiceth and... Is 64:5 6293

MEETETH {3}
When Esau my brother *m* thee .... Gen 32:17 6298
when he *m* him, he shall slay him .... Num 35:19 6293
slay the murderer, when he *m* him .... Num 35:21 6293

MEETING {2}
was afraid at the *m* of David 1Sa 21:1 7125
it is iniquity, even the solemn *m* .... Is 1:13 6116

MEGIDDO *(me-ghid'-do)* {11} See MEGIDDON. *A city on the plain of Jezreel.*
the king of *M*, one .... Josh 12:21 4023
towns, and the inhabitants of *M* .... Josh 17:11 4023
towns, nor the inhabitants of *M* .... Judg 1:27 4023
in Taanach by the waters of *M* .... Judg 5:19 4023
to him pertained Taanach and *M* 1Kin 4:12 4023
wall of Jerusalem, and Hazor, and *M* 1Kin 9:15 4023
And he fled to *M*, and died there 2Kin 9:27 4023
and he slew him at *M*, when he had 2Kin 23:29 4023
him in a chariot dead from *M* 2Kin 23:30 4023
towns, Taanach and her towns, *M* 1Chr 7:29 4023
came to fight in the valley of *M* 2Chr 35:22 4023

MEGIDDON *(me-ghid'-don)* {1} See ARMAGEDDON, MEGIDDO. *Same as Megiddo.*
of Hadadrimmon in the valley of *M* .... Zec 12:11 4023

MEHETABEEL *(me-het'-a-be-el)* {1} See MEHETABEL. *Father of Delaiah.*
the son of Delaiah the son of *M* .... Neh 6:10 4105

MEHETABEL *(me-het'-a-bel)* {2} See MEHETABEEL. *Wife of Hadar.*
and his wife's name was *M*, the .... Gen 36:39 4105
and his wife's name was *M*, the 1Chr 1:50 4105

MEHIDA *(me-hi'-dah)* {2} *A family of exiles.*
of Bazlith, the children of *M* .... Ezr 2:52 4240
of Bazlith, the children of *M* .... Neh 7:54 4240

MEHIR *(me'-hur)* {1} *A son of Chelub.*
the brother of Shuah begat *M* 1Chr 4:11 4243

MEHOLATHITE *(me-ho'-lath-ite)* {2} *An inhabitant of a city in Issachar.*
given unto Adriel the *M* to wife 1Sa 18:19 4259
Adriel the son of Barzillai the *M* 2Sa 21:8 4259

MEHUJAEL *(me-hu'-ja-el)* {2} *Son of Irad.*
and Irad begat *M* .... Gen 4:18 4232
and *M* begat Methusael .... Gen 4:18 4232

MEHUMAN *(me-hu'-man)* {1} *A servant of King Ahasuerus.*
merry with wine, he commanded *M* .... Est 1:10 4104

MEHUNIM *(me-hu'-nim)* {1} See MAONITE, MEHUNIMS, MEUNIM. *A family of exiles.*
of Asnah, the children of *M* .... Ezr 2:50 4586

MEHUNIMS *(me-hu'-nims)* {1} See MEHUNIM. *A people who lived in Arabia.*
that dwelt in Gur-baal, and the *M* 2Chr 26:7 4586

ME-JARKON *(me-jar'-kon)* {1} *A city in Dan.*
And *M*, and Rakkon, with the border .... Josh 19:46 4313

MEKERATHITE See MECHERATHITE.

MEKONAH *(me-ko'-nah)* {1} *A city in Judah.*
And at Ziklag, and at *M*, and in the .... Neh 11:28 4368

MELATIAH *(mel-a-ti'-ah)* {1} *A repairer of Jerusalem's wall.*
them repaired *M* the Gibeonite .... Neh 3:7 4424

MELCHI *(mel'-ki)* {2} See MELCHI-SHUA, MELCHIZEDEK.
1. Son of Janna; ancestor of Jesus.
of Levi, which was the son of *M* .... Lk 3:24 *3197*
2. Son of Addi; ancestor of Jesus.
Which was the son of *M*, which was .... Lk 3:28 *3197*

MELCHIAH *(mel-ki'-ah)* {1} See MALCHIAH. *Father of Pashur.*
sent unto him Pashur the son of *M* .... Jer 21:1 4441

MELCHISEDEC *(mel-kis'-e-dek)* {9} See MELCHIZEDEK. *Greek form of Melchizedek.*
for ever after the order of *M* .... Heb 5:6 *3198*
high priest after the order of *M* .... Heb 5:10 *3198*
for ever after the order of *M* .... Heb 6:20 *3198*
For this *M*, king of Salem, priest .... Heb 7:1 *3198*
of his father, when *M* met him .... Heb 7:10 *3198*
should rise after the order of *M* .... Heb 7:11 *3198*
of *M* there ariseth another priest .... Heb 7:15 *3198*
for ever after the order of *M* .... Heb 7:17 *3198*
for ever after the order of *M* .... Heb 7:21 *3198*

MELCHI-SHUA *(mel'-ki-shu'-ah)* {2} See MALCHI-SHUA. *A son of King Saul.*
were Jonathan, and Ishui, and *M* 1Sa 14:49 4444
slew Jonathan, and Abinadab, and *M* 1Sa 31:2 4444

MELCHIZEDEK *(mel-kiz'-e-dek)* {2} See MELCHISEDEC. *King and priest of Salem.*
M king of Salem brought forth .... Gen 14:18 4442
for ever after the order of *M* .... Ps 110:4 4442

MELEA *(mel'-e-ah)* {1} *Son of Menan; an ancestor of Jesus.*
Which was the son of *M*, which was .... Lk 3:31 *3190*

MELECH *(me'-lek)* {2} See EBED-MELECH, HAMMELECH, NATHAN-MELECH, REGEM-MELECH. *A son of Micah.*
sons of Micah were, Pithon, and *M* 1Chr 8:35 4429
sons of Micah were, Pithon, and *M* 1Chr 9:41 4429

MELICHU See MELICU.

MELICU *(mel'-i-cu)* {1} See MALLUCH. *A priest.*
Of *M*, Jonathan .... Neh 12:14 4409

MELITA *(mel'-i-tah)* {1} *A Mediterranean island.*
knew that the island was called *M* .... Acts 28:1 *3194*

MELODY {4}
make sweet *m*, sing many songs, ... Is 23:16 5059
thanksgiving, and the voice of *m* .... Is 51:3 2172
will not hear the *m* of thy viols .... Amos 5:23 2172
making *m* in your heart to the .... Eph 5:19 *5567*

MELONS {1}
the cucumbers, and the *m*, and the .... Num 11:5 20

MELT {17}
of Canaan shall *m* away .... Ex 15:15 4127
these things, our hearts did *m* .... Josh 2:11 4549
me made the heart of the people *m* .... Josh 14:8 4529
heart of a lion, shall utterly *m* 2Sa 17:10 4549
Let them *m* away as waters which .... Ps 58:7 3988
gnash with his teeth, and *m* away .... Ps 112:10 4549
and every man's heart shall *m* .... Is 13:7 4549
Egypt shall *m* in the midst of it .... Is 19:1 4549
of hosts, Behold, I will *m* them .... Jer 9:7 6884
and every heart shall *m*, and all .... Eze 21:7 4549
to blow the fire upon it, to *m* it .... Eze 22:20 5413
I will leave you there, and *m* you .... Eze 22:20 5413
toucheth the land, and it shall *m* .... Amos 9:5 4127
wine, and all the hills shall *m* .... Amos 9:13 4127
quake at him, and the hills *m* .... Nah 1:5 4127
shall *m* with fervent heat 2Pet 3:10 *3089*
shall *m* with fervent heat 2Pet 3:12 *5080*

MELTED {13}
and when the sun waxed hot, it *m* .... Ex 16:21 4549
passed over, that their heart *m* .... Josh 5:1 4549
the hearts of the people *m* .... Josh 7:5 4549
The mountains *m* from before the .... Judg 5:5 5140
and, behold, the multitude *m* away 1Sa 14:16 4127
it is *m* in the midst of my bowels .... Ps 22:14 4549
he uttered his voice, the earth *m* .... Ps 46:6 4127
The hills *m* like wax at the .... Ps 97:5 4549
their soul is *m* because of .... Ps 107:26 4127
shall be *m* with their blood .... Is 34:3 4549
ye shall be *m* in the midst .... Eze 22:21 5413
As silver is *m* in the midst of .... Eze 22:22 2046
so shall ye be *m* in the midst .... Eze 22:22 5413

MELTETH {7}
As a snail which *m*, let every one .... Ps 58:8 8557
as wax *m* before the fire, so let .... Ps 68:2 4549
My soul *m* for heaviness .... Ps 119:28 1811
sendeth out his word, and *m* them .... Ps 147:18 4549
The workman *m* a graven image, and .... Is 40:19 5258
the founder *m* in vain .... Jer 6:29 6884
and the heart *m*, and the knees .... Nah 2:10 4549

MELTING {1}
As when the *m* fire burneth, the .... Is 64:2 2003

MELZAR *(mel'-zar)* {2} *Babylonian officer charged with Daniel and his companions.*
Then said Daniel to *M*, whom the .... Dan 1:11 4453
Thus *M* took away the portion of .... Dan 1:16 4453

MEMBER {6}
or hath his privy *m* cut off .... Deut 23:1
For the body is not one *m* 1Cor 12:14 *3196*
And if they were all one *m* 1Cor 12:19 *3196*
And whether one *m* suffer, all the 1Cor 12:26 *3196*
or one *m* be honoured, all the 1Cor 12:26 *3196*
Even so the tongue is a little *m* .... Jas 3:5 *3196*

MEMBERS {32}
and all my *m* are as a shadow .... Job 17:7 3338
in thy book all my *m* were written .... Ps 139:16
that one of thy *m* should perish .... Mt 5:29 *3196*
that one of thy *m* should perish .... Mt 5:30 *3196*
yield ye your *m* as instruments of .... Rom 6:13 *3196*
dead, and your *m* as instruments of .... Rom 6:13 *3196*
your *m* servants to uncleanness .... Rom 6:19 *3196*
even so now yield your *m* servants .... Rom 6:19 *3196*
did work in our *m* to bring forth .... Rom 7:5 *3196*
But I see another law in my *m* .... Rom 7:23 *3196*
the law of sin which is in my *m* .... Rom 7:23 *3196*
For as we have many *m* in one body .... Rom 12:4 *3196*
all *m* have not the same office .... Rom 12:4 *3196*
every one *m* one of another .... Rom 12:5 *3196*
your bodies are the *m* of Christ 1Cor 6:15 *3196*
shall I then take the *m* of Christ 1Cor 6:15 *3196*
and make them the *m* of an harlot 1Cor 6:15 *3196*
the body is one, and hath many *m* 1Cor 12:12 *3196*
all the *m* of that one body, being 1Cor 12:12 *3196*
But now hath God set the *m* every 1Cor 12:18 *3196*
But now are they many *m*, yet but 1Cor 12:20 *3196*
much more those *m* of the body 1Cor 12:22 *3196*
those *m* of the body, which we 1Cor 12:23
but that the *m* should have the 1Cor 12:25 *3196*
suffer, all the *m* suffer with it 1Cor 12:26 *3196*
all the *m* rejoice with it 1Cor 12:26 *3196*
of Christ, and *m* in particular 1Cor 12:27 *3196*
for we are *m* one of another .... Eph 4:25 *3196*
For we are *m* of his body, of his .... Eph 5:30 *3196*
Mortify therefore your *m* which .... Col 3:5 *3196*
so is the tongue among our *m* .... Jas 3:6 *3196*
of your lusts that war in your *m* .... Jas 4:1 *3196*

MEMORIAL {32}
this is my *m* unto all generations .... Ex 3:15 2143
day shall be unto you for a *m* .... Ex 12:14 2146
for a *m* between thine eyes, that .... Ex 13:9 2146
Write this for a *m* in a book .... Ex 17:14 2146
of the ephod for stones of *m* unto .... Ex 28:12 2146
upon his two shoulders for a *m* .... Ex 28:12 2146
place, for a *m* before the LORD .... Ex 28:29 2146
that it may be a *m* unto the .... Ex 30:16 2146
for a *m* to the children of Israel .... Ex 39:7 2146
burn the *m* of it upon the altar .... Lev 2:2 234
the meat offering a *m* thereof .... Lev 2:9 234
the priest shall burn the *m* of it .... Lev 2:16 234
even a *m* thereof, and burn it on .... Lev 5:12 234
a sweet savour, even the *m* of it .... Lev 6:15 234
a *m* of blowing of trumpets, an .... Lev 23:24 2146
it may be on the bread for a *m* .... Lev 24:7 234
of jealousy, an offering of *m* .... Num 5:15 2146
the offering of *m* in her hands .... Num 5:18 2146
the offering, even the *m* thereof .... Num 5:26 234
be to you for a *m* before your God .... Num 10:10 2146
To be a *m* unto the children of .... Num 16:40 2146
for a *m* for the children of .... Num 31:54 2146
these stones shall be for a *m* .... Josh 4:7 2146
have no portion, nor right, nor *m* .... Neh 2:20 2146
nor the *m* of them perish from .... Est 9:28 2143
their *m* is perished with them .... Ps 9:6 2143
and thy *m*, O LORD, throughout all .... Ps 135:13 2143
the LORD is his *m* .... Hos 12:5 2143
for a *m* in the temple of the LORD .... Zec 6:14 2146
hath done, be told for a *m* of her .... Mt 26:13 *3422*
shall be spoken of for a *m* of her .... Mk 14:9 *3422*
are come up for a *m* before God .... Acts 10:4 *3422*

MEMORY {6}
off the *m* of them from the earth .... Ps 109:15 2143
utter the *m* of thy great goodness .... Ps 145:7 2143
The *m* of the just is blessed .... Prov 10:7 2143
for the *m* of them is forgotten .... Eccl 9:5 2143
and made all their *m* to perish .... Is 26:14 2143
if ye keep in *m* what I preached 1Cor 15:2

MEMPHIS *(mem'-fis)* {1} See NOPH. *A city in Egypt.*
gather them up, *M* shall bury them .... Hos 9:6 4644

MEMUCAN *(mem-u'-can)* {3} *A prince of Media and Persia.*
Tarshish, Meres, Marsena, and *M* .... Est 1:14 4462
M answered before the king and the .... Est 1:16 4462
did according to the word of *M* .... Est 1:21 4462

MEN {1656}
then began *m* to call upon the .... Gen 4:26 582
when *m* began to multiply on the .... Gen 6:1 120
of *m* that they were fair .... Gen 6:2 120
came in unto the daughters of *m* .... Gen 6:4 120
became mighty *m* which were of old .... Gen 6:4 120
which were of old, *m* of renown .... Gen 6:4 582
which the children of *m* builded .... Gen 11:5 120
commanded his *m* concerning him .... Gen 12:20 582
But the *m* of Sodom were wicked and .... Gen 13:13 582
that which the young *m* have eaten .... Gen 14:24 5288
of the *m* which went with me .... Gen 14:24 582
among the *m* of Abraham's house .... Gen 17:23 582
all the *m* of his house, born in .... Gen 17:27 582
and, lo, three *m* stood by him .... Gen 18:2 582
the *m* rose up from thence, and .... Gen 18:16 582
the *m* turned their faces from .... Gen 18:22 582
the *m* of the city, even the *m* .... Gen 19:4 582
Where are the *m* which came in to .... Gen 19:5 582
only unto these *m* do nothing .... Gen 19:8 582
But the *m* put forth their hand, ... Gen 19:10 582
they smote the *m* that were at the .... Gen 19:11 582
the *m* said unto Lot, Hast thou .... Gen 19:12 582
the *m* laid hold upon his hand, and .... Gen 19:16 582
and the *m* were sore afraid .... Gen 20:8 582
took two of his young *m* with him .... Gen 22:3 5288
And Abraham said unto his young *m* .... Gen 22:5 5288
Abraham returned unto his young *m* .... Gen 22:19 5288
the daughters of the *m* of the .... Gen 24:13 582
the *m* that were with him, and .... Gen 24:54 582
and Abraham's servant, and his *m* .... Gen 24:59 582
the *m* of the place asked him of .... Gen 26:7 582
the *m* of the place should kill me .... Gen 26:7 582
together all the *m* of the place .... Gen 29:22 582
thee, and four hundred *m* with him .... Gen 32:6 376
thou power with God and with *m* .... Gen 32:28 582
came, and with him four hundred *m* .... Gen 33:1 376
if *m* should overdrive them one .... Gen 33:13
the *m* were grieved, and they were .... Gen 34:7 582
communed with the *m* of their city .... Gen 34:20 582
These *m* are peaceable with us .... Gen 34:21 582
Only herein will the *m* consent .... Gen 34:22 582
Then he asked the *m* of that place .... Gen 38:21 582
also the *m* of the place said, ... Gen 38:22 582
there was none of the *m* of the .... Gen 39:11 582
called unto the *m* of her house .... Gen 39:14 582
Egypt, and all the wise *m* thereof .... Gen 41:8 2450
we are true *m*, thy servants are .... Gen 42:11
If ye be true *m*, let one of your .... Gen 42:19
we said unto him, We are true *m* .... Gen 42:31
shall I know that ye are true *m* .... Gen 42:33
no spies, but that ye are true *m* .... Gen 42:34
the *m* took that present, and they .... Gen 43:15 582
of his house, Bring these *m* home .... Gen 43:16 582
for these *m* shall dine with me at .... Gen 43:16 582
brought the *m* into Joseph's house .... Gen 43:17 582
the *m* were afraid, because they .... Gen 43:18 582
brought the *m* into Joseph's house .... Gen 43:24 582
the *m* marvelled one at another .... Gen 43:33 582
the *m* were sent away, they and .... Gen 44:3 582
steward, Up, follow after the *m* .... Gen 44:4 582
the *m* are shepherds, for their .... Gen 46:32 582
some of his brethren, even five *m* .... Gen 47:2 582
if thou knowest any *m* of activity .... Gen 47:6 582
but saved the *m* children alive .... Ex 1:17 3206
have saved the *m* children alive .... Ex 1:18 3206
two *m* of the Hebrews strove .... Ex 2:13 582
for all the *m* are dead which .... Ex 4:19 582
more work be laid upon the *m* .... Ex 5:9 582
Pharaoh also called the wise *m* .... Ex 7:11 2450
let the *m* go, that they may serve .... Ex 10:7 582

M

go now ye that are *m*, and serve	Ex 10:11	1397
for they said, We be all dead *m*	Ex 12:33	
thousand on foot that were *m*	Ex 12:37	1397
the mighty *m* of Moab, trembling	Ex 15:15	
said unto Joshua, Choose us out *m*	Ex 17:9	582
out of all the people able *m*	Ex 18:21	582
m of truth, hating covetousness	Ex 18:21	582
Moses chose able *m* out of all	Ex 18:25	582
if *m* strive together, and one	Ex 21:18	582
If *m* strive, and hurt a woman with	Ex 21:22	582
And ye shall be holy *m* unto me	Ex 22:31	582
he sent young *m* of the children	Ex 24:5	5288
that day about three thousand *m*	Ex 32:28	376
in the year shall all your *m*	Ex 34:23	582
And they came, both *m* and women, as	Ex 35:22	582
And all the wise *m*, that wrought	Ex 36:4	2450
and five hundred and fifty *m*	Ex 38:26	
of which *m* offer an offering made	Lev 7:25	
have the *m* of the land done	Lev 18:27	582
whereof *m* bring an offering unto	Lev 27:9	
which shall be devoted of *m*	Lev 27:29	120
the *m* that shall stand with you	Num 1:5	582
Aaron took these *m* which are	Num 1:17	582
princes of Israel, being twelve *m*	Num 1:44	376
commit any sin that *m* commit	Num 5:6	120
And there were certain *m*, who were	Num 9:6	582
those *m* said unto him, We are	Num 9:7	582
Gather unto me seventy *m* of the	Num 11:16	376
gathered the seventy *m* of the	Num 11:24	376
remained two of the *m* in the camp	Num 11:26	582
of Moses, one of his young *m*	Num 11:28	979
above all the *m* which were upon	Num 12:3	120
Send thou *m*, that they may search	Num 13:2	582
all those *m* were heads of the	Num 13:3	582
These are the names of the *m*	Num 13:16	582
unto Rehob, as *m* come to Hamath	Num 13:21	
But the *m* that went up with him	Num 13:31	582
in it are *m* of a great stature	Num 13:32	582
Because all those *m* which have	Num 14:22	582
And the *m*, which Moses sent to	Num 14:36	582
Even those *m* that did bring up	Num 14:37	582
which were of the *m* that went to	Num 14:38	582
of Peleth, sons of Reuben, took *m*	Num 16:1	
in the congregation, *m* of renown	Num 16:2	582
thou put out the eyes of these *m*	Num 16:14	582
from the tents of these wicked *m*	Num 16:26	582
If these *m* die the common death	Num 16:29	
die the common death of all *m*	Num 16:29	120
after the visitation of all *m*	Num 16:29	120
these *m* have provoked the LORD	Num 16:30	582
all the *m* that appertained unto	Num 16:32	120
fifty *m* that offered incense	Num 16:35	376
whether it be of *m* or beasts	Num 18:15	120
What *m* are these with thee	Num 22:9	582
If the *m* come to call thee, rise	Num 22:20	582
said unto Balaam, Go with the *m*	Num 22:35	582
Slay ye every one his *m* that were	Num 25:5	582
devoured two hundred and fifty *m*	Num 26:10	376
spoil, and all the prey, both of *m*	Num 31:11	120
the priest said unto the *m* of war	Num 31:21	582
a tribute unto the LORD of the *m*	Num 31:28	582
which the *m* of war had caught	Num 31:32	582
divided from the *m* that warred	Num 31:42	582
have taken the sum of the *m* of	Num 31:49	582
(For the *m* of war had taken spoil	Num 31:53	582
Surely none of the *m* that came up	Num 32:11	582
stead, an increase of sinful *m*	Num 32:14	582
These are the names of the *m*	Num 34:17	582
And the names of the *m* are these	Num 34:19	582
Take you wise *m*, and understanding	Deut 1:13	582
the chief of your tribes, wise *m*	Deut 1:15	582
and said, We will send *m* before us	Deut 1:22	582
and I took twelve *m* of you	Deut 1:23	582
m of this evil generation see	Deut 1:35	582
the *m* of war were wasted out from	Deut 2:14	582
when all the *m* of war were	Deut 2:16	582
time, and utterly destroyed the *m*	Deut 2:34	4962
Heshbon, utterly destroying the *m*	Deut 3:6	4962
for all the *m* that followed	Deut 4:3	376
Certain *m*, the children of Belial	Deut 13:13	582
Then both the *m*, between whom the	Deut 19:17	582
all the *m* of his city shall stone	Deut 21:21	582
the *m* of her city shall stone her	Deut 22:21	582
there be a controversy between *m*	Deut 25:1	582
When *m* strive together one with	Deut 25:11	582
say unto all the *m* of Israel with	Deut 27:14	376
with all the *m* of Israel	Deut 29:10	376
Then *m* shall say, Because they	Deut 29:25	
Gather the people together, *m*	Deut 31:12	582
of them to cease from among *m*	Deut 32:26	582
and let not his *m* be few	Deut 33:6	4962
armed, all the mighty *m* of valour	Josh 1:14	1368
of Shittim two *m* to spy secretly	Josh 2:1	582
there came *m* in hither to night	Josh 2:2	582
Bring forth the *m* that are come	Josh 2:3	582
And the woman took the two *m*	Josh 2:4	582
said thus, There came *m* unto me	Josh 2:4	582
it was dark, that the *m* went out	Josh 2:5	582
whither the *m* went I wot not	Josh 2:5	582
the *m* pursued after them the way	Josh 2:7	582
And she said unto the *m*, I know	Josh 2:9	582
the *m* answered her, Our life for	Josh 2:14	582
the *m* said unto her, We will be	Josh 2:17	582
So the two *m* returned, and	Josh 2:23	582
m out of the tribes of Israel	Josh 3:12	376
Take you twelve *m* out of the	Josh 4:2	582
Then Joshua called the twelve *m*	Josh 4:4	376
were males, even all the *m* of war	Josh 5:4	582
all the people that were *m* of war	Josh 5:6	582
and the mighty *m* of valour	Josh 6:2	1368
compass the city, all ye *m* of war	Josh 6:3	582
the armed *m* went before the	Josh 6:9	
the armed *m* went before them	Josh 6:13	
Joshua had said unto the two *m*	Josh 6:22	582
the young *m* that were spies went	Josh 6:23	5288
Joshua sent *m* from Jericho to Ai,	Josh 7:2	582
the *m* went up and viewed Ai	Josh 7:2	582
two or three thousand *m* go up	Josh 7:3	376
the people about three thousand *m*	Josh 7:4	376
and they fled before the *m* of Ai	Josh 7:4	582
the *m* of Ai smote of them about	Josh 7:5	582
of them about thirty and six *m*	Josh 7:5	376
thousand mighty *m* of valour	Josh 8:3	376
And he took about five thousand *m*	Josh 8:12	376
the *m* of the city went out	Josh 8:14	582
when the *m* of Ai looked behind	Josh 8:20	582
turned again, and slew the *m* of Ai	Josh 8:21	582
all that fell that day, both of *m*	Josh 8:25	376
thousand, even all the *m* of Ai	Josh 8:25	582
to the *m* of Israel, We be come	Josh 9:6	376
the *m* of Israel said unto the	Josh 9:7	376
the *m* took of their victuals, and	Josh 9:14	582
all the *m* thereof were mighty	Josh 10:2	582
the *m* of Gibeon sent unto Joshua	Josh 10:6	582
and all the mighty *m* of valour	Josh 10:7	1368
set *m* by it for to keep them	Josh 10:18	582
called for all the *m* of Israel	Josh 10:24	376
the *m* of war which went with him	Josh 10:24	582
among you three *m* for each tribe	Josh 18:4	582
the *m* arose, and went away	Josh 18:8	582
the *m* went and passed through the	Josh 18:9	582
the *m* of Jericho fought against	Josh 24:11	1167
of them in Bezek ten thousand *m*	Judg 1:4	376
at that time about ten thousand *m*	Judg 3:29	376
all lusty, and all *m* of valour	Judg 3:29	376
six hundred *m* with an ox goad	Judg 3:31	376
m of the children of Naphtali	Judg 4:6	376
with ten thousand *m* at his feet	Judg 4:10	376
and ten thousand *m* after him	Judg 4:14	376
Gideon took ten *m* of his servants	Judg 6:27	582
the *m* of the city, that he could	Judg 6:27	582
when the *m* of the city arose	Judg 6:28	582
Then the *m* of the city said unto	Judg 6:30	582
their mouth, were three hundred *m*	Judg 7:6	376
By the three hundred *m* that	Judg 7:7	376
and retained those three hundred *m*	Judg 7:8	376
the armed *m* that were in the host	Judg 7:11	
hundred *m* into three companies	Judg 7:16	376
the hundred *m* that were with him,	Judg 7:19	376
And the *m* of Israel gathered	Judg 7:23	376
Then all the *m* of Ephraim	Judg 7:24	376
the *m* of Ephraim said unto him,	Judg 8:1	376
the three hundred *m* that were	Judg 8:4	376
And he said unto the *m* of Succoth	Judg 8:5	582
the *m* of Penuel answered him as	Judg 8:8	582
the *m* of Succoth had answered him	Judg 8:8	582
spake also unto the *m* of Penuel	Judg 8:9	582
them, about fifteen thousand *m*	Judg 8:10	
twenty thousand *m* that drew sword	Judg 8:10	376
a young man of the *m* of Succoth	Judg 8:14	582
even threescore and seventeen *m*	Judg 8:14	376
And he came unto the *m* of Succoth	Judg 8:15	582
bread unto thy *m* that are weary	Judg 8:15	582
them he taught the *m* of Succoth	Judg 8:16	582
Penuel, and slew the *m* of the city	Judg 8:17	582
What manner of *m* were they whom	Judg 8:18	582
Then the *m* of Israel said unto	Judg 8:22	376
the ears of all the *m* of Shechem	Judg 9:2	1167
the *m* of Shechem all these words	Judg 9:3	1167
all the *m* of Shechem gathered	Judg 9:6	1167
ye *m* of Shechem, that God may	Judg 9:7	1167
king over the *m* of Shechem	Judg 9:18	1167
and devour the *m* of Shechem	Judg 9:20	1167
come out from the *m* of Shechem	Judg 9:20	1167
Abimelech and the *m* of Shechem	Judg 9:23	1167
and the *m* of Shechem dealt	Judg 9:23	1167
upon the *m* of Shechem, which	Judg 9:24	1167
the *m* of Shechem set liers in	Judg 9:25	1167
the *m* of Shechem put their	Judg 9:26	1167
serve the *m* of Hamor the father	Judg 9:28	582
the mountains as if they were *m*	Judg 9:36	582
went out before the *m* of Shechem	Judg 9:39	1167
when all the *m* of the tower of	Judg 9:46	1167
that all the *m* of the tower of	Judg 9:47	1167
so that all the *m* of the tower of	Judg 9:49	582
died also, about a thousand *m*	Judg 9:49	376
city, and thither fled all the *m*	Judg 9:51	582
that *m* say not of me, A woman	Judg 9:54	
when the *m* of Israel saw that	Judg 9:55	376
all the evil of the *m* of Shechem	Judg 9:57	582
were gathered vain *m* to Jephthah	Judg 11:3	582
the *m* of Ephraim gathered	Judg 12:1	376
together all the *m* of Gilead	Judg 12:4	582
the *m* of Gilead smote Ephraim,	Judg 12:4	582
that the *m* of Gilead said unto	Judg 12:5	582
for so used the young *m* to do	Judg 14:10	970
the *m* of the city said unto him	Judg 14:18	582
and slew thirty *m* of them	Judg 14:19	376
the *m* of Judah said, Why are ye	Judg 15:10	376
Then three thousand *m* of Judah	Judg 15:11	376
and slew a thousand *m* therewith	Judg 15:15	376
an ass have I slain a thousand *m*	Judg 15:16	376
Now there were *m* lying in wait	Judg 16:9	
Now the house was full of *m*	Judg 16:27	582
the roof about three thousand *m*	Judg 16:27	376
family five *m* from their coasts	Judg 18:2	582
m of valour, from Zorah, and from	Judg 18:2	1121
Then the five *m* departed, and came	Judg 18:7	582
six hundred *m* appointed with	Judg 18:11	376
Then answered the five *m* that	Judg 18:14	582
the six hundred *m* appointed with	Judg 18:16	376
the five *m* that went to spy out	Judg 18:17	582
m that were appointed with	Judg 18:17	376
the *m* that were in the houses	Judg 18:22	582
but the *m* of the place were	Judg 19:16	582
the *m* of the city, certain sons	Judg 19:22	582
But the *m* would not hearken to	Judg 19:25	582
the *m* of Gibeah rose against me,	Judg 20:5	1167
we will take ten *m* of an hundred	Judg 20:10	582
So all the *m* of Israel were	Judg 20:11	376
sent *m* through all the tribe of	Judg 20:12	582
Now therefore deliver us the *m*	Judg 20:13	582
six thousand *m* that drew sword,	Judg 20:15	376
numbered seven hundred chosen *m*	Judg 20:15	376
seven hundred chosen *m* lefthanded	Judg 20:16	376
the *m* of Israel, beside Benjamin,	Judg 20:17	376
thousand *m* that drew sword	Judg 20:17	376
all these were *m* of war	Judg 20:17	376
the *m* of Israel went out to	Judg 20:20	376
the *m* of Israel put themselves in	Judg 20:20	376
that day twenty and two thousand *m*	Judg 20:21	376
the people the *m* of Israel	Judg 20:22	376
Israel again eighteen thousand *m*	Judg 20:25	376
field, about thirty *m* of Israel	Judg 20:31	376
all the *m* of Israel rose up out	Judg 20:33	376
chosen *m* out of all Israel	Judg 20:34	376
and five thousand and an hundred *m*	Judg 20:35	376
for the *m* of Israel gave place to	Judg 20:36	376
sign between the *m* of Israel	Judg 20:38	376
when the *m* of Israel retired in	Judg 20:39	376
kill of the *m* of Israel about	Judg 20:39	376
when the *m* of Israel turned again	Judg 20:41	376
the *m* of Benjamin were amazed	Judg 20:41	376
m of Israel unto the way of the	Judg 20:42	376
of Benjamin eighteen thousand *m*	Judg 20:44	376
all these were *m* of valour	Judg 20:44	582
in the highways five thousand *m*	Judg 20:45	376
and slew two thousand *m* of them	Judg 20:45	376
five thousand *m* that drew the	Judg 20:46	376
all these were *m* of valour	Judg 20:46	582
But six hundred *m* turned and fled	Judg 20:47	376
the *m* of Israel turned again upon	Judg 20:48	376
as well the *m* of every city, as	Judg 20:48	4974
Now the *m* of Israel had sworn in	Judg 21:1	376
thousand *m* of the valiantest	Judg 21:10	376
have I not charged the young *m*	Ruth 2:9	5288
that which the young *m* have drawn	Ruth 2:9	5288
glean, Boaz commanded his young *m*	Ruth 2:15	5288
shalt keep fast by my young *m*	Ruth 2:21	5288
as thou followedst not young *m*	Ruth 3:10	970
he took ten *m* of the elders of	Ruth 4:2	582
bows of the mighty *m* are broken	1Sa 2:4	
m was very great before the LORD	1Sa 2:17	5288
for *m* abhorred the offering of	1Sa 2:17	582
with the LORD, and also with *m*	1Sa 2:26	582
the field about four thousand *m*	1Sa 4:2	376
strong, and quit yourselves like *m*	1Sa 4:9	582
quit yourselves like *m*, and fight	1Sa 4:9	582
when the *m* of Ashdod saw that it	1Sa 5:7	582
and he smote the *m* of the city	1Sa 5:9	582
the *m* that died not were smitten	1Sa 5:12	582
And the *m* did so	1Sa 6:10	582
the *m* of Beth-shemesh offered	1Sa 6:15	582
he smote the *m* of Beth-shemesh,	1Sa 6:19	376
thousand and threescore and ten *m*	1Sa 6:19	376
the *m* of Beth-shemesh said, Who	1Sa 6:20	582
the *m* of Kirjath-jearim came, and	1Sa 7:1	582
the *m* of Israel went out of	1Sa 7:11	582
and your goodliest young *m*	1Sa 8:16	970
Samuel said unto the *m* of Israel	1Sa 8:22	582
then thou shalt find two *m* by	1Sa 10:2	582
m going up to God to Beth-el	1Sa 10:3	582
there went with him a band of *m*	1Sa 10:26	2428
all the *m* of Jabesh said unto	1Sa 11:1	582
the tidings of the *m* of Jabesh	1Sa 11:5	582
the *m* of Judah thirty thousand	1Sa 11:8	376
say unto the *m* of Jabesh-gilead	1Sa 11:9	376
and shewed it to the *m* of Jabesh	1Sa 11:9	582
Therefore the *m* of Jabesh said,	1Sa 11:10	582
bring the *m*, that we may put them	1Sa 11:12	582
all the *m* of Israel rejoiced	1Sa 11:15	582
him three thousand *m* of Israel	1Sa 13:2	
When the *m* of Israel saw that	1Sa 13:6	376
with him, about six hundred *m*	1Sa 13:15	376
with him were about six hundred *m*	1Sa 14:2	376
we will pass over unto these *m*	1Sa 14:8	582
the *m* of the garrison answered	1Sa 14:12	582
made, was about twenty *m*, within	1Sa 14:14	376
Likewise all the *m* of Israel	1Sa 14:22	376
the *m* of Israel were distressed	1Sa 14:24	376
and ten thousand *m* of Judah	1Sa 15:4	376
the *m* of Israel were gathered	1Sa 17:2	376
the man went among *m* for an old	1Sa 17:12	582
all the *m* of Israel, were in the	1Sa 17:19	376
all the *m* of Israel, when they	1Sa 17:24	376
the *m* of Israel said, Have ye	1Sa 17:25	376
spake to the *m* that stood by him	1Sa 17:26	582
heard when he spake unto the *m*	1Sa 17:28	582
the *m* of Israel and of Judah arose	1Sa 17:52	582
and Saul set him over the *m* of war	1Sa 18:5	582
David arose and went, he and his *m*	1Sa 18:27	582
of the Philistines two hundred *m*	1Sa 18:27	376
if the young *m* have kept	1Sa 21:4	5288
vessels of the young *m* are holy	1Sa 21:5	5288

Have I need of mad *m*, that ye	1Sa 21:15	7696
with him about four hundred *m*	1Sa 22:2	376
the *m* that were with him, (now	1Sa 22:6	582
the edge of the sword, both *m*	1Sa 22:19	376
David's *m* said unto him, Behold,	1Sa 23:3	582
his *m* went to Keilah, and fought	1Sa 23:5	582
Keilah, to besiege David and his *m*	1Sa 23:8	582
Will the *m* of Keilah deliver me	1Sa 23:11	1167
Will the *m* of Keilah deliver me	1Sa 23:12	1167
my *m* into the hand of Saul	1Sa 23:12	582
Then David and his *m*, which were	1Sa 23:13	582
his *m* were in the wilderness of	1Sa 23:24	582
also and his *m* went to seek him	1Sa 23:25	582
his *m* on that side of the	1Sa 23:26	582
his *m* compassed David and his *m*	1Sa 23:26	582
chosen *m* out of all Israel	1Sa 24:2	376
his *m* upon the rocks of the wild	1Sa 24:2	582
his *m* remained in the sides of	1Sa 24:3	582
the *m* of David said unto him,	1Sa 24:4	582
And he said unto his *m*, The LORD	1Sa 24:6	582
his *m* got them up unto the hold	1Sa 24:22	582
And David sent out ten young *m*	1Sa 25:5	5288
and David said unto the young *m*	1Sa 25:5	5288
Ask thy young *m*, and they will	1Sa 25:8	5288
Wherefore let the young *m* find	1Sa 25:8	5288
And when David's young *m* came	1Sa 25:9	5288
my shearers, and give it unto *m*	1Sa 25:11	582
David's young *m* turned their way	1Sa 25:12	5288
And David said unto his *m*, Gird ye	1Sa 25:13	582
after David about four hundred *m*	1Sa 25:13	376
one of the young *m* told Abigail	1Sa 25:14	5288
But the *m* were very good unto us,	1Sa 25:15	582
his *m* came down against her	1Sa 25:20	582
saw not the young *m* of my lord	1Sa 25:25	5288
the young *m* that follow my lord	1Sa 25:27	5288
chosen *m* of Israel with him	1Sa 26:2	376
but if they be the children of *m*	1Sa 26:19	120
let one of the young *m* come over	1Sa 26:22	5288
over with the six hundred *m* that	1Sa 27:2	376
with Achish at Gath, he and his *m*	1Sa 27:3	582
his *m* went up, and invaded the	1Sa 27:8	582
with me to battle, thou and thy *m*	1Sa 28:1	582
two *m* with him, and they came to	1Sa 28:8	582
his *m* passed on in the rereward	1Sa 29:2	582
not be with the heads of these *m*	1Sa 29:4	582
his *m* rose up early to depart in	1Sa 29:11	582
his *m* were come to Ziklag on the	1Sa 30:1	582
his *m* came to the city, and,	1Sa 30:3	582
the six hundred *m* that were with	1Sa 30:9	376
pursued, he and four hundred *m*	1Sa 30:10	376
them, save four hundred young *m*	1Sa 30:17	376
David came to the two hundred *m*	1Sa 30:21	582
Then answered all the wicked *m*	1Sa 30:22	376
m of Belial, of those that went	1Sa 30:22	
and his *m* were wont to haunt	1Sa 30:31	582
the *m* of Israel fled from before	1Sa 31:1	582
and his armourbearer, and all his *m*	1Sa 31:6	582
when the *m* of Israel that were on	1Sa 31:7	582
saw that the *m* of Israel fled, and	1Sa 31:7	582
All the valiant *m* arose, and went	1Sa 31:12	376
likewise all the *m* that were with	2Sa 1:11	582
David called one of the young *m*	2Sa 1:15	5288
his *m* that were with him did	2Sa 2:3	582
the *m* of Judah came, and there	2Sa 2:4	582
That the *m* of Jabesh-gilead were	2Sa 2:4	582
unto the *m* of Jabesh-gilead	2Sa 2:5	582
Joab, Let the young *m* now arise	2Sa 2:14	5288
the *m* of Israel, before the	2Sa 2:17	582
thee hold on one of the young *m*	2Sa 2:21	5288
his *m* walked all that night	2Sa 2:29	582
of David's servants nineteen *m*	2Sa 2:30	376
of Benjamin, and of Abner's *m*	2Sa 2:31	582
hundred and threescore *m* died	2Sa 2:31	376
his *m* went all night, and they	2Sa 2:32	582
to Hebron, and twenty *m* with him	2Sa 3:20	582
the *m* that were with him a feast	2Sa 3:20	582
as a man falleth before wicked *m*	2Sa 3:34	1121
these *m* the sons of Zeruiah be	2Sa 3:39	582
Saul's son had two *m* that were	2Sa 4:2	582
when wicked *m* have slain a	2Sa 4:11	582
And David commanded his young *m*	2Sa 4:12	5288
his *m* went to Jerusalem unto the	2Sa 5:6	582
and David and his *m* burned them	2Sa 5:21	582
all the chosen *m* of Israel	2Sa 6:1	977
Israel, as well to the women as *m*	2Sa 6:19	376
the great *m* that are in the earth	2Sa 7:9	
chasten him with the rod of *m*	2Sa 7:14	582
the stripes of the children of *m*	2Sa 7:14	120
Syrians two and twenty thousand *m*	2Sa 8:5	376
salt, being eighteen thousand *m*	2Sa 8:13	
because the *m* were greatly	2Sa 10:5	582
and of king Maacah a thousand *m*	2Sa 10:6	376
and of Ish-tob twelve thousand *m*	2Sa 10:6	376
and all the host of the mighty *m*	2Sa 10:7	1368
of all the choice *m* of Israel	2Sa 10:9	977
let us play the *m* for our people	2Sa 10:12	2388
David slew the *m* of seven hundred	2Sa 10:18	
where he knew that valiant *m* were	2Sa 11:16	582
the *m* of the city went out, and	2Sa 11:17	582
Surely the *m* prevailed against us	2Sa 11:23	582
him, There were two *m* in one city	2Sa 12:1	582
said, Have out all *m* from me	2Sa 13:9	376
all the young *m* the king's sons	2Sa 13:32	5288
fifty *m* to run before him	2Sa 15:1	376
the hearts of the *m* of Israel	2Sa 15:6	582
two hundred *m* out of Jerusalem	2Sa 15:11	376
The hearts of the *m* of Israel are	2Sa 15:13	376
six hundred *m* which came after	2Sa 15:18	376

Gittite passed over, and all his *m*	2Sa 15:22	582
fruit for the young *m* to eat	2Sa 16:2	5288
all the mighty *m* were on his	2Sa 16:6	1368
his *m* went by the way, Shimei	2Sa 16:13	582
and all the people the *m* of Israel	2Sa 16:15	376
all the *m* of Israel, choose, his	2Sa 16:18	376
now choose out twelve thousand *m*	2Sa 17:1	376
thou knowest thy father and his *m*	2Sa 17:8	582
that they be mighty *m*	2Sa 17:8	1368
which be with him are valiant *m*	2Sa 17:10	1121
of all the *m* that are with him	2Sa 17:12	582
all the *m* of Israel said, The	2Sa 17:14	376
all the *m* of Israel with him	2Sa 17:24	376
that day of twenty thousand *m*	2Sa 18:7	
ten young *m* that bare Joab's	2Sa 18:15	5288
the *m* that lifted up their hand	2Sa 18:28	582
the heart of all the *m* of Judah	2Sa 19:14	376
came down with the *m* of Judah to	2Sa 19:16	376
a thousand *m* of Benjamin with him	2Sa 19:17	376
dead *m* before my lord the king	2Sa 19:28	582
any more the voice of singing *m*	2Sa 19:35	582
all the *m* of Israel came to the	2Sa 19:41	376
the *m* of Judah stolen thee away	2Sa 19:41	376
and all David's *m* with him	2Sa 19:41	582
all the *m* of Judah answered the	2Sa 19:42	376
of Judah answered the *m* of Israel	2Sa 19:42	376
the *m* of Israel answered the *m*	2Sa 19:43	376
the words of the *m* of Judah were	2Sa 19:43	376
than the words of the *m* of Israel	2Sa 19:43	376
but the *m* of Judah clave unto	2Sa 20:2	376
Assemble me the *m* of Judah within	2Sa 20:4	376
went to assemble the *m* of Judah	2Sa 20:5	
there went out after him Joab's *m*	2Sa 20:7	582
Pelethites, and all the mighty *m*	2Sa 20:7	1368
And one of Joab's *m* stood by him	2Sa 20:11	376
Let seven *m* of his sons be	2Sa 21:6	582
son from the *m* of Jabesh-gilead	2Sa 21:12	1167
Then the *m* of David sware unto	2Sa 21:17	582
of ungodly *m* made me afraid	2Sa 22:5	
that ruleth over *m* must be just	2Sa 23:3	120
of the mighty *m* whom David had	2Sa 23:8	1368
of the three mighty *m* with David	2Sa 23:9	1368
the *m* of Israel were gone away	2Sa 23:9	376
the three mighty *m* brake through	2Sa 23:16	1368
is not this the blood of the *m*	2Sa 23:17	582
things did these three mighty *m*	2Sa 23:17	1368
he slew two lionlike *m* of Moab	2Sa 23:20	739
had the name among three mighty *m*	2Sa 23:22	1368
valiant *m* that drew the sword	2Sa 24:9	376
the *m* of Judah were five hundred	2Sa 24:9	376
were five hundred thousand *m*	2Sa 24:9	376
to Beer-sheba seventy thousand *m*	2Sa 24:15	376
fifty *m* to run before him	1Kin 1:5	376
the mighty *m* which belonged to	1Kin 1:8	1368
all the *m* of Judah the king's	1Kin 1:9	582
and Benaiah, and the mighty *m*	1Kin 1:10	1368
fell upon two *m* more righteous	1Kin 2:32	582
For he was wiser than all *m*	1Kin 4:31	120
and the levy was thirty thousand *m*	1Kin 5:13	376
all the *m* of Israel assembled	1Kin 8:2	376
hearts of all the children of *m*	1Kin 8:39	120
but they were *m* of war, and his	1Kin 9:22	582
Happy are thy *m*, happy are these	1Kin 10:8	582
they took *m* with them out of	1Kin 11:18	582
And he gathered *m* unto him	1Kin 11:24	582
Rehoboam consulted with the old *m*	1Kin 12:6	2205
forsook the counsel of the old *m*	1Kin 12:8	2205
consulted with the young *m* that	1Kin 12:8	3206
the young *m* that were grown up	1Kin 12:10	3206
after the counsel of the young *m*	1Kin 12:14	3206
and fourscore thousand chosen *m*	1Kin 12:21	1368
m passed by, and saw the carcase	1Kin 13:25	582
how I hid an hundred *m* of the	1Kin 18:13	376
are four hundred and fifty *m*	1Kin 18:22	376
Even by the young *m* of the	1Kin 20:14	5288
Then he numbered the young *m* of	1Kin 20:15	5288
the young *m* of the princes of the	1Kin 20:17	5288
There are *m* come out of Samaria	1Kin 20:17	582
So these young *m* of the princes	1Kin 20:19	5288
thousand of the *m* that were left	1Kin 20:30	376
Now the *m* did diligently observe	1Kin 20:33	582
And set two *m*, sons of Belial,	1Kin 21:10	582
the *m* of his city, even the	1Kin 21:11	582
And there came in two *m*, children	1Kin 21:13	582
the *m* of Belial witnessed against	1Kin 21:13	582
together, about four hundred *m*	1Kin 22:6	376
fifty *m* of the sons of the	2Kin 2:7	376
with thy servants fifty strong *m*	2Kin 2:16	582
They sent therefore fifty *m*	2Kin 2:17	376
the *m* of the city said unto	2Kin 2:19	582
seven hundred *m* that drew swords	2Kin 3:26	376
I pray thee, one of the young *m*	2Kin 4:22	5288
they poured out for the *m* to eat	2Kin 4:40	582
I set this before an hundred *m*	2Kin 4:43	376
m of the sons of the prophets	2Kin 5:22	5288
and he let the *m* go, and they	2Kin 5:24	582
LORD, open the eyes of these *m*	2Kin 6:20	
there were four leprous *m* at the	2Kin 7:3	582
their young *m* wilt thou slay with	2Kin 8:12	970
heads of the *m* your master's sons	2Kin 10:6	582
were with the great *m* of the city	2Kin 10:6	
in Jezreel, and all his great *m*	2Kin 10:11	
house, even two and forty *m*	2Kin 10:14	376
appointed fourscore *m* without	2Kin 10:24	376
If any of the *m* whom I have	2Kin 10:24	582
they took every man his *m* that	2Kin 11:9	582
they reckoned not with the *m*	2Kin 12:15	582
behold, they spied a band of *m*	2Kin 13:21	

of all the mighty *m* of wealth	2Kin 15:20	1368
Arieh, and with him fifty *m* of the	2Kin 15:25	376
of Assyria brought *m* from Babylon	2Kin 17:24	
And the *m* of Babylon made	2Kin 17:30	582
the *m* of Cuth made Nergal, and the	2Kin 17:30	582
the *m* of Hamath made Ashima,	2Kin 17:30	582
me to the *m* which sit on the wall	2Kin 18:27	582
said unto him, What said these *m*	2Kin 20:14	582
all the *m* of Judah and all the	2Kin 23:2	376
their places with the bones of *m*	2Kin 23:14	120
the *m* of the city told him, It is	2Kin 23:17	582
and all the mighty *m* of valour	2Kin 24:14	1368
all the *m* of might, even seven	2Kin 24:16	582
all the *m* of war fled by night by	2Kin 25:4	582
that was set over the *m* of war	2Kin 25:19	582
five *m* of them that were in the	2Kin 25:19	582
threescore *m* of the people of the	2Kin 25:19	376
of the armies, they and their *m*	2Kin 25:23	582
of a Maachathite, they and their *m*	2Kin 25:23	582
sware to them, and to their *m*	2Kin 25:24	582
ten *m* with him, and smote Gedaliah	2Kin 25:25	582
These are the *m* of Rechah	1Chr 4:12	582
the *m* of Chozeba, and Joash, and	1Chr 4:22	582
sons of Simeon, five hundred *m*	1Chr 4:42	582
tribe of Manasseh, of valiant *m*	1Chr 5:18	1368
m able to bear buckler and sword,	1Chr 5:18	582
and of *m* an hundred thousand	1Chr 5:21	120
mighty *m* of valour, famous *m*,	1Chr 5:24	582
they were valiant *m* of might in	1Chr 7:2	1368
all of them chief *m*	1Chr 7:3	
for war, six and thirty thousand *m*	1Chr 7:4	
Issachar were valiant *m* of might	1Chr 7:5	1368
their fathers, mighty *m* of valour	1Chr 7:7	1368
mighty *m* of valour, was twenty	1Chr 7:9	1368
fathers, mighty *m* of valour, were	1Chr 7:11	1368
whom the *m* of Gath that were born	1Chr 7:21	582
mighty *m* of valour, chief of the	1Chr 7:40	1368
was twenty and six thousand *m*	1Chr 7:40	582
by their generations, chief *m*	1Chr 8:28	
of Ulam were mighty *m* of valour	1Chr 8:40	582
All these *m* were chief of the	1Chr 9:9	582
very able *m* for the work of the	1Chr 9:13	1368
the *m* of Israel fled from before	1Chr 10:1	376
when all the *m* of Israel that	1Chr 10:7	376
They arose, all the valiant *m*	1Chr 10:12	376
of the mighty *m* whom David had	1Chr 11:10	1368
of the mighty *m* whom David had	1Chr 11:11	1368
I drink the blood of these *m* that	1Chr 11:19	582
he slew two lionlike *m* of Moab	1Chr 11:22	582
Also the valiant *m* of the armies	1Chr 11:26	1368
and they were among the mighty *m*	1Chr 12:1	1368
hold to the wilderness *m* of might	1Chr 12:8	1368
m of war fit for the battle, that	1Chr 12:8	582
they were all mighty *m* of valour	1Chr 12:21	1368
mighty *m* of valour for the war,	1Chr 12:25	1368
mighty *m* of valour, famous	1Chr 12:30	1368
Issachar, which were *m* that had	1Chr 12:32	582
All these *m* of war, that could	1Chr 12:38	582
let *m* say among the nations, The	1Chr 16:31	
the great *m* that are in the earth	1Chr 17:8	
Syrians two and twenty thousand *m*	1Chr 18:5	376
told David how the *m* were served	1Chr 19:5	582
for the *m* were greatly ashamed	1Chr 19:5	582
and all the host of the mighty *m*	1Chr 19:8	1368
m which fought in chariots	1Chr 19:18	
thousand *m* that drew sword	1Chr 21:5	376
ten thousand *m* that drew sword	1Chr 21:5	376
fell of Israel seventy thousand *m*	1Chr 21:14	376
all manner of cunning *m* for every	1Chr 22:15	
there were more chief *m* found of	1Chr 24:4	1397
there were sixteen chief *m* of the	1Chr 24:4	
for they were mighty *m* of valour	1Chr 26:6	1368
whose brethren were strong *m*	1Chr 26:7	1121
able *m* for strength for the	1Chr 26:8	376
had sons and brethren, strong *m*	1Chr 26:9	1121
porters, even among the chief *m*	1Chr 26:12	1397
m of valour, a thousand and seven	1Chr 26:30	1121
m of valour at Jazer of Gilead	1Chr 26:31	1368
m of valour, were two thousand and	1Chr 26:32	1121
officers, and with the mighty *m*	1Chr 28:1	1368
and with all the valiant *m*	1Chr 28:1	1368
all the princes, and the mighty *m*	1Chr 29:24	1368
ten thousand *m* to bear burdens,	2Chr 2:2	376
m that are with me in Judah	2Chr 2:7	
be put to him, with thy cunning *m*	2Chr 2:14	
with the cunning *m* of my lord	2Chr 2:14	
Wherefore all the *m* of Israel	2Chr 5:3	376
deed dwell with *m* on the earth	2Chr 6:18	120
the hearts of the children of *m*	2Chr 6:30	120
but they were *m* of war, and chief	2Chr 8:9	582
Happy are thy *m*, and happy are	2Chr 9:7	582
took counsel with the old *m* that	2Chr 10:6	
counsel which the old *m* gave him	2Chr 10:8	
took counsel with the young *m*	2Chr 10:8	3206
the young *m* that were brought up	2Chr 10:10	3206
forsook the counsel of the old *m*	2Chr 10:13	
after the advice of the young *m*	2Chr 10:14	3206
and fourscore thousand chosen *m*	2Chr 11:1	977
with an army of valiant *m* of war	2Chr 13:3	1368
four hundred thousand chosen *m*	2Chr 13:3	376
eight hundred thousand chosen *m*	2Chr 13:3	376
being mighty *m* of valour	2Chr 13:3	1368
are gathered unto him vain *m*	2Chr 13:7	582
Then the *m* of Judah gave a shout	2Chr 13:15	376
as the *m* of Judah shouted, it	2Chr 13:15	376
five hundred thousand chosen *m*	2Chr 13:17	376
an army of *m* that bare targets	2Chr 14:8	
all these were mighty *m* of valour	2Chr 14:8	1368

M

the *m* of war, mighty *m* of ... 2Chr 17:13 582
mighty *m* of valour, were in ... 2Chr 17:13 1368
with him mighty *m* of valour three ... 2Chr 17:14 1368
thousand mighty *m* of valour ... 2Chr 17:16 1368
and with him armed *m* with bow ... 2Chr 17:17
of prophets four hundred *m* ... 2Chr 18:5 376
for the band of *m* that came with ... 2Chr 22:1 582
took every man his *m* that were to ... 2Chr 23:8 582
came with a small company of *m* ... 2Chr 24:24 582
three hundred thousand choice *m* ... 2Chr 25:5 977
m of valour out of Israel for an ... 2Chr 25:6
Uzziah had an host of fighting *m* ... 2Chr 26:11 1368
m of valour were two thousand ... 2Chr 26:12 1368
engines, invented by cunning *m* ... 2Chr 26:15
of the LORD, that were valiant *m* ... 2Chr 26:17 1121
one day, which were all valiant *m* ... 2Chr 28:6 1121
So the armed *m* left the captives ... 2Chr 28:14
the *m* which were expressed by ... 2Chr 28:15 582
the *m* that were expressed by name ... 2Chr 31:19 582
his mighty *m* to stop the waters ... 2Chr 32:3 1368
off all the mighty *m* of valour ... 2Chr 32:21 1368
the *m* did the work faithfully ... 2Chr 34:12 582
all the *m* of Judah, and the ... 2Chr 34:30 376
and all the singing *m* and the ... 2Chr 35:25 7891
who slew their young *m* with the ... 2Chr 36:17 970
let the *m* of his place help him ... Ezr 1:4 582
The number of the *m* of the people ... Ezr 2:2 582
The *m* of Netophah, fifty and six ... Ezr 2:22 582
The *m* of Anathoth, an hundred ... Ezr 2:23 582
The *m* of Michmas, an hundred ... Ezr 2:27 582
The *m* of Beth-el and Ai, two ... Ezr 2:28 582
among them two hundred singing *m* ... Ezr 2:65 582
the fathers, who were ancient *m* ... Ezr 3:12
Thy servants the *m* on this side ... Ezr 4:11 606
to cause these *m* to cease ... Ezr 4:21 1400
of the *m* that make this building ... Ezr 5:4 1400
the *m* that were the chief of them ... Ezr 5:10 1400
expences be given unto these *m* ... Ezr 6:8 1400
Israel chief *m* to go up with me ... Ezr 7:28 582
and for Meshullam, chief *m* ... Ezr 8:16 1400
for Elnathan, *m* of understanding ... Ezr 8:16 582
a very great congregation of *m* ... Ezr 10:1 582
Then all the *m* of Judah and ... Ezr 10:9 582
they made an end with all the *m* ... Ezr 10:17 582
came, he and certain *m* of Judah ... Neh 1:2 582
night, I and some few *m* with me ... Neh 2:12 582
unto him builded the *m* of Jericho ... Neh 3:2 582
the *m* of Gibeon, and of Mizpah, ... Neh 3:7 582
the priests, the *m* of the plain ... Neh 3:22 582
nor the *m* of the guard which ... Neh 4:23 582
for other *m* have our lands and ... Neh 5:5 582
of the *m* of the people of Israel ... Neh 7:7 582
The *m* of Beth-lehem and Netophah, ... Neh 7:26 582
The *m* of Anathoth, an hundred ... Neh 7:27 582
The *m* of Beth-azmaveth, forty and ... Neh 7:28 582
The *m* of Kirjath-jearim, ... Neh 7:29 582
The *m* of Ramah and Gaba, six ... Neh 7:30 582
The *m* of Michmas, an hundred and ... Neh 7:31 582
The *m* of Beth-el and Ai, an ... Neh 7:32 582
The *m* of the other Nebo, fifty and ... Neh 7:33 582
hundred forty and five singing *m* ... Neh 7:67 7891
before the congregation both of *m* ... Neh 8:2 376
until midday, before the *m* ... Neh 8:3 582
And the people blessed all the *m* ... Neh 11:2 582
threescore and eight valiant *m* ... Neh 11:6 582
mighty *m* of valour, an hundred ... Neh 11:14 1368
the son of one of the great *m* ... Neh 11:14
There dwelt *m* of Tyre also ... Neh 13:16 582
Then the king said to the wise *m* ... Est 1:13 2450
Then said his wise *m* and Zeresh ... Est 6:13 2450
slew and destroyed five hundred *m* ... Est 9:6 376
hundred *m* in Shushan the palace ... Est 9:12 376
slew three hundred *m* at Shushan ... Est 9:15 376
greatest of all the *m* of the east ... Job 1:3 1121
and it fell upon the young *m* ... Job 1:19 5288
when deep sleep falleth on *m* ... Job 4:13 582
unto thee, O thou preserver of *m* ... Job 7:20 120
thy lies make *m* hold their peace ... Job 11:3 4962
For he knoweth vain *m* ... Job 11:11 4962
the grayheaded and very aged *m* ... Job 15:10
Which wise *m* have told from their ... Job 15:18 2450
Upright *m* shall be astonied at ... Job 17:8
way which wicked *m* have trodden ... Job 22:15 4962
When *m* are cast down, then thou ... Job 22:29
M groan from out of the city, and ... Job 24:12 4962
M shall clap their hands at him, ... Job 27:23
up, they are gone away from *m* ... Job 28:4 582
The young *m* saw me, and hid ... Job 29:8 5288
Unto me *m* gave ear, and waited, and ... Job 29:21
were driven forth from among *m* ... Job 30:5
of fools, yea, children of base *m* ... Job 30:8
If the *m* of my tabernacle said ... Job 31:31 4962
So these three *m* ceased to answer ... Job 32:1 582
in the mouth of these three *m* ... Job 32:5 582
Great *m* are not always wise ... Job 32:9
when deep sleep falleth upon *m* ... Job 33:15 582
Then he openeth the ears of *m* ... Job 33:16 582
He looketh upon *m*, and if any say, ... Job 33:27 582
Hear my words, O ye wise *m* ... Job 34:2 2450
and walketh with wicked *m* ... Job 34:8 582
unto me, ye *m* of understanding ... Job 34:10 582
in pieces mighty *m* without number ... Job 34:24 3524
He striketh them as wicked *m* in ... Job 34:26 3524
Let *m* of understanding tell me, ... Job 34:34 582
of his answers for wicked *m* ... Job 34:36 582
because of the pride of evil *m* ... Job 35:12
magnify his work, which *m* behold ... Job 36:24 582
that all *m* may know his work ... Job 37:7 582
now *m* see not the bright light ... Job 37:21
M do therefore fear him ... Job 37:24 582
he goeth on to meet the armed *m* ... Job 39:21
O ye sons of *m*, how long will ye ... Ps 4:2 376
may know themselves to be but *m* ... Ps 9:20 582
eyelids try, the children of *m* ... Ps 11:4 120
fail from among the children of *m* ... Ps 12:1 120
when the vilest *m* are exalted ... Ps 12:8
heaven upon the children of *m* ... Ps 14:2 120
Concerning the words of *m* ... Ps 17:4 120
From *m* which are thy hand, O LORD ... Ps 17:14 4962
from *m* of the world, which have ... Ps 17:14 4962
of ungodly *m* made me afraid ... Ps 18:4
seed from among the children of *m* ... Ps 21:10 120
a reproach of *m*, and despised of ... Ps 22:6 120
nor my life with bloody *m* ... Ps 26:9 582
in thee before the sons of *m* ... Ps 31:19 120
he beholdeth all the sons of *m* ... Ps 33:13 120
of *m* put their trust under the ... Ps 36:7 120
art fairer than the children of *m* ... Ps 45:2 120
For he seeth that wise *m* die ... Ps 49:10
m will praise thee, when thou ... Ps 49:18
heaven upon the children of *m* ... Ps 53:2 120
deceitful *m* shall not live out ... Ps 55:23 582
set on fire, even the sons of *m* ... Ps 57:4 120
judge uprightly, O ye sons of *m* ... Ps 58:1 120
and save me from bloody *m* ... Ps 59:2 582
Surely *m* of low degree are vanity ... Ps 62:9 120,1121
m of high degree are a lie ... Ps 62:9 376,1121
all *m* shall fear, and shall ... Ps 64:9 120
doing toward the children of *m* ... Ps 66:5 120
Thou hast caused *m* to ride over ... Ps 66:12 582
thou hast received gifts for *m* ... Ps 68:18 120
m shall be blessed in him ... Ps 72:17
are not in trouble as other *m* ... Ps 73:5 582
are they plagued like other *m* ... Ps 73:5 120
none of the *m* of might have found ... Ps 76:5 582
smote down the chosen *m* of Israel ... Ps 78:31 970
the tent which he placed among *m* ... Ps 78:60 120
The fire consumed their young *m* ... Ps 78:63 970
But ye shall die like *m*, and fall ... Ps 82:7 120
That *m* may know that thou, whose ... Ps 83:18
m have sought after my soul ... Ps 86:14
hast thou made all *m* in vain ... Ps 89:47 120,1121
sayest, Return, ye children of *m* ... Ps 90:3 120
they were but a few *m* in number ... Ps 105:12 4962
Oh that *m* would praise the LORD ... Ps 107:8
works to the children of *m* ... Ps 107:8 120
Oh that *m* would praise the LORD ... Ps 107:15
works to the children of *m* ... Ps 107:15 120
Oh that *m* would praise the LORD ... Ps 107:21
works to the children of *m* ... Ps 107:21 120
Oh that *m* would praise the LORD ... Ps 107:31
works to the children of *m* ... Ps 107:31 120
he given to the children of *m* ... Ps 115:16 120
said in my haste, All *m* are liars ... Ps 116:11 120
when *m* rose up against us ... Ps 124:2 120
from me therefore, ye bloody *m* ... Ps 139:19 582
works with *m* that work iniquity ... Ps 141:4 376
m shall speak of the might of thy ... Ps 145:6
to the sons of *m* his mighty acts ... Ps 145:12 120
Both young *m*, and maidens ... Ps 148:12 970
old *m*, and children ... Ps 148:12
mayest walk in the way of good *m* ... Prov 2:20
and go not in the way of evil *m* ... Prov 4:14
M do not despise a thief, if he ... Prov 6:30
many strong *m* have been slain by ... Prov 7:26 582
Unto you, O *m*, I call ... Prov 8:4 376
delights were with the sons of *m* ... Prov 8:31 120
Wise *m* lay up knowledge ... Prov 10:14
and the hope of unjust *m* perisheth ... Prov 11:7
and strong *m* retain riches ... Prov 11:16
wicked desireth the net of evil *m* ... Prov 12:12
walketh with wise *m* shall be wise ... Prov 13:20
the hearts of the children of *m* ... Prov 15:11 120
of the LORD *m* depart from evil ... Prov 16:6
children are the crown of old *m* ... Prov 17:6
and bringeth him before great *m* ... Prov 18:16
Most *m* will proclaim every one ... Prov 20:6 120
of young *m* is their strength ... Prov 20:29
beauty of old *m* is the grey head ... Prov 20:29
he shall not stand before mean *m* ... Prov 22:29
the transgressors among *m* ... Prov 23:28 120
not thou envious against evil *m* ... Prov 24:1 582
scorner is an abomination to *m* ... Prov 24:9 120
not thyself because of evil *m* ... Prov 24:19
which the *m* of Hezekiah king of ... Prov 25:1 582
stand not in the place of great *m* ... Prov 25:6
so for *m* to search their own ... Prov 25:27
seven *m* that can render a reason ... Prov 26:16
Evil *m* understand not judgment ... Prov 28:5 582
of riotous *m* shameth his father ... Prov 28:7
When righteous *m* do rejoice ... Prov 28:12
wicked rise, *m* hide themselves ... Prov 28:28 120
Scornful *m* bring a city into a ... Prov 29:8 582
but wise *m* turn away wrath ... Prov 29:8
earth, and the needy from among *m* ... Prov 30:14 120
was that good for the sons of *m* ... Eccl 2:3 120
I gat me *m* singers and women ... Eccl 2:8 7891
and the delights of the sons of *m* ... Eccl 2:8 120
sons of *m* to be exercised in it ... Eccl 3:10 120
that *m* should fear before him ... Eccl 3:14 582
the estate of the sons of *m* ... Eccl 3:18 120
the sons of *m* befalleth beasts ... Eccl 3:19 120
the sun, and it is common among *m* ... Eccl 6:1 120
for that is the end of all *m* ... Eccl 7:2 120
mighty *m* which are in the city ... Eccl 7:19
the heart of the sons of *m* is ... Eccl 8:11 120
that there be just *m*, unto whom ... Eccl 8:14
again, there be wicked *m*, to whom ... Eccl 8:14
of the sons of *m* is full of evil ... Eccl 9:3 120
yet riches to *m* of understanding ... Eccl 9:11
nor yet favour to *m* of skill ... Eccl 9:11
so are the sons of *m* snared in an ... Eccl 9:12 120
a little city, and few *m* within it ... Eccl 9:14 582
The words of wise *m* are heard in ... Eccl 9:17
the strong *m* shall bow themselves ... Eccl 12:3 582
threescore valiant *m* are about it ... Song 3:7 1368
bucklers, all shields of mighty *m* ... Song 4:4 1368
the haughtiness of *m* shall be ... Is 2:11 582
of *m* shall be made low ... Is 2:17 582
Thy *m* shall fall by the sword, and ... Is 3:25 4962
m of Judah, judge, I pray you, ... Is 5:3 376
the *m* of Judah his pleasant plant ... Is 5:7 376
their honourable *m* are famished ... Is 5:13 4962
m of strength to mingle strong ... Is 5:22 582
the LORD have removed *m* far away ... Is 6:12 120
a small thing for you to weary *m* ... Is 7:13 582
and with bows shall *m* come thither ... Is 7:24
as *m* rejoice when they divide the ... Is 9:3
have no joy in their young *m* ... Is 9:17 970
and make *m* go over dryshod ... Is 11:15
shall dash the young *m* to pieces ... Is 13:18 5288
where are thy wise *m* ... Is 19:12
here cometh a chariot of *m* ... Is 21:9 376
the mighty *m* of the children of ... Is 21:17 1368
thy slain *m* are not slain with ... Is 22:2
the quiver with chariots of *m* ... Is 22:6 120
neither do I nourish up young *m* ... Is 23:4 970
earth are burned, and few *m* left ... Is 24:6 582
Thy dead *m* shall live, together ... Is 26:19
word of the LORD, ye scornful *m* ... Is 28:14 582
which *m* deliver to one that is ... Is 29:11
me is taught by the precept of *m* ... Is 29:13 582
of their wise *m* shall perish ... Is 29:14
of their prudent *m* shall be hid ... Is 29:14
the poor among *m* shall rejoice in ... Is 29:19 120
Now the Egyptians are *m*, and not ... Is 31:3 120
his young *m* shall be discomfited ... Is 31:8 970
the wayfaring *m*, though fools, ... Is 35:8 582
to the *m* that sit upon the wall ... Is 36:12 582
O Lord, by these things *m* live ... Is 38:16
said unto him, What said these *m* ... Is 39:3 582
the young *m* shall utterly fall ... Is 40:30 970
thee from the chief *m* thereof ... Is 41:9
worm Jacob, and ye *m* of Israel ... Is 41:14 4962
therefore will I give *m* for thee ... Is 43:4 120
and the workmen, they are of *m* ... Is 44:11 120
that turneth wise *m* backward ... Is 44:25
m of stature, shall come over ... Is 45:14 582
even to him shall *m* come ... Is 45:24
this, and shew yourselves *m* ... Is 46:8 376
fear ye not the reproach of *m* ... Is 51:7 582
his form more than the sons of *m* ... Is 52:14 120
He is despised and rejected of *m* ... Is 53:3 376
merciful *m* are taken away, none ... Is 57:1 582
are in desolate places as dead *m* ... Is 59:10
that *m* may bring unto thee the ... Is 60:11
m, shall call you the Ministers ... Is 61:6
of the world *m* have not heard ... Is 64:4
look upon the carcases of the *m* ... Is 66:24 582
saith the LORD to the *m* of Judah ... Jer 4:3 376
ye *m* of Judah and inhabitants of ... Jer 4:4 376
I will get me unto the great *m* ... Jer 5:5
sepulchre, they are all mighty *m* ... Jer 5:16 1368
my people are found wicked *m* ... Jer 5:26
they set a trap, they catch *m* ... Jer 5:26 582
the assembly of young *m* together ... Jer 6:11 970
set in array as *m* for war against ... Jer 6:23 376
silver shall *m* call them, because ... Jer 6:30
The wise *m* are ashamed, they are ... Jer 8:9
a lodging place of wayfaring *m* ... Jer 9:2
an assembly of treacherous *m* ... Jer 9:2
neither can *m* hear the voice of ... Jer 9:10
the young *m* from the streets ... Jer 9:21 970
Even the carcases of *m* shall fall ... Jer 9:22 120
all the wise *m* of the nations ... Jer 10:7
are all the work of cunning *m* ... Jer 10:9
and speak unto the *m* of Judah ... Jer 11:2 376
is found among the *m* of Judah ... Jer 11:9 376
the LORD of the *m* of Anathoth ... Jer 11:21 582
the young *m* shall die by the ... Jer 11:22 970
bring evil upon the *m* of Anathoth ... Jer 11:23 582
the young *m* a spoiler at noonday ... Jer 15:8 970
nor *m* have lent to me on usury ... Jer 15:10
neither shall *m* lament for them, ... Jer 16:6
Neither shall *m* tear themselves ... Jer 16:7
neither shall *m* give them the cup ... Jer 16:7
princes, the *m* of Judah, and the ... Jer 17:25 376
go to, speak to the *m* of Judah ... Jer 18:11 376
let their *m* be put to death ... Jer 18:21 582
let their young *m* be slain by the ... Jer 18:21 970
sight of the *m* that go with thee ... Jer 19:10 582
the king, with all his mighty *m* ... Jer 26:21 1368
the king sent *m* into Egypt ... Jer 26:22 582
certain *m* with him into Egypt ... Jer 26:22 582
in the dance, both young *m* ... Jer 31:13 970
all the ways of the sons of *m* ... Jer 32:19 120
and in Israel, and among other *m* ... Jer 32:20 120
and the *m* of Judah, and the ... Jer 32:32 376
M shall buy fields for money, and ... Jer 32:44
them with the dead bodies of *m* ... Jer 33:5 120
I will give the *m* that have ... Jer 34:18 582
Go and tell the *m* of Judah ... Jer 35:13 376
Jerusalem, and upon the *m* of Judah ... Jer 36:31 376
remained but wounded *m* among them ... Jer 37:10 582

he weakeneth the hands of the *m* Jer 38:4 582
these *m* have done evil in all Jer 38:9 582
from hence thirty *m* with thee Jer 38:10 582
Ebed-melech took the *m* with him Jer 38:11 582
of these *m* that seek thy life Jer 38:16 582
saw them, and all the *m* of war Jer 39:4 582
of the *m* of whom thou art afraid Jer 39:17 582
the fields, even they and their *m* Jer 40:7 582
land, and had committed unto him *m* Jer 40:7 582
of a Maachathite, they and their *m* Jer 40:8 582
sware unto them and to their *m* Jer 40:9 582
of the king, even ten *m* with him Jer 41:1 582
the ten *m* that were with him, and Jer 41:2 582
were found there, and the *m* of war Jer 41:3 582
and from Samaria, even fourscore *m* Jer 41:5 376
he, and the *m* that were with him Jer 41:7 582
But ten *m* were found among them Jer 41:8 582
cast all the dead bodies of the *m* Jer 41:9 582
Then they took all the *m*, and went Jer 41:12 582
escaped from Johanan with eight *m* Jer 41:15 582
of Ahikam, even mighty *m* of war Jer 41:16 582
So shall it be with all the *m* Jer 42:17 582
son of Kareah, and all the proud *m* Jer 43:2 582
Even *m*, and women, and children, and Jer 43:6 1397
in the sight of the *m* of Judah Jer 43:9 582
Then all the *m* which knew that Jer 44:15 582
offerings unto her, without our *m* Jer 44:19 582
unto all the people, to the *m* Jer 44:20 1397
all the *m* of Judah that are in Jer 44:27 376
and let the mighty *m* come forth Jer 46:9 1368
Why are thy valiant *m* swept away Jer 46:15
Also her hired *m* are in the midst Jer 46:21
then the *m* shall cry, and all the Jer 47:2 120
mighty and strong *m* for the war Jer 48:14 582
his chosen young *m* are gone down Jer 48:15 970
mourn for the *m* of Kir-heres Jer 48:31 582
like pipes for the *m* of Kir-heres Jer 48:36 582
the heathen, and despised among *m* Jer 49:15 120
m of Edom be as the heart of a Jer 49:22 1368
Therefore her young *m* shall fall Jer 49:26 970
all the *m* of war shall be cut off Jer 49:26 582
Kedar, and spoil the *m* of the east Jer 49:28 1121
her young *m* fall in the streets Jer 50:30 970
all her *m* of war shall be cut off Jer 50:30 582
her princes, and upon her wise *m* Jer 50:35
a sword is upon her mighty *m* Jer 50:36 1368
and spare ye not her young *m* Jer 51:3 970
Surely I will fill thee with *m* Jer 51:14 120
The mighty *m* of Babylon have Jer 51:30 1368
the *m* of war are affrighted Jer 51:32 582
and her mighty *m* are taken Jer 51:56 1368
drunk her princes, and her wise *m* Jer 51:57
and her rulers, and her mighty *m* Jer 51:57 1368
all the *m* of war fled, and went Jer 52:7 582
and all the houses of the great *m* Jer 52:13
had the charge of the *m* of war Jer 52:25 582
seven *m* of them that were near Jer 52:25 582
threescore *m* of the people of the Jer 52:25 376
my mighty *m* in the midst of me Lam 1:15
against me to crush my young *m* Lam 1:15 970
and my young *m* are gone into Lam 1:18 970
Is this the city that *m* call The Lam 2:15
my young *m* are fallen by the Lam 2:21 970
nor grieve the children of *m* Lam 3:33 376
as blind *m* in the streets Lam 4:14
so that *m* could not touch their Lam 4:14
They took the young *m* to grind Lam 5:13 970
the young *m* from their musick Lam 5:14 970
your slain *m* before your idols Eze 6:4
when their slain *m* shall be among Eze 6:13
m of the ancients of the house of Eze 8:11 376
were about five and twenty *m* Eze 8:16 376
six *m* came from the way of the Eze 9:2 582
the foreheads of the *m* that sigh Eze 9:4 582
m which were before the house Eze 9:6 582
door of the gate five and twenty *m* Eze 11:1 376
these are the *m* that devise Eze 11:2 582
the *m* of thy kindred, and all the Eze 11:15 582
a few *m* of them from the sword Eze 12:16 582
these *m* have set up their idols Eze 14:3 582
Though these three *m*, Noah, Eze 14:14 582
Though these three *m* were in it Eze 14:16 582
Though these three *m* were in it Eze 14:18 582
or will *m* take a pin of it to Eze 15:3
and madest to thyself images of *m* Eze 16:17 2145
it devoured *m* Eze 19:3 120
to catch the prey, and devoured *m* Eze 19:6 120
of the great *m* that are slain Eze 21:14
thee into the hand of brutish *m* Eze 21:31 582
In thee are *m* that carry tales to Eze 22:9 582
all of them desirable young *m* Eze 23:6 970
that were the chosen *m* of Assyria Eze 23:7 1121
all of them desirable young *m* Eze 23:12 970
for when she saw *m* pourtrayed Eze 23:14 582
all of them desirable young *m* Eze 23:23 970
have sent for *m* to come from far Eze 23:40 582
with the *m* of the common sort Eze 23:42 582
And the righteous *m*, they shall Eze 23:45 582
lips, and eat not the bread of *m* Eze 24:17 582
your lips, nor eat the bread of *m* Eze 24:22 582
I will deliver thee to the *m* of Eze 25:4 1121
Unto the *m* of the east with the Eze 25:10 1121
as *m* enter into a city wherein is Eze 26:10
wast inhabited of seafaring *m* Eze 26:17
thy wise *m*, O Tyrus, that were in Eze 27:8
the wise *m* thereof were in thee Eze 27:9
were in thine army, thy *m* of war Eze 27:10 582
The *m* of Arvad with thine army Eze 27:11 1121

they traded the persons of *m* Eze 27:13 120
The *m* of Dedan were thy merchants Eze 27:15 1121
merchandise, and all thy *m* of war Eze 27:27 582
the *m* of the land that is in Eze 30:5 1121
The young *m* of Aven and of Eze 30:17 970
in the midst of the children of *m* Eze 31:14 120
the flock of my pasture, are *m* Eze 34:31 120
his mountains with his slain *m* Eze 35:8
And I will multiply *m* upon you Eze 36:10 120
I will cause *m* to walk upon you, Eze 36:12 120
more henceforth bereave them of *m* Eze 36:12
you, Thou land devourest up *m* Eze 36:13 120
thou shalt devour *m* no more Eze 36:14 120
Neither will I cause *m* to hear in Eze 36:15
increase them with *m* like a flock Eze 36:37 120
cities be filled with flocks of *m* Eze 36:38 120
all the *m* that are upon the face Eze 38:20 120
they shall sever out *m* of Eze 39:14 582
horses and chariots, with mighty *m* Eze 39:20 1368
and with all *m* of war Eze 39:20 376
way of Hethlon, as *m* go to Zedad Eze 47:15
destroy all the wise *m* of Babylon Dan 2:12 2445
that the wise *m* should be slain Dan 2:13 2445
to slay the wise *m* of Babylon Dan 2:14 2445
the rest of the wise *m* of Babylon Dan 2:18 2445
to destroy the wise *m* of Babylon Dan 2:24 2445
Destroy not the wise *m* of Babylon Dan 2:24 2445
hath demanded cannot the wise *m* Dan 2:27 2445
the children of *m* dwell, the Dan 2:38 606
themselves with the seed of *m* Dan 2:43 606
over all the wise *m* of Babylon Dan 2:48 2445
these *m*, O king, have not Dan 3:12 1400
brought these *m* before the king Dan 3:13 1400
he commanded the most mighty *m* Dan 3:20 1400
Then these *m* were bound in their Dan 3:21 1400
those *m* that took up Shadrach Dan 3:22 1400
And these three *m*, Shadrach, Dan 3:23 1400
Did not we cast three *m* bound Dan 3:24 1400
and said, Lo, I see four *m* loose Dan 3:25 1400
gathered together, saw these *m* Dan 3:27 1400
the wise *m* of Babylon before me Dan 4:6 2445
High ruleth in the kingdom of *m* Dan 4:17 606
up over it the basest of *m* Dan 4:17 606
forasmuch as all the wise *m* of my Dan 4:18 2445
That they shall drive thee from *m* Dan 4:25 606
High ruleth in the kingdom of *m* Dan 4:25 606
And they shall drive thee from *m* Dan 4:32 606
High ruleth in the kingdom of *m* Dan 4:32 606
and he was driven from *m*, and did Dan 4:33 606
and said to the wise *m* of Babylon Dan 5:7 2445
came in all the king's wise *m* Dan 5:8 2445
And now the wise *m*, the Dan 5:15 2445
he was driven from the sons of *m* Dan 5:21 606
God ruled in the kingdom of *m* Dan 5:21 606
Then said these *m*, We shall not Dan 6:5 1400
Then these *m* assembled, and found Dan 6:11 1400
Then these *m* assembled unto the Dan 6:15 1400
they brought those *m* which had Dan 6:24 1400
dominion of my kingdom *m* tremble Dan 6:26
to the *m* of Judah, and to the Dan 9:7 376
for the *m* that were with me saw Dan 10:7 582
of the sons of *m* touched my lips Dan 10:16 120
But they like *m* have transgressed Hos 6:7 120
in the multitude of thy mighty *m* Hos 10:13 1368
Let the *m* that sacrifice kiss the Hos 13:2 120
Hear this, ye old *m*, and give ear, Joel 1:2
withered away from the sons of *m* Joel 1:12 120
They shall run like mighty *m* Joel 2:7 1368
climb the wall like *m* of war Joel 2:7 582
your old *m* shall dream dreams, Joel 2:28
your young *m* shall see visions Joel 2:28 970
Prepare war, wake up the mighty *m* Joel 3:9 582
let all the *m* of war draw near Joel 3:9 582
and of your young *m* for Nazarites Amos 2:11 970
your young *m* have I slain with Amos 4:10 970
there remain ten *m* in one house Amos 6:9 582
and young *m* faint for thirst Amos 8:13 970
All the *m* of thy confederacy have Obad 7 582
the *m* that were at peace with Obad 7 582
destroy the wise *m* out of Edom Obad 8
And thy mighty *m*, O Teman, shall Obad 9 1368
Then were the *m* exceedingly Jonah 1:10 582
For the *m* knew that he fled from Jonah 1:10 582
Nevertheless the *m* rowed hard to Jonah 1:13 582
Then the *m* feared the LORD Jonah 1:16 582
by securely as *m* averse from war Mic 2:8
by reason of the multitude of *m* Mic 2:12 120
shepherds, and eight principal *m* Mic 5:5 120
nor waiteth for the sons of *m* Mic 5:7 120
For the rich *m* thereof are full Mic 6:12
and there is none upright among *m* Mic 7:2 120
are the *m* of his own house Mic 7:6 582
of his mighty *m* is made red Nah 2:3 1368
the valiant *m* are in scarlet Nah 2:3 582
cast lots for her honourable *m* Nah 3:10
all her great *m* were bound in Nah 3:10
makest *m* as the fishes of the sea Hab 1:14 120
punish the *m* that are settled on Zeph 1:12 582
And I will bring distress upon *m* Zeph 1:17 120
that they shall walk like blind *m* Zeph 1:17
m shall worship him, every one Zeph 2:11
ground bringeth forth, and upon *m* Hag 1:11 120
walls for the multitude of *m* Zec 2:4 120
for they are *m* wondered at Zec 3:8 582
and Regem-melech, and their *m* Zec 7:2 582
when *m* inhabited the south and the Zec 7:7
There shall yet old *m* and old Zec 8:4
for I set all *m* every one against Zec 8:10 120

that ten *m* shall take hold out of Zec 8:23 582
shall make the young *m* cheerful Zec 9:17 970
And they shall be as mighty *m* Zec 10:5 1368
I will deliver the *m* every one Zec 11:6 120
m shall dwell in it, and there Zec 14:11
there came wise *m* from the east Mt 2:1 *3097*
he had privily called the wise *m* Mt 2:7 *3097*
that he was mocked of the wise *m* Mt 2:16 *3097*
diligently enquired of the wise *m* Mt 2:16 *3097*
and I will make you fishers of *m* Mt 4:19 *444*
when *m* shall revile you, and Mt 5:11
and to be trodden under foot of *m* Mt 5:13 *444*
Neither do *m* light a candle, and Mt 5:15
Let your light so shine before *m* Mt 5:16 *444*
commandments, and shall teach *m* so Mt 5:19 *444*
that ye do not your alms before *m* Mt 6:1 *444*
that they may have glory of *m* Mt 6:2 *444*
that they may be seen of *m* Mt 6:5 *444*
if ye forgive *m* their trespasses Mt 6:14 *444*
ye forgive not *m* their trespasses Mt 6:15 *444*
they may appear unto *m* to fast Mt 6:16 *444*
thou appear not unto *m* to fast Mt 6:18 *444*
ye would that *m* should do to you Mt 7:12 *444*
Do *m* gather grapes of thorns, or Mt 7:16
But the *m* marvelled, saying, What Mt 8:27 *444*
which had given such power unto *m* Mt 9:8 *444*
Neither do *m* put new wine into Mt 9:17
two blind *m* followed him, crying, Mt 9:27
house, the blind *m* came to him Mt 9:28
But beware of *m* Mt 10:17 *444*
hated of all *m* for my name's sake Mt 10:22
shall confess me before *m* Mt 10:32 *444*
whosoever shall deny me before *m* Mt 10:33 *444*
shall be forgiven unto *m* Mt 12:31 *444*
shall not be forgiven unto *m* Mt 12:31 *444*
idle word that *m* shall speak Mt 12:36 *444*
The *m* of Nineveh shall rise in Mt 12:41 *435*
righteous *m* have desired to see Mt 13:17
But while *m* slept, his enemy came Mt 13:25 *444*
eaten were about five thousand *m* Mt 14:21 *435*
when the *m* of that place had Mt 14:35 *435*
doctrines the commandments of *m* Mt 15:9 *444*
that did eat were four thousand *m* Mt 15:38 *435*
Whom do *m* say that I the Son of Mt 16:13 *444*
be of God, but those that be of *m* Mt 16:23 *444*
be betrayed into the hands of *m* Mt 17:22 *444*
All *m* cannot receive this saying, Mt 19:11
which were made eunuchs of *m* Mt 19:12 *444*
With *m* this is impossible Mt 19:26 *444*
two blind *m* sitting by the way Mt 20:30
from heaven, or of *m* Mt 21:25 *444*
But if we shall say, Of *m* Mt 21:26 *444*
miserably destroy those wicked *m* Mt 21:41
regardest not the person of *m* Mt 22:16 *444*
works they do for to be seen of *m* Mt 23:5 *444*
the markets, and to be called of *m* Mt 23:7 *444*
the kingdom of heaven against *m* Mt 23:13 *444*
outwardly appear righteous unto *m* Mt 23:28 *444*
send unto you prophets, and wise *m* Mt 23:34
Though all *m* shall be offended Mt 26:33
did shake, and became as dead *m* Mt 28:4
make you to become fishers of *m* Mk 1:17 *444*
unto him, All *m* seek for thee Mk 1:37
be forgiven unto the sons of *m* Mk 3:28 *444*
and all *m* did marvel Mk 5:20
and preached that *m* should repent Mk 6:12
loaves were about five thousand *m* Mk 6:44 *435*
doctrines the commandments of *m* Mk 7:7 *444*
God, ye hold the tradition of *m* Mk 7:8 *444*
within, out of the heart of *m* Mk 7:21 *444*
these *m* with bread here in the Mk 8:4
I see *m* as trees, walking Mk 8:24 *444*
them, Whom do *m* say that I am Mk 8:27 *444*
God, but the things that be of *m* Mk 8:33 *444*
is delivered into the hands of *m* Mk 9:31 *444*
With *m* it is impossible, but not Mk 10:27 *444*
John, was it from heaven, or of *m* Mk 11:30 *444*
But if we shall say, Of *m* Mk 11:32 *444*
for all *m* counted John, that he Mk 11:32
regardest not the person of *m* Mk 12:14 *444*
hated of all *m* for my name's sake Mk 13:13
the young *m* laid hold on him Mk 14:51 *3495*
to take away my reproach among *m* Lk 1:25 *444*
earth peace, good will toward *m* Lk 2:14 *444*
all *m* mused in their hearts of Lk 3:15
henceforth thou shalt catch *m* Lk 5:10 *444*
m brought in a bed a man which Lk 5:18 *435*
when *m* shall hate you, and when Lk 6:22 *444*
when all *m* shall speak well of Lk 6:26 *444*
ye would that *m* should do to you Lk 6:31 *444*
shall *m* give into your bosom Lk 6:38
For of thorns *m* do not gather Lk 6:44
When the *m* were come unto him, Lk 7:20 *435*
I liken the *m* of this generation Lk 7:31 *444*
they were about five thousand *m* Lk 9:14 *435*
there talked with him two *m* Lk 9:30 *435*
the two *m* that stood with him Lk 9:32 *435*
be delivered into the hands of *m* Lk 9:44 *444*
with the *m* of this generation Lk 11:31 *435*
The *m* of Nineve shall rise up in Lk 11:32 *435*
the *m* that walk over them are not Lk 11:44 *444*
for ye lade *m* with burdens Lk 11:46 *444*
shall confess me before *m* Lk 12:8 *444*
m shall be denied before the Lk 12:9 *444*
ye yourselves like unto *m* that Lk 12:36 *444*
to whom *m* have committed much, of Lk 12:48
all *m* that dwelt in Jerusalem Lk 13:4 *444*
six days in which *m* ought to work Lk 13:14

M

That none of those *m* which were Lk 14:24 *435*
but *m* cast it out Lk 14:35
which justify yourselves before *m* Lk 16:15 *444*
m is abomination in the sight of Lk 16:15 *444*
met him ten *m* that were lepers Lk 17:12 *435*
there shall be two *m* in one bed Lk 17:34
Two *m* shall be in the field Lk 17:36
that *m* ought always to pray, and Lk 18:1
Two *m* went up into the temple to Lk 18:10 *444*
that I am not as other *m* are Lk 18:11 *444*
with *m* are possible with God Lk 18:27 *444*
John, was it from heaven, or of *m* Lk 20:4 *444*
But and if we say, Of *m* Lk 20:6 *444*
should feign themselves just *m* Lk 20:20
saw the rich *m* casting their Lk 21:1
hated of all *m* for my name's sake Lk 21:17
the *m* that held Jesus mocked him, Lk 22:63 *435*
Herod with his *m* of war set him Lk 23:11 *4753*
two *m* stood by them in shining Lk 24:4 *435*
into the hands of sinful *m* Lk 24:7 *444*
and the life was the light of *m* Jn 1:4 *444*
that all *m* through him might Jn 1:7
when *m* have well drunk, then that Jn 2:10
unto them, because he knew all *m* Jn 2:24
m loved darkness rather than Jn 3:19 *444*
baptizeth, and all *m* come to him Jn 3:26
place where *m* ought to worship Jn 4:20
into the city, and saith to the *m* Jn 4:28 *444*
other *m* laboured, and ye are Jn 4:38
That all *m* should honour the Son, Jn 5:23
I receive not honour from *m* Jn 5:41 *444*
Jesus said, Make the *m* sit down Jn 6:10 *444*
So the *m* sat down, in number Jn 6:10 *435*
Then those *m*, when they had seen Jn 6:14 *444*
the testimony of two *m* is true Jn 8:17 *444*
all *m* will believe on him Jn 11:48
earth, will draw all *m* unto me Jn 12:32
of *m* more than the praise of God Jn 12:43 *444*
By this shall all *m* know that ye Jn 13:35
m gather them, and cast them into Jn 15:6
manifested thy name unto the *m* Jn 17:6 *444*
then, having received a band of *m* Jn 18:3
two *m* stood by them in white Acts 1:10 *435*
Ye *m* of Galilee, why stand ye Acts 1:11 *435*
M and brethren, this scripture Acts 1:16 *435*
Wherefore of these *m* which have Acts 1:21 *435*
which knowest the hearts of all *m* Acts 1:24
at Jerusalem Jews, devout *m* Acts 2:5 *435*
These *m* are full of new wine Acts 2:13
Ye *m* of Judaea, and all ye that Acts 2:14 *435*
your young *m* shall see visions, Acts 2:17 *3495*
your old *m* shall dream dreams Acts 2:17
Ye *m* of Israel, hear these words Acts 2:22 *435*
M and brethren, let me freely Acts 2:29 *435*
and to the rest of the apostles, *M* Acts 2:37 *435*
and goods, and parted them to all *m* Acts 2:45
Ye *m* of Israel, why marvel ye at Acts 3:12 *435*
the number of the *m* was about Acts 4:4 *435*
name under heaven given among *m* Acts 4:12 *444*
they were unlearned and ignorant *m* Acts 4:13 *444*
What shall we do to these *m* Acts 4:16 *444*
for all *m* glorified God for that Acts 4:21
thou hast not lied unto *m* Acts 5:4 *444*
And the young *m* arose, wound him Acts 5:6
and the young *m* came in, and found Acts 5:10 *3495*
to the Lord, multitudes both of *m* Acts 5:14 *435*
the *m* whom ye put in prison are Acts 5:25 *435*
ought to obey God rather than *m* Acts 5:29 *444*
Ye *m* of Israel, take heed to Acts 5:35 *435*
intend to do as touching these *m* Acts 5:35 *444*
to whom a number of *m*, about four Acts 5:36 *435*
unto you, Refrain from these *m* Acts 5:38 *444*
this counsel or this work be of *m* Acts 5:38 *444*
you seven *m* of honest report Acts 6:3 *435*
Then they suborned *m*, which said, Acts 6:11 *435*
And he said, *M*, brethren, and Acts 7:2 *435*
devout *m* carried Stephen to his Acts 8:2 *435*
into every house, and haling *m* Acts 8:3 *435*
they were baptized, both *m* Acts 8:12 *435*
way, whether they were *m* or women Acts 9:2 *435*
the *m* which journeyed with him Acts 9:7 *435*
there, they sent unto him two *m* Acts 9:38 *435*
And now send *m* to Joppa, and call Acts 10:5 *435*
the *m* which were sent from Acts 10:17 *435*
him, Behold, three *m* seek thee Acts 10:19 *435*
Then Peter went down to the *m* Acts 10:21 *435*
wentest in to *m* uncircumcised Acts 11:3 *435*
m already come unto the house Acts 11:11 *435*
Send *m* to Joppa, and call for Acts 11:13 *435*
And some of them were *m* of Cyprus Acts 11:20 *435*
sent unto them, saying, Ye *m* Acts 13:15 *435*
M of Israel, and ye that fear God, Acts 13:16 *435*
M and brethren, children of the Acts 13:26 *435*
Be it known unto you therefore, *m* Acts 13:38 *435*
the chief *m* of the city, and Acts 13:50
down to us in the likeness of *m* Acts 14:11 *444*
We also are *m* of like passions Acts 14:15 *444*
certain *m* which came down from Acts 15:1
rose up, and said unto them, *M* Acts 15:7 *435*
peace, James answered, saying, *M* Acts 15:13 *435*
That the residue of *m* might seek Acts 15:17 *444*
to send chosen *m* of their own Acts 15:22 *435*
chief *m* among the brethren Acts 15:22 *435*
to send chosen *m* unto you with Acts 15:25 *435*
M that have hazarded their lives Acts 15:26 *444*
These *m* are the servants of the Acts 16:17 *444*
the magistrates, saying, These *m* Acts 16:20 *444*
serjeants, saying, Let those *m* go Acts 16:35 *444*
women which were Greeks, and of *m* Acts 17:12 *435*
Ye *m* of Athens, I perceive that Acts 17:22 *435*
of one blood all nations of *m* for Acts 17:26 *444*
all *m* every where to repent Acts 17:30 *444*
hath given assurance unto all *m* Acts 17:31
Howbeit certain *m* clave unto him Acts 17:34 *435*
This fellow persuadeth *m* to Acts 18:13 *444*
all the *m* were about twelve Acts 19:7 *435*
and burned them before all *m* Acts 19:19
m of Macedonia, Paul's companions Acts 19:29
Ye *m* of Ephesus, what man is Acts 19:35 *435*
ye have brought hither these *m* Acts 19:37 *435*
I am pure from the blood of all *m* Acts 20:26
of your own selves shall *m* arise Acts 20:30 *435*
We have four *m* which have a vow Acts 21:23 *435*
Then Paul took the *m*, and the next Acts 21:26 *435*
Crying out, *M* of Israel, help Acts 21:28 *435*
that teacheth all *m* every where Acts 21:28
thousand *m* that were murderers Acts 21:38 *435*
M, brethren, and fathers, hear ye Acts 22:1 *435*
and delivering into prisons both *m* Acts 22:4 *435*
unto all *m* of what thou hast seen Acts 22:15 *444*
beholding the council, said, *M* Acts 23:1 *435*
he cried out in the council, *M* Acts 23:6 *435*
for him of them more than forty *m* Acts 23:21 *435*
offence toward God, and toward *m* Acts 24:16 *444*
principal *m* of the city, at Acts 25:23 *435*
all *m* which are here present with Acts 25:24 *435*
together, he said unto them, *M* Acts 28:17 *435*
and unrighteousness of *m*, who hold Rom 1:18 *444*
And likewise also the *m*, leaving Rom 1:27 *730*
m with *m* working that which is Rom 1:27 *730*
m with *m* working that which is Rom 1:27 *730*
God shall judge the secrets of *m* Rom 2:16 *444*
whose praise is not of *m*, but of Rom 2:29 *444*
and so death passed upon all *m* Rom 5:12 *444*
came upon all *m* to condemnation Rom 5:18 *444*
all *m* unto justification of life Rom 5:18 *444*
of *m* because of the infirmity of Rom 6:19 *442*
to myself seven thousand *m* Rom 11:4 *435*
but condescend to *m* of low estate Rom 12:16
honest in the sight of all *m* Rom 12:17 *444*
in you, live peaceably with all *m* Rom 12:18 *444*
to God, and approved of *m* Rom 14:18 *444*
is come abroad unto all *m* Rom 16:19
of God is wiser than *m* 1Cor 1:25 *444*
of God is stronger than *m* 1Cor 1:25 *444*
not many wise *m* after the flesh 1Cor 1:26
not stand in the wisdom of *m* 1Cor 2:5 *444*
are ye not carnal, and walk as *m* 1Cor 3:3 *444*
Therefore let no man glory in *m* 1Cor 3:21 *444*
of *m* above that which is written 1Cor 4:6
the world, and to angels, and to *m* 1Cor 4:9 *444*
For I would that all *m* were even 1Cor 7:7 *444*
be not ye the servants of *m* 1Cor 7:23 *444*
For though I be free from all *m* 1Cor 9:19
I am made all things to all *m* 1Cor 9:22
I speak as to wise *m* 1Cor 10:15
as I please all *m* in all things 1Cor 10:33
I speak with the tongues of *m* 1Cor 13:1 *444*
tongue speaketh not unto *m* 1Cor 14:2 *444*
speaketh unto *m* to edification 1Cor 14:3 *444*
but in understanding be *m* 1Cor 14:20 *5046*
With *m* of other tongues and other 1Cor 14:21
we are of all *m* most miserable 1Cor 15:19 *444*
If after the manner of *m* I have 1Cor 15:32 *444*
there is one kind of flesh of *m* 1Cor 15:39 *444*
in the faith, quit you like *m* 1Cor 16:13 *407*
hearts, known and read of all *m* 2Cor 3:2 *444*
terror of the Lord, we persuade *m* 2Cor 5:11 *444*
I mean not that other *m* be eased 2Cor 8:13
Lord, but also in the sight of *m* 2Cor 8:21 *444*
unto them, and unto all *m* 2Cor 9:13
Paul, an apostle, (not of *m* Gal 1:1 *444*
For do I now persuade *m*, or God Gal 1:10 *444*
or do I seek to please *m* Gal 1:10 *444*
for if I yet pleased *m*, I should Gal 1:10 *444*
I speak after the manner of *m* Gal 3:15 *444*
let us do good unto all *m* Gal 6:10
not made known unto the sons of *m* Eph 3:5 *444*
to make all *m* see what is the Eph 3:9
captive, and gave gifts unto *m* Eph 4:8 *444*
of doctrine, by the sleight of *m* Eph 4:14 *444*
So ought *m* to love their wives as Eph 5:28 *435*
as to the Lord, and not to *m* Eph 6:7 *444*
and was made in the likeness of *m* Phil 2:7 *444*
moderation be known unto all *m* Phil 4:5 *444*
deceit, after the tradition of *m* Col 2:8 *444*
commandments and doctrines of *m* Col 2:22 *444*
as to the Lord, and not unto *m* Col 3:23 *444*
as ye know what manner of *m* we 1Th 1:5
not as pleasing *m*, but God, which 1Th 2:4 *444*
Nor of *m* sought we glory, neither 1Th 2:6 *444*
received it not as the word of *m* 1Th 2:13 *444*
not God, and are contrary to all *m* 1Th 2:15 *444*
toward another, and toward all *m* 1Th 3:12
the weak, be patient toward all *m* 1Th 5:14
among yourselves, and to all *m* 1Th 5:15
from unreasonable and wicked *m* 2Th 3:2 *444*
for all *m* have not faith 2Th 3:2
of thanks, be made for all *m* 1Ti 2:1 *444*
Who will have all *m* to be saved 1Ti 2:4 *444*
and one mediator between God and *m* 1Ti 2:5 *444*
therefore that *m* pray every where 1Ti 2:8 *435*
God, who is the Saviour of all *m* 1Ti 4:10 *444*
and the younger *m* as brethren 1Ti 5:1
and some *m* they follow after 1Ti 5:24 *444*
disputings of *m* of corrupt minds 1Ti 6:5 *444*
which drown *m* in destruction and 1Ti 6:9 *444*
same commit thou to faithful *m* 2Ti 2:2 *444*
but be gentle unto all *m*, apt to 2Ti 2:24
For *m* shall be lovers of their 2Ti 3:2 *444*
m of corrupt minds, reprobate 2Ti 3:8 *444*
shall be manifest unto all *m* 2Ti 3:9
But evil *m* and seducers shall wax 2Ti 3:13 *444*
with me, but all *m* forsook me 2Ti 4:16
of hospitality, a lover of good *m* Titus 1:8
fables, and commandments of *m* Titus 1:14 *444*
That the aged *m* be sober, grave, Titus 2:2
Young *m* likewise exhort to be Titus 2:6
salvation hath appeared to all *m* Titus 2:11 *444*
shewing all meekness unto all *m* Titus 3:2 *444*
are good and profitable unto *m* Titus 3:8 *444*
high priest taken from among *m* is Heb 5:1 *444*
for *m* in things pertaining to God Heb 5:1 *444*
For *m* verily swear by the greater Heb 6:16 *444*
here *m* that die receive tithes Heb 7:8 *444*
For the law maketh *m* high priests Heb 7:28 *444*
is of force after *m* are dead Heb 9:17
is appointed unto *m* once to die Heb 9:27 *444*
Follow peace with all *m*, and Heb 12:14
spirits of just *m* made perfect Heb 12:23
that giveth to all *m* liberally Jas 1:5
Do not rich *m* oppress you Jas 2:6
and therewith curse we *m*, which Jas 3:9 *444*
Go to now, ye rich *m*, weep and Jas 5:1
stone, disallowed indeed of *m* 1Pet 2:4 *444*
the ignorance of foolish *m* 1Pet 2:15 *444*
Honour all *m* 1Pet 2:17
in the flesh to the lusts of *m* 1Pet 4:2 *444*
according to *m* in the flesh 1Pet 4:6 *444*
but holy *m* of God spake as they 2Pet 1:21 *444*
and perdition of ungodly *m* 2Pet 3:7 *444*
as some *m* count slackness 2Pet 3:9
I write unto you, young *m* 1Jn 2:13 *3495*
I have written unto you, young *m* 1Jn 2:14 *3495*
If we receive the witness of *m* 1Jn 5:9 *444*
hath good report of all *m* 3Jn 12
are certain *m* crept in unawares Jude 4 *444*
to this condemnation, ungodly *m* Jude 4
and the great *m*, and the rich *m* Rev 6:15
chief captains, and the mighty *m* Rev 6:15
many *m* died of the waters, Rev 8:11 *444*
but only those *m* which have not Rev 9:4 *444*
in those days shall *m* seek death Rev 9:6 *444*
faces were as the faces of *m* Rev 9:7 *444*
power was to hurt *m* five months Rev 9:10 *444*
for to slay the third part of *m* Rev 9:15 *444*
was the third part of *m* killed Rev 9:18 *444*
the rest of the *m* which were not Rev 9:20 *444*
were slain of *m* seven thousand Rev 11:13 *444*
on the earth in the sight of *m* Rev 13:13 *444*
These were redeemed from among *m* Rev 14:4 *444*
grievous sore upon the *m* which Rev 16:2 *444*
unto him to scorch *m* with fire Rev 16:8 *444*
m were scorched with great heat, Rev 16:9 *444*
not since *m* were upon the earth Rev 16:18 *444*
there fell upon *m* a great hail Rev 16:21 *444*
m blasphemed God because of the Rev 16:21 *444*
and slaves, and souls of *m* Rev 18:13 *444*
were the great *m* of the earth Rev 18:23
and the flesh of mighty *m* Rev 19:18
on them, and the flesh of all *m* Rev 19:18
the tabernacle of God is with *m* Rev 21:3 *444*

MENAHEM *(men'-a-hem)* {8} *Son of Gadi.*
For *M* the son of Gadi went up 2Kin 15:14 4505
Then *M* smote Tiphsah, and all that 2Kin 15:16 4505
M the son of Gadi to reign over 2Kin 15:17 4505
M gave Pul a thousand talents of 2Kin 15:19 4505
M exacted the money of Israel, 2Kin 15:20 4505
And the rest of the acts of *M* 2Kin 15:21 4505
And *M* slept with his fathers 2Kin 15:22 4505
of Judah Pekahiah the son of *M* 2Kin 15:23 4505

MENAN *(me'-nan)* {1} *Father of Melea; ancestor of Jesus.*
of Melea, which was the son of *M* Lk 3:31 *3104*

MEND {1}
brass to *m* the house of the LORD 2Chr 24:12 2388

MENDING {2}
their father, *m* their nets Mt 4:21 *2675*
were in the ship *m* their nets Mk 1:19 *2675*

MENE *(me'-ne)* {3} *Part of "the handwriting on the wall".*
writing that was written, *M*, *M* Dan 5:25 4484
M; God hath numbered Dan 5:26 4484

MENI See MENAN.

MENNA See MENAN.

MENPLEASERS {2}
Not with eyeservice, as *m* Eph 6:6 *441*
not with eyeservice, as *m* Col 3:22 *441*

MEN'S {24}
the *m* feet that were with him Gen 24:32 582
Fill the *m* sacks with food, as Gen 44:1 582
serve gods, the work of *m* hands Deut 4:28 120
Wherefore hearest thou *m* words 1Sa 24:9 120
forsook the old *m* counsel that 1Kin 12:13
m bones shall be burnt upon thee 1Kin 13:2 120
no gods, but the work of *m* hands 2Kin 19:18 120
burned *m* bones upon them, and 2Kin 23:20 120
and gold, the work of *m* hands Ps 115:4 120
and gold, the work of *m* hands Ps 135:15 120
no gods, but the work of *m* hands Is 37:19 120
the mighty *m* hearts in Moab at Jer 48:41 1368
because of *m* blood, and for the Hab 2:8 120

them afraid, because of *m* blood Hab 2:17 120
borne, and lay them on *m* shoulders Mt 23:4 *444*
are within full of dead *m* bones Mt 23:27
is not come to destroy *m* lives Lk 9:56 *444*
M hearts failing them for fear, Lk 21:26 *444*
is worshipped with *m* hands Acts 17:25 *444*
that is, of other *m* labours 2Cor 10:15
be partaker of other *m* sins 1Ti 5:22
Some *m* sins are open beforehand, 1Ti 5:24 *444*
as a busybody in other *m* matters 1Pet 4:15
having *m* persons in admiration Jude 16 *4283*

MENSERVANTS {10}
sheep, and oxen, and he asses, and *m* Gen 12:16 5650
took sheep, and oxen, and *m* Gen 20:14 5650
herds, and silver, and gold, and *m* Gen 24:35 5650
cattle, and maidservants, and *m* Gen 30:43 5650
have oxen, and asses, flocks, and *m* Gen 32:5 5650
she shall not go out as the *m* do Ex 21:7 5650
and your daughters, and your *m* Deut 12:12 5650
And he will take your *m*, and your 1Sa 8:16 5650
and sheep, and oxen, and *m*, and 2Kin 5:26 5650
and shall begin to beat the *m* Lk 12:45 *3816*

MENSTEALERS {1}
themselves with mankind, for *m* 1Ti 1:10 *405*

MENSTRUOUS {3}
shalt cast them away as a *m* cloth Is 30:22 1739
is as a *m* woman among them Lam 1:17 5079
hath come near to a *m* woman Eze 18:6 5079

MENTION {23}
make *m* of me unto Pharaoh, and Gen 40:14 2142
make no *m* of the name of other Ex 23:13 2142
neither make *m* of the names of Josh 23:7 2142
when he made *m* of the ark of God, 1Sa 4:18 2142
No *m* shall be made of coral, or Job 28:18 2142
I will make *m* of thy Ps 71:16 2142
I will make *m* of Rahab and Babylon Ps 87:4 2142
make *m* that his name is exalted Is 12:4 2142
every one that maketh *m* thereof Is 19:17 2142
only will we make *m* of thy name Is 26:13 2142
make *m* of the God of Israel, but Is 48:1 2142
mother hath he made *m* of my name Is 49:1 2142
ye that make *m* of the LORD Is 62:6 2142
I will *m* the lovingkindnesses of Is 63:7 2142
Make ye *m* to the nations Jer 4:16 2142
I said, I will not make *m* of him Jer 20:9 2142
of the LORD shall ye *m* no more Jer 23:36 2142
for we may not make *m* of the name Amos 6:10 2142
m of you always in my prayers Rom 1:9 *3417*
making *m* of you in my prayers Eph 1:16 *3417*
making *m* of you in our prayers 1Th 1:2 *3417*
making *m* of thee always in my Philem 4 *3417*
made *m* of the departing of the Heb 11:22 *3421*

MENTIONED {7}
cities which are here *m* by name Josh 21:9 7121
These *m* by their names were 1Chr 4:38 935
who is *m* in the book of the kings 2Chr 20:34 5927
For thy sister Sodom was not *m* by Eze 16:56 8052
they shall not be *m* unto him Eze 18:22 2142
that he hath done shall not be *m* Eze 18:24 2142
committed shall be *m* unto him Eze 33:16 2142

MENUHOTH See MANAHETHITES.

MEONENIM *(me-on'-e-nim)* {1} *A place near Shechem.*
come along by the plain of *M* Judg 9:37 6049

MEONOTHAI *(me-on'-o-thahee)* {1} *Descendant of Judah.*
And *M* begat Ophrah 1Chr 4:14 4587

MEPHAATH *(mef'-a-ath)* {4} *A Levitical city in Reuben.*
And Jahaza, and Kedemoth, and *M* Josh 13:18 4158
suburbs, and *M* with her suburbs Josh 21:37 4158
suburbs, and *M* with her suburbs 1Chr 6:79 4158
Holon, and upon Jahazah, and upon *M* Jer 48:21 4158

MEPHIBOSHETH *(me-fib'-o-sheth)* {15} See MERIBBAAL.
1. Son of Jonathan.
And his name was *M* 2Sa 4:4 4648
Now when *M*, the son of Jonathan, 2Sa 9:6 4648
And David said, *M* 2Sa 9:6 4648
but *M* thy master's son shall eat 2Sa 9:10 4648
As for *M*, said the king, he shall 2Sa 9:11 4648
M had a young son, whose name was 2Sa 9:12 4648
of Ziba were servants unto *M* 2Sa 9:12 4648
So *M* dwelt in Jerusalem 2Sa 9:13 4648
Ziba the servant of *M* met him 2Sa 16:1 4648
are all that pertained unto *M* 2Sa 16:4 4648
M the son of Saul came down to 2Sa 19:24 4648
wentest not thou with me, *M* 2Sa 19:25 4648
M said unto the king, Yea, let 2Sa 19:30 4648
But the king spared *M*, the son of 2Sa 21:7 4648
2. Son of Rizpah.
she bare unto Saul, Armoni and *M* 2Sa 21:8 4648

MERAB *(me'-rab)* {3} *Daughter of King Saul.*
the name of the firstborn *M* 1Sa 14:49 4764
David, Behold my elder daughter *M* 1Sa 18:17 4764
M Saul's daughter should have 1Sa 18:19 4764

MERAIAH *(mer-a-i'-ah)* {1} *A priest.*
fathers: of Seraiah, *M* Neh 12:12 4811

MERAIOTH *(me-rah'-yoth)* {7} See MEREMOTH.
1. An ancestor of Azariah.
Zerahiah, and Zerahiah begat *M* 1Chr 6:6 4812
M begat Amariah, and Amariah begat 1Chr 6:7 4812
M his son, Amariah his son, 1Chr 6:52 4812
the son of Azariah, the son of *M* Ezr 7:3 4812
2. Another ancestor of Azariah.
the son of Zadok, the son of *M* 1Chr 9:11 4812
the son of Zadok, the son of *M* Neh 11:11 4812
3. A priest in exile.
of *M*, Helkai Neh 12:15 4812

MERARI *(me-ra'-ri)* {39} See MERARITES. *A son of Levi.*
Gershon, Kohath, and *M* Gen 46:11 4847
Gershon, and Kohath, and *M* Ex 6:16 4847
And the sons of *M* Ex 6:19 4847
Gershon, and Kohath, and *M* Num 3:17 4847
the sons of *M* by their families Num 3:20 4847
Of *M* was the family of the Num 3:33 4847
these are the families of *M* Num 3:33 4847
M was Zuriel the son of Abihail Num 3:35 4847
charge of the sons of *M* shall be Num 3:36 4847
As for the sons of *M*, thou shalt Num 4:29 4847
of the families of the sons of *M* Num 4:33 4847
of the families of the sons of *M* Num 4:42 4847
of the families of the sons of *M* Num 4:45 4847
oxen he gave unto the sons of *M* Num 7:8 4847
and the sons of *M* set forward Num 10:17 4847
of *M*, the family of the Merarites Num 26:57 4847
The children of *M* by their Josh 21:7 4847
the families of the children of *M* Josh 21:34 4847
children of *M* by their families Josh 21:40 4847
Gershon, Kohath, and *M* 1Chr 6:1 4847
Gershom, Kohath, and *M* 1Chr 6:16 4847
The sons of *M*; Mahli, and 1Chr 6:19 4847
The sons of *M*; Mahli, Libni 1Chr 6:29 4847
sons of *M* stood on the left hand 1Chr 6:44 4847
the son of Mushi, the son of *M* 1Chr 6:47 4847
Unto the sons of *M* were given by 1Chr 6:63 4847
the rest of the children of *M* 1Chr 6:77 4847
of Hashabiah, of the sons of *M* 1Chr 9:14 4847
Of the sons of *M* 1Chr 15:6 4847
of the sons of *M* their brethren 1Chr 15:17 4847
namely, Gershon, Kohath, and *M* 1Chr 23:6 4847
The sons of *M*; Mahli, and 1Chr 23:21 4847
The sons of *M* were Mahli and Mushi 1Chr 24:26 4847
The sons of *M* by Jaaziah 1Chr 24:27 4847
Also Hosah, of the children of *M* 1Chr 26:10 4847
of Kore, and among the sons of *M* 1Chr 26:19 4847
and of the sons of *M*, Kish the son 2Chr 29:12 4847
the Levites, of the sons of *M* 2Chr 34:12 4847
him Jeshaiah of the sons of *M* Ezr 8:19 4847

MERARITES *(me-ra'-rites)* {1} *Descendants of Merari.*
of Merari, the family of the *M* Num 26:57 4848

MERATHAIM *(mer-a-tha'-im)* {1} *A symbolic name for Babylon.*
Go up against the land of *M* Jer 50:21 4850

MERCHANDISE {22}
thou shalt not make *m* of her Deut 21:14 6014
of Israel, and maketh *m* of him Deut 24:7 6014
For the *m* of it is better than Prov 3:14 5504
it is better than the *m* of silver Prov 3:14 5505
She perceiveth that her *m* is good Prov 31:18 5504
And her *m* and her hire shall be Is 23:18 5504
for her *m* shall be for them that Is 23:18 5504
m of Ethiopia and of the Sabeans, Is 45:14 5505
riches, and make a prey of thy *m* Eze 26:12 7404
were in thee to occupy thy *m* Eze 27:9 4627
isles were the *m* of thine hand Eze 27:15 5506
and made of cedar, among thy *m* Eze 27:24 4819
Thy riches, and thy fairs, thy *m* Eze 27:27 4627
and the occupiers of thy *m* Eze 27:27 4267
of thy riches and of thy *m* Eze 27:33 4627
in the depths of the waters thy *m* Eze 27:34 4627
By the multitude of thy *m* they Eze 28:16 7404
one to his farm, another to his *m* Mt 22:5 *1711*
my Father's house an house of *m* Jn 2:16 *1712*
with feigned words make *m* of you 2Pet 2:3
no man buyeth their *m* any more Rev 18:11 *1117*
The *m* of gold, and silver, and Rev 18:12 *1117*

MERCHANT {12}
silver, current money with the *m* Gen 23:16
and delivereth girdles unto the *m* Prov 31:24 5503
with all powders of the *m* Song 3:6 7402
a commandment against the *m* city Is 23:11 3667
which art a *m* of the people for Eze 27:3 7402
Tarshish was thy *m* by reason of Eze 27:12 5503
Syria was thy *m* by reason of the Eze 27:16 5503
Damascus was thy *m* in the Eze 27:18 5503
Dedan was thy *m* in precious Eze 27:20 7402
He is a *m*, the balances of deceit Hos 12:7 3667
for all the *m* people are cut down Zeph 1:11 3667
of heaven is like unto a *m* man Mt 13:45 *1713*

MERCHANTMEN {2}
Then there passed by Midianites *m* Gen 37:28 5503
Beside that he had of the *m* 1Kin 10:15 8446

MERCHANTS {28}
and of the traffick of the spice *m* 1Kin 10:15 7402
the king's *m* received the linen 1Kin 10:28 5503
the king's *m* received the linen 2Chr 1:16 5503
that which chapmen and *m* brought 2Chr 9:14 5503
of the Nethinims, and of the *m* Neh 3:31 7402
repaired the goldsmiths and the *m* Neh 3:32 7402
So the *m* and sellers of all kind Neh 13:20 7402
shall they part him among the *m* Job 41:6 3669
thou whom the *m* of Zidon, that Is 23:2 5503
whose *m* are princes, whose Is 23:8 5503
thou hast laboured, even thy *m* Is 47:15 5503
he set it in a city of *m* Eze 17:4 7402
and Meshech, they were thy *m* Eze 27:13 7402
The men of Dedan were thy *m* Eze 27:15 7402
land of Israel, they were thy *m* Eze 27:17 7402
in these were they thy *m* Eze 27:21 5503
The *m* of Sheba and Raamah Eze 27:22 7402
Sheba and Raamah, they were thy *m* Eze 27:22 7402
the *m* of Sheba, Asshur, and Eze 27:23 7402
and Chilmad, were thy *m* Eze 27:23 7402
These were thy *m* in all sorts of Eze 27:24 7402
The *m* among the people shall hiss Eze 27:36 5503
the *m* of Tarshish, with all the Eze 38:13 5503
Thou hast multiplied thy *m* above Nah 3:16 7402
the *m* of the earth are waxed rich Rev 18:3 *1713*
the *m* of the earth shall weep and Rev 18:11 *1713*
The *m* of these things, which were Rev 18:15 *1713*
for thy *m* were the great men of Rev 18:23 *1713*

MERCHANTS' {1}
She is like the *m* ships Prov 31:14 5503

MERCIES {40}
worthy of the least of all the *m* Gen 32:10 2617
for his *m* are great 2Sa 24:14 7356
for very great are his *m* 1Chr 21:13 7356
remember the *m* of David thy 2Chr 6:42 2617
Yet thou in thy manifold *m* Neh 9:19 7356
m thou gavest them saviours Neh 9:27 7356
deliver them according to thy *m* Neh 9:28 7356
Remember, O LORD, thy tender *m* Ps 25:6 7356
not thou thy tender *m* from me Ps 40:11 7356
m blot out my transgressions Ps 51:1 7356
to the multitude of thy tender *m* Ps 69:16 7356
he in anger shut up his tender *m* Ps 77:9 7356
let thy tender *m* speedily prevent Ps 79:8 7356
I will sing of the *m* of the LORD Ps 89:1 2617
with lovingkindness and tender *m* Ps 103:4 7356
not the multitude of thy *m* Ps 106:7 2617
to the multitude of his *m* Ps 106:45 2617
Let thy *m* come also unto me, O Ps 119:41 2617
Let thy tender *m* come unto me Ps 119:77 7356
Great are thy tender *m*, O LORD Ps 119:156 7356
his tender *m* are over all his Ps 145:9 7356
but the tender *m* of the wicked Prov 12:10 7356
but with great *m* will I gather Is 54:7 7356
you, even the sure *m* of David Is 55:3 2617
on them according to his *m* Is 63:7 7356
thy bowels and of thy *m* toward me Is 63:15 7356
LORD, even lovingkindness and *m* Jer 16:5 7356
And I will shew *m* unto you Jer 42:12 7356
It is of the LORD's *m* that we are Lam 3:22 2617
to the multitude of his *m* Lam 3:32 2617
That they would desire *m* of the Dan 2:18 7359
To the Lord our God belong *m* Dan 9:9 7356
but for thy great *m* Dan 9:18 7356
and in lovingkindness, and in *m* Hos 2:19 7356
I am returned to Jerusalem with *m* Zec 1:16 7356
will give you the sure *m* of David Acts 13:34 *3741*
brethren, by the *m* of God Rom 12:1 *3628*
Jesus Christ, the Father of *m* 2Cor 1:3 *3628*
of the Spirit, if any bowels and *m* Phil 2:1 *3628*
God, holy and beloved, bowels of *m* Col 3:12 *3628*

MERCIES' {4}
Nevertheless for thy great *m* sake Neh 9:31 7356
oh save me for thy *m* sake Ps 6:4 2617
save me for thy *m* sake Ps 31:16 2617
help, and redeem us for thy *m* sake Ps 44:26 2617

MERCIFUL {40}
the LORD being *m* unto him Gen 19:16 2551
The LORD, The LORD God, *m* Ex 34:6 7349
(For the LORD thy God is a *m* God Deut 4:31 7349
Be *m*, O LORD, unto thy people Deut 21:8 3722
will be *m* unto his land, and to Deut 32:43 3722
With the *m* thou wilt shew thyself 2Sa 22:26 2623
thou wilt shew thyself *m* 2Sa 22:26 2616
the house of Israel are *m* kings 1Kin 20:31 2617
LORD your God is gracious and *m* 2Chr 30:9 7349
ready to pardon, gracious and *m* Neh 9:17 7349
for thou art a gracious and *m* God Neh 9:31 7349
With the *m* thou wilt shew thyself Ps 18:25 2623
thou wilt shew thyself *m* Ps 18:25 2616
redeem me, and be *m* unto me Ps 26:11 2603
He is ever *m*, and lendeth Ps 37:26 2603
I said, LORD, be *m* unto me Ps 41:4 2603
be *m* unto me, and raise me up, Ps 41:10 2603
Be *m* unto me, O God Ps 56:1 2603
Be *m* unto me, O God, be *m* Ps 57:1 2603
be not *m* to any wicked Ps 59:5 2603
God be *m* unto us, and bless us Ps 67:1 2603
Be *m* unto me, O Lord Ps 86:3 2603
The LORD is *m* and gracious, slow Ps 103:8 7349
yea, our God is *m* Ps 116:5 7355
For his *m* kindness is great Ps 117:2 2617
be *m* unto me according to thy Ps 119:58 2603
thy *m* kindness be for my comfort, Ps 119:76 2617
be *m* unto me, as thou usest to do Ps 119:132 2603
The *m* man doeth good to his own Prov 11:17 2617
m men are taken away, none Is 57:1 2617
for I am *m*, saith the LORD, and I Jer 3:12 2623
for he is gracious and *m*, slow to Joel 2:13 7349
thou art a gracious God, and *m* Jonah 4:2 7349
Blessed are the *m* Mt 5:7 *1655*
Be ye therefore *m*, as your Father Lk 6:36 *3629*
as your Father also is *m* Lk 6:36 *3629*
saying, God be *m* to me a sinner Lk 18:13 *2433*
brethren, that he might be a *m* Heb 2:17 *1655*
For I will be *m* to their Heb 8:12 *2436*

MERCURIUS *(mer-cu'-re-us)* {1} *A Roman god.*
and Paul, *M*, because he was the Acts 14:12 *2060*

MERCY {277}
and thou hast magnified thy *m* Gen 19:19 2617
left destitute my master of his *m* Gen 24:27 2617

M

was with Joseph, and shewed him *m* ... Gen 39:21 2617
give you *m* before the man ... Gen 43:14 7356
Thou in thy *m* hast led forth the ... Ex 15:13 2617
shewing *m* unto thousands of them ... Ex 20:6 2617
shalt make a *m* seat of pure gold ... Ex 25:17 3727
in the two ends of the *m* seat ... Ex 25:18 3727
even of the *m* seat shall ye make ... Ex 25:19 3727
covering the *m* seat with their ... Ex 25:20 3727
toward the *m* seat shall the faces ... Ex 25:20 3727
thou shalt put the *m* seat above ... Ex 25:21 3727
with thee from above the *m* seat ... Ex 25:22 3727
thou shalt put the *m* seat upon ... Ex 26:34 3727
before the *m* seat that is over ... Ex 30:6 3727
the *m* seat that is thereupon, and ... Ex 31:7 3727
shew *m* on whom I will shew *m* ... Ex 33:19 7355
Keeping *m* for thousands, ... Ex 34:7 2617
staves thereof, with the *m* seat ... Ex 35:12 3727
he made the *m* seat of pure gold ... Ex 37:6 3727
on the two ends of the *m* seat ... Ex 37:7 3727
out of the *m* seat made he the ... Ex 37:8 3727
with their wings over the *m* seat ... Ex 37:9 3727
even to the *m* seatward were the ... Ex 37:9 3727
staves thereof, and the *m* seat, ... Ex 39:35 3727
put the *m* seat above upon the ark ... Ex 40:20 3727
within the vail before the *m* seat ... Lev 16:2 3727
in the cloud upon the *m* seat ... Lev 16:2 3727
of the incense may cover the *m* ... Lev 16:13 3727
finger upon the *m* seat eastward ... Lev 16:14 3727
before the *m* seat shall he ... Lev 16:14 3727
and sprinkle it upon the *m* seat ... Lev 16:15 3727
and before the *m* seat ... Lev 16:15 3727
m seat that was upon the ark of ... Num 7:89 3727
is longsuffering, and of great *m* ... Num 14:18 2617
unto the greatness of thy *m* ... Num 14:19 2617
shewing *m* unto thousands of them ... Deut 5:10 2617
with them, nor shew *m* unto them ... Deut 7:2 2603
m with them that love him and keep ... Deut 7:9 2617
the *m* which he sware unto thy ... Deut 7:12 2617
of his anger, and shew thee *m* ... Deut 13:17 7356
the city, and we will shew thee *m* ... Judg 1:24 2617
But my *m* shall not depart away ... 2Sa 7:15 2617
m and truth be with thee ... 2Sa 15:20 2617
sheweth *m* to his anointed, unto ... 2Sa 22:51 2617
servant David my father great *m* ... 1Kin 3:6 2617
m with thy servants that walk ... 1Kin 8:23 2617
for his *m* endureth for ever ... 1Chr 16:34 2617
because his *m* endureth for ever ... 1Chr 16:41 2617
will not take my *m* away from him ... 1Chr 17:13 2617
and of the place of the *m* seat ... 1Chr 28:11 3727
great *m* unto David my father ... 2Chr 1:8 2617
for his *m* endureth for ever ... 2Chr 5:13 2617
shewest *m* unto thy servants, that ... 2Chr 6:14 2617
for his *m* endureth for ever ... 2Chr 7:3 2617
because his *m* endureth for ever, ... 2Chr 7:6 2617
for his *m* endureth for ever ... 2Chr 20:21 2617
for his *m* endureth for ever ... Ezr 3:11 2617
hath extended *m* unto me before ... Ezr 7:28 2617
but hath extended *m* unto us in ... Ezr 9:9 2617
m for them that love him and ... Neh 1:5 2617
grant him *m* in the sight of this ... Neh 1:11 7356
God, who keepest covenant and *m* ... Neh 9:32 2617
to the greatness of thy *m* ... Neh 13:22 2617
or for his land, or for *m* ... Job 37:13 2617
have *m* upon me, and hear my prayer ... Ps 4:1 2603
house in the multitude of thy *m* ... Ps 5:7 2617
Have *m* upon me, O LORD ... Ps 6:2 2603
Have *m* upon me, O LORD ... Ps 9:13 2603
But I have trusted in thy *m* ... Ps 13:5 2617
sheweth *m* to his anointed, to ... Ps 18:50 2617
through the *m* of the most High he ... Ps 21:7 2617
m shall follow me all the days of ... Ps 23:6 2617
according to thy *m* remember thou ... Ps 25:7 2617
All the paths of the LORD are *m* ... Ps 25:10 2617
thee unto me, and have *m* upon me ... Ps 25:16 2603
have *m* also upon me, and answer me ... Ps 27:7 2603
Hear, O LORD, and have *m* upon me ... Ps 30:10 2603
will be glad and rejoice in thy *m* ... Ps 31:7 2617
Have *m* upon me, O LORD, for I am ... Ps 31:9 2603
m shall compass him about ... Ps 32:10 2617
him, upon them that hope in his *m* ... Ps 33:18 2617
Let thy *m*, O LORD, be upon us, ... Ps 33:22 2617
Thy *m*, O LORD, is in the heavens ... Ps 36:5 2617
but the righteous sheweth *m* ... Ps 37:21 2603
Have *m* upon me, O God, according ... Ps 51:1 2603
I trust in the *m* of God for ever ... Ps 52:8 2617
God shall send forth his *m* ... Ps 57:3 2617
For thy *m* is great unto the ... Ps 57:10 2617
The God of my *m* shall prevent me ... Ps 59:10 2617
aloud of thy *m* in the morning ... Ps 59:16 2617
is my defence, and the God of my *m* ... Ps 59:17 2617
O prepare *m* and truth, which may ... Ps 61:7 2617
unto thee, O Lord, belongeth *m* ... Ps 62:12 2617
away my prayer, nor his *m* from me ... Ps 66:20 2617
in the multitude of thy *m* hear me ... Ps 69:13 2617
Is his *m* clean gone for ever ... Ps 77:8 2617
Shew us thy *m*, O LORD, and grant ... Ps 85:7 2617
M and truth are met together ... Ps 85:10 2617
plenteous in *m* unto all them that ... Ps 86:5 2617
For great is thy *m* toward me ... Ps 86:13 2617
longsuffering, and plenteous in *m* ... Ps 86:15 2617
O turn unto me, and have *m* upon me ... Ps 86:16 2603
M shall be built up for ever ... Ps 89:2 2617
m and truth shall go before thy ... Ps 89:14 2617
and my *m* shall be with him ... Ps 89:24 2617
My *m* will I keep for him for ... Ps 89:28 2617
O satisfy us early with thy *m* ... Ps 90:14 2617
thy *m*, O LORD, held me up ... Ps 94:18 2617
He hath remembered his *m* and his ... Ps 98:3 2617

his *m* is everlasting ... Ps 100:5 2617
I will sing of *m* and judgment ... Ps 101:1 2617
shalt arise, and have *m* upon Zion ... Ps 102:13 7355
slow to anger, and plenteous in *m* ... Ps 103:8 2617
so great is his *m* toward them ... Ps 103:11 2617
But the *m* of the LORD is from ... Ps 103:17 2617
for his *m* endureth for ever ... Ps 106:1 2617
for his *m* endureth for ever ... Ps 107:1 2617
For thy *m* is great above the ... Ps 108:4 2617
be none to extend *m* unto him ... Ps 109:12 2617
that he remembered not to shew *m* ... Ps 109:16 2617
because thy *m* is good, deliver ... Ps 109:21 2617
O save me according to thy *m* ... Ps 109:26 2617
thy name give glory, for thy *m* ... Ps 115:1 2617
because his *m* endureth for ever ... Ps 118:1 2617
that his *m* endureth for ever ... Ps 118:2 2617
that his *m* endureth for ever ... Ps 118:3 2617
that his *m* endureth for ever ... Ps 118:4 2617
for his *m* endureth for ever ... Ps 118:29 2617
earth, O LORD, is full of thy *m* ... Ps 119:64 2617
thy servant according unto thy *m* ... Ps 119:124 2617
God, until that he have *m* upon us ... Ps 123:2 2603
Have *m* upon us, O LORD, have ... Ps 123:3 2603
upon us, O LORD, have *m* upon us ... Ps 123:3 2603
for with the LORD there is *m* ... Ps 130:7 2617
for his *m* endureth for ever ... Ps 136:1 2617
for his *m* endureth for ever ... Ps 136:2 2617
for his *m* endureth for ever ... Ps 136:3 2617
for his *m* endureth for ever ... Ps 136:4 2617
for his *m* endureth for ever ... Ps 136:5 2617
for his *m* endureth for ever ... Ps 136:6 2617
for his *m* endureth for ever ... Ps 136:7 2617
for his *m* endureth for ever ... Ps 136:8 2617
for his *m* endureth for ever ... Ps 136:9 2617
for his *m* endureth for ever ... Ps 136:10 2617
for his *m* endureth for ever ... Ps 136:11 2617
for his *m* endureth for ever ... Ps 136:12 2617
for his *m* endureth for ever ... Ps 136:13 2617
for his *m* endureth for ever ... Ps 136:14 2617
for his *m* endureth for ever ... Ps 136:15 2617
for his *m* endureth for ever ... Ps 136:16 2617
for his *m* endureth for ever ... Ps 136:17 2617
for his *m* endureth for ever ... Ps 136:18 2617
for his *m* endureth for ever ... Ps 136:19 2617
for his *m* endureth for ever ... Ps 136:20 2617
for his *m* endureth for ever ... Ps 136:21 2617
for his *m* endureth for ever ... Ps 136:22 2617
for his *m* endureth for ever ... Ps 136:23 2617
for his *m* endureth for ever ... Ps 136:24 2617
for his *m* endureth for ever ... Ps 136:25 2617
for his *m* endureth for ever ... Ps 136:26 2617
thy *m*, O LORD, endureth for ever ... Ps 138:8 2617
of thy *m* cut off mine enemies, and ... Ps 143:12 2617
slow to anger, and of great *m* ... Ps 145:8 2617
him, in those that hope in his *m* ... Ps 147:11 2617
Let not *m* and truth forsake thee ... Prov 3:3 2617
but he that hath *m* on the poor ... Prov 14:21 2603
but *m* and truth shall be to them ... Prov 14:22 2617
honoureth him hath *m* on the poor ... Prov 14:31 2603
By *m* and truth iniquity is purged ... Prov 16:6 2617
M and truth preserve the king ... Prov 20:28 2617
and his throne is upholden by *m* ... Prov 20:28 2617
m findeth life, righteousness, and ... Prov 21:21 2617
and forsaketh them shall have *m* ... Prov 28:13 7355
neither shall have *m* on their ... Is 9:17 7355
For the LORD will have *m* on Jacob ... Is 14:1 7355
And in *m* shall the throne be ... Is 16:5 2617
made them will not have *m* on them ... Is 27:11 7355
that he may have *m* upon you ... Is 30:18 7355
thou didst shew them no *m* ... Is 47:6 7356
for he that hath *m* on them shall ... Is 49:10 7355
will have *m* upon his afflicted ... Is 49:13 7355
kindness will I have *m* on thee ... Is 54:8 7355
the LORD that hath *m* on thee ... Is 54:10 7355
LORD, and he will have *m* upon him ... Is 55:7 7355
in my favour have I had *m* on thee ... Is 60:10 7355
they are cruel, and have no *m* ... Jer 6:23 7355
not pity, nor spare, nor have *m* ... Jer 13:14 7355
neither have pity, nor have *m* ... Jer 21:7 7355
have *m* on his dwellingplaces ... Jer 30:18 7355
I will surely have *m* upon him ... Jer 31:20 7355
for his *m* endureth for ever ... Jer 33:11 2617
to return, and have *m* on them ... Jer 33:26 7355
you, that he may have *m* upon you ... Jer 42:12 7355
are cruel, and will not shew *m* ... Jer 50:42 7355
have *m* upon the whole house of ... Eze 39:25 7355
by shewing *m* to the poor ... Dan 4:27 2604
m to them that love him, and to ... Dan 9:4 2617
for I will no more have *m* upon ... Hos 1:6 7355
But I will have *m* upon the house ... Hos 1:7 7355
I will not have *m* upon her ... Hos 2:4 7355
I will have *m* upon her that had ... Hos 2:23 7355
upon her that had not obtained *m* ... Hos 2:23 7355
because there is no truth, nor *m* ... Hos 4:1 2617
For I desired *m*, and not sacrifice ... Hos 6:6 2617
in righteousness, reap in *m* ... Hos 10:12 2617
keep *m* and judgment, and wait on ... Hos 12:6 2617
in thee the fatherless findeth *m* ... Hos 14:3 7355
vanities forsake their own *m* ... Jonah 2:8 2617
but to do justly, and to love *m* ... Mic 6:8 2617
ever, because he delighteth in *m* ... Mic 7:18 2617
the *m* to Abraham, which thou hast ... Mic 7:20 2617
in wrath remember *m* ... Hab 3:2 7355
wilt thou not have *m* on Jerusalem ... Zec 1:12 7355
Execute true judgment, and shew *m* ... Zec 7:9 2617
for I have *m* upon them ... Zec 10:6 7355
for they shall obtain *m* ... Mt 5:7 *1653*
what that meaneth, I will have *m* ... Mt 9:13 *1656*

Thou son of David, have *m* on us ... Mt 9:27 *1653*
what this meaneth, I will have *m* ... Mt 12:7 *1656*
Have *m* on me, O Lord, thou son of ... Mt 15:22 *1653*
Lord, have *m* on my son ... Mt 17:15 *1653*
Have *m* on us, O Lord, thou son of ... Mt 20:30 *1653*
Have *m* on us, O Lord, thou son of ... Mt 20:31 *1653*
matters of the law, judgment, *m* ... Mt 23:23 *1656*
thou son of David, have *m* on me ... Mk 10:47 *1653*
Thou son of David, have *m* on me ... Mk 10:48 *1653*
his *m* is on them that fear him ... Lk 1:50 *1656*
Israel, in remembrance of his *m* ... Lk 1:54 *1656*
Lord had shewed great *m* upon her ... Lk 1:58 *1656*
To perform the *m* promised to our ... Lk 1:72 *1656*
Through the tender *m* of our God ... Lk 1:78 *1656*
he said, He that shewed *m* on him ... Lk 10:37 *1656*
have *m* on me, and send Lazarus, ... Lk 16:24 *1653*
said, Jesus, Master, have *m* on us ... Lk 17:13 *1653*
thou son of David, have *m* on me ... Lk 18:38 *1653*
Thou son of David, have *m* on me ... Lk 18:39 *1653*
I will have *m* on whom I will have ... Rom 9:15 *1653*
have *m* on whom I will have *m* ... Rom 9:15 *1653*
but of God that sheweth *m* ... Rom 9:16 *1653*
Therefore hath he *m* on whom he ... Rom 9:18 *1653*
on whom he will have *m* ... Rom 9:18
of his glory on the vessels of *m* ... Rom 9:23 *1656*
yet have now obtained *m* through ... Rom 11:30 *1653*
that through your *m* they also may ... Rom 11:31 *1656*
they also may obtain *m* ... Rom 11:31 *1653*
that he might have *m* upon all ... Rom 11:32 *1653*
he that sheweth *m*, with ... Rom 12:8 *1653*
might glorify God for his *m* ... Rom 15:9 *1656*
as one that hath obtained *m* of ... 1Cor 7:25 *1653*
ministry, as we have received *m* ... 2Cor 4:1 *1653*
this rule, peace be on them, and *m* ... Gal 6:16 *1656*
But God, who is rich in *m* ... Eph 2:4 *1656*
but God had *m* on him ... Phil 2:27 *1653*
Grace, *m*, and peace, from God our ... 1Ti 1:2 *1656*
but I obtained *m*, because I did ... 1Ti 1:13 *1653*
for this cause I obtained *m* ... 1Ti 1:16 *1653*
Grace, *m*, and peace, from God the ... 2Ti 1:2 *1656*
The Lord give *m* unto the house of ... 2Ti 1:16 *1656*
find *m* of the Lord in that day ... 2Ti 1:18 *1656*
Grace, *m*, and peace, from God the ... Titus 1:4 *1656*
according to his *m* he saved us ... Titus 3:5 *1656*
of grace, that we may obtain *m* ... Heb 4:16 *1656*
Moses' law died without *m* under ... Heb 10:28 *3628*
he shall have judgment without *m* ... Jas 2:13 *448*
that hath shewed no *m* ... Jas 2:13 *1656*
m rejoiceth against judgment ... Jas 2:13 *1656*
easy to be intreated, full of *m* ... Jas 3:17 *1656*
is very pitiful, and of tender *m* ... Jas 5:11 *3629*
m hath begotten us again unto a ... 1Pet 1:3 *1656*
which had not obtained *m* ... 1Pet 2:10 *1653*
but now have obtained *m* ... 1Pet 2:10 *1653*
Grace be with you, *m*, and peace, ... 2Jn 3 *1656*
M unto you, and peace, and love, be ... Jude 2 *1656*
looking for the *m* of our Lord ... Jude 21 *1656*

MERCYSEAT {1}
of glory shadowing the *m* ... Heb 9:5 *2435*

MERED *(me'-red)* {2} *A descendant of Judah.*
sons of Ezra were, Jether, and *M* ... 1Chr 4:17 4778
daughter of Pharaoh, which *M* took ... 1Chr 4:18 4778

MEREMOTH *(mer'-e-moth)* {6} See MERAIOTH.
1. Son of Uriah the priest.
of *M* the son of Uriah the priest ... Ezr 8:33 4822
them repaired *M* the son of Urijah ... Neh 3:4 4822
After him repaired *M* the son of ... Neh 3:21 4822
2. Married a foreigner in exile.
Vaniah, *M*, Eliashib, ... Ezr 10:36 4822
3. A priest who renewed the covenant.
Harim, *M*, Obadiah, ... Neh 10:5 4822
Shechaniah, Rehum, *M*, ... Neh 12:3 4822

MERES *(me'-res)* {1} *A prince of Media and Persia.*
Shethar, Admatha, Tarshish, *M* ... Est 1:14 4825

MERIBAH *(mer'-i-bah)* {6} See MASSAH, MERIBAH-KADESH. *Same as Meribah-Kadesh.*
name of the place Massah, and *M* ... Ex 17:7 4809
This is the water of *M* ... Num 20:13 4809
against my word at the water of *M* ... Num 20:24 4809
that is the water of *M* in Kadesh ... Num 27:14 4809
didst strive at the waters of *M* ... Deut 33:8 4809
I proved thee at the waters of *M* ... Ps 81:7 4809

MERIBAH-KADESH *(mer'-i-bah-ka'-desh)* {1} *A place between Zin and Sinai.*
of Israel at the waters of *M* ... Deut 32:51

MERIBATH-KADESH See MERIBAH-KADESH.

MERIB-BAAL *(me-rib'-ba-al)* {4} See MEPHIBOSHETH. *Son of Jonathan.*
And the son of Jonathan was *M* ... 1Chr 8:34 4807
and *M* begat Micah ... 1Chr 8:34 4807
And the son of Jonathan was *M* ... 1Chr 9:40 4807
and *M* begat Micah ... 1Chr 9:40 4810

MERODACH *(mer'-o-dak)* {1} See BERODACH, EVIL-MERODACH, MERODACH-BALADAN. *A Babylonian god of war.*
confounded, *M* is broken in pieces ... Jer 50:2 4781

MERODACH-BALADAN *(mer'-o-dak-bal'-a-dan)* {1} See BERODACH-BALADAN. *A king of Babylon.*
At that time *M*, the son of ... Is 39:1 4757

MEROM *(me'-rom)* {2} *A small lake north of the Sea of Chinneroth.*
together at the waters of *M* ... Josh 11:5 4792
them by the waters of *M* suddenly ... Josh 11:7 4792

MERONOTHITE *(me-ron'-o-thite)* {2} *An inhabitant of a district of Zebulun.*
over the asses was Jehdeiah the *M* ... 1Chr 27:30 4824
the Gibeonite, and Jadon the *M* ... Neh 3:7 4824

MEROZ *(me'-roz)* {1} *A place near Lake Merom.*
Curse ye *M*, said the angel of the ... Judg 5:23 4789

MERRILY {1}
then go thou in *m* with the king ... Est 5:14 8056

MERRY {28}
And they drank, and were *m* with him ... Gen 43:34 7937
and trode the grapes, and made *m* ... Judg 9:27 1974
to pass, when their hearts were *m* ... Judg 16:25 2896
night, and let thine heart be *m* ... Judg 19:6 3190
here, that thine heart may be *m* ... Judg 19:9 3190
they were making their hearts *m* ... Judg 19:22 3190
and drunk, and his heart was *m* ... Ruth 3:7 3190
Nabal's heart was *m* within him ... 1Sa 25:36 2896
when Amnon's heart is *m* with wine ... 2Sa 13:28 2896
eating and drinking, and making *m* ... 1Kin 4:20 8056
bread, and let thine heart be *m* ... 1Kin 21:7 3190
m in heart for the goodness that ... 2Chr 7:10 2896
heart of the king was *m* with wine ... Est 1:10 2896
A *m* heart maketh a cheerful ... Prov 15:13 8056
but he that is of a *m* heart hath ... Prov 15:15 2896
A *m* heart doeth good like a ... Prov 17:22 8056
to eat, and to drink, and to be *m* ... Eccl 8:15 8055
and drink thy wine with a *m* heart ... Eccl 9:7 2896
for laughter, and wine maketh *m* ... Eccl 10:19 8055
and the voice of them that make *m* ... Jer 30:19 7832
in the dances of them that make *m* ... Jer 31:4 7832
thine ease, eat, drink, and be *m* ... Lk 12:19 *2165*
and let us eat, and be *m* ... Lk 15:23 *2165*
And they began to be *m* ... Lk 15:24 *2165*
I might make *m* with my friends ... Lk 15:29 *2165*
It was meet that we should make *m* ... Lk 15:32 *2165*
Is any *m*? ... Jas 5:13 *2114*
rejoice over them, and make *m* ... Rev 11:10 *2165*

MERRYHEARTED {1}
languisheth, all the *m* do sigh ... Is 24:7

MESECH *(me'-sek)* {1} See MESHECH. *A tribe joined to Kedar.*
Woe is me, that I sojourn in *M* ... Ps 120:5 4902

MESHA *(me'-shah)* {4}
1. A place in southeastern Arabia.
And their dwelling was from *M* ... Gen 10:30 4852
2. A king of Moab.
M king of Moab was a sheepmaster, ... 2Kin 3:4 4337
3. A son of Caleb.
M his firstborn, which was the ... 1Chr 2:42 4338
4. A son of Shaharaim.
his wife, Jobab, and Zibia, and *M* ... 1Chr 8:9 4331

MESHACH *(me'-shak)* {15} *A companion of Daniel.*
and to Mishael, of *M* ... Dan 1:7 4335
the king, and he set Shadrach, *M* ... Dan 2:49 4336
province of Babylon, Shadrach, *M* ... Dan 3:12 4336
commanded to bring Shadrach, *M* ... Dan 3:13 4336
them, Is it true, O Shadrach, *M* ... Dan 3:14 4336
Shadrach, *M*, and Abed-nego, ... Dan 3:16 4336
was changed against Shadrach, *M* ... Dan 3:19 4336
in his army to bind Shadrach, *M* ... Dan 3:20 4336
men that took up Shadrach, *M* ... Dan 3:22 4336
And these three men, Shadrach, *M* ... Dan 3:23 4336
and spake, and said, Shadrach, *M* ... Dan 3:26 4336
Then Shadrach, *M*, and Abed-nego ... Dan 3:26 4336
Blessed be the God of Shadrach, *M* ... Dan 3:28 4336
against the God of Shadrach, *M* ... Dan 3:29 4336
the king promoted Shadrach, *M* ... Dan 3:30 4336

MESHECH *(me'-shek)* {8} See MESECH.
1. A son of Japheth.
Madai, and Javan, and Tubal, and *M* ... Gen 10:2 4902
Madai, and Javan, and Tubal, and *M* ... 1Chr 1:5 4902
2. A son of Shem.
and Uz, and Hul, and Gether, and *M* ... 1Chr 1:17 4902
3. Descendants of Meschech 1.
Javan, Tubal, and *M*, they were thy ... Eze 27:13 4902
There is *M*, Tubal, and all her ... Eze 32:26 4902
of Magog, the chief prince of *M* ... Eze 38:2 4902
O Gog, the chief prince of *M* ... Eze 38:3 4902
O Gog, the chief prince of *M* ... Eze 39:1 4902

MESHELEMIAH *(me-shel-e-mi'-ah)* {4} See MESHULLAM, SHELEMIAH, SHALLUM. *Father of Zechariah.*
Zechariah the son of *M* was porter ... 1Chr 9:21 4920
Korhites was *M* the son of Kore ... 1Chr 26:1 4920
And the sons of *M* were, Zechariah ... 1Chr 26:2 4920
M had sons and brethren, strong ... 1Chr 26:9 4920

MESHEZABEEL *(me-shez'-a-be-el)* {3}
1. Father of Berechiah.
son of Berechiah, the son of *M* ... Neh 3:4 4898
2. An Israelite who renewed the covenant.
M, Zadok, Jaddua, ... Neh 10:21 4898
And Pethahiah the son of *M* ... Neh 11:24 4898

MESHEZABEL See MESHEZABEEL.

MESHILLEMITH *(me-shil'-le-mith)* {1} See MESHILLEMOTH. *A family of exiles.*
son of Meshullam, the son of *M* ... 1Chr 9:12 4921

MESHILLEMOTH *(me-shil'-le-moth)* {2} See MESHILLEMITH.
1. Father of Berechiah.
Johanan, Berechiah the son of *M* ... 2Chr 28:12 4919
2. A family of exiles.
the son of Ahasai, the son of *M* ... Neh 11:13 4919

MESHOBAB *(me-sho'-bab)* {1} *A chief of Simeon.*
And *M*, and Jamlech, and Joshah the ... 1Chr 4:34 4877

MESHULLAM *(me-shul'-lam)* {25} See MESHELEMIAH.
1. A scribe in Josiah's time.
the son of Azaliah, the son of *M* ... 2Kin 22:3 4918
2. A descendant of Jeconiah.
M, and Hananiah, and Shelomith ... 1Chr 3:19 4918
3. Head of a Gadite family.
their fathers were, Michael, and *M* ... 1Chr 5:13 4918
4. A Benjamite of the Elpaal family.
Zebadiah, and *M*, and Hezeki, and ... 1Chr 8:17 4918
5. Father of Sallu.
Sallu the son of *M*, the son of ... 1Chr 9:7 4918
6. Son of Shephathiah.
M the son of Shephatiah, the son ... 1Chr 9:8 4918
7. Father of Hilkiah.
the son of Hilkiah, the son of *M* ... 1Chr 9:11 4918
the son of Hilkiah, the son of *M* ... Neh 11:11 4918
8. Son of Meshillemith.
the son of Jahzerah, the son of *M* ... 1Chr 9:12 4918
9. A Kohathite repairer of the wall.
and Zechariah and *M*, of the sons of ... 2Chr 34:12 4918
10. A clan leader with Ezra.
and for Zechariah, and for *M* ... Ezr 8:16 4918
11. A priest who accounted for the foreign wives.
and *M* and Shabbethai the Levite ... Ezr 10:15 4918
12. A son of Bani.
M, Malluch, and Adaiah, Jashub, and ... Ezr 10:29 4918
13. A son of Berechiah.
repaired *M* the son of Berechiah ... Neh 3:4 4918
After him repaired *M* the son of ... Neh 3:30 4918
of *M* the son of Berechiah ... Neh 6:18 4918
14. A son of Besodeiah.
Paseah, and *M* the son of Besodeiah ... Neh 3:6 4918
15. A Levite who aided Ezra.
and Hashbadana, Zechariah, and *M* ... Neh 8:4 4918
16. A priest who renewed the covenant.
M, Abijah, Mijamin, ... Neh 10:7 4918
17. A clan leader who renewed the covenant.
Magpiash, *M*, Hezir, ... Neh 10:20 4918
18. A family of exiles.
Sallu the son of *M*, the son of ... Neh 11:7 4918
19. A priest who dedicated the wall.
Of Ezra, *M* ... Neh 12:13 4918
And Azariah, Ezra, and *M*, ... Neh 12:33 4918
20. A descendant of Ginnethon.
of Ginnethon, *M* ... Neh 12:16 4918
21. A Levite gatekeeper.
and Bakbukiah, Obadiah, *M* ... Neh 12:25 4918

MESHULLEMETH *(me-shul'-le-meth)* {1} *Mother of King Amon.*
And his mother's name was *M* ... 2Kin 21:19 4922

MESOBAITE *(me-so'-ba-ite)* {1} *Family name of Jasiel.*
Eliel, and Obed, and Jasiel the *M* ... 1Chr 11:47 4677

MESOPOTAMIA *(mes-o-po-ta'-me-ah)* {7} See ARAM, NAHARAIM. *Land between the Tigris and Euphrates Rivers.*
and he arose, and went to *M* ... Gen 24:10 763
the son of Beor of Pethor of *M* ... Deut 23:4 763
of Chushan-rishathaim king of *M* ... Judg 3:8 763
king of *M* into his hand ... Judg 3:10 763
chariots and horsemen out of *M* ... 1Chr 19:6 763
and Elamites, and the dwellers in *M* ... Acts 2:9 *3318*
father Abraham, when he was in *M* ... Acts 7:2 *3318*

MESS {2}
but Benjamin's *m* was five times ... Gen 43:34 4864
there followed him a *m* of meat ... 2Sa 11:8 4864

MESSAGE {7}
I have a *m* from God unto thee ... Judg 3:20 1697
pass, when Ben-hadad heard this *m* ... 1Kin 20:12 1697
He that sendeth a *m* by the hand ... Prov 26:6 1697
in the LORD's *m* unto the people ... Hag 1:13 4400
sent a *m* after him, saying, We ... Lk 19:14 *4242*
This then is the *m* which we have ... 1Jn 1:5 *1860*
For this is the *m* that ye heard ... 1Jn 3:11 *31*

MESSENGER {34}
And they sent a *m* unto Joseph ... Gen 50:16 6680
the *m* answered and said, Israel is ... 1Sa 4:17 1319
But there came a *m* unto Saul ... 1Sa 23:27 4397
And charged the *m*, saying, When ... 2Sa 11:19 4397
So the *m* went, and came and shewed ... 2Sa 11:22 4397
the *m* said unto David, Surely the ... 2Sa 11:23 4397
Then David said unto the *m* ... 2Sa 11:25 4397
And there came a *m* to David ... 2Sa 15:13 5046
Then Jezebel sent a *m* unto Elijah ... 1Kin 19:2 4397
the *m* that was gone to call ... 1Kin 22:13 4397
And Elisha sent a *m* unto him ... 2Kin 5:10 4397
but ere the *m* came to him ... 2Kin 6:32 4397
look, when the *m* cometh, shut the ... 2Kin 6:32 4397
behold, the *m* came down unto him ... 2Kin 6:33 4397
The *m* came to them, but he cometh ... 2Kin 9:18 4397
And there came a *m*, and told him, ... 2Kin 10:8 4397
the *m* that went to call Micaiah ... 2Chr 18:12 4397
And there came a *m* unto Job ... Job 1:14 4397
If there be a *m* with him, an ... Job 33:23 4397
A wicked *m* falleth into mischief ... Prov 13:17 4397
therefore a cruel *m* shall be sent ... Prov 17:11 4397
so is a faithful *m* to them that ... Prov 25:13 6735
or deaf, as my *m* that I sent ... Is 42:19 4397
one *m* to meet another, to shew ... Jer 51:31 5046
from far, unto whom a *m* was sent ... Eze 23:40 4397
Then spake Haggai the LORD's *m* in ... Hag 1:13 4397
for he is the *m* of the LORD of ... Mal 2:7 4397
Behold, I will send my *m*, and he ... Mal 3:1 4397
even the *m* of the covenant, whom ... Mal 3:1 4397
I send my *m* before thy face, ... Mt 11:10 *32*
I send my *m* before thy face, ... Mk 1:2 *32*
I send my *m* before thy face, ... Lk 7:27 *32*
the *m* of Satan to buffet me, lest ... 2Cor 12:7 *32*
and fellow soldier, but your *m* ... Phil 2:25 *652*

MESSENGERS {79}
Jacob sent *m* before him to Esau ... Gen 32:3 4397
the *m* returned to Jacob, saying, ... Gen 32:6 4397
Moses sent *m* from Kadesh unto the ... Num 20:14 4397
Israel sent *m* unto Sihon king of ... Num 21:21 4397
He sent *m* therefore unto Balaam ... Num 22:5 4397
Spake I not also to thy *m* which ... Num 24:12 4397
I sent *m* out of the wilderness of ... Deut 2:26 4397
she hid the *m* that we sent ... Josh 6:17 4397
because she hid the *m*, which ... Josh 6:25 4397
So Joshua sent *m*, and they ran ... Josh 7:22 4397
he sent *m* throughout all Manasseh ... Judg 6:35 4397
he sent *m* unto Asher, and unto ... Judg 6:35 4397
Gideon sent *m* throughout all ... Judg 7:24 4397
he sent *m* unto Abimelech privily, ... Judg 9:31 4397
Jephthah sent *m* unto the king of ... Judg 11:12 4397
answered unto the *m* of Jephthah ... Judg 11:13 4397
Jephthah sent *m* again unto the ... Judg 11:14 4397
Then Israel sent *m* unto the king ... Judg 11:17 4397
Israel sent *m* unto Sihon king of ... Judg 11:19 4397
they sent *m* to the inhabitants of ... 1Sa 6:21 4397
that we may send *m* unto all the ... 1Sa 11:3 4397
Then came the *m* to Gibeah of Saul ... 1Sa 11:4 4397
of Israel by the hands of *m* ... 1Sa 11:7 4397
And they said unto the *m* that came ... 1Sa 11:9 4397
the *m* came and shewed it to the ... 1Sa 11:9 4397
Wherefore Saul sent *m* unto Jesse ... 1Sa 16:19 4397
Saul also sent *m* unto David's ... 1Sa 19:11 4397
And when Saul sent *m* to take David ... 1Sa 19:14 4397
Saul sent the *m* again to see ... 1Sa 19:15 4397
when the *m* were come in, behold, ... 1Sa 19:16 4397
Saul sent *m* to take David ... 1Sa 19:20 4397
of God was upon the *m* of Saul ... 1Sa 19:20 4397
it was told Saul, he sent other *m* ... 1Sa 19:21 4397
Saul sent *m* again the third time, ... 1Sa 19:21 4397
Behold, David sent *m* out of the ... 1Sa 25:14 4397
and she went after the *m* of David ... 1Sa 25:42 4397
David sent *m* unto the men of ... 2Sa 2:5 4397
Abner sent *m* to David on his ... 2Sa 3:12 4397
David sent *m* to Ish-bosheth ... 2Sa 3:14 4397
he sent *m* after Abner, which ... 2Sa 3:26 4397
king of Tyre sent *m* to David ... 2Sa 5:11 4397
And David sent *m*, and took her ... 2Sa 11:4 4397
And Joab sent *m* to David, and said, ... 2Sa 12:27 4397
he sent *m* to Ahab king of Israel ... 1Kin 20:2 4397
the *m* came again, and said, Thus ... 1Kin 20:5 4397
he said unto the *m* of Ben-hadad ... 1Kin 20:9 4397
the *m* departed, and brought him ... 1Kin 20:9 4397
and he sent *m*, and said unto them, ... 2Kin 1:2 4397
go up to meet the *m* of the king ... 2Kin 1:3 4397
when the *m* turned back unto him, ... 2Kin 1:5 4397
Forasmuch as thou hast sent *m* to ... 2Kin 1:16 4397
the *m* returned, and told the king ... 2Kin 7:15 4397
Then Amaziah sent *m* to Jehoash ... 2Kin 14:8 4397
So Ahaz sent *m* to Tiglath-pileser ... 2Kin 16:7 4397
for he had sent *m* to So king of ... 2Kin 17:4 4397
he sent *m* again unto Hezekiah, ... 2Kin 19:9 4397
the letter of the hand of the *m* ... 2Kin 19:14 4397
By thy *m* thou hast reproached the ... 2Kin 19:23 4397
king of Tyre sent *m* to David ... 1Chr 14:1 4397
David sent *m* to comfort him ... 1Chr 19:2 4397
worse before Israel, they sent *m* ... 1Chr 19:16 4397
fathers sent to them by his *m* ... 2Chr 36:15 4397
But they mocked the *m* of God ... 2Chr 36:16 4397
I sent *m* unto them, saying, I am ... Neh 6:3 4397
wrath of a king is as *m* of death ... Prov 16:14 4397
then answer the *m* of the nation ... Is 14:32 4397
waters, saying, Go, ye swift *m* ... Is 18:2 4397
he sent *m* to Hezekiah, saying, ... Is 37:9 4397
the letter from the hand of the *m* ... Is 37:14 4397
performeth the counsel of his *m* ... Is 44:26 4397
and didst send thy *m* far off ... Is 57:9 6735
by the hand of the *m* which come ... Jer 27:3 4397
sent *m* unto them into Chaldea ... Eze 23:16 4397
In that day shall *m* go forth from ... Eze 30:9 4397
the voice of thy *m* shall no more ... Nah 2:13 4397
when the *m* of John were departed, ... Lk 7:24 *32*
And sent *m* before his face ... Lk 9:52 *32*
they are the *m* of the churches, ... 2Cor 8:23 *652*
when she had received the *m* ... Jas 2:25 *32*

MESSES {1}
sent *m* unto them from before him ... Gen 43:34 4864

MESSIAH *(mes-si'-ah)* {2} See MESSIAS. *The great Deliverer of Israel.*
to build Jerusalem unto the *M* the ... Dan 9:25 4899
and two weeks shall *M* be cut off ... Dan 9:26 4899

MESSIAS *(mes-si'-as)* {2} See MESSIAH. *Greek form of Messiah.*
unto him, We have found the *M* ... Jn 1:41 *3323*
unto him, I know that *M* cometh ... Jn 4:25 *3323*

MET {45}
way, and the angels of God *m* him ... Gen 32:1 6293
thou by all this drove which I *m* ... Gen 33:8 6298
God of the Hebrews hath *m* with us ... Ex 3:18 7136
in the inn, that the LORD *m* him ... Ex 4:24 6298
m him in the mount of God, and ... Ex 4:27 6298
God of the Hebrews hath *m* with us ... Ex 5:3 7122
they *m* Moses and Aaron, who stood ... Ex 5:20 6293
And God *m* Balaam ... Num 23:4 7136
And the LORD *m* Balaam, and put a ... Num 23:16 7136
Because they *m* you not with bread ... Deut 23:4 6923
How he *m* thee by the way, and ... Deut 25:18 7136
all these kings were *m* together ... Josh 11:5 3259

M

they *m* together in Asher on the... Josh 17:10 6293
a company of prophets *m* him... 1Sa 10:10 7125
and she *m* them... 1Sa 25:20 6298
m together by the pool of Gibeon... 2Sa 2:13 6298
the servant of Mephibosheth *m* him... 2Sa 16:1 7135
Absalom *m* the servants of David... 2Sa 18:9 7122
a lion *m* him by the way, and slew... 1Kin 13:24 4672
in the way, behold, Elijah *m* him... 1Kin 18:7 7125
m him in the portion of Naboth... 2Kin 9:21 4672
Jehu *m* with the brethren of... 2Kin 10:13 4672
Because they *m* not the children... Neh 13:2 6923
Mercy and truth are *m* together... Ps 85:10 6298
there *m* him a woman with the... Prov 7:10 7125
and it came to pass, as he *m* them... Jer 41:6 6298
flee from a lion, and a bear *m* him... Amos 5:19 6293
there *m* him two possessed with... Mt 8:28 *5221*
disciples, behold, Jesus *m* them... Mt 28:9 *528*
immediately there *m* him out of... Mk 5:2 *528*
in a place where two ways *m*... Mk 11:4 *296*
there *m* him out of the city a... Lk 8:27 *5221*
from the hill, much people *m* him... Lk 9:37 *4876*
there *m* him ten men that were... Lk 17:12 *528*
going down, his servants *m* him... Jn 4:51 *528*
Jesus was coming, went and *m* him... Jn 11:20 *5221*
in that place where Martha *m* him... Jn 11:30 *5221*
this cause the people also *m* him... Jn 12:18 *5221*
was coming in, Cornelius *m* him... Acts 10:25 *4876*
with a spirit of divination *m* us... Acts 16:16 *528*
daily with them that *m* with him... Acts 17:17 *3909*
when he *m* with us at Assos, we... Acts 20:14 *4820*
into a place where two seas *m*... Acts 27:41
who *m* Abraham returning from the... Heb 7:1 *4876*
father, when Melchisedec *m* him... Heb 7:10 *4876*

METE {6}
when they did *m* it with an omer,... Ex 16:18 4058
m out the valley of Succoth... Ps 60:6 4058
m out the valley of Succoth... Ps 108:7 4058
and with what measure ye *m*... Mt 7:2 *3354*
with what measure ye *m*, it shall... Mk 4:24 *3354*
with the same measure that ye *m*... Lk 6:38 *3354*

METED {3}
a nation *m* out and trodden down,... Is 18:2 6978
a nation *m* out and trodden under... Is 18:7 6978
m out heaven with the span, and... Is 40:12 8505

METEYARD {1}
unrighteousness in judgment, in *m*... Lev 19:35 4060

METHEG-AMMAH *(me'-theg-am'-mah)* {1} *A place in Philistia.*
David took *M* out of the hand of... 2Sa 8:1 4965

METHUSAEL *(me-thu'-sa-el)* {2} *A descendant of Cain.*
and Mehujael begat *M*... Gen 4:18 4967
and *M* begat Lamech... Gen 4:18 4967

METHUSELAH *(me-thu'-se-lah)* {6} See Mathusala. *Son of Enoch.*
sixty and five years, and begat *M*... Gen 5:21 4968
he begat *M* three hundred years... Gen 5:22 4968
M lived an hundred eighty and... Gen 5:25 4968
M lived after he begat Lamech... Gen 5:26 4968
all the days of *M* were nine... Gen 5:27 4968
Henoch, *M*, Lamech,... 1Chr 1:3 4968

METHUSHAEL See Methusael.

MEUNIM *(me-u'-nim)* {1} See Mehunim. *A family of exiles.*
of Besai, the children of *M*... Neh 7:52 4586

MEUNITES See Mehunims.

MEZAHAB *(mez'-a-hab)* {2} *Grandmother of Mehetabel.*
of Matred, the daughter of *M*... Gen 36:39 4314
of Matred, the daughter of *M*... 1Chr 1:50 4314

MEZOBAITE See Mesobaite.

MIAMIN *(mi'-a-min)* {2} See Mijamin, Miniamin.
1. Married a foreigner in exile.
and Jeziah, and Malchiah, and *M*... Ezr 10:25 4326
2. A priest with Zerubbabel.
M, Maadiah, Bilgah,... Neh 12:5 4326

MIBHAR *(mib'-har)* {1} *A "mighty man" of David.*
of Nathan, *M* the son of Haggeri,... 1Chr 11:38 4006

MIBSAM *(mib'-sam)* {3}
1. A son of Ishmael.
and Kedar, and Adbeel, and *M*... Gen 25:13 4017
then Kedar, and Adbeel, and *M*... 1Chr 1:29 4017
2. A son of Simeon.
M his son, Mishma his son... 1Chr 4:25 4017

MIBZAR *(mib'-zar)* {2} *A descendant of Esau.*
Duke Kenaz, duke Teman, duke *M*... Gen 36:42 4014
Duke Kenaz, duke Teman, duke *M*... 1Chr 1:53 4014

MICA See Micha.

MICAH *(mi'-cah)* {28} See Micaiah, Micah's, Michah.
1. An Ephraimite who set up idols.
mount Ephraim, whose name was *M*... Judg 17:1 4319
and they were in the house of *M*,... Judg 17:4 4319
the man *M* had an house of gods,... Judg 17:5 4318
mount Ephraim to the house of *M*... Judg 17:8 4318
M said unto him, Whence comest... Judg 17:9 4319
M said unto him, Dwell with me,... Judg 17:10 4319
And *M* consecrated the Levite... Judg 17:12 4318
priest, and was in the house of *M*... Judg 17:12 4318
Then said *M*, Now know I that the... Judg 17:13 4318
mount Ephraim, to the house of *M*... Judg 18:2 4318
When they were by the house of *M*... Judg 18:3 4318
Thus and thus dealeth *M* with me... Judg 18:4 4318
and came unto the house of *M*... Judg 18:13 4318
Levite, even unto the house of *M*... Judg 18:15 4318
a good way from the house of *M*... Judg 18:22 4318
their faces, and said unto *M*... Judg 18:23 4318
when *M* saw that they were too... Judg 18:26 4318
took the things which *M* had made... Judg 18:27 4318
2. Head of a Reubenite family.
M his son, Reaia his son, Baal... 1Chr 5:5 4318
3. Son of Merib-baal.
and Merib-baal begat *M*... 1Chr 8:34 4318
And the sons of *M* were, Pithon, and... 1Chr 8:35 4318
and Merib-baal begat *M*... 1Chr 9:40 4318
And the sons of *M* were, Pithon, and... 1Chr 9:41 4318
4. A family of exiles.
Galal, and Mattaniah the son of *M*... 1Chr 9:15 4316
5. A sanctuary servant.
M the first, and Jesiah the second... 1Chr 23:20 4318
6. Father of Abdon.
of Shaphan, and Abdon the son of *M*... 2Chr 34:20 4318
7. A prophet.
M the Morasthite prophesied in... Jer 26:18 4320
M the Morasthite in the days of... Mic 1:1 4318

MICAH'S *(mi'-cahs)* {3} *Refers to Micah 1.*
And these went into *M* house... Judg 18:18 4318
to *M* house were gathered together... Judg 18:22 4318
they set them up *M* graven image... Judg 18:31 4318

MICAIAH *(mi-ka-i'-ah)* {18} See Micha, Michaiah. *A prophet who foretold Ahab's fall.*
M the son of Imlah, by whom we... 1Kin 22:8 4321
Hasten hither *M* the son of Imlah... 1Kin 22:9 4321
was gone to call *M* spake unto him... 1Kin 22:13 4321
M said, As the Lord liveth, what... 1Kin 22:14 4321
And the king said unto him, *M*... 1Kin 22:15 4321
smote *M* on the cheek, and said,... 1Kin 22:24 4321
M said, Behold, thou shalt see in... 1Kin 22:25 4321
the king of Israel said, Take *M*... 1Kin 22:26 4321
M said, If thou return at all in... 1Kin 22:28 4321
the same is *M* the son of Imla... 2Chr 18:7 4321
Fetch quickly *M* the son of Imla... 2Chr 18:8 4319
that went to call *M* spake to him... 2Chr 18:12 4321
M said, As the Lord liveth, even... 2Chr 18:13 4321
king, the king said unto him, *M*... 2Chr 18:14 4318
smote *M* upon the cheek, and said,... 2Chr 18:23 4321
M said, Behold, thou shalt see on... 2Chr 18:24 4321
king of Israel said, Take ye *M*... 2Chr 18:25 4321
M said, If thou certainly return... 2Chr 18:27 4321

MICE {4}
golden emerods, and five golden *m*... 1Sa 6:4 5909
images of your *m* that mar the... 1Sa 6:5 5909
and the coffer with the *m* of gold... 1Sa 6:11 5909
And the golden *m*, according to the... 1Sa 6:18 5909

MICHA *(mi'-cah)* {4} See Micah, Micaiah.
1. Son of Mephibosheth.
had a young son, whose name was *M*... 2Sa 9:12 4316
2. A Levite who renewed the covenant.
M, Rehob, Hashabiah,... Neh 10:11 4316
3. A family of exiles.
And Mattaniah the son of *M*... Neh 11:17 4316
son of Mattaniah, the son of *M*... Neh 11:22 4316

MICHAEL *(mi'-ka-el)* {15}
1. Father of Sethur.
of Asher, Sethur the son of *M*... Num 13:13 4317
2. A Gadite who settled in Bashan.
house of their fathers were, *M*... 1Chr 5:13 4317
3. Son of Jeshishai.
the son of Gilead, the son of *M*... 1Chr 5:14 4317
4. Son of Baaseiah.
The son of *M*, the son of Baaseiah... 1Chr 6:40 4317
5. A chief man of Issachar.
M, and Obadiah, and Joel, Ishiah,... 1Chr 7:3 4317
6. A Benjamite in Jerusalem.
And *M*, and Ispah, and Joha, the sons... 1Chr 8:16 4317
7. A warrior in David's army.
and Jozabad, and Jediael, and *M*... 1Chr 12:20 4317
8. Father of Omri.
of Issachar, Omri the son of *M*... 1Chr 27:18 4317
9. A son of Jehoshaphat.
and Zechariah, and Azariah, and *M*... 2Chr 21:2 4317
10. A family of exiles.
Zebadiah the son of *M*, and with... Ezr 8:8 4317
11. Angelic messenger who came to Daniel.
but, lo, *M*, one of the chief... Dan 10:13 4317
these things, but *M* your prince... Dan 10:21 4317
And at that time shall *M* stand up... Dan 12:1 4317
Yet *M* the archangel, when... Jude 9 *3413*
M and his angels fought against... Rev 12:7 *3413*

MICHAH *(mi'-cah)* {3} See Micah, Michaiah. *A sanctuary servant.*
sons of Uzziel; *M*... 1Chr 24:24 4318
of the sons of *M*... 1Chr 24:24 4318
The brother of *M* was Isshiah... 1Chr 24:25 4318

MICHAIAH *(mi-ka-i'-ah)* {7} See Micah, Micaiah.
1. Father of Achbor.
Shaphan, and Achbor the son of *M*... 2Kin 22:12 4320
2. Wife of King Rehoboam.
His mother's name also was *M* the... 2Chr 13:2 4322
3. A prince of Judah.
and to Nethaneel, and to *M*... 2Chr 17:7 4322
4. A priest with Zerubbabel.
son of Mattaniah, the son of *M*... Neh 12:35 4320
Eliakim, Maaseiah, Miniamin, *M*... Neh 12:41 4320
5. Son of Gemariah.
When *M* the son of Gemariah, the... Jer 36:11 4321
Then *M* declared unto them all the... Jer 36:13 4321

MICHAL *(mi'-kal)* {18} See Eglah. *A wife of David.*
and the name of the younger *M*... 1Sa 14:49 4324
M Saul's daughter loved David... 1Sa 18:20 4324
Saul gave him *M* his daughter to... 1Sa 18:27 4324
that *M* Saul's daughter loved him... 1Sa 18:28 4324
M David's wife told him, saying,... 1Sa 19:11 4324
So *M* let David down through a... 1Sa 19:12 4324
M took an image, and laid it in... 1Sa 19:13 4324
And Saul said unto *M*, Why hast... 1Sa 19:17 4324
M answered Saul, He said unto me,... 1Sa 19:17 4324
But Saul had given *M* his daughter... 1Sa 25:44 4324
first bring *M* Saul's daughter... 2Sa 3:13 4324
son, saying, Deliver me my wife *M*... 2Sa 3:14 4324
M Saul's daughter looked through... 2Sa 6:16 4324
M the daughter of Saul came out... 2Sa 6:20 4324
And David said unto *M*, It was... 2Sa 6:21 4324
Therefore *M* the daughter of Saul... 2Sa 6:23 4324
the five sons of *M* the daughter... 2Sa 21:8 4324
that *M* the daughter of Saul... 1Chr 15:29 4324

MICHMAS *(mik'-mas)* {2} See Michmash. *Home of some exiles.*
The men of *M*, an hundred twenty... Ezr 2:27 4363
The men of *M*, an hundred and... Neh 7:31 4363

MICHMASH *(mik'-mash)* {9} See Michmas. *A city near Jerusalem.*
two thousand were with Saul in *M*... 1Sa 13:2 4363
and they came up, and pitched in *M*... 1Sa 13:5 4363
gathered themselves together at *M*... 1Sa 13:11 4363
but the Philistines encamped in *M*... 1Sa 13:16 4363
went out to the passage of *M*... 1Sa 13:23 4363
situate northward over against *M*... 1Sa 14:5 4363
that day from *M* to Aijalon... 1Sa 14:31 4363
of Benjamin from Geba dwelt at *M*... Neh 11:31 4363
at *M* he hath laid up his... Is 10:28 4363

MICHMETHAH *(mik'-me-thah)* {2} *A city between Ephraim and Manasseh.*
the sea to *M* on the north side... Josh 16:6 4366
of Manasseh was from Asher to *M*... Josh 17:7 4366

MICHMETHATH See Michmethah.

MICHRI *(mik'-ri)* {1} *Father of Uzzi.*
the son of Uzzi, the son of *M*... 1Chr 9:8 4381

MICHTAM *(mik'-tam)* {6} *A type of psalm.*
M of David... Ps 16:*t* 4387
a *M* of David, when the... Ps 56:*t* 4387
M of David, when he fled from... Ps 57:*t* 4387
Musician, Altaschith, *M* of David... Ps 58:*t* 4387
Musician, Altaschith, *M* of David... Ps 59:*t* 4387
M of David, to teach... Ps 60:*t* 4387

MICMASH See Michmash.

MICMETHAH See Michmethah.

MICRI See Michri.

MIDDAY {3}
to pass, when *m* was past, and they... 1Kin 18:29 6672
gate from the morning until *m*... Neh 8:3 4276,3117
At *m*, O king, I saw in the way a... Acts 26:13 *2250,3319*

MIDDIN *(mid'-din)* {1} *A city in the wilderness south of Judah.*
In the wilderness, Beth-arabah, *M*... Josh 15:61 4081

MIDDLE {18}
the *m* bar in the midst of the... Ex 26:28 8432
he made the *m* bar to shoot... Ex 36:33 8484
from the *m* of the river, and from... Josh 12:2 8432
in the beginning of the *m* watch... Judg 7:19 8484
people down by the *m* of the land... Judg 9:37 2872
Samson took hold of the two *m*... Judg 16:29 8432
out, as out of the *m* of a sling... 1Sa 25:29 8432
cut off their garments in the *m*... 2Sa 10:4 2677
the *m* was six cubits broad, and... 1Kin 6:6 8484
The door for the *m* chamber was in... 1Kin 6:8 8484
winding stairs into the *m* chamber... 1Kin 6:8 8484
out of the *m* into the third... 1Kin 6:8 8484
day did the king hallow the *m* of... 1Kin 8:64 8432
was gone out into the *m* court... 2Kin 20:4 8484
m of the court that was before... 2Chr 7:7 8484
came in, and sat in the *m* gate... Jer 39:3 8484
were a wheel in the *m* of a wheel... Eze 1:16 8432
hath broken down the *m* wall of... Eph 2:14 *3320*

MIDDLEMOST {2}
than the *m* of the building... Eze 42:5 8484
lowest and the *m* from the ground... Eze 42:6 8484

MIDIAN *(mid'-e-an)* {39} See Madian, Midianite.
1. A son of Abraham.
and Jokshan, and Medan, and *M*... Gen 25:2 4080
And the sons of *M*... Gen 25:4 4080
and Jokshan, and Medan, and *M*... 1Chr 1:32 4080
And the sons of *M*... 1Chr 1:33 4080
2. A nation on the southern border of Israel.
who smote *M* in the field of Moab,... Gen 36:35 4080
and dwelt in the land of *M*... Ex 2:15 4080
Now the priest of *M* had seven... Ex 2:16 4080
father in law, the priest of *M*... Ex 3:1 4080
And the Lord said unto Moses in *M*... Ex 4:19 4080
When Jethro, the priest of *M*... Ex 18:1 4080
And Moab said unto the elders of *M*... Num 22:4 4080
the elders of *M* departed with the... Num 22:7 4080
people, and of a chief house in *M*... Num 25:15 4080
the daughter of a prince of *M*... Num 25:18 4080
and avenge the Lord of *M*... Num 31:3 4080
And they slew the kings of *M*... Num 31:8 4080
and Hur, and Reba, five kings of *M*... Num 31:8 4080
took all the women of *M* captives... Num 31:9 4080
Moses smote with the princes of *M*... Josh 13:21 4080
into the hand of *M* seven years... Judg 6:1 4080
the hand of *M* prevailed against... Judg 6:2 4080
the host of *M* was beneath him in... Judg 7:8 4080
bread tumbled into the host of *M*... Judg 7:13 4080

his hand hath God delivered *M* ... Judg 7:14 4080
into your hand the host of *M* ... Judg 7:15 4080
winepress of Zeeb, and pursued *M* ... Judg 7:25 4080
into your hands the princes of *M* ... Judg 8:3 4080
Zebah and Zalmunna, kings of *M* ... Judg 8:5 4080
them, and took the two kings of *M* ... Judg 8:12 4080
delivered us from the hand of *M* ... Judg 8:22 4080
that was on the kings of *M* ... Judg 8:26 4080
Thus was *M* subdued before the ... Judg 8:28 4080
you out of the hand of *M* ... Judg 9:17 4080
And they arose out of *M*, and came ... 1Kin 11:18 4080
which smote *M* in the field of ... 1Chr 1:46 4080
his oppressor, as in the day of *M* ... Is 9:4 4080
of *M* at the rock of Oreb ... Is 10:26 4080
cover thee, the dromedaries of *M* ... Is 60:6 4080
of the land of *M* did tremble ... Hab 3:7 4080

MIDIANITE *(mid'-e-an-ite)* {1} See MIDIANITES, MIDIANITISH. *A descendant of Midian.*
Hobab, the son of Raguel the *M* ... Num 10:29 4084

MIDIANITES *(mid'-e-an-ites)* {34} See KENITES.
there passed by *M* merchantmen ... Gen 37:28 4084
the *M* sold him into Egypt unto ... Gen 37:36 4092
Vex the *M*, and smite them ... Num 25:17 4084
the children of Israel of the *M* ... Num 31:2 4084
war, and let them go against the *M* ... Num 31:3 4080
And they warred against the *M* ... Num 31:7 4080
because of the *M* the children of ... Judg 6:2 4080
had sown, that the *M* came up ... Judg 6:3 4080
impoverished because of the *M* ... Judg 6:6 4080
unto the LORD because of the *M* ... Judg 6:7 4080
winepress, to hide it from the *M* ... Judg 6:11 4080
us into the hands of the *M* ... Judg 6:13 4080
Israel from the hand of the *M* ... Judg 6:14 4080
thou shalt smite the *M* as one man ... Judg 6:16 4080
Then all the *M* and the Amalekites ... Judg 6:33 4080
so that the host of the *M* were on ... Judg 7:1 4080
me to give the *M* into their hands ... Judg 7:2 4080
deliver the *M* into thine hand ... Judg 7:7 4080
And the *M* and the Amalekites and all ... Judg 7:12 4080
Manasseh, and pursued after the *M* ... Judg 7:23 4080
saying, Come down against the *M* ... Judg 7:24 4080
And they took two princes of the *M* ... Judg 7:25 4080
thou wentest to fight with the *M* ... Judg 8:1 4080
Do unto them as unto the *M* ... Ps 83:9 4080

MIDIANITISH *(mid'-e-an-i'-tish)* {3} *Belonging to the land of Midian.*
a *M* woman in the sight of Moses ... Num 25:6 4084
that was slain with the *M* woman ... Num 25:14 4084
the name of the *M* woman that was ... Num 25:15 4084

MIDNIGHT {14}
About *m* will I go out into the ... Ex 11:4 2676,3915
at *m* the LORD smote all the ... Ex 12:29 2677,3915
lay till *m*, and arose at *m* ... Judg 16:3 2677,3915
it came to pass at *m*, that the ... Ruth 3:8 2677,3915
arose at *m*, and took my son ... 1Kin 3:20 8432,3915
the people shall be troubled at *m* ... Job 34:20 2676,3915
At *m* I will rise to give thanks ... Ps 119:62 2676,3915
m there was a cry made, Behold ... Mt 25:6 *3319,3571*
house cometh, at even, or at *m* ... Mk 13:35 *3317*
and shall go unto him at *m* ... Lk 11:5 *3317*
at *m* Paul and Silas prayed, and ... Acts 16:25 *3317*
and continued his speech until *m* ... Acts 20:7 *3317*
about *m* the shipmen deemed ... Acts 27:27 *3319,3571*

MIDST See APPENDIX.

MIDWIFE {3}
that the *m* said unto her, Fear ... Gen 35:17 3205
the *m* took and bound upon his hand ... Gen 38:28 3205
office of a *m* to the Hebrew women ... Ex 1:16 3205

MIDWIVES {7}
of Egypt spake to the Hebrew *m* ... Ex 1:15 3205
But the *m* feared God, and did not ... Ex 1:17 3205
king of Egypt called for the *m* ... Ex 1:18 3205
the *m* said unto Pharaoh, Because ... Ex 1:19 3205
ere the *m* come in unto them ... Ex 1:19 3205
God dealt well with the *m* ... Ex 1:20 3205
to pass, because the *m* feared God ... Ex 1:21 3205

MIGDAL EDER See EDAR.

MIGDAL-EL *(mig'-dal-el)* {1} *A city in Naphtali.*
And Iron, and *M*, Horem, and ... Josh 19:38 4027

MIGDAL-GAD *(mig'-dal-gad)* {1} *A city in Judah.*
Zenan, and Hadashah, and *M*, ... Josh 15:37 4028

MIGDOL *(mig' dol)* {4}
1. A place west of the Red Sea.
before Pi-hahiroth, between *M* ... Ex 14:2 4024
and they pitched before *M* ... Num 33:7 4024
2. A place in northern Egypt.
land of Egypt, which dwell at *M* ... Jer 44:1 4024
ye in Egypt, and publish in *M* ... Jer 46:14 4024

MIGHT {475}
so I *m* have taken her to me to ... Gen 12:19
that they *m* dwell together ... Gen 13:6
O that Ishmael *m* live before thee ... Gen 17:18
one of the people *m* lightly have ... Gen 26:10
I would it *m* be according to thy ... Gen 30:34
that they *m* conceive among the ... Gen 30:41
that I *m* have sent thee away with ... Gen 31:27
than that they *m* dwell together ... Gen 36:7
that he *m* rid him out of their ... Gen 37:22
because the Egyptians *m* not eat ... Gen 43:32 3201
thou art my firstborn, my *m* ... Gen 49:3 3581
that I *m* shew these my signs ... Ex 10:1
that they *m* send them out of the ... Ex 12:33
tent together, that it *m* be one ... Ex 36:18
that it *m* be above the curious ... Ex 39:21
that the breastplate *m* not be ... Ex 39:21
mind of the LORD *m* be shewed them ... Lev 24:12
heathen, that I *m* be their God ... Lev 26:45
all that *m* do service in the ... Num 4:37
of all that *m* do service in the ... Num 4:41
people in thy *m* from among them ... Num 14:13 3581
that thence he *m* see the utmost ... Num 22:41
that he *m* deliver him into thy ... Deut 2:30
thy works, and according to thy *m* ... Deut 3:24 1369
that ye *m* do them in the land ... Deut 4:14
voice, that he *m* instruct thee ... Deut 4:36
That the slayer *m* flee thither ... Deut 4:42
one of these cities he *m* live ... Deut 4:42
that it *m* be well with them, and ... Deut 5:29
that ye *m* do them in the land ... Deut 6:1
all thy soul, and with all thy *m* ... Deut 6:5 3966
that he *m* bring us in, to give us ... Deut 6:23
that he *m* preserve us alive, as ... Deut 6:24
that he *m* make thee know that man ... Deut 8:3
that he *m* humble thee, and that he ... Deut 8:16
that he *m* prove thee, to do thee ... Deut 8:16
the *m* of mine hand hath gotten me ... Deut 8:17 6108
there shall be no *m* in thine hand ... Deut 28:32 410
that ye *m* know that I am the LORD ... Deut 29:6
that he *m* eat the increase of the ... Deut 32:13
earth *m* know the hand of the LORD ... Josh 4:24
that ye *m* fear the LORD your God ... Josh 4:24
that he *m* destroy them utterly, ... Josh 11:20
that they *m* have no favour ... Josh 11:20
but that he *m* destroy them, as ... Josh 11:20
person at unawares *m* flee thither ... Josh 20:9
that ye *m* rebel this day against ... Josh 22:16
m speak unto our children ... Josh 22:24
that we *m* do the service of the ... Josh 22:27
that ye *m* possess their land ... Josh 24:8
of the children of Israel *m* know ... Judg 3:2
sun when he goeth forth in his *m* ... Judg 5:31 1369
him, and said, Go in this thy *m* ... Judg 6:14 3581
and ten sons of Jerubbaal *m* come ... Judg 9:24
he bowed himself with all his *m* ... Judg 16:30 3581
that *m* put them to shame in any ... Judg 18:7
that she *m* return from the ... Ruth 1:6
that they *m* bring from thence the ... 1Sa 4:4
to meet him, that he *m* salute him ... 1Sa 13:10
land, which a yoke of oxen *m* plow ... 1Sa 14:14
that he *m* be the king's son in ... 1Sa 18:27
asked leave of me that he *m* run ... 1Sa 20:6
before the LORD with all his *m* ... 2Sa 6:14 5797
that he *m* put them in array ... 2Sa 10:10
any suit or cause *m* come unto me ... 2Sa 15:4
LORD *m* bring evil upon Absalom ... 2Sa 17:14
for they *m* not be seen to come ... 2Sa 17:17 3201
that I *m* destroy them that hate ... 2Sa 22:41
that he *m* fulfil the word of the ... 1Kin 2:27
for the throne where he *m* judge ... 1Kin 7:7
that they *m* bring up the ark of ... 1Kin 8:1
house, that my name *m* be therein ... 1Kin 8:16
that he *m* perform his saying, ... 1Kin 12:15
that he *m* not suffer any to go ... 1Kin 15:17
all the acts of Asa, and all his *m* ... 1Kin 15:23 1369
Baasha, and what he did, and his *m* ... 1Kin 16:5 1369
his *m* that he shewed, are they ... 1Kin 16:27 1369
for himself that he *m* die ... 1Kin 19:4
besides, that we *m* enquire of him ... 1Kin 22:7
his *m* that he shewed, and how he ... 1Kin 22:45 1369
in heaven, *m* this thing be ... 2Kin 7:2
in heaven, *m* such a thing be ... 2Kin 7:19
to the intent that he *m* destroy ... 2Kin 10:19
and all that he did, and all his *m* ... 2Kin 10:34 1369
and all that he did, and his *m* ... 2Kin 13:8 1369
his *m* wherewith he fought against ... 2Kin 13:12 1369
of Jehoash which he did, and his *m* ... 2Kin 14:15 1369
and all that he did, and his *m* ... 2Kin 14:28 1369
that his hand *m* be with him to ... 2Kin 15:19
acts of Hezekiah, and all his *m* ... 2Kin 20:20 1369
that they *m* provoke me to anger ... 2Kin 22:17
that no man *m* make his son or his ... 2Kin 23:10
that he *m* perform the words of ... 2Kin 23:24
all his soul, and with all his *m* ... 2Kin 23:25 3966
that he *m* not reign in Jerusalem ... 2Kin 23:33
And all the men of *m*, even seven ... 2Kin 24:16 2428
and that thine hand *m* be with me ... 1Chr 4:10
men of *m* in their generations ... 1Chr 7:2 2428
of Issachar were valiant men of *m* ... 1Chr 7:5 2428
hold to the wilderness men of *m* ... 1Chr 12:8 2428
before God with all their *m* ... 1Chr 13:8 5797
my *m* for the house of my God the ... 1Chr 29:2 3581
and in thine hand is power and *m* ... 1Chr 29:12 1369
With all his reign and his *m* ... 1Chr 29:30 1369
that *m* build an house for the ... 2Chr 2:12
house in, that my name *m* be there ... 2Chr 6:5
that my name *m* be there ... 2Chr 6:6
that the LORD *m* perform his word, ... 2Chr 10:15
that he *m* bring the kingdom again ... 2Chr 11:1
to the intent that he *m* let none ... 2Chr 16:1
besides, that we *m* enquire of him ... 2Chr 18:6
hand is there not power and *m* ... 2Chr 20:6 1369
for we have no *m* against this ... 2Chr 20:12 3581
that he *m* deliver them into the ... 2Chr 25:20
that they *m* be encouraged in the ... 2Chr 31:4
that they *m* take the city ... 2Chr 32:18
that he *m* know all that was in ... 2Chr 32:31
that they *m* provoke me to anger ... 2Chr 34:25
that they *m* give according to the ... 2Chr 35:12
they *m* not depart from their ... 2Chr 35:15
that he *m* fight with him, and ... 2Chr 35:22
of Jeremiah *m* be accomplished ... 2Chr 36:22
mouth of Jeremiah *m* be fulfilled ... Ezr 1:1
that we *m* write the names of the ... Ezr 5:10
that we *m* afflict ourselves ... Ezr 8:21
that we *m* buy corn, because of ... Neh 5:3
m exact of them money and corn ... Neh 5:10
that they *m* have matter for an ... Neh 6:13
report, that they *m* reproach me ... Neh 6:13
that they *m* be reckoned by ... Neh 7:5
that they *m* do with them as they ... Neh 9:24
that the same Levites *m* have the ... Neh 10:37
for none *m* enter into the king's ... Est 4:2
the acts of his power and of his *m* ... Est 10:2 1369
Oh that I *m* have my request ... Job 6:8
that *m* lay his hand upon us both ... Job 9:33
Oh that one *m* plead for a man ... Job 16:21
Oh that I knew where I *m* find him ... Job 23:3
that I *m* come even to his seat ... Job 23:3
the righteous *m* dispute with him ... Job 23:7
whereto *m* the strength of their ... Job 30:2
That it *m* take hold of the ends ... Job 38:13
that the wicked *m* be shaken out ... Job 38:13
that I *m* destroy them that hate ... Ps 18:40
the LORD God *m* dwell among them ... Ps 68:18
none of the men of *m* have found ... Ps 76:5 2428
generation to come *m* know them ... Ps 78:6
That they *m* set their hope in God ... Ps 78:7
m not be as their fathers, a ... Ps 78:8
That they *m* observe his statutes, ... Ps 105:45
that he *m* make his mighty power ... Ps 106:8
that they *m* go to a city of ... Ps 107:7
that he *m* even slay the broken in ... Ps 109:16
thrust sore at me that I *m* fall ... Ps 118:13
that I *m* not sin against thee ... Ps 119:11
that I *m* learn thy statutes ... Ps 119:71
evil way, that I *m* keep thy word ... Ps 119:101
that I *m* meditate in thy word ... Ps 119:148
of the *m* of thy terrible acts ... Ps 145:6 5807
That I *m* make thee know the ... Prov 22:21
till I *m* see what was that good ... Eccl 2:3
that God *m* manifest them, and that ... Eccl 3:18
that they *m* see that they ... Eccl 3:18
findeth to do, do it with thy *m* ... Eccl 9:10 3581
the spirit of counsel and *m* ... Is 11:2 1369
that they *m* go, and fall backward, ... Is 28:13
that are near, acknowledge my *m* ... Is 33:13 1369
names by the greatness of his *m* ... Is 40:26 202
to them that have no *m* he ... Is 40:29 202
that they *m* be called trees of ... Is 61:3
the LORD, that he *m* be glorified ... Is 61:3
that the mountains *m* flow down at ... Is 64:1
that I *m* weep day and night for ... Jer 9:1
that I *m* leave my people, and go ... Jer 9:2
let the mighty man glory in his *m* ... Jer 9:23 1369
great, and thy name is great in *m* ... Jer 10:6 1369
that they *m* be unto me for a ... Jer 13:11
them to know mine hand and my *m* ... Jer 16:21 1369
neck stiff, that they *m* not hear ... Jer 17:23
that they *m* not hear my words ... Jer 19:15
or that my mother *m* have been my ... Jer 20:17
that ye *m* provoke me to anger ... Jer 25:7
Thus *m* we procure great evil ... Jer 26:19
that I *m* drive you out, and that ... Jer 27:15
you out, and that ye *m* perish ... Jer 27:15
that they *m* put us to death, and ... Jer 43:3
that ye *m* cut yourselves off, and ... Jer 44:8
that ye *m* be a curse and a ... Jer 44:8
bow of Elam, the chief of their *m* ... Jer 49:35 1369
their *m* hath failed ... Jer 51:30 1369
that he *m* water it by the furrows ... Eze 17:7
that it *m* bring forth branches, ... Eze 17:8
that it *m* bear fruit ... Eze 17:8
that it *m* be a goodly vine ... Eze 17:8
That the kingdom *m* be base ... Eze 17:14
that it *m* not lift itself up, but ... Eze 17:14
of his covenant it *m* stand ... Eze 17:14
that they *m* give him horses and ... Eze 17:15
that they *m* know that I am the ... Eze 20:12
that I *m* make them desolate ... Eze 20:26
to the end that they *m* know that ... Eze 20:26
That it *m* cause fury to come up ... Eze 24:8
which with their *m* are laid by ... Eze 32:29 1369
they are ashamed of their *m* ... Eze 32:30 1369
that ye *m* be a possession unto ... Eze 36:3
for to the intent that I *m* shew ... Eze 40:4
about, that they *m* have hold ... Eze 41:6
whom they *m* teach the learning and ... Dan 1:4
they *m* stand before the king ... Dan 1:5
that he *m* not defile himself ... Dan 1:8
for wisdom and *m* are his ... Dan 2:20 1370
who hast given me wisdom and *m* ... Dan 2:23 1370
that they *m* not serve nor worship ... Dan 3:28
that they *m* make known unto me ... Dan 4:6
the kingdom by the *m* of my power ... Dan 4:30 8632
his concubines, *m* drink therein ... Dan 5:2
that the princes *m* give accounts ... Dan 6:2
that the purpose *m* not be changed ... Dan 6:17
that no beasts *m* stand before him ... Dan 8:4
that they *m* not obey thy voice ... Dan 9:11
our God, that we *m* turn from our ... Dan 9:13
girl for wine, that they *m* drink ... Joel 3:3
that ye *m* remove them far from ... Joel 3:6
that they *m* enlarge their border ... Amos 1:13
till he *m* see what would become ... Jonah 4:5
that it *m* be a shadow over his ... Jonah 4:6
the LORD, and of judgment, and of *m* ... Mic 3:8 1369
and be confounded at all their *m* ... Mic 7:16 1369
that I *m* rest in the day of ... Hab 3:16
unto Zerubbabel, saying, Not by *m* ... Zec 4:6 2428
sought to go that they *m* walk to ... Zec 6:7

laid, that the temple *m* be built Zec 8:9
that I *m* break my covenant which Zec 11:10
that I *m* break the brotherhood Zec 11:14
that my covenant *m* be with Levi Mal 2:4
That he *m* seek a godly seed Mal 2:15
that it *m* be fulfilled which was Mt 1:22
that it *m* be fulfilled which was Mt 2:15
that it *m* be fulfilled which was Mt 2:23
That it *m* be fulfilled which was Mt 4:14
That it *m* be fulfilled which was Mt 8:17
so that no man *m* pass by that way Mt 8:28 *2480*
that they *m* accuse him Mt 12:10
him, how they *m* destroy him Mt 12:14
That it *m* be fulfilled which was Mt 12:17
That it *m* be fulfilled which was Mt 13:35
besought him that they *m* only Mt 14:36
that it *m* be fulfilled which was Mt 21:4
afterward, that ye *m* believe him Mt 21:32
that they *m* receive the fruits of Mt 21:34
took counsel how they *m* entangle Mt 22:15
consulted that they *m* take Jesus Mt 26:4
For this ointment *m* have been Mt 26:9 *1410*
of the prophets *m* be fulfilled Mt 26:56
that it *m* be fulfilled which was Mt 27:35
that they *m* accuse him Mk 3:2
him, how they *m* destroy him Mk 3:6
that he *m* send them forth to Mk 3:14
prayed him that he *m* be with him Mk 5:18
besought him that they *m* touch if Mk 6:56
that I *m* receive my sight Mk 10:51
if haply he *m* find any thing Mk 11:13
and sought how they *m* destroy him Mk 11:18
that he *m* receive from the Mk 12:2
how they *m* take him by craft Mk 14:1
For it *m* have been sold for more Mk 14:5 *1410*
he sought how he *m* conveniently Mk 14:11
the hour *m* pass from him Mk 14:35
sweet spices, that they *m* come Mk 16:1
enemies *m* serve him without fear Lk 1:74
that they *m* cast him down Lk 4:29
m bring him in because of the Lk 5:19
that they *m* find an accusation Lk 6:7
another what they *m* do to Jesus Lk 6:11
saying, What *m* this parable be Lk 8:9
that seeing they *m* not see Lk 8:10
hearing they *m* not understand Lk 8:10
him that he *m* be with him Lk 8:38
his mouth, that they *m* accuse him Lk 11:54
that I *m* make merry with my Lk 15:29
ye *m* say unto this sycamine tree, Lk 17:6
that he *m* know how much every man Lk 19:15
that at my coming I *m* have Lk 19:23
And could not find what they *m* do Lk 19:48
that they *m* take hold of his Lk 20:20
that so they *m* deliver him unto Lk 20:20
sought how they *m* kill him Lk 22:2
how he *m* betray him unto them Lk 22:4
requiring that he *m* be crucified Lk 23:23
that he *m* bear it after Jesus Lk 23:26
that they *m* understand the Lk 24:45
all men through him *m* believe Jn 1:7
the world through him *m* be saved Jn 3:17
things I say, that ye *m* be saved Jn 5:34
come to me, that ye *m* have life Jn 5:40
that we *m* work the works of God Jn 6:28
that they *m* have to accuse him Jn 8:6
he, Lord, that I *m* believe on him Jn 9:36
that they which see not *m* see Jn 9:39
they which see *m* be made blind Jn 9:39
I am come that they *m* have life Jn 10:10
life, and that they *m* have it more Jn 10:10
my life, that I *m* take it again Jn 10:17
of God, that the Son of God *m* be Jn 11:4
shew it, that they *m* take him Jn 11:57
but that they *m* see Lazarus also, Jn 12:9
they *m* put Lazarus also to death Jn 12:10
Esaias the prophet *m* be fulfilled Jn 12:38
it is come to pass, ye *m* believe Jn 14:29
that my joy *m* remain in you, and Jn 15:11
you, and that your joy *m* be full Jn 15:11
that the word *m* be fulfilled that Jn 15:25
you, that in me ye *m* have peace Jn 16:33
that they *m* know thee the only Jn 17:3
that the scripture *m* be fulfilled Jn 17:12
that they *m* have my joy fulfilled Jn 17:13
that they also *m* be sanctified Jn 17:19
That the saying *m* be fulfilled Jn 18:9
but that they *m* eat the passover Jn 18:28
saying of Jesus *m* be fulfilled Jn 18:32
that the scripture *m* be fulfilled Jn 19:24
that the scripture *m* be fulfilled Jn 19:28
that their legs *m* be broken Jn 19:31
that they *m* be taken away Jn 19:31
he saith true, that ye *m* believe Jn 19:35
besought Pilate that he *m* take Jn 19:38
that ye *m* believe that Jesus is Jn 20:31
that believing ye *m* have life Jn 20:31
that he *m* go to his own place Acts 1:25
nothing how they *m* punish them Acts 4:21
by *m* overshadow some of them Acts 5:15
to the end they *m* not live Acts 7:19
that they *m* receive the Holy Acts 8:15
he *m* bring them bound unto Acts 9:2
that he *m* receive his sight Acts 9:12
that he *m* bring them bound unto Acts 9:21
besought that these words *m* be Acts 13:42
of men *m* seek after the Lord Acts 15:17
if haply they *m* feel after him, Acts 17:27
so that I *m* finish my course with Acts 20:24
that he *m* know wherefore they Acts 22:24
him of Paul, that he *m* loose him Acts 24:26
kept till I *m* send him to Caesar Acts 25:21
I *m* have somewhat to write Acts 25:26
This man *m* have been set at Acts 26:32 *1410*
means they *m* attain to Phenice Acts 27:12 *1410*
I *m* have a prosperous journey by Rom 1:10
that I *m* have some fruit among Rom 1:13
that he *m* be just, and the Rom 3:26
that he *m* be the father of all Rom 4:11
that righteousness *m* be imputed Rom 4:11
of faith, that it *m* be by grace Rom 4:16
to the end the promise *m* be sure Rom 4:16
that he *m* become the father of Rom 4:18
that the offence *m* abound Rom 5:20
even so *m* grace reign through Rom 5:21
the body of sin *m* be destroyed Rom 6:6
that it *m* appear sin, working Rom 7:13
m become exceeding sinful Rom 7:13
of the law *m* be fulfilled in us Rom 8:4
that he *m* be the firstborn among Rom 8:29
God according to election *m* stand Rom 9:11
that I *m* shew my power in thee, Rom 9:17
that my name *m* be declared Rom 9:17
that he *m* make known the riches Rom 9:23
Israel is, that they *m* be saved Rom 10:1
my flesh, and *m* save some of them Rom 11:14
off, that I *m* be graffed in Rom 11:19
that he *m* have mercy upon all Rom 11:32
that he *m* be Lord both of the Rom 14:9
of the scriptures *m* have hope Rom 15:4
that the Gentiles *m* glorify God Rom 15:9
of the Gentiles *m* be acceptable Rom 15:16
that we *m* know the things that 1Cor 2:12
that ye *m* learn in us not to 1Cor 4:6
that we also *m* reign with you 1Cor 4:8
he that hath done this deed *m* be 1Cor 5:2
unto all, that I *m* gain the more 1Cor 9:19
as a Jew, that I *m* gain the Jews 1Cor 9:20
that I *m* gain them that are under 1Cor 9:20
that I *m* gain them that are 1Cor 9:21
I as weak, that I *m* gain the weak 1Cor 9:22
that I *m* by all means save some 1Cor 9:22
that I *m* be partaker thereof with 1Cor 9:23
by my voice I *m* teach others also 1Cor 14:19
that ye *m* have a second benefit 2Cor 1:15
but that ye *m* know the love which 2Cor 2:4
that I *m* know the proof of you, 2Cor 2:9
that the life also of Jesus *m* be 2Cor 4:10
that the life also of Jesus *m* be 2Cor 4:11
that the abundant grace *m* through 2Cor 4:15
that mortality *m* be swallowed up 2Cor 5:4
that we *m* be made the 2Cor 5:21
that ye *m* receive damage by us in 2Cor 7:9
sight of God *m* appear unto you 2Cor 7:12
ye through his poverty *m* be rich 2Cor 8:9
before, that the same *m* be ready 2Cor 9:5
accepted, ye *m* well bear with him 2Cor 11:4
myself that ye *m* be exalted 2Cor 11:7
thrice, that it *m* depart from me 2Cor 12:8
that he *m* deliver us from this Gal 1:4
that I *m* preach him among the Gal 1:16
that they *m* bring us into bondage Gal 2:4
of the gospel *m* continue with you Gal 2:5
that we *m* be justified by the Gal 2:16
the law, that I *m* live unto God Gal 2:19
m come on the Gentiles through Gal 3:14
that we *m* receive the promise of Gal 3:14
by faith of Jesus Christ *m* be Gal 3:22
that we *m* be justified by faith Gal 3:24
that we *m* receive the adoption of Gal 4:5
you, that ye *m* affect them Gal 4:17
he *m* gather together in one all Eph 1:10
all principality, and power, and *m* Eph 1:21 1411
That in the ages to come he *m* Eph 2:7
that he *m* reconcile both unto God Eph 2:16
powers in heavenly places *m* be Eph 3:10
to be strengthened with *m* by his Eph 3:16 1411
that ye *m* be filled with all the Eph 3:19
that he *m* fill all things Eph 4:10
That he *m* sanctify and cleanse it Eph 5:26
That he *m* present it to himself a Eph 5:27
Lord, and in the power of his *m* Eph 6:10 2479
that ye *m* know our affairs, and Eph 6:22
that he *m* comfort your hearts Eph 6:22
Though I *m* also have confidence Phil 3:4
whereof he *m* trust in the flesh Phil 3:4
If by any means I *m* attain unto Phil 3:11
to desire that ye *m* be filled Col 1:9
That ye *m* walk worthy of the Lord Col 1:10
Strengthened with all *m*, Col 1:11 1411
things he *m* have the preeminence Col 1:18
That their hearts *m* be comforted Col 2:2
that he *m* know your estate, and Col 4:8
when we *m* have been burdensome, 1Th 2:6 1410
the Gentiles that they *m* be saved 1Th 2:16
that we *m* see your face 1Th 3:10
m perfect that which is lacking 1Th 3:10
that he *m* be revealed in his time 2Th 2:6
the truth, that they *m* be saved 2Th 2:10
That they all *m* be damned who 2Th 2:12
that we *m* not be chargeable to 2Th 3:8
m shew forth all longsuffering 1Ti 1:16
me the preaching *m* be fully known 2Ti 4:17
and that all the Gentiles *m* hear 2Ti 4:17
that he *m* redeem us from all Titus 2:14
God *m* be careful to maintain good Titus 3:8
though I *m* be much bold in Christ Philem 8
that in thy stead he *m* have Philem 13
that through death he *m* destroy Heb 2:14
that he *m* be a merciful and Heb 2:17
we *m* have a strong consolation, Heb 6:18
they which are called *m* receive Heb 9:15
of God, ye *m* receive the promise Heb 10:36
they *m* have had opportunity to Heb 11:15
that they *m* obtain a better Heb 11:35
that we *m* be partakers of his Heb 12:10
unto the mount that *m* be touched Heb 12:18
that he *m* sanctify the people Heb 13:12
earnestly that it *m* not rain Jas 5:17
m be found unto praise and honour 1Pet 1:7
your faith and hope *m* be in God 1Pet 1:21
that he *m* bring us to God, being 1Pet 3:18
that they *m* be judged according 1Pet 4:6
that by these ye *m* be partakers 2Pet 1:4
which are greater in power and *m* 2Pet 2:11 *1411*
that they *m* be made manifest that 1Jn 2:19
that he *m* destroy the works of 1Jn 3:8
that we *m* live through him 1Jn 4:9
that we *m* be fellowhelpers to the 3Jn 8
and honour, and power, and *m* Rev 7:12 *2479*
eagle, that she *m* fly into the Rev 12:14
that he *m* cause her to be carried Rev 12:15
And that no man *m* buy or sell Rev 13:17 *1410*
kings of the east *m* be prepared Rev 16:12

MIGHTEST {19}
that thou *m* know that the LORD he Deut 4:35
That thou *m* fear the LORD thy God Deut 6:2
wherewith thou *m* be bound to Judg 16:6
thee, wherewith thou *m* be bound Judg 16:10
tell me wherewith thou *m* be bound Judg 16:13
down that thou *m* see the battle 1Sa 17:28
that thou *m* bring them again unto Neh 9:29
that thou *m* still the enemy and Ps 8:2
that thou *m* be justified when Ps 51:4
that thou *m* answer the words of Prov 22:21
that thou *m* know the thoughts of Dan 2:30
thou *m* be profited by me Mt 15:5
thou *m* be profited by me Mk 7:11
That thou *m* know the certainty of Lk 1:4
that thou *m* receive thy sight, and Acts 9:17
That thou *m* be justified in thy Rom 3:4
m overcome when thou art judged Rom 3:4
that thou *m* charge some that they 1Ti 1:3
that thou by them *m* war a good 1Ti 1:18

MIGHTIER {3}
for thou art much *m* than we Gen 26:16 6105
of Israel are more and *m* than we Ex 1:9 6099
a greater nation and *m* than they Num 14:12 6099
m than thou art, to bring thee in Deut 4:38 6099
nations greater and *m* than thou Deut 7:1 6099
m than thyself, cities great and Deut 9:1 6099
and I will make of thee a nation *m* Deut 9:14 6099
nations and *m* than yourselves Deut 11:23 6099
The LORD on high is *m* than the Ps 93:4 117
with him that is *m* than he Eccl 6:10 8623
that cometh after me is *m* than I Mt 3:11 *2478*
cometh one *m* than I after me Mk 1:7 *2478*
but one *m* than I cometh, the Lk 3:16 *2478*

MIGHTIES {2}
who was one of the three *m* 1Chr 11:12 1368
and had the name among the three *m* 1Chr 11:24 1368

MIGHTIEST {1}
These things did these three *m* 1Chr 11:19 1368

MIGHTILY {11}
thee, and that ye may increase *m* Deut 6:3 3966
twenty years he *m* oppressed the Judg 4:3 2393
of the LORD came *m* upon him Judg 14:6
of the LORD came *m* upon him Judg 15:14
he shall *m* roar upon his Jer 25:30
with sackcloth, and cry *m* unto God Jonah 3:8 2393
loins strong, fortify thy power *m* Nah 2:1 3966
For he *m* convinced the Jews, and Acts 18:28 *2159*
So *m* grew the word of God and Acts 19:20 *2596,2904*
which worketh in me *m* Col 1:29 *1722,1411*
he cried *m* with a strong voice, Rev 18:2 *1722,2479*

MIGHTY {284}
the same became *m* men which were Gen 6:4 1368
began to be a *m* one in the earth Gen 10:8 1368
He was a *m* hunter before the LORD Gen 10:9 1368
Even as Nimrod the *m* hunter Gen 10:9 1368
m nation, and all the nations of Gen 18:18 6099
thou art a *m* prince among us Gen 23:6 430
the hands of the *m* God of Jacob Gen 49:24 46
multiplied, and waxed exceeding *m* Ex 1:7 6105
multiplied, and waxed very *m* Ex 1:20 6105
let you go, no, not by a *m* hand Ex 3:19 2389
there be no more *m* thunderings Ex 9:28 430
LORD turned a *m* strong west wind Ex 10:19 3966
they sank as lead in the *m* waters Ex 15:10 117
the *m* men of Moab, trembling Ex 15:15 352
great power, and with a *m* hand Ex 32:11 2389
nor honour the person of the *m* Lev 19:15 1419
for they are too *m* for me Num 22:6 6099
thy greatness, and thy *m* hand Deut 3:24 2389
and by war, and by a *m* hand Deut 4:34 2389
with his *m* power out of Egypt Deut 4:37 1419
thee out thence through a *m* hand Deut 5:15 2389
us out of Egypt with a *m* hand Deut 6:21 2389
brought you out with a *m* hand Deut 7:8 2389
the *m* hand, and the stretched out Deut 7:19 2389
is among you, a *m* God and terrible Deut 7:21 1419
destroy them with a *m* destruction Deut 7:23 1419

forth out of Egypt with a *m* hand ... Deut 9:26 2389
broughtest out by thy *m* power ... Deut 9:29 1419
Lord of lords, a great God, a *m* ... Deut 10:17 1368
his *m* hand, and his stretched out ... Deut 11:2 2389
became there a nation, great, *m* ... Deut 26:5 6099
forth out of Egypt with a *m* hand ... Deut 26:8 2389
And in all that *m* hand, and in all ... Deut 34:12 2389
all the *m* men of valour, and help ... Josh 1:14 1368
hand of the LORD, that it is *m* ... Josh 4:24 2389
thereof, and the *m* men of valour ... Josh 6:2 1368
thirty thousand *m* men of valour ... Josh 8:3 1368
Ai, and all the men thereof were *m* ... Josh 10:2 1368
him, and all the *m* men of valour ... Josh 10:7 1368
made me have dominion over the *m* ... Judg 5:13 1368
the pransings of their *m* ones ... Judg 5:22 47
help of the LORD against the *m* ... Judg 5:23 1368
with thee, thou *m* man of valour ... Judg 6:12 1368
Gileadite was a *m* man of valour ... Judg 11:1 1368
a *m* man of wealth, of the family ... Ruth 2:1 1368
The bows of the *m* men are broken ... 1Sa 2:4 1368
out of the hand of these *m* Gods ... 1Sa 4:8 117
a Benjamite, a *m* man of power ... 1Sa 9:1 1368
a *m* valiant man, and a man of war, ... 1Sa 16:18 1368
how are the *m* fallen ... 2Sa 1:19 1368
of the *m* is vilely cast away ... 2Sa 1:21 1368
the slain, from the fat of the *m* ... 2Sa 1:22 1368
How are the *m* fallen in the midst ... 2Sa 1:25 1368
How are the *m* fallen, and the ... 2Sa 1:27 1368
and all the host of the *m* men ... 2Sa 10:7 1368
all the *m* men were on his right ... 2Sa 16:6 1368
and his men, that they be *m* men ... 2Sa 17:8 1368
that thy father is a *m* man ... 2Sa 17:10 1368
the Pelethites, and all the *m* men ... 2Sa 20:7 1368
names of the *m* men whom David had ... 2Sa 23:8 1368
one of the three *m* men with David ... 2Sa 23:9 1368
the three *m* men brake through the ... 2Sa 23:16 1368
things did these three *m* men ... 2Sa 23:17 1368
had the name among three *m* men ... 2Sa 23:22 1368
the *m* men which belonged to David ... 1Kin 1:8 1368
prophet, and Benaiah, and the *m* men ... 1Kin 1:10 1368
Jeroboam was a *m* man of valour ... 1Kin 11:28 1368
he was also a *m* man in valour ... 2Kin 5:1 1368
even of all the *m* men of wealth ... 2Kin 15:20 1368
all the *m* men of valour, even ten ... 2Kin 24:14 1368
the *m* of the land, those carried ... 2Kin 24:15 193
he began to be *m* upon the earth ... 1Chr 1:10 1368
m men of valour, famous men, and ... 1Chr 5:24 1368
of their fathers, *m* men of valour ... 1Chr 7:7 1368
m men of valour, was twenty ... 1Chr 7:9 1368
m men of valour, were seventeen ... 1Chr 7:11 1368
m men of valour, chief of the ... 1Chr 7:40 1368
sons of Ulam were *m* men of valour ... 1Chr 8:40 1368
chief of the *m* men whom David had ... 1Chr 11:10 1368
of the *m* men whom David had ... 1Chr 11:11 1368
and they were among the *m* men ... 1Chr 12:1 1368
a *m* man among the thirty, and over ... 1Chr 12:4 1368
for they were all *m* men of valour ... 1Chr 12:21 1368
m men of valour for the war, ... 1Chr 12:25 1368
And Zadok, a young man *m* of valour ... 1Chr 12:28 1368
hundred, *m* men of valour, famous ... 1Chr 12:30 1368
and all the host of the *m* men ... 1Chr 19:8 1368
for they were *m* men of valour ... 1Chr 26:6 1368
them *m* men of valour at Jazer of ... 1Chr 26:31 1368
who was *m* among the thirty, and ... 1Chr 27:6 1368
the officers, and with the *m* men ... 1Chr 28:1 1368
And all the princes, and the *m* men ... 1Chr 29:24 1368
thy *m* hand, and thy stretched out ... 2Chr 6:32 2389
chosen men, being *m* men of valour ... 2Chr 13:3 1368
But Abijah waxed *m*, and married ... 2Chr 13:21 2388
all these were *m* men of valour ... 2Chr 14:8 1368
of war, *m* men of valour, were in ... 2Chr 17:13 1368
with him *m* men of valour three ... 2Chr 17:14 1368
hundred thousand *m* men of valour ... 2Chr 17:16 1368
Eliada a *m* man of valour, and with ... 2Chr 17:17 1368
hired also an hundred thousand *m* ... 2Chr 25:6 1368
m men of valour were two thousand ... 2Chr 26:12 1368
that made war with *m* power ... 2Chr 26:13 2428
So Jotham became *m*, because he ... 2Chr 27:6 2388
a *m* man of Ephraim, slew Maaseiah ... 2Chr 28:7 1368
his *m* men to stop the waters of ... 2Chr 32:3 1368
cut off all the *m* men of valour ... 2Chr 32:21 1368
There have been *m* kings also over ... Ezr 4:20 8624
before all the king's *m* princes ... Ezr 7:28 1368
made, and unto the house of the *m* ... Neh 3:16 1368
as a stone into the *m* waters ... Neh 9:11 5794
our God, the great, the *m* ... Neh 9:32 1368
m men of valour, an hundred ... Neh 11:14 1368
mouth, and from the hand of the *m* ... Job 5:15 2389
Redeem me from the hand of the *m* ... Job 6:23 6184
wise in heart, and *m* in strength ... Job 9:4 533
spoiled, and overthroweth the *m* ... Job 12:19 386
weakeneth the strength of the *m* ... Job 12:21 650
become old, yea, are *m* in power ... Job 21:7 1396
But as for the *m* man, he had the ... Job 22:8 2220
draweth also the *m* with his power ... Job 24:22 47
the *m* shall be taken away without ... Job 34:20 47
in pieces *m* men without number ... Job 34:24 3524
out by reason of the arm of the *m* ... Job 35:9 7227
Behold, God is *m*, and despiseth ... Job 36:5 3524
he is *m* in strength and wisdom ... Job 36:5 3524
up himself, the *m* are afraid ... Job 41:25 410
and *m*, the LORD *m* in battle ... Ps 24:8 1368
Give unto the LORD, O ye *m* ... Ps 29:1 1121,410
a *m* man is not delivered by much ... Ps 33:16 1368
sword upon thy thigh, O most *m* ... Ps 45:3 1368
The *m* God, even the LORD, hath ... Ps 50:1 410
thou thyself in mischief, O *m* man ... Ps 52:1 1368
the *m* are gathered against me ... Ps 59:3 5794

out his voice, and that a *m* voice ... Ps 68:33 5797
mine enemies wrongfully, are *m* ... Ps 69:4 6105
thou driedst up *m* rivers ... Ps 74:15 386
like a *m* man that shouteth by ... Ps 78:65 1368
in the congregation of the *m* ... Ps 82:1 410
who among the sons of the *m* can ... Ps 89:6 410
Thou hast a *m* arm ... Ps 89:13 1369
have laid help upon one that is *m* ... Ps 89:19 1368
the reproach of all the *m* people ... Ps 89:50 7227
than the *m* waves of the sea ... Ps 93:4 117
can utter the *m* acts of the LORD ... Ps 106:2 1369
make his *m* power to be known ... Ps 106:8 1369
His seed shall be *m* upon earth ... Ps 112:2 1368
Sharp arrows of the *m*, with coals ... Ps 120:4 1368
arrows are in the hand of a *m* man ... Ps 127:4 1368
and vowed unto the *m* God of Jacob ... Ps 132:2 46
habitation for the *m* God of Jacob ... Ps 132:5 46
great nations, and slew *m* kings ... Ps 135:10 6099
and shall declare thy *m* acts ... Ps 145:4 1369
to the sons of men his *m* acts ... Ps 145:12 1369
Praise him for his *m* acts ... Ps 150:2 1369
to anger is better than the *m* ... Prov 16:32 1368
cease, and parteth between the *m* ... Prov 18:18 6099
man scaleth the city of the *m* ... Prov 21:22 1368
For their redeemer is *m* ... Prov 23:11 2389
the wise more than ten *m* men ... Eccl 7:19 7989
bucklers, all shields of *m* men ... Song 4:4 1368
the *m* One of Israel, Ah, I will ... Is 1:24 46
The *m* man, and the man of war, the ... Is 3:2 1368
by the sword, and thy *m* in the war ... Is 3:25 1369
the *m* man shall be humbled, and ... Is 5:15 376
them that are *m* to drink wine ... Is 5:22 1368
Wonderful, Counsellor, The *m* God ... Is 9:6 1368
remnant of Jacob, unto the *m* God ... Is 10:21 1368
and Lebanon shall fall by a *m* one ... Is 10:34 117
with his *m* wind shall he shake ... Is 11:15 5868
called my *m* ones for mine anger ... Is 13:3 1368
like the rushing of *m* waters ... Is 17:12 3524
the *m* men of the children of ... Is 21:17 1368
thee away with a *m* captivity ... Is 22:17 1397
Behold, the Lord hath a *m* ... Is 28:2 2389
storm, as a flood of *m* waters ... Is 28:2 3524
the LORD, to the *m* One of Israel ... Is 30:29 6697
with the sword, not of a *m* man ... Is 31:8 376
LORD shall go forth as a *m* man ... Is 42:13 1368
sea, and a path in the *m* waters ... Is 43:16 5794
the prey be taken from the *m* ... Is 49:24 1368
of the *m* shall be taken away ... Is 49:25 1368
thy Redeemer, the *m* One of Jacob ... Is 49:26 46
thy Redeemer, the *m* One of Jacob ... Is 60:16 46
speak in righteousness, *m* to save ... Is 63:1 7227
it is a *m* nation, it is an ... Jer 5:15 386
sepulchre, they are all *m* men ... Jer 5:16 1368
neither let the *m* man glory in ... Jer 9:23 1368
as a *m* man that cannot save ... Jer 14:9 1368
is with me as a *m* terrible one ... Jer 20:11 1368
the king, with all his *m* men ... Jer 26:21 1368
the Great, the *M* God, the LORD of ... Jer 32:18 1368
Great in counsel, and *m* in work ... Jer 32:19 7227
m things, which thou knowest not ... Jer 33:3 1219
even *m* men of war, and the women, ... Jer 41:16 1397
their *m* ones are beaten down, and ... Jer 46:5 1368
flee away, nor the *m* man escape ... Jer 46:6 1368
and let the *m* men come forth ... Jer 46:9 1368
for the *m* man hath stumbled ... Jer 46:12 1368
man hath stumbled against the *m* ... Jer 46:12 1368
How say ye, We are *m* and strong ... Jer 48:14 1368
the *m* men's hearts in Moab at ... Jer 48:41 1368
m men of Edom be as the heart of ... Jer 49:22 1368
shall be as of a *m* expert man ... Jer 50:9 1368
a sword is upon her *m* men ... Jer 50:36 1368
The *m* men of Babylon have forborn ... Jer 51:30 1368
her *m* men are taken, every one of ... Jer 51:56 1368
and her rulers, and her *m* men ... Jer 51:57 1368
all my *m* men in the midst of me ... Lam 1:15 47
hath also taken the *m* of the land ... Eze 17:13 352
shall Pharaoh with his *m* army ... Eze 17:17 1419
Lord GOD, surely with a *m* hand ... Eze 20:33 2389
ye are scattered, with a *m* hand ... Eze 20:34 2389
hand of the *m* one of the heathen ... Eze 31:11 410
By the swords of the *m* will I ... Eze 32:12 1368
The strong among the *m* shall ... Eze 32:21 1368
with the *m* that are fallen of the ... Eze 32:27 1368
the *m* in the land of the living ... Eze 32:27 1368
a great company, and a *m* army ... Eze 38:15 7227
Ye shall eat the flesh of the *m* ... Eze 39:18 1368
horses and chariots, with *m* men ... Eze 39:20 1368
he commanded the most *m* men that ... Dan 3:20 1401
and how *m* are his wonders ... Dan 4:3 8624
And his power shall be *m*, but not ... Dan 8:24 6105
practise, and shall destroy the *m* ... Dan 8:24 6099
the land of Egypt with a *m* hand ... Dan 9:15 2389
a *m* king shall stand up, that ... Dan 11:3 1368
with a very great and *m* army ... Dan 11:25 6099
in the multitude of thy *m* men ... Hos 10:13 1368
They shall run like *m* men ... Joel 2:7 1368
Prepare war, wake up the *m* men ... Joel 3:9 1368
cause thy *m* ones to come down ... Joel 3:11 1368
shall the *m* deliver himself ... Amos 2:14 1368
m shall flee away naked in that ... Amos 2:16 1368
transgressions and your *m* sins ... Amos 5:12 6099
and righteousness as a *m* stream ... Amos 5:24 386
And thy *m* men, O Teman, shall be ... Obad 9 1368
there was a *m* tempest in the sea, ... Jonah 1:4 1419
shield of his *m* men is made red ... Nah 2:3 1368
O *m* God, thou hast established ... Hab 1:12 6697
the *m* man shall cry there ... Zeph 1:14 1368
thy God in the midst of thee is *m* ... Zeph 3:17 1368

made thee as the sword of a *m* man ... Zec 9:13 1368
And they shall be as *m* men ... Zec 10:5 1368
of Ephraim shall be like a *m* man ... Zec 10:7 1368
because the *m* are spoiled ... Zec 11:2 117
most of his *m* works were done ... Mt 11:20 *1411*
for if the *m* works, which were ... Mt 11:21 *1411*
for if the *m* works, which have ... Mt 11:23 *1411*
man this wisdom, and these *m* works ... Mt 13:54 *1411*
he did not many *m* works there ... Mt 13:58 *1411*
therefore *m* works do shew forth ... Mt 14:2 *1411*
that even such *m* works are ... Mk 6:2 *1411*
And he could there do no *m* work ... Mk 6:5 *1411*
therefore *m* works do shew forth ... Mk 6:14 *1411*
For he that is *m* hath done to me ... Lk 1:49 *1415*
put down the *m* from their seats ... Lk 1:52 *1413*
all amazed at the *m* power of God ... Lk 9:43 *3168*
for if the *m* works had been done ... Lk 10:13 *1411*
there arose a *m* famine in that ... Lk 15:14 *2478*
the *m* works that they had seen ... Lk 19:37 *1411*
which was a prophet *m* in deed ... Lk 24:19 *1415*
heaven as of a rushing *m* wind ... Acts 2:2 *972*
was *m* in words and in deeds ... Acts 7:22 *1415*
m in the scriptures, came to ... Acts 18:24 *1415*
Through *m* signs and wonders, by ... Rom 15:19 *1411*
men after the flesh, not many *m* ... 1Cor 1:26 *1415*
confound the things which are *m* ... 1Cor 1:27 *2478*
but *m* through God to the pulling ... 2Cor 10:4 *1415*
in signs, and wonders, and *m* deeds ... 2Cor 12:12 *1411*
is not weak, but is *m* in you ... 2Cor 13:3 *1414*
the same was *m* in me toward the ... Gal 2:8 *1754*
to the working of his *m* power ... Eph 1:19 *2479*
from heaven with his *m* angels ... 2Th 1:7 *1411*
therefore under the *m* hand of God ... 1Pet 5:6 *2900*
when she is shaken of a *m* wind ... Rev 6:13 *3173*
the chief captains, and the *m* men ... Rev 6:15 *1415*
I saw another *m* angel come down ... Rev 10:1 *2478*
so *m* an earthquake, and so great ... Rev 16:18 *5082*
great city Babylon, that *m* city ... Rev 18:10 *2478*
a *m* angel took up a stone like a ... Rev 18:21 *2478*
and as the voice of *m* thunderings ... Rev 19:6 *2478*
captains, and the flesh of *m* men ... Rev 19:18 *2478*

MIGRON *(mi'-gron)* {2} *A city in Benjamin.*
a pomegranate tree which is in *M* ... 1Sa 14:2 4051
come to Aiath, he is passed to *M* ... Is 10:28 4051

MIJAMIN *(mij'-a-min)* {2} See MIAMIN.
1. A priest in David's time.
to Malchijah, the sixth to *M* ... 1Chr 24:9 4326
2. A priest who renewed the covenant.
Meshullam, Abijah, *M*, ... Neh 10:7 4326

M

MIKLOTH *(mik'-loth)* {4}
1. A Benjamite in Jerusalem.
And *M* begat Shimeah ... 1Chr 8:32 4732
and Ahio, and Zechariah, and *M* ... 1Chr 9:37 4732
And *M* begat Shimeam ... 1Chr 9:38 4732
2. A ruler of David's guard.
his course was *M* also the ruler ... 1Chr 27:4 4732

MIKNEIAH *(mik-ne-i'-ah)* {2} *A Levite musician.*
and Mattithiah, and Elipheleh, and *M* ... 1Chr 15:18 4737
And Mattithiah, and Elipheleh, and *M* ... 1Chr 15:21 4737

MILALAI *(mil'-a-lahee)* {1} *A priest who purified the wall.*
brethren, Shemaiah, and Azarael, *M* ... Neh 12:36 4450

MILCAH *(mil'-cah)* {11}
1. Daughter of Haran.
and the name of Nahor's wife, *M* ... Gen 11:29 4435
of Haran, the father of *M* ... Gen 11:29 4435
told Abraham, saying, Behold, *M* ... Gen 22:20 4435
these eight *M* did bear to Nahor, ... Gen 22:23 4435
who was born to Bethuel, son of *M* ... Gen 24:15 4435
daughter of Bethuel the son of *M* ... Gen 24:24 4435
Nahor's son, whom *M* bare unto him ... Gen 24:47 4435
2. A daughter of Zelophehad.
were Mahlah, and Noah, Hoglah, *M* ... Num 26:33 4435
Mahlah, Noah, and Hoglah, and *M* ... Num 27:1 4435
Mahlah, Tirzah, and Hoglah, and *M* ... Num 36:11 4435
Mahlah, and Noah, Hoglah, *M* ... Josh 17:3 4435

MILCH {3}
Thirty *m* camels with their colts, ... Gen 32:15 3243
a new cart, and take two *m* kine ... 1Sa 6:7 5763
and took two *m* kine, and tied them ... 1Sa 6:10 5763

MILCHAM See MILCOM.

MILCOM *(mil'-com)* {3} See MALCHAM, MOLECH. *Chief god of the Ammonites.*
after *M* the abomination of the ... 1Kin 11:5 4445
M the god of the children of ... 1Kin 11:33 4445
for *M* the abomination of the ... 2Kin 23:13 4445

MILDEW {5}
and with blasting, and with *m* ... Deut 28:22 3420
there be pestilence, blasting, *m* ... 1Kin 8:37 3420
if there be blasting, or *m* ... 2Chr 6:28 3420
smitten you with blasting and *m* ... Amos 4:9 3420
smote you with blasting and with *m* ... Hag 2:17 3420

MILE {1}
shall compel thee to go a *m* ... Mt 5:41 *3400*

MILETUM *(mi-le'-tum)* {1} See MILETUS. *A city in the Roman province of Caria.*
Trophimus have I left at *M* sick ... 2Ti 4:20 *3399*

MILETUS *(mi-le-tus)* {2} See MILETUM. *Same as Miletum.*
and the next day we came to *M* ... Acts 20:15 *3399*
from *M* he sent to Ephesus, and ... Acts 20:17 *3399*

MILK {48}
And he took butter, and *m*, and the ... Gen 18:8 2461
wine, and his teeth white with *m* ... Gen 49:12 2461
large, unto a land flowing with *m* ... Ex 3:8 2461
unto a land flowing with *m* ... Ex 3:17 2461
give thee, a land flowing with *m* ... Ex 13:5 2461
seethe a kid in his mother's *m* ... Ex 23:19 2461
Unto a land flowing with *m* ... Ex 33:3 2461
seethe a kid in his mother's *m* ... Ex 34:26 2461
it, a land that floweth with *m* ... Lev 20:24 2461
us, and surely it floweth with *m* ... Num 13:27 2461
a land which floweth with *m* ... Num 14:8 2461
out of a land that floweth with *m* ... Num 16:13 2461
into a land that floweth with *m* ... Num 16:14 2461
in the land that floweth with *m* ... Deut 6:3 2461
seed, a land that floweth with *m* ... Deut 11:9 2461
seethe a kid in his mother's *m* ... Deut 14:21 2461
even a land that floweth with *m* ... Deut 26:9 2461
a land that floweth with *m* ... Deut 26:15 2461
thee, a land that floweth with *m* ... Deut 27:3 2461
fathers, that floweth with *m* ... Deut 31:20 2461
m of sheep, with fat of lambs, and ... Deut 32:14 2461
us, a land that floweth with *m* ... Josh 5:6 2461
And she opened a bottle of *m* ... Judg 4:19 2461
He asked water, and she gave him *m* ... Judg 5:25 2461
Hast thou not poured me out as *m* ... Job 10:10 2461
His breasts are full of *m* ... Job 21:24 2461
have goats' *m* enough for thy food ... Prov 27:27 2461
of *m* bringeth forth butter ... Prov 30:33 2461
honey and *m* are under thy tongue ... Song 4:11 2461
I have drunk my wine with my *m* ... Song 5:1 2461
rivers of waters, washed with *m* ... Song 5:12 2461
of *m* that they shall give ... Is 7:22 2461
them that are weaned from the *m* ... Is 28:9 2461
m without money and without price ... Is 55:1 2461
also suck the *m* of the Gentiles ... Is 60:16 2461
that ye may *m* out, and be ... Is 66:11 4711
give them a land flowing with *m* ... Jer 11:5 2461
give them, a land flowing with *m* ... Jer 32:22 2461
snow, they were whiter than *m* ... Lam 4:7 2461
espied for them, flowing with *m* ... Eze 20:6 2461
I had given them, flowing with *m* ... Eze 20:15 2461
fruit, and they shall drink thy *m* ... Eze 25:4 2461
and the hills shall flow with *m* ... Joel 3:18 2461
I have fed you with *m*, and not ... 1Cor 3:2 *1051*
eateth not of the *m* of the flock ... 1Cor 9:7 *1051*
are become such as have need of *m* ... Heb 5:12 *1051*
For every one that useth *m* is ... Heb 5:13 *1051*
desire the sincere *m* of the word ... 1Pet 2:2 *1051*

MILL {2}
maidservant that is behind the *m* ... Ex 11:5 7347
women shall be grinding at the *m* ... Mt 24:41 *3459*

MILLET {1}
and beans, and lentiles, and *m* ... Eze 4:9 1764

MILLIONS {1}
thou the mother of thousands of *m* ... Gen 24:60 7233

MILLO *(mil'-lo)* {10}
1. A fort near Shechem.
together, and all the house of *M* ... Judg 9:6 4407
men of Shechem, and the house of *M* ... Judg 9:20 4407
Shechem, and from the house of *M* ... Judg 9:20 4407
2. A fort near Jerusalem.
And David built round about from *M* ... 2Sa 5:9 4407
the LORD, and his own house, and *M* ... 1Kin 9:15 4407
then did he build *M* ... 1Kin 9:24 4407
Solomon built *M*, and repaired the ... 1Kin 11:27 4407
and slew Joash in the house of *M* ... 2Kin 12:20 4407
about, even from *M* round about ... 1Chr 11:8 4407
repaired *M* in the city of David, ... 2Chr 32:5 4407

MILLS {1}
and gathered it, and ground it in *m* ... Num 11:8 7347

MILLSTONE {9}
nether or the upper *m* to pledge ... Deut 24:6 7347
of a *m* upon Abimelech's head ... Judg 9:53 7393
of a *m* upon him from the wall ... 2Sa 11:21 7393
hard as a piece of the nether *m* ... Job 41:24
m were hanged about his neck ... Mt 18:6 *3458,3684*
m were hanged about his neck ... Mk 9:42 *3037,3457*
m were hanged about his neck ... Lk 17:2 *3458,3684*
took up a stone like a great *m* ... Rev 18:21 *3458*
the sound of a *m* shall be heard ... Rev 18:22 *3458*

MILLSTONES {2}
Take the *m*, and grind meal ... Is 47:2 7347
of the bride, the sound of the *m* ... Jer 25:10 7347

MINCING {1}
m as they go, and making a ... Is 3:16 2952

MIND {95}
If it be your *m* that I should ... Gen 23:8 5315
were a grief of *m* unto Isaac ... Gen 26:35 7307
that the *m* of the LORD might be ... Lev 24:12 6310
have not done them of mine own *m* ... Num 16:28 3820
either good or bad of mine own *m* ... Num 24:13 3820
m unto the place which the LORD ... Deut 18:6 5315
failing of eyes, and sorrow of *m* ... Deut 28:65 5315
them to *m* among all the nations ... Deut 30:1 3824
which is in mine heart and in my *m* ... 1Sa 2:35 5315
days ago, set not thy *m* on them ... 1Sa 9:20 3820
it was in my *m* to build an house ... 1Chr 22:7 3824
perfect heart and with a willing *m* ... 1Chr 28:9 5315
for the people had a *m* to work ... Neh 4:6 3820
But he is in one *m*, and who can ... Job 23:13
Should it be according to thy *m* ... Job 34:33 5973
forgotten as a dead man out of *m* ... Ps 31:12 3820
he bringeth it with a wicked *m* ... Prov 21:27
A fool uttereth all his *m* ... Prov 29:11 7307
whose *m* is stayed on thee ... Is 26:3 3336
bring it again to *m*, O ye ... Is 46:8 3820
be remembered, nor come into *m* ... Is 65:17 3820
neither shall it come to *m* ... Jer 3:16 3820
yet my *m* could not be toward this ... Jer 15:1 5315
it, neither came it into my *m* ... Jer 19:5 3820
not, neither came it into my *m* ... Jer 32:35 3820
them, and came it not into his *m* ... Jer 44:21 3820
and let Jerusalem come into your *m* ... Jer 51:50 3824
This I recall to my *m*, therefore ... Lam 3:21 3820
the things that come into your *m* ... Eze 11:5 7307
into your *m* shall not be at all ... Eze 20:32 7307
her *m* was alienated from them ... Eze 23:17 5315
then my *m* was alienated from her, ... Eze 23:18 5315
like as my *m* was alienated from ... Eze 23:18 5315
from whom thy *m* is alienated ... Eze 23:22 5315
them from whom thy *m* is alienated ... Eze 23:28 5315
time shall things come into thy *m* ... Eze 38:10 3824
came into thy *m* upon thy bed ... Dan 2:29
his *m* hardened in pride, he was ... Dan 5:20 7307
Then shall his *m* change, and he ... Hab 1:11 7307
all thy soul, and with all thy *m* ... Mt 22:37 *1271*
and clothed, and in his right *m* ... Mk 5:15 *4993*
all thy soul, and with all thy *m* ... Mk 12:30 *1271*
Peter called to *m* the word that ... Mk 14:72 *363*
cast in her *m* what manner of ... Lk 1:29
Jesus, clothed, and in his right *m* ... Lk 8:35 *4993*
thy strength, and with all thy *m* ... Lk 10:27 *1271*
neither be ye of doubtful *m* ... Lk 12:29
the word with all readiness of *m* ... Acts 17:11 *4288*
the Lord with all humility of *m* ... Acts 20:19
gave them over to a reprobate *m* ... Rom 1:28 *3563*
warring against the law of my *m* ... Rom 7:23 *3563*
So then with the *m* I myself serve ... Rom 7:25 *3563*
do *m* the things of the flesh ... Rom 8:5 *5426*
Because the carnal *m* is enmity ... Rom 8:7 *5427*
what is the *m* of the Spirit ... Rom 8:27 *5427*
who hath known the *m* of the Lord ... Rom 11:34 *3563*
by the renewing of your *m* ... Rom 12:2 *3563*
Be of the same *m* one toward ... Rom 12:16 *5426*
M not high things, but condescend ... Rom 12:16 *5426*
be fully persuaded in his own *m* ... Rom 14:5 *3563*
That ye may with one *m* and one ... Rom 15:6 *3661*
in some sort, as putting you in *m* ... Rom 15:15 *1878*
joined together in the same *m* ... 1Cor 1:10 *3563*
who hath known the *m* of the Lord ... 1Cor 2:16 *3563*
But we have the *m* of Christ ... 1Cor 2:16 *3563*
your fervent *m* toward me ... 2Cor 7:7
For if there be first a willing *m* ... 2Cor 8:12 *4288*
and declaration of your ready *m* ... 2Cor 8:19 *4288*
I know the forwardness of your *m* ... 2Cor 9:2 *4288*
be of good comfort, be of one *m* ... 2Cor 13:11 *5426*
desires of the flesh and of the *m* ... Eph 2:3 *1271*
walk, in the vanity of their *m* ... Eph 4:17 *3563*
renewed in the spirit of your *m* ... Eph 4:23 *3563*
with one *m* striving together for ... Phil 1:27 *5590*
being of one accord, of one *m* ... Phil 2:2 *5426*
but in lowliness of *m* let each ... Phil 2:3 *5012*
Let this *m* be in you, which was ... Phil 2:5 *5426*
rule, let us *m* the same thing ... Phil 3:16 *5426*
their shame, who *m* earthly things ... Phil 3:19 *5426*
they be of the same *m* in the Lord ... Phil 4:2 *5426*
enemies in your *m* by wicked works ... Col 1:21 *1271*
vainly puffed up by his fleshly *m* ... Col 2:18 *3563*
kindness, humbleness of *m* ... Col 3:12
That ye be not soon shaken in *m* ... 2Th 2:2 *3563*
and of love, and of a sound *m* ... 2Ti 1:7 *4995*
but even their *m* and conscience is ... Titus 1:15 *3563*
Put them in *m* to be subject to ... Titus 3:1 *5279*
But without thy *m* would I do ... Philem 14 *1106*
I will put my laws into their *m* ... Heb 8:10 *1271*
gird up the loins of your *m* ... 1Pet 1:13 *1271*
Finally, be ye all of one *m* ... 1Pet 3:8 *3675*
likewise with the same *m* ... 1Pet 4:1 *1771*
filthy lucre, but of a ready *m* ... 1Pet 5:2 *4290*
here is the *m* which hath wisdom ... Rev 17:9 *3563*
These have one *m*, and shall give ... Rev 17:13 *1106*

MINDED {15}
was stedfastly *m* to go with her ... Ruth 1:18
Joash was *m* to repair the ... 2Chr 24:4 5973,3820
which are *m* of their own freewill ... Ezr 7:13
was *m* to put her away privily ... Mt 1:19 *1014*
shore, into the which they were *m* ... Acts 27:39 *1014*
For to be carnally *m* is death ... Rom 8:6 *5427*
but to be spiritually *m* is life ... Rom 8:6 *5427*
I was *m* to come unto you before ... 2Cor 1:15 *1014*
When I therefore was thus *m* ... 2Cor 1:17 *1011*
that ye will be none otherwise *m* ... Gal 5:10 *5426*
as many as be perfect, be thus *m* ... Phil 3:15 *5426*
if in any thing ye be otherwise *m* ... Phil 3:15 *5426*
men likewise exhort to be sober *m* ... Titus 2:6 *4993*
A double *m* man is unstable in all ... Jas 1:8 *1374*
purify your hearts, ye double *m* ... Jas 4:8 *1374*

MINDFUL {10}
Be ye *m* always of his covenant ... 1Chr 16:15 2142
neither were *m* of thy wonders ... Neh 9:17 2142
is man, that thou art *m* of him ... Ps 8:4 2142
he will ever be *m* of his covenant ... Ps 111:5 2142
The LORD hath been *m* of us ... Ps 115:12 2142
hast not been *m* of the rock of ... Is 17:10 2142
being *m* of thy tears, that I may ... 2Ti 1:4 *3403*
is man, that thou art *m* of him ... Heb 2:6 *3403*
if they had been *m* of that ... Heb 11:15 *3421*
That ye may be *m* of the words ... 2Pet 3:2 *3403*

MINDING {1}
appointed, *m* himself to go afoot ... Acts 20:13 *3195*

MINDS {16}
it, take advice, and speak your *m* ... Judg 19:30
men, and they be chafed in their *m* ... 2Sa 17:8 5315
And Jehu said, If it be your *m* ... 2Kin 9:15 5315
that whereupon they set their *m* ... Eze 24:25 5315
their heart, with despiteful *m* ... Eze 36:5 5315
made their *m* evil affected ... Acts 14:2 *5590*
come to him, they changed their *m* ... Acts 28:6
But their *m* were blinded ... 2Cor 3:14 *3540*
the *m* of them which believe not ... 2Cor 4:4 *3540*
so your *m* should be corrupted ... 2Cor 11:3 *3540*
hearts and *m* through Christ Jesus ... Phil 4:7 *3540*
disputings of men of corrupt *m* ... 1Ti 6:5 *3563*
men of corrupt *m*, reprobate ... 2Ti 3:8 *3563*
in their *m* will I write them ... Heb 10:16 *1271*
ye be wearied and faint in your *m* ... Heb 12:3 *5590*
your pure *m* by way of remembrance ... 2Pet 3:1 *1271*

MINE See APPENDIX.

MINGLE {2}
men of strength to *m* strong drink ... Is 5:22 4537
they shall *m* themselves with the ... Dan 2:43 6151

MINGLED {55}
fire *m* with the hail, very ... Ex 9:24 3947
m with the fourth part of an hin ... Ex 29:40 1101
cakes of fine flour *m* with oil ... Lev 2:4 1101
fine flour unleavened, *m* with oil ... Lev 2:5 1101
m with oil, and dry, shall all the ... Lev 7:10 1101
unleavened cakes *m* with oil ... Lev 7:12 1101
cakes *m* with oil, of fine flour, ... Lev 7:12 1101
and a meat offering *m* with oil ... Lev 9:4 1101
m with oil, and one log of oil ... Lev 14:10 1101
m with oil for a meat offering ... Lev 14:21 1101
not sow thy field with *m* seed ... Lev 19:19 3610
shall a garment *m* of linen ... Lev 19:19 3610
deals of fine flour *m* with oil ... Lev 23:13 1101
cakes of fine flour *m* with oil ... Num 6:15 1101
m with oil for a meat offering ... Num 7:13 1101
m with oil for a meat offering ... Num 7:19 1101
m with oil for a meat offering ... Num 7:25 1101
m with oil for a meat offering ... Num 7:31 1101
m with oil for a meat offering ... Num 7:37 1101
m with oil for a meat offering ... Num 7:43 1101
m with oil for a meat offering ... Num 7:49 1101
m with oil for a meat offering ... Num 7:55 1101
m with oil for a meat offering ... Num 7:61 1101
m with oil for a meat offering ... Num 7:67 1101
m with oil for a meat offering ... Num 7:73 1101
m with oil for a meat offering ... Num 7:79 1101
even fine flour *m* with oil ... Num 8:8 1101
of a tenth deal of flour *m* with ... Num 15:4 1101
two tenth deals of flour *m* with ... Num 15:6 1101
flour *m* with half an hin of oil ... Num 15:9 1101
m with the fourth part of an hin ... Num 28:5 1101
m with oil, and the drink offering ... Num 28:9 1101
m with oil, for one bullock ... Num 28:12 1101
offering, *m* with oil, for one ram ... Num 28:12 1101
m with oil for a meat offering ... Num 28:13 1101
shall be of flour *m* with oil ... Num 28:20 1101
meat offering of flour *m* with oil ... Num 28:28 1101
shall be of flour *m* with oil ... Num 29:3 1101
shall be of flour *m* with oil ... Num 29:9 1101
shall be of flour *m* with oil ... Num 29:14 1101
so that the holy seed have *m* ... Ezr 9:2 6148
and *m* my drink with weeping, ... Ps 102:9 4537
But were *m* among the heathen, and ... Ps 106:35 6148
she hath *m* her wine ... Prov 9:2 4537
drink of the wine which I have *m* ... Prov 9:5 4537
The LORD hath *m* a perverse spirit ... Is 19:14 4537
And all the *m* people, and all the ... Jer 25:20 6154
all the kings of the *m* people ... Jer 25:24 6154
upon all the *m* people that are in ... Jer 50:37 6154
and Lydia, and all the *m* people ... Eze 30:5 6154
him vinegar to drink *m* with gall ... Mt 27:34 *3396*
him to drink wine *m* with myrrh ... Mk 15:23
had *m* with their sacrifices ... Lk 13:1 *3396*
fire *m* with blood, and they were ... Rev 8:7 *3396*
were a sea of glass *m* with fire ... Rev 15:2 *3396*

MINIAMIN *(min'-e-a-min)* {3} See MIAMIN.
1. A Levite.
And next him were Eden, and *M* ... 2Chr 31:15 4509
2. A priest with Zerubbabel.
of *M*, of Moadiah, Piltai ... Neh 12:17 4509
Eliakim, Maaseiah, *M*, Michaiah, ... Neh 12:41 4509

MINISH {1}
Ye shall not *m* ought from your ... Ex 5:19 1639

MINISHED {1}
Again, they are *m* and brought low ... Ps 107:39 4591

MINISTER {100}
And Moses rose up, and his *m* Joshua ... Ex 24:13 8334
that he may *m* unto me in the ... Ex 28:1
that he may *m* unto me in the ... Ex 28:3
that he may *m* unto me in the ... Ex 28:4
And it shall be upon Aaron to *m* ... Ex 28:35 8334
that they may *m* unto me in the ... Ex 28:41
the altar to *m* in the holy place ... Ex 28:43 8334
to *m* unto me in the priest's ... Ex 29:1
to *m* in the holy place ... Ex 29:30 8334
to *m* to me in the priest's office ... Ex 29:44
they come near to the altar to *m* ... Ex 30:20 8334
that they may *m* unto me in the ... Ex 30:30
to *m* in the priest's office, ... Ex 31:10
to *m* in the priest's office ... Ex 35:19 8334
about the hem of the robe to *m* in ... Ex 39:26 8334
to *m* in the priest's office ... Ex 39:41 8334
that he may *m* unto me in the ... Ex 40:13

that they may *m* unto me in the ... Ex 40:15
m unto the LORD in the priest's ... Lev 7:35
whom he shall consecrate to *m* in ... Lev 16:32
and they shall *m* unto it, and shall ... Num 1:50 8334
to *m* in the priest's office ... Num 3:3
priest, that they may *m* unto him ... Num 3:6 8334
of the sanctuary wherewith they *m* ... Num 3:31 8334
thereof, wherewith they *m* unto it ... Num 4:9 8334
wherewith they *m* in the sanctuary ... Num 4:12 8334
wherewith they *m* about it ... Num 4:14 8334
But shall *m* with their brethren ... Num 8:26 8334
the congregation to *m* unto them ... Num 16:9 8334
joined unto thee, and *m* unto thee ... Num 18:2 8334
shall *m* before the tabernacle of ... Num 18:2
before the LORD to *m* unto him ... Deut 10:8 8334
the priest that standeth to *m* ... Deut 17:12 8334
to stand to *m* in the name of the ... Deut 18:5 8334
Then he shall *m* in the name of ... Deut 18:7 8334
thy God hath chosen to *m* unto him ... Deut 21:5 8334
Joshua the son of Nun, Moses' *m* ... Josh 1:1 8334
the child did *m* unto the LORD ... 1Sa 2:11 8334
stand to *m* because of the cloud ... 1Kin 8:11 8334
of God, and to *m* unto him for ever ... 1Chr 15:2 8334
certain of the Levites to *m* ... 1Chr 16:4 8334
to *m* before the ark continually, ... 1Chr 16:37 8334
to *m* unto him, and to bless in his ... 1Chr 23:13 8334
to *m* in the house of the LORD ... 1Chr 26:12 8334
stand to *m* by reason of the cloud ... 2Chr 5:14 8334
m before the priests, as the duty ... 2Chr 8:14 8334
which *m* unto the LORD, are the ... 2Chr 13:10 8334
they that *m* of the Levites ... 2Chr 23:6 8334
of the LORD, even vessels to *m* ... 2Chr 24:14 8335
him, and that ye should *m* unto him ... 2Chr 29:11 8334
and for peace offerings, to *m* ... 2Chr 31:2 8334
unto the priests that *m* in the ... Neh 10:36 8334
sanctuary, and the priests that *m* ... Neh 10:39 8334
he shall *m* judgment to the people ... Ps 9:8 1777
of Nebaioth shall *m* unto thee ... Is 60:7 8334
and their kings shall *m* unto thee ... Is 60:10 8334
and the Levites that *m* unto me ... Jer 33:22 8334
near to the LORD to *m* unto him ... Eze 40:46 8334
lay their garments wherein they *m* ... Eze 42:14 8334
to *m* unto me, saith the Lord GOD, ... Eze 43:19 8334
stand before them to *m* unto them ... Eze 44:11 8334
come near to me to *m* unto me ... Eze 44:15 8334
to *m* unto me, and they shall keep ... Eze 44:16 8334
whiles they *m* in the gates of the ... Eze 44:17 8334
to *m* in the sanctuary, he shall ... Eze 44:27 8334
come near to *m* unto the LORD ... Eze 45:4 8334
among you, let him be your *m* ... Mt 20:26 *1249*
to be ministered unto, but to *m* ... Mt 20:28 *1247*
in prison, and did not *m* unto thee ... Mt 25:44 *1247*
great among you, shall be your *m* ... Mk 10:43 *1249*
to be ministered unto, but to *m* ... Mk 10:45 *1247*
and he gave it again to the *m* ... Lk 4:20 *5257*
and they had also John to their *m* ... Acts 13:5 *5257*
to *m* or come unto him ... Acts 24:23 *5256*
this purpose, to make thee a *m* ... Acts 26:16 *5257*
For he is the *m* of God to thee ... Rom 13:4 *1249*
for he is the *m* of God, a ... Rom 13:4 *1249*
a *m* of the circumcision for the ... Rom 15:8 *1249*
That I should be the *m* of Jesus ... Rom 15:16 *3011*
Jerusalem to *m* unto the saints ... Rom 15:25 *1247*
their duty is also to *m* unto them ... Rom 15:27 *3008*
m about holy things live of the ... 1Cor 9:13 *2038*
sower both *m* bread for your food ... 2Cor 9:10 *5524*
is therefore Christ the *m* of sin ... Gal 2:17 *1249*
Whereof I was made a *m*, according ... Eph 3:7 *1249*
that it may *m* grace unto the ... Eph 4:29 *1325*
faithful *m* in the Lord, shall ... Eph 6:21 *1249*
is for you a faithful *m* of Christ ... Col 1:7 *1249*
whereof I Paul am made a *m* ... Col 1:23 *1249*
Whereof I am made a *m*, according ... Col 1:25 *1249*
beloved brother, and a faithful *m* ... Col 4:7 *1249*
m of God, and our fellowlabourer ... 1Th 3:2 *1249*
which *m* questions, rather than ... 1Ti 1:4 *3930*
shalt be a good *m* of Jesus Christ ... 1Ti 4:6 *1249*
sent forth to *m* for them who ... Heb 1:14 *1248*
ministered to the saints, and do *m* ... Heb 6:10 *1247*
A *m* of the sanctuary, and of the ... Heb 8:2 *3011*
but unto us they did *m* the things ... 1Pet 1:12 *1247*
even so *m* the same one to another ... 1Pet 4:10 *1247*
if any man *m*, let him do it as of ... 1Pet 4:11 *1247*

MINISTERED {37}
Ithamar *m* in the priest's office ... Num 3:4
Eleazar his son *m* in the priest's ... Deut 10:6
But Samuel *m* before the LORD, ... 1Sa 2:18 8334
the child Samuel *m* unto the LORD ... 1Sa 3:1 8334
his servant that *m* unto him ... 2Sa 13:17 8334
cherished the king, and *m* to him ... 1Kin 1:4 8334
the Shunammite *m* unto the king ... 1Kin 1:15 8334
went after Elijah, and *m* unto him ... 1Kin 19:21 8334
vessels of brass wherewith they *m* ... 2Kin 25:14 8334
they *m* before the dwelling place ... 1Chr 6:32 8334
that *m* to the king by course ... 1Chr 28:1 8334
that *m* to Ahaziah, he slew them ... 2Chr 22:8 8334
king's servants that *m* unto him ... Est 2:2 8334
king's servants that *m* unto him ... Est 6:3 8334
vessels of brass wherewith they *m* ... Jer 52:18 8334
Because they *m* unto them before ... Eze 44:12 8334
off their garments wherein they *m* ... Eze 44:19 8334
thousand thousands *m* unto him ... Dan 7:10 8120
behold, angels came and *m* unto him ... Mt 4:11 *1247*
and she arose, and *m* unto them ... Mt 8:15 *1247*
Son of man came not to be *m* unto ... Mt 20:28 *1247*
and the angels *m* unto him ... Mk 1:13 *1247*
left her, and she *m* unto them ... Mk 1:31 *1247*
Son of man came not to be *m* unto ... Mk 10:45 *1247*
followed him, and *m* unto him ... Mk 15:41 *1247*
she arose and *m* unto them ... Lk 4:39 *1247*
which *m* unto him of their ... Lk 8:3 *1247*
As they *m* to the Lord, and fasted, ... Acts 13:2 *3008*
two of them that *m* unto him ... Acts 19:22 *1247*
hands have *m* unto my necessities ... Acts 20:34 *5256*
be the epistle of Christ *m* by us ... 2Cor 3:3 *1247*
and he that *m* to my wants ... Phil 2:25 *3011*
and bands having nourishment *m* ... Col 2:19 *2023*
things he *m* unto me at Ephesus ... 2Ti 1:18 *1247*
m unto me in the bonds of the ... Philem 13 *1247*
in that ye have *m* to the saints ... Heb 6:10 *1247*
For so an entrance shall be *m* ... 2Pet 1:11 *2023*

MINISTERETH {2}
Now he that *m* seed to the sower ... 2Cor 9:10 *2023*
that *m* to you the Spirit, and ... Gal 3:5 *2023*

MINISTERING {9}
had the charge of the *m* vessels ... 1Chr 9:28 5656
of the house, and *m* to the house ... Eze 44:11 8334
Jesus from Galilee, *m* unto him ... Mt 27:55 *1247*
Or ministry, let us wait on our *m* ... Rom 12:7 *1248*
m the gospel of God, that the ... Rom 15:16 *2418*
fellowship of the *m* to the saints ... 2Cor 8:4 *1248*
as touching the *m* to the saints ... 2Cor 9:1 *1248*
Are they not all *m* spirits ... Heb 1:14 *3010*
And every priest standeth daily *m* ... Heb 10:11 *3008*

MINISTERS {26}
and the attendance of his *m* ... 1Kin 10:5 8334
and the attendance of his *m* ... 2Chr 9:4 8334
or *m* of this house of God, it ... Ezr 7:24 6399
us *m* for the house of our God ... Ezr 8:17 8334
ye *m* of his, that do his pleasure ... Ps 103:21 8334
his *m* a flaming fire ... Ps 104:4 8334
shall call you the *M* of our God ... Is 61:6 8334
the Levites the priests, my *m* ... Jer 33:21 8334
they shall be *m* in my sanctuary ... Eze 44:11 8334
priests the *m* of the sanctuary ... Eze 45:4 8334
the *m* of the house, have for ... Eze 45:5 8334
where the *m* of the house shall ... Eze 46:24 8334
the priests, the LORD's *m* ... Joel 1:9 8334
howl, ye *m* of the altar ... Joel 1:13 8334
in sackcloth, ye *m* of my God ... Joel 1:13 8334
the *m* of the LORD, weep between ... Joel 2:17 8334
eyewitnesses, and *m* of the word ... Lk 1:2 *5257*
for they are God's *m*, attending ... Rom 13:6 *3011*
but *m* by whom ye believed, even ... 1Cor 3:5 *1249*
of us, as of the *m* of Christ ... 1Cor 4:1 *5257*
us able *m* of the new testament ... 2Cor 3:6 *1249*
ourselves as the *m* of God ... 2Cor 6:4 *1249*
his *m* also be transformed as the ... 2Cor 11:15 *1249*
as the *m* of righteousness ... 2Cor 11:15 *1249*
Are they *m* of Christ? ... 2Cor 11:23 *1249*
spirits, and his *m* a flame of fire ... Heb 1:7 *3011*

MINISTRATION {7}
days of his *m* were accomplished ... Lk 1:23 *3009*
were neglected in the daily *m* ... Acts 6:1 *1248*
But if the *m* of death, written and ... 2Cor 3:7 *1248*
How shall not the *m* of the spirit ... 2Cor 3:8 *1248*
For if the *m* of condemnation be ... 2Cor 3:9 *1248*
be glory, much more doth the *m* of ... 2Cor 3:9 *1248*
this *m* they glorify God for your ... 2Cor 9:13 *1248*

MINISTRY {22}
take all the instruments of *m* ... Num 4:12 8335
came to do the service of the *m* ... Num 4:47 5656
when David praised by their *m* ... 2Chr 7:6 3027
by the *m* of the prophets ... Hos 12:10 3027
and had obtained part of this *m* ... Acts 1:17 *1248*
That he may take part of this *m* ... Acts 1:25 *1248*
prayer, and to the *m* of the word ... Acts 6:4 *1248*
when they had fulfilled their *m* ... Acts 12:25 *1248*
my course with joy, and the *m* ... Acts 20:24 *1248*
among the Gentiles by his *m* ... Acts 21:19 *1248*
Or *m*, let us wait on our ... Rom 12:7 *1248*
themselves to the *m* of the saints ... 1Cor 16:15 *1248*
Therefore, seeing we have this *m* ... 2Cor 4:1 *1248*
to us the *m* of reconciliation ... 2Cor 5:18 *1248*
thing, that the *m* be not blamed ... 2Cor 6:3 *1248*
the saints, for the work of the *m* ... Eph 4:12 *1248*
Take heed to the *m* which thou ... Col 4:17 *1248*
faithful, putting me into the *m* ... 1Ti 1:12 *1248*
make full proof of thy *m* ... 2Ti 4:5 *1248*
he is profitable to me for the *m* ... 2Ti 4:11 *1248*
he obtained a more excellent *m* ... Heb 8:6 *3009*
and all the vessels of the *m* ... Heb 9:21 *3009*

MINJAMIN See MINIAMIN.

MINNI *(min'-ni)* {1} *A district in Armenia.*
her the kingdoms of Ararat, *M* ... Jer 51:27 4508

MINNITH *(min'-nith)* {2} *An Ammonite city.*
Aroer, even till thou come to *M* ... Judg 11:33 4511
traded in thy market wheat of *M* ... Eze 27:17 4511

MINSTREL {2}
But now bring me a *m* ... 2Kin 3:15 5059
came to pass, when the *m* played ... 2Kin 3:15 5059

MINSTRELS {1}
the ruler's house, and saw the *m* ... Mt 9:23 *834*

MINT {2}
for ye pay tithe of *m* and anise and ... Mt 23:23 *2238*
for ye tithe *m* and rue and all ... Lk 11:42 *2238*

MIPHKAD *(mif'-kad)* {1} *A gate of Jerusalem.*
over against the gate *M*, and to ... Neh 3:31 4663

MIRACLE {10}
you, saying, Shew a *m* for you ... Ex 7:9 4159
not the *m* of the loaves ... Mk 6:52
man which shall do a *m* in my name ... Mk 9:39 *1411*
to have seen some *m* done by him ... Lk 23:8 *4592*
again the second *m* that Jesus did ... Jn 4:54 *4592*
had seen the *m* that Jesus did ... Jn 6:14 *4592*
unto him, and said, John did no *m* ... Jn 10:41 *4592*
heard that he had done this *m* ... Jn 12:18 *4592*
m hath been done by them is ... Acts 4:16 *4592*
on whom this *m* of healing was ... Acts 4:22 *4592*

MIRACLES {27}
which have seen my glory, and my *m* ... Num 14:22 226
And his *m*, and his acts, which he ... Deut 11:3 226
seen, the signs, and those great *m* ... Deut 29:3 4159
where be all his *m* which our ... Judg 6:13 6381
This beginning of *m* did Jesus in ... Jn 2:11 *4592*
when they saw the *m* which he did ... Jn 2:23 *4592*
can do these *m* that thou doest ... Jn 3:2 *4592*
because they saw his *m* which he ... Jn 6:2 *4592*
seek me, not because ye saw the *m* ... Jn 6:26 *4592*
will he do more *m* than these ... Jn 7:31 *4592*
a man that is a sinner do such *m* ... Jn 9:16 *4592*
for this man doeth many *m* ... Jn 11:47 *4592*
he had done so many *m* before them ... Jn 12:37 *4592*
approved of God among you by *m* ... Acts 2:22 *1411*
wonders and *m* among the people ... Acts 6:8 *4592*
seeing the *m* which he did ... Acts 8:6 *4592*
and wondered, beholding the *m* ... Acts 8:13 *1411*
and Paul, declaring what *m* ... Acts 15:12 *4592*
God wrought special *m* by the ... Acts 19:11 *1411*
To another the working of *m* ... 1Cor 12:10 *1411*
thirdly teachers, after that *m* ... 1Cor 12:28 *1411*
are all workers of *m*? ... 1Cor 12:29 *1411*
worketh *m* among you, doeth he it ... Gal 3:5 *1411*
and wonders, and with divers *m* ... Heb 2:4 *1411*
m which he had power to do in the ... Rev 13:14 *4592*
the spirits of devils, working *m* ... Rev 16:14 *4592*
prophet that wrought *m* before him ... Rev 19:20 *4592*

MIRE {15}
stamp them as the *m* of the street ... 2Sa 22:43 2916
Can the rush grow up without *m* ... Job 8:11 1207
He hath cast me into the *m* ... Job 30:19 2563
sharp pointed things upon the *m* ... Job 41:30 2916
I sink in deep *m*, where there is ... Ps 69:2 3121
Deliver me out of the *m*, and let ... Ps 69:14 2916
down like the *m* of the streets ... Is 10:6 2563
rest, whose waters cast up *m* ... Is 57:20 7516
dungeon there was no water, but *m* ... Jer 38:6 2916
so Jeremiah sunk in the *m* ... Jer 38:6 2916
thy feet are sunk in the *m* ... Jer 38:22 1206
down as the *m* of the streets ... Mic 7:10 2916
fine gold as the *m* of the streets ... Zec 9:3 2916
m of the streets in the battle ... Zec 10:5 2916
washed to her wallowing in the *m* ... 2Pet 2:22 *1004*

MIRIAM *(mir'-e-am)* {15} See MARY.
1. *Sister of Aaron.*
M the prophetess, the sister of ... Ex 15:20 4813
M answered them, Sing ye to the ... Ex 15:21 4813
M and Aaron spake against Moses ... Num 12:1 4813
Moses, and unto Aaron, and unto *M* ... Num 12:4 4813
tabernacle, and called Aaron and *M* ... Num 12:5 4813
M became leprous, white as snow ... Num 12:10 4813
and Aaron looked upon *M*, and, ... Num 12:10 4813
M was shut out from the camp ... Num 12:15 4813
not till *M* was brought in again ... Num 12:15 4813
M died there, and was buried there ... Num 20:1 4813
Aaron and Moses, and *M* their sister ... Num 26:59 4813
thy God did unto *M* by the way ... Deut 24:9 4813
Aaron, and Moses, and *M* ... 1Chr 6:3 4813
before thee Moses, Aaron, and *M* ... Mic 6:4 4813
2. *A daughter of Ezra.*
and she bare *M*, and Shammai, and ... 1Chr 4:17 4813

MIRMA *(mur'-mah)* {1} *Son of Shaharaim.*
And Jeuz, and Shachia, and *M* ... 1Chr 8:10 4821

MIRMAH See MIRMA.

MIRTH {15}
might have sent thee away with *m* ... Gen 31:27 8057
send portions, and to make great *m* ... Neh 8:12 8057
that wasted us required of us *m* ... Ps 137:3 8057
and the end of that *m* is heaviness ... Prov 14:13 8057
to now, I will prove thee with *m* ... Eccl 2:1 8057
and of *m*, What doeth it ... Eccl 2:2 8057
of fools is in the house of *m* ... Eccl 7:4 8057
Then I commended *m*, because a man ... Eccl 8:15 8057
The *m* of tabrets ceaseth, the ... Is 24:8 4885
the *m* of the land is gone ... Is 24:11 4885
of Jerusalem, the voice of *m* ... Jer 7:34 8342
and in your days, the voice of *m* ... Jer 16:9 8342
take from them the voice of *m* ... Jer 25:10 8342
should we then make *m*? ... Eze 21:10 7797
also cause all her *m* to cease ... Hos 2:11 4885

MIRY {4}
horrible pit, out of the *m* clay ... Ps 40:2 3121
But the *m* places thereof and the ... Eze 47:11 1207
sawest the iron mixed with *m* clay ... Dan 2:41 2917
sawest iron mixed with *m* clay ... Dan 2:43 2917

MISCARRYING {1}
give them a *m* womb and dry breasts ... Hos 9:14 7921

MISCHIEF {47}
Lest peradventure *m* befall him ... Gen 42:4 611
if *m* befall him by the way in the ... Gen 42:38 611
m befall him, ye shall bring down ... Gen 44:29 611
from her, and yet no *m* follow ... Ex 21:22 611
And if any *m* follow, then thou ... Ex 21:23 611
For *m* did he bring them out, to ... Ex 32:12 7451
people, that they are set on *m* ... Ex 32:22 7451
secretly practised *m* against him ... 1Sa 23:9 7451

M

behold, thou art taken in thy *m* 2Sa 16:8 7451
beside the *m* that Hadad did 1Kin 11:25 7451
and see how this man seeketh *m* 1Kin 20:7 7451
light, some *m* will come upon us 2Kin 7:9 5771
But they thought to do me *m* Neh 6:2 7451
away the *m* of Haman the Agagite Est 8:3 7451
They conceive *m*, and bring forth Job 15:35 5999
iniquity, and hath conceived *m* Ps 7:14 5999
His *m* shall return upon his own Ps 7:16 5999
under his tongue is *m* and vanity Ps 10:7 5999
for thou beholdest *m* and spite, to Ps 10:14 5999
In whose hands is *m*, and their Ps 26:10 2154
but *m* is in their hearts Ps 28:3 7451
He deviseth *m* upon his bed Ps 36:4 205
Why boastest thou thyself in *m* Ps 52:1 7451
m also and sorrow are in the midst Ps 55:10 205
will ye imagine *m* against a man Ps 62:3 205
thee, which frameth *m* by a law Ps 94:20 5999
draw nigh that follow after *m* Ps 119:150 2154
let the *m* of their own lips cover Ps 140:9 5999
not, except they have done *m* Prov 4:16 7489
heart, he deviseth *m* continually Prov 6:14 7451
that be swift in running to *m* Prov 6:18 7451
It is as sport to a fool to do *m* Prov 10:23 2154
but he that seeketh *m*, it shall Prov 11:27 7451
the wicked shall be filled with *m* Prov 12:21 7451
A wicked messenger falleth into *m* Prov 13:17 7451
a perverse tongue falleth into *m* Prov 17:20 7451
and their lips talk of *m* Prov 24:2 5999
but the wicked shall fall into *m* Prov 24:16 7451
his heart shall fall into *m* Prov 28:14 7451
and *m* shall fall upon thee Is 47:11 1943
they conceive *m*, and bring forth Is 59:4 5999
M shall come upon *m* Eze 7:26 1943
these are the men that devise *m* Eze 11:2 205
kings' hearts shall be to do *m* Dan 11:27 4827
yet do they imagine *m* against me Hos 7:15 7451
O full of all subtilty and all *m* Acts 13:10 *4468*

MISCHIEFS {3}
I will heap *m* upon them Deut 32:23 7451
Thy tongue deviseth *m* Ps 52:2 1942
Which imagine *m* in their heart Ps 140:2 7451

MISCHIEVOUS {5}
they imagined a *m* device, which Ps 21:11 4209
that seek my hurt speak *m* things Ps 38:12 1942
evil shall be called a *m* person Prov 24:8 4209
the end of his talk is *m* madness Eccl 10:13 7451
man, he uttereth his *m* desire Mic 7:3 1942

MISERABLE {3}
m comforters are ye all Job 16:2 5999
Christ, we are of all men most *m* 1Cor 15:19 *1652*
not that thou art wretched, and *m* Rev 3:17 *1652*

MISERABLY {1}
He will *m* destroy those wicked Mt 21:41 *2560*

MISERIES {2}
of her *m* all her pleasant things Lam 1:7 4788
howl for your *m* that shall come Jas 5:1 *5004*

MISERY {7}
was grieved for the *m* of Israel Judg 10:16 5999
light given to him that is in *m* Job 3:20 6001
Because thou shalt forget thy *m* Job 11:16 5999
and remember his *m* no more Prov 31:7 5999
therefore the *m* of man is great Eccl 8:6 7451
mine affliction and my *m*, the Lam 3:19 4788
and *m* are in their ways Rom 3:16 *5004*

MISGAB *(mis'-gab)* {1} *The mountainous area in Moab.*
M is confounded and dismayed Jer 48:1 4869

MISHAEL *(mish'-a-el)* {8} See MISHAL.
1. A son of Uzziel.
M, and Elzaphan, and Zithri Ex 6:22 4332
Moses called *M* and Elzaphan, and Lev 10:4 4332
of Judah, Daniel, Hananiah, *M* Dan 1:6 4332
and to *M*, of Meshach Dan 1:7 4332
had set over Daniel, Hananiah, *M* Dan 1:11 4332
none like Daniel, Hananiah, *M* Dan 1:19 4332
the thing known to Hananiah, *M* Dan 2:17 4332
2. A priest who aided Ezra.
on his left hand, Pedaiah, and *M* Neh 8:4 4332

MISHAL *(mi'-shal)* {1} See MISHAEL. *A Levitical city in Asher.*
M with her suburbs, Abdon with Josh 21:30 4861

MISHAM *(mi'-sham)* {1} *Son of Elpaal.*
Eber, and *M*, and Shamed, who built 1Chr 8:12 4936

MISHEAL *(mish'-e-al)* {1} *Same as Mishal.*
And Alammelech, and Amad, and *M* Josh 19:26 4861

MISHMA *(mish'-mah)* {4} *A son of Ishmeal.*
And *M*, and Dumah, and Massa, Gen 25:14 4927
M, and Dumah, Massa, Hadad, and 1Chr 1:30 4927
son, Mibsam his son, *M* his son 1Chr 4:25 4927
And the sons of *M* 1Chr 4:26 4927

MISHMANNAH *(mish-man'-nah)* {1} *A warrior in David's army.*
M the fourth, Jeremiah the fifth, 1Chr 12:10 4925

MISHRAITES *(mish'-ra-ites)* {1} *A family of Kirjath-jearim.*
and the Shumathites, and the *M* 1Chr 2:53 4954

MISPAR See MIZPAR.

MISPERETH *(mis-pe'-reth)* {1} See MIZPAR. *An exile with Ezra.*
Nahamani, Mordecai, Bilshan, *M* Neh 7:7 4559

MISREPHOTH-MAIM {2} *Same as Zarephath.*
them unto great Zidon, and unto *M* Josh 11:8 4956
hill country from Lebanon unto *M* Josh 13:6 4956

MISS {2}
at an hair breadth, and not *m* Judg 20:16 2398
If thy father at all *m* me 1Sa 20:6 6485

MISSED {3}
and thou shalt be *m*, because thy 1Sa 20:18 6485
neither *m* we any thing, as long 1Sa 25:15 6485
so that nothing was *m* of all that 1Sa 25:21 6485

MISSING {2}
was there ought *m* unto them 1Sa 25:7 6485
if by any means he be *m*, then 1Kin 20:39 6485

MIST {3}
there went up a *m* from the earth Gen 2:6 108
immediately there fell on him a *m* Acts 13:11 *887*
to whom the *m* of darkness is 2Pet 2:17 *2217*

MISTRESS {9}
her *m* was despised in her eyes Gen 16:4 1404
flee from the face of my *m* Sarai Gen 16:8 1404
said unto her, Return to thy *m* Gen 16:9 1404
the *m* of the house, fell sick 1Kin 17:17 1172
And she said unto her *m*, Would God 2Kin 5:3 1404
a maiden unto the hand of her *m* Ps 123:2 1404
an handmaid that is heir to her *m* Prov 30:23 1404
as with the maid, so with her *m* Is 24:2 1404
the *m* of witchcrafts, that Nah 3:4 1172

MISUSED {1}
m his prophets, until the wrath 2Chr 36:16 8591

MITE {1}
thou hast paid the very last *m* Lk 12:59 *3016*

MITES {2}
poor widow, and she threw in two *m* Mk 12:42 *3016*
widow casting in thither two *m* Lk 21:2 *3016*

MITHCAH *(mith'-cah)* {2} *An Israelite encampment in the wilderness.*
from Tarah, and pitched in *M* Num 33:28 4989
And they went from *M*, and pitched Num 33:29 4989

MITHCAK See MITHCAH.

MITHKAH See MITHCAH.

MITHNITE *(mith'-nite)* {1} *Family name of Joshaphat.*
of Maachah, and Joshaphat the *M* 1Chr 11:43 4981

MITHREDATH *(mith'-re-dath)* {2} *Treasurer for King Cyrus of Persia.*
by the hand of *M* the treasurer Ezr 1:8 4990
of Artaxerxes wrote Bishlam, *M* Ezr 4:7 4990

MITRE {13}
a robe, and a broidered coat, a *m* Ex 28:4 4701
lace, that it may be upon the *m* Ex 28:37 4701
forefront of the *m* it shall be Ex 28:37 4701
shalt make the *m* of fine linen Ex 28:39 4701
shalt put the *m* upon his head Ex 29:6 4701
and put the holy crown upon the *m* Ex 29:6 4701
a *m* of fine linen, and goodly Ex 39:28 4701
to fasten it on high upon the *m* Ex 39:31 4701
he put the *m* upon his head Lev 8:9 4701
also upon the *m*, even upon his Lev 8:9 4701
with the linen *m* shall he be Lev 16:4 4701
them set a fair *m* upon his head Zec 3:5 6797
they set a fair *m* upon his head Zec 3:5 6797

MITYLENE *(mit-i-le'-ne)* {1} *Major city of the island of Lesbos.*
we took him in, and came to *M* Acts 20:14 *3412*

MIXED {9}
a *m* multitude went up also with Ex 12:38 6154
from Israel all the *m* multitude Neh 13:3 6154
they that go to seek *m* wine Prov 23:30 4469
dross, thy wine *m* with water Is 1:22 4107
sawest the iron *m* with miry clay Dan 2:41 6151
thou sawest iron *m* with miry clay Dan 2:43 6151
even as iron is not *m* with clay Dan 2:43 6151
he hath *m* himself among the Hos 7:8 1101
not being *m* with faith in them Heb 4:2 *4786*

MIXT {1}
the *m* multitude that was among Num 11:4

MIXTURE {3}
it is full of *m* Ps 75:8 4538
by night, and brought a *m* of myrrh Jn 19:39 *3395*
which is poured out without *m* Rev 14:10 *194*

MIZAR *(mi'-zar)* {1} *A hill near Hermon.*
the Hermonites, from the hill *M* Ps 42:6 4706

MIZPAH *(miz'-pah)* {23} See MIZPEH.
1. A city in Gad.
And *M*; for he said Gen 31:49 4709
2. A city in Benjamin.
with them Geba of Benjamin, and *M* 1Kin 15:22 4709
the men of Gibeon, and of *M* Neh 3:7 4709
3. A city in Judah.
there came to Gedaliah to *M* 2Kin 25:23 4709
Chaldees that were with him at *M* 2Kin 25:25 4709
and he built therewith Geba and *M* 2Chr 16:6 4709
Gedaliah the son of Ahikam to *M* Jer 40:6 4708
Then they came to Gedaliah to *M* Jer 40:8 4708
I will dwell at *M* to serve the Jer 40:10 4708
of Judah, to Gedaliah, unto *M* Jer 40:12 4708
the fields, came to Gedaliah to *M* Jer 40:13 4708
spake to Gedaliah in *M* secretly Jer 40:15 4709
Gedaliah the son of Ahikam to *M* Jer 41:1 4709
they did eat bread together in *M* Jer 41:1 4709
him, even with Gedaliah, at *M* Jer 41:3 4709
went forth from *M* to meet them Jer 41:6 4709
of the people that were in *M* Jer 41:10 4709
all the people that remained in *M* Jer 41:10 4709
away captive from *M* cast about Jer 41:14 4709
the son of Nethaniah, from *M* Jer 41:16 4709
because ye have been a snare on *M* Hos 5:1 4709
4. A district ruled by Shallum.
Colhozeh, the ruler of part of *M* Neh 3:15 4709
5. A place ruled by Ezer.
the son of Jeshua, the ruler of *M* Neh 3:19 4709

MIZPAR *(miz'-par)* {1} See MISPERETH. *A clan leader with Zerubbabel.*
Reelaiah, Mordecai, Bilshan, *M* Ezr 2:2 4558

MIZPEH *(miz'-peh)* {23} See MIZPAH, RAMATH-MIZPEH.
1. A valley near Mt. Hermon.
under Hermon in the land of *M* Josh 11:3 4709
and unto the valley of *M* eastward Josh 11:8 4708
2. A city in Judah.
And Dilean, and *M*, and Joktheel, Josh 15:38 4708
of Gilead, unto the LORD in *M* Judg 20:1 4709
of Israel were gone up to *M* Judg 20:3 4709
the men of Israel had sworn in *M* Judg 21:1 4709
that came not up to the LORD to *M* Judg 21:5 4709
that came not up to *M* to the LORD Judg 21:8 4709
said, Gather all Israel to *M* 1Sa 7:5 4708
And they gathered together to *M* 1Sa 7:6 4709
the children of Israel in *M* 1Sa 7:6 4708
were gathered together to *M* 1Sa 7:7 4708
the men of Israel went out of *M* 1Sa 7:11 4709
took a stone, and set it between *M* 1Sa 7:12 4709
to Beth-el, and Gilgal, and *M* 1Sa 7:16 4709
together unto the LORD to *M* 1Sa 10:17 4709
3. A city in Benjamin.
And *M*, and Chephirah, and Mozah, Josh 18:26 4708
4. A city in Gad.
together, and encamped in *M* Judg 10:17 4709
his words before the LORD in *M* Judg 11:11 4709
and passed over *M* of Gilead Judg 11:29 4708
from *M* of Gilead he passed over Judg 11:29 4708
Jephthah came to *M* unto his house Judg 11:34 4709
5. A city in Moab.
And David went thence to *M* of Moab 1Sa 22:3 4708

MIZRAIM *(miz'-ra-im)* {4} See ABEL-MIZRAIM. *Son of Ham.*
Cush, and *M*, and Phut, and Canaan Gen 10:6 4714
M begat Ludim, and Anamim, and Gen 10:13 4714
Cush, and *M*, Put, and Canaan 1Chr 1:8 4714
M begat Ludim, and Anamim, and 1Chr 1:11 4714

MIZZAH *(miz'-zah)* {3} *Son of Reuel.*
Nahath, and Zerah, Shammah, and *M* Gen 36:13 4199
duke Zerah, duke Shammah, duke *M* Gen 36:17 4199
Nahath, Zerah, Shammah, and *M* 1Chr 1:37 4199

MNASON *(na'-son)* {1} *A Christian in Jerusalem.*
brought with them one *M* of Cyprus Acts 21:16 *3416*

MOAB *(mo'-ab)* {170}
1. A nation east of Israel.
smote Midian in the field of *M* Gen 36:35 4124
the mighty men of *M*, trembling Ex 15:15 4124
the wilderness which is before *M* Num 21:11 4124
is the border of *M*, between *M* Num 21:13 4124
Ar, and lieth upon the border of *M* Num 21:15 4124
that is in the country of *M* Num 21:20 4124
against the former king of *M* Num 21:26 4124
it hath consumed Ar of *M*, and the Num 21:28 4124
Woe to thee, *M* Num 21:29 4124
pitched in the plains of *M* on Num 22:1 4124
M was sore afraid of the people, Num 22:3 4124
M was distressed because of the Num 22:3 4124
M said unto the elders of Midian, Num 22:4 4124
And the elders of *M* and the elders Num 22:7 4124
the princes of *M* abode with Num 22:8 4124
the son of Zippor, king of *M* Num 22:10 4124
And the princes of *M* rose up Num 22:14 4124
and went with the princes of *M* Num 22:21 4124
out to meet him unto a city of *M* Num 22:36 4124
he, and all the princes of *M* Num 23:6 4124
Balak the king of *M* hath brought Num 23:7 4124
and the princes of *M* with him Num 23:17 4124
and shall smite the corners of *M* Num 24:17 4124
whoredom with the daughters of *M* Num 25:1 4124
of *M* by Jordan near Jericho Num 26:3 4124
of *M* by Jordan near Jericho Num 26:63 4124
unto the camp at the plains of *M* Num 31:12 4124
in Ije-abarim, in the border of *M* Num 33:44 4124
of *M* by Jordan near Jericho Num 33:48 4124
Abel-shittim in the plains of *M* Num 33:49 4124
in the plains of *M* by Jordan Num 33:50 4124
of *M* by Jordan near Jericho Num 35:1 4124
of *M* by Jordan near Jericho Num 36:13 4124
side Jordan, in the land of *M* Deut 1:5 4124
by the way of the wilderness of *M* Deut 2:8 4124
over through Ar, the coast of *M* Deut 2:18 4124
of Israel in the land of *M* Deut 29:1 4124
Nebo, which is in the land of *M* Deut 32:49 4124
of *M* unto the mountain of Nebo Deut 34:1 4124
LORD died there in the land of *M* Deut 34:5 4124
him in a valley in the land of *M* Deut 34:6 4124
in the plains of *M* thirty days Deut 34:8 4124
inheritance in the plains of *M* Josh 13:32 4124
the son of Zippor, king of *M* Josh 24:9 4124
the king of *M* against Israel Judg 3:12 4124
the king of *M* eighteen years Judg 3:14 4124
present unto Eglon the king of *M* Judg 3:15 4124
the present unto Eglon king of *M* Judg 3:17 4124
took the fords of Jordan toward *M* Judg 3:28 4124
they slew of *M* at that time about Judg 3:29 4124

So *M* was subdued that day under ... Judg 3:30 4124
gods of Zidon, and the gods of *M* ... Judg 10:6 4124
took not away the land of *M* ... Judg 11:15 4124
they sent unto the king of *M* ... Judg 11:17 4124
land of Edom, and the land of *M* ... Judg 11:18 4124
by the east side of the land of *M* ... Judg 11:18 4124
came not within the border of *M* ... Judg 11:18 4124
for Arnon was the border of *M* ... Judg 11:18 4124
the son of Zippor, king of *M* ... Judg 11:25 4124
to sojourn in the country of *M* ... Ruth 1:1 4124
they came into the country of *M* ... Ruth 1:2 4124
took them wives of the women of *M* ... Ruth 1:4 4125
return from the country of *M* ... Ruth 1:6 4124
M how that the LORD had visited ... Ruth 1:6 4124
returned out of the country of *M* ... Ruth 1:22 4124
Naomi out of the country of *M* ... Ruth 2:6 4124
again out of the country of *M* ... Ruth 4:3 4124
and into the hand of the king of *M* ... 1Sa 12:9 4124
enemies on every side, against *M* ... 1Sa 14:47 4124
David went thence to Mizpeh of *M* ... 1Sa 22:3 4124
and he said unto the king of *M* ... 1Sa 22:3 4124
brought them before the king of *M* ... 1Sa 22:4 4124
And he smote *M*, and measured them ... 2Sa 8:2 4124
Of Syria, and of *M*, and of the ... 2Sa 8:12 4124
he slew two lionlike men of *M* ... 2Sa 23:20 4124
for Chemosh, the abomination of *M* ... 1Kin 11:7 4124
Then *M* rebelled against Israel ... 2Kin 1:1 4124
Mesha king of *M* was a sheepmaster ... 2Kin 3:4 4124
that the king of *M* rebelled ... 2Kin 3:5 4124
The king of *M* hath rebelled ... 2Kin 3:7 4124
go with me against *M* to battle ... 2Kin 3:7 4124
deliver them into the hand of *M* ... 2Kin 3:10 4124
deliver them into the hand of *M* ... 2Kin 3:13 4124
now therefore, *M*, to the spoil ... 2Kin 3:23 4124
when the king of *M* saw that the ... 2Kin 3:26 4124
smote Midian in the field of *M* ... 1Chr 1:46 4124
Saraph, who had the dominion in *M* ... 1Chr 4:22 4124
children in the country of *M* ... 1Chr 8:8 4124
he slew two lionlike men of *M* ... 1Chr 11:22 4124
And he smote *M* ... 1Chr 18:2 4124
from Edom, and from *M*, and from the ... 1Chr 18:11 4124
this also, that the children of *M* ... 2Chr 20:1 4124
the children of Ammon and *M* ... 2Chr 20:10 4124
against the children of Ammon, *M* ... 2Chr 20:22 4124
Ammon and *M* stood up against the ... 2Chr 20:23 4124
of Ashdod, of Ammon, and of *M* ... Neh 13:23 4125
M is my washpot ... Ps 60:8 4124
of *M*, and the Hagarenes ... Ps 83:6 4124
M is my washpot ... Ps 108:9 4124
lay their hand upon Edom and *M* ... Is 11:14 4124
The burden of *M* ... Is 15:1 4124
the night Ar of *M* is laid waste ... Is 15:1 4124
the night Kir of *M* is laid waste ... Is 15:1 4124
M shall howl over Nebo, and over ... Is 15:2 4124
armed soldiers of *M* shall cry out ... Is 15:4 4124
My heart shall cry out for *M* ... Is 15:5 4124
gone round about the borders of *M* ... Is 15:8 4124
lions upon him that escapeth of *M* ... Is 15:9 4124
so the daughters of *M* shall be at ... Is 16:2 4124
mine outcasts dwell with thee, *M* ... Is 16:4 4124
We have heard of the pride of *M* ... Is 16:6 4124
Therefore shall *M* howl for *M* ... Is 16:7 4124
Therefore shall *M* howl for *M* ... Is 16:7 4124
shall sound like an harp for *M* ... Is 16:11 4124
when it is seen that *M* is weary ... Is 16:12 4124
concerning *M* since that time ... Is 16:13 4124
the glory of *M* shall be contemned ... Is 16:14 4124
M shall be trodden down under him ... Is 25:10 4124
and the children of Ammon, and *M* ... Jer 9:26 4124
Edom, and *M*, and the children of ... Jer 25:21 4124
king of Edom, and to the king of *M* ... Jer 27:3 4124
when all the Jews that were in *M* ... Jer 40:11 4124
Against *M* thus saith the LORD of ... Jer 48:1 4124
shall be no more praise of *M* ... Jer 48:2 4124
M is destroyed ... Jer 48:4 4124
Give wings unto *M*, that it may ... Jer 48:9 4124
M hath been at ease from his ... Jer 48:11 4124
M shall be ashamed of Chemosh, as ... Jer 48:13 4124
M is spoiled, and gone up out of ... Jer 48:15 4124
The calamity of *M* is near to come ... Jer 48:16 4124
for the spoiler of *M* shall come ... Jer 48:18 4124
M is confounded ... Jer 48:20 4124
it in Arnon, that *M* is spoiled ... Jer 48:20 4124
all the cities of the land of *M* ... Jer 48:24 4124
The horn of *M* is cut off, and his ... Jer 48:25 4124
M also shall wallow in his vomit ... Jer 48:26 4124
O ye that dwell in *M*, leave the ... Jer 48:28 4124
We have heard the pride of *M* ... Jer 48:29 4124
Therefore will I howl for *M* ... Jer 48:31 4124
and I will cry out for all *M* ... Jer 48:31 4124
field, and from the land of *M* ... Jer 48:33 4124
I will cause to cease in *M* ... Jer 48:35 4124
shall sound for *M* like pipes ... Jer 48:36 4124
upon all the housetops of *M* ... Jer 48:38 4124
for I have broken *M* like a vessel ... Jer 48:38 4124
how hath *M* turned the back with ... Jer 48:39 4124
so shall *M* be a derision and a ... Jer 48:39 4124
and shall spread his wings over *M* ... Jer 48:40 4124
the mighty men's hearts in *M* at ... Jer 48:41 4124
M shall be destroyed from being a ... Jer 48:42 4124
be upon thee, O inhabitant of *M* ... Jer 48:43 4124
I will bring upon it, even upon *M* ... Jer 48:44 4124
and shall devour the corner of *M* ... Jer 48:45 4124
Woe be unto thee, O *M* ... Jer 48:46 4124
captivity of *M* in the latter days ... Jer 48:47 4124
Thus far is the judgment of *M* ... Jer 48:47 4124
Because that *M* and Seir do say ... Eze 25:8 4124
the side of *M* from the cities ... Eze 25:9 4124
I will execute judgments upon *M* ... Eze 25:11 4124
out of his hand, even Edom, and *M* ... Dan 11:41 4124
For three transgressions of *M* ... Amos 2:1 4124
But I will send a fire upon *M* ... Amos 2:2 4124
M shall die with tumult, with ... Amos 2:2 4124
what Balak king of *M* consulted ... Mic 6:5 4124
I have heard the reproach of *M* ... Zeph 2:8 4124
Surely *M* shall be as Sodom, and ... Zeph 2:9 4124
2. *Son of Lot.*
bare a son, and called his name *M* ... Gen 19:37 4124

MOABITE *(mo'-ab-ite)* {3} See MOABITES, MOABITESS, MOABITISH. *An inhabitant of Moab.*
An Ammonite or *M* shall not enter ... Deut 23:3 4125
sons of Elnaam, and Ithmah the *M* ... 1Chr 11:46 4125
the *M* should not come into the ... Neh 13:1 4125

MOABITES *(mo'-ab-ites)* {19}
the father of the *M* unto this day ... Gen 19:37 4124
was king of the *M* at that time ... Num 22:4 4124
said unto me, Distress not the *M* ... Deut 2:9 4124
but the *M* call them Emims ... Deut 2:11 4125
the *M* which dwell in Ar, did unto ... Deut 2:29 4125
your enemies the *M* into your hand ... Judg 3:28 4124
so the *M* became David's servants ... 2Sa 8:2 4124
of Pharaoh, women of the *M* ... 1Kin 11:1 4125
Chemosh the god of the *M* ... 1Kin 11:33 4124
deliver the *M* also into your hand ... 2Kin 3:18 4124
when all the *M* heard that the ... 2Kin 3:21 4124
the *M* saw the water on the other ... 2Kin 3:22 4124
Israelites rose up and smote the *M* ... 2Kin 3:24 4124
they went forward smiting the *M* ... 2Kin 3:24 4124
the bands of the *M* invaded the ... 2Kin 13:20 4124
Chemosh the abomination of the *M* ... 2Kin 23:13 4124
of the Syrians, and bands of the *M* ... 2Kin 24:2 4124
the *M* became David's servants, and ... 1Chr 18:2 4124
Jebusites, the Ammonites, the *M* ... Ezr 9:1 4124

MOABITESS *(mo'-ab-i-tess)* {6} *A female Moabite.*
So Naomi returned, and Ruth the *M* ... Ruth 1:22 4125
Ruth the *M* said unto Naomi, Let ... Ruth 2:2 4125
And Ruth the *M* said, He said unto ... Ruth 2:21 4125
must buy it also of Ruth the *M* ... Ruth 4:5 4125
Moreover Ruth the *M*, the wife of ... Ruth 4:10 4125
Jehozabad the son of Shimrith a *M* ... 2Chr 24:26 4125

MOABITISH *(mo'-ab-i-tish)* {1} *Belonging to the Moabites.*
It is the *M* damsel that came back ... Ruth 2:6 4125

MOADIAH *(mo-ad-i'-ah)* {1} See MAADIAH. *A priest.*
of Miniamin, of *M*, Piltai ... Neh 12:17 4153

MOCK {12}
in an Hebrew unto us to *m* us ... Gen 39:14 6711
unto us, came in unto me to *m* me ... Gen 39:17 6711
mocketh another, do ye so *m* him ... Job 13:9 2048
and after that I have spoken, *m* on ... Job 21:3 3932
I will *m* when your fear cometh ... Prov 1:26 3932
Fools make a *m* at sin ... Prov 14:9 3887
me into their hand, and they *m* me ... Jer 38:19 5953
saw her, and did *m* at her sabbaths ... Lam 1:7 7832
be far from thee, shall *m* thee ... Eze 22:5 7046
deliver him to the Gentiles to *m* ... Mt 20:19 *1702*
And they shall *m* him, and shall ... Mk 10:34 *1702*
all that behold it begin to *m* him ... Lk 14:29 *1702*

MOCKED {21}
one that *m* unto his sons in law ... Gen 19:14 6711
the ass, Because thou hast *m* me ... Num 22:29 5953
Samson, Behold, thou hast *m* me ... Judg 16:10 2048
Samson, Hitherto thou hast *m* me ... Judg 16:13 2048
thou hast *m* me these three times ... Judg 16:15 2048
pass at noon, that Elijah *m* them ... 1Kin 18:27 2048
m him, and said unto him, Go up ... 2Kin 2:23 7046
laughed them to scorn, and *m* them ... 2Chr 30:10 3932
But they *m* the messengers of God ... 2Chr 36:16 3931
great indignation, and *m* the Jews ... Neh 4:1 3932
I am as one *m* of his neighbour ... Job 12:4 7832
saw that he was *m* of the wise men ... Mt 2:16 *1702*
m him, saying, Hail, King of the ... Mt 27:29 *1702*
And after that they had *m* him ... Mt 27:31 *1702*
And when they had *m* him, they took ... Mk 15:20 *1702*
unto the Gentiles, and shall be *m* ... Lk 18:32 *1702*
And the men that held Jesus *m* him ... Lk 22:63 *1702*
m him, and arrayed him in a ... Lk 23:11 *1702*
And the soldiers also *m* him ... Lk 23:36 *1702*
resurrection of the dead, some *m* ... Acts 17:32 *5512*
God is not *m* ... Gal 6:7 *3456*

MOCKER {1}
Wine is a *m*, strong drink is ... Prov 20:1 3887

MOCKERS {5}
Are there not *m* with me ... Job 17:2 2049
With hypocritical *m* in feasts ... Ps 35:16 3934
Now therefore be ye not *m* ... Is 28:22 3887
sat not in the assembly of the *m* ... Jer 15:17 7832
should be *m* in the last time ... Jude 18 *1703*

MOCKEST {1}
and when thou *m*, shall no man make ... Job 11:3 3932

MOCKETH {5}
or as one man *m* another, do ye so ... Job 13:9 2048
He *m* at fear, and is not ... Job 39:22 7832
Whoso *m* the poor reproacheth his ... Prov 17:5 3932
The eye that *m* at his father, and ... Prov 30:17 3932
in derision daily, every one *m* me ... Jer 20:7 3932

MOCKING {5}
she had born unto Abraham, *m* ... Gen 21:9 6711
heathen, and a *m* to all countries ... Eze 22:4 7048
also the chief priests *m* him ... Mt 27:41 *1702*
m said among themselves with the ... Mk 15:31 *1702*
Others *m* said, These men are full ... Acts 2:13 *5512*

MOCKINGS {1}
And others had trial of cruel *m* ... Heb 11:36 *1701*

MODERATELY {1}
hath given you the former rain *m* ... Joel 2:23 6666

MODERATION {1}
Let your *m* be known unto all men ... Phil 4:5 *1933*

MODEST {1}
adorn themselves in *m* apparel ... 1Ti 2:9 *2887*

MOIST {1}
of grapes, nor eat *m* grapes ... Num 6:3 3892

MOISTENED {1}
and his bones are *m* with marrow ... Job 21:24 8248

MOISTURE {2}
my *m* is turned into the drought ... Ps 32:4 3955
away, because it lacked *m* ... Lk 8:6 *2429*

MOLADAH *(mo-la'-dah)* {4} *A city in Judah.*
Amam, and Shema, and *M* ... Josh 15:26 4137
Beer-sheba, or Sheba, and *M* ... Josh 19:2 4137
And they dwelt at Beer-sheba, and *M* ... 1Chr 4:28 4137
And at Jeshua, and at *M*, and at ... Neh 11:26 4137

MOLE {1}
lizard, and the snail, and the *m* ... Lev 11:30 8580

MOLECH *(mo'-lek)* {8} See MALCHAM, MOLOCH. *An Ammonite god.*
seed pass through the fire to *M* ... Lev 18:21 4432
giveth any of his seed unto *M* ... Lev 20:2 4432
he hath given of his seed unto *M* ... Lev 20:3 4432
when he giveth of his seed unto *M* ... Lev 20:4 4432
him, to commit whoredom with *M* ... Lev 20:5 4432
is before Jerusalem, and for *M* ... 1Kin 11:7 4432
to pass through the fire to *M* ... 2Kin 23:10 4432
to pass through the fire unto *M* ... Jer 32:35 4432

MOLES {1}
for himself to worship, to the *m* ... Is 2:20 2661

MOLID *(mo'-lid)* {1} *A descendant of Jerahmeel.*
and she bare him Ahban, and *M* ... 1Chr 2:29 4140

MOLLIFIED {1}
bound up, neither *m* with ointment ... Is 1:6 7401

MOLOCH *(mo'-loch)* {2} See MILCHOM, MOLECH. *Same as Molech.*
borne the tabernacle of your *M* ... Amos 5:26 4432
ye took up the tabernacle of *M* ... Acts 7:43 *3434*

MOLTEN {39}
after he had made it a *m* calf ... Ex 32:4 4541
they have made them a *m* calf ... Ex 32:8 4541
Thou shalt make thee no *m* gods ... Ex 34:17 4541
nor make to yourselves *m* gods ... Lev 19:4 4541
and destroy all their *m* images ... Num 33:52 4541
they have made them a *m* image ... Deut 9:12 4541
God, and had made you a *m* calf ... Deut 9:16 4541
that maketh any graven or *m* image ... Deut 27:15 4541
make a graven image and a *m* image ... Judg 17:3 4541
a graven image and a *m* image ... Judg 17:4 4541
and a graven image, and a *m* image ... Judg 18:14 4541
and the teraphim, and the *m* image ... Judg 18:17 4541
and the teraphim, and the *m* image ... Judg 18:18 4541
he made two chapiters of *m* brass ... 1Kin 7:16 3332
And he made a *m* sea, ten cubits ... 1Kin 7:23 3332
the laver were undersetters *m* ... 1Kin 7:30 3332
and their spokes, were all *m* ... 1Kin 7:33 3332
m images, to provoke me to anger ... 1Kin 14:9 4541
their God, and made them *m* images ... 2Kin 17:16 4541
Also he made a *m* sea of ten ... 2Chr 4:2 3332
made also *m* images for Baalim ... 2Chr 28:2 4541
carved images, and the *m* images ... 2Chr 34:3 4541
the *m* images, he brake in pieces ... 2Chr 34:4 4541
when they had made them a *m* calf ... Neh 9:18 4541
brass is *m* out of the stone ... Job 28:2 6694
strong, and as a *m* looking glass ... Job 37:18 3332
Horeb, and worshipped the *m* image ... Ps 106:19 4541
ornament of thy *m* images of gold ... Is 30:22 4541
their *m* images are wind and ... Is 41:29 5262
images, that say to the *m* images ... Is 42:17 4541
or *m* a graven image that is ... Is 44:10 5258
my *m* image, hath commanded them ... Is 48:5 5262
for his *m* image is falsehood, and ... Jer 10:14 5262
for his *m* image is falsehood, and ... Jer 51:17 5262
filthiness of it may be *m* in it ... Eze 24:11 5413
have made them *m* images of their ... Hos 13:2 4541
mountains shall be *m* under him ... Mic 1:4 4549
the graven image and the *m* image ... Nah 1:14 4541
the *m* image, and a teacher of lies ... Hab 2:18 4541

MOMENT {22}
up into the midst of thee in a *m* ... Ex 33:5 7281
that I may consume them in a *m* ... Num 16:21 7281
that I may consume them as in a *m* ... Num 16:45 7281
every morning, and try him every *m* ... Job 7:18 7281
joy of the hypocrite but for a *m* ... Job 20:5 7281
in a *m* go down to the grave ... Job 21:13 7281
In a *m* shall they die, and the ... Job 34:20 7281
For his anger endureth but a *m* ... Ps 30:5 7281
into desolation, as in a *m* ... Ps 73:19 7281
but a lying tongue is but for a *m* ... Prov 12:19 7281
thyself as it were for a little *m* ... Is 26:20 7281
I will water it every *m* ... Is 27:3 7281
come to thee in a *m* in one day ... Is 47:9 7281
For a small *m* have I forsaken ... Is 54:7 7281
I hid my face from thee for a *m* ... Is 54:8 7281
spoiled, and my curtains in a *m* ... Jer 4:20 7281
that was overthrown as in a *m* ... Lam 4:6 7281
and shall tremble at every *m* ... Eze 26:16 7281
and they shall tremble at every *m* ... Eze 32:10 7281
of the world in a *m* of time ... Lk 4:5 *4743*

M

In a *m*, in the twinkling of an ... 1Cor 15:52 *823*
affliction, which is but for a *m* ... 2Cor 4:17 *3901*

MONEY {140}

or bought with *m* of any stranger, ... Gen 17:12 3701
and he that is bought with thy *m* ... Gen 17:13 3701
all that were bought with his *m* ... Gen 17:23 3701
bought with *m* of the stranger, ... Gen 17:27 3701
for as much *m* as it is worth he ... Gen 23:9 3701
I will give thee *m* for the field ... Gen 23:13 3701
current *m* with the merchant ... Gen 23:16 3701
and hath quite devoured also our *m* ... Gen 31:15 3701
for an hundred pieces of *m* ... Gen 33:19 7192
every man's *m* into his sack ... Gen 42:25 3701
in the inn, he espied his *m* ... Gen 42:27 3701
his brethren, My *m* is restored ... Gen 42:28 3701
man's bundle of *m* was in his sack ... Gen 42:35 3701
their father saw the bundles of *m* ... Gen 42:35 3701
take double *m* in your hand ... Gen 43:12 3701
the *m* that was brought again in ... Gen 43:12 3701
they took double *m* in their hand ... Gen 43:15 3701
Because of the *m* that was ... Gen 43:18 3701
every man's *m* was in the mouth of ... Gen 43:21 3701
of his sack, our *m* in full weight ... Gen 43:21 3701
other *m* have we brought down in ... Gen 43:22 3701
tell who put our *m* in our sacks ... Gen 43:22 3701
I had your *m* ... Gen 43:23 3701
put every man's *m* in his sack's ... Gen 44:1 3701
of the youngest, and his corn *m* ... Gen 44:2 3701
Behold, the *m*, which we found in ... Gen 44:8 3701
Joseph gathered up all the *m* that ... Gen 47:14 3701
Joseph brought the *m* into ... Gen 47:14 3701
when *m* failed in the land of ... Gen 47:15 3701
for the *m* faileth ... Gen 47:15 3701
you for your cattle, if *m* fail ... Gen 47:16 3701
my lord, how that our *m* is spent ... Gen 47:18 3701
servant that is bought for *m* ... Ex 12:44 3701
shall she go out free without *m* ... Ex 21:11 3701
for he is his *m* ... Ex 21:21 3701
there be laid on him a sum of *m* ... Ex 21:30
give *m* unto the owner of them ... Ex 21:34 3701
live ox, and divide the *m* of it ... Ex 21:35 3701
his neighbour *m* or stuff to keep ... Ex 22:7 3701
he shall pay *m* according to the ... Ex 22:17 3701
If thou lend *m* to any of my ... Ex 22:25 3701
m of the children of Israel ... Ex 30:16 3701
priest buy any soul with his *m* ... Lev 22:11 3701
not give him thy *m* upon usury ... Lev 25:37 3701
of the *m* that he was bought for ... Lev 25:51 3701
the *m* of thy estimation unto it ... Lev 27:15 3701
shall reckon unto him the *m* ... Lev 27:18 3701
the *m* of thy estimation unto it ... Lev 27:19 3701
And thou shalt give the *m*, ... Num 3:48 3701
m of them that were over and above ... Num 3:49 3701
children of Israel took he the *m* ... Num 3:50 3701
Moses gave the *m* of them that ... Num 3:51 3701
for the *m* of five shekels, after ... Num 18:16 3701
Ye shall buy meat of them for *m* ... Deut 2:6 3701
also buy water of them for *m* ... Deut 2:6 3701
Thou shalt sell me meat for *m* ... Deut 2:28 3701
and give me water for *m*, that I ... Deut 2:28 3701
Then shalt thou turn it into *m* ... Deut 14:25 3701
bind up the *m* in thine hand, and ... Deut 14:25 3701
thou shalt bestow that *m* for ... Deut 14:26 3701
shalt not sell her at all for *m* ... Deut 21:14 3701
usury of *m*, usury of victuals, ... Deut 23:19 3701
they took no gain of *m* ... Judg 5:19 3701
her, and brought *m* in their hand ... Judg 16:18 3701
he restored the *m* unto his mother ... Judg 17:4 3701
give thee the worth of it in *m* ... 1Kin 21:2 3701
him, Give me thy vineyard for *m* ... 1Kin 21:6 3701
he refused to give thee for *m* ... 1Kin 21:15 3701
Is it a time to receive *m* ... 2Kin 5:26 3701
All the *m* of the dedicated things ... 2Kin 12:4 3701
even the *m* of every one that ... 2Kin 12:4 3701
the *m* that every man is set at, ... 2Kin 12:4 3701
all the *m* that cometh into any ... 2Kin 12:4 3701
no more *m* of your acquaintance ... 2Kin 12:7 3701
receive no more *m* of the people ... 2Kin 12:8 3701
the door put therein all the *m* ... 2Kin 12:9 3701
there was much *m* in the chest ... 2Kin 12:10 3701
told the *m* that was found in the ... 2Kin 12:10 3701
And they gave the *m*, being told, ... 2Kin 12:11 3701
of the *m* that was brought into ... 2Kin 12:13 3701
the *m* to be bestowed on workmen ... 2Kin 12:15 3701
The trespass *m* and sin *m* was ... 2Kin 12:16 3701
Menahem exacted the *m* of Israel ... 2Kin 15:20 3701
m that was delivered into their ... 2Kin 22:7 3701
the *m* that was found in the house ... 2Kin 22:9 3701
he taxed the land to give the *m* ... 2Kin 23:35 3701
gather of all Israel *m* to repair ... 2Chr 24:5 3701
they saw that there was much *m* ... 2Chr 24:11 3701
day, and gathered *m* in abundance ... 2Chr 24:11 3701
the rest of the *m* before the king ... 2Chr 24:14 3701
they delivered the *m* that was ... 2Chr 34:9 3701
when they brought out the *m* that ... 2Chr 34:14 3701
m that was found in the house of ... 2Chr 34:17 3701
They gave *m* also unto the masons, ... Ezr 3:7 3701
buy speedily with this *m* bullocks ... Ezr 7:17 3702
We have borrowed *m* for the king's ... Neh 5:4 3701
servants, might exact of them *m* ... Neh 5:10 3701
also the hundredth part of the *m* ... Neh 5:11 3701
of the sum of the *m* that Haman ... Est 4:7 3701
the fruits thereof without *m* ... Job 31:39 3701
man also gave him a piece of *m* ... Job 42:11 7192
putteth not out his *m* to usury ... Ps 15:5 3701
He hath taken a bag of *m* with him ... Prov 7:20 3701
is a defence, and *m* is a defence ... Eccl 7:12 3701
but *m* answereth all things ... Eccl 10:19 3701
bought me no sweet cane with *m* ... Is 43:24 3701
and ye shall be redeemed without *m* ... Is 52:3 3701
the waters, and he that hath no *m* ... Is 55:1 3701
come, buy wine and milk without *m* ... Is 55:1 3701
Wherefore do ye spend *m* for that ... Is 55:2 3701
in Anathoth, and weighed him the *m* ... Jer 32:9 3701
weighed him the *m* in the balances ... Jer 32:10 3701
God, Buy thee the field for *m* ... Jer 32:25 3701
Men shall buy fields for *m* ... Jer 32:44 3701
We have drunken our water for *m* ... Lam 5:4 3701
the prophets thereof divine for *m* ... Mic 3:11 3701
received tribute *m* came to Peter ... Mt 17:24
thou shalt find a piece of *m* ... Mt 17:27 *4715*
Shew me the tribute *m* ... Mt 22:19 *3546*
in the earth, and hid his lord's *m* ... Mt 25:18 *694*
have put my *m* to the exchangers ... Mt 25:27 *694*
they gave large *m* unto the ... Mt 28:12 *694*
So they took the *m*, and did as ... Mt 28:15 *694*
no bread, no *m* in their purse ... Mk 6:8 *5475*
people cast *m* into the treasury ... Mk 12:41 *5475*
glad, and promised to give him *m* ... Mk 14:11 *694*
scrip, neither bread, neither *m* ... Lk 9:3 *694*
him, to whom he had given the *m* ... Lk 19:15 *694*
not thou my *m* into the bank ... Lk 19:23 *694*
glad, and covenanted to give him *m* ... Lk 22:5 *694*
and the changers of *m* sitting ... Jn 2:14 *2773*
and poured out the changers' *m* ... Jn 2:15 *2772*
land, sold it, and brought the *m* ... Acts 4:37 *5536*
Abraham bought for a sum of *m* of ... Acts 7:16 *694*
was given, he offered them *m* ... Acts 8:18 *5536*
Thy *m* perish with thee, because ... Acts 8:20 *694*
of God may be purchased with *m* ... Acts 8:20 *5536*
He hoped also that *m* should have ... Acts 24:26 *5536*
For the love of *m* is the root of ... 1Ti 6:10 *5365*

MONEYCHANGERS {2}

and overthrew the tables of the *m* ... Mt 21:12 *2855*
and overthrew the tables of the *m* ... Mk 11:15 *2855*

MONSTERS {1}

Even the sea *m* draw out the ... Lam 4:3 8577

MONTH {258}

of Noah's life, in the second *m* ... Gen 7:11 2320
the seventeenth day of the *m* ... Gen 7:11 2320
the ark rested in the seventh *m* ... Gen 8:4 2320
on the seventeenth day of the *m* ... Gen 8:4 2320
continually until the tenth *m* ... Gen 8:5 2320
in the tenth *m*, on the first day ... Gen 8:5
on the first day of the *m* ... Gen 8:5 2320
and first year, in the first *m* ... Gen 8:13
the first day of the *m* ... Gen 8:13 2320
And in the second *m*, on the seven ... Gen 8:14 2320
seven and twentieth day of the *m* ... Gen 8:14 2320
abode with him the space of a *m* ... Gen 29:14 2320
This *m* shall be unto you the ... Ex 12:2 2320
be the first *m* of the year to you ... Ex 12:2 2320
In the tenth day of this *m* they ... Ex 12:3 2320
the fourteenth day of the same *m* ... Ex 12:6 2320
In the first *m*, on the fourteenth ... Ex 12:18
fourteenth day of the *m* at even ... Ex 12:18 2320
and twentieth day of the *m* at even ... Ex 12:18 2320
day came ye out in the *m* Abib ... Ex 13:4 2320
shalt keep this service in this *m* ... Ex 13:5 2320
m after their departing out of ... Ex 16:1 2320
In the third *m*, when the children ... Ex 19:1 2320
the time appointed of the *m* Abib ... Ex 23:15 2320
thee, in the time of the *m* Abib ... Ex 34:18 2320
for in the *m* Abib thou camest out ... Ex 34:18 2320
the first *m* shalt thou set up the ... Ex 40:2 2320
in the first *m* in the second year ... Ex 40:17 2320
on the first day of the *m* ... Ex 40:17 2320
that in the seventh *m*, on the ... Lev 16:29 2320
m, on the tenth day of the *m* ... Lev 16:29 2320
m at even is the Lord's passover ... Lev 23:5 2320
same *m* is the feast of unleavened ... Lev 23:6 2320
Israel, saying, In the seventh *m* ... Lev 23:24 2320
in the first day of the *m* ... Lev 23:24 2320
seventh *m* there shall be a day of ... Lev 23:27 2320
in the ninth day of the *m* at even ... Lev 23:32 2320
seventh *m* shall be the feast of ... Lev 23:34 2320
fifteenth day of the seventh *m* ... Lev 23:39 2320
celebrate it in the seventh *m* ... Lev 23:41 2320
on the tenth day of the seventh *m* ... Lev 25:9 2320
if it be from a *m* old even unto ... Lev 27:6 2320
on the first day of the second *m* ... Num 1:1 2320
on the first day of the second *m* ... Num 1:18 2320
every male from a *m* old and upward ... Num 3:15 2320
of all the males, from a *m* old ... Num 3:22 2320
of all the males, from a *m* old ... Num 3:28 2320
of all the males, from a *m* old ... Num 3:34 2320
all the males from a *m* old ... Num 3:39 2320
children of Israel from a *m* old ... Num 3:40 2320
the number of names, from a *m* old ... Num 3:43 2320
in the first *m* of the second year ... Num 9:1 2320
In the fourteenth day of this *m* ... Num 9:3 2320
m at even in the wilderness of ... Num 9:5 2320
m at even they shall keep it ... Num 9:11 2320
whether it were two days, or a *m* ... Num 9:22 2320
the twentieth day of the second *m* ... Num 10:11 2320
But even a whole *m*, until it come ... Num 11:20 2320
that they may eat a whole *m* ... Num 11:21 2320
from a *m* old shalt thou redeem ... Num 18:16 2320
the desert of Zin in the first *m* ... Num 20:1 2320
thousand, all males from a *m* old ... Num 26:62 2320
m throughout the months of the ... Num 28:14 2320
m is the passover of the Lord ... Num 28:16 2320
day of this *m* is the feast ... Num 28:17 2320
And in the seventh *m*, on the first ... Num 29:1 2320
m, on the first day of the *m* ... Num 29:1 2320
the burnt offering of the *m* ... Num 29:6 2320
seventh *m* an holy convocation ... Num 29:7 2320
seventh *m* ye shall have an holy ... Num 29:12 2320
from Rameses in the first *m* ... Num 33:3 2320
the fifteenth day of the first *m* ... Num 33:3 2320
in the first day of the fifth *m* ... Num 33:38 2320
fortieth year, in the eleventh *m* ... Deut 1:3 2320
m, on the first day of the *m* ... Deut 1:3 2320
Observe the *m* of Abib, and keep ... Deut 16:1 2320
for in the *m* of Abib the Lord thy ... Deut 16:1 2320
her father and her mother a full *m* ... Deut 21:13 3391
on the tenth day of the first *m* ... Josh 4:19 2320
of the *m* at even in the plains of ... Josh 5:10 2320
which was the second day of the *m* ... 1Sa 20:27 2320
no meat the second day of the *m* ... 1Sa 20:34 2320
each man his *m* in a year made ... 1Kin 4:7 2320
table, every man in his *m* ... 1Kin 4:27 2320
ten thousand a *m* by courses ... 1Kin 5:14 2320
a *m* they were in Lebanon, and two ... 1Kin 5:14 2320
reign over Israel, in the *m* Zif ... 1Kin 6:1 2320
m Zif, which is the second *m* ... 1Kin 6:1 2320
of the Lord laid, in the *m* Zif ... 1Kin 6:37 3391
the eleventh year, in the *m* Bul ... 1Kin 6:38 3391
which is the eighth *m* ... 1Kin 6:38 2320
at the feast in the *m* Ethanim ... 1Kin 8:2 3391
which is the seventh *m* ... 1Kin 8:2 2320
ordained a feast in the eighth *m* ... 1Kin 12:32 2320
on the fifteenth day of the *m* ... 1Kin 12:32 2320
the fifteenth day of the eighth *m* ... 1Kin 12:33 2320
even in the *m* which he had ... 1Kin 12:33 2320
and he reigned a full *m* in Samaria ... 2Kin 15:13 3391
year of his reign, in the tenth *m* ... 2Kin 25:1 2320
in the tenth day of the *m* ... 2Kin 25:1 2320
m the famine prevailed in the ... 2Kin 25:3 2320
And in the fifth *m*, on the seventh ... 2Kin 25:8 2320
on the seventh day of the *m* ... 2Kin 25:8 2320
it came to pass in the seventh *m* ... 2Kin 25:25 2320
king of Judah, in the twelfth *m* ... 2Kin 25:27 2320
seven and twentieth day of the *m* ... 2Kin 25:27 2320
went over Jordan in the first *m* ... 1Chr 12:15 2320
went out *m* by *m* throughout ... 1Chr 27:1 2320
first *m* was Jashobeam the son of ... 1Chr 27:2 2320
of the host for the first *m* ... 1Chr 27:3 2320
the second *m* was Dodai an Ahohite ... 1Chr 27:4 2320
of the host for the third *m* was ... 1Chr 27:5 2320
fourth captain for the fourth *m* ... 1Chr 27:7 2320
fifth *m* was Shamhuth the Izrahite ... 1Chr 27:8 2320
m was Ira the son of Ikkesh the ... 1Chr 27:9 2320
seventh *m* was Helez the Pelonite ... 1Chr 27:10 2320
m was Sibbecai the Hushathite ... 1Chr 27:11 2320
m was Abiezer the Anetothite ... 1Chr 27:12 2320
m was Maharai the Netophathite ... 1Chr 27:13 2320
captain for the eleventh *m* was ... 1Chr 27:14 2320
m was Heldai the Netophathite ... 1Chr 27:15 2320
in the second day of the second *m* ... 2Chr 3:2 2320
feast which was in the seventh *m* ... 2Chr 5:3 2320
m he sent the people away into ... 2Chr 7:10 2320
at Jerusalem in the third *m* ... 2Chr 15:10 2320
year of his reign, in the first *m* ... 2Chr 29:3 2320
day of the first *m* to sanctify ... 2Chr 29:17 2320
on the eighth day of the *m* came ... 2Chr 29:17 2320
of the first *m* they made an end ... 2Chr 29:17 2320
keep the passover in the second *m* ... 2Chr 30:2 2320
unleavened bread in the second *m* ... 2Chr 30:13 2320
fourteenth day of the second *m* ... 2Chr 30:15 2320
In the third *m* they began to lay ... 2Chr 31:7 2320
and finished them in the seventh *m* ... 2Chr 31:7 2320
the fourteenth day of the first *m* ... 2Chr 35:1 2320
And when the seventh *m* was come ... Ezr 3:1 2320
m began they to offer burnt ... Ezr 3:6 2320
God at Jerusalem, in the second *m* ... Ezr 3:8 2320
on the third day of the *m* Adar ... Ezr 6:15 3393
the fourteenth day of the first *m* ... Ezr 6:19 2320
came to Jerusalem in the fifth *m* ... Ezr 7:8 2320
m began he to go up from Babylon ... Ezr 7:9 2320
the fifth *m* came he to Jerusalem ... Ezr 7:9 2320
on the twelfth day of the first *m* ... Ezr 8:31 2320
It was the ninth *m*, on the ... Ezr 10:9 2320
on the twentieth day of the *m* ... Ezr 10:9 2320
the tenth *m* to examine the matter ... Ezr 10:16 2320
by the first day of the first *m* ... Ezr 10:17 2320
it came to pass in the *m* Chisleu ... Neh 1:1 2320
And it came to pass in the *m* Nisan ... Neh 2:1 2320
twenty and fifth day of the *m* Elul ... Neh 6:15
and when the seventh *m* came ... Neh 7:73 2320
the first day of the seventh *m* ... Neh 8:2 2320
in the feast of the seventh *m* ... Neh 8:14 2320
fourth day of this *m* the children ... Neh 9:1 2320
his house royal in the tenth *m* ... Est 2:16 2320
which is the *m* Tebeth ... Est 2:16 2320
In the first *m*, that is ... Est 3:7 2320
the *m* Nisan, in the twelfth year ... Est 3:7 2320
m to *m*, to the twelfth *m* ... Est 3:7
that is, the *m* Adar ... Est 3:7 2320
the thirteenth day of the first *m* ... Est 3:12 2320
thirteenth day of the twelfth *m* ... Est 3:13 2320
which is the *m* Adar ... Est 3:13 2320
at that time in the third *m* ... Est 8:9 2320
the *m* Sivan, on the three and ... Est 8:9 2320
thirteenth day of the twelfth *m* ... Est 8:12 2320
which is the *m* Adar ... Est 8:12 2320
Now in the twelfth *m*, that is, ... Est 9:1 2320
the *m* Adar, on the thirteenth day ... Est 9:1 2320
fourteenth day also of the *m* Adar ... Est 9:15 2320
the thirteenth day of the *m* Adar ... Est 9:17 2320
of the *m* Adar a day of gladness ... Est 9:19 2320
the fourteenth day of the *m* Adar ... Est 9:21 2320

the *m* which was turned unto them .... Est 9:22 2320
Jerusalem captive in the fifth *m*............. Jer 1:3 2320
in her *m* they shall find her .... Jer 2:24 2320
fourth year, and in the fifth *m* .... Jer 28:1 2320
the same year in the seventh *m* .... Jer 28:17 2320
king of Judah, in the ninth *m*................ Jer 36:9 2320
in the winterhouse in the ninth *m*.......... Jer 36:22 2320
king of Judah, in the tenth *m*................ Jer 39:1 2320
year of Zedekiah, in the fourth *m* .... Jer 39:2 2320
the ninth day of the *m*........................... Jer 39:2 2320
it came to pass in the seventh *m* .... Jer 41:1 2320
year of his reign, in the tenth *m*........... Jer 52:4 2320
m, in the tenth day of the *m*................. Jer 52:4 2320
And in the fourth *m*, in the ninth .... Jer 52:6 2320
m, in the ninth day of the *m*................. Jer 52:6 2320
Now in the fifth *m*, in the tenth............. Jer 52:12 2320
m, in the tenth day of the *m*................. Jer 52:12 2320
king of Judah, in the twelfth *m*............. Jer 52:31 2320
five and twentieth day of the *m* .... Jer 52:31 2320
thirtieth year, in the fourth *m* .... Eze 1:1
in the fifth day of the *m* .... Eze 1:1 2320
in the fifth day of the *m*......................... Eze 1:2 2320
in the sixth year, in the sixth *m* .... Eze 8:1
in the fifth day of the *m* .... Eze 8:1 2320
the seventh year, in the fifth *m* .... Eze 20:1
the tenth day of the *m*............................. Eze 20:1 2320
in the ninth year, in the tenth *m* .... Eze 24:1 2320
in the tenth day of the *m*....................... Eze 24:1 2320
year, in the first day of the *m*................ Eze 26:1 2320
In the tenth year, in the tenth *m* .... Eze 29:1
in the twelfth day of the *m*.................... Eze 29:1 2320
and twentieth year, in the first *m*.......... Eze 29:17
in the first day of the *m* .... Eze 29:17 2320
the eleventh year, in the first *m* .... Eze 30:20 2320
in the seventh day of the *m* .... Eze 30:20 2320
the eleventh year, in the third *m* .... Eze 31:1
in the first day of the *m* .... Eze 31:1 2320
twelfth year, in the twelfth *m*................ Eze 32:1 2320
in the first day of the *m* .... Eze 32:1 2320
in the fifteenth day of the *m* .... Eze 32:17 2320
of our captivity, in the tenth *m* .... Eze 33:21
in the fifth day of the *m*......................... Eze 33:21 2320
year, in the tenth day of the *m* .... Eze 40:1 2320
In the first *m*, in the first day .... Eze 45:18
in the first day of the *m* .... Eze 45:18 2320
the *m* for every one that erreth .... Eze 45:20 2320
In the first *m*, in the fourteenth .... Eze 45:21
in the fourteenth day of the *m* .... Eze 45:21 2320
In the seventh *m*, in the......................... Eze 45:25
in the fifteenth day of the *m* .... Eze 45:25 2320
and twentieth day of the first *m* .... Dan 10:4 2320
now shall a *m* devour them with............. Hos 5:7 2320
and the latter rain in the first *m*........... Joel 2:23
Darius the king, in the sixth *m*.............. Hag 1:1 2320
m, in the first day of the *m* .... Hag 1:1 2320
and twentieth day of the sixth *m*............ Hag 1:15 2320
In the seventh *m*, in the one and............. Hag 2:1
the one and twentieth day of the *m* .... Hag 2:1 2320
and twentieth day of the ninth *m*............ Hag 2:10
and twentieth day of the ninth *m*............ Hag 2:18
four and twentieth day of the *m* .... Hag 2:20 2320
In the eighth *m*, in the second................ Zec 1:1 2320
twentieth day of the eleventh *m*.............. Zec 1:7 2320
which is the *m* Sebat............................... Zec 1:7 2320
in the fourth day of the ninth *m* .... Zec 7:1 2320
Should I weep in the fifth *m*................... Zec 7:3 2320
mourned in the fifth and seventh *m*......... Zec 7:5
The fast of the fourth *m*, and the............. Zec 8:19
shepherds also I cut off in one *m* .... Zec 11:8 3391
in the sixth *m* the angel Gabriel .... Lk 1:26 3376
and this is the sixth *m* with her............... Lk 1:36 3376
for an hour, and a day, and a *m*.............. Rev 9:15 3376
and yielded her fruit every *m*................. Rev 22:2 3376

MONTHLY {1}

the *m* prognosticators, stand up,............. Is 47:13 2320

MONTHS {59}

came to pass about three *m* after........... Gen 38:24 2320
goodly child, she hid him three *m*.......... Ex 2:2 3391
be unto you the beginning of *m* .... Ex 12:2 2320
and in the beginnings of your *m* .... Num 10:10 2320
in the beginnings of your *m* ye................ Num 28:11 2320
throughout the *m* of the year .... Num 28:14 2320
let me alone two *m*, that I may go........... Judg 11:37 2320
And he sent her away for two *m* .... Judg 11:38 2320
came to pass at the end of two *m*............ Judg 11:39 2320
and was there four whole *m*..................... Judg 19:2 2320
abode in the rock Rimmon four *m* .... Judg 20:47 2320
of the Philistines seven *m*....................... 1Sa 6:1 2320
was a full year and four *m* 1Sa 27:7 2320
of Judah was seven years and six *m* 2Sa 2:11 2320
over Judah seven years and six *m*............ 2Sa 5:5 2320
of Obed-edom the Gittite three *m*............ 2Sa 6:11 2320
to Jerusalem at the end of nine *m*........... 2Sa 24:8 2320
flee three *m* before thine enemies 2Sa 24:13 2320
were in Lebanon, and two *m* at home...... 1Kin 5:14 2320
(For six *m* did Joab remain there 1Kin 11:16 2320
over Israel in Samaria six *m* 2Kin 15:8 2320
he reigned three *m* in Jerusalem 2Kin 23:31 2320
he reigned in Jerusalem three *m* 2Kin 24:8 2320
he reigned seven years and six *m*........... 1Chr 3:4 2320
of Obed-edom in his house three *m* 1Chr 13:14 2320
or three *m* to be destroyed before........... 1Chr 21:12 2320
throughout all the *m* of the year 1Chr 27:1 2320
he reigned three *m* in Jerusalem 2Chr 36:2 2320
to reign, and he reigned three *m* 2Chr 36:9 2320
after that she had been twelve *m*............. Est 2:12 2320
six *m* with oil of myrrh, and six.............. Est 2:12 2320
six *m* with sweet odours, and with .... Est 2:12 2320
not come into the number of the *m*......... Job 3:6 3391
am I made to possess *m* of vanity .... Job 7:3 3391
the number of his *m* are with thee......... Job 14:5 2320
when the number of his *m* is cut............. Job 21:21 2320
Oh that I were as in *m* past .... Job 29:2 3391
number the *m* that they fulfil .... Job 39:2 3391
seven *m* shall the house of Israel .... Eze 39:12 2320
end of seven *m* shall they search............ Eze 39:14 2320
new fruit according to his *m*.................. Eze 47:12 2320
At the end of twelve *m* he walked........... Dan 4:29 3393
were yet three *m* to the harvest.............. Amos 4:7 2320
conceived, and hid herself five *m*............ Lk 1:24 3376
Mary abode with her about three *m* .... Lk 1:56 3376
was shut up three years and six *m* .... Lk 4:25 3376
Say not ye, There are yet four *m* .... Jn 4:35 5072
up in his father's house three *m*............. Acts 7:20 3370
continued there a year and six *m*............ Acts 18:11 3376
boldly for the space of three *m* .... Acts 19:8 3376
And there abode three *m*......................... Acts 20:3 3376
after three *m* we departed in a............... Acts 28:11 3376
Ye observe days, and *m*, and times,......... Gal 4:10 3376
was hid three *m* of his parents,............... Heb 11:23 5150
the space of three years and six *m*......... Jas 5:17 3376
they should be tormented five *m*............ Rev 9:5 3376
power was to hurt men five *m*................. Rev 9:10 3376
tread under foot forty and two *m*........... Rev 11:2 3376
him to continue forty and two *m* .... Rev 13:5 3376

MONUMENTS {1}

the graves, and lodge in the *m* .... Is 65:4 5341

MOON {51}

and, behold, the sun and the *m*............... Gen 37:9 3394
when thou seest the sun, and the *m*........ Deut 4:19 3394
them, either the sun, or *m* .... Deut 17:3 3394
things put forth by the *m* .... Deut 33:14 3391
and thou, *M*, in the valley of.................... Josh 10:12 3394
the *m* stayed, until the people................. Josh 10:13 3394
Behold, to morrow is the new *m* 1Sa 20:5 2320
to David, To morrow is the new *m*........... 1Sa 20:18 2320
and when the new *m* was come................ 1Sa 20:24 2320
it is neither new *m*, nor sabbath 2Kin 4:23 2320
Baal, to the sun, and to the *m*................. 2Kin 23:5 3394
Behold even to the *m*, and it .... Job 25:5 3394
or the *m* walking in brightness .... Job 31:26 3394
the work of thy fingers, the *m*................ Ps 8:3 3394
sun and *m* endure, throughout all........... Ps 72:5 3394
peace so long as the *m* endureth .... Ps 72:7 3394
Blow up the trumpet in the new *m* .... Ps 81:3 2320
be established for ever as the *m*.............. Ps 89:37 3394
He appointed the *m* for seasons .... Ps 104:19 3394
thee by day, nor the *m* by night............... Ps 121:6 3394
The *m* and stars to rule by night............. Ps 136:9 3394
Praise ye him, sun and *m* .... Ps 148:3 3394
the sun, or the light, or the *m* .... Eccl 12:2 3394
as the morning, fair as the *m* .... Song 6:10 3842
and their round tires like the *m* .... Is 3:18
the *m* shall not cause her light................. Is 13:10 3394
Then the *m* shall be confounded,............. Is 24:23 3842
Moreover the light of the *m* shall............. Is 30:26 3842
shall the *m* give light unto thee............... Is 60:19 3394
shall thy *m* withdraw itself...................... Is 60:20 3391
that from one new *m* to another .... Is 66:23 2320
them before the sun, and the *m*............... Jer 8:2 3394
day, and the ordinances of the *m* .... Jer 31:35 3394
the *m* shall not give her light .... Eze 32:7 3394
of the new *m* it shall be opened............... Eze 46:1 2320
in the day of the new *m* it shall .... Eze 46:6 2320
the *m* shall be dark, and the stars............ Joel 2:10 3394
the *m* into blood, before the .... Joel 2:31 3394
the *m* shall be darkened, and the............. Joel 3:15 3394
When will the new *m* be gone .... Amos 8:5 2320
m stood still in their habitation .... Hab 3:11 3394
the *m* shall not give her light, ... Mt 24:29 4582
the *m* shall not give her light, ... Mk 13:24 4582
be signs in the sun, and in the *m* .... Lk 21:25 4582
the *m* into blood, before that .... Acts 2:20 4582
sun, and another glory of the *m*.............. 1Cor 15:41 4582
of an holyday, or of the new *m* .... Col 2:16 3561
of hair, and the *m* became as blood .... Rev 6:12 4582
and the third part of the *m* .... Rev 8:12 4582
the *m* under her feet, and upon her .... Rev 12:1 4582
need of the sun, neither of the *m* .... Rev 21:23 4582

MOONS {11}

in the sabbaths, in the new *m* 1Chr 23:31 2320
on the sabbaths, and on the new *m*......... 2Chr 2:4 2320
on the sabbaths, and on the new *m*......... 2Chr 8:13 2320
the sabbaths, and for the new *m*............. 2Chr 31:3 2320
burnt offering, both of the new *m*............ Ezr 3:5 2320
of the sabbaths, of the new *m* .... Neh 10:33 2320
the new *m* and sabbaths, the.................... Is 1:13 2320
Your new *m* and your appointed............... Is 1:14 2320
in the feasts, and in the new *m* .... Eze 45:17 2320
in the sabbaths and in the new *m*............ Eze 46:3 2320
cease, her feast days, her new *m* .... Hos 2:11 2320

MORASTHITE *(mo'-ras-thite)* {2} *Family name of Micah the prophet.*

Micah the *M* prophesied in the .... Jer 26:18 4183
Micah the *M* in the days of Jotham......... Mic 1:1 4183

MORDECAI *(mor'-de-cahee)* {58} See MORDECAI'S.

1. A clan leader with Zerubbabel.

Nehemiah, Seraiah, Reelaiah, *M*............. Ezr 2:2 4782
Azariah, Raamiah, Nahamani, *M*............ Neh 7:7 4782

2. Cousin of Esther.

a certain Jew, whose name was *M*........... Est 2:5 4782
whom *M*, when her father and mother .... Est 2:7 4782
for *M* had charged her that she............... Est 2:10 4782
M walked every day before the .... Est 2:11 4782
of Abihail the uncle of *M* .... Est 2:15 4782
then *M* sat in the king's gate.................... Est 2:19 4782
as *M* had charged her............................... Est 2:20 4782
Esther did the commandment of *M*......... Est 2:20 4782
while *M* sat in the king's gate, ... Est 2:21 4782
And the thing was known to *M*............... Est 2:22 4782
But *M* bowed not, nor did him................ Est 3:2 4782
in the king's gate, said unto *M*................ Est 3:3 4782
when Haman saw that *M* bowed not....... Est 3:5 4782
scorn to lay hands on *M* alone .... Est 3:6 4782
had shewed him the people of *M* .... Est 3:6 4782
Ahasuerus, even the people of *M* .... Est 3:6 4782
When *M* perceived all that was.............. Est 4:1 4782
M rent his clothes, and put on .... Est 4:1 4782
and she sent raiment to clothe *M*............ Est 4:4 4782
and gave him a commandment to *M*........ Est 4:5 4782
So Hatach went forth to *M* unto .... Est 4:6 4782
M told him of all that had........................ Est 4:7 4782
and told Esther the words of *M* .... Est 4:9 4782
and gave him commandment unto *M*...... Est 4:10 4782
they told to *M* Esther's words .... Est 4:12 4782
Then *M* commanded to answer Esther.... Est 4:13 4782
bade them return *M* this answer .... Est 4:15 4782
So *M* went his way, and did .... Est 4:17 4782
Haman saw *M* in the king's gate .... Est 5:9 4782
was full of indignation against *M* .... Est 5:9 4782
so long as I see *M* the Jew .... Est 5:13 4782
king that *M* may be hanged thereon .... Est 5:14 4782
that *M* had told of Bigthana and .... Est 6:2 4782
hath been done to *M* for this................... Est 6:3 4782
hang *M* on the gallows that he had......... Est 6:4 4782
said, and do even so to *M* the Jew........... Est 6:10 4782
and the horse, and arrayed *M* .... Est 6:11 4782
M came again to the king's gate.............. Est 6:12 4782
If *M* be of the seed of the Jews,............... Est 6:13 4782
high, which Haman had made for *M*......... Est 7:9 4782
that he had prepared for *M*..................... Est 7:10 4782
And *M* came before the king.................... Est 8:1 4782
from Haman, and gave it unto *M*............ Est 8:2 4782
Esther set *M* over the house of................ Est 8:2 4782
to *M* the Jew, Behold, I have .... Est 8:7 4782
that *M* commanded unto the Jews .... Est 8:9 4782
M went out from the presence of .... Est 8:15 4782
the fear of *M* fell upon them.................. Est 9:3 4782
For *M* was great in the king's.................. Est 9:4 4782
for this man *M* waxed greater and.......... Est 9:4 4782
M wrote these things, and sent .... Est 9:20 4782
as *M* had written unto them.................... Est 9:23 4782
M the Jew, wrote with all......................... Est 9:29 4782
appointed, according as *M* the Jew .... Est 9:31 4782
declaration of the greatness of *M*........... Est 10:2 4782
For *M* the Jew was next unto king.......... Est 10:3 4782

MORDECAI'S *(mor'-de-cahees)* {2} *Refers to Mordecai 2.*

the king thereof in *M* name..................... Est 2:22 4782
to see whether *M* matters would............. Est 3:4 4782

MORE See APPENDIX.

MOREH *(mo'-reh)* {3}

1. A place in Ephraim.

of Sichem, unto the plain of *M* .... Gen 12:6 4176
Gilgal, beside the plains of *M* .... Deut 11:30 4176

2. A place in Issachar.

side of them, by the hill of *M*.................. Judg 7:1 4176

MOREOVER See APPENDIX.

MORESHETH See MORASTHITE.

MORESHETH-GATH *(mor'-e-sheth-gath)* {1} See MORASTHITE. *A city in Judah.*

shalt thou give presents to *M* .... Mic 1:14 4182

MORIAH *(mo-ri'-ah)* {2} *The Temple Mount.*

and get thee into the land of *M*............... Gen 22:2 4179
the LORD at Jerusalem in mount *M*......... 2Chr 3:1 4179

MORNING {228}

and the *m* were the first day .... Gen 1:5 1242
the *m* were the second day .... Gen 1:8 1242
and the *m* were the third day.................. Gen 1:13 1242
the *m* were the fourth day....................... Gen 1:19 1242
and the *m* were the fifth day................... Gen 1:23 1242
and the *m* were the sixth day.................. Gen 1:31 1242
And when the *m* arose, then the .... Gen 19:15 7837
the *m* to the place where he stood .... Gen 19:27 1242
Abimelech rose early in the *m* .... Gen 20:8 1242
And Abraham rose up early in the *m*...... Gen 21:14 1242
And Abraham rose up early in the *m*...... Gen 22:3 1242
and they rose up in the *m*, and he........... Gen 24:54 1242
And they rose up betimes in the *m* .... Gen 26:31 1242
And Jacob rose up early in the *m*............ Gen 28:18 1242
And it came to pass, that in the *m*.......... Gen 29:25 1242
early in the *m* Laban rose up, and .... Gen 31:55 1242
Joseph came in unto them in the *m*......... Gen 40:6 1242
it came to pass in the *m* that his............ Gen 41:8 1242
As soon as the *m* was light....................... Gen 44:3 1242
in the *m* he shall devour the prey .... Gen 49:27 1242
Get thee unto Pharaoh in the *m*.............. Ex 7:15 1242
Moses, Rise up early in the *m*................. Ex 8:20 1242
Moses, Rise up early in the *m*................. Ex 9:13 1242
and when it was *m*, the east wind........... Ex 10:13 1242
nothing of it remain until the *m* .... Ex 12:10 1242
the *m* ye shall burn with fire................... Ex 12:10 1242
the door of his house until the *m* .... Ex 12:22 1242
that in the *m* watch the LORD .... Ex 14:24 1242
his strength when the *m* appeared.......... Ex 14:27 1242
And in the *m*, then ye shall see .... Ex 16:7 1242
in the *m* bread to the full .... Ex 16:8 1242
in the *m* ye shall be filled with .... Ex 16:12 1242

M

in the *m* the dew lay round about ... Ex 16:13 1242
Let no man leave of it till the *m* ... Ex 16:19 1242
of them left of it until the *m* ... Ex 16:20 1242
And they gathered it every *m* ... Ex 16:21 1242
up for you to be kept until the *m* ... Ex 16:23 1242
And they laid it up till the *m* ... Ex 16:24 1242
Moses from the *m* unto the evening ... Ex 18:13 1242
stand by thee from *m* unto even ... Ex 18:14 1242
to pass on the third day in the *m* ... Ex 19:16 1242
my sacrifice remain until the *m* ... Ex 23:18 1242
LORD, and rose up early in the *m* ... Ex 24:4 1242
from evening to *m* before the LORD ... Ex 27:21 1242
of the bread, remain unto the *m* ... Ex 29:34 1242
lamb thou shalt offer in the *m* ... Ex 29:39 1242
to the meat offering of the *m* ... Ex 29:41 1242
thereon sweet incense every *m* ... Ex 30:7 1242
And be ready in the *m*, and come up ... Ex 34:2 1242
come up in the *m* unto mount Sinai ... Ex 34:2 1242
and Moses rose up early in the *m* ... Ex 34:4 1242
the passover be left unto the *m* ... Ex 34:25 1242
unto him free offerings every *m* ... Ex 36:3 1242
the altar all night unto the *m* ... Lev 6:9 1242
shall burn wood on it every *m* ... Lev 6:12 1242
perpetual, half of it in the *m* ... Lev 6:20 1242
not leave any of it until the *m* ... Lev 7:15 1242
the burnt sacrifice of the *m* ... Lev 9:17 1242
with thee all night until the *m* ... Lev 19:13 1242
the *m* before the LORD continually ... Lev 24:3 1242
shall leave none of it unto the *m* ... Num 9:12 1242
appearance of fire, until the *m* ... Num 9:15 1242
cloud abode from even unto the *m* ... Num 9:21 1242
the cloud was taken up in the *m* ... Num 9:21 1242
And they rose up early in the *m* ... Num 14:40 1242
And Balaam rose up in the *m* ... Num 22:13 1242
And Balaam rose up in the *m* ... Num 22:21 1242
lamb shalt thou offer in the *m* ... Num 28:4 1242
as the meat offering of the *m* ... Num 28:8 1242
the burnt offering in the *m* ... Num 28:23 1242
remain all night until the *m* ... Deut 16:4 1242
and thou shalt turn in the *m* ... Deut 16:7 1242
In the *m* thou shalt say, Would ... Deut 28:67 1242
shalt say, Would God it were *m* ... Deut 28:67 1242
And Joshua rose early in the *m* ... Josh 3:1 1242
And Joshua rose early in the *m* ... Josh 6:12 1242
In the *m* therefore ye shall be ... Josh 7:14 1242
So Joshua rose up early in the *m* ... Josh 7:16 1242
And Joshua rose up early in the *m* ... Josh 8:10 1242
of the city arose early in the *m* ... Judg 6:28 1242
put to death whilst it is yet *m* ... Judg 6:31 1242
And it shall be, that in the *m* ... Judg 9:33 1242
all the night, saying, In the *m* ... Judg 16:2 1242
when they arose early in the *m* ... Judg 19:5 1242
he arose early in the *m* on the ... Judg 19:8 1242
her all the night until the *m* ... Judg 19:25 1242
And her lord rose up in the *m* ... Judg 19:27 1242
of Israel rose up in the *m* ... Judg 20:19 1242
even from the *m* until now ... Ruth 2:7 1242
night, and it shall be in the *m* ... Ruth 3:13 1242
lie down until the *m* ... Ruth 3:13 1242
she lay at his feet until the *m* ... Ruth 3:14 1242
And they rose up in the *m* early ... 1Sa 1:19 1242
And Samuel lay until the *m* ... 1Sa 3:15 1242
they arose early on the morrow *m* ... 1Sa 5:4 1242
midst of the host in the *m* watch ... 1Sa 11:11 1242
and spoil them until the *m* light ... 1Sa 14:36 1242
rose early to meet Saul in the *m* ... 1Sa 15:12 1242
And the Philistine drew near *m* ... 1Sa 17:16 7925
And David rose up early in the *m* ... 1Sa 17:20 1242
take heed to thyself until the *m* ... 1Sa 19:2 1242
him, and to slay him in the *m* ... 1Sa 19:11 1242
And it came to pass in the *m* ... 1Sa 20:35 1242
m light any that pisseth against ... 1Sa 25:22 1242
m light any that pisseth against ... 1Sa 25:34 1242
less or more, until the *m* light ... 1Sa 25:36 1242
But it came to pass in the *m* ... 1Sa 25:37 1242
now rise up early in the *m* with ... 1Sa 29:10 1242
soon as ye be up early in the *m* ... 1Sa 29:10 1242
rose up early to depart in the *m* ... 1Sa 29:11 1242
surely then in the *m* the people ... 2Sa 2:27 1242
And it came to pass in the *m* ... 2Sa 11:14 1242
by the *m* light there lacked not ... 2Sa 17:22 1242
he shall be as the light of the *m* ... 2Sa 23:4 1242
riseth, even a *m* without clouds ... 2Sa 23:4 1242
For when David was up in the *m* ... 2Sa 24:11 1242
the *m* even to the time appointed ... 2Sa 24:15 1242
when I rose in the *m* to give my ... 1Kin 3:21 1242
when I had considered it in the *m* ... 1Kin 3:21 1242
him bread and flesh in the *m* ... 1Kin 17:6 1242
of Baal from *m* even until noon ... 1Kin 18:26 1242
And it came to pass in the *m* ... 2Kin 3:20 1242
And they rose up early in the *m* ... 2Kin 3:22 1242
if we tarry till the *m* light ... 2Kin 7:9 1242
in of the gate until the *m* ... 2Kin 10:8 1242
And it came to pass in the *m* ... 2Kin 10:9 1242
altar burn the *m* burnt offering ... 2Kin 16:15 1242
and when they arose early in the *m* ... 2Kin 19:35 1242
thereof every *m* pertained to them ... 1Chr 9:27 1242
the burnt offering continually *m* ... 1Chr 16:40 1242
And to stand every *m* to thank ... 1Chr 23:30 1242
and for the burnt offerings *m* ... 2Chr 2:4 1242
they burn unto the LORD every *m* ... 2Chr 13:11 1242
And they rose early in the *m* ... 2Chr 20:20 1242
offerings, to wit, for the *m* ... 2Chr 31:3 1242
the LORD, even burnt offerings *m* ... Ezr 3:3 1242
of the *m* till the stars appeared ... Neh 4:21 7837
gate from the *m* until midday ... Neh 8:3 216
them, and rose up early in the *m* ... Job 1:5 1242
are destroyed from *m* to evening ... Job 4:20 1242
thou shouldest visit him every *m* ... Job 7:18 1242
and thou shalt seek me in the *m* ... Job 7:21 7836
forth, thou shalt be as the *m* ... Job 11:17 1242
For the *m* is to them even as the ... Job 24:17 1242
When the *m* stars sang together, ... Job 38:7 1242
commanded the *m* since thy days ... Job 38:12 1242
are like the eyelids of the *m* ... Job 41:18 7837
My voice shalt thou hear in the *m* ... Ps 5:3 1242
in the *m* will I direct my prayer ... Ps 5:3 1242
a night, but joy cometh in the *m* ... Ps 30:5 1242
have dominion over them in the *m* ... Ps 49:14 1242
Evening, and *m*, and at noon, will I ... Ps 55:17 1242
sing aloud of thy mercy in the *m* ... Ps 59:16 1242
makest the outgoings of the *m* ... Ps 65:8 1242
plagued, and chastened every *m* ... Ps 73:14 1242
in the *m* shall my prayer prevent ... Ps 88:13 1242
in the *m* they are like grass ... Ps 90:5 1242
In the *m* it flourisheth, and ... Ps 90:6 1242
forth thy lovingkindness in the *m* ... Ps 92:2 1242
holiness from the womb of the *m* ... Ps 110:3 4891
I prevented the dawning of the *m* ... Ps 119:147
than they that watch for the *m* ... Ps 130:6 1242
than they that watch for the *m* ... Ps 130:6 1242
If I take the wings of the *m* ... Ps 139:9 7837
hear thy lovingkindness in the *m* ... Ps 143:8 1242
take our fill of love until the *m* ... Prov 7:18 1242
loud voice, rising early in the *m* ... Prov 27:14 1242
and thy princes eat in the *m* ... Eccl 10:16 1242
In the *m* sow thy seed, and in the ... Eccl 11:6 1242
she that looketh forth as the *m* ... Song 6:10 7837
them that rise up early in the *m* ... Is 5:11 1242
heaven, O Lucifer, son of the *m* ... Is 14:12 7837
in the *m* shalt thou make thy seed ... Is 17:11 1242
and before the *m* he is not ... Is 17:14 1242
The *m* cometh, and also the night ... Is 21:12 1242
for *m* by *m* shall it pass ... Is 28:19 1242
be thou their arm every *m* ... Is 33:2 1242
and when they arose early in the *m* ... Is 37:36 1242
I reckoned till *m*, that, as a ... Is 38:13 1242
he wakeneth *m* by *m*, he ... Is 50:4 1242
thy light break forth as the *m* ... Is 58:8 7837
They were as fed horses in the *m* ... Jer 5:8 7904
and let him hear the cry in the *m* ... Jer 20:16 1242
Execute judgment in the *m* ... Jer 21:12 1242
They are new every *m* ... Lam 3:23 1242
The *m* is come unto thee, O thou ... Eze 7:7 6843
the *m* is gone forth ... Eze 7:10 6843
in the *m* came the word of the ... Eze 12:8 1242
I spake unto the people in the *m* ... Eze 24:18 1242
I did in the *m* as I was commanded ... Eze 24:18 1242
until he came to me in the *m* ... Eze 33:22 1242
thou shalt prepare it every *m* ... Eze 46:13 1242
a meat offering for it every *m* ... Eze 46:14 1242
every *m* for a continual burnt ... Eze 46:15 1242
king arose very early in the *m* ... Dan 6:19 5053
the *m* which was told is true ... Dan 8:26 1242
going forth is prepared as the *m* ... Hos 6:3 7837
for your goodness is as a *m* cloud ... Hos 6:4 1242
in the *m* it burneth as a flaming ... Hos 7:6 1242
in a *m* shall the king of Israel ... Hos 10:15 7837
they shall be as the *m* cloud ... Hos 13:3 1242
as the *m* spread upon the ... Joel 2:2 7837
and bring your sacrifices every *m* ... Amos 4:4 1242
that maketh the *m* darkness ... Amos 4:13 7837
the shadow of death into the *m* ... Amos 5:8 1242
worm when the *m* rose the next day ... Jonah 4:7 7837
when the *m* is light, they ... Mic 2:1 1242
every *m* doth he bring his ... Zeph 3:5 1242
And in the *m*, It will be foul ... Mt 16:3 *4404*
the *m* to hire labourers into his ... Mt 20:1
Now in the *m* as he returned into ... Mt 21:18 *4405*
When the *m* was come, all the ... Mt 27:1 *4405*
And in the *m*, rising up a great ... Mk 1:35 *4404*
And in the *m*, as they passed by, ... Mk 11:20 *4404*
at the cockcrowing, or in the *m* ... Mk 13:35 *4404*
straightway in the *m* the chief ... Mk 15:1 *4404*
very early in the *m* the first day ... Mk 16:2
in the *m* to him in the temple ... Lk 21:38
of the week, very early in the *m* ... Lk 24:1
And early in the *m* he came ... Jn 8:1
early in the *m* he came again into ... Jn 8:2
But when the *m* was now come ... Jn 21:4 *4405*
into the temple early in the *m* ... Acts 5:21
the prophets, from *m* till evening ... Acts 28:23 *4404*
And I will give him the *m* star ... Rev 2:28 *4407*
of David, and the bright and *m* star ... Rev 22:16 *3720*

MORROW {103}

And it came to pass on the *m* ... Gen 19:34 4283
And he said, To *m* ... Ex 8:10 4279
to *m* shall this sign be ... Ex 8:23 4279
and from his people, to *m* ... Ex 8:29 4279
To *m* the LORD shall do this thing ... Ex 9:5 4279
the LORD did that thing on the *m* ... Ex 9:6 4283
to *m* about this time I will cause ... Ex 9:18 4279
to *m* will I bring the locusts ... Ex 10:4 4279
To *m* is the rest of the holy ... Ex 16:23 4279
to *m* I will stand on the top of ... Ex 17:9 4279
And it came to pass on the *m* ... Ex 18:13 4283
and sanctify them to day and to *m* ... Ex 19:10 4279
To *m* is a feast to the LORD ... Ex 32:5 4279
And they rose up early on the *m* ... Ex 32:6 4283
And it came to pass on the *m* ... Ex 32:30 4283
on the *m* also the remainder of it ... Lev 7:16 4283
same day ye offer it, and on the *m* ... Lev 19:6 4283
leave none of it until the *m* ... Lev 22:30 1242
on the *m* after the sabbath the ... Lev 23:11 4283
you from the *m* after the sabbath ... Lev 23:15 4283
Even unto the *m* after the seventh ... Lev 23:16 4283
Sanctify yourselves against to *m* ... Num 11:18 4279
) To *m* turn you, and get you into ... Num 14:25 4279
Even to *m* the LORD will shew who ... Num 16:5 1242
in them before the LORD to *m* ... Num 16:7 4279
thou, and they, and Aaron, to *m* ... Num 16:16 4279
But on the *m* all the congregation ... Num 16:41 4283
that on the *m* Moses went into the ... Num 17:8 4283
And it came to pass on the *m* ... Num 22:41 1242
on the *m* after the passover the ... Num 33:3 4283
for to *m* the LORD will do wonders ... Josh 3:5 4279
land on the *m* after the passover ... Josh 5:11 4283
the manna ceased on the *m* after ... Josh 5:12 4283
Sanctify yourselves against to *m* ... Josh 7:13 4279
for to *m* about this time will I ... Josh 11:6 4279
that to *m* he will be wroth with ... Josh 22:18 4279
for he rose up early on the *m* ... Judg 6:38 4283
And it came to pass on the *m* ... Judg 9:42 4283
to *m* get you early on your way, ... Judg 19:9 4279
for to *m* I will deliver them into ... Judg 20:28 4279
And it came to pass on the *m* ... Judg 21:4 4279
of Ashdod arose early on the *m* ... 1Sa 5:3 4283
they arose early on the *m* morning ... 1Sa 5:4 4283
To *m* about this time I will send ... 1Sa 9:16 4279
to *m* I will let thee go, and will ... 1Sa 9:19 1242
the men of Jabesh-gilead, To *m* ... 1Sa 11:9 4279
To *m* we will come out unto you, ... 1Sa 11:10 4279
And it was so on the *m*, that Saul ... 1Sa 11:11 4283
And it came to pass on the *m* ... 1Sa 18:10 4283
night, to *m* thou shalt be slain ... 1Sa 19:11 4279
to *m* is the new moon, and I should ... 1Sa 20:5 4279
my father about to *m* any time ... 1Sa 20:12 4279
to David, To *m* is the new moon ... 1Sa 20:18 4279
And it came to pass on the *m* ... 1Sa 20:27 4283
to *m* shalt thou and thy sons be ... 1Sa 28:19 4279
And it came to pass on the *m* ... 1Sa 31:8 4283
to *m* I will let thee depart ... 2Sa 11:12 4279
in Jerusalem that day, and the *m* ... 2Sa 11:12 4283
of them by to *m* about this time ... 1Kin 19:2 4279
unto thee to *m* about this time ... 1Kin 20:6 4279
day, and we will eat my son to *m* ... 2Kin 6:28 4279
To *m* about this time shall a ... 2Kin 7:1 4279
shall be to *m* about this time in ... 2Kin 7:18 4279
And it came to pass on the *m* ... 2Kin 8:15 4283
me to Jezreel by to *m* this time ... 2Kin 10:6 4279
And it came to pass on the *m* ... 1Chr 10:8 4283
on the *m* after that day, even a ... 1Chr 29:21 4283
To *m* go ye down against them ... 2Chr 20:16 4279
to *m* go out against them ... 2Chr 20:17 4279
on the *m* she returned into the ... Est 2:14 1242
I will do to *m* as the king hath ... Est 5:8 4279
to *m* am I invited unto her also ... Est 5:12 4279
to *m* speak thou unto the king ... Est 5:14 1242
which are in Shushan to do to *m* ... Est 9:13 4279
come again, and to *m* I will give ... Prov 3:28 4279
Boast not thyself of to *m* ... Prov 27:1 4279
for to *m* we shall die ... Is 22:13 4279
to *m* shall be as this day, and ... Is 56:12 4279
And it came to pass on the *m* ... Jer 20:3 4283
gnaw not the bones till the *m* ... Zeph 3:3 1242
to *m* is cast into the oven, shall ... Mt 6:30 *839*
therefore no thought for the *m* ... Mt 6:34 *839*
for the *m* shall take thought for ... Mt 6:34 *839*
And on the *m*, when they were come ... Mk 11:12 *1887*
on the *m* when he departed, he ... Lk 10:35 *839*
to *m* is cast into the oven ... Lk 12:28 *839*
and I do cures to day and to *m* ... Lk 13:32 *839*
I must walk to day, and to *m* ... Lk 13:33 *839*
And it came to pass on the *m* ... Acts 4:5 *839*
On the *m*, as they went on their ... Acts 10:9 *1887*
on the *m* Peter went away with ... Acts 10:23 *1887*
the *m* after they entered into ... Acts 10:24 *1887*
them, ready to depart on the *m* ... Acts 20:7 *1887*
On the *m*, because he would have ... Acts 22:30 *1887*
he bring him down unto you to *m* ... Acts 23:15 *839*
down Paul to *m* into the council ... Acts 23:20 *839*
On the *m* they left the horsemen ... Acts 23:32 *1887*
without any delay on the *m* I sat ... Acts 25:17 *1836*
To *m*, said he, thou shalt hear ... Acts 25:22 *839*
And on the *m*, when Agrippa was ... Acts 25:23 *1887*
for to *m* we die ... 1Cor 15:32 *839*
To day or to *m* we will go into ... Jas 4:13 *839*
know not what shall be on the *m* ... Jas 4:14 *839*

MORSEL {10}

And I will fetch a *m* of bread ... Gen 18:5 6595
thine heart with a *m* of bread ... Judg 19:5 6595
and dip thy *m* in the vinegar ... Ruth 2:14 6595
a *m* of bread, and shall say, Put ... 1Sa 2:36 3603
let me set a *m* of bread before ... 1Sa 28:22 6595
a *m* of bread in thine hand ... 1Kin 17:11 6595
Or have eaten my *m* myself alone ... Job 31:17 6595
Better is a dry *m*, and quietness ... Prov 17:1 6595
The *m* which thou hast eaten shalt ... Prov 23:8 6595
who for one *m* of meat sold his ... Heb 12:16 *1035*

MORSELS {1}

He casteth forth his ice like *m* ... Ps 147:17 6595

MORTAL {6}

Shall *m* man be more just than God ... Job 4:17 582
therefore reign in your *m* body ... Rom 6:12 *2349*
your *m* bodies by his Spirit that ... Rom 8:11 *2349*
this *m* must put on immortality ... 1Cor 15:53 *2349*
and this *m* shall have put on ... 1Cor 15:54 *2349*
be made manifest in our *m* flesh ... 2Cor 4:11 *2349*

MORTALITY {1}

that *m* might be swallowed up of ... 2Cor 5:4 *2349*

MORTALLY {1}
smite him *m* that he die, and ... Deut 19:11 5315

MORTAR {2}
it in mills, or beat it in a *m* ... Num 11:8 4085
in a *m* among wheat with a pestle ... Prov 27:22 4388

MORTER {11}
stone, and slime had they for *m* ... Gen 11:3 2563
bitter with hard bondage, in *m* ... Ex 1:14 2563
and he shall take other *m*, and ... Lev 14:42 6083
and all the *m* of the house ... Lev 14:45 6083
shall come upon princes as upon *m* ... Is 41:25 2563
daubed it with untempered *m* ... Eze 13:10
which daub it with untempered *m* ... Eze 13:11
ye have daubed with untempered *m* ... Eze 13:14
have daubed it with untempered *m* ... Eze 13:15
daubed them with untempered *m* ... Eze 22:28
go into clay, and tread the *m* ... Nah 3:14 2563

MORTGAGED {1}
We have *m* our lands, vineyards, ... Neh 5:3 6148

MORTIFY {2}
Spirit do *m* the deeds of the body ... Rom 8:13 *2289*
M therefore your members which ... Col 3:5 *3499*

MOSERA *(mo-se'-rah)* {1} See MOSEROTH. *Where Aaron was buried.*
of the children of Jaakan to *M* ... Deut 10:6 4149

MOSERAH See MOSERA.

MOSEROTH *(mo-se'-roth)* {2} See MOSERA. *An Israelite encampment in the wilderness.*
from Hashmonah, and encamped at *M* ... Num 33:30 4149
And they departed from *M*, and ... Num 33:31 4149

MOSES *(mo'-zez)* {829} See MOSES'. *Led Israel out of Egypt.*
And she called his name *M* ... Ex 2:10 4872
when *M* was grown, that he went ... Ex 2:11 4872
M feared, and said, Surely this ... Ex 2:14 4872
this thing, he sought to slay *M* ... Ex 2:15 4872
But *M* fled from the face of ... Ex 2:15 4872
but *M* stood up and helped them, and ... Ex 2:17 4872
M was content to dwell with the ... Ex 2:21 4872
he gave *M* Zipporah his daughter ... Ex 2:21 4872
Now *M* kept the flock of Jethro ... Ex 3:1 4872
M said, I will now turn aside, and ... Ex 3:3 4872
of the bush, and said, *M*, *M* ... Ex 3:4 4872
And *M* hid his face ... Ex 3:6 4872
M said unto God, Who am I, that I ... Ex 3:11 4872
M said unto God, Behold, when I ... Ex 3:13 4872
And God said unto *M*, I AM THAT I ... Ex 3:14 4872
And God said moreover unto *M* ... Ex 3:15 4872
M answered and said, But, behold, ... Ex 4:1 4872
and *M* fled from before it ... Ex 4:3 4872
And the LORD said unto *M*, Put ... Ex 4:4 4872
M said unto the LORD, O my Lord, ... Ex 4:10 4872
of the LORD was kindled against *M* ... Ex 4:14 4872
M went and returned to Jethro his ... Ex 4:18 4872
And Jethro said to *M*, Go in peace ... Ex 4:18 4872
And the LORD said unto *M* in Midian ... Ex 4:19 4872
M took his wife and his sons, and ... Ex 4:20 4872
M took the rod of God in his hand ... Ex 4:20 4872
And the LORD said unto *M*, When ... Ex 4:21 4872
Go into the wilderness to meet *M* ... Ex 4:27 4872
M told Aaron all the words of the ... Ex 4:28 4872
And *M* and Aaron went and gathered ... Ex 4:29 4872
which the LORD had spoken unto *M* ... Ex 4:30 4872
And afterward *M* and Aaron went in, ... Ex 5:1 4872
unto them, Wherefore do ye, *M* ... Ex 5:4 4872
And they met *M* and Aaron, who stood ... Ex 5:20 4872
M returned unto the LORD, and said ... Ex 5:22 4872
Then the LORD said unto *M* ... Ex 6:1 4872
And God spake unto *M*, and said unto ... Ex 6:2 4872
M spake so unto the children of ... Ex 6:9 4872
not unto *M* for anguish of spirit ... Ex 6:9 4872
And the LORD spake unto *M*, saying, ... Ex 6:10 4872
M spake before the LORD, saying, ... Ex 6:12 4872
And the LORD spake unto *M* and unto ... Ex 6:13 4872
and she bare him Aaron and *M* ... Ex 6:20 4872
These are that Aaron and *M* ... Ex 6:26 4872
these are that *M* and Aaron ... Ex 6:27 4872
spake unto *M* in the land of Egypt ... Ex 6:28 4872
That the LORD spake unto *M* ... Ex 6:29 4872
M said before the LORD, Behold, I ... Ex 6:30 4872
And the LORD said unto *M*, See, I ... Ex 7:1 4872
And *M* and Aaron did as the LORD ... Ex 7:6 4872
M was fourscore years old, and ... Ex 7:7 4872
And the LORD spake unto *M* and unto ... Ex 7:8 4872
And *M* and Aaron went in unto ... Ex 7:10 4872
And the LORD said unto *M*, ... Ex 7:14 4872
And the LORD spake unto *M*, Say ... Ex 7:19 4872
And *M* and Aaron did so, as the LORD ... Ex 7:20 4872
And the LORD spake unto *M*, Go unto ... Ex 8:1 4872
And the LORD spake unto *M*, Say ... Ex 8:5 4872
Then Pharaoh called for *M* ... Ex 8:8 4872
M said unto Pharaoh, Glory over ... Ex 8:9 4872
And *M* and Aaron went out from ... Ex 8:12 4872
M cried unto the LORD because of ... Ex 8:12 4872
did according to the word of *M* ... Ex 8:13 4872
And the LORD said unto *M*, Say unto ... Ex 8:16 4872
And the LORD said unto *M*, Rise up ... Ex 8:20 4872
And Pharaoh called for *M* and for ... Ex 8:25 4872
M said, It is not meet so to do ... Ex 8:26 4872
M said, Behold, I go out from ... Ex 8:29 4872
M went out from Pharaoh, and ... Ex 8:30 4872
did according to the word of *M* ... Ex 8:31 4872
Then the LORD said unto *M* ... Ex 9:1 4872
And the LORD said unto *M* and unto ... Ex 9:8 4872
let *M* sprinkle it toward the ... Ex 9:8 4872
M sprinkled it up toward heaven ... Ex 9:10 4872
before *M* because of the boils ... Ex 9:11 4872
as the LORD had spoken unto *M* ... Ex 9:12 4872
And the LORD said unto *M*, Rise up ... Ex 9:13 4872
And the LORD said unto *M*, Stretch ... Ex 9:22 4872
M stretched forth his rod toward ... Ex 9:23 4872
And Pharaoh sent, and called for *M* ... Ex 9:27 4872
M said unto him, As soon as I am ... Ex 9:29 4872
M went out of the city from ... Ex 9:33 4872
as the LORD had spoken by *M* ... Ex 9:35 4872
And the LORD said unto *M*, Go in ... Ex 10:1 4872
And *M* and Aaron came in unto ... Ex 10:3 4872
And *M* and Aaron were brought again ... Ex 10:8 4872
M said, We will go with our young ... Ex 10:9 4872
And the LORD said unto *M*, Stretch ... Ex 10:12 4872
M stretched forth his rod over ... Ex 10:13 4872
Then Pharaoh called for *M* ... Ex 10:16 4872
And the LORD said unto *M*, Stretch ... Ex 10:21 4872
M stretched forth his hand toward ... Ex 10:22 4872
And Pharaoh called unto *M*, and said ... Ex 10:24 4872
M said, Thou must give us also ... Ex 10:25 4872
M said, Thou hast spoken well, I ... Ex 10:29 4872
And the LORD said unto *M*, Yet will ... Ex 11:1 4872
Moreover the man *M* was very great ... Ex 11:3 4872
M said, Thus saith the LORD, ... Ex 11:4 4872
And the LORD said unto *M*, Pharaoh ... Ex 11:9 4872
And *M* and Aaron did all these ... Ex 11:10 4872
the LORD spake unto *M* and Aaron ... Ex 12:1 4872
Then *M* called for all the elders ... Ex 12:21 4872
did as the LORD had commanded *M* ... Ex 12:28 4872
And he called for *M* and Aaron by ... Ex 12:31 4872
did according to the word of *M* ... Ex 12:35 4872
And the LORD said unto *M* and Aaron, ... Ex 12:43 4872
the LORD commanded *M* and Aaron, ... Ex 12:50 4872
And the LORD spake unto *M*, saying, ... Ex 13:1 4872
M said unto the people, Remember ... Ex 13:3 4872
M took the bones of Joseph with ... Ex 13:19 4872
And the LORD spake unto *M*, saying, ... Ex 14:1 4872
And they said unto *M*, Because ... Ex 14:11 4872
M said unto the people, Fear ye ... Ex 14:13 4872
And the LORD said unto *M* ... Ex 14:15 4872
M stretched out his hand over the ... Ex 14:21 4872
And the LORD said unto *M*, Stretch ... Ex 14:26 4872
M stretched forth his hand over ... Ex 14:27 4872
the LORD, and his servant *M* ... Ex 14:31 4872
Then sang *M* and the children of ... Ex 15:1 4872
So *M* brought Israel from the Red ... Ex 15:22 4872
And the people murmured against *M* ... Ex 15:24 4872
of Israel murmured against *M* ... Ex 16:2 4872
Then said the LORD unto *M* ... Ex 16:4 4872
And *M* and Aaron said unto all the ... Ex 16:6 4872
M said, This shall be, when the ... Ex 16:8 4872
M spake unto Aaron, Say unto all ... Ex 16:9 4872
And the LORD spake unto *M*, saying, ... Ex 16:11 4872
M said unto them, This is the ... Ex 16:15 4872
M said, Let no man leave of it ... Ex 16:19 4872
they hearkened not unto *M* ... Ex 16:20 4872
and *M* was wroth with them ... Ex 16:20 4872
the congregation came and told *M* ... Ex 16:22 4872
it up till the morning, as *M* bade ... Ex 16:24 4872
And *M* said, Eat that to day ... Ex 16:25 4872
And the LORD said unto *M*, How long ... Ex 16:28 4872
M said, This is the thing which ... Ex 16:32 4872
M said unto Aaron, Take a pot, and ... Ex 16:33 4872
As the LORD commanded *M*, so Aaron ... Ex 16:34 4872
the people did chide with *M* ... Ex 17:2 4872
M said unto them, Why chide ye ... Ex 17:2 4872
and the people murmured against *M* ... Ex 17:3 4872
M cried unto the LORD, saying, ... Ex 17:4 4872
And the LORD said unto *M*, Go on ... Ex 17:5 4872
M did so in the sight of the ... Ex 17:6 4872
M said unto Joshua, Choose us out ... Ex 17:9 4872
Joshua did as *M* had said to him ... Ex 17:10 4872
and *M*, Aaron, and Hur went up to ... Ex 17:10 4872
when *M* held up his hand, that ... Ex 17:11 4872
And the LORD said unto *M*, Write ... Ex 17:14 4872
M built an altar, and called the ... Ex 17:15 4872
of all that God had done for *M* ... Ex 18:1 4872
sons and his wife unto *M* into the ... Ex 18:5 4872
And he said unto *M*, I thy father ... Ex 18:6 4872
M went out to meet his father in ... Ex 18:7 4872
M told his father in law all that ... Ex 18:8 4872
that *M* sat to judge the people ... Ex 18:13 4872
the people stood by *M* from the ... Ex 18:13 4872
M said unto his father in law, ... Ex 18:15 4872
So *M* hearkened to the voice of ... Ex 18:24 4872
M chose able men out of all ... Ex 18:25 4872
hard causes they brought unto *M* ... Ex 18:26 4872
M let his father in law depart ... Ex 18:27 4872
M went up unto God, and the LORD ... Ex 19:3 4872
M came and called for the elders ... Ex 19:7 4872
M returned the words of the ... Ex 19:8 4872
And the LORD said unto *M*, Lo, I ... Ex 19:9 4872
M told the words of the people ... Ex 19:9 4872
And the LORD said unto *M*, Go unto ... Ex 19:10 4872
M went down from the mount unto ... Ex 19:14 4872
M brought forth the people out of ... Ex 19:17 4872
M spake, and God answered him by a ... Ex 19:19 4872
the LORD called *M* up to the top ... Ex 19:20 4872
and *M* went up ... Ex 19:20 4872
And the LORD said unto *M*, Go down, ... Ex 19:21 4872
M said unto the LORD, The people ... Ex 19:23 4872
So *M* went down unto the people, ... Ex 19:25 4872
And they said unto *M*, Speak thou ... Ex 20:19 4872
M said unto the people, Fear not ... Ex 20:20 4872
M drew near unto the thick ... Ex 20:21 4872
And the LORD said unto *M*, Thus ... Ex 20:22 4872
And he said unto *M*, Come up unto ... Ex 24:1 4872
M alone shall come near the LORD ... Ex 24:2 4872
M came and told the people all the ... Ex 24:3 4872
M wrote all the words of the LORD ... Ex 24:4 4872
M took half of the blood, and put ... Ex 24:6 4872
M took the blood, and sprinkled it ... Ex 24:8 4872
Then went up *M*, and Aaron, Nadab, ... Ex 24:9 4872
And the LORD said unto *M*, Come up ... Ex 24:12 4872
M rose up, and his minister Joshua ... Ex 24:13 4872
M went up into the mount of God ... Ex 24:13 4872
M went up into the mount, and a ... Ex 24:15 4872
M out of the midst of the cloud ... Ex 24:16 4872
M went into the midst of the ... Ex 24:18 4872
M was in the mount forty days and ... Ex 24:18 4872
And the LORD spake unto *M*, saying, ... Ex 25:1 4872
And the LORD spake unto *M*, saying, ... Ex 30:11 4872
And the LORD spake unto *M*, saying, ... Ex 30:17 4872
Moreover the LORD spake unto *M* ... Ex 30:22 4872
And the LORD said unto *M*, Take ... Ex 30:34 4872
And the LORD spake unto *M*, saying, ... Ex 31:1 4872
And the LORD spake unto *M*, saying, ... Ex 31:12 4872
And he gave unto *M*, when he had ... Ex 31:18 4872
when the people saw that *M* ... Ex 32:1 4872
for as for this *M*, the man that ... Ex 32:1 4872
And the LORD said unto *M*, Go, get ... Ex 32:7 4872
And the LORD said unto *M*, I have ... Ex 32:9 4872
M besought the LORD his God, and ... Ex 32:11 4872
M turned, and went down from the ... Ex 32:15 4872
as they shouted, he said unto *M* ... Ex 32:17 4872
M said unto Aaron, What did this ... Ex 32:21 4872
for as for this *M*, the man that ... Ex 32:23 4872
when *M* saw that the people were ... Ex 32:25 4872
Then *M* stood in the gate of the ... Ex 32:26 4872
did according to the word of *M* ... Ex 32:28 4872
For *M* had said, Consecrate ... Ex 32:29 4872
that *M* said unto the people, Ye ... Ex 32:30 4872
M returned unto the LORD, and said ... Ex 32:31 4872
And the LORD said unto *M*, ... Ex 32:33 4872
And the LORD said unto *M*, Depart, ... Ex 33:1 4872
For the LORD had said unto *M* ... Ex 33:5 4872
M took the tabernacle, and pitched ... Ex 33:7 4872
to pass, when *M* went out unto the ... Ex 33:8 4872
his tent door, and looked after *M* ... Ex 33:8 4872
as *M* entered into the tabernacle, ... Ex 33:9 4872
and the LORD talked with *M* ... Ex 33:9 4872
LORD spake unto *M* face to face ... Ex 33:11 4872
M said unto the LORD, See, thou ... Ex 33:12 4872
And the LORD said unto *M*, I will ... Ex 33:17 4872
And the LORD said unto *M*, Hew thee ... Ex 34:1 4872
M rose up early in the morning, ... Ex 34:4 4872
M made haste, and bowed his head ... Ex 34:8 4872
And the LORD said unto *M*, Write ... Ex 34:27 4872
when *M* came down from mount Sinai ... Ex 34:29 4872
that *M* wist not that the skin of ... Ex 34:29 4872
all the children of Israel saw *M* ... Ex 34:30 4872
And *M* called unto them ... Ex 34:31 4872
and *M* talked with them ... Ex 34:31 4872
till *M* had done speaking with ... Ex 34:33 4872
But when *M* went in before the ... Ex 34:34 4872
of Israel saw the face of *M* ... Ex 34:35 4872
M put the vail upon his face ... Ex 34:35 4872
M gathered all the congregation ... Ex 35:1 4872
M spake unto all the congregation ... Ex 35:4 4872
departed from the presence of *M* ... Ex 35:20 4872
to be made by the hand of *M* ... Ex 35:29 4872
M said unto the children of ... Ex 35:30 4872
M called Bezaleel and Aholiab, and ... Ex 36:2 4872
received of *M* all the offering ... Ex 36:3 4872
And they spake unto *M*, saying, The ... Ex 36:5 4872
M gave commandment, and they ... Ex 36:6 4872
according to the commandment of *M* ... Ex 38:21 4872
all that the LORD commanded *M* ... Ex 38:22 4872
as the LORD commanded *M* ... Ex 39:1 4872
as the LORD commanded *M* ... Ex 39:5 4872
as the LORD commanded *M* ... Ex 39:7 4872
as the LORD commanded *M* ... Ex 39:21 4872
as the LORD commanded *M* ... Ex 39:26 4872
as the LORD commanded *M* ... Ex 39:29 4872
as the LORD commanded *M* ... Ex 39:31 4872
to all that the LORD commanded *M* ... Ex 39:32 4872
brought the tabernacle unto *M* ... Ex 39:33 4872
to all that the LORD commanded *M* ... Ex 39:42 4872
M did look upon all the work ... Ex 39:43 4872
and *M* blessed them ... Ex 39:43 4872
And the LORD spake unto *M*, saying, ... Ex 40:1 4872
Thus did *M* ... Ex 40:16 4872
M reared up the tabernacle, and ... Ex 40:18 4872
as the LORD commanded *M* ... Ex 40:19 4872
as the LORD commanded *M* ... Ex 40:21 4872
as the LORD had commanded *M* ... Ex 40:23 4872
as the LORD commanded *M* ... Ex 40:25 4872
as the LORD commanded *M* ... Ex 40:27 4872
as the LORD commanded *M* ... Ex 40:29 4872
M and Aaron and his sons washed ... Ex 40:31 4872
as the LORD commanded *M* ... Ex 40:32 4872
So *M* finished the work ... Ex 40:33 4872
M was not able to enter into the ... Ex 40:35 4872
And the LORD called unto *M* ... Lev 1:1 4872
And the LORD spake unto *M*, saying, ... Lev 4:1 4872
And the LORD spake unto *M*, saying, ... Lev 5:14 4872
And the LORD spake unto *M*, saying, ... Lev 6:1 4872
And the LORD spake unto *M*, saying, ... Lev 6:8 4872
And the LORD spake unto *M*, saying, ... Lev 6:19 4872
And the LORD spake unto *M*, saying, ... Lev 6:24 4872
And the LORD spake unto *M*, saying, ... Lev 7:22 4872
And the LORD spake unto *M*, saying, ... Lev 7:28 4872
LORD commanded *M* in mount Sinai ... Lev 7:38 4872
And the LORD spake unto *M*, saying, ... Lev 8:1 4872
M did as the LORD commanded him ... Lev 8:4 4872

M

M said unto the congregation, Lev 8:5 4872
M brought Aaron and his sons, and Lev 8:6 4872
as the LORD commanded *M* Lev 8:9 4872
M took the anointing oil, and Lev 8:10 4872
M brought Aaron's sons, and put Lev 8:13 4872
as the LORD commanded *M* Lev 8:13 4872
M took the blood, and put it upon Lev 8:15 4872
M burned it upon the altar Lev 8:16 4872
as the LORD commanded *M* Lev 8:17 4872
M sprinkled the blood upon the Lev 8:19 4872
M burnt the head, and the pieces, Lev 8:20 4872
M burnt the whole ram upon the Lev 8:21 4872
as the LORD commanded *M* Lev 8:21 4872
M took of the blood of it, and put Lev 8:23 4872
M put of the blood upon the tip Lev 8:24 4872
M sprinkled the blood upon the Lev 8:24 4872
M took them from off their hands, Lev 8:28 4872
M took the breast, and waved it Lev 8:29 4872
as the LORD commanded *M* Lev 8:29 4872
M took of the anointing oil, and Lev 8:30 4872
M said unto Aaron and to his sons, Lev 8:31 4872
LORD commanded by the hand of *M* Lev 8:36 4872
that *M* called Aaron and his sons, Lev 9:1 4872
they brought that which *M* Lev 9:5 4872
M said, This is the thing which Lev 9:6 4872
M said unto Aaron, Go unto the Lev 9:7 4872
as the LORD commanded *M* Lev 9:10 4872
as *M* commanded Lev 9:21 4872
And *M* and Aaron went into the Lev 9:23 4872
Then *M* said unto Aaron, This is Lev 10:3 4872
M called Mishael and Elzaphan, and Lev 10:4 4872
as *M* had said Lev 10:5 4872
M said unto Aaron, and unto Lev 10:6 4872
did according to the word of *M* Lev 10:7 4872
spoken unto them by the hand of *M* Lev 10:11 4872
M spake unto Aaron, and unto Lev 10:12 4872
M diligently sought the goat of Lev 10:16 4872
And Aaron said unto *M*, Behold, Lev 10:19 4872
when *M* heard that, he was content Lev 10:20 4872
And the LORD spake unto *M* and to Lev 11:1 4872
And the LORD spake unto *M*, saying, Lev 12:1 4872
the LORD spake unto *M* and Aaron Lev 13:1 4872
And the LORD spake unto *M*, saying, Lev 14:1 4872
And the LORD spake unto *M* and unto Lev 14:33 4872
And the LORD spake unto *M* and to Lev 15:1 4872
the LORD spake unto *M* after the Lev 16:1 4872
And the LORD said unto *M*, Speak Lev 16:2 4872
he did as the LORD commanded *M* Lev 16:34 4872
And the LORD spake unto *M*, saying, Lev 17:1 4872
And the LORD spake unto *M*, saying, Lev 18:1 4872
And the LORD spake unto *M*, saying, Lev 19:1 4872
And the LORD spake unto *M*, saying, Lev 20:1 4872
And the LORD said unto *M*, Speak Lev 21:1 4872
And the LORD spake unto *M*, saying, Lev 21:16 4872
M told it unto Aaron, and to his Lev 21:24 4872
And the LORD spake unto *M*, saying, Lev 22:1 4872
And the LORD spake unto *M*, saying, Lev 22:17 4872
And the LORD spake unto *M*, saying, Lev 22:26 4872
And the LORD spake unto *M*, saying, Lev 23:1 4872
And the LORD spake unto *M*, saying, Lev 23:9 4872
And the LORD spake unto *M*, saying, Lev 23:23 4872
And the LORD spake unto *M*, saying, Lev 23:26 4872
And the LORD spake unto *M*, saying, Lev 23:33 4872
M declared unto the children of Lev 23:44 4872
And the LORD spake unto *M*, saying, Lev 24:1 4872
And they brought him unto *M* Lev 24:11 4872
And the LORD spake unto *M*, saying, Lev 24:13 4872
M spake to the children of Israel Lev 24:23 4872
did as the LORD commanded *M* Lev 24:23 4872
LORD spake unto *M* in mount Sinai Lev 25:1 4872
in mount Sinai by the hand of *M* Lev 26:46 4872
And the LORD spake unto *M*, saying, Lev 27:1 4872
which the LORD commanded *M* for Lev 27:34 4872
the LORD spake unto *M* in the Num 1:1 4872
And *M* and Aaron took these men Num 1:17 4872
As the LORD commanded *M*, so he Num 1:19 4872
those that were numbered, which *M* Num 1:44 4872
For the LORD had spoken unto *M* Num 1:48 4872
to all that the LORD commanded *M* Num 1:54 4872
And the LORD spake unto *M* and unto Num 2:1 4872
as the LORD commanded *M* Num 2:33 4872
to all that the LORD commanded *M* Num 2:34 4872
M in the day that the LORD spake Num 3:1 4872
LORD spake with *M* in mount Sinai Num 3:1 4872
And the LORD spake unto *M*, saying, Num 3:5 4872
And the LORD spake unto *M*, saying, Num 3:11 4872
the LORD spake unto *M* in the Num 3:14 4872
M numbered them according to the Num 3:16 4872
congregation eastward, shall be *M* Num 3:38 4872
numbered of the Levites, which *M* Num 3:39 4872
And the LORD said unto *M*, Number Num 3:40 4872
M numbered, as the LORD commanded Num 3:42 4872
And the LORD spake unto *M*, saying, Num 3:44 4872
M took the redemption money of Num 3:49 4872
M gave the money of them that Num 3:51 4872
the LORD, as the LORD commanded *M* Num 3:51 4872
And the LORD spake unto *M* and unto Num 4:1 4872
And the LORD spake unto *M* and unto Num 4:17 4872
And the LORD spake unto *M*, saying, Num 4:21 4872
And *M* and Aaron and the chief of the Num 4:34 4872
of the congregation, which *M* Num 4:37 4872
of the LORD by the hand of *M* Num 4:37 4872
of the congregation, whom *M* Num 4:41 4872
of the sons of Merari, whom *M* Num 4:45 4872
word of the LORD by the hand of *M* Num 4:45 4872
numbered of the Levites, whom *M* Num 4:46 4872
were numbered by the hand of *M* Num 4:49 4872
of him, as the LORD commanded *M* Num 4:49 4872
And the LORD spake unto *M*, saying, Num 5:1 4872
as the LORD spake unto *M*, so did Num 5:4 4872
And the LORD spake unto *M*, saying, Num 5:5 4872
And the LORD spake unto *M*, saying, Num 5:11 4872
And the LORD spake unto *M*, saying, Num 6:1 4872
And the LORD spake unto *M*, saying, Num 6:22 4872
M had fully set up the tabernacle Num 7:1 4872
And the LORD spake unto *M*, saying, Num 7:4 4872
M took the wagons and the oxen, and Num 7:6 4872
And the LORD said unto *M*, They Num 7:11 4872
And when *M* was gone into the Num 7:89 4872
And the LORD spake unto *M*, saying, Num 8:1 4872
as the LORD commanded *M* Num 8:3 4872
which the LORD had shewed *M* Num 8:4 4872
And the LORD spake unto *M*, saying, Num 8:5 4872
And *M*, and Aaron, and all the Num 8:20 4872
M concerning the Levites, so did Num 8:20 4872
M concerning the Levites, so did Num 8:22 4872
And the LORD spake unto *M*, saying, Num 8:23 4872
the LORD spake unto *M* in the Num 9:1 4872
M spake unto the children of Num 9:4 4872
to all that the LORD commanded *M* Num 9:5 4872
and they came before *M* and before Num 9:6 4872
M said unto them, Stand still, and Num 9:8 4872
And the LORD spake unto *M*, saying, Num 9:9 4872
of the LORD by the hand of *M* Num 9:23 4872
And the LORD spake unto *M*, saying, Num 10:1 4872
of the LORD by the hand of *M* Num 10:13 4872
M said unto Hobab, the son of Num 10:29 4872
the ark set forward, that *M* said Num 10:35 4872
And the people cried unto *M* Num 11:2 4872
when *M* prayed unto the LORD, the Num 11:2 4872
Then *M* heard the people weep Num 11:10 4872
M also was displeased Num 11:10 4872
M said unto the LORD, Wherefore Num 11:11 4872
And the LORD said unto *M*, Gather Num 11:16 4872
M said, The people, among whom I Num 11:21 4872
And the LORD said unto *M*, Is the Num 11:23 4872
M went out, and told the people Num 11:24 4872
there ran a young man, and told *M* Num 11:27 4872
the son of Nun, the servant of *M* Num 11:28 4872
men, answered and said, My lord *M* Num 11:28 4872
M said unto him, Enviest thou for Num 11:29 4872
M gat him into the camp, he and Num 11:30 4872
Aaron spake against *M* because of Num 12:1 4872
the LORD indeed spoken only by *M* Num 12:2 4872
(Now the man *M* was very meek, Num 12:3 4872
And the LORD spake suddenly unto *M* Num 12:4 4872
My servant *M* is not so, who is Num 12:7 4872
to speak against my servant *M* Num 12:8 4872
And Aaron said unto *M*, Alas, my Num 12:11 4872
M cried unto the LORD, saying, Num 12:13 4872
And the LORD said unto *M*, If her Num 12:14 4872
And the LORD spake unto *M*, saying, Num 13:1 4872
M by the commandment of the LORD Num 13:3 4872
which *M* sent to spy out the land Num 13:16 4872
M called Oshea the son of Nun Num 13:16 4872
M sent them to spy out the land Num 13:17 4872
And they went and came to *M* Num 13:26 4872
Caleb stilled the people before *M* Num 13:30 4872
of Israel murmured against *M* Num 14:2 4872
Then *M* and Aaron fell on their Num 14:5 4872
And the LORD said unto *M*, How long Num 14:11 4872
M said unto the LORD, Then the Num 14:13 4872
And the LORD spake unto *M* and unto Num 14:26 4872
which *M* sent to search the land, Num 14:36 4872
M told these sayings unto all the Num 14:39 4872
M said, Wherefore now do ye Num 14:41 4872
of the covenant of the LORD, and *M* Num 14:44 4872
And the LORD spake unto *M*, saying, Num 15:1 4872
And the LORD spake unto *M*, saying, Num 15:17 4872
which the LORD hath spoken unto *M* Num 15:22 4872
commanded you by the hand of *M* Num 15:23 4872
the day that the LORD commanded *M* Num 15:23
sticks brought him unto *M* Num 15:33 4872
And the LORD said unto *M*, The man Num 15:35 4872
as the LORD commanded *M* Num 15:36 4872
And the LORD spake unto *M*, saying, Num 15:37 4872
And they rose up before *M*, with Num 16:2 4872
themselves together against *M* Num 16:3 4872
when *M* heard it, he fell upon his Num 16:4 4872
M said unto Korah, Hear, I pray Num 16:8 4872
M sent to call Dathan and Abiram, Num 16:12 4872
M was very wroth, and said unto Num 16:15 4872
M said unto Korah, Be thou and all Num 16:16 4872
of the congregation with *M* Num 16:18 4872
And the LORD spake unto *M* and unto Num 16:20 4872
And the LORD spake unto *M*, saying, Num 16:23 4872
M rose up and went unto Dathan and Num 16:25 4872
M said, Hereby ye shall know that Num 16:28 4872
And the LORD spake unto *M*, saying, Num 16:36 4872
LORD said to him by the hand of *M* Num 16:40 4872
of Israel murmured against *M* Num 16:41 4872
was gathered against *M* and against Num 16:42 4872
And *M* and Aaron came before the Num 16:43 4872
And the LORD spake unto *M*, saying, Num 16:44 4872
M said unto Aaron, Take a censer, Num 16:46 4872
And Aaron took as *M* commanded Num 16:47 4872
Aaron returned unto *M* unto the Num 16:50 4872
And the LORD spake unto *M*, saying, Num 17:1 4872
M spake unto the children of Num 17:6 4872
M laid up the rods before the Num 17:7 4872
that on the morrow *M* went into Num 17:8 4872
M brought out all the rods from Num 17:9 4872
And the LORD said unto *M*, Bring Num 17:10 4872
And *M* did so Num 17:11 4872
children of Israel spake unto *M* Num 17:12 4872
And the LORD spake unto *M*, saying, Num 18:25 4872
And the LORD spake unto *M* and unto Num 19:1 4872
themselves together against *M* Num 20:2 4872
And the people chode with *M* Num 20:3 4872
And *M* and Aaron went from the Num 20:6 4872
And the LORD spake unto *M*, saying, Num 20:7 4872
M took the rod from before the Num 20:9 4872
And *M* and Aaron gathered the Num 20:10 4872
M lifted up his hand, and with his Num 20:11 4872
the LORD spake unto *M* and Aaron Num 20:12 4872
M sent messengers from Kadesh Num 20:14 4872
the LORD spake unto *M* and Aaron Num 20:23 4872
M did as the LORD commanded Num 20:27 4872
M stripped Aaron of his garments, Num 20:28 4872
and *M* and Eleazar came down from Num 20:28 4872
spake against God, and against *M* Num 21:5 4872
Therefore the people came to *M* Num 21:7 4872
And *M* prayed for the people Num 21:7 4872
And the LORD said unto *M*, Make Num 21:8 4872
M made a serpent of brass, and put Num 21:9 4872
whereof the LORD spake unto *M* Num 21:16 4872
M sent to spy out Jaazer, and they Num 21:32 4872
And the LORD said unto *M*, Fear him Num 21:34 4872
And the LORD said unto *M*, Take all Num 25:4 4872
M said unto the judges of Israel, Num 25:5 4872
woman in the sight of *M*, and in Num 25:6 4872
And the LORD spake unto *M*, saying, Num 25:10 4872
And the LORD spake unto *M*, saying, Num 25:16 4872
that the LORD spake unto *M* Num 26:1 4872
And *M* and Eleazar the priest spake Num 26:3 4872
as the LORD commanded *M* and the Num 26:4 4872
who strove against *M* and against Num 26:9 4872
And the LORD spake unto *M*, saying, Num 26:52 4872
she bare unto Amram Aaron and *M* Num 26:59 4872
are they that were numbered by *M* Num 26:63 4872
was not a man of them whom *M* Num 26:64 4872
And they stood before *M*, and before Num 27:2 4872
M brought their cause before the Num 27:5 4872
And the LORD spake unto *M*, saying, Num 27:6 4872
judgment, as the LORD commanded *M* Num 27:11 4872
And the LORD said unto *M*, Get thee Num 27:12 4872
M spake unto the LORD, saying, Num 27:15 4872
And the LORD said unto *M*, Take Num 27:18 4872
M did as the LORD commanded him Num 27:22 4872
LORD commanded by the hand of *M* Num 27:23 4872
And the LORD spake unto *M*, saying, Num 28:1 4872
M told the children of Israel Num 29:40 4872
to all that the LORD commanded *M* Num 29:40 4872
M spake unto the heads of the Num 30:1 4872
which the LORD commanded *M* Num 30:16 4872
And the LORD spake unto *M*, saying, Num 31:1 4872
M spake unto the people, saying, Num 31:3 4872
M sent them to the war, a Num 31:6 4872
as the LORD commanded *M* Num 31:7 4872
and the prey, and the spoil, unto *M* Num 31:12 4872
And *M*, and Eleazar the priest, and Num 31:13 4872
M was wroth with the officers of Num 31:14 4872
M said unto them, Have ye saved Num 31:15 4872
law which the LORD commanded *M* Num 31:21 4872
And the LORD spake unto *M*, saying, Num 31:25 4872
And *M* and Eleazar the priest did as Num 31:31 4872
did as the LORD commanded *M* Num 31:31 4872
M gave the tribute, which was the Num 31:41 4872
priest, as the LORD commanded *M* Num 31:41 4872
which *M* divided from the men that Num 31:42 4872
M took one portion of fifty, both Num 31:47 4872
as the LORD commanded *M* Num 31:47 4872
of hundreds, came near unto *M* Num 31:48 4872
And they said unto *M*, Thy servants Num 31:49 4872
And *M* and Eleazar the priest took Num 31:51 4872
And *M* and Eleazar the priest took Num 31:54 4872
of Reuben came and spake unto *M* Num 32:2 4872
M said unto the children of Gad Num 32:6 4872
M said unto them, If ye will do Num 32:20 4872
children of Reuben spake unto *M* Num 32:25 4872
So concerning them *M* commanded Num 32:28 4872
M said unto them, If the children Num 32:29 4872
M gave unto them, even to the Num 32:33 4872
M gave Gilead unto Machir the son Num 32:40 4872
their armies under the hand of *M* Num 33:1 4872
And *M* wrote their goings out Num 33:2 4872
the LORD spake unto *M* in the Num 33:50 4872
And the LORD spake unto *M*, saying, Num 34:1 4872
M commanded the children of Num 34:13 4872
And the LORD spake unto *M*, saying, Num 34:16 4872
the LORD spake unto *M* in the Num 35:1 4872
And the LORD spake unto *M*, saying, Num 35:9 4872
came near, and spake before *M* Num 36:1 4872
M commanded the children of Num 36:5 4872
Even as the LORD commanded *M* Num 36:10 4872
LORD commanded by the hand of *M* Num 36:13 4872
These be the words which *M* spake Deut 1:1 4872
that *M* spake unto the children of Deut 1:3 4872
began *M* to declare this law, Deut 1:5 4872
Then *M* severed three cities on Deut 4:41 4872
this is the law which *M* set Deut 4:44 4872
which *M* spake unto the children Deut 4:45 4872
who dwelt at Heshbon, whom *M* Deut 4:46 4872
M called all Israel, and said unto Deut 5:1 4872
M with the elders of Israel Deut 27:1 4872
And *M* and the priests the Levites Deut 27:9 4872
M charged the people the same day Deut 27:11 4872
which the LORD commanded *M* to Deut 29:1 4872
M called unto all Israel, and said Deut 29:2 4872
M went and spake these words unto Deut 31:1 4872
M called unto Joshua, and said Deut 31:7 4872
M wrote this law, and delivered it Deut 31:9 4872
M commanded them, saying, At the Deut 31:10 4872
And the LORD said unto *M*, Behold, Deut 31:14 4872

M and Joshua went, and presented ... Deut 31:14 4872
And the LORD said unto *M*, Behold, ... Deut 31:16 4872
M therefore wrote this song the ... Deut 31:22 4872
when *M* had made an end of writing ... Deut 31:24 4872
That *M* commanded the Levites, ... Deut 31:25 4872
M spake in the ears of all the ... Deut 31:30 4872
M came and spake all the words of ... Deut 32:44 4872
M made an end of speaking all ... Deut 32:45 4872
spake unto *M* that selfsame day ... Deut 32:48 4872
wherewith *M* the man of God ... Deut 33:1 4872
M commanded us a law, even the ... Deut 33:4 4872
M went up from the plains of Moab ... Deut 34:1 4872
So *M* the servant of the LORD died ... Deut 34:5 4872
M was an hundred and twenty years ... Deut 34:7 4872
M in the plains of Moab thirty ... Deut 34:8 4872
and mourning for *M* were ended ... Deut 34:8 4872
for *M* had laid his hands upon him ... Deut 34:9 4872
and did as the LORD commanded *M* ... Deut 34:9 4872
since in Israel like unto *M* ... Deut 34:10 4872
M shewed in the sight of all ... Deut 34:12 4872
Now after the death of *M* the ... Josh 1:1 4872
M my servant is dead ... Josh 1:2 4872
given unto you, as I said unto *M* ... Josh 1:3 4872
as I was with *M*, so I will be ... Josh 1:5 4872
which *M* my servant commanded thee ... Josh 1:7 4872
which *M* the servant of the LORD ... Josh 1:13 4872
M gave you on this side Jordan ... Josh 1:14 4872
which *M* the LORD's servant gave ... Josh 1:15 4872
we hearkened unto *M* in all things ... Josh 1:17 4872
be with thee, as he was with *M* ... Josh 1:17 4872
may know that, as I was with *M* ... Josh 3:7 4872
to all that *M* commanded Joshua ... Josh 4:10 4872
of Israel, as *M* spake unto them ... Josh 4:12 4872
they feared him, as they feared *M* ... Josh 4:14 4872
As *M* the servant of the LORD ... Josh 8:31 4872
in the book of the law of *M* ... Josh 8:31 4872
the stones a copy of the law of *M* ... Josh 8:32 4872
as *M* the servant of the LORD had ... Josh 8:33 4872
a word of all that *M* commanded ... Josh 8:35 4872
M to give you all the land ... Josh 9:24 4872
as *M* the servant of the LORD ... Josh 11:12 4872
the LORD commanded *M* his servant ... Josh 11:15 4872
so did *M* command Joshua, and so ... Josh 11:15 4872
of all that the LORD commanded *M* ... Josh 11:15 4872
them, as the LORD commanded *M* ... Josh 11:20 4872
to all that the LORD said unto *M* ... Josh 11:23 4872
Them did *M* the servant of the ... Josh 12:6 4872
M the servant of the LORD gave it ... Josh 12:6 4872
which *M* gave them, beyond Jordan ... Josh 13:8 4872
even as *M* the servant of the LORD ... Josh 13:8 4872
for these did *M* smite, and cast ... Josh 13:12 4872
M gave unto the tribe of the ... Josh 13:15 4872
whom *M* smote with the princes of ... Josh 13:21 4872
M gave inheritance unto the tribe ... Josh 13:24 4872
M gave inheritance unto the half ... Josh 13:29 4872
These are the countries which *M* ... Josh 13:32 4872
Levi *M* gave not any inheritance ... Josh 13:33 4872
LORD commanded by the hand of *M* ... Josh 14:2 4872
For *M* had given the inheritance ... Josh 14:3 4872
As the LORD commanded *M*, so the ... Josh 14:5 4872
M the man of God concerning me ... Josh 14:6 4872
Forty years old was I when *M* the ... Josh 14:7 4872
M sware on that day, saying, ... Josh 14:9 4872
the LORD spake this word unto *M* ... Josh 14:10 4872
I was in the day that *M* sent me ... Josh 14:11 4872
The LORD commanded *M* to give us ... Josh 17:4 4872
which *M* the servant of the LORD ... Josh 18:7 4872
I spake unto you by the hand of *M* ... Josh 20:2 4872
M to give us cities to dwell in ... Josh 21:2 4872
LORD commanded by the hand of *M* ... Josh 21:8 4872
Ye have kept all that *M* the ... Josh 22:2 4872
which *M* the servant of the LORD ... Josh 22:4 4872
which *M* the servant of the LORD ... Josh 22:5 4872
half of the tribe of Manasseh *M* ... Josh 22:7 4872
word of the LORD by the hand of *M* ... Josh 22:9 4872
in the book of the law of *M* ... Josh 23:6 4872
I sent *M* also and Aaron, and I ... Josh 24:5 4872
gave Hebron unto Caleb, as *M* said ... Judg 1:20 4872
their fathers by the hand of *M* ... Judg 3:4 4872
of Hobab the father in law of *M* ... Judg 4:11 4872
It is the LORD that advanced *M* ... 1Sa 12:6 4872
the LORD, then the LORD sent *M* ... 1Sa 12:8 4872
as it is written in the law of *M* ... 1Kin 2:3 4872
which *M* put there at Horeb, when ... 1Kin 8:9 4872
by the hand of *M* thy servant ... 1Kin 8:53 4872
by the hand of *M* his servant ... 1Kin 8:56 4872
in the book of the law of *M* ... 2Kin 14:6 4872
brasen serpent that *M* had made ... 2Kin 18:4 4872
which the LORD commanded *M* ... 2Kin 18:6 4872
all that *M* the servant of the ... 2Kin 18:12 4872
that my servant *M* commanded them ... 2Kin 21:8 4872
according to all the law of *M* ... 2Kin 23:25 4872
Aaron, and *M*, and Miriam ... 1Chr 6:3 4872
according to all that *M* the ... 1Chr 6:49 4872
as *M* commanded according to the ... 1Chr 15:15 4872
which *M* made in the wilderness, ... 1Chr 21:29 4872
charged *M* with concerning Israel ... 1Chr 22:13 4872
of Amram; Aaron and *M* ... 1Chr 23:13 4872
Now concerning *M* the man of God ... 1Chr 23:14 4872
The sons of *M* were, Gershom, and ... 1Chr 23:15 4872
the son of Gershom, the son of *M* ... 1Chr 26:24 4872
which *M* the servant of the LORD ... 2Chr 1:3 4872
which *M* put therein at Horeb ... 2Chr 5:10 4872
according to the commandment of *M* ... 2Chr 8:13 4872
as it is written in the law of *M* ... 2Chr 23:18 4872
of *M* the servant of the LORD ... 2Chr 24:6 4872
M the servant of God laid upon ... 2Chr 24:9 4872
in the law in the book of *M* ... 2Chr 25:4 4872
to the law of *M* the man of God ... 2Chr 30:16 4872
the ordinances by the hand of *M* ... 2Chr 33:8 4872
of the law of the LORD given by *M* ... 2Chr 34:14 4872
word of the LORD by the hand of *M* ... 2Chr 35:6 4872
as it is written in the book of *M* ... 2Chr 35:12 4872
in the law of *M* the man of God ... Ezr 3:2 4872
as it is written in the book of *M* ... Ezr 6:18 4873
a ready scribe in the law of *M* ... Ezr 7:6 4872
thou commandedst thy servant *M* ... Neh 1:7 4872
thou commandedst thy servant *M* ... Neh 1:8 4872
to bring the book of the law of *M* ... Neh 8:1 4872
which the LORD had commanded by *M* ... Neh 8:14 4872
by the hand of *M* thy servant ... Neh 9:14 4872
was given by *M* the servant of God ... Neh 10:29 4872
day they read in the book of *M* in ... Neh 13:1 4872
like a flock by the hand of *M* ... Ps 77:20 4872
A Prayer of *M*, the man of God ... Ps 90:*t* 4872
M and Aaron among his priests, and ... Ps 99:6 4872
He made known his ways unto *M* ... Ps 103:7 4872
He sent *M* his servant ... Ps 105:26 4872
They envied *M* also in the camp, ... Ps 106:16 4872
had not *M* his chosen stood before ... Ps 106:23 4872
went ill with *M* for their sakes ... Ps 106:32 4872
he remembered the days of old, *M* ... Is 63:11 4872
hand of *M* with his glorious arm ... Is 63:12 4872
said the LORD unto me, Though *M* ... Jer 15:1 4872
the law of *M* the servant of God ... Dan 9:11 4872
As it is written in the law of *M* ... Dan 9:13 4872
and I sent before thee *M*, Aaron, ... Mic 6:4 4872
ye the law of *M* my servant ... Mal 4:4 4872
offer the gift that *M* commanded ... Mt 8:4 *3475*
there appeared unto them *M* ... Mt 17:3 *3475*
one for thee, and one for *M* ... Mt 17:4 *3475*
Why did *M* then command to give a ... Mt 19:7 *3475*
M because of the hardness of your ... Mt 19:8 *3475*
M said, If a man die, having no ... Mt 22:24 *3475*
those things which *M* commanded ... Mk 1:44 *3475*
For *M* said, Honour thy father and ... Mk 7:10 *3475*
appeared unto them Elias with *M* ... Mk 9:4 *3475*
one for thee, and one for *M* ... Mk 9:5 *3475*
unto them, What did *M* command you ... Mk 10:3 *3475*
M suffered to write a bill of ... Mk 10:4 *3475*
M wrote unto us, If a man's ... Mk 12:19 *3475*
have ye not read in the book of *M* ... Mk 12:26 *3475*
to the law of *M* were accomplished ... Lk 2:22 *3475*
according as *M* commanded ... Lk 5:14 *3475*
with him two men, which were *M* ... Lk 9:30 *3475*
one for thee, and one for *M* ... Lk 9:33 *3475*
saith unto him, They have *M* ... Lk 16:29 *3475*
said unto him, If they hear not *M* ... Lk 16:31 *3475*
M wrote unto us, If any man's ... Lk 20:28 *3475*
even *M* shewed at the bush, when ... Lk 20:37 *3475*
And beginning at *M* and all the ... Lk 24:27 *3475*
were written in the law of *M* ... Lk 24:44 *3475*
For the law was given by *M* ... Jn 1:17 *3475*
of whom *M* in the law, and the ... Jn 1:45 *3475*
as *M* lifted up the serpent in the ... Jn 3:14 *3475*
is one that accuseth you, even *M* ... Jn 5:45 *3475*
For had ye believed *M*, ye would ... Jn 5:46 *3475*
M gave you not that bread from ... Jn 6:32 *3475*
Did not *M* give you the law, and ... Jn 7:19 *3475*
M therefore gave unto you ... Jn 7:22 *3475*
(not because it is of *M*, but of ... Jn 7:22 *3475*
that the law of *M* should not be ... Jn 7:23 *3475*
Now *M* in the law commanded us, ... Jn 8:5 *3475*
We know that God spake unto *M* ... Jn 9:29 *3475*
For *M* truly said unto the fathers ... Acts 3:22 *3475*
speak blasphemous words against *M* ... Acts 6:11 *3475*
the customs which *M* delivered us ... Acts 6:14 *3475*
In which time *M* was born, and was ... Acts 7:20 *3475*
M was learned in all the wisdom ... Acts 7:22 *3475*
Then fled *M* at this saying, and ... Acts 7:29 *3475*
When *M* saw it, he wondered at the ... Acts 7:31 *3475*
Then *M* trembled, and durst not ... Acts 7:32 *3475*
This *M* whom they refused, saying, ... Acts 7:35 *3475*
This is that *M*, which said unto ... Acts 7:37 *3475*
for as for this *M*, which brought ... Acts 7:40 *3475*
he had appointed, speaking unto *M* ... Acts 7:44 *3475*
not be justified by the law of *M* ... Acts 13:39 *3475*
circumcised after the manner of *M* ... Acts 15:1 *3475*
command them to keep the law of *M* ... Acts 15:5 *3475*
For *M* of old time hath in every ... Acts 15:21 *3475*
among the Gentiles to forsake *M* ... Acts 21:21 *3475*
prophets and *M* did say should come ... Acts 26:22 *3475*
Jesus, both out of the law of *M* ... Acts 28:23 *3475*
death reigned from Adam to *M* ... Rom 5:14 *3475*
For he saith to *M*, I will have ... Rom 9:15 *3475*
For *M* describeth the ... Rom 10:5 *3475*
First *M* saith, I will provoke you ... Rom 10:19 *3475*
For it is written in the law of *M* ... 1Cor 9:9 *3475*
all baptized unto *M* in the cloud ... 1Cor 10:2 *3475*
face of *M* for the glory of his ... 2Cor 3:7 *3475*
And not as *M*, which put a vail ... 2Cor 3:13 *3475*
when *M* is read, the vail is upon ... 2Cor 3:15 *3475*
as Jannes and Jambres withstood *M* ... 2Ti 3:8 *3475*
as also *M* was faithful in all his ... Heb 3:2 *3475*
worthy of more glory than *M* ... Heb 3:3 *3475*
M verily was faithful in all his ... Heb 3:5 *3475*
all that came out of Egypt by *M* ... Heb 3:16 *3475*
of which tribe *M* spake nothing ... Heb 7:14 *3475*
as *M* was admonished of God when ... Heb 8:5 *3475*
For when *M* had spoken every ... Heb 9:19 *3475*
By faith *M*, when he was born, was ... Heb 11:23 *3475*
By faith *M*, when he was come to ... Heb 11:24 *3475*
was the sight, that *M* said ... Heb 12:21 *3475*
he disputed about the body of *M* ... Jude 9 *3475*
the song of *M* the servant of God ... Rev 15:3 *3475*

MOSES' {19}
But *M* hands were heavy ... Ex 17:12 4872
M father in law, heard of all ... Ex 18:1 4872
M father in law, took Zipporah, ... Ex 18:2 4872
M wife, after he had sent her ... Ex 18:2 4872
M father in law, came with his ... Ex 18:5 4872
M father in law, took a burnt ... Ex 18:12 4872
to eat bread with *M* father in law ... Ex 18:12 4872
when *M* father in law saw all that ... Ex 18:14 4872
M father in law said unto him, ... Ex 18:17 4872
M anger waxed hot, and he cast the ... Ex 32:19 4872
two tables of testimony in *M* hand ... Ex 34:29 4872
that the skin of *M* face shone ... Ex 34:35 4872
ram of consecration it was *M* part ... Lev 8:29 4872
M father in law, We are ... Num 10:29 4872
son of Nun, *M* minister, saying, ... Josh 1:1 4872
M father in law, went up out of ... Judg 1:16 4872
and the Pharisees sit in *M* seat ... Mt 23:2 *3475*
but we are *M* disciples ... Jn 9:28 *3475*
He that despised *M* law died ... Heb 10:28 *3475*

MOST See APPENDIX.

MOTE {6}
why beholdest thou the *m* that is ... Mt 7:3 *2595*
pull out the *m* out of thine eye ... Mt 7:4 *2595*
the *m* out of thy brother's eye ... Mt 7:5 *2595*
why beholdest thou the *m* that is ... Lk 6:41 *2595*
let me pull out the *m* that is in ... Lk 6:42 *2595*
see clearly to pull out the *m* ... Lk 6:42 *2595*

MOTH {10}
which are crushed before the *m* ... Job 4:19 6211
as a garment that is *m* eaten ... Job 13:28 6211
He buildeth his house as a *m* ... Job 27:18 6211
beauty to consume away like a *m* ... Ps 39:11 6211
the *m* shall eat them up ... Is 50:9 6211
For the *m* shall eat them up like ... Is 51:8 6211
will I be unto Ephraim as a *m* ... Hos 5:12 6211
treasures upon earth, where *m* ... Mt 6:19 *4597*
where neither *m* nor rust doth ... Mt 6:20 *4597*
approacheth, neither *m* corrupteth ... Lk 12:33 *4597*

MOTHEATEN {1}
corrupted, and your garments are *m* ... Jas 5:2 *4598*

MOTHER {245}
a man leave his father and his *m* ... Gen 2:24 517
she was the *m* of all living ... Gen 3:20 517
and she shall be a *m* of nations ... Gen 17:16
but not the daughter of my *m* ... Gen 20:12 517
his *m* took him a wife out of the ... Gen 21:21 517
and to her *m* precious things ... Gen 24:53 517
her *m* said, Let the damsel abide ... Gen 24:55 517
be thou the *m* of thousands of ... Gen 24:60
her into his *m* Sarah's tent ... Gen 24:67 517
And Jacob said to Rebekah his *m* ... Gen 27:11 517
his *m* said unto him, Upon me be ... Gen 27:13 517
fetched, and brought them to his *m* ... Gen 27:14 517
his *m* made savoury meat, such as ... Gen 27:14 517
of Rebekah, Jacob's and Esau's *m* ... Gen 28:5 517
Jacob obeyed his father and his *m* ... Gen 28:7 517
and brought them unto his *m* Leah ... Gen 30:14 517
me, and the *m* with the children ... Gen 32:11 517
Shall I and thy *m* and thy brethren ... Gen 37:10 517
and he alone is left of his *m* ... Gen 44:20 517
maid went and called the child's *m* ... Ex 2:8 517
Honour thy father and thy *m* ... Ex 20:12 517
that smiteth his father, or his *m* ... Ex 21:15 517
that curseth his father, or his *m* ... Ex 21:17 517
father, or the nakedness of thy *m* ... Lev 18:7 517
she is thy *m* ... Lev 18:7 517
thy father, or daughter of thy *m* ... Lev 18:9 517
Ye shall fear every man his *m* ... Lev 19:3 517
m shall be surely put to death ... Lev 20:9 517
hath cursed his father or his *m* ... Lev 20:9 517
And if a man take a wife and her *m* ... Lev 20:14 517
near unto him, that is, for his *m* ... Lev 21:2 517
for his father, or for his *m* ... Lev 21:11 517
for his father, or for his *m* ... Num 6:7 517
whom her *m* bare to Levi in Egypt ... Num 26:59 517
Honour thy father and thy *m* ... Deut 5:16 517
If thy brother, the son of thy *m* ... Deut 13:6 517
her father and her *m* a full month ... Deut 21:13 517
his father, or the voice of his *m* ... Deut 21:18 517
his *m* lay hold on him, and bring ... Deut 21:19 517
father of the damsel, and her *m* ... Deut 22:15 517
light by his father or his *m* ... Deut 27:16 517
father, or the daughter of his *m* ... Deut 27:22 517
he that lieth with his *m* in law ... Deut 27:23 2059
said unto his father and to his *m* ... Deut 33:9 517
save alive my father, and my *m* ... Josh 2:13 517
shalt bring thy father, and thy *m* ... Josh 2:18 517
Rahab, and her father, and her *m* ... Josh 6:23 517
arose, that I arose a *m* in Israel ... Judg 5:7 517
The *m* of Sisera looked out at a ... Judg 5:28 517
brethren, even the sons of my *m* ... Judg 8:19 517
up, and told his father and his *m* ... Judg 14:2 517
his *m* said unto him, Is there ... Judg 14:3 517
his *m* knew not that it was of the ... Judg 14:4 517
down, and his father and his *m* ... Judg 14:5 517
father or his *m* what he had done ... Judg 14:6 517
and came to his father and *m* ... Judg 14:9 517
not told it my father nor my *m* ... Judg 14:16 517
And he said unto his *m*, The eleven ... Judg 17:2 517
his *m* said, Blessed be thou of ... Judg 17:2 517
shekels of silver to his *m* ... Judg 17:3 517
his *m* said, I had wholly ... Judg 17:3 517
he restored the money unto his *m* ... Judg 17:4 517
his *m* took two hundred shekels of ... Judg 17:4 517
and Orpah kissed her *m* in law ... Ruth 1:14 2545

M

that thou hast done unto thy *m* in ... Ruth 2:11 2545
hast left thy father and thy *m* ... Ruth 2:11 517
her *m* in law saw what she had ... Ruth 2:18 2545
her *m* in law said unto her, Where ... Ruth 2:19 2545
she shewed her *m* in law with whom ... Ruth 2:19 2545
and dwelt with her *m* in law ... Ruth 2:23 2545
Then Naomi her *m* in law said unto ... Ruth 3:1 2545
to all that her *m* in law bade her ... Ruth 3:6 2545
And when she came to her *m* in law ... Ruth 3:16 2545
Go not empty unto thy *m* in law ... Ruth 3:17 2545
Moreover his *m* made him a little ... 1Sa 2:19 517
so shall thy *m* be childless among ... 1Sa 15:33 517
of Moab, Let my father and my *m* ... 1Sa 22:3 517
sister to Zeruiah Joab's *m* ... 2Sa 17:25 517
the grave of my father and of my *m* ... 2Sa 19:37 517
destroy a city and a *m* in Israel ... 2Sa 20:19 517
his *m* bare him after Absalom ... 1Kin 1:6
unto Bath-sheba the *m* of Solomon ... 1Kin 1:11 517
to Bath-sheba the *m* of Solomon ... 1Kin 2:13 517
a seat to be set for the king's *m* ... 1Kin 2:19 517
king said unto her, Ask on, my *m* ... 1Kin 2:20 517
answered and said unto his *m* ... 1Kin 2:22 517
she is the *m* thereof ... 1Kin 3:27 517
And also Maachah his *m*, even her ... 1Kin 15:13 517
and delivered him unto his *m* ... 1Kin 17:23 517
pray thee, kiss my father and my *m* ... 1Kin 19:20 517
father, and in the way of his *m* ... 1Kin 22:52 517
like his father, and like his *m* ... 2Kin 3:2 517
and to the prophets of thy *m* ... 2Kin 3:13 517
said to a lad, Carry him to his *m* ... 2Kin 4:19 517
him, and brought him to his *m* ... 2Kin 4:20 517
the *m* of the child said, As the ... 2Kin 4:30 517
as the whoredoms of thy *m* Jezebel ... 2Kin 9:22 517
when Athaliah the *m* of Ahaziah ... 2Kin 11:1 517
the king of Babylon, he, and his *m* ... 2Kin 24:12 517
to Babylon, and the king's *m* ... 2Kin 24:15 517
she was the *m* of Onam ... 1Chr 2:26 517
his *m* called his name Jabez, ... 1Chr 4:9 517
Maachah the *m* of Asa the king ... 2Chr 15:16 517
for his *m* was his counsellor to ... 2Chr 22:3 517
But when Athaliah the *m* of ... 2Chr 22:10 517
for she had neither father nor *m* ... Est 2:7 517
m were dead, took for his own ... Est 2:7 517
to the worm, Thou art my *m* ... Job 17:14 517
my *m* forsake me, then the LORD ... Ps 27:10 517
as one that mourneth for his *m* ... Ps 35:14 517
and in sin did my *m* conceive me ... Ps 51:5 517
the sin of his *m* be blotted out ... Ps 109:14 517
and to be a joyful *m* of children ... Ps 113:9 517
a child that is weaned of his *m* ... Ps 131:2 517
and forsake not the law of thy *m* ... Prov 1:8 517
only beloved in the sight of my *m* ... Prov 4:3 517
and forsake not the law of thy *m* ... Prov 6:20 517
son is the heaviness of his *m* ... Prov 10:1 517
but a foolish man despiseth his *m* ... Prov 15:20 517
his father, and chaseth away his *m* ... Prov 19:26 517
Whoso curseth his father or his *m* ... Prov 20:20 517
despise not thy *m* when she is old ... Prov 23:22 517
thy *m* shall be glad, and she that ... Prov 23:25 517
Whoso robbeth his father or his *m* ... Prov 28:24 517
himself bringeth his *m* to shame ... Prov 29:15 517
father, and doth not bless their *m* ... Prov 30:11 517
and despiseth to obey his *m* ... Prov 30:17 517
prophecy that his *m* taught him ... Prov 31:1 517
with the crown wherewith his *m* ... Song 3:11 517
she is the only one of her *m* ... Song 6:9 517
that sucked the breasts of my *m* ... Song 8:1 517
there thy *m* brought thee forth ... Song 8:5 517
to cry, My father, and my *m* ... Is 8:4 517
from the bowels of my *m* hath he ... Is 49:1 517
transgressions is your *m* put away ... Is 50:1 517
As one whom his *m* comforteth ... Is 66:13 517
m of the young men a spoiler at ... Jer 15:8 517
Woe is me, my *m*, that thou hast ... Jer 15:10 517
for their father or for their *m* ... Jer 16:7 517
wherein my *m* bare me be blessed ... Jer 20:14 517
or that my *m* might have been my ... Jer 20:17 517
thy *m* that bare thee, into ... Jer 22:26 517
Your *m* shall be sore confounded ... Jer 50:12 517
an Amorite, and thy *m* an Hittite ... Eze 16:3 517
against thee, saying, As is the *m* ... Eze 16:44 517
your *m* was an Hittite, and your ... Eze 16:45 517
And say, What is thy *m* ... Eze 19:2 517
Thy *m* is like a vine in thy blood ... Eze 19:10 517
they set light by father and *m* ... Eze 22:7 517
two women, the daughters of one *m* ... Eze 23:2 517
but for father, or for *m*, or for ... Eze 44:25 517
Plead with your *m*, plead ... Hos 2:2 517
For their *m* hath played the ... Hos 2:5 517
night, and I will destroy thy *m* ... Hos 4:5 517
the *m* was dashed in pieces upon ... Hos 10:14 517
daughter riseth up against her *m* ... Mic 7:6 517
in law against her *m* in law ... Mic 7:6 2545
his *m* that begat him shall say ... Zec 13:3 517
his *m* that begat him shall thrust ... Zec 13:3 517
When as his *m* Mary was espoused ... Mt 1:18 3384
the young child with Mary his *m* ... Mt 2:11 3384
and take the young child and his *m* ... Mt 2:13 3384
his *m* by night, and departed into ... Mt 2:14 3384
and take the young child and his *m* ... Mt 2:20 3384
and took the young child and his *m* ... Mt 2:21 3384
house, he saw his wife's *m* laid ... Mt 8:14 3994
and the daughter against her *m* ... Mt 10:35 3384
in law against her *m* in law ... Mt 10:35 3994
He that loveth father or *m* more ... Mt 10:37 3384
to the people, behold, his *m* ... Mt 12:46 3384
one said unto him, Behold, thy *m* ... Mt 12:47 3384
him that told him, Who is my *m* ... Mt 12:48 3384
disciples, and said, Behold my *m* ... Mt 12:49 3384
is my brother, and sister, and *m* ... Mt 12:50 3384
is not his *m* called Mary ... Mt 13:55 3384
being before instructed of her *m* ... Mt 14:8 3384
and she brought it to her *m* ... Mt 14:11 3384
saying, Honour thy father and *m* ... Mt 15:4 3384
and, He that curseth father or *m* ... Mt 15:4 3384
shall say to his father or his *m* ... Mt 15:5 3384
And honour not his father or his *m* ... Mt 15:6 3384
shall a man leave father and *m* ... Mt 19:5 3384
Honour thy father and thy *m* ... Mt 19:19 3384
or sisters, or father, or *m* ... Mt 19:29 3384
Then came to him the *m* of ... Mt 20:20 3384
Magdalene, and Mary the *m* of James ... Mt 27:56 3384
the *m* of Zebedee's children ... Mt 27:56 3384
But Simon's wife's *m* lay sick of ... Mk 1:30 3994
came then his brethren and his *m* ... Mk 3:31 3384
they said unto him, Behold, thy *m* ... Mk 3:32 3384
them, saying, Who is my *m* ... Mk 3:33 3384
about him, and said, Behold my *m* ... Mk 3:34 3384
is my brother, and my sister, and *m* ... Mk 3:35 3384
the *m* of the damsel, and them that ... Mk 5:40 3384
went forth, and said unto her *m* ... Mk 6:24 3384
and the damsel gave it to her *m* ... Mk 6:28 3384
said, Honour thy father and thy *m* ... Mk 7:10 3384
and, Whoso curseth father or *m* ... Mk 7:10 3384
man shall say to his father or *m* ... Mk 7:11 3384
do ought for his father or his *m* ... Mk 7:12 3384
shall a man leave his father and *m* ... Mk 10:7 3384
not, Honour thy father and *m* ... Mk 10:19 3384
or sisters, or father, or *m* ... Mk 10:29 3384
Mary the *m* of James the less and ... Mk 15:40 3384
Mary the *m* of Joses beheld where ... Mk 15:47
Magdalene, and Mary the *m* of James ... Mk 16:1
that the *m* of my Lord should come ... Lk 1:43 3384
his *m* answered and said, Not so ... Lk 1:60 3384
his *m* marvelled at those things ... Lk 2:33 3384
them, and said unto Mary his *m* ... Lk 2:34 3384
and Joseph and his *m* knew not of it ... Lk 2:43 3384
his *m* said unto him, Son, why ... Lk 2:48 3384
but his *m* kept all these sayings ... Lk 2:51 3384
Simon's wife's *m* was taken with a ... Lk 4:38 3994
out, the only son of his *m* ... Lk 7:12 3384
And he delivered him to his *m* ... Lk 7:15 3384
Then came to him his *m* and his ... Lk 8:19 3384
him by certain which said, Thy *m* ... Lk 8:20 3384
answered and said unto them, My *m* ... Lk 8:21 3384
the father and the *m* of the maiden ... Lk 8:51 3384
the *m* against the daughter ... Lk 12:53 3384
and the daughter against the *m* ... Lk 12:53 3384
the *m* in law against her daughter ... Lk 12:53 3994
in law against her *m* in law ... Lk 12:53 3994
me, and hate not his father, and *m* ... Lk 14:26 3384
Honour thy father and thy *m* ... Lk 18:20 3384
and Joanna, and Mary the *m* of James ... Lk 24:10
and the *m* of Jesus was there ... Jn 2:1 3384
the *m* of Jesus saith unto him, ... Jn 2:3 3384
His *m* saith unto the servants, ... Jn 2:5 3384
down to Capernaum, he, and his *m* ... Jn 2:12 3384
Joseph, whose father and *m* we know ... Jn 6:42 3384
stood by the cross of Jesus his *m* ... Jn 19:25 3384
When Jesus therefore saw his *m* ... Jn 19:26 3384
he loved, he saith unto his *m* ... Jn 19:26 3384
he to the disciple, Behold thy *m* ... Jn 19:27 3384
the women, and Mary the *m* of Jesus ... Acts 1:14 3384
the house of Mary the *m* of John ... Acts 12:12 3384
chosen in the Lord, and his *m* ... Rom 16:13 3384
is free, which is the *m* of us all ... Gal 4:26 3384
shall a man leave his father and *m* ... Eph 5:31 3384
Honour thy father and *m* ... Eph 6:2 3384
grandmother Lois, and thy *m* Eunice ... 2Ti 1:5 3384
Without father, without *m* ... Heb 7:3 282
THE *M* OF HARLOTS AND ... Rev 17:5 3384

MOTHER'S {75}

told them of her *m* house these ... Gen 24:28 517
was comforted after his *m* death ... Gen 24:67 517
let thy *m* sons bow down to thee ... Gen 27:29 517
the house of Bethuel thy *m* father ... Gen 28:2 517
daughters of Laban thy *m* brother ... Gen 28:2 517
daughter of Laban his *m* brother ... Gen 29:10 517
the sheep of Laban his *m* brother ... Gen 29:10 517
the flock of Laban his *m* brother ... Gen 29:10 517
his brother Benjamin, his *m* son ... Gen 43:29 517
not seethe a kid in his *m* milk ... Ex 23:19 517
not seethe a kid in his *m* milk ... Ex 34:26 517
the nakedness of thy *m* sister ... Lev 18:13 517
for she is thy *m* near kinswoman ... Lev 18:13 517
or his *m* daughter, and see her ... Lev 20:17 517
the nakedness of thy *m* sister ... Lev 20:19 517
his *m* name was Shelomith, the ... Lev 24:11 517
when he cometh out of his *m* womb ... Num 12:12 517
not seethe a kid in his *m* milk ... Deut 14:21 517
to Shechem unto his *m* brethren ... Judg 9:1 517
of the house of his *m* father ... Judg 9:1 517
his *m* brethren spake of him in ... Judg 9:3 517
Nazarite unto God from my *m* womb ... Judg 16:17 517
Go, return each to her *m* house ... Ruth 1:8 517
the confusion of thy *m* nakedness ... 1Sa 20:30 517
whose *m* name was Zeruah, a widow ... 1Kin 11:26 517
And his *m* name was Naamah an ... 1Kin 14:21 517
And his *m* name was Naamah an ... 1Kin 14:31 517
his *m* name was Maachah, the ... 1Kin 15:2 517
his *m* name was Maachah, the ... 1Kin 15:10 517
his *m* name was Azubah the ... 1Kin 22:42 517
his *m* name was Athaliah, the ... 2Kin 8:26 517
And his *m* name was Zibiah of ... 2Kin 12:1 517
his *m* name was Jehoaddan of ... 2Kin 14:2 517
his *m* name was Jecholiah of ... 2Kin 15:2 517
his *m* name was Jerusha, the ... 2Kin 15:33 517
His *m* name also was Abi, the ... 2Kin 18:2 517
his *m* name was Hephzi-bah ... 2Kin 21:1 517
his *m* name was Meshullemeth, the ... 2Kin 21:19 517
his *m* name was Jedidah, the ... 2Kin 22:1 517
his *m* name was Hamutal, the ... 2Kin 23:31 517
his *m* name was Zebudah, the ... 2Kin 23:36 517
his *m* name was Nehushta, the ... 2Kin 24:8 517
his *m* name was Hamutal, the ... 2Kin 24:18 517
And his *m* name was Naamah an ... 2Chr 12:13 517
His *m* name also was Michaiah the ... 2Chr 13:2 517
his *m* name was Azubah the ... 2Chr 20:31 517
His *m* name also was Athaliah the ... 2Chr 22:2 517
His *m* name also was Zibiah of ... 2Chr 24:1 517
his *m* name was Jehoaddan of ... 2Chr 25:1 517
His *m* name also was Jecoliah of ... 2Chr 26:3 517
His *m* name also was Jerushah, the ... 2Chr 27:1 517
his *m* name was Abijah, the ... 2Chr 29:1 517
Naked came I out of my *m* womb ... Job 1:21 517
not up the doors of my *m* womb ... Job 3:10
I have guided her from my *m* womb ... Job 31:18 517
hope when I was upon my *m* breasts ... Ps 22:9 517
thou art my God from my *m* belly ... Ps 22:10 517
thou slanderest thine own *m* son ... Ps 50:20 517
and an alien unto my *m* children ... Ps 69:8 517
that took me out of my *m* bowels ... Ps 71:6 517
thou hast covered me in my *m* womb ... Ps 139:13 517
As he came forth of his *m* womb ... Eccl 5:15 517
my *m* children were angry with me ... Song 1:6 517
I had brought him into my *m* house ... Song 3:4 517
and bring thee into my *m* house ... Song 8:2 517
is the bill of your *m* divorcement ... Is 50:1 517
his *m* name was Hamutal the ... Jer 52:1 517
Thou art thy *m* daughter, that ... Eze 16:45 517
were so born from their *m* womb ... Mt 19:12 3384
Holy Ghost, even from his *m* womb ... Lk 1:15 3384
the second time into his *m* womb ... Jn 3:4 3384
his *m* sister, Mary the wife of ... Jn 19:25 3384
lame from his *m* womb was carried ... Acts 3:2 3384
being a cripple from his *m* womb ... Acts 14:8 3384
who separated me from my *m* womb ... Gal 1:15 3384

MOTHERS {7}

and their queens thy nursing *m* ... Is 49:23
concerning their *m* that bare them ... Jer 16:3 517
They say to their *m*, Where is ... Lam 2:12 517
fatherless, our *m* are as widows ... Lam 5:3 517
and brethren, and sisters, and *m* ... Mk 10:30 3384
of fathers and murderers of *m* ... 1Ti 1:9 3389
The elder women as *m* ... 1Ti 5:2 3384

MOTHERS' {1}

was poured out into their *m* bosom ... Lam 2:12 517

MOTIONS {1}

the *m* of sins, which were by the ... Rom 7:5 3804

MOULDY {2}

of their provision was dry and *m* ... Josh 9:5 5350
behold, it is dry, and it is *m* ... Josh 9:12 5350

MOUNT {264}

goest unto Sephar a *m* of the east ... Gen 10:30 2022
And the Horites in their *m* Seir ... Gen 14:6 2042
In the *m* of the LORD it shall be ... Gen 22:14 2022
set his face toward the *m* Gilead ... Gen 31:21 2022
they overtook him in the *m* Gilead ... Gen 31:23 2022
had pitched his tent in the *m* ... Gen 31:25 2022
pitched in the *m* of Gilead ... Gen 31:25 2022
offered sacrifice upon the *m* ... Gen 31:54 2022
and tarried all night in the *m* ... Gen 31:54 2022
Thus dwelt Esau in *m* Seir ... Gen 36:8 2022
father of the Edomites in *m* Seir ... Gen 36:9 2022
went, and met him in the *m* of God ... Ex 4:27 2022
where he encamped at the *m* of God ... Ex 18:5 2022
there Israel camped before the *m* ... Ex 19:2 2022
of all the people upon *m* Sinai ... Ex 19:11 2022
that ye go not up into the *m* ... Ex 19:12 2022
whosoever toucheth the *m* shall be ... Ex 19:12 2022
long, they shall come up to the *m* ... Ex 19:13 2022
down from the *m* unto the people ... Ex 19:14 2022
and a thick cloud upon the *m* ... Ex 19:16 2022
stood at the nether part of the *m* ... Ex 19:17 2022
m Sinai was altogether on a smoke ... Ex 19:18 2022
the whole *m* quaked greatly ... Ex 19:18 2022
m Sinai, on the top of the *m* ... Ex 19:20 2022
Moses up to the top of the *m* ... Ex 19:20 2022
people cannot come up to *m* Sinai ... Ex 19:23 2022
saying, Set bounds about the *m* ... Ex 19:23 2022
Moses, Come up to me into the *m* ... Ex 24:12 2022
Moses went up into the *m* of God ... Ex 24:13 2022
And Moses went up into the *m* ... Ex 24:15 2022
and a cloud covered the *m* ... Ex 24:15 2022
of the LORD abode upon *m* Sinai ... Ex 24:16 2022
fire on the top of the *m* in the ... Ex 24:17 2022
cloud, and gat him up into the *m* ... Ex 24:18 2022
and Moses was in the *m* forty days ... Ex 24:18 2022
which was shewed thee in the *m* ... Ex 25:40 2022
which was shewed thee in the *m* ... Ex 26:30 2022
as it was shewed thee in the *m* ... Ex 27:8 2022
communing with him upon *m* Sinai ... Ex 31:18 2022
delayed to come down out of the *m* ... Ex 32:1 2022
turned, and went down from the *m* ... Ex 32:15 2022
and brake them beneath the *m* ... Ex 32:19 2022
of their ornaments by the *m* Horeb ... Ex 33:6 2022
up in the morning unto *m* Sinai ... Ex 34:2 2022
there to me in the top of the *m* ... Ex 34:2 2022
man be seen throughout all the *m* ... Ex 34:3 2022
nor herds feed before that *m* ... Ex 34:3 2022
morning, and went up unto *m* Sinai ... Ex 34:4 2022

when Moses came down from *m* Sinai	Ex 34:29	2022
when he came down from the *m*	Ex 34:29	2022
had spoken with him in *m* Sinai	Ex 34:32	2022
LORD commanded Moses in *m* Sinai	Lev 7:38	2022
LORD spake unto Moses in *m* Sinai	Lev 25:1	2022
the children of Israel in *m* Sinai	Lev 26:46	2022
the children of Israel in *m* Sinai	Lev 27:34	2022
LORD spake with Moses in *m* Sinai	Num 3:1	2022
they departed from the *m* of the	Num 10:33	2022
from Kadesh, and came unto *m* Hor	Num 20:22	2022
unto Moses and Aaron in *m* Hor	Num 20:23	2022
son, and bring them up unto *m* Hor	Num 20:25	2022
they went up into *m* Hor in the	Num 20:27	2022
died there in the top of the *m*	Num 20:28	2022
and Eleazar came down from the *m*	Num 20:28	2022
they journeyed from *m* Hor by the	Num 21:4	2022
Get thee up into this *m* Abarim	Num 27:12	2022
which was ordained in *m* Sinai for	Num 28:6	2022
and pitched in *m* Shapher	Num 33:23	2022
And they removed from *m* Shapher	Num 33:24	2022
from Kadesh, and pitched in *m* Hor	Num 33:37	2022
m Hor at the commandment of the	Num 33:38	2022
years old when he died in *m* Hor	Num 33:39	2022
And they departed from *m* Hor	Num 33:41	2022
ye shall point out for you *m* Hor	Num 34:7	2022
From *m* Hor ye shall point out	Num 34:8	2022
way of *m* Seir unto Kadesh-barnea	Deut 1:2	2022
have dwelt long enough in this *m*	Deut 1:6	2022
go to the *m* of the Amorites, and	Deut 1:7	2022
we compassed *m* Seir many days	Deut 2:1	2022
because I have given *m* Seir unto	Deut 2:5	2022
the river of Arnon unto *m* Hermon	Deut 3:8	2022
half *m* Gilead, and the cities	Deut 3:12	2022
even unto *m* Sion which is Hermon,	Deut 4:48	2022
m out of the midst of the fire	Deut 5:4	2022
fire, and went not up into the *m*	Deut 5:5	2022
m out of the midst of the fire	Deut 5:22	2022
When I was gone up into the *m* to	Deut 9:9	2022
then I abode in the *m* forty days	Deut 9:9	2022
the LORD spake with you in the *m*	Deut 9:10	2022
I turned and came down from the *m*	Deut 9:15	2022
and the *m* burned with fire	Deut 9:15	2022
brook that descended out of the *m*	Deut 9:21	2022
and come up unto me into the *m*	Deut 10:1	2022
the first, and went up into the *m*	Deut 10:3	2022
the LORD spake unto you in the *m*	Deut 10:4	2022
myself and came down from the *m*	Deut 10:5	2022
And I stayed in the *m*, according	Deut 10:10	2022
put the blessing upon *m* Gerizim	Deut 11:29	2022
and the curse upon *m* Ebal	Deut 11:29	2022
in *m* Ebal, and thou shalt plaister	Deut 27:4	2022
These shall stand upon *m* Gerizim	Deut 27:12	2022
shall stand upon *m* Ebal to curse	Deut 27:13	2022
this mountain Abarim, unto *m* Nebo	Deut 32:49	2022
die in the *m* whither thou goest	Deut 32:50	2022
Aaron thy brother died in *m* Hor	Deut 32:50	2022
he shined forth from *m* Paran	Deut 33:2	2022
the LORD God of Israel in *m* Ebal	Josh 8:30	2022
of them over against *m* Gerizim	Josh 8:33	2022
half of them over against *m* Ebal	Josh 8:33	2022
Even from the *m* Halak, that goeth	Josh 11:17	2022
valley of Lebanon under *m* Hermon	Josh 11:17	2022
the river Arnon unto *m* Hermon	Josh 12:1	2022
And reigned in *m* Hermon, and in	Josh 12:5	2022
of Lebanon even unto the *m* Halak	Josh 12:7	2022
from Baal-gad under *m* Hermon unto	Josh 13:5	2022
all *m* Hermon, and all Bashan unto	Josh 13:11	2022
in the *m* of the valley,	Josh 13:19	2022
out to the cities of *m* Ephron	Josh 15:9	2022
from Baalah westward unto *m* Seir	Josh 15:10	2022
along unto the side of *m* Jearim	Josh 15:10	2022
and passed along to *m* Baalah	Josh 15:11	2022
from Jericho throughout *m* Beth-el	Josh 16:1	2022
if *m* Ephraim be too narrow for	Josh 17:15	2022
even Timnath-serah in *m* Ephraim	Josh 19:50	2022
Kedesh in Galilee in *m* Naphtali	Josh 20:7	2022
and Shechem in *m* Ephraim	Josh 20:7	2022
with her suburbs in *m* Ephraim	Josh 21:21	2022
and I gave unto Esau *m* Seir	Josh 24:4	2022
which is in *m* Ephraim, on the	Josh 24:30	2022
which was given him in *m* Ephraim	Josh 24:33	2022
would dwell in *m* Heres in Aijalon	Judg 1:35	2022
in the *m* of Ephraim, on the north	Judg 2:9	2022
Hivites that dwelt in *m* Lebanon	Judg 3:3	2022
from *m* Baal-hermon unto the	Judg 3:3	2022
went down with him from the *m*	Judg 3:27	2022
Ramah and Beth-el in *m* Ephraim	Judg 4:5	2022
saying, Go and draw toward *m* Tabor	Judg 4:6	2022
of Abinoam was gone up to *m* Tabor	Judg 4:12	2022
So Barak went down from *m* Tabor	Judg 4:14	2022
and depart early from *m* Gilead	Judg 7:3	2022
throughout all *m* Ephraim, saying,	Judg 7:24	2022
and stood in the top of *m* Gerizim	Judg 9:7	2022
Abimelech gat him up to *m* Zalmon	Judg 9:48	2022
he dwelt in Shamir in *m* Ephraim	Judg 10:1	2022
in the *m* of the Amalekites	Judg 12:15	2022
And there was a man of *m* Ephraim	Judg 17:1	2022
he came to *m* Ephraim to the house	Judg 17:8	2022
who when they came to *m* Ephraim	Judg 18:2	2022
they passed thence unto *m* Ephraim	Judg 18:13	2022
on the side of *m* Ephraim, who	Judg 19:1	2022
even, which was also of *m* Ephraim	Judg 19:16	2022
toward the side of *m* Ephraim	Judg 19:18	2022
of *m* Ephraim, and his name was	1Sa 1:1	2022
And he passed through *m* Ephraim	1Sa 9:4	2022
in *m* Beth-el, and a thousand were	1Sa 13:2	2022
had hid themselves in *m* Ephraim	1Sa 14:22	2022
and fell down slain in *m* Gilboa	1Sa 31:1	2022

his three sons fallen in *m* Gilboa	1Sa 31:8	2022
happened by chance upon *m* Gilboa	2Sa 1:6	2022
went up by the ascent of *m* Olivet	2Sa 15:30	
was come to the top of the *m*	2Sa 15:32	
but a man of *m* Ephraim, Sheba the	2Sa 20:21	2022
The son of Hur, in *m* Ephraim	1Kin 4:8	2022
built Shechem in *m* Ephraim	1Kin 12:25	2022
to me all Israel unto *m* Carmel	1Kin 18:19	2022
prophets together unto *m* Carmel	1Kin 18:20	2022
nights unto Horeb the *m* of God	1Kin 19:8	2022
stand upon the *m* before the LORD	1Kin 19:11	2022
he went from thence to *m* Carmel	2Kin 2:25	2022
unto the man of God to *m* Carmel	2Kin 4:25	2022
m Ephraim two young men of the	2Kin 5:22	2022
and they that escape out of *m* Zion	2Kin 19:31	2022
right hand of the *m* of corruption	2Kin 23:13	2022
that were there in the *m*, and sent	2Kin 23:16	2022
five hundred men, went to *m* Seir	1Chr 4:42	2022
and Senir, and unto *m* Hermon	1Chr 5:23	2022
Shechem in *m* Ephraim with her	1Chr 6:67	2022
and fell down slain in *m* Gilboa	1Chr 10:1	2022
and his sons fallen in *m* Gilboa	1Chr 10:8	2022
the LORD at Jerusalem in *m* Moriah	2Chr 3:1	2022
Abijah stood up upon *m* Zemaraim	2Chr 13:4	2022
Zemaraim, which is in *m* Ephraim	2Chr 13:4	2022
which he had taken from *m* Ephraim	2Chr 15:8	2022
from Beer-sheba to *m* Ephraim	2Chr 19:4	2022
m Seir, whom thou wouldest not	2Chr 20:10	2022
m Seir, which were come against	2Chr 20:22	2022
against the inhabitants of *m* Seir	2Chr 20:23	2022
in the *m* of the house of the LORD	2Chr 33:15	2022
saying, Go forth unto the *m*	Neh 8:15	2022
camest down also upon *m* Sinai	Neh 9:13	2022
excellency *m* up to the heavens	Job 20:6	5927
Doth the eagle *m* up at thy	Job 39:27	1361
is *m* Zion, on the sides of the	Ps 48:2	2022
Let *m* Zion rejoice, let the	Ps 48:11	2022
this *m* Zion, wherein thou hast	Ps 74:2	2022
the *m* Zion which he loved	Ps 78:68	2022
They *m* up to the heaven, they go	Ps 107:26	5927
in the LORD shall be as *m* Zion	Ps 125:1	2022
goats, that appear from *m* Gilead	Song 4:1	2022
every dwelling place of *m* Zion	Is 4:5	2022
hosts, which dwelleth in *m* Zion	Is 8:18	2022
they shall *m* up like the lifting	Is 9:18	55
his whole work upon *m* Zion	Is 10:12	2022
the *m* of the daughter of Zion	Is 10:32	2022
upon the *m* of the congregation	Is 14:13	2022
unto the *m* of the daughter of	Is 16:1	2022
of the LORD of hosts, the *m* Zion	Is 18:7	2022
of hosts shall reign in *m* Zion	Is 24:23	2022
LORD in the holy *m* at Jerusalem	Is 27:13	2022
shall rise up as in *m* Perazim	Is 28:21	2022
lay siege against thee with a *m*	Is 29:3	4674
be, that fight against *m* Zion	Is 29:8	2022
come down to fight for *m* Zion	Is 31:4	2022
and they that escape out of *m* Zion	Is 37:32	2022
they shall *m* up with wings as	Is 40:31	5927
affliction from *m* Ephraim	Jer 4:15	2022
cast a *m* against Jerusalem	Jer 6:6	5550
upon the *m* Ephraim shall cry	Jer 31:6	2022
shall be satisfied upon *m* Ephraim	Jer 50:19	2022
Babylon should *m* up to heaven	Jer 51:53	5927
it, and cast a *m* against it	Eze 4:2	5550
wings to *m* up from the earth	Eze 10:16	7311
against the gates, to cast a *m*	Eze 21:22	5550
cast a *m* against thee, and lift up	Eze 26:8	5550
man, set thy face against *m* Seir	Eze 35:2	2022
O *m* Seir, I am against thee, and I	Eze 35:3	2022
Thus will I make *m* Seir most	Eze 35:7	2022
O *m* Seir, and all Idumea, even all	Eze 35:15	2022
north shall come, and cast up a *m*	Dan 11:15	5550
for in *m* Zion and in Jerusalem	Joel 2:32	2022
out of the *m* of Esau	Obad 8	2022
the *m* of Esau may be cut off by	Obad 9	2022
But upon *m* Zion shall be	Obad 17	2022
south shall possess the *m* of Esau	Obad 19	2022
m Zion to judge the *m* of Esau	Obad 21	2022
them in *m* Zion from henceforth	Mic 4:7	2022
and the Holy One from *m* Paran	Hab 3:3	2022
in that day upon the *m* of Olives	Zec 14:4	2022
the *m* of Olives shall cleave in	Zec 14:4	2022
unto the *m* of Olives, then sent	Mt 21:1	*3735*
And as he sat upon the *m* of Olives	Mt 24:3	*3735*
went out into the *m* of Olives	Mt 26:30	*3735*
at the *m* of Olives, he sendeth	Mk 11:1	*3735*
as he sat upon the *m* of Olives	Mk 13:3	*3735*
went out into the *m* of Olives	Mk 14:26	*3735*
at the *m* called the *m* of	Lk 19:29	*3735*
called the *m* of Olives	Lk 19:29	
at the descent of the *m* of Olives	Lk 19:37	*3735*
abode in the *m* that is called the	Lk 21:37	*3735*
that is called the *m* of Olives	Lk 21:37	
he was wont, to the *m* of Olives	Lk 22:39	*3735*
Jesus went unto the *m* of Olives	Jn 8:1	*3735*
from the *m* called Olivet, which	Acts 1:12	*3735*
to him in the wilderness of *m*	Acts 7:30	*3735*
which spake to him in the *m* Sina	Acts 7:38	*3735*
the one from the *m* Sinai, which	Gal 4:24	*3735*
this Agar is *m* Sinai in Arabia	Gal 4:25	*3735*
pattern shewed to thee in the *m*	Heb 8:5	*3735*
unto the *m* that might be touched	Heb 12:18	*3735*
But ye are come unto *m* Sion	Heb 12:22	*3735*
we were with him in the holy *m*	2Pet 1:18	*3735*
lo, a Lamb stood on the *m* Sion	Rev 14:1	*3735*

MOUNTAIN {137}

unto a *m* on the east of Beth-el	Gen 12:8	2022
they that remained fled to the *m*	Gen 14:10	2022
escape to the *m*, lest thou be	Gen 19:17	2022
and I cannot escape to the *m*	Gen 19:19	2022
up out of Zoar, and dwelt in the *m*	Gen 19:30	2022
desert, and came to the *m* of God	Ex 3:1	2022
ye shall serve God upon this *m*	Ex 3:12	2022
plant them in the *m* of thine	Ex 15:17	2022
LORD called unto him out of the *m*	Ex 19:3	2022
of the trumpet, and the *m* smoking	Ex 20:18	2022
southward, and go up into the *m*	Num 13:17	2022
gat them up into the top of the *m*	Num 14:40	2022
the way of the *m* of the Amorites	Deut 1:19	2022
come unto the *m* of the Amorites	Deut 1:20	2022
they turned and went up into the *m*	Deut 1:24	2022
Amorites, which dwelt in that *m*	Deut 1:44	2022
have compassed this *m* long enough	Deut 2:3	2022
is beyond Jordan, that goodly *m*	Deut 3:25	2022
ye came near and stood under the *m*	Deut 4:11	2022
the *m* burned with fire unto the	Deut 4:11	2022
(for the *m* did burn with fire,)	Deut 5:23	2022
Get thee up into this *m* Abarim	Deut 32:49	2022
shall call the people unto the *m*	Deut 33:19	2022
plains of Moab unto the *m* of Nebo	Deut 34:1	2022
said unto them, Get you to the *m*	Josh 2:16	2022
And they went, and came unto the *m*	Josh 2:22	2022
returned, and descended from the *m*	Josh 2:23	2022
the *m* of Israel, and the valley of	Josh 11:16	2022
Now therefore give me this *m*	Josh 14:12	2022
went up to the top of the *m* that	Josh 15:8	2022
But the *m* shall be thine	Josh 17:18	2022
came down to the end of the *m*	Josh 18:16	2022
is Hebron, in the *m* of Judah	Josh 20:7	2022
Canaanites, that dwelt in the *m*	Judg 1:9	2022
out the inhabitants of the *m*	Judg 1:19	2022
the children of Dan into the *m*	Judg 1:34	2022
a trumpet in the *m* of Ephraim	Judg 3:27	2022
stood on a *m* on the one side	1Sa 17:3	2022
stood on a *m* on the other side	1Sa 17:3	2022
remained in a *m* in the wilderness	1Sa 23:14	2022
Saul went on this side of the *m*	1Sa 23:26	2022
and his men on that side of the *m*	1Sa 23:26	2022
him up, and cast him upon some *m*	2Kin 2:16	2022
the *m* was full of horses and	2Kin 6:17	2022
thousand to hew in the *m*, and	2Chr 2:2	2022
thousand to be hewers in the *m*	2Chr 2:18	2022
surely the *m* falling cometh to	Job 14:18	2022
my soul, Flee as a bird to your *m*	Ps 11:1	2022
hast made my *m* to stand strong	Ps 30:7	2042
our God, in the *m* of his holiness	Ps 48:1	2022
of his sanctuary, even to this *m*	Ps 78:54	2022
I will get me to the *m* of myrrh	Song 4:6	2022
that the *m* of the LORD's house	Is 2:2	2022
let us go up to the *m* of the LORD	Is 2:3	2022
hurt nor destroy in all my holy *m*	Is 11:9	2022
ye up a banner upon the high *m*	Is 13:2	2022
in this *m* shall the LORD of hosts	Is 25:6	2022
he will destroy in this *m* the	Is 25:7	2022
For in this *m* shall the hand of	Is 25:10	2022
as a beacon upon the top of a *m*	Is 30:17	2022
there shall be upon every high *m*	Is 30:25	2022
to come into the *m* of the LORD	Is 30:29	2022
shall be exalted, and every *m*	Is 40:4	2022
get thee up into the high *m*	Is 40:9	2022
them will I bring to my holy *m*	Is 56:7	2022
high *m* hast thou set thy bed	Is 57:7	2022
land, and shall inherit my holy *m*	Is 57:13	2022
the LORD, that forget my holy *m*	Is 65:11	2022
hurt nor destroy in all my holy *m*	Is 65:25	2022
beasts, to my holy *m* Jerusalem	Is 66:20	2022
she is gone up upon every high *m*	Jer 3:6	2022
they shall hunt them from every *m*	Jer 16:16	2022
O my *m* in the field, I will give	Jer 17:3	2042
the *m* of the house as the high	Jer 26:18	2022
of justice, and *m* of holiness	Jer 31:23	2022
they have gone from *m* to hill	Jer 50:6	2022
I am against thee, O destroying *m*	Jer 51:25	2022
and will make thee a burnt *m*	Jer 51:25	2022
Because of the *m* of Zion, which	Lam 5:18	2022
stood upon the *m* which is on the	Eze 11:23	2022
and will plant it upon an high *m*	Eze 17:22	2022
In the *m* of the height of Israel	Eze 17:23	2022
For in mine holy *m*	Eze 20:40	2022
in the *m* of the height of Israel,	Eze 20:40	2022
thou wast upon the holy *m* of God	Eze 28:14	2022
as profane out of the *m* of God	Eze 28:16	2022
and set me upon a very high *m*	Eze 40:2	2022
Upon the top of the *m* the whole	Eze 43:12	2022
smote the image became a great *m*	Dan 2:35	2906
cut out of the *m* without hands	Dan 2:45	2906
thy city Jerusalem, thy holy *m*	Dan 9:16	2022
my God for the holy *m* of my God	Dan 9:20	2022
the seas in the glorious holy *m*	Dan 11:45	2022
and sound an alarm in my holy *m*	Joel 2:1	2022
God dwelling in Zion, my holy *m*	Joel 3:17	2022
that are in the *m* of Samaria	Amos 4:1	2022
and trust in the *m* of Samaria	Amos 6:1	2022
as ye have drunk upon my holy *m*	Obad 16	2022
the *m* of the house as the high	Mic 3:12	2022
that the *m* of the house of the	Mic 4:1	2022
let us go up to the *m* of the LORD	Mic 4:2	2022
sea to sea, and from *m* to *m*	Mic 7:12	2022
be haughty because of my holy *m*	Zeph 3:11	2022
Go up to the *m*, and bring wood, and	Hag 1:8	2022
Who art thou, O great *m*	Zec 4:7	2022
the *m* of the LORD of hosts the	Zec 8:3	2022
of the LORD of hosts the holy *m*	Zec 8:3	2022

M

half of the *m* shall remove toward ... Zec 14:4 2022
him up into an exceeding high *m* ... Mt 4:8 *3735*
multitudes, he went up into a *m* ... Mt 5:1 *3735*
When he was come down from the *m* ... Mt 8:1 *3735*
he went up into a *m* apart to pray ... Mt 14:23 *3735*
and went up into a *m*, and sat down ... Mt 15:29 *3735*
them up into an high *m* apart ... Mt 17:1 *3735*
And as they came down from the *m* ... Mt 17:9 *3735*
seed, ye shall say unto this *m* ... Mt 17:20 *3735*
also if ye shall say unto this *m* ... Mt 21:21 *3735*
Galilee, into a *m* where Jesus had ... Mt 28:16 *3735*
And he goeth up into a *m*, and ... Mk 3:13 *3735*
he departed into a *m* to pray ... Mk 6:46 *3735*
an high *m* apart by themselves ... Mk 9:2 *3735*
And as they came down from the *m* ... Mk 9:9 *3735*
whosoever shall say unto this *m* ... Mk 11:23 *3735*
shall be filled, and every *m* ... Lk 3:5 *3735*
taking him up into an high *m* ... Lk 4:5 *3735*
that he went out into a *m* to pray ... Lk 6:12 *3735*
of many swine feeding on the *m* ... Lk 8:32 *3735*
and went up into a *m* to pray ... Lk 9:28 *3735*
Our fathers worshipped in this *m* ... Jn 4:20 *3735*
when ye shall neither in this *m* ... Jn 4:21 *3735*
And Jesus went up into a *m* ... Jn 6:3 *3735*
again into a *m* himself alone ... Jn 6:15 *3735*
if so much as a beast touch the *m* ... Heb 12:20 *3735*
and every *m* and island were moved ... Rev 6:14 *3735*
as it were a great *m* burning with ... Rev 8:8 *3735*
the spirit to a great and high *m* ... Rev 21:10 *3735*

MOUNTAINS {177}
and the *m* were covered ... Gen 7:20 2022
the month, upon the *m* of Ararat ... Gen 8:4 2022
were the tops of the *m* seen ... Gen 8:5 2022
the *m* which I will tell thee of ... Gen 22:2 2022
them out, to slay them in the *m* ... Ex 32:12 2022
and the Amorites, dwell in the *m* ... Num 13:29 2022
out of the *m* of the east, saying, ... Num 23:7 2042
and pitched in the *m* of Abarim ... Num 33:47 2022
departed from the *m* of Abarim ... Num 33:48 2022
nor unto the cities in the *m* ... Deut 2:37 2022
their gods, upon the high *m* ... Deut 12:2 2022
on fire the foundations of the *m* ... Deut 32:22 2022
the chief things of the ancient *m* ... Deut 33:15 2042
m are gathered together against ... Josh 10:6 2022
that were on the north of the *m* ... Josh 11:2 2022
and the Jebusite in the *m* ... Josh 11:3 2022
and cut off the Anakims from the *m* ... Josh 11:21 2022
Anab, and from all the *m* of Judah ... Josh 11:21 2022
and from all the *m* of Israel ... Josh 11:21 2022
In the *m*, and in the valleys, and ... Josh 12:8 2022
And in the *m*, Shamir, and Jattir, ... Josh 15:48 2022
and went up through the *m* westward ... Josh 18:12 2022
The *m* melted from before the LORD ... Judg 5:5 2022
them the dens which are in the *m* ... Judg 6:2 2022
wait for him in the top of the *m* ... Judg 9:25 2022
people down from the top of the *m* ... Judg 9:36 2022
of the *m* as if they were men ... Judg 9:36 2022
I may go up and down upon the *m* ... Judg 11:37 2022
bewailed her virginity upon the *m* ... Judg 11:38 2022
doth hunt a partridge in the *m* ... 1Sa 26:20 2022
Ye *m* of Gilboa, let there be no ... 2Sa 1:21 2022
thousand hewers in the *m* ... 1Kin 5:15 2022
a great and strong wind rent the *m* ... 1Kin 19:11 2022
am come up to the height of the *m* ... 2Kin 19:23 2022
as swift as the roes upon the *m* ... 1Chr 12:8 2022
all Israel scattered upon the *m* ... 2Chr 18:16 2022
high places in the *m* of Judah ... 2Chr 21:11 2022
also, and vine dressers in the *m* ... 2Chr 26:10 2022
he built cities in the *m* of Judah ... 2Chr 27:4 2022
Which removeth the *m*, and they ... Job 9:5 2022
are wet with the showers of the *m* ... Job 24:8 2022
he overturneth the *m* by the roots ... Job 28:9 2022
The range of the *m* is his pasture ... Job 39:8 2022
Surely the *m* bring him forth food ... Job 40:20 2022
righteousness is like the great *m* ... Ps 36:6 2042
though the *m* be carried into the ... Ps 46:2 2022
though the *m* shake with the ... Ps 46:3 2022
I know all the fowls of the *m* ... Ps 50:11 2022
his strength setteth fast the *m* ... Ps 65:6 2022
The *m* shall bring peace to the ... Ps 72:3 2022
the earth upon the top of the *m* ... Ps 72:16 2022
and excellent than the *m* of prey ... Ps 76:4 2042
the flame setteth the *m* on fire ... Ps 83:14 2022
His foundation is in the holy *m* ... Ps 87:1 2042
Before the *m* were brought forth, ... Ps 90:2 2022
the waters stood above the *m* ... Ps 104:6 2022
They go up by the *m* ... Ps 104:8 2022
The *m* skipped like rams, and the ... Ps 114:4 2022
Ye *m*, that ye skipped like rams ... Ps 114:6 2022
As the *m* are round about ... Ps 125:2 2022
that descended upon the *m* of Zion ... Ps 133:3 2042
touch the *m*, and they shall smoke ... Ps 144:5 2022
maketh grass to grow upon the *m* ... Ps 147:8 2022
M, and all hills ... Ps 148:9 2022
Before the *m* were settled, before ... Prov 8:25 2022
and herbs of the *m* are gathered ... Prov 27:25 2022
he cometh leaping upon the *m* ... Song 2:8 2022
a young hart upon the *m* of Bether ... Song 2:17 2022
from the *m* of the leopards ... Song 4:8 2042
a young hart upon the *m* of spices ... Song 8:14 2022
established in the top of the *m* ... Is 2:2 2022
And upon all the high *m*, and upon ... Is 2:14 2022
The noise of a multitude in the *m* ... Is 13:4 2022
upon my *m* tread him under foot ... Is 14:25 2022
chaff of the *m* before the wind ... Is 17:13 2022
he lifteth up an ensign on the *m* ... Is 18:3 2022
together unto the fowls of the *m* ... Is 18:6 2022
the walls, and of crying to the *m* ... Is 22:5 2022
the *m* shall be melted with their ... Is 34:3 2022
I come up to the height of the *m* ... Is 37:24 2022
and weighed the *m* in scales ... Is 40:12 2022
thou shalt thresh the *m*, and beat ... Is 41:15 2022
them shout from the top of the *m* ... Is 42:11 2022
I will make waste *m* and hills, and ... Is 42:15 2022
break forth into singing, ye *m* ... Is 44:23 2022
And I will make all my *m* a way ... Is 49:11 2022
and break forth into singing, O *m* ... Is 49:13 2022
How beautiful upon the *m* are the ... Is 52:7 2022
For the *m* shall depart, and the ... Is 54:10 2022
the *m* and the hills shall break ... Is 55:12 2022
that the *m* might flow down at thy ... Is 64:1 2022
the *m* flowed down at thy presence ... Is 64:3 2022
have burned incense upon the *m* ... Is 65:7 2022
out of Judah an inheritor of my *m* ... Is 65:9 2022
hills, and from the multitude of *m* ... Jer 3:23 2022
I beheld the *m*, and, lo, they ... Jer 4:24 2022
For the *m* will I take up a ... Jer 9:10 2022
your feet stumble upon the dark *m* ... Jer 13:16 2022
and from the plain, and from the *m* ... Jer 17:26 2022
plant vines upon the *m* of Samaria ... Jer 31:5 2022
Judah, and in the cities of the *m* ... Jer 32:44 2022
In the cities of the *m*, in the ... Jer 33:13 2022
Surely as Tabor is among the *m* ... Jer 46:18 2022
have turned them away on the *m* ... Jer 50:6 2022
they pursued us upon the *m* ... Lam 4:19 2022
thy face toward the *m* of Israel ... Eze 6:2 2022
Ye *m* of Israel, hear the word of ... Eze 6:3 2022
Thus saith the Lord GOD to the *m* ... Eze 6:3 2022
hill, in all the tops of the *m* ... Eze 6:13 2022
not the sounding again of the *m* ... Eze 7:7 2022
shall be on the *m* like doves of ... Eze 7:16 2022
And hath not eaten upon the *m* ... Eze 18:6 2022
but even hath eaten upon the *m* ... Eze 18:11 2022
That hath not eaten upon the *m* ... Eze 18:15 2022
be heard upon the *m* of Israel ... Eze 19:9 2022
and in thee they eat upon the *m* ... Eze 22:9 2022
upon the *m* and in all the valleys ... Eze 31:12 2022
I will lay thy flesh upon the *m* ... Eze 32:5 2022
thou swimmest, even to the *m* ... Eze 32:6 2022
the *m* of Israel shall be desolate ... Eze 33:28 2022
sheep wandered through all the *m* ... Eze 34:6 2022
feed them upon the *m* of Israel by ... Eze 34:13 2022
upon the high *m* of Israel shall ... Eze 34:14 2022
they feed upon the *m* of Israel ... Eze 34:14 2022
I will fill his *m* with his slain ... Eze 35:8 2022
spoken against the *m* of Israel ... Eze 35:12 2022
prophesy unto the *m* of Israel ... Eze 36:1 2022
Ye *m* of Israel, hear the word of ... Eze 36:1 2022
ye *m* of Israel, hear the word of ... Eze 36:4 2022
Thus saith the Lord GOD to the *m* ... Eze 36:4 2022
land of Israel, and say unto the *m* ... Eze 36:6 2022
O *m* of Israel, ye shall shoot ... Eze 36:8 2022
in the land upon the *m* of Israel ... Eze 37:22 2022
people, against the *m* of Israel ... Eze 38:8 2022
the *m* shall be thrown down, and ... Eze 38:20 2022
against him throughout all my *m* ... Eze 38:21 2022
bring thee upon the *m* of Israel ... Eze 39:2 2022
shalt fall upon the *m* of Israel ... Eze 39:4 2022
sacrifice upon the *m* of Israel ... Eze 39:17 2022
sacrifice upon the tops of the *m* ... Hos 4:13 2022
and they shall say to the *m* ... Hos 10:8 2022
as the morning spread upon the *m* ... Joel 2:2 2022
on the tops of *m* shall they leap ... Joel 2:5 2022
that the *m* shall drop down new ... Joel 3:18 2022
yourselves upon the *m* of Samaria ... Amos 3:9 2022
For, lo, he that formeth the *m* ... Amos 4:13 2022
the *m* shall drop sweet wine, and ... Amos 9:13 2022
went down to the bottoms of the *m* ... Jonah 2:6 2022
the *m* shall be molten under him, ... Mic 1:4 2022
established in the top of the *m* ... Mic 4:1 2022
Arise, contend thou before the *m* ... Mic 6:1 2022
Hear ye, O *m*, the LORD's ... Mic 6:2 2022
The *m* quake at him, and the hills ... Nah 1:5 2022
Behold upon the *m* the feet of him ... Nah 1:15 2022
people is scattered upon the *m* ... Nah 3:18 2022
the everlasting *m* were scattered ... Hab 3:6 2042
The *m* saw thee, and they trembled ... Hab 3:10 2022
upon the land, and upon the *m* ... Hag 1:11 2022
chariots out from between two *m* ... Zec 6:1 2022
and the *m* were *m* of brass ... Zec 6:1 2022
shall flee to the valley of the *m* ... Zec 14:5 2022
of the *m* shall reach unto Azal ... Zec 14:5 2022
And I hated Esau, and laid his *m* ... Mal 1:3 2022
and nine, and goeth into the *m* ... Mt 18:12 *3735*
be in Judaea flee into the *m* ... Mt 24:16 *3735*
night and day, he was in the *m* ... Mk 5:5 *3735*
m a great herd of swine feeding ... Mk 5:11 *3735*
that be in Judaea flee to the *m* ... Mk 13:14 *3735*
which are in Judaea flee to the *m* ... Lk 21:21 *3735*
shall they begin to say to the *m* ... Lk 23:30 *3735*
faith, so that I could remove *m* ... 1Cor 13:2 *3735*
they wandered in deserts, and in *m* ... Heb 11:38 *3735*
the dens and in the rocks of the *m* ... Rev 6:15 *3735*
And said to the *m* and rocks, Fall ... Rev 6:16 *3735*
away, and the *m* were not found ... Rev 16:20 *3735*
The seven heads are seven *m* ... Rev 17:9 *3735*

MOUNTED {1}
m up from the earth in my sight ... Eze 10:19 7426

MOUNTING {1}
for by the *m* up of Luhith with ... Is 15:5 4608

MOUNTS {3}
Behold the *m*, they are come unto ... Jer 32:24 5550
which are thrown down by the *m* ... Jer 33:4 5550
him in the war, by casting up *m* ... Eze 17:17 5550

MOURN {45}
and Abraham came to *m* for Sarah ... Gen 23:2 5594
How long wilt thou *m* for Saul ... 1Sa 16:1 56
with sackcloth, and *m* before Abner ... 2Sa 3:31 5594
prophet came to the city, to *m* ... 1Kin 13:29 5594
And all Israel shall *m* for him ... 1Kin 14:13 5594
m not, nor weep ... Neh 8:9 56
together to come to *m* with him ... Job 2:11 5110
that those which *m* may be exalted ... Job 5:11 6937
and his soul within him shall *m* ... Job 14:22 56
I *m* in my complaint, and make a ... Ps 55:2 7300
thou *m* at the last, when thy ... Prov 5:11 5098
wicked beareth rule, the people *m* ... Prov 29:2 584
a time to *m*, and a time to dance ... Eccl 3:4 5594
And her gates shall lament and *m* ... Is 3:26 56
of Kir-hareseth shall ye *m* ... Is 16:7 1897
The fishers also shall *m*, and all ... Is 19:8 578
I did *m* as a dove ... Is 38:14 1897
like bears, and *m* sore like doves ... Is 59:11 1897
to comfort all that *m* ... Is 61:2 57
appoint unto them that *m* in Zion ... Is 61:3 57
with her, all ye that *m* for her ... Is 66:10 56
For this shall the earth *m* ... Jer 4:28 56
How long shall the land *m* ... Jer 12:4 56
mine heart shall *m* for the men of ... Jer 48:31 1897
The ways of Zion do *m*, because ... Lam 1:4 57
buyer rejoice, nor the seller *m* ... Eze 7:12 56
The king shall *m*, and the prince ... Eze 7:27 56
yet neither shalt thou *m* nor weep ... Eze 24:16 5594
ye shall not *m* nor weep ... Eze 24:23 5594
and *m* one toward another ... Eze 24:23 5098
and I caused Lebanon to *m* for him ... Eze 31:15 6937
Therefore shall the land *m* ... Hos 4:3 56
people thereof shall *m* over it ... Hos 10:5 56
priests, the LORD's ministers, *m* ... Joel 1:9 56
of the shepherds shall *m*, and the ... Amos 1:2 56
every one *m* that dwelleth therein ... Amos 8:8 56
and all that dwell therein shall *m* ... Amos 9:5 56
pierced, and they shall *m* for him ... Zec 12:10 5594
And the land shall *m*, every family ... Zec 12:12 5594
Blessed are they that *m* ... Mt 5:4 *3996*
children of the bridechamber *m* ... Mt 9:15 *3996*
all the tribes of the earth *m* ... Mt 24:30 *2875*
for ye shall *m* and weep ... Lk 6:25 *3996*
Be afflicted, and *m*, and weep ... Jas 4:9 *3996*
earth shall weep and *m* over her ... Rev 18:11 *3996*

MOURNED {22}
loins, and *m* for his son many days ... Gen 37:34 56
and the Egyptians *m* for him ... Gen 50:3 1058
there they *m* with a great and very ... Gen 50:10 5594
heard these evil tidings, they *m* ... Ex 33:4 56
and the people *m* greatly ... Num 14:39 56
they *m* for Aaron thirty days, ... Num 20:29 1058
nevertheless Samuel *m* for Saul ... 1Sa 15:35 56
And they *m*, and wept, and fasted ... 2Sa 1:12 5594
was dead, she *m* for her husband ... 2Sa 11:26 5594
David *m* for his son every day ... 2Sa 13:37 56
had a long time *m* for the dead ... 2Sa 14:2 56
they *m* over him, saying, Alas, my ... 1Kin 13:30 5594
and all Israel *m* for him, ... 1Kin 14:18 5594
Ephraim their father *m* many days ... 1Chr 7:22 56
Judah and Jerusalem *m* for Josiah ... 2Chr 35:24 56
for he *m* because of the ... Ezr 10:6 56
m certain days, and fasted, and ... Neh 1:4 56
m in the fifth and seventh month, ... Zec 7:5 5594
we have *m* unto you, and ye have ... Mt 11:17 *2354*
that had been with him, as they *m* ... Mk 16:10 *3996*
we have *m* to you, and ye have not ... Lk 7:32 *2354*
puffed up, and have not rather *m* ... 1Cor 5:2 *3996*

MOURNER {1}
thee, feign thyself to be a *m* ... 2Sa 14:2 56

MOURNERS {4}
as one that comforteth the *m* ... Job 29:25 57
the *m* go about the streets ... Eccl 12:5 5594
comforts unto him and to his *m* ... Is 57:18 57
be unto them as the bread of *m* ... Hos 9:4 205

MOURNETH {11}
the king weepeth and *m* for Absalom ... 2Sa 19:1 56
as one that *m* for his mother ... Ps 35:14 57
Mine eye *m* by reason of ... Ps 88:9 1669
The earth *m* and fadeth away, the ... Is 24:4 56
The new wine *m*, the vine ... Is 24:7 56
The earth *m* and languisheth ... Is 33:9 56
and being desolate it *m* unto me ... Jer 12:11 56
Judah *m*, and the gates thereof ... Jer 14:2 56
because of swearing the land *m* ... Jer 23:10 56
The field is wasted, the land *m* ... Joel 1:10 56
as one *m* for his only son, and ... Zec 12:10 5594

MOURNFULLY {1}
that we have walked *m* before the ... Mal 3:14 6941

MOURNING {51}
The days of *m* for my father are ... Gen 27:41 60
down into the grave unto my son *m* ... Gen 37:35 57
when the days of his *m* were past ... Gen 50:4 1086
he made a *m* for his father seven ... Gen 50:10 60
saw the *m* in the floor of Atad, ... Gen 50:11 60
is a grievous *m* to the Egyptians ... Gen 50:11 60
I have not eaten thereof in my *m* ... Deut 26:14 205
weeping and *m* for Moses were ended ... Deut 34:8 60
And when the *m* was past, David ... 2Sa 11:27 60
mourner, and put on now *m* apparel ... 2Sa 14:2 60
turned into *m* unto all the people ... 2Sa 19:2 60
there was great *m* among the Jews ... Est 4:3 60
But Haman hasted to his house *m* ... Est 6:12 57
to joy, and from *m* into a good day ... Est 9:22 60
who are ready to raise up their *m* ... Job 3:8 3382

I went *m* without the sun	Job 30:28	6937
My harp also is turned to *m*	Job 30:31	60
turned for me my *m* into dancing	Ps 30:11	4553
I go *m* all the day long	Ps 38:6	6937
why go I *m* because of the	Ps 42:9	6937
Why go I *m* because of the	Ps 43:2	6937
is better to go to the house of *m*	Eccl 7:2	60
of the wise is in the house of *m*	Eccl 7:4	60
of hosts call to weeping, and to *m*	Is 22:12	4553
and sorrow and *m* shall flee away	Is 51:11	585
the days of thy *m* shall be ended	Is 60:20	60
for ashes, the oil of joy for *m*	Is 61:3	60
make thee *m*, as for an only son,	Jer 6:26	60
ye, and call for the *m* women	Jer 9:17	6969
Enter not into the house of *m*	Jer 16:5	4798
men tear themselves for them in *m*	Jer 16:7	60
for I will turn their *m* into joy	Jer 31:13	60
in the daughter of Judah *m*	Lam 2:5	8386
our dance is turned into *m*	Lam 5:15	60
therein lamentations, and *m*	Eze 2:10	1899
of the valleys, all of them *m*	Eze 7:16	1993
make no *m* for the dead, bind the	Eze 24:17	60
down to the grave I caused a *m*	Eze 31:15	56
I Daniel was *m* three full weeks	Dan 10:2	56
and with weeping, and with *m*	Joel 2:12	4553
shall call the husbandman to *m*	Amos 5:16	60
And I will turn your feasts into *m*	Amos 8:10	60
make it as the *m* of an only son	Amos 8:10	60
the dragons, and *m* as the owls	Mic 1:8	60
not forth in the *m* of Beth-ezel	Mic 1:11	4553
there be a great *m* in Jerusalem	Zec 12:11	4553
as the *m* of Hadadrimmon in the	Zec 12:11	4553
and weeping, and great *m*, Rachel	Mt 2:18	*3602*
us your earnest desire, your *m*	2Cor 7:7	*3602*
let your laughter be turned to *m*	Jas 4:9	*3997*
come in one day, death, and *m*	Rev 18:8	*3997*

MOUSE {2}

the weasel, and the *m*, and the	Lev 11:29	5909
and the abomination, and the *m*	Is 66:17	5909

MOUTH {428}

which hath opened her *m* to	Gen 4:11	6310
in her *m* was an olive leaf pluckt	Gen 8:11	6310
the damsel, and enquire at her *m*	Gen 24:57	6310
great stone was upon the well's *m*	Gen 29:2	6310
the stone from the well's *m*	Gen 29:3	6310
upon the well's *m* in his place	Gen 29:3	6310
roll the stone from the well's *m*	Gen 29:8	6310
the stone from the well's *m*	Gen 29:10	6310
behold, it was in his sack's *m*	Gen 42:27	6310
again in the *m* of your sacks	Gen 43:12	6310
money was in the *m* of his sack	Gen 43:21	6310
every man's money in his sack's *m*	Gen 44:1	6310
in the sack's *m* of the youngest,	Gen 44:2	6310
that it is my *m* that speaketh	Gen 45:12	6310
unto him, Who hath made man's *m*	Ex 4:11	6310
go, and I will be with thy *m*	Ex 4:12	6310
unto him, and put words in his *m*	Ex 4:15	6310
be with thy *m*, and with his *m*	Ex 4:15	6310
shall be to thee instead of a *m*	Ex 4:16	6310
the LORD's law may be in thy *m*	Ex 13:9	6310
let it be heard out of thy *m*	Ex 23:13	6310
With him will I speak *m* to *m*	Num 12:8	6310
With him will I speak *m* to *m*	Num 12:8	6310
thing, and the earth open her *m*	Num 16:30	6310
And the earth opened her *m*	Num 16:32	6310
the LORD opened the *m* of the ass	Num 22:28	6310
the word that God putteth in my *m*	Num 22:38	6310
the LORD put a word in Balaam's *m*	Num 23:5	6310
which the LORD hath put in my *m*	Num 23:12	6310
Balaam, and put a word in his *m*	Num 23:16	6310
And the earth opened her *m*	Num 26:10	6310
all that proceedeth out of his *m*	Num 30:2	6310
hath proceeded out of your *m*	Num 32:24	6310
to death by the *m* of witnesses	Num 35:30	6310
the *m* of the LORD doth man live	Deut 8:3	6310
how the earth opened her *m*	Deut 11:6	6310
At the *m* of two witnesses, or	Deut 17:6	6310
but at the *m* of one witness he	Deut 17:6	6310
and will put my words in his *m*	Deut 18:18	6310
at the *m* of two witnesses	Deut 19:15	6310
or at the *m* of three witnesses,	Deut 19:15	6310
thou hast promised with thy *m*	Deut 23:23	6310
is very nigh unto thee, in thy *m*	Deut 30:14	6310
hear, O earth, the words of my *m*	Deut 32:1	6310
law shall not depart out of thy *m*	Josh 1:8	6310
any word proceed out of your *m*	Josh 6:10	6310
not counsel at the *m* of the LORD	Josh 9:14	6310
stones upon the *m* of the cave	Josh 10:18	6310
Open the *m* of the cave, and bring	Josh 10:22	6310
laid great stones in the cave's *m*	Josh 10:27	6310
putting their hand to their *m*	Judg 7:6	6310
unto him, Where is now thy *m*	Judg 9:38	6310
I have opened my *m* unto the LORD	Judg 11:35	6310
hast opened thy *m* unto the LORD	Judg 11:36	6310
which hath proceeded out of thy *m*	Judg 11:36	6310
peace, lay thine hand upon thy *m*	Judg 18:19	6310
the LORD, that Eli marked her *m*	1Sa 1:12	6310
my *m* is enlarged over mine	1Sa 2:1	6310
not arrogancy come out of your *m*	1Sa 2:3	6310
but no man put his hand to his *m*	1Sa 14:26	6310
and put his hand to his *m*	1Sa 14:27	6310
him, and delivered it out of his *m*	1Sa 17:35	6310
for thy *m* hath testified against	2Sa 1:16	6310
So Joab put the words in her *m*	2Sa 14:3	6310
words in the *m* of thine handmaid	2Sa 14:19	6310
a covering over the well's *m*	2Sa 17:19	6310
alone, there is tidings in his *m*	2Sa 18:25	6310
and fire out of his *m* devoured	2Sa 22:9	6310
the *m* of it within the chapiter	1Kin 7:31	6310
but the *m* thereof was round after	1Kin 7:31	6310
also upon the *m* of it were	1Kin 7:31	6310
with his *m* unto David my father	1Kin 8:15	6310
thou spakest also with thy *m*	1Kin 8:24	6310
hast disobeyed the *m* of the LORD	1Kin 13:21	6310
of the LORD in thy *m* is truth	1Kin 17:24	6310
every *m* which hath not kissed him	1Kin 19:18	6310
good unto the king with one *m*	1Kin 22:13	6310
in the *m* of all his prophets	1Kin 22:22	6310
the *m* of all these thy prophets	1Kin 22:23	6310
and put his *m* upon his *m*	2Kin 4:34	6310
and the judgments of his *m*	1Chr 16:12	6310
with his *m* to my father David	2Chr 6:4	6310
and spakest with thy *m*, and hast	2Chr 6:15	6310
in the *m* of all his prophets	2Chr 18:21	6310
in the *m* of these thy prophets	2Chr 18:22	6310
words of Necho from the *m* of God	2Chr 35:22	6310
speaking from the *m* of the LORD	2Chr 36:12	6310
of the LORD by the *m* of Jeremiah	2Chr 36:21	6310
by the *m* of Jeremiah might be	2Chr 36:22	6310
the word of the LORD by the *m* of	Ezr 1:1	6310
not thy manna from their *m*	Neh 9:20	6310
the word went out of the king's *m*	Est 7:8	6310
After this opened Job his *m*	Job 3:1	6310
poor from the sword, from their *m*	Job 5:15	6310
hope, and iniquity stoppeth her *m*	Job 5:16	6310
Therefore I will not refrain my *m*	Job 7:11	6310
of thy *m* be like a strong wind	Job 8:2	6310
Till he fill thy *m* with laughing	Job 8:21	6310
mine own *m* shall condemn me	Job 9:20	6310
and the *m* taste his meat	Job 12:11	2441
For thy *m* uttereth thine iniquity	Job 15:5	6310
Thine own *m* condemneth thee, and	Job 15:6	6310
such words go out of thy *m*	Job 15:13	6310
breath of his *m* shall he go away	Job 15:30	6310
I would strengthen you with my *m*	Job 16:5	6310
have gaped upon me with their *m*	Job 16:10	6310
I intreated him with my *m*	Job 19:16	6310
wickedness be sweet in his *m*	Job 20:12	6310
but keep it still within his *m*	Job 20:13	2441
and lay your hand upon your *m*	Job 21:5	6310
I pray thee, the law from his *m*	Job 22:22	6310
him, and fill my *m* with arguments	Job 23:4	6310
his *m* more than my necessary food	Job 23:12	6310
and laid their hand on their *m*	Job 29:9	6310
cleaved to the roof of their *m*	Job 29:10	2441
they opened their *m* wide as for	Job 29:23	6310
or my *m* hath kissed my hand	Job 31:27	6310
(Neither have I suffered my *m* to	Job 31:30	2441
in the *m* of these three men	Job 32:5	6310
Behold, now I have opened my *m*	Job 33:2	6310
my tongue hath spoken in my *m*	Job 33:2	2441
words, as the *m* tasteth meat	Job 34:3	2441
doth Job open his *m* in vain	Job 35:16	6310
the sound that goeth out of his *m*	Job 37:2	6310
I will lay mine hand upon my *m*	Job 40:4	6310
he can draw up Jordan into his *m*	Job 40:23	6310
Out of his *m* go burning lamps, and	Job 41:19	6310
and a flame goeth out of his *m*	Job 41:21	6310
is no faithfulness in their *m*	Ps 5:9	6310
Out of the *m* of babes and	Ps 8:2	6310
His *m* is full of cursing and	Ps 10:7	6310
that my *m* shall not transgress	Ps 17:3	6310
with their *m* they speak proudly	Ps 17:10	6310
and fire out of his *m* devoured	Ps 18:8	6310
Let the words of my *m*, and the	Ps 19:14	6310
Save me from the lion's *m*	Ps 22:21	6310
whose *m* must be held in with bit	Ps 32:9	5716
of them by the breath of his *m*	Ps 33:6	6310
shall continually be in my *m*	Ps 34:1	6310
opened their *m* wide against me	Ps 35:21	6310
The words of his *m* are iniquity	Ps 36:3	6310
The *m* of the righteous speaketh	Ps 37:30	6310
a dumb man that openeth not his *m*	Ps 38:13	6310
in whose *m* are no reproofs	Ps 38:14	6310
I will keep my *m* with a bridle	Ps 39:1	6310
I was dumb, I opened not my *m*	Ps 39:9	6310
And he hath put a new song in my *m*	Ps 40:3	6310
My *m* shall speak of wisdom	Ps 49:3	6310
take my covenant in thy *m*	Ps 50:16	6310
Thou givest thy *m* to evil	Ps 50:19	6310
my *m* shall shew forth thy praise	Ps 51:15	6310
give ear to the words of my *m*	Ps 54:2	6310
The words of his *m* were smoother	Ps 55:21	6310
their teeth, O God, in their *m*	Ps 58:6	6310
they belch out with their *m*	Ps 59:7	6310
For the sin of their *m* and the	Ps 59:12	6310
they bless with their *m*, but they	Ps 62:4	6310
my *m* shall praise thee with	Ps 63:5	6310
but the *m* of them that speak lies	Ps 63:11	6310
my *m* hath spoken, when I was in	Ps 66:14	6310
I cried unto him with my *m*	Ps 66:17	6310
not the pit shut her *m* upon me	Ps 69:15	6310
Let my *m* be filled with thy	Ps 71:8	6310
My *m* shall shew forth thy	Ps 71:15	6310
They set their *m* against the	Ps 73:9	6310
your ears to the words of my *m*	Ps 78:1	6310
I will open my *m* in a parable	Ps 78:2	6310
they did flatter him with their *m*	Ps 78:36	6310
open thy *m* wide, and I will fill	Ps 81:10	6310
with my *m* will I make known thy	Ps 89:1	6310
satisfieth thy *m* with good things	Ps 103:5	5716
and the judgments of his *m*	Ps 105:5	6310
and all iniquity shall stop her *m*	Ps 107:42	6310
For the *m* of the wicked and the	Ps 109:2	6310
the *m* of the deceitful are opened	Ps 109:2	6310
greatly praise the LORD with my *m*	Ps 109:30	6310
all the judgments of thy *m*	Ps 119:13	6310
word of truth utterly out of my *m*	Ps 119:43	6310
The law of thy *m* is better unto	Ps 119:72	6310
I keep the testimony of thy *m*	Ps 119:88	6310
yea, sweeter than honey to my *m*	Ps 119:103	6310
the freewill offerings of my *m*	Ps 119:108	6310
I opened my *m*, and panted	Ps 119:131	6310
Then was our *m* filled with	Ps 126:2	6310
tongue cleave to the roof of my *m*	Ps 137:6	2441
when they hear the words of thy *m*	Ps 138:4	6310
Set a watch, O LORD, before my *m*	Ps 141:3	6310
are scattered at the grave's *m*	Ps 141:7	6310
Whose *m* speaketh vanity, and their	Ps 144:8	6310
whose *m* speaketh vanity, and their	Ps 144:11	6310
My *m* shall speak the praise of	Ps 145:21	6310
high praises of God be in their *m*	Ps 149:6	1627
out of his *m* cometh knowledge and	Prov 2:6	6310
decline from the words of my *m*	Prov 4:5	6310
Put away from thee a froward *m*	Prov 4:24	6310
her *m* is smoother than oil	Prov 5:3	2441
depart not from the words of my *m*	Prov 5:7	6310
snared with the words of thy *m*	Prov 6:2	6310
art taken with the words of thy *m*	Prov 6:2	6310
man, walketh with a froward *m*	Prov 6:12	6310
and attend to the words of my *m*	Prov 7:24	6310
For my *m* shall speak truth	Prov 8:7	2441
All the words of my *m* are in	Prov 8:8	6310
and the evil way, and the froward *m*	Prov 8:13	6310
covereth the *m* of the wicked	Prov 10:6	6310
The *m* of a righteous man is a	Prov 10:11	6310
covereth the *m* of the wicked	Prov 10:11	6310
but the *m* of the foolish is near	Prov 10:14	6310
The *m* of the just bringeth forth	Prov 10:31	6310
but the *m* of the wicked speaketh	Prov 10:32	6310
An hypocrite with his *m*	Prov 11:9	6310
overthrown by the *m* of the wicked	Prov 11:11	6310
but the *m* of the upright shall	Prov 12:6	6310
with good by the fruit of his *m*	Prov 12:14	6310
eat good by the fruit of his *m*	Prov 13:2	6310
keepeth his *m* keepeth his life	Prov 13:3	6310
In the *m* of the foolish is a rod	Prov 14:3	6310
but the *m* of fools poureth out	Prov 15:2	6310
but the *m* of fools feedeth on	Prov 15:14	6310
hath joy by the answer of his *m*	Prov 15:23	6310
but the *m* of the wicked poureth	Prov 15:28	6310
his *m* transgresseth not in	Prov 16:10	6310
heart of the wise teacheth his *m*	Prov 16:23	6310
for his *m* craveth it of him	Prov 16:26	6310
of a man's *m* are as deep waters	Prov 18:4	6310
his *m* calleth for strokes	Prov 18:6	6310
A fool's *m* is his destruction, and	Prov 18:7	6310
satisfied with the fruit of his *m*	Prov 18:20	6310
much as bring it to his *m* again	Prov 19:24	6310
the *m* of the wicked devoureth	Prov 19:28	6310
but afterwards his *m* shall be	Prov 20:17	6310
Whoso keepeth his *m* and his tongue	Prov 21:23	6310
The *m* of strange women is a deep	Prov 22:14	6310
he openeth not his *m* in the gate	Prov 24:7	6310
so is a parable in the *m* of fools	Prov 26:7	6310
so is a parable in the *m* of fools	Prov 26:9	6310
him to bring it again to his *m*	Prov 26:15	6310
and a flattering *m* worketh ruin	Prov 26:28	6310
praise thee, and not thine own *m*	Prov 27:2	6310
she eateth, and wipeth her *m*	Prov 30:20	6310
evil, lay thine hand upon thy *m*	Prov 30:32	6310
Open thy *m* for the dumb in the	Prov 31:8	6310
Open thy *m*, judge righteously, and	Prov 31:9	6310
She openeth her *m* with wisdom	Prov 31:26	6310
Be not rash with thy *m*, and let	Eccl 5:2	6310
Suffer not thy *m* to cause thy	Eccl 5:6	6310
the labour of man is for his *m*	Eccl 6:7	6310
of a wise man's *m* are gracious	Eccl 10:12	6310
the words of his *m* is foolishness	Eccl 10:13	6310
kiss me with the kisses of his *m*	Song 1:2	6310
His *m* is most sweet	Song 5:16	2441
the roof of thy *m* like the best	Song 7:9	2441
for the *m* of the LORD hath spoken	Is 1:20	6310
opened her *m* without measure	Is 5:14	6310
And he laid it upon my *m*, and said,	Is 6:7	6310
shall devour Israel with open *m*	Is 9:12	6310
and every *m* speaketh folly	Is 9:17	6310
moved the wing, or opened the *m*	Is 10:14	6310
the earth with the rod of his *m*	Is 11:4	6310
by the *m* of the brooks, and every	Is 19:7	6310
people draw near me with their *m*	Is 29:13	6310
Egypt, and have not asked at my *m*	Is 30:2	6310
for my *m* it hath commanded, and	Is 34:16	6310
for the *m* of the LORD hath spoken	Is 40:5	6310
gone out of my *m* in righteousness	Is 45:23	6310
and they went forth out of my *m*	Is 48:3	6310
he hath made my *m* like a sharp	Is 49:2	6310
And I have put my words in thy *m*	Is 51:16	6310
yet he opened not his *m*	Is 53:7	6310
is dumb, so he openeth not his *m*	Is 53:7	6310
neither was any deceit in his *m*	Is 53:9	6310
be that goeth forth out of my *m*	Is 55:11	6310
against whom make ye a wide *m*	Is 57:4	6310
for the *m* of the LORD hath spoken	Is 58:14	6310
words which I have put in thy *m*	Is 59:21	6310
shall not depart out of thy *m*	Is 59:21	6310
nor out of the *m* of thy seed	Is 59:21	6310
nor out of the *m* of thy seed's	Is 59:21	6310
which the *m* of the LORD shall	Is 62:2	6310
forth his hand, and touched my *m*	Jer 1:9	6310
I have put my words in thy *m*	Jer 1:9	6310
will make my words in thy *m* fire	Jer 5:14	6310
and is cut off from their *m*	Jer 7:28	6310

M

to his neighbour with his *m* ... Jer 9:8 6310
who is he to whom the *m* of the ... Jer 9:12 6310
ear receive the word of his *m* ... Jer 9:20 6310
thou art near in their *m*, and far ... Jer 12:2 6310
the vile, thou shalt be as my *m* ... Jer 15:19 6310
and not out of the *m* of the LORD ... Jer 23:16 6310
shall speak with him *m* to *m* ... Jer 32:4 6310
shall speak with thee *m* to *m* ... Jer 34:3 6310
Baruch wrote from the *m* of ... Jer 36:4 6310
which thou hast written from my *m* ... Jer 36:6 6310
write all these words at his *m* ... Jer 36:17 6310
these words unto me with his *m* ... Jer 36:18 6310
Baruch wrote at the *m* of Jeremiah ... Jer 36:27 6310
who wrote therein from the *m* of ... Jer 36:32 6310
goeth forth out of our own *m* ... Jer 44:17 6310
shall no more be named in the *m* ... Jer 44:26 6310
in a book at the *m* of Jeremiah ... Jer 45:1 6310
nest in the sides of the hole's *m* ... Jer 48:28 6310
I will bring forth out of his *m* ... Jer 51:44 6310
have opened their *m* against thee ... Lam 2:16 6310
He putteth his *m* in the dust ... Lam 3:29 6310
Out of the *m* of the most High ... Lam 3:38 6310
to the roof of his *m* for thirst ... Lam 4:4 2441
open thy *m*, and eat that I give ... Eze 2:8 6310
So I opened my *m*, and he caused me ... Eze 3:2 6310
it was in my *m* as honey for ... Eze 3:3 6310
therefore hear the word at my *m* ... Eze 3:17 6310
cleave to the roof of thy *m* ... Eze 3:26 2441
with thee, I will open thy *m* ... Eze 3:27 6310
there abominable flesh into my *m* ... Eze 4:14 6310
by thy *m* in the day of thy pride ... Eze 16:56 6310
never open thy *m* any more because ... Eze 16:63 6310
to open the *m* in the slaughter, ... Eze 21:22 6310
In that day shall thy *m* be opened ... Eze 24:27 6310
of the *m* in the midst of them ... Eze 29:21 6310
thou shalt hear the word at my *m* ... Eze 33:7 6310
and had opened my *m*, until he came ... Eze 33:22 6310
my *m* was opened, and I was no more ... Eze 33:22 6310
for with their *m* they shew much ... Eze 33:31 6310
deliver my flock from their *m* ... Eze 34:10 6310
Thus with your *m* ye have boasted ... Eze 35:13 6310
m of the burning fiery furnace ... Dan 3:26 8651
the word was in the king's *m* ... Dan 4:31 6433
and laid upon the *m* of the den ... Dan 6:17 6433
it had three ribs in the *m* of it ... Dan 7:5 6433
a *m* speaking great things ... Dan 7:8 6433
a *m* that spake very great things, ... Dan 7:20 6433
came flesh nor wine in my *m* ... Dan 10:3 6310
then I opened my *m*, and spake, and ... Dan 10:16 6310
the names of Baalim out of her *m* ... Hos 2:17 6310
slain them by the words of my *m* ... Hos 6:5 6310
Set the trumpet to thy *m* ... Hos 8:1 2441
for it is cut off from your *m* ... Joel 1:5 6310
out of the *m* of the lion two legs ... Amos 3:12 6310
for the *m* of the LORD of hosts ... Mic 4:4 6310
tongue is deceitful in their *m* ... Mic 6:12 6310
keep the doors of thy *m* from her ... Mic 7:5 6310
shall lay their hand upon their *m* ... Mic 7:16 6310
even fall into the *m* of the eater ... Nah 3:12 6310
tongue be found in their *m* ... Zeph 3:13 6310
weight of lead upon the *m* thereof ... Zec 5:8 6310
words by the *m* of the prophets ... Zec 8:9 6310
take away his blood out of his *m* ... Zec 9:7 6310
shall consume away in their *m* ... Zec 14:12 6310
The law of truth was in his *m* ... Mal 2:6 6310
they should seek the law at his *m* ... Mal 2:7 6310
proceedeth out of the *m* of God ... Mt 4:4 *4750*
And he opened his *m*, and taught ... Mt 5:2 *4750*
of the heart the *m* speaketh ... Mt 12:34 *4750*
I will open my *m* in parables ... Mt 13:35 *4750*
draweth nigh unto me with their *m* ... Mt 15:8 *4750*
goeth into the *m* defileth a man ... Mt 15:11 *4750*
that which cometh out of the *m* ... Mt 15:11 *4750*
in at the *m* goeth into the belly ... Mt 15:17 *4750*
the *m* come forth from the heart ... Mt 15:18 *4750*
and when thou hast opened his *m* ... Mt 17:27 *4750*
that in the *m* of two or three ... Mt 18:16 *4750*
never read, Out of the *m* of babes ... Mt 21:16 *4750*
his *m* was opened immediately, and ... Lk 1:64 *4750*
As he spake by the *m* of his holy ... Lk 1:70 *4750*
which proceeded out of his *m* ... Lk 4:22 *4750*
of the heart his *m* speaketh ... Lk 6:45 *4750*
to catch something out of his *m* ... Lk 11:54 *4750*
Out of thine own *m* will I judge ... Lk 19:22 *4750*
For I will give you a *m* and wisdom ... Lk 21:15 *4750*
ourselves have heard of his own *m* ... Lk 22:71 *4750*
upon hyssop, and put it to his *m* ... Jn 19:29 *4750*
by the *m* of David spake before ... Acts 1:16 *4750*
by the *m* of all his prophets ... Acts 3:18 *4750*
which God hath spoken by the *m* of ... Acts 3:21 *4750*
Who by the *m* of thy servant David ... Acts 4:25 *4750*
shearer, so opened he not his *m* ... Acts 8:32 *4750*
Then Philip opened his *m*, and ... Acts 8:35 *4750*
Then Peter opened his *m*, and said, ... Acts 10:34 *4750*
at any time entered into my *m* ... Acts 11:8 *4750*
that the Gentiles by my *m* should ... Acts 15:7 *4750*
tell you the same things by *m* ... Acts 15:27 *3056*
Paul was now about to open his *m* ... Acts 18:14 *4750*
shouldest hear the voice of his *m* ... Acts 22:14 *4750*
by him to smite him on the *m* ... Acts 23:2 *4750*
Whose *m* is full of cursing and ... Rom 3:14 *4750*
that every *m* may be stopped, and ... Rom 3:19 *4750*
word is nigh thee, even in thy *m* ... Rom 10:8 *4750*
confess with thy *m* the Lord Jesus ... Rom 10:9 *4750*
with the *m* confession is made ... Rom 10:10 *4750*
one *m* glorify God, even the ... Rom 15:6 *4750*
Thou shalt not muzzle the *m* of ... 1Cor 9:9
our *m* is open unto you, our heart ... 2Cor 6:11 *4750*
In the *m* of two or three ... 2Cor 13:1 *4750*
proceed out of your *m*, but that ... Eph 4:29 *4750*
me, that I may open my *m* boldly ... Eph 6:19 *4750*
communication out of your *m* ... Col 3:8 *4750*
consume with the spirit of his *m* ... 2Th 2:8 *4750*
out of the *m* of the lion ... 2Ti 4:17 *4750*
Out of the same *m* proceedeth ... Jas 3:10 *4750*
neither was guile found in his *m* ... 1Pet 2:22 *4750*
their *m* speaketh great swelling ... Jude 16 *4750*
out of his *m* went a sharp ... Rev 1:16 *4750*
them with the sword of my *m* ... Rev 2:16 *4750*
hot, I will spue thee out of my *m* ... Rev 3:16 *4750*
For their power is in their *m* ... Rev 9:19 *4750*
shall be in thy *m* sweet as honey ... Rev 10:9 *4750*
it was in my *m* sweet as honey ... Rev 10:10 *4750*
fire proceedeth out of their *m* ... Rev 11:5 *4750*
his *m* water as a flood after the ... Rev 12:15 *4750*
woman, and the earth opened her *m* ... Rev 12:16 *4750*
the dragon cast out of his *m* ... Rev 12:16 *4750*
his *m* as the *m* of a lion ... Rev 13:2 *4750*
and his *m* as the *m* of a lion ... Rev 13:2 *4750*
him a *m* speaking great things ... Rev 13:5 *4750*
he opened his *m* in blasphemy ... Rev 13:6 *4750*
in their *m* was found no guile ... Rev 14:5 *4750*
come out of the *m* of the dragon ... Rev 16:13 *4750*
out of the *m* of the beast ... Rev 16:13 *4750*
out of the *m* of the false prophet ... Rev 16:13 *4750*
out of his *m* goeth a sharp sword, ... Rev 19:15 *4750*
sword proceeded out of his *m* ... Rev 19:21 *4750*

MOUTHS {18}
which we found in our sacks' *m* ... Gen 44:8 6310
put it in their *m*, that this song ... Deut 31:19 6310
out of the *m* of their seed ... Deut 31:21 6310
They gaped upon me with their *m* ... Ps 22:13 6310
their meat was yet in their *m* ... Ps 78:30 6310
They have *m*, but they speak not ... Ps 115:5 6310
They have *m*, but they speak not ... Ps 135:16 6310
is there any breath in their *m* ... Ps 135:17 6310
kings shall shut their *m* at him ... Is 52:15 6310
have both spoken with your *m* ... Jer 44:25 6310
have opened their *m* against us ... Lam 3:46 6310
angel, and hath shut the lions' *m* ... Dan 6:22 6433
he that putteth not into their *m* ... Mic 3:5 6310
Whose *m* must be stopped, who ... Titus 1:11 *1993*
promises, stopped the *m* of lions ... Heb 11:33 *4750*
we put bits in the horses' *m* ... Jas 3:3 *4750*
and out of their *m* issued fire ... Rev 9:17 *4750*
which issued out of their *m* ... Rev 9:18 *4750*

MOVE {13}
shall not a dog *m* his tongue ... Ex 11:7 2782
of all that *m* in the waters, and ... Lev 11:10 8318
but thou shalt not *m* a sickle ... Deut 23:25 5130
I will *m* them to jealousy with ... Deut 32:21
m him at times in the camp of Dan ... Judg 13:25 6470
place of their own, and *m* no more ... 2Sa 7:10 7264
m any more out of the land which ... 2Kin 21:8 5110
let no man *m* his bones ... 2Kin 23:18 5128
and with hammers, that it *m* not ... Jer 10:4 6328
they shall *m* out of their holes ... Mic 7:17 7264
but they themselves will not *m* ... Mt 23:4 *2795*
For in him we live, and *m*, and have ... Acts 17:28 *2795*
But none of these things *m* me ... Acts 20:24 *3056,4160*

MOVEABLE {1}
the path of life, her ways are *m* ... Prov 5:6 5128

MOVED {75}
the Spirit of God *m* upon the face ... Gen 1:2 7363
flesh died that *m* upon the earth ... Gen 7:21 7430
They have *m* me to jealousy with ... Deut 32:21
none *m* his tongue against any of ... Josh 10:21 2782
that she *m* him to ask of her ... Josh 15:18 5496
that she *m* him to ask of her ... Judg 1:14 5496
all the city was *m* about them ... Ruth 1:19 1949
only her lips *m*, but her voice ... 1Sa 1:13 5128
And the king was much *m*, and went ... 2Sa 18:33 7264
the foundations of heaven *m* ... 2Sa 22:8 7264
he *m* David against them to say, ... 2Sa 24:1 5496
shall be stable, that it be not *m* ... 1Chr 16:30 4131
place, and shall be *m* no more ... 1Chr 17:9 7264
God *m* them to depart from him ... 2Chr 18:31 5496
that they have *m* sedition within ... Ezr 4:15 5648
nor *m* for him, he was full of ... Est 5:9 2111
and is *m* out of his place ... Job 37:1 5425
they cannot be *m* ... Job 41:23 4131
in his heart, I shall not be *m* ... Ps 10:6 4131
trouble me rejoice when I am *m* ... Ps 13:4 4131
these things shall never be *m* ... Ps 15:5 4131
my right hand, I shall not be *m* ... Ps 16:8 4131
foundations also of the hills *m* ... Ps 18:7 7264
the most High he shall not be *m* ... Ps 21:7 4131
I said, I shall never be *m* ... Ps 30:6 4131
she shall not be *m* ... Ps 46:5 4131
raged, the kingdoms were *m* ... Ps 46:6 4131
suffer the righteous to be *m* ... Ps 55:22 4131
I shall not be greatly *m* ... Ps 62:2 4131
I shall not be *m* ... Ps 62:6 4131
and suffereth not our feet to be *m* ... Ps 66:9 4132
even Sinai itself was *m* at the ... Ps 68:8
m him to jealousy with their ... Ps 78:58
stablished, that it cannot be *m* ... Ps 93:1 4131
that it shall not be *m* ... Ps 96:10 4131
let the earth be *m* ... Ps 99:1 5120
Surely he shall not be *m* for ever ... Ps 112:6 4131
will not suffer thy foot to be *m* ... Ps 121:3 4132
of the righteous shall not be *m* ... Prov 12:3 4131
door, and my bowels were *m* for him ... Song 5:4 1993
the posts of the door *m* at the ... Is 6:4 5128
And his heart was *m*, and the heart ... Is 7:2 5128
of the wood are *m* with the wind ... Is 7:2 5128
and there was none that *m* the wing ... Is 10:14 5074
Hell from beneath is *m* for thee ... Is 14:9 7264
Egypt shall be *m* at his presence ... Is 19:1 5128
the earth is *m* exceedingly ... Is 24:19 4132
graven image, that shall not be *m* ... Is 40:20 4131
nails, that it should not be *m* ... Is 41:7 4131
and all the hills *m* lightly ... Jer 4:24 7043
And they shall drink, and be *m* ... Jer 25:16 1607
whose waters are *m* as the rivers ... Jer 46:7 1607
his waters are *m* like the rivers ... Jer 46:8 1607
The earth is *m* at the noise of ... Jer 49:21 7493
taking of Babylon the earth is *m* ... Jer 50:46 7493
he was *m* with choler against him, ... Dan 8:7
the south shall be *m* with choler ... Dan 11:11
he was *m* with compassion on them, ... Mt 9:36 *4697*
was *m* with compassion toward them ... Mt 14:14 *4697*
servant was *m* with compassion ... Mt 18:27 *4697*
they were *m* with indignation ... Mt 20:24 *23*
Jerusalem, all the city was *m* ... Mt 21:10 *4579*
m with compassion, put forth his ... Mk 1:41 *4697*
was *m* with compassion toward them ... Mk 6:34 *4697*
the chief priests *m* the people ... Mk 15:11 *383*
hand, that I should not be *m* ... Acts 2:25 *4531*
m with envy, sold Joseph into ... Acts 7:9 *2206*
m with envy, took unto them ... Acts 17:5 *2206*
And all the city was *m*, and the ... Acts 21:30 *2795*
be not *m* away from the hope of ... Col 1:23 *3334*
should be *m* by these afflictions ... 1Th 3:3 *4525*
m with fear, prepared an ark to ... Heb 11:7 *2125*
a kingdom which cannot be *m* ... Heb 12:28 *761*
as they were *m* by the Holy Ghost ... 2Pet 1:21 *5342*
island were *m* out of their places ... Rev 6:14 *2795*

MOVEDST {1}
although thou *m* me against him, ... Job 2:3 5496

MOVER {1}
a *m* of sedition among all the ... Acts 24:5 *2795*

MOVETH {8}
and every living creature that *m* ... Gen 1:21 7430
thing that *m* upon the earth ... Gen 1:28 7430
upon all that *m* upon the earth, ... Gen 9:2 7430
creature that *m* in the waters ... Lev 11:46 7430
He *m* his tail like a cedar ... Job 40:17 2654
and every thing that *m* therein ... Ps 69:34 7430
the cup, when it *m* itself aright ... Prov 23:31 1980
every thing that liveth, which *m* ... Eze 47:9 8317

MOVING {5}
the *m* creature that hath life ... Gen 1:20 8318
Every *m* thing that liveth shall ... Gen 9:3 7430
the *m* of my lips should asswage ... Job 16:5 5205
m his lips he bringeth evil to ... Prov 16:30 7169
waiting for the *m* of the water ... Jn 5:3 *2796*

MOWER {1}
Wherewith the *m* filleth not his ... Ps 129:7 7114

MOWINGS {1}
latter growth after the king's *m* ... Amos 7:1 1488

MOWN {1}
down like rain upon the *m* grass ... Ps 72:6 1488

MOZA *(mo'-zah)* {5}
1. A son of Caleb.
concubine, bare Haran, and *M* ... 1Chr 2:46 4162
2. Descendant of King Saul.
and Zimri begat *M*, ... 1Chr 8:36 4162
And *M* begat Binea ... 1Chr 8:37 4162
and Zimri begat *M* ... 1Chr 9:42 4162
And *M* begat Binea ... 1Chr 9:43 4162

MOZAH *(mo'-zah)* {1} *A city in Benjamin.*
And Mizpeh, and Chephirah, and *M* ... Josh 18:26 4681

MUCH See APPENDIX.

MUFFLERS {1}
and the bracelets, and the *m* ... Is 3:19 7479

MULBERRY {4}
them over against the *m* trees ... 2Sa 5:23 1057
going in the tops of the *m* trees ... 2Sa 5:24 1057
them over against the *m* trees ... 1Chr 14:14 1057
going in the tops of the *m* trees ... 1Chr 14:15 1057

MULE {9}
every man gat him up upon his *m* ... 2Sa 13:29 6505
And Absalom rode upon a *m*, and the ... 2Sa 18:9 6505
the *m* went under the thick boughs ... 2Sa 18:9 6505
the *m* that was under him went ... 2Sa 18:9 6505
my son to ride upon mine own *m* ... 1Kin 1:33 6506
to ride upon king David's *m* ... 1Kin 1:38 6506
him to ride upon the king's *m* ... 1Kin 1:44 6506
ye not as the horse, or as the *m* ... Ps 32:9 6505
the plague of the horse, of the *m* ... Zec 14:15 6505

MULES {11}
found the *m* in the wilderness ... Gen 36:24 3222
armour, and spices, horses, and *m* ... 1Kin 10:25 6505
m alive, that we lose not all the ... 1Kin 18:5 6505
on asses, and on camels, and on *m* ... 1Chr 12:40 6505
harness, and spices, horses, and *m* ... 2Chr 9:24 6505
their *m*, two hundred forty and ... Ezr 2:66 6505
their *m*, two hundred forty and ... Neh 7:68 6505
on horseback, and riders on *m* ... Est 8:10 7409
So the posts that rode upon *m* ... Est 8:14 7409
and in litters, and upon *m* ... Is 66:20 6505
with horses and horsemen and *m* ... Eze 27:14 6505

MULES' {1}
thy servant two *m* burden of earth ... 2Kin 5:17 6505

MULTIPLIED {44}
and grew, and *m* exceedingly ..... Gen 47:27 7235
and increased abundantly, and *m* ..... Ex 1:7 7235
afflicted them, the more they *m* ..... Ex 1:12 7235
and the people *m*, and waxed very ..... Ex 1:20 7235
may be *m* in the land of Egypt ..... Ex 11:9 7235
The LORD your God hath *m* you ..... Deut 1:10 7235
and thy silver and thy gold is *m* ..... Deut 8:13 7235
and all that thou hast is *m* ..... Deut 8:13 7235
That your days may be *m*, and the ..... Deut 11:21 7235
m his seed, and gave him Isaac ..... Josh 24:3 7235
were *m* in the land of Gilead 1Chr 5:9 7235
If his children be *m*, it is for ..... Job 27:14 7235
or if thy transgressions be *m* ..... Job 35:6 7231
Their sorrows shall be *m* that ..... Ps 16:4 7235
that hate me wrongfully are *m* ..... Ps 38:19 7231
also, so that they are *m* greatly ..... Ps 107:38 7235
For by me thy days shall be *m* ..... Prov 9:11 7235
When the wicked are *m*, ... Prov 29:16 7235
Thou hast *m* the nation, and not ..... Is 9:3 7235
transgressions are *m* before thee ..... Is 59:12 7231
shall come to pass, when ye be *m* ..... Jer 3:16 7235
Because ye *m* more than the ..... Eze 5:7 1995
Ye have *m* your slain in this city ..... Eze 11:6 7235
passed by, and *m* thy whoredoms ..... Eze 16:25 7235
Thou hast moreover *m* thy ..... Eze 16:29 7235
but thou hast *m* thine ..... Eze 16:51 7235
may faint, and their ruins be *m* ..... Eze 21:15 7235
Yet she *m* her whoredoms, in ..... Eze 23:19 7235
the field, and his boughs were *m* ..... Eze 31:5 7235
have *m* your words against me ..... Eze 35:13 6280
Peace be *m* unto you ..... Dan 4:1 7680
Peace be *m* unto you ..... Dan 6:25 7680
m her silver and gold, which they ..... Hos 2:8 7235
Judah hath *m* fenced cities ..... Hos 8:14 7235
I have *m* visions, and used ..... Hos 12:10 7235
Thou hast *m* thy merchants above ..... Nah 3:16 7235
the number of the disciples was *m* ..... Acts 6:1 *4129*
disciples *m* in Jerusalem greatly ..... Acts 6:7 *4129*
the people grew and *m* in Egypt, ... Acts 7:17 *4129*
comfort of the Holy Ghost, were *m* ..... Acts 9:31 *4129*
But the word of God grew and *m* ..... Acts 12:24 *4129*
Grace unto you, and peace, be *m* 1Pet 1:2 *4129*
peace be *m* unto you through the 2Pet 1:2 *4129*
unto you, and peace, and love, be *m* ..... Jude 2 *4129*

MULTIPLIEDST {1}
Their children also *m* thou as the ..... Neh 9:23 7235

MULTIPLIETH {3}
m my wounds without cause ..... Job 9:17 7235
us, and *m* his words against God ..... Job 34:37 7235
he *m* words without knowledge ..... Job 35:16 3527

MULTIPLY {46}
them, saying, Be fruitful, and *m* ..... Gen 1:22 7235
seas, and let fowl *m* in the earth ..... Gen 1:22 7235
said unto them, Be fruitful, and *m* ..... Gen 1:28 7235
said, I will greatly *m* thy sorrow ..... Gen 3:16 7235
when men began to *m* on the face ..... Gen 6:1 7231
be fruitful, and *m* upon the earth ..... Gen 8:17 7235
said unto them, Be fruitful, and *m* ..... Gen 9:1 7235
And you, be ye fruitful, and *m* ..... Gen 9:7 7235
in the earth, and *m* therein ..... Gen 9:7 7235
I will *m* thy seed exceedingly, ... Gen 16:10 7235
thee, and will *m* thee exceedingly ..... Gen 17:2 7235
and will *m* him exceedingly ..... Gen 17:20 7235
in multiplying I will *m* thy seed ..... Gen 22:17 7235
seed to *m* as the stars of heaven ..... Gen 26:4 7235
m thy seed for my servant ..... Gen 26:24 7235
m thee, that thou mayest be a ..... Gen 28:3 7235
be fruitful and *m* ..... Gen 35:11 7235
m thee, and I will make of thee a ..... Gen 48:4 7235
lest they *m*, and it come to pass, ... Ex 1:10 7235
m my signs and my wonders in the ..... Ex 7:3 7235
beast of the field *m* against thee ..... Ex 23:29 7227
I will *m* your seed as the stars ..... Ex 32:13 7235
m you, and establish my covenant ..... Lev 26:9 7235
thee, and bless thee, and *m* thee ..... Deut 7:13 7235
to do, that ye may live, and *m* ..... Deut 8:1 7235
And when thy herds and thy flocks *m* ..... Deut 8:13 7235
m thee, as he hath sworn unto thy ..... Deut 13:17 7235
But he shall not *m* horses to ..... Deut 17:16 7235
the end that he should *m* horses ..... Deut 17:16 7235
shall he *m* wives to himself ..... Deut 17:17 7235
he greatly *m* to himself silver ..... Deut 17:17 7235
you to do you good, and to *m* you ..... Deut 28:63 7235
good, and *m* thee above thy fathers ..... Deut 30:5 7235
that thou mayest live and *m* ..... Deut 30:16 7235
neither did all their family *m* 1Chr 4:27 7235
I shall *m* my days as the sand ..... Job 29:18 7235
and I will *m* them, and they shall ..... Jer 30:19 7235
so will I *m* the seed of David my ..... Jer 33:22 7235
I have caused thee to *m* as the ..... Eze 16:7 7233
I will *m* men upon you, all the ..... Eze 36:10 7235
I will *m* upon you man and beast ..... Eze 36:11 7235
I will *m* the fruit of the tree, ... Eze 36:30 7235
m them, and will set my sanctuary ..... Eze 37:26 7235
at Gilgal *m* transgression ..... Amos 4:4 7235
m your seed sown, and increase the 2Cor 9:10 *4129*
and multiplying I will *m* thee ..... Heb 6:14 *4129*

MULTIPLYING {2}
in *m* I will multiply thy seed as ..... Gen 22:17 7235
thee, and I will multiply thee ..... Heb 6:14 *4129*

MULTITUDE {243}
it shall not be numbered for *m* ..... Gen 16:10 7230
that thou mayest be a *m* of people ..... Gen 28:3 6951
and it is now increased unto a *m* ..... Gen 30:30 7230
which cannot be numbered for *m* ..... Gen 32:12 7230
I will make of thee a *m* of people ..... Gen 48:4 6951
let them grow into a *m* in the ..... Gen 48:16 7230
seed shall become a *m* of nations ..... Gen 48:19 4393
a mixed *m* went up also with them ..... Ex 12:38 7227
shalt not follow a *m* to do evil ..... Ex 23:2 7227
According to the *m* of years thou ..... Lev 25:16 7230
the mixt *m* that was among them ..... Num 11:4 628
Gad had a very great *m* of cattle ..... Num 32:1 7227
day as the stars of heaven for *m* ..... Deut 1:10 7230
thee as the stars of heaven for *m* ..... Deut 10:22 7230
were as the stars of heaven for *m* ..... Deut 28:62 7230
that is upon the sea shore in *m* ..... Josh 11:4 7230
army, with his chariots and his *m* ..... Judg 4:7 1995
they came as grasshoppers for *m* ..... Judg 6:5 7230
valley like grasshoppers for *m* ..... Judg 7:12 7230
as the sand by the sea side for *m* ..... Judg 7:12 7230
which is on the sea shore in *m* 1Sa 13:5 7230
the *m* melted away, and they went 1Sa 14:16 1995
even among the whole *m* of Israel 2Sa 6:19 1995
the sand that is by the sea for *m* 2Sa 17:11 7230
be numbered nor counted for *m* 1Kin 3:8 7230
the sand which is by the sea in *m* 1Kin 4:20 7230
not be told nor numbered for *m* 1Kin 8:5 7230
Hast thou seen all this great *m* 1Kin 20:13 1995
all this great *m* into thine hand 1Kin 20:28
they are as all the *m* of Israel 2Kin 7:13 1995
they are even as all the *m* of the 2Kin 7:13 1995
With the *m* of my chariots I am 2Kin 19:23 7393
with the remnant of the *m* 2Kin 25:11 1995
like the dust of the earth in *m* 2Chr 1:9 7227
not be told nor numbered for *m* 2Chr 5:6 7230
and ye be a great *m*, and there are 2Chr 13:8 1995
in thy name we go against this *m* 2Chr 14:11 1995
There cometh a great *m* against 2Chr 20:2 1995
by reason of this great *m* 2Chr 20:15 1995
they looked unto the *m*, and, ... 2Chr 20:24 1995
away a great *m* of them captives 2Chr 28:5
For a *m* of the people, even many 2Chr 30:18 4768
nor for all the *m* that is with 2Chr 32:7 1995
from Israel all the mixed *m* ..... Neh 13:3 6154
the *m* of his children, and all the ..... Est 5:11 7230
accepted of the *m* of his brethren ..... Est 10:3 7230
Should not the *m* of words be ..... Job 11:2 7230
Did I fear a great *m*, or did the ..... Job 31:34 1995
m of years should teach wisdom ..... Job 32:7 7230
the *m* of his bones with strong ..... Job 33:19 7379
By reason of the *m* of oppressions ..... Job 35:9 7230
He scorneth the *m* of the city ..... Job 39:7 1995
thy house in the *m* of thy mercy ..... Ps 5:7 7230
cast them out in the *m* of their ..... Ps 5:10 7230
no king saved by the *m* of an host ..... Ps 33:16 7230
for I had gone with the *m* ..... Ps 42:4 5519
with a *m* that kept holyday ..... Ps 42:4 1995
in the *m* of their riches ..... Ps 49:6 7230
according unto the *m* of thy ..... Ps 51:1 7230
the *m* of the bulls, with the ..... Ps 68:30 5712
in the *m* of thy mercy hear me, in ..... Ps 69:13 7230
to the *m* of thy tender mercies ..... Ps 69:16 7230
unto the *m* of the wicked ..... Ps 74:19 2416
In the *m* of my thoughts within me ..... Ps 94:19 7230
let the *m* of isles be glad ..... Ps 97:1 7227
not the *m* of thy mercies ..... Ps 106:7 7230
according to the *m* of his mercies ..... Ps 106:45 7230
I will praise him among the *m* ..... Ps 109:30 7227
In the *m* of words there wanteth ..... Prov 10:19 7230
but in the *m* of counsellors there ..... Prov 11:14 7230
In the *m* of people is the king's ..... Prov 14:28 7230
but in the *m* of counsellors they ..... Prov 15:22 7230
There is gold, and a *m* of rubies ..... Prov 20:15 7230
in *m* of counsellors there is ..... Prov 24:6 7230
cometh through the *m* of business ..... Eccl 5:3 7230
voice is known by *m* of words ..... Eccl 5:3 7230
For in the *m* of dreams and many ..... Eccl 5:7 7230
To what purpose is the *m* of your ..... Is 1:11 7230
their *m* dried up with thirst ..... Is 5:13 1995
and their glory, and their *m* ..... Is 5:14 1995
The noise of a *m* in the mountains ..... Is 13:4 1995
contemned, with all that great *m* ..... Is 16:14 1995
Woe to the *m* of many people, ... Is 17:12 1995
Moreover the *m* of thy strangers ..... Is 29:5 1995
the *m* of the terrible ones shall ..... Is 29:5 1995
the *m* of all the nations that ..... Is 29:7 1995
so shall the *m* of all the nations ..... Is 29:8 1995
when a *m* of shepherds is called ..... Is 31:4 4393
the *m* of the city shall be left ..... Is 32:14 1995
By the *m* of my chariots am I come ..... Is 37:24 7230
for the *m* of thy sorceries ..... Is 47:9 7230
with the *m* of thy sorceries, ... Is 47:12 7230
wearied in the *m* of thy counsels ..... Is 47:13 7230
The *m* of camels shall cover thee, ... Is 60:6 8229
according to the *m* of his ..... Is 63:7 7230
hills, and from the *m* of mountains ..... Jer 3:23 1995
there is a *m* of waters in the ..... Jer 10:13 1995
they have called a *m* after thee ..... Jer 12:6 4392
for the *m* of thine iniquity ..... Jer 30:14 7230
for the *m* of thine iniquity ..... Jer 30:15 7230
women that stood by, a great *m* ..... Jer 44:15 6951
Behold, I will punish the *m* of No ..... Jer 46:25 582
the *m* of their cattle a spoil ..... Jer 49:32 527
there is a *m* of waters in the ..... Jer 51:16 527
with the *m* of the waves thereof ..... Jer 51:42 527
of Babylon, and the rest of the *m* ..... Jer 52:15 527
for the *m* of her transgressions ..... Lam 1:5 7230
according to the *m* of his mercies ..... Lam 3:32 7230
them shall remain, nor of their *m* ..... Eze 7:11 1995
wrath is upon all the *m* thereof ..... Eze 7:12 1995
is touching the whole *m* thereof ..... Eze 7:13 1995
wrath is upon all the *m* thereof ..... Eze 7:14 1995
according to the *m* of his idols ..... Eze 14:4 7230
height with the *m* of her branches ..... Eze 19:11 7230
a voice of a *m* being at ease was ..... Eze 23:42 1995
of the *m* of all kind of riches ..... Eze 27:12 7230
the *m* of the wares of thy making ..... Eze 27:16 7230
was thy merchant in the *m* of the ..... Eze 27:18 7230
making, for the *m* of all riches ..... Eze 27:18 7230
earth with the *m* of thy riches ..... Eze 27:33 7230
By the *m* of thy merchandise they ..... Eze 28:16 7230
by the *m* of thine iniquities ..... Eze 28:18 7230
and he shall take her *m*, and take ..... Eze 29:19 1995
and they shall take away her *m* ..... Eze 30:4 1995
I will also make the *m* of Egypt ..... Eze 30:10 1995
and I will cut off the *m* of No ..... Eze 30:15 1995
king of Egypt, and to his *m* ..... Eze 31:2 1995
long because of the *m* of waters ..... Eze 31:5 7227
him fair by the *m* of his branches ..... Eze 31:9 7230
This is Pharaoh and all his *m* ..... Eze 31:18 1995
mighty will I cause thy *m* to fall ..... Eze 32:12 1995
all the *m* thereof shall be ..... Eze 32:12 1995
even for Egypt, and for all her *m* ..... Eze 32:16 1995
of man, wail for the *m* of Egypt ..... Eze 32:18 1995
all her *m* round about her grave, ... Eze 32:24 1995
midst of the slain with all her *m* ..... Eze 32:25 1995
is Meshech, Tubal, and all her *m* ..... Eze 32:26 1995
shall be comforted over all his *m* ..... Eze 32:31 1995
sword, even Pharaoh and all his *m* ..... Eze 32:32 1995
shall they bury Gog and all his *m* ..... Eze 39:11 1995
shall be a very great *m* of fish ..... Eze 47:9
his words like the voice of a *m* ..... Dan 10:6 1995
assemble a *m* of great forces ..... Dan 11:10 1995
and he shall set forth a great *m* ..... Dan 11:11 1995
but the *m* shall be given into his ..... Dan 11:11 1995
And when he hath taken away the *m* ..... Dan 11:12 1995
shall set forth a *m* greater than ..... Dan 11:13 1995
for the *m* of thine iniquity, and ..... Hos 9:7 7230
according to the *m* of his fruit ..... Hos 10:1 7230
in the *m* of thy mighty men ..... Hos 10:13 7230
noise by reason of the *m* of men ..... Mic 2:12
and there is a *m* of slain, and a ..... Nah 3:3 7230
Because of the *m* of the whoredoms ..... Nah 3:4 7230
without walls for the *m* of men ..... Zec 2:4 7230
the whole *m* stood on the shore ..... Mt 13:2 *3793*
Jesus unto the *m* in parables ..... Mt 13:34 *3793*
Then Jesus sent the *m* away ..... Mt 13:36 *3793*
put him to death, he feared the *m* ..... Mt 14:5 *3793*
went forth, and saw a great *m* ..... Mt 14:14 *3793*
send the *m* away, that they may go ..... Mt 14:15 *3793*
he commanded the *m* to sit down on ..... Mt 14:19 *3793*
and the disciples to the *m* ..... Mt 14:19 *3793*
And he called the *m*, and said unto ..... Mt 15:10 *3793*
Insomuch that the *m* wondered ..... Mt 15:31 *3793*
said, I have compassion on the *m* ..... Mt 15:32 *3793*
as to fill so great a *m* ..... Mt 15:33 *3793*
he commanded the *m* to sit down on ..... Mt 15:35 *3793*
and the disciples to the *m* ..... Mt 15:36 *3793*
And he sent away the *m*, and took ..... Mt 15:39 *3793*
And when they were come to the *m* ..... Mt 17:14 *3793*
Jericho, a great *m* followed him ..... Mt 20:29 *3793*
the *m* rebuked them, because they ..... Mt 20:31 *3793*
a very great *m* spread their ..... Mt 21:8 *3793*
the *m* said, This is Jesus the ..... Mt 21:11 *3793*
hands on him, they feared the *m* ..... Mt 21:46 *3793*
when the *m* heard this, they were ..... Mt 22:33 *3793*
Then spake Jesus to the *m* ..... Mt 23:1 *3793*
and with him a great *m* with swords ..... Mt 26:47 *3793*
elders persuaded the *m* that they ..... Mt 27:20 *3793*
and washed his hands before the *m* ..... Mt 27:24 *3793*
all the *m* resorted unto him, and ..... Mk 2:13 *3793*
a great *m* from Galilee followed ..... Mk 3:7 *4128*
about Tyre and Sidon, a great *m* ..... Mk 3:8 *4128*
wait on him because of the *m* ..... Mk 3:9 *3793*
the *m* cometh together again, so ..... Mk 3:20 *3793*
the *m* sat about him, and they said ..... Mk 3:32 *3793*
was gathered unto him a great *m* ..... Mk 4:1 *3793*
the whole *m* was by the sea on the ..... Mk 4:1 *3793*
And when they had sent away the *m* ..... Mk 4:36 *3793*
Thou seest the *m* thronging thee ..... Mk 5:31 *3793*
And he took him aside from the *m* ..... Mk 7:33 *3793*
those days the *m* being very great ..... Mk 8:1 *3793*
I have compassion on the *m* ..... Mk 8:2 *3793*
he saw a great *m* about them ..... Mk 9:14 *3793*
And one of the *m* answered and said, ... Mk 9:17 *3793*
and with him a great *m* with swords ..... Mk 14:43 *3793*
the *m* crying aloud began to ..... Mk 15:8 *3793*
the whole *m* of the people were ..... Lk 1:10 *4128*
there was with the angel a *m* of ..... Lk 2:13 *4128*
Then said he to the *m* that came ..... Lk 3:7 *3793*
they inclosed a great *m* of fishes ..... Lk 5:6 *4128*
bring him in because of the *m* ..... Lk 5:19 *3793*
a great *m* of people out of all ..... Lk 6:17 *4128*
the whole *m* sought to touch him ..... Lk 6:19 *3793*
Then the whole *m* of the country ..... Lk 8:37 *4128*
the *m* throng thee and press thee, ... Lk 8:45 *3793*
and said unto him, Send the *m* away ..... Lk 9:12 *3793*
the disciples to set before the *m* ..... Lk 9:16 *3793*
an innumerable *m* of people ..... Lk 12:1 *3461*
And hearing the *m* pass by, he ..... Lk 18:36 *3793*
the whole *m* of the disciples ..... Lk 19:37 *4128*
from among the *m* said unto him ..... Lk 19:39 *3793*
unto them in the absence of the *m* ..... Lk 22:6 *3793*
And while he yet spake, behold a *m* ..... Lk 22:47 *3793*
the whole *m* of them arose, and led ..... Lk 23:1 *4128*
lay a great *m* of impotent folk ..... Jn 5:3 *4128*
away, a *m* being in that place ..... Jn 5:13 *3793*
a great *m* followed him, because ..... Jn 6:2 *3793*
to draw it for the *m* of fishes ..... Jn 21:6 *4128*
the *m* came together, and were ..... Acts 2:6 *4128*

M

the *m* of them that believed were ... Acts 4:32 *4128*
There came also a *m* out of the ... Acts 5:16 *4128*
the *m* of the disciples unto them ... Acts 6:2 *4128*
And the saying pleased the whole *m* ... Acts 6:5 *4128*
that a great *m* both of the Jews ... Acts 14:1 *4128*
But the *m* of the city was divided ... Acts 14:4 *4128*
Then all the *m* kept silence ... Acts 15:12 *4128*
they had gathered the *m* together ... Acts 15:30 *4128*
the *m* rose up together against ... Acts 16:22 *3793*
and of the devout Greeks a great *m* ... Acts 17:4 *4128*
evil of that way before the *m* ... Acts 19:9 *4128*
they drew Alexander out of the *m* ... Acts 19:33 *3793*
the *m* must needs come together ... Acts 21:22 *4128*
thing, some another, among the *m* ... Acts 21:34 *3793*
For the *m* of the people followed ... Acts 21:36 *4128*
and the *m* was divided ... Acts 23:7 *4128*
in the temple, neither with *m* ... Acts 24:18 *3793*
about whom all the *m* of the Jews ... Acts 25:24 *4128*
many as the stars of the sky in *m* ... Heb 11:12 *4128*
death, and shall hide a *m* of sins ... Jas 5:20 *4128*
charity shall cover the *m* of sins ... 1Pet 4:8 *4128*
this I beheld, and, lo, a great *m* ... Rev 7:9 *3793*
as it were the voice of a great *m* ... Rev 19:6 *3793*

MULTITUDES {24}
draw her and all her *m* ... Eze 32:20 1995
M, *m* in the valley of ... Joel 3:14 1995
great *m* of people from Galilee ... Mt 4:25 *3793*
And seeing the *m*, he went up into ... Mt 5:1 *3793*
mountain, great *m* followed him ... Mt 8:1 *3793*
when Jesus saw great *m* about him ... Mt 8:18 *3793*
But when the *m* saw it, they ... Mt 9:8 *3793*
the *m* marvelled, saying, It was ... Mt 9:33 *3793*
But when he saw the *m*, he was ... Mt 9:36 *3793*
to say unto the *m* concerning John ... Mt 11:7 *3793*
great *m* followed him, and he ... Mt 12:15 *3793*
great *m* were gathered together ... Mt 13:2 *3793*
side, while he sent the *m* away ... Mt 14:22 *3793*
And when he had sent the *m* away ... Mt 14:23 *3793*
great *m* came unto him, having ... Mt 15:30 *3793*
And great *m* followed him ... Mt 19:2 *3793*
the *m* that went before, and that ... Mt 21:9 *3793*
same hour said Jesus to the *m* ... Mt 26:55 *3793*
great *m* came together to hear, and ... Lk 5:15 *3793*
And there went great *m* with him ... Lk 14:25 *3793*
the Lord, *m* both of men and women ... Acts 5:14 *4128*
But when the Jews saw the *m* ... Acts 13:45 *3793*
whore sitteth, are peoples, and *m* ... Rev 17:15 *3793*

MUNITION {2}
that fight against [illegible] and her *m* ... Is 29:7 4685
keep the *m*, watch [illegible] way, make ... Nah 2:1 4694

MUNITIONS {1}
defence shall be the *m* of rocks ... Is 33:16 4679

MUPPIM *(mup'-pim)* {1} See SHUPPIM. *A son of Benjamin.*
Gera, and Naaman, Ehi, and Rosh, *M* ... Gen 46:21 4649

MURDER {9}
places doth he *m* the innocent ... Ps 10:8 2026
the stranger, and *m* the fatherless ... Ps 94:6 7523
Will ye steal, *m*, and commit ... Jer 7:9 7523
priests *m* in the way by consent ... Hos 6:9 7523
Jesus said, Thou shalt do no *m* ... Mt 19:18 *5407*
who had committed *m* in the ... Mk 15:7 *5408*
made in the city, and for *m* ... Lk 23:19 *5408*
m was cast into prison, whom they ... Lk 23:25 *5408*
full of envy, *m*, debate, deceit, ... Rom 1:29 *5408*

MURDERER {20}
iron, so that he die, he is a *m* ... Num 35:16 7523
the *m* shall surely be put to ... Num 35:16 7523
he may die, and he die, he is a *m* ... Num 35:17 7523
the *m* shall surely be put to ... Num 35:17 7523
he may die, and he die, he is a *m* ... Num 35:18 7523
the *m* shall surely be put to ... Num 35:18 7523
of blood himself shall slay the *m* ... Num 35:19 7523
for he is a *m* ... Num 35:21 7523
of blood shall slay the *m* ... Num 35:21 7523
the *m* shall be put to death by ... Num 35:30 7523
satisfaction for the life of a *m* ... Num 35:31 7523
See ye how this son of a *m* hath ... 2Kin 6:32 7523
The *m* rising with the light ... Job 24:14 7523
bring forth his children to the *m* ... Hos 9:13 2026
He was a *m* from the beginning, and ... Jn 8:44 *443*
desired a *m* to be granted unto ... Acts 3:14 *5406*
No doubt this man is a *m* ... Acts 28:4 *5406*
But let none of you suffer as a *m* ... 1Pet 4:15 *5406*
hateth his brother is a *m* ... 1Jn 3:15 *443*
ye know that no *m* hath eternal ... 1Jn 3:15 *443*

MURDERERS {11}
the children of the *m* he slew not ... 2Kin 14:6 5221
lodged in it; but now *m* ... Is 1:21 7523
my soul is wearied because of *m* ... Jer 4:31 2026
his armies, and destroyed those *m* ... Mt 22:7 *5406*
have been now the betrayers and *m* ... Acts 7:52 *5406*
four thousand men that were *m* ... Acts 21:38 *4607*
for *m* of fathers and *m* of ... 1Ti 1:9 *3964*
m of mothers, for manslayers, ... 1Ti 1:9 *3389*
and the abominable, and *m*, and ... Rev 21:8 *5406*
sorcerers, and whoremongers, and *m* ... Rev 22:15 *5406*

MURDERS {4}
heart proceed evil thoughts, *m* ... Mt 15:19 *5408*
adulteries, fornications, *m* ... Mk 7:21 *5408*
Envyings, *m*, drunkenness, ... Gal 5:21 *5408*
Neither repented they of their *m* ... Rev 9:21 *5408*

MURMUR {9}
what are we, that ye *m* against us ... Ex 16:7 3885
murmurings which ye *m* against him ... Ex 16:8 3885
congregation, which *m* against me ... Num 14:27 3885
Israel, which they *m* against me ... Num 14:27 3885
the congregation to *m* against him ... Num 14:36 3885
is Aaron, that ye *m* against him ... Num 16:11 3885
whereby they *m* against you ... Num 17:5 3885
unto them, *M* not among yourselves ... Jn 6:43 *1111*
Neither *m* ye, as some of them ... 1Cor 10:10 *1111*

MURMURED {19}
the people *m* against Moses, ... Ex 15:24 3885
of Israel *m* against Moses ... Ex 16:2 3885
the people *m* against Moses, and ... Ex 17:3 3885
of Israel *m* against Moses ... Num 14:2 3885
upward, which have *m* against me ... Num 14:29 3885
of Israel *m* against Moses ... Num 16:41 3885
ye *m* in your tents, and said, ... Deut 1:27 7279
m against the princes ... Josh 9:18 3885
But *m* in their tents, and ... Ps 106:25 7279
they that *m* shall learn doctrine ... Is 29:24 7279
they *m* against the goodman of the ... Mt 20:11 *1111*
And they *m* against her ... Mk 14:5 *1690*
Pharisees *m* against his disciples ... Lk 5:30 *1111*
And the Pharisees and scribes *m* ... Lk 15:2 *1234*
And when they saw it, they all *m* ... Lk 19:7 *1234*
The Jews then *m* at him, because ... Jn 6:41 *1111*
that his disciples *m* at it ... Jn 6:61 *1111*
m such things concerning him ... Jn 7:32 *1111*
murmur ye, as some of them also *m* ... 1Cor 10:10 *1111*

MURMURERS {1}
These are *m*, complainers, walking ... Jude 16 *1113*

MURMURING {2}
there was much *m* among the people ... Jn 7:12 *1112*
there arose a *m* of the Grecians ... Acts 6:1 *1112*

MURMURINGS {9}
heareth your *m* against the LORD ... Ex 16:7 8519
m which ye murmur against him ... Ex 16:8 8519
your *m* are not against us, but ... Ex 16:8 8519
for he hath heard your *m* ... Ex 16:9 8519
I have heard the *m* of the ... Ex 16:12 8519
I have heard the *m* of the ... Num 14:27 8519
the *m* of the children of Israel ... Num 17:5 8519
quite take away their *m* from me ... Num 17:10 8519
Do all things without *m* and ... Phil 2:14 *1112*

MURRAIN {1}
there shall be a very grievous *m* ... Ex 9:3 1698

MUSE {1}
I *m* on the work of thy hands ... Ps 143:5 7878

MUSED {1}
all men *m* in their hearts of John ... Lk 3:15 *1260*

MUSHI *(mu'-shi)* {8} See MUSHITES. *A son of Merari.*
of Merari; Mahali and *M* ... Ex 6:19 4187
families; Mahli, and *M* ... Num 3:20 4187
Merari; Mahli, and *M* ... 1Chr 6:19 4187
The son of Mahli, the son of *M* ... 1Chr 6:47 4187
Merari; Mahli, and *M* ... 1Chr 23:21 4187
The sons of *M*; Mahli ... 1Chr 23:23 4187
sons of Merari were Mahli and *M* ... 1Chr 24:26 4187
The sons also of *M* ... 1Chr 24:30 4187

MUSHITES *(mu'-shites)* {2} *The family of Mushi.*
Mahlites, and the family of the *M* ... Num 3:33 4188
the Mahlites, the family of the *M* ... Num 26:58 4188

MUSICAL {3}
with *m* instruments of God ... 1Chr 16:42 7892
with the *m* instruments of David ... Neh 12:36 7892
as *m* instruments, and that of all ... Eccl 2:8 7705

MUSICIAN {55}
To the chief *M* on Neginoth ... Ps 4:*t* 5329
To the chief *M* upon Nehiloth, A ... Ps 5:*t* 5329
To the chief *M* on Neginoth upon ... Ps 6:*t* 5329
To the chief *M* upon Gittith ... Ps 8:*t* 5329
To the chief *M* upon Muth-labben, ... Ps 9:*t* 5329
To the chief *M*, A Psalm of David ... Ps 11:*t* 5329
To the chief *M* upon Sheminith, A ... Ps 12:*t* 5329
To the chief *M*, A Psalm of David ... Ps 13:*t* 5329
To the chief *M*, A Psalm of David ... Ps 14:*t* 5329
To the chief *M*, A Psalm of David, ... Ps 18:*t* 5329
To the chief *M*, A Psalm of David ... Ps 19:*t* 5329
To the chief *M*, A Psalm of David ... Ps 20:*t* 5329
To the chief *M*, A Psalm of David ... Ps 21:*t* 5329
To the chief *M* upon Aijeleth ... Ps 22:*t* 5329
To the chief *M*, A Psalm of David ... Ps 31:*t* 5329
To the chief *M*, A Psalm of David, ... Ps 36:*t* 5329
To the chief *M*, even to Jeduthun, ... Ps 39:*t* 5329
To the chief *M*, A Psalm of David ... Ps 40:*t* 5329
To the chief *M*, A Psalm of David ... Ps 41:*t* 5329
To the chief *M*, Maschil, for the ... Ps 42:*t* 5329
To the chief *M* for the sons of ... Ps 44:*t* 5329
To the chief *M* upon Shoshannim, ... Ps 45:*t* 5329
To the chief *M* for the sons of ... Ps 46:*t* 5329
To the chief *M*, A Psalm for the ... Ps 47:*t* 5329
To the chief *M*, A Psalm for the ... Ps 49:*t* 5329
To the chief *M*, A Psalm of David, ... Ps 51:*t* 5329
To the chief *M*, Maschil, A Psalm ... Ps 52:*t* 5329
To the chief *M* upon Mahalath, ... Ps 53:*t* 5329
To the chief *M* on Neginoth ... Ps 54:*t* 5329
To the chief *M* on Neginoth ... Ps 55:*t* 5329
To the chief *M* upon ... Ps 56:*t* 5329
To the chief *M*, Altaschith, ... Ps 57:*t* 5329
To the chief *M*, Altaschith, ... Ps 58:*t* 5329
To the chief *M*, Altaschith, ... Ps 59:*t* 5329
To the chief *M* upon Shushan-eduth ... Ps 60:*t* 5329
To the chief *M* upon Neginah ... Ps 61:*t* 5329
To the chief *M*, to Jeduthun, A ... Ps 62:*t* 5329
To the chief *M*, A Psalm of David ... Ps 64:*t* 5329
To the chief *M*, A Psalm and Song ... Ps 65:*t* 5329
To the chief *M*, A Song or Psalm ... Ps 66:*t* 5329
To the chief *M* on Neginoth ... Ps 67:*t* 5329
To the chief *M*, A Psalm or Song ... Ps 68:*t* 5329
To the chief *M* upon Shoshannim, A ... Ps 69:*t* 5329
To the chief *M*, A Psalm of David, ... Ps 70:*t* 5329
To the chief *M*, Altaschith, A ... Ps 75:*t* 5329
To the chief *M* on Neginoth ... Ps 76:*t* 5329
To the chief *M*, to Jeduthun, A ... Ps 77:*t* 5329
To the chief *M* upon ... Ps 80:*t* 5329
To the chief *M* upon Gittith ... Ps 81:*t* 5329
To the chief *M* upon Gittith ... Ps 84:*t* 5329
To the chief *M*, A Psalm for the ... Ps 85:*t* 5329
chief *M* upon Mahalath Leannoth ... Ps 88:*t* 5329
To the chief *M*, A Psalm of David ... Ps 109:*t* 5329
To the chief *M*, A Psalm of David ... Ps 139:*t* 5329
To the chief *M*, A Psalm of David ... Ps 140:*t* 5329

MUSICIANS {1}
And the voice of harpers, and *m* ... Rev 18:22 *3451*

MUSICK {16}
joy, and with instruments of *m* ... 1Sa 18:6
the singers with instruments of *m* ... 1Chr 15:16 7892
and cymbals and instruments of *m* ... 2Chr 5:13 7892
with instruments of *m* of the LORD ... 2Chr 7:6 7892
the singers with instruments of *m* ... 2Chr 23:13 7892
could skill of instruments of *m* ... 2Chr 34:12 7892
of *m* shall be brought low ... Eccl 12:4 7892
I am their *m* ... Lam 3:63 4485
gate, the young men from their *m* ... Lam 5:14 5058
dulcimer, and all kinds of *m* ... Dan 3:5 2170
psaltery, and all kinds of *m* ... Dan 3:7 2170
and dulcimer, and all kinds of *m* ... Dan 3:10 2170
and dulcimer, and all kinds of *m* ... Dan 3:15 2170
of *m* brought before him ... Dan 6:18
to themselves instruments of *m* ... Amos 6:5 7892
nigh to the house, he heard *m* ... Lk 15:25 *4858*

MUSING {1}
while I was *m* the fire burned ... Ps 39:3 1901

MUST {132}
thy money, *m* needs be circumcised ... Gen 17:13
m I needs bring thy son again ... Gen 24:5
It *m* not be so done in our ... Gen 29:26
and said, Thou *m* come in unto me ... Gen 30:16
If it *m* be so now, do this ... Gen 43:11
time drew nigh that Israel *m* die ... Gen 47:29
for we *m* hold a feast unto the ... Ex 10:9
Thou *m* give us also sacrifices and ... Ex 10:25
for thereof *m* we take to serve ... Ex 10:26
not with what we *m* serve the LORD ... Ex 10:26
save that which every man *m* eat ... Ex 12:16
them the way wherein they *m* walk ... Ex 18:20
walk, and the work that they *m* do ... Ex 18:20
it *m* be put into water, and it ... Lev 11:32
seven days ye *m* eat unleavened ... Lev 23:6
so he *m* do after the law of his ... Num 6:21
Neither *m* the children of Israel ... Num 18:22
m we fetch you water out of this ... Num 20:10
M I not take heed to speak that ... Num 23:12
the LORD speaketh, that I *m* do ... Num 23:26
word again by what way we *m* go up ... Deut 1:22
But I *m* die in this land, I *m* ... Deut 4:22
But thou *m* eat them before the ... Deut 12:18
for thou *m* go with this people ... Deut 31:7
thy days approach that thou *m* die ... Deut 31:14
may know the way by which ye *m* go ... Josh 3:4
But that ye *m* turn away this day ... Josh 22:18
thou *m* offer it unto the LORD ... Judg 13:16
There *m* be an inheritance for ... Judg 21:17
thou *m* buy it also of Ruth the ... Ruth 4:5
was in mine hand, and, lo, I *m* die ... 1Sa 14:43
For we *m* needs die, and are as ... 2Sa 14:14
He that ruleth over men *m* be just ... 2Sa 23:3
touch them *m* be fenced with iron ... 2Sa 23:7
he sleepeth, and *m* be awaked ... 1Kin 18:27
thou *m* go to be with thy fathers ... 1Chr 17:11
LORD *m* be exceeding magnifical ... 1Chr 22:5
As thou hast said, so *m* we do ... Ezr 10:12
whose mouth *m* be held in with bit ... Ps 32:9
friends *m* shew himself friendly ... Prov 18:24
him, yet thou *m* do it again ... Prov 19:19
then *m* he put to more strength ... Eccl 10:10
m have a thousand, and those that ... Song 8:12
For precept *m* be upon precept, ... Is 28:10
they *m* needs be borne, because ... Jer 10:5
this is a grief, and I *m* bear it ... Jer 10:19
but ye *m* tread down with your ... Eze 34:18
but ye *m* foul the residue with ... Eze 34:18
how that he *m* go unto Jerusalem, ... Mt 16:21 *1163*
scribes that Elias *m* first come ... Mt 17:10 *1163*
for it *m* needs be that offences ... Mt 18:7 *318*
all these things *m* come to pass ... Mt 24:6 *1163*
be fulfilled, that thus it *m* be ... Mt 26:54 *1163*
but new wine *m* be put into new ... Mk 2:22
Son of man *m* suffer many things ... Mk 8:31 *1163*
scribes that Elias *m* first come ... Mk 9:11 *1163*
that he *m* suffer many things, and ... Mk 9:12
for such things *m* needs be ... Mk 13:7 *1163*
the gospel *m* first be published ... Mk 13:10 *1163*
but the scriptures *m* be fulfilled ... Mk 14:49 *2443*
wist ye not that I *m* be about my ... Lk 2:49 *1163*
I *m* preach the kingdom of God to ... Lk 4:43 *1163*
But new wine *m* be put into new ... Lk 5:38
The Son of man *m* suffer many ... Lk 9:22 *1163*
Nevertheless I *m* walk to day ... Lk 13:33 *1163*
ground, and I *m* needs go and see it ... Lk 14:18 *2192*
But first *m* he suffer many things ... Lk 17:25 *1163*
for to day I *m* abide at thy house ... Lk 19:5 *1163*

for these things *m* first come to Lk 21:9 *1163*
when the passover *m* be killed Lk 22:7 *1163*
m yet be accomplished in me Lk 22:37 *1163*
(For of necessity he *m* release Lk 23:17
The Son of man *m* be delivered Lk 24:7 *1163*
that all things *m* be fulfilled Lk 24:44 *1163*
unto thee, Ye *m* be born again Jn 3:7 *1163*
even so *m* the Son of man be Jn 3:14 *1163*
He *m* increase, but I Jn 3:30 *1163*
increase, but I *m* decrease Jn 3:30
he *m* needs go through Samaria Jn 4:4
him *m* worship him in spirit Jn 4:24 *1163*
I *m* work the works of him that Jn 9:4 *1163*
them also I *m* bring, and they Jn 10:16 *1163*
The Son of man *m* be lifted up Jn 12:34 *1163*
that he *m* rise again from the Jn 20:9 *1163*
this scripture *m* needs have been Acts 1:16 *1163*
m one be ordained to be a witness Acts 1:22 *1163*
Whom the heaven *m* receive until Acts 3:21 *1163*
among men, whereby we *m* be saved Acts 4:12 *1163*
shall be told thee what thou *m* do Acts 9:6 *1163*
he *m* suffer for my name's sake Acts 9:16 *1163*
faith, and that we *m* through much Acts 14:22 *1163*
Ye *m* be circumcised, and keep the Acts 15:24
Sirs, what *m* I do to be saved Acts 16:30 *1163*
that Christ *m* needs have suffered Acts 17:3 *1163*
I *m* by all means keep this feast Acts 18:21 *1163*
been there, I *m* also see Rome Acts 19:21 *1163*
the multitude *m* needs come Acts 21:22 *1163*
so *m* thou bear witness also at Acts 23:11 *1163*
thou *m* be brought before Caesar Acts 27:24 *1163*
Howbeit we *m* be cast upon a Acts 27:26 *1163*
Wherefore ye *m* needs be subject, Rom 13:5
for then *m* ye needs go out of the 1Cor 5:10 *3784*
For there *m* be also heresies 1Cor 11:19 *1163*
For he *m* reign, till he hath put 1Cor 15:25 *1163*
corruptible *m* put on incorruption 1Cor 15:53 *1163*
this mortal *m* put on immortality 1Cor 15:53
For we *m* all appear before the 2Cor 5:10 *1163*
If I *m* needs glory, I will glory 2Cor 11:30 *1163*
A bishop then *m* be blameless 1Ti 3:2 *1163*
Moreover he *m* have a good report 1Ti 3:7 *1163*
Likewise *m* the deacons be grave, 1Ti 3:8
Even so *m* their wives be grave, 1Ti 3:11
The husbandman that laboureth *m* 2Ti 2:6 *1163*
servant of the Lord *m* not strive 2Ti 2:24 *1163*
For a bishop *m* be blameless Titus 1:7 *1163*
Whose mouths *m* be stopped Titus 1:11 *1163*
that some *m* enter therein Heb 4:6
there *m* also of necessity be the Heb 9:16
For then *m* he often have suffered Heb 9:26 *1163*
to God *m* believe that he is Heb 11:6 *1163*
as they that *m* give account Heb 13:17
m begin at the house of God 1Pet 4:17
Knowing that shortly I *m* put off 2Pet 1:14
which *m* shortly come to pass Rev 1:1 *1163*
thee things which *m* be hereafter Rev 4:1 *1163*
Thou *m* prophesy again before many Rev 10:11 *1163*
he *m* in this manner be killed Rev 11:5 *1163*
sword *m* be killed with the sword Rev 13:10 *1163*
he *m* continue a short space Rev 17:10 *1163*
after that he *m* be loosed a Rev 20:3 *1163*
things which *m* shortly be done Rev 22:6 *1163*

MUSTARD {5}
is like to a grain of *m* seed Mt 13:31 *4615*
have faith as a grain of *m* seed Mt 17:20 *4615*
It is like a grain of *m* seed Mk 4:31 *4615*
It is like a grain of *m* seed Lk 13:19 *4615*
ye had faith as a grain of *m* seed Lk 17:6 *4615*

MUSTERED {2}
which *m* the people of the land, 2Kin 25:19 6633
who *m* the people of the land Jer 52:25 6633

MUSTERETH {1}
the LORD of hosts *m* the host of Is 13:4 6485

MUTH-LABBEN *(muth-lab'-ben)* {1} *A muscial notation.*
To the chief Musician upon *M* Ps 9:*t* 4192

MUTTER {1}
unto wizards that peep, and that *m* Is 8:19 1897

MUTTERED {1}
your tongue hath *m* perverseness Is 59:3 1897

MUTUAL {1}
you by the *m* faith both of you Rom 1:12 *1722,240*

MUZZLE {3}
Thou shalt not *m* the ox when he Deut 25:4 2629
Thou shalt not *m* the mouth of the 1Cor 9:9 *5392*
Thou shalt not *m* the ox that 1Ti 5:18 *5392*

MY See APPENDIX.

MYRA *(mi'-rah)* {1} *A city in Lycia.*
and Pamphylia, we came to *M* Acts 27:5 *3460*

MYRRH {17}
bearing spicery and balm and *m* Gen 37:25 3910
and a little honey, spices, and *m* Gen 43:11 3910
of pure *m* five hundred shekels Ex 30:23 4753
to wit, six months with oil of *m* Est 2:12 4753
All thy garments smell of *m* Ps 45:8 4753
I have perfumed my bed with *m* Prov 7:17 4753
A bundle of *m* is my wellbeloved Song 1:13 4753
pillars of smoke, perfumed with *m* Song 3:6 4753
will get me to the mountain of *m* Song 4:6 4753
m and aloes, with all the chief Song 4:14 4753
have gathered my *m* with my spice Song 5:1 4753
and my hands dropped with *m* Song 5:5 4753
my fingers with sweet smelling *m* Song 5:5 4753
lilies, dropping sweet smelling *m* Song 5:13 4753
gold, and frankincense, and *m* Mt 2:11 *4666*
him to drink wine mingled with *m* Mk 15:23 *4669*
night, and brought a mixture of *m* Jn 19:39 *4666*

MYRTLE {6}
m branches, and palm branches, and Neh 8:15 1918
cedar, the shittah tree, and the *m* Is 41:19 1918
brier shall come up the *m* tree Is 55:13 1918
he stood among the *m* trees that Zec 1:8 1918
stood among the *m* trees answered Zec 1:10 1918
LORD that stood among the *m* trees Zec 1:11 1918

MYSELF See APPENDIX.

MYSIA *(miz'-ye-ah)* {2} *A Roman province in Asia Minor.*
After they were come to *M* Acts 16:7 *3463*
they passing by *M* came down to Acts 16:8 *3463*

MYSTERIES {5}
the *m* of the kingdom of heaven Mt 13:11 *3466*
know the *m* of the kingdom of God Lk 8:10 *3466*
and stewards of the *m* of God 1Cor 4:1 *3466*
of prophecy, and understand all *m* 1Cor 13:2 *3466*
in the spirit he speaketh *m* 1Cor 14:2 *3466*

MYSTERY {22}
know the *m* of the kingdom of God Mk 4:11 *3466*
ye should be ignorant of this *m* Rom 11:25 *3466*
to the revelation of the *m* Rom 16:25 *3466*
we speak the wisdom of God in a *m* 1Cor 2:7 *3466*
Behold, I shew you a *m* 1Cor 15:51 *3466*
known unto us the *m* of his will Eph 1:9 *3466*
he made known unto me the *m* Eph 3:3 *3466*
my knowledge in the *m* of Christ) Eph 3:4 *3466*
what is the fellowship of the *m* Eph 3:9 *3466*
This is a great *m* Eph 5:32 *3466*
to make known the *m* of the gospel Eph 6:19 *3466*
Even the *m* which hath been hid Col 1:26 *3466*
of this *m* among the Gentiles Col 1:27 *3466*
acknowledgement of the *m* of God Col 2:2 *3466*
to speak the *m* of Christ Col 4:3 *3466*
For the *m* of iniquity doth 2Th 2:7 *3466*
Holding the *m* of the faith in a 1Ti 3:9 *3466*
great is the *m* of godliness 1Ti 3:16 *3466*
The *m* of the seven stars which Rev 1:20 *3466*
the *m* of God should be finished, Rev 10:7 *3466*
forehead was a name written, *M* Rev 17:5 *3466*
will tell thee the *m* of the woman Rev 17:7 *3466*

N

NAAM *(na'-am)* {1} *A son of Caleb.*
Iru, Elah, and *N* 1Chr 4:15 5277

NAAMAH *(na'-a-mah)* {5} See NAAMATHITE.
1. Sister of Tubal-cain.
and the sister of Tubal-cain was *N* Gen 4:22 5279
2. Mother of King Rehoboam.
mother's name was *N* an Ammonitess 1Kin 14:21 5279
mother's name was *N* an Ammonitess 1Kin 14:31 5279
mother's name was *N* an Ammonitess 2Chr 12:13 5279
3. A city in Judah.
And Gederoth, Beth-dagon, and *N* Josh 15:41 5279

NAAMAN *(na'-a-man)* {16} See NAAMAN'S, NAAMITES.
1. A son of Benjamin.
and Becher, and Ashbel, Gera, and *N* Gen 46:21 5283
2. A son of Bela.
And the sons of Bela were Ard and *N* Num 26:40 5283
and of *N*, the family of the Num 26:40 5283
And Abishua, and *N*, and Ahoah, 1Chr 8:4 5283
3. A son of Ehud.
And *N*, and Ahiah, and Gera, he 1Chr 8:7 5283
4. A Syrian captain.
Now *N*, captain of the host of the 2Kin 5:1 5283
sent *N* my servant to thee 2Kin 5:6 5283
So *N* came with his horses and with 2Kin 5:9 5283
But *N* was wroth, and went away, and 2Kin 5:11 5283
N said, Shall there not then, I 2Kin 5:17 5283
master hath spared *N* this Syrian 2Kin 5:20 5283
So Gehazi followed after *N* 2Kin 5:21 5283
when *N* saw him running after him, 2Kin 5:21 5283
N said, Be content, take two 2Kin 5:23 5283
of *N* shall cleave unto thee 2Kin 5:27 5283
was cleansed, saving *N* the Syrian Lk 4:27 *3497*

NAAMAN'S *(na'-a-mans)* {1} *Refers to Naaman 4.*
and she waited on *N* wife 2Kin 5:2 5283

NAAMATHITE *(na'-a-math-ite)* {4} *Family name of Zophar.*
the Shuhite, and Zophar the *N* Job 2:11 5284
Then answered Zophar the *N* Job 11:1 5284
Then answered Zophar the *N* Job 20:1 5284
the Shuhite and Zophar the *N* went Job 42:9 5284

NAAMITES *(na'-a-mites)* {1} *Descendants of Naaman 3.*
and of Naaman, the family of the *N* Num 26:40 5280

NAARAH *(na'-a-rah)* {3} See NAARAN, NAARATH. *A wife of Ashur.*
Tekoa had two wives, Helah and *N* 1Chr 4:5 5292
N bare him Ahuzam, and Hepher, and 1Chr 4:6 5292
These were the sons of *N* 1Chr 4:6 5292

NAARAI *(na'-a-rahee)* {1} See PAARAI. *A "mighty man" of David.*
Carmelite, *N* the son of Ezbai, 1Chr 11:37 5293

NAARAN *(na'-a-ran)* {1} *A city in Ephraim.*
the towns thereof, and eastward *N* 1Chr 7:28 5295

NAARATH *(na'-a-rath)* {1} See NAARAH, NAARAN. *Same as Naaran.*
from Janohah to Ataroth, and to *N* Josh 16:7 5292

NAASHON *(na'-a-shon)* {1} See NAHSHON. *Brother of Elisheba.*
of Amminadab, sister of *N* Ex 6:23 5177

NAASSON *(na'-as-son)* {3} See NAASHON. *Father of Salmon.*
and Aminadab begat *N* Mt 1:4 *3476*
and *N* begat Salmon Mt 1:4 *3476*
of Salmon, which was the son of *N* Lk 3:32 *3476*

NABAJOTH See NABOTH.

NABAL *(na'-bal)* {18} See NABAL'S. *A wife of David.*
Now the name of the man was *N* 1Sa 25:3 5037
that *N* did shear his sheep 1Sa 25:4 5037
Get you up to Carmel, and go to *N* 1Sa 25:5 5037
they spake to *N* according to all 1Sa 25:9 5037
N answered David's servants, and 1Sa 25:10 5037
But she told not her husband *N* 1Sa 25:19 5037
regard this man of Belial, even *N* 1Sa 25:25 5037
N is his name, and folly is with 1Sa 25:25 5037
seek evil to my lord, be as *N* 1Sa 25:26 5037
there had not been left unto *N* by 1Sa 25:34 5037
And Abigail came to *N* 1Sa 25:36 5037
when the wine was gone out of *N* 1Sa 25:37 5037
days after, that the LORD smote *N* 1Sa 25:38 5037
when David heard that *N* was dead 1Sa 25:39 5037
of my reproach from the hand of *N* 1Sa 25:39 5037
wickedness of *N* upon his own head 1Sa 25:39 5037
the wife of *N* the Carmelite 1Sa 30:5 5037
the wife of *N* the Carmelite 2Sa 3:3 5037

NABAL'S *(na'-balz)* {4}
N wife, saying, Behold, David 1Sa 25:14 5037
N heart was merry within him for 1Sa 25:36 5037
Abigail the Carmelitess, *N* wife 1Sa 27:3 5037
Abigail *N* wife the Carmelite 2Sa 2:2 5037

NABOTH *(na'-both)* {22} *A Jezreelite of Issachar.*
that *N* the Jezreelite had a 1Kin 21:1 5022
And Ahab spake unto *N*, saying, 1Kin 21:2 5022
N said to Ahab, The LORD forbid 1Kin 21:3 5022
because of the word which *N* the 1Kin 21:4 5022
I spake unto *N* the Jezreelite 1Kin 21:6 5022
the vineyard of *N* the Jezreelite 1Kin 21:7 5022
were in his city, dwelling with *N* 1Kin 21:8 5022
set *N* on high among the people 1Kin 21:9 5022
set *N* on high among the people 1Kin 21:12 5022
against him, even against *N* 1Kin 21:13 5022
N did blaspheme God and the king 1Kin 21:13 5022
saying, *N* is stoned, and is dead 1Kin 21:14 5022
Jezebel heard that *N* was stoned 1Kin 21:15 5022
the vineyard of *N* the Jezreelite 1Kin 21:15 5022
for *N* is not alive, but dead 1Kin 21:15 5022
when Ahab heard that *N* was dead 1Kin 21:16 5022
the vineyard of *N* the Jezreelite 1Kin 21:16 5022
he is in the vineyard of *N* 1Kin 21:18 5022
of *N* shall dogs lick thy blood 1Kin 21:19 5022
the portion of *N* the Jezreelite 2Kin 9:21 5022
of the field of *N* the Jezreelite 2Kin 9:25 5022
seen yesterday the blood of *N* 2Kin 9:26 5022

NACHON See NACHON'S.

NACHON'S *(na'-kons)* {1}
they came to *N* threshingfloor 2Sa 6:6 5225

NACHOR *(na'-kor)* {2} See NAHOR.
1. Brother of Abraham.
of Abraham, and the father of *N* Josh 24:2 5152
2. Father of Thara; ancestor of Jesus.
of Thara, which was the son of *N* Lk 3:34 *3493*

NACON See NACHON'S.

NADAB *(na'-dab)* {20}
1. Son of Aaron.
and she bare him *N*, and Abihu, Ex 6:23 5070
unto the LORD, thou, and Aaron, *N* Ex 24:1 5070
Then went up Moses, and Aaron, *N* Ex 24:9 5070
priest's office, even Aaron, *N* Ex 28:1 5070
And *N* and Abihu, the sons of Aaron, Lev 10:1 5070
N the firstborn, and Abihu, Num 3:2 5070
And *N* and Abihu died before the Num 3:4 5070
And unto Aaron was born *N*, and Num 26:60 5070
And *N* and Abihu died, when they Num 26:61 5070
N, and Abihu, Eleazar, and Ithamar 1Chr 6:3 5070
N, and Abihu, Eleazar, and Ithamar 1Chr 24:1 5070
But *N* and Abihu died before their 1Chr 24:2 5070
2. Son of King Jeroboam 1.
N his son reigned in his stead 1Kin 14:20 5070
N the son of Jeroboam began to 1Kin 15:25 5070
for *N* and all Israel laid siege to 1Kin 15:27 5070
Now the rest of the acts of *N* 1Kin 15:31 5070

3. Great-grandson of Jerahmeel.
Shammai; *N*, and ... 1Chr 2:28 5070
And the sons of *N* ... 1Chr 2:30 5070
4. A descendant of King Saul.
and Zur, and Kish, and Baal, and *N* ... 1Chr 8:30 5070
and Kish, and Baal, and Ner, and *N* ... 1Chr 9:36 5070

NAGGAI See NAGGE.

NAGGE *(nag'-e)* {1} See NEARIAH. *Father of Esli; ancestor of Jesus.*
of Esli, which was the son of *N* ... Lk 3:25 *3477*

NAHALAL *(na'-ha-lal)* {1} *A Levitical city in Zebulun.*
her suburbs, *N* with her suburbs ... Josh 21:35 5096

NAHALIEL *(na-ha'-le-el)* {2} *An Israelite encampment in the wilderness.*
And from Mattanah to *N* ... Num 21:19 5160
and from *N* to Bamoth ... Num 21:19 5160

NAHALLAL *(na'-hal-el)* {1} See NAHALAL. *Same as Nahalal.*
And Kattath, and *N*, and Shimron, and .. Josh 19:15 5096

NAHALOL *(na'-ha-lol)* {1} *Same as Nahalal.*
Kitron, nor the inhabitants of *N* ... Judg 1:30 5096

NAHAM *(na'-ham)* {1} See ISHBAH. *A descendant of Caleb.*
his wife Hodiah the sister of *N* ... 1Chr 4:19 5163

NAHAMANI *(na-ham'-a-ni)* {1} *A clan chief with Zerubbabel.*
Nehemiah, Azariah, Raamiah, *N* ... Neh 7:7 5167

NAHARAI *(na'-ha-rahee)* {1} See NAHARI. *A "mighty man" of David.*
N the Berothite, the armourbearer ... 1Chr 11:39 5171

NAHARI *(na'-ha-ri)* {1} See NAHARAI. *Same as Naharai.*
N the Beerothite, armourbearer to ... 2Sa 23:37 5171

NAHASH *(na'-hash)* {9} See IR-NAHASH.
1. An Ammonite king.
Then *N* the Ammonite came up, and ... 1Sa 11:1 5176
all the men of Jabesh said unto *N* ... 1Sa 11:1 5176
N the Ammonite answered them, On ... 1Sa 11:2 5176
when ye saw that *N* the king of ... 1Sa 12:12 5176
2. Father of Shobi and Hanun.
kindness unto Hanun the son of *N* ... 2Sa 10:2 5176
that Shobi the son of *N* of Rabbah ... 2Sa 17:27 5176
that *N* the king of the children ... 1Chr 19:1 5176
kindness unto Hanun the son of *N* ... 1Chr 19:2 5176
3. Mother of Abigail.
in to Abigail the daughter of *N* ... 2Sa 17:25 5176

NAHATH *(na'-hath)* {5} See TOHU.
1. A son of Reuel.
N, and Zerah, Shammah, and Mizzah ... Gen 36:13 5184
duke *N*, duke Zerah, duke Shammah, ... Gen 36:17 5184
N, Zerah, Shammah, and Mizzah ... 1Chr 1:37 5184
2. Son of Zophi.
Zophai his son, and *N* his son, ... 1Chr 6:26 5184
3. A Temple servant.
And Jehiel, and Azaziah, and *N* ... 2Chr 31:13 5184

NAHBI *(nah'-bi)* {1} *A spy sent to the Promised Land.*
of Naphtali, *N* the son of Vophsi ... Num 13:14 5147

NAHOR *(na'-hor)* {15} See NACHOR, NAHOR'S.
1. Grandfather of Abraham.
lived thirty years, and begat *N* ... Gen 11:22 5152
he begat *N* two hundred years ... Gen 11:23 5152
N lived nine and twenty years, and ... Gen 11:24 5152
N lived after he begat Terah an ... Gen 11:25 5152
Serug, *N*, Terah, ... 1Chr 1:26 5152
2. Son of Terah.
seventy years, and begat Abram, *N* ... Gen 11:26 5152
Terah begat Abram, *N*, and Haran ... Gen 11:27 5152
And Abram and *N* took them wives ... Gen 11:29 5152
born children unto thy brother *N* ... Gen 22:20 5152
these eight Milcah did bear to *N* ... Gen 22:23 5152
Mesopotamia, unto the city of *N* ... Gen 24:10 5152
son of Milcah, the wife of *N* ... Gen 24:15 5152
of Milcah, which she bare unto *N* ... Gen 24:24 5152
them, Know ye Laban the son of *N* ... Gen 29:5 5152
God of Abraham, and the God of *N* ... Gen 31:53 5152

NAHOR'S *(na'-hors)* {2} *Refers to Nahor 2.*
and the name of *N* wife, Milcah, ... Gen 11:29 5152
N son, whom Milcah bare unto him ... Gen 24:47 5152

NAHSHON *(nah'-shon)* {11} See NAASHON, NAASSON. *Son of Amminadab.*
N the son of Amminadab ... Num 1:7 5177
N the son of Amminadab shall be ... Num 2:3 5177
day was *N* the son of Amminadab ... Num 7:12 5177
of *N* the son of Amminadab ... Num 7:17 5177
over his host was *N* the son of ... Num 10:14 5177
And Amminadab begat *N*, and *N* ... Ruth 4:20 5177
begat *N*, and *N* begat Salmon, ... Ruth 4:20 5177
and Amminadab begat *N*, prince of ... 1Chr 2:10 5177
N begat Salma, and Salma begat ... 1Chr 2:11 5177

NAHUM *(na'-hum)* {1} See NAUM. *A prophet who spoke against Nineveh.*
of the vision of *N* the Elkoshite ... Nah 1:1 5151

NAIL {8}
Heber's wife took a *n* of the tent ... Judg 4:21 3489
smote the *n* into his temples, and ... Judg 4:21 3489
dead, and the *n* was in his temples ... Judg 4:22 3489
She put her hand to the *n* ... Judg 5:26 3489
to give us a *n* in his holy place, ... Ezr 9:8 3489
fasten him as a *n* in a sure place ... Is 22:23 3489
shall the *n* that is fastened in ... Is 22:25 3489
the corner, out of him the *n* ... Zec 10:4 3489

NAILING {1}
out of the way, *n* it to his cross ... Col 2:14 *4338*

NAILS {10}
shave her head, and pare her *n* ... Deut 21:12 6856
iron in abundance for the *n* for ... 1Chr 22:3 4548
the weight of the *n* was fifty ... 2Chr 3:9 4548
as *n* fastened by the masters of ... Eccl 12:11 4930
and he fastened it with *n*, that it ... Is 41:7 4548
they fasten it with *n* and with ... Jer 10:4 4548
and his *n* like birds' claws ... Dan 4:33 2953
were of iron, and his *n* of brass ... Dan 7:19 2953
in his hands the print of the *n* ... Jn 20:25 *2247*
my finger into the print of the *n* ... Jn 20:25 *2247*

NAIN *(nane)* {1} *A city in Galilee.*
that he went into a city called *N* ... Lk 7:11 *3484*

NAIOTH *(nay'-yoth)* {6} *A place in Ramah.*
he and Samuel went and dwelt in *N* ... 1Sa 19:18 5121
Behold, David is at *N* in Ramah ... 1Sa 19:19 5121
Behold, they be at *N* in Ramah ... 1Sa 19:22 5121
And he went thither to *N* in Ramah ... 1Sa 19:23 5121
until he came to *N* in Ramah ... 1Sa 19:23 5121
And David fled from *N* in Ramah ... 1Sa 20:1 5121

NAKED {47}
And they were both *n*, the man and ... Gen 2:25 6174
and they knew that they were *n* ... Gen 3:7 5903
and I was afraid, because I was *n* ... Gen 3:10 5903
Who told thee that thou wast *n* ... Gen 3:11 5903
Moses saw that the people were *n* ... Ex 32:25 6544
(for Aaron had made them *n* unto ... Ex 32:25 6544
lay down *n* all that day and all ... 1Sa 19:24 6174
all that were *n* among them ... 2Chr 28:15 4636
for he made Judah *n*, and ... 2Chr 28:19 6544
N came I out of my mother's womb, ... Job 1:21 6174
and *n* shall I return thither ... Job 1:21 6174
stripped the *n* of their clothing ... Job 22:6 6174
They cause the *n* to lodge without ... Job 24:7 6174
him to go *n* without clothing ... Job 24:10 6174
Hell is *n* before him, and ... Job 26:6 6174
n shall he return to go as he ... Eccl 5:15 6174
And he did so, walking *n* and ... Is 20:2 6174
my servant Isaiah hath walked *n* ... Is 20:3 6174
captives, young and old, *n* ... Is 20:4 6174
when thou seest the *n*, that thou ... Is 58:7 6174
drunken, and shalt make thyself *n* ... Lam 4:21 6168
is grown, whereas thou wast *n* ... Eze 16:7 5903
of thy youth, when thou wast *n* ... Eze 16:22 5903
thy fair jewels, and leave thee *n* ... Eze 16:39 5903
hath covered the *n* with a garment ... Eze 18:7 5903
hath covered the *n* with a garment ... Eze 18:16 5903
thy labour, and shall leave thee *n* ... Eze 23:29 5903
Lest I strip her *n*, and set her as ... Hos 2:3 6174
shall flee away *n* in that day ... Amos 2:16 6174
and howl, I will go stripped and *n* ... Mic 1:8 6174
of Saphir, having thy shame *n* ... Mic 1:11 6181
Thy bow was made quite *n*, ... Hab 3:9 5783
N, and ye clothed me ... Mt 25:36 *1131*
or *n*, and clothed thee ... Mt 25:38 *1131*
n, and ye clothed me not ... Mt 25:43 *1131*
or athirst, or a stranger, or *n* ... Mt 25:44 *1131*
linen cloth cast about his *n* body ... Mk 14:51 *1131*
linen cloth, and fled from them *n* ... Mk 14:52 *1131*
coat unto him, (for he was *n* ... Jn 21:7 *1131*
they fled out of that house *n* ... Acts 19:16 *1131*
both hunger, and thirst, and are *n* ... 1Cor 4:11 *1130*
clothed we shall not be found *n* ... 2Cor 5:3 *1131*
but all things are *n* and opened ... Heb 4:13 *1131*
If a brother or sister be *n* ... Jas 2:15 *1131*
and poor, and blind, and *n* ... Rev 3:17 *1131*
his garments, lest he walk *n* ... Rev 16:15 *1131*
and shall make her desolate and *n* ... Rev 17:16 *1131*

NAKEDNESS {57}
saw the *n* of his father, and told ... Gen 9:22 6172
covered the *n* of their father ... Gen 9:23 6172
and they saw not their father's *n* ... Gen 9:23 6172
to see the *n* of the land ye are ... Gen 42:9 6172
but to see the *n* of the land ye ... Gen 42:12 6172
that thy *n* be not discovered ... Ex 20:26 6172
linen breeches to cover their *n* ... Ex 28:42 6172
of kin to him, to uncover their *n* ... Lev 18:6 6172
The *n* of thy father ... Lev 18:7 6172
or the *n* of thy mother, shalt ... Lev 18:7 6172
thou shalt not uncover her *n* ... Lev 18:7 6172
The *n* of thy father's wife shalt ... Lev 18:8 6172
it is thy father's *n* ... Lev 18:8 6172
The *n* of thy sister, the daughter ... Lev 18:9 6172
even their *n* thou shalt not ... Lev 18:9 6172
The *n* of thy son's daughter, or ... Lev 18:10 6172
even their *n* thou shalt not ... Lev 18:10 6172
for theirs is thine own *n* ... Lev 18:10 6172
The *n* of thy father's wife's ... Lev 18:11 6172
thou shalt not uncover her *n* ... Lev 18:11 6172
the *n* of thy father's sister ... Lev 18:12 6172
the *n* of thy mother's sister ... Lev 18:13 6172
the *n* of thy father's brother ... Lev 18:14 6172
the *n* of thy daughter in law ... Lev 18:15 6172
thou shalt not uncover her *n* ... Lev 18:15 6172
the *n* of thy brother's wife ... Lev 18:16 6172
it is thy brother's *n* ... Lev 18:16 6172
not uncover the *n* of a woman ... Lev 18:17 6172
daughter, to uncover her *n* ... Lev 18:17 6172
to vex her, to uncover her *n* ... Lev 18:18 6172
unto a woman to uncover her *n* ... Lev 18:19 6172
hath uncovered his father's *n* ... Lev 20:11 6172
her *n*, and she see his *n* ... Lev 20:17 6172
he hath uncovered his sister's *n* ... Lev 20:17 6172
sickness, and shall uncover her *n* ... Lev 20:18 6172
the *n* of thy mother's sister ... Lev 20:19 6172
he hath uncovered his uncle's *n* ... Lev 20:20 6172
he hath uncovered his brother's *n* ... Lev 20:21 6172
in hunger, and in thirst, and in *n* ... Deut 28:48 5903
the confusion of thy mother's *n* ... 1Sa 20:30 6172
Thy *n* shall be uncovered, yea, ... Is 47:3 6172
her, because they have seen her *n* ... Lam 1:8 6172
skirt over thee, and covered thy *n* ... Eze 16:8 6172
thy *n* discovered through thy ... Eze 16:36 6172
and will discover thy *n* unto them ... Eze 16:37 6172
that they may see all thy *n* ... Eze 16:37 6172
they discovered their fathers' *n* ... Eze 22:10 6172
These discovered her *n* ... Eze 23:10 6172
whoredoms, and discovered her *n* ... Eze 23:18 6172
the *n* of thy whoredoms shall be ... Eze 23:29 6172
and my flax given to cover her *n* ... Hos 2:9 6172
and I will shew the nations thy *n* ... Nah 3:5 4626
that thou mayest look on their *n* ... Hab 2:15 4589
or persecution, or famine, or *n* ... Rom 8:35 *1132*
in fastings often, in cold and *n* ... 2Cor 11:27 *1132*
the shame of thy *n* do not appear ... Rev 3:18 *1132*

NAME {927}
The *n* of the first is Pison ... Gen 2:11 8034
the *n* of the second river is ... Gen 2:13 8034
the *n* of the third river is ... Gen 2:14 8034
creature, that was the *n* thereof ... Gen 2:19 8034
And Adam called his wife's *n* Eve ... Gen 3:20 8034
called the *n* of the city ... Gen 4:17 8034
after the *n* of his son, Enoch ... Gen 4:17 8034
the *n* of the one was Adah, and the ... Gen 4:19 8034
the *n* of the other Zillah ... Gen 4:19 8034
And his brother's *n* was Jubal ... Gen 4:21 8034
bare a son, and called his *n* Seth ... Gen 4:25 8034
and he called his *n* Enos ... Gen 4:26 8034
to call upon the *n* of the LORD ... Gen 4:26 8034
them, and called their *n* Adam ... Gen 5:2 8034
and called his *n* Seth ... Gen 5:3 8034
And he called his *n* Noah, saying, ... Gen 5:29 8034
the *n* of one was Peleg ... Gen 10:25 8034
and his brother's *n* was Joktan ... Gen 10:25 8034
and let us make us a *n*, lest we be ... Gen 11:4 8034
Therefore is the *n* of it called ... Gen 11:9 8034
the *n* of Abram's wife was Sarai ... Gen 11:29 8034
the *n* of Nahor's wife, Milcah, ... Gen 11:29 8034
bless thee, and make thy *n* great ... Gen 12:2 8034
and called upon the *n* of the LORD ... Gen 12:8 8034
Abram called on the *n* of the LORD ... Gen 13:4 8034
an Egyptian, whose *n* was Hagar ... Gen 16:1 8034
son, and shalt call his *n* Ishmael ... Gen 16:11 8034
she called the *n* of the LORD that ... Gen 16:13 8034
and Abram called his son's *n* ... Gen 16:15 8034
Neither shall thy *n* any more be ... Gen 17:5 8034
but thy *n* shall be Abraham ... Gen 17:5 8034
thou shalt not call her *n* Sarai ... Gen 17:15 8034
Sarai, but Sarah shall her *n* be ... Gen 17:15 8034
and thou shalt call his *n* Isaac ... Gen 17:19 8034
Therefore the *n* of the city was ... Gen 19:22 8034
bare a son, and called his *n* Moab ... Gen 19:37 8034
a son, and called his *n* Ben-ammi ... Gen 19:38 8034
Abraham called the *n* of his son ... Gen 21:3 8034
called there on the *n* of the LORD ... Gen 21:33 8034
Abraham called the *n* of that ... Gen 22:14 8034
whose *n* was Reumah, she bare also ... Gen 22:24 8034
had a brother, and his *n* was Laban ... Gen 24:29 8034
took a wife, and her *n* was Keturah ... Gen 25:1 8034
and they called his *n* Esau ... Gen 25:25 8034
and his *n* was called Jacob ... Gen 25:26 8034
therefore was his *n* called Edom ... Gen 25:30 8034
he called the *n* of the well Esek ... Gen 26:20 8034
and he called the *n* of it Sitnah ... Gen 26:21 8034
he called the *n* of it Rehoboth ... Gen 26:22 8034
and called upon the *n* of the LORD ... Gen 26:25 8034
therefore the *n* of the city is ... Gen 26:33 8034
he called the *n* of that place ... Gen 28:19 8034
but the *n* of that city was called ... Gen 28:19 8034
the *n* of the elder was Leah, and ... Gen 29:16 8034
the *n* of the younger was Rachel ... Gen 29:16 8034
a son, and she called his *n* Reuben ... Gen 29:32 8034
and she called his *n* Simeon ... Gen 29:33 8034
therefore was his *n* called Levi ... Gen 29:34 8034
therefore she called his *n* Judah ... Gen 29:35 8034
therefore called she his *n* Dan ... Gen 30:6 8034
and she called his *n* Naphtali ... Gen 30:8 8034
and she called his *n* Gad ... Gen 30:11 8034
and she called his *n* Asher ... Gen 30:13 8034
and she called his *n* Issachar ... Gen 30:18 8034
and she called his *n* Zebulun ... Gen 30:20 8034
a daughter, and called her *n* Dinah ... Gen 30:21 8034
And she called his *n* Joseph ... Gen 30:24 8034
Therefore was the *n* of it called ... Gen 31:48 8034
he called the *n* of that place ... Gen 32:2 8034
he said unto him, What is thy *n* ... Gen 32:27 8034
Thy *n* shall be called no more ... Gen 32:28 8034
said, Tell me, I pray thee, thy *n* ... Gen 32:29 8034
it that thou dost ask after my *n* ... Gen 32:29 8034
Jacob called the *n* of the place ... Gen 32:30 8034
therefore the *n* of the place is ... Gen 33:17 8034
and the *n* of it was called ... Gen 35:8 8034
God said unto him, Thy *n* is Jacob ... Gen 35:10 8034
thy *n* shall not be called any ... Gen 35:10 8034
Jacob, but Israel shall be thy *n* ... Gen 35:10 8034
and he called his *n* Israel ... Gen 35:10 8034
Jacob called the *n* of the place ... Gen 35:15 8034
that she called his *n* Ben-oni ... Gen 35:18 8034
the *n* of his city was Dinhabah ... Gen 36:32 8034
the *n* of his city was Avith ... Gen 36:35 8034
the *n* of his city was Pau ... Gen 36:39 8034
his wife's *n* was Mehetabel, the ... Gen 36:39 8034
Adullamite, whose *n* was Hirah ... Gen 38:1 8034

Canaanite, whose *n* was Shuah .... Gen 38:2 8034
and he called his *n* Er .... Gen 38:3 8034
and she called his *n* Onan .... Gen 38:4 8034
and called his *n* Shelah .... Gen 38:5 8034
his firstborn, whose *n* was Tamar .... Gen 38:6 8034
therefore his *n* was called Pharez .... Gen 38:29 8034
and his *n* was called Zarah .... Gen 38:30 8034
Joseph's *n* Zaphnath-paaneah .... Gen 41:45 8034
Joseph called the *n* of the .... Gen 41:51 8034
the *n* of the second called he .... Gen 41:52 8034
shall be called after the *n* of .... Gen 48:6 8034
let my *n* be named on them, and the .... Gen 48:16 8034
the *n* of my fathers Abraham and .... Gen 48:16 8034
wherefore the *n* of it was called .... Gen 50:11 8034
of which the *n* of the one was .... Ex 1:15 8034
and the *n* of the other Puah .... Ex 1:15 8034
And she called his *n* Moses .... Ex 2:10 8034
a son, and he called his *n* Gershom .... Ex 2:22 8034
shall say to me, What is his *n* .... Ex 3:13 8034
this is my *n* for ever, and this is .... Ex 3:15 8034
came to Pharaoh to speak in thy *n* .... Ex 5:23 8034
by the *n* of God Almighty, but by .... Ex 6:3
but by my *n* JEHOVAH was I not .... Ex 6:3 8034
that my *n* may be declared .... Ex 9:16 8034
the LORD is his *n* .... Ex 15:3 8034
therefore the *n* of it was called .... Ex 15:23 8034
Israel called the *n* thereof Manna .... Ex 16:31 8034
he called the *n* of the place .... Ex 17:7 8034
called the *n* of it Jehovah-nissi .... Ex 17:15 8034
of which the *n* of the one was .... Ex 18:3 8034
the *n* of the other was Eliezer .... Ex 18:4 8034
Thou shalt not take the *n* of the .... Ex 20:7 8034
that taketh his *n* in vain .... Ex 20:7 8034
record my *n* I will come unto thee .... Ex 20:24 8034
no mention of the *n* of other gods .... Ex 23:13 8034
for my *n* is in him .... Ex 23:21 8034
every one with his *n* shall they .... Ex 28:21 8034
I have called by *n* Bezaleel the .... Ex 31:2 8034
thou hast said, I know thee by *n* .... Ex 33:12 8034
in my sight, and I know thee by *n* .... Ex 33:17 8034
I will proclaim the *n* of the LORD .... Ex 33:19 8034
and proclaimed the *n* of the LORD .... Ex 34:5 8034
whose *n* is Jealous, is a jealous .... Ex 34:14 8034
by *n* Bezaleel the son of Uri .... Ex 35:30 8034
of a signet, every one with his *n* .... Ex 39:14 8034
thou profane the *n* of thy God .... Lev 18:21 8034
shall not swear by my *n* falsely .... Lev 19:12 8034
thou profane the *n* of thy God .... Lev 19:12 8034
and to profane my holy *n* .... Lev 20:3 8034
and not profane the *n* of their God .... Lev 21:6 8034
holy *n* in those things which they .... Lev 22:2 8034
shall ye profane my holy *n* .... Lev 22:32 8034
son blasphemed the *n* of the LORD .... Lev 24:11 8034
his mother's *n* was Shelomith, the .... Lev 24:11 8034
blasphemeth the *n* of the LORD .... Lev 24:16 8034
he blasphemeth the *n* of the LORD .... Lev 24:16 8034
and by *n* ye shall reckon the .... Num 4:32 8034
they shall put my *n* upon the .... Num 6:27 8034
he called the *n* of the place .... Num 11:3 8034
the *n* of the one was Eldad .... Num 11:26 8034
and the *n* of the other Medad .... Num 11:26 8034
he called the *n* of that place .... Num 11:34 8034
thou every man's *n* upon his rod .... Num 17:2 8034
Aaron's *n* upon the rod of Levi .... Num 17:3 8034
he called the *n* of the place .... Num 21:3 8034
Now the *n* of the Israelite that .... Num 25:14 8034
the *n* of the Midianitish woman .... Num 25:15 8034
the *n* of the daughter of Asher .... Num 26:46 8034
the *n* of Amram's wife was .... Num 26:59 8034
Why should the *n* of our father be .... Num 27:4 8034
called it Nobah, after his own *n* .... Num 32:42 8034
and called them after his own *n* .... Deut 3:14 8034
Thou shalt not take the *n* of the .... Deut 5:11 8034
that taketh his *n* in vain .... Deut 5:11 8034
him, and shalt swear by his *n* .... Deut 6:13 8034
destroy their *n* from under heaven .... Deut 7:24 8034
blot out their *n* from under .... Deut 9:14 8034
unto him, and to bless in his *n* .... Deut 10:8 8034
thou cleave, and swear by his *n* .... Deut 10:20 8034
your tribes to put his *n* there .... Deut 12:5 8034
to cause his *n* to dwell there .... Deut 12:11 8034
his *n* there be too far from thee .... Deut 12:21 8034
shall choose to place his *n* there .... Deut 14:23 8034
shall choose to set his *n* there .... Deut 14:24 8034
shall choose to place his *n* there .... Deut 16:2 8034
shall choose to place his *n* in .... Deut 16:6 8034
hath chosen to place his *n* there .... Deut 16:11 8034
to minister in the *n* of the LORD .... Deut 18:5 8034
in the *n* of the LORD his God .... Deut 18:7 8034
which he shall speak in my *n* .... Deut 18:19 8034
presume to speak a word in my *n* .... Deut 18:20 8034
speak in the *n* of other gods .... Deut 18:20 8034
speaketh in the *n* of the LORD .... Deut 18:22 8034
and to bless in the *n* of the LORD .... Deut 21:5 8034
and bring up an evil *n* upon her .... Deut 22:14 8034
an evil *n* upon a virgin of Israel .... Deut 22:19 8034
n of his brother which is dead .... Deut 25:6 8034
that his *n* be not put out of .... Deut 25:6 8034
up unto his brother a *n* in Israel .... Deut 25:7 8034
his *n* shall be called in Israel, ... Deut 25:10 8034
shall choose to place his *n* there .... Deut 26:2 8034
he hath made, in praise, and in *n* .... Deut 26:19 8034
art called by the *n* of the LORD .... Deut 28:10 8034
fear this glorious and fearful *n* .... Deut 28:58 8034
blot out his *n* from under heaven .... Deut 29:20 8034
I will publish the *n* of the LORD .... Deut 32:3 8034
Wherefore the *n* of the place is .... Josh 5:9 8034
cut off our *n* from the earth .... Josh 7:9 8034

wilt thou do unto thy great *n* .... Josh 7:9 8034
Wherefore the *n* of that place was .... Josh 7:26 8034
of the *n* of the LORD thy God .... Josh 9:9 8034
the *n* of Hebron before was .... Josh 14:15 8034
the *n* of Debir before was .... Josh 15:15 8034
after the *n* of Dan their father .... Josh 19:47 8034
which are here mentioned by *n* .... Josh 21:9 8034
(now the *n* of Hebron before was .... Judg 1:10 8034
the *n* of Debir before was .... Judg 1:11 8034
the *n* of the city was called .... Judg 1:17 8034
(Now the *n* of the city before was .... Judg 1:23 8034
city, and called the *n* thereof Luz .... Judg 1:26 8034
which is the *n* thereof unto this .... Judg 1:26 8034
they called the *n* of that place .... Judg 2:5 8034
whose *n* he called Abimelech .... Judg 8:31 8034
the Danites, whose *n* was Manoah .... Judg 13:2 8034
he was, neither told he me his *n* .... Judg 13:6 8034
angel of the LORD, What is thy *n* .... Judg 13:17 8034
Why askest thou thus after my *n* .... Judg 13:18 8034
a son, and called his *n* Samson .... Judg 13:24 8034
called the *n* thereof En-hakkore .... Judg 15:19 8034
of Sorek, whose *n* was Delilah .... Judg 16:4 8034
mount Ephraim, whose *n* was Micah .... Judg 17:1 8034
they called the *n* of the city Dan .... Judg 18:29 8034
after the *n* of Dan their father, ... Judg 18:29 8034
howbeit the *n* of the city was .... Judg 18:29 8034
the *n* of the man was Elimelech, ... Ruth 1:2 8034
the *n* of his wife Naomi, and the .... Ruth 1:2 8034
the *n* of his two sons Mahlon and .... Ruth 1:2 8034
the *n* of the one was Orpah .... Ruth 1:4 8034
and the *n* of the other Ruth .... Ruth 1:4 8034
and his *n* was Boaz .... Ruth 2:1 8034
The man's *n* with whom I wrought .... Ruth 2:19 8034
to raise up the *n* of the dead .... Ruth 4:5 8034
to raise up the *n* of the dead .... Ruth 4:10 8034
that the *n* of the dead be not cut .... Ruth 4:10 8034
that his *n* may be famous in .... Ruth 4:14 8034
women her neighbours gave it a *n* .... Ruth 4:17 8034
and they called his *n* Obed .... Ruth 4:17 8034
his *n* was Elkanah, the son of 1Sa 1:1 8034
the *n* of the one was Hannah, and 1Sa 1:2 8034
the *n* of the other Peninnah 1Sa 1:2 8034
a son, and called his *n* Samuel 1Sa 1:20 8034
called the *n* of it Eben-ezer, ... 1Sa 7:12 8034
Now the *n* of his firstborn was 1Sa 8:2 8034
the *n* of his second, Abiah 1Sa 8:2 8034
whose *n* was Kish, the son of 1Sa 9:1 8034
whose *n* was Saul, a choice young 1Sa 9:2 8034
the *n* of the one was Bozez 1Sa 14:4 8034
and the *n* of the other Seneh 1Sa 14:4 8034
the *n* of the firstborn Merab, and 1Sa 14:49 8034
the *n* of the younger Michal 1Sa 14:49 8034
the *n* of Saul's wife was Ahinoam, ... 1Sa 14:50 8034
the *n* of the captain of his host 1Sa 14:50 8034
unto me him whom I *n* unto thee 1Sa 16:3 559
whose *n* was Jesse 1Sa 17:12 8034
Philistine of Gath, Goliath by *n* 1Sa 17:23 8034
in the *n* of the LORD of hosts 1Sa 17:45 8034
so that his *n* was much set by 1Sa 18:30 8034
both of us in the *n* of the LORD 1Sa 20:42 8034
his *n* was Doeg, an Edomite, the 1Sa 21:7 8034
my *n* out of my father's house 1Sa 24:21 8034
Now the *n* of the man was Nabal 1Sa 25:3 8034
the *n* of his wife Abigail 1Sa 25:3 8034
go to Nabal, and greet him in my *n* 1Sa 25:5 8034
all those words in the *n* of David 1Sa 25:9 8034
for as his *n* is, so is he 1Sa 25:25 8034
Nabal is his *n*, and folly is with 1Sa 25:25 8034
him up, whom I shall *n* unto thee 1Sa 28:8 559
whose *n* was Rizpah, the daughter 2Sa 3:7 8034
the *n* of the one was Baanah, and 2Sa 4:2 8034
the *n* of the other Rechab, the 2Sa 4:2 8034
And his *n* was Mephibosheth 2Sa 4:4 8034
Therefore he called the *n* of that 2Sa 5:20 8034
whose *n* is called by the *n* of 2Sa 6:2 8034
he called the *n* of the place 2Sa 6:8
in the *n* of the LORD of hosts 2Sa 6:18 8034
and have made thee a great *n* 2Sa 7:9 8034
like unto the *n* of the great men 2Sa 7:9 8034
He shall build an house for my *n* 2Sa 7:13 8034
to himself, and to make him a *n* 2Sa 7:23 8034
let thy *n* be magnified for ever, ... 2Sa 7:26 8034
David gat him a *n* when he 2Sa 8:13 8034
Saul a servant whose *n* was Ziba 2Sa 9:2 8034
a young son, whose *n* was Micha 2Sa 9:12 8034
a son, and he called his *n* Solomon 2Sa 12:24 8034
and he called his *n* Jedidiah 2Sa 12:25 8034
city, and it be called after my *n* 2Sa 12:28 8034
a fair sister, whose *n* was Tamar 2Sa 13:1 8034
whose *n* was Jonadab, the son of 2Sa 13:3 8034
n nor remainder upon the earth 2Sa 14:7 8034
one daughter, whose *n* was Tamar 2Sa 14:27 8034
whose *n* was Shimei, the son of 2Sa 16:5 8034
whose *n* was Ithra an Israelite, ... 2Sa 17:25 8034
son to keep my *n* in remembrance 2Sa 18:18 8034
called the pillar after his own *n* 2Sa 18:18 8034
whose *n* was Sheba, the son of 2Sa 20:1 8034
Sheba the son of Bichri by *n* 2Sa 20:21 8034
them, and had the *n* among three 2Sa 23:18 8034
had the *n* among three mighty men 2Sa 23:22 8034
n of Solomon better than thy *n* 1Kin 1:47 8034
built unto the *n* of the LORD 1Kin 3:2 8034
the *n* of the LORD his God for the 1Kin 5:3 8034
unto the *n* of the LORD my God 1Kin 5:5 8034
he shall build an house unto my *n* 1Kin 5:5 8034
called the *n* thereof Jachin 1Kin 7:21 8034
called the *n* thereof Boaz 1Kin 7:21 8034
that my *n* might be therein 1Kin 8:16 8034

the *n* of the LORD God of Israel 1Kin 8:17 8034
heart to build an house unto my *n* 1Kin 8:18 8034
shall build the house unto my *n* 1Kin 8:19 8034
the *n* of the LORD God of Israel 1Kin 8:20 8034
hast said, My *n* shall be there 1Kin 8:29 8034
again to thee, and confess thy *n* 1Kin 8:33 8034
this place, and confess thy *n* 1Kin 8:35 8034
they shall hear of thy great *n* 1Kin 8:42 8034
of the earth may know thy *n* 1Kin 8:43 8034
have builded, is called by thy *n* 1Kin 8:43 8034
house that I have built for thy *n* 1Kin 8:44 8034
which I have built for thy *n* 1Kin 8:48 8034
to put my *n* there for ever 1Kin 9:3 8034
which I have hallowed for my *n* 1Kin 9:7 8034
concerning the *n* of the LORD 1Kin 10:1 8034
whose mother's *n* was Zeruah 1Kin 11:26 8034
have chosen me to put my *n* there 1Kin 11:36 8034
the house of David, Josiah by *n* 1Kin 13:2 8034
of Israel, to put his *n* there 1Kin 14:21 8034
his mother's *n* was Naamah an 1Kin 14:21 8034
his mother's *n* was Naamah an 1Kin 14:31 8034
And his mother's *n* was Maachah 1Kin 15:2 8034
And his mother's *n* was Maachah 1Kin 15:10 8034
called the *n* of the city which he 1Kin 16:24 8034
he built, after the *n* of Shemer 1Kin 16:24 8034
And call ye on the *n* of your gods 1Kin 18:24 8034
I will call on the *n* of the LORD 1Kin 18:24 8034
call on the *n* of your gods, but 1Kin 18:25 8034
called on the *n* of Baal from 1Kin 18:26 8034
saying, Israel shall be thy *n* 1Kin 18:31 8034
an altar in the *n* of the LORD 1Kin 18:32 8034
So she wrote letters in Ahab's *n* 1Kin 21:8 8034
is true in the *n* of the LORD 1Kin 22:16 8034
his mother's *n* was Azubah the 1Kin 22:42 8034
cursed them in the *n* of the LORD 2Kin 2:24 8034
call on the *n* of the LORD his God 2Kin 5:11 8034
And his mother's *n* was Athaliah 2Kin 8:26 8034
his mother's *n* was Zibiah of 2Kin 12:1 8034
his mother's *n* was Jehoaddan of 2Kin 14:2 8034
called the *n* of it Joktheel unto 2Kin 14:7 8034
the *n* of Israel from under heaven 2Kin 14:27 8034
his mother's *n* was Jecholiah of 2Kin 15:2 8034
And his mother's *n* was Jerusha 2Kin 15:33 8034
His mother's *n* also was Abi 2Kin 18:2 8034
his mother's *n* was Hephzi-bah 2Kin 21:1 8034
In Jerusalem will I put my *n* 2Kin 21:4 8034
Israel, will I put my *n* for ever 2Kin 21:7 8034
his mother's *n* was Meshullemeth, ... 2Kin 21:19 8034
And his mother's *n* was Jedidah 2Kin 22:1 8034
which I said, My *n* shall be there 2Kin 23:27 8034
And his mother's *n* was Hamutal 2Kin 23:31 8034
turned his *n* to Jehoiakim, and 2Kin 23:34 8034
And his mother's *n* was Zebudah 2Kin 23:36 8034
And his mother's *n* was Nehushta 2Kin 24:8 8034
and changed his *n* to Zedekiah 2Kin 24:17 8034
And his mother's *n* was Hamutal 2Kin 24:18 8034
the *n* of the one was Peleg 1Chr 1:19 8034
and his brother's *n* was Joktan 1Chr 1:19 8034
the *n* of his city was Dinhabah 1Chr 1:43 8034
the *n* of his city was Avith 1Chr 1:46 8034
the *n* of his city was Pai 1Chr 1:50 8034
his wife's *n* was Mehetabel, the 1Chr 1:50 8034
another wife, whose *n* was Atarah 1Chr 2:26 8034
the *n* of the wife of Abishur was 1Chr 2:29 8034
an Egyptian, whose *n* was Jarha 1Chr 2:34 8034
the *n* of their sister was 1Chr 4:3 8034
and his mother called his *n* Jabez 1Chr 4:9 8034
these written by *n* came in the 1Chr 4:41 8034
whose sister's *n* was Maachah 1Chr 7:15 8034
and the *n* of the second was 1Chr 7:15 8034
a son, and she called his *n* Peresh 1Chr 7:16 8034
the *n* of his brother was Sheresh 1Chr 7:16 8034
a son, and he called his *n* Beriah 1Chr 7:23 8034
whose wife's *n* was Maachah 1Chr 8:29 8034
whose wife's *n* was Maachah 1Chr 9:35 8034
them, and had a *n* among the three 1Chr 11:20 8034
had the *n* among the three 1Chr 11:24 8034
which were expressed by *n* 1Chr 12:31 8034
whose *n* is called on it 1Chr 13:6 8034
therefore they called the *n* of 1Chr 14:11 8034
the people in the *n* of the LORD 1Chr 16:2 8034
unto the LORD, call upon his *n* 1Chr 16:8 8034
Glory ye in his holy *n* 1Chr 16:10 8034
the LORD the glory due unto his *n* 1Chr 16:29 8034
we may give thanks to thy holy *n* 1Chr 16:35 8034
chosen, who were expressed by *n* 1Chr 16:41 8034
have made thee a *n* like the *n* 1Chr 17:8 8034
n of the great men that are in 1Chr 17:8 8034
to make thee a *n* of greatness 1Chr 17:21 8034
that thy *n* may be magnified for 1Chr 17:24 8034
he spake in the *n* of the LORD 1Chr 21:19 8034
unto the *n* of the LORD my God 1Chr 22:7 8034
not build an house unto my *n* 1Chr 22:8 8034
for his *n* shall be Solomon, and I 1Chr 22:9 8034
He shall build an house for my *n* 1Chr 22:10 8034
to be built to the *n* of the LORD 1Chr 22:19 8034
and to bless in his *n* for ever 1Chr 23:13 8034
shalt not build an house for my *n* 1Chr 28:3 8034
thee, and praise thy glorious *n* 1Chr 29:13 8034
thine holy *n* cometh of thine hand 1Chr 29:16 8034
an house for the *n* of the LORD 2Chr 2:1 8034
house to the *n* of the LORD my God 2Chr 2:4 8034
called the *n* of that on the right 2Chr 3:17 8034
the *n* of that on the left Boaz 2Chr 3:17 8034
in, that my *n* might be there 2Chr 6:5 8034
that my *n* might be there 2Chr 6:6 8034
the *n* of the LORD God of Israel 2Chr 6:7 8034
heart to build an house for my *n* 2Chr 6:8 8034

he shall build the house for my *n* 2Chr 6:9 8034
the *n* of the LORD God of Israel 2Chr 6:10 8034
thou wouldest put thy *n* there 2Chr 6:20 8034
and shall return and confess thy *n* 2Chr 6:24 8034
this place, and confess thy *n* 2Chr 6:26 8034
of the earth may know thy *n* 2Chr 6:33 8034
I have built is called by thy *n* 2Chr 6:33 8034
which I have built for thy *n* 2Chr 6:34 8034
which I have built for thy *n* 2Chr 6:38 8034
people, which are called by my *n* 2Chr 7:14 8034
that my *n* may be there for ever 2Chr 7:16 8034
which I have sanctified for my *n* 2Chr 7:20 8034
of Israel, to put his *n* there 2Chr 12:13 8034
his mother's *n* was Naamah an 2Chr 12:13 8034
His mother's *n* also was Michaiah 2Chr 13:2 8034
in thy *n* we go against this 2Chr 14:11 8034
truth to me in the *n* of the LORD 2Chr 18:15 8034
a sanctuary therein for thy *n* 2Chr 20:8 8034
(for thy *n* is in this house,) and 2Chr 20:9 8034
therefore the *n* of the same place 2Chr 20:26 8034
his mother's *n* was Azubah the 2Chr 20:31 8034
His mother's *n* also was Athaliah 2Chr 22:2 8034
His mother's *n* also was Zibiah of 2Chr 24:1 8034
his mother's *n* was Jehoaddan of 2Chr 25:1 8034
His mother's *n* also was Jecoliah 2Chr 26:3 8034
his *n* spread abroad even to the 2Chr 26:8 8034
And his *n* spread far abroad 2Chr 26:15 8034
His mother's *n* also was Jerushah 2Chr 27:1 8034
LORD was there, whose *n* was Oded 2Chr 28:9 8034
which were expressed by *n* rose up 2Chr 28:15 8034
And his mother's *n* was Abijah 2Chr 29:1 8034
the men that were expressed by *n* 2Chr 31:19 8034
Jerusalem shall my *n* be for ever 2Chr 33:4 8034
Israel, will I put my *n* for ever 2Chr 33:7 8034
the *n* of the LORD God of Israel 2Chr 33:18 8034
turned his *n* to Jehoiakim 2Chr 36:4 8034
and was called after their *n* Ezr 2:61 8034
Jerusalem in the *n* of the God of Ezr 5:1 8036
whose *n* was Sheshbazzar, whom he Ezr 5:14 8036
his *n* to dwell there destroy all Ezr 6:12 8036
all of them were expressed by *n* Ezr 8:20 8034
I have chosen to set my *n* there Neh 1:9 8034
who desire to fear thy *n* Neh 1:11 8034
wife, and was called after their *n* Neh 7:63 8034
and blessed be thy glorious *n* Neh 9:5 8034
and gavest him the *n* of Abraham Neh 9:7 8034
So didst thou get thee a *n* Neh 9:10 8034
whose *n* was Mordecai, the son of Est 2:5 8034
her, and that she were called by *n* Est 2:14 8034
the king thereof in Mordecai's *n* Est 2:22 8034
in the *n* of king Ahasuerus was it Est 3:12 8034
as it liketh you, in the king's *n* Est 8:8 8034
which is written in the king's *n* Est 8:8 8034
he wrote in the king Ahasuerus' *n* Est 8:10 8034
days Purim after the *n* of Pur Est 9:26 8034
the land of Uz, whose *n* was Job Job 1:1 8034
blessed be the *n* of the LORD Job 1:21 8034
he shall have no *n* in the street Job 18:17 8034
And he called the *n* of the first Job 42:14 8034
the *n* of the second, Kezia Job 42:14 8034
the *n* of the third, Keren-happuch Job 42:14 8034
that love thy *n* be joyful in thee Ps 5:11 8034
to the *n* of the LORD most high Ps 7:17 8034
is thy *n* in all the earth Ps 8:1 8034
is thy *n* in all the earth Ps 8:9 8034
I will sing praise to thy *n* Ps 9:2 8034
hast put out their *n* for ever Ps 9:5 8034
they that know thy *n* will put Ps 9:10 8034
and sing praises unto thy *n* Ps 18:49 8034
the *n* of the God of Jacob defend Ps 20:1 8034
in the *n* of our God we will set Ps 20:5 8034
the *n* of the LORD our God Ps 20:7 8034
declare thy *n* unto my brethren Ps 22:22 8034
the LORD the glory due unto his *n* Ps 29:2 8034
we have trusted in his holy *n* Ps 33:21 8034
and let us exalt his *n* together Ps 34:3 8034
shall he die, and his *n* perish Ps 41:5 8034
through thy *n* will we tread them Ps 44:5 8034
long, and praise thy *n* for ever Ps 44:8 8034
have forgotten the *n* of our God Ps 44:20 8034
I will make thy *n* to be Ps 45:17 8034
According to thy *n*, O God, so is Ps 48:10 8034
and I will wait on thy *n* Ps 52:9 8034
Save me, O God, by thy *n*, and Ps 54:1 8034
I will praise thy *n*, O LORD Ps 54:6 8034
heritage of those that fear thy *n* Ps 61:5 8034
I sing praise unto thy *n* for ever Ps 61:8 8034
I will lift up my hands in thy *n* Ps 63:4 8034
Sing forth the honour of his *n* Ps 66:2 8034
they shall sing to thy *n* Ps 66:4 8034
unto God, sing praises to his *n* Ps 68:4 8034
upon the heavens by his *n* JAH Ps 68:4 8034
I will praise the *n* of God with a Ps 69:30 8034
they that love his *n* shall dwell Ps 69:36 8034
His *n* shall endure for ever Ps 72:17 8034
his *n* shall be continued as long Ps 72:17 8034
be his glorious *n* for ever Ps 72:19 8034
place of thy *n* to the ground Ps 74:7 8034
enemy blaspheme thy *n* for ever Ps 74:10 8034
people have blasphemed thy *n* Ps 74:18 8034
the poor and needy praise thy *n* Ps 74:21 8034
for that thy *n* is near thy Ps 75:1 8034
his *n* is great in Israel Ps 76:1 8034
that have not called upon thy *n* Ps 79:6 8034
salvation, for the glory of thy *n* Ps 79:9 8034
us, and we will call upon thy *n* Ps 80:18 8034
that the *n* of Israel may be no Ps 83:4 8034
that they may seek thy *n*, O LORD Ps 83:16 8034

whose *n* alone is JEHOVAH, art the Ps 83:18 8034
and shall glorify thy *n* Ps 86:9 8034
unite my heart to fear thy *n* Ps 86:11 8034
I will glorify thy *n* for evermore Ps 86:12 8034
and Hermon shall rejoice in thy *n* Ps 89:12 8034
In thy *n* shall they rejoice all Ps 89:16 8034
in my *n* shall his horn be exalted Ps 89:24 8034
high, because he hath known my *n* Ps 91:14 8034
and to sing praises unto thy *n* Ps 92:1 8034
Sing unto the LORD, bless his *n* Ps 96:2 8034
the LORD the glory due unto his *n* Ps 96:8 8034
praise thy great and terrible *n* Ps 99:3 8034
among them that call upon his *n* Ps 99:6 8034
thankful unto him, and bless his *n* Ps 100:4 8034
shall fear the *n* of the LORD Ps 102:15 8034
To declare the *n* of the LORD in Ps 102:21 8034
is within me, bless his holy *n* Ps 103:1 8034
call upon his *n* Ps 105:1 8034
Glory ye in his holy *n* Ps 105:3 8034
to give thanks unto thy holy *n* Ps 106:47 8034
let their *n* be blotted out Ps 109:13 8034
holy and reverend is his *n* Ps 111:9 8034
LORD, praise the *n* of the LORD Ps 113:1 8034
Blessed be the *n* of the LORD from Ps 113:2 8034
the LORD's *n* is to be praised Ps 113:3 8034
us, but unto thy *n* give glory Ps 115:1 8034
called I upon the *n* of the LORD Ps 116:4 8034
and call upon the *n* of the LORD Ps 116:13 8034
will call upon the *n* of the LORD Ps 116:17 8034
but in the *n* of the LORD will I Ps 118:10 8034
but in the *n* of the LORD I will Ps 118:11 8034
for in the *n* of the LORD I will Ps 118:12 8034
that cometh in the *n* of the LORD Ps 118:26 8034
I have remembered thy *n*, O LORD, Ps 119:55 8034
to do unto those that love thy *n* Ps 119:132 8034
thanks unto the *n* of the LORD Ps 122:4 8034
Our help is in the *n* of the LORD Ps 124:8 8034
we bless you in the *n* of the LORD Ps 129:8 8034
Praise ye the *n* of the LORD Ps 135:1 8034
sing praises unto his *n* Ps 135:3 8034
Thy *n*, O LORD, endureth for ever Ps 135:13 8034
temple, and praise thy *n* for thy Ps 138:2 8034
thy word above all thy *n* Ps 138:2 8034
thine enemies take thy *n* in vain Ps 139:20
shall give thanks unto thy *n* Ps 140:13 8034
prison, that I may praise thy *n* Ps 142:7 8034
and I will bless thy *n* for ever Ps 145:1 8034
and I will praise thy *n* for ever Ps 145:2 8034
flesh bless his holy *n* for ever Ps 145:21 8034
Let them praise the *n* of the LORD Ps 148:5 8034
Let them praise the *n* of the LORD Ps 148:13 8034
for his *n* alone is excellent Ps 148:13 8034
them praise his *n* in the dance Ps 149:3 8034
but the *n* of the wicked shall rot Prov 10:7 8034
The *n* of the LORD is a strong Prov 18:10 8034
Proud and haughty scorner is his *n* Prov 21:24 8034
A good *n* is rather to be chosen Prov 22:1 8034
his *n*, and what is his son's *n* Prov 30:4
take the *n* of my God in vain Prov 30:9
his *n* shall be covered with Eccl 6:4 8034
A good *n* is better than precious Eccl 7:1 8034
of thy good ointments thy *n* is as Song 1:3 8034
only let us be called by thy *n* Is 4:1 8034
son, and shall call his *n* Immanuel Is 7:14 8034
Call his *n* Maher-shalal-hash-baz Is 8:3 8034
his *n* shall be called Wonderful, Is 9:6 8034
Praise the LORD, call upon his *n* Is 12:4 8034
mention that his *n* is exalted Is 12:4 8034
and cut off from Babylon the *n* Is 14:22 8034
to the place of the *n* of the LORD Is 18:7 8034
even the *n* of the LORD God of Is 24:15 8034
exalt thee, I will praise thy *n* Is 25:1 8034
desire of our soul is to thy *n* Is 26:8 8034
will we make mention of thy *n* Is 26:13 8034
of him, they shall sanctify my *n* Is 29:23 8034
the *n* of the LORD cometh from far Is 30:27 8034
the sun shall he call upon my *n* Is 41:25 8034
that is my *n* Is 42:8 8034
thee, I have called thee by thy *n* Is 43:1 8034
every one that is called by my *n* Is 43:7 8034
call himself by the *n* of Jacob Is 44:5 8034
himself by the *n* of Israel Is 44:5 8034
LORD, which call thee by thy *n* Is 45:3 8034
I have even called thee by thy *n* Is 45:4 8034
the LORD of hosts is his *n* Is 47:4 8034
are called by the *n* of Israel Is 48:1 8034
which swear by the *n* of the LORD Is 48:1 8034
The LORD of hosts is his *n* Is 48:2 8034
for how should my *n* be polluted Is 48:11
his *n* should not have been cut Is 48:19 8034
hath he made mention of my *n* Is 49:1 8034
him trust in the *n* of the LORD Is 50:10 8034
The LORD of hosts is his *n* Is 51:15 8034
my *n* continually every day is Is 52:5 8034
my people shall know my *n* Is 52:6 8034
the LORD of hosts is his *n* Is 54:5 8034
it shall be to the LORD for a *n* Is 55:13 8034
a *n* better than of sons and of Is 56:5 8034
I will give them an everlasting *n* Is 56:5 8034
him, and to love the *n* of the LORD Is 56:6 8034
eternity, whose *n* is Holy Is 57:15 8034
So shall they fear the *n* of the Is 59:19 8034
unto the *n* of the LORD thy God, Is 60:9 8034
thou shalt be called by a new *n* Is 62:2 8034
the mouth of the LORD shall *n* Is 62:2 8034
to make himself an everlasting *n* Is 63:12 8034
to make thyself a glorious *n* Is 63:14 8034
thy *n* is from everlasting Is 63:16

they were not called by thy *n* Is 63:19 8034
to make thy *n* known to thine Is 64:2 8034
is none that calleth upon thy *n* Is 64:7 8034
that was not called by my *n* Is 65:1 8034
ye shall leave your *n* for a curse Is 65:15 8034
and call his servants by another *n* Is 65:15 8034
shall your seed and your *n* remain Is 66:22 8034
unto it, to the *n* of the LORD, to Jer 3:17 8034
house, which is called by my *n* Jer 7:10 8034
house, which is called by my *n* Jer 7:11 8034
where I set my *n* at the first Jer 7:12 8034
house, which is called by my *n* Jer 7:14 8034
the house which is called by my *n* Jer 7:30 8034
great, and thy *n* is great in might Jer 10:6 8034
The LORD of hosts is his *n* Jer 10:16 8034
families that call not on thy *n* Jer 10:25 8034
The LORD called thy *n*, A green Jer 11:16 8034
that his *n* may be no more Jer 11:19 8034
Prophesy not in the *n* of the LORD Jer 11:21 8034
of my people, to swear by my *n* Jer 12:16 8034
unto me for a people, and for a *n* Jer 13:11 8034
of us, and we are called by thy *n* Jer 14:9 8034
prophets prophesy lies in my *n* Jer 14:14 8034
prophets that prophesy in my *n* Jer 14:15 8034
for I am called by thy *n*, O LORD Jer 15:16 8034
shall know that my *n* is The LORD Jer 16:21 8034
LORD hath not called thy *n* Pashur Jer 20:3 8034
him, nor speak any more in his *n* Jer 20:9 8034
this is his *n* whereby he shall be Jer 23:6 8034
said, that prophesy lies in my *n* Jer 23:25 8034
n by their dreams which they tell Jer 23:27 8034
have forgotten my *n* for Baal Jer 23:27 8034
the city which is called by my *n* Jer 25:29 8034
prophesied in the *n* of the LORD Jer 26:9 8034
us in the *n* of the LORD our God Jer 26:16 8034
prophesied in the *n* of the LORD Jer 26:20 8034
yet they prophesy a lie in my *n* Jer 27:15 8034
prophesy falsely unto you in my *n* Jer 29:9 8034
prophesy a lie unto you in my *n* Jer 29:21 8034
have spoken lying words in my *n* Jer 29:23 8034
thou hast sent letters in thy *n* Jer 29:25 8034
The LORD of hosts is his *n* Jer 31:35 8034
God, the LORD of hosts, is his *n* Jer 32:18 8034
and hast made thee a *n*, as at this Jer 32:20 8034
house, which is called by my *n* Jer 32:34 8034
the LORD is his *n* Jer 33:2 8034
And it shall be to me a *n* of joy Jer 33:9 8034
this is the *n* wherewith she shall Jer 33:16
the house which is called by my *n* Jer 34:15 8034
But ye turned and polluted my *n* Jer 34:16 8034
whose *n* was Irijah, the son of Jer 37:13 8034
unto us in the *n* of the LORD Jer 44:16 8034
I have sworn by my great *n* Jer 44:26 8034
that my *n* shall no more be named Jer 44:26 8034
whose *n* is the LORD of hosts, Jer 46:18 8034
whose *n* is the LORD of hosts Jer 48:15 8034
and all ye that know his *n* Jer 48:17 8034
the LORD of hosts is his *n* Jer 50:34 8034
the LORD of hosts is his *n* Jer 51:19 8034
whose *n* is the LORD of hosts Jer 51:57 8034
his mother's *n* was Hamutal the Jer 52:1 8034
I called upon thy *n*, O LORD, out Lam 3:55 8034
the *n* thereof is called Bamah Eze 20:29 8034
but pollute ye my holy *n* no more Eze 20:39 8034
man, write thee the *n* of the day Eze 24:2 8034
went, they profaned my holy *n* Eze 36:20 8034
But I had pity for mine holy *n* Eze 36:21 8034
And I will sanctify my great *n* Eze 36:23 8034
So will I make my holy *n* known in Eze 39:7 8034
them pollute my holy *n* any more Eze 39:7 8034
also the *n* of the city shall be Eze 39:16 8034
and will be jealous for my holy *n* Eze 39:25 8034
of Israel for ever, and my holy *n* Eze 43:7 8034
they have even defiled my holy *n* Eze 43:8 8034
the *n* of the city from that day Eze 48:35 8034
unto Daniel the *n* of Belteshazzar Dan 1:7 8034
Blessed be the *n* of God for ever Dan 2:20 8036
whose *n* was Belteshazzar, Art Dan 2:26 8036
whose *n* was Belteshazzar, Dan 4:8 8036
according to the *n* of my god Dan 4:8 8036
whose *n* was Belteshazzar, was Dan 4:19 8036
which spake in thy *n* to our kings Dan 9:6 8034
the city which is called by thy *n* Dan 9:18 8034
and thy people are called by thy *n* Dan 9:19 8034
whose *n* was called Belteshazzar Dan 10:1 8034
said unto him, Call his *n* Jezreel Hos 1:4 8034
unto him, Call her *n* Lo-ruhamah Hos 1:6 8034
Then said God, Call his *n* Lo-ammi Hos 1:9 8034
no more be remembered by their *n* Hos 2:17 8034
praise the *n* of the LORD your God Joel 2:26 8034
whosoever shall call on the *n* of Joel 2:32 8034
same maid, to profane my holy *n* Amos 2:7 8034
LORD, The God of hosts, is his *n* Amos 4:13 8034
The LORD is his *n* Amos 5:8 8034
whose *n* is The God of hosts Amos 5:27 8034
make mention of the *n* of the LORD Amos 6:10 8034
The LORD is his *n* Amos 9:6 8034
heathen, which are called by my *n* Amos 9:12 8034
every one in the *n* of his god Mic 4:5 8034
we will walk in the *n* of the LORD Mic 4:5 8034
of the *n* of the LORD his God Mic 5:4 8034
the man of wisdom shall see thy *n* Mic 6:9 8034
that no more of thy *n* be sown Nah 1:14 8034
the *n* of the Chemarims with the Zeph 1:4 8034
all call upon the *n* of the LORD Zeph 3:9 8034
shall trust in the *n* of the LORD Zeph 3:12 8034
for I will make you a *n* and a Zeph 3:20 8034
him that sweareth falsely by my *n* Zec 5:4 8034

the man whose *n* is The BRANCH .... Zec 6:12 8034
shall walk up and down in his *n* .... Zec 10:12 8034
lies in the *n* of the LORD .... Zec 13:3 8034
they shall call on my *n*, and I .... Zec 13:9 8034
there be one LORD, and his *n* one .... Zec 14:9 8034
you, O priests, that despise my *n* .... Mal 1:6 8034
Wherein have we despised thy *n* .... Mal 1:6 8034
my *n* shall be great among the .... Mal 1:11 8034
shall be offered unto my *n* .... Mal 1:11 8034
for my *n* shall be great among the .... Mal 1:11 8034
my *n* is dreadful among the .... Mal 1:14 8034
to heart, to give glory unto my *n* .... Mal 2:2 8034
me, and was afraid before my *n* .... Mal 2:5 8034
LORD, and that thought upon his *n* .... Mal 3:16 8034
But unto you that fear my *n* shall .... Mal 4:2 8034
and thou shalt call his *n* JESUS .... Mt 1:21 *3686*
and they shall call his *n* Emmanuel .... Mt 1:23 *3686*
and he called his *n* JESUS .... Mt 1:25 *3686*
art in heaven, Hallowed be thy *n* .... Mt 6:9 *3686*
have we not prophesied in thy *n* .... Mt 7:22 *3686*
in thy *n* have cast out devils .... Mt 7:22 *3686*
in thy *n* done many wonderful .... Mt 7:22 *3686*
n of a prophet shall receive a .... Mt 10:41 *3686*
a righteous man in the *n* of a .... Mt 10:41 *3686*
water only in the *n* of a disciple .... Mt 10:42 *3686*
in his *n* shall the Gentiles trust .... Mt 12:21 *3686*
little child in my *n* receiveth me .... Mt 18:5 *3686*
are gathered together in my *n* .... Mt 18:20 *3686*
that cometh in the *n* of the Lord .... Mt 21:9 *3686*
that cometh in the *n* of the Lord .... Mt 23:39 *3686*
For many shall come in my *n* .... Mt 24:5 *3686*
found a man of Cyrene, Simon by *n* .... Mt 27:32 *3686*
them in the *n* of the Father .... Mt 28:19 *3686*
And he asked him, What is thy *n* .... Mk 5:9 *3686*
answered, saying, My *n* is Legion .... Mk 5:9 *3686*
of the synagogue, Jairus by *n* .... Mk 5:22 *3686*
(for his *n* was spread abroad .... Mk 6:14 *3686*
one of such children in my *n* .... Mk 9:37 *3686*
one casting out devils in thy *n* .... Mk 9:38 *3686*
which shall do a miracle in my *n* .... Mk 9:39 *3686*
a cup of water to drink in my *n* .... Mk 9:41 *3686*
that cometh in the *n* of the Lord .... Mk 11:9 *3686*
that cometh in the *n* of the Lord .... Mk 11:10 *3686*
For many shall come in my *n* .... Mk 13:6 *3686*
In my *n* shall they cast out .... Mk 16:17 *3686*
of Aaron, and her *n* was Elisabeth .... Lk 1:5 *3686*
and thou shalt call his *n* John .... Lk 1:13 *3686*
to a man whose *n* was Joseph .... Lk 1:27 *3686*
and the virgin's *n* was Mary .... Lk 1:27 *3686*
a son, and shalt call his *n* JESUS .... Lk 1:31 *3686*
and holy is his *n* .... Lk 1:49 *3686*
after the *n* of his father .... Lk 1:59 *3686*
kindred that is called by this *n* .... Lk 1:61 *3686*
and wrote, saying, His *n* is John .... Lk 1:63 *3686*
his *n* was called JESUS, which was .... Lk 2:21 *3686*
in Jerusalem, whose *n* was Simeon .... Lk 2:25 *3686*
you, and cast out your *n* as evil .... Lk 6:22 *3686*
asked him, saying, What is thy *n* .... Lk 8:30 *3686*
this child in my *n* receiveth me .... Lk 9:48 *3686*
one casting out devils in thy *n* .... Lk 9:49 *3686*
are subject unto us through thy *n* .... Lk 10:17 *3686*
art in heaven, Hallowed be thy *n* .... Lk 11:2 *3686*
that cometh in the *n* of the Lord .... Lk 13:35 *3686*
that cometh in the *n* of the Lord .... Lk 19:38 *3686*
for many shall come in my *n* .... Lk 21:8 *3686*
whose *n* was Cleopas, answering .... Lk 24:18 *3686*
in his *n* among all nations .... Lk 24:47 *3686*
sent from God, whose *n* was John .... Jn 1:6 *3686*
to them that believe on his *n* .... Jn 1:12 *3686*
feast day, many believed in his *n* .... Jn 2:23 *3686*
he hath not believed in the *n* of .... Jn 3:18 *3686*
I am come in my Father's *n* .... Jn 5:43 *3686*
another shall come in his own *n* .... Jn 5:43 *3686*
and he calleth his own sheep by *n* .... Jn 10:3 *3686*
works that I do in my Father's *n* .... Jn 10:25 *3686*
that cometh in the *n* of the Lord .... Jn 12:13 *3686*
Father, glorify thy *n* .... Jn 12:28 *3686*
whatsoever ye shall ask in my *n* .... Jn 14:13 *3686*
If ye shall ask any thing in my *n* .... Jn 14:14 *3686*
whom the Father will send in my *n* .... Jn 14:26 *3686*
shall ask of the Father in my *n* .... Jn 15:16 *3686*
ye shall ask the Father in my *n* .... Jn 16:23 *3686*
have ye asked nothing in my *n* .... Jn 16:24 *3686*
At that day ye shall ask in my *n* .... Jn 16:26 *3686*
I have manifested thy *n* unto the .... Jn 17:6 *3686*
keep through thine own *n* those .... Jn 17:11 *3686*
the world, I kept them in thy *n* .... Jn 17:12 *3686*
I have declared unto them thy *n* .... Jn 17:26 *3686*
The servant's *n* was Malchus .... Jn 18:10 *3686*
ye might have life through his *n* .... Jn 20:31 *3686*
the *n* of the Lord shall be saved .... Acts 2:21 *3686*
in the *n* of Jesus Christ for the .... Acts 2:38 *3686*
In the *n* of Jesus Christ of .... Acts 3:6 *3686*
his *n* through faith in his *n* .... Acts 3:16 *3686*
By what power, or by what *n* .... Acts 4:7 *3686*
that by the *n* of Jesus Christ of .... Acts 4:10 *3686*
for there is none other *n* under .... Acts 4:12 *3686*
henceforth to no man in this *n* .... Acts 4:17 *3686*
all nor teach in the *n* of Jesus .... Acts 4:18 *3686*
by the *n* of thy holy child Jesus .... Acts 4:30 *3686*
ye should not teach in this *n* .... Acts 5:28 *3686*
not speak in the *n* of Jesus .... Acts 5:40 *3686*
worthy to suffer shame for his *n* .... Acts 5:41 *3686*
man's feet, whose *n* was Saul .... Acts 7:58 *2564*
the *n* of Jesus Christ, they were .... Acts 8:12 *3686*
in the *n* of the Lord Jesus .... Acts 8:16 *3686*
to bind all that call on thy *n* .... Acts 9:14 *3686*
to bear my *n* before the Gentiles .... Acts 9:15 *3686*
called on this *n* in Jerusalem .... Acts 9:21 *3686*
at Damascus in the *n* of Jesus .... Acts 9:27 *3686*
boldly in the *n* of the Lord Jesus .... Acts 9:29 *3686*
that through his *n* whosoever .... Acts 10:43 *3686*
be baptized in the *n* of the Lord .... Acts 10:48 *3686*
a Jew, whose *n* was Bar-jesus .... Acts 13:6 *3686*
the sorcerer (for so is his *n* by .... Acts 13:8 *3686*
out of them a people for his *n* .... Acts 15:14 *3686*
upon whom my *n* is called .... Acts 15:17 *3686*
the *n* of our Lord Jesus Christ .... Acts 15:26 *3686*
I command thee in the *n* of Jesus .... Acts 16:18 *3686*
in the *n* of the Lord Jesus .... Acts 19:5 *3686*
spirits the *n* of the Lord Jesus .... Acts 19:13 *3686*
the *n* of the Lord Jesus was .... Acts 19:17 *3686*
for the *n* of the Lord Jesus .... Acts 21:13 *3686*
calling on the *n* of the Lord .... Acts 22:16 *3686*
to the *n* of Jesus of Nazareth .... Acts 26:9 *3686*
the island, whose *n* was Publius .... Acts 28:7 *3686*
among all nations, for his *n* .... Rom 1:5 *3686*
For the *n* of God is blasphemed .... Rom 2:24 *3686*
that my *n* might be declared .... Rom 9:17 *3686*
the *n* of the Lord shall be saved .... Rom 10:13 *3686*
the Gentiles, and sing unto thy *n* .... Rom 15:9 *3686*
the *n* of Jesus Christ our Lord 1Cor 1:2 *3686*
by the *n* of our Lord Jesus Christ 1Cor 1:10 *3686*
were ye baptized in the *n* of Paul 1Cor 1:13 *3686*
that I had baptized in mine own *n* 1Cor 1:15 *3686*
In the *n* of our Lord Jesus Christ 1Cor 5:4 *3686*
in the *n* of the Lord Jesus 1Cor 6:11 *3686*
every *n* that is named, not only .... Eph 1:21 *3686*
the Father in the *n* of our Lord .... Eph 5:20 *3686*
him a *n* which is above every *n* .... Phil 2:9 *3686*
That at the *n* of Jesus every knee .... Phil 2:10 *3686*
do all in the *n* of the Lord Jesus .... Col 3:17 *3686*
That the *n* of our Lord Jesus 2Th 1:12 *3686*
in the *n* of our Lord Jesus Christ 2Th 3:6 *3686*
of all honour, that the *n* of God 1Ti 6:1 *3686*
Let every one that nameth the *n* 2Ti 2:19 *3686*
a more excellent *n* than they .... Heb 1:4 *3686*
declare thy *n* unto my brethren .... Heb 2:12 *3686*
which ye have shewed toward his *n* .... Heb 6:10 *3686*
our lips giving thanks to his *n* .... Heb 13:15 *3686*
n by the which ye are called .... Jas 2:7 *3686*
have spoken in the *n* of the Lord .... Jas 5:10 *3686*
him with oil in the *n* of the Lord .... Jas 5:14 *3686*
be reproached for the *n* of Christ 1Pet 4:14 *3686*
on the *n* of his Son Jesus Christ 1Jn 3:23 *3686*
on the *n* of the Son of God 1Jn 5:13 *3686*
on the *n* of the Son of God 1Jn 5:13 *3686*
Greet the friends by *n* 3Jn 14 *3686*
and thou holdest fast my *n* .... Rev 2:13 *3686*
and in the stone a new *n* written .... Rev 2:17 *3686*
thou hast a *n* that thou livest .... Rev 3:1 *3686*
out his *n* out of the book of life .... Rev 3:5 *3686*
confess his *n* before my Father .... Rev 3:5 *3686*
my word, and hast not denied my *n* .... Rev 3:8 *3686*
write upon him the *n* of my God .... Rev 3:12 *3686*
the *n* of the city of my God .... Rev 3:12 *3686*
and I will write upon him my new *n* .... Rev 3:12 *3686*
his *n* that sat on him was Death .... Rev 6:8 *3686*
the *n* of the star is called .... Rev 8:11 *3686*
whose *n* in the Hebrew tongue is .... Rev 9:11 *3686*
Greek tongue hath his *n* Apollyon .... Rev 9:11 *3686*
saints, and them that fear thy *n* .... Rev 11:18 *3686*
upon his heads the *n* of blasphemy .... Rev 13:1 *3686*
against God, to blaspheme his *n* .... Rev 13:6 *3686*
or the *n* of the beast, or the .... Rev 13:17 *3686*
the beast, or the number of his *n* .... Rev 13:17 *3686*
having his Father's *n* written in .... Rev 14:1 *3686*
receiveth the mark of his *n* .... Rev 14:11 *3686*
mark, and over the number of his *n* .... Rev 15:2 *3686*
thee, O Lord, and glorify thy *n* .... Rev 15:4 *3686*
heat, and blasphemed the *n* of God .... Rev 16:9 *3686*
upon her forehead was a *n* written .... Rev 17:5 *3686*
and he had a *n* written, that no .... Rev 19:12 *3686*
his *n* is called The Word of God .... Rev 19:13 *3686*
and on his thigh a *n* written .... Rev 19:16 *3686*
his *n* shall be in their foreheads .... Rev 22:4 *3686*

NAMED {57}
which he had *n* in the audience of .... Gen 23:16 1696
said, Is not he rightly *n* Jacob .... Gen 27:36 7121,8034
and let my name be *n* on them .... Gen 48:16 7121
house, *n* Rahab, and lodged there .... Josh 2:1 8034
she *n* the child I-chabod, saying 1Sa 4:21 7121
n Goliath, of Gath, whose height 1Sa 17:4 8034
n Abiathar, escaped, and fled 1Sa 22:20 8034
of Jacob, whom he *n* Israel 2Kin 17:34 8034
his sons were *n* of the tribe of 1Chr 23:14 7121
That which hath been is *n* already .. Eccl 6:10 8034,7121
But ye shall be *n* the Priests of .... Is 61:6 7121
be *n* in the mouth of any man of .... Jer 44:26 7121
whom the king *n* Belteshazzar .... Dan 5:12 8036
which are *n* chief of the nations .... Amos 6:1 5344
O thou that art *n* the house of .... Mic 2:7 559
n Matthew, sitting at the receipt .... Mt 9:9 *3004*
n Joseph, who also himself was .... Mt 27:57 *3686*
to a place which was *n* Gethsemane .... Mk 14:32 *3686*
And there was one *n* Barabbas .... Mk 15:7 *3004*
a certain priest *n* Zacharias .... Lk 1:5 *3686*
a city of Galilee, *n* Nazareth .... Lk 1:26 *3686*
which was so *n* of the angel .... Lk 2:21 *2564*
n Levi, sitting at the receipt of .... Lk 5:27 *3686*
twelve, whom also he *n* apostles .... Lk 6:13 *3687*
Simon, (whom he also *n* Peter .... Lk 6:14 *3687*
behold, there came a man *n* Jairus .... Lk 8:41 *3686*
a certain woman *n* Martha received .... Lk 10:38 *3686*
was a certain beggar *n* Lazarus .... Lk 16:20 *3686*
there was a man *n* Zacchaeus .... Lk 19:2 *2564*
behold, there was a man *n* Joseph .... Lk 23:50 *3686*
n Nicodemus, a ruler of the Jews .... Jn 3:1 *3686*
n Lazarus, of Bethany, the town .... Jn 11:1
n Caiaphas, being the high priest .... Jn 11:49
But a certain man *n* Ananias .... Acts 5:1 *3686*
n Gamaliel, a doctor of the law .... Acts 5:34 *3686*
disciple at Damascus, *n* Ananias .... Acts 9:10 *3686*
vision a man *n* Ananias coming in .... Acts 9:12 *3686*
he found a certain man *n* Aeneas .... Acts 9:33 *3686*
a certain disciple *n* Tabitha .... Acts 9:36 *3686*
stood up one of them *n* Agabus .... Acts 11:28 *3686*
a damsel came to hearken, *n* Rhoda .... Acts 12:13 *3686*
n Timotheus, the son of a certain .... Acts 16:1 *3686*
And a certain woman *n* Lydia .... Acts 16:14 *3686*
Areopagite, and a woman *n* Damaris .... Acts 17:34 *3686*
And found a certain Jew *n* Aquila .... Acts 18:2 *3686*
n Justus, one that worshipped God .... Acts 18:7 *3686*
And a certain Jew *n* Apollos .... Acts 18:24 *3686*
For a certain man *n* Demetrius .... Acts 19:24 *3686*
a certain young man *n* Eutychus .... Acts 20:9 *3686*
a certain prophet, *n* Agabus .... Acts 21:10 *3686*
with a certain orator *n* Tertullus .... Acts 24:1
other prisoners unto one *n* Julius .... Acts 27:1 *3686*
gospel, not where Christ was *n* .... Rom 15:20 *3687*
so much as *n* among the Gentiles 1Cor 5:1 *3687*
dominion, and every name that is *n* .... Eph 1:21 *3687*
family in heaven and earth is *n* .... Eph 3:15 *3687*
let it not be once *n* among you .... Eph 5:3 *3687*

NAMELY See APPENDIX.

NAME'S {30}
his people for his great *n* sake 1Sa 12:22 8034
of a far country for thy *n* sake 1Kin 8:41 8034
far country for thy great *n* sake 2Chr 6:32 8034
of righteousness for his *n* sake .... Ps 23:3 8034
For thy *n* sake, O LORD, pardon .... Ps 25:11 8034
therefore for thy *n* sake lead me .... Ps 31:3 8034
away our sins, for thy *n* sake .... Ps 79:9 8034
he saved them for his *n* sake .... Ps 106:8 8034
O GOD the Lord, for thy *n* sake .... Ps 109:21 8034
me, O LORD, for thy *n* sake .... Ps 143:11 8034
For my *n* sake will I defer mine .... Is 48:9 8034
that cast you out for my *n* sake .... Is 66:5 8034
us, do thou it for thy *n* sake .... Jer 14:7 8034
Do not abhor us, for thy *n* sake .... Jer 14:21 8034
But I wrought for my *n* sake .... Eze 20:9 8034
But I wrought for my *n* sake .... Eze 20:14 8034
hand, and wrought for my *n* sake .... Eze 20:22 8034
wrought with you for my *n* sake .... Eze 20:44 8034
Israel, but for mine holy *n* sake .... Eze 36:22 8034
be hated of all men for my *n* sake .... Mt 10:22 *3686*
children, or lands, for my *n* sake .... Mt 19:29 *3686*
of all nations for my *n* sake .... Mt 24:9 *3686*
be hated of all men for my *n* sake .... Mk 13:13 *3686*
kings and rulers for my *n* sake .... Lk 21:12 *3686*
be hated of all men for my *n* sake .... Lk 21:17 *3686*
they do unto you for my *n* sake .... Jn 15:21 *3686*
he must suffer for my *n* sake .... Acts 9:16 *3686*
are forgiven you for his *n* sake 1Jn 2:12 *3686*
for his *n* sake they went forth 3Jn 7 *3686*
for my *n* sake hast laboured, and .... Rev 2:3 *3686*

NAMES {98}
Adam gave *n* to all cattle, and to .... Gen 2:20 8034
these are the *n* of the sons of .... Gen 25:13 8034
the sons of Ishmael, by their *n* .... Gen 25:13 8034
of Ishmael, and these are their *n* .... Gen 25:16 8034
he called their *n* after the *n* .... Gen 26:18 8034
These are the *n* of Esau's sons .... Gen 36:10 8034
these are the *n* of the dukes that .... Gen 36:40 8034
after their places, by their *n* .... Gen 36:40 8034
these are the *n* of the children .... Gen 46:8 8034
Now these are the *n* of the .... Ex 1:1 8034
these are the *n* of the sons of .... Ex 6:16 8034
grave on them the *n* of the .... Ex 28:9 8034
Six of their *n* on one stone .... Ex 28:10 8034
the other six *n* of the rest on .... Ex 28:10 8034
the *n* of the children of Israel .... Ex 28:11 8034
Aaron shall bear their *n* before .... Ex 28:12 8034
the *n* of the children of Israel .... Ex 28:21 8034
twelve, according to their *n* .... Ex 28:21 8034
Aaron shall bear the *n* of the .... Ex 28:29 8034
with the *n* of the children of .... Ex 39:6 8034
the *n* of the children of Israel .... Ex 39:14 8034
twelve, according to their *n* .... Ex 39:14 8034
with the number of their *n* .... Num 1:2 8034
these are the *n* of the men that .... Num 1:5 8034
which are expressed by their *n* .... Num 1:17 8034
according to the number of the *n* .... Num 1:18 8034
according to the number of the *n* .... Num 1:20 8034
according to the number of the *n* .... Num 1:22 8034
according to the number of the *n* .... Num 1:24 8034
according to the number of the *n* .... Num 1:26 8034
according to the number of the *n* .... Num 1:28 8034
according to the number of the *n* .... Num 1:30 8034
according to the number of the *n* .... Num 1:32 8034
according to the number of the *n* .... Num 1:34 8034
according to the number of the *n* .... Num 1:36 8034
according to the number of the *n* .... Num 1:38 8034
according to the number of the *n* .... Num 1:40 8034
according to the number of the *n* .... Num 1:42 8034
these are the *n* of the sons of .... Num 3:2 8034
These are the *n* of the sons of .... Num 3:3 8034
were the sons of Levi by their *n* .... Num 3:17 8034
these are the *n* of the sons of .... Num 3:18 8034
and take the number of their *n* .... Num 3:40 8034
males by the number of *n*, from a .... Num 3:43 8034
And these were their *n* .... Num 13:4 8034

N

These are the *n* of the men which ... Num 13:16 8034
the *n* of the daughters of ... Num 26:33 8034
according to the number of *n* ... Num 26:53 8034
according to the *n* of the tribes ... Num 26:55 8034
these are the *n* of his daughters ... Num 27:1 8034
(their *n* being changed,) and ... Num 32:38 8034
gave other *n* unto the cities ... Num 32:38 8034
These are the *n* of the men which ... Num 34:17 8034
the *n* of the men are these ... Num 34:19 8034
destroy the *n* of them out of that ... Deut 12:3 8034
these are the *n* of his daughters, ... Josh 17:3 8034
mention of the *n* of their gods ... Josh 23:7 8034
the *n* of his two daughters were ... 1Sa 14:49 8034
the *n* of his three sons that went ... 1Sa 17:13 8034
these be the *n* of those that were ... 2Sa 5:14 8034
These be the *n* of the mighty men ... 2Sa 23:8 8034
And these are their *n* ... 1Kin 4:8 8034
These mentioned by their *n* were ... 1Chr 4:38 8034
these be the *n* of the sons of ... 1Chr 6:17 8034
which are called by their *n* ... 1Chr 6:65 8034
whose *n* are these, Azrikam, ... 1Chr 8:38 8034
whose *n* are these, Azrikam, ... 1Chr 9:44 8034
Now these are the *n* of his ... 1Chr 14:4 8034
by number of *n* by their polls ... 1Chr 23:24 8034
What are the *n* of the men that ... Ezr 5:4 8036
We asked their *n* also, to certify ... Ezr 5:10 8036
that we might write the *n* of the ... Ezr 5:10 8036
whose *n* are these, Eliphelet, ... Ezr 8:13 8034
and all of them by their *n* ... Ezr 10:16 8034
nor take up their *n* into my lips ... Ps 16:4 8034
their lands after their own *n* ... Ps 49:11 8034
he calleth them all by their *n* ... Ps 147:4 8034
he calleth them all by *n* by the ... Is 40:26 8034
the *n* of them were Aholah the ... Eze 23:4 8034
Thus were their *n* ... Eze 23:4 8034
Now these are the *n* of the tribes ... Eze 48:1 8034
the *n* of the tribes of Israel ... Eze 48:31 8034
the prince of the eunuchs gave *n* ... Dan 1:7 8034
For I will take away the *n* of ... Hos 2:17 8034
that I will cut off the *n* of the ... Zec 13:2 8034
Now the *n* of the twelve apostles ... Mt 10:2 *3686*
because your *n* are written in ... Lk 10:20 *3686*
(the number of *n* together were ... Acts 1:15 *3686*
if it be a question of words and *n* ... Acts 18:15 *3686*
whose *n* are in the book of life ... Phil 4:3 *3686*
Thou hast a few *n* even in Sardis ... Rev 3:4 *3686*
whose *n* are not written in the ... Rev 13:8 *3686*
full of *n* of blasphemy, having ... Rev 17:3 *3686*
whose *n* were not written in the ... Rev 17:8 *3686*
n written thereon, which are the ... Rev 21:12 *3686*
which are the *n* of the twelve ... Rev 21:12
in them the *n* of the twelve ... Rev 21:14 *3686*

NAMETH {1}
Let every one that *n* the name of ... 2Ti 2:19 *3687*

NAOMI *(na'-o-mee)* {20} See NAOMI'S. *Mother-in-law of Ruth.*
and the name of his wife *N* ... Ruth 1:2 *5281*
N said unto her two daughters in ... Ruth 1:8 *5281*
N said, Turn again, my daughters ... Ruth 1:11 *5281*
them, and they said, Is this *N* ... Ruth 1:19 *5281*
she said unto them, Call me not *N* ... Ruth 1:20 *5281*
why then call ye me *N*, seeing the ... Ruth 1:21 *5281*
So *N* returned, and Ruth the ... Ruth 1:22 *5281*
N had a kinsman of her husband's, ... Ruth 2:1 *5281*
And Ruth the Moabitess said unto *N* ... Ruth 2:2 *5281*
with *N* out of the country of Moab ... Ruth 2:6 *5281*
N said unto her daughter in law, ... Ruth 2:20 *5281*
N said unto her, The man is near ... Ruth 2:20 *5281*
N said unto Ruth her daughter in ... Ruth 2:22 *5281*
Then *N* her mother in law said ... Ruth 3:1 *5281*
And he said unto the kinsman, *N* ... Ruth 4:3 *5281*
buyest the field of the hand of *N* ... Ruth 4:5 *5281*
and Mahlon's, of the hand of *N* ... Ruth 4:9 *5281*
And the women said unto *N*, Blessed ... Ruth 4:14 *5281*
N took the child, and laid it in ... Ruth 4:16 *5281*
saying, There is a son born to *N* ... Ruth 4:17 *5281*

NAOMI'S *(na'-o-meze)* {1}
And Elimelech *N* husband died ... Ruth 1:3 5281

NAPHATH See DOR.

NAPHATH DOR See DOR.

NAPHETH See DOR.

NAPHISH *(na'-fish)* {2} See NEPHISH. *A son of Ishmael.*
Hadar, and Tema, Jetur, *N*, and ... Gen 25:15 5305
Jetur, *N*, and Kedemah ... 1Chr 1:31 5305

NAPHTALI *(naf'-ta-li)* {49} See NEPHTHALIM.
1. A son of Jacob.
and she called his name *N* ... Gen 30:8 5321
handmaid; Dan, and *N* ... Gen 35:25 5321
And the sons of *N* ... Gen 46:24 5321
N is a hind let loose ... Gen 49:21 5321
Dan, and *N*, Gad, and Asher ... Ex 1:4 5321
Dan, Joseph, and Benjamin, *N* ... 1Chr 2:2 5321
The sons of *N* ... 1Chr 7:13 5321
one gate of Asher, one gate of *N* ... Eze 48:34 5321
2. The tribe and land.
Of *N*; Ahira the son ... Num 1:15 5321
Of the children of *N*, throughout ... Num 1:42 5321
of them, even of the tribe of *N* ... Num 1:43 5321
Then the tribe of *N* ... Num 2:29 5321
N shall be Ahira the son of Enan ... Num 2:29 5321
Enan, prince of the children of *N* ... Num 7:78 5321
of *N* was Ahira the son of Enan ... Num 10:27 5321
Of the tribe of *N*, Nahbi the son ... Num 13:14 5321
Of the sons of *N* after their ... Num 26:48 5321
These are the families of *N* ... Num 26:50 5321
of the tribe of the children of *N* ... Num 34:28 5321
and Asher, and Zebulun, Dan, and *N* ... Deut 27:13 5321
And of Naphtali he said, O *N* ... Deut 33:23 5321
And all *N*, and the land of Ephraim, ... Deut 34:2 5321
lot came out to the children of *N* ... Josh 19:32 5321
even for the children of *N* ... Josh 19:32 5321
of *N* according to their families ... Josh 19:39 5321
Kedesh in Galilee in mount *N* ... Josh 20:7 5321
Asher, and out of the tribe of *N* ... Josh 21:6 5321
And out of the tribe of *N*, Kedesh ... Josh 21:32 5321
Neither did *N* drive out the ... Judg 1:33 5321
thousand men of the children of *N* ... Judg 4:6 5321
called Zebulun and *N* to Kedesh ... Judg 4:10 5321
N were a people that jeoparded ... Judg 5:18 5321
Asher, and unto Zebulun, and unto *N* ... Judg 6:35 5321
themselves together out of *N* ... Judg 7:23 5321
Ahimaaz was in *N* ... 1Kin 4:15 5321
a widow's son of the tribe of *N* ... 1Kin 7:14 5321
Cinneroth, with all the land of *N* ... 1Kin 15:20 5321
and Galilee, all the land of *N* ... 2Kin 15:29 5321
Asher, and out of the tribe of *N* ... 1Chr 6:62 5321
And out of the tribe of *N* ... 1Chr 6:76 5321
of *N* a thousand captains, and with ... 1Chr 12:34 5321
unto Issachar and Zebulun and *N* ... 1Chr 12:40 5321
of *N*, Jerimoth the son of Azriel ... 1Chr 27:19 5321
and all the store cities of *N* ... 2Chr 16:4 5321
Ephraim, and Simeon, even unto *N* ... 2Chr 34:6 5321
of Zebulun, and the princes of *N* ... Ps 68:27 5321
land of Zebulun and the land of *N* ... Is 9:1 5321
the west side, a portion for *N* ... Eze 48:3 5321
And by the border of *N*, from the ... Eze 48:4 5321

NAPHTUHIM *(naf'-too-him)* {1} *Inhabitants of central Egypt.*
and Anamim, and Lehabim, and *N* ... Gen 10:13 5320

NAPKIN {3}
which I have kept laid up in a *n* ... Lk 19:20 *4676*
his face was bound about with a *n* ... Jn 11:44 *4676*
And the *n*, that was about his head ... Jn 20:7 *4676*

NAPHTUHIM {1}
and Anamim, and Lehabim, and *N* ... 1Chr 1:11 5320

NARCISSUS *(nar-sis'-sus)* {1} *A Christian in Rome.*
that be of the household of *N* ... Rom 16:11 *3488*

NARROW {9}
further, and stood in a *n* place ... Num 22:26 6862
mount Ephraim be too *n* for thee ... Josh 17:15 213
house he made windows of *n* lights ... 1Kin 6:4 331
and a strange woman is a *n* pit ... Prov 23:27 6862
shall even now be too *n* by reason ... Is 49:19 3334
there were *n* windows to the ... Eze 40:16 331
the *n* windows, and the galleries ... Eze 41:16 331
And there were *n* windows and palm ... Eze 41:26 331
n is the way, which leadeth unto ... Mt 7:14 *2346*

NARROWED {1}
house he made *n* rests round about ... 1Kin 6:6 4052

NARROWER {1}
the covering *n* than that he can ... Is 28:20 6887

NARROWLY {2}
lookest *n* unto all my paths ... Job 13:27 8104
see thee shall *n* look upon thee ... Is 14:16

NATHAN *(na'-than)* {43} See NATHAN-MELECH.
1. A son of David.
Shammuah, and Shobab, and *N* ... 2Sa 5:14 5416
Shimea, and Shobab, and *N*, and ... 1Chr 3:5 5416
and Shobab, *N*, and Solomon ... 1Chr 14:4 5416
Mattatha, which was the son of *N* ... Lk 3:31 *3481*
2. A prophet in David's court.
the king said unto *N* the prophet ... 2Sa 7:2 5416
N said to the king, Go, do all ... 2Sa 7:3 5416
the word of the LORD came unto *N* ... 2Sa 7:4 5416
so did *N* speak unto David ... 2Sa 7:17 5416
And the LORD sent *N* unto David ... 2Sa 12:1 5416
and he said to *N*, As the LORD ... 2Sa 12:5 5416
N said to David, Thou art the man ... 2Sa 12:7 5416
And David said unto *N*, I have ... 2Sa 12:13 5416
N said unto David, The LORD also ... 2Sa 12:13 5416
N departed unto his house ... 2Sa 12:15 5416
sent by the hand of *N* the prophet ... 2Sa 12:25 5416
N the prophet, and Shimei, and Rei, ... 1Kin 1:8 5416
But *N* the prophet, and Benaiah, and ... 1Kin 1:10 5416
Wherefore *N* spake unto Bath-sheba ... 1Kin 1:11 5416
N the prophet also came in ... 1Kin 1:22 5416
saying, Behold *N* the prophet ... 1Kin 1:23 5416
N said, My lord, O king, hast ... 1Kin 1:24 5416
N the prophet, and Benaiah the son ... 1Kin 1:32 5416
N the prophet anoint him there ... 1Kin 1:34 5416
N the prophet, and Benaiah the son ... 1Kin 1:38 5416
N the prophet, and Benaiah the son ... 1Kin 1:44 5416
N the prophet have anointed him ... 1Kin 1:45 5416
that David said to *N* the prophet ... 1Chr 17:1 5416
Then *N* said unto David, Do all ... 1Chr 17:2 5416
that the word of God came to *N* ... 1Chr 17:3 5416
so did *N* speak unto David ... 1Chr 17:15 5416
and in the book of *N* the prophet ... 1Chr 29:29 5416
in the book of *N* the prophet ... 2Chr 9:29 5416
the king's seer, and *N* the prophet ... 2Chr 29:25 5416
when *N* the prophet came unto him, ... Ps 51:*t* 5416
3. Father of Igal.
Igal the son of *N* of Zobah ... 2Sa 23:36 5416
4. Father of Azariah.
Azariah the son of *N* was over the ... 1Kin 4:5 5416
5. Father of Zebud.
Zabud the son of *N* was principal ... 1Kin 4:5 5416
6. Son of Attai.
And Attai begat *N* ... 1Chr 2:36 5416
and *N* begat Zabad ... 1Chr 2:36 5416
7. Brother of Joel.
Joel the brother of *N*, Mibhar the ... 1Chr 11:38 5416
8. A clan leader with Ezra.
Jarib, and for Elnathan, and for *N* ... Ezr 8:16 5416
9. Married a foreigner in exile.
And Shelemiah, and *N*, and Adaiah, ... Ezr 10:39 5416
10. A family leader.
family of the house of *N* apart ... Zec 12:12 5416

NATHANAEL *(na-than'-a-el)* {6} See BARTHOLOMEW. *A disciple of Jesus.*
Philip findeth *N*, and saith unto ... Jn 1:45 *3482*
N said unto him, Can there any ... Jn 1:46 *3482*
Jesus saw *N* coming to him, and ... Jn 1:47 *3482*
N saith unto him, Whence knowest ... Jn 1:48 *3482*
N answered and saith unto him, ... Jn 1:49 *3482*
N of Cana in Galilee, and the sons ... Jn 21:2 *3482*

NATHAN-MELECH *(na'-than-me'-lek)* {1} *A servant of King Josiah.*
the chamber of *N* the chamberlain ... 2Kin 23:11 5419

NATION {145}
And I will make of thee a great *n* ... Gen 12:2 1471
And also that *n*, whom they shall ... Gen 15:14 1471
and I will make him a great *n* ... Gen 17:20 1471
surely become a great and mighty *n* ... Gen 18:18 1471
wilt thou slay also a righteous *n* ... Gen 20:4 1471
of the bondwoman will I make a *n* ... Gen 21:13 1471
for I will make him a great *n* ... Gen 21:18 1471
a *n* and a company of nations shall ... Gen 35:11 1471
will there make of thee a great *n* ... Gen 46:3 1471
land of Egypt since it became a *n* ... Ex 9:24 1471
kingdom of priests, and an holy *n* ... Ex 19:6 1471
strange *n* he shall have no power ... Ex 21:8 5971
and I will make of thee a great *n* ... Ex 32:10 1471
that this *n* is thy people ... Ex 33:13 1471
in all the earth, nor in any *n* ... Ex 34:10 1471
neither any of your own *n* ... Lev 18:26 249
not walk in the manners of the *n* ... Lev 20:23 1471
and will make of thee a greater *n* ... Num 14:12 1471
Surely this great *n* is a wise ... Deut 4:6 1471
For what *n* is there so great, who ... Deut 4:7 1471
what *n* is there so great, that ... Deut 4:8 1471
take him a *n* from the midst of ... Deut 4:34 1471
from the midst of another *n* ... Deut 4:34 1471
I will make of thee a *n* mightier ... Deut 9:14 1471
with a few, and became there a *n* ... Deut 26:5 1471
shall a *n* which thou knowest not ... Deut 28:33 5971
unto a *n* which neither thou nor ... Deut 28:36 1471
bring a *n* against thee from far ... Deut 28:49 1471
a *n* whose tongue thou shalt not ... Deut 28:49 1471
A *n* of fierce countenance, which ... Deut 28:50 1471
them to anger with a foolish *n* ... Deut 32:21 1471
For they are a *n* void of counsel, ... Deut 32:28 1471
what one *n* in the earth is like ... 2Sa 7:23 1471
liveth, there is no *n* or kingdom ... 1Kin 18:10 1471
took an oath of the kingdom and *n* ... 1Kin 18:10 1471
Howbeit every *n* made gods of ... 2Kin 17:29 1471
every *n* in their cities wherein ... 2Kin 17:29 1471
when they went from *n* to *n* ... 1Chr 16:20 1471
what one *n* in the earth is like ... 1Chr 17:21 1471
And *n* was destroyed of *n* ... 2Chr 15:6 1471
for no god of any *n* or kingdom ... 2Chr 32:15 1471
whether it be done against a *n* ... Job 34:29 1471
Blessed is the *n* whose God is the ... Ps 33:12 1471
my cause against an ungodly *n* ... Ps 43:1 1471
us cut them off from being a *n* ... Ps 83:4 1471
they went from one *n* to another ... Ps 105:13 1471
rejoice in the gladness of thy *n* ... Ps 106:5 1471
He hath not dealt so with any *n* ... Ps 147:20 1471
Righteousness exalteth a *n* ... Prov 14:34 1471
Ah sinful *n*, a people laden with ... Is 1:4 1471
n shall not lift up sword against ... Is 2:4 1471
shall not lift up sword against *n* ... Is 2:4 1471
Thou hast multiplied the *n* ... Is 9:3 1471
him against an hypocritical *n* ... Is 10:6 1471
answer the messengers of the *n* ... Is 14:32 1471
to a *n* scattered and peeled, to a ... Is 18:2 1471
a *n* meted out and trodden down, ... Is 18:2 1471
a *n* meted out and trodden under ... Is 18:7 1471
that the righteous *n* which ... Is 26:2 1471
Thou hast increased the *n* ... Is 26:15 1471
O LORD, thou hast increased the *n* ... Is 26:15 1471
to him whom the *n* abhorreth ... Is 49:7 1471
and give ear unto me, O my *n* ... Is 51:4 3816
thou shalt call a *n* that thou ... Is 55:5 1471
as a *n* that did righteousness, and ... Is 58:2 1471
For the *n* and kingdom that will ... Is 60:12 1471
and a small one a strong *n* ... Is 60:22 1471
unto a *n* that was not called by ... Is 65:1 1471
or shall a *n* be born at once ... Is 66:8 1471
Hath a *n* changed their gods, ... Jer 2:11 1471
be avenged on such a *n* as this ... Jer 5:9 1471
I will bring a *n* upon you from ... Jer 5:15 1471
mighty *n*, it is an ancient *n* ... Jer 5:15 1471
a *n* whose language thou knowest ... Jer 5:15 1471
be avenged on such a *n* as this ... Jer 5:29 1471
a great *n* shall be raised from ... Jer 6:22 1471
This is a *n* that obeyeth not the ... Jer 7:28 1471
be avenged on such a *n* as this ... Jer 9:9 1471
pluck up and destroy that *n* ... Jer 12:17 1471
I shall speak concerning a *n* ... Jer 18:7 1471
If that *n*, against whom I have ... Jer 18:8 1471
I shall speak concerning a *n* ... Jer 18:9 1471
the king of Babylon, and that *n* ... Jer 25:12 1471
shall go forth from *n* to *n* ... Jer 25:32 1471
it shall come to pass, that the *n* ... Jer 27:8 1471
that *n* will I punish, saith the ... Jer 27:8 1471
LORD hath spoken against the *n* ... Jer 27:13 1471

from being a *n* before me for ever ... Jer 31:36 1471
should be no more a *n* before them ... Jer 33:24 1471
let us cut it off from being a *n* ... Jer 48:2 1471
get you up unto the wealthy *n* ... Jer 49:31 1471
there shall be no *n* whither the ... Jer 49:36 1471
there cometh up a *n* against her ... Jer 50:3 1471
come from the north, and a great *n* ... Jer 50:41 1471
for a *n* that could not save us ... Lam 4:17 1471
to a rebellious *n* that hath ... Eze 2:3 1471
I will make them one *n* in the ... Eze 37:22 1471
a decree, That every people, *n* ... Dan 3:29 524
shall stand up out of the *n* ... Dan 8:22 1471
was a *n* even to that same time ... Dan 12:1 1471
For a *n* is come up upon my land, ... Joel 1:6 1471
I will raise up against you a *n* ... Amos 6:14 1471
n shall not lift up a sword ... Mic 4:3 1471
not lift up a sword against *n* ... Mic 4:3 1471
that was cast far off a strong *n* ... Mic 4:7 1471
Chaldeans, that bitter and hasty *n* ... Hab 1:6 1471
gather together, O *n* not desired ... Zeph 2:1 1471
coast, the *n* of the Cherethites ... Zeph 2:5 1471
people, and so is this *n* before me ... Hag 2:14 1471
have robbed me, even this whole *n* ... Mal 3:9 1471
given to a *n* bringing forth the ... Mt 21:43 *1484*
For *n* shall rise against *n*, ... Mt 24:7 *1484*
was a Greek, a Syrophenician by *n* ... Mk 7:26 *1085*
For *n* shall rise against *n*, ... Mk 13:8 *1484*
For he loveth our *n*, and he hath ... Lk 7:5 *1484*
N shall rise against *n*, and ... Lk 21:10 *1484*
this fellow perverting the *n* ... Lk 23:2 *1484*
and take away both our place and *n* ... Jn 11:48 *1484*
and that the whole *n* perish not ... Jn 11:50 *1484*
that Jesus should die for that *n* ... Jn 11:51 *1484*
And not for that *n* only, but that ... Jn 11:52 *1484*
Thine own *n* and the chief priests ... Jn 18:35 *1484*
men, out of every *n* under heaven ... Acts 2:5 *1484*
the *n* to whom they shall be in ... Acts 7:7 *1484*
among all the *n* of the Jews ... Acts 10:22 *1484*
or come unto one of another *n* ... Acts 10:28 *246*
But in every *n* he that feareth ... Acts 10:35 *1484*
unto this *n* by thy providence ... Acts 24:2 *1484*
of many years a judge unto this *n* ... Acts 24:10 *1484*
I came to bring alms to my *n* ... Acts 24:17 *1484*
among mine own *n* at Jerusalem ... Acts 26:4 *1484*
I had ought to accuse my *n* of ... Acts 28:19 *1484*
by a foolish *n* I will anger you ... Rom 10:19 *1484*
many my equals in mine own *n* ... Gal 1:14 *1085*
midst of a crooked and perverse *n* ... Phil 2:15 *1074*
a royal priesthood, an holy *n* ... 1Pet 2:9 *1484*
and tongue, and people, and *n* ... Rev 5:9 *1484*
dwell on the earth, and to every *n* ... Rev 14:6 *1484*

NATIONS {336}

after their families, in their *n* ... Gen 10:5 1471
in their countries, and in their *n* ... Gen 10:20 1471
in their lands, after their *n* ... Gen 10:31 1471
their generations, in their *n* ... Gen 10:32 1471
by these were the *n* divided in ... Gen 10:32 1471
king of Elam, and Tidal king of *n* ... Gen 14:1 1471
of Elam, and with Tidal king of *n* ... Gen 14:9 1471
thou shalt be a father of many *n* ... Gen 17:4 1471
father of many *n* have I made thee ... Gen 17:5 1471
and I will make *n* of thee ... Gen 17:6 1471
and she shall be a mother of *n* ... Gen 17:16 1471
all the *n* of the earth shall be ... Gen 18:18 1471
all the *n* of the earth be blessed ... Gen 22:18 1471
princes according to their *n* ... Gen 25:16 523
Two *n* are in thy womb, and two ... Gen 25:23 1471
all the *n* of the earth be blessed ... Gen 26:4 1471
serve thee, and *n* bow down to thee ... Gen 27:29 3816
a company of *n* shall be of thee, ... Gen 35:11 1471
shall become a multitude of *n* ... Gen 48:19 1471
I will cast out the *n* before thee ... Ex 34:24 1471
for in all these the *n* are ... Lev 18:24 1471
as it spued out the *n* that were ... Lev 18:28 1471
then the *n* which have heard the ... Num 14:15 1471
shall not be reckoned among the *n* ... Num 23:9 1471
he shall eat up the *n* his enemies ... Num 24:8 1471
Amalek was the first of the *n* ... Num 24:20 1471
the fear of thee upon the *n* that ... Deut 2:25 5971
in the sight of the *n*, which ... Deut 4:6 5971
unto all *n* under the whole heaven ... Deut 4:19 5971
shall scatter you among the *n* ... Deut 4:27 5971
To drive out *n* from before thee ... Deut 4:38 1471
hath cast out many *n* before thee ... Deut 7:1 1471
seven *n* greater and mightier than ... Deut 7:1 1471
heart, These *n* are more than I ... Deut 7:17 1471
out those *n* before thee by little ... Deut 7:22 1471
As the *n* which the LORD ... Deut 8:20 1471
to go in to possess *n* greater ... Deut 9:1 1471
n the LORD doth drive them out ... Deut 9:4 1471
n the LORD thy God doth drive ... Deut 9:5 1471
out all these *n* from before you ... Deut 11:23 1471
and ye shall possess greater *n* ... Deut 11:23 1471
wherein the *n* which ye shall ... Deut 12:2 1471
cut off the *n* from before thee ... Deut 12:29 1471
How did these *n* serve their gods ... Deut 12:30 1471
above all the *n* that are upon the ... Deut 14:2 5971
and thou shalt lend unto many *n* ... Deut 15:6 1471
and thou shalt reign over many *n* ... Deut 15:6 1471
like as all the *n* that are about ... Deut 17:14 1471
after the abominations of those *n* ... Deut 18:9 1471
For these *n*, which thou shalt ... Deut 18:14 1471
LORD thy God hath cut off the *n* ... Deut 19:1 1471
are not of the cities of these *n* ... Deut 20:15 1471
above all *n* which he hath made ... Deut 26:19 1471
on high above all *n* of the earth ... Deut 28:1 1471
and thou shalt lend unto many *n* ... Deut 28:12 1471
among all *n* whither the LORD ... Deut 28:37 5971
among these *n* shalt thou find no ... Deut 28:65 1471
through the *n* which ye passed by ... Deut 29:16 1471
go and serve the gods of these *n* ... Deut 29:18 1471
Even all *n* shall say, Wherefore ... Deut 29:24 1471
call them to mind among all the *n* ... Deut 30:1 1471
and gather thee from all the *n* ... Deut 30:3 5971
destroy these *n* from before thee ... Deut 31:3 1471
to the *n* their inheritance ... Deut 32:8 1471
Rejoice, O ye *n*, with his people ... Deut 32:43 1471
the king of the *n* of Gilgal ... Josh 12:23 1471
unto all these *n* because of you ... Josh 23:3 1471
you by lot these *n* that remain ... Josh 23:4 1471
with all the *n* that I have cut ... Josh 23:4 1471
That ye come not among these *n* ... Josh 23:7 1471
out from before you great *n* ... Josh 23:9 1471
unto the remnant of these *n* ... Josh 23:12 1471
any of these *n* from before you ... Josh 23:13 1471
n which Joshua left when he died ... Judg 2:21 1471
Therefore the LORD left those *n* ... Judg 2:23 1471
Now these are the *n* which the ... Judg 3:1 1471
a king to judge us like all the *n* ... 1Sa 8:5 1471
we also may be like all the *n* ... 1Sa 8:20 1471
for those *n* were of old the ... 1Sa 27:8
to thee from Egypt, from the *n* ... 2Sa 7:23 1471
of all *n* which he subdued ... 2Sa 8:11 1471
his fame was in all *n* round about ... 1Kin 4:31 1471
Of the *n* concerning which the ... 1Kin 11:2 1471
n which the LORD cast out before ... 1Kin 14:24 1471
The *n* which thou hast removed, and ... 2Kin 17:26 1471
after the manner of the *n* whom ... 2Kin 17:33 1471
So these *n* feared the LORD, and ... 2Kin 17:41 1471
Hath any of the gods of the *n* ... 2Kin 18:33 1471
Have the gods of the *n* delivered ... 2Kin 19:12 1471
of Assyria have destroyed the *n* ... 2Kin 19:17 1471
to do more evil than did the *n* ... 2Kin 21:9 1471
the fear of him upon all *n* ... 1Chr 14:17 1471
his marvellous works among all *n* ... 1Chr 16:24 5971
and let men say among the *n* ... 1Chr 16:31 1471
by driving out *n* from before thy ... 1Chr 17:21 1471
that he brought from all these *n* ... 1Chr 18:11 1471
a proverb and a byword among all *n* ... 2Chr 7:20 5971
manner of the *n* of other lands ... 2Chr 13:9 5971
were the gods of the *n* of those ... 2Chr 32:13 1471
those *n* that my fathers utterly ... 2Chr 32:14 1471
As the gods of the *n* of other ... 2Chr 32:17 1471
sight of all *n* from thenceforth ... 2Chr 32:23 1471
the rest of the *n* whom the great ... Ezr 4:10 524
scatter you abroad among the *n* ... Neh 1:8 5971
thou gavest them kingdoms and *n* ... Neh 9:22 5971
yet among many *n* was there no ... Neh 13:26 1471
He increaseth the *n*, and ... Job 12:23 1471
he enlargeth the *n*, and ... Job 12:23 1471
all the *n* that forget God ... Ps 9:17 1471
that the *n* may know themselves to ... Ps 9:20 1471
all the kindreds of the *n* shall ... Ps 22:27 1471
and he is the governor among the *n* ... Ps 22:28 1471
under us, and the *n* under our feet ... Ps 47:3 3816
I will sing unto thee among the *n* ... Ps 57:9 3816
his eyes behold the *n* ... Ps 66:7 1471
thy saving health among all *n* ... Ps 67:2 1471
O let the *n* be glad and sing for ... Ps 67:4 3816
and govern the *n* upon earth ... Ps 67:4 3816
all *n* shall serve him ... Ps 72:11 1471
all *n* shall call him blessed ... Ps 72:17 1471
for thou shalt inherit all *n* ... Ps 82:8 1471
All *n* whom thou hast made shall ... Ps 86:9 1471
all the gods of the *n* are idols ... Ps 96:5 5971
their seed also among the *n* ... Ps 106:27 1471
They did not destroy the *n* ... Ps 106:34 5971
praises unto thee among the *n* ... Ps 108:3 3816
The LORD is high above all *n* ... Ps 113:4 1471
O praise the LORD, all ye *n* ... Ps 117:1 1471
All *n* compassed me about ... Ps 118:10 1471
Who smote great *n*, and slew mighty ... Ps 135:10 1471
people curse, *n* shall abhor him ... Prov 24:24 3816
and all *n* shall flow unto it ... Is 2:2 1471
And he shall judge among the *n* ... Is 2:4 1471
up an ensign to the *n* from far ... Is 5:26 1471
Jordan, in Galilee of the *n* ... Is 9:1 1471
to destroy and cut off *n* not a few ... Is 10:7 1471
shall set up an ensign for the *n* ... Is 11:12 1471
kingdoms of *n* gathered together ... Is 13:4 1471
he that ruled the *n* in anger ... Is 14:6 1471
thrones all the kings of the *n* ... Is 14:9 1471
ground, which didst weaken the *n* ... Is 14:12 1471
All the kings of the *n*, even all ... Is 14:18 1471
is stretched out upon all the *n* ... Is 14:26 1471
and to the rushing of *n*, that make ... Is 17:12 3816
The *n* shall rush like the rushing ... Is 17:13 3816
and she is a mart of *n* ... Is 23:3 1471
of the terrible *n* shall fear thee ... Is 25:3 1471
vail that is spread over all *n* ... Is 25:7 1471
the *n* that fight against Ariel ... Is 29:7 1471
the multitude of all the *n* be ... Is 29:8 1471
to sift the *n* with the sieve of ... Is 30:28 1471
of thyself the *n* were scattered ... Is 33:3 1471
Come near, ye *n*, to hear ... Is 34:1 1471
of the LORD is upon all *n* ... Is 34:2 1471
Hath any of the gods of the *n* ... Is 36:18 1471
Have the gods of the *n* delivered ... Is 37:12 1471
Assyria have laid waste all the *n* ... Is 37:18 776
the *n* are as a drop of a bucket, ... Is 40:15 1471
All *n* before him are as nothing ... Is 40:17 1471
gave the *n* before him, and made ... Is 41:2 1471
Let all the *n* be gathered ... Is 43:9 1471
holden, to subdue *n* before him ... Is 45:1 1471
ye that are escaped of the *n* ... Is 45:20 1471
holy arm in the eyes of all the *n* ... Is 52:10 1471
So shall he sprinkle many *n* ... Is 52:15 1471
n that knew not thee shall run ... Is 55:5 1471
those *n* shall be utterly wasted ... Is 60:12 1471
to spring forth before all the *n* ... Is 61:11 1471
that the *n* may tremble at thy ... Is 64:2 1471
come, that I will gather all *n* ... Is 66:18 1471
that escape of them unto the *n* ... Is 66:19 1471
the LORD out of all *n* upon horses ... Is 66:20 1471
thee a prophet unto the *n* ... Jer 1:5 1471
have this day set thee over the *n* ... Jer 1:10 1471
all the *n* shall be gathered unto ... Jer 3:17 1471
goodly heritage of the hosts of *n* ... Jer 3:19 1471
the *n* shall bless themselves in ... Jer 4:2 1471
Make ye mention to the *n* ... Jer 4:16 1471
Therefore hear, ye *n*, and know, O ... Jer 6:18 1471
for all these *n* are uncircumcised ... Jer 9:26 1471
would not fear thee, O King of *n* ... Jer 10:7 1471
among all the wise men of the *n* ... Jer 10:7 1471
the *n* shall not be able to abide ... Jer 10:10 1471
many *n* shall pass by this city, ... Jer 22:8 1471
against all these *n* round about ... Jer 25:9 1471
these *n* shall serve the king of ... Jer 25:11 1471
hath prophesied against all the *n* ... Jer 25:13 1471
For many *n* and great kings shall ... Jer 25:14 1471
at my hand, and cause all the *n* ... Jer 25:15 1471
hand, and made all the *n* to drink ... Jer 25:17 1471
hath a controversy with the *n* ... Jer 25:31 1471
a curse to all the *n* of the earth ... Jer 26:6 1471
all *n* shall serve him, and his son ... Jer 27:7 1471
and then many *n* and great kings ... Jer 27:7 1471
But the *n* that bring their neck ... Jer 27:11 1471
n within the space of two full ... Jer 28:11 1471
iron upon the neck of all these *n* ... Jer 28:14 1471
I will gather you from all the *n* ... Jer 29:14 1471
among all the *n* whither I have ... Jer 29:18 1471
n whither I have scattered thee ... Jer 30:11 1471
and shout among the chief of the *n* ... Jer 31:7 1471
Hear the word of the LORD, O ye *n* ... Jer 31:10 1471
before all the *n* of the earth ... Jer 33:9 1471
Judah, and against all the *n* ... Jer 36:2 1471
that were returned from all *n* ... Jer 43:5 1471
among all the *n* of the earth ... Jer 44:8 1471
The *n* have heard of thy shame, and ... Jer 46:12 1471
the *n* whither I have driven thee ... Jer 46:28 1471
Declare ye among the *n*, and ... Jer 50:2 1471
of great *n* from the north country ... Jer 50:9 1471
of the *n* shall be a wilderness ... Jer 50:12 1471
become a desolation among the *n* ... Jer 50:23 1471
and the cry is heard among the *n* ... Jer 50:46 1471
the *n* have drunken of her wine ... Jer 51:7 1471
therefore the *n* are mad ... Jer 51:7 1471
thee will I break in pieces the *n* ... Jer 51:20 1471
blow the trumpet among the *n* ... Jer 51:27 1471
prepare the *n* against her ... Jer 51:27 1471
Prepare against her the *n* with ... Jer 51:28 1471
an astonishment among the *n* ... Jer 51:41 1471
the *n* shall not flow together any ... Jer 51:44 1471
she that was great among the *n* ... Lam 1:1 1471
have set it in the midst of the *n* ... Eze 5:5 1471
into wickedness more than the *n* ... Eze 5:6 1471
the *n* that are round about you ... Eze 5:7 1471
to the judgments of the *n* that ... Eze 5:7 1471
of thee in the sight of the *n* ... Eze 5:8 1471
a reproach among the *n* that are ... Eze 5:14 1471
an astonishment unto the *n* that ... Eze 5:15 1471
escape the sword among the *n* ... Eze 6:8 1471
n whither they shall be carried ... Eze 6:9 1471
I shall scatter them among the *n* ... Eze 12:15 1471
The *n* also heard of him ... Eze 19:4 1471
Then the *n* set against him on ... Eze 19:8 1471
may not be remembered among the *n* ... Eze 25:10 1471
will cause many *n* to come up ... Eze 26:3 1471
it shall become a spoil to the *n* ... Eze 26:5 1471
upon thee, the terrible of the *n* ... Eze 28:7 1471
scatter the Egyptians among the *n* ... Eze 29:12 1471
exalt itself any more above the *n* ... Eze 29:15 1471
shall no more rule over the *n* ... Eze 29:15 1471
with him, the terrible of the *n* ... Eze 30:11 1471
scatter the Egyptians among the *n* ... Eze 30:23 1471
scatter the Egyptians among the *n* ... Eze 30:26 1471
his shadow dwelt all great *n* ... Eze 31:6 1471
strangers, the terrible of the *n* ... Eze 31:12 1471
I made the *n* to shake at the ... Eze 31:16 1471
art like a young lion of the *n* ... Eze 32:2 1471
bring thy destruction among the *n* ... Eze 32:9 1471
to fall, the terrible of the *n* ... Eze 32:12 1471
of the *n* shall lament her ... Eze 32:16 1471
and the daughters of the famous *n* ... Eze 32:18 1471
thou hast said, These two *n* ... Eze 35:10 1471
up men, and hast bereaved thy *n* ... Eze 36:13 1471
neither bereave thy *n* any more ... Eze 36:14 1471
thou cause thy *n* to fall any more ... Eze 36:15 1471
and they shall be no more two *n* ... Eze 37:22 1471
it is brought forth out of the *n* ... Eze 38:8 1471
that are gathered out of the *n* ... Eze 38:12 1471
be known in the eyes of many *n* ... Eze 38:23 1471
in them in the sight of many *n* ... Eze 39:27 1471
you it is commanded, O people, *n* ... Dan 3:4 524
of musick, all the people, the *n* ... Dan 3:7 524
the king, unto all people, *n* ... Dan 4:1 524
that he gave him, all people, *n* ... Dan 5:19 524
Darius wrote unto all people, *n* ... Dan 6:25 524
and a kingdom, that all people, *n* ... Dan 7:14 524
they have hired among the *n* ... Hos 8:10 1471
shall be wanderers among the *n* ... Hos 9:17 1471
I will also gather all *n*, and will ... Joel 3:2 1471
they have scattered among the *n* ... Joel 3:2 1471

which are named chief of the *n* ... Amos 6:1 1471
the house of Israel among all *n* ... Amos 9:9 1471
many *n* shall come, and say, Come, ... Mic 4:2 1471
and rebuke strong *n* afar off ... Mic 4:3 1471
Now also many *n* are gathered ... Mic 4:11 1471
The *n* shall see and be confounded ... Mic 7:16 1471
that selleth *n* through her ... Nah 3:4 1471
I will shew the *n* thy nakedness ... Nah 3:5 1471
spare continually to slay the *n* ... Hab 1:17 1471
but gathereth unto him all *n* ... Hab 2:5 1471
Because thou hast spoiled many *n* ... Hab 2:8 1471
he beheld, and drove asunder the *n* ... Hab 3:6 1471
of her, all the beasts of the *n* ... Zeph 2:14 1471
I have cut off the *n* ... Zeph 3:6 1471
determination is to gather the *n* ... Zeph 3:8 1471
I will shake all *n* ... Hag 2:7 1471
and the desire of all *n* shall come ... Hag 2:7 1471
me unto the *n* which spoiled you ... Zec 2:8 1471
many *n* shall be joined to the ... Zec 2:11 1471
all the *n* whom they knew not ... Zec 7:14 1471
strong *n* shall come to seek the ... Zec 8:22 1471
out of all languages of the *n* ... Zec 8:23 1471
the *n* that come against Jerusalem ... Zec 12:9 1471
For I will gather all *n* against ... Zec 14:2 1471
forth, and fight against those *n* ... Zec 14:3 1471
one that is left of all the *n* ... Zec 14:16 1471
the punishment of all *n* that come ... Zec 14:19 1471
all *n* shall call you blessed ... Mal 3:12 1471
hated of all *n* for my name's sake ... Mt 24:9 *1484*
world for a witness unto all *n* ... Mt 24:14 *1484*
him shall be gathered all *n* ... Mt 25:32 *1484*
Go ye therefore, and teach all *n* ... Mt 28:19 *1484*
of all *n* the house of prayer ... Mk 11:17 *1484*
first be published among all *n* ... Mk 13:10 *1484*
do the *n* of the world seek after ... Lk 12:30 *1484*
be led away captive into all *n* ... Lk 21:24 *1484*
and upon the earth distress of *n* ... Lk 21:25 *1484*
preached in his name among all *n* ... Lk 24:47 *1484*
seven *n* in the land of Chanaan ... Acts 13:19 *1484*
all *n* to walk in their own ways ... Acts 14:16 *1484*
hath made of one blood all *n* of ... Acts 17:26 *1484*
to the faith among all *n*, for his ... Rom 1:5 *1484*
have made thee a father of many *n* ... Rom 4:17 *1484*
might become the father of many *n* ... Rom 4:18 *1484*
made known to all *n* for the ... Rom 16:26 *1484*
In thee shall all *n* be blessed ... Gal 3:8 *1484*
him will I give power over the *n* ... Rev 2:26 *1484*
no man could number, of all *n* ... Rev 7:9 *1484*
again before many peoples, and *n* ... Rev 10:11 *1484*
n shall see their dead bodies ... Rev 11:9 *1484*
the *n* were angry, and thy wrath is ... Rev 11:18 *1484*
to rule all *n* with a rod of iron ... Rev 12:5 *1484*
all kindreds, and tongues, and *n* ... Rev 13:7 *1484*
because she made all *n* drink of ... Rev 14:8 *1484*
for all *n* shall come and worship ... Rev 15:4 *1484*
and the cities of the *n* fell ... Rev 16:19 *1484*
are peoples, and multitudes, and *n* ... Rev 17:15 *1484*
For all *n* have drunk of the wine ... Rev 18:3 *1484*
thy sorceries were all *n* deceived ... Rev 18:23 *1484*
with it he should smite the *n* ... Rev 19:15 *1484*
he should deceive the *n* no more ... Rev 20:3 *1484*
shall go out to deceive the *n* ... Rev 20:8 *1484*
the *n* of them which are saved ... Rev 21:24 *1484*
glory and honour of the *n* into it ... Rev 21:26 *1484*
were for the healing of the *n* ... Rev 22:2 *1484*

NATIVE {1}
no more, nor see his *n* country ... Jer 22:10 4138

NATIVITY {7}
father Terah in the land of his *n* ... Gen 11:28 4138
thy mother, and the land of thy *n* ... Ruth 2:11 4138
people, and to the land of our *n* ... Jer 46:16 4138
thy *n* is of the land of Canaan ... Eze 16:3 4138
And as for thy *n*, in the day thou ... Eze 16:4 4138
created, in the land of thy *n* ... Eze 21:30 4351
of Chaldea, the land of their *n* ... Eze 23:15 4138

NATURAL {13}
not dim, nor his *n* force abated ... Deut 34:7 3893
n use into that which is against ... Rom 1:26 *5446*
leaving the *n* use of the woman, ... Rom 1:27 *5446*
without *n* affection, implacable, ... Rom 1:31
if God spared not the *n* branches ... Rom 11:21 *2596,6449*
these, which be the *n* branches ... Rom 11:24 *2596,6449*
But the *n* man receiveth not the ... 1Cor 2:14 *5591*
It is sown a *n* body ... 1Cor 15:44 *5591*
There is a *n* body, and there is a ... 1Cor 15:44 *5591*
is spiritual, but that which is *n* ... 1Cor 15:46 *5591*
Without *n* affection, ... 2Ti 3:3
beholding his *n* face in a glass ... Jas 1:23 *1083*
as *n* brute beasts, made to be ... 2Pet 2:12 *5446*

NATURALLY {2}
who will *n* care for your state ... Phil 2:20 *1103*
but what they know *n*, as brute ... Jude 10 *5447*

NATURE {12}
use into that which is against *n* ... Rom 1:26 *5449*
do by *n* the things contained in ... Rom 2:14 *5449*
not uncircumcision which is by *n* ... Rom 2:27 *5449*
the olive tree which is wild by *n* ... Rom 11:24 *5449*
to *n* into a good olive tree ... Rom 11:24 *5449*
Doth not even *n* itself teach you, ... 1Cor 11:14 *5449*
We who are Jews by *n*, and not ... Gal 2:15 *5449*
unto them which by *n* are no gods ... Gal 4:8 *5449*
were by *n* the children of wrath, ... Eph 2:3 *5449*
took not on him the *n* of angels ... Heb 2:16
setteth on fire the course of *n* ... Jas 3:6 *1078*
be partakers of the divine *n* ... 2Pet 1:4 *5449*

NAUGHT {3}
but the water is *n*, and the ground ... 2Kin 2:19 7451
It is *n*, it is *n*, saith the ... Prov 20:14 7451

NAUGHTINESS {3}
pride, and the *n* of thine heart ... 1Sa 17:28 7455
shall be taken in their own *n* ... Prov 11:6 1942
filthiness and superfluity of *n* ... Jas 1:21 *2549*

NAUGHTY {3}
A *n* person, a wicked man, walketh ... Prov 6:12 1100
a liar giveth ear to a *n* tongue ... Prov 17:4 1942
the other basket had very *n* figs ... Jer 24:2 7451

NAUM *(na'-um)* {1} See NAHUM. *Father of Amos; ancestor of Jesus.*
of Amos, which was the son of *N* ... Lk 3:25 *3486*

NAVEL {4}
force is in the *n* of his belly ... Job 40:16 8306
It shall be health to thy *n* ... Prov 3:8 8270
Thy *n* is like a round goblet, ... Song 7:2 8326
thou wast born thy *n* was not cut ... Eze 16:4 8270

NAVES {1}
their axletrees, and their *n* ... 1Kin 7:33 1354

NAVY {6}
king Solomon made a *n* of ships in ... 1Kin 9:26 590
Hiram sent in the *n* his servants ... 1Kin 9:27 590
the *n* also of Hiram, that brought ... 1Kin 10:11 590
For the king had at sea a *n* of ... 1Kin 10:22 590
of Tharshish with the *n* of Hiram ... 1Kin 10:22 590
years came the *n* of Tharshish ... 1Kin 10:22 590

NAY {55}
And he said, *N*; but thou didst ... Gen 18:15 3808
And they said, *N*; but we will ... Gen 19:2
N, my lord, hear me ... Gen 23:11 3808
And Jacob said, *N*, I pray thee, if ... Gen 33:10 408
And they said unto him, *N*, my lord ... Gen 42:10 3808
And he said unto them, *N*, but to ... Gen 42:12 3808
And he said, *N*. ... Num 22:30 3808
And he said, *N*; but as captain ... Josh 5:14 3808
And the people said unto Joshua, *N* ... Josh 24:21 3808
If he said, *N* ... Judg 12:5 3808
unto them, and said unto them, *N* ... Judg 19:23 408
my brethren, *n*, I pray you ... Judg 19:23
n, my daughters; for it ... Ruth 1:13 408
then he would answer him, *N* ... 1Sa 2:16
N, my sons; for it is ... 1Sa 2:24 408
and they said, *N*; but we will ... 1Sa 8:19 3808
and ye have said unto him, *N* ... 1Sa 10:19
against you, ye said unto me, *N* ... 1Sa 12:12 3808
And she answered him, *N*, my ... 2Sa 13:12 408
And the king said to Absalom, *N* ... 2Sa 13:25 408
And Hushai said unto Absalom, *N* ... 2Sa 16:18 3808
And the king said unto Araunah, *N* ... 2Sa 24:24 3808
king, (for he will not say thee *n* ... 1Kin 2:17
I pray thee, say me not *n* ... 1Kin 2:20 6440
for I will not say thee *n* ... 1Kin 2:20
And he said, *N*; but I ... 1Kin 2:30 3808
And the other woman said, *N* ... 1Kin 3:22 3808
and the other saith, *N* ... 1Kin 3:23 3808
king of Israel said unto him, *N* ... 2Kin 3:13 408
And she said, *N*, my lord, thou man ... 2Kin 4:16 408
n, but let the shadow return ... 2Kin 20:10 3808
And king David said to Ornan, *N* ... 1Chr 21:24 3808
n, they were not at all ashamed, ... Jer 6:15 1571
n, they were not at all ashamed, ... Jer 8:12 1571
be, Yea, yea; *N*, *n* ... Mt 5:37 *3756*
But he said, *N*; lest while ... Mt 13:29 *3756*
I tell you, *N*; but rather ... Lk 12:51 *3780*
I tell you, *N*: but, except ... Lk 13:3 *3780*
I tell you, *N*: but, except ... Lk 13:5 *3780*
And he said, *N*, father Abraham ... Lk 16:30 *3780*
others said, *N*; but he ... Jn 7:12 *3756*
n verily; but let them ... Acts 16:37 *3756*
N: but by the law ... Rom 3:27 *3780*
N, I had not known sin, but by ... Rom 7:7 *235*
N, in all these things we are ... Rom 8:37 *235*
N but, O man, who art thou that ... Rom 9:20 *3304*
N, ye do wrong, and defraud, and ... 1Cor 6:8 *235*
N, much more those members of the ... 1Cor 12:22 *235*
there should be yea yea, and *n* *n* ... 2Cor 1:17 *3756*
word toward you was not yea and *n* ... 2Cor 1:18 *3756*
and Timotheus, was not yea and *n* ... 2Cor 1:19 *3756*
be yea; and your *n*, *n* ... Jas 5:12 *3756*

NAZARENE *(naz-a-reen')* {1} See NAZARENES. *Native to Nazareth.*
prophets, He shall be called a *N* ... Mt 2:23 *3480*

NAZARENES *(naz-a-reens')* {1}
a ringleader of the sect of the *N* ... Acts 24:5 *3480*

NAZARETH *(naz'-a-reth)* {29} See NAZARENE. *A city in Galilee.*
came and dwelt in a city called *N* ... Mt 2:23 *3478*
And leaving *N*, he came and dwelt in ... Mt 4:13 *3478*
Jesus the prophet of *N* of Galilee ... Mt 21:11 *3478*
fellow was also with Jesus of *N* ... Mt 26:71 *3478*
that Jesus came from *N* of Galilee ... Mk 1:9 *3478*
to do with thee, thou Jesus of *N* ... Mk 1:24 *3478*
he heard that it was Jesus of *N* ... Mk 10:47 *3478*
And thou also wast with Jesus of *N* ... Mk 14:67 *3478*
Ye seek Jesus of *N*, which was ... Mk 16:6 *3478*
unto a city of Galilee, named *N* ... Lk 1:26 *3478*
Galilee, out of the city of *N* ... Lk 2:4 *3478*
into Galilee, to their own city *N* ... Lk 2:39 *3478*
went down with them, and came to *N* ... Lk 2:51 *3478*
And he came to *N*, where he had ... Lk 4:16 *3478*
to do with thee, thou Jesus of *N* ... Lk 4:34 *3478*
him, that Jesus of *N* passeth by ... Lk 18:37 *3478*
unto him, Concerning Jesus of *N* ... Lk 24:19 *3478*
prophets, did write, Jesus of *N* ... Jn 1:45 *3478*
any good thing come out of *N* ... Jn 1:46 *3478*
They answered him, Jesus of *N* ... Jn 18:5 *3478*
And they said, Jesus of *N* ... Jn 18:7 *3478*
JESUS OF *N* THE KING OF THE ... Jn 19:19 *3478*
Jesus of *N*, a man approved of God ... Acts 2:22 *3478*
name of Jesus Christ of *N* rise up ... Acts 3:6 *3478*
by the name of Jesus Christ of *N* ... Acts 4:10 *3478*
that this Jesus of *N* shall ... Acts 6:14 *3478*
Jesus of *N* with the Holy Ghost ... Acts 10:38 *3478*
he said unto me, I am Jesus of *N* ... Acts 22:8 *3478*
to the name of Jesus of *N* ... Acts 26:9 *3478*

NAZARITE *(naz'-a-rite)* {9} See NAZARITES. *Title applied to one making a special vow of abstention.*
themselves to vow a vow of a *N* ... Num 6:2 5139
And this is the law of the *N* ... Num 6:13 5139
the *N* shall shave the head of his ... Num 6:18 5139
put them upon the hands of the *N* ... Num 6:19 5139
after that the *N* may drink wine ... Num 6:20 5139
the law of the *N* who hath vowed ... Num 6:21 5139
be a *N* unto God from the womb ... Judg 13:5 5139
for the child shall be a *N* to God ... Judg 13:7 5139
for I have been a *N* unto God from ... Judg 16:17 5139

NAZARITES *(naz'-a-rites)* {3}
Her *N* were purer than snow, they ... Lam 4:7 5139
and of your young men for *N* ... Amos 2:11 5139
But ye gave the *N* wine to drink ... Amos 2:12 5139

NEAH *(ne'-ah)* {1} *A city in Zebulun.*
goeth out to Remmon-methoar to *N* ... Josh 19:13 5269

NEAPOLIS *(ne-ap'-o-lis)* {1} *A Macedonian seaport.*
Samothracia, and the next day to *N* ... Acts 16:11 *3496*

NEAR See APPENDIX.

NEARER See APPENDIX.

NEARIAH *(ne-a-ri'-ah)* {3} See NAGGE.
1. A son of Shemiah.
and Igeal, and Bariah, and *N* ... 1Chr 3:22 5294
And the sons of *N* ... 1Chr 3:23 5294
2. A son of Ishi.
for their captains Pelatiah, and *N* ... 1Chr 4:42 5294

NEBAI *(ne'-bahee)* {1} *A renewer of the covenant.*
Hariph, Anathoth, *N*, ... Neh 10:19 5109

NEBAIOTH *(ne-bah'-yoth)* {2} See NEBAJOTH.
1. A son of Ishmael.
The firstborn of Ishmael, *N* ... 1Chr 1:29 5032
2. Descendants of Ishmael.
the rams of *N* shall minister unto ... Is 60:7 5032

NEBAJOTH *(ne-ba'-joth)* {3} See NEBAIOTH. *Same as Nebaioth 1.*
the firstborn of Ishmael, *N* ... Gen 25:13 5032
Abraham's son, the sister of *N* ... Gen 28:9 5032
Ishmael's daughter, sister of *N* ... Gen 36:3 5032

NEBALLAT *(ne-bal'-lat)* {1} *A Benjamite city.*
Hadid, Zeboim, *N*, ... Neh 11:34 5041

NEBAT *(ne'-bat)* {25} *Father of King Jeroboam.*
And Jeroboam the son of *N*, an ... 1Kin 11:26 5028
pass, when Jeroboam the son of *N* ... 1Kin 12:2 5028
unto Jeroboam the son of *N* ... 1Kin 12:15 5028
of *N* reigned Abijam over Judah ... 1Kin 15:1 5028
house of Jeroboam the son of *N* ... 1Kin 16:3 5028
the way of Jeroboam the son of *N* ... 1Kin 16:26 5028
the sins of Jeroboam the son of *N* ... 1Kin 16:31 5028
house of Jeroboam the son of *N* ... 1Kin 21:22 5028
the way of Jeroboam the son of *N* ... 1Kin 22:52 5028
the sins of Jeroboam the son of *N* ... 2Kin 3:3 5028
house of Jeroboam the son of *N* ... 2Kin 9:9 5028
the sins of Jeroboam the son of *N* ... 2Kin 10:29 5028
the sins of Jeroboam the son of *N* ... 2Kin 13:2 5028
the sins of Jeroboam the son of *N* ... 2Kin 13:11 5028
the sins of Jeroboam the son of *N* ... 2Kin 14:24 5028
the sins of Jeroboam the son of *N* ... 2Kin 15:9 5028
the sins of Jeroboam the son of *N* ... 2Kin 15:18 5028
the sins of Jeroboam the son of *N* ... 2Kin 15:24 5028
the sins of Jeroboam the son of *N* ... 2Kin 15:28 5028
made Jeroboam the son of *N* king ... 2Kin 17:21 5028
place which Jeroboam the son of *N* ... 2Kin 23:15 5028
against Jeroboam the son of *N* ... 2Chr 9:29 5028
pass, when Jeroboam the son of *N* ... 2Chr 10:2 5028
to Jeroboam the son of *N* ... 2Chr 10:15 5028
Yet Jeroboam the son of *N* ... 2Chr 13:6 5028

NEBO *(ne'-bo)* {13} See PISGAH, SAMGAR-NEBO.
1. A city in Reuben.
and Elealeh, and Shebam, and *N* ... Num 32:3 5015
And *N*, and Baal-meon, (their names ... Num 32:38 5015
the mountains of Abarim, before *N* ... Num 33:47 5015
who dwelt in Aroer, even unto *N* ... 1Chr 5:8 5015
Moab shall howl over *N*, and over ... Is 15:2 5015
Woe unto *N* ... Jer 48:1 5015
And upon Dibon, and upon *N*, ... Jer 48:22 5015
2. A mountain east of the Jordan.
mountain Abarim, unto mount *N* ... Deut 32:49 5015
of Moab unto the mountain of *N* ... Deut 34:1 5015
3. A city in Judah.
The children of *N*, fifty and two ... Ezr 2:29 5015
The men of the other *N*, fifty and ... Neh 7:33 5015
4. A Chaldean idol.
N stoopeth, their idols were upon ... Is 46:1 5015
5. Father of several who married foreigners.
Of the sons of *N* ... Ezr 10:43 5015

NEBO-SARSEKIM See SARSECHIM.

NEBUCHADNEZZAR *(neb-u-kad-nez'-zar)* {60} See NEBUCHADREZZAR. *King of Babylon.*
In his days *N* king of Babylon ... 2Kin 24:1 5019
At that time the servants of *N* ... 2Kin 24:10 5019
N king of Babylon came against ... 2Kin 24:11 5019
that *N* king of Babylon came, he, ... 2Kin 25:1 5019
year of king *N* king of Babylon ... 2Kin 25:8 5019
whom *N* king of Babylon had left, ... 2Kin 25:22 5019
and Jerusalem by the hand of *N* ... 1Chr 6:15 5019
him came up *N* king of Babylon ... 2Chr 36:6 5019
N also carried of the vessels of ... 2Chr 36:7 5019
the year was expired, king *N* sent ... 2Chr 36:10 5019
he also rebelled against king *N* ... 2Chr 36:13 5019
which *N* had brought forth out of ... Ezr 1:7 5019
whom *N* the king of Babylon had ... Ezr 2:1 5019
the hand of *N* the king of Babylon ... Ezr 5:12 5020
which *N* took out of the temple ... Ezr 5:14 5020
which *N* took forth out of the ... Ezr 6:5 5020
whom *N* the king of Babylon had ... Neh 7:6 5019
whom *N* the king of Babylon had ... Est 2:6 5019
the hand of *N* the king of Babylon ... Jer 27:6 5019
the same *N* the king of Babylon ... Jer 27:8 5019
Which *N* king of Babylon took not, ... Jer 27:20 5019
that *N* king of Babylon took away ... Jer 28:3 5019
so will I break the yoke of *N* ... Jer 28:11 5019
they may serve *N* king of Babylon ... Jer 28:14 5019
to all the people whom *N* had ... Jer 29:1 5019
to *N* king of Babylon) saying ... Jer 29:3 5019
when *N* king of Babylon, and all ... Jer 34:1 5019
they brought him up to *N* king of ... Jer 39:5 5019
N king of Babylon unto Jerusalem ... Dan 1:1 5019
eunuchs brought them in before *N* ... Dan 1:18 5019
the second year of the reign of *N* ... Dan 2:1 5019
N dreamed dreams, wherewith his ... Dan 2:1 5019
maketh known to the king *N* what ... Dan 2:28 5020
Then the king *N* fell upon his ... Dan 2:46 5020
N the king made an image of gold, ... Dan 3:1 5020
Then *N* the king sent to gather ... Dan 3:2 5020
image which *N* the king had set up ... Dan 3:2 5020
image that *N* the king had set up ... Dan 3:3 5020
the image that *N* had set up ... Dan 3:3 5020
image that *N* the king hath set up ... Dan 3:5 5020
image that *N* the king had set up ... Dan 3:7 5020
They spake and said to the king *N* ... Dan 3:9 5020
Then *N* in his rage and fury ... Dan 3:13 5020
N spake and said unto them, Is it ... Dan 3:14 5020
answered and said to the king, O *N* ... Dan 3:16 5020
Then was *N* full of fury, and the ... Dan 3:19 5020
Then *N* the king was astonied, and ... Dan 3:24 5020
Then *N* came near to the mouth of ... Dan 3:26 5020
Then *N* spake, and said, Blessed be ... Dan 3:28 5020
N the king, unto all people, ... Dan 4:1 5020
I *N* was at rest in mine house, and ... Dan 4:4 5020
This dream I king *N* have seen ... Dan 4:18 5020
All this came upon the king *N* ... Dan 4:28 5020
from heaven, saying, O king *N* ... Dan 4:31 5020
was the thing fulfilled upon *N* ... Dan 4:33 5020
at the end of the days I *N* lifted ... Dan 4:34 5020
Now I *N* praise and extol and honour ... Dan 4:37 5020
N had taken out of the temple ... Dan 5:2 5020
whom the king *N* thy father ... Dan 5:11 5020
God gave *N* thy father a kingdom ... Dan 5:18 5020

NEBUCHADREZZAR *(neb-u-kad-rez'-zar)* {31} See NEBUCHADNEZZAR. *Same as Nebuchadnezzar.*
for *N* king of Babylon maketh war ... Jer 21:2 5019
the hand of *N* king of Babylon ... Jer 21:7 5019
the hand of *N* king of Babylon ... Jer 22:25 5019
after that *N* king of Babylon had ... Jer 24:1 5019
first year of *N* king of Babylon ... Jer 25:1 5019
N the king of Babylon, my servant ... Jer 25:9 5019
the hand of *N* king of Babylon ... Jer 29:21 5019
was the eighteenth year of *N* ... Jer 32:1 5019
the hand of *N* king of Babylon ... Jer 32:28 5019
when *N* king of Babylon came up ... Jer 35:11 5019
whom *N* king of Babylon made king ... Jer 37:1 5019
came *N* king of Babylon and all his ... Jer 39:1 5019
Now *N* king of Babylon gave charge ... Jer 39:11 5019
take *N* the king of Babylon, my ... Jer 43:10 5019
the hand of *N* king of Babylon ... Jer 44:30 5019
which *N* king of Babylon smote in ... Jer 46:2 5019
how *N* king of Babylon should come ... Jer 46:13 5019
the hand of *N* king of Babylon ... Jer 46:26 5019
which *N* king of Babylon shall ... Jer 49:28 5019
for *N* king of Babylon hath taken ... Jer 49:30 5019
last this *N* king of Babylon hath ... Jer 50:17 5019
N the king of Babylon hath ... Jer 51:34 5019
that *N* king of Babylon came, he ... Jer 52:4 5019
year of *N* king of Babylon ... Jer 52:12 5019
whom *N* carried away captive ... Jer 52:28 5019
In the eighteenth year of *N* he ... Jer 52:29 5019
twentieth year of *N* Nebuzar-adan ... Jer 52:30 5019
upon Tyrus *N* king of Babylon ... Eze 26:7 5019
N king of Babylon caused his army ... Eze 29:18 5019
of Egypt unto *N* king of Babylon ... Eze 29:19 5019
by the hand of *N* king of Babylon ... Eze 30:10 5019

NEBUSHASBAN *(neb-u-shas'-ban)* {1} *A Babylonian prince.*
captain of the guard sent, and *N* ... Jer 39:13 5021

NEBUSHAZBAN See NEBUSHASBAN.

NEBUZAR-ADAN *(neb-u-zar'-a-dan)* {15} *Commander of Nebuchadnezzar's army.*
king of Babylon, came *N*, captain ... 2Kin 25:8 5018
did *N* the captain of the guard ... 2Kin 25:11 5018
N captain of the guard took these ... 2Kin 25:20 5018
Then *N* the captain of the guard ... Jer 39:9 5018
But *N* the captain of the guard ... Jer 39:10 5018
to *N* the captain of the guard ... Jer 39:11 5018
So *N* the captain of the guard ... Jer 39:13 5018
after that *N* the captain of the ... Jer 40:1 5018
whom *N* the captain of the guard ... Jer 41:10 5018
every person that *N* the captain ... Jer 43:6 5018
king of Babylon, came *N*, captain ... Jer 52:12 5018
Then *N* the captain of the guard ... Jer 52:15 5018
But *N* the captain of the guard ... Jer 52:16 5018
So *N* the captain of the guard ... Jer 52:26 5018
year of Nebuchadrezzar *N* the ... Jer 52:30 5018

NEBUZARADAN See NEBUZAR-ADAN.

NECESSARY {9}
of his mouth more than my *n* food ... Job 23:12 2706
It was *n* that the word of God ... Acts 13:46 *316*
burden than these *n* things ... Acts 15:28 *1876*
us with such things as were *n* ... Acts 28:10 *4311,3688,5532*
seem to be more feeble, are *n* ... 1Cor 12:22 *316*
it *n* to exhort the brethren ... 2Cor 9:5 *316*
Yet I supposed it *n* to send to ... Phil 2:25 *316*
to maintain good works for *n* uses ... Titus 3:14 *316*
It was therefore *n* that the ... Heb 9:23 *316*

NECESSITIES {3}
hands have ministered unto my *n* ... Acts 20:34 *5532*
patience, in afflictions, in *n* ... 2Cor 6:4 *318*
infirmities, in reproaches, in *n* ... 2Cor 12:10 *318*

NECESSITY {10}
(For of *n* he must release one ... Lk 23:17 *2192,318*
Distributing to the *n* of saints ... Rom 12:13 *5532*
in his heart, having no *n* ... 1Cor 7:37 *318*
for *n* is laid upon me ... 1Cor 9:16 *318*
not grudgingly, or of *n* ... 2Cor 9:7 *318*
ye sent once and again unto my *n* ... Phil 4:16 *5532*
should not be as it were of *n* ... Philem 14 *318*
there is made of *n* a change also ... Heb 7:12 *318*
wherefore it is of *n* that this ... Heb 8:3 *316*
there must also of *n* be the death ... Heb 9:16 *318*

NECHO *(ne'-ko)* {3} See PHARAOH-NECHOH. *A king of Egypt.*
N king of Egypt came up to fight ... 2Chr 35:20 5224
words of *N* from the mouth of God ... 2Chr 35:22 5224
N took Jehoahaz his brother, and ... 2Chr 36:4 5224

NECK {62}
and upon the smooth of his *n* ... Gen 27:16 6677
break his yoke from off thy *n* ... Gen 27:40 6677
and embraced him, and fell on his *n* ... Gen 33:4 6677
and put a gold chain about his *n* ... Gen 41:42 6677
upon his brother Benjamin's *n* ... Gen 45:14 6677
and Benjamin wept upon his *n* ... Gen 45:14 6677
and he fell on his *n*, and wept on ... Gen 46:29 6677
wept on his *n* a good while ... Gen 46:29 6677
be in the *n* of thine enemies ... Gen 49:8 6203
it, then thou shalt break his *n* ... Ex 13:13 6203
not, then shalt thou break his *n* ... Ex 34:20 6203
and wring off his head from his *n* ... Lev 5:8 6203
heifer's *n* there in the valley ... Deut 21:4 6203
put a yoke of iron upon thy *n* ... Deut 28:48 6677
thy rebellion, and thy stiff *n* ... Deut 31:27 6203
gate, and his *n* brake, and he died ... 1Sa 4:18 4665
like to the *n* of their fathers, ... 2Kin 17:14 6203
but he stiffened his *n*, and ... 2Chr 36:13 6203
the shoulder, and hardened their *n* ... Neh 9:29 6203
runneth upon him, even on his *n* ... Job 15:26 6677
he hath also taken me by my *n* ... Job 16:12 6203
thou clothed his *n* with thunder ... Job 39:19 6677
In his *n* remaineth strength, and ... Job 41:22 6677
speak not with a stiff *n* ... Ps 75:5 6677
thy head, and chains about thy *n* ... Prov 1:9 1621
bind them about thy *n* ... Prov 3:3 1621
unto thy soul, and grace to thy *n* ... Prov 3:22 1621
heart, and tie them about thy *n* ... Prov 6:21 1621
often reproved hardeneth his *n* ... Prov 29:1 6203
thy *n* with chains of gold ... Song 1:10 6677
Thy *n* is like the tower of David ... Song 4:4 6677
eyes, with one chain of thy *n* ... Song 4:9 6677
Thy *n* is as a tower of ivory ... Song 7:4 6677
he shall reach even to the *n* ... Is 8:8 6677
and his yoke from off thy *n* ... Is 10:27 6677
shall reach to the midst of the *n* ... Is 30:28 6677
thy *n* is an iron sinew, and thy ... Is 48:4 6203
thyself from the bands of thy *n* ... Is 52:2 6677
lamb, as if he cut off a dog's *n* ... Is 66:3 6202
their ear, but hardened their *n* ... Jer 7:26 6202
their ear, but made their *n* stiff ... Jer 17:23 6202
and yokes, and put them upon thy *n* ... Jer 27:2 6677
that will not put their *n* under ... Jer 27:8 6677
the nations that bring their *n* ... Jer 27:11 6677
from off the prophet Jeremiah's *n* ... Jer 28:10 6677
king of Babylon from the *n* of all ... Jer 28:11 6677
off the *n* of the prophet Jeremiah ... Jer 28:12 6677
upon the *n* of all these nations ... Jer 28:14 6677
break his yoke from off thy *n* ... Jer 30:8 6677
wreathed, and come up upon my *n* ... Lam 1:14 6677
thy hands, and a chain on thy *n* ... Eze 16:11 1627
have a chain of gold about his *n* ... Dan 5:7 6676
have a chain of gold about thy *n* ... Dan 5:16 6676
put a chain of gold about his *n* ... Dan 5:29 6676
but I passed over upon her fair *n* ... Hos 10:11 6676
the foundation unto the *n* ... Hab 3:13 6676
millstone were hanged about his *n* ... Mt 18:6 *5137*
millstone were hanged about his *n* ... Mk 9:42 *5137*
and ran, and fell on his *n* ... Lk 15:20 *5137*
millstone were hanged about his *n* ... Lk 17:2 *5137*
yoke upon the *n* of the disciples ... Acts 15:10 *5137*
wept sore, and fell on Paul's *n* ... Acts 20:37 *5137*

NECKS {18}
feet upon the *n* of these kings ... Josh 10:24 6677
put their feet upon the *n* of them ... Josh 10:24 6677
meet for the *n* of them that take ... Judg 5:30 6677
that were on their camels' *n* ... Judg 8:21 6677
that were about their camels' *n* ... Judg 8:26 6677
given me the *n* of mine enemies ... 2Sa 22:41 6203
not hear, but hardened their *n* ... 2Kin 17:14 6203
their *n* to the work of their Lord ... Neh 3:5 6677
proudly, and hardened their *n* ... Neh 9:16 6203
but hardened their *n*, and in their ... Neh 9:17 6203
given me the *n* of mine enemies ... Ps 18:40 6203
and walk with stretched forth *n* ... Is 3:16 1627
they have hardened their *n* ... Jer 19:15 6203
Bring your *n* under the yoke of ... Jer 27:12 6677
Our *n* are under persecution ... Lam 5:5 6677
upon the *n* of them that are slain ... Eze 21:29 6677
which ye shall not remove your *n* ... Mic 2:3 6677
for my life laid down their own *n* ... Rom 16:4 *5137*

NECO See NECHOH.

NECROMANCER {1}
spirits, or a wizard, or a *n* ... Deut 18:11 1875,4191

NEDABIAH *(ned-a-bi'-ah)* {1} *Son of Jeconiah.*
Shenazar, Jecamiah, Hoshama, and *N* ... 1Chr 3:18 5072

NEED {49}
lend him sufficient for his *n* ... Deut 15:8 4270
Have I *n* of mad men, that ye have ... 1Sa 21:15 2638
Lebanon, as much as thou shalt *n* ... 2Chr 2:16 6878
Ye shall not *n* to fight in this ... 2Chr 20:17
And that which they have *n* of ... Ezr 6:9 2818
that he shall have no *n* of spoil ... Prov 31:11 2637
I have *n* to be baptized of thee, ... Mt 3:14 *5532*
knoweth what things ye have *n* of ... Mt 6:8 *5532*
ye have *n* of all these things ... Mt 6:32 *5535*
that be whole *n* not a physician ... Mt 9:12 *2192,5532*
said unto them, They *n* not depart ... Mt 14:16 *2192,5532*
say, The Lord hath *n* of them ... Mt 21:3 *5532*
what further *n* have we of ... Mt 26:65 *5532*
whole have no *n* of the physician ... Mk 2:17 *5532*
what David did, when he had *n* ... Mk 2:25 *5532*
ye that the Lord hath *n* of him ... Mk 11:3 *5532*
What *n* we any further witnesses ... Mk 14:63 *2192,5532*
that are whole *n* not a physician ... Lk 5:31 *2192,5532*
healed them that had *n* of healing ... Lk 9:11 *5532*
that ye have *n* of these things ... Lk 12:30 *5535*
persons, which *n* no repentance ... Lk 15:7 *2192,5532*
Because the Lord hath *n* of him ... Lk 19:31 *5532*
they said, The Lord hath *n* of him ... Lk 19:34 *5532*
What *n* we any further witness ... Lk 22:71 *2192,5532*
we have *n* of against the feast ... Jn 13:29 *5532*
to all men, as every man had *n* ... Acts 2:45 *5532*
every man according as he had *n* ... Acts 4:35 *5532*
business she hath *n* of you ... Rom 16:2 *5535*
n so require, let him do what he ... 1Cor 7:36 *3784*
the hand, I have no *n* of thee ... 1Cor 12:21 *5532*
to the feet, I have no *n* of you ... 1Cor 12:21 *5532*
For our comely parts have no *n* ... 1Cor 12:24 *5532*
or *n* we, as some others, epistles ... 2Cor 3:1 *5535*
both to abound and to suffer *n* ... Phil 4:12
your *n* according to his riches in ... Phil 4:19 *5532*
so that we *n* not to speak any ... 1Th 1:8 *2192,5532*
ye *n* not that I write unto you ... 1Th 4:9 *5532*
ye have no *n* that I write unto ... 1Th 5:1 *5532*
find grace to help in time of *n* ... Heb 4:16 *2121*
ye have *n* that one teach you ... Heb 5:12 *5532*
are become such as have *n* of milk ... Heb 5:12 *5532*
what further *n* was there that ... Heb 7:11 *5532*
For ye have *n* of patience ... Heb 10:36 *5532*
though now for a season, if *n* be ... 1Pet 1:6 *1163*
ye *n* not that any man teach you ... 1Jn 2:27 *2192,5532*
good, and seeth his brother have *n* ... 1Jn 3:17 *5532*
with goods, and have *n* of nothing ... Rev 3:17 *5532*
And the city had no *n* of the sun ... Rev 21:23 *5532*
they *n* no candle, neither light ... Rev 22:5

NEEDED {2}
n not that any should testify of ... Jn 2:25 *2192,5532*
hands, as though he *n* any thing ... Acts 17:25 *4326*

NEEDEST {1}
n not that any man should ask ... Jn 16:30 *2192,5532*

NEEDETH {6}
And he said, What *n* it ... Gen 33:15
rise and give him as many as he *n* ... Lk 11:8 *5535*
He that is washed *n* not save to ... Jn 13:10 *2192,5532*
he may have to give to him that *n* ... Eph 4:28 *5532*
a workman that *n* not to be ... 2Ti 2:15 *422*
Who *n* not daily, as those high ... Heb 7:27 *2192,318*

NEEDFUL {6}
be *n* for the house of thy God ... Ezr 7:20 2819
But one thing is *n* ... Lk 10:42 *5532*
That it was *n* to circumcise them, ... Acts 15:5 *1163*
in the flesh is more *n* for you ... Phil 1:24 *316*
things which are *n* to the body ... Jas 2:16 *2006*
it was *n* for me to write unto you ... Jude 3 *318*

NEEDLE {2}
to go through the eye of a *n* ... Mt 19:24 *4476*
to go through the eye of a *n* ... Mk 10:25 *4476*

NEEDLE'S {1}
for a camel to go through a *n* eye ... Lk 18:25 *4476*

NEEDLEWORK {9}
fine twined linen, wrought with *n* ... Ex 26:36 4639,7551
fine twined linen, wrought with *n* ... Ex 27:16 7551
thou shalt make the girdle of *n* ... Ex 28:39 7551
and fine twined linen, of *n* ... Ex 36:37 7551
for the gate of the court was *n* ... Ex 38:18 7551

blue, and purple, and scarlet, of *n* .... Ex 39:29 7551
a prey of divers colours of *n* .... Judg 5:30 7553
divers colours of *n* on both sides .... Judg 5:30 7553
unto the king in raiment of *n* .... Ps 45:14 7553

NEEDS {16}
thy money, must *n* be circumcised .... Gen 17:13
sojourn, and he will *n* be a judge .... Gen 19:9
must I *n* bring thy son again unto .... Gen 24:5
though thou wouldest *n* be gone .... Gen 31:30
For we must *n* die, and are as 2Sa 14:14
they must *n* be borne, because .... Jer 10:5
for it must *n* be that offences .... Mt 18:7 *318*
for such things must *n* be .... Mk 13:7
a piece of ground, and I must *n* go .... Lk 14:18 *318*
he must *n* go through Samaria .... Jn 4:4
must *n* have been fulfilled .... Acts 1:16
that Christ must *n* have suffered .... Acts 17:3
multitude must *n* come together .... Acts 21:22 *3843*
Wherefore ye must *n* be subject .... Rom 13:5 *318*
for then must ye *n* go out of the 1Cor 5:10
If I must *n* glory, I will glory 2Cor 11:30

NEEDY {38}
brother, to thy poor, and to thy *n* .... Deut 15:11 34
hired servant that is poor and *n* .... Deut 24:14 34
They turn the *n* out of the way .... Job 24:4 34
the light killeth the poor and *n* .... Job 24:14 34
For the *n* shall not alway be .... Ps 9:18 34
poor, for the sighing of the *n* .... Ps 12:5 34
the *n* from him that spoileth him .... Ps 35:10 34
bow, to cast down the poor and *n* .... Ps 37:14 34
But I am poor and *n* .... Ps 40:17 34
But I am poor and *n* .... Ps 70:5 34
shall save the children of the *n* .... Ps 72:4 34
deliver the *n* when he crieth .... Ps 72:12 34
He shall spare the poor and *n* .... Ps 72:13 34
and shall save the souls of the *n* .... Ps 72:13 34
let the poor and *n* praise thy name .... Ps 74:21 34
do justice to the afflicted and *n* .... Ps 82:3 7326
Deliver the poor and *n* .... Ps 82:4 34
for I am poor and *n* .... Ps 86:1 34
n man, that he might even slay .... Ps 109:16 34
For I am poor and *n*, and my heart .... Ps 109:22 34
lifteth the *n* out of the dunghill .... Ps 113:7 34
earth, and the *n* from among men .... Prov 30:14 34
plead the cause of the poor and *n* .... Prov 31:9 34
reacheth forth her hands to the *n* .... Prov 31:20 34
To turn aside the *n* from judgment .... Is 10:2 1800
the *n* shall lie down in safety .... Is 14:30 34
strength to the *n* in his distress .... Is 25:4 34
the poor, and the steps of the *n* .... Is 26:6 1800
even when the *n* speaketh right .... Is 32:7 34
n seek water, and there is none, ... Is 41:17 34
the right of the *n* do they not .... Jer 5:28 34
judged the cause of the poor and *n* .... Jer 22:16 34
the hand of the poor and *n* .... Eze 16:49 34
Hath oppressed the poor and *n* .... Eze 18:12 34
and have vexed the poor and *n* .... Eze 22:29 34
the poor, which crush the *n* .... Amos 4:1 34
this, O ye that swallow up the *n* .... Amos 8:4 34
the *n* for a pair of shoes .... Amos 8:6 34

NEESINGS {1}
By his *n* a light doth shine, and .... Job 41:18 5846

NEGEV See SOUTH.

NEGINAH *(neg'-i-nah)* {1} See NEGINOTH. *A stringed instrument.*
To the chief Musician upon *N* .... Ps 61:*t* 5058

NEGINOTH *(neg'-i-noth)* {6} See NEGINAH. *Same as Neginah.*
To the chief Musician on *N* .... Ps 4:*t* 5058
Musician on *N* upon Sheminith .... Ps 6:*t* 5058
To the chief Musician on *N* .... Ps 54:*t* 5058
To the chief Musician on *N* .... Ps 55:*t* 5058
To the chief Musician on *N* .... Ps 67:*t* 5058
To the chief Musician on *N* .... Ps 76:*t* 5058

NEGLECT {4}
if he shall *n* to hear them, tell .... Mt 18:17 *3878*
but if he *n* to hear the church, ... Mt 18:17 *3878*
N not the gift that is in thee, ... 1Ti 4:14 *272*
if we *n* so great salvation .... Heb 2:3 *272*

NEGLECTED {1}
were *n* in the daily ministration .... Acts 6:1 *3865*

NEGLECTING {1}
and humility, and *n* of the body .... Col 2:23 *857*

NEGLIGENT {2}
My sons, be not now *n* 2Chr 29:11 7952
not be *n* to put you always in 2Pet 1:12 *272*

NEHELAM See NEHELAMITE.

NEHELAMITE *(ne-hel'-am-ite)* {3} *Family name of Shemaiah.*
thou also speak to Shemaiah the *N* .... Jer 29:24 5161
LORD concerning Shemaiah the *N* .... Jer 29:31 5161
I will punish Shemaiah the *N* .... Jer 29:32 5161

NEHEMIAH *(ne-he-mi'-ah)* {8}
1. A clan leader with Zerubbabel.
Jeshua, *N*, Seraiah, Reelaiah, ... Ezr 2:2 5166
came with Zerubbabel, Jeshua, *N* .... Neh 7:7 5166
2. Governor of Jerusalem.
The words of *N* the son of .... Neh 1:1 5166
And *N*, which is the Tirshatha, and .... Neh 8:9 5166
Now those that sealed were, *N* .... Neh 10:1 5166
and in the days of *N* the governor .... Neh 12:26 5166
Zerubbabel, and in the days of *N* .... Neh 12:47 5166
3. A rebuilder of Jerusalem's wall.
him repaired *N* the son of Azbuk .... Neh 3:16 5166

NEHILOTH *(ne'-hi-loth)* {1} *A musical choir or instrument.*
To the chief Musician upon *N* .... Ps 5:*t* 5155

NEHUM *(ne'-hum)* {1} See REHUM. *A clan leader with Zerubbabel.*
Bilshan, Mispereth, Bigvai, *N* .... Neh 7:7 5149

NEHUSHTA *(ne-hush'-tah)* {1} *Mother of King Jehoiachin.*
And his mother's name was *N* 2Kin 24:8 5179

NEHUSHTAN *(ne-hush'-tan)* {1} *Name given to the brazen serpents.*
and he called it *N* 2Kin 18:4 5180

NEIEL *(ne-i'-el)* {1} *A city in Asher.*
the north side of Beth-emek, and *N* .... Josh 19:27 5272

NEIGHBOUR {107}
every woman shall borrow of her *n* .... Ex 3:22 7934
and let every man borrow of his *n* .... Ex 11:2 7453
and every woman of her *n*, jewels .... Ex 11:2 7468
his *n* next unto his house take it .... Ex 12:4 7934
bear false witness against thy *n* .... Ex 20:16 7453
come presumptuously upon his *n* .... Ex 21:14 7453
unto his *n* money or stuff to keep .... Ex 22:7 7453
he shall pay double unto his *n* .... Ex 22:9 7453
a man deliver unto his *n* an ass .... Ex 22:10 7453
And if a man borrow ought of his *n* .... Ex 22:14 7453
his companion, and every man his *n* .... Ex 32:27 7138
lie unto his *n* in that which was .... Lev 6:2 5997
violence, or hath deceived his *n* .... Lev 6:2 5997
Thou shalt not defraud thy *n* .... Lev 19:13 7453
shalt thou judge thy *n* .... Lev 19:15 5997
stand against the blood of thy *n* .... Lev 19:16 7453
shalt in any wise rebuke thy *n* .... Lev 19:17 5997
thou shalt love thy *n* as thyself .... Lev 19:18 7453
if a man cause a blemish in his *n* .... Lev 24:19 5997
And if thou sell ought unto thy *n* .... Lev 25:14 5997
jubile thou shalt buy of thy *n* .... Lev 25:15 5997
which should kill his *n* unawares .... Deut 4:42 7453
bear false witness against thy *n* .... Deut 5:20 7453
ought unto his *n* shall release it .... Deut 15:2 7453
he shall not exact it of his *n* .... Deut 15:2 7453
Whoso killeth his *n* ignorantly .... Deut 19:4 7453
the wood with his *n* to hew wood .... Deut 19:5 7453
the helve, and lighteth upon his *n* .... Deut 19:5 7453
But if any man hate his *n* .... Deut 19:11 7453
when a man riseth against his *n* .... Deut 22:26 7453
into the standing corn of thy *n* .... Deut 23:25 7453
be he that smiteth his *n* secretly .... Deut 27:24 7453
he smote his *n* unwittingly .... Josh 20:5 7453
off his shoe, and gave it to his *n* .... Ruth 4:7 7453
and hath given it to a *n* of thine 1Sa 15:28 7453
thine hand, and given it to thy *n* 1Sa 28:17 7453
eyes, and give them unto thy *n* 2Sa 12:11 7453
If any man trespass against his *n* 1Kin 8:31 7453
his *n* in the word of the LORD 1Kin 20:35 7453
If a man sin against his *n* 2Chr 6:22 7453
I am as one mocked of his *n* .... Job 12:4 7453
God, as a man pleadeth for his *n* .... Job 16:21 7453
speak vanity every one with his *n* .... Ps 12:2 7453
tongue, nor doeth evil to his *n* .... Ps 15:3 7453
up a reproach against his *n* .... Ps 15:3 7138
Whoso privily slandereth his *n* .... Ps 101:5 7453
Say not unto thy *n*, Go, and come .... Prov 3:28 7453
Devise not evil against thy *n* .... Prov 3:29 7453
with his mouth destroyeth his *n* .... Prov 11:9 7453
is void of wisdom despiseth his *n* .... Prov 11:12 7453
is more excellent than his *n* .... Prov 12:26 7453
poor is hated even of his own *n* .... Prov 14:20 7453
He that despiseth his *n* sinneth .... Prov 14:21 7453
A violent man enticeth his *n* .... Prov 16:29 7453
but his *n* cometh and searcheth him .... Prov 18:17 7453
the poor is separated from his *n* .... Prov 19:4 7453
his *n* findeth no favour in his .... Prov 21:10 7453
against thy *n* without cause .... Prov 24:28 7453
when thy *n* hath put thee to shame .... Prov 25:8 7453
thy cause with thy *n* himself .... Prov 25:9 7453
witness against his *n* is a maul .... Prov 25:18 7453
is the man that deceiveth his *n* .... Prov 26:19 7453
for better is a *n* that is near .... Prov 27:10 7934
A man that flattereth his *n* .... Prov 29:5 7453
for this a man is envied of his *n* .... Eccl 4:4 7453
by another, and every one by his *n* .... Is 3:5 7453
and every one against his *n* .... Is 19:2 7453
They helped every one his *n* .... Is 41:6 7453
the *n* and his friend shall perish .... Jer 6:21 7934
judgment between a man and his *n* .... Jer 7:5 7453
Take ye heed every one of his *n* .... Jer 9:4 7453
every *n* will walk with slanders .... Jer 9:4 7453
they will deceive every one his *n* .... Jer 9:5 7453
peaceably to his *n* with his mouth .... Jer 9:8 7453
and every one her *n* lamentation .... Jer 9:20 7468
they shall say every man to his *n* .... Jer 22:8 7453
they tell every man to his *n* .... Jer 23:27 7453
my words every one from his *n* .... Jer 23:30 7453
shall ye say every one to his *n* .... Jer 23:35 7453
teach no more every man his *n* .... Jer 31:34 7453
liberty every man to his *n* .... Jer 34:15 7453
brother, and every man to his *n* .... Jer 34:17 7453
the *n* cities thereof, saith the .... Jer 49:18 7934
the *n* cities thereof, saith the .... Jer 50:40 7934
unto him that giveth his *n* drink .... Hab 2:15 7453
every man his *n* under the vine .... Zec 3:10 7453
all men every one against his *n* .... Zec 8:10 7453
ye every man the truth to his *n* .... Zec 8:16 7453
evil in your hearts against his *n* .... Zec 8:17 7453
every one on the hand of his *n* .... Zec 14:13 7453
rise up against the hand of his *n* .... Zec 14:13 7453
been said, Thou shalt love thy *n* .... Mt 5:43 *4139*
Thou shalt love thy *n* as thyself .... Mt 19:19 *4139*
Thou shalt love thy *n* as thyself .... Mt 22:39 *4139*
Thou shalt love thy *n* as thyself .... Mk 12:31 *4139*
and to love his *n* as himself .... Mk 12:33 *4139*
and thy *n* as thyself .... Lk 10:27 *4139*
said unto Jesus, And who is my *n* .... Lk 10:29 *4139*
was *n* unto him that fell among .... Lk 10:36 *4139*
But he that did his *n* wrong .... Acts 7:27 *4139*
Thou shalt love thy *n* as thyself .... Rom 13:9 *4139*
Love worketh no ill to his *n* .... Rom 13:10 *4139*
his *n* for his good to edification .... Rom 15:2 *4139*
Thou shalt love thy *n* as thyself .... Gal 5:14 *4139*
speak every man truth with his *n* .... Eph 4:25 *4139*
shall not teach every man his *n* .... Heb 8:11 *4139*
Thou shalt love thy *n* as thyself .... Jas 2:8 *4139*

NEIGHBOUR'S {28}
Thou shalt not covet thy *n* house .... Ex 20:17 7453
thou shalt not covet thy *n* wife .... Ex 20:17 7453
ass, nor any thing that is thy *n* .... Ex 20:17 7453
put his hand unto his *n* goods .... Ex 22:8 7453
not put his hand unto his *n* goods .... Ex 22:11 7453
all take thy *n* raiment to pledge .... Ex 22:26 7453
not lie carnally with thy *n* wife .... Lev 18:20 5997
adultery with his *n* wife, the .... Lev 20:10 7453
or buyest ought of thy *n* hand .... Lev 25:14 5997
shalt thou desire thy *n* wife .... Deut 5:21 7453
shalt thou covet thy *n* house .... Deut 5:21 7453
ass, or any thing that is thy *n* .... Deut 5:21 7453
shalt not remove thy *n* landmark .... Deut 19:14 7453
he hath humbled his *n* wife .... Deut 22:24 7453
thou comest into thy *n* vineyard .... Deut 23:24 7453
a sickle unto thy *n* standing corn .... Deut 23:25 7453
he that removeth his *n* landmark .... Deut 27:17 7453
if I have laid wait at my *n* door .... Job 31:9 7453
So he that goeth in to his *n* wife .... Prov 6:29 7453
thy foot from thy *n* house .... Prov 25:17 7453
one neighed after his *n* wife .... Jer 5:8 7453
that useth his *n* service without .... Jer 22:13 7453
neither hath defiled his *n* wife .... Eze 18:6 7453
mountains, and defiled his *n* wife .... Eze 18:11 7453
hath not defiled his *n* wife .... Eze 18:15 7453
abomination with his *n* wife .... Eze 22:11 7453
and ye defile every one his *n* wife .... Eze 33:26 7453
the men every one into his *n* hand .... Zec 11:6 7453

NEIGHBOURS {21}
they heard that they were their *n* .... Josh 9:16 7138
the women her *n* gave it a name, ... Ruth 4:17 7934
thee vessels abroad of all thy *n* 2Kin 4:3 7934
which speak peace to their *n* .... Ps 28:3 7453
but especially among my *n* .... Ps 31:11 7934
makest us a reproach to our *n* .... Ps 44:13 7934
We are become a reproach to our *n* .... Ps 79:4 7934
render unto our *n* sevenfold into .... Ps 79:12 7934
makest us a strife unto our *n* .... Ps 80:6 7934
he is a reproach to his *n* .... Ps 89:41 7934
the LORD against all mine evil *n* .... Jer 12:14 7934
and his brethren, and his *n* .... Jer 49:10 7934
with the Egyptians thy *n*, great .... Eze 16:26 7934
gained of thy *n* by extortion .... Eze 22:12 7453
lovers, on the Assyrians her *n* .... Eze 23:5 7138
doted upon the Assyrians her *n* .... Eze 23:12 7138
And her *n* and her cousins heard how .... Lk 1:58 *4040*
thy kinsmen, nor thy rich *n* .... Lk 14:12 *1069*
calleth together his friends and *n* .... Lk 15:6 *1069*
her *n* together, saying, Rejoice .... Lk 15:9 *1069*
The *n* therefore, and they which .... Jn 9:8 *1069*

NEIGHBOURS' {1}
adultery with their *n* wives .... Jer 29:23 7453

NEIGHED {1}
every one *n* after his neighbour's .... Jer 5:8 6670

NEIGHING {1}
sound of the *n* of his strong ones .... Jer 8:16 4684

NEIGHINGS {1}
seen thine adulteries, and thy *n* .... Jer 13:27 4684

NEITHER See APPENDIX.

NEKEB *(ne'-keb)* {1} *A city in Naphtali.*
Allon to Zaanannim, and Adami, *N* .... Josh 19:33 5346

NEKODA *(ne-ko'-dah)* {4}
1. A family of exiles.
of Rezin, the children of *N* .... Ezr 2:48 5353
of Rezin, the children of *N* .... Neh 7:50 5353
2. A family of uncertain origin.
of Tobiah, the children of *N* .... Ezr 2:60 5353
of Tobiah, the children of *N* .... Neh 7:62 5353

NEMUEL *(ne-mu'-el)* {3} See JEMUEL, NEMUELITES.
1. Son of Eliab.
N, and Dathan, and Abiram .... Num 26:9 5241
2. A son of Simeon.
of *N*, the family of the .... Num 26:12 5241
The sons of Simeon were, *N* 1Chr 4:24 5241

NEMUELITES *(ne-mu'-el-ites)* {1} *Descendants of Nemuel 2.*
of Nemuel, the family of the *N* .... Num 26:12 5242

NEPHEG *(ne'-feg)* {4}
1. A son of Izhar.
Korah, and *N*, and Zichri .... Ex 6:21 5298
2. A son of David.
Ibhar also, and Elishua, and *N* 2Sa 5:15 5298
And Nogah, and *N*, and Japhia, ... 1Chr 3:7 5298
And Nogah, and *N*, and Japhia, ... 1Chr 14:6 5298

NEPHEW {2}
have son nor *n* among his people .... Job 18:19 5220
name, and remnant, and son, and *n* .... Is 14:22 5220

NEPHEWS {2}
And he had forty sons and thirty *n*........Judg 12:14 1121
if any widow have children or *n*..............1Ti 5:4 *1549*

NEPHILIM See GIANTS.

NEPHISH *(ne'-fish)* {1} See NAPHISH. *Descendants of Naphish.*
the Hagarites, with Jetur, and *N*............1Chr 5:19 5305

NEPHISHESIM *(ne-fish'-e-sim)* {1} See NEPHUSIM. *A family of exiles.*
of Meunim, the children of *N*.................Neh 7:52 5300

NEPHISIM See NEPHUSIM.

NEPHTHALIM *(nef'-tha-lim)* {2} See NAPHTALI. *Country and tribe of Naphtali.*
in the borders of Zabulon and *N*............Mt 4:13 *3508*
land of Zabulon, and the land of *N*...........Mt 4:15 *3508*

NEPHTOAH *(nef-to'-ah)* {2} *A stream near Jerusalem.*
the fountain of the water of *N*................Josh 15:9 5318
out to the well of waters of *N*................Josh 18:15 5318

NEPHUSHESIM See NEPHISHESIM.

NEPHUSIM *(ne-fu'-sim)* {1} See NEPHISHESIM. *A family of exiles.*
of Mehunim, the children of *N*...............Ezr 2:50 5304

NEPTHALIM {1}
Of the tribe of *N* were sealed ....Rev 7:6 *3508*

NER *(nur)* {16} *Grandfather of King Saul.*
his host was Abner, the son of *N*............1Sa 14:50 5369
N the father of Abner was the son..........1Sa 14:51 5369
Saul lay, and Abner the son of *N*............1Sa 26:5 5369
people, and to Abner the son of *N*..........1Sa 26:14 5369
But Abner the son of *N*, captain..............2Sa 2:8 5369
And Abner the son of *N*, and the.............2Sa 2:12 5369
the son of *N* came to the king.................2Sa 3:23 5369
Thou knowest Abner the son of *N*.............2Sa 3:25 5369
the blood of Abner the son of *N*..............2Sa 3:28 5369
king to slay Abner the son of *N*..............2Sa 3:37 5369
Israel, unto Abner the son of *N*...............1Kin 2:5 5369
to wit, Abner the son of *N*......................1Kin 2:32 5369
N begat Kish, and Kish begat Saul,..........1Chr 8:33 5369
then Zur, and Kish, and Baal, and *N*.......1Chr 9:36 5369
And *N* begat Kish...................................1Chr 9:39 5369
of Kish, and Abner the son of *N*.............1Chr 26:28 5369

NERAIAH See NERIAH.

NEREUS *(ne'-re-us)* {1} *A Christian acquaintance of Paul.*
Salute Philologus, and Julia, *N*...............Rom 16:15 *3517*

NERGAL *(nur'-gal)* {1} See NERGAL-SHAREZER. *War god of Cuth.*
and the men of Cuth made *N*..................2Kin 17:30 5370

NERGAL-SHAREZER *(nur'-gal-sha-re'-zur)* {3}
1. A Babylonian prince.
and sat in the middle gate, even *N*..........Jer 39:3 5371
2. Another Babylonian prince.
Sarsechim, Rab-saris, *N*, Rab-mag..........Jer 39:3 5371
and Nebushasban, Rab-saris, and *N*.......Jer 39:13 5371

NERI *(ne'-ri)* {1} *Father of Salathiel; ancestor of Jesus.*
Salathiel, which was the son of *N*...........Lk 3:27 *3518*

NERIAH *(ne-ri'-ah)* {10} *Father of Baruch.*
purchase unto Baruch the son of *N*..........Jer 32:12 5374
purchase unto Baruch the son of *N*..........Jer 32:16 5374
called Baruch the son of *N*......................Jer 36:4 5374
Baruch the son of *N* did according............Jer 36:8 5374
So Baruch the son of *N* took the...............Jer 36:14 5374
Baruch the scribe, the son of *N*...............Jer 36:32 5374
But Baruch the son of *N* setteth...............Jer 43:3 5374
prophet, and Baruch the son of *N*.............Jer 43:6 5374
spake unto Baruch the son of *N*...............Jer 45:1 5374
commanded Seraiah the son of *N*.............Jer 51:59 5374

NERO *(ne'-ro)* {1} *Emperor of Rome.*
brought before *N* the second time...........2Ti s *3505*

NEST {15}
and thou puttest thy *n* in a rock ....Num 24:21 7064
If a bird's *n* chance to be before..............Deut 22:6 7064
As an eagle stirreth up her *n*..................Deut 32:11 7064
Then I said, I shall die in my *n*...............Job 29:18 7064
command, and make her *n* on high..........Job 39:27 7064
and the swallow a *n* for herself................Ps 84:3 7064
a bird that wandereth from her *n*..............Prov 27:8 7064
my hand hath found as a *n* the ....Is 10:14 7064
wandering bird cast out of the *n*...............Is 16:2 7064
shall the great owl make her *n*.................Is 34:15 7077
that makest thy *n* in the cedars................Jer 22:23 7077
her *n* in the sides of the hole's.................Jer 48:28 7077
make thy *n* as high as the eagle ....Jer 49:16 7064
thou set thy *n* among the stars..................Obad 4 7064
that he may set his *n* on high..................Hab 2:9 7064

NESTS {4}
Where the birds make their *n*...................Ps 104:17 7077
heaven made their *n* in his boughs............Eze 31:6 7077
and the birds of the air have *n*.................Mt 8:20 *2682*
holes, and birds of the air have *n*..............Lk 9:58 *2682*

NET {39}
upon the *n* shalt thou make four.............Ex 27:4 7568
that the *n* may be even to the..................Ex 27:5 7568
is cast into a *n* by his own feet................Job 18:8 7568
and hath compassed me with his *n*...........Job 19:6 4685
in the *n* which they hid is their.................Ps 9:15 7568
when he draweth him into his *n*................Ps 10:9 7568
shall pluck my feet out of the *n* ....Ps 25:15 7568
Pull me out of the *n* that they..................Ps 31:4 7568
they hid for me their *n* in a pit................Ps 35:7 7568
let his *n* that he hath hid catch................Ps 35:8 7568
have prepared a *n* for my steps ....Ps 57:6 7568
Thou broughtest us into the *n*..................Ps 66:11 4685
have spread a *n* by the wayside................Ps 140:5 7568
Surely in vain the *n* is spread in ....Prov 1:17 7568
wicked desireth the *n* of evil men ....Prov 12:12 4686
spreadeth a *n* for his feet ....Prov 29:5 7568
that are taken in an evil *n*.......................Eccl 9:12 4686
streets, as a wild bull in a *n*.....................Is 51:20 4364
he hath spread a *n* for my feet ....Lam 1:13 7568
My *n* also will I spread upon him, ...Eze 12:13 7568
And I will spread my *n* upon him ....Eze 17:20 7568
and spread their *n* over him.....................Eze 19:8 7568
my *n* over thee with a company of ....Eze 32:3 7568
they shall bring thee up in my *n*...............Eze 32:3 2764
Mizpah, and a *n* spread upon Tabor ....Hos 5:1 7568
go, I will spread my *n* upon them...............Hos 7:12 7568
every man his brother with a *n*..................Mic 7:2 2764
angle, they catch them in their *n* ....Hab 1:15 2764
they sacrifice unto their *n* ....Hab 1:16 2764
they therefore empty their *n* ....Hab 1:17 2764
brother, casting a *n* into the sea...............Mt 4:18 *293*
of heaven is like unto a *n*.........................Mt 13:47 *4522*
brother casting a *n* into the sea.................Mk 1:16 *293*
at thy word I will let down the *n* ....Lk 5:5 *1350*
and their *n* brake......................................Lk 5:6 *1350*
Cast the *n* on the right side of..................Jn 21:6 *1350*
dragging the *n* with fishes.........................Jn 21:8 *1350*
drew the *n* to land full of great...................Jn 21:11 *1350*
so many, yet was not the *n* broken ....Jn 21:11 *1350*

NETAIM See PLANTS.

NETHANEAL See NETHANEEL.

NETHANEEL *(ne-than'-e-el)* {14}
1. A son of Zuar.
N the son of Zuar ....Num 1:8 5417
N the son of Zuar shall be.........................Num 2:5 5417
the second day *N* the son of Zuar ....Num 7:18 5417
the offering of *N* the son of Zuar ....Num 7:23 5417
of Issachar was *N* the son of Zuar...............Num 10:15 5417
2. A brother of David.
N the fourth, Raddai the fifth, ...1Chr 2:14 5417
3. A priest who relocated the Ark.
Shebaniah, and Jehoshaphat, and *N*.......1Chr 15:24 5417
4. A sanctuary servant.
Shemaiah the son of *N* the scribe 1Chr 24:6 5417
5. A son of Obed-edom.
Sacar the fourth, and *N* the fifth, ...1Chr 26:4 5417
6. A prince of Judah.
Obadiah, and to Zechariah, and to *N*.......2Chr 17:7 5417
7. A chief Levite.
Conaniah also, and Shemaiah and *N*.......2Chr 35:9 5417
8. Married a foreigner in exile.
Elioenai, Maaseiah, Ishmael, *N*................Ezr 10:22 5417
9. A priest with Zerubbabel.
of Jedaiah, *N* ....Neh 12:21 5417
10. A priest who dedicated the wall.
Milalai, Gilalai, Maai, *N*...........................Neh 12:36 5417

NETHANEL See NETHANEEL.

NETHANIAH *(neth-a-ni'-ah)* {20}
1. Father of Ishmael.
Mizpah, even Ishmael the son of *N*..........2Kin 25:23 5418
month, that Ishmael the son of *N*..............2Kin 25:25 5418
Mizpah, even Ishmael the son of *N* ....Jer 40:8 5418
Ishmael the son of *N* to slay thee ....Jer 40:14 5418
I will slay Ishmael the son of *N*...................Jer 40:15 5418
the son of *N* the son of Elishama ....Jer 41:1 5418
Then arose Ishmael the son of *N*.................Jer 41:2 5418
Ishmael the son of *N* went forth..................Jer 41:6 5418
Ishmael the son of *N* slew them ....Jer 41:7 5418
Ishmael the son of *N* filled it......................Jer 41:9 5418
Ishmael the son of *N* carried them ....Jer 41:10 5418
Ishmael the son of *N* had done....................Jer 41:11 5418
fight with Ishmael the son of *N* ....Jer 41:12 5418
But Ishmael the son of *N* escaped ....Jer 41:15 5418
from Ishmael the son of *N*...........................Jer 41:16 5418
because Ishmael the son of *N* had................Jer 41:18 5418
2. A sanctuary servant.
Zaccur, and Joseph, and *N*, and.................1Chr 25:2 5418
The fifth to *N*, he, his sons, and 1Chr 25:12 5418
3. A Levite.
sent Levites, even Shemaiah, and *N*.........2Chr 17:8 5418
4. Father of Jehudi.
princes sent Jehudi the son of *N* ....Jer 36:14 5418

NETHER {15}
stood at the *n* part of the mount ....Ex 19:17 8482
No man shall take the *n* or the..................Deut 24:6 7347
upper springs, and the *n* springs.................Josh 15:19 8482
the coast of Beth-horon the *n* ....Josh 16:3 8481
south side of the *n* Beth-horon ....Josh 18:13 8481
upper springs and the *n* springs..................Judg 1:15 8482
built Gezer, and Beth-horon the *n* 1Kin 9:17 8481
who built Beth-horon the *n*..........................1Chr 7:24 8481
the upper, and Beth-horon the *n*..................2Chr 8:5 8481
as a piece of the *n* millstone.......................Job 41:24 8482
to the *n* parts of the earth, in.....................Eze 31:14 8482
in the *n* parts of the earth ....Eze 31:16 8482
unto the *n* parts of the earth ....Eze 31:18 8482
unto the *n* parts of the earth,......................Eze 32:18 8482
into the *n* parts of the earth ....Eze 32:24 8482

NETHERMOST {1}
The *n* chamber was five cubits...................1Kin 6:6 8481

NETHINIM See NETHINIMS.

NETHINIMS *(neth'-in-ims)* {18} *Assistants to the Levites.*
the priests, Levites, and the *N* 1Chr 9:2 5411
The *N*: the children of Ziha ....Ezr 2:43 5411
All the *N*, and the children of......................Ezr 2:58 5411
singers, and the porters, and the *N*..........Ezr 2:70 5411
singers, and the porters, and the *N*..........Ezr 7:7 5411
and Levites, singers, porters, *N*.................Ezr 7:24 5412
Iddo, and to his brethren the *N*..................Ezr 8:17 5411
Also of the *N*, whom David and the ....Ezr 8:20 5411
Levites, two hundred and twenty *N*...........Ezr 8:20 5411
Moreover the *N* dwelt in Ophel, ...Neh 3:26 5411
son unto the place of the *N*........................Neh 3:31 5411
The *N*: the children of Ziha ....Neh 7:46 5411
All the *N*, and the children of.....................Neh 7:60 5411
and some of the people, and the *N*............Neh 7:73 5411
the porters, the singers, the *N*...................Neh 10:28 5411
priests, and the Levites, and the *N* ....Neh 11:3 5411
But the *N* dwelt in Ophel ....Neh 11:21 5411
and Ziha and Gispa were over the *N* ....Neh 11:21 5411

NETOPHAH *(ne-to'-fah)* {2} See NETOPHATHITE. *A city in Judah.*
The men of *N*, fifty and six ....Ezr 2:22 5199
The men of Beth-lehem and *N* ....Neh 7:26 5199

NETOPHATHI *(ne-to'-fa-thi)* {1} See NETOPHATHITE. *An inhabitant of Netophah.*
and from the villages of *N*..........................Neh 12:28 5200

NETOPHATHITE *(ne-to'-fa-thite)* {8} See NETOPHATHI, NETHOPHATHITES. *Same as Netophathi.*
Zalmon the Ahohite, Maharai the *N*.......2Sa 23:28 5200
Heleb the son of Baanah, a *N*...................2Sa 23:29 5200
the son of Tanhumeth the *N*.....................2Kin 25:23 5200
Maharai the *N*, Heled the son of 1Chr 11:30 5200
Heled the son of Baanah the *N* 1Chr 11:30 5200
the tenth month was Maharai the *N*.........1Chr 27:13 5200
twelfth month was Heldai the *N*...............1Chr 27:15 5200
and the sons of Ephai the *N*......................Jer 40:8 5200

NETOPHATHITES *(ne-to'-fa-thites)* {2}
Beth-lehem, and the *N*, Ataroth, ...1Chr 2:54 5200
dwelt in the villages of the *N*....................1Chr 9:16 5200

NETS {13}
n of checker work, and wreaths of..........1Kin 7:17 7638
the wicked fall into their own *n*.................Ps 141:10 4365
woman, whose heart is snares and *n*.......Eccl 7:26 2764
they that spread *n* upon the ....Is 19:8 4364
of *n* in the midst of the sea ....Eze 26:5 2764
shalt be a place to spread *n* upon ....Eze 26:14 2764
be a place to spread forth *n* ....Eze 47:10 2764
And they straightway left their *n*.............Mt 4:20 *1350*
their father, mending their *n*....................Mt 4:21 *1350*
straightway they forsook their *n*..............Mk 1:18 *1350*
were in the ship mending their *n*..............Mk 1:19 *1350*
of them, and were washing their *n*............Lk 5:2 *1350*
and let down your *n* for a draught............Lk 5:4 *1350*

NETTLES {5}
under the *n* they were gathered ....Job 30:7 2738
n had covered the face thereof,..............Prov 24:31 2738
shall come up in her palaces, *n* ....Is 34:13 7057
silver, *n* shall possess them......................Hos 9:6 7057
Gomorrah, even the breeding of *n* ....Zeph 2:9 2738

NETWORK {7}
make for it a grate of *n* of brass......Ex 27:4 4640,7568
of *n* under the compass thereof.......Ex 38:4 4640,7568
rows round about upon the one *n* 1Kin 7:18 7639
the belly which was by the *n*....................1Kin 7:20 7639
rows of pomegranates for one *n* 1Kin 7:42 7639
chapiter was five cubits, with *n* ....Jer 52:22 7639
the *n* were an hundred round about..........Jer 52:23 7639

NETWORKS {3}
and the two *n*, to cover the two................1Kin 7:41 7639
pomegranates for the two *n* 1Kin 7:42 7639
fine flax, and they that weave *n*.................Is 19:9 2355

NEVER See APPENDIX.

NEVERTHELESS See APPENDIX.

NEW {150}
arose up a *n* king over Egypt ....Ex 1:8 2319
ye shall offer a *n* meat offering ....Lev 23:16 2319
forth the old because of the *n* ....Lev 26:10 2319
But if the LORD make a *n* thing ....Num 16:30 1278
when ye bring a *n* meat offering ....Num 28:26 2319
there that hath built a *n* house ....Deut 20:5 2319
When thou buildest a *n* house..................Deut 22:8 2319
When a man hath taken a *n* wife ....Deut 24:5 2319
to *n* gods that came newly up,..................Deut 32:17 2319
of wine, which we filled, were *n* ....Josh 9:13 2319
They chose *n* gods.....................................Judg 5:8 2319
they bound him with two *n* cords ....Judg 15:13 2319
he found a *n* jawbone of an ass,................Judg 15:15 2961
If they bind me fast with *n* ropes..............Judg 16:11 2319
Delilah therefore took *n* ropes ....Judg 16:12 2319
Now therefore make a *n* cart.....................1Sa 6:7 2319
Behold, to morrow is the *n* moon...............1Sa 20:5 2320
to David, To morrow is the *n* moon............1Sa 20:18 2320
when the *n* moon was come, the 1Sa 20:24 2320
set the ark of God upon a *n* cart................2Sa 6:3 2319
of Abinadab, drave the *n* cart 2Sa 6:3 2319
he being girded with a *n* sword..................2Sa 21:16 2319
had clad himself with a *n* garment 1Kin 11:29 2319
Ahijah caught the *n* garment that...............1Kin 11:30 2319
And he said, Bring me a *n* cruse 2Kin 2:20 2319
it is neither *n* moon, nor sabbath 2Kin 4:23 2320
in a *n* cart out of the house of....................1Chr 13:7 2319
in the sabbaths, in the *n* moons 1Chr 23:31 2320
the sabbaths, and on the *n* moons..............2Chr 2:4 2320
the sabbaths, and on the *n* moons..............2Chr 8:13 2320
of the LORD, before the *n* court 2Chr 20:5 2319
the sabbaths, and for the *n* moons 2Chr 31:3 2320
offering, both of the *n* moons.....................Ezr 3:5 2320

N

stones, and a row of *n* timber ... Ezr 6:4 2323
of the sabbaths, of the *n* moons ... Neh 10:33 2320
of the corn, of the *n* wine ... Neh 10:39 8492
the *n* wine, and the oil, which was ... Neh 13:5 8492
the *n* wine and the oil unto the ... Neh 13:12 8492
is ready to burst like *n* bottles ... Job 32:19 2319
Sing unto him a *n* song ... Ps 33:3 2319
he hath put a *n* song in my mouth, ... Ps 40:3 2319
Blow up the trumpet in the *n* moon ... Ps 81:3 2320
O sing unto the LORD a *n* song ... Ps 96:1 2319
O sing unto the LORD a *n* song ... Ps 98:1 2319
I will sing a *n* song unto thee, O ... Ps 144:9 2319
Sing unto the LORD a *n* song ... Ps 149:1 2319
shall burst out with *n* wine ... Prov 3:10 8492
there is no *n* thing under the sun ... Eccl 1:9 2319
it may be said, See, this is *n* ... Eccl 1:10 2319
all manner of pleasant fruits, *n* ... Song 7:13 2319
the *n* moons and sabbaths, the ... Is 1:13 2320
Your *n* moons and your appointed ... Is 1:14 2320
The *n* wine mourneth, the vine ... Is 24:7 8492
I will make thee a *n* sharp ... Is 41:15 2319
to pass, and *n* things do I declare ... Is 42:9 2319
Sing unto the LORD a *n* song ... Is 42:10 2319
Behold, I will do a *n* thing ... Is 43:19 2319
I have shewed thee *n* things from ... Is 48:6 2319
thou shalt be called by a *n* name ... Is 62:2 2319
As the *n* wine is found in the ... Is 65:8 8492
I create *n* heavens and a *n* earth ... Is 65:17 2319
For as the *n* heavens ... Is 66:22 2319
the *n* earth, which I will make, ... Is 66:22 2319
that from one *n* moon to another, ... Is 66:23 2320
of the *n* gate of the LORD's house ... Jer 26:10 2319
created a *n* thing in the earth ... Jer 31:22 2319
that I will make a *n* covenant ... Jer 31:31 2319
at the entry of the *n* gate of the ... Jer 36:10 2319
They are *n* every morning ... Lam 3:23 2319
I will put a *n* spirit within you ... Eze 11:19 2319
you a *n* heart and a *n* spirit ... Eze 18:31 2319
A *n* heart also will I give you, ... Eze 36:26 2319
a *n* spirit will I put within you ... Eze 36:26 2319
in the feasts, and in the *n* moons ... Eze 45:17 2320
in the day of the *n* moon it shall ... Eze 46:1 2320
in the sabbaths and in the *n* moons ... Eze 46:3 2320
in the day of the *n* moon it shall ... Eze 46:6 2320
it shall bring forth *n* fruit ... Eze 47:12 1069
her *n* moons, and her sabbaths, and ... Hos 2:11 2320
n wine take away the heart ... Hos 4:11 8492
the *n* wine shall fail in her ... Hos 9:2 8492
of wine, because of the *n* wine ... Joel 1:5
the *n* wine is dried up, the oil ... Joel 1:10 8492
mountains shall drop down *n* wine ... Joel 3:18
When will the *n* moon be gone ... Amos 8:5 2320
upon the corn, and upon the *n* wine ... Hag 1:11 8492
men cheerful, and *n* wine the maids ... Zec 9:17 8492
of *n* cloth unto an old garment ... Mt 9:16 *46*
Neither do men put *n* wine into ... Mt 9:17 *3501*
but they put *n* wine into ... Mt 9:17 *3501*
wine into *n* bottles ... Mt 9:17 *2537*
out of his treasure things *n* ... Mt 13:52 *2537*
is my blood of the *n* testament ... Mt 26:28 *2537*
until that day when I drink it *n* ... Mt 26:29 *2537*
And laid it in his own *n* tomb ... Mt 27:60 *2537*
what *n* doctrine is this ... Mk 1:27 *2537*
of *n* cloth on an old garment ... Mk 2:21 *46*
else the *n* piece that filled it ... Mk 2:21 *2537*
no man putteth *n* wine into old ... Mk 2:22 *3501*
else the *n* wine doth burst the ... Mk 2:22 *3501*
but *n* wine must be put into ... Mk 2:22 *3501*
wine must be put into *n* bottles ... Mk 2:22 *2537*
is my blood of the *n* testament ... Mk 14:24 *2537*
drink it *n* in the kingdom of God ... Mk 14:25 *2537*
they shall speak with *n* tongues ... Mk 16:17 *2537*
piece of a *n* garment upon an old ... Lk 5:36 *2537*
then both the *n* maketh a rent ... Lk 5:36 *2537*
of the *n* agreeth not with the old ... Lk 5:36 *2537*
no man putteth *n* wine into old ... Lk 5:37 *3501*
else the *n* wine will burst the ... Lk 5:37 *3501*
But *n* wine must be put into ... Lk 5:38 *3501*
wine must be put into *n* bottles ... Lk 5:38 *2537*
old wine straightway desireth *n* ... Lk 5:39 *2537*
This cup is the *n* testament in my ... Lk 22:20 *2537*
A *n* commandment I give unto you, ... Jn 13:34 *2537*
and in the garden a *n* sepulchre ... Jn 19:41 *2537*
These men are full of *n* wine ... Acts 2:13 *1098*
May we know what this *n* doctrine ... Acts 17:19 *2537*
to tell, or to hear some *n* thing ... Acts 17:21 *2537*
leaven, that ye may be a *n* lump ... 1Cor 5:7 *3501*
This cup is the *n* testament in my ... 1Cor 11:25 *2537*
able ministers of the *n* testament ... 2Cor 3:6 *2537*
be in Christ, he is a *n* creature ... 2Cor 5:17 *2537*
behold, all things are become *n* ... 2Cor 5:17 *2537*
uncircumcision, but a *n* creature ... Gal 6:15 *2537*
in himself of twain one *n* man ... Eph 2:15 *2537*
And that ye put on the *n* man ... Eph 4:24 *2537*
of an holyday, or of the *n* moon ... Col 2:16 *3561*
And have put on the *n* man, which ... Col 3:10 *3501*
when I will make a *n* covenant ... Heb 8:8 *2537*
A *n* covenant, he hath made the ... Heb 8:13 *2537*
the mediator of the *n* testament ... Heb 9:15 *2537*
By a *n* and living way, which he ... Heb 10:20 *4372*
the mediator of the *n* covenant ... Heb 12:24 *3501*
his promise, look for *n* heavens ... 2Pet 3:13 *2537*
a *n* earth, wherein dwelleth ... 2Pet 3:13 *2537*
I write no *n* commandment unto you ... 1Jn 2:7 *2537*
a *n* commandment I write unto you, ... 1Jn 2:8 *2537*
I wrote a *n* commandment unto thee ... 2Jn 5 *2537*
and in the stone a *n* name written ... Rev 2:17 *2537*
which is *n* Jerusalem, which ... Rev 3:12 *2537*
I will write upon him my *n* name ... Rev 3:12 *2537*
And they sung a *n* song, saying, ... Rev 5:9 *2537*
were a *n* song before the throne ... Rev 14:3 *2537*
I saw a *n* heaven and a *n* earth ... Rev 21:1 *2537*
n Jerusalem, coming down from God ... Rev 21:2 *2537*
said, Behold, I make all things *n* ... Rev 21:5 *2537*

NEWBORN {1}
As *n* babes, desire the sincere ... 1Pet 2:2 *738*

NEWLY {2}
not, to new gods that came *n* up ... Deut 32:17 7138
they had but *n* set the watch ... Judg 7:19 6965

NEWNESS {2}
we also should walk in *n* of life ... Rom 6:4 *2538*
we should serve in *n* of spirit ... Rom 7:6 *2538*

NEWS {1}
so is good *n* from a far country ... Prov 25:25 8052

NEXT See APPENDIX.

NEZIAH *(ne-zi'-ah)* {2} *A family of exiles.*
The children of *N*, the children ... Ezr 2:54 5335
The children of *N*, the children ... Neh 7:56 5335

NEZIB *(ne'-zib)* {1} *A city in Judah.*
And Jiphtah, and Ashnah, and *N* ... Josh 15:43 5334

NIBHAZ *(nib'-haz)* {1} *A god of the Avites.*
And the Avites made *N* and Tartak, ... 2Kin 17:31 5026

NIBSHAN *(nib'-shan)* {1} *A city in Judah.*
And *N*, and the city of Salt, and ... Josh 15:62 5044

NICANOR *(ni-ca'-nor)* {1} *A leader in the Jerusalem church.*
and Philip, and Prochorus, and *N* ... Acts 6:5 *3527*

NICODEMUS *(nic-o-de'-mus)* {5} *A Pharisee sympathetic to Jesus.*
a man of the Pharisees, named *N* ... Jn 3:1 *3530*
N saith unto him, How can a man ... Jn 3:4 *3530*
N answered and said unto him, How ... Jn 3:9 *3530*
N saith unto them, (he that came ... Jn 7:50 *3530*
And there came also *N*, which at ... Jn 19:39 *3530*

NICOLAITANES *(nic-o-la'-i-tans)* {2} *A group condemned in Revelation.*
thou hatest the deeds of the *N* ... Rev 2:6 *3531*
that hold the doctrine of the *N* ... Rev 2:15 *3531*

NICOLAITANS See NICOLAITANES.

NICOLAS *(nic'-o-las)* {1} *A leader in the Jerusalem church.*
and *N* a proselyte of Antioch ... Acts 6:5 *3532*

NICOLAUS See NICOLAS.

NICOPOLIS *(ni-cop'-o-lis)* {2} *A city in Thrace.*
be diligent to come unto me to *N* ... Titus 3:12 *3533*
the Cretians, from *N* of Macedonia ... Titus *s* *3533*

NIGER *(ni'-jur)* {1} See SIMEON. *A Christian teacher and prophet at Antioch.*
and Simeon that was called *N* ... Acts 13:1 *3526*

NIGH {100}
the time drew *n* that Israel must ... Gen 47:29 7126
And he said, Draw not *n* hither ... Ex 3:5 7126
And when Pharaoh drew *n*, the ... Ex 14:10 7126
but they shall not come *n* ... Ex 24:2 5066
soon as he came *n* unto the camp ... Ex 32:19 7126
and they were afraid to come *n* him ... Ex 34:30 5066
all the children of Israel came *n* ... Ex 34:32 5066
sanctified in them that come *n* me ... Lev 10:3 7138
that is *n* unto him, which hath ... Lev 21:3 7138
n to offer the offerings of the ... Lev 21:21 5066
he shall not come *n* to offer the ... Lev 21:21 5066
nor come *n* unto the altar, ... Lev 21:23 5066
or any that is *n* of kin unto him ... Lev 25:49 7607
cometh *n* shall be put to death ... Num 1:51 7126
cometh *n* shall be put to death ... Num 3:10 7126
cometh *n* shall be put to death ... Num 3:38 7126
Israel come *n* unto the sanctuary ... Num 8:19 5066
only they shall not come *n* the ... Num 18:3 7126
shall not come *n* unto you ... Num 18:4 7126
cometh *n* shall be put to death ... Num 18:7 7126
come *n* the tabernacle of the ... Num 18:22 7126
I shall behold him, but not *n* ... Num 24:17 7126
unto all the places *n* thereunto ... Deut 1:7 7934
when thou comest *n* over against ... Deut 2:19 7126
who hath God so *n* unto them ... Deut 4:7 7126
n unto thee, or far off from thee ... Deut 13:7 7126
ye are come *n* unto the battle ... Deut 20:2 7126
When thou comest *n* unto a city to ... Deut 20:10 7126
if thy brother be not *n* unto thee ... Deut 22:2 7126
But the word is very *n* unto thee ... Deut 30:14 7126
were with him, went up, and drew *n* ... Josh 8:11 5066
drew *n* to meet David, that David ... 1Sa 17:48 7126
And Joab drew *n*, and the people ... 2Sa 10:13 5066
Wherefore approached ye so *n* unto ... 2Sa 11:20
why went ye *n* the wall ... 2Sa 11:21 5066
that when any man came *n* to him ... 2Sa 15:5 7126
David drew *n* that he should die ... 1Kin 2:1 7126
be *n* unto the LORD our God day and ... 1Kin 8:59 7126
Moreover they that were *n* them ... 1Chr 12:40 7126
n before the Syrians unto the ... 1Chr 19:14 5066
of the king Ahasuerus, both *n* ... Est 9:20 7126
they shall not come *n* unto him ... Ps 32:6 5060
The LORD is *n* unto them that are ... Ps 34:18 7126
Draw *n* unto my soul, and redeem it ... Ps 69:18 7126
my steps had well *n* slipped ... Ps 73:2 4952
salvation is *n* them that fear him ... Ps 85:9 7126
my life draweth *n* unto the grave ... Ps 88:3 5060
but it shall not come *n* thee ... Ps 91:7 5066
any plague come *n* thy dwelling ... Ps 91:10 7126
They draw *n* that follow after ... Ps 119:150 7126
The LORD is *n* unto all them that ... Ps 145:18 7138
come not *n* the door of her house ... Prov 5:8 7126
come not, nor the years draw *n* ... Eccl 12:1 5060
of the Holy One of Israel draw *n* ... Is 5:19 7126
LORD cometh, for it is *n* at hand ... Joel 2:1 7126
This people draweth *n* unto me ... Mt 15:8 *1448*
came *n* unto the sea of Galilee ... Mt 15:29 *3844*
when they drew *n* unto Jerusalem ... Mt 21:1 *1448*
leaves, ye know that summer is *n* ... Mt 24:32 *1451*
not come *n* unto him for the press ... Mk 2:4
Now there was there *n* unto the ... Mk 5:11 *4314*
and he was *n* unto the sea ... Mk 5:21 *3844*
And when they came *n* to Jerusalem ... Mk 11:1
come to pass, know that it is *n* ... Mk 13:29 *1451*
Now when he came *n* to the gate of ... Lk 7:12 *1448*
kingdom of God is come *n* unto you ... Lk 10:9 *1448*
kingdom of God is come *n* unto you ... Lk 10:11 *1448*
drew *n* to the house, he heard ... Lk 15:25 *1448*
as he was come *n* unto Jericho ... Lk 18:35 *1448*
because he was *n* to Jerusalem ... Lk 19:11 *1451*
when he was come *n* to Bethphage ... Lk 19:29 *1448*
And when he was come *n*, even now ... Lk 19:37 *1448*
that the desolation thereof is *n* ... Lk 21:20 *1448*
for your redemption draweth *n* ... Lk 21:28 *1448*
that summer is now *n* at hand ... Lk 21:30 *1451*
the kingdom of God is *n* at hand ... Lk 21:31 *1451*
feast of unleavened bread drew *n* ... Lk 22:1 *1448*
they drew *n* unto the village, ... Lk 24:28 *1448*
a feast of the Jews, was *n* ... Jn 6:4 *1451*
sea, and drawing *n* unto the ship ... Jn 6:19 *1451*
n unto the place where they did ... Jn 6:23 *1451*
Now Bethany was *n* unto Jerusalem ... Jn 11:18 *1451*
the Jews' passover was *n* at hand ... Jn 11:55 *1451*
was crucified was *n* to the city ... Jn 19:20 *1451*
for the sepulchre was *n* at hand ... Jn 19:42 *1451*
the time of the promise drew *n* ... Acts 7:17 *1448*
forasmuch as Lydda was *n* to Joppa ... Acts 9:38 *1451*
drew *n* unto the city, Peter went ... Acts 10:9 *1448*
was come *n* unto Damascus about ... Acts 22:6 *1448*
n whereunto was the city of Lasea ... Acts 27:8 *1451*
The word is *n* thee, even in thy ... Rom 10:8 *1451*
are made *n* by the blood of Christ ... Eph 2:13 *1451*
afar off, and to them that were *n* ... Eph 2:17 *1451*
indeed he was sick *n* unto death ... Phil 2:27 *3897*
of Christ he was *n* unto death ... Phil 2:30 *1448*
is rejected, and is *n* unto cursing ... Heb 6:8 *1451*
by the which we draw *n* unto God ... Heb 7:19 *1448*
Draw *n* to God, and he will draw ... Jas 4:8 *1448*
to God, and he will draw *n* to you ... Jas 4:8 *1448*
the coming of the Lord draweth *n* ... Jas 5:8 *1448*

NIGHT {307}
Day, and the darkness he called *N* ... Gen 1:5 3915
to divide the day from the *n* ... Gen 1:14 3915
and the lesser light to rule the *n* ... Gen 1:16 3915
rule over the day and over the *n* ... Gen 1:18 3915
and day and *n* shall not cease ... Gen 8:22 3915
them, he and his servants, by *n* ... Gen 14:15 3915
servant's house, and tarry all *n* ... Gen 19:2
we will abide in the street all *n* ... Gen 19:2
men which came in to thee this *n* ... Gen 19:5 3915
their father drink wine that *n* ... Gen 19:33 3915
make him drink wine this *n* also ... Gen 19:34 3915
father drink wine that *n* also ... Gen 19:35 3915
came to Abimelech in a dream by *n* ... Gen 20:3 3915
were with him, and tarried all *n* ... Gen 24:54
LORD appeared unto him the same *n* ... Gen 26:24 3915
place, and tarried there all *n* ... Gen 28:11
thee to *n* for thy son's mandrakes ... Gen 30:15 3915
And he lay with her that *n* ... Gen 30:16 3915
Laban the Syrian in a dream by *n* ... Gen 31:24 3915
stolen by day, or stolen by *n* ... Gen 31:39 3915
consumed me, and the frost by *n* ... Gen 31:40 3915
tarried all *n* in the mount ... Gen 31:54
And he lodged there that same *n* ... Gen 32:13 3915
lodged that *n* in the company ... Gen 32:21 3915
And he rose up that *n*, and took his ... Gen 32:22 3915
them, each man his dream in one *n* ... Gen 40:5 3915
And we dreamed a dream in one *n* ... Gen 41:11 3915
Israel in the visions of the *n* ... Gen 46:2 3915
at *n* he shall divide the spoil ... Gen 49:27 6153
land all that day, and all that *n* ... Ex 10:13 3915
shall eat the flesh in that *n* ... Ex 12:8 3915
through the land of Egypt this *n* ... Ex 12:12 3915
And Pharaoh rose up in the *n* ... Ex 12:30 3915
he called for Moses and Aaron by *n* ... Ex 12:31 3915
It is a *n* to be much observed ... Ex 12:42 3915
this is that *n* of the LORD to be ... Ex 12:42 3915
by *n* in a pillar of fire, to give ... Ex 13:21 3915
to go by day and *n* ... Ex 13:21 3915
day, nor the pillar of fire by *n* ... Ex 13:22 3915
but it gave light by *n* to these ... Ex 14:20 3915
came not near the other all the *n* ... Ex 14:20 3915
by a strong east wind all that *n* ... Ex 14:21 3915
by day, and fire was on it by *n* ... Ex 40:38 3915
the altar all *n* unto the morning ... Lev 6:9 3915
the morning, and half thereof at *n* ... Lev 6:20 6153
n seven days, and keep the charge ... Lev 8:35 3915
the *n* hawk, and the cuckow, and the ... Lev 11:16 8464
with thee all *n* until the morning ... Lev 19:13
and the appearance of fire by *n* ... Num 9:16 3915
by *n* that the cloud was taken up ... Num 9:21 3915
dew fell upon the camp in the *n* ... Num 11:9 3915
up all that day, and all that *n* ... Num 11:32 3915
and the people wept that *n* ... Num 14:1 3915
and in a pillar of fire by *n* ... Num 14:14 3915
said unto them, Lodge here this *n* ... Num 22:8 3915
you, tarry ye also here this *n* ... Num 22:19 3915

And God came unto Balaam at *n* ... Num 22:20 3915
pitch your tents in, in fire by *n* ... Deut 1:33 3915
the *n* hawk, and the cuckow, and the ... Deut 14:15 8464
thee forth out of Egypt by *n* ... Deut 16:1 3915
remain all *n* until the morning ... Deut 16:4
not remain all *n* upon the tree ... Deut 21:23
that chanceth him by *n*, then ... Deut 23:10 3915
and thou shalt fear day and *n* ... Deut 28:66 3915
shalt meditate therein day and *n* ... Josh 1:8 3915
there came men in hither to *n* of ... Josh 2:2 3915
where ye shall lodge this *n* ... Josh 4:3 3915
of valour, and sent them away by *n* ... Josh 8:3 3915
lodged that *n* among the people ... Josh 8:9 3915
Joshua went that *n* into the midst ... Josh 8:13 3915
and went up from Gilgal all *n* ... Josh 10:9 3915
And it came to pass the same *n* ... Judg 6:25 3915
do it by day, that he did it by *n* ... Judg 6:27 3915
And God did so that *n* ... Judg 6:40 3915
And it came to pass the same *n* ... Judg 7:9 3915
Now therefore up by *n*, thou and ... Judg 9:32 3915
people that were with him, by *n* ... Judg 9:34 3915
laid wait for him all *n* in the ... Judg 16:2 3915
the city, and were quiet all the *n* ... Judg 16:2 3915
I pray thee, and tarry all *n* ... Judg 19:6
evening, I pray you tarry all *n* ... Judg 19:9
the man would not tarry that *n* ... Judg 19:10
of these places to lodge all *n* ... Judg 19:13
her all the *n* until the morning ... Judg 19:25 3915
house round about upon me by *n* ... Judg 20:5 3915
should have an husband also to *n* ... Ruth 1:12 3915
barley to *n* in the threshingfloor ... Ruth 3:2 3915
Tarry this *n*, and it shall be in ... Ruth 3:13 3915
every man his ox with him that *n* ... 1Sa 14:34 3915
down after the Philistines by *n* ... 1Sa 14:36 3915
and he cried unto the LORD all *n* ... 1Sa 15:11 3915
the LORD hath said to me this *n* ... 1Sa 15:16 3915
and David fled, and escaped that *n* ... 1Sa 19:10 3915
saying, If thou save not thy to *n* ... 1Sa 19:11 3915
naked all that day and all that *n* ... 1Sa 19:24 3915
were a wall unto us both by *n* ... 1Sa 25:16 3915
Abishai came to the people by *n* ... 1Sa 26:7 3915
and they came to the woman by *n* ... 1Sa 28:8 3915
bread all the day, nor all the *n* ... 1Sa 28:20 3915
they rose up, and went away that *n* ... 1Sa 28:25 3915
valiant men arose, and went all *n* ... 1Sa 31:12 3915
all that *n* through the plain ... 2Sa 2:29 3915
And Joab and his men went all *n* ... 2Sa 2:32 3915
them away through the plain all *n* ... 2Sa 4:7 3915
And it came to pass that *n* ... 2Sa 7:4 3915
in, and lay all *n* upon the earth ... 2Sa 12:16
and pursue after David this *n* ... 2Sa 17:1 3915
Lodge not this *n* in the plains of ... 2Sa 17:16 3915
not tarry one with thee this *n* ... 2Sa 19:7 3915
nor the beasts of the field by *n* ... 2Sa 21:10 3915
to Solomon in a dream by *n* ... 1Kin 3:5 3915
this woman's child died in the *n* ... 1Kin 3:19 3915
may be open toward this house *n* ... 1Kin 8:29 3915
unto the LORD our God day and *n* ... 1Kin 8:59 3915
and they came by *n*, and compassed ... 2Kin 6:14 3915
And the king arose in the *n* ... 2Kin 7:12 3915
and he rose by *n*, and smote the ... 2Kin 8:21 3915
And it came to pass that *n* ... 2Kin 19:35 3915
all the men of war fled by *n* by ... 2Kin 25:4 3915
employed in that work day and *n* ... 1Chr 9:33 3915
And it came to pass the same *n* ... 1Chr 17:3 3915
In that *n* did God appear unto ... 2Chr 1:7 3915
be open upon this house day and *n* ... 2Chr 6:20 3915
the LORD appeared to Solomon by *n* ... 2Chr 7:12 3915
and he rose up by *n*, and smote the ... 2Chr 21:9 3915
offerings and the fat until *n* ... 2Chr 35:14 3915
I pray before thee now, day and *n* ... Neh 1:6 3915
And I arose in the *n*, I and some ... Neh 2:12 3915
I went out by *n* by the gate of ... Neh 2:13 3915
went I up in the *n* by the brook ... Neh 2:15 3915
set a watch against them day and *n* ... Neh 4:9 3915
that in the *n* they may be a guard ... Neh 4:22 3915
in the *n* will they come to slay ... Neh 6:10 3915
in the *n* by a pillar of fire, to ... Neh 9:12 3915
neither the pillar of fire by *n* ... Neh 9:19 3915
nor drink three days, *n* or day ... Est 4:16 3915
On that *n* could not the king ... Est 6:1 3915
the *n* in which it was said, There ... Job 3:3 3915
As for that *n*, let darkness seize ... Job 3:6 3915
Lo, let that *n* be solitary ... Job 3:7 3915
from the visions of the *n* ... Job 4:13 3915
grope in the noonday as in the *n* ... Job 5:14 3915
shall I arise, and the *n* be gone ... Job 7:4 6153
They change the *n* into day ... Job 17:12 3915
chased away as a vision of the *n* ... Job 20:8 3915
needy, and in the *n* is as a thief ... Job 24:14 3915
until the day and *n* come to an end ... Job 26:10 2822
stealeth him away in the *n* ... Job 27:20 3915
the dew lay all *n* upon my branch ... Job 29:19
are pierced in me in the *n* season ... Job 30:17 3915
In a dream, in a vision of the *n* ... Job 33:15 3915
and he overturneth them in the *n* ... Job 34:25 3915
maker, who giveth songs in the *n* ... Job 35:10 3915
Desire not the *n*, when people are ... Job 36:20 3915
his law doth he meditate day and *n* ... Ps 1:2 3915
all the *n* make I my bed to swim ... Ps 6:6 3915
also instruct me in the *n* seasons ... Ps 16:7 3915
thou hast visited me in the *n* ... Ps 17:3 3915
n unto *n* sheweth knowledge ... Ps 19:2 3915
and in the *n* season, and am not ... Ps 22:2 3915
weeping may endure for a *n* ... Ps 30:5 6153
n thy hand was heavy upon me ... Ps 32:4 3915
tears have been my meat day and *n* ... Ps 42:3 3915
in the *n* his song shall be with ... Ps 42:8 3915
n they go about it upon the walls ... Ps 55:10 3915
meditate on thee in the *n* watches ... Ps 63:6
day is thine, the *n* also is thine ... Ps 74:16 3915
my sore ran in the *n*, and ceased ... Ps 77:2 3915
to remembrance my song in the *n* ... Ps 77:6 3915
all the *n* with a light of fire ... Ps 78:14 3915
I have cried day and *n* before thee ... Ps 88:1 3915
is past, and as a watch in the *n* ... Ps 90:4 3915
not be afraid for the terror by *n* ... Ps 91:5 3915
and thy faithfulness every *n* ... Ps 92:2 3915
Thou makest darkness, and it is *n* ... Ps 104:20 3915
and fire to give light in the *n* ... Ps 105:39 3915
thy name, O LORD, in the *n* ... Ps 119:55 3915
Mine eyes prevent the *n* watches ... Ps 119:148
thee by day, nor the moon by *n* ... Ps 121:6 3915
which by *n* stand in the house of ... Ps 134:1 3915
The moon and stars to rule by *n* ... Ps 136:9 3915
even the *n* shall be light about ... Ps 139:11 3915
but the *n* shineth as the day ... Ps 139:12 3915
evening, in the black and dark *n* ... Prov 7:9 3915
She riseth also while it is yet *n* ... Prov 31:15 3915
her candle goeth not out by *n* ... Prov 31:18 3915
heart taketh not rest in the *n* ... Eccl 2:23 3915
nor *n* seeth sleep with his eyes ... Eccl 8:16 3915
he shall lie all *n* betwixt my ... Song 1:13
By *n* on my bed I sought him whom ... Song 3:1 3915
thigh because of fear in the *n* ... Song 3:8 3915
my locks with the drops of the *n* ... Song 5:2 3915
shining of a flaming fire by *n* ... Is 4:5 3915
that continue until *n*, till wine ... Is 5:11 5399
Because in the *n* Ar of Moab is ... Is 15:1 3915
because in the *n* Kir of Moab is ... Is 15:1 3915
make thy shadow as the *n* in the ... Is 16:3 3915
the *n* of my pleasure hath he ... Is 21:4 5399
of Seir, Watchman, what of the *n* ... Is 21:11 3915
Watchman, what of the *n* ... Is 21:11 3915
The morning cometh, and also the *n* ... Is 21:12 3915
soul have I desired thee in the *n* ... Is 26:9 3915
any hurt it, I will keep it *n* ... Is 27:3 3915
it pass over, by day and by *n* ... Is 28:19 3915
shall be as a dream of a *n* vision ... Is 29:7 3915
as in the *n* when a holy solemnity ... Is 30:29 3915
shall not be quenched *n* nor day ... Is 34:10 3915
from day even to *n* wilt thou make ... Is 38:12 3915
from day even to *n* wilt thou make ... Is 38:13 3915
we stumble at noonday as in the *n* ... Is 59:10 5399
they shall not be shut day nor *n* ... Is 60:11 3915
never hold their peace day nor *n* ... Is 62:6 3915
Arise, and let us go by *n*, and let ... Jer 6:5 3915
n for the slain of the daughter ... Jer 9:1 3915
turneth aside to tarry for a *n* ... Jer 14:8
mine eyes run down with tears *n* ... Jer 14:17 3915
ye serve other gods day and *n* ... Jer 16:13 3915
and of the stars for a light by *n* ... Jer 31:35 3915
the day, and my covenant of the *n* ... Jer 33:20 3915
not be day and *n* in their season ... Jer 33:20 3915
my covenant be not with day and *n* ... Jer 33:25 3915
heat, and in the *n* to the frost ... Jer 36:30 3915
went forth out of the city by *n* ... Jer 39:4 3915
if thieves by *n*, they will ... Jer 49:9 3915
went forth out of the city by *n* ... Jer 52:7 3915
She weepeth sore in the *n* ... Lam 1:2 3915
run down like a river day and *n* ... Lam 2:18 3915
Arise, cry out in the *n* ... Lam 2:19 3915
unto Daniel in a *n* vision ... Dan 2:19 3916
In that *n* was Belshazzar the king ... Dan 5:30 3916
palace, and passed the *n* fasting ... Dan 6:18 956
and said, I saw in my vision by *n* ... Dan 7:2 3916
After this I saw in the *n* visions ... Dan 7:7 3916
I saw in the *n* visions, and, ... Dan 7:13 6916
shall fall with thee in the *n* ... Hos 4:5 3915
their baker sleepeth all the *n* ... Hos 7:6 3915
lie all *n* in sackcloth, ye ... Joel 1:13
and maketh the day dark with *n* ... Amos 5:8 3915
came to thee, if robbers by *n* ... Obad 5 3915
up in a *n*, and perished in a *n* ... Jonah 4:10 3915
Therefore *n* shall be unto you, ... Mic 3:6 3915
I saw by *n*, and behold a man ... Zec 1:8 3915
known to the LORD, not day, nor *n* ... Zec 14:7 3915
young child and his mother by *n* ... Mt 2:14 3571
of the *n* Jesus went unto them ... Mt 14:25 3571
be offended because of me this *n* ... Mt 26:31 3571
I say unto thee, That this *n* ... Mt 26:34 3571
day, lest his disciples come by *n* ... Mt 27:64 3571
Say ye, His disciples came by *n* ... Mt 28:13 3571
And should sleep, and rise *n* ... Mk 4:27 3571
And always, *n* and day, he was in ... Mk 5:5 3571
of the *n* he cometh unto them ... Mk 6:48 3571
be offended because of me this *n* ... Mk 14:27 3571
That this day, even in this *n* ... Mk 14:30 3571
watch over their flock by *n* ... Lk 2:8 3571
God with fastings and prayers *n* ... Lk 2:37 3571
Master, we have toiled all the *n* ... Lk 5:5 3571
continued all *n* in prayer to God ... Lk 6:12 1273
this *n* thy soul shall be required ... Lk 12:20 3571
in that *n* there shall be two men ... Lk 17:34 3571
n unto him, though he bear long ... Lk 18:7 3571
at *n* he went out, and abode in the ... Lk 21:37 3571
The same came to Jesus by *n* ... Jn 3:2 3571
them, (he that came to Jesus by *n* ... Jn 7:50 3571
the *n* cometh, when no man can ... Jn 9:4 3571
But if a man walk in the *n* ... Jn 11:10 3571
and it was *n* ... Jn 13:30 3571
at the first came to Jesus by *n* ... Jn 19:39 3571
that *n* they caught nothing ... Jn 21:3 3571
Lord by *n* opened the prison doors ... Acts 5:19 3571
the gates day and *n* to kill him ... Acts 9:24 3571
Then the disciples took him by *n* ... Acts 9:25 3571
the same *n* Peter was sleeping ... Acts 12:6 3571
vision appeared to Paul in the *n* ... Acts 16:9 3571
took them the same hour of the *n* ... Acts 16:33 3571
Paul and Silas by *n* unto Berea ... Acts 17:10 3571
Lord to Paul in the *n* by a vision ... Acts 18:9 3571
I ceased not to warn every one *n* ... Acts 20:31 3571
the *n* following the Lord stood by ... Acts 23:11 3571
at the third hour of the *n* ... Acts 23:23 3571
and brought him by *n* to Antipatris ... Acts 23:31 3571
instantly serving God day and *n* ... Acts 26:7 3571
by me this *n* the angel of God ... Acts 27:23 3571
when the fourteenth *n* was come ... Acts 27:27 3571
The *n* is far spent, the day is at ... Rom 13:12 3571
That the Lord Jesus the same *n* in ... 1Cor 11:23 3571
thrice I suffered shipwreck, a *n* ... 2Cor 11:25 3574
for labouring *n* and day, because ... 1Th 2:9 3571
N and day praying exceedingly that ... 1Th 3:10 3571
so cometh as a thief in the *n* ... 1Th 5:2 3571
we are not of the *n*, nor of ... 1Th 5:5 3571
they that sleep sleep in the *n* ... 1Th 5:7 3571
be drunken are drunken in the *n* ... 1Th 5:7 3571
wrought with labour and travail *n* ... 2Th 3:8 3571
in supplications and prayers *n* ... 1Ti 5:5 3571
of thee in my prayers *n* and day ... 2Ti 1:3 3571
will come as a thief in the *n* ... 2Pet 3:10 3571
and they rest not day and *n* ... Rev 4:8 3571
serve him day and *n* in his temple ... Rev 7:15 3571
part of it, and the *n* likewise ... Rev 8:12 3571
them before our God day and *n* ... Rev 12:10 3571
and they have no rest day nor *n* ... Rev 14:11 3571
day and *n* for ever and ever ... Rev 20:10 3571
for there shall be no *n* there ... Rev 21:25 3571
And there shall be no *n* there ... Rev 22:5 3571

NIGHTS {18}
the earth forty days and forty *n* ... Gen 7:4 3915
the earth forty days and forty *n* ... Gen 7:12 3915
the mount forty days and forty *n* ... Ex 24:18 3915
the LORD forty days and forty *n* ... Ex 34:28 3915
the mount forty days and forty *n* ... Deut 9:9 3915
the end of forty days and forty *n* ... Deut 9:11 3915
the first, forty days and forty *n* ... Deut 9:18 3915
the LORD forty days and forty *n* ... Deut 9:25 3915
first time, forty days and forty *n* ... Deut 10:10 3915
any water, three days and three *n* ... 1Sa 30:12 3915
forty *n* unto Horeb the mount of ... 1Kin 19:8 3915
the ground seven days and seven *n* ... Job 2:13 3915
wearisome *n* are appointed to me ... Job 7:3 3915
and I am set in my ward whole *n* ... Is 21:8 3915
of the fish three days and three *n* ... Jonah 1:17 3915
had fasted forty days and forty *n* ... Mt 4:2 3571
three *n* in the whale's belly ... Mt 12:40 3571
three *n* in the heart of the earth ... Mt 12:40 3571

NILE See BROOKS, FLOOD, RIVER.

NIMRAH *(nim'-rah)* {1} See BETH-NIMRAH. *A city in Gad.*
Ataroth, and Dibon, and Jazer, and *N* ... Num 32:3 5247

NIMRIM *(nim'-rim)* {2} *A body of water on the border of Gad.*
the waters of *N* shall be desolate ... Is 15:6 5249
also of *N* shall be desolate ... Jer 48:34 5249

NIMROD *(nim'-rod)* {4} *Son of Cush.*
And Cush begat *N* ... Gen 10:8 5248
Even as *N* the mighty hunter ... Gen 10:9 5248
And Cush begat *N* ... 1Chr 1:10 5248
the land of *N* in the entrances ... Mic 5:6 5248

NIMSHI *(nim'-shi)* {5} *Grandfather of Jehu.*
Jehu the son of *N* shalt thou ... 1Kin 19:16 5250
son of Jehoshaphat the son of *N* ... 2Kin 9:2 5250
son of *N* conspired against Joram ... 2Kin 9:14 5250
the driving of Jehu the son of *N* ... 2Kin 9:20 5250
Jehoram against Jehu the son of *N* ... 2Chr 22:7 5250

NINE {50}
that Adam lived were *n* hundred ... Gen 5:5 8672
the days of Seth were *n* hundred ... Gen 5:8 8672
the days of Enos were *n* hundred ... Gen 5:11 8672
the days of Cainan were *n* hundred ... Gen 5:14 8672
of Jared were *n* hundred sixty ... Gen 5:20 8672
n hundred sixty and *n* years ... Gen 5:27 8672
the days of Noah were *n* hundred ... Gen 9:29 8672
n years, and begat sons and ... Gen 11:19 8672
And Nahor lived *n* and twenty years, ... Gen 11:24 8672
Abram was ninety years old and *n* ... Gen 17:1 8672
Abraham was ninety years old and *n* ... Gen 17:24 8672
n talents, and seven hundred and ... Ex 38:24 8672
be unto thee forty and *n* years ... Lev 25:8 8672
n thousand and three hundred ... Num 1:23 8672
n thousand and three hundred ... Num 2:13 8672
And on the fifth day *n* bullocks ... Num 29:26 8672
to give unto the *n* tribes ... Num 34:13 8672
n cubits was the length thereof, ... Deut 3:11 8672
an inheritance unto the *n* tribes ... Josh 13:7 8672
hand of Moses, for the *n* tribes ... Josh 14:2 8672
all the cities are twenty and *n* ... Josh 15:32 8672
n cities with their villages ... Josh 15:44 8672
n cities with their villages ... Josh 15:54 8672
n cities out of those two tribes ... Josh 21:16 8672
for he had *n* hundred chariots of ... Judg 4:3 8672
even *n* hundred chariots of iron, ... Judg 4:13 8672
Jerusalem at the end of *n* months ... 2Sa 24:8 8672
twenty and *n* years in Jerusalem ... 2Kin 14:2 8672
of Jabesh began to reign in the *n* ... 2Kin 15:13 8672
In the *n* and thirtieth year of ... 2Kin 15:17 8672
in Samaria over Israel *n* years ... 2Kin 17:1 8672
twenty and *n* years in Jerusalem ... 2Kin 18:2 8672
and Eliada, and Eliphelet, *n* ... 1Chr 3:8 8672

n hundred and fifty and six ... 1Chr 9:9 8672
twenty and *n* years in Jerusalem ... 2Chr 25:1 8672
twenty years old, and he reigned *n* ... 2Chr 29:1 8672
a thousand chargers of silver, *n* ... Ezr 1:9 8672
of Zattu, *n* hundred forty and five ... Ezr 2:8 8672
n hundred seventy and three ... Ezr 2:36 8672
in all an hundred thirty and *n* ... Ezr 2:42 8672
Senaah, three thousand *n* hundred ... Neh 7:38 8672
n hundred seventy and three ... Neh 7:39 8672
n parts to dwell in other cities ... Neh 11:1 8672
n hundred twenty and eight ... Neh 11:8 8672
doth he not leave the ninety and *n* ... Mt 18:12 *1768*
ninety and *n* which went not astray ... Mt 18:13 *1768*
n* in the wilderness, and go after ... Lk 15:4 *1768
n* just persons, which need no ... Lk 15:7 *1768
but where are the *n* ... Lk 17:17 *1767*

NINETEEN {3}
n years, and begat sons and ... Gen 11:25 8672,6240
n cities with their villages ... Josh 19:38 8672,6240
lacked of David's servants *n* men ... 2Sa 2:30 8672,6240

NINETEENTH {4}
which is the *n* year of king ... 2Kin 25:8 8672,6240
The *n* to Pethahiah, the twentieth ... 1Chr 24:16 8672,6240
The *n* to Mallothi, he, his sons, ... 1Chr 25:26 8672,6240
month, which was the *n* year of ... Jer 52:12 8672,6240

NINETY {24}
And Enos lived *n* years, and begat ... Gen 5:9 8673
Mahalaleel were eight hundred *n* ... Gen 5:17 8673
he begat Noah five hundred *n* ... Gen 5:30 8673
And when Abram was *n* years old ... Gen 17:1 8673
that is *n* years old, bear ... Gen 17:17 8673
And Abraham was *n* years old ... Gen 17:24 8673
Now Eli was *n* and eight years old ... 1Sa 4:15 8673
their brethren, six hundred and *n* ... 1Chr 9:6 8673
children of Ater of Hezekiah, *n* ... Ezr 2:16 8673
The children of Gibbar, *n* ... Ezr 2:20 8673
servants, were three hundred *n* ... Ezr 2:58 8673
twelve bullocks for all Israel, *n* ... Ezr 8:35 8673
children of Ater of Hezekiah, *n* ... Neh 7:21 8673
The children of Gibeon, *n* ... Neh 7:25 8673
servants, were three hundred *n* ... Neh 7:60 8673
And there were *n* and six ... Jer 52:23 8673
the days, three hundred and *n* days ... Eze 4:5 8673
n days shalt thou eat thereof ... Eze 4:9 8673
and the length thereof *n* cubits ... Eze 41:12 8673
a thousand two hundred and *n* days ... Dan 12:11 8673
astray, doth he not leave the *n* ... Mt 18:12 *1768*
more of that sheep, than of the *n* ... Mt 18:13 *1768*
one of them, doth not leave the *n* ... Lk 15:4 *1768*
that repenteth, more than over *n* ... Lk 15:7 *1768*

NINEVE *(nen'-e-ve)* {1} See NINEVEH, NINEVITES. *Same as Nineveh.*
The men of *N* shall rise up in the ... Lk 11:32 *3535*

NINEVEH *(nin'-e-veh)* {18} See NINEVE. *Capital of Assyria.*
went forth Asshur, and builded *N* ... Gen 10:11 5210
And Resen between *N* and Calah ... Gen 10:12 5210
went and returned, and dwelt at *N* ... 2Kin 19:36 5210
went and returned, and dwelt at *N* ... Is 37:37 5210
Arise, go to *N*, that great city, ... Jonah 1:2 5210
Arise, go unto *N*, that great city ... Jonah 3:2 5210
So Jonah arose, and went unto *N* ... Jonah 3:3 5210
Now *N* was an exceeding great city ... Jonah 3:3 5210
days, and *N* shall be overthrown ... Jonah 3:4 5210
So the people of *N* believed God ... Jonah 3:5 5210
For word came unto the king of *N* ... Jonah 3:6 5210
published through *N* by the decree ... Jonah 3:7 5210
And should not I spare *N*, that ... Jonah 4:11 5210
The burden of *N* ... Nah 1:1 5210
But *N* is of old like a pool of ... Nah 2:8 5210
thee, and say, *N* is laid waste ... Nah 3:7 5210
will make *N* a desolation, and dry ... Zeph 2:13 5210
The men of *N* shall rise in ... Mt 12:41 *3536*

NINEVITES *(nin'-e-vites)* {1} *Inhabitants of Nineveh.*
as Jonas was a sign unto the *N* ... Lk 11:30 *3536*

NINTH {35}
in the *n* day of the month at even ... Lev 23:32 8672
yet of old fruit until the *n* year ... Lev 25:22 8671
On the *n* day Abidan the son of ... Num 7:60 8671
In the *n* year of Hoshea the king ... 2Kin 17:6 8671
that is the *n* year of Hoshea king ... 2Kin 18:10 8672
pass in the *n* year of his reign ... 2Kin 25:1 8671
on the *n* day of the fourth month ... 2Kin 25:3 8672
Johanan the eighth, Elzabad the *n* ... 1Chr 12:12 8671
The *n* to Jeshua, the tenth to ... 1Chr 24:11 8671
The *n* to Mattaniah, he, his sons, ... 1Chr 25:16 8671
The *n* captain for the *n* month ... 1Chr 27:12 8671
for the *n* month was Abiezer the ... 1Chr 27:12 8671
n year of his reign was diseased ... 2Chr 16:12 8672
It was the *n* month, on the ... Ezr 10:9 8671
king of Judah, in the *n* month ... Jer 36:9 8671
in the winterhouse in the *n* month ... Jer 36:22 8671
In the *n* year of Zedekiah king of ... Jer 39:1 8671
the *n* day of the month, the city ... Jer 39:2 8672
pass in the *n* year of his reign ... Jer 52:4 8671
in the *n* day of the month, the ... Jer 52:6 8672
Again in the *n* year, in the tenth ... Eze 24:1 8671
and twentieth day of the *n* month ... Hag 2:10 8671
and twentieth day of the *n* month ... Hag 2:18 8671
in the fourth day of the *n* month ... Zec 7:1 8671
sixth and *n* hour, and did likewise ... Mt 20:5 *1766*
over all the land unto the *n* hour ... Mt 27:45 *1766*
about the *n* hour Jesus cried with ... Mt 27:46 *1766*
the whole land until the *n* hour ... Mk 15:33 *1766*
at the *n* hour Jesus cried with a ... Mk 15:34 *1766*
all the earth until the *n* hour ... Lk 23:44 *1766*
hour of prayer, being the *n* hour ... Acts 3:1 *1766*
n hour of the day an angel of God ... Acts 10:3 *1766*
at the *n* hour I prayed in my ... Acts 10:30 *1766*
the *n*, a topaz ... Rev 21:20 *1766*

NISAN *(ni'-san)* {2} See ABIB. *First month of the Hebrew year.*
And it came to pass in the month *N* ... Neh 2:1 5212
first month, that is, the month *N* ... Est 3:7 5212

NISROCH *(nis'-rok)* {2} *An Assyrian god.*
in the house of *N* his god ... 2Kin 19:37 5268
in the house of *N* his god ... Is 37:38 5268

NITRE {2}
weather, and as vinegar upon *n* ... Prov 25:20 5427
For though thou wash thee with *n* ... Jer 2:22 5427

NO *(Also see* APPENDIX.) {5} *A city on the Nile.*
I will punish the multitude of *N* ... Jer 46:25 4996
and will execute judgments in *N* ... Eze 30:14 4996
I will cut off the multitude of *N* ... Eze 30:15 4996
N shall be rent asunder, and Noph ... Eze 30:16 4996
Art thou better than populous *N* ... Nah 3:8 4996

NOADIAH *(no-a-di'-ah)* {2}
1. Son of Binnui.
N the son of Binnui, Levites ... Ezr 8:33 5129
2. An opponent of Nehemiah.
works, and on the prophetess *N* ... Neh 6:14 5129

NOAH *(no'-ah)* {51} See NOAH'S, NOE.
1. Son of Lamech; built the ark.
And he called his name *N*, saying, ... Gen 5:29 5146
he begat *N* five hundred ninety ... Gen 5:30 5146
N was five hundred years old ... Gen 5:32 5146
N begat Shem, Ham, and Japheth ... Gen 5:32 5146
But *N* found grace in the eyes of ... Gen 6:8 5146
These are the generations of *N* ... Gen 6:9 5146
N was a just man and perfect in ... Gen 6:9 5146
generations, and *N* walked with God ... Gen 6:9 5146
N begat three sons, Shem, Ham, and ... Gen 6:10 5146
And God said unto *N*, The end of ... Gen 6:13 5146
Thus did *N* ... Gen 6:22 5146
And the LORD said unto *N*, Come ... Gen 7:1 5146
N did according unto all that the ... Gen 7:5 5146
N was six hundred years old when ... Gen 7:6 5146
N went in, and his sons, and his ... Gen 7:7 5146
two unto *N* into the ark, the male ... Gen 7:9 5146
female, as God had commanded *N* ... Gen 7:9 5146
In the selfsame day entered *N* ... Gen 7:13 5146
and Ham, and Japheth, the sons of *N* ... Gen 7:13 5146
they went in unto *N* into the ark ... Gen 7:15 5146
N only remained alive, and they ... Gen 7:23 5146
And God remembered *N*, and every ... Gen 8:1 5146
that *N* opened the window of the ... Gen 8:6 5146
so *N* knew that the waters were ... Gen 8:11 5146
N removed the covering of the ark ... Gen 8:13 5146
And God spake unto *N*, saying, ... Gen 8:15 5146
N went forth, and his sons, and his ... Gen 8:18 5146
N builded an altar unto the LORD ... Gen 8:20 5146
And God blessed *N* and his sons, and ... Gen 9:1 5146
And God spake unto *N*, and to his ... Gen 9:8 5146
And God said unto *N*, This is the ... Gen 9:17 5146
And the sons of *N*, that went forth ... Gen 9:18 5146
These are the three sons of *N* ... Gen 9:19 5146
N began to be an husbandman, and ... Gen 9:20 5146
N awoke from his wine, and knew ... Gen 9:24 5146
N lived after the flood three ... Gen 9:28 5146
all the days of *N* were nine ... Gen 9:29 5146
the generations of the sons of *N* ... Gen 10:1 5146
are the families of the sons of *N* ... Gen 10:32 5146
N, Shem, Ham, and Japheth ... 1Chr 1:4 5146
is as the waters of *N* unto me ... Is 54:9 5146
of *N* should no more go over the ... Is 54:9 5146
Though these three men, *N* ... Eze 14:14 5146
Though *N*, Daniel, and Job, were in ... Eze 14:20 5146
By faith *N*, being warned of God ... Heb 11:7 *3575*
of God waited in the days of *N* ... 1Pet 3:20 *3575*
but saved *N* the eighth person, a ... 2Pet 2:5 *3575*
2. A daughter of Zelophehad.
of Zelophehad were Mahlah, and *N* ... Num 26:33 5270
Mahlah, *N*, and Hoglah, and Milcah, ... Num 27:1 5270
and Hoglah, and Milcah, and *N* ... Num 36:11 5270
of his daughters, Mahlah, and *N* ... Josh 17:3 5270

NOAH'S *(no'-ahz)* {2} *Refers to Noah 1.*
the six hundredth year of *N* life ... Gen 7:11 5146
N wife, and the three wives of his ... Gen 7:13 5146

NO-AMON See NO.

NOB *(nob)* {6} *A Levitical city in Benjamin.*
Then came David to *N* to Ahimelech ... 1Sa 21:1 5011
saw the son of Jesse coming to *N* ... 1Sa 22:9 5011
house, the priests that were in *N* ... 1Sa 22:11 5011
And *N*, the city of the priests, ... 1Sa 22:19 5011
And at Anathoth, *N*, Ananiah, ... Neh 11:32 5011
yet shall he remain at *N* that day ... Is 10:32 5011

NOBAH *(no'-bah)* {3} See KENAH, NOPHAH.
1. A Manassite who captured an Amorite city.
N went and took Kenath, and the ... Num 32:42 5025
villages thereof, and called it *N* ... Num 32:42 5025
2. A city in the Trachonitis.
dwelt in tents on the east of *N* ... Judg 8:11 5025

NOBLE {7}
n Asnapper brought over, and set ... Ezr 4:10 3358
one of the king's most *n* princes ... Est 6:9 6579
Yet I had planted thee a *n* vine ... Jer 2:21
These were more *n* than those in ... Acts 17:11 *2104*
places, most *n* Felix, with all ... Acts 24:3 *2908*
said, I am not mad, most *n* Festus ... Acts 26:25 *2908*
not many mighty, not many *n* ... 1Cor 1:26 *2104*

NOBLEMAN {3}
A certain *n* went into a far ... Lk 19:12 *2104,444*
And there was a certain *n*, whose ... Jn 4:46 *937*
The *n* saith unto him, Sir, come ... Jn 4:49 *937*

NOBLES {30}
upon the *n* of the children of ... Ex 24:11 678
the *n* of the people digged it, by ... Num 21:18 5081
over the *n* among the people ... Judg 5:13 117
to the *n* that were in his city, ... 1Kin 21:8 2715
the *n* who were the inhabitants in ... 1Kin 21:11 2715
captains of hundreds, and the *n* ... 2Chr 23:20 117
nor to the priests, nor to the *n* ... Neh 2:16 2715
but their *n* put not their necks ... Neh 3:5 117
and rose up, and said unto the *n* ... Neh 4:14 2715
And I said unto the *n*, and to the ... Neh 4:19 2715
with myself, and I rebuked the *n* ... Neh 5:7 2715
Moreover in those days the *n* of ... Neh 6:17 2715
heart to gather together the *n* ... Neh 7:5 2715
clave to their brethren, their *n* ... Neh 10:29 117
I contended with the *n* of Judah ... Neh 13:17 2715
power of Persia and Media, the *n* ... Est 1:3 6579
The *n* held their peace, and their ... Job 29:10 5057
Make their *n* like Oreb, and like ... Ps 83:11 5081
their *n* with fetters of iron ... Ps 149:8 3513
By me princes rule, and *n*, even ... Prov 8:16 5081
when thy king is the son of *n* ... Eccl 10:17 2715
may go into the gates of the *n* ... Is 13:2 5081
They shall call the *n* thereof to ... Is 34:12 2715
and have brought down all their *n* ... Is 43:14 1281
their *n* have sent their little ... Jer 14:3 117
all the *n* of Judah and Jerusalem ... Jer 27:20 2715
their *n* shall be of themselves, ... Jer 30:21 117
Babylon slew all the *n* of Judah ... Jer 39:6 2715
the decree of the king and his *n* ... Jonah 3:7 1419
thy *n* shall dwell in the dust ... Nah 3:18 117

NOD *(nod)* {1} *A land east of Eden.*
LORD, and dwelt in the land of *N* ... Gen 4:16 5113

NODAB *(no'-dab)* {1} *Name of tribe east of the Jordan.*
with Jetur, and Nephish, and *N* ... 1Chr 5:19 5114

NOE *(no'-e)* {5} See NOAH. *Greek form of Noah.*
But as the days of *N* were ... Mt 24:37 *3575*
until the day that *N* entered into ... Mt 24:38 *3575*
of Sem, which was the son of *N* ... Lk 3:36 *3575*
And as it was in the days of *N* ... Lk 17:26 *3575*
until the day that *N* entered into ... Lk 17:27 *3575*

NOGAH *(no'-gah)* {2} *A son of David.*
And *N*, and Nepheg, and Japhia, ... 1Chr 3:7 5052
And *N*, and Nepheg, and Japhia, ... 1Chr 14:6 5052

NOHAH *(no'-hah)* {1} *A son of Benjamin.*
N the fourth, and Rapha the fifth ... 1Chr 8:2 5119

NOISE {88}
the *n* of the trumpet, and the ... Ex 20:18 6963
when Joshua heard the *n* of the ... Ex 32:17 6963
There is a *n* of war in the camp ... Ex 32:17 6963
but the *n* of them that sing do I ... Ex 32:18 6963
nor make any *n* with your voice, ... Josh 6:10 8085
the *n* of archers in the places of ... Judg 5:11 6963
heard the *n* of the shout, they ... 1Sa 4:6 6963
What meaneth the *n* of this great ... 1Sa 4:6 6963
Eli heard the *n* of the crying ... 1Sa 4:14 6963
What meaneth the *n* of this tumult ... 1Sa 4:14 6963
that the *n* that was in the host ... 1Sa 14:19 1995
Wherefore is this *n* of the city ... 1Kin 1:41 6963
This is the *n* that ye have heard ... 1Kin 1:45 6963
Syrians to hear a *n* of chariots ... 2Kin 7:6 6963
a *n* of horses, even the *n* of ... 2Kin 7:6 6963
Athaliah heard the *n* of the guard ... 2Kin 11:13 6963
making a *n* with psalteries and ... 1Chr 15:28 8085
heard the *n* of the people running ... 2Chr 23:12 6963
n of the shout of joy from the ... Ezr 3:13 6963
n of the weeping of the people ... Ezr 3:13 6963
and the *n* was heard afar off ... Ezr 3:13 6963
or the *n* of his tabernacle ... Job 36:29 8663
The *n* thereof sheweth concerning ... Job 36:33 7452
attentively the *n* of his voice ... Job 37:2 7267
play skilfully with a loud *n* ... Ps 33:3 8643
deep at the *n* of thy waterspouts ... Ps 42:7 6963
in my complaint, and make a *n* ... Ps 55:2 1949
they make a *n* like a dog, and go ... Ps 59:6 1993
and let them make a *n* like a dog ... Ps 59:14 1993
Which stilleth the *n* of the seas ... Ps 65:7 7588
the *n* of their waves, and the ... Ps 65:7 7588
Make a joyful *n* unto God, all ye ... Ps 66:1
make a joyful *n* unto the God of ... Ps 81:1
than the *n* of many waters ... Ps 93:4 6963
let us make a joyful *n* to the ... Ps 95:1
make a joyful *n* unto him with ... Ps 95:2
Make a joyful *n* unto the LORD ... Ps 98:4
make a loud *n*, and rejoice, and ... Ps 98:4 6476
make a joyful *n* before the LORD ... Ps 98:6
Make a joyful *n* unto the LORD ... Ps 100:1
of the warrior is with confused *n* ... Is 9:5
The *n* of a multitude in the ... Is 13:4 6963
a tumultuous *n* of the kingdoms of ... Is 13:4 6963
the grave, and the *n* of thy viols ... Is 14:11 1998
a *n* like the *n* of the seas ... Is 17:12 1993
the *n* of them that rejoice endeth ... Is 24:8 7588
that he who fleeth from the *n* of ... Is 24:18 6963
bring down the *n* of strangers ... Is 25:5 7588
and with earthquake, and great *n* ... Is 29:6 6963
abase himself for the *n* of them ... Is 31:4 1995
At the *n* of the tumult the people ... Is 33:3 6963
A voice of *n* from the city, a ... Is 66:6 7588

my heart maketh a *n* in me ... Jer 4:19 1993
flee for the *n* of the horsemen ... Jer 4:29 6963
the *n* of the bruit is come, and a ... Jer 10:22 6963
with the *n* of a great tumult he ... Jer 11:16 6963
A *n* shall come even to the ends ... Jer 25:31 7588
Pharaoh king of Egypt is but a *n* ... Jer 46:17 7588
At the *n* of the stamping of the ... Jer 47:3 6963
is moved at the *n* of their fall ... Jer 49:21 6963
at the cry the *n* thereof was ... Jer 49:21 6963
At the *n* of the taking of Babylon ... Jer 50:46 6963
a *n* of their voice is uttered ... Jer 51:55 7588
they have made a *n* in the house ... Lam 2:7 6963
I heard the *n* of their wings, ... Eze 1:24 6963
like the *n* of great waters, as ... Eze 1:24 6963
of speech, as the *n* of an host ... Eze 1:24 6963
I heard also the *n* of the wings ... Eze 3:13 6963
the *n* of the wheels over against ... Eze 3:13 6963
them, and a *n* of a great rushing ... Eze 3:13 6963
thereof, by the *n* of his roaring ... Eze 19:7 6963
shake at the *n* of the horsemen ... Eze 26:10 6963
I will cause the *n* of thy songs ... Eze 26:13 1995
and as I prophesied, there was a *n* ... Eze 37:7 6963
voice was like a *n* of many waters ... Eze 43:2 6963
Like the *n* of chariots on the ... Joel 2:5 6963
like the *n* of a flame of fire ... Joel 2:5 6963
away from me the *n* of thy songs ... Amos 5:23 1995
they shall make great *n* by reason ... Mic 2:12 1949
The *n* of a whip, and the *n* of ... Nah 3:2 6963
that there shall be the *n* of a ... Zeph 1:10 6963
and make a *n* as through wine ... Zec 9:15 6963
and the people making a *n*, ... Mt 9:23 *2350*
shall pass away with a great *n* ... 2Pet 3:10 *4500*
as it were the *n* of thunder ... Rev 6:1 *5456*

NOISED {4}
his fame was *n* throughout all the ... Josh 6:27
it was *n* that he was in the house ... Mk 2:1 *191*
all these sayings were *n* abroad ... Lk 1:65 *1255*
Now when this was *n* abroad ... Acts 2:6 *1096,5408*

NOISOME {4}
fowler, and from the *n* pestilence ... Ps 91:3 1942
If I cause *n* beasts to pass ... Eze 14:15 7451
the *n* beast, and the pestilence, ... Eze 14:21 7451
and there fell a *n* and grievous ... Rev 16:2 *2556*

NON *(non)* {1} See NUN. *Son of Elishama.*
N his son, Jehoshuah his son ... 1Chr 7:27 5126

NONE {358}
n of us shall withhold from thee ... Gen 23:6 376,3808
this is *n* other but the house of ... Gen 28:17 369
There is *n* greater in this house ... Gen 39:9 369
there was *n* of the men of the ... Gen 39:11 369
but there was *n* that could ... Gen 41:8 369
there is *n* that can interpret it ... Gen 41:15 369
but there was *n* that could ... Gen 41:24 369
there is *n* so discreet and wise as ... Gen 41:39 369
is *n* like unto the LORD our God ... Ex 8:10 369
is *n* like me in all the earth ... Ex 9:14 369
such as there was *n* like it in ... Ex 9:24 3808
such as there was *n* like it ... Ex 11:6 3808
n of you shall go out at the door ... Ex 12:22 3808
I will put *n* of these diseases ... Ex 15:26 3808
sabbath, in it there shall be *n* ... Ex 16:26 3808
for to gather, and they found *n* ... Ex 16:27 3808
n shall appear before me empty ... Ex 23:15 3808
n shall appear before me empty ... Ex 34:20 3808
N of you shall approach to any ... Lev 18:6 376,3808
There shall *n* be defiled for the ... Lev 21:1 3808
ye shall leave *n* of it until the ... Lev 22:30 3808
And if the man have *n* to redeem it ... Lev 25:26 3808
down, and *n* shall make you afraid ... Lev 26:6 369
ye shall flee when *n* pursueth you ... Lev 26:17 369
they shall fall when *n* pursueth ... Lev 26:36 369
before a sword, when *n* pursueth ... Lev 26:37 369
N devoted, which shall be devoted ... Lev 27:29 376,3808
unto the sons of Kohath he gave *n* ... Num 7:9 3808
They shall leave *n* of it unto the ... Num 9:12 3808
until there was *n* left him alive ... Num 21:35 1115
she bound her soul, of *n* effect ... Num 30:8 6565
Surely *n* of the men that came up ... Num 32:11
every city, we left *n* to remain ... Deut 2:34 3808
we smote him until *n* was left to ... Deut 3:3 1115
there is *n* else beside him ... Deut 4:35 369
there is *n* else ... Deut 4:39 369
Thou shalt have *n* other gods ... Deut 5:7 3808
will put *n* of the evil diseases ... Deut 7:15 3808
cried, and there was *n* to save her ... Deut 22:27 369
thou shalt have *n* to rescue them ... Deut 28:31 369
shalt have *n* assurance of thy ... Deut 28:66 3808
is gone, and there is *n* shut up ... Deut 32:36 657
There is *n* like unto the God of ... Deut 33:26 369
n went out, and *n* came in ... Josh 6:1 369
so that they let *n* of them remain ... Josh 8:22 1115
there shall *n* of you be freed ... Josh 9:23 3808
n moved his tongue against any of ... Josh 10:21 3808
he let *n* remain ... Josh 10:28 3808
he let *n* remain in it ... Josh 10:30 3808
until he had left him *n* remaining ... Josh 10:33 1115
he left *n* remaining, according to ... Josh 10:37 3808
he left *n* remaining ... Josh 10:39 3808
he left *n* remaining, but utterly ... Josh 10:40 3808
until they left them *n* remaining ... Josh 11:8 1115
strength, Israel burned *n* of them ... Josh 11:13 3808
There was *n* of the Anakims left ... Josh 11:22 3808
of Levi he gave *n* inheritance ... Josh 13:14 3808
he gave *n* inheritance among them ... Josh 14:3 3808
But *n* answered ... Judg 19:28 369
there came *n* to the camp from ... Judg 21:8 376,3808
there were *n* of the inhabitants ... Judg 21:9 369,376
for there is *n* to redeem it ... Ruth 4:4 369
There is *n* holy as the LORD ... 1Sa 2:2 369
for there is *n* beside thee ... 1Sa 2:2 369
did let *n* of his words fall to ... 1Sa 3:19 3808
that there is *n* like him among ... 1Sa 10:24 369
So *n* of the people tasted any ... 1Sa 14:24 3808
David said, There is *n* like that ... 1Sa 21:9 369
there is *n* that sheweth me that ... 1Sa 22:8 369
there is *n* of you that is sorry ... 1Sa 22:8 369
for there is *n* like thee, neither ... 2Sa 7:22 369
there was *n* to part them, but the ... 2Sa 14:6 369
n can turn to the right hand or ... 2Sa 14:19 376
was *n* to be so much praised as ... 2Sa 14:25 376,3808
Beware that *n* touch the young man ... 2Sa 18:12
looked, but there was *n* to save ... 2Sa 22:42 369
so that there was *n* like thee ... 1Kin 3:12 3808
is God, and that there is *n* else ... 1Kin 8:60 369
n were of silver ... 1Kin 10:21 369
there was *n* that followed the ... 1Kin 12:20 3808
n was exempted ... 1Kin 15:22 369
But there was *n* like unto Ahab, ... 1Kin 21:25 3808
whom I stand, I will receive *n* ... 2Kin 5:16
And one of his servants said, *N* ... 2Kin 6:12 3808
and there shall be *n* to bury her ... 2Kin 9:10 369
then let *n* go forth nor escape ... 2Kin 9:15 408
until he left him *n* remaining ... 2Kin 10:11 1115
let *n* be wanting ... 2Kin 10:19 376,408
you *n* of the servants of the LORD ... 2Kin 10:23
let *n* come forth ... 2Kin 10:25 408
there was *n* left but the tribe of ... 2Kin 17:18 3808
so that after him was *n* like him ... 2Kin 18:5 3808
n remained, save the poorest sort ... 2Kin 24:14 3808
N ought to carry the ark of God ... 1Chr 15:2 3808
there is *n* like thee, neither is ... 1Chr 17:20 369
And Eliezer had *n* other sons ... 1Chr 23:17 3808
a shadow, and there is *n* abiding ... 1Chr 29:15 369
such as *n* of the kings have had ... 2Chr 1:12 3808
there were *n* such seen before in ... 2Chr 9:11 3808
n were of silver ... 2Chr 9:20 369
we have *n* inheritance in the son ... 2Chr 10:16 3808
n go out or come in to Asa king ... 2Chr 16:1 1115
so that *n* is able to withstand ... 2Chr 20:6 369
fallen to the earth, and *n* escaped ... 2Chr 20:24 369
But let *n* come into the house of ... 2Chr 23:6 408
that *n* which was unclean in any ... 2Chr 23:19 3808
found there *n* of the sons of Levi ... Ezr 8:15 3808
n of us put off our clothes, ... Neh 4:23 369
to the law; *n* did compel ... Est 1:8 369
for *n* might enter into the king's ... Est 4:2 369
that there is *n* like him in the ... Job 1:8 369
that there is *n* like him in the ... Job 2:3 369
and *n* spake a word unto him ... Job 2:13 369
let it look for light, but have *n* ... Job 3:9 369
there is *n* that can deliver out ... Job 10:7 369
down, and *n* shall make thee afraid ... Job 11:19 369
because it is *n* of his ... Job 18:15 1097
There shall *n* of his meat be left ... Job 20:21 369
and him that had *n* to help him ... Job 29:12 3808
there was *n* of you that convinced ... Job 32:12 369
But *n* saith, Where is God my ... Job 35:10 3808
but *n* giveth answer, because of ... Job 35:12 3808
N is so fierce that dare stir him ... Job 41:10 3808
while there is *n* to deliver ... Ps 7:2 369
his wickedness till thou find *n* ... Ps 10:15 1077
there is *n* that doeth good ... Ps 14:1 369
there is *n* that doeth good, no, ... Ps 14:3 369
but there was *n* to save them ... Ps 18:41 369
for there is *n* to help ... Ps 22:11 369
n can keep alive his own soul ... Ps 22:29 3808
let *n* that wait on thee be ... Ps 25:3 3808
devices of the people of *n* effect ... Ps 33:10 5106
n of them that trust in him shall ... Ps 34:22 3808
n of his steps shall slide ... Ps 37:31 3808
N of them can by any means ... Ps 49:7 25,3808
pieces, and there be *n* to deliver ... Ps 50:22 369
there is *n* that doeth good ... Ps 53:1 369
there is *n* that doeth good, no, ... Ps 53:3 369
to take pity, but there was *n* ... Ps 69:20 369
and for comforters, but I found *n* ... Ps 69:20 3808
let *n* dwell in their tents ... Ps 69:25 408
for there is *n* to deliver him ... Ps 71:11 369
there is *n* upon earth that I ... Ps 73:25 3808
n of the men of might have found ... Ps 76:5 3808
and there was *n* to bury them ... Ps 79:3 369
and Israel would *n* of me ... Ps 81:11 3808
gods there is *n* like unto thee ... Ps 86:8 369
fell down, and there was *n* to help ... Ps 107:12 369
Let there be *n* to extend mercy ... Ps 109:12 408
when as yet there was *n* of them ... Ps 139:16 259,3808
counsel, and would *n* of my reproof ... Prov 1:25 3808
They would *n* of my counsel ... Prov 1:30 3808
N that go unto her return again, ... Prov 2:19 3808
and choose *n* of his ways ... Prov 3:31 408
twins, and *n* is barren among them ... Song 4:2 369
together, and *n* shall quench them ... Is 1:31 369
N shall be weary nor stumble ... Is 5:27 369
n shall slumber nor sleep ... Is 5:27 3808
away safe, and *n* shall deliver it ... Is 5:29 369
there was *n* that moved the wing, ... Is 10:14 3808
is persecuted, and *n* hindereth ... Is 14:6 1097
n shall be alone in his appointed ... Is 14:31 369
down, and *n* shall make them afraid ... Is 17:2 369
so he shall open, and *n* shall shut ... Is 22:22 369
and he shall shut, and *n* shall open ... Is 22:22 369
n shall pass through it for ever ... Is 34:10 369
but *n* shall be there, and all her ... Is 34:12 369
shall fail, *n* shall want her mate ... Is 34:16 802,3808
needy seek water, and there is *n* ... Is 41:17 369
there is *n* that sheweth, yea, ... Is 41:26 369
there is *n* that declareth, yea, ... Is 41:26 369
there is *n* that heareth your ... Is 41:26 369
are for a prey, and *n* delivereth ... Is 42:22 369
for a spoil, and *n* saith, Restore ... Is 42:22 369
there is *n* that can deliver out ... Is 43:13 369
n considereth in his heart, ... Is 44:19 3808
I am the LORD, and there is *n* else ... Is 45:5 369
west, that there is *n* beside me ... Is 45:6 657
I am the LORD, and there is *n* else ... Is 45:6 369
and there is *n* else, there is no ... Is 45:14 369
and there is *n* else ... Is 45:18 369
there is *n* beside me ... Is 45:21 369
for I am God, and there is *n* else ... Is 45:22 369
for I am God, and there is *n* else ... Is 46:9 369
I am God, and there is *n* like me ... Is 46:9 657
heart, I am, and *n* else beside me ... Is 47:8 657
thou hast said, *N* seeth me ... Is 47:10 369
heart, I am, and *n* else beside me ... Is 47:10 657
n shall save thee ... Is 47:15 369
I called, was there *n* to answer ... Is 50:2 369
There is *n* to guide her among all ... Is 51:18 369
n considering that the righteous ... Is 57:1 369
N calleth for justice, nor any ... Is 59:4 369
look for judgment, but there is *n* ... Is 59:11 369
of the people there was *n* with me ... Is 63:3 369,376
I looked, and there was *n* to help ... Is 63:5 369
that there was *n* to uphold ... Is 63:5 369
there is *n* that calleth upon thy ... Is 64:7 369
when I called, *n* did answer ... Is 66:4 369
burn that *n* can quench it because ... Jer 4:4 369
they have *n* understanding ... Jer 4:22 3808
and *n* shall fray them away ... Jer 7:33 369
so that *n* can pass through them ... Jer 9:10 376,1097
that *n* passeth through ... Jer 9:12 1997
and *n* shall gather them ... Jer 9:22 369
as there is *n* like unto thee ... Jer 10:6 369
there is *n* like unto thee ... Jer 10:7 369
there is *n* to stretch forth my ... Jer 10:20 369
be shut up, and *n* shall open them ... Jer 13:19 369
and they shall have *n* to bury them ... Jer 14:16 369
burn that *n* can quench it, ... Jer 21:12 369
that *n* doth return from his ... Jer 23:14 1115
is great, so that *n* is like it ... Jer 30:7 369
quiet, and *n* shall make him afraid ... Jer 30:10 369
There is *n* to plead thy cause, ... Jer 30:13 369
that *n* should serve himself of ... Jer 34:9 1115
that *n* should serve themselves of ... Jer 34:10 1115
for unto this day they drink *n* ... Jer 35:14 3808
He shall have *n* to sit upon the ... Jer 36:30 3808
n of them shall remain or escape ... Jer 42:17 3808
Judah, to leave you *n* to remain ... Jer 44:7 1115
So that *n* of the remnant of Judah ... Jer 44:14 3808
for *n* shall return but such as ... Jer 44:14 3808
ease, and *n* shall make him afraid ... Jer 46:27 369
n shall tread with shouting ... Jer 48:33 3808
n shall gather up him that ... Jer 49:5 369
and *n* shall dwell therein ... Jer 50:3 3808
n shall return in vain ... Jer 50:9 3808
sought for, and there shall be *n* ... Jer 50:20 369
let *n* thereof escape ... Jer 50:29 408
and fall, and *n* shall raise him up ... Jer 50:32 369
that *n* shall remain in it, ... Jer 51:62 1115
lovers she hath *n* to comfort her ... Lam 1:2 369
because *n* come to the solemn ... Lam 1:4 1997
of the enemy, and *n* did help her ... Lam 1:7 369
there is *n* to comfort her ... Lam 1:17 369
there is *n* to comfort me ... Lam 1:21 369
anger *n* escaped nor remained ... Lam 2:22 3808
there is *n* that doth deliver us ... Lam 5:8 369
n of them shall remain, nor of ... Eze 7:11 3808
but *n* goeth to the battle ... Eze 7:14 369
seek peace, and there shall be *n* ... Eze 7:25 369
There shall *n* of my words be ... Eze 12:28 3808
N eye pitied thee, to do any of ... Eze 16:5 3808
whereas *n* followeth thee to ... Eze 16:34 3808
hath spoiled *n* by violence ... Eze 18:7 3808
but I found *n* ... Eze 22:30 3808
To the end that *n* of all the ... Eze 31:14 3808
N of his sins that he hath ... Eze 33:16 3808
that *n* shall pass through ... Eze 33:28 369
n did search or seek after them ... Eze 34:6 369
and *n* shall make them afraid ... Eze 34:28 369
their land, and *n* made them afraid ... Eze 39:26 369
have left *n* of them any more ... Eze 39:28 3808
them all was found *n* like Daniel ... Dan 1:19 3808
there is *n* other that can shew it ... Dan 2:11 3809
n can stay his hand, or say unto ... Dan 4:35 3809
could find *n* occasion nor fault ... Dan 6:4 3809
there was *n* that could deliver ... Dan 8:7 3808
the vision, but *n* understood it ... Dan 8:27 369
there is *n* that holdeth with me ... Dan 10:21 369
will, and *n* shall stand before him ... Dan 11:16 369
to his end, and *n* shall help him ... Dan 11:45 369
n of the wicked shall understand ... Dan 12:10 3808
n shall deliver her out of mine ... Hos 2:10 3808
take away, and *n* shall rescue him ... Hos 5:14 369
there is *n* among them that ... Hos 7:7 369
High, *n* at all would exalt him ... Hos 11:7 3808
n iniquity in me that were sin ... Hos 12:8 3808
I am the LORD your God, and *n* else ... Joel 2:27 369
there is *n* to raise her up ... Amos 5:2 369
there be *n* to quench it in ... Amos 5:6 369
there is *n* understanding in him ... Obad 7 369
Therefore thou shalt have *n* that ... Mic 2:5 3808
n evil can come upon us ... Mic 3:11 3808
and *n* shall make them afraid ... Mic 4:4 369

N

in pieces, and *n* can deliver ... Mic 5:8 369
there is *n* upright among men ... Mic 7:2 369
but *n* shall look back ... Nah 2:8 369
for there is *n* end of the store ... Nah 2:9 369
whelp, and *n* made them afraid ... Nah 2:11 369
there is *n* end of their corpses ... Nah 3:3 369
I am, and there is *n* beside me ... Zeph 2:15 657
streets waste, that *n* passeth by ... Zeph 3:6 1097
man, that there is *n* inhabitant ... Zeph 3:6 369
down, and *n* shall make them afraid ... Zeph 3:13 369
clothe you, but there is *n* warm ... Hag 1:6 369
let *n* of you imagine evil against ... Zec 7:10 408
let *n* of you imagine evil in your ... Zec 8:17 408
let *n* deal treacherously against ... Mal 2:15 408
seeking rest, and findeth *n* ... Mt 12:43 *3756*
God of *n* effect by your tradition ... Mt 15:6 *208*
there is *n* good but one, that is, ... Mt 19:17 *3762*
But found *n*: yea, though ... Mt 26:60 *3756*
witnesses came, yet found they *n* ... Mt 26:60 *3756*
Making the word of God of *n* ... Mk 7:13 *208*
there is *n* good but one, that is, ... Mk 10:18 *3762*
There is *n* other commandment ... Mk 12:31 *3756*
and there is *n* other but he ... Mk 12:32 *3756*
and found *n*. ... Mk 14:55 *3756*
There is *n* of thy kindred that is ... Lk 1:61 *3762*
let him impart to him that hath *n* ... Lk 3:11 *3361*
But unto *n* of them was Elias sent ... Lk 4:26 *3762*
n of them was cleansed, saving ... Lk 4:27 *3762*
and finding *n*, he saith, I will ... Lk 11:24 *3361*
sought fruit thereon, and found *n* ... Lk 13:6 *3756*
fruit on this fig tree, and find *n* ... Lk 13:7 *3756*
That *n* of those men which were ... Lk 14:24 *3762*
n is good, save one, that is, God ... Lk 18:19 *3762*
they understood *n* of these things ... Lk 18:34 *3762*
that there was *n* other boat there ... Jn 6:22 *3756*
yet *n* of you keepeth the law ... Jn 7:19 *3762*
saw *n* but the woman, he said unto ... Jn 8:10 *3367*
the works which *n* other man did ... Jn 15:24 *3762*
n of you asketh me, Whither goest ... Jn 16:5 *3762*
n of them is lost, but the son of ... Jn 17:12 *3762*
thou gavest me have I lost *n* ... Jn 18:9 *3762*
n of the disciples durst ask him, ... Jn 21:12 *3762*
said, Silver and gold have I *n* ... Acts 3:6 *3756*
for there is *n* other name under ... Acts 4:12 *3777*
he gave him *n* inheritance in it, ... Acts 7:5 *3756*
yet he was fallen upon *n* of them ... Acts 8:16 *3762*
that *n* of these things which ye ... Acts 8:24 *3367*
preaching the word to *n* but unto ... Acts 11:19 *3367*
cared for *n* of those things ... Acts 18:17 *3762*
But *n* of these things move me, ... Acts 20:24 *3762*
that he should forbid *n* of his ... Acts 24:23 *3367*
but if there be *n* of these things ... Acts 25:11 *3762*
they brought *n* accusation of such ... Acts 25:18 *3762*
saying *n* other things than those ... Acts 26:22 *3762*
for I am persuaded that *n* of ... Acts 26:26 3762
There is *n* righteous, no, not one ... Rom 3:10 *3756*
There is *n* that understandeth, ... Rom 3:11 *3756*
there is *n* that seeketh after God ... Rom 3:11 *3756*
there is *n* that doeth good, no, ... Rom 3:12 *3756*
and the promise made of *n* effect ... Rom 4:14 *2673*
Spirit of Christ, he is *n* of his ... Rom 8:9 *3756*
word of God hath taken *n* effect ... Rom 9:6 *1601*
For *n* of us liveth to himself, and ... Rom 14:7 *3762*
God that I baptized *n* of you ... 1Cor 1:14 *3762*
Christ should be made of *n* effect ... 1Cor 1:17 *2758*
Which *n* of the princes of this ... 1Cor 2:8 *3762*
wives be as though they had *n* ... 1Cor 7:29 *3361*
that there is *n* other God but one ... 1Cor 8:4 *3762*
But I have used *n* of these things ... 1Cor 9:15 *3762*
Give *n* offence, neither to the ... 1Cor 10:32 *677*
world, and *n* of them is without ... 1Cor 14:10 *3762*
For we write *n* other things unto ... 2Cor 1:13 *3756*
But other of the apostles saw I *n* ... Gal 1:19 *3756*
make the promise of *n* effect ... Gal 3:17 *208*
that ye will be *n* otherwise ... Gal 5:10 *3762*
See that *n* render evil for evil ... 1Th 5:15 3361,5100
give *n* occasion to the adversary ... 1Ti 5:14 *3361*
But let *n* of you suffer as a ... 1Pet 4:15 *3387*
there is *n* occasion of stumbling ... 1Jn 2:10 *3756*
Fear *n* of those things which thou ... Rev 2:10 *3367*
will put upon you *n* other burden ... Rev 2:24 *3367*

NOON {12}
these men shall dine with me at *n* ... Gen 43:16 6672
present against Joseph came at *n* ... Gen 43:25 6672
who lay on a bed at *n* ... 2Sa 4:5 6672
of Baal from morning even until *n* ... 1Kin 18:26 6672
And it came to pass at *n*, that ... 1Kin 18:27 6672
And they went out at *n* ... 1Kin 20:16 6672
he sat on her knees till *n* ... 2Kin 4:20 6672
Evening, and morning, and at *n* ... Ps 55:17 6672
makest thy flock to rest at *n* ... Song 1:7 6672
arise, and let us go up at *n* ... Jer 6:4 6672
cause the sun to go down at *n* ... Amos 8:9 6672
come nigh unto Damascus about *n* ... Acts 22:6 *3314*

NOONDAY {10}
And thou shalt grope at *n*, as the ... Deut 28:29 6672
grope in the *n* as in the night ... Job 5:14 6672
age shall be clearer than the *n* ... Job 11:17 6672
light, and thy judgment as the *n* ... Ps 37:6 6672
the destruction that wasteth at *n* ... Ps 91:6 6672
the night in the midst of the *n* ... Is 16:3 6672
and thy darkness be as the *n* ... Is 58:10 6672
we stumble at *n* as in the night ... Is 59:10 6672
of the young men a spoiler at *n* ... Jer 15:8 6672
shall drive out Ashdod at the *n* ... Zeph 2:4 6672

NOONTIDE {1}
morning, and the shouting at *n* ... Jer 20:16 6256,6672

NOPH (*nof*) {7} See MEMPHIS. *Same as Memphis.*
the princes of *N* are deceived ... Is 19:13 5297
Also the children of *N* and ... Jer 2:16 5297
Migdol, and at Tahpanhes, and at *N* ... Jer 44:1 5297
in Migdol, and publish in *N* ... Jer 46:14 5297
for *N* shall be waste and desolate ... Jer 46:19 5297
their images to cease out of *N* ... Eze 30:13 5297
N shall have distresses daily ... Eze 30:16 5297

NOPHAH (*no'-fah*) {1} See NOBAH. *A city in Sihon.*
have laid them waste even unto *N* ... Num 21:30 5302

NOR See APPENDIX.

NORTH {132}
west, and to the east, and to the *n* ... Gen 28:14 6828
the *n* side there shall be twenty ... Ex 26:20 6828
shalt put the table on the *n* side ... Ex 26:35 6828
likewise for the *n* side in length ... Ex 27:11 6828
which is toward the *n* corner ... Ex 36:25 6828
for the *n* side the hangings were ... Ex 38:11 6828
be on the *n* side by their armies ... Num 2:25 6828
And this shall be your *n* border ... Num 34:7 6828
this shall be your *n* border ... Num 34:9 6828
on the *n* side two thousand cubits ... Num 35:5 6828
and pitched on the *n* side of Ai ... Josh 8:11 6828
that was on the *n* of the city ... Josh 8:13 6828
were on the *n* of the mountains ... Josh 11:2 6828
their border in the *n* quarter was ... Josh 15:5 6828
along by the *n* of Beth-arabah ... Josh 15:6 6828
which is Chesalon, on the *n* side ... Josh 15:10 6828
sea to Michmethah on the *n* side ... Josh 16:6 6828
was on the *n* side of the river ... Josh 17:9 6828
met together in Asher on the *n* ... Josh 17:10 6828
abide in their coasts on the *n* ... Josh 18:5 6828
their border on the *n* side was ... Josh 18:12 6828
the side of Jericho on the *n* side ... Josh 18:12 6828
the valley of the giants on the *n* ... Josh 18:16 6828
And was drawn from the *n*, and went ... Josh 18:17 6828
of the border were at the *n* bay ... Josh 18:19 6828
it on the *n* side to Hannathon ... Josh 19:14 6828
toward the *n* side of Beth-emek ... Josh 19:27 6828
on the *n* side of the hill of ... Josh 24:30 6828
on the *n* side of the hill Gaash ... Judg 2:9 6828
were on the *n* side of them ... Judg 7:1 6828
which is on the *n* side of Beth-el ... Judg 21:19 6828
oxen, three looking toward the *n* ... 1Kin 7:25 6828
put it on the *n* side of the altar ... 2Kin 16:14 6828
porters, toward the east, west, *n* ... 1Chr 9:24 6828
oxen, three looking toward the *n* ... 2Chr 4:4 6828
out the *n* over the empty place ... Job 26:7 6828
and cold out of the *n* ... Job 37:9 4215
Fair weather cometh out of the *n* ... Job 37:22 6828
mount Zion, on the sides of the *n* ... Ps 48:2 6828
The *n* and the south thou hast ... Ps 89:12 6828
and from the west, from the *n* ... Ps 107:3 6828
The *n* wind driveth away rain ... Prov 25:23 6828
and turneth about unto the *n* ... Eccl 1:6 6828
toward the south, or toward the *n* ... Eccl 11:3 6828
Awake, O *n* wind ... Song 4:16 6828
in the sides of the *n* ... Is 14:13 6828
shall come from the *n* a smoke ... Is 14:31 6828
I have raised up one from the *n* ... Is 41:25 6828
I will say to the *n*, Give up ... Is 43:6 6828
and, lo, these from the *n* and from ... Is 49:12 6828
the face thereof is toward the *n* ... Jer 1:13 6828
Out of the *n* an evil shall break ... Jer 1:14 6828
families of the kingdoms of the *n* ... Jer 1:15 6828
proclaim these words toward the *n* ... Jer 3:12 6828
n to the land that I have given ... Jer 3:18 6828
for I will bring evil from the *n* ... Jer 4:6 6828
for evil appeareth out of the *n* ... Jer 6:1 6828
people cometh from the *n* country ... Jer 6:22 6828
commotion out of the *n* country ... Jer 10:22 6828
behold them that come from the *n* ... Jer 13:20 6828
of Israel from the land of the *n* ... Jer 16:15 6828
of Israel out of the *n* country ... Jer 23:8 6828
and take all the families of the *n* ... Jer 25:9 6828
And all the kings of the *n* ... Jer 25:26 6828
bring them from the *n* country ... Jer 31:8 6828
fall toward the *n* by the river ... Jer 46:6 6828
hosts hath a sacrifice in the *n* ... Jer 46:10 6828
it cometh out of the *n* ... Jer 46:20 6828
the hand of the people of the *n* ... Jer 46:24 6828
waters rise up out of the *n* ... Jer 47:2 6828
For out of the *n* there cometh up ... Jer 50:3 6828
great nations from the *n* country ... Jer 50:9 6828
a people shall come from the *n* ... Jer 50:41 6828
shall come unto her from the *n* ... Jer 51:48 6828
a whirlwind came out of the *n* ... Eze 1:4 6828
gate, that looketh toward the *n* ... Eze 8:3 6828
eyes now the way toward the *n* ... Eze 8:5 6828
up mine eyes the way toward the *n* ... Eze 8:5 6828
house which was toward the *n* ... Eze 8:14 6828
gate, which lieth toward the *n* ... Eze 9:2 6828
to the *n* shall be burned therein ... Eze 20:47 6828
all flesh from the south to the *n* ... Eze 21:4 6828
a king of kings, from the *n* ... Eze 26:7 6828
There be the princes of the *n* ... Eze 32:30 6828
of Togarmah of the *n* quarters ... Eze 38:6 6828
from thy place out of the *n* parts ... Eze 38:15 6828
thee to come up from the *n* parts ... Eze 39:2 6828
court that looked toward the *n* ... Eze 40:20 6828
against the gate toward the *n* ... Eze 40:23 6828
And he brought me to the *n* gate ... Eze 40:35 6828
up to the entry of the *n* gate ... Eze 40:40 6828
was at the side of the *n* gate ... Eze 40:44 6828
having the prospect toward the *n* ... Eze 40:44 6828
toward the *n* is for the priests ... Eze 40:46 6828
was left, one door toward the *n* ... Eze 41:11 6828
utter court, the way toward the *n* ... Eze 42:1 6828
before the building toward the *n* ... Eze 42:1 6828
an hundred cubits was the *n* door ... Eze 42:2 6828
and their doors toward the *n* ... Eze 42:4 6828
chambers which were toward the *n* ... Eze 42:11 6828
The *n* chambers and the south ... Eze 42:13 6828
He measured the *n* side, five ... Eze 42:17 6828
of the *n* gate before the house ... Eze 44:4 6828
entereth in by the way of the *n* ... Eze 46:9 6828
go forth by the way of the *n* gate ... Eze 46:9 6828
which looked toward the *n* ... Eze 46:19 6828
of the land toward the *n* side ... Eze 47:15 6828
the *n* northward, and the border of ... Eze 47:17 6828
And this is the *n* side ... Eze 47:17 6828
From the *n* end to the coast of ... Eze 48:1 6828
toward the *n* five and twenty ... Eze 48:10 6828
the *n* side four thousand and five ... Eze 48:16 6828
shall be toward the *n* two hundred ... Eze 48:17 6828
out of the city on the *n* side ... Eze 48:30 6828
of the *n* to make an agreement ... Dan 11:6 6828
the fortress of the king of the *n* ... Dan 11:7 6828
more years than the king of the *n* ... Dan 11:8 6828
him, even with the king of the *n* ... Dan 11:11 6828
the king of the *n* shall return ... Dan 11:13 6828
So the king of the *n* shall come ... Dan 11:15 6828
the king of the *n* shall come ... Dan 11:40 6828
out of the *n* shall trouble him ... Dan 11:44 6828
from the *n* even to the east, they ... Amos 8:12 6828
out his hand against the *n* ... Zeph 2:13 6828
and flee from the land of the *n* ... Zec 2:6 6828
go forth into the *n* country ... Zec 6:6 6828
these that go toward the *n* ... Zec 6:8 6828
my spirit in the *n* country ... Zec 6:8 6828
shall remove toward the *n* ... Zec 14:4 6828
and from the west, and from the *n* ... Lk 13:29 *1005*
toward the south west and *n* west ... Acts 27:12 *5566*
on the *n* three gates ... Rev 21:13 *1005*

NORTHERN {2}
Shall iron break the *n* iron ... Jer 15:12 6828
far off from you the *n* army ... Joel 2:20 6830

NORTHWARD {24}
from the place where thou art *n* ... Gen 13:14 6828
upon the side of the tabernacle *n* ... Ex 40:22 6828
of the altar *n* before the LORD ... Lev 1:11 6828
on the side of the tabernacle *n* ... Num 3:35 6828
turn you *n* ... Deut 2:3 6828
lift up thine eyes westward, and *n* ... Deut 3:27 6828
even unto the borders of Ekron *n* ... Josh 13:3 6828
from the valley of Achor, and so *n* ... Josh 15:7 6828
end of the valley of the giants *n* ... Josh 15:8 6828
went out unto the side of Ekron *n* ... Josh 15:11 6828
n it was Manasseh's, and the sea ... Josh 17:10 6828
the side over against Arabah *n* ... Josh 18:18 6828
to the side of Beth-hoglah *n* ... Josh 18:19 6828
themselves together, and went *n* ... Judg 12:1 6828
situate *n* over against Michmash ... 1Sa 14:5 6828
and his lot came out *n* ... 1Chr 26:14 6828
n four a day, southward four a ... 1Chr 26:17 6828
behold *n* at the gate of the altar ... Eze 8:5 6828
an hundred cubits eastward and *n* ... Eze 40:19 6828
me out of the way of the gate *n* ... Eze 47:2 6828
of Damascus, and the north *n* ... Eze 47:17 6828
the border of Damascus *n* ... Eze 48:1 6828
three gates *n*; one gate ... Eze 48:31 6828
the ram pushing westward, and *n* ... Dan 8:4 6828

NOSE {12}
a lame, or he that hath a flat *n* ... Lev 21:18 2763
I will put my hook in thy *n* ... 2Kin 19:28 639
his *n* pierceth through snares ... Job 40:24 639
Canst thou put an hook into his *n* ... Job 41:2 639
the wringing of the *n* bringeth ... Prov 30:33 639
thy *n* is as the tower of Lebanon ... Song 7:4 639
and the smell of thy *n* like apples ... Song 7:8 639
The rings, and *n* jewels, ... Is 3:21 639
will I put my hook in thy *n* ... Is 37:29 639
These are a smoke in my *n* ... Is 65:5 639
they put the branch to their *n* ... Eze 8:17 639
they shall take away thy *n* ... Eze 23:25 639

NOSES {2}
n have they, but they smell not ... Ps 115:6 639
stop the *n* of the passengers ... Eze 39:11

NOSTRILS {15}
breathed into his *n* the breath of ... Gen 2:7 639
All in whose *n* was the breath of ... Gen 7:22 639
with the blast of thy *n* the ... Ex 15:8 639
until it come out at your *n* ... Num 11:20 639
went up a smoke out of his *n* ... 2Sa 22:9 639
the blast of the breath of his *n* ... 2Sa 22:16 639
breath of his *n* are they consumed ... Job 4:9 639
and the spirit of God is in my *n* ... Job 27:3 639
the glory of his *n* is terrible ... Job 39:20 5170
Out of his *n* goeth smoke, as out ... Job 41:20 5156
went up a smoke out of his *n* ... Ps 18:8 639
the blast of the breath of thy *n* ... Ps 18:15 639
man, whose breath is in his *n* ... Is 2:22 639
The breath of our *n*, the anointed ... Lam 4:20 639
your camps to come up unto your *n* ... Amos 4:10 639

NOT See APPENDIX.

NOTABLE {5}
the goat had a *n* horn between his ... Dan 8:5 2380
for it came up four *n* ones toward ... Dan 8:8 2380
And they had then a *n* prisoner ... Mt 27:16 *1978*
great and *n* day of the Lord come ... Acts 2:20 *2016*
for that indeed a *n* miracle hath ... Acts 4:16 *1110*

NOTE {3}
n it in a book, that it may be ... Is 30:8 2710
who are of *n* among the apostles, ... Rom 16:7 *1978*
n that man, and have no company ... 2Th 3:14 *4593*

NOTED {1}
is *n* in the scripture of truth ... Dan 10:21 7559

NOTHING See APPENDIX.

NOTICE {2}
And all the people took *n* of it ... 2Sa 3:36 5234
bounty, whereof ye had *n* before ... 2Cor 9:5 *4293*

NOTWITHSTANDING {36}
N they hearkened not unto Moses ... Ex 16:20
N, if he continue a day or two, ... Ex 21:21 389
N the cities of the Levites, and ... Lev 25:32
N no devoted thing, that a man ... Lev 27:28 389
N the children of Korah died not ... Num 26:11
N the land shall be divided by ... Num 26:55
N ye would not go up, but ... Deut 1:26
N thou mayest kill and eat flesh ... Deut 12:15 7535
N, if the land of your possession ... Josh 22:19 389
n the journey that thou takest ... Judg 4:9 657
n yet Jotham the youngest son of ... Judg 9:5
N they hearkened not unto the ... 1Sa 2:25
n, if there be in me iniquity, ... 1Sa 20:8
n the princes of the Philistines ... 1Sa 29:9 389
N the king's word prevailed ... 2Sa 24:4
N in thy days I will not do it ... 1Kin 11:12 389
N they would not hear, but ... 2Kin 17:14
N the LORD turned not from the ... 2Kin 23:26 389
N thou shalt not build the house ... 2Chr 6:9 7535
N Hezekiah humbled himself for ... 2Chr 32:26
n I have spoken unto you, rising ... Jer 35:14
N the children rebelled against ... Eze 20:21
N the land shall be desolate ... Mic 7:13
n, being warned of God in a dream ... Mt 2:22
n he that is least in the kingdom ... Mt 11:11
N, lest we should offend them, go ... Mt 17:27
n be ye sure of this, that the ... Lk 10:11 *4133*
N in this rejoice not, that the ... Lk 10:20 *4133*
N it pleased Silas to abide there ... Acts 15:34
N, that I be not further tedious ... Acts 24:4
n, every way, whether in pretence ... Phil 1:18 *4133*
N ye have well done, that ye did ... Phil 4:14 *4133*
N she shall be saved in ... 1Ti 2:15
N the Lord stood with me, and ... 2Ti 4:17
n ye give them not those things ... Jas 2:16
N I have a few things against ... Rev 2:20 *235*

NOUGHT {36}
thou therefore serve me for *n* ... Gen 29:15 2600
there shall cleave *n* of the ... Deut 13:17 408,3972
brother, and thou givest him *n* ... Deut 15:9 3808
destroy you, and to bring you to *n* ... Deut 28:63 8045
had brought their counsel to *n* ... Neh 4:15 6565
and said, Doth Job fear God for *n* ... Job 1:9 2600
of the wicked shall come to *n* ... Job 8:22 369
the mountain falling cometh to *n* ... Job 14:18 5034
a pledge from thy brother for *n* ... Job 22:6 2600
the counsel of the heathen to *n* ... Ps 33:10 6331
Thou sellest thy people for *n* ... Ps 44:12 3808,1952
ye have set at *n* all my counsel ... Prov 1:25 6544
together, and it shall come to *n* ... Is 8:10 6565
the terrible one is brought to *n* ... Is 29:20 656
aside the just for a thing of *n* ... Is 29:21 8414
be as nothing, and as a thing of *n* ... Is 41:12 657
are of nothing, and your work of *n* ... Is 41:24 659
I have spent my strength for *n* ... Is 49:4 8414
Ye have sold yourselves for *n* ... Is 52:3 2600
my people is taken away for *n* ... Is 52:5 2600
and divination, and a thing of *n* ... Jer 14:14 434
and Beth-el shall come to *n* ... Amos 5:5 205
Ye which rejoice in a thing of *n* ... Amos 6:13 3808,1697
that would shut the doors for *n* ... Mal 1:10
kindle fire on mine altar for *n* ... Mal 1:10 2600
many things, and be set at *n* ... Mk 9:12 *1847*
with his men of war set him at *n* ... Lk 23:11 *1848*
was set at *n* of you builders ... Acts 4:11 *1848*
were scattered, and brought to *n* ... Acts 5:36 *3762*
work be of men, it will come to *n* ... Acts 5:38 *2647*
craft is in danger to be set at *n* ... Acts 19:27 *557*
dost thou set at *n* thy brother ... Rom 14:10 *1848*
to bring to *n* things that are ... 1Cor 1:28 *2673*
of this world, that come to *n* ... 1Cor 2:6 *2673*
did we eat any man's bread for *n* ... 2Th 3:8 *1432*
hour so great riches is come to *n* ... Rev 18:17 *2049*

NOURISH {5}
And there will I *n* thee ... Gen 45:11 3557
I will *n* you, and your little ones ... Gen 50:21 3557
that a man shall *n* a young cow ... Is 7:21 2421
neither do I *n* up young men ... Is 23:4 1431
an ash, and the rain doth *n* it ... Is 44:14 1431

NOURISHED {10}
Joseph *n* his father, and his ... Gen 47:12 3557
lamb, which he had bought and *n* up ... 2Sa 12:3 2421
the LORD hath spoken, I have *n* ... Is 1:2 1431
she *n* her whelps among young ... Eze 19:2 7235
n up in his father's house three ... Acts 7:20 *397*
him up, and *n* him for her own son ... Acts 7:21 *397*
was *n* by the king's country ... Acts 12:20 *5142*
n up in the words of faith and of ... 1Ti 4:6 *1789*
ye have *n* your hearts, as in a ... Jas 5:5 *5142*
place, where she is *n* for a time ... Rev 12:14 *5142*

NOURISHER {1}
thy life, and a *n* of thine old age ... Ruth 4:15 3557

NOURISHETH {1}
but *n* and cherisheth it, even as ... Eph 5:29 *1625*

NOURISHING {1}
so *n* them three years, that at ... Dan 1:5 1431

NOURISHMENT {1}
and bands having *n* ministered ... Col 2:19 *2023*

NOVICE {1}
Not a *n*, lest being lifted up ... 1Ti 3:6 *3504*

NOW See APPENDIX.

NUMBER {178}
so that if a man can *n* the dust ... Gen 13:16 4487
stars, if thou be able to *n* them ... Gen 15:5 5608
and I being few in *n*, they shall ... Gen 34:30 4557
for it was without *n* ... Gen 41:49 4557
according to the *n* of the souls ... Ex 12:4 4373
to the *n* of your persons ... Ex 16:16 4557
the *n* of thy days I will fulfil ... Ex 23:26 4557
children of Israel after their *n* ... Ex 30:12 6485
then he shall *n* to himself seven ... Lev 15:13 5608
then she shall *n* to herself seven ... Lev 15:28 5608
sabbath shall ye *n* fifty days ... Lev 23:16 5608
thou shalt *n* seven sabbaths of ... Lev 25:8 5608
According to the *n* of years after ... Lev 25:15 4557
according unto the *n* of years of ... Lev 25:15 4557
for according to the *n* of the ... Lev 25:16 4557
be according unto the *n* of years ... Lev 25:50 4557
your cattle, and make you few in *n* ... Lev 26:22
with the *n* of their names, every ... Num 1:2 4557
Aaron shall *n* them by their ... Num 1:3 6485
according to the *n* of the names ... Num 1:18 4557
according to the *n* of the names ... Num 1:20 4557
according to the *n* of the names ... Num 1:22 4557
according to the *n* of the names ... Num 1:24 4557
according to the *n* of the names ... Num 1:26 4557
according to the *n* of the names ... Num 1:28 4557
according to the *n* of the names ... Num 1:30 4557
according to the *n* of the names ... Num 1:32 4557
according to the *n* of the names ... Num 1:34 4557
according to the *n* of the names ... Num 1:36 4557
according to the *n* of the names ... Num 1:38 4557
according to the *n* of the names ... Num 1:40 4557
according to the *n* of the names ... Num 1:42 4557
shalt not *n* the tribe of Levi ... Num 1:49 6485
N the children of Levi after the ... Num 3:15 6485
old and upward shalt thou *n* them ... Num 3:15 6485
to the *n* of all the males ... Num 3:22 4557
In the *n* of all the males, from a ... Num 3:28 4557
to the *n* of all the males ... Num 3:34 4557
N all the firstborn of the males ... Num 3:40 6485
take the *n* of their names ... Num 3:40 4557
firstborn males by the *n* of names ... Num 3:43 4557
wherewith the odd *n* of them is to ... Num 3:48 5736
fifty years old shalt thou *n* them ... Num 4:23 6485
thou shalt *n* them after their ... Num 4:29 6485
fifty years old shalt thou *n* them ... Num 4:30 6485
Aaron did *n* according to the ... Num 4:37 6485
Aaron did *n* according to the ... Num 4:41 6485
of you, according to your whole *n* ... Num 14:29 4557
After the *n* of the days in which ... Num 14:34 4557
According to the *n* that ye shall ... Num 15:12 4557
to every one according to their *n* ... Num 15:12 4557
the *n* of the fourth part of ... Num 23:10 4557
according to the *n* of names ... Num 26:53 4557
shall be according to their *n* ... Num 29:18 4557
shall be according to their *n* ... Num 29:21 4557
shall be according to their *n* ... Num 29:24 4557
shall be according to their *n* ... Num 29:27 4557
shall be according to their *n* ... Num 29:30 4557
shall be according to their *n* ... Num 29:33 4557
shall be according to their *n* ... Num 29:37 4557
was in *n* three hundred thousand ... Num 31:36 4557
left few in *n* among the heathen ... Deut 4:27 4557
ye were more in *n* than any people ... Deut 7:7
weeks shalt thou *n* unto thee ... Deut 16:9 5608
begin to *n* the seven weeks from ... Deut 16:9 5608
to his fault, by a certain *n* ... Deut 25:2 4557
And ye shall be left few in *n* ... Deut 28:62
the *n* of the children of Israel ... Deut 32:8 4557
according unto the *n* of the ... Josh 4:5 4557
according to the *n* of the tribes ... Josh 4:8 4557
and their camels were without *n* ... Judg 6:5 4557
the *n* of them that lapped, ... Judg 7:6 4557
and their camels were without *n* ... Judg 7:12 4557
them wives, according to their *n* ... Judg 21:23 4557
according to the *n* of the lords ... 1Sa 6:4 4557
according to the *n* of all the ... 1Sa 6:18 4557
N now, and see who is gone from us ... 1Sa 14:17 6485
went over by *n* twelve of Benjamin ... 2Sa 2:15 4557
six toes, four and twenty in *n* ... 2Sa 21:20 4557
to say, Go, *n* Israel and Judah ... 2Sa 24:1 4487
n ye the people, that I may know ... 2Sa 24:2 6485
I may know the *n* of the people ... 2Sa 24:2 4557
to *n* the people of Israel ... 2Sa 24:4 6485
the *n* of the people unto the king ... 2Sa 24:9 4662
according to the *n* of the tribes ... 1Kin 18:31 4557
n thee an army, like the army ... 1Kin 20:25 4487
whose *n* was in the days of David ... 1Chr 7:2 4557
the *n* of them, after their ... 1Chr 7:9 3187
the *n* throughout the genealogy of ... 1Chr 7:40 4557,3187
this is the *n* of the mighty men ... 1Chr 11:11 4557
and provoked David to *n* Israel ... 1Chr 21:1 4487
n Israel from Beer-sheba even to ... 1Chr 21:2 5608
bring the *n* of them to me, that I ... 1Chr 21:2 4557
of the *n* of the people unto David ... 1Chr 21:5 4662
brass, and the iron, there is no *n* ... 1Chr 22:16 4557
their *n* by their polls, man by ... 1Chr 23:3 4557
by *n* of names by their polls ... 1Chr 23:24 4557
moons, and on the set feasts, by *n* ... 1Chr 23:31 4557
the *n* of the workmen according to ... 1Chr 25:1 4557
So the *n* of them, with their ... 1Chr 25:7 4557
children of Israel after their *n* ... 1Chr 27:1 4557
But David took not the *n* of them ... 1Chr 27:23 4557
the son of Zeruiah began to *n* ... 1Chr 27:24 4487
neither was the *n* put in the ... 1Chr 27:24 4557
the people were without *n* that ... 2Chr 12:3 4557
according to the *n* of their ... 2Chr 26:11 4557
The whole *n* of the chief of the ... 2Chr 26:12 4557
the *n* of the burnt offerings, ... 2Chr 29:32 4557
a great *n* of priests sanctified ... 2Chr 30:24
to the *n* of thirty thousand, and ... 2Chr 35:7 4557
And this is the *n* of them ... Ezr 1:9 4557
The *n* of the men of the people of ... Ezr 2:2 4557
the daily burnt offerings by *n* ... Ezr 3:4 4557
according to the *n* of the tribes ... Ezr 6:17 4510
By *n* and by weight of every one ... Ezr 8:34 4557
The *n*, I say, of the men of the ... Neh 7:7 4557
On that day the *n* of those that ... Est 9:11 4557
according to the *n* of them all ... Job 1:5 4557
not come into the *n* of the months ... Job 3:6 4557
marvellous things without *n* ... Job 5:9 4557
yea, and wonders without *n* ... Job 9:10 4557
the *n* of his months are with thee ... Job 14:5 4557
the *n* of years is hidden to the ... Job 15:20 4557
when the *n* of his months is cut ... Job 21:21 4557
Is there any *n* of his armies ... Job 25:3 4557
unto him the *n* of my steps ... Job 31:37 4557
in pieces mighty men without *n* ... Job 34:24 2714
neither can the *n* of his years be ... Job 36:26 4557
or because the *n* of thy days is ... Job 38:21 4557
Who can *n* the clouds in wisdom ... Job 38:37 5608
Canst thou *n* the months that they ... Job 39:2 5608
So teach us to *n* our days ... Ps 90:12 4487
When they were but a few men in *n* ... Ps 105:12 4557
caterpillers, and that without *n* ... Ps 105:34 4557
they are more in *n* than the sand ... Ps 139:18
He telleth the *n* of the stars ... Ps 147:4 4557
concubines, and virgins without *n* ... Song 6:8 4557
the residue of the *n* of archers ... Is 21:17 4557
that bringeth out their host by *n* ... Is 40:26 4557
the drink offering unto that *n* ... Is 65:11 4507
will I *n* you to the sword ... Is 65:12 4487
for according to the *n* of thy ... Jer 2:28 4557
have forgotten me days without *n* ... Jer 2:32 4557
For according to the *n* of thy ... Jer 11:13 4557
according to the *n* of the streets ... Jer 11:13 4557
Yet a small *n* that escape the ... Jer 44:28 4557
according to the *n* of the days ... Eze 4:4 4557
according to the *n* of the days ... Eze 4:5 4557
according to the *n* of the days ... Eze 4:9 4557
also take thereof a few in *n* ... Eze 5:3 4557
by books the *n* of the years ... Dan 9:2 4557
Yet the *n* of the children of ... Hos 1:10 4557
my land, strong, and without *n* ... Joel 1:6 4557
slain, and a great *n* of carcases ... Nah 3:3
a great *n* of people, blind ... Mk 10:46 *3793*
being of the *n* of the twelve ... Lk 22:3 *706*
down, in *n* about five thousand ... Jn 6:10 *706*
(the *n* of names together were ... Acts 1:15 *3793*
the *n* of the men was about five ... Acts 4:4 *706*
to whom a *n* of men, about four ... Acts 5:36 *706*
when the *n* of the disciples was ... Acts 6:1
the *n* of the disciples multiplied ... Acts 6:7 *706*
a great *n* believed, and turned ... Acts 11:21 *706*
faith, and increased in *n* daily ... Acts 16:5 *706*
Though the *n* of the children of ... Rom 9:27 *706*
dare not make ourselves of the *n* ... 2Cor 10:12 *1469*
the *n* under threescore years old ... 1Ti 5:9 *2639*
the *n* of them was ten thousand ... Rev 5:11 *706*
I heard the *n* of them which were ... Rev 7:4 *706*
multitude, which no man could *n* ... Rev 7:9 *705*
the *n* of the army of the horsemen ... Rev 9:16 *706*
and I heard the *n* of them ... Rev 9:16 *706*
the beast, or the *n* of his name ... Rev 13:17 *706*
count the *n* of the beast ... Rev 13:18 *706*
for it is the *n* of a man ... Rev 13:18 *706*
his *n* is six hundred threescore ... Rev 13:18 *706*
over the *n* of his name, stand on ... Rev 15:2 *706*
the *n* of whom is as the sand of ... Rev 20:8 *706*

NUMBERED {128}
then shall thy seed also be *n* ... Gen 13:16 4487
it shall not be *n* for multitude ... Gen 16:10 5608
which cannot be *n* for multitude ... Gen 32:12 5608
passeth among them that are *n* ... Ex 30:13 6485
passeth among them that are *n* ... Ex 30:14 6485
were *n* of the congregation was an ... Ex 38:25 6485
for every one that went to be *n* ... Ex 38:26 6485
so he *n* them in the wilderness of ... Num 1:19 6485
Those that were *n* of them ... Num 1:21 6485
those that were *n* of them ... Num 1:22 6485
Those that were *n* of them ... Num 1:23 6485
Those that were *n* of them ... Num 1:25 6485
Those that were *n* of them ... Num 1:27 6485
Those that were *n* of them ... Num 1:29 6485
Those that were *n* of them ... Num 1:31 6485
Those that were *n* of them ... Num 1:33 6485
Those that were *n* of them ... Num 1:35 6485
Those that were *n* of them ... Num 1:37 6485
Those that were *n* of them ... Num 1:39 6485
Those that were *n* of them ... Num 1:41 6485
Those that were *n* of them ... Num 1:43 6485
n, which Moses and Aaron *n* ... Num 1:44 6485
were *n* of the children of Israel ... Num 1:45 6485
Even all they that were *n* were ... Num 1:46 6485
fathers were not *n* among them ... Num 1:47 6485
and those that were *n* of them ... Num 2:4 6485

N

- and those that were *n* thereof ... Num 2:6 6485
- and those that were *n* thereof ... Num 2:8 6485
- All that were *n* in the camp of ... Num 2:9 6485
- and those that were *n* thereof ... Num 2:11 6485
- and those that were *n* of them ... Num 2:13 6485
- and those that were *n* of them ... Num 2:15 6485
- All that were *n* in the camp of ... Num 2:16 6485
- and those that were *n* of them ... Num 2:19 6485
- and those that were *n* of them ... Num 2:21 6485
- and those that were *n* of them ... Num 2:23 6485
- All that were *n* of the camp of ... Num 2:24 6485
- and those that were *n* of them ... Num 2:26 6485
- and those that were *n* of them ... Num 2:28 6485
- and those that were *n* of them ... Num 2:30 6485
- All they that were *n* in the camp ... Num 2:31 6485
- These are those which were *n* of ... Num 2:32 6485
- all those that were *n* of the ... Num 2:32 6485
- But the Levites were not *n* among ... Num 2:33 6485
- Moses *n* them according to the ... Num 3:16 6485
- Those that were *n* of them ... Num 3:22 6485
- even those that were *n* of them ... Num 3:22 6485
- And those that were *n* of them ... Num 3:34 6485
- All that were *n* of the Levites, ... Num 3:39 6485
- Aaron *n* at the commandment of the ... Num 3:39 6485
- Moses *n*, as the LORD commanded ... Num 3:42 6485
- of those that were *n* of them ... Num 3:43 6485
- *n* the sons of the Kohathites ... Num 4:34 6485
- those that were *n* of them by ... Num 4:36 6485
- were *n* of the families of the ... Num 4:37 6485
- those that were *n* of the sons of ... Num 4:38 6485
- Even those that were *n* of them ... Num 4:40 6485
- These are they that were *n* of the ... Num 4:41 6485
- those that were *n* of the families ... Num 4:42 6485
- Even those that were *n* of them ... Num 4:44 6485
- These be those that were *n* of the ... Num 4:45 6485
- Aaron *n* according to the word of ... Num 4:45 6485
- those that were *n* of the Levites ... Num 4:46 6485
- and Aaron and the chief of Israel *n* ... Num 4:46 6485
- Even those that were *n* of them ... Num 4:48 6485
- they were *n* by the hand of Moses ... Num 4:49 6485
- thus were they *n* of him, as the ... Num 4:49 6485
- and were over them that were *n* ... Num 7:2 6485
- and all that were *n* of you ... Num 14:29 6485
- they that were *n* of them were ... Num 26:7 6485
- to those that were *n* of them ... Num 26:18 6485
- to those that were *n* of them ... Num 26:22 6485
- to those that were *n* of them ... Num 26:25 6485
- to those that were *n* of them ... Num 26:27 6485
- and those that were *n* of them ... Num 26:34 6485
- to those that were *n* of them ... Num 26:37 6485
- they that were *n* of them were ... Num 26:41 6485
- to those that were *n* of them ... Num 26:43 6485
- to those that were *n* of them ... Num 26:47 6485
- they that were *n* of them were ... Num 26:50 6485
- These were the *n* of the children ... Num 26:51 6485
- to those that were *n* of him ... Num 26:54 6485
- these are they that were *n* of the ... Num 26:57 6485
- those that were *n* of them were ... Num 26:62 6485
- for they were not *n* among the ... Num 26:62 6485
- are they that were *n* by Moses ... Num 26:63 6485
- who *n* the children of Israel in ... Num 26:63 6485
- whom Moses and Aaron the priest *n* ... Num 26:64 6485
- when they *n* the children of ... Num 26:64 6485
- *n* the people, and went up, he and ... Josh 8:10 6485
- the children of Benjamin were *n* ... Judg 20:15 6485
- which were *n* seven hundred chosen ... Judg 20:15 6485
- were *n* four hundred thousand men ... Judg 20:17 6485
- For the people were *n*, and, behold ... Judg 21:9 6485
- when he *n* them in Bezek, the ... 1Sa 11:8 6485
- Saul *n* the people that were ... 1Sa 13:15 6485
- And when they had *n*, behold, ... 1Sa 14:17 6485
- *n* them in Telaim, two hundred ... 1Sa 15:4 6485
- David *n* the people that were with ... 2Sa 18:1 6485
- after that he had *n* the people ... 2Sa 24:10 5608
- that cannot be *n* nor counted for ... 1Kin 3:8 4487
- not be told nor *n* for multitude ... 1Kin 8:5 4487
- Then he *n* the young men of the ... 1Kin 20:15 6485
- after them he *n* all the people, ... 1Kin 20:15 6485
- that Ben-hadad *n* the Syrians ... 1Kin 20:26 6485
- And the children of Israel were *n* ... 1Kin 20:27 6485
- the same time, and *n* all Israel ... 2Kin 3:6 6485
- that commanded the people to be *n* ... 1Chr 21:17 4487
- Now the Levites were *n* from the ... 1Chr 23:3 5608
- were *n* from twenty years old ... 1Chr 23:27 4557
- Solomon *n* all the strangers that ... 2Chr 2:17 5608
- David his father had *n* them ... 2Chr 2:17 5608
- not be told nor *n* for multitude ... 2Chr 5:6 4487
- he *n* them from twenty years old ... 2Chr 25:5 6485
- *n* them unto Sheshbazzar, the ... Ezr 1:8 5608
- them, they are more than can be *n* ... Ps 40:5 5608
- that which is wanting cannot be *n* ... Eccl 1:15 4487
- ye have *n* the houses of Jerusalem ... Is 22:10 5608
- he was *n* with the transgressors ... Is 53:12 4487
- As the host of heaven cannot be *n* ... Jer 33:22 5608
- God hath *n* thy kingdom, and ... Dan 5:26 4483
- which cannot be measured nor *n* ... Hos 1:10 5608
- very hairs of your head are all *n* ... Mt 10:30 *705*
- he was *n* with the transgressors ... Mk 15:28 *3049*
- very hairs of your head are all *n* ... Lk 12:7 *705*
- For he was *n* with us, and had ... Acts 1:17 *2674*
- he was *n* with the eleven apostles ... Acts 1:26 *4785*

NUMBEREST {3}
- unto the LORD, when thou *n* them ... Ex 30:12 6485
- among them, when thou *n* them ... Ex 30:12 6485
- For now thou *n* my steps ... Job 14:16 5608

NUMBERING {2}
- sea, very much, until he left *n* ... Gen 41:49 5608
- after the *n* wherewith David his ... 2Chr 2:17 5610

NUMBERS {3}
- these are the *n* of the bands that ... 1Chr 12:23 4557
- these are the *n* of them according ... 2Chr 17:14 6486
- for I know not the *n* thereof ... Ps 71:15 5615

NUN *(nun)* {29} See NON. *Father of Joshua.*
- his servant Joshua, the son of *N* ... Ex 33:11 5126
- And Joshua the son of *N*, the ... Num 11:28 5126
- of Ephraim, Oshea the son of *N* ... Num 13:8 5126
- Oshea the son of *N* Jehoshua ... Num 13:16 5126
- And Joshua the son of *N*, and Caleb ... Num 14:6 5126
- Jephunneh, and Joshua the son of *N* ... Num 14:30 5126
- But Joshua the son of *N*, and Caleb ... Num 14:38 5126
- Jephunneh, and Joshua the son of *N* ... Num 26:65 5126
- Take thee Joshua the son of *N* ... Num 27:18 5126
- Kenezite, and Joshua the son of *N* ... Num 32:12 5126
- priest, and Joshua the son of *N* ... Num 32:28 5126
- priest, and Joshua the son of *N* ... Num 34:17 5126
- But Joshua the son of *N*, which ... Deut 1:38 5126
- gave Joshua the son of *N* a charge ... Deut 31:23 5126
- he, and Hoshea the son of *N* ... Deut 32:44 5126
- Joshua the son of *N* was full of ... Deut 34:9 5126
- spake unto Joshua the son of *N* ... Josh 1:1 5126
- Joshua the son of *N* sent out of ... Josh 2:1 5126
- and came to Joshua the son of *N* ... Josh 2:23 5126
- Joshua the son of *N* called the ... Josh 6:6 5126
- priest, and Joshua the son of *N* ... Josh 14:1 5126
- and before Joshua the son of *N* ... Josh 17:4 5126
- to Joshua the son of *N* among them ... Josh 19:49 5126
- priest, and Joshua the son of *N* ... Josh 19:51 5126
- and unto Joshua the son of *N* ... Josh 21:1 5126
- things, that Joshua the son of *N* ... Josh 24:29 5126
- And Joshua the son of *N*, the ... Judg 2:8 5126
- he spake by Joshua the son of *N* ... 1Kin 16:34 5126
- of *N* unto that day had not the ... Neh 8:17 5126

NURSE {10}
- Rebekah their sister, and her *n* ... Gen 24:59 3243
- But Deborah Rebekah's *n* died ... Gen 35:8 3243
- call to thee a *n* of the Hebrew ... Ex 2:7 3243
- that she may *n* the child for thee ... Ex 2:7 3243
- *n* it for me, and I will give thee ... Ex 2:9 3243
- in her bosom, and became *n* unto it ... Ruth 4:16 539
- his *n* took him up, and fled ... 2Sa 4:4 539
- they hid him, even him and his *n* ... 2Kin 11:2 3243
- put him and his *n* in a bedchamber ... 2Chr 22:11 3243
- even as a *n* cherisheth her ... 1Th 2:7 *5162*

NURSED {2}
- the woman took the child, and *n* it ... Ex 2:9 5134
- daughters shall be *n* at thy side ... Is 60:4 539

NURSING {3}
- as a *n* father beareth the sucking ... Num 11:12 539
- And kings shall be thy *n* fathers ... Is 49:23 539
- and their queens thy *n* mothers ... Is 49:23 3243

NURTURE {1}
- but bring them up in the *n* ... Eph 6:4 *3809*

NUTS {2}
- little honey, spices, and myrrh, *n* ... Gen 43:11 992
- I went down into the garden of *n* ... Song 6:11 93

NYMPHA See NYMPHAS.

NYMPHAS *(nim'-fas)* {1} *A Christian at Colosse.*
- which are in Laodicea, and *N* ... Col 4:15 *3564*

O

O See APPENDIX.

OAK {15}
- under the *o* which was by Shechem ... Gen 35:4 424
- buried beneath Beth-el under an *o* ... Gen 35:8 437
- and set it up there under an *o* ... Josh 24:26 427
- sat under an *o* which was in ... Judg 6:11 424
- it out unto him under the *o* ... Judg 6:19 424
- the thick boughs of a great *o* ... 2Sa 18:9 424
- and his head caught hold of the *o* ... 2Sa 18:9 424
- I saw Absalom hanged in an *o* ... 2Sa 18:10 424
- yet alive in the midst of the *o* ... 2Sa 18:14 424
- and found him sitting under an *o* ... 1Kin 13:14 424
- their bones under the *o* in Jabesh ... 1Chr 10:12 424
- be as an *o* whose leaf fadeth ... Is 1:30 424
- as a teil tree, and as an *o* ... Is 6:13 437
- and taketh the cypress and the *o* ... Is 44:14 437
- tree, and under every thick *o* ... Eze 6:13 424

OAKS {6}
- of the *o* which ye have desired ... Is 1:29 352
- up, and upon all the *o* of Bashan ... Is 2:13 437
- Of the *o* of Bashan have they made ... Eze 27:6 437
- incense upon the hills, under *o* ... Hos 4:13 437
- cedars, and he was strong as the *o* ... Amos 2:9 437
- howl, O ye *o* of Bashan ... Zec 11:2 437

OAR {1}
- And all that handle the *o*, the ... Eze 27:29 4880

OARS {2}
- wherein shall go no galley with *o* ... Is 33:21 7885
- of Bashan have they made thine *o* ... Eze 27:6 4880

OATH {59}
- shalt be clear from this my *o* ... Gen 24:8 7621
- thou be clear from this my *o* ... Gen 24:41 423
- thou shalt be clear from my *o* ... Gen 24:41 423
- I will perform the *o* which I ... Gen 26:3 7621
- Let there be now an *o* betwixt us ... Gen 26:28 423
- Joseph took an *o* of the children ... Gen 50:25 7650
- Then shall an *o* of the LORD be ... Ex 22:11 7621
- a man shall pronounce with an *o* ... Lev 5:4 7621
- priest shall charge her by an *o* ... Num 5:19 7650
- the woman with an *o* of cursing ... Num 5:21 7621
- an *o* among thy people, when the ... Num 5:21 7621
- or swear an *o* to bind his soul ... Num 30:2 7621
- her soul by a bond with an *o* ... Num 30:10 7621
- every binding *o* to afflict the ... Num 30:13 7621
- because he would keep the *o* which ... Deut 7:8 7621
- the LORD thy God, and into his *o* ... Deut 29:12 423
- do I make this covenant and this *o* ... Deut 29:14 423
- *o* which thou hast made us swear ... Josh 2:17 7621
- *o* which thou hast made us to ... Josh 2:20 7621
- because of the *o* which we sware ... Josh 9:20 7621
- For they had made a great *o* ... Judg 21:5 7621
- for the people feared the *o* ... 1Sa 14:26 7621
- charged the people with the *o* ... 1Sa 14:27 7650
- charged the people with an *o* ... 1Sa 14:28 7650
- LORD's *o* that was between them ... 2Sa 21:7 7621
- thou not kept the *o* of the LORD ... 1Kin 2:43 7621
- an *o* be laid upon him to cause ... 1Kin 8:31 423
- the *o* come before thine altar in ... 1Kin 8:31 423
- he took an *o* of the kingdom and ... 1Kin 18:10 7650
- took an *o* of them in the house of ... 2Kin 11:4 7650
- Abraham, and of his *o* unto Isaac ... 1Chr 16:16 7621
- an *o* be laid upon him to make him ... 2Chr 6:22 423
- the *o* come before thine altar in ... 2Chr 6:22 423
- And all Judah rejoiced at the *o* ... 2Chr 15:15 7621
- the priests, and took an *o* of them ... Neh 5:12 7650
- into a curse, and into an *o* ... Neh 10:29 7621
- with Abraham, and his *o* unto Isaac ... Ps 105:9 7621
- and that in regard of the *o* of God ... Eccl 8:2 7621
- sweareth, as he that feareth an *o* ... Eccl 9:2 7621
- That I may perform the *o* which I ... Jer 11:5 7621
- which hast despised the *o* in ... Eze 16:59 423
- him, and hath taken an *o* of him ... Eze 17:13 423
- whose *o* he despised, and whose ... Eze 17:16 423
- Seeing he despised the *o* by ... Eze 17:18 423
- surely mine *o* that he hath ... Eze 17:19 423
- the *o* that is written in the law ... Dan 9:11 7621
- and love no false *o* ... Zec 8:17 7621
- an *o* to give her whatsoever she ... Mt 14:7 *3727*
- And again he denied with an *o* ... Mt 26:72 *3727*
- The *o* which he sware to our ... Lk 1:73 *3727*
- God had sworn with an *o* to him ... Acts 2:30 *3727*
- have bound themselves with an *o* ... Acts 23:21 *332*
- an *o* for confirmation is to them ... Heb 6:16 *3727*
- his counsel, confirmed it by an *o* ... Heb 6:17 *3727*
- without an *o* he was made priest ... Heb 7:20 *3728*
- priests were made without an *o* ... Heb 7:21 *3728*
- but this with an *o* by him that ... Heb 7:21 *3728*
- but the word of the *o*, which was ... Heb 7:28 *3728*
- the earth, neither by any other *o* ... Jas 5:12 *3727*

OATH'S {2}
- nevertheless for the *o* sake ... Mt 14:9 *3727*
- yet for his *o* sake, and for their ... Mk 6:26 *3727*

OATHS {3}
- sight, to them that have sworn *o* ... Eze 21:23 7621
- according to the *o* of the tribes ... Hab 3:9 7621
- perform unto the Lord thine *o* ... Mt 5:33 *3727*

OBADIAH *(o-ba-di'-ah)* {20}

1. An officer in Ahab's court.
- And Ahab called *O*, which was the ... 1Kin 18:3 5662
- (Now *O* feared the LORD greatly ... 1Kin 18:3 5662
- that *O* took an hundred prophets, ... 1Kin 18:4 5662
- And Ahab said unto *O*, Go into the ... 1Kin 18:5 5662
- *O* went another way by himself ... 1Kin 18:6 5662
- as *O* was in the way, behold, ... 1Kin 18:7 5662
- So *O* went to meet Ahab, and told ... 1Kin 18:16 5662

2. A descendant of David.
- the sons of Arnan, the sons of *O* ... 1Chr 3:21 5662

3. A descendant of Tola.
- Michael, and *O*, and Joel, Ishiah, ... 1Chr 7:3 5662

4. Son of Azel.
- and Ishmael, and Sheariah, and *O* ... 1Chr 8:38 5662
- and Ishmael, and Sheariah, and *O* ... 1Chr 9:44 5662

5. Son of Shemaiah.
- *O* the son of Shemaiah, the son of ... 1Chr 9:16 5662

6. A warrior in David's army.
- *O* the second, Eliab the third, ... 1Chr 12:9 5662

7. A prince of Zebulun.
- Of Zebulun, Ishmaiah the son of *O* ... 1Chr 27:19 5662

8. A prince of Judah.
- even to Ben-hail, and to *O* ... 2Chr 17:7 5662

9. A Levite in Josiah's time.
- of them were Jahath and *O*, the ... 2Chr 34:12 5662

10. A clan leader with Ezra.
O the son of Jehiel, and with him .... Ezr 8:9 5662
11. A priest who renewed the covenant.
Harim, Meremoth, *O*,....... Neh 10:5 5662
12. A Temple gatekeeper.
Mattaniah, and Bakbukiah, *O*....... Neh 12:25 5662
13. A prophet.
The vision of *O*....... Obad 1 5662

OBAL *(o'-bal)* {1} *A son of Joktan.*
And *O*, and Abimael, and Sheba,....... Gen 10:28 5745

OBED *(o'-bed)* {13} See OBED-EDOM.
1. Father of Jesse.
and they called his name *O*....... Ruth 4:17 5744
begat Boaz, and Boaz begat *O*....... Ruth 4:21 5744
O begat Jesse, and Jesse begat....... Ruth 4:22 5744
And Boaz begat *O*, and *O* begat....... 1Chr 2:12 5744
and Booz begat *O* of Ruth....... Mt 1:5 *5601*
and *O* begat Jesse....... Mt 1:5 *5601*
of Jesse, which was the son of *O*....... Lk 3:32 *5601*
2. A descendant of Judah.
begat Ephlal, and Ephlal begat *O*....... 1Chr 2:37 5744
O begat Jehu, and Jehu begat....... 1Chr 2:38 5744
3. A "mighty man" of David.
Eliel, and *O*, and Jasiel the....... 1Chr 11:47 5744
4. A sanctuary servant.
Othni, and Rephael, and *O*, Elzabad,....... 1Chr 26:7 5744
5. Father of Azariah.
and Azariah the son of *O*, and....... 2Chr 23:1 5744

OBED-EDOM *(o'-bed-e'-dom)* {20}
1. A Levite.
into the house of *O* the Gittite....... 2Sa 6:10 5654
of *O* the Gittite three months....... 2Sa 6:11 5654
and the LORD blessed *O*, and all his....... 2Sa 6:11 5654
LORD hath blessed the house of *O*....... 2Sa 6:12 5654
of *O* into the city of David with....... 2Sa 6:12 5654
into the house of *O* the Gittite....... 1Chr 13:13 5654
of *O* in his house three months....... 1Chr 13:14 5654
the LORD blessed the house of *O*....... 1Chr 13:14 5654
and *O* and Jehiah were doorkeepers....... 1Chr 15:24 5654
out of the house of *O* with joy....... 1Chr 15:25 5654
2. A priest who relocated the Ark.
and Elipheleh, and Mikneiah, and *O*....... 1Chr 15:18 5654
and Elipheleh, and Mikneiah, and *O*....... 1Chr 15:21 5654
Moreover the sons of *O* were....... 1Chr 26:4 5654
All these of the sons of *O*....... 1Chr 26:8 5654
were threescore and two of *O*....... 1Chr 26:8 5654
To *O* southward....... 1Chr 26:15 5654
3. Another priest who relocated the Ark.
and Eliab, and Benaiah, and *O*....... 1Chr 16:5 5654
O with their brethren, threescore....... 1Chr 16:38 5654
4. Son of Jeduthun.
O also the son of Jeduthun and....... 1Chr 16:38 5654
5. A Temple servant.
found in the house of God with *O*....... 2Chr 25:24 5654

OBEDIENCE {12}
for *o* to the faith among all....... Rom 1:5 *5218*
so by the *o* of one shall many be....... Rom 5:19 *5218*
or of *o* unto righteousness....... Rom 6:16 *5218*
For your *o* is come abroad unto....... Rom 16:19 *5218*
to all nations for the *o* of faith....... Rom 16:26 *5218*
they are commanded to be under *o*....... 1Cor 14:34 *5293*
he remembereth the *o* of you all....... 2Cor 7:15 *5218*
every thought to the *o* of Christ....... 2Cor 10:5 *5218*
when your *o* is fulfilled....... 2Cor 10:6 *5218*
in thy *o* I wrote unto thee....... Philem 21 *5218*
yet learned he *o* by the things....... Heb 5:8 *5218*
of the Spirit, unto *o* and....... 1Pet 1:2 *5218*

OBEDIENT {16}
hath said will we do, and be *o*....... Ex 24:7 8085
the children of Israel may be *o*....... Num 27:20 8085
shalt be *o* unto his voice....... Deut 4:30 8085
because ye would not be *o* unto....... Deut 8:20 8085
hear, they shall be *o* unto me....... 2Sa 22:45 8085
is a wise reprover upon an *o* ear....... Prov 25:12 8085
If ye be willing and *o*, ye shall....... Is 1:19 8085
neither were they *o* unto his law....... Is 42:24 8085
the priests were *o* to the faith....... Acts 6:7 *5219*
by me, to make the Gentiles *o*....... Rom 15:18 *5218*
whether ye be *o* in all things....... 2Cor 2:9 *5255*
be *o* to them that are your....... Eph 6:5 *5219*
became *o* unto death, even the....... Phil 2:8 *5255*
o to their own husbands, that the....... Titus 2:5 *5293*
Exhort servants to be *o* unto....... Titus 2:9 *5293*
As *o* children, not fashioning....... 1Pet 1:14 *5218*

OBEISANCE {9}
about, and made *o* to my sheaf....... Gen 37:7 7812
and the eleven stars made *o* to me....... Gen 37:9 7812
bowed down their heads, and made *o*....... Gen 43:28 7812
meet his father in law, and did *o*....... Ex 18:7 7812
he fell to the earth, and did *o*....... 2Sa 1:2 7812
her face to the ground, and did *o*....... 2Sa 14:4 7812
man came nigh to him to do him *o*....... 2Sa 15:5 7812
bowed, and did *o* unto the king....... 1Kin 1:16 7812
of Judah, and made *o* to the king....... 2Chr 24:17 7812

OBEY {69}
o my voice according to that....... Gen 27:8 8085
only *o* my voice, and go fetch me....... Gen 27:13 8085
Now therefore, my son, *o* my voice....... Gen 27:43 8085
that I should *o* his voice to let....... Ex 5:2 8085
if ye will *o* my voice indeed, and....... Ex 19:5 8085
o his voice, provoke him not....... Ex 23:21 8085
if thou shalt indeed *o* his voice....... Ex 23:22 8085
if ye *o* the commandments of the....... Deut 11:27 8085
if ye will not *o* the commandments....... Deut 11:28 8085
o his voice, and ye shall serve....... Deut 13:4 8085
which will not *o* the voice of his....... Deut 21:18 8085
he will not *o* our voice....... Deut 21:20 8085
Thou shalt therefore *o* the voice....... Deut 27:10 8085
because thou wouldest not *o* the....... Deut 28:62 8085
shalt *o* his voice according to....... Deut 30:2 8085
o the voice of the LORD, and do....... Deut 30:8 8085
and that thou mayest *o* his voice....... Deut 30:20 8085
we serve, and his voice will we *o*....... Josh 24:24 8085
refused to *o* the voice of Samuel....... 1Sa 8:19 8085
o his voice, and not rebel against....... 1Sa 12:14 8085
But if ye will not *o* the voice of....... 1Sa 12:15 8085
thou not *o* the voice of the LORD....... 1Sa 15:19 8085
to *o* is better than sacrifice, and....... 1Sa 15:22 8085
And refused to *o*, neither were....... Neh 9:17 8085
If they *o* and serve him, they....... Job 36:11 8085
But if they *o* not, they shall....... Job 36:12 8085
they hear of me, they shall *o* me....... Ps 18:44 8085
and despiseth to *o* his mother....... Prov 30:17 3349
children of Ammon shall *o* them....... Is 11:14 4928
O my voice, and I will be your God....... Jer 7:23 8085
O my voice, and do them, according....... Jer 11:4 8085
and protesting, saying, *O* my voice....... Jer 11:7 8085
But if they will not *o*, I will....... Jer 12:17 8085
that it *o* not my voice, then I....... Jer 18:10 8085
o the voice of the LORD your God....... Jer 26:13 8085
but *o* their father's commandment....... Jer 35:14 8085
O, I beseech thee, the voice of....... Jer 38:20 8085
we will *o* the voice of the LORD....... Jer 42:6 8085
when we *o* the voice of the LORD....... Jer 42:6 8085
neither *o* the voice of the LORD....... Jer 42:13 8085
dominions shall serve and *o* him....... Dan 7:27 8086
that they might not *o* thy voice....... Dan 9:11 8085
if ye will diligently *o* the voice....... Zec 6:15 8085
even the winds and the sea *o* him....... Mt 8:27 *5219*
unclean spirits, and they do *o* him....... Mk 1:27 *5219*
even the wind and the sea *o* him....... Mk 4:41 *5219*
the winds and water, and they *o* him....... Lk 8:25 *5219*
and it should *o* you....... Lk 17:6 *5219*
We ought to *o* God rather than men....... Acts 5:29 *3980*
God hath given to them that *o* him....... Acts 5:32 *3980*
To whom our fathers would not *o*... Acts 7:39 *5255,1036*
do not *o* the truth....... Rom 2:8 *544*
but *o* unrighteousness....... Rom 2:8 *3982*
that ye should *o* it in the lusts....... Rom 6:12 *5219*
ye yield yourselves servants to *o*....... Rom 6:16 *5218*
his servants ye are to whom ye *o*....... Rom 6:16 *5219*
that ye should not *o* the truth....... Gal 3:1 *3982*
that ye should not *o* the truth....... Gal 5:7 *3982*
o your parents in the Lord....... Eph 6:1 *5219*
o your parents in all things....... Col 3:20 *5219*
o in all things your masters....... Col 3:22 *5219*
that *o* not the gospel of our Lord....... 2Th 1:8 *5219*
if any man *o* not our word by this....... 2Th 3:14 *5219*
to *o* magistrates, to be ready to....... Titus 3:1 *3980*
unto all them that *o* him....... Heb 5:9 *5219*
O them that have the rule over....... Heb 13:17 *3982*
mouths, that they may *o* us....... Jas 3:3 *3982*
if any *o* not the word, they also....... 1Pet 3:1 *544*
them that *o* not the gospel of God....... 1Pet 4:17 *544*

OBEYED {41}
because thou hast *o* my voice....... Gen 22:18 8085
Because that Abraham *o* my voice....... Gen 26:5 8085
And that Jacob *o* his father....... Gen 28:7 8085
because they *o* not the voice of....... Josh 5:6 8085
have *o* my voice in all that I....... Josh 22:2 8085
but ye have not *o* my voice....... Judg 2:2 8085
but ye have not *o* my voice....... Judg 6:10 8085
I have *o* the voice of the LORD,....... 1Sa 15:20 8085
the people, and *o* their voice....... 1Sa 15:24 8085
thine handmaid hath *o* thy voice....... 1Sa 28:21 8085
hast not *o* the voice of the LORD....... 1Kin 20:36 8085
Because they *o* not the voice of....... 2Kin 18:12 8085
and all Israel *o* him....... 1Chr 29:23 8085
they *o* the words of the LORD, and....... 2Chr 11:4 8085
have not *o* the voice of my....... Prov 5:13 8085
tree, and ye have not *o* my voice....... Jer 3:13 8085
have not *o* the voice of the LORD....... Jer 3:25 8085
them, and have not *o* my voice....... Jer 9:13 8085
Yet they *o* not, nor inclined....... Jer 11:8 8085
But they *o* not, neither inclined....... Jer 17:23 8085
but they *o* not thy voice, neither....... Jer 32:23 8085
of them any more, then they *o*....... Jer 34:10 8085
Thus have we *o* the voice of....... Jer 35:8 8085
we have dwelt in tents, and have *o*....... Jer 35:10 8085
Because ye have *o* the commandment....... Jer 35:18 8085
have not *o* his voice, therefore....... Jer 40:3 8085
but ye have not *o* the voice of....... Jer 42:21 8085
o not the voice of the LORD, to....... Jer 43:4 8085
for they *o* not the voice of the....... Jer 43:7 8085
have not *o* the voice of the LORD,....... Jer 44:23 8085
Neither have we *o* the voice of....... Dan 9:10 8085
for we *o* not his voice....... Dan 9:14 8085
She *o* not the voice....... Zeph 3:2 8085
o the voice of the LORD their God....... Hag 1:12 8085
and all, as many as *o* him, were....... Acts 5:36 *3982*
and all, even as many as *o* him....... Acts 5:37 *3982*
but ye have *o* from the heart that....... Rom 6:17 *5219*
they have not all *o* the gospel....... Rom 10:16 *5219*
my beloved, as ye have always *o*....... Phil 2:12 *5219*
receive for an inheritance, *o*....... Heb 11:8 *5219*
Even as Sarah *o* Abraham, calling....... 1Pet 3:6 *5219*

OBEYEDST {2}
Because thou *o* not the voice of....... 1Sa 28:18 8085
youth, that thou *o* not my voice....... Jer 22:21 8085

OBEYETH {3}
that *o* the voice of his servant,....... Is 50:10 8085
This is a nation that *o* not the....... Jer 7:28 8085
Cursed be the man that *o* not the....... Jer 11:3 8085

OBEYING {3}
o the commandments of the LORD....... Judg 2:17 8085
as in *o* the voice of the LORD....... 1Sa 15:22 8085
in *o* the truth through the Spirit....... 1Pet 1:22 *5218*

OBIL *(o'-bil)* {1} *An Ishmaelite camel driver.*
camels also was *O* the Ishmaelite....... 1Chr 27:30 179

OBJECT {1}
have been here before thee, and *o*....... Acts 24:19 *2723*

OBLATION {35}
if thou bring an *o* of a meat....... Lev 2:4 7133
if thy *o* be a meat offering baken....... Lev 2:5 7133
if thy *o* be a meat offering baken....... Lev 2:7 7133
As for the *o* of the firstfruits,....... Lev 2:12 7133
every *o* of thy meat offering....... Lev 2:13 7133
if his *o* be a sacrifice of peace....... Lev 3:1 7133
offer one out of the whole *o* for....... Lev 7:14 7133
unto the LORD shall bring his *o*....... Lev 7:29 7133
will offer his *o* for all his vows....... Lev 22:18 7133
every *o* of theirs, every meat....... Num 18:9 7133
brought an *o* for the LORD....... Num 31:50 7133
day, and shall do sacrifice and *o*....... Is 19:21 4503
o chooseth a tree that will not....... Is 40:20 8641
he that offereth an *o*, as if he....... Is 66:3 4503
they offer burnt offering and an *o*....... Jer 14:12 4503
every *o* of all, of every sort of....... Eze 44:30 8641
ye shall offer an *o* unto the LORD....... Eze 45:1 8641
over against the *o* of the holy....... Eze 45:6 8641
side of the *o* of the holy portion....... Eze 45:7 8641
before the *o* of the holy portion,....... Eze 45:7 8641
This is the *o* that ye shall offer....... Eze 45:13 8641
this *o* for the prince in Israel....... Eze 45:16 8641
The *o* that ye shall offer unto....... Eze 48:9 8641
the priests, shall be this holy *o*....... Eze 48:10 8641
this *o* of the land that is....... Eze 48:12 8642
in length over against the *o* of....... Eze 48:18 8641
against the *o* of the holy portion....... Eze 48:18 8641
All the *o* shall be five and twenty....... Eze 48:20 8641
shall offer the holy *o* foursquare....... Eze 48:20 8641
and on the other of the holy *o*....... Eze 48:21 8641
of the *o* toward the east border....... Eze 48:21 8641
and it shall be the holy *o*....... Eze 48:21 8641
that they should offer an *o*....... Dan 2:46 4541
about the time of the evening *o*....... Dan 9:21 4503
the *o* to cease, and for the....... Dan 9:27 4503

OBLATIONS {5}
to offer their *o* unto the LORD....... Lev 7:38 7133
to distribute the *o* of the LORD....... 2Chr 31:14 8641
Bring no more vain *o*....... Is 1:13 4503
and the firstfruits of your *o*....... Eze 20:40 4864
of all, of every sort of your *o*....... Eze 44:30 8641

OBOTH *(o'-both)* {4} *An Israelite encampment in the wilderness.*
set forward, and pitched in *O*....... Num 21:10 88
And they journeyed from *O*, and....... Num 21:11 88
from Punon, and pitched in *O*....... Num 33:43 88
And they departed from *O*, and....... Num 33:44 88

OBSCURE {1}
shall be put out in *o* darkness....... Prov 20:20 380

OBSCURITY {3}
of the blind shall see out of *o*....... Is 29:18 652
then shall thy light rise in *o*....... Is 58:10 2822
we wait for light, but behold *o*....... Is 59:9 2822

OBSERVATION {1}
kingdom of God cometh not with *o*....... Lk 17:20 *3907*

OBSERVE {55}
And ye shall *o* the feast of....... Ex 12:17 8104
therefore shall ye *o* this day in....... Ex 12:17 8104
ye shall *o* this thing for an....... Ex 12:24 8104
to *o* the sabbath throughout their....... Ex 31:16 6213
O thou that which I command thee....... Ex 34:11 8104
thou shalt *o* the feast of weeks,....... Ex 34:22 6213
ye use enchantment, nor *o* times....... Lev 19:26 6049
shall ye *o* all my statutes....... Lev 19:37 8104
shall ye *o* to offer unto me in....... Num 28:2 8104
Ye shall *o* to do therefore as the....... Deut 5:32 8104
O Israel, and *o* to do it....... Deut 6:3 8104
if we *o* to do all these....... Deut 6:25 8104
thee this day shall ye *o* to do....... Deut 8:1 8104
ye shall *o* to do all the statutes....... Deut 11:32 8104
which ye shall *o* to do in the....... Deut 12:1 8104
O and hear all these words which I....... Deut 12:28 8104
soever I command you, *o* to do it....... Deut 12:32 8104
to *o* to do all these commandments....... Deut 15:5 8104
O the month of Abib, and keep the....... Deut 16:1 8104
and thou shalt *o* and do these....... Deut 16:12 8104
Thou shalt *o* the feast of....... Deut 16:13 6213
thou shalt *o* to do according to....... Deut 17:10 8104
that thou *o* diligently, and do....... Deut 24:8 8104
them, so ye shall *o* to do....... Deut 24:8 8104
voice of the LORD thy God, to *o*....... Deut 28:1 8104
I command thee this day, to *o*....... Deut 28:13 8104
to *o* to do all his commandments....... Deut 28:15 8104
If thou wilt not *o* to do all the....... Deut 28:58 8104
o to do all the words of this law....... Deut 31:12 8104
command your children to *o* to do....... Deut 32:46 8104
that thou mayest *o* to do....... Josh 1:7 8104
night, that thou mayest *o* to do....... Josh 1:8 8104
that I commanded her let her *o*....... Judg 13:14 8104
Now the men did diligently *o*....... 1Kin 20:33 5172
ye shall *o* to do for evermore....... 2Kin 17:37 8104

O

only if they will *o* to do ... 2Kin 21:8 8104
shalt *o* my statutes and my ... 2Chr 7:17 8104
love him and *o* his commandments ... Neh 1:5 8104
Moses the servant of God, and to *o* ... Neh 10:29 8104
That they might *o* his statutes ... Ps 105:45 8104
will *o* these things, even they ... Ps 107:43 8104
I shall *o* it with my whole heart ... Ps 119:34 8104
and let thine eyes *o* my ways ... Prov 23:26 5341
the swallow *o* the time of their ... Jer 8:7 8104
neither *o* their judgments, nor ... Eze 20:18 8104
o my statutes, and do them ... Eze 37:24 8104
leopard by the way will I *o* them ... Hos 13:7 7789
They that *o* lying vanities ... Jonah 2:8 8104
they bid you *o*, that *o* ... Mt 23:3 *5083*
Teaching them to *o* all things ... Mt 28:20 *5083*
for us to receive, neither to *o* ... Acts 16:21 *4160*
that they *o* no such thing ... Acts 21:25 *5083*
Ye *o* days, and months, and times, ... Gal 4:10 *3906*
that thou *o* these things without ... 1Ti 5:21 *5442*

OBSERVED {11}
but his father *o* the saying ... Gen 37:11 8104
It is a night to be much *o* unto ... Ex 12:42 8107
o of all the children of Israel ... Ex 12:42 8107
not *o* all these commandments, ... Num 15:22 6213
for they have *o* thy word, and kept ... Deut 33:9 8104
to pass, when Joab *o* the city ... 2Sa 11:16 8104
o times, and used enchantments, and ... 2Kin 21:6 6049
also he *o* times, and used ... 2Chr 33:6 6049
I have heard him, and *o* him ... Hos 14:8 7789
a just man and an holy, and *o* him ... Mk 6:20 *4933*
all these have I *o* from my youth ... Mk 10:20 *5442*

OBSERVER {1}
or an *o* of times, or an enchanter ... Deut 18:10 6049

OBSERVERS {1}
hearkened unto *o* of times ... Deut 18:14 6049

OBSERVEST {1}
many things, but thou *o* not ... Is 42:20 8104

OBSERVETH {1}
He that *o* the wind shall not sow ... Eccl 11:4 8104

OBSTINATE {2}
his spirit, and made his heart *o* ... Deut 2:30 553
Because I knew that thou art *o* ... Is 48:4 7186

OBTAIN {15}
be that I may *o* children by her ... Gen 16:2 1129
shall *o* favour of the LORD ... Prov 8:35 6329
they shall *o* joy and gladness, and ... Is 35:10 5381
they shall *o* gladness and joy ... Is 51:11 5381
o the kingdom by flatteries ... Dan 11:21 2388
for they shall *o* mercy ... Mt 5:7 *1653*
accounted worthy to *o* that world ... Lk 20:35 *5177*
your mercy they also may *o* mercy ... Rom 11:31 *1653*
So run, that ye may *o* ... 1Cor 9:24 *2638*
Now they do it to *o* a corruptible ... 1Cor 9:25 *2983*
but to *o* salvation by our Lord ... 1Th 5:9 *4047*
sakes, that they may also *o* the ... 2Ti 2:10 *5177*
of grace, that we may *o* mercy ... Heb 4:16 *2983*
that they might *o* a better ... Heb 11:35 *5177*
and desire to have, and cannot *o* ... Jas 4:2 *2013*

OBTAINED {28}
after certain days *o* I leave of ... Neh 13:6 7592
him, and she *o* kindness of him ... Est 2:9 5375
Esther *o* favour in the sight of ... Est 2:15 5375
she *o* grace and favour in his ... Est 2:17 5375
that she *o* favour in his sight ... Est 5:2 5375
upon her that had not *o* mercy ... Hos 2:23 5375
had *o* part of this ministry ... Acts 1:17 *2975*
With a great sum *o* I this freedom ... Acts 22:28 *2932*
Having therefore *o* help of God ... Acts 26:22 *5177*
that they had *o* their purpose ... Acts 27:13 *2902*
Israel hath not *o* that which he ... Rom 11:7 *2013*
but the election hath *o* it ... Rom 11:7 *2013*
yet have now *o* mercy through ... Rom 11:30 *1653*
as one that hath *o* mercy of the ... 1Cor 7:25 *1653*
also we have *o* an inheritance ... Eph 1:11 *2820*
but I *o* mercy, because I did it ... 1Ti 1:13 *1653*
Howbeit for this cause I *o* mercy ... 1Ti 1:16 *1653*
as he hath by inheritance *o* a ... Heb 1:4 *2816*
endured, he *o* the promise ... Heb 6:15 *2013*
But now hath he *o* a more ... Heb 8:6 *5177*
having *o* eternal redemption for ... Heb 9:12 *2147*
by it the elders *o* a good report ... Heb 11:2 *3140*
by which he *o* witness that he was ... Heb 11:4 *3140*
o promises, stopped the mouths of ... Heb 11:33 *2013*
having *o* a good report through ... Heb 11:39 *3140*
which had not *o* mercy ... 1Pet 2:10 *1653*
but now have *o* mercy ... 1Pet 2:10 *1653*
to them that have *o* like precious ... 2Pet 1:1 *2975*

OBTAINETH {2}
A good man *o* favour of the LORD ... Prov 12:2 6329
thing, and *o* favour of the LORD ... Prov 18:22 6329

OBTAINING {1}
to the *o* of the glory of our Lord ... 2Th 2:14 *4047*

OCCASION {21}
that he may seek *o* against us ... Gen 43:18 1556
do to them as thou shalt find *o* ... Judg 9:33 4672
that he sought an *o* against the ... Judg 14:4 8385
that thou do as *o* serve thee ... 1Sa 10:7 4672
o to the enemies of the LORD to ... 2Sa 12:14 ...
which thou shalt have *o* to bestow ... Ezr 7:20 5308
in her *o* who can turn her away ... Jer 2:24 8385
ye shall not have *o* any more to ... Eze 18:3 ...
princes sought to find *o* against ... Dan 6:4 5931
they could find none *o* nor fault ... Dan 6:4 5931
find any *o* against this Daniel ... Dan 6:5 5931
taking *o* by the commandment, ... Rom 7:8 *874*
taking *o* by the commandment, ... Rom 7:11 *874*
an *o* to fall in his brother's way ... Rom 14:13 *4625*
but give you *o* to glory on our ... 2Cor 5:12 *874*
but by *o* of the forwardness of ... 2Cor 8:8 *1223*
o from them which desire *o* ... 2Cor 11:12 *874*
not liberty for an *o* to the flesh ... Gal 5:13 *874*
give none *o* to the adversary to ... 1Ti 5:14 *874*
there is none *o* of stumbling in ... 1Jn 2:10 *4625*

OCCASIONED {1}
I have *o* the death of all the ... 1Sa 22:22 5437

OCCASIONS {3}
give *o* of speech against her, and ... Deut 22:14 5949
he hath given *o* of speech against ... Deut 22:17 5949
Behold, he findeth *o* against me ... Job 33:10 8569

OCCUPATION {5}
you, and shall say, What is your *o* ... Gen 46:33 4639
unto his brethren, What is your *o* ... Gen 47:3 4639
What is thine *o* ... Jonah 1:8 4399
for by their *o* they were ... Acts 18:3 *5078*
with the workmen of like *o* ... Acts 19:25

OCCUPIED {7}
All the gold that was *o* for the ... Ex 38:24 6213
with new ropes that never were *o* ... Judg 16:11 6213,4399
they *o* in thy fairs with emeralds ... Eze 27:16 5414
going to and fro *o* in thy fairs ... Eze 27:19 5414
they *o* with thee in lambs, and ... Eze 27:21 5503
they *o* in thy fairs with chief of ... Eze 27:22 5414
them that have been *o* therein ... Heb 13:9 *4043*

OCCUPIERS {1}
the *o* of thy merchandise, and all ... Eze 27:27 6148

OCCUPIETH {1}
how shall he that *o* the room of ... 1Cor 14:16 *378*

OCCUPY {2}
were in thee to *o* thy merchandise ... Eze 27:9 6148
and said unto them, *O* till I come ... Lk 19:13 *4231*

OCCURRENT {1}
is neither adversary nor evil *o* ... 1Kin 5:4 6294

OCHRAN See OCRAN.

OCRAN *(o'-cran)* {5} *An Asherite who counted the people.*
Pagiel the son of *O* ... Num 1:13 5918
shall be Pagiel the son of *O* ... Num 2:27 5918
eleventh day Pagiel the son of *O* ... Num 7:72 5918
offering of Pagiel the son of *O* ... Num 7:77 5918
of Asher was Pagiel the son of *O* ... Num 10:26 5918

ODD {1}
wherewith the *o* number of them is ... Num 3:48 5736

ODED *(o'-ded)* {3}
1. Father of Azariah.
came upon Azariah the son of *O* ... 2Chr 15:1 5752
and the prophecy of *O* the prophet ... 2Chr 15:8 5752
2. A prophet of Samaria.
LORD was there, whose name was *O* ... 2Chr 28:9 5752

ODIOUS {2}
had made themselves *o* to David ... 1Chr 19:6 887
For an *o* woman when she is ... Prov 30:23 8130

ODOUR {2}
filled with the *o* of the ointment ... Jn 12:3 *3744*
you, an *o* of a sweet smell, a ... Phil 4:18 *3744*

ODOURS {7}
smell the savour of your sweet *o* ... Lev 26:31 5207
bed which was filled with sweet *o* ... 2Chr 16:14 1314
myrrh, and six months with sweet *o* ... Est 2:12 1314
so shall they burn *o* for thee ... Jer 34:5
an oblation and sweet *o* unto him ... Dan 2:46 5208
harps, and golden vials full of *o* ... Rev 5:8 *2368*
And cinnamon, and *o*, and ointments, ... Rev 18:13 *2368*

OF See APPENDIX.

OFF See APPENDIX.

OFFENCE {19}
nor *o* of heart unto my lord, ... 1Sa 25:31 4383
for a rock of *o* to both the ... Is 8:14 4383
till they acknowledge their *o* ... Hos 5:15 816
thou art an *o* unto me ... Mt 16:23 *4625*
to that man by whom the *o* cometh ... Mt 18:7 *4625*
a conscience void of *o* toward God ... Acts 24:16 *677*
But not as the *o*, so also is the ... Rom 5:15 *3900*
For if through the *o* of one many ... Rom 5:15 *3900*
For if by one man's *o* death ... Rom 5:17 *3900*
Therefore as by the *o* of one ... Rom 5:18 *3900*
entered, that the *o* might abound ... Rom 5:20 *3900*
a stumblingstone and rock of *o* ... Rom 9:33 *4625*
for that man who eateth with *o* ... Rom 14:20 *4348*
Give none *o*, neither to the Jews, ... 1Cor 10:32 *677*
Giving no *o* in any thing, that ... 2Cor 6:3 *4349*
Have I committed an *o* in abasing ... 2Cor 11:7 *266*
then is the *o* of the cross ceased ... Gal 5:11 *4625*
without *o* till the day of Christ ... Phil 1:10 *677*
of stumbling, and a rock of *o* ... 1Pet 2:8 *4625*

OFFENCES {7}
for yielding pacifieth great *o* ... Eccl 10:4 2399
Woe unto the world because of *o* ... Mt 18:7 *4625*
for it must needs be that *o* come ... Mt 18:7 *4625*
impossible but that *o* will come ... Lk 17:1 *4625*
Who was delivered for our *o* ... Rom 4:25 *3900*
is of many *o* unto justification ... Rom 5:16 *3900*
o contrary to the doctrine which ... Rom 16:17 *4625*

OFFEND {25}
I will not *o* any more ... Job 34:31 2254
I should *o* against the generation ... Ps 73:15 898
and nothing shall *o* them ... Ps 119:165 4383
all that devour him shall *o* ... Jer 2:3 816
We *o* not, because they have ... Jer 50:7 816
the harlot, yet let not Judah *o* ... Hos 4:15 816
and he shall pass over, and *o* ... Hab 1:11 816
And if thy right eye *o* thee ... Mt 5:29 *4624*
And if thy right hand *o* thee ... Mt 5:30 *4624*
of his kingdom all things that *o* ... Mt 13:41 *4625*
lest we should *o* them, go thou ... Mt 17:27 *4624*
But whoso shall *o* one of these ... Mt 18:6 *4624*
if thy hand or thy foot *o* thee ... Mt 18:8 *4624*
And if thine eye *o* thee, pluck it ... Mt 18:9 *4624*
whosoever shall *o* one of these ... Mk 9:42 *4624*
And if thy hand *o* thee, cut it off ... Mk 9:43 *4624*
And if thy foot *o* thee, cut it off ... Mk 9:45 *4624*
And if thine eye *o* thee, pluck it ... Mk 9:47 *4624*
than that he should *o* one of ... Lk 17:2 *4624*
said unto them, Doth this *o* you ... Jn 6:61 *4624*
if meat make my brother to *o* ... 1Cor 8:13 *4624*
lest I make my brother to *o* ... 1Cor 8:13 *4624*
yet *o* in one point, he is guilty ... Jas 2:10 *4417*
For in many things we *o* all ... Jas 3:2 *4417*
If any man *o* not in word, the ... Jas 3:2 *4417*

OFFENDED {25}
and what have I *o* thee, that thou ... Gen 20:9 2398
his baker had *o* their lord the ... Gen 40:1 2398
to Lachish, saying, I have *o* ... 2Kin 18:14 2398
for whereas we have *o* against the ... 2Chr 28:13 819
A brother *o* is harder to be won ... Prov 18:19 6586
What have I *o* against thee, or ... Jer 37:18 2398
vengeance, and hath greatly *o* ... Eze 25:12 816
but when he *o* in Baal, he died ... Hos 13:1 816
whosoever shall not be *o* in me ... Mt 11:6 *4624*
of the word, by and by he is *o* ... Mt 13:21 *4624*
And they were *o* in him ... Mt 13:57 *4624*
thou that the Pharisees were *o* ... Mt 15:12 *4624*
And then shall many be *o*, and shall ... Mt 24:10 *4624*
All ye shall be *o* because of me ... Mt 26:31 *4624*
men shall be *o* because of thee ... Mt 26:33 *4624*
yet will I never be *o* ... Mt 26:33 *4624*
sake, immediately they are *o* ... Mk 4:17 *4624*
And they were *o* at him ... Mk 6:3 *4624*
All ye shall be *o* because of me ... Mk 14:27 *4624*
unto him, Although all shall be *o* ... Mk 14:29 *4624*
whosoever shall not be *o* in me ... Lk 7:23 *4624*
unto you, that ye should not be *o* ... Jn 16:1 *4624*
have I *o* any thing at all ... Acts 25:8 *264*
thy brother stumbleth, or is *o* ... Rom 14:21 *4624*
who is *o*, and I burn not ... 2Cor 11:29 *4624*

OFFENDER {2}
That make a man an *o* for a word ... Is 29:21 2398
For if I be an *o*, or have ... Acts 25:11 *91*

OFFENDERS {1}
my son Solomon shall be counted *o* ... 1Kin 1:21 2400

OFFER {236}
o him there for a burnt offering ... Gen 22:2 5927
Thou shalt not delay to *o* the ... Ex 22:29
Thou shalt not *o* the blood of my ... Ex 23:18 2076
thou shalt *o* every day a bullock ... Ex 29:36 6213
which thou shalt *o* upon the altar ... Ex 29:38 6213
lamb thou shalt *o* in the morning ... Ex 29:39 6213
other lamb thou shalt *o* at even ... Ex 29:39 6213
other lamb thou shalt *o* at even ... Ex 29:41 6213
Ye shall *o* no strange incense ... Ex 30:9 5927
Thou shalt not *o* the blood of my ... Ex 34:25 7819
Every one that did *o* an offering ... Ex 35:24 7311
let him *o* a male without blemish ... Lev 1:3 7126
he shall *o* it of his own ... Lev 1:3 7126
when any will *o* a meat offering ... Lev 2:1 7126
ye shall *o* them unto the LORD ... Lev 2:12 7126
thine offerings thou shalt *o* salt ... Lev 2:13 7126
if thou *o* a meat offering of thy ... Lev 2:14 7126
thou shalt *o* for the meat ... Lev 2:14 7126
offering, if he *o* it of the herd ... Lev 3:1 7126
he shall *o* it without blemish ... Lev 3:1 7126
he shall *o* of the sacrifice of ... Lev 3:3 7126
he shall *o* it without blemish ... Lev 3:6 7126
If he *o* a lamb for his offering, ... Lev 3:7 7126
then shall he *o* it before the ... Lev 3:7 7126
he shall *o* of the sacrifice of ... Lev 3:9 7126
then he shall *o* it before the ... Lev 3:12 7126
he shall *o* thereof his offering, ... Lev 3:14 7126
o a young bullock for the sin ... Lev 4:14 7126
who shall *o* that which is for the ... Lev 5:8 7126
he shall *o* the second for a burnt ... Lev 5:10 6213
Aaron shall *o* it before the LORD ... Lev 6:14 7126
which they shall *o* unto the LORD ... Lev 6:20 7126
o for a sweet savour unto the ... Lev 6:21 7126
anointed in his stead shall *o* it ... Lev 6:22 6213
he shall *o* of it all the fat ... Lev 7:3 7126
which he shall *o* unto the LORD ... Lev 7:11 7126
If he *o* it for a thanksgiving, ... Lev 7:12 7126
then he shall *o* with the ... Lev 7:12 7126
he shall *o* for his offering ... Lev 7:13 7126
of it he shall *o* one out of the ... Lev 7:14 7126
of which men *o* an offering made ... Lev 7:25 7126
the children of Israel to *o* their ... Lev 7:38 7126
and *o* them before the LORD ... Lev 9:2 7126
o thy sin offering, and thy burnt ... Lev 9:7 6213
o the offering of the people, and ... Lev 9:7 6213
Who shall *o* it before the LORD, ... Lev 12:7 7126
o him for a trespass offering, and ... Lev 14:12 7126
priest shall *o* the sin offering ... Lev 14:19 6213
the priest shall *o* the burnt ... Lev 14:20 5927
he shall *o* the one of the ... Lev 14:30 6213
And the priest shall *o* them ... Lev 15:15 6213

the priest shall *o* the one for a ... Lev 15:30 6213
Aaron shall *o* his bullock of the ... Lev 16:6 7126
fell, and *o* him for a sin offering ... Lev 16:9 6213
o his burnt offering, and the ... Lev 16:24 6213
to *o* an offering unto the LORD ... Lev 17:4 7126
which they *o* in the open field, ... Lev 17:5 2076
o them for peace offerings unto ... Lev 17:5 2076
they shall no more *o* their ... Lev 17:7 2076
to *o* it unto the LORD ... Lev 17:9 6213
if ye *o* a sacrifice of peace ... Lev 19:5 2076
ye shall *o* it at your own will ... Lev 19:5 2076
be eaten the same day ye *o* it ... Lev 19:6 2077
the bread of their God, they do *o* ... Lev 21:6 7126
to *o* the bread of his God ... Lev 21:17 7126
the priest shall come nigh to *o* ... Lev 21:21 7126
nigh to *o* the bread of his God ... Lev 21:21 7126
which they *o* unto the LORD ... Lev 22:15 7311
that will *o* his oblation for all ... Lev 22:18 7126
which they will *o* unto the LORD ... Lev 22:18 7126
Ye shall *o* at your own will a ... Lev 22:19
a blemish, that shall ye not *o* ... Lev 22:20 7126
ye shall not *o* these unto the ... Lev 22:22 7126
that mayest thou *o* for a freewill ... Lev 22:23 6213
Ye shall not *o* unto the LORD that ... Lev 22:24 7126
o the bread of your God of any of ... Lev 22:25 7126
when ye will *o* a sacrifice of ... Lev 22:29 2076
the LORD, *o* it at your own will ... Lev 22:29 2076
But ye shall *o* an offering made ... Lev 23:8 7126
ye shall *o* that day when ye wave ... Lev 23:12 6213
ye shall *o* a new meat offering ... Lev 23:16 7126
ye shall *o* with the bread seven ... Lev 23:18 7126
but ye shall *o* an offering made ... Lev 23:25 7126
o an offering made by fire unto ... Lev 23:27 7126
Seven days ye shall *o* an offering ... Lev 23:36 7126
ye shall *o* an offering made by ... Lev 23:36 7126
to *o* an offering made by fire ... Lev 23:37 7126
beast, of which they do not *o* a ... Lev 27:11 7126
the LORD, and *o* it upon the altar ... Num 5:25 7126
the priest shall *o* the one for a ... Num 6:11 6213
he shall *o* his offering unto the ... Num 6:14 7126
shall *o* his sin offering, and his ... Num 6:16 6213
And he shall *o* the ram for a ... Num 6:17 6213
the priest shall *o* also his meat ... Num 6:17 6213
They shall *o* their offering, each ... Num 7:11 7126
Zuar, prince of Issachar, did *o* ... Num 7:18 7126
of the children of Zebulun, did *o* ... Num 7:24
of the children of Reuben, did *o* ... Num 7:30
of the children of Simeon, did *o* ... Num 7:36
Aaron shall *o* the Levites before ... Num 8:11 5130
thou shalt *o* the one for a sin ... Num 8:12 6213
o them for an offering unto the ... Num 8:13 5130
them, and *o* them for an offering ... Num 8:15 5130
that we may not *o* an offering of ... Num 9:7 7126
o the third part of an hin of ... Num 15:7 7126
will *o* an offering made by fire, ... Num 15:14 6213
ye shall *o* up an heave offering ... Num 15:19 7311
Ye shall *o* up a cake of the first ... Num 15:20 7311
o one young bullock for a burnt ... Num 15:24 6213
come near to *o* incense before the ... Num 16:40
which they shall *o* unto the LORD ... Num 18:12 5414
of Israel *o* unto the LORD ... Num 18:19 7311
which they *o* as an heave offering ... Num 18:24 7311
then ye shall *o* up an heave ... Num 18:26 7311
Thus ye also shall *o* an heave ... Num 18:28 7311
o every heave offering of the ... Num 18:29 7311
shall ye observe to *o* unto me in ... Num 28:2 7126
which ye shall *o* unto the LORD ... Num 28:3 7126
lamb shalt thou *o* in the morning ... Num 28:4 6213
other lamb shalt thou *o* at even ... Num 28:4 6213
other lamb shalt thou *o* at even ... Num 28:8 6213
offering thereof, thou shalt *o* it ... Num 28:8 6213
of your months ye shall *o* a burnt ... Num 28:11 7126
But ye shall *o* a sacrifice made ... Num 28:19 7126
deals shall ye *o* for a bullock ... Num 28:20 6213
deal shalt thou *o* for every lamb ... Num 28:21 6213
Ye shall *o* these beside the burnt ... Num 28:23 6213
this manner ye shall *o* daily ... Num 28:24 6213
But ye shall *o* the burnt offering ... Num 28:27 7126
Ye shall *o* them beside the ... Num 28:31 6213
ye shall *o* a burnt offering for a ... Num 29:2 6213
But ye shall *o* a burnt offering ... Num 29:8 7126
ye shall *o* a burnt offering, a ... Num 29:13 7126
ye shall *o* twelve young bullocks ... Num 29:17
But ye shall *o* a burnt offering, ... Num 29:36 7126
thou *o* not thy burnt offerings in ... Deut 12:13 5927
there thou shalt *o* thy burnt ... Deut 12:14 5927
thou shalt *o* thy burnt offerings, ... Deut 12:27 6213
from them that *o* a sacrifice ... Deut 18:3 2076
thou shalt *o* burnt offerings ... Deut 27:6 5927
thou shalt *o* peace offerings, and ... Deut 27:7 2076
there they shall *o* sacrifices of ... Deut 33:19 2076
or if to *o* thereon burnt offering ... Josh 22:23 5927
or if to *o* peace offerings ... Josh 22:23 6213
had made an end to *o* the present ... Judg 3:18 7126
o a burnt sacrifice with the wood ... Judg 6:26 5927
I will *o* it up for a burnt ... Judg 11:31 5927
if thou wilt *o* a burnt offering, ... Judg 13:16 6213
thou must *o* it unto the LORD ... Judg 13:16 5927
to *o* a great sacrifice unto Dagon ... Judg 16:23 2076
went up to *o* unto the LORD the ... 1Sa 1:21 2076
husband to *o* the yearly sacrifice ... 1Sa 2:19 2076
to *o* upon mine altar, to burn ... 1Sa 2:28 5927
to *o* burnt offerings, and to ... 1Sa 10:8 5927
the LORD, I *o* thee three things ... 2Sa 24:12 5190
o up what seemeth good unto him ... 2Sa 24:22 5927
neither will I *o* burnt offerings ... 2Sa 24:24 5927
did Solomon *o* upon that altar ... 1Kin 3:4 5927
did Solomon *o* burnt offerings ... 1Kin 9:25 5927
upon thee shall he *o* the priests ... 1Kin 13:2 2076
o neither burnt offering nor ... 2Kin 5:17 6213
when they went in to *o* sacrifices ... 2Kin 10:24 6213
To *o* burnt offerings unto the ... 1Chr 16:40 5927
the LORD, I *o* thee three things ... 1Chr 21:10 5186
nor *o* burnt offerings without ... 1Chr 21:24 5927
to *o* all burnt sacrifices unto ... 1Chr 23:31 5927
that we should be able to *o* so ... 1Chr 29:14
here, to *o* willingly unto thee ... 1Chr 29:17
to *o* the burnt offerings of the ... 2Chr 23:18 5927
to *o* withal, and spoons, and ... 2Chr 24:14 5927
priests the sons of Aaron to *o* ... 2Chr 29:21 5927
Hezekiah commanded to *o* the burnt ... 2Chr 29:27 5927
to *o* unto the LORD, as it is ... 2Chr 35:12 7126
to *o* burnt offerings upon the ... 2Chr 35:16 5927
to *o* burnt offerings thereon, as ... Ezr 3:2 5927
o burnt offerings unto the LORD ... Ezr 3:6 5927
That they may *o* sacrifices of ... Ezr 6:10 7127
o them upon the altar of the ... Ezr 7:17 7127
o up for yourselves a burnt ... Job 42:8 5927
O the sacrifices of righteousness ... Ps 4:5 2076
offerings of blood will I not *o* ... Ps 16:4 5258
therefore will I *o* in his ... Ps 27:6 2076
O unto God thanksgiving ... Ps 50:14 2076
then shall they *o* bullocks upon ... Ps 51:19 5927
I will *o* unto thee burnt ... Ps 66:15 5927
I will *o* bullocks with goats ... Ps 66:15 6213
of Sheba and Seba shall *o* gifts ... Ps 72:10 7126
I will *o* to thee the sacrifice of ... Ps 116:17 2076
wentest thou up to *o* sacrifice ... Is 57:7 2076
the gods unto whom they *o* incense ... Jer 11:12
when they *o* burnt offering and an ... Jer 14:12 5927
before me to *o* burnt offerings ... Jer 33:18 5927
the place where they did *o* sweet ... Eze 6:13 5414
For when ye *o* your gifts, when ye ... Eze 20:31 5375
to *o* burnt offerings thereon, and ... Eze 43:18 5927
o a kid of the goats without ... Eze 43:22 7126
thou shalt *o* a young bullock ... Eze 43:23 7126
thou shalt *o* them before the LORD ... Eze 43:24 7126
they shall *o* them up for a burnt ... Eze 43:24 5927
when ye *o* my bread, the fat and ... Eze 44:7 7126
before me to *o* unto me the fat ... Eze 44:15 7126
he shall *o* his sin offering, ... Eze 44:27 7126
ye shall *o* an oblation unto the ... Eze 45:1 7311
is the oblation that ye shall *o* ... Eze 45:13 7311
ye shall *o* the tenth part of a ... Eze 45:14
o unto the LORD in the sabbath ... Eze 46:4 7126
offering which ye shall *o* of five ... Eze 48:8 7311
The oblation that ye shall *o* unto ... Eze 48:9 7311
ye shall *o* the holy oblation ... Eze 48:20 7311
that they should *o* an oblation ... Dan 2:46 5260
They shall not *o* wine offerings ... Hos 9:4 5258
o a sacrifice of thanksgiving ... Amos 4:5 6999
Though ye *o* me burnt offerings and ... Amos 5:22 5927
that which they *o* there is ... Hag 2:14 7126
Ye *o* polluted bread upon mine ... Mal 1:7 5066
if ye *o* the blind for sacrifice, ... Mal 1:8 5066
if ye *o* the lame and sick, is it ... Mal 1:8 5066
o it now unto thy governor ... Mal 1:8 7126
that they may *o* unto the LORD an ... Mal 3:3 5066
and then come and *o* thy gift ... Mt 5:24 *4374*
o the gift that Moses commanded, ... Mt 8:4 *4374*
o for thy cleansing those things ... Mk 1:44 *4374*
to *o* a sacrifice according to ... Lk 2:24 *1325*
o for thy cleansing, according as ... Lk 5:14 *4374*
on the one cheek *o* also the other ... Lk 6:29 *3930*
an egg, will he *o* him a scorpion ... Lk 11:12 *1929*
to God, that he may *o* both gifts ... Heb 5:1 *4374*
also for himself, to *o* for sins ... Heb 5:3 *4374*
to *o* up sacrifice, first for his ... Heb 7:27 *399*
priest is ordained to *o* gifts ... Heb 8:3 *4374*
this man have somewhat also to *o* ... Heb 8:3 *4374*
that *o* gifts according to the law ... Heb 8:4 *4374*
that he should *o* himself often ... Heb 9:25 *4374*
By him therefore let us *o* the ... Heb 13:15 *399*
to *o* up spiritual sacrifices, ... 1Pet 2:5 *399*
that he should *o* it with the ... Rev 8:3 *1325*

OFFERED {143}

o burnt offerings on the altar ... Gen 8:20 5927
o him up for a burnt offering in ... Gen 22:13 5927
Then Jacob *o* sacrifice upon the ... Gen 31:54 2076
o sacrifices unto the God of his ... Gen 46:1 2076
which *o* burnt offerings, and ... Ex 24:5 5927
o burnt offerings, and brought ... Ex 32:6 5927
every man that *o* ... Ex 35:22 5130
o an offering of gold ... Ex 35:22
o upon it the burnt offering and ... Ex 40:29 5927
burnt offering which he hath *o* ... Lev 7:8 7126
eaten the same day that it is *o* ... Lev 7:15 7133
o it for sin, as the first ... Lev 9:15 2398
o it according to the manner ... Lev 9:16 6213
o strange fire before the LORD, ... Lev 10:1 7126
have they *o* their sin offering ... Lev 10:19 7126
when they *o* before the LORD, and ... Lev 16:1 7126
when they *o* strange fire before ... Num 3:4 7126
over them that were numbered, *o* ... Num 7:2 7126
the princes *o* for dedicating of ... Num 7:10 7126
even the princes *o* their offering ... Num 7:10 7126
he that *o* his offering the first ... Num 7:12 7126
He *o* for his offering one silver ... Num 7:19 7126
prince of the children of Gad, *o* ... Num 7:42
of the children of Ephraim, *o* ... Num 7:48
On the eighth day *o* Gamaliel the ... Num 7:54
of the children of Benjamin, *o* ... Num 7:60
prince of the children of Dan, *o* ... Num 7:66
of the children of Asher, *o* ... Num 7:72
of the children of Naphtali, *o* ... Num 7:78
Aaron *o* them as an offering ... Num 8:21 5130
and fifty men that *o* incense ... Num 16:35 7126
for they *o* them before the LORD, ... Num 16:38 7126
they that were burnt had *o* ... Num 16:39 7126
And Balak *o* oxen and sheep, and sent ... Num 22:40 2076
Balaam *o* on every altar a bullock ... Num 23:2 5927
I have *o* upon every altar a ... Num 23:4 5927
o a bullock and a ram on every ... Num 23:14 5927
o a bullock and a ram on every ... Num 23:30 5927
when they *o* strange fire before ... Num 26:61 7126
offering unto the LORD shall be *o* ... Num 28:15 6213
it shall be *o* beside the ... Num 28:24 6213
that they *o* up to the LORD ... Num 31:52 7311
they *o* thereon burnt offerings ... Josh 8:31 5927
the people willingly *o* themselves ... Judg 5:2
that *o* themselves willingly among ... Judg 5:9
the second bullock was *o* upon the ... Judg 6:28 5927
o it upon a rock unto the LORD ... Judg 13:19 5927
o burnt offerings and peace ... Judg 20:26 5927
o burnt offerings and peace ... Judg 21:4 5927
when the time was that Elkanah *o* ... 1Sa 1:4 2076
that, when any man *o* sacrifice ... 1Sa 2:13 2076
o the kine a burnt offering unto ... 1Sa 6:14 5927
of Beth-shemesh *o* burnt offerings ... 1Sa 6:15 5927
o it for a burnt offering wholly ... 1Sa 7:9 5927
And he *o* the burnt offering ... 1Sa 13:9 5927
therefore, and *o* a burnt offering ... 1Sa 13:12 5927
David *o* burnt offerings and peace ... 2Sa 6:17 5927
from Giloh, while he *o* sacrifices ... 2Sa 15:12 2076
o burnt offerings and peace ... 2Sa 24:25 5927
o up burnt offerings ... 1Kin 3:15 5927
o peace offerings, and made a ... 1Kin 3:15 6213
o sacrifice before the LORD ... 1Kin 8:62 2076
Solomon *o* a sacrifice of peace ... 1Kin 8:63 2076
which he *o* unto the LORD, two and ... 1Kin 8:63 2076
for there he *o* burnt offerings, ... 1Kin 8:64 6213
in Judah, and he *o* upon the altar ... 1Kin 12:32 5927
So he *o* upon the altar which he ... 1Kin 12:33 5927
he *o* upon the altar, and burnt ... 1Kin 12:33 5927
for the people *o* and burnt incense ... 1Kin 22:43 2076
when the meat offering was *o* ... 2Kin 3:20 5927
o him for a burnt offering upon ... 2Kin 3:27 5927
to the altar, and *o* thereon ... 2Kin 16:12 5927
his sons *o* upon the altar of the ... 1Chr 6:49 6999
that they *o* seven bullocks and ... 1Chr 15:26 2076
they *o* burnt sacrifices and peace ... 1Chr 16:1 7126
o burnt offerings and peace ... 1Chr 21:26 5927
of the king's work, *o* willingly, ... 1Chr 29:6
for that they *o* willingly ... 1Chr 29:9
they *o* willingly to the LORD ... 1Chr 29:9
have willingly *o* all these things ... 1Chr 29:17
o burnt offerings unto the LORD, ... 1Chr 29:21 5927
o a thousand burnt offerings upon ... 2Chr 1:6 5927
such things as they *o* for the ... 2Chr 4:6 4639
all the people *o* sacrifices ... 2Chr 7:4 2076
king Solomon *o* a sacrifice of ... 2Chr 7:5 2076
for there he *o* burnt offerings, ... 2Chr 7:7 6213
Then Solomon *o* burnt offerings ... 2Chr 8:12 5927
they *o* unto the LORD the same ... 2Chr 15:11 2076
who willingly *o* himself unto the ... 2Chr 17:16
they *o* burnt offerings in the ... 2Chr 24:14 5927
nor *o* burnt offerings in the holy ... 2Chr 29:7 5927
beside all that was willingly *o* ... Ezr 1:6
o freely for the house of God to ... Ezr 2:68
they *o* burnt offerings thereon ... Ezr 3:3 5927
o the daily burnt offerings by ... Ezr 3:4
afterward *o* the continual burnt ... Ezr 3:5
of every one that willingly *o* a ... Ezr 3:5 5068
the place where they *o* sacrifices ... Ezr 6:3 1684
o at the dedication of this house ... Ezr 6:17 7127
freely *o* unto the God of Israel ... Ezr 7:15 5069
all Israel there present, had *o* ... Ezr 8:25 7311
o burnt offerings unto the God of ... Ezr 8:35 7126
they *o* a ram of the flock for ... Ezr 10:19
that willingly *o* themselves to ... Neh 11:2
that day they *o* great sacrifices ... Neh 12:43 2076
o burnt offerings according to ... Job 1:5 5927
thou hast *o* a meat offering ... Is 57:6 5927
as if he *o* swine's blood ... Is 66:3 5927
they have *o* incense unto Baal ... Jer 32:29 6999
they *o* there their sacrifices, and ... Eze 20:28 2076
oblation of the land that is *o* ... Eze 48:12 8641
the reproach *o* by him to cease ... Dan 11:18
Have ye *o* unto me sacrifices and ... Amos 5:25 5066
o a sacrifice unto the LORD, and ... Jonah 1:16 2076
incense shall be *o* unto my name ... Mal 1:11 5066
o sacrifice unto the idol, and ... Acts 7:41 *321*
have ye *o* to me slain beasts and ... Acts 7:42 *4374*
Ghost was given, he *o* them money, ... Acts 8:18 *4374*
ye abstain from meats *o* to idols ... Acts 15:29 *1494*
themselves from things *o* to idols ... Acts 21:25 *1494*
should be *o* for every one of them ... Acts 21:26 *4374*
as touching things *o* unto idols ... 1Cor 8:1 *1494*
are *o* in sacrifice unto idols ... 1Cor 8:4 *1494*
eat it as a thing *o* unto an idol ... 1Cor 8:7 *1494*
those things which are *o* to idols ... 1Cor 8:10 *1494*
or that which is *o* in sacrifice ... 1Cor 10:19 *1494*
This is *o* in sacrifice unto idols ... 1Cor 10:28 *1494*
if I be *o* upon the sacrifice and ... Phil 2:17 *4689*
For I am now ready to be *o* ... 2Ti 4:6 *4689*
flesh, when he had *o* up prayers ... Heb 5:7 *4374*
he did once, when he *o* up himself ... Heb 7:27
which he *o* for himself, and for ... Heb 9:7 *4374*
in which were *o* both gifts ... Heb 9:9
o himself without spot to God ... Heb 9:14 *4374*
So Christ was once *o* to bear the ... Heb 9:28 *4374*
those sacrifices which they *o* ... Heb 10:1 *4374*
they not have ceased to be *o* ... Heb 10:2 *4374*

which are *o* by the law .... Heb 10:8 4374
after he had *o* one sacrifice for .... Heb 10:12 4374
By faith Abel *o* unto God a more .... Heb 11:4 4374
when he was tried, *o* up Isaac .... Heb 11:17 4374
o up his only begotten son .... Heb 11:17 4374
when he had *o* Isaac his son upon .... Jas 2:21 399

OFFERETH {15}
The priest that *o* it for sin .... Lev 6:26 2398
the priest that *o* any man's burnt .... Lev 7:8 7126
shall be the priest's that *o* it .... Lev 7:9 7126
same day that he *o* his sacrifice .... Lev 7:16 7126
it be imputed unto him that *o* it .... Lev 7:18 7126
He that *o* the sacrifice of his .... Lev 7:29 7126
that *o* the blood of the peace .... Lev 7:33 7126
that *o* a burnt offering or .... Lev 17:8 5926
for he *o* the bread of thy God .... Lev 21:8 7126
whosoever *o* a sacrifice of peace .... Lev 22:21 7126
Then shall he that *o* his offering .... Num 15:4 7126
Whoso *o* praise glorifieth me .... Ps 50:23 2076
he that *o* an oblation, as if he .... Is 66:3 5927
him that *o* in the high places, and .... Jer 48:35 5927
him that *o* an offering unto the .... Mal 2:12 5066

OFFERING {724}
of the ground an *o* unto the LORD .... Gen 4:3 4503
had respect unto Abel and to his *o* .... Gen 4:4 4503
to his *o* he had not respect .... Gen 4:5 4503
offer him there for a burnt *o* .... Gen 22:2
and clave the wood for the burnt *o* .... Gen 22:3
took the wood of the burnt *o* .... Gen 22:6
where is the lamb for a burnt *o* .... Gen 22:7
himself a lamb for a burnt *o* .... Gen 22:8
a burnt *o* in the stead of his son .... Gen 22:13
and he poured a drink *o* thereon .... Gen 35:14
father in law, took a burnt *o* .... Ex 18:12
Israel, that they bring me an *o* .... Ex 25:2 8641
with his heart ye shall take my *o* .... Ex 25:2 8641
this is the *o* which ye shall take .... Ex 25:3 8641
it is a sin *o* .... Ex 29:14
it is a burnt *o* unto the LORD .... Ex 29:18
an *o* made by fire unto the LORD .... Ex 29:18
them for a wave *o* before the LORD .... Ex 29:24
them upon the altar for a burnt *o* .... Ex 29:25
it is an *o* made by fire unto the .... Ex 29:25
it for a wave *o* before the LORD .... Ex 29:26
sanctify the breast of the wave *o* .... Ex 29:27
and the shoulder of the heave *o* .... Ex 29:27 8641
for it is an heave *o* .... Ex 29:28 8641
it shall be an heave *o* from the .... Ex 29:28 8641
even their heave *o* unto the LORD .... Ex 29:28 8641
bullock for a sin *o* for atonement .... Ex 29:36
of an hin of wine for a drink *o* .... Ex 29:40
to the meat *o* of the morning .... Ex 29:41 4503
according to the drink *o* thereof .... Ex 29:41
an *o* made by fire unto the LORD .... Ex 29:41
o throughout your generations at .... Ex 29:42
nor burnt sacrifice, nor meat *o* .... Ex 30:9 4503
shall ye pour drink *o* thereon .... Ex 30:9
blood of the sin *o* of atonements .... Ex 30:10
shekel shall be the *o* of the LORD .... Ex 30:13 8641
shall give an *o* unto the LORD .... Ex 30:14 8641
when they give an *o* unto the LORD .... Ex 30:15 8641
to burn *o* made by fire unto the .... Ex 30:20
the altar of burnt *o* with all his .... Ex 30:28
the altar of burnt *o* with all his .... Ex 31:9
from among you an *o* unto the LORD .... Ex 35:5 8641
him bring it, an *o* of the LORD .... Ex 35:5 8641
The altar of burnt *o*, with his .... Ex 35:16
they brought the LORD's *o* to the .... Ex 35:21 8641
an *o* of gold unto the LORD .... Ex 35:22
one that did offer an *o* of silver .... Ex 35:24 8641
and brass brought the LORD's *o* .... Ex 35:24 8641
brought a willing *o* unto the LORD .... Ex 35:29
they received of Moses all the *o* .... Ex 36:3 8641
work for the *o* of the sanctuary .... Ex 36:6 8641
altar of burnt *o* of shittim wood .... Ex 38:1
place, even the gold of the *o* .... Ex 38:24 8573
the brass of the *o* was seventy .... Ex 38:29 8573
burnt *o* before the door of the .... Ex 40:6
anoint the altar of the burnt *o* .... Ex 40:10
he put the altar of burnt *o* by .... Ex 40:29
and offered upon it the burnt *o* .... Ex 40:29
and the meat *o* .... Ex 40:29 4503
of you bring an *o* unto the LORD .... Lev 1:2 7133
shall bring your *o* of the cattle .... Lev 1:2 7133
If his *o* be a burnt sacrifice of .... Lev 1:3 7133
hand upon the head of the burnt *o* .... Lev 1:4
And he shall flay the burnt *o* .... Lev 1:6
an *o* made by fire, of a sweet .... Lev 1:9
if his *o* be of the flocks, namely .... Lev 1:10 7133
an *o* made by fire, of a sweet .... Lev 1:13
for his *o* to the LORD be of fowls .... Lev 1:14 7133
shall bring his *o* of turtledoves .... Lev 1:14 7133
an *o* made by fire, of a sweet .... Lev 1:17
will offer a meat *o* unto the LORD .... Lev 2:1 7133
his *o* shall be of fine flour .... Lev 2:1 7133
to be an *o* made by fire, of a .... Lev 2:2
of a meat *o* baken in the oven .... Lev 2:4 4503
be a meat *o* baken in a pan .... Lev 2:5 4503
it is a meat *o* .... Lev 2:6 4503
a meat *o* baken in the frying pan .... Lev 2:7 4503
thou shalt bring the meat *o* that .... Lev 2:8 4503
the meat *o* a memorial thereof .... Lev 2:9 4503
it is an *o* made by fire, of a .... Lev 2:9
of the meat *o* shall be Aaron's .... Lev 2:10 4503
No meat *o*, which ye shall bring .... Lev 2:11 4503
in any *o* of the LORD made by fire .... Lev 2:11
every oblation of thy meat *o* .... Lev 2:13 4503

God to be lacking from thy meat *o* .... Lev 2:13 4503
if thou offer a meat *o* of thy .... Lev 2:14 4503
o of thy firstfruits green ears .... Lev 2:14 4503
it is a meat *o* .... Lev 2:15 4503
it is an *o* made by fire unto the .... Lev 2:16
be a sacrifice of peace *o* .... Lev 3:1
his hand upon the head of his *o* .... Lev 3:2 7133
of the peace *o* an *o* made .... Lev 3:3
it is an *o* made by fire, of a .... Lev 3:5
if his *o* for a sacrifice of peace .... Lev 3:6 7133
for a sacrifice of peace *o* unto .... Lev 3:6
If he offer a lamb for his *o* .... Lev 3:7 7133
his hand upon the head of his *o* .... Lev 3:8 7133
of the peace *o* an *o* made .... Lev 3:9
it is the food of the *o* made by .... Lev 3:11
if his *o* be a goat, then he shall .... Lev 3:12 7133
And he shall offer thereof his *o* .... Lev 3:14 7133
even an *o* made by fire unto the .... Lev 3:14
it is the food of the *o* made by .... Lev 3:16
blemish unto the LORD for a sin *o* .... Lev 4:3
of the altar of the burnt *o* .... Lev 4:7
fat of the bullock for the sin *o* .... Lev 4:8
upon the altar of the burnt *o* .... Lev 4:10
of the altar of the burnt *o* .... Lev 4:18
did with the bullock for a sin *o* .... Lev 4:20
it is a sin *o* for the .... Lev 4:21
he shall bring his *o*, a kid of .... Lev 4:23 7133
kill the burnt *o* before the LORD .... Lev 4:24
it is a sin *o* .... Lev 4:24
of the sin *o* with his finger .... Lev 4:25
the horns of the altar of burnt *o* .... Lev 4:25
bottom of the altar of burnt *o* .... Lev 4:25
then he shall bring his *o* .... Lev 4:28 7133
hand upon the head of the sin *o* .... Lev 4:29
slay the sin *o* in the place of .... Lev 4:29
in the place of the burnt *o* .... Lev 4:29
the horns of the altar of burnt *o* .... Lev 4:30
And if he bring a lamb for a sin *o* .... Lev 4:32 7133
hand upon the head of the sin *o* .... Lev 4:33
slay it for a sin *o* in the place .... Lev 4:33
place where they kill the burnt *o* .... Lev 4:33
of the sin *o* with his finger .... Lev 4:34
the horns of the altar of burnt *o* .... Lev 4:34
he shall bring his trespass *o* .... Lev 5:6 817
a kid of the goats, for a sin *o* .... Lev 5:6
one for a sin *o*, and the other for .... Lev 5:7
and the other for a burnt *o* .... Lev 5:7
that which is for the sin *o* first .... Lev 5:8
of the blood of the sin *o* upon .... Lev 5:9
it is a sin *o* .... Lev 5:9
offer the second for a burnt *o* .... Lev 5:10
o the tenth part of an ephah of .... Lev 5:11 7133
ephah of fine flour for a sin *o* .... Lev 5:11
for it is a sin *o* .... Lev 5:11
it is a sin *o* .... Lev 5:12
be the priest's, as a meat *o* .... Lev 5:13 4503
the sanctuary, for a trespass *o* .... Lev 5:15
with the ram of the trespass *o* .... Lev 5:16
thy estimation, for a trespass *o* .... Lev 5:18
It is a trespass *o* .... Lev 5:19
in the day of his trespass *o* .... Lev 6:5
his trespass *o* unto the LORD .... Lev 6:6
thy estimation, for a trespass *o* .... Lev 6:6
This is the law of the burnt *o* .... Lev 6:9
It is the burnt *o*, because of the .... Lev 6:9
with the burnt *o* on the altar .... Lev 6:10
lay the burnt *o* in order upon it .... Lev 6:12
And this is the law of the meat *o* .... Lev 6:14 4503
of the flour of the meat *o* .... Lev 6:15 4503
which is upon the meat *o*, and .... Lev 6:15 4503
it is most holy, as is the sin *o* .... Lev 6:17
and as the trespass *o* .... Lev 6:17
This is the *o* of Aaron and of his .... Lev 6:20 7133
fine flour for a meat *o* perpetual .... Lev 6:20 4503
o shalt thou offer for a sweet .... Lev 6:21 4503
For every meat *o* for the priest .... Lev 6:23 4503
This is the law of the sin *o* .... Lev 6:25
burnt *o* is killed shall the sin .... Lev 6:25
is killed shall the sin *o* be .... Lev 6:25
And no sin *o*, whereof any of the .... Lev 6:30
this is the law of the trespass *o* .... Lev 7:1
o shall they kill the trespass .... Lev 7:2
shall they kill the trespass *o* .... Lev 7:2
an *o* made by fire unto the LORD .... Lev 7:5
it is a trespass *o* .... Lev 7:5
o is, so is the trespass *o* .... Lev 7:7
that offereth any man's burnt .... Lev 7:8
the burnt *o* which he hath offered .... Lev 7:8
all the meat *o* that is baken in .... Lev 7:9 4503
And every meat *o*, mingled with oil .... Lev 7:10 4503
he shall offer for his *o* leavened .... Lev 7:13 7133
for an heave *o* unto the LORD .... Lev 7:14 8641
the sacrifice of his *o* be a vow .... Lev 7:16 7133
be a vow, or a voluntary *o* .... Lev 7:16
of which men offer an *o* made by .... Lev 7:25
for a wave *o* before the LORD .... Lev 7:30
unto the priest for an heave *o* of .... Lev 7:32 8641
This is the law of the burnt *o* .... Lev 7:37
of the meat *o* .... Lev 7:37 4503
o, and of the trespass *o* .... Lev 7:37
oil, and a bullock for the sin *o* .... Lev 8:2
brought the bullock for the sin *o* .... Lev 8:14
head of the bullock for the sin *o* .... Lev 8:14
brought the ram for the burnt *o* .... Lev 8:18 5930
an *o* made by fire unto the LORD .... Lev 8:21
them for a wave *o* before the LORD .... Lev 8:27
on the altar upon the burnt *o* .... Lev 8:28
it is an *o* made by fire unto the .... Lev 8:28

it for a wave *o* before the LORD .... Lev 8:29
o, and a ram for a burnt *o* .... Lev 9:2
ye a kid of the goats for a sin *o* .... Lev 9:3
without blemish, for a burnt *o* .... Lev 9:3
a meat *o* mingled with oil .... Lev 9:4 4503
the altar, and offer thy sin *o* .... Lev 9:7
and thy burnt *o* .... Lev 9:7
offer the *o* of the people, and .... Lev 9:7 7133
and slew the calf of the sin *o* .... Lev 9:8
caul above the liver of the sin *o* .... Lev 9:10
And he slew the burnt *o* .... Lev 9:12
presented the burnt *o* unto him .... Lev 9:13
upon the burnt *o* on the altar .... Lev 9:14
And he brought the people's *o* .... Lev 9:15 7133
was the sin *o* for the people .... Lev 9:15
And he brought the burnt *o* .... Lev 9:16
And he brought the meat *o*, and took .... Lev 9:17 4503
for a wave *o* before the LORD .... Lev 9:21
came down from *o* of the sin .... Lev 9:22 6213
the sin *o*, and the burnt *o* .... Lev 9:22
upon the altar the burnt *o* .... Lev 9:24
Take the meat *o* that remaineth of .... Lev 10:12 4503
it for a wave *o* before the LORD .... Lev 10:15
sought the goat of the sin *o* .... Lev 10:16
eaten the sin *o* in the holy place .... Lev 10:17
day have they offered their sin *o* .... Lev 10:19
their burnt *o* before the LORD .... Lev 10:19
if I had eaten the sin *o* to day .... Lev 10:19
of the first year for a burnt *o* .... Lev 12:6
or a turtledove, for a sin *o* .... Lev 12:6
the one for the burnt *o* .... Lev 12:8
and the other for a sin *o* .... Lev 12:8
deals of fine flour for a meat *o* .... Lev 14:10
and offer him for a trespass *o* .... Lev 14:12
them for a wave *o* before the LORD .... Lev 14:12
the sin *o* and the burnt *o* .... Lev 14:13
for as the sin *o* is the priest's .... Lev 14:13
so is the trespass *o* .... Lev 14:13
of the blood of the trespass *o* .... Lev 14:14
upon the blood of the trespass *o* .... Lev 14:17
the priest shall offer the sin *o* .... Lev 14:19
he shall kill the burnt *o* .... Lev 14:19
priest shall offer the burnt *o* .... Lev 14:20
the meat *o* upon the altar .... Lev 14:20 4503
lamb for a trespass *o* to be waved .... Lev 14:21
mingled with oil for a meat *o* .... Lev 14:21 4503
o, and the other a burnt *o* .... Lev 14:22
take the lamb of the trespass *o* .... Lev 14:24
them for a wave *o* before the LORD .... Lev 14:24
kill the lamb of the trespass *o* .... Lev 14:25
of the blood of the trespass *o* .... Lev 14:25
of the blood of the trespass *o* .... Lev 14:28
able to get, the one for a sin *o* .... Lev 14:31
and the other for a burnt *o* .... Lev 14:31
with the meat *o* .... Lev 14:31 4503
offer them, the one for a sin *o* .... Lev 15:15
and the other for a burnt *o* .... Lev 15:15
shall offer the one for a sin *o* .... Lev 15:30
and the other for a burnt *o* .... Lev 15:30
o, and a ram for a burnt *o* .... Lev 16:3
two kids of the goats for a sin *o* .... Lev 16:5
and one ram for a burnt *o* .... Lev 16:5
offer his bullock of the sin *o* .... Lev 16:6
fell, and offer him for a sin *o* .... Lev 16:9
bring the bullock of the sin *o* .... Lev 16:11
of the sin *o* which is for himself .... Lev 16:11
he kill the goat of the sin *o* .... Lev 16:15
come forth, and offer his burnt *o* .... Lev 16:24
the burnt *o* of the people, and .... Lev 16:24
the fat of the sin *o* shall he .... Lev 16:25
And the bullock for the sin *o* .... Lev 16:27
and the goat for the sin *o* .... Lev 16:27
to offer an *o* unto the LORD .... Lev 17:4 7133
offereth a burnt *o* or sacrifice .... Lev 17:8
his trespass *o* unto the LORD .... Lev 19:21
even a ram for a trespass *o* .... Lev 19:21
o before the LORD for his sin .... Lev 19:22
eat of an *o* of the holy things .... Lev 22:12 8641
offer unto the LORD for a burnt *o* .... Lev 22:18
or a freewill *o* in beeves or .... Lev 22:21
nor make an *o* by fire of them .... Lev 22:22
thou offer for a freewill *o* .... Lev 22:23
make any *o* thereof in your land .... Lev 22:24
an *o* made by fire unto the LORD .... Lev 22:27
But ye shall offer an *o* made by .... Lev 23:8
year for a burnt *o* unto the LORD .... Lev 23:12
the meat *o* thereof shall be two .... Lev 23:13 4503
an *o* made by fire unto the LORD .... Lev 23:13
the drink *o* thereof shall be of .... Lev 23:13
have brought an *o* unto your God .... Lev 23:14 7133
brought the sheaf of the wave *o* .... Lev 23:15
offer a new meat *o* unto the LORD .... Lev 23:16 4503
be for a burnt *o* unto the LORD .... Lev 23:18
unto the LORD, with their meat *o* .... Lev 23:18 4503
even an *o* made by fire, of sweet .... Lev 23:18
one kid of the goats for a sin *o* .... Lev 23:19
for a wave *o* before the LORD .... Lev 23:20
but ye shall offer an *o* made by .... Lev 23:25
offer an *o* made by fire unto the .... Lev 23:27
an *o* made by fire unto the LORD .... Lev 23:36
ye shall offer an *o* made by fire .... Lev 23:36
to offer an *o* made by fire unto .... Lev 23:37
by fire unto the LORD, a burnt *o* .... Lev 23:37
and a meat *o* .... Lev 23:37 4503
even an *o* made by fire unto the .... Lev 24:7
men bring an *o* unto the LORD .... Lev 27:9 7133
incense, and the daily meat *o* .... Num 4:16 4503
every *o* of all the holy things of .... Num 5:9 8641

and he shall bring her *o* for her Num 5:15 7133
for it is an *o* of jealousy Num 5:15 4503
an *o* of memorial, bringing Num 5:15 4503
put the *o* of memorial in her Num 5:18 4503
hands, which is the jealousy *o* Num 5:18 4503
o out of the woman's hand Num 5:25 4503
shall wave the *o* before the LORD, Num 5:25 4503
shall take an handful of the *o* Num 5:26 4503
shall offer the one for a sin *o* Num 6:11
and the other for a burnt *o* Num 6:11
the first year for a trespass *o* Num 6:12
shall offer his *o* unto the LORD Num 6:14 7133
without blemish for a burnt *o* Num 6:14
year without blemish for a sin *o* Num 6:14
with oil, and their meat *o* Num 6:15 4503
his sin *o*, and his burnt *o* Num 6:16
shall offer also his meat *o* Num 6:17 4503
and his drink *o* Num 6:17
them for a wave before the LORD Num 6:20
of his *o* unto the LORD for his Num 6:21 7133
brought their *o* before the LORD Num 7:3 7133
offered their *o* before the altar Num 7:10 7133
Moses, They shall offer their *o* Num 7:11 7133
he that offered his *o* the first Num 7:12 7133
his *o* was one silver charger, the Num 7:13 7133
mingled with oil for a meat *o* Num 7:13 4503
of the first year, for a burnt *o* Num 7:15
One kid of the goats for a sin *o* Num 7:16
this was the *o* of Nahshon the son Num 7:17 7133
for his *o* one silver charger Num 7:19 7133
mingled with oil for a meat *o* Num 7:19 4503
of the first year, for a burnt *o* Num 7:21
One kid of the goats for a sin *o* Num 7:22
this was the *o* of Nethaneel the Num 7:23 7133
His *o* was one silver charger, the Num 7:25 7133
mingled with oil for a meat *o* Num 7:25 4503
of the first year, for a burnt *o* Num 7:27
One kid of the goats for a sin *o* Num 7:28
this was the *o* of Eliab the son Num 7:29 7133
His *o* was one silver charger of Num 7:31 7133
mingled with oil for a meat *o* Num 7:31 4503
of the first year, for a burnt *o* Num 7:33
One kid of the goats for a sin *o* Num 7:34
this was the *o* of Elizur the son Num 7:35 7133
His *o* was one silver charger, the Num 7:37 7133
mingled with oil for a meat *o* Num 7:37 4503
of the first year, for a burnt *o* Num 7:39
One kid of the goats for a sin *o* Num 7:40
this was the *o* of Shelumiel the Num 7:41 7133
His *o* was one silver charger of Num 7:43 7133
mingled with oil for a meat *o* Num 7:43 4503
of the first year, for a burnt *o* Num 7:45
One kid of the goats for a sin *o* Num 7:46
this was the *o* of Eliasaph the Num 7:47 7133
His *o* was one silver charger, the Num 7:49 7133
mingled with oil for a meat *o* Num 7:49 4503
of the first year, for a burnt *o* Num 7:51
One kid of the goats for a sin *o* Num 7:52
this was the *o* of Elishama the Num 7:53 7133
His *o* was one silver charger of Num 7:55 7133
mingled with oil for a meat *o* Num 7:55 4503
of the first year, for a burnt *o* Num 7:57
One kid of the goats for a sin *o* Num 7:58
this was the *o* of Gamaliel the Num 7:59 7133
His *o* was one silver charger, the Num 7:61 7133
mingled with oil for a meat *o* Num 7:61 4503
of the first year, for a burnt *o* Num 7:63
One kid of the goats for a sin *o* Num 7:64
this was the *o* of Abidan the son Num 7:65 7133
His *o* was one silver charger, the Num 7:67 7133
mingled with oil for a meat *o* Num 7:67 4503
of the first year, for a burnt *o* Num 7:69
One kid of the goats for a sin *o* Num 7:70
this was the *o* of Ahiezer the son Num 7:71 7133
His *o* was one silver charger, the Num 7:73 7133
mingled with oil for a meat *o* Num 7:73 4503
of the first year, for a burnt *o* Num 7:75
One kid of the goats for a sin *o* Num 7:76
this was the *o* of Pagiel the son Num 7:77 7133
His *o* was one silver charger, the Num 7:79 7133
mingled with oil for a meat *o* Num 7:79 4503
of the first year, for a burnt *o* Num 7:81
One kid of the goats for a sin *o* Num 7:82
this was the *o* of Ahira the son Num 7:83 7133
the burnt *o* were twelve bullocks Num 7:87
year twelve, with their meat *o* Num 7:87 4503
of the goats for sin *o* twelve Num 7:87
a young bullock with his meat *o* Num 8:8 4503
shalt thou take for a sin *o* Num 8:8
an *o* of the children of Israel Num 8:11 8573
shalt offer the one for a sin *o* Num 8:12
and the other for a burnt *o* Num 8:12
offer them for an *o* unto the LORD Num 8:13 8573
them, and offer them for an *o* Num 8:15 8573
them as an *o* before the LORD Num 8:21 8573
that we may not offer an *o* of the Num 9:7 7133
because he brought not the *o* of Num 9:13 7133
will make an *o* by fire unto the Num 15:3
by fire unto the LORD, a burnt *o* Num 15:3
a vow, or in a freewill *o* Num 15:3
his *o* unto the LORD bring a meat Num 15:4 7133
a meat *o* of a tenth deal of flour Num 15:4 4503
o shalt thou prepare with the Num 15:5
with the burnt *o* or sacrifice Num 15:5
a meat *o* two tenth deals of flour Num 15:6 4503
for a drink *o* thou shalt offer Num 15:7
preparest a bullock for a burnt *o* Num 15:8
o of three tenth deals of flour Num 15:9 4503

for a drink *o* half an hin of wine Num 15:10
for an *o* made by fire, of a sweet Num 15:10
after this manner, in *o* Num 15:13 7126
an *o* made by fire Num 15:13
and will offer an *o* made by fire Num 15:14
offer up an heave *o* unto the LORD Num 15:19 8641
of your dough for an heave *o* Num 15:20 8641
as ye do the heave *o* of the Num 15:20 8641
an heave *o* in your generations Num 15:21 8641
one young bullock for a burnt *o* Num 15:24
unto the LORD, with his meat *o* Num 15:24 4503
and his drink *o* Num 15:24
one kid of the goats for a sin *o* Num 15:24
and they shall bring their *o* Num 15:25 7133
their sin *o* before the LORD, for Num 15:25
of the first year for a sin *o* Num 15:27
LORD, Respect not thou their *o* Num 16:15 4503
of theirs, every meat *o* of theirs Num 18:9 4503
and every sin *o* of theirs Num 18:9
and every trespass *o* of theirs Num 18:9
the heave *o* of their gift, with Num 18:11 8641
their fat for an *o* made by fire Num 18:17
offer as an heave *o* unto the LORD Num 18:24 8641
up an heave *o* of it for the LORD Num 18:26 8641
this your heave *o* shall be Num 18:27 8641
heave *o* unto the LORD of all your Num 18:28 8641
heave *o* to Aaron the priest Num 18:28 8641
offer every heave *o* of the LORD Num 18:29 8641
unto Balak, Stand by thy burnt *o* Num 23:3
Balak, Stand here by thy burnt *o* Num 23:15
behold, he stood by his burnt *o* Num 23:17
of Israel, and say unto them, My *o* Num 28:2 7133
This is the *o* made by fire which Num 28:3
by day, for a continual burnt *o* Num 28:3
of an ephah of flour for a meat *o* Num 28:5 4503
It is a continual burnt *o* Num 28:6
the drink *o* thereof shall be the Num 28:7
unto the LORD for a drink *o* Num 28:7
as the meat *o* of the morning, and Num 28:8 4503
and as the drink *o* thereof Num 28:8
tenth deals of flour for a meat *o* Num 28:9 4503
with oil, and the drink *o* thereof Num 28:9
is the burnt *o* of every sabbath Num 28:10
burnt *o*, and his drink *o* Num 28:10
offer a burnt *o* unto the LORD Num 28:11
tenth deals of flour for a meat *o* Num 28:12 4503
tenth deals of flour for a meat *o* Num 28:12 4503
oil for a meat *o* unto one lamb Num 28:13 4503
for a burnt *o* of a sweet savour, Num 28:13
this is the burnt *o* of every Num 28:14
o unto the LORD shall be offered Num 28:15
burnt *o*, and his drink *o* Num 28:15
fire for a burnt *o* unto the LORD Num 28:19
their meat *o* shall be of flour Num 28:20 4503
And one goat for a sin *o*, to make Num 28:22
beside the burnt *o* in the morning Num 28:23
which is for a continual burnt *o* Num 28:23
burnt *o*, and his drink *o* Num 28:24
bring a new meat *o* unto the LORD Num 28:26 4503
o for a sweet savour unto the Num 28:27
their meat *o* of flour mingled Num 28:28 4503
them beside the continual burnt *o* Num 28:31
and his meat *o* Num 28:31 4503
ye shall offer a burnt *o* for a Num 29:2
their meat *o* shall be of flour Num 29:3 4503
one kid of the goats for a sin *o* Num 29:5
Beside the burnt *o* of the month Num 29:6
of the month, and his meat *o* Num 29:6 4503
and the daily burnt *o* Num 29:6
and his meat *o* Num 29:6 4503
burnt *o* unto the LORD for a sweet Num 29:8
their meat *o* shall be of flour Num 29:9 4503
One kid of the goats for a sin *o* Num 29:11
beside the sin *o* of atonement Num 29:11
and the continual burnt *o* Num 29:11
and the meat *o* of it Num 29:11 4503
And ye shall offer a burnt *o* Num 29:13
their meat *o* shall be of flour Num 29:14 4503
one kid of the goats for a sin *o* Num 29:16
beside the continual burnt *o* Num 29:16
his meat *o* Num 29:16 4503
his meat *o*, and his drink *o* Num 29:16
And their meat *o* and their drink Num 29:18 4503
one kid of the goats for a sin *o* Num 29:19
beside the continual burnt *o* Num 29:19
and the meat *o* thereof Num 29:19 4503
And their meat *o* and their drink Num 29:21 4503
And one goat for a sin *o* Num 29:22
beside the continual burnt *o* Num 29:22
and his meat *o* Num 29:22 4503
and his drink *o* Num 29:22
Their meat *o* and their drink Num 29:24 4503
one kid of the goats for a sin *o* Num 29:25
beside the continual burnt *o* Num 29:25
his meat *o*, and his drink Num 29:25 4503
and his drink *o*. Num 29:25
And their meat *o* and their drink Num 29:27 4503
And one goat for a sin *o* Num 29:28
beside the continual burnt *o* Num 29:28
and his meat *o* Num 29:28 4503
and his drink *o* Num 29:28
And their meat *o* and their drink Num 29:30 4503
And one goat for a sin *o* Num 29:31
beside the continual burnt *o* Num 29:31
his meat *o*, and his drink Num 29:31 4503
and his drink *o* Num 29:31
And their meat *o* and their drink Num 29:33 4503
And one goat for a sin *o* Num 29:34

beside the continual burnt *o* Num 29:34
his meat *o*, and his drink Num 29:34 4503
and his drink *o* Num 29:34
But ye shall offer a burnt *o* Num 29:36
Their meat *o* and their drink Num 29:37 4503
And one goat for a sin *o* Num 29:38
beside the continual burnt *o* Num 29:38
and his meat *o* Num 29:38 4503
and his drink *o* Num 29:38
for an heave *o* of the LORD Num 31:29 8641
which was the LORD's heave *o* Num 31:41 8641
all the gold of the *o* that they Num 31:52 8641
the heave *o* of your hand, and all Deut 12:11 8641
or heave *o* of thine hand Deut 12:17 8641
of a freewill *o* of thine hand Deut 16:10
even a freewill *o*, according as Deut 23:23
thereon burnt *o* or meat Josh 22:23
or meat *o*, or if Josh 22:23 4503
us an altar, not for burnt *o* Josh 22:26
I will offer it up for a burnt *o* Judg 11:31
and if thou wilt offer a burnt *o* Judg 13:16
Manoah took a kid with a meat *o* Judg 13:19 4503
would not have received a burnt *o* Judg 13:23
a meat *o* at our hands, neither Judg 13:23 4503
men abhorred the *o* of the LORD 1Sa 2:17 4503
ye at my sacrifice and at mine *o* 1Sa 2:29 4503
with sacrifice nor *o* for ever 1Sa 3:14 4503
any wise return him a trespass *o* 1Sa 6:3
What shall be the trespass *o* 1Sa 6:4
ye return him for a trespass *o* 1Sa 6:8
the kine a burnt *o* unto the LORD 1Sa 6:14
for a trespass *o* unto the LORD 1Sa 6:17
a burnt *o* wholly unto the LORD 1Sa 7:9
as Samuel was *o* up the burnt 1Sa 7:10 5927
up the burnt *o* 1Sa 7:10
Bring hither a burnt *o* to me 1Sa 13:9
And he offered the burnt *o* 1Sa 13:9
an end of *o* the burnt 1Sa 13:10 5927
the burnt *o*, behold 1Sa 13:10
therefore, and offered a burnt *o* 1Sa 13:12
against me, let him accept an *o* 1Sa 26:19 4503
made an end of *o* burnt offerings 2Sa 6:18 5927
until the time of the *o* of the 1Kin 18:29 5927
of the *o* of the evening sacrifice 1Kin 18:36 5927
when the meat *o* was offered 2Kin 3:20 4503
him for a burnt *o* upon the wall 2Kin 3:27
o nor sacrifice unto other gods 2Kin 5:17
an end of *o* the burnt 2Kin 10:25 6213
the burnt *o*, that Jehu 2Kin 10:25
And he burnt his burnt *o* and his 2Kin 16:13
and his meat *o* 2Kin 16:13 4503
and poured his drink *o* 2Kin 16:13
altar burn the morning burnt *o* 2Kin 16:15
and the evening meat *o* 2Kin 16:15 4503
burnt sacrifice, and his meat *o* 2Kin 16:15
with the burnt *o* of all the 2Kin 16:15
of the land, and their meat *o* 2Kin 16:15 4503
it all the blood of the burnt *o* 2Kin 16:15
upon the altar of the burnt *o* 1Chr 6:49
an end of *o* the burnt offerings 1Chr 16:2 5927
bring an *o*, and come before him 1Chr 16:29 4503
the burnt *o* continually morning 1Chr 16:40
wood, and the wheat for the meat *o* 1Chr 21:23 4503
by fire upon the altar of burnt *o* 1Chr 21:26
and the altar of the burnt *o* 1Chr 21:29
altar of the burnt *o* for Israel 1Chr 22:1
and for the fine flour for meat *o* 1Chr 23:29 4503
the burnt *o* they washed in them 2Chr 4:6
heaven, and consumed the burnt *o* 2Chr 7:1
o according to the commandment of 2Chr 8:13 5927
the LORD, and the altar of burnt *o* 2Chr 29:18
for a sin *o* for the kingdom, and 2Chr 29:21
for the sin *o* before the king 2Chr 29:23
king commanded that the burnt *o* 2Chr 29:24
the sin *o* should be made for all 2Chr 29:24
offer the burnt *o* upon the altar 2Chr 29:27
And when the burnt *o* began 2Chr 29:27
until the burnt *o* was finished 2Chr 29:28
And when they had made an end of *o* 2Chr 29:29 5927
were for a burnt *o* to the LORD 2Chr 29:32
drink offerings for every burnt *o* 2Chr 29:35
o peace offerings, and making 2Chr 30:22 2076
busied in *o* of burnt offerings 2Chr 35:14 5927
beside the freewill *o* for the Ezr 1:4
offered the continual burnt *o* Ezr 3:5
a freewill *o* unto the LORD Ezr 3:5
for a sin *o* for all Israel, Ezr 6:17
with the freewill *o* of the people Ezr 7:16
o willingly for the house of Ezr 7:16
even the *o* of the house of our Ezr 8:25 8641
the gold are a freewill *o* unto Ezr 8:28
twelve he goats for a sin *o* Ezr 8:35
this was a burnt *o* unto the LORD Ezr 8:35
and for the continual meat *o* Neh 10:33 4503
and for the continual burnt *o* Neh 10:33
and the people, for the wood *o* Neh 10:34 7133
shall bring the *o* of the corn Neh 10:39 8641
the house of God, with the meat *o* Neh 13:9 4503
And for the wood *o*, at times Neh 13:31 7133
offer up for yourselves a burnt *o* Job 42:8
and *o* thou didst not desire Ps 40:6 4503
burnt *o* and sin *o* hast thou Ps 40:6
thou delightest not in burnt *o* Ps 51:16
burnt *o* and whole burnt *o* Ps 51:19
bring an *o*, and come into his Ps 96:8 4503
thereof sufficient for a burnt *o* Is 40:16
caused thee to serve with an *o* Is 43:23 4503
shalt make his soul an *o* for sin Is 53:10

them hast thou poured a drink *o*	Is 57:6	
thou hast offered a meat *o*	Is 57:6	4503
I hate robbery for burnt *o*	Is 61:8	
the drink *o* unto that number	Is 65:11	
for an *o* unto the LORD out of all	Is 66:20	4503
an *o* in a clean vessel into the	Is 66:20	4503
to anger in *o* incense unto Baal	Jer 11:17	
and when they offer burnt *o*	Jer 14:12	
the provocation of their *o*	Eze 20:28	7133
where they washed the burnt *o*	Eze 40:38	
side, to slay thereon the burnt *o*	Eze 40:39	
sin *o* and the trespass *o*	Eze 40:39	
of hewn stone for the burnt *o*	Eze 40:42	
wherewith they slew the burnt *o*	Eze 40:42	
the tables was the flesh of the *o*	Eze 40:43	7133
most holy things, and the meat *o*	Eze 42:13	4503
sin *o*, and the trespass *o*	Eze 42:13	
GOD, a young bullock for a sin *o*	Eze 43:19	
the bullock also of the sin *o*	Eze 43:21	
goats without blemish for a sin *o*	Eze 43:22	
up for a burnt *o* unto the LORD	Eze 43:24	
every day a goat for a sin *o*	Eze 43:25	
they shall slay the burnt *o*	Eze 44:11	
he shall offer his sin *o*	Eze 44:27	
They shall eat the meat *o*	Eze 44:29	4503
sin *o*, and the trespass *o*	Eze 44:29	
for a meat *o*, and for a burnt	Eze 45:15	4503
and for a burnt *o*	Eze 45:15	
he shall prepare the sin *o*	Eze 45:17	
and the meat *o*	Eze 45:17	4503
and the burnt *o*	Eze 45:17	
take of the blood of the sin *o*	Eze 45:19	
of the land a bullock for a sin *o*	Eze 45:22	
prepare a burnt *o* to the LORD	Eze 45:23	
of the goats daily for a sin *o*	Eze 45:23	
he shall prepare a meat *o* of an	Eze 45:24	4503
days, according to the sin *o*	Eze 45:25	
according to the burnt *o*	Eze 45:25	
and according to the meat *o*	Eze 45:25	4503
priests shall prepare his burnt *o*	Eze 46:2	
the burnt *o* that the prince shall	Eze 46:4	
the meat *o* shall be an ephah for	Eze 46:5	4503
the meat *o* for the lambs as he	Eze 46:5	4503
And he shall prepare a meat *o*	Eze 46:7	4503
in the solemnities the meat *o*	Eze 46:11	4503
o or peace offerings voluntarily	Eze 46:12	
and he shall prepare his burnt *o*	Eze 46:12	
shalt daily prepare a burnt *o*	Eze 46:13	
a meat *o* for it every morning	Eze 46:14	4503
a meat *o* continually by a	Eze 46:14	4503
prepare the lamb, and the meat *o*	Eze 46:15	4503
morning for a continual burnt *o*	Eze 46:15	
trespass *o* and the sin *o*	Eze 46:20	
where they shall bake the meat *o*	Eze 46:20	4503
shall be the *o* which ye shall	Eze 48:8	8641
The meat *o* and the drink	Joel 1:9	4503
the drink *o* is cut off from the	Joel 1:9	
for the meat *o* and the drink	Joel 1:13	4503
the drink *o* is withholden from	Joel 1:13	
even a meat *o* and a drink	Joel 2:14	4503
a drink *o* unto the LORD your God	Joel 2:14	
my dispersed, shall bring mine *o*	Zeph 3:10	4503
will I accept an *o* at your hand	Mal 1:10	4503
offered unto my name, and a pure *o*	Mal 1:11	4503
thus ye brought an *o*	Mal 1:13	4503
him that offereth an *o* unto the	Mal 2:12	4503
he regardeth not the *o* any more	Mal 2:13	4503
the LORD an *o* in righteousness	Mal 3:3	4503
Then shall the *o* of Judah	Mal 3:4	4503
coming to him, and *o* him vinegar,	Lk 23:36	*4374*
until that an *o* should be offered	Acts 21:26	*4376*
that the *o* up of the Gentiles	Rom 15:16	*4376*
and hath given himself for us an *o*	Eph 5:2	*4376*
o thou wouldest not, but a body	Heb 10:5	*4376*
when he said, Sacrifice and *o*	Heb 10:8	*4376*
o for sin thou wouldest not,	Heb 10:8	
the *o* of the body of Jesus Christ	Heb 10:10	*4376*
o oftentimes the same sacrifices,	Heb 10:11	*4374*
For by one *o* he hath perfected	Heb 10:14	*4376*
is, there is no more *o* for sin	Heb 10:18	*4376*

OFFERINGS {270}

and offered burnt *o* on the altar	Gen 8:20	
us also sacrifices and burnt *o*	Ex 10:25	
sacrifice thereon thy burnt *o*	Ex 20:24	
burnt *o*, and thy peace *o*	Ex 20:24	
of Israel, which offered burnt *o*	Ex 24:5	
sacrificed peace *o* of oxen unto	Ex 24:5	2077
of the sacrifice of their peace *o*	Ex 29:28	
on the morrow, and offered burnt *o*	Ex 32:6	
o, and brought peace *o*	Ex 32:6	
yet unto him free *o* every morning	Ex 36:3	
of the meat *o* shall be Aaron's	Lev 2:3	
of the *o* of the LORD made by fire	Lev 2:3	
of the *o* of the LORD made by fire	Lev 2:10	
with all thine *o* thou shalt offer	Lev 2:13	7133
of the sacrifice of peace *o*	Lev 4:10	
fat of the sacrifice of peace *o*	Lev 4:26	
from off the sacrifice of peace *o*	Lev 4:31	
from the sacrifice of the peace *o*	Lev 4:35	
according to the *o* made by fire	Lev 4:35	
according to the *o* made by fire	Lev 5:12	
thereon the fat of the peace *o*	Lev 6:12	
portion of my *o* made by fire	Lev 6:17	
the *o* of the LORD made by fire	Lev 6:18	
law of the sacrifice of peace *o*	Lev 7:11	
of thanksgiving of his peace *o*	Lev 7:13	
the blood of the peace *o*	Lev 7:14	
of the sacrifice of his peace *o*	Lev 7:15	
o be eaten at all on the third	Lev 7:18	
flesh of the sacrifice of peace *o*	Lev 7:20	
flesh of the sacrifice of peace *o*	Lev 7:21	
the sacrifice of his peace *o* unto	Lev 7:29	
of the sacrifice of his peace *o*	Lev 7:29	
the *o* of the LORD made by fire	Lev 7:30	
of the sacrifices of your peace *o*	Lev 7:32	
offereth the blood of the peace *o*	Lev 7:33	
the sacrifices of their peace *o*	Lev 7:34	
out of the *o* of the LORD made by	Lev 7:35	
of the sacrifice of the peace *o*	Lev 7:37	
a bullock and a ram for peace *o*	Lev 9:4	
ram for a sacrifice of peace *o*	Lev 9:18	
and the burnt offering, and peace *o*	Lev 9:22	
of the *o* of the LORD made by fire	Lev 10:12	
peace *o* of the children of Israel	Lev 10:14	
the *o* made by fire of the fat	Lev 10:15	
them for peace *o* unto the LORD	Lev 17:5	2077
of peace *o* unto the LORD, ye	Lev 19:5	
for the *o* of the LORD made by	Lev 21:6	
the *o* of the LORD made by fire	Lev 21:21	
vows, and for all his freewill *o*	Lev 22:18	
offereth a sacrifice of peace *o*	Lev 22:21	
meat offering, and their drink *o*	Lev 23:18	
year for a sacrifice of peace *o*	Lev 23:19	
offering, a sacrifice, and drink *o*	Lev 23:37	
and beside all your freewill *o*	Lev 23:38	
o of the LORD made by fire by a	Lev 24:9	
ram without blemish for peace *o*	Num 6:14	
meat offering, and their drink *o*	Num 6:15	
of peace *o* unto the LORD, with	Num 6:17	
the sacrifice of the peace *o*	Num 6:18	
And for a sacrifice of peace *o*	Num 7:17	
And for a sacrifice of peace *o*	Num 7:23	
And for a sacrifice of peace *o*	Num 7:29	
And for a sacrifice of peace *o*	Num 7:35	
And for a sacrifice of peace *o*	Num 7:41	
And for a sacrifice of peace *o*	Num 7:47	
And for a sacrifice of peace *o*	Num 7:53	
And for a sacrifice of peace *o*	Num 7:59	
And for a sacrifice of peace *o*	Num 7:65	
And for a sacrifice of peace *o*	Num 7:71	
And for a sacrifice of peace *o*	Num 7:77	
And for a sacrifice of peace *o*	Num 7:83	
of the peace *o* were twenty	Num 7:88	
the trumpets over your burnt *o*	Num 10:10	
the sacrifices of your peace *o*	Num 10:10	
a vow, or peace *o* unto the LORD	Num 15:8	
o of all the hallowed things of	Num 18:8	8641
with all the wave *o* of the	Num 18:11	
All the heave *o* of the holy	Num 18:19	8641
their drink *o* shall be half an	Num 28:14	
without blemish) and their drink *o*	Num 28:31	
meat offering, and their drink *o*	Num 29:6	
offering of it, and their drink *o*	Num 29:11	
their drink *o* for the bullocks,	Num 29:18	
thereof, and their drink *o*	Num 29:19	
their drink *o* for the bullocks,	Num 29:21	
their drink *o* for the bullocks,	Num 29:24	
their drink *o* for the bullocks,	Num 29:27	
their drink *o* for the bullocks,	Num 29:30	
their drink *o* for the bullocks,	Num 29:33	
their drink *o* for the bullock,	Num 29:37	
your vows, and your freewill *o*	Num 29:39	
for your burnt *o*	Num 29:39	
and for your meat *o*	Num 29:39	4503
and for your drink *o*	Num 29:39	
and for your peace *o*	Num 29:39	
ye shall bring your burnt *o*	Deut 12:6	
heave *o* of your hand, and your	Deut 12:6	
and your vows, and your freewill *o*	Deut 12:6	
your burnt *o*, and your sacrifices,	Deut 12:11	
that thou offer not thy burnt *o*	Deut 12:13	
thou shalt offer thy burnt *o*	Deut 12:14	
thou vowest, nor thy freewill *o*	Deut 12:17	
And thou shalt offer thy burnt *o*	Deut 12:27	
they shall eat the *o* of the LORD	Deut 18:1	
thou shalt offer burnt *o* thereon	Deut 27:6	
And thou shalt offer peace *o*	Deut 27:7	
drank the wine of their drink *o*	Deut 32:38	
thereon burnt *o* unto the LORD	Josh 8:31	
the LORD, and sacrificed peace *o*	Josh 8:31	
or if to offer peace *o* thereon	Josh 22:23	2077
LORD before him with our burnt *o*	Josh 22:27	
sacrifices, and with our peace *o*	Josh 22:27	
our fathers made, not for burnt *o*	Josh 22:28	
to build an altar for burnt *o*	Josh 22:29	
for burnt *o*, for meat *o*	Josh 22:29	4503
until even, and offered burnt *o*	Judg 20:26	
and peace *o* before the LORD	Judg 20:26	
burnt *o* and peace *o*	Judg 21:4	
o made by fire of the children of	1Sa 2:28	
of all the *o* of Israel my people	1Sa 2:29	4503
of Beth-shemesh offered burnt *o*	1Sa 6:15	
down unto thee, to offer burnt *o*	1Sa 10:8	
sacrifice sacrifices of peace *o*	1Sa 10:8	
of peace *o* before the LORD	1Sa 11:15	
burnt offering to me, and peace *o*	1Sa 13:9	
LORD as great delight in burnt *o*	1Sa 15:22	
rain, upon you, nor fields of *o*	2Sa 1:21	8641
and David offered burnt *o* and peace	2Sa 6:17	
and peace *o* before the LORD	2Sa 6:17	
burnt *o* and peace *o*	2Sa 6:18	
neither will I offer burnt *o* unto	2Sa 24:24	
burnt *o* and peace *o*	2Sa 24:25	
a thousand burnt *o* did Solomon	1Kin 3:4	
the LORD, and offered up burnt *o*	1Kin 3:15	
o, and offered peace *o*	1Kin 3:15	
offered a sacrifice of peace *o*	1Kin 8:63	
for there he offered burnt *o*	1Kin 8:64	
and meat *o*	1Kin 8:64	4503
and the fat of the peace *o*	1Kin 8:64	
too little to receive the burnt *o*	1Kin 8:64	
and meat *o*	1Kin 8:64	4503
and the fat of the peace *o*	1Kin 8:64	
a year did Solomon offer burnt *o*	1Kin 9:25	
peace *o* upon the altar which he	1Kin 9:25	
in to offer sacrifices and burnt *o*	2Kin 10:24	
the blood of his peace *o*, upon	2Kin 16:13	
meat offering, and their drink *o*	2Kin 16:15	
sacrifices and peace *o* before God	1Chr 16:1	
burnt *o* and the peace *o*	1Chr 16:2	
To offer burnt *o* unto the LORD	1Chr 16:40	
thee the oxen also for burnt *o*	1Chr 21:23	
nor offer burnt *o* without cost	1Chr 21:24	
burnt *o* and peace *o*	1Chr 21:26	
and offered burnt *o* unto the LORD	1Chr 29:21	
lambs, with their drink *o*	1Chr 29:21	
a thousand burnt *o* upon it	2Chr 1:6	
and for the burnt *o* morning	2Chr 2:4	
for there he offered burnt *o*	2Chr 7:7	
and the fat of the peace *o*	2Chr 7:7	
not able to receive the burnt *o*	2Chr 7:7	
and the meat *o*	2Chr 7:7	4503
Then Solomon offered burnt *o* unto	2Chr 8:12	
to offer the burnt *o* of the LORD	2Chr 23:18	
they offered burnt *o* in the house	2Chr 24:14	
incense nor offered burnt *o* in	2Chr 29:7	
thank *o* into the house of the	2Chr 29:31	
brought in sacrifices and thank *o*	2Chr 29:31	
as were of a free heart burnt *o*	2Chr 29:31	
And the number of the burnt *o*	2Chr 29:32	
could not flay all the burnt *o*	2Chr 29:34	
And also the burnt *o* were in	2Chr 29:35	
with the fat of the peace *o*	2Chr 29:35	
the drink *o* for every burnt	2Chr 29:35	
brought in the burnt *o* into the	2Chr 30:15	
seven days, offering peace *o*	2Chr 30:22	2077
priests and Levites for burnt *o*	2Chr 31:2	
and for peace *o*	2Chr 31:2	
of his substance for the burnt *o*	2Chr 31:3	
the morning and evening burnt *o*	2Chr 31:3	
the burnt *o* for the sabbaths, and	2Chr 31:3	
the *o* into the house of the LORD	2Chr 31:10	8641
And brought in the *o* and the tithes	2Chr 31:12	8641
was over the freewill *o* of God	2Chr 31:14	8641
and sacrificed thereon peace *o*	2Chr 33:16	2077
and thank *o*, and commanded	2Chr 33:16	
and kids, all for the passover *o*	2Chr 35:7	
for the passover *o* two thousand	2Chr 35:8	
o five thousand small cattle	2Chr 35:9	
And they removed the burnt *o*	2Chr 35:12	
the other holy *o* sod they in pots	2Chr 35:13	
busied in offering of burnt *o*	2Chr 35:14	
to offer burnt *o* upon the altar	2Chr 35:16	
Israel, to offer burnt *o* thereon	Ezr 3:2	
they offered burnt *o* thereon unto	Ezr 3:3	
the LORD, even burnt *o* morning	Ezr 3:3	
the daily burnt *o* by number	Ezr 3:4	
to offer burnt *o* unto the LORD	Ezr 3:6	
for the burnt *o* of the God of	Ezr 6:9	
rams, lambs, with their meat *o*	Ezr 7:17	4503
and their drink *o*	Ezr 7:17	
offered burnt *o* unto the God of	Ezr 8:35	
and for the sin *o* to make an	Neh 10:33	
of our dough, and our *o*, and the	Neh 10:37	8641
for the treasures, for the *o*	Neh 12:44	8641
aforetime they laid the meat *o*	Neh 13:5	4503
and the *o* of the priests	Neh 13:5	4503
offered burnt *o* according to the	Job 1:5	
their drink *o* of blood will I not	Ps 16:4	
Remember all thy *o*, and accept thy	Ps 20:3	4503
for thy sacrifices or thy burnt *o*	Ps 50:8	
go into thy house with burnt *o*	Ps 66:13	
thee, the freewill *o* of my mouth	Ps 119:108	
I have peace *o* with me	Prov 7:14	
I am full of the burnt *o* of rams	Is 1:11	
the small cattle of thy burnt *o*	Is 43:23	
their burnt *o* and their sacrifices	Is 56:7	
your burnt *o* are not acceptable,	Jer 6:20	
pour out drink *o* unto other gods	Jer 7:18	5262
Put your burnt *o* unto your	Jer 7:21	
concerning burnt *o* or sacrifices	Jer 7:22	
from the south, bringing burnt *o*	Jer 17:26	
and sacrifices, and meat *o*	Jer 17:26	4503
with fire for burnt *o* unto Baal	Jer 19:5	
out drink *o* unto other gods	Jer 19:13	
out drink *o* unto other gods	Jer 32:29	
a man before me to offer burnt *o*	Jer 33:18	
and to kindle meat *o*	Jer 33:18	4503
and having cut themselves, with *o*	Jer 41:5	4503
and to pour out drink *o* unto her	Jer 44:17	
and to pour out drink *o* unto her	Jer 44:18	
and poured out drink *o* unto her	Jer 44:19	
and pour out drink *o* unto her	Jer 44:19	
and to pour out drink *o* unto her	Jer 44:25	
and poured out there their drink *o*	Eze 20:28	
and there will I require your *o*	Eze 20:40	8641
make it, to offer burnt *o* thereon	Eze 43:18	
make your burnt *o* upon the altar	Eze 43:27	
upon the altar, and your peace *o*	Eze 43:27	
a burnt offering, and for peace *o*	Eze 45:15	
the prince's part to give burnt *o*	Eze 45:17	
and meat *o*, and drink	Eze 45:17	4503
and drink *o*, in the	Eze 45:17	

burnt offering, and the peace *o* ... Eze 45:17
his burnt offering and his peace *o* ... Eze 46:2
burnt offering or peace *o* ... Eze 46:12
his burnt offering and his peace *o* ... Eze 46:12
of God more than burnt *o* ... Hos 6:6
for the sacrifices of mine *o* ... Hos 8:13 1890
not offer wine *o* to the LORD ... Hos 9:4
and proclaim and publish the free *o* ... Amos 4:5
Though ye offer me burnt *o* ... Amos 5:22
and your meat *o* ... Amos 5:22 4503
the peace *o* of your fat beasts ... Amos 5:22
o in the wilderness forty years, ... Amos 5:25 4503
I come before him with burnt *o* ... Mic 6:6
In tithes and *o* ... Mal 3:8 8641
is more than all whole burnt *o* ... Mk 12:33 *3646*
cast in unto the *o* of God ... Lk 21:4 *1435*
to bring alms to my nation, and *o* ... Acts 24:17 *4376*
In burnt *o* and sacrifices for sin ... Heb 10:6 *3646*
Sacrifice and offering and burnt *o* ... Heb 10:8 *3646*

OFFICE {46}
me he restored unto mine *o* ... Gen 41:13 3653
When ye do the *o* of a midwife to ... Ex 1:16
unto me in the priest's *o* ... Ex 28:1
unto me in the priest's *o* ... Ex 28:3
unto me in the priest's *o* ... Ex 28:4
unto me in the priest's *o* ... Ex 28:41
unto me in the priest's *o* ... Ex 29:1
the priest's *o* shall be theirs ... Ex 29:9
minister to me in the priest's *o* ... Ex 29:44
unto me in the priest's *o* ... Ex 30:30
to minister in the priest's *o* ... Ex 31:10
to minister in the priest's *o* ... Ex 35:19
to minister in the priest's *o* ... Ex 39:41
unto me in the priest's *o* ... Ex 40:13
unto me in the priest's *o* ... Ex 40:15
unto the LORD in the priest's *o* ... Lev 7:35
priest's *o* in his father's stead ... Lev 16:32
to minister in the priest's *o* ... Num 3:3
ministered in the priest's *o* in ... Num 3:4
shall wait on their priest's *o* ... Num 3:10
to the *o* of Eleazar the son of ... Num 4:16 6486
o for every thing of the altar ... Num 18:7
I have given your priest's *o* unto ... Num 18:7
in the priest's *o* in his stead ... Deut 10:6
o in the temple that Solomon ... 1Chr 6:10
their *o* according to their order ... 1Chr 6:32 5656
seer did ordain in their set *o* ... 1Chr 9:22
porters, were in their set *o* ... 1Chr 9:26
had the set *o* over the things ... 1Chr 9:31
Because their *o* was to wait on ... 1Chr 23:28 4612
Ithamar executed the priest's *o* ... 1Chr 24:2
the priest's *o* unto the LORD ... 2Chr 11:14
o by the hand of the Levites ... 2Chr 24:11 6486
of the priests, in their set *o* ... 2Chr 31:15
for in their set *o* they ... 2Chr 31:18
their *o* was to distribute unto ... Neh 13:13
and let another take his *o* ... Ps 109:8 6486
to do the *o* of a priest unto me, ... Eze 44:13
o before God in the order of his ... Lk 1:8 *2407*
to the custom of the priest's *o* ... Lk 1:9 *2405*
of the Gentiles, I magnify mine *o* ... Rom 11:13 *1248*
all members have not the same *o* ... Rom 12:4 *4234*
If a man desire the *o* of a bishop ... 1Ti 3:1 *1984*
let them use the *o* of a deacon ... 1Ti 3:10 *1247*
For they that have used the *o* of ... 1Ti 3:13 *1247*
of Levi, who receive the *o* of the ... Heb 7:5 *2405*

OFFICER {12}
an *o* of Pharaoh's, and captain of ... Gen 37:36 5631
an *o* of Pharaoh, captain of the ... Gen 39:1 5631
and Zebul his *o* ... Judg 9:28 6496
the son of Nathan was principal *o* ... 1Kin 4:5 5324
he was the only *o* which was in ... 1Kin 4:19 5333
the king of Israel called an *o* ... 1Kin 22:9 5631
appointed unto her a certain *o* ... 2Kin 8:6 5631
out of the city he took an *o* that ... 2Kin 25:19 5631
and the high priest's *o* came ... 2Chr 24:11 6496
the judge deliver thee to the *o* ... Mt 5:25 *5257*
the judge deliver thee to the *o* ... Lk 12:58 *4233*
the *o* cast thee into prison ... Lk 12:58 *4233*

OFFICERS {58}
was wroth against two of his *o* ... Gen 40:2 5631
he asked Pharaoh's *o* that were ... Gen 40:7 5631
let him appoint *o* over the land ... Gen 41:34 6496
of the people, and their *o* ... Ex 5:6 7860
the people went out, and their *o* ... Ex 5:10 7860
the *o* of the children of Israel, ... Ex 5:14 7860
Then the *o* of the children of ... Ex 5:15 7860
the *o* of the children of Israel ... Ex 5:19 7860
of the people, and *o* over them ... Num 11:16 7860
was wroth with the *o* of the host ... Num 31:14 6485
the *o* which were over thousands ... Num 31:48 6485
over tens, and *o* among your tribes ... Deut 1:15 7860
o shalt thou make thee in all thy ... Deut 16:18 7860
the *o* shall speak unto the people ... Deut 20:5 7860
the *o* shall speak further unto ... Deut 20:8 7860
when the *o* have made an end of ... Deut 20:9 7860
tribes, your elders, and your *o* ... Deut 29:10 7860
elders of your tribes, and your *o* ... Deut 31:28 7860
commanded the *o* of the people ... Josh 1:10 7860
that the *o* went through the host ... Josh 3:2 7860
all Israel, and their elders, and *o* ... Josh 8:33 7860
for their judges, and for their *o* ... Josh 23:2 7860
for their judges, and for their *o* ... Josh 24:1 7860
your vineyards, and give to his *o* ... 1Sa 8:15 5631
the son of Nathan was over the *o* ... 1Kin 4:5 5324
had twelve *o* over all Israel ... 1Kin 4:7 5324
those *o* provided victual for king ... 1Kin 4:27 5324
unto the place where the *o* were ... 1Kin 4:28
o which were over the work ... 1Kin 5:16 5324
These were the chief of the *o* ... 1Kin 9:23 5324
the *o* of the host, and said unto ... 2Kin 11:15 6485
the priest appointed *o* over the ... 2Kin 11:18 6486
and his princes, and his *o* ... 2Kin 24:12 5631
and the king's wives, and his *o* ... 2Kin 24:15 5631
and six thousand were *o* and judges ... 1Chr 23:4 7860
business over Israel, for *o* ... 1Chr 26:29 7860
were *o* among them of Israel on ... 1Chr 26:30 6486
their *o* that served the king in ... 1Chr 27:1 7860
king, and of his sons, with the *o* ... 1Chr 28:1 5631
the chief of king Solomon's *o* ... 2Chr 8:10 5324
of Israel called for one of his *o* ... 2Chr 18:8 5631
the Levites shall be *o* before you ... 2Chr 19:11 7860
Levites there were scribes, and *o* ... 2Chr 34:13 7860
to all the *o* of his house ... Est 1:8 7227
let the king appoint *o* in all the ... Est 2:3 6496
o of the king, helped the Jews ... Est 9:3 6213
I will also make thy *o* peace ... Is 60:17 6486
that ye should be *o* in the house ... Jer 29:26 6496
chief priests sent *o* to take him ... Jn 7:32 *5257*
Then came the *o* to the chief ... Jn 7:45 *5257*
The *o* answered, Never man spake ... Jn 7:46 *5257*
o from the chief priests and ... Jn 18:3 *5257*
o of the Jews took Jesus, and ... Jn 18:12 *5257*
o stood there, who had made a ... Jn 18:18 *5257*
one of the *o* which stood by ... Jn 18:22 *5257*
o saw him, they cried out, saying ... Jn 19:6 *5257*
But when the *o* came, and found ... Acts 5:22 *5257*
Then went the captain with the *o* ... Acts 5:26 *5257*

OFFICES {5}
thee, into one of the priests' *o* ... 1Sa 2:36
to their *o* in their service ... 1Chr 24:3 6486
And the priests waited on their *o* ... 2Chr 7:6 4931
Also Jehoiada appointed the *o* of ... 2Chr 23:18 6486
of my God, and for the *o* thereof ... Neh 13:14 4929

OFFSCOURING {2}
Thou hast made us as the *o* ... Lam 3:45 5501
are the *o* of all things unto this ... 1Cor 4:13 *4067*

OFFSPRING {12}
thine *o* as the grass of the earth ... Job 5:25 6631
their *o* before their eyes ... Job 21:8 6631
his *o* shall not be satisfied with ... Job 27:14 6631
yea, let my *o* be rooted out ... Job 31:8 6631
of his father's house, the *o* ... Is 22:24 6631
seed, and my blessing upon thine *o* ... Is 44:3 6631
the *o* of thy bowels like the ... Is 48:19 6631
and their *o* among the people ... Is 61:9 6631
of the LORD, and their *o* with them ... Is 65:23 6631
have said, For we are also his *o* ... Acts 17:28 *1085*
then as we are the *o* of God ... Acts 17:29 *1085*
the *o* of David, and the bright and ... Rev 22:16 *1085*

OFT {13}
that as *o* as he passed by, he ... 2Kin 4:8 1767
How *o* is the candle of the wicked ... Job 21:17
how *o* cometh their destruction ... Job 21:17
How *o* did they provoke him in the ... Ps 78:40
Why do we and the Pharisees fast *o* ... Mt 9:14 *4183*
the fire, and *o* into the water ... Mt 17:15 *4178*
how *o* shall my brother sin ... Mt 18:21 *4212*
except they wash their hands *o* ... Mk 7:3 *4435*
I punished them *o* in every ... Acts 26:11 *4178*
do ye, as *o* as ye drink it, in ... 1Cor 11:25 *3740*
more frequent, in deaths *o* ... 2Cor 11:23 *4178*
for he *o* refreshed me, and was not ... 2Ti 1:16 *4178*
in the rain that cometh *o* upon it ... Heb 6:7 *4178*

OFTEN See APPENDIX.

OFTENER {1}
wherefore he sent for him the *o* ... Acts 24:26 *4437*

OFTENTIMES {6}
things worketh God *o* with man ... Job 33:29 6471,7969
For *o* also thine own heart ... Eccl 7:22 6471,7227
For *o* it had caught him ... Lk 8:29 *4183,5550*
that *o* I purposed to come unto ... Rom 1:13 *4178*
whom we have *o* proved diligent in ... 2Cor 8:22 *4178*
offering *o* the same sacrifices, ... Heb 10:11 *4178*

OFTTIMES {3}
for *o* he falleth into the fire, ... Mt 17:15 *4178*
o it hath cast him into the fire, ... Mk 9:22 *4178*
for Jesus *o* resorted thither with ... Jn 18:2 *4178*

OG *(og)* {22} *An Amorite king.*
O the king of Bashan went out ... Num 21:33 5747
the kingdom of *O* king of Bashan ... Num 32:33 5747
O the king of Bashan, which dwelt ... Deut 1:4 5747
O the king of Bashan came out ... Deut 3:1 5747
delivered into our hands *O* also ... Deut 3:3 5747
Argob, the kingdom of *O* in Bashan ... Deut 3:4 5747
of the kingdom of *O* in Bashan ... Deut 3:10 5747
For only *O* king of Bashan ... Deut 3:11 5747
Bashan, being the kingdom of *O* ... Deut 3:13 5747
the land of *O* king of Bashan, two ... Deut 4:47 5747
O the king of Bashan, came out ... Deut 29:7 5747
them as he did to Sihon and to *O* ... Deut 31:4 5747
the other side Jordan, Sihon and *O* ... Josh 2:10 5747
to *O* king of Bashan, which was at ... Josh 9:10 5747
the coast of *O* king of Bashan, ... Josh 12:4 5747
All the kingdom of *O* in Bashan ... Josh 13:12 5747
the kingdom of *O* king of Bashan ... Josh 13:30 5747
of the kingdom of *O* in Bashan ... Josh 13:31 5747
Amorites, and of *O* king of Bashan ... 1Kin 4:19 5747
the land of *O* king of Bashan ... Neh 9:22 5747
O king of Bashan, and all the ... Ps 135:11 5747
And *O* the king of Bashan ... Ps 136:20 5747

OH See APPENDIX.

OHAD *(o'-had)* {2} *A son of Simeon.*
Jemuel, and Jamin, and *O*, and Jachin ... Gen 46:10 161
Jemuel, and Jamin, and *O*, and Jachin ... Ex 6:15 161

OHEL *(o'-hel)* {1} *A son of Zerubbabel.*
And Hashubah, and *O*, and Berechiah, ... 1Chr 3:20 169

OHOLAH See AHOLAH.

OHOLIAB See AHOLIAB.

OHOLIBAH See AHOLIBAH.

OHOLIBAMAH See AHOLIBAMAH.

OIL {202}
poured *o* upon the top of it ... Gen 28:18 8081
thereon, and he poured *o* thereon ... Gen 35:14 8081
O for the light, spices for ... Ex 25:6 8081
the light, spices for anointing *o* ... Ex 25:6 8081
that they bring thee pure *o* olive ... Ex 27:20 8081
cakes unleavened tempered with *o* ... Ex 29:2 8081
wafers unleavened anointed with *o* ... Ex 29:2 8081
shalt thou take the anointing *o* ... Ex 29:7 8081
the altar, and of the anointing *o* ... Ex 29:21 8081
fourth part of an hin of beaten *o* ... Ex 29:40 8081
sanctuary, and of *o* olive an hin ... Ex 30:24 8081
make it an *o* of holy ointment ... Ex 30:25 8081
it shall be an holy anointing *o* ... Ex 30:25 8081
o unto me throughout your ... Ex 30:31 8081
And the anointing *o*, and sweet ... Ex 31:11 8081
o for the light, and spices for ... Ex 35:8 8081
light, and spices for anointing *o* ... Ex 35:8 8081
with the *o* for the light, ... Ex 35:14 8081
and his staves, and the anointing *o* ... Ex 35:15 8081
o for the light, and for the ... Ex 35:28 8081
the light, and for the anointing *o* ... Ex 35:28 8081
And he made the holy anointing *o* ... Ex 37:29 8081
thereof, and the *o* for light, ... Ex 39:37 8081
golden altar, and the anointing *o* ... Ex 39:38 8081
thou shalt take the anointing *o* ... Ex 40:9 8081
and he shall pour *o* upon it ... Lev 2:1 8081
of the *o* thereof, with all the ... Lev 2:2 8081
of fine flour mingled with *o* ... Lev 2:4 8081
unleavened wafers anointed with *o* ... Lev 2:4 8081
flour unleavened, mingled with *o* ... Lev 2:5 8081
it in pieces, and pour *o* thereon ... Lev 2:6 8081
be made of fine flour with *o* ... Lev 2:7 8081
And thou shalt put *o* upon it ... Lev 2:15 8081
thereof, and part of the *o* thereof ... Lev 2:16 8081
he shall put no *o* upon it ... Lev 5:11 8081
of the *o* thereof, and all the ... Lev 6:15 8081
In a pan it shall be made with *o* ... Lev 6:21 8081
meat offering, mingled with *o* ... Lev 7:10 8081
unleavened cakes mingled with *o* ... Lev 7:12 8081
with *o*, and cakes mingled with *o* ... Lev 7:12 8081
the garments, and the anointing *o* ... Lev 8:2 8081
And Moses took the anointing *o* ... Lev 8:10 8081
the anointing *o* upon Aaron's head ... Lev 8:12 8081
And Moses took of the anointing *o* ... Lev 8:30 8081
and a meat offering mingled with *o* ... Lev 9:4 8081
for the anointing *o* of the LORD ... Lev 10:7 8081
mingled with *o*, and one log of *o* ... Lev 14:10 8081
offering, and the log of *o* ... Lev 14:12 8081
shall take some of the log of *o* ... Lev 14:15 8081
in the *o* that is in his left hand ... Lev 14:16 8081
shall sprinkle of the *o* with his ... Lev 14:16 8081
of the rest of the *o* that is in ... Lev 14:17 8081
the remnant of the *o* that is in ... Lev 14:18 8081
with *o* for a meat offering ... Lev 14:21 8081
a meat offering, and a log of *o* ... Lev 14:21 8081
offering, and the log of *o* ... Lev 14:24 8081
the priest shall pour of the *o* ... Lev 14:26 8081
his right finger some of the *o* ... Lev 14:27 8081
the priest shall put of the *o* ... Lev 14:28 8081
the rest of the *o* that is in the ... Lev 14:29 8081
head the anointing *o* was poured ... Lev 21:10 8081
o of his God is upon him ... Lev 21:12 8081
of fine flour mingled with *o* ... Lev 23:13 8081
pure *o* olive beaten for the light ... Lev 24:2 8081
all the *o* vessels thereof, ... Num 4:9 8081
pertaineth the *o* for the light ... Num 4:16 8081
meat offering, and the anointing *o* ... Num 4:16 8081
he shall pour no *o* upon it ... Num 5:15 8081
of fine flour mingled with *o* ... Num 6:15 8081
unleavened bread anointed with *o* ... Num 6:15 8081
with *o* for a meat offering ... Num 7:13 8081
with *o* for a meat offering ... Num 7:19 8081
with *o* for a meat offering ... Num 7:25 8081
with *o* for a meat offering ... Num 7:31 8081
with *o* for a meat offering ... Num 7:37 8081
with *o* for a meat offering ... Num 7:43 8081
with *o* for a meat offering ... Num 7:49 8081
with *o* for a meat offering ... Num 7:55 8081
with *o* for a meat offering ... Num 7:61 8081
with *o* for a meat offering ... Num 7:67 8081
with *o* for a meat offering ... Num 7:73 8081
with *o* for a meat offering ... Num 7:79 8081
even fine flour mingled with *o* ... Num 8:8 8081
of it was as the taste of fresh *o* ... Num 11:8 8081
the fourth part of an hin of *o* ... Num 15:4 8081
the third part of an hin of *o* ... Num 15:6 8081
mingled with half an hin of *o* ... Num 15:9 8081
All the best of the *o*, and all the ... Num 18:12 8081
fourth part of an hin of beaten *o* ... Num 28:5 8081
a meat offering, mingled with *o* ... Num 28:9 8081
a meat offering, mingled with *o* ... Num 28:12 8081
a meat offering, mingled with *o* ... Num 28:12 8081
deal of flour mingled with *o* for ... Num 28:13 8081
shall be of flour mingled with *o* ... Num 28:20 8081

offering of flour mingled with *o*	Num 28:28	8081
shall be of flour mingled with *o*	Num 29:3	8081
shall be of flour mingled with *o*	Num 29:9	8081
shall be of flour mingled with *o*	Num 29:14	8081
was anointed with the holy *o*	Num 35:25	8081
thy corn, and thy wine, and thine *o*	Deut 7:13	3323
a land of *o* olive, and honey	Deut 8:8	8081
thy corn, and thy wine, and thine *o*	Deut 11:14	3323
corn, or of thy wine, or of thy *o*	Deut 12:17	3323
corn, of thy wine, and of thine *o*	Deut 14:23	3323
corn, of thy wine, and of thine *o*	Deut 18:4	3323
not anoint thyself with the *o*	Deut 28:40	8081
thee either corn, wine, or *o*	Deut 28:51	3323
rock, and *o* out of the flinty rock	Deut 32:13	8081
and let him dip his foot in *o*	Deut 33:24	8081
Then Samuel took a vial of *o*	1Sa 10:1	8081
fill thine horn with *o*, and go, I	1Sa 16:1	8081
Then Samuel took the horn of *o*	1Sa 16:13	8081
he had not been anointed with *o*	2Sa 1:21	8081
and anoint not thyself with *o*	2Sa 14:2	8081
horn of *o* out of the tabernacle	1Kin 1:39	8081
and twenty measures of pure *o*	1Kin 5:11	8081
barrel, and a little *o* in a cruse	1Kin 17:12	8081
neither shall the cruse of *o* fail	1Kin 17:14	8081
neither did the cruse of *o* fail	1Kin 17:16	8081
in the house, save a pot of *o*	2Kin 4:2	8081
And the *o* stayed	2Kin 4:6	8081
And he said, Go, sell the *o*	2Kin 4:7	8081
take this box of *o* in thine hand	2Kin 9:1	8081
Then take the box of *o*, and pour	2Kin 9:3	8081
and he poured the *o* on his head	2Kin 9:6	8081
and vineyards, a land of *o* olive	2Kin 18:32	3323
fine flour, and the wine, and the *o*	1Chr 9:29	8081
bunches of raisins, and wine, and *o*	1Chr 12:40	8081
over the cellars of *o* was Joash	1Chr 27:28	8081
and twenty thousand baths of *o*	2Chr 2:10	8081
the wheat, and the barley, the *o*	2Chr 2:15	8081
and store of victual, and of *o*	2Chr 11:11	8081
firstfruits of corn, wine, and *o*	2Chr 31:5	3323
increase of corn, and wine, and *o*	2Chr 32:28	3323
and meat, and drink, and *o*, unto	Ezr 3:7	8081
heaven, wheat, salt, wine, and *o*	Ezr 6:9	4887
wine, and to an hundred baths of *o*	Ezr 7:22	4887
of the corn, the wine, and the *o*	Neh 5:11	3323
manner of trees, of wine and of *o*	Neh 10:37	3323
corn, of the new wine, and the *o*	Neh 10:39	3323
the corn, the new wine, and the *o*	Neh 13:5	3323
the *o* unto the treasuries	Neh 13:12	3323
wit, six months with *o* of myrrh	Est 2:12	8081
Which make *o* within their walls,	Job 24:11	6671
rock poured me out rivers of *o*	Job 29:6	8081
thou anointest my head with *o*	Ps 23:5	8081
hath anointed thee with the *o* of	Ps 45:7	8081
his words were softer than *o*	Ps 55:21	8081
with my holy *o* have I anointed	Ps 89:20	8081
I shall be anointed with fresh *o*	Ps 92:10	8081
o to make his face to shine, and	Ps 104:15	8081
water, and like *o* into his bones	Ps 109:18	8081
it shall be an excellent *o*	Ps 141:5	8081
and her mouth is smoother than *o*	Prov 5:3	8081
wine and *o* shall not be rich	Prov 21:17	8081
o in the dwelling of the wise	Prov 21:20	8081
and the myrtle, and the *o* tree	Is 41:19	8081
the *o* of joy for mourning, the	Is 61:3	8081
for wheat, and for wine, and for *o*	Jer 31:12	3323
ye wine, and summer fruits, and *o*	Jer 40:10	8081
of wheat, and of barley, and of *o*	Jer 41:8	8081
thee, and I anointed thee with *o*	Eze 16:9	8081
eat fine flour, and honey, and *o*	Eze 16:13	8081
and thou hast set mine *o* and mine	Eze 16:18	8081
I gave thee, fine flour, and *o*	Eze 16:19	8081
hast set mine incense and mine *o*	Eze 23:41	8081
and Pannag, and honey, and *o*	Eze 27:17	8081
cause their rivers to run like *o*	Eze 32:14	8081
ordinance of *o*, the bath of *o*	Eze 45:14	8081
ram, and an hin of *o* for an ephah	Eze 45:24	8081
offering, and according to the *o*	Eze 45:25	8081
give, and an hin of *o* to an ephah	Eze 46:5	8081
unto, and an hin of *o* to an ephah	Eze 46:7	8081
give, and an hin of *o* to an ephah	Eze 46:11	8081
and the third part of an hin of *o*	Eze 46:14	8081
and the meat offering, and the *o*	Eze 46:15	8081
water, my wool and my flax, mine *o*	Hos 2:5	8081
I gave her corn, and wine, and *o*	Hos 2:8	3323
the corn, and the wine, and the *o*	Hos 2:22	3323
and *o* is carried into Egypt	Hos 12:1	8081
is dried up, the *o* languisheth	Joel 1:10	3323
will send you corn, and wine, and *o*	Joel 2:19	3323
shall overflow with wine and *o*	Joel 2:24	3323
with ten thousands of rivers of *o*	Mic 6:7	8081
thou shalt not anoint thee with *o*	Mic 6:15	8081
upon the new wine, and upon the *o*	Hag 1:11	3323
bread, or pottage, or wine, or *o*	Hag 2:12	8081
the golden *o* out of themselves	Zec 4:12	
lamps, and took no *o* with them	Mt 25:3	*1637*
But the wise took *o* in their	Mt 25:4	*1637*
unto the wise, Give us of your *o*	Mt 25:8	*1637*
anointed with *o* many that were	Mk 6:13	*1637*
My head with *o* thou didst not	Lk 7:46	*1637*
bound up his wounds, pouring in *o*	Lk 10:34	*1637*
he said, An hundred measures of *o*	Lk 16:6	*1637*
hath anointed thee with the *o* of	Heb 1:9	*1637*
anointing him with *o* in the name	Jas 5:14	*1637*
and see thou hurt not the *o*	Rev 6:6	*1637*
and frankincense, and wine, and *o*	Rev 18:13	*1637*

OILED {2}

of bread, and one cake of *o* bread	Ex 29:23	8081
cake, and a cake of *o* bread	Lev 8:26	8081

OINTMENT {27}

shalt make it an oil of holy *o*	Ex 30:25	4888
an *o* compound after the art of	Ex 30:25	7545
and the spices, and the precious *o*	2Kin 20:13	8081
priests made the *o* of the spices	1Chr 9:30	4842
he maketh the sea like a pot of *o*	Job 41:31	4841
like the precious *o* upon the head	Ps 133:2	8081
O and perfume rejoice the heart	Prov 27:9	8081
the *o* of his right hand, which	Prov 27:16	8081
name is better than precious *o*	Eccl 7:1	8081
and let thy head lack no *o*	Eccl 9:8	8081
Dead flies cause the *o* of the	Eccl 10:1	8081
thy name is as *o* poured forth	Song 1:3	8081
up, neither mollified with *o*	Is 1:6	8081
and the spices, and the precious *o*	Is 39:2	8081
thou wentest to the king with *o*	Is 57:9	8081
alabaster box of very precious *o*	Mt 26:7	*3464*
For this *o* might have been sold	Mt 26:9	*3464*
she hath poured this *o* on my body	Mt 26:12	*3464*
of *o* of spikenard very precious	Mk 14:3	*3464*
Why was this waste of the *o* made	Mk 14:4	*3464*
brought an alabaster box of *o*	Lk 7:37	*3464*
feet, and anointed them with the *o*	Lk 7:38	*3464*
hath anointed my feet with *o*	Lk 7:46	*3464*
which anointed the Lord with *o*	Jn 11:2	*3464*
Mary a pound of *o* of spikenard	Jn 12:3	*3464*
filled with the odour of the *o*	Jn 12:3	*3464*
Why was not this *o* sold for three	Jn 12:5	*3464*

OINTMENTS {5}

of the savour of thy good *o* thy	Song 1:3	8081
smell of thine *o* than all spices	Song 4:10	8081
themselves with the chief *o*	Amos 6:6	8081
returned, and prepared spices and *o*	Lk 23:56	*3464*
And cinnamon, and odours, and *o*	Rev 18:13	*3464*

OLD {380}

And Noah was five hundred years *o*	Gen 5:32	1121
became mighty men which were of *o*	Gen 6:4	5769
Noah was six hundred years *o* when	Gen 7:6	1121
Shem was an hundred years *o*	Gen 11:10	1121
five years *o* when he departed out	Gen 12:4	1121
me an heifer of three years *o*	Gen 15:9	8027
and a she goat of three years *o*	Gen 15:9	8027
and a ram of three years *o*	Gen 15:9	8027
shalt be buried in a good *o* age	Gen 15:15	7872
was fourscore and six years *o*	Gen 16:16	1121
And when Abram was ninety years *o*	Gen 17:1	1121
he that is eight days *o* shall be	Gen 17:12	1121
him that is an hundred years *o*	Gen 17:17	1121
Sarah, that is ninety years *o*	Gen 17:17	1323
And Abraham was ninety years *o*	Gen 17:24	1121
his son was thirteen years *o*	Gen 17:25	1121
Now Abraham and Sarah were *o*	Gen 18:11	2205
After I am waxed *o* shall I have	Gen 18:12	1086
pleasure, my lord being *o* also	Gen 18:12	2204
a surety bear a child, which am *o*	Gen 18:13	2204
compassed the house round, both *o*	Gen 19:4	2205
unto the younger, Our father is *o*	Gen 19:31	2204
bare Abraham a son in his *o* age	Gen 21:2	2208
his son Isaac being eight days *o*	Gen 21:4	1121
And Abraham was an hundred years *o*	Gen 21:5	1121
have born him a son in his *o* age	Gen 21:7	2208
and seven and twenty years *o*	Gen 23:1	2416
And Abraham was *o*, and well	Gen 24:1	2204
a son to my master when she was *o*	Gen 24:36	2209
ghost, and died in a good *o* age	Gen 25:8	7872
an *o* man, and full of years	Gen 25:8	2205
Isaac was forty years *o* when he	Gen 25:20	1121
years *o* when she bare them	Gen 25:26	1121
Esau was forty years *o* when he	Gen 26:34	1121
to pass, that when Isaac was *o*	Gen 27:1	2204
And he said, Behold now, I am *o*	Gen 27:2	2204
gathered unto his people, being *o*	Gen 35:29	2205
Joseph, being seventeen years *o*	Gen 37:2	1121
he was the son of his *o* age	Gen 37:3	2208
Joseph was thirty years *o* when he	Gen 41:46	1121
the *o* man of whom ye spake	Gen 43:27	2205
o man, and a child of his *o* age	Gen 44:20	2208
unto Jacob, How *o* art thou	Gen 47:8	3117,8140,3117
as a lion, and as an *o* lion	Gen 49:9	3833
being an hundred and ten years *o*	Gen 50:26	1121
And Moses was fourscore years *o*	Ex 7:7	1121
Aaron fourscore and three years *o*	Ex 7:7	1121
go with our young and with our *o*	Ex 10:9	2205
are numbered, from twenty years *o*	Ex 30:14	1121
be numbered, from twenty years *o*	Ex 38:26	1121
It is an *o* leprosy in the skin of	Lev 13:11	3462
and honour the face of the *o* man	Lev 19:32	2205
eat yet of *o* fruit until the	Lev 25:22	3465
in ye shall eat of the *o* store	Lev 25:22	3465
And ye shall eat *o* store	Lev 26:10	3462
bring forth the *o* because of the	Lev 26:10	3465
years *o* even unto sixty years *o*	Lev 27:3	1121
o even unto twenty years	Lev 27:5	1121
month *o* even unto five years *o*	Lev 27:6	1121
And if it be from sixty years *o*	Lev 27:7	1121
From twenty years *o* and upward,	Num 1:3	1121
of the names, from twenty years *o*	Num 1:18	1121
every male from twenty years *o*	Num 1:20	1121
every male from twenty years *o*	Num 1:22	1121
of the names, from twenty years *o*	Num 1:24	1121
of the names, from twenty years *o*	Num 1:26	1121
of the names, from twenty years *o*	Num 1:28	1121
of the names, from twenty years *o*	Num 1:30	1121
of the names, from twenty years *o*	Num 1:32	1121
of the names, from twenty years *o*	Num 1:34	1121
of the names, from twenty years *o*	Num 1:36	1121
of the names, from twenty years *o*	Num 1:38	1121
of the names, from twenty years *o*	Num 1:40	1121
of the names, from twenty years *o*	Num 1:42	1121
fathers, from twenty years *o*	Num 1:45	1121
every male from a month *o*	Num 3:15	1121
of all the males, from a month *o*	Num 3:22	1121
of all the males, from a month *o*	Num 3:28	1121
of all the males, from a month *o*	Num 3:34	1121
all the males from a month *o*	Num 3:39	1121
children of Israel from a month *o*	Num 3:40	1121
number of names, from a month *o*	Num 3:43	1121
From thirty years *o* and upward	Num 4:3	1121
upward even until fifty years *o*	Num 4:3	1121
From thirty years *o* and upward	Num 4:23	1121
years *o* shalt thou number them	Num 4:23	1121
From thirty years *o* and upward	Num 4:30	1121
years *o* shalt thou number them	Num 4:30	1121
From thirty years *o* and upward	Num 4:35	1121
and upward even unto fifty years *o*	Num 4:35	1121
From thirty years *o* and upward	Num 4:39	1121
and upward even unto fifty years *o*	Num 4:39	1121
From thirty years *o* and upward	Num 4:43	1121
and upward even unto fifty years *o*	Num 4:43	1121
From thirty years *o* and upward	Num 4:47	1121
and upward even unto fifty years *o*	Num 4:47	1121
from twenty and five years *o*	Num 8:24	1121
whole number, from twenty years *o*	Num 14:29	1121
from a month *o* shalt thou redeem	Num 18:16	1121
of Israel, from twenty years *o*	Num 26:2	1121
the people, from twenty years *o*	Num 26:4	1121
all males from a month *o*	Num 26:62	1121
out of Egypt, from twenty years *o*	Num 32:11	1121
three years *o* when he died in	Num 33:39	1121
giants dwelt therein in *o* time	Deut 2:20	6440
Thy raiment waxed not *o* upon thee	Deut 8:4	1086
which they of *o* time have set in	Deut 19:14	7223
not regard the person of the *o*	Deut 28:50	2205
clothes are not waxen *o* upon you	Deut 29:5	1086
shoe is not waxen *o* upon thy foot	Deut 29:5	1086
and twenty years *o* this day	Deut 31:2	1121
Remember the days of *o*, consider	Deut 32:7	5769
and twenty years *o* when he died	Deut 34:7	1121
they did eat of the *o* corn of the	Josh 5:11	5669
eaten of the *o* corn of the land	Josh 5:12	5669
both man and woman, young and *o*	Josh 6:21	5288
took *o* sacks upon their asses, and	Josh 9:4	1087
their asses, and wine bottles, *o*	Josh 9:4	1087
o shoes and clouted upon their	Josh 9:5	1087
feet, and *o* garments upon them	Josh 9:5	1087
our shoes are become *o* by reason	Josh 9:13	1086
Now Joshua was *o* and stricken in	Josh 13:1	2204
LORD said unto him, Thou art *o*	Josh 13:1	2204
Forty years *o* was I when Moses	Josh 14:7	1121
day fourscore and five years *o*	Josh 14:10	1121
round about, that Joshua waxed *o*	Josh 23:1	2204
and said unto them, I am *o*	Josh 23:2	2204
other side of the flood in *o* time	Josh 24:2	5769
being an hundred and ten years *o*	Josh 24:29	1121
being an hundred and ten years *o*	Judg 2:8	1121
second bullock of seven years *o*	Judg 6:25	
son of Joash died in a good *o* age	Judg 8:32	7872
there came an *o* man from his work	Judg 19:16	2205
the *o* man said, Whither goest	Judg 19:17	2205
the *o* man said, Peace be with	Judg 19:20	2205
master of the house, the *o* man	Judg 19:22	2205
for I am too *o* to have an husband	Ruth 1:12	2204
and a nourisher of thine *o* age	Ruth 4:15	7872
Now Eli was very *o*, and heard all	1Sa 2:22	2204
not be an *o* man in thine house	1Sa 2:31	2205
there shall not be an *o* man in	1Sa 2:32	2205
Eli was ninety and eight years *o*	1Sa 4:15	1121
for he was an *o* man, and heavy	1Sa 4:18	2204
came to pass, when Samuel was *o*	1Sa 8:1	2204
said unto him, Behold, thou art *o*	1Sa 8:5	2204
and I am *o* and grayheaded	1Sa 12:2	2204
for an *o* man in the days of Saul	1Sa 17:12	2204
for those nations were of *o* the	1Sa 27:8	5769
And she said, An *o* man cometh up	1Sa 28:14	2205
Saul's son was forty years *o* when	2Sa 2:10	1121
He was five years *o* when the	2Sa 4:4	1121
years *o* when he began to reign	2Sa 5:4	1121
aged man, even fourscore years *o*	2Sa 19:32	1121
I am this day fourscore years *o*	2Sa 19:35	1121
They were wont to speak in *o* time	2Sa 20:18	7223
Now king David was *o* and stricken	1Kin 1:1	2204
and the king was very *o*	1Kin 1:15	2204
came to pass, when Solomon was *o*	1Kin 11:4	2209
Rehoboam consulted with the *o* men	1Kin 12:6	2205
forsook the counsel of the *o* men	1Kin 12:8	2205
forsook the *o* men's counsel that	1Kin 12:13	2205
dwelt an *o* prophet in Beth-el	1Kin 13:11	2205
city where the *o* prophet dwelt	1Kin 13:25	2205
the *o* prophet came to the city,	1Kin 13:29	2205
one years *o* when he began to	1Kin 14:21	1121
o age he was diseased in his feet	1Kin 15:23	2209
five years *o* when he began to	1Kin 22:42	1121
no child, and her husband is *o*	2Kin 4:14	2204
two years *o* was he when he began	2Kin 8:17	1121
twenty years *o* was Ahaziah when	2Kin 8:26	1121
Seven years *o* was Jehoash when he	2Kin 11:21	1121
five years *o* when he began to	2Kin 14:2	1121
which was sixteen years *o*	2Kin 14:21	1121
Sixteen years *o* was he when he	2Kin 15:2	1121
twenty years *o* was he when he	2Kin 15:33	1121
Twenty years *o* was Ahaz when he	2Kin 16:2	1121
five years *o* was he when he began	2Kin 18:2	1121

years *o* when he began to reign 2Kin 21:1 1121
two years *o* when he began to 2Kin 21:19 1121
years *o* when he began to reign 2Kin 22:1 1121
three years *o* when he began to 2Kin 23:31 1121
five years *o* when he began to 2Kin 23:36 1121
years *o* when he began to reign 2Kin 24:8 1121
one years *o* when he began to 2Kin 24:18 1121
when he was threescore years *o* 1Chr 2:21 1121
they of Ham had dwelt there of *o* 1Chr 4:40 6440
So when David was *o* and full of 1Chr 23:1 2204
were numbered from twenty years *o* 1Chr 23:27 1121
of them from twenty years *o* 1Chr 27:23 1121
And he died in a good *o* age 1Chr 29:28 7872
the *o* men that had stood before 2Chr 10:6 2205
counsel which the *o* men gave him 2Chr 10:8 2205
forsook the counsel of the *o* men 2Chr 10:13 2205
forty years *o* when he began to 2Chr 12:13 1121
five years *o* when he began to 2Chr 20:31 1121
two years *o* when he began to 2Chr 21:5 1121
two years *o* was he when he began 2Chr 21:20 1121
two years *o* was Ahaziah when he 2Chr 22:2 1121
Joash was seven years *o* when he 2Chr 24:1 1121
But Jehoiada waxed *o*, and was full 2Chr 24:15 2204
thirty years *o* was he when he 2Chr 24:15 1121
five years *o* when he began to 2Chr 25:1 1121
numbered them from twenty years *o* 2Chr 25:5 1121
Uzziah, who was sixteen years *o* 2Chr 26:1 1121
Sixteen years *o* was Uzziah when 2Chr 26:3 1121
five years *o* when he began to 2Chr 27:1 1121
twenty years *o* when he began to 2Chr 27:8 1121
Ahaz was twenty years *o* when he 2Chr 28:1 1121
he was five and twenty years *o* 2Chr 29:1 1121
of males, from three years *o* 2Chr 31:16 1121
the Levites from twenty years *o* 2Chr 31:17 1121
years *o* when he began to reign 2Chr 33:1 1121
twenty years *o* when he began to 2Chr 33:21 1121
years *o* when he began to reign 2Chr 34:1 1121
three years *o* when he began to 2Chr 36:2 1121
five years *o* when he began to 2Chr 36:5 1121
years *o* when he began to reign 2Chr 36:9 1121
twenty years *o* when he began to 2Chr 36:11 1121
o man, or him that stooped for 2Chr 36:17 2205
the Levites, from twenty years *o* Ezr 3:8 1121
within the same of *o* time Ezr 4:15 5957
of *o* time hath made insurrection Ezr 4:19 5957
Moreover the *o* gate repaired Neh 3:6 3465
their clothes waxed not *o* Neh 9:21 1086
of Ephraim, and above the *o* gate Neh 12:39 3465
Asaph of *o* there were chief of Neh 12:46 6924
perish, all Jews, both young and *o* Est 3:13 2205
The *o* lion perisheth for lack of Job 4:11
root thereof wax *o* in the earth Job 14:8 2204
Knowest thou not this of *o* Job 20:4 5703
do the wicked live, become *o* Job 21:7 6275
Hast thou marked the *o* way which Job 22:15 5769
in whom *o* age was perished Job 30:2
I am young, and ye are very *o* Job 32:6 3453
So Job died, being *o* and full of Job 42:17 2205
it waxeth *o* because of all mine Ps 6:7 6275
for they have been ever of *o* Ps 25:6 5769
my bones waxed *o* through my Ps 32:3 1086
I have been young, and now am *o* Ps 37:25 2204
in their days, in the times of *o* Ps 44:1 6924
them, even he that abideth of *o* Ps 55:19 6924
of heavens, which were of *o* Ps 68:33 6924
me not off in the time of *o* age Ps 71:9 2209
Now also when I am *o* and Ps 71:18 2209
which thou hast purchased of *o* Ps 74:2 6924
For God is my King of *o*, working Ps 74:12 6924
I have considered the days of *o* Ps 77:5 6924
I will remember thy wonders of *o* Ps 77:11 6924
I will utter dark sayings of *o* Ps 78:2 6924
still bring forth fruit in *o* age Ps 92:14 7872
Thy throne is established of *o* Ps 93:2 227
Of *o* hast thou laid the Ps 102:25 6440
them shall wax *o* like a garment Ps 102:26 1086
I remembered thy judgments of *o* Ps 119:52 5769
I have known of *o* that thou hast Ps 119:152 6924
I remember the days of *o* Ps 143:5 6924
o men, and children Ps 148:12 2205
of his way, before his works of *o* Prov 8:22 227
children are the crown of *o* men Prov 17:6 2205
the beauty of *o* men is the grey Prov 20:29 2205
and when he is *o*, he will not Prov 22:6 2204
Remove not the *o* landmark Prov 23:10 5769
not thy mother when she is *o* Prov 23:22 2204
it hath been already of *o* time Eccl 1:10 5769
a poor and a wise child than an *o* Eccl 4:13 2205
of pleasant fruits, new and *o* Song 7:13 3465
Zoar, an heifer of three years *o* Is 15:5 7992
Ethiopians captives, young and *o* Is 20:4 2205
walls for the water of the *o* pool Is 22:11 3465
thy counsels of *o* are Is 25:1 7350
o lion, the viper and fiery flying Is 30:6 3918
For Tophet is ordained of *o* Is 30:33 865
neither consider the things of *o* Is 43:18 6931
And even to your *o* age I am he Is 46:4 2209
Remember the former things of *o* Is 46:9 5769
they all shall wax *o* as a garment Is 50:9 1086
earth shall wax *o* like a garment Is 51:6 1086
days, in the generations of *o* Is 51:9 5769
not I held my peace even of *o* Is 57:11 5769
shall build the *o* waste places Is 58:12 5769
And they shall build the *o* wastes Is 61:4 5769
and carried them all the days of *o* Is 63:9 5769
Then he remembered the days of *o* Is 63:11 5769
nor an *o* man that hath not filled Is 65:20 2205
shall die an hundred years *o* Is 65:20 1121
hundred years *o* shall be accursed Is 65:20 1121
For of *o* time I have broken thy Jer 2:20 5769
and see, and ask for the *o* paths Jer 6:16 5769
before thee of *o* prophesied both Jer 28:8 5769
LORD hath appeared of *o* unto me Jer 31:3 7350
both young men and *o* together Jer 31:13 2205
and took thence *o* cast clouts Jer 38:11 1094
o rotten rags, and let them down Jer 38:11 1094
Put now these *o* cast clouts Jer 38:12 1094
be inhabited, as in the days of *o* Jer 46:26 6924
as an heifer of three years *o* Jer 48:34 7992
thee will I break in pieces *o* Jer 51:22 2205
twenty years *o* when he began to Jer 52:1 1121
that she had in the days of *o* Lam 1:7 6924
he had commanded in the days of *o* Lam 2:17 6924
the *o* lie on the ground in the Lam 2:21 2205
flesh and my skin hath he made *o* Lam 3:4 1086
places, as they that be dead of *o* Lam 3:6 5769
renew our days as of *o* Lam 5:21 6924
Slay utterly *o* and young, both Eze 9:6 2205
unto her that was *o* in adulteries Eze 23:43 1087
to destroy it for the *o* hatred Eze 25:15 5769
pit, with the people of *o* time Eze 26:20 5769
earth, in places desolate of *o* Eze 26:20 5769
settle you after your *o* estates Eze 36:11 6927
in *o* time by my servants the Eze 38:17 6931
about threescore and two years *o* Dan 5:31 1247
ye *o* men, and give ear, all ye Joel 1:2 2205
your *o* men shall dream dreams, Joel 2:28 2205
will build it as in the days of *o* Amos 9:11 5769
goings forth have been from of *o* Mic 5:2 6924
with calves of a year *o* Mic 6:6 1121
and Gilead, as in the days of *o* Mic 7:14 5769
our fathers from the days of *o* Mic 7:20 6924
But Nineveh is of *o* like a pool Nah 2:8 3117
where the lion, even the *o* lion Nah 2:11
There shall yet *o* men Zec 8:4 2205
o women dwell in the streets of Zec 8:4 2205
the LORD, as in the days of *o* Mal 3:4 5769
coasts thereof, from two years *o* Mt 2:16 *1332*
it was said by them of *o* time Mt 5:21 *744*
it was said by them of *o* time Mt 5:27 *744*
hath been said by them of *o* time Mt 5:33 *744*
of new cloth unto an *o* garment Mt 9:16 *3820*
men put new wine into *o* bottles Mt 9:17 *3820*
of his treasure things new and *o* Mt 13:52 *3820*
of new cloth on an *o* garment Mk 2:21 *3820*
it up taketh away from the *o* Mk 2:21 *3820*
putteth new wine into *o* bottles Mk 2:22 *3820*
for I am an *o* man, and my wife Lk 1:18 *4246*
also conceived a son in her *o* age Lk 1:36 *1094*
And when he was twelve years *o* Lk 2:42
piece of a new garment upon an *o* Lk 5:36 *3820*
of the new agreeth not with the *o* Lk 5:36 *3820*
putteth new wine into *o* bottles Lk 5:37 *3820*
No man also having drunk *o* wine Lk 5:39 *3820*
for he saith, The *o* is better Lk 5:39 *3820*
that one of the *o* prophets was Lk 9:8 *744*
that one of the *o* prophets is Lk 9:19 *744*
yourselves bags which wax not *o* Lk 12:33 *3822*
can a man be born when he is *o* Jn 3:4 *1088*
Thou art not yet fifty years *o* Jn 8:57
but when thou shalt be *o*, thou Jn 21:18 *1095*
your *o* men shall dream dreams Acts 2:17 *4245*
the man was above forty years *o* Acts 4:22
And when he was full forty years *o* Acts 7:23 *5550*
For Moses of *o* time hath in every Acts 15:21 *744*
an *o* disciple, with whom we Acts 21:16 *744*
he was about an hundred years *o* Rom 4:19 *1541*
that our *o* man is crucified with Rom 6:6 *3820*
Purge out therefore the *o* leaven 1Cor 5:7 *3820*
keep the feast, not with *o* leaven 1Cor 5:8 *3820*
in the reading of the *o* testament 2Cor 3:14 *3820*
o things are passed away 2Cor 5:17 *744*
the former conversation the *o* man Eph 4:22 *3820*
put off the *o* man with his deeds Col 3:9 *3820*
o wives' fables, and exercise 1Ti 4:7 *1126*
number under threescore years *o* 1Ti 5:9
all shall wax *o* as doth a garment Heb 1:11 *3822*
he hath made the first *o* Heb 8:13 *3822*
waxeth *o* is ready to vanish away Heb 8:13 *1095*
in the *o* time the holy women also 1Pet 3:5 *4218*
he was purged from his *o* sins 2Pet 1:9 *3819*
not in *o* time by the will of man 2Pet 1:21 *4218*
And spared not the *o* world 2Pet 2:5 *744*
word of God the heavens were of *o* 2Pet 3:5 *1597*
but an *o* commandment which ye had 1Jn 2:7 *3820*
The *o* commandment is the word 1Jn 2:7 *3820*
who were before of *o* ordained to Jude 4 *3819*
that *o* serpent, called the Devil, Rev 12:9 *744*
that *o* serpent, which is the Rev 20:2 *744*

OLDNESS {1}
not in the *o* of the letter Rom 7:6 *3821*

OLIVE {38}
mouth was an *o* leaf pluckt off Gen 8:11 2132
pure oil *o* beaten for the light Ex 27:20 2132
the sanctuary, and of oil *o* an hin Ex 30:24 2132
pure oil *o* beaten for the light Lev 24:2 2132
o trees, which thou plantedst not Deut 6:11 2132
a land of oil *o*, and honey Deut 8:8 2132
When thou beatest thine *o* tree Deut 24:20 2132
Thou shalt have *o* trees Deut 28:40 2132
for thine *o* shall cast his fruit Deut 28:40 2132
and they said unto the *o* tree Judg 9:8 2132
But the *o* tree said unto them, Judg 9:9 2132
he made two cherubims of *o* tree 1Kin 6:23 8081
oracle he made doors of *o* tree 1Kin 6:31 8081
The two doors also were of *o* tree 1Kin 6:32 8081
of the temple posts of *o* tree 1Kin 6:33 8081
and vineyards, a land of oil *o* 2Kin 18:32 2132
And over the *o* trees and the 1Chr 27:28 2132
fetch *o* branches, and pine Neh 8:15 2132
cast off his flower as the *o* Job 15:33 2132
But I am like a green *o* tree in Ps 52:8 2132
thy children like *o* plants round Ps 128:3 2132
it, as the shaking of an *o* tree Is 17:6 2132
be as the shaking of an *o* tree Is 24:13 2132
called thy name, A green *o* tree Jer 11:16 2132
his beauty shall be as the *o* tree Hos 14:6 2132
your *o* trees increased, the Amos 4:9 2132
the labour of the *o* shall fail Hab 3:17 2132
the *o* tree, hath not brought Hag 2:19 2132
two *o* trees by it, one upon the Zec 4:3 2132
What are these two *o* trees upon Zec 4:11 2132
What be these two *o* branches Zec 4:12 2132
off, and thou, being a wild *o* tree Rom 11:17 *65*
the root and fatness of the *o* tree Rom 11:17 *1636*
o tree which is wild by nature Rom 11:24 *65*
to nature into a good *o* tree Rom 11:24 *2565*
be graffed into their own *o* tree Rom 11:24 *1636*
tree, my brethren, bear *o* berries Jas 3:12 *1636*
These are the two *o* trees Rev 11:4 *1636*

OLIVES {15}
corn, with the vineyards and *o* Judg 15:5 2132
thou shalt tread the *o*, but thou Mic 6:15 2132
in that day upon the mount of *O* Zec 14:4 2132
the mount of *O* shall cleave in Zec 14:4 2132
to Bethphage, unto the mount of *O* Mt 21:1 *1636*
And as he sat upon the mount of *O* Mt 24:3 *1636*
they went out into the mount of *O* Mt 26:30 *1636*
and Bethany, at the mount of *O* Mk 11:1 *1636*
of *O* over against the temple Mk 13:3 *1636*
they went out into the mount of *O* Mk 14:26 *1636*
the mount called the mount of *O* Lk 19:29 *1636*
at the descent of the mount of *O* Lk 19:37 *1636*
that is called the mount of *O* Lk 21:37 *1636*
as he was wont, to the mount of *O* Lk 22:39 *1636*
Jesus went unto the mount of *O* Jn 8:1 *1636*

OLIVET See MOUNT, OLIVES.{2} *Hills east of Jerusalem.*
went up by the ascent of mount *O* 2Sa 15:30 2132
Jerusalem from the mount called *O* Acts 1:12 *1638*

OLIVEYARD {1}
with thy vineyard, and with thy *o* Ex 23:11 2132

OLIVEYARDS {5}
o which ye planted not do ye eat Josh 24:13 2132
and your vineyards, and your *o* 1Sa 8:14 2132
and to receive garments, and *o* 2Kin 5:26 2132
lands, their vineyards, their *o* Neh 5:11 2132
wells digged, vineyards, and *o* Neh 9:25 2132

OLYMPAS *(o-lim'-pas)* {1} *A Christian acquaintance of Paul.*
Nereus, and his sister, and *O* Rom 16:15 *3632*

OMAR *(o'-mar)* {3} *A son of Eliphaz.*
the sons of Eliphaz were Teman, *O* Gen 36:11 201
duke Teman, duke *O*, duke Zepho, Gen 36:15 201
Teman, and *O*, Zephi, and Gatam, 1Chr 1:36 201

OMEGA *(o'-me-gah)* {4} *Last letter of Greek alphabet; a title applied to Jesus.*
I am Alpha and *O*, the beginning and Rev 1:8 *5598*
Saying, I am Alpha and *O*, the Rev 1:11 *5598*
I am Alpha and *O*, the beginning and Rev 21:6 *5598*
I am Alpha and *O*, the beginning and Rev 22:13 *5598*

OMER {5}
an *o* for every man, according to Ex 16:16 6016
when they did mete it with an *o* Ex 16:18 6016
Fill an *o* of it to be kept for Ex 16:32 6016
put an *o* full of manna therein, Ex 16:33 6016
Now an *o* is the tenth part of an Ex 16:36 6016

OMERS {1}
as much bread, two *o* for one man Ex 16:22 6016

OMITTED {1}
have *o* the weightier matters of Mt 23:23 *863*

OMNIPOTENT {1}
for the Lord God *o* reigneth Rev 19:6 *3841*

OMRI *(om'-ri)* {18}
1. A king of Israel.
wherefore all Israel made *O* 1Kin 16:16 6018
O went up from Gibbethon, and all 1Kin 16:17 6018
and half followed *O* 1Kin 16:21 6018
O prevailed against the people 1Kin 16:22 6018
so Tibni died, and *O* reigned 1Kin 16:22 6018
began *O* to reign over Israel 1Kin 16:23 6018
But *O* wrought evil in the eyes of 1Kin 16:25 6018
of the acts of *O* which he did 1Kin 16:27 6018
So *O* slept with his fathers, and 1Kin 16:28 6018
the son of *O* to reign over Israel 1Kin 16:29 6018
Ahab the son of *O* reigned over 1Kin 16:29 6018
Ahab the son of *O* did evil in the 1Kin 16:30 6018
the daughter of *O* king of Israel 2Kin 8:26 6018
was Athaliah the daughter of *O* 2Chr 22:2 6018
For the statutes of *O* are kept Mic 6:16 6018
2. Son of Becher.
and Eliezer, and Elioenai, and *O* 1Chr 7:8 6018
3. A descendant of Pharez.
the son of Ammihud, the son of *O* 1Chr 9:4 6018
4. A ruler of Issachar.
of Issachar, *O* the son of Michael 1Chr 27:18 6018

O

ON {4} (*Also see* APPENDIX.)
1. Capital of Lower Egypt.
of Poti-pherah priest of *O* ... Gen 41:45 204
priest of *O* bare unto him ... Gen 41:50 204
priest of *O* bare unto him ... Gen 46:20 204
2. Son of Peleth.
Abiram, the sons of Eliab, and *O* ... Num 16:1 203

ONAM *(o'-nam)* {4}
1. A son of Shobal.
Manahath, and Ebal, Shepho, and *O* ... Gen 36:23 208
Manahath, and Ebal, Shephi, and *O* ... 1Chr 1:40 208
2. A son of Jerahmeel.
she was the mother of *O* ... 1Chr 2:26 208
And the sons of *O* were, Shammai, ... 1Chr 2:28 208

ONAN *(o'-nan)* {8} *A son of Judah.*
and she called his name *O* ... Gen 38:4 209
And Judah said unto *O*, Go in unto ... Gen 38:8 209
O knew that the seed should not ... Gen 38:9 209
Er, and *O*, and Shelah, and Pharez, ... Gen 46:12 209
O died in the land of Canaan ... Gen 46:12 209
The sons of Judah were Er and *O* ... Num 26:19 209
O died in the land of Canaan ... Num 26:19 209
Er, and *O*, and Shelah ... 1Chr 2:3 209

ONCE {59}
and I will speak yet but this *o* ... Gen 18:32 6471
I pray thee, my sin only this *o* ... Ex 10:17 6471
atonement upon the horns of it *o* ... Ex 30:10 259
o in the year shall he make ... Ex 30:10 259
for all their sins *o* a year ... Lev 16:34 259
Moses, and said, Let us go up at *o* ... Num 13:30
thou mayest not consume them at *o* ... Deut 7:22 4118
war, and go round about the city *o* ... Josh 6:3 259
the city, going about it *o* ... Josh 6:11 259
day they compassed the city *o* ... Josh 6:14 259
me, and I will speak but this *o* ... Judg 6:39 6471
but this *o* with the fleece ... Judg 6:39 6471
saying, Come up this *o*, for he ... Judg 16:18 6471
me, I pray thee, only this *o* ... Judg 16:28 6471
that I may be at *o* avenged of the ... Judg 16:28
the spear even to the earth at *o* ... 1Sa 26:8 6471,259
o in three years came the navy of ... 1Kin 10:22 259
himself there, not *o* nor twice ... 2Kin 6:10 259
every three years *o* came the ... 2Chr 9:21 259
o in ten days store of all sorts ... Neh 5:18 996
without Jerusalem *o* or twice ... Neh 13:20 6471
For God speaketh *o*, yea twice, ... Job 33:14 259
O have I spoken ... Job 40:5 259
God hath spoken *o* ... Ps 62:11 259
work thereof at *o* with axes ... Ps 74:6
thy sight when *o* thou art angry ... Ps 76:7 227
O have I sworn by my holiness ... Ps 89:35 259
in his ways shall fall at *o* ... Prov 28:18 259
I will destroy and devour at *o* ... Is 42:14 3162
or shall a nation be born at *o* ... Is 66:8 6471
inhabitants of the land at this *o* ... Jer 10:18 6471
when shall it *o* be ... Jer 13:27 5750
I will this *o* cause them to know, ... Jer 16:21 6471
Yet *o*, it is a little while, and I ... Hag 2:6 259
When *o* the master of the house is ... Lk 13:25
And they cried out all at *o* ... Lk 23:18 *3826*
that he died, he died unto sin *o* ... Rom 6:10 *2178*
For I was alive without the law *o* ... Rom 7:9 *4218*
above five hundred brethren at *o* ... 1Cor 15:6 *2178*
o was I stoned, thrice I suffered ... 2Cor 11:25 *530*
the faith which *o* he destroyed ... Gal 1:23 *4218*
let it not be *o* named among you, ... Eph 5:3 *3366*
even in Thessalonica ye sent *o* ... Phil 4:16 *530*
come unto you, even I Paul, *o* ... 1Th 2:18 *530*
for those who were *o* enlightened ... Heb 6:4 *530*
for this he did *o*, when he ... Heb 7:27 *2178*
high priest alone *o* every year ... Heb 9:7 *530*
entered in *o* into the holy place ... Heb 9:12 *2178*
but now *o* in the end of the world ... Heb 9:26 *530*
it is appointed unto men *o* to die ... Heb 9:27 *530*
So Christ was *o* offered to bear ... Heb 9:28 *530*
because that the worshippers *o* ... Heb 10:2 *530*
body of Jesus Christ *o* for all ... Heb 10:10 *2178*
Yet *o* more I shake not the earth ... Heb 12:26 *530*
Yet *o* more, signifieth the ... Heb 12:27 *530*
also hath *o* suffered for sins ... 1Pet 3:18 *530*
when *o* the longsuffering of God ... 1Pet 3:20 *530*
was *o* delivered unto the saints ... Jude 3 *530*
though ye *o* knew this, how that ... Jude 5 *530*

ONE See APPENDIX.

ONE'S See APPENDIX.

ONES See APPENDIX.

ONESIMUS *(o-nes'-i-mus)* {4} *A Christian of Colosse.*
With *O*, a faithful and beloved ... Col 4:9 *3682*
the Colossians by Tychicus and *O* ... Col *s* *3682*
I beseech thee for my son *O* ... Philem 10 *3682*
from Rome to Philemon, by *O* ... Philem *s* *3682*

ONESIPHORUS *(o-ne-sif'-o-rus)* {2} *A Christian of Ephesus.*
give mercy unto the house of *O* ... 2Ti 1:16 *3683*
and Aquila, and the household of *O* ... 2Ti 4:19 *3683*

ONIONS {1}
melons, and the leeks, and the *o* ... Num 11:5 1211

ONLY See APPENDIX.

ONO *(o'-no)* {5}
1. A city in Benjamin.
Misham, and Shamed, who built *O* ... 1Chr 8:12 207
The children of Lod, Hadid, and *O* ... Ezr 2:33 207
The children of Lod, Hadid, and *O* ... Neh 7:37 207
Lod, and *O*, the valley of ... Neh 11:35 207
2. A valley near Jerusalem.
of the villages in the plain of *O* ... Neh 6:2 207

ONWARD {1}
went *o* in all their journeys ... Ex 40:36

ONYCHA {1}
thee sweet spices, stacte, and *o* ... Ex 30:34 7827

ONYX {11}
there is bdellium and the *o* stone ... Gen 2:12 7718
O stones, and stones to be set in ... Ex 25:7 7718
And thou shalt take two *o* stones ... Ex 28:9 7718
the fourth row a beryl, and an *o* ... Ex 28:20 7718
o stones, and stones to be set for ... Ex 35:9 7718
And the rulers brought *o* stones ... Ex 35:27 7718
they wrought *o* stones inclosed in ... Ex 39:6 7718
And the fourth row, a beryl, an *o* ... Ex 39:13 7718
o stones, and stones to be set, ... 1Chr 29:2 7718
of Ophir, with the precious *o* ... Job 28:16 7718
and the diamond, the beryl, the *o* ... Eze 28:13 7718

OPEN {124}
in the *o* firmament of heaven ... Gen 1:20 6440
herself, and sat in an *o* place ... Gen 38:14 5869
And if a man shall *o* a pit ... Ex 21:33 6605
bird loose into the *o* field ... Lev 14:7 6440
out of the city into the *o* fields ... Lev 14:53 6440
which they offer in the *o* field ... Lev 17:5 6440
instead of such as *o* every womb ... Num 8:16 6363
thing, and the earth *o* her mouth ... Num 16:30 6475
every *o* vessel, which hath no ... Num 19:15 6605
with a sword in the *o* fields ... Num 19:16 6440
man whose eyes are *o* hath said ... Num 24:3 8365
a trance, but having his eyes *o* ... Num 24:4 1540
man whose eyes are *o* hath said ... Num 24:15 8365
a trance, but having his eyes *o* ... Num 24:16 1540
But thou shalt *o* thine hand wide ... Deut 15:8 6605
Thou shalt *o* thine hand wide unto ... Deut 15:11 6605
o unto thee, then it shall be, ... Deut 20:11 6605
The LORD shall *o* unto thee his ... Deut 28:12 6605
and they left the city *o*, and ... Josh 8:17 6605
O the mouth of the cave, and bring ... Josh 10:22 6605
there was no *o* vision ... 1Sa 3:1 6555
are encamped in the *o* fields ... 2Sa 11:11 6440
carved with knops and *o* flowers ... 1Kin 6:18 6358
o flowers, within and without ... 1Kin 6:29 6358
o flowers, and overlaid them with ... 1Kin 6:32 6358
and palm trees and *o* flowers ... 1Kin 6:35 6358
That thine eyes may be *o* toward ... 1Kin 8:29 6605
That thine eyes may be *o* unto the ... 1Kin 8:52 6605
o his eyes, that he may see ... 2Kin 6:17 6491
o the eyes of these men, that ... 2Kin 6:20 6491
Then *o* the door, and flee, and ... 2Kin 9:3 6605
And he said, *O* the window eastward ... 2Kin 13:17 6605
o, LORD, thine eyes, and see ... 2Kin 19:16 6491
eyes may be *o* upon this house day ... 2Chr 6:20 6605
I beseech thee, thine eyes be *o* ... 2Chr 6:40 6605
Now mine eyes shall be *o*, and mine ... 2Chr 7:15 6605
now be attentive, and thine eyes *o* ... Neh 1:6 6605
time with an *o* letter in his hand ... Neh 6:5 6605
speak, and *o* his lips against thee ... Job 11:5 6605
dost thou *o* thine eyes upon such ... Job 14:3 6491
I will *o* my lips and answer ... Job 32:20 6605
men in the *o* sight of others ... Job 34:26 4725
doth Job *o* his mouth in vain ... Job 35:16 6475
Who can *o* the doors of his face ... Job 41:14 6605
their throat is an *o* sepulchre ... Ps 5:9 6605
his ears are *o* unto their cry ... Ps 34:15
I will *o* my dark saying upon the ... Ps 49:4 6605
O Lord, *o* thou my lips ... Ps 51:15 6605
I will *o* my mouth in a parable ... Ps 78:2 6605
o thy mouth wide, and I will fill ... Ps 81:10
O to me the gates of ... Ps 118:19 6605
O thou mine eyes, that I may ... Ps 119:18 1540
but a fool layeth *o* his folly ... Prov 13:16 6566
o thine eyes, and thou shalt be ... Prov 20:13 6491
O rebuke is better than secret ... Prov 27:5 1540
O thy mouth for the dumb in the ... Prov 31:8 6605
O thy mouth, judge righteously, ... Prov 31:9 6605
O to me, my sister, my love, my ... Song 5:2 6605
I rose up to *o* to my beloved ... Song 5:5 6605
shall devour Israel with *o* mouth ... Is 9:12 3605
so he shall *o*, and none shall shut ... Is 22:22 6605
and he shall shut, and none shall *o* ... Is 22:22 6605
the windows from on high are *o* ... Is 24:18 6605
O ye the gates, that the ... Is 26:2 6605
doth he *o* and break the clods of ... Is 28:24 6605
o thine eyes, O LORD, and see ... Is 37:17 6491
I will *o* rivers in high places, ... Is 41:18 6605
To *o* the blind eyes, to bring out ... Is 42:7 6491
to *o* before him the two leaved ... Is 45:1 6605
let the earth *o*, and let them ... Is 45:8 6605
thy gates shall be *o* continually ... Is 60:11 6605
Their quiver is as an *o* sepulchre ... Jer 5:16 6605
fall as dung upon the *o* field ... Jer 9:22 6440
be shut up, and none shall *o* them ... Jer 13:19 6605
and custom, and that which was *o* ... Jer 32:11 1540
and this evidence which is *o* ... Jer 32:14 1540
for thine eyes are *o* upon all the ... Jer 32:19 6491
utmost border, *o* her storehouses ... Jer 50:26 6605
o thy mouth, and eat that I give ... Eze 2:8 6475
I will *o* thy mouth, and thou shalt ... Eze 3:27 6605
thou wast cast out in the *o* field ... Eze 16:5 6440
never *o* thy mouth any more ... Eze 16:63 6610
to *o* the mouth in the slaughter, ... Eze 21:22 6605
I will *o* the side of Moab from ... Eze 25:9 6605
thou shalt fall upon the *o* fields ... Eze 29:5 6440
cast thee forth upon the *o* field ... Eze 32:4 6440
him that is in the *o* field will I ... Eze 33:27 6440
were very many in the *o* valley ... Eze 37:2 6440
I will *o* your graves, and cause ... Eze 37:12 6605
Thou shalt fall upon the *o* field ... Eze 39:5 6440
one shall then *o* him the gate ... Eze 46:12 6605
his windows being *o* in his ... Dan 6:10 6606
o thine eyes, and behold our ... Dan 9:18 6491
be set wide *o* unto thine enemies ... Nah 3:13 6605
O thy doors, O Lebanon, that the ... Zec 11:1 6605
I will *o* mine eyes upon the house ... Zec 12:4 6491
if I will not *o* you the windows ... Mal 3:10 6605
I will *o* my mouth in parables ... Mt 13:35 *455*
saying, Lord, Lord, *o* to us ... Mt 25:11 *455*
they may *o* unto him immediately ... Lk 12:36 *455*
saying, Lord, Lord, *o* unto us ... Lk 13:25 *455*
Hereafter ye shall see heaven *o* ... Jn 1:51 *455*
Can a devil *o* the eyes of the ... Jn 10:21 *455*
and seeing the prison doors *o* ... Acts 16:27 *455*
Paul was now about to *o* his mouth ... Acts 18:14 *455*
against any man, the law is *o* ... Acts 19:38 *71*
To *o* their eyes, and to turn them ... Acts 26:18 *455*
Their throat is an *o* sepulchre ... Rom 3:13 *455*
with *o* face beholding as in a ... 2Cor 3:18 *343*
our mouth is *o* unto you, our ... 2Cor 6:11 *455*
that I may *o* my mouth boldly, to ... Eph 6:19 *1722,457*
that God would *o* unto us a door ... Col 4:3 *455*
Some men's sins are *o* beforehand ... 1Ti 5:24 *4271*
afresh, and put him to an *o* shame ... Heb 6:6 *3856*
his ears are *o* unto their prayers ... 1Pet 3:12
I have set before thee an *o* door ... Rev 3:8 *455*
o the door, I will come in to him ... Rev 3:20 *455*
Who is worthy to *o* the book ... Rev 5:2 *455*
the earth, was able to *o* the book ... Rev 5:3 *455*
no man was found worthy to *o* ... Rev 5:4 *455*
hath prevailed to *o* the book ... Rev 5:5 *455*
book, and to *o* the seals thereof ... Rev 5:9 *455*
had in his hand a little book *o* ... Rev 10:2 *455*
take the little book which is *o* ... Rev 10:8 *455*

OPENED {137}
then your eyes shall be *o* ... Gen 3:5 6491
And the eyes of them both were *o* ... Gen 3:7 6491
which hath *o* her mouth to receive ... Gen 4:11 6475
and the windows of heaven were *o* ... Gen 7:11 6605
that Noah *o* the window of the ark ... Gen 8:6 6605
God *o* her eyes, and she saw a well ... Gen 21:19 6491
Leah was hated, he *o* her womb ... Gen 29:31 6605
hearkened to her, and *o* her womb ... Gen 30:22 6605
Joseph *o* all the storehouses, and ... Gen 41:56 6605
as one of them *o* his sack to give ... Gen 42:27 6605
that we *o* our sacks, and, behold, ... Gen 43:21 6605
ground, and *o* every man his sack ... Gen 44:11 6605
And when she had *o* it, she saw the ... Ex 2:6 6605
And the earth *o* her mouth, and ... Num 16:32 6605
the LORD *o* the mouth of the ass, ... Num 22:28 6605
Then the LORD *o* the eyes of ... Num 22:31 1540
And the earth *o* her mouth, and ... Num 26:10 6605
how the earth *o* her mouth ... Deut 11:6 6475
he *o* not the doors of the parlour ... Judg 3:25 6605
they took a key, and *o* them ... Judg 3:25 6605
she *o* a bottle of milk, and gave ... Judg 4:19 6605
for I have *o* my mouth unto the ... Judg 11:35 6475
if thou hast *o* thy mouth unto the ... Judg 11:36 6475
o the doors of the house, and went ... Judg 19:27 6605
o the doors of the house of the ... 1Sa 3:15 6605
times, and the child *o* his eyes ... 2Kin 4:35 6491
the LORD *o* the eyes of the young ... 2Kin 6:17 6491
the LORD *o* their eyes, and they ... 2Kin 6:20 6491
And he *o* the door, and fled ... 2Kin 9:10 6605
And he *o* it ... 2Kin 13:17 6605
because they *o* not to him ... 2Kin 15:16 6605
o the doors of the house of the ... 2Chr 29:3 6605
be *o* until the sun be hot ... Neh 7:3 6605
Ezra *o* the book in the sight of ... Neh 8:5 6605
and when he *o* it, all the people ... Neh 8:5 6605
not be *o* till after the sabbath ... Neh 13:19 6605
After this *o* Job his mouth, and ... Job 3:1 6605
they *o* their mouth wide as for ... Job 29:23 6473
but I *o* my doors to the traveller ... Job 31:32 6605
Behold, now I have *o* my mouth ... Job 33:2 6605
gates of death been *o* unto thee ... Job 38:17 1540
they *o* their mouth wide against ... Ps 35:21
I was dumb, I *o* not my mouth ... Ps 39:9 6605
mine ears hast thou *o* ... Ps 40:6 3738
above, and *o* the doors of heaven, ... Ps 78:23 6605
He *o* the rock, and the waters ... Ps 105:41 6605
The earth *o* and swallowed up ... Ps 106:17 6605
of the deceitful are *o* against me ... Ps 109:2 6605
I *o* my mouth, and panted ... Ps 119:131 6473
I *o* to my beloved ... Song 5:6 6605
o her mouth without measure ... Is 5:14 6473
or *o* the mouth, or peeped ... Is 10:14 6475
that *o* not the house of his ... Is 14:17 6605
the eyes of the blind shall be *o* ... Is 35:5 6491
time that thine ear was not *o* ... Is 48:8 6605
The Lord GOD hath *o* mine ear ... Is 50:5 6605
afflicted, yet he *o* not his mouth ... Is 53:7 6605
for unto thee have I *o* my cause ... Jer 20:12 1540
The LORD hath *o* his armoury ... Jer 50:25 6605
All thine enemies have *o* their ... Lam 2:16 6475
All our enemies have *o* their ... Lam 3:46 6475
Chebar, that the heavens were *o* ... Eze 1:1 6605
So I *o* my mouth, and he caused me ... Eze 3:2 6605
hast *o* thy feet to every one that ... Eze 16:25 6589
be *o* to him which is escaped ... Eze 24:27 6605
had *o* my mouth, until he came to ... Eze 33:22 6605
and my mouth was *o*, and I was no ... Eze 33:22 6605
LORD, when I have *o* your graves ... Eze 37:13 6605
shall be shut, it shall not be *o* ... Eze 44:2 6605

but on the sabbath it shall be *o* .... Eze 46:1 6605
day of the new moon it shall be *o* .... Eze 46:1 6605
was set, and the books were *o* .... Dan 7:10 6606
then I *o* my mouth, and spake, and .... Dan 10:16 6605
gates of the rivers shall be *o* .... Nah 2:6 6605
fountain *o* to the house of David .... Zec 13:1 6605
when they had *o* their treasures, ... Mt 2:11 *455*
lo, the heavens were *o* unto him .... Mt 3:16 *455*
he *o* his mouth, and taught them, ... Mt 5:2 *455*
knock, and it shall be *o* unto you .... Mt 7:7 *455*
him that knocketh it shall be *o* .... Mt 7:8 *455*
And their eyes were *o* .... Mt 9:30 *455*
and when thou hast *o* his mouth .... Mt 17:27 *455*
him, Lord, that our eyes may be *o* .... Mt 20:33 *455*
And the graves were *o* .... Mt 27:52 *455*
the water, he saw the heavens *o* .... Mk 1:10 *4977*
him, Ephphatha, that is, Be *o* .... Mk 7:34 *1272*
And straightway his ears were *o* .... Mk 7:35 *1272*
And his mouth was *o* immediately .... Lk 1:64 *455*
and praying, the heaven was *o* .... Lk 3:21 *455*
And when he had *o* the book .... Lk 4:17 *380*
knock, and it shall be *o* unto you .... Lk 11:9 *455*
him that knocketh it shall be *o* .... Lk 11:10 *455*
And their eyes were *o*, and they .... Lk 24:31 *1272*
while he *o* to us the scriptures .... Lk 24:32 *1272*
Then *o* he their understanding, ... Lk 24:45 *1272*
unto him, How were thine eyes *o* .... Jn 9:10 *455*
made the clay, and *o* his eyes .... Jn 9:14 *455*
of him, that he hath *o* thine eyes .... Jn 9:17 *455*
or who hath *o* his eyes, we know .... Jn 9:21 *455*
how *o* he thine eyes .... Jn 9:26 *455*
he is, and yet he hath *o* mine eyes .... Jn 9:30 *455*
o the eyes of one that was born .... Jn 9:32 *455*
which *o* the eyes of the blind, ... Jn 11:37 *455*
Lord by night *o* the prison doors .... Acts 5:19 *455*
but when we had *o*, we found no .... Acts 5:23 *455*
said, Behold, I see the heavens *o* .... Acts 7:56 *455*
shearer, so *o* he not his mouth .... Acts 8:32 *455*
Then Philip *o* his mouth, and began .... Acts 8:35 *455*
and when his eyes were *o*, he saw .... Acts 9:8 *455*
And she *o* her eyes .... Acts 9:40 *455*
And saw heaven *o*, and a certain .... Acts 10:11 *455*
Then Peter *o* his mouth, and said, ... Acts 10:34 *455*
which *o* to them of his own accord .... Acts 12:10 *455*
she *o* not the gate for gladness, ... Acts 12:14 *455*
and when they had *o* the door .... Acts 12:16 *455*
how he had *o* the door of faith .... Acts 14:27 *455*
whose heart the Lord *o*, that she .... Acts 16:14 *1272*
immediately all the doors were *o* .... Acts 16:26 *455*
door and effectual is *o* unto me 1Cor 16:9 *455*
a door was *o* unto me of the Lord, ... 2Cor 2:12 *455*
o unto the eyes of him with whom .... Heb 4:13 *5136*
behold, a door was *o* in heaven .... Rev 4:1 *455*
when the Lamb *o* one of the seals .... Rev 6:1 *455*
when he had *o* the second seal, I .... Rev 6:3 *455*
when he had *o* the third seal, I .... Rev 6:5 *455*
when he had *o* the fourth seal, I .... Rev 6:7 *455*
when he had *o* the fifth seal, I .... Rev 6:9 *455*
when he had *o* the sixth seal .... Rev 6:12 *455*
when he had *o* the seventh seal, ... Rev 8:1 *455*
And he *o* the bottomless pit .... Rev 9:2 *455*
the temple of God was *o* in heaven .... Rev 11:19 *455*
woman, and the earth *o* her mouth .... Rev 12:16 *455*
he *o* his mouth in blasphemy .... Rev 13:6 *455*
of the testimony in heaven was *o* .... Rev 15:5 *455*
And I saw heaven *o*, and behold a .... Rev 19:11 *455*
and the books were *o* .... Rev 20:12 *455*
and another book was *o*, which is .... Rev 20:12 *455*

OPENEST {2}
thou *o* thine hand, they are .... Ps 104:28 6605
Thou *o* thine hand, and satisfiest .... Ps 145:16 6605

OPENETH {21}
whatsoever *o* the womb among the .... Ex 13:2 6363
the LORD all that *o* the matrix .... Ex 13:12 6363
to the LORD all that *o* the matrix .... Ex 13:15 6363
All that *o* the matrix is mine .... Ex 34:19 6363
of all the firstborn that *o* the .... Num 3:12 6363
Every thing that *o* the matrix in .... Num 18:15 6363
he *o* his eyes, and he is not .... Job 27:19 6491
Then he *o* the ears of men, and .... Job 33:16 1540
He *o* also their ear to discipline .... Job 36:10 1540
o their ears in oppression .... Job 36:15 1540
a dumb man that *o* not his mouth .... Ps 38:13 6605
The LORD *o* the eyes of the blind .... Ps 146:8 6491
but he that *o* wide his lips shall .... Prov 13:3 6589
he *o* not his mouth in the gate .... Prov 24:7 6605
She *o* her mouth with wisdom .... Prov 31:26 6605
is dumb, so he *o* not his mouth .... Is 53:7 6605
the fire all that *o* the womb .... Eze 20:26 6363
Every male that *o* the womb shall .... Lk 2:23 *1272*
To him the porter *o* .... Jn 10:3 *455*
hath the key of David, he that *o* .... Rev 3:7 *455*
and shutteth, and no man *o* .... Rev 3:7 *455*

OPENING {7}
the *o* thereof every morning 1Chr 9:27 4668
up a man, and there can be no *o* .... Job 12:14 6605
the *o* of my lips shall be right .... Prov 8:6 4669
o the ears, but he heareth not .... Is 42:20 6491
the *o* of the prison to them that .... Is 61:1 6495
I will give thee the *o* of the .... Eze 29:21 6610
O and alleging, that Christ must .... Acts 17:3 *1272*

OPENINGS {1}
concourse, in the *o* of the gates .... Prov 1:21 6607

OPENLY {15}
that was *o* by the way side .... Gen 38:21 5879
his righteousness hath he *o* .... Ps 98:2
himself shall reward thee *o* .... Mt 6:4 *1722,3588,5318*
in secret shall reward thee *o* .... Mt 6:6 *1722,3588,5318*
in secret, shall reward thee *o* .... Mt 6:18 *1722,3588,5318*
no more *o* enter into the city .... Mk 1:45 *5320*
And he spake that saying *o* .... Mk 8:32 *3954*
he himself seeketh to be known *o* ... Jn 7:4 *1722,3954*
he also up unto the feast, not *o* .... Jn 7:10 *5320*
Howbeit no man spake *o* of him for .... Jn 7:13 *3954*
walked no more *o* among the Jews .... Jn 11:54 *3954*
him, I spake *o* to the world .... Jn 18:20 *3954*
up the third day, and shewed him *o* .... Acts 10:40 *1717*
They have beaten us *o* uncondemned .... Acts 16:37 *1219*
powers, he made a shew of them *o*.. Col 2:15 *1722,3954*

OPERATION {3}
nor the *o* of his hands, he shall .... Ps 28:5 4639
consider the *o* of his hands .... Is 5:12 4639
through the faith of the *o* of God .... Col 2:12 *1753*

OPERATIONS {1}
And there are diversities of *o* 1Cor 12:6 *1755*

OPHEL *(o'-fel)* {5} *A fortified place near Jerusalem.*
and on the wall of *O* he built much 2Chr 27:3 6077
fish gate, and compassed about *O* 2Chr 33:14 6077
Moreover the Nethinims dwelt in *O* .... Neh 3:26 6077
out, even unto the wall of *O* .... Neh 3:27 6077
But the Nethinims dwelt in *O* .... Neh 11:21 6077

OPHIR *(o'-fur)* {13}
1. A son of Joktan.
And *O*, and Havilah, and Jobab .... Gen 10:29 211
And *O*, and Havilah, and Jobab 1Chr 1:23 211
2. A place in southern Arabia.
And they came to *O*, and fetched 1Kin 9:28 211
Hiram, that brought gold from *O* 1Kin 10:11 211
brought in from *O* great plenty of 1Kin 10:11 211
of Tharshish to go to *O* for gold 1Kin 22:48 211
talents of gold, of the gold of *O* 1Chr 29:4 211
with the servants of Solomon to *O* 2Chr 8:18 211
which brought gold from *O* 2Chr 9:10 211
the gold of *O* as the stones of .... Job 22:24 211
be valued with the gold of *O* .... Job 28:16 211
did stand the queen in gold of *O* .... Ps 45:9 211
a man than the golden wedge of *O* .... Is 13:12 211

OPHNI *(of'-ni)* {1} *A place in Benjamin.*
And Chephar-haammonai, and *O* .... Josh 18:24 6078

OPHRAH *(of'-rah)* {8} See APHRAH.
1. A city in Benjamin.
And Avim, and Parah, and *O*, ... Josh 18:23 6084
unto the way that leadeth to *O* 1Sa 13:17 6084
2. A city in Manasseh.
sat under an oak which was in *O* .... Judg 6:11 6084
it is yet in *O* of the Abi-ezrites .... Judg 6:24 6084
and put it in his city, even in *O* .... Judg 8:27 6084
father, in *O* of the Abi-ezrites .... Judg 8:32 6084
went unto his father's house at *O* .... Judg 9:5 6084
3. Head of a family in Judah.
And Meonothai begat *O* 1Chr 4:14 6084

OPINION {3}
and durst not shew you mine *o* .... Job 32:6 1843
I also will shew mine *o* .... Job 32:10 1843
my part, I also will shew mine *o* .... Job 32:17 1843

OPINIONS {1}
How long halt ye between two *o* 1Kin 18:21 5587

OPPORTUNITY {5}
time he sought *o* to betray him .... Mt 26:16 *2120*
sought *o* to betray him unto them .... Lk 22:6 *2120*
As we have therefore *o*, let us do .... Gal 6:10 *2540*
also careful, but ye lacked *o* .... Phil 4:10 *170*
might have had *o* to have returned .... Heb 11:15 *2540*

OPPOSE {1}
those that *o* themselves 2Ti 2:25 *475*

OPPOSED {1}
when they *o* themselves, and .... Acts 18:6 *498*

OPPOSEST {1}
hand thou *o* thyself against me .... Job 30:21 7852

OPPOSETH {1}
Who *o* and exalteth himself above 2Th 2:4 *480*

OPPOSITIONS {1}
o of science falsely so called 1Ti 6:20 *477*

OPPRESS {23}
wherewith the Egyptians *o* them .... Ex 3:9 3905
neither vex a stranger, nor *o* him .... Ex 22:21 3905
Also thou shalt not *o* a stranger .... Ex 23:9 3905
hand, ye shall not *o* one another .... Lev 25:14 3238
shall not therefore *o* one another .... Lev 25:17 3238
thou shalt not *o* him .... Deut 23:16 3238
Thou shalt not *o* an hired servant .... Deut 24:14 6231
and the Maonites, did *o* you .... Judg 10:12 3905
unto thee that thou shouldest *o* .... Job 10:3 6231
man of the earth may no more *o* .... Ps 10:18 6206
From the wicked that *o* me .... Ps 17:9 7703
let not the proud *o* me .... Ps 119:122 6231
neither *o* the afflicted in the .... Prov 22:22 1792
I will feed them that *o* thee with .... Is 49:26 3238
If ye *o* not the stranger, the .... Jer 7:6 6231
and I will punish all that *o* them .... Jer 30:20 3905
princes shall no more *o* my people .... Eze 45:8 3238
he loveth to *o* .... Hos 12:7 6231
which *o* the poor, which crush the .... Amos 4:1 6231
so they *o* a man and his house, ... Mic 2:2 6231
And *o* not the widow, nor the .... Zec 7:10 6231
against those that *o* the hireling .... Mal 3:5 6231
Do not rich men *o* you, and draw .... Jas 2:6 *2616*

OPPRESSED {38}
and thou shalt be only *o* and .... Deut 28:29 6231
and thou shalt be only *o* and .... Deut 28:33 6231
by reason of them that *o* them .... Judg 2:18 3905
mightily *o* the children of Israel .... Judg 4:3 3905
out of the hand of all that *o* you .... Judg 6:9 3905
vexed and *o* the children of Israel .... Judg 10:8 7533
kingdoms, and of them that *o* you 1Sa 10:18 3905
whom have I *o* 1Sa 12:3 7533
hast not defrauded us, nor *o* us 1Sa 12:4 7533
because the king of Syria *o* them 2Kin 13:4 3905
But Hazael king of Syria *o* Israel 2Kin 13:22 3905
Asa *o* some of the people the same 2Chr 16:10 7533
Because he hath *o* and hath .... Job 20:19 7533
they make the *o* to cry .... Job 35:9
also will be a refuge for the *o* .... Ps 9:9 1790
To judge the fatherless and the *o* .... Ps 10:18 1790
O let not the *o* return ashamed .... Ps 74:21 1790
and judgment for all that are *o* .... Ps 103:6 6231
Their enemies also *o* them .... Ps 106:42 3905
executeth judgment for the *o* .... Ps 146:7 6231
the tears of such as were *o* .... Eccl 4:1 6231
seek judgment, relieve the *o* .... Is 1:17 2541
And the people shall be *o*, every .... Is 3:5 5065
no more rejoice, O thou *o* virgin .... Is 23:12 6231
O LORD, I am *o* .... Is 38:14 6234
the Assyrian *o* them without cause .... Is 52:4 6231
He was *o*, and he was afflicted, ... Is 53:7 5065
burdens, and to let the *o* go free .... Is 58:6 7533
children of Judah were *o* together .... Jer 50:33 6231
And hath not *o* any, but hath .... Eze 18:7 3238
Hath *o* the poor and needy, hath .... Eze 18:12 3238
Neither hath *o* any, hath not .... Eze 18:16 3238
his father, because he cruelly *o* .... Eze 18:18 6231
yea, they have *o* the stranger .... Eze 22:29 6231
Ephraim is *o* and broken in .... Hos 5:11 6231
the *o* in the midst thereof .... Amos 3:9 6217
him, and avenged him that was *o* .... Acts 7:24 *2669*
all that were *o* of the devil .... Acts 10:38 *2616*

OPPRESSETH {5}
land against the enemy that *o* you .... Num 10:9 6887
he fighting daily *o* me .... Ps 56:1 3905
He that *o* the poor reproacheth .... Prov 14:31 6231
He that *o* the poor to increase .... Prov 22:16 6231
A poor man that *o* the poor is .... Prov 28:3 6231

OPPRESSING {3}
of our nativity, from the *o* sword .... Jer 46:16 3238
for fear of the *o* sword they .... Jer 50:16 3238
filthy and polluted, to the *o* city .... Zeph 3:1 3238

OPPRESSION {24}
I have also seen the *o* wherewith .... Ex 3:9 3906
and our labour, and our *o* .... Deut 26:7 3906
for he saw the *o* of Israel 2Kin 13:4 3906
and openeth their ears in *o* .... Job 36:15 3906
For the *o* of the poor, for the .... Ps 12:5 7701
because of the *o* of the enemy .... Ps 42:9 3906
because of the *o* of the enemy .... Ps 43:2 3906
our affliction and our *o* .... Ps 44:24 3906
because of the *o* of the wicked .... Ps 55:3 6125
Trust not in *o*, and become not .... Ps 62:10 6233
and speak wickedly concerning *o* .... Ps 73:8 6233
minished and brought low through *o* .... Ps 107:39 6115
Deliver me from the *o* of man .... Ps 119:134 6233
If thou seest the *o* of the poor .... Eccl 5:8 6233
Surely *o* maketh a wise man mad .... Eccl 7:7 6233
looked for judgment, but behold *o* .... Is 5:7 4939
despise this word, and trust in *o* .... Is 30:12 6233
thou shalt be far from *o* .... Is 54:14 6233
away from our God, speaking *o* .... Is 59:13 6233
she is wholly *o* in the midst of .... Jer 6:6 6233
to shed innocent blood, and for *o* .... Jer 22:17 6233
they dealt by *o* with the stranger .... Eze 22:7 6233
people of the land have used *o* .... Eze 22:29 6233
of the people's inheritance by *o* .... Eze 46:18 3238

OPPRESSIONS {3}
By reason of the multitude of *o* .... Job 35:9 6217
considered all the *o* that are .... Eccl 4:1 6217
he that despiseth the gain of *o* .... Is 33:15 4642

OPPRESSOR {14}
they hear not the voice of the *o* .... Job 3:18 5065
of years is hidden to the *o* .... Job 15:20 6184
and shall break in pieces the *o* .... Ps 72:4 6231
Envy thou not the *o*, and choose .... Prov 3:31 376,2555
understanding is also a great *o* .... Prov 28:16 4642
of his shoulder, the rod of his *o* .... Is 9:4 5065
and say, How hath the *o* ceased .... Is 14:4 5065
day because of the fury of the *o* .... Is 51:13 6693
and where is the fury of the *o* .... Is 51:13 6693
spoiled out of the hand of the *o* .... Jer 21:12 6231
spoiled out of the hand of the *o* .... Jer 22:3 6216
of the fierceness of the *o* .... Jer 25:38 3238
no *o* shall pass through them any .... Zec 9:8 5065
bow, out of him every *o* together .... Zec 10:4 5065

OPPRESSORS {8}
with God, and the heritage of *o* .... Job 27:13 6184
me, and *o* seek after my soul .... Ps 54:3 6184
leave me not to mine *o* .... Ps 119:121 6231
side of their *o* there was power .... Eccl 4:1 6231
my people, children are their *o* .... Is 3:12 5065
and they shall rule over their *o* .... Is 14:2 5065
the *o* are consumed out of the .... Is 16:4 7429
unto the LORD because of the *o* .... Is 19:20 3905

OR See APPENDIX.

O

ORACLE {17}
man had enquired at the *o* of God 2Sa 16:23 1697
both of the temple and of the *o* 1Kin 6:5 1687
for it within, even for the *o* 1Kin 6:16 1687
the *o* he prepared in the house 1Kin 6:19 1687
the *o* in the forepart was twenty 1Kin 6:20 1687
the chains of gold before the *o* 1Kin 6:21 1687
by the *o* he overlaid with gold 1Kin 6:22 1687
And within the *o* he made two 1Kin 6:23 1687
for the entering of the *o* he made 1Kin 6:31 1687
and five on the left, before the *o* 1Kin 7:49 1687
into the *o* of the house, to the 1Kin 8:6 1687
in the holy place before the *o* 1Kin 8:8 1687
And he made chains, as in the *o* 2Chr 3:16 1687
after the manner before the *o* 2Chr 4:20 1687
to the *o* of the house, into the 2Chr 5:7 1687
seen from the ark before the *o* 2Chr 5:9 1687
up my hands toward thy holy *o* Ps 28:2 1687

ORACLES {4}
the lively *o* to give unto us Acts 7:38 *3051*
them were committed the *o* of God Rom 3:2 *3051*
first principles of the *o* of God Heb 5:12 *3051*
let him speak as the *o* of God 1Pet 4:11 *3051*

ORATION {1}
throne, and made an *o* unto them Acts 12:21 *1215*

ORATOR {2}
artificer, and the eloquent *o* Is 3:3 3908
with a certain *o* named Tertullus, Acts 24:1 *4489*

ORCHARD {1}
plants are an *o* of pomegranates Song 4:13 6508

ORCHARDS {1}
I made me gardens and *o*, and I Eccl 2:5 6508

ORDAIN {5}
seer did *o* in their set office 1Chr 9:22 3245
Also I will *o* a place for my 1Chr 17:9 7760
LORD, thou wilt *o* peace for us Is 26:12 8239
And so *o* I in all churches 1Cor 7:17 *1299*
o elders in every city, as I had Titus 1:5 *2525*

ORDAINED {37}
which was *o* in mount Sinai for a Num 28:6 6213
Jeroboam *o* a feast in the eighth 1Kin 12:32 6213
o a feast unto the children of 1Kin 12:33 6213
had *o* to burn incense in the high 2Kin 23:5 5414
he *o* him priests for the high 2Chr 11:15 5975
singing, as it was *o* by David 2Chr 23:18
with the instruments *o* by David 2Chr 29:27
The Jews *o*, and took upon them, and Est 9:27 6965
sucklings hast thou *o* strength Ps 8:2 3245
and the stars, which thou hast *o* Ps 8:3 3559
This he *o* in Joseph for a Ps 81:5 7760
I have *o* a lamp for mine anointed Ps 132:17 6186
For Tophet is *o* of old Is 30:33 6186
I *o* thee a prophet unto the Jer 1:5 5414
whom the king had *o* to destroy Dan 2:24 4483
thou hast *o* them for judgment Hab 1:12 7760
he *o* twelve, that they should be Mk 3:14 *4160*
o you, that ye should go and bring Jn 15:16 *5087*
must one be *o* to be a witness Acts 1:22 *1096*
o of God to be the Judge of quick Acts 10:42 *3724*
as many as were *o* to eternal life Acts 13:48 *5021*
when they had *o* them elders in Acts 14:23 *5500*
that were *o* of the apostles and Acts 16:4 *2919*
by that man whom he hath *o* Acts 17:31 *3724*
commandment, which was *o* to life Rom 7:10
the powers that be are *o* of God Rom 13:1 *5021*
which God *o* before the world unto 1Cor 2:7 *4304*
Even so hath the Lord *o* that they 1Cor 9:14 *1299*
it was *o* by angels in the hand of Gal 3:19 *1299*
which God hath before *o* that we Eph 2:10 *4282*
Whereunto I am *o* a preacher 1Ti 2:7 *5087*
o the first bishop of the church 2Ti *s* *5500*
o the first bishop of the church Titus *s* *5500*
priest taken from among men is *o* Heb 5:1 *2525*
high priest is *o* to offer gifts Heb 8:3 *2525*
Now when these things were thus *o* Heb 9:6 *2680*
of old *o* to this condemnation Jude 4 *4270*

ORDAINETH {1}
he *o* his arrows against the Ps 7:13 6466

ORDER {61}
there, and laid the wood in *o* Gen 22:9
set in *o* one against another Ex 26:17 7947
his sons shall *o* it from evening Ex 27:21 6186
with the lamps to be set in *o* Ex 39:37 4634
set in *o* the things that are to Ex 40:4 6186
that are to be set in *o* upon it Ex 40:4 6187
he set the bread in *o* upon it Ex 40:23 6186
lay the wood in *o* upon the fire Lev 1:7 6186
in *o* upon the wood that is on the Lev 1:8 6186
the priest shall lay them in *o* on Lev 1:12 6186
the burnt offering in *o* upon it Lev 6:12 6186
shall Aaron *o* it from the evening Lev 24:3 6186
He shall *o* the lamps upon the Lev 24:4 6186
sabbath he shall set it in *o* Lev 24:8 6186
she had laid in *o* upon the roof Josh 2:6 6186
How shall we *o* the child, and how Judg 13:12 4941
city, and put his household in *o* 2Sa 17:23 6680
And he put the wood in *o*, and cut 1Kin 18:33 6186
he said, Who shall *o* the battle 1Kin 20:14 631
the LORD, Set thine house in *o* 2Kin 20:1 6680
and the priests of the second *o* 2Kin 23:4
their office according to their *o* 1Chr 6:32 4941
we sought him not after the due *o* 1Chr 15:13 4941
according to the *o* commanded unto 1Chr 23:31 4941
according to the *o* of the king 1Chr 25:2 3027
to the king's *o* to Asaph, 1Chr 25:6 3027
according to the *o* of David his 2Chr 8:14 4941
set they in *o* upon the pure table 2Chr 13:11
house of the LORD was set in *o* 2Chr 29:35 3559
shadow of death, without any *o* Job 10:22 5468
I would *o* my cause before him, and Job 23:4 6186
me, set thy words in *o* before me Job 33:5 6186
for we cannot *o* our speech by Job 37:19 6186
be reckoned up in *o* unto thee Ps 40:5 6186
set them in *o* before thine eyes Ps 50:21 6186
ever after the *o* of Melchizedek Ps 110:4 1700
O my steps in thy word Ps 119:133 3559
out, and set in *o* many proverbs Eccl 12:9 8626
and upon his kingdom, to *o* it Is 9:7 3559
the LORD, Set thine house in *o* Is 38:1 6680
declare it, and set it in *o* for me Is 44:7 6186
O ye the buckler and shield, and Jer 46:3 6186
one over another, and thirty in *o* Eze 41:6 6471
o a declaration of those things Lk 1:1 *1299*
first, to write unto thee in *o* Lk 1:3 *2517*
before God in the *o* of his course Lk 1:8 *5010*
and expounded it by *o* unto them Acts 11:4 *2517*
of Galatia and Phrygia in *o* Acts 18:23 *2517*
rest will I set in *o* when I come 1Cor 11:34 *1299*
things be done decently and in *o* 1Cor 14:40 *5010*
But every man in his own *o* 1Cor 15:23 *5001*
as I have given *o* to the churches 1Cor 16:1 *1299*
joying and beholding your *o* Col 2:5 *5010*
that thou shouldest set in *o* the Titus 1:5 *1930*
ever after the *o* of Melchisedec Heb 5:6 *5010*
priest after the *o* of Melchisedec Heb 5:10 *5010*
ever after the *o* of Melchisedec Heb 6:20 *5010*
rise after the *o* of Melchisedec Heb 7:11 *5010*
be called after the *o* of Aaron Heb 7:11 *5010*
ever after the *o* of Melchisedec Heb 7:17 *5010*
ever after the *o* of Melchisedec Heb 7:21 *5010*

ORDERED {4}
top of this rock, in the *o* place Judg 6:26 4634
o in all things, and sure 2Sa 23:5 6186
Behold now, I have *o* my cause Job 13:18 6186
of a good man are *o* by the LORD Ps 37:23 3559

ORDERETH {1}
to him that *o* his conversation Ps 50:23 7760

ORDERINGS {1}
These were the *o* of them in their 1Chr 24:19 6486

ORDERLY {1}
that thou thyself also walkest *o* Acts 21:24 *4748*

ORDINANCE {30}
keep it a feast by an *o* for ever Ex 12:14 2708
your generations by an *o* for ever Ex 12:17 2708
this thing for an *o* to thee Ex 12:24 2706
This is the *o* of the passover Ex 12:43 2708
Thou shalt therefore keep this *o* Ex 13:10 2708
made for them a statute and an *o* Ex 15:25 4941
Therefore shall ye keep mine *o* Lev 18:30 4931
They shall therefore keep mine *o* Lev 22:9 4931
to the *o* of the passover, and Num 9:14 2708
ye shall have one *o*, both for the Num 9:14 2708
for an *o* for ever throughout your Num 10:8 2708
One *o* shall be both for you of Num 15:15 2708
an *o* for ever in your generations Num 15:15 2708
and to thy sons, by an *o* for ever Num 18:8 2706
This is the *o* of the law which Num 19:2 2708
This is the *o* of the law which Num 31:21 2708
them a statute and an *o* in Shechem Josh 24:25 4941
an *o* for Israel unto this day 1Sa 30:25 4941
This is an *o* for ever to Israel 2Chr 2:4
with fire according to the *o* 2Chr 35:13 4941
day, and made them an *o* in Israel 2Chr 35:25 2706
after the *o* of David king of Ezr 3:10 3027
and the *o* that he gave them Ps 99:7 2706
the laws, changed the *o*, broken Is 24:5 2706
and forsook not the *o* of their God Is 58:2 4941
Concerning the *o* of oil, the bath Eze 45:14 2706
by a perpetual *o* unto the LORD Eze 46:14 2708
is it that we have kept his *o* Mal 3:14 4931
the power, resisteth the *o* of God Rom 13:2 *1296*
o of man for the Lord's sake 1Pet 2:13 *2937*

ORDINANCES {27}
And thou shalt teach them *o* Ex 18:20 2706
neither shall ye walk in their *o* Lev 18:3 2708
do my judgments, and keep mine *o* Lev 18:4 2708
according to all the *o* of the Num 9:12 2708
their statutes, or after their *o* 2Kin 17:34 4941
And the statutes, and the *o* 2Kin 17:37 4941
the *o* by the hand of Moses 2Chr 33:8 4941
Also we made *o* for us, to charge Neh 10:32 4687
Knowest thou the *o* of heaven Job 38:33 2708
this day according to thine *o* Ps 119:91 4941
they ask of me the *o* of justice Is 58:2 4941
the *o* of the moon and of the stars Jer 31:35 2708
If those *o* depart from before me, Jer 31:36 2706
not appointed the *o* of heaven Jer 33:25 2708
in my statutes, and keep mine *o* Eze 11:20 4941
thereof, and all the *o* thereof Eze 43:11 2708
thereof, and all the *o* thereof Eze 43:11 2708
These are the *o* of the altar in Eze 43:18 2708
the *o* of the house of the LORD Eze 44:5 2708
ye are gone away from mine *o* Mal 3:7 2706
and *o* of the Lord blameless Lk 1:6 *1345*
me in all things, and keep the *o* 1Cor 11:2 *3862*
of commandments contained in *o* Eph 2:15 *1378*
of *o* that was against us, which Col 2:14 *1378*
in the world, are ye subject to *o* Col 2:20 *1379*
had also *o* of divine service Heb 9:1 *1345*
and divers washings, and carnal *o* Heb 9:10 *1345*

ORDINARY {1}
and have diminished thine *o* food Eze 16:27 2706

OREB *(o'-reb)* {7}
1. A prince of Midian.
two princes of the Midianites, *O* Judg 7:25 6157
they slew *O* upon the rock *O*, Judg 7:25 6157
Midian, and brought the heads of *O* Judg 7:25 6157
hands the princes of Midian, *O* Judg 8:3 6157
Make their nobles like *O*, and like Ps 83:11 6157
2. A rock east of the Jordan.
of Midian at the rock of *O* Is 10:26 6157

OREN *(o'-ren)* {1} *A son of Jerahmeel.*
Ram the firstborn, and Bunah, and *O* 1Chr 2:25 767

ORGAN {3}
all such as handle the harp and *o* Gen 4:21 5748
and rejoice at the sound of the *o* Job 21:12 5748
my *o* into the voice of them that Job 30:31 5748

ORGANS {1}
with stringed instruments and *o* Ps 150:4 5748

ORION *(o'-ri'-on)* {3} *A constellation of stars.*
Which maketh Arcturus, *O*, and Job 9:9 3685
Pleiades, or loose the bands of *O* Job 38:31 3685
that maketh the seven stars and *O* Amos 5:8 3685

ORNAMENT {7}
For they shall be an *o* of grace Prov 1:9 3880
give to thine head an *o* of grace Prov 4:9 3880
an *o* of fine gold, so is a wise Prov 25:12 2481
the *o* of thy molten images of Is 30:22 642
thee with them all, as with an *o* Is 49:18 5716
As for the beauty of his *o* Eze 7:20 5716
even the *o* of a meek and quiet 1Pet 3:4

ORNAMENTS {14}
and no man did put on him his *o* Ex 33:4 5716
now put off thy *o* from thee Ex 33:5 5716
of their *o* by the mount Horeb Ex 33:6 5716
took away the *o* that were on Judg 8:21 7720
beside *o*, and collars, and purple Judg 8:26 7720
who put on *o* of gold upon your 2Sa 1:24 5716
their tinkling *o* about their feet Is 3:18 5914
the *o* of the legs, and the Is 3:20 6807
bridegroom decketh himself with *o* Is 61:10 6287
Can a maid forget her *o*, or a Jer 2:32 5716
thou deckest thee with *o* of gold Jer 4:30 5716
and thou art come to excellent *o* Eze 16:7 5716
I decked thee also with *o* Eze 16:11 5716
eyes, and deckedst thyself with *o* Eze 23:40 5716

ORNAN *(or'-nan)* {12} See ARAUNAH. *A Jebusite prince.*
threshingfloor of *O* the Jebusite 1Chr 21:15 771
threshingfloor of *O* the Jebusite 1Chr 21:18 771
O turned back, and saw the angel 1Chr 21:20 771
Now *O* was threshing wheat 1Chr 21:20 771
And as David came to *O*, *O* 1Chr 21:21 771
Then David said to *O*, Grant me 1Chr 21:22 771
O said unto David, Take it to 1Chr 21:23 771
And king David said to *O*, Nay 1Chr 21:24 771
So David gave to *O* for the place 1Chr 21:25 771
threshingfloor of *O* the Jebusite 1Chr 21:28 771
threshingfloor of *O* the Jebusite 2Chr 3:1 771

ORPAH *(or'-pah)* {2} *Daughter-in-law of Naomi.*
the name of the one was *O* Ruth 1:4 6204
O kissed her mother in law Ruth 1:14 6204

ORPHANS {1}
We are *o* and fatherless, our Lam 5:3 3490

OSEE *(o'-see)* {1} See HOSEA, JOSHUA, OSHEA. *Greek form of Hoshea.*
As he saith also in *O*, I will Rom 9:25 *5617*

OSHEA *(o-she'-ah)* {2} See HOSHEA, OSEE. *Same as Joshua, son of Nun.*
of Ephraim, *O* the son of Nun Num 13:8 1954
Moses called *O* the son of Nun Num 13:16 1954

OSNAPPAR See ASNAPPER.

OSPRAY {2}
eagle, and the ossifrage, and the *o* Lev 11:13 5822
eagle, and the ossifrage, and the *o* Deut 14:12 5822

OSSIFRAGE {2}
the eagle, and the *o*, and the Lev 11:13 6538
the eagle, and the *o*, and the Deut 14:12 6538

OSTRICH {1}
or wings and feathers unto the *o* Job 39:13 5133

OSTRICHES {1}
like the *o* in the wilderness Lam 4:3 3283

OTHER See APPENDIX.

OTHERS See APPENDIX.

OTHERWISE See APPENDIX.

OTHNI *(oth'-ni)* {1} *A son of Shemiah.*
O, and Rephael, and Obed, Elzabad, 1Chr 26:7 6273

OTHNIEL *(oth'-ne-el)* {7}
1. A brother of Caleb.
O the son of Kenaz, the brother Josh 15:17 6274
O the son of Kenaz, Caleb's Judg 1:13 6274
even *O* the son of Kenaz, Caleb's Judg 3:9 6274
And *O* the son of Kenaz died Judg 3:11 6274
O, and Seraiah 1Chr 4:13 6274
and the sons of *O* 1Chr 4:13 6274
2. Tribe or family of Othniel 1.
was Heldai the Netophathite, of *O* 1Chr 27:15 6274

OUCHES {8}
make them to be set in *o* of gold Ex 28:11 4865
And thou shalt make *o* of gold Ex 28:13 4865
the wreathen chains to the *o* Ex 28:14 4865

thou shalt fasten in the two *o* ... Ex 28:25 4865
onyx stones inclosed in *o* of gold ... Ex 39:6 4865
they were inclosed in *o* of gold ... Ex 39:13 4865
And they made two *o* of gold ... Ex 39:16 4865
chains they fastened in the two *o* ... Ex 39:18 4865

OUGHT See APPENDIX.

OUGHTEST {4}
what thou *o* to do unto him ... 1Kin 2:9
Thou *o* therefore to have put my ... Mt 25:27 *1163*
shall tell thee what thou *o* to do ... Acts 10:6 *1163*
o to behave thyself in the house ... 1Ti 3:15 *1163*

OUR See APPENDIX.

OURS See APPENDIX.

OURSELVES See APPENDIX.

OUT See APPENDIX.

OUTCAST {1}
because they called thee an *O* ... Jer 30:17 5080

OUTCASTS {7}
together the *o* of Israel ... Ps 147:2 1760
and shall assemble the *o* of Israel ... Is 11:12 1760
hide the *o* ... Is 16:3 5080
Let mine *o* dwell with thee, Moab ... Is 16:4 5080
the *o* in the land of Egypt, and ... Is 27:13 5080
gathereth the *o* of Israel saith ... Is 56:8 1760
the *o* of Elam shall not come ... Jer 49:36 5080

OUTER {4}
was heard even to the *o* court ... Eze 10:5 2435
shall be cast out into *o* darkness ... Mt 8:12 *1857*
away, and cast him into *o* darkness ... Mt 22:13 *1857*
servant into *o* darkness ... Mt 25:30 *1857*

OUTGOINGS {8}
the *o* of it were at the sea ... Josh 17:9 8444
the *o* of it shall be thine ... Josh 17:18 8444
the *o* of the border were at the ... Josh 18:19 8444
the *o* thereof are in the valley ... Josh 19:14 8444
the *o* of their border were at ... Josh 19:22 8444
the *o* thereof are at the sea from ... Josh 19:29 8444
the *o* thereof were at Jordan ... Josh 19:33 8444
thou makest the *o* of the morning ... Ps 65:8 4161

OUTLANDISH {1}
even him did *o* women cause to sin ... Neh 13:26 5237

OUTLIVED {1}
of the elders that *o* Joshua ... Judg 2:7 748,3117,310

OUTMOST {4}
curtain that is *o* in the coupling ... Ex 26:10 7020
o coast of the salt sea eastward ... Num 34:3 7097
out unto the *o* parts of heaven ... Deut 30:4 7097
four or five in the *o* fruitful ... Is 17:6

OUTRAGEOUS {1}
Wrath is cruel, and anger is *o* ... Prov 27:4 7858

OUTRUN {1}
and the other disciple did *o* Peter ... Jn 20:4 *4370,5032*

OUTSIDE See APPENDIX.

OUTSTRETCHED {3}
a mighty hand, and with an *o* arm ... Deut 26:8 5186
fight against you with an *o* hand ... Jer 21:5 5186
by my great power and by my *o* arm ... Jer 27:5 5186

OUTWARD {14}
o a thousand cubits round about ... Num 35:4 2435
man looketh on the *o* appearance ... 1Sa 16:7 5869
for the *o* business over Israel ... 1Chr 26:29 2435
had the oversight of the *o* ... Neh 11:16 2435
the *o* court of the king's house ... Est 6:4 2435
brought he me into the *o* court ... Eze 40:17 2435
the gate of the *o* court that ... Eze 40:20 2435
thereof were toward the *o* court ... Eze 40:34 2435
o sanctuary which looketh toward ... Eze 44:1 2435
which indeed appear beautiful *o* ... Mt 23:27 *1855*
which is *o* in the flesh ... Rom 2:28 *1722,3588,5318*
but though our *o* man perish ... 2Cor 4:16 *1854*
on things after the *o* appearance ... 2Cor 10:7 *4383*
adorning let it not be that *o* ... 1Pet 3:3 *1855*

OUTWARDLY {2}
Even so ye also *o* appear ... Mt 23:28 *1855*
he is not a Jew, which is one *o* ... Rom 2:28 *1722,5318*

OUTWENT {1}
o them, and came together unto him ... Mk 6:33 *4281*

OVEN {12}
of a meat offering baken in the *o* ... Lev 2:4 8574
offering that is baken in the *o* ... Lev 7:9 8574
whether it be *o*, or ranges for ... Lev 11:35 8574
shall bake your bread in one *o* ... Lev 26:26 8574
o in the time of thine anger ... Ps 21:9 8574
Our skin was black like an *o* ... Lam 5:10 8574
as an *o* heated by the baker, who ... Hos 7:4 8574
made ready their heart like an *o* ... Hos 7:6 8574
They are all hot as an *o*, and have ... Hos 7:7 8574
cometh, that shall burn as an *o* ... Mal 4:1 8574
and to morrow is cast into the *o* ... Mt 6:30 *2823*
and to morrow is cast into the *o* ... Lk 12:28 *2823*

OVENS {1}
upon thy people, and into thine *o* ... Ex 8:3 8574

OVER See APPENDIX.

OVERCAME {3}
o them, and prevailed against them ... Acts 19:16 *2634*
me in my throne, even as I also *o* ... Rev 3:21 *3528*
they *o* him by the blood of the ... Rev 12:11 *3528*

OVERCHARGE {1}
that I may not *o* you all ... 2Cor 2:5 *1912*

OVERCHARGED {1}
your hearts be *o* with surfeiting ... Lk 21:34 *925*

OVERCOME {22}
Gad, a troop shall *o* him ... Gen 49:19 1464
but he shall *o* at the last ... Gen 49:19 1464
of them that cry for being *o* ... Ex 32:18 2476
for we are well able to *o* it ... Num 13:30 3201
I shall be able to *o* them ... Num 22:11 3898
Ahaz, but could not *o* him ... 2Kin 16:5 3898
eyes from me, for they have *o* me ... Song 6:5 7292
of them that are *o* with wine ... Is 28:1 1986
and like a man whom wine hath *o* ... Jer 23:9 5674
o him, he taketh from him all his ... Lk 11:22 *3528*
I have *o* the world ... Jn 16:33 *3528*
mightest *o* when thou art judged ... Rom 3:4 *3528*
Be not *o* of evil, but *o* ... Rom 12:21 *3528*
for of whom a man is *o*, of the ... 2Pet 2:19 *2274*
are again entangled therein, and *o* ... 2Pet 2:20 *2274*
because ye have *o* the wicked one ... 1Jn 2:13 *3528*
you, and ye have *o* the wicked one ... 1Jn 2:14 *3528*
little children, and have *o* them ... 1Jn 4:4 *3528*
war against them, and shall *o* them ... Rev 11:7 *3528*
war with the saints, and to *o* them ... Rev 13:7 *3528*
Lamb, and the Lamb shall *o* them ... Rev 17:14 *3528*

OVERCOMETH {11}
is born of God *o* the world ... 1Jn 5:4 *3528*
is the victory that *o* the world ... 1Jn 5:4 *3528*
Who is he that *o* the world ... 1Jn 5:5 *3528*
To him that *o* will I give to eat ... Rev 2:7 *3528*
He that *o* shall not be hurt of ... Rev 2:11 *3528*
To him that *o* will I give to eat ... Rev 2:17 *3528*
And he that *o*, and keepeth my works ... Rev 2:26 *3528*
He that *o*, the same shall be ... Rev 3:5 *3528*
Him that *o* will I make a pillar ... Rev 3:12 *3528*
To him that *o* will I grant to sit ... Rev 3:21 *3528*
He that *o* shall inherit all ... Rev 21:7 *3528*

OVERDRIVE {1}
and if men should *o* them one day ... Gen 33:13 1849

OVERFLOW {13}
the water of the Red sea to *o* ... Deut 11:4 6687
waters, where the floods *o* me ... Ps 69:2 7857
Let not the waterflood *o* me ... Ps 69:15 7857
he shall *o* and go over, he shall ... Is 8:8 7857
shall *o* with righteousness ... Is 10:22 7857
waters shall *o* the hiding place ... Is 28:17 7857
the rivers, they shall not *o* thee ... Is 43:2 7857
shall *o* the land, and all that is ... Jer 47:2 7857
and one shall certainly come, and *o* ... Dan 11:10 7857
destroy him, and his army shall *o* ... Dan 11:26 7857
into the countries, and shall *o* ... Dan 11:40 7857
and the fats shall *o* with wine ... Joel 2:24 7783
for the press is full, the fats *o* ... Joel 3:13 7783

OVERFLOWED {2}
gushed out, and the streams *o* ... Ps 78:20 7857
being *o* with water, perished ... 2Pet 3:6 *2626*

OVERFLOWETH {1}
(for Jordan *o* all his banks all ... Josh 3:15 4390

OVERFLOWING {11}
He bindeth the floods from *o* ... Job 28:11 1065
a watercourse for the *o* of waters ... Job 38:25 7858
as a flood of mighty waters *o* ... Is 28:2 7857
when the *o* scourge shall pass ... Is 28:15 7857
when the *o* scourge shall pass ... Is 28:18 7857
as an *o* stream, shall reach to ... Is 30:28 7857
the north, and shall be an *o* flood ... Jer 47:2 7857
there shall be an *o* shower ... Eze 13:11 7857
there shall be an *o* shower in ... Eze 13:13 7857
o rain, and great hailstones, fire ... Eze 38:22 7857
the *o* of the water passed by ... Hab 3:10 2230

OVERFLOWN {3}
when it had *o* all his banks ... 1Chr 12:15 4390
foundation was *o* with a flood ... Job 22:16 3332
shall they be *o* from before him ... Dan 11:22 7857

OVERLAID {35}
of shittim wood *o* with gold ... Ex 26:32 6823
he *o* the boards with gold, and ... Ex 36:34 6823
the bars, and *o* the bars with gold ... Ex 36:34 6823
shittim wood, and *o* them with gold ... Ex 36:36 6823
he *o* their chapiters and their ... Ex 36:38 6823
he *o* it with pure gold within and ... Ex 37:2 6823
shittim wood, and *o* them with gold ... Ex 37:4 6823
he *o* it with pure gold, and made ... Ex 37:11 6823
o them with gold, to bear the ... Ex 37:15 6823
he *o* it with pure gold, both the ... Ex 37:26 6823
shittim wood, and *o* them with gold ... Ex 37:28 6823
and he *o* it with brass ... Ex 38:2 6823
wood, and *o* them with brass ... Ex 38:6 6823
o their chapiters, and filleted ... Ex 38:28 6823
because she *o* it ... 1Kin 3:19 7901
and he *o* it with pure gold ... 1Kin 6:20 6823
So Solomon *o* the house within ... 1Kin 6:21 6823
and he *o* it with gold ... 1Kin 6:21 6823
And the whole house he *o* with gold ... 1Kin 6:22 6823
was by the oracle he *o* with gold ... 1Kin 6:22 6823
he *o* the cherubims with gold ... 1Kin 6:28 6823
floor of the house he *o* with gold ... 1Kin 6:30 6823
o them with gold, and spread gold ... 1Kin 6:32 6823
ivory, and *o* it with the best gold ... 1Kin 10:18 6823
Hezekiah king of Judah had *o* ... 2Kin 18:16 6823
he *o* it within with pure gold ... 2Chr 3:4 6823
which he *o* with fine gold, and set ... 2Chr 3:5 2645
He *o* also the house, the beams, ... 2Chr 3:7 2645
he *o* it with fine gold, amounting ... 2Chr 3:8 2645
he *o* the upper chambers with gold ... 2Chr 3:9 2645
image work, and *o* them with gold ... 2Chr 3:10 6823
o the doors of them with brass ... 2Chr 4:9 6823
of ivory, and *o* it with pure gold ... 2Chr 9:17 6823
as bright ivory *o* with sapphires ... Song 5:14 5968
covenant *o* round about with gold ... Heb 9:4 *4028*

OVERLAY {13}
thou shalt *o* it with pure gold, ... Ex 25:11 6823
within and without shalt thou *o* it ... Ex 25:11 6823
shittim wood, and *o* them with gold ... Ex 25:13 6823
thou shalt *o* it with pure gold, ... Ex 25:24 6823
o them with gold, that the table ... Ex 25:28 6823
thou shalt *o* the boards with gold ... Ex 26:29 6823
thou shalt *o* the bars with gold ... Ex 26:29 6823
o them with gold, and their hooks ... Ex 26:37 6823
thou shalt *o* it with brass ... Ex 27:2 6823
wood, and *o* them with brass ... Ex 27:6 6823
thou shalt *o* it with pure gold, ... Ex 30:3 6823
shittim wood, and *o* them with gold ... Ex 30:5 6823
to *o* the walls of the houses ... 1Chr 29:4 2902

OVERLAYING {2}
the *o* of their chapiters of ... Ex 38:17 6826
the *o* of their chapiters and their ... Ex 38:19 6826

OVERLIVED {1}
days of the elders that *o* Joshua ... Josh 24:31

OVERMUCH {1}
be swallowed up with *o* sorrow ... 2Cor 2:7 *4055*

OVERPASS {1}
they *o* the deeds of the wicked ... Jer 5:28 5674

OVERPAST {2}
until these calamities be *o* ... Ps 57:1 5674
until the indignation be *o* ... Is 26:20 5674

OVERPLUS {1}
restore the *o* unto the man to ... Lev 25:27 5736

OVERRAN {1}
the way of the plain, and *o* Cushi ... 2Sa 18:23 5674

OVERRUNNING {1}
But with an *o* flood he will make ... Nah 1:8 5674

OVERSEE {2}
were appointed to *o* the vessels ... 1Chr 9:29
thousand and six hundred to *o* them ... 2Chr 2:2 5329

OVERSEER {7}
he made him *o* over his house, and ... Gen 39:4 6485
he had made him *o* in his house ... Gen 39:5 6485
the son of Zichri was their *o* ... Neh 11:9 6496
their *o* was Zabdiel, the son of ... Neh 11:14 6496
The *o* also of the Levites at ... Neh 11:22 6496
sang loud, with Jezrahiah their *o* ... Neh 12:42 6496
Which having no guide, *o*, or ... Prov 6:7 7860

OVERSEERS {6}
six hundred *o* to set the people a ... 2Chr 2:18 5329
were *o* under the hand of Cononiah ... 2Chr 31:13 6496
the *o* of them were Jahath and ... 2Chr 34:12 6485
were *o* of all that wrought the ... 2Chr 34:13 5329
it into the hand of the *o* ... 2Chr 34:17 6485
the Holy Ghost hath made you *o* ... Acts 20:28 *1985*

O

OVERSHADOW {2}
power of the Highest shall *o* thee ... Lk 1:35 *1982*
passing by might *o* some of them ... Acts 5:15 *1982*

OVERSHADOWED {3}
behold, a bright cloud *o* them ... Mt 17:5 *1982*
And there was a cloud that *o* them ... Mk 9:7 *1982*
there came a cloud, and *o* them ... Lk 9:34 *1982*

OVERSIGHT {11}
peradventure it was an *o* ... Gen 43:12 4870
have the *o* of them that keep the ... Num 3:32 6486
the *o* of all the tabernacle, and ... Num 4:16 6486
that had the *o* of the house of ... 2Kin 12:11 6485
that have the *o* of the house of ... 2Kin 22:5 6485
that have the *o* of the house of ... 2Kin 22:9 6485
their children had the *o* of the ... 1Chr 9:23 5921
the *o* of the house of the LORD ... 2Chr 34:10 6485
had the *o* of the outward business ... Neh 11:16 5921
having the *o* of the chamber of ... Neh 13:4 5414
among you, taking the *o* thereof ... 1Pet 5:2 *1983*

OVERSPREAD {1}
and of them was the whole earth *o* ... Gen 9:19 5310

OVERSPREADING {1}
for the *o* of abominations he ... Dan 9:27 3671

OVERTAKE {17}
and when thou dost *o* them, say ... Gen 44:4 5381
said, I will pursue, I will *o* ... Ex 15:9 5381
o him, because the way is long, ... Deut 19:6 5381
o thee, if thou shalt hearken ... Deut 28:2 5381
shall come upon thee, and *o* thee ... Deut 28:15 5381
o thee, till thou be destroyed ... Deut 28:45 5381
for ye shall *o* them ... Josh 2:5 5381
shall I *o* them ... 1Sa 30:8 5381
for thou shalt surely *o* them ... 1Sa 30:8 5381
lest he *o* us suddenly, and bring ... 2Sa 15:14 5381
us, neither doth justice *o* us ... Is 59:9 5381
shall *o* you there in the land of ... Jer 42:16 5381
lovers, but she shall not *o* them ... Hos 2:7 5381
of iniquity did not *o* them ... Hos 10:9 5381
evil shall not *o* nor prevent us ... Amos 9:10 5066
the plowman shall *o* the reaper ... Amos 9:13 5066
that day should *o* you as a thief ... 1Th 5:4 *2638*

OVERTAKEN {2}
pursued mine enemies, and *o* them ... Ps 18:37 5381
if a man be *o* in a fault ... Gal 6:1 *4301*

OVERTAKETH {1}
the sword of thine enemies *o* thee ... 1Chr 21:12 5381

OVERTHREW {12}
he *o* those cities, and all the ... Gen 19:25 2015
when he *o* the cities in the which ... Gen 19:29 2015
the LORD *o* the Egyptians in the ... Ex 14:27 5287
which the LORD *o* in his anger ... Deut 29:23 2015
But *o* Pharaoh and his host in the ... Ps 136:15 5286
shall be as when God *o* Sodom ... Is 13:19 4114
be as the cities which the LORD *o* ... Jer 20:16 2015
As God *o* Sodom and Gomorrah ... Jer 50:40 4114
some of you, as God *o* Sodom ... Amos 4:11 4114
o the tables of the moneychangers ... Mt 21:12 *2690*
o the tables of the moneychangers ... Mk 11:15 *2690*
changers' money, and *o* the tables ... Jn 2:15 *390*

OVERTHROW {19}
also, that I will not *o* this city ... Gen 19:21 2015
Lot out of the midst of the *o* ... Gen 19:29 2018
but thou shalt utterly *o* them ... Ex 23:24 2040
ye shall *o* their altars, and break ... Deut 12:3 5422
therein, like the *o* of Sodom ... Deut 29:23 4114
and to spy it out, and to *o* it ... 2Sa 10:3 2015
strong against the city, and *o* it ... 2Sa 11:25 2040
unto thee for to search, and to *o* ... 1Chr 19:3 2015
to *o* them in the wilderness ... Ps 106:26 5307
To *o* their seed also among the ... Ps 106:27 5307
who have purposed to *o* my goings ... Ps 140:4 1760
hunt the violent man to *o* him ... Ps 140:11 4073
to *o* the righteous in judgment ... Prov 18:5 5186
As in the *o* of Sodom and Gomorrah ... Jer 49:18 4114
I will *o* the throne of kingdoms, ... Hag 2:22 2015
I will *o* the chariots, and those ... Hag 2:22 2015
if it be of God, ye cannot *o* it ... Acts 5:39 *2647*
and *o* the faith of some ... 2Ti 2:18 *396*
ashes condemned them with an *o* ... 2Pet 2:6 *2692*

OVERTHROWETH {5}
away spoiled, and *o* the mighty ... Job 12:19 5557
but wickedness *o* the sinner ... Prov 13:6 5557
but God *o* the wicked for their ... Prov 21:12 5557
and he *o* the words of the ... Prov 22:12 5557
but he that receiveth gifts *o* it ... Prov 29:4 2040

OVERTHROWN {16}
of thine excellency thou hast *o* ... Ex 15:7 2040
fled before him, and many were *o* ... Judg 9:40 5307
some of them be *o* at the first ... 2Sa 17:9 5307
and the Ethiopians were *o*, that ... 2Chr 14:13 5307
Know now that God hath *o* me ... Job 19:6 5791
judges are *o* in stony places ... Ps 141:6 8058
but it is *o* by the mouth of the ... Prov 11:11 2040
The wicked are *o*, and are not ... Prov 12:7 2015
house of the wicked shall be *o* ... Prov 14:11 8045
it is desolate, as *o* by strangers ... Is 1:7 4114
but let them be *o* before thee ... Jer 18:23 3782
that was *o* as in a moment, and no ... Lam 4:6 2015
and many countries shall be *o* ... Dan 11:41 3782
I have *o* some of you, as God ... Amos 4:11 2015
forty days, and Nineveh shall be *o* ... Jonah 3:4 2015
for they were *o* in the wilderness ... 1Cor 10:5 *2693*

OVERTOOK {10}
they *o* him in the mount Gilead ... Gen 31:23 1692
Then Laban *o* Jacob ... Gen 31:25 5381
he *o* them, and he spake unto them ... Gen 44:6 5381
o them encamping by the sea, ... Ex 14:9 5381
and *o* the children of Dan ... Judg 18:22 1692
but the battle *o* them ... Judg 20:42 1692
o him in the plains of Jericho ... 2Kin 25:5 5381
o Zedekiah in the plains of ... Jer 39:5 5381
o Zedekiah in the plains of ... Jer 52:8 5381
all her persecutors *o* her between ... Lam 1:3 5381

OVERTURN {4}
them out, and they *o* the earth ... Job 12:15 2015
I will *o*, *o*, *o* ... Eze 21:27 5754

OVERTURNED {1}
o it, that the tent lay along ... Judg 7:13 2015

OVERTURNETH {3}
which *o* them in his anger ... Job 9:5 2015
he *o* the mountains by the roots ... Job 28:9 2015
he *o* them in the night, so that ... Job 34:25 2015

OVERWHELM {1}
ye *o* the fatherless, and ye dig a ... Job 6:27 5307

OVERWHELMED {8}
come upon me, and horror hath *o* me ... Ps 55:5 3680
cry unto thee, when my heart is *o* ... Ps 61:2 5848
I complained, and my spirit was *o* ... Ps 77:3 5848
but the sea *o* their enemies ... Ps 78:53 3680
of the afflicted, when he is *o* ... Ps 102:*t* 5848
Then the waters had *o* us, the ... Ps 124:4 7857
When my spirit was *o* within me ... Ps 142:3 5848
is my spirit *o* within me ... Ps 143:4 5848

OWE {1}
O no man any thing, but to love ... Rom 13:8 *3784*

OWED {3}
which *o* him ten thousand talents ... Mt 18:24 *3781*
which *o* him an hundred pence ... Mt 18:28 *3784*
the one *o* five hundred pence, and ... Lk 7:41 *3784*

OWEST {4}
saying, Pay me that thou *o* ... Mt 18:28 *3784*
How much *o* thou unto my lord ... Lk 16:5 *3784*
he to another, And how much *o* thou ... Lk 16:7 *3784*
o unto me even thine own self ... Philem 19 *4359*

OWETH {1}
or *o* thee ought, put that on mine ... Philem 18 *3784*

OWL {10}
And the *o*, and the night hawk, and Lev 11:16 1323,3284
And the little *o*, and the cormorant ... Lev 11:17 3563
and the cormorant, and the great *o* ... Lev 11:17 3244
And the *o*, and the night hawk ... Deut 14:15 1323,3284
The little *o*, and the great ... Deut 14:16 3563
and the great *o* ... Deut 14:16 3244
I am like an *o* of the desert ... Ps 102:6 3563
the *o* also and the raven shall ... Is 34:11 3244
the screech *o* also shall rest ... Is 34:14 3917
shall the great *o* make her nest ... Is 34:15 7091

OWLS {6}
to dragons, and a companion to *o* ... Job 30:29 1323,3284
o shall dwell there, and satyrs ... Is 13:21 1323,3284
of dragons, and a court for *o* ... Is 34:13 1323,3284
honour me, the dragons and the *o* ... Is 43:20 1323,3284
the *o* shall dwell therein ... Jer 50:39 1323,3284
dragons, and mourning as the *o* ... Mic 1:8 1323,3284

OWN {599}
So God created man in his *o* image ... Gen 1:27
and begat a son in his *o* likeness ... Gen 5:3 249
servants, born in his *o* house ... Gen 14:14 249
o bowels shall be thine heir ... Gen 15:4 249
that I may go unto mine *o* place ... Gen 30:25
I provide for mine *o* house also ... Gen 30:30
he put his *o* flocks by themselves ... Gen 30:40
and four parts shall be your *o* ... Gen 47:24
the fault is in thine *o* people ... Ex 5:16
he went his way into his *o* land ... Ex 18:27
and the dead shall be his *o* ... Ex 21:36
of the best of his *o* field ... Ex 22:5
and of the best of his *o* vineyard ... Ex 22:5
whom thou swarest by thine *o* self ... Ex 32:13
he shall offer it of his *o* ... Lev 1:3
His *o* hands shall bring the ... Lev 7:30
into the palm of his *o* left hand ... Lev 14:15 3548
into the palm of his *o* left hand ... Lev 14:26 3548
it be one of your *o* country ... Lev 16:29 249
it be one of your *o* country ... Lev 17:15 249
for theirs is thine *o* nakedness ... Lev 18:10
neither any of your *o* nation ... Lev 18:26 249
ye shall offer it at your *o* will ... Lev 19:5
a virgin of his *o* people to wife ... Lev 21:14
Ye shall offer at your *o* will a ... Lev 22:19
the LORD, offer it at your *o* will ... Lev 22:29
as for one of your *o* country ... Lev 24:22 249
That which groweth of its *o* ... Lev 25:5
and shall return unto his *o* family ... Lev 25:41
tents, every man by his *o* camp ... Num 1:52
and every man by his *o* standard ... Num 1:52
shall pitch by his *o* standard ... Num 2:2
but I will depart to mine *o* land ... Num 10:30
we were in our *o* sight as ... Num 13:33
ye seek not after your *o* heart ... Num 15:39
your *o* heart and your *o* eyes ... Num 15:39
have not done them of mine *o* mind ... Num 16:28
sinners against their *o* souls ... Num 16:38
either good or bad of mine *o* mind ... Num 24:13
but died in his *o* sin, and had no ... Num 27:3
called it Nobah, after his *o* name ... Num 32:42
keep himself to his *o* inheritance ... Num 36:9
and called them after his *o* name ... Deut 3:14
whatsoever is right in his *o* eyes ... Deut 12:8
friend, which is as thine *o* soul ... Deut 13:6
shalt bring it unto thine *o* house ... Deut 22:2
thy fill at thine *o* pleasure ... Deut 23:24
he may sleep in his *o* raiment ... Deut 24:13
be put to death for his *o* sin ... Deut 24:16
eat the fruit of thine *o* body ... Deut 28:53
brethren, nor knew his *o* children ... Deut 33:9
put it even among their *o* stuff ... Josh 7:11
his *o* city, and unto his *o* house ... Josh 20:6
ceased not from their *o* doings ... Judg 2:19
Mine *o* hand hath saved me ... Judg 7:2
went and dwelt in his *o* house ... Judg 8:29
which was right in his *o* eyes ... Judg 17:6
which was right in his *o* eyes ... Judg 21:25
lest I mar mine *o* inheritance ... Ruth 4:6
And they went unto their *o* home ... 1Sa 2:20
and let it go again to his *o* place ... 1Sa 5:11
of his *o* coast to Beth-shemesh ... 1Sa 6:9
him a man after his *o* heart ... 1Sa 13:14
Philistines went to their *o* place ... 1Sa 14:46
thou wast little in thine *o* sight ... 1Sa 15:17
Jonathan loved him as his *o* soul ... 1Sa 18:1
he loved him as his *o* soul ... 1Sa 18:3
loved him as he loved his *o* soul ... 1Sa 20:17
son of Jesse to thine *o* confusion ... 1Sa 20:30
thyself with thine *o* hand ... 1Sa 25:26
avenging myself with mine *o* hand ... 1Sa 25:33
of Nabal upon his *o* head ... 1Sa 25:39
him in Ramah, even in his *o* city ... 1Sa 28:3
in his *o* house upon his bed ... 2Sa 4:11
and will be base in mine *o* sight ... 2Sa 6:22
may dwell in a place of their *o* ... 2Sa 7:10
and according to thine *o* heart ... 2Sa 7:21
o meat, and drank of his *o* cup ... 2Sa 12:3
of his *o* flock and of his *o* herd ... 2Sa 12:4
against thee out of thine *o* house ... 2Sa 12:11
then he came to his *o* house ... 2Sa 12:20
said, Let him turn to his *o* house ... 2Sa 14:24
Absalom returned to his *o* house ... 2Sa 14:24
go to battle in thine *o* person ... 2Sa 17:11
falsehood against mine *o* life ... 2Sa 18:13
the pillar after his *o* name ... 2Sa 18:18
that did eat at thine *o* table ... 2Sa 19:28
again in peace unto his *o* house ... 2Sa 19:30
that I may die in mine *o* city ... 2Sa 19:37
and he returned unto his *o* place ... 2Sa 19:39
and slew him with his *o* spear ... 2Sa 23:21
thou mayest save thine *o* life ... 1Kin 1:12
my son to ride upon mine *o* mule ... 1Kin 1:33
this word against his *o* life ... 1Kin 2:23
to Anathoth, unto thine *o* fields ... 1Kin 2:26
return his blood upon his *o* head ... 1Kin 2:32
he was buried in his *o* house in ... 1Kin 2:34
blood shall be upon thine *o* head ... 1Kin 2:37
thy wickedness upon thine *o* head ... 1Kin 2:44
an end of building his *o* house ... 1Kin 3:1
his *o* house thirteen years ... 1Kin 7:1
man the plague of his *o* heart ... 1Kin 8:38
his *o* house, and Millo, and the ... 1Kin 9:15
heard in mine *o* land of thy acts ... 1Kin 10:6
turned and went to her *o* country ... 1Kin 10:13 249
to wife the sister of his *o* wife ... 1Kin 11:19
that I may go to mine *o* country ... 1Kin 11:21
seekest to go to thine *o* country ... 1Kin 11:22
now see to thine *o* house, David ... 1Kin 12:16
he had devised of his *o* heart ... 1Kin 12:33
laid his carcase in his *o* grave ... 1Kin 13:30
get thee to thine *o* house ... 1Kin 14:12
abode, and laid him upon his *o* bed ... 1Kin 17:19
and every man to his *o* country ... 1Kin 22:36
and he took hold of his *o* clothes ... 2Kin 2:12 249
him, and returned to their *o* land ... 2Kin 3:27
I dwell among mine *o* people ... 2Kin 4:13
his *o* hallowed things, and all the ... 2Kin 12:18
be put to death for his *o* sin ... 2Kin 14:6
carried away out of their *o* land ... 2Kin 17:23
every nation made gods of their *o* ... 2Kin 17:29
the LORD, and served their *o* gods ... 2Kin 17:33
that they may eat their *o* dung ... 2Kin 18:27
drink their *o* piss with you ... 2Kin 18:27
eat ye every man of his *o* vine ... 2Kin 18:31
away to a land like your *o* land ... 2Kin 18:32
and shall return to his *o* land ... 2Kin 19:7
fall by the sword in his *o* land ... 2Kin 19:7
city, to save it, for mine *o* sake ... 2Kin 19:34
defend this city for mine *o* sake ... 2Kin 20:6
in the garden of his *o* house ... 2Kin 21:18
and slew the king in his *o* house ... 2Kin 21:23
and buried him in his *o* sepulchre ... 2Kin 23:30
and slew him with his *o* spear ... 1Chr 11:23
and according to thine *o* heart ... 1Chr 17:19
went to redeem to be his *o* people ... 1Chr 17:21
thou make thine *o* people for ever ... 1Chr 17:22
God, I have of mine *o* proper good ... 1Chr 29:3
of thine *o* have we given thee ... 1Chr 29:14
of thine hand, and is all thine *o* ... 1Chr 29:16
his way upon his *o* head ... 2Chr 6:23
every one shall know his *o* sore ... 2Chr 6:29
his *o* grief, and shall spread ... 2Chr 6:29
of the LORD, and in his *o* house ... 2Chr 7:11
of the LORD, and his *o* house, ... 2Chr 8:1
in mine *o* land of thine acts ... 2Chr 9:5
and went away to her *o* land ... 2Chr 9:12
now, David, see to thine *o* house ... 2Chr 10:16
buried him in his *o* sepulchres ... 2Chr 16:14
his *o* servants conspired against ... 2Chr 24:25 249
every man shall die for his *o* sin ... 2Chr 25:4
their *o* people out of thine hand ... 2Chr 25:15
possession, into their *o* cities ... 2Chr 31:1
with shame of face to his *o* land ... 2Chr 32:21
they that came forth of his *o* ... 2Chr 32:21
and they buried him in his *o* house ... 2Chr 33:20
him, and slew him in his *o* house ... 2Chr 33:24
which are minded of their *o* ... Ezr 7:13
their reproach upon their *o* head ... Neh 4:4
them out of thine *o* heart ... Neh 6:8
much cast down in their *o* eyes ... Neh 6:16
should bear rule in his *o* house ... Est 1:22
dead, took for his *o* daughter ... Est 2:7
should return upon his *o* head ... Est 9:25
came every one from his *o* place ... Job 2:11
the wise in their *o* craftiness ... Job 5:13
mine *o* mouth shall condemn me ... Job 9:20
mine *o* clothes shall abhor me ... Job 9:31
maintain mine *o* ways before him ... Job 13:15
Thine *o* mouth condemneth thee, and ... Job 15:6
thine *o* lips testify against thee ... Job 15:6
his *o* counsel shall cast him down ... Job 18:7
is cast into a net by his *o* feet ... Job 18:8
children's sake of mine *o* body ... Job 19:17
perish for ever like his *o* dung ... Job 20:7
he was righteous in his *o* eyes ... Job 32:1
thine *o* right hand can save thee ... Job 40:14
commune with your *o* heart upon ... Ps 4:4
let them fall by their *o* counsels ... Ps 5:10
shall return upon his *o* head ... Ps 7:16
shall come down upon his *o* pate ... Ps 7:16
they hid is their *o* foot taken ... Ps 9:15
snared in the work of his *o* hands ... Ps 9:16
our lips are our *o* ... Ps 12:4
He that sweareth to his *o* hurt ... Ps 15:4
They are inclosed in their *o* fat ... Ps 17:10 249
thee according to thine *o* heart ... Ps 20:4
LORD, in thine *o* strength ... Ps 21:13
and none can keep alive his *o* soul ... Ps 22:29
hath chosen for his *o* inheritance ... Ps 33:12
prayer returned into mine *o* bosom ... Ps 35:13
flattereth himself in his *o* eyes ... Ps 36:2
shall enter into their *o* heart ... Ps 37:15
mine *o* familiar friend, in whom I ... Ps 41:9
in possession by their *o* sword ... Ps 44:3
neither did their *o* arm save them ... Ps 44:3
forget also thine *o* people ... Ps 45:10
their lands after their *o* names ... Ps 49:11
slanderest thine *o* mother's son ... Ps 50:20

So they shall make their *o* tongue.......... Ps 64:8
and God, even our *o* God, shall.......... Ps 67:6
Arise, O God, plead thine *o* cause.......... Ps 74:22
I commune with mine *o* heart.......... Ps 77:6
for he gave them their *o* desire.......... Ps 78:29
But made his *o* people to go forth.......... Ps 78:52
them up unto their *o* hearts' lust.......... Ps 81:12
they walked in their *o* counsels.......... Ps 81:12
bring upon them their *o* iniquity.......... Ps 94:23
them off in their *o* wickedness.......... Ps 94:23
they defiled with their *o* works.......... Ps 106:39
a whoring with their *o* inventions.......... Ps 106:39
he abhorred his *o* inheritance.......... Ps 106:40
themselves with their *o* confusion.......... Ps 109:29
not the works of thine *o* hands.......... Ps 138:8
of their *o* lips cover them.......... Ps 140:9
the wicked fall into their *o* nets.......... Ps 141:10 249
they lay wait for their *o* blood.......... Prov 1:18
lurk privily for their *o* lives.......... Prov 1:18
eat of the fruit of their *o* way.......... Prov 1:31
and be filled with their *o* devices.......... Prov 1:31
not unto thine *o* understanding.......... Prov 3:5
Be not wise in thine *o* eyes.......... Prov 3:7
waters out of thine *o* cistern.......... Prov 5:15
waters out of thine *o* well.......... Prov 5:15
Let them be only thine *o*, and not.......... Prov 5:17 249
His *o* iniquities shall take the.......... Prov 5:22 249
doeth it destroyeth his *o* soul.......... Prov 6:32
against me wrongeth his *o* soul.......... Prov 8:36
shall fall by his *o* wickedness.......... Prov 11:5
be taken in their *o* naughtiness.......... Prov 11:6
man doeth good to his *o* soul.......... Prov 11:17
is cruel troubleth his *o* flesh.......... Prov 11:17
evil pursueth it to his *o* death.......... Prov 11:19
He that troubleth his *o* house.......... Prov 11:29
of a fool is right in his *o* eyes.......... Prov 12:15
heart knoweth his *o* bitterness.......... Prov 14:10 5315
shall be filled with his *o* ways.......... Prov 14:14
is hated even of his *o* neighbour.......... Prov 14:20
of gain troubleth his *o* house.......... Prov 15:27
instruction despiseth his *o* soul.......... Prov 15:32
of a man are clean in his *o* eyes.......... Prov 16:2
as an high wall in his *o* conceit.......... Prov 18:11
first in his *o* cause seemeth just.......... Prov 18:17
getteth wisdom loveth his *o* soul.......... Prov 19:8
commandment keepeth his *o* soul.......... Prov 19:16
anger sinneth against his *o* soul.......... Prov 20:2
proclaim every one his *o* goodness.......... Prov 20:6
a man then understand his *o* way.......... Prov 20:24
of a man is right in his *o* eyes.......... Prov 21:2
cease from thine *o* wisdom.......... Prov 23:4
search their *o* glory is not glory.......... Prov 25:27
o spirit is like a city that is.......... Prov 25:28
lest he be wise in his *o* conceit.......... Prov 26:5
thou a man wise in his *o* conceit.......... Prov 26:12
The sluggard is wiser in his *o*.......... Prov 26:16
praise thee, and not thine *o* mouth.......... Prov 27:2
a stranger, and not thine *o* lips.......... Prov 27:2
Thine *o* friend, and thy father's.......... Prov 27:10
shall fall himself into his *o* pit.......... Prov 28:10
rich man is wise in his *o* conceit.......... Prov 28:11
trusteth in his *o* heart is a fool.......... Prov 28:26
with a thief hateth his *o* soul.......... Prov 29:24
that are pure in their *o* eyes.......... Prov 30:12
let her *o* works praise her in the.......... Prov 31:31
I communed with mine *o* heart.......... Eccl 1:16
man should rejoice in his *o* works.......... Eccl 3:22
together, and eateth his *o* flesh.......... Eccl 4:5
For oftentimes also thine *o* heart.......... Eccl 7:22
ruleth over another to his *o* hurt.......... Eccl 8:9
but mine *o* vineyard have I not.......... Song 1:6
worship the work of their *o* hands.......... Is 2:8
that which their *o* fingers have.......... Is 2:8
saying, We will eat our *o* bread.......... Is 4:1
o bread, and wear our *o* apparel.......... Is 4:1
that are wise in their *o* eyes.......... Is 5:21
and prudent in their *o* sight.......... Is 5:21
every man the flesh of his *o* arm.......... Is 9:20
every man turn to his *o* people.......... Is 13:14
and flee every one into his *o* land.......... Is 13:14
and set them in their *o* land.......... Is 14:1
glory, every one in his *o* house.......... Is 14:18
her *o* feet shall carry her afar.......... Is 23:7
which your *o* hands have made unto.......... Is 31:7
that they may eat their *o* dung.......... Is 36:12
drink their *o* piss with you.......... Is 36:12
one the waters of his *o* cistern.......... Is 36:16
away to a land like your *o* land.......... Is 36:17
a rumour, and return to his *o* land.......... Is 37:7
fall by the sword in his *o* land.......... Is 37:7
city to save it for mine *o* sake.......... Is 37:35
transgressions for mine *o* sake.......... Is 43:25
and they are their *o* witnesses.......... Is 44:9
o sake, even for mine *o* sake.......... Is 48:11
oppress thee with their *o* flesh.......... Is 49:26
be drunken with their *o* blood.......... Is 49:26
turned every one to his *o* way.......... Is 53:6
they all look to their *o* way.......... Is 56:11
not thyself from thine *o* flesh.......... Is 58:7
him, not doing thine *o* ways.......... Is 58:13
nor finding thine *o* pleasure.......... Is 58:13
nor speaking thine *o* words.......... Is 58:13
therefore mine *o* arm brought.......... Is 63:5
not good, after their *o* thoughts.......... Is 65:2
they have chosen their *o* ways.......... Is 66:3
the works of their *o* hands.......... Jer 1:16 249
Thine *o* wickedness shall correct.......... Jer 2:19
your *o* sword hath devoured your.......... Jer 2:30

to the confusion of their *o* faces.......... Jer 7:19
the imagination of their *o* heart.......... Jer 9:14
we will walk after our *o* devices.......... Jer 18:12
they shall dwell in their *o* land.......... Jer 23:8
speak a vision of their *o* heart.......... Jer 23:16
the imagination of his *o* heart.......... Jer 23:17
of the deceit of their *o* heart.......... Jer 23:26
of your hands to your *o* hurt.......... Jer 25:7
to the works of their *o* hands.......... Jer 25:14
let remain still in their *o* land.......... Jer 27:11
shall be builded upon her *o* heap.......... Jer 30:18
come again to their *o* border.......... Jer 31:17
one shall die for his *o* iniquity.......... Jer 31:30
return to Egypt into their *o* land.......... Jer 37:7
you to return to your *o* land.......... Jer 42:12
your *o* wickedness, and the.......... Jer 44:9
goeth forth out of our *o* mouth.......... Jer 44:17
let us go again to our *o* people.......... Jer 46:16
flee every one to his *o* land.......... Jer 50:16
go every one into his *o* country.......... Jer 51:9
away captive out of his *o* land.......... Jer 52:27
have sodden their *o* children.......... Lam 4:10
their way upon their *o* heads.......... Eze 11:21
prophesy out of their *o* hearts.......... Eze 13:2
that follow their *o* spirit.......... Eze 13:3
prophesy out of their *o* heart.......... Eze 13:17
house of Israel in their *o* heart.......... Eze 14:5
o souls by their righteousness.......... Eze 14:14
o souls by their righteousness.......... Eze 14:20
thee polluted in thine *o* blood.......... Eze 16:6
didst trust in thine *o* beauty.......... Eze 16:15
bear thine *o* shame for thy sins.......... Eze 16:52
thou mayest bear thine *o* shame.......... Eze 16:54
will I recompense upon his *o* head.......... Eze 17:19
I polluted them in their *o* gifts.......... Eze 20:26
o sight for all your evils that.......... Eze 20:43
their *o* way have I recompensed.......... Eze 22:31
and pluck off thine *o* breasts.......... Eze 23:34
hath said, My river is mine *o*.......... Eze 29:3
moment, every man for his *o* life.......... Eze 32:10
blood shall be upon his *o* head.......... Eze 33:4
he trust to his *o* righteousness.......... Eze 33:13
will bring them to their *o* land.......... Eze 34:13
of Israel dwelt in their *o* land.......... Eze 36:17
they defiled it by their *o* way.......... Eze 36:17
will bring you into your *o* land.......... Eze 36:24
ye remember your *o* evil ways.......... Eze 36:31
your *o* sight for your iniquities.......... Eze 36:31
and confounded for your *o* ways.......... Eze 36:32
I shall place you in your *o* land.......... Eze 37:14
and bring them into their *o* land.......... Eze 37:21
gathered them unto their *o* land.......... Eze 39:28
out of his *o* possession.......... Eze 46:18
any god, except their *o* God.......... Dan 3:28
king sealed it with his *o* signet.......... Dan 6:17
be mighty, but not by his *o* power.......... Dan 8:24
defer not, for thine *o* sake.......... Dan 9:19
and shall return into his *o* land.......... Dan 11:9
shall do according to his *o* will.......... Dan 11:16 7522
but a prince for his *o* behalf.......... Dan 11:18
without his *o* reproach he shall.......... Dan 11:18
toward the fort of his *o* land.......... Dan 11:19
exploits, and return to his *o* land.......... Dan 11:28
now their *o* doings have beset.......... Hos 7:2
shall be ashamed of his *o* counsel.......... Hos 10:6
them, because of their *o* counsels.......... Hos 11:6
to their *o* understanding, all of.......... Hos 13:2
your recompence upon your *o* head.......... Joel 3:4
your recompence upon your *o* head.......... Joel 3:7
to us horns by our *o* strength.......... Amos 6:13
away captive out of their *o* land.......... Amos 7:11
shall return upon thine *o* head.......... Obad 15
vanities forsake their *o* mercy.......... Jonah 2:8
are the men of his *o* house.......... Mic 7:6
ye run every man unto his *o* house.......... Hag 1:9
and set there upon her *o* base.......... Zec 5:11
their *o* shepherds pity them not.......... Zec 11:5
be inhabited again in her *o* place.......... Zec 12:6
his *o* son that serveth him.......... Mal 3:17
into their *o* country another way.......... Mt 2:12
the beam that is in thine *o* eye.......... Mt 7:3
behold, a beam is in thine *o* eye.......... Mt 7:4
out the beam out of thine *o* eye.......... Mt 7:5
over, and came into his *o* city.......... Mt 9:1 *2398*
shall be they of his *o* household.......... Mt 10:36
he was come into his *o* country.......... Mt 13:54
o country, and in his *o* house.......... Mt 13:57
whole world, and lose his *o* soul.......... Mt 16:26
of their *o* children, or of.......... Mt 17:25
me to do what I will with mine *o*.......... Mt 20:15
who called his *o* servants.......... Mt 25:14 *2398*
have received mine *o* with usury.......... Mt 25:27
put his *o* raiment on him, and led.......... Mt 27:31
And laid it in his *o* new tomb.......... Mt 27:60
and came into his *o* country.......... Mk 6:1
honour, but in his *o* country.......... Mk 6:4
his *o* kin, and in his *o* house.......... Mk 6:4
that ye may keep your *o* tradition.......... Mk 7:9
away fasting to their *o* houses.......... Mk 8:3
whole world, and lose his *o* soul.......... Mk 8:36
put his *o* clothes on him, and led.......... Mk 15:20 *2398*
he departed to his *o* house.......... Lk 1:23
and returned to her *o* house.......... Lk 1:56
taxed, every one into his *o* city.......... Lk 2:3 *2398*
pierce through thy *o* soul also.......... Lk 2:35
Galilee, to their *o* city Nazareth.......... Lk 2:39
is accepted in his *o* country.......... Lk 4:24
lay, and departed to his *o* house.......... Lk 5:25

him a great feast in his *o* house.......... Lk 5:29
the beam that is in thine *o* eye.......... Lk 6:41 *2398*
the beam that is in thine *o* eye.......... Lk 6:42
first the beam out of thine *o* eye.......... Lk 6:42
tree is known by his *o* fruit.......... Lk 6:44 *2398*
Return to thine *o* house, and shew.......... Lk 8:39
when he shall come in his *o* glory.......... Lk 9:26
wine, and set him on his *o* beast.......... Lk 10:34 *2398*
his *o* life also, he cannot be my.......... Lk 14:26 *1438*
give you that which is your *o*.......... Lk 16:12
shall not God avenge his *o* elect.......... Lk 18:7
Out of thine *o* mouth will I judge.......... Lk 19:22
have required mine *o* with usury.......... Lk 19:23
know of your *o* selves that summer.......... Lk 21:30
have heard of his *o* mouth.......... Lk 22:71 *1438*
He came unto his *o*.......... Jn 1:11
and his *o* received him not.......... Jn 1:11
first findeth his *o* brother Simon.......... Jn 1:41
believed because of his *o* word.......... Jn 4:41
hath no honour in his *o* country.......... Jn 4:44 *2398*
I can of mine *o* self do nothing.......... Jn 5:30
because I seek not mine *o* will.......... Jn 5:30
another shall come in his *o* name.......... Jn 5:43 *2398*
heaven, not to do mine *o* will.......... Jn 6:38
of himself seeketh his *o* glory.......... Jn 7:18 *2398*
every man went unto his *o* house.......... Jn 7:53
convicted by their *o* conscience.......... Jn 8:9
a lie, he speaketh of his *o*.......... Jn 8:44 *2398*
And I seek not mine *o* glory.......... Jn 8:50
and he calleth his *o* sheep by name.......... Jn 10:3 *2398*
when he putteth forth his *o* sheep.......... Jn 10:4 *2398*
whose *o* the sheep are not, seeth.......... Jn 10:12 *2398*
having loved his *o* which were in.......... Jn 13:1 *2398*
world, the world would love his *o*.......... Jn 15:19 *2398*
be scattered, every man to his *o*.......... Jn 16:32 *2398*
glorify thou me with thine *o* self.......... Jn 17:5 *4572*
keep through thine *o* name those.......... Jn 17:11
Thine *o* nation and the chief.......... Jn 18:35
disciple took her unto his *o* home.......... Jn 19:27 *2398*
went away again unto their *o* home.......... Jn 20:10 *1438*
Father hath put in his *o* power.......... Acts 1:7 *2398*
that he might go to his *o* place.......... Acts 1:25 *2398*
them speak in his *o* language.......... Acts 2:6 *2398*
hear we every man in our *o* tongue.......... Acts 2:8 *2398*
as though by our *o* power or.......... Acts 3:12 *2398*
go, they went to their *o* company.......... Acts 4:23 *2398*
which he possessed was his *o*.......... Acts 4:32 *2398*
it remained, was it not thine *o*.......... Acts 5:4
sold, was it not in thine *o* power.......... Acts 5:4
and nourished him for her *o* son.......... Acts 7:21 *1438*
in the works of their *o* hands.......... Acts 7:41
opened to them of his *o* accord.......... Acts 12:10 *848*
Jesse, a man after mine *o* heart.......... Acts 13:22
after he had served his *o*.......... Acts 13:36 *2398*
nations to walk in their *o* ways.......... Acts 14:16 *848*
to send chosen men of their *o*.......... Acts 15:22
also of your *o* poets have said.......... Acts 17:28 *2596*
Your blood be upon your *o* heads.......... Acts 18:6
hath purchased with his *o* blood.......... Acts 20:28 *2398*
Also of your *o* selves shall men.......... Acts 20:30
girdle, and bound his *o* hands.......... Acts 21:11 *848*
him of their *o* superstition.......... Acts 25:19 *2398*
among mine *o* nation at Jerusalem.......... Acts 26:4
o hands the tackling of the ship.......... Acts 27:19 *849*
whole years in his *o* hired house.......... Acts 28:30 *2398*
the lusts of their *o* hearts.......... Rom 1:24
to dishonour their *o* bodies.......... Rom 1:24
not his *o* body now dead, when he.......... Rom 4:19 *1438*
God sending his *o* Son in the.......... Rom 8:3 *1438*
He that spared not his *o* Son.......... Rom 8:32 *2398*
establish their *o* righteousness.......... Rom 10:3 *2398*
graffed into their *o* olive tree.......... Rom 11:24 *2398*
should be wise in your *o* conceits.......... Rom 11:25 *1438*
Be not wise in your *o* conceits.......... Rom 12:16 *1438*
to his *o* master he standeth or.......... Rom 14:4 *2398*
be fully persuaded in his *o* mind.......... Rom 14:5 *2398*
my life laid down their *o* necks.......... Rom 16:4 *1438*
Jesus Christ, but their *o* belly.......... Rom 16:18 *1438*
I had baptized in mine *o* name.......... 1Cor 1:15
his *o* reward according to his *o*.......... 1Cor 3:8 *2398*
reward according to his *o* labour.......... 1Cor 3:8 *2398*
the wise in their *o* craftiness.......... 1Cor 3:19
yea, I judge not mine *o* self.......... 1Cor 4:3 *1683*
labour, working with our *o* hands.......... 1Cor 4:12 *2398*
also raise up us by his *o* power.......... 1Cor 6:14 *848*
sinneth against his *o* body.......... 1Cor 6:18 *2398*
have of God, and ye are not your *o*.......... 1Cor 6:19 *1438*
let every man have his *o* wife.......... 1Cor 7:2 *1438*
every woman have her *o* husband.......... 1Cor 7:2 *2398*
wife hath not power of her *o* body.......... 1Cor 7:4 *2398*
hath not power of his *o* body.......... 1Cor 7:4 *2398*
And this I speak for your *o* profit.......... 1Cor 7:35 *846*
but hath power over his *o* will.......... 1Cor 7:37 *2398*
warfare any time at his *o* charges.......... 1Cor 9:7 *2398*
Let no man seek his *o*, but every.......... 1Cor 10:24 *1438*
Conscience, I say, not thine *o*.......... 1Cor 10:29 *1438*
things, not seeking mine *o* profit.......... 1Cor 10:33 *1683*
taketh before other his *o* supper.......... 1Cor 11:21 *2398*
unseemly, seeketh not her *o*.......... 1Cor 13:5 *1438*
But every man in his *o* order.......... 1Cor 15:23 *2398*
him, and to every seed his *o* body.......... 1Cor 15:38 *2398*
of me Paul with mine *o* hand.......... 1Cor 16:21 *1699*
are straitened in your *o* bowels.......... 2Cor 6:12
gave their *o* selves to the Lord.......... 2Cor 8:5
of his *o* accord he went unto you.......... 2Cor 8:17 *830*
in perils by mine *o* countrymen.......... 2Cor 11:26
prove your *o* selves.......... 2Cor 13:5
Know ye not your *o* selves.......... 2Cor 13:5

many my equals in mine *o* nation ... Gal 1:14
have plucked out your *o* eyes ... Gal 4:15
let every man prove his *o* work ... Gal 6:4 *1438*
every man shall bear his *o* burden ... Gal 6:5 *2398*
written unto you with mine *o* hand ... Gal 6:11
after the counsel of his *o* will ... Eph 1:11 *848*
set him at his *o* right hand in ... Eph 1:20 *848*
yourselves unto your *o* husbands ... Eph 5:22 *2398*
their *o* husbands in every thing ... Eph 5:24 *2398*
their wives as their *o* bodies ... Eph 5:28 *1438*
no man ever yet hated his *o* flesh ... Eph 5:29 *1438*
not every man on his *o* things ... Phil 2:4 *1438*
work out your *o* salvation with ... Phil 2:12 *1438*
For all seek their *o*, not the ... Phil 2:21
not having mine *o* righteousness ... Phil 3:9 *1699*
yourselves unto your *o* husbands ... Col 3:18 *2398*
of God only, but also our *o* souls ... 1Th 2:8 *1438*
like things of your *o* countrymen ... 1Th 2:14 *2398*
their *o* prophets, and have ... 1Th 2:15 *2398*
quiet, and to do your *o* business ... 1Th 4:11 *2398*
and to work with your *o* hands ... 1Th 4:11 *2398*
they work, and eat their *o* bread ... 2Th 3:12 *1438*
of Paul with mine *o* hand, which ... 2Th 3:17
Timothy, my *o* son in the faith ... 1Ti 1:2 *1103*
One that ruleth well his *o* house ... 1Ti 3:4 *2398*
know not how to rule his *o* house ... 1Ti 3:5 *2398*
children and their *o* houses well ... 1Ti 3:12 *2398*
But if any provide not for his *o* ... 1Ti 5:8 *2398*
for those of his *o* house, he hath ... 1Ti 5:8 *2398*
o masters worthy of all honour ... 1Ti 6:1 *2398*
but according to his *o* purpose ... 2Ti 1:9 *2398*
shall be lovers of their *o* selves ... 2Ti 3:2
but after their *o* lusts shall ... 2Ti 4:3 *2398*
mine *o* son after the common faith ... Titus 1:4 *1103*
even a prophet of their *o* ... Titus 1:12 *2398*
obedient to their *o* husbands ... Titus 2:5 *2398*
be obedient unto their *o* masters ... Titus 2:9 *2398*
him, that is, mine *o* bowels ... Philem 12
have written it with mine *o* hand ... Philem 19
unto me even thine *o* self besides ... Philem 19 *4572*
Ghost, according to his *o* will ... Heb 2:4
Christ as a son over his *o* house ... Heb 3:6 *848*
also hath ceased from his *o* works ... Heb 4:10 *848*
sacrifice, first for his *o* sins ... Heb 7:27 *2398*
but by his *o* blood he entered in ... Heb 9:12 *2398*
us after their *o* pleasure ... Heb 12:10 *848*
the people with his *o* blood ... Heb 13:12 *2398*
he is drawn away of his *o* lust ... Jas 1:14 *2398*
Of his *o* will begat he us with ... Jas 1:18
only, deceiving your *o* selves ... Jas 1:22
tongue, but deceiveth his *o* heart ... Jas 1:26 *848*
Who his *o* self bare our sins in ... 1Pet 2:24 *848*
sins in his *o* body on the tree ... 1Pet 2:24
in subjection to your *o* husbands ... 1Pet 3:1 *2398*
subjection unto their *o* husbands ... 1Pet 3:5 *2398*
perish in their *o* corruption ... 2Pet 2:12 *848*
o deceivings while they feast ... 2Pet 2:13 *848*
is turned to his *o* vomit again ... 2Pet 2:22 *2398*
walking after their *o* lusts ... 2Pet 3:3 *2398*
unto their *o* destruction ... 2Pet 3:16 *2398*
fall from your *o* stedfastness ... 2Pet 3:17 *2398*
Because his *o* works were evil, and ... 1Jn 3:12
but left their *o* habitation ... Jude 6 *2398*
sea, foaming out their *o* shame ... Jude 13 *1438*
walking after their *o* lusts ... Jude 16 *848*
walk after their *o* ungodly lusts ... Jude 18 *1438*
us from our sins in his *o* blood ... Rev 1:5 *848*

OWNER {13}
but the *o* of the ox shall be quit ... Ex 21:28 1167
it hath been testified to his *o* ... Ex 21:29 1167
his *o* also shall be put to death ... Ex 21:29 1167
The *o* of the pit shall make it ... Ex 21:34 1167
and give money unto the *o* of them ... Ex 21:34 1167
his *o* hath not kept him in ... Ex 21:36 1167
the *o* of it shall accept thereof, ... Ex 22:11 1167
restitution unto the *o* thereof ... Ex 22:12 1167
the *o* thereof being not with it, ... Ex 22:14 1167
But if the *o* thereof be with it, ... Ex 22:15 1167
of Shemer, *o* of the hill, Samaria ... 1Kin 16:24 113
The ox knoweth his *o*, and the ass ... Is 1:3 7069
the *o* of the ship, more than ... Acts 27:11 *3490*

OWNERS {5}
or have caused the *o* thereof to ... Job 31:39 1167
away the life of the *o* thereof ... Prov 1:19 1167
good is there to the *o* thereof ... Eccl 5:11 1167
riches kept for the *o* thereof to ... Eccl 5:13 1167
the *o* thereof said unto them, Why ... Lk 19:33 *2962*

OWNETH {2}
he that *o* the house shall come and ... Lev 14:35
bind the man that *o* this girdle ... Acts 21:11 *2076*

OX {64}
nor his maidservant, nor his *o* ... Ex 20:17 7794
If an *o* gore a man or a woman, ... Ex 21:28 7794
then the *o* shall be surely stoned ... Ex 21:28 7794
the owner of the *o* shall be quit ... Ex 21:28 7794
But if the *o* were wont to push ... Ex 21:29 7794
the *o* shall be stoned, and his ... Ex 21:29 7794
If the *o* shall push a manservant ... Ex 21:32 7794
silver, and the *o* shall be stoned ... Ex 21:32 7794
an *o* or an ass fall therein ... Ex 21:33 7794
if one man's *o* hurt another's, ... Ex 21:35 7794
then they shall sell the live *o* ... Ex 21:35 7794
the dead *o* also they shall divide ... Ex 21:35
Or if it be known that the *o* hath ... Ex 21:36 7794
he shall surely pay *o* for *o* ... Ex 21:36 7794
If a man shall steal an *o* ... Ex 22:1 7794
shall restore five oxen for an *o* ... Ex 22:1 7794
his hand alive, whether it be *o* ... Ex 22:4 7794
of trespass, whether it be for *o* ... Ex 22:9 7794
his neighbour an ass, or an *o* ... Ex 22:10 7794
enemy's *o* or his ass going astray ... Ex 23:4 7794
that thine *o* and thine ass may ... Ex 23:12 7794
whether *o* or sheep, that is male ... Ex 34:19 7794
shall eat no manner of fat, of *o* ... Lev 7:23 7794
of Israel, that killeth an *o* ... Lev 17:3 7794
whether it be *o*, or sheep ... Lev 27:26 7794
the princes, and for each one an *o* ... Num 7:3 7794
as the *o* licketh up the grass of ... Num 22:4 7794
nor thy maidservant, nor thine *o* ... Deut 5:14 7794
or his maidservant, his *o* ... Deut 5:21 7794
the *o*, the sheep, and the goat, ... Deut 14:4 7794
and the pygarg, and the wild *o* ... Deut 14:5 8377
whether it be *o* or sheep ... Deut 18:3 7794
o or his sheep go astray, and hide ... Deut 22:1 7794
ass or his *o* fall down by the way ... Deut 22:4 7794
Thou shalt not plow with an *o* ... Deut 22:10 7794
Thou shalt not muzzle the *o* when ... Deut 25:4 7794
Thine *o* shall be slain before ... Deut 28:31 7794
man and woman, young and old, and *o* .. Josh 6:21 7794
six hundred men with an *o* goad ... Judg 3:31 1241
for Israel, neither sheep, nor *o* ... Judg 6:4 7794
whose *o* have I taken ... 1Sa 12:3 7794
Bring me hither every man his *o* ... 1Sa 14:34 7794
man his *o* with him that night ... 1Sa 14:34 7794
and woman, infant and suckling, *o* ... 1Sa 15:3 7794
prepared for me daily was one *o* ... Neh 5:18 7794
or loweth the *o* over his fodder ... Job 6:5 7794
take the widow's *o* for a pledge ... Job 24:3 7794
he eateth grass as an *o* ... Job 40:15 1241
an *o* or bullock that hath horns ... Ps 69:31 7794
of an *o* that eateth grass ... Ps 106:20 7794
as an *o* goeth to the slaughter, ... Prov 7:22 7794
is by the strength of the *o* ... Prov 14:4 7794
where love is, than a stalled *o* ... Prov 15:17 7794
The *o* knoweth his owner, and the ... Is 1:3 7794
lion shall eat straw like the *o* ... Is 11:7 1241
forth thither the feet of the *o* ... Is 32:20 7794
He that killeth an *o* is as if he ... Is 66:3 7794
or an *o* that is brought to the ... Jer 11:19 441
the face of an *o* on the left side ... Eze 1:10 7794
his *o* or his ass from the stall ... Lk 13:15 *1016*
an ass or an *o* fallen into a pit ... Lk 14:5 *1016*
the *o* that treadeth out the corn ... 1Cor 9:9 *1016*
Thou shalt not muzzle the *o* that ... 1Ti 5:18 *1016*

OXEN {102}
and he had sheep, and *o*, and he ... Gen 12:16 1241
And Abimelech took sheep, and *o* ... Gen 20:14 1241
And Abraham took sheep and *o* ... Gen 21:27 1241
And I have *o*, and asses, flocks, and ... Gen 32:5 7794
They took their sheep, and their *o* ... Gen 34:28 1241
upon the camels, upon the *o* ... Ex 9:3 1241
offerings, thy sheep, and thine *o* ... Ex 20:24 1241
he shall restore five *o* for an ox ... Ex 22:1 1241
shalt thou do with thine *o* ... Ex 22:30 7794
offerings of *o* unto the LORD ... Ex 24:5 6499
six covered wagons, and twelve *o* ... Num 7:3 1241
And Moses took the wagons and the *o* ... Num 7:6 1241
four *o* he gave unto the sons of ... Num 7:7 1241
eight *o* he gave unto the sons of ... Num 7:8 1241
of peace offerings, two *o* ... Num 7:17 1241
of peace offerings, two *o* ... Num 7:23 1241
of peace offerings, two *o* ... Num 7:29 1241
of peace offerings, two *o* ... Num 7:35 1241
of peace offerings, two *o* ... Num 7:41 1241
of peace offerings, two *o* ... Num 7:47 1241
of peace offerings, two *o* ... Num 7:53 1241
of peace offerings, two *o* ... Num 7:59 1241
of peace offerings, two *o* ... Num 7:65 1241
of peace offerings, two *o* ... Num 7:71 1241
of peace offerings, two *o* ... Num 7:77 1241
of peace offerings, two *o* ... Num 7:83 1241
All the *o* for the burnt offering ... Num 7:87 1241
all the *o* for the sacrifice of ... Num 7:88 1241
And Balak offered *o* and sheep, and ... Num 22:40 1241
and prepare me here seven *o* ... Num 23:1 6499
thy soul lusteth after, for *o* ... Deut 14:26 1241
sons, and his daughters, and his *o* ... Josh 7:24 7794
And he took a yoke of *o*, and hewed ... 1Sa 11:7 1241
so shall it be done unto his *o* ... 1Sa 11:7 1241
which a yoke of *o* might plow ... 1Sa 14:14
the spoil, and took sheep, and *o* ... 1Sa 14:32 1241
best of the sheep, and of the *o* ... 1Sa 15:9 1241
the lowing of the *o* which I hear ... 1Sa 15:14 1241
the best of the sheep and of the *o* ... 1Sa 15:15 1241
took of the spoil, sheep and *o* ... 1Sa 15:21 1241
children and sucklings, and *o* ... 1Sa 22:19 7794
and took away the sheep, and the *o* ... 1Sa 27:9 1241
for the *o* shook it ... 2Sa 6:6 1241
gone six paces, he sacrificed *o* ... 2Sa 6:13 7794
here be *o* for burnt sacrifice, and ... 2Sa 24:22 1241
instruments of the *o* for wood ... 2Sa 24:22 1241
the *o* for fifty shekels of silver ... 2Sa 24:24 1241
And Adonijah slew sheep and *o* ... 1Kin 1:9 1241
And he hath slain *o* and fat cattle ... 1Kin 1:19 7794
down this day, and hath slain *o* ... 1Kin 1:25 7794
Ten fat *o*, and twenty *o* out of ... 1Kin 4:23 1241
It stood upon twelve *o*, three ... 1Kin 7:25 1241
between the ledges were lions, *o* ... 1Kin 7:29 1241
o were certain additions made of ... 1Kin 7:29 1241
sea, and twelve *o* under the sea ... 1Kin 7:44 1241
the ark, sacrificing sheep and *o* ... 1Kin 8:5 1241
LORD, two and twenty thousand *o* ... 1Kin 8:63 1241
with twelve yoke of *o* before him ... 1Kin 19:19
And he left the *o*, and ran after ... 1Kin 19:20 1241
from him, and took a yoke of *o* ... 1Kin 19:21 1241
with the instruments of the *o* ... 1Kin 19:21 1241
and vineyards, and sheep, and *o* ... 2Kin 5:26 1241
the brasen *o* that were under it ... 2Kin 16:17 1241
on camels, and on mules, and on *o* ... 1Chr 12:40 1241
of raisins, and wine, and oil, and *o* ... 1Chr 12:40 1241
for the *o* stumbled ... 1Chr 13:9 1241
I give thee the *o* also for burnt ... 1Chr 21:23 1241
under it was the similitude of *o* ... 2Chr 4:3 1241
Two rows of *o* were cast, when it ... 2Chr 4:3 1241
It stood upon twelve *o*, three ... 2Chr 4:4 1241
One sea, and twelve *o* under it ... 2Chr 4:15 1241
the ark, sacrificed sheep and *o* ... 2Chr 5:6 1241
of twenty and two thousand *o* ... 2Chr 7:5 1241
they had brought, seven hundred *o* ... 2Chr 15:11 1241
o for him in abundance, and for ... 2Chr 18:2 1241
things were six hundred *o* ... 2Chr 29:33 1241
also brought in the tithe of *o* ... 2Chr 31:6 1241
small cattle, and three hundred *o* ... 2Chr 35:8 1241
small cattle, and five hundred *o* ... 2Chr 35:9 1241
And so did they with the *o* ... 2Chr 35:12 1241
camels, and five hundred yoke of *o* ... Job 1:3 1241
The *o* were plowing, and the asses ... Job 1:14 1241
camels, and a thousand yoke of *o* ... Job 42:12 1241
All sheep and *o*, yea, and the ... Ps 8:7 504
That our *o* may be strong to ... Ps 144:14 441
Where no *o* are, the crib is clean ... Prov 14:4 5091
be for the sending forth of *o* ... Is 7:25 7794
behold joy and gladness, slaying *o* ... Is 22:13 1241
The *o* likewise and the young asses ... Is 30:24 504
the husbandman and his yoke of *o* ... Jer 51:23
shall make thee to eat grass as *o* ... Dan 4:25 8450
shall make thee to eat grass as *o* ... Dan 4:32 8450
from men, and did eat grass as *o* ... Dan 4:33 8450
they fed him with grass like *o* ... Dan 5:21 8450
will one plow there with *o* ... Amos 6:12 1241
my *o* and my fatlings are killed, ... Mt 22:4 *5022*
I have bought five yoke of *o* ... Lk 14:19 *1016*
in the temple those that sold *o* ... Jn 2:14 *1016*
temple, and the sheep, and the *o* ... Jn 2:15 *1016*
was before their city, brought *o* ... Acts 14:13 *5022*
Doth God take care for *o* ... 1Cor 9:9 *1016*

OZEM *(o'-zem)* {2}
1. Son of Jesse.
O the sixth, David the seventh ... 1Chr 2:15 684
2. Son of Jerahmeel.
and Bunah, and Oren, and *O*, and ... 1Chr 2:25 684

OZIAS *(o-zi'-as)* {2} See UZZIAH. *Son of Joram; ancestor of Jesus.*
and Joram begat *O* ... Mt 1:8 *3604*
And *O* begat Joatham ... Mt 1:9 *3604*

OZNI *(oz'-ni)* {1} See OZNITES. *A son of Gad.*
Of *O*, the family of the Oznites ... Num 26:16 244

OZNITES *(oz'-nites)* {1} *Descendants of Ozni.*
Of Ozni, the family of the *O* ... Num 26:16 244

P

PAARAI *(pa'-ar-ahee)* {1} See NOARAI. *A "mighty man" of David.*
the Carmelite, *P* the Arbite, ... 2Sa 23:35 6474

PACATIANA *(pa-ca-she-a'-nah)* {1} *A region of Phrygia in Asia Minor.*
is the chiefest city of Phrygia *P* ... 1Ti *s* *3818*

PACES {1}
ark of the LORD had gone six *p* ... 2Sa 6:13 6806

PACIFIED {2}
Then was the king's wrath *p* ... Est 7:10 7918
when I am *p* toward thee for all ... Eze 16:63 3722

PACIFIETH {2}
A gift in secret *p* anger ... Prov 21:14 3711
for yielding *p* great offences ... Eccl 10:4 3240

PACIFY {1}
but a wise man will *p* it ... Prov 16:14 3722

PADAN *(pa'-dan)* {1} See PADAN-ARAM. *Same as Padan-aram.*
And as for me, when I came from *P* ... Gen 48:7 6307

PADAN-ARAM *(pa'-dan-a'-ram)* {10} *The plains of Mesopotamia.*
of Bethuel the Syrian of *P* ... Gen 25:20 6307
Arise, go to *P*, to the house of ... Gen 28:2 6307
and he went to *P* unto Laban ... Gen 28:5 6307

Jacob, and sent him away to *P* .... Gen 28:6 6307
and his mother, and was gone to *P* .... Gen 28:7 6307
getting, which he had gotten in *P* .... Gen 31:18 6307
of Canaan, when he came from *P* .... Gen 33:18 6307
again, when he came out of *P* .... Gen 35:9 6307
which were born to him in *P* .... Gen 35:26 6307
which she bare unto Jacob in *P* .... Gen 46:15 6307

PADDLE {1}
shalt have a *p* upon thy weapon .... Deut 23:13 3489

PADON *(pa'-don)* {2} *A family of exiles.*
of Siaha, the children of *P* .... Ezr 2:44 6303
of Sia, the children of *P* .... Neh 7:47 6303

PAGIEL *(pa'-ghe-el)* {5} *An Asherite who counted the people.*
P the son of Ocran .... Num 1:13 6295
Asher shall be *P* the son of Ocran .... Num 2:27 6295
eleventh day *P* the son of Ocran .... Num 7:72 6295
offering of *P* the son of Ocran .... Num 7:77 6295
of Asher was *P* the son of Ocran .... Num 10:26 6295

PAHATH-MOAB *(pa'-hath-mo'-ab)* {6}
1. A family of exiles.
The children of *P*, of the .... Ezr 2:6 6355
And of the sons of *P* .... Ezr 10:30 6355
of Harim, and Hashub the son of *P* .... Neh 3:11 6355
The children of *P*, of the .... Neh 7:11 6355
2. Another family of exiles.
Of the sons of *P* .... Ezr 8:4 6355
3. A family who renewed the covenant.
Parosh, *P*, Elam, Zatthu, Bani, ... Neh 10:14 6355

PAI *(pa'-i)* {1} See PAU. *A city in Edom.*
and the name of his city was *P* 1Chr 1:50 6464

PAID {4}
and custom, was *p* unto them .... Ezr 4:20 3052
so he *p* the fare thereof, and went .... Jonah 1:3 5414
till thou hast *p* the uttermost .... Mt 5:26 *591*
till thou hast *p* the very last .... Lk 12:59 *591*

PAIN {25}
his flesh upon him shall have *p* .... Job 14:22 3510
travaileth with *p* all his days .... Job 15:20
also with *p* upon his bed, and the .... Job 33:19 4341
of his bones with strong *p* .... Job 33:19
Look upon mine affliction and my *p* .... Ps 25:18 5999
took hold upon them there, and *p* .... Ps 48:6 2427
they shall be in *p* as a woman .... Is 13:8 2342
are my loins filled with *p* .... Is 21:3 2479
the time of her delivery, is in *p* .... Is 26:17 2342
with child, we have been in *p* .... Is 26:18 2342
before her *p* came, she was .... Is 66:7 2256
hath taken hold of us, and *p* .... Jer 6:24 2427
they have put themselves to *p* .... Jer 12:13 2470
Why is my *p* perpetual, and my .... Jer 15:18 3511
the *p* as of a woman in travail .... Jer 22:23 2427
it shall fall with *p* upon the .... Jer 30:23 2342
take balm for her *p*, if so be she .... Jer 51:8 4341
great *p* shall be in Ethiopia, ... Eze 30:4 2479
great *p* shall come upon them, as .... Eze 30:9 2479
Sin shall have great *p*, and No .... Eze 30:16 2342
Be in *p*, and labour to bring forth .... Mic 4:10 2342
much *p* is in all loins, and the .... Nah 2:10 2479
travaileth in *p* together until .... Rom 8:22
they gnawed their tongues for *p* .... Rev 16:10 *4192*
neither shall there be any more *p* .... Rev 21:4 *4192*

PAINED {5}
My heart is sore *p* within me .... Ps 55:4 2342
be sorely *p* at the report of Tyre .... Is 23:5 2342
I am *p* at my very heart .... Jer 4:19 3176
face the people shall be much *p* .... Joel 2:6 2342
in birth, and *p* to be delivered .... Rev 12:2 *928*

PAINFUL {1}
to know this, it was too *p* for me .... Ps 73:16 5999

PAINFULNESS {1}
In weariness and *p*, in watchings 2Cor 11:27 *3449*

PAINS {4}
for her *p* came upon her 1Sa 4:19 6735
the *p* of hell gat hold upon me .... Ps 116:3 4712
up, having loosed the *p* of death .... Acts 2:24 *5604*
God of heaven because of their *p* .... Rev 16:11 *4192*

PAINTED {2}
she *p* her face, and tired her head ... 2Kin 9:30 7760,6320
with cedar, and *p* with vermilion .... Jer 22:14 4886

PAINTEDST {1}
p thy eyes, and deckedst thyself .... Eze 23:40 3583

PAINTING {1}
thou rentest thy face with *p* .... Jer 4:30 6320

PAIR {4}
and the poor for a *p* of shoes .... Amos 2:6
and the needy for a *p* of shoes .... Amos 8:6
A *p* of turtledoves, or two young .... Lk 2:24 *2201*
had a *p* of balances in his hand .... Rev 6:5 *2218*

PALACE {48}
into the *p* of the king's house 1Kin 16:18 759
hard by the *p* of Ahab king of 1Kin 21:1 1964
in the *p* of the king's house, ... 2Kin 15:25 759
in the *p* of the king of Babylon 2Kin 20:18 1964
for the *p* is not for man, but for 1Chr 29:1 1002
these things, and to build the *p* 1Chr 29:19 1002
of the LORD, and to the king's *p* 2Chr 9:11 1004
maintenance from the king's *p* .... Ezr 4:14 1964
in the *p* that is in the province .... Ezr 6:2 1002
year, as I was in Shushan the *p* .... Neh 1:1 1002
p which appertained to the house .... Neh 2:8 1002
and Hananiah the ruler of the *p* .... Neh 7:2 1002
which was in Shushan the *p* .... Est 1:2 1002
were present in Shushan the *p* .... Est 1:5 1002
of the garden of the king's *p* .... Est 1:5 1055
young virgins unto Shushan the *p* .... Est 2:3 1002
Now in Shushan the *p* there was a .... Est 2:5 1002
together unto Shushan the *p* .... Est 2:8 1002
decree was given in Shushan the *p* .... Est 3:15 1002
his wrath went into the *p* garden .... Est 7:7 1055
p garden into the place of the .... Est 7:8 1055
decree was given at Shushan the *p* .... Est 8:14 1002
And in Shushan the *p* the Jews slew .... Est 9:6 1002
the *p* was brought before the king .... Est 9:11 1002
five hundred men in Shushan the *p* .... Est 9:12 1002
shall enter into the king's *p* .... Ps 45:15 1964
after the similitude of a *p* .... Ps 144:12 1964
will build upon her a *p* of silver .... Song 8:9 2918
a *p* of strangers to be no city .... Is 25:2 759
in the *p* of the king of Babylon .... Is 39:7 1964
the *p* shall remain after the .... Jer 30:18 759
in them to stand in the king's *p* .... Dan 1:4 1964
house, and flourishing in my *p* .... Dan 4:4 1965
the *p* of the kingdom of Babylon .... Dan 4:29 1965
of the wall of the king's *p* .... Dan 5:5 1965
Then the king went to his *p* .... Dan 6:18 1965
that I was at Shushan in the *p* .... Dan 8:2 1002
of his *p* between the seas in the .... Dan 11:45 643
and ye shall cast them into the *p* .... Amos 4:3 2038
and the *p* shall be dissolved .... Nah 2:6 1964
unto the *p* of the high priest, ... Mt 26:3 *833*
afar off unto the high priest's *p* .... Mt 26:58 *833*
Now Peter sat without in the *p* .... Mt 26:69 *833*
even into the *p* of the high .... Mk 14:54 *833*
And as Peter was beneath in the *p* .... Mk 14:66 *833*
a strong man armed keepeth his *p* .... Lk 11:21 *833*
into the *p* of the high priest .... Jn 18:15 *833*
Christ are manifest in all the *p* .... Phil 1:13 *4232*

PALACES {33}
burnt all the *p* thereof with fire 2Chr 36:19 759
and cassia, out of the ivory *p* .... Ps 45:8 1964
is known in her *p* for a refuge .... Ps 48:3 759
well her bulwarks, consider her *p* .... Ps 48:13 759
built his sanctuary like high *p* .... Ps 78:69
walls, and prosperity within thy *p* .... Ps 122:7 759
with her hands, and is in kings' *p* .... Prov 30:28 1964
and dragons in their pleasant *p* .... Is 13:22 1964
they raised up the *p* thereof .... Is 23:13 759
Because the *p* shall be forsaken .... Is 32:14 759
And thorns shall come up in her *p* .... Is 34:13 759
by night, and let us destroy her *p* .... Jer 6:5 759
windows, and is entered into our *p* .... Jer 9:21 759
shall devour the *p* of Jerusalem .... Jer 17:27 759
shall consume the *p* of Ben-hadad .... Jer 49:27 759
he hath swallowed up all her *p* .... Lam 2:5 759
of the enemy the walls of her *p* .... Lam 2:7 759
And he knew their desolate *p* .... Eze 19:7 759
and they shall set their *p* in thee .... Eze 25:4 2918
and it shall devour the *p* thereof .... Hos 8:14 759
shall devour the *p* of Ben-hadad .... Amos 1:4 759
which shall devour the *p* thereof .... Amos 1:7 759
which shall devour the *p* thereof .... Amos 1:10 759
shall devour the *p* of Bozrah .... Amos 1:12 759
and it shall devour the *p* thereof .... Amos 1:14 759
it shall devour the *p* of Kirioth .... Amos 2:2 759
shall devour the *p* of Jerusalem .... Amos 2:5 759
Publish in the *p* at Ashdod .... Amos 3:9 759
in the *p* in the land of Egypt, and .... Amos 3:9 759
up violence and robbery in their *p* .... Amos 3:10 759
thee, and thy *p* shall be spoiled .... Amos 3:11 759
of Jacob, and hate his *p* .... Amos 6:8 759
and when he shall tread in our *p* .... Mic 5:5 759

PALAL *(pa'-lal)* {1} *A rebuilder of Jerusalem's wall.*
P the son of Uzai, over against .... Neh 3:25 6420

PALE {2}
neither shall his face now wax *p* .... Is 29:22 2357
And I looked, and behold a *p* horse .... Rev 6:8 *5515*

PALENESS {1}
and all faces are turned into *p* .... Jer 30:6 3420

PALESTINA *(pal-es-ti'-nah)* {3} See PALESTINE, PHILISTIA. *The west coast of Canaan.*
take hold on the inhabitants of *P* .... Ex 15:14 6429
Rejoice not thou, whole *P* .... Is 14:29 6429
thou, whole *P*, art dissolved .... Is 14:31 6429

PALESTINE *(pal'-es-tine)* {1} See PALESTINA. *Same as Palestina.*
and Zidon, and all the coasts of *P* .... Joel 3:4 6429

PALLU *(pal'-lu)* {4} See PALLUITES, PHALLU. *A son of Reuben.*
Hanoch, and *P*, Hezron, and Carmi .... Ex 6:14 6396
of *P*, the family of the Palluites .... Num 26:5 6396
And the sons of *P* .... Num 26:8 6396
of Israel were, Hanoch, and *P* 1Chr 5:3 6396

PALLUITES *(pal'-lu-ites)* {1} *Descendants of Pallu.*
of Pallu, the family of the *P* .... Num 26:5 6384

PALM {35}
and threescore and ten *p* trees .... Ex 15:27 8558
pour it into the *p* of his own .... Lev 14:15 3709
into the *p* of his own left hand .... Lev 14:26 3709
goodly trees, branches of *p* trees .... Lev 23:40 8558
and threescore and ten *p* trees .... Num 33:9 8558
of Jericho, the city of *p* trees .... Deut 34:3 8558
of *p* trees with the children of .... Judg 1:16 8558
and possessed the city of *p* trees .... Judg 3:13 8558
she dwelt under the *p* tree of .... Judg 4:5 8560
p trees and open flowers, within 1Kin 6:29 8561
p trees and open flowers, and 1Kin 6:32 8561
cherubims, and upon the *p* trees 1Kin 6:32 8561
and *p* trees and open flowers 1Kin 6:35 8561
p trees, according to the 1Kin 7:36 8561
fine gold, and set thereon *p* trees 2Chr 3:5 8561
to Jericho, the city of *p* trees 2Chr 28:15 8558
p branches, and branches of thick .... Neh 8:15 8558
shall flourish like the *p* tree .... Ps 92:12 8558
thy stature is like to a *p* tree .... Song 7:7 8558
said, I will go up to the *p* tree .... Song 7:8 8558
They are upright as the *p* tree .... Jer 10:5 8560
and upon each post were *p* trees .... Eze 40:16 8561
and their arches, and their *p* trees .... Eze 40:22 8561
and it had *p* trees, one on this .... Eze 40:26 8561
p trees were upon the posts .... Eze 40:31 8561
p trees were upon the posts .... Eze 40:34 8561
p trees were upon the posts .... Eze 40:37 8561
toward the *p* tree on the one side .... Eze 41:19 8561
the *p* tree on the other side .... Eze 41:19 8561
p trees made, and on the wall of .... Eze 41:20 8561
p trees, like as were made upon .... Eze 41:25 8561
p trees on the one side and on the .... Eze 41:26 8561
the *p* tree also, and the apple .... Joel 1:12 8558
Took branches of *p* trees, and went .... Jn 12:13 *5404*
Jesus with the *p* of his hand .... Jn 18:22 *4475*

PALMERWORM {3}
That which the *p* hath left hath .... Joel 1:4 1501
and the caterpiller, and the *p* .... Joel 2:25 1501
increased, the *p* devoured them .... Amos 4:9 1501

PALMS {7}
both the *p* of his hands were cut 1Sa 5:4 3709
the feet, and the *p* of her hands 2Kin 9:35 3709
thee upon the *p* of my hands .... Is 49:16 3709
knees and upon the *p* of my hands .... Dan 10:10 3709
him with the *p* of their hands .... Mt 26:67 *4474*
him with the *p* of their hands .... Mk 14:65 *4475*
white robes, and *p* in their hands .... Rev 7:9 *5404*

PALSIES {1}
and many taken with *p*, and that .... Acts 8:7 *3886*

PALSY {13}
lunatick, and those that had the *p* .... Mt 4:24 *3885*
lieth at home sick of the *p* .... Mt 8:6 *3885*
to him a man sick of the *p* .... Mt 9:2 *3885*
faith said unto the sick of the *p* .... Mt 9:2 *3885*
saith he to the sick of the *p* .... Mt 9:6 *3885*
him, bringing one sick of the *p* .... Mk 2:3 *3885*
bed wherein the sick of the *p* lay .... Mk 2:4 *3885*
he said unto the sick of the *p* .... Mk 2:5 *3885*
to say to the sick of the *p* .... Mk 2:9 *3885*
(he saith to the sick of the *p* .... Mk 2:10 *3885*
a man which was taken with a *p* .... Lk 5:18 *3886*
(he said unto the sick of the *p* .... Lk 5:24 *3886*
eight years, and was sick of the *p* .... Acts 9:33 *3886*

PALTI *(pal'-ti)* {1} *A spy sent to the Promised Land.*
of Benjamin, *P* the son of Raphu .... Num 13:9 6406

PALTIEL *(pal'-te-el)* {1} See PHALTIEL. *A chief of Issachar.*
of Issachar, *P* the son of Azzan .... Num 34:26 6409

PALTITE *(pal'-tite)* {1} See PELONITE. *A resident of Beth-palet.*
Helez the *P*, Ira the son of 2Sa 23:26 6407

PAMPHYLIA *(pam-fil'-e-ah)* {5} *A province of Asia Minor.*
Phrygia, and *P*, in Egypt, and in .... Acts 2:10 *3828*
Paphos, they came to Perga in *P* .... Acts 13:13 *3828*
Pisidia, they came to *P* .... Acts 14:24 *3828*
who departed from them from *P* .... Acts 15:38 *3828*
over the sea of Cilicia and *P* .... Acts 27:5 *3828*

PAN {8}
be a meat offering baken in a *p* .... Lev 2:5 4227
offering baken in the frying *p* .... Lev 2:7 4227
In a *p* it shall be made with oil .... Lev 6:21 4227
in the fryingpan, and in the *p* .... Lev 7:9 4227
And he struck it into the *p* 1Sa 2:14 3595
And she took a *p*, and poured them 2Sa 13:9 4958
for that which is baked in the *p* 1Chr 23:29 4227
take thou unto thee an iron *p* .... Eze 4:3 4227

PANGS {9}
p and sorrows shall take hold of .... Is 13:8 6735
p have taken hold upon me, as the .... Is 21:3 6735
upon me, as the *p* of a woman that .... Is 21:3 6735
in pain, and crieth out in her *p* .... Is 26:17 2256
thou be when *p* come upon thee .... Jer 22:23 2256
as the heart of a woman in her *p* .... Jer 48:41 6887
as the heart of a woman in her *p* .... Jer 49:22 6887
p as of a woman in travail .... Jer 50:43 2427
for *p* have taken thee as a woman .... Mic 4:9 2427

PANNAG *(pan'-nag)* {1} *A place on the Damascus-Baalbeck road.*
thy market wheat of Minnith, and *P* .... Eze 27:17 6436

PANS {4}
thou shalt make his *p* to receive .... Ex 27:3 5518
it in a mortar, and baked it in *p* .... Num 11:8 6517
things that were made in the *p* 1Chr 9:31 2281
in pots, and in caldrons, and in *p* 2Chr 35:13 6745

PANT {1}
That *p* after the dust of the .... Amos 2:7 7602

PANTED {2}
I opened my mouth, and *p* .... Ps 119:131 7602
My heart *p*, fearfulness .... Is 21:4 8582

PANTETH {3}
My heart *p*, my strength faileth .... Ps 38:10 5503
As the hart *p* after the water .... Ps 42:1 6165
so *p* my soul after thee, O God .... Ps 42:1 6165

PAPER {2}
The p reeds by the brooks, by the ... Is 19:7 6169
you, I would not write with p ... 2Jn 12 5489

PAPHOS *(pa'-fos)* {2} *Capital of Cyprus.*
had gone through the isle unto P ... Acts 13:6 3974
Paul and his company loosed from P ... Acts 13:13 3974

PAPS {4}
Egyptians for the p of thy youth ... Eze 23:21 7699
the p which thou hast sucked ... Lk 11:27 3149
the p which never gave suck ... Lk 23:29 3149
girt about the p with a golden ... Rev 1:13 3149

PARABLE {49}
And he took up his p, and said, ... Num 23:7 4912
And he took up his p, and said, ... Num 23:18 4912
And he took up his p, and said, ... Num 24:3 4912
And he took up his p, and said, ... Num 24:15 4912
on Amalek, he took up his p ... Num 24:20 4912
on the Kenites, and took up his p ... Num 24:21 4912
And he took up his p, and said, ... Num 24:23 4912
Moreover Job continued his p ... Job 27:1 4912
Moreover Job continued his p ... Job 29:1 4912
I will incline mine ear to a p ... Ps 49:4 4912
I will open my mouth in a p ... Ps 78:2 4912
so is a p in the mouth of fools ... Prov 26:7 4912
so is a p in the mouth of fools ... Prov 26:9 4912
speak a p unto the house of ... Eze 17:2 4912
utter a p unto the rebellious ... Eze 24:3 4912
shall one take up a p against you ... Mic 2:4 4912
all these take up a p against him ... Hab 2:6 4912
ye therefore the p of the sower ... Mt 13:18 3850
Another p put he forth unto them, ... Mt 13:24 3850
Another p put he forth unto them, ... Mt 13:31 3850
Another p spake he unto them ... Mt 13:33 3850
without a p spake he not unto ... Mt 13:34 3850
Declare unto us the p of the ... Mt 13:36 3850
unto him, Declare unto us this p ... Mt 15:15 3850
Hear another p ... Mt 21:33 3850
Now learn a p of the fig tree ... Mt 24:32 3850
the twelve asked of him the p ... Mk 4:10 3850
unto them, Know ye not this p ... Mk 4:13 3850
But without a p spake he not unto ... Mk 4:34 3850
asked him concerning the p ... Mk 7:17 3850
he had spoken the p against them ... Mk 12:12 3850
Now learn a p of the fig tree ... Mk 13:28 3850
And he spake also a p unto them ... Lk 5:36 3850
And he spake a p unto them ... Lk 6:39 3850
of every city, he spake by a p ... Lk 8:4 3850
him, saying, What might this p be ... Lk 8:9 3850
Now the p is this ... Lk 8:11 3850
And he spake a p unto them ... Lk 12:16 3850
speakest thou this p unto us ... Lk 12:41 3850
He spake also this p ... Lk 13:6 3850
he put forth a p to those which ... Lk 14:7 3850
And he spake this p unto them ... Lk 15:3 3850
he spake a p unto them to this ... Lk 18:1 3850
he spake this p unto certain ... Lk 18:9 3850
things, he added and spake a p ... Lk 19:11 3850
he to speak to the people this p ... Lk 20:9 3850
he had spoken this p against them ... Lk 20:19 3850
And he spake to them a p ... Lk 21:29 3850
This p spake Jesus unto them ... Jn 10:6 3942

PARABLES {16}
say of me, Doth he not speak p ... Eze 20:49 4912
spake many things unto them in p ... Mt 13:3 3850
Why speakest thou unto them in p ... Mt 13:10 3850
Therefore speak I to them in p ... Mt 13:13 3850
Jesus unto the multitude in p ... Mt 13:34 3850
saying, I will open my mouth in p ... Mt 13:35 3850
when Jesus had finished these p ... Mt 13:53 3850
and Pharisees had heard his p ... Mt 21:45 3850
and spake unto them again by p ... Mt 22:1 3850
unto him, and said unto them in p ... Mk 3:23 3850
he taught them many things by p ... Mk 4:2 3850
all these things are done in p ... Mk 4:11 3850
and how then will ye know all p ... Mk 4:13 3850
with many such p spake he the ... Mk 4:33 3850
he began to speak unto them by p ... Mk 12:1 3850
but to others in p ... Lk 8:10 3850

PARADISE {3}
To day shalt thou be with me in p ... Lk 23:43 3857
How that he was caught up into p ... 2Cor 12:4 3857
is in the midst of the p of God ... Rev 2:7 3857

PARAH *(pa'-rah)* {1} *A city in Benjamin.*
And Avim, and P, and Ophrah, ... Josh 18:23 6511

PARAMOURS {1}
For she doted upon their p ... Eze 23:20 6370

PARAN *(pa'-ran)* {11} *A wilderness south of Canaan.*
he dwelt in the wilderness of P ... Gen 21:21 6290
rested in the wilderness of P ... Num 10:12 6290
and pitched in the wilderness of P ... Num 12:16 6290
them from the wilderness of P ... Num 13:3 6290
Israel, unto the wilderness of P ... Num 13:26 6290
against the Red sea, between P ... Deut 1:1 6290
he shined forth from mount P ... Deut 33:2 6290
went down to the wilderness of P ... 1Sa 25:1 6290
arose out of Midian, and came to P ... 1Kin 11:18 6290
they took men with them out of P ... 1Kin 11:18 6290
and the Holy One from mount P ... Hab 3:3 6290

PARBAR *(par'-bar)* {2} *A place near the Temple in Jerusalem.*
At P westward, four at the ... 1Chr 26:18 6503
four at the causeway, and two at P ... 1Chr 26:18 6503

PARCEL {6}
And he bought a p of a field ... Gen 33:19 2513
in a p of ground which Jacob ... Josh 24:32 2513
of Moab, selleth a p of land ... Ruth 4:3 2513
where was a p of ground full of ... 1Chr 11:13 2513
themselves in the midst of that p ... 1Chr 11:14 2513
near to the p of ground that ... Jn 4:5 5564

PARCHED {9}
nor p corn, nor green ears, until ... Lev 23:14 7039
p corn in the selfsame day ... Josh 5:11
and he reached her p corn, and she ... Ruth 2:14 7039
brethren an ephah of this p corn ... 1Sa 17:17 7039
and five measures of p corn ... 1Sa 25:18 7039
p corn, and beans, and lentiles, and ... 2Sa 17:28 7039
beans, and lentiles, and p pulse, ... 2Sa 17:28 7039
the p ground shall become a pool, ... Is 35:7 8273
but shall inhabit the p places in ... Jer 17:6 2788

PARCHMENTS {1}
the books, but especially the p ... 2Ti 4:13 3200

PARDON {16}
for he will not p your ... Ex 23:21 5375
p our iniquity and our sin, and ... Ex 34:9 5545
P, I beseech thee, the iniquity ... Num 14:19 5545
p my sin, and turn again with me, ... 1Sa 15:25 5375
this thing the LORD p thy servant ... 2Kin 5:18 5545
the LORD p thy servant in this ... 2Kin 5:18 5545
which the LORD would not p ... 2Kin 24:4 5545
saying, The good LORD p every one ... 2Chr 30:18 3722
but thou art a God ready to p ... Neh 9:17 5547
dost thou not p my transgression ... Job 7:21 5375
sake, O LORD, p mine iniquity ... Ps 25:11 5545
our God, for he will abundantly p ... Is 55:7 5545
and I will p it ... Jer 5:1 5545
How shall I p thee for this ... Jer 5:7 5545
I will p all their iniquities, ... Jer 33:8 5545
for I will p them whom I reserve ... Jer 50:20 5545

PARDONED {3}
I have p according to thy word ... Num 14:20 5545
that her iniquity is p ... Is 40:2 7521
thou hast not p ... Lam 3:42 5545

PARDONETH {1}
that p iniquity, and passeth by ... Mic 7:18 5375

PARE {1}
shave her head, and p her nails ... Deut 21:12 6213

PARENTS {21}
shall rise up against their p ... Mt 10:21 1118
shall rise up against their p ... Mk 13:12 1118
when the p brought in the child ... Lk 2:27 1118
Now his p went to Jerusalem every ... Lk 2:41 1118
And her p were astonished ... Lk 8:56 1118
no man that hath left house, or p ... Lk 18:29 1118
And ye shall be betrayed both by p ... Lk 21:16 1118
who did sin, this man, or his p ... Jn 9:2 1118
hath this man sinned, nor his p ... Jn 9:3 1118
until they called the p of him ... Jn 9:18 1118
His p answered them and said, We ... Jn 9:20 1118
These words spake his p, because ... Jn 9:22 1118
Therefore said his p, He is of ... Jn 9:23 1118
of evil things, disobedient to p ... Rom 1:30 1118
ought not to lay up for the p ... 2Cor 12:14 1118
but the p for the children ... 2Cor 12:14 1118
Children, obey your p in the Lord ... Eph 6:1 1118
obey your p in all things ... Col 3:20 1118
at home, and to requite their p ... 1Ti 5:4 4269
blasphemers, disobedient to p ... 2Ti 3:2 1118
was hid three months of his p ... Heb 11:23 3962

PARLOUR {5}
and he was sitting in a summer p ... Judg 3:20 5944
shut the doors of the p upon him ... Judg 3:23 5944
the doors of the p were locked ... Judg 3:24 5944
he opened not the doors of the p ... Judg 3:25 5944
and brought them into the p ... 1Sa 9:22 3957

PARLOURS {1}
and of the inner p thereof ... 1Chr 28:11 2315

PARMASHTA *(par-mash'-tah)* {1} *A son of Haman.*
And P, and Arisai, and Aridai, and ... Est 9:9 6534

PARMENAS *(par'-me-nas)* {1} *A leader in the Jerusalem church.*
and Nicanor, and Timon, and P ... Acts 6:5 3937

PARNACH *(par'-nak)* {1} *A Zebulunite who apportioned the Promised Land.*
Zebulun, Elizaphan the son of P ... Num 34:25 6535

PAROSH *(pa'-rosh)* {5} See PHAROSH.
1. A family of exiles.
The children of P, two thousand ... Ezr 2:3 6551
The children of P, two thousand ... Neh 7:8 6551
2. Married a foreigner in exile.
of the sons of P ... Ezr 10:25 6551
3. Father of Pedaiah.
After him Pedaiah the son of P ... Neh 3:25 6551
4. A family who renewed the covenant.
P, Pahath-moab, Elam, Zatthu, ... Neh 10:14 6551

PARSHANDATHA *(par-shan'-da-thah)* {1} *A son of Haman.*
And P, and Dalphon, and Aspatha, ... Est 9:7 6577

PART See APPENDIX.

PARTAKER {9}
hast been p with adulterers ... Ps 50:18 2506
in hope should be p of his hope ... 1Cor 9:10 3348
that I might be p thereof with ... 1Cor 9:23 4791
For if I by grace be a p, why am ... 1Cor 10:30 3348
neither be p of other men's sins ... 1Ti 5:22 2841
but be thou p of the afflictions ... 2Ti 1:8 4777
must be first p of the fruits ... 2Ti 2:6 3335
also a p of the glory that shall ... 1Pet 5:1 2844
God speed is p of his evil deeds ... 2Jn 11 2841

PARTAKERS {22}
we would not have been p with ... Mt 23:30 2844
made p of their spiritual things ... Rom 15:27 2841
If others be p of this power over ... 1Cor 9:12 3348
at the altar are p with the altar ... 1Cor 9:13 4829
for we are all p of that one ... 1Cor 10:17 3348
of the sacrifices p of the altar ... 1Cor 10:18 2844
ye cannot be p of the Lord's ... 1Cor 10:21 3348
knowing, that as ye are p of the ... 2Cor 1:7 2844
p of his promise in Christ by the ... Eph 3:6 4830
Be not ye therefore p with them ... Eph 5:7 4830
gospel, ye all are p of my grace ... Phil 1:7 4791
to be p of the inheritance of the ... Col 1:12 3310
and beloved, p of the benefit ... 1Ti 6:2 482
as the children are p of flesh ... Heb 2:14 2841
p of the heavenly calling, ... Heb 3:1 3353
For we are made p of Christ ... Heb 3:14 3353
were made p of the Holy Ghost, ... Heb 6:4 3353
chastisement, whereof all are p ... Heb 12:8 3353
we might be p of his holiness ... Heb 12:10 3335
inasmuch as ye are p of Christ's ... 1Pet 4:13 2841
might be p of the divine nature ... 2Pet 1:4 2844
that ye be not p of her sins ... Rev 18:4 4790

PARTAKEST {1}
with them p of the root and ... Rom 11:17 1096,4791

PARTED {12}
and from thence it was p, and ... Gen 2:10 6504
of fire, and p them both asunder ... 2Kin 2:11 6504
waters, they p hither and thither ... 2Kin 2:14 2673
By what way is the light p ... Job 38:24 2505
among the nations, and p my land ... Joel 3:2 2505
p his garments, casting lots ... Mt 27:35 1266
They p my garments among them, and ... Mt 27:35 1266
they p his garments, casting lots ... Mk 15:24 1266
they p his raiment, and cast lots ... Lk 23:34 1266
he was p from them, and carried up ... Lk 24:51 1339
They p my raiment among them, and ... Jn 19:24 1266
p them to all men, as every man ... Acts 2:45 1266

PARTETH {3}
Whatsoever p the hoof, and is ... Lev 11:3 6536
And every beast that p the hoof ... Deut 14:6 6536
to cease, and p between the mighty ... Prov 18:18 6504

PARTHIANS *(par-the'-uns)* {1} *Inhabitants of Parthia, now Iran.*
P, and Medes, and Elamites, and the ... Acts 2:9 3934

PARTIAL {2}
ways, but have been p in the law ... Mal 2:9 5375,6440
Are ye not then p in yourselves ... Jas 2:4 1252

PARTIALITY {2}
another, doing nothing by p ... 1Ti 5:21 4346
mercy and good fruits, without p ... Jas 3:17 87

PARTICULAR {2}
body of Christ, and members in p ... 1Cor 12:27 3313
let every one of you in p so love ... Eph 5:33 3588,1520

PARTICULARLY {2}
declared p what things God ... Acts 21:19 1520,1538,2596
of which we cannot now speak p ... Heb 9:5 2596,3313

PARTIES {1}
the cause of both p shall come ... Ex 22:9

PARTING {1}
Babylon stood at the p of the way ... Eze 21:21 517

PARTITION {2}
he made a p by the chains of gold ... 1Kin 6:21 5674
the middle wall of p between us ... Eph 2:14 5418

PARTLY {5}
be p strong, and p broken ... Dan 2:42 7118
and I p believe it ... 1Cor 11:18 3313,5100
P, whilst ye were made a ... Heb 10:33 5124,3303
and p, whilst ye became companions ... Heb 10:33 1161

PARTNER {3}
Whoso is p with a thief hateth ... Prov 29:24 2505
do enquire of Titus, he is my p ... 2Cor 8:23 2844
If thou count me therefore a p ... Philem 17 2844

PARTNERS {2}
And they beckoned unto their p ... Lk 5:7 3353
Zebedee, which were p with Simon ... Lk 5:10 2844

PARTRIDGE {2}
doth hunt a p in the mountains ... 1Sa 26:20 7124
As the p sitteth on eggs, and ... Jer 17:11 7124

PARTS See APPENDIX.

PARUAH *(par'-u-ah)* {1} *Father of Jehoshaphat.*
Jehoshaphat the son of P, in ... 1Kin 4:17 6515

PARVAIM *(par-va'-im)* {1} *A place rich in gold.*
and the gold was gold of P ... 2Chr 3:6 6516

PARZITES See PHARZITES.

PASACH *(pa'-sak)* {1} *A son of Japhet.*
P, and Bimhal, and Ashvath ... 1Chr 7:33 6457

PAS-DAMMIM *(pas-dam'-mim)* {1} *A place in Judah.*
He was with David at P, and there ... 1Chr 11:13 6450

PASEAH *(pa-se'-ah)* {3} See PHASEAH.
1. A son of Eshton.
And Eshton begat Beth-rapha, and P ... 1Chr 4:12 6454
2. A family of exiles.
of Uzza, the children of P ... Ezr 2:49 6454
3. Father of Jehoiada.
repaired Jehoiada the son of P ... Neh 3:6 6454

PASHUR *(pash'-ur)* {14}
1. Head of a priestly family.
the son of Jeroham, the son of *P* 1Chr 9:12 6583
The children of *P*, a thousand two .... Ezr 2:38 6583
And of the sons of *P* .... Ezr 10:22 6583
The children of *P*, a thousand two .... Neh 7:41 6583
son of Zechariah, the son of *P* .... Neh 11:12 6583
2. A priest who renewed the covenant.
P, Amariah, Malchijah, ... Neh 10:3 6583
3. A son of Immer.
Now *P* the son of Immer the priest .... Jer 20:1 6583
Then *P* smote Jeremiah the prophet .... Jer 20:2 6583
that *P* brought forth Jeremiah out .... Jer 20:3 6583
LORD hath not called thy name *P* .... Jer 20:3 6583
And thou, *P*, and all that dwell in .... Jer 20:6 6583
Mattan, and Gedaliah the son of *P* .... Jer 38:1 6583
4. A son of Melchiah/Malchiah.
unto him *P* the son of Melchiah .... Jer 21:1 6583
P the son of Malchiah, heard the .... Jer 38:1 6583

PASS {830}
in process of time it came to *p* .... Gen 4:3
and it came to *p*, when they were .... Gen 4:8
and it shall come to *p*, that every .... Gen 4:14
And it came to *p*, when men began .... Gen 6:1
it came to *p* after seven days, ... Gen 7:10
made a wind to *p* over the earth .... Gen 8:1 5674
it came to *p* at the end of forty .... Gen 8:6
it came to *p* in the six hundredth .... Gen 8:13
And it shall come to *p*, when I .... Gen 9:14
And it came to *p*, as they .... Gen 11:2
And it came to *p*, when he was come .... Gen 12:11
Therefore it shall come to *p* .... Gen 12:12
And it came to *p*, that, when Abram .... Gen 12:14
it came to *p* in the days of .... Gen 14:1
And it came to *p*, that, when the .... Gen 15:17
p not away, I pray thee, from thy .... Gen 18:3 5674
after that ye shall *p* on .... Gen 18:5 5674
And it came to *p*, when they had .... Gen 19:17
And it came to *p*, when God .... Gen 19:29
it came to *p* on the morrow, that .... Gen 19:34
And it came to *p*, when God caused .... Gen 20:13
it came to *p* at that time, that .... Gen 21:22
it came to *p* after these things, ... Gen 22:1
it came to *p* after these things, ... Gen 22:20
And let it come to *p*, that the .... Gen 24:14
And it came to *p*, before he had .... Gen 24:15
And it came to *p*, as the camels .... Gen 24:22
And it came to *p*, when he saw the .... Gen 24:30
and it shall come to *p*, that when .... Gen 24:43
And it came to *p*, that, when .... Gen 24:52
it came to *p* after the death of .... Gen 25:11
And it came to *p*, when he had been .... Gen 26:8
it came to *p* the same day, that .... Gen 26:32
And it came to *p*, that when Isaac .... Gen 27:1
And it came to *p*, as soon as Isaac .... Gen 27:30
it shall come to *p* when thou .... Gen 27:40
And it came to *p*, when Jacob saw .... Gen 29:10
And it came to *p*, when Laban heard .... Gen 29:13
it came to *p* in the evening, that .... Gen 29:23
And it came to *p*, that in the .... Gen 29:25
And it came to *p*, when Rachel had .... Gen 30:25
I will *p* through all thy flock to .... Gen 30:32 5674
And it came to *p*, whensoever the .... Gen 30:41
it came to *p* at the time that the .... Gen 31:10
that I will not *p* over this heap .... Gen 31:52 5674
thou shalt not *p* over this heap .... Gen 31:52 5674
P over before me, and put a space .... Gen 32:16 5674
p over before his servant .... Gen 33:14 5674
it came to *p* on the third day, ... Gen 34:25
And it came to *p*, when she was in .... Gen 35:17
And it came to *p*, as her soul was .... Gen 35:18
And it came to *p*, when Israel .... Gen 35:22
And it came to *p*, when Joseph was .... Gen 37:23
it came to *p* at that time, that .... Gen 38:1
and it came to *p*, when he went in .... Gen 38:9
it came to *p* about three months .... Gen 38:24
it came to *p* in the time of her .... Gen 38:27
And it came to *p*, when she .... Gen 38:28
And it came to *p*, as he drew back .... Gen 38:29
it came to *p* from the time that .... Gen 39:5
it came to *p* after these things, ... Gen 39:7
And it came to *p*, as she spake to .... Gen 39:10
it came to *p* about this time, ... Gen 39:11
And it came to *p*, when she saw .... Gen 39:13
And it came to *p*, when he heard .... Gen 39:15
And it came to *p*, as I lifted up .... Gen 39:18
And it came to *p*, when his master .... Gen 39:19
it came to *p* after these things, ... Gen 40:1
it came to *p* the third day, which .... Gen 40:20
it came to *p* at the end of two .... Gen 41:1
it came to *p* in the morning that .... Gen 41:8
And it came to *p*, as he .... Gen 41:13
and God will shortly bring it to *p* .... Gen 41:32 6213
it came to *p* as they emptied .... Gen 42:35
And it came to *p*, when they had .... Gen 43:2
And it came to *p*, when we came to .... Gen 43:21
it came to *p* when we came up unto .... Gen 44:24
It shall come to *p*, when he seeth .... Gen 44:31
And it shall come to *p*, when .... Gen 46:33
shall come to *p* in the increase .... Gen 47:24
it came to *p* after these things, ... Gen 48:1
meant it unto good, to bring to *p* .... Gen 50:20 6213
they multiply, and it come to *p* .... Ex 1:10
And it came to *p*, because the .... Ex 1:21
it came to *p* in those days, when .... Ex 2:11
it came to *p* in process of time, ... Ex 2:23
and it shall come to *p*, that, when .... Ex 3:21
And it shall come to *p*, if they .... Ex 4:8
And it shall come to *p*, if they .... Ex 4:9
it came to *p* by the way in the .... Ex 4:24
it came to *p* on the day when the .... Ex 6:28
For I will *p* through the land of .... Ex 12:12 5674
I will *p* over you, and the plague .... Ex 12:13 6452
For the LORD will *p* through to .... Ex 12:23 5674
the LORD will *p* over the door .... Ex 12:23 6452
And it shall come to *p*, when ye be .... Ex 12:25
And it shall come to *p*, when your .... Ex 12:26
And it came to *p*, that at midnight .... Ex 12:29
it came to *p* at the end of the .... Ex 12:41
the selfsame day it came to *p* .... Ex 12:41
it came to *p* the selfsame day, ... Ex 12:51
And it came to *p*, when Pharaoh .... Ex 13:15
And it came to *p*, when Pharaoh had .... Ex 13:17
And it came to *p*, that in the .... Ex 14:24
till thy people *p* over, O LORD, ... Ex 15:16 5674
O LORD, till the people *p* over .... Ex 15:16 5674
And it shall come to *p*, that on .... Ex 16:5
And it came to *p*, as Aaron spake .... Ex 16:10
And it came to *p*, that at even the .... Ex 16:13
And it came to *p*, that on the .... Ex 16:22
And it came to *p*, that there went .... Ex 16:27
And it came to *p*, when Moses held .... Ex 17:11
it came to *p* on the morrow, that .... Ex 18:13
it came to *p* on the third day in .... Ex 19:16
and it shall come to *p*, when he .... Ex 22:27
And it came to *p*, as soon as he .... Ex 32:19
it came to *p* on the morrow, that .... Ex 32:30
And it came to *p*, that every one .... Ex 33:7
And it came to *p*, when Moses went .... Ex 33:8
And it came to *p*, as Moses entered .... Ex 33:9
all my goodness *p* before thee .... Ex 33:19 5674
And it shall come to *p*, while my .... Ex 33:22
thee with my hand while I *p* by .... Ex 33:22 5674
And it came to *p*, when Moses came .... Ex 34:29
it came to *p* in the first month .... Ex 40:17
it came to *p* on the eighth day, ... Lev 9:1
seed *p* through the fire to Molech .... Lev 18:21 5674
water, then it shall come to *p* .... Num 5:27
it came to *p* on the day that .... Num 7:1
it came to *p* on the twentieth day .... Num 10:11
And it came to *p*, when the ark set .... Num 10:35
shall come to *p* unto thee or not .... Num 11:23
and it came to *p*, that, when the .... Num 11:25
And it came to *p*, as he had made .... Num 16:31
And it came to *p*, when the .... Num 16:42
And it shall come to *p*, that the .... Num 17:5
And it came to *p*, that on the .... Num 17:8
Let us *p*, I pray thee, through .... Num 20:17 5674
we will not *p* through the fields, ... Num 20:17 5674
unto him, Thou shalt not *p* by me .... Num 20:18 5674
and it shall come to *p*, that every .... Num 21:8
it upon a pole, and it came to *p* .... Num 21:9
Let me *p* through thy land .... Num 21:22 5674
Israel to *p* through his border .... Num 21:23 5674
it came to *p* on the morrow, that .... Num 22:41
it came to *p* after the plague, ... Num 26:1
of their father to *p* unto them .... Num 27:7 5674
to *p* unto his daughter .... Num 27:8 5674
But thy servants will *p* over .... Num 32:27 5674
will *p* with you over Jordan .... Num 32:29 5674
will not *p* over with you armed .... Num 32:30 5674
We will *p* over armed before the .... Num 32:32 5674
then it shall come to *p*, that .... Num 33:55
Moreover it shall come to *p* .... Num 33:56
of Akrabbim, and *p* on to Zin .... Num 34:4 5674
to Hazar-addar, and *p* on to Azmon .... Num 34:4 5674
it came to *p* in the fortieth year .... Deut 1:3
Ye are to *p* through the coast of .... Deut 2:4 5674
So it came to *p*, when all the men .... Deut 2:16
Thou art to *p* over through Ar, ... Deut 2:18 5674
and *p* over the river Arnon .... Deut 2:24 5674
Let me *p* through thy land .... Deut 2:27 5674
only I will *p* through on my feet .... Deut 2:28 5674
until I shall *p* over Jordan into .... Deut 2:29 5674
Heshbon would not let us *p* by him .... Deut 2:30 5674
ye shall *p* over armed before your .... Deut 3:18 5674
And it came to *p*, when ye heard .... Deut 5:23
Wherefore it shall come to *p* .... Deut 7:12
Thou art to *p* over Jordan this .... Deut 9:1 5674
it came to *p* at the end of forty .... Deut 9:11
And it shall come to *p*, if ye .... Deut 11:13
And it shall come to *p*, when the .... Deut 11:29
For ye shall *p* over Jordan to go .... Deut 11:31 5674
the sign or the wonder come to *p* .... Deut 13:2
daughter to *p* through the fire .... Deut 18:10 5674
And it shall come to *p*, that .... Deut 18:19
thing follow not, nor come to *p* .... Deut 18:22
it come to *p* that she find no .... Deut 24:1
be on the day when ye shall *p* .... Deut 27:2 5674
And it shall come to *p*, if thou .... Deut 28:1
But it shall come to *p*, if thou .... Deut 28:15
And it shall come to *p*, that as .... Deut 28:63
And it come to *p*, when he heareth .... Deut 29:19
And it shall come to *p*, when all .... Deut 30:1
And it shall come to *p*, when many .... Deut 31:21
And it came to *p*, when Moses had .... Deut 31:24
servant of the LORD it came to *p* .... Josh 1:1
P through the host, and command .... Josh 1:11 5674
days ye shall *p* over this Jordan .... Josh 1:11 5674
but ye shall *p* before your .... Josh 1:14 5674
it came to *p* about the time of .... Josh 2:5
it came to *p* after three days, ... Josh 3:2
and *p* over before the people .... Josh 3:6 5674
And it shall come to *p*, as soon as .... Josh 3:13
And it came to *p*, when the people .... Josh 3:14
to *p* over Jordan, and the priests .... Josh 3:14 5674
And it came to *p*, when all the .... Josh 4:1
P over before the ark of the LORD .... Josh 4:5 5674
And it came to *p*, when all the .... Josh 4:11
And it came to *p*, when the priests .... Josh 4:18
And it came to *p*, when all the .... Josh 5:1
And it came to *p*, when they had .... Josh 5:8
And it came to *p*, when Joshua was .... Josh 5:13
And it shall come to *p*, that when .... Josh 6:5
P on, and compass the city, and let .... Josh 6:7 5674
let him that is armed *p* on before .... Josh 6:7 5674
And it came to *p*, when Joshua had .... Josh 6:8
it came to *p* on the seventh day, ... Josh 6:15
it came to *p* at the seventh time, ... Josh 6:16
and it came to *p*, when the people .... Josh 6:20
and it shall come to *p*, when they .... Josh 8:5
And it came to *p*, when the king of .... Josh 8:14
And it came to *p*, when Israel had .... Josh 8:24
And it came to *p*, when all the .... Josh 9:1
it came to *p* at the end of three .... Josh 9:16
Now it came to *p*, when .... Josh 10:1
And it came to *p*, as they fled .... Josh 10:11
And it came to *p*, when Joshua and .... Josh 10:20
And it came to *p*, when they .... Josh 10:24
it came to *p* at the time of the .... Josh 10:27
And it came to *p*, when Jabin king .... Josh 11:1
And it came to *p*, as she came unto .... Josh 15:18
Yet it came to *p*, when the .... Josh 17:13
all came to *p* .... Josh 21:45 935
then *p* ye over unto the land of .... Josh 22:19 5674
it came to *p* a long time after .... Josh 23:1
all are come to *p* unto you .... Josh 23:14
Therefore it shall come to *p* .... Josh 23:15
it came to *p* after these things, ... Josh 24:29
the death of Joshua it came to *p* .... Judg 1:1
And it came to *p*, when she came to .... Judg 1:14
And it came to *p*, when Israel was .... Judg 1:28
And it came to *p*, when the angel .... Judg 2:4
And it came to *p*, when the judge .... Judg 2:19
And it came to *p*, when he was come .... Judg 3:27
and suffered not a man to *p* over .... Judg 3:28 5674
And it came to *p*, when the .... Judg 6:7
it came to *p* the same night, that .... Judg 6:25
it came to *p* the same night, that .... Judg 7:9
And it came to *p*, as soon as .... Judg 8:33
it came to *p* on the morrow, that .... Judg 9:42
it came to *p* in process of time, ... Judg 11:4
I pray thee, *p* through thy land .... Judg 11:17 5674
and Israel said unto him, Let us *p* .... Judg 11:19 5674
not Israel to *p* through his coast .... Judg 11:20 5674
And it came to *p*, when he saw her, ... Judg 11:35
it came to *p* at the end of two .... Judg 11:39
said, Now let thy words come to *p* .... Judg 13:12 935
come to *p* we may do thee honour .... Judg 13:17 935
For it came to *p*, when the flame .... Judg 13:20
And it came to *p*, when they saw .... Judg 14:11
it came to *p* on the seventh day, ... Judg 14:15
it came to *p* on the seventh day, ... Judg 14:17
But it came to *p* within a while .... Judg 15:1
And it came to *p*, when he had made .... Judg 15:17
And it came to *p* afterward .... Judg 16:4
And it came to *p*, when she pressed .... Judg 16:16
And it came to *p*, when their .... Judg 16:25
it came to *p* in those days, when .... Judg 19:1
it came to *p* on the fourth day, ... Judg 19:5
we will *p* over to Gibeah .... Judg 19:12 5674
why is this come to *p* in Israel .... Judg 21:3
it came to *p* on the morrow, that .... Judg 21:4
Now it came to *p* in the days when .... Ruth 1:1
And it came to *p*, when they were .... Ruth 1:19
it came to *p* at midnight, that .... Ruth 3:8
And it came to *p*, as she continued 1Sa 1:12
Wherefore it came to *p*, when the 1Sa 1:20
And it shall come to *p*, that every 1Sa 2:36
it came to *p* at that time, when 1Sa 3:2
And it came to *p*, when he made 1Sa 4:18
And it came to *p*, as the ark of 1Sa 5:10
And it came to *p*, while the ark 1Sa 7:2
And it came to *p*, when Samuel was 1Sa 8:1
that he saith cometh surely to *p* 1Sa 9:6
it came to *p* about the spring of 1Sa 9:26
Bid the servant *p* on before us 1Sa 9:27 5674
and it shall come to *p*, when thou 1Sa 10:5
those signs came to *p* that day 1Sa 10:9
And it came to *p*, when all that 1Sa 10:11
and it came to *p*, that they which 1Sa 11:11
And it came to *p*, that as soon as 1Sa 13:10
So it came to *p* in the day of 1Sa 13:22
Now it came to *p* upon a day 1Sa 14:1
we will *p* over unto these men, and 1Sa 14:8 5674
And it came to *p*, while Saul 1Sa 14:19
And it came to *p*, when they were 1Sa 16:6
and made him *p* before Samuel 1Sa 16:8 5674
Then Jesse made Shammah to *p* by 1Sa 16:9 5674
of his sons to *p* before Samuel 1Sa 16:10 5674
and it shall come to *p*, when the 1Sa 16:16
And it came to *p*, when the evil 1Sa 16:23
And it came to *p*, when the 1Sa 17:48
And it came to *p*, when he had made 1Sa 18:1
it came to *p* as they came, when 1Sa 18:6
it came to *p* on the morrow, that 1Sa 18:10
But it came to *p* at the time when 1Sa 18:19
and it came to *p*, after they went 1Sa 18:30
it came to *p* on the morrow, which 1Sa 20:27
it came to *p* in the morning, that 1Sa 20:35
And it came to *p*, when Abiathar 1Sa 23:6
and it shall come to *p*, if he be 1Sa 23:23
And it came to *p*, when Saul was 1Sa 24:1

P

And it came to *p* afterward 1Sa 24:5
And it came to *p*, when David had 1Sa 24:16
And it shall come to *p*, when the 1Sa 25:30
But it came to *p* in the morning 1Sa 25:37
it came to *p* about ten days after 1Sa 25:38
it came to *p* in those days, that 1Sa 28:1
And it came to *p*, when David and 1Sa 30:1
it came to *p* on the morrow, when 1Sa 31:8
Now it came to *p* after the death 2Sa 1:1
It came even to *p* on the third 2Sa 1:2
And it came to *p* after this 2Sa 2:1
and it came to *p*, that as many as 2Sa 2:23
And it came to *p*, while there was 2Sa 3:6
and it came to *p*, as she made 2Sa 4:4
And it came to *p*, when the king 2Sa 7:1
And it came to *p* that night 2Sa 7:4
And after this it came to *p* 2Sa 8:1
And it came to *p* after this 2Sa 10:1
And it came to *p*, after the year 2Sa 11:1
it came to *p* in an eveningtide, 2Sa 11:2
it came to *p* in the morning, that 2Sa 11:14
And it came to *p*, when Joab 2Sa 11:16
it came to *p* on the seventh day, 2Sa 12:18
made them *p* through the brickkiln 2Sa 12:31 5674
And it came to *p* after this 2Sa 13:1
it came to *p* after two full years 2Sa 13:23
And it came to *p*, while they were 2Sa 13:30
And it came to *p*, as soon as he 2Sa 13:36
And it came to *p* after this 2Sa 15:1
it came to *p* after forty years, 2Sa 15:7
David said to Ittai, Go and *p* over 2Sa 15:22 5674
And it came to *p*, that when David 2Sa 15:32
And it came to *p*, when Hushai the 2Sa 16:16
and it will come to *p*, when some 2Sa 17:9
wilderness, but speedily *p* over 2Sa 17:16 5674
And it came to *p*, after they were 2Sa 17:21
and *p* quickly over the water 2Sa 17:21 5674
And it came to *p*, when David was 2Sa 17:27
And it came to *p*, when he was come 2Sa 19:25
And it came to *p* after this 2Sa 21:18
Otherwise it shall come to *p* 1Kin 1:21
it came to *p* at the end of three 1Kin 2:39
it came to *p* the third day after 1Kin 3:18
And it came to *p*, when Hiram heard 1Kin 5:7
it came to *p* in the four hundred 1Kin 6:1
And it came to *p*, when the priests 1Kin 8:10
And it came to *p*, when Solomon had 1Kin 9:1
it came to *p* at the end of twenty 1Kin 9:10
For it came to *p*, when Solomon 1Kin 11:4
For it came to *p*, when David was 1Kin 11:15
it came to *p* at that time when 1Kin 11:29
And it came to *p*, when Jeroboam 1Kin 12:2
And it came to *p*, when all Israel 1Kin 12:20
And it came to *p*, when king 1Kin 13:4
And it came to *p*, as they sat at 1Kin 13:20
And it came to *p*, after he had 1Kin 13:23
And it came to *p*, after he had 1Kin 13:31
Samaria, shall surely come to *p* 1Kin 13:32
it came to *p* in the fifth year of 1Kin 14:25
And it came to *p*, when Baasha 1Kin 15:21
And it came to *p*, when he reigned, 1Kin 15:29
And it came to *p*, when he began to 1Kin 16:11
And it came to *p*, when Zimri saw 1Kin 16:18
And it came to *p*, as if it had 1Kin 16:31
it came to *p* after a while, that 1Kin 17:7
it came to *p* after these things, 1Kin 17:17
it came to *p* after many days, 1Kin 18:1
between them to *p* throughout it 1Kin 18:6 5674
And it shall come to *p*, as soon as 1Kin 18:12
And it came to *p*, when Ahab saw 1Kin 18:17
And it came to *p* at noon, that 1Kin 18:27
And it came to *p*, when midday was 1Kin 18:29
it came to *p* at the time of the 1Kin 18:36
it came to *p* at the seventh time, 1Kin 18:44
it came to *p* in the mean while, 1Kin 18:45
And it shall come to *p*, that him 1Kin 19:17
And it came to *p*, when Ben-hadad 1Kin 20:12
it came to *p* at the return of the 1Kin 20:26
it came to *p* after these things, 1Kin 21:1
And it came to *p*, when Jezebel 1Kin 21:15
And it came to *p*, when Ahab heard 1Kin 21:16
And it came to *p*, when Ahab heard 1Kin 21:27
it came to *p* in the third year, 1Kin 22:2
And it came to *p*, when the 1Kin 22:32
And it came to *p*, when the 1Kin 22:33
And it came to *p*, when the LORD 2Kin 2:1
And it came to *p*, when they were 2Kin 2:9
And it came to *p*, as they still 2Kin 2:11
But it came to *p*, when Ahab was 2Kin 3:5
And it came to *p*, when the 2Kin 3:15
it came to *p* in the morning, when 2Kin 3:20
And it came to *p*, when the vessels 2Kin 4:6
And it came to *p*, when the man of 2Kin 4:25
And it came to *p*, as they were 2Kin 4:40
And it came to *p*, when the king of 2Kin 5:7
that thou *p* not such a place 2Kin 6:9 5674
And it came to *p*, when they were 2Kin 6:20
And it came to *p* after this 2Kin 6:24
And it came to *p*, when the king 2Kin 6:30
it came to *p* as the man of God 2Kin 7:18
it came to *p* at the seven years' 2Kin 8:3
And it came to *p*, as he was 2Kin 8:5
it came to *p* on the morrow, that 2Kin 8:15
And it came to *p*, when Joram saw 2Kin 9:22
And it came to *p*, when the letter 2Kin 10:7
it came to *p* in the morning, that 2Kin 10:9
And it came to *p*, as soon as he 2Kin 10:25
And it came to *p*, as they were 2Kin 13:21
And it came to *p*, as soon as the 2Kin 14:5
And so it came to *p* 2Kin 15:12
made his son to *p* through the 2Kin 16:3 5674
daughters to *p* through the fire 2Kin 17:17 5674
Now it came to *p* in the third 2Kin 18:1
it came to *p* in the fourth year 2Kin 18:9
And it came to *p*, when king 2Kin 19:1
now have I brought it to *p* 2Kin 19:25
And it came to *p* that night 2Kin 19:35
And it came to *p*, as he was 2Kin 19:37
And it came to *p*, afore Isaiah was 2Kin 20:4
he made his son *p* through the 2Kin 21:6 5674
it came to *p* in the eighteenth 2Kin 22:3
And it came to *p*, when the king 2Kin 22:11
to *p* through the fire to Molech 2Kin 23:10 5674
LORD it came to *p* in Jerusalem 2Kin 24:20
it came to *p* in the ninth year of 2Kin 25:1
But it came to *p* in the seventh 2Kin 25:25
it came to *p* in the seven and 2Kin 25:27
it came to *p* on the morrow, when 1Chr 10:8
And it came to *p*, when God helped 1Chr 15:26
And it came to *p*, as the ark of 1Chr 15:29
Now it came to *p*, as David sat in 1Chr 17:1
it came to *p* the same night, that 1Chr 17:3
And it shall come to *p*, when thy 1Chr 17:11
Now after this it came to *p* 1Chr 18:1
Now it came to *p* after this 1Chr 19:1
And it came to *p*, that after the 1Chr 20:1
And it came to *p* after this 1Chr 20:4
And it came to *p*, when the priests 2Chr 5:11
It came even to *p*, as the 2Chr 5:13
it came to *p* at the end of twenty 2Chr 8:1
And it came to *p*, when Jeroboam 2Chr 10:2
And it came to *p*, when Rehoboam 2Chr 12:1
And it came to *p*, that in the 2Chr 12:2
of Judah shouted, it came to *p* 2Chr 13:15
And it came to *p*, when Baasha 2Chr 16:5
And it came to *p*, when the 2Chr 18:31
For it came to *p*, that, when the 2Chr 18:32
It came to *p* after this also, 2Chr 20:1
And it came to *p*, that in process 2Chr 21:19
And it came to *p*, that, when Jehu 2Chr 22:8
And it came to *p* after this 2Chr 24:4
Now it came to *p*, that at what 2Chr 24:11
it came to *p* at the end of the 2Chr 24:23
Now it came to *p*, when the 2Chr 25:3
Now it came to *p*, after that 2Chr 25:14
And it came to *p*, as he talked 2Chr 25:16
he caused his children to *p* 2Chr 33:6 5674
And it came to *p*, when the king 2Chr 34:19
it came to *p* in the month Chisleu Neh 1:1
And it came to *p*, when I heard Neh 1:4
it came to *p* in the month Nisan, Neh 2:1
the beast that was under me to *p* Neh 2:14 5674
But it came to *p*, that when Neh 4:1
But it came to *p*, that when Neh 4:7
And it came to *p*, that when the Neh 4:12
And it came to *p*, when our enemies Neh 4:15
it came to *p* from that time forth Neh 4:16
Now it came to *p*, when Sanballat, Neh 6:1
And it came to *p*, that when all Neh 6:16
Now it came to *p*, when the wall Neh 7:1
Now it came to *p*, when they had Neh 13:3
And it came to *p*, that when the Neh 13:19
Now it came to *p* in the days of Est 1:1
So it came to *p*, when the king's Est 2:8
Now it came to *p*, when they spake Est 3:4
Now it came to *p* on the third day Est 5:1
the stream of brooks they *p* away Job 6:15 5674
remember it as waters that *p* away Job 11:16 5674
his bounds that he cannot *p* Job 14:5 5674
fenced up my way that I cannot *p* Job 19:8 5674
troubled at midnight, and *p* away Job 34:20 5674
and he shall bring it to *p* Ps 37:5 6213
who bringeth wicked devices to *p* Ps 37:7 6213
let every one of them *p* away Ps 58:8 1980
sea, and caused them to *p* through Ps 78:13 5674
so that all they which *p* by the Ps 80:12 5674
All that *p* by the way spoil him Ps 89:41 5674
a bound that they may not *p* over Ps 104:9 5674
made Israel to *p* through the Ps 136:14 5674
made a decree which shall not *p* Ps 148:6 5674
p not by it, turn from it, and Prov 4:15 5674
by it, turn from it, and *p* away Prov 4:15 5674
should not *p* his commandment Prov 8:29 5674
his lips he bringeth evil to *p* Prov 16:30 3615
it is his glory to *p* over a Prov 19:11 5674
but the simple *p* on, and are Prov 22:3 5674
but the simple *p* on, and are Prov 27:12 5674
shall come to *p* in the last days Is 2:2
And it shall come to *p*, that Is 3:24
And it shall come to *p*, that he Is 4:3
it came to *p* in the days of Ahaz Is 7:1
stand, neither shall it come to *p* Is 7:7
And it shall come to *p* in that day Is 7:18
And it shall come to *p* in that day Is 7:21
And it shall come to *p*, for the Is 7:22
And it shall come to *p* in that day Is 7:23
And he shall *p* through Judah Is 8:8 2498
And they shall *p* through it Is 8:21 5674
and it shall come to *p*, that when Is 8:21
Wherefore it shall come to *p* Is 10:12
And it shall come to *p* in that day Is 10:20
And it shall come to *p* in that day Is 10:27
And it shall come to *p* in that day Is 11:11
it shall come to *p* in the day Is 14:3
thought, so shall it come to *p* Is 14:24
And it shall come to *p*, when it is Is 16:12
And in that day it shall come to *p* Is 17:4
whirlwinds in the south *p* through Is 21:1 2498
And it shall come to *p*, that thy Is 22:7
And it shall come to *p* in that day Is 22:20
that *p* over the sea, have Is 23:2 5674
P ye over to Tarshish Is 23:6 5674
P through thy land as a river, O Is 23:10 5674
arise, *p* over to Chittim Is 23:12 5674
And it shall come to *p* in that day Is 23:15
it shall come to *p* after the end Is 23:17
And it shall come to *p*, that he Is 24:18
And it shall come to *p* in that day Is 24:21
And it shall come to *p* in that day Is 27:12
And it shall come to *p* in that day Is 27:13
scourge shall *p* through, it shall Is 28:15 5674
scourge shall *p* through, then ye Is 28:18 5674
by morning shall it *p* over Is 28:19 5674
and bring to *p* his act, his Is 28:21 5674
where the grounded staff shall *p* Is 30:32 4569
he shall *p* over to his strong Is 31:9 5674
shall gallant ship *p* thereby Is 33:21 5674
none shall *p* through it for ever Is 34:10 5674
the unclean shall not *p* over it Is 35:8 5674
Now it came to *p* in the Is 36:1
And it came to *p*, when king Is 37:1
now have I brought it to *p* Is 37:26
And it came to *p*, as he was Is 37:38
the former things are come to *p* Is 42:9
it, I will also bring it to *p* Is 46:11
the thigh, *p* over the rivers Is 47:2 5674
them suddenly, and they came to *p* Is 48:3
it came to *p* I shewed it thee Is 48:5
a way for the ransomed to *p* over Is 51:10 5674
And it shall come to *p*, that Is 65:24
And it shall come to *p*, that from Is 66:23
For *p* over the isles of Chittim, Jer 2:10 5674
And it came to *p* through the Jer 3:9
And it shall come to *p*, when ye be Jer 3:16
And it shall come to *p* at that day Jer 4:9
And it shall come to *p*, when ye Jer 5:19
decree, that it cannot *p* it Jer 5:22 5674
roar, yet can they not *p* over it Jer 5:22 5674
given them shall *p* away from them Jer 8:13 5674
so that none can *p* through them Jer 9:10 5674
And it shall come to *p*, after that Jer 12:15
And it shall come to *p*, if they Jer 12:16
it came to *p* after many days, Jer 13:6
And it shall come to *p*, if they Jer 15:2
I will make thee to *p* with thine Jer 15:14 5674
And it shall come to *p*, when thou Jer 16:10
And it shall come to *p*, if ye Jer 17:24
it came to *p* on the morrow, that Jer 20:3
many nations shall *p* by this city Jer 22:8 5674
And it shall come to *p*, when Jer 25:12
Now it came to *p*, when Jeremiah Jer 26:8
And it shall come to *p*, that the Jer 27:8
it came to *p* the same year, in Jer 28:1
of the prophet shall come to *p* Jer 28:9
it shall come to *p* in that day Jer 30:8
And it shall come to *p*, that like Jer 31:28
thou hast spoken is come to *p* Jer 32:24
their daughters to *p* through the Jer 32:35 5674
shall the flocks *p* again under Jer 33:13 5674
But it came to *p*, when Jer 35:11
it came to *p* in the fourth year Jer 36:1
it came to *p* in the fifth year of Jer 36:9
Now it came to *p*, when they had Jer 36:16
And it came to *p*, that when Jehudi Jer 36:23
And it came to *p*, that when the Jer 37:11
And it came to *p*, that when Jer 39:4
Now it came to *p* in the seventh Jer 41:1
it came to *p* the second day after Jer 41:4
and it came to *p*, as he met them, Jer 41:6
Now it came to *p*, that when all Jer 41:13
and it shall come to *p*, that Jer 42:4
it came to *p* after ten days, that Jer 42:7
Then it shall come to *p*, that the Jer 42:16
And it came to *p*, that when Jer 43:1
come to *p* in the latter days Jer 49:39
doth any son of man *p* thereby Jer 51:43 5674
LORD it came to *p* in Jerusalem Jer 52:3
it came to *p* in the ninth year of Jer 52:4
it came to *p* in the seven and Jer 52:31
nothing to you, all ye that *p* by Lam 1:12 5674
All that *p* by clap their hands at Lam 2:15 5674
he that saith, and it cometh to *p* Lam 3:37
our prayer should not *p* through Lam 3:44 5674
also shall *p* through unto thee Lam 4:21 5674
Now it came to *p* in the thirtieth Eze 1:1
it came to *p* at the end of seven Eze 3:16
cause it to *p* upon thine head and Eze 5:1 5674
in the sight of all that *p* by Eze 5:14 5674
blood shall *p* through thee Eze 5:17 5674
it came to *p* in the sixth year, Eze 8:1
And it came to *p*, while they were Eze 9:8
And it came to *p*, that when he had Eze 10:6
And it came to *p*, when I Eze 11:13
I shall speak shall come to *p* Eze 12:25 6213
beasts to *p* through the land Eze 14:15 5674
that no man may *p* through because Eze 14:15 5674
to *p* through the fire for them Eze 16:21 5674
it came to *p* after all thy Eze 16:23
it came to *p* in the seventh year, Eze 20:1
in that they caused to *p* through Eze 20:26 5674
your sons to *p* through the fire Eze 20:31 5674
will cause you to *p* under the rod Eze 20:37 5674
cometh, and shall be brought to *p* Eze 21:7
to *p* for them through the fire, Eze 23:37 5674

it shall come to *p*, and I will do ... Eze 24:14
it came to *p* in the eleventh year ... Eze 26:1
No foot of man shall *p* through it ... Eze 29:11 5674
foot of beast shall *p* through it ... Eze 29:11 5674
it came to *p* in the seven and ... Eze 29:17
it came to *p* in the eleventh year ... Eze 30:20
it came to *p* in the eleventh year ... Eze 31:1
it came to *p* in the twelfth year, ... Eze 32:1
It came to *p* also in the twelfth ... Eze 32:17
Whom dost thou *p* in beauty ... Eze 32:19
it came to *p* in the twelfth year ... Eze 33:21
that none shall *p* through ... Eze 33:28 5674
And when this cometh to *p*, (lo, it ... Eze 33:33
caused me to *p* by them round ... Eze 37:2 5674
It shall also come to *p*, that at ... Eze 38:10
It shall come to *p* at the same time ... Eze 38:18
And it shall come to *p* in that day ... Eze 39:11
that *p* through the land, when any ... Eze 39:15 5674
And it shall come to *p*, that when ... Eze 44:17
caused me to *p* by the four ... Eze 46:21 5674
a river that I could not *p* over ... Eze 47:5 5674
And it shall come to *p*, that every ... Eze 47:9
And it shall come to *p*, that the ... Eze 47:10
And it shall come to *p*, that ye ... Eze 47:22
And it shall come to *p*, that in ... Eze 47:23
what should come to *p* hereafter ... Dan 2:29
to thee what shall come to *p* ... Dan 2:29
what shall come to *p* hereafter ... Dan 2:45
and let seven times *p* over him ... Dan 4:16 2499
till seven times *p* over him ... Dan 4:23 2499
and seven times shall *p* over thee ... Dan 4:25 2499
and seven times shall *p* over thee ... Dan 4:32 2499
dominion, which shall not *p* away ... Dan 7:14 5709
and it came to *p*, when I saw, that ... Dan 8:2
And it came to *p*, when I, even I ... Dan 8:15
come, and overflow, and *p* through ... Dan 11:10 5674
and shall overflow and *p* over ... Dan 11:40 5674
And it shall come to *p* at that day ... Hos 1:5
and it shall come to *p*, that in ... Hos 1:10
And it shall come to *p* in that day ... Hos 2:21
And it shall come to *p* afterward ... Joel 2:28
And it shall come to *p*, that ... Joel 2:32
strangers *p* through her any more ... Joel 3:17 5674
And it shall come to *p* in that day ... Joel 3:18
Gilgal, and *p* not to Beer-sheba ... Amos 5:5 5674
for I will *p* through thee, saith ... Amos 5:17 5674
P ye unto Calneh, and see ... Amos 6:2 5674
And it shall come to *p*, if there ... Amos 6:9
And it came to *p*, that when they ... Amos 7:2
will not again *p* by them any more ... Amos 7:8 5674
will not again *p* by them any more ... Amos 8:2 5674
And it shall come to *p* in that day ... Amos 8:9
And it came to *p*, when the sun did ... Jonah 4:8
P ye away, thou inhabitant of ... Mic 1:11 5674
p by securely as men averse from ... Mic 2:8 5674
and their king shall *p* before them ... Mic 2:13 5674
the last days it shall come to *p* ... Mic 4:1
And it shall come to *p* in that day ... Mic 5:10
cut down, when he shall *p* through ... Nah 1:12 5674
shall no more *p* through thee ... Nah 1:15 5674
And it shall come to *p*, that all ... Nah 3:7
mind change, and he shall *p* over ... Hab 1:11 5674
it shall come to *p* in the day of ... Zeph 1:8
And it shall come to *p* in that day ... Zeph 1:10
it shall come to *p* at that time ... Zeph 1:12
before the day *p* as the chaff ... Zeph 2:2 5674
thine iniquity to *p* from thee ... Zec 3:4 5674
And this shall come to *p*, if ye ... Zec 6:15
it came to *p* in the fourth year ... Zec 7:1
Therefore it is come to *p* ... Zec 7:13
And it shall come to *p*, that as ye ... Zec 8:13
It shall yet come to *p*, that ... Zec 8:20
In those days it shall come to *p* ... Zec 8:23
no oppressor shall *p* through them ... Zec 9:8 5674
he shall *p* through the sea with ... Zec 10:11 5674
And it shall come to *p* in that day ... Zec 12:9
And it shall come to *p* in that day ... Zec 13:2
spirit to *p* out of the land ... Zec 13:2 5674
And it shall come to *p*, that when ... Zec 13:3
And it shall come to *p* in that day ... Zec 13:4
And it shall come to *p*, that in ... Zec 13:8
And it shall come to *p* in that day ... Zec 14:6
but it shall come to *p*, that at ... Zec 14:7
And it shall come to *p* in that day ... Zec 14:13
And it shall come to *p*, that every ... Zec 14:16
unto you, Till heaven and earth *p* ... Mt 5:18 *3928*
shall in no wise *p* from the law ... Mt 5:18 *3928*
And it came to *p*, when Jesus had ... Mt 7:28
that no man might *p* by that way ... Mt 8:28 *3928*
And it came to *p*, as Jesus sat at ... Mt 9:10
And it came to *p*, when Jesus had ... Mt 11:1
And it came to *p*, that when Jesus ... Mt 13:53
And it came to *p*, that when Jesus ... Mt 19:1
all these things must come to *p* ... Mt 24:6
you, This generation shall not *p* ... Mt 24:34 *3928*
Heaven and earth shall *p* away ... Mt 24:35 *3928*
but my words shall not *p* away ... Mt 24:35 *3928*
And it came to *p*, when Jesus had ... Mt 26:1
possible, let this cup *p* from me ... Mt 26:39 *3928*
this cup may not *p* away from me ... Mt 26:42 *3928*
it came to *p* in those days, that ... Mk 1:9
And it came to *p*, that, as Jesus ... Mk 2:15
And it came to *p*, that he went ... Mk 2:23
And it came to *p*, as he sowed, ... Mk 4:4
Let us *p* over unto the other side ... Mk 4:35 *1330*
which he saith shall come to *p* ... Mk 11:23
shall see these things come to *p* ... Mk 13:29
that this generation shall not *p* ... Mk 13:30 *3928*

Heaven and earth shall *p* away ... Mk 13:31 *3928*
but my words shall not *p* away ... Mk 13:31 *3928*
the hour might *p* from him ... Mk 14:35 *3928*
And it came to *p*, that while he ... Lk 1:8
And it came to *p*, that, as soon as ... Lk 1:23
And it came to *p*, that, when ... Lk 1:41
And it came to *p*, that on the ... Lk 1:59
it came to *p* in those days, that ... Lk 2:1
And it came to *p*, as the angels ... Lk 2:15
see this thing which is come to *p* ... Lk 2:15
And it came to *p*, that after three ... Lk 2:46
were baptized, it came to *p* ... Lk 3:21
And it came to *p*, that, as the ... Lk 5:1
And it came to *p*, when he was in a ... Lk 5:12
it came to *p* on a certain day, as ... Lk 5:17
it came to *p* on the second ... Lk 6:1
it came to *p* also on another ... Lk 6:6
it came to *p* in those days, that ... Lk 6:12
it came to *p* the day after, that ... Lk 7:11
And it came to *p* afterward ... Lk 8:1
Now it came to *p* on a certain day ... Lk 8:22
And it came to *p*, that, when Jesus ... Lk 8:40
And it came to *p*, as he was alone ... Lk 9:18
it came to *p* about an eight days ... Lk 9:28
And it came to *p*, as they departed ... Lk 9:33
And it came to *p*, that on the next ... Lk 9:37
And it came to *p*, when the time ... Lk 9:51
And it came to *p*, that, as they ... Lk 9:57
Now it came to *p*, as they went, ... Lk 10:38
And it came to *p*, that, as he was ... Lk 11:1
And it came to *p*, when the devil ... Lk 11:14
And it came to *p*, as he spake ... Lk 11:27
p over judgment and the love of ... Lk 11:42 *3928*
and it cometh to *p* ... Lk 12:55
And it came to *p*, as he went into ... Lk 14:1
easier for heaven and earth to *p* ... Lk 16:17 *3928*
And it came to *p*, that the beggar ... Lk 16:22
would *p* from hence to you cannot ... Lk 16:26 *1224*
neither can they *p* to us, that ... Lk 16:26 *1276*
And it came to *p*, as he went to ... Lk 17:11
And it came to *p*, that, as they ... Lk 17:14
And it came to *p*, that as he was ... Lk 18:35
And hearing the multitude *p* by ... Lk 18:36 *1279*
for he was to *p* that way ... Lk 19:4 *1330*
And it came to *p*, that when he was ... Lk 19:15
And it came to *p*, when he was come ... Lk 19:29
And it came to *p*, that on one of ... Lk 20:1
when these things shall come to *p* ... Lk 21:7
these things must first come to *p* ... Lk 21:9
these things begin to come to *p* ... Lk 21:28
ye see these things come to *p* ... Lk 21:31
This generation shall not *p* away ... Lk 21:32 *3928*
Heaven and earth shall *p* away ... Lk 21:33 *3928*
but my words shall not *p* away ... Lk 21:33 *3928*
these things that shall come to *p* ... Lk 21:36
And it came to *p*, as they were ... Lk 24:4
at that which was come to *p* ... Lk 24:12
And it came to *p*, that, while they ... Lk 24:15
are come to *p* there in these days ... Lk 24:18
And it came to *p*, as he sat at ... Lk 24:30
And it came to *p*, while he blessed ... Lk 24:51
come, that, when it is come to *p* ... Jn 13:19
have told you before it come to *p* ... Jn 14:29
that, when it is come to *p* ... Jn 14:29
But this cometh to *p*, that the ... Jn 15:25
shall come to *p* in the last days ... Acts 2:17
And it shall come to *p*, that ... Acts 2:21
And it shall come to *p*, that every ... Acts 3:23
it came to *p* on the morrow, that ... Acts 4:5
And it came to *p*, as Peter passed ... Acts 9:32
it came to *p* in those days, that ... Acts 9:37
And it came to *p*, that he tarried ... Acts 9:43
And it came to *p*, that a whole ... Acts 11:26
which came to *p* in the days of ... Acts 11:28
And it came to *p* in Iconium ... Acts 14:1
And it came to *p*, as we went to ... Acts 16:16
he was disposed to *p* into Achaia ... Acts 18:27 *1330*
And it came to *p*, that, while ... Acts 19:1
And it came to *p*, that after we ... Acts 21:1
And it came to *p*, that, as I made ... Acts 22:6
And it came to *p*, that, when I was ... Acts 22:17
And so it came to *p*, that they ... Acts 27:44
And it came to *p*, that the father ... Acts 28:8
And it came to *p*, that after three ... Acts 28:17
And it shall come to *p*, that in ... Rom 9:26
if she *p* the flower of her age, ... 1Cor 7:36 *5230*
then shall be brought to *p* the ... 1Cor 15:54
when I shall *p* through Macedonia ... 1Cor 16:5 *1330*
for I do *p* through Macedonia ... 1Cor 16:5 *1330*
to *p* by you into Macedonia, and to ... 2Cor 1:16 *1330*
even as it came to *p*, and ye know ... 1Th 3:4
of the grass he shall *p* away ... Jas 1:10 *3928*
p the time of your sojourning ... 1Pet 1:17 *390*
shall *p* away with a great noise ... 2Pet 3:10 *3928*
which must shortly come to *p* ... Rev 1:1

PASSAGE {4}
give Israel *p* through his border ... Num 20:21 5674
at the *p* of the children of ... Josh 22:11 1552
went out to the *p* of Michmash ... 1Sa 13:23 4569
They are gone over the *p* ... Is 10:29 4569

PASSAGES {5}
took the *p* of Jordan before the ... Judg 12:5 4569
and slew him at the *p* of Jordan ... Judg 12:6 4569
And between the *p*, by which ... 1Sa 14:4 4569
in Bashan, and cry from the *p* ... Jer 22:20 5676
that the *p* are stopped, and the ... Jer 51:32 4569

PASSED {161}
Abram *p* through the land unto the ... Gen 12:6 5674
a burning lamp that *p* between ... Gen 15:17 5674
p over the river, and set his face ... Gen 31:21 5674
my staff I *p* over this Jordan ... Gen 32:10 5674
sons, and *p* over the ford Jabbok ... Gen 32:22 5674
as he *p* over Penuel the sun rose ... Gen 32:31 5674
he *p* over before them, and bowed ... Gen 33:3 5674
Then there *p* by Midianites ... Gen 37:28 5674
who *p* over the houses of the ... Ex 12:27 6452
the LORD *p* by before him, and ... Ex 34:6 5674
which we *p* through to search it, ... Num 14:7 5674
left, until we have *p* thy borders ... Num 20:17 5674
p through the midst of the sea ... Num 33:8 5674
When ye are *p* over Jordan into ... Num 33:51 5674
when we *p* by from our brethren ... Deut 2:8 5674
p by the way of the wilderness of ... Deut 2:8 5674
of this law, when thou art *p* over ... Deut 27:3 5674
through the nations which ye *p* by ... Deut 29:16 5674
p over, and came to Joshua the son ... Josh 2:23 5674
lodged there before they *p* over ... Josh 3:1 5674
for ye have not *p* this way ... Josh 3:4 5674
the people *p* over right against ... Josh 3:16 5674
Israelites *p* over on dry ground ... Josh 3:17 5674
people were *p* clean over Jordan ... Josh 3:17 5674
people were clean *p* over Jordan ... Josh 4:1 5674
when it *p* over Jordan, the waters ... Josh 4:7 5674
and the people hasted and *p* over ... Josh 4:10 5674
all the people were clean *p* over ... Josh 4:11 5674
that the ark of the LORD *p* over ... Josh 4:11 5674
p over armed before the children ... Josh 4:12 5674
war *p* over before the LORD unto ... Josh 4:13 5674
before you, until ye were *p* over ... Josh 4:23 5674
of Israel, until we were *p* over ... Josh 5:1 5674
rams' horns *p* on before the LORD ... Josh 6:8 5674
Then Joshua *p* from Makkedah, and ... Josh 10:29 5674
Joshua *p* from Libnah, and all ... Josh 10:31 5674
from Lachish Joshua *p* unto Eglon ... Josh 10:34 5674
p along to Zin, and ascended up on ... Josh 15:3 5674
p along to Hezron, and went up to ... Josh 15:3 5674
From thence it *p* toward Azmon ... Josh 15:4 5674
and *p* along by the north of ... Josh 15:6 5674
the border *p* toward the waters of ... Josh 15:7 5674
p along unto the side of mount ... Josh 15:10 5674
Beth-shemesh, and *p* on to Timnah ... Josh 15:10 5674
p along to mount Baalah, and went ... Josh 15:11 5674
p by it on the east to Janohah ... Josh 16:6 5674
p through the land, and described ... Josh 18:9 5674
p along toward the side over ... Josh 18:18 5674
the border *p* along to the side of ... Josh 18:19 5674
all the people through whom we *p* ... Josh 24:17 5674
p beyond the quarries, and escaped ... Judg 3:26 5674
p over, he, and the three hundred ... Judg 8:4 5674
Ammon *p* over Jordan to fight also ... Judg 10:9 5674
he *p* over Gilead, and Manasseh, and ... Judg 11:29 5674
p over Mizpeh of Gilead, and from ... Judg 11:29 5674
from Mizpeh of Gilead he *p* over ... Judg 11:29 5674
So Jephthah *p* over unto the ... Judg 11:32 5674
p over against the children of ... Judg 12:3 5674
they *p* thence unto mount Ephraim, ... Judg 18:13 5674
And they *p* on and went their way ... Judg 19:14 5674
he *p* through mount Ephraim, and ... 1Sa 9:4 5674
p through the land of Shalisha, ... 1Sa 9:4 5674
then they *p* through the land of ... 1Sa 9:4 5674
he *p* through the land of the ... 1Sa 9:4 5674
pass on before us, (and he *p* on ... 1Sa 9:27 5674
the battle *p* over unto Beth-aven ... 1Sa 14:23 5674
p on, and gone down to Gilgal ... 1Sa 15:12 5674
he *p* over with the six hundred ... 1Sa 27:2 5674
the Philistines *p* on by hundreds ... 1Sa 29:2 5674
his men *p* on in the rereward with ... 1Sa 29:2 5674
p over Jordan, and went through ... 2Sa 2:29 5674
p over Jordan, and came to Helam ... 2Sa 10:17 5674
all his servants *p* on beside him ... 2Sa 15:18 5674
from Gath, *p* on before the king ... 2Sa 15:18 5674
And Ittai the Gittite *p* over ... 2Sa 15:22 5674
voice, and all the people *p* over ... 2Sa 15:23 5674
himself *p* over the brook Kidron ... 2Sa 15:23 5674
and all the people *p* over ... 2Sa 15:23 5674
with him, and they *p* over Jordan ... 2Sa 17:22 5674
Absalom *p* over Jordan, he and all ... 2Sa 17:24 5674
they *p* over Jordan, and pitched in ... 2Sa 24:5 5674
And, behold, men *p* by, and saw the ... 1Kin 13:25 5674
And, behold, the LORD *p* by ... 1Kin 19:11 5674
and Elijah *p* by him, and cast his ... 1Kin 19:19 5674
And as the king *p* by, he cried ... 1Kin 20:39 5674
on a day, that Elisha *p* to Shunem ... 2Kin 4:8 5674
so it was, that as oft as he *p* by ... 2Kin 4:8 5674
Gehazi *p* on before them, and laid ... 2Kin 4:31 5674
he *p* by upon the wall, and the ... 2Kin 6:30 5674
there *p* by a wild beast that was ... 2Kin 14:9 5674
p over Jordan, and came upon them, ... 1Chr 19:17 5674
king Solomon *p* all the kings of ... 2Chr 9:22 1431
there *p* by a wild beast that was ... 2Chr 25:18 5674
So the posts *p* from city to city ... 2Chr 30:10 5674
Then a spirit *p* before my face ... Job 4:15 2498
They are *p* away as the swift ... Job 9:26 2498
and no stranger *p* among them ... Job 15:19 5674
it, nor the fierce lion *p* by it ... Job 28:8 5710
was before him his thick clouds *p* ... Ps 18:12 5674
Yet he *p* away, and, lo, he was not ... Ps 37:36 5674
assembled, they *p* by together ... Ps 48:4 5674
our days are *p* away in thy wrath ... Ps 90:9 6437
but a little that I *p* from them ... Song 3:4 5674
come to Aiath, he is *p* to Migron ... Is 10:28 5674
my judgment is *p* over from my God ... Is 40:27 5674
He pursued them, and *p* safely ... Is 41:3 5674
a land that no man *p* through ... Jer 2:6 5674

and the holy flesh is *p* from thee ... Jer 11:15 5674
p between the parts thereof, ... Jer 34:18 5674
which *p* between the parts of the ... Jer 34:19 5674
he hath *p* the time appointed ... Jer 46:17 5674
when I *p* by thee, and saw thee ... Eze 16:6 5674
Now when I *p* by thee, and looked ... Eze 16:8 5674
on every one that *p* by ... Eze 16:15 5674
thy feet to every one that *p* by ... Eze 16:25 5674
in the sight of all that *p* by ... Eze 36:34 5674
a river that could not be *p* over ... Eze 47:5 5674
the smell of fire had *p* on them ... Dan 3:27 5709
palace, and *p* the night fasting ... Dan 6:18 956
but I *p* over upon her fair neck ... Hos 10:11 5674
billows and thy waves *p* over me ... Jonah 2:3 5674
have *p* through the gate, and are ... Mic 2:13 5674
not thy wickedness *p* continually ... Nah 3:19 5674
the overflowing of the water *p* by ... Hab 3:10 5674
that no man *p* through nor ... Zec 7:14 5674
p over, and came into his own city ... Mt 9:1 *1276*
as Jesus *p* forth from thence, he ... Mt 9:9 *3855*
when they heard that Jesus *p* by ... Mt 20:30 *3855*
they that *p* by reviled him, ... Mt 27:39 *3899*
And as he *p* by, he saw Levi the ... Mk 2:14 *3855*
when Jesus was *p* over again by ... Mk 5:21 *1276*
place, and now the time is far *p* ... Mk 6:35
the sea, and would have *p* by them ... Mk 6:48 *3928*
And when they had *p* over, they ... Mk 6:53 *1276*
thence, and *p* through Galilee ... Mk 9:30 *3899*
And in the morning, as they *p* by ... Mk 11:20 *3899*
one Simon a Cyrenian, who *p* by ... Mk 15:21 *3855*
they that *p* by railed on him, ... Mk 15:29 *3899*
he *p* by on the other side ... Lk 10:31 *492*
on him, and *p* by on the other side ... Lk 10:32 *492*
that he *p* through the midst of ... Lk 17:11 *1330*
entered and *p* through Jericho ... Lk 19:1 *1330*
but is *p* from death unto life ... Jn 5:24 *3327*
the midst of them, and so *p* by ... Jn 8:59 *3855*
And as Jesus *p* by, he saw a man ... Jn 9:1 *3855*
as Peter *p* throughout all ... Acts 9:32 *1330*
out, and *p* on through one street ... Acts 12:10 *4281*
after they had *p* throughout ... Acts 14:24 *1330*
they *p* through Phenice and Samaria ... Acts 15:3 *1330*
Now when they had *p* through ... Acts 17:1 *1353*
For as I *p* by, and beheld your ... Acts 17:23 *1330*
Paul having *p* through the upper ... Acts 19:1 *1330*
when he had *p* through Macedonia ... Acts 19:21 *1330*
so death *p* upon all men, for that ... Rom 5:12 *1330*
cloud, and all *p* through the sea ... 1Cor 10:1 *1330*
old things are *p* away ... 2Cor 5:17 *3928*
that is *p* into the heavens, Jesus ... Heb 4:14 *1330*
By faith they *p* through the Red ... Heb 11:29 *1224*
we have *p* from death unto life ... 1Jn 3:14 *3327*
and the first earth were *p* away ... Rev 21:1 *3928*
for the former things are *p* away ... Rev 21:4 *565*

PASSEDST {1}
Wherefore *p* thou over to fight ... Judg 12:1 5674

PASSENGERS {5}
To call *p* who go right on their ... Prov 9:15 5674,1870
the valley of the *p* on the east ... Eze 39:11 5674
it shall stop the noses of the *p* ... Eze 39:11 5674
the land to bury with the *p* those ... Eze 39:14 5674
the *p* that pass through the land, ... Eze 39:15 5674

PASSEST {5}
all the kingdoms whither thou *p* ... Deut 3:21 5674
whither thou *p* over Jordan to go ... Deut 30:18 5674
If thou *p* on with me, then thou ... 2Sa 15:33 5674
p over the brook Kidron, thou ... 1Kin 2:37 5674
When thou *p* through the waters, I ... Is 43:2 5674

PASSETH {38}
every one that *p* among them that ... Ex 30:13 5674
Every one that *p* among them that ... Ex 30:14 5674
come to pass, while my glory *p* by ... Ex 33:22 5674
of whatsoever *p* under the rod ... Lev 27:32 5674
p over before you into Jordan ... Josh 3:11 5674
p along unto the borders of Archi ... Josh 16:2 5674
from thence *p* on along on the ... Josh 19:13 5674
every one that *p* by it shall be ... 1Kin 9:8 5674
which *p* by us continually ... 2Kin 4:9 5674
of every one that *p* the account ... 2Kin 12:4 5674
to every one that *p* by it ... 2Chr 7:21 5674
he *p* on also, but I perceive him ... Job 9:11 2498
for ever against him, and he *p* ... Job 14:20 1980
my welfare *p* away as a cloud ... Job 30:15 5674
but the wind *p*, and cleanseth them ... Job 37:21 5674
whatsoever *p* through the paths of ... Ps 8:8 5674
a wind that *p* away, and cometh not ... Ps 78:39 1980
For the wind *p* over it, and it is ... Ps 103:16 5674
days are as a shadow that *p* away ... Ps 144:4 5674
As the whirlwind *p*, so is the ... Prov 10:25 5674
He that *p* by, and meddleth with ... Prov 26:17 5674
One generation *p* away, and another ... Eccl 1:4 1980
shall be as chaff that *p* away ... Is 29:5 5674
a wilderness, that none *p* through ... Jer 9:12 5674
that *p* away by the wind of the ... Jer 13:24 5674
every one that *p* thereby shall be ... Jer 18:16 5674
every one that *p* thereby shall be ... Jer 19:8 5674
and cut off from it him that *p* out ... Eze 35:7 5674
and as the early dew that *p* away ... Hos 13:3 1980
p by the transgression of the ... Mic 7:18 5674
every one that *p* by her shall ... Zeph 2:15 5674
streets waste, that none *p* by ... Zeph 3:6 5674
army, because of him that *p* by ... Zec 9:8 5674
him, that Jesus of Nazareth *p* by ... Lk 18:37 *3928*
the fashion of this world *p* away ... 1Cor 7:31 *3855*
which *p* knowledge, that ye might ... Eph 3:19 *5235*
which *p* all understanding, shall ... Phil 4:7 *5242*
And the world *p* away, and the lust ... 1Jn 2:17 *3855*

PASSING {13}
We are *p* from Beth-lehem-judah ... Judg 19:18 5674
wonderful, *p* the love of women ... 2Sa 1:26
people had done *p* out of the city ... 2Sa 15:24 5674
of Israel was *p* by upon the wall ... 2Kin 6:26 5674
Who *p* through the valley of Baca ... Ps 84:6 5674
P through the street near her ... Prov 7:8 5674
p over he will preserve it ... Is 31:5 5674
p through the land to bury with ... Eze 39:14 5674
But he *p* through the midst of ... Lk 4:30 *1330*
p by might overshadow some of ... Acts 5:15 *2064*
p through he preached in all the ... Acts 8:40 *1330*
they *p* by Mysia came down to ... Acts 16:8 *3928*
And, hardly *p* it, came unto a ... Acts 27:8 *3881*

PASSION {1}
his *p* by many infallible proofs ... Acts 1:3 *3958*

PASSIONS {2}
also are men of like *p* with you ... Acts 14:15 *3663*
a man subject to like *p* as we are ... Jas 5:17 *3663*

PASSOVER {76}
it is the LORD's *p* ... Ex 12:11 6453
to your families, and kill the *p* ... Ex 12:21 6453
is the sacrifice of the LORD's *p* ... Ex 12:27 6453
This is the ordinance of the *p* ... Ex 12:43 6453
and will keep the *p* to the LORD ... Ex 12:48 6453
of the *p* be left unto the morning ... Ex 34:25 6453
month at even is the LORD's *p* ... Lev 23:5 6453
the *p* at his appointed season ... Num 9:2 6453
that they should keep the *p* ... Num 9:4 6453
they kept the *p* on the fourteenth ... Num 9:5 6453
could not keep the *p* on that day ... Num 9:6 6453
he shall keep the *p* unto the LORD ... Num 9:10 6453
of the *p* they shall keep it ... Num 9:12 6453
and forbeareth to keep the *p* ... Num 9:13 6453
and will keep the *p* unto the LORD ... Num 9:14 6453
to the ordinance of the *p* ... Num 9:14 6453
first month is the *p* of the LORD ... Num 28:16 6453
on the morrow after the *p* the ... Num 33:3 6453
keep the *p* unto the LORD thy God ... Deut 16:1 6453
the *p* unto the LORD thy God ... Deut 16:2 6453
the *p* within any of thy gates ... Deut 16:5 6453
shalt sacrifice the *p* at even ... Deut 16:6 6453
kept the *p* on the fourteenth day ... Josh 5:10 6453
land on the morrow after the *p* ... Josh 5:11 6453
Keep the *p* unto the LORD your God ... 2Kin 23:21 6453
a *p* from the days of the judges ... 2Kin 23:22 6453
wherein this *p* was holden to the ... 2Kin 23:23 6453
to keep the *p* unto the LORD God ... 2Chr 30:1 6453
to keep the *p* in the second month ... 2Chr 30:2 6453
they should come to keep the *p* ... 2Chr 30:5 6453
Then they killed the *p* on the ... 2Chr 30:15 6453
yet did they eat the *p* otherwise ... 2Chr 30:18 6453
Moreover Josiah kept a *p* unto the ... 2Chr 35:1 6453
and they killed the *p* on the ... 2Chr 35:1 6453
So kill the *p*, and sanctify ... 2Chr 35:6 6453
and kids, all for the *p* offerings ... 2Chr 35:7 6453
for the *p* offerings two thousand ... 2Chr 35:8 6453
gave unto the Levites for *p* ... 2Chr 35:9 6453
And they killed the *p*, and the ... 2Chr 35:11 6453
they roasted the *p* with fire ... 2Chr 35:13 6453
the same day, to keep the *p* ... 2Chr 35:16 6453
present kept the *p* at that time ... 2Chr 35:17 6453
there was no *p* like to that kept ... 2Chr 35:18 6453
keep such a *p* as Josiah kept ... 2Chr 35:18 6453
reign of Josiah was this *p* kept ... 2Chr 35:19 6453
of the captivity kept the *p* upon ... Ezr 6:19 6453
killed the *p* for all the children ... Ezr 6:20 6453
of the month, ye shall have the *p* ... Eze 45:21 6453
two days is the feast of the *p* ... Mt 26:2 *3957*
we prepare for thee to eat the *p* ... Mt 26:17 *3957*
I will keep the *p* at thy house ... Mt 26:18 *3957*
and they made ready the *p* ... Mt 26:19 *3957*
two days was the feast of the *p* ... Mk 14:1 *3957*
bread, when they killed the *p* ... Mk 14:12 *3957*
that thou mayest eat the *p* ... Mk 14:12 *3957*
shall eat the *p* with my disciples ... Mk 14:14 *3957*
and they made ready the *p* ... Mk 14:16 *3957*
every year at the feast of the *p* ... Lk 2:41 *3957*
drew nigh, which is called the *P* ... Lk 22:1 *3957*
when the *p* must be killed ... Lk 22:7 *3957*
saying, Go and prepare us the *p* ... Lk 22:8 *3957*
shall eat the *p* with my disciples ... Lk 22:11 *3957*
and they made ready the *p* ... Lk 22:13 *3957*
this *p* with you before I suffer ... Lk 22:15 *3957*
the Jews' *p* was at hand, and Jesus ... Jn 2:13 *3957*
when he was in Jerusalem at the *p* ... Jn 2:23 *3957*
And the *p*, a feast of the Jews, ... Jn 6:4 *3957*
the Jews' *p* was nigh at hand ... Jn 11:55 *3957*
up to Jerusalem before the *p* ... Jn 11:55 *3957*
days before the *p* came to Bethany ... Jn 12:1 *3957*
Now before the feast of the *p* ... Jn 13:1 *3957*
but that they might eat the *p* ... Jn 18:28 *3957*
release unto you one at the *p* ... Jn 18:39 *3957*
it was the preparation of the *p* ... Jn 19:14 *3957*
For even Christ our *p* is ... 1Cor 5:7 *3957*
Through faith he kept the *p* ... Heb 11:28 *3957*

PASSOVERS {1}
the *p* for every one that was not ... 2Chr 30:17 6453

PAST {51}
the days of his mourning were *p* ... Gen 50:4 5674
to push with his horn in time *p* ... Ex 21:29 8032
ox hath used to push in time *p* ... Ex 21:36 8032
way, until we be *p* thy borders ... Num 21:22 5674
Emims dwelt therein in times *p* ... Deut 2:10
ask now of the days that are *p* ... Deut 4:32 7223
and hated him not in times *p* ... Deut 4:42 8032
whom he hated not in time *p* ... Deut 19:4 8032
as he hated him not in time *p* ... Deut 19:6 8032
the bitterness of death is *p* ... 1Sa 15:32 5493
in his presence, as in times *p* ... 1Sa 19:7 8032
in times *p* to be king over you ... 2Sa 3:17 8032
Also in time *p*, when Saul was ... 2Sa 5:2 8032
And when the mourning was *p* ... 2Sa 11:27 5493
a little *p* the top of the hill ... 2Sa 16:1 5674
came to pass, when midday was *p* ... 1Kin 18:29 5674
was the ruler over them in time *p* ... 1Chr 9:20
And moreover in time *p*, even when ... 1Chr 11:2 8032
doeth great things *p* finding out ... Job 9:10 369
me secret, until thy wrath be *p* ... Job 14:13 7725
My days are *p*, my purposes are ... Job 17:11 5674
Oh that I were as in months *p* ... Job 29:2 6924
are but as yesterday when it is *p* ... Ps 90:4 5674
and God requireth that which is *p* ... Eccl 3:15 7291
For, lo, the winter is *p*, the ... Song 2:11 5674
The harvest is *p*, the summer is ... Jer 8:20 5674
place, and the time is now *p* ... Mt 14:15 *3928*
And when the sabbath was *p* ... Mk 16:1 *1230*
And when the voice was *p*, Jesus ... Lk 9:36 *1096*
When they were *p* the first ... Acts 12:10 *1330*
Who in times *p* suffered all ... Acts 14:16 *3944*
the fast was now already *p* ... Acts 27:9 *3928*
the remission of sins that are *p* ... Rom 3:25 *4266*
For as ye in times *p* have not ... Rom 11:30
and his ways *p* finding out ... Rom 11:33 *421*
in time *p* in the Jews' religion ... Gal 1:13
p now preacheth the faith which ... Gal 1:23
as I have also told you in time *p* ... Gal 5:21 *4302*
Wherein in time *p* ye walked ... Eph 2:2
times *p* in the lusts of our flesh ... Eph 2:3
in time *p* Gentiles in the flesh ... Eph 2:11
Who being *p* feeling have given ... Eph 4:19 *524*
the resurrection is *p* already ... 2Ti 2:18 *1096*
Which in time *p* was to thee ... Philem 11
in time *p* unto the fathers by the ... Heb 1:1 *3819*
of a child when she was *p* age ... Heb 11:11 *3844*
Which in time *p* were not a people ... 1Pet 2:10
For the time *p* of our life may ... 1Pet 4:3 *3928*
because the darkness is *p* ... 1Jn 2:8 *3855*
One woe is *p* ... Rev 9:12 *565*
The second woe is *p* ... Rev 11:14 *565*

PASTOR {1}
from being a *p* to follow thee ... Jer 17:16 7462

PASTORS {8}
the *p* also transgressed against ... Jer 2:8 7462
I will give you *p* according to ... Jer 3:15 7462
For the *p* are become brutish, and ... Jer 10:21 7462
Many *p* have destroyed my vineyard ... Jer 12:10 7462
The wind shall eat up all thy *p* ... Jer 22:22 7462
Woe be unto the *p* that destroy ... Jer 23:1 7462
against the *p* that feed my people ... Jer 23:2 7462
and some, *p* and teachers ... Eph 4:11 *4166*

PASTURE {20}
have no *p* for their flocks ... Gen 47:4 4829
to seek *p* for their flocks ... 1Chr 4:39 4829
And they found fat *p* and good, and ... 1Chr 4:40 4829
because there was *p* there for ... 1Chr 4:41 4829
range of the mountains is his *p* ... Job 39:8 4829
smoke against the sheep of thy *p* ... Ps 74:1 4830
sheep of thy *p* will give thee ... Ps 79:13 4830
and we are the people of his *p* ... Ps 95:7 4830
his people, and the sheep of his *p* ... Ps 100:3 4830
joy of wild asses, a *p* of flocks ... Is 32:14 4829
and scatter the sheep of my *p* ... Jer 23:1 4830
for the LORD hath spoiled their *p* ... Jer 25:36 4830
become like harts that find no *p* ... Lam 1:6 4829
I will feed them in a good *p* ... Eze 34:14 4829
in a fat *p* shall they feed upon ... Eze 34:14 4829
you to have eaten up the good *p* ... Eze 34:18 4829
And ye my flock, the flock of my *p* ... Eze 34:31 4830
According to their *p*, so were ... Hos 13:6 4830
perplexed, because they have no *p* ... Joel 1:18 4829
and shall go in and out, and find *p* ... Jn 10:9 *3542*

PASTURES {11}
oxen, and twenty oxen out of the *p* ... 1Kin 4:23 7471
maketh me to lie down in green *p* ... Ps 23:2 4999
drop upon the *p* of the wilderness ... Ps 65:12 4999
The *p* are clothed with flocks ... Ps 65:13 3733
shall thy cattle feed in large *p* ... Is 30:23 3733
their *p* shall be in all high ... Is 49:9 4830
your feet the residue of your *p* ... Eze 34:18 4829
out of the fat *p* of Israel ... Eze 45:15 4945
devoured the *p* of the wilderness ... Joel 1:19 4999
devoured the *p* of the wilderness ... Joel 1:20 4999
for the *p* of the wilderness do ... Joel 2:22 4999

PATARA *(pat'-a-rah)* {1} *A city in Lycia in Asia Minor.*
Rhodes, and from thence unto *P* ... Acts 21:1 *3959*

PATE {1}
shall come down upon his own *p* ... Ps 7:16 6936

PATH {23}
by the way, an adder in the *p* ... Gen 49:17 734
stood in a *p* of the vineyards ... Num 22:24 4934
There is a *p* which no fowl ... Job 28:7 5410
They mar my *p*, they set forward ... Job 30:13 5410
He maketh a *p* to shine after him ... Job 41:32 5410
Thou wilt shew me the *p* of life ... Ps 16:11 734
O LORD, and lead me in a plain *p* ... Ps 27:11 734
thy *p* in the great waters, and thy ... Ps 77:19 7635
go in the *p* of thy commandments ... Ps 119:35 5410
my feet, and a light unto my *p* ... Ps 119:105 5410

Thou compassest my *p* and my lying ... Ps 139:3 734
within me, then thou knewest my *p* ... Ps 142:3 5410
refrain thy foot from their *p* ... Prov 1:15 5410
yea, every good *p* ... Prov 2:9 4570
not into the *p* of the wicked ... Prov 4:14 734
But the *p* of the just is as the ... Prov 4:18 734
Ponder the *p* of thy feet, and let ... Prov 4:26 4570
shouldest ponder the *p* of life ... Prov 5:6 734
dost weigh the *p* of the just ... Is 26:7 4570
the way, turn aside out of the *p* ... Is 30:11 734
taught him in the *p* of judgment ... Is 40:14 734
sea, and a *p* in the mighty waters ... Is 43:16 5410
shall walk every one in his *p* ... Joel 2:8 4546

PATHROS *(path'-ros)* {5} See PATHRUSIM. *A name for Upper Egypt.*
Assyria, and from Egypt, and from *P* ... Is 11:11 6624
at Noph, and in the country of *P* ... Jer 44:1 6624
dwelt in the land of Egypt, in *P* ... Jer 44:15 6624
them to return into the land of *P* ... Eze 29:14 6624
And I will make *P* desolate ... Eze 30:14 6624

PATHRUS See PATHROS.

PATHRUSIM *(path-ru'-sim)* {2} *A descendant of Mizraim.*
And *P*, and Casluhim, (out of whom ... Gen 10:14 6625
And *P*, and Casluhim, (of whom came ... 1Chr 1:12 6625

PATHS {43}
The *p* of their way are turned ... Job 6:18 734
So are the *p* of all that forget ... Job 8:13 734
and lookest narrowly unto all my *p* ... Job 13:27 734
and he hath set darkness in my *p* ... Job 19:8 5410
nor abide in the *p* thereof ... Job 24:13 5410
the stocks, he marketh all my *p* ... Job 33:11 734
know the *p* to the house thereof ... Job 38:20 5410
passeth through the *p* of the seas ... Ps 8:8 734
me from the *p* of the destroyer ... Ps 17:4 734
Hold up my goings in thy *p* ... Ps 17:5 4570
he leadeth me in the *p* of ... Ps 23:3 4570
teach me thy *p* ... Ps 25:4 734
All the *p* of the LORD are mercy ... Ps 25:10 734
and thy *p* drop fatness ... Ps 65:11 4570
He keepeth the *p* of judgment ... Prov 2:8 734
Who leave the *p* of uprightness, ... Prov 2:13 734
and they froward in their *p* ... Prov 2:15 4570
death, and her *p* unto the dead ... Prov 2:18 4570
take they hold of the *p* of life ... Prov 2:19 734
keep the *p* of the righteous ... Prov 2:20 734
him, and he shall direct thy *p* ... Prov 3:6 734
and all her *p* are peace ... Prov 3:17 5410
I have led thee in right *p* ... Prov 4:11 4570
her ways, go not astray in her *p* ... Prov 7:25 5410
by the way in the places of the *p* ... Prov 8:2 5410
in the midst of the *p* of judgment ... Prov 8:20 5410
ways, and we will walk in his *p* ... Is 2:3 734
err, and destroy the way of thy *p* ... Is 3:12 734
I will lead them in *p* that they ... Is 42:16 5410
The restorer of *p* to dwell in ... Is 58:12 5410
and destruction are in their *p* ... Is 59:7 4546
they have made them crooked *p* ... Is 59:8 5410
and see, and ask for the old *p* ... Jer 6:16 5410
in their ways from the ancient *p* ... Jer 18:15 7635
the ancient *p*, to walk in *p* ... Jer 18:15 5410
stone, he hath made my *p* crooked ... Lam 3:9 5410
that she shall not find her *p* ... Hos 2:6 5410
ways, and we will walk in his *p* ... Mic 4:2 734
of the Lord, make his *p* straight ... Mt 3:3 *5147*
of the Lord, make his *p* straight ... Mk 1:3 *5147*
of the Lord, make his *p* straight ... Lk 3:4 *5147*
And make straight *p* for your feet ... Heb 12:13 *5163*

PATHWAY {1}
in the *p* thereof there is no ... Prov 12:28 1870,5410

PATIENCE {34}
have *p* with me, and I will pay ... Mt 18:26 *3114*
Have *p* with me, and I will pay ... Mt 18:29 *3114*
it, and bring forth fruit with *p* ... Lk 8:15 *5281*
In your *p* possess ye your souls ... Lk 21:19 *5281*
that tribulation worketh *p* ... Rom 5:3 *5281*
And *p*, experience ... Rom 5:4 *5281*
then do we with *p* wait for it ... Rom 8:25 *5281*
our learning, that we through *p* ... Rom 15:4 *5281*
Now the God of *p* and consolation ... Rom 15:5 *5281*
the ministers of God, in much *p* ... 2Cor 6:4 *5281*
were wrought among you in all *p* ... 2Cor 12:12 *5281*
to his glorious power, unto all *p* ... Col 1:11 *5281*
p of hope in our Lord Jesus ... 1Th 1:3 *5281*
in the churches of God for your *p* ... 2Th 1:4 *5281*
godliness, faith, love, *p* ... 1Ti 6:11 *5281*
faith, longsuffering, charity, *p* ... 2Ti 3:10 *5281*
sound in faith, in charity, in *p* ... Titus 2:2 *5281*
faith and *p* inherit the promises ... Heb 6:12 *3115*
For ye have need of *p*, that, ... Heb 10:36 *5281*
let us run with *p* the race that ... Heb 12:1 *5281*
trying of your faith worketh *p* ... Jas 1:3 *5281*
But let *p* have her perfect work, ... Jas 1:4 *5281*
the earth, and hath long *p* for it ... Jas 5:7 *3114*
of suffering affliction, and of *p* ... Jas 5:10 *3115*
Ye have heard of the *p* of Job ... Jas 5:11 *5281*
and to temperance *p* ... 2Pet 1:6 *5281*
and to *p* godliness ... 2Pet 1:6 *5281*
p of Jesus Christ, was in the ... Rev 1:9 *5281*
works, and thy labour, and thy *p* ... Rev 2:2 *5281*
And hast borne, and hast *p*, and for ... Rev 2:3 *5281*
and service, and faith, and thy *p* ... Rev 2:19 *5281*
thou hast kept the word of my *p* ... Rev 3:10 *5281*
Here is the *p* and the faith of the ... Rev 13:10 *5281*
Here is the *p* of the saints ... Rev 14:12 *5281*

PATIENT {9}
the *p* in spirit is better than ... Eccl 7:8 750
To them who by *p* continuance in ... Rom 2:7 *5281*
p in tribulation ... Rom 12:12 *5278*
the weak, be *p* toward all men ... 1Th 5:14 *3114*
into the *p* waiting for Christ ... 2Th 3:5 *5281*
but *p*, not a brawler, not ... 1Ti 3:3 *1933*
unto all men, apt to teach, *p* ... 2Ti 2:24 *420*
Be *p* therefore, brethren, unto ... Jas 5:7 *3114*
Be ye also *p* ... Jas 5:8 *3114*

PATIENTLY {6}
in the LORD, and wait *p* for him ... Ps 37:7 2342
I waited *p* for the LORD ... Ps 40:1 6960
I beseech thee to hear me *p* ... Acts 26:3 *3116*
And so, after he had *p* endured ... Heb 6:15 *3114*
your faults, ye shall take it *p* ... 1Pet 2:20 *5278*
and suffer for it, ye take it *p* ... 1Pet 2:20 *5278*

PATMOS *(pat'-mos)* {1} *An island off the west coast of Asia Minor.*
was in the isle that is called *P* ... Rev 1:9 *3963*

PATRIARCH {2}
speak unto you of the *p* David ... Acts 2:29 *3966*
unto whom even the *p* Abraham gave ... Heb 7:4 *3966*

PATRIARCHS {2}
and Jacob begat the twelve *p* ... Acts 7:8 *3966*
And the *p*, moved with envy, sold ... Acts 7:9 *3966*

PATRIMONY {1}
which cometh of the sale of his *p* ... Deut 18:8

PATROBAS *(pat'-ro-bas)* {1} *A Christian in Rome.*
Asyncritus, Phlegon, Hermas, *P* ... Rom 16:14 *3969*

PATTERN {14}
after the *p* of the tabernacle, and ... Ex 25:9 8403
the *p* of all the instruments ... Ex 25:9 8403
that thou make them after their *p* ... Ex 25:40 8403
according unto the *p* which the ... Num 8:4 4758
Behold the *p* of the altar of the ... Josh 22:28 8403
the *p* of it, according to all the ... 2Kin 16:10 8403
his son the *p* of the porch ... 1Chr 28:11 8403
the *p* of all that he had by the ... 1Chr 28:12 8403
gold for the *p* of the chariot of ... 1Chr 28:18 8403
me, even all the works of this *p* ... 1Chr 28:19 8403
and let them measure the *p* ... Eze 43:10 8508
for a *p* to them which should ... 1Ti 1:16 *5296*
shewing thyself a *p* of good works ... Titus 2:7 *5179*
the *p* shewed to thee in the mount ... Heb 8:5 *5179*

PATTERNS {1}
therefore necessary that the *p* of ... Heb 9:23 *5262*

PAU *(pa'-u)* {1} See PAI. *City of King Hagar of Edom.*
and the name of his city was *P* ... Gen 36:39 6464

PAUL *(pawl)* {157} See PAUL'S, PAULUS, SAUL. *The apostle to the Gentiles.*
Then Saul, (who also is called *P* ... Acts 13:9 *3972*
Now when *P* and his company loosed ... Acts 13:13 *3972*
Then *P* stood up, and beckoning ... Acts 13:16 *3972*
religious proselytes followed *P* ... Acts 13:43 *3972*
things which were spoken by *P* ... Acts 13:45 *3972*
Then *P* and Barnabas waxed bold, and ... Acts 13:46 *3972*
and raised persecution against *P* ... Acts 13:50 *3972*
The same heard *P* speak ... Acts 14:9 *3972*
the people saw what *P* had done ... Acts 14:11 *3972*
and *P*, Mercurius, because he was ... Acts 14:12 *3972*
when the apostles, Barnabas and *P* ... Acts 14:14 *3972*
the people, and, having stoned *P* ... Acts 14:19 *3972*
When therefore *P* and Barnabas had ... Acts 15:2 *3972*
with them, they determined that *P* ... Acts 15:2 *3972*
and gave audience to Barnabas and *P* ... Acts 15:12 *3972*
own company to Antioch with *P* ... Acts 15:22 *3972*
with our beloved Barnabas and *P* ... Acts 15:25 *3972*
P also and Barnabas continued in ... Acts 15:35 *3972*
some days after *P* said unto ... Acts 15:36 *3972*
But *P* thought not good to take ... Acts 15:38 *3972*
P chose Silas, and departed, being ... Acts 15:40 *3972*
Him would *P* have to go forth with ... Acts 16:3 *3972*
vision appeared to *P* in the night ... Acts 16:9 *3972*
the things which were spoken of *P* ... Acts 16:14 *3972*
The same followed *P* and us, and ... Acts 16:17 *3972*
But *P*, being grieved, turned and ... Acts 16:18 *3972*
gains was gone, they caught *P* ... Acts 16:19 *3972*
And at midnight *P* and Silas prayed, ... Acts 16:25 *3972*
But *P* cried with a loud voice, ... Acts 16:28 *3972*
trembling, and fell down before *P* ... Acts 16:29 *3972*
the prison told this saying to *P* ... Acts 16:36 *3972*
But *P* said unto them, They have ... Acts 16:37 *3972*
And *P*, as his manner was, went in ... Acts 17:2 *3972*
believed, and consorted with *P* ... Acts 17:4 *3972*
brethren immediately sent away *P* ... Acts 17:10 *3972*
of God was preached of *P* at Berea ... Acts 17:13 *3972*
the brethren sent away *P* to go as ... Acts 17:14 *3972*
they that conducted *P* brought him ... Acts 17:15 *3972*
Now while *P* waited for them at ... Acts 17:16 *3972*
Then *P* stood in the midst of ... Acts 17:22 *3972*
So *P* departed from among them ... Acts 17:33 *3972*
After these things *P* departed ... Acts 18:1 *3972*
P was pressed in the spirit, and ... Acts 18:5 *3972*
Then spake the Lord to *P* in the ... Acts 18:9 *3972*
with one accord against *P* ... Acts 18:12 *3972*
when *P* was now about to open his ... Acts 18:14 *3972*
P after this tarried there yet a ... Acts 18:18 *3972*
P having passed through the upper ... Acts 19:1 *3972*
Then said *P*, John verily baptized ... Acts 19:4 *3972*
when *P* had laid his hands upon ... Acts 19:6 *3972*
miracles by the hands of *P* ... Acts 19:11 *3972*
you by Jesus whom *P* preacheth ... Acts 19:13 *3972*
said, Jesus I know, and *P* I know ... Acts 19:15 *3972*
P purposed in the spirit, when he ... Acts 19:21 *3972*
this *P* hath persuaded and turned ... Acts 19:26 *3972*
when *P* would have entered in unto ... Acts 19:30 *3972*
P called unto him the disciples, ... Acts 20:1 *3972*
P preached unto them, ready to ... Acts 20:7 *3972*
as *P* was long preaching, he sunk ... Acts 20:9 *3972*
P went down, and fell on him, and ... Acts 20:10 *3972*
there intending to take in *P* ... Acts 20:13 *3972*
For *P* had determined to sail by ... Acts 20:16 *3972*
who said to *P* through the Spirit, ... Acts 21:4 *3972*
Then *P* answered, What mean ye to ... Acts 21:13 *3972*
the day following *P* went in with ... Acts 21:18 *3972*
Then *P* took the men, and the next ... Acts 21:26 *3972*
whom they supposed that *P* had ... Acts 21:29 *3972*
and they took *P*, and drew him out ... Acts 21:30 *3972*
soldiers, they left beating of *P* ... Acts 21:32 *3972*
as *P* was to be led into the ... Acts 21:37 *3972*
But *P* said, I am a man which am a ... Acts 21:39 *3972*
P stood on the stairs, and ... Acts 21:40 *3972*
P said unto the centurion that ... Acts 22:25 *3972*
P said, But I was free born ... Acts 22:28 *3972*
to appear, and brought *P* down ... Acts 22:30 *3972*
And *P*, earnestly beholding the ... Acts 23:1 *3972*
Then said *P* unto him, God shall ... Acts 23:3 *3972*
Then said *P*, I wist not, brethren ... Acts 23:5 *3972*
But when *P* perceived that the one ... Acts 23:6 *3972*
fearing lest *P* should have been ... Acts 23:10 *3972*
him, and said, Be of good cheer, *P* ... Acts 23:11 *3972*
nor drink till they had killed *P* ... Acts 23:12 *3972*
eat nothing until we have slain *P* ... Acts 23:14 *3972*
into the castle, and told *P* ... Acts 23:16 *3972*
Then *P* called one of the ... Acts 23:17 *3972*
P the prisoner called me unto him ... Acts 23:18 *3972*
down *P* to morrow into the council ... Acts 23:20 *3972*
beasts, that they may set *P* on ... Acts 23:24 *3972*
as it was commanded them, took *P* ... Acts 23:31 *3972*
presented *P* also before him ... Acts 23:33 *3972*
informed the governor against *P* ... Acts 24:1 *3972*
Then *P*, after that the governor ... Acts 24:10 *3972*
commanded a centurion to keep *P* ... Acts 24:23 *3972*
which was a Jewess, he sent for *P* ... Acts 24:24 *3972*
should have been given him of *P* ... Acts 24:26 *3972*
the Jews a pleasure, left *P* bound ... Acts 24:27 *3972*
the Jews informed him against *P* ... Acts 25:2 *3972*
that *P* should be kept at Caesarea ... Acts 25:4 *3972*
seat commanded *P* to be brought ... Acts 25:6 *3972*
and grievous complaints against *P* ... Acts 25:7 *3972*
the Jews a pleasure, answered *P* ... Acts 25:9 *3972*
Then said *P*, I stand at Caesar's ... Acts 25:10 *3972*
whom *P* affirmed to be alive ... Acts 25:19 *3972*
But when *P* had appealed to be ... Acts 25:21 *3972*
commandment *P* was brought forth ... Acts 25:23 *3972*
Then Agrippa said unto *P*, Thou ... Acts 26:1 *3972*
Then *P* stretched forth the hand, ... Acts 26:1 *3972*
Festus said with a loud voice, *P* ... Acts 26:24 *3972*
Then Agrippa said unto *P*, Almost ... Acts 26:28 *3972*
P said, I would to God, that not ... Acts 26:29 *3972*
sail into Italy, they delivered *P* ... Acts 27:1 *3972*
And Julius courteously entreated *P* ... Acts 27:3 *3972*
already past, *P* admonished them, ... Acts 27:9 *3972*
things which were spoken by *P* ... Acts 27:11 *3972*
But after long abstinence *P* stood ... Acts 27:21 *3972*
Saying, Fear not, *P* ... Acts 27:24 *3972*
P said to the centurion and to the ... Acts 27:31 *3972*
P besought them all to take meat, ... Acts 27:33 *3972*
the centurion, willing to save *P* ... Acts 27:43 *3972*
when *P* had gathered a bundle of ... Acts 28:3 *3972*
to whom *P* entered in, and prayed, ... Acts 28:8 *3972*
whom when *P* saw, he thanked God, ... Acts 28:15 *3972*
but *P* was suffered to dwell by ... Acts 28:16 *3972*
that after three days *P* called ... Acts 28:17 *3972*
after that *P* had spoken one word, ... Acts 28:25 *3972*
P dwelt two whole years in his ... Acts 28:30 *3972*
P, a servant of Jesus Christ, ... Rom 1:1 *3972*
P, called to be an apostle of ... 1Cor 1:1 *3972*
every one of you saith, I am of *P* ... 1Cor 1:12 *3972*
was *P* crucified for you ... 1Cor 1:13 *3972*
were ye baptized in the name of *P* ... 1Cor 1:13 *3972*
For while one saith, I am of *P* ... 1Cor 3:4 *3972*
Who then is *P*, and who is Apollos, ... 1Cor 3:5 *3972*
Whether *P*, or Apollos, or Cephas, ... 1Cor 3:22 *3972*
of me *P* with mine own hand ... 1Cor 16:21 *3972*
P, an apostle of Jesus Christ by ... 2Cor 1:1 *3972*
Now I *P* myself beseech you by the ... 2Cor 10:1 *3972*
P, an apostle, (not of men, ... Gal 1:1 *3972*
I *P* say unto you, that if ye be ... Gal 5:2 *3972*
P, an apostle of Jesus Christ by ... Eph 1:1 *3972*
For this cause I *P*, the prisoner ... Eph 3:1 *3972*
P and Timotheus, the servants of ... Phil 1:1 *3972*
P, an apostle of Jesus Christ by ... Col 1:1 *3972*
whereof I *P* am made a minister ... Col 1:23 *3972*
salutation by the hand of me *P* ... Col 4:18 *3972*
P, and Silvanus, and Timotheus, ... 1Th 1:1 *3972*
have come unto you, even I *P* ... 1Th 2:18 *3972*
P, and Silvanus, and Timotheus, ... 2Th 1:1 *3972*
The salutation of *P* with mine own ... 2Th 3:17 *3972*
P, an apostle of Jesus Christ by ... 1Ti 1:1 *3972*
P, an apostle of Jesus Christ by ... 2Ti 1:1 *3972*
when *P* was brought before Nero ... 2Ti *s* *3972*
P, a servant of God, and an ... Titus 1:1 *3972*
P, a prisoner of Jesus Christ, and ... Philem 1 *3972*
being such an one as *P* the aged ... Philem 9 *3972*
I *P* have written it with mine own ... Philem 19 *3972*
even as our beloved brother *P* ... 2Pet 3:15 *3972*

PAUL'S *(pawls)* {6}
P companions in travel, they ... Acts 19:29 *3972*
all wept sore, and fell on *P* neck ... Acts 20:37 *3972*

P

that were of *P* company departed ... Acts 21:8 *3972*
come unto us, he took *P* girdle ... Acts 21:11 *3972*
when *P* sister's son heard of ... Acts 23:16 *3972*
Festus declared *P* cause unto the ... Acts 25:14 *3972*

PAULUS {1} See Paul. *A Roman proconsul.*
deputy of the country, Sergius *P* ... Acts 13:7 *3972*

PAVED {2}
were a *p* work of a sapphire stone ... Ex 24:10 3840
midst thereof being *p* with love ... Song 3:10 7528

PAVEMENT {9}
it, and put it upon a *p* of stones ... 2Kin 16:17 4837
faces to the ground upon the *p* ... 2Chr 7:3 7531
gold and silver, upon a *p* of red ... Est 1:6 7531
a *p* made for the court round ... Eze 40:17 7531
thirty chambers were upon the *p* ... Eze 40:17 7531
the *p* by the side of the gates ... Eze 40:18 7531
of the gates was the lower *p* ... Eze 40:18 7531
over against the *p* which was for ... Eze 42:3 7531
in a place that is called the *P* ... Jn 19:13 *3037*

PAVILION {4}
his *p* round about him were dark ... Ps 18:11 5521
trouble he shall hide me in his *p* ... Ps 27:5 5520
in a *p* from the strife of tongues ... Ps 31:20 5521
spread his royal *p* over them ... Jer 43:10 8237

PAVILIONS {3}
made darkness *p* round about him ... 2Sa 22:12 5521
he and the kings in the *p* ... 1Kin 20:12 5521
drinking himself drunk in the *p* ... 1Kin 20:16 5521

PAW {2}
me out of the *p* of the lion ... 1Sa 17:37 3027
out of the *p* of the bear, he will ... 1Sa 17:37 3027

PAWETH {1}
He *p* in the valley, and rejoiceth ... Job 39:21 2658

PAWS {1}
And whatsoever goeth upon his *p* ... Lev 11:27 3709

PAY {39}
only he shall *p* for the loss of ... Ex 21:19 5414
and he shall *p* as the judges ... Ex 21:22 5414
he shall surely *p* ox for ox ... Ex 21:36 7999
thief be found, let him *p* double ... Ex 22:7 7999
he shall *p* double unto his ... Ex 22:9 7999
he shall *p* money according to the ... Ex 22:17 8254
thy water, then I will *p* for it ... Num 20:19 5414,4377
God, thou shalt not slack to *p* it ... Deut 23:21 7999
p my vow, which I have vowed unto ... 2Sa 15:7 7999
thou shalt *p* a talent of silver ... 1Kin 20:39 8254
p thy debt, and live thou and thy ... 2Kin 4:7 7999
make to *p* tribute until this day ... 2Chr 8:8 5927
the children of Ammon *p* unto him ... 2Chr 27:5 7725
again, then will they not *p* toll ... Ezr 4:13 5415
I will *p* ten thousand talents of ... Est 3:9 8254
that Haman had promised to *p* to ... Est 4:7 8254
thee, and thou shalt *p* thy vows ... Job 22:27 7999
I will *p* my vows before them that ... Ps 22:25 7999
p thy vows unto the most High ... Ps 50:14 7999
I will *p* thee my vows, ... Ps 66:13 7999
Vow, and *p* unto the Lord your God ... Ps 76:11 7999
I will *p* my vows unto the Lord ... Ps 116:14 7999
I will *p* my vows unto the Lord ... Ps 116:18 7999
he hath given will he *p* him again ... Prov 19:17 7999
If thou hast nothing to *p* ... Prov 22:27 7999
a vow unto God, defer not to *p* it ... Eccl 5:4 7999
p that which thou hast vowed ... Eccl 5:4 7999
that thou shouldest vow and not *p* ... Eccl 5:5 7999
I will *p* that that I have vowed ... Jonah 2:9 7999
Doth not your master *p* tribute ... Mt 17:24 *5055*
But forasmuch as he had not to *p* ... Mt 18:25 *591*
with me, and I will *p* thee all ... Mt 18:26 *591*
saying, *P* me that thou owest ... Mt 18:28 *591*
with me, and I will *p* thee all ... Mt 18:29 *591*
prison, till he should *p* the debt ... Mt 18:30 *591*
till he should *p* all that was due ... Mt 18:34 *591*
for ye *p* tithe of mint and anise ... Mt 23:23 *586*
And when they had nothing to *p* ... Lk 7:42 *591*
for this cause *p* ye tribute also ... Rom 13:6 *5055*

PAYED {2}
this day have I *p* my vows ... Prov 7:14 7999
tithes, *p* tithes in Abraham ... Heb 7:9 *1183*

PAYETH {1}
wicked borroweth, and *p* not again ... Ps 37:21 7999

PAYMENT {1}
all that he had, and *p* to be made ... Mt 18:25 *591*

PEACE {430}
thou shalt go to thy fathers in *p* ... Gen 15:15 7965
man wondering at her held his *p* ... Gen 24:21 2790
good, and have sent thee away in *p* ... Gen 26:29 7965
and they departed from him in *p* ... Gen 26:31 7965
again to my father's house in *p* ... Gen 28:21 7965
Jacob held his *p* until they were ... Gen 34:5 2790
shall give Pharaoh an answer of *p* ... Gen 41:16 7965
And he said, *P* be to you, fear not ... Gen 43:23 7965
get you up in *p* unto your father ... Gen 44:17 7965
And Jethro said to Moses, Go in *p* ... Ex 4:18 7965
for you, and ye shall hold your *p* ... Ex 14:14 2790
shall also go to their place in *p* ... Ex 18:23 7965
thy *p* offerings, thy sheep, and ... Ex 20:24 8002
sacrificed *p* offerings of oxen ... Ex 24:5 8002
sacrifice of their *p* offerings ... Ex 29:28 8002
offerings, and brought *p* offerings ... Ex 32:6 8002
be a sacrifice of *p* offering ... Lev 3:1 8002
p offering an offering made by ... Lev 3:3 8002
of *p* offering unto the Lord be of ... Lev 3:6 8002
p offering an offering made by ... Lev 3:9 8002
of the sacrifice of *p* offerings ... Lev 4:10 8002
of the sacrifice of *p* offerings ... Lev 4:26 8002
off the sacrifice of *p* offerings ... Lev 4:31 8002
the sacrifice of the *p* offerings ... Lev 4:35 8002
the fat of the *p* offerings ... Lev 6:12 8002
of the sacrifice of *p* offerings ... Lev 7:11 8002
thanksgiving of his *p* offerings ... Lev 7:13 8002
the blood of the *p* offerings ... Lev 7:14 8002
his *p* offerings for thanksgiving ... Lev 7:15 8002
p offerings be eaten at all on ... Lev 7:18 8002
of the sacrifice of *p* offerings ... Lev 7:20 8002
of the sacrifice of *p* offerings ... Lev 7:21 8002
p offerings unto the Lord shall ... Lev 7:29 8002
the sacrifice of his *p* offerings ... Lev 7:29 8002
sacrifices of your *p* offerings ... Lev 7:32 8002
the blood of the *p* offerings ... Lev 7:33 8002
sacrifices of their *p* offerings ... Lev 7:34 8002
the sacrifice of the *p* offerings ... Lev 7:37 8002
bullock and a ram for *p* offerings ... Lev 9:4 8002
for a sacrifice of *p* offerings ... Lev 9:18 8002
burnt offering, and *p* offerings ... Lev 9:22 8002
And Aaron held his *p* ... Lev 10:3 1826
of *p* offerings of the children of ... Lev 10:14 8002
offer them for *p* offerings unto ... Lev 17:5 8002
of *p* offerings unto the Lord ... Lev 19:5 8002
offereth a sacrifice of *p* ... Lev 22:21 8002
for a sacrifice of *p* offerings ... Lev 23:19 8002
And I will give *p* in the land ... Lev 26:6 7965
without blemish for *p* offerings ... Num 6:14 8002
of *p* offerings unto the Lord ... Num 6:17 8002
the sacrifice of the *p* offerings ... Num 6:18 8002
upon thee, and give thee *p* ... Num 6:26 7965
And for a sacrifice of *p* offerings ... Num 7:17 8002
And for a sacrifice of *p* offerings ... Num 7:23 8002
And for a sacrifice of *p* offerings ... Num 7:29 8002
And for a sacrifice of *p* offerings ... Num 7:35 8002
And for a sacrifice of *p* offerings ... Num 7:41 8002
And for a sacrifice of *p* offerings ... Num 7:47 8002
And for a sacrifice of *p* offerings ... Num 7:53 8002
And for a sacrifice of *p* offerings ... Num 7:59 8002
And for a sacrifice of *p* offerings ... Num 7:65 8002
And for a sacrifice of *p* offerings ... Num 7:71 8002
And for a sacrifice of *p* offerings ... Num 7:77 8002
And for a sacrifice of *p* offerings ... Num 7:83 8002
of the *p* offerings were twenty ... Num 7:88 8002
sacrifices of your *p* offerings ... Num 10:10 8002
or *p* offerings unto the Lord ... Num 15:8 8002
I give unto him my covenant of *p* ... Num 25:12 7965
and for your *p* offerings ... Num 29:39 8002
father shall hold his *p* at her ... Num 30:4 2790
held his *p* at her in the day that ... Num 30:7 2790
heard it, and held his *p* at her ... Num 30:11 2790
hold his *p* at her from day to day ... Num 30:14 2790
because he held his *p* at her in ... Num 30:14 2790
king of Heshbon with words of *p* ... Deut 2:26 7965
it, then proclaim *p* unto it ... Deut 20:10 7965
be, if it make thee answer of *p* ... Deut 20:11 7965
And if it will make no *p* with thee ... Deut 20:12 7999
Thou shalt not seek their *p* nor ... Deut 23:6 7965
And thou shalt offer *p* offerings ... Deut 27:7 8002
his heart, saying, I shall have *p* ... Deut 29:19 7965
Lord, and sacrificed *p* offerings ... Josh 8:31 8002
And Joshua made *p* with them ... Josh 9:15 7965
of Gibeon had made *p* with Israel ... Josh 10:1 7999
for it hath made *p* with Joshua ... Josh 10:4 7999
camp to Joshua at Makkedah in *p* ... Josh 10:21 7965
p with the children of Israel ... Josh 11:19 7999
or if to offer *p* offerings ... Josh 22:23 8002
and with our *p* offerings ... Josh 22:27 8002
for there was *p* between Jabin the ... Judg 4:17 7965
said unto him, *P* be unto thee ... Judg 6:23 7965
saying, When I come again in *p* ... Judg 8:9 7965
when I return in *p* from the ... Judg 11:31 7965
priest said unto them, Go in *p* ... Judg 18:6 7965
And they said unto him, Hold thy *p* ... Judg 18:19 2790
the old man said, *P* be with thee ... Judg 19:20 7965
p offerings before the Lord ... Judg 20:26 8002
burnt offerings and *p* offerings ... Judg 21:4 8002
Eli answered and said, Go in *p* ... 1Sa 1:17 7965
there was *p* between Israel and the ... 1Sa 7:14 7965
sacrifices of *p* offerings ... 1Sa 10:8 8002
But he held his *p* ... 1Sa 10:27 2790
of *p* offerings before the Lord ... 1Sa 11:15 8002
offering to me, and *p* offerings ... 1Sa 13:9 8002
thy servant shall have *p* ... 1Sa 20:7 7965
away, that thou mayest go in *p* ... 1Sa 20:13 7965
for there is *p* to thee, and no ... 1Sa 20:21 7965
Jonathan said to David, Go in *p* ... 1Sa 20:42 7965
P be both to thee ... 1Sa 25:6 7965
p be to thine house ... 1Sa 25:6 7965
p be unto all that thou hast ... 1Sa 25:6 7965
Go up in *p* to thine house ... 1Sa 25:35 7965
Wherefore now return, and go in *p* ... 1Sa 29:7 7965
and he went in *p* ... 2Sa 3:21 7965
him away, and he was gone in *p* ... 2Sa 3:22 7965
sent him away, and he is gone in *p* ... 2Sa 3:23 7965
p offerings before the Lord ... 2Sa 6:17 8002
p offerings, he blessed the ... 2Sa 6:18 8002
they made *p* with Israel, and ... 2Sa 10:19 7999
but hold now thy *p*, my sister ... 2Sa 13:20 2790
the king said unto him, Go in *p* ... 2Sa 15:9 7965
return into the city in *p* ... 2Sa 15:27 7965
so all the people shall be in *p* ... 2Sa 17:3 7965
until the day he came again in *p* ... 2Sa 19:24 7965
again in *p* unto his own house ... 2Sa 19:30 7965
burnt offerings and *p* offerings ... 2Sa 24:25 8002
and shed the blood of war in *p* ... 1Kin 2:5 7965
head go down to the grave in *p* ... 1Kin 2:6 7965
shall there be *p* for ever from ... 1Kin 2:33 7965
offered *p* offerings, and made a ... 1Kin 3:15 8002
he had *p* on all sides round about ... 1Kin 4:24 7965
there was *p* between Hiram and ... 1Kin 5:12 7965
a sacrifice of *p* offerings ... 1Kin 8:63 8002
and the fat of the *p* offerings ... 1Kin 8:64 8002
and the fat of the *p* offerings ... 1Kin 8:64 8002
p offerings upon the altar which ... 1Kin 9:25 8002
Whether they be come out for *p* ... 1Kin 20:18 7965
every man to his house in *p* ... 1Kin 22:17 7965
of affliction, until I come in *p* ... 1Kin 22:27 7965
said, If thou return at all in *p* ... 1Kin 22:28 7965
Jehoshaphat made *p* with the king ... 1Kin 22:44 7999
hold ye your *p* ... 2Kin 2:3 2814
hold ye your *p* ... 2Kin 2:5 2814
And he said unto him, Go in *p* ... 2Kin 5:19 7965
of good tidings, and we hold our *p* ... 2Kin 7:9 2814
them, and let him say, Is it *p* ... 2Kin 9:17 7965
Thus saith the king, Is it *p* ... 2Kin 9:18 7965
said, What hast thou to do with *p* ... 2Kin 9:18 7965
Thus saith the king, Is it *p* ... 2Kin 9:19 7965
What hast thou to do with *p* ... 2Kin 9:19 7965
saw Jehu, that he said, Is it *p* ... 2Kin 9:22 7965
And he answered, What *p*, so long ... 2Kin 9:22 7965
the gate, she said, Had Zimri *p* ... 2Kin 9:31 7965
the blood of his *p* offerings ... 2Kin 16:13 8002
But the people held their *p* ... 2Kin 18:36 2790
And he said, Is it not good, if *p* ... 2Kin 20:19 7965
be gathered into thy grave in *p* ... 2Kin 22:20 7965
p, *p* be unto thee, and *p* ... 1Chr 12:18 7965
thee, and *p* be to thine helpers ... 1Chr 12:18 7965
and *p* offerings before God ... 1Chr 16:1 8002
the *p* offerings, he blessed the ... 1Chr 16:2 8002
they made *p* with David, and became ... 1Chr 19:19 7999
p offerings, and called upon the ... 1Chr 21:26 8002
be Solomon, and I will give *p* ... 1Chr 22:9 7965
and the fat of the *p* offerings ... 2Chr 7:7 8002
was no *p* to him that went out ... 2Chr 15:5 7965
every man to his house in *p* ... 2Chr 18:16 7965
affliction, until I return in *p* ... 2Chr 18:26 7965
If thou certainly return in *p* ... 2Chr 18:27 7965
to his house in *p* to Jerusalem ... 2Chr 19:1 7965
with the fat of the *p* offerings ... 2Chr 29:35 8002
offering *p* offerings, and making ... 2Chr 30:22 8002
for *p* offerings, to minister, and ... 2Chr 31:2 8002
and sacrificed thereon *p* offerings ... 2Chr 33:16 8002
be gathered to thy grave in *p* ... 2Chr 34:28 7965
unto the rest beyond the river, *P* ... Ezr 4:17 8001
Unto Darius the king, all *p* ... Ezr 5:7 8001
of the God of heaven, perfect *p* ... Ezr 7:12
nor seek their *p* or their wealth ... Ezr 9:12 7965
Then held they their *p*, and found ... Neh 5:8 2790
the people, saying, Hold your *p* ... Neh 8:11 2013
holdest thy *p* at this time ... Est 4:14 2790
of Ahasuerus, with words of *p* ... Est 9:30 7965
speaking *p* to all his seed ... Est 10:3 7965
the field shall be at *p* with thee ... Job 5:23 7999
that thy tabernacle shall be in *p* ... Job 5:24 7965
thy lies make men hold their *p* ... Job 11:3 2790
ye would altogether hold your *p* ... Job 13:5 2790
Hold your *p*, let me alone, that I ... Job 13:13 2790
now thyself with him, and be at *p* ... Job 22:21 7999
he maketh *p* in his high places ... Job 25:2 7965
The nobles held their *p*, and their ... Job 29:10 6963
hold thy *p*, and I will speak ... Job 33:31 2790
hold thy *p*, and I shall teach thee ... Job 33:33 2790
I will both lay me down in *p* ... Ps 4:8 7965
unto him that was at *p* with me ... Ps 7:4 7999
which speak *p* to their neighbours ... Ps 28:3 7965
Lord will bless his people with *p* ... Ps 29:11 7965
seek *p*, and pursue it ... Ps 34:14 7965
For they speak not *p* ... Ps 35:20 7965
themselves in the abundance of *p* ... Ps 37:11 7965
for the end of that man is *p* ... Ps 37:37 7965
dumb with silence, I held my *p* ... Ps 39:2 2814
hold not thy *p* at my tears ... Ps 39:12 2790
in *p* from the battle that was ... Ps 55:18 7965
against such as be at *p* with him ... Ps 55:20 7965
shall bring *p* to the people ... Ps 72:3 7965
abundance of *p* so long as the ... Ps 72:7 7965
hold not thy *p*, and be not still, ... Ps 83:1 2790
he will speak *p* unto his people ... Ps 85:8 7965
and *p* have kissed each other ... Ps 85:10 7965
Hold not thy *p*, O God of my ... Ps 109:1 2790
Great *p* have they which love thy ... Ps 119:165 7965
long dwelt with him that hateth *p* ... Ps 120:6 7965
I am for *p* ... Ps 120:7 7965
Pray for the *p* of Jerusalem ... Ps 122:6 7965
P be within thy walls, and ... Ps 122:7 7965
I will now say, *P* be within thee ... Ps 122:8 7965
but *p* shall be upon Israel ... Ps 125:5 7965
children, and *p* upon Israel ... Ps 128:6 7965
He maketh *p* in thy borders, and ... Ps 147:14 7965
of days, and long life, and *p* ... Prov 3:2 7965
and all her paths are *p* ... Prov 3:17 7965
I have *p* offerings with me ... Prov 7:14 8002
of understanding holdeth his *p* ... Prov 11:12 2790
to the counsellors of *p* is joy ... Prov 12:20 7965
his enemies to be at *p* with him ... Prov 16:7 7999
a fool, when he holdeth his *p* ... Prov 17:28 2790
a time of war, and a time of *p* ... Eccl 3:8 7965
Father, The Prince of *P* ... Is 9:6 7965
p there shall be no end, upon the ... Is 9:7 7965
Thou wilt keep him in perfect *p* ... Is 26:3 7965
Lord, thou wilt ordain *p* for us ... Is 26:12 7965
that he may make *p* with me ... Is 27:5 7965
and he shall make *p* with me ... Is 27:5 7965
work of righteousness shall be *p* ... Is 32:17 7965
the ambassadors of *p* shall weep ... Is 33:7 7965

But they held their p, and ... Is 36:21 2790
for p I had great bitterness ... Is 38:17 7965
moreover, For there shall be p ... Is 39:8 7965
I have long time holden my p ... Is 42:14 2814
I make p, and create evil ... Is 45:7 7965
then had thy p been as a river, ... Is 48:18 7965
There is no p, saith the LORD, ... Is 48:22 7965
good tidings, that publisheth p ... Is 52:7 7965
of our p was upon him ... Is 53:5 7965
the covenant of my p be removed ... Is 54:10 7965
shall be the p of thy children ... Is 54:13 7965
with joy, and be led forth with p ... Is 55:12 7965
He shall enter into p ... Is 57:2 7965
have not I held my p even of old ... Is 57:11 2814
P, p to him that is far off, ... Is 57:19 7965
There is no p, saith my God, to ... Is 57:21 7965
The way of p they know not ... Is 59:8 7965
goeth therein shall not know p ... Is 59:8 7965
I will also make thy officers p ... Is 60:17 7965
Zion's sake will I not hold my p ... Is 62:1 2814
never hold their p day nor night ... Is 62:6 2814
wilt thou hold thy p, and afflict ... Is 64:12 2814
I will extend p to her like a ... Is 66:12 7965
saying, Ye shall have p ... Jer 4:10 7965
I cannot hold my p, because thou ... Jer 4:19 2790
people slightly, saying, P, p ... Jer 6:14 7965
when there is no p ... Jer 6:14 7965
people slightly, saying, P, p ... Jer 8:11 7965
when there is no p ... Jer 8:11 7965
We looked for p, but no good came ... Jer 8:15 7965
and if in the land of p, wherein ... Jer 12:5 7965
no flesh shall have p ... Jer 12:12 7965
give you assured p in this place ... Jer 14:13 7965
we looked for p, and there is no ... Jer 14:19 7965
taken away my p from this people ... Jer 16:5 7965
LORD hath said, Ye shall have p ... Jer 23:17 7965
prophet which prophesieth of p ... Jer 28:9 7965
seek the p of the city whither I ... Jer 29:7 7965
the p thereof shall ye have p ... Jer 29:7 7965
saith the LORD, thoughts of p ... Jer 29:11 7965
trembling, of fear, and not of p ... Jer 30:5 7965
unto them the abundance of p ... Jer 33:6 7965
But thou shalt die in p ... Jer 34:5 7965
shall go forth from thence in p ... Jer 43:12 7965
removed my soul far off from p ... Lam 3:17 7965
and they shall seek p, and there ... Eze 7:25 7965
have seduced my people, saying, P ... Eze 13:10 7965
and there was no p ... Eze 13:10 7965
p for her, and there is no p ... Eze 13:16 7965
make with them a covenant of p ... Eze 34:25 7965
make a covenant of p with them ... Eze 37:26 7965
the altar, and your p offerings ... Eze 43:27 8002
and for p offerings, to make ... Eze 45:15 8002
and the p offerings, to make ... Eze 45:17 8002
his p offerings, and he shall ... Eze 46:2 8002
a voluntary burnt offering or p ... Eze 46:12 8002
his p offerings, as he did on the ... Eze 46:12 8002
P be multiplied unto you ... Dan 4:1 8001
P be multiplied unto you ... Dan 6:25 8001
heart, and by p shall destroy many ... Dan 8:25 7962
p be unto thee, be strong, yea, ... Dan 10:19 7965
neither will I regard the p ... Amos 5:22 8002
the men that were at p with thee ... Obad 7 7965
bite with their teeth, and cry, P ... Mic 3:5 7965
And this man shall be the p ... Mic 5:5 7965
good tidings, that publisheth p ... Nah 1:15 7965
Hold thy p at the presence of the ... Zeph 1:7 2013
and in this place will I give p ... Hag 2:9 7965
the counsel of p shall be between ... Zec 6:13 7965
neither was there any p to him ... Zec 8:10 7965
of truth and p in your gates ... Zec 8:16 7965
therefore love the truth and p ... Zec 8:19 7965
he shall speak p unto the heathen ... Zec 9:10 7965
was with him of life and p ... Mal 2:5 7965
he walked with me in p and equity, ... Mal 2:6 7965
worthy, let your p come upon it ... Mt 10:13 1515
worthy, let your p return to you ... Mt 10:13 1515
that I am come to send p on earth ... Mt 10:34 1515
I came not to send p, but a sword ... Mt 10:34 1515
because they should hold their p ... Mt 20:31 4623
But Jesus held his p ... Mt 26:63 4623
rebuked him, saying, Hold thy p ... Mk 1:25 5392
But they held their p ... Mk 3:4 4623
the wind, and said unto the sea, P ... Mk 4:39 4623
go in p, and be whole of thy ... Mk 5:34 1515
But they held their p ... Mk 9:34 4623
and have p one with another ... Mk 9:50 1518
him that he should hold his p ... Mk 10:48 4623
But he held his p, and answered ... Mk 14:61 4623
guide our feet into the way of p ... Lk 1:79 1515
God in the highest, and on earth p ... Lk 2:14 1515
thou thy servant depart in p ... Lk 2:29 1515
rebuked him, saying, Hold thy p ... Lk 4:35 5392
go in p ... Lk 7:50 1515
go in p ... Lk 8:48 1515
first say, P be to this house ... Lk 10:5 1515
And if the son of p be there ... Lk 10:6 1515
your p shall rest upon it ... Lk 10:6 1515
his palace, his goods are in p ... Lk 11:21 1515
that I am come to give p on earth ... Lk 12:51 1515
And they held their p ... Lk 14:4 2270
and desireth conditions of p ... Lk 14:32 1515
him, that he should hold his p ... Lk 18:39 4623
p in heaven, and glory in the ... Lk 19:38 1515
if these should hold their p ... Lk 19:40 4623
things which belong unto thy p ... Lk 19:42 1515
at his answer, and held their p ... Lk 20:26 4601
and saith unto them, P be unto you ... Lk 24:36 1515
P I leave with you, my p I ... Jn 14:27 1515
you, that in me ye might have p ... Jn 16:33 1515
and saith unto them, P be unto you ... Jn 20:19 1515
to them again, P be unto you ... Jn 20:21 1515
the midst, and said, P be unto you ... Jn 20:26 1515
preaching p by Jesus Christ ... Acts 10:36 1515
these things, they held their p ... Acts 11:18 2270
with the hand to hold their p ... Acts 12:17 4601
their friend, desired p ... Acts 12:20 1515
And after they had held their p ... Acts 15:13 4601
they were let go in p from the ... Acts 15:33 1515
now therefore depart, and go in p ... Acts 16:36 1515
but speak, and hold not thy p ... Acts 18:9 4623
p from God our Father, and the ... Rom 1:7 1515
But glory, honour, and p, to every ... Rom 2:10 1515
the way of p have they not known ... Rom 3:17 1515
we have p with God through our ... Rom 5:1 1515
spiritually minded is life and p ... Rom 8:6 1515
them that preach the gospel of p ... Rom 10:15 1515
but righteousness, and p, and joy ... Rom 14:17 1515
after the things which make for p ... Rom 14:19 1515
p in believing, that ye may ... Rom 15:13 1515
Now the God of p be with you all ... Rom 15:33 1515
the God of p shall bruise Satan ... Rom 16:20 1515
Grace be unto you, and p, from God ... 1Cor 1:3 1515
but God hath called us to p ... 1Cor 7:15 1515
by, let the first hold his p ... 1Cor 14:30 4601
the author of confusion, but of p ... 1Cor 14:33 1515
but conduct him forth in p ... 1Cor 16:11 1515
p from God our Father, and from ... 2Cor 1:2 1515
be of one mind, live in p ... 2Cor 13:11 1518
of love and p shall be with you ... 2Cor 13:11 1515
p from God the Father, and from ... Gal 1:3 1515
of the Spirit is love, joy, p ... Gal 5:22 1515
p be on them, and mercy, and upon ... Gal 6:16 1515
Grace be to you, and p, from God ... Eph 1:2 1515
For he is our p, who hath made ... Eph 2:14 1515
of twain one new man, so making p ... Eph 2:15 1515
preached p to you which were afar ... Eph 2:17 1515
of the Spirit in the bond of p ... Eph 4:3 1515
preparation of the gospel of p ... Eph 6:15 1515
P be to the brethren, and love ... Eph 6:23 1515
Grace be unto you, and p, from God ... Phil 1:2 1515
the p of God, which passeth all ... Phil 4:7 1515
the God of p shall be with you ... Phil 4:9 1515
Grace be unto you, and p, from God ... Col 1:2 1515
having made p through the blood ... Col 1:20 1517
let the p of God rule in your ... Col 3:15 1515
Grace be unto you, and p, from God ... 1Th 1:1 1515
For when they shall say, P ... 1Th 5:3 1515
And be at p among yourselves ... 1Th 5:13 1518
the very God of p sanctify you ... 1Th 5:23 1515
Grace unto you, and p, from God ... 2Th 1:2 1515
Now the Lord of p himself give ... 2Th 3:16 1515
give you p always by all means ... 2Th 3:16 1515
Grace, mercy, and p, from God our ... 1Ti 1:2 1515
Grace, mercy, and p, from God the ... 2Ti 1:2 1515
righteousness, faith, charity, p ... 2Ti 2:22 1515
Grace, mercy, and p, from God the ... Titus 1:4 1515
Grace to you, and p, from God our ... Philem 3 1515
of Salem, which is, King of p ... Heb 7:2 1515
she had received the spies with p ... Heb 11:31 1515
Follow p with all men, and ... Heb 12:14 1515
Now the God of p, that brought ... Heb 13:20 1515
of you say unto them, Depart in p ... Jas 2:16 1515
sown in p of them that make p ... Jas 3:18 1515
Grace unto you, and p, be ... 1Pet 1:2 1515
let him seek p, and ensue it ... 1Pet 3:11 1515
P be with you all that are in ... 1Pet 5:14 1515
p be multiplied unto you through ... 2Pet 1:2 1515
that ye may be found of him in p ... 2Pet 3:14 1515
Grace be with you, mercy, and p ... 2Jn 3 1515
P be to thee ... 3Jn 14 1515
Mercy unto you, and p, and love, be ... Jude 2 1515
Grace be unto you, and p, from him ... Rev 1:4 1515
thereon to take p from the earth ... Rev 6:4 1515

PEACEABLE {8}
These men are p with us ... Gen 34:21 8003
I am one of them that are p ... 2Sa 20:19 7999
the land was wide, and quiet, and p ... 1Chr 4:40 7961
shall dwell in a p habitation ... Is 32:18 7965
the p habitations are cut down ... Jer 25:37 7965
p life in all godliness and ... 1Ti 2:2 2272
afterward it yieldeth the p fruit ... Heb 12:11 1516
from above is first pure, then p ... Jas 3:17 1516

PEACEABLY {12}
and could not speak p unto him ... Gen 37:4 7965
restore those lands again p ... Judg 11:13 7965
Rimmon, and to call p unto them ... Judg 21:13 7965
coming, and said, Comest thou p ... 1Sa 16:4 7965
And he said, P ... 1Sa 16:5 7965
And she said, Comest thou p ... 1Kin 2:13 7965
And he said, P ... 1Kin 2:13 7965
If ye be come p unto me to help ... 1Chr 12:17 7965
one speaketh p to his neighbour ... Jer 9:8 7965
but he shall come in p, and obtain ... Dan 11:21 7962
He shall enter p even upon the ... Dan 11:24 7962
lieth in you, live p with all men ... Rom 12:18 1518

PEACEMAKERS {1}
Blessed are the p ... Mt 5:9 1518

PEACOCKS {3}
and silver, ivory, and apes, and p ... 1Kin 10:22 8500
and silver, ivory, and apes, and p ... 2Chr 9:21 8500
thou the goodly wings unto the p ... Job 39:13 7443

PEARL {2}
he had found one p of great price ... Mt 13:46 3135
every several gate was of one p ... Rev 21:21 3135

PEARLS {8}
shall be made of coral, or of p ... Job 28:18 1378
cast ye your p before swine ... Mt 7:6 3135
a merchant man, seeking goodly p ... Mt 13:45 3135
with broided hair, or gold, or p ... 1Ti 2:9 3135
with gold and precious stones and p ... Rev 17:4 3135
and precious stones, and of p ... Rev 18:12 3135
gold, and precious stones, and p ... Rev 18:16 3135
And the twelve gates were twelve p ... Rev 21:21 3135

PECULIAR {7}
then ye shall be a p treasure ... Ex 19:5 5459
to be a p people unto himself ... Deut 14:2 5459
thee this day to be his p people ... Deut 26:18 5459
and Israel for his p treasure ... Ps 135:4 5459
the p treasure of kings and of the ... Eccl 2:8 5459
and purify unto himself a p people ... Titus 2:14 4041
an holy nation, a p people ... 1Pet 2:9 1519,4047

PEDAHEL (ped'-a-hel) {1} *A Naphtalite who apportioned the Promised Land.*
of Naphtali, P the son of Ammihud ... Num 34:28 6300

PEDAHZUR (pe-dah'-zur) {5} *Father of Gamaliel.*
Gamaliel the son of P ... Num 1:10 6301
shall be Gamaliel the son of P ... Num 2:20 6301
day offered Gamaliel the son of P ... Num 7:54 6301
offering of Gamaliel the son of P ... Num 7:59 6301
was Gamaliel the son of P ... Num 10:23 6301

PEDAIAH (pe-dah'-yah) {8}
1. Grandfather of King Josiah.
the daughter of P of Rumah ... 2Kin 23:36 6305
2. Descendant of Jeconiah.
Malchiram also, and P, and Shenazar ... 1Chr 3:18 6305
And the sons of P were, Zerubbabel ... 1Chr 3:19 6305
3. Father of Joel.
of Manasseh, Joel the son of P ... 1Chr 27:20 6305
4. Son of Parosh.
After him P the son of Parosh ... Neh 3:25 6305
5. A priest who aided Ezra.
and on his left hand, P, and ... Neh 8:4 6305
the scribe, and of the Levites, P ... Neh 13:13 6305
6. A family of exiles.
the son of Joed, the son of P ... Neh 11:7 6305

PEDIGREES {1}
they declared their p after their ... Num 1:18 3205

PEELED {3}
to a nation scattered and p ... Is 18:2 4178
hosts of a people scattered and p ... Is 18:7 4178
bald, and every shoulder was p ... Eze 29:18 4803

PEEP {1}
spirits, and unto wizards that p ... Is 8:19 6850

PEEPED {1}
wing, or opened the mouth, or p ... Is 10:14 6850

PEKAH (pe'-kah) {11} *A king of Israel.*
But P the son of Remaliah, a ... 2Kin 15:25 6492
P the son of Remaliah began to ... 2Kin 15:27 6492
In the days of P king of Israel ... 2Kin 15:29 6492
against P the son of Remaliah ... 2Kin 15:30 6492
And the rest of the acts of P ... 2Kin 15:31 6492
In the second year of P the son ... 2Kin 15:32 6492
Syria, and P the son of Remaliah ... 2Kin 15:37 6492
In the seventeenth year of P the ... 2Kin 16:1 6492
P son of Remaliah king of Israel ... 2Kin 16:5 6492
For P the son of Remaliah slew in ... 2Chr 28:6 6492
P the son of Remaliah, king of ... Is 7:1 6492

PEKAHIAH (pe-ka-hi'-ah) {3} *Son of King Menahem.*
P his son reigned in his stead ... 2Kin 15:22 6494
P the son of Menahem began to ... 2Kin 15:23 6494
And the rest of the acts of P ... 2Kin 15:26 6494

PEKOD (pe'-kod) {2} *Symbolic name for Chaldea.*
and against the inhabitants of P ... Jer 50:21 6489
and all the Chaldeans, P, and Shoa ... Eze 23:23 6489

PELAIAH (pel-a-i'-ah) {3}
1. A son of Elioenai.
were, Hodaiah, and Eliashib, and P ... 1Chr 3:24 6411
2. A priest who aided Ezra.
Azariah, Jozabad, Hanan, P ... Neh 8:7 6411
3. A Levite who renewed the covenant.
Shebaniah, Hodijah, Kelita, P ... Neh 10:10 6411

PELALIAH (pel-a-li'-ah) {1} *A family of exiles.*
the son of Jeroham, the son of P ... Neh 11:12 6421

PELATIAH (pel-a-ti'-ah) {5}
1. Son of Hananiah.
of Hananiah; P, and Jesaiah ... 1Chr 3:21 6410
2. A Simeonite captain.
Seir, having for their captains P ... 1Chr 4:42 6410
3. A family who renewed the covenant.
P, Hanan, Anaiah, ... Neh 10:22 6410
4. Son of Benaiah.
P the son of Benaiah, princes of ... Eze 11:1 6410
that P the son of Benaiah died ... Eze 11:13 6410

PELEG (pe'-leg) {7} See PHALEC. *A son of Eber.*
the name of one was P ... Gen 10:25 6389
four and thirty years, and begat P ... Gen 11:16 6389
after he begat P four hundred ... Gen 11:17 6389
P lived thirty years, and begat ... Gen 11:18 6389
P lived after he begat Reu two ... Gen 11:19 6389
the name of the one was P ... 1Chr 1:19 6389
Eber, P, Reu, ... 1Chr 1:25 6389

PELET *(pe'-let)* {2} See BETH-PALET.
1. A son of Jahdai.
Jotham, and Gesham, and P 1Chr 2:47 6404
2. A captain in David's army.
and Jeziel, and P, the sons of 1Chr 12:3 6404

PELETH *(pe'-leth)* {2}
1. Father of On.
of Eliab, and On, the son of P .... Num 16:1 6431
of Jonathan; P, and Zaza 1Chr 2:33 6431

PELETHITES *(pel'-e-thites)* {7} *A company of David's bodyguards.*
both the Cherethites and the P 2Sa 8:18 6432
all the Cherethites, and all the P 2Sa 15:18 6432
men, and the Cherethites, and the P 2Sa 20:7 6432
the Cherethites and over the P 2Sa 20:23 6432
and the Cherethites, and the P 1Kin 1:38 6432
and the Cherethites, and the P 1Kin 1:44 6432
was over the Cherethites and the P 1Chr 18:17 6432

PELICAN {3}
And the swan, and the p, and the .... Lev 11:18 6893
And the p, and the gier eagle, and .... Deut 14:17 6893
I am like a p of the wilderness .... Ps 102:6 6893

PELONITE *(pel'-o-nite)* {3} See PALTITE.
1. Family name of Helez.
the Harorite, Helez the P 1Chr 11:27 6397
the seventh month was Helez the P 1Chr 27:10 6397
2. Family name of Ahijah.
the Mecherathite, Ahijah the P 1Chr 11:36 6397

PELUSIUM See SIN.

PEN {7}
that handle the p of the writer .... Judg 5:14 7626
they were graven with an iron p .... Job 19:24 5842
my tongue is the p of a ready .... Ps 45:1 5842
in it with a man's p concerning .... Is 8:1 2747
the p of the scribes is in vain .... Jer 8:8 5842
Judah is written with a p of iron .... Jer 17:1 5842
not with ink and p write unto thee 3Jn 13 *2563*

PENCE {5}
which owed him an hundred p .... Mt 18:28 *1220*
for more than three hundred p .... Mk 14:5 *1220*
the one owed five hundred p .... Lk 7:41 *1220*
he departed, he took out two p .... Lk 10:35 *1220*
ointment sold for three hundred p .... Jn 12:5 *1220*

PENIEL *(pe-ni'-el)* {1} See PENUEL. *Same as Penuel.*
called the name of the place P .... Gen 32:30 6439

PENINNAH *(pe-nin'-nah)* {3} *A wife of Elkanah.*
and the name of the other P 1Sa 1:2 6444
P had children, but Hannah had no 1Sa 1:2 6444
offered, he gave to P his wife 1Sa 1:4 6444

PENKNIFE {1}
four leaves, he cut it with the p .... Jer 36:23 8593

PENNY {9}
with the labourers for a p a day .... Mt 20:2 *1220*
hour, they received every man a p .... Mt 20:9 *1220*
likewise received every man a p .... Mt 20:10 *1220*
not thou agree with me for a p .... Mt 20:13 *1220*
And they brought unto him a p .... Mt 22:19 *1220*
bring me a p, that I may see it .... Mk 12:15 *1220*
Shew me a p .... Lk 20:24 *1220*
say, A measure of wheat for a p .... Rev 6:6 *1220*
three measures of barley for a p .... Rev 6:6 *1220*

PENNYWORTH {2}
go and buy two hundred p of bread .... Mk 6:37 *1220*
Two hundred p of bread is not .... Jn 6:7 *1220*

PENTECOST *(pen'-te-cost)* {3} *Greek name for Passover.*
when the day of P was fully come .... Acts 2:1 *4005*
to be at Jerusalem the day of P .... Acts 20:16 *4005*
I will tarry at Ephesus until P 1Cor 16:8 *4005*

PENUEL *(pe-nu'-el)* {7} See PENIEL.
1. Where Jacob wrestled God.
as he passed over P the sun rose .... Gen 32:31 6439
And he went up thence to P .... Judg 8:8 6439
the men of P answered him as the .... Judg 8:8 6439
he spake also unto the men of P .... Judg 8:9 6439
And he beat down the tower of P .... Judg 8:17 6439
2. Father of Gedor.
P the father of Gedor, and Ezer 1Chr 4:4 6439
3. A son of Shashak.
And Iphedeiah, and P, the sons of 1Chr 8:25 6439

PENURY {2}
of the lips tendeth only to p .... Prov 14:23 4270
but she of her p hath cast in all .... Lk 21:4 *5303*

PEOPLE {2139}
the p is one, and they have all .... Gen 11:6 5971
and the women also, and the p .... Gen 14:16 5971
soul shall be cut off from his p .... Gen 17:14 5971
kings of p shall be of her .... Gen 17:16 5971
all the p from every quarter .... Gen 19:4 5971
himself to the p of the land .... Gen 23:7 5971
the sons of my p give I it thee .... Gen 23:11 5971
himself before the p of the land .... Gen 23:12 5971
the audience of the p of the land .... Gen 23:13 5971
and was gathered to his p .... Gen 25:8 5971
and was gathered unto his p .... Gen 25:17 5971
womb, and two manner of p shall be .... Gen 25:23 3816
the one p shall be stronger than .... Gen 25:23 3816
be stronger than the other p .... Gen 25:23 3816
one of the p might lightly have .... Gen 26:10 5971
And Abimelech charged all his p .... Gen 26:11 5971
Let p serve thee, and nations bow .... Gen 27:29 5971
thou mayest be a multitude of p .... Gen 28:3 5971
the land of the p of the east .... Gen 29:1 1121
he divided the p that was with .... Gen 32:7 5971
with you, and we will become one p .... Gen 34:16 5971
for to dwell with us, to be one p .... Gen 34:22 5971
all the p that were with him .... Gen 35:6 5971
died, and was gathered unto his p .... Gen 35:29 5971
thy word shall all my p be ruled .... Gen 41:40 5971
the p cried to Pharaoh for bread .... Gen 41:55 5971
sold to all the p of the land .... Gen 42:6 5971
And as for the p, he removed them .... Gen 47:21 5971
Then Joseph said unto the p .... Gen 47:23 5971
make of thee a multitude of p .... Gen 48:4 5971
he also shall become a p, and he .... Gen 48:19 5971
shall the gathering of the p be .... Gen 49:10 5971
Dan shall judge his p, as one of .... Gen 49:16 5971
I am to be gathered unto my p .... Gen 49:29 5971
ghost, and was gathered unto his p .... Gen 49:33 5971
is this day, to save much p alive .... Gen 50:20 5971
And he said unto his p, Behold, ... Ex 1:9 5971
the p of the children of Israel .... Ex 1:9 5971
the p multiplied, and waxed very .... Ex 1:20 5971
And Pharaoh charged all his p .... Ex 1:22 5971
of my p which are in Egypt .... Ex 3:7 5971
p the children of Israel out of .... Ex 3:10 5971
brought forth the p out of Egypt .... Ex 3:12 5971
I will give this p favour in the .... Ex 3:21 5971
shall be thy spokesman unto the p .... Ex 4:16 5971
that he shall not let the p go .... Ex 4:21 5971
the signs in the sight of the p .... Ex 4:30 5971
And the p believed .... Ex 4:31 5971
LORD God of Israel, Let my p go .... Ex 5:1 5971
let the p from their works .... Ex 5:4 5971
the p of the land now are many, ... Ex 5:5 5971
same day the taskmasters of the p .... Ex 5:6 5971
give the p straw to make brick .... Ex 5:7 5971
the taskmasters of the p went out .... Ex 5:10 5971
officers, and they spake to the p .... Ex 5:10 5971
So the p were scattered abroad .... Ex 5:12 5971
but the fault is in thine own p .... Ex 5:16 5971
thou so evil entreated this p .... Ex 5:22 5971
name, he hath done evil to this p .... Ex 5:23 5971
hast thou delivered thy p at all .... Ex 5:23 5971
And I will take you to me for a p .... Ex 6:7 5971
my p the children of Israel, out .... Ex 7:4 5971
he refuseth to let the p go .... Ex 7:14 5971
me unto thee, saying, Let my p go .... Ex 7:16 5971
Thus saith the LORD, Let my p go .... Ex 8:1 5971
of thy servants, and upon thy p .... Ex 8:3 5971
up both on thee, and upon thy p .... Ex 8:4 5971
the frogs from me, and from my p .... Ex 8:8 5971
and I will let the p go, that they .... Ex 8:8 5971
and for thy servants, and for thy p .... Ex 8:9 5971
from thy servants, and from thy p .... Ex 8:11 5971
Thus saith the LORD, Let my p go .... Ex 8:20 5971
if thou wilt not let my p go .... Ex 8:21 5971
upon thy servants, and upon thy p .... Ex 8:21 5971
of Goshen, in which my p dwell .... Ex 8:22 5971
between my p and thy p .... Ex 8:23 5971
from his servants, and from his p .... Ex 8:29 5971
the p go to sacrifice to the LORD .... Ex 8:29 5971
from his servants, and from his p .... Ex 8:31 5971
neither would he let the p go .... Ex 8:32 5971
God of the Hebrews, Let my p go .... Ex 9:1 5971
and he did not let the p go .... Ex 9:7 5971
God of the Hebrews, Let my p go .... Ex 9:13 5971
upon thy servants, and upon thy p .... Ex 9:14 5971
thee and thy p with pestilence .... Ex 9:15 5971
thou thyself against my p .... Ex 9:17 5971
and I and my p are wicked .... Ex 9:27 5971
let my p go, that they may serve .... Ex 10:3 5971
if thou refuse to let my p go .... Ex 10:4 5971
Speak now in the ears of the p .... Ex 11:2 5971
the LORD gave the p favour in the .... Ex 11:3 5971
and in the sight of the p .... Ex 11:3 5971
all the p that follow thee .... Ex 11:8 5971
And the p bowed the head and .... Ex 12:27 5971
and get you forth from among my p .... Ex 12:31 5971
Egyptians were urgent upon the p .... Ex 12:33 5971
the p took their dough before it .... Ex 12:34 5971
the LORD gave the p favour in the .... Ex 12:36 5971
And Moses said unto the p, ... Ex 13:3 5971
when Pharaoh had let the p go .... Ex 13:17 5971
Lest peradventure the p repent .... Ex 13:17 5971
But God led the p about, through .... Ex 13:18 5971
fire by night, from before the p .... Ex 13:22 5971
the king of Egypt that the p fled .... Ex 14:5 5971
servants was turned against the p .... Ex 14:5 5971
chariot, and took his p with him .... Ex 14:6 5971
And Moses said unto the p, Fear ye .... Ex 14:13 5971
the p feared the LORD, and .... Ex 14:31 5971
the p which thou hast redeemed .... Ex 15:13 5971
The p shall hear, and be afraid .... Ex 15:14 5971
till thy p pass over, O LORD, ... Ex 15:16 5971
till the p pass over, which thou .... Ex 15:16 5971
the p murmured against Moses, ... Ex 15:24 5971
the p shall go out and gather a .... Ex 16:4 5971
the p on the seventh day for to .... Ex 16:27 5971
So the p rested on the seventh .... Ex 16:30 5971
was no water for the p to drink .... Ex 17:1 5971
Wherefore the p did chide with .... Ex 17:2 5971
the p thirsted there for water .... Ex 17:3 5971
the p murmured against Moses, and .... Ex 17:3 5971
What shall I do unto this p .... Ex 17:4 5971
unto Moses, Go on before the p .... Ex 17:5 5971
out of it, that the p may drink .... Ex 17:6 5971
his p with the edge of the sword .... Ex 17:13 5971
for Moses, and for Israel his p .... Ex 18:1 5971
who hath delivered the p from .... Ex 18:10 5971
that Moses sat to judge the p .... Ex 18:13 5971
the p stood by Moses from the .... Ex 18:13 5971
law saw all that he did to the p .... Ex 18:14 5971
thing that thou doest to the p .... Ex 18:14 5971
all the p stand by thee from .... Ex 18:14 5971
Because the p come unto me to .... Ex 18:15 5971
thou, and this p that is with thee .... Ex 18:18 5971
Be thou for the p to God-ward .... Ex 18:19 5971
provide out of all the p able men .... Ex 18:21 5971
them judge the p at all seasons .... Ex 18:22 5971
all this p shall also go to their .... Ex 18:23 5971
and made them heads over the p .... Ex 18:25 5971
they judged the p at all seasons .... Ex 18:26 5971
treasure unto me above all p .... Ex 19:5 5971
and called for the elders of the p .... Ex 19:7 5971
all the p answered together, and .... Ex 19:8 5971
the words of the p unto the LORD .... Ex 19:8 5971
that the p may hear when I speak .... Ex 19:9 5971
the words of the p unto the LORD .... Ex 19:9 5971
said unto Moses, Go unto the p .... Ex 19:10 5971
of all the p upon mount Sinai .... Ex 19:11 5971
set bounds unto the p round about .... Ex 19:12 5971
down from the mount unto the p .... Ex 19:14 5971
and sanctified the p .... Ex 19:14 5971
And he said unto the p, Be ready .... Ex 19:15 5971
so that all the p that was in the .... Ex 19:16 5971
Moses brought forth the p out of .... Ex 19:17 5971
unto Moses, Go down, charge the p .... Ex 19:21 5971
The p cannot come up to mount .... Ex 19:23 5971
the p break through to come up .... Ex 19:24 5971
So Moses went down unto the p .... Ex 19:25 5971
all the p saw the thunderings, and .... Ex 20:18 5971
and when the p saw it, they .... Ex 20:18 5971
And Moses said unto the p, Fear .... Ex 20:20 5971
the p stood afar off, and Moses .... Ex 20:21 5971
any of my p that is poor by thee .... Ex 22:25 5971
nor curse the ruler of thy p .... Ex 22:28 5971
that the poor of thy p may eat .... Ex 23:11 5971
will destroy all the p to whom .... Ex 23:27 5971
shall the p go up with him .... Ex 24:2 5971
told the p all the words of the .... Ex 24:3 5971
all the p answered with one voice .... Ex 24:3 5971
and read in the audience of the p .... Ex 24:7 5971
blood, and sprinkled it on the p .... Ex 24:8 5971
shall even be cut off from his p .... Ex 30:33 5971
shall even be cut off from his p .... Ex 30:38 5971
shall be cut off from among his p .... Ex 31:14 5971
when the p saw that Moses delayed .... Ex 32:1 5971
the p gathered themselves .... Ex 32:1 5971
all the p brake off the golden .... Ex 32:3 5971
the p sat down to eat and to drink .... Ex 32:6 5971
for thy p, which thou broughtest .... Ex 32:7 5971
unto Moses, I have seen this p .... Ex 32:9 5971
and, behold, it is a stiffnecked p .... Ex 32:9 5971
thy wrath wax hot against thy p .... Ex 32:11 5971
repent of this evil against thy p .... Ex 32:12 5971
which he thought to do unto his p .... Ex 32:14 5971
noise of the p as they shouted .... Ex 32:17 5971
Aaron, What did this p unto thee .... Ex 32:21 5971
thou knowest the p, that they are .... Ex 32:22 5971
Moses saw that the p were naked .... Ex 32:25 5971
there fell of the p that day .... Ex 32:28 5971
that Moses said unto the p .... Ex 32:30 5971
this p have sinned a great sin, ... Ex 32:31 5971
lead the p unto the place of .... Ex 32:34 5971
And the LORD plagued the p .... Ex 32:35 5971
the p which thou hast brought up .... Ex 33:1 5971
for thou art a stiffnecked p .... Ex 33:3 5971
when the p heard these evil .... Ex 33:4 5971
of Israel, Ye are a stiffnecked p .... Ex 33:5 5971
that all the p rose up, and stood .... Ex 33:8 5971
all the p saw the cloudy pillar .... Ex 33:10 5971
and all the p rose up and .... Ex 33:10 5971
sayest unto me, Bring up this p .... Ex 33:12 5971
that this nation is thy p .... Ex 33:13 5971
thy p have found grace in thy .... Ex 33:16 5971
shall we be separated, I and thy p .... Ex 33:16 5971
from all the p that are upon the .... Ex 33:16 5971
for it is a stiffnecked p .... Ex 34:9 5971
before all thy p I will do .... Ex 34:10 5971
all the p among which thou art .... Ex 34:10 5971
The p bring much more than enough .... Ex 36:5 5971
So the p were restrained from .... Ex 36:6 5971
sin according to the sin of the p .... Lev 4:3 5971
common p sin through ignorance .... Lev 4:27 5971
soul shall be cut off from his p .... Lev 7:20 5971
soul shall be cut off from his p .... Lev 7:21 5971
it shall be cut off from his p .... Lev 7:25 5971
soul shall be cut off from his p .... Lev 7:27 5971
for thyself, and for the p .... Lev 9:7 5971
and offer the offering of the p .... Lev 9:7 5971
was the sin offering for the p .... Lev 9:15 5971
offerings, which was for the p .... Lev 9:18 5971
lifted up his hand toward the p .... Lev 9:22 5971
and came out, and blessed the p .... Lev 9:23 5971
the LORD appeared unto all the p .... Lev 9:23 5971
which when all the p saw, they .... Lev 9:24 5971
before all the p I will be .... Lev 10:3 5971
and lest wrath come upon all the p .... Lev 10:6 5712
sin offering, that is for the p .... Lev 16:15 5971
and the burnt offering of the p .... Lev 16:24 5971
for himself, and for the p .... Lev 16:24 5971
for all the p of the congregation .... Lev 16:33 5971
shall be cut off from among his p .... Lev 17:4 5971
shall be cut off from among his p .... Lev 17:9 5971
will cut him off from among his p .... Lev 17:10 5971
be cut off from among their p .... Lev 18:29 5971
shall be cut off from among his p .... Lev 19:8 5971
down as a talebearer among thy p .... Lev 19:16 5971

against the children of thy *p*	Lev 19:18	5971
the *p* of the land shall stone him	Lev 20:2	5971
will cut him off from among his *p*	Lev 20:3	5971
if the *p* of the land do any ways	Lev 20:4	5971
with Molech, from among their *p*	Lev 20:5	5971
will cut him off from among his *p*	Lev 20:6	5971
cut off in the sight of their *p*	Lev 20:17	5971
be cut off from among their *p*	Lev 20:18	5971
have separated you from other *p*	Lev 20:24	5971
and have severed you from other *p*	Lev 20:26	5971
defiled for the dead among his *p*	Lev 21:1	5971
being a chief man among his *p*	Lev 21:4	5971
a virgin of his own *p* to wife	Lev 21:14	5971
he profane his seed among his *p*	Lev 21:15	5971
shall be cut off from among his *p*	Lev 23:29	5971
will I destroy from among his *p*	Lev 23:30	5971
be your God, and ye shall be my *p*	Lev 26:12	5971
a curse and an oath among thy *p*	Num 5:21	5971
shall be a curse among her *p*	Num 5:27	5971
shall be cut off from among his *p*	Num 9:13	5971
when the *p* complained, it	Num 11:1	5971
And the *p* cried unto Moses	Num 11:2	5971
the *p* went about, and gathered it,	Num 11:8	5971
Then Moses heard the *p* weep	Num 11:10	5971
the burden of all this *p* upon me	Num 11:11	5971
Have I conceived all this *p*	Num 11:12	5971
flesh to give unto all this *p*	Num 11:13	5971
not able to bear all this *p* alone	Num 11:14	5971
knowest to be the elders of the *p*	Num 11:16	5971
the burden of the *p* with thee	Num 11:17	5971
And say thou unto the *p*, Sanctify	Num 11:18	5971
And Moses said, The *p*, among whom	Num 11:21	5971
told the *p* the words of the LORD,	Num 11:24	5971
men of the elders of the *p*	Num 11:24	5971
all the LORD's *p* were prophets	Num 11:29	5971
the *p* stood up all that day, and	Num 11:32	5971
LORD was kindled against the *p*	Num 11:33	5971
the LORD smote the *p* with a very	Num 11:33	5971
they buried the *p* that lusted	Num 11:34	5971
And the *p* journeyed from	Num 11:35	5971
the *p* journeyed not till Miriam	Num 12:15	5971
afterward the *p* removed from	Num 12:16	5971
the *p* that dwelleth therein,	Num 13:18	5971
Nevertheless the *p* be strong that	Num 13:28	5971
Caleb stilled the *p* before Moses	Num 13:30	5971
not able to go up against the *p*	Num 13:31	5971
all the *p* that we saw in it are	Num 13:32	5971
and the *p* wept that night	Num 14:1	5971
neither fear ye the *p* of the land	Num 14:9	5971
How long will this *p* provoke me	Num 14:11	5971
p in thy might from among them	Num 14:13	5971
that thou LORD art among this *p*	Num 14:14	5971
shalt kill all this *p* as one man	Num 14:15	5971
p into the land which he sware	Num 14:16	5971
the iniquity of this *p* according	Num 14:19	5971
and as thou hast forgiven this *p*	Num 14:19	5971
and the *p* mourned greatly	Num 14:39	5971
seeing all the *p* were in	Num 15:26	5971
shall be cut off from among his *p*	Num 15:30	5971
Ye have killed the *p* of the LORD	Num 16:41	5971
the plague was begun among the *p*	Num 16:47	5971
and made an atonement for the *p*	Num 16:47	5971
and the *p* abode in Kadesh	Num 20:1	5971
the *p* chode with Moses, and spake,	Num 20:3	5971
came out against him with much *p*	Num 20:20	5971
shall be gathered unto his *p*	Num 20:24	5971
shall be gathered unto his *p*	Num 20:26	5971
deliver this *p* into my hand	Num 21:2	5971
the soul of the *p* was much	Num 21:4	5971
the *p* spake against God, and	Num 21:5	5971
sent fiery serpents among the *p*	Num 21:6	5971
and they bit the *p*	Num 21:6	5971
and much *p* of Israel died	Num 21:6	5971
Therefore the *p* came to Moses	Num 21:7	5971
And Moses prayed for the *p*	Num 21:7	5971
unto Moses, Gather the *p* together	Num 21:16	5971
the nobles of the *p* digged it	Num 21:18	5971
Sihon gathered all his *p* together	Num 21:23	5971
thou art undone, O *p* of Chemosh	Num 21:29	5971
against them, he, and all his *p*	Num 21:33	5971
him into thy hand, and all his *p*	Num 21:34	5971
him, and his sons, and all his *p*	Num 21:35	5971
And Moab was sore afraid of the *p*	Num 22:3	5971
the land of the children of his *p*	Num 22:5	5971
there is a *p* come out from Egypt	Num 22:5	5971
I pray thee, curse me this *p*	Num 22:6	5971
there is a *p* come out of Egypt,	Num 22:11	5971
thou shalt not curse the *p*	Num 22:12	5971
I pray thee, curse me this *p*	Num 22:17	5971
see the utmost part of the *p*	Num 22:41	5971
the *p* shall dwell alone, and shall	Num 23:9	5971
the *p* shall rise up as a great	Num 23:24	5971
And now, behold, I go unto my *p*	Num 24:14	5971
p shall do to thy *p* in the	Num 24:14	5971
the *p* began to commit whoredom	Num 25:1	5971
they called the *p* unto the	Num 25:2	5971
the *p* did eat, and bowed down to	Num 25:2	5971
Take all the heads of the *p*	Num 25:4	5971
he was head over a *p*, and of a	Num 25:15	523
Take the sum of the *p*, from	Num 26:4	
also shalt be gathered unto thy *p*	Num 27:13	5971
shalt thou be gathered unto thy *p*	Num 31:2	5971
And Moses spake unto the *p*	Num 31:3	5971
and ye shall destroy all this *p*	Num 32:15	5971
was no water for the *p* to drink	Num 33:14	5971
The *p* is greater and taller than	Deut 1:28	5971
And command thou the *p*, saying, Ye	Deut 2:4	5971
a *p* great, and many, and tall, as	Deut 2:10	5971
consumed and dead from among the *p*	Deut 2:16	5971
A *p* great, and many, and tall, as	Deut 2:21	5971
out against us, he and all his *p*	Deut 2:32	5971
him, and his sons, and all his *p*	Deut 2:33	5971
out against us, he and all his *p*	Deut 3:1	5971
I will deliver him, and all his *p*	Deut 3:2	5971
the king of Bashan, and all his *p*	Deut 3:3	5971
he shall go over before this *p*	Deut 3:28	5971
is a wise and understanding *p*	Deut 4:6	5971
unto me, Gather me the *p* together	Deut 4:10	5971
to be unto him a *p* of inheritance	Deut 4:20	5971
Did ever *p* hear the voice of God	Deut 4:33	5971
the voice of the words of this *p*	Deut 5:28	5971
of the gods of the *p* which are	Deut 6:14	5971
For thou art an holy *p* unto the	Deut 7:6	5971
to be a special *p* unto himself	Deut 7:6	5971
above all *p* that are upon the	Deut 7:6	5971
ye were more in number than any *p*	Deut 7:7	5971
for ye were the fewest of all *p*	Deut 7:7	5971
Thou shalt be blessed above all *p*	Deut 7:14	5971
thou shalt consume all the *p*	Deut 7:16	5971
all the *p* of whom thou art afraid	Deut 7:19	5971
A *p* great and tall, the children	Deut 9:2	5971
for thou art a stiffnecked *p*	Deut 9:6	5971
for thy *p* which thou hast brought	Deut 9:12	5971
me, saying, I have seen this *p*	Deut 9:13	5971
and, behold, it is a stiffnecked *p*	Deut 9:13	5971
O Lord GOD, destroy not thy *p*	Deut 9:26	5971
unto the stubbornness of this *p*	Deut 9:27	5971
Yet they are thy *p* and thine	Deut 9:29	5971
take thy journey before the *p*	Deut 10:11	5971
after them, even you above all *p*	Deut 10:15	5971
of the gods of the *p* which are	Deut 13:7	5971
afterwards the hand of all the *p*	Deut 13:9	5971
For thou art an holy *p* unto the	Deut 14:2	5971
to be a peculiar *p* unto himself	Deut 14:2	5971
for thou art an holy *p* unto the	Deut 14:21	5971
judge the *p* with just judgment	Deut 16:18	5971
afterward the hands of all the *p*	Deut 17:7	5971
all the *p* shall hear, and fear, and	Deut 17:13	5971
nor cause the *p* to return to	Deut 17:16	5971
be the priest's due from the *p*	Deut 18:3	5971
a *p* more than thou, be not afraid	Deut 20:1	5971
approach and speak unto the *p*	Deut 20:2	5971
officers shall speak unto the *p*	Deut 20:5	5971
shall speak further unto the *p*	Deut 20:8	5971
an end of speaking unto the *p*	Deut 20:9	5971
of the armies to lead the *p*	Deut 20:9	5971
that all the *p* that is found	Deut 20:11	5971
But of the cities of these *p*	Deut 20:16	5971
O LORD, unto thy *p* Israel	Deut 21:8	5971
unto thy *p* of Israel's charge	Deut 21:8	5971
heaven, and bless thy *p* Israel	Deut 26:15	5971
this day to be his peculiar *p*	Deut 26:18	5971
an holy *p* unto the LORD thy God	Deut 26:19	5971
elders of Israel commanded the *p*	Deut 27:1	5971
become the *p* of the LORD thy God	Deut 27:9	5971
Moses charged the *p* the same day	Deut 27:11	5971
upon mount Gerizim to bless the *p*	Deut 27:12	5971
all the *p* shall answer and say,	Deut 27:15	5971
all the *p* shall say, Amen	Deut 27:16	5971
all the *p* shall say, Amen	Deut 27:17	5971
all the *p* shall say, Amen	Deut 27:18	5971
all the *p* shall say, Amen	Deut 27:19	5971
all the *p* shall say, Amen	Deut 27:20	5971
all the *p* shall say, Amen	Deut 27:21	5971
all the *p* shall say, Amen	Deut 27:22	5971
all the *p* shall say, Amen	Deut 27:23	5971
all the *p* shall say, Amen	Deut 27:24	5971
all the *p* shall say, Amen	Deut 27:25	5971
all the *p* shall say, Amen	Deut 27:26	5971
thee an holy *p* unto himself	Deut 28:9	5971
all *p* of the earth shall see that	Deut 28:10	5971
shall be given unto another *p*	Deut 28:32	5971
shall scatter thee among all *p*	Deut 28:64	5971
thee to day for a *p* unto himself	Deut 29:13	5971
for thou must go with this *p* unto	Deut 31:7	5971
Gather the *p* together, men, and	Deut 31:12	5971
this *p* will rise up, and go a	Deut 31:16	5971
requite the LORD, O foolish *p*	Deut 32:6	5971
he set the bounds of the *p*	Deut 32:8	5971
For the LORD's portion is his *p*	Deut 32:9	5971
with those which are not a *p*	Deut 32:21	5971
For the LORD shall judge his *p*	Deut 32:36	5971
Rejoice, O ye nations, with his *p*	Deut 32:43	5971
unto his land, and to his *p*	Deut 32:43	5971
of this song in the ears of the *p*	Deut 32:44	5971
up, and be gathered unto thy *p*	Deut 32:50	5971
Hor, and was gathered unto his *p*	Deut 32:50	5971
Yea, he loved the *p*	Deut 33:3	5971
Jeshurun, when the heads of the *p*	Deut 33:5	5971
of Judah, and bring him unto his *p*	Deut 33:7	5971
the *p* together to the ends of the	Deut 33:17	5971
call the *p* unto the mountain	Deut 33:19	5971
he came with the heads of the *p*	Deut 33:21	5971
O *p* saved by the LORD, the shield	Deut 33:29	5971
this Jordan, thou, and all this *p*	Josh 1:2	5971
for unto this *p* shalt thou divide	Josh 1:6	5971
commanded the officers of the *p*	Josh 1:10	5971
the host, and command the *p*	Josh 1:11	5971
And they commanded the *p*, saying,	Josh 3:3	5971
And Joshua said unto the *p*	Josh 3:5	5971
and pass over before the *p*	Josh 3:6	5971
covenant, and went before the *p*	Josh 3:6	5971
when the *p* removed from their	Josh 3:14	5971
ark of the covenant before the *p*	Josh 3:14	5971
the *p* passed over right against	Josh 3:16	5971
until all the *p* were passed clean	Josh 3:17	1471
when all the *p* were clean passed	Josh 4:1	1471
Take you twelve men out of the *p*	Josh 4:2	5971
Joshua to speak unto the *p*	Josh 4:10	5971
the *p* hasted and passed over	Josh 4:10	5971
when all the *p* were clean passed	Josh 4:11	5971
priests, in the presence of the *p*	Josh 4:11	5971
the *p* came up out of Jordan on	Josh 4:19	5971
That all the *p* of the earth might	Josh 4:24	5971
All the *p* that came out of Egypt,	Josh 5:4	5971
Now all the *p* that came out were	Josh 5:5	5971
but all the *p* that were born in	Josh 5:5	5971
till all the *p* that were men of	Josh 5:6	1471
had done circumcising all the *p*	Josh 5:8	1471
all the *p* shall shout with a	Josh 6:5	5971
the *p* shall ascend up every man	Josh 6:5	5971
And he said unto the *p*, Pass on,	Josh 6:7	5971
when Joshua had spoken unto the *p*	Josh 6:8	5971
And Joshua had commanded the *p*	Josh 6:10	5971
trumpets, Joshua said unto the *p*	Josh 6:16	5971
So the *p* shouted when the priests	Josh 6:20	5971
when the *p* heard the sound of the	Josh 6:20	5971
the *p* shouted with a great shout,	Josh 6:20	5971
so that the *p* went up into the	Josh 6:20	5971
unto him, Let not all the *p* go up	Josh 7:3	5971
make not all the *p* to labour	Josh 7:3	5971
of the *p* about three thousand men	Josh 7:4	5971
the hearts of the *p* melted	Josh 7:5	5971
at all brought this *p* over Jordan	Josh 7:7	5971
Up, sanctify the *p*, and say,	Josh 7:13	5971
take all the *p* of war with thee,	Josh 8:1	5971
thy hand the king of Ai, and his *p*	Josh 8:1	5971
Joshua arose, and all the *p* of war	Josh 8:3	5971
all the *p* that are with me, will	Josh 8:5	5971
lodged that night among the *p*	Josh 8:9	5971
in the morning, and numbered the *p*	Josh 8:10	5971
of Israel, before the *p* to Ai	Josh 8:10	5971
And all the *p*, even the	Josh 8:11	5971
even the *p* of war that were with	Josh 8:11	
And when they had set the *p*	Josh 8:13	5971
Israel to battle, he and all his *p*	Josh 8:14	5971
all the *p* that were in Ai were	Josh 8:16	5971
the *p* that fled to the wilderness	Josh 8:20	5971
they should bless the *p* of Israel	Josh 8:33	5971
all the *p* of war with him, and all	Josh 10:7	5971
stayed, until the *p* had avenged	Josh 10:13	1471
all the *p* returned to the camp to	Josh 10:21	5971
and Joshua smote him and his *p*	Josh 10:33	5971
all their hosts with them, much *p*	Josh 11:4	5971
all the *p* of war with him,	Josh 11:7	5971
me made the heart of the *p* melt	Josh 14:8	5971
to inherit, seeing I am a great *p*	Josh 17:14	5971
them, If thou be a great *p*	Josh 17:15	5971
saying, Thou art a great *p*	Josh 17:17	5971
And Joshua said unto all the *p*	Josh 24:2	5971
the *p* answered and said, God	Josh 24:16	5971
among all the *p* through whom we	Josh 24:17	5971
out from before us all the *p*	Josh 24:18	5971
And Joshua said unto the *p*	Josh 24:19	5971
the *p* said unto Joshua, Nay	Josh 24:21	5971
And Joshua said unto the *p*	Josh 24:22	5971
the *p* said unto Joshua, The LORD	Josh 24:24	5971
a covenant with the *p* that day	Josh 24:25	5971
And Joshua said unto all the *p*	Josh 24:27	5971
So Joshua let the *p* depart	Josh 24:28	5971
and they went and dwelt among the *p*	Judg 1:16	5971
that the *p* lifted up their voice,	Judg 2:4	5971
And when Joshua had let the *p* go	Judg 2:6	5971
the *p* served the LORD all the	Judg 2:7	5971
of the gods of the *p* that were	Judg 2:12	5971
he said, Because that this *p* hath	Judg 2:20	1471
he sent away the *p* that bare the	Judg 3:18	5971
all the *p* that were with him,	Judg 4:13	5971
when the *p* willingly offered	Judg 5:2	5971
themselves willingly among the *p*	Judg 5:9	5971
then shall the *p* of the LORD go	Judg 5:11	5971
over the nobles among the *p*	Judg 5:13	5971
after thee, Benjamin, among thy *p*	Judg 5:14	5971
Naphtali were a *p* that jeoparded	Judg 5:18	5971
all the *p* that were with him,	Judg 7:1	5971
The *p* that are with thee are too	Judg 7:2	5971
to, proclaim in the ears of the *p*	Judg 7:3	5971
And there returned of the *p* twenty	Judg 7:3	5971
Gideon, The *p* are yet too many	Judg 7:4	5971
brought down the *p* unto the water	Judg 7:5	5971
but all the rest of the *p* bowed	Judg 7:6	5971
let all the other *p* go every man	Judg 7:7	5971
So the *p* took victuals in their	Judg 7:8	5971
bread unto the *p* that follow me	Judg 8:5	5971
would to God this *p* were under my	Judg 9:29	5971
the *p* that is with thee, and lie	Judg 9:32	5971
the *p* that is with him come out	Judg 9:33	5971
all the *p* that were with him, by	Judg 9:34	5971
the *p* that were with him, from	Judg 9:35	5971
And when Gaal saw the *p*, he said	Judg 9:36	5971
there come *p* down from the top of	Judg 9:36	5971
See there come *p* down by the	Judg 9:37	5971
is not this the *p* that thou hast	Judg 9:38	5971
that the *p* went out into the	Judg 9:42	5971
And he took the *p*, and divided them	Judg 9:43	5971
the *p* were come forth out of the	Judg 9:43	5971
all the *p* that were in the fields	Judg 9:44	
slew the *p* that was therein, and	Judg 9:45	5971
all the *p* that were with him	Judg 9:48	5971
said unto the *p* that were with	Judg 9:48	5971
all the *p* likewise cut down every	Judg 9:49	5971
And the *p* and princes of Gilead	Judg 10:18	5971
the *p* made him head and captain	Judg 11:11	5971
Sihon gathered all his *p* together	Judg 11:20	5971

all his *p* into the hand of Israel	Judg 11:21	5971
Amorites from before his *p* Israel	Judg 11:23	5971
my *p* were at great strife with	Judg 12:2	5971
thy brethren, or among all my *p*	Judg 14:3	5971
riddle unto the children of my *p*	Judg 14:16	5971
riddle to the children of her *p*	Judg 14:17	5971
And when the *p* saw him, they	Judg 16:24	5971
upon all the *p* that were therein	Judg 16:30	5971
saw the *p* that were therein, how	Judg 18:7	5971
go, ye shall come unto a *p* secure	Judg 18:10	5971
and went in the midst of the *p*	Judg 18:20	5971
unto a *p* that were at quiet and	Judg 18:27	5971
And the chief of all the *p*	Judg 20:2	5971
in the assembly of the *p* of God	Judg 20:2	5971
all the *p* arose as one man,	Judg 20:8	5971
to fetch victual for the *p*	Judg 20:10	5971
Among all this *p* there were seven	Judg 20:16	5971
And the *p* the men of Israel	Judg 20:22	5971
children of Israel, and all the *p*	Judg 20:26	5971
Benjamin went out against the *p*	Judg 20:31	5971
and they began to smite of the *p*	Judg 20:31	5971
the *p* came to the house of God,	Judg 21:2	5971
that the *p* rose early, and built	Judg 21:4	5971
For the *p* were numbered, and,	Judg 21:9	5971
the *p* repented them for Benjamin,	Judg 21:15	5971
his *p* in giving them bread	Ruth 1:6	5971
will return with thee unto thy *p*	Ruth 1:10	5971
in law is gone back unto her *p*	Ruth 1:15	5971
thy *p* shall be my *p*, and thy	Ruth 1:16	5971
art come unto a *p* which thou	Ruth 2:11	5971
for all the city of my *p* doth	Ruth 3:11	5971
and before the elders of my *p*	Ruth 4:4	5971
the elders, and unto all the *p*	Ruth 4:9	5971
all the *p* that were in the gate,	Ruth 4:11	5971
priest's custom with the *p* was	1Sa 2:13	5971
your evil dealings by all this *p*	1Sa 2:23	5971
make the LORD's *p* to transgress	1Sa 2:24	5971
all the offerings of Israel my *p*	1Sa 2:29	5971
when the *p* were come into the	1Sa 4:3	5971
So the *p* sent to Shiloh, that	1Sa 4:4	5971
a great slaughter among the *p*	1Sa 4:17	5971
Israel to us, to slay us and our *p*	1Sa 5:10	5971
that it slay us not, and our *p*	1Sa 5:11	5971
them, did they not let the *p* go	1Sa 6:6	
he smote of the *p* fifty thousand	1Sa 6:19	5971
the *p* lamented, because the LORD	1Sa 6:19	5971
of the *p* with a great slaughter	1Sa 6:19	5971
Hearken unto the voice of the *p*	1Sa 8:7	5971
the *p* that asked of him a king	1Sa 8:10	5971
Nevertheless the *p* refused to	1Sa 8:19	5971
heard all the words of the *p*	1Sa 8:21	5971
he was higher than any of the *p*	1Sa 9:2	5971
of the *p* to day in the high place	1Sa 9:12	5971
for the *p* will not eat until he	1Sa 9:13	5971
to be captain over my *p* Israel	1Sa 9:16	5971
that he may save my *p* out of the	1Sa 9:16	5971
for I have looked upon my *p*	1Sa 9:16	5971
this same shall reign over my *p*	1Sa 9:17	5971
I said, I have invited the *p*	1Sa 9:24	5971
then the *p* said one to another,	1Sa 10:11	5971
Samuel called the *p* together unto	1Sa 10:17	5971
and when he stood among the *p*	1Sa 10:23	5971
any of the *p* from his shoulders	1Sa 10:23	5971
And Samuel said to all the *p*	1Sa 10:24	5971
is none like him among all the *p*	1Sa 10:24	5971
And all the *p* shouted, and said,	1Sa 10:24	5971
Then Samuel told the *p* the manner	1Sa 10:25	5971
And Samuel sent all the *p* away	1Sa 10:25	5971
the tidings in the ears of the *p*	1Sa 11:4	5971
all the *p* lifted up their voices,	1Sa 11:4	5971
What aileth the *p* that they weep	1Sa 11:5	5971
fear of the LORD fell on the *p*	1Sa 11:7	5971
that Saul put the *p* in three	1Sa 11:11	5971
the *p* said unto Samuel, Who is he	1Sa 11:12	5971
Then said Samuel to the *p*	1Sa 11:14	5971
And all the *p* went to Gilgal	1Sa 11:15	5971
And Samuel said unto the *p*	1Sa 12:6	5971
all the *p* greatly feared the LORD	1Sa 12:18	5971
all the *p* said unto Samuel, Pray	1Sa 12:19	5971
And Samuel said unto the *p*	1Sa 12:20	5971
his *p* for his great name's sake	1Sa 12:22	5971
the LORD to make you his *p*	1Sa 12:22	5971
the rest of the *p* he sent every	1Sa 13:2	5971
the *p* were called together after	1Sa 13:4	5971
p as the sand which is on the sea	1Sa 13:5	5971
(for the *p* were distressed,)	1Sa 13:6	5971
then the *p* did hide themselves	1Sa 13:6	5971
all the *p* followed him trembling	1Sa 13:7	5971
the *p* were scattered from him	1Sa 13:8	5971
that the *p* were scattered from me	1Sa 13:11	5971
him to be captain over his *p*	1Sa 13:14	5971
Saul numbered the *p* that were	1Sa 13:15	5971
the *p* that were present with them	1Sa 13:16	5971
any of the *p* that were with Saul	1Sa 13:22	5971
the *p* that were with him were	1Sa 14:2	5971
the *p* knew not that Jonathan was	1Sa 14:3	5971
in the field, and among all the *p*	1Sa 14:15	5971
unto the *p* that were with him	1Sa 14:17	5971
all the *p* that were with him	1Sa 14:20	5971
for Saul had adjured the *p*	1Sa 14:24	5971
So none of the *p* tasted any food	1Sa 14:24	5971
when the *p* were come into the	1Sa 14:26	5971
for the *p* feared the oath	1Sa 14:26	5971
charged the *p* with the oath	1Sa 14:27	5971
Then answered one of the *p*	1Sa 14:28	5971
charged the *p* with an oath	1Sa 14:28	5971
And the *p* were faint	1Sa 14:28	5971
if haply the *p* had eaten freely	1Sa 14:30	5971
and the *p* were very faint	1Sa 14:31	5971
the *p* flew upon the spoil, and	1Sa 14:32	5971
the *p* did eat them with the blood	1Sa 14:32	5971
the *p* sin against the LORD, in	1Sa 14:33	5971
Disperse yourselves among the *p*	1Sa 14:34	5971
all the *p* brought every man his	1Sa 14:34	5971
hither, all the chief of the *p*	1Sa 14:38	5971
among all the *p* that answered him	1Sa 14:39	5971
the *p* said unto Saul, Do what	1Sa 14:40	5971
but the *p* escaped	1Sa 14:41	5971
the *p* said unto Saul, Shall	1Sa 14:45	5971
So the *p* rescued Jonathan, that	1Sa 14:45	5971
anoint thee to be king over his *p*	1Sa 15:1	5971
And Saul gathered the *p* together	1Sa 15:4	5971
utterly destroyed all the *p* with	1Sa 15:8	5971
the *p* spared Agag, and the best of	1Sa 15:9	5971
for the *p* spared the best of the	1Sa 15:15	5971
But the *p* took of the spoil,	1Sa 15:21	5971
because I feared the *p*, and obeyed	1Sa 15:24	5971
thee, before the elders of my *p*	1Sa 15:30	5971
the *p* answered him after this	1Sa 17:27	5971
the *p* answered him again after	1Sa 17:30	5971
in the sight of all the *p*	1Sa 18:5	5971
went out and came in before the *p*	1Sa 18:13	5971
called all the *p* together to war	1Sa 23:8	5971
the *p* pitched round about him	1Sa 26:5	5971
and Abishai came to the *p* by night	1Sa 26:7	5971
the *p* lay round about him	1Sa 26:7	5971
And David cried to the *p*, and to	1Sa 26:14	5971
for there came one of the *p* in to	1Sa 26:15	5971
He hath made his *p* Israel utterly	1Sa 27:12	5971
the *p* that were with him lifted	1Sa 30:4	5971
for the *p* spake of stoning him,	1Sa 30:6	5971
the soul of all the *p* was grieved	1Sa 30:6	5971
to meet the *p* that were with him	1Sa 30:21	5971
and when David came near to the *p*	1Sa 30:21	5971
of their idols, and among the *p*	1Sa 31:9	5971
That the *p* are fled from the	2Sa 1:4	5971
many of the *p* also are fallen and	2Sa 1:4	5971
for the *p* of the LORD, and for the	2Sa 1:12	5971
ere thou bid the *p* return from	2Sa 2:26	5971
the *p* had gone up every one from	2Sa 2:27	5971
all the *p* stood still, and pursued	2Sa 2:28	5971
had gathered all the *p* together	2Sa 2:30	5971
p Israel out of the hand of the	2Sa 3:18	5971
to all the *p* that were with him,	2Sa 3:31	5971
and all the *p* wept	2Sa 3:32	5971
all the *p* wept again over him	2Sa 3:34	5971
when all the *p* came to cause	2Sa 3:35	5971
all the *p* took notice of it, and	2Sa 3:36	5971
the king did pleased all the *p*	2Sa 3:36	5971
For all the *p* and all Israel	2Sa 3:37	5971
thee, Thou shalt feed my *p* Israel	2Sa 5:2	5971
kingdom for his *p* Israel's sake	2Sa 5:12	5971
went with all the *p* that were	2Sa 6:2	5971
he blessed the *p* in the name of	2Sa 6:18	5971
And he dealt among all the *p*	2Sa 6:19	5971
So all the *p* departed every one	2Sa 6:19	5971
me ruler over the *p* of the LORD	2Sa 6:21	5971
I commanded to feed my *p* Israel	2Sa 7:7	5971
the sheep, to be ruler over my *p*	2Sa 7:8	5971
appoint a place for my *p* Israel	2Sa 7:10	5971
judges to be over my *p* Israel	2Sa 7:11	5971
nation in the earth is like thy *p*	2Sa 7:23	5971
went to redeem for a *p* to himself	2Sa 7:23	5971
for thy land, before thy *p*	2Sa 7:23	5971
hast confirmed to thyself thy *p*	2Sa 7:24	5971
to be a *p* unto thee for ever	2Sa 7:24	5971
and justice unto all his *p*	2Sa 8:15	5971
the rest of the *p* he delivered	2Sa 10:10	5971
and let us play the men for our *p*	2Sa 10:12	5971
the *p* that were with him, unto	2Sa 10:13	5971
how Joab did, and how the *p* did	2Sa 11:7	5971
there fell some of the *p* of the	2Sa 11:17	5971
gather the rest of the *p* together	2Sa 12:28	5971
David gathered all the *p* together	2Sa 12:29	5971
forth the *p* that were therein	2Sa 12:31	5971
all the *p* returned unto Jerusalem	2Sa 12:31	5971
there came much *p* by the way of	2Sa 13:34	5971
such a thing against the *p* of God	2Sa 14:13	5971
it is because the *p* have made me	2Sa 14:15	5971
for the *p* increased continually	2Sa 15:12	5971
all the *p* after him, and tarried	2Sa 15:17	5971
voice, and all the *p* passed over	2Sa 15:23	5971
all the *p* passed over, toward the	2Sa 15:23	5971
until all the *p* had done passing	2Sa 15:24	5971
all the *p* that was with him	2Sa 15:30	5971
and all the *p* and all the mighty	2Sa 16:6	5971
all the *p* that were with him,	2Sa 16:14	5971
all the *p* the men of Israel, came	2Sa 16:15	5971
but whom the LORD, and this *p*	2Sa 16:18	5971
all the *p* that are with him shall	2Sa 17:2	5971
bring back all the *p* unto thee	2Sa 17:3	5971
so all the *p* shall be in peace	2Sa 17:3	5971
war, and will not lodge with the *p*	2Sa 17:8	5971
among the *p* that follow Absalom	2Sa 17:9	5971
all the *p* that are with him	2Sa 17:16	5971
all the *p* that were with him, and	2Sa 17:22	5971
for the *p* that were with him, to	2Sa 17:29	5971
The *p* is hungry, and weary, and	2Sa 17:29	5971
numbered the *p* that were with him	2Sa 18:1	5971
of the *p* under the hand of Joab	2Sa 18:2	5971
And the king said unto the *p*	2Sa 18:2	5971
But the *p* answered, Thou shalt	2Sa 18:3	5971
all the *p* came out by hundreds and	2Sa 18:4	5971
all the *p* heard when the king	2Sa 18:5	5971
So the *p* went out into the field	2Sa 18:6	5971
Where the *p* of Israel were slain	2Sa 18:7	5971
the wood devoured more *p* that day	2Sa 18:8	5971
the *p* returned from pursuing	2Sa 18:16	5971
for Joab held back the *p*	2Sa 18:16	5971
into mourning unto all the *p*	2Sa 19:2	5971
for the *p* heard say that day how	2Sa 19:2	5971
the *p* gat them by stealth that	2Sa 19:3	5971
as *p* being ashamed steal away	2Sa 19:3	5971
And they told unto all the *p*	2Sa 19:8	5971
all the *p* came before the king	2Sa 19:8	5971
And all the *p* were at strife	2Sa 19:9	5971
all the *p* went over Jordan	2Sa 19:39	5971
all the *p* of Judah conducted the	2Sa 19:40	5971
and also half the *p* of Israel	2Sa 19:40	5971
saw that all the *p* stood still	2Sa 20:12	5971
all the *p* went on after Joab, to	2Sa 20:13	376
all the *p* that were with Joab	2Sa 20:15	5971
went unto all the *p* in her wisdom	2Sa 20:22	5971
the afflicted *p* thou wilt save	2Sa 22:28	5971
me from the strivings of my *p*	2Sa 22:44	5971
a *p* which I knew not shall serve	2Sa 22:44	5971
that bringeth down the *p* under me	2Sa 22:48	5971
the *p* returned after him only to	2Sa 23:10	5971
the *p* fled from the Philistines	2Sa 23:11	5971
to Beer-sheba, and number ye the *p*	2Sa 24:2	5971
I may know the number of the *p*	2Sa 24:2	5971
the LORD thy God add unto the *p*	2Sa 24:3	5971
king, to number the *p* of Israel	2Sa 24:4	5971
the number of the *p* unto the king	2Sa 24:9	5971
after that he had numbered the *p*	2Sa 24:10	5971
there died of the *p* from Dan even	2Sa 24:15	5971
to the angel that destroyed the *p*	2Sa 24:16	5971
he saw the angel that smote the *p*	2Sa 24:17	5971
plague may be stayed from the *p*	2Sa 24:21	5971
and all the *p* said, God save king	1Kin 1:39	5971
all the *p* came up after him, and	1Kin 1:40	5971
the *p* piped with pipes, and	1Kin 1:40	5971
Only the *p* sacrificed in high	1Kin 3:2	5971
of thy *p* which thou hast chosen	1Kin 3:8	5971
which thou hast chosen, a great *p*	1Kin 3:8	5971
heart to judge thy *p*, that I may	1Kin 3:9	5971
to judge this thy so great a *p*	1Kin 3:9	5971
there came of all *p* to hear the	1Kin 4:34	5971
a wise son over this great *p*	1Kin 5:7	5971
which ruled over the *p* that	1Kin 5:16	5971
and will not forsake my *p* Israel	1Kin 6:13	5971
forth my *p* Israel out of Egypt	1Kin 8:16	5971
David to be over my *p* Israel	1Kin 8:16	5971
thy servant, and of thy *p* Israel	1Kin 8:30	5971
When thy *p* Israel be smitten down	1Kin 8:33	5971
forgive the sin of thy *p* Israel	1Kin 8:34	5971
thy servants, and of thy *p* Israel	1Kin 8:36	5971
given to thy *p* for an inheritance	1Kin 8:36	5971
any man, or by all thy *p* Israel	1Kin 8:38	5971
that is not of thy *p* Israel	1Kin 8:41	5971
that all *p* of the earth may know	1Kin 8:43	5971
to fear thee, as do thy *p* Israel	1Kin 8:43	5971
If thy *p* go out to battle against	1Kin 8:44	5971
forgive thy *p* that have sinned	1Kin 8:50	5971
For they be thy *p*, and thine	1Kin 8:51	5971
the supplication of thy *p* Israel	1Kin 8:52	5971
from among all the *p* of the earth	1Kin 8:53	5971
hath given rest unto his *p* Israel	1Kin 8:56	5971
the cause of his *p* Israel at all	1Kin 8:59	5971
That all the *p* of the earth may	1Kin 8:60	5971
the eighth day he sent the *p* away	1Kin 8:66	5971
his servant, and for Israel his *p*	1Kin 8:66	5971
a proverb and a byword among all *p*	1Kin 9:7	5971
all the *p* that were left of the	1Kin 9:20	5971
the *p* that wrought in the work	1Kin 9:23	5971
And the *p* departed	1Kin 12:5	5971
advise that I may answer this *p*	1Kin 12:6	5971
be a servant unto this *p* this day	1Kin 12:7	5971
give ye that we may answer this *p*	1Kin 12:9	5971
unto this *p* that spake unto thee	1Kin 12:10	5971
all the *p* came to Rehoboam the	1Kin 12:12	5971
the king answered the *p* roughly	1Kin 12:13	5971
the king hearkened not unto the *p*	1Kin 12:15	5971
the *p* answered the king, saying,	1Kin 12:16	5971
and to the remnant of the *p*	1Kin 12:23	5971
If this *p* go up to do sacrifice	1Kin 12:27	5971
this *p* turn again unto their lord	1Kin 12:27	5971
for the *p* went to worship before	1Kin 12:30	5971
priests of the lowest of the *p*	1Kin 12:31	5971
the *p* priests of the high places	1Kin 13:33	5971
that I should be king over this *p*	1Kin 14:2	5971
I exalted thee from among the *p*	1Kin 14:7	5971
made thee prince over my *p* Israel	1Kin 14:7	5971
made thee prince over my *p* Israel	1Kin 16:2	5971
hast made my *p* Israel to sin, to	1Kin 16:2	5971
the *p* were encamped against	1Kin 16:15	5971
the *p* that were encamped heard	1Kin 16:16	5971
Then were the *p* of Israel divided	1Kin 16:21	5971
half of the *p* followed Tibni the	1Kin 16:21	5971
But the *p* that followed Omri	1Kin 16:22	5971
Omri prevailed against the *p* that	1Kin 16:22	5971
And Elijah came unto all the *p*	1Kin 18:21	5971
the *p* answered him not a word	1Kin 18:21	5971
Then said Elijah unto the *p*	1Kin 18:22	5971
all the *p* answered and said, It is	1Kin 18:24	5971
And Elijah said unto all the *p*	1Kin 18:30	5971
all the *p* came near unto him	1Kin 18:30	5971
that this *p* may know that thou	1Kin 18:37	5971
And when all the *p* saw it, they	1Kin 18:39	5971
of the oxen, and gave unto the *p*	1Kin 19:21	5971
all the *p* said unto him, Hearken	1Kin 20:8	5971
for all the *p* that follow me	1Kin 20:10	5971
after them he numbered all the *p*	1Kin 20:15	5971
his life, and thy *p* for his *p*	1Kin 20:42	5971

and set Naboth on high among the p	1Kin 21:9	5971
and set Naboth on high among the p	1Kin 21:12	5971
Naboth, in the presence of the p	1Kin 21:13	5971
as thou art, my p as thy p	1Kin 22:4	5971
And he said, Hearken, O p, every	1Kin 22:28	5971
for the p offered and burnt	1Kin 22:43	5971
as thou art, my p as thy p	2Kin 3:7	5971
I dwell among mine own p	2Kin 4:13	5971
and he said, Pour out for the p	2Kin 4:41	5971
And he said, Give unto the p	2Kin 4:42	5971
He said again, Give the p	2Kin 4:43	5971
the LORD, and said, Smite this p	2Kin 6:18	1471
the p looked, and, behold, he had	2Kin 6:30	5971
the p went out, and spoiled the	2Kin 7:16	5971
the p trode upon him in the gate,	2Kin 7:17	5971
for the p trode upon him in the	2Kin 7:20	5971
the p fled into their tents	2Kin 8:21	5971
thee king over the p of the LORD	2Kin 9:6	5971
and stood, and said to all the p	2Kin 10:9	5971
Jehu gathered all the p together	2Kin 10:18	5971
noise of the guard and of the p	2Kin 11:13	5971
she came to the p into the temple	2Kin 11:13	5971
all the p of the land rejoiced,	2Kin 11:14	5971
the LORD and the king and the p	2Kin 11:17	5971
that they should be the LORD's p	2Kin 11:17	5971
between the king also and the p	2Kin 11:17	5971
all the p of the land went into	2Kin 11:18	5971
guard, and all the p of the land	2Kin 11:19	5971
all the p of the land rejoiced,	2Kin 11:20	5971
the p still sacrificed and burnt	2Kin 12:3	5971
to receive no more money of the p	2Kin 12:8	5971
Neither did he leave of the p to	2Kin 13:7	5971
as yet the p did sacrifice and	2Kin 14:4	5971
all the p of Judah took Azariah,	2Kin 14:21	5971
the p sacrificed and burnt incense	2Kin 15:4	5971
house, judging the p of the land	2Kin 15:5	5971
him, and smote him before the p	2Kin 15:10	5971
the p sacrificed and burned	2Kin 15:35	5971
carried the p of it captive to	2Kin 16:9	
offering of all the p of the land	2Kin 16:15	5971
of the p that are on the wall	2Kin 18:26	5971
But the p held their peace, and	2Kin 18:36	5971
tell Hezekiah the captain of my p	2Kin 20:5	5971
the p of the land slew all them	2Kin 21:24	5971
the p of the land made Josiah his	2Kin 21:24	5971
the door have gathered of the p	2Kin 22:4	5971
of the LORD for me, and for the p	2Kin 22:13	5971
and the prophets, and all the p	2Kin 23:2	5971
all the p stood to the covenant	2Kin 23:3	5971
graves of the children of the p	2Kin 23:6	5971
And the king commanded all the p	2Kin 23:21	5971
the p of the land took Jehoahaz	2Kin 23:30	5971
and the gold of the p of the land	2Kin 23:35	5971
poorest sort of the p of the land	2Kin 24:14	5971
no bread for the p of the land	2Kin 25:3	5971
Now the rest of the p that were	2Kin 25:11	5971
which mustered the p of the land	2Kin 25:19	5971
threescore men of the p of the	2Kin 25:19	5971
as for the p that remained in the	2Kin 25:22	5971
And all the p, both small and great	2Kin 25:26	5971
the gods of the p of the land	1Chr 5:25	5971
unto their idols, and to the p	1Chr 10:9	5971
thee, Thou shalt feed my p Israel	1Chr 11:2	5971
shalt be ruler over my p Israel	1Chr 11:2	5971
the p fled from before the	1Chr 11:13	5971
right in the eyes of all the p	1Chr 13:4	5971
on high, because of his p Israel	1Chr 14:2	5971
he blessed the p in the name of	1Chr 16:2	5971
make known his deeds among the p	1Chr 16:8	5971
and from one kingdom to another p	1Chr 16:20	5971
all the gods of the p are idols	1Chr 16:26	5971
the LORD, ye kindreds of the p	1Chr 16:28	5971
And all the p said, Amen, and	1Chr 16:36	5971
all the p departed every man to	1Chr 16:43	5971
whom I commanded to feed my p	1Chr 17:6	5971
be ruler over my p Israel	1Chr 17:7	5971
ordain a place for my p Israel	1Chr 17:9	5971
judges to be over my p Israel	1Chr 17:10	5971
in the earth is like thy p Israel	1Chr 17:21	5971
went to redeem to be his own p	1Chr 17:21	5971
out nations from before thy p	1Chr 17:21	5971
For thy p Israel didst thou make	1Chr 17:22	5971
thou make thine own p for ever	1Chr 17:22	5971
and justice among all his p	1Chr 18:14	5971
and the king of Maachah and his p	1Chr 19:7	5971
the rest of the p he delivered	1Chr 19:11	5971
ourselves valiantly for our p	1Chr 19:13	5971
the p that were with him drew	1Chr 19:14	5971
brought out the p that were in it	1Chr 20:3	5971
all the p returned to Jerusalem	1Chr 20:3	5971
to Joab and to the rulers of the p	1Chr 21:2	5971
The LORD make his p an hundred	1Chr 21:3	5971
of the number of the p unto David	1Chr 21:5	5971
commanded the p to be numbered	1Chr 21:17	5971
but not on thy p, that they	1Chr 21:17	5971
plague may be stayed from the p	1Chr 21:22	5971
before the LORD, and before his p	1Chr 22:18	5971
Israel hath given rest unto his p	1Chr 23:25	5971
Hear me, my brethren, and my p	1Chr 28:2	5971
all the p will be wholly at thy	1Chr 28:21	5971
Then the p rejoiced, for that	1Chr 29:9	5971
But who am I, and what is my p	1Chr 29:14	5971
and now have I seen with joy thy p	1Chr 29:17	5971
thoughts of the heart of thy p	1Chr 29:18	5971
a p like the dust of the earth in	2Chr 1:9	5971
go out and come in before this p	2Chr 1:10	5971
for who can judge this thy p	2Chr 1:10	5971
that thou mayest judge my p	2Chr 1:11	5971
Because the LORD hath loved his p	2Chr 2:11	5971
overseers to set the p a work	2Chr 2:18	5971
my p out of the land of Egypt I	2Chr 6:5	5971
to be a ruler over my p Israel	2Chr 6:5	5971
David to be over my p Israel	2Chr 6:6	5971
thy servant, and of thy p Israel	2Chr 6:21	5971
if thy p Israel be put to the	2Chr 6:24	5971
forgive the sin of thy p Israel	2Chr 6:25	5971
thy servants, and of thy p Israel	2Chr 6:27	5971
unto thy p for an inheritance	2Chr 6:27	5971
any man, or of all thy p Israel	2Chr 6:29	5971
which is not of thy p Israel	2Chr 6:32	5971
that all p of the earth may know	2Chr 6:33	5971
fear thee, as doth thy p Israel	2Chr 6:33	5971
If thy p go out to war against	2Chr 6:34	5971
forgive thy p which have sinned	2Chr 6:39	5971
all the p offered sacrifices	2Chr 7:4	5971
all the p dedicated the house of	2Chr 7:5	5971
sent the p away into their tents	2Chr 7:10	5971
and to Solomon, and to Israel his p	2Chr 7:10	5971
if I send pestilence among my p	2Chr 7:13	5971
If my p, which are called by my	2Chr 7:14	5971
As for all the p that were left	2Chr 8:7	5971
fifty, that bare rule over the p	2Chr 8:10	5971
And the p departed	2Chr 10:5	5971
ye me to return answer to this p	2Chr 10:6	5971
saying, If thou be kind to this p	2Chr 10:7	5971
we may return answer to this p	2Chr 10:9	5971
answer the p that spake unto thee	2Chr 10:10	5971
all the p came to Rehoboam on the	2Chr 10:12	5971
the king hearkened not unto the p	2Chr 10:15	5971
the p answered the king, saying,	2Chr 10:16	5971
the p were without number that	2Chr 12:3	5971
his p slew them with a great	2Chr 13:17	5971
the p that were with him pursued	2Chr 14:13	5971
some of the p the same time	2Chr 16:10	5971
cities of Judah, and taught the p	2Chr 17:9	5971
for the p that he had with him,	2Chr 18:2	5971
thou art, and my p as thy p	2Chr 18:3	5971
And he said, Hearken, all ye p	2Chr 18:27	5971
the p from Beer-sheba to mount	2Chr 19:4	5971
of this land before thy p Israel	2Chr 20:7	5971
when he had consulted with the p	2Chr 20:21	5971
his p came to take away the spoil	2Chr 20:25	5971
for as yet the p had not prepared	2Chr 20:33	5971
plague will the LORD smite thy p	2Chr 21:14	5971
his p made no burning for him,	2Chr 21:19	5971
all the p shall be in the courts	2Chr 23:5	5971
but all the p shall keep the	2Chr 23:6	5971
And he set all the p, every man	2Chr 23:10	5971
heard the noise of the p running	2Chr 23:12	5971
she came to the p into the house	2Chr 23:12	5971
all the p of the land rejoiced,	2Chr 23:13	5971
between him, and between all the p	2Chr 23:16	5971
that they should be the LORD's p	2Chr 23:16	5971
Then all the p went to the house	2Chr 23:17	5971
nobles, and the governors of the p	2Chr 23:20	5971
all the p of the land, and brought	2Chr 23:20	5971
all the p of the land rejoiced	2Chr 23:21	5971
all the p rejoiced, and brought in	2Chr 24:10	5971
priest, which stood above the p	2Chr 24:20	5971
of the p from among the p	2Chr 24:23	5971
himself, and led forth his p	2Chr 25:11	5971
sought after the gods of the p	2Chr 25:15	5971
their own p out of thine hand	2Chr 25:15	5971
Then all the p of Judah took	2Chr 26:1	5971
house, judging the p of the land	2Chr 26:21	5971
And the p did yet corruptly	2Chr 27:2	5971
Hezekiah rejoiced, and all the p	2Chr 29:36	5971
that God had prepared the p	2Chr 29:36	5971
neither had the p gathered	2Chr 30:3	5971
assembled at Jerusalem much p to	2Chr 30:13	5971
For a multitude of the p, even	2Chr 30:18	5971
to Hezekiah, and healed the p	2Chr 30:20	5971
Levites arose and blessed the p	2Chr 30:27	5971
Moreover he commanded the p that	2Chr 31:4	5971
blessed the LORD, and his p Israel	2Chr 31:8	5971
Since the p began to bring the	2Chr 31:10	
for the LORD hath blessed his p	2Chr 31:10	5971
was gathered much p together	2Chr 32:4	5971
he set captains of war over the p	2Chr 32:6	5971
the p rested themselves upon the	2Chr 32:8	5971
unto all the p of other lands	2Chr 32:13	5971
deliver his p out of mine hand	2Chr 32:14	5971
to deliver his p out of mine hand	2Chr 32:15	5971
their p out of mine hand, so	2Chr 32:17	5971
deliver his p out of mine hand	2Chr 32:17	5971
in the Jews' speech unto the p of	2Chr 32:18	5971
the gods of the p of the earth	2Chr 32:19	5971
spake to Manasseh, and to his p	2Chr 33:10	5971
Nevertheless the p did sacrifice	2Chr 33:17	5971
But the p of the land slew all	2Chr 33:25	5971
the p of the land made Josiah his	2Chr 33:25	5971
and the Levites, and all the p	2Chr 34:30	5971
LORD your God, and his p Israel,	2Chr 35:3	5971
fathers of your brethren the p	2Chr 35:5	
And Josiah gave to the p, of the	2Chr 35:7	
princes gave willingly unto the p	2Chr 35:8	5971
of the families of the p, to	2Chr 35:12	
them speedily among all the p	2Chr 35:13	
Then the p of the land took	2Chr 36:1	5971
chief of the priests, and the p	2Chr 36:14	5971
he had compassion on his p	2Chr 36:15	5971
of the LORD arose against his p	2Chr 36:16	5971
is there among you of all his p	2Chr 36:23	5971
is there among you of all his p	Ezr 1:3	5971
of the men of the p of Israel	Ezr 2:2	5971
and the Levites, and some of the p	Ezr 2:70	5971
the p gathered themselves	Ezr 3:1	5971
of the p of those countries	Ezr 3:3	5971
all the p shouted with a great	Ezr 3:11	5971
So that the p could not discern	Ezr 3:13	5971
the noise of the weeping of the p	Ezr 3:13	5971
for the p shouted with a loud	Ezr 3:13	5971
Then the p of the land weakened	Ezr 4:4	5971
the hands of the p of Judah	Ezr 4:4	5971
carried the p away into Babylon	Ezr 5:12	5972
there destroy all kings and p	Ezr 6:12	5972
that all they of the p of Israel	Ezr 7:13	5972
the freewill offering of the p	Ezr 7:16	5972
which may judge all the p that	Ezr 7:25	5972
and I viewed the p, and the priests	Ezr 8:15	5971
and they furthered the p, and the	Ezr 8:36	5971
The p of Israel, and the priests,	Ezr 9:1	5971
from the p of the lands, doing	Ezr 9:1	5971
with the p of those lands	Ezr 9:2	5971
filthiness of the p of the lands	Ezr 9:11	5971
with the p of these abominations	Ezr 9:14	5971
for the p wept very sore	Ezr 10:1	5971
wives of the p of the land	Ezr 10:2	5971
all the p sat in the street of	Ezr 10:9	5971
yourselves from the p of the land	Ezr 10:11	5971
But the p are many, and it is a	Ezr 10:13	5971
these are thy servants and thy p	Neh 1:10	5971
for the p had a mind to work	Neh 4:6	5971
I even set the p after their	Neh 4:13	5971
rulers, and to the rest of the p	Neh 4:14	5971
rulers, and to the rest of the p	Neh 4:19	5971
the same time said I unto the p	Neh 4:22	5971
And there was a great cry of the p	Neh 5:1	5971
the p did according to this	Neh 5:13	5971
me were chargeable unto the p	Neh 5:15	5971
servants bare rule over the p	Neh 5:15	5971
the bondage was heavy upon this p	Neh 5:18	5971
all that I have done for this p	Neh 5:19	5971
but the p were few therein, and	Neh 7:4	5971
nobles, and the rulers, and the p	Neh 7:5	5971
of the men of the p of Israel was	Neh 7:7	5971
that which the rest of the p gave	Neh 7:72	5971
and the singers, and some of the p	Neh 7:73	5971
all the p gathered themselves	Neh 8:1	5971
the ears of all the p were	Neh 8:3	5971
the book in the sight of all p	Neh 8:5	5971
(for he was above all the p	Neh 8:5	5971
he opened it, all the p stood up	Neh 8:5	5971
all the p answered, Amen, Amen,	Neh 8:6	5971
caused the p to understand the	Neh 8:7	5971
the p stood in their place	Neh 8:7	5971
and the Levites that taught the p	Neh 8:9	5971
said unto all the p	Neh 8:9	5971
For all the p wept, when they	Neh 8:9	5971
So the Levites stilled all the p	Neh 8:11	5971
all the p went their way to eat,	Neh 8:12	5971
chief of the fathers of all the p	Neh 8:13	5971
So the p went forth, and brought	Neh 8:16	5971
and on all the p of his land	Neh 9:10	5971
the p of the land, that they	Neh 9:24	5971
the hand of the p of the lands	Neh 9:30	5971
on our fathers, and on all thy p	Neh 9:32	5971
The chief of the p	Neh 10:14	5971
And the rest of the p, the priests	Neh 10:28	5971
p of the lands unto the law of	Neh 10:28	5971
daughters unto the p of the land	Neh 10:30	5971
if the p of the land bring ware	Neh 10:31	5971
priests, the Levites, and the p	Neh 10:34	5971
the rulers of the p dwelt at	Neh 11:1	5971
the rest of the p also cast lots	Neh 11:1	5971
the p blessed all the men, that	Neh 11:2	5971
in all matters concerning the p	Neh 11:24	5971
themselves, and purified the p	Neh 12:30	5971
the half of the p upon the wall	Neh 12:38	5971
of Moses in the audience of the p	Neh 13:1	5971
to the language of each p	Neh 13:24	5971
p that were present in Shushan	Est 1:5	5971
the crown royal, to shew the p	Est 1:11	5971
to all the p that are in all the	Est 1:16	5971
to every p after their language,	Est 1:22	5971
to the language of every p	Est 1:22	5971
not shewed her p nor her kindred	Est 2:10	5971
yet shewed her kindred nor her p	Est 2:20	5971
had shewed him the p of Mordecai	Est 3:6	5971
Ahasuerus, even the p of Mordecai	Est 3:6	5971
is a certain p scattered abroad	Est 3:8	5971
dispersed among the p in all the	Est 3:8	5971
their laws are diverse from all p	Est 3:8	5971
the p also, to do with them as it	Est 3:11	5971
to the rulers of every p of every	Est 3:12	5971
to every p after their language	Est 3:12	5971
province was published unto all p	Est 3:14	5971
make request before him for her p	Est 4:8	5971
the p of the king's provinces, do	Est 4:11	5971
petition, and my p at my request	Est 7:3	5971
For we are sold, I and my p	Est 7:4	5971
evil that shall come unto my p	Est 8:6	5971
unto every p after their language	Est 8:9	5971
to perish, all the power of the p	Est 8:11	5971
province was published unto all p	Est 8:13	5971
many of the p of the land became	Est 8:17	5971
the fear of them fell upon all p	Est 9:2	5971
seeking the wealth of his p	Est 10:3	5971
No doubt but ye are the p	Job 12:2	5971
the chief of the p of the earth	Job 12:24	5971
made me also a byword of the p	Job 17:6	5971
have son nor nephew among his p	Job 18:19	5971
the p shall be troubled at	Job 34:20	5971
reign not, lest the p be ensnared	Job 34:30	5971

when *p* are cut off in their place ... Job 36:20 5971
For by them judgeth he the *p* ... Job 36:31 5971
the *p* imagine a vain thing ... Ps 2:1 3816
be afraid of ten thousands of *p* ... Ps 3:6 5971
thy blessing is upon thy *p* ... Ps 3:8 5971
of the *p* compass thee about ... Ps 7:7 3816
The LORD shall judge the *p* ... Ps 7:8 5971
judgment to the *p* in uprightness ... Ps 9:8 3816
declare among the *p* his doings ... Ps 9:11 5971
who eat up my *p* as they eat bread ... Ps 14:4 5971
back the captivity of his *p* ... Ps 14:7 5971
thou wilt save the afflicted *p* ... Ps 18:27 5971
me from the strivings of the *p* ... Ps 18:43 5971
a *p* whom I have not known shall ... Ps 18:43 5971
me, and subdueth the *p* under me ... Ps 18:47 5971
of men, and despised of the *p* ... Ps 22:6 5971
unto a *p* that shall be born ... Ps 22:31 5971
Save thy *p*, and bless thine ... Ps 28:9 5971
will give strength unto his *p* ... Ps 29:11 5971
LORD will bless his *p* with peace ... Ps 29:11 5971
devices of the *p* of none effect ... Ps 33:10 5971
the *p* whom he hath chosen for his ... Ps 33:12 5971
I will praise thee among much *p* ... Ps 35:18 5971
how thou didst afflict the *p* ... Ps 44:2 3816
Thou sellest thy *p* for nought ... Ps 44:12 5971
a shaking of the head among the *p* ... Ps 44:14 3816
whereby the *p* fall under thee ... Ps 45:5 5971
forget also thine own *p*, and thy ... Ps 45:10 5971
even the rich among the *p* shall ... Ps 45:12 5971
therefore shall the *p* praise thee ... Ps 45:17 5971
O clap your hands, all ye *p* ... Ps 47:1 5971
He shall subdue the *p* under us ... Ps 47:3 5971
The princes of the *p* are gathered ... Ps 47:9 5971
even the *p* of the God of Abraham ... Ps 47:9 5971
Hear this, all ye *p* ... Ps 49:1 5971
earth, that he may judge his *p* ... Ps 50:4 5971
Hear, O my *p*, and I will speak ... Ps 50:7 5971
who eat up my *p* as they eat bread ... Ps 53:4 5971
back the captivity of his *p* ... Ps 53:6 5971
in thine anger cast down the *p* ... Ps 56:7 5971
praise thee, O Lord, among the *p* ... Ps 57:9 5971
Slay them not, lest my *p* forget ... Ps 59:11 5971
hast shewed thy *p* hard things ... Ps 60:3 5971
ye *p*, pour out your heart before ... Ps 62:8 5971
waves, and the tumult of the *p* ... Ps 65:7 3816
O bless our God, ye *p*, and make ... Ps 66:8 5971
Let the *p* praise thee, O God ... Ps 67:3 5971
let all the *p* praise thee ... Ps 67:3 5971
shalt judge the *p* righteously ... Ps 67:4 5971
Let the *p* praise thee, O God ... Ps 67:5 5971
let all the *p* praise thee ... Ps 67:5 5971
thou wentest forth before thy *p* ... Ps 68:7 5971
I will bring my *p* again from the ... Ps 68:22
bulls, with the calves of the *p* ... Ps 68:30 5971
scatter thou the *p* that delight ... Ps 68:30 5971
strength and power unto his *p* ... Ps 68:35 5971
judge thy *p* with righteousness ... Ps 72:2 5971
shall bring peace to the *p* ... Ps 72:3 5971
He shall judge the poor of the *p* ... Ps 72:4 5971
Therefore his *p* return hither ... Ps 73:10 5971
the *p* inhabiting the wilderness ... Ps 74:14 5971
LORD, and that the foolish *p* have ... Ps 74:18 5971
declared thy strength among the *p* ... Ps 77:14 5971
with thine arm redeemed thy *p* ... Ps 77:15 5971
Thou leddest thy *p* like a flock ... Ps 77:20 5971
Give ear, O my *p*, to my law ... Ps 78:1 5971
can he provide flesh for his *p* ... Ps 78:20 5971
But made his own *p* to go forth ... Ps 78:52 5971
He gave his *p* over also unto the ... Ps 78:62 5971
brought him to feed Jacob his *p* ... Ps 78:71 5971
So we thy *p* and sheep of thy ... Ps 79:13 5971
angry against the prayer of thy *p* ... Ps 80:4 5971
Hear, O my *p*, and I will testify ... Ps 81:8 5971
But my *p* would not hearken to my ... Ps 81:11 5971
Oh that my *p* had hearkened unto ... Ps 81:13 5971
crafty counsel against thy *p* ... Ps 83:3 5971
forgiven the iniquity of thy *p* ... Ps 85:2 5971
that thy *p* may rejoice in thee ... Ps 85:6 5971
he will speak peace unto his *p* ... Ps 85:8 5971
count, when he writeth up the *p* ... Ps 87:6 5971
Blessed is the *p* that know the ... Ps 89:15 5971
exalted one chosen out of the *p* ... Ps 89:19 5971
the reproach of all the mighty *p* ... Ps 89:50 5971
They break in pieces thy *p* ... Ps 94:5 5971
ye brutish among the *p* ... Ps 94:8 5971
the LORD will not cast off his *p* ... Ps 94:14 5971
we are the *p* of his pasture, and ... Ps 95:7 5971
It is a *p* that do err in their ... Ps 95:10 5971
heathen, his wonders among all *p* ... Ps 96:3 5971
the LORD, O ye kindreds of the *p* ... Ps 96:7 5971
he shall judge the *p* righteously ... Ps 96:10 5971
and the *p* with his truth ... Ps 96:13 5971
and all the *p* see his glory ... Ps 97:6 5971
the world, and the *p* with equity ... Ps 98:9 5971
let the *p* tremble ... Ps 99:1 5971
and he is high above all the *p* ... Ps 99:2 5971
we are his *p*, and the sheep of his ... Ps 100:3 5971
the *p* which shall be created ... Ps 102:18 5971
When the *p* are gathered together, ... Ps 102:22 5971
make known his deeds among the *p* ... Ps 105:1 5971
from one kingdom to another *p* ... Ps 105:13 5971
even the ruler of the *p*, and let ... Ps 105:20 5971
And he increased his *p* greatly ... Ps 105:24 5971
turned their heart to hate his *p* ... Ps 105:25 5971
The *p* asked, and he brought quails ... Ps 105:40
he brought forth his *p* with joy ... Ps 105:43 5971
inherited the labour of the *p* ... Ps 105:44 3816
that thou bearest unto thy *p* ... Ps 106:4 5971

of the LORD kindled against his *p* ... Ps 106:40 5971
and let all the *p* say, Amen ... Ps 106:48 5971
also in the congregation of the *p* ... Ps 107:32 5971
praise thee, O LORD, among the *p* ... Ps 108:3 5971
Thy *p* shall be willing in the day ... Ps 110:3 5971
He hath shewed his *p* the power of ... Ps 111:6 5971
He sent redemption unto his *p* ... Ps 111:9 5971
even with the princes of his *p* ... Ps 113:8 5971
from a *p* of strange language ... Ps 114:1 5971
now in the presence of all his *p* ... Ps 116:14 5971
now in the presence of all his *p* ... Ps 116:18 5971
praise him, all ye *p* ... Ps 117:1 528
p from henceforth even for ever ... Ps 125:2 5971
an heritage unto Israel his *p* ... Ps 135:12 5971
For the LORD will judge his *p* ... Ps 135:14 5971
To him which led his *p* through ... Ps 136:16 5971
who subdueth my *p* under me ... Ps 144:2 5971
Happy is that *p*, that is in such ... Ps 144:15 5971
yea, happy is that *p*, whose God ... Ps 144:15 5971
Kings of the earth, and all *p* ... Ps 148:11 3816
also exalteth the horn of his *p* ... Ps 148:14 5971
of Israel, a *p* near unto him ... Ps 148:14 5971
the LORD taketh pleasure in his *p* ... Ps 149:4 5971
and punishments upon the *p* ... Ps 149:7 3816
Where no counsel is, the *p* fall ... Prov 11:14 5971
corn, the *p* shall curse him ... Prov 11:26 3816
In the multitude of *p* is the ... Prov 14:28 5971
but in the want of *p* is the ... Prov 14:28 3816
but sin is a reproach to any *p* ... Prov 14:34 3816
him shall the *p* curse, nations ... Prov 24:24 5971
is a wicked ruler over the poor *p* ... Prov 28:15 5971
are in authority, the *p* rejoice ... Prov 29:2 5971
wicked beareth rule, the *p* mourn ... Prov 29:2 5971
there is no vision, the *p* perish ... Prov 29:18 5971
The ants are a *p* not strong ... Prov 30:25 5971
There is no end of all the *p* ... Eccl 4:16 5971
he still taught the *p* knowledge ... Eccl 12:9 5971
not know, my *p* doth not consider ... Is 1:3 5971
a *p* laden with iniquity, a seed ... Is 1:4 5971
law of our God, ye *p* of Gomorrah ... Is 1:10 5971
many *p* shall go and say, Come ye, ... Is 2:3 5971
nations, and shall rebuke many *p* ... Is 2:4 5971
forsaken thy *p* the house of Jacob ... Is 2:6 5971
the *p* shall be oppressed, every ... Is 3:5 5971
make me not a ruler of the *p* ... Is 3:7 5971
As for my *p*, children are their ... Is 3:12 5971
O my *p*, they which lead thee ... Is 3:12 5971
plead, and standeth to judge the *p* ... Is 3:13 5971
with the ancients of his *p* ... Is 3:14 5971
ye that ye beat my *p* to pieces ... Is 3:15 5971
Therefore my *p* are gone into ... Is 5:13 5971
of the LORD kindled against his *p* ... Is 5:25 5971
the midst of a *p* of unclean lips ... Is 6:5 5971
And he said, Go, and tell this *p* ... Is 6:9 5971
Make the heart of this *p* fat ... Is 6:10 5971
was moved, and the heart of his *p* ... Is 7:2 5971
be broken, that it be not a *p* ... Is 7:8 5971
bring upon thee, and upon thy *p* ... Is 7:17 5971
Forasmuch as this *p* refuseth the ... Is 8:6 5971
Associate yourselves, O ye *p* ... Is 8:9 5971
not walk in the way of this *p* ... Is 8:11 5971
all them to whom this *p* shall say ... Is 8:12 5971
should not a *p* seek unto their ... Is 8:19 5971
The *p* that walked in darkness ... Is 9:2 5971
all the *p* shall know, even ... Is 9:9 5971
For the *p* turneth not unto him ... Is 9:13 5971
of this *p* cause them to err ... Is 9:16 5971
the *p* shall be as the fuel of the ... Is 9:19 5971
the right from the poor of my *p* ... Is 10:2 5971
against the *p* of my wrath will I ... Is 10:6 5971
have removed the bounds of the *p* ... Is 10:13 5971
as a nest the riches of the *p* ... Is 10:14 5971
For though thy *p* Israel be as the ... Is 10:22 5971
O my *p* that dwellest in Zion, be ... Is 10:24 5971
stand for an ensign of the *p* ... Is 11:10 5971
to recover the remnant of his *p* ... Is 11:11 5971
highway for the remnant of his *p* ... Is 11:16 5971
declare his doings among the *p* ... Is 12:4 5971
mountains, like as of a great *p* ... Is 13:4 5971
shall every man turn to his own *p* ... Is 13:14 5971
the *p* shall take them, and bring ... Is 14:2 5971
He who smote the *p* in wrath with ... Is 14:6 5971
thy land, and slain thy *p* ... Is 14:20 5971
the poor of his *p* shall trust in ... Is 14:32 5971
Woe to the multitude of many *p* ... Is 17:12 5971
to a *p* terrible from their ... Is 18:2 5971
LORD of hosts of a *p* scattered ... Is 18:7 5971
from a *p* terrible from their ... Is 18:7 5971
saying, Blessed be Egypt my *p* ... Is 19:25 5971
spoiling of the daughter of my *p* ... Is 22:4 5971
this *p* was not, til the Assyrian ... Is 23:13 5971
And it shall be, as with the *p* ... Is 24:2 5971
the haughty *p* of the earth do ... Is 24:4 5971
the midst of the land among the *p* ... Is 24:13 5971
shall the strong *p* glorify thee ... Is 25:3 5971
unto all *p* a feast of fat things ... Is 25:6 5971
of the covering cast over all *p* ... Is 25:7 5971
the rebuke of his *p* shall he take ... Is 25:8 5971
ashamed for their envy at the *p* ... Is 26:11 5971
Come, my *p*, enter thou into thy ... Is 26:20 5971
for it is a *p* of no understanding ... Is 27:11 5971
beauty, unto the residue of his *p* ... Is 28:5 5971
tongue will he speak to this *p* ... Is 28:11 5971
that rule this *p* which is in ... Is 28:14 5971
Forasmuch as this *p* draw near me ... Is 29:13 5971
do a marvellous work among this *p* ... Is 29:14 5971
of a *p* that could not profit them ... Is 30:5 5971
to a *p* that shall not profit them ... Is 30:6 5971

That this is a rebellious *p* ... Is 30:9 5971
For the *p* shall dwell in Zion at ... Is 30:19 5971
bindeth up the breach of his *p* ... Is 30:26 5971
be a bridle in the jaws of the *p* ... Is 30:28 5971
Upon the land of my *p* shall come ... Is 32:13 5971
my *p* shall dwell in a peaceable ... Is 32:18 5971
noise of the tumult the *p* fled ... Is 33:3 5971
the *p* shall be as the burnings of ... Is 33:12 5971
Thou shalt not see a fierce *p* ... Is 33:19 5971
a *p* of a deeper speech than thou ... Is 33:19 5971
the *p* that dwell therein shall be ... Is 33:24 5971
and hearken, ye *p* ... Is 34:1 3816
upon the *p* of my curse, to ... Is 34:5 5971
in the ears of the *p* that are on ... Is 36:11 5971
Comfort ye, comfort ye my *p* ... Is 40:1 5971
surely the *p* is grass ... Is 40:7 5971
let the *p* renew their strength ... Is 41:1 3816
giveth breath unto the *p* upon it ... Is 42:5 5971
give thee for a covenant of the *p* ... Is 42:6 5971
But this is a *p* robbed and spoiled ... Is 42:22 5971
men for thee, and *p* for thy life ... Is 43:4 3816
forth the blind *p* that have eyes ... Is 43:8 5971
and let the *p* be assembled ... Is 43:9 3816
the desert, to give drink to my *p* ... Is 43:20 5971
This *p* have I formed for myself ... Is 43:21 5971
since I appointed the ancient *p* ... Is 44:7 5971
I was wroth with my *p*, I have ... Is 47:6 5971
and hearken, ye *p*, from far ... Is 49:1 3816
give thee for a covenant of the *p* ... Is 49:8 5971
for the LORD hath comforted his *p* ... Is 49:13 5971
and set up my standard to the *p* ... Is 49:22 5971
Hearken unto me, my *p* ... Is 51:4 5971
to rest for a light of the *p* ... Is 51:4 5971
and mine arms shall judge the *p* ... Is 51:5 5971
the *p* in whose heart is my law ... Is 51:7 5971
and say unto Zion, Thou art my *p* ... Is 51:16 5971
that pleadeth the cause of his *p* ... Is 51:22 5971
My *p* went down aforetime into ... Is 52:4 5971
that my *p* is taken away for ... Is 52:5 5971
Therefore my *p* shall know my name ... Is 52:6 5971
for the LORD hath comforted his *p* ... Is 52:9 5971
of my *p* was he stricken ... Is 53:8 5971
given him for a witness to the *p* ... Is 55:4 3816
a leader and commander to the *p* ... Is 55:4 3816
utterly separated me from his *p* ... Is 56:3 5971
an house of prayer for all *p* ... Is 56:7 5971
out of the way of my *p* ... Is 57:14 5971
shew my *p* their transgression, and ... Is 58:1 5971
earth, and gross darkness the *p* ... Is 60:2 3816
Thy *p* also shall be all righteous ... Is 60:21 5971
and their offspring among the *p* ... Is 61:9 5971
prepare ye the way of the *p* ... Is 62:10 5971
lift up a standard for the *p* ... Is 62:10 5971
they shall call them, The holy *p* ... Is 62:12 5971
of the *p* there was none with me ... Is 63:3 5971
tread down the *p* in mine anger ... Is 63:6 5971
For he said, Surely they are my *p* ... Is 63:8 5971
the days of old, Moses, and his *p* ... Is 63:11 5971
so didst thou lead thy *p*, to make ... Is 63:14 5971
The *p* of thy holiness have ... Is 63:18 5971
we beseech thee, we are all thy *p* ... Is 64:9 5971
all the day unto a rebellious *p* ... Is 65:2 5971
A *p* that provoketh me to anger ... Is 65:3 5971
for my *p* that have sought me ... Is 65:10 5971
a rejoicing, and her *p* a joy ... Is 65:18 5971
in Jerusalem, and joy in my *p* ... Is 65:19 5971
of a tree are the days of my *p* ... Is 65:22 5971
and against the *p* of the land ... Jer 1:18 5971
but my *p* have changed their glory ... Jer 2:11 5971
For my *p* have committed two evils ... Jer 2:13 5971
wherefore say my *p*, We are lords ... Jer 2:31 5971
yet my *p* have forgotten me days ... Jer 2:32 5971
thou hast greatly deceived this *p* ... Jer 4:10 5971
time shall it be said to this *p* ... Jer 4:11 5971
toward the daughter of my *p* ... Jer 4:11 5971
For my *p* is foolish, they have ... Jer 4:22 5971
in thy mouth fire, and this *p* wood ... Jer 5:14 5971
Hear now this, O foolish *p* ... Jer 5:21 5971
But this *p* hath a revolting and a ... Jer 5:23 5971
For among my *p* are found wicked ... Jer 5:26 5971
and my *p* love to have it so ... Jer 5:31 5971
of the daughter of my *p* slightly ... Jer 6:14 5971
I will bring evil upon this *p* ... Jer 6:19 5971
lay stumblingblocks before this *p* ... Jer 6:21 5971
a *p* cometh from the north country ... Jer 6:22 5971
O daughter of my *p*, gird thee ... Jer 6:26 5971
a tower and a fortress among my *p* ... Jer 6:27 5971
for the wickedness of my *p* Israel ... Jer 7:12 5971
pray not thou for this *p*, neither ... Jer 7:16 5971
be your God, and ye shall be my *p* ... Jer 7:23 5971
the carcases of this *p* shall be ... Jer 7:33 5971
Why then is this *p* of Jerusalem ... Jer 8:5 5971
but my *p* know not the judgment of ... Jer 8:7 5971
of the daughter of my *p* slightly ... Jer 8:11 5971
the cry of the daughter of my *p* ... Jer 8:19 5971
of the daughter of my *p* am I hurt ... Jer 8:21 5971
of the daughter of my *p* recovered ... Jer 8:22 5971
the slain of the daughter of my *p* ... Jer 9:1 5971
that I might leave my *p*, and go ... Jer 9:2 5971
I do for the daughter of my *p* ... Jer 9:7 5971
I will feed them, even this *p* ... Jer 9:15 5971
For the customs of the *p* are vain ... Jer 10:3 5971
so shall ye be my *p*, and I will be ... Jer 11:4 5971
pray not thou for this *p*, neither ... Jer 11:14 5971
caused my *p* Israel to inherit ... Jer 12:14 5971
diligently learn the ways of my *p* ... Jer 12:16 5971
they taught my *p* to swear by Baal ... Jer 12:16 5971
be built in the midst of my *p* ... Jer 12:16 5971

This evil *p*, which refuse to hear	Jer 13:10	5971
they might be unto me for a *p*	Jer 13:11	5971
Thus saith the LORD unto this *p*	Jer 14:10	5971
not for this *p* for their good	Jer 14:11	5971
the *p* to whom they prophesy shall	Jer 14:16	5971
p is broken with a great breach	Jer 14:17	5971
mind could not be toward this *p*	Jer 15:1	5971
of children, I will destroy my *p*	Jer 15:7	5971
unto this *p* a fenced brasen wall	Jer 15:20	5971
taken away my peace from this *p*	Jer 16:5	5971
shalt shew this *p* all these words	Jer 16:10	5971
the gate of the children of the *p*	Jer 17:19	5971
Because my *p* hath forgotten me,	Jer 18:15	5971
and take of the ancients of the *p*	Jer 19:1	5971
Even so will I break this *p*	Jer 19:11	5971
and said to all the *p*,	Jer 19:14	5971
Judah, and his servants, and the *p*	Jer 21:7	5971
unto this *p* thou shalt say, Thus	Jer 21:8	5971
thy *p* that enter in by these	Jer 22:2	5971
he, and his servants, and his *p*	Jer 22:4	5971
the pastors that feed my *p*	Jer 23:2	5971
caused my *p* Israel to err	Jer 23:13	5971
had caused my *p* to hear my words,	Jer 23:22	5971
Which think to cause my *p* to	Jer 23:27	5971
cause my *p* to err by their lies,	Jer 23:32	5971
shall not profit this *p* at all	Jer 23:32	5971
And when this *p*, or the prophet,	Jer 23:33	5971
prophet, and the priest, and the *p*	Jer 23:34	5971
and they shall be my *p*, and I will	Jer 24:7	5971
p of Judah in the fourth year of	Jer 25:1	5971
spake unto all the *p* of Judah	Jer 25:2	5971
and his princes, and all his *p*	Jer 25:19	5971
And all the mingled *p*, and all the	Jer 25:20	
p that dwell in the desert	Jer 25:24	
all the *p* heard Jeremiah speaking	Jer 26:7	5971
him to speak unto all the *p*	Jer 26:8	5971
all the *p* took him, saying, Thou	Jer 26:8	5971
all the *p* were gathered against	Jer 26:9	5971
unto the princes and to all the *p*	Jer 26:11	5971
all the princes and to all the *p*	Jer 26:12	5971
all the *p* unto the priests and to	Jer 26:16	5971
to all the assembly of the *p*	Jer 26:17	5971
and spake to all the *p* of Judah	Jer 26:18	5971
into the graves of the common *p*	Jer 26:23	5971
hand of the *p* to put him to death	Jer 26:24	5971
of Babylon, and serve him and his *p*	Jer 27:12	5971
Why will ye die, thou and thy *p*	Jer 27:13	5971
to the priests and to all this *p*	Jer 27:16	5971
of the priests and of all the *p*	Jer 28:1	5971
in the presence of all the *p* that	Jer 28:5	5971
ears, and in the ears of all the *p*	Jer 28:7	5971
in the presence of all the *p*	Jer 28:11	5971
makest this *p* to trust in a lie	Jer 28:15	5971
to all the *p* whom Nebuchadnezzar	Jer 29:1	5971
of all the *p* that dwelleth in	Jer 29:16	5971
all the *p* that are at Jerusalem	Jer 29:25	5971
have a man to dwell among this *p*	Jer 29:32	5971
the good that I will do for my *p*	Jer 29:32	5971
the captivity of my *p* Israel	Jer 30:3	5971
And ye shall be my *p*, and I will be	Jer 30:22	5971
of Israel, and they shall be my *p*	Jer 31:1	5971
The *p* which were left of the	Jer 31:2	5971
ye, and say, O LORD, save thy *p*	Jer 31:7	5971
my *p* shall be satisfied with my	Jer 31:14	5971
their God, and they shall be my *p*	Jer 31:33	5971
hast brought forth thy *p* Israel	Jer 32:21	5971
And they shall be my *p*, and I will	Jer 32:38	5971
all this great evil upon this *p*	Jer 32:42	5971
thou not what this *p* have spoken	Jer 33:24	5971
thus they have despised my *p*	Jer 33:24	5971
of his dominion, and all the *p*	Jer 34:1	5971
all the *p* which were at Jerusalem	Jer 34:8	5971
all the princes, and all the *p*	Jer 34:10	5971
all the *p* of the land, which	Jer 34:19	5971
but this *p* hath not hearkened	Jer 35:16	5971
p in the LORD's house upon the	Jer 36:6	5971
hath pronounced against this *p*	Jer 36:7	5971
LORD to all the *p* in Jerusalem	Jer 36:9	5971
to all the *p* that came from the	Jer 36:9	5971
house, in the ears of all the *p*	Jer 36:10	5971
the book in the ears of the *p*	Jer 36:13	5971
hast read in the ears of the *p*	Jer 36:14	5971
nor the *p* of the land, did	Jer 37:2	5971
came in and went out among the *p*	Jer 37:4	5971
thence in the midst of the *p*	Jer 37:12	5971
thy servants, or against this *p*	Jer 37:18	5971
had spoken unto all the *p*	Jer 38:1	5971
city, and the hands of all the *p*	Jer 38:4	5971
seeketh not the welfare of this *p*	Jer 38:4	5971
house, and the houses of the *p*	Jer 39:8	5971
the *p* that remained in the city	Jer 39:9	5971
the rest of the *p* that remained	Jer 39:9	5971
guard left of the poor of the *p*	Jer 39:10	5971
so he dwelt among the *p*	Jer 39:14	5971
and dwell with him among the *p*	Jer 40:5	5971
dwelt with him among the *p* that	Jer 40:6	5971
of the *p* that were in Mizpah	Jer 41:10	5971
all the *p* that remained in Mizpah	Jer 41:10	5971
that when all the *p* which were	Jer 41:13	5971
So all the *p* that Ishmael had	Jer 41:14	5971
all the remnant of the *p* whom he	Jer 41:16	5971
all the *p* from the least even	Jer 42:1	5971
all the *p* from the least even to	Jer 42:8	5971
p all the words of the LORD their	Jer 43:1	5971
of the forces, and all the *p*	Jer 43:4	5971
even all the *p* that dwelt in the	Jer 44:15	5971
Then Jeremiah said unto all the *p*	Jer 44:20	5971
to all the *p* which had given him	Jer 44:20	5971
the *p* of the land, did not the	Jer 44:21	5971
Jeremiah said unto all the *p*	Jer 44:24	5971
and let us go again to our own *p*	Jer 46:16	5971
the hand of the *p* of the north	Jer 46:24	5971
shall be destroyed from being a *p*	Jer 48:42	5971
the *p* of Chemosh perisheth	Jer 48:46	5971
his *p* dwell in his cities	Jer 49:1	5971
My *p* hath been lost sheep	Jer 50:6	5971
shall turn every one to his *p*	Jer 50:16	5971
upon all the mingled *p* that are	Jer 50:37	
a *p* shall come from the north, and	Jer 50:41	5971
My *p*, go ye out of the midst of	Jer 51:45	5971
the *p* shall labour in vain, and	Jer 51:58	5971
no bread for the *p* of the land	Jer 52:6	5971
certain of the poor of the *p*	Jer 52:15	5971
the residue of the *p* that	Jer 52:15	5971
who mustered the *p* of the land	Jer 52:25	5971
men of the *p* of the land, that	Jer 52:25	5971
This is the *p* whom Nebuchadrezzar	Jer 52:28	5971
sit solitary, that was full of *p*	Lam 1:1	5971
when her *p* fell into the hand of	Lam 1:7	5971
All her *p* sigh, they seek bread	Lam 1:11	5971
hear, I pray you, all *p*, and	Lam 1:18	5971
of the daughter of my *p*	Lam 2:11	5971
I was a derision to all my *p*	Lam 3:14	5971
and refuse in the midst of the *p*	Lam 3:45	5971
of the daughter of my *p*	Lam 3:48	5971
daughter of my *p* is become cruel	Lam 4:3	5971
p is greater than the punishment	Lam 4:6	5971
of the daughter of my *p*	Lam 4:10	5971
sent to a *p* of a strange speech	Eze 3:5	5971
Not to many *p* of a strange speech	Eze 3:6	5971
unto the children of thy *p*	Eze 3:11	5971
the hands of the *p* of the land	Eze 7:27	5971
son of Benaiah, princes of the *p*	Eze 11:1	5971
I will even gather you from the *p*	Eze 11:17	5971
and they shall be my *p*, and I will	Eze 11:20	5971
And say unto the *p* of the land	Eze 12:19	5971
not be in the assembly of my *p*	Eze 13:9	5971
because they have seduced my *p*	Eze 13:10	5971
against the daughters of thy *p*	Eze 13:17	5971
Will ye hunt the souls of my *p*	Eze 13:18	5971
among my *p* for handfuls of barley	Eze 13:19	5971
lying to my *p* that hear your lies	Eze 13:19	5971
deliver my *p* out of your hand, and	Eze 13:21	5971
deliver my *p* out of your hand	Eze 13:23	5971
him off from the midst of my *p*	Eze 14:8	5971
him from the midst of my *p* Israel	Eze 14:9	5971
but that they may be my *p*	Eze 14:11	5971
p to pluck it up by the roots	Eze 17:9	5971
might give him horses and much *p*	Eze 17:15	5971
which is not good among his *p*	Eze 18:18	5971
I will bring you out from the *p*	Eze 20:34	5971
you into the wilderness of the *p*	Eze 20:35	5971
when I bring you out from the *p*	Eze 20:41	5971
for it shall be upon my *p*	Eze 21:12	5971
of the sword shall be upon my *p*	Eze 21:12	5971
The *p* of the land have used	Eze 22:29	5971
wheels, and with an assembly of *p*	Eze 23:24	5971
I spake unto the *p* in the morning	Eze 24:18	5971
the *p* said unto me, Wilt thou not	Eze 24:19	5971
and I will cut thee off from the *p*	Eze 25:7	5971
Edom by the hand of my *p* Israel	Eze 25:14	5971
that was the gates of the *p*	Eze 26:2	5971
horsemen, and companies, and much *p*	Eze 26:7	5971
he shall slay thy *p* by the sword	Eze 26:11	5971
with the *p* of old time, and shall	Eze 26:20	5971
merchant of the *p* for many isles	Eze 27:3	5971
of the seas, thou filledst many *p*	Eze 27:33	5971
among the *p* shall hiss at thee	Eze 27:36	5971
the *p* shall be astonished at thee	Eze 28:19	5971
the house of Israel from the *p*	Eze 28:25	5971
the *p* whither they were scattered	Eze 29:13	5971
and Lydia, and all the mingled *p*	Eze 30:5	
his *p* with him, the terrible of	Eze 30:11	5971
all the *p* of the earth are gone	Eze 31:12	5971
thee with a company of many *p*	Eze 32:3	5971
also vex the hearts of many *p*	Eze 32:9	5971
I will make many *p* amazed at thee	Eze 32:10	5971
speak to the children of thy *p*	Eze 33:2	5971
if the *p* of the land take a man	Eze 33:2	5971
blow the trumpet, and warn the *p*	Eze 33:3	5971
trumpet, and the *p* be not warned	Eze 33:6	5971
say unto the children of thy *p*	Eze 33:12	5971
Yet the children of thy *p* say	Eze 33:17	5971
the children of thy *p* still are	Eze 33:30	5971
come unto thee as the *p* cometh	Eze 33:31	5971
and they sit before thee as my *p*	Eze 33:31	5971
I will bring them out from the *p*	Eze 34:13	5971
the house of Israel, are my *p*	Eze 34:30	5971
and are an infamy of the *p*	Eze 36:3	5971
your fruit to my *p* of Israel	Eze 36:8	5971
walk upon you, even my *p* Israel	Eze 36:12	5971
the reproach of the *p* any more	Eze 36:15	5971
them, These are the *p* of the LORD	Eze 36:20	5971
and ye shall be my *p*, and I will be	Eze 36:28	5971
Behold, O my *p*, I will open your	Eze 37:12	5971
I have opened your graves, O my *p*	Eze 37:13	5971
of thy *p* shall speak unto thee	Eze 37:18	5971
so shall they be my *p*, and I will	Eze 37:23	5971
their God, and they shall be my *p*	Eze 37:27	5971
and many *p* with thee	Eze 38:6	5971
and is gathered out of many *p*	Eze 38:8	5971
thy bands, and many *p* with thee	Eze 38:9	5971
upon the *p* that are gathered out	Eze 38:12	5971
In that day when my *p* of Israel	Eze 38:14	5971
many *p* with thee, all of them	Eze 38:15	5971
come up against my *p* of Israel	Eze 38:16	5971
upon the many *p* that are with him	Eze 38:22	5971
bands, and the *p* that is with thee	Eze 39:4	5971
known in the midst of my *p* Israel	Eze 39:7	5971
all the *p* of the land shall bury	Eze 39:13	5971
brought them again from the *p*	Eze 39:27	5971
those things which are for the *p*	Eze 42:14	5971
and the sacrifice for the *p*	Eze 44:11	5971
into the utter court to the *p*	Eze 44:19	5971
the *p* with their garments	Eze 44:19	5971
they shall teach my *p* the	Eze 44:23	5971
shall no more oppress my *p*	Eze 45:8	5971
away your exactions from my *p*	Eze 45:9	5971
All the *p* of the land shall give	Eze 45:16	5971
for all the *p* of the land a	Eze 45:22	5971
Likewise the *p* of the land shall	Eze 46:3	5971
But when the *p* of the land shall	Eze 46:9	5971
that my *p* be not scattered every	Eze 46:18	5971
utter court, to sanctify the *p*	Eze 46:20	5971
shall boil the sacrifice of the *p*	Eze 46:24	5971
shall not be left to other *p*	Dan 2:44	5972
To you it is commanded, O *p*	Dan 3:4	5972
when all the *p* heard the sound of	Dan 3:7	5972
and all kinds of musick, all the *p*	Dan 3:7	5972
I make a decree, That every *p*	Dan 3:29	5972
the king, unto all *p*, nations, and	Dan 4:1	5972
majesty that he gave him, all *p*	Dan 5:19	5972
Then king Darius wrote unto all *p*	Dan 6:25	5972
glory, and a kingdom, that all *p*	Dan 7:14	5972
shall be given to the *p* of the	Dan 7:27	5972
destroy the mighty and the holy *p*	Dan 8:24	5971
and to all the *p* of the land	Dan 9:6	5971
that hast brought thy *p* forth out	Dan 9:15	5971
thy *p* are become a reproach to	Dan 9:16	5971
thy *p* are called by thy name	Dan 9:19	5971
my sin and the sin of my *p* Israel	Dan 9:20	5971
weeks are determined upon thy *p*	Dan 9:24	5971
the *p* of the prince that shall	Dan 9:26	5971
befall thy *p* in the latter days	Dan 10:14	5971
also the robbers of thy *p* shall	Dan 11:14	5971
withstand, neither his chosen *p*	Dan 11:15	5971
become strong with a small *p*	Dan 11:23	1471
but the *p* that do know their God	Dan 11:32	5971
among the *p* shall instruct many	Dan 11:33	5971
for the children of thy *p*	Dan 12:1	5971
at that time thy *p* shall be	Dan 12:1	5971
scatter the power of the holy *p*	Dan 12:7	5971
for ye are not my *p*, and I will	Hos 1:9	5971
said unto them, Ye are not my *p*	Hos 1:10	5971
were not my *p*, Thou art my *p*	Hos 2:23	5971
for thy *p* are as they that strive	Hos 4:4	5971
My *p* are destroyed for lack of	Hos 4:6	5971
They eat up the sin of my *p*	Hos 4:8	5971
And there shall be, like *p*	Hos 4:9	5971
My *p* ask counsel at their stocks,	Hos 4:12	5971
therefore the *p* that doth not	Hos 4:14	5971
I returned the captivity of my *p*	Hos 6:11	5971
he hath mixed himself among the *p*	Hos 7:8	5971
O Israel, for joy, as other *p*	Hos 9:1	5971
for the *p* thereof shall mourn	Hos 10:5	5971
the *p* shall be gathered against	Hos 10:10	5971
shall a tumult arise among thy *p*	Hos 10:14	5971
my *p* are bent to backsliding from	Hos 11:7	5971
a great *p* and a strong	Joel 2:2	5971
as a strong *p* set in battle array	Joel 2:5	5971
face the *p* shall be much pained	Joel 2:6	5971
Gather the *p*, sanctify the	Joel 2:16	5971
and let them say, Spare thy *p*	Joel 2:17	5971
should they say among the *p*	Joel 2:17	5971
for his land, and pity his *p*	Joel 2:18	5971
will answer and say unto his *p*	Joel 2:19	5971
my *p* shall never be ashamed	Joel 2:26	5971
my *p* shall never be ashamed	Joel 2:27	5971
plead with them there for my *p*	Joel 3:2	5971
And they have cast lots for my *p*	Joel 3:3	5971
to the Sabeans, to a *p* far off	Joel 3:8	1471
LORD will be the hope of his *p*	Joel 3:16	5971
the *p* of Syria shall go into	Amos 1:5	5971
the city, and the *p* not be afraid	Amos 3:6	5971
in the midst of my *p* Israel	Amos 7:8	5971
me, Go, prophesy unto my *p* Israel	Amos 7:15	5971
end is come upon my *p* of Israel	Amos 8:2	5971
All the sinners of my *p* shall die	Amos 9:10	5971
the captivity of my *p* of Israel	Amos 9:14	5971
entered into the gate of my *p* in	Obad 13	5971
and of what *p* art thou	Jonah 1:8	5971
So the *p* of Nineveh believed God,	Jonah 3:5	582
Hear, all ye *p*	Mic 1:2	5971
he is come unto the gate of my *p*	Mic 1:9	5971
hath changed the portion of my *p*	Mic 2:4	5971
Even of late my *p* is risen up as	Mic 2:8	5971
The women of my *p* have ye cast	Mic 2:9	5971
even be the prophet of this *p*	Mic 2:11	5971
Who also eat the flesh of my *p*	Mic 3:3	5971
the prophets that make my *p* err	Mic 3:5	5971
and *p* shall flow unto it	Mic 4:1	5971
And he shall judge among many *p*	Mic 4:3	5971
For all *p* will walk every one in	Mic 4:5	5971
thou shalt beat in pieces many *p*	Mic 4:13	5971
of many *p* as a dew from the LORD	Mic 5:7	5971
p as a lion among the beasts of	Mic 5:8	5971
hath a controversy with his *p*	Mic 6:2	5971
O my *p*, what have I done unto	Mic 6:3	5971
O my *p*, remember now what Balak	Mic 6:5	5971
shall bear the reproach of my *p*	Mic 6:16	5971
Feed thy *p* with thy rod, the	Mic 7:14	5971
thy *p* in the midst of thee are	Nah 3:13	5971
thy *p* is scattered upon the	Nah 3:18	5971
and heapeth unto him all *p*	Hab 2:5	5971

P

remnant of the p shall spoil thee ... Hab 2:8 5971
thy house by cutting off many p ... Hab 2:10 5971
p shall labour in the very fire ... Hab 2:13 5971
the p shall weary themselves for ... Hab 2:13 3816
forth for the salvation of thy p ... Hab 3:13 5971
when he cometh up unto the p ... Hab 3:16 5971
all the merchant p are cut down ... Zeph 1:11 5971
whereby they have reproached my p ... Zeph 2:8 5971
residue of my p shall spoil them ... Zeph 2:9 5971
the remnant of my p shall possess ... Zeph 2:9 1471
the p of the LORD of hosts ... Zeph 2:10 5971
I turn to the p a pure language ... Zeph 3:9 5971
of thee an afflicted and poor p ... Zeph 3:12 5971
a praise among all p of the earth ... Zeph 3:20 5971
LORD of hosts, saying, This p say ... Hag 1:2 5971
with all the remnant of the p ... Hag 1:12 5971
the p did fear before the LORD ... Hag 1:12 5971
in the LORD's message unto the p ... Hag 1:13 5971
of all the remnant of the p ... Hag 1:14 5971
and to the residue of the p ... Hag 2:2 5971
all ye p of the land, saith the ... Hag 2:4 5971
Haggai, and said, So is this p ... Hag 2:14 5971
in that day, and shall be my p ... Zec 2:11 5971
Speak unto all the p of the land ... Zec 7:5 5971
remnant of this p in these days ... Zec 8:6 5971
I will save my p from the east ... Zec 8:7 5971
and they shall be my p, and I will ... Zec 8:8 5971
of this p as in the former days ... Zec 8:11 5971
p to possess all these things ... Zec 8:12 5971
to pass, that there shall come p ... Zec 8:20 5971
Yea, many p and strong nations ... Zec 8:22 5971
in that day as the flock of his p ... Zec 9:16 5971
And I will sow them among the p ... Zec 10:9 5971
which I had made with all the p ... Zec 11:10 5971
unto all the p round about ... Zec 12:2 5971
a burdensome stone for all p ... Zec 12:3 5971
though all the p of the earth be ... Zec 12:3 1471
horse of the p with blindness ... Zec 12:4 5971
devour all the p round about ... Zec 12:6 5971
I will say, It is my p ... Zec 13:9 5971
the residue of the p shall not be ... Zec 14:2 5971
the p that have fought against ... Zec 14:12 5971
The p against whom the LORD hath ... Mal 1:4 5971
and base before all the p, ... Mal 2:9 5971
shall save his p from their sins ... Mt 1:21 2992
and scribes of the p together ... Mt 2:4 2992
that shall rule my p Israel ... Mt 2:6 2992
The p which sat in darkness saw ... Mt 4:16 2992
all manner of disease among the p ... Mt 4:23 2992
p that were taken with divers ... Mt 4:24
multitudes of p from Galilee ... Mt 4:25
the p were astonished at his ... Mt 7:28 3793
and the p making a noise, ... Mt 9:23 3793
But when the p were put forth, he ... Mt 9:25 3793
and every disease among the p ... Mt 9:35 2992
all the p were amazed, and said, ... Mt 12:23 3793
While he yet talked to the p ... Mt 12:46 3793
when the p had heard thereof, ... Mt 14:13 3793
This p draweth nigh unto me with ... Mt 15:8 2992
the elders of the p came unto him ... Mt 21:23 2992
we fear the p ... Mt 21:26 3793
scribes, and the elders of the p ... Mt 26:3 2992
there be an uproar among the p ... Mt 26:5 2992
chief priests and elders of the p ... Mt 26:47 2992
elders of the p took counsel ... Mt 27:1 2992
to release unto the p a prisoner ... Mt 27:15 3793
Then answered all the p, and said, ... Mt 27:25 2992
steal him away, and say unto the p ... Mt 27:64 2992
side, much p gathered unto him ... Mk 5:21 3793
much p followed him, and thronged ... Mk 5:24 3793
the p saw them departing, and many ... Mk 6:33 3793
when he came out, saw much p ... Mk 6:34 3793
while he sent away the p ... Mk 6:45 3793
This p honoureth me with their ... Mk 7:6 2992
he had called all the p unto him ... Mk 7:14 3793
entered into the house from the p ... Mk 7:17 3793
he commanded the p to sit down on ... Mk 8:6 3793
and they did set them before the p ... Mk 8:6 3793
when he had called the p unto him ... Mk 8:34 3793
And straightway all the p, when ... Mk 9:15 3793
that the p came running together ... Mk 9:25 3793
the p resort unto him again ... Mk 10:1 3793
disciples and a great number of p ... Mk 10:46 3793
because all the p was astonished ... Mk 11:18 3793
they feared the p ... Mk 11:32 2992
lay hold on him, but feared the p ... Mk 12:12 3793
the common p heard him gladly ... Mk 12:37 3793
beheld how the p cast money into ... Mk 12:41 3793
lest there be an uproar of the p ... Mk 14:2 2992
But the chief priests moved the p ... Mk 15:11 3793
Pilate, willing to content the p ... Mk 15:15 3793
the whole multitude of the p were ... Lk 1:10 2992
to make ready a p prepared for ... Lk 1:17 2992
the p waited for Zacharias, and ... Lk 1:21 2992
he hath visited and redeemed his p ... Lk 1:68 2992
p by the remission of their sins ... Lk 1:77 2992
joy, which shall be to all p ... Lk 2:10 2992
prepared before the face of all p ... Lk 2:31 2992
and the glory of thy p Israel ... Lk 2:32 2992
the p asked him, saying, What ... Lk 3:10 3793
as the p were in expectation, and ... Lk 3:15 2992
preached he unto the p ... Lk 3:18 2992
Now when all the p were baptized ... Lk 3:21 2992
the p sought him, and came unto ... Lk 4:42 3793
as the p pressed upon him to hear ... Lk 5:1 3793
taught the p out of the ship ... Lk 5:3 3793
multitude of p out of all Judaea ... Lk 6:17 2992
sayings in the audience of the p ... Lk 7:1 2992
said unto the p that followed him ... Lk 7:9 3793
went with him, and much p ... Lk 7:11 3793
much p of the city was with her ... Lk 7:12 3793
and, That God hath visited his p ... Lk 7:16 2992
speak unto the p concerning John ... Lk 7:24 3793
all the p that heard him, and the ... Lk 7:29 2992
when much p were gathered ... Lk 8:4 3793
the p gladly received him ... Lk 8:40 3793
But as he went the p thronged him ... Lk 8:42 3793
unto him before all the p for ... Lk 8:47 2992
And the p, when they knew it, ... Lk 9:11 3793
go and buy meat for all this p ... Lk 9:13 2992
saying, Whom say the p that I am ... Lk 9:18 3793
from the hill, much p met him ... Lk 9:37 3793
and the p wondered ... Lk 11:14 3793
when the p were gathered thick ... Lk 11:29 3793
an innumerable multitude of p ... Lk 12:1 3793
And he said also to the p, When ye ... Lk 12:54 3793
sabbath day, and said unto the p ... Lk 13:14 3793
all the p rejoiced for all the ... Lk 13:17 3793
and all the p, when they saw it, ... Lk 18:43 2992
the chief of the p sought to ... Lk 19:47 2992
for all the p were very attentive ... Lk 19:48 2992
as he taught the p in the temple ... Lk 20:1 2992
all the p will stone us ... Lk 20:6 2992
he to speak to the p this parable ... Lk 20:9 2992
and they feared the p ... Lk 20:19 2992
hold of his words before the p ... Lk 20:26 2992
the p he said unto his disciples ... Lk 20:45 2992
in the land, and wrath upon this p ... Lk 21:23 2992
all the p came early in the ... Lk 21:38 2992
for they feared the p ... Lk 22:2 2992
it was day, the elders of the p ... Lk 22:66 2992
to the chief priests and to the p ... Lk 23:4 3793
saying, He stirreth up the p ... Lk 23:5 2992
priests and the rulers and the p ... Lk 23:13 2992
me, as one that perverteth the p ... Lk 23:14 2992
followed him a great company of p ... Lk 23:27 2992
And the p stood beholding ... Lk 23:35 2992
all the p that came together to ... Lk 23:48 3793
and word before God and all the p ... Lk 24:19 2992
when the p which stood on the ... Jn 6:22 3793
When the p therefore saw that ... Jn 6:24 3793
among the p concerning him ... Jn 7:12 3793
but he deceiveth the p ... Jn 7:12 3793
The p answered and said, Thou hast ... Jn 7:20 3793
many of the p believed on him, and ... Jn 7:31 3793
The Pharisees heard that the p ... Jn 7:32 3793
Many of the p therefore, when ... Jn 7:40 3793
among the p because of him ... Jn 7:43 3793
But this p who knoweth not the ... Jn 7:49 3793
and all the p came unto him ... Jn 8:2 2992
but because of the p which stand ... Jn 11:42 3793
that one man should die for the p ... Jn 11:50 2992
Much p of the Jews therefore knew ... Jn 12:9 3793
On the next day much p that were ... Jn 12:12 3793
The p therefore that was with him ... Jn 12:17 3793
For this cause the p also met him ... Jn 12:18 3793
The p therefore, that stood by, ... Jn 12:29 3793
The p answered him, We have heard ... Jn 12:34 3793
that one man should die for the p ... Jn 18:14 2992
and having favour with all the p ... Acts 2:47 2992
all the p saw him walking and ... Acts 3:9 2992
all the p ran together unto them ... Acts 3:11 2992
saw it, he answered unto the p ... Acts 3:12 2992
be destroyed from among the p ... Acts 3:23 2992
And as they spake unto the p ... Acts 4:1 2992
grieved that they taught the p ... Acts 4:2 2992
unto them, Ye rulers of the p ... Acts 4:8 2992
all, and to all the p of Israel ... Acts 4:10 2992
it spread no further among the p ... Acts 4:17 2992
punish them, because of the p ... Acts 4:21 2992
the p imagine vain things ... Acts 4:25 2992
the p of Israel, were gathered ... Acts 4:27 2992
and wonders wrought among the p ... Acts 5:12 2992
but the p magnified them ... Acts 5:13 2992
the p all the words of this life ... Acts 5:20 2992
in the temple, and teaching the p ... Acts 5:25 2992
for they feared the p, lest they ... Acts 5:26 2992
had in reputation among all the p ... Acts 5:34 2992
and drew away much p after him ... Acts 5:37 2992
wonders and miracles among the p ... Acts 6:8 2992
And they stirred up the p, and the ... Acts 6:12 2992
the p grew and multiplied in Egypt ... Acts 7:17 2992
of my p which is in Egypt ... Acts 7:34 2992
the p with one accord gave heed ... Acts 8:6 3793
and bewitched the p of Samaria ... Acts 8:9 1484
which gave much alms to the p ... Acts 10:2 2992
Not to all the p, but unto ... Acts 10:41 2992
commanded us to preach unto the p ... Acts 10:42 2992
much p was added unto the Lord ... Acts 11:24 3793
with the church, and taught much p ... Acts 11:26 3793
to bring him forth to the p ... Acts 12:4 2992
expectation of the p of the Jews ... Acts 12:11 2992
the p gave a shout, saying, It is ... Acts 12:22 1218
any word of exhortation for the p ... Acts 13:15 2992
The God of this p of Israel chose ... Acts 13:17 2992
exalted the p when they dwelt as ... Acts 13:17 2992
repentance to all the p of Israel ... Acts 13:24 2992
who are his witnesses unto the p ... Acts 13:31 2992
when the p saw what Paul had done ... Acts 14:11 3793
have done sacrifice with the p ... Acts 14:13 3793
clothes, and ran in among the p ... Acts 14:14 3793
scarce restrained they the p ... Acts 14:18 3793
and Iconium, who persuaded the p ... Acts 14:19 3793
take out of them a p for his name ... Acts 15:14 2992
sought to bring them out to the p ... Acts 17:5 1218
And they troubled the p and the ... Acts 17:8 3793
thither also, and stirred up the p ... Acts 17:13 3793
for I have much p in this city ... Acts 18:10 2992
of repentance, saying unto the p ... Acts 19:4 2992
persuaded and turned away much p ... Acts 19:26 3793
would have entered in unto the p ... Acts 19:30 1218
have made his defence unto the p ... Acts 19:33 1218
the townclerk had appeased the p ... Acts 19:35 3793
the temple, stirred up all the p ... Acts 21:27 3793
all men every where against the p ... Acts 21:28 2992
was moved, and the p ran together ... Acts 21:30 2992
for the violence of the p ... Acts 21:35 3793
multitude of the p followed after ... Acts 21:36 2992
suffer me to speak unto the p ... Acts 21:39 2992
beckoned with the hand unto the p ... Acts 21:40 2992
speak evil of the ruler of thy p ... Acts 23:5 2992
any man, neither raising up the p ... Acts 24:12 3793
Delivering thee from the p ... Acts 26:17 2992
and should shew light unto the p ... Acts 26:23 2992
the barbarous p shewed us no ... Acts 28:2
committed nothing against the p ... Acts 28:17 2992
Saying, Go unto this p, and say, ... Acts 28:26 2992
heart of this p is waxed gross ... Acts 28:27 2992
my p, which were not my p ... Rom 9:25 2992
said unto them, Ye are not my p ... Rom 9:26 2992
to jealousy by them that are no p ... Rom 10:19 1484
a disobedient and gainsaying p ... Rom 10:21 2992
then, Hath God cast away his p ... Rom 11:1 2992
cast away his p which he foreknew ... Rom 11:2 2992
Rejoice, ye Gentiles, with his p ... Rom 15:10 2992
and laud him, all ye p ... Rom 15:11 2992
The p sat down to eat and drink, ... 1Cor 10:7 2992
lips will I speak unto this p ... 1Cor 14:21 2992
their God, and they shall be my p ... 2Cor 6:16 2992
purify unto himself a peculiar p ... Titus 2:14 2992
for the sins of the p ... Heb 2:17 2992
therefore a rest to the p of God ... Heb 4:9 2992
hereof he ought, as for the p ... Heb 5:3 2992
of the p according to the law ... Heb 7:5 2992
under it the p received the law ... Heb 7:11 2992
a God, and they shall be to me a p ... Heb 8:10 2992
and for the errors of the p ... Heb 9:7 2992
to all the p according to the law ... Heb 9:19 2992
both the book, and all the p ... Heb 9:19 2992
again, The Lord shall judge his p ... Heb 10:30 2992
affliction with the p of God ... Heb 11:25 2992
sanctify the p with his own blood ... Heb 13:12 2992
an holy nation, a peculiar p ... 1Pet 2:9 2992
Which in time past were not a p ... 1Pet 2:10 2992
but are now the p of God ... 1Pet 2:10 2992
false prophets also among the p ... 2Pet 2:1 2992
having saved the p out of the ... Jude 5 2992
of every kindred, and tongue, and p ... Rev 5:9 2992
of all nations, and kindreds, and p ... Rev 7:9 2992
And they of the p and kindreds and ... Rev 11:9 2992
and kindred, and tongue, and p ... Rev 14:6 2992
saying, Come out of her, my p ... Rev 18:4 2992
a great voice of much p in heaven ... Rev 19:1 3793
with them, and they shall be his p ... Rev 21:3 2992

PEOPLE'S See APPENDIX.

PEOPLES See APPENDIX.

PEOR *(pe'-or)* {4} See BAAL-PEOR, BETH-PEOR, PEOR'S.
1. A Moabite god.
beguiled you in the matter of P ... Num 25:18 6465
the LORD in the matter of P ... Num 31:16 6465
iniquity of P too little for us ... Josh 22:17 6465
2. A mountain.
brought Balaam unto the top of P ... Num 23:28 6465

PEOR'S {1}
the day of the plague for P sake ... Num 25:18 6465

PERADVENTURE {32}
P there be fifty righteous within ... Gen 18:24 194
P there shall lack five of the ... Gen 18:28 194
P there shall be forty found ... Gen 18:29 194
P there shall thirty be found ... Gen 18:30 194
P there shall be twenty found ... Gen 18:31 194
P ten shall be found there ... Gen 18:32 194
P the woman will not be willing ... Gen 24:5 194
P the woman will not follow me ... Gen 24:39 194
My father p will feel me, and I ... Gen 27:12 194
P thou wouldest take by force thy ... Gen 31:31 6435
p he will accept of me ... Gen 32:20 194
Lest p he die also, as his ... Gen 38:11
Lest p mischief befall him ... Gen 42:4
p it was an oversight ... Gen 43:12 194
lest p I see the evil that shall ... Gen 44:34
they said, Joseph will p hate us ... Gen 50:15 3863
Lest p the people repent when ... Ex 13:17
p I shall make an atonement for ... Ex 32:30 194
p I shall prevail, that we may ... Num 22:6 194
p I shall be able to overcome ... Num 22:11 194
p the LORD will come to meet me ... Num 23:3 194
p it will please God that thou ... Num 23:27 194
the Hivites, P ye dwell among us ... Josh 9:7 194
p he will lighten his hand from ... 1Sa 6:5 194
p he can shew us our way that we ... 1Sa 9:6 194
p we may find grass to save the ... 1Kin 18:5 194
or p he sleepeth, and must be ... 1Kin 18:27 194
p he will save thy life ... 1Kin 20:31 194
lest p the Spirit of the LORD ... 2Kin 2:16
P he will be enticed, and we shall ... Jer 20:10 194
yet p for a good man some would ... Rom 5:7 5029
if God p will give them ... 2Ti 2:25 3379

PERAZIM *(per'-a-zim)* {1} *Where David defeated the Philistines.*
LORD shall rise up as in mount P ... Is 28:21

PERCEIVE {25}
hath not given you an heart to p ... Deut 29:4 3045
This day we p that the LORD is ... Josh 22:31 3045
that ye may p and see that your ... 1Sa 12:17 3045
for this day I p, that if Absalom ... 2Sa 19:6 3045
I p that this is an holy man of ... 2Kin 4:9 3045
passeth on also, but I p him not ... Job 9:11 995
and backward, but I cannot p him ... Job 23:8 3045
to p the words of understanding ... Prov 1:2
Wherefore I p that there is ... Eccl 3:22 7200
and see ye indeed, but p not ... Is 6:9 3045
a deeper speech than thou canst p ... Is 33:19 8085
ye shall see, and shall not p ... Mt 13:14 1492
seeing they may see, and not p ... Mk 4:12 1492
Do ye not p, that whatsoever ... Mk 7:18 3539
p ye not yet, neither understand ... Mk 8:17 3539
for I p that virtue is gone out ... Lk 8:46 1097
I p that thou art a prophet ... Jn 4:19 2334
P ye how ye prevail nothing ... Jn 12:19 2334
For I p that thou art in the gall ... Acts 8:23 3708
Of a truth I p that God is no ... Acts 10:34 2638
I p that in all things ye are too ... Acts 17:22 2334
I p that this voyage will be with ... Acts 27:10 2334
and seeing ye shall see, and not p ... Acts 28:26 1492
for I p that the same epistle ... 2Cor 7:8 991
Hereby p we the love of God, ... 1Jn 3:16 1097

PERCEIVED {35}
he p not when she lay down, nor ... Gen 19:33 3045
he p not when she lay down, nor ... Gen 19:35 3045
when Gideon p that he was an ... Judg 6:22 7200
Eli p that the LORD had called ... 1Sa 3:8 995
Saul p that it was Samuel, and he ... 1Sa 28:14 3045
David p that the LORD had ... 2Sa 5:12 3045
David p that the child was dead ... 2Sa 12:19 995
p that the king's heart was ... 2Sa 14:1 3045
p that it was not the king of ... 1Kin 22:33 7200
David p that the LORD had ... 1Chr 14:2 3045
p that it was not the king of ... 2Chr 18:32 7200
I p that God had not sent him ... Neh 6:12 5234
for they p that this work was ... Neh 6:16 3045
I p that the portions of the ... Neh 13:10 3045
When Mordecai p all that was done ... Est 4:1 3045
Hast thou p the breadth of the ... Job 38:18 995
I p that this also is vexation of ... Eccl 1:17 3045
I myself p also that one event ... Eccl 2:14 3045
nor p by the ear, neither hath ... Is 64:4 238
counsel of the LORD, and hath p ... Jer 23:18 7200
for the matter was not p ... Jer 38:27 8085
Which when Jesus p, he said unto ... Mt 16:8 1097
they p that he spake of them ... Mt 21:45 1097
But Jesus p their wickedness, and ... Mt 22:18 1097
immediately when Jesus p in his ... Mk 2:8 1921
they p that he had seen a vision ... Lk 1:22 1921
But when Jesus p their thoughts ... Lk 5:22 1921
hid from them, that they p it not ... Lk 9:45 143
for they p that he had spoken ... Lk 20:19 1097
But he p their craftiness, and ... Lk 20:23 2657
therefore p that they would come ... Jn 6:15 1097
p that they were unlearned and ... Acts 4:13 2638
But when Paul p that the one part ... Acts 23:6 1097
Whom I p to be accused of ... Acts 23:29 2147
p the grace that was given unto ... Gal 2:9 1097

PERCEIVEST {2}
when thou p not in him the lips ... Prov 14:7 3045
but p not the beam that is in ... Lk 6:41 2657

PERCEIVETH {3}
low, but he p it not of them ... Job 14:21 995
once, yea twice, yet man p it not ... Job 33:14 7789
She p that her merchandise is ... Prov 31:18 2938

PERCEIVING {3}
p that he had answered them well, ... Mk 12:28 1492
p the thought of their heart, ... Lk 9:47 1492
p that he had faith to be healed, ... Acts 14:9 1492

PERDITION {8}
of them is lost, but the son of p ... Jn 17:12 684
is to them an evident token of p ... Phil 1:28 684
of sin be revealed, the son of p ... 2Th 2:3 684
drown men in destruction and p ... 1Ti 6:9 684
not of them who draw back unto p ... Heb 10:39 684
of judgment and p of ungodly men ... 2Pet 3:7 684
the bottomless pit, and go into p ... Rev 17:8 684
is of the seven, and goeth into p ... Rev 17:11 684

PERES *(pe'-res)* {1} *Portion of "the handwriting on the wall."*
P; Thy kingdom is ... Dan 5:28 6537

PERESH *(pe'-resh)* {1} *A son of Machir.*
a son, and she called his name P ... 1Chr 7:16 6570

PEREZ *(pe'-rez)* {3} See PEREZ-UZZAH, PHARES.
1. An ancestor of Jashobeam.
Of the children of P was the ... 1Chr 27:3 6557
2. A son of Judah; same as Pharez.
Mahalaleel, of the children of P ... Neh 11:4 6557
All the sons of P that dwelt at ... Neh 11:6 6557

PEREZITES See PHARZITES.

PEREZ-UZZA *(pe'-rez-uz'-zah)* {1} See PEREZ-UZZAH. *Where Uzza died.*
place is called P to this day ... 1Chr 13:11 6560

PEREZ-UZZAH *(pe'-rez-uz'-zah)* {1} See PEREZ-UZZA. *Same as Perez-uzza.*
name of the place P to this day ... 2Sa 6:8 6560

PERFECT {99}
p in his generations, and Noah ... Gen 6:9 8549
walk before me, and be thou p ... Gen 17:1 8549
it shall be p to be accepted ... Lev 22:21 8549
Thou shalt be p with the LORD thy ... Deut 18:13 8549
a p and just weight, a p ... Deut 25:15 8003
He is the Rock, his work is p ... Deut 32:4 8549
LORD God of Israel, Give a p lot ... 1Sa 14:41 8549
As for God, his way is p ... 2Sa 22:31 8549
and he maketh my way p ... 2Sa 22:33 8549
be p with the LORD our God ... 1Kin 8:61 8003
his heart was not p with the LORD ... 1Kin 11:4 8003
his heart was not p with the LORD ... 1Kin 15:3 8003
was p with the LORD all his days ... 1Kin 15:14 8003
thee in truth and with a p heart ... 2Kin 20:3 8003
came with a p heart to Hebron, to ... 1Chr 12:38 8003
and serve him with a p heart ... 1Chr 28:9 8003
because with p heart they offered ... 1Chr 29:9 8003
unto Solomon my son a p heart ... 1Chr 29:19 8003
made he of gold, and that p gold ... 2Chr 4:21 4357
heart of Asa was p all his days ... 2Chr 15:17 8003
them whose heart is p toward him ... 2Chr 16:9 8003
faithfully, and with a p heart ... 2Chr 19:9 8003
the LORD, but not with a p heart ... 2Chr 25:2 8003
p peace, and at such a time ... Ezr 7:12 1585
and that man was p and upright, and ... Job 1:1 8535
none like him in the earth, a p ... Job 1:8 8535
none like him in the earth, a p ... Job 2:3 8535
God will not cast away a p man ... Job 8:20 8535
if I say, I am p, it shall also ... Job 9:20 8535
Though I were p, yet would I not ... Job 9:21 8535
I said it, He destroyeth the p ... Job 9:22 8535
him, that thou makest thy ways p ... Job 22:3 8552
he that is p in knowledge is with ... Job 36:4 8549
of him which is p in knowledge ... Job 37:16 8549
As for God, his way is p ... Ps 18:30 8549
with strength, and maketh my way p ... Ps 18:32 8549
The law of the LORD is p, ... Ps 19:7 8549
Mark the p man, and behold the ... Ps 37:37 8535
they may shoot in secret at the p ... Ps 64:4 8535
behave myself wisely in a p way ... Ps 101:2 8549
within my house with a p heart ... Ps 101:2 8537
he that walketh in a p way ... Ps 101:6 8549
The LORD will p that which ... Ps 138:8 1584
I hate them with p hatred ... Ps 139:22 8503
land, and the p shall remain in it ... Prov 2:21 8549
more and more unto the p day ... Prov 4:18 3559
of the p shall direct his way ... Prov 11:5 8549
the harvest, when the bud is p ... Is 18:5 8552
Thou wilt keep him in p peace ... Is 26:3
thee in truth and with a p heart ... Is 38:3 8003
who is blind as he that is p ... Is 42:19 7999
for it was p through my ... Eze 16:14 3632
thou hast said, I am of p beauty ... Eze 27:3 3632
they have made thy beauty p ... Eze 27:11 3634
full of wisdom, and p in beauty ... Eze 28:12 3632
Thou wast p in thy ways from the ... Eze 28:15 8549
Be ye therefore p, even as your ... Mt 5:48 5046
Father which is in heaven is p ... Mt 5:48 5046
said unto him, If thou wilt be p ... Mt 19:21 5046
having had p understanding of all ... Lk 1:3 199
but every one that is p shall be ... Lk 6:40 2675
that they may be made p in one ... Jn 17:23 5048
p soundness in the presence of ... Acts 3:16 3647
taught according to the p manner ... Acts 22:3 195
having more p knowledge of that ... Acts 24:22 197
is that good, and acceptable, and p ... Rom 12:2 5046
wisdom among them that are p ... 1Cor 2:6 5046
But when that which is p is come ... 1Cor 13:10 5046
my strength is made p in weakness ... 2Cor 12:9 5048
Be p, be of good comfort, be of ... 2Cor 13:11 2675
are ye now made p by the flesh ... Gal 3:3 2005
of the Son of God, unto a p man ... Eph 4:13 5046
attained, either were already p ... Phil 3:12 5048
Let us therefore, as many as be p ... Phil 3:15 5046
every man p in Christ Jesus ... Col 1:28 5046
in prayers, that ye may stand p ... Col 4:12 5046
might p that which is lacking in ... 1Th 3:10 2675
That the man of God may be p ... 2Ti 3:17 739
salvation p through sufferings ... Heb 2:10 5048
And being made p, he became the ... Heb 5:9 5048
For the law made nothing p ... Heb 7:19 5048
make him that did the service p ... Heb 9:9 5048
more p tabernacle, not made with ... Heb 9:11 5046
make the comers thereunto p ... Heb 10:1 5048
without us should not be made p ... Heb 11:40 5048
to the spirits of just men made p ... Heb 12:23 5048
Make you p in every good work to ... Heb 13:21 2675
But let patience have her p work ... Jas 1:4 5046
that ye may be p ... Jas 1:4 5046
every p gift is from above, and ... Jas 1:17 5046
looketh into the p law of liberty ... Jas 1:25 5046
and by works was faith made p ... Jas 2:22 5048
not in word, the same is a p man ... Jas 3:2 5046
have suffered a while, make you p ... 1Pet 5:10 2675
Herein is our love made p ... 1Jn 4:17 5048
but p love casteth out fear ... 1Jn 4:18 5046
feareth is not made p in love ... 1Jn 4:18 5048
not found thy works p before God ... Rev 3:2 4137

PERFECTED {8}
So the house of the LORD was p ... 2Chr 8:16 8003
and the work was p by them ... 2Chr 24:13 5927,724
thy builders have p thy beauty ... Eze 27:4 3634
and sucklings thou hast p praise ... Mt 21:16 2675
and the third day I shall be p ... Lk 13:32 5048
he hath p for ever them that are ... Heb 10:14 5048
him verily is the love of God p ... 1Jn 2:5 5048
in us, and his love is p in us ... 1Jn 4:12 5048

PERFECTING {2}
p holiness in the fear of God ... 2Cor 7:1 2005
For the p of the saints, for the ... Eph 4:12 2677

PERFECTION {11}
thou find out the Almighty unto p ... Job 11:7 8503
the p thereof upon the earth ... Job 15:29 4512
darkness, and searcheth out all p ... Job 28:3 8503
the p of beauty, God hath shined ... Ps 50:2 4359
I have seen an end of all p ... Ps 119:96 8502
their p for the multitude of thy ... Is 47:9 8537
that men call The p of beauty ... Lam 2:15 3632
this life, and bring no fruit to p ... Lk 8:14 5052
and this also we wish, even your p ... 2Cor 13:9 2676
of Christ, let us go on unto p ... Heb 6:1 5051
If therefore p were by the ... Heb 7:11 5050

PERFECTLY {7}
days ye shall consider it p ... Jer 23:20 998
many as touched were made p whole ... Mt 14:36 1295
unto him the way of God more p ... Acts 18:26 197
something more p concerning him ... Acts 23:15 197
enquire somewhat of him more p ... Acts 23:20 197
but that ye be p joined together ... 1Cor 1:10 2675
For yourselves know p that the ... 1Th 5:2 199

PERFECTNESS {1}
charity, which is the bond of p ... Col 3:14 5047

PERFORM {42}
I will p the oath which I sware ... Gen 26:3 6965
not able to p it thyself alone ... Ex 18:18 6213
that enter in to p the service ... Num 4:23 6633
which he commanded you to p ... Deut 4:13 6213
that he may p the word which the ... Deut 9:5 6965
of thy lips thou shalt keep and p ... Deut 23:23 6213
p the duty of an husband's ... Deut 25:5
he will not p the duty of my ... Deut 25:7
that if he will p unto thee the ... Ruth 3:13
In that day I will p against Eli ... 1Sa 3:12 6965
p the request of his handmaid ... 2Sa 14:15 6213
then will I p my word with thee, ... 1Kin 6:12 6965
LORD, that he might p his saying ... 1Kin 12:15 6965
to p the words of this covenant ... 2Kin 23:3 6965
that he might p the words of the ... 2Kin 23:24 6965
that the LORD might p his word ... 2Chr 10:15 6965
to p the words of the covenant ... 2Chr 34:31 6213
to p my request, let the king and ... Est 5:8 6213
hands cannot p their enterprise ... Job 5:12
which they are not able to p ... Ps 21:11
ever, that I may daily p my vows ... Ps 61:8 7999
I have sworn, and I will p it ... Ps 119:106 6965
heart to p thy statutes alway ... Ps 119:112 6213
of the LORD of hosts will p this ... Is 9:7 6213
vow a vow unto the LORD, and p it ... Is 19:21 7999
and shall p all my pleasure ... Is 44:28 7999
for I will hasten my word to p it ... Jer 1:12 6213
That I may p the oath which I ... Jer 11:5 6965
the LORD p thy words which thou ... Jer 28:6 6965
p my good word toward you, in ... Jer 29:10 6965
that I will p that good thing ... Jer 33:14 6965
We will surely p our vows that we ... Jer 44:25 6213
your vows, and surely p your vows ... Jer 44:25 6213
will I say the word, and will p it ... Eze 12:25 6213
Thou wilt p the truth to Jacob, ... Mic 7:20 5414
thy solemn feasts, p thy vows ... Nah 1:15 7999
but shalt p unto the Lord thine ... Mt 5:33 591
To p the mercy promised to our ... Lk 1:72 4160
promised, he was able also to p ... Rom 4:21 4160
but how to p that which is good I ... Rom 7:18 2716
Now therefore p the doing of it ... 2Cor 8:11 2005
will p it until the day of Jesus ... Phil 1:6 2005

PERFORMANCE {2}
for there shall be a p of those ... Lk 1:45 5050
so there may be a p also out of ... 2Cor 8:11 2005

PERFORMED {21}
hath not p my commandments ... 1Sa 15:11 6965
I have p the commandment of the ... 1Sa 15:13 6965
and they p all that the king ... 2Sa 21:14 6213
the LORD hath p his word that he ... 1Kin 8:20 6965
The LORD therefore hath p his ... 2Chr 6:10 6965
to his seed, and hast p thy words ... Neh 9:8 6965
because she hath not p the ... Est 1:15 6213
half of the kingdom it shall be p ... Est 5:6 6213
and it shall be p, even to the ... Est 7:2 6213
and unto thee shall the vow be p ... Ps 65:1 7999
that when the Lord hath p his ... Is 10:12 1214
till he have p the thoughts of ... Jer 23:20 6965
until he have p the intents of ... Jer 30:24 6965
which have not p the words of the ... Jer 34:18 6965
his sons not to drink wine, are p ... Jer 35:14 6965
Jonadab the son of Rechab have p ... Jer 35:16 6965
LORD shall be p against Babylon ... Jer 51:29 6965
it, and p it, saith the LORD ... Eze 37:14 6213
day that these things shall be p ... Lk 1:20 1096
when they had p all things ... Lk 2:39 5055
When therefore I have p this ... Rom 15:28 2005

PERFORMETH {4}
that p not this promise, even ... Neh 5:13 6965
For he p the thing that is ... Job 23:14 7999
unto God that p all things for me ... Ps 57:2 1584
p the counsel of his messengers ... Is 44:26 7999

PERFORMING {2}
or a sacrifice in p a vow ... Num 15:3 6381
or for a sacrifice in p a vow ... Num 15:8 6381

PERFUME {3}
And thou shalt make it a p ... Ex 30:35 7004
as for the p which thou shalt ... Ex 30:37 7004
Ointment and p rejoice the heart ... Prov 27:9 7004

PERFUMED {2}
I have p my bed with myrrh, aloes ... Prov 7:17 5130
p with myrrh and frankincense, ... Song 3:6 6999

P

PERFUMES {1}
ointment, and didst increase thy *p*.......... Is 57:9 7547

PERGA *(pur'-gah)* {3} *Capital of Pamphylia.*
they came to *P* in Pamphylia .... Acts 13:13 *4011*
But when they departed from *P*............ Acts 13:14 *4011*
they had preached the word in *P*.......... Acts 14:25 *4011*

PERGAMOS *(pur'-ga-mos)* {2} *A city in Mysia in Asia Minor.*
and unto Smyrna, and unto *P*................ Rev 1:11 *4010*
angel of the church in *P* write.............. Rev 2:12 *4010*

PERGAMUM See PERGAMOS.

PERHAPS See APPENDIX.

PERIDA *(per-i'-dah)* {1} *A family of exiles.*
of Sophereth, the children of *P*.............. Neh 7:57 6514

PERIL {2}
We gat our bread with the *p* of .... Lam 5:9
or famine, or nakedness, or *p*.................. Rom 8:35 *2794*

PERILOUS {1}
the last days *p* times shall come............. 2Ti 3:1 *5467*

PERILS {8}
in *p* of waters... 2Cor 11:26 *2794*
in *p* of robbers 2Cor 11:26 *2794*
in *p* by mine own countrymen.................. 2Cor 11:26 *2794*
in *p* by the heathen.................................. 2Cor 11:26 *2794*
in *p* in the city... 2Cor 11:26 *2794*
in *p* in the wilderness.............................. 2Cor 11:26 *2794*
in *p* in the sea.. 2Cor 11:26 *2794*
in *p* among false brethren 2Cor 11:26 *2794*

PERISH {120}
that the land *p* not through the................ Gen 41:36 3772
LORD to gaze, and many of them *p* .... Ex 19:21 5307
or the eye of his maid, that it *p*............. Ex 21:26 7843
ye shall *p* among the heathen, and.......... Lev 26:38 6
we die, we *p*, we all *p* .... Num 17:12 6
end shall be that he *p* for ever .... Num 24:20 8
Eber, and he also shall *p* for ever........... Num 24:24 8
that ye shall soon utterly *p* from............ Deut 4:26 6
this day that ye shall surely *p* .... Deut 8:19 6
before your face, so shall ye *p*................ Deut 8:20 6
lest ye *p* quickly from off the .... Deut 11:17 6
A Syrian ready to *p* was my father.......... Deut 26:5 6
and until thou *p* quickly.......................... Deut 28:20 6
shall pursue thee until thou *p* .... Deut 28:22 6
this day, that ye shall surely *p*............... Deut 30:18 6
until ye *p* from off this good .... Josh 23:13 6
ye shall *p* quickly from off the .... Josh 23:16 6
So let all thine enemies *p*........................ Judg 5:31 6
shall descend into battle, and *p* 1Sa 26:10 5595
I shall now *p* one day by the hand 1Sa 27:1 5595
the whole house of Ahab shall *p*............. 2Kin 9:8 6
to kill, and to cause to *p*......................... Est 3:13 6
and if I *p*, I *p* .... Est 4:16 6
destroyed, to be slain, and to *p* .... Est 7:4 6
to slay, and to cause to *p* .... Est 8:11 6
of them *p* from their seed........................ Est 9:28 5486
Let the day *p* wherein I was born, ... Job 3:3 6
By the blast of God they *p* .... Job 4:9 6
they *p* for ever without any..................... Job 4:20 6
they go to nothing, and *p* .... Job 6:18 6
and the hypocrite's hope shall *p*............. Job 8:13 6
shall *p* from the earth, and he................ Job 18:17 6
Yet he shall *p* for ever like his............... Job 20:7 6
that was ready to *p* came upon me .... Job 29:13 6
If I have seen any *p* for want of .... Job 31:19 6
All flesh shall *p* together........................ Job 34:15 1478
they shall *p* by the sword, and................ Job 36:12 5674
the way of the ungodly shall *p* .... Ps 1:6 6
ye *p* from the way, when his wrath .... Ps 2:12 6
shall fall and *p* at thy presence .... Ps 9:3 6
of the poor shall not *p* for ever .... Ps 9:18 6
But the wicked shall *p*, and the............... Ps 37:20 6
When shall he die, and his name *p* .... Ps 41:5 6
the fool and the brutish person *p*............ Ps 49:10 6
he is like the beasts that *p* .... Ps 49:12 1820
not, is like the beasts that *p* .... Ps 49:20 1820
so let the wicked *p* at the .... Ps 68:2 6
that are far from thee shall *p* .... Ps 73:27 6
they *p* at the rebuke of thy..................... Ps 80:16 6
let them be put to shame, and *p*.............. Ps 83:17 6
for, lo, thine enemies shall *p*.................. Ps 92:9 6
They shall *p*, but thou shalt .... Ps 102:26 6
the desire of the wicked shall *p* .... Ps 112:10 6
in that very day his thoughts *p* .... Ps 146:4 6
expectation of the wicked shall *p* .... Prov 10:28 6
dieth, his expectation shall *p* .... Prov 11:7 6
and when the wicked *p*, there is............... Prov 11:10 6
and he that speaketh lies shall *p* .... Prov 19:9 6
A false witness shall *p*............................. Prov 21:28 6
but when they *p*, the righteous .... Prov 28:28 6
there is no vision, the people *p* .... Prov 29:18 6544
drink unto him that is ready to *p*............ Prov 31:6 6
those riches *p* by evil travail .... Eccl 5:14 6
and made all their memory to *p*.............. Is 26:14 6
ready to *p* in the land of Assyria............. Is 27:13 6
wisdom of their wise men shall *p* .... Is 29:14 6
that strive with thee shall *p* .... Is 41:11 6
that will not serve thee shall *p*.............. Is 60:12 6
the heart of the king shall *p*.................... Jer 4:9 6
neighbour and his friend shall *p*............. Jer 6:21 6
even they shall *p* from the earth .... Jer 10:11 7
of their visitation they shall *p*............... Jer 10:15 6
law shall not *p* from the priest................ Jer 18:18 6
drive you out, and ye should *p* .... Jer 27:10 6
drive you out, and that ye might *p*.......... Jer 27:15 6
and the remnant in Judah *p* .... Jer 40:15 6
the valley also shall *p*, and the................ Jer 48:8 6
of their visitation they shall *p*............... Jer 51:18 6
the law shall *p* from the priest................ Eze 7:26 6
thee to *p* out of the countries .... Eze 25:7 6
his fellows should not *p* with the............ Dan 2:18 7
of the Philistines shall *p*......................... Amos 1:8 6
the flight shall *p* from the swift.............. Amos 2:14 6
and the houses of ivory shall *p*............... Amos 3:15 6
will think upon us, that we *p* not............ Jonah 1:6 6
let us not *p* for this man's life,............... Jonah 1:14 6
his fierce anger, that we *p* not............... Jonah 3:9 6
and the king shall *p* from Gaza.............. Zec 9:5 6
that one of thy members should *p*.......... Mt 5:29 *622*
that one of thy members should *p*.......... Mt 5:30 *622*
Lord, save us: we *p* .... Mt 8:25 *622*
runneth out, and the bottles *p*................ Mt 9:17 *622*
one of these little ones should *p*............ Mt 18:14 *622*
the sword shall *p* with the sword............ Mt 26:52 *622*
Master, carest thou not that we *p*........... Mk 4:38 *622*
spilled, and the bottles shall *p*.............. Lk 5:37 *622*
him, saying, Master, master, we *p*........... Lk 8:24 *622*
repent, ye shall all likewise *p*................. Lk 13:3 *622*
repent, ye shall all likewise *p*................. Lk 13:5 *622*
that a prophet *p* out of Jerusalem........... Lk 13:33 *622*
and to spare, and I *p* with hunger........... Lk 15:17 *622*
shall not an hair of your head *p*............. Lk 21:18 *622*
believeth in him should not *p*................. Jn 3:15 *622*
believeth in him should not *p*................. Jn 3:16 *622*
and they shall never *p*, neither............... Jn 10:28 *622*
and that the whole nation *p* not.............. Jn 11:50 *622*
him, Thy money *p* with thee..... Acts 8:20 *1510,1519,604*
ye despisers, and wonder, and *p*............. Acts 13:41 *853*
law shall also *p* without law .... Rom 2:12 *622*
is to them that *p* foolishness 1Cor 1:18 *622*
shall the weak brother *p*, for................... 1Cor 8:11 *622*
that are saved, and in them that *p* 2Cor 2:15 *622*
but though our outward man *p*................ 2Cor 4:16 *1311*
Which all are to *p* with the using............ Col 2:22 *5356*
of unrighteousness in them that *p* 2Th 2:10 *622*
They shall *p*; but thou .... Heb 1:11 *622*
shall utterly *p* in their own 2Pet 2:12 *2704*
not willing that any should *p* 2Pet 3:9 *622*

PERISHED {26}
and they *p* from among the .... Num 16:33 6
Heshbon is *p* even unto Dibon, and .... Num 21:30 6
that man *p* not alone in his .... Josh 22:20 1478
fallen, and the weapons of war *p*............. 2Sa 1:27 6
Remember, I pray thee, who ever *p*.......... Job 4:7 6
profit me, in whom old age was *p*........... Job 30:2 6
their memorial is *p* with them................. Ps 9:6 6
the heathen are *p* out of his land .... Ps 10:16 6
Which *p* at En-dor................................... Ps 83:10 8045
then have *p* in mine affliction .... Ps 119:92 6
hatred, and their envy, is now *p*............. Eccl 9:6 6
truth is *p*, and is cut off from.................. Jer 7:28 6
riches that he hath gotten are *p*.............. Jer 48:36 6
is counsel *p* from the prudent .... Jer 49:7 6
my hope is *p* from the LORD .... Lam 3:18 6
the harvest of the field is *p* .... Joel 1:11 6
up in a night, and *p* in a night .... Jonah 4:10 6
is thy counsellor *p* .... Mic 4:9 6
The good man is *p* out of the .... Mic 7:2 6
into the sea, and *p* in the waters.............. Mt 8:32 *599*
which *p* between the altar and the.......... Lk 11:51 *622*
after him: he also *p*................................. Acts 5:37 *622*
are fallen asleep in Christ are *p* 1Cor 15:18 *622*
By faith the harlot Rahab *p* not............... Heb 11:31 *4881*
being overflowed with water, *p*.............. 2Pet 3:6 *622*
p in the gainsaying of Core .... Jude 11 *622*

PERISHETH {9}
The old lion *p* for lack of prey,................ Job 4:11 6
and the hope of unjust men *p* .... Prov 11:7 6
man that *p* in his righteousness .... Eccl 7:15 6
The righteous *p*, and no man layeth......... Is 57:1 6
declare it, for what the land *p* .... Jer 9:12 6
the people of Chemosh *p* .... Jer 48:46 6
Labour not for the meat which *p*............. Jn 6:27 *622*
the grace of the fashion of it *p*................ Jas 1:11 *622*
more precious than of gold that *p*........... 1Pet 1:7 *622*

PERISHING {1}
and his life from *p* by the sword .... Job 33:18 5674

PERIZZITE *(per'-iz-zite)* {5} See PERIZZITES. *A tribe in Judah.*
the *P* dwelled then in the land................. Gen 13:7 6522
Amorite, and the Hittite, and the *P*......... Ex 33:2 6522
and the Hittite, and the *P* .... Ex 34:11 6522
the Amorite, the Canaanite, the *P* .... Josh 9:1 6522
Amorite, and the Hittite, and the *P*......... Josh 11:3 6522

PERIZZITES *(per'-iz-zites)* {18}
And the Hittites, and the *P*..................... Gen 15:20 6522
among the Canaanites and the *P* .... Gen 34:30 6522
and the Amorites, and the *P* .... Ex 3:8 6522
and the Amorites, and the *P* .... Ex 3:17 6522
and the Hittites, and the *P*...................... Ex 23:23 6522
and the Canaanites, and the *P* .... Deut 7:1 6522
the Canaanites, and the *P*....................... Deut 20:17 6522
and the Hivites, and the *P*....................... Josh 3:10 6522
and the Canaanites, the *P* .... Josh 12:8 6522
there in the land of the *P* .... Josh 17:15 6522
you, the Amorites, and the *P*................... Josh 24:11 6522
and the *P* into their hand........................ Judg 1:4 6522
they slew the Canaanites and the *P*........ Judg 1:5 6522
Hittites, and Amorites, and *P* .... Judg 3:5 6522
left of the Amorites, Hittites, *P*.............. 1Kin 9:20 6522
and the Amorites, and the *P* 2Chr 8:7 6522
Canaanites, the Hittites, the *P* .... Ezr 9:1 6522
Hittites, the Amorites, and the *P* .... Neh 9:8 6522

PERJURED {1}
for *p* persons, and if there be any 1Ti 1:10 *1965*

PERMISSION {1}
But I speak this by *p*, and not of............. 1Cor 7:6 *4774*

PERMIT {2}
a while with you, if the Lord *p* 1Cor 16:7 *2010*
And this will we do, if God *p*.................. Heb 6:3 *2010*

PERMITTED {2}
Thou art *p* to speak for thyself................ Acts 26:1 *2010*
for it is not *p* unto them to...................... 1Cor 14:34 *2010*

PERNICIOUS {1}
And many shall follow their *p* ways......... 2Pet 2:2 *684*

PERPETUAL {28}
is with you, for *p* generations................. Gen 9:12 5769
shall be theirs for a *p* statute .... Ex 29:9 5769
a *p* incense before the LORD..................... Ex 30:8 8548
generations, for a *p* covenant .... Ex 31:16 5769
It shall be a *p* statute for your .... Lev 3:17 5769
fine flour for a meat offering *p* .... Lev 6:20 8548
LORD made by fire by a *p* statute............ Lev 24:9 5769
for it is their *p* possession .... Lev 25:34 5769
it shall be a *p* statute unto them .... Num 19:21 5769
destructions are come to a *p* end .... Ps 9:6 5331
thy feet unto the *p* desolations................ Ps 74:3 5331
he put them to a *p* reproach..................... Ps 78:66 5769
bound of the sea by a *p* decree................. Jer 5:22 5769
slidden back by a *p* backsliding................ Jer 8:5 5331
Why is my pain *p*, and my wound............ Jer 15:18 5331
land desolate, and a *p* hissing.................. Jer 18:16 5769
a *p* shame, which shall not be.................... Jer 23:40 5769
and an hissing, and *p* desolations .... Jer 25:9 5769
and will make it *p* desolations .... Jer 25:12 5769
cities thereof shall be *p* wastes .... Jer 49:13 5769
in a *p* covenant that shall not be.............. Jer 50:5 5769
may rejoice, and sleep a *p* sleep.............. Jer 51:39 5769
and they shall sleep a *p* sleep.................. Jer 51:57 5769
Because thou hast had a *p* hatred............ Eze 35:5 5769
I will make thee *p* desolations................. Eze 35:9 5769
by a *p* ordinance unto the LORD............... Eze 46:14 5769
scattered, the *p* hills did bow.................. Hab 3:6 5769
and saltpits, and a *p* desolation .... Zeph 2:9 5769

PERPETUALLY {3}
and mine heart shall be there *p*....... 1Kin 9:3 3605,3711
and mine heart shall be there *p*....... 2Chr 7:16 3605,3711
all pity, and his anger did tear *p*............. Amos 1:11 5703

PERPLEXED {5}
but the city Shushan was *p*...................... Est 3:15 943
the herds of cattle are *p* .... Joel 1:18 943
and he was *p*, because that it was............. Lk 9:7 *1280*
as they were much *p* thereabout .... Lk 24:4 *1280*
we are *p*, but not in despair 2Cor 4:8 *639*

PERPLEXITY {3}
of *p* by the Lord GOD of hosts in............. Is 22:5 3998
now shall be their *p*................................. Mic 7:4 3998
earth distress of nations, with *p*............. Lk 21:25 *640*

PERSECUTE {25}
Why do ye *p* me as God, and are not ...... Job 19:22 7291
Why *p* we him, seeing the root of............ Job 19:28 7291
save me from all them that *p* me.............. Ps 7:1 7291
Let the enemy *p* my soul, and take .... Ps 7:5 7291
in his pride doth *p* the poor .... Ps 10:2 1814
enemies, and from them that *p* me.......... Ps 31:15 7291
the way against them that *p* me.............. Ps 35:3 7291
let the angel of the LORD *p* them .... Ps 35:6 7291
For they *p* him whom thou hast.............. Ps 69:26 7291
p and take him .... Ps 71:11 7291
So *p* them with thy tempest, and............. Ps 83:15 7291
judgment on them that *p* me .... Ps 119:84 7291
they *p* me wrongfully .... Ps 119:86 7291
Let them be confounded that *p* me........... Jer 17:18 7291
I will *p* them with the sword,.......... Jer 29:18 7921,310
P and destroy them in anger from .... Lam 3:66 7291
p you, and shall say all manner of........... Mt 5:11 *1377*
despitefully use you, and *p* you.............. Mt 5:44 *1377*
But when they *p* you in this city,............ Mt 10:23 *1377*
and *p* them from city to city .... Mt 23:34 *1377*
some of them they shall slay and *p*......... Lk 11:49 *1559*
p you, delivering you up to the............... Lk 21:12 *1377*
And therefore did the Jews *p* Jesus......... Jn 5:16 *1377*
me, they will also *p* you........................... Jn 15:20 *1377*
Bless them which *p* you............................. Rom 12:14 *1377*

PERSECUTED {20}
them that hate thee, which *p* thee........... Deut 30:7 7291
but *p* the poor and needy man, that......... Ps 109:16 7291
Princes have *p* me without a cause .... Ps 119:161 7291
For the enemy hath *p* my soul .... Ps 143:3 7291
ruled the nations in anger, is *p*................ Is 14:6 4783
hast covered with anger, and *p* us........... Lam 3:43 7291
are *p* for righteousness' sake.................... Mt 5:10 *1377*
for so *p* they the prophets which.............. Mt 5:12 *1377*
If they have *p* me, they will also............... Jn 15:20 *1377*
prophets have not your fathers *p* .... Acts 7:52 *1377*
I *p* this way unto the death, ... Acts 22:4 *1377*
I *p* them even unto strange cities .... Acts 26:11 *1377*
being *p*, we suffer it................................. 1Cor 4:12 *1377*
because I *p* the church of God................. 1Cor 15:9 *1377*
P, but not forsaken 2Cor 4:9 *1377*
measure I *p* the church of God................. Gal 1:13 *1377*
That he which *p* us in times past .... Gal 1:23 *1377*
p him that was born after the .... Gal 4:29 *1377*
their own prophets, and have *p* us 1Th 2:15 *1559*
he *p* the woman which brought................. Rev 12:13 *1377*

PERSECUTEST {6}
him, Saul, Saul, why p thou me ... Acts 9:4 1377
Lord said, I am Jesus whom thou p ... Acts 9:5 1377
me, Saul, Saul, why p thou me ... Acts 22:7 1377
am Jesus of Nazareth, whom thou p ... Acts 22:8 1377
tongue, Saul, Saul, why p thou me ... Acts 26:14 1377
he said, I am Jesus whom thou p ... Acts 26:15 1377

PERSECUTING {1}
Concerning zeal, p the church ... Phil 3:6 1377

PERSECUTION {10}
Our necks are under p ... Lam 5:5 7291
for when tribulation or p ariseth ... Mt 13:21 1375
when affliction or p ariseth for ... Mk 4:17 1375
at that time there was a great p ... Acts 8:1 1375
the p that arose about Stephen ... Acts 11:19 2347
raised p against Paul and Barnabas ... Acts 13:50 1375
tribulation, or distress, or p ... Rom 8:35 1375
why do I yet suffer p ... Gal 5:11 1377
suffer p for the cross of Christ ... Gal 6:12 1377
in Christ Jesus shall suffer p ... 2Ti 3:12 1377

PERSECUTIONS {5}
and children, and lands, with p ... Mk 10:30 1375
reproaches, in necessities, in p ... 2Cor 12:10 1375
patience and faith in all your p ... 2Th 1:4 1375
P, afflictions, which came unto ... 2Ti 3:11 1375
what p I endured ... 2Ti 3:11 1375

PERSECUTOR {1}
was before a blasphemer, and a p ... 1Ti 1:13 1376

PERSECUTORS {8}
their p thou threwest into the ... Neh 9:11 7291
his arrows against the p ... Ps 7:13 1814
Many are my p and mine enemies ... Ps 119:157 7291
deliver me from my p ... Ps 142:6 7291
visit me, and revenge me of my p ... Jer 15:15 7291
therefore my p shall stumble, and ... Jer 20:11 7291
all her p overtook her between ... Lam 1:3 7291
Our p are swifter than the eagles ... Lam 4:19 7291

PERSEVERANCE {1}
and watching thereunto with all p ... Eph 6:18 4343

PERSIA *(per'-she-ah)* {29} See ELAM, PERSIAN. *An ancient world power located in present-day Iran.*
the reign of the kingdom of P ... 2Chr 36:20 6539
the first year of Cyrus king of P ... 2Chr 36:22 6539
up the spirit of Cyrus king of P ... 2Chr 36:22 6539
Thus saith Cyrus king of P ... 2Chr 36:23 6539
the first year of Cyrus king of P ... Ezr 1:1 6539
up the spirit of Cyrus king of P ... Ezr 1:1 6539
Thus saith Cyrus king of P ... Ezr 1:2 6539
of P bring forth by the hand of ... Ezr 1:8 6539
that they had of Cyrus king of P ... Ezr 3:7 6539
the king of P hath commanded us ... Ezr 4:3 6539
all the days of Cyrus king of P ... Ezr 4:5 6539
the reign of Darius king of P ... Ezr 4:5 6539
unto Artaxerxes king of P ... Ezr 4:7 6539
of the reign of Darius king of P ... Ezr 4:24 6540
Darius, and Artaxerxes king of P ... Ezr 6:14 6540
the reign of Artaxerxes king of P ... Ezr 7:1 6539
us in the sight of the kings of P ... Ezr 9:9 6539
the power of P and Media, the ... Est 1:3 6539
Memucan, the seven princes of P ... Est 1:14 6539
Likewise shall the ladies of P ... Est 1:18 6539
of the kings of Media and P ... Est 10:2 6539
They of P and of Lud and of Phut ... Eze 27:10 6539
P, Ethiopia, and Libya with them ... Eze 38:5 6539
horns are the kings of Media and P ... Dan 8:20 6539
of P a thing was revealed unto ... Dan 10:1 6539
the kingdom of P withstood me one ... Dan 10:13 6539
there with the kings of P ... Dan 10:13 6539
to fight with the prince of P ... Dan 10:20 6539
stand up yet three kings in P ... Dan 11:2 6539

PERSIAN *(per'-she-un)* {2} *A native of Persia.*
to the reign of Darius the P ... Neh 12:22 6542
and in the reign of Cyrus the P ... Dan 6:28 6523

PERSIANS *(per'-she-uns)* {5} See ELAMITES.
written among the laws of the P ... Est 1:19 6539
and given to the Medes and P ... Dan 5:28 6540
to the law of the Medes and P ... Dan 6:8 6540
to the law of the Medes and P ... Dan 6:12 6540
P is, That no decree nor statute ... Dan 6:15 6540

PERSIS *(pur'-sis)* {1} *A Christian in Rome.*
Salute the beloved P, which ... Rom 16:12 4069

PERSON {56}
And Joseph was a goodly p, and well ... Gen 39:6
uncircumcised p shall eat thereof ... Ex 12:48
not respect the p of the poor ... Lev 19:15 6440
nor honour the p of the mighty ... Lev 19:15 6440
the LORD, and that p be guilty ... Num 5:6 5315
for an unclean p they shall take ... Num 19:17
a clean p shall take hyssop, and ... Num 19:18 376,120
the clean p shall sprinkle upon ... Num 19:19
whatsoever the unclean p toucheth ... Num 19:22
whosoever hath killed any p ... Num 31:19 5315
which killeth any p at unawares ... Num 35:11 5315
any p unawares may flee thither ... Num 35:15 5315
Whoso killeth any p, the murderer ... Num 35:30 5315
against any p to cause him to die ... Num 35:30 5315
the clean p shall eat it alike ... Deut 15:22
reward to slay an innocent p ... Deut 27:25 5315
shall not regard the p of the old ... Deut 28:50 6440
that killeth any p unawares ... Josh 20:3 5315
that whosoever killeth any p at ... Josh 20:9 5315
of Israel a goodlier p than he ... 1Sa 9:2 376
prudent in matters, and a comely p ... 1Sa 16:18 376
thy voice, and have accepted thy p ... 1Sa 25:35 6440
men have slain a righteous p in ... 2Sa 4:11 376
neither doth God respect any p ... 2Sa 14:14 5315
thou go to battle in thine own p ... 2Sa 17:11 6440
Will ye accept his p ... Job 13:8 6440
and he shall save the humble p ... Job 22:29
I pray you, accept any man's p ... Job 32:21 6440
whose eyes a vile p is contemned ... Ps 15:4
the fool and the brutish p perish ... Ps 49:10
I will not know a wicked p ... Ps 101:4
one feeble p among their tribes ... Ps 105:37
A naughty p, a wicked man ... Prov 6:12 120
to accept the p of the wicked ... Prov 18:5 6440
shall be called a mischievous p ... Prov 24:8 1167
of any p shall flee to the pit ... Prov 28:17 5315
The vile p shall be no more ... Is 32:5
For the vile p will speak villany ... Is 32:6
every p that Nebuzar-adan the ... Jer 43:6 5315
them that were near the king's p ... Jer 52:25 6440
field, to the lothing of thy p ... Eze 16:5 5315
take any p from among them, he is ... Eze 33:6 5315
at no dead p to defile themselves ... Eze 44:25 120
estate shall stand up a vile p ... Dan 11:21
with thee, or accept thy p ... Mal 1:8 6440
thou regardest not the p of men ... Mt 22:16 4383
of the blood of this just p ... Mt 27:24
thou regardest not the p of men ... Mk 12:14 4383
acceptest thou the p of any ... Lk 20:21 4383
among yourselves that wicked p ... 1Cor 5:13
forgave I it in the p of Christ ... 2Cor 2:10 4383
God accepteth no man's p ... Gal 2:6 4383
no whoremonger, nor unclean p ... Eph 5:5
and the express image of his p ... Heb 1:3 5287
be any fornicator, or profane p ... Heb 12:16
but saved Noah the eighth p ... 2Pet 2:5

PERSONS {56}
said unto Abram, Give me the p ... Gen 14:21 5315
all the p of his house, and his ... Gen 36:6 5315
according to the number of your p ... Ex 16:16 5315
the p shall be for the LORD by ... Lev 27:2 5315
upon the p that were there, and ... Num 19:18 5315
of five hundred, both of the p ... Num 31:28 120
one portion of fifty, of the p ... Num 31:30 120
thirty and two thousand p in all ... Num 31:35 5315,120
the p were sixteen thousand ... Num 31:40 5315,120
tribute was thirty and two p ... Num 31:40 5315,120
And sixteen thousand p ... Num 31:46 5315,120
shall not respect p in judgment ... Deut 1:17 6440
a terrible, which regardeth not p ... Deut 10:17 6440
Egypt with threescore and ten p ... Deut 10:22 5315
thou shalt not respect p, neither ... Deut 16:19 6440
which are threescore and ten p ... Judg 9:2 376
Abimelech hired vain and light p ... Judg 9:4 582
being threescore and ten p ... Judg 9:5 376
his sons, threescore and ten p ... Judg 9:18 376
the men of Israel about thirty p ... Judg 20:39 376
bidden, which were about thirty p ... 1Sa 9:22 376
five p that did wear a linen ... 1Sa 22:18 376
all the p of thy father's house ... 1Sa 22:22 5315
the king's sons, being seventy p ... 2Kin 10:6 376
king's sons, and slew seventy p ... 2Kin 10:7 376
LORD our God, nor respect of p ... 2Chr 19:7 6440
you, if ye do secretly accept p ... Job 13:10 6440
accepteth not the p of princes ... Job 34:19 6440
I have not sat with vain p ... Ps 26:4 4962
accept the p of the wicked ... Ps 82:2 6440
vain p is void of understanding ... Prov 12:11
to have respect of p in judgment ... Prov 24:23 6440
vain p shall have poverty enough ... Prov 28:19
To have respect of p is not good ... Prov 28:21 6440
eight hundred thirty and two p ... Jer 52:29 5315
seven hundred forty and five p ... Jer 52:30 5315
all the p were four thousand and ... Jer 52:30 5315
not the p of the priests, they ... Lam 4:16 6440
building forts, to cut off many p ... Eze 17:17 5315
they traded the p of men and ... Eze 27:13 5315
p that cannot discern between ... Jonah 4:11 120
are light and treacherous p ... Zeph 3:4 582
will he regard your p ... Mal 1:9 6440
than over ninety and nine just p ... Lk 15:7
that God is no respecter of p ... Acts 10:34 4381
the Jews, and with the devout p ... Acts 17:17
there is no respect of p with God ... Rom 2:11 4382
upon us by the means of many p ... 2Cor 1:11 4383
is there respect of p with him ... Eph 6:9 4382
and there is no respect of p ... Col 3:25 4382
for liars, for perjured p ... 1Ti 1:10 678
Lord of glory, with respect of p ... Jas 2:1 4382
But if ye have respect to p ... Jas 2:9 4380
who without respect of p judgeth ... 1Pet 1:17 678
what manner of p ought ye to be ... 2Pet 3:11
having men's p in admiration ... Jude 16 4383

PERSUADE {9}
the LORD said, Who shall p Ahab ... 1Kin 22:20 6601
the LORD, and said, I will p him ... 1Kin 22:21 6601
And he said, Thou shalt p him ... 1Kin 22:22 6601
Doth not Hezekiah p you to give ... 2Chr 32:11 5496
nor p you on this manner, neither ... 2Chr 32:15 5496
Beware lest Hezekiah p you ... Is 36:18 5496
governor's ears, we will p him ... Mt 28:14 3982
the terror of the Lord, we p men ... 2Cor 5:11 3982
For do I now p men, or God ... Gal 1:10 3982

PERSUADED {20}
p him to go up with him to ... 2Chr 18:2 5496
By long forbearing is a prince p ... Prov 25:15 6601
elders p the multitude that they ... Mt 27:20 3982
prophets, neither will they be p ... Lk 16:31 3982
for they be p that John was a ... Lk 20:6 3982
p them to continue in the grace ... Acts 13:43 3982
who p the people, and, having ... Acts 14:19 3982
and p the Jews and the Greeks ... Acts 18:4 3982
all Asia, this Paul hath p ... Acts 19:26 3982
And when he would not be p ... Acts 21:14 3982
for I am p that none of these ... Acts 26:26 3982
And being fully p that, what he ... Rom 4:21 4135
For I am p, that neither death ... Rom 8:38 3982
man be fully p in his own mind ... Rom 14:5 4135
am p by the Lord Jesus, that ... Rom 14:14 3982
And I myself also am p of you ... Rom 15:14 3982
and I am p that in thee also ... 2Ti 1:5 3982
am p that he is able to keep that ... 2Ti 1:12 3982
we are p better things of you, and ... Heb 6:9 3982
were p of them, and embraced them ... Heb 11:13 3982

PERSUADEST {1}
Paul, Almost thou p me to be a ... Acts 26:28 3982

PERSUADETH {2}
not unto Hezekiah, when he p you ... 2Kin 18:32 5496
This fellow p men to worship God ... Acts 18:13 374

PERSUADING {2}
p the things concerning the ... Acts 19:8 3982
p them concerning Jesus, both out ... Acts 28:23 3982

PERSUASION {1}
This p cometh not of him that ... Gal 5:8 3988

PERTAIN {6}
that p unto the LORD, having his ... Lev 7:20
which p unto the LORD, even that ... Lev 7:21
if I leave of all that p to him ... 1Sa 25:22
in those things which p to God ... Rom 15:17
more things that p to this life ... 1Cor 6:3
us all things that p unto life ... 2Pet 1:3

PERTAINED {17}
(Now the half that p unto the ... Num 31:43
a hill that p to Phinehas his son ... Josh 24:33
that p unto Joash the Abi-ezrite ... Judg 6:11
was missed of all that p unto him ... 1Sa 25:21
which p to Ish-bosheth the son of ... 2Sa 2:15
master's son all that p to Saul ... 2Sa 9:9 1961
are all that p unto Mephibosheth ... 2Sa 16:4
to him p Sochoh, and all the land ... 1Kin 4:10
to him p Taanach and Megiddo, and ... 1Kin 4:12
to him p the towns of Jair the ... 1Kin 4:13
to him also p the region of Argob ... 1Kin 4:13
made all the vessels that p unto ... 1Kin 7:48
all that p to the king of Egypt ... 2Kin 24:7
thereof every morning p to them ... 1Chr 9:27
that p to the children of ... 1Chr 11:31
fenced cities which p to Judah ... 2Chr 12:4
that p to the children of Israel ... 2Chr 34:33

PERTAINETH {7}
get that which p to his cleansing ... Lev 14:32
priest p the oil for the light ... Num 4:16
not wear that which p unto a man ... Deut 22:5 3627
wherefore Ziklag p unto the kings ... 1Sa 27:6 1961
Obed-edom, and all that p unto him ... 2Sa 6:12
to whom p the adoption, and the ... Rom 9:4
are spoken p to another tribe ... Heb 7:13 3348

PERTAINING {8}
were p unto the children of ... Josh 13:31
for every matter p to God ... 1Chr 26:32
things p to the kingdom of God ... Acts 1:3 4012
as p to the flesh, hath found ... Rom 4:1
of things p to this life, set ... 1Cor 6:4
high priest in things p to God ... Heb 2:17
for men in things p to God ... Heb 5:1
perfect, as p to the conscience ... Heb 9:9

PERUDA *(per'-u-dah)* {1} See PERIDA. *A family of exiles.*
of Sophereth, the children of P ... Ezr 2:55 6514

PERVERSE {20}
because thy way is p before me ... Num 22:32 3399
they are a p and crooked ... Deut 32:5 6141
Thou son of the p rebellious ... 1Sa 20:30 5753
cannot my taste discern p things ... Job 6:30 1942
perfect, it shall also prove me p ... Job 9:20 6140
and p lips put far from thee ... Prov 4:24 3891
is nothing froward or p in them ... Prov 8:8 6141
but he that is of a p heart shall ... Prov 12:8 5753
but he that is p in his ways ... Prov 14:2 3868
he that hath a p tongue falleth ... Prov 17:20 2015
than he that is p in his lips ... Prov 19:1 6141
thine heart shall utter p things ... Prov 23:33 8419
than he that is p in his ways ... Prov 28:6 6141
but he that is p in his ways ... Prov 28:18 6140
The LORD hath mingled a p spirit ... Is 19:14 5773
p generation, how long shall I be ... Mt 17:17 1294
p generation, how long shall I be ... Lk 9:41 1294
men arise, speaking p things ... Acts 20:30 1294
p nation, among whom ye shine as ... Phil 2:15 1294
P disputings of men of corrupt ... 1Ti 6:5 3859

PERVERSELY {3}
that which thy servant did p the ... 2Sa 19:19 5753
We have sinned, and have done p ... 1Kin 8:47 5753
for they dealt p with me without ... Ps 119:78 5791

PERVERSENESS {6}
neither hath he seen p in Israel ... Num 23:21 5999
but the p of transgressors shall ... Prov 11:3 5558
but p therein is a breach in the ... Prov 15:4 5558
word, and trust in oppression and p ... Is 30:12 3868
lies, your tongue hath muttered p ... Is 59:3 5766
of blood, and the city full of p ... Eze 9:9 4297

PERVERT {10}
p the words of the righteous ... Deut 16:19 5557
Thou shalt not *p* the judgment of ... Deut 24:17 5186
Doth God *p* judgment ... Job 8:3 5791
or doth the Almighty *p* justice ... Job 8:3 5791
will the Almighty *p* judgment ... Job 34:12 5791
bosom to *p* the ways of judgment ... Prov 17:23 5186
p the judgment of any of the ... Prov 31:5 8138
abhor judgment, and *p* all equity ... Mic 3:9 6140
wilt thou not cease to *p* the ... Acts 13:10 *1294*
would *p* the gospel of Christ ... Gal 1:7 *3344*

PERVERTED {5}
and took bribes, and *p* judgment ... 1Sa 8:3 5186
p that which was right, and it ... Job 33:27 5753
and thy knowledge, it hath *p* thee ... Is 47:10 7725
for they have *p* their way ... Jer 3:21 5753
for ye have *p* the words of the ... Jer 23:36 2015

PERVERTETH {5}
p the words of the righteous ... Ex 23:8 5557
Cursed be he that *p* the judgment ... Deut 27:19 5186
but he that *p* his ways shall be ... Prov 10:9 6140
The foolishness of man *p* his way ... Prov 19:3 5557
unto me, as one that *p* the people ... Lk 23:14 *654*

PERVERTING {2}
violent *p* of judgment and justice ... Eccl 5:8
We found this fellow *p* the nation ... Lk 23:2 *1294*

PESTILENCE {47}
lest he fall upon us with *p* ... Ex 5:3 1698
smite thee and thy people with *p* ... Ex 9:15 1698
I will send the *p* among you ... Lev 26:25 1698
I will smite them with the *p* ... Num 14:12 1698
shall make the *p* cleave unto thee ... Deut 28:21 1698
be three days' *p* in thy land ... 2Sa 24:13 1698
So the LORD sent a *p* upon Israel ... 2Sa 24:15 1698
in the land famine, if there be *p* ... 1Kin 8:37 1698
the sword of the LORD, even the *p* ... 1Chr 21:12 1698
So the LORD sent *p* upon Israel ... 1Chr 21:14 1698
dearth in the land, if there be *p* ... 2Chr 6:28 1698
or if I send *p* among my people ... 2Chr 7:13 1698
us, as the sword, judgment, or *p* ... 2Chr 20:9 1698
but gave their life over to the *p* ... Ps 78:50 1698
the fowler, and from the noisome *p* ... Ps 91:3 1698
Nor for the *p* that walketh in ... Ps 91:6 1698
and by the famine, and by the *p* ... Jer 14:12 1698
they shall die of a great *p* ... Jer 21:6 1698
are left in this city from the *p* ... Jer 21:7 1698
and by the famine, and by the *p* ... Jer 21:9 1698
the sword, the famine, and the *p* ... Jer 24:10 1698
and with the famine, and with the *p* ... Jer 27:8 1698
sword, by the famine, and by the *p* ... Jer 27:13 1698
of war, and of evil, and of *p* ... Jer 28:8 1698
the sword, the famine, and the *p* ... Jer 29:17 1698
with the famine, and with the *p* ... Jer 29:18 1698
and of the famine, and of the *p* ... Jer 32:24 1698
and by the famine, and by the *p* ... Jer 32:36 1698
the LORD, to the sword, to the *p* ... Jer 34:17 1698
sword, by the famine, and by the *p* ... Jer 38:2 1698
sword, by the famine, and by the *p* ... Jer 42:17 1698
sword, by the famine, and by the *p* ... Jer 42:22 1698
sword, by the famine, and by the *p* ... Jer 44:13 1698
part of thee shall die with the *p* ... Eze 5:12 1698
and *p* and blood shall pass through ... Eze 5:17 1698
sword, by the famine, and by the *p* ... Eze 6:11 1698
is far off shall die of the *p* ... Eze 6:12 1698
The sword is without, and the *p* ... Eze 7:15 1698
famine and *p* shall devour him ... Eze 7:15 1698
from the famine, and from the *p* ... Eze 12:16 1698
Or if I send a *p* into that land ... Eze 14:19 1698
and the noisome beast, and the *p* ... Eze 14:21 1698
For I will send into her *p* ... Eze 28:23 1698
in the caves shall die of the *p* ... Eze 33:27 1698
I will plead against him with *p* ... Eze 38:22 1698
the *p* after the manner of Egypt ... Amos 4:10 1698
Before him went the *p*, and burning ... Hab 3:5 1698

PESTILENCES {2}
and there shall be famines, and *p* ... Mt 24:7 *3061*
divers places, and famines, and *p* ... Lk 21:11 *3061*

PESTILENT {1}
we have found this man a *p* fellow ... Acts 24:5 *3061*

PESTLE {1}
in a mortar among wheat with a *p* ... Prov 27:22 5940

PETER *(pe'-tur)* {158} See CEPHAS, PETER'S, SIMON. *A disciple of Jesus.*
saw two brethren, Simon called *P* ... Mt 4:18 *4074*
The first, Simon, who is called *P* ... Mt 10:2 *4074*
P answered him and said, Lord, if ... Mt 14:28 *4074*
when *P* was come down out of the ... Mt 14:29 *4074*
Then answered *P* and said unto him, ... Mt 15:15 *4074*
Simon *P* answered and said, Thou ... Mt 16:16 *4074*
also unto thee, That thou art *P* ... Mt 16:18 *4074*
Then *P* took him, and began to ... Mt 16:22 *4074*
But he turned, and said unto *P* ... Mt 16:23 *4074*
And after six days Jesus taketh *P* ... Mt 17:1 *4074*
Then answered *P*, and said unto ... Mt 17:4 *4074*
received tribute money came to *P* ... Mt 17:24 *4074*
P saith unto him, Of strangers ... Mt 17:26 *4074*
Then came *P* to him, and said, Lord ... Mt 18:21 *4074*
Then answered *P* and said unto him, ... Mt 19:27 *4074*
P answered and said unto him, ... Mt 26:33 *4074*
P said unto him, Though I should ... Mt 26:35 *4074*
And he took with him *P* and the two ... Mt 26:37 *4074*
them asleep, and saith unto *P* ... Mt 26:40 *4074*
But *P* followed him afar off unto ... Mt 26:58 *4074*
Now *P* sat without in the palace ... Mt 26:69 *4074*
they that stood by, and said to *P* ... Mt 26:73 *4074*
P remembered the word of Jesus, ... Mt 26:75 *4074*
And Simon he surnamed *P* ... Mk 3:16 *4074*
no man to follow him, save *P* ... Mk 5:37 *4074*
P answereth and saith unto him, ... Mk 8:29 *4074*
P took him, and began to rebuke ... Mk 8:32 *4074*
on his disciples, he rebuked *P* ... Mk 8:33 *4074*
six days Jesus taketh with him *P* ... Mk 9:2 *4074*
P answered and said to Jesus, ... Mk 9:5 *4074*
Then *P* began to say unto him, Lo, ... Mk 10:28 *4074*
P calling to remembrance saith ... Mk 11:21 *4074*
Olives over against the temple, *P* ... Mk 13:3 *4074*
But *P* said unto him, Although all ... Mk 14:29 *4074*
And he taketh with him *P* and James ... Mk 14:33 *4074*
them sleeping, and saith unto *P* ... Mk 14:37 *4074*
P followed him afar off, even ... Mk 14:54 *4074*
as *P* was beneath in the palace, ... Mk 14:66 *4074*
when she saw *P* warming himself, ... Mk 14:67 *4074*
that stood by said again to *P* ... Mk 14:70 *4074*
P called to mind the word that ... Mk 14:72 *4074*
P that he goeth before you into ... Mk 16:7 *4074*
When Simon *P* saw it, he fell down ... Lk 5:8 *4074*
Simon, (whom he also named *P* ... Lk 6:14 *4074*
When all denied, *P* and they that ... Lk 8:45 *4074*
suffered no man to go in, save *P* ... Lk 8:51 *4074*
P answering said, The Christ of ... Lk 9:20 *4074*
after these sayings, he took *P* ... Lk 9:28 *4074*
But *P* and they that were with him ... Lk 9:32 *4074*
P said unto Jesus, Master, it is ... Lk 9:33 *4074*
Then *P* said unto him, Lord, ... Lk 12:41 *4074*
Then *P* said, Lo, we have left all ... Lk 18:28 *4074*
And he sent *P* and John, saying, Go ... Lk 22:8 *4074*
And he said, I tell thee, *P* ... Lk 22:34 *4074*
And *P* followed afar off ... Lk 22:54 *4074*
together, *P* sat down among them ... Lk 22:55 *4074*
And *P* said, Man, I am not ... Lk 22:58 *4074*
P said, Man, I know not what thou ... Lk 22:60 *4074*
the Lord turned, and looked upon *P* ... Lk 22:61 *4074*
P remembered the word of the Lord ... Lk 22:61 *4074*
P went out, and wept bitterly ... Lk 22:62 *4074*
Then arose *P*, and ran unto the ... Lk 24:12 *4074*
the city of Andrew and *P* ... Jn 1:44 *4074*
Then Simon *P* answered him, Lord, ... Jn 6:68 *4074*
Then cometh he to Simon *P* ... Jn 13:6 *4074*
P saith unto him, Lord, dost thou ... Jn 13:6
P saith unto him, Thou shalt ... Jn 13:8 *4074*
Simon *P* saith unto him, Lord, not ... Jn 13:9 *4074*
Simon *P* therefore beckoned to him ... Jn 13:24 *4074*
Simon *P* said unto him, Lord, ... Jn 13:36 *4074*
P said unto him, Lord, why cannot ... Jn 13:37 *4074*
Then Simon *P* having a sword drew ... Jn 18:10 *4074*
Then said Jesus unto *P*, Put up ... Jn 18:11 *4074*
Simon *P* followed Jesus, and so did ... Jn 18:15 *4074*
But *P* stood at the door without ... Jn 18:16 *4074*
kept the door, and brought in *P* ... Jn 18:16 *4074*
damsel that kept the door unto *P* ... Jn 18:17 *4074*
P stood with them, and warmed ... Jn 18:18 *4074*
And Simon *P* stood and warmed ... Jn 18:25 *4074*
his kinsman whose ear *P* cut off ... Jn 18:26 *4074*
P then denied again ... Jn 18:27 *4074*
she runneth, and cometh to Simon *P* ... Jn 20:2 *4074*
P therefore went forth, and that ... Jn 20:3 *4074*
the other disciple did outrun *P* ... Jn 20:4 *4074*
Then cometh Simon *P* following him ... Jn 20:6 *4074*
There were together Simon *P* ... Jn 21:2 *4074*
Simon *P* saith unto them, I go a ... Jn 21:3 *4074*
whom Jesus loved saith unto *P* ... Jn 21:7 *4074*
Now when Simon *P* heard that it ... Jn 21:7 *4074*
Simon *P* went up, and drew the net ... Jn 21:11 *4074*
had dined, Jesus saith to Simon *P* ... Jn 21:15 *4074*
P was grieved because he said ... Jn 21:17 *4074*
Then *P*, turning about, seeth the ... Jn 21:20 *4074*
P seeing him saith to Jesus, Lord ... Jn 21:21 *4074*
an upper room, where abode both *P* ... Acts 1:13 *4074*
in those days *P* stood up in the ... Acts 1:15 *4074*
But *P*, standing up with the ... Acts 2:14 *4074*
in their heart, and said unto *P* ... Acts 2:37 *4074*
Then *P* said unto them, Repent, and ... Acts 2:38 *4074*
Now *P* and John went up together ... Acts 3:1 *4074*
Who seeing *P* and John about to go ... Acts 3:3 *4074*
And *P*, fastening his eyes upon him ... Acts 3:4 *4074*
Then *P* said, Silver and gold have ... Acts 3:6 *4074*
lame man which was healed held *P* ... Acts 3:11 *4074*
when *P* saw it, he answered unto ... Acts 3:12 *4074*
Then *P*, filled with the Holy ... Acts 4:8 *4074*
when they saw the boldness of *P* ... Acts 4:13 *4074*
But *P* and John answered and said ... Acts 4:19 *4074*
But *P* said, Ananias, why hath ... Acts 5:3 *4074*
P answered unto her, Tell me ... Acts 5:8 *4074*
Then *P* said unto her, How is it ... Acts 5:9 *4074*
of *P* passing by might overshadow ... Acts 5:15 *4074*
Then *P* and the other apostles ... Acts 5:29 *4074*
of God, they sent unto them *P* ... Acts 8:14 *4074*
But *P* said unto him, Thy money ... Acts 8:20 *4074*
as *P* passed throughout all ... Acts 9:32 *4074*
P said unto him, Aeneas, Jesus ... Acts 9:34 *4074*
had heard that *P* was there ... Acts 9:38 *4074*
Then *P* arose and went with them ... Acts 9:39 *4074*
But *P* put them all forth, and ... Acts 9:40 *4074*
and when she saw *P*, she sat up ... Acts 9:40 *4074*
for one Simon, whose surname is *P* ... Acts 10:5 *4074*
P went up upon the housetop to ... Acts 10:9 *4074*
came a voice to him, Rise, *P* ... Acts 10:13 *4074*
But *P* said, Not so, Lord ... Acts 10:14 *4074*
Now while *P* doubted in himself ... Acts 10:17 *4074*
Simon, which was surnamed *P* ... Acts 10:18 *4074*
While *P* thought on the vision, ... Acts 10:19 *4074*
Then *P* went down to the men which ... Acts 10:21 *4074*
on the morrow *P* went away with ... Acts 10:23 *4074*
as *P* was coming in, Cornelius met ... Acts 10:25 *4074*
But *P* took him up, saying, Stand ... Acts 10:26 *4074*
hither Simon, whose surname is *P* ... Acts 10:32 *4074*
Then *P* opened his mouth, and said, ... Acts 10:34 *4074*
While *P* yet spake these words, ... Acts 10:44 *4074*
as many as came with *P*, because ... Acts 10:45 *4074*
Then answered *P*, ... Acts 10:46 *4074*
when *P* was come up to Jerusalem, ... Acts 11:2 *4074*
But *P* rehearsed the matter from ... Acts 11:4 *4074*
a voice saying unto me, Arise, *P* ... Acts 11:7 *4074*
for Simon, whose surname is *P* ... Acts 11:13 *4074*
proceeded further to take *P* also ... Acts 12:3 *4074*
P therefore was kept in prison ... Acts 12:5 *4074*
the same night *P* was sleeping ... Acts 12:6 *4074*
he smote *P* on the side, and raised ... Acts 12:7 *4074*
when *P* was come to himself, he ... Acts 12:11 *4074*
as *P* knocked at the door of the ... Acts 12:13 *4074*
told how *P* stood before the gate ... Acts 12:14 *4074*
But *P* continued knocking ... Acts 12:16 *4074*
soldiers, what was become of *P* ... Acts 12:18 *4074*
P rose up, and said unto them, Men ... Acts 15:7 *4074*
I went up to Jerusalem to see *P* ... Gal 1:18 *4074*
of the circumcision was unto *P* ... Gal 2:7 *4074*
in *P* to the apostleship of the ... Gal 2:8 *4074*
But when *P* was come to Antioch, I ... Gal 2:11 *4074*
I said unto *P* before them all, If ... Gal 2:14 *4074*
P, an apostle of Jesus Christ, to ... 1Pet 1:1 *4074*
Simon *P*, a servant and an apostle ... 2Pet 1:1 *4074*

PETER'S *(pe'-turz)* {4}
when Jesus was come into *P* house ... Mt 8:14 *4074*
him, was Andrew, Simon *P* brother ... Jn 1:40 *4074*
Simon *P* brother, saith unto him, ... Jn 6:8 *4074*
And when she knew *P* voice, she ... Acts 12:14 *4074*

PETHAHIAH *(peth-a-hi'-ah)* {4}
1. A sanctuary servant.
The nineteenth to *P*, the ... 1Chr 24:16 6611
2. Married a foreigner.
Kelaiah, (the same is Kelita,) *P* ... Ezr 10:23 6611
3. A Levite who helped Ezra.
Hodijah, Shebaniah, and *P* ... Neh 9:5 6611
4. An aide to Nehemiah.
P the son of Meshezabeel, of the ... Neh 11:24 6611

PETHOR *(pe'-thor)* {2} *A city in Mesopotamia.*
unto Balaam the son of Beor to *P* ... Num 22:5 6604
son of Beor of *P* of Mesopotamia ... Deut 23:4 6604

PETHUEL {1} *Father of Joel the prophet.*
that came to Joel the son of *P* ... Joel 1:1 6602

PETITION {13}
thy *p* that thou hast asked of him ... 1Sa 1:17 7596
me my *p* which I asked of him ... 1Sa 1:27 7596
And now I ask one *p* of thee ... 1Kin 2:16 7596
I desire one small *p* of thee ... 1Kin 2:20 7596
banquet of wine, What is thy *p* ... Est 5:6 7596
answered Esther, and said, My *p* ... Est 5:7 7596
it please the king to grant my *p* ... Est 5:8 7596
banquet of wine, What is thy *p* ... Est 7:2 7596
let my life be given me at my *p* ... Est 7:3 7596
now what is thy *p* ... Est 9:12 7596
that whosoever shall ask a *p* of ... Dan 6:7 1159
p of any God or man within thirty ... Dan 6:12
but maketh his *p* three times a ... Dan 6:13 1159

PETITIONS {2}
the LORD fulfil all thy *p* ... Ps 20:5 4862
have the *p* that we desired of him ... 1Jn 5:15 *155*

PEULLETHAI See PEULTHAI.

PEULTHAI *(pe-ul'-thahee)* {1} *A sanctuary servant.*
the seventh, *P* the eighth ... 1Chr 26:5 6469

PHALEC *(fa'-lek)* {1} See PELEG. *Father of Ragau; ancestor of Jesus.*
of Ragau, which was the son of *P* ... Lk 3:35 *5317*

PHALLU *(fal'-lu)* {1} *Son of Reuben.*
and *P*, and Hezron, and Carmi ... Gen 46:9 6396

PHALTI *(fal'-ti)* {1} See PHALTIEL. *Son of Laish.*
to *P* the son of Laish, which was ... 1Sa 25:44 6406

PHALTIEL *(fal'-te-el)* {1} See PHALTI. *Same as Phalti.*
even from *P* the son of Laish ... 2Sa 3:15 6409

PHANUEL *(fan-u'-el)* {1} *Mother of Anna.*
a prophetess, the daughter of *P* ... Lk 2:36 *5323*

PHARAOH *(fa'-ra-o)* {224} See PHARAOH'S, PHARAOH-HOPHRA, PHARAOH-NECHO.
1. Ruler of Egypt in Abraham's time.
The princes also of *P* saw her ... Gen 12:15 6547
and commended her before *P* ... Gen 12:15 6547
And the LORD plagued *P* and his ... Gen 12:17 6547
P called Abram, and said, What is ... Gen 12:18 6547
P commanded his men concerning ... Gen 12:20 6547
2. Ruler of Egypt in Joseph's time.
and Potiphar, an officer of *P* ... Gen 39:1 6547
P was wroth against two of his ... Gen 40:2 6547
days shall *P* lift up thine head ... Gen 40:13 6547
me, and make mention of me unto *P* ... Gen 40:14 6547
of all manner of bakemeats for *P* ... Gen 40:17 6547
Yet within three days shall *P* ... Gen 40:19 6547
of two full years, that *P* dreamed ... Gen 41:1 6547
So *P* awoke ... Gen 41:4 6547
P awoke, and, behold, it was a ... Gen 41:7 6547
and *P* told them his dream ... Gen 41:8 6547
that could interpret them unto *P* ... Gen 41:8 6547
spake the chief butler unto *P* ... Gen 41:9 6547
P was wroth with his servants, and ... Gen 41:10 6547
Then *P* sent and called Joseph, and ... Gen 41:14 6547
his raiment, and came in unto *P* ... Gen 41:14 6547
P said unto Joseph, I have ... Gen 41:15 6547

And Joseph answered P, saying, It ... Gen 41:16 6547
God shall give P an answer of ... Gen 41:16 6547
P said unto Joseph, In my dream, ... Gen 41:17 6547
And Joseph said unto P ... Gen 41:25 6547
The dream of P is one ... Gen 41:25 6547
God hath shewed P what he is ... Gen 41:25 6547
thing which I have spoken unto P ... Gen 41:28 6547
is about to do he sheweth unto P ... Gen 41:28 6547
dream was doubled unto P twice ... Gen 41:32 6547
Now therefore let P look out a ... Gen 41:33 6547
Let P do this, and let him appoint ... Gen 41:34 6547
lay up corn under the hand of P ... Gen 41:35 6547
thing was good in the eyes of P ... Gen 41:37 6547
P said unto his servants, Can we ... Gen 41:38 6547
P said unto Joseph, Forasmuch as ... Gen 41:39 6547
P said unto Joseph, See, I have ... Gen 41:41 6547
P took off his ring from his hand ... Gen 41:42 6547
P said unto Joseph, I am Pharaoh, ... Gen 41:44 6547
And P called Joseph's name ... Gen 41:45 6547
he stood before P king of Egypt ... Gen 41:46 6547
went out from the presence of P ... Gen 41:46 6547
the people cried to P for bread ... Gen 41:55 6547
P said unto all the Egyptians, Go ... Gen 41:55 6547
By the life of P ye shall not go ... Gen 42:15 6547
the life of P surely ye are spies ... Gen 42:16 6547
for thou art even as P ... Gen 44:18 6547
Egyptians and the house of P heard ... Gen 45:2 6547
and he hath made me a father to P ... Gen 45:8 6547
and it pleased P well, and his ... Gen 45:16 6547
P said unto Joseph, Say unto thy ... Gen 45:17 6547
according to the commandment of P ... Gen 45:21 6547
in the wagons which P had sent to ... Gen 46:5 6547
house, I will go up, and shew P ... Gen 46:31 6547
when P shall call you, and shall ... Gen 46:33 6547
Then Joseph came and told P ... Gen 47:1 6547
men, and presented them unto P ... Gen 47:2 6547
P said unto his brethren, What is ... Gen 47:3 6547
And they said unto P, Thy servants ... Gen 47:3 6547
They said moreover unto P ... Gen 47:4 6547
P spake unto Joseph, saying, Thy ... Gen 47:5 6547
his father, and set him before P ... Gen 47:7 6547
and Jacob blessed P ... Gen 47:7 6547
P said unto Jacob, How old art ... Gen 47:8 6547
And Jacob said unto P, The days of ... Gen 47:9 6547
And Jacob blessed P ... Gen 47:10 6547
and went out from before P ... Gen 47:10 6547
of Rameses, as P had commanded ... Gen 47:11 6547
our land will be servants unto P ... Gen 47:19 6547
all the land of Egypt for P ... Gen 47:20 6547
had a portion assigned them of P ... Gen 47:22 6547
their portion which P gave them ... Gen 47:22 6547
you this day and your land for P ... Gen 47:23 6547
shall give the fifth part unto P ... Gen 47:24 6547
that P should have the fifth part ... Gen 47:26 6547
Joseph spake unto the house of P ... Gen 50:4 6547
I pray you, in the ears of P ... Gen 50:4 6547
P said, Go up, and bury thy father ... Gen 50:6 6547
him went up all the servants of P ... Gen 50:7 6547
in the sight of P king of Egypt ... Acts 7:10 *5328*
kindred was made known unto P ... Acts 7:13 *5328*
3. Ruler of Egypt during Moses' infancy.
they built for P treasure cities, ... Ex 1:11 6547
And the midwives said unto P ... Ex 1:19 6547
P charged all his people, saying, ... Ex 1:22 6547
the daughter of P came down to ... Ex 2:5 6547
4. Ruler of Egypt during Moses' adulthood.
Now when P heard this thing, he ... Ex 2:15 6547
But Moses fled from the face of P ... Ex 2:15 6547
5. Ruler of Egypt when Moses returned to Egypt.
and I will send thee unto P ... Ex 3:10 6547
Who am I, that I should go unto P ... Ex 3:11 6547
do all those wonders before P ... Ex 4:21 6547
And thou shalt say unto P, Thus ... Ex 4:22 6547
Moses and Aaron went in, and told P ... Ex 5:1 6547
P said, Who is the LORD, that I ... Ex 5:2 6547
P said, Behold, the people of the ... Ex 5:5 6547
P commanded the same day the ... Ex 5:6 6547
the people, saying, Thus saith P ... Ex 5:10 6547
of Israel came and cried unto P ... Ex 5:15 6547
way, as they came forth from P ... Ex 5:20 6547
to be abhorred in the eyes of P ... Ex 5:21 6547
For since I came to P to speak in ... Ex 5:23 6547
thou see what I will do to P ... Ex 6:1 6547
speak unto P king of Egypt, that ... Ex 6:11 6547
how then shall P hear me, who am ... Ex 6:12 6547
unto P king of Egypt, to bring ... Ex 6:13 6547
which spake to P king of Egypt ... Ex 6:27 6547
speak thou unto P king of Egypt ... Ex 6:29 6547
how shall P hearken unto me ... Ex 6:30 6547
See, I have made thee a god to P ... Ex 7:1 6547
thy brother shall speak unto P ... Ex 7:2 6547
But P shall not hearken unto you, ... Ex 7:4 6547
years old, when they spake unto P ... Ex 7:7 6547
When P shall speak unto you, ... Ex 7:9 6547
Take thy rod, and cast it before P ... Ex 7:9 6547
And Moses and Aaron went in unto P ... Ex 7:10 6547
Aaron cast down his rod before P ... Ex 7:10 6547
Then P also called the wise men ... Ex 7:11 6547
Get thee unto P in the morning ... Ex 7:15 6547
in the river, in the sight of P ... Ex 7:20 6547
P turned and went into his house, ... Ex 7:23 6547
LORD spake unto Moses, Go unto P ... Ex 8:1 6547
Then P called for Moses and Aaron, ... Ex 8:8 6547
And Moses said unto P, Glory over ... Ex 8:9 6547
And Moses and Aaron went out from P ... Ex 8:12 6547
which he had brought against P ... Ex 8:12 6547
But when P saw that there was ... Ex 8:15 6547
Then the magicians said unto P ... Ex 8:19 6547
in the morning, and stand before P ... Ex 8:20 6547
of flies into the house of P ... Ex 8:24 6547
P called for Moses and for Aaron, ... Ex 8:25 6547
P said, I will let you go, that ... Ex 8:28 6547
swarms of flies may depart from P ... Ex 8:29 6547
but let not P deal deceitfully ... Ex 8:29 6547
And Moses went out from P, and ... Ex 8:30 6547
the swarms of flies from P ... Ex 8:31 6547
P hardened his heart at this time ... Ex 8:32 6547
said unto Moses, Go in unto P ... Ex 9:1 6547
P sent, and, behold, there was not ... Ex 9:7 6547
And the heart of P was hardened ... Ex 9:7 6547
the heaven in the sight of P ... Ex 9:8 6547
of the furnace, and stood before P ... Ex 9:10 6547
the LORD hardened the heart of P ... Ex 9:12 6547
in the morning, and stand before P ... Ex 9:13 6547
servants of P made his servants ... Ex 9:20 6547
P sent, and called for Moses and ... Ex 9:27 6547
Moses went out of the city from P ... Ex 9:33 6547
when P saw that the rain and the ... Ex 9:34 6547
And the heart of P was hardened ... Ex 9:35 6547
said unto Moses, Go in unto P ... Ex 10:1 6547
And Moses and Aaron came in unto P ... Ex 10:3 6547
himself, and went out from P ... Ex 10:6 6547
Aaron were brought again unto P ... Ex 10:8 6547
Then P called for Moses and Aaron ... Ex 10:16 6547
And he went out from P, and ... Ex 10:18 6547
P called unto Moses, and said, Go ... Ex 10:24 6547
P said unto him, Get thee from me ... Ex 10:28 6547
I bring one plague more upon P ... Ex 11:1 6547
from the firstborn of P that ... Ex 11:5 6547
went out from P in a great anger ... Ex 11:8 6547
P shall not hearken unto you ... Ex 11:9 6547
did all these wonders before P ... Ex 11:10 6547
from the firstborn of P that sat ... Ex 12:29 6547
P rose up in the night, he, and ... Ex 12:30 6547
when P would hardly let us go, ... Ex 13:15 6547
when P had let the people go, ... Ex 13:17 6547
For P will say of the children of ... Ex 14:3 6547
and I will be honoured upon P ... Ex 14:4 6547
and the heart of P and of his ... Ex 14:5 6547
the heart of P king of Egypt ... Ex 14:8 6547
all the horses and chariots of P ... Ex 14:9 6547
when P drew nigh, the children of ... Ex 14:10 6547
and I will get me honour upon P ... Ex 14:17 6547
I have gotten me honour upon P ... Ex 14:18 6547
all the host of P that came into ... Ex 14:28 6547
For the horse of P went in with ... Ex 15:19 6547
delivered me from the sword of P ... Ex 18:4 6547
all that the LORD had done unto P ... Ex 18:8 6547
and out of the hand of P, who ... Ex 18:10 6547
great and sore, upon Egypt, upon P ... Deut 6:22 6547
from the hand of P king of Egypt ... Deut 7:8 6547
what the LORD thy God did unto P ... Deut 7:18 6547
of Egypt unto P the king of Egypt ... Deut 11:3 6547
eyes in the land of Egypt unto P ... Deut 29:2 6547
to do in the land of Egypt to P ... Deut 34:11 6547
and P hardened their hearts ... 1Sa 6:6 6547
under the hand of P king of Egypt ... 2Kin 17:7 6547
shewedst signs and wonders upon P ... Neh 9:10 6547
midst of thee, O Egypt, upon P ... Ps 135:9 6547
But overthrew P and his host in ... Ps 136:15 6547
For the scripture saith unto P ... Rom 9:17 *5328*
6. Ruler of Egypt in Solomon's time.
affinity with P king of Egypt ... 1Kin 3:1 6547
For P king of Egypt had gone up, ... 1Kin 9:16 6547
together with the daughter of P ... 1Kin 11:1 6547
to Egypt, unto P king of Egypt ... 1Kin 11:18 6547
great favour in the sight of P ... 1Kin 11:19 6547
household among the sons of P ... 1Kin 11:20 6547
host was dead, Hadad said to P ... 1Kin 11:21 6547
Then P said unto him, But what ... 1Kin 11:22 6547
brought up the daughter of P out ... 2Chr 8:11 6547
7. Ruler of Egypt in Isaiah's time.
of P is become brutish ... Is 19:11 6547
how say ye unto P, I am the son ... Is 19:11 6547
themselves in the strength of P ... Is 30:2 6547
the strength of P be your shame ... Is 30:3 6547
so is P king of Egypt to all that ... Is 36:6 6547
8. Ruler of Egypt in Jeremiah's time.
so is P king of Egypt unto all ... 2Kin 18:21 6547
gave the silver and the gold to P ... 2Kin 23:35 6547
according to the commandment of P ... 2Kin 23:35 6547
sons of Bithiah the daughter of P ... 1Chr 4:18 6547
P king of Egypt, and his servants, ... Jer 25:19 6547
P king of Egypt is but a noise ... Jer 46:17 6547
punish the multitude of No, and P ... Jer 46:25 6547
even P, and all them that trust in ... Jer 46:25 6547
before that P smote Gaza ... Jer 47:1 6547
Neither shall P with his mighty ... Eze 17:17 6547
thy face against P king of Egypt ... Eze 29:2 6547
P king of Egypt, the great dragon ... Eze 29:3 6547
broken the arm of P king of Egypt ... Eze 30:21 6547
I am against P king of Egypt, and ... Eze 30:22 6547
the arms of P shall fall down ... Eze 30:25 6547
speak unto P king of Egypt, and to ... Eze 31:2 6547
This is P and all his multitude, ... Eze 31:18 6547
a lamentation for P king of Egypt ... Eze 32:2 6547
P shall see them, and shall be ... Eze 32:31 6547
over all his multitude, even P ... Eze 32:31 6547
are slain with the sword, even P ... Eze 32:32 6547

PHARAOH-HOPHRA *(fa'-ra-o-hof'-rah)* {1} *Same as Pharaoh 8.*
I will give P king of Egypt into ... Jer 44:30 6548

PHARAOH-NECHO *(fa'-ra-o-ne'-ko)* {1} See PHARAOH-NECHOH. *Egyptian ruler during Josiah's time.*
the army of P king of Egypt ... Jer 46:2 6549

PHARAOH-NECHOH *(fa'-ra-o-ne'-ko)* {4} See PHARAOH-NECHO. *Same as Pharaoh-necho.*
In his days P king of Egypt went ... 2Kin 23:29 6549
P put him in bands at Riblah in ... 2Kin 23:33 6549
P made Eliakim the son of Josiah ... 2Kin 23:34 6549
his taxation, to give it unto P ... 2Kin 23:35 6549

PHARAOH'S *(fa'-ra-oze)* {48}
the woman was taken into P house ... Gen 12:15 6547
unto Potiphar, an officer of P ... Gen 37:36 6547
he asked P officers that were ... Gen 40:7 6547
And P cup was in my hand ... Gen 40:11 6547
and pressed them into P cup ... Gen 40:11 6547
and I gave the cup into P hand ... Gen 40:11 6547
shalt deliver P cup into his hand ... Gen 40:13 6547
third day, which was P birthday ... Gen 40:20 6547
and he gave the cup into P hand ... Gen 40:21 6547
fame thereof was heard in P house ... Gen 45:16 6547
brought the money into P house ... Gen 47:14 6547
so the land became P ... Gen 47:20 6547
my lord, and we will be P servants ... Gen 47:25 6547
priests only, which became not P ... Gen 47:26 6547
said his sister to P daughter ... Ex 2:7 6547
P daughter said to her, Go ... Ex 2:8 6547
P daughter said unto her, Take ... Ex 2:9 6547
she brought him unto P daughter ... Ex 2:10 6547
which P taskmasters had set over ... Ex 5:14 6547
And I will harden P heart, and ... Ex 7:3 6547
And he hardened P heart, that he ... Ex 7:13 6547
P heart is hardened, he refuseth ... Ex 7:14 6547
P heart was hardened, neither did ... Ex 7:22 6547
P heart was hardened, and he ... Ex 8:19 6547
P servants said unto him, How ... Ex 10:7 6547
were driven out from P presence ... Ex 10:11 6547
But the LORD hardened P heart ... Ex 10:20 6547
But the LORD hardened P heart ... Ex 10:27 6547
Egypt, in the sight of P servants ... Ex 11:3 6547
and the LORD hardened P heart ... Ex 11:10 6547
And I will harden P heart, that he ... Ex 14:4 6547
of the sea, even all P horses ... Ex 14:23 6547
P chariots and his host hath he ... Ex 15:4 6547
We were P bondmen in Egypt ... Deut 6:21 6547
they were in Egypt in P house ... 1Sa 2:27 6547
took P daughter, and brought her ... 1Kin 3:1 6547
made also an house for P daughter ... 1Kin 7:8 6547
But P daughter came up out of the ... 1Kin 9:24 6547
whom Tahpenes weaned in P house ... 1Kin 11:20 6547
Genubath was in P household among ... 1Kin 11:20 6547
a company of horses in P chariots ... Song 1:9 6547
Then P army was come forth out of ... Jer 37:5 6547
P army, which is come forth to ... Jer 37:7 6547
from Jerusalem for fear of P army ... Jer 37:11 6547
the entry of P house in Tahpanhes ... Jer 43:9 6547
but I will break P arms, and he ... Eze 30:24 6547
P daughter took him up, and ... Acts 7:21 *5328*
be called the son of P daughter ... Heb 11:24 *5328*

PHARES *(fa'-rez)* {3} See PHAREZ. *Same as Pharez.*
And Judas begat P and Zara of ... Mt 1:3 *5329*
and P begat Esrom ... Mt 1:3 *5329*
of Esrom, which was the son of P ... Lk 3:33 *5329*

PHAREZ *(fa'-rez)* {12} See PEREZ, PHARES, PHARZITES. *A son of Judah.*
therefore his name was called P ... Gen 38:29 6557
Er, and Onan, and Shelah, and P ... Gen 46:12 6557
And the sons of P were Hezron ... Gen 46:12 6557
of P, the family of the Pharzites ... Num 26:20 6557
And the sons of P were ... Num 26:21 6557
thy house be like the house of P ... Ruth 4:12 6557
these are the generations of P ... Ruth 4:18 6557
P begat Hezron, ... Ruth 4:18 6557
his daughter in law bare him P ... 1Chr 2:4 6557
The sons of P ... 1Chr 2:5 6557
P, Hezron, and Carmi, and Hur, and ... 1Chr 4:1 6557
children of P the son of Judah ... 1Chr 9:4 6557

PHARISAIC See PHARISEES.

PHARISEE *(far'-i-see)* {11} See PHARISEE'S, PHARISEES. *A member of a Jewish sect.*
Thou blind P, cleanse first that ... Mt 23:26 *5330*
Now when the P which had bidden ... Lk 7:39 *5330*
a certain P besought him to dine ... Lk 11:37 *5330*
And when the P saw it, he ... Lk 11:38 *5330*
the one a P, and the other a ... Lk 18:10 *5330*
The P stood and prayed thus with ... Lk 18:11 *5330*
there up one in the council, a P ... Acts 5:34 *5330*
I am a P, the son of a P ... Acts 23:6 *5330*
sect of our religion I lived a P ... Acts 26:5 *5330*
as touching the law, a P ... Phil 3:5 *5330*

PHARISEE'S *(far'-i-seze)* {2}
And he went into the P house ... Lk 7:36 *5330*
Jesus sat at meat in the P house ... Lk 7:37 *5330*

PHARISEES *(far'-i-seze)* {86} See PHARISEES'. *A Jewish sect.*
But when he saw many of the P ... Mt 3:7 *5330*
righteousness of the scribes and P ... Mt 5:20 *5330*
And when the P saw it, they said ... Mt 9:11 *5330*
the P fast oft, but thy disciples ... Mt 9:14 *5330*
But the P said, He casteth out ... Mt 9:34 *5330*
But when the P saw it, they said ... Mt 12:2 *5330*
Then the P went out, and held a ... Mt 12:14 *5330*
But when the P heard it, they ... Mt 12:24 *5330*
of the P answered, saying, Master ... Mt 12:38 *5330*
Then came to Jesus scribes and P ... Mt 15:1 *5330*
thou that the P were offended ... Mt 15:12 *5330*
The P also with the Sadducees ... Mt 16:1 *5330*
and beware of the leaven of the P ... Mt 16:6 *5330*
beware of the leaven of the P ... Mt 16:11 *5330*

but of the doctrine of the *P* .... Mt 16:12 5330
The *P* also came unto him, ... Mt 19:3 5330
P had heard his parables, they .... Mt 21:45 5330
Then went the *P*, and took counsel .... Mt 22:15 5330
But when the *P* had heard that he .... Mt 22:34 5330
While the *P* were gathered .... Mt 22:41 5330
and the *P* sit in Moses' seat .... Mt 23:2 5330
But woe unto you, scribes and *P* .... Mt 23:13 5330
Woe unto you, scribes and *P* .... Mt 23:14 5330
Woe unto you, scribes and *P* .... Mt 23:15 5330
Woe unto you, scribes and *P* .... Mt 23:23 5330
Woe unto you, scribes and *P* .... Mt 23:25 5330
Woe unto you, scribes and *P* .... Mt 23:27 5330
Woe unto you, scribes and *P* .... Mt 23:29 5330
P came together unto Pilate, ... Mt 27:62 5330
P saw him eat with publicans and .... Mk 2:16 5330
of John and of the *P* used to fast .... Mk 2:18 5330
of John and of the *P* fast, but thy .... Mk 2:18 5330
the *P* said unto him, Behold, why .... Mk 2:24 5330
the *P* went forth, and straightway .... Mk 3:6 5330
Then came together unto him the *P* .... Mk 7:1 5330
For the *P*, and all the Jews, ... Mk 7:3 5330
Then the *P* and scribes asked him, ... Mk 7:5 5330
the *P* came forth, and began to .... Mk 8:11 5330
beware of the leaven of the *P* .... Mk 8:15 5330
the *P* came to him, and asked him, ... Mk 10:2 5330
send unto him certain of the *P* .... Mk 12:13 5330
was teaching, that there were *P* .... Lk 5:17 5330
the *P* began to reason, saying, ... Lk 5:21 5330
P murmured against his disciples, ... Lk 5:30 5330
likewise the disciples of the *P* .... Lk 5:33 5330
certain of the *P* said unto them .... Lk 6:2 5330
P watched him, whether he would .... Lk 6:7 5330
But the *P* and lawyers rejected the .... Lk 7:30 5330
one of the *P* desired him that he .... Lk 7:36 5330
Now do ye *P* make clean the .... Lk 11:39 5330
But woe unto you, *P* .... Lk 11:42 5330
Woe unto you, *P* .... Lk 11:43 5330
Woe unto you, scribes and *P* .... Lk 11:44 5330
and the *P* began to urge him .... Lk 11:53 5330
Beware ye of the leaven of the *P* .... Lk 12:1 5330
day there came certain of the *P* .... Lk 13:31 5330
the house of one of the chief *P* .... Lk 14:1 5330
spake unto the lawyers and *P* .... Lk 14:3 5330
And the *P* and scribes murmured, ... Lk 15:2 5330
the *P* also, who were covetous, ... Lk 16:14 5330
And when he was demanded of the *P* .... Lk 17:20 5330
some of the *P* from among the .... Lk 19:39 5330
which were sent were of the *P* .... Jn 1:24 5330
There was a man of the *P*, named .... Jn 3:1 5330
the *P* had heard that Jesus made .... Jn 4:1 5330
The *P* heard that the people .... Jn 7:32 5330
and the *P* and the chief priests .... Jn 7:32 5330
to the chief priests and *P* .... Jn 7:45 5330
Then answered them the *P*, Are ye .... Jn 7:47 5330
or of the *P* believed on him .... Jn 7:48 5330
P brought unto him a woman taken .... Jn 8:3 5330
The *P* therefore said unto him, ... Jn 8:13 5330
They brought to the *P* him that .... Jn 9:13 5330
Then again the *P* also asked him .... Jn 9:15 5330
Therefore said some of the *P* .... Jn 9:16 5330
some of the *P* which were with him .... Jn 9:40 5330
of them went their ways to the *P* .... Jn 11:46 5330
the *P* a council, and said, What do .... Jn 11:47 5330
the *P* had given a commandment, ... Jn 11:57 5330
The *P* therefore said among .... Jn 12:19 5330
but because of the *P* they did not .... Jn 12:42 5330
from the chief priests and *P* .... Jn 18:3 5330
the sect of the *P* which believed .... Acts 15:5 5330
were Sadducees, and the other *P* .... Acts 23:6 5330
arose a dissension between the *P* .... Acts 23:7 5330
but the *P* confess both .... Acts 23:8 5330

PHARISEES' *(far'-i-seez)* {1}
that were of the *P* part arose .... Acts 23:9 5330

PHAROSH *(fa'-rosh)* {1} *A family of exiles.*
of Shechaniah, of the sons of *P* .... Ezr 8:3 6551

PHARPAR *(far'-par)* {1} *A river near Damascus.*
Are not Abana and *P*, rivers of 2Kin 5:12 6554

PHARZITES *(far'-zites)* {1} *Descendants of Pharez.*
of Pharez, the family of the *P* .... Num 26:20 6558

PHASEAH *(fa-se'-ah)* {1} See PASEAH. *A family of exiles.*
of Uzza, the children of *P* .... Neh 7:51 6454

PHEBE *(fe'-be)* {2} *A Christian acquaintance of Paul.*
I commend unto you *P* our sister .... Rom 16:1 5402
sent by *P* servant of the church .... Rom *s* 5402

PHENICE *(fe-ni'-se)* {3} See PHENICIA.
1. Same as Phenecia.
Stephen travelled as far as *P* .... Acts 11:19 5403
the church, they passed through *P* .... Acts 15:3 5403
2. A harbor on Crete.
any means they might attain to *P* .... Acts 27:12 5405

PHENICIA *(fe-nish'-e-ah)* {1} See PHENICE. *Coastal region of northern Palestine.*
a ship sailing over unto *P* .... Acts 21:2 5403

PHICHOL *The commander of Abimelech's army.*
P the chief captain of his host .... Gen 21:22 6369
P the chief captain of his host, ... Gen 21:32 6369
P the chief captain of his army .... Gen 26:26 6369

PHICOL *(fi'-col)* {3} See PHICHOL. *A Philistine commander.*

PHILADELPHIA *(fil-a-del'-fe-ah)* {2} *A city in Lydia in Asia Minor.*
and unto Sardis, and unto *P* .... Rev 1:11 5359
angel of the church in *P* write .... Rev 3:7 5359

PHILEMON *(fi-le'-mon)* {2} *A recipient of a New Testament epistle.*
unto *P* our dearly beloved, and .... Philem 1 5371
Written from Rome to *P*, by .... Philem *s* 5371

PHILETUS *(fi-le'tus)* {1} *A false Christian teacher.*
of whom is Hymenaeus and *P* 2Ti 2:17 5372

PHILIP *(fil'-ip)* {33} See PHILIP'S.
1. An apostle.
P, and Bartholomew .... Mt 10:3 5376
And Andrew, and *P*, and Bartholomew, .. Mk 3:18 5376
his brother, James and John, *P* .... Lk 6:14 5376
forth into Galilee, and findeth *P* .... Jn 1:43 5376
Now *P* was of Bethsaida, the city .... Jn 1:44 5376
P findeth Nathanael, and saith .... Jn 1:45 5376
P saith unto him, Come and see .... Jn 1:46 5376
him, Before that *P* called thee .... Jn 1:48 5376
come unto him, he saith unto *P* .... Jn 6:5 5376
P answered him, Two hundred .... Jn 6:7 5376
The same came therefore to *P* .... Jn 12:21 5376
P cometh and telleth Andrew .... Jn 12:22 5376
and again Andrew and *P* tell Jesus .... Jn 12:22 5376
P saith unto him, Lord, shew us .... Jn 14:8 5376
and yet hast thou not known me, *P* .... Jn 14:9 5376
and James, and John, and Andrew, *P* .... Acts 1:13 5376
2. A son of Herod the Great.
his brother *P* tetrarch of Ituraea .... Lk 3:1 5376
3. The evangelist.
faith and of the Holy Ghost, and *P* .... Acts 6:5 5376
Then *P* went down to the city of .... Acts 8:5 5376
unto those things which *P* spake .... Acts 8:6 5376
But when they believed *P* .... Acts 8:12 5376
was baptized, he continued with *P* .... Acts 8:13 5376
angel of the Lord spake unto *P* .... Acts 8:26 5376
Then the Spirit said unto *P* .... Acts 8:29 5376
P ran thither to him, and heard .... Acts 8:30 5376
he desired *P* that he would come .... Acts 8:31 5376
And the eunuch answered *P*, and said .... Acts 8:34 5376
Then *P* opened his mouth, and began .... Acts 8:35 5376
P said, If thou believest with .... Acts 8:37 5376
down both into the water, both *P* .... Acts 8:38 5376
Spirit of the Lord caught away *P* .... Acts 8:39 5376
But *P* was found at Azotus .... Acts 8:40 5376
the house of *P* the evangelist .... Acts 21:8 5376

PHILIPPI *(fil-ip'-pi)* {8} See PHILIPPIANS.
1. A town in northern Palestine.
into the coasts of Caesarea *P* .... Mt 16:13 5375
into the towns of Caesarea *P* .... Mk 8:27 5375
2. A Macedonian city.
And from thence to *P*, which is the .... Acts 16:12 5375
we sailed away from *P* after the .... Acts 20:6 5375
was written from *P* by Stephanus .... 1Cor *s* 5375
Corinthians was written from *P* .... 2Cor *s* 5375
in Christ Jesus which are at *P* .... Phil 1:1 5375
entreated, as ye know, at *P* 1Th 2:2 5375

PHILIPPIANS *(fil-ip'-pe-uns)* {2} *Residents of Philippi 2.*
Now ye *P* know also, that in the .... Phil 4:15 5374
It was written to the *P* from Rome .... Phil *s*

PHILIP'S *(fil'-ips)* {3} *Refers to Philip 2.*
sake, his brother *P* wife .... Mt 14:3 5376
sake, his brother *P* wife .... Mk 6:17 5376
for Herodias his brother *P* wife .... Lk 3:19 5376

PHILISTIA *(fil-is'-te-ah)* {3} See PALESTINE, PHILISTINE. *Land of the Philistines.*
P, triumph thou because of me .... Ps 60:8 6429
behold *P*, and Tyre, with Ethiopia .... Ps 87:4 6429
over *P* will I triumph .... Ps 108:9 6429

PHILISTIM *(fil-is'-tim)* {1} See PHILISTINES. *Descendents of Casluhim.*
and Casluhim, (out of whom came *P* .... Gen 10:14 6430

PHILISTINE *(fil-is'-tin)* {33} See PHILISTINES. *An inhabitant of Philistia.*
am not I a *P*, and ye servants to 1Sa 17:8 6430
the *P* said, I defy the armies of 1Sa 17:10 6430
Israel heard those words of the *P* 1Sa 17:11 6430
the *P* drew near morning and 1Sa 17:16 6430
the *P* of Gath, Goliath by name, ... 1Sa 17:23 6430
to the man that killeth this *P* 1Sa 17:26 6430
for who is this uncircumcised *P* 1Sa 17:26 6430
will go and fight with this *P* 1Sa 17:32 6430
against this *P* to fight with him 1Sa 17:33 6430
this uncircumcised *P* shall be as 1Sa 17:36 6430
me out of the hand of this *P* 1Sa 17:37 6430
and he drew near to the *P* 1Sa 17:40 6430
the *P* came on and drew near unto 1Sa 17:41 6430
when the *P* looked about, and saw 1Sa 17:42 6430
the *P* said unto David, Am I a dog 1Sa 17:43 6430
the *P* cursed David by his gods 1Sa 17:43 6430
the *P* said to David, Come to me, ... 1Sa 17:44 6430
Then said David to the *P*, Thou 1Sa 17:45 6430
it came to pass, when the *P* arose 1Sa 17:48 6430
ran toward the army to meet the *P* 1Sa 17:48 6430
smote the *P* in his forehead, that 1Sa 17:49 6430
prevailed over the *P* with a sling 1Sa 17:50 6430
and with a stone, and smote the *P* 1Sa 17:50 6430
David ran, and stood upon the *P* 1Sa 17:51 6430
And David took the head of the *P* 1Sa 17:54 6430
saw David go forth against the *P* 1Sa 17:55 6430
from the slaughter of the *P* 1Sa 17:57 6430
the head of the *P* in his hand 1Sa 17:57 6430
from the slaughter of the *P* 1Sa 18:6 6430
life in his hand, and slew the *P* 1Sa 19:5 6430
said, The sword of Goliath the *P* 1Sa 21:9 6430
him the sword of Goliath the *P* 1Sa 22:10 6430
succoured him, and smote the *P* 2Sa 21:17 6430

PHILISTINES *(fil-is'-tinz)* {251} See PHILISTIM, PHILISTINES'.
returned into the land of the *P* .... Gen 21:32 6430
king of the *P* unto Gerar .... Gen 26:1 6430
of the *P* looked out at a window .... Gen 26:8 6430
and the *P* envied him .... Gen 26:14 6430
the *P* had stopped them, and filled .... Gen 26:15 6430
for the *P* had stopped them after .... Gen 26:18 6430
the way of the land of the *P* .... Ex 13:17 6430
sea even unto the sea of the *P* .... Ex 23:31 6430
all the borders of the *P*, and all .... Josh 13:2 6430
five lords of the *P* .... Josh 13:3 6430
Namely, five lords of the *P* .... Judg 3:3 6430
which slew of the *P* six hundred .... Judg 3:31 6430
of Ammon, and the gods of the *P* .... Judg 10:6 6430
sold them into the hands of the *P* .... Judg 10:7 6430
children of Ammon, and from the *P* .... Judg 10:11 6430
the hand of the *P* forty years .... Judg 13:1 6430
Israel out of the hand of the *P* .... Judg 13:5 6430
Timnath of the daughters of the *P* .... Judg 14:1 6430
Timnath of the daughters of the *P* .... Judg 14:2 6430
a wife of the uncircumcised *P* .... Judg 14:3 6430
sought an occasion against the *P* .... Judg 14:4 6430
for at that time the *P* had .... Judg 14:4 6430
I be more blameless than the *P* .... Judg 15:3 6430
into the standing corn of the *P* .... Judg 15:5 6430
Then the *P* said, Who hath done .... Judg 15:6 6430
the *P* came up, and burnt her and .... Judg 15:6 6430
Then the *P* went up, and pitched in .... Judg 15:9 6430
not that the *P* are rulers over us .... Judg 15:11 6430
thee into the hand of the *P* .... Judg 15:12 6430
the *P* shouted against him .... Judg 15:14 6430
in the days of the *P* twenty years .... Judg 15:20 6430
lords of the *P* came up unto her .... Judg 16:5 6430
Then the lords of the *P* brought .... Judg 16:8 6430
The *P* be upon thee, Samson .... Judg 16:9 6430
The *P* be upon thee, Samson .... Judg 16:12 6430
The *P* be upon thee, Samson .... Judg 16:14 6430
and called for the lords of the *P* .... Judg 16:18 6430
lords of the *P* came up unto her .... Judg 16:18 6430
The *P* be upon thee, Samson .... Judg 16:20 6430
But the *P* took him, and put out .... Judg 16:21 6430
Then the lords of the *P* gathered .... Judg 16:23 6430
all the lords of the *P* were there .... Judg 16:27 6430
avenged of the *P* for my two eyes .... Judg 16:28 6430
said, Let me die with the *P* .... Judg 16:30 6430
went out against the *P* to battle 1Sa 4:1 6430
and the *P* pitched in Aphek 1Sa 4:1 6430
the *P* put themselves in array 1Sa 4:2 6430
Israel was smitten before the *P* 1Sa 4:2 6430
smitten us to day before the *P* 1Sa 4:3 6430
when the *P* heard the noise of the 1Sa 4:6 6430
the *P* were afraid, for they said, ... 1Sa 4:7 6430
quit yourselves like men, O ye *P* 1Sa 4:9 6430
the *P* fought, and Israel was 1Sa 4:10 6430
said, Israel is fled before the *P* 1Sa 4:17 6430
the *P* took the ark of God, and 1Sa 5:1 6430
When the *P* took the ark of God, ... 1Sa 5:2 6430
all the lords of the *P* unto them 1Sa 5:8 6430
together all the lords of the *P* 1Sa 5:11 6430
the country of the *P* seven months 1Sa 6:1 6430
the *P* called for the priests and 1Sa 6:2 6430
the number of the lords of the *P* 1Sa 6:4 6430
the lords of the *P* went after 1Sa 6:12 6430
five lords of the *P* had seen it 1Sa 6:16 6430
the *P* returned for a trespass 1Sa 6:17 6430
the *P* belonging to the five lords 1Sa 6:18 6430
The *P* have brought again the ark 1Sa 6:21 6430
you out of the hand of the *P* 1Sa 7:3 6430
when the *P* heard that the 1Sa 7:7 6430
the lords of the *P* went up 1Sa 7:7 6430
it, they were afraid of the *P* 1Sa 7:7 6430
save us out of the hand of the *P* 1Sa 7:8 6430
the *P* drew near to battle against 1Sa 7:10 6430
thunder on that day upon the *P* 1Sa 7:10 6430
out of Mizpeh, and pursued the *P* 1Sa 7:11 6430
So the *P* were subdued, and they 1Sa 7:13 6430
the *P* all the days of Samuel 1Sa 7:13 6430
the cities which the *P* had taken 1Sa 7:14 6430
deliver out of the hands of the *P* 1Sa 7:14 6430
people out of the hand of the *P* 1Sa 9:16 6430
where is the garrison of the *P* 1Sa 10:5 6430
Hazor, and into the hand of the *P* 1Sa 12:9 6430
of the *P* that was in Geba 1Sa 13:3 6430
and the *P* heard of it 1Sa 13:3 6430
had smitten a garrison of the *P* 1Sa 13:4 6430
was had in abomination with the *P* 1Sa 13:4 6430
the *P* gathered themselves 1Sa 13:5 6430
that the *P* gathered themselves 1Sa 13:11 6430
The *P* will come down now upon me 1Sa 13:12 6430
but the *P* encamped in Michmash 1Sa 13:16 6430
camp of the *P* in three companies 1Sa 13:17 6430
for the *P* said, Lest the Hebrews 1Sa 13:19 6430
the Israelites went down to the *P* 1Sa 13:20 6430
the garrison of the *P* went out to 1Sa 13:23 6430
unto the garrison of the *P* 1Sa 14:1 6430
the *P* said, Behold, the Hebrews 1Sa 14:11 6430
was in the host of the *P* went on 1Sa 14:19 6430
were with the *P* before that time 1Sa 14:21 6430
when they heard that the *P* fled 1Sa 14:22 6430
greater slaughter among the *P* 1Sa 14:30 6430
they smote the *P* that day from 1Sa 14:31 6430
us go down after the *P* by night 1Sa 14:36 6430

God, Shall I go down after the *P* 1Sa 14:37 6430
Saul went up from following the *P* 1Sa 14:46 6430
the *P* went to their own place 1Sa 14:46 6430
kings of Zobah, and against the *P* 1Sa 14:47 6430
the *P* all the days of Saul 1Sa 14:52 6430
Now the *P* gathered together their 1Sa 17:1 6430
the battle in array against the *P* 1Sa 17:2 6430
the *P* stood on a mountain on the 1Sa 17:3 6430
champion out of the camp of the *P* 1Sa 17:4 6430
of Elah, fighting with the *P* 1Sa 17:19 6430
the *P* had put the battle in array 1Sa 17:21 6430
name, out of the armies of the *P* 1Sa 17:23 6430
P this day unto the fowls of the 1Sa 17:46 6430
when the *P* saw their champion was 1Sa 17:51 6430
and shouted, and pursued the *P* 1Sa 17:52 6430
the wounded of the *P* fell down by 1Sa 17:52 6430
returned from chasing after the *P* 1Sa 17:53 6430
let the hand of the *P* be upon him 1Sa 18:17 6430
hand of the *P* may be against him 1Sa 18:21 6430
but an hundred foreskins of the *P* 1Sa 18:25 6430
David fall by the hand of the *P* 1Sa 18:25 6430
slew of the *P* two hundred men 1Sa 18:27 6430
the princes of the *P* went forth 1Sa 18:30 6430
went out, and fought with the *P* 1Sa 19:8 6430
the *P* fight against Keilah, and 1Sa 23:1 6430
Shall I go and smite these *P* 1Sa 23:2 6430
unto David, Go, and smite the *P* 1Sa 23:2 6430
against the armies of the *P* 1Sa 23:3 6430
deliver the *P* into thine hand 1Sa 23:4 6430
to Keilah, and fought with the *P* 1Sa 23:5 6430
for the *P* have invaded the land 1Sa 23:27 6430
David, and went against the *P* 1Sa 23:28 6430
was returned from following the *P* 1Sa 24:1 6430
escape into the land of the *P* 1Sa 27:1 6430
country of the *P* was a full year 1Sa 27:7 6430
dwelleth in the country of the *P* 1Sa 27:11 6430
that the *P* gathered their armies 1Sa 28:1 6430
the *P* gathered themselves 1Sa 28:4 6430
when Saul saw the host of the *P* 1Sa 28:5 6430
for the *P* make war against me, and 1Sa 28:15 6430
with thee into the hand of the *P* 1Sa 28:19 6430
of Israel into the hand of the *P* 1Sa 28:19 6430
Now the *P* gathered together all 1Sa 29:1 6430
the lords of the *P* passed on by 1Sa 29:2 6430
Then said the princes of the *P* 1Sa 29:3 6430
said unto the princes of the *P* 1Sa 29:3 6430
the princes of the *P* were wroth 1Sa 29:4 6430
princes of the *P* said unto him 1Sa 29:4 6430
displease not the lords of the *P* 1Sa 29:7 6430
the princes of the *P* have said 1Sa 29:9 6430
to return into the land of the *P* 1Sa 29:11 6430
And the *P* went up to Jezreel 1Sa 29:11 6430
taken out of the land of the *P* 1Sa 30:16 6430
Now the *P* fought against Israel 1Sa 31:1 6430
of Israel fled from before the *P* 1Sa 31:1 6430
the *P* followed hard upon Saul and 1Sa 31:2 6430
the *P* slew Jonathan, and Abinadab, 1Sa 31:2 6430
the *P* came and dwelt in them 1Sa 31:7 6430
when the *P* came to strip the 1Sa 31:8 6430
the land of the *P* round about 1Sa 31:9 6430
that which the *P* had done to Saul 1Sa 31:11 6430
the daughters of the *P* rejoice 2Sa 1:20 6430
for an hundred foreskins of the *P* 2Sa 3:14 6430
Israel out of the hand of the *P* 2Sa 3:18 6430
But when the *P* heard that they 2Sa 5:17 6430
all the *P* came up to seek David 2Sa 5:17 6430
The *P* also came and spread 2Sa 5:18 6430
saying, Shall I go up to the *P* 2Sa 5:19 6430
deliver the *P* into thine hand 2Sa 5:19 6430
the *P* came up yet again, and 2Sa 5:22 6430
thee, to smite the host of the *P* 2Sa 5:24 6430
smote the *P* from Geba until thou 2Sa 5:25 6430
to pass, that David smote the *P* 2Sa 8:1 6430
out of the hand of the *P* 2Sa 8:1 6430
children of Ammon, and of the *P* 2Sa 8:12 6430
us out of the hand of the *P* 2Sa 19:9 6430
where the *P* had hanged them 2Sa 21:12 6430
when the *P* had slain Saul in 2Sa 21:12 6430
Moreover the *P* had yet war again 2Sa 21:15 6430
with him, and fought against the *P* 2Sa 21:15 6430
again a battle with the *P* at Gob 2Sa 21:18 6430
again a battle in Gob with the *P* 2Sa 21:19 6430
when they defied the *P* that were 2Sa 23:9 6430
smote the *P* until his hand was 2Sa 23:10 6430
the *P* were gathered together into 2Sa 23:11 6430
and the people fled from the *P* 2Sa 23:11 6430
and defended it, and slew the *P* 2Sa 23:12 6430
the troop of the *P* pitched in the 2Sa 23:13 6430
the garrison of the *P* was then in 2Sa 23:14 6430
brake through the host of the *P* 2Sa 23:16 6430
the river unto the land of the *P* 1Kin 4:21 6430
which belonged to the *P* 1Kin 15:27 6430
which belonged to the *P* 1Kin 16:15 6430
in the land of the *P* seven years 2Kin 8:2 6430
returned out of the land of the *P* 2Kin 8:3 6430
He smote the *P*, even unto Gaza 2Kin 18:8 6430
and Casluhim, (of whom came the *P* 1Chr 1:12 6430
Now the *P* fought against Israel 1Chr 10:1 6430
of Israel fled from before the *P* 1Chr 10:1 6430
the *P* followed hard after Saul, 1Chr 10:2 6430
the *P* slew Jonathan, and Abinadab, 1Chr 10:2 6430
the *P* came and dwelt in them 1Chr 10:7 6430
when the *P* came to strip the 1Chr 10:8 6430
the land of the *P* round about 1Chr 10:9 6430
all that the *P* had done to Saul 1Chr 10:11 6430
there the *P* were gathered 1Chr 11:13 6430
the people fled from before the *P* 1Chr 11:13 6430
and delivered it, and slew the *P* 1Chr 11:14 6430
the host of the *P* encamped in the 1Chr 11:15 6430
brake through the host of the *P* 1Chr 11:18 6430
when he came with the *P* against 1Chr 12:19 6430
for the lords of the *P* upon 1Chr 12:19 6430
when the *P* heard that David was 1Chr 14:8 6430
all the *P* went up to seek David 1Chr 14:8 6430
the *P* came and spread themselves 1Chr 14:9 6430
Shall I go up against the *P* 1Chr 14:10 6430
the *P* yet again spread themselves 1Chr 14:13 6430
thee to smite the host of the *P* 1Chr 14:15 6430
the *P* from Gibeon even to Gazer 1Chr 14:16 6430
to pass, that David smote the *P* 1Chr 18:1 6430
towns out of the hand of the *P* 1Chr 18:1 6430
children of Ammon, and from the *P* 1Chr 18:11
arose war at Gezer with the *P* 1Chr 20:4 6430
And there was war again with the *P* 1Chr 20:5 6430
river even unto the land of the *P* 2Chr 9:26 6430
Also some of the *P* brought 2Chr 17:11 6430
Jehoram the spirit of the *P* 2Chr 21:16 6430
forth and warred against the *P* 2Chr 26:6 6430
about Ashdod, and among the *P* 2Chr 26:6 6430
And God helped him against the *P* 2Chr 26:7 6430
The *P* also had invaded the cities 2Chr 28:18 6430
when the *P* took him in Gath Ps 56:*t* 6430
the *P* with the inhabitants of Ps 83:7 6430
and are soothsayers like the *P* Is 2:6 6430
Syrians before, and the *P* behind Is 9:12 6430
of the *P* toward the west Is 11:14 6430
the kings of the land of the *P* Jer 25:20 6430
the prophet against the *P* Jer 47:1 6430
that cometh to spoil all the *P* Jer 47:4 6430
for the LORD will spoil the *P* Jer 47:4 6430
hate thee, the daughters of the *P* Eze 16:27 6430
about her, the daughters of the *P* Eze 16:57 6430
Because the *P* have dealt by Eze 25:15 6430
stretch out mine hand upon the *P* Eze 25:16 6430
the remnant of the *P* shall perish Amos 1:8 6430
then go down to Gath of the *P* Amos 6:2 6430
the *P* from Caphtor, and the Amos 9:7 6430
and they of the plain the *P* Obad 19 6430
O Canaan, the land of the *P* Zeph 2:5 6430
I will cut off the pride of the *P* Zec 9:6 6430

PHILISTINES' *(fil-is'-tinz)* {4}
sojourned in the *P* land many days Gen 21:34 6430
let us go over to the *P* garrison 1Sa 14:1 6430
to go over unto the *P* garrison 1Sa 14:4 6430
the *P* garrison was then at 1Chr 11:16 6430

PHILOLOGUS *(fil-ol'-o-gus)* {1} *A Christian in Rome.*
Salute *P*, and Julia, Nereus, and Rom 16:15 *5378*

PHILOSOPHERS {1}
Then certain *p* of the Epicureans, Acts 17:18 *5386*

PHILOSOPHY {1}
lest any man spoil you through *p* Col 2:8 *5385*

PHINEHAS *(fin'-e-has)* {17} See PHINEHAS'.
1. A son of Eleazar.
and she bare him *P* Ex 6:25 6372
And when *P*, the son of Eleazar, Num 25:7 6372
P, the son of Eleazar, the son of Num 25:11 6372
P the son of Eleazar the priest, Num 31:6 6372
P the son of Eleazar the priest, Josh 22:13 6372
when *P* the priest, and the princes Josh 22:30 6372
P the son of Eleazar the priest Josh 22:31 6372
P the son of Eleazar the priest, Josh 22:32 6372
hill that pertained to *P* his son Josh 24:33 6372
And *P*, the son of Eleazar, the son Judg 20:28 6372
Eleazar begat *P* 1Chr 6:4 6372
P begat Abishua 1Chr 6:4 6372
P his son, Abishua his son, 1Chr 6:50 6372
P the son of Eleazar was the 1Chr 9:20 6372
The son of Abishua, the son of *P* Ezr 7:5 6372
Of the sons of *P* Ezr 8:2 6372
Then stood up *P*, and executed Ps 106:30 6372
2. A son of Eli.
the two sons of Eli, Hophni and *P* 1Sa 1:3 6372
upon thy two sons, on Hophni and *P* 1Sa 2:34 6372
the two sons of Eli, Hophni and *P* 1Sa 4:4 6372
the two sons of Eli, Hophni and *P* 1Sa 4:11 6372
and thy two sons also, Hophni and *P* 1Sa 4:17 6372
I-chabod's brother, the son of *P* 1Sa 14:3 6372
3. Father of Eleazar.
with him was Eleazar the son of *P* Ezr 8:33 6372

PHINEHAS' *(fin'-e-has)* {1} *Refers to Phinehas 2.*
P wife, was with child, near to 1Sa 4:19 6372

PHLEGON *(fle'-gon)* {1} *A Christian in Rome.*
Salute Asyncritus, *P*, Hermas, Rom 16:14 *5393*

PHOENIX See PHENICE.

PHRYGIA *(frij'-e-ah)* {4} *A Roman province in Asia Minor.*
P, and Pamphylia, in Egypt, and in Acts 2:10 *5435*
when they had gone throughout *P* Acts 16:6 *5435*
P in order, strengthening all the Acts 18:23 *5435*
the chiefest city of *P* Pacatiana 1Ti *s* *5435*

PHURAH *(fu'-rah)* {2} *A servant of Gideon.*
go thou with *P* thy servant down Judg 7:10 6513
Then went he down with *P* his Judg 7:11 6513

PHUT *(fut)* {2} See PUT.
1. A son of Ham.
and Mizraim, and *P*, and Canaan Gen 10:6 6316
2. Land of Phut's descendants.
of *P* were in thine army, thy men Eze 27:10 6316

PHUVAH *(fu'-vah)* {1} See PUAH. *A son of Issachar.*
Tola, and *P*, and Job, and Shimron Gen 46:13 6312

PHYGELLUS *(fi-jel'-lus)* {1} *An unfaithful Christian.*
of whom are *P* and Hermogenes 2Ti 1:15 *5436*

PHYGELUS See PHYGELLUS.

PHYLACTERIES {1}
they make broad their *p*, and Mt 23:5 *5440*

PHYSICIAN {6}
is there no *p* there Jer 8:22 7495
They that be whole need not a *p* Mt 9:12 *2395*
are whole have no need of the *p* Mk 2:17 *2395*
say unto me this proverb, *P* Lk 4:23 *2395*
They that are whole need not a *p* Lk 5:31 *2395*
Luke, the beloved *p*, and Demas, Col 4:14 *2395*

PHYSICIANS {6}
the *p* to embalm his father Gen 50:2 7495
and the *p* embalmed Israel Gen 50:2 7495
not to the LORD, but to the *p* 2Chr 16:12 7495
of lies, ye are all *p* of no value Job 13:4 7495
suffered many things of many *p* Mk 5:26 *2395*
had spent all her living upon *p* Lk 8:43 *2395*

PI-BESETH {1} A city in Egypt.
of *P* shall fall by the sword Eze 30:17 6364

PICK {1}
of the valley shall *p* it out Prov 30:17 5365

PICTURES {3}
you, and destroy all their *p* Num 33:52 4906
apples of gold in *p* of silver Prov 25:11 4906
Tarshish, and upon all pleasant *p* Is 2:16 7914

PIECE {43}
laid each *p* one against another Gen 15:10 1335
beaten out of one *p* made he them Ex 37:7 4749
of a whole *p* shalt thou make them Num 10:2
a certain woman cast a *p* of a Judg 9:53 6400
crouch to him for a *p* of silver 1Sa 2:36 95
that I may eat a *p* of bread 1Sa 2:36 6595
they gave him a *p* of a cake of 1Sa 30:12 6400
a good *p* of flesh, and a flagon of 2Sa 6:19 829
did not a woman cast a *p* of a 2Sa 11:21 6400
where was a *p* of ground full of 2Sa 23:11 2513
mar every good *p* of land with 2Kin 3:19 2513
on every good *p* of land cast 2Kin 3:25 2513
a good *p* of flesh, and a flagon of 1Chr 16:3 829
Pahath-moab, repaired the other *p* Neh 3:11 4060
another *p* over against the going Neh 3:19 4060
earnestly repaired the other *p* Neh 3:20 4060
Urijah the son of Koz another *p* Neh 3:21 4060
the son of Henadad another *p* Neh 3:24 4060
the Tekoites repaired another *p* Neh 3:27 4060
sixth son of Zalaph, another *p* Neh 3:30 4060
as hard as a *p* of the nether Job 41:24 6400
man also gave him a *p* of money Job 42:11
a man is brought to a *p* of bread Prov 6:26 3603
for for a *p* of bread that man Prov 28:21 6595
thy temples are like a *p* of a Song 4:3 6400
As a *p* of a pomegranate are thy Song 6:7 6400
a *p* of bread out of the bakers' Jer 37:21 3603
into it, even every good *p* Eze 24:4 5409
bring it out *p* by *p* Eze 24:6 5409
lion two legs, or a *p* of an ear Amos 3:12 915
one *p* was rained upon Amos 4:7
the *p* whereupon it rained not Amos 4:7
No man putteth a *p* of new cloth Mt 9:16 *1915*
thou shalt find a *p* of money Mt 17:27
No man also seweth a *p* of new Mk 2:21 *1915*
else the new *p* that filled it up Mk 2:21 *4138*
No man putteth a *p* of a new Lk 5:36 *1915*
the *p* that was taken out of the Lk 5:36 *1915*
him, I have bought a *p* of ground Lk 14:18
of silver, if she lose one *p* Lk 15:8 *1406*
have found the *p* which I had lost Lk 15:9 *1406*
they gave him a *p* of a broiled Lk 24:42 *3313*

PIECES {121}
lamp that passed between those *p* Gen 15:17 1506
brother a thousand *p* of silver Gen 20:16
father, for an hundred *p* of money Gen 33:19
for twenty *p* of silver Gen 37:28
Joseph is without doubt rent in *p* Gen 37:33
and I said, Surely he is torn in *p* Gen 44:28
he gave three hundred *p* of silver Gen 45:22
LORD, hath dashed in *p* the enemy Ex 15:6
If it be torn in *p*, then let him Ex 22:13
And thou shalt cut the ram in *p* Ex 29:17 5409
his legs, and put them unto his *p* Ex 29:17 5409
offering, and cut it into his *p* Lev 1:6 5409
And he shall cut it into his *p* Lev 1:12 5409
Thou shalt part it in *p*, and pour Lev 2:6 6595
the baken *p* of the meat offering Lev 6:21 6595
And he cut the ram into *p* Lev 8:20 5409
and Moses burnt the head, and the *p* Lev 8:20 5409
unto him, with the *p* thereof Lev 9:13 5409
for an hundred *p* of silver Josh 24:32
ten *p* of silver out of the house Judg 9:4
of us eleven hundred *p* of silver Judg 16:5
with her bones, into twelve *p* Judg 19:29 5409
my concubine, and cut her in *p* Judg 20:6
of the LORD shall be broken to *p* 1Sa 2:10
yoke of oxen, and hewed them in *p* 1Sa 11:7
Samuel hewed Agag in *p* before the 1Sa 15:33
on him, and rent it in twelve *p* 1Kin 11:30 7168
said to Jeroboam, Take thee ten *p* 1Kin 11:31 7168
for themselves, and cut it in *p* 1Kin 18:23
in order, and cut the bullock in *p* 1Kin 18:33
brake in *p* the rocks before the 1Kin 19:11
clothes, and rent them in two *p* 2Kin 2:12 7168
silver, and six thousand *p* of gold 2Kin 5:5
sold for fourscore *p* of silver 2Kin 6:25
dove's dung for five *p* of silver 2Kin 6:25
images brake they in *p* thoroughly 2Kin 11:18

P

brake in *p* the brasen serpent 2Kin 18:4
And he brake in *p* the images 2Kin 23:14
cut in *p* all the vessels of gold 2Kin 24:13
LORD, did the Chaldees break in *p* 2Kin 25:13
his altars and his images in *p* 2Chr 23:17
that they all were broken in *p* 2Chr 25:12
cut in *p* the vessels of the house 2Chr 28:24
Judah, and brake the images in *p* 2Chr 31:1
the molten images, he brake in *p* 2Chr 34:4
me by my neck, and shaken me to *p* Job 16:12
soul, and break me in *p* with words Job 19:2
He shall break in *p* mighty men Job 34:24
bones are as strong *p* of brass Job 40:18
them in *p* like a potter's vessel Ps 2:9
soul like a lion, rending it in *p* Ps 7:2
forget God, lest I tear you in *p* Ps 50:22
arrows, let them be as cut in *p* Ps 58:7
submit himself with *p* of silver Ps 68:30 7518
and shall break in *p* the oppressor Ps 72:4
the heads of leviathan in *p* Ps 74:14
Thou hast broken Rahab in *p* Ps 89:10
They break in *p* thy people Ps 94:5
to bring a thousand *p* of silver Song 8:11
ye that ye beat my people to *p* Is 3:15
and ye shall be broken in *p* Is 8:9
and ye shall be broken in *p* Is 8:9
and ye shall be broken in *p* Is 8:9
be dashed to *p* before their eyes Is 13:16
shall dash the young men to *p* Is 13:18
vessel that is broken in *p* Is 30:14
I will break in *p* the gates of Is 45:2
out thence shall be torn in *p* Jer 5:6
that breaketh the rock in *p* Jer 23:29
Merodach is broken in *p* Jer 50:2
her images are broken in *p* Jer 50:2
will I break in *p* the nations Jer 51:20
thee will I break in *p* the horse Jer 51:21
will I break in *p* the chariot Jer 51:21
thee also will I break in *p* man Jer 51:22
with thee will I break in *p* old Jer 51:22
will I break in *p* the young man Jer 51:22
I will also break in *p* with thee Jer 51:23
will I break in *p* the husbandman Jer 51:23
thee will I break in *p* captains Jer 51:23
aside my ways, and pulled me in *p* Lam 3:11
dieth of itself, or is torn in *p* Eze 4:14
for *p* of bread, to slay the souls Eze 13:19 6595
Gather the *p* thereof into it, Eze 24:4 5409
thereof, ye shall be cut in *p* Dan 2:5 1917
iron and clay, and brake them to *p* Dan 2:34
and the gold, broken to *p* together Dan 2:35
forasmuch as iron breaketh in *p* Dan 2:40
all these, shall it break in *p* Dan 2:40
people, but it shall break in *p* Dan 2:44
and that it brake in *p* the iron Dan 2:45
and Abed-nego, shall be cut in *p* Dan 3:29 1917
brake all their bones in *p* or Dan 6:24
it devoured and brake in *p* Dan 7:7
which devoured, brake in *p* Dan 7:19
tread it down, and break it in *p* Dan 7:23
her to me for fifteen *p* of silver Hos 3:2
of Samaria shall be broken in *p* Hos 8:6
was dashed in *p* upon her children Hos 10:14
infants shall be dashed in *p* Hos 13:16
thereof shall be beaten to *p* Mic 1:7
their bones, and chop them in *p* Mic 3:3
thou shalt beat in *p* many people Mic 4:13
treadeth down, and teareth in *p* Mic 5:8
He that dasheth in *p* is come up Nah 2:1
The lion did tear in *p* enough for Nah 2:12
children also were dashed in *p* at Nah 3:10
for my price thirty *p* of silver Zec 11:12
And I took the thirty *p* of silver Zec 11:13
the fat, and tear their claws in *p* Zec 11:16
with it shall be cut in *p* Zec 12:3
with him for thirty *p* of silver Mt 26:15
brought again the thirty *p* of Mt 27:3
he cast down the *p* of silver in Mt 27:5
chief priests took the silver *p* Mt 27:6
they took the thirty *p* of silver Mt 27:9
him, and the fetters broken in *p* Mk 5:4
what woman having ten *p* of silver Lk 15:8 *1406*
it fifty thousand *p* of silver Acts 19:19
have been pulled in *p* of them Acts 23:10 *1288*
and some on broken *p* of the ship Acts 27:44

PIERCE {4}
p them through with his arrows Num 24:8 4272
it will go into his hand, and *p* it 2Kin 18:21 5344
it will go into his hand, and *p* it Is 36:6 5344
a sword shall *p* through thy own Lk 2:35 *1330*

PIERCED {8}
off his head, when she had *p* Judg 5:26 4272
My bones are *p* in me in the night Job 30:17 5365
they *p* my hands and my feet Ps 22:16 738
look upon me whom they have *p* Zec 12:10 1856
soldiers with a spear *p* his side Jn 19:34 *3572*
shall look on him whom they *p* Jn 19:37 *1574*
p themselves through with many 1Ti 6:10 *4044*
see him, and they also which *p* him Rev 1:7 *1574*

PIERCETH {1}
his nose *p* through snares Job 40:24 5344

PIERCING {2}
punish leviathan the *p* serpent Is 27:1 1281
p even to the dividing asunder of Heb 4:12 *1338*

PIERCINGS {1}
speaketh like the *p* of a sword Prov 12:18 4094

PIETY {1}
learn first to shew *p* at home 1Ti 5:4 *2151*

PIGEON {2}
and a turtledove, and a young *p* Gen 15:9 1469
a burnt offering, and a young *p* Lev 12:6 3123

PIGEONS {10}
of turtledoves, or of young *p* Lev 1:14 3123
two turtledoves, or two young *p* Lev 5:7 3123
two turtledoves, or two young *p* Lev 5:11 3123
bring two turtles, or two young *p* Lev 12:8 3123
two turtledoves, or two young *p* Lev 14:22 3123
turtledoves, or of the young *p* Lev 14:30 3123
two turtledoves, or two young *p* Lev 15:14 3123
her two turtles, or two young *p* Lev 15:29 3123
bring two turtles, or two young *p* Num 6:10 3123
of turtledoves, or two young *p* Lk 2:24 *4058*

PI-HAHIROTH {4} *A wilderness encampment.*
that they turn and encamp before *P* Ex 14:2 6367
encamping by the sea, beside *P* Ex 14:9 6367
Etham, and turned again unto *P* Num 33:7 6367
And they departed from before *P* Num 33:8 6367

PILATE *(pi'-lut)* {56} *A Roman procurator of Judea.*
him to Pontius *P* the governor Mt 27:2 *4091*
Then said *P* unto him, Hearest Mt 27:13 *4091*
P said unto them, Whom will ye Mt 27:17 *4091*
P saith unto them, What shall I Mt 27:22 *4091*
When *P* saw that he could prevail Mt 27:24 *4091*
He went to *P*, and begged the body Mt 27:58 *4091*
Then *P* commanded the body to be Mt 27:58 *4091*
and Pharisees came together unto *P* Mt 27:62 *4091*
P said unto them, Ye have a watch Mt 27:65 *4091*
him away, and delivered him to *P* Mk 15:1 *4091*
P asked him, Art thou the King of Mk 15:2 *4091*
P asked him again, saying, Mk 15:4 *4091*
so that *P* marvelled Mk 15:5 *4091*
But *P* answered them, saying, Will Mk 15:9 *4091*
P answered and said again unto Mk 15:12 *4091*
Then *P* said unto them, Why, what Mk 15:14 *4091*
And so *P*, willing to content the Mk 15:15 *4091*
came, and went in boldly unto *P* Mk 15:43 *4091*
P marvelled if he were already Mk 15:44 *4091*
Pontius *P* being governor of Lk 3:1 *4091*
whose blood *P* had mingled with Lk 13:1 *4091*
of them arose, and led him unto *P* Lk 23:1 *4091*
P asked him, saying, Art thou the Lk 23:3 *4091*
Then said *P* to the chief priests Lk 23:4 *4091*
When *P* heard of Galilee, he asked Lk 23:6 *4091*
robe, and sent him again to *P* Lk 23:11 *4091*
And the same day *P* and Herod were Lk 23:12 *4091*
And *P*, when he had called together Lk 23:13 *4091*
P therefore, willing to release Lk 23:20 *4091*
P gave sentence that it should be Lk 23:24 *4091*
This man went unto *P*, and begged Lk 23:52 *4091*
P then went out unto them, and Jn 18:29 *4091*
Then said *P* unto them, Take ye Jn 18:31 *4091*
Then *P* entered into the judgment Jn 18:33 *4091*
P answered, Am I a Jew Jn 18:35 *4091*
P therefore said unto him, Art Jn 18:37 *4091*
P saith unto him, What is truth Jn 18:38 *4091*
Then *P* therefore took Jesus, and Jn 19:1 *4091*
P therefore went forth again, and Jn 19:4 *4091*
P saith unto them, Behold the man Jn 19:5
P saith unto them, Take ye him, Jn 19:6 *4091*
When *P* therefore heard that Jn 19:8 *4091*
Then saith *P* unto him, Speakest Jn 19:10 *4091*
from thenceforth *P* sought to Jn 19:12 *4091*
When *P* therefore heard that Jn 19:13 *4091*
P saith unto them, Shall I Jn 19:15 *4091*
P wrote a title, and put it on the Jn 19:19 *4091*
chief priests of the Jews to *P* Jn 19:21 *4091*
P answered, What I have written I Jn 19:22 *4091*
besought *P* that their legs might Jn 19:31 *4091*
besought *P* that he might take Jn 19:38 *4091*
and *P* gave him leave Jn 19:38 *4091*
denied him in the presence of *P* Acts 3:13 *4091*
both Herod, and Pontius *P* Acts 4:27 *4091*
yet desired they *P* that he should Acts 13:28 *4091*
who before Pontius *P* witnessed a 1Ti 6:13 *4091*

PILDASH *(pil'-dash)* {1} *A son of Nahor.*
And Chesed, and Hazo, and *P*, and Gen 22:22 6394

PILE {2}
the *p* thereof is fire and much Is 30:33 4071
even make the *p* for fire great Eze 24:9 4071

PILEHA *(pil'-e-hah)* {1} *A renewer of the covenant.*
Hallohesh, *P*, Shobek, Neh 10:24 6401

PILGRIMAGE {4}
the years of my *p* are an hundred Gen 47:9 4033
my fathers in the days of their *p* Gen 47:9 4033
of Canaan, the land of their *p* Ex 6:4 4033
my songs in the house of my *p* Ps 119:54 4033

PILGRIMS {2}
were strangers and *p* on the earth Heb 11:13 *3927*
I beseech you as strangers and *p* 1Pet 2:11 *3927*

PILHA See PILEHA.

PILLAR {47}
him, and she became a *p* of salt Gen 19:26 5333
his pillows, and set it up for a *p* Gen 28:18 4676
stone, which I have set for a *p* Gen 28:22 4676
where thou anointedst the *p* Gen 31:13 4676
a stone, and set it up for a *p* Gen 31:45 4676
this heap, and behold this *p* Gen 31:51 4676
this *p* be witness, that I will Gen 31:52 4676
heap and this *p* unto me, for harm Gen 31:52 4676
Jacob set up a *p* in the place Gen 35:14 4676
with him, even a *p* of stone Gen 35:14 4678
Jacob set a *p* upon her grave Gen 35:20 4676
that is the *p* of Rachel's grave Gen 35:20 4678
them by day in a *p* of a cloud Ex 13:21 5982
and by night in a *p* of fire Ex 13:21 5982
away the *p* of the cloud by day Ex 13:22 5982
nor the *p* of fire by night, from Ex 13:22 5982
the *p* of the cloud went from Ex 14:19 5982
Egyptians through the *p* of fire Ex 14:24 5982
the cloudy *p* descended, and stood Ex 33:9 5982
p stand at the tabernacle door Ex 33:10 5982
came down in the *p* of the cloud Num 12:5 5982
by daytime in a *p* of a cloud Num 14:14 5982
and in a *p* of fire by night Num 14:14 5982
the tabernacle in a *p* of a cloud Deut 31:15 5982
the *p* of the cloud stood over the Deut 31:15 5982
of the *p* that was in Shechem Judg 9:6 5324
out of the city with a *p* of smoke Judg 20:40 5982
and reared up for himself a *p* 2Sa 18:18 4678
he called the *p* after his own 2Sa 18:18 4678
and he set up the right *p*, and 1Kin 7:21 5982
and he set up the left *p*, and 1Kin 7:21 5982
behold, the king stood by a *p* 2Kin 11:14 5982
And the king stood by a *p*, and made 2Kin 23:3 5982
of the one *p* was eighteen cubits 2Kin 25:17 5982
the second *p* with wreathen work 2Kin 25:17 5982
stood at his *p* at the entering in 2Chr 23:13 5982
them in the day by a cloudy *p* Neh 9:12 5982
and in the night by a *p* of fire Neh 9:12 5982
the *p* of the cloud departed not Neh 9:19 5982
neither the *p* of fire by night, Neh 9:19 5982
spake unto them in the cloudy *p* Ps 99:7 5982
a *p* at the border thereof to the Is 19:19 4676
day a defenced city, and an iron *p* Jer 1:18 5982
the height of one *p* was eighteen Jer 52:21 5982
The second *p* also and the Jer 52:22 5982
church of the living God, the *p* 1Ti 3:15 *4769*
make a *p* in the temple of my God Rev 3:12 *4769*

PILLARS {89}
altar under the hill, and twelve *p* Ex 24:4 4676
thou shalt hang it upon four *p* of Ex 26:32 5982
hanging five *p* of shittim wood Ex 26:37 5982
And the twenty *p* thereof and their Ex 27:10 5982
the hooks of the *p* and their Ex 27:10 5982
cubits long, and his twenty *p* Ex 27:11 5982
the hooks of the *p* and their Ex 27:11 5982
their *p* ten, and their sockets ten Ex 27:12 5982
their *p* three, and their sockets Ex 27:14 5982
their *p* three, and their sockets Ex 27:15 5982
their *p* shall be four, and their Ex 27:16 5982
All the *p* round about the court Ex 27:17 5982
and his boards, his bars, his *p* Ex 35:11 5982
The hangings of the court, his *p* Ex 35:17 5982
thereunto four *p* of shittim wood Ex 36:36 5982
the five *p* of it with their hooks Ex 36:38 5982
Their *p* were twenty, and their Ex 38:10 5982
the hooks of the *p* and their Ex 38:10 5982
their *p* were twenty, and their Ex 38:11 5982
the hooks of the *p* and their Ex 38:11 5982
of fifty cubits, their *p* ten Ex 38:12 5982
the hooks of the *p* and their Ex 38:12 5982
their *p* three, and their sockets Ex 38:14 5982
their *p* three, and their sockets Ex 38:15 5982
sockets for the *p* were of brass Ex 38:17 5982
the hooks of the *p* and their Ex 38:17 5982
all the *p* of the court were Ex 38:17 5982
their *p* were four, and their Ex 38:19 5982
shekels he made hooks for the *p* Ex 38:28 5982
his boards, his bars, and his *p* Ex 39:33 5982
The hangings of the court, his *p* Ex 39:40 5982
bars thereof, and reared up his *p* Ex 40:18 5982
the *p* thereof, and the sockets Num 3:36 5982
the *p* of the court round about, Num 3:37 5982
the *p* thereof, and sockets thereof Num 4:31 5982
the *p* of the court round about, Num 4:32 5982
their altars, and break their *p* Deut 12:3 4676
and they set him between the *p* Judg 16:25 5982
p whereupon the house standeth Judg 16:26 5982
p upon which the house stood Judg 16:29 5982
for the *p* of the earth are the 1Sa 2:8 4690
cubits, upon four rows of cedar *p* 1Kin 7:2 5982
with cedar beams upon the *p* 1Kin 7:2 5982
beams, that lay on forty five *p* 1Kin 7:3 5982
And he made a porch of *p* 1Kin 7:6 5982
and the other *p* and the thick beam 1Kin 7:6 5982
For he cast two *p* of brass 1Kin 7:15 5982
to set upon the tops of the *p* 1Kin 7:16 5982
which were upon the top of the *p* 1Kin 7:17 5982
And he made the *p*, and two rows 1Kin 7:18 5982
that were upon the top of the *p* 1Kin 7:19 5982
the chapiters upon the two *p* had 1Kin 7:20 5982
he set up the *p* in the porch of 1Kin 7:21 5982
the top of the *p* was lily work 1Kin 7:22 5982
so was the work of the *p* finished 1Kin 7:22 5982
The two *p*, and the two bowls of 1Kin 7:41 5982
that were on the top of the two *p* 1Kin 7:41 5982
which were upon the top of the *p* 1Kin 7:41 5982
chapiters that were upon the *p* 1Kin 7:42 5982
trees *p* for the house of the LORD 1Kin 10:12 4552
from the *p* which Hezekiah king of 2Kin 18:16 547
the *p* of brass that were in the 2Kin 25:13 5982
The two *p*, one sea, and the bases 2Kin 25:16 5982
made the brasen sea, and the *p* 1Chr 18:8 5982
before the house two *p* of thirty 2Chr 3:15 5982
and put them on the heads of the *p* 2Chr 3:16 5982
he reared up the *p* before the 2Chr 3:17 5982
To wit, the two *p*, and the pommels 2Chr 4:12 5982

were on the top of the two p ... 2Chr 4:12 5982
which were on the top of the p ... 2Chr 4:12 5982
chapiters which were upon the p ... 2Chr 4:13 5982
to silver rings and p of marble ... Est 1:6 5982
place, and the p thereof tremble ... Job 9:6 5982
The p of heaven tremble, and are ... Job 26:11 5982
I bear up the p of it ... Ps 75:3 5982
she hath hewn out her seven p ... Prov 9:1 5982
of the wilderness like p of smoke ... Song 3:6 8490
He made the p thereof of silver, ... Song 3:10 5982
His legs are as p of marble ... Song 5:15 5982
LORD of hosts concerning the p ... Jer 27:19 5982
Also the p of brass that were in ... Jer 52:17 5982
The two p, one sea, and twelve ... Jer 52:20 5982
And concerning the p, the height ... Jer 52:21 5982
there were p by the posts, one on ... Eze 40:49 5982
p as the p of the courts ... Eze 42:6 5982
blood, and fire, and p of smoke ... Joel 2:30 8490
and John, who seemed to be p ... Gal 2:9 *4769*
the sun, and his feet as p of fire ... Rev 10:1 *4769*

PILLED {2}
p white strakes in them, and made ... Gen 30:37 6478
he had p before the flocks in the ... Gen 30:38 6478

PILLOW {3}
put a p of goats' hair for his ... 1Sa 19:13 3523
with a p of goats' hair for his ... 1Sa 19:16 3523
part of the ship, asleep on a p ... Mk 4:38 *4344*

PILLOWS {4}
that place, and put them for his p ... Gen 28:11 4763
stone that he had put for his p ... Gen 28:18 4763
women that sew p to all armholes ... Eze 13:18 3704
Behold, I am against your p ... Eze 13:20 3704

PILOTS {4}
that were in thee, were thy p ... Eze 27:8 2259
thy mariners, and thy p, thy ... Eze 27:27 2259
at the sound of the cry of thy p ... Eze 27:28 2259
all the p of the sea, shall come ... Eze 27:29 2259

PILTAI *(pil'-tahee)* {1} *A priest.*
of Miniamin, of Moadiah, P ... Neh 12:17 6408

PIN {3}
And she fastened it with the p ... Judg 16:14 3489
went away with the p of the beam ... Judg 16:14 3489
or will men take a p of it to ... Eze 15:3 3489

PINE {8}
p away in their iniquity in your ... Lev 26:39 4743
shall they p away with them ... Lev 26:39 4743
p branches, and myrtle branches, ... Neh 8:15 6086,8081
the desert the fir tree, and the p ... Is 41:19 8410
the p tree, and the box together, ... Is 60:13 8410
for these p away, stricken ... Lam 4:9 2100
but ye shall p away for your ... Eze 24:23 4743
we p away in them, how should we ... Eze 33:10 4743

PINETH {1}
with his teeth, and p away ... Mk 9:18 *3583*

PINING {1}
will cut me off with p sickness ... Is 38:12 1803

PINNACLE {2}
setteth him on a p of the temple ... Mt 4:5 *4419*
set him on a p of the temple, and ... Lk 4:9 *4419*

PINON {2}
Aholibamah, duke Elah, duke P ... Gen 36:41 6373
Aholibamah, duke Elah, duke P ... 1Chr 1:52 6373

PINS {11}
thereof, and all the p thereof ... Ex 27:19 3489
all the p of the court, shall be ... Ex 27:19 3489
The p of the tabernacle, and the ... Ex 35:18 3489
the p of the court, and their ... Ex 35:18 3489
all the p of the tabernacle, and ... Ex 38:20 3489
all the p of the tabernacle, and ... Ex 38:31 3489
all the p of the court round ... Ex 38:31 3489
court gate, his cords, and his p ... Ex 39:40 3489
and their sockets, and their p ... Num 3:37 3489
and their sockets, and their p ... Num 4:32 3489
and the wimples, and the crisping p ... Is 3:22

PIPE {4}
a psaltery, and a tabret, and a p ... 1Sa 10:5 2485
and the viol, the tabret, and p ... Is 5:12 2485
as when one goeth with a p to ... Is 30:29 2485
giving sound, whether p or harp ... 1Cor 14:7 *836*

PIPED {4}
him, and the people p with pipes ... 1Kin 1:40 2490
We have p unto you, and ye have ... Mt 11:17 *832*
We have p unto you, and ye have ... Lk 7:32 *832*
it be known what is p or harped ... 1Cor 14:7 *832*

PIPERS {1}
of harpers, and musicians, and of p ... Rev 18:22 *834*

PIPES {6}
him, and the people piped with p ... 1Kin 1:40 2485
heart shall sound for Moab like p ... Jer 48:36 2485
like p for the men of Kir-heres ... Jer 48:36 2485
of thy p was prepared in thee in ... Eze 28:13 5345
seven p to the seven lamps, which ... Zec 4:2 4166
p empty the golden oil out of ... Zec 4:12 6804

PIRAM *(pi'-ram)* {1} *An Amorite king.*
unto P king of Jarmuth, and unto ... Josh 10:3 6502

PIRATHON *(pir'-a-thon)* {1} See PIRATHONITE. *A place in Ephraim.*
was buried in P in the land of ... Judg 12:15 6552

PIRATHONITE *(pir'-a-thon-ite)* {5} *An inhabitant of Pirathon.*
him Abdon the son of Hillel, a P ... Judg 12:13 6553
the son of Hillel the P died ... Judg 12:15 6553
Benaiah the P, Hiddai of the ... 2Sa 23:30 6553
of Benjamin, Benaiah the P ... 1Chr 11:31 6553
eleventh month was Benaiah the P ... 1Chr 27:14 6553

PISGAH *(piz'-gah)* {5} *A mountain peak in Moab.*
country of Moab, to the top of P ... Num 21:20 6449
field of Zophim, to the top of P ... Num 23:14 6449
Get thee up into the top of P ... Deut 3:27 6449
the plain, under the springs of P ... Deut 4:49 6449
mountain of Nebo, to the top of P ... Deut 34:1 6449

PISHON See PISON.

PISIDIA *(pi-sid'-e-ah)* {2} *A Roman province in Asia Minor.*
Perga, they came to Antioch in P ... Acts 13:14 *4099*
they had passed throughout P ... Acts 14:24 *4099*

PISIDIAN ANTIOCH See PISIDIA.

PISON *(pi'-son)* {1} *A river of Eden.*
The name of the first is P ... Gen 2:11 6376

PISPA See PISPAH.

PISPAH *(piz'-pah)* {1} *A son of Jether.*
Jephunneh, and P, and Ara ... 1Chr 7:38 6462

PISS {2}
and drink their own p with you ... 2Kin 18:27 7890
and drink their own p with you ... Is 36:12 7890

PISSETH {6}
light any that p against the wall ... 1Sa 25:22 8366
light any that p against the wall ... 1Sa 25:34 8366
him that p against the wall ... 1Kin 14:10 8366
him not one that p against a wall ... 1Kin 16:11 8366
Ahab him that p against the wall ... 1Kin 21:21 8366
Ahab him that p against the wall ... 2Kin 9:8 8366

PIT {88}
slay him, and cast him into some p ... Gen 37:20 953
but cast him into this p that is ... Gen 37:22 953
took him, and cast him into a p ... Gen 37:24 953
the p was empty, there was no ... Gen 37:24 953
and lifted up Joseph out of the p ... Gen 37:28 953
And Reuben returned unto the p ... Gen 37:29 953
behold, Joseph was not in the p ... Gen 37:29 953
And if a man shall open a p ... Ex 21:33 953
or if a man shall dig a p ... Ex 21:33 953
The owner of the p shall make it ... Ex 21:34 953
Nevertheless a fountain or p ... Lev 11:36 953
and they go down quick into the p ... Num 16:30 7585
them, went down alive into the p ... Num 16:33 7585
Behold, he is hid now in some p ... 2Sa 17:9 6354
him into a great p in the wood ... 2Sa 18:17 6354
the midst of a p in time of snow ... 2Sa 23:20 953
slew them at the p of the ... 2Kin 10:14 953
slew a lion in a p in a snowy day ... 1Chr 11:22 953
ye dig a p for your friend ... Job 6:27
go down to the bars of the p ... Job 17:16 7585
keepeth back his soul from the p ... Job 33:18 7845
him from going down to the p ... Job 33:24 7845
his soul from going into the p ... Job 33:28 7845
To bring back his soul from the p ... Job 33:30 7845
He made a p, and digged it, and is ... Ps 7:15 953
sunk down in the p that they made ... Ps 9:15 7845
like them that go down into the p ... Ps 28:1 953
I should not go down to the p ... Ps 30:3 953
my blood, when I go down to the p ... Ps 30:9 7845
they hid for me their net in a p ... Ps 35:7 7845
me up also out of an horrible p ... Ps 40:2 953
down into the p of destruction ... Ps 55:23 875
they have digged a p before me ... Ps 57:6 7882
let not the p shut her mouth upon ... Ps 69:15 875
with them that go down into the p ... Ps 88:4 953
Thou hast laid me in the lowest p ... Ps 88:6 953
until the p be digged for the ... Ps 94:13 7845
unto them that go down into the p ... Ps 143:7 953
as those that go down into the p ... Prov 1:12 953
of strange women is a deep p ... Prov 22:14 7745
and a strange woman is a narrow p ... Prov 23:27 875
Whoso diggeth a p shall fall ... Prov 26:27 7845
shall fall himself into his own p ... Prov 28:10 7816
of any person shall flee to the p ... Prov 28:17 953
He that diggeth a p shall fall ... Eccl 10:8 1475
to hell, to the sides of the p ... Is 14:15 953
go down to the stones of the p ... Is 14:19 953
Fear, and the p, and the snare, are ... Is 24:17 6354
of the fear shall fall into the p ... Is 24:18 6354
up out of the midst of the p ... Is 24:18 6354
prisoners are gathered in the p ... Is 24:22 953
to take water withal out of the p ... Is 30:14 1360
it from the p of corruption ... Is 38:17 7845
the p cannot hope for thy truth ... Is 38:18 953
to the hole of the p whence ye ... Is 51:1 953
that he should not die in the p ... Is 51:14 7845
they have digged a p for my soul ... Jer 18:20 7745
they have digged a p to take me ... Jer 18:22 7743,7882
cast them into the midst of the p ... Jer 41:7 953
Now the p wherein Ishmael had ... Jer 41:9 953
Fear, and the p, and the snare, ... Jer 48:43 6354
the fear shall fall into the p ... Jer 48:44 6354
the p shall be taken in the snare ... Jer 48:44 6354
he was taken in their p, and they ... Eze 19:4 7845
he was taken in their p ... Eze 19:8 7845
with them that descend into the p ... Eze 26:20 953
with them that go down to the p ... Eze 26:20 953
shall bring thee down to the p ... Eze 28:8 7845
with them that go down to the p ... Eze 31:14 953
with them that descend into the p ... Eze 31:16 953
with them that go down into the p ... Eze 32:18 953
are set in the sides of the p ... Eze 32:23 953
with them that go down to the p ... Eze 32:24 953
with them that go down to the p ... Eze 32:25 953
with them that go down to the p ... Eze 32:29 953
with them that go down to the p ... Eze 32:30 953
out of the p wherein is no water ... Zec 9:11 953
if it fall into a p on the ... Mt 12:11 *999*
an ass or an ox fallen into a p ... Lk 14:5 *5421*
given the key of the bottomless p ... Rev 9:1 *5421*
And he opened the bottomless p ... Rev 9:2 *5421*
there arose a smoke out of the p ... Rev 9:2 *5421*
by reason of the smoke of the p ... Rev 9:2 *5421*
is the angel of the bottomless p ... Rev 9:11
p shall make war against them ... Rev 11:7
ascend out of the bottomless p ... Rev 17:8
the key of the bottomless p ... Rev 20:1
And cast him into the bottomless p ... Rev 20:3

PITCH {19}
p it within and without with p ... Gen 6:14 3724
and daubed it with slime and with p ... Ex 2:3 2203
of Israel shall p their tents ... Num 1:52 2583
But the Levites shall p round ... Num 1:53 2583
shall p by his own standard ... Num 2:2 2583
of the congregation shall they p ... Num 2:2 2583
Judah p throughout their armies ... Num 2:3 2583
those that do p next unto him ... Num 2:5 2583
those which p by him shall be the ... Num 2:12 2583
of the Gershonites shall p behind ... Num 3:23 2583
of the sons of Kohath shall p on ... Num 3:29 2583
these shall p on the side of the ... Num 3:35 2583
out a place to p your tents in ... Deut 1:33 2583
of Jordan, did Joshua p in Gilgal ... Josh 4:20 6965
shall the Arabian p tent there ... Is 13:20 167
thereof shall be turned into p ... Is 34:9 2203
thereof shall become burning p ... Is 34:9 2203
they shall p their tents against ... Jer 6:3 8628

PITCHED {82}
p his tent, having Beth-el on the ... Gen 12:8 5186
plain, and p his tent toward Sodom ... Gen 13:12 167
p his tent in the valley of Gerar ... Gen 26:17 2583
of the LORD, and p his tent there ... Gen 26:25 5186
Now Jacob had p his tent in the ... Gen 31:25 8628
brethren p in the mount of Gilead ... Gen 31:25 8628
p his tent before the city ... Gen 33:18 2583
of the LORD, and p in Rephidim ... Ex 17:1 2583
Sinai, and had p in the wilderness ... Ex 19:2 2583
p it without the camp, afar off ... Ex 33:7 5186
and when the tabernacle is to be p ... Num 1:51 2583
so they p by their standards, and ... Num 2:34 2583
children of Israel p their tents ... Num 9:17 2583
commandment of the LORD they p ... Num 9:18 2583
p in the wilderness of Paran ... Num 12:16 2583
Israel set forward, and p in Oboth ... Num 21:10 2583
Oboth, and p at Ije-abarim, in the ... Num 21:11 2583
and p in the valley of Zared ... Num 21:12 2583
p on the other side of Arnon, ... Num 21:13 2583
p in the plains of Moab on this ... Num 22:1 2583
from Rameses, and p in Succoth ... Num 33:5 2583
p in Etham, which is in the edge ... Num 33:6 2583
and they p before Migdol ... Num 33:7 2583
of Etham, and p in Marah ... Num 33:8 2583
and they p there ... Num 33:9 2583
p in the wilderness of Sinai ... Num 33:15 2583
Sinai, and p at Kibroth-hattaavah ... Num 33:16 2583
from Hazeroth, and p in Rithmah ... Num 33:18 2583
Rithmah, and p at Rimmon-parez ... Num 33:19 2583
from Rimmon-parez, and p in Libnah ... Num 33:20 2583
from Libnah, and p at Rissah ... Num 33:21 2583
from Rissah, and p in Kehelathah ... Num 33:22 2583
Kehelathah, and p in mount Shapher ... Num 33:23 2583
from Haradah, and p in Makheloth ... Num 33:25 2583
from Tahath, and p at Tarah ... Num 33:27 2583
from Tarah, and p in Mithcah ... Num 33:28 2583
from Mithcah, and p in Hashmonah ... Num 33:29 2583
Moseroth, and p in Bene-jaakan ... Num 33:31 2583
Hor-hagidgad, and p in Jotbathah ... Num 33:33 2583
p in the wilderness of Zin, which ... Num 33:36 2583
p in mount Hor, in the edge of ... Num 33:37 2583
from mount Hor, and p in Zalmonah ... Num 33:41 2583
from Zalmonah, and p in Punon ... Num 33:42 2583
from Punon, and p in Oboth ... Num 33:43 2583
p in Ije-abarim, in the border of ... Num 33:44 2583
from Iim, and p in Dibon-gad ... Num 33:45 2583
p in the mountains of Abarim, ... Num 33:47 2583
p in the plains of Moab by Jordan ... Num 33:48 2583
And they p by Jordan, from ... Num 33:49 2583
p on the north side of Ai ... Josh 8:11 2583
p together at the waters of Merom ... Josh 11:5 2583
p his tent unto the plain of ... Judg 4:11 5186
p in the valley of Jezreel ... Judg 6:33 2583
p beside the well of Harod ... Judg 7:1 2583
p on the other side of Arnon, but ... Judg 11:18 2583
p in Jahaz, and fought against ... Judg 11:20 2583
p in Judah, and spread themselves ... Judg 15:9 2583
p in Kirjath-jearim, in Judah ... Judg 18:12 2583
to battle, and p beside Eben-ezer ... 1Sa 4:1 2583
and the Philistines p in Aphek ... 1Sa 4:1 2583
p in Michmash, eastward from ... 1Sa 13:5 2583
p between Shochoh and Azekah, in ... 1Sa 17:1 2583
p by the valley of Elah, and set ... 1Sa 17:2 2583
Saul p in the hill of Hachilah, ... 1Sa 26:3 2583
to the place where Saul had p ... 1Sa 26:5 2583
the people p round about him ... 1Sa 26:5 2583
together, and came and p in Shunem ... 1Sa 28:4 2583
together, and they p in Gilboa ... 1Sa 28:4 2583
the Israelites p by a fountain ... 1Sa 29:1 2583
that David had p for it ... 2Sa 6:17 5186
Absalom p in the land of Gilead ... 2Sa 17:26 2583
p in the valley of Rephaim ... 2Sa 23:13 2583

p in Aroer, on the right side of 2Sa 24:5 2583
the children of Israel *p* before 1Kin 20:27 2583
they *p* one over against the other 1Kin 20:29 2583
Jerusalem, and *p* against it 2Kin 25:1 2583
ark of God, and *p* for it a tent 1Chr 15:1 5186
the tent that David had *p* for it 1Chr 16:1 5186
who came and *p* before Medeba 1Chr 19:7 2583
for he had *p* a tent for it at 2Chr 1:4 5186
p against it, and built forts Jer 52:4 2583
true tabernacle, which the Lord *p* Heb 8:2 *4078*

PITCHER {12}
whom I shall say, Let down thy *p* Gen 24:14 3537
with her *p* upon her shoulder Gen 24:15 3537
down to the well, and filled her *p* Gen 24:16 3537
drink a little water of thy *p* Gen 24:17 3537
let down her *p* upon her hand, and Gen 24:18 3537
emptied her *p* into the trough, and Gen 24:20 3537
a little water of thy *p* to drink Gen 24:43 3537
forth with her *p* on her shoulder Gen 24:45 3537
let down her *p* from her shoulder, Gen 24:46 3537
or the *p* be broken at the Eccl 12:6 3537
you a man bearing a *p* of water Mk 14:13 *2765*
meet you, bearing a *p* of water Lk 22:10 *2765*

PITCHERS {5}
in every man's hand, with empty *p* Judg 7:16 3537
and lamps within the *p* Judg 7:16 3537
brake the *p* that were in their Judg 7:19 3537
blew the trumpets, and brake the *p* Judg 7:20 3537
are they esteemed as earthen *p* Lam 4:2 5035

PITHOM *(pi'-thom)* {1} *A city in Lower Egypt.*
for Pharaoh treasure cities, *P.* Ex 1:11 6619

PITHON *(pi'-thon)* {2} *A son of Micah.*
And the sons of Micah were, *P.* 1Chr 8:35 6377
And the sons of Micah were, *P.* 1Chr 9:41 6377

PITIED {6}
He made them also to be *p* of all Ps 106:46 7356
of Jacob, and hath not *p* Lam 2:2 2550
hath thrown down, and hath not *p* Lam 2:17 2550
thou hast killed, and not *p* Lam 2:21 2550
thou hast slain, thou hast not *p* Lam 3:43 2550
None eye *p* thee, to do any of Eze 16:5 2347

PITIETH {3}
Like as a father *p* his children Ps 103:13 7355
so the LORD *p* them that fear him Ps 103:13 7355
eyes, and that which your soul *p* Eze 24:21 4263

PITIFUL {3}
The hands of the *p* women have Lam 4:10 7362
that the Lord is very *p*, and of Jas 5:11 *4184*
another, love as brethren, be *p* 1Pet 3:8 *2155*

PITS {6}
rocks, and in high places, and in *p* 1Sa 13:6 953
The proud have digged *p* for me Ps 119:85 7882
into deep *p*, that they rise not Ps 140:10
through a land of deserts and of *p* Jer 2:6 7745
they came to the *p*, and found no Jer 14:3 1356
of the LORD, was taken in their *p* Lam 4:20 7825

PITY {30}
eye shall have no *p* upon them Deut 7:16 2347
neither shall thine eye *p* him Deut 13:8 2347
Thine eye shall not *p* him Deut 19:13 2347
And thine eye shall not *p* Deut 19:21 2347
hand, thine eye shall not *p* her Deut 25:12 2347
thing, and because he had no *p* 2Sa 12:6 2550
To him that is afflicted *p* should Job 6:14 2617
Have *p* upon me, have *p* upon me Job 19:21 2603
and I looked for some to take *p* Ps 69:20 5110
He that hath *p* upon the poor Prov 19:17 2603
it for him that will *p* the poor Prov 28:8 2603
they shall have no *p* on the fruit Is 13:18 7355
in his *p* he redeemed them Is 63:9 2551
I will not *p*, nor spare, nor have Jer 13:14 2550
For who shall have *p* upon thee Jer 15:5 2550
not spare them, neither have *p* Jer 21:7 2550
spare, neither will I have any *p* Eze 5:11 2550
spare thee, neither will I have *p* Eze 7:4 2550
not spare, neither will I have *p* Eze 7:9 2550
not spare, neither will I have *p* Eze 8:18 2550
your eye spare, neither have ye *p* Eze 9:5 2550
not spare, neither will I have *p* Eze 9:10 2550
But I had *p* for mine holy name, Eze 36:21 2550
for his land, and *p* his people Joel 2:18 2550
the sword, and did cast off all *p* Amos 1:11 7356
Thou hast had *p* on the gourd Jonah 4:10 2347
and their own shepherds *p* them not Zec 11:5 2550
For I will no more *p* the Zec 11:6 2550
even as I had *p* on thee Mt 18:33 *1653*

PLACE {718}
be gathered together unto one *p* Gen 1:9 4725
the land unto the *p* of Sichem Gen 12:6 4725
unto the *p* where his tent had Gen 13:3 4725
Unto the *p* of the altar, which he Gen 13:4 4725
look from the *p* where thou art Gen 13:14 4725
not spare the *p* for the fifty Gen 18:24 4725
spare all the *p* for their sakes Gen 18:26 4725
and Abraham returned unto his *p* Gen 18:33 4725
city, bring them out of this *p* Gen 19:12 4725
For we will destroy this *p* Gen 19:13 4725
said, Up, get you out of this *p* Gen 19:14 4725
p where he stood before the LORD Gen 19:27 4725
the fear of God is not in this *p* Gen 20:11 4725
at every *p* whither we shall come, Gen 20:13 4725
he called that *p* Beer-sheba Gen 21:31 4725
went unto the *p* of which God had Gen 22:3 4725
his eyes, and saw the *p* afar off Gen 22:4 4725
they came to the *p* which God had Gen 22:9 4725
the name of that *p* Jehovah-jireh Gen 22:14 4725
the men of the *p* asked him of his Gen 26:7 4725
the men of the *p* should kill me Gen 26:7 4725
And he lighted upon a certain *p* Gen 28:11 4725
he took of the stones of that *p* Gen 28:11 4725
and lay down in that *p* to sleep Gen 28:11 4725
Surely the LORD is in this *p* Gen 28:16 4725
and said, How dreadful is this *p* Gen 28:17 4725
called the name of that *p* Beth-el Gen 28:19 4725
upon the well's mouth in his *p* Gen 29:3 4725
together all the men of the *p* Gen 29:22 4725
that I may go unto mine own *p* Gen 30:25 4725
departed, and returned unto his *p* Gen 31:55 4725
the name of that *p* Mahanaim Gen 32:2 4725
called the name of the *p* Peniel Gen 32:30 4725
name of the *p* is called Succoth Gen 33:17 4725
altar, and called the *p* El-beth-el Gen 35:7 4725
in the *p* where he talked with him Gen 35:13 4725
in the *p* where he talked with him Gen 35:14 4725
of the *p* where God spake with him Gen 35:15 4725
herself, and sat in an open *p* Gen 38:14 6607
Then he asked the men of that *p* Gen 38:21 4725
There was no harlot in this *p* Gen 38:21
and also the men of the *p* said Gen 38:22 4725
there was no harlot in this *p* Gen 38:22
a *p* where the king's prisoners Gen 39:20 4725
the *p* where Joseph was bound Gen 40:3 4725
head, and restore thee unto thy *p* Gen 40:13 3653
whom God hath given me in this *p* Gen 48:9
for am I in the *p* of God Gen 50:19 8478
for the *p* whereon thou standest Ex 3:5 4725
unto the *p* of the Canaanites, and Ex 3:8 4725
any from his *p* for three days Ex 10:23 8478
LORD brought you out from this *p* Ex 13:3
of thine inheritance, in the *p* Ex 15:17 4349
abide ye every man in his *p* Ex 16:29 8478
out of his *p* on the seventh day Ex 16:29 4725
called the name of the *p* Massah Ex 17:7 4725
p such over them, to be rulers of Ex 18:21 7760
shall also go to their *p* in peace Ex 18:23 4725
thee a *p* whither he shall flee Ex 21:13 4725
into the *p* which I have prepared Ex 23:20 4725
unto you between the holy *p* Ex 26:33 6944
the testimony in the most holy *p* Ex 26:34 6944
when he goeth in unto the holy *p* Ex 28:29 6944
unto the holy *p* before the LORD Ex 28:35 6944
altar to minister in the holy *p* Ex 28:43 6944
to minister in the holy *p* Ex 29:30 6944
and seethe his flesh in the holy *p* Ex 29:31 4725
and sweet incense for the holy *p* Ex 31:11 6944
lead the people unto the *p* of Ex 32:34
said, Behold, there is a *p* by me Ex 33:21 4725
to do service in the holy *p* Ex 35:19 6944
in all the work of the holy *p* Ex 38:24 6944
to do service in the holy *p* Ex 39:1 6944
to do service in the holy *p* Ex 39:41 6944
east part, by the *p* of the ashes Lev 1:16 4725
without the camp unto a clean *p* Lev 4:12 4725
kill it in the *p* where they kill Lev 4:24 4725
in the *p* of the burnt offering Lev 4:29 4725
the *p* where they kill the burnt Lev 4:33 4725
without the camp unto a clean *p* Lev 6:11 4725
shall it be eaten in the holy *p* Lev 6:16 4725
In the *p* where the burnt offering Lev 6:25 4725
in the holy *p* shall it be eaten, Lev 6:26 4725
it was sprinkled in the holy *p* Lev 6:27 4725
to reconcile withal in the holy *p* Lev 6:30 6944
In the *p* where they kill the Lev 7:2 4725
it shall be eaten in the holy *p* Lev 7:6 4725
And ye shall eat it in the holy *p* Lev 10:13 4725
shall ye eat in a clean *p* Lev 10:14 4725
the sin offering in the holy *p* Lev 10:17 4725
not brought in within the holy *p* Lev 10:18 6944
have eaten it in the holy *p* Lev 10:18 6944
in the *p* of the boil there be a Lev 13:19 4725
if the bright spot stay in his *p* Lev 13:23 8478
if the bright spot stay in his *p* Lev 13:28 8478
the *p* where he shall kill the sin Lev 14:13 4725
the burnt offering, in the holy *p* Lev 14:13 4725
upon the *p* of the blood of the Lev 14:28 4725
an unclean *p* without the city Lev 14:40 4725
the city into an unclean *p* Lev 14:41 4725
put them in the *p* of those stones Lev 14:42 8478
out of the city into an unclean *p* Lev 14:45 4725
holy *p* within the vail before the Lev 16:2 6944
shall Aaron come into the holy *p* Lev 16:3 6944
make an atonement for the holy *p* Lev 16:16 6944
make an atonement in the holy *p* Lev 16:17 6944
an end of reconciling the holy *p* Lev 16:20 6944
on when he went into the holy *p* Lev 16:23 6944
flesh with water in the holy *p* Lev 16:24 4725
to make atonement in the holy *p* Lev 16:27 6944
they shall eat it in the holy *p* Lev 24:9 4725
every man in his *p* by their Num 2:17 3027
in the *p* where the cloud abode, Num 9:17 4725
In the first *p* went the standard Num 10:14
unto the *p* of which the LORD said Num 10:29 4725
search out a resting *p* for them Num 10:33
called the name of the *p* Taberah Num 11:3 4725
name of that *p* Kibroth-hattaavah Num 11:34 4725
The *p* was called the brook Eshcol Num 13:24 4725
will go up unto the *p* which the Num 14:40 4725
In the most holy *p* shalt thou eat Num 18:10 6944
And ye shall eat it in every *p* Num 18:31 4725
up without the camp in a clean *p* Num 19:9 4725
to bring us in unto this evil *p* Num 20:5 4725
it is no *p* of seed, or of figs, Num 20:5 4725
called the name of the *p* Hormah Num 21:3 4725
further, and stood in a narrow *p* Num 22:26 4725
And he went to an high *p* Num 23:3 8205
pray thee, with me unto another *p* Num 23:13 4725
I will bring thee unto another *p* Num 23:27 4725
Therefore now flee thou to thy *p* Num 24:11 4725
up, and went and returned to his *p* Num 24:25 4725
in the holy *p* shalt thou cause Num 28:7 6944
the *p* was a *p* for cattle Num 32:1 4725
we have brought them unto their *p* Num 32:17 4725
be in the *p* where his lot falleth Num 33:54
went, until ye came into this *p* Deut 1:31 4725
to search you out a *p* to pitch Deut 1:33 4725
nor unto any *p* of the river Deut 2:37 3027
Egypt, until ye came unto this *p* Deut 9:7 4725
until ye came into this *p* Deut 11:5 4725
Every *p* whereon the soles of your Deut 11:24 4725
the names of them out of that *p* Deut 12:3 4725
But unto the *p* which the LORD Deut 12:5 4725
Then there shall be a *p* which the Deut 12:11 4725
in every *p* that thou seest Deut 12:13 4725
But in the *p* which the LORD shall Deut 12:14 4725
p which the LORD thy God shall Deut 12:18 4725
If the *p* which the LORD thy God Deut 12:21 4725
go unto the *p* which the LORD Deut 12:26 4725
in the *p* which he shall choose to Deut 14:23 4725
shall choose to *p* his name there Deut 14:23 7931
or if the *p* be too far from thee, Deut 14:24 4725
shalt go unto the *p* which the Deut 14:25 4725
the *p* which the LORD shall choose Deut 15:20 4725
in the *p* which the LORD shall Deut 16:2 4725
shall choose to *p* his name there Deut 16:2 7931
But at the *p* which the LORD thy Deut 16:6 4724
God shall choose to *p* his name in Deut 16:6 7931
eat it in the *p* which the LORD Deut 16:7 4725
in the *p* which the LORD thy God Deut 16:11 4725
hath chosen to *p* his name there Deut 16:11 7931
the *p* which the LORD shall choose Deut 16:15 4725
in the *p* which he shall choose Deut 16:16 4725
get thee up into the *p* which the Deut 17:8 4725
which they of that *p* which the Deut 17:10 4725
the *p* which the LORD shall choose Deut 18:6 4725
city, and unto the gate of his *p* Deut 21:19 4725
Thou shalt have a *p* also without Deut 23:12 4725
in that *p* which he shall choose Deut 23:16 4725
shalt go unto the *p* which the Deut 26:2 4725
shall choose to *p* his name there Deut 26:2 7931
And he hath brought us into this *p* Deut 26:9 4725
and putteth it in a secret *p* Deut 27:15
And when ye came unto this *p* Deut 29:7 4725
in the *p* which he shall choose Deut 31:11 4725
Every *p* that the sole of your Josh 1:3 4725
then ye shall remove from your *p* Josh 3:3 4725
out of the *p* where the priests' Josh 4:3 6944
and leave them in the lodging *p* Josh 4:3
them unto the *p* where they lodged Josh 4:8
in the *p* where the feet of the Josh 4:9
of Jordan returned unto their *p* Josh 4:18 4725
Wherefore the name of the *p* is Josh 5:9 4725
for the *p* whereon thou standest Josh 5:15 4725
the name of that *p* was called Josh 7:26 4725
arose quickly out of their *p* Josh 8:19 4725
in the *p* which he should choose Josh 9:27 4725
city unto them, and give him a *p* Josh 20:4 4725
called the name of that *p* Bochim Judg 2:5 4725
of this rock, in the ordered *p* Judg 6:26 4634
people go every man unto his *p* Judg 7:7 4725
man in his *p* round about the camp Judg 7:21 8478
departed every man unto his *p* Judg 9:55 4725
thee, through thy land into my *p* Judg 11:19 4725
and called that *p* Ramath-lehi Judg 15:17 4725
an hollow *p* that was in the jaw Judg 15:19
sojourn where he could find a *p* Judg 17:8
to sojourn where I may find a *p* Judg 17:9
and what makest thou in this *p* Judg 18:3
a *p* where there is no want of any Judg 18:10 4725
that *p* Mahaneh-dan unto this day Judg 18:12 4725
the men of the *p* were Benjamites Judg 19:16 4725
rose up, and gat him unto his *p* Judg 19:28 4725
p where they put themselves in Judg 20:22 4725
of Israel rose up out of their *p* Judg 20:33 4725
Israel gave *p* to the Benjamites Judg 20:36 4725
a *p* which is on the north side of Judg 21:19
forth out of the *p* where she was Ruth 1:7 4725
mark the *p* where he shall lie Ruth 3:4 4725
and from the gate of his *p* Ruth 4:10 4725
when Eli was laid down in his *p* 1Sa 3:2 4725
Samuel went and lay down in his *p* 1Sa 3:9 4725
Dagon, and set him in his *p* again 1Sa 5:3 4725
and let it go again to his own *p* 1Sa 5:11 4725
we shall send it to his *p* 1Sa 6:2 4725
the people to day in the high *p* 1Sa 9:12 1116
he go up to the high *p* to eat 1Sa 9:13 1116
them, for to go up to the high *p* 1Sa 9:14 1116
go up before me unto the high *p* 1Sa 9:19 1116
p among them that were bidden 1Sa 9:22 4725
from the high *p* into the city 1Sa 9:25 1116
from the high *p* with a psaltery 1Sa 10:5 1116
And one of the same *p* answered 1Sa 10:12
he came to the high *p* 1Sa 10:13 1116
and made them dwell in this *p* 1Sa 12:8 4725
then we will stand still in our *p* 1Sa 14:9 8478
Philistines went to their own *p* 1Sa 14:46 4725
and, behold, he set him up a *p* 1Sa 15:12 3027
morning, and abide in a secret *p* 1Sa 19:2
come to the *p* where thou didst 1Sa 20:19 4725
side, and David's *p* was empty 1Sa 20:25 4725
month, that David's *p* was empty 1Sa 20:27 4725

when the lad was come to the *p* of	1Sa 20:37	4725
arose out of a *p* toward the south	1Sa 20:41	
my servants to such and such a *p*	1Sa 21:2	4725
see his *p* where his haunt is, and	1Sa 23:22	4725
called that *p* Sela-hammahlekoth	1Sa 23:28	4725
came to the *p* where Saul had	1Sa 26:5	4725
David beheld the *p* where Saul lay	1Sa 26:5	4725
way, and Saul returned to his *p*	1Sa 26:25	4725
let them give me a *p* in some town	1Sa 27:5	4725
that he may go again to his *p*	1Sa 29:4	4725
wherefore that *p* was called	2Sa 2:16	4725
down there, and died in the same *p*	2Sa 2:23	8478
to the *p* where Asahel fell down	2Sa 2:23	4725
the name of that *p* Baal-perazim	2Sa 5:20	4725
of the *p* Perez-uzzah to this day	2Sa 6:8	4725
of the LORD, and set it in his *p*	2Sa 6:17	4725
appoint a *p* for my people Israel	2Sa 7:10	4725
may dwell in a *p* of their own	2Sa 7:10	8478
that he assigned Uriah unto a *p*	2Sa 11:16	4725
tarried in a *p* that was far off	2Sa 15:17	1004
return to thy *p*, and abide with	2Sa 15:19	4725
surely in what *p* my lord the king	2Sa 15:21	4725
in some pit, or in some other *p*	2Sa 17:9	4725
in some *p* where he shall be found	2Sa 17:12	4725
called unto this day, Absalom's *p*	2Sa 18:18	3027
and he returned unto his own *p*	2Sa 19:39	4725
me forth also into a large *p*	2Sa 22:20	4800
burned with fire in the same *p*	2Sa 23:7	7675
for that was the great high *p*	1Kin 3:4	1116
even unto the *p* that is beyond	1Kin 4:12	
brought they unto the *p* where the	1Kin 4:28	4725
the *p* that thou shalt appoint me	1Kin 5:9	4725
oracle, even for the most holy *p*	1Kin 6:16	6944
the inner house, the most holy *p*	1Kin 7:50	6944
covenant of the LORD unto his *p*	1Kin 8:6	4725
of the house, to the most holy *p*	1Kin 8:6	6944
two wings over the *p* of the ark	1Kin 8:7	4725
in the holy *p* before the oracle	1Kin 8:8	6944
were come out of the holy *p*	1Kin 8:10	6944
a settled *p* for thee to abide in	1Kin 8:13	4349
I have set there a *p* for the ark	1Kin 8:21	4725
even toward the *p* of which thou	1Kin 8:29	4725
servant shall make toward this *p*	1Kin 8:29	4725
they shall pray toward this *p*	1Kin 8:30	4725
thou in heaven thy dwelling *p*	1Kin 8:30	4725
if they pray toward this *p*	1Kin 8:35	4725
thou in heaven thy dwelling *p*	1Kin 8:39	4349
thou in heaven thy dwelling *p*	1Kin 8:43	4349
in heaven thy dwelling *p*, and	1Kin 8:49	4349
either side on the *p* of the seat	1Kin 10:19	4725
build an high *p* for Chemosh	1Kin 11:7	1116
bread nor drink water in this *p*	1Kin 13:8	4725
drink water with thee in this *p*	1Kin 13:16	4725
bread and drunk water in the *p*	1Kin 13:22	4725
away, every man out of his *p*	1Kin 20:24	4725
In the *p* where dogs licked the	1Kin 21:19	4725
in a void *p* in the entrance of	1Kin 22:10	4725
and strike his hand over the *p*	2Kin 5:11	4725
the *p* where we dwell with thee is	2Kin 6:1	4725
beam, and let us make us a *p* there	2Kin 6:2	4725
And he shewed him the *p*	2Kin 6:6	4725
such a *p* shall be my camp	2Kin 6:8	4725
that thou pass not such a *p*	2Kin 6:9	4725
p which the man of God told him	2Kin 6:10	4725
LORD against this *p* to destroy it	2Kin 18:25	4725
I will bring evil upon this *p*	2Kin 22:16	4725
shall be kindled against this *p*	2Kin 22:17	4725
what I spake against this *p*	2Kin 22:19	4725
which I will bring upon this *p*	2Kin 22:20	4725
the high *p* which Jeroboam the son	2Kin 23:15	1116
the high *p* he brake down	2Kin 23:15	1116
and burned the high *p*	2Kin 23:15	1116
p of the tabernacle of the	1Chr 6:32	
all the work of the *p* most holy	1Chr 6:49	
wherefore that *p* is called	1Chr 13:11	4725
the name of that *p* Baal-perazim	1Chr 14:11	4725
prepared a *p* for the ark of God,	1Chr 15:1	4725
up the ark of the LORD unto his *p*	1Chr 15:3	4725
the *p* that I have prepared for it	1Chr 15:12	
strength and gladness are in his *p*	1Chr 16:27	4725
in the high *p* that was at Gibeon	1Chr 16:39	1116
ordain a *p* for my people Israel	1Chr 17:9	4725
and they shall dwell in their *p*	1Chr 17:9	8478
to Ornan, Grant me the *p* of this	1Chr 21:22	4725
p six hundred shekels of gold by	1Chr 21:25	4725
season in the high *p* at Gibeon	1Chr 21:29	1116
and the charge of the holy *p*	1Chr 23:32	6944
of the *p* of the mercy seat,	1Chr 28:11	1004
went to the high *p* that was at	2Chr 1:3	1116
up from Kirjath-jearim to the *p*	2Chr 1:4	
from his journey to the high *p*	2Chr 1:13	1116
in the *p* that David had prepared	2Chr 3:1	4725
doors thereof for the most holy *p*	2Chr 4:22	6944
covenant of the LORD unto his *p*	2Chr 5:7	4725
the house, into the most holy *p*	2Chr 5:7	6944
their wings over the *p* of the ark	2Chr 5:8	4725
were come out of the holy *p*	2Chr 5:11	6944
a *p* for thy dwelling for ever	2Chr 6:2	4349
upon the *p* whereof thou hast said	2Chr 6:20	4725
thy servant prayeth toward this *p*	2Chr 6:20	4725
they shall make toward this *p*	2Chr 6:21	4725
hear thou from thy dwelling *p*	2Chr 6:21	4725
yet if they pray toward this *p*	2Chr 6:26	4725
thou from heaven thy dwelling *p*	2Chr 6:30	4349
heavens, even from thy dwelling *p*	2Chr 6:33	4349
heavens, even from thy dwelling *p*	2Chr 6:39	4349
the prayer that is made in this *p*	2Chr 6:40	4725
O LORD God, into thy resting *p*	2Chr 6:41	
have chosen this *p* to myself for	2Chr 7:12	4725
the prayer that is made in this *p*	2Chr 7:15	4725
on each side of the sitting *p*	2Chr 9:18	4725
they sat in a void *p* at the	2Chr 18:9	
the name of the same *p* was called	2Chr 20:26	4725
it, and carried it to his *p* again	2Chr 24:11	4725
the filthiness out of the holy *p*	2Chr 29:5	6944
the holy *p* unto the God of Israel	2Chr 29:7	6944
in their *p* after their manner	2Chr 30:16	5977
came up to his holy dwelling *p*	2Chr 30:27	
I will bring evil upon this *p*	2Chr 34:24	4725
shall be poured out upon this *p*	2Chr 34:25	4725
heardest his words against this *p*	2Chr 34:27	4725
that I will bring upon this *p*	2Chr 34:28	4725
And the king stood in his *p*	2Chr 34:31	5977
stand in the holy *p* according to	2Chr 35:5	6944
and the priests stood in their *p*	2Chr 35:10	5977
the sons of Asaph were in their *p*	2Chr 35:15	4612
his people, and on his dwelling *p*	2Chr 36:15	
in any *p* where he sojourneth	Ezr 1:4	4725
let the men of his *p* help him	Ezr 1:4	4725
of God to set it up in his *p*	Ezr 2:68	4349
house of God be builded in his *p*	Ezr 5:15	870
builded, the *p* where they offered	Ezr 6:3	870
at Jerusalem, every one to his *p*	Ezr 6:5	870
p them in the house of God	Ezr 6:5	5182
build this house of God in his *p*	Ezr 6:7	870
Iddo the chief at the *p* Casiphia	Ezr 8:17	4725
at the *p* Casiphia, that they	Ezr 8:17	4725
to give us a nail in his holy *p*	Ezr 9:8	4725
will bring them unto the *p* that I	Neh 1:9	4725
the *p* of my fathers' sepulchres,	Neh 2:3	1004
but there was no *p* for the beast	Neh 2:14	4725
unto the *p* over against the	Neh 3:16	
unto the *p* over against the water	Neh 3:26	
son unto the *p* of the Nethinims	Neh 3:31	1004
In what *p* therefore ye hear the	Neh 4:20	4725
and the people stood in their *p*	Neh 8:7	5977
And they stood up in their *p*	Neh 9:3	5977
together, and set them in their *p*	Neh 13:11	5977
her maids unto the best *p* of the	Est 2:9	
arise to the Jews from another *p*	Est 4:14	4725
into the *p* of the banquet of wine	Est 7:8	1004
came every one from his own *p*	Job 2:11	4725
they are consumed out of their *p*	Job 6:17	4725
shall his *p* know him any more	Job 7:10	4725
heap, and seeth the *p* of stones	Job 8:17	1004
If he destroy him from his *p*	Job 8:18	4725
the dwelling *p* of the wicked	Job 8:22	
shaketh the earth out of her *p*	Job 9:6	4725
the rock is removed out of his *p*	Job 14:18	4725
my blood, and let my cry have no *p*	Job 16:18	4725
the rock be removed out of his *p*	Job 18:4	4725
this is the *p* of him that knoweth	Job 18:21	4725
neither shall his *p* any more	Job 20:9	4725
out the north over the empty *p*	Job 26:7	8414
a storm hurleth him out of his *p*	Job 27:21	4725
and shall hiss him out of his *p*	Job 27:23	4725
a *p* for gold where they fine it	Job 28:1	4725
of it are the *p* of sapphires	Job 28:6	4725
where is the *p* of understanding	Job 28:12	4725
where is the *p* of understanding	Job 28:20	4725
and he knoweth the *p* thereof	Job 28:23	4725
out of the strait into a broad *p*	Job 36:16	7338
people are cut off in their *p*	Job 36:20	8478
and is moved out of his *p*	Job 37:1	4725
And brake up for it my decreed *p*	Job 38:10	
the dayspring to know his *p*	Job 38:12	4725
darkness, where is the *p* thereof	Job 38:19	4725
crag of the rock, and the strong *p*	Job 39:28	
tread down the wicked in their *p*	Job 40:12	8478
He made darkness his secret *p*	Ps 18:11	
me forth also into a large *p*	Ps 18:19	4800
or who shall stand in his holy *p*	Ps 24:3	4725
the *p* where thine honour dwelleth	Ps 26:8	4725
My foot standeth in an even *p*	Ps 26:12	
Thou art my hiding *p*	Ps 32:7	
From the *p* of his habitation he	Ps 33:14	4349
shalt diligently consider his *p*	Ps 37:10	4725
broken us in the *p* of dragons	Ps 44:19	4725
the holy *p* of the tabernacles of	Ps 46:4	
pluck thee out of thy dwelling *p*	Ps 52:5	
us out into a wealthy *p*	Ps 66:12	
them, as in Sinai, in the holy *p*	Ps 68:17	6944
p of thy name to the ground	Ps 74:7	
and his dwelling *p* in Zion	Ps 76:2	
and laid waste his dwelling *p*	Ps 79:7	
thee in the secret *p* of thunder	Ps 81:7	
our dwelling *p* in all generations	Ps 90:1	
p of the most High shall abide	Ps 91:1	
the *p* thereof shall know it no	Ps 103:16	4725
the *p* which thou hast founded for	Ps 104:8	4725
me, and set me in a large *p*	Ps 118:5	
Thou art my hiding *p* and my shield	Ps 119:114	
Until I find out a *p* for the LORD	Ps 132:5	4725
in the chief *p* of concourse	Prov 1:21	
children shall have a *p* of refuge	Prov 14:26	
eyes of the LORD are in every *p*	Prov 15:3	4725
spoil not his resting *p*	Prov 24:15	
stand not in the *p* of great men	Prov 25:6	4725
a man that wandereth from his *p*	Prov 27:8	4725
hasteth to his *p* where he arose	Eccl 1:5	4725
unto the *p* from whence the rivers	Eccl 1:7	4725
under the sun the *p* of judgment	Eccl 3:16	4725
the *p* of righteousness, that	Eccl 3:16	4725
All go unto one *p*	Eccl 3:20	4725
do not all go to one *p*	Eccl 6:6	4725
and gone from the *p* of the holy	Eccl 8:10	4725
up against thee, leave not thy *p*	Eccl 10:4	4725
dignity, and the rich sit in low *p*	Eccl 10:6	
in the *p* where the tree falleth,	Eccl 11:3	4725
every dwelling *p* of mount Zion	Is 4:5	
for a *p* of refuge, and for a	Is 4:6	
to field, till there be no *p*	Is 5:8	4725
that day, that every *p* shall be	Is 7:23	4725
earth shall remove out of her *p*	Is 13:13	4725
them, and bring them to their *p*	Is 14:2	4725
that Moab is weary on the high *p*	Is 16:12	1116
p like a clear heat upon herbs	Is 18:4	
to the *p* of the name of the LORD	Is 18:7	4725
fasten him as a nail in a sure *p*	Is 22:23	4725
fastened in the sure *p* be removed	Is 22:25	4725
strangers, as the heat in a dry *p*	Is 25:5	
the LORD cometh out of his *p* to	Is 26:21	4725
so that there is no *p* clean	Is 28:8	4725
shall overflow the hiding *p*	Is 28:17	
barley and the rie in their *p*	Is 28:25	1367
in every *p* where the grounded	Is 30:32	
be as an hiding *p* from the wind	Is 32:2	
as rivers of water in a dry *p*	Is 32:2	
the city shall be low in a low *p*	Is 32:19	
his *p* of defence shall be the	Is 33:16	
be unto us a *p* of broad rivers	Is 33:21	4725
and find for herself a *p* of rest	Is 34:14	
the solitary *p* shall be glad for	Is 35:1	
secret, in a dark *p* of the earth	Is 45:19	4725
carry him, and set him in his *p*	Is 46:7	8478
from his *p* shall he not remove	Is 46:7	4725
I will *p* salvation in Zion for	Is 46:13	5414
The *p* is too strait for me	Is 49:20	4725
give *p* to me that I may dwell	Is 49:20	4725
Enlarge the *p* of thy tent	Is 54:2	4725
mine house and within my walls a *p*	Is 56:5	3027
I dwell in the high and holy *p*	Is 57:15	6944
to beautify the *p* of my sanctuary	Is 60:13	4725
I will make the *p* of my feet	Is 60:13	4725
the valley of Achor a *p* for the	Is 65:10	
and where is the *p* of my rest	Is 66:1	4725
his *p* to make thy land desolate	Jer 4:7	4725
the fruitful *p* was a wilderness,	Jer 4:26	
shall feed every one in his *p*	Jer 6:3	3027
will cause you to dwell in this *p*	Jer 7:3	4725
shed not innocent blood in this *p*	Jer 7:6	4725
I cause you to dwell in this *p*	Jer 7:7	4725
now unto my *p* which was in Shiloh	Jer 7:12	4725
unto the *p* which I gave to you and	Jer 7:14	4725
shall be poured out upon this *p*	Jer 7:20	4725
in Tophet, till there be no *p*	Jer 7:32	4725
a lodging *p* of wayfaring men	Jer 9:2	
from the *p* where I had hid it	Jer 13:7	4725
give you assured peace in this *p*	Jer 14:13	4725
have sons or daughters in this *p*	Jer 16:2	4725
daughters that are born in this *p*	Jer 16:3	4725
cease out of this *p* in your eyes	Jer 16:9	4725
is the *p* of our sanctuary	Jer 17:12	4725
come from another *p* be forsaken	Jer 18:14	2114
I will bring evil upon this *p*	Jer 19:3	4725
me, and have estranged this *p*	Jer 19:4	4725
have filled this *p* with the blood	Jer 19:4	4725
that this *p* shall no more be	Jer 19:6	4725
of Judah and Jerusalem in this *p*	Jer 19:7	4725
till there be no *p* to bury	Jer 19:11	4725
Thus will I do unto this *p*	Jer 19:12	4725
be defiled as the *p* of Tophet	Jer 19:13	4725
shed innocent blood in this *p*	Jer 22:3	4725
which went forth out of this *p*	Jer 22:11	4725
But he shall die in the *p* whither	Jer 22:12	4725
whom I have sent out of this *p*	Jer 24:5	4725
up, and restore them to this *p*	Jer 27:22	4725
will I bring again into this *p*	Jer 28:3	4725
of Babylon took away from this *p*	Jer 28:3	4725
I will bring again to this *p*	Jer 28:4	4725
captive, from Babylon into this *p*	Jer 28:6	4725
causing you to return to this *p*	Jer 29:10	4725
the *p* whence I caused you to be	Jer 29:14	4725
will bring them again unto this *p*	Jer 32:37	4725
there shall be heard in this *p*	Jer 33:10	4725
Again in this *p*, which is	Jer 33:12	4725
for hunger in the *p* where he is	Jer 38:9	8478
pronounced this evil upon this *p*	Jer 40:2	4725
and ye shall see this *p* no more	Jer 42:18	4725
in the *p* whither ye desire to go	Jer 42:22	4725
that I will punish you in this *p*	Jer 44:29	4725
a dwelling *p* for dragons, an	Jer 51:37	4725
thou hast spoken against this *p*	Jer 51:62	4725
the glory of the LORD from his *p*	Eze 3:12	4725
the *p* where they did offer sweet	Eze 6:13	4725
and they shall pollute my secret *p*	Eze 7:22	
but to the *p* whither the head	Eze 10:11	4725
thou shalt remove from thy *p*	Eze 12:3	4725
to another *p* in their sight	Eze 12:3	4725
also built unto thee an eminent *p*	Eze 16:24	
thee an high *p* in every street	Eze 16:24	
high *p* at every head of the way	Eze 16:25	
p in the head of every way	Eze 16:31	
thine high *p* in every street	Eze 16:31	
shall throw down thine eminent *p*	Eze 16:39	
surely in the *p* where the king	Eze 17:16	4725
is the high *p* whereunto ye go	Eze 20:29	1116
and choose thou a *p*, choose it at	Eze 21:19	3027
in the *p* where thou wast created	Eze 21:30	4725
It shall be a *p* for the spreading	Eze 26:5	
thou shalt be a *p* to spread nets	Eze 26:14	
I shall *p* you in your own land	Eze 37:14	3241
and I will *p* them, and multiply	Eze 37:26	5414
from thy *p* out of the north parts	Eze 38:15	4725

Gog a *p* there of graves in Israel ... Eze 39:11 4725
unto me, This is the most holy *p* ... Eze 41:4 6944
that which was left was the *p* of ... Eze 41:9 1004
were toward the *p* that was left ... Eze 41:11
the breadth of the *p* that was ... Eze 41:11 4725
that was before the separate *p* at ... Eze 41:12
and the separate *p*, and the ... Eze 41:13
of the separate *p* toward the east ... Eze 41:14
separate *p* which was behind it ... Eze 41:15
was over against the separate *p* ... Eze 42:1
east, over against the separate *p* ... Eze 42:10
which are before the separate *p* ... Eze 42:13
for the *p* is holy ... Eze 42:13 4725
the holy *p* into the utter court ... Eze 42:14 6944
the sanctuary and the profane *p* ... Eze 42:20
the *p* of my throne ... Eze 43:7 4725
the *p* of the soles of my feet, ... Eze 43:7 4725
be the higher *p* of the altar ... Eze 43:13
in the appointed *p* of the house ... Eze 43:21
holy things, in the most holy *p* ... Eze 44:13 6944
the sanctuary and the most holy *p* ... Eze 45:3 6944
it shall be a *p* for their houses, ... Eze 45:4 4725
an holy *p* for the sanctuary ... Eze 45:4 6944
there was a *p* on the two sides ... Eze 46:19 4725
This is the *p* where the priests ... Eze 46:20 4725
they shall be a *p* to spread forth ... Eze 47:10 4725
shall be a profane *p* for the city ... Eze 48:15
that no *p* was found for them ... Dan 2:35 870
the *p* of his sanctuary was cast ... Dan 8:11 4349
they shall *p* the abomination that ... Dan 11:31 5414
that in the *p* where it was said ... Hos 1:10 4725
feed them as a lamb in a large *p* ... Hos 4:16
I will go and return to my *p* ... Hos 5:15 4725
Tyrus, is planted in a pleasant *p* ... Hos 9:13
I will *p* them in their houses, ... Hos 11:11 3427
in the *p* of the breaking forth of ... Hos 13:13
the *p* whither ye have sold them ... Joel 3:7 4725
be many dead bodies in every *p* ... Amos 8:3 4725
LORD cometh forth out of his *p* ... Mic 1:3 4725
that are poured down a steep *p* ... Mic 1:4
an utter end of the *p* thereof ... Nah 1:8 4725
the feeding *p* of the young lions, ... Nah 2:11 4725
their *p* is not known where they ... Nah 3:17 4725
the remnant of Baal from this *p* ... Zeph 1:4 4725
worship him, every one from his *p* ... Zeph 2:11 4725
a *p* for beasts to lie down in ... Zeph 2:15
in this *p* will I give peace, ... Hag 2:9 4725
and he shall grow up out of his *p* ... Zec 6:12 8478
I will bring them again to *p* them ... Zec 10:6 3427
p shall not be found for them ... Zec 10:10
be inhabited again in her own *p* ... Zec 12:6 8478
lifted up, and inhabited in her *p* ... Zec 14:10 8478
gate unto the *p* of the first gate ... Zec 14:10 4725
in every *p* incense shall be ... Mal 1:11 4725
down a steep *p* into the sea ... Mt 8:32
He said unto them, Give *p* ... Mt 9:24 *402*
That in this *p* is one greater ... Mt 12:6 *5602*
by ship into a desert *p* apart ... Mt 14:13 *5117*
him, saying, This is a desert *p* ... Mt 14:15 *5117*
of that *p* had knowledge of him ... Mt 14:35 *5117*
Remove hence to yonder *p* ... Mt 17:20
the prophet, stand in the holy *p* ... Mt 24:15 *5117*
them unto a *p* called Gethsemane ... Mt 26:36 *5564*
Put up again thy sword into his *p* ... Mt 26:52 *5117*
come unto a *p* called Golgotha ... Mt 27:33 *5117*
that is to say, a *p* of a skull, ... Mt 27:33 *5117*
see the *p* where the Lord lay ... Mt 28:6 *5117*
and departed into a solitary *p* ... Mk 1:35 *5117*
down a steep *p* into the sea ... Mk 5:13
In what *p* soever ye enter into a ... Mk 6:10 *3699*
abide till ye depart from that *p* ... Mk 6:10 *1564*
yourselves apart into a desert *p* ... Mk 6:31 *5117*
into a desert *p* by ship privately ... Mk 6:32 *5117*
him, and said, This is a desert *p* ... Mk 6:35 *5117*
without in a *p* where two ways met ... Mk 11:4 *296*
digged a *p* for the winefat, and ... Mk 12:1
they came to a *p* which was named ... Mk 14:32 *5564*
bring him unto the *p* Golgotha ... Mk 15:22 *5117*
interpreted, The *p* of a skull ... Mk 15:22 *5117*
behold the *p* where they laid him ... Mk 16:6 *5117*
he found the *p* where it was ... Lk 4:17 *5117*
p of the country round about ... Lk 4:37 *5117*
departed and went into a desert *p* ... Lk 4:42 *5117*
down a steep *p* into the lake ... Lk 8:33
p belonging to the city called ... Lk 9:10 *5117*
for we are here in a desert *p* ... Lk 9:12 *5117*
his face into every city and *p* ... Lk 10:1 *5117*
a Levite, when he was at the *p* ... Lk 10:32 *5117*
as he was praying in a certain *p* ... Lk 11:1 *5117*
candle, putteth it in a secret *p* ... Lk 11:33
and say to thee, Give this man *p* ... Lk 14:9 *5117*
also come into this *p* of torment ... Lk 16:28 *5117*
And when Jesus came to the *p* ... Lk 19:5 *5117*
And when he was at the *p*, he said ... Lk 22:40 *5117*
beginning from Galilee to this *p* ... Lk 23:5 *5602*
And when they were come to the *p* ... Lk 23:33 *5117*
that in Jerusalem is the *p* where ... Jn 4:20 *5117*
away, a multitude being in that *p* ... Jn 5:13 *5117*
Now there was much grass in the *p* ... Jn 6:10 *5117*
the *p* where they did eat bread ... Jn 6:23 *5117*
because my word hath no *p* in you ... Jn 8:37 *5562*
p where John at first baptized ... Jn 10:40 *5117*
still in the same *p* where he was ... Jn 11:6 *5117*
but was in that *p* where Martha ... Jn 11:30 *5117*
the *p* where the dead was laid ... Jn 11:41
come and take away both our *p* ... Jn 11:48 *5117*
I go to prepare a *p* for you ... Jn 14:2 *5117*
And if I go and prepare a *p* for you ... Jn 14:3 *5117*
which betrayed him, knew the *p* ... Jn 18:2 *5117*
a *p* that is called the Pavement ... Jn 19:13 *5117*
a *p* called the *p* of a skull ... Jn 19:17 *5117*
for the *p* where Jesus was ... Jn 19:20 *5117*
Now in the *p* where he was ... Jn 19:41 *5117*
wrapped together in a *p* by itself ... Jn 20:7 *5117*
that he might go to his own *p* ... Acts 1:25 *5117*
were all with one accord in one *p* ... Acts 2:1
the *p* was shaken where they were ... Acts 4:31 *5117*
words against this holy *p* ... Acts 6:13 *5117*
of Nazareth shall destroy this *p* ... Acts 6:14 *5117*
come forth, and serve me in this *p* ... Acts 7:7 *5117*
for the *p* where thou standest is ... Acts 7:33 *5117*
or what is the *p* of my rest ... Acts 7:49 *5117*
The *p* of the scripture which he ... Acts 8:32 *4042*
departed, and went into another *p* ... Acts 12:17 *5117*
both we, and they of that *p* ... Acts 21:12 *1786*
the people, and the law, and this *p* ... Acts 21:28 *5117*
and hath polluted this holy *p* ... Acts 21:28 *5117*
was entered into the *p* of hearing ... Acts 25:23 *201*
came unto a *p* which is called The ... Acts 27:8 *5117*
falling into a *p* where two seas ... Acts 27:41 *5117*
that in the *p* where it was said ... Rom 9:26 *5117*
but rather give *p* unto wrath ... Rom 12:19 *5117*
having no more *p* in these parts ... Rom 15:23 *5117*
with all that in every *p* call ... 1Cor 1:2 *5117*
have no certain dwellingplace *p* ... 1Cor 4:11 *5117*
together therefore into one *p* ... 1Cor 11:20
be come together into one *p* ... 1Cor 14:23
of his knowledge by us in every *p* ... 2Cor 2:14 *5117*
To whom we gave *p* by subjection ... Gal 2:5 *1502*
Neither give *p* to the devil ... Eph 4:27 *5117*
but also in every *p* your faith to ... 1Th 1:8 *5117*
But one in a certain *p* testified ... Heb 2:6
For he spake in a certain *p* of ... Heb 4:4
And in this *p* again, If they shall ... Heb 4:5
As he saith also in another *p* ... Heb 5:6
then should no *p* have been sought ... Heb 8:7 *5117*
entered in once into the holy *p* ... Heb 9:12 *39*
priest entereth into the holy *p* ... Heb 9:25 *39*
a *p* which he should after receive ... Heb 11:8 *5117*
for he found no *p* of repentance ... Heb 12:17 *5117*
him, Sit thou here in a good *p* ... Jas 2:3
forth at the same *p* sweet water ... Jas 3:11 *3692*
a light that shineth in a dark *p* ... 2Pet 1:19 *5117*
thy candlestick out of his *p* ... Rev 2:5 *5117*
she hath a *p* prepared of God ... Rev 12:6 *5117*
neither was their *p* found any ... Rev 12:8 *5117*
into the wilderness, into her *p* ... Rev 12:14 *5117*
a *p* called in the Hebrew tongue ... Rev 16:16 *5117*
and there was found no *p* for them ... Rev 20:11 *5117*

PLACED {14}

he *p* at the east of the garden of ... Gen 3:24 7931
Joseph *p* his father and his ... Gen 47:11 3427
he *p* in Beth-el the priests of ... 1Kin 12:32 5975
p them in Halah and in Habor by ... 2Kin 17:6 3427
p them in the cities of Samaria ... 2Kin 17:24 3427
p in the cities of Samaria, know ... 2Kin 17:26 3427
which he *p* in the chariot cities, ... 2Chr 1:14 3240
p them in the temple, five on the ... 2Chr 4:8 3240
he *p* forces in all the fenced ... 2Chr 17:2 5414
old, since man was *p* upon earth ... Job 20:4 7760
the tent which he *p* among men ... Ps 78:60 7931
that they may be *p* alone in the ... Is 5:8 3427
which have *p* the sand for the ... Jer 5:22 776
he *p* it by great waters, and set ... Eze 17:5 3947

PLACES {216}

thee in all *p* whither thou goest ... Gen 28:15
to their families, after their *p* ... Gen 36:40 4725
in all *p* where I record my name I ... Ex 20:24 4725
border shall the rings be for *p* ... Ex 25:27 1004
rings of gold for *p* for the bars ... Ex 26:29 1004
they shall be for *p* for the ... Ex 30:4 1004
of gold to be *p* for the bars ... Ex 36:34 1004
the *p* for the staves to bear the ... Ex 37:14 1004
to be *p* for the staves to bear it ... Ex 37:27 1004
of brass, to be *p* for the staves ... Ex 38:5 1004
And I will destroy your high *p* ... Lev 26:30
the lords of the high *p* of Arnon ... Num 21:28
him up into the high *p* of Baal ... Num 22:41
quite pluck down all their high *p* ... Num 33:52
unto all the *p* nigh thereunto, in ... Deut 1:7
shall utterly destroy all the *p* ... Deut 12:2 4725
ride on the high *p* of the earth ... Deut 32:13
shalt tread upon their high *p* ... Deut 33:29
they abode in their *p* in the camp ... Josh 5:8 8478
archers in the *p* of drawing water ... Judg 5:11
death in the high *p* of the field ... Judg 5:18
one of these *p* to lodge all night ... Judg 19:13 4725
Israel came forth out of their *p* ... Judg 20:33 4725
and judged Israel in all those *p* ... 1Sa 7:16 4725
and in rocks, and in high *p* ... 1Sa 13:6
lurking *p* where he hideth himself ... 1Sa 23:23
to all the *p* where David himself ... 1Sa 30:31 4725
Israel is slain upon thy high *p* ... 2Sa 1:19
thou wast slain in thine high *p* ... 2Sa 1:25
In all the *p* wherein I have ... 2Sa 7:7
and setteth me upon my high *p* ... 2Sa 22:34
be afraid out of their close *p* ... 2Sa 22:46
the people sacrificed in high *p* ... 1Kin 3:2
and burnt incense in high *p* ... 1Kin 3:3
And he made an house of high *p* ... 1Kin 12:31
of the high *p* which he had made ... 1Kin 12:32
p that burn incense upon thee ... 1Kin 13:2
high *p* which are in the cities of ... 1Kin 13:32
the people priests of the high *p* ... 1Kin 13:33
one of the priests of the high *p* ... 1Kin 13:33
For they also built them high *p* ... 1Kin 14:23
But the high *p* were not removed ... 1Kin 15:14
the high *p* were not taken away ... 1Kin 22:43
burnt incense yet in the high *p* ... 1Kin 22:43
But the high *p* were not taken ... 2Kin 12:3
and burnt incense in the high *p* ... 2Kin 12:3
Howbeit the high *p* were not taken ... 2Kin 14:4
and burnt incense on the high *p* ... 2Kin 14:4
that the high *p* were not removed ... 2Kin 15:4
burnt incense still on the high *p* ... 2Kin 15:4
the high *p* were not removed ... 2Kin 15:35
incense still in the high *p* ... 2Kin 15:35
and burnt incense in the high *p* ... 2Kin 16:4
them high *p* in all their cities ... 2Kin 17:9
burnt incense in all the high *p* ... 2Kin 17:11
p which the Samaritans had made ... 2Kin 17:29
of them priests of the high *p* ... 2Kin 17:32
them in the houses of the high *p* ... 2Kin 17:32
He removed the high *p*, and brake ... 2Kin 18:4
is not that he, whose high *p* ... 2Kin 18:22
up all the rivers of besieged *p* ... 2Kin 19:24
p which Hezekiah his father had ... 2Kin 21:3
the high *p* in the cities of Judah ... 2Kin 23:5
in the *p* round about Jerusalem ... 2Kin 23:5
defiled the high *p* where the ... 2Kin 23:8
brake down the high *p* of the ... 2Kin 23:8
the priests of the high *p* came ... 2Kin 23:9
the high *p* that were before ... 2Kin 23:13
filled their *p* with the bones of ... 2Kin 23:14 4725
high *p* that were in the cities of ... 2Kin 23:19
all the priests of the high *p* ... 2Kin 23:20
p throughout their castles in ... 1Chr 6:54
of Israel, because the *p* are holy ... 2Chr 8:11
him priests for the high *p* ... 2Chr 11:15
the strange gods, and the high *p* ... 2Chr 14:3
the cities of Judah the high *p* ... 2Chr 14:5
But the high *p* were not taken ... 2Chr 15:17
moreover he took away the high *p* ... 2Chr 17:6
Howbeit the high *p* were not taken ... 2Chr 20:33
Moreover he made high *p* in the ... 2Chr 21:11
and burnt incense in the high *p* ... 2Chr 28:4
city of Judah he made high *p* to ... 2Chr 28:25
groves, and threw down the high *p* ... 2Chr 31:1
Hezekiah taken away his high *p* ... 2Chr 32:12
For he built again the high *p* ... 2Chr 33:3
did sacrifice still in the high *p* ... 2Chr 33:17
the *p* wherein he built high ... 2Chr 33:19 4725
wherein he built high *p* ... 2Chr 33:19
and Jerusalem from the high *p* ... 2Chr 34:3
From all *p* whence ye shall return ... Neh 4:12 4725
I in the lower *p* behind the wall ... Neh 4:13 4725
the wall, and on the higher *p* ... Neh 4:13
the Levites out of all their *p* ... Neh 12:27 4725
built desolate *p* for themselves ... Job 3:14 2723
shall be hid in his secret *p* ... Job 20:26
are the dwelling *p* of the wicked ... Job 21:28 168
he maketh peace in his high *p* ... Job 25:2
into dens, and remain in their *p* ... Job 37:8 4585
in the lurking *p* of the villages ... Ps 10:8
in the secret *p* doth he murder ... Ps 10:8
are fallen unto me in pleasant *p* ... Ps 16:6
a young lion lurking in secret *p* ... Ps 17:12
and setteth me upon my high *p* ... Ps 18:33
and be afraid out of their close *p* ... Ps 18:45
ever, and their dwelling *p* to all ... Ps 49:11
art terrible out of thy holy *p* ... Ps 68:35
thou didst set them in slippery *p* ... Ps 73:18
for the dark *p* of the earth are ... Ps 74:20
him to anger with their high *p* ... Ps 78:58
hand are the deep *p* of the earth ... Ps 95:4
works in all *p* of his dominion ... Ps 103:22 4725
ran in the dry *p* like a river ... Ps 105:41
also out of their desolate *p* ... Ps 109:10
he shall fill the *p* with the dead ... Ps 110:6
earth, in the seas, and all deep *p* ... Ps 135:6
judges are overthrown in stony *p* ... Ps 141:6 3027
She standeth in the top of high *p* ... Prov 8:2
by the way in the *p* of the paths ... Prov 8:2 1004
upon the highest *p* of the city ... Prov 9:3
a seat in the high *p* of the city ... Prov 9:14
in the secret *p* of the stairs ... Song 2:14
the waste *p* of the fat ones shall ... Is 5:17
Bajith, and to Dibon, the high *p* ... Is 15:2
dwellings, and in quiet resting *p* ... Is 32:18
is it not he, whose high *p* ... Is 36:7
all the rivers of the besieged *p* ... Is 37:25
straight, and the rough *p* plain ... Is 40:4
I will open rivers in high *p* ... Is 41:18
raise up the decayed *p* thereof ... Is 44:26
and make the crooked *p* straight ... Is 45:2
and hidden riches of secret *p* ... Is 45:3
pastures shall be in all high *p* ... Is 49:9
For thy waste and thy desolate *p* ... Is 49:19
he will comfort all her waste *p* ... Is 51:3
together, ye waste *p* of Jerusalem ... Is 52:9
thee shall build the old waste *p* ... Is 58:12
ride upon the high *p* of the earth ... Is 58:14
we are in desolate *p* as dead men ... Is 59:10
up thine eyes unto the high *p* ... Jer 3:2
A voice was heard upon the high *p* ... Jer 3:21
A dry wind of the high *p* in the ... Jer 4:11
from those *p* shall come unto me ... Jer 4:12
and seek in the broad *p* thereof ... Jer 5:1
take up a lamentation on high *p* ... Jer 7:29
have built the high *p* of Tophet ... Jer 7:31
which remain in all the *p* whither ... Jer 8:3 4725
all high *p* through the wilderness ... Jer 12:12
weep in secret *p* for your pride ... Jer 13:17

asses did stand in the high *p*...... Jer 14:6
the spoil, and thy high *p* for sin...... Jer 17:3
the parched *p* in the wilderness...... Jer 17:6
from the *p* about Jerusalem, and...... Jer 17:26 5439
built also the high *p* of Baal...... Jer 19:5
the pleasant *p* of the wilderness...... Jer 23:10
secret *p* that I shall not see him...... Jer 23:24
in all *p* whither I shall drive...... Jer 24:9 4725
house as the high *p* of a forest...... Jer 26:18
from all the *p* whither I have...... Jer 29:14 4725
And they built the high *p* of Baal...... Jer 32:35
in the *p* about Jerusalem, and in...... Jer 32:44
in the *p* about Jerusalem, and in...... Jer 33:13
of all *p* whither they were driven...... Jer 40:12 4725
prey in all *p* whither thou goest...... Jer 45:5 4725
him that offereth in the high *p*...... Jer 48:35
I have uncovered his secret *p*...... Jer 49:10
destroyed his *p* of the assembly...... Lam 2:6
He hath set me in dark *p*, as they...... Lam 3:6
in wait, and as a lion in secret *p*...... Lam 3:10
and I will destroy your high *p*...... Eze 6:3
the high *p* shall be desolate...... Eze 6:6
their holy *p* shall be defiled...... Eze 7:24
deckedst thy high *p* with divers...... Eze 16:16
and shall break down thy high *p*...... Eze 16:39
drop thy word toward the holy *p*...... Eze 21:2
in *p* desolate of old, with them...... Eze 26:20
will deliver them out of all *p*...... Eze 34:12 4725
the inhabited *p* of the country...... Eze 34:13
the *p* round about my hill a...... Eze 34:26
even the ancient high *p* are ours...... Eze 36:2
I the LORD build the ruined *p*...... Eze 36:36
desolate *p* that are now inhabited...... Eze 38:12
the steep *p* shall fall, and every...... Eze 38:20
of their kings in their high *p*...... Eze 43:7
it was made with boiling *p* under...... Eze 46:23
These are the *p* of them that boil...... Eze 46:24 1004
But the miry *p* thereof and the...... Eze 47:11
the fattest *p* of the province...... Dan 11:24
the pleasant *p* for their silver,...... Hos 9:6
The high *p* also of Aven, the sin...... Hos 10:8
and want of bread in all your *p*...... Amos 4:6 4725
upon the high *p* of the earth...... Amos 4:13
the high *p* of Isaac shall be...... Amos 7:9
upon the high *p* of the earth...... Mic 1:3
and what are the high *p* of Judah...... Mic 1:5
house as the high *p* of the forest...... Mic 3:12
make me to walk upon mine high *p*...... Hab 3:19
I will give thee *p* to walk among...... Zec 3:7
return and build the desolate *p*...... Mal 1:4
a man, he walketh through dry *p*...... Mt 12:43 *5117*
Some fell upon stony *p*, where...... Mt 13:5
received the seed into stony *p*...... Mt 13:20
and earthquakes, in divers *p*...... Mt 24:7 *5117*
city, but was without in desert *p*...... Mk 1:45 *5117*
shall be earthquakes in divers *p*...... Mk 13:8 *5117*
a man, he walketh through dry *p*...... Lk 11:24 *5117*
earthquakes shall be in divers *p*...... Lk 21:11 *5117*
We accept it always, and in all *p*...... Acts 24:3 *3837*
blessings in heavenly *p* in Christ...... Eph 1:3
own right hand in the heavenly *p*...... Eph 1:20
in heavenly *p* in Christ Jesus...... Eph 2:6
powers in heavenly *p* might be...... Eph 3:10
spiritual wickedness in high *p*...... Eph 6:12
all the palace, and in all other *p*...... Phil 1:13
into the holy *p* made with hands...... Heb 9:24
island were moved out of their *p*...... Rev 6:14 *5117*

PLAGUE {98}
I bring one *p* more upon Pharaoh...... Ex 11:1 5061
the *p* shall not be upon you to...... Ex 12:13 5063
that there be no *p* among them...... Ex 30:12 5063
his flesh like the *p* of leprosy...... Lev 13:2 5061
on the *p* in the skin of the flesh...... Lev 13:3 5061
the hair in the *p* is turned white...... Lev 13:3 5061
the *p* in sight be deeper than the...... Lev 13:3 5061
his flesh, it is a *p* of leprosy...... Lev 13:3 5061
up him that hath the *p* seven days...... Lev 13:4 5061
if the *p* in his sight be at a...... Lev 13:5 5061
the *p* spread not in the skin...... Lev 13:5 5061
if the *p* be somewhat dark...... Lev 13:6 5061
the *p* spread not in the skin...... Lev 13:6 5061
When the *p* of leprosy is in a man...... Lev 13:9 5061
the skin of him that hath the *p*...... Lev 13:12 5061
him clean that hath the *p*...... Lev 13:13 5061
if the *p* be turned into white...... Lev 13:17 5061
him clean that hath the *p*...... Lev 13:17 5061
it is a *p* of leprosy broken out...... Lev 13:20 5061
it is a *p*...... Lev 13:22 5061
it is the *p* of leprosy...... Lev 13:25 5061
it is the *p* of leprosy...... Lev 13:27 5061
If a man or woman have a *p* upon...... Lev 13:29 5061
Then the priest shall see the *p*...... Lev 13:30 5061
priest look on the *p* of the scall...... Lev 13:31 5061
the *p* of the scall seven days...... Lev 13:31 5061
the priest shall look on the *p*...... Lev 13:32 5061
his *p* is in his head...... Lev 13:44 5061
And the leper in whom the *p* is...... Lev 13:45 5061
All the days wherein the *p* shall...... Lev 13:46 5061
also that the *p* of leprosy is in...... Lev 13:47 5061
if the *p* be greenish or reddish...... Lev 13:49 5061
it is a *p* of leprosy, and shall be...... Lev 13:49 5061
the priest shall look upon the *p*...... Lev 13:50 5061
up it that hath the *p* seven days...... Lev 13:50 5061
look on the *p* on the seventh day...... Lev 13:51 5061
if the *p* be spread in the garment...... Lev 13:51 5061
the *p* is a fretting leprosy...... Lev 13:51 5061
thing of skin, wherein the *p* is...... Lev 13:52 5061
the *p* be not spread in the...... Lev 13:53 5061
wash the thing wherein the *p* is...... Lev 13:54 5061
And the priest shall look on the *p*...... Lev 13:55 5061
if the *p* have not changed his...... Lev 13:55 5061
colour, and the *p* be not spread...... Lev 13:55 5061
the *p* be somewhat dark after the...... Lev 13:56 5061
it is a spreading *p*...... Lev 13:57
that wherein the *p* is with fire...... Lev 13:57 5061
if the *p* be departed from them,...... Lev 13:58 5061
This is the law of the *p* of...... Lev 13:59 5061
if the *p* of leprosy be healed in...... Lev 14:3 5061
him in whom is the *p* of leprosy...... Lev 14:32 5061
I put the *p* of leprosy in a house...... Lev 14:34 5061
is as it were a *p* in the house...... Lev 14:35 5061
priest go into it to see the *p*...... Lev 14:36 5061
And he shall look on the *p*...... Lev 14:37 5061
if the *p* be in the walls of the...... Lev 14:37 5061
if the *p* be spread in the walls...... Lev 14:39 5061
away the stones in which the *p* is...... Lev 14:40 5061
if the *p* come again, and break out...... Lev 14:43 5061
if the *p* be spread in the house,...... Lev 14:44 5061
the *p* hath not spread in the...... Lev 14:48 5061
clean, because the *p* is healed...... Lev 14:48 5061
for all manner of *p* of leprosy...... Lev 14:54 5061
that there be no *p* among the...... Num 8:19 5063
the people with a very great *p*...... Num 11:33 4347
died by the *p* before the LORD...... Num 14:37 4046
the *p* is begun...... Num 16:46 5063
the *p* was begun among the people...... Num 16:47 5063
and the *p* was stayed...... Num 16:48 4046
in the *p* were fourteen thousand...... Num 16:49 4046
and the *p* was stayed...... Num 16:50 4046
So the *p* was stayed from the...... Num 25:8 4046
that died in the *p* were twenty...... Num 25:9 4046
the day of the *p* for Peor's sake...... Num 25:18 4046
And it came to pass after the *p*...... Num 26:1 4046
Peor, and there was a *p* among the...... Num 31:16 4046
Take heed in the *p* of leprosy...... Deut 24:8 5061
Also every sickness, and every *p*...... Deut 28:61 4347
although there was a *p* in the...... Josh 22:17 5063
for one *p* was on you all, and on...... 1Sa 6:4 4046
that the *p* may be stayed from the...... 2Sa 24:21 4046
the *p* was stayed from Israel...... 2Sa 24:25 4046
whatsoever *p*, whatsoever sickness...... 1Kin 8:37 5061
every man the *p* of his own heart...... 1Kin 8:38 5061
that the *p* may be stayed from the...... 1Chr 21:22 4046
with a great *p* will the LORD...... 2Chr 21:14 4046
his face, and *p* them that hate him...... Ps 89:23 5063
neither shall any *p* come nigh thy...... Ps 91:10 5061
and the *p* brake in upon them...... Ps 106:29 4046
and so the *p* was stayed...... Ps 106:30 4046
this shall be the *p* wherewith the...... Zec 14:12 4046
And so shall be the *p* of the horse...... Zec 14:15 4046
be in these tents, as this *p*...... Zec 14:15 4046
there shall be the *p*, wherewith...... Zec 14:18 4046
that she was healed of that *p*...... Mk 5:29 *3148*
go in peace, and be whole of thy *p*...... Mk 5:34 *3148*
God because of the *p* of the hail...... Rev 16:21 *4127*
for the *p* thereof was exceeding...... Rev 16:21 *4127*

PLAGUED {6}
And the LORD *p* Pharaoh and his...... Gen 12:17 5060
the LORD *p* the people, because...... Ex 32:35 5062
I *p* Egypt, according to that...... Josh 24:5 5062
thy people, that they should be *p*...... 1Chr 21:17 4046
neither are they *p* like other men...... Ps 73:5 5060
all the day long have I been *p*...... Ps 73:14 5060

PLAGUES {24}
his house with great *p* because of...... Gen 12:17 5061
send all my *p* upon thine heart...... Ex 9:14 4046
I will bring seven times more *p*...... Lev 26:21 4347
LORD will make thy *p* wonderful...... Deut 28:59 4347
p of thy seed, even great *p*...... Deut 28:59 4347
when they see the *p* of that land...... Deut 29:22 4347
with all the *p* in the wilderness...... 1Sa 4:8 4347
hiss because of all the *p* thereof...... Jer 19:8 4347
shall hiss at all the *p* thereof...... Jer 49:17 4347
astonished, and hiss at all her *p*...... Jer 50:13 4347
O death, I will be thy *p*...... Hos 13:14 1698
to touch him, as many as had *p*...... Mk 3:10 *3148*
many of their infirmities and *p*...... Lk 7:21 *3148*
p yet repented not of the works...... Rev 9:20 *4127*
and to smite the earth with all *p*...... Rev 11:6 *4127*
angels having the seven last *p*...... Rev 15:1 *4127*
of the temple, having the seven *p*...... Rev 15:6 *4127*
till the seven *p* of the seven...... Rev 15:8 *4127*
which hath power over these *p*...... Rev 16:9 *4127*
and that ye receive not of her *p*...... Rev 18:4 *4127*
shall her *p* come in one day...... Rev 18:8 *4127*
vials full of the seven last *p*...... Rev 21:9 *4127*
God shall add unto him the *p* that...... Rev 22:18 *4127*

PLAIN {75}
that they found a *p* in the land...... Gen 11:2 1237
of Sichem, unto the *p* of Moreh...... Gen 12:6 436
and beheld all the *p* of Jordan...... Gen 13:10 3603
Lot chose him all the *p* of Jordan...... Gen 13:11 3603
dwelled in the cities of the *p*...... Gen 13:12 3603
came and dwelt in the *p* of Mamre...... Gen 13:18 436
for he dwelt in the *p* of Mamre...... Gen 14:13 436
neither stay thou in all the *p*...... Gen 19:17 3603
those cities, and all the *p*...... Gen 19:25 3603
and toward all the land of the *p*...... Gen 19:28 3603
God destroyed the cities of the *p*...... Gen 19:29 3603
and Jacob was a *p* man, dwelling in...... Gen 25:27 8535
in the *p* over against the Red sea...... Deut 1:1 6160
places nigh thereunto, in the *p*...... Deut 1:7 6160
the way of the *p* from Elath...... Deut 2:8 6160
All the cities of the *p*, and all...... Deut 3:10 4334
The *p* also, and Jordan, and the...... Deut 3:17 6160
even unto the sea of the *p*...... Deut 3:17 6160
in the *p* country, of the...... Deut 4:43 4334
all the *p* on this side Jordan...... Deut 4:49 6160
even unto the sea of the *p*...... Deut 4:49 6160
the *p* of the valley of Jericho,...... Deut 34:3 3603
came down toward the sea of the *p*...... Josh 3:16 6160
at a time appointed, before the *p*...... Josh 8:14 6160
Goshen, and the valley, and the *p*...... Josh 11:16 6160
Hermon, and all the *p* on the east...... Josh 12:1 6160
And from the *p* to the sea of...... Josh 12:3 6160
east, and unto the sea of the *p*...... Josh 12:3 6160
all the *p* of Medeba unto Dibon...... Josh 13:9 4334
the river, and all the *p* by Medeba...... Josh 13:16 4334
all her cities that are in the *p*...... Josh 13:17 4334
And all the cities of the *p*...... Josh 13:21 4334
the *p* out of the tribe of Reuben...... Josh 20:8 4334
his tent unto the *p* of Zaanaim...... Judg 4:11 436
by the *p* of the pillar that was...... Judg 9:6 436
come along by the *p* of Meonenim...... Judg 9:37 436
unto the *p* of the vineyards, with...... Judg 11:33 58
thou shalt come to the *p* of Tabor...... 1Sa 10:3 436
in the *p* on the south of Jeshimon...... 1Sa 23:24 6160
all that night through the *p*...... 2Sa 2:29 6160
them away through the *p* all night...... 2Sa 4:7 6160
tarry in the *p* of the wilderness...... 2Sa 15:28 6160
Ahimaaz ran by the way of the *p*...... 2Sa 18:23 3603
In the *p* of Jordan did the king...... 1Kin 7:46 3603
us fight against them in the *p*...... 1Kin 20:23 4334
will fight against them in the *p*...... 1Kin 20:25 4334
of Hamath unto the sea of the *p*...... 2Kin 14:25 6160
king went the way toward the *p*...... 2Kin 25:4 6160
In the *p* of Jordan did the king...... 2Chr 4:17 3603
the priests, the men of the *p*...... Neh 3:22 3603
of the villages in the *p* of Ono...... Neh 6:2 1237
both out of the *p* country round...... Neh 12:28 3603
O LORD, and lead me in a *p* path...... Ps 27:11 4334
They are all *p* to him that...... Prov 8:9 5228
way of the righteous is made *p*...... Prov 15:19 5549
he hath made *p* the face thereof...... Is 28:25 7737
straight, and the rough places *p*...... Is 40:4 1237
land of Benjamin, and from the *p*...... Jer 17:26 8219
of the valley, and rock of the *p*...... Jer 21:13 4334
and he went out the way of the *p*...... Jer 39:4 6160
the *p* shall be destroyed, as the...... Jer 48:8 4334
is come upon the *p* country...... Jer 48:21 4334
) and they went by the way of the *p*...... Jer 52:7 6160
me, Arise, go forth into the *p*...... Eze 3:22 1237
I arose, and went forth into the *p*...... Eze 3:23 1237
to the vision that I saw in the *p*...... Eze 8:4 1237
he set it up in the *p* of Dura...... Dan 3:1 1236
the inhabitant from the *p* of Aven...... Amos 1:5 1237
they of the *p* the Philistines...... Obad 19 8219
make it *p* upon tables, that he...... Hab 2:2 874
Zerubbabel thou shalt become a *p*...... Zec 4:7 4334
men inhabited the south and the *p*...... Zec 7:7 8219
a *p* from Geba to Rimmon south of...... Zec 14:10 6160
tongue was loosed, and he spake *p*...... Mk 7:35 *3723*
with them, and stood in the *p*...... Lk 6:17 *5117,3977*

PLAINLY {11}
And if the servant shall *p* say...... Ex 21:5 559
all the words of this law very *p*...... Deut 27:8 874
Did I *p* appear unto the house of...... 1Sa 2:27 1540
He told us *p* that the asses were...... 1Sa 10:16 5046
us hath been *p* read before me...... Ezr 4:18 6568
shall be ready to speak *p*...... Is 32:4 6703
If thou be the Christ, tell us *p*...... Jn 10:24 *3954*
Then said Jesus unto them *p*...... Jn 11:14 *3954*
I shall shew you *p* of the Father...... Jn 16:25 *3954*
unto him, Lo, now speakest thou *p*...... Jn 16:29 *3954*
p that they seek a country...... Heb 11:14 *1718*

PLAINNESS {1}
hope, we use great *p* of speech...... 2Cor 3:12 *3954*

PLAINS {25}
unto him in the *p* of Mamre...... Gen 18:1 436
pitched in the *p* of Moab on this...... Num 22:1 6160
priest spake with them in the *p*...... Num 26:3 6160
the children of Israel in the *p*...... Num 26:63 6160
unto the camp at the *p* of Moab...... Num 31:12 6160
pitched in the *p* of Moab by...... Num 33:48 6160
Abel-shittim in the *p* of Moab...... Num 33:49 6160
Moses in the *p* of Moab by Jordan...... Num 33:50 6160
LORD spake unto Moses in the *p* of...... Num 35:1 6160
the children of Israel in the *p*...... Num 36:13 6160
Gilgal, beside the *p* of Moreh...... Deut 11:30 436
Moses went up from the *p* of Moab...... Deut 34:1 6160
in the *p* of Moab thirty days...... Deut 34:8 6160
unto battle, to the *p* of Jericho...... Josh 4:13 6160
month at even in the *p* of Jericho...... Josh 5:10 6160
of the *p* south of Chinneroth, and...... Josh 11:2 6160
and in the valleys, and in the *p*...... Josh 12:8 6160
for inheritance in the *p* of Moab...... Josh 13:32 6160
night in the *p* of the wilderness...... 2Sa 17:16 6160
overtook him in the *p* of Jericho...... 2Kin 25:5 6160
trees that were in the low *p* was...... 1Chr 27:28 8219
are in the low *p* in abundance...... 2Chr 9:27 8219
in the low country, and in the *p*...... 2Chr 26:10 4334
Zedekiah in the *p* of Jericho...... Jer 39:5 6160
Zedekiah in the *p* of Jericho...... Jer 52:8 6160

PLAISTER {7}
morter, and shall *p* the house...... Lev 14:42 2902
stones, and *p* them with *p*...... Deut 27:2 7874
thou shalt *p* them with *p*...... Deut 27:4 7874
lay it for a *p* upon the boil, and...... Is 38:21 4799
the candlestick upon the *p* of the...... Dan 5:5 1528

PLAISTERED {2}
the house, and after it is *p* .... Lev 14:43 2902
the house, after the house was *p* .... Lev 14:48 2902

PLAITING {1}
outward adorning of *p* the hair.......... 1Pet 3:3 *1708*

PLANES {1}
he fitteth it with *p*, and he.......... Is 44:13 4741

PLANETS {1}
sun, and to the moon, and to the *p* 2Kin 23:5 4208

PLANKS {3}
floor of the house with *p* of fir.......... 1Kin 6:15 6763
there were thick *p* upon the face.......... Eze 41:25 6086
chambers of the house, and thick *p* .... Eze 41:26 5646

PLANT {42}
every *p* of the field before it.......... Gen 2:5 7880
p them in the mountain of thine .... Ex 15:17 5193
Thou shalt not *p* thee a grove of .... Deut 16:21 5193
thou shalt *p* a vineyard, and shalt .... Deut 28:30 5193
Thou shalt *p* vineyards, and dress.......... Deut 28:39 5193
my people Israel, and will *p* them.......... 2Sa 7:10 5193
p vineyards, and eat the fruits 2Kin 19:29 5193
my people Israel, and will *p* them.......... 1Chr 17:9 5193
and bring forth boughs like a *p* .... Job 14:9 5194
p vineyards, which may yield.......... Ps 107:37 5193
a time to *p*, and a time to pluck .... Eccl 3:2 5193
the men of Judah his pleasant *p* .... Is 5:7 5194
shalt thou *p* pleasant plants.......... Is 17:10 5193
day shalt thou make thy *p* to grow .... Is 17:11 5194
p vineyards, and eat the fruit.......... Is 37:30 5193
I will *p* in the wilderness the .... Is 41:19 5414
that I may *p* the heavens, and lay .... Is 51:16 5193
grow up before him as a tender *p* .... Is 53:2
and they shall *p* vineyards .... Is 65:21 5193
they shall not *p*, and another eat .... Is 65:22 5193
to throw down, to build, and to *p* .... Jer 1:10 5193
p of a strange vine unto me.......... Jer 2:21
a kingdom, to build and to *p* it .... Jer 18:9 5193
and I will *p* them, and not pluck.......... Jer 24:6 5193
p gardens, and eat the fruit of .... Jer 29:5 5193
p gardens, and eat the fruit of .... Jer 29:28 5193
Thou shalt yet *p* vines upon the.......... Jer 31:5 5193
the planters shall *p*, and shall .... Jer 31:5 5193
over them, to build, and to *p*.......... Jer 31:28 5193
I will *p* them in this land .... Jer 32:41 5193
nor *p* vineyard, nor have any.......... Jer 35:7 5193
pull you down, and I will *p* you .... Jer 42:10 5193
will *p* it upon an high mountain .... Eze 17:22 8362
the height of Israel will I *p* it.......... Eze 17:23 8362
build houses, and *p* vineyards .... Eze 28:26 5193
raise up for them a *p* of renown.......... Eze 34:29 4302
and *p* that that was desolate .... Eze 36:36 5193
he shall *p* the tabernacles of his.......... Dan 11:45 5193
and they shall *p* vineyards .... Amos 9:14 5193
I will *p* them upon their land, and.......... Amos 9:15 5193
and they shall *p* vineyards .... Zeph 1:13 5193
But he answered and said, Every *p* .... Mt 15:13 *5451*

PLANTATION {1}
water it by the furrows of her *p*.......... Eze 17:7 4302

PLANTED {39}
the LORD God *p* a garden eastward .... Gen 2:8 5193
an husbandman, and he *p* a vineyard .... Gen 9:20 5193
Abraham *p* a grove in Beer-sheba, ... Gen 21:33 5193
shall have *p* all manner of trees .... Lev 19:23 5193
lign aloes which the LORD hath *p* .... Num 24:6 5193
man is he that hath *p* a vineyard .... Deut 20:6 5193
which ye *p* not do ye eat.......... Josh 24:13 5193
a tree *p* by the rivers of water .... Ps 1:3 8362
cast out the heathen, and *p* it .... Ps 80:8 5193
which thy right hand hath *p* .... Ps 80:15 5193
Those that be *p* in the house of.......... Ps 92:13 8362
He that *p* the ear, shall he not.......... Ps 94:9 5193
of Lebanon, which he hath *p* .... Ps 104:16 5193
I *p* me vineyards .... Eccl 2:4 5193
I *p* trees in them of all kind of .... Eccl 2:5 5193
time to pluck up that which is *p*.......... Eccl 3:2 5193
p it with the choicest vine, and.......... Is 5:2 5193
Yea, they shall not be *p* .... Is 40:24 5193
Yet I had *p* thee a noble vine,.......... Jer 2:21 5193
the LORD of hosts, that *p* thee.......... Jer 11:17 5193
Thou hast *p* them, yea, they have.......... Jer 12:2 5193
be as a tree *p* by the waters.......... Jer 17:8 8362
which I have *p* I will pluck up .... Jer 45:4 5193
land, and *p* it in a fruitful field.......... Eze 17:5
It was *p* in a good soil by great.......... Eze 17:8 8362
Yea, behold, being *p*, shall it .... Eze 17:10 8362
in thy blood, *p* by the waters.......... Eze 19:10 8362
now she is *p* in the wilderness, ... Eze 19:13 8362
Tyrus, is *p* in a pleasant place .... Hos 9:13 8362
ye have *p* pleasant vineyards, but .... Amos 5:11 5193
my heavenly Father hath not *p* .... Mt 15:13 *5452*
which *p* a vineyard, and hedged it .... Mt 21:33 *5452*
A certain man *p* a vineyard .... Mk 12:1 *5452*
had a fig tree *p* in his vineyard .... Lk 13:6 *5452*
the root, and be thou *p* in the sea .... Lk 17:6 *5452*
they bought, they sold, they *p* .... Lk 17:28 *5452*
A certain man *p* a vineyard .... Lk 20:9 *5452*
For if we have been *p* together in.......... Rom 6:5 *4854*
I have *p*, Apollos watered.......... 1Cor 3:6 *5452*

PLANTEDST {2}
and olive trees, which thou *p* not.......... Deut 6:11 5193
heathen with thy hand, and *p* them.......... Ps 44:2 5193

PLANTERS {1}
the *p* shall plant, and shall eat.......... Jer 31:5 5193

PLANTETH {5}
of her hands she *p* a vineyard .... Prov 31:16 5192
he *p* an ash, and the rain doth .... Is 44:14 5192
neither is he that *p* any thing.......... 1Cor 3:7 *5452*
Now he that *p* and he that watereth 1Cor 3:8 *5452*
who *p* a vineyard, and eateth not.......... 1Cor 9:7 *5452*

PLANTING {2}
land for ever, the branch of my *p*.......... Is 60:21 4302
the *p* of the LORD, that he might.......... Is 61:3 4302

PLANTINGS {1}
the field, and as *p* of a vineyard.......... Mic 1:6 4302

PLANTS {8}
and those that dwelt among *p*.......... 1Chr 4:23 5194
olive *p* round about thy table.......... Ps 128:3 8363
be as *p* grown up in their youth.......... Ps 144:12 5195
Thy *p* are an orchard of.......... Song 4:13 7973
down the principal *p* thereof.......... Is 16:8 8291
shalt thou plant pleasant *p* .... Is 17:10 5194
thy *p* are gone over the sea, they.......... Jer 48:32 5189
rivers running round about his *p* .... Eze 31:4 4302

PLAT {2}
and I will requite thee in this *p* 2Kin 9:26 2513
and cast him into the *p* of ground.......... 2Kin 9:26 2513

PLATE {3}
thou shalt make a *p* of pure gold .... Ex 28:36 6731
they made the *p* of the holy crown.......... Ex 39:30 6731
did he put the golden *p*, the .... Lev 8:9 6731

PLATES {6}
did beat the gold into thin *p* .... Ex 39:3 6341
let them make them broad *p* for a.......... Num 16:38 6341
they were made broad *p* for a .... Num 16:39
four brasen wheels, and *p* of brass 1Kin 7:30 5633
For on the *p* of the ledges.......... 1Kin 7:36 3871
Silver spread into *p* is brought.......... Jer 10:9

PLATTED {3}
when they had *p* a crown of thorns .... Mt 27:29 *4120*
p a crown of thorns, and put it .... Mk 15:17 *4120*
the soldiers *p* a crown of thorns,.......... Jn 19:2 *4120*

PLATTER {3}
outside of the cup and of the *p* .... Mt 23:25 *3953*
that which is within the cup and *p* .... Mt 23:26 *3953*
the outside of the cup and the *p* .... Lk 11:39 *4094*

PLAY {17}
eat and to drink, and rose up to *p*.......... Ex 32:6 6711
to *p* the whore in her father's.......... Deut 22:21
that he shall *p* with his hand 1Sa 16:16 5059
me now a man that can *p* well 1Sa 16:17 5059
to *p* the mad man in my presence 1Sa 21:15
men now arise, and *p* before us.......... 2Sa 2:14 7832
will I *p* before the LORD 2Sa 6:21 7832
let us *p* the men for our people, ... 2Sa 10:12
all the beasts of the field *p*.......... Job 40:20 7832
Wilt thou *p* with him as with a.......... Job 41:5 7832
p skilfully with a loud noise.......... Ps 33:3 5059
whom thou hast made to *p* therein .... Ps 104:26 7832
shall *p* on the hole of the asp .... Is 11:8 8173
can *p* well on an instrument.......... Eze 33:32 5059
thou shalt not *p* the harlot .... Hos 3:3
p the harlot, yet let not Judah.......... Hos 4:15
to eat and drink, and rose up to *p*.......... 1Cor 10:7 *3815*

PLAYED {18}
daughter in law hath *p* the harlot.......... Gen 38:24
his concubine *p* the whore against.......... Judg 19:2
took an harp, and *p* with his hand.......... 1Sa 16:23 5059
answered one another as they *p*.......... 1Sa 18:7 7832
David *p* with his hand, as at 1Sa 18:10 5059
and David *p* with his hand.......... 1Sa 19:9 5059
I have *p* the fool, and have erred.......... 1Sa 26:21
all the house of Israel *p* before.......... 2Sa 6:5 7832
came to pass, when the minstrel *p* 2Kin 3:15 5059
all Israel *p* before God with all.......... 1Chr 13:8 7832
but thou hast *p* the harlot with.......... Jer 3:1
tree, and there hath *p* the harlot.......... Jer 3:6
but went and *p* the harlot also.......... Jer 3:8
Thou hast *p* the whore also with.......... Eze 16:28
thou hast *p* the harlot with them, ... Eze 16:28
Aholah *p* the harlot when she was.......... Eze 23:5
wherein she had *p* the harlot in .... Eze 23:19
their mother hath *p* the harlot .... Hos 2:5

PLAYEDST {2}
p the harlot because of thy.......... Eze 16:15
and *p* the harlot thereupon .... Eze 16:16

PLAYER {1}
who is a cunning *p* on an harp.......... 1Sa 16:16 5059

PLAYERS {2}
the *p* on instruments followed.......... Ps 68:25 5059
As well the singers as the *p* on.......... Ps 87:7 2490

PLAYETH {1}
in unto a woman that *p* the harlot.......... Eze 23:44

PLAYING {7}
profane herself by *p* the whore .... Lev 21:9
that is cunning in *p*, and a 1Sa 16:18 5059
saw king David dancing and *p*.......... 1Chr 15:29 7832
were the damsels *p* with timbrels .... Ps 68:25
tree thou wanderest, *p* the harlot.......... Jer 2:20
thee to cease from *p* the harlot .... Eze 16:41
girls *p* in the streets thereof .... Zec 8:5 7832

PLEA {2}
blood and blood, between *p* and *p*.......... Deut 17:8 1779

PLEAD {39}
against him, Will ye *p* for Baal .... Judg 6:31 7378
he that will *p* for him, let him.......... Judg 6:31 7378
let him *p* for himself, because .... Judg 6:31 7378
Let Baal *p* against him, because .... Judg 6:32 7378
p my cause, and deliver me out of.......... 1Sa 24:15 7378
who shall set me a time to *p* .... Job 9:19
Who is he that will *p* with me.......... Job 13:19 7378
Oh that one might *p* for a man.......... Job 16:21 3198
me, and *p* against me my reproach .... Job 19:5 3198
Will he *p* against me with his.......... Job 23:6 7378
P my cause, O LORD, with them .... Ps 35:1 7378
p my cause against an ungodly .... Ps 43:1 7378
Arise, O God, *p* thine own cause.......... Ps 74:22 7378
P my cause, and deliver me.......... Ps 119:154 7378
For the LORD will *p* their cause.......... Prov 22:23 7378
he shall *p* their cause with thee .... Prov 23:11 7378
p the cause of the poor and needy.......... Prov 31:9 1777
the fatherless, *p* for the widow .... Is 1:17 7378
The LORD standeth up to *p*.......... Is 3:13 7378
let us *p* together.......... Is 43:26 8199
will the LORD *p* with all flesh .... Is 66:16 8199
Wherefore I will yet *p* with you .... Jer 2:9 7378
your children's children will I *p* .... Jer 2:9 7378
Wherefore will ye *p* with me .... Jer 2:29 7378
I will *p* with thee, because thou.......... Jer 2:35 8199
thou, O LORD, when I *p* with thee.......... Jer 12:1 7378
nations, he will *p* with all flesh .... Jer 25:31 8199
There is none to *p* thy cause.......... Jer 30:13 1777
he shall throughly *p* their cause .... Jer 50:34 7378
I will *p* thy cause, and take.......... Jer 51:36 7378
will *p* with him there for his .... Eze 17:20 8199
there will I *p* with you face to.......... Eze 20:35 8199
of Egypt, so will I *p* with you.......... Eze 20:36 8199
I will *p* against him with.......... Eze 38:22 8199
P with your mother, *p* .... Hos 2:2 7378
will *p* with them there for my .... Joel 3:2 8199
people, and he will *p* with Israel.......... Mic 6:2 3198
against him, until he *p* my cause.......... Mic 7:9 7378

PLEADED {3}
that hath *p* the cause of my.......... 1Sa 25:39 7378
thou hast *p* the causes of my soul .... Lam 3:58 7378
Like as I *p* with your fathers in .... Eze 20:36 8199

PLEADETH {3}
as a man *p* for his neighbour .... Job 16:21
thy God that *p* the cause of his.......... Is 51:22 7378
for justice, nor any *p* for truth .... Is 59:4 8199

PLEADINGS {1}
and hearken to the *p* of my lips .... Job 13:6 7379

PLEASANT {56}
every tree that is *p* to the sight .... Gen 2:9 2530
and that it was *p* to the eyes .... Gen 3:6 8378
good, and the land that it was *p* .... Gen 49:15 5276
p in their lives, and in their 2Sa 1:23 5273
very *p* hast thou been unto me.......... 2Sa 1:26 5276
whatsoever is *p* in thine eyes 1Kin 20:6 4261
the situation of this city is *p* 2Kin 2:19 2896
and for all manner of *p* jewels 2Chr 32:27 2532
are fallen unto me in *p* places.......... Ps 16:6 5273
the *p* harp with the psaltery.......... Ps 81:2 5273
Yea, they despised the *p* land .... Ps 106:24 2532
how *p* it is for brethren to dwell .... Ps 133:1 5273
for it is *p*.......... Ps 135:3 5273
knowledge is *p* unto thy soul.......... Prov 2:10 5276
be as the loving hind and *p* roe.......... Prov 5:19 2580
and bread eaten in secret is *p* .... Prov 9:17 5276
the words of the pure are *p* words .... Prov 15:26 5278
P words are as an honeycomb,.......... Prov 16:24 5278
For it is a *p* thing if thou keep .... Prov 22:18 5273
with all precious and *p* riches .... Prov 24:4 5273
a *p* thing it is for the eyes to .... Eccl 11:7 2896
thou art fair, my beloved, yea, *p*.......... Song 1:16 5273
of pomegranates, with *p* fruits.......... Song 4:13 4022
his garden, and eat his *p* fruits .... Song 4:16 4022
how *p* art thou, O love, for.......... Song 7:6 5276
gates are all manner of *p* fruits.......... Song 7:13 4022
Tarshish, and upon all *p* pictures.......... Is 2:16 2532
and the men of Judah his *p* plant .... Is 5:7 8191
and dragons in their *p* palaces.......... Is 13:22 6027
shalt thou plant *p* plants.......... Is 17:10 5194
for the teats, for the *p* fields .... Is 32:12 2531
and all thy borders of *p* stones.......... Is 54:12 2656
all our *p* things are laid waste .... Is 64:11 4261
children, and give thee a *p* land .... Jer 3:19 2532
they have made my *p* portion a .... Jer 12:10 2532
the *p* places of the wilderness .... Jer 23:10 4999
and ye shall fall like a *p* vessel .... Jer 25:34 2532
is he a *p* child .... Jer 31:20 8191
of her miseries all her *p* things .... Lam 1:7 4262
his hand upon all her *p* things .... Lam 1:10 4261
they have given their *p* things.......... Lam 1:11 4262
slew all that were *p* to the eye .... Lam 2:4 4261
walls, and destroy thy *p* houses.......... Eze 26:12 2532
song of one that hath a *p* voice .... Eze 33:32 3303
the east, and toward the *p* land .... Dan 8:9 6643
I ate no *p* bread, neither came .... Dan 10:3 2530
with precious stones, and *p* things.......... Dan 11:38 2530
the *p* places for their silver,.......... Hos 9:6 4261
Tyrus, is planted in a *p* place .... Hos 9:13 5116
the treasure of all *p* vessels .... Hos 13:15 2532
your temples my goodly *p* things .... Joel 3:5 4261
ye have planted *p* vineyards.......... Amos 5:11 2531
ye cast out from their *p* houses .... Mic 2:9 8588
glory out of all the *p* furniture.......... Nah 2:9 2532
for they laid the *p* land desolate .... Zec 7:14 2532
Jerusalem be *p* unto the LORD, as .... Mal 3:4 6148

PLEASANTNESS {1}
Her ways are ways of *p*, and all .... Prov 3:17 5278

PLEASE {39}
If she *p* not her master, who hath ... Ex 21:8 7451,5869
peradventure it will *p* God that ... Num 23:27 3477,5869
but if it *p* my father to do thee ... 1Sa 20:13 3190
Therefore now let it *p* thee to ... 2Sa 7:29 2894
or else, if it *p* thee, I will ... 1Kin 21:6 2655
Now therefore let it *p* thee to ... 1Chr 17:27 2894
p them, and speak good words to ... 2Chr 10:7 7521
If it *p* the king, and if thy ... Neh 2:5 2895
If it *p* the king, let letters be ... Neh 2:7 2895
If it *p* the king, let there go a ... Est 1:19 2895
If it *p* the king, let it be ... Est 3:9 2895
if it *p* the king to grant my ... Est 5:8 2895
if it *p* the king, let my life be ... Est 7:3 2895
If it *p* the king, and if I have ... Est 8:5 2896
If it *p* the king, let it be ... Est 9:13 2896
that it would *p* God to destroy me ... Job 6:9 2894
children shall seek to *p* the poor ... Job 20:10 7521
This also shall *p* the LORD better ... Ps 69:31 3190
When a man's ways *p* the LORD ... Prov 16:7 7521
up, nor awake my love, till he *p* ... Song 2:7 2654
up, nor awake my love, till he *p* ... Song 3:5 2654
up, nor awake my love, until he *p* ... Song 8:4 2654
they *p* themselves in the children ... Is 2:6 5606
shall accomplish that which I *p* ... Is 55:11 2654
and choose the things that *p* me ... Is 56:4 2654
do always those things that *p* him ... Jn 8:29 *701*
are in the flesh cannot *p* God ... Rom 8:8 *700*
the weak, and not to *p* ourselves ... Rom 15:1 *700*
Let every one of us *p* his ... Rom 15:2 *700*
the Lord, how he may *p* the Lord ... 1Cor 7:32 *700*
the world, how he may *p* his wife ... 1Cor 7:33 *700*
world, how she may *p* her husband ... 1Cor 7:34 *700*
Even as I *p* all men in all things ... 1Cor 10:33 *700*
or do I seek to *p* men ... Gal 1:10 *700*
they *p* not God, and are contrary ... 1Th 2:15 *700*
to *p* God, so ye would abound more ... 1Th 4:1 *700*
that he may *p* him who hath chosen ... 2Ti 2:4 *700*
to *p* them well in all things ... Titus 2:9 *2001,1511*
faith it is impossible to *p* him ... Heb 11:6 *2100*

PLEASED {62}
of Canaan *p* not Isaac his father ... Gen 28:8 7451,5869
of God, and thou wast *p* with me ... Gen 33:10 7521
And their words *p* Hamor, and ... Gen 34:18 3190,5869
it *p* Pharaoh well, and his ... Gen 45:16 3190,5869
when Balaam saw that it *p* the ... Num 24:1 2895
And the saying *p* me well ... Deut 1:23 3190,5869
of Manasseh spake, it *p* them ... Josh 22:30 3190,5869
the thing *p* the children of ... Josh 22:33 3190,5869
If the LORD were *p* to kill us ... Judg 13:23 2654
and she *p* Samson well ... Judg 14:7 3477,5869
because it hath *p* the LORD to ... 1Sa 12:22 2974
told Saul, and the thing *p* him ... 1Sa 18:20 3477,5869
it *p* David well to be the king's ... 1Sa 18:26 3477,5869
took notice of it, and it *p* them ... 2Sa 3:36 3190,5869
the king did *p* all the people ... 2Sa 3:36 2896,5869
the saying *p* Absalom well, and all ... 2Sa 17:4 3477,5869
this day, then it had *p* thee well ... 2Sa 19:6 3477,5869
And the speech *p* the Lord, that ... 1Kin 3:10 3190,5869
desire which he was *p* to do ... 1Kin 9:1 2654
and they *p* him not ... 1Kin 9:12 3477,5869
And the thing *p* the king and all ... 2Chr 30:4 3477,5869
So it *p* the king to send me ... Neh 2:6 3190
And the saying *p* the king and the ... Est 1:21 3190,5869
And the thing *p* the king ... Est 2:4 3190,5869
And the maiden *p* him, and she ... Est 2:9 3190,5869
And the thing *p* Haman ... Est 5:14 3190
Be *p*, O LORD, to deliver me ... Ps 40:13 7521
Then shalt thou be *p* with the ... Ps 51:19 2654
he hath done whatsoever he hath *p* ... Ps 115:3 2654
Whatsoever the LORD *p*, that did ... Ps 135:6 2654
The LORD is well *p* for his ... Is 42:21 2654
Yet it *p* the LORD to bruise him ... Is 53:10 2654
It *p* Darius to set over the ... Dan 6:1 8232
O LORD, hast done as it *p* thee ... Jonah 1:14 2654
Will the LORD be *p* with thousands ... Mic 6:7 7521
will he be *p* with thee, or accept ... Mal 1:8 7521
beloved Son, in whom I am well *p* ... Mt 3:17 *2106*
in whom my soul is well *p* ... Mt 12:18 *2106*
danced before them, and *p* Herod ... Mt 14:6 *700*
beloved Son, in whom I am well *p* ... Mt 17:5 *2106*
beloved Son, in whom I am well *p* ... Mk 1:11 *2106*
p Herod and them that sat with him ... Mk 6:22 *700*
in thee I am well *p* ... Lk 3:22 *2106*
the saying *p* the whole multitude ... Acts 6:5 *700*
And because he saw it *p* the Jews ... Acts 12:3 *701*
Then *p* it the apostles and elders, ... Acts 15:22 *1380*
Notwithstanding it *p* Silas to ... Acts 15:34 *1380*
For even Christ *p* not himself ... Rom 15:3 *700*
For it hath *p* them of Macedonia ... Rom 15:26 *2106*
It hath *p* them verily ... Rom 15:27 *2106*
it *p* God by the foolishness of ... 1Cor 1:21 *2106*
she be *p* to dwell with him, let ... 1Cor 7:12 *4909*
if he be *p* to dwell with her, let ... 1Cor 7:13 *4909*
many of them God was not well *p* ... 1Cor 10:5 *2106*
in the body, as it hath *p* him ... 1Cor 12:18 *2309*
giveth it a body as it hath *p* him ... 1Cor 15:38 *2309*
for if I yet *p* men, I should not ... Gal 1:10 *700*
But when it *p* God, who separated ... Gal 1:15 *2106*
For it *p* the Father that in him ... Col 1:19 *2106*
had this testimony, that he *p* God ... Heb 11:5 *2100*
such sacrifices God is well *p* ... Heb 13:16 *2100*
beloved Son, in whom I am well *p* ... 2Pet 1:17 *2106*

PLEASETH {6}
do to her as it *p* thee ... Gen 16:6 2896,5869
dwell where it *p* thee ... Gen 20:15 2896,5869
for she *p* me well ... Judg 14:3 3477,5869
let the maiden which *p* the king ... Est 2:4 3190,5869
p God shall escape from her ... Eccl 7:26 2896,6440
for he doeth whatsoever *p* him ... Eccl 8:3 2654

PLEASING {6}
I be *p* in his eyes, let it be ... Est 8:5 2896
neither shall they be *p* unto him ... Hos 9:4 6148
worthy of the Lord unto all *p* ... Col 1:10 *699*
for this is well *p* unto the Lord ... Col 3:20 *700*
not as *p* men, but God, which ... 1Th 2:4 *700*
things that are *p* in his sight ... 1Jn 3:22 *701*

PLEASURE {61}
I am waxed old shall I have *p* ... Gen 18:12 5730
grapes thy fill at thine own *p* ... Deut 23:24 5315
heart, and hast *p* in uprightness ... 1Chr 29:17 7521
let the king send his *p* to us ... Ezr 5:17 7470
God of your fathers, and do his *p* ... Ezr 10:11 7522
and over our cattle, at their *p* ... Neh 9:37 7522
do according to every man's *p* ... Est 1:8 7522
For what *p* hath he in his house ... Job 21:21 2656
his soul, and never eateth with *p* ... Job 21:25 2896
Is it any *p* to the Almighty, that ... Job 22:3 2656
a God that hath *p* in wickedness ... Ps 5:4 2655
which hath *p* in the prosperity of ... Ps 35:27 2655
Do good in thy good *p* unto Zion ... Ps 51:18 7522
thy servants take *p* in her stones ... Ps 102:14 7521
ministers of his, that do his *p* ... Ps 103:21 7522
To bind his princes at his *p* ... Ps 105:22 5315
of all them that have *p* therein ... Ps 111:2 2656
he taketh not *p* in the legs of a ... Ps 147:10 7521
The LORD taketh *p* in them that ... Ps 147:11 7521
the LORD taketh *p* in his people ... Ps 149:4 7521
He that loveth *p* shall be a poor ... Prov 21:17 8057
with mirth, therefore enjoy *p* ... Eccl 2:1 2896
for he hath no *p* in fools ... Eccl 5:4 2656
shalt say, I have no *p* in them ... Eccl 12:1 2656
the night of my *p* hath he turned ... Is 21:4 2837
and shall perform all my *p* ... Is 44:28 2656
stand, and I will do all my *p* ... Is 46:10 2656
he will do his *p* on Babylon ... Is 48:14 2656
the *p* of the LORD shall prosper ... Is 53:10 2656
in the day of your fast ye find *p* ... Is 58:3 2656
from doing thy *p* on my holy day ... Is 58:13 2656
own ways, nor finding thine own *p* ... Is 58:13 2656
snuffeth up the wind at her *p* ... Jer 2:24 185,5315
is he a vessel wherein is no *p* ... Jer 22:28 2656
he had set at liberty at their *p* ... Jer 34:16 5315
like a vessel wherein is no *p* ... Jer 48:38 2656
with whom thou hast taken *p* ... Eze 16:37 6148
Have I any *p* at all that the ... Eze 18:23 2654
For I have no *p* in the death of ... Eze 18:32 2654
I have no *p* in the death of the ... Eze 33:11 2654
as a vessel wherein is not *p* ... Hos 8:8 2656
and I will take *p* in it, and I will ... Hag 1:8 7521
I have no *p* in you, saith the ... Mal 1:10 2656
good *p* to give you the kingdom ... Lk 12:32 *2106*
willing to shew the Jews a *p* ... Acts 24:27 *5485*
willing to do the Jews a *p* ... Acts 25:9 *5485*
but have *p* in them that do them ... Rom 1:32 *4909*
Therefore I take *p* in infirmities ... 2Cor 12:10 *2106*
to the good *p* of his will ... Eph 1:5 *2107*
according to his good *p* which he ... Eph 1:9 *2107*
to will and to do of his good *p* ... Phil 2:13 *2107*
all the good *p* of his goodness ... 2Th 1:11 *2107*
but had *p* in unrighteousness ... 2Th 2:12 *2106*
But she that liveth in *p* is dead ... 1Ti 5:6 *4684*
for sin thou hast had no *p* ... Heb 10:6 *2106*
not, neither hadst *p* therein ... Heb 10:8 *2106*
my soul shall have no *p* in him ... Heb 10:38 *2106*
chastened us after their own *p* ... Heb 12:10 *3588,1380*
Ye have lived in *p* on the earth ... Jas 5:5 *5171*
as they that count it *p* to riot ... 2Pet 2:13 *2237*
for thy *p* they are and were ... Rev 4:11 *2307*

PLEASURES {8}
prosperity, and their years in *p* ... Job 36:11 5273
hand there are *p* for evermore ... Ps 16:11 5273
them drink of the river of thy *p* ... Ps 36:8 5730
this, thou that art given to *p* ... Is 47:8 5719
p of this life, and bring no fruit ... Lk 8:14 *2237*
lovers of *p* more than lovers of ... 2Ti 3:4 *5569*
serving divers lusts and *p* ... Titus 3:3 *2237*
than to enjoy the *p* of sin for a ... Heb 11:25

PLEDGE {22}
she said, Wilt thou give me a *p* ... Gen 38:17 6162
he said, What *p* shall I give thee ... Gen 38:18 6162
to receive his *p* from the woman's ... Gen 38:20 6162
take thy neighbour's raiment to *p* ... Ex 22:26 2254
or the upper millstone to *p* ... Deut 24:6 2254
for he taketh a man's life to *p* ... Deut 24:6 2254
go into his house to fetch his *p* ... Deut 24:10 5667
bring out the *p* abroad unto thee ... Deut 24:11 5667
thou shalt not sleep with his *p* ... Deut 24:12 5667
p again when the sun goeth down ... Deut 24:13 5667
nor take a widow's raiment to *p* ... Deut 24:17 2254
brethren fare, and take their *p* ... 1Sa 17:18 6161
For thou hast taken a *p* from thy ... Job 22:6 2254
they take the widow's ox for a *p* ... Job 24:3 2254
breast, and take a *p* of the poor ... Job 24:9 2254
take a *p* of him for a strange ... Prov 20:16 2254
take a *p* of him for a strange ... Prov 27:13 2254
hath restored to the debtor his *p* ... Eze 18:7 2258
violence, hath not restored the *p* ... Eze 18:12 2258
any, hath not withholden the *p* ... Eze 18:16 2258
If the wicked restore the *p* ... Eze 33:15 2258
clothes laid to *p* by every altar ... Amos 2:8 2254

PLEDGES {2}
give *p* to my lord the king of ... 2Kin 18:23 6148
Now therefore give *p*, I pray thee ... Is 36:8 6148

PLEIADES *(ple'-ya-dez)* {2} *A constellation of stars.*
maketh Arcturus, Orion, and *P* ... Job 9:9 3598
bind the sweet influences of *P* ... Job 38:31 3598

PLENTEOUS {12}
of Egypt in the seven *p* years ... Gen 41:34 7647
in the seven *p* years the earth ... Gen 41:47 7647
LORD shall make thee *p* in goods ... Deut 28:11 3498
p in every work of thine hand ... Deut 30:9 3498
gold at Jerusalem as *p* as stones ... 2Chr 1:15
p in mercy unto all them that ... Ps 86:5 7227
and *p* in mercy and truth ... Ps 86:15 7227
slow to anger, and *p* in mercy ... Ps 103:8 7227
and with him is *p* redemption ... Ps 130:7 7235
earth, and it shall be fat and *p* ... Is 30:23 8082
portion is fat, and their meat *p* ... Hab 1:16 1277
disciples, The harvest truly is *p* ... Mt 9:37 *4180*

PLENTEOUSNESS {2}
And the seven years of *p*, that was ... Gen 41:53 7647
of the diligent tend only to *p* ... Prov 21:5 4195

PLENTIFUL {4}
Thou, O God, didst send a *p* rain ... Ps 68:9 5071
away, and joy out of the *p* field ... Is 16:10 3759
And I brought you into a *p* country ... Jer 2:7 3759
is taken from the *p* field ... Jer 48:33 3759

PLENTIFULLY {3}
how hast thou *p* declared the ... Job 26:3 7230
p rewardeth the proud doer ... Ps 31:23 3499
certain rich man brought forth *p* ... Lk 12:16 *2164*

PLENTY {13}
the earth, and *p* of corn and wine ... Gen 27:28 7230
p throughout all the land of ... Gen 41:29 7647
all the *p* shall be forgotten in ... Gen 41:30 7647
the *p* shall not be known in the ... Gen 41:31 7647
pit, wherein there is *p* of water ... Lev 11:36 4723
from Ophir great *p* of almug trees ... 1Kin 10:11 7235
had enough to eat, and have left *p* ... 2Chr 31:10 7230
and thou shalt have *p* of silver ... Job 22:25 8443
in judgment, and in *p* of justice ... Job 37:23 7230
shall thy barns be filled with *p* ... Prov 3:10 7647
his land shall have *p* of bread ... Prov 28:19 7646
for then had we *p* of victuals ... Jer 44:17 7646
And ye shall eat in *p*, and be ... Joel 2:26 398

PLOTTETH {1}
The wicked *p* against the just, and ... Ps 37:12 2161

PLOUGH {1}
man, having put his hand to the *p* ... Lk 9:62 *723*

PLOW {8}
Thou shalt not *p* with an ox ... Deut 22:10 2790
which a yoke of oxen might *p* ... 1Sa 14:14
I have seen, they that *p* iniquity ... Job 4:8 2790
will not *p* by reason of the cold ... Prov 20:4 2790
Doth the plowman *p* all day to sow ... Is 28:24 2790
Judah shall *p*, and Jacob shall ... Hos 10:11 2790
will one *p* there with oxen ... Amos 6:12 2790
he that ploweth should *p* in hope ... 1Cor 9:10 *722*

PLOWED {5}
If ye had not *p* with my heifer, ... Judg 14:18 2790
The plowers *p* upon my back ... Ps 129:3 2790
Zion shall be *p* like a field ... Jer 26:18 2790
Ye have *p* wickedness, ye have ... Hos 10:13 2790
for your sake be *p* as a field ... Mic 3:12 2790

PLOWERS {1}
The *p* plowed upon my back ... Ps 129:3 2790

PLOWETH {1}
that he that *p* should plow in ... 1Cor 9:10

PLOWING {4}
who was *p* with twelve yoke of ... 1Kin 19:19 2790
Job, and said, The oxen were *p* ... Job 1:14 2790
the *p* of the wicked, is sin ... Prov 21:4 5215
having a servant *p* or feeding ... Lk 17:7 *722*

PLOWMAN {2}
Doth the *p* plow all day to sow ... Is 28:24 2790
that the *p* shall overtake the ... Amos 9:13 2790

PLOWMEN {2}
sons of the alien shall be your *p* ... Is 61:5 406
the *p* were ashamed, they covered ... Jer 14:4 406

PLOWSHARES {3}
shall beat their swords into *p* ... Is 2:4 855
Beat your *p* into swords, and your ... Joel 3:10 855
shall beat their swords into *p* ... Mic 4:3 855

PLUCK {30}
he shall *p* away his crop with his ... Lev 1:16 5493
quite *p* down all their high ... Num 33:52 8045
then thou mayest *p* the ears with ... Deut 23:25 6998
Then will I *p* them up by the ... 2Chr 7:20 5428
They *p* the fatherless from the ... Job 24:9 1497
for he shall *p* my feet out of the ... Ps 25:15 3318
p thee out of thy dwelling place, ... Ps 52:5 5255
p it out of thy bosom ... Ps 74:11 3615
which pass by the way do *p* her ... Ps 80:12 717
a time to *p* up that which is ... Eccl 3:2 6131
I will *p* them out of their land, ... Jer 12:14 5428
p out the house of Judah from ... Jer 12:14 5428
not obey, I will utterly *p* up ... Jer 12:17 5428
and concerning a kingdom, to *p* up ... Jer 18:7 5428
hand, yet would I *p* thee thence ... Jer 22:24 5423
will plant them, and not *p* them up ... Jer 24:6 5428
I have watched over them, to *p* up ... Jer 31:28 5428
I will plant you, and not *p* you up ... Jer 42:10 5428

P

which I have planted I will *p* up — Jer 45:4 — 5428
to *p* it up by the roots thereof — Eze 17:9 — 5375
and *p* off thine own breasts — Eze 23:34 — 5423
who *p* off their skin from off — Mic 3:2 — 1497
I will *p* up thy groves out of the — Mic 5:14 — 5428
p it out, and cast it from thee — Mt 5:29 — *1808*
began to *p* the ears of corn, and — Mt 12:1 — *5089*
p it out, and cast it from thee — Mt 18:9 — *1807*
they went, to *p* the ears of corn — Mk 2:23 — *5089*
thine eye offend thee, *p* it out — Mk 9:47 — *1544*
any man *p* them out of my hand — Jn 10:28 — *726*
no man is able to *p* them out of — Jn 10:29 — *726*

PLUCKED {23}
p it out of his bosom, and, behold — Ex 4:7 — 3318
ye shall be *p* from off the land — Deut 28:63 — 5255
a man *p* off his shoe, and gave it — Ruth 4:7 — 8025
p the spear out of the Egyptian's — 2Sa 23:21 — 1497
p the spear out of the Egyptian's — 1Chr 11:23 — 1497
p off the hair of my head and of — Ezr 9:3 — 4803
p off their hair, and made them — Neh 13:25 — 4803
p the spoil out of his teeth — Job 29:17 — 7993
to them that *p* off the hair — Is 50:6 — 4803
for the wicked are not *p* away — Jer 6:29 — 5423
after that I have *p* them out I — Jer 12:15 — 5428
it shall not be *p* up, nor thrown — Jer 31:40 — 5428
But she was *p* up in fury, she was — Eze 19:12 — 5428
till the wings thereof were *p* — Dan 7:4 — 4804
the first horns *p* up by the roots — Dan 7:8 — 6132
for his kingdom shall be *p* up — Dan 11:4 — 5428
a firebrand *p* out of the burning — Amos 4:11 — 5337
this a brand *p* out of the fire — Zec 3:2 — 5337
chains had been *p* asunder by him — Mk 5:4 — *1288*
his disciples *p* the ears of corn, — Lk 6:1 — *5089*
Be thou *p* up by the root, and be — Lk 17:6 — *1610*
ye would have *p* out your own eyes — Gal 4:15 — *1846*
twice dead, *p* up by the roots — Jude 12 — *1610*

PLUCKETH {1}
but the foolish *p* it down with — Prov 14:1 — 2040

PLUCKT {1}
her mouth was an olive leaf *p* off — Gen 8:11 — 2965

PLUMBLINE {4}
stood upon a wall made by a *p* — Amos 7:7 — 594
with a *p* in his hand — Amos 7:7 — 594
And I said, A *p* — Amos 7:8 — 594
I will set a *p* in the midst of my — Amos 7:8 — 594

PLUMMET {3}
the *p* of the house of Ahab — 2Kin 21:13 — 4949
line, and righteousness to the *p* — Is 28:17 — 4949
shall see the *p* in the hand of — Zec 4:10 — 68,913

PLUNGE {1}
Yet shalt thou *p* me in the ditch, — Job 9:31 — 2881

POCHERETH *(po-ke'-reth)* {2} *A family of exiles.*
the children of *P* of Zebaim — Ezr 2:57 — 6380
the children of *P* of Zebaim — Neh 7:59 — 6380

POETS {1}
also of your own *p* have said — Acts 17:28 — *4163*

POINT {9}
Behold, I am at the *p* to die — Gen 25:32 — 1980
ye shall *p* out for you mount Hor — Num 34:7 — 8376
From mount Hor ye shall *p* out — Num 34:8 — 8376
ye shall *p* out your east border — Num 34:10 — 184
iron, and with the *p* of a diamond — Jer 17:1 — 6856
I have set the *p* of the sword — Eze 21:15 — 19
daughter lieth at the *p* of death — Mk 5:23 — *2079*
for he was at the *p* of death — Jn 4:47 — *3195*
whole law, and yet offend in one *p* — Jas 2:10

POINTED {1}
he spreadeth sharp *p* things upon — Job 41:30 — 2742

POINTS {2}
evil, that in all *p* as he came — Eccl 5:16 — 5980
but was in all *p* tempted like as — Heb 4:15

POISON {9}
with the *p* of serpents of the — Deut 32:24 — 2534
Their wine is the *p* of dragons — Deut 32:33 — 2534
the *p* whereof drinketh up my — Job 6:4 — 2534
He shall suck the *p* of asps — Job 20:16 — 7219
p is like the *p* of a serpent — Ps 58:4 — 2534
adders' *p* is under their lips — Ps 140:3 — 2534
the *p* of asps is under their lips — Rom 3:13 — *2447*
an unruly evil, full of deadly *p* — Jas 3:8 — *2447*

POLE {2}
fiery serpent, and set it upon a *p* — Num 21:8 — 5251
of brass, and put it upon a *p* — Num 21:9 — 5251

POLICY {1}
through his *p* also he shall cause — Dan 8:25 — 7922

POLISHED {3}
p after the similitude of a — Ps 144:12 — 2404
he hid me, and made me a *p* shaft — Is 49:2 — 1305
feet like in colour to *p* brass — Dan 10:6 — 7044

POLISHING {1}
rubies, their *p* was of sapphire — Lam 4:7 — 1508

POLL {3}
take five shekels apiece by the *p* — Num 3:47 — 1538
they shall only *p* their heads — Eze 44:20 — 3697
p thee for thy delicate children — Mic 1:16 — 1494

POLLED {3}
when he *p* his head, (for it was — 2Sa 14:26 — 1548
at every year's end that he *p* it — 2Sa 14:26 — 1548
heavy on him, therefore he *p* it — 2Sa 14:26 — 1548

POLLS {6}
names, every male by their *p* — Num 1:2 — 1538
years old and upward, by their *p* — Num 1:18 — 1538
number of the names, by their *p* — Num 1:20 — 1538
number of the names, by their *p* — Num 1:22 — 1538
and their number by their *p* — 1Chr 23:3 — 1538
by number of names by their *p* — 1Chr 23:24 — 1538

POLLUTE {11}
neither shall ye *p* the holy — Num 18:32 — 2490
So ye shall not *p* the land — Num 35:33 — 2610
is called by my name, to *p* it — Jer 7:30 — 2930
and they shall *p* it — Eze 7:21 — 2490
they shall *p* my secret place — Eze 7:22 — 2490
will ye *p* me among my people for — Eze 13:19 — 2490
ye *p* yourselves with all your — Eze 20:31 — 2930
but *p* ye my holy name no more — Eze 20:39 — 2490
I will not let them *p* my holy — Eze 39:7 — 2490
to be in my sanctuary, to *p* it — Eze 44:7 — 2490
they shall *p* the sanctuary of — Dan 11:31 — 2490

POLLUTED {40}
thy tool upon it, thou hast *p* it — Ex 20:25 — 2490
p it, according to the word of — 2Kin 23:16 — 2930
p the house of the LORD which he — 2Chr 36:14 — 2930
therefore were they, as *p* — Ezr 2:62 — 1351
therefore were they, as *p* — Neh 7:64 — 1351
and the land was *p* with blood — Ps 106:38 — 2610
I have *p* mine inheritance, and — Is 47:6 — 2490
for how should my name be *p* — Is 48:11 — 2490
How canst thou say, I am not *p* — Jer 2:23 — 2930
shall not that land be greatly *p* — Jer 3:1 — 2610
thou hast *p* the land with thy — Jer 3:2 — 2610
p my name, and caused every man — Jer 34:16 — 2490
he hath *p* the kingdom and the — Lam 2:2 — 2490
they have *p* themselves with blood — Lam 4:14 — 1351
behold, my soul hath not been *p* — Eze 4:14 — 2930
neither be *p* any more with all — Eze 14:11 — 2930
saw thee *p* in thine own blood, I — Eze 16:6 — 947
and bare, and wast *p* in thy blood — Eze 16:22 — 947
not be *p* before the heathen — Eze 20:9 — 2490
and my sabbaths they greatly *p* — Eze 20:13 — 2490
not be *p* before the heathen — Eze 20:14 — 2490
in my statutes, but *p* my sabbaths — Eze 20:16 — 2490
they *p* my sabbaths — Eze 20:21 — 2490
that it should not be *p* in the — Eze 20:22 — 2490
had *p* my sabbaths, and their eyes — Eze 20:24 — 2490
I *p* them in their own gifts, in — Eze 20:26 — 2930
Are ye *p* after the manner of your — Eze 20:30 — 2930
she was *p* with them, and her mind — Eze 23:17 — 2930
thou art *p* with their idols — Eze 23:30 — 2930
idols wherewith they had *p* it — Eze 36:18 — 2930
work iniquity, and is *p* with blood — Hos 6:8 — 6121
all that eat thereof shall be *p* — Hos 9:4 — 2930
and thou shalt die in a *p* land — Amos 7:17 — 2931
because it is *p*, it shall destroy — Mic 2:10 — 2930
Woe to her that is filthy and *p* — Zeph 3:1 — 1351
her priests have *p* the sanctuary — Zeph 3:4 — 2490
Ye offer *p* bread upon mine altar — Mal 1:7 — 1351
and ye say, Wherein have we *p* thee — Mal 1:7 — 1351
say, The table of the LORD is *p* — Mal 1:12 — 1351
temple, and hath *p* this holy place — Acts 21:28 — *2840*

POLLUTING {2}
keepeth the sabbath from *p* it — Is 56:2 — 2490
keepeth the sabbath from *p* it — Is 56:6 — 2490

POLLUTION {1}
her that was set apart for *p* — Eze 22:10 — 2931

POLLUTIONS {2}
that they abstain from *p* of idols — Acts 15:20 — *234*
the *p* of the world through the — 2Pet 2:20 — *3393*

POLLUX {1} *A Roman god.*
isle, whose sign was Castor and *P* — Acts 28:11 — *1359*

POMEGRANATE {12}
A golden bell and a *p*, a golden — Ex 28:34 — 7416
p, a golden bell and a *p* — Ex 28:34 — 7416
A bell and a *p*, a bell and a — Ex 39:26 — 7416
and a *p*, a bell and a *p* — Ex 39:26 — 7416
part of Gibeah under a *p* tree — 1Sa 14:2 — 7416
a piece of a *p* within thy locks — Song 4:3 — 7416
As a piece of a *p* are thy temples — Song 6:7 — 7416
spiced wine of the juice of my *p* — Song 8:2 — 7416
the *p* tree, the palm tree also, — Joel 1:12 — 7416
vine, and the fig tree, and the *p* — Hag 2:19 — 7416

POMEGRANATES {23}
of it thou shalt make *p* of blue — Ex 28:33 — 7416
the hems of the robe *p* of blue — Ex 39:24 — 7416
the *p* upon the hem of the robe — Ex 39:25 — 7416
robe, round about between the *p* — Ex 39:25 — 7416
and they brought of the *p*, and of — Num 13:23 — 7416
or of figs, or of vines, or of *p* — Num 20:5 — 7416
and vines, and fig trees, and *p* — Deut 8:8 — 7416
that were upon the top, with *p* — 1Kin 7:18 — 7416
the two pillars had *p* also above — 1Kin 7:20
the *p* were two hundred in rows — 1Kin 7:20 — 7416
four hundred *p* for the two — 1Kin 7:42 — 7416
two rows of *p* for one network — 1Kin 7:42 — 7416
p upon the chapiter round about, — 2Kin 25:17 — 7416
and made an hundred *p*, and put them — 2Chr 3:16 — 7416
four hundred *p* on the two wreaths — 2Chr 4:13 — 7416
two rows of *p* on each wreath, to — 2Chr 4:13 — 7416
Thy plants are an orchard of *p* — Song 4:13 — 7416
vine flourished, and the *p* budded — Song 6:11 — 7416
grape appear, and the *p* bud forth — Song 7:12 — 7416
p upon the chapiters round about, — Jer 52:22 — 7416
the *p* were like unto these — Jer 52:22 — 7416
were ninety and six *p* on a side — Jer 52:23 — 7416
all the *p* upon the network were — Jer 52:23 — 7416

POMMELS {3}
To wit, the two pillars, and the *p* — 2Chr 4:12 — 1543
two wreaths to cover the two *p* of — 2Chr 4:12 — 1543
to cover the two *p* of the — 2Chr 4:13 — 1543

POMP {7}
and their multitude, and their *p* — Is 5:14 — 7588
Thy *p* is brought down to the — Is 14:11 — 1347
I will also make the *p* of the — Eze 7:24 — 1347
the *p* of her strength shall cease — Eze 30:18 — 1347
they shall spoil the *p* of Egypt — Eze 32:12 — 1347
the *p* of her strength shall cease — Eze 33:28 — 1347
come, and Bernice, with great *p* — Acts 25:23 — *5325*

PONDER {2}
P the path of thy feet, and let — Prov 4:26 — 6424
thou shouldest *p* the path of life — Prov 5:6 — 6424

PONDERED {1}
things, and *p* them in her heart — Lk 2:19 — *4820*

PONDERETH {3}
the LORD, and he *p* all his goings — Prov 5:21 — 6424
but the LORD *p* the hearts — Prov 21:2 — 8505
doth not he that *p* the heart — Prov 24:12 — 8505

PONDS {3}
their rivers, and upon their *p* — Ex 7:19 — 98
over the rivers, and over the *p* — Ex 8:5 — 98
that make sluices and *p* for fish — Is 19:10 — 99

PONTIUS *(pon'-she-us)* {4} *The family name of Pilate.*
delivered him to *P* Pilate the — Mt 27:2 — *4194*
P Pilate being governor of Judaea — Lk 3:1 — *4194*
P Pilate, with the Gentiles, and — Acts 4:27 — *4194*
who before *P* Pilate witnessed a — 1Ti 6:13 — *4194*

PONTUS *(pon'-tus)* {3} *A Roman province in Asia Minor.*
and in Judaea, and Cappadocia, in *P* — Acts 2:9 — *4195*
Jew named Aquila, born in *P* — Acts 18:2 — *4195*
strangers scattered throughout *P* — 1Pet 1:1 — *4195*

POOL {22}
met together by the *p* of Gibeon — 2Sa 2:13 — 1295
the one on the one side of the *p* — 2Sa 2:13 — 1295
other on the other side of the *p* — 2Sa 2:13 — 1295
them up over the *p* in Hebron — 2Sa 4:12 — 1295
the chariot in the *p* of Samaria — 1Kin 22:38 — 1295
by the conduit of the upper *p* — 2Kin 18:17 — 1295
all his might, and how he made a *p* — 2Kin 20:20 — 1295
the fountain, and to the king's *p* — Neh 2:14 — 1295
the wall of the *p* of Siloah by — Neh 3:15 — 1295
to the *p* that was made, and unto — Neh 3:16 — 1295
p in the highway of the fuller's — Is 7:3 — 1295
the waters of the lower *p* — Is 22:9 — 1295
walls for the water of the old *p* — Is 22:11 — 1295
parched ground shall become a *p* — Is 35:7 — 98
by the conduit of the upper *p* in — Is 36:2 — 1295
make the wilderness a *p* of water — Is 41:18 — 98
is of old like a *p* of water — Nah 2:8 — 1295
Jerusalem by the sheep market a *p* — Jn 5:2 — *2861*
at a certain season into the *p* — Jn 5:4 — *2861*
is troubled, to put me into the *p* — Jn 5:7 — *2861*
him, Go, wash in the *p* of Siloam — Jn 9:7 — *2861*
unto me, Go to the *p* of Siloam — Jn 9:11 — *2861*

POOLS {5}
and upon all their *p* of water — Ex 7:19 — 4723
the rain also filleth the *p* — Ps 84:6 — 1293
I made me *p* of water, to water — Eccl 2:6 — 1295
for the bittern, and *p* of water — Is 14:23 — 98
islands, and I will dry up the *p* — Is 42:15 — 98

POOR {205}
other kine came up after them, *p* — Gen 41:19 — 1800
of my people that is *p* by thee — Ex 22:25 — 6041
countenance a *p* man in his cause — Ex 23:3 — 1800
judgment of thy *p* in his cause — Ex 23:6 — 34
that the *p* of thy people may eat — Ex 23:11 — 34
the *p* shall not give less than — Ex 30:15 — 1800
And if he be *p*, and cannot get so — Lev 14:21 — 1800
thou shalt leave them for the *p* — Lev 19:10 — 6041
not respect the person of the *p* — Lev 19:15 — 1800
thou shalt leave them unto the *p* — Lev 23:22 — 6041
If thy brother be waxen *p* — Lev 25:25 — 4134
And if thy brother be waxen *p* — Lev 25:35 — 4134
that dwelleth by thee be waxen *p* — Lev 25:39 — 4134
that dwelleth by him wax *p* — Lev 25:47 — 4134
there shall be no *p* among you — Deut 15:4 — 34
If there be among you a *p* man of — Deut 15:7 — 34
thine hand from thy *p* brother — Deut 15:7 — 34
eye be evil against thy *p* brother — Deut 15:9 — 34
For the *p* shall never cease out — Deut 15:11 — 34
wide unto thy brother, to thy *p* — Deut 15:11 — 6041
And if the man be *p*, thou shalt — Deut 24:12 — 6041
an hired servant that is *p* — Deut 24:14 — 6041
for he is *p*, and setteth his heart — Deut 24:15 — 6041
my family is *p* in Manasseh — Judg 6:15 — 1800
not young men, whether *p* or rich — Ruth 3:10 — 1800
The LORD maketh *p*, and maketh rich — 1Sa 2:7 — 3423
raiseth up the *p* out of the dust — 1Sa 2:8 — 1800
in law, seeing that I am a *p* man — 1Sa 18:23 — 7326
the one rich, and the other *p* — 2Sa 12:1 — 7326
But the *p* man had nothing, save — 2Sa 12:3 — 7326
but took the *p* man's lamb — 2Sa 12:4 — 7326
of the guard left of the *p* of the — 2Kin 25:12 — 1803
one to another, and gifts to the *p* — Est 9:22 — 34
he saveth the *p* from the sword — Job 5:15 — 34
So the *p* hath hope, and iniquity — Job 5:16 — 1800
shall seek to please the *p* — Job 20:10 — 1800
oppressed and hath forsaken the *p* — Job 20:19 — 1800
the *p* of the earth hide — Job 24:4 — 6035
breast, and take a pledge of the *p* — Job 24:9 — 6041

with the light killeth the *p* ... Job 24:14 6041
I delivered the *p* that cried ... Job 29:12 6041
I was a father to the *p* ... Job 29:16 34
was not my soul grieved for the *p* ... Job 30:25 34
withheld the *p* from their desire ... Job 31:16 1800
or any *p* without covering ... Job 31:19 34
the rich more than the *p* ... Job 34:19 1800
the cry of the *p* to come unto him ... Job 34:28 1800
but giveth right to the *p* ... Job 36:6 6041
the *p* in his affliction, and ... Job 36:15 6041
the expectation of the *p* shall ... Ps 9:18 6041
in his pride doth persecute the *p* ... Ps 10:2 6041
are privily set against the *p* ... Ps 10:8 2489
he lieth in wait to catch the *p* ... Ps 10:9 6041
he doth catch the *p*, when he ... Ps 10:9 6041
that the *p* may fall by his strong ... Ps 10:10 2489
the *p* committeth himself unto ... Ps 10:14 2489
For the oppression of the *p* ... Ps 12:5 6041
have shamed the counsel of the *p* ... Ps 14:6 6041
This *p* man cried, and the LORD ... Ps 34:6 6041
which deliverest the *p* from him ... Ps 35:10 6041
is too strong for him, yea, the *p* ... Ps 35:10 6041
their bow, to cast down the *p* ... Ps 37:14 6041
But I am *p* and needy ... Ps 40:17 6041
is he that considereth the *p* ... Ps 41:1 1800
Both low and high, rich and *p* ... Ps 49:2 34
of thy goodness for the *p* ... Ps 68:10 6041
But I am *p* and sorrowful ... Ps 69:29 6041
For the LORD heareth the *p* ... Ps 69:33 34
But I am *p* and needy ... Ps 70:5 6041
and thy *p* with judgment ... Ps 72:2 6041
shall judge the *p* of the people ... Ps 72:4 6041
the *p* also, and him that hath no ... Ps 72:12 6041
He shall spare the *p* and needy, and ... Ps 72:13 1800
congregation of thy *p* for ever ... Ps 74:19 6041
let the *p* and needy praise thy ... Ps 74:21 6041
Defend the *p* and fatherless ... Ps 82:3 1800
Deliver the *p* and needy ... Ps 82:4 1800
for I am *p* and needy ... Ps 86:1 6041
Yet setteth he the *p* on high from ... Ps 107:41 34
shew mercy, but persecuted the *p* ... Ps 109:16 6041
For I am *p* and needy, and my heart ... Ps 109:22 6041
stand at the right hand of the *p* ... Ps 109:31 34
dispersed, he hath given to the *p* ... Ps 112:9 34
raiseth up the *p* out of the dust ... Ps 113:7 1800
I will satisfy her *p* with bread ... Ps 132:15 34
afflicted, and the right of the *p* ... Ps 140:12 34
He becometh *p* that dealeth with a ... Prov 10:4 7326
of the *p* is their poverty ... Prov 10:15 1800
there is that maketh himself *p* ... Prov 13:7 7326
but the *p* heareth not rebuke ... Prov 13:8 7326
food is in the tillage of the *p* ... Prov 13:23 7326
The *p* is hated even of his own ... Prov 14:20 7326
but he that hath mercy on the *p* ... Prov 14:21 6035,6041
the *p* reproacheth his Maker ... Prov 14:31 1800
honoureth him hath mercy on the *p* ... Prov 14:31 34
Whoso mocketh the *p* reproacheth ... Prov 17:5 7326
The *p* useth intreaties ... Prov 18:23 7326
Better is the *p* that walketh in ... Prov 19:1 7326
but the *p* is separated from his ... Prov 19:4 1800
the brethren of the *p* do hate him ... Prov 19:7 7326
upon the *p* lendeth unto the LORD ... Prov 19:17 1800
a *p* man is better than a liar ... Prov 19:22 7326
his ears at the cry of the *p* ... Prov 21:13 1800
loveth pleasure shall be a *p* man ... Prov 21:17 4270
The rich and *p* meet together ... Prov 22:2 7326
The rich ruleth over the *p* ... Prov 22:7 7326
he giveth of his bread to the *p* ... Prov 22:9 1800
the *p* to increase his riches ... Prov 22:16 1800
Rob not the *p*, because he is *p* ... Prov 22:22 1800
A *p* man that oppresseth the ... Prov 28:3 7326
p is like a sweeping rain which ... Prov 28:3 1800
Better is the *p* that walketh in ... Prov 28:6 1800
it for him that will pity the *p* ... Prov 28:8 1800
but the *p* that hath understanding ... Prov 28:11 1800
a wicked ruler over the *p* people ... Prov 28:15 1800
giveth unto the *p* shall not lack ... Prov 28:27 7326
considereth the cause of the *p* ... Prov 29:7 1800
The *p* and the deceitful man meet ... Prov 29:13 7326
that faithfully judgeth the *p* ... Prov 29:14 1800
or lest I be *p*, and steal, and take ... Prov 30:9 3423
to devour the *p* from off the ... Prov 30:14 6041
and plead the cause of the *p* ... Prov 31:9 6041
stretcheth out her hand to the *p* ... Prov 31:20 6041
Better is a *p* and a wise child ... Eccl 4:13 4542
is born in his kingdom becometh *p* ... Eccl 4:14 7326
seest the oppression of the *p* ... Eccl 5:8 7326
what hath the *p*, that knoweth to ... Eccl 6:8 6041
was found in it a *p* wise man ... Eccl 9:15 4542
no man remembered that same *p* man ... Eccl 9:15 4542
nevertheless the *p* man's wisdom ... Eccl 9:16 4542
the spoil of the *p* is in your ... Is 3:14 6041
and grind the faces of the *p* ... Is 3:15 6041
the right from the *p* of my people ... Is 10:2 6041
be heard unto Laish, O *p* Anathoth ... Is 10:30 6041
shall he judge the *p*, and reprove ... Is 11:4 1800
the firstborn of the *p* shall feed ... Is 14:30 1800
the *p* of his people shall trust ... Is 14:32 6041
hast been a strength to the *p* ... Is 25:4 1800
it down, even the feet of the *p* ... Is 26:6 6041
the *p* among men shall rejoice in ... Is 29:19 34
to destroy the *p* with lying words ... Is 32:7 6035,6041
When the *p* and needy seek water, ... Is 41:17 6041
that thou bring the *p* that are ... Is 58:7 6041
I look, even to him that is *p* ... Is 66:2 6041
of the souls of the *p* innocents ... Jer 2:34 34
I said, Surely these are *p* ... Jer 5:4 1800
the *p* from the hand of evildoers ... Jer 20:13 34
He judged the cause of the *p* ... Jer 22:16 6041
guard left of the *p* of the people ... Jer 39:10 1800
of the *p* of the land, of them ... Jer 40:7 1803
certain of the *p* of the people ... Jer 52:15 1803
p of the land for vinedressers ... Jer 52:16 1803
she strengthen the hand of the *p* ... Eze 16:49 6041
Hath oppressed the *p* and needy, ... Eze 18:12 6041
taken off his hand from the *p* ... Eze 18:17 6041
robbery, and have vexed the *p* ... Eze 22:29 6041
by shewing mercy to the *p* ... Dan 4:27 6033
the *p* for a pair of shoes ... Amos 2:6 34
of the earth on the head of the *p* ... Amos 2:7 1800
of Samaria, which oppress the *p* ... Amos 4:1 1800
as your treading is upon the *p* ... Amos 5:11 1800
they turn aside the *p* in the gate ... Amos 5:12 34
even to make the *p* of the land to ... Amos 8:4 6035,6041
That we may buy the *p* for silver ... Amos 8:6 1800
was as to devour the *p* secretly ... Hab 3:14 6041
p people, and they shall trust in ... Zeph 3:12 1800
the stranger, nor the *p* ... Zec 7:10 6041
even you, O *p* of the flock ... Zec 11:7 6041
so the *p* of the flock that waited ... Zec 11:11 6041
Blessed are the *p* in spirit ... Mt 5:3 *4434*
the *p* have the gospel preached to ... Mt 11:5 *4434*
that thou hast, and give to the *p* ... Mt 19:21 *4434*
sold for much, and given to the *p* ... Mt 26:9 *4434*
For ye have the *p* always with you ... Mt 26:11 *4434*
thou hast, and give to the *p* ... Mk 10:21 *4434*
And there came a certain *p* widow ... Mk 12:42 *4434*
That this *p* widow hath cast more ... Mk 12:43 *4434*
and have been given to the *p* ... Mk 14:5 *4434*
For ye have the *p* with you always ... Mk 14:7 *4434*
me to preach the gospel to the *p* ... Lk 4:18 *4434*
and said, Blessed be ye *p* ... Lk 6:20 *4434*
to the *p* the gospel is preached ... Lk 7:22 *4434*
thou makest a feast, call the *p* ... Lk 14:13 *4434*
city, and bring in hither the *p* ... Lk 14:21 *4434*
hast, and distribute unto the *p* ... Lk 18:22 *4434*
half of my goods I give to the *p* ... Lk 19:8 *4434*
he saw also a certain *p* widow ... Lk 21:2 *3998*
that this *p* widow hath cast in ... Lk 21:3 *4434*
hundred pence, and given to the *p* ... Jn 12:5 *4434*
said, not that he cared for the *p* ... Jn 12:6 *4434*
For the *p* always ye have with you ... Jn 12:8 *4434*
he should give something to the *p* ... Jn 13:29 *4434*
p saints which are at Jerusalem ... Rom 15:26 *4434*
bestow all my goods to feed the *p* ... 1Cor 13:3
as *p*, yet making many rich ... 2Cor 6:10 *4434*
yet for your sakes he became *p* ... 2Cor 8:9 *4433*
he hath given to the *p* ... 2Cor 9:9 *3993*
that we should remember the *p* ... Gal 2:10 *4434*
in also a *p* man in vile raiment ... Jas 2:2 *4434*
and say to the *p*, Stand thou there ... Jas 2:3 *4434*
Hath not God chosen the *p* of this ... Jas 2:5 *4434*
But ye have despised the *p* ... Jas 2:6 *4434*
art wretched, and miserable, and *p* ... Rev 3:17 *4434*
both small and great, rich and *p* ... Rev 13:16 *4434*

POORER {1}
But if he be *p* than thy ... Lev 27:8 4134

POOREST {1}
save the *p* sort of the people of ... 2Kin 24:14 1803

POPLAR {1}
And Jacob took him rods of green *p* ... Gen 30:37 3839

POPLARS {1}
upon the hills, under oaks and *p* ... Hos 4:13 3839

POPULOUS {2}
a nation, great, mighty, and *p* ... Deut 26:5 7227
Art thou better than *p* No ... Nah 3:8 527

PORATHA *(por'-a-thah)* {1} *A son of Haman.*
And *P*, and Adalia, and Aridatha, ... Est 9:8 6334

PORCH {39}
Ehud went forth through the *p* ... Judg 3:23 4528
the *p* before the temple of the ... 1Kin 6:3 197
And he made a *p* of pillars ... 1Kin 7:6 197
and the *p* was before them ... 1Kin 7:6 197
Then he made a *p* for the throne ... 1Kin 7:7 197
judge, even the *p* of judgment ... 1Kin 7:7 197
had another court within the *p* ... 1Kin 7:8 197
taken to wife, like unto this *p* ... 1Kin 7:8 197
LORD, and for the *p* of the house ... 1Kin 7:12 197
were of lily work in the *p* ... 1Kin 7:19 197
pillars in the *p* of the temple ... 1Kin 7:21 197
his son the pattern of the *p* ... 1Chr 28:11 197
the *p* that was in the front of ... 2Chr 3:4 197
which he had built before the *p* ... 2Chr 8:12 197
that was before the *p* of the LORD ... 2Chr 15:8 197
have shut up the doors of the *p* ... 2Chr 29:7 197
came they to the *p* of the LORD ... 2Chr 29:17 197
temple of the LORD, between the *p* ... Eze 8:16 197
threshold of the gate by the *p* of ... Eze 40:7 197
also the *p* of the gate within ... Eze 40:8 197
measured he the *p* of the gate ... Eze 40:9 197
the *p* of the gate was inward ... Eze 40:9 197
p of the inner gate were fifty ... Eze 40:15 197
in the *p* of the gate were two ... Eze 40:39 197
which was at the *p* of the gate ... Eze 40:40 197
brought me to the *p* of the house ... Eze 40:48 197
and measured each post of the *p* ... Eze 40:48 197
length of the *p* was twenty cubits ... Eze 40:49 197
upon the face of the *p* without ... Eze 41:25 197
other side, on the sides of the *p* ... Eze 41:26 197
by the way of the *p* of that gate ... Eze 44:3 197
way of the *p* of that gate without ... Eze 46:2 197
by the way of the *p* of that gate ... Eze 46:8 197
of the LORD, weep between the *p* ... Joel 2:17 197
when he was gone out into the *p* ... Mt 26:71 *4440*
And he went out into the *p* ... Mk 14:68 *4259*
in the temple in Solomon's *p* ... Jn 10:23 *4745*
in the *p* that is called Solomon's ... Acts 3:11 *4745*
with one accord in Solomon's *p* ... Acts 5:12 *4745*

PORCHES {2}
temple, and the *p* of the court ... Eze 41:15 197
tongue Bethesda, having five *p* ... Jn 5:2 *4745*

PORCIUS *(por'-she-us)* {1} *Family name of Festus.*
But after two years *P* Festus came ... Acts 24:27 *4201*

PORT {1}
the dragon well, and to the dung *p* ... Neh 2:13 8179

PORTER {6}
and the watchman called unto the *p* ... 2Sa 18:26 7778
and called unto the *p* of the city ... 2Kin 7:10 7778
the son of Meshelemiah was *p* of ... 1Chr 9:21 7778
the *p* toward the east, was over ... 2Chr 31:14 7778
work, and commanded the *p* to watch ... Mk 13:34 *2377*
To him the *p* openeth ... Jn 10:3 *2377*

PORTERS {33}
And he called the *p* ... 2Kin 7:11 7778
the *p* were, Shallum, and Akkub, and ... 1Chr 9:17 7778
they were *p* in the companies of ... 1Chr 9:18 7778
p in the gates were two hundred ... 1Chr 9:22 7778
In four quarters were the *p* ... 1Chr 9:24 7778
these Levites, the four chief *p* ... 1Chr 9:26 7778
and Obed-edom, and Jeiel, the *p* ... 1Chr 15:18 7778
son of Jeduthun and Hosah to be *p* ... 1Chr 16:38 7778
And the sons of Jeduthun were *p* ... 1Chr 16:42 8179
Moreover four thousand were *p* ... 1Chr 23:5 7778
Concerning the divisions of the *p* ... 1Chr 26:1 7778
these were the divisions of the *p* ... 1Chr 26:12 7778
of the *p* among the sons of Kore ... 1Chr 26:19 7778
the *p* also by their courses at ... 2Chr 8:14 7778
Levites, shall be *p* of the doors ... 2Chr 23:4 7778
he set the *p* at the gates of the ... 2Chr 23:19 7778
were scribes, and officers, and *p* ... 2Chr 34:13 7778
the *p* waited at every gate ... 2Chr 35:15 7778
The children of the *p* ... Ezr 2:42 7778
people, and the singers, and the *p* ... Ezr 2:70 7778
Levites, and the singers, and the *p* ... Ezr 7:7 7778
priests and Levites, singers, *p* ... Ezr 7:24 8652
the *p*; Shallum, and Telem ... Ezr 10:24 7778
I had set up the doors, and the *p* ... Neh 7:1 7778
The *p*: the children of Shallum ... Neh 7:45 7778
priests, and the Levites, and the *p* ... Neh 7:73 7778
the priests, the Levites, the *p* ... Neh 10:28 7778
priests that minister, and the *p* ... Neh 10:39 7778
Moreover the *p*, Akkub, Talmon, and ... Neh 11:19 7778
were *p* keeping the ward at the ... Neh 12:25 7778
the *p* kept the ward of their God, ... Neh 12:45 7778
portions of the singers and the *p* ... Neh 12:47 7778
Levites, and the singers, and the *p* ... Neh 13:5 7778

PORTION {100}
the *p* of the men which went with ... Gen 14:24 2506
let them take their *p* ... Gen 14:24 2506
Is there yet any *p* or inheritance ... Gen 31:14 2506
for the priests had a *p* assigned ... Gen 47:22 2706
did eat their *p* which Pharaoh ... Gen 47:22 2706
to thee one *p* above thy brethren ... Gen 48:22 7926
p of my offerings made by fire ... Lev 6:17 2506
This is the *p* of the anointing of ... Lev 7:35
thou shalt take one *p* of fifty ... Num 31:30 270
which was the *p* of them that went ... Num 31:36 2506
half, Moses took one *p* of fifty ... Num 31:47 270
a double *p* of all that he hath ... Deut 21:17 6310
For the LORD's *p* is his people ... Deut 32:9 2506
in a *p* of the lawgiver, was he ... Deut 33:21 2513
one *p* to inherit, seeing I am a ... Josh 17:14 2256
Out of the *p* of the children of ... Josh 19:9 2256
unto Hannah he gave a worthy *p* ... 1Sa 1:5 4490
Bring the *p* which I gave thee, of ... 1Sa 9:23 4490
saying, What *p* have we in David ... 1Kin 12:16 2506
let a double *p* of thy spirit be ... 2Kin 2:9 6310
eat Jezebel in the *p* of Jezreel ... 2Kin 9:10 2506
met him in the *p* of Naboth the ... 2Kin 9:21 2513
cast him in the *p* of the field of ... 2Kin 9:25 2513
In the *p* of Jezreel shall dogs ... 2Kin 9:36 2506
of the field in the *p* of Jezreel ... 2Kin 9:37 2506
saying, What *p* have we in David ... 2Chr 10:16 2506
For Ahaz took away a *p* out of the ... 2Chr 28:21 2505
He appointed also the king's *p* of ... 2Chr 31:3 4521
to give the *p* of the priests ... 2Chr 31:4 4521
his daily *p* for their service in ... 2Chr 31:16 1697
have no *p* on this side the river ... Ezr 4:16 2508
but ye have no *p*, nor right, nor ... Neh 2:20 2506
that a certain *p* should be for ... Neh 11:23
and the porters, every day his *p* ... Neh 12:47 1697
This is the *p* of a wicked man ... Job 20:29 2506
their *p* is cursed in the earth ... Job 24:18 2513
how little a *p* is heard of him ... Job 26:14 1697
This is the *p* of a wicked man ... Job 27:13 2506
For what *p* of God is there from ... Job 31:2 2506
this shall be the *p* of their cup ... Ps 11:6 4521
The LORD is the *p* of mine ... Ps 16:5 4490
which have their *p* in this life ... Ps 17:14 2506
they shall be a *p* for foxes ... Ps 63:10 4521
of my heart, and my *p* for ever ... Ps 73:26 2506
Thou art my *p*, O LORD ... Ps 119:57 2506
my *p* in the land of the living ... Ps 142:5 2506
household, and a *p* to her maidens ... Prov 31:15 2706
this was my *p* of all my labour ... Eccl 2:10 2506
shall he leave it for his *p* ... Eccl 2:21 2506
for that is his *p* ... Eccl 3:22 2506
for it is his *p* ... Eccl 5:18 2506
to eat thereof, and to take his *p* ... Eccl 5:19 2506

neither have they any more a *p* ... Eccl 9:6 2506
for that is thy *p* in this life ... Eccl 9:9 2506
Give a *p* to seven, and also to ... Eccl 11:2 2506
This is the *p* of them that spoil ... Is 17:14 2506
I divide him a *p* with the great ... Is 53:12
stones of the stream is thy *p* ... Is 57:6 2506
they shall rejoice in their *p* ... Is 61:7 2506
The *p* of Jacob is not like them ... Jer 10:16 2506
they have trodden my *p* under foot ... Jer 12:10 2513
pleasant *p* a desolate wilderness ... Jer 12:10 2513
the *p* of thy measures from me, ... Jer 13:25 4490
The *p* of Jacob is not like them ... Jer 51:19 2506
every day a *p* until the day of ... Jer 52:34 1697
The LORD is my *p*, saith my soul ... Lam 3:24 2506
the LORD, an holy *p* of the land ... Eze 45:1
The holy *p* of the land shall be ... Eze 45:4
the oblation of the holy *p* ... Eze 45:6
a *p* shall be for the prince on ... Eze 45:7
of the oblation of the holy *p* ... Eze 45:7
before the oblation of the holy *p* ... Eze 45:7
a *p* for Dan ... Eze 48:1
unto the west side, a *p* for Asher ... Eze 48:2
the west side, a *p* for Naphtali ... Eze 48:3
the west side, a *p* for Manasseh ... Eze 48:4
the west side, a *p* for Ephraim ... Eze 48:5
the west side, a *p* for Reuben ... Eze 48:6
unto the west side, a *p* for Judah ... Eze 48:7
the oblation of the holy *p* shall ... Eze 48:18
the oblation of the holy *p* ... Eze 48:18
side, Benjamin shall have a *p* ... Eze 48:23
west side, Simeon shall have a *p* ... Eze 48:24
unto the west side, Issachar a *p* ... Eze 48:25
unto the west side, Zebulun a *p* ... Eze 48:26
side unto the west side, Gad a *p* ... Eze 48:27
with the *p* of the king's meat ... Dan 1:8 6598
eat of the *p* of the king's meat ... Dan 1:13 6598
did eat the *p* of the king's meat ... Dan 1:15 6598
took away the *p* of their meat ... Dan 1:16 6598
let his *p* be with the beasts in ... Dan 4:15 2508
let his *p* be with the beasts of ... Dan 4:23 2508
they that feed of the *p* of his ... Dan 11:26 6598
hath changed the *p* of my people ... Mic 2:4 2506
because by them their *p* is fat ... Hab 1:16 2506
Judah his *p* in the holy land ... Zec 2:12 2506
appoint him his *p* with the ... Mt 24:51 *3313*
to give them their *p* of meat in ... Lk 12:42 *4620*
him his *p* with the unbelievers ... Lk 12:46 *3313*
give me the *p* of goods that ... Lk 15:12 *3313*

PORTIONS {16}
They shall have like *p* to eat ... Deut 18:8 2506
And there fell ten *p* to Manasseh ... Josh 17:5 2256
all her sons and her daughters, *p* ... 1Sa 1:4 4490
to give *p* to all the males among ... 2Chr 31:19 4490
send *p* unto them for whom nothing ... Neh 8:10 4490
to eat, and to drink, and to send *p* ... Neh 8:12 4490
the *p* of the law for the priests ... Neh 12:44 4521
gave the *p* of the singers and the ... Neh 12:47 4521
I perceived that the *p* of the ... Neh 13:10 4521
of sending *p* one to another ... Est 9:19 4490
of sending *p* one to another, and ... Est 9:22 4490
be over against one of the *p* ... Eze 45:7 2506
Joseph shall have two *p* ... Eze 47:13 2256
over against the *p* for the prince ... Eze 48:21 2506
inheritance, and these are their *p* ... Eze 48:29 4256
a month devour them with their *p* ... Hos 5:7 2506

POSSESS {106}
thy seed shall *p* the gate of his ... Gen 22:17 3423
let thy seed *p* the gate of those ... Gen 24:60 3423
I will give it unto you to *p* it ... Lev 20:24 3423
Let us go up at once, and *p* it ... Num 13:30 3423
and his seed shall *p* it ... Num 14:24 3423
of his family, and he shall *p* it ... Num 27:11 3423
I have given you the land to *p* it ... Num 33:53 3423
p the land which the LORD sware ... Deut 1:8 3423
p it, as the LORD God of thy ... Deut 1:21 3423
I give it, and they shall *p* it ... Deut 1:39 3423
begin to *p* it, and contend with ... Deut 2:24 3423
begin to *p*, that thou mayest ... Deut 2:31 3423
hath given you this land to *p* it ... Deut 3:18 3423
until they also *p* the land which ... Deut 3:20 3423
p the land which the LORD God of ... Deut 4:1 3423
in the land whither ye go to *p* it ... Deut 4:5 3423
land whither ye go over to *p* it ... Deut 4:14 3423
go over, and *p* that good land ... Deut 4:22 3423
ye go over Jordan to *p* it ... Deut 4:26 3423
land which I give them to *p* it ... Deut 5:31 3423
days in the land which ye shall *p* ... Deut 5:33 3423
in the land whither ye go to *p* it ... Deut 6:1 3423
p the good land which the LORD ... Deut 6:18 3423
land whither thou goest to *p* it ... Deut 7:1 3423
p the land which the LORD sware ... Deut 8:1 3423
to go in to *p* nations greater and ... Deut 9:1 3423
hath brought me in to *p* this land ... Deut 9:4 3423
dost thou go to *p* their land ... Deut 9:5 3423
to *p* it for thy righteousness ... Deut 9:6 3423
p the land which I have given you ... Deut 9:23 3423
p the land, which I sware unto ... Deut 10:11 3423
p the land, whither ye go to ... Deut 11:8 3423
the land, whither ye go to *p* it ... Deut 11:8 3423
whither thou goest in to *p* it ... Deut 11:10 3423
the land, whither ye go to *p* it ... Deut 11:11 3423
ye shall *p* greater nations and ... Deut 11:23 3423
land whither thou goest to *p* it ... Deut 11:29 3423
to *p* the land which the LORD your ... Deut 11:31 3423
God giveth you, and ye shall *p* it ... Deut 11:31 3423
thy fathers giveth thee to *p* it ... Deut 12:1 3423
ye shall *p* served their gods ... Deut 12:2 3423
whither thou goest to *p* them ... Deut 12:29 3423
thee for an inheritance to *p* it ... Deut 15:4 3423
God giveth thee, and shalt *p* it ... Deut 17:14 3423
these nations, which thou shalt *p* ... Deut 18:14 3423
LORD thy God giveth thee to *p* it ... Deut 19:2 3423
LORD thy God giveth thee to *p* it ... Deut 19:14 3423
LORD thy God giveth thee to *p* it ... Deut 21:1 3423
land whither thou goest to *p* it ... Deut 23:20 3423
thee for an inheritance to *p* it ... Deut 25:19 3423
land, whither thou goest to *p* it ... Deut 28:21 3423
land whither thou goest to *p* it ... Deut 28:63 3423
possessed, and thou shalt *p* it ... Deut 30:5 3423
land whither thou goest to *p* it ... Deut 30:16 3423
passest over Jordan to go to *p* it ... Deut 30:18 3423
before thee, and thou shalt *p* them ... Deut 31:3 3423
whither ye go over Jordan to *p* it ... Deut 31:13 3423
whither ye go over Jordan to *p* it ... Deut 32:47 3423
p thou the west and the south ... Deut 33:23 3423
Jordan, to go in to *p* the land ... Josh 1:11 3423
LORD your God giveth you to *p* it ... Josh 1:11 3423
are ye slack to go to *p* the land ... Josh 18:3 3423
ye shall *p* their land, as the ... Josh 23:5 3423
unto Esau mount Seir, to *p* it ... Josh 24:4 3423
hand, that ye might *p* their land ... Josh 24:8 3423
his inheritance to *p* the land ... Judg 2:6 3423
Israel, and shouldest thou *p* it ... Judg 11:23 3423
Wilt not thou *p* that which ... Judg 11:24 3423
Chemosh thy god giveth thee to *p* ... Judg 11:24 3423
from before us, them will we *p* ... Judg 11:24 3423
to go, and to enter to *p* the land ... Judg 18:9 3423
whither he is gone down to *p* it ... 1Kin 21:18 3423
that ye may *p* this good land, and ... 1Chr 28:8 3423
land, unto which ye go to *p* it ... Ezr 9:11 3423
them that they should go in to *p* ... Neh 9:15 3423
that they should go in to *p* it ... Neh 9:23 3423
So am I made to *p* months of ... Job 7:3 5157
makest me to *p* the iniquities of ... Job 13:26 3423
the house of Israel shall *p* them ... Is 14:2 5157
nor *p* the land, nor fill the face ... Is 14:21 3423
and the bittern shall *p* it ... Is 34:11 3423
they shall *p* it for ever, from ... Is 34:17 3423
his trust in me shall *p* the land ... Is 57:13 5157
land they shall *p* the double ... Is 61:7 3423
their fathers, and they shall *p* it ... Jer 30:3 3423
they shall *p* their houses ... Eze 7:24 3423
and shall ye *p* the land ... Eze 33:25 3423
and shall ye *p* the land ... Eze 33:26 3423
shall be mine, and we will *p* it ... Eze 35:10 3423
and they shall *p* thee, and thou ... Eze 36:12 3423
p the kingdom for ever, even for ... Dan 7:18 2631
silver, nettles shall *p* them ... Hos 9:6 3423
to *p* the land of the Amorite ... Amos 2:10 3423
That they may *p* the remnant of ... Amos 9:12 3423
Jacob shall *p* their possessions ... Obad 17 3423
south shall *p* the mount of Esau ... Obad 19 3423
they shall *p* the fields of ... Obad 19 3423
and Benjamin shall *p* Gilead ... Obad 19
shall *p* that of the Canaanites ... Obad 20
shall *p* the cities of the south ... Obad 20 423
to *p* the dwellingplaces that are ... Hab 1:6 423
remnant of my people shall *p* them ... Zeph 2:9 5157
this people to *p* all these things ... Zec 8:12 5157
I give tithes of all that I *p* ... Lk 18:12 *2932*
In your patience *p* ye your souls ... Lk 21:19 *2932*
to *p* his vessel in sanctification ... 1Th 4:4 *2932*

POSSESSED {39}
p his land from Arnon unto Jabbok ... Num 21:24 3423
and they *p* his land ... Num 21:35 3423
which we *p* at that time, from ... Deut 3:12 3423
they *p* his land, and the land of ... Deut 4:47 3423
into the land which thy fathers *p* ... Deut 30:5 3423
they also have *p* the land which ... Josh 1:15 3423
p their land on the other side ... Josh 12:1 3423
yet very much land to be *p* ... Josh 13:1 3423
p it, and dwelt therein, and called ... Josh 19:47 3423
and they *p* it, and dwelt therein ... Josh 21:43 3423
possession, whereof they were *p* ... Josh 22:9 270
and *p* the city of palm trees ... Judg 3:13 3423
so Israel *p* all the land of the ... Judg 11:21 3423
they *p* all the coasts of the ... Judg 11:22 3423
they *p* Samaria, and dwelt in the ... 2Kin 17:24 3423
so they *p* the land of Sihon, and ... Neh 9:22 3423
p the land, and thou subduedst ... Neh 9:24 3423
p houses full of all goods, wells ... Neh 9:25 3423
For thou hast *p* my reins ... Ps 139:13 7069
The LORD *p* me in the beginning of ... Prov 8:22 7069
have *p* it but a little while ... Is 63:18 3423
shall be *p* again in this land ... Jer 32:15 7069
And they came in, and *p* it ... Jer 32:23 3423
that the saints *p* the kingdom ... Dan 7:22 2631
and those which were *p* with devils ... Mt 4:24 *1139*
him many that were *p* with devils ... Mt 8:16 *1139*
there met him two *p* with devils ... Mt 8:28 *1139*
befallen to the *p* of the devils ... Mt 8:33 *1139*
to him a dumb man *p* with a devil ... Mt 9:32 *1139*
unto him one *p* with a devil ... Mt 12:22 *1139*
and them that were *p* with devils ... Mk 1:32 *1139*
see him that was *p* with the devil ... Mk 5:15 *1139*
to him that was *p* with the devil ... Mk 5:16 *1139*
he that had been *p* with the devil ... Mk 5:18 *1139*
was *p* of the devils was healed ... Lk 8:36 *1139*
the things which he *p* was his own ... Acts 4:32 *5224*
out of many that were *p* with them ... Acts 8:7 *2192*
a certain damsel *p* with a spirit ... Acts 16:16 *2192*
that buy, as though they *p* not ... 1Cor 7:30 *2722*

POSSESSEST {1}
p it, and dwellest therein ... Deut 26:1 3423

POSSESSETH {2}
that *p* an inheritance in any ... Num 36:8 3423
of the things which he *p* ... Lk 12:15 *5224*

POSSESSING {1}
nothing, and yet *p* all things ... 2Cor 6:10 *2722*

POSSESSION {104}
of Canaan, for an everlasting *p* ... Gen 17:8 272
give me a *p* of a buryingplace ... Gen 23:4 272
a *p* of a buryingplace amongst you ... Gen 23:9 272
Unto Abraham for a *p* in the ... Gen 23:18 4736
made sure unto Abraham for a *p* of ... Gen 23:20 272
For he had *p* of flocks, and ... Gen 26:14 4735
p of herds, and great store of ... Gen 26:14 4735
in the land of their *p* ... Gen 36:43 272
gave them a *p* in the land of ... Gen 47:11 272
after thee for an everlasting *p* ... Gen 48:4 272
Hittite for a *p* of a buryingplace ... Gen 49:30 272
bought with the field for a *p* of ... Gen 50:13 272
which I give to you for a *p* ... Lev 14:34 272
in a house of the land of your *p* ... Lev 14:34 272
shall return every man unto his *p* ... Lev 25:10 272
shall return every man unto his *p* ... Lev 25:13 272
in all the land of your *p* ye ... Lev 25:24 272
and hath sold away some of his *p* ... Lev 25:25 272
that he may return unto his *p* ... Lev 25:27 272
and he shall return unto his *p* ... Lev 25:28 272
houses of the cities of their *p* ... Lev 25:32 272
was sold, and the city of his *p* ... Lev 25:33 272
p among the children of Israel ... Lev 25:33 272
for it is their perpetual *p* ... Lev 25:34 272
unto the *p* of his fathers shall ... Lev 25:41 272
and they shall be your *p* ... Lev 25:45 272
you, to inherit them for a *p* ... Lev 25:46 272
some part of a field of his *p* ... Lev 27:16 272
the *p* thereof shall be the ... Lev 27:21 272
is not of the fields of his *p* ... Lev 27:22 272
whom the *p* of the land did belong ... Lev 27:24 272
beast, and of the field of his *p* ... Lev 27:28 272
And Edom shall be a *p* ... Num 24:18 3424
also shall be a *p* for his enemies ... Num 24:18 3424
According to the lot shall the *p* ... Num 26:56 5159
Give unto us therefore a *p* among ... Num 27:4 272
a *p* of an inheritance among their ... Num 27:7 272
given unto thy servants for a *p* ... Num 32:5 272
shall be your *p* before the LORD ... Num 32:22 272
them the land of Gilead for a *p* ... Num 32:29 272
that the *p* of our inheritance on ... Num 32:32 272
of their *p* cities to dwell in ... Num 35:2 272
the *p* of the children of Israel ... Num 35:8 272
return into the land of his *p* ... Num 35:28 272
mount Seir unto Esau for a *p* ... Deut 2:5 3425
give thee of their land for a *p* ... Deut 2:9 3425
unto the children of Lot for a *p* ... Deut 2:9 3425
Israel did unto the land of his *p* ... Deut 2:12 3425
of the children of Ammon any *p* ... Deut 2:19 3425
unto the children of Lot for a *p* ... Deut 2:19 3425
ye return every man unto his *p* ... Deut 3:20 3425
the substance that was in their *p* ... Deut 11:6 7272
the children of Israel for a *p* ... Deut 32:49 272
return unto the land of your *p* ... Josh 1:15 3425
it for a *p* unto the Reubenites ... Josh 12:6 3425
a *p* according to their divisions ... Josh 12:7 3425
this was the *p* of the half tribe ... Josh 13:29
the son of Jephunneh for his *p* ... Josh 21:12 272
of the Levites within the *p* of ... Josh 21:41 272
tents, and unto the land of your *p* ... Josh 22:4 272
Moses had given *p* in Bashan ... Josh 22:7
of Gilead, to the land of their *p* ... Josh 22:9 272
if the land of your *p* be unclean ... Josh 22:19 272
the land of the *p* of the LORD ... Josh 22:19 272
dwelleth, and take *p* among us ... Josh 22:19 270
take *p* of the vineyard of Naboth ... 1Kin 21:15 3423
the Jezreelite, to take *p* of it ... 1Kin 21:16 3423
Hast thou killed, and also taken *p* ... 1Kin 21:19 3423
p of the king, and of his sons, ... 1Chr 28:1 4735
left their suburbs and their *p* ... 2Chr 11:14 272
to come to cast us out of thy *p* ... 2Chr 20:11 3425
returned, every man to his *p* ... 2Chr 31:1 272
one in his *p* in their cities ... Neh 11:3 272
parts of the earth for thy *p* ... Ps 2:8 272
the land in *p* by their own sword ... Ps 44:3 3423
may dwell there, and have it in *p* ... Ps 69:35 3423
ourselves the houses of God in *p* ... Ps 83:12 3423
shall have good things in *p* ... Prov 28:10 5157
also make it a *p* for the bittern ... Is 14:23 4180
unto us is this land given in *p* ... Eze 11:15 4181
to the men of the east for a *p* ... Eze 25:4 4181
Ammonites, and will give them in *p* ... Eze 25:10 4181
ancient high places are ours in *p* ... Eze 36:2 4181
that ye might be a *p* unto the ... Eze 36:3 4181
appointed my land into their *p* ... Eze 36:5 4181
ye shall give them no *p* in Israel ... Eze 44:28 272
I am their *p* ... Eze 44:28 272
for a *p* for twenty chambers ... Eze 45:5 272
ye shall appoint the *p* of the ... Eze 45:6 272
of the *p* of the city, before the ... Eze 45:7 272
before the *p* of the city, from ... Eze 45:7 272
the land shall be his *p* in Israel ... Eze 45:8 272
shall be their *p* by inheritance ... Eze 46:16 272
to thrust them out of their *p* ... Eze 46:18 272
sons inheritance out of his own *p* ... Eze 46:18 272
scattered every man from his *p* ... Eze 46:18 272
with the *p* of the city ... Eze 48:20 272
of the *p* of the city, over ... Eze 48:21 272
from the *p* of the Levites ... Eze 48:22 272
from the *p* of the city, being in ... Eze 48:22 272
with Sapphira his wife, sold a *p* ... Acts 5:1 *2933*

he would give it to him for a *p* ... Acts 7:5 *2697*
Jesus into the *p* of the Gentiles ... Acts 7:45 *2697*
the redemption of the purchased *p* ... Eph 1:14 *4047*

POSSESSIONS {13}
ye therein, and get you *p* therein ... Gen 34:10 270
and they had *p* therein, and grew, ... Gen 47:27 270
they shall have *p* among you in ... Num 32:30 270
in Maon, whose *p* were in Carmel ... 1Sa 25:2 4639
And their *p* and habitations were, ... 1Chr 7:28 272
in their *p* in their cities were ... 1Chr 9:2 272
p of flocks and herds in abundance ... 2Chr 32:29 4735
also I had great *p* of great ... Eccl 2:7 4735
of Jacob shall possess their *p* ... Obad 17 4180
for he had great *p* ... Mt 19:22 *2933*
for he had great *p* ... Mk 10:22 *2933*
And sold their *p* and goods, and ... Acts 2:45 *2933*
In the same quarters were *p* of ... Acts 28:7 *5564*

POSSESSOR {2}
high God, *p* of heaven and earth ... Gen 14:19 7069
the *p* of heaven and earth, ... Gen 14:22 7069

POSSESSORS {2}
Whose *p* slay them, and hold ... Zec 11:5 7069
for as many as were *p* of lands or ... Acts 4:34 *2935*

POSSIBLE {15}
but with God all things are *p* ... Mt 19:26 *1415*
insomuch that, if it were *p* ... Mt 24:24 *1415*
saying, O my Father, if it be *p* ... Mt 26:39 *1415*
all things are *p* to him that ... Mk 9:23 *1415*
for with God all things are *p* ... Mk 10:27 *1415*
wonders, to seduce, if it were *p* ... Mk 13:22 *1415*
and prayed that, if it were *p* ... Mk 14:35 *1415*
all things are *p* unto thee ... Mk 14:36 *1415*
with men are *p* with God ... Lk 18:27 *1415*
because it was not *p* that he ... Acts 2:24 *1415*
he hasted, if it were *p* for him ... Acts 20:16 *1415*
they were minded, if it were *p* ... Acts 27:39 *1410*
If it be *p*, as much as lieth in ... Rom 12:18 *1415*
record, that, if it had been *p* ... Gal 4:15 *1415*
For it is not *p* that the blood of ... Heb 10:4 *102*

POST {11}
on the upper door *p* of the houses ... Ex 12:7 4947
to the door, or unto the door *p* ... Ex 21:6 4201
by a *p* of the temple of the LORD ... 1Sa 1:9 4201
Now my days are swifter than a *p* ... Job 9:25 7323
One *p* shall run to meet another, ... Jer 51:31 7323
even unto the *p* of the court ... Eze 40:14 352
upon each *p* were palm trees ... Eze 40:16 352
and measured each *p* of the porch ... Eze 40:48 352
and measured the *p* of the door ... Eze 41:3 352
their *p* by my posts, and the wall ... Eze 43:8 4201
shall stand by the *p* of the gate ... Eze 46:2 4201

POSTERITY {9}
to preserve you a *p* in the earth ... Gen 45:7 7611
If any man of you or of your *p* ... Num 9:10 1755
I will take away the *p* of Baasha ... 1Kin 16:3 310
of Baasha, and the *p* of his house ... 1Kin 16:3 310
thee, and will take away thy *p* ... 1Kin 21:21 310
yet their *p* approve their sayings ... Ps 49:13 310
Let his *p* be cut off ... Ps 109:13 319
and not to his *p*, nor according to ... Dan 11:4 319
hooks, and your *p* with fishhooks ... Amos 4:2 319

POSTS {42}
and strike it on the two side *p* ... Ex 12:7 4201
the two side *p* with the blood ... Ex 12:22 4201
the lintel, and on the two side *p* ... Ex 12:23 4201
them upon the *p* of thy house ... Deut 6:9 4201
upon the door *p* of thine house ... Deut 11:20 4201
gate of the city, and the two *p* ... Judg 16:3 4201
side *p* were a fifth part of the ... 1Kin 6:31 4201
of the temple *p* of olive tree ... 1Kin 6:33 4201
p were square, with the windows ... 1Kin 7:5 4201
also the house, the beams, the *p* ... 2Chr 3:7 5592
So the *p* went with the letters ... 2Chr 30:6 7323
So the *p* passed from city to city ... 2Chr 30:10 7323
the letters were sent by *p* into ... Est 3:13 7323
The *p* went out, being hastened by ... Est 3:15 7323
and sent letters by *p* on horseback ... Est 8:10 7323
So the *p* that rode upon mules and ... Est 8:14 7323
waiting at the *p* of my doors ... Prov 8:34 4201
the *p* of the door moved at the ... Is 6:4 520
the *p* hast thou set up thy ... Is 57:8 4201
the *p* thereof, two cubits ... Eze 40:9 352
the *p* had one measure on this ... Eze 40:10 352
He made also *p* of threescore ... Eze 40:14 352
to their *p* within the gate round ... Eze 40:16 352
the *p* thereof and the arches ... Eze 40:21 352
and he measured the *p* thereof ... Eze 40:24 352
on that side, upon the *p* thereof ... Eze 40:26 352
the *p* thereof, and the arches ... Eze 40:29 352
trees were upon the *p* thereof ... Eze 40:31 352
the *p* thereof, and the arches ... Eze 40:33 352
trees were upon the *p* thereof ... Eze 40:34 352
the *p* thereof, and the arches ... Eze 40:36 352
the *p* thereof were toward the ... Eze 40:37 352
trees were upon the *p* thereof ... Eze 40:37 352
were by the *p* of the gates ... Eze 40:38 352
and there were pillars by the *p* ... Eze 40:49 352
to the temple, and measured the *p* ... Eze 41:1 352
The door *p*, and the narrow windows ... Eze 41:16 5592
The *p* of the temple were squared, ... Eze 41:21 4201
thresholds, and their post by my *p* ... Eze 43:8 4201
and put it upon the *p* of the house ... Eze 45:19 4201
upon the *p* of the gate of the ... Eze 45:19 4201
of the door, that the *p* may shake ... Amos 9:1 5592

POT {22}
Moses said unto Aaron, Take a *p* ... Ex 16:33 6803
and if it be sodden in a brasen *p* ... Lev 6:28 3627
and he put the broth in a *p* ... Judg 6:19 6517
pan, or kettle, or caldron, or *p* ... 1Sa 2:14 6517
in the house, save a *p* of oil ... 2Kin 4:2 610
his servant, Set on the great *p* ... 2Kin 4:38 5518
shred them into the *p* of pottage ... 2Kin 4:39 5518
of God, there is death in the *p* ... 2Kin 4:40 5518
And he cast it into the *p* ... 2Kin 4:41 5518
And there was no harm in the *p* ... 2Kin 4:41 5518
as out of a seething *p* or caldron ... Job 41:20 1731
maketh the deep to boil like a *p* ... Job 41:31 5518
the sea like a *p* of ointment ... Job 41:31
The fining *p* is for silver, and ... Prov 17:3 4715
As the fining *p* for silver ... Prov 27:21 4715
the crackling of thorns under a *p* ... Eccl 7:6 5518
and I said, I see a seething *p* ... Jer 1:13 5518
Set on a *p*, set it on, and also ... Eze 24:3 5518
to the *p* whose scum is therein, ... Eze 24:6 5518
chop them in pieces, as for the *p* ... Mic 3:3 5518
every *p* in Jerusalem and in Judah ... Zec 14:21 5518
was the golden *p* that had manna ... Heb 9:4 *4713*

POTENTATE {1}
who is the blessed and only *P* ... 1Ti 6:15 *1413*

POTIPHAR *(pot'i-far)* {2} *A captain of Pharaoh's guard.*
sold him into Egypt unto *P* ... Gen 37:36 6318
and *P*, an officer of Pharaoh, ... Gen 39:1 6318

POTI-PHERAH {3} *Priest of On.*
the daughter of *P* priest of On ... Gen 41:45 6319
of *P* priest of On bare unto him ... Gen 41:50 6319
of *P* priest of On bare unto him ... Gen 46:20 6319

POTS {15}
Egypt, when we sat by the flesh *p* ... Ex 16:3 5518
the vessels of the altar, the *p* ... Ex 38:3 5518
it be oven, or ranges for *p* ... Lev 11:35
And the *p*, and the shovels, and the ... 1Kin 7:45 5518
And the *p*, and the shovels, and the ... 2Kin 25:14 5518
And Huram made the *p*, and the ... 2Chr 4:11 5518
The *p* also, and the shovels, and ... 2Chr 4:16 5518
holy offerings sod they in *p* ... 2Chr 35:13 5518
Before your *p* can feel the thorns ... Ps 58:9 5518
Though ye have lien among the *p* ... Ps 68:13 8240
hands were delivered from the *p* ... Ps 81:6 1731
of the Rechabites *p* full of wine ... Jer 35:5 1375
the *p* in the LORD's house shall ... Zec 14:20 5518
as the washing of cups, and *p* ... Mk 7:4 *3582*
of men, as the washing of *p* ... Mk 7:8 *3582*

POTSHERD {4}
he took him a *p* to scrape himself ... Job 2:8 2789
My strength is dried up like a *p* ... Ps 22:15 2789
a *p* covered with silver dross ... Prov 26:23 2789
Let the *p* strive with the ... Is 45:9 2789

POTSHERDS {1}
strive with the *p* of the earth ... Is 45:9 2789

POTTAGE {7}
And Jacob sod *p* ... Gen 25:29 5138
I pray thee, with that same red *p* ... Gen 25:30
gave Esau bread and *p* of lentiles ... Gen 25:34 5138
seethe *p* for the sons of the ... 2Kin 4:38 5138
and shred them into the pot of *p* ... 2Kin 4:39 5138
as they were eating of the *p* ... 2Kin 4:40 5138
his skirt do touch bread, or *p* ... Hag 2:12 5138

POTTER {10}
morter, and as the *p* treadeth clay ... Is 41:25 3335
we are the clay, and thou our *p* ... Is 64:8 3335
was marred in the hand of the *p* ... Jer 18:4 3335
seemed good to the *p* to make it ... Jer 18:4 3335
cannot I do with you as this *p* ... Jer 18:6 3335
the work of the hands of the *p* ... Lam 4:2 3335
said unto me, Cast it unto the *p* ... Zec 11:13 3335
cast them to the *p* in the house ... Zec 11:13 3335
Hath not the *p* power over the ... Rom 9:21 *2763*
as the vessels of a *p* shall they ... Rev 2:27 *2764*

POTTER'S {9}
them in pieces like a *p* vessel ... Ps 2:9 3335
shall be esteemed as the *p* clay ... Is 29:16 3335
Arise, and go down to the *p* house ... Jer 18:2 3335
Then I went down to the *p* house ... Jer 18:3 3335
as the clay is in the *p* hand ... Jer 18:6 3335
get a *p* earthen bottle, and take ... Jer 19:1 3335
city, as one breaketh a *p* vessel ... Jer 19:11 3335
and bought with them the *p* field ... Mt 27:7 *2763*
And gave them for the *p* field ... Mt 27:10 *2763*

POTTERS {1}
These were the *p*, and those that ... 1Chr 4:23 3335

POTTERS' {2}
p vessel that is broken in pieces ... Is 30:14 3335
the feet and toes, part of *p* clay ... Dan 2:41 6353

POUND {8}
three *p* of gold went to one ... 1Kin 10:17 4488
and five thousand *p* of silver ... Ezr 2:69 4488
thy *p* hath gained ten pounds ... Lk 19:16 *3414*
thy *p* hath gained five pounds ... Lk 19:18 *3414*
Lord, behold, here is thy *p* ... Lk 19:20 *3414*
stood by, Take from him the *p* ... Lk 19:24 *3414*
Then took Mary a *p* of ointment of ... Jn 12:3 *3046*
aloes, about an hundred *p* weight ... Jn 19:39 *3046*

POUNDS {7}
and two hundred *p* of silver ... Neh 7:71 4488
gold, and two thousand *p* of silver ... Neh 7:72 4488
servants, and delivered them ten *p* ... Lk 19:13 *3414*
Lord, thy pound hath gained ten *p* ... Lk 19:16 *3414*
thy pound hath gained five *p* ... Lk 19:18 *3414*
and give it to him that hath ten *p* ... Lk 19:24 *3414*
unto him, Lord, he hath ten *p* ... Lk 19:25 *3414*

POUR {63}
river, and *p* it upon the dry land ... Ex 4:9 8210
p it upon his head, and anoint him ... Ex 29:7 3332
p all the blood beside the bottom ... Ex 29:12 8210
neither shall ye *p* drink offering ... Ex 30:9 5258
he shall *p* oil upon it, and put ... Lev 2:1 3332
it in pieces, and *p* oil thereon ... Lev 2:6 3332
shall *p* all the blood of the ... Lev 4:7 8210
shall *p* out all the blood at the ... Lev 4:18 8210
shall *p* out his blood at the ... Lev 4:25 8210
shall *p* out all the blood thereof ... Lev 4:30 8210
shall *p* out all the blood thereof ... Lev 4:34 8210
p it into the palm of his own ... Lev 14:15 3332
in the priest's hand he shall *p* ... Lev 14:18 5414
the priest shall *p* of the oil ... Lev 14:26 3332
they shall *p* out the dust that ... Lev 14:41 8210
he shall even *p* out the blood ... Lev 17:13 8210
he shall *p* no oil upon it, nor ... Num 5:15 3332
He shall *p* the water out of his ... Num 24:7 5140
ye shall *p* it upon the earth as ... Deut 12:16 8210
thou shalt *p* it upon the earth as ... Deut 12:24 8210
thou shalt *p* it upon the ground ... Deut 15:23 8210
this rock, and *p* out the broth ... Judg 6:20 8210
p it on the burnt sacrifice, and ... 1Kin 18:33 3332
shalt *p* out into all those ... 2Kin 4:4 3332
P out for the people, that they ... 2Kin 4:41 3332
p it on his head, and say, Thus ... 2Kin 9:3 3332
they *p* down rain according to the ... Job 36:27 2212
things, I *p* out my soul in me ... Ps 42:4 8210
p out your heart before him ... Ps 62:8 8210
P out thine indignation upon them ... Ps 69:24 8210
P out thy wrath upon the heathen ... Ps 79:6 8210
I will *p* out my spirit unto you, ... Prov 1:23 5042
For I will *p* water upon him that ... Is 44:3 3332
I will *p* my spirit upon thy seed, ... Is 44:3 3332
above, and let the skies *p* down ... Is 45:8 5140
I will *p* it out upon the children ... Jer 6:11 8210
to *p* out drink offerings unto ... Jer 7:18 5258
P out thy fury upon the heathen ... Jer 10:25 8210
for I will *p* their wickedness ... Jer 14:16 8210
p out their blood by the force of ... Jer 18:21 5064
to *p* out drink offerings unto her ... Jer 44:17 5258
to *p* out drink offerings unto her ... Jer 44:18 5258
p out drink offerings unto her, ... Jer 44:19 5258
to *p* out drink offerings unto her ... Jer 44:25 5258
p out thine heart like water ... Lam 2:19 8210
Now will I shortly *p* out my fury ... Eze 7:8 8210
p out my fury upon it in blood, ... Eze 14:19 8210
I will *p* out my fury upon them, ... Eze 20:8 8210
I would *p* out my fury upon them ... Eze 20:13 8210
I would *p* out my fury upon them, ... Eze 20:21 8210
I will *p* out mine indignation ... Eze 21:31 8210
it on, and also *p* water into it ... Eze 24:3 3332
I will *p* my fury upon Sin, the ... Eze 30:15 8210
therefore I will *p* out my wrath ... Hos 5:10 8210
that I will *p* out my spirit upon ... Joel 2:28 8210
those days will I *p* out my spirit ... Joel 2:29 8210
I will *p* down the stones thereof ... Mic 1:6 5064
to *p* upon them mine indignation, ... Zeph 3:8 8210
I will *p* upon the house of David, ... Zec 12:10 8210
p you out a blessing, that there ... Mal 3:10 7324
I will *p* out of my Spirit upon ... Acts 2:17 *1632*
on my handmaidens I will *p* out in ... Acts 2:18 *1632*
p out the vials of the wrath of ... Rev 16:1 *1632*

POURED {84}
and *p* oil upon the top of it ... Gen 28:18 3332
he *p* a drink offering thereon ... Gen 35:14 5258
and he *p* oil thereon ... Gen 35:14 3332
the rain was not *p* upon the earth ... Ex 9:33 5413
man's flesh shall it not be *p* ... Ex 30:32 3251
place, where the ashes are *p* out ... Lev 4:12 8211
where the ashes are *p* out shall ... Lev 4:12 8211
he *p* of the anointing oil upon ... Lev 8:12 3332
p the blood at the bottom of the ... Lev 8:15 3332
p out the blood at the bottom of ... Lev 9:9 3332
head the anointing oil was *p* ... Lev 21:10 3332
to be *p* unto the LORD for a drink ... Num 28:7 5258
of thy sacrifices shall be *p* out ... Deut 12:27 8210
but have *p* out my soul before the ... 1Sa 1:15 8210
p it out before the LORD, and ... 1Sa 7:6 8210
p it upon his head, and kissed him ... 1Sa 10:1 3332
a pan, and *p* them out before him ... 2Sa 13:9 3332
but *p* it out unto the LORD ... 2Sa 23:16 5258
that are upon it shall be *p* out ... 1Kin 13:3 8210
the ashes *p* out from the altar, ... 1Kin 13:5 8210
which *p* water on the hands of ... 2Kin 3:11 3332
and she *p* out ... 2Kin 4:5 3332
So they *p* out for the men to eat ... 2Kin 4:40 3332
he *p* the oil on his head, and said ... 2Kin 9:6 3332
and *p* his drink offering, and ... 2Kin 16:13 5258
but *p* it out to the LORD, ... 1Chr 11:18 5258
my wrath shall not be *p* out upon ... 2Chr 12:7 5413
of the LORD that is *p* out upon us ... 2Chr 34:21 5413
shall be *p* out upon this place ... 2Chr 34:25 5413
my roarings are *p* out like the ... Job 3:24 5413
Hast thou not *p* me out as milk, ... Job 10:10 5413
the rock *p* me out rivers of oil ... Job 29:6 6694
And now my soul is *p* out upon me ... Job 30:16 8210
I am *p* out like water, and all my ... Ps 22:14 8210
grace is *p* into thy lips ... Ps 45:2 3332
The clouds *p* out water ... Ps 77:17 2229
I *p* out my complaint before him ... Ps 142:2 8210
thy name is as ointment *p* forth ... Song 1:3 7324
they *p* out a prayer when thy ... Is 26:16 6694
For the LORD hath *p* out upon you ... Is 29:10 5258

P

Until the spirit be *p* upon us ... Is 32:15 6168
Therefore he hath *p* upon him the ... Is 42:25 8210
because he hath *p* out his soul ... Is 53:12 6168
them hast thou *p* a drink offering ... Is 57:6 8210
my fury shall be *p* out upon this ... Jer 7:20 5413
have *p* out drink offerings unto ... Jer 19:13 5258
p out drink offerings unto other ... Jer 32:29 5258
my fury hath been *p* forth upon ... Jer 42:18 5413
shall my fury be *p* forth upon you ... Jer 42:18 5413
my fury and mine anger was *p* forth ... Jer 44:6 5413
p out drink offerings unto her, ... Jer 44:19 5258
he *p* out his fury like fire ... Lam 2:4 8210
my liver is *p* upon the earth, for ... Lam 2:11 8210
when their soul was *p* out into ... Lam 2:12 8210
p out in the top of every street ... Lam 4:1 8210
he hath *p* out his fierce anger, ... Lam 4:11 8210
Because thy filthiness was *p* out ... Eze 16:36 8210
p out there their drink offerings ... Eze 20:28 5258
out arm, and with fury *p* out ... Eze 20:33 8210
out arm, and with fury *p* out ... Eze 20:34 8210
LORD have *p* out my fury upon you ... Eze 22:22 8210
Therefore have I *p* out mine ... Eze 22:31 8210
p their whoredom upon her ... Eze 23:8 8210
she *p* it not upon the ground, to ... Eze 24:7 8210
Wherefore I *p* my fury upon them ... Eze 36:18 8210
for I have *p* out my spirit upon ... Eze 39:29 8210
therefore the curse is *p* upon us ... Dan 9:11 5413
shall be *p* upon the desolate ... Dan 9:27 5413
that are *p* down a steep place ... Mic 1:4 5064
his fury is *p* out like fire, and ... Nah 1:6 5413
blood shall be *p* out as dust ... Zeph 1:17 8210
p it on his head, as he sat at ... Mt 26:7 *2708*
For in that she hath *p* this ... Mt 26:12 *906*
the box, and *p* it on his head ... Mk 14:3 *2708*
p out the changers' money, and ... Jn 2:15 *1632*
that on the Gentiles also was *p* ... Acts 10:45 *1632*
which is *p* out without mixture ... Rev 14:10 *2767*
p out his vial upon the earth ... Rev 16:2 *1632*
the second angel *p* out his vial ... Rev 16:3 *1632*
the third angel *p* out his vial ... Rev 16:4 *1632*
the fourth angel *p* out his vial ... Rev 16:8 *1632*
the fifth angel *p* out his vial ... Rev 16:10 *1632*
the sixth angel *p* out his vial ... Rev 16:12 *1632*
the seventh angel *p* out his vial ... Rev 16:17 *1632*

POUREDST {1}
p out thy fornications on every ... Eze 16:15 8210

POURETH {11}
He *p* contempt upon princes, and ... Job 12:21 8210
he *p* out my gall upon the ground ... Job 16:13 8210
but mine eye *p* out tears unto God ... Job 16:20 1811
and he *p* out of the same ... Ps 75:8 5064
p out his complaint before the ... Ps 102:*t* 8210
He *p* contempt upon princes, and ... Ps 107:40 8210
mouth of fools *p* out foolishness ... Prov 15:2 5042
of the wicked *p* out evil things ... Prov 15:28 5042
p them out upon the face of the ... Amos 5:8 8210
p them out upon the face of the ... Amos 9:6 8210
After that he *p* water into a ... Jn 13:5 *906*

POURING {2}
the residue of Israel in thy *p* ... Eze 9:8 8210
p in oil and wine, and set him on ... Lk 10:34

POURTRAY {1}
thee, and *p* upon it the city, even ... Eze 4:1 2710

POURTRAYED {3}
p upon the wall round about ... Eze 8:10 2707
when she saw men *p* upon the wall ... Eze 23:14 2707
of the Chaldeans *p* with vermilion ... Eze 23:14 2710

POVERTY {15}
and all that thou hast, come to *p* ... Gen 45:11 3423
So shall thy *p* come as one that ... Prov 6:11 7389
of the poor is their *p* ... Prov 10:15 7389
than is meet, but it tendeth to *p* ... Prov 11:24 4270
P and shame shall be to him that ... Prov 13:18 7389
not sleep, lest thou come to *p* ... Prov 20:13 3423
and the glutton shall come to *p* ... Prov 23:21 3423
So shall thy *p* come as one that ... Prov 24:34 7389
vain persons shall have *p* enough ... Prov 28:19 7389
not that *p* shall come upon him ... Prov 28:22 2639
give me neither *p* nor riches ... Prov 30:8 7389
Let him drink, and forget his *p* ... Prov 31:7 7389
their deep *p* abounded unto the ... 2Cor 8:2 *4432*
ye through his *p* might be rich ... 2Cor 8:9 *4432*
thy works, and tribulation, and *p* ... Rev 2:9 *4432*

POWDER {8}
it in the fire, and ground it to *p* ... Ex 32:20 1854
shall make the rain of thy land *p* ... Deut 28:24 80
Kidron, and stamped it small to *p* ... 2Kin 23:6 6083
cast the *p* thereof upon the ... 2Kin 23:6 6083
place, and stamped it small to *p* ... 2Kin 23:15 6083
beaten the graven images into *p* ... 2Chr 34:7 1854
fall, it will grind him to *p* ... Mt 21:44 *3039*
fall, it will grind him to *p* ... Lk 20:18 *3039*

POWDERS {1}
with all *p* of the merchant ... Song 3:6 81

POWER {272}
ye know that with all my *p* I have ... Gen 31:6 3581
It is in the *p* of my hand to do ... Gen 31:29 410
as a prince hast thou *p* with God ... Gen 32:28 8280
dignity, and the excellency of *p* ... Gen 49:3 5794
thee up, for to shew in thee my *p* ... Ex 9:16 3581
O LORD, is become glorious in *p* ... Ex 15:6 3581
strange nation he shall have no *p* ... Ex 21:8 4910
of the land of Egypt with great *p* ... Ex 32:11 3581
I will break the pride of your *p* ... Lev 26:19 5797
ye shall have no *p* to stand ... Lev 26:37 8617
let the *p* of my LORD be great, ... Num 14:17 3581
have I now any *p* at all to say ... Num 22:38 3201
with his mighty *p* out of Egypt ... Deut 4:37 3581
And thou say in thine heart, My *p* ... Deut 8:17 3581
that giveth thee *p* to get wealth ... Deut 8:18 3581
broughtest out by thy mighty *p* ... Deut 9:29 3581
he seeth that their *p* is gone ... Deut 32:36 3027
they had no *p* to flee this way or ... Josh 8:20 3027
a great people, and hast great *p* ... Josh 17:17 3581
a Benjamite, a mighty man of *p* ... 1Sa 9:1 2428
until they had no more *p* to weep ... 1Sa 30:4 3581
God is my strength and *p* ... 2Sa 22:33 2428
of the land of Egypt with great *p* ... 2Kin 17:36 3581
their inhabitants were of small *p* ... 2Kin 19:26 3027
Joab led forth the *p* of the army ... 1Chr 20:1 2428
LORD, is the greatness, and the *p* ... 1Chr 29:11 1369
and in thine hand is *p* and might ... 1Chr 29:12 3581
many, or with them that have no *p* ... 2Chr 14:11 3581
and in thine hand is there not *p* ... 2Chr 20:6 3581
no *p* to keep still the kingdom ... 2Chr 22:9 3581
for God hath *p* to help, and to ... 2Chr 25:8 3581
that made war with mighty *p* ... 2Chr 26:13 3581
all his *p* with him,) unto ... 2Chr 32:9 4475
made them to cease by force and *p* ... Ezr 4:23 2429
but his *p* and his wrath is against ... Ezr 8:22 5797
thou hast redeemed by thy great *p* ... Neh 1:10 3581
is it in our *p* to redeem them ... Neh 5:5 3027
the *p* of Persia and Media, the ... Est 1:3 2428
all the *p* of the people and ... Est 8:11 2428
Jews hoped to have *p* over them ... Est 9:1 7980
And all the acts of his *p* and of ... Est 10:2 8633
all that he hath is in thy *p* ... Job 1:12 3027
and in war from the *p* of the sword ... Job 5:20 3027
become old, yea, are mighty in *p* ... Job 21:7 2428
plead against me with his great *p* ... Job 23:6 3581
also the mighty with his *p* ... Job 24:22 3581
thou helped him that is without *p* ... Job 26:2 3581
He divideth the sea with his *p* ... Job 26:12 3581
of his *p* who can understand ... Job 26:14 1369
Behold, God exalteth by his *p* ... Job 36:22 3581
he is excellent in *p*, and in ... Job 37:23 3581
not conceal his parts, nor his *p* ... Job 41:12 1369
so will we sing and praise thy *p* ... Ps 21:13 1369
my darling from the *p* of the dog ... Ps 22:20 3027
I have seen the wicked in great *p* ... Ps 37:35 6184
my soul from the *p* of the grave ... Ps 49:15 3027
scatter them by thy *p* ... Ps 59:11 2428
But I will sing of thy *p* ... Ps 59:16 5797
that *p* belongeth unto God ... Ps 62:11 5797
To see thy *p* and thy glory, so as ... Ps 63:2 5797
being girded with *p* ... Ps 65:6 1369
thy *p* shall thine enemies submit ... Ps 66:3 5797
He ruleth by his *p* for ever ... Ps 66:7 1369
strength and *p* unto his people ... Ps 68:35 8592
thy *p* to every one that is to ... Ps 71:18 1369
by his *p* he brought in the south ... Ps 78:26 5797
to the greatness of thy *p* ... Ps 79:11 2220
Who knoweth the *p* of thine anger ... Ps 90:11 5797
make his mighty *p* to be known ... Ps 106:8 1369
be willing in the day of thy *p* ... Ps 110:3 2428
his people the *p* of his works ... Ps 111:6 3581
of thy kingdom, and talk of thy *p* ... Ps 145:11 1369
Great is our Lord, and of great *p* ... Ps 147:5 3581
him in the firmament of his *p* ... Ps 150:1 5797
when it is in the *p* of thine hand ... Prov 3:27 410
life are in the *p* of the tongue ... Prov 18:21 3027
of their oppressors there was *p* ... Eccl 4:1 3581
hath given him *p* to eat thereof ... Eccl 5:19 7980
giveth him not *p* to eat thereof ... Eccl 6:2 7980
the word of a king is, there is *p* ... Eccl 8:4 7983
There is no man that hath *p* over ... Eccl 8:8 7989
neither hath he *p* in the day of ... Eccl 8:8 7983
their inhabitants were of small *p* ... Is 37:27 3027
might, for that he is strong in *p* ... Is 40:26 3581
He giveth *p* to the faint ... Is 40:29 3581
and horse, the army and the *p* ... Is 43:17 5808
from the *p* of the flame ... Is 47:14 3027
or have I no *p* to deliver ... Is 50:2 3581
He hath made the earth by his *p* ... Jer 10:12 3581
upon the ground, by my great *p* ... Jer 27:5 3581
and the earth by thy great *p* ... Jer 32:17 3581
He hath made the earth by his *p* ... Jer 51:15 3581
even without great *p* or many ... Eze 17:9 2220
in thee to their *p* to shed blood ... Eze 22:6 2220
pride of her *p* shall come down ... Eze 30:6 5797
hath given thee a kingdom, *p* ... Dan 2:37 2632
whose bodies the fire had no *p* ... Dan 3:27 7981
the kingdom by the might of my *p* ... Dan 4:30 2632
Daniel from the *p* of the lions ... Dan 6:27 3028
ran unto him in the fury of his *p* ... Dan 8:6 3581
there was no *p* in the ram to ... Dan 8:7 3581
of the nation, but not in his *p* ... Dan 8:22 3581
his *p* shall be mighty ... Dan 8:24 3581
but not by his own *p* ... Dan 8:24 3581
shall not retain the *p* of the arm ... Dan 11:6 3581
And he shall stir up his *p* ... Dan 11:25 3581
But he shall have *p* over the ... Dan 11:43 4910
scatter the *p* of the holy people ... Dan 12:7 3027
by his strength he had *p* with God ... Hos 12:3 8280
he had *p* over the angel, and ... Hos 12:4 7786
them from the *p* of the grave ... Hos 13:14 3027
it is in the *p* of their hand ... Mic 2:1 410
But truly I am full of *p* by the ... Mic 3:8 3581
is slow to anger, and great in *p* ... Nah 1:3 3581
strong, fortify thy *p* mightily ... Nah 2:1 3581
imputing this his *p* unto his god ... Hab 1:11 3581
be delivered from the *p* of evil ... Hab 2:9 3709
and there was the hiding of his *p* ... Hab 3:4 5797
saying, Not by might, nor by *p* ... Zec 4:6 3581
and he will smite her *p* in the sea ... Zec 9:4 2428
thine is the kingdom, and the *p* ... Mt 6:13 *1411*
hath *p* on earth to forgive sins ... Mt 9:6 *1849*
which had given such *p* unto men ... Mt 9:8 *1849*
he gave them *p* against unclean ... Mt 10:1 *1849*
the scriptures, nor the *p* of God ... Mt 22:29 *1411*
in the clouds of heaven with *p* ... Mt 24:30 *1411*
sitting on the right hand of *p* ... Mt 26:64 *1411*
All *p* is given unto me in heaven ... Mt 28:18 *1849*
hath *p* on earth to forgive sins ... Mk 2:10 *1849*
to have *p* to heal sicknesses, and ... Mk 3:15 *1849*
gave them *p* over unclean spirits ... Mk 6:7 *1849*
the kingdom of God come with *p* ... Mk 9:1 *1411*
scriptures, neither the *p* of God ... Mk 12:24 *1411*
coming in the clouds with great *p* ... Mk 13:26 *1411*
sitting on the right hand of *p* ... Mk 14:62 *1411*
p of Elias, to turn the hearts of ... Lk 1:17 *1411*
the *p* of the Highest shall ... Lk 1:35 *1411*
All this *p* will I give thee, and ... Lk 4:6 *1849*
Jesus returned in the *p* of the ... Lk 4:14 *1411*
for his word was with *p* ... Lk 4:32 *1849*
p he commandeth the unclean ... Lk 4:36 *1411*
the *p* of the Lord was present to ... Lk 5:17 *1411*
hath *p* upon earth to forgive sins ... Lk 5:24 *1849*
together, and gave them *p* and ... Lk 9:1 *1411*
all amazed at the mighty *p* of God ... Lk 9:43 *3168*
I give unto you *p* to tread on ... Lk 10:19 *1849*
and over all the *p* of the enemy ... Lk 10:19 *1411*
killed hath *p* to cast into hell ... Lk 12:5 *1849*
they might deliver him unto the *p* ... Lk 20:20 *746*
of man coming in a cloud with *p* ... Lk 21:27 *1411*
your hour, and the *p* of darkness ... Lk 22:53 *1849*
on the right hand of the *p* of God ... Lk 22:69 *1411*
ye be endued with *p* from on high ... Lk 24:49 *1411*
to them gave he *p* to become the ... Jn 1:12 *1849*
I have *p* to lay it down, and I ... Jn 10:18 *1849*
I have *p* to take it again ... Jn 10:18 *1849*
hast given him *p* over all flesh ... Jn 17:2 *1849*
not that I have *p* to crucify thee ... Jn 19:10 *1849*
and have *p* to release thee ... Jn 19:10 *1849*
have no *p* at all against me ... Jn 19:11 *1849*
the Father hath put in his own *p* ... Acts 1:7 *1849*
But ye shall receive *p*, after ... Acts 1:8 *1411*
as though by our own *p* or ... Acts 3:12 *1411*
the midst, they asked, By what *p* ... Acts 4:7 *1411*
with great *p* gave the apostles ... Acts 4:33 *1411*
sold, was it not in thine own *p* ... Acts 5:4 *1849*
And Stephen, full of faith and *p* ... Acts 6:8 *1411*
This man is the great *p* of God ... Acts 8:10 *1411*
Saying, Give me also this *p* ... Acts 8:19 *1849*
with the Holy Ghost and with *p* ... Acts 10:38 *1411*
from the *p* of Satan unto God, ... Acts 26:18 *1849*
to be the Son of God with *p* ... Rom 1:4 *1411*
for it is the *p* of God unto ... Rom 1:16 *1411*
that are made, even his eternal *p* ... Rom 1:20 *1411*
that I might shew my *p* in thee ... Rom 9:17 *1411*
not the potter *p* over the clay ... Rom 9:21 *1849*
his wrath, and to make his *p* known ... Rom 9:22 *1415*
For there is no *p* but of God ... Rom 13:1 *1849*
therefore resisteth the *p* ... Rom 13:2 *1849*
thou then not be afraid of the *p* ... Rom 13:3 *1849*
through the *p* of the Holy Ghost ... Rom 15:13 *1411*
by the *p* of the Spirit of God ... Rom 15:19 *1411*
Now to him that is of *p* to ... Rom 16:25 *1410*
are saved it is the *p* of God ... 1Cor 1:18 *1411*
and Greeks, Christ the *p* of God ... 1Cor 1:24 *1411*
of the Spirit and of *p* ... 1Cor 2:4 *1411*
of men, but in the *p* of God ... 1Cor 2:5 *1411*
which are puffed up, but the *p* ... 1Cor 4:19 *1411*
of God is not in word, but in *p* ... 1Cor 4:20 *1411*
with the *p* of our Lord Jesus ... 1Cor 5:4 *1411*
not be brought under the *p* of any ... 1Cor 6:12 *1850*
also raise up us by his own *p* ... 1Cor 6:14 *1411*
wife hath not *p* of her own body ... 1Cor 7:4 *1850*
hath not *p* of his own body ... 1Cor 7:4 *1850*
but hath *p* over his own will, and ... 1Cor 7:37 *1849*
Have we not *p* to eat and to drink ... 1Cor 9:4 *1849*
Have we not *p* to lead about a ... 1Cor 9:5 *1849*
have not we *p* to forbear working ... 1Cor 9:6 *1849*
be partakers of this *p* over you ... 1Cor 9:12 *1849*
we have not used this *p* ... 1Cor 9:12 *1849*
I abuse not my *p* in the gospel ... 1Cor 9:18 *1849*
have *p* on her head because of the ... 1Cor 11:10 *1849*
all rule and all authority and *p* ... 1Cor 15:24 *1411*
it is raised in *p* ... 1Cor 15:43 *1411*
excellency of the *p* may be of God ... 2Cor 4:7 *1411*
word of truth, by the *p* of God ... 2Cor 6:7 *1411*
For to their *p*, I bear record, ... 2Cor 8:3 *1411*
beyond their *p* they were willing ... 2Cor 8:3 *1411*
that the *p* of Christ may rest ... 2Cor 12:9 *1411*
yet he liveth by the *p* of God ... 2Cor 13:4 *1411*
him by the *p* of God toward you ... 2Cor 13:4 *1411*
according to the *p* which the Lord ... 2Cor 13:10 *1849*
of his *p* to us-ward who believe ... Eph 1:19 *1411*
to the working of his mighty *p* ... Eph 1:19 *2904*
Far above all principality, and *p* ... Eph 1:21 *1849*
to the prince of the *p* of the air ... Eph 2:2 *1849*
by the effectual working of his *p* ... Eph 3:7 *1411*
according to the *p* that worketh ... Eph 3:20 *1411*
Lord, and in the *p* of his might ... Eph 6:10 *2904*
the *p* of his resurrection, and the ... Phil 3:10 *1411*
according to his glorious *p* ... Col 1:11 *2904*
us from the *p* of darkness ... Col 1:13 *1849*
the head of all principality and *p* ... Col 2:10 *1849*
you in word only, but also in *p* ... 1Th 1:5 *1411*
Lord, and from the glory of his *p* ... 2Th 1:9 *2479*
and the work of faith with *p* ... 2Th 1:11 *1411*

the working of Satan with all p 2Th 2:9 1411
Not because we have not p 2Th 3:9 1849
whom be honour and p everlasting 1Ti 6:16 2904
but of p, and of love, and of a 2Ti 1:7 1411
gospel according to the p of God 2Ti 1:8 1411
but denying the p thereof 2Ti 3:5 1411
all things by the word of his p Heb 1:3 1411
him that had the p of death Heb 2:14 2904
but after the p of an endless Heb 7:16 1411
Who are kept by the p of God 1Pet 1:5 1411
According as his divine p hath 2Pet 1:3 1411
when we made known unto you the p 2Pet 1:16 1411
angels, which are greater in p 2Pet 2:11 2479
glory and majesty, dominion and p Jude 25 1849
will I give p over the nations Rev 2:26 1849
to receive glory and honour and p Rev 4:11 1411
Lamb that was slain to receive p Rev 5:12 1411
and honour, and glory, and p Rev 5:13 2904
p was given to him that sat Rev 6:4
p was given unto them over the Rev 6:8 1849
and thanksgiving, and honour, and p Rev 7:12 1411
and unto them was given p, as the Rev 9:3 1849
the scorpions of the earth have p Rev 9:3 1849
their p was to hurt men five Rev 9:10 1849
For their p is in their mouth, and Rev 9:19 1849
I will give p unto my two Rev 11:3
These have p to shut heaven, that Rev 11:6 1849
have p over waters to turn them Rev 11:6 1849
hast taken to thee thy great p Rev 11:17 1411
our God, and the p of his Christ Rev 12:10 1849
and the dragon gave him his p Rev 13:2 1411
which gave p unto the beast Rev 13:4 1849
p was given unto him to continue Rev 13:5 1849
p was given him over all kindreds Rev 13:7 1849
he exerciseth all the p of the Rev 13:12 1849
of those miracles which he had p Rev 13:14 1325
he had p to give life unto the Rev 13:15 1325
the altar, which had p over fire Rev 14:18 1849
the glory of God, and from his p Rev 15:8 1411
p was given unto him to scorch Rev 16:8
which hath p over these plagues Rev 16:9 1849
but receive p as kings one hour Rev 17:12 1849
one mind, and shall give their p Rev 17:13 1411
down from heaven, having great p Rev 18:1 1849
and glory, and honour, and p Rev 19:1 1411
such the second death hath no p Rev 20:6 1849

POWERFUL {3}
The voice of the LORD is p Ps 29:4 3581
say they, are weighty and p 2Cor 10:10 2478
the word of God is quick, and p Heb 4:12 1756

POWERS {14}
the p of the heavens shall be Mt 24:29 1411
the p that are in heaven shall be Mk 13:25 1411
and unto magistrates, and p Lk 12:11 1849
for the p of heaven shall be Lk 21:26 1411
angels, nor principalities, nor p Rom 8:38 1411
soul be subject unto the higher p Rom 13:1 1849
the p that be are ordained of God Rom 13:1 1849
p in heavenly places might be Eph 3:10 1849
against principalities, against p Eph 6:12 1849
or principalities, or p Col 1:16 1849
spoiled principalities and p Col 2:15 1849
be subject to principalities and p Titus 3:1 1849
the p of the world to come, Heb 6:5 1411
p being made subject unto him 1Pet 3:22 1411

PRACTICES {1}
have exercised with covetous p 2Pet 2:14

PRACTISE {4}
to p wicked works with men that Ps 141:4 5953
to p hypocrisy, and to utter error Is 32:6 6213
and shall prosper, and p, and shall Dan 8:24 6213
the morning is light, they p it Mic 2:1 6213

PRACTISED {2}
secretly p mischief against him 1Sa 23:9 2790
and it p, and prospered Dan 8:12 6213

PRAETORIUM *(pre-to'-re-um)* {1} *Palace of the Roman procurator in Jerusalem.*
him away into the hall, called P Mk 15:16 4232

PRAISE {248}
she said, Now will I p the LORD Gen 29:35 3034
art he whom thy brethren shall p Gen 49:8 3034
be holy to p the LORD withal Lev 19:24 1974
He is thy p, and he is thy God, Deut 10:21 8416
nations which he hath made, in p Deut 26:19 8416
P ye the LORD for the avenging of Judg 5:2 1288
I will sing p to the LORD God of Judg 5:3
thank and p the LORD God of Israel 1Chr 16:4 1984
thy holy name, and glory in thy p 1Chr 16:35 8416
made, said David, to p therewith 1Chr 23:5 1984
p the LORD, and likewise at even 1Chr 23:30 1984
to give thanks and to p the LORD 1Chr 25:3 1984
thee, and p thy glorious name 1Chr 29:13 1984
the king had made to p the LORD 2Chr 7:6 3034
Levites to their charges, to p 2Chr 8:14 1984
stood up to p the LORD God of 2Chr 20:19 1984
that should p the beauty of 2Chr 20:21 1984
the army, and to say, P the LORD 2Chr 20:21 3034
when they began to sing and to p 2Chr 20:22 8416
and such as taught to sing p 2Chr 23:13 1984
commanded the Levites to sing p 2Chr 29:30 1984
to p in the gates of the tents of 2Chr 31:2 1984
cymbals, to p the LORD, after the Ezr 3:10 1984
exalted above all blessing and p Neh 9:5 8416
brethren over against them, to p Neh 12:24 1984
of the singers, and songs of p Neh 12:46 8416
I will p the LORD according to Ps 7:17 3034
will sing p to the name of the Ps 7:17
I will p thee, O LORD, with my Ps 9:1 3034
I will sing p to thy name Ps 9:2
That I may shew forth all thy p Ps 9:14 8416
so will we sing and p thy power Ps 21:13 2167
of the congregation will I p thee Ps 22:22 1984
Ye that fear the LORD, p him Ps 22:23 1984
My p shall be of thee in the Ps 22:25 8416
they shall p the LORD that seek Ps 22:26 1984
and with my song will I p him Ps 28:7 3034
shall the dust p thee Ps 30:9 3034
that my glory may sing p to thee Ps 30:12
for p is comely for the upright Ps 33:1 8416
P the LORD with harp Ps 33:2 3034
his p shall continually be in my Ps 34:1 8416
I will p thee among much people Ps 35:18 1984
of thy p all the day long Ps 35:28 8416
in my mouth, even p unto our God Ps 40:3 8416
God, with the voice of joy and p Ps 42:4 8426
for I shall yet p him for the Ps 42:5 3034
for I shall yet p him, who is the Ps 42:11 3034
yea, upon the harp will I p thee Ps 43:4 3034
for I shall yet p him, who is the Ps 43:5 3034
day long, and p thy name for ever Ps 44:8 3034
shall the people p thee for ever Ps 45:17 3034
so is thy p unto the ends of the Ps 48:10 8416
his soul, and men will p thee Ps 49:18 3034
Whoso offereth p glorifieth me Ps 50:23 8426
my mouth shall shew forth thy p Ps 51:15 8416
I will p thee for ever, because Ps 52:9 3034
I will p thy name, O LORD Ps 54:6 3034
In God I will p his word, in God Ps 56:4 1984
In God will I p his word Ps 56:10 1984
in the LORD will I p his word Ps 56:10 1984
I will sing and give p Ps 57:7 2167
I will p thee, O Lord, among the Ps 57:9 3034
So will I sing p unto thy name Ps 61:8
than life, my lips shall p thee Ps 63:3 7623
my mouth shall p thee with joyful Ps 63:5 1984
P waiteth for thee, O God in Sion Ps 65:1 8416
make his p glorious Ps 66:2 8416
the voice of his p to be heard Ps 66:8 8416
Let the people p thee, O God Ps 67:3 3034
let all the people p thee Ps 67:3 3034
Let the people p thee, O God Ps 67:5 3034
let all the people p thee Ps 67:5 3034
I will p the name of God with a Ps 69:30 1984
Let the heaven and earth p him Ps 69:34 1984
my p shall be continually of thee Ps 71:6 8416
Let my mouth be filled with thy p Ps 71:8 8416
will yet p thee more and more Ps 71:14 8416
I will also p thee with the Ps 71:22 3034
let the poor and needy p thy name Ps 74:21 1984
the wrath of man shall p thee Ps 76:10 3034
forth thy p to all generations Ps 79:13 8416
I will p thee, O Lord my God, Ps 86:12 3034
shall the dead arise and p thee Ps 88:10 3034
the heavens shall p thy wonders Ps 89:5 3034
loud noise, and rejoice, and sing p Ps 98:4
Let them p thy great and terrible Ps 99:3 3034
A Psalm of p Ps 100:t 8426
and into his courts with p Ps 100:4 8416
shall be created shall p the LORD Ps 102:18 1984
in Zion, and his p in Jerusalem Ps 102:21 8416
I will sing p to my God while I Ps 104:33
P ye the LORD Ps 104:35 1984
P ye the LORD Ps 105:45 1984
P ye the LORD Ps 106:1 1984
who can shew forth all his p Ps 106:2 8416
they sang his p Ps 106:12 8416
holy name, and to triumph in thy p Ps 106:47 8416
P ye the LORD Ps 106:48 1984
Oh that men would p the LORD for Ps 107:8 3034
Oh that men would p the LORD for Ps 107:15 3034
Oh that men would p the LORD for Ps 107:21 3034
Oh that men would p the LORD for Ps 107:31 3034
p him in the assembly of the Ps 107:32 1984
I will sing and give p, even with Ps 108:1 2167
I will p thee, O LORD, among the Ps 108:3 3034
Hold not thy peace, O God of my p Ps 109:1 8416
I will greatly p the LORD with my Ps 109:30 3034
I will p him among the multitude Ps 109:30 1984
P ye the LORD Ps 111:1 1984
I will p the LORD with my whole Ps 111:1 3034
his p endureth for ever Ps 111:10 8416
P ye the LORD Ps 112:1 1984
P ye the LORD Ps 113:1 1984
P, O ye servants of the LORD, Ps 113:1 1984
p the name of the LORD Ps 113:1 1984
P ye the LORD Ps 113:9 1984
The dead p not the LORD, neither Ps 115:17 1984
P the LORD Ps 115:18 1984
P ye the LORD Ps 116:19 1984
O p the LORD, all ye nations Ps 117:1 1984
p him, all ye people Ps 117:1 7623
P ye the LORD Ps 117:2 1984
into them, and I will p the LORD Ps 118:19 3034
I will p thee Ps 118:21 3034
Thou art my God, and I will p thee Ps 118:28 3034
I will p thee with uprightness of Ps 119:7 3034
Seven times a day do I p thee Ps 119:164 1984
My lips shall utter p, when thou Ps 119:171 8416
my soul live, and it shall p thee Ps 119:175 1984
P ye the LORD Ps 135:1 1984
P ye the name of the LORD Ps 135:1 1984
p him, O ye servants of the LORD Ps 135:1 1984
P the LORD Ps 135:3 1984
P ye the LORD Ps 135:21 1984
I will p thee with my whole heart Ps 138:1 3034
the gods will I sing p unto thee Ps 138:1 2167
p thy name for thy lovingkindness Ps 138:2 3034
kings of the earth shall p thee Ps 138:4 3034
I will p thee Ps 139:14 3034
of prison, that I may p thy name Ps 142:7 3034
David's Psalm of p Ps 145:t 8416
I will p thy name for ever and Ps 145:2 1984
shall p thy works to another Ps 145:4 7623
All thy works shall p thee Ps 145:10 3034
shall speak the p of the LORD Ps 145:21 8416
P ye the LORD Ps 146:1 1984
P the LORD, O my soul Ps 146:1 1984
While I live will I p the LORD Ps 146:2 1984
P ye the LORD Ps 146:10 1984
P ye the LORD Ps 147:1 1984
and p is comely Ps 147:1 8416
sing p upon the harp unto our God Ps 147:7
P the LORD, O Jerusalem Ps 147:12 7623
p thy God, O Zion Ps 147:12 1984
P ye the LORD Ps 147:20 1984
P ye the LORD Ps 148:1 1984
P ye the LORD from the heavens Ps 148:1 1984
p him in the heights Ps 148:1 1984
P ye him, all his angels Ps 148:2 1984
p ye him, all his hosts Ps 148:2 1984
P ye him, sun and moon Ps 148:3 1984
p him, all ye stars of light Ps 148:3 1984
P him, ye heavens of heavens, and Ps 148:4 1984
Let them p the name of the LORD Ps 148:5 1984
P the LORD from the earth, ye Ps 148:7 1984
Let them p the name of the LORD Ps 148:13 1984
people, the p of all his saints Ps 148:14 8416
P ye the LORD Ps 148:14 1984
P ye the LORD Ps 149:1 1984
his p in the congregation of Ps 149:1 8416
Let them p his name in the dance Ps 149:3 1984
P ye the LORD Ps 149:9 1984
P ye the LORD Ps 150:1 1984
P God in his sanctuary Ps 150:1 1984
p him in the firmament of his Ps 150:1 1984
P him for his mighty acts Ps 150:2 1984
p him according to his excellent Ps 150:2 1984
P him with the sound of the Ps 150:3 1984
p him with the psaltery and harp Ps 150:3 1984
P him with the timbrel and dance Ps 150:4 1984
p him with stringed instruments Ps 150:4 1984
P him upon the loud cymbals Ps 150:5 1984
p him upon the high sounding Ps 150:5 1984
thing that hath breath p the LORD Ps 150:6 1984
P ye the LORD Ps 150:6 1984
Let another man p thee, and not Prov 27:2 1984
so is a man to his p Prov 27:21 4110
that forsake the law p the wicked Prov 28:4 1984
her own works p her in the gates Prov 31:31 1984
shalt say, O LORD, I will p thee Is 12:1 3034
P the LORD, call upon his name, Is 12:4 3034
exalt thee, I will p thy name Is 25:1 3034
For the grave cannot p thee Is 38:18 3034
the living, he shall p thee Is 38:19 3034
neither my p to graven images Is 42:8 8416
his p from the end of the earth, Is 42:10 8416
declare his p in the islands Is 42:12 8416
they shall shew forth my p Is 43:21 8416
for my p will I refrain for thee, Is 48:9 8416
walls Salvation, and thy gates P Is 60:18 8416
the garment of p for the spirit Is 61:3 8416
p to spring forth before all the Is 61:11 8416
make Jerusalem a p in the earth Is 62:7 8416
it shall eat it, and p the LORD Is 62:9 1984
people, and for a name, and for a p Jer 13:11 8416
for thou art my p Jer 17:14 8416
and bringing sacrifices of p Jer 17:26 8426
Sing unto the LORD, p ye the LORD Jer 20:13 1984
p ye, and say, O LORD, save thy Jer 31:7 1984
shall be to me a name of joy, a p Jer 33:9 8416
shall say, P the LORD of hosts Jer 33:11 3034
of p into the house of the LORD Jer 33:11 8426
There shall be no more p of Moab Jer 48:2 8416
How is the city of p not left Jer 49:25 8416
how is the p of the whole earth Jer 51:41 8416
p thee, O thou God of my fathers, Dan 2:23 7624
Now I Nebuchadnezzar p and extol Dan 4:37 7624
p the name of the LORD your God, Joel 2:26 1984
and the earth was full of his p Hab 3:3 8416
and I will get them p and fame in Zeph 3:19 8416
a p among all people of the earth Zeph 3:20 8416
sucklings thou hast perfected p Mt 21:16 136
when they saw it, gave p unto God Lk 18:43 136
p God with a loud voice for all Lk 19:37 134
and said unto him, Give God the p Jn 9:24 1391
For they loved the p of men more Jn 12:43 1391
of men more than the p of God Jn 12:43 1391
whose p is not of men, but of God Rom 2:29 1868
and thou shalt have p of the same Rom 13:3 1868
P the Lord, all ye Gentiles Rom 15:11 134
shall every man have p of God 1Cor 4:5 1868
Now I p you, brethren, that ye 1Cor 11:2 1867
I declare unto you I p you not 1Cor 11:17 1867
shall I p you in this 1Cor 11:22 1867
I p you not 1Cor 11:22 1868
brother, whose p is in the gospel 2Cor 8:18 1868
To the p of the glory of his Eph 1:6 1868
should be to the p of his glory Eph 1:12 1868
unto the p of his glory Eph 1:14 1868
unto the glory and p of God Phil 1:11 1868
any virtue, and if there be any p Phil 4:8 1868

church will I sing *p* unto thee ... Heb 2:12 *5214*
sacrifice of *p* to God continually ... Heb 13:15 *133*
with fire, might be found unto *p* ... 1Pet 1:7 *1868*
for the *p* of them that do well ... 1Pet 2:14 *1868*
Jesus Christ, to whom be *p* ... 1Pet 4:11 *1391*
P our God, all ye his servants, ... Rev 19:5 *134*

PRAISED {26}
people saw him, they *p* their god ... Judg 16:24 1984
much *p* as Absalom for his beauty ... 2Sa 14:25 1984
the LORD, who is worthy to be *p* ... 2Sa 22:4 1984
is the LORD, and greatly to be *p* ... 1Chr 16:25 1984
people said, Amen, and *p* the LORD ... 1Chr 16:36 1984
four thousand *p* the LORD with the ... 1Chr 23:5 1984
p the LORD, saying, For he is ... 2Chr 5:13 1984
p the LORD, saying, For he is ... 2Chr 7:3 3034
when David *p* by their ministry ... 2Chr 7:6 1984
the priests *p* the LORD day by day ... 2Chr 30:21 1984
great shout, when they *p* the LORD ... Ezr 3:11 1984
said, Amen, and *p* the LORD ... Neh 5:13 1984
the LORD, who is worthy to be *p* ... Ps 18:3 1984
greatly to be *p* in the city of ... Ps 48:1 1984
and daily shall he be *p* ... Ps 72:15 1288
LORD is great, and greatly to be *p* ... Ps 96:4 1984
same the LORD's name is to be *p* ... Ps 113:3 1984
is the LORD, and greatly to be *p* ... Ps 145:3 1984
feareth the LORD, she shall be *p* ... Prov 31:30 1984
Wherefore I *p* the dead which are ... Eccl 4:2 7623
and the concubines, and they *p* her ... Song 6:9 1984
house, where our fathers *p* thee ... Is 64:11 1984
I blessed the most High, and I *p* ... Dan 4:34 7624
p the gods of gold, and of silver, ... Dan 5:4 7624
thou hast *p* the gods of silver, ... Dan 5:23 7624
loosed, and he spake, and *p* God ... Lk 1:64 *2127*

PRAISES {28}
in holiness, fearful in *p* ... Ex 15:11 8416
they sang *p* with gladness, and ... 2Chr 29:30 1984
Sing *p* to the LORD, which ... Ps 9:11
heathen, and sing *p* unto thy name ... Ps 18:49
that inhabitest the *p* of Israel ... Ps 22:3 8416
I will sing *p* unto the LORD ... Ps 27:6
Sing *p* to God, sing *p* ... Ps 47:6
p unto our King, sing *p* ... Ps 47:6
sing ye *p* with understanding ... Ps 47:7
I will render *p* unto thee ... Ps 56:12 8426
Sing unto God, sing *p* to his name ... Ps 68:4
O sing *p* unto the Lord ... Ps 68:32
I will sing *p* to the God of Jacob ... Ps 75:9
to come the *p* of the LORD ... Ps 78:4 8416
to sing *p* unto thy name, O most ... Ps 92:1
I will sing *p* unto thee among the ... Ps 108:3
sing *p* unto his name ... Ps 135:3
strings will I sing *p* unto thee ... Ps 144:9
I will sing *p* unto my God while I ... Ps 146:2
it is good to sing *p* unto our God ... Ps 147:1
let them sing *p* unto him with the ... Ps 149:3
Let the high *p* of God be in their ... Ps 149:6
shew forth the *p* of the LORD ... Is 60:6 8416
the *p* of the LORD, according to ... Is 63:7 8416
Silas prayed, and sang *p* unto God ... Acts 16:25
that ye should shew forth the *p* ... 1Pet 2:9 *703*

PRAISETH {1}
her husband also, and he *p* her ... Prov 31:28 1984

PRAISING {10}
make one sound to be heard in *p* ... 2Chr 5:13 1984
p the king, she came to the ... 2Chr 23:12 1984
they sang together by course in *p* ... Ezr 3:11 1984
they will be still *p* thee ... Ps 84:4 1984
of the heavenly host *p* God ... Lk 2:13 *134*
p God for all the things that ... Lk 2:20 *134*
were continually in the temple, *p* ... Lk 24:53 *134*
P God, and having favour with all ... Acts 2:47 *134*
walking, and leaping, and *p* God ... Acts 3:8 *134*
people saw him walking and *p* God ... Acts 3:9 *134*

PRANSING {1}
of the wheels, and of the *p* horses ... Nah 3:2 1725

PRANSINGS {2}
broken by the means of the *p* ... Judg 5:22 1726
the *p* of their mighty ones ... Judg 5:22 1726

PRATING {3}
but a *p* fool shall fall ... Prov 10:8 8193
but a *p* fool shall fall ... Prov 10:10 8193
p against us with malicious words ... 3Jn 10 *5396*

PRAY {313}
I *p* thee, thou art my sister ... Gen 12:13 4994
I *p* thee, between me and thee, and ... Gen 13:8 4994
thyself, I *p* thee, from me ... Gen 13:9 4994
I *p* thee, go in unto my maid ... Gen 16:2 4994
I *p* thee, from thy servant ... Gen 18:3 4994
I *p* you, be fetched, and wash your ... Gen 18:4 4994
I *p* you, into your servant's ... Gen 19:2 4994
I *p* you, brethren, do not so ... Gen 19:7 4994
I *p* you, bring them out unto you, ... Gen 19:8 4994
a prophet, and he shall *p* for thee ... Gen 20:7 6419
wilt give it, I *p* thee, hear me ... Gen 23:13 3863
I *p* thee, thy hand under my thigh ... Gen 24:2 4994
I *p* thee, send me good speed this ... Gen 24:12 4994
I *p* thee, that I may drink ... Gen 24:14 4994
I *p* thee, drink a little water of ... Gen 24:17 4994
tell me, I *p* thee ... Gen 24:23 4994
I *p* thee, a little water of thy ... Gen 24:43 4994
unto her, Let me drink, I *p* thee ... Gen 24:45 4994
I *p* thee, with that same red ... Gen 25:30 4994
I *p* thee, thy weapons, thy quiver ... Gen 27:3 4994
I *p* thee, sit and eat of my ... Gen 27:19 4994
I *p* thee, that I may feel thee, ... Gen 27:21 4994
I *p* thee, of thy son's mandrakes ... Gen 30:14 4994
I *p* thee, if I have found favour ... Gen 30:27 4994
I *p* thee, from the hand of my ... Gen 32:11 4994
said, Tell me, I *p* thee, thy name ... Gen 32:29 4994
I *p* thee, if now I have found ... Gen 33:10 4994
I *p* thee, my blessing that is ... Gen 33:11 4994
I *p* thee, pass over before his ... Gen 33:14 4994
I *p* you give her him to wife ... Gen 34:8 4994
I *p* you, this dream which I have ... Gen 37:6 4994
I *p* thee, see whether it be well ... Gen 37:14 4994
I *p* thee, where they feed their ... Gen 37:16 4994
I *p* thee, let me come in unto ... Gen 38:16 4994
I *p* thee, whose are these, the ... Gen 38:25 4994
tell me them, I *p* you ... Gen 40:8 4994
I *p* thee, unto me, and make ... Gen 40:14 4994
I *p* thee, speak a word in my ... Gen 44:18 4994
I *p* thee, let thy servant abide ... Gen 44:33 4994
Come near to me, I *p* you ... Gen 45:4 4994
we *p* thee, let thy servants dwell ... Gen 47:4 4994
I *p* thee, thy hand under my thigh ... Gen 47:29 4994
bury me not, I *p* thee, in Egypt ... Gen 47:29 4994
I *p* thee, unto me, and I will ... Gen 48:9 4994
I *p* you, in the ears of Pharaoh, ... Gen 50:4 4994
I *p* thee, and bury my father, and I ... Gen 50:5 4994
I *p* thee now, the trespass of thy ... Gen 50:17 577
we *p* thee, forgive the trespass ... Gen 50:17 4994
I *p* thee, by the hand of him whom ... Ex 4:13 4994
I *p* thee, and return unto my ... Ex 4:18 4994
we *p* thee, three days' journey ... Ex 5:3 4994
I *p* thee, my sin only this once, ... Ex 10:17 4994
I *p* thee, out of thy book which ... Ex 32:32 4994
I *p* thee, if I have found grace ... Ex 33:13 4994
my Lord, I *p* thee, go among us ... Ex 34:9 4994
he said, Leave us not, I *p* thee ... Num 10:31 4994
I *p* thee, out of hand, if I have ... Num 11:15 4994
Hear, I *p* you, ye sons of Levi ... Num 16:8 4994
I *p* you, from the tents of these ... Num 16:26 4994
I *p* thee, through thy country ... Num 20:17 4994
p unto the LORD, that he take ... Num 21:7 6419
I *p* thee, curse me this people ... Num 22:6 4994
I *p* thee, hinder thee from coming ... Num 22:16 4994
I *p* thee, curse me this people ... Num 22:17 4994
I *p* you, tarry ye also here this ... Num 22:19 4994
I *p* thee, with me unto another ... Num 23:13 4994
I *p* thee, I will bring thee unto ... Num 23:27 4994
I *p* thee, let me go over, and see ... Deut 3:25 4994
I *p* you, swear unto me by the ... Josh 2:12 4994
I *p* thee, glory to the LORD God ... Josh 7:19 4994
we *p* thee, the entrance into the ... Judg 1:24 4994
I *p* thee, a little water to drink ... Judg 4:19 4994
I *p* thee, until I come unto thee, ... Judg 6:18 4994
I *p* thee, but this once with the ... Judg 6:39 4994
I *p* you, loaves of bread unto the ... Judg 8:5 4994
I *p* you, in the ears of all the ... Judg 9:2 4994
I *p* now, and fight with them ... Judg 9:38 4994
us only, we *p* thee, this day ... Judg 10:15 4994
I *p* thee, pass through thy land ... Judg 11:17 4994
we *p* thee, through thy land into ... Judg 11:19 4994
I *p* thee, and drink not wine nor ... Judg 13:4 4994
I *p* thee, let us detain thee, ... Judg 13:15 4994
her, I *p* thee, instead of her ... Judg 15:2 4994
I *p* thee, wherein thy great ... Judg 16:6 4994
I *p* thee, wherewith thou mightest ... Judg 16:10 4994
I *p* thee, and strengthen me ... Judg 16:28 4994
I *p* thee, only this once, O God, ... Judg 16:28 4994
we *p* thee, of God, that we may ... Judg 18:5 4994
I *p* thee, and tarry all night, and ... Judg 19:6 4994
Comfort thine heart, I *p* thee ... Judg 19:8 4994
evening, I *p* you tarry all night ... Judg 19:9 4994
I *p* thee, and let us turn in into ... Judg 19:11 4994
I *p* you, do not so wickedly ... Judg 19:23 4994
I *p* you, let me glean and gather ... Ruth 2:7 4994
I *p* thee, into one of the ... 1Sa 2:36 4994
I *p* thee hide it not from me ... 1Sa 3:17 4994
I will *p* for you unto the LORD ... 1Sa 7:5 6419
I *p* thee, where the seer's house ... 1Sa 9:18 4994
I *p* thee, what Samuel said unto ... 1Sa 10:15 4994
P for thy servants unto the LORD ... 1Sa 12:19 6419
the LORD in ceasing to *p* for you ... 1Sa 12:23 6419
I *p* you, how mine eyes have been ... 1Sa 14:29 4994
I *p* thee, pardon my sin, and turn ... 1Sa 15:25 4994
I *p* thee, before the elders of my ... 1Sa 15:30 4994
I *p* thee, stand before me ... 1Sa 16:22 4994
I *p* thee, take heed to thyself ... 1Sa 19:2 4994
And he said, Let me go, I *p* thee ... 1Sa 20:29 4994
I *p* thee, and see my brethren ... 1Sa 20:29 4994
I *p* thee, come forth, and be with ... 1Sa 22:3 4994
I *p* you, prepare yet, and know and ... 1Sa 23:22 4994
I *p* thee, whatsoever cometh to ... 1Sa 25:8 4994
I *p* thee, speak in thine audience ... 1Sa 25:24 4994
I *p* thee, regard this man of ... 1Sa 25:25 4994
I *p* thee, forgive the trespass of ... 1Sa 25:28 4994
I *p* thee, with the spear even to ... 1Sa 26:8 4994
I *p* thee, take thou now the spear ... 1Sa 26:11 4994
I *p* thee, let my lord the king ... 1Sa 26:19 4994
I *p* thee, divine unto me by the ... 1Sa 28:8 4994
I *p* thee, hearken thou also unto ... 1Sa 28:22 4994
I *p* thee, bring me hither the ... 1Sa 30:7 4994
I *p* thee, tell me ... 2Sa 1:4 4994
I *p* thee, upon me, and slay me ... 2Sa 1:9 4994
heart to *p* this prayer unto thee ... 2Sa 7:27 6419
I *p* thee, let my sister Tamar ... 2Sa 13:5 4994
I *p* thee, let Tamar my sister ... 2Sa 13:6 4994
I *p* thee, speak unto the king ... 2Sa 13:13 4994
I *p* thee, let my brother Amnon go ... 2Sa 13:26 4994
I *p* thee, feign thyself to be a ... 2Sa 14:2 4994
I *p* thee, let the king remember ... 2Sa 14:11 4994
I *p* thee, speak one word unto my ... 2Sa 14:12 4994
I *p* thee, the thing that I shall ... 2Sa 14:18 4994
I *p* thee, let me go and pay my vow ... 2Sa 15:7 4994
I *p* thee, turn the counsel of ... 2Sa 15:31 4994
I *p* thee, and take off his head ... 2Sa 16:9 4994
I *p* thee, also run after Cushi ... 2Sa 18:22 4994
I *p* thee, turn back again, that I ... 2Sa 19:37 4994
I *p* you, unto Joab, Come near ... 2Sa 20:16 4994
I *p* thee, be against me, and ... 2Sa 24:17 4994
I *p* thee, give thee counsel, that ... 1Kin 1:12 4994
I *p* thee, unto Solomon the king, ... 1Kin 2:17 4994
I *p* thee, say me not nay ... 1Kin 2:20
I *p* thee, be verified, which thou ... 1Kin 8:26 4994
when they shall *p* toward this ... 1Kin 8:30 6419
thee, and confess thy name, and *p* ... 1Kin 8:33 6419
if they *p* toward this place, and ... 1Kin 8:35 6419
shall come and *p* toward this house ... 1Kin 8:42 6419
shall *p* unto the LORD toward the ... 1Kin 8:44 6419
p unto thee toward their land, ... 1Kin 8:48 6419
p for me, that my hand may be ... 1Kin 13:6 6419
I *p* thee, and disguise thyself, ... 1Kin 14:2 4994
I *p* thee, a little water in a ... 1Kin 17:10 4994
I *p* thee, a morsel of bread in ... 1Kin 17:11 4994
I *p* thee, let this child's soul ... 1Kin 17:21 4994
I *p* thee, kiss my father and my ... 1Kin 19:20 4994
I *p* you, and see how this man ... 1Kin 20:7 4994
I *p* thee, put sackcloth on our ... 1Kin 20:31 4994
saith, I *p* thee, let me live ... 1Kin 20:32 4994
of the LORD, Smite me, I *p* thee ... 1Kin 20:35 4994
man, and said, Smite me, I *p* thee ... 1Kin 20:37 4994
I *p* thee, at the word of the LORD ... 1Kin 22:5 4994
I *p* thee, be like the word of one ... 1Kin 22:13 4994
I *p* thee, let my life, and the ... 2Kin 1:13 4994
unto Elisha, Tarry here, I *p* thee ... 2Kin 2:2 4994
him, Elisha, tarry here, I *p* thee ... 2Kin 2:4 4994
unto him, Tarry, I *p* thee, here ... 2Kin 2:6 4994
I *p* thee, let a double portion of ... 2Kin 2:9 4994
we *p* thee, and seek thy master ... 2Kin 2:16 4994
I *p* thee, the situation of this ... 2Kin 2:19 4994
chamber, I *p* thee, on the wall ... 2Kin 4:10 4994
I *p* thee, one of the young men, ... 2Kin 4:22 4994
I *p* thee, to meet her, and say ... 2Kin 4:26 4994
I *p* you, and see how he seeketh a ... 2Kin 5:7 4994
I *p* thee, take a blessing of thy ... 2Kin 5:15 4994
I *p* thee, be given to thy servant ... 2Kin 5:17 4994
I *p* thee, a talent of silver, and ... 2Kin 5:22 4994
we *p* thee, unto Jordan, and take ... 2Kin 6:2 4994
I *p* thee, and go with thy servants ... 2Kin 6:3 4994
I *p* thee, open his eyes, that he ... 2Kin 6:17 4994
people, I *p* thee, with blindness ... 2Kin 6:18 4994
I *p* thee, five of the horses that ... 2Kin 7:13 4994
I *p* thee, all the great things ... 2Kin 8:4 4994
I *p* thee, give pledges to my lord ... 2Kin 18:23 4994
I *p* thee, to thy servants in the ... 2Kin 18:26 4994
in his heart to *p* before thee ... 1Chr 17:25 6419
I *p* thee, O LORD my God, be on me ... 1Chr 21:17 4994
return and confess thy name, and *p* ... 2Chr 6:24 6419
yet if they *p* toward this place, ... 2Chr 6:26 6419
if they come and *p* in this house ... 2Chr 6:32 6419
they *p* unto thee toward this city ... 2Chr 6:34
p unto thee in the land of their ... 2Chr 6:37 2603
p toward their land, which thou ... 2Chr 6:38 6419
shall humble themselves, and *p* ... 2Chr 7:14 6419
I *p* thee, at the word of the LORD ... 2Chr 18:4 4994
I *p* thee, be like one of theirs, ... 2Chr 18:12 4994
p for the life of the king, and of ... Ezr 6:10 6739
which I *p* before thee now, day and ... Neh 1:6 6419
I *p* thee, thy servant this day, ... Neh 1:11 4994
I *p* you, let us leave off this ... Neh 5:10 4994
I *p* you, to them, even this day, ... Neh 5:11 4994
I *p* thee, who ever perished, ... Job 4:7 4994
I *p* you, let it not be iniquity ... Job 6:29 4994
I *p* thee, of the former age, and ... Job 8:8 4994
should we have, if we *p* unto him ... Job 21:15 6293
I *p* thee, the law from his mouth, ... Job 22:22 4994
I *p* you, accept any man's person, ... Job 32:21 4994
I *p* thee, hear my speeches, and ... Job 33:1 4994
He shall *p* unto God, and he will ... Job 33:26 6279
and my servant Job shall *p* for you ... Job 42:8 6419
for unto thee will I *p* ... Ps 5:2 6419
p unto thee in a time when thou ... Ps 32:6 6419
and morning, and at noon, will I *p* ... Ps 55:17 7878
I *p* thee, thy merciful kindness ... Ps 119:76 7592
P for the peace of Jerusalem ... Ps 122:6 7592
I *p* you, betwixt me and my ... Is 5:3 4994
shall come to his sanctuary to *p* ... Is 16:12 6419
saying, Read this, I *p* thee ... Is 29:11 4994
saying, Read this, I *p* thee ... Is 29:12 4994
I *p* thee, to my master the king ... Is 36:8 4994
I *p* thee, unto thy servants in ... Is 36:11 4994
p unto a god that cannot save ... Is 45:20 6419
Therefore *p* not thou for this ... Jer 7:16 6419
Therefore *p* not thou for this ... Jer 11:14 6419
P not for this people for their ... Jer 14:11 6419
I *p* thee, of the LORD for us ... Jer 21:2 4994
and *p* unto the LORD for it ... Jer 29:7 6419
p unto me, and I will hearken unto ... Jer 29:12 6419
I *p* thee, that is in Anathoth, ... Jer 32:8 4994
P now unto the LORD our God for ... Jer 37:3 6419
I *p* thee, O my lord the king ... Jer 37:20 4994
I *p* thee, be accepted before thee ... Jer 37:20 4994
I *p* thee, and I will slay Ishmael ... Jer 40:15
p for us unto the LORD thy God, ... Jer 42:2 6419
I will *p* unto the LORD your God ... Jer 42:4 6419
P for us unto the LORD our God ... Jer 42:20 6419
I *p* you, all people, and behold my ... Lam 1:18 4994
I *p* you, and hear what is the word ... Eze 33:30 4994
we *p* thee, for whose cause this ... Jonah 1:8 4994
I *p* thee, O LORD, was not this my ... Jonah 4:2 577

I *p* you, O heads of Jacob, and ye	Mic 3:1	4994
I *p* you, ye heads of the house of	Mic 3:9	4994
I *p* you, consider from this day	Hag 2:15	4994
their men, to *p* before the LORD,	Zec 7:2	2470
go speedily to *p* before the LORD	Zec 8:21	2470
and to *p* before the LORD	Zec 8:22	2470
I *p* you, beseech God that he will	Mal 1:9	4994
p for them which despitefully use	Mt 5:44	*4336*
for they love to *p* standing in	Mt 6:5	*4336*
p to thy Father which is in	Mt 6:6	*4336*
But when ye *p*, use not vain	Mt 6:7	*4336*
After this manner therefore *p* ye	Mt 6:9	*4336*
P ye therefore the Lord of the	Mt 9:38	*1189*
up into a mountain apart to *p*	Mt 14:23	*4336*
put his hands on them, and *p*	Mt 19:13	*4336*
But *p* ye that your flight be not	Mt 24:20	*4336*
ye here, while I go and *p* yonder	Mt 26:36	*4336*
Watch and *p*, that ye enter not	Mt 26:41	*4336*
that I cannot now *p* to my Father	Mt 26:53	*3870*
they began to *p* him to depart out	Mk 5:17	*3870*
I *p* thee, come and lay thy hands	Mk 5:23	
he departed into a mountain to *p*	Mk 6:46	*4336*
soever ye desire, when ye *p*	Mk 11:24	*4336*
p ye that your flight be not in	Mk 13:18	*4336*
Take ye heed, watch and *p*	Mk 13:33	*4336*
Sit ye here, while I shall *p*	Mk 14:32	*4336*
Watch ye and *p*, lest ye enter into	Mk 14:38	*4336*
he went out into a mountain to *p*	Lk 6:12	*4336*
p for them which despitefully use	Lk 6:28	*4336*
and went up into a mountain to *p*	Lk 9:28	*4336*
p ye therefore the Lord of the	Lk 10:2	*1189*
unto him, Lord, teach us to *p*	Lk 11:1	*4336*
And he said unto them, When ye *p*	Lk 11:2	*4336*
I *p* thee have me excused	Lk 14:18	*2065*
I *p* thee have me excused	Lk 14:19	*2065*
I *p* thee therefore, father, that	Lk 16:27	*2065*
end, that men ought always to *p*	Lk 18:1	*4336*
men went up into the temple to *p*	Lk 18:10	*4336*
and *p* always, that ye may be	Lk 21:36	*1189*
them, *P* that ye enter not into	Lk 22:40	*4336*
rise and *p*, lest ye enter into	Lk 22:46	*4336*
I will *p* the Father, and he shall	Jn 14:16	*2065*
that I will *p* the Father for you	Jn 16:26	*2065*
I *p* for them	Jn 17:9	*2065*
I *p* not for the world, but for	Jn 17:9	*2065*
I *p* not that thou shouldest take	Jn 17:15	*2065*
Neither *p* I for these alone, but	Jn 17:20	*2065*
p God, if perhaps the thought of	Acts 8:22	*1189*
P ye to the Lord for me, that	Acts 8:24	*1189*
I *p* thee, of whom speaketh the	Acts 8:34	*1189*
to *p* about the sixth hour	Acts 10:9	*4336*
I *p* thee that thou wouldest hear	Acts 24:4	*3870*
Wherefore I *p* you to take some	Acts 27:34	*3870*
what we should *p* for as we ought	Rom 8:26	*4336*
that a woman *p* unto God uncovered	1Cor 11:13	*4336*
tongue *p* that he may interpret	1Cor 14:13	*4336*
For if I *p* in an unknown tongue,	1Cor 14:14	*4336*
I will *p* with the spirit, and I	1Cor 14:15	*4336*
I will *p* with the understanding	1Cor 14:15	*4336*
we *p* you in Christ's stead, be ye	2Cor 5:20	*1189*
Now I *p* to God that ye do no evil	2Cor 13:7	*2172*
And this I *p*, that your love may	Phil 1:9	*4336*
it, do not cease to *p* for you	Col 1:9	*4336*
P without ceasing	1Th 5:17	*4336*
I *p* God your whole spirit and soul	1Th 5:23	
Brethren, *p* for us	1Th 5:25	*4336*
also we *p* always for you, that	2Th 1:11	*4336*
p for us, that the word of the	2Th 3:1	*4336*
therefore that men *p* every where	1Ti 2:8	*4336*
I *p* God that it may not be laid	2Ti 4:16	
P for us	Heb 13:18	*4336*
let him *p*	Jas 5:13	*4336*
and let them *p* over him, anointing	Jas 5:14	*4336*
p one for another, that ye may be	Jas 5:16	*2172*
do not say that he shall *p* for it	1Jn 5:16	*2065*

PRAYED {65}

So Abraham *p* unto God	Gen 20:17	6419
when Moses *p* unto the LORD, the	Num 11:2	6419
And Moses *p* for the people	Num 21:7	6419
I *p* for Aaron also the same time	Deut 9:20	6419
I *p* therefore unto the LORD, and	Deut 9:26	6419
p unto the LORD, and wept sore	1Sa 1:10	6419
For this child I *p*	1Sa 1:27	6419
And Hannah *p*, and said, My heart	1Sa 2:1	6419
And Samuel *p* unto the LORD	1Sa 8:6	6419
them twain, and *p* unto the LORD	2Kin 4:33	6419
And Elisha *p*, and said, LORD, I	2Kin 6:17	6419
Elisha *p* unto the LORD, and said,	2Kin 6:18	6419
Hezekiah *p* before the LORD, and	2Kin 19:15	6419
That which thou hast *p* to me	2Kin 19:20	6419
wall, and *p* unto the LORD, saying,	2Kin 20:2	6419
But Hezekiah *p* for them, saying,	2Chr 30:18	6419
prophet Isaiah the son of Amoz, *p*	2Chr 32:20	6419
to the death, and *p* unto the LORD	2Chr 32:24	6419
And *p* unto him	2Chr 33:13	6419
Now when Ezra had *p*, and when he	Ezr 10:1	6419
p before the God of heaven,	Neh 1:4	6419
So I *p* to the God of heaven	Neh 2:4	6419
when he *p* for his friends	Job 42:10	6419
Hezekiah *p* unto the LORD, saying,	Is 37:15	6419
Whereas thou hast *p* to me against	Is 37:21	6419
the wall, and *p* unto the LORD,	Is 38:2	6419
I *p* unto the LORD, saying,	Jer 32:16	6419
his knees three times a day, and *p*	Dan 6:10	6739
I *p* unto the LORD my God, and made	Dan 9:4	6419
Then Jonah *p* unto the LORD his	Jonah 2:1	6419
he *p* unto the LORD, and said, I	Jonah 4:2	6419
and fell on his face, and *p*	Mt 26:39	*4336*
away again the second time, and *p*	Mt 26:42	*4336*
p the third time, saying the same	Mt 26:44	*4336*
into a solitary place, and there *p*	Mk 1:35	*4336*
p him that he might be with him	Mk 5:18	*3870*
p that, if it were possible, the	Mk 14:35	*4336*
And again he went away, and *p*	Mk 14:39	*4336*
p him that he would thrust out a	Lk 5:3	*2065*
himself into the wilderness, and *p*	Lk 5:16	*4336*
And as he *p*, the fashion of his	Lk 9:29	*4336*
p thus with himself, God, I thank	Lk 18:11	*4336*
But I have *p* for thee, that thy	Lk 22:32	*1189*
cast, and kneeled down, and *p*	Lk 22:41	*4336*
in an agony he *p* more earnestly	Lk 22:44	*4336*
mean while his disciples *p* him	Jn 4:31	*2065*
And they *p*, and said, Thou, Lord,	Acts 1:24	*4336*
And when they had *p*, the place was	Acts 4:31	*1189*
and when they had *p*, they laid	Acts 6:6	*4336*
p for them, that they might	Acts 8:15	*4336*
all forth, and kneeled down, and *p*	Acts 9:40	*4336*
to the people, and *p* to God alway	Acts 10:2	*1189*
at the ninth hour I *p* in my house	Acts 10:30	*4336*
Then *p* they him to tarry certain	Acts 10:48	*2065*
And when they had fasted and *p*	Acts 13:3	*4336*
and had *p* with fasting, they	Acts 14:23	*4336*
p him, saying, Come over into	Acts 16:9	*3870*
And at midnight Paul and Silas *p*	Acts 16:25	*4336*
kneeled down, and *p* with them all	Acts 20:36	*4336*
kneeled down on the shore, and *p*	Acts 21:5	*4336*
even while I *p* in the temple, I	Acts 22:17	*4336*
p me to bring this young man unto	Acts 23:18	*2065*
to whom Paul entered in, and *p*	Acts 28:8	*4336*
he *p* earnestly that it might not	Jas 5:17	*4336*
he *p* again, and the heaven gave	Jas 5:18	*4336*

PRAYER {114}

heart to pray this *p* unto thee	2Sa 7:27	8605
respect unto the *p* of thy servant	1Kin 8:28	8605
hearken unto the cry and to the *p*	1Kin 8:28	8605
p which thy servant shall make	1Kin 8:29	8605
What *p* and supplication soever be	1Kin 8:38	8605
Then hear thou in heaven their *p*	1Kin 8:45	8605
Then hear thou their *p* and their	1Kin 8:49	8605
made an end of praying all this *p*	1Kin 8:54	8605
said unto him, I have heard thy *p*	1Kin 9:3	8605
wherefore lift up thy *p* for the	2Kin 19:4	8605
thy father, I have heard thy *p*	2Kin 20:5	8605
therefore to the *p* of thy servant	2Chr 6:19	8605
the *p* which thy servant prayeth	2Chr 6:19	8605
to hearken unto the *p* which thy	2Chr 6:20	8605
Then what *p* or what supplication	2Chr 6:29	8605
thou from the heavens their *p*	2Chr 6:35	8605
from thy dwelling place, their *p*	2Chr 6:39	8605
the *p* that is made in this place	2Chr 6:40	8605
said unto him, I have heard thy *p*	2Chr 7:12	8605
mine ears attent unto the *p* that	2Chr 7:15	8605
their *p* came up to his holy	2Chr 30:27	8605
his *p* unto his God, and the words	2Chr 33:18	8605
His *p* also, and how God was	2Chr 33:19	8605
mayest hear the *p* of thy servant	Neh 1:6	8605
attentive to the *p* of thy servant	Neh 1:11	8605
to the *p* of thy servants, who	Neh 1:11	8605
we made our *p* unto our God	Neh 4:9	6419
to begin the thanksgiving in *p*	Neh 11:17	8605
fear, and restrainest *p* before God	Job 15:4	7878
also my *p* is pure	Job 16:17	8605
Thou shalt make thy *p* unto him	Job 22:27	6279
have mercy upon me, and hear my *p*	Ps 4:1	8605
will I direct my *p* unto thee	Ps 5:3	
the LORD will receive my *p*	Ps 6:9	8605
A *P* of David	Ps 17:*t*	8605
unto my cry, give ear unto my *p*	Ps 17:1	8605
my *p* returned into mine own bosom	Ps 35:13	8605
Hear my *p*, O LORD, and give ear	Ps 39:12	8605
my *p* unto the God of my life	Ps 42:8	8605
Hear my *p*, O God	Ps 54:2	8605
Give ear to my *p*, O God	Ps 55:1	8605
attend unto my *p*	Ps 61:1	8605
Hear my voice, O God, in my *p*	Ps 64:1	7879
O thou that hearest *p*, unto thee	Ps 65:2	8605
attended to the voice of my *p*	Ps 66:19	8605
which hath not turned away my *p*	Ps 66:20	8605
my *p* is unto thee, O LORD, in an	Ps 69:13	8605
p also shall be made for him	Ps 72:15	6419
angry against the *p* of thy people	Ps 80:4	8605
O LORD God of hosts, hear my *p*	Ps 84:8	8605
A *P* of David	Ps 86:*t*	8605
Give ear, O LORD, unto my *p*	Ps 86:6	8605
Let my *p* come before thee	Ps 88:2	8605
morning shall my *p* prevent thee	Ps 88:13	8605
A *P* of Moses, the man of God	Ps 90:*t*	8605
A *P* of the afflicted, when he is	Ps 102:*t*	8605
Hear my *p*, O LORD, and let my cry	Ps 102:1	8605
regard the *p* of the destitute	Ps 102:17	8605
and not despise their *p*	Ps 102:17	8605
but I give myself unto *p*	Ps 109:4	8605
and let his *p* become sin	Ps 109:7	8605
Let my *p* be set forth before thee	Ps 141:2	8605
for yet my *p* also shall be in	Ps 141:5	8605
A *P* when he was in the cave	Ps 142:*t*	8605
Hear my *p*, O LORD, give ear to my	Ps 143:1	8605
but the *p* of the upright is his	Prov 15:8	8605
he heareth the *p* of the righteous	Prov 15:29	8605
even his *p* shall be abomination	Prov 28:9	8605
they poured out a *p* when thy	Is 26:16	3908
wherefore lift up thy *p* for the	Is 37:4	8605
thy father, I have heard thy *p*	Is 38:5	8605
make them joyful in my house of *p*	Is 56:7	8605
an house of *p* for all people	Is 56:7	8605
lift up cry nor *p* for them	Jer 7:16	8605
lift up a cry or *p* for them	Jer 11:14	8605
and shout, he shutteth out my *p*	Lam 3:8	8605
that our *p* should not pass	Lam 3:44	8605
unto the Lord God, to seek by *p*	Dan 9:3	8605
yet made we not our *p* before the	Dan 9:13	2470
hear the *p* of thy servant, and his	Dan 9:17	8605
Yea, whiles I was speaking in *p*	Dan 9:21	8605
my *p* came in unto thee, into	Jonah 2:7	8605
A *p* of Habakkuk the prophet upon	Hab 3:1	8605
this kind goeth not out but by *p*	Mt 17:21	*4335*
shall be called the house of *p*	Mt 21:13	*4335*
whatsoever ye shall ask in *p*	Mt 21:22	*4335*
and for a pretence make long *p*	Mt 23:14	*4336*
come forth by nothing, but by *p*	Mk 9:29	*4335*
of all nations the house of *p*	Mk 11:17	*4335*
for thy *p* is heard	Lk 1:13	*1162*
continued all night in *p* to God	Lk 6:12	*4335*
My house is the house of *p*	Lk 19:46	*4335*
And when he rose up from *p*	Lk 22:45	*4335*
continued with one accord in *p*	Acts 1:14	*4335*
into the temple at the hour of *p*	Acts 3:1	*4335*
give ourselves continually to *p*	Acts 6:4	*4335*
thy *p* is heard, and thine alms are	Acts 10:31	*4335*
but *p* was made without ceasing of	Acts 12:5	*4335*
where *p* was wont to be made	Acts 16:13	*4335*
it came to pass, as we went to *p*	Acts 16:16	*4335*
p to God for Israel is, that they	Rom 10:1	*1162*
continuing instant in *p*	Rom 12:12	*4335*
give yourselves to fasting and *p*	1Cor 7:5	*4335*
also helping together by *p* for us	2Cor 1:11	*1162*
And by their *p* for you, which long	2Cor 9:14	*1162*
Praying always with all *p*	Eph 6:18	*4335*
Always in every *p* of mine for you	Phil 1:4	*1162*
to my salvation through your *p*	Phil 1:19	*1162*
but in every thing by *p* and	Phil 4:6	*4335*
Continue in *p*, and watch in the	Col 4:2	*4335*
by the word of God and *p*	1Ti 4:5	*1783*
the *p* of faith shall save the	Jas 5:15	*2171*
The effectual fervent *p* of a	Jas 5:16	*1162*
therefore sober, and watch unto *p*	1Pet 4:7	*4335*

PRAYERS {24}

The *p* of David the son of Jesse	Ps 72:20	8605
you, when ye make many *p*, I will	Is 1:15	8605
and for a pretence make long *p*	Mk 12:40	*4336*
with fastings and *p* night and day	Lk 2:37	*1162*
of John fast often, and make *p*	Lk 5:33	*1162*
houses, and for a shew make long *p*	Lk 20:47	*4336*
and in breaking of bread, and in *p*	Acts 2:42	*4335*
And he said unto him, Thy *p*	Acts 10:4	*4335*
mention of you always in my *p*	Rom 1:9	*4335*
with me in your *p* to God for me	Rom 15:30	*4335*
making mention of you in my *p*	Eph 1:16	*4335*
labouring fervently for you in *p*	Col 4:12	*4335*
making mention of you in our *p*	1Th 1:2	*4335*
first of all, supplications, *p*	1Ti 2:1	*4335*
supplications and *p* night and day	1Ti 5:5	*4335*
remembrance of thee in my *p* night	2Ti 1:3	*1162*
mention of thee always in my *p*	Philem 4	*4335*
your *p* I shall be given unto you	Philem 22	*4335*
flesh, when he had offered up *p*	Heb 5:7	*1162*
that your *p* be not hindered	1Pet 3:7	*4335*
and his ears are open unto their *p*	1Pet 3:12	*1162*
odours, which are the *p* of saints	Rev 5:8	*4335*
he should offer it with the *p* of	Rev 8:3	*4335*
came with the *p* of the saints	Rev 8:4	*4335*

PRAYEST {2}

And when thou *p*, thou shalt not be	Mt 6:5	*4336*
But thou, when thou *p*, enter into	Mt 6:6	*4336*

PRAYETH {7}

which thy servant *p* before thee	1Kin 8:28	6419
which thy servant *p* before thee	2Chr 6:19	6419
thy servant *p* toward this place	2Chr 6:20	6419
p unto it, and saith, Deliver me	Is 44:17	6419
for, behold, he *p*,	Acts 9:11	*4336*
But every woman that *p* or	1Cor 11:5	*4336*
in an unknown tongue, my spirit *p*	1Cor 14:14	*4336*

PRAYING {20}

she continued *p* before the LORD	1Sa 1:12	6419
by thee here, *p* unto the LORD	1Sa 1:26	6419
made an end of *p* all this prayer	1Kin 8:54	6419
when Solomon had made an end of *p*	2Chr 7:1	6419
men assembled, and found Daniel *p*	Dan 6:11	1156
And whiles I was speaking, and *p*	Dan 9:20	6419
And when ye stand *p*, forgive, if	Mk 11:25	*4336*
multitude of the people were *p*	Lk 1:10	*4336*
Jesus also being baptized, and *p*	Lk 3:21	*4336*
came to pass, as he was alone *p*	Lk 9:18	*4336*
as he was *p* in a certain place,	Lk 11:1	*4336*
I was in the city of Joppa *p*	Acts 11:5	*4336*
many were gathered together *p*	Acts 12:12	*4336*
Every man *p* or prophesying,	1Cor 11:4	*4336*
P us with much intreaty that we	2Cor 8:4	*1189*
P always with all prayer and	Eph 6:18	*4336*
Jesus Christ, *p* always for you,	Col 1:3	*4336*
Withal *p* also for us, that God	Col 4:3	*4336*
day *p* exceedingly that we might	1Th 3:10	*1189*
holy faith, *p* in the Holy Ghost,	Jude 20	*4336*

PREACH {50}

to *p* of thee at Jerusalem	Neh 6:7	7121
to *p* good tidings unto the meek	Is 61:1	1319
p unto it the preaching that I	Jonah 3:2	7121
From that time Jesus began to *p*	Mt 4:17	*2784*
And as ye go, *p*, saying, The	Mt 10:7	*2784*
that *p* ye upon the housetops	Mt 10:27	*2784*

to teach and to *p* in their cities ... Mt 11:1 *2784*
p the baptism of repentance for ... Mk 1:4 *2784*
towns, that I may *p* there also ... Mk 1:38 *2784*
he might send them forth to *p* ... Mk 3:14 *2784*
p the gospel to every creature ... Mk 16:15 *2784*
me to *p* the gospel to the poor ... Lk 4:18 *2097*
to *p* deliverance to the captives, ... Lk 4:18 *2784*
To *p* the acceptable year of the ... Lk 4:19 *2784*
I must *p* the kingdom of God to ... Lk 4:43 *2097*
he sent them to *p* the kingdom of ... Lk 9:2 *2784*
go thou and *p* the kingdom of God ... Lk 9:60 *1229*
not to teach and *p* Jesus Christ ... Acts 5:42 *2097*
commanded us to *p* unto the people ... Acts 10:42 *2784*
p unto you that ye should turn ... Acts 14:15 *2097*
in every city them that *p* him ... Acts 15:21 *2784*
Holy Ghost to *p* the word in Asia ... Acts 16:6 *2980*
us for to *p* the gospel unto them ... Acts 16:10 *2097*
whom I *p* unto you, is Christ ... Acts 17:3 *2605*
I am ready to *p* the gospel to you ... Rom 1:15 *2097*
is, the word of faith, which we *p* ... Rom 10:8 *2784*
And how shall they *p*, except they ... Rom 10:15 *2784*
them that *p* the gospel of peace ... Rom 10:15 *2097*
so have I strived to *p* the gospel ... Rom 15:20 *2097*
to baptize, but to *p* the gospel ... 1Cor 1:17 *2097*
But we *p* Christ crucified, unto ... 1Cor 1:23 *2784*
p the gospel should live of the ... 1Cor 9:14 *2605*
For though I *p* the gospel ... 1Cor 9:16 *2097*
is unto me, if I *p* not the gospel ... 1Cor 9:16 *2097*
when I *p* the gospel, I may make ... 1Cor 9:18 *2097*
it were I or they, so we *p* ... 1Cor 15:11 *2784*
to Troas to *p* Christ's gospel ... 2Cor 2:12
For we *p* not ourselves, but ... 2Cor 4:5 *2784*
To *p* the gospel in the regions ... 2Cor 10:16 *2097*
p any other gospel unto you than ... Gal 1:8 *2097*
If any man *p* any other gospel ... Gal 1:9 *2097*
that I might *p* him among the ... Gal 1:16 *2097*
which I *p* among the Gentiles ... Gal 2:2 *2784*
if I yet *p* circumcision, why do I ... Gal 5:11 *2784*
that I should *p* among the ... Eph 3:8 *2097*
Some indeed *p* Christ even of envy ... Phil 1:15 *2784*
The one *p* Christ of contention, ... Phil 1:16 *2605*
Whom we *p*, warning every man, and ... Col 1:28 *2605*
P the word ... 2Ti 4:2 *2784*
the everlasting gospel to *p* unto ... Rev 14:6 *2097*

PREACHED {61}
I have *p* righteousness in the ... Ps 40:9 1319
poor have the gospel *p* to them ... Mt 11:5 *2097*
p in all the world for a witness ... Mt 24:14 *2784*
shall be *p* in the whole world ... Mt 26:13 *2784*
And *p*, saying, There cometh one ... Mk 1:7 *2784*
And he *p* in their synagogues ... Mk 1:39 *2784*
and he *p* the word unto them ... Mk 2:2 *2980*
out, and *p* that men should repent ... Mk 6:12 *2784*
this gospel shall be *p* throughout ... Mk 14:9 *2784*
p every where, the Lord working ... Mk 16:20 *2784*
exhortation *p* he unto the people ... Lk 3:18 *2097*
he *p* in the synagogues of Galilee ... Lk 4:44 *2784*
to the poor the gospel is *p* ... Lk 7:22 *2097*
that time the kingdom of God is *p* ... Lk 16:16 *2097*
p the gospel, the chief priests ... Lk 20:1 *2097*
remission of sins should be *p* in ... Lk 24:47 *2784*
which before was *p* unto you ... Acts 3:20 *4296*
p through Jesus the resurrection ... Acts 4:2 *2605*
of Samaria, and *p* Christ unto them ... Acts 8:5 *2784*
p the word of the Lord, returned ... Acts 8:25 *2980*
p the gospel in many villages of ... Acts 8:25 *2097*
scripture, and *p* unto him Jesus ... Acts 8:35 *2097*
through he *p* in all the cities ... Acts 8:40 *2097*
straightway he *p* Christ in the ... Acts 9:20 *2784*
how he had *p* boldly at Damascus ... Acts 9:27 *3954*
after the baptism which John *p* ... Acts 10:37 *2784*
they *p* the word of God in the ... Acts 13:5 *2605*
When John had first *p* before his ... Acts 13:24 *4296*
that through this man is *p* unto ... Acts 13:38 *2605*
be *p* to them the next sabbath ... Acts 13:42 *2980*
And there they *p* the gospel ... Acts 14:7 *2097*
when they had *p* the gospel to ... Acts 14:21 *2097*
when they had *p* the word in Perga ... Acts 14:25 *2980*
we have *p* the word of the Lord ... Acts 15:36 *2605*
of God was *p* of Paul at Berea ... Acts 17:13 *2605*
because he *p* unto them Jesus, and ... Acts 17:18 *2907*
Paul *p* unto them, ready to depart ... Acts 20:7 *1256*
I have fully *p* the gospel of ... Rom 15:19 *4137*
means, when I have *p* to others ... 1Cor 9:27 *2784*
you the gospel which I *p* unto you ... 1Cor 15:1 *2097*
keep in memory what I *p* unto you ... 1Cor 15:2 *2097*
Now if Christ be *p* that he rose ... 1Cor 15:12 *2784*
who was *p* among you by us, even ... 2Cor 1:19 *2784*
another Jesus, whom we have not *p* ... 2Cor 11:4 *2784*
because I have *p* to you the ... 2Cor 11:7 *2097*
that which we have *p* unto you ... Gal 1:8 *2097*
was *p* of me is not after man ... Gal 1:11 *2097*
p before the gospel unto Abraham, ... Gal 3:8 *4283*
infirmity of the flesh I *p* the ... Gal 4:13 *2097*
p peace to you which were afar ... Eph 2:17 *2097*
or in truth, Christ is *p* ... Phil 1:18 *2605*
which was *p* to every creature ... Col 1:23 *2784*
we *p* unto you the gospel of God ... 1Th 2:9 *2784*
p unto the Gentiles, believed on ... 1Ti 3:16 *2784*
For unto us was the gospel *p* ... Heb 4:2 *2097*
but the word *p* did not profit ... Heb 4:2 *189*
first *p* entered not in because of ... Heb 4:6 *2097*
unto you by them that have *p* the ... 1Pet 1:12 *2097*
which by the gospel is *p* unto you ... 1Pet 1:25 *2097*
p unto the spirits in prison ... 1Pet 3:19 *2784*
p also to them that are dead ... 1Pet 4:6 *2097*

PREACHER {11}
The words of the *P*, the son of ... Eccl 1:1 6953
Vanity of vanities, saith the *P* ... Eccl 1:2 6953
I the *P* was king over Israel in ... Eccl 1:12 6953
this have I found, saith the *p* ... Eccl 7:27 6953
Vanity of vanities, saith the *p* ... Eccl 12:8 6953
moreover, because the *p* was wise ... Eccl 12:9 6953
The *p* sought to find out ... Eccl 12:10 6953
how shall they hear without a *p* ... Rom 10:14 *2784*
Whereunto I am ordained a *p* ... 1Ti 2:7 *2783*
Whereunto I am appointed a *p* ... 2Ti 1:11 *2783*
a *p* of righteousness, bringing in ... 2Pet 2:5 *2783*

PREACHEST {1}
thou that *p* a man should not ... Rom 2:21 *2784*

PREACHETH {3}
adjure you by Jesus whom Paul *p* ... Acts 19:13 *2784*
if he that cometh *p* another Jesus ... 2Cor 11:4 *2784*
now *p* the faith which once he ... Gal 1:23 *2097*

PREACHING {27}
unto it the *p* that I bid thee ... Jonah 3:2 7150
p in the wilderness of Judaea, ... Mt 3:1 *2784*
p the gospel of the kingdom, and ... Mt 4:23 *2784*
p the gospel of the kingdom, and ... Mt 9:35 *2784*
they repented at the *p* of Jonas ... Mt 12:41 *2782*
p the gospel of the kingdom of ... Mk 1:14 *2784*
p the baptism of repentance for ... Lk 3:3 *2784*
every city and village, *p* and ... Lk 8:1 *2784*
p the gospel, and healing every ... Lk 9:6 *2097*
they repented at the *p* of Jonas ... Lk 11:32 *2782*
went every where *p* the word ... Acts 8:4 *2097*
p the things concerning the ... Acts 8:12 *2097*
Israel, *p* peace by Jesus Christ ... Acts 10:36 *2097*
p the word to none but unto the ... Acts 11:19 *2980*
the Grecians, *p* the Lord Jesus ... Acts 11:20 *2097*
p the word of the Lord, with many ... Acts 15:35 *2097*
and as Paul was long *p*, he sunk ... Acts 20:9 *1256*
I have gone *p* the kingdom of God ... Acts 20:25 *2784*
P the kingdom of God, and teaching ... Acts 28:31 *2784*
the *p* of Jesus Christ, according ... Rom 16:25 *2782*
For the *p* of the cross is to them ... 1Cor 1:18 *3056*
of *p* to save them that believe ... 1Cor 1:21 *2782*
my *p* was not with enticing words ... 1Cor 2:4 *2782*
be not risen, then is our *p* vain ... 1Cor 15:14 *2782*
also in *p* the gospel of Christ ... 2Cor 10:14
that by me the *p* might be fully ... 2Ti 4:17 *2782*
manifested his word through *p* ... Titus 1:3 *2782*

PRECEPT {11}
For *p* must be upon *p*, ... Is 28:10 6673
p upon *p*; line upon line ... Is 28:10 6673
LORD was unto them *p* upon *p* ... Is 28:13 6673
p upon *p*; line upon line ... Is 28:13 6673
me is taught by the *p* of men ... Is 29:13 4687
of your heart he wrote you this *p* ... Mk 10:5 *1785*
p to all the people according to ... Heb 9:19 *1785*

PRECEPTS {24}
sabbath, and commandedst them *p* ... Neh 9:14 4687
us to keep thy *p* diligently ... Ps 119:4 6490
I will meditate in thy *p*, and have ... Ps 119:15 6490
me to understand the way of thy *p* ... Ps 119:27 6490
Behold, I have longed after thy *p* ... Ps 119:40 6490
for I seek thy *p* ... Ps 119:45 6490
This I had, because I kept thy *p* ... Ps 119:56 6490
thee, and of them that keep thy *p* ... Ps 119:63 6490
keep thy *p* with my whole heart ... Ps 119:69 6490
but I will meditate in thy *p* ... Ps 119:78 6490
but I forsook not thy *p* ... Ps 119:87 6490
I will never forget thy *p* ... Ps 119:93 6490
for I have sought thy *p* ... Ps 119:94 6490
ancients, because I keep thy *p* ... Ps 119:100 6490
Through thy *p* I get understanding ... Ps 119:104 6490
yet I erred not from thy *p* ... Ps 119:110 6490
Therefore I esteem all thy *p* ... Ps 119:128 6490
so will I keep thy *p* ... Ps 119:134 6490
yet do not I forget thy *p* ... Ps 119:141 6490
Consider how I love thy *p* ... Ps 119:159 6490
I have kept thy *p* and thy ... Ps 119:168 6490
for I have chosen thy *p* ... Ps 119:173 6490
your father, and kept all his *p* ... Jer 35:18 4687
even by departing from thy *p* ... Dan 9:5 4687

PRECIOUS {76}
brother and to her mother *p* things ... Gen 24:53 4030
for the *p* things of heaven, for ... Deut 33:13 4022
for the *p* fruits brought forth by ... Deut 33:14 4022
for the *p* things put forth by the ... Deut 33:14 4022
for the *p* things of the lasting ... Deut 33:15 4022
for the *p* things of the earth and ... Deut 33:16 4022
of the LORD was *p* in those days ... 1Sa 3:1 3368
because my soul was *p* in thine ... 1Sa 26:21 3365
talent of gold with the *p* stones ... 2Sa 12:30 3368
and very much gold, and *p* stones ... 1Kin 10:2 3368
very great store, and *p* stones ... 1Kin 10:10 3368
of almug trees, and *p* stones ... 1Kin 10:11 3368
thy servants, be *p* in thy sight ... 2Kin 1:13 3365
let my life now be *p* in thy sight ... 2Kin 1:14 3365
all the house of his *p* things ... 2Kin 20:13 5238
the *p* ointment, and all the house ... 2Kin 20:13 2896
there were *p* stones in it ... 1Chr 20:2 3368
and all manner of *p* stones ... 1Chr 29:2 3368
they with whom *p* stones were ... 1Chr 29:8
house with *p* stones for beauty ... 2Chr 3:6 3368
and gold in abundance, and *p* stones ... 2Chr 9:1 3368
great abundance, and *p* stones ... 2Chr 9:9 3368
brought algum trees and *p* stones ... 2Chr 9:10 3368
p jewels, which they stripped off ... 2Chr 20:25 2530
of *p* things, with fenced cities ... 2Chr 21:3 4030
for *p* stones, and for spices, and ... 2Chr 32:27 3368
with *p* things, beside all that ... Ezr 1:6 4030
vessels of fine copper, *p* as gold ... Ezr 8:27 2530
and his eye seeth every *p* thing ... Job 28:10 3366
gold of Ophir, with the *p* onyx ... Job 28:16 3368
the redemption of their soul is *p* ... Ps 49:8 3365
p shall their blood be in his ... Ps 72:14 3365
P in the sight of the LORD is the ... Ps 116:15 3368
forth and weepeth, bearing *p* seed ... Ps 126:6 4901
It is like the *p* ointment upon ... Ps 133:2 2896
How *p* also are thy thoughts unto ... Ps 139:17 3365
We shall find all *p* substance ... Prov 1:13 3368
She is more *p* than rubies ... Prov 3:15 3368
will hunt for the *p* life ... Prov 6:26 3368
substance of a diligent man is *p* ... Prov 12:27 3368
A gift is as a *p* stone in the ... Prov 17:8 2580
lips of knowledge are a *p* jewel ... Prov 20:15 3366
the chambers be filled with all *p* ... Prov 24:4 3368
name is better than *p* ointment ... Eccl 7:1 2896
make a man more *p* than fine gold ... Is 13:12 3365
stone, a *p* corner stone, a sure ... Is 28:16 3368
them the house of his *p* things ... Is 39:2 5238
the *p* ointment, and all the house ... Is 39:2 2896
Since thou wast *p* in my sight ... Is 43:4 3365
take forth the *p* from the vile ... Jer 15:19 3368
all the *p* things thereof, and all ... Jer 20:5 3366
The *p* sons of Zion, comparable to ... Lam 4:2 3368
taken the treasure and *p* things ... Eze 22:25 3366
in *p* clothes for chariots ... Eze 27:20 2667
all spices, and with all *p* stones ... Eze 27:22 3368
every *p* stone was thy covering, ... Eze 28:13 3368
with their *p* vessels of silver and ... Dan 11:8 2532
with *p* stones, and pleasant things ... Dan 11:38 3368
over all the *p* things of Egypt ... Dan 11:43 2530
alabaster box of very *p* ointment ... Mt 26:7 *927*
of ointment of spikenard very *p* ... Mk 14:3 *4185*
p stones, wood, hay, stubble ... 1Cor 3:12 *5093*
for the *p* fruit of the earth ... Jas 5:7 *5093*
being much more *p* than of gold ... 1Pet 1:7 *5093*
But with the *p* blood of Christ, ... 1Pet 1:19 *5093*
of men, but chosen of God, and *p* ... 1Pet 2:4 *1784*
a chief corner stone, elect, *p* ... 1Pet 2:6 *1784*
therefore which believe he is *p* ... 1Pet 2:7 *5092*
like *p* faith with us through the ... 2Pet 1:1 *2472*
us exceeding great and *p* promises ... 2Pet 1:4 *5093*
p stones and pearls, having a ... Rev 17:4 *5093*
p stones, and of pearls, and fine ... Rev 18:12 *5093*
all manner vessels of most *p* wood ... Rev 18:12 *5093*
with gold, and *p* stones, and pearls ... Rev 18:16 *5093*
was like unto a stone most *p* ... Rev 21:11 *5093*
with all manner of *p* stones ... Rev 21:19 *5093*

PREDESTINATE {2}
he also did *p* to be conformed to ... Rom 8:29 *4309*
Moreover whom he did *p*, them he ... Rom 8:30 *4309*

PREDESTINATED {2}
Having *p* us unto the adoption of ... Eph 1:5 *4309*
being *p* according to the purpose ... Eph 1:11 *4309*

PREEMINENCE {3}
a man hath no *p* above a beast ... Eccl 3:19 4195
in all things he might have the *p* ... Col 1:18 *4409*
loveth to have the *p* among them ... 3Jn 9 *5383*

PREFER {1}
if I *p* not Jerusalem above my ... Ps 137:6 5927

PREFERRED {5}
he *p* her and her maids unto the ... Est 2:9 8138
Daniel was *p* above the presidents ... Dan 6:3 5330
cometh after me is *p* before me ... Jn 1:15 *1096*
coming after me is *p* before me ... Jn 1:27 *1096*
cometh a man which is *p* before me ... Jn 1:30 *1096*

PREFERRING {2}
in honour *p* one another ... Rom 12:10 *4285*
without *p* one before another ... 1Ti 5:21 *4299*

PREMEDITATE {1}
ye shall speak, neither do ye *p* ... Mk 13:11 *3191*

PREPARATION {9}
will therefore now make *p* for it ... 1Chr 22:5 3559
torches in the day of his *p* ... Nah 2:3 3559
that followed the day of the *p* ... Mt 27:62 *3904*
was come, because it was the *p* ... Mk 15:42 *3904*
And that day was the *p*, and the ... Lk 23:54 *3904*
it was the *p* of the passover, and ... Jn 19:14 *3904*
therefore, because it was the *p* ... Jn 19:31 *3904*
because of the Jews' *p* day ... Jn 19:42 *3904*
with the *p* of the gospel of peace ... Eph 6:15 *2091*

PREPARATIONS {1}
The *p* of the heart in man, and the ... Prov 16:1 4633

PREPARE {81}
I will *p* him an habitation ... Ex 15:2
shall *p* that which they bring in ... Ex 16:5 3559
thou *p* with the burnt offering or ... Num 15:5 6213
thou shalt *p* for a meat offering ... Num 15:6 6213
to the number that ye shall *p* ... Num 15:12 6213
p me here seven oxen and seven ... Num 23:1 3559
p me here seven bullocks and seven ... Num 23:29 3559
Thou shalt *p* thee a way, and ... Deut 19:3 3559
people, saying, *P* you victuals ... Josh 1:11 3559
Let us now *p* to build us an altar ... Josh 22:26 6213
p your hearts unto the LORD, and ... 1Sa 7:3 3559
p yet, and know and see his place ... 1Sa 23:22 3559
P thy chariot, and get thee down, ... 1Kin 18:44 631
shewbread, to *p* it every sabbath ... 1Chr 9:32 3559
and *p* their heart unto thee ... 1Chr 29:18 3559
Even to *p* me timber in abundance ... 2Chr 2:9 3559
Then Hezekiah commanded to *p* ... 2Chr 31:11 3559
p yourselves by the houses of ... 2Chr 35:4 3559

p your brethren, that they may do ... 2Chr 35:6 3559
banquet that I shall *p* for them ... Est 5:8 6213
p thyself to the search of their ... Job 8:8 3559
If thou *p* thine heart, and stretch ... Job 11:13 3559
dust, and *p* raiment as the clay ... Job 27:16 3559
He may *p* it, but the just shall ... Job 27:17 3559
thou wilt *p* their heart, thou ... Ps 10:17 3559
p themselves without my fault ... Ps 59:4 3559
O *p* mercy and truth, which may ... Ps 61:7 4487
that they may *p* a city for ... Ps 107:36 3559
P thy work without, and make it ... Prov 24:27 3559
yet they *p* their meat in the ... Prov 30:25 3559
P slaughter for his children for ... Is 14:21 3559
P the table, watch in the ... Is 21:5 6186
P ye the way of the LORD, make ... Is 40:3 6437
workman to *p* a graven image ... Is 40:20 3559
ye up, *p* the way, take up the ... Is 57:14 6437
p ye the way of the people ... Is 62:10 6437
that *p* a table for that troop, and ... Is 65:11 6186
P ye war against her ... Jer 6:4 6942
p them for the day of slaughter ... Jer 12:3 6942
I will *p* destroyers against thee, ... Jer 22:7 6942
say ye, Stand fast, and *p* thee ... Jer 46:14 3559
up the watchmen, *p* the ambushes ... Jer 51:12 3559
p the nations against her, call ... Jer 51:27 6942
P against her the nations with ... Jer 51:28 6942
thou shalt *p* thy bread therewith ... Eze 4:15 6213
p thee stuff for removing, and ... Eze 12:3 6213
I will *p* thee unto blood, and ... Eze 35:6 6213
p for thyself, thou, and all thy ... Eze 38:7 3559
Seven days shalt thou *p* every day ... Eze 43:25 6213
they shall also *p* a young bullock ... Eze 43:25 3559
he shall *p* the sin offering, and ... Eze 45:17 3559
shall the prince *p* for himself ... Eze 45:22 3559
days of the feast he shall *p* a ... Eze 45:23 3559
he shall *p* a meat offering of an ... Eze 45:24 3559
the priests shall *p* his burnt ... Eze 46:2 3559
he shall *p* a meat offering, an ... Eze 46:7 3559
Now when the prince shall *p* a ... Eze 46:12 3559
he shall *p* his burnt offering and ... Eze 46:12 3559
Thou shalt daily *p* a burnt ... Eze 46:13 3559
thou shalt *p* it every morning ... Eze 46:13 3559
thou shalt *p* a meat offering for ... Eze 46:14 3559
Thus shall they *p* the lamb ... Eze 46:15 3559
P war, wake up the mighty men, ... Joel 3:9 6942
p to meet thy God, O Israel ... Amos 4:12 3559
they even *p* war against him ... Mic 3:5 6942
he shall *p* the way before me ... Mal 3:1 6437
P ye the way of the Lord, make ... Mt 3:3 *2090*
which shall *p* thy way before thee ... Mt 11:10 *2680*
Where wilt thou that we *p* for ... Mt 26:17 *2090*
which shall *p* thy way before thee ... Mk 1:2 *2680*
P ye the way of the Lord, make ... Mk 1:3 *2090*
p that thou mayest eat the ... Mk 14:12 *2090*
face of the Lord to *p* his ways ... Lk 1:76 *2090*
P ye the way of the Lord, make ... Lk 3:4 *2090*
which shall *p* thy way before thee ... Lk 7:27 *2680*
p us the passover, that we may ... Lk 22:8 *2090*
him, Where wilt thou that we *p* ... Lk 22:9 *2090*
I go to *p* a place for you ... Jn 14:2 *2090*
p a place for you, I will come ... Jn 14:3 *2090*
who shall *p* himself to the battle ... 1Cor 14:8 *3903*
But withal *p* me also a lodging ... Philem 22 *2090*

PREPARED {101}
for I have *p* the house, and room ... Gen 24:31 6437
and the bread, which she had *p* ... Gen 27:17 6213
neither had they *p* for themselves ... Ex 12:39 6213
into the place which I have *p* ... Ex 23:20 3559
the city of Sihon be built and *p* ... Num 21:27 3559
I have *p* seven altars, and I have ... Num 23:4 6186
whom he had *p* of the children of ... Josh 4:4 3559
About forty thousand *p* for war ... Josh 4:13 2502
this, that Absalom *p* him chariots ... 2Sa 15:1 6213
he *p* him chariots and horsemen, and ... 1Kin 1:5 6213
so they *p* timber and stones to ... 1Kin 5:18 3559
the oracle he *p* in the house ... 1Kin 6:19 3559
he *p* great provision for them ... 2Kin 6:23 3739
for their brethren had *p* for them ... 1Chr 12:39 3559
p a place for the ark of God, and ... 1Chr 15:1 3559
his place, which he had *p* for it ... 1Chr 15:3 3559
the place that I have *p* for it ... 1Chr 15:12 3559
David *p* iron in abundance for the ... 1Chr 22:3 3559
So David *p* abundantly before his ... 1Chr 22:5 3559
in my trouble I have *p* for the ... 1Chr 22:14 3559
timber also and stone have I *p* ... 1Chr 22:14 3559
Now I have *p* with all my might ... 1Chr 29:2 3559
that I have *p* for the holy house ... 1Chr 29:3 3559
have *p* to build thee an house for ... 1Chr 29:16 3559
place which David had *p* for it ... 2Chr 1:4 3559
in the place that David had *p* in ... 2Chr 3:1 3559
p unto the day of the foundation ... 2Chr 8:16 3559
because he *p* not his heart to ... 2Chr 12:14 3559
divers kinds of spices *p* by the ... 2Chr 16:14 7543
thousand ready *p* for the war ... 2Chr 17:18 2502
hast *p* thine heart to seek God ... 2Chr 19:3 3559
p their hearts unto the God of ... 2Chr 20:33 3559
Uzziah *p* for them throughout all ... 2Chr 26:14 3559
because he *p* his ways before the ... 2Chr 27:6 3559
in his transgression, have we *p* ... 2Chr 29:19 3559
people, that God had *p* the people ... 2Chr 29:36 3559
and they *p* them, ... 2Chr 31:11 3559
So the service was *p*, and the ... 2Chr 35:10 3559
the Levites *p* for themselves ... 2Chr 35:14 3559
brethren the Levites *p* for them ... 2Chr 35:15 3559
of the LORD was *p* the same day ... 2Chr 35:16 3559
when Josiah had *p* the temple ... 2Chr 35:20 3559
For Ezra had *p* his heart to seek ... Ezr 7:10 3559
Now that which was *p* for me daily ... Neh 5:18 6213
also fowls were *p* for me, and once ... Neh 5:18 6213
unto them for whom nothing is *p* ... Neh 8:10 3559
he had *p* for him a great chamber, ... Neh 13:5 6213
the banquet that I have *p* for him ... Est 5:4 6213
to the banquet that Esther had *p* ... Est 5:5 6213
banquet that she had *p* but myself ... Est 5:12 6213
the gallows that he had *p* for him ... Est 6:4 3559
the banquet that Esther had *p* ... Est 6:14 6213
that he had *p* for Mordecai ... Est 7:10 3559
he *p* it, yea, and searched it out ... Job 28:27 3559
when I *p* my seat in the street ... Job 29:7 3559
He hath also *p* for him the ... Ps 7:13 3559
he hath *p* his throne for judgment ... Ps 9:7 3559
They have *p* a net for my steps ... Ps 57:6 3559
hast *p* of thy goodness for the ... Ps 68:10 3559
thou hast *p* the light and the sun ... Ps 74:16 3559
The LORD hath *p* his throne in the ... Ps 103:19 3559
When he *p* the heavens, I was ... Prov 8:27 3559
Judgments are *p* for scorners ... Prov 19:29 3559
The horse is *p* against the day of ... Prov 21:31 3559
yea, for the king it is *p* ... Is 30:33 3559
what he hath *p* for him that ... Is 64:4 6213
a table *p* before it, whereupon ... Eze 23:41 6186
of thy pipes was *p* in thee in the ... Eze 28:13 3559
Be thou *p*, and prepare for thyself ... Eze 38:7 3559
for ye have *p* lying and corrupt ... Dan 2:9 2164
and gold, which they *p* for Baal ... Hos 2:8 6213
going forth is *p* as the morning ... Hos 6:3 3559
Now the LORD had *p* a great fish ... Jonah 1:17 4487
And the LORD God *p* a gourd ... Jonah 4:6 4487
But God *p* a worm when the morning ... Jonah 4:7 4487
that God *p* a vehement east wind ... Jonah 4:8 4487
and the defence shall be *p* ... Nah 2:5 3559
for the LORD hath *p* a sacrifice ... Zeph 1:7 3559
for whom it is *p* of my Father ... Mt 20:23 *2090*
Behold, I have *p* my dinner ... Mt 22:4 *2090*
inherit the kingdom *p* for you ... Mt 25:34 *2090*
p for the devil and his angels ... Mt 25:41 *2090*
be given to them for whom it is *p* ... Mk 10:40 *2090*
a large upper room furnished and *p* ... Mk 14:15 *2092*
ready a people *p* for the Lord ... Lk 1:17 *2680*
Which thou hast *p* before the face ... Lk 2:31 *2090*
p not himself, neither did ... Lk 12:47 *2090*
and *p* spices and ointments ... Lk 23:56 *2090*
the spices which they had *p* ... Lk 24:1 *2090*
which he had afore *p* unto glory ... Rom 9:23 *4282*
God hath *p* for them that love him ... 1Cor 2:9 *2090*
use, and *p* unto every good work ... 2Ti 2:21 *2090*
not, but a body hast thou *p* me ... Heb 10:5 *2675*
p an ark to the saving of his ... Heb 11:7 *2680*
for he hath *p* for them a city ... Heb 11:16 *2090*
trumpets *p* themselves to sound ... Rev 8:6 *2090*
like unto horses *p* unto battle ... Rev 9:7 *2090*
which were *p* for an hour, and a ... Rev 9:15 *2090*
where she hath a place *p* of God ... Rev 12:6 *2090*
the kings of the east might be *p* ... Rev 16:12 *2090*
p as a bride adorned for her ... Rev 21:2 *2090*

PREPAREDST {1}
Thou *p* room before it, and didst ... Ps 80:9 6437

PREPAREST {3}
when thou *p* a bullock for a burnt ... Num 15:8 6213
Thou *p* a table before me in the ... Ps 23:5 6186
thou *p* them corn, when thou hast ... Ps 65:9 3559

PREPARETH {3}
That *p* his heart to seek God, the ... 2Chr 30:19 3559
vanity, and their belly *p* deceit ... Job 15:35 3559
who *p* rain for the earth, who ... Ps 147:8 3559

PREPARING {2}
in *p* him a chamber in the courts ... Neh 13:7 6213
of Noah, while the ark was a *p* ... 1Pet 3:20 *2680*

PRESBYTERY {1}
laying on of the hands of the *p* ... 1Ti 4:14 *4244*

PRESCRIBED {1}
grievousness which they have *p* ... Is 10:1 3789

PRESCRIBING {1}
oil, and salt without *p* how much ... Ezr 7:22 3792

PRESENCE {116}
the *p* of the LORD God amongst the ... Gen 3:8 6440
went out from the *p* of the LORD ... Gen 4:16 6440
in the *p* of all his brethren ... Gen 16:12 6440
in the *p* of the sons of my people ... Gen 23:11 5869
in the *p* of the children of Heth ... Gen 23:18 5869
he died in the *p* of all his ... Gen 25:18 6440
from the *p* of Isaac his father ... Gen 27:30 6440
went out from the *p* of Pharaoh ... Gen 41:46 6440
for they were troubled at his *p* ... Gen 45:3 6440
for why should we die in thy *p* ... Gen 47:15 5048
were driven out from Pharaoh's *p* ... Ex 10:11 6440
My *p* shall go with thee, and I ... Ex 33:14 6440
If thy *p* go not with me, carry us ... Ex 33:15 6440
departed from the *p* of Moses ... Ex 35:20 6440
soul shall be cut off from my *p* ... Lev 22:3 6440
Aaron went from the *p* of the ... Num 20:6 6440
unto him in the *p* of the elders ... Deut 25:9 5869
priests, in the *p* of the people ... Josh 4:11 6440
which he wrote in the *p* of the ... Josh 8:32 6440
David avoided out of his *p* twice ... 1Sa 18:11 6440
David to Saul, and he was in his *p* ... 1Sa 19:7 6440
he slipped away out of Saul's *p* ... 1Sa 19:10 6440
to play the mad man in my *p* ... 1Sa 21:15 5921
I not serve in the *p* of his son ... 2Sa 16:19 6440
I have served in thy father's *p* ... 2Sa 16:19 6440
so will I be in thy *p* ... 2Sa 16:19 6440
went out from the *p* of the king ... 2Sa 24:4 6440
And she came into the king's *p* ... 1Kin 1:28 6440
the *p* of all the congregation of ... 1Kin 8:22 5048
fled from the *p* of king Solomon ... 1Kin 12:2 6440
in the *p* of the people, saying, ... 1Kin 21:13 5048
the *p* of Jehoshaphat the king of ... 2Kin 3:14 6440
he went out from his *p* a leper as ... 2Kin 5:27 6440
cast he them from his *p* as yet ... 2Kin 13:23 6440
he had cast them out from his *p* ... 2Kin 24:20 6440
of them that were in the king's *p* ... 2Kin 25:19 6440
Glory and honour are in his *p* ... 1Chr 16:27 6440
sing out at the *p* of the LORD ... 1Chr 16:33 6440
Aaron in the *p* of David the king ... 1Chr 24:31 6440
the *p* of all the congregation of ... 2Chr 6:12 5048
the earth sought the *p* of Solomon ... 2Chr 9:23 6440
from the *p* of Solomon the king ... 2Chr 10:2 6440
before this house, and in thy *p* ... 2Chr 20:9 6440
the altars of Baalim in his *p* ... 2Chr 34:4 6440
not been beforetime sad in his *p* ... Neh 2:1 6440
in the *p* of Ahasuerus the king ... Est 1:10 6440
Mordecai went out from the *p* of ... Est 8:15 6440
went forth from the *p* of the LORD ... Job 1:12 6440
forth from the *p* of the LORD ... Job 2:7 6440
Therefore am I troubled at his *p* ... Job 23:15 6440
shall fall and perish at thy *p* ... Ps 9:3 6440
in thy *p* is fulness of joy ... Ps 16:11 6440
my sentence come forth from thy *p* ... Ps 17:2 6440
me in the *p* of mine enemies ... Ps 23:5 5048
of thy *p* from the pride of man ... Ps 31:20 6440
Cast me not away from thy *p* ... Ps 51:11 6440
the wicked perish at the *p* of God ... Ps 68:2 6440
also dropped at the *p* of God ... Ps 68:8 6440
itself was moved at the *p* of God ... Ps 68:8 6440
before his *p* with thanksgiving ... Ps 95:2 6440
like wax at the *p* of the LORD ... Ps 97:5 6440
at the *p* of the LORD of the whole ... Ps 97:5 6440
come before his *p* with singing ... Ps 100:2 6440
at the *p* of the Lord ... Ps 114:7 6440
at the *p* of the God of Jacob ... Ps 114:7 6440
now in the *p* of all his people ... Ps 116:14 5048
now in the *p* of all his people ... Ps 116:18 6440
whither shall I flee from thy *p* ... Ps 139:7 6440
the upright shall dwell in thy *p* ... Ps 140:13 6440
Go from the *p* of a foolish man, ... Prov 14:7 5048
surety in the *p* of his friend ... Prov 17:18 6440
thyself in the *p* of the king ... Prov 25:6 6440
p of the prince whom thine eyes ... Prov 25:7 6440
strangers devour it in your *p* ... Is 1:7 5048
of Egypt shall be moved at his *p* ... Is 19:1 6440
and the angel of his *p* saved them ... Is 63:9 6440
might flow down at thy *p*, ... Is 64:1 6440
the nations may tremble at thy *p* ... Is 64:2 6440
mountains flowed down at thy *p* ... Is 64:3 6440
broken down at the *p* of the LORD ... Jer 4:26 6440
will ye not tremble at my *p* ... Jer 5:22 6440
fathers, and cast you out of my *p* ... Jer 23:39 6440
in the *p* of the priests and of all ... Jer 28:1 5869
Hananiah in the *p* of the priests ... Jer 28:5 5869
in the *p* of all the people that ... Jer 28:5 5869
spake in the *p* of all the people ... Jer 28:11 5869
in the *p* of the witnesses that ... Jer 32:12 5869
he had cast them out from his *p* ... Jer 52:3 6440
of the earth, shall shake at my *p* ... Eze 38:20 6440
answered in the *p* of the king ... Dan 2:27 6925
Tarshish from the *p* of the LORD ... Jonah 1:3 6440
Tarshish from the *p* of the LORD ... Jonah 1:3 6440
he fled from the *p* of the LORD ... Jonah 1:10 6440
and the earth is burned at his *p* ... Nah 1:5 6440
peace at the *p* of the Lord GOD ... Zeph 1:7 6440
that stand in the *p* of God ... Lk 1:19 *1799*
We have eaten and drunk in thy *p* ... Lk 13:26 *1799*
p of them that sit at meat with ... Lk 14:10 *1799*
there is joy in the *p* of the ... Lk 15:10 *1799*
Jesus in the *p* of his disciples ... Jn 20:30 *1799*
and denied him in the *p* of Pilate ... Acts 3:13 *4383*
soundness in the *p* of you all ... Acts 3:16 *561*
shall come from the *p* of the Lord ... Acts 3:19 *4383*
from the *p* of the council ... Acts 5:41 *4383*
thanks to God in *p* of them all ... Acts 27:35 *1799*
no flesh should glory in his *p* ... 1Cor 1:29 *1799*
who in *p* am base among you, but ... 2Cor 10:1 *4383*
but his bodily *p* is weak, and his ... 2Cor 10:10 *3952*
obeyed, not as in my *p* only ... Phil 2:12 *3952*
from you for a short time in *p* ... 1Th 2:17 *4383*
Are not even ye in the *p* of our ... 1Th 2:19 *1715*
from the *p* of the Lord, and from ... 2Th 1:9 *4383*
to appear in the *p* of God for us ... Heb 9:24 *4383*
you faultless before the *p* of his ... Jude 24 *2714*
brimstone in the *p* of the holy ... Rev 14:10 *1799*
angels, and in the *p* of the Lamb ... Rev 14:10 *1799*

PRESENT {106}
his hand a *p* for Esau his brother ... Gen 32:13 4503
it is a *p* sent unto my lord Esau ... Gen 32:18 4503
with the *p* that goeth before me ... Gen 32:20 4503
So went the *p* over before him ... Gen 32:21 4503
then receive my *p* at my hand ... Gen 33:10 4503
and carry down the man a *p* ... Gen 43:11 4503
And the men took that *p*, and they ... Gen 43:15 4503
they made ready the *p* against ... Gen 43:25 4503
they brought him the *p* which was ... Gen 43:26 4503
p thyself there to me in the top ... Ex 34:2 5324
p the man that is to be made ... Lev 14:11 5975
p them before the LORD at the ... Lev 16:7 5975
then he shall *p* himself before ... Lev 27:8 5975
then he shall *p* the beast before ... Lev 27:11 5975
p them before Aaron the priest, ... Num 3:6 5975
p yourselves in the tabernacle of ... Deut 31:14 3320
a *p* unto Eglon the king of Moab ... Judg 3:15 4503

P

he brought the *p* unto Eglon king ... Judg 3:17 4503
he had made an end to offer the *p* ... Judg 3:18 4503
away the people that bare the *p* ... Judg 3:18 4503
unto thee, and bring forth my *p* ... Judg 6:18 4503
there is not a *p* to bring to the ... 1Sa 9:7 8670
Now therefore *p* yourselves before ... 1Sa 10:19 3320
the people that were *p* with him ... 1Sa 13:15 4672
the people that were *p* with them ... 1Sa 13:16 4672
in mine hand, or what there is *p* ... 1Sa 21:3 4672
Behold a *p* for you of the spoil ... 1Sa 30:26 1293
three days, and be thou here *p* ... 2Sa 20:4 5975
given it for a *p* unto his ... 1Kin 9:16 7964
And they brought every man his *p* ... 1Kin 10:25 4503
have sent unto thee a *p* of silver ... 1Kin 15:19 7810
were numbered, and were all *p* ... 1Kin 20:27 3557
Take a *p* in thine hand, and go, ... 2Kin 8:8 4503
took a *p* with him, even of every ... 2Kin 8:9 4503
sent it for a *p* to the king of ... 2Kin 16:8 7810
brought no *p* to the king of ... 2Kin 17:4 4503
Make an agreement with me by a *p* ... 2Kin 18:31 1293
sent letters and a *p* unto Hezekiah ... 2Kin 20:12 4503
joy thy people, which are *p* here ... 1Chr 29:17 4672
that were *p* were sanctified ... 2Chr 5:11 4672
And they brought every man his *p* ... 2Chr 9:24 4503
all that were *p* with him bowed ... 2Chr 29:29 4672
children of Israel that were *p* at ... 2Chr 30:21 4672
all Israel that were *p* went out ... 2Chr 31:1 4672
all that were *p* in Jerusalem ... 2Chr 34:32 4672
that were *p* in Israel to serve ... 2Chr 34:33 4672
offerings, for all that were *p* ... 2Chr 35:7 4672
children of Israel that were *p* ... 2Chr 35:17 4672
all Judah and Israel that were *p* ... 2Chr 35:18 4672
his lords, and all Israel there *p* ... Ezr 8:25 4672
that were *p* in Shushan the palace ... Est 1:5 4672
the Jews that are *p* in Shushan ... Est 4:16 4672
to *p* themselves before the LORD ... Job 1:6 3320
to *p* themselves before the LORD ... Job 2:1 3320
them to *p* himself before the LORD ... Job 2:1 3320
a very *p* help in trouble ... Ps 46:1 4672
In that time shall the *p* be ... Is 18:7 7862
Make an agreement with me by a *p* ... Is 36:16 1293
sent letters and a *p* to Hezekiah ... Is 39:1 4503
It may be they will *p* their ... Jer 36:7 5307
unto whom ye sent me to *p* your ... Jer 42:9 5307
thee for a *p* horns of ivory ... Eze 27:15 814
for we do not *p* our supplications ... Dan 9:18 5307
Assyria for a *p* to king Jareb ... Hos 10:6 4503
Jerusalem, to *p* him to the Lord ... Lk 2:22 *3936*
of the Lord was *p* to heal them ... Lk 5:17
There were *p* at that season some ... Lk 13:1 *3918*
manifold more in this *p* time ... Lk 18:30 *3918*
unto you, being yet *p* with you ... Jn 14:25 *3306*
are we all here *p* before God ... Acts 10:33 *3918*
and all the elders were *p* ... Acts 21:18 *3854*
all men which are here *p* with us ... Acts 25:24 *4840*
every one, because of the *p* rain ... Acts 28:2 *2186*
for to will is *p* with me ... Rom 7:18 *3873*
would do good, evil is *p* with me ... Rom 7:21 *3873*
this *p* time are not worthy to be ... Rom 8:18 *3568*
nor powers, nor things *p* ... Rom 8:38 *1764*
Even so then at this *p* time also ... Rom 11:5 *3568*
that ye *p* your bodies a living ... Rom 12:1 *3936*
or life, or death, or things *p* ... 1Cor 3:22 *1764*
Even unto this *p* hour we both ... 1Cor 4:11 *737*
but *p* in spirit, have judged ... 1Cor 5:3 *3918*
already, as though I were *p* ... 1Cor 5:3 *3918*
this is good for the *p* distress ... 1Cor 7:26 *1764*
greater part remain unto this *p* ... 1Cor 15:6 *737*
by Jesus, and shall *p* us with you ... 2Cor 4:14 *3936*
body, and to be *p* with the Lord ... 2Cor 5:8 *1736*
whether *p* or absent, we may be ... 2Cor 5:9 *1736*
when I am *p* with that confidence ... 2Cor 10:2 *3918*
we be also in deed when we are *p* ... 2Cor 10:11 *3918*
that I may *p* you as a chaste ... 2Cor 11:2 *3936*
And when I was *p* with you, and ... 2Cor 11:9 *3918*
and foretell you, as if I were *p* ... 2Cor 13:2 *3918*
lest being *p* I should use ... 2Cor 13:10 *3918*
deliver us from this *p* evil world ... Gal 1:4 *1764*
and not only when I am *p* with you ... Gal 4:18 *3918*
I desire to be *p* with you now ... Gal 4:20 *3918*
That he might *p* it to himself a ... Eph 5:27 *3936*
to *p* you holy and unblameable and ... Col 1:22 *3936*
that we may *p* every man perfect ... Col 1:28 *3936*
me, having loved this *p* world ... 2Ti 4:10 *3568*
and godly, in this *p* world ... Titus 2:12 *3568*
was a figure for the time then *p* ... Heb 9:9 *1764*
for the *p* seemeth to be joyous ... Heb 12:11 *3918*
and be established in the *p* truth ... 2Pet 1:12 *3918*
to *p* you faultless before the ... Jude 24 *2476*

PRESENTED {18}
to Goshen, and *p* himself unto him ... Gen 46:29 7200
five men, and *p* them unto Pharaoh ... Gen 47:2 3322
when it is *p* unto the priest, he ... Lev 2:8 7126
in the day when he *p* them to ... Lev 7:35 7126
Aaron's sons *p* unto him the blood ... Lev 9:12 4672
they *p* the burnt offering unto ... Lev 9:13 4672
Aaron's sons *p* unto him the blood ... Lev 9:18 4672
shall be *p* alive before the LORD, ... Lev 16:10 5975
p themselves in the tabernacle of ... Deut 31:14 3320
they *p* themselves before God ... Josh 24:1 3320
unto him under the oak, and *p* it ... Judg 6:19 5066
p themselves in the assembly of ... Judg 20:2 3320
evening, and *p* himself forty days ... 1Sa 17:16 3320
I *p* my supplication before the ... Jer 38:26 5307
there they *p* the provocation of ... Eze 20:28 5414
treasures, they *p* unto him gifts ... Mt 2:11 *4374*
the saints and widows, *p* her alive ... Acts 9:41 *3936*
governor, *p* Paul also before him ... Acts 23:33 *3936*

PRESENTING {1}
p my supplication before the LORD ... Dan 9:20 5307

PRESENTLY {5}
them not fail to burn the fat *p* ... 1Sa 2:16 3117
A fool's wrath is *p* known ... Prov 12:16 3117
p the fig tree withered away ... Mt 21:19 *3916*
he shall *p* give me more than ... Mt 26:53 *3936*
Him therefore I hope to send *p* ... Phil 2:23 *1824*

PRESENTS {10}
despised him, and brought him no *p* ... 1Sa 10:27 4503
they brought *p*, and served Solomon ... 1Kin 4:21 4503
became his servant, and gave him *p* ... 2Kin 17:3 4503
Judah brought to Jehoshaphat *p* ... 2Chr 17:5 4503
Philistines brought Jehoshaphat *p* ... 2Chr 17:11 4503
p to Hezekiah king of Judah ... 2Chr 32:23 4030
shall kings bring *p* unto thee ... Ps 68:29 7862
and of the isles shall bring *p* ... Ps 72:10 4503
bring *p* unto him that ought to be ... Ps 76:11 7862
thou give *p* to Moresheth-gath ... Mic 1:14 7964

PRESERVE {30}
that we may *p* seed of our father ... Gen 19:32 2421
that we may *p* seed of our father ... Gen 19:34 2421
did send me before you to *p* life ... Gen 45:5 4241
God sent me before you to *p* you a ... Gen 45:7 7760
always, that he might *p* us alive ... Deut 6:24 2421
thou shalt *p* them from this ... Ps 12:7 5341
P me, O God ... Ps 16:1 8104
Let integrity and uprightness *p* me ... Ps 25:21 5341
thou shalt *p* me from trouble ... Ps 32:7 5341
and thy truth continually *p* me ... Ps 40:11 5341
The LORD will *p* him, and keep him ... Ps 41:2 8104
mercy and truth, which may *p* him ... Ps 61:7 5341
p my life from fear of the enemy ... Ps 64:1 5341
p thou those that are appointed ... Ps 79:11 3498
P my soul ... Ps 86:2 8104
The LORD shall *p* thee from all ... Ps 121:7 8104
he shall *p* thy soul ... Ps 121:7 8104
The LORD shall *p* thy going out ... Ps 121:8 8104
p me from the violent man ... Ps 140:1 5341
p me from the violent man ... Ps 140:4 5341
Discretion shall *p* thee, ... Prov 2:11 8104
her not, and she shall *p* thee ... Prov 4:6 8104
the lips of the wise shall *p* them ... Prov 14:3 8104
Mercy and truth *p* the king ... Prov 20:28 5341
The eyes of the LORD *p* knowledge ... Prov 22:12 5341
and passing over he will *p* it ... Is 31:5 4422
and I will *p* thee, and give thee ... Is 49:8 5341
children, I will *p* them alive ... Jer 49:11 2421
shall lose his life shall *p* it ... Lk 17:33 *2225*
will *p* me unto his heavenly ... 2Ti 4:18 *4982*

PRESERVED {16}
God face to face, and my life is *p* ... Gen 32:30 5337
p us in all the way wherein we ... Josh 24:17 8104
LORD hath given us, who hath *p* us ... 1Sa 30:23 8104
the LORD *p* David whithersoever he ... 2Sa 8:6 3467
the LORD *p* David whithersoever he ... 2Sa 8:14 3467
Thus the LORD *p* David ... 1Chr 18:6 3467
Thus the LORD *p* David ... 1Chr 18:13 3467
thy visitation hath *p* my spirit ... Job 10:12 8104
as in the days when God *p* me ... Job 29:2 8104
they are *p* for ever ... Ps 37:28 8104
and to restore the *p* of Israel ... Is 49:6 5336
Egypt, and by a prophet was he *p* ... Hos 12:13 8104
into new bottles, and both are *p* ... Mt 9:17 *4933*
and both are *p* ... Lk 5:38 *4933*
body be *p* blameless unto the ... 1Th 5:23 *5083*
p in Jesus Christ, and called ... Jude 1 *5083*

PRESERVER {1}
I do unto thee, O thou *p* of men ... Job 7:20 5314

PRESERVEST {2}
is therein, and thou *p* them all ... Neh 9:6 2421
O LORD, thou *p* man and beast ... Ps 36:6 3467

PRESERVETH {8}
He *p* not the life of the wicked ... Job 36:6 2421
for the LORD *p* the faithful ... Ps 31:23 5341
he *p* the souls of his saints ... Ps 97:10 8104
The LORD *p* the simple ... Ps 116:6 8104
The LORD *p* all them that love him ... Ps 145:20 8104
The LORD *p* the strangers ... Ps 146:9 8104
and *p* the way of his saints ... Prov 2:8 8104
that keepeth his way *p* his soul ... Prov 16:17 8104

PRESIDENTS {5}
And over these three *p* ... Dan 6:2 5632
Daniel was preferred above the *p* ... Dan 6:3 5632
Then the *p* and princes sought to ... Dan 6:4 5632
Then these *p* and princes assembled ... Dan 6:6 5632
All the *p* of the kingdom, the ... Dan 6:7 5632

PRESS {9}
for the *p* is full, the fats ... Joel 3:13 1660
out fifty vessels out of the *p* ... Hag 2:16 6333
not come nigh unto him for the *p* ... Mk 2:4 *3793*
of Jesus, came in the *p* behind ... Mk 5:27 *3793*
of him, turned him about in the *p* ... Mk 5:30 *3793*
could not come at him for the *p* ... Lk 8:19 *3793*
p thee, and sayest thou, Who ... Lk 8:45 *598*
and could not for the *p*, because ... Lk 19:3 *3793*
I *p* toward the mark for the prize ... Phil 3:14 *1377*

PRESSED {15}
And he *p* upon them greatly ... Gen 19:3 6484
they *p* sore upon the man, even ... Gen 19:9 6484
p them into Pharaoh's cup, and I ... Gen 40:11 7818
when she *p* him daily with her ... Judg 16:16 6693
And he *p* him ... 2Sa 13:25 6555
But Absalom *p* him, that he let ... 2Sa 13:27 6555
p on by the king's commandment ... Est 8:14 1765
there were their breasts *p* ... Eze 23:3 4600
I am *p* under you, as a cart is ... Amos 2:13 5781
as a cart is *p* that is full of ... Amos 2:13 5781
insomuch that they *p* upon him for ... Mk 3:10 *1968*
as the people *p* upon him to hear ... Lk 5:1 *1945*
p down, and shaken together, and ... Lk 6:38 *4085*
Paul was *p* in the spirit, and ... Acts 18:5 *4912*
that we were *p* out of measure, ... 2Cor 1:8 *916*

PRESSES {2}
thy *p* shall burst out with new ... Prov 3:10 3342
tread out no wine in their *p* ... Is 16:10 3342

PRESSETH {2}
fast in me, and thy hand *p* me sore ... Ps 38:2 5181
preached, and every man *p* into it ... Lk 16:16 *971*

PRESSFAT {1}
when one came to the *p* for to ... Hag 2:16 3342

PRESUME {2}
which shall *p* to speak a word in ... Deut 18:20 2102
that durst *p* in his heart to do ... Est 7:5 4390

PRESUMED {1}
But they *p* to go up unto the hill ... Num 14:44 6075

PRESUMPTUOUS {2}
back thy servant also from *p* sins ... Ps 19:13 2086
P are they, selfwilled, they are ... 2Pet 2:10 *5113*

PRESUMPTUOUSLY {6}
But if a man come *p* upon his ... Ex 21:14 2102
But the soul that doeth ought *p* ... Num 15:30 3027
LORD, and went *p* up into the hill ... Deut 1:43 2102
And the man that will do *p* ... Deut 17:12 2087
hear, and fear, and do no more *p* ... Deut 17:13 2102
but the prophet hath spoken it *p* ... Deut 18:22 2087

PRETENCE {3}
and for a *p* make long prayer ... Mt 23:14 *4392*
for a *p* make long prayers ... Mk 12:40 *4392*
every way, whether in *p*, or in ... Phil 1:18 *4392*

PREVAIL {29}
cubits upward did the waters *p* ... Gen 7:20 1396
peradventure I shall *p*, that we ... Num 22:6 3201
what means we may *p* against him ... Judg 16:5 3201
for by strength shall no man *p* ... 1Sa 2:9 1396
but if I *p* against him, and kill ... 1Sa 17:9 3201
things, and also shalt still *p* ... 1Sa 26:25 3201
shalt persuade him, and *p* also ... 1Kin 22:22 3201
let not man *p* against thee ... 2Chr 14:11 6113
entice him, and thou shalt also *p* ... 2Chr 18:21 3201
thou shalt not *p* against him ... Est 6:13 3201
they shall *p* against him, as a ... Job 15:24 8630
and the robber shall *p* against him ... Job 18:9 2388
let not man *p* ... Ps 9:19 5810
said, With our tongue will we *p* ... Ps 12:4 1396
Iniquities *p* against me ... Ps 65:3 1396
if one *p* against him, two shall ... Eccl 4:12 8630
it, but could not *p* against it ... Is 7:1 3898
but he shall not *p* ... Is 16:12 3201
he shall *p* against his enemies ... Is 42:13 1396
to profit, if so be thou mayest *p* ... Is 47:12 6206
but they shall not *p* against thee ... Jer 1:19 3201
themselves, yet can they not *p* ... Jer 5:22 3201
but they shall not *p* against thee ... Jer 15:20 3201
we shall *p* against him, and we ... Jer 20:10 3201
stumble, and they shall not *p* ... Jer 20:11 3201
deal against them, and shall *p* ... Dan 11:7 2388
of hell shall not *p* against it ... Mt 16:18 *2729*
saw that he could *p* nothing ... Mt 27:24 *5623*
Perceive ye how ye *p* nothing ... Jn 12:19 *5623*

PREVAILED {37}
And the waters *p*, and were ... Gen 7:18 1396
the waters *p* exceedingly upon the ... Gen 7:19 1396
the waters *p* upon the earth an ... Gen 7:24 1396
with my sister, and I have *p* ... Gen 30:8 3201
he saw that he *p* not against him ... Gen 32:25 3201
with God and with men, and hast *p* ... Gen 32:28 3201
because the famine *p* over them ... Gen 47:20 2388
have *p* above the blessings of my ... Gen 49:26 1396
held up his hand, that Israel *p* ... Ex 17:11 1396
he let down his hand, Amalek *p* ... Ex 17:11 1396
the hand of the house of Joseph *p* ... Judg 1:35 3513
and his hand *p* against ... Judg 3:10 5810
p against Jabin the king of ... Judg 4:24 7186
hand of Midian *p* against Israel ... Judg 6:2 5810
So David *p* over the Philistine ... 1Sa 17:50 2388
Surely the men *p* against us ... 2Sa 11:23 1396
the king's word *p* against Joab ... 2Sa 24:4 2388
Omri *p* against the people that ... 1Kin 16:22 2388
month the famine *p* in the city ... 2Kin 25:3 2388
For Judah *p* above his brethren, ... 1Chr 5:2 1396
the king's word *p* against Joab ... 1Chr 21:4 2388
to Hamath-zobah, and *p* against it ... 2Chr 8:3 2388
time, and the children of Judah *p* ... 2Chr 13:18 553
the Ammonites, and *p* against them ... 2Chr 27:5 2388
enemy say, I have *p* against him ... Ps 13:4 3201
yet they have not *p* against me ... Ps 129:2 3201
art stronger than I, and hast *p* ... Jer 20:7 3201
thee on, and have *p* against thee ... Jer 38:22 3201
are desolate, because the enemy *p* ... Lam 1:16 1396
the saints, and *p* against them ... Dan 7:21 3202
he had power over the angel, and *p* ... Hos 12:4 3201
deceived thee, and *p* against thee ... Obad 7 3201
of them and of the chief priests *p* ... Lk 23:23 *2729*
p against them, so that they fled ... Acts 19:16 *2480*
grew the word of God and *p* ... Acts 19:20 *2480*

hath *p* to open the book, and to ... Rev 5:5 *3528*
And *p* not ... Rev 12:8 *2480*

PREVAILEST {1}
Thou *p* for ever against him, and ... Job 14:20 8630

PREVAILETH {1}
my bones, and it *p* against them ... Lam 1:13 7287

PREVENT {7}
Why did the knees *p* me ... Job 3:12 6923
The God of my mercy shall *p* me ... Ps 59:10 6923
thy tender mercies speedily *p* us ... Ps 79:8 6923
morning shall my prayer *p* thee ... Ps 88:13 6923
Mine eyes *p* the night watches, ... Ps 119:148 6923
evil shall not overtake nor *p* us ... Amos 9:10 6923
shall not *p* them which are asleep ... 1Th 4:15 *5348*

PREVENTED {9}
the snares of death *p* me ... 2Sa 22:6 6923
They *p* me in the day of my ... 2Sa 22:19 6923
the days of affliction *p* me ... Job 30:27 6923
Who hath *p* me, that I should ... Job 41:11 6923
the snares of death *p* me ... Ps 18:5 6923
They *p* me in the day of my ... Ps 18:18 6923
I *p* the dawning of the morning, ... Ps 119:147 6923
they *p* with their bread him that ... Is 21:14 6923
come into the house, Jesus *p* him ... Mt 17:25 *4399*

PREVENTEST {1}
For thou *p* him with the blessings ... Ps 21:3 6923

PREY {73}
from the *p*, my son, thou art gone ... Gen 49:9 2964
the morning he shall devour the *p* ... Gen 49:27 5706
and our children should be a *p* ... Num 14:3 957
ones, which ye said should be a *p* ... Num 14:31 957
lie down until he eat of the *p* ... Num 23:24 2964
took all the spoil, and all the *p* ... Num 31:11 4455
brought the captives, and the *p* ... Num 31:12 4455
the sum of the *p* that was taken ... Num 31:26 4455
divide the *p* into two parts ... Num 31:27 4455
being the rest of the *p* which the ... Num 31:32 957
ones, which ye said should be a *p* ... Deut 1:39 957
we took for a *p* unto ourselves ... Deut 2:35 962
we took for a *p* to ourselves ... Deut 3:7 962
ye take for a *p* unto yourselves ... Josh 8:2 962
took for a *p* unto themselves ... Josh 8:27 962
took for a *p* unto themselves ... Josh 11:14 962
have they not divided the *p* ... Judg 5:30 7998
to Sisera a *p* of divers colours, ... Judg 5:30 7998
a *p* of divers colours of ... Judg 5:30 7998
every man the earrings of his *p* ... Judg 8:24 7998
every man the earrings of his *p* ... Judg 8:25 7998
and they shall become a *p* and a ... 2Kin 21:14 957
give them for a *p* in the land of ... Neh 4:4 961
to take the spoil of them for a *p* ... Est 3:13 962
to take the spoil of them for a *p* ... Est 8:11 962
but on the *p* they laid not their ... Est 9:15 961
laid not their hands on the *p* ... Est 9:16 961
old lion perisheth for lack of *p* ... Job 4:11 2964
the eagle that hasteth to the *p* ... Job 9:26 400
rising betimes for a *p* ... Job 24:5 2964
Wilt thou hunt the *p* for the lion ... Job 38:39 2964
From thence she seeketh the *p* ... Job 39:29 400
as a lion that is greedy of his *p* ... Ps 17:12 2963
excellent than the mountains of *p* ... Ps 76:4 2964
young lions roar after their *p* ... Ps 104:21 2964
given us as a *p* to their teeth ... Ps 124:6 2964
She also lieth in wait as for a *p* ... Prov 23:28 2863
shall roar, and lay hold of the *p* ... Is 5:29 2964
that widows may be their *p* ... Is 10:2 7998
take the spoil, and to take the *p* ... Is 10:6 957
the young lion roaring on his *p* ... Is 31:4 2964
then is the *p* of a great spoil ... Is 33:23 5706
the lame take the *p* ... Is 33:23 957
they are for a *p*, and none ... Is 42:22 957
Shall the *p* be taken from the ... Is 49:24 4455
the *p* of the terrible shall be ... Is 49:25 4455
from evil maketh himself a *p* ... Is 59:15 7997
life shall be unto him for a *p* ... Jer 21:9 7998
all that *p* upon thee will I give ... Jer 30:16 962
upon thee will I give for a *p* ... Jer 30:16 7998
he shall have his life for a *p* ... Jer 38:2 7998
life shall be for a *p* unto thee ... Jer 39:18 7998
a *p* in all places whither thou ... Jer 45:5 7998
hands of the strangers for a *p* ... Eze 7:21 957
and it learned to catch the *p* ... Eze 19:3 2964
lion, and learned to catch the *p* ... Eze 19:6 2964
a roaring lion ravening the *p* ... Eze 22:25 2964
are like wolves ravening the *p* ... Eze 22:27 2964
make a *p* of thy merchandise ... Eze 26:12 962
and take her spoil, and take her *p* ... Eze 29:19 957
because my flock became a *p* ... Eze 34:8 957
and they shall no more be a *p* ... Eze 34:22 957
no more be a *p* to the heathen ... Eze 34:28 957
are forsaken, which became a *p* ... Eze 36:4 957
minds, to cast it out for a *p* ... Eze 36:5 957
To take a spoil, and to take a *p* ... Eze 38:12 957
gathered thy company to take a *p* ... Eze 38:13 957
he shall scatter among them the *p* ... Dan 11:24 961
in the forest, when he hath no *p* ... Amos 3:4 2964
and filled his holes with *p* ... Nah 2:12 2964
will cut off thy *p* from the earth ... Nah 2:13 2964
the *p* departeth not ... Nah 3:1 2964
the day that I rise up to the *p* ... Zeph 3:8 5706

PRICE {33}
thou shalt increase the *p* thereof ... Lev 25:16 4736
thou shalt diminish the *p* of it ... Lev 25:16 4736
the *p* of his sale shall be ... Lev 25:50 3701
p of his redemption out of the ... Lev 25:51
him again the *p* of his redemption ... Lev 25:52
or the *p* of a dog, into the house ... Deut 23:18 4242
will surely buy it of thee at a *p* ... 2Sa 24:24 4242
received the linen yarn at a *p* ... 1Kin 10:28 4242
shalt grant it me for the full *p* ... 1Chr 21:22 3701
will verily buy it for the full *p* ... 1Chr 21:24 3701
received the linen yarn at a *p* ... 2Chr 1:16 4242
Man knoweth not the *p* thereof ... Job 28:13 6187
be weighed for the *p* thereof ... Job 28:15 4242
for the *p* of wisdom is above ... Job 28:18 4901
increase thy wealth by their *p* ... Ps 44:12 4242
Wherefore is there a *p* in the ... Prov 17:16 4242
the goats are the *p* of the field ... Prov 27:26 4242
for her *p* is far above rubies ... Prov 31:10 4377
not for *p* nor reward, saith the ... Is 45:13 4242
milk without money and without *p* ... Is 55:1 4242
I give to the spoil without *p* ... Jer 15:13 4242
If ye think good, give me my *p* ... Zec 11:12 7939
So they weighed for my *p* thirty ... Zec 11:12 7939
a goodly *p* that I was prised at ... Zec 11:13 3365
he had found one pearl of great *p* ... Mt 13:46 *4186*
because it is the *p* of blood ... Mt 27:6 *5092*
the *p* of him that was valued, ... Mt 27:9 *5092*
And kept back part of the *p* ... Acts 5:2 *5092*
back part of the *p* of the land ... Acts 5:3 *5092*
and they counted the *p* of them ... Acts 19:19 *5092*
For ye are bought with a *p* ... 1Cor 6:20 *5092*
Ye are bought with a *p* ... 1Cor 7:23 *5092*
is in the sight of God of great *p* ... 1Pet 3:4 *4185*

PRICES {1}
brought the *p* of the things that ... Acts 4:34 *5092*

PRICKED {2}
grieved, and I was *p* in my reins ... Ps 73:21 8150
they were *p* in their heart, and ... Acts 2:37 *2669*

PRICKING {1}
there shall be no more a *p* brier ... Eze 28:24 3992

PRICKS {3}
of them shall be *p* in your eyes ... Num 33:55 7899
for thee to kick against the *p* ... Acts 9:5 *2759*
for thee to kick against the *p* ... Acts 26:14 *2759*

PRIDE {49}
I will break the *p* of your power ... Lev 26:19 1347
I know thy *p*, and the naughtiness ... 1Sa 17:28 2087
himself for the *p* of his heart ... 2Chr 32:26 1363
his purpose, and hide *p* from man ... Job 33:17 1466
because of the *p* of evil men ... Job 35:12 1347
His scales are his *p*, shut up ... Job 41:15 1346
a king over all the children of *p* ... Job 41:34 7830
The wicked in his *p* doth ... Ps 10:2 1346
through the *p* of his countenance, ... Ps 10:4 1363
of thy presence from the *p* of man ... Ps 31:20 7407
not the foot of *p* come against me ... Ps 36:11 1346
let them even be taken in their *p* ... Ps 59:12 1347
Therefore *p* compasseth them about ... Ps 73:6 1346
p, and arrogancy, and the evil way, ... Prov 8:13 1344
When *p* cometh, then cometh shame ... Prov 11:2 2087
Only by *p* cometh contention ... Prov 13:10 2087
of the foolish is a rod of *p* ... Prov 14:3 1346
P goeth before destruction, and an ... Prov 16:18 1347
A man's *p* shall bring him low ... Prov 29:23 1346
of Samaria, that say in the *p* ... Is 9:9 1346
We have heard of the *p* of Moab ... Is 16:6 1347
even of his haughtiness, and his *p* ... Is 16:6 1347
it, to stain the *p* of all glory ... Is 23:9 1347
he shall bring down their *p* ... Is 25:11 1346
Woe to the crown of *p*, to the ... Is 28:1 1348
The crown of *p*, the drunkards of ... Is 28:3 1348
manner will I mar the *p* of Judah ... Jer 13:9 1347
and the great *p* of Jerusalem ... Jer 13:9 1347
weep in secret places for your *p* ... Jer 13:17 1466
We have heard the *p* of Moab ... Jer 48:29 1347
and his arrogancy, and his *p* ... Jer 48:29 1347
the *p* of thine heart, O thou that ... Jer 49:16 2087
rod hath blossomed, *p* hath budded ... Eze 7:10 2087
iniquity of thy sister Sodom, *p* ... Eze 16:49 1347
by thy mouth in the day of thy *p* ... Eze 16:56 1347
the *p* of her power shall come ... Eze 30:6 1347
those that walk in *p* he is able ... Dan 4:37 1466
up, and his mind hardened in *p* ... Dan 5:20 2103
the *p* of Israel doth testify to ... Hos 5:5 1347
the *p* of Israel testifieth to his ... Hos 7:10 1347
The *p* of thine heart hath ... Obad 3 2087
This shall they have for their *p* ... Zeph 2:10 1347
thee them that rejoice in thy *p* ... Zeph 3:11 1346
cut off the *p* of the Philistines ... Zec 9:6 1347
the *p* of Assyria shall be brought ... Zec 10:11 1347
for the *p* of Jordan is spoiled ... Zec 11:3 1347
an evil eye, blasphemy, *p* ... Mk 7:22 *5243*
lest being lifted up with *p* he ... 1Ti 3:6 *5187*
the *p* of life, is not of the ... 1Jn 2:16 *212*

PRIEST {498}
he was the *p* of the most high God ... Gen 14:18 3548
daughter of Poti-pherah *p* of On ... Gen 41:45 3548
Poti-pherah *p* of On bare unto him ... Gen 41:50 3548
Poti-pherah *p* of On bare unto him ... Gen 46:20 3548
Now the *p* of Midian had seven ... Ex 2:16 3548
father in law, the *p* of Midian ... Ex 3:1 3548
the *p* of Midian, Moses' father in ... Ex 18:1 3548
that son that is *p* in his stead ... Ex 29:30 3548
the holy garments for Aaron the *p* ... Ex 31:10 3548
the holy garments for Aaron the *p* ... Ex 35:19 3548
of Ithamar, son to Aaron the *p* ... Ex 38:21 3548
the holy garments for Aaron the *p* ... Ex 39:41 3548
the sons of Aaron the *p* shall put ... Lev 1:7 3548
the *p* shall burn all on the altar ... Lev 1:9 3548
the *p* shall lay them in order on ... Lev 1:12 3548
the *p* shall bring it all, and burn ... Lev 1:13 3548
the *p* shall bring it unto the ... Lev 1:15 3548
the *p* shall burn it upon the ... Lev 1:17 3548
the *p* shall burn the memorial of ... Lev 2:2 3548
when it is presented unto the *p* ... Lev 2:8 3548
the *p* shall take from the meat ... Lev 2:9 3548
the *p* shall burn the memorial of ... Lev 2:16 3548
the *p* shall burn it upon the ... Lev 3:11 3548
the *p* shall burn them upon the ... Lev 3:16 3548
If the *p* that is anointed do sin ... Lev 4:3 3548
the *p* that is anointed shall take ... Lev 4:5 3548
the *p* shall dip his finger in the ... Lev 4:6 3548
the *p* shall put some of the blood ... Lev 4:7 3548
the *p* shall burn them upon the ... Lev 4:10 3548
the *p* that is anointed shall ... Lev 4:16 3548
the *p* shall dip his finger in ... Lev 4:17 3548
the *p* shall make an atonement for ... Lev 4:20 3548
the *p* shall take of the blood of ... Lev 4:25 3548
the *p* shall make an atonement for ... Lev 4:26 3548
the *p* shall take of the blood ... Lev 4:30 3548
the *p* shall burn it upon the ... Lev 4:31 3548
the *p* shall make an atonement for ... Lev 4:31 3548
the *p* shall take of the blood of ... Lev 4:34 3548
the *p* shall burn them upon the ... Lev 4:35 3548
the *p* shall make an atonement for ... Lev 4:35 3548
the *p* shall make an atonement for ... Lev 5:6 3548
And he shall bring them unto the *p* ... Lev 5:8 3548
the *p* shall make an atonement for ... Lev 5:10 3548
Then shall he bring it to the *p* ... Lev 5:12 3548
the *p* shall take his handful of ... Lev 5:12 3548
the *p* shall make an atonement for ... Lev 5:13 3548
thereto, and give it unto the *p* ... Lev 5:16 3548
the *p* shall make an atonement for ... Lev 5:16 3548
a trespass offering, unto the *p* ... Lev 5:18 3548
the *p* shall make an atonement for ... Lev 5:18 3548
a trespass offering, unto the *p* ... Lev 6:6 3548
the *p* shall make an atonement for ... Lev 6:7 3548
the *p* shall put on his linen ... Lev 6:10 3548
the *p* shall burn wood on it every ... Lev 6:12 3548
the *p* of his sons that is ... Lev 6:22 3548
for the *p* shall be wholly burnt ... Lev 6:23 3548
The *p* that offereth it for sin ... Lev 6:26 3548
the *p* shall burn them upon the ... Lev 7:5 3548
the *p* that maketh atonement ... Lev 7:7 3548
the *p* that offereth any man's ... Lev 7:8 3548
even the *p* shall have to himself ... Lev 7:8 3548
the *p* shall burn the fat upon the ... Lev 7:31 3548
p for an heave offering of the ... Lev 7:32 3548
have given them unto Aaron the *p* ... Lev 7:34 3548
of the congregation, unto the *p* ... Lev 12:6 3548
the *p* shall make an atonement for ... Lev 12:8 3548
shall be brought unto Aaron the *p* ... Lev 13:2 3548
the *p* shall look on the plague in ... Lev 13:3 3548
the *p* shall look on him, and ... Lev 13:3 3548
then the *p* shall shut up him that ... Lev 13:4 3548
the *p* shall look on him the ... Lev 13:5 3548
then the *p* shall shut him up ... Lev 13:5 3548
the *p* shall look on him again the ... Lev 13:6 3548
the *p* shall pronounce him clean ... Lev 13:6 3548
seen of the *p* for his cleansing ... Lev 13:7 3548
he shall be seen of the *p* again ... Lev 13:7 3548
if the *p* see that, behold, the ... Lev 13:8 3548
then the *p* shall pronounce him ... Lev 13:8 3548
he shall be brought unto the *p* ... Lev 13:9 3548
And the *p* shall see him ... Lev 13:10 3548
the *p* shall pronounce him unclean ... Lev 13:11 3548
foot, wheresoever the *p* looketh ... Lev 13:12 3548
Then the *p* shall consider ... Lev 13:13 3548
the *p* shall see the raw flesh, and ... Lev 13:15 3548
white, he shall come unto the *p* ... Lev 13:16 3548
And the *p* shall see him ... Lev 13:17 3548
then the *p* shall pronounce him ... Lev 13:17 3548
reddish, and it be shewed to the *p* ... Lev 13:19 3548
And if, when the *p* seeth it ... Lev 13:20 3548
the *p* shall pronounce him unclean ... Lev 13:20 3548
But if the *p* look on it, and, ... Lev 13:21 3548
then the *p* shall shut him up ... Lev 13:21 3548
then the *p* shall pronounce him ... Lev 13:22 3548
the *p* shall pronounce him clean ... Lev 13:23 3548
Then the *p* shall look upon it ... Lev 13:25 3548
wherefore the *p* shall pronounce ... Lev 13:25 3548
But if the *p* look on it, and, ... Lev 13:26 3548
then the *p* shall shut him up ... Lev 13:26 3548
the *p* shall look upon him the ... Lev 13:27 3548
then the *p* shall pronounce him ... Lev 13:27 3548
the *p* shall pronounce him clean ... Lev 13:28 3548
Then the *p* shall see the plague ... Lev 13:30 3548
then the *p* shall pronounce him ... Lev 13:30 3548
if the *p* look on the plague of ... Lev 13:31 3548
then the *p* shall shut up him that ... Lev 13:31 3548
in the seventh day the *p* shall ... Lev 13:32 3548
the *p* shall shut up him that hath ... Lev 13:33 3548
in the seventh day the *p* shall ... Lev 13:34 3548
then the *p* shall pronounce him ... Lev 13:34 3548
Then the *p* shall look on him ... Lev 13:36 3548
the *p* shall not seek for yellow ... Lev 13:36 3548
the *p* shall pronounce him clean ... Lev 13:37 3548
Then the *p* shall look ... Lev 13:39 3548
Then the *p* shall look upon it ... Lev 13:43 3548
the *p* shall pronounce him utterly ... Lev 13:44 3548
and shall be shewed unto the *p* ... Lev 13:49 3548
the *p* shall look upon the plague, ... Lev 13:50 3548
if the *p* shall look, and, behold, ... Lev 13:53 3548
Then the *p* shall command that ... Lev 13:54 3548
the *p* shall look on the plague, ... Lev 13:55 3548
And if the *p* look, and, behold, the ... Lev 13:56 3548
He shall be brought unto the *p* ... Lev 14:2 3548
the *p* shall go forth out of the ... Lev 14:3 3548

P

the *p* shall look, and, behold, if	Lev 14:3	3548
Then shall the *p* command to take	Lev 14:4	3548
the *p* shall command that one of	Lev 14:5	3548
the *p* that maketh him clean shall	Lev 14:11	3548
the *p* shall take one he lamb, and	Lev 14:12	3548
the *p* shall take some of the	Lev 14:14	3548
the *p* shall put it upon the tip	Lev 14:14	3548
the *p* shall take some of the log	Lev 14:15	3548
the *p* shall dip his right finger	Lev 14:16	3548
p put upon the tip of the right	Lev 14:17	3548
the *p* shall make an atonement for	Lev 14:18	3548
the *p* shall offer the sin	Lev 14:19	3548
the *p* shall offer the burnt	Lev 14:20	3548
the *p* shall make an atonement for	Lev 14:20	3548
day for his cleansing unto the *p*	Lev 14:23	3548
the *p* shall take the lamb of the	Lev 14:24	3548
the *p* shall wave them for a wave	Lev 14:24	3548
the *p* shall take some of the	Lev 14:25	3548
the *p* shall pour of the oil into	Lev 14:26	3548
the *p* shall sprinkle with his	Lev 14:27	3548
the *p* shall put of the oil that	Lev 14:28	3548
the *p* shall make an atonement for	Lev 14:31	3548
house shall come and tell the *p*	Lev 14:35	3548
Then the *p* shall command that	Lev 14:36	3548
before the *p* go into it to see	Lev 14:36	3548
afterward the *p* shall go in to	Lev 14:36	3548
Then the *p* shall go out of the	Lev 14:38	3548
the *p* shall come again the	Lev 14:39	3548
Then the *p* shall command that	Lev 14:40	3548
Then the *p* shall come and look, and	Lev 14:44	3548
if the *p* shall come in, and look	Lev 14:48	3548
then the *p* shall pronounce the	Lev 14:48	3548
and give them unto the *p*	Lev 15:14	3548
the *p* shall offer them, the one	Lev 15:15	3548
the *p* shall make an atonement for	Lev 15:15	3548
pigeons, and bring them unto the *p*	Lev 15:29	3548
the *p* shall offer the one for a	Lev 15:30	3548
the *p* shall make an atonement for	Lev 15:30	3548
the *p* make an atonement for you	Lev 16:30	3548
And the *p*, whom he shall anoint,	Lev 16:32	3548
of the congregation, unto the *p*	Lev 17:5	3548
the *p* shall sprinkle the blood	Lev 17:6	3548
the *p* shall make an atonement for	Lev 19:22	3548
And the daughter of any *p*, if she	Lev 21:9	3548
is the high *p* among his brethren	Lev 21:10	3548
of the seed of Aaron the *p* shall	Lev 21:21	3548
a sojourner of the *p*, or an hired	Lev 22:10	3548
But if the *p* buy any soul with	Lev 22:11	3548
it unto the *p* with the holy thing	Lev 22:14	3548
of your harvest unto the *p*	Lev 23:10	3548
the sabbath the *p* shall wave it	Lev 23:11	3548
the *p* shall wave them with the	Lev 23:20	3548
be holy to the LORD for the *p*	Lev 23:20	3548
present himself before the *p*	Lev 27:8	3548
and the *p* shall value him	Lev 27:8	3548
that vowed shall the *p* value him	Lev 27:8	3548
present the beast before the *p*	Lev 27:11	3548
the *p* shall value it, whether it	Lev 27:12	3548
as thou valuest it, who art the *p*	Lev 27:12	3548
then the *p* shall estimate it,	Lev 27:14	3548
as the *p* shall estimate it, so	Lev 27:14	3548
then the *p* shall reckon unto him	Lev 27:18	3548
Then the *p* shall reckon unto him	Lev 27:23	3548
present them before Aaron the *p*	Num 3:6	3548
Eleazar the son of Aaron the *p*	Num 3:32	3548
the *p* pertaineth the oil for the	Num 4:16	3548
of Ithamar the son of Aaron the *p*	Num 4:28	3548
of Ithamar the son of Aaron the *p*	Num 4:33	3548
unto the LORD, even to the *p*	Num 5:8	3548
which they bring unto the *p*	Num 5:9	3548
whatsoever any man giveth the *p*	Num 5:10	3548
the man bring his wife unto the *p*	Num 5:15	3548
the *p* shall bring her near, and	Num 5:16	3548
the *p* shall take holy water in an	Num 5:17	3548
the tabernacle the *p* shall take	Num 5:17	3548
the *p* shall set the woman before	Num 5:18	3548
the *p* shall have in his hand the	Num 5:18	3548
the *p* shall charge her by an oath	Num 5:19	3548
Then the *p* shall charge the woman	Num 5:21	3548
the *p* shall say unto the woman,	Num 5:21	3548
the *p* shall write these curses in	Num 5:23	3548
Then the *p* shall take the	Num 5:25	3548
the *p* shall take an handful of	Num 5:26	3548
the *p* shall execute upon her all	Num 5:30	3548
or two young pigeons, to the *p*	Num 6:10	3548
the *p* shall offer the one for a	Num 6:11	3548
the *p* shall bring them before the	Num 6:16	3548
the *p* shall offer also his meat	Num 6:17	3548
the *p* shall take the sodden	Num 6:19	3548
the *p* shall wave them for a wave	Num 6:20	3548
this is holy for the *p*, with the	Num 6:20	3548
of Ithamar the son of Aaron the *p*	Num 7:8	3548
the *p* shall make an atonement for	Num 15:25	3548
the *p* shall make an atonement for	Num 15:28	3548
Eleazar the son of Aaron the *p*	Num 16:37	3548
Eleazar the *p* took the brasen	Num 16:39	3548
heave offering to Aaron the *p*	Num 18:28	3548
shall give her unto Eleazar the *p*	Num 19:3	3548
Eleazar the *p* shall take of her	Num 19:4	3548
the *p* shall take cedar wood, and	Num 19:6	3548
Then the *p* shall wash his clothes	Num 19:7	3548
the *p* shall be unclean until the	Num 19:7	3548
Eleazar, the son of Aaron the *p*	Num 25:7	3548
Eleazar, the son of Aaron the *p*	Num 25:11	3548
Eleazar the son of Aaron the *p*	Num 26:1	3548
Eleazar the *p* spake with them in	Num 26:3	3548
by Moses and Eleazar the *p*	Num 26:63	3548
Moses and Aaron the *p* numbered	Num 26:64	3548
Moses, and before Eleazar the *p*	Num 27:2	3548
And set him before Eleazar the *p*	Num 27:19	3548
shall stand before Eleazar the *p*	Num 27:21	3548
and set him before Eleazar the *p*	Num 27:22	3548
Phinehas the son of Eleazar the *p*	Num 31:6	3548
unto Moses, and Eleazar the *p*	Num 31:12	3548
And Moses, and Eleazar the *p*	Num 31:13	3548
Eleazar the *p* said unto the men	Num 31:21	3548
of beast, thou, and Eleazar the *p*	Num 31:26	3548
and give it unto Eleazar the *p*	Num 31:29	3548
Eleazar the *p* did as the LORD	Num 31:31	3548
offering, unto Eleazar the *p*	Num 31:41	3548
Eleazar the *p* took the gold of	Num 31:51	3548
Eleazar the *p* took the gold of	Num 31:54	3548
unto Moses, and to Eleazar the *p*	Num 32:2	3548
Moses commanded Eleazar the *p*	Num 32:28	3548
Aaron the *p* went up into mount	Num 33:38	3548
Eleazar the *p*, and Joshua the son	Num 34:17	3548
it unto the death of the high *p*	Num 35:25	3548
until the death of the high *p*	Num 35:28	3548
p the slayer shall return into	Num 35:28	3548
land, until the death of the *p*	Num 35:32	3548
will not hearken unto the *p* that	Deut 17:12	3548
give unto the *p* the shoulder	Deut 18:3	3548
that the *p* shall approach and	Deut 20:2	3548
thou shalt go unto the *p* that	Deut 26:3	3548
the *p* shall take the basket out	Deut 26:4	3548
of Canaan, which Eleazar the *p*	Josh 14:1	3548
came near before Eleazar the *p*	Josh 17:4	3548
inheritances, which Eleazar the *p*	Josh 19:51	3548
p that shall be in those days	Josh 20:6	3548
of the Levites unto Eleazar the *p*	Josh 21:1	3548
and the children of Aaron the *p*	Josh 21:4	3548
the *p* Hebron with her suburbs	Josh 21:13	3548
Phinehas the son of Eleazar the *p*	Josh 22:13	3548
And when Phinehas the *p*, and the	Josh 22:30	3548
the *p* said unto the children of	Josh 22:31	3548
Phinehas the son of Eleazar the *p*	Josh 22:32	3548
one of his sons, who became his *p*	Judg 17:5	3548
me, and be unto me a father and a *p*	Judg 17:10	3548
and the young man became his *p*	Judg 17:12	3548
seeing I have a Levite to my *p*	Judg 17:13	3548
and hath hired me, and I am his *p*	Judg 18:4	3548
the *p* said unto them, Go in peace	Judg 18:6	3548
the *p* stood in the entering of	Judg 18:17	3548
Then said the *p* unto them	Judg 18:18	3548
us, and be to us a father and a *p*	Judg 18:19	3548
be a *p* unto the house of one man	Judg 18:19	3548
or that thou be a *p* unto a tribe	Judg 18:19	3548
my gods which I made, and the *p*	Judg 18:24	3548
the *p* which he had, and came unto	Judg 18:27	3548
Now Eli the *p* sat upon a seat by	1Sa 1:9	3548
unto the LORD before Eli the *p*	1Sa 2:11	3548
brought up the *p* took for himself	1Sa 2:14	3548
Give flesh to roast for the *p*	1Sa 2:15	3548
the tribes of Israel to be my *p*	1Sa 2:28	3548
I will raise me up a faithful *p*	1Sa 2:35	3548
of Eli, the LORD's *p* in Shiloh	1Sa 14:3	3548
while Saul talked unto the *p*	1Sa 14:19	3548
and Saul said unto the *p*, Withdraw	1Sa 14:19	3548
Then said the *p*, Let us draw near	1Sa 14:36	3548
David to Nob to Ahimelech the *p*	1Sa 21:1	3548
David said unto Ahimelech the *p*	1Sa 21:2	3548
the *p* answered David, and said,	1Sa 21:4	3548
And David answered the *p*, and said	1Sa 21:5	3548
So the *p* gave him hallowed bread	1Sa 21:6	3548
the *p* said, The sword of Goliath	1Sa 21:9	3548
king sent to call Ahimelech the *p*	1Sa 22:11	3548
and he said to Abiathar the *p*	1Sa 23:9	3548
And David said to Abiathar the *p*	1Sa 30:7	3548
king said also unto Zadok the *p*	2Sa 15:27	3548
Zeruiah, and with Abiathar the *p*	1Kin 1:7	3548
But Zadok the *p*, and Benaiah the	1Kin 1:8	3548
of the king, and Abiathar the *p*	1Kin 1:19	3548
of the host, and Abiathar the *p*	1Kin 1:25	3548
me thy servant, and Zadok the *p*	1Kin 1:26	3548
David said, Call me Zadok the *p*	1Kin 1:32	3548
And let Zadok the *p* and Nathan the	1Kin 1:34	3548
So Zadok the *p*, and Nathan the	1Kin 1:38	3548
Zadok the *p* took an horn of oil	1Kin 1:39	3548
the son of Abiathar the *p* came	1Kin 1:42	3548
hath sent with him Zadok the *p*	1Kin 1:44	3548
And Zadok the *p* and Nathan the	1Kin 1:45	3548
for him, and for Abiathar the *p*	1Kin 2:22	3548
unto Abiathar the *p* said the king	1Kin 2:26	3548
from being *p* unto the LORD	1Kin 2:27	3548
Zadok the *p* did the king put in	1Kin 2:35	3548
Azariah the son of Zadok the *p*	1Kin 4:2	3548
that Jehoiada the *p* commanded	2Kin 11:9	3548
and came to Jehoiada the *p*	2Kin 11:9	3548
the *p* give king David's spears	2Kin 11:10	3548
But Jehoiada the *p* commanded the	2Kin 11:15	3548
For the *p* had said, Let her not	2Kin 11:15	3548
slew Mattan the *p* of Baal before	2Kin 11:18	3548
the *p* appointed officers over the	2Kin 11:18	3548
Jehoiada the *p* instructed him	2Kin 12:2	3548
Jehoash called for Jehoiada the *p*	2Kin 12:7	3548
But Jehoiada the *p* took a chest	2Kin 12:9	3548
scribe and the high *p* came up	2Kin 12:10	3548
the *p* the fashion of the altar	2Kin 16:10	3548
Urijah the *p* built an altar	2Kin 16:11	3548
so Urijah the *p* made it against	2Kin 16:11	3548
king Ahaz commanded Urijah the *p*	2Kin 16:15	3548
Thus did Urijah the *p*, according	2Kin 16:16	3548
Go up to Hilkiah the high *p*	2Kin 22:4	3548
Hilkiah the high *p* said unto	2Kin 22:8	3548
Hilkiah the *p* hath delivered me a	2Kin 22:10	3548
the king commanded Hilkiah the *p*	2Kin 22:12	3548
So Hilkiah the *p*, and Ahikam, and	2Kin 22:14	3548
king commanded Hilkiah the high *p*	2Kin 23:4	3548
in the book that Hilkiah the *p*	2Kin 23:24	3548
guard took Seraiah the chief *p*	2Kin 25:18	3548
and Zephaniah the second *p*	2Kin 25:18	3548
And Zadok the *p*, and his brethren	1Chr 16:39	3548
and the princes, and Zadok the *p*	1Chr 24:6	3548
the son of Jehoiada, a chief *p*	1Chr 27:5	3548
chief governor, and Zadok to be *p*	1Chr 29:22	3548
the same may be a *p* of them that	2Chr 13:9	3548
true God, and without a teaching *p*	2Chr 15:3	3548
Amariah the chief *p* is over you	2Chr 19:11	3548
the wife of Jehoiada the *p*	2Chr 22:11	3548
that Jehoiada the *p* had commanded	2Chr 23:8	3548
for Jehoiada the *p* dismissed not	2Chr 23:8	3548
Moreover Jehoiada the *p* delivered	2Chr 23:9	3548
Then Jehoiada the *p* brought out	2Chr 23:14	3548
For the *p* said, Slay her not in	2Chr 23:14	3548
slew Mattan the *p* of Baal before	2Chr 23:17	3548
all the days of Jehoiada the *p*	2Chr 24:2	3548
the son of Jehoiada the *p*	2Chr 24:20	3548
of the sons of Jehoiada the *p*	2Chr 24:25	3548
Azariah the *p* went in after him,	2Chr 26:17	3548
And Azariah the chief *p*, and all	2Chr 26:20	3548
Azariah the chief *p* of the house	2Chr 31:10	3548
they came to Hilkiah the high *p*	2Chr 34:9	3548
Hilkiah the *p* found a book of the	2Chr 34:14	3548
Hilkiah the *p* hath given me a	2Chr 34:18	3548
till there stood up a *p* with Urim	Ezr 2:63	3548
the son of Aaron the chief *p*	Ezr 7:5	3548
Artaxerxes gave unto Ezra the *p*	Ezr 7:11	3548
king of kings, unto Ezra the *p*	Ezr 7:12	3549
river, that whatsoever Ezra the *p*	Ezr 7:21	3548
Meremoth the son of Uriah the *p*	Ezr 8:33	3548
And Ezra the *p* stood up, and said	Ezr 10:10	3548
And Ezra the *p*, with certain chief	Ezr 10:16	3548
Then Eliashib the high *p* rose up	Neh 3:1	3548
the house of Eliashib the high *p*	Neh 3:20	3548
till there stood up a *p* with Urim	Neh 7:65	3548
Ezra the *p* brought the law before	Neh 8:2	3548
Ezra the *p* the scribe, and the	Neh 8:9	3548
the *p* the son of Aaron shall be	Neh 10:38	3548
the governor, and of Ezra the *p*	Neh 12:26	3548
And before this, Eliashib the *p*	Neh 13:4	3548
the treasuries, Shelemiah the *p*	Neh 13:13	3548
the son of Eliashib the high *p*	Neh 13:28	3548
Thou art a *p* for ever after the	Ps 110:4	3548
witnesses to record, Uriah the *p*	Is 8:2	3548
as with the people, so with the *p*	Is 24:2	3548
the *p* and the prophet have erred	Is 28:7	3548
the *p* every one dealeth falsely	Jer 6:13	3548
the *p* every one dealeth falsely	Jer 8:10	3548
the *p* go about into a land that	Jer 14:18	3548
law shall not perish from the *p*	Jer 18:18	3548
Now Pashur the son of Immer the *p*	Jer 20:1	3548
the son of Maaseiah the *p*	Jer 21:1	3548
For both prophet and *p* are profane	Jer 23:11	3548
people, or the prophet, or a *p*	Jer 23:33	3548
And as for the prophet, and the *p*	Jer 23:34	3548
the son of Maaseiah the *p*	Jer 29:25	3548
The LORD hath made thee *p* in the	Jer 29:26	3548
in the stead of Jehoiada the *p*	Jer 29:26	3548
Zephaniah the *p* read this letter	Jer 29:29	3548
the *p* to the prophet Jeremiah	Jer 37:3	3548
guard took Seraiah the chief *p*	Jer 52:24	3548
and Zephaniah the second *p*	Jer 52:24	3548
of his anger the king and the *p*	Lam 2:6	3548
shall the *p* and the prophet be	Lam 2:20	3548
came expressly unto Ezekiel the *p*	Eze 1:3	3548
the law shall perish from the *p*	Eze 7:26	3548
to do the office of a *p* unto me	Eze 44:13	3547
Neither shall any *p* drink wine	Eze 44:21	3548
or a widow that had a *p* before	Eze 44:22	3548
the *p* the first of your dough	Eze 44:30	3548
the *p* shall take of the blood of	Eze 45:19	3548
as they that strive with the *p*	Hos 4:4	3548
that thou shalt be no *p* to me	Hos 4:6	3547
shall be, like people, like *p*	Hos 4:9	3548
Then Amaziah the *p* of Beth-el	Amos 7:10	3548
the son of Josedech, the high *p*	Hag 1:1	3548
the son of Josedech, the high *p*	Hag 1:12	3548
the son of Josedech, the high *p*	Hag 1:14	3548
the son of Josedech, the high *p*	Hag 2:2	3548
son of Josedech, the high *p*	Hag 2:4	3548
p standing before the angel of	Zec 3:1	3548
Hear now, O Joshua the high *p*	Zec 3:8	3548
the son of Josedech, the high *p*	Zec 6:11	3548
he shall be a *p* upon his throne	Zec 6:13	3548
go thy way, shew thyself to the *p*	Mt 8:4	*2409*
unto the palace of the high *p*	Mt 26:3	*749*
him away to Caiaphas the high *p*	Mt 26:57	*749*
And the high *p* arose, and said unto	Mt 26:62	*749*
And the high *p* answered and said	Mt 26:63	*749*
Then the high *p* rent his clothes,	Mt 26:65	*749*
go thy way, shew thyself to the *p*	Mk 1:44	*2409*
the days of Abiathar the high *p*	Mk 2:26	*749*
and staves, from the chief *p*	Mk 14:43	*749*
and smote a servant of the high *p*	Mk 14:47	*749*
they led Jesus away to the high *p*	Mk 14:53	*749*
into the palace of the high *p*	Mk 14:54	*749*
the high *p* stood up in the midst,	Mk 14:60	*749*
Again the high *p* asked him	Mk 14:61	*749*
Then the high *p* rent his clothes,	Mk 14:63	*749*
one of the maids of the high *p*	Mk 14:66	*749*
a certain *p* named Zacharias, of	Lk 1:5	*2409*
but go, and shew thyself to the *p*	Lk 5:14	*2409*
came down a certain *p* that way	Lk 10:31	*2409*
smote the servant of the high *p*	Lk 22:50	*749*

being the high *p* that same year... Jn 11:49 *749*
but being high *p* that year... Jn 11:51 *749*
was the high *p* that same year... Jn 18:13 *749*
was known unto the high *p*... Jn 18:15 *749*
into the palace of the high *p*... Jn 18:15 *749*
which was known unto the high *p*... Jn 18:16 *749*
The high *p* then asked Jesus of... Jn 18:19 *749*
Answerest thou the high *p* so... Jn 18:22 *749*
bound unto Caiaphas the high *p*... Jn 18:24 *749*
One of the servants of the high *p*... Jn 18:26 *749*
And Annas the high *p*, and Caiaphas,... Acts 4:6 *749*
were of the kindred of the high *p*... Acts 4:6 *748*
Then the high *p* rose up, and all... Acts 5:17 *749*
But the high *p* came, and they that... Acts 5:21 *749*
Now when the high *p* and the... Acts 5:24 *749*
and the high *p* asked them,... Acts 5:27 *749*
Then said the high *p*, Are these... Acts 7:1 *749*
of the Lord, went unto the high *p*... Acts 9:1 *749*
Then the *p* of Jupiter, which was... Acts 14:13 *2409*
As also the high *p* doth bear me... Acts 22:5 *749*
the high *p* Ananias commanded them... Acts 23:2 *749*
said, Revilest thou God's high *p*... Acts 23:4 *749*
brethren, that he was the high *p*... Acts 23:5 *749*
high *p* descended with the elders... Acts 24:1 *749*
Then the high *p* and the chief of... Acts 25:2 *749*
faithful high *p* in things... Heb 2:17 *749*
High *P* of our profession, Christ... Heb 3:1 *749*
then that we have a great high *p*... Heb 4:14 *749*
For we have not an high *p* which... Heb 4:15 *749*
For every high *p* taken from among... Heb 5:1 *749*
not himself to be made an high *p*... Heb 5:5 *749*
Thou art a *p* for ever after the... Heb 5:6 *2409*
Called of God an high *p* after the... Heb 5:10 *749*
made an high *p* for ever after the... Heb 6:20 *749*
p of the most high God, who met... Heb 7:1 *2409*
abideth a *p* continually... Heb 7:3 *2409*
need was there that another *p*... Heb 7:11 *2409*
there ariseth another *p*,... Heb 7:15 *2409*
Thou art a *p* for ever after the... Heb 7:17 *2409*
not without an oath he was made *p*... Heb 7:20
Thou art a *p* for ever after the... Heb 7:21 *2409*
For such an high *p* became us... Heb 7:26 *749*
We have such an high *p*, who is... Heb 8:1 *749*
For every high *p* is ordained to... Heb 8:3 *749*
on earth, he should not be a *p*... Heb 8:4 *2409*
the high *p* alone once every year... Heb 9:7 *749*
an high *p* of good things to come... Heb 9:11 *749*
as the high *p* entereth into the... Heb 9:25 *749*
And every *p* standeth daily... Heb 10:11 *2409*
having an high *p* over the house... Heb 10:21 *2409*
sanctuary by the high *p* for sin... Heb 13:11 *749*

PRIESTHOOD {16}
p throughout their generations... Ex 40:15 3550
and seek ye the *p* also... Num 16:10 3550
shall bear the iniquity of your *p*... Num 18:1 3550
the covenant of an everlasting *p*... Num 25:13 3550
for the *p* of the LORD is their... Josh 18:7 3550
they, as polluted, put from the *p*... Ezr 2:62 3550
they, as polluted, put from the *p*... Neh 7:64 3550
because they have defiled the *p*... Neh 13:29 3550
and the covenant of the *p*... Neh 13:29 3550
who receive the office of the *p*... Heb 7:5 *2405*
were by the Levitical *p*, (for... Heb 7:11 *2420*
For the *p* being changed, there is... Heb 7:12 *2420*
Moses spake nothing concerning *p*... Heb 7:14 *2420*
ever, hath an unchangeable *p*... Heb 7:24 *2420*
up a spiritual house, an holy *p*... 1Pet 2:5 *2406*
a chosen generation, a royal *p*... 1Pet 2:9 *2406*

PRIEST'S {47}
minister unto me in the *p* office... Ex 28:1 3547
minister unto me in the *p* office... Ex 28:3 3547
minister unto me in the *p* office... Ex 28:4 3547
minister unto me in the *p* office... Ex 28:41 3547
minister unto me in the *p* office... Ex 29:1 3547
the *p* office shall be theirs for... Ex 29:9 3550
to minister to me in the *p* office... Ex 29:44 3547
minister unto me in the *p* office... Ex 30:30 3547
sons, to minister in the *p* office... Ex 31:10 3547
sons, to minister in the *p* office... Ex 35:19 3547
to minister in the *p* office... Ex 39:41 3547
minister unto me in the *p* office... Ex 40:13 3547
minister unto me in the *p* office... Ex 40:15 3547
and the remnant shall be the *p*... Lev 5:13 3548
shall be the *p* that offereth it... Lev 7:9 3548
it shall be the *p* that sprinkleth... Lev 7:14 3548
unto the LORD in the *p* office... Lev 7:35 3547
for as the sin offering is the *p*... Lev 14:13 3548
of the oil that is in the *p* hand... Lev 14:18 3548
rest of the oil that is in the *p*... Lev 14:29 3548
p office in his father's stead... Lev 16:32 3547
If the *p* daughter also be married... Lev 22:12 3548
But if the *p* daughter be a widow,... Lev 22:13 3548
possession thereof shall be the *p*... Lev 27:21 3548
to minister in the *p* office... Num 3:3 3547
Ithamar ministered in the *p*... Num 3:4 3547
they shall wait on their *p* office... Num 3:10 3550
p office for every thing of the... Num 18:7 3550
I have given your *p* office unto... Num 18:7 3550
in the *p* office in his stead... Deut 10:6 3547
this shall be the *p* due from the... Deut 18:3 3548
the *p* heart was glad, and he took... Judg 18:20 3548
the *p* custom with the people was,... 1Sa 2:13 3548
the *p* servant came, while the... 1Sa 2:13 3548
the *p* servant came, and said to... 1Sa 2:15 3548
the *p* office in the temple that... 1Chr 6:10 3547
and Ithamar executed the *p* office... 1Chr 24:2 3547
the *p* office unto the LORD... 2Chr 11:14 3547
the high *p* officer came and... 2Chr 24:11 3548
of your oblations, shall be the *p*... Eze 44:30 3548
For the *p* lips should keep... Mal 2:7 3548
and struck a servant of the high *p*... Mt 26:51 *749*
afar off unto the high *p* palace... Mt 26:58 *749*
that while he executed the *p*... Lk 1:8 *2407*
to the custom of the *p* office... Lk 1:9 *2405*
brought him into the high *p* house... Lk 22:54 *749*
it, and smote the high *p* servant... Jn 18:10 *749*

PRIESTS {391}
the land of the *p* bought he not... Gen 47:22 3548
for the *p* had a portion assigned... Gen 47:22 3548
except the land of the *p* only... Gen 47:26 3548
shall be unto me a kingdom of *p*... Ex 19:6 3548
And let the *p* also, which come... Ex 19:22 3548
but let not the *p* and the people... Ex 19:24 3548
and the *p*, Aaron's sons, shall... Lev 1:5 3548
And the *p*, Aaron's sons, shall lay... Lev 1:8 3548
and the *p*, Aaron's sons, shall... Lev 1:11 3548
bring it to Aaron's sons the *p*... Lev 2:2 3548
Aaron's sons the *p* shall sprinkle... Lev 3:2 3548
among the *p* shall eat thereof... Lev 6:29 3548
among the *p* shall eat thereof... Lev 7:6 3548
or unto one of his sons the *p*... Lev 13:2 3548
shall make an atonement for the *p*... Lev 16:33 3548
Speak unto the *p* the sons of... Lev 21:1 3548
the *p* which were anointed, whom... Num 3:3 3548
And the sons of Aaron, the *p*... Num 10:8 3548
shalt come unto the *p* the Levites... Deut 17:9 3548
which is before the *p* the Levites... Deut 17:18 3548
The *p* the Levites, and all the... Deut 18:1 3548
before the LORD, before the *p*... Deut 19:17 3548
the *p* the sons of Levi shall come... Deut 21:5 3548
the *p* the Levites shall teach you... Deut 24:8 3548
the *p* the Levites spake unto all... Deut 27:9 3548
it unto the *p* the sons of Levi... Deut 31:9 3548
the *p* the Levites bearing it,... Josh 3:3 3548
And Joshua spake unto the *p*... Josh 3:6 3548
thou shalt command the *p* that... Josh 3:8 3548
p that bear the ark of the LORD... Josh 3:13 3548
the *p* bearing the ark of the... Josh 3:14 3548
the feet of the *p* that bare the... Josh 3:15 3548
the *p* that bare the ark of the... Josh 3:17 3548
the *p* which bare the ark of the... Josh 4:9 3548
For the *p* which bare the ark... Josh 4:10 3548
of the LORD passed over, and the *p*... Josh 4:11 3548
Command the *p* that bear the ark... Josh 4:16 3548
Joshua therefore commanded the *p*... Josh 4:17 3548
when the *p* that bare the ark of... Josh 4:18 3548
seven *p* shall bear before the ark... Josh 6:4 3548
the *p* shall blow with the... Josh 6:4 3548
the son of Nun called the *p*... Josh 6:6 3548
let seven *p* bear seven trumpets... Josh 6:6 3548
that the seven *p* bearing the... Josh 6:8 3548
the *p* that blew with the trumpets... Josh 6:9 3548
the *p* going on, and blowing with... Josh 6:9 3548
the *p* took up the ark of the LORD... Josh 6:12 3548
seven *p* bearing seven trumpets of... Josh 6:13 3548
the *p* going on, and blowing with... Josh 6:13 3548
when the *p* blew with the trumpets... Josh 6:16 3548
when the *p* blew with the trumpets... Josh 6:20 3548
side before the *p* the Levites... Josh 8:33 3548
of the children of Aaron, the *p*... Josh 21:19 3548
his sons were *p* to the tribe of... Judg 18:30 3548
the *p* of the LORD, were there... 1Sa 1:3 3548
Therefore neither the *p* of Dagon... 1Sa 5:5 3548
the Philistines called for the *p*... 1Sa 6:2 3548
house, the *p* that were in Nob... 1Sa 22:11 3548
Turn, and slay the *p* of the LORD... 1Sa 22:17 3548
to fall upon the *p* of the LORD... 1Sa 22:17 3548
Turn thou, and fall upon the *p*... 1Sa 22:18 3548
turned, and he fell upon the *p*... 1Sa 22:18 3548
And Nob, the city of the *p*... 1Sa 22:19 3548
that Saul had slain the LORD's *p*... 1Sa 22:21 3548
the son of Abiathar, were the *p*... 2Sa 8:17 3548
with thee Zadok and Abiathar the *p*... 2Sa 15:35 3548
it to Zadok and Abiathar the *p*... 2Sa 15:35 3548
unto Zadok and to Abiathar the *p*... 2Sa 17:15 3548
to Zadok and to Abiathar the *p*... 2Sa 19:11 3548
and Zadok and Abiathar were the *p*... 2Sa 20:25 3548
and Zadok and Abiathar were the *p*... 1Kin 4:4 3548
came, and the *p* took up the ark... 1Kin 8:3 3548
tabernacle, even those did the *p*... 1Kin 8:4 3548
the *p* brought in the ark of the... 1Kin 8:6 3548
when the *p* were come out of the... 1Kin 8:10 3548
So that the *p* could not stand to... 1Kin 8:11 3548
made *p* of the lowest of the... 1Kin 12:31 3548
he placed in Beth-el the *p* of the... 1Kin 12:32 3548
p of the high places that burn... 1Kin 13:2 3548
the people *p* of the high places... 1Kin 13:33 3548
one of the *p* of the high places... 1Kin 13:33 3548
men, and his kinsfolks, and his *p*... 2Kin 10:11 3548
all his servants, and all his *p*... 2Kin 10:19 3548
And Jehoash said to the *p*, All the... 2Kin 12:4 3548
Let the *p* take it to them, every... 2Kin 12:5 3548
year of king Jehoash the *p* had... 2Kin 12:6 3548
the priest, and the other *p*... 2Kin 12:7 3548
the *p* consented to receive no... 2Kin 12:8 3548
the *p* that kept the door put... 2Kin 12:9 3548
Carry thither one of the *p* whom... 2Kin 17:27 3548
Then one of the *p* whom they had... 2Kin 17:28 3548
of them *p* of the high places... 2Kin 17:32 3548
scribe, and the elders of the *p*... 2Kin 19:2 3548
of Jerusalem with him, and the *p*... 2Kin 23:2 3548
the *p* of the second order, and the... 2Kin 23:4 3548
And he put down the idolatrous *p*... 2Kin 23:5
he brought all the *p* out of the... 2Kin 23:8 3548
where the *p* had burned incense... 2Kin 23:8 3548
Nevertheless the *p* of the high... 2Kin 23:9 3548
he slew all the *p* of the high... 2Kin 23:20 3548
were, the Israelites, the *p*... 1Chr 9:2 3548
And of the *p*; Jedaiah... 1Chr 9:10 3548
some of the sons of the *p* made... 1Chr 9:30 3548
and with them also to the *p*... 1Chr 13:2 3548
for Zadok and Abiathar the *p*... 1Chr 15:11 3548
So the *p* and the Levites... 1Chr 15:14 3548
and Benaiah, and Eliezer, the *p*... 1Chr 15:24 3548
Jahaziel the *p* with trumpets... 1Chr 16:6 3548
the priest, and his brethren the *p*... 1Chr 16:39 3548
the son of Abiathar, were the *p*... 1Chr 18:16 3548
the princes of Israel, with the *p*... 1Chr 23:2 3548
the chief of the fathers of the *p*... 1Chr 24:6 3548
the chief of the fathers of the *p*... 1Chr 24:31 3548
Also for the courses of the *p*... 1Chr 28:13 3548
And, behold, the courses of the *p*... 1Chr 28:21 3548
the sea was for the *p* to wash in... 2Chr 4:6 3548
he made the court of the *p*... 2Chr 4:9 3548
the tabernacle, these did the *p*... 2Chr 5:5 3548
the *p* brought in the ark of the... 2Chr 5:7 3548
when the *p* were come out of the... 2Chr 5:11 3548
(for all the *p* that were present... 2Chr 5:11 3548
twenty *p* sounding with trumpets... 2Chr 5:12 3548
So that the *p* could not stand to... 2Chr 5:14 3548
let thy *p*, O LORD God, be clothed... 2Chr 6:41 3548
the *p* could not enter into the... 2Chr 7:2 3548
the *p* waited on their offices... 2Chr 7:6 3548
the *p* sounded trumpets before... 2Chr 7:6 3548
courses of the *p* to their service... 2Chr 8:14 3548
praise and minister before the *p*... 2Chr 8:14 3548
of the king unto the *p* and Levites... 2Chr 8:15 3548
And the *p* and the Levites that were... 2Chr 11:13 3548
he ordained him *p* for the high... 2Chr 11:15 3548
ye not cast out the *p* of the LORD... 2Chr 13:9 3548
have made you *p* after the manner... 2Chr 13:9 3548
and the *p*, which minister unto the... 2Chr 13:10 3548
his *p* with sounding trumpets to... 2Chr 13:12 3548
the *p* sounded with the trumpets... 2Chr 13:14 3548
with them Elishama and Jehoram, *p*... 2Chr 17:8 3548
set of the Levites, and of the *p*... 2Chr 19:8 3548
entering on the sabbath, of the *p*... 2Chr 23:4 3548
the house of the LORD, save the *p*... 2Chr 23:6 3548
by the hand of the *p* the Levites... 2Chr 23:18 3548
And he gathered together the *p*... 2Chr 24:5 3548
with him fourscore *p* of the LORD... 2Chr 26:17 3548
but to the *p* the sons of Aaron,... 2Chr 26:18 3548
and while he was wroth with the *p*... 2Chr 26:19 3548
the *p* in the house of the LORD... 2Chr 26:19 3548
the chief priest, and all the *p*... 2Chr 26:20 3548
And he brought in the *p* and the... 2Chr 29:4 3548
the *p* went into the inner part of... 2Chr 29:16 3548
he commanded the *p* the sons of... 2Chr 29:21 3548
the *p* received the blood, and... 2Chr 29:22 3548
the *p* killed them, and they made... 2Chr 29:24 3548
David, and the *p* with the trumpets... 2Chr 29:26 3548
But the *p* were too few, so that... 2Chr 29:34 3548
until the other *p* had sanctified... 2Chr 29:34 3548
to sanctify themselves than the *p*... 2Chr 29:34 3548
because the *p* had not sanctified... 2Chr 30:3 3548
and the *p* and the Levites were... 2Chr 30:15 3548
the *p* sprinkled the blood, which... 2Chr 30:16 3548
the *p* praised the LORD day by day... 2Chr 30:21 3548
a great number of *p* sanctified... 2Chr 30:24 3548
congregation of Judah, with the *p*... 2Chr 30:25 3548
Then the *p* the Levites arose and... 2Chr 30:27 3548
appointed the courses of the *p*... 2Chr 31:2 3548
according to his service, the *p*... 2Chr 31:2 3548
to give the portion of the *p*... 2Chr 31:4 3548
Hezekiah questioned with the *p*... 2Chr 31:9 3548
Shecaniah, in the cities of the *p*... 2Chr 31:15 3548
Both to the genealogy of the *p* by... 2Chr 31:17 3548
Also of the sons of Aaron the *p*... 2Chr 31:19 3548
to all the males among the *p*... 2Chr 31:19 3548
bones of the *p* upon their altars... 2Chr 34:5 3548
of Jerusalem, and the *p*, and the... 2Chr 34:30 3548
he set the *p* in their charges, and... 2Chr 35:2 3548
unto the people, to the *p*... 2Chr 35:8 3548
gave unto the *p* for the passover... 2Chr 35:8 3548
the *p* stood in their place, and... 2Chr 35:10 3548
the *p* sprinkled the blood from... 2Chr 35:11 3548
for themselves, and for the *p*... 2Chr 35:14 3548
because the *p* the sons of Aaron... 2Chr 35:14 3548
for the *p* the sons of Aaron... 2Chr 35:14 3548
passover as Josiah kept, and the *p*... 2Chr 35:18 3548
Moreover all the chief of the *p*... 2Chr 36:14 3548
of Judah and Benjamin, and the *p*... Ezr 1:5 3548
The *p*: the children of... Ezr 2:36 3548
And of the children of the *p*... Ezr 2:61 3548
So the *p*, and the Levites, and some... Ezr 2:70 3548
of Jozadak, and his brethren the *p*... Ezr 3:2 3548
remnant of their brethren the *p*... Ezr 3:8 3548
they set the *p* in their apparel... Ezr 3:10 3548
But many of the *p* and Levites and... Ezr 3:12 3548
of the *p* which are at Jerusalem... Ezr 6:9 3549
And the children of Israel, the *p*... Ezr 6:16 3549
they set the *p* in their divisions... Ezr 6:18 3549
For the *p* and the Levites were... Ezr 6:20 3548
and for their brethren the *p*... Ezr 6:20 3548
children of Israel, and of the *p*... Ezr 7:7 3548
the people of Israel, and of his *p*... Ezr 7:13 3549
of the people, and of the *p*... Ezr 7:16 3549
you, that touching any of the *p*... Ezr 7:24 3549
and I viewed the people, and the *p*... Ezr 8:15 3548
twelve of the chief of the *p*... Ezr 8:24 3548
them before the chief of the *p*... Ezr 8:29 3548
So took the *p* and the Levites the... Ezr 8:30 3548

P

The people of Israel, and the *p* Ezr 9:1 3548
have we, our kings, and our *p* Ezr 9:7 3548
arose Ezra, and made the chief *p* Ezr 10:5 3548
among the sons of the *p* there Ezr 10:18 3548
told it to the Jews, nor to the *p* Neh 2:16 3548
rose up with his brethren the *p* Neh 3:1 3548
And after him repaired the *p* Neh 3:22 3548
the horse gate repaired the *p* Neh 3:28 3548
Then I called the *p*, and took an Neh 5:12 3548
The *p*: the children of Neh 7:39 3548
And of the *p*: the children Neh 7:63 3548
So the *p*, and the Levites, and the Neh 7:73 3548
fathers of all the people, the *p* Neh 8:13 3548
on our princes, and on our *p* Neh 9:32 3548
our kings, our princes, our *p* Neh 9:34 3548
and our princes, Levites, and *p* Neh 9:38 3548
these were the *p* Neh 10:8 3548
And the rest of the people, the *p* Neh 10:28 3548
And we cast the lots among the *p* Neh 10:34 3548
unto the *p* that minister in the Neh 10:36 3548
of wine and of oil, unto the *p* Neh 10:37 3548
the *p* that minister, and the Neh 10:39 3548
cities, to wit, Israel, the *p* Neh 11:3 3548
Of the *p*: Jedaiah Neh 11:10 3548
the residue of Israel, of the *p* Neh 11:20 3548
Now these are the *p* and the Neh 12:1 3548
These were the chief of the *p* Neh 12:7 3548
And in the days of Joiakim were *p* Neh 12:12 3548
also the *p*, to the reign of Neh 12:22 3548
And the *p* and the Levites purified Neh 12:30 3548
And the *p*; Eliakim Neh 12:41 3548
the portions of the law for the *p* Neh 12:44 3548
for Judah rejoiced for the *p* Neh 12:44 3548
and the offerings of the *p* Neh 13:5 3548
and appointed the wards of the *p* Neh 13:30 3548
Their *p* fell by the sword Ps 78:64 3548
Moses and Aaron among his *p* Ps 99:6 3548
Let thy *p* be clothed with Ps 132:9 3548
also clothe her *p* with salvation Ps 132:16 3548
the elders of the *p* covered with Is 37:2 3548
shall be named the *P* of the LORD Is 61:6 3548
And I will also take of them for *p* Is 66:21 3548
of the *p* that were in Anathoth in Jer 1:1 3548
thereof, against the *p* thereof Jer 1:18 3548
The *p* said not, Where is the LORD Jer 2:8 3548
kings, their princes, and their *p* Jer 2:26 3548
the *p* shall be astonished, and the Jer 4:9 3548
the *p* bear rule by their means Jer 5:31 3548
princes, and the bones of the *p* Jer 8:1 3548
sit upon David's throne, and the *p* Jer 13:13 3548
and of the ancients of the *p* Jer 19:1 3548
So the *p* and the prophets and all Jer 26:7 3548
unto all the people, that the *p* Jer 26:8 3548
Then spake the *p* and the prophets Jer 26:11 3548
and all the people unto the *p* Jer 26:16 3548
Also I spake to the *p* and to all Jer 27:16 3548
LORD, in the presence of the *p* Jer 28:1 3548
Hananiah in the presence of the *p* Jer 28:5 3548
away captives, and to the *p* Jer 29:1 3548
the priest, and to all the *p* Jer 29:25 3548
the soul of the *p* with fatness Jer 31:14 3548
kings, their princes, their *p* Jer 32:32 3548
Neither shall the *p* the Levites Jer 33:18 3548
and with the Levites the *p* Jer 33:21 3548
Jerusalem, the eunuchs, and the *p* Jer 34:19 3548
forth into captivity with his *p* Jer 48:7 3548
shall go into captivity, and his *p* Jer 49:3 3548
her *p* sigh, her virgins are Lam 1:4 3548
my *p* and mine elders gave up the Lam 1:19 3548
and the iniquities of her *p* Lam 4:13 3548
not the persons of the *p*, they Lam 4:16 3548
Her *p* have violated my law, and Eze 22:26 3548
is toward the south, is for the *p* Eze 40:45 3548
is toward the north is for the *p* Eze 40:46 3548
where the *p* that approach unto Eze 42:13 3548
When the *p* enter therein, then Eze 42:14 3548
thou shalt give to the *p* the Eze 43:19 3548
the *p* shall cast salt upon them, Eze 43:24 3548
the *p* shall make your burnt Eze 43:27 3548
But the *p* the Levites, the sons Eze 44:15 3548
The *p* shall not eat of any thing Eze 44:31 3548
of the land shall be for the *p* Eze 45:4 3548
the *p* shall prepare his burnt Eze 46:2 3548
into the holy chambers of the *p* Eze 46:19 3548
the *p* shall boil the trespass Eze 46:20 3548
And for them, even for the *p* Eze 48:10 3548
It shall be for the *p* that are Eze 48:11 3548
the *p* the Levites shall have five Eze 48:13 3548
Hear ye this, O *p* Hos 5:1 3548
so the company of *p* murder in the Hos 6:9 3548
the *p* thereof that rejoiced on it Hos 10:5 3649
the *p*, the LORD's ministers, Joel 1:9 3548
Gird yourselves, and lament, ye *p* Joel 1:13 3548
Let the *p*, the ministers of the Joel 2:17 3548
the *p* thereof teach for hire, and Mic 3:11 3548
name of the Chemarims with the *p* Zeph 1:4 3548
her *p* have polluted the sanctuary Zeph 3:4 3548
Ask now the *p* concerning the law, Hag 2:11 3548
the *p* answered and said, No Hag 2:12 3548
the *p* answered and said, It shall Hag 2:13 3548
to speak unto the *p* which were in Zec 7:3 3548
people of the land, and to the *p* Zec 7:5 3548
the LORD of hosts unto you, O *p* Mal 1:6 3548
And now, O ye *p*, this commandment Mal 2:1 3548
he had gathered all the chief *p* Mt 2:4 *749*
were with him, but only for the *p* Mt 12:4 *2409*
the *p* in the temple profane the Mt 12:5 *2409*
things of the elders and chief *p* Mt 16:21 *749*
be betrayed unto the chief *p* Mt 20:18 *749*
And when the chief *p* and scribes Mt 21:15 *749*
come into the temple, the chief *p* Mt 21:23 *749*
And when the chief *p* and Pharisees Mt 21:45 *749*
assembled together the chief *p* Mt 26:3 *749*
Iscariot, went unto the chief *p* Mt 26:14 *749*
and staves, from the chief *p* Mt 26:47 *749*
Now the chief *p*, and elders, and Mt 26:59 *749*
morning was come, all the chief *p* Mt 27:1 *749*
pieces of silver to the chief *p* Mt 27:3 *749*
the chief *p* took the silver Mt 27:6 *749*
he was accused of the chief *p* Mt 27:12 *749*
But the chief *p* and elders Mt 27:20 *749*
also the chief *p* mocking him Mt 27:41 *749*
of the preparation, the chief *p* Mt 27:62 *749*
shewed unto the chief *p* all the Mt 28:11 *749*
not lawful to eat but for the *p* Mk 2:26 *2409*
of the elders, and of the chief *p* Mk 8:31 *749*
be delivered unto the chief *p* Mk 10:33 *749*
chief *p* heard it, and sought how Mk 11:18 *749*
there come to him the chief *p* Mk 11:27 *749*
and the chief *p* and the scribes Mk 14:1 *749*
the twelve, went unto the chief *p* Mk 14:10 *749*
were assembled all the chief *p* Mk 14:53 *749*
And the chief *p* and all the council Mk 14:55 *749*
in the morning the chief *p* held a Mk 15:1 *749*
the chief *p* accused him of many Mk 15:3 *749*
p had delivered him for envy Mk 15:10 *749*
But the chief *p* moved the people, Mk 15:11 *749*
Likewise also the chief *p* mocking Mk 15:31 *749*
and Caiaphas being the high *p* Lk 3:2 *749*
lawful to eat but for the *p* alone Lk 6:4 *2409*
rejected of the elders and chief *p* Lk 9:22 *749*
Go shew yourselves unto the *p* Lk 17:14 *2409*
But the chief *p* and the scribes and Lk 19:47 *749*
preached the gospel, the chief *p* Lk 20:1 *749*
And the chief *p* and the scribes the Lk 20:19 *749*
And the chief *p* and scribes sought Lk 22:2 *749*
way, and communed with the chief *p* Lk 22:4 *749*
Then Jesus said unto the chief *p* Lk 22:52 *749*
of the people and the chief *p* Lk 22:66 *749*
Then said Pilate to the chief *p* Lk 23:4 *749*
And the chief *p* and scribes stood Lk 23:10 *749*
had called together the chief *p* Lk 23:13 *749*
them and of the chief *p* prevailed Lk 23:23 *749*
And how the chief *p* and our rulers Lk 24:20 *749*
of John, when the Jews sent *p* Jn 1:19 *2409*
the chief *p* sent officers to take Jn 7:32 *749*
came the officers to the chief *p* Jn 7:45 *749*
Then gathered the chief *p* Jn 11:47 *749*
Now both the chief *p* and the Jn 11:57 *749*
But the chief *p* consulted that Jn 12:10 *749*
men and officers from the chief *p* Jn 18:3 *749*
the chief *p* have delivered thee Jn 18:35 *749*
When the chief *p* therefore Jn 19:6 *749*
The chief *p* answered, We have no Jn 19:15 *749*
Then said the chief *p* of the Jews Jn 19:21 *749*
they spake unto the people, the *p* Acts 4:1 *2409*
and reported all that the chief *p* Acts 4:23 *749*
the chief *p* heard these things, Acts 5:24 *749*
a great company of the *p* were Acts 6:7 *2409*
p to bind all that call on thy Acts 9:14 *749*
bring them bound unto the chief *p* Acts 9:21 *749*
Sceva, a Jew, and chief of the *p* Acts 19:14 *749*
bands, and commanded the chief *p* Acts 22:30 *749*
And they came to the chief *p* Acts 23:14 *749*
I was at Jerusalem, the chief *p* Acts 25:15 *749*
authority from the chief *p* Acts 26:10 *749*
and commission from the chief *p* Acts 26:12 *749*
(For those *p* were made without an Heb 7:21 *2409*
And they truly were many *p* Heb 7:23 *2409*
not daily, as those high *p* Heb 7:27 *749*
men high *p* which have infirmity Heb 7:28 *749*
seeing that there are *p* that Heb 8:4 *2409*
the *p* went always into the first Heb 9:6 *2409*
kings and *p* unto God and his Father Rev 1:6 *2409*
made us unto our God kings and *p* Rev 5:10 *2409*
power, but they shall be *p* of God Rev 20:6 *2409*

PRIESTS' {8}

place where the *p* feet stood firm Josh 4:3 3548
the soles of the *p* feet were Josh 4:18 3548
thee, into one of the *p* offices 1Sa 2:36 3548
it was the *p* 2Kin 12:16 3548
silver, and one hundred *p* garments Ezr 2:69 3548
five hundred and thirty *p* garments Neh 7:70 3548
and threescore and seven *p* garments Neh 7:72 3548
certain of the *p* sons with Neh 12:35 3548

PRINCE {102}

thou art a mighty *p* among us Gen 23:6 5387
for as a *p* hast thou power with Gen 32:28
p of the country, saw her, he Gen 34:2 5387
And he said, Who made thee a *p* Ex 2:14 8269
each *p* on his day, for the Num 7:11 5387
of Zuar, *p* of Issachar, did offer Num 7:18 5387
p of the children of Zebulun, did Num 7:24 5387
p of the children of Reuben, did Num 7:30 5387
p of the children of Simeon, did Num 7:36 5387
p of the children of Gad, offered Num 7:42 5387
p of the children of Ephraim, Num 7:48 5387
p of the children of Manasseh Num 7:54 5387
p of the children of Benjamin, Num 7:60 5387
p of the children of Dan, offered Num 7:66 5387
p of the children of Asher, Num 7:72 5387
p of the children of Naphtali, Num 7:78 5387
thyself altogether a *p* over us Num 16:13 8323
him a rod apiece, for each *p* one Num 17:6 5387
a *p* of a chief house among the Num 25:14 5387
the daughter of a *p* of Midian Num 25:18 5387
shall take one *p* of every tribe Num 34:18 5387
the *p* of the tribe of the Num 34:22 5387
The *p* of the children of Joseph, Num 34:23 5387
the *p* of the tribe of the Num 34:24 5387
the *p* of the tribe of the Num 34:25 5387
the *p* of the tribe of the Num 34:26 5387
the *p* of the tribe of the Num 34:27 5387
the *p* of the tribe of the Num 34:28 5387
princes, of each chief house a *p* Josh 22:14 5387
Know ye not that there is a *p* 2Sa 3:38 8269
but I will make him *p* all the 1Kin 11:34 5387
made thee *p* over my people Israel 1Kin 14:7 5057
made thee *p* over my people Israel 1Kin 16:2 5057
p of the children of Judah 1Chr 2:10 5387
he was *p* of the Reubenites 1Chr 5:6 5387
unto Sheshbazzar, the *p* of Judah Ezr 1:8 5387
say, Where is the house of the *p* Job 21:28 5081
as a *p* would I go near unto him Job 31:37 5057
is the destruction of the *p* Prov 14:28 7333
much less do lying lips a *p* Prov 17:7 5081
will intreat the favour of the *p* Prov 19:6 5081
the *p* whom thine eyes have seen Prov 25:7 5081
long forbearing is a *p* persuaded Prov 25:15 7101
The *p* that wanteth understanding Prov 28:16 5057
Father, The *P* of Peace Is 9:6 8269
And this Seraiah was a quiet *p* Jer 51:59 8269
the *p* shall be clothed with Eze 7:27 5387
concerneth the *p* in Jerusalem Eze 12:10 5387
the *p* that is among them shall Eze 12:12 5387
thou, profane wicked *p* of Israel Eze 21:25 5387
of man, say unto the *p* of Tyrus Eze 28:2 5057
no more a *p* of the land of Egypt Eze 30:13 5387
my servant David a *p* among them Eze 34:24 5387
David shall be their *p* for ever Eze 37:25 5387
the chief *p* of Meshech and Tubal, Eze 38:2 5387
the chief *p* of Meshech and Tubal Eze 38:3 5387
the chief *p* of Meshech and Tubal Eze 39:1 5387
It is for the *p* Eze 44:3 5387
the *p*, he shall sit in it to eat Eze 44:3 5387
be for the *p* on the one side Eze 45:7 5387
this oblation for the *p* in Israel Eze 45:16 5387
shall the *p* prepare for himself Eze 45:22 5387
the *p* shall enter by the way of Eze 46:2 5387
the burnt offering that the *p* Eze 46:4 5387
when the *p* shall enter, he shall Eze 46:8 5387
the *p* in the midst of them, when Eze 46:10 5387
Now when the *p* shall prepare a Eze 46:12 5387
If the *p* give a gift unto any of Eze 46:16 5387
after, it shall return to the *p* Eze 46:17 5387
Moreover the *p* shall not take of Eze 46:18 5387
And the residue shall be for the *p* Eze 48:21 5387
against the portions for the *p* Eze 48:21 5387
of Benjamin, shall be for the *p* Eze 48:22 5387
Unto whom the *p* of the eunuchs Dan 1:7 8269
p of the eunuchs that he might Dan 1:8 8269
love with the *p* of the eunuchs Dan 1:9 8269
the *p* of the eunuchs said unto Dan 1:10 8269
whom the *p* of the eunuchs had set Dan 1:11 8269
then the *p* of the eunuchs brought Dan 1:18 8269
himself even to the *p* of the host Dan 8:11 8269
stand up against the *P* of princes Dan 8:25 8269
the *P* shall be seven weeks Dan 9:25 5057
the people of the *p* that shall Dan 9:26 5057
But the *p* of the kingdom of Dan 10:13 8269
to fight with the *p* of Persia Dan 10:20 8269
the *p* of Grecia shall come Dan 10:20 8269
these things, but Michael your *p* Dan 10:21 8269
but a *p* for his own behalf shall Dan 11:18 7101
also the *p* of the covenant Dan 11:22 5057
the great *p* which standeth for Dan 12:1 8269
without a king, and without a *p* Hos 3:4 8269
the *p* asketh, and the judge asketh Mic 7:3 8269
through the *p* of the devils Mt 9:34 *758*
by Beelzebub the *p* of the devils Mt 12:24 *758*
by the *p* of the devils casteth he Mk 3:22 *758*
now shall the *p* of this world be Jn 12:31 *758*
for the *p* of this world cometh, Jn 14:30 *758*
because the *p* of this world is Jn 16:11 *758*
And killed the *P* of life, whom God Acts 3:15 *747*
with his right hand to be a *P* Acts 5:31 *747*
according to the *p* of the power Eph 2:2 *758*
the *p* of the kings of the earth Rev 1:5 *758*

PRINCE'S {3}

thy feet with shoes, O *p* daughter Song 7:1 5081
it shall be the *p* part to give Eze 45:17 5387
the midst of that which is the *p* Eze 48:22 5387

PRINCES {273}

The *p* also of Pharaoh saw her, and Gen 12:15 8269
twelve *p* shall he beget, and I Gen 17:20 5387
twelve *p* according to their Gen 25:16 5387
p of the tribes of their fathers, Num 1:16 5387
the *p* of Israel, being twelve men Num 1:44 5387
That the *p* of Israel, heads of Num 7:2 5387
who were the *p* of the tribes, and Num 7:2 5387
a wagon for two of the *p*, and for Num 7:3 5387
the *p* offered for dedicating of Num 7:10 5387
even the *p* offered their offering Num 7:10 5387
was anointed, by the *p* of Israel Num 7:84 5387
but with one trumpet, then the *p* Num 10:4 5387
fifty *p* of the assembly, famous Num 16:2 5387
of all their *p* according to the Num 17:2 5387
every one of their *p* gave him a Num 17:6 5387
The *p* digged the well, the nobles Num 21:18 8269
the *p* of Moab abode with Balaam Num 22:8 8269
and said unto the *p* of Balak Num 22:13 8269
the *p* of Moab rose up, and they Num 22:14 8269

And Balak sent yet again *p* ... Num 22:15 8269
ass, and went with the *p* of Moab ... Num 22:21 8269
Balaam went with the *p* of Balak ... Num 22:35 8269
to the *p* that were with him ... Num 22:40 8269
he, and all the *p* of Moab ... Num 23:6 8269
and the *p* of Moab with him ... Num 23:17 8269
the priest, and before the *p* ... Num 27:2 5387
all the *p* of the congregation, ... Num 31:13 5387
unto the *p* of the congregation, ... Num 32:2 5387
before Moses, and before the *p* ... Num 36:1 5387
the *p* of the congregation sware ... Josh 9:15 5387
because the *p* of the congregation ... Josh 9:18 5387
murmured against the *p* ... Josh 9:18 5387
But all the *p* said unto all the ... Josh 9:19 5387
the *p* said unto them, Let them ... Josh 9:21 5387
as the *p* had promised them ... Josh 9:21 5387
Moses smote with the *p* of Midian ... Josh 13:21 5387
the son of Nun, and before the *p* ... Josh 17:4 5387
And with him ten *p*, of each chief ... Josh 22:14 5387
the *p* of the congregation and ... Josh 22:30 5387
of Eleazar the priest, and the *p* ... Josh 22:32 5387
give ear, O ye *p* ... Judg 5:3 7336
the *p* of Issachar were with ... Judg 5:15 8269
they took two *p* of the Midianites ... Judg 7:25 8269
into your hands the *p* of Midian ... Judg 8:3 8269
the *p* of Succoth said, Are the ... Judg 8:6 8269
unto him the *p* of Succoth ... Judg 8:14 8269
p of Gilead said one to another, ... Judg 10:18 8269
the dunghill, to set them among *p* ... 1Sa 2:8 5081
Then the *p* of the Philistines ... 1Sa 18:30 8269
Then said the *p* of the ... 1Sa 29:3 8269
unto the *p* of the Philistines ... 1Sa 29:3 8269
the *p* of the Philistines were ... 1Sa 29:4 8269
the *p* of the Philistines said ... 1Sa 29:4 8269
notwithstanding the *p* of the ... 1Sa 29:9 8269
the *p* of the children of Ammon ... 2Sa 10:3 8269
regardest neither *p* nor servants ... 2Sa 19:6 8269
And these were the *p* which he had ... 1Kin 4:2 8269
of war, and his servants, and his *p* ... 1Kin 9:22 8269
men of the *p* of the provinces ... 1Kin 20:14 8269
men of the *p* of the provinces ... 1Kin 20:15 8269
the young men of the *p* of the ... 1Kin 20:17 8269
So these young men of the *p* of ... 1Kin 20:19 8269
as the manner was, and the *p* ... 2Kin 11:14 8269
mother, and his servants, and his *p* ... 2Kin 24:12 8269
away all Jerusalem, and all the *p* ... 2Kin 24:14 8269
names were *p* in their families ... 1Chr 4:38 5387
men of valour, chief of the *p* ... 1Chr 7:40 5387
But the *p* of the children of ... 1Chr 19:3 8269
David also commanded all the *p* of ... 1Chr 22:17 8269
together all the *p* of Israel ... 1Chr 23:2 8269
them before the king, and the *p* ... 1Chr 24:6 8269
These were the *p* of the tribes of ... 1Chr 27:22 8269
assembled all the *p* of Israel ... 1Chr 28:1 8269
the *p* of the tribes, and the ... 1Chr 28:1 8269
also the *p* and all the people will ... 1Chr 28:21 8269
p of the tribes of Israel, and the ... 1Chr 29:6 8269
And all the *p*, and the mighty men, ... 1Chr 29:24 8269
to the *p* of Judah, that were ... 2Chr 12:5 8269
Whereupon the *p* of Israel ... 2Chr 12:6 8269
of his reign he sent to his *p* ... 2Chr 17:7 8269
and divers also of the *p* of Israel ... 2Chr 21:4 8269
Jehoram went forth with his *p* ... 2Chr 21:9 8269
of Ahab, and found the *p* of Judah ... 2Chr 22:8 8269
at the entering in, and the *p* ... 2Chr 23:13 8269
And all the *p* and all the people ... 2Chr 24:10 8269
of Jehoiada came the *p* of Judah ... 2Chr 24:17 8269
destroyed all the *p* of the people ... 2Chr 24:23 8269
and the spoil before the *p* ... 2Chr 28:14 8269
house of the king, and of the *p* ... 2Chr 28:21 8269
the *p* commanded the Levites to ... 2Chr 29:30 8269
king had taken counsel, and his *p* ... 2Chr 30:2 8269
his *p* throughout all Israel and ... 2Chr 30:6 8269
of the king and of the *p*, by the ... 2Chr 30:12 8269
the *p* gave to the congregation a ... 2Chr 30:24 8269
the *p* came and saw the heaps, they ... 2Chr 31:8 8269
He took counsel with his *p* ... 2Chr 32:3 8269
ambassadors of the *p* of Babylon ... 2Chr 32:31 8269
his *p* gave willingly unto the ... 2Chr 35:8 8269
of the king, and of his *p* ... 2Chr 36:18 8269
and before all the king's mighty *p* ... Ezr 7:28 8269
the *p* had appointed for the ... Ezr 8:20 8269
the *p* came to me, saying, The ... Ezr 9:1 8269
yea, the hand of the *p* and rulers ... Ezr 9:2 8269
according to the counsel of the *p* ... Ezr 10:8 8269
upon us, on our kings, on our *p* ... Neh 9:32 8269
Neither have our kings, our *p* ... Neh 9:34 8269
and our *p*, Levites, and priests, ... Neh 9:38 8269
Then I brought up the *p* of Judah ... Neh 12:31 8269
and half of the *p* of Judah ... Neh 12:32 8269
he made a feast unto all his *p* ... Est 1:3 8269
p of the provinces, being before ... Est 1:3 8269
the people and the *p* her beauty ... Est 1:11 8269
and Memucan, the seven *p* of Persia ... Est 1:14 8269
answered before the king and the *p* ... Est 1:16 8269
king only, but also to all the *p* ... Est 1:16 8269
this day unto all the king's *p* ... Est 1:18 8269
saying pleased the king and the *p* ... Est 1:21 8269
made a great feast unto all his *p* ... Est 2:18 8269
all the *p* that were with him ... Est 3:1 8269
he had advanced him above the *p* ... Est 5:11 8269
of one of the king's most noble *p* ... Est 6:9 8269
Or with *p* that had gold, who ... Job 3:15 8269
He leadeth *p* away spoiled, and ... Job 12:19 3548
He poureth contempt upon *p* ... Job 12:21 5081
The *p* refrained talking, and laid ... Job 29:9 8269
and to *p*, Ye are ungodly ... Job 34:18 5081
accepteth not the persons of *p* ... Job 34:19 8269
mayest make *p* in all the earth ... Ps 45:16 8269
The *p* of the people are gathered ... Ps 47:9 5081
the *p* of Judah and their council, ... Ps 68:27 8269
the *p* of Zebulun ... Ps 68:27 8269
and the *p* of Naphtali ... Ps 68:27 8269
P shall come out of Egypt ... Ps 68:31 2831
He shall cut off the spirit of *p* ... Ps 76:12 5057
men, and fall like one of the *p* ... Ps 82:7 8269
yea, all their *p* as Zebah ... Ps 83:11 5257
To bind his *p* at his pleasure ... Ps 105:22 8269
He poureth contempt upon *p* ... Ps 107:40 5081
That he may set him with *p* ... Ps 113:8 5081
even with the *p* of his people ... Ps 113:8 5081
LORD than to put confidence in *p* ... Ps 118:9 5081
P also did sit and speak against ... Ps 119:23 8269
P have persecuted me without a ... Ps 119:161 8269
Put not your trust in *p*, nor in ... Ps 146:3 5081
p, and all judges of the earth ... Ps 148:11 8269
kings reign, and *p* decree justice ... Prov 8:15 7336
By me *p* rule, and nobles, even all ... Prov 8:16 8269
good, nor to strike *p* for equity ... Prov 17:26 5081
for a servant to have rule over *p* ... Prov 19:10 8269
of a land many are the *p* thereof ... Prov 28:2 8269
nor for *p* strong drink ... Prov 31:4 7336
p walking as servants upon the ... Eccl 10:7 8269
and thy *p* eat in the morning ... Eccl 10:16 8269
thy *p* eat in due season, for ... Eccl 10:17 8269
Thy *p* are rebellious, and ... Is 1:23 8269
will give children to be their *p* ... Is 3:4 8269
of his people, and the *p* thereof ... Is 3:14 8269
Are not my *p* altogether kings ... Is 10:8 8269
Surely the *p* of Zoan are fools, ... Is 19:11 8269
The *p* of Zoan are become fools, ... Is 19:13 8269
the *p* of Noph are deceived ... Is 19:13 8269
arise, ye *p*, and anoint the shield ... Is 21:5 8269
city, whose merchants are *p* ... Is 23:8 8269
For his *p* were at Zoan, and his ... Is 30:4 8269
his *p* shall be afraid of the ... Is 31:9 8269
and *p* shall rule in judgment ... Is 32:1 8269
all her *p* shall be nothing ... Is 34:12 8269
That bringeth the *p* to nothing ... Is 40:23 7336
shall come upon *p* as upon morter ... Is 41:25 5461
profaned the *p* of the sanctuary ... Is 43:28 8269
p also shall worship, because of ... Is 49:7 8269
of Judah, against the *p* thereof ... Jer 1:18 8269
they, their kings, their *p* ... Jer 2:26 8269
perish, and the heart of the *p* ... Jer 4:9 8269
of Judah, and the bones of his *p* ... Jer 8:1 8269
p sitting upon the throne of ... Jer 17:25 8269
and on horses, they, and their *p* ... Jer 17:25 8269
and the *p* of Judah, with the ... Jer 24:1 8269
the king of Judah, and his *p* ... Jer 24:8 8269
the *p* thereof, to make them a ... Jer 25:18 8269
Egypt, and his servants, and his *p* ... Jer 25:19 8269
When the *p* of Judah heard these ... Jer 26:10 8269
and the prophets unto the *p* ... Jer 26:11 8269
spake Jeremiah unto all the *p* ... Jer 26:12 8269
Then said the *p* and all the people ... Jer 26:16 8269
all his mighty men, and all the *p* ... Jer 26:21 8269
the *p* of Judah and Jerusalem, and ... Jer 29:2 8269
anger, they, their kings, their *p* ... Jer 32:32 8269
Now when all the *p*, and all the ... Jer 34:10 8269
The *p* of Judah ... Jer 34:19 8269
the *p* of Jerusalem, the eunuchs, ... Jer 34:19 8269
his *p* will I give into the hand ... Jer 34:21 8269
which was by the chamber of the *p* ... Jer 35:4 8269
all the *p* sat there, even ... Jer 36:12 8269
the son of Hananiah, and all the *p* ... Jer 36:12 8269
Therefore all the *p* sent Jehudi ... Jer 36:14 8269
Then said the *p* unto Baruch ... Jer 36:19 8269
in the ears of all the *p* which ... Jer 36:21 8269
Jeremiah, and brought him to the *p* ... Jer 37:14 8269
Wherefore the *p* were wroth with ... Jer 37:15 8269
Therefore the *p* said unto the ... Jer 38:4 8269
unto the king of Babylon's *p* ... Jer 38:17 8269
forth to the king of Babylon's *p* ... Jer 38:18 8269
forth to the king of Babylon's *p* ... Jer 38:22 8269
But if the *p* hear that I have ... Jer 38:25 8269
Then came all the *p* unto Jeremiah ... Jer 38:27 8269
all the *p* of the king of Babylon ... Jer 39:3 8269
of the *p* of the king of Babylon ... Jer 39:3 8269
and all the king of Babylon's *p* ... Jer 39:13 7227
the *p* of the king, even ten men ... Jer 41:1 7227
our fathers, our kings, and our *p* ... Jer 44:17 8269
fathers, your kings, and your *p* ... Jer 44:21 8269
his priests and his *p* together ... Jer 48:7 8269
and his priests and his *p* together ... Jer 49:3 8269
from thence the king and the *p* ... Jer 49:38 8269
of Babylon, and upon her *p* ... Jer 50:35 8269
And I will make drunk her *p* ... Jer 51:57 8269
also all the *p* of Judah in Riblah ... Jer 52:10 8269
her *p* are become like harts that ... Lam 1:6 8269
the kingdom and the *p* thereof ... Lam 2:2 8269
her *p* are among the Gentiles ... Lam 2:9 8269
P are hanged up by their hand ... Lam 5:12 8269
son of Benaiah, *p* of the people ... Eze 11:1 8269
the *p* thereof, and led them with ... Eze 17:12 8269
a lamentation for the *p* of Israel ... Eze 19:1 5387
shall be upon all the *p* of Israel ... Eze 21:12 5387
the *p* of Israel, every one were ... Eze 22:6 5387
Her *p* in the midst thereof are ... Eze 22:27 8269
heads, all of them *p* to look to ... Eze 23:15 7991
Then all the *p* of the sea shall ... Eze 26:16 5387
all the *p* of Kedar, they occupied ... Eze 27:21 5387
is Edom, her kings, and all her *p* ... Eze 32:29 5387
There be the *p* of the north ... Eze 32:30 5257
the blood of the *p* of the earth ... Eze 39:18 5387
my *p* shall no more oppress my ... Eze 45:8 5387
Let it suffice you, O *p* of Israel ... Eze 45:9 5387
of the king's seed, and of the *p* ... Dan 1:3 6579
sent to gather together the *p* ... Dan 3:2 324
Then the *p*, the governors, and ... Dan 3:3 324
And the *p*, governors, and captains, ... Dan 3:27 324
that the king, and his *p*, his ... Dan 5:2 7261
and the king, and his *p*, his wives, ... Dan 5:3 7261
kingdom an hundred and twenty *p* ... Dan 6:1 324
that the *p* might give accounts ... Dan 6:2 324
above the presidents and *p* ... Dan 6:3 324
p sought to find occasion against ... Dan 6:4 324
p assembled together to the king, ... Dan 6:6 324
kingdom, the governors, and the *p* ... Dan 6:7 324
stand up against the Prince of *p* ... Dan 8:25 8269
in thy name to our kings, our *p* ... Dan 9:6 8269
of face, to our kings, to our *p* ... Dan 9:8 8269
lo, Michael, one of the chief *p* ... Dan 10:13 8269
shall be strong, and one of his *p* ... Dan 11:5 8269
Egypt their gods, with their *p* ... Dan 11:8 5257
The *p* of Judah were like them ... Hos 5:10 8269
and the *p* with their lies ... Hos 7:3 8269
In the day of our king the *p* have ... Hos 7:5 8269
their *p* shall fall by the sword ... Hos 7:16 8269
they have made *p*, and I knew it ... Hos 8:4 8269
for the burden of the king of *p* ... Hos 8:10 8269
all their *p* are revolters ... Hos 9:15 8269
thou saidst, Give me a king and *p* ... Hos 13:10 8269
his *p* together, saith the LORD ... Amos 1:15 8269
slay all the *p* thereof with him ... Amos 2:3 8269
ye *p* of the house of Israel ... Mic 3:1 7101
p of the house of Israel, that ... Mic 3:9 7101
the *p* shall be a scorn unto them ... Hab 1:10 7336
that I will punish the *p* ... Zeph 1:8 8269
Her *p* within her are roaring ... Zeph 3:3 8269
not the least among the *p* of Juda ... Mt 2:6 *2232*
Ye know that the *p* of the ... Mt 20:25 *758*
nor of the *p* of this world, that ... 1Cor 2:6 *758*
Which none of the *p* of this world ... 1Cor 2:8 *758*

PRINCESS {1}
p among the provinces, how is she ... Lam 1:1 8282

PRINCESSES {1}
And he had seven hundred wives, *p* ... 1Kin 11:3 8282

PRINCIPAL {17}
Take thou also unto thee *p* spices ... Ex 30:23 7218
he shall even restore it in the *p* ... Lev 6:5 7218
his trespass with the *p* thereof ... Num 5:7 7218
the son of Nathan was *p* officer ... 1Kin 4:5 3548
the *p* scribe of the host, which ... 2Kin 25:19 8269
one *p* household being taken for ... 1Chr 24:6 1
even the *p* fathers over against ... 1Chr 24:31 7218
of Asaph, was the *p* to begin the ... Neh 11:17 7218
Wisdom is the *p* thing ... Prov 4:7 7225
broken down the *p* plants thereof ... Is 16:8 8291
cummin, and cast in the *p* wheat ... Is 28:25 7795
in the ashes, ye *p* of the flock ... Jer 25:34 117
nor the *p* of the flock to escape ... Jer 25:35 117
an howling of the *p* of the flock ... Jer 25:36 117
the *p* scribe of the host, who ... Jer 52:25 8269
seven shepherds, and eight *p* men ... Mic 5:5 5257
p men of the city, at ... Acts 25:23 *3588,2596,1851,5607*

PRINCIPALITIES {7}
for your *p* shall come down, even ... Jer 13:18 4761
nor life, nor angels, nor *p* ... Rom 8:38 *746*
To the intent that now unto the *p* ... Eph 3:10 *746*
flesh and blood, but against *p* ... Eph 6:12 *746*
be thrones, or dominions, or *p* ... Col 1:16 *746*
And having spoiled *p* and powers, he ... Col 2:15 *746*
them in mind to be subject to *p* ... Titus 3:1 *746*

PRINCIPALITY {2}
Far above all *p*, and power, and ... Eph 1:21 *746*
him, which is the head of all *p* ... Col 2:10 *746*

PRINCIPLES {2}
the first *p* of the oracles of God ... Heb 5:12 *4747*
Therefore leaving the *p* of the ... Heb 6:1 *746*

PRINT {4}
dead, nor *p* any marks upon you ... Lev 19:28 5414
thou settest a *p* upon the heels ... Job 13:27 2707
in his hands the *p* of the nails ... Jn 20:25 *5179*
my finger into the *p* of the nails ... Jn 20:25 *5179*

PRINTED {1}
oh that they were *p* in a book ... Job 19:23 2710

PRISCA (*pris'-cah*) {1} See PRISCILLA. *Same as Priscilla.*
Salute *P* and Aquila, and the ... 2Ti 4:19 *4251*

PRISCILLA (*pris-sil'-lah*) {5} See PRISCA. *Wife of Aquila and co-worker of Paul.*
come from Italy, with his wife *P* ... Acts 18:2 *4252*
thence into Syria, and with him *P* ... Acts 18:18 *4252*
P had heard, they took him unto ... Acts 18:26 *4252*
Greet *P* and Aquila my helpers in ... Rom 16:3 *4252*
P salute you much in the Lord, ... 1Cor 16:19 *4252*

PRISED {1}
price that I was *p* at of them ... Zec 11:13 3365

PRISON {90}
took him, and put him into the *p* ... Gen 39:20 1004,5470
and he was there in the *p* ... Gen 39:20 1004,5470
the sight of the keeper of the *p* ... Gen 39:21 1004,5470
the keeper of the *p* committed to ... Gen 39:22 1004,5470
the prisoners that were in the *p* ... Gen 39:22 1004,5470
The keeper of the *p* looked not to ... Gen 39:23 1004,5470
captain of the guard, into the *p* ... Gen 40:3 1004,5470
Egypt, which were bound in the *p* .. Gen 40:5 1004,5470
brother, and ye shall be kept in *p* ... Gen 42:16
be bound in the house of your *p* ... Gen 42:19 4929

P

and he did grind in the *p* house ... Judg 16:21 631
for Samson out of the *p* house ... Judg 16:25 631
king, Put this fellow in the *p* ... 1Kin 22:27 1004,3608
shut him up, and bound him in *p* ... 2Kin 17:4 1004,3608
Jehoiachin king of Judah out of *p* ... 2Kin 25:27 1004,3608
And changed his *p* garments ... 2Kin 25:29 3608
the seer, and put him in a *p* house ... 2Chr 16:10 4115
king, Put this fellow in the *p* ... 2Chr 18:26 1004,612
that was by the court of the *p* ... Neh 3:25 4307
and they stood still in the *p* gate ... Neh 12:39 4307
Bring my soul out of *p*, that I ... Ps 142:7 4525
For out of *p* he cometh to reign ... Eccl 4:14 1004,612
pit, and shall be shut up in the *p* ... Is 24:22 4525
out the prisoners from the *p* ... Is 42:7 4525
in darkness out of the *p* house ... Is 42:7 3608
and they are hid in *p* houses ... Is 42:22 3608
He was taken from *p* and from ... Is 53:8 6115
the opening of the *p* to them that ... Is 61:1 6495
that thou shouldest put him in *p* ... Jer 29:26 4115
was shut up in the court of the *p* ... Jer 32:2 4307
p according to the word of the ... Jer 32:8 4307
that sat in the court of the *p* ... Jer 32:12 4307
yet shut up in the court of the *p* ... Jer 33:1 4307
for they had not put him into *p* ... Jer 37:4 1004,3608
put him in *p* in the house of ... Jer 37:15 1004,612
for they had made that the *p* ... Jer 37:15 1004,3608
people, that ye have put me in *p* ... Jer 37:18 1004,3608
Jeremiah into the court of the *p* ... Jer 37:21 4307
remained in the court of the *p* ... Jer 37:21 4307
that was in the court of the *p* ... Jer 38:6 4307
remained in the court of the *p* ... Jer 38:13 4307
abode in the court of the *p* until ... Jer 38:28 4307
out of the court of the *p* ... Jer 39:14 4307
was shut up in the court of the *p* ... Jer 39:15 4307
put him in *p* till the day of his ... Jer 52:11 1004,6486
and brought him forth out of *p* ... Jer 52:31 1004,3608
And changed his *p* garments ... Jer 52:33 3608
heard that John was cast into *p* ... Mt 4:12 *3860*
officer, and thou be cast into *p* ... Mt 5:25 *5438*
in the *p* the works of Christ ... Mt 11:2 *1201*
put him in *p* for Herodias' sake, ... Mt 14:3 *5438*
sent, and beheaded John in the *p* ... Mt 14:10 *5438*
but went and cast him into *p* ... Mt 18:30 *5438*
I was in *p*, and ye came unto me ... Mt 25:36 *5438*
Or when saw we thee sick, or in *p* ... Mt 25:39 *5438*
sick, and in *p*, and ye visited me ... Mt 25:43 *5438*
or naked, or sick, or in *p* ... Mt 25:44 *5438*
Now after that John was put in *p* ... Mk 1:14 *3860*
bound him in *p* for Herodias' sake ... Mk 6:17 *5438*
he went and beheaded him in the *p* ... Mk 6:27 *5438*
all, that he shut up John in *p* ... Lk 3:20 *5438*
and the officer cast thee into *p* ... Lk 12:58 *5438*
to go with thee, both into *p* ... Lk 22:33 *5438*
and for murder, was cast into *p* ... Lk 23:19 *5438*
and murder was cast into *p* ... Lk 23:25 *5438*
For John was not yet cast into *p* ... Jn 3:24 *5438*
and put them in the common *p* ... Acts 5:18 *5084*
Lord by night opened the *p* doors ... Acts 5:19 *5438*
sent to the *p* to have them ... Acts 5:21 *1201*
came, and found them not in the *p* ... Acts 5:22 *5438*
The *p* truly found we shut with ... Acts 5:23 *1201*
the men whom ye put in *p* are ... Acts 5:25 *5438*
men and women committed them to *p* ... Acts 8:3 *5438*
apprehended him, he put him in *p* ... Acts 12:4 *5438*
Peter therefore was kept in *p* ... Acts 12:5 *5438*
before the door kept the *p* ... Acts 12:6 *5438*
him, and a light shined in the *p* ... Acts 12:7 *3612*
Lord had brought him out of the *p* ... Acts 12:17 *5438*
upon them, they cast them into *p* ... Acts 16:23 *5438*
thrust them into the inner *p* ... Acts 16:24 *5438*
foundations of the *p* were shaken ... Acts 16:26 *1201*
the keeper of the *p* awaking out ... Acts 16:27 *1200*
sleep, and seeing the *p* doors open ... Acts 16:27 *5438*
the keeper of the *p* told this ... Acts 16:36 *1200*
Romans, and have cast us into *p* ... Acts 16:37 *5438*
And they went out of the *p* ... Acts 16:40 *5438*
of the saints did I shut up in *p* ... Acts 26:10 *5438*
and preached unto the spirits in *p* ... 1Pet 3:19 *5438*
shall cast some of you into *p* ... Rev 2:10 *5438*
shall be loosed out of his *p* ... Rev 20:7 *5438*

PRISONER {13}
sighing of the *p* come before thee ... Ps 79:11 616
To hear the groaning of the *p* ... Ps 102:20 615
to release unto the people a *p* ... Mt 27:15 *1198*
And they had then a notable *p* ... Mt 27:16 *1198*
feast he released unto them one *p* ... Mk 15:6 *1198*
Paul the *p* called me unto him, and ... Acts 23:18 *1198*
to me unreasonable to send a *p* ... Acts 25:27 *1198*
yet was I delivered *p* from ... Acts 28:17 *1198*
the *p* of Jesus Christ for you ... Eph 3:1 *1198*
the *p* of the Lord, beseech you ... Eph 4:1 *1198*
of our Lord, nor of me his *p* ... 2Ti 1:8 *1198*
a *p* of Jesus Christ, and Timothy ... Philem 1 *1198*
now also a *p* of Jesus Christ ... Philem 9 *1198*

PRISONERS {20}
where the king's *p* were bound ... Gen 39:20 615
all the *p* that were in the prison ... Gen 39:22 615
Israel, and took some of them *p* ... Num 21:1 7628
There the *p* rest together ... Job 3:18 615
the poor, and despiseth not his *p* ... Ps 69:33 615
The LORD looseth the *p* ... Ps 146:7 631
they shall bow down under the *p* ... Is 10:4 616
opened not the house of his *p* ... Is 14:17 615
Assyria lead away the Egyptians *p* ... Is 20:4 7628
as *p* are gathered in the pit, and ... Is 24:22 616
bring out the *p* from the prison ... Is 42:7 616
That thou mayest say to the *p* ... Is 49:9 631

his feet all the *p* of the earth ... Lam 3:34 615
p out of the pit wherein is no ... Zec 9:11 615
to the strong hold, ye *p* of hope ... Zec 9:12 615
and the *p* heard them ... Acts 16:25 *1198*
that the *p* had been fled ... Acts 16:27 *1198*
certain other *p* unto one named ... Acts 27:1 *1202*
counsel was to kill the *p* ... Acts 27:42 *1202*
the *p* to the captain of the guard ... Acts 28:16 *1198*

PRISONS {3}
up to the synagogues, and into *p* ... Lk 21:12 *5438*
and delivering into *p* both men ... Acts 22:4 *5438*
in *p* more frequent, in deaths oft ... 2Cor 11:23 *5438*

PRIVATE {1}
is of any *p* interpretation ... 2Pet 1:20 *2398*

PRIVATELY {8}
the disciples came unto him *p* ... Mt 24:3 *2596,2398*
into a desert place by ship *p* ... Mk 6:32 *2596,2398*
house, his disciples asked him *p* ... Mk 9:28 *2596,2398*
John and Andrew asked him *p* ... Mk 13:3 *2596,2398*
went aside *p* into a desert place ... Lk 9:10 *2596,2398*
him unto his disciples, and said *p* ... Lk 10:23 *2596,2398*
hand, and went with him aside *p* ... Acts 23:19 *2596,2398*
but *p* to them which were of ... Gal 2:2 *2596,2398*

PRIVILY {15}
sent messengers unto Abimelech *p* ... Judg 9:31 8649
off the skirt of Saul's robe *p* ... 1Sa 24:4 3909
his eyes are *p* set against the ... Ps 10:8 6845
that they may *p* shoot at the ... Ps 11:2 652
net that they have laid *p* for me ... Ps 31:4 2934
they commune of laying snares *p* ... Ps 64:5 2934
Whoso *p* slandereth his neighbour, ... Ps 101:5 5643
have they *p* laid a snare for me ... Ps 142:3 2934
let us lurk *p* for the innocent ... Prov 1:11
they lurk *p* for their own lives ... Prov 1:18
was minded to put her away *p* ... Mt 1:19 *2977*
when he had *p* called the wise men ... Mt 2:7 *2977*
and now do they thrust us out *p* ... Acts 16:37 *2977*
who came in *p* to spy out our ... Gal 2:4 *3922*
who *p* shall bring in damnable ... 2Pet 2:1 *3918*

PRIVY {4}
or hath his *p* member cut off, ... Deut 23:1 8212
which thine heart is *p* to ... 1Kin 2:44 3045
entereth into their *p* chambers ... Eze 21:14 2314
his wife also being *p* to it ... Acts 5:2 *4894*

PRIZE {2}
run all, but one receiveth the *p* ... 1Cor 9:24 *1017*
p of the high calling of God in ... Phil 3:14 *1017*

PROCEED {15}
that *p* out of the candlestick ... Ex 25:35 3318
any word *p* out of your mouth ... Josh 6:10 3318
which shall *p* out of thy bowels, ... 2Sa 7:12 3318
but I will *p* no further ... Job 40:5 3254
I will *p* to do a marvellous work ... Is 29:14 3254
for a law shall *p* from me ... Is 51:4 3318
for they *p* from evil to evil, and ... Jer 9:3 3318
out of them shall *p* thanksgiving ... Jer 30:19 3318
their governor shall *p* from the ... Jer 30:21 3318
dignity shall *p* of themselves ... Hab 1:7 3318
But those things which *p* out of ... Mt 15:18 *1607*
out of the heart *p* evil thoughts ... Mt 15:19 *1831*
p evil thoughts, adulteries, ... Mk 7:21 *1607*
communication *p* out of your mouth ... Eph 4:29 *1607*
But they shall *p* no further ... 2Ti 3:9 *4298*

PROCEEDED {9}
then whatsoever *p* out of her lips ... Num 30:12 4161
which hath *p* out of your mouth ... Num 32:24 3318
which hath *p* out of thy mouth ... Judg 11:36 3318
Elihu also *p*, and said, ... Job 36:1 3254
words which *p* out of his mouth ... Lk 4:22 *1607*
for I *p* forth and came from God ... Jn 8:42 *1831*
he *p* further to take Peter also ... Acts 12:3 *4369*
And out of the throne *p* lightnings ... Rev 4:5 *1607*
which sword *p* out of his mouth ... Rev 19:21 *1607*

PROCEEDETH {11}
The thing *p* from the LORD ... Gen 24:50 3318
to all that *p* out of his mouth ... Num 30:2 3318
but by every word that *p* out of ... Deut 8:3 4161
Wickedness *p* from the wicked ... 1Sa 24:13 3318
an error which *p* from the ruler ... Eccl 10:5 3318
mouth of the most High *p* not evil ... Lam 3:38 3318
therefore wrong judgment *p* ... Hab 1:4 3318
but by every word that *p* out of ... Mt 4:4 *1607*
which *p* from the Father, he shall ... Jn 15:26 *1607*
Out of the same mouth *p* blessing ... Jas 3:10 *1831*
fire *p* out of their mouth, and ... Rev 11:5 *1607*

PROCEEDING {1}
p out of the throne of God and of ... Rev 22:1 *1607*

PROCESS {5}
in *p* of time it came to pass, ... Gen 4:3 7093
in *p* of time the daughter of ... Gen 38:12 7235
And it came to pass in *p* of time ... Ex 2:23 7227
And it came to pass in *p* of time ... Judg 11:4
came to pass, that in *p* of time ... 2Chr 21:19

PROCHORUS *(prok'-o-rus)* {1} *A leader in the Jerusalem church.*
the Holy Ghost, and Philip, and *P* ... Acts 6:5 *4402*

PROCLAIM {23}
I will *p* the name of the LORD ... Ex 33:19 7121
which ye shall *p* to be holy ... Lev 23:2 7121
which ye shall *p* in their seasons ... Lev 23:4 7121
ye shall *p* on the selfsame day, ... Lev 23:21 7121
which ye shall *p* to be holy ... Lev 23:37 7121
p liberty throughout all the land ... Lev 25:10 7121
against it, then *p* peace unto it ... Deut 20:10 7121

p in the ears of the people, ... Judg 7:3 7121
P a fast, and set Naboth on high ... 1Kin 21:9 7121
P a solemn assembly for Baal ... 2Kin 10:20 6942
p in all their cities, and in ... Neh 8:15 5674
p before him, Thus shall it be ... Est 6:9 7121
Most men will *p* every one his own ... Prov 20:6 7121
to *p* liberty to the captives, and ... Is 61:1 7121
To *p* the acceptable year of the ... Is 61:2 7121
p these words toward the north, ... Jer 3:12 7121
p there this word, and say, Hear ... Jer 7:2 7121
P all these words in the cities ... Jer 11:6 7121
p there the words that I shall ... Jer 19:2 7121
Jerusalem, to *p* liberty unto them ... Jer 34:8 7121
I *p* a liberty for you, saith the ... Jer 34:17 7121
P ye this among the Gentiles ... Joel 3:9 7121
of thanksgiving with leaven, and *p* ... Amos 4:5 7121

PROCLAIMED {16}
there, and *p* the name of the LORD ... Ex 34:5 7121
LORD passed by before him, and *p* ... Ex 34:6 7121
it to be *p* throughout the camp ... Ex 36:6 5674
They *p* a fast, and set Naboth on ... 1Kin 21:12 7121
And they *p* it ... 2Kin 10:20 7121
God *p*, who *p* these words ... 2Kin 23:16 7121
p these things that thou hast ... 2Kin 23:17 7121
p a fast throughout all Judah ... 2Chr 20:3 7121
Then I *p* a fast there, at the ... Ezr 8:21 7121
p before him, Thus shall it be ... Est 6:11 7121
the LORD hath *p* unto the end of ... Is 62:11 8085
that they *p* a fast before the ... Jer 36:9 7121
p a fast, and put on sackcloth, ... Jonah 3:5 7121
And he caused it to be *p* and ... Jonah 3:7 2199
shall be *p* upon the housetops ... Lk 12:3 *2784*

PROCLAIMETH {1}
the heart of fools *p* foolishness ... Prov 12:23 7121

PROCLAIMING {3}
in *p* liberty every man to his ... Jer 34:15 7121
in *p* liberty, every one to his ... Jer 34:17 7121
strong angel *p* with a loud voice ... Rev 5:2 *2784*

PROCLAMATION {9}
and Aaron made *p*, and said, To ... Ex 32:5 7121
Asa made a *p* throughout all Judah ... 1Kin 15:22 8085
there went a *p* throughout the ... 1Kin 22:36 7440
they made a *p* through Judah and ... 2Chr 24:9 6963
to make *p* throughout all Israel ... 2Chr 30:5 5674,6963
that he made a *p* throughout all ... 2Chr 36:22 5674,6963
that he made a *p* throughout all ... Ezr 1:1 5674,6963
they made *p* throughout Judah ... Ezr 10:7 5674,6963
made a *p* concerning him, that he ... Dan 5:29 3745

PROCURE {2}
Thus might we *p* great evil ... Jer 26:19 6213
the prosperity that I *p* unto it ... Jer 33:9 6213

PROCURED {2}
Hast thou not *p* this unto thyself ... Jer 2:17 6213
thy doings have *p* these things ... Jer 4:18 6213

PROCURETH {1}
diligently seeketh good *p* favour ... Prov 11:27 1245

PRODUCE {1}
P your cause, saith the LORD ... Is 41:21 7126

PROFANE {33}
neither shalt thou *p* the name of ... Lev 18:21 2490
neither shalt thou *p* the name of ... Lev 19:12 2490
sanctuary, and to *p* my holy name ... Lev 20:3 2490
among his people, to *p* himself ... Lev 21:4 2490
not *p* the name of their God ... Lev 21:6 2490
take a wife that is a whore, or *p* ... Lev 21:7 2491
if she *p* herself by playing the ... Lev 21:9 2490
nor *p* the sanctuary of his God ... Lev 21:12 2490
widow, or a divorced woman, or *p* ... Lev 21:14 2491
Neither shall he *p* his seed among ... Lev 21:15 2490
that he *p* not my sanctuaries ... Lev 21:23 2490
that they *p* not my holy name in ... Lev 22:2 2490
and die therefore, if they *p* it ... Lev 22:9 2490
they shall not *p* the holy things ... Lev 22:15 2490
Neither shall ye *p* my holy name ... Lev 22:32 2490
that ye do, and *p* the sabbath day ... Neh 13:17 2490
For both prophet and priest are *p* ... Jer 23:11 2610
p wicked prince of Israel, whose ... Eze 21:25 2491
difference between the holy and *p* ... Eze 22:26 2455
day into my sanctuary to *p* it ... Eze 23:39 2490
I will *p* my sanctuary, the ... Eze 24:21 2490
as *p* out of the mountain of God ... Eze 28:16 2490
the sanctuary and the *p* place ... Eze 42:20 2455
difference between the holy and *p* ... Eze 44:23 2455
shall be a *p* place for the city, ... Eze 48:15 2455
the same maid, to *p* my holy name ... Amos 2:7 2490
in the temple *p* the sabbath ... Mt 12:5 *953*
hath gone about to *p* the temple ... Acts 24:6 *953*
and for sinners, for unholy and *p* ... 1Ti 1:9 *952*
But refuse *p* and old wives' fables ... 1Ti 4:7 *952*
to thy trust, avoiding *p* and vain ... 1Ti 6:20 *952*
But shun *p* and vain babblings ... 2Ti 2:16 *952*
or *p* person, as Esau, who for one ... Heb 12:16 *952*

PROFANED {15}
because he hath *p* the hallowed ... Lev 19:8 2490
thou hast *p* his crown by casting ... Ps 89:39 2490
Therefore I have *p* the princes of ... Is 43:28 2490
things, and hast *p* my sabbaths ... Eze 22:8 2490
law, and have *p* mine holy things ... Eze 22:26 2490
my sabbaths, and I am *p* among them ... Eze 22:26 2490
same day, and have *p* my sabbaths ... Eze 23:38 2490
my sanctuary, when it was *p* ... Eze 25:3 2490
they *p* my holy name, when they ... Eze 36:20 2490
of Israel had *p* among the heathen ... Eze 36:21 2490
which ye have *p* among the heathen ... Eze 36:22 2490

which was *p* among the heathen, ... Eze 36:23 2490
which ye have *p* in the midst of ..... Eze 36:23 2490
But ye have *p* it, in that ye say, ... Mal 1:12 2490
for Judah hath *p* the holiness of ..... Mal 2:11 2490

PROFANENESS {1}
is *p* gone forth into all the land ..... Jer 23:15 2613

PROFANETH {1}
the whore, she *p* her father ..... Lev 21:9 2490

PROFANING {2}
upon Israel by *p* the sabbath ..... Neh 13:18 2490
by *p* the covenant of our fathers ..... Mal 2:10 2490

PROFESS {3}
I *p* this day unto the LORD thy ..... Deut 26:3 5046
And then will I *p* unto them ..... Mt 7:23 *3670*
They *p* that they know God ..... Titus 1:16 *3670*

PROFESSED {2}
they glorify God for your *p* 2Cor 9:13 *3671*
hast *p* a good profession before 1Ti 6:12 *3670*

PROFESSING {3}
P themselves to be wise, they ..... Rom 1:22 *5335*
But (which becometh women *p* 1Ti 2:10 *1861*
Which some *p* have erred 1Ti 6:21 *1861*

PROFESSION {4}
a good *p* before many witnesses 1Ti 6:12 *3671*
Apostle and High Priest of our *p* ..... Heb 3:1 *3671*
of God, let us hold fast our *p* ..... Heb 4:14 *3671*
Let us hold fast the *p* of our ..... Heb 10:23 *3671*

PROFIT {45}
what *p* shall this birthright do ..... Gen 25:32
What *p* is it if we slay our ..... Gen 37:26 1215
which cannot *p* nor deliver 1Sa 12:21 3276
for the king's *p* to suffer them ..... Est 3:8 7737
what *p* should we have, if we pray ..... Job 21:15 3276
the strength of their hands *p* me ..... Job 30:2
What *p* shall I have, if I be ..... Job 35:3 3276
may *p* the son of man ..... Job 35:8
What *p* is there in my blood, when ..... Ps 30:9 1215
Treasures of wickedness *p* nothing ..... Prov 10:2 3276
Riches *p* not in the day of wrath ..... Prov 11:4 3276
In all labour there is *p* ..... Prov 14:23 4195
What *p* hath a man of all his ..... Eccl 1:3 3504
there was no *p* under the sun ..... Eccl 2:11 3504
What *p* hath he that worketh in ..... Eccl 3:9 3504
Moreover the *p* of the earth is ..... Eccl 5:9 3504
what *p* hath he that hath laboured ..... Eccl 5:16 3504
by it there is *p* to them that see ..... Eccl 7:11 3148
of a people that could not *p* them ..... Is 30:5 3276
nor be an help nor *p* ..... Is 30:5 3276
to a people that shall not *p* them ..... Is 30:6 3276
delectable things shall not *p* ..... Is 44:9 3276
if so be thou shalt be able to *p* ..... Is 47:12 3276
thy God which teacheth thee to *p* ..... Is 48:17 3276
for they shall not *p* thee ..... Is 57:12 3276
walked after things that do not *p* ..... Jer 2:8 3276
glory for that which doth not *p* ..... Jer 2:11 3276
in lying words, that cannot *p* ..... Jer 7:8 3276
to pain, but shall not *p* ..... Jer 12:13 3276
and things wherein there is no *p* ..... Jer 16:19 3276
shall not *p* this people at all ..... Jer 23:32 3276
what *p* is it that we have kept ..... Mal 3:14 1215
For what shall it *p* a man ..... Mk 8:36 *5623*
or what *p* is there of ..... Rom 3:1 *5622*
And this I speak for your own *p* 1Cor 7:35 *4851*
own *p*, but the *p* of many 1Cor 10:33 *4851*
is given to every man to *p* withal 1Cor 12:7 *4851*
with tongues, what shall I *p* you 1Cor 14:6 *5623*
Christ shall *p* you nothing ..... Gal 5:2 *5623*
strive not about words to no *p* 2Ti 2:14 *5539*
the word preached did not *p* them ..... Heb 4:2 *5623*
but he for our *p*, that we might ..... Heb 12:10 *4851*
What doth it *p*, my brethren, ... Jas 2:14 *3786*
what doth it *p* ..... Jas 2:16 *3786*

PROFITABLE {13}
Can a man be *p* unto God, as he ..... Job 22:2 5532
is wise may be *p* unto himself ..... Job 22:2 5532
but wisdom is *p* to direct ..... Eccl 10:10 3504
image that is *p* for nothing ..... Is 44:10 3276
was marred, it was *p* for nothing ..... Jer 13:7 6743
for it is *p* for thee that one of ..... Mt 5:29 *4851*
for it is *p* for thee that one of ..... Mt 5:30 *4851*
back nothing that was *p* unto you ..... Acts 20:20 *4851*
godliness is *p* unto all things 1Ti 4:8 *5624*
is *p* for doctrine, for reproof, ... 2Ti 3:16 *5624*
for he is *p* to me for the 2Ti 4:11 *2173*
things are good and *p* unto men ..... Titus 3:8 *5624*
unprofitable, but now *p* to thee ..... Philem 11 *2173*

PROFITED {6}
which was right, and it *p* me not ..... Job 33:27 7737
thou mightest be *p* by me ..... Mt 15:5 *5623*
For what is a man *p*, if he shall ..... Mt 16:26 *5623*
thou mightest be *p* by me ..... Mk 7:11 *5623*
p in the Jews' religion above ..... Gal 1:14 *4298*
which have not *p* them that have ..... Heb 13:9 *5623*

PROFITETH {6}
It *p* a man nothing that he should ..... Job 34:9 5532
What *p* the graven image that the ..... Hab 2:18 3276
the flesh *p* nothing ..... Jn 6:63 *5623*
For circumcision verily *p* ..... Rom 2:25 *5623*
have not charity, it *p* me nothing 1Cor 13:3 *5623*
For bodily exercise *p* little 1Ti 4:8 *5624,2076*

PROFITING {1}
that thy *p* may appear to all 1Ti 4:15 *4297*

PROFOUND {1}
revolters are *p* to make slaughter ..... Hos 5:2 6009

PROGENITORS {1}
above the blessings of my *p* unto ..... Gen 49:26 2029

PROGNOSTICATORS {1}
the stargazers, the monthly *p* ..... Is 47:13 3045

PROLONG {14}
ye shall not *p* your days upon it, ... Deut 4:26 748
that thou mayest *p* thy days upon ..... Deut 4:40 748
that ye may *p* your days in the ..... Deut 5:33 748
that ye may *p* your days in the ..... Deut 11:9 748
to the end that he may *p* his days ..... Deut 17:20 748
and that thou mayest *p* thy days ..... Deut 22:7 748
that ye shall not *p* your days ..... Deut 30:18 748
ye shall *p* your days in the land ..... Deut 32:47 748
mine end, that I should *p* my life ..... Job 6:11 748
neither shall he *p* the perfection ..... Job 15:29 5186
Thou wilt *p* the king's life ..... Ps 61:6 3254
covetousness shall *p* his days ..... Prov 28:16 748
neither shall he *p* his days ..... Eccl 8:13 748
see his seed, he shall *p* his days ..... Is 53:10 748

PROLONGED {9}
that thy days may be *p*, and that ..... Deut 5:16 748
and that thy days may be *p* ..... Deut 6:2 748
the state thereof shall be *p* ..... Prov 28:2 748
hundred times, and his days be *p* ..... Eccl 8:12 748
come, and her days shall not be *p* ..... Is 13:22 4900
of Israel, saying, The days are *p* ..... Eze 12:22 748
it shall be no more *p* ..... Eze 12:25 4900
none of my words be *p* any more ..... Eze 12:28 4900
their lives were *p* for a season ..... Dan 7:12 754,3052

PROLONGETH {2}
The fear of the LORD *p* days ..... Prov 10:27 3254
that *p* his life in his wickedness ..... Eccl 7:15 748

PROMISE {53}
and ye shall know my breach of *p* ..... Num 14:34
failed one word of all his good *p* 1Kin 8:56 1697
let thy *p* unto David my father be 2Chr 1:9 1697
should do according to this *p* ..... Neh 5:12 1697
that performeth not this *p* ..... Neh 5:13 1697
people did according to this *p* ..... Neh 5:13 1697
doth his *p* fail for evermore ..... Ps 77:8 562
For he remembered his holy *p* ..... Ps 105:42 1697
I send the *p* of my Father upon ..... Lk 24:49 *1860*
but wait for the *p* of the Father ..... Acts 1:4 *1860*
Father the *p* of the Holy Ghost ..... Acts 2:33 *1860*
For the *p* is unto you, and to your ..... Acts 2:39 *1860*
when the time of the *p* drew nigh ..... Acts 7:17 *1860*
p raised unto Israel a Saviour ..... Acts 13:23 *1860*
how that the *p* which was made ..... Acts 13:32 *1860*
ready, looking for a *p* from thee ..... Acts 23:21 *1860*
p made of God unto our fathers ..... Acts 26:6 *1860*
Unto which *p* our twelve tribes, ... Acts 26:7
For the *p*, that he should be the ..... Rom 4:13 *1860*
the *p* made of none effect ..... Rom 4:14 *1860*
to the end the *p* might be sure to ..... Rom 4:16 *1860*
at the *p* of God through unbelief ..... Rom 4:20 *1860*
but the children of the *p* are ..... Rom 9:8 *1860*
For this is the word of *p* ..... Rom 9:9 *1860*
that we might receive the *p* of ..... Gal 3:14 *1860*
should make the *p* of none effect ..... Gal 3:17 *1860*
be of the law, it is no more of *p* ..... Gal 3:18 *1860*
but God gave it to Abraham by *p* ..... Gal 3:18 *1860*
come to whom the *p* was made ..... Gal 3:19 *1861*
that the *p* by faith of Jesus ..... Gal 3:22 *1860*
seed, and heirs according to the *p* ..... Gal 3:29 *1860*
but he of the freewoman was by *p* ..... Gal 4:23 *1860*
Isaac was, are the children of *p* ..... Gal 4:28 *1860*
sealed with that holy Spirit of *p* ..... Eph 1:13 *1860*
strangers from the covenants of *p* ..... Eph 2:12 *1860*
partakers of his *p* in Christ by ..... Eph 3:6 *1860*
is the first commandment with *p* ..... Eph 6:2 *1860*
having *p* of the life that now is, ... 1Ti 4:8 *1860*
according to the *p* of life which 2Ti 1:1 *1860*
a *p* being left us of entering ..... Heb 4:1 *1860*
For when God made *p* to Abraham ..... Heb 6:13 *1861*
endured, he obtained the *p* ..... Heb 6:15 *1860*
to shew unto the heirs of *p* the ..... Heb 6:17 *1860*
the *p* of eternal inheritance ..... Heb 9:15 *1860*
of God, ye might receive the *p* ..... Heb 10:36 *1860*
he sojourned in the land of *p* ..... Heb 11:9 *1860*
the heirs with him of the same *p* ..... Heb 11:9 *1860*
through faith, received not the *p* ..... Heb 11:39 *1860*
While they *p* them liberty, they 2Pet 2:19 *1861*
Where is the *p* of his coming 2Pet 3:4 *1860*
is not slack concerning his *p* 2Pet 3:9 *1860*
we, according to his *p*, look for 2Pet 3:13 *1862*
this is the *p* that he hath 1Jn 2:25 *1860*

PROMISED {48}
give you, according as he hath *p* ..... Ex 12:25 1696
the place which the LORD hath *p* ..... Num 14:40 559
and bless you, as he hath *p* you ..... Deut 1:11 1696
God of thy fathers hath *p* thee ..... Deut 6:3 1696
into the land which he *p* them ..... Deut 9:28 1696
as the LORD thy God *p* him ..... Deut 10:9 1696
thy border, as he hath *p* thee ..... Deut 12:20 1696
God blesseth thee, as he *p* thee ..... Deut 15:6 1696
he *p* to give unto thy fathers ..... Deut 19:8 1696
which thou hast *p* with thy mouth ..... Deut 23:23 1696
people, as he hath *p* thee ..... Deut 26:18 1696
God of thy fathers hath *p* thee ..... Deut 27:3 1696
as the princes had *p* them ..... Josh 9:21 1696
unto your brethren, as he *p* them ..... Josh 22:4 1696
the LORD your God hath *p* unto you ..... Josh 23:5 1696
for you, as he hath *p* you ..... Josh 23:10 1696
which the LORD your God *p* you ..... Josh 23:15 1696
thou hast *p* this goodness unto 2Sa 7:28 1696
hath made me an house, as he *p* 1Kin 2:24 1696
gave Solomon wisdom, as he *p* him 1Kin 5:12 1696
throne of Israel, as the LORD *p* 1Kin 8:20 1696
according to all that he *p* 1Kin 8:56 1696
which he *p* by the hand of Moses 1Kin 8:56 1696
as I *p* to David thy father, ... 1Kin 9:5 1696
as he *p* him to give him alway a 2Kin 8:19 559
hast *p* this goodness unto thy 1Chr 17:26 1696
throne of Israel, as the LORD *p* 2Chr 6:10 1696
father that which thou hast *p* him 2Chr 6:15 1696
father that which thou hast *p* him 2Chr 6:16 1696
as he *p* to give a light to him and 2Chr 21:7 559
thou hadst *p* to their fathers ..... Neh 9:23 559
p to pay to the king's treasuries ..... Est 4:7 559
all the good that I have *p* them ..... Jer 32:42 1696
I have *p* unto the house of Israel ..... Jer 33:14 1696
Whereupon he *p* with an oath to ..... Mt 14:7 *3670*
were glad, and *p* to give him money ..... Mk 14:11 *1861*
the mercy *p* to our fathers ..... Lk 1:72
And he *p*, and sought opportunity to ..... Lk 22:6 *1843*
yet he *p* that he would give it to ..... Acts 7:5 *1861*
(Which he had *p* afore by his ..... Rom 1:2 *4279*
persuaded that, what he had *p* ..... Rom 4:21 *1861*
lie, *p* before the world began ..... Titus 1:2 *1861*
(for he is faithful that *p* ..... Heb 10:23 *1861*
she judged him faithful who had *p* ..... Heb 11:11 *1861*
but now he hath *p*, saying, Yet ..... Heb 12:26 *1861*
which the Lord hath *p* to them ..... Jas 1:12 *1861*
he hath *p* to them that love him ..... Jas 2:5 *1861*
is the promise that he hath *p* us 1Jn 2:25 *1861*

PROMISEDST {3}
David my father that thou *p* him 1Kin 8:24 1696
David my father that thou *p* him 1Kin 8:25 1696
p them that they should go in to ..... Neh 9:15 559

PROMISES {13}
and the service of God, and the *p* ..... Rom 9:4 *1860*
to confirm the *p* made unto the ..... Rom 15:8 *1860*
For all the *p* of God in him are 2Cor 1:20 *1860*
therefore these *p* dearly beloved 2Cor 7:1 *1860*
and his seed were the *p* made ..... Gal 3:16 *1860*
the law then against the *p* of God ..... Gal 3:21 *1860*
faith and patience inherit the *p* ..... Heb 6:12 *1860*
and blessed him that had the *p* ..... Heb 7:6 *1860*
was established upon better *p* ..... Heb 8:6 *1860*
faith, not having received the *p* ..... Heb 11:13 *1860*
he that had received the *p* ..... Heb 11:17 *1860*
wrought righteousness, obtained *p* ..... Heb 11:33 *1860*
us exceeding great and precious *p* 2Pet 1:4 *1862*

PROMISING {1}
his wicked way, by *p* him life ..... Eze 13:22 2421

PROMOTE {5}
For I will *p* thee unto very great ..... Num 22:17 3513
able indeed to *p* thee to honour ..... Num 22:37 3513
I thought to *p* thee unto great ..... Num 24:11 3513
p Haman the son of Hammedatha the ..... Est 3:1 1431
Exalt her, and she shall *p* thee ..... Prov 4:8 7311

PROMOTED {5}
go to be *p* over the trees ..... Judg 9:9 5128
go to be *p* over the trees ..... Judg 9:11 5128
go to be *p* over the trees ..... Judg 9:13 5128
things wherein the king had *p* him ..... Est 5:11 1431
Then the king *p* Shadrach, Meshach ..... Dan 3:30 6744

PROMOTION {2}
For *p* cometh neither from the ..... Ps 75:6 7311
but shame shall be the *p* of fools ..... Prov 3:35 7311

PRONOUNCE {23}
that a man shall *p* with an oath ..... Lev 5:4 981
look on him, and *p* him unclean ..... Lev 13:3
the priest shall *p* him clean ..... Lev 13:6
the priest shall *p* him unclean ..... Lev 13:8
and the priest shall *p* him unclean ..... Lev 13:11
he shall *p* him clean that hath ..... Lev 13:13
raw flesh, and *p* him to be unclean ..... Lev 13:15
then the priest shall *p* him clean ..... Lev 13:17
the priest shall *p* him unclean ..... Lev 13:20
the priest shall *p* him unclean ..... Lev 13:22
and the priest shall *p* him clean ..... Lev 13:23
the priest shall *p* him unclean ..... Lev 13:25
the priest shall *p* him unclean ..... Lev 13:27
and the priest shall *p* him clean ..... Lev 13:28
the priest shall *p* him unclean ..... Lev 13:30
then the priest shall *p* him clean ..... Lev 13:34
and the priest shall *p* him clean ..... Lev 13:37
the priest shall *p* him utterly ..... Lev 13:44
to *p* it clean, or to *p* it ..... Lev 13:59
shall *p* him clean, and shall let ..... Lev 14:7
priest shall *p* the house clean ..... Lev 14:48
he could not frame to *p* it right ..... Judg 12:6 1696

PRONOUNCED {14}
but that he *p* this prophecy ..... Neh 6:12 1696
hath *p* evil against thee, for the ..... Jer 11:17 1696
Wherefore hath the LORD *p* all ..... Jer 16:10 1696
nation, against whom I have *p* ..... Jer 18:8 1696
the evil that I have *p* against it ..... Jer 19:15 1696
words which I have *p* against it ..... Jer 25:13 1696
evil that he hath *p* against you ..... Jer 26:13 1696
evil which he had *p* against them ..... Jer 26:19 1696
for I have *p* the word, saith the ..... Jer 34:5 1696
evil that I have *p* against them ..... Jer 35:17 1696
LORD hath *p* against this people ..... Jer 36:7 1696
He *p* all these words unto me with ..... Jer 36:18 7126
evil that I have *p* against them ..... Jer 36:31 1691
The LORD thy God hath *p* this evil ..... Jer 40:2 1691

PRONOUNCING {1}
p with his lips to do evil, or to ..... Lev 5:4 981

P

PROOF {5}
that I might know the *p* of you ... 2Cor 2:9 *1382*
the *p* of your love, and of our ... 2Cor 8:24 *1732*
Since ye seek a *p* of Christ ... 2Cor 13:3 *1382*
But ye know the *p* of him, that, ... Phil 2:22 *1382*
make full *p* of thy ministry ... 2Ti 4:5 *4135*

PROOFS {1}
his passion by many infallible *p* ... Acts 1:3 *5039*

PROPER {4}
my God, I have of mine own *p* good ... 1Chr 29:3 5459
field is called in their *p* tongue ... Acts 1:19 *2398*
every man hath his *p* gift of God ... 1Cor 7:7 *2398*
because they saw he was a *p* child ... Heb 11:23 *791*

PROPHECIES {2}
but whether there be *p*, they ... 1Cor 13:8 *4394*
according to the *p* which went ... 1Ti 1:18 *4394*

PROPHECY {21}
in the *p* of Ahijah the Shilonite, ... 2Chr 9:29 5016
the *p* of Oded the prophet, he ... 2Chr 15:8 5016
he pronounced this *p* against me ... Neh 6:12 5016
Agur the son of Jakeh, even the *p* ... Prov 30:1 4853
the *p* that his mother taught him ... Prov 31:1 4853
and to seal up the vision and *p* ... Dan 9:24 5030
them is fulfilled the *p* of Esaias ... Mt 13:14 *4394*
that is given to us, whether *p* ... Rom 12:6 *4394*
to another *p* ... 1Cor 12:10 *4394*
And though I have the gift of *p* ... 1Cor 13:2 *4394*
thee, which was given thee by *p* ... 1Ti 4:14 *4394*
have also a more sure word of *p* ... 2Pet 1:19 *4397*
that no *p* of the scripture is of ... 2Pet 1:20 *4394*
For the *p* came not in old time by ... 2Pet 1:21 *4394*
that hear the words of this *p* ... Rev 1:3 *4394*
rain not in the days of their *p* ... Rev 11:6 *4394*
of Jesus is the spirit of *p* ... Rev 19:10 *4394*
the sayings of the *p* of this book ... Rev 22:7 *4394*
the sayings of the *p* of this book ... Rev 22:10 *4394*
the words of the *p* of this book ... Rev 22:18 *4394*
the words of the book of this *p* ... Rev 22:19 *4394*

PROPHESIED {50}
spirit rested upon them, they *p* ... Num 11:25 5012
and they *p* in the camp ... Num 11:26 5012
came upon him, and he *p* among them ... 1Sa 10:10 5012
he *p* among the prophets, then the ... 1Sa 10:11 5012
he *p* in the midst of the house ... 1Sa 18:10 5012
of Saul, and they also *p* ... 1Sa 19:20 5012
messengers, and they *p* likewise ... 1Sa 19:21 5012
the third time, and they *p* also ... 1Sa 19:21 5012
him also, and he went on, and *p* ... 1Sa 19:23 5012
p before Samuel in like manner, ... 1Sa 19:24 5012
they *p* until the time of the ... 1Kin 18:29 5012
and all the prophets *p* before them ... 1Kin 22:10 5012
And all the prophets *p* so, saying, ... 1Kin 22:12 5012
which *p* according to the order of ... 1Chr 25:2 5012
who *p* with a harp, to give thanks ... 1Chr 25:3 5012
for he never *p* good unto me ... 2Chr 18:7 5012
and all the prophets *p* before them ... 2Chr 18:9 5012
And all the prophets *p* so, saying, ... 2Chr 18:11 5012
of Mareshah *p* against Jehoshaphat ... 2Chr 20:37 5012
p unto the Jews that were in ... Ezr 5:1 5013
me, and the prophets *p* by Baal ... Jer 2:8 5012
that Jeremiah *p* these things ... Jer 20:1 5012
friends, to whom thou hast *p* lies ... Jer 20:6 5012
they *p* in Baal, and caused my ... Jer 23:13 5012
not spoken to them, yet they *p* ... Jer 23:21 5012
which Jeremiah hath *p* against all ... Jer 25:13 5012
Why hast thou *p* in the name of ... Jer 26:9 5012
for he hath *p* against this city, ... Jer 26:11 5012
Micah the Morasthite *p* in the ... Jer 26:18 5012
that *p* in the name of the LORD ... Jer 26:20 5012
who *p* against this city and ... Jer 26:20 5012
thy words which thou hast *p* ... Jer 28:6 5012
before thee of old *p* both against ... Jer 28:8 5012
that Shemaiah hath *p* unto you ... Jer 29:31 5012
your prophets which *p* unto you ... Jer 37:19 5012
And it came to pass, when I *p* ... Eze 11:13 5012
So I *p* as I was commanded ... Eze 37:7 5012
and as I *p*, there was a noise, and ... Eze 37:7 5012
So I *p* as he commanded me, and the ... Eze 37:10 5012
which *p* in those days many years ... Eze 38:17 5012
one of his vision, when he hath *p* ... Zec 13:4 5012
Lord, have we not *p* in thy name ... Mt 7:22 *4395*
prophets and the law *p* until John ... Mt 11:13 *4395*
Well hath Esaias *p* of you ... Mk 7:6 *4395*
filled with the Holy Ghost, and *p* ... Lk 1:67 *4395*
he *p* that Jesus should die for ... Jn 11:51 *4395*
and they spake with tongues, and *p* ... Acts 19:6 *4395*
tongues, but rather that ye *p* ... 1Cor 14:5 *4395*
who *p* of the grace that should ... 1Pet 1:10 *4395*
p of these, saying, Behold, the ... Jude 14 *4395*

PROPHESIETH {7}
The prophet which *p* of peace ... Jer 28:9 5012
he *p* of the times that are far ... Eze 12:27 5012
thrust him through when he *p* ... Zec 13:3 5012
or *p* with her head uncovered ... 1Cor 11:5 *4395*
But he that *p* speaketh unto men ... 1Cor 14:3 *4395*
but he that *p* edifieth the church ... 1Cor 14:4 *4395*
for greater is he that *p* than he ... 1Cor 14:5 *4395*

PROPHESY {90}
Eldad and Medad do *p* in the camp ... Num 11:27 5012
and they shall *p* ... 1Sa 10:5 5012
thee, and thou shalt *p* with them ... 1Sa 10:6 5012
for he doth not *p* good concerning ... 1Kin 22:8 5012
he would *p* no good concerning me ... 1Kin 22:18 5012
Jeduthun, who should *p* with harps ... 1Chr 25:1 5012
that he would not *p* good unto me ... 2Chr 18:17 5012
P not unto us right things, speak ... Is 30:10 2372
unto us smooth things, *p* deceits ... Is 30:10 2372
The prophets *p* falsely, and the ... Jer 5:31 5012
P not in the name of the LORD, ... Jer 11:21 5012
The prophets *p* lies in my name ... Jer 14:14 5012
they *p* unto you a false vision and ... Jer 14:14 5012
the prophets that *p* in my name ... Jer 14:15 5012
the people to whom they *p* shall ... Jer 14:16 5012
the LORD had sent him to *p* ... Jer 19:14 5012
of the prophets that *p* unto you ... Jer 23:16 5012
that *p* lies in my name, saying, I ... Jer 23:25 5012
heart of the prophets that *p* lies ... Jer 23:26 5012
against them that *p* false dreams ... Jer 23:32 5012
Therefore *p* thou against them all ... Jer 25:30 5012
sent me to *p* against this house ... Jer 26:12 5012
For they *p* a lie unto you, to ... Jer 27:10 5012
for they *p* a lie unto you ... Jer 27:14 5012
yet they *p* a lie in my name ... Jer 27:15 5012
and the prophets that *p* unto you ... Jer 27:15 5012
of your prophets that *p* unto you ... Jer 27:16 5012
for they *p* a lie unto you ... Jer 27:16 5012
For they *p* falsely unto you in my ... Jer 29:9 5012
which *p* a lie unto you in my name ... Jer 29:21 5012
up, saying, Wherefore dost thou *p* ... Jer 32:3 5012
and thou shalt *p* against it ... Eze 4:7 5012
of Israel, and *p* against them, ... Eze 6:2 5012
p against them, *p*, O son ... Eze 11:4 5012
p against the prophets of Israel ... Eze 13:2 5012
the prophets of Israel that *p* ... Eze 13:2 5012
that *p* out of their own hearts ... Eze 13:2 5012
which *p* concerning Jerusalem ... Eze 13:16 5012
which *p* out of their own heart ... Eze 13:17 5012
and *p* thou against them, ... Eze 13:17 5012
p against the forest of the south ... Eze 20:46 5012
p against the land of Israel, ... Eze 21:2 5012
Son of man, *p*, and say, Thus saith ... Eze 21:9 5012
Thou therefore, son of man, *p* ... Eze 21:14 5012
And thou, son of man, *p* and say, ... Eze 21:28 5012
the Ammonites, and *p* against them ... Eze 25:2 5012
against Zidon, and *p* against it, ... Eze 28:21 5012
p against him, and against all ... Eze 29:2 5012
Son of man, *p* and say, Thus saith ... Eze 30:2 5012
p against the shepherds of Israel ... Eze 34:2 5012
the shepherds of Israel, *p* ... Eze 34:2 5012
mount Seir, and *p* against it, ... Eze 35:2 5012
p unto the mountains of Israel, ... Eze 36:1 5012
Therefore *p* and say, Thus saith ... Eze 36:3 5012
P therefore concerning the land ... Eze 36:6 5012
P upon these bones, and say unto ... Eze 37:4 5012
P unto the wind, *p*, son of ... Eze 37:9 5012
Therefore *p* and say unto them, ... Eze 37:12 5012
and Tubal, and *p* against him, ... Eze 38:2 5012
Therefore, son of man, and *p* and say ... Eze 38:14 5012
p against Gog, and say, Thus saith ... Eze 39:1 5012
sons and your daughters shall *p* ... Joel 2:28 5012
the prophets, saying, *P* not ... Amos 2:12 5012
GOD hath spoken, who can but *p* ... Amos 3:8 5012
and there eat bread, and *p* there ... Amos 7:12 5012
But *p* not again any more at ... Amos 7:13 5012
me, Go, *p* unto my people Israel ... Amos 7:15 5012
P not against Israel, and drop not ... Amos 7:16 5012
P ye not, say they to them that ... Mic 2:6 5197
ye not, say they to them that *p* ... Mic 2:6 5197
they shall not *p* to them, that ... Mic 2:6 5197
I will *p* unto thee of wine and of ... Mic 2:11 5197
pass, that when any shall yet *p* ... Zec 13:3 5197
well did Esaias *p* of you ... Mt 15:7 *4395*
P unto us, thou Christ, Who is he ... Mt 26:68 *4395*
buffet him, and to say unto him, *P* ... Mk 14:65 *4395*
the face, and asked him, saying, *P* ... Lk 22:64 *4395*
sons and your daughters shall *p* ... Acts 2:17 *4395*
and they shall *p* ... Acts 2:18 *4395*
daughters, virgins, which did *p* ... Acts 21:9 *4395*
let us *p* according to the ... Rom 12:6
we know in part, and we *p* in part ... 1Cor 13:9 *4395*
gifts, but rather that ye may *p* ... 1Cor 14:1 *4395*
But if all *p*, and there come in ... 1Cor 14:24 *4395*
For ye may all *p* one by one ... 1Cor 14:31 *4395*
Wherefore, brethren, covet to *p* ... 1Cor 14:39 *4395*
Thou must *p* again before many ... Rev 10:11 *4395*
they shall *p* a thousand two ... Rev 11:3 *4395*

PROPHESYING {6}
And when he had made an end of *p* ... 1Sa 10:13 5012
saw the company of the prophets *p* ... 1Sa 19:20 5012
the *p* of Haggai the prophet ... Ezr 6:14 5017
Every man praying or *p*, having ... 1Cor 11:4 *4395*
or by knowledge, or by *p* ... 1Cor 14:6 *4394*
but *p* serveth not for them that ... 1Cor 14:22 *4394*

PROPHESYINGS {1}
Despise not *p* ... 1Th 5:20 *4394*

PROPHET {242}
for he is a *p*, and he shall pray ... Gen 20:7 5030
Aaron thy brother shall be thy *p* ... Ex 7:1 5030
If there be a *p* among you ... Num 12:6 5030
If there arise among you a *p* ... Deut 13:1 5030
hearken unto the words of that *p* ... Deut 13:3 5030
And that *p*, or that dreamer of ... Deut 13:5 5030
thee a *P* from the midst of thee ... Deut 18:15 5030
I will raise them up a *P* from ... Deut 18:18 5030
But the *p*, which shall presume to ... Deut 18:20 5030
other gods, even that *p* shall die ... Deut 18:20 5030
When a *p* speaketh in the name of ... Deut 18:22 5030
spoken, but the *p* hath spoken it ... Deut 18:22 5030
there arose not a *p* since in ... Deut 34:10 5030
That the LORD sent a *p* unto the ... Judg 6:8 5030
established to be a *p* of the LORD ... 1Sa 3:20 5030
for he that is now called a *P* was ... 1Sa 9:9 5030
the *p* Gad said unto David, Abide ... 1Sa 22:5 5030
the king said unto Nathan the *p* ... 2Sa 7:2 5030
sent by the hand of Nathan the *p* ... 2Sa 12:25 5030
of the LORD came unto the *p* Gad ... 2Sa 24:11 5030
son of Jehoiada, and Nathan the *p* ... 1Kin 1:8 5030
But Nathan the *p*, and Benaiah, and ... 1Kin 1:10 5030
Nathan the *p* also came in ... 1Kin 1:22 5030
king, saying, Behold Nathan the *p* ... 1Kin 1:23 5030
Zadok the priest, and Nathan the *p* ... 1Kin 1:32 5030
Nathan the *p* anoint him there ... 1Kin 1:34 5030
Zadok the priest, and Nathan the *p* ... 1Kin 1:38 5030
Zadok the priest, and Nathan the *p* ... 1Kin 1:44 5030
Nathan the *p* have anointed him ... 1Kin 1:45 5030
that the *p* Ahijah the Shilonite ... 1Kin 11:29 5030
there dwelt an old *p* in Beth-el ... 1Kin 13:11 5030
I am a *p* also as thou art ... 1Kin 13:18 5030
unto the *p* that brought him back ... 1Kin 13:20 5030
for the *p* whom he had brought ... 1Kin 13:23 5030
in the city where the old *p* dwelt ... 1Kin 13:25 5030
when the *p* that brought him back ... 1Kin 13:26 5030
the *p* took up the carcase of the ... 1Kin 13:29 5030
the old *p* came to the city, to ... 1Kin 13:29 5030
behold, there is Ahijah the *p* ... 1Kin 14:2 5030
hand of his servant Ahijah the *p* ... 1Kin 14:18 5030
also by the hand of the *p* Jehu ... 1Kin 16:7 5030
against Baasha by Jehu the *p* ... 1Kin 16:12 5030
I only, remain a *p* of the LORD ... 1Kin 18:22 5030
that Elijah the *p* came near ... 1Kin 18:36 5030
thou anoint to be *p* in thy room ... 1Kin 19:16 5030
there came a *p* unto Ahab king of ... 1Kin 20:13 5030
the *p* came to the king of Israel, ... 1Kin 20:22 5030
So the *p* departed, and waited for ... 1Kin 20:38 5030
not here a *p* of the LORD besides ... 1Kin 22:7 5030
Is there not here a *p* of the LORD ... 2Kin 3:11 5030
with the *p* that is in Samaria ... 2Kin 5:3 5030
know that there is a *p* in Israel ... 2Kin 5:8 5030
if the *p* had bid thee do some ... 2Kin 5:13 5030
the *p* that is in Israel, telleth ... 2Kin 6:12 5030
Elisha the *p* called one of the ... 2Kin 9:1 5030
man, even the young man the *p* ... 2Kin 9:4 5030
Jonah, the son of Amittai, the *p* ... 2Kin 14:25 5030
to Isaiah the *p* the son of Amoz ... 2Kin 19:2 5030
the *p* Isaiah the son of Amoz came ... 2Kin 20:1 5030
Isaiah the *p* cried unto the LORD ... 2Kin 20:11 5030
Isaiah the *p* unto king Hezekiah ... 2Kin 20:14 5030
with the bones of the *p* that came ... 2Kin 23:18 5030
that David said to Nathan the *p* ... 1Chr 17:1 5030
and in the book of Nathan the *p* ... 1Chr 29:29 5030
in the book of Nathan the *p* ... 2Chr 9:29 5030
came Shemaiah the *p* to Rehoboam ... 2Chr 12:5 5030
in the book of Shemaiah the *p* ... 2Chr 12:15 5030
in the story of the *p* Iddo ... 2Chr 13:22 5030
and the prophecy of Oded the *p* ... 2Chr 15:8 5030
not here a *p* of the LORD besides ... 2Chr 18:6 5030
writing to him from Elijah the *p* ... 2Chr 21:12 5030
Amaziah, and he sent unto him a *p* ... 2Chr 25:15 5030
Then the *p* forbare, and said, I ... 2Chr 25:16 5030
first and last, did Isaiah the *p* ... 2Chr 26:22 5030
But a *p* of the LORD was there, ... 2Chr 28:9 5030
the king's seer, and Nathan the *p* ... 2Chr 29:25 5030
the *p* Isaiah the son of Amoz, ... 2Chr 32:20 5030
in the vision of Isaiah the *p* ... 2Chr 32:32 5030
from the days of Samuel the *p* ... 2Chr 35:18 5030
p speaking from the mouth of the ... 2Chr 36:12 5030
Then the prophets, Haggai the *p* ... Ezr 5:1 5029
the prophesying of Haggai the *p* ... Ezr 6:14 5029
when Nathan the *p* came unto him ... Ps 51:*t* 5030
there is no more any *p* ... Ps 74:9 5030
man of war, the judge, and the *p* ... Is 3:2 5030
the *p* that teacheth lies, he is ... Is 9:15 5030
the *p* have erred through strong ... Is 28:7 5030
unto Isaiah the *p* the son of Amoz ... Is 37:2 5030
Isaiah the *p* the son of Amoz came ... Is 38:1 5030
Isaiah the *p* unto king Hezekiah ... Is 39:3 5030
thee a *p* unto the nations ... Jer 1:5 5030
from the *p* even unto the priest ... Jer 6:13 5030
from the *p* even unto the priest ... Jer 8:10 5030
yea, both the *p* and the priest go ... Jer 14:18 5030
the wise, nor the word from the *p* ... Jer 18:18 5030
Then Pashur smote Jeremiah the *p* ... Jer 20:2 5030
For both *p* and priest are profane ... Jer 23:11 5030
The *p* that hath a dream, let him ... Jer 23:28 5030
And when this people, or the *p* ... Jer 23:33 5030
And as for the *p*, and the priest, ... Jer 23:34 5030
Thus shalt thou say to the *p* ... Jer 23:37 5030
The which Jeremiah the *p* spake ... Jer 25:2 5030
Hananiah the son of Azur the *p* ... Jer 28:1 5030
p Jeremiah said unto the *p* ... Jer 28:5 5030
Even the *p* Jeremiah said, Amen ... Jer 28:6 5030
The *p* which prophesieth of peace, ... Jer 28:9 5030
word of the *p* shall come to pass ... Jer 28:9 5030
then shall the *p* be known ... Jer 28:9 5030
Then Hananiah the *p* took the yoke ... Jer 28:10 5030
from off the *p* Jeremiah's neck ... Jer 28:10 5030
the *p* Jeremiah went his way ... Jer 28:11 5030
the LORD came unto Jeremiah the *p* ... Jer 28:12
after that Hananiah the *p* had ... Jer 28:12 5030
off the neck of the *p* Jeremiah ... Jer 28:12 5030
Then said the *p* Jeremiah unto ... Jer 28:15 5030
Jeremiah unto Hananiah the *p* ... Jer 28:15 5030
So Hananiah the *p* died the same ... Jer 28:17 5030
p sent from Jerusalem unto the ... Jer 29:1 5030
is mad, and maketh himself a *p* ... Jer 29:26 5012
which maketh himself a *p* to you ... Jer 29:27 5012
in the ears of Jeremiah the *p* ... Jer 29:29 5030
Jeremiah the *p* was shut up in the ... Jer 32:2 5030
Then Jeremiah the *p* spake all ... Jer 34:6 5030
that Jeremiah the *p* commanded him ... Jer 36:8 5030

the scribe and Jeremiah the *p*	Jer 36:26	5030
which he spake by the *p* Jeremiah	Jer 37:2	5030
the priest to the *p* Jeremiah	Jer 37:3	5030
of the LORD unto the *p* Jeremiah	Jer 37:6	5030
and he took Jeremiah the *p*	Jer 37:13	5030
they have done to Jeremiah the *p*	Jer 38:9	5030
Jeremiah the *p* out of the dungeon	Jer 38:10	5030
took Jeremiah the *p* unto him into	Jer 38:14	5030
And said unto Jeremiah the *p*	Jer 42:2	5030
Jeremiah the *p* said unto them	Jer 42:4	5030
son of Shaphan, and Jeremiah the *p*	Jer 43:6	5030
The word that Jeremiah the *p*	Jer 45:1	5030
the *p* against the Gentiles	Jer 46:1	5030
the LORD spake to Jeremiah the *p*	Jer 46:13	5030
the *p* against the Philistines	Jer 47:1	5030
p against Elam in the beginning	Jer 49:34	5030
the Chaldeans by Jeremiah the *p*	Jer 50:1	5030
The word which Jeremiah the *p*	Jer 51:59	5030
the *p* be slain in the sanctuary	Lam 2:20	5030
there hath been a *p* among them	Eze 2:5	5030
shall they seek a vision of the *p*	Eze 7:26	5030
his face, and cometh to the *p*	Eze 14:4	5030
cometh to a *p* to enquire of him	Eze 14:7	5030
if the *p* be deceived when he hath	Eze 14:9	5030
I the LORD have deceived that *p*	Eze 14:9	5030
the punishment of the *p* shall be	Eze 14:10	5030
that a *p* hath been among them	Eze 33:33	5030
the LORD came to Jeremiah the *p*	Dan 9:2	5030
the *p* also shall fall with thee	Hos 4:5	5030
the *p* is a fool, the spiritual	Hos 9:7	5030
but the *p* is a snare of a fowler	Hos 9:8	5030
by a *p* the LORD brought Israel	Hos 12:13	5030
Egypt, and by a *p* was he preserved	Hos 12:13	5030
and said to Amaziah, I was no *p*	Amos 7:14	5030
even be the *p* of this people	Mic 2:11	5197
which Habakkuk the *p* did see	Hab 1:1	5030
of Habakkuk the *p* upon Shigionoth	Hab 3:1	5030
the *p* unto Zerubbabel the son of	Hag 1:1	5030
word of the LORD by Haggai the *p*	Hag 1:3	5030
God, and the words of Haggai the *p*	Hag 1:12	5030
word of the LORD by the *p* Haggai	Hag 2:1	5030
word of the LORD by Haggai the *p*	Hag 2:10	5030
Berechiah, the son of Iddo the *p*	Zec 1:1	5030
Berechiah, the son of Iddo the *p*	Zec 1:7	5030
But he shall say, I am no *p*	Zec 13:5	5030
I will send you Elijah the *p*	Mal 4:5	5030
was spoken of the Lord by the *p*	Mt 1:22	*4396*
for thus it is written by the *p*	Mt 2:5	*4396*
was spoken of the Lord by the *p*	Mt 2:15	*4396*
which was spoken by Jeremy the *p*	Mt 2:17	*4396*
was spoken of by the *p* Esaias	Mt 3:3	*4396*
which was spoken by Esaias the *p*	Mt 4:14	*4396*
which was spoken by Esaias the *p*	Mt 8:17	*4396*
He that receiveth a *p* in the name	Mt 10:41	*4396*
of a *p* shall receive a prophet's	Mt 10:41	*4396*
for to see? A *p*?	Mt 11:9	*4396*
I say unto you, and more than a *p*	Mt 11:9	*4396*
which was spoken by Esaias the *p*	Mt 12:17	*4396*
it, but the sign of the *p* Jonas	Mt 12:39	*4396*
which was spoken by the *p*	Mt 13:35	*4396*
A *p* is not without honour, save	Mt 13:57	*4396*
because they counted him as a *p*	Mt 14:5	*4396*
it, but the sign of the *p* Jonas	Mt 16:4	*4396*
which was spoken by the *p*	Mt 21:4	*4396*
This is Jesus the *p* of Nazareth	Mt 21:11	*4396*
for all hold John as a *p*	Mt 21:26	*4396*
because they took him for a *p*	Mt 21:46	*4396*
spoken of by Daniel the *p*	Mt 24:15	*4396*
which was spoken by Jeremy the *p*	Mt 27:9	*4396*
which was spoken by the *p*	Mt 27:35	*4396*
A *p* is not without honour, but in	Mk 6:4	*4396*
And others said, That it is a *p*	Mk 6:15	*4396*
John, that he was a *p* indeed	Mk 11:32	*4396*
spoken of by Daniel the *p*	Mk 13:14	*4396*
be called the *p* of the Highest	Lk 1:76	*4396*
book of the words of Esaias the *p*	Lk 3:4	*4396*
unto him the book of the *p* Esaias	Lk 4:17	*4396*
No *p* is accepted in his own	Lk 4:24	*4396*
in the time of Eliseus the *p*	Lk 4:27	*4396*
That a great *p* is risen up among	Lk 7:16	*4396*
for to see? A *p*?	Lk 7:26	*4396*
unto you, and much more than a *p*	Lk 7:26	*4396*
a greater *p* than John the Baptist	Lk 7:28	*4396*
saying, This man, if he were a *p*	Lk 7:39	*4396*
it, but the sign of Jonas the *p*	Lk 11:29	*4396*
that a *p* perish out of Jerusalem	Lk 13:33	*4396*
be persuaded that John was a *p*	Lk 20:6	*4396*
which was a *p* mighty in deed and	Lk 24:19	*4396*
Art thou that *p*	Jn 1:21	*4396*
of the Lord, as said the *p* Esaias	Jn 1:23	*4396*
Christ, nor Elias, neither that *p*	Jn 1:25	*4396*
Sir, I perceive that thou art a *p*	Jn 4:19	*4396*
that a *p* hath no honour in his	Jn 4:44	*4396*
This is of a truth that *p* that	Jn 6:14	*4396*
said, Of a truth this is the *P*	Jn 7:40	*4396*
for out of Galilee ariseth no *p*	Jn 7:52	*4396*
He said, He is a *p*	Jn 9:17	*4396*
Esaias the *p* might be fulfilled	Jn 12:38	*4396*
which was spoken by the *p* Joel	Acts 2:16	*4396*
Therefore being a *p*, and knowing	Acts 2:30	*4396*
A *p* shall the Lord your God raise	Acts 3:22	*4396*
soul, which will not hear that *p*	Acts 3:23	*4396*
A *p* shall the Lord your God raise	Acts 7:37	*4396*
as saith the *p*,	Acts 7:48	*4396*
in his chariot read Esaias the *p*	Acts 8:28	*4396*
and heard him read the *p* Esaias	Acts 8:30	*4396*
thee, of whom speaketh the *p* this	Acts 8:34	*4396*
a certain sorcerer, a false *p*	Acts 13:6	*5578*
fifty years, until Samuel the *p*	Acts 13:20	*4396*
came down from Judaea a certain *p*	Acts 21:10	*4396*
by Esaias the *p* unto our fathers	Acts 28:25	*4396*
any man think himself to be a *p*	1Cor 14:37	*4396*
even a *p* of their own, said, The	Titus 1:12	*4396*
voice forbad the madness of the *p*	2Pet 2:16	*4396*
out of the mouth of the false *p*	Rev 16:13	*5578*
with him the false *p* that wrought	Rev 19:20	*5578*
the beast and the false *p* are	Rev 20:10	*5578*

PROPHETESS {8}

And Miriam the *p*, the sister of	Ex 15:20	5031
And Deborah, a *p*, the wife of	Judg 4:4	5031
Asahiah, went unto Huldah the *p*	2Kin 22:14	5031
appointed, went to Huldah the *p*	2Chr 34:22	5031
on the *p* Noadiah, and the rest of	Neh 6:14	5031
And I went unto the *p*	Is 8:3	5031
And there was one Anna, a *p*	Lk 2:36	*4398*
which calleth herself a *p*	Rev 2:20	*4398*

PROPHET'S {2}

prophet, neither was I an *p* son	Amos 7:14	5030
prophet shall receive a *p* reward	Mt 10:41	*4396*

PROPHETS {239}

that all the LORD's people were *p*	Num 11:29	5030
thou shalt meet a company of *p*	1Sa 10:5	5030
behold, a company of *p* met him	1Sa 10:10	5030
behold, he prophesied among the *p*	1Sa 10:11	5030
Is Saul also among the *p*	1Sa 10:11	5030
proverb, Is Saul also among the *p*	1Sa 10:12	5030
the company of the *p* prophesying	1Sa 19:20	5030
say, Is Saul also among the *p*	1Sa 19:24	5030
by dreams, nor by Urim, nor by *p*	1Sa 28:6	5030
me no more, neither by *p*, nor by	1Sa 28:15	5030
Jezebel cut off the *p* of the LORD	1Kin 18:4	5030
that Obadiah took an hundred *p*	1Kin 18:4	5030
Jezebel slew the *p* of the LORD	1Kin 18:13	5030
the LORD's *p* by fifty in a cave	1Kin 18:13	5030
the *p* of Baal four hundred and	1Kin 18:19	5030
the *p* of the groves four hundred,	1Kin 18:19	5030
gathered the *p* together unto	1Kin 18:20	5030
but Baal's *p* are four hundred and	1Kin 18:22	5030
And Elijah said unto the *p* of Baal	1Kin 18:25	5030
unto them, Take the *p* of Baal	1Kin 18:40	5030
slain all the *p* with the sword	1Kin 19:1	5030
slain thy *p* with the sword	1Kin 19:10	5030
slain thy *p* with the sword	1Kin 19:14	5030
p said unto his neighbour in the	1Kin 20:35	5030
him that he was of the *p*	1Kin 20:41	5030
of Israel gathered the *p* together	1Kin 22:6	5030
all the *p* prophesied before them	1Kin 22:10	5030
all the *p* prophesied so, saying,	1Kin 22:12	5030
the words of the *p* declare good	1Kin 22:13	5030
spirit in the mouth of all his *p*	1Kin 22:22	5030
in the mouth of all these thy *p*	1Kin 22:23	5030
the sons of the *p* that were at	2Kin 2:3	5030
the sons of the *p* that were at	2Kin 2:5	5030
men of the sons of the *p* went	2Kin 2:7	5030
when the sons of the *p* which were	2Kin 2:15	5030
get thee to the *p* of thy father	2Kin 3:13	5030
and to the *p* of thy mother	2Kin 3:13	5030
of the sons of the *p* unto Elisha	2Kin 4:1	5030
the sons of the *p* were sitting	2Kin 4:38	5030
pottage for the sons of the *p*	2Kin 4:38	5030
young men of the sons of the *p*	2Kin 5:22	5030
the sons of the *p* said unto	2Kin 6:1	5030
one of the children of the *p*	2Kin 9:1	5030
the blood of my servants the *p*	2Kin 9:7	5030
call unto me all the *p* of Baal	2Kin 10:19	5030
and against Judah, by all the *p*	2Kin 17:13	5030
sent to you by my servants the *p*	2Kin 17:13	5030
said by all his servants the *p*	2Kin 17:23	5030
LORD spake by his servants the *p*	2Kin 21:10	5030
him, and the priests, and the *p*	2Kin 23:2	5030
he spake by his servants the *p*	2Kin 24:2	5030
mine anointed, and do my *p* no harm	1Chr 16:22	5030
together of *p* four hundred men	2Chr 18:5	5030
all the *p* prophesied before them	2Chr 18:9	5030
all the *p* prophesied so, saying,	2Chr 18:11	5030
the words of the *p* declare good	2Chr 18:12	5030
spirit in the mouth of all his *p*	2Chr 18:21	5030
in the mouth of these thy *p*	2Chr 18:22	5030
believe his *p*, so shall ye	2Chr 20:20	5030
Yet he sent *p* to them, to bring	2Chr 24:19	5030
commandment of the LORD by his *p*	2Chr 29:25	5030
his words, and misused his *p*	2Chr 36:16	5030
Then the *p*, Haggai the prophet,	Ezr 5:1	5029
with them were the *p* of God	Ezr 5:2	5029
commanded by thy servants the *p*	Ezr 9:11	5030
thou hast also appointed *p* to	Neh 6:7	5030
Noadiah, and the rest of the *p*	Neh 6:14	5030
slew thy *p* which testified	Neh 9:26	5030
them by thy spirit in thy *p*	Neh 9:30	5030
and on our priests, and on our *p*	Neh 9:32	5030
mine anointed, and do my *p* no harm	Ps 105:15	5030
the *p* and your rulers, the seers	Is 29:10	5030
and to the *p*, Prophesy not unto us	Is 30:10	2374
the *p* prophesied by Baal, and	Jer 2:8	5030
and their priests, and their *p*	Jer 2:26	5030
own sword hath devoured your *p*	Jer 2:30	5030
astonished, and the *p* shall wonder	Jer 4:9	5030
the *p* shall become wind, and the	Jer 5:13	5030
The *p* prophesy falsely, and the	Jer 5:31	5030
unto you all my servants the *p*	Jer 7:25	5030
priests, and the bones of the *p*	Jer 8:1	5030
throne, and the priests, and the *p*	Jer 13:13	5030
the *p* say unto them, Ye shall not	Jer 14:13	5030
The *p* prophesy lies in my name	Jer 14:14	5030
the *p* that prophesy in my name	Jer 14:15	5030
famine shall those *p* be consumed	Jer 14:15	5030
me is broken because of the *p*	Jer 23:9	5030
seen folly in the *p* of Samaria	Jer 23:13	5030
I have seen also in the *p* of	Jer 23:14	5030
LORD of hosts concerning the *p*	Jer 23:15	5030
for from the *p* of Jerusalem is	Jer 23:15	5030
of the *p* that prophesy unto you	Jer 23:16	5030
I have not sent these *p*, yet they	Jer 23:21	5030
I have heard what the *p* said	Jer 23:25	5030
heart of the *p* that prophesy lies	Jer 23:26	5030
they are *p* of the deceit of their	Jer 23:26	5030
behold, I am against the *p*	Jer 23:30	5030
Behold, I am against the *p*	Jer 23:31	5030
unto you all his servants the *p*	Jer 25:4	5030
to the words of my servants the *p*	Jer 26:5	5030
So the priests and the *p* and all	Jer 26:7	5030
people, that the priests and the *p*	Jer 26:8	5030
the *p* unto the princes and to all	Jer 26:11	5030
unto the priests and to the *p*	Jer 26:16	5030
hearken not ye to your *p*, nor to	Jer 27:9	5030
of the *p* that speak unto you	Jer 27:14	5030
the *p* that prophesy unto you	Jer 27:15	5030
of your *p* that prophesy unto you	Jer 27:16	5030
But if they be *p*, and if the word	Jer 27:18	5030
The *p* that have been before me and	Jer 28:8	5030
and to the priests, and to the *p*	Jer 29:1	5030
Let not your *p* and your diviners,	Jer 29:8	5030
hath raised us up *p* in Babylon	Jer 29:15	5030
unto them by my servants the *p*	Jer 29:19	5030
their priests, and their *p*	Jer 32:32	5030
unto you all my servants the *p*	Jer 35:15	5030
Where are now your *p* which	Jer 37:19	5030
unto you all my servants the *p*	Jer 44:4	5030
her *p* also find no vision from	Lam 2:9	5030
Thy *p* have seen vain and foolish	Lam 2:14	5030
For the sins of her *p*, and the	Lam 4:13	5030
prophesy against the *p* of Israel	Eze 13:2	5030
Woe unto the foolish *p*, that	Eze 13:3	5030
thy *p* are like the foxes in the	Eze 13:4	5030
be upon the *p* that see vanity	Eze 13:9	5030
the *p* of Israel which prophesy	Eze 13:16	5030
of her *p* in the midst thereof	Eze 22:25	5030
her *p* have daubed them with	Eze 22:28	5030
by my servants the *p* of Israel	Eze 38:17	5030
hearkened unto thy servants the *p*	Dan 9:6	5030
before us by his servants the *p*	Dan 9:10	5030
have I hewed them by the *p*	Hos 6:5	5030
I have also spoken by the *p*	Hos 12:10	5030
by the ministry of the *p*	Hos 12:10	5030
And I raised up of your sons for *p*	Amos 2:11	5030
and commanded the *p*, saying,	Amos 2:12	5030
secret unto his servants the *p*	Amos 3:7	5030
the *p* that make my people err	Mic 3:5	5030
the sun shall go down over the *p*	Mic 3:6	5030
the *p* thereof divine for money	Mic 3:11	5030
Her *p* are light and treacherous	Zeph 3:4	5030
unto whom the former *p* have cried	Zec 1:4	5030
and the *p*, do they live for ever	Zec 1:5	5030
I commanded my servants the *p*	Zec 1:6	5030
of the LORD of hosts, and to the *p*	Zec 7:3	5030
LORD hath cried by the former *p*	Zec 7:7	5030
in his spirit by the former *p*	Zec 7:12	5030
these words by the mouth of the *p*	Zec 8:9	5030
and also I will cause the *p*	Zec 13:2	5030
that the *p* shall be ashamed every	Zec 13:4	5030
which was spoken by the *p*	Mt 2:23	*4396*
they the *p* which were before you	Mt 5:12	*4396*
come to destroy the law, or the *p*	Mt 5:17	*4396*
for this is the law and the *p*	Mt 7:12	*4396*
Beware of false *p*, which come to	Mt 7:15	*5578*
For all the *p* and the law	Mt 11:13	*4396*
I say unto you, That many *p*	Mt 13:17	*4396*
others, Jeremias, or one of the *p*	Mt 16:14	*4396*
hang all the law and the *p*	Mt 22:40	*4396*
ye build the tombs of the *p*	Mt 23:29	*4396*
with them in the blood of the *p*	Mt 23:30	*4396*
of them which killed the *p*	Mt 23:31	*4396*
behold, I send unto you *p*	Mt 23:34	*4396*
thou that killest the *p*, and	Mt 23:37	*4396*
And many false *p* shall rise	Mt 24:11	*5578*
arise false Christs, and false *p*	Mt 24:24	*5578*
of the *p* might be fulfilled	Mt 26:56	*4396*
As it is written in the *p*	Mk 1:2	*4396*
is a prophet, or as one of the *p*	Mk 6:15	*4396*
and others, One of the *p*	Mk 8:28	*4396*
false *p* shall rise, and shall shew	Mk 13:22	*5578*
spake by the mouth of his holy *p*	Lk 1:70	*4396*
did their fathers unto the *p*	Lk 6:23	*4396*
did their fathers to the false *p*	Lk 6:26	*5578*
one of the old *p* was risen again	Lk 9:8	*4396*
one of the old *p* is risen again	Lk 9:19	*4396*
For I tell you, that many *p*	Lk 10:24	*4396*
ye build the sepulchres of the *p*	Lk 11:47	*4396*
wisdom of God, I will send them *p*	Lk 11:49	*4396*
That the blood of all the *p*	Lk 11:50	*4396*
and Isaac, and Jacob, and all the *p*	Lk 13:28	*4396*
Jerusalem, which killest the *p*	Lk 13:34	*4396*
The law and the *p* were until John	Lk 16:16	*4396*
him, They have Moses and the *p*	Lk 16:29	*4396*
If they hear not Moses and the *p*	Lk 16:31	*4396*
things that are written by the *p*	Lk 18:31	*4396*
all that the *p* have spoken	Lk 24:25	*4396*
beginning at Moses and all the *p*	Lk 24:27	*4396*
in the law of Moses, and in the *p*	Lk 24:44	*4396*
whom Moses in the law, and the *p*	Jn 1:45	*4396*
It is written in the *p*, And they	Jn 6:45	*4396*
Abraham is dead, and the *p*	Jn 8:52	*4396*
and the *p* are dead	Jn 8:53	*4396*

shewed by the mouth of all his *p* ... Acts 3:18 *4396*
his holy *p* since the world began ... Acts 3:21 *4396*
all the *p* from Samuel and those ... Acts 3:24 *4396*
Ye are the children of the *p* ... Acts 3:25 *4396*
is written in the book of the *p* ... Acts 7:42 *4396*
Which of the *p* have not your ... Acts 7:52 *4396*
To him give all the *p* witness ... Acts 10:43 *4396*
in these days came *p* from ... Acts 11:27 *4396*
that was at Antioch certain *p* ... Acts 13:1 *4396*
the *p* the rulers of the synagogue ... Acts 13:15 *4396*
nor yet the voices of the *p* which ... Acts 13:27 *4396*
you, which is spoken of in the *p* ... Acts 13:40 *4396*
to this agree the words of the *p* ... Acts 15:15 *4396*
being *p* also themselves, exhorted ... Acts 15:32 *4396*
written in the law and in the *p* ... Acts 24:14 *4396*
things than those which the *p* ... Acts 26:22 *4396*
Agrippa, believest thou the *p* ... Acts 26:27 *4396*
the law of Moses, and out of the *p* ... Acts 28:23 *4396*
by his *p* in the holy scriptures ... Rom 1:2 *4396*
witnessed by the law and the *p* ... Rom 3:21 *4396*
Lord, they have killed thy *p* ... Rom 11:3 *4396*
and by the scriptures of the *p* ... Rom 16:26 *4397*
first apostles, secondarily *p* ... 1Cor 12:28 *4396*
are all *p*? ... 1Cor 12:29 *4396*
Let the *p* speak two or three, and ... 1Cor 14:29 *4396*
the *p* are subject to the *p* ... 1Cor 14:32 *4396*
foundation of the apostles and *p* ... Eph 2:20 *4396*
holy apostles and *p* by the Spirit ... Eph 3:5 *4396*
and some, *p* ... Eph 4:11 *4396*
the Lord Jesus, and their own *p* ... 1Th 2:15 *4396*
past unto the fathers by the *p* ... Heb 1:1 *4396*
also, and Samuel, and of the *p* ... Heb 11:32 *4396*
Take, my brethren, the *p*, who ... Jas 5:10 *4396*
salvation the *p* have enquired ... 1Pet 1:10 *4396*
But there were false *p* also among ... 2Pet 2:1 *5578*
were spoken before by the holy *p* ... 2Pet 3:2 *4396*
because many false *p* are gone out ... 1Jn 4:1 *5578*
declared to his servants the *p* ... Rev 10:7 *4396*
because these two *p* tormented ... Rev 11:10 *4396*
reward unto thy servants the *p* ... Rev 11:18 *4396*
shed the blood of saints and *p* ... Rev 16:6 *4396*
heaven, and ye holy apostles and *p* ... Rev 18:20 *4396*
in her was found the blood of *p* ... Rev 18:24 *4396*
the Lord God of the holy *p* sent ... Rev 22:6 *4396*
and of thy brethren the *p* ... Rev 22:9 *4396*

PROPITIATION {3}
be a *p* through faith in his blood ... Rom 3:25 *2435*
And he is the *p* for our sins ... 1Jn 2:2 *2434*
his Son to be the *p* for our sins ... 1Jn 4:10 *2434*

PROPORTION {3}
according to the *p* of every one ... 1Kin 7:36 4626
nor his power, nor his comely *p* ... Job 41:12 6187
according to the *p* of faith ... Rom 12:6 *356*

PROSELYTE {2}
compass sea and land to make one *p* ... Mt 23:15 *4339*
and Nicolas a *p* of Antioch ... Acts 6:5 *4339*

PROSELYTES {2}
and strangers of Rome, Jews and *p* ... Acts 2:10 *4339*
religious *p* followed Paul and ... Acts 13:43 *4339*

PROSPECT {6}
their *p* was toward the south ... Eze 40:44 6440
having the *p* toward the north ... Eze 40:44 6440
whose *p* is toward the south, is ... Eze 40:45 6440
the chamber whose *p* is toward the ... Eze 40:46 6440
gate whose *p* is toward the east ... Eze 42:15 6440
gate whose *p* is toward the east ... Eze 43:4 6440

PROSPER {49}
his angel with thee, and *p* thy way ... Gen 24:40 6743
if now thou do *p* my way which I ... Gen 24:42 6743
all that he did to *p* in his hand ... Gen 39:3 6743
he did, the LORD made it to *p* ... Gen 39:23 6743
but it shall not *p* ... Num 14:41 6743
and thou shalt not *p* in thy ways ... Deut 28:29 6743
that ye may *p* in all that ye do ... Deut 29:9 7919
that thou mayest *p* whithersoever ... Josh 1:7 7919
that thou mayest *p* in all that ... 1Kin 2:3 7919
Go up to Ramoth-gilead, and *p* ... 1Kin 22:12 6743
And he answered him, Go, and *p* ... 1Kin 22:15 6743
p thou, and build the house of the ... 1Chr 22:11 6743
Then shalt thou *p*, if thou takest ... 1Chr 22:13 6743
for ye shall not *p* ... 2Chr 13:12 6743
Go up to Ramoth-gilead, and *p* ... 2Chr 18:11 6743
And he said, Go ye up, and *p* ... 2Chr 18:14 6743
his prophets, so shall ye *p* ... 2Chr 20:20 6743
of the LORD, that ye cannot *p* ... 2Chr 24:20 6743
the LORD, God made him to *p* ... 2Chr 26:5 6743
and *p*, I pray thee, thy servant ... Neh 1:11 6743
The God of heaven, he will *p* us ... Neh 2:20 6743
The tabernacles of robbers *p* ... Job 12:6 7951
and whatsoever he doeth shall *p* ... Ps 1:3 6743
the ungodly, who *p* in the world ... Ps 73:12 7951
they shall *p* that love thee ... Ps 122:6 7951
covereth his sins shall not *p* ... Prov 28:13 6743
thou knowest not whether shall *p* ... Eccl 11:6 3787
of the LORD shall *p* in his hand ... Is 53:10 6743
is formed against thee shall *p* ... Is 54:17 6743
it shall *p* in the thing whereto I ... Is 55:11 6743
and thou shalt not *p* in them ... Jer 2:37 6743
of the fatherless, yet they *p* ... Jer 5:28 6743
therefore they shall not *p* ... Jer 10:21 7919
doth the way of the wicked *p* ... Jer 12:1 6743
for they shall not *p* ... Jer 20:11 7919
man that shall not *p* in his days ... Jer 22:30 6743
for no man of his seed shall *p* ... Jer 22:30 6743
and a King shall reign and *p* ... Jer 23:5 7919
the Chaldeans, ye shall not *p* ... Jer 32:5 6743
are the chief, her enemies *p* ... Lam 1:5 7919
thou didst *p* into a kingdom ... Eze 16:13 6743
Shall it *p*? ... Eze 17:9 6743
behold, being planted, shall it *p* ... Eze 17:10 6743
Shall he *p*? ... Eze 17:15 6743
destroy wonderfully, and shall *p* ... Dan 8:24 6743
cause craft to *p* in his hand ... Dan 8:25 6743
but it shall not *p* ... Dan 11:27 6743
shall *p* till the indignation be ... Dan 11:36 6743
all things that thou mayest *p* ... 3Jn 2 *2137*

PROSPERED {13}
seeing the LORD hath *p* my way ... Gen 24:56 6743
hand of the children of Israel *p* ... Judg 4:24 1980
the people did, and how the war *p* ... 2Sa 11:7 7965
he *p* whithersoever he went forth ... 2Kin 18:7 7919
instead of David his father, and *p* ... 1Chr 29:23 6743
So they built and *p* ... 2Chr 14:7 6743
did it with all his heart, and *p* ... 2Chr 31:21 6743
Hezekiah *p* in all his works ... 2Chr 32:30 6743
they *p* through the prophesying of ... Ezr 6:14 6744
himself against him, and hath *p* ... Job 9:4 7999
So this Daniel *p* in the reign of ... Dan 6:28 6744
and it practised, and *p* ... Dan 8:12 6743
him in store, as God hath *p* him ... 1Cor 16:2 *2137*

PROSPERETH {4}
fast on, and *p* in their hands ... Ezr 5:8 6744
because of him who *p* in his way ... Ps 37:7 6743
whithersoever it turneth, it *p* ... Prov 17:8 7919
be in health, even as thy soul *p* ... 3Jn 2 *2137*

PROSPERITY {17}
nor their *p* all thy days for ever ... Deut 23:6 2896
ye say to him that liveth in *p* ... 1Sa 25:6
p exceedeth the fame which I ... 1Kin 10:7 2896
in *p* the destroyer shall come ... Job 15:21 7965
they shall spend their days in *p* ... Job 36:11 2896
in my *p* I said, I shall never be ... Ps 30:6 7961
pleasure in the *p* of his servant ... Ps 35:27 7965
when I saw the *p* of the wicked ... Ps 73:3 7965
LORD, I beseech thee, send now *p* ... Ps 118:25 6743
walls, and *p* within thy palaces ... Ps 122:7 7962
the *p* of fools shall destroy them ... Prov 1:32 7962
In the day of *p* be joyful ... Eccl 7:14 2896
I spake unto thee in thy *p* ... Jer 22:21 7962
for all the *p* that I procure unto ... Jer 33:9 7965
I forgat *p* ... Lam 3:17 2896
My cities through *p* shall yet be ... Zec 1:17 2896
Jerusalem was inhabited and in *p* ... Zec 7:7 7961

PROSPEROUS {8}
had made his journey *p* or not ... Gen 24:21 6743
with Joseph, and he was a *p* man ... Gen 39:2 6743
then thou shalt make thy way *p* ... Josh 1:8 6743
our way which we go shall be *p* ... Judg 18:5 6743
habitation of thy righteousness *p* ... Job 8:6 7999
him, and he shall make his way *p* ... Is 48:15 6743
For the seed shall be *p* ... Zec 8:12 7965
now at length I might have a *p* ... Rom 1:10 *2137*

PROSPEROUSLY {2}
in his own house, he *p* effected ... 2Chr 7:11 6743
majesty ride *p* because of truth ... Ps 45:4 6743

PROSTITUTE {1}
Do not *p* thy daughter, to cause ... Lev 19:29 2490

PROTECTION {1}
rise up and help you, and be your *p* ... Deut 32:38 5643

PROTEST {3}
The man did solemnly *p* unto us ... Gen 43:3 5749
howbeit yet *p* solemnly unto them, ... 1Sa 8:9 5749
I *p* by your rejoicing which I ... 1Cor 15:31 *3513*

PROTESTED {3}
p unto thee, saying, Know for a ... 1Kin 2:42 5749
For I earnestly *p* unto your ... Jer 11:7 5749
angel of the LORD *p* unto Joshua ... Zec 3:6 5749

PROTESTING {1}
unto this day, rising early and *p* ... Jer 11:7 5749

PROUD {48}
the *p* helpers do stoop under him ... Job 9:13 7293
he smiteth through the *p* ... Job 26:12 7293
here shall thy *p* waves be stayed ... Job 38:11 1347
and behold every one that is *p* ... Job 40:11 1343
Look on every one that is *p* ... Job 40:12 1343
the tongue that speaketh *p* things ... Ps 12:3 1419
plentifully rewardeth the *p* doer ... Ps 31:23 1346
trust, and respecteth not the *p* ... Ps 40:4 7295
the *p* are risen against me, and ... Ps 86:14 2086
render a reward to the *p* ... Ps 94:2 1343
a *p* heart will not I suffer ... Ps 101:5 7342
rebuked the *p* that are cursed ... Ps 119:21 2086
The *p* have had me greatly in ... Ps 119:51 2086
The *p* have forged a lie against ... Ps 119:69 2086
Let the *p* be ashamed ... Ps 119:78 2086
The *p* have digged pits for me, ... Ps 119:85 2086
let not the *p* oppress me ... Ps 119:122 2086
and with the contempt of the *p* ... Ps 123:4 1349
Then the *p* waters had gone over ... Ps 124:5 2121
but the *p* he knoweth afar off ... Ps 138:6 1364
The *p* have hid a snare for me, and ... Ps 140:5 1343
A *p* look, a lying tongue, and ... Prov 6:17 7311
will destroy the house of the *p* ... Prov 15:25 1343
Every one that is *p* in heart is ... Prov 16:5 1362
to divide the spoil with the *p* ... Prov 16:19 1343
a *p* heart, and the plowing of the ... Prov 21:4 7342
P and haughty scorner is his name, ... Prov 21:24 2086
who dealeth in *p* wrath ... Prov 21:24 2087
He that is of a *p* heart stirreth ... Prov 28:25 7342
is better than the *p* in spirit ... Eccl 7:8 1362
shall be upon every one that is *p* ... Is 2:12 1343
the arrogancy of the *p* to cease ... Is 13:11 2086
he is very *p* ... Is 16:6 1341
be not *p* ... Jer 13:15 1341
son of Kareah, and all the *p* men ... Jer 43:2 2086
(he is exceeding *p*) his loftiness ... Jer 48:29 1343
she hath been *p* against the LORD ... Jer 50:29 2102
I am against thee, O thou most *p* ... Jer 50:31 2087
the most *p* shall stumble and fall, ... Jer 50:32 2087
by wine, he is a *p* man, neither ... Hab 2:5 3093
And now we call the *p* happy ... Mal 3:15 2086
and all the *p*, yea, and all that do ... Mal 4:1 2086
he hath scattered the *p* in the ... Lk 1:51 *5244*
haters of God, despiteful, *p* ... Rom 1:30 *5244*
He is *p*, knowing nothing, but ... 1Ti 6:4 *5187*
own selves, covetous, boasters, *p* ... 2Ti 3:2 *5244*
he saith, God resisteth the *p* ... Jas 4:6 *5244*
for God resisteth the *p*, and ... 1Pet 5:5 *5244*

PROUDLY {9}
they dealt *p* he was above them ... Ex 18:11 2102
Talk no more so exceeding *p* ... 1Sa 2:3 1364
that they dealt *p* against them ... Neh 9:10 2102
But they and our fathers dealt *p* ... Neh 9:16 2102
yet they dealt *p*, and hearkened ... Neh 9:29 2102
with their mouth they speak *p* ... Ps 17:10 1348
which speak grievous things *p* ... Ps 31:18 1346
himself *p* against the ancient ... Is 3:5 7292
spoken *p* in the day of distress ... Obad 12 1431

PROVE {25}
rate every day, that I may *p* them ... Ex 16:4 5254
for God is come to *p* you, and that ... Ex 20:20 5254
to *p* thee, to know what was in ... Deut 8:2 5254
thee, and that he might *p* thee ... Deut 8:16 5254
one, whom thou didst *p* at Massah ... Deut 33:8 5254
That through them I may *p* Israel ... Judg 2:22 5254
to *p* Israel by them, even as many ... Judg 3:1 5254
they were to *p* Israel by them, to ... Judg 3:4 5254
let me *p*, I pray thee, but this ... Judg 6:39 5254
she came to *p* him with hard ... 1Kin 10:1 5254
she came to *p* Solomon with hard ... 2Chr 9:1 5254
it shall also *p* me perverse ... Job 9:20
Examine me, O LORD, and *p* me ... Ps 26:2 5254
I will *p* thee with mirth, ... Eccl 2:1 5254
P thy servants, I beseech thee, ... Dan 1:12 5254
p me now herewith, saith the LORD ... Mal 3:10 974
yoke of oxen, and I go to *p* them ... Lk 14:19 *1381*
And this he said to *p* him ... Jn 6:6 *3985*
Neither can they *p* the things ... Acts 24:13 *3936*
Paul, which they could not *p* ... Acts 25:7 *584*
that ye may *p* what is that good, ... Rom 12:2 *1381*
to *p* the sincerity of your love ... 2Cor 8:8 *1381*
p your own selves ... 2Cor 13:5 *1381*
But let every man *p* his own work ... Gal 6:4 *1381*
P all things ... 1Th 5:21 *1381*

PROVED {15}
Hereby ye shall be *p* ... Gen 42:15 974
prison, that your words may be *p* ... Gen 42:16 974
an ordinance, and there he *p* them ... Ex 15:25 5254
for he had not *p* it ... 1Sa 17:39 5254
for I have not *p* them ... 1Sa 17:39 5254
Thou hast *p* mine heart ... Ps 17:3 974
For thou, O God, hast *p* us ... Ps 66:10 974
I *p* thee at the waters of Meribah ... Ps 81:7 974
tempted me, *p* me, and saw my work ... Ps 95:9 974
All this have I *p* by wisdom ... Eccl 7:23 5254
this matter, and *p* them ten days ... Dan 1:14 5254
for we have before *p* both Jews ... Rom 3:9 *4256*
p diligent in many things ... 2Cor 8:22 *1381*
And let these also first be *p* ... 1Ti 3:10 *1381*
p me, and saw my works forty years ... Heb 3:9 *1381*

PROVENDER {7}
p enough, and room to lodge in ... Gen 24:25 4554
p for the camels, and water to ... Gen 24:32 4554
sack to give his ass *p* in the inn ... Gen 42:27 4554
and he gave their asses *p* ... Gen 43:24 4554
is both straw and *p* for our asses ... Judg 19:19 4554
house, and gave *p* unto the asses ... Judg 19:21 1101
ear the ground shall eat clean *p* ... Is 30:24 1098

PROVERB {20}
shalt become an astonishment, a *p* ... Deut 28:37 4912
Therefore it became a *p*, Is Saul ... 1Sa 10:12 4912
As saith the *p* of the ancients, ... 1Sa 24:13 4912
and Israel shall be a *p* and a ... 1Kin 9:7 4912
sight, and will make it to be a *p* ... 2Chr 7:20 4912
and I became a *p* to them ... Ps 69:11 4912
To understand a *p*, and the ... Prov 1:6 4912
p against the king of Babylon ... Is 14:4 4912
hurt, to be a reproach and a *p* ... Jer 24:9 4912
what is that *p* that ye have in ... Eze 12:22 4912
I will make this *p* to cease ... Eze 12:23 4912
no more use it as a *p* in Israel ... Eze 12:23 4911
and will make him a sign and a *p* ... Eze 14:8 4912
shall use this *p* against thee ... Eze 16:44 4911
that ye use this *p* concerning the ... Eze 18:2 4911
any more to use this *p* in Israel ... Eze 18:3 4911
a taunting *p* against him, and say, ... Hab 2:6 2420
Ye will surely say unto me this *p* ... Lk 4:23 *3850*
thou plainly, and speakest no *p* ... Jn 16:29 *3942*
unto them according to the true *p* ... 2Pet 2:22 *3942*

PROVERBS {9}
they that speak in *p* say, Come ... Num 21:27 4911
And he spake three thousand *p* ... 1Kin 4:32 4912
The *P* of Solomon the son of David ... Prov 1:1 4912
The *p* of Solomon ... Prov 10:1 4912
These are also *p* of Solomon ... Prov 25:1 4912
out, and set in order many *p* ... Eccl 12:9 4912

every one that useth *p* shall use ... Eze 16:44 4911
have I spoken unto you in *p* ... Jn 16:25 *3942*
shall no more speak unto you in *p* ... Jn 16:25 *3942*

PROVETH {1}
for the LORD your God *p* you ... Deut 13:3 5254

PROVIDE {11}
God will *p* himself a lamb for a ... Gen 22:8 7200
now when shall I *p* for mine own ... Gen 30:30 6213
Moreover thou shalt *p* out of all ... Ex 18:21 2372
P me now a man that can play well ... 1Sa 16:17 7200
whom David my father did *p* ... 2Chr 2:7 3559
can he *p* flesh for his people ... Ps 78:20 3559
P neither gold, nor silver, nor ... Mt 10:9 *2532*
p yourselves bags which wax not ... Lk 12:33 *4160*
p them beasts, that they may set ... Acts 23:24 *3936*
P things honest in the sight of ... Rom 12:17 *4306*
But if any *p* not for his own, and ... 1Ti 5:8 *4306*

PROVIDED {9}
he *p* the first part for himself, ... Deut 33:21 7200
for I have *p* me a king among his ... 1Sa 16:1 7200
he had *p* the king of sustenance ... 2Sa 19:32
which *p* victuals for the king and ... 1Kin 4:7
those officers *p* victual for king ... 1Kin 4:27
Moreover he *p* him cities, and ... 2Chr 32:29 6213
corn, when thou hast so *p* for it ... Ps 65:9 3559
things be, which thou hast *p* ... Lk 12:20 *2090*
God having *p* some better thing ... Heb 11:40 *4265*

PROVIDENCE {1}
done unto this nation by thy *p* ... Acts 24:2 *4307*

PROVIDETH {2}
Who *p* for the raven his food ... Job 38:41 3559
P her meat in the summer, and ... Prov 6:8 3559

PROVIDING {1}
P for honest things, not only in ... 2Cor 8:21 *4306*

PROVINCE {27}
of the *p* that went up out of the ... Ezr 2:1 4082
that we went into the *p* of Judea ... Ezr 5:8 4083
that is in the *p* of the Medes ... Ezr 6:2 4082
find in all the *p* of Babylon ... Ezr 7:16 4082
in the *p* are in great affliction ... Neh 1:3 4082
These are the children of the *p* ... Neh 7:6 4082
of the *p* that dwelt in Jerusalem ... Neh 11:3 4082
into every *p* according to the ... Est 1:22 4082
governors that were over every *p* ... Est 3:12 4082
every *p* according to the writing ... Est 3:12 4082
to be given in every *p* was ... Est 3:14 4082
And in every *p*, whithersoever the ... Est 4:3 4082
unto every *p* according to the ... Est 8:9 4082
p that would assault them, both ... Est 8:11 4082
to be given in every *p* was ... Est 8:13 4082
And in every *p*, and in every city, ... Est 8:17 4082
generation, every family, every *p* ... Est 9:28 4082
of judgment and justice in a *p* ... Eccl 5:8 4082
ruler over the whole *p* of Babylon ... Dan 2:48 4083
the affairs of the *p* of Babylon ... Dan 2:49 4083
of Dura, in the *p* of Babylon ... Dan 3:1 4083
the affairs of the *p* of Babylon ... Dan 3:12 4083
and Abed-nego, in the *p* of Babylon ... Dan 3:30 4082
palace, which is in the *p* of Elam ... Dan 8:2 4082
upon the fattest places of the *p* ... Dan 11:24 4082
letter, he asked of what *p* he was ... Acts 23:34 *1885*
when Festus was come into the *p* ... Acts 25:1 *1885*

PROVINCES {30}
young men of the princes of the *p* ... 1Kin 20:14 4082
young men of the princes of the *p* ... 1Kin 20:15 4082
princes of the *p* went out first ... 1Kin 20:17 4082
of the *p* came out of the city ... 1Kin 20:19 4082
city, and hurtful unto kings and *p* ... Ezr 4:15 4083
an hundred and seven and twenty *p* ... Est 1:1 4082
the nobles and princes of the *p* ... Est 1:3 4082
all the *p* of the king Ahasuerus ... Est 1:16 4082
letters into all the king's *p* ... Est 1:22 4082
in all the *p* of his kingdom ... Est 2:3 4082
and he made a release to the *p* ... Est 2:18 4082
in all the *p* of thy kingdom ... Est 3:8 4082
by posts into all the king's *p* ... Est 3:13 4082
and the people of the king's *p* ... Est 4:11 4082
which are in all the king's *p* ... Est 8:5 4082
rulers of the *p* which are from ... Est 8:9 4082
an hundred twenty and seven *p* ... Est 8:9 4082
in all the *p* of king Ahasuerus ... Est 8:12 4082
all the *p* of the king Ahasuerus ... Est 9:2 4082
And all the rulers of the *p* ... Est 9:3 4082
went out throughout all the *p* ... Est 9:4 4082
done in the rest of the king's *p* ... Est 9:12 4082
p gathered themselves together ... Est 9:16 4082
all the *p* of the king Ahasuerus ... Est 9:20 4082
seven *p* of the kingdom of ... Est 9:30 4082
treasure of kings and of the *p* ... Eccl 2:8 4082
nations, and princess among the *p* ... Lam 1:1 4082
him on every side from the *p* ... Eze 19:8 4082
and all the rulers of the *p* ... Dan 3:2 4082
and all the rulers of the *p* ... Dan 3:3 4082

PROVING {2}
p that this is very Christ ... Acts 9:22 *4822*
P what is acceptable unto the ... Eph 5:10 *1381*

PROVISION {11}
and to give them *p* for the way ... Gen 42:25 6720
and gave them *p* for the way ... Gen 45:21 6720
all the bread of their *p* was dry ... Josh 9:5 6718
our bread we took hot for our *p* ... Josh 9:12 6679
man his month in a year made *p* ... 1Kin 4:7 3557
Solomon's *p* for one day was ... 1Kin 4:22 3899
And he prepared great *p* for them ... 2Kin 6:23 3740
for the which I have made *p* ... 1Chr 29:19 3559
I will abundantly bless her *p* ... Ps 132:15 6718
them a daily *p* of the king's meat ... Dan 1:5 1697
make not *p* for the flesh, to ... Rom 13:14 *4307*

PROVOCATION {8}
by his *p* wherewith he provoked ... 1Kin 15:30 3708
for the *p* wherewith thou hast ... 1Kin 21:22 3708
not mine eye continue in their *p* ... Job 17:2 4784
not your heart, as in the *p* ... Ps 95:8 4808
been to me as a *p* of mine anger ... Jer 32:31 3708
presented the *p* of their offering ... Eze 20:28 3708
not your hearts, as in the *p* ... Heb 3:8 *3894*
not your hearts, as in the *p* ... Heb 3:15 *3894*

PROVOCATIONS {3}
because of all the *p* that ... 2Kin 23:26 3708
of Egypt, and had wrought great *p* ... Neh 9:18 5007
to thee, and they wrought great *p* ... Neh 9:26 5007

PROVOKE {42}
him, and obey his voice, *p* him not ... Ex 23:21 4843
How long will this people *p* me ... Num 14:11 5006
LORD thy God, to *p* him to anger ... Deut 4:25
of the LORD, to *p* him to anger ... Deut 9:18
p me, and break my covenant ... Deut 31:20 5006
to *p* him to anger through the ... Deut 31:29
I will *p* them to anger with a ... Deut 32:21
to *p* me to anger, and hast cast me ... 1Kin 14:9
to *p* me to anger with their sins ... 1Kin 16:2
to *p* the LORD God of Israel to ... 1Kin 16:26
Ahab did more to *p* the LORD God ... 1Kin 16:33
things to *p* the LORD to anger ... 2Kin 17:11
of the LORD, to *p* him to anger ... 2Kin 17:17
of the LORD, to *p* him to anger ... 2Kin 21:6
that they might *p* me to anger ... 2Kin 22:17
had made to *p* the LORD to anger ... 2Kin 23:19
of the LORD, to *p* him to anger ... 2Chr 33:6
that they might *p* me to anger ... 2Chr 34:25
they that *p* God are secure ... Job 12:6 7264
How oft did they *p* him in the ... Ps 78:40 4784
to *p* the eyes of his glory ... Is 3:8 4784
gods, that they may *p* me to anger ... Jer 7:18
Do they *p* me to anger ... Jer 7:19
do they not *p* themselves to the ... Jer 7:19
p me to anger in offering incense ... Jer 11:17
p me not to anger with the works ... Jer 25:6
that ye might *p* me to anger with ... Jer 25:7
unto other gods, to *p* me to anger ... Jer 32:29
they have done to *p* me to anger ... Jer 32:32
have committed to *p* me to anger ... Jer 44:3
In that ye *p* me unto wrath with ... Jer 44:8
and have returned to *p* me to anger ... Eze 8:17
thy whoredoms, to *p* me to anger ... Eze 16:26
to *p* him to speak of many things ... Lk 11:53 *653*
I will *p* you to jealousy by them ... Rom 10:19 *3863*
for to *p* them to jealousy ... Rom 11:11 *3863*
If by any means I may *p* to ... Rom 11:14 *3863*
Do we *p* the Lord to jealousy ... 1Cor 10:22 *3863*
p not your children to wrath ... Eph 6:4 *3949*
p not your children to anger, ... Col 3:21 *2042*
some, when they had heard, did *p* ... Heb 3:16 *3893*
one another to *p* unto love ... Heb 10:24 *3948*

PROVOKED {33}
any of them that *p* me see it ... Num 14:23 5006
that these men have *p* the LORD ... Num 16:30 5006
Also in Horeb ye *p* the LORD to ... Deut 9:8
ye *p* the LORD to wrath ... Deut 9:22
They *p* him to jealousy with ... Deut 32:16 3707
abominations *p* they him to anger ... Deut 32:16
they have *p* me to anger with ... Deut 32:21
unto them, and *p* the LORD to anger ... Judg 2:12
And her adversary also *p* her sore ... 1Sa 1:6 3707
house of the LORD, so she *p* her ... 1Sa 1:7 3707
they *p* him to jealousy with their ... 1Kin 14:22
p the LORD God of Israel to anger ... 1Kin 15:30
wherewith thou hast *p* me to anger ... 1Kin 21:22
p to anger the LORD God of Israel ... 1Kin 22:53
have *p* me to anger, since the day ... 2Kin 21:15
that Manasseh had *p* him withal ... 2Kin 23:26 3707
and *p* David to number Israel ... 1Chr 21:1 5496
p to anger the LORD God of his ... 2Chr 28:25
p the God of heaven unto wrath ... Ezr 5:12 7265
for they have *p* thee to anger ... Neh 4:5
p the most high God, and kept not ... Ps 78:56 4784
For they *p* him to anger with ... Ps 78:58
but *p* him at the sea, even at the ... Ps 106:7 4784
Thus they *p* him to anger with ... Ps 106:29
Because they *p* his spirit ... Ps 106:33 4784
but they *p* him with their counsel ... Ps 106:43 4784
they have *p* the Holy One of ... Is 1:4 5006
Why have they *p* me to anger with ... Jer 8:19
p me to anger with the work of ... Jer 32:30
Ephraim *p* him to anger most ... Hos 12:14
when your fathers *p* me to wrath ... Zec 8:14
not her own, is not easily *p* ... 1Cor 13:5 *3947*
and your zeal hath *p* very many ... 2Cor 9:2 *2042*

PROVOKEDST {1}
how thou *p* the LORD thy God to ... Deut 9:7

PROVOKETH {3}
whoso *p* him to anger sinneth ... Prov 20:2 5674
A people that *p* me to anger ... Is 65:3
of jealousy, which *p* to jealousy ... Eze 8:3

PROVOKING {6}
because of the *p* of his sons ... Deut 32:19 3707
their groves, *p* the LORD to anger ... 1Kin 14:15
in *p* him to anger with the work ... 1Kin 16:7
in *p* the LORD God of Israel to ... 1Kin 16:13
sinned yet more against him by *p* ... Ps 78:17 4784
p one another, envying one ... Gal 5:26 *4292*

PRUDENCE {3}
king a wise son, endued with *p* ... 2Chr 2:12 7922
I wisdom dwell with *p*, and find ... Prov 8:12 6195
toward us in all wisdom and *p* ... Eph 1:8 *5428*

PRUDENT {24}
p in matters, and a comely person, ... 1Sa 16:18 995
but a *p* man covereth shame ... Prov 12:16 6175
A *p* man concealeth knowledge ... Prov 12:23 6175
Every *p* man dealeth with ... Prov 13:16 6175
The wisdom of the *p* is to ... Prov 14:8 6175
but the *p* man looketh well to his ... Prov 14:15 6175
but the *p* are crowned with ... Prov 14:18 6175
he that regardeth reproof is *p* ... Prov 15:5 6191
wise in heart shall be called *p* ... Prov 16:21 995
The heart of the *p* getteth ... Prov 18:15 995
a *p* wife is from the LORD ... Prov 19:14 7919
A *p* man foreseeth the evil, and ... Prov 22:3 6175
A *p* man foreseeth the evil, and ... Prov 27:12 6175
judge, and the prophet, and the *p* ... Is 3:2 7080
own eyes, and *p* in their own sight ... Is 5:21 995
for I am *p* ... Is 10:13 995
of their *p* men shall be hid ... Is 29:14 995
is counsel perished from the *p* ... Jer 49:7 995
p, and he shall know them ... Hos 14:9 995
Therefore the *p* shall keep ... Amos 5:13 7919
these things from the wise and *p* ... Mt 11:25 *4908*
these things from the wise and *p* ... Lk 10:21 *4908*
country, Sergius Paulus, a *p* man ... Acts 13:7 *4908*
the understanding of the *p* ... 1Cor 1:19 *4908*

PRUDENTLY {1}
Behold, my servant shall deal *p* ... Is 52:13 7919

PRUNE {2}
years thou shalt *p* thy vineyard ... Lev 25:3 2168
sow thy field, nor *p* thy vineyard ... Lev 25:4 2168

PRUNED {1}
it shall not be *p*, nor digged ... Is 5:6 2167

PRUNINGHOOKS {4}
and their spears into *p* ... Is 2:4 4211
both cut off the sprigs with *p* ... Is 18:5 4211
swords, and your *p* into spears ... Joel 3:10 4211
and their spears into *p* ... Mic 4:3 4211

PSALM {88}
day David delivered first this *p* ... 1Chr 16:7
A *P* of David, when he fled from ... Ps 3:*t* 4210
on Neginoth, A *P* of David ... Ps 4:*t* 4210
upon Nehiloth, A *P* of David ... Ps 5:*t* 4210
upon Sheminith, A *P* of David ... Ps 6:*t* 4210
upon Gittith, A *P* of David ... Ps 8:*t* 4210
upon Muth-labben, A *P* of David ... Ps 9:*t* 4210
the chief Musician, A *P* of David ... Ps 11:*t*
upon Sheminith, A *P* of David ... Ps 12:*t* 4210
the chief Musician, A *P* of David ... Ps 13:*t* 4210
the chief Musician, A *P* of David ... Ps 14:*t*
A *P* of David ... Ps 15:*t* 4210
A *P* of David, the servant of the ... Ps 18:*t* 4210
the chief Musician, A *P* of David ... Ps 19:*t* 4210
the chief Musician, A *P* of David ... Ps 20:*t* 4210
the chief Musician, A *P* of David ... Ps 21:*t* 4210
Aijeleth Shahar, A *P* of David ... Ps 22:*t* 4210
A *P* of David ... Ps 23:*t* 4210
A *P* of David ... Ps 24:*t*
A *P* of David ... Ps 25:*t*
A *P* of David ... Ps 26:*t*
A *P* of David ... Ps 27:*t*
A *P* of David ... Ps 28:*t*
A *P* of David ... Ps 29:*t* 4210
A *P* and Song at the dedication of ... Ps 30:*t* 4210
the chief Musician, A *P* of David ... Ps 31:*t* 4210
A *P* of David, A Maschil ... Ps 32:*t*
A *P* of David, when he changed his ... Ps 34:*t*
A *P* of David ... Ps 35:*t*
A *P* of David, the servant of the ... Ps 36:*t*
A *P* of David ... Ps 37:*t*
A *P* of David, to bring to ... Ps 38:*t* 4210
even to Jeduthun, A *P* of David ... Ps 39:*t* 4210
the chief Musician, A *P* of David ... Ps 40:*t* 4210
the chief Musician, A *P* of David ... Ps 41:*t* 4210
A *P* for the sons of Korah ... Ps 47:*t* 4210
A Song and *P* for the sons of Korah ... Ps 48:*t* 4210
A *P* for the sons of Korah ... Ps 49:*t* 4210
A *P* of Asaph ... Ps 50:*t* 4210
A *P* of David, when Nathan the ... Ps 51:*t* 4210
A *P* of David, when Doeg the ... Ps 52:*t*
Mahalath, Maschil, A *P* of David ... Ps 53:*t*
A *P* of David, when the Ziphims ... Ps 54:*t*
Neginoth, Maschil, A *P* of David ... Ps 55:*t*
upon Neginah, A *P* of David ... Ps 61:*t*
to Jeduthun, A *P* of David ... Ps 62:*t* 4210
A *P* of David, when he was in the ... Ps 63:*t* 4210
the chief Musician, A *P* of David ... Ps 64:*t* 4210
To the chief Musician, A *P* ... Ps 65:*t* 4210
the chief Musician, A Song or *P* ... Ps 66:*t* 4210
Musician on Neginoth, A *P* or Song ... Ps 67:*t* 4210
Musician, A *P* or Song of David ... Ps 68:*t* 4210
upon Shoshannim, A *P* of David ... Ps 69:*t*
A *P* of David, to bring to ... Ps 70:*t*
A *P* for Solomon ... Ps 72:*t* 4210
A *P* of Asaph ... Ps 73:*t* 4210
Altaschith, A *P* or Song of Asaph ... Ps 75:*t* 4210
on Neginoth, A *P* or Song of Asaph ... Ps 76:*t* 4210
to Jeduthun, A *P* of Asaph ... Ps 77:*t* 4210
A *P* of Asaph ... Ps 79:*t* 4210
Shoshannim-Eduth, A *P* of Asaph ... Ps 80:*t* 4210

P

upon Gittith, A *P* of Asaph ... Ps 81:*t*
Take a *p*, and bring hither the ... Ps 81:2 2172
A *P* of Asaph ... Ps 82:*t* 4210
A Song or *P* of Asaph ... Ps 83:*t* 4210
A *P* for the sons of Korah ... Ps 84:*t* 4210
A *P* for the sons of Korah ... Ps 85:*t* 4210
A *P* or Song for the sons of Korah ... Ps 87:*t* 4210
A Song or *P* for the sons of Korah ... Ps 88:*t* 4210
A *P* or Song for the sabbath day ... Ps 92:*t* 4210
A *P* ... Ps 98:*t* 4210
the harp, and the voice of a *p* ... Ps 98:5 2172
A *P* of praise ... Ps 100:*t* 4210
A *P* of David ... Ps 101:*t* 4210
A *P* of David ... Ps 103:*t*
A Song or *P* of David ... Ps 108:*t* 4210
the chief Musician, A *P* of David ... Ps 109:*t* 4210
A *P* of David ... Ps 110:*t* 4210
A *P* of David ... Ps 138:*t*
the chief Musician, A *P* of David ... Ps 139:*t* 4210
the chief Musician, A *P* of David ... Ps 140:*t* 4210
A *P* of David ... Ps 141:*t* 4210
A *P* of David ... Ps 143:*t* 4210
A *P* of David ... Ps 144:*t*
David's *P* of praise ... Ps 145:*t*
is also written in the second *p* ... Acts 13:33 *5568*
he saith also in another *p* ... Acts 13:35
every one of you hath a *p* ... 1Cor 14:26 *5568*

PSALMIST {1}
Jacob, and the sweet *p* of Israel ... 2Sa 23:1 2158

PSALMS {9}
sing *p* unto him, talk ye of all ... 1Chr 16:9 2167
a joyful noise unto him with *p* ... Ps 95:2 2158
Sing unto him, sing *p* unto him ... Ps 105:2 2167
himself saith in the book of *P* ... Lk 20:42 *5568*
and in the prophets, and in the *p* ... Lk 24:44 *5568*
it is written in the book of *P* ... Acts 1:20 *5568*
Speaking to yourselves in *p* ... Eph 5:19 *5568*
and admonishing one another in *p* ... Col 3:16 *5568*
let him sing *p* ... Jas 5:13 *5567*

PSALTERIES {14}
fir wood, even on harps, and on *p* ... 2Sa 6:5 5035
harps also and *p* for singers ... 1Kin 10:12 5035
singing, and with harps, and with *p* ... 1Chr 13:8 5035
with instruments of musick, *p* ... 1Chr 15:16 5035
and Benaiah, with *p* on Alamoth ... 1Chr 15:20 5035
cymbals, making a noise with *p* ... 1Chr 15:28 5035
and Jeiel with *p* and with harps ... 1Chr 16:5 3627
prophesy with harps, with *p* ... 1Chr 25:1 5035
of the LORD, with cymbals, *p* ... 1Chr 25:6 5035
white linen, having cymbals and *p* ... 2Chr 5:12 5035
palace, and harps and *p* for singers ... 2Chr 9:11 5035
And they came to Jerusalem with *p* ... 2Chr 20:28 5035
of the LORD with cymbals, with *p* ... 2Chr 29:25 5035
and with singing, with cymbals, *p* ... Neh 12:27 5035

PSALTERY {13}
down from the high place with a *p* ... 1Sa 10:5 5035
sing unto him with the *p* and an ... Ps 33:2 5035
awake, *p* and harp ... Ps 57:8 5035
will also praise thee with the *p* ... Ps 71:22 3627
the pleasant harp with the *p* ... Ps 81:2 5035
of ten strings, and upon the *p* ... Ps 92:3 5035
Awake, *p* and harp ... Ps 108:2 5035
upon a *p* and an instrument of ten ... Ps 144:9 5035
praise him with the *p* and harp ... Ps 150:3 5035
cornet, flute, harp, sackbut, *p* ... Dan 3:5 6460
cornet, flute, harp, sackbut, *p* ... Dan 3:7 6460
cornet, flute, harp, sackbut, *p* ... Dan 3:10 6460
cornet, flute, harp, sackbut, *p* ... Dan 3:15 6460

PTOLEMAIS *(tol-e-ma'-is)* {1} See ACCHO. *A seaport between Carmel and Tyre.*
course from Tyre, we came to *P* ... Acts 21:7 *4424*

PUA *(pu'ah)* {1} See PUAH. *A son of Issachar.*
of *P*, the family of the Punites ... Num 26:23 6312

PUAH *(pu'-ah)* {3} See PHUVAH, PUA, PUNITES.
1. Same as Pua.
sons of Issachar were, Tola, and *P* ... 1Chr 7:1 6312
2. Father of Tola.
defend Israel Tola the son of *P* ... Judg 10:1 6312
3. A Hebrew midwife in Egypt.
and the name of the other *P* ... Ex 1:15 6326

PUBLICAN {6}
Thomas, and Matthew the *p* ... Mt 10:3 *5057*
thee as an heathen man and a *p* ... Mt 18:17 *5057*
things he went forth, and saw a *p* ... Lk 5:27 *5057*
one a Pharisee, and the other a *p* ... Lk 18:10 *5057*
adulterers, or even as this *p* ... Lk 18:11 *5057*
And the *p*, standing afar off ... Lk 18:13 *5057*

PUBLICANS {17}
do not even the *p* the same ... Mt 5:46 *5057*
do not even the *p* so ... Mt 5:47 *5057*
meat in the house, behold, many *p* ... Mt 9:10 *5057*
Why eateth your Master with *p* ... Mt 9:11 *5057*
and a winebibber, a friend of *p* ... Mt 11:19 *5057*
Verily I say unto you, That the *p* ... Mt 21:31 *5057*
but the *p* and the harlots believed ... Mt 21:32 *5057*
sat at meat in his house, many *p* ... Mk 2:15 *5057*
and Pharisees saw him eat with *p* ... Mk 2:16 *5057*
that he eateth and drinketh with *p* ... Mk 2:16 *5057*
Then came also *p* to be baptized ... Lk 3:12 *5057*
and there was a great company of *p* ... Lk 5:29 *5057*
Why do ye eat and drink with *p* ... Lk 5:30 *5057*
people that heard him, and the *p* ... Lk 7:29 *5057*
and a winebibber, a friend of *p* ... Lk 7:34 *5057*
Then drew near unto him all the *p* ... Lk 15:1 *5057*
which was the chief among the *p* ... Lk 19:2 *754*

PUBLICK {1}
willing to make her a *p* example ... Mt 1:19 *3856*

PUBLICKLY {2}
convinced the Jews, and that *p* ... Acts 18:28 *1219*
shewed you, and have taught you *p* ... Acts 20:20 *1219*

PUBLISH {17}
Because I will *p* the name of the ... Deut 32:3 7121
to *p* it in the house of their ... 1Sa 31:9 1319
p it not in the streets of ... 2Sa 1:20 1319
And that they should *p* and proclaim ... Neh 8:15 8085
That I may *p* with the voice of ... Ps 26:7 8085
ye in Judah, and *p* in Jerusalem ... Jer 4:5 8085
p against Jerusalem, that ... Jer 4:16 8085
Jacob, and *p* it in Judah, saying ... Jer 5:20 8085
p ye, praise ye, and say, O LORD ... Jer 31:7 8085
p in Migdol, and *p* in Noph ... Jer 46:14 8085
ye among the nations, and *p* ... Jer 50:2 8085
p, and conceal not ... Jer 50:2 8085
P in the palaces at Ashdod, and in ... Amos 3:9 8085
proclaim and *p* the free offerings ... Amos 4:5 8085
went out, and began to *p* it much ... Mk 1:45 *2784*
began to *p* in Decapolis how great ... Mk 5:20 *2784*

PUBLISHED {11}
be *p* throughout all his empire ... Est 1:20 8085
that it should be *p* according to ... Est 1:22 1696
province was *p* unto all people ... Est 3:14 1540
province was *p* unto all people ... Est 8:13 1540
the company of those that *p* it ... Ps 68:11 1319
p through Nineveh by the decree ... Jonah 3:7 559
the more a great deal they *p* it ... Mk 7:36 *2784*
must first be *p* among all nations ... Mk 13:10 *2784*
p throughout the whole city how ... Lk 8:39 *2784*
which was *p* throughout all Judaea ... Acts 10:37 *1096*
the word of the Lord was *p* ... Acts 13:49 *1308*

PUBLISHETH {4}
good tidings, that *p* peace ... Is 52:7 8085
tidings of good, that *p* salvation ... Is 52:7 8085
p affliction from mount Ephraim ... Jer 4:15 8085
good tidings, that *p* peace ... Nah 1:15 8085

PUBLIUS *(pub'-le-us)* {2} *A chief man on Melita.*
of the island, whose name was *P* ... Acts 28:7 *4196*
that the father of *P* lay sick of ... Acts 28:8 *4196*

PUDENS *(pu'-denz)* {1} *A Christian in Rome.*
Eubulus greeteth thee, and *P* ... 2Ti 4:21 *4227*

PUFFED {6}
that no one of you be *p* up for ... 1Cor 4:6 *5448*
Now some are *p* up, as though I ... 1Cor 4:18 *5448*
the speech of them which are *p* up ... 1Cor 4:19 *5448*
And ye are *p* up, and have not ... 1Cor 5:2 *5448*
vaunteth not itself, is not *p* up ... 1Cor 13:4 *5448*
vainly *p* up by his fleshly mind ... Col 2:18 *5448*

PUFFETH {3}
for all his enemies, he *p* at them ... Ps 10:5 6315
in safety from him that *p* at him ... Ps 12:5 6315
Knowledge *p* up, but charity ... 1Cor 8:1 *5448*

PUHITES *(pu'-hites)* {1} *A family descended from Caleb.*
the Ithrites, and the *P*, and the ... 1Chr 2:53 6336

PUL *(pul)* {4}
1. Same as Tiglath-pileser.
P the king of Assyria came ... 2Kin 15:19 6322
Menahem gave *P* a thousand talents ... 2Kin 15:19 6322
the spirit of *P* king of Assyria ... 1Chr 5:26 6322
2. A place near Libya.
unto the nations, to Tarshish, *P* ... Is 66:19 6322

PULL {15}
he could not *p* it in again to him ... 1Kin 13:4 7725
P me out of the net that they ... Ps 31:4 3318
thy state shall he *p* thee down ... Is 22:19 2040
to *p* down, and to destroy, and to ... Jer 1:10 5422
p them out like sheep for the ... Jer 12:3 5423
to *p* down, and to destroy it ... Jer 18:7 5422
build them, and not *p* them down ... Jer 24:6 2040
not *p* you down, and I will plant ... Jer 42:10 2040
shall he not *p* up the roots ... Eze 17:9 5423
ye *p* off the robe with the ... Mic 2:8 6584
Let me *p* out the mote out of ... Mt 7:4 *1544*
let me *p* out the mote that is in ... Lk 6:42 *1544*
to *p* out the mote that is in thy ... Lk 6:42 *1544*
I will *p* down my barns, and build ... Lk 12:18 *2507*
will not straightway *p* him out on ... Lk 14:5 *385*

PULLED {7}
p her in unto him into the ark ... Gen 8:9 4026
p Lot into the house to them, and ... Gen 19:10 935
let timber be *p* down from his ... Ezr 6:11 5256
aside my ways, and *p* me in pieces ... Lam 3:11 6582
they shall no more be *p* up out of ... Amos 9:15 5428
p away the shoulder, and stopped ... Zec 7:11 5414
have been *p* in pieces of them ... Acts 23:10 *1288*

PULLING {2}
God to the *p* down of strong holds ... 2Cor 10:4 *2506*
with fear, *p* them out of the fire ... Jude 23 *726*

PULPIT {1}
the scribe stood upon a *p* of wood ... Neh 8:4 4026

PULSE {3}
beans, and lentiles, and parched *p* ... 2Sa 17:28
and let them give us *p* to eat ... Dan 1:12 2235
and gave them *p* ... Dan 1:16 2235

PUNISH {32}
then I will *p* you seven times ... Lev 26:18 3256
will *p* you yet seven times for ... Lev 26:24 5221
Also to *p* the just is not good ... Prov 17:26 6064
I will *p* the fruit of the stout ... Is 10:12 6485
I will *p* the world for their evil ... Is 13:11 6485
that the LORD shall *p* the host of ... Is 24:21 6485
to *p* the inhabitants of the earth ... Is 26:21 6485
strong sword shall *p* leviathan ... Is 27:1 6485
that I will *p* all them which are ... Jer 9:25 6485
of hosts, Behold, I will *p* them ... Jer 11:22 6485
thou say when he shall *p* thee ... Jer 13:21 6485
But I will *p* you according to the ... Jer 21:14 6485
the LORD, I will even *p* that man ... Jer 23:34 6485
that I will *p* the king of Babylon ... Jer 25:12 6485
of Babylon, that nation will I *p* ... Jer 27:8 6485
I will *p* Shemaiah the Nehelamite ... Jer 29:32 6485
I will *p* all that oppress them ... Jer 30:20 6485
And I will *p* him and his seed and ... Jer 36:31 6485
For I will *p* them that dwell in ... Jer 44:13 6485
that I will *p* you in this place ... Jer 44:29 6485
I will *p* the multitude of No, and ... Jer 46:25 6485
I will *p* the king of Babylon and ... Jer 50:18 6485
I will *p* Bel in Babylon, and I ... Jer 51:44 6485
I will *p* them for their ways, and ... Hos 4:9 6485
I will not *p* your daughters when ... Hos 4:14 6485
will *p* Jacob according to his ... Hos 12:2 6485
therefore I will *p* you for all ... Amos 3:2 6485
that I will *p* the princes ... Zeph 1:8 6485
I *p* all those that leap on the ... Zeph 1:9 6485
p the men that are settled on ... Zeph 1:12 6485
As I thought to *p* you, when your ... Zec 8:14 7489
nothing how they might *p* them ... Acts 4:21 *2849*

PUNISHED {17}
he shall be surely *p* ... Ex 21:20 5358
a day or two, he shall not be *p* ... Ex 21:21 5358
he shall be surely *p*, according ... Ex 21:22 6064
p us less than our iniquities ... Ezr 9:13 2820
an iniquity to be *p* by the judges ... Job 31:11
an iniquity to be *p* by the judge ... Job 31:28
When the scorner is *p*, the simple ... Prov 21:11 6064
but the simple pass on, and are *p* ... Prov 22:3 6064
but the simple pass on, and are *p* ... Prov 27:12 6064
of Egypt, as I have *p* Jerusalem ... Jer 44:13 6485
as I have *p* the king of Assyria ... Jer 50:18 6485
be cut off, howsoever I *p* them ... Zeph 3:7 6485
the shepherds, and I *p* the goats ... Zec 10:3 6485
bound unto Jerusalem, for to be *p* ... Acts 22:5 *5097*
I *p* them oft in every synagogue ... Acts 26:11 *5097*
Who shall be *p* with everlasting ... 2Th 1:9 *1349,5099*
unto the day of judgment to be *p* ... 2Pet 2:9 *2849*

PUNISHMENT {27}
My *p* is greater than I can bear ... Gen 4:13 5771
accept of the *p* of their iniquity ... Lev 26:41 5771
accept of the *p* of their iniquity ... Lev 26:43 5771
there shall no *p* happen to thee ... 1Sa 28:10 5771
a strange *p* to the workers of ... Job 31:3
man of great wrath shall suffer *p* ... Prov 19:19 6066
a man for the *p* of his sins ... Lam 3:39 2399
For the *p* of the iniquity of the ... Lam 4:6 5771
than the *p* of the sin of Sodom ... Lam 4:6 2403
The *p* of thine iniquity is ... Lam 4:22 5771
bear the *p* of their iniquity ... Eze 14:10 5771
the *p* of the prophet shall be ... Eze 14:10 5771
p of him that seeketh unto him ... Eze 14:10 5771
will not turn away the *p* thereof ... Amos 1:3
will not turn away the *p* thereof ... Amos 1:6
will not turn away the *p* thereof ... Amos 1:9
will not turn away the *p* thereof ... Amos 1:11
will not turn away the *p* thereof ... Amos 1:13
will not turn away the *p* thereof ... Amos 2:1
will not turn away the *p* thereof ... Amos 2:4
will not turn away the *p* thereof ... Amos 2:6
This shall be the *p* of Egypt ... Zec 14:19 2403
the *p* of all nations that come ... Zec 14:19 2403
shall go away into everlasting *p* ... Mt 25:46 *2851*
to such a man is this *p*, which ... 2Cor 2:6 *2009*
Of how much sorer *p*, suppose ye ... Heb 10:29 *5098*
by him for the *p* of evildoers ... 1Pet 2:14 *1557*

PUNISHMENTS {2}
wrath bringeth the *p* of the sword ... Job 19:29 5771
the heathen, and *p* upon the people ... Ps 149:7 5771

PUNITES *(pu'-nites)* {1} *Descendents of Pua.*
of Pua, the family of the *P* ... Num 26:23 6324

PUNON *(pu'-non)* {2} *An Edomite city.*
from Zalmonah, and pitched in *P* ... Num 33:42 6325
And they departed from *P*, and ... Num 33:43 6325

PUR *(pur)* {3} See PURIM. *Same as Purim.*
of king Ahasuerus, they cast *P* ... Est 3:7 6332
to destroy them, and had cast *P* ... Est 9:24 6332
days Purim after the name of *P* ... Est 9:26 6332

PURAH See PHURAH.

PURCHASE {8}
The *p* of the field and of the cave ... Gen 49:32 4736
if a man *p* of the Levites, then ... Lev 25:33 1350
So I took the evidence of the *p* ... Jer 32:11 4736
I gave the evidence of the *p* unto ... Jer 32:12 4736
that subscribed the book of the *p* ... Jer 32:12 4736
evidences, this evidence of the *p* ... Jer 32:14 4736
p unto Baruch the son of Neriah ... Jer 32:16 4736
p to themselves a good degree ... 1Ti 3:13 *4046*

PURCHASED {9}
Abraham *p* of the sons of Heth ... Gen 25:10 7069
pass over, which thou hast *p* ... Ex 15:16 7069
have I *p* to be my wife, to raise ... Ruth 4:10 7069
which thou hast *p* of old ... Ps 74:2 7069
which his right hand had *p* ... Ps 78:54 7069
Now this man *p* a field with the ... Acts 1:18 *2932*
gift of God may be *p* with money ... Acts 8:20 *2932*
which he hath *p* with his own ... Acts 20:28 *4046*
redemption of the *p* possession ... Eph 1:14 *4047*

PURE {97}
thou shalt overlay it with *p* gold ... Ex 25:11 2889
shalt make a mercy seat of *p* gold ... Ex 25:17 2889
thou shalt overlay it with *p* gold ... Ex 25:24 2889
of *p* gold shalt thou make them ... Ex 25:29 2889
make a candlestick of *p* gold ... Ex 25:31 2889
be one beaten work of *p* gold ... Ex 25:36 2889
thereof, shall be of *p* gold ... Ex 25:38 2889
Of a talent of *p* gold shall he ... Ex 25:39 2889
that they bring thee *p* oil olive ... Ex 27:20 2134
two chains of *p* gold at the ends ... Ex 28:14 2889
ends of wreathen work of *p* gold ... Ex 28:22 2889
thou shalt make a plate of *p* gold ... Ex 28:36 2889
thou shalt overlay it with *p* gold ... Ex 30:3 2889
of *p* myrrh five hundred shekels ... Ex 30:23 1865
sweet spices with *p* frankincense ... Ex 30:34 2134
apothecary, tempered together, *p* ... Ex 30:35 2889
the *p* candlestick with all his ... Ex 31:8 2889
he overlaid it with *p* gold within ... Ex 37:2 2889
he made the mercy seat of *p* gold ... Ex 37:6 2889
And he overlaid it with *p* gold ... Ex 37:11 2889
covers to cover withal, of *p* gold ... Ex 37:16 2889
he made the candlestick of *p* gold ... Ex 37:17 2889
it was one beaten work of *p* gold ... Ex 37:22 2889
and his snuffdishes, of *p* gold ... Ex 37:23 2889
Of a talent of *p* gold made he it, ... Ex 37:24 2889
And he overlaid it with *p* gold ... Ex 37:26 2889
the *p* incense of sweet spices, ... Ex 37:29 2889
ends, of wreathen work of *p* gold ... Ex 39:15 2889
And they made bells of *p* gold ... Ex 39:25 2889
plate of the holy crown of *p* gold ... Ex 39:30 2889
The *p* candlestick, with the lamps ... Ex 39:37 2889
that they bring unto thee *p* oil ... Lev 24:2 2134
the *p* candlestick before the LORD ... Lev 24:4 2888
upon the *p* table before the LORD ... Lev 24:6 2888
thou shalt put *p* frankincense ... Lev 24:7 2134
drink the *p* blood of the grape ... Deut 32:14 2561
With the *p* thou wilt shew thyself ... 2Sa 22:27 2889
thou wilt shew thyself *p* ... 2Sa 22:27 1305
and twenty measures of *p* oil ... 1Kin 5:11 3795
and he overlaid it with *p* gold ... 1Kin 6:20 5462
the house within with *p* gold ... 1Kin 6:21 5462
And the candlesticks of *p* gold ... 1Kin 7:49 5462
spoons, and the censers of *p* gold ... 1Kin 7:50 5462
forest of Lebanon were of *p* gold ... 1Kin 10:21 5462
Also *p* gold for the fleshhooks, ... 1Chr 28:17 2889
he overlaid it within with *p* gold ... 2Chr 3:4 2889
before the oracle, of *p* gold ... 2Chr 4:20 5462
spoons, and the censers, of *p* gold ... 2Chr 4:22 5462
ivory, and overlaid it with *p* gold ... 2Chr 9:17 2889
forest of Lebanon were of *p* gold ... 2Chr 9:20 5462
they in order upon the *p* table ... 2Chr 13:11 2889
together, all of them were *p* ... Ezr 6:20 2889
a man be more *p* than his maker ... Job 4:17 2891
If thou wert *p* and upright ... Job 8:6 2134
thou hast said, My doctrine is *p* ... Job 11:4 2134
also my prayer is *p* ... Job 16:17 2134
the stars are not *p* in his sight ... Job 25:5 2141
shall it be valued with *p* gold ... Job 28:19 2889
The words of the LORD are *p* words ... Ps 12:6 2889
With the *p* thou wilt shew thyself ... Ps 18:26 2889
thou wilt shew thyself *p* ... Ps 18:26 1305
the commandment of the LORD is *p* ... Ps 19:8 1249
a crown of *p* gold on his head ... Ps 21:3 6337
hath clean hands, and a *p* heart ... Ps 24:4 1249
Thy word is very *p* ... Ps 119:140 6884
words of the *p* are pleasant words ... Prov 15:26 2889
heart clean, I am *p* from my sin ... Prov 20:9 2891
his doings, whether his work be *p* ... Prov 20:11 2134
but as for the *p*, his work is ... Prov 21:8 2134
Every word of God is *p* ... Prov 30:5 6884
that are *p* in their own eyes ... Prov 30:12 2889
hair of his head like the *p* wool ... Dan 7:9 5343
Shall I count them *p* with the ... Mic 6:11 2135
I turn to the people a *p* language ... Zeph 3:9 1305
unto my name, and a *p* offering ... Mal 1:11 2889
Blessed are the *p* in heart ... Mt 5:8 *2513*
that I am *p* from the blood of all ... Acts 20:26 *2513*
All things indeed are *p* ... Rom 14:20 *2513*
are just, whatsoever things are *p* ... Phil 4:8 *53*
is charity out of a *p* heart ... 1Ti 1:5 *2513*
of the faith in a *p* conscience ... 1Ti 3:9 *2513*
keep thyself *p* ... 1Ti 5:22 *53*
my forefathers with *p* conscience ... 2Ti 1:3 *2513*
call on the Lord out of a *p* heart ... 2Ti 2:22 *2513*
Unto the *p* all things are *p* ... Titus 1:15 *2513*
and unbelieving is nothing *p* ... Titus 1:15 *2513*
and our bodies washed with *p* water ... Heb 10:22 *2513*
P religion and undefiled before ... Jas 1:27 *2513*
that is from above is first *p* ... Jas 3:17 *53*
another with a *p* heart fervently ... 1Pet 1:22 *2513*
p minds by way of remembrance ... 2Pet 3:1 *1506*
himself, even as he is *p* ... 1Jn 3:3 *53*
the seven plagues, clothed in *p* ... Rev 15:6 *2513*
and the city was *p* gold, like unto ... Rev 21:18 *2513*
the street of the city was *p* gold ... Rev 21:21 *2513*
he shewed me a *p* river of water ... Rev 22:1 *2513*

PURELY {1}
p purge away thy dross, and take ... Is 1:25 1252

PURENESS {3}
delivered by the *p* of thine hands ... Job 22:30 1252
He that loveth *p* of heart ... Prov 22:11 2890
By *p*, by knowledge, by ... 2Cor 6:6 *54*

PURER {2}
Her Nazarites were *p* than snow ... Lam 4:7 2141
Thou art of *p* eyes than to behold ... Hab 1:13 2889

PURGE {15}
twelfth year he began to *p* Judah ... 2Chr 34:3 2891
P me with hyssop, and I shall be ... Ps 51:7 2398
thou shalt *p* them away ... Ps 65:3 3722
p away our sins, for thy name's ... Ps 79:9 3722
purely *p* away thy dross, and take ... Is 1:25 6884
I will *p* out from among you the ... Eze 20:38 1305
thus shalt thou cleanse and *p* it ... Eze 43:20 3722
Seven days shall they *p* the altar ... Eze 43:26 3722
shall fall, to try them, and to *p* ... Dan 11:35 1305
p them as gold and silver, that ... Mal 3:3 2212
and he will throughly *p* his floor ... Mt 3:12 *1245*
and he will throughly *p* his floor ... Lk 3:17 *1245*
P out therefore the old leaven, ... 1Cor 5:7 *1571*
therefore *p* himself from these ... 2Ti 2:21 *1571*
p your conscience from dead works ... Heb 9:14 *2511*

PURGED {14}
of Eli's house shall not be *p* ... 1Sa 3:14 3722
his reign, when he had *p* the land ... 2Chr 34:8 2891
By mercy and truth iniquity is *p* ... Prov 16:6 3722
shall have *p* the blood of ... Is 4:4 1740
is taken away, and thy sin *p* ... Is 6:7 3722
not be *p* from you till ye die ... Is 22:14 3722
shall the iniquity of Jacob be *p* ... Is 27:9 3722
because I have *p* thee ... Eze 24:13 2891
and thou wast not *p* ... Eze 24:13 2891
thou shalt not be *p* from thy ... Eze 24:13 2891
when he had by himself *p* our sins .. Heb 1:3 *4160,2512*
are by the law *p* with blood ... Heb 9:22 *2511*
once *p* should have had no more ... Heb 10:2 *2508*
that he was *p* from his old sins ... 2Pet 1:9 *2512*

PURGETH {1}
that beareth fruit, he *p* it ... Jn 15:2 *2508*

PURGING {1}
out into the draught, *p* all meats ... Mk 7:19 *2511*

PURIFICATION {8}
it is a *p* for sin ... Num 19:9 2403
of the burnt heifer of *p* for sin ... Num 19:17 2403
to the *p* of the sanctuary ... 2Chr 30:19 2893
their God, and the ward of the *p* ... Neh 12:45 2893
their things for *p* be given them ... Est 2:3 8562
gave her her things for *p* ... Est 2:9 8562
when the days of her *p* according ... Lk 2:22 *2512*
accomplishment of the days of *p* ... Acts 21:26 *49*

PURIFICATIONS {1}
the days of their *p* accomplished ... Est 2:12 4795

PURIFIED {12}
p the altar, and poured the blood ... Lev 8:15 2398
And the Levites were *p*, and they ... Num 8:21 2398
nevertheless it shall be *p* with ... Num 31:23 2398
for she was *p* from her ... 2Sa 11:4 6942
and the Levites were *p* together ... Ezr 6:20 2891
and the Levites *p* themselves ... Neh 12:30 2891
p the people, and the gates, and ... Neh 12:30 2891
a furnace of earth, *p* seven times ... Ps 12:6 2212
Many shall be *p*, and made white, ... Dan 12:10 1305
Asia found me *p* in the temple ... Acts 24:18 *48*
heavens should be *p* with these ... Heb 9:23 *2511*
Seeing ye have *p* your souls in ... 1Pet 1:22 *48*

PURIFIER {1}
sit as a refiner and *p* of silver ... Mal 3:3 2891

PURIFIETH {2}
p not himself, defileth the ... Num 19:13 2398
hath this hope in him *p* himself ... 1Jn 3:3 *48*

PURIFY {14}
He shall *p* himself with it on the ... Num 19:12 2398
but if he *p* not himself the third ... Num 19:12 2398
seventh day he shall *p* himself ... Num 19:19 2398
unclean, and shall not *p* himself ... Num 19:20 2398
p both yourselves and your ... Num 31:19 2398
p all your raiment, and all that ... Num 31:20 2398
of breakings they *p* themselves ... Job 41:25 2398
p themselves in the gardens ... Is 66:17 2891
they purge the altar and *p* it ... Eze 43:26 2891
he shall *p* the sons of Levi, and ... Mal 3:3 2891
the passover, to *p* themselves ... Jn 11:55 *48*
p thyself with them, and be at ... Acts 21:24 *48*
p unto himself a peculiar people, ... Titus 2:14 *2511*
p your hearts, ye double minded ... Jas 4:8 *48*

PURIFYING {12}
in the blood of her *p* three ... Lev 12:4 2893
the days of her *p* be fulfilled ... Lev 12:4 2892
in the blood of her *p* threescore ... Lev 12:5 2893
the days of her *p* are fulfilled ... Lev 12:6 2892
Sprinkle water of *p* upon them ... Num 8:7 2403
in the *p* of all holy things, and ... 1Chr 23:28 2893
things for the *p* of the women ... Est 2:12 8562
the manner of the *p* of the Jews ... Jn 2:6 *2512*
disciples and the Jews about *p* ... Jn 3:25 *2512*
and them, *p* their hearts by faith ... Acts 15:9 *2511*
the next day *p* himself with them ... Acts 21:26 *48*
sanctifieth to the *p* of the flesh ... Heb 9:13 *2514*

PURIM *(pu'-rim)* {5} See PUR. *A Jewish festival celebrating the deliverance from Haman.*
days *P* after the name of Pur ... Est 9:26 6332
that these days of *P* should not ... Est 9:28 6332
confirm this second letter of *P* ... Est 9:29 6332
of *P* in their times appointed ... Est 9:31 6332
confirmed these matters of *P* ... Est 9:32 6332

PURITY {2}
in spirit, in faith, in *p* ... 1Ti 4:12 *47*
younger as sisters, with all *p* ... 1Ti 5:2 *47*

PURLOINING {1}
Not *p*, but shewing all good ... Titus 2:10 *3557*

PURPLE {48}
And blue, and *p*, and scarlet, and ... Ex 25:4 713
fine twined linen, and blue, and *p* ... Ex 26:1 713
shalt make a vail of blue, and *p* ... Ex 26:31 713
door of the tent, of blue, and *p* ... Ex 26:36 713
of twenty cubits, of blue, and *p* ... Ex 27:16 713
shall take gold, and blue, and *p* ... Ex 28:5 713
ephod of gold, of blue, and of *p* ... Ex 28:6 713
even of gold, of blue, and *p* ... Ex 28:8 713
of gold, of blue, and of *p* ... Ex 28:15 713
pomegranates of blue, and of *p* ... Ex 28:33 713
And blue, and *p*, and scarlet, and ... Ex 35:6 713
with whom was found blue, and *p* ... Ex 35:23 713
had spun, both of blue, and of *p* ... Ex 35:25 713
the embroiderer, in blue, and in *p* ... Ex 35:35 713
fine twined linen, and blue, and *p* ... Ex 36:8 713
And he made a vail of blue, and *p* ... Ex 36:35 713
the tabernacle door of blue, and *p* ... Ex 36:37 713
was needlework, of blue, and *p* ... Ex 38:18 713
an embroiderer in blue, and in *p* ... Ex 38:23 713
And of the blue, and *p*, and scarlet, ... Ex 39:1 713
the ephod of gold, blue, and *p* ... Ex 39:2 713
work it in the blue, and in the *p* ... Ex 39:3 713
of gold, blue, and *p*, and scarlet, ... Ex 39:5 713
of gold, blue, and *p*, and scarlet, ... Ex 39:8 713
robe pomegranates of blue, and *p* ... Ex 39:24 713
fine twined linen, and blue, and *p* ... Ex 39:29 713
and spread a *p* cloth thereon ... Num 4:13 713
p raiment that was on the kings ... Judg 8:26 713
and in brass, and in iron, and in *p* ... 2Chr 2:7 710
in stone, and in timber, in *p* ... 2Chr 2:14 713
And he made the vail of blue, and *p* ... 2Chr 3:14 713
p to silver rings and pillars of ... Est 1:6 713
with a garment of fine linen and *p* ... Est 8:15 713
her clothing is silk and *p* ... Prov 31:22 713
of gold, the covering of it of *p* ... Song 3:10 713
and the hair of thine head like *p* ... Song 7:5 713
blue and *p* is their clothing ... Jer 10:9 713
p from the isles of Elishah was ... Eze 27:7 713
in thy fairs with emeralds, *p* ... Eze 27:16 713
And they clothed him with *p* ... Mk 15:17 *4209*
him, they took off the *p* from him ... Mk 15:20 *4209*
rich man, which was clothed in *p* ... Lk 16:19 *4209*
head, and they put on him a *p* robe ... Jn 19:2 *4210*
crown of thorns, and the *p* robe ... Jn 19:5 *4210*
woman named Lydia, a seller of *p* ... Acts 16:14 *4211*
And the woman was arrayed in *p* ... Rev 17:4 *4209*
and of pearls, and fine linen, and *p* ... Rev 18:12 *4209*
was clothed in fine linen, and *p* ... Rev 18:16 *4210*

PURPOSE {36}
some of the handfuls of *p* for her ... Ruth 2:16 7997
I *p* to build an house unto the ... 1Kin 5:5 559
now ye *p* to keep under the ... 2Chr 28:10 559
them, to frustrate their *p* ... Ezr 4:5 6098
which they had made for the *p* ... Neh 8:4 1697
he may withdraw man from his *p* ... Job 33:17 4639
Every *p* is established by counsel ... Prov 20:18 4284
a time to every *p* under the ... Eccl 3:1 2656
there is a time there for every *p* ... Eccl 3:17 2656
Because to every *p* there is time ... Eccl 8:6 2656
To what *p* is the multitude of ... Is 1:11
This is the *p* that is purposed ... Is 14:26 6098
shall help in vain, and to no *p* ... Is 30:7 7385
To what *p* cometh there to me ... Jer 6:20
which I *p* to do unto them because ... Jer 26:3 2803
evil which I *p* to do unto them ... Jer 36:3 2803
and hath conceived a *p* against you ... Jer 49:30 4284
for every *p* of the LORD shall be ... Jer 51:29 4284
that the *p* might not be changed ... Dan 6:17 6640
saying, To what *p* is this waste ... Mt 26:8
that with *p* of heart they would ... Acts 11:23 *4286*
appeared unto thee for this *p* ... Acts 26:16
that they had obtained their *p* ... Acts 27:13 *4286*
save Paul, kept them from their *p* ... Acts 27:43 *1013*
are the called according to his *p* ... Rom 8:28 *4286*
that the *p* of God according to ... Rom 9:11 *4286*
Even for this same *p* have I ... Rom 9:17
or the things that I *p* ... 2Cor 1:17 *1011*
do I *p* according to the flesh, ... 2Cor 1:17 *1011*
p of him who worketh all things ... Eph 1:11 *4286*
According to the eternal *p* which ... Eph 3:11 *4286*
have sent unto you for the same *p* ... Eph 6:22
have sent unto you for the same *p* ... Col 4:8
works, but according to his own *p* ... 2Ti 1:9 *4286*
my doctrine, manner of life, *p* ... 2Ti 3:10 *4286*
For this *p* the Son of God was ... 1Jn 3:8

PURPOSED {19}
that he was *p* to fight against ... 2Chr 32:2 6440
I am *p* that my mouth shall not ... Ps 17:3 2161
who have *p* to overthrow my goings ... Ps 140:4 2803
and as I have *p*, so shall it stand ... Is 14:24 3289
that is *p* upon the whole earth ... Is 14:26 3289
For the LORD of hosts hath *p* ... Is 14:27 3289
LORD of hosts hath *p* upon Egypt ... Is 19:12 3289
The LORD of hosts hath *p* it ... Is 23:9 3289
I have *p* it, I will also do it ... Is 46:11 3335
I have spoken it, I have *p* it ... Jer 4:28 2161
that he hath *p* against the ... Jer 49:20 2803
that he hath *p* against the land ... Jer 50:45 2803
The LORD hath *p* to destroy the ... Lam 2:8 2803
But Daniel *p* in his heart that he ... Dan 1:8 7760
Paul *p* in the spirit, when he had ... Acts 19:21 *5087*
he *p* to return through Macedonia .. Acts 20:3 *1096,1106*
oftentimes I *p* to come unto you ... Rom 1:13 *4388*
which he hath *p* in himself ... Eph 1:9 *4388*
he *p* in Christ Jesus our Lord ... Eph 3:11 *4160*

PURPOSES {5}
my *p* are broken off, even the ... Job 17:11 2154
Without counsel *p* are ... Prov 15:22 4284
shall be broken in the *p* thereof ... Is 19:10 8356
and his *p*, that he hath purposed ... Jer 49:20 4284
and his *p*, that he hath purposed ... Jer 50:45 4284

PURPOSETH {1}
according as he *p* in his heart ... 2Cor 9:7 *4255*

PURPOSING {1}
comfort himself, *p* to kill thee ... Gen 27:42

PURSE {5}
let us all have one *p* ... Prov 1:14 3599
no bread, no money in their *p* ... Mk 6:8 *2223*
Carry neither *p*, nor scrip, nor ... Lk 10:4 *905*
them, When I sent you without *p* ... Lk 22:35 *905*
them, But now, he that hath a *p* ... Lk 22:36 *905*

PURSES {1}
nor silver, nor brass in your *p* ... Mt 10:9 *2223*

PURSUE {29}
they did not *p* after the sons of ... Gen 35:5 7291
The enemy said, I will *p*, I will ... Ex 15:9 7291
avenger of the blood *p* the slayer ... Deut 19:6 7291
they shall *p* thee until thou ... Deut 28:22 7291
come upon thee, and shall *p* thee ... Deut 28:45 7291
p after them quickly ... Josh 2:5 7291
called together to *p* after them ... Josh 8:16 7291
but *p* after your enemies, and ... Josh 10:19 7291
the avenger of blood *p* after him ... Josh 20:5 7291
after whom dost thou *p* ... 1Sa 24:14 7291
Yet a man is risen to *p* thee ... 1Sa 25:29 7291
my lord thus *p* after his servant ... 1Sa 26:18 7291
Shall I *p* after this troop ... 1Sa 30:8 7291
And he answered him, *P* ... 1Sa 30:8 7291
arise and *p* after David this night ... 2Sa 17:1 7291
p after him, lest he get him ... 2Sa 20:6 7291
to *p* after Sheba the son of ... 2Sa 20:7 7291
to *p* after Sheba the son of ... 2Sa 20:13 7291
thine enemies, while they *p* thee ... 2Sa 24:13 7291
wilt thou *p* the dry stubble ... Job 13:25 7291
they *p* my soul as the wind ... Job 30:15 7291
seek peace, and *p* it ... Ps 34:14 7291
shall they that *p* you be swift ... Is 30:16 7291
the sword shall *p* thee ... Jer 48:2 3212
unto blood, and blood shall *p* thee ... Eze 35:6 7291
blood, even blood shall *p* thee ... Eze 35:6 7291
the enemy shall *p* him ... Hos 8:3 7291
because he did *p* his brother with ... Amos 1:11 7291
and darkness shall *p* his enemies ... Nah 1:8 7291

PURSUED {38}
and eighteen, and *p* them unto Dan ... Gen 14:14 7291
p them unto Hobah, which is on ... Gen 14:15 7291
p after him seven days' journey ... Gen 31:23 7291
thou hast so hotly *p* after me ... Gen 31:36 1814
he *p* after the children of Israel ... Ex 14:8 7291
But the Egyptians *p* after them ... Ex 14:9 7291
And the Egyptians *p*, and went in ... Ex 14:23 7291
overflow them as they *p* after you ... Deut 11:4 7291
the men *p* after them the way to ... Josh 2:7 7291
as soon as they which *p* after ... Josh 2:7 7291
they *p* after Joshua, and were ... Josh 8:16 7291
the city open, and *p* after Israel ... Josh 8:17 7291
the Egyptians *p* after your ... Josh 24:6 7291
they *p* after him, and caught him, ... Judg 1:6 7291
But Barak *p* after the chariots, ... Judg 4:16 7291
And, behold, as Barak *p* Sisera ... Judg 4:22 7291
and *p* after the Midianites ... Judg 7:23 7291
p Midian, and brought the heads of ... Judg 7:25 7291
he *p* after them, and took the two ... Judg 8:12 7291
p hard after them unto Gidom, and ... Judg 20:45 1692
p the Philistines, and smote them, ... 1Sa 7:11 7291
p the Philistines, until thou ... 1Sa 17:52 7291
that, he *p* after David in the ... 1Sa 23:25 7291
But David *p*, he and four hundred ... 1Sa 30:10 7291
And Asahel *p* after Abner ... 2Sa 2:19 7291
also and Abishai *p* after Abner ... 2Sa 2:24 7291
p after Israel no more, neither ... 2Sa 2:28 7291
Abishai his brother *p* after Sheba ... 2Sa 20:10 7291
I have *p* mine enemies, and ... 2Sa 22:38 7291
and Israel *p* them ... 1Kin 20:20 7291
of the Chaldees *p* after the king ... 2Kin 25:5 7291
Abijah *p* after Jeroboam, and took ... 2Chr 13:19 7291
were with him *p* them unto Gerar ... 2Chr 14:13 7291
I have *p* mine enemies, and ... Ps 18:37 7291
He *p* them, and passed safely ... Is 41:3 7291
the Chaldeans' army *p* after them ... Jer 39:5 7291
of the Chaldeans *p* after the king ... Jer 52:8 7291
they *p* us upon the mountains, ... Lam 4:19 1814

PURSUER {1}
without strength before the *p* ... Lam 1:6 7291

PURSUERS {5}
the mountain, lest the *p* meet you ... Josh 2:16 7291
days, until the *p* be returned ... Josh 2:16 7291
until the *p* were returned ... Josh 2:22 7291
the *p* sought them throughout all ... Josh 2:22 7291
wilderness turned back upon the *p* ... Josh 8:20 7291

PURSUETH {9}
and ye shall flee when none *p* you ... Lev 26:17 7291
and they shall fall when none *p* ... Lev 26:36 7291
were before a sword, when none *p* ... Lev 26:37 7291
so he that *p* evil *p* it to ... Prov 11:19 7291
evil *p* it to his own death ... Prov 11:19
Evil *p* sinners ... Prov 13:21 7291
he *p* them with words, yet they ... Prov 19:7 7291
The wicked flee when no man *p* ... Prov 28:1 7291

PURSUING {8}
were with him, faint, yet *p* them ... Judg 8:4 7291
I am *p* after Zebah and Zalmunna, ... Judg 8:5 7291
Saul returned from *p* after David ... 1Sa 23:28 7291
David and Joab came from *p* a troop ... 2Sa 3:22
returned from *p* after Israel ... 2Sa 18:16 7291
either he is talking, or he is *p* ... 1Kin 18:27 7873
that they turned back from *p* him ... 1Kin 22:33 310
they turned back again from *p* him ... 2Chr 18:32 310

PURTENANCE {1}
his legs, and with the *p* thereof ... Ex 12:9 7130

PUSH {9}
to *p* with his horn in time past ... Ex 21:29 5056
If the ox shall *p* a manservant or ... Ex 21:32 5055
ox hath used to *p* in time past ... Ex 21:36 5056
with them he shall *p* the people ... Deut 33:17 5055
these shalt thou *p* the Syrians ... 1Kin 22:11 5055
With these thou shalt *p* Syria ... 2Chr 18:10 5055
they *p* away my feet, and they ... Job 30:12 7971
thee will we *p* down our enemies ... Ps 44:5 5055
the king of the south *p* at him ... Dan 11:40 5055

PUSHED {1}
p all the diseased with your ... Eze 34:21 5055

PUSHING {1}
I saw the ram *p* westward, and ... Dan 8:4 5055

PUT *(put)* {916} See PHUT.
1. A verb.
there he *p* the man whom he had ... Gen 2:8 7760
p him into the garden of Eden to ... Gen 2:15 3240
I will *p* enmity between thee and ... Gen 3:15 7896
lest he *p* forth his hand, and take ... Gen 3:22 7971
then he *p* forth his hand, and took ... Gen 8:9 7971
But the men *p* forth their hand, ... Gen 19:10 7971
ruled over all that he had, *P* ... Gen 24:2 7760
the servant *p* his hand under the ... Gen 24:9 7760
I *p* the earring upon her face, and ... Gen 24:47 7760
wife shall surely be *p* to death ... Gen 26:11
p them upon Jacob her younger son ... Gen 27:15 3847
she *p* the skins of the kids of ... Gen 27:16 3847
p them for his pillows, and lay ... Gen 28:11 7760
that he had *p* for his pillows ... Gen 28:18 7760
bread to eat, and raiment to *p* on ... Gen 28:20 3847
p the stone again upon the well's ... Gen 29:3 7725
he *p* his own flocks by themselves ... Gen 30:40 7896
p them not unto Laban's cattle ... Gen 30:40 7896
were feeble, he *p* them not in ... Gen 30:42 7760
p them in the camel's furniture, ... Gen 31:34 7760
p a space betwixt drove and drove ... Gen 32:16 7760
he *p* the handmaids and their ... Gen 33:2 7760
P away the strange gods that are ... Gen 35:2 5493
p sackcloth upon his loins, and ... Gen 37:34 7760
she *p* her widow's garments off ... Gen 38:14 5493
her, and *p* on the garments of her ... Gen 38:19 3847
that the one *p* out his hand ... Gen 38:28 5414
that he had he *p* into his hand ... Gen 39:4 5414
p him into the prison, a place ... Gen 39:20 5414
he *p* them in ward in the house of ... Gen 40:3 5414
they should *p* me into the dungeon ... Gen 40:15 7760
p me in ward in the captain of ... Gen 41:10 5414
p it upon Joseph's hand, and ... Gen 41:42 5414
p a gold chain about his neck ... Gen 41:42 7760
he *p* them all together into ward ... Gen 42:17 622
we cannot tell who *p* our money in ... Gen 43:22 7760
p every man's money in his sack's ... Gen 44:1 7760
p my cup, the silver cup, in the ... Gen 44:2 7760
Joseph shall *p* his hand upon ... Gen 46:4 7896
have found grace in thy sight, *p* ... Gen 47:29 7760
p thy right hand upon his head ... Gen 48:18 7760
he was *p* in a coffin in Egypt ... Gen 50:26 3455
pitch, and *p* the child therein ... Ex 2:3 7760
p off thy shoes from off thy feet ... Ex 3:5 5394
ye shall *p* them upon your sons, ... Ex 3:22 7760
P forth thine hand, and take it by ... Ex 4:4 7971
he *p* forth his hand, and caught it ... Ex 4:4 7971
P now thine hand into thy bosom ... Ex 4:6 935
he *p* his hand into his bosom ... Ex 4:6 935
P thine hand into thy bosom again ... Ex 4:7 7725
he *p* his hand into his bosom ... Ex 4:7 7725
unto him, and *p* words in his mouth ... Ex 4:15 7760
which I have *p* in thine hand ... Ex 4:21 7760
to *p* a sword in their hand to ... Ex 5:21 5414
I will *p* a division between my ... Ex 8:23 7760
doth *p* a difference between the ... Ex 11:7
even the first day ye shall *p* ... Ex 12:15 7673
I will *p* none of these diseases ... Ex 15:26 7760
p an omer full of manna therein, ... Ex 16:33 5414
p it under him, and he sat thereon ... Ex 17:12 7760
for I will utterly *p* out the ... Ex 17:14 4229
mount shall be surely *p* to death ... Ex 19:12
die, shall be surely *p* to death ... Ex 21:12
shall be surely *p* to death ... Ex 21:15
he shall surely be *p* to death ... Ex 21:16
shall surely be *p* to death ... Ex 21:17
owner also shall be *p* to death ... Ex 21:29
shall *p* in his beast, and shall ... Ex 22:5 7971
to see whether he have *p* his hand ... Ex 22:8 7971
that he hath not *p* his hand unto ... Ex 22:11 7971
beast shall surely be *p* to death ... Ex 22:19
p not thine hand with the wicked ... Ex 23:1 7896
of the blood, and *p* it in basons ... Ex 24:6 7760
p them in the four corners ... Ex 25:12 5414
thou shalt *p* the staves into the ... Ex 25:14 935
thou shalt *p* into the ark the ... Ex 25:16 5414
thou shalt *p* the mercy seat above ... Ex 25:21 5414
in the ark thou shalt *p* the ... Ex 25:21 5414
p the rings in the four corners ... Ex 25:26 5414
p the taches into the loops, and ... Ex 26:11 935
thou shalt *p* the mercy seat upon ... Ex 26:34 5414
thou shalt *p* the table on the ... Ex 26:35 5414
thou shalt *p* it under the compass ... Ex 27:5 5414
staves shall be *p* into the rings ... Ex 27:7 935
thou shalt *p* the two stones upon ... Ex 28:12 7760
shalt *p* the two rings on the two ... Ex 28:23 5414
thou shalt *p* the two wreathen ... Ex 28:24 5414
p them on the shoulderpieces of ... Ex 28:25 5414
thou shalt *p* them upon the two ... Ex 28:26 7760
shalt *p* them on the two sides of ... Ex 28:27 5414
thou shalt *p* in the breastplate ... Ex 28:30 5414
thou shalt *p* it on a blue lace, ... Ex 28:37 7760
thou shalt *p* them upon Aaron thy ... Ex 28:41 3847
thou shalt *p* them into one basket ... Ex 29:3 5414
p upon Aaron the coat, and the ... Ex 29:5 3847
thou shalt *p* the mitre upon his ... Ex 29:6 7760
p the holy crown upon the mitre ... Ex 29:6 5414
his sons, and *p* coats upon them ... Ex 29:8 3847
sons, and *p* the bonnets on them ... Ex 29:9 2280
his sons shall *p* their hands upon ... Ex 29:10 5564
p it upon the horns of the altar ... Ex 29:12 5414
his sons shall *p* their hands upon ... Ex 29:15 5564
p them unto his pieces, and unto ... Ex 29:17 5414
his sons shall *p* their hands upon ... Ex 29:19 5564
p it upon the tip of the right ... Ex 29:20 5414
thou shalt *p* all in the hands of ... Ex 29:24 7760
stead shall *p* them on seven days ... Ex 29:30 3847
thou shalt *p* it before the vail ... Ex 30:6 5414
thou shalt *p* it between the ... Ex 30:18 5414
thou shalt *p* water therein ... Ex 30:18 5414
p of it before the testimony in ... Ex 30:36 5414
are wise hearted I have *p* wisdom ... Ex 31:6 5414
it shall surely be *p* to death ... Ex 31:14
he shall surely be *p* to death ... Ex 31:15
P every man his sword by his side ... Ex 32:27 7760
no man did *p* on him his ornaments ... Ex 33:4 7896
therefore now *p* off thy ornaments ... Ex 33:5 3381
that I will *p* thee in a clift of ... Ex 33:22 7760
them, he *p* a vail on his face ... Ex 34:33 5414
Moses *p* the vail upon his face ... Ex 34:35 7725
work therein shall be *p* to death ... Ex 35:2
he hath *p* in his heart that he ... Ex 35:34 5414
man, in whom the LORD *p* wisdom ... Ex 36:1 5414
whose heart the LORD had *p* wisdom ... Ex 36:2 5414
he *p* the staves into the rings by ... Ex 37:5 935
p the rings upon the four corners ... Ex 37:13 5414
he *p* the staves into the rings on ... Ex 38:7 935
he *p* them on the shoulders of the ... Ex 39:7 7760
p the two rings in the two ends ... Ex 39:16 5414
they *p* the two wreathen chains of ... Ex 39:17 5414
p them on the shoulderpieces of ... Ex 39:18 5414
p them on the two ends of the ... Ex 39:19 7760
p them on the two sides of the ... Ex 39:20 5414
gold, and *p* the bells between the ... Ex 39:25 5414
thou shalt *p* therein the ark of ... Ex 40:3 7760
p the hanging of the door to the ... Ex 40:5 7760
altar, and shalt *p* water therein ... Ex 40:7 5414
thou shalt *p* upon Aaron the holy ... Ex 40:13 3847
p in the bars thereof, and reared ... Ex 40:18 5414
p the covering of the tent above ... Ex 40:19 7760
p the testimony into the ark, and ... Ex 40:20 5114
p the mercy seat above upon the ... Ex 40:20 5114
he *p* the table in the tent of the ... Ex 40:22 5114
he *p* the candlestick in the tent ... Ex 40:24 7760
he *p* the golden altar in the tent ... Ex 40:26 7760
he *p* the altar of burnt offering ... Ex 40:29 7760
p water there, to wash withal ... Ex 40:30 5414
he shall *p* his hand upon the head ... Lev 1:4 5564
shall *p* fire upon the altar ... Lev 1:7 5414
it, and *p* frankincense thereon ... Lev 2:1 5414
thou shalt *p* oil upon it, and lay ... Lev 2:15 5414
the priest shall *p* some of the ... Lev 4:7 5414
he shall *p* some of the blood upon ... Lev 4:18 5414
p it upon the horns of the altar ... Lev 4:25 5414
p it upon the horns of the altar ... Lev 4:30 5414
p it upon the horns of the altar ... Lev 4:34 5414
he shall *p* no oil upon it, ... Lev 5:11 7760
upon it, neither shall he *p* any ... Lev 5:11 5414
the priest shall *p* on his linen ... Lev 6:10 3847
shall he *p* upon his flesh ... Lev 6:10 3847
he shall *p* them beside the altar ... Lev 6:10 7760
he shall *p* off his garments, and ... Lev 6:11 6584
p on other garments, and carry ... Lev 6:11 3847
it shall not be *p* out ... Lev 6:12 3518
he *p* upon him the coat, and girded ... Lev 8:7 5414
p the ephod upon him, and he ... Lev 8:7 5414
he *p* the breastplate upon him ... Lev 8:8 7760
also he *p* in the breastplate the ... Lev 8:8 5414
he *p* the mitre upon his head ... Lev 8:9 7760
did he *p* the golden plate, the ... Lev 8:9 7760
p coats upon them, and girded them ... Lev 8:13 3847
girdles, and *p* bonnets upon them ... Lev 8:13 2280
p it upon the horns of the altar ... Lev 8:15 5414
p it upon the tip of Aaron's ... Lev 8:23 5414
Moses *p* of the blood upon the tip ... Lev 8:24 5414
p them on the fat, and upon the ... Lev 8:26 7760
he *p* all upon Aaron's hands, and ... Lev 8:27 5414
p it upon the horns of the altar, ... Lev 9:9 5414
they *p* the fat upon the breasts, ... Lev 9:20 7760
p fire therein, and *p* incense ... Lev 10:1 5414
p incense thereon, and offered ... Lev 10:1 7760
that ye may *p* difference between ... Lev 10:10
is done, it must be *p* into water ... Lev 11:32 935
if any water be *p* upon the seed ... Lev 11:38 5414
he shall *p* a covering upon his ... Lev 13:45
the priest shall *p* it upon the ... Lev 14:14 5414
p upon the tip of the right ear ... Lev 14:17 5414

p it upon the tip of the right ... Lev 14:25 5414
the priest shall *p* of the oil ... Lev 14:28 5414
in the priest's hand he shall *p* ... Lev 14:29 5414
I *p* the plague of leprosy in a ... Lev 14:34 5414
p them in the place of those ... Lev 14:42 935
she shall be *p* apart seven days ... Lev 15:19 5079
He shall *p* on the holy linen coat ... Lev 16:4 3847
flesh in water, and so *p* them on ... Lev 16:4 3847
he shall *p* the incense upon the ... Lev 16:13 5414
p it upon the horns of the altar ... Lev 16:18 5414
shall *p* off the linen garments, ... Lev 16:23 6584
which he *p* on when he went into ... Lev 16:23 3847
p on his garments, and come forth, ... Lev 16:24 3847
shall *p* on the linen clothes, ... Lev 16:32 3847
as long as she is *p* apart for her ... Lev 18:19 5079
nor *p* a stumblingblock before the ... Lev 19:14 5414
they shall not be *p* to death ... Lev 19:20
he shall surely be *p* to death ... Lev 20:2
mother shall be surely *p* to death ... Lev 20:9
shall surely be *p* to death ... Lev 20:10
them shall surely be *p* to death ... Lev 20:11
them shall surely be *p* to death ... Lev 20:12
they shall surely be *p* to death ... Lev 20:13
he shall surely be *p* to death ... Lev 20:15
they shall surely be *p* to death ... Lev 20:16
Ye shall therefore *p* difference ... Lev 20:25
shall surely be *p* to death ... Lev 20:27
a woman *p* away from her husband ... Lev 21:7 1644
consecrated to *p* on the garments ... Lev 21:10 3847
then he shall *p* the fifth part ... Lev 22:14 3254
thou shalt *p* pure frankincense ... Lev 24:7 5414
they *p* him in ward, that the mind ... Lev 24:12 3240
he shall surely be *p* to death ... Lev 24:16
of the LORD, shall be *p* to death ... Lev 24:16
man shall surely be *p* to death ... Lev 24:17
a man, he shall be *p* to death ... Lev 24:21
shall *p* ten thousand to flight ... Lev 26:8
but shall surely be *p* to death ... Lev 27:29
cometh nigh shall be *p* to death ... Num 1:51
cometh nigh shall be *p* to death ... Num 3:10
cometh nigh shall be *p* to death ... Num 3:38
shall *p* thereon the covering of ... Num 4:6 5414
shall *p* in the staves thereof ... Num 4:6 7760
p thereon the dishes, and the ... Num 4:7 5414
shall *p* in the staves thereof ... Num 4:8 7760
And they shall *p* it and all the ... Num 4:10 5414
skins, and shall *p* it upon a bar ... Num 4:10 5414
shall *p* to the staves thereof ... Num 4:11 7725
p them in a cloth of blue, and ... Num 4:12 5414
skins, and shall *p* them on a bar ... Num 4:12 5414
they shall *p* upon it all the ... Num 4:14 5414
skins, and *p* to the staves of it ... Num 4:14 7760
that they *p* out of the camp every ... Num 5:2 7971
male and female shall ye *p* out ... Num 5:3 7971
without the camp shall ye *p* them ... Num 5:3 7971
p them out without the camp ... Num 5:4 7971
nor *p* frankincense thereon ... Num 5:15 5414
take, and *p* it into the water ... Num 5:17 5414
p the offering of memorial in her ... Num 5:18 5414
p it in the fire which is under ... Num 6:18 5414
shall *p* them upon the hands of ... Num 6:19 5414
they shall *p* my name upon the ... Num 6:27 7760
p their hands upon the Levites ... Num 8:10 5564
upon thee, and will *p* it upon them ... Num 11:17 7760
that the LORD would *p* his spirit ... Num 11:29 5414
they *p* him in ward, because it ... Num 15:34 3240
man shall be surely *p* to death ... Num 15:35
that they *p* upon the fringe of ... Num 15:38 5414
p fire therein, and *p* incense in ... Num 16:7 5414
p incense in them before the LORD ... Num 16:7 7760
wilt thou *p* out the eyes of these ... Num 16:14 5365
p incense in them, and bring ye ... Num 16:17 5414
p fire in them, and laid incense ... Num 16:18 5414
p fire therein from off the altar ... Num 16:46 5414
p on incense, and go quickly unto ... Num 16:46 7760
he *p* on incense, and made an ... Num 16:47 5414
cometh nigh shall be *p* to death ... Num 18:7
shall be *p* thereto in a vessel ... Num 19:17 5414
p them upon Eleazar his son ... Num 20:26 3847
p them upon Eleazar his son ... Num 20:28 3847
p it upon a pole, and it came to ... Num 21:9 7760
the LORD *p* a word in Balaam's ... Num 23:5 7760
which the LORD hath *p* in my mouth ... Num 23:12 7760
p a word in his mouth, and said, ... Num 23:16 7760
thou shalt *p* some of thine honour ... Num 27:20 5414
shall surely be *p* to death ... Num 35:16
shall surely be *p* to death ... Num 35:17
shall surely be *p* to death ... Num 35:18
him shall surely be *p* to death ... Num 35:21
the murderer shall be *p* to death ... Num 35:30
but he shall be surely *p* to death ... Num 35:31
shall be *p* to the inheritance of ... Num 36:3 3254
be *p* unto the inheritance of the ... Num 36:4 3254
I begin to *p* the dread of thee ... Deut 2:25 5414
will *p* none of the evil diseases ... Deut 7:15 7760
the LORD thy God will *p* out those ... Deut 7:22 5394
thou shalt *p* them in the ark ... Deut 10:2 7760
p the tables in the ark which I ... Deut 10:5 7760
that thou shalt *p* the blessing ... Deut 11:29 5414
your tribes to *p* his name there ... Deut 12:5 7760
in all that ye *p* your hand unto ... Deut 12:7 4916
p his name there be too far from ... Deut 12:21 7760
of dreams, shall be *p* to death ... Deut 13:5
So shalt thou *p* the evil away ... Deut 13:5 1197
first upon him to *p* him to death ... Deut 13:9
to *p* the sickle to the corn ... Deut 16:9
is worthy of death be *p* to death ... Deut 17:6
he shall not be *p* to death ... Deut 17:6
first upon him to *p* him to death ... Deut 17:7
So thou shalt *p* the evil away ... Deut 17:7 1197
thou shalt *p* away the evil from ... Deut 17:12 1197
will *p* my words in his mouth ... Deut 18:18 5414
but thou shalt *p* away the guilt ... Deut 19:13 1197
so shalt thou *p* the evil away ... Deut 19:19 1197
So shalt thou *p* away the guilt of ... Deut 21:9 1197
she shall *p* the raiment of her ... Deut 21:13 5493
so shalt thou *p* evil away from ... Deut 21:21 1197
death, and he be to be *p* to death ... Deut 21:22
neither shall a man *p* on a ... Deut 22:5 3847
he may not *p* her away all his ... Deut 22:19 7971
so shalt thou *p* evil away from ... Deut 22:21 1197
so shalt thou *p* away evil from ... Deut 22:22 1197
so thou shalt *p* away evil from ... Deut 22:24 1197
he may not *p* her away all his ... Deut 22:29 7971
shalt not *p* any in thy vessel ... Deut 23:24 5414
thou shalt *p* evil away from among ... Deut 24:7 1197
The fathers shall not be *p* to ... Deut 24:16
be *p* to death for the fathers ... Deut 24:16
every man shall be *p* to death for ... Deut 24:16
his name be not *p* out of Israel ... Deut 25:6 4229
shalt *p* it in a basket, and shalt ... Deut 26:2 7760
he shall *p* a yoke of iron upon ... Deut 28:48 5414
the LORD thy God will *p* all these ... Deut 30:7 5414
p it in their mouths, that this ... Deut 31:19 7760
p it in the side of the ark of ... Deut 31:26 7760
two *p* ten thousand to flight, ... Deut 32:30
they shall *p* incense before thee, ... Deut 33:10 7760
things *p* forth by the moon ... Deut 33:14 1645
him, he shall be *p* to death ... Josh 1:18
they *p* into the treasury of the ... Josh 6:24 5414
and *p* dust upon their heads ... Josh 7:6 5927
they have *p* it even among their ... Josh 7:11 7760
p your feet upon the necks of ... Josh 10:24 7760
p their feet upon the necks of ... Josh 10:24 7760
that they *p* the Canaanites to ... Josh 17:13 5414
he *p* darkness between you and the ... Josh 24:7 7760
p away the gods which your ... Josh 24:14 5493
Now therefore *p* away, said he, ... Josh 24:23 5493
that they *p* the Canaanites to ... Judg 1:28 7760
Ehud *p* forth his left hand, and ... Judg 3:21 7971
She *p* her hand to the nail, and ... Judg 5:26 7971
the flesh he *p* in a basket ... Judg 6:19 7760
he *p* the broth in a pot, and ... Judg 6:19 7760
Then the angel of the LORD *p* ... Judg 6:21 7971
let him be *p* to death whilst it ... Judg 6:31
I will *p* a fleece of wool in the ... Judg 6:37 3322
he *p* a trumpet in every man's ... Judg 7:16 5414
p it in his city, even in Ophrah ... Judg 8:27 3322
p your trust in my shadow ... Judg 9:15
the men of Shechem *p* their ... Judg 9:26
p them to the hold, and set the ... Judg 9:49 7760
they *p* away the strange gods from ... Judg 10:16 5493
I *p* my life in my hands, and ... Judg 12:3 7760
I will now *p* forth a riddle unto ... Judg 14:12 2330
P forth thy riddle, that we may ... Judg 14:13 2330
thou hast *p* forth a riddle unto ... Judg 14:16 2330
p a firebrand in the midst ... Judg 15:4 7760
p forth his hand, and took it, and ... Judg 15:15 7971
p them upon his shoulders, and ... Judg 16:3 7760
p out his eyes, and brought him ... Judg 16:21 5365
that might *p* them to shame in any ... Judg 18:7 3637
p the little ones and the cattle ... Judg 18:21 7760
that we may *p* them to death, and ... Judg 20:13
death, and *p* away evil from Israel ... Judg 20:13 1197
the men of Israel *p* themselves in ... Judg 20:20
p themselves in array the first ... Judg 20:22
p themselves in array against ... Judg 20:30
and *p* themselves in array at ... Judg 20:33
He shall surely be *p* to death ... Judg 21:5
p thy raiment upon thee, and get ... Ruth 3:3 7760
p away thy wine from thee ... 1Sa 1:14 5493
P me, I pray thee, into one of ... 1Sa 2:36 5596
the Philistines *p* themselves in ... 1Sa 4:2
p the jewels of gold, which ye ... 1Sa 6:8 7760
p them on the great stone ... 1Sa 6:15 7760
then *p* away the strange gods and ... 1Sa 7:3 5493
of Israel did *p* away Baalim ... 1Sa 7:4 5493
your asses, and *p* them to his work ... 1Sa 8:16 6213
that Saul *p* the people in three ... 1Sa 11:11 7760
that we may *p* them to death ... 1Sa 11:12
not a man be *p* to death this day ... 1Sa 11:13
but no man *p* his hand to his ... 1Sa 14:26 5381
wherefore he *p* forth the end of ... 1Sa 14:27 7971
and *p* his hand to his mouth ... 1Sa 14:27 7725
had *p* the battle in array ... 1Sa 17:21
he *p* an helmet of brass upon his ... 1Sa 17:38 5414
And David *p* them off him ... 1Sa 17:39 5493
p them in a shepherd's bag which ... 1Sa 17:40 7760
David *p* his hand in his bag, and ... 1Sa 17:49 7971
but he *p* his armour in his tent ... 1Sa 17:54 7760
For he did *p* his life in his hand ... 1Sa 19:5 7760
p a pillow of goats' hair for his ... 1Sa 19:13 7760
to *p* hot bread in the day when it ... 1Sa 21:6 7760
p forth their hand to fall upon ... 1Sa 22:17 7971
I will not *p* forth mine hand ... 1Sa 24:10 7971
Saul had *p* away those that had ... 1Sa 28:3 5493
p on other raiment, and he went, ... 1Sa 28:8 3847
I have *p* my life in my hand, and ... 1Sa 28:21 7760
they *p* his armour in the house of ... 1Sa 31:10 7760
who *p* on ornaments of gold upon ... 2Sa 1:24 5927
nor thy feet *p* into fetters ... 2Sa 3:34 5056
Uzzah *p* forth his hand to the ark ... 2Sa 6:6 7971
whom I *p* away before thee ... 2Sa 7:15 5493
lines measured he to *p* to death ... 2Sa 8:2
Then David *p* garrisons in Syria ... 2Sa 8:6 7760
And he *p* garrisons in Edom ... 2Sa 8:14 7760
all Edom *p* he garrisons, and all ... 2Sa 8:14 7760
p the battle in array at the ... 2Sa 10:8
p them in array against the ... 2Sa 10:9
that he might *p* them in array ... 2Sa 10:10
The LORD also hath *p* away thy sin ... 2Sa 12:13 5674
p them under saws, and under ... 2Sa 12:31 7760
P now this woman out from me, and ... 2Sa 13:17 7971
Tamar *p* ashes on her head, and ... 2Sa 13:19 3947
p on now mourning apparel, and ... 2Sa 14:2 3847
So Joab *p* the words in her mouth ... 2Sa 14:3 7760
he *p* all these words in the mouth ... 2Sa 14:19 7760
he *p* forth his hand, and took him, ... 2Sa 15:5 7971
p his household in order, and ... 2Sa 17:23
yet would I not *p* forth mine hand ... 2Sa 18:12 7971
not Shimei be *p* to death for this ... 2Sa 19:21
shall there any man be *p* to death ... 2Sa 19:22
p them in ward, and fed them, but ... 2Sa 20:3 5414
he had *p* on was girded unto him ... 2Sa 20:8 5414
were *p* to death in the days of ... 2Sa 21:9
p the blood of war upon his ... 1Kin 2:5 5414
I will not *p* thee to death with ... 1Kin 2:8
shall be *p* to death this day ... 1Kin 2:24
not at this time *p* thee to death ... 1Kin 2:26
the king *p* Benaiah the son of ... 1Kin 2:35 5414
king *p* in the room of Abiathar ... 1Kin 2:35 5414
until the LORD *p* them under the ... 1Kin 5:3 5414
he *p* five bases on the right side ... 1Kin 7:39 5414
did he *p* among the treasures of ... 1Kin 7:51 5414
which Moses *p* there at Horeb, ... 1Kin 8:9 3240
to *p* my name there for ever ... 1Kin 9:3 7760
the king *p* them in the house of ... 1Kin 10:17 5414
which God had *p* in his heart ... 1Kin 10:24 5414
have chosen me to *p* my name there ... 1Kin 11:36 7760
his heavy yoke which he *p* upon us ... 1Kin 12:4 5414
thy father did *p* upon us lighter ... 1Kin 12:9 5414
Beth-el, and the other *p* he in Dan ... 1Kin 12:29 5414
that he *p* forth his hand from the ... 1Kin 13:4 7971
which he *p* forth against him, ... 1Kin 13:4 7971
of Israel, to *p* his name there ... 1Kin 14:21 7760
it on wood, and *p* no fire under ... 1Kin 18:23 7760
it on wood, and *p* no fire under ... 1Kin 18:23 7760
of your gods, but *p* no fire under ... 1Kin 18:25 7760
he *p* the wood in order, and cut ... 1Kin 18:33 6186
p his face between his knees, ... 1Kin 18:42 7760
they shall *p* it in their hand, and ... 1Kin 20:6 7760
p captains in their rooms ... 1Kin 20:24 7760
p sackcloth on our loins, and ... 1Kin 20:31 7760
p ropes on their heads, and came ... 1Kin 20:32
p sackcloth upon his flesh, and ... 1Kin 21:27 7760
having *p* on their robes, in a ... 1Kin 22:10 3847
the LORD hath *p* a lying spirit in ... 1Kin 22:23 5414
P this fellow in the prison, and ... 1Kin 22:27 7760
but *p* thou on thy robes ... 1Kin 22:30 3847
me a new cruse, and *p* salt therein ... 2Kin 2:20 7760
for he *p* away the image of Baal ... 2Kin 3:2 5493
all that were able to *p* on armour ... 2Kin 3:21 2296
p his mouth upon his mouth, and ... 2Kin 4:34 7760
he *p* out his hand, and took it ... 2Kin 6:7 7971
p it under him on the top of the ... 2Kin 9:13 7760
p their heads in baskets, and sent ... 2Kin 10:7 7760
p the crown upon him, and gave him ... 2Kin 11:12 5414
p therein all the money that was ... 2Kin 12:9 5414
they *p* up in bags, and told the ... 2Kin 12:10 6695
P thine hand upon the bow ... 2Kin 13:16 7392
And he *p* his hand upon it ... 2Kin 13:16 7760
Elisha *p* his hands upon the ... 2Kin 13:16 7760
The fathers shall not be *p* to ... 2Kin 14:6 4191
nor the children be *p* to death ... 2Kin 14:6 4191
but every man shall be *p* to death ... 2Kin 14:6 4191
Judah was *p* to the worse before ... 2Kin 14:12
p it on the north side of the ... 2Kin 16:14 5414
p it upon a pavement of stones ... 2Kin 16:17 5414
p them in the houses of the high ... 2Kin 17:29 3240
p them in Halah and in Habor by ... 2Kin 18:11 5148
p thy trust on Egypt for chariots ... 2Kin 18:24
therefore I will *p* my hook in thy ... 2Kin 19:28 7760
In Jerusalem will I *p* my name ... 2Kin 21:4 7760
will I *p* my name for ever ... 2Kin 21:7 7760
he *p* down the idolatrous priests, ... 2Kin 23:5 7673
in Jerusalem, did Josiah *p* away ... 2Kin 23:24 1197
Pharaoh-nechoh *p* him in bands at ... 2Kin 23:33
p the land to a tribute of an ... 2Kin 23:33 5414
p out the eyes of Zedekiah, and ... 2Kin 25:7 5786
because they *p* their trust in him ... 1Chr 5:20
they *p* his armour in the house of ... 1Chr 10:10 7760
have *p* their lives in jeopardy ... 1Chr 11:19 5414
they *p* to flight all them of the ... 1Chr 12:15 7760
Uzza *p* forth his hand to hold the ... 1Chr 13:9 7971
because he *p* his hand to the ark ... 1Chr 13:10 7971
Then David *p* garrisons in ... 1Chr 18:6 7760
And he *p* garrisons in Edom ... 1Chr 18:13 7760
p the battle in array before the ... 1Chr 19:9
p them in array against the ... 1Chr 19:10
were *p* to the worse before Israel ... 1Chr 19:16
So when David had *p* the battle in ... 1Chr 19:17
were *p* to the worse before Israel ... 1Chr 19:19
he *p* up his sword again into the ... 1Chr 21:27 7725
number *p* in the account of the ... 1Chr 27:24 5927
he *p* before the tabernacle of the ... 2Chr 1:5 7760
device which shall be *p* to him ... 2Chr 2:14 5414
p them on the heads of the ... 2Chr 3:16 5414
and *p* them on the chains ... 2Chr 3:16 5414
p five on the right hand, and five ... 2Chr 4:6 5414
p he among the treasures of the ... 2Chr 5:1 5414
which Moses *p* therein at Horeb ... 2Chr 5:10 5414
And in it have I *p* the ark ... 2Chr 6:11 7760
thou wouldest *p* thy name there ... 2Chr 6:20 7760
if thy people Israel be *p* to the ... 2Chr 6:24

P

the king *p* them in the house of	2Chr 9:16	5414
that God had *p* in his heart	2Chr 9:23	5414
his heavy yoke that he *p* upon us	2Chr 10:4	5414
that thy father did *p* upon us	2Chr 10:9	5414
my father *p* a heavy yoke upon you	2Chr 10:11	6006
I will *p* more to your yoke	2Chr 10:11	3254
p captains in them, and store of	2Chr 11:11	5414
every several city he *p* shields	2Chr 11:12	
of Israel, to *p* his name there	2Chr 12:13	7760
p away the abominable idols out	2Chr 15:8	5674
of Israel should be *p* to death	2Chr 15:13	
seer, and *p* him in a prison house	2Chr 16:10	5414
beside those whom the king *p* in	2Chr 17:19	5414
the LORD hath *p* a lying spirit in	2Chr 18:22	5414
P this fellow in the prison, and	2Chr 18:26	7760
but *p* thou on thy robes	2Chr 18:29	3847
slain, and *p* him and his nurse in a	2Chr 22:11	5414
the house, he shall be *p* to death	2Chr 23:7	
p upon him the crown, and gave him	2Chr 23:11	5414
Judah was *p* to the worse before	2Chr 25:22	
p out the lamps, and have not	2Chr 29:7	3518
will I *p* my name for ever	2Chr 33:7	7760
p captains of war in all the	2Chr 33:14	7760
they *p* it in the hand of the	2Chr 34:10	5414
P the holy ark in the house which	2Chr 35:3	5414
p him in the second chariot that	2Chr 35:24	7392
the king of Egypt *p* him down at	2Chr 36:3	5493
p them in his temple at Babylon	2Chr 36:7	5414
p it also in writing, saying,	2Chr 36:22	
p it also in writing, saying,	Ezr 1:1	
had *p* them in the house of his	Ezr 1:7	5414
polluted, *p* from the priesthood	Ezr 2:62	
that shall *p* to their hand to	Ezr 6:12	7972
which hath *p* such a thing as this	Ezr 7:27	5414
our God to *p* away all the wives	Ezr 10:3	3318
they would *p* away their wives	Ezr 10:19	3318
p in my heart to do at Jerusalem	Neh 2:12	5414
but their nobles *p* not their	Neh 3:5	935
none of us *p* off our clothes,	Neh 4:23	6584
every one *p* them off for washing	Neh 4:23	7973
that would have *p* me in fear	Neh 6:14	
sent letters to *p* me in fear	Neh 6:19	
my God *p* into mine heart to	Neh 7:5	5414
polluted, *p* from the priesthood	Neh 7:64	
p on sackcloth with ashes, and	Est 4:1	3847
one law of his to *p* him to death	Est 4:11	
that Esther *p* on her royal	Est 5:1	3847
besought him with tears to *p* away	Est 8:3	5674
drew near to be *p* in execution	Est 9:1	
But *p* forth thine hand now, and	Job 1:11	7971
only upon himself *p* not forth	Job 1:12	7971
But *p* forth thine hand now, and	Job 2:5	7971
he *p* no trust in his servants	Job 4:18	
p it far away, and let not	Job 11:14	
teeth, and *p* my life in mine hand	Job 13:14	7760
p me in a surety with thee	Job 17:3	
of the wicked shall be *p* out	Job 18:5	1846
candle shall be *p* out with him	Job 18:6	1846
He hath *p* my brethren far from me	Job 19:13	
is the candle of the wicked *p* out	Job 21:17	1846
thou shalt *p* away iniquity far	Job 22:23	
but he would *p* strength in me	Job 23:6	7760
it, but the just shall *p* it on	Job 27:17	3847
I *p* on righteousness, and it	Job 29:14	3847
Who hath *p* wisdom in the inward	Job 38:36	7896
Canst thou *p* an hook into his	Job 41:2	7760
they that *p* their trust in him	Ps 2:12	
and *p* your trust in the LORD	Ps 4:5	
Thou hast *p* gladness in my heart,	Ps 4:7	5414
But let all those that *p* their	Ps 5:11	
my God, in thee do I *p* my trust	Ps 7:1	
thou hast *p* all things under his	Ps 8:6	7896
thou hast *p* out their name for	Ps 9:5	4229
name will *p* their trust in thee	Ps 9:10	
P them in fear, O LORD	Ps 9:20	7896
In the LORD *p* I my trust	Ps 11:1	
for in thee do I *p* my trust	Ps 16:1	
by thy right hand them which *p*	Ps 17:7	
I did not *p* away his statutes	Ps 18:22	5493
for I *p* my trust in thee	Ps 25:20	
p not thy servant away in anger	Ps 27:9	5186
thou hast *p* off my sackcloth, and	Ps 30:11	6605
IN thee, O LORD, do I *p* my trust	Ps 31:1	
the lying lips be *p* to silence	Ps 31:18	
p to shame that seek after my	Ps 35:4	
therefore the children of men *p*	Ps 36:7	
he hath *p* a new song in my mouth,	Ps 40:3	5414
p to shame that wish me evil	Ps 40:14	
hast *p* them to shame that hated	Ps 44:7	
hast cast off, and *p* us to shame	Ps 44:9	
thou hast *p* them to shame,	Ps 53:5	
He hath *p* forth his hands against	Ps 55:20	7971
word, in God I have *p* my trust	Ps 56:4	
p thou my tears into thy bottle	Ps 56:8	5414
In God have I *p* my trust	Ps 56:11	
p to confusion, that desire my	Ps 70:2	
In thee, O LORD, do I *p* my trust	Ps 71:1	
let me never be *p* to confusion	Ps 71:1	
I have *p* my trust in the Lord GOD	Ps 73:28	7896
he *p* them to a perpetual reproach	Ps 78:66	5414
yea, let them be *p* to shame	Ps 83:17	
Thou hast *p* away mine	Ps 88:8	7368
and friend hast thou *p* far from me	Ps 88:18	7368
LORD than to *p* confidence in man	Ps 118:8	
than to *p* confidence in princes	Ps 118:9	
O LORD, *p* me not to shame	Ps 119:31	
lest the righteous *p* forth their	Ps 125:3	7971
P not your trust in princes, nor	Ps 146:3	
P away from thee a froward mouth,	Prov 4:24	5493
and perverse lips *p* far from thee	Prov 4:24	7368
understanding *p* forth her voice	Prov 8:1	5414
lamp of the wicked shall be *p* out	Prov 13:9	1846
his lamp shall be *p* out in	Prov 20:20	1846
p a knife to thy throat, if thou	Prov 23:2	7760
of the wicked shall be *p* out	Prov 24:20	1846
P not forth thyself in the	Prov 25:6	1921
than that thou shouldest be *p*	Prov 25:7	
neighbour hath *p* thee to shame	Prov 25:8	
that heareth it *p* thee to shame	Prov 25:10	
them that *p* their trust in him	Prov 30:5	
nothing can be *p* to it, nor any	Eccl 3:14	3254
then must he *p* to more strength	Eccl 10:10	1396
p away evil from thy flesh	Eccl 11:10	5674
I have *p* off my coat	Song 5:3	6584
how shall I *p* it on	Song 5:3	3847
My beloved *p* in his hand by the	Song 5:4	7971
p away the evil of your doings	Is 1:16	5493
that *p* darkness for light, and	Is 5:20	7760
that *p* bitter for sweet, and sweet	Is 5:20	7760
I have *p* down the inhabitants	Is 10:13	3381
the weaned child shall *p* his hand	Is 11:8	1911
p off thy shoe from thy foot	Is 20:2	2502
p thy trust on Egypt for chariots	Is 36:9	
therefore will I *p* my hook in thy	Is 37:29	7760
I have *p* my spirit upon him	Is 42:1	5414
P me in remembrance	Is 43:26	
shalt not be able to *p* if off	Is 47:11	3722
divorcement, whom I have *p* away	Is 50:1	7971
is your mother *p* away	Is 50:1	7971
p on strength, O arm of the LORD	Is 51:9	3847
I have *p* my words in thy mouth,	Is 51:16	7760
But I will *p* it into the hand of	Is 51:23	7760
p on thy strength, O Zion	Is 52:1	3847
p on thy beautiful garments, O	Is 52:1	3847
he hath *p* him to grief	Is 53:10	
for thou shalt not be *p* to shame	Is 54:4	
For he *p* on righteousness as a	Is 59:17	3847
he *p* on the garments of vengeance	Is 59:17	3847
words which I have *p* in thy mouth	Is 59:21	7760
where is he that *p* his holy	Is 63:11	7760
Then the LORD *p* forth his hand,	Jer 1:9	7971
I have *p* my words in thy mouth	Jer 1:9	5414
If a man *p* away his wife, and she	Jer 3:1	7971
adultery I had *p* her away	Jer 3:8	7971
How shall I *p* thee among the	Jer 3:19	7896
if thou wilt *p* away thine	Jer 4:1	5493
P your burnt offerings unto your	Jer 7:21	5595
LORD our God hath *p* us to silence	Jer 8:14	
they have *p* themselves to pain,	Jer 12:13	
p it upon thy loins, and *p* it	Jer 13:1	7760
thy loins, and *p* it not in water	Jer 13:1	7760
of the LORD, and *p* it on my loins	Jer 13:2	7760
and let their men be *p* to death	Jer 18:21	2026
p him in the stocks that were in	Jer 20:2	5414
that if ye *p* me to death, ye	Jer 26:15	
all Judah *p* him at all to death	Jer 26:19	
the king sought to *p* him to death	Jer 26:21	
of the people to *p* him to death	Jer 26:24	
yokes, and *p* them upon thy neck,	Jer 27:2	5414
that will not *p* their neck under	Jer 27:8	5414
I have *p* a yoke of iron upon the	Jer 28:14	5414
thou shouldest *p* him in prison	Jer 29:26	5414
I will *p* my law in their inward	Jer 31:33	5414
p them in an earthen vessel, that	Jer 32:14	5414
but I will *p* my fear in their	Jer 32:40	5414
they had not *p* him into prison	Jer 37:4	5414
p him in prison in the house of	Jer 37:15	5414
that ye have *p* me in prison	Jer 37:18	5414
thee, let this man be *p* to death	Jer 38:4	
heard that they had *p* Jeremiah in	Jer 38:7	5414
P now these old cast clouts and	Jer 38:12	7760
thou not surely *p* me to death	Jer 38:15	
I will not *p* thee to death,	Jer 38:16	
we will not *p* thee to death	Jer 38:25	
Moreover he *p* out Zedekiah's eyes	Jer 39:7	5786
thou hast *p* thy trust in me	Jer 39:18	
p them in your vessels, and dwell	Jer 40:10	7760
that they might *p* us to death	Jer 43:3	
spears, and *p* on the brigandines	Jer 46:4	3847
p up thyself into thy scabbard,	Jer 47:6	622
P yourselves in array against	Jer 50:14	
upon horses, every one *p* in array	Jer 50:42	
Then he *p* out the eyes of	Jer 52:11	5786
p him in prison till the day of	Jer 52:11	5411
p them to death in Riblah in the	Jer 52:27	
they shall *p* bands upon thee, and	Eze 3:25	5414
p them in one vessel, and make	Eze 4:9	5414
he *p* forth the form of an hand,	Eze 8:3	7971
they *p* the branch to their nose	Eze 8:17	7971
p it into the hands of him that	Eze 10:7	5414
I will *p* a new spirit within you	Eze 11:19	5414
p the stumblingblock of their	Eze 14:3	5414
I *p* bracelets upon thy hands, and	Eze 16:11	5414
I *p* a jewel on thy forehead, and	Eze 16:12	5414
which I had *p* upon thee, saith	Eze 16:14	7760
p forth a riddle, and speak a	Eze 17:2	2330
they *p* him in ward in chains, and	Eze 19:9	5414
they have *p* no difference between	Eze 22:26	
which *p* bracelets upon their	Eze 23:42	5414
p on thy shoes upon thy feet, and	Eze 24:17	7760
p off their broidered garments	Eze 26:16	6584
But I will *p* hooks in thy jaws,	Eze 29:4	5414
I will *p* a fear in the land of	Eze 30:13	5414
to *p* a roller to bind it, to make	Eze 30:21	7760
and *p* my sword in his hand	Eze 30:24	5414
when I shall *p* my sword into the	Eze 30:25	5414
And when I shall *p* thee out	Eze 32:7	3518
he is *p* in the midst of them that	Eze 32:25	5414
a new spirit will I *p* within you	Eze 36:26	5414
I will *p* my spirit within you, and	Eze 36:27	5414
p breath in you, and ye shall live	Eze 37:6	5414
shall *p* my spirit in you, and ye	Eze 37:14	5414
will *p* them with him, even with	Eze 37:19	5414
p hooks into thy jaws, and I will	Eze 38:4	5414
shall *p* on other garments, and	Eze 42:14	3847
Now let them *p* away their	Eze 43:9	7368
p it on the four horns of it, and	Eze 43:20	5414
they shall *p* off their garments	Eze 44:19	6584
they shall *p* on other garments	Eze 44:19	3847
a widow, nor her that is *p* away	Eze 44:22	1644
p it upon the posts of the house,	Eze 45:19	5414
and whom he would he *p* down	Dan 5:19	8214
p a chain of gold about his neck,	Dan 5:29	
let her therefore *p* away her	Hos 2:2	5493
P ye in the sickle, for the	Joel 3:13	7971
Ye that *p* far away the evil day,	Amos 6:3	
p on sackcloth, from the greatest	Jonah 3:5	3847
I will *p* them together as the	Mic 2:12	7760
p ye not confidence in a guide	Mic 7:5	
where they have been *p* to shame	Zeph 3:19	
to *p* it into a bag with holes	Hag 1:6	
was minded to *p* her away privily	Mt 1:19	630
p it under a bushel, but on a	Mt 5:15	5087
Whosoever shall *p* away his wife	Mt 5:31	630
whosoever shall *p* away his wife	Mt 5:32	*630*
for your body, what ye shall *p* on	Mt 6:25	*1749*
Jesus *p* forth his hand, and	Mt 8:3	*1614*
for that which is *p* in to fill it	Mt 9:16	
Neither do men *p* new wine into	Mt 9:17	*906*
but they *p* new wine into new	Mt 9:17	*906*
But when the people were *p* forth	Mt 9:25	*1544*
and cause them to be *p* to death	Mt 10:21	*2289*
I will *p* my Spirit upon him, and	Mt 12:18	*5087*
Another parable *p* he forth unto	Mt 13:24	*3908*
Another parable *p* he forth unto	Mt 13:31	*3908*
p him in prison for Herodias'	Mt 14:3	*5087*
when he would have *p* him to death	Mt 14:5	*615*
Is it lawful for a man to *p* away	Mt 19:3	*630*
together, let not man *p* asunder	Mt 19:6	*5562*
of divorcement, and to *p* her away	Mt 19:7	*630*
suffered you to *p* away your wives	Mt 19:8	*630*
Whosoever shall *p* away his wife	Mt 19:9	*630*
is *p* away doth commit adultery	Mt 19:9	*630*
that he should *p* his hands on	Mt 19:13	*2007*
p on them their clothes, and they	Mt 21:7	*2007*
he had *p* the Sadducees to silence	Mt 22:34	
have *p* my money to the exchangers	Mt 25:27	*906*
P up again thy sword into his	Mt 26:52	*654*
against Jesus, to *p* him to death	Mt 26:59	*2289*
against Jesus to *p* him to death	Mt 27:1	*2289*
for to *p* them into the treasury	Mt 27:6	*906*
him, and *p* on him a scarlet robe	Mt 27:28	*4060*
they *p* it upon his head, and a	Mt 27:29	*2007*
p his own raiment on him, and led	Mt 27:31	*1746*
p it on a reed, and gave him to	Mt 27:48	*4060*
after that John was *p* in prison	Mk 1:14	*3860*
p forth his hand, and touched him,	Mk 1:41	*1614*
wine must be *p* into new bottles	Mk 2:22	*906*
brought to be *p* under a bushel	Mk 4:21	*5087*
But when he had *p* them all out	Mk 5:40	*1544*
and not *p* on two coats	Mk 6:9	*1746*
him to *p* his hand upon him	Mk 7:32	*2007*
p his fingers into his ears, and	Mk 7:33	*906*
p his hands upon him, he asked	Mk 8:23	*2007*
After that he *p* his hands again	Mk 8:25	*2007*
for a man to *p* away his wife	Mk 10:2	*630*
of divorcement, and to *p* her away	Mk 10:4	*630*
together, let not man *p* asunder	Mk 10:9	*5562*
Whosoever shall *p* away his wife	Mk 10:11	*630*
a woman shall *p* away her husband	Mk 10:12	*630*
p his hands upon them, and blessed	Mk 10:16	*5087*
shall cause them to be *p* to death	Mk 13:12	*2289*
him by craft, and *p* him to death	Mk 14:1	*615*
against Jesus to *p* him to death	Mk 14:55	*2289*
thorns, and *p* it about his head,	Mk 15:17	*4060*
p his own clothes on him, and led	Mk 15:20	*1746*
p it on a reed, and gave him to	Mk 15:36	*4060*
He hath *p* down the mighty from	Lk 1:52	*2507*
he *p* forth his hand, and touched	Lk 5:13	*1614*
wine must be *p* into new bottles	Lk 5:38	*906*
he *p* them all out, and took her by	Lk 8:54	*1544*
having *p* his hand to the plough,	Lk 9:62	*1911*
for the body, what ye shall *p* on	Lk 12:22	*1746*
he *p* forth a parable to those	Lk 14:7	*3004*
the best robe, and *p* it on him	Lk 15:22	*1746*
p a ring on his hand, and shoes on	Lk 15:22	*1325*
do, that, when I am *p* out of the	Lk 16:4	*3179*
that is *p* away from her husband	Lk 16:18	*630*
scourge him, and *p* him to death	Lk 18:33	*615*
shall they cause to be *p* to death	Lk 21:16	*2289*
led with him to be *p* to death	Lk 23:32	*337*
troubled, to *p* me into the pool	Jn 5:7	*906*
He *p* clay upon mine eyes, and I	Jn 9:15	*2007*
he should be *p* out of the	Jn 9:22	
together for to *p* him to death	Jn 11:53	*615*
bag, and bare what was *p* therein	Jn 12:6	*906*
might *p* Lazarus also to death	Jn 12:10	*615*
lest they should be *p* out of the	Jn 12:42	*1096*
the devil having now *p* into the	Jn 13:2	*906*
They shall *p* you out of the	Jn 16:2	*4160*
P up thy sword into the sheath	Jn 18:11	*906*
for us to *p* any man to death	Jn 18:31	*615*
p it on his head, and they *p* on	Jn 19:2	*2007*
they *p* on him a purple robe,	Jn 19:2	*4016*

a title, and *p* it on the cross Jn 19:19 *5087*
p it upon hyssop, and *p* it to Jn 19:29 *4060*
upon hyssop, and *p* it to his mouth Jn 19:29 *4374*
p my finger into the print of the Jn 20:25 *906*
Father hath *p* in his own power Acts 1:7 *5087*
p them in hold unto the next day Acts 4:3 *5087*
p them in the common prison Acts 5:18 *5087*
the men whom ye *p* in prison are Acts 5:25 *5087*
commanded to *p* the apostles forth Acts 5:34 *4160*
P off thy shoes from thy feet Acts 7:33 *3089*
But Peter *p* them all forth, and Acts 9:40 *1544*
he *p* him in prison, and delivered Acts 12:4 *5087*
that they should be *p* to death Acts 12:19 *520*
but seeing ye *p* it from you Acts 13:46 *683*
p no difference between us and Acts 15:9 *1252*
to *p* a yoke upon the neck of the Acts 15:10 *2007*
and when they were *p* to death Acts 26:10 *337*
and he *p* us therein Acts 27:6 *1688*
let us *p* on the armour of light Rom 13:12 *1746*
But *p* ye on the Lord Jesus Christ Rom 13:14 *1746*
that no man *p* a stumblingblock or Rom 14:13 *5087*
Therefore *p* away from among 1Cor 5:13 *1808*
not the husband *p* away his wife 1Cor 7:11 *863*
with him, let him not *p* her away 1Cor 7:12 *863*
a man, I *p* away childish things 1Cor 13:11 *2673*
he shall have *p* down all rule 1Cor 15:24 *2673*
till he hath *p* all enemies under 1Cor 15:25 *5087*
For he hath *p* all things under 1Cor 15:27 *5293*
saith all things are *p* under him 1Cor 15:27 *5293*
which did *p* all things under him 1Cor 15:27 *5293*
him that *p* all things under him 1Cor 15:28 *5293*
must *p* on incorruption, and this 1Cor 15:53 *1746*
this mortal must *p* on immortality 1Cor 15:53 *1746*
shall have *p* on incorruption 1Cor 15:54 *1746*
shall have *p* on immortality 1Cor 15:54 *1746*
which *p* a vail over his face, 2Cor 3:13 *5087*
which *p* the same earnest care 2Cor 8:16 *1325*
into Christ have *p* on Christ Gal 3:27 *1746*
hath *p* all things under his feet, Eph 1:22 *5293*
That ye *p* off concerning the Eph 4:22 *659*
that ye *p* on the new man, which Eph 4:24 *1746*
be *p* away from you, with all Eph 4:31 *142*
P on the whole armour of God, Eph 6:11 *1746*
But now ye also *p* off all these Col 3:8 *659*
seeing that ye have *p* off the old Col 3:9 *554*
have *p* on the new man, which is Col 3:10 *1746*
P on therefore, as the elect of Col 3:12 *1746*
all these things *p* on charity Col 3:14
to be *p* in trust with the gospel 1Th 2:4 *4160*
which some having *p* away 1Ti 1:19 *683*
If thou *p* the brethren in 1Ti 4:6 *5294*
Wherefore I *p* thee in remembrance 2Ti 1:6 *363*
Of these things *p* them in 2Ti 2:14 *5279*
P them in mind to be subject to Titus 3:1 *5279*
ought, *p* that on mine account Philem 18 *1677*
p in subjection the world to come Heb 2:5 *5293*
Thou hast *p* all things in Heb 2:8 *5293*
For in that he *p* all in Heb 2:8 *5293*
nothing that is not *p* under him Heb 2:8 *506*
not yet all things *p* under him Heb 2:8 *5293*
again, I will *p* my trust in him Heb 2:13 *3982*
afresh, and *p* him to an open shame Heb 6:6 *3856*
I will *p* my laws into their mind, Heb 8:10 *1325*
to *p* away sin by the sacrifice of Heb 9:26 *115*
I will *p* my laws into their Heb 10:16 *1325*
we *p* bits in the horses' mouths, Jas 3:3 *906*
may *p* to silence the ignorance of 1Pet 2:15 *5392*
being *p* to death in the flesh, 1Pet 3:18 *2289*
I will not be negligent to *p* you 2Pet 1:12 *5279*
I must *p* off this my tabernacle 2Pet 1:14 *595*
I will therefore *p* you in Jude 5 *5279*
I will *p* upon you none other Rev 2:24 *906*
dead bodies to be *p* in graves Rev 11:9 *5087*
For God hath *p* in their hearts to Rev 17:17 *1325*
2. *Descendant of Put 3.*
P and Lubim were thy helpers Nah 3:9 6316
3. *Son of Ham.*
Cush, and Mizraim, *P*, and Canaan 1Chr 1:8 6319

PUTEOLI *(pu-te'-o-li)* {1} *A seaport in Italy.*
and we came the next day to *P* Acts 28:13 *4223*

PUTHITES See PUHITES.

PUTIEL *(pu'-te-el)* {1} *Father-in-law of Eleazar.*
one of the daughters of *P* to wife Ex 6:25 6317

PUTRIFYING {1}
wounds, and bruises, and *p* sores Is 1:6 2961

PUTTEST {7}
thou *p* thy nest in a rock Num 24:21 7760
all that thou *p* thine hand unto Deut 12:18 4916
all that thou *p* thine hand unto Deut 15:10 4916
that which thou *p* on me will I 2Kin 18:14 5414
Thou *p* my feet also in the stocks Job 13:27 7760
Thou *p* away all the wicked of the Ps 119:119 7673
that *p* thy bottle to him, and Hab 2:15 5596

PUTTETH {30}
or whosoever *p* any of it upon a Ex 30:33 5414
the word that God *p* in my mouth Num 22:38 7760
p forth her hand, and taketh him Deut 25:11 7971
and *p* it in a secret place Deut 27:15 7760
boast himself as he that *p* it off 1Kin 20:11 6605
he *p* no trust in his saints Job 15:15
He *p* forth his hand upon the rock Job 28:9 7971
He *p* my feet in the stocks, he Job 33:11 7760
He that *p* not out his money to Ps 15:5 5414
he *p* down one, and setteth up Ps 75:7 8213
but he that *p* his trust in the Prov 28:25
but whoso *p* his trust in the LORD Prov 29:25
The fig tree *p* forth her green Song 2:13 2590
but he that *p* his trust in me Is 57:13
as a shepherd *p* on his garment Jer 43:12 5844
He *p* his mouth in the dust Lam 3:29 5414
p the stumblingblock of his Eze 14:4 7760
p the stumblingblock of his Eze 14:7 7760
he that *p* not into their mouths, Mic 3:5 5414
No man *p* a piece of new cloth Mt 9:16 *1911*
p forth leaves, ye know that Mt 24:32 *1631*
no man *p* new wine into old Mk 2:22 *906*
immediately he *p* in the sickle Mk 4:29 *649*
p forth leaves, ye know that Mk 13:28 *1631*
No man *p* a piece of a new garment Lk 5:36 *1911*
no man *p* new wine into old Lk 5:37 *906*
a vessel, or *p* it under a bed Lk 8:16 *5087*
p it in a secret place, neither Lk 11:33 *5087*
Whosoever *p* away his wife, and Lk 16:18 *630*
when he *p* forth his own sheep, he Jn 10:4 *1544*

PUTTING {17}
p it on her shoulder, and the Gen 21:14 7760
p them upon the head of the goat, Lev 16:21 5414
p their hand to their mouth, were Judg 7:6
the *p* forth of the finger, and Is 58:9 7971
saith that he hateth *p* away Mal 2:16 7971
p his hand on him, that he might Acts 9:12 *2007*
p his hands on him said, Brother Acts 9:17 *2007*
multitude, the Jews *p* him forward Acts 19:33 *4261*
as *p* you in mind, because of the Rom 15:15 *1878*
Wherefore *p* away lying, speak Eph 4:25 *659*
in *p* off the body of the sins of Col 2:11 *555*
p on the breastplate of faith and 1Th 5:8 *1746*
faithful, *p* me into the ministry 1Ti 1:12 *5087*
in thee by the *p* on of my hands 2Ti 1:6 *1936*
of gold, or of *p* on of apparel 1Pet 3:3 *1745*
p away of the filth of the flesh 1Pet 3:21 *595*
to stir you up by *p* you in 2Pet 1:13 *5279*

PUVAH See PUA.

PUVVAH See PHUVAH.

PYGARG {1}
deer, and the wild goat, and the *p* Deut 14:5 1787

PYRRHUS Not in KJV.

QUAILS {4}
pass, that at even the *q* came up Ex 16:13 7958
brought *q* from the sea, and let Num 11:31 7958
next day, and they gathered the *q* Num 11:32 7958
The people asked, and he brought *q* Ps 105:40 7958

QUAKE {4}
The earth shall *q* before them Joel 2:10 7264
The mountains *q* at him, and the Nah 1:5 7493
and the earth did *q*, and the rocks Mt 27:51 *4579*
said, I exceedingly fear and *q* Heb 12:21 *1790*

QUAKED {2}
and the whole mount *q* greatly Ex 19:18 2729
also trembled, and the earth *q* 1Sa 14:15 7264

QUAKING {2}
Son of man, eat thy bread with *q* Eze 12:18 7494
but a great *q* fell upon them, so Dan 10:7 2731

QUANTITY {1}
the issue, all vessels of small *q* Is 22:24

QUARREL 4}
shall avenge the *q* of my covenant Lev 26:25 5359
see how he seeketh a *q* against me 2Kin 5:7 579
Herodias had a *q* against him Mk 6:19 *1758*
if any man have a *q* against any Col 3:13 *3437*

QUARRIES {2}
from the *q* that were by Gilgal Judg 3:19 6456
tarried, and passed beyond the *q* Judg 3:26 6456

QUARTER {8}
all the people from every *q* Gen 19:4 7098
Then your south *q* shall be from Num 34:3 6285
their border in the north *q* was Josh 15:5 6285
this was the west *q* Josh 18:14 6285
the south *q* was from the end of Josh 18:15 6285
shall wander every one to his *q* Is 47:15 5676
one for his gain, from his *q* Is 56:11 7098
and they came to him from every *q* Mk 1:45 *3836*

QUARTERS {9}
seen with thee in all thy *q* Ex 13:7 1366
upon the four *q* of thy vesture Deut 22:12 3671
In four *q* were the porters, 1Chr 9:24 7307
winds from the four *q* of heaven Jer 49:36 7098
house of Togarmah of the north *q* Eze 38:6 3411
as Peter passed throughout all *q* Acts 9:32
of the Jews which were in those *q* Acts 16:3 *5117*
In the same *q* were possessions of Acts 28:7 *5117*
are in the four *q* of the earth Rev 20:8 *1137*

QUARTUS *(quar'-tus)* {1} *A Christian in Rome.*
city saluteth you, and *Q* a brother Rom 16:23 *2890*

QUATERNIONS {1}
delivered him to four *q* of Acts 12:4 *5069*

QUEEN {54}
when the *q* of Sheba heard of the 1Kin 10:1 4436
when the *q* of Sheba had seen all 1Kin 10:4 4436
of spices as these which the *q* of 1Kin 10:10 4436
the *q* of Sheba all her desire 1Kin 10:13 4436
the sister of Tahpenes the *q* 1Kin 11:19 1377
even her he removed from being *q* 1Kin 15:13 1377
the king and the children of the *q* 2Kin 10:13 1377
when the *q* of Sheba heard of the 2Chr 9:1 4436
when the *q* of Sheba had seen the 2Chr 9:3 4436
the *q* of Sheba gave king Solomon 2Chr 9:9 4436
to the *q* of Sheba all her desire 2Chr 9:12 4436
king, he removed her from being *q* 2Chr 15:16 1377
(the *q* also sitting by him,) For Neh 2:6 7694
Also Vashti the *q* made a feast Est 1:9 4436
To bring Vashti the *q* before the Est 1:11 4436
But the *q* Vashti refused to come Est 1:12 4436
the *q* Vashti according to law Est 1:15 4436
Vashti the *q* hath not done wrong Est 1:16 4436
For this deed of the *q* shall come Est 1:17 4436
the *q* to be brought in before him Est 1:17 4436
have heard of the deed of the *q* Est 1:18 4436
the king be *q* instead of Vashti Est 2:4 4427
made her *q* instead of Vashti Est 2:17 4427
who told it unto Esther the *q* Est 2:22 4436
Then was the *q* exceedingly Est 4:4 4436
the *q* standing in the court Est 5:2 4436
her, What wilt thou, *q* Esther Est 5:3 4436
Esther the *q* did let no man come Est 5:12 4436
came to banquet with Esther the *q* Est 7:1 4436
What is thy petition, *q* Esther Est 7:2 4436
Then Esther the *q* answered Est 7:3 4436
and said unto Esther the *q* Est 7:5 4436
afraid before the king and the *q* Est 7:6 4436
for his life to Esther the *q* Est 7:7 4436
Will he force the *q* also before Est 7:8 4436
the Jews' enemy unto Esther the *q* Est 8:1 4436
Ahasuerus said unto Esther the *q* Est 8:7 4436
the king said unto Esther the *q* Est 9:12 4436
Then Esther the *q*, the daughter Est 9:29 4436
Esther the *q* had enjoined them, Est 9:31 4436
did stand the *q* in gold of Ophir Ps 45:9 7694
to make cakes to the *q* of heaven Jer 7:18 4446
Say unto the king and to the *q* Jer 13:18 1377
that Jeconiah the king, and the *q* Jer 29:2 1377
burn incense unto the *q* of heaven Jer 44:17 4446
burn incense to the *q* of heaven Jer 44:18 4446
burned incense to the *q* of heaven Jer 44:19 4446
burn incense to the *q* of heaven Jer 44:25 4446
Now the *q*, by reason of the words Dan 5:10 4433
the *q* spake and said, O king, live Dan 5:10 4433
The *q* of the south shall rise up Mt 12:42 *938*
The *q* of the south shall rise up Lk 11:31 *938*
under Candace *q* of the Ethiopians Acts 8:27 *938*
she saith in her heart, I sit a *q* Rev 18:7 *938*

QUEENS {3}
There are threescore *q*, and Song 6:8 4436
yea, the *q* and the concubines, and Song 6:9 4436
their *q* thy nursing mothers Is 49:23 8282

QUENCH {12}
so they shall *q* my coal which is 2Sa 14:7 3518
that thou *q* not the light of 2Sa 21:17 3518
the wild asses *q* their thirst Ps 104:11 7665
Many waters cannot *q* love Song 8:7 3518
together, and none shall *q* them Is 1:31 3518
the smoking flax shall he not *q* Is 42:3 3518
burn that none can *q* it because Jer 4:4 3518
fire, and burn that none can *q* it Jer 21:12 3518
there be none to *q* it in Beth-el Amos 5:6 3518
and smoking flax shall he not *q* Mt 12:20 *4570*
to *q* all the fiery darts of the Eph 6:16 *4570*
Q not the Spirit 1Th 5:19 *4570*

QUENCHED {17}
unto the LORD, the fire was *q* Num 11:2 8257
this place, and shall not be *q* 2Kin 22:17 3518
this place, and shall not be *q* 2Chr 34:25 3518
they are *q* as the fire of thorns Ps 118:12 1846
It shall not be *q* night nor day Is 34:10 3518
are extinct, they are *q* as tow Is 43:17 3518
neither shall their fire be *q* Is 66:24 3518
it shall burn, and shall not be *q* Jer 7:20 3518
Jerusalem, and it shall not be *q* Jer 17:27 3518
the flaming flame shall not be *q* Eze 20:47 3518
it shall not be *q* Eze 20:48 3518
the fire that never shall be *q* Mk 9:43 *762*
dieth not, and the fire is not *q* Mk 9:44 *4570*
the fire that never shall be *q* Mk 9:45 *762*
dieth not, and the fire is not *q* Mk 9:46 *4570*
dieth not, and the fire is not *q* Mk 9:48 *4570*
Q the violence of fire, escaped Heb 11:34 *4570*

QUESTION {14}
which was a lawyer, asked him a *q* Mt 22:35
forth, and began to *q* with him Mk 8:11 *4802*

the scribes, What *q* ye with them ... Mk 9:16 *4802*
I will also ask of you one *q* ... Mk 11:29 *3056*
after that durst ask him any *q* ... Mk 12:34
durst not ask him any *q* at all ... Lk 20:40
Then there arose a *q* between some ... Jn 3:25 *2214*
apostles and elders about this *q* ... Acts 15:2 *2213*
But if it be a *q* of words ... Acts 18:15 *2213*
called in *q* for this day's uproar ... Acts 19:40 *1458*
of the dead I am called in *q* ... Acts 23:6 *2919*
I am called in *q* by you this day ... Acts 24:21 *2919*
asking no *q* for conscience sake ... 1Cor 10:25
asking no *q* for conscience sake ... 1Cor 10:27

QUESTIONED {3}
Then Hezekiah *q* with the priests ... 2Chr 31:9 1875
that they *q* among themselves ... Mk 1:27 *4802*
Then he *q* with him in many words ... Lk 23:9 *1905*

QUESTIONING {2}
q one with another what the ... Mk 9:10 *4802*
them, and the scribes *q* with them ... Mk 9:14 *4802*

QUESTIONS {14}
she came to prove him with hard *q* ... 1Kin 10:1 2420
And Solomon told her all her *q* ... 1Kin 10:3 1697
Solomon with hard *q* at Jerusalem ... 2Chr 9:1 2420
And Solomon told her all her *q* ... 2Chr 9:2 1697
that day forth ask him any more *q* ... Mt 22:46
hearing them, and asking them *q* ... Lk 2:46 *1905*
to be accused of *q* of their law ... Acts 23:29 *2213*
But had certain *q* against him of ... Acts 25:19 *2213*
I doubted of such manner of *q* ... Acts 25:20 *2214*
q which are among the Jews ... Acts 26:3 *2213*
genealogies, which minister *q* ... 1Ti 1:4 *2214*
nothing, but doting about *q* ... 1Ti 6:4 *2214*
But foolish and unlearned *q* avoid ... 2Ti 2:23 *2214*
But avoid foolish *q*, and ... Titus 3:9 *2214*

QUICK {10}
there be *q* raw flesh in the ... Lev 13:10 4241
the *q* flesh that burneth have a ... Lev 13:24 4241
and they go down *q* into the pit ... Num 16:30 2416
and let them go down *q* into hell ... Ps 55:15 2416
Then they had swallowed us up *q* ... Ps 124:3 2416
shall make him of *q* understanding ... Is 11:3
of God to be the Judge of *q* ... Acts 10:42 *2198*
Christ, who shall judge the *q* ... 2Ti 4:1 *2198*
For the word of God is *q*, and ... Heb 4:12 *2198*
him that is ready to judge the *q* ... 1Pet 4:5 *2198*

QUICKEN {13}
shalt *q* me again, and shalt bring ... Ps 71:20 2421
q us, and we will call upon thy ... Ps 80:18 2421
q thou me according to thy word ... Ps 119:25 2421
and *q* thou me in thy way ... Ps 119:37 2421
q me in thy righteousness ... Ps 119:40 2421
Q me after thy lovingkindness ... Ps 119:88 2421
q me, O LORD, according unto thy ... Ps 119:107 2421
q me according to thy judgment ... Ps 119:149 2421
q me according to thy word ... Ps 119:154 2421
q me according to thy judgments ... Ps 119:156 2421
q me, O LORD, according to thy ... Ps 119:159 2421
Q me, O LORD, for thy name's sake ... Ps 143:11 2421
also *q* your mortal bodies by his ... Rom 8:11 *2227*

QUICKENED {7}
for thy word hath *q* me ... Ps 119:50 2421
for with them thou hast *q* me ... Ps 119:93 2421
that which thou sowest is not *q* ... 1Cor 15:36 *2227*
And you hath he *q*, who were dead ... Eph 2:1
hath *q* us together with Christ, ... Eph 2:5 *4806*
hath he *q* together with him, ... Col 2:13 *4806*
in the flesh, but *q* by the Spirit ... 1Pet 3:18 *2227*

QUICKENETH {5}
raiseth up the dead, and *q* them ... Jn 5:21 *2227*
even so the Son *q* whom he will ... Jn 5:21 *2227*
It is the spirit that *q* ... Jn 6:63 *2227*
who *q* the dead, and calleth those ... Rom 4:17 *2227*
who *q* all things, and before ... 1Ti 6:13 *2227*

QUICKENING {1}
the last Adam was made a *q* spirit ... 1Cor 15:45 *2227*

QUICKLY {39}
Make ready *q* three measures of ... Gen 18:6 4116
it that thou hast found it so *q* ... Gen 27:20 4116
aside *q* out of the way which I ... Ex 32:8 4118
go *q* unto the congregation, and ... Num 16:46 4120
drive them out, and destroy them *q* ... Deut 9:3 4118
Arise, get thee down *q* from hence ... Deut 9:12 4118
they are *q* turned aside out of ... Deut 9:12 4118
ye had turned aside *q* out of the ... Deut 9:16 4118
lest ye perish *q* from off the ... Deut 11:17 4120
destroyed, and until thou perish *q* ... Deut 28:20 4118
pursue after them *q* ... Josh 2:5 4118
the ambush arose *q* out of their ... Josh 8:19 4120
come up to us *q*, and save us, and ... Josh 10:6 4120
ye shall perish *q* from off the ... Josh 23:16 4120
they turned *q* out of the way ... Judg 2:17 4118
days, then thou shalt go down *q* ... 1Sa 20:19 3966
Now therefore send *q*, and tell ... 2Sa 17:16 4120
but they went both of them away *q* ... 2Sa 17:18 4120
Arise, and pass *q* over the water ... 2Sa 17:21 4120
Come down *q* ... 2Kin 1:11 4120
Fetch *q* Micaiah the son of Imla ... 2Chr 18:8 4116
a threefold cord is not *q* broken ... Eccl 4:12 4120
Agree with thine adversary *q* ... Mt 5:25 *5035*
And go *q*, and tell his disciples ... Mt 28:7 *5035*
And they departed *q* from the ... Mt 28:8 *5035*
And they went out *q*, and fled from ... Mk 16:8 *5035*
Go out *q* into the streets and ... Lk 14:21 *5030*
him, Take thy bill, and sit down *q* ... Lk 16:6 *5030*
as she heard that, she arose *q* ... Jn 11:29 *5035*
unto him, That thou doest, do *q* ... Jn 13:27 *5032*
raised him up, saying, Arise up *q* ... Acts 12:7 *1722,5034*
get thee *q* out of Jerusalem ... Acts 22:18 *1722,5034*
or else I will come unto thee *q* ... Rev 2:5 *5035*
or else I will come unto thee *q* ... Rev 2:16 *5035*
Behold, I come *q* ... Rev 3:11 *5035*
behold, the third woe cometh *q* ... Rev 11:14 *5035*
Behold, I come *q* ... Rev 22:7 *5035*
And, behold, I come *q* ... Rev 22:12 *5035*
things saith, Surely I come *q* ... Rev 22:20 *5035*

QUICKSANDS {1}
lest they should fall into the *q* ... Acts 27:17 *4950*

QUIET {31}
were *q* all the night, saying, In ... Judg 16:2 2790
the manner of the Zidonians, *q* ... Judg 18:7 8252
unto a people that were at *q* ... Judg 18:27 8252
rejoiced, and the city was in *q* ... 2Kin 11:20 8252
good, and the land was wide, and *q* ... 1Chr 4:40 8252
his days the land was *q* ten years ... 2Chr 14:1 8252
and the kingdom was *q* before him ... 2Chr 14:5 8252
So the realm of Jehoshaphat was *q* ... 2Chr 20:30 8252
and the city was *q*, after that ... 2Chr 23:21 8252
I have lain still and been *q* ... Job 3:13 8252
had I rest, neither was I *q* ... Job 3:26 5117
being wholly at ease and *q* ... Job 21:23 7961
them that are *q* in the land ... Ps 35:20 7282
are they glad because they be *q* ... Ps 107:30 8367
shall be *q* from fear of evil ... Prov 1:33 7599
q more than the cry of him that ... Eccl 9:17 5183
say unto him, Take heed, and be *q* ... Is 7:4 8252
whole earth is at rest, and is *q* ... Is 14:7 8252
dwellings, and in *q* resting places ... Is 32:18 7600
see Jerusalem a *q* habitation ... Is 33:20 7600
and shall be in rest, and be *q* ... Jer 30:10 7599
how long will it be ere thou be *q* ... Jer 47:6 8252
How can it be *q*, seeing the LORD ... Jer 47:7 8252
it cannot be *q* ... Jer 49:23 8252
And this Seraiah was a *q* prince ... Jer 51:59 4496
depart from thee, and I will be *q* ... Eze 16:42 8252
Though they be *q*, and likewise ... Nah 1:12 8003
spoken against, ye ought to be *q* ... Acts 19:36 *2687*
And that ye study to be *q*, and to ... 1Th 4:11 *2270*
that we may lead a *q* and peaceable ... 1Ti 2:2 *2263*
q spirit, which is in the sight ... 1Pet 3:4 *2272*

QUIETED {2}
q myself, as a child that is ... Ps 131:2 1826
toward the north country have *q* ... Zec 6:8 5117

QUIETETH {1}
when he *q* the earth by the south ... Job 37:17 8252

QUIETLY {2}
in the gate to speak with him *q* ... 2Sa 3:27 7987
q wait for the salvation of the ... Lam 3:26

QUIETNESS {10}
the country was in *q* forty years ... Judg 8:28 8252
q unto Israel in his days ... 1Chr 22:9 8253
he shall not feel *q* in his belly ... Job 20:20 7961
When he giveth *q*, who then can ... Job 34:29 8252
q therewith, than an house full ... Prov 17:1 7962
Better is an handful with *q* ... Eccl 4:6 5183
in *q* and in confidence shall be ... Is 30:15 8252
and the effect of righteousness *q* ... Is 32:17 8252
that by thee we enjoy great *q* ... Acts 24:2 *1515*
Christ, that with *q* they work ... 2Th 3:12 *2271*

QUIRINIUS See CYRENIUS.

QUIT {6}
then shall he that smote him be *q* ... Ex 21:19 5352
the owner of the ox shall be *q* ... Ex 21:28 5355
then we will be *q* of thine oath ... Josh 2:20 5355
q yourselves like men, O ye ... 1Sa 4:9 1961
q yourselves like men, and fight ... 1Sa 4:9
q you like men, be strong ... 1Cor 16:13 *407*

QUITE {7}
hath *q* devoured also our money ... Gen 31:15
q break down their images ... Ex 23:24
thou shalt *q* take away their ... Num 17:10 3615
q pluck down all their high ... Num 33:52
sent him away, and he is *q* gone ... 2Sa 3:24
and is wisdom driven *q* from me ... Job 6:13 5080
Thy bow was made *q* naked, ... Hab 3:9 6181

QUIVER {7}
I pray thee, thy weapons, thy *q* ... Gen 27:3 8522
The *q* rattleth against him, the ... Job 39:23 827
man that hath his *q* full of them ... Ps 127:5 827
Elam bare the *q* with chariots of ... Is 22:6 827
in his *q* hath he hid me ... Is 49:2 827
Their *q* is as an open sepulchre, ... Jer 5:16 827
of his *q* to enter into my reins ... Lam 3:13 827

QUIVERED {1}
my lips *q* at the voice ... Hab 3:16 6750

R

RAAMA See RAAMAH.

RAAMAH *(ra'-a-mah)* {5}
1. A son of Cush.
Seba, and Havilah, and Sabtah, and *R* ... Gen 10:7 7484
and the sons of *R* ... Gen 10:7 7484
Seba, and Havilah, and Sabta, and *R* ... 1Chr 1:9 7484
And the sons of *R* ... 1Chr 1:9 7484
2. A place in Arabia.
The merchants of Sheba and *R* ... Eze 27:22 7484

RAAMIAH *(ra-a-mi'-ah)* {1} *A clan leader in exile.*
Jeshua, Nehemiah, Azariah, *R* ... Neh 7:7 7485

RAAMSES *(ra-am'-seze)* {1} See RAMESES. *An Egyptian city.*
treasure cities, Pithom and *R* ... Ex 1:11 7486

RABBAH *(rab'-bah)* {13} See RABBATH.
1. An Ammonite city.
unto Aroer that is before *R* ... Josh 13:25 7237
children of Ammon, and besieged *R* ... 2Sa 11:1 7237
Joab fought against *R* of the ... 2Sa 12:26 7237
and said, I have fought against *R* ... 2Sa 12:27 7237
the people together, and went to *R* ... 2Sa 12:29 7237
of *R* of the children of Ammon ... 2Sa 17:27 7237
of Ammon, and came and besieged *R* ... 1Chr 20:1 7237
And Joab smote *R*, and destroyed it ... 1Chr 20:1 7237
to be heard in *R* of the Ammonites ... Jer 49:2 7237
cry, ye daughters of *R*, gird you ... Jer 49:3 7237
I will make *R* a stable for camels ... Eze 25:5 7237
kindle a fire in the wall of *R* ... Amos 1:14 7237
2. A city in Judah.
which is Kirjath-jearim, and *R* ... Josh 15:60 7237

RABBATH *(rab'-bath)* {2} See RABBAH. *Same as Rabbah 1.*
is it not in *R* of the children of ... Deut 3:11 7237
may come to *R* of the Ammonites ... Eze 21:20 7237

RABBI *(rab'-bi)* {8} See RABBONI. *A Jewish title meaning "teacher."*
and to be called of men, *R*, *R* ... Mt 23:7 *4461*
But be not ye called *R* ... Mt 23:8 *4461*
They said unto him, *R*, (which is ... Jn 1:38 *4461*
answered and saith unto him, *R* ... Jn 1:49 *4461*
by night, and said unto him, *R* ... Jn 3:2 *4461*
unto John, and said unto him, *R* ... Jn 3:26 *4461*
of the sea, they said unto him, *R* ... Jn 6:25 *4461*

RABBITH *(rab'-bith)* {1} *A city in Issachar.*
And *R*, and Kishion, and Abez, ... Josh 19:20 7245

RABBONI *(rab-bo'-ni)* {1} See RABBI. *A Jewish title of respect.*
herself, and saith unto him, *R* ... Jn 20:16 *4462*

RAB-MAG *A Babylonian prince.*
Rab-saris, Nergal-sharezer, *R* ... Jer 39:3 7248
Rab-saris, and Nergal-sharezer, *R* ... Jer 39:13 7248

RAB-SARIS {3}
1. A Babylonian prince.
Samgar-nebo, Sarsechim, *R* ... Jer 39:3 7249
the guard sent, and Nebushasban, *R* ... Jer 39:13 7249
2. An Assyrian officer.
king of Assyria sent Tartan and *R* ... 2Kin 18:17 7249

RAB-SHAKEH *(rab'-sha-keh)* {8} See RABSHAKEH. *An Assyrian officer.*
R from Lachish to king Hezekiah ... 2Kin 18:17 7262
R said unto them, Speak ye now to ... 2Kin 18:19 7262
and Shebna, and Joah, unto *R* ... 2Kin 18:26 7262
But *R* said unto them, Hath my ... 2Kin 18:27 7262
Then *R* stood and cried with a loud ... 2Kin 18:28 7262
rent, and told him the words of *R* ... 2Kin 18:37 7262
God will hear all the words of *R* ... 2Kin 19:4 7262
So *R* returned, and found the king ... 2Kin 19:8 7262

RABSHAKEH *(rab'-sha-keh)* {8} See RAB-SHAKEH. *Same as Rab-shakeh.*
the king of Assyria sent *R* from ... Is 36:2 7262
R said unto them, Say ye now to ... Is 36:4 7262
Eliakim and Shebna and Joah unto *R* ... Is 36:11 7262
But *R* said, Hath my master sent ... Is 36:12 7262
Then *R* stood, and cried with a ... Is 36:13 7262
rent, and told him the words of *R* ... Is 36:22 7262
thy God will hear the words of *R* ... Is 37:4 7262
So *R* returned, and found the king ... Is 37:8 7262

RACA *(ra'-cah)* {1} *A Jewish term of disrespect.*
shall say to his brother, *R* ... Mt 5:22 *4469*

RACAL See RACHAL.

RACE {4}
as a strong man to run a *r* ... Ps 19:5 734
that the *r* is not to the swift, ... Eccl 9:11 4793
they which run in a *r* run all ... 1Cor 9:24 *4712*
the *r* that is set before us ... Heb 12:1 *73*

RACHAB *(ra'kab)* {1} See RAHAB. *Same as Rahab; ancestor of Jesus.*
And Salmon begat Booz of *R* ... Mt 1:5 *4477*

RACHAL *(ra'-kal)* {1} *A city in Judah.*
And to them which were in *R* ... 1Sa 30:29 7403

RACHEL *(ra'-chel)* {42} See RACHEL'S, RAHEL. *Wife of Jacob.*
R his daughter cometh with the ... Gen 29:6 7354
R came with her father's sheep ... Gen 29:9 7354
when Jacob saw *R* the daughter of ... Gen 29:10 7354
And Jacob kissed *R*, and lifted up ... Gen 29:11 7354
Jacob told *R* that he was her ... Gen 29:12 7354
and the name of the younger was *R* ... Gen 29:16 7354
but *R* was beautiful and well ... Gen 29:17 7354
And Jacob loved *R* ... Gen 29:18 7354
years for *R* thy younger daughter ... Gen 29:18 7354
And Jacob served seven years for *R* ... Gen 29:20 7354
did not I serve with thee for *R* ... Gen 29:25 7354
he gave him *R* his daughter to ... Gen 29:28 7354
Laban gave to *R* his daughter ... Gen 29:29 7354
And he went in also unto *R* ... Gen 29:30 7354
he loved also *R* more than Leah, ... Gen 29:30 7354
but *R* was barren ... Gen 29:31 7354
when *R* saw that she bare Jacob no ... Gen 30:1 7354
no children, *R* envied her sister ... Gen 30:1 7354
anger was kindled against *R* ... Gen 30:2 7354
R said, God hath judged me, and ... Gen 30:6 7354
R said, With great wrestlings ... Gen 30:8 7354
Then *R* said to Leah, Give me, I ... Gen 30:14 7354
R said, Therefore he shall lie ... Gen 30:15 7354
And God remembered *R*, and God ... Gen 30:22 7354
when *R* had born Joseph, that ... Gen 30:25 7354
And Jacob sent and called *R* ... Gen 31:4 7354
And *R* and Leah answered and said ... Gen 31:14 7354
R had stolen the images that were ... Gen 31:19 7354
knew not that *R* had stolen them ... Gen 31:32 7354
Now *R* had taken the images, and ... Gen 31:34 7354
the children unto Leah, and unto *R* ... Gen 33:1 7354
Leah and her children after, and *R* ... Gen 33:2 7354
and after came Joseph near and *R* ... Gen 33:7 7354
R travailed, and she had hard ... Gen 35:16 7354
R died, and was buried in the way ... Gen 35:19 7354
The sons of *R* ... Gen 35:24 7354
The sons of *R* Jacob's wife ... Gen 46:19 7354
These are the sons of *R*, which ... Gen 46:22 7354
Laban gave unto *R* his daughter ... Gen 46:25 7354
R died by me in the land of ... Gen 48:7 7354
is come into thine house like *R* ... Ruth 4:11 7354
R weeping for her children, and ... Mt 2:18 *4478*

RACHEL'S *(ra'-chelz)* {5}
Bilhah *R* maid conceived again, and ... Gen 30:7 7354
tent, and entered into *R* tent ... Gen 31:33 7354
pillar of *R* grave unto this day ... Gen 35:20 7354
And the sons of Bilhah, *R* handmaid ... Gen 35:25 7354
by *R* sepulchre in the border of ... 1Sa 10:2 7354

RADDAI *(rad'-dahee)* {1} *Son of Jesse.*
the fourth, *R* the fifth, ... 1Chr 2:14 7288

RAFTERS {1}
house are cedar, and our *r* of fir ... Song 1:17 7351

RAGAU *(ra'-gaw)* {1} See REU. *Father of Saruch; ancestor of Jesus.*
of Saruch, which was the son of *R* ... Lk 3:35 *4466*

RAGE {18}
So he turned and went away in a *r* ... 2Kin 5:12 2534
coming in, and thy *r* against me ... 2Kin 19:27 7264
Because thy *r* against me and thy ... 2Kin 19:28 7264
for he was in a *r* with him ... 2Chr 16:10 2197
ye have slain them in a *r* that ... 2Chr 28:9 2197
the ground with fierceness and *r* ... Job 39:24 7267
Cast abroad the *r* of thy wrath ... Job 40:11 5678
Why do the heathen *r*, and the ... Ps 2:1 7283
because of the *r* of mine enemies ... Ps 7:6 5678
For jealousy is the *r* of a man ... Prov 6:34 2534
man, whether he *r* or laugh ... Prov 29:9 7264
coming in, and thy *r* against me ... Is 37:28 7264
Because thy *r* against me, and thy ... Is 37:29 7264
and *r*, ye chariots ... Jer 46:9 1984
Then Nebuchadnezzar in his *r* ... Dan 3:13 7266
sword for the *r* of their tongue ... Hos 7:16 2195
chariots shall *r* in the streets ... Nah 2:4 1984
hast said, Why did the heathen *r* ... Acts 4:25 *5433*

RAGED {1}
The heathen *r*, the kingdoms were ... Ps 46:6 1993

RAGETH {1}
but the fool *r*, and is confident ... Prov 14:16 5674

RAGGED {1}
and into the tops of the *r* rocks ... Is 2:21

RAGING {5}
Thou rulest the *r* of the sea ... Ps 89:9 1348
is a mocker, strong drink is *r* ... Prov 20:1 1993
and the sea ceased from her *r* ... Jonah 1:15 2197
the wind and the *r* of the water ... Lk 8:24 *2830*
R waves of the sea, foaming out ... Jude 13 *66*

RAGS {4}
shall clothe a man with *r* ... Prov 23:21 7168
righteousnesses are as filthy *r* ... Is 64:6 899
old cast clouts and old rotten *r* ... Jer 38:11 4418
rotten *r* under thine armholes ... Jer 38:12 4418

RAGUEL *(ra-gu'-el)* {1} *Father-in-law of Moses.*
the son of *R* the Midianite, ... Num 10:29 7467

RAHAB *(ra'-hab)* {10} See RACHAB.
1. A Jericho woman who befriended the spies.
into an harlot's house, named *R* ... Josh 2:1 7343
the king of Jericho sent unto *R* ... Josh 2:3 7343
only *R* the harlot shall live, she ... Josh 6:17 7343
spies went in, and brought out *R* ... Josh 6:23 7343
Joshua saved *R* the harlot alive, ... Josh 6:25 7343
By faith the harlot *R* perished ... Heb 11:31 *4460*
Likewise also was not *R* the ... Jas 2:25 *4460*
2. A symbolic name for Egypt.
I will make mention of *R* and ... Ps 87:4 7294
Thou hast broken *R* in pieces ... Ps 89:10 7294
Art thou not it that hath cut *R* ... Is 51:9 7294

RAHAM *(ra'-ham)* {1} *Son of Shema.*
And Shema begat *R*, the father of ... 1Chr 2:44 7357

RAHEL *(ra'-hel)* {1} See RACHEL. *Same as Rachel.*
R weeping for her children ... Jer 31:15 7354

RAIL {1}
He wrote also letters to *r* on the ... 2Chr 32:17 2778

RAILED {3}
and he *r* on them ... 1Sa 25:14 5860
And they that passed by *r* on him ... Mk 15:29 *987*
which were hanged *r* on him ... Lk 23:39 *987*

RAILER {1}
covetous, or an idolater, or a *r* ... 1Cor 5:11 *3060*

RAILING {4}
evil for evil, or *r* for *r* ... 1Pet 3:9 *3059*
bring not *r* accusation against ... 2Pet 2:11 *989*
bring against him a *r* accusation ... Jude 9 *988*

RAILINGS {1}
whereof cometh envy, strife, *r* ... 1Ti 6:4 *988*

RAIMENT {57}
silver, and jewels of gold, and *r* ... Gen 24:53 899
Rebekah took goodly *r* of her ... Gen 27:15 899
and he smelled the smell of his *r* ... Gen 27:27 899
me bread to eat, and *r* to put on, ... Gen 28:20 899
shaved himself, and changed his *r* ... Gen 41:14 8071
he gave each man changes of *r* ... Gen 45:22 8071
of silver, and five changes of *r* ... Gen 45:22 8071
silver, and jewels of gold, and *r* ... Ex 3:22 8071
silver, and jewels of gold, and *r* ... Ex 12:35 8071
her food, her *r*, and her duty of ... Ex 21:10 3682
for ox, for ass, for sheep, for *r* ... Ex 22:9 8008
take thy neighbour's *r* to pledge ... Ex 22:26 8008
only, it is his *r* for his skin ... Ex 22:27 8071
it be any vessel of wood, or *r* ... Lev 11:32 899
And purify all your *r*, and all that ... Num 31:20 899
Thy *r* waxed not old upon thee, ... Deut 8:4 8071
stranger, in giving him food and *r* ... Deut 10:18 8071
she shall put the *r* of her ... Deut 21:13 8071
and so shalt thou do with his *r* ... Deut 22:3 8071
that he may sleep in his own *r* ... Deut 24:13 8008
nor take a widow's *r* to pledge ... Deut 24:17 899
and with iron, and with very much *r* ... Josh 22:8 8008
under his *r* upon his right thigh ... Judg 3:16 4055
purple *r* that was on the kings of ... Judg 8:26 899
put thy *r* upon thee, and get thee ... Ruth 3:3 8071
himself, and put on other *r* ... 1Sa 28:8 899
of gold, and ten changes of *r* ... 2Kin 5:5 899
thence silver, and gold, and *r* ... 2Kin 7:8 899
silver, and vessels of gold, and *r* ... 2Chr 9:24 8008
she sent *r* to clothe Mordecai, and ... Est 4:4 899
dust, and prepare *r* as the clay ... Job 27:16 4403
unto the king in *r* of needlework ... Ps 45:14 7553
as the *r* of those that are slain, ... Is 14:19 3830
and I will stain all my *r* ... Is 63:3 4403
thy *r* was of fine linen, and silk, ... Eze 16:13 4403
will clothe thee with change of *r* ... Zec 3:4 4254
John had his *r* of camel's hair ... Mt 3:4 *1742*
than meat, and the body than *r* ... Mt 6:25 *1742*
And why take ye thought for *r* ... Mt 6:28 *1742*
A man clothed in soft *r* ... Mt 11:8 *2440*
his *r* was white as the light ... Mt 17:2 *2440*
from him, and put his own *r* on him ... Mt 27:31 *2440*
lightning, and his *r* white as snow ... Mt 28:3 *1742*
his *r* became shining, exceeding ... Mk 9:3 *2440*
A man clothed in soft *r* ... Lk 7:25 *2440*
his *r* was white and glistering ... Lk 9:29 *2441*
which stripped him of his *r* ... Lk 10:30 *2441*
meat, and the body is more than *r* ... Lk 12:23 *1742*
And they parted his *r*, and cast ... Lk 23:34 *2440*
They parted my *r* among them ... Jn 19:24 *2440*
and blasphemed, he shook his *r* ... Acts 18:6 *2440*
kept the *r* of them that slew him ... Acts 22:20 *2440*
r let us be therewith content ... 1Ti 6:8 *4629*
come in also a poor man in vile *r* ... Jas 2:2 *2066*
same shall be clothed in white *r* ... Rev 3:5 *2440*
and white *r*, that thou mayest be ... Rev 3:18 *2440*
sitting, clothed in white *r* ... Rev 4:4 *2440*

RAIN {104}
not caused it to *r* upon the earth ... Gen 2:5 4305
I will cause it to *r* upon the ... Gen 7:4 4305
the *r* was upon the earth forty ... Gen 7:12 1653
the *r* from heaven was restrained ... Gen 8:2 1653
it to *r* a very grievous hail ... Ex 9:18 4305
the *r* was not poured upon the ... Ex 9:33 4306
And when Pharaoh saw that the *r* ... Ex 9:34 4306
I will *r* bread from heaven for ... Ex 16:4 4305
I will give you *r* in due season ... Lev 26:4 1653
drinketh water of the *r* of heaven ... Deut 11:11 4306
That I will give you the *r* of ... Deut 11:14 4306
in his due season, the first *r* ... Deut 11:14 4456
and the latter *r* ... Deut 11:14 3138
up the heaven, that there be no *r* ... Deut 11:17 4306
the heaven to give the *r* unto thy ... Deut 28:12 4306
make the *r* of thy land powder ... Deut 28:24 4306
My doctrine shall drop as the *r* ... Deut 32:2 4306
as the small *r* upon the tender ... Deut 32:2 8164
and he shall send thunder and *r* ... 1Sa 12:17 4306
LORD sent thunder and *r* that day ... 1Sa 12:18 4306
be no dew, neither let there be *r* ... 2Sa 1:21 4306
earth by clear shining after *r* ... 2Sa 23:4 4306
is shut up, and there is no *r* ... 1Kin 8:35 4306
give *r* upon thy land, which thou ... 1Kin 8:36 4306
not be dew nor *r* these years ... 1Kin 17:1 4306
there had been no *r* in the land ... 1Kin 17:7 1653
the LORD sendeth *r* upon the earth ... 1Kin 17:14 1653
I will send *r* upon the earth ... 1Kin 18:1 4306
is a sound of abundance of *r* ... 1Kin 18:41 1653
down, that the *r* stop thee not ... 1Kin 18:44 1653
and wind, and there was a great *r* ... 1Kin 18:45 1653
see wind, neither shall ye see *r* ... 2Kin 3:17 1653
is shut up, and there is no *r* ... 2Chr 6:26 4306
send *r* upon thy land, which thou ... 2Chr 6:27 4306
shut up heaven that there be no *r* ... 2Chr 7:13 4306
this matter, and for the great *r* ... Ezr 10:9 1653
many, and it is a time of much *r* ... Ezr 10:13 1653
Who giveth *r* upon the earth, and ... Job 5:10 4306
shall *r* it upon him while he is ... Job 20:23 4305
When he made a decree for the *r* ... Job 28:26 4306
they waited for me as for the *r* ... Job 29:23 4306
mouth wide as for the latter *r* ... Job 29:23 4456
they pour down *r* according to the ... Job 36:27 4306
likewise to the small *r*, and to ... Job 37:6 1653
to the great *r* of his strength ... Job 37:6 1653
To cause it to *r* on the earth ... Job 38:26 4305
Hath the *r* a father ... Job 38:28 4306
Upon the wicked he shall *r* snares ... Ps 11:6 4305
O God, didst send a plentiful *r* ... Ps 68:9 1653
down like *r* upon the mown grass ... Ps 72:6 4306
the *r* also filleth the pools ... Ps 84:6 4175
He gave them hail for *r*, and ... Ps 105:32 1653
he maketh lightnings for the *r* ... Ps 135:7 4306
who prepareth *r* for the earth ... Ps 147:8 4306
is as a cloud of the latter *r* ... Prov 16:15 4456
is like clouds and wind without *r* ... Prov 25:14 1653
The north wind driveth away *r* ... Prov 25:23 1653
as *r* in harvest, so honour is not ... Prov 26:1 4306
sweeping *r* which leaveth no food ... Prov 28:3 4306
If the clouds be full of *r* ... Eccl 11:3 1653
nor the clouds return after the *r* ... Eccl 12:2 1653
is past, the *r* is over and gone ... Song 2:11 1653
for a covert from storm and from *r* ... Is 4:6 4306
that they *r* no *r* upon it ... Is 5:6 4305
that they *r* no *r* upon it ... Is 5:6 4306
shall he give the *r* of thy seed ... Is 30:23 4306
an ash, and the *r* doth nourish it ... Is 44:14 1653
For as the *r* cometh down, and the ... Is 55:10 1653
and there hath been no latter *r* ... Jer 3:3 4456
the LORD our God, that giveth *r* ... Jer 5:24 1653
he maketh lightnings with *r* ... Jer 10:13 4306
for there was no *r* in the earth ... Jer 14:4 1653
of the Gentiles that can cause *r* ... Jer 14:22 1653
he maketh lightnings with *r* ... Jer 51:16 4306
is in the cloud in the day of *r* ... Eze 1:28 1653
I will *r* upon him, and upon his ... Eze 38:22 4305
are with him, and overflowing *r* ... Eze 38:22 1653
and he shall come unto us as the *r* ... Hos 6:3 1653
latter and former *r* unto the earth ... Hos 6:3 3384
come and *r* righteousness upon you ... Hos 10:12 3384
given you the former *r* moderately ... Joel 2:23 4175
cause to come down for you the *r* ... Joel 2:23 1653
the former *r*, and the latter ... Joel 2:23 4175
the latter *r* in the first month ... Joel 2:23 4456
I have withholden the *r* from you ... Amos 4:7 1653
and I caused it to *r* upon one city ... Amos 4:7 4305
caused it not to *r* upon another ... Amos 4:7 4305
Ask ye of the LORD *r* in the time ... Zec 10:1 4306
in the time of the latter *r* ... Zec 10:1 4456
clouds, and give them showers of *r* ... Zec 10:1 4306
even upon them shall be no *r* ... Zec 14:17 4306
up, and come not, that have no *r* ... Zec 14:18
sendeth *r* on the just and on the ... Mt 5:45 *1026*
the *r* descended, and the floods ... Mt 7:25 *1028*
the *r* descended, and the floods ... Mt 7:27 *1028*
gave us *r* from heaven, and ... Acts 14:17 *5205*
one, because of the present *r* ... Acts 28:2 *5205*
in the *r* that cometh oft upon it ... Heb 6:7 *5205*
he receive the early and latter *r* ... Jas 5:7 *5205*
earnestly that it might not *r* ... Jas 5:17 *1026*
again, and the heaven gave *r* ... Jas 5:18 *5205*
that it *r* not in the days of ... Rev 11:6 *1026,5205*

RAINBOW {2}
there was a *r* round about the ... Rev 4:3 *2463*
a *r* was upon his head, and his ... Rev 10:1 *2463*

RAINED {9}
Then the LORD *r* upon Sodom ... Gen 19:24 4305
the LORD *r* hail upon the land of ... Ex 9:23 4305
had *r* down manna upon them to eat ... Ps 78:24 4305
He *r* flesh also upon them as dust ... Ps 78:27 4305
nor *r* upon in the day of ... Eze 22:24 1656
one piece was *r* upon, and the ... Amos 4:7 4305
piece whereupon it *r* not withered ... Amos 4:7 4305
Lot went out of Sodom it *r* fire ... Lk 17:29 *1026*
it *r* not on the earth by the ... Jas 5:17 *1026*

RAINY {1}
dropping in a very *r* day and a ... Prov 27:15 5464

RAISE {59}
her, and *r* up seed to thy brother ... Gen 38:8 6965
Thou shalt not *r* a false report ... Ex 23:1 5375
The LORD thy God will *r* up unto ... Deut 18:15 6965
I will *r* them up a Prophet from ... Deut 18:18 6965
r up unto his brother a name in ... Deut 25:7 6965
r thereon a great heap of stones, ... Josh 8:29 6965
to *r* up the name of the dead upon ... Ruth 4:5 6965
to *r* up the name of the dead upon ... Ruth 4:10 6965
I will *r* me up a faithful priest, ... 1Sa 2:35 6965
I will *r* up evil against thee out ... 2Sa 12:11 6965
to *r* him up from the earth ... 2Sa 12:17 6965
Moreover the LORD shall *r* him up ... 1Kin 14:14 6965

R

that I will *r* up thy seed after 1Chr 17:11 6965
who are ready to *r* up their Job 3:8 5782
r up their way against me, and Job 19:12 5549
they *r* up against me the ways of Job 30:12 5549
r me up, that I may requite them Ps 41:10 6965
shall *r* up a cry of destruction Is 15:5 5782
I will *r* forts against thee Is 29:3 6965
I will *r* up the decayed places Is 44:26 6965
to *r* up the tribes of Jacob Is 49:6 6965
thou shalt *r* up the foundations Is 58:12 6965
they shall *r* up the former Is 61:4 6965
that I will *r* unto David a Jer 23:5 6965
whom I will *r* up unto them Jer 30:9 6965
For, lo, I will *r* and cause to Jer 50:9 5782
and fall, and none shall *r* him up Jer 50:32 6965
I will *r* up against Babylon, and Jer 51:1 5782
I will *r* up thy lovers against Eze 23:22 5782
I will *r* up for them a plant of Eze 34:29 6965
in the third day he will *r* us up Hos 6:2 6965
I will *r* them out of the place Joel 3:7 5782
there is none to *r* her up Amos 5:2 6965
I will *r* up against you a nation, Amos 6:14 6965
In that day will I *r* up the Amos 9:11 6965
I will *r* up his ruins, and I will Amos 9:11 6965
then shall we *r* against him seven Mic 5:5 6965
and there are that *r* up strife Hab 1:3 5375
I *r* up the Chaldeans, that bitter Hab 1:6 6965
I will *r* up a shepherd in the Zec 11:16 6965
to *r* up children unto Abraham Mt 3:9 *1453*
r the dead, cast out devils Mt 10:8 *1453*
r up seed unto his brother Mt 22:24 *450*
r up seed unto his brother Mk 12:19 *1817*
to *r* up children unto Abraham Lk 3:8 *1453*
r up seed unto his brother Lk 20:28 *1817*
and in three days I will *r* it up Jn 2:19 *1453*
but should *r* it up again at the Jn 6:39 *450*
I will *r* him up at the last day Jn 6:40 *450*
I will *r* him up at the last day Jn 6:44 *450*
I will *r* him up at the last day Jn 6:54 *450*
he would *r* up Christ to sit on Acts 2:30 *450*
r up unto you of your brethren Acts 3:22 *450*
r up unto you of your brethren Acts 7:37 *450*
you, that God should *r* the dead Acts 26:8 *1453*
will also *r* up us by his own 1Cor 6:14 *1825*
Jesus shall *r* up us also by Jesus 2Cor 4:14 *1453*
that God was able to *r* him up Heb 11:19 *1453*
sick, and the Lord shall *r* him up Jas 5:15 *1453*

RAISED {85}
for this cause have I *r* thee up Ex 9:16 5975
whom he *r* up in their stead, them Josh 5:7 6965
they *r* over him a great heap of Josh 7:26 6965
Nevertheless the LORD *r* up judges Judg 2:16 6965
when the LORD *r* them up judges, Judg 2:18 6965
the LORD *r* up a deliverer to the Judg 3:9 6965
the LORD *r* them up a deliverer, Judg 3:15 6965
and the man who was *r* up on high 2Sa 23:1 6965
king Solomon *r* a levy out of all 1Kin 5:13 5927
of the levy which king Solomon *r* 1Kin 9:15 5927
r it up to the towers, and another 2Chr 32:5 5927
r it up a very great height, and 2Chr 33:14 1361
all them whose spirit God had *r* Ezr 1:5 5782
nor be *r* out of their sleep Job 14:12 5782
I *r* thee up under the apple tree Song 8:5 5782
it hath *r* up from their thrones Is 14:9 6965
they *r* up the palaces thereof Is 23:13 6209
Who *r* up the righteous man from Is 41:2 5782
I have *r* up one from the north, Is 41:25 5782
I have *r* him up in righteousness, Is 45:13 5782
a great nation shall be *r* from Jer 6:22 5782
a great whirlwind shall be *r* up Jer 25:32 5782
The LORD hath *r* us up prophets in Jer 29:15 6965
many kings shall be *r* up from the Jer 50:41 5782
the LORD hath *r* up the spirit of Jer 51:11 5782
it *r* up itself on one side, and it Dan 7:5 6966
I *r* up of your sons for prophets, Amos 2:11 6965
for he is *r* up out of his holy Zec 2:13 5782
r up thy sons, O Zion, against Zec 9:13 5782
Then Joseph being *r* from sleep Mt 1:24 *1326*
the deaf hear, the dead are *r* up Mt 11:5 *1453*
and be *r* again the third day Mt 16:21 *1453*
the third day he shall be *r* again Mt 17:23 *1453*
hath *r* up an horn of salvation Lk 1:69 *1453*
the deaf hear, the dead are *r* Lk 7:22 *1453*
be slain, and be *r* the third day Lk 9:22 *1453*
Now that the dead are *r*, even Lk 20:37 *1453*
dead, whom he *r* from the dead Jn 12:1 *1453*
whom he had *r* from the dead Jn 12:9 *1453*
r him from the dead, bare record Jn 12:17 *1453*
Whom God hath *r* up, having loosed Acts 2:24 *450*
This Jesus hath God *r* up, whereof Acts 2:32 *450*
whom God hath *r* from the dead Acts 3:15 *1453*
having *r* up his Son Jesus, sent Acts 3:26 *450*
whom God *r* from the dead, even by Acts 4:10 *1453*
The God of our fathers *r* up Jesus Acts 5:30 *1453*
Him God *r* up the third day, and Acts 10:40 *1453*
r him up, saying, Arise up Acts 12:7 *1453*
he *r* up unto them David to be Acts 13:22 *1453*
promise *r* unto Israel a Saviour Acts 13:23 *1453*
But God *r* him from the dead Acts 13:30 *1453*
in that he hath *r* up Jesus again Acts 13:33 *450*
that he *r* him up from the dead Acts 13:34 *450*
But he, whom God *r* again, saw no Acts 13:37 *1453*
r persecution against Paul and Acts 13:50 *1892*
in that he hath *r* him from the Acts 17:31 *450*
if we believe on him that *r* up Rom 4:24 *1453*
was *r* again for our justification Rom 4:25 *1453*
that like as Christ was *r* up from Rom 6:4 *1453*
Knowing that Christ being *r* from Rom 6:9 *1453*
to him who is *r* from the dead Rom 7:4 *1453*
But if the Spirit of him that *r* Rom 8:11 *1453*
he that *r* up Christ from the dead Rom 8:11 *1453*
same purpose have I *r* thee up Rom 9:17 *1825*
that God hath *r* him from the dead Rom 10:9 *1453*
And God hath both *r* up the Lord 1Cor 6:14 *1453*
of God that he *r* up Christ 1Cor 15:15 *1453*
whom he *r* not up, if so be that 1Cor 15:15 *1453*
rise not, then is not Christ *r* 1Cor 15:16 *1453*
And if Christ be not *r*, your faith 1Cor 15:17 *1453*
will say, How are the dead *r* up 1Cor 15:35 *1453*
it is *r* in incorruption 1Cor 15:42 *1453*
it is *r* in glory 1Cor 15:43 *1453*
it is *r* in power 1Cor 15:43 *1453*
it is *r* a spiritual body 1Cor 15:44 *1453*
the dead shall be *r* incorruptible 1Cor 15:52 *1453*
Knowing that he which *r* up the 2Cor 4:14 *1453*
Father, who *r* him from the dead Gal 1:1 *1453*
when he *r* him from the dead, and Eph 1:20 *1453*
hath *r* us up together, and made us Eph 2:6 *4891*
who hath *r* him from the dead Col 2:12 *1453*
whom he *r* from the dead, even 1Th 1:10 *1453*
r from the dead according to my 2Ti 2:8 *1453*
their dead *r* to life again Heb 11:35 *386*
that *r* him up from the dead, and 1Pet 1:21 *1453*

RAISER {1}
a *r* of taxes in the glory of the Dan 11:20 5674

RAISETH {8}
He *r* up the poor out of the dust, 1Sa 2:8 6965
When he *r* up himself, the mighty Job 41:25 7613
r the stormy wind, which lifteth Ps 107:25 5975
He *r* up the poor out of the dust, Ps 113:7 6965
r up all those that be bowed down Ps 145:14 2210
the LORD *r* them that are bowed Ps 146:8 2210
For as the Father *r* up the dead Jn 5:21 *1453*
but in God which *r* the dead 2Cor 1:9 *1453*

RAISING {2}
who ceaseth from *r* after he hath Hos 7:4 5872
neither *r* up the people, neither Acts 24:12 *4160,1999*

RAISINS {4}
corn, and an hundred clusters of *r* 1Sa 25:18 6778
of figs, and two clusters of *r* 1Sa 30:12 6778
bread, and an hundred bunches of *r* 2Sa 16:1 6778
cakes of figs, and bunches of *r* 1Chr 12:40 6778

RAKEM *(ra'-kem)* {1} *Son of Sheresh.*
and his sons were Ulam and *R* 1Chr 7:16 7552

RAKKATH *(rah'-kath)* {1} *A city in Naphtali.*
are Ziddim, Zer, and Hammath, *R* Josh 19:35 7557

RAKKON *(rak'-kon)* {1} *A city in Dan.*
And Me-jarkon, and *R*, with the Josh 19:46 7542

RAM *(ram)* {96}
1. Father of Aminadab.
And Hezron begat *R* Ruth 4:19 7410
and *R* begat Amminadab Ruth 4:19 7410
Jerahmeel, and *R*, and Chelubai 1Chr 2:9 7410
And *R* begat Amminadab 1Chr 2:10 7410
2. Son of Jerahmeel.
R the firstborn, and Bunah, and 1Chr 2:25 7410
the sons of *R* the firstborn of 1Chr 2:27 7410
3. Head of Elihu's family.
the Buzite, of the kindred of *R* Job 32:2 7410
4. Male sheep.
a *r* of three years old, and a Gen 15:9 352
behold behind him a *r* caught in a Gen 22:13 352
and Abraham went and took the *r* Gen 22:13 352
Thou shalt also take one *r* Ex 29:15 352
hands upon the head of the *r* Ex 29:15 352
And thou shalt slay the *r*, and thou Ex 29:16 352
And thou shalt cut the *r* in pieces Ex 29:17 352
burn the whole *r* upon the altar Ex 29:18 352
And thou shalt take the other *r* Ex 29:19 352
hands upon the head of the *r* Ex 29:19 352
Then shalt thou kill the *r* Ex 29:20 352
thou shalt take of the *r* the fat Ex 29:22 352
for it is a *r* of consecration Ex 29:22 352
of the *r* of Aaron's consecration Ex 29:26 352
of the *r* of the consecration, Ex 29:27 352
take the *r* of the consecration Ex 29:31 352
sons shall eat the flesh of the *r* Ex 29:32 352
a *r* without blemish out of the Lev 5:15 352
the *r* of the trespass offering Lev 5:16 352
he shall bring a *r* without Lev 5:18 352
a *r* without blemish out of the Lev 6:6 352
he brought the *r* for the burnt Lev 8:18 352
hands upon the head of the *r* Lev 8:18 352
And he cut the *r* into pieces Lev 8:20 352
burnt the whole *r* upon the altar Lev 8:21 352
other ram, the *r* of consecration Lev 8:22 352
hands upon the head of the *r* Lev 8:22 352
for of the *r* of consecration it Lev 8:29 352
a *r* for a burnt offering, without Lev 9:2 352
a *r* for peace offerings, to Lev 9:4 352
the *r* for a sacrifice of peace Lev 9:18 352
fat of the bullock and of the *r* Lev 9:19 352
and a *r* for a burnt offering Lev 16:3 352
one *r* for a burnt offering Lev 16:5 352
even a *r* for a trespass offering Lev 19:21 352
an atonement for him with the *r* Lev 19:22 352
beside the *r* of the atonement, Num 5:8 352
one *r* without blemish for peace Num 6:14 352
he shall offer the *r* for a Num 6:17 352
take the sodden shoulder of the *r* Num 6:19 352
One young bullock, one *r*, one Num 7:15 352
One young bullock, one *r*, one Num 7:21 352
One young bullock, one *r*, one Num 7:27 352
One young bullock, one *r*, one Num 7:33 352
One young bullock, one *r*, one Num 7:39 352
One young bullock, one *r*, one Num 7:45 352
One young bullock, one *r*, one Num 7:51 352
One young bullock, one *r*, one Num 7:57 352
One young bullock, one *r*, one Num 7:63 352
One young bullock, one *r*, one Num 7:69 352
One young bullock, one *r*, one Num 7:75 352
One young bullock, one *r*, one Num 7:81 352
Or for a *r*, thou shalt prepare Num 15:6 352
for one bullock, or for one *r* Num 15:11 352
on every altar a bullock and a *r* Num 23:2 352
upon every altar a bullock and a *r* Num 23:4 352
a bullock and a *r* on every altar Num 23:14 352
a bullock and a *r* on every altar Num 23:30 352
two young bullocks, and one *r* Num 28:11 352
mingled with oil, for one *r* Num 28:12 352
the third part of an hin unto a *r* Num 28:14 352
two young bullocks, and one *r* Num 28:19 352
and two tenth deals for a *r* Num 28:20 352
two young bullocks, one *r* Num 28:27 352
two tenth deals unto one *r* Num 28:28 352
one young bullock, one *r*, and Num 29:2 352
and two tenth deals for a *r* Num 29:3 352
one young bullock, one *r*, and Num 29:8 352
and two tenth deals to one *r* Num 29:9 352
deals to each *r* of the two rams Num 29:14 352
one bullock, one *r*, seven lambs Num 29:36 352
for the bullock, for the *r* Num 29:37 352
they offered a *r* of the flock for Ezr 10:19 352
a *r* out of the flock without Eze 43:23 352
a *r* out of the flock, without Eze 43:25 352
a bullock, and an ephah for a *r* Eze 45:24 352
blemish, and a *r* without blemish Eze 46:4 352
shall be an ephah for a *r* Eze 46:5 352
blemish, and six lambs, and a *r* Eze 46:6 352
a bullock, and an ephah for a *r* Eze 46:7 352
to a bullock, and an ephah to a *r* Eze 46:11 352
the river a *r* which had two horns Dan 8:3 352
I saw the *r* pushing westward, and Dan 8:4 352
he came to the *r* that had two Dan 8:6 352
I saw him come close unto the *r* Dan 8:7 352
against him, and smote the *r* Dan 8:7 352
in the *r* to stand before him Dan 8:7 352
deliver the *r* out of his hand Dan 8:7 352
The *r* which thou sawest having Dan 8:20 352

RAMA *(ra-mah)* {1} See RAMAH. *Same as Ramah 1.*
In *R* was there a voice heard, Mt 2:18 *4471*

RAMAH *(ra'-mah)* {36} See RAMA, RAMATH.
1. A city in Benjamin.
Gibeon, and *R*, and Beeroth, Josh 18:25 7414
palm tree of Deborah between *R* Judg 4:5 7414
all night, in Gibeah, or in *R* Judg 19:13 7414
went up against Judah, and built *R* 1Kin 15:17 7414
that he left off building of *R* 1Kin 15:21 7414
and they took away the stones of *R* 1Kin 15:22 7414
came up against Judah, and built *R* 2Chr 16:1 7414
that he left off building of *R* 2Chr 16:5 7414
they carried away the stones of *R* 2Chr 16:6 7414
The children of *R* and Gaba, six Ezr 2:26 7414
The men of *R* and Gaba, six hundred Neh 7:30 7414
Hazor, *R*, Gittaim, Neh 11:33 7414
R is afraid Is 10:29 7414
the guard had let him go from *R* Jer 40:1 7414
in Gibeah, and the trumpet in *R* Hos 5:8 7414
2. A city in Naphtali.
And then the coast turneth to *R* Josh 19:29 7414
And Adamah, and *R*, and Hazor, Josh 19:36 7414
3. A city in Ephraim.
and came to their house to *R* 1Sa 1:19 7414
And Elkanah went to *R* to his house 1Sa 2:11 7414
And his return was to *R* 1Sa 7:17 7414
and came to Samuel unto *R* 1Sa 8:4 7414
Then Samuel went to *R* 1Sa 15:34 7414
So Samuel rose up, and went to *R* 1Sa 16:13 7414
escaped, and came to Samuel to *R* 1Sa 19:18 7414
Behold, David is at Naioth in *R* 1Sa 19:19 7414
Then went he also to *R*, and came 1Sa 19:22 7414
Behold, they be at Naioth in *R* 1Sa 19:22 7414
And he went thither to Naioth in *R* 1Sa 19:23 7414
until he came to Naioth in *R* 1Sa 19:23 7414
And David fled from Naioth in *R* 1Sa 20:1 7414
abode in Gibeah under a tree in *R* 1Sa 22:6 7414
and buried him in his house at *R* 1Sa 25:1 7414
lamented him, and buried him in *R* 1Sa 28:3 7414
A voice was heard in *R*, Jer 31:15 7414
4. A short form of Ramoth-Gilead.
the Syrians had given him at *R* 2Kin 8:29 7414
wounds which were given him at *R* 2Chr 22:6 7414

RAMATH *(ra-math)* {1} *A city in Simeon.*
to Baalath-beer, *R* of the south Josh 19:8 7418

RAMATHAIM-ZOPHIM *(ram-a-tha'-im-zo'-fim)* {1} *A city on Mt. Ephraim.*
Now there was a certain man of *R* 1Sa 1:1 7436

RAMATHITE *(ra'-math-ite)* {1} *An inhabitant of Ramah 1.*
the vineyards was Shimei the *R* 1Chr 27:27 7435

RAMATH-LEHI *(ra'-math-le'-hi)* {1} *A place in Judah.*
his hand, and called that place *R* Judg 15:17 7437

RAMATH MIZPAH See RAMATH-MIZPEH.

RAMATH-MIZPEH *(ra'-math-miz'-peh)* {1} *A city in Gad.*
And from Heshbon unto *R*, and Josh 13:26 7434

RAMESES *(ram'-e-seze)* {4} See RAAMSES. *A city in Goshen.*
of the land, in the land of *R* ... Gen 47:11 7486
journeyed from *R* to Succoth ... Ex 12:37 7486
from *R* in the first month ... Num 33:3 7486
children of Israel removed from *R* ... Num 33:5 7486

RAMIAH *(ra'-mi-ah)* {1} *Married a foreigner while in exile.*
R, and Jeziah, and Malchiah, and ... Ezr 10:25 7422

RAMOTH *(ra'-moth)* {8} See JARMUTH, RAMAH, RAMOTH-GILEAD, REMETH.
1. A Levitical city in Gad.
R in Gilead, of the Gadites ... Deut 4:43 7216
R in Gilead out of the tribe of ... Josh 20:8 7216
R in Gilead with her suburbs, to ... Josh 21:38 7216
R in Gilead with her suburbs, and ... 1Chr 6:80 7216
2. A Levitical city in Issachar.
R with her suburbs, and Anem with ... 1Chr 6:73 7216
3. Married a foreigner in exile.
and Adaiah, Jashub, and Sheal, and *R* ... Ezr 10:29 3406
4. A city in Simeon.
and to them which were in south *R* ... 1Sa 30:27 7418
5. Same as Ramoth-gilead.
Know ye that *R* in Gilead is ours, ... 1Kin 22:3 7216

RAMOTH-GILEAD *(ra'-moth-ghil'-e-ad)* {19} *A city in Gad.*
The son of Geber, in *R* ... 1Kin 4:13 7433
thou go with me to battle to *R* ... 1Kin 22:4 7433
Shall I go against *R* to battle ... 1Kin 22:6 7433
prophesied so, saying, Go up to *R* ... 1Kin 22:12 7433
shall we go against *R* to battle ... 1Kin 22:15 7433
that he may go up and fall at *R* ... 1Kin 22:20 7433
the king of Judah went up to *R* ... 1Kin 22:29 7433
against Hazael king of Syria in *R* ... 2Kin 8:28 7433
of oil in thine hand, and go to *R* ... 2Kin 9:1 7433
young man the prophet, went to *R* ... 2Kin 9:4 7433
(Now Joram had kept *R*, he and all ... 2Kin 9:14 7433
him to go up with him to *R* ... 2Chr 18:2 7433
Judah, Wilt thou go with me to *R* ... 2Chr 18:3 7433
them, Shall we go to *R* to battle ... 2Chr 18:5 7433
prophesied so, saying, Go up to *R* ... 2Chr 18:11 7433
shall we go to *R* to battle ... 2Chr 18:14 7433
that he may go up and fall at *R* ... 2Chr 18:19 7433
the king of Judah went up to *R* ... 2Chr 18:28 7433
against Hazael king of Syria at *R* ... 2Chr 22:5 7433

RAMOTH NEGEV See RAMOTH-GILEAD.

RAMPART {2}
therefore he made the *r* and the ... Lam 2:8 2426
whose *r* was the sea, and her wall ... Nah 3:8 2426

RAM'S {1}
make a long blast with the *r* horn ... Josh 6:5 3104

RAMS {68}
the *r* which leaped upon the ... Gen 31:10 6260
all the *r* which leap upon the ... Gen 31:12 6260
the *r* of thy flock have I not ... Gen 31:38 352
two hundred ewes, and twenty *r* ... Gen 32:14 352
and two *r* without blemish, ... Ex 29:1 352
with the bullock and the two *r* ... Ex 29:3 352
and goats' hair, and red skins of *r* ... Ex 35:23 352
for the sin offering, and two *r* ... Lev 8:2 352
and one young bullock, and two *r* ... Lev 23:18 352
peace offerings, two oxen, five *r* ... Num 7:17 352
peace offerings, two oxen, five *r* ... Num 7:23 352
peace offerings, two oxen, five *r* ... Num 7:29 352
peace offerings, two oxen, five *r* ... Num 7:35 352
peace offerings, two oxen, five *r* ... Num 7:41 352
peace offerings, two oxen, five *r* ... Num 7:47 352
peace offerings, two oxen, five *r* ... Num 7:53 352
peace offerings, two oxen, five *r* ... Num 7:59 352
peace offerings, two oxen, five *r* ... Num 7:65 352
peace offerings, two oxen, five *r* ... Num 7:71 352
peace offerings, two oxen, five *r* ... Num 7:77 352
peace offerings, two oxen, five *r* ... Num 7:83 352
the *r* twelve, the lambs of the ... Num 7:87 352
the *r* sixty, the he goats sixty, ... Num 7:88 352
me here seven oxen and seven *r* ... Num 23:1 352
me here seven bullocks and seven *r* ... Num 23:29 352
thirteen young bullocks, two *r* ... Num 29:13 352
deals to each ram of the two *r* ... Num 29:14 352
twelve young bullocks, two *r* ... Num 29:17 352
for the bullocks, for the *r* ... Num 29:18 352
third day eleven bullocks, two *r* ... Num 29:20 352
for the bullocks, for the *r* ... Num 29:21 352
fourth day ten bullocks, two *r* ... Num 29:23 352
for the bullocks, for the *r* ... Num 29:24 352
fifth day nine bullocks, two *r* ... Num 29:26 352
for the bullocks, for the *r* ... Num 29:27 352
sixth day eight bullocks, two *r* ... Num 29:29 352
for the bullocks, for the *r* ... Num 29:30 352
seventh day seven bullocks, two *r* ... Num 29:32 352
for the bullocks, for the *r* ... Num 29:33 352
r of the breed of Bashan, and ... Deut 32:14 352
and to hearken than the fat of *r* ... 1Sa 15:22 352
lambs, and an hundred thousand *r* ... 2Kin 3:4 352
offered seven bullocks and seven *r* ... 1Chr 15:26 352
a thousand bullocks, a thousand *r* ... 1Chr 29:21 352
with a young bullock and seven *r* ... 2Chr 13:9 352
seven thousand and seven hundred *r* ... 2Chr 17:11 352
seven bullocks, and seven *r* ... 2Chr 29:21 352
when they had killed the *r* ... 2Chr 29:22 352
and ten bullocks, an hundred *r* ... 2Chr 29:32 352
of, both young bullocks, and *r* ... Ezr 6:9 1798
hundred bullocks, two hundred *r* ... Ezr 6:17 1798
with this money bullocks, *r* ... Ezr 7:17 1798
for all Israel, ninety and six *r* ... Ezr 8:35 352
you now seven bullocks and seven *r* ... Job 42:8 352
fatlings, with the incense of *r* ... Ps 66:15 352
The mountains skipped like *r* ... Ps 114:4 352
mountains, that ye skipped like *r* ... Ps 114:6 352
full of the burnt offerings of *r* ... Is 1:11 352
with the fat of the kidneys of *r* ... Is 34:6 352
the *r* of Nebaioth shall minister ... Is 60:7 352
slaughter, like *r* with he goats ... Jer 51:40 352
set battering *r* against it round ... Eze 4:2 3733
battering *r* against the gates ... Eze 21:22 3733
occupied with thee in lambs, and *r* ... Eze 27:21 352
cattle and cattle, between the *r* ... Eze 34:17 352
of the princes of the earth, of *r* ... Eze 39:18 352
seven *r* without blemish daily the ... Eze 45:23 352
be pleased with thousands of *r* ... Mic 6:7 352

RAMS' {9}
r skins dyed red, and badgers' ... Ex 25:5 352
for the tent of *r* skins dyed red ... Ex 26:14 352
r skins dyed red, and badgers' ... Ex 35:7 352
for the tent of *r* skins dyed red ... Ex 36:19 352
the covering of *r* skins dyed red ... Ex 39:34 352
the ark seven trumpets of *r* horns ... Josh 6:4 3104
of *r* horns before the ark of the ... Josh 6:6 3104
bearing the seven trumpets of *r* ... Josh 6:8 3104
bearing seven trumpets of *r* horns ... Josh 6:13 3104

RAN {61}
he *r* to meet them from the tent ... Gen 18:2 7323
Abraham *r* unto the herd, and ... Gen 18:7 7323
And the servant *r* to meet her ... Gen 24:17 7323
r again unto the well to draw ... Gen 24:20 7323
And the damsel *r*, and told them of ... Gen 24:28 7323
Laban *r* out unto the man, unto ... Gen 24:29 7323
and she *r* and told her father ... Gen 29:12 7323
that he *r* to meet him, and ... Gen 29:13 7323
Esau *r* to meet him, and embraced ... Gen 33:4 7323
the fire *r* along upon the ground ... Ex 9:23 1980
there *r* a young man, and told ... Num 11:27 7323
and *r* into the midst of the ... Num 16:47 7323
and they *r* unto the tent ... Josh 7:22 7323
and they *r* as soon as he had ... Josh 8:19 7323
and all the host *r*, and cried, and ... Judg 7:21 7323
And Jotham *r* away, and fled, and ... Judg 9:21 7323
the two other companies *r* upon ... Judg 9:44 6584
And the woman made haste, and *r* ... Judg 13:10 7323
he *r* unto Eli, and said, Here am I ... 1Sa 3:5 7323
there *r* a man of Benjamin out of ... 1Sa 4:12 7323
And they *r* and fetched him thence ... 1Sa 10:23 7323
r into the army, and came and ... 1Sa 17:22 7323
r toward the army to meet the ... 1Sa 17:48 7323
Therefore David *r*, and stood upon ... 1Sa 17:51 7323
And as the lad *r*, he shot an arrow ... 1Sa 20:36 7323
bowed himself unto Joab, and *r* ... 2Sa 18:21 7323
Then Ahimaaz *r* by the way of the ... 2Sa 18:23 7323
two of the servants of Shimei *r* ... 1Kin 2:39 1272
the water *r* round about the altar ... 1Kin 18:35 7323
r before Ahab to the entrance of ... 1Kin 18:46 7323
r after Elijah, and said, Let me, ... 1Kin 19:20 7323
the blood *r* out of the wound into ... 1Kin 22:35 3332
the brook that *r* through the ... 2Chr 32:4 7857
my sore *r* in the night, and ceased ... Ps 77:2 5064
they *r* in the dry places like a ... Ps 105:41 1980
that *r* down upon the beard, even ... Ps 133:2 3331
sent these prophets, yet they *r* ... Jer 23:21 7323
And the living creatures *r* ... Eze 1:14 7519
there *r* out waters on the right ... Eze 47:2 6379
r unto him in the fury of his ... Dan 8:6 7323
the whole herd of swine *r* ... Mt 8:32 *3729*
And straightway one of them *r* ... Mt 27:48 *5143*
when he saw Jesus afar off, he *r* ... Mk 5:6 *5143*
the herd *r* violently down a steep ... Mk 5:13 *3729*
r afoot thither out of all cities ... Mk 6:33 *4936*
r through that whole region round ... Mk 6:55 *4063*
And one *r* and filled a spunge full ... Mk 15:36 *5143*
the herd *r* violently down a steep ... Lk 8:33 *3729*
saw him, and had compassion, and *r* ... Lk 15:20 *5143*
he *r* before, and climbed up into a ... Lk 19:4 *4390*
Peter, and *r* unto the sepulchre ... Lk 24:12 *5143*
So they *r* both together ... Jn 20:4 *5143*
all the people *r* together unto ... Acts 3:11 *4936*
r upon him with one accord, ... Acts 7:57 *3729*
Philip *r* thither to him, and heard ... Acts 8:30 *4370*
the gate for gladness, but *r* in ... Acts 12:14 *1532*
r in among the people, crying out ... Acts 14:14 *1530*
moved, and the people *r* together ... Acts 21:30 *4890*
centurions, and *r* down unto them ... Acts 21:32 *2701*
seas met, they *r* the ship aground ... Acts 27:41 *2027*
r greedily after the error of ... Jude 11 *1632*

RANG {2}
shout, so that the earth *r* again ... 1Sa 4:5 1949
so that the city *r* again ... 1Kin 1:45 1949

RANGE {1}
The *r* of the mountains is his ... Job 39:8 3491

RANGES {4}
or *r* for pots, they shall be ... Lev 11:35 3600
and he that cometh within the *r* ... 2Kin 11:8 7713
Have her forth without the *r* ... 2Kin 11:15 7713
them, Have her forth of the *r* ... 2Chr 23:14 7713

RANGING {1}
As a roaring lion, and a *r* bear ... Prov 28:15 8264

RANK {6}
of corn came up upon one stalk, *r* ... Gen 41:5 1277
thin ears devoured the seven *r* ... Gen 41:7 1277
shall set forth in the second *r* ... Num 2:16
shall go forward in the third *r* ... Num 2:24
thousand, which could keep *r* ... 1Chr 12:33 5737
men of war, that could keep *r* ... 1Chr 12:38 4634

RANKS {4}
was against light in three *r* ... 1Kin 7:4 6471
was against light in three *r* ... 1Kin 7:5 6471
and they shall not break their *r* ... Joel 2:7 734
And they sat down in *r*, by ... Mk 6:40 *4237*

RANSOM {13}
then he shall give for the *r* of ... Ex 21:30 6306
a *r* for his soul unto the LORD ... Ex 30:12 3724
I have found a *r* ... Job 33:24 3724
then a great *r* cannot deliver ... Job 36:18 3724
nor give to God a *r* for him ... Ps 49:7 3724
He will not regard any *r* ... Prov 6:35 3724
The *r* of a man's life are his ... Prov 13:8 3724
shall be a *r* for the righteous ... Prov 21:18 3724
I gave Egypt for thy *r*, Ethiopia ... Is 43:3 3724
I will *r* them from the power of ... Hos 13:14 6299
and to give his life a *r* for many ... Mt 20:28 *3083*
and to give his life a *r* for many ... Mk 10:45 *3083*
Who gave himself a *r* for all ... 1Ti 2:6 *487*

RANSOMED {3}
the *r* of the LORD shall return, ... Is 35:10 6299
sea a way for the *r* to pass over ... Is 51:10 1350
r him from the hand of him that ... Jer 31:11 1350

RAPHA *(ra'-fah)* {2} See BETH-RAPHA, REPHAIAH.
1. Son of Benjamin.
Nohah the fourth, and *R* the fifth ... 1Chr 8:2 7498
2. A member of Saul's family.
R was his son, Eleasah his son, ... 1Chr 8:37 7498

RAPHAIN See RAPHA.

RAPHU *(ra'-fu)* {1} *A Benjamite spy sent to the Promised Land.*
of Benjamin, Palti the son of *R* ... Num 13:9 7505

RARE {1}
it is a *r* thing that the king ... Dan 2:11 3358

RASE {2}
R it, *r* it, even to the ... Ps 137:7 6168

RASH {2}
Be not *r* with thy mouth, and let ... Eccl 5:2 926
The heart also of the *r* shall ... Is 32:4 4116

RASHLY {1}
to be quiet, and to do nothing *r* ... Acts 19:36 *4312*

RASOR {1}
like a sharp *r*, working ... Ps 52:2 8593

RATE {5}
and gather a certain *r* every day ... Ex 16:4 1697
and mules, a *r* year by year ... 1Kin 10:25 1697
a daily *r* for every day, all the ... 2Kin 25:30 1697
Even after a certain *r* every day ... 2Chr 8:13 1697
and mules, a *r* year by year ... 2Chr 9:24 1697

RATHER See APPENDIX.

RATTLETH {1}
The quiver *r* against him, the ... Job 39:23 7439

RATTLING {1}
the noise of the *r* of the wheels ... Nah 3:2 7494

RAVEN {6}
And he sent forth a *r*, which went ... Gen 8:7 6158
Every *r* after his kind ... Lev 11:15 6158
And every *r* after his kind, ... Deut 14:14 6158
Who provideth for the *r* his food ... Job 38:41 6158
locks are bushy, and black as a *r* ... Song 5:11 6158
also and the *r* shall dwell in it ... Is 34:11 6158

RAVENING {5}
upon me with their mouths, as a *r* ... Ps 22:13 2963
like a roaring lion *r* the prey ... Eze 22:25 2963
are like wolves *r* the prey ... Eze 22:27 2963
but inwardly they are *r* wolves ... Mt 7:15 *727*
but your inward part is full of *r* ... Lk 11:39 *724*

RAVENOUS {3}
nor any *r* beast shall go up ... Is 35:9 6530
Calling a *r* bird from the east, ... Is 46:11 5861
unto the *r* birds of every sort ... Eze 39:4 5861

RAVENS {5}
the *r* to feed thee there ... 1Kin 17:4 6158
the *r* brought him bread and flesh ... 1Kin 17:6 6158
food, and to the young *r* which cry ... Ps 147:9 6158
the *r* of the valley shall pick it ... Prov 30:17 6158
Consider the *r* ... Lk 12:24 *2876*

RAVIN {2}
Benjamin shall *r* as a wolf ... Gen 49:27 2963
with prey, and his dens with *r* ... Nah 2:12 2966

RAVISHED {7}
be thou *r* always with her love ... Prov 5:19 7686
be *r* with a strange woman, and ... Prov 5:20 7686
Thou hast *r* my heart, my sister, ... Song 4:9 3823
thou hast *r* my heart with one of ... Song 4:9 3823
be spoiled, and their wives *r* ... Is 13:16 7693
They *r* the women in Zion, and the ... Lam 5:11 6031
the houses rifled, and the women *r* ... Zec 14:2 7693

RAW {7}
Eat not of it *r*, nor sodden at ... Ex 12:9 4995
there be quick *r* flesh in the ... Lev 13:10 2416
But when *r* flesh appeareth in him ... Lev 13:14 2416
the priest shall see the *r* flesh ... Lev 13:15 2416
for the *r* flesh is unclean ... Lev 13:15 2416
Or if the *r* flesh turn again, and ... Lev 13:16 2416
have sodden flesh of thee, but *r* ... 1Sa 2:15 2416

R

RAZOR {6}
shall no *r* come upon his head ... Num 6:5
no *r* shall come on his head ... Judg 13:5 4177
hath not come a *r* upon mine head ... Judg 16:17 4177
there shall no *r* come upon his ... 1Sa 1:11 4177
Lord shave with a *r* that is hired ... Is 7:20 8593
knife, take thee a barber's *r* ... Eze 5:1 8593

REACH See APPENDIX.

REACHED See APPENDIX.

REACHETH See APPENDIX.

REACHING See APPENDIX.

READ {70}
r in the audience of the people ... Ex 24:7 7121
he shall *r* therein all the days ... Deut 17:19 7121
thou shalt *r* this law before all ... Deut 31:11 7121
afterward he *r* all the words of ... Josh 8:34 7121
which Joshua *r* not before all the ... Josh 8:35 7121
king of Israel had *r* the letter ... 2Kin 5:7 7121
hand of the messengers, and *r* it ... 2Kin 19:14 7121
the book to Shaphan, and he *r* it ... 2Kin 22:8 7121
Shaphan *r* it before the king ... 2Kin 22:10 7121
which the king of Judah hath *r* ... 2Kin 22:16 7121
he *r* in their ears all the words ... 2Kin 23:2 7121
Shaphan *r* it before the king ... 2Chr 34:18 7121
have *r* before the king of Judah ... 2Chr 34:24 7121
he *r* in their ears all the words ... 2Chr 34:30 7121
us hath been plainly *r* before me ... Ezr 4:18 7123
letter was *r* before Rehum ... Ezr 4:23 7123
he *r* therein before the street ... Neh 8:3 7121
So they *r* in the book in the law ... Neh 8:8 7121
he *r* in the book of the law of ... Neh 8:18 7121
r in the book of the law of the ... Neh 9:3 7121
On that day they *r* in the book of ... Neh 13:1 7121
they were *r* before the king ... Est 6:1 7121
saying, *R* this, I pray thee ... Is 29:11 7121
saying, *R* this, I pray thee ... Is 29:12 7121
out of the book of the LORD, and *r* ... Is 34:16 7121
hand of the messengers, and *r* it ... Is 37:14 7121
Zephaniah the priest *r* this ... Jer 29:29 7121
r in the roll, which thou hast ... Jer 36:6 7121
also thou shalt *r* them in the ... Jer 36:6 7121
Then *r* Baruch in the book the ... Jer 36:10 7121
when Baruch *r* the book in the ... Jer 36:13 7121
hast *r* in the ears of the people ... Jer 36:14 7121
Sit down now, and *r* it in our ears ... Jer 36:15 7121
So Baruch *r* it in their ears ... Jer 36:15 7121
Jehudi *r* it in the ears of the ... Jer 36:21 7121
Jehudi had *r* three or four leaves ... Jer 36:23 7121
see, and shalt *r* all these words ... Jer 51:61 7121
Whosoever shall *r* this writing ... Dan 5:7 7123
but they could not *r* the writing ... Dan 5:8 7123
that they should *r* this writing ... Dan 5:15 7123
now if thou canst *r* the writing ... Dan 5:16 7123
yet I will *r* the writing unto the ... Dan 5:17 7123
Have ye not *r* what David did, ... Mt 12:3 *314*
Or have ye not *r* in the law ... Mt 12:5 *314*
and said unto them, Have ye not *r* ... Mt 19:4 *314*
have ye never *r*, Out of the mouth ... Mt 21:16 *314*
Did ye never *r* in the scriptures, ... Mt 21:42 *314*
have ye not *r* that which was ... Mt 22:31 *314*
Have ye never *r* what David did, ... Mk 2:25 *314*
have ye not *r* this scripture ... Mk 12:10 *314*
have ye not *r* in the book of ... Mk 12:26 *314*
sabbath day, and stood up for to *r* ... Lk 4:16 *314*
Have ye not *r* so much as this, ... Lk 6:3 *314*
This title then *r* many of the ... Jn 19:20 *314*
his chariot *r* Esaias the prophet ... Acts 8:28 *314*
heard him *r* the prophet Esaias, ... Acts 8:30 *314*
the scripture which he *r* was this ... Acts 8:32 *314*
which are *r* every sabbath day ... Acts 13:27 *314*
being *r* in the synagogues every ... Acts 15:21 *314*
Which when they had *r*, they ... Acts 15:31 *314*
the governor had *r* the letter ... Acts 23:34 *314*
than what ye *r* or acknowledge ... 2Cor 1:13 *314*
our hearts, known and *r* of all men ... 2Cor 3:2 *314*
unto this day, when Moses is *r* ... 2Cor 3:15 *314*
Whereby, when ye *r*, ye may ... Eph 3:4 *314*
when this epistle is *r* among you ... Col 4:16 *314*
cause that it be *r* also in the ... Col 4:16 *314*
that ye likewise *r* the epistle ... Col 4:16 *314*
be *r* unto all the holy brethren ... 1Th 5:27 *314*
to *r* the book, neither to look ... Rev 5:4 *314*

READEST {2}
how *r* thou ... Lk 10:26 *314*
Understandest thou what thou *r* ... Acts 8:30 *314*

READETH {4}
tables, that he may run that *r* it ... Hab 2:2 7121
stand in the holy place, (whoso *r* ... Mt 24:15 *314*
not, (let him that *r* understand ... Mk 13:14 *314*
Blessed is he that *r*, and they ... Rev 1:3 *314*

READINESS {3}
the word with all *r* of mind ... Acts 17:11 *4288*
that as there was a *r* to will ... 2Cor 8:11 *4288*
having in a *r* to revenge all ... 2Cor 10:6 *2092*

READING {6}
caused them to understand the *r* ... Neh 8:8 4744
r in the book the words of the ... Jer 36:8 7121
hast made an end of *r* this book ... Jer 51:63 7121
after the *r* of the law and the ... Acts 13:15 *320*
in the *r* of the old testament ... 2Cor 3:14 *320*
Till I come, give attendance to *r* ... 1Ti 4:13 *320*

READY {100}
Make *r* quickly three measures of ... Gen 18:6 4116
men home, and slay, and make *r* ... Gen 43:16 3559
they made *r* the present against ... Gen 43:25 3559
And Joseph made *r* his chariot ... Gen 46:29 631
he made *r* his chariot, and took ... Ex 14:6 631
they be almost *r* to stone me ... Ex 17:4 5750
be *r* against the third day ... Ex 19:11 3559
Be *r* against the third day ... Ex 19:15 3559
be *r* in the morning, and come up ... Ex 34:2 3559
But we ourselves will go *r* armed ... Num 32:17 2363
ye were *r* to go up into the hill ... Deut 1:41 1951
A Syrian *r* to perish was my ... Deut 26:5
from the city, but be ye all *r* ... Josh 8:4 3559
made *r* a kid, and unleavened cakes ... Judg 6:19
shall have made *r* a kid for thee ... Judg 13:15
of wine, and five sheep *r* dressed ... 1Sa 25:18
Behold, thy servants are *r* to do ... 2Sa 15:15
that thou hast no tidings *r* ... 2Sa 18:22 4672
was built of stone made *r* before ... 1Kin 6:7 8003
And Joram said, Make *r* ... 2Kin 9:21 631
And his chariot was made *r* ... 2Kin 9:21 631
that were *r* armed to the war ... 1Chr 12:23
eight hundred, *r* armed to the war ... 1Chr 12:24
had made *r* for the building ... 1Chr 28:2 3559
fourscore thousand *r* prepared for ... 2Chr 17:18
they made *r* for themselves ... 2Chr 35:14 3559
he was a *r* scribe in the law of ... Ezr 7:6 4106
but thou art a God *r* to pardon ... Neh 9:17
they should be *r* against that day ... Est 3:14 6264
that the Jews should be *r* against ... Est 8:13 6264
who are *r* to raise up their ... Job 3:8 6264
He that is *r* to slip with his ... Job 12:5 3559
day of darkness is *r* at his hand ... Job 15:23 3559
as a king *r* to the battle ... Job 15:24 6264
which are *r* to become heaps ... Job 15:28 6257
extinct, the graves are *r* for me ... Job 17:1
shall be *r* at his side ... Job 18:12 3559
that was *r* to perish came upon me ... Job 29:13
it is *r* to burst like new bottles ... Job 32:19
hath bent his bow, and made it *r* ... Ps 7:12 3559
they make *r* their arrow upon the ... Ps 11:2 3559
when thou shalt make *r* thine ... Ps 21:12 3559
For I am *r* to halt, and my sorrow ... Ps 38:17 3559
tongue is the pen of a *r* writer ... Ps 45:1 4106
Lord, art good, and *r* to forgive ... Ps 86:5
r to die from my youth up ... Ps 88:15
and those that are *r* to be slain ... Prov 24:11 4131
unto him that is *r* to perish ... Prov 31:6
of God, and be more *r* to hear ... Eccl 5:1 7138
were *r* to perish in the land of ... Is 27:13
be to you as a breach *r* to fall ... Is 30:13
shall be *r* to speak plainly ... Is 32:4 4116
The LORD was *r* to save me ... Is 38:20
saying, It is *r* for the sodering ... Is 41:7 2896
as if he were *r* to destroy ... Is 51:13 3559
the trumpet, even to make all *r* ... Eze 7:14 3559
Now if ye be *r* that at what time ... Dan 3:15 6263
For they have made *r* their heart ... Hos 7:6 7126
are killed, and all things are *r* ... Mt 22:4 *2092*
to his servants, The wedding is *r* ... Mt 22:8 *2092*
Therefore be ye also *r* ... Mt 24:44 *2092*
they that were *r* went in with him ... Mt 25:10 *2092*
and they made *r* the passover ... Mt 26:19 *2090*
there make *r* for us ... Mk 14:15 *2090*
and they made *r* the passover ... Mk 14:16 *2090*
The spirit truly is *r*, but the ... Mk 14:38 *4289*
to make *r* a people prepared for ... Lk 1:17 *2090*
unto him, was sick, and *r* to die ... Lk 7:2 *3195*
the Samaritans, to make *r* for him ... Lk 9:52 *2090*
Be ye therefore *r* also ... Lk 12:40 *2092*
for all things are now *r* ... Lk 14:17 *2092*
Make *r* wherewith I may sup, and ... Lk 17:8 *2090*
there make *r* ... Lk 22:12 *2090*
and they made *r* the passover ... Lk 22:13 *2090*
I am *r* to go with thee, both into ... Lk 22:33 *2092*
but your time is alway *r* ... Jn 7:6 *2092*
but while they made *r*, he fell ... Acts 10:10 *3903*
r to depart on the morrow ... Acts 20:7 *3195*
for I am *r* not to be bound only, ... Acts 21:13 *2093*
he come near, are *r* to kill him ... Acts 23:15 *2092*
and now are they *r*, looking for a ... Acts 23:21 *2092*
Make *r* two hundred soldiers to go ... Acts 23:23 *2090*
I am *r* to preach the gospel to ... Rom 1:15 *4289*
and declaration of your *r* mind ... 2Cor 8:19 *4288*
that Achaia was *r* a year ago ... 2Cor 9:2 *3903*
that, as I said, ye may be *r* ... 2Cor 9:3 *3903*
before, that the same might be *r* ... 2Cor 9:5 *2092*
line of things made *r* to our hand ... 2Cor 10:16 *2092*
third time I am *r* to come to you ... 2Cor 12:14 *2093*
r to distribute, willing to ... 1Ti 6:18 *2130*
For I am now *r* to be offered, and ... 2Ti 4:6 *4689*
to be *r* to every good work, ... Titus 3:1 *2092*
waxeth old is *r* to vanish away ... Heb 8:13 *1451*
through faith unto salvation *r* to ... 1Pet 1:5 *2092*
be *r* always to give an answer to ... 1Pet 3:15 *2092*
him that is *r* to judge the quick ... 1Pet 4:5 *2093*
for filthy lucre, but of a *r* mind ... 1Pet 5:2 *4289*
which remain, that are *r* to die ... Rev 3:2 *3195*
woman which was *r* to be delivered ... Rev 12:4 *3195*
and his wife hath made herself *r* ... Rev 19:7 *2090*

REAIA *(re-ah'-yah)* {1} *Grandfather of Beerah.*
his son, *R* his son, Baal his son, ... 1Chr 5:5 7211

REAIAH *(re-ah'-yah)* {3} See REAIA.
1. Son of Shobal.
R the son of Shobal begat Jahath ... 1Chr 4:2 7211
2. A family of exiles.
of Gahar, the children of *R* ... Ezr 2:47 7211
The children of *R*, the children ... Neh 7:50 7211

REALM {7}
So the *r* of Jehoshaphat was quiet ... 2Chr 20:30 4438
his priests and Levites, in my *r* ... Ezr 7:13 4437
wrath against the *r* of the king ... Ezr 7:23 4437
that were in all his *r* ... Dan 1:20 4438
to set him over the whole *r* ... Dan 6:3 4437
king over the *r* of the Chaldeans ... Dan 9:1 4438
up all against the *r* of Grecia ... Dan 11:2 4438

REAP {32}
when ye *r* the harvest of your ... Lev 19:9 7114
thou shalt not wholly *r* the ... Lev 19:9
shall *r* the harvest thereof, then ... Lev 23:10 7114
when ye *r* the harvest of your ... Lev 23:22 7114
of thy harvest thou shalt not *r* ... Lev 25:5 7114
neither *r* that which groweth of ... Lev 25:11 7114
be on the field that they do *r* ... Ruth 2:9 7114
to *r* his harvest, and to make his ... 1Sa 8:12 7114
and in the third year sow ye, and *r* ... 2Kin 19:29 7114
and sow wickedness, *r* the same ... Job 4:8 7114
They *r* every one his corn in the ... Job 24:6 7114
that sow in tears shall *r* in joy ... Ps 126:5 7114
soweth iniquity shall *r* vanity ... Prov 22:8 7114
regardeth the clouds shall not *r* ... Eccl 11:4 7114
and in the third year sow ye, and *r* ... Is 37:30 7114
sown wheat, but shall *r* thorns ... Jer 12:13 7114
they shall *r* the whirlwind ... Hos 8:7 7114
in righteousness, *r* in mercy ... Hos 10:12 7114
shalt sow, but thou shalt not *r* ... Mic 6:15 7114
they sow not, neither do they *r* ... Mt 6:26 *2325*
that I *r* where I sowed not ... Mt 25:26 *2325*
for they neither sow nor *r* ... Lk 12:24 *2325*
I sent you to *r* that whereon ye ... Jn 4:38 *2325*
if we shall *r* your carnal things ... 1Cor 9:11 *2325*
sparingly shall *r* also sparingly ... 2Cor 9:6 *2325*
shall *r* also bountifully ... 2Cor 9:6 *2325*
man soweth, that shall he also *r* ... Gal 6:7 *2325*
shall of the flesh *r* corruption ... Gal 6:8 *2325*
of the Spirit *r* life everlasting ... Gal 6:8 *2325*
for in due season we shall *r* ... Gal 6:9 *2325*
cloud, Thrust in thy sickle, and *r* ... Rev 14:15 *2325*
the time is come for thee to *r* ... Rev 14:15 *2325*

REAPED {4}
wickedness, ye have *r* iniquity ... Hos 10:13 7114
who have *r* down your fields ... Jas 5:4 *270*
r are entered into the ears of ... Jas 5:4 *2325*
and the earth was *r* ... Rev 14:16 *2325*

REAPER {1}
the plowman shall overtake the *r* ... Amos 9:13 7114

REAPERS {9}
gleaned in the field after the *r* ... Ruth 2:3 7114
Beth-lehem, and said unto the *r* ... Ruth 2:4 7114
servant that was set over the *r* ... Ruth 2:5 7114
that was set over the *r* answered ... Ruth 2:6 7114
gather after the *r* among the ... Ruth 2:7 7114
And she sat beside the *r* ... Ruth 2:14 7114
went out to his father to the *r* ... 2Kin 4:18 7114
of harvest I will say to the *r* ... Mt 13:30 *2327*
and the *r* are the angels ... Mt 13:39 *2327*

REAPEST {2}
corners of thy field when thou *r* ... Lev 23:22 7114
r that thou didst not sow ... Lk 19:21 *2325*

REAPETH {4}
corn, and *r* the ears with his arm ... Is 17:5 7114
he that *r* receiveth wages, and ... Jn 4:36 *2325*
he that *r* may rejoice together ... Jn 4:36 *2325*
true, One soweth, and another *r* ... Jn 4:37 *2325*

REAPING {3}
they of Beth-shemesh were *r* their ... 1Sa 6:13 7114
r where thou hast not sown, and ... Mt 25:24 *2325*
not down, and *r* that I did not sow ... Lk 19:22 *2325*

REAR {4}
thou shalt *r* up the tabernacle ... Ex 26:30 6965
neither *r* you up a standing image ... Lev 26:1 6965
r an altar unto the LORD in the ... 2Sa 24:18 6965
wilt thou *r* it up in three days ... Jn 2:20 *1453*

REARED {10}
that the tabernacle was *r* up ... Ex 40:17 6965
Moses *r* up the tabernacle, and ... Ex 40:18 6965
bars thereof, and *r* up his pillars ... Ex 40:18 6965
he *r* up the court round about the ... Ex 40:33 6965
was *r* up the cloud covered the ... Num 9:15 6965
r up for himself a pillar, which ... 2Sa 18:18 5324
he *r* up an altar for Baal in the ... 1Kin 16:32 6965
he *r* up altars for Baal, and made ... 2Kin 21:3 6965
he *r* up the pillars before the ... 2Chr 3:17 6965
he *r* up altars for Baalim, and ... 2Chr 33:3 6965

REASON {71}
by *r* of that famine following ... Gen 41:31 6440
Canaan fainted by *r* of the famine ... Gen 47:13 6440
Israel sighed by *r* of the bondage ... Ex 2:23 4480
up unto God by *r* of the bondage ... Ex 2:23 4480
cry by *r* of their taskmasters ... Ex 3:7 6440
by *r* of the swarm of flies ... Ex 8:24 6440
be unclean by *r* of a dead body ... Num 9:10
given them by *r* of the anointing ... Num 18:8
ye shall bear no sin by *r* of it ... Num 18:32 5921
ye were afraid by *r* of the fire ... Deut 5:5 6440
that is not clean by *r* of ... Deut 23:10
old by *r* of the very long journey ... Josh 9:13
by *r* of them that oppressed them ... Judg 2:18
that I may *r* with you before the ... 1Sa 12:7 8199
this is the *r* of the levy which ... 1Kin 9:15 1697
his eyes were set by *r* of his age ... 1Kin 14:4
to minister by *r* of the cloud ... 2Chr 5:14 6440

by *r* of this great multitude ... 2Chr 20:15 6440
by *r* of the sickness day by day ... 2Chr 21:15 4480
fell out by *r* of his sickness ... 2Chr 21:19 5973
are blackish by *r* of the ice ... Job 6:16 4480
choose out my words to *r* with him ... Job 9:14
and I desire to *r* with God ... Job 13:3 3198
Should he *r* with unprofitable ... Job 15:3 3198
eye also is dim by *r* of sorrow ... Job 17:7
by *r* of his highness I could not ... Job 31:23
By *r* of the multitude of ... Job 35:9
they cry out by *r* of the arm of ... Job 35:9
order our speech by *r* of darkness ... Job 37:19 6440
by *r* of breakings they purify ... Job 41:25
I have roared by *r* of the ... Ps 38:8
by *r* of the enemy and avenger ... Ps 44:16 6440
man that shouteth by *r* of wine ... Ps 78:65
eye mourneth by *r* of affliction ... Ps 88:9 4480
if by *r* of strength they be ... Ps 90:10
By *r* of the voice of my groaning ... Ps 102:5
will not plow by *r* of the cold ... Prov 20:4
seven men that can render a *r* ... Prov 26:16 2940
the *r* of things, and to know the ... Eccl 7:25 2808
let us *r* together, saith the LORD ... Is 1:18 3198
narrow by *r* of the inhabitants ... Is 49:19
of branches by *r* of many waters ... Eze 19:10
terrors by *r* of the sword shall ... Eze 21:12 413
By *r* of the abundance of his ... Eze 26:10
Tarshish was thy merchant by *r* of ... Eze 27:12
Syria was thy merchant by *r* of ... Eze 27:16
thy wisdom by *r* of thy brightness ... Eze 28:17 5921
same time my *r* returned unto me ... Dan 4:36 4486
by *r* of the words of the king and ... Dan 5:10 6903
sacrifice by *r* of transgression ... Dan 8:12
I cried by *r* of mine affliction ... Jonah 2:2
by *r* of the multitude of men ... Mic 2:12
why *r* ye among yourselves, ... Mt 16:8 *1260*
Why *r* ye these things in your ... Mk 2:8 *1260*
it, he saith unto them, Why *r* ye ... Mk 8:17 *1260*
and the Pharisees began to *r* ... Lk 5:21 *1260*
them, What *r* ye in your hearts ... Lk 5:22 *1260*
the sea arose by *r* of a great ... Jn 6:18
Because that by *r* of him many of ... Jn 12:11 *1223*
It is not *r* that we should leave ... Acts 6:2 *701*
r would that I should bear with ... Acts 18:14 *3056*
but by *r* of him who hath ... Rom 8:20 *1223*
by *r* of the glory that excelleth ... 2Cor 3:10 *1752*
by *r* hereof he ought, as for the ... Heb 5:3 *1223*
even those who by *r* of use have ... Heb 5:14 *1223*
to continue by *r* of death ... Heb 7:23
to every man that asketh you a *r* ... 1Pet 3:15 *3056*
by *r* of whom the way of truth ... 2Pet 2:2 *1223*
by *r* of the other voices of the ... Rev 8:13 *1537*
by *r* of the smoke of the pit ... Rev 9:2 *1537*
in the sea by *r* of her costliness ... Rev 18:19 *1537*

REASONABLE {1}
unto God, which is your *r* service ... Rom 12:1 *3050*

REASONED {12}
they *r* among themselves, saying, ... Mt 16:7 *1260*
they *r* with themselves, saying, ... Mt 21:25 *1260*
that they so *r* within themselves ... Mk 2:8 *1260*
they *r* among themselves, saying, ... Mk 8:16 *1260*
they *r* with themselves, saying, ... Mk 11:31 *3049*
they *r* with themselves, saying, ... Lk 20:5 *4817*
they *r* among themselves, saying, ... Lk 20:14 *1260*
while they communed together and *r* ... Lk 24:15 *4802*
three sabbath days *r* with them ... Acts 17:2 *1256*
he *r* in the synagogue every ... Acts 18:4 *1256*
the synagogue, and *r* with the Jews ... Acts 18:19 *1256*
as he *r* of righteousness, ... Acts 24:25 *1256*

REASONING {5}
Hear now my *r*, and hearken to the ... Job 13:6 8433
there, and *r* in their hearts, ... Mk 2:6 *1260*
and having heard them *r* together ... Mk 12:28 *4802*
Then there arose a *r* among them ... Lk 9:46 *1261*
had great *r* among themselves ... Acts 28:29 *4803*

REASONS {2}
I gave ear to your *r*, whilst ye ... Job 32:11 8394
bring forth your strong *r* ... Is 41:21

REBA *(re'-bah)* {2} *A king of Midian.*
and Rekem, and Zur, and Hur, and *R* ... Num 31:8 7254
and Rekem, and Zur, and Hur, and *R* ... Josh 13:21 7254

REBECCA *(re-bek'-kah)* {1} See REBEKAH. *Greek form of Rebekah.*
but when *R* also had conceived by ... Rom 9:10 *4479*

REBEKAH *(re-bek'-kah)* {28} See REBECCA, REBEKAH'S. *Wife of Isaac.*
And Bethuel begat *R* ... Gen 22:23 7259
R came out, who was born to ... Gen 24:15 7259
R had a brother, and his name was ... Gen 24:29 7259
heard the words of *R* his sister ... Gen 24:30 7259
R came forth with her pitcher on ... Gen 24:45 7259
R is before thee, take her, and go ... Gen 24:51 7259
and raiment, and gave them to *R* ... Gen 24:53 7259
And they called *R*, and said unto ... Gen 24:58 7259
And they sent away *R* their sister ... Gen 24:59 7259
And they blessed *R*, and said unto ... Gen 24:60 7259
R arose, and her damsels, and they ... Gen 24:61 7259
and the servant took *R*, and went ... Gen 24:61 7259
R lifted up her eyes, and when she ... Gen 24:64 7259
mother Sarah's tent, and took *R* ... Gen 24:67 7259
years old when he took *R* to wife ... Gen 25:20 7259
of him, and *R* his wife conceived ... Gen 25:21 7259
but *R* loved Jacob ... Gen 25:28 7259
of the place should kill me for *R* ... Gen 26:7 7259
was sporting with *R* his wife ... Gen 26:8 7259
grief of mind unto Isaac and to *R* ... Gen 26:35 7259
R heard when Isaac spake to Esau ... Gen 27:5 7259
R spake unto Jacob her son, ... Gen 27:6 7259
And Jacob said to *R* his mother ... Gen 27:11 7259
R took goodly raiment of her ... Gen 27:15 7259
Esau her elder son were told to *R* ... Gen 27:42 7259
R said to Isaac, I am weary of my ... Gen 27:46 7259
the Syrian, the brother of *R* ... Gen 28:5 7259
they buried Isaac and *R* his wife ... Gen 49:31 7259

REBEKAH'S *(re-bek'-kahz)* {2}
brother, and that he was *R* son ... Gen 29:12 7259
But Deborah *R* nurse died, and she ... Gen 35:8 7259

REBEL {14}
Only *r* not ye against the LORD, ... Num 14:9 4775
doth *r* against thy commandment ... Josh 1:18 4784
that ye might *r* this day against ... Josh 22:16 4775
seeing ye *r* to day against the ... Josh 22:18 4775
but *r* not against the LORD ... Josh 22:19 4775
nor *r* against us, in building you ... Josh 22:19 4775
that we should *r* against the LORD ... Josh 22:29 4775
not *r* against the commandment of ... 1Sa 12:14 4784
but *r* against the commandment of ... 1Sa 12:15 4784
will ye *r* against the king ... Neh 2:19 4775
that thou and the Jews think to *r* ... Neh 6:6 4775
of those that *r* against the light ... Job 24:13 4775
But if ye refuse and *r*, ye shall ... Is 1:20 4784
and wine, and they *r* against me ... Hos 7:14 5493

REBELLED {34}
and in the thirteenth year they *r* ... Gen 14:4 4775
because ye *r* against my word at ... Num 20:24 4784
For ye *r* against my commandment ... Num 27:14 4784
but *r* against the commandment of ... Deut 1:26 4784
but *r* against the commandment of ... Deut 1:43 4784
then ye *r* against the commandment ... Deut 9:23 4784
So Israel *r* against the house of ... 1Kin 12:19 6586
Then Moab *r* against Israel after ... 2Kin 1:1 6586
that the king of Moab *r* against ... 2Kin 3:5 6586
king of Moab hath *r* against me ... 2Kin 3:7 6586
he *r* against the king of Assyria, ... 2Kin 18:7 4775
then he turned and *r* against him ... 2Kin 24:1 4775
that Zedekiah *r* against the king ... 2Kin 24:20 4775
Israel *r* against the house of ... 2Chr 10:19 6856
up, and hath *r* against his lord ... 2Chr 13:6 4775
And he also *r* against king ... 2Chr 36:13 4775
r against thee, and cast thy law ... Neh 9:26 4775
for they have *r* against thee ... Ps 5:10 4784
for they *r* not against his word ... Ps 105:28 4784
Because they *r* against the words ... Ps 107:11 4784
and they have *r* against me ... Is 1:2 6586
But they *r*, and vexed his holy ... Is 63:10 4784
that Zedekiah *r* against the king ... Jer 52:3 4775
for I have *r* against his ... Lam 1:18 4784
for I have grievously *r* ... Lam 1:20 4784
We have transgressed and have *r* ... Lam 3:42 4784
nation that hath *r* against me ... Eze 2:3 4775
But he *r* against him in sending ... Eze 17:15 4775
But they *r* against me, and would ... Eze 20:8 4784
But the house of Israel *r* against ... Eze 20:13 4784
the children *r* against me ... Eze 20:21 4784
and have done wickedly, and have *r* ... Dan 9:5 4775
though we have *r* against him ... Dan 9:9 4775
for she hath *r* against her God ... Hos 13:16 4784

REBELLEST {2}
trust, that thou *r* against me ... 2Kin 18:20 4775
trust, that thou *r* against me ... Is 36:5 4775

REBELLION {9}
For I know thy *r*, and thy stiff ... Deut 31:27 4805
if it be in *r*, or if in ... Josh 22:22 4779
For *r* is as the sin of witchcraft ... 1Sa 15:23 4805
against kings, and that *r* and ... Ezr 4:19 4776
in their *r* appointed a captain to ... Neh 9:17 4805
For he addeth *r* unto his sin ... Job 34:37 6588
An evil man seeketh only *r* ... Prov 17:11 4805
hast taught *r* against the LORD ... Jer 28:16 5627
he hath taught *r* against the LORD ... Jer 29:32 5627

REBELLIOUS {36}
ye have been *r* against the LORD ... Deut 9:7 4784
Ye have been *r* against the LORD ... Deut 9:24 4784
r son, which will not obey the ... Deut 21:18 4784
This our son is stubborn and *r* ... Deut 21:20 4784
ye have been *r* against the LORD ... Deut 31:27 4784
Thou son of the perverse *r* woman ... 1Sa 20:30 4780
unto Jerusalem, building the *r* ... Ezr 4:12 4779
know that this city is a *r* city ... Ezr 4:15 4779
let not the *r* exalt themselves ... Ps 66:7 5637
but the *r* dwell in a dry land ... Ps 68:6 5637
yea, for the *r* also, that the ... Ps 68:18 5637
a stubborn and *r* generation ... Ps 78:8 4784
Thy princes are *r*, and companions ... Is 1:23 5637
Woe to the *r* children, saith the ... Is 30:1 5637
That this is a *r* people, lying ... Is 30:9 4805
opened mine ear, and I was not *r* ... Is 50:5 4784
hands all the day unto a *r* people ... Is 65:2 5637
she hath been *r* against me ... Jer 4:17 4784
hath a revolting and a *r* heart ... Jer 5:23 4784
to a *r* nation that hath rebelled ... Eze 2:3 4775
forbear, (for they are a *r* house ... Eze 2:5 4805
looks, though they be a *r* house ... Eze 2:6 4805
for they are most *r* ... Eze 2:7 4805
Be not thou *r* like that ... Eze 2:8 4805
like that *r* house ... Eze 2:8 4805
looks, though they be a *r* house ... Eze 3:9 4805
for they are a *r* house ... Eze 3:26 4805
for they are a *r* house ... Eze 3:27 4805
in the midst of a *r* house ... Eze 12:2 4805
for they are a *r* house ... Eze 12:2 4805
though they be a *r* house ... Eze 12:3 4805
the *r* house, said unto thee, What ... Eze 12:9 4805
O *r* house, will I say the word, ... Eze 12:25 4805
Say now to the *r* house, Know ye ... Eze 17:12 4805
utter a parable unto the *r* house ... Eze 24:3 4805
And thou shalt say to the *r* ... Eze 44:6 4805

REBELS {3}
be kept for a token against the *r* ... Num 17:10 4805
he said unto them, Hear now, ye *r* ... Num 20:10 4784
purge out from among you the *r* ... Eze 20:38 4775

REBUKE {46}
shalt in any wise *r* thy neighbour ... Lev 19:17 3198
upon thee cursing, vexation, and *r* ... Deut 28:20 4045
she may glean them, and *r* her not ... Ruth 2:16 1605
day is a day of trouble, and of *r* ... 2Kin 19:3 8433
our fathers look thereon, and *r* it ... 1Chr 12:17 3198
r me not in thine anger, neither ... Ps 6:1 3198
world were discovered at thy *r* ... Ps 18:15 1606
O LORD, *r* me not in thy wrath ... Ps 38:1 3198
R the company of spearmen, the ... Ps 68:30 1605
At thy *r*, O God of Jacob, both ... Ps 76:6 1606
at the *r* of thy countenance ... Ps 80:16 1606
At thy *r* they fled ... Ps 104:7 1606
r a wise man, and he will love ... Prov 9:8 3198
but a scorner heareth not *r* ... Prov 13:1 1606
but the poor heareth not *r* ... Prov 13:8 1606
But to them that *r* him shall be ... Prov 24:25 3198
Open *r* is better than secret love ... Prov 27:5 8433
better to hear the *r* of the wise ... Eccl 7:5 1606
nations, and shall *r* many people ... Is 2:4 3198
but God shall *r* them, and they ... Is 17:13 1605
the *r* of his people shall he take ... Is 25:8 2781
shall flee at the *r* of one ... Is 30:17 1606
at the *r* of five shall ye flee ... Is 30:17 1606
day is a day of trouble, and of *r* ... Is 37:3 8433
at my *r* I dry up the sea, I make ... Is 50:2 1606
of the LORD, the *r* of thy God ... Is 51:20 1606
be wroth with thee, nor *r* thee ... Is 54:9 1605
his *r* with flames of fire ... Is 66:15 1606
for thy sake I have suffered *r* ... Jer 15:15 2781
shall be desolate in the day of *r* ... Hos 5:9 8433
r strong nations afar off ... Mic 4:3 3198
said unto Satan, The LORD *r* thee ... Zec 3:2 1605
that hath chosen Jerusalem *r* thee ... Zec 3:2 1605
I will *r* the devourer for your ... Mal 3:11 1605
Peter took him, and began to *r* him ... Mt 16:22 *2008*
Peter took him, and began to *r* him ... Mk 8:32 *2008*
trespass against thee, *r* him ... Lk 17:3 *2008*
unto him, Master, *r* thy disciples ... Lk 19:39 *2008*
the sons of God, without *r* ... Phil 2:15 *298*
R not an elder, but intreat him ... 1Ti 5:1 *1969*
Them that sin *r* before all ... 1Ti 5:20 *1651*
reprove, *r*, exhort with all ... 2Ti 4:2 *2008*
Wherefore *r* them sharply, that ... Titus 1:13 *1651*
exhort, and *r* with all authority ... Titus 2:15 *1651*
but said, The Lord *r* thee ... Jude 9 *2008*
As many as I love, I *r* and chasten ... Rev 3:19 *1651*

REBUKED {25}
my hands, and *r* thee yesternight ... Gen 31:42 3198
and his father *r* him, and said unto ... Gen 37:10 1605
I *r* the nobles, and the rulers, and ... Neh 5:7 7378
Thou hast *r* the heathen, thou ... Ps 9:5 1605
He *r* the Red sea also, and it was ... Ps 106:9 1605
Thou hast *r* the proud that are ... Ps 119:21 1605
arose, and *r* the winds and the sea ... Mt 8:26 *2008*
And Jesus *r* the devil ... Mt 17:18 *2008*
and the disciples *r* them ... Mt 19:13 *2008*
And the multitude *r* them, because ... Mt 20:31 *2008*
And Jesus *r* him, saying, Hold thy ... Mk 1:25 *2008*
r the wind, and said unto the sea, ... Mk 4:39 *2008*
he *r* Peter, saying, Get thee ... Mk 8:33 *2008*
he *r* the foul spirit, saying unto ... Mk 9:25 *2008*
his disciples *r* those that ... Mk 10:13 *2008*
And Jesus *r* him, saying, Hold thy ... Lk 4:35 *2008*
he stood over her, and *r* the fever ... Lk 4:39 *2008*
r the wind and the raging of the ... Lk 8:24 *2008*
Jesus *r* the unclean spirit, and ... Lk 9:42 *2008*
r them, and said, Ye know not what ... Lk 9:55 *2008*
his disciples saw it, they *r* them ... Lk 18:15 *2008*
And they which went before *r* him ... Lk 18:39 *2008*
But the other answering *r* him ... Lk 23:40 *2008*
nor faint when thou art *r* of him ... Heb 12:5 *1651*
But was *r* for his iniquity ... 2Pet 2:16 *2192,1649*

REBUKER {1}
I have been a *r* of them all ... Hos 5:2 4148

REBUKES {3}
When thou with *r* dost correct man ... Ps 39:11 8433
anger and in fury and in furious *r* ... Eze 5:15 8433
upon them with furious *r* ... Eze 25:17 8433

REBUKETH {4}
he that *r* a wicked man getteth ... Prov 9:7 3198
He that *r* a man afterwards shall ... Prov 28:23 3198
They hate him that *r* in the gate ... Amos 5:10 3198
He *r* the sea, and maketh it dry, ... Nah 1:4 1605

REBUKING {2}
at the *r* of the LORD, at the ... 2Sa 22:16 1606
he *r* them suffered them not to ... Lk 4:41 *2008*

RECALL {1}
This I *r* to my mind, therefore ... Lam 3:21 7725

RECEIPT {3}
sitting at the *r* of custom ... Mt 9:9 *5058*
sitting at the *r* of custom ... Mk 2:14 *5058*
Levi, sitting at the *r* of custom ... Lk 5:27 *5058*

RECEIVE {176}

to *r* thy brother's blood from thy	Gen 4:11	3947
then *r* my present at my hand	Gen 33:10	3947
to *r* his pledge from the woman's	Gen 38:20	3947
make his pans to *r* his ashes	Ex 27:3	1878
thou shalt *r* them of their hands,	Ex 29:25	3947
which ye *r* of the children of	Num 18:28	3947
mount to *r* the tables of stone	Deut 9:9	3947
every one shall *r* of thy words	Deut 33:3	5375
which thou shalt *r* of their hands	1Sa 10:4	3947
Though I should *r* a thousand	2Sa 18:12	8254
there, and thou shalt *r* them	1Kin 5:9	5375
little to *r* the burnt offerings	1Kin 8:64	3557
whom I stand, I will *r* none	2Kin 5:16	3947
Is it a time to *r* money	2Kin 5:26	3947
to *r* garments, and oliveyards, and	2Kin 5:26	3947
now therefore *r* no more money of	2Kin 12:7	3947
the priests consented to *r* no	2Kin 12:8	3947
not able to *r* the burnt offerings	2Chr 7:7	3557
shall we *r* good at the hand of	Job 2:10	6901
of God, and shall we not *r* evil	Job 2:10	6901
R, I pray thee, the law from his	Job 22:22	3947
they shall *r* of the Almighty	Job 27:13	3947
the LORD will *r* my prayer	Ps 6:9	3947
He shall *r* the blessing from the	Ps 24:5	5375
for he shall *r* me	Ps 49:15	3947
and afterward *r* me to glory	Ps 73:24	3947
When I shall *r* the congregation I	Ps 75:2	3947
To *r* the instruction of wisdom,	Prov 1:3	3947
My son, if thou wilt *r* my words	Prov 2:1	3947
Hear, O my son, and *r* my sayings	Prov 4:10	3947
R my instruction, and not silver	Prov 8:10	3947
wise in heart will *r* commandments	Prov 10:8	3947
r instruction, that thou mayest	Prov 19:20	6901
Should I *r* comfort in these	Is 57:6	5162
they have refused to *r* correction	Jer 5:3	3947
let your ear *r* the word of his	Jer 9:20	3947
might not hear, nor *r* instruction	Jer 17:23	3947
not hearkened to *r* instruction	Jer 32:33	3947
Will ye not *r* instruction to	Jer 35:13	3947
speak unto thee *r* in thine heart	Eze 3:10	3947
when thou shalt *r* thy sisters	Eze 16:61	3947
that ye shall *r* no more reproach	Eze 36:30	3947
ye shall *r* of me gifts and rewards	Dan 2:6	6902
Ephraim shall *r* shame, and Israel	Hos 10:6	3947
all iniquity, and *r* us graciously	Hos 14:2	3947
he shall *r* of you his standing	Mic 1:11	3947
fear me, thou wilt *r* instruction	Zeph 3:7	3947
shall not be room enough to *r* it	Mal 3:10	
And whosoever shall not *r* you	Mt 10:14	*1209*
shall *r* a prophet's reward	Mt 10:41	*2983*
shall *r* a righteous man's reward	Mt 10:41	*2983*
The blind *r* their sight, and the	Mt 11:5	*308*
And if ye will *r* it, this is Elias	Mt 11:14	*1209*
whoso shall *r* one such little	Mt 18:5	*1209*
All men cannot *r* this saying	Mt 19:11	*5562*
He that is able to *r* it	Mt 19:12	*5562*
let him *r* it	Mt 19:12	*5562*
shall *r* an hundredfold, and shall	Mt 19:29	*2983*
is right, that shall ye *r*	Mt 20:7	*2983*
in prayer, believing, ye shall *r*	Mt 21:22	*2983*
that they might *r* the fruits of	Mt 21:34	*2983*
therefore ye shall *r* the greater	Mt 23:14	*2983*
that there was no room to *r* them	Mk 2:2	*5562*
immediately *r* it with gladness	Mk 4:16	*2983*
r it, and bring forth fruit, some	Mk 4:20	*3858*
And whosoever shall not *r* you	Mk 6:11	*1209*
Whosoever shall *r* one of such	Mk 9:37	*1209*
and whosoever shall *r* me,	Mk 9:37	*1209*
Whosoever shall not *r* the kingdom	Mk 10:15	*1209*
But he shall *r* an hundredfold now	Mk 10:30	*2983*
Lord, that I might *r* my sight	Mk 10:51	*308*
ye pray, believe that ye *r* them	Mk 11:24	*2983*
servant, that he might *r* from the	Mk 12:2	*2983*
these shall *r* greater damnation	Mk 12:40	*2983*
lend to them of whom ye hope to *r*	Lk 6:34	*618*
to sinners, to *r* as much again	Lk 6:34	*618*
they hear, *r* the word with joy	Lk 8:13	*1209*
And whosoever will not *r* you	Lk 9:5	*1209*
Whosoever shall *r* this child in	Lk 9:48	*1209*
whosoever shall *r* me receiveth	Lk 9:48	*1209*
And they did not *r* him, because	Lk 9:53	*1209*
city ye enter, and they *r* you	Lk 10:8	*1209*
they *r* you not, go your ways out	Lk 10:10	*1209*
they may *r* me into their houses	Lk 16:4	*1209*
they may *r* you into everlasting	Lk 16:9	*1209*
Whosoever shall not *r* the kingdom	Lk 18:17	*1209*
Who shall not *r* manifold more in	Lk 18:30	*618*
said, Lord, that I may *r* my sight	Lk 18:41	*308*
Jesus said unto him, *R* thy sight	Lk 18:42	*308*
to *r* for himself a kingdom	Lk 19:12	*2983*
the same shall *r* greater	Lk 20:47	*2983*
for we *r* the due reward of our	Lk 23:41	*618*
and ye *r* not our witness	Jn 3:11	*2983*
and said, A man can *r* nothing	Jn 3:27	*2983*
But I *r* not testimony from man	Jn 5:34	*2983*
I *r* not honour from men	Jn 5:41	*2983*
my Father's name, and ye *r* me not	Jn 5:43	*2983*
in his own name, him ye will *r*	Jn 5:43	*2983*
which *r* honour one of another, and	Jn 5:44	*2983*
on the sabbath day *r* circumcision	Jn 7:23	*2983*
they that believe on him should *r*	Jn 7:39	*2983*
come again, and *r* you unto myself	Jn 14:3	*3880*
whom the world cannot *r*, because	Jn 14:17	*2983*
for he shall *r* of mine, and shall	Jn 16:14	*2983*
ask, and ye shall *r*, that your joy	Jn 16:24	*2983*
unto them, *R* ye the Holy Ghost	Jn 20:22	*2983*
But ye shall *r* power, after that	Acts 1:8	*2983*
ye shall *r* the gift of the Holy	Acts 2:38	*2983*
expecting to *r* something of them	Acts 3:5	*2983*
Whom the heaven must *r* until the	Acts 3:21	*1209*
saying, Lord Jesus, *r* my spirit	Acts 7:59	*1209*
that they might *r* the Holy Ghost	Acts 8:15	*2983*
hands, he may *r* the Holy Ghost	Acts 8:19	*2983*
on him, that he might *r* his sight	Acts 9:12	*308*
that thou mightest *r* thy sight	Acts 9:17	*308*
in him shall *r* remission of sins	Acts 10:43	*2983*
which are not lawful for us to *r*	Acts 16:21	*3858*
exhorting the disciples to *r* him	Acts 18:27	*588*
is more blessed to give than to *r*	Acts 20:35	*2983*
me, Brother Saul, *r* thy sight	Acts 22:13	*308*
for they will not *r* thy testimony	Acts 22:18	*3858*
that they may *r* forgiveness of	Acts 26:18	*2983*
they which *r* abundance of grace	Rom 5:17	*2983*
they that resist shall *r* to	Rom 13:2	*2983*
that is weak in the faith *r* ye	Rom 14:1	*4355*
Wherefore *r* ye one another, as	Rom 15:7	*4355*
That ye *r* her in the Lord, as	Rom 16:2	*4327*
every man shall *r* his own reward	1Cor 3:8	*2983*
thereupon, he shall *r* a reward	1Cor 3:14	*2983*
hast thou that thou didst not *r*	1Cor 4:7	*2983*
now if thou didst *r* it, why dost	1Cor 4:7	*2983*
that the church may *r* edifying	1Cor 14:5	*2983*
that every one may *r* the things	2Cor 5:10	*2865*
beseech you also that ye *r* not	2Cor 6:1	*1209*
and I will *r* you,	2Cor 6:17	*1523*
R us; we have wronged	2Cor 7:2	*5562*
that ye might *r* damage by us in	2Cor 7:9	*2210*
intreaty that we would *r* the gift	2Cor 8:4	*1209*
or if ye *r* another spirit, which	2Cor 11:4	*2983*
if otherwise, yet as a fool *r* me	2Cor 11:16	*1209*
that we might *r* the promise of	Gal 3:14	*2983*
that we might *r* the adoption of	Gal 4:5	*618*
the same shall he *r* of the Lord	Eph 6:8	*2865*
R him therefore in the Lord with	Phil 2:29	*4327*
that of the Lord ye shall *r* the	Col 3:24	*618*
r for the wrong which he hath	Col 3:25	*2865*
if he come unto you, *r* him	Col 4:10	*1209*
Against an elder *r* not an	1Ti 5:19	*3858*
thou therefore *r* him, that is,	Philem 12	*4355*
thou shouldest *r* him for ever	Philem 15	*568*
a partner, *r* him as myself	Philem 17	*4355*
of Levi, who *r* the office of the	Heb 7:5	*2983*
And here men that die *r* tithes	Heb 7:8	*2983*
might *r* the promise of eternal	Heb 9:15	*2983*
of God, ye might *r* the promise	Heb 10:36	*2865*
should after *r* for an inheritance	Heb 11:8	*2983*
he shall *r* any thing of the Lord	Jas 1:7	*2983*
he shall *r* the crown of life,	Jas 1:12	*2983*
r with meekness the engrafted	Jas 1:21	*1209*
knowing that we shall *r* the	Jas 3:1	*2983*
r not, because ye ask amiss, that	Jas 4:3	*2983*
until he *r* the early and latter	Jas 5:7	*2983*
ye shall *r* a crown of glory that	1Pet 5:4	*2865*
And shall *r* the reward of	2Pet 2:13	*2865*
we *r* of him, because we keep his	1Jn 3:22	*2983*
If we *r* the witness of men, the	1Jn 5:9	*2983*
but that we *r* a full reward	2Jn 8	*618*
r him not into your house,	2Jn 10	*2983*
We therefore ought to *r* such	3Jn 8	*618*
doth he himself *r* the brethren	3Jn 10	*1926*
to *r* glory and honour and power	Rev 4:11	*2983*
Lamb that was slain to *r* power	Rev 5:12	*2983*
to *r* a mark in their right hand,	Rev 13:16	*1325*
r his mark in his forehead, or in	Rev 14:9	*2983*
but *r* power as kings one hour	Rev 17:12	*2983*
that ye *r* not of her plagues	Rev 18:4	*2983*

RECEIVED {160}

r in the same year an hundredfold	Gen 26:12	4672
he *r* them at their hand, and	Ex 32:4	3947
they *r* of Moses all the offering,	Ex 36:3	3947
after that let her be *r* in again	Num 12:14	622
I have *r* commandment to bless	Num 23:20	3947
fathers, have *r* their inheritance	Num 34:14	3947
Manasseh have *r* their inheritance	Num 34:14	3947
the half tribe have *r* their	Num 34:15	3947
of the tribe whereunto they are *r*	Num 36:3	1961
of the tribe whereunto they are *r*	Num 36:4	1961
and the Gadites have *r* their	Josh 13:8	3947
had not yet *r* their inheritance	Josh 18:2	2505
have *r* their inheritance beyond	Josh 18:7	3947
would not have *r* a burnt offering	Judg 13:23	3947
or of whose hand have I *r* any	1Sa 12:3	3947
So David *r* of her hand that which	1Sa 25:35	3947
the king's merchants *r* the linen	1Kin 10:28	3947
Hezekiah *r* the letter of the hand	2Kin 19:14	3947
Then David *r* them, and made them	1Chr 12:18	6901
the king's merchants *r* the linen	2Chr 1:16	3947
and it *r* and held three thousand	2Chr 4:5	2388
and the priests *r* the blood	2Chr 29:22	6901
which they *r* of the hand of the	2Chr 30:16	
but he *r* it not	Est 4:4	6901
mine ear *r* a little thereof	Job 4:12	3947
thou hast *r* gifts for men	Ps 68:18	3947
looked upon it, and *r* instruction	Prov 24:32	3947
Hezekiah *r* the letter from the	Is 37:14	3947
for she hath *r* of the LORD's hand	Is 40:2	3947
they *r* no correction	Jer 2:30	3947
that hath not *r* usury nor	Eze 18:17	3947
she *r* not correction	Zeph 3:2	3947
freely ye have *r*, freely give	Mt 10:8	*2983*
This is he which *r* seed by the	Mt 13:19	*4687*
But he that *r* the seed into stony	Mt 13:20	*4687*
He also that *r* seed among the	Mt 13:22	*4687*
But he that *r* seed into the good	Mt 13:23	*4687*
they that *r* tribute money came to	Mt 17:24	*2983*
hour, they *r* every man a penny	Mt 20:9	*2983*
that they should have *r* more	Mt 20:10	*2983*
they likewise *r* every man a penny	Mt 20:10	*2983*
And when they had *r* it, they	Mt 20:11	*2983*
and immediately their eyes *r* sight	Mt 20:34	*308*
Then he that had *r* the five	Mt 25:16	*2983*
And likewise he that had *r* two	Mt 25:17	
But he that had *r* one went	Mt 25:18	*2983*
so he that had *r* five talents	Mt 25:20	*2983*
also that had *r* two talents came	Mt 25:22	*2983*
Then he which had *r* the one	Mt 25:24	*2983*
should have *r* mine own with usury	Mt 25:27	*2865*
be, which they have *r* to hold	Mk 7:4	*3880*
And immediately he *r* his sight	Mk 10:52	*308*
but he *r* it not	Mk 15:23	*2983*
he was *r* up into heaven, and sat	Mk 16:19	*353*
for ye have *r* your consolation	Lk 6:24	*568*
returned, the people gladly *r* him	Lk 8:40	*588*
he *r* them, and spake unto them of	Lk 9:11	*1209*
was come that he should be *r* up	Lk 9:51	*354*
named Martha *r* him into her house	Lk 10:38	*5264*
calf, because he hath *r* him safe	Lk 15:27	*618*
And immediately he *r* his sight	Lk 18:43	*308*
and came down, and *r* him joyfully	Lk 19:6	*5264*
having *r* the kingdom, then he	Lk 19:15	*2983*
his own, and his own *r* him not	Jn 1:11	*3880*
But as many as *r* him, to them	Jn 1:12	*2983*
And of his fulness have all we *r*	Jn 1:16	*2983*
He that hath *r* his testimony hath	Jn 3:33	*2983*
Galilee, the Galilaeans *r* him	Jn 4:45	*1209*
willingly *r* him into the ship	Jn 6:21	*2983*
and I went and washed, and I *r* sight	Jn 9:11	*308*
asked him how he had *r* his sight	Jn 9:15	*308*
r his sight, until they called	Jn 9:18	*308*
of him that had *r* his sight	Jn 9:18	*308*
commandment have I *r* of my Father	Jn 10:18	*2983*
He then having *r* the sop went	Jn 13:30	*2983*
and they have *r* them, and have	Jn 17:8	*2983*
having *r* a band of men and	Jn 18:3	*2983*
Jesus therefore had *r* the vinegar	Jn 19:30	*2983*
a cloud *r* him out of their sight	Acts 1:9	*5274*
having *r* of the Father the	Acts 2:33	*2983*
Then they that gladly *r* his word	Acts 2:41	*588*
feet and ancle bones *r* strength	Acts 3:7	*4732*
who *r* the lively oracles to give	Acts 7:38	*1209*
Who have *r* the law by the	Acts 7:53	*2983*
Samaria had *r* the word of God	Acts 8:14	*1209*
on them, and they *r* the Holy Ghost	Acts 8:17	*2983*
he *r* sight forthwith, and arose,	Acts 9:18	*308*
And when he had *r* meat, he was	Acts 9:19	*2983*
the vessel was *r* up again into	Acts 10:16	*353*
which have *r* the Holy Ghost as	Acts 10:47	*2983*
had also *r* the word of God	Acts 11:1	*1209*
they were *r* of the church, and of	Acts 15:4	*588*
having *r* such a charge, thrust	Acts 16:24	*2983*
Whom Jason hath *r*	Acts 17:7	*5264*
in that they *r* the word with all	Acts 17:11	*1209*
Have ye *r* the Holy Ghost since ye	Acts 19:2	*2983*
which I have *r* of the Lord Jesus,	Acts 20:24	*2983*
the brethren *r* us gladly	Acts 21:17	*1209*
from whom also I *r* letters unto	Acts 22:5	*1209*
having *r* authority from the chief	Acts 26:10	*2983*
r us every one, because of the	Acts 28:2	*4355*
who *r* us, and lodged us three days	Acts 28:7	*324*
We neither *r* letters out of	Acts 28:21	*1209*
r all that came in unto him,	Acts 28:30	*588*
By whom we have *r* grace and	Rom 1:5	*2983*
he *r* the sign of circumcision, a	Rom 4:11	*2983*
whom we have now *r* the atonement	Rom 5:11	*2983*
For ye have not *r* the spirit of	Rom 8:15	*2983*
but ye have *r* the Spirit of	Rom 8:15	*2983*
for God hath *r* him	Rom 14:3	*4355*
as Christ also *r* us to the glory	Rom 15:7	*4355*
Now we have *r*, not the spirit of	1Cor 2:12	*2983*
glory, as if thou hadst not *r* it	1Cor 4:7	*2983*
For I have *r* of the Lord that	1Cor 11:23	*3880*
unto you, which also ye have *r*	1Cor 15:1	*3880*
first of all that which I also *r*	1Cor 15:3	*3880*
this ministry, as we have *r* mercy	2Cor 4:1	*1653*
with fear and trembling ye *r* him	2Cor 7:15	*1209*
spirit, which ye have not *r*	2Cor 11:4	*2983*
Of the Jews five times *r* I forty	2Cor 11:24	*2983*
unto you than that ye have *r*	Gal 1:9	*3880*
For I neither *r* it of man	Gal 1:12	*3880*
R ye the Spirit by the works of	Gal 3:2	*2983*
but *r* me as an angel of God, even	Gal 4:14	*1209*
which ye have both learned, and *r*	Phil 4:9	*3880*
having *r* of Epaphroditus the	Phil 4:18	*1209*
As ye have therefore *r* Christ	Col 2:6	*3880*
(touching whom ye *r* commandments	Col 4:10	*2983*
which thou hast *r* in the Lord	Col 4:17	*3880*
having *r* the word in much	1Th 1:6	*1209*
when ye *r* the word of God which	1Th 2:13	*3880*
ye *r* it not as the word of men,	1Th 2:13	*1209*
that as ye have *r* of us how ye	1Th 4:1	*3880*
because they *r* not the love of	2Th 2:10	*1209*
the tradition which he *r* of us	2Th 3:6	*3880*
on in the world, *r* up into glory	1Ti 3:16	*353*
which God hath created to be *r*	1Ti 4:3	*3336*
if it be *r* with thanksgiving	1Ti 4:4	*2983*
disobedience *r* a just recompence	Heb 2:2	*2983*
from them *r* tithes of Abraham	Heb 7:6	*1183*
for under it the people *r* the law	Heb 7:11	*3549*
have *r* the knowledge of the truth	Heb 10:26	*2983*
r strength to conceive seed	Heb 11:11	*2983*
not having *r* the promises, but	Heb 11:13	*2983*
he that had *r* the promises	Heb 11:17	*324*

whence also he *r* him in a figure ... Heb 11:19 *2865*
when she had *r* the spies with ... Heb 11:31 *1209*
Women *r* their dead raised to life ... Heb 11:35 *2983*
through faith, *r* not the promise ... Heb 11:39 *2865*
when she had *r* the messengers, and ... Jas 2:25 *5264*
from your vain conversation *r* by ... 1Pet 1:18
As every man hath *r* the gift ... 1Pet 4:10 *2983*
For he *r* from God the Father ... 2Pet 1:17 *2983*
ye have *r* of him abideth in you ... 1Jn 2:27 *2983*
as we have *r* a commandment from ... 2Jn 4 *2983*
even as I *r* of my Father ... Rev 2:27 *2983*
therefore how thou hast *r* ... Rev 3:3 *2983*
which have *r* no kingdom as yet ... Rev 17:12 *2983*
that had *r* the mark of the beast ... Rev 19:20 *2983*
neither had *r* his mark upon their ... Rev 20:4

RECEIVEDST {1}
in thy lifetime *r* thy good things ... Lk 16:25 *618*

RECEIVER {1}
where is the *r* ... Is 33:18 8254

RECEIVETH {37}
is no man that *r* me to house ... Judg 19:18 622
or what *r* he of thine hand ... Job 35:7 3947
is instructed, he *r* knowledge ... Prov 21:11 3947
but he that *r* gifts overthroweth ... Prov 29:4
LORD their God, nor *r* correction ... Jer 7:28 3947
or *r* it with good will at your ... Mal 2:13 3947
For every one that asketh *r* ... Mt 7:8 *2983*
He that *r* you *r* me, and he ... Mt 10:40 *1209*
r me *r* him that sent me ... Mt 10:40 *1209*
He that *r* a prophet in the name ... Mt 10:41 *2983*
he that *r* a righteous man in the ... Mt 10:41 *2983*
the word, and anon with joy *r* it ... Mt 13:20 *2983*
such little child in my name *r* me ... Mt 18:5 *1209*
of such children in my name, *r* me ... Mk 9:37 *1209*
r not me, but him that sent me ... Mk 9:37 *1209*
this child in my name *r* me ... Lk 9:48 *1209*
receive me *r* him that sent me ... Lk 9:48 *1209*
For every one that asketh *r* ... Lk 11:10 *2983*
saying, This man *r* sinners ... Lk 15:2 *4327*
and no man *r* his testimony ... Jn 3:32 *2983*
And he that reapeth *r* wages ... Jn 4:36 *2983*
r not my words, hath one that ... Jn 12:48 *2983*
r whomsoever I send *r* me ... Jn 13:20 *2983*
r me *r* him that sent me ... Jn 13:20 *2983*
But the natural man *r* not the ... 1Cor 2:14 *1209*
race run all, but one *r* the prize ... 1Cor 9:24 *2983*
is dressed, *r* blessing from God ... Heb 6:7 *3335*
but there he *r* them, of whom it ... Heb 7:8
who *r* tithes, payed tithes in ... Heb 7:9 *2983*
and scourgeth every son whom he *r* ... Heb 12:6 *3858*
preeminence among them, *r* us not ... 3Jn 9 *1926*
man knoweth saving he that *r* it ... Rev 2:17 *2983*
whosoever *r* the mark of his name ... Rev 14:11 *2983*

RECEIVING {7}
in not *r* at his hands that which ... 2Kin 5:20 3947
r a commandment unto Silas and ... Acts 17:15 *2983*
r in themselves that recompence ... Rom 1:27 *618*
what shall the *r* of them be ... Rom 11:15 *4356*
with me as concerning giving and *r* ... Phil 4:15 *3028*
Wherefore we *r* a kingdom which ... Heb 12:28 *3880*
R the end of your faith, even the ... 1Pet 1:9 *2865*

RECHAB *(re'-kab)* {13} See RECHABITES.
1. A son of Rimmon.
and the name of the other *R* ... 2Sa 4:2 7394
sons of Rimmon the Beerothite, *R* ... 2Sa 4:5 7394
and *R* and Baanah his brother ... 2Sa 4:6 7394
And David answered *R* and Baanah ... 2Sa 4:9 7394
2. Founder of the Rechabites.
the son of *R* coming to meet him ... 2Kin 10:15 7394
went, and Jehonadab the son of *R* ... 2Kin 10:23 7394
for Jonadab the son of *R* our ... Jer 35:6 7394
R our father in all that he hath ... Jer 35:8 7394
The words of Jonadab the son of *R* ... Jer 35:14 7394
R have performed the commandment ... Jer 35:16 7394
Jonadab the son of *R* shall not ... Jer 35:19 7394
3. A descendant of Hemath.
the father of the house of *R* ... 1Chr 2:55 7394
4. Father of Malchiah.
repaired Malchiah the son of *R* ... Neh 3:14 7394

RECHABITES *(rek'-ab-ites)* {4} *Descendants of Rechab 2.*
Go unto the house of the *R* ... Jer 35:2 7397
sons, and the whole house of the *R* ... Jer 35:3 7397
house of the *R* pots full of wine ... Jer 35:5 7397
said unto the house of the *R* ... Jer 35:18 7397

RECHAH {1} *A family of Judah.*
These are the men of *R* ... 1Chr 4:12 7397

RECKON {8}
he shall *r* with him that bought ... Lev 25:50 2803
then the priest shall *r* unto him ... Lev 27:18 2803
Then the priest shall *r* unto him ... Lev 27:23 2803
and by name ye shall *r* the ... Num 4:32 6485
they shall *r* unto him seven days ... Eze 44:26 5608
And when he had begun to *r* ... Mt 18:24 *4868*
Likewise *r* ye also yourselves to ... Rom 6:11 *3049*
For I *r* that the sufferings of ... Rom 8:18 *3049*

RECKONED {22}
offering shall be *r* unto you ... Num 18:27 2803
shall not be *r* among the nations ... Num 23:9 2803
Beeroth also was *r* to Benjamin ... 2Sa 4:2 2803
Moreover they *r* not with the men ... 2Kin 12:15 2803
not to be *r* after the birthright ... 1Chr 5:1 3187
of their generations was *r* ... 1Chr 5:7 3187
All these were *r* by genealogies ... 1Chr 5:17 3187
r in all by their genealogies ... 1Chr 7:5 3187
were *r* by their genealogies ... 1Chr 7:7 3187
all Israel were *r* by genealogies ... 1Chr 9:1 3187
These were *r* by their genealogy ... 1Chr 9:22 3187
to all that were *r* by genealogies ... 2Chr 31:19 3187
those that were *r* by genealogy ... Ezr 2:62 3187
with him were *r* by genealogy of ... Ezr 8:3 3187
that they might be *r* by genealogy ... Neh 7:5 3187
those that were *r* by genealogy ... Neh 7:64 3187
they cannot be *r* up in order unto ... Ps 40:5
I *r* till morning, that, as a lion ... Is 38:13 7737
he was *r* among the transgressors ... Lk 22:37 *3049*
is the reward not *r* of grace ... Rom 4:4 *3049*
for we say that faith was *r* to ... Rom 4:9 *3049*
How was it then *r* ... Rom 4:10 *3049*

RECKONETH {1}
servants cometh, and *r* with them ... Mt 25:19 *4868,3056*

RECKONING {2}
Howbeit there was no *r* made with ... 2Kin 22:7 2803
therefore they were in one *r* ... 1Chr 23:11 6486

RECOMMENDED {2}
from whence they had been *r* to ... Acts 14:26 *3860*
being *r* by the brethren unto the ... Acts 15:40 *3860*

RECOMPENCE {19}
To me belongeth vengeance, and *r* ... Deut 32:35 8005
for vanity shall be his *r* ... Job 15:31 8545
with vengeance, even God with a *r* ... Is 35:4 1576
his adversaries, *r* to his enemies ... Is 59:18 1576
to the islands he will repay *r* ... Is 59:18 1576
that rendereth *r* to his enemies ... Is 66:6 1576
he will render unto her a *r* ... Jer 51:6 1576
Render unto them a *r*, O LORD, ... Lam 3:64 1576
are come, the days of *r* are come ... Hos 9:7 7966
will ye render me a *r* ... Joel 3:4 1576
return your *r* upon your own head ... Joel 3:4 1576
will return your *r* upon your own ... Joel 3:7 1576
thee again, and a *r* be made thee ... Lk 14:12 *468*
receiving in themselves that *r* of ... Rom 1:27 *489*
stumblingblock, and a *r* unto them ... Rom 11:9 *468*
Now for a *r* in the same, (I speak ... 2Cor 6:13 *489*
received a just *r* of reward ... Heb 2:2 *3405*
which hath great *r* of reward ... Heb 10:35 *3405*
respect unto the *r* of the reward ... Heb 11:26 *3405*

RECOMPENCES {2}
the year of *r* for the controversy ... Is 34:8 7966
for the LORD God of *r* shall ... Jer 51:56 1578

RECOMPENSE {27}
he shall *r* his trespass with the ... Num 5:7 7725
no kinsman to *r* the trespass unto ... Num 5:8 7725
The LORD *r* thy work, and a full ... Ruth 2:12 7999
why should the king *r* it me with ... 2Sa 19:36 1580
he will *r* it, whether thou refuse ... Job 34:33 7999
the *r* of a man's hands shall be ... Prov 12:14
Say not thou, I will *r* evil ... Prov 20:22 7999
will not keep silence, but will *r* ... Is 65:6 7999
even *r* into their bosom, ... Is 65:6
first I will *r* their iniquity and ... Jer 16:18 7999
I will *r* them according to their ... Jer 25:14 7999
r her according to her work ... Jer 50:29 7999
will *r* upon thee all thine ... Eze 7:3 5414
but I will *r* thy ways upon thee, ... Eze 7:4 5414
will *r* thee for all thine ... Eze 7:8 5414
I will *r* thee according to thy ... Eze 7:9 5414
but I will *r* their way upon their ... Eze 9:10 5414
I will *r* their way upon their own ... Eze 11:21 5414
therefore I also will *r* thy way ... Eze 16:43 5414
even it will I *r* upon his own ... Eze 17:19 5414
they shall *r* your lewdness upon ... Eze 23:49 5414
to his doings will he *r* him ... Hos 12:2 7725
and if ye *r* me, swiftly and ... Joel 3:4 1580
for they cannot *r* thee ... Lk 14:14 *467*
R to no man evil for evil ... Rom 12:17 *591*
God to *r* tribulation to them that ... 2Th 1:6 *467*
belongeth unto me, I will *r* ... Heb 10:30 *467*

RECOMPENSED {10}
the trespass be *r* unto the LORD ... Num 5:8 7725
of my hands hath he *r* me ... 2Sa 22:21 7725
LORD hath *r* me according to my ... 2Sa 22:25 7725
of my hands hath he *r* me ... Ps 18:20 7725
the LORD *r* me according to my ... Ps 18:24 7725
righteous shall be *r* in the earth ... Prov 11:31 7999
Shall evil be *r* for good ... Jer 18:20 7999
own way have I *r* upon their heads ... Eze 22:31 5414
for thou shalt be *r* at the ... Lk 14:14 *467*
it shall be *r* unto him again ... Rom 11:35 *467*

RECOMPENSEST {1}
r the iniquity of the fathers ... Jer 32:18 7999

RECOMPENSING {1}
by *r* his way upon his own head ... 2Chr 6:23 5414

RECONCILE {5}
of the congregation to *r* withal ... Lev 6:30 3722
he *r* himself unto his master ... 1Sa 29:4 7521
so shall ye *r* the house ... Eze 45:20 3722
that he might *r* both unto God in ... Eph 2:16 *604*
by him to *r* all things unto ... Col 1:20 *604*

RECONCILED {7}
first be *r* to thy brother, and ... Mt 5:24 *1259*
we were *r* to God by the death of ... Rom 5:10 *2644*
of his Son, much more, being *r* ... Rom 5:10 *2644*
unmarried, or be *r* to her husband ... 1Cor 7:11 *2644*
who hath *r* us to himself by Jesus ... 2Cor 5:18 *2644*
in Christ's stead, be ye *r* to God ... 2Cor 5:20 *2644*
wicked works, yet now hath he *r* ... Col 1:21 *604*

RECONCILIATION {8}
sanctified it, to make *r* upon it ... Lev 8:15 3722
they made *r* with their blood upon ... 2Chr 29:24 2398
to make *r* for them, saith the ... Eze 45:15 3722
to make *r* for the house of Israel ... Eze 45:17 3722
to make *r* for iniquity, and to ... Dan 9:24 3722
given to us the ministry of *r* ... 2Cor 5:18 *2643*
committed unto us the word of *r* ... 2Cor 5:19 *2643*
to make *r* for the sins of the ... Heb 2:17 *2433*

RECONCILING {3}
made an end of *r* the holy place ... Lev 16:20 3722
of them be the *r* of the world ... Rom 11:15 *2643*
r the world unto himself, not ... 2Cor 5:19 *2644*

RECORD {30}
in all places where I *r* my name I ... Ex 20:24 2142
earth to *r* this day against you, ... Deut 30:19 5749
heaven and earth to *r* against them ... Deut 31:28 5749
the ark of the LORD, and to *r* ... 1Chr 16:4 2142
and therein was a *r* thus written ... Ezr 6:2 1799
is in heaven, and my *r* is on high ... Job 16:19 7717
unto me faithful witnesses to *r* ... Is 8:2 5749
And this is the *r* of John, when ... Jn 1:19 *3141*
And John bare *r*, saying, I saw the ... Jn 1:32 *3140*
bare *r* that this is the Son of ... Jn 1:34 *3140*
him, Thou bearest *r* of thyself ... Jn 8:13 *3140*
thy *r* is not true ... Jn 8:13 *3141*
them, Though I bear *r* of myself ... Jn 8:14 *3140*
yet my *r* is true ... Jn 8:14 *3141*
raised him from the dead, bare *r* ... Jn 12:17 *3140*
And he that saw it bare *r*, and his ... Jn 19:35 *3140*
and his *r* is true ... Jn 19:35 *3141*
I take you to *r* this day, that I ... Acts 20:26 *3143*
For I bear them *r* that they have ... Rom 10:2 *3140*
I call God for a *r* upon my soul ... 2Cor 1:23 *3144*
For to their power, I bear *r* ... 2Cor 8:3 *3140*
for I bear you *r*, that, if it had ... Gal 4:15 *3140*
For God is my *r*, how greatly I ... Phil 1:8 *3144*
For I bear him *r*, that he hath a ... Col 4:13 *3140*
are three that bear *r* in heaven ... 1Jn 5:7 *3140*
the *r* that God gave of his Son ... 1Jn 5:10 *3141*
And this is the *r*, that God hath ... 1Jn 5:11 *3141*
yea, and we also bear *r* ... 3Jn 12 *3140*
and ye know that our *r* is true ... 3Jn 12 *3141*
Who bare *r* of the word of God, and ... Rev 1:2 *3140*

RECORDED {1}
were *r* chief of the fathers ... Neh 12:22 3789

RECORDER {9}
the son of Ahilud was *r* ... 2Sa 8:16 2142
the son of Ahilud was *r* ... 2Sa 20:24 2142
the son of Ahilud, the *r* ... 1Kin 4:3 2142
and Joah the son of Asaph the *r* ... 2Kin 18:18 2142
and Joah the son of Asaph the *r* ... 2Kin 18:37 2142
Jehoshaphat the son of Ahilud, *r* ... 1Chr 18:15 2142
and Joah the son of Joahaz the *r* ... 2Chr 34:8 2142
and Joah, Asaph's son, the *r* ... Is 36:3 2142
and Joah, the son of Asaph, the *r* ... Is 36:22 2142

RECORDS {3}
the book of the *r* of thy fathers ... Ezr 4:15 1799
thou find in the book of the *r* ... Ezr 4:15 1799
the book of *r* of the chronicles ... Est 6:1 2146

RECOUNT {1}
He shall *r* his worthies ... Nah 2:5 2142

RECOVER {21}
ye not *r* them within that time ... Judg 11:26 5337
them, and without fail *r* all ... 1Sa 30:8 5337
as he went to *r* his border at the ... 2Sa 8:3 7725
whether I shall *r* of this disease ... 2Kin 1:2 2421
for he would *r* him of his leprosy ... 2Kin 5:3 622
that thou mayest *r* him of his ... 2Kin 5:6 622
unto me to *r* a man of his leprosy ... 2Kin 5:7 622
over the place, and *r* the leper ... 2Kin 5:11 622
Shall I *r* of this disease ... 2Kin 8:8 2421
Shall I *r* of this disease ... 2Kin 8:9 2421
unto him, Thou mayest certainly *r* ... 2Kin 8:10 2421
me that thou shouldest surely *r* ... 2Kin 8:14 2421
Neither did Jeroboam *r* strength ... 2Chr 13:20 6113
that they could not *r* themselves ... 2Chr 14:13 4241
O spare me, that I may *r* strength ... Ps 39:13 1082
to *r* the remnant of his people ... Is 11:11 7069
so wilt thou *r* me, and make me to ... Is 38:16 2492
upon the boil, and he shall *r* ... Is 38:21 2421
will *r* my wool and my flax given ... Hos 2:9 5337
on the sick, and they shall *r* ... Mk 16:18 *2192,2573*
that they may *r* themselves out of ... 2Ti 2:26 *366*

RECOVERED {11}
David *r* all that the Amalekites ... 1Sa 30:18 5337
David *r* all ... 1Sa 30:19 7725
ought of the spoil that we have *r* ... 1Sa 30:22 5337
him, and *r* the cities of Israel ... 2Kin 13:25 7725
how he *r* Damascus, and Hamath, ... 2Kin 14:28 7725
king of Syria *r* Elath to Syria ... 2Kin 16:6 7725
and laid it on the boil, and he *r* ... 2Kin 20:7 2421
sick, and was *r* of his sickness ... Is 38:9 2421
that he had been sick, and was *r* ... Is 39:1 2388
of the daughter of my people *r* ... Jer 8:22 5927
he had *r* from Ishmael the son of ... Jer 41:16 7725

RECOVERING {1}
r of sight to the blind, to set ... Lk 4:18 *309*

RED {53} *The sea dividing Egypt and Arabia.*
And the first came out *r*, all over ... Gen 25:25 132
thee, with that same *r* pottage ... Gen 25:30 122
His eyes shall be *r* with wine ... Gen 49:12 2447
and cast them into the *R* sea ... Ex 10:19 5488
of the wilderness of the *R* sea ... Ex 13:18 5488

R

also are drowned in the *R* sea ... Ex 15:4 5488
brought Israel from the *R* sea ... Ex 15:22 5488
R sea even unto the sea of the ... Ex 23:31 5488
And rams' skins dyed *r*, and ... Ex 25:5 119
the tent of rams' skins dyed *r* ... Ex 26:14 119
And rams' skins dyed *r*, and ... Ex 35:7 119
r skins of rams, and badgers' ... Ex 35:23 119
the tent of rams' skins dyed *r* ... Ex 36:19 119
covering of rams' skins dyed *r* ... Ex 39:34 119
by the way of the *R* sea ... Num 14:25 5488
thee a *r* heifer without spot ... Num 19:2 122
mount Hor by the way of the *R* sea ... Num 21:4 5488
LORD, What he did in the *R* sea ... Num 21:14 5492
Elim, and encamped by the *R* sea ... Num 33:10 5488
And they removed from the *R* sea ... Num 33:11 5488
the plain over against the *R* sea ... Deut 1:1 5489
by the way of the *R* sea ... Deut 1:40 5488
by the way of the *R* sea, as the ... Deut 2:1 5488
R sea to overflow them as they ... Deut 11:4 5488
up the water of the *R* sea for you ... Josh 2:10 5488
LORD your God did to the *R* sea ... Josh 4:23 5488
and horsemen unto the *R* sea ... Josh 24:6 5488
the wilderness unto the *R* sea ... Judg 11:16 5488
Eloth, on the shore of the *R* sea ... 1Kin 9:26 5488
on the other side as *r* as blood ... 2Kin 3:22 122
heardest their cry by the *R* sea ... Neh 9:9 5488
and silver, upon a pavement of *r* ... Est 1:6 923
there is a cup, and the wine is *r* ... Ps 75:8 2560
him at the sea, even at the *R* sea ... Ps 106:7 5488
He rebuked the *R* sea also ... Ps 106:9 5488
and terrible things by the *R* sea ... Ps 106:22 5488
divided the *R* sea into parts ... Ps 136:13 5488
Pharaoh and his host in the *R* sea ... Ps 136:15 5488
thou upon the wine when it is *r* ... Prov 23:31 119
though they be *r* like crimson ... Is 1:18 119
ye unto her, A vineyard of *r* wine ... Is 27:2 2561
art thou *r* in thine apparel ... Is 63:2 122
thereof was heard in the *R* sea ... Jer 49:21 5488
of his mighty men is made *r* ... Nah 2:3 119
a man riding upon a *r* horse ... Zec 1:8 122
and behind him were there *r* horses ... Zec 1:8 122
the first chariot were *r* horses ... Zec 6:2 122
for the sky is *r* ... Mt 16:2 *4449*
for the sky is *r* and lowring ... Mt 16:3 *4449*
land of Egypt, and in the *R* sea ... Acts 7:36 *2281*
through the *R* sea as by dry land ... Heb 11:29 *2281*
went out another horse that was *r* ... Rev 6:4 *4450*
and behold a great *r* dragon ... Rev 12:3 *4450*

REDDISH {6}
bright spot, white, and somewhat *r* ... Lev 13:19 125
a white bright spot, somewhat *r* ... Lev 13:24 125
or bald forehead, a white *r* sore ... Lev 13:42 125
sore be white *r* in his bald head ... Lev 13:43 125
be greenish or *r* in the garment ... Lev 13:49 125
hollow strakes, greenish or *r* ... Lev 14:37 125

REDEEM {56}
I will *r* you with a stretched out ... Ex 6:6 1350
an ass thou shalt *r* with a lamb ... Ex 13:13 6299
and if thou wilt not *r* it, then ... Ex 13:13 6299
among thy children shalt thou *r* ... Ex 13:13 6299
the firstborn of my children I *r* ... Ex 13:15 6299
an ass thou shalt *r* with a lamb ... Ex 34:20 6299
and if thou *r* him not, then shalt ... Ex 34:20 6299
of thy sons thou shalt *r* ... Ex 34:20 6299
and if any of his kin come to *r* it ... Lev 25:25 1350
then shall he *r* that which his ... Lev 25:25 1350
And if the man have none to *r* it ... Lev 25:26 1350
and himself be able to *r* it ... Lev 25:26 1353
then he may *r* it within a whole ... Lev 25:29 1353
within a full year may he *r* it ... Lev 25:29 1353
may the Levites *r* at any time ... Lev 25:32 1353
one of his brethren may *r* him ... Lev 25:48 1350
or his uncle's son, may *r* him ... Lev 25:49 1350
unto him of his family may *r* him ... Lev 25:49 1350
if he be able, he may *r* himself ... Lev 25:49 1353
But if he will at all *r* it ... Lev 27:13 1350
sanctified it will *r* his house ... Lev 27:15 1350
the field will in any wise *r* it ... Lev 27:19 1350
And if he will not *r* the field ... Lev 27:20 1350
then he shall *r* it according to ... Lev 27:27 6299
will at all *r* ought of his tithes ... Lev 27:31 1350
of man shalt thou surely *r* ... Num 18:15 6299
of unclean beasts shalt thou *r* ... Num 18:15 6299
from a month old shalt thou *r* ... Num 18:16 6299
of a goat, thou shalt not *r* ... Num 18:17 6299
If thou wilt *r* it ... Ruth 4:4 1350
r it: but if thou wilt ... Ruth 4:4 6299
but if thou wilt not *r* it ... Ruth 4:4 1350
there is none to *r* it beside thee ... Ruth 4:4 1350
And he said, I will *r* it ... Ruth 4:4 1350
I cannot *r* it for myself, lest I ... Ruth 4:6 1350
r thou my right to thyself ... Ruth 4:6 1350
for I cannot *r* it ... Ruth 4:6 1350
whom God went to *r* for a people ... 2Sa 7:23 6299
whom God went to *r* to be his own ... 1Chr 17:21 6299
is it in our power to *r* them ... Neh 5:5
famine he shall *r* thee from death ... Job 5:20 6299
R me from the hand of the mighty ... Job 6:23 6299
R Israel, O God, out of all his ... Ps 25:22 6299
r me, and be merciful unto me ... Ps 26:11 6299
r us for thy mercies' sake ... Ps 44:26 6299
can by any means *r* his brother ... Ps 49:7 6299
But God will *r* my soul from the ... Ps 49:15 6299
Draw nigh unto my soul, and *r* it ... Ps 69:18 1350
He shall *r* their soul from deceit ... Ps 72:14 1350
he shall *r* Israel from all his ... Ps 130:8 6299
at all, that it cannot *r* ... Is 50:2 6304
I will *r* thee out of the hand of ... Jer 15:21 6299
I will *r* them from death ... Hos 13:14 1350
there the LORD shall *r* thee from ... Mic 4:10 1350
To *r* them that were under the law ... Gal 4:5 *1805*
that he might *r* us from all ... Titus 2:14 *3084*

REDEEMED {62}
The angel which *r* me from all ... Gen 48:16 1350
the people which thou hast *r* ... Ex 15:13 1350
then shall he let her be *r* ... Ex 21:8 6299
to an husband, and not at all *r* ... Lev 19:20 6299
if it be not *r* within the space ... Lev 25:30 1350
they may be *r*, and they shall go ... Lev 25:31 1353
that he is sold he may be *r* again ... Lev 25:48 1353
if he be not *r* in these years ... Lev 25:54 1350
man, it shall not be *r* any more ... Lev 27:20 1350
or if it be not *r*, then it shall ... Lev 27:27 1350
possession, shall be sold or *r* ... Lev 27:28 1350
be devoted of men, shall be *r* ... Lev 27:29 6299
it shall not be *r* ... Lev 27:33 1350
are to be *r* of the two hundred ... Num 3:46 6302
the odd number of them is to be *r* ... Num 3:48 6302
them that were *r* by the Levites ... Num 3:49 6306
of them that were *r* unto Aaron ... Num 3:51 6306
those that are to be *r* from a ... Num 18:16 6299
r you out of the house of bondmen ... Deut 7:8 6299
which thou hast *r* through thy ... Deut 9:26 6299
r you out of the house of bondage ... Deut 13:5 6299
Egypt, and the LORD thy God *r* thee ... Deut 15:15 6299
people Israel, whom thou hast *r* ... Deut 21:8 6299
and the LORD thy God *r* thee thence ... Deut 24:18 6299
who hath *r* my soul out of all ... 2Sa 4:9 6299
that hath *r* my soul out of all ... 1Kin 1:29 6299
whom thou hast *r* out of Egypt ... 1Chr 17:21 6299
whom thou hast *r* by thy great ... Neh 1:10 6299
have *r* our brethren the Jews ... Neh 5:8 7069
thou hast *r* me, O LORD God of ... Ps 31:5 6299
and my soul, which thou hast *r* ... Ps 71:23 6299
inheritance, which thou hast *r* ... Ps 74:2 1350
hast with thine arm *r* thy people ... Ps 77:15 1350
r them from the hand of the enemy ... Ps 106:10 1350
Let the *r* of the LORD say so ... Ps 107:2 1350
whom he hath *r* from the hand of ... Ps 107:2 1350
hath *r* us from our enemies ... Ps 136:24 6561
Zion shall be *r* with judgment ... Is 1:27 6299
who *r* Abraham, concerning the ... Is 29:22 6299
but the *r* shall walk there ... Is 35:9 1350
for I have *r* thee, I have called ... Is 43:1 1350
for I have *r* thee ... Is 44:22 1350
for the LORD hath *r* Jacob ... Is 44:23 1350
The LORD hath *r* his servant Jacob ... Is 48:20 1350
Therefore the *r* of the LORD shall ... Is 51:11 6299
ye shall be *r* without money ... Is 52:3 1350
his people, he hath *r* Jerusalem ... Is 52:9 1350
holy people, The *r* of the LORD ... Is 62:12 1350
and the year of my *r* is come ... Is 63:4 1350
his love and in his pity he *r* them ... Is 63:9 1350
For the LORD hath *r* Jacob ... Jer 31:11 6299
thou hast *r* my life ... Lam 3:58 1350
though I have *r* them, yet they ... Hos 7:13 6299
r thee out of the house of ... Mic 6:4 6299
for I have *r* them ... Zec 10:8 6299
he hath visited and *r* his people, ... Lk 1:68 *4160,3085*
he which should have *r* Israel ... Lk 24:21 *3084*
Christ hath *r* us from the curse ... Gal 3:13 *1805*
not *r* with corruptible things ... 1Pet 1:18 *3084*
hast *r* us to God by thy blood out ... Rev 5:9 *59*
which were *r* from the earth ... Rev 14:3 *59*
These were *r* from among men, ... Rev 14:4 *59*

REDEEMEDST {1}
which thou *r* to thee from Egypt, ... 2Sa 7:23 6299

REDEEMER {18}
For I know that my *r* liveth ... Job 19:25 1350
O LORD, my strength, and my *r* ... Ps 19:14 1350
rock, and the high God their *r* ... Ps 78:35 1350
For their *r* is mighty ... Prov 23:11 1350
thee, saith the LORD, and thy *r* ... Is 41:14 1350
Thus saith the LORD, your *r* ... Is 43:14 1350
and his *r* the LORD of hosts ... Is 44:6 1350
Thus saith the LORD, thy *r* ... Is 44:24 1350
As for our *r*, the LORD of hosts ... Is 47:4 1350
Thus saith the LORD, thy *R* ... Is 48:17 1350
the *R* of Israel, and his Holy One, ... Is 49:7 1350
the LORD am thy Saviour and thy *R* ... Is 49:26 1350
thy *R* the Holy One of Israel ... Is 54:5 1350
on thee, saith the LORD thy *R* ... Is 54:8 1350
the *R* shall come to Zion, and unto ... Is 59:20 1350
the LORD am thy Saviour and thy *R* ... Is 60:16 1350
O LORD, art our father, our *r* ... Is 63:16 1350
Their *R* is strong ... Jer 50:34 1350

REDEEMETH {2}
The LORD *r* the soul of his ... Ps 34:22 6299
Who *r* thy life from destruction ... Ps 103:4 1350

REDEEMING {3}
time in Israel concerning *r* ... Ruth 4:7 1353
R the time, because the days are ... Eph 5:16 *1805*
them that are without, *r* the time ... Col 4:5 *1805*

REDEMPTION {20}
ye shall grant a *r* for the land ... Lev 25:24 1353
give again the price of his *r* out ... Lev 25:51 1353
give him again the price of his *r* ... Lev 25:52 1353
Moses took the *r* money of them ... Num 3:49 6306
(For the *r* of their soul is ... Ps 49:8 6306
He sent *r* unto his people ... Ps 111:9 6304
mercy, and with him is plenteous *r* ... Ps 130:7 6304
for the right of *r* is thine to ... Jer 32:7 1353
is thine, and the *r* is thine ... Jer 32:8 1353
that looked for *r* in Jerusalem ... Lk 2:38 *3085*
for your *r* draweth nigh ... Lk 21:28 *629*
the *r* that is in Christ Jesus ... Rom 3:24 *629*
to wit, the *r* of our body ... Rom 8:23 *629*
and sanctification, and *r* ... 1Cor 1:30 *629*
In whom we have *r* through his ... Eph 1:7 *629*
the *r* of the purchased possession ... Eph 1:14 *629*
ye are sealed unto the day of *r* ... Eph 4:30 *629*
In whom we have *r* through his ... Col 1:14 *629*
having obtained eternal *r* for us ... Heb 9:12 *3085*
for the *r* of the transgressions ... Heb 9:15 *629*

REDNESS {1}
who hath *r* of eyes ... Prov 23:29 2498

REDOUND {1}
of many *r* to the glory of God ... 2Cor 4:15 *4052*

REED {33}
as a *r* is shaken in the water, and ... 1Kin 14:15 7070
upon the staff of this bruised *r* ... 2Kin 18:21 7070
trees, in the covert of the *r* ... Job 40:21 7070
in the staff of this broken *r* ... Is 36:6 7070
A bruised *r* shall he not break, ... Is 42:3 7070
staff of *r* to the house of Israel ... Eze 29:6 7070
in his hand, and a measuring *r* ... Eze 40:3 7070
in the man's hand a measuring *r* ... Eze 40:5 7070
breadth of the building, one *r* ... Eze 40:5 7070
and the height, one *r* ... Eze 40:5 7070
the gate, which was one *r* broad ... Eze 40:6 7070
the gate, which was one *r* broad ... Eze 40:6 7070
was one *r* long, and one *r* broad ... Eze 40:7 7070
of the gate within was one *r* ... Eze 40:7 7070
porch of the gate within, one *r* ... Eze 40:8 7070
were a full *r* of six great cubits ... Eze 41:8 7070
east side with the measuring *r* ... Eze 42:16 7070
with the measuring *r* round about ... Eze 42:16 7070
with the measuring *r* round about ... Eze 42:17 7070
reeds, with the measuring *r* ... Eze 42:18 7070
reeds with the measuring *r* ... Eze 42:19 7070
A *r* shaken with the wind ... Mt 11:7 *2563*
A bruised *r* shall he not break, ... Mt 12:20 *2563*
head, and a *r* in his right hand ... Mt 27:29 *2563*
they spit upon him, and took the *r* ... Mt 27:30 *2563*
it with vinegar, and put it on a *r* ... Mt 27:48 *2563*
smote him on the head with a *r* ... Mk 15:19 *2563*
full of vinegar, and put it on a *r* ... Mk 15:36 *2563*
A *r* shaken with the wind ... Lk 7:24 *2563*
was given me a *r* like unto a rod ... Rev 11:1 *2563*
a golden *r* to measure the city ... Rev 21:15 *2563*
he measured the city with the *r* ... Rev 21:16 *2563*

REEDS {11}
the *r* and flags shall wither ... Is 19:6 7070
The paper *r* by the brooks, by the ... Is 19:7
each lay, shall be grass with *r* ... Is 35:7 7070
the *r* they have burned with fire, ... Jer 51:32 98
measuring reed, five hundred *r* ... Eze 42:16 7070
the north side, five hundred *r* ... Eze 42:17 7070
the south side, five hundred *r* ... Eze 42:18 7070
measured five hundred *r* with the ... Eze 42:19 7070
round about, five hundred *r* long ... Eze 42:20
of five and twenty thousand *r* ... Eze 45:1
and twenty thousand *r* in breadth ... Eze 48:8

REEL {2}
They *r* to and fro, and stagger like ... Ps 107:27 2287
The earth shall *r* to and fro like ... Is 24:20 5128

REELAIAH *(re-el-ah'-yah)* {1} *A clan leader with Zerubbabel.*
Jeshua, Nehemiah, Seraiah, *R* ... Ezr 2:2 7480

REFINE {1}
will *r* them as silver is refined, ... Zec 13:9 6884

REFINED {5}
altar of incense *r* gold by weight ... 1Chr 28:18 2212
thousand talents of *r* silver ... 1Chr 29:4 2212
of wines on the lees well *r* ... Is 25:6 2212
Behold, I have *r* thee, but not ... Is 48:10 6884
will refine them as silver is *r* ... Zec 13:9 6884

REFINER {1}
And he shall sit as a *r* and ... Mal 3:3 6884

REFINER'S {1}
for he is like a *r* fire, and like ... Mal 3:2 6884

REFORMATION {1}
on them until the time of *r* ... Heb 9:10 *1357*

REFORMED {1}
if ye will not be *r* by me by ... Lev 26:23 3256

REFRAIN {9}
Then Joseph could not *r* himself ... Gen 45:1 662
Therefore I will not *r* my mouth ... Job 7:11 2820
r thy foot from their path ... Prov 1:15 4513
a time to *r* from embracing ... Eccl 3:5 7368
for my praise will I *r* for thee ... Is 48:9 2413
Wilt thou *r* thyself for these ... Is 64:12 662
R thy voice from weeping, and ... Jer 31:16 4513
R from these men, and let them ... Acts 5:38 *868*
let him *r* his tongue from evil, ... 1Pet 3:10 *3973*

REFRAINED {7}
r himself, and said, Set on bread ... Gen 43:31 662
Nevertheless Haman *r* himself ... Est 5:10 662
The princes *r* talking, and laid ... Job 29:9 6113
lo, I have not *r* my lips, O LORD, ... Ps 40:9 3607
I have *r* my feet from every evil ... Ps 119:101 3601
I have been still, and *r* myself ... Is 42:14 662
they have not *r* their feet ... Jer 14:10 2820

REFRAINETH {1}
but he that *r* his lips is wise ... Prov 10:19 2820

R slept with his fathers, and was 2Chr 12:16 7346
against *R* the son of Solomon 2Chr 13:7 7346
when *R* was young and tenderhearted 2Chr 13:7 7346

REHOBOTH *(re'-ho-both)* {4}
1. A city in Assyria.
and builded Nineveh, and the city *R* Gen 10:11 7344
Saul of *R* by the river reigned in Gen 36:37 7344
Shaul of *R* by the river reigned 1Chr 1:48 7344
2. A well Isaac dug.
and he called the name of it *R* Gen 26:22 7344

REHOBOTH-BY-THE-WATER See REHOBOTH.

REHOBOTH-IR See REHOBOTH.

REHUM *(re'-hum)* {8} See NEHUM.
1. A clan leader with Zerubbabel.
Bilshan, Mizpar, Bigvai, *R* Ezr 2:2 7348
Shechaniah, *R*, Meremoth, Neh 12:3 7348
2. An officer of King Artaxerxes.
R the chancellor and Shimshai the Ezr 4:8 7348
Then wrote *R* the chancellor, and Ezr 4:9 7348
an answer unto *R* the chancellor Ezr 4:17 7348
letter was read before *R*, and Ezr 4:23 7348
3. A Levite rebuilder of Jerusalem's wall.
the Levites, *R* the son of Bani Neh 3:17 7348
4. A renewer of the covenant.
R, Hashabnah, Maaseiah, Neh 10:25 7348

REI *(re'-i)* {1} *A friend of David.*
the prophet, and Shimei, and *R* 1Kin 1:8 7472

REIGN {168}
him, Shalt thou indeed *r* over us Gen 37:8 4427
The LORD shall *r* for ever Ex 15:18 4427
that hate you shall *r* over you Lev 26:17 7287
thou shalt *r* over many nations, Deut 15:6 4910
but they shall not *r* over thee Deut 15:6 4910
r over you, or that one *r* Judg 9:2 4910
the olive tree, *R* thou over us Judg 9:8 4427
fig tree, Come thou, and *r* over us Judg 9:10 4427
the vine, Come thou, and *r* over us Judg 9:12 4427
bramble, Come thou, and *r* over us Judg 9:14 4427
me, that I should not *r* over them 1Sa 8:7 4427
the king that shall *r* over them 1Sa 8:9 4427
of the king that shall *r* over you 1Sa 8:11 4427
this same shall *r* over my people 1Sa 9:17 6113
that said, Shall Saul *r* over us 1Sa 11:12 4427
but a king shall *r* over us 1Sa 12:12 4427
when he began to *r* over Israel 2Sa 2:10 4427
that thou mayest *r* over all that 2Sa 3:21 4427
years old when he began to *r* 2Sa 5:4 4427
the son of Haggith doth *r* 1Kin 1:11 4427
Solomon thy son shall *r* after me 1Kin 1:13 4427
why then doth Adonijah *r* 1Kin 1:13 4427
Solomon thy son shall *r* after me 1Kin 1:17 4427
said, Adonijah shall *r* after me 1Kin 1:24 4427
Solomon thy son shall *r* after me 1Kin 1:30 4427
faces on me, that I should *r* 1Kin 2:15 4427
year of Solomon's *r* over Israel 1Kin 6:1 4427
thou shalt *r* according to all 1Kin 11:37 4427
one years old when he began to *r* 1Kin 14:21 4427
the son of Jeroboam began to *r* 1Kin 15:25 4427
to *r* over all Israel in Tirzah 1Kin 15:33 4427
Baasha to *r* over Israel in Tirzah 1Kin 16:8 4427
came to pass, when he began to *r* 1Kin 16:11 4427
did Zimri *r* seven days in Tirzah 1Kin 16:15 4427
Judah began Omri to *r* over Israel 1Kin 16:23 4427
the son of Omri to *r* over Israel 1Kin 16:29 4427
the son of Asa began to *r* over 1Kin 22:41 4427
five years old when he began to *r* 1Kin 22:42 4427
the son of Ahab began to *r* over 1Kin 22:51 4427
the son of Ahab began to *r* over 2Kin 3:1 4427
king of Judah began to *r* 2Kin 8:16 4427
old was he when he began to *r* 2Kin 8:17 4427
Jehoram king of Judah begin to *r* 2Kin 8:25 4427
was Ahaziah when he began to *r* 2Kin 8:26 4427
began Ahaziah to *r* over Judah 2Kin 9:29 4427
Athaliah did *r* over the land 2Kin 11:3 4427
was Jehoash when he began to *r* 2Kin 11:21 4427
year of Jehu Jehoash began to *r* 2Kin 12:1 4427
began to *r* over Israel in Samaria 2Kin 13:1 4427
to *r* over Israel in Samaria 2Kin 13:10 4427
five years old when he began to *r* 2Kin 14:2 4427
of Israel began to *r* in Samaria 2Kin 14:23 4427
son of Amaziah king of Judah to *r* 2Kin 15:1 4427
old was he when he began to *r* 2Kin 15:2 4427
r over Israel in Samaria six 2Kin 15:8 4427
of Jabesh began to *r* in the nine 2Kin 15:13 4427
the son of Gadi to *r* over Israel 2Kin 15:17 4427
began to *r* over Israel in Samaria 2Kin 15:23 4427
began to *r* over Israel in Samaria 2Kin 15:27 4427
son of Uzziah king of Judah to *r* 2Kin 15:32 4427
old was he when he began to *r* 2Kin 15:33 4427
Jotham king of Judah began to *r* 2Kin 16:1 4427
old was Ahaz when he began to *r* 2Kin 16:2 4427
to *r* in Samaria over Israel nine 2Kin 17:1 4427
of Ahaz king of Judah began to *r* 2Kin 18:1 4427
old was he when he began to *r* 2Kin 18:2 4427
years old when he began to *r* 2Kin 21:1 4427
two years old when he began to *r* 2Kin 21:19 4427
years old when he began to *r* 2Kin 22:1 4427
years old when he began to *r* 2Kin 23:31 4427
that he might not *r* in Jerusalem 2Kin 23:33 4427
five years old when he began to *r* 2Kin 23:36 4427
years old when he began to *r* 2Kin 24:8 4427
him in the eighth year of his *r* 2Kin 24:12 4427
one years old when he began to *r* 2Kin 24:18 4427
pass in the ninth year of his *r* 2Kin 25:1 4427
to *r* did lift up the head of 2Kin 25:27 4427
their cities unto the *r* of David 1Chr 4:31 4427
In the fortieth year of the *r* of 1Chr 26:31 4438
With all his *r* and his might, and 1Chr 29:30 4438
and hast made me to *r* in his stead 2Chr 1:8 4427
in the fourth year of his *r* 2Chr 3:2 4438
years old when he began to *r* 2Chr 12:13 4427
began Abijah to *r* over Judah 2Chr 13:1 4427
fifteenth year of the *r* of Asa 2Chr 15:10 4438
and thirtieth year of the *r* of Asa 2Chr 15:19 4438
thirtieth year of the *r* of Asa 2Chr 16:1 4438
ninth year of his *r* was diseased 2Chr 16:12 4438
the one and fortieth year of his *r* 2Chr 16:13 4427
of his *r* he sent to his princes 2Chr 17:7 4427
five years old when he began to *r* 2Chr 20:31 4427
two years old when he began to *r* 2Chr 21:5 4427
old was he when he began to *r* 2Chr 21:20 4427
was Ahaziah when he began to *r* 2Chr 22:2 4427
Behold, the king's son shall *r* 2Chr 23:3 4427
years old when he began to *r* 2Chr 24:1 4427
five years old when he began to *r* 2Chr 25:1 4427
old was Uzziah when he began to *r* 2Chr 26:3 4427
five years old when he began to *r* 2Chr 27:1 4427
years old when he began to *r* 2Chr 27:8 4427
years old when he began to *r* 2Chr 28:1 4427
began to *r* when he was five 2Chr 29:1 4427
He in the first year of his *r* 2Chr 29:3 4427
in his *r* did cast away in his 2Chr 29:19 4438
years old when he began to *r* 2Chr 33:1 4427
years old when he began to *r* 2Chr 33:21 4427
years old when he began to *r* 2Chr 34:1 4427
For in the eighth year of his *r* 2Chr 34:3 4427
in the eighteenth year of his *r* 2Chr 34:8 4427
the *r* of Josiah was this passover 2Chr 35:19 4438
years old when he began to *r* 2Chr 36:2 4427
five years old when he began to *r* 2Chr 36:5 4427
years old when he began to *r* 2Chr 36:9 4427
years old when he began to *r* 2Chr 36:11 4427
his sons until the *r* of the 2Chr 36:20 4427
even until the *r* of Darius king Ezr 4:5 4438
in the *r* of Ahasuerus, in the Ezr 4:6 4438
in the beginning of his *r* Ezr 4:6 4438
of the *r* of Darius king of Persia Ezr 4:24 4437
year of the *r* of Darius the king Ezr 6:15 4437
in the *r* of Artaxerxes king of Ezr 7:1 4438
in the *r* of Artaxerxes the king Ezr 8:1 4438
to the *r* of Darius the Persian Neh 12:22 4438
In the third year of his *r* Est 1:3 4427
in the seventh year of his *r* Est 2:16 4438
That the hypocrite *r* not, lest Job 34:30 4427
The LORD shall *r* for ever Ps 146:10 4427
By me kings *r*, and princes decree Prov 8:15 4427
For out of prison he cometh to *r* Eccl 4:14 4427
of hosts shall *r* in mount Zion Is 24:23 4427
a king shall *r* in righteousness, Is 32:1 4427
in the thirteenth year of his *r* Jer 1:2 4427
Shalt thou *r*, because thou Jer 22:15 4427
Branch, and a King shall *r* Jer 23:5 4427
In the beginning of the *r* of Jer 26:1 4468
In the beginning of the *r* of Jer 27:1 4467
in the beginning of the *r* of Jer 28:1 4467
have a son to *r* upon his throne Jer 33:21 4427
the *r* of Zedekiah king of Judah Jer 49:34 4438
in the fourth year of his *r* Jer 51:59 4427
years old when he began to *r* Jer 52:1 4427
pass in the ninth year of his *r* Jer 52:4 4427
of his *r* lifted up the head of Jer 52:31 4438
In the third year of the *r* of Dan 1:1 4438
year of the *r* of Nebuchadnezzar Dan 2:1 4438
prospered in the *r* of Darius Dan 6:28 4437
in the *r* of Cyrus the Persian Dan 6:28 4437
In the third year of the *r* of Dan 8:1 4438
In the first year of his *r* I Dan 9:2 4427
the LORD shall *r* over them in Mic 4:7 4427
he heard that Archelaus did *r* in Mt 2:22 *936*
he shall *r* over the house of Lk 1:33 *936*
year of the *r* of Tiberius Caesar Lk 3:1 *2231*
not have this man to *r* over us Lk 19:14 *936*
not that I should *r* over them Lk 19:27 *936*
shall *r* in life by one, Jesus Rom 5:17 *936*
even so might grace *r* through Rom 5:21 *936*
therefore *r* in your mortal body Rom 6:12 *936*
shall rise to *r* over the Gentiles Rom 15:12 *757*
and I would to God ye did *r* 1Cor 4:8 *936*
that we also might *r* with you 1Cor 4:8 *4821*
For he must *r*, till he hath put 1Cor 15:25 *936*
suffer, we shall also *r* with him 2Ti 2:12 *4821*
and we shall *r* on the earth Rev 5:10 *936*
and he shall *r* for ever and ever Rev 11:15 *936*
shall *r* with him a thousand years Rev 20:6 *936*
and they shall *r* for ever and ever Rev 22:5 *936*

REIGNED {176}
kings that *r* in the land of Edom Gen 36:31 4427
before there *r* any king over the Gen 36:31 4427
And Bela the son of Beor *r* in Edom Gen 36:32 4427
of Zerah of Bozrah *r* in his stead Gen 36:33 4427
the land of Temani *r* in his stead Gen 36:34 4427
the field of Moab, *r* in his stead Gen 36:35 4427
Samlah of Masrekah *r* in his stead Gen 36:36 4427
by the river *r* in his stead Gen 36:37 4427
the son of Achbor *r* in his stead Gen 36:38 4427
died, and Hadar *r* in his stead Gen 36:39 4427
r in mount Hermon, and in Salcah, Josh 12:5 4910
which *r* in Heshbon, unto the Josh 13:10 4427
which *r* in Ashtaroth and in Edrei, Josh 13:12 4427
which *r* in Heshbon, whom Moses Josh 13:21 4427
king of Canaan, that *r* in Hazor Judg 4:2 4427
When Abimelech had *r* three years Judg 9:22 7786
Saul *r* one year 1Sa 13:1 4427
when he had *r* two years over 1Sa 13:1 4427
reign over Israel, and *r* two years 2Sa 2:10 4427
to reign, and he *r* forty years 2Sa 5:4 4427
In Hebron he *r* over Judah seven 2Sa 5:5 4427
and in Jerusalem he *r* thirty 2Sa 5:5 4427
And David *r* over all Israel 2Sa 8:15 4427
and Hanun his son *r* in his stead 2Sa 10:1 4427
Saul, in whose stead thou hast *r* 2Sa 16:8 4427
the days that David *r* over Israel 1Kin 2:11 4427
seven years *r* he in Hebron, and 1Kin 2:11 4427
three years *r* he in Jerusalem 1Kin 2:11 4427
Solomon *r* over all kingdoms from 1Kin 4:21 4910
dwelt therein, and *r* in Damascus 1Kin 11:24 4427
abhorred Israel, and *r* over Syria 1Kin 11:25 4427
the time that Solomon *r* in 1Kin 11:42 4427
Rehoboam his son *r* in his stead 1Kin 11:43 4427
of Judah, Rehoboam *r* over them 1Kin 12:17 4427
how he warred, and how he *r* 1Kin 14:19 4427
days which Jeroboam *r* were two 1Kin 14:20 4427
and Nadab his son *r* in his stead 1Kin 14:20 4427
the son of Solomon *r* in Judah 1Kin 14:21 4427
he *r* seventeen years in Jerusalem 1Kin 14:21 4427
And Abijam his son *r* in his stead 1Kin 14:31 4427
son of Nebat *r* Abijam over Judah 1Kin 15:1 4427
Three years *r* he in Jerusalem 1Kin 15:2 4427
Asa his son *r* in his stead 1Kin 15:8 4427
king of Israel *r* Asa over Judah 1Kin 15:9 4427
one years *r* he in Jerusalem 1Kin 15:10 4427
his son *r* in his stead 1Kin 15:24 4427
Judah, and *r* over Israel two years 1Kin 15:25 4427
slay him, and *r* in his stead 1Kin 15:28 4427
And it came to pass, when he *r* 1Kin 15:29 4427
and Elah his son *r* in his stead 1Kin 16:6 4427
king of Judah, and *r* in his stead 1Kin 16:10 4427
so Tibni died, and Omri *r* 1Kin 16:22 4427
six years *r* he in Tirzah 1Kin 16:23 4427
and Ahab his son *r* in his stead 1Kin 16:28 4427
Ahab the son of Omri *r* over 1Kin 16:29 4427
and Ahaziah his son *r* in his stead 1Kin 22:40 4427
he *r* twenty and five years in 1Kin 22:42 4427
and Jehoram his son *r* in his stead 1Kin 22:50 4427
Judah, and *r* two years over Israel 1Kin 22:51 4427
Jehoram *r* in his stead in the 2Kin 1:17 4427
king of Judah, and *r* twelve years 2Kin 3:1 4427
that should have *r* in his stead 2Kin 3:27 4427
and Hazael *r* in his stead 2Kin 8:15 4427
he *r* eight years in Jerusalem 2Kin 8:17 4427
and Ahaziah his son *r* in his stead 2Kin 8:24 4427
he *r* one year in Jerusalem 2Kin 8:26
Jehoahaz his son *r* in his stead 2Kin 10:35 4427
the time that Jehu *r* over Israel 2Kin 10:36 4427
forty years *r* he in Jerusalem 2Kin 12:1 4427
and Amaziah his son *r* in his stead 2Kin 12:21 4427
in Samaria, and *r* seventeen years 2Kin 13:1
and Joash his son *r* in his stead 2Kin 13:9 4427
in Samaria, and *r* sixteen years 2Kin 13:10
Ben-hadad his son *r* in his stead 2Kin 13:24 4427
r Amaziah the son of Joash king 2Kin 14:1 4427
r twenty and nine years in 2Kin 14:2 4427
Jeroboam his son *r* in his stead 2Kin 14:16 4427
Samaria, and *r* forty and one years 2Kin 14:23
Zachariah his son *r* in his stead 2Kin 14:29 4427
he *r* two and fifty years in 2Kin 15:2 4427
and Jotham his son *r* in his stead 2Kin 15:7 4427
and slew him, and *r* in his stead 2Kin 15:10 4427
he *r* a full month in Samaria 2Kin 15:13 4427
and slew him, and *r* in his stead 2Kin 15:14 4427
Israel, and *r* ten years in Samaria 2Kin 15:17
Pekahiah his son *r* in his stead 2Kin 15:22 4427
Israel in Samaria, and *r* two years 2Kin 15:23
he killed him, and *r* in his room 2Kin 15:25 4427
in Samaria, and *r* twenty years 2Kin 15:27
r in his stead, in the twentieth 2Kin 15:30 4427
he *r* sixteen years in Jerusalem 2Kin 15:33 4427
and Ahaz his son *r* in his stead 2Kin 15:38 4427
r sixteen years in Jerusalem, and 2Kin 16:2 4427
Hezekiah his son *r* in his stead 2Kin 16:20 4427
he *r* twenty and nine years in 2Kin 18:2 4427
his son *r* in his stead 2Kin 19:37 4427
Manasseh his son *r* in his stead 2Kin 20:21 4427
and *r* fifty and five years in 2Kin 21:1 4427
and Amon his son *r* in his stead 2Kin 21:18 4427
he *r* two years in Jerusalem 2Kin 21:19 4427
and Josiah his son *r* in his stead 2Kin 21:26 4427
he *r* thirty and one years in 2Kin 22:1 4427
he *r* three months in Jerusalem 2Kin 23:31 4427
he *r* eleven years in Jerusalem 2Kin 23:36 4427
Jehoiachin his son *r* in his stead 2Kin 24:6 4427
he *r* in Jerusalem three months 2Kin 24:8 4427
he *r* eleven years in Jerusalem 2Kin 24:18 4427
Now these are the kings that *r* in 1Chr 1:43 4427
r over the children of Israel 1Chr 1:43 4427
of Zerah of Bozrah *r* in his stead 1Chr 1:44 4427
of the Temanites *r* in his stead 1Chr 1:45 4427
the field of Moab, *r* in his stead 1Chr 1:46 4427
Samlah of Masrekah *r* in his stead 1Chr 1:47 4427
by the river *r* in his stead 1Chr 1:48 4427
the son of Achbor *r* in his stead 1Chr 1:49 4427
was dead, Hadad *r* in his stead 1Chr 1:50 4427
there he *r* seven years and six 1Chr 3:4 4427
and in Jerusalem he *r* thirty 1Chr 3:4 4427
So David *r* over all Israel, and 1Chr 18:14 4427
died, and his son *r* in his stead 1Chr 19:1 4427
son of Jesse *r* over all Israel 1Chr 29:26 4427
the time that he *r* over Israel 1Chr 29:27 4427
seven years *r* he in Hebron, and 1Chr 29:27 4427
three years *r* he in Jerusalem 1Chr 29:27 4427
and Solomon his son *r* in his stead 1Chr 29:28 4427

congregation, and *r* over Israel 2Chr 1:13 4427
he *r* over all the kings from the 2Chr 9:26 4910
Solomon *r* in Jerusalem over all 2Chr 9:30 4427
Rehoboam his son *r* in his stead 2Chr 9:31 4427
of Judah, Rehoboam *r* over them 2Chr 10:17 4427
himself in Jerusalem, and *r* 2Chr 12:13 4427
he *r* seventeen years in Jerusalem 2Chr 12:13 4427
and Abijah his son *r* in his stead 2Chr 12:16 4427
He *r* three years in Jerusalem 2Chr 13:2 4427
Asa his son *r* in his stead 2Chr 14:1 4427
his son *r* in his stead, and 2Chr 17:1 4427
And Jehoshaphat *r* over Judah 2Chr 20:31 4427
he *r* twenty and five years in 2Chr 20:31 4427
And Jehoram his son *r* in his stead 2Chr 21:1 4427
he *r* eight years in Jerusalem 2Chr 21:5 4427
he *r* in Jerusalem eight years, and 2Chr 21:20 4427
son of Jehoram king of Judah *r* 2Chr 22:1 4427
he *r* one year in Jerusalem 2Chr 22:2 4427
and Athaliah *r* over the land 2Chr 22:12 4427
he *r* forty years in Jerusalem 2Chr 24:1 4427
And Amaziah his son *r* in his stead 2Chr 24:27 4427
he *r* twenty and nine years in 2Chr 25:1 4427
he *r* fifty and two years in 2Chr 26:3 4427
and Jotham his son *r* in his stead 2Chr 26:23 4427
he *r* sixteen years in Jerusalem 2Chr 27:1 4427
r sixteen years in Jerusalem 2Chr 27:8 4427
and Ahaz his son *r* in his stead 2Chr 27:9 4427
he *r* sixteen years in Jerusalem 2Chr 28:1 4427
Hezekiah his son *r* in his stead 2Chr 28:27 4427
he *r* nine and twenty years in 2Chr 29:1 4427
Manasseh his son *r* in his stead 2Chr 32:33 4427
he *r* fifty and five years in 2Chr 33:1 4427
and Amon his son *r* in his stead 2Chr 33:20 4427
and *r* two years in Jerusalem 2Chr 33:21 4427
he *r* in Jerusalem one and thirty 2Chr 34:1 4427
he *r* three months in Jerusalem 2Chr 36:2 4427
he *r* eleven years in Jerusalem 2Chr 36:5 4427
Jehoiachin his son *r* in his stead 2Chr 36:8 4427
he *r* three months and ten days in 2Chr 36:9 4427
r eleven years in Jerusalem 2Chr 36:11 4427
(this is Ahasuerus which *r* from .... Est 1:1 4427
his son *r* in his stead .... Is 37:38 4427
which *r* instead of Josiah his .... Jer 22:11 4427
r instead of Coniah the son of .... Jer 37:1 4427
he *r* eleven years in Jerusalem .... Jer 52:1 4427
death *r* from Adam to Moses .... Rom 5:14 *936*
one man's offence death *r* by one .... Rom 5:17 *936*
That as sin hath *r* unto death .... Rom 5:21 *936*
ye have *r* as kings without us 1Cor 4:8 *936*
thee thy great power, and hast *r* .... Rev 11:17 *936*
r with Christ a thousand years .... Rev 20:4 *936*

REIGNEST {1}
come of thee, and thou *r* over all 1Chr 29:12 4910

REIGNETH {13}
also the king that *r* over you 1Sa 12:14 4427
ye shall say, Absalom *r* in Hebron 2Sa 15:10 4427
And now, behold, Adonijah *r* 1Kin 1:18 4427
say among the nations, The LORD *r* 1Chr 16:31 4427
God *r* over the heathen .... Ps 47:8 4427
The LORD *r*, he is clothed with .... Ps 93:1 4427
among the heathen that the LORD *r* .... Ps 96:10 4427
The LORD *r* .... Ps 97:1 4427
The LORD *r* .... Ps 99:1 4427
For a servant when he *r* .... Prov 30:22 4427
that saith unto Zion, Thy God *r* .... Is 52:7 4427
which *r* over the kings of the .... Rev 17:18 *2192,932*
for the Lord God omnipotent *r* .... Rev 19:6 *936*

REIGNING {1}
rejected him from *r* over Israel 1Sa 16:1 4427

REINS {15}
about, he cleaveth my *r* asunder .... Job 16:13 3629
though my *r* be consumed within me .... Job 19:27 3629
God trieth the hearts and *r* .... Ps 7:9 3629
my *r* also instruct me in the .... Ps 16:7 3629
try my *r* and my heart .... Ps 26:2 3629
grieved, and I was pricked in my *r* .... Ps 73:21 3629
For thou hast possessed my *r* .... Ps 139:13 3629
my *r* shall rejoice, when thy lips .... Prov 23:16 3629
faithfulness the girdle of his *r* .... Is 11:5 2504
righteously, that triest the *r* .... Jer 11:20 3629
their mouth, and far from their *r* .... Jer 12:2 3629
search the heart, I try the *r* .... Jer 17:10 3629
the righteous, and seest the *r* .... Jer 20:12 3629
of his quiver to enter into my *r* .... Lam 3:13 3629
I am he which searcheth the *r* .... Rev 2:23 *3510*

REJECT {4}
knowledge, I will also *r* thee .... Hos 4:6 3988
sat with him, he would not *r* her .... Mk 6:26 *114*
Full well ye *r* the commandment of .... Mk 7:9 *114*
the first and second admonition *r* .... Titus 3:10 *3868*

REJECTED {29}
r thee, but they have *r* me 1Sa 8:7 3988
And ye have this day *r* your God 1Sa 10:19 3988
Because thou hast *r* the word of 1Sa 15:23 3988
he hath also *r* thee from being 1Sa 15:23 3988
for thou hast *r* the word of the 1Sa 15:26 3988
the LORD hath *r* thee from being 1Sa 15:26 3988
seeing I have *r* him from reigning 1Sa 16:1 3988
they *r* his statutes, and his 2Kin 17:15 3988
the LORD *r* all the seed of Israel 2Kin 17:20 3988
He is despised and *r* of men .... Is 53:3 2310
the LORD hath *r* thy confidences .... Jer 2:37 3988
my words, nor to my law, but *r* it .... Jer 6:19 3988
because the LORD hath *r* them .... Jer 6:30 3988
for the LORD hath *r* and forsaken .... Jer 7:29 3988
they have *r* the word of the LORD .... Jer 8:9 3988
Hast thou utterly *r* Judah .... Jer 14:19 3988
But thou hast utterly *r* us .... Lam 5:22 3988
because thou hast *r* knowledge .... Hos 4:6 3988
The stone which the builders *r* .... Mt 21:42 *593*
be *r* of the elders, and of the .... Mk 8:31 *593*
r is become the head of the .... Mk 12:10 *593*
lawyers *r* the counsel of God .... Lk 7:30 *114*
be *r* of the elders and chief .... Lk 9:22 *593*
and be *r* of this generation .... Lk 17:25 *593*
The stone which the builders *r* .... Lk 20:17 *593*
my flesh ye despised not, nor *r* .... Gal 4:14 *1609*
beareth thorns and briers is *r* .... Heb 6:8 *96*
inherited the blessing, he was *r* .... Heb 12:17 *593*

REJECTETH {1}
He that *r* me, and receiveth not my .... Jn 12:48 *14*

REJOICE {192}
ye shall *r* before the LORD your .... Lev 23:40 8055
ye shall *r* in all that ye put .... Deut 12:7 8055
ye shall *r* before the LORD your .... Deut 12:12 8055
thou shalt *r* before the LORD thy .... Deut 12:18 8055
the LORD thy God, and thou shalt *r* .... Deut 14:26 8055
thou shalt *r* before the LORD thy .... Deut 16:11 8055
thou shalt *r* in thy feast, thou, ... Deut 16:14 8055
therefore thou shalt surely *r* .... Deut 16:15 8055
thou shalt *r* in every good thing .... Deut 26:11 8056
r before the LORD thy God .... Deut 27:7 8055
so the LORD will *r* over you to .... Deut 28:63 7797
will again *r* over thee for good .... Deut 30:9 7797
R, O ye nations, with his people .... Deut 32:43 7442
And of Zebulun he said, *R*, Zebulun .... Deut 33:18 8055
then *r* ye in Abimelech .... Judg 9:19 8055
and let him also *r* in you .... Judg 9:19 8055
unto Dagon their god, and to *r* .... Judg 16:23 8057
because I *r* in thy salvation 1Sa 2:1 8055
thou sawest it, and didst *r* 1Sa 19:5 8055
daughters of the Philistines *r* 2Sa 1:20 8055
of them *r* that seek the LORD 1Chr 16:10 8055
be glad, and let the earth *r* 1Chr 16:31 1523
let the fields *r*, and all that is 1Chr 16:32 5970
and let thy saints *r* in goodness 2Chr 6:41 8055
made them to *r* over their enemies 2Chr 20:27 8055
had made them *r* with great joy .... Neh 12:43 8055
Which *r* exceedingly, and are glad, ... Job 3:22 8055
be, and he shall not *r* therein .... Job 20:18 5965
r at the sound of the organ .... Job 21:12 8055
with fear, and *r* with trembling .... Ps 2:11 1523
that put their trust in thee *r* .... Ps 5:11 8055
I will be glad and *r* in thee .... Ps 9:2 5970
I will *r* in thy salvation .... Ps 9:14 1523
that trouble me *r* when I am moved .... Ps 13:4 1523
my heart shall *r* in thy salvation .... Ps 13:5 1523
of his people, Jacob shall *r* .... Ps 14:7 1523
We will *r* in thy salvation, and in .... Ps 20:5 7442
salvation how greatly shall he *r* .... Ps 21:1 1523
not made my foes to *r* over me .... Ps 30:1 8055
I will be glad and *r* in thy mercy .... Ps 31:7 8055
Be glad in the LORD, and *r* .... Ps 32:11 1524
R in the LORD, O ye righteous .... Ps 33:1 7442
For our heart shall *r* in him .... Ps 33:21 8055
it shall *r* in his salvation .... Ps 35:9 7797
mine enemies wrongfully *r* over me .... Ps 35:19 8055
and let them not *r* over me .... Ps 35:24 8055
together that *r* at mine hurt .... Ps 35:26 8055
otherwise they should *r* over me .... Ps 38:16 8055
Let all those that seek thee *r* .... Ps 40:16 7797
Let mount Zion *r*, let the .... Ps 48:11 8055
which thou hast broken may *r* .... Ps 51:8 1523
of his people, Jacob shall *r* .... Ps 53:6 1523
The righteous shall *r* when he .... Ps 58:10 8055
I will *r*, I will divide Shechem, ... Ps 60:6 5937
the shadow of thy wings will I *r* .... Ps 63:7 7442
But the king shall *r* in God .... Ps 63:11 8055
of the morning and evening to *r* .... Ps 65:8 7442
the little hills *r* on every side .... Ps 65:12 1524
there did we *r* in him .... Ps 66:6 8055
let them *r* before God .... Ps 68:3 5970
yea, let them exceedingly *r* .... Ps 68:3 7797
by his name JAH, and *r* before him .... Ps 68:4 5937
Let all those that seek thee *r* .... Ps 70:4 7797
greatly *r* when I sing unto thee .... Ps 71:23 7442
that thy people may *r* in thee .... Ps 85:6 8055
R the soul of thy servant .... Ps 86:4 8055
and Hermon shall *r* in thy name .... Ps 89:12 7442
thy name shall they *r* all the day .... Ps 89:16 1523
hast made all his enemies to *r* .... Ps 89:42 8055
that we may *r* and be glad all our .... Ps 90:14 7442
Let the heavens *r*, and let the .... Ps 96:11 8056
shall all the trees of the wood *r* .... Ps 96:12 7442
let the earth *r* .... Ps 97:1 1523
R in the LORD, ye righteous .... Ps 97:12 8055
make a loud noise, and *r*, and sing .... Ps 98:4 7442
the LORD shall *r* in his works .... Ps 104:31 8055
of them *r* that seek the LORD .... Ps 105:3 8055
that I may *r* in the gladness of .... Ps 106:5 8055
The righteous shall see it, and *r* .... Ps 107:42 8055
I will *r*, I will divide Shechem, ... Ps 108:7 5937
but let thy servant *r* .... Ps 109:28 8055
we will *r* and be glad in it .... Ps 118:24 1523
I *r* at thy word, as one that .... Ps 119:162 7797
Let Israel *r* in him that made him .... Ps 149:2 8055
Who *r* to do evil, and delight in .... Prov 2:14 8056
r with the wife of thy youth .... Prov 5:18 8055
heart be wise, my heart shall *r* .... Prov 23:15 8055
Yea, my reins shall *r*, when thy .... Prov 23:16 5937
of the righteous shall greatly *r* .... Prov 23:24 1523
and she that bare thee shall *r* .... Prov 23:25 1523
R not when thine enemy falleth, ... Prov 24:17 8055
Ointment and perfume *r* the heart .... Prov 27:9 8055
When righteous men do *r*, there is .... Prov 28:12 5970
are in authority, the people *r* .... Prov 29:2 8055
but the righteous doth sing and *r* .... Prov 29:6 8055
she shall *r* in time to come .... Prov 31:25 7832
good in them, but for a man to *r* .... Eccl 3:12 8055
a man should *r* in his own works .... Eccl 3:22 8055
come after shall not *r* in him .... Eccl 4:16 8055
portion, and to *r* in his labour .... Eccl 5:19 8055
live many years, and *r* in them all .... Eccl 11:8 8055
R, O young man, in thy youth .... Eccl 11:9 8055
r in thee, we will remember thy .... Song 1:4 8055
r in Rezin and Remaliah's son .... Is 8:6 4885
as men *r* when they divide the .... Is 9:3 1523
even them that *r* in my highness .... Is 13:3 5947
Yea, the fir trees *r* at thee .... Is 14:8 8055
R not thou, whole Palestina, ... Is 14:29 8055
And he said, Thou shalt no more *r* .... Is 23:12 5937
the noise of them that *r* endeth .... Is 24:8 5947
be glad and *r* in his salvation .... Is 25:9 8055
the poor among men shall *r* in the .... Is 29:19 1523
and the desert shall *r*, and blossom .... Is 35:1 1523
r even with joy and singing .... Is 35:2 1523
thou shalt *r* in the LORD, and .... Is 41:16 1523
they shall *r* in their portion .... Is 61:7 7442
I will greatly *r* in the LORD .... Is 61:10 7797
so shall thy God *r* over thee .... Is 62:5 7797
behold, my servants shall *r* .... Is 65:13 8055
r for ever in that which I create .... Is 65:18 1523
I will *r* in Jerusalem, and joy in .... Is 65:19 1523
R ye with Jerusalem, and be glad .... Is 66:10 8055
r for joy with her, all ye that .... Is 66:10 7797
ye see this, your heart shall *r* .... Is 66:14 7797
shall the virgin *r* in the dance .... Jer 31:13 8055
make them *r* from their sorrow .... Jer 31:13 8055
I will *r* over them to do them .... Jer 32:41 7797
them drunken, that they may *r* .... Jer 51:39 5937
caused thine enemy to *r* over thee .... Lam 2:17 8055
R and be glad, O daughter of Edom, ... Lam 4:21 7797
let not the buyer *r*, nor the .... Eze 7:12 8055
As thou didst *r* at the .... Eze 35:15 8057
R not, O Israel, for joy, as .... Hos 9:1 8055
be glad and *r* .... Joel 2:21 8055
Zion, and *r* in the LORD your God .... Joel 2:23 8055
Ye which *r* in a thing of nought, ... Amos 6:13 8055
R not against me, O mine enemy .... Mic 7:8 8055
therefore they *r* and are glad .... Hab 1:15 8055
Yet I will *r* in the LORD, I will .... Hab 3:18 5937
of thee them that *r* in thy pride .... Zeph 3:11 5947
r with all the heart, O daughter .... Zeph 3:14 5937
he will *r* over thee with joy .... Zeph 3:17 7797
Sing and *r*, O daughter of Zion .... Zec 2:10 8055
for they shall *r*, and shall see .... Zec 4:10 8055
R greatly, O daughter of Zion .... Zec 9:9 1523
heart shall *r* as through wine .... Zec 10:7 8055
their heart shall *r* in the LORD .... Zec 10:7 1523
R, and be exceeding glad .... Mt 5:12 *5463*
many shall *r* at his birth .... Lk 1:14 *5463*
R ye in that day, and leap for joy .... Lk 6:23 *5463*
Notwithstanding in this *r* not .... Lk 10:20 *5463*
but rather *r*, because your names .... Lk 10:20 *5463*
saying unto them, *R* with me .... Lk 15:6 *4796*
together, saying, *R* with me .... Lk 15:9 *4796*
of the disciples began to *r* .... Lk 19:37 *5463*
and he that reapeth may *r* together .... Jn 4:36 *5463*
for a season to *r* in his light .... Jn 5:35 *21*
If ye loved me, ye would *r* .... Jn 14:28 *5463*
and lament, but the world shall *r* .... Jn 16:20 *5463*
you again, and your heart shall *r* .... Jn 16:22 *5463*
Therefore did my heart *r*, and my .... Acts 2:26 *2165*
r in hope of the glory of God .... Rom 5:2 *2744*
R with them that do *r* .... Rom 12:15 *5463*
And again he saith, *R*, ye Gentiles .... Rom 15:10 *2165*
and they that *r*, as though they 1Cor 7:30 *5463*
all the members *r* with it 1Cor 12:26 *4796*
from them of whom I ought to *r* 2Cor 2:3 *5463*
Now I *r*, not that ye were made 2Cor 7:9 *5463*
I *r* therefore that I have 2Cor 7:16 *5463*
For it is written, *R*, thou barren .... Gal 4:27 *2165*
do *r*, yea, and will *r* .... Phil 1:18 *5463*
that I may *r* in the day of Christ .... Phil 2:16 *2745*
faith, I joy, and *r* with you all .... Phil 2:17 *4796*
also do ye joy, and *r* with me .... Phil 2:18 *4796*
when ye see him again, ye may *r* .... Phil 2:28 *5463*
my brethren, *r* in the Lord .... Phil 3:1 *5463*
r in Christ Jesus, and have no .... Phil 3:3 *2744*
R in the Lord alway .... Phil 4:4 *5463*
and again I say, *R* .... Phil 4:4 *5463*
Who now *r* in my sufferings for .... Col 1:24 *5463*
R evermore 1Th 5:16 *5463*
degree *r* in that he is exalted .... Jas 1:9 *2744*
But now ye *r* in your boastings .... Jas 4:16 *2744*
Wherein ye greatly *r*, though now 1Pet 1:6 *21*
ye *r* with joy unspeakable and full 1Pet 1:8 *21*
But *r*, inasmuch as ye are 1Pet 4:13 *5463*
upon the earth shall *r* over them .... Rev 11:10 *5463*
Therefore *r*, ye heavens, and ye .... Rev 12:12 *2165*
R over her, thou heaven, and ye .... Rev 18:20 *2165*
Let us be glad and *r*, and give .... Rev 19:7 *21*

REJOICED {47}
Jethro *r* for all the goodness .... Ex 18:9 2302
that as the LORD *r* over you to do .... Deut 28:63 7797
good, as he *r* over thy fathers .... Deut 30:9 7797
damsel saw him, he *r* to meet him .... Judg 19:3 8055
and saw the ark, and *r* to see it 1Sa 6:13 8055
all the men of Israel *r* greatly 1Sa 11:15 8055
r with great joy, so that the 1Kin 1:40 8056

R

of Solomon, that he *r* greatly 1Kin 5:7 8055
and all the people of the land *r* 2Kin 11:14 8056
And all the people of the land *r* 2Kin 11:20 8055
Then the people *r*, for that they 1Chr 29:9 8055
the king also *r* with great joy 1Chr 29:9 8055
And all Judah *r* at the oath 2Chr 15:15 8055
and all the people of the land *r* 2Chr 23:13 8056
And all the people of the land *r* 2Chr 23:21 8055
the princes and all the people *r* 2Chr 24:10 8055
And Hezekiah *r*, and all the people, 2Chr 29:36 8055
Israel, and that dwelt in Judah, *r* 2Chr 30:25 8055
offered great sacrifices, and *r* Neh 12:43 8055
the wives also and the children *r* Neh 12:43 8055
for Judah *r* for the priests and Neh 12:44 8057
and the city of Shushan *r* and was Est 8:15 6670
If I *r* because my wealth was Job 31:25 8055
If I *r* at the destruction of him Job 31:29 8055
But in mine adversity they *r* Ps 35:15 8055
the daughters of Judah *r* because Ps 97:8 1523
I have *r* in the way of thy Ps 119:14 7797
for my heart *r* in all my labour Eccl 2:10 8055
assembly of the mockers, nor *r* Jer 15:17 5937
ye were glad, because ye *r* Jer 50:11 5937
r in heart with all thy despite Eze 25:6 8055
the priests thereof that *r* on it Hos 10:5 1523
neither shouldest thou have *r* Obad 12 8055
they *r* with exceeding great joy Mt 2:10 *5463*
my spirit hath *r* in God my Lk 1:47 *21*
and they *r* with her Lk 1:58 *4796*
In that hour Jesus *r* in spirit Lk 10:21 *21*
all the people *r* for all the Lk 13:17 *5463*
father Abraham *r* to see my day Jn 8:56 *21*
r in the works of their own hands Acts 7:41 *2165*
they *r* for the consolation Acts 15:31 *5463*
he set meat before them, and *r* Acts 16:34 *21*
rejoice, as though they *r* not 1Cor 7:30 *5463*
so that I *r* the more 2Cor 7:7 *5463*
But I *r* in the Lord greatly, that Phil 4:10 *5463*
I *r* greatly that I found of thy 2Jn 4 *5463*
For I *r* greatly, when the 3Jn 3 *5463*

REJOICEST {1}
when thou doest evil, then thou *r* Jer 11:15 5937

REJOICETH {18}
My heart *r* in the LORD, mine horn 1Sa 2:1 5970
the valley, and *r* in his strength Job 39:21 7797
my heart is glad, and my glory *r* Ps 16:9 1523
r as a strong man to run a race Ps 19:5 7797
therefore my heart greatly *r* Ps 28:7 5937
with the righteous, the city *r* Prov 11:10 5970
The light of the righteous *r* Prov 13:9 8055
The light of the eyes *r* the heart Prov 15:30 8055
Whoso loveth wisdom *r* his father Prov 29:3 8055
and their pomp, and he that *r* Is 5:14 5938
the bridegroom *r* over the bride Is 62:5 4885
Thou meetest him that *r* and Is 64:5 7797
When the whole earth *r*, I will Eze 35:14 8055
he *r* more of that sheep, than of Mt 18:13 *5463*
him, *r* greatly because of the Jn 3:29 *5463*
R not in iniquity 1Cor 13:6 *5463*
but *r* in the truth 1Cor 13:6 *4796*
and mercy *r* against judgment Jas 2:13 *2620*

REJOICING {28}
and they are come up from thence *r* 1Kin 1:45 8056
in the law of Moses, with *r* 2Chr 23:18 8057
with laughing, and thy lips with *r* Job 8:21 8643
the LORD are right, *r* the heart Ps 19:8 8055
and *r* shall they be brought Ps 45:15 1524
and declare his works with *r* Ps 107:22 7440
The voice of *r* and salvation is in Ps 118:15 7440
for they are the *r* of my heart Ps 119:111 8342
shall doubtless come again with *r* Ps 126:6 7440
his delight, *r* always before him Prov 8:30 7832
R in the habitable part of his Prov 8:31 7832
behold, I create Jerusalem a *r* Is 65:18 1525
me the joy and *r* of mine heart Jer 15:16 8057
their *r* was as to devour the poor Hab 3:14 5951
This is the *r* city that dwelt Zeph 2:15 5947
he layeth it on his shoulders, *r* Lk 15:5 *5463*
r that they were counted worthy Acts 5:41 *5463*
and he went on his way *r* Acts 8:39 *5463*
R in hope Rom 12:12 *5463*
I protest by your *r* which I have 1Cor 15:31 *2746*
For our *r* is this, the testimony 2Cor 1:12 *2746*
us in part, that we are your *r* 2Cor 1:14 *2745*
As sorrowful, yet alway *r* 2Cor 6:10 *5463*
shall he have *r* in himself alone Gal 6:4 *2745*
That your *r* may be more abundant Phil 1:26 *2745*
our hope, or joy, or crown of *r* 1Th 2:19 *2746*
the *r* of the hope firm unto the Heb 3:6 *2745*
all such *r* is evil Jas 4:16 *2746*

REKEM *(re'-kem)* {5}
1. A prince of Midian.
namely, Evi, and *R*, and Zur, and Hur Num 31:8 7552
the princes of Midian, Evi, and *R* Josh 13:21 7552
2. A son of Hebron.
Korah, and Tappuah, and *R*, 1Chr 2:43 7552
and *R* begat Shammai 1Chr 2:44 7552
3. A city in Benjamin.
And *R*, and Irpeel, and Taralah, Josh 18:27 7552

RELEASE {21}
seven years thou shalt make a *r* Deut 15:1 8059
And this is the manner of the *r* Deut 15:2 8059
unto his neighbour shall *r* it Deut 15:2 8058
because it is called the LORD's *r* Deut 15:2 8059
thy brother thine hand shall *r* Deut 15:3 8058
The seventh year, the year of *r* Deut 15:9 8059
in the solemnity of the year of *r* Deut 31:10 8059
he made a *r* to the provinces, and Est 2:18 2010
to *r* unto the people a prisoner Mt 27:15 *630*
Whom will ye that I *r* unto you Mt 27:17 *630*
twain will ye that I *r* unto you Mt 27:21 *630*
Will ye that I *r* unto you the Mk 15:9 *630*
rather *r* Barabbas unto them Mk 15:11 *630*
therefore chastise him, and *r* him Lk 23:16 *630*
(For of necessity he must *r* one Lk 23:17 *630*
this man, and *r* unto us Barabbas Lk 23:18 *630*
therefore, willing to *r* Jesus Lk 23:20 *630*
that I should *r* unto you one at Jn 18:39 *630*
will ye therefore that I *r* unto Jn 18:39 *630*
thee, and have power to *r* thee Jn 19:10 *630*
Pilate sought to *r* him Jn 19:12 *630*

RELEASED {4}
Then *r* he Barabbas unto them Mt 27:26 *630*
Now at that feast he *r* unto them Mk 15:6 *630*
people, *r* Barabbas unto them, and Mk 15:15 *630*
he *r* unto them him that for Lk 23:25 *630*

RELIED {3}
because they *r* upon the LORD God 2Chr 13:18 8172
Because thou hast *r* on the king 2Chr 16:7 8172
not *r* on the LORD thy God, 2Chr 16:7 8172

RELIEF {1}
determined to send *r* unto the Acts 11:29 *1248*

RELIEVE {7}
then thou shalt *r* him Lev 25:35 2388
r the oppressed, judge the Is 1:17 833
things for meat to *r* the soul Lam 1:11 7725
should *r* my soul is far from me Lam 1:16 7725
their meat to *r* their souls Lam 1:19 7725
have widows, let them *r* them 1Ti 5:16 *1884*
that it may *r* them that are 1Ti 5:16 *1884*

RELIEVED {1}
if she have *r* the afflicted, if 1Ti 5:10 *1884*

RELIEVETH {1}
he *r* the fatherless and widow Ps 146:9 5749

RELIGION {5}
sect of our *r* I lived a Pharisee Acts 26:5 *2356*
in time past in the Jews' *r* Gal 1:13 *2454*
profited in the Jews' *r* above Gal 1:14 *2454*
own heart, this man's *r* is vain Jas 1:26 *2356*
Pure *r* and undefiled before God and Jas 1:27 *2356*

RELIGIOUS {2}
r proselytes followed Paul and Acts 13:43 *4576*
If any man among you seem to be *r* Jas 1:26 *2357*

RELY {1}
because thou didst *r* on the LORD 2Chr 16:8 8172

REMAIN {79}
R a widow at thy father's house, Gen 38:11 3427
that they may *r* in the river only Ex 8:9 7604
they shall *r* in the river only Ex 8:11 7604
nothing of it *r* until the morning Ex 12:10 3498
my sacrifice *r* until the morning Ex 23:18 3885
r unto the morning, then thou Ex 29:34 3498
if ought *r* until the third day, Lev 19:6 3498
r in the hand of him that hath Lev 25:28 1961
if there *r* but few years unto the Lev 25:52 7604
according to the years that *r* Lev 27:18 3498
that those which ye let *r* of them Num 33:55 3498
of every city, we left none to *r* Deut 2:34 8300
r all night until the morning Deut 16:4 3885
And those which *r* shall hear Deut 19:20 7604
shall *r* in thine house, and bewail Deut 21:13 3427
His body shall not *r* all night Deut 21:23 3885
shall *r* in the land which Moses Josh 1:14 3427
neither did there *r* any more Josh 2:11 6965
they let none of them *r* or escape Josh 8:22 8300
which *r* until this very day Josh 10:27
he let none *r* Josh 10:28 8300
he let none *r* in it Josh 10:30 8300
you by lot these nations that *r* Josh 23:4 7604
nations, these that *r* among you Josh 23:7 7604
even these that *r* among you Josh 23:12 7604
and why did Dan *r* in ships Judg 5:17 1481
we do for wives for them that *r* Judg 21:7 3498
we do for wives for them that *r* Judg 21:16 3498
shalt *r* by the stone Ezel 1Sa 20:19 3427
did Joab *r* there with all Israel 1Kin 11:16 3427
I only, *r* a prophet of the LORD 1Kin 18:22 3498
thee, five of the horses that *r* 2Kin 7:13 7604
for we *r* yet escaped, as it is Ezr 9:15 7604
the grave, and shall *r* in the tomb Job 21:32 8245
Those that *r* of him shall be Job 27:15 8300
into dens, and *r* in their places Job 37:8 7931
far off, and *r* in the wilderness Ps 55:7 3885
and the perfect shall *r* in it Prov 2:21 3498
the way of understanding shall *r* Prov 21:16 5117
As yet shall he *r* at Nob that day Is 10:32 5975
righteousness *r* in the fruitful Is 32:16 3427
that it may *r* in the house Is 44:13 3427
Which *r* among the graves, and Is 65:4 3427
shall *r* before me, saith the LORD Is 66:22 5975
so shall your seed and your name *r* Is 66:22 5975
them that *r* of this evil family Jer 8:3 7604
which *r* in all the places whither Jer 8:3 7604
and this city shall *r* for ever Jer 17:25 3427
that *r* in this land, and them that Jer 24:8 7604
those will I let *r* still in their Jer 27:11 3241
the vessels that *r* in this city Jer 27:19 3498
that *r* in the house of the LORD Jer 27:21 3498
the palace shall *r* after the Jer 30:18 3427
men of war that *r* in this city Jer 38:4 7604
none of them shall *r* or escape Jer 42:17 8300
of Judah, to leave you none to *r* Jer 44:7 7611
sojourn there, shall escape or *r* Jer 44:14 8300
it off, that none shall *r* in it Jer 51:62 3427
none of them shall *r*, nor of Eze 7:11
they that *r* shall be scattered Eze 17:21 7604
all the fowls of the heaven *r* Eze 31:13 7931
of the heaven to *r* upon thee Eze 32:4 7931
that *r* upon the face of the earth Eze 39:14 3498
if there *r* ten men in one house, Amos 6:9 3498
that did *r* in the day of distress Obad 14 8300
it shall *r* in the midst of his Zec 5:4 3885
All the families that *r*, every Zec 12:14 7604
And in the same house *r*, eating and Lk 10:7 *3306*
Gather up the fragments that *r* Jn 6:12 *4052*
you, that my joy might *r* in you Jn 15:11 *3306*
and that your fruit should *r* Jn 15:16 *3306*
that the bodies should not *r* upon Jn 19:31 *3306*
let her *r* unmarried, or be 1Cor 7:11 *3306*
greater part *r* unto this present 1Cor 15:6 *3306*
r unto the coming of the Lord 1Th 4:15 *4035*
r shall be caught up together 1Th 4:17 *4035*
which cannot be shaken may *r* Heb 12:27 *3306*
from the beginning shall *r* in you 1Jn 2:24 *3306*
and strengthen the things which *r* Rev 3:2 *3062*

REMAINDER {6}
thou shalt burn the *r* with fire Ex 29:34 3498
the *r* thereof shall Aaron and his Lev 6:16 3498
also the *r* of it shall be eaten Lev 7:16 3498
But the *r* of the flesh of the Lev 7:17 3498
neither name nor *r* upon the earth 2Sa 14:7 7611
the *r* of wrath shalt thou Ps 76:10 7611

REMAINED {53}
and Noah only *r* alive, and they Gen 7:23 7604
they that *r* fled to the mountain Gen 14:10 7604
there *r* not one Ex 8:31 7604
there *r* not any green thing in Ex 10:15 3498
there *r* not one locust in all the Ex 10:19 7604
there *r* not so much as one of Ex 14:28 7604
But there *r* two of the men in the Num 11:26 7604
Because he should have *r* in the Num 35:28 3427
their inheritance *r* in the tribe Num 36:12 1961
Bashan *r* of the remnant of giants Deut 3:11 7604
ye shall have *r* long in the land, Deut 4:25 3462
that the rest which *r* of them Josh 10:20 8277
in Gath, and in Ashdod, there *r* Josh 11:22 7604
who *r* of the remnant of the Josh 13:12 7604
there *r* among the children of Josh 18:2 3498
the Levites which *r* of the Josh 21:20 3498
of the children of Kohath that *r* Josh 21:26 3498
and there *r* ten thousand Judg 7:3 7604
that they which *r* were scattered 1Sa 11:11 7604
r in a mountain in the wilderness 1Sa 23:14 3427
his men *r* in the sides of the 1Sa 24:3 3427
So Tamar *r* desolate in her 2Sa 13:20 3427
which *r* in the days of his father 1Kin 22:46 7604
So Jehu slew all that *r* of the 2Kin 10:11 7604
he slew all that *r* unto Ahab in 2Kin 10:17 7604
there *r* the grove also in Samaria 2Kin 13:6 5975
none *r*, save the poorest sort of 2Kin 24:14 7604
that *r* in the land of Judah 2Kin 25:22 7604
the ark of God *r* with the family 1Chr 13:14 3427
also my wisdom *r* with me Eccl 2:9 5975
cities *r* of the cities of Judah Jer 34:7 7604
there *r* but wounded men among Jer 37:10 7604
Jeremiah had *r* there many days Jer 37:16 3427
Thus Jeremiah *r* in the court of Jer 37:21 3427
Jeremiah *r* in the court of the Jer 38:13 3427
of the people that *r* in the city Jer 39:9 7604
the rest of the people that *r* Jer 39:9 7604
all the people that *r* in Mizpah Jer 41:10 7604
therefore his taste *r* in him Jer 48:11 5975
they have *r* in their holds Jer 51:30 3427
of the people that *r* in the city Jer 52:15 7604
LORD's anger none escaped nor *r* Lam 2:22 8300
r there astonished among them Eze 3:15 3427
there *r* no strength in me Dan 10:8 7604
I *r* there with the kings of Dan 10:13 3498
there *r* no strength in me Dan 10:17 5975
it would have *r* until this day Mt 11:23 *3306*
that *r* twelve baskets full Mt 14:20 *4052*
unto them, and *r* speechless Lk 1:22 *1265*
that *r* to them twelve baskets Lk 9:17 *4052*
five barley loaves, which *r* over Jn 6:13 *4052*
Whiles it *r*, was it not thine own Acts 5:4 *3306*
r unmoveable, but the hinder part Acts 27:41 *3306*

REMAINEST {2}
Thou, O LORD, *r* for ever Lam 5:19 3427
but thou *r* Heb 1:11 *1265*

REMAINETH {37}
While the earth *r*, seedtime and Gen 8:22 3117
which *r* unto you from the hail, Ex 10:5 7604
that which *r* of it until the Ex 12:10 3498
that which *r* over lay up for you Ex 16:23 5736
the remnant that *r* of the Ex 26:12 5736
the tent, the half curtain that *r* Ex 26:12 5736
r in the length of the curtains Ex 26:13 5736
that which *r* of the flesh and of Lev 8:32 3498
Take the meat offering that *r* of Lev 10:12 3498
that *r* among them in the midst of Lev 16:16 7931
destroy him that *r* of the city Num 24:19 8300
of stones, that *r* unto this day Josh 8:29
there *r* yet very much land to be Josh 13:1 7604
This is the land that yet *r* Josh 13:2 7604
Then he made him that *r* have Judg 5:13 8300
which stone *r* unto this day in 1Sa 6:18

There *r* yet the youngest, and, — 1Sa 16:11 — 7604
of the LORD *r* under curtains — 1Chr 17:1
whosoever *r* in any place where he — Ezr 1:4 — 7604
erred, mine error *r* with myself — Job 19:4 — 3885
in your answers there *r* falsehood — Job 21:34 — 7604
In his neck *r* strength, and sorrow — Job 41:22 — 3885
he that *r* in Jerusalem, shall be — Is 4:3 — 3498
He that *r* in this city shall die — Jer 38:2 — 3427
and Zidon every helper that *r* — Jer 47:4 — 8300
and he that *r* and is besieged shall — Eze 6:12 — 7604
Egypt, so my spirit *r* among you — Hag 2:5 — 5975
but he that *r*, even he, shall be — Zec 9:7 — 7604
therefore your sin *r* — Jn 9:41 — 3306
it *r*, that both they that have — 1Cor 7:29 — 3588,3063
more that which *r* is glorious — 2Cor 3:11 — 3306
for until this day *r* the same — 2Cor 3:14 — 3306
his righteousness *r* for ever — 2Cor 9:9 — 3306
Seeing therefore it *r* that some — Heb 4:6 — 620
There *r* therefore a rest to the — Heb 4:9 — 620
there *r* no more sacrifice for — Heb 10:26 — 620
for his seed *r* in him — 1Jn 3:9 — 3306

REMAINING {14}
r thereon, the children of Israel — Num 9:22 — 7931
him until none was left to him *r* — Deut 3:3 — 8300
until he had left him none *r* — Josh 10:33 — 8300
he left none *r*, according to all — Josh 10:37 — 8300
he left none *r* — Josh 10:39 — 8300
he left none *r*, but utterly — Josh 10:40 — 8300
them, until they left them none *r* — Josh 11:8 — 8300
which were *r* of the families of — Josh 21:40 — 3498
we should be destroyed from *r* in — 2Sa 21:5 — 3320
priests, until he left him none *r* — 2Kin 10:11 — 8300
who *r* in the chambers were free — 1Chr 9:33
nor any *r* in his dwellings — Job 18:19 — 8300
not be any *r* of the house of Esau — Obad 18 — 8300
r on him, the same is he which — Jn 1:33 — 3306

REMALIAH *(rem-a-li'-ah)* {11} See REMALIAH'S. *Father of Pekah.*
But Pekah the son of *R*, a captain — 2Kin 15:25 — 7425
R began to reign over Israel in — 2Kin 15:27 — 7425
against Pekah the son of *R* — 2Kin 15:30 — 7425
R king of Israel began Jotham the — 2Kin 15:32 — 7425
of Syria, and Pekah the son of *R* — 2Kin 15:37 — 7425
year of Pekah the son of *R* Ahaz — 2Kin 16:1 — 7425
Pekah son of *R* king of Israel — 2Kin 16:5 — 7425
For Pekah the son of *R* slew in — 2Chr 28:6 — 7425
of Syria, and Pekah the son of *R* — Is 7:1 — 7425
with Syria, and of the son of *R* — Is 7:4 — 7425
Syria, Ephraim, and the son of *R* — Is 7:5 — 7425

REMALIAH'S *(rem-a-li'-ahs)* {2}
and the head of Samaria is *R* son — Is 7:9 — 7425
and rejoice in Rezin and *R* son — Is 8:6 — 7425

REMEDY {3}
his people, till there was no *r* — 2Chr 36:16 — 4832
shall he be broken without *r* — Prov 6:15 — 4832
be destroyed, and that without *r* — Prov 29:1 — 4832

REMEMBER {148}
I will *r* my covenant, which is — Gen 9:15 — 2142
that I may *r* the everlasting — Gen 9:16 — 2142
did not the chief butler *r* Joseph — Gen 40:23 — 2142
I do *r* my faults this day — Gen 41:9 — 2142
R this day, in which ye came out — Ex 13:3 — 2142
R the sabbath day, to keep it — Ex 20:8 — 2142
R Abraham, Isaac, and Israel, thy — Ex 32:13 — 2142
Then will I *r* my covenant with — Lev 26:42 — 2142
my covenant with Abraham will I *r* — Lev 26:42 — 2142
and I will *r* the land — Lev 26:42 — 2142
But I will for their sakes *r* the — Lev 26:45 — 2142
We *r* the fish, which we did eat — Num 11:5 — 2142
r all the commandments of the — Num 15:39 — 2142
That ye may *r*, and do all my — Num 15:40 — 2142
r that thou wast a servant in the — Deut 5:15 — 2142
but shalt well *r* what the LORD — Deut 7:18 — 2142
thou shalt *r* all the way which — Deut 8:2 — 2142
But thou shalt *r* the LORD thy God — Deut 8:18 — 2142
R, and forget not, how thou — Deut 9:7 — 2142
R thy servants, Abraham, Isaac, — Deut 9:27 — 2142
thou shalt *r* that thou wast a — Deut 15:15 — 2142
that thou mayest *r* the day when — Deut 16:3 — 2142
thou shalt *r* that thou wast a — Deut 16:12 — 2142
R what the LORD thy God did unto — Deut 24:9 — 2142
But thou shalt *r* that thou wast a — Deut 24:18 — 2142
thou shalt *r* that thou wast a — Deut 24:22 — 2142
R what Amalek did unto thee by — Deut 25:17 — 2142
R the days of old, consider the — Deut 32:7 — 2142
R the word which Moses the — Josh 1:13 — 2142
r also that I am your bone and — Judg 9:2 — 2142
r me, I pray thee, and strengthen — Judg 16:28 — 2142
r me, and not forget thine — 1Sa 1:11 — 2142
I *r* that which Amalek did to — 1Sa 15:2 — 6485
my lord, then *r* thine handmaid — 1Sa 25:31 — 2142
let the king *r* the LORD thy God, — 2Sa 14:11 — 2142
neither do thou *r* that which thy — 2Sa 19:19 — 2142
for *r* how that, when I and thou — 2Kin 9:25 — 2142
r now how I have walked before — 2Kin 20:3 — 2142
R his marvellous works that he — 1Chr 16:12 — 2142
r the mercies of David thy — 2Chr 6:42 — 2142
R, I beseech thee, the word that — Neh 1:8 — 2142
r the LORD, which is great and — Neh 4:14 — 2142
R me, O my God, concerning this, — Neh 13:14 — 2142
R me, O my God, concerning this — Neh 13:22 — 2142
R them, O my God, because they — Neh 13:29 — 2142
R me, O my God, for good — Neh 13:31 — 2142
R, I pray thee, who ever perished — Job 4:7 — 2142
O *r* that my life is wind — Job 7:7 — 2142
R, I beseech thee, that thou hast — Job 10:9 — 2142
r it as waters that pass away — Job 11:16 — 2142
appoint me a set time, and *r* me — Job 14:13 — 2142
Even when I *r* I am afraid — Job 21:6 — 2142
R that thou magnify his work, — Job 36:24 — 2142
him, *r* the battle, do no more — Job 41:8 — 2142
R all thy offerings, and accept — Ps 20:3 — 2142
but we will *r* the name of the — Ps 20:7 — 2142
All the ends of the world shall *r* — Ps 22:27 — 2142
R, O LORD, thy tender mercies and — Ps 25:6 — 2142
R not the sins of my youth, nor — Ps 25:7 — 2142
according to thy mercy *r* thou me — Ps 25:7 — 2142
When I *r* these things, I pour out — Ps 42:4 — 2142
therefore will I *r* thee from the — Ps 42:6 — 2142
When I *r* thee upon my bed, and — Ps 63:6 — 2142
R thy congregation, which thou — Ps 74:2 — 2142
R this, that the enemy hath — Ps 74:18 — 2142
r how the foolish man reproacheth — Ps 74:22 — 2142
but I will *r* the years of the — Ps 77:10 — 2142
I will *r* the works of the LORD — Ps 77:11 — 2142
surely I will *r* thy wonders of — Ps 77:11 — 2142
O *r* not against us former — Ps 79:8 — 2142
R how short my time is — Ps 89:47 — 2142
R, Lord, the reproach of thy — Ps 89:50 — 2142
to those that *r* his commandments — Ps 103:18 — 2142
R his marvellous works that he — Ps 105:5 — 2142
R me, O LORD, with the favour — Ps 106:4 — 2142
R the word unto thy servant, upon — Ps 119:49 — 2142
r David, and all his afflictions — Ps 132:1 — 2142
If I do not *r* thee, let my tongue — Ps 137:6 — 2142
R, O LORD, the children of Edom — Ps 137:7 — 2142
I *r* the days of old — Ps 143:5 — 2142
poverty, and *r* his misery no more — Prov 31:7 — 2142
not much *r* the days of his life — Eccl 5:20 — 2142
yet let him *r* the days of — Eccl 11:8 — 2142
R now thy Creator in the days of — Eccl 12:1 — 2142
we will *r* thy love more than wine — Song 1:4 — 2142
R now, O LORD, I beseech thee, — Is 38:3 — 2142
R ye not the former things, — Is 43:18 — 2142
own sake, and will not *r* thy sins — Is 43:25 — 2142
R these, O Jacob and Israel — Is 44:21 — 2142
R this, and shew yourselves men — Is 46:8 — 2142
R the former things of old — Is 46:9 — 2142
neither didst *r* the latter end of — Is 47:7 — 2142
shalt not *r* the reproach of thy — Is 54:4 — 2142
those that *r* thee in thy ways — Is 64:5 — 2142
neither *r* iniquity for ever — Is 64:9 — 2142
I *r* thee, the kindness of thy — Jer 2:2 — 2142
neither shall they *r* it — Jer 3:16 — 2142
he will now *r* their iniquity, and — Jer 14:10 — 2142
r, break not thy covenant with us — Jer 14:21 — 2142
r me, and visit me, and revenge me — Jer 15:15 — 2142
their children *r* their altars — Jer 17:2 — 2142
R that I stood before thee to — Jer 18:20 — 2142
him, I do earnestly *r* him still — Jer 31:20 — 2142
I will *r* their sin no more — Jer 31:34 — 2142
the land, did not the LORD *r* them — Jer 44:21 — 2142
r the LORD afar off, and let — Jer 51:50 — 2142
R, O LORD, what is come upon us — Lam 5:1 — 2142
r me among the nations whither — Eze 6:9 — 2142
Nevertheless I will *r* my covenant — Eze 16:60 — 2142
Then thou shalt *r* thy ways — Eze 16:61 — 2142
That thou mayest *r*, and be — Eze 16:63 — 2142
And there shall ye *r* your ways — Eze 20:43 — 2142
unto them, nor *r* Egypt any more — Eze 23:27 — 2142
Then shall ye *r* your own evil — Eze 36:31 — 2142
that I *r* all their wickedness — Hos 7:2 — 2142
now will he *r* their iniquity, and — Hos 8:13 — 2142
he will *r* their iniquity, he will — Hos 9:9 — 2142
r now what Balak king of Moab — Mic 6:5 — 2142
in wrath *r* mercy — Hab 3:2 — 2142
they shall *r* me in far countries — Zec 10:9 — 2142
R ye the law of Moses my servant, — Mal 4:4 — 2142
neither *r* the five loaves of the — Mt 16:9 — *3421*
we *r* that that deceiver said, — Mt 27:63 — *3415*
and do ye not *r* — Mk 8:18 — *3421*
and to *r* his holy covenant — Lk 1:72 — *3415*
r that thou in thy lifetime — Lk 16:25 — *3415*
R Lot's wife — Lk 17:32 — *3421*
r me when thou comest into thy — Lk 23:42 — *3415*
r how he spake unto you when he — Lk 24:6 — *3415*
R the word that I said unto you, — Jn 15:20 — *3421*
ye may *r* that I told you of them — Jn 16:4 — *3421*
Therefore watch, and *r*, that by — Acts 20:31 — *3421*
to *r* the words of the Lord Jesus, — Acts 20:35 — *3421*
that ye *r* me in all things, and — 1Cor 11:2 — *3415*
would that we should *r* the poor — Gal 2:10 — *3421*
Wherefore *r*, that ye being in — Eph 2:11 — *3421*
R my bonds — Col 4:18 — *3421*
For ye *r*, brethren, our labour and — 1Th 2:9 — *3421*
R ye not, that, when I was yet — 2Th 2:5 — *3421*
R that Jesus Christ of the seed — 2Ti 2:8 — *3421*
their iniquities will I *r* no more — Heb 8:12 — *3415*
and iniquities will I *r* no more — Heb 10:17 — *3415*
R them that are in bonds, as — Heb 13:3 — *3403*
R them which have the rule over — Heb 13:7 — *3421*
I will *r* his deeds which he doeth — 3Jn 10 — *5279*
r ye the words which were spoken — Jude 17 — *3415*
R therefore from whence thou art — Rev 2:5 — *3421*
R therefore how thou hast — Rev 3:3 — *3421*

REMEMBERED {57}
God *r* Noah, and every living thing — Gen 8:1 — 2142
of the plain, that God *r* Abraham — Gen 19:29 — 2142
God *r* Rachel, and God hearkened to — Gen 30:22 — 2142
Joseph *r* the dreams which he — Gen 42:9 — 2142
God *r* his covenant with Abraham, — Ex 2:24 — 2142
and I have *r* my covenant — Ex 6:5 — 2142
ye shall be *r* before the LORD — Num 10:9 — 2142
Israel *r* not the LORD their God — Judg 8:34 — 2142
and the LORD *r* her — 1Sa 1:19 — 2142
Thus Joash the king *r* not the — 2Chr 24:22 — 2142
he *r* Vashti, and what she had done — Est 2:1 — 2142
And that these days should be *r* — Est 9:28 — 2142
he shall be no more *r* — Job 24:20 — 2142
name to be *r* in all generations — Ps 45:17 — 2142
I *r* God, and was troubled — Ps 77:3 — 2142
they *r* that God was their rock, — Ps 78:35 — 2142
For he *r* that they were but flesh — Ps 78:39 — 2142
They *r* not his hand, nor the day — Ps 78:42 — 2142
He hath *r* his mercy and his truth — Ps 98:3 — 2142
He hath *r* his covenant for ever, — Ps 105:8 — 2142
For he *r* his holy promise, and — Ps 105:42 — 2142
they *r* not the multitude of thy — Ps 106:7 — 2142
he *r* for them his covenant, and — Ps 106:45 — 2142
of his fathers be *r* with the LORD — Ps 109:14 — 2142
Because that he *r* not to shew — Ps 109:16 — 2142
made his wonderful works to be *r* — Ps 111:4 — 2143
I *r* thy judgments of old, O LORD — Ps 119:52 — 2142
I have *r* thy name, O LORD, in the — Ps 119:55 — 2142
Who *r* us in our low estate — Ps 136:23 — 2142
yea, we wept, when we *r* Zion — Ps 137:1 — 2142
yet no man *r* that same poor man — Eccl 9:15 — 2142
many songs, that thou mayest be *r* — Is 23:16 — 2142
thou hast lied, and hast not *r* me — Is 57:11 — 2142
Then he *r* the days of old, Moses, — Is 63:11 — 2142
and the former shall not be *r* — Is 65:17 — 2142
that his name may be no more *r* — Jer 11:19 — 2142
Jerusalem *r* in the days of her — Lam 1:7 — 2142
r not his footstool in the day of — Lam 2:1 — 2142
which he hath done shall not be *r* — Eze 3:20 — 2142
hast not *r* the days of thy youth — Eze 16:22 — 2142
hast not *r* the days of thy youth — Eze 16:43 — 2142
have made your iniquity to be *r* — Eze 21:24 — 2142
thou shalt be no more *r* — Eze 21:32 — 2142
may not be *r* among the nations — Eze 25:10 — 2142
righteousnesses shall not be *r* — Eze 33:13 — 2142
shall no more be *r* by their name — Hos 2:17 — 2142
r not the brotherly covenant — Amos 1:9 — 2142
fainted within me I *r* the LORD — Jonah 2:7 — 2142
land, and they shall no more be *r* — Zec 13:2 — 2142
Peter *r* the word of Jesus, which — Mt 26:75 — *3415*
Peter *r* the word of the Lord, how — Lk 22:61 — *5279*
And they *r* his words, — Lk 24:8 — *3415*
his disciples *r* that it was — Jn 2:17 — *3415*
his disciples *r* that he had said — Jn 2:22 — *3415*
then *r* they that these things — Jn 12:16 — *3415*
Then *r* I the word of the Lord, — Acts 11:16 — *3415*
God hath *r* her iniquities — Rev 18:5 — *3421*

REMEMBEREST {2}
in the grave, whom thou *r* no more — Ps 88:5 — 2142
there *r* that thy brother hath — Mt 5:23 — *3415*

REMEMBERETH {5}
inquisition for blood, he *r* them — Ps 9:12 — 2142
he *r* that we are dust — Ps 103:14 — 2142
she *r* not her last end — Lam 1:9 — 2142
she *r* no more the anguish, for — Jn 16:21 — *3421*
whilst he *r* the obedience of you — 2Cor 7:15 — *363*

REMEMBERING {2}
R mine affliction and my misery, — Lam 3:19 — 2142
R without ceasing your work of — 1Th 1:3 — *3421*

REMEMBRANCE {53}
the *r* of Amalek from under heaven — Ex 17:14 — 2143
memorial, bringing iniquity to *r* — Num 5:15 — 2142
the *r* of Amalek from under heaven — Deut 25:19 — 2143
I would make the *r* of them to — Deut 32:26 — 2143
have no son to keep my name in *r* — 2Sa 18:18 — 2142
come unto me to call my sin to *r* — 1Kin 17:18 — 2142
His *r* shall perish from the earth — Job 18:17 — 2143
in death there is no *r* of thee — Ps 6:5 — 2143
thanks at the *r* of his holiness — Ps 30:4 — 2143
to cut off the *r* of them from the — Ps 34:16 — 2143
A Psalm of David, to bring to *r* — Ps 38:*t* — 2142
A Psalm of David, to bring to *r* — Ps 70:*t* — 2142
I call to *r* my song in the night — Ps 77:6 — 2142
of Israel may be no more in *r* — Ps 83:4 — 2142
thanks at the *r* of his holiness — Ps 97:12 — 2143
thy *r* unto all generations — Ps 102:12 — 2143
shall be in everlasting *r* — Ps 112:6 — 2143
There is no *r* of former things — Eccl 1:11 — 2146
neither shall there be any *r* of — Eccl 1:11 — 2146
For there is no *r* of the wise — Eccl 2:16 — 2146
to thy name, and to the *r* of thee — Is 26:8 — 2143
Put me in *r* — Is 43:26 — 2142
the posts hast thou set up thy *r* — Is 57:8 — 2146
My soul hath them still in *r* — Lam 3:20 — 2142
he will call to *r* the iniquity — Eze 21:23 — 2142
I say, that ye are come to *r* — Eze 21:24 — 2142
in calling to *r* the days of her — Eze 23:19 — 2142
Thus thou calledst to *r* the — Eze 23:21 — 6485
bringeth their iniquity to *r* — Eze 29:16 — 2142
a book of *r* was written before — Mal 3:16 — 2146
Peter calling to *r* saith unto him — Mk 11:21 — *364*
servant Israel, in *r* of his mercy — Lk 1:54 — *3415*
this do in *r* of me — Lk 22:19 — *364*
and bring all things to your *r* — Jn 14:26 — *5279*
are had in *r* in the sight of God — Acts 10:31 — *3415*
who shall bring you into *r* of my — 1Cor 4:17 — *363*
this do in *r* of me — 1Cor 11:24 — *364*
as oft as ye drink it, in *r* of me — 1Cor 11:25 — *364*
thank my God upon every *r* of you — Phil 1:3 — *3417*
that ye have good *r* of us always — 1Th 3:6 — *3417*
the brethren in *r* of these things — 1Ti 4:6 — *5294*
r of thee in my prayers night — 2Ti 1:3 — *3417*
When I call to *r* the unfeigned — 2Ti 1:5 — *5280*

Wherefore I put thee in *r* that ... 2Ti 1:6 *363*
Of these things put them in *r* ... 2Ti 2:14 *5279*
a *r* again made of sins every year ... Heb 10:3 *364*
But call to *r* the former days, in ... Heb 10:32 *363*
you always in *r* of these things ... 2Pet 1:12 *5179*
stir you up by putting you in *r* ... 2Pet 1:13 *5280*
to have these things always in *r* ... 2Pet 1:15 *3418*
up your pure minds by way of *r* ... 2Pet 3:1 *5280*
I will therefore put you in *r* ... Jude 5 *5179*
Babylon came in *r* before God ... Rev 16:19 *3415*

REMEMBRANCES {1}
Your *r* are like unto ashes, your ... Job 13:12 2146

REMETH *(re'-meth)* {1} See RAMOTH, JARMUTH. *A Levitical city in Issachar.*
And *R*, and En-gannim, ... Josh 19:21 7432

REMISSION {10}
shed for many for the *r* of sins ... Mt 26:28 *859*
of repentance for the *r* of sins ... Mk 1:4 *859*
his people by the *r* of their sins ... Lk 1:77 *859*
of repentance for the *r* of sins ... Lk 3:3 *859*
r of sins should be preached in ... Lk 24:47 *859*
of Jesus Christ for the *r* of sins ... Acts 2:38 *859*
in him shall receive *r* of sins ... Acts 10:43 *859*
for the *r* of sins that are past ... Rom 3:25 *3929*
without shedding of blood is no *r* ... Heb 9:22 *859*
Now where *r* of these is, there is ... Heb 10:18 *859*

REMIT {1}
Whose soever sins ye *r*, they are ... Jn 20:23 *863*

REMITTED {1}
ye remit, they are *r* unto them ... Jn 20:23 *863*

REMMON *(rem'-mon)* {1} See RIMMON. *A city in Judah.*
Ain, *R*, and Ether, and Ashan ... Josh 19:7 7417

REMMON-METHOAR *(rem'-mon-meth'-o-ar)* {1} *A city in Zebulun.*
and goeth out to *R* to Neah ... Josh 19:13 7417

REMNANT {92}
the *r* that remaineth of the ... Ex 26:12 5629
the *r* of the meat offerings shall ... Lev 2:3 3498
the *r* shall be the priest's, as a ... Lev 5:13
the *r* of the oil that is in the ... Lev 14:18 3498
remained of the *r* of giants ... Deut 3:11 3499
toward the *r* of his children ... Deut 28:54 3499
which was of the *r* of the giants ... Josh 12:4 3499
remained of the *r* of the giants ... Josh 13:12 3499
cleave unto the *r* of these ... Josh 23:12 3499
but of the *r* of the Amorites ... 2Sa 21:2 3499
to the *r* of the people, saying, ... 1Kin 12:23 3499
will take away the *r* of the house ... 1Kin 14:10 310
the *r* of the sodomites, which ... 1Kin 22:46 3499
prayer for the *r* that are left ... 2Kin 19:4 7611
the *r* that is escaped of the ... 2Kin 19:30 7604
of Jerusalem shall go forth a *r* ... 2Kin 19:31 7611
I will forsake the *r* of mine ... 2Kin 21:14 7611
with the *r* of the multitude, did ... 2Kin 25:11 3499
of the *r* of the sons of Kohath ... 1Chr 6:70 3498
and he will return to the *r* of you ... 2Chr 30:6 7604
and of all the *r* of Israel ... 2Chr 34:9 7611
the *r* of their brethren the ... Ezr 3:8 7605
God, to leave us a *r* to escape ... Ezr 9:8
there should be no *r* nor escaping ... Ezr 9:14 7611
The *r* that are left of the ... Neh 1:3 7604
but the *r* of them the fire ... Job 22:20 3499
had left unto us a very small *r* ... Is 1:9 8300
that the *r* of Israel, and such as ... Is 10:20 7605
The *r* shall return, even the ... Is 10:21 7605
shall return, even the *r* of Jacob ... Is 10:21 7605
yet a *r* of them shall return ... Is 10:22 7605
to recover the *r* of his people ... Is 11:11 7605
highway for the *r* of his people ... Is 11:16 7605
off from Babylon the name, and *r* ... Is 14:22 7605
famine, and he shall slay thy *r* ... Is 14:30 7611
Moab, and upon the *r* of the land ... Is 15:9 7611
the *r* shall be very small and ... Is 16:14 7605
from Damascus, and the *r* of Syria ... Is 17:3 7605
thy prayer for the *r* that is left ... Is 37:4 7611
the *r* that is escaped of the ... Is 37:31 7604
of Jerusalem shall go forth a *r* ... Is 37:32 7611
all the *r* of the house of Israel, ... Is 46:3 7611
glean the *r* of Israel as a vine ... Jer 6:9 7611
And there shall be no *r* of them ... Jer 11:23 7611
it shall be well with thy *r* ... Jer 15:11 8293
I will gather the *r* of my flock ... Jer 23:3 7611
and Ekron, and the *r* of Ashdod, ... Jer 25:20 7611
save thy people, the *r* of Israel ... Jer 31:7 7611
away captive into Babylon the *r* ... Jer 39:9 3499
of Babylon had left a *r* of Judah ... Jer 40:11 7611
and the *r* in Judah perish ... Jer 40:15 7611
all the *r* of the people whom he ... Jer 41:16 7611
LORD thy God, even for all this *r* ... Jer 42:2 7611
word of the LORD, ye *r* of Judah ... Jer 42:15 7611
concerning you, O ye *r* of Judah ... Jer 42:19 7611
forces, took all the *r* of Judah ... Jer 43:5 7611
And I will take the *r* of Judah ... Jer 44:12 7611
So that none of the *r* of Judah ... Jer 44:14 7611
all the *r* of Judah, that are gone ... Jer 44:28 7611
the *r* of the country of Caphtor ... Jer 47:4 7611
off with the *r* of their valley ... Jer 47:5 7611
the whole *r* of thee will I ... Eze 5:10 7611
Yet will I leave a *r*, that ye may ... Eze 6:8 3498
a full end of the *r* of Israel ... Eze 11:13 7611
therein shall be left a *r* that ... Eze 14:22 6413
thy *r* shall fall by the sword ... Eze 23:25 319
destroy the *r* of the sea coast ... Eze 25:16 7611
in the *r* whom the LORD shall call ... Joel 2:32 8300
the *r* of the Philistines shall ... Amos 1:8 7611
be gracious unto the *r* of Joseph ... Amos 5:15 7611
they may possess the *r* of Edom ... Amos 9:12 7611
surely gather the *r* of Israel ... Mic 2:12 7611
I will make her that halted a *r* ... Mic 4:7 7611
then the *r* of his brethren shall ... Mic 5:3 3499
the *r* of Jacob shall be in the ... Mic 5:7 7611
the *r* of Jacob shall be among the ... Mic 5:8 7611
of the *r* of his heritage ... Mic 7:18 7611
all the *r* of the people shall ... Hab 2:8 3499
I will cut off the *r* of Baal from ... Zeph 1:4 7605
for the *r* of the house of Judah ... Zeph 2:7 7611
the *r* of my people shall possess ... Zeph 2:9 3499
The *r* of Israel shall not do ... Zeph 3:13 7611
with all the *r* of the people, ... Hag 1:12 7611
spirit of all the *r* of the people ... Hag 1:14 7611
r of this people in these days ... Zec 8:6 7611
I will cause the *r* of this people ... Zec 8:12 7611
the *r* took his servants, and ... Mt 22:6 *3062*
of the sea, a *r* shall be saved ... Rom 9:27 *2640*
a *r* according to the election of ... Rom 11:5 *3005*
the *r* were affrighted, and gave ... Rev 11:13 *3062*
make war with the *r* of her seed ... Rev 12:17 *3062*
the *r* were slain with the sword ... Rev 19:21 *3062*

REMOVE {45}
to *r* it from Ephraim's head unto ... Gen 48:17 5493
of Israel *r* from tribe to tribe ... Num 36:7 5437
Neither shall the inheritance *r* ... Num 36:9 5437
Thou shalt not *r* thy neighbour's ... Deut 19:14 5253
then ye shall *r* from your place, ... Josh 3:3 5265
then would I *r* Abimelech ... Judg 9:29 5493
So David would not *r* the ark of ... 2Sa 6:10 5493
I will *r* Judah also out of my ... 2Kin 23:27 5493
to *r* them out of his sight, for ... 2Kin 24:3 5493
Neither will I any more *r* the ... 2Chr 33:8 5493
Some *r* the landmarks ... Job 24:2 5472
till I die I will not *r* mine ... Job 27:5 5493
not the hand of the wicked *r* me ... Ps 36:11 5110
R thy stroke away from me ... Ps 39:10 5493
R from me reproach and contempt ... Ps 119:22 1556
R from me the way of lying ... Ps 119:29 5493
r thy foot from evil ... Prov 4:27 5493
R thy way far from her, and come ... Prov 5:8 7368
R not the ancient landmark, which ... Prov 22:28 5253
R not the old landmark ... Prov 23:10 5253
R far from me vanity and lies ... Prov 30:8 7368
Therefore *r* sorrow from thy heart ... Eccl 11:10 5493
the earth shall *r* out of her ... Is 13:13 7493
from his place shall he not *r* ... Is 46:7 4185
my sight, then shalt thou not *r* ... Jer 4:1 5110
to *r* you far from your land ... Jer 27:10 7368
that I should *r* it from before my ... Jer 32:31 5493
they shall *r*, they shall depart, ... Jer 50:3 5110
R out of the midst of Babylon, and ... Jer 50:8 5110
and *r* by day in their sight ... Eze 12:3 1540
thou shalt *r* from thy place to ... Eze 12:3 1540
they shall *r* and go into captivity ... Eze 12:11 5493
R the diadem, and take off the ... Eze 21:26 5493
r violence and spoil, and execute ... Eze 45:9 5493
were like them that *r* the bound ... Hos 5:10 5253
But I will *r* far off from you the ... Joel 2:20 7368
that ye might *r* them far from ... Joel 3:6 7368
which ye shall not *r* your necks ... Mic 2:3 4185
I will *r* the iniquity of that ... Zec 3:9 4185
mountain shall *r* toward the north ... Zec 14:4 4185
mountain, *R* hence to yonder place ... Mt 17:20 *3327*
and it shall *r* ... Mt 17:20 *3327*
be willing, *r* this cup from me ... Lk 22:42 *3911*
so that I could *r* mountains ... 1Cor 13:2 *3179*
will *r* thy candlestick out of his ... Rev 2:5 *2795*

REMOVED {91}
Noah *r* the covering of the ark, ... Gen 8:13 5493
he *r* from thence unto a mountain ... Gen 12:8 6275
Then Abram *r* his tent, and came and ... Gen 13:18 167
he *r* from thence, and digged ... Gen 26:22 6275
he *r* that day the he goats that ... Gen 30:35 5493
he *r* them to cities from one end ... Gen 47:21 5674
he *r* the swarms of flies from ... Ex 8:31 5493
went before the camp of Israel, *r* ... Ex 14:19 5265
and when the people saw it, they *r* ... Ex 20:18 5128
the people *r* from Hazeroth ... Num 12:16 5265
From thence they *r*, and pitched in ... Num 21:12 5265
From thence they *r*, and pitched on ... Num 21:13 5265
children of Israel *r* from Rameses ... Num 33:5 5265
they *r* from Etham, and turned ... Num 33:7 5265
they *r* from Marah, and came unto ... Num 33:9 5265
they *r* from Elim, and encamped by ... Num 33:10 5265
they *r* from the Red sea, and ... Num 33:11 5265
they *r* from Alush, and encamped at ... Num 33:14 5265
they *r* from the desert of Sinai, ... Num 33:16 5265
they *r* from Libnah, and pitched at ... Num 33:21 5265
they *r* from mount Shapher, and ... Num 33:24 5265
they *r* from Haradah, and pitched ... Num 33:25 5265
they *r* from Makheloth, and ... Num 33:26 5265
they *r* from Tarah, and pitched in ... Num 33:28 5265
they *r* from Bene-jaakan, and ... Num 33:32 5265
they *r* from Jotbathah, and ... Num 33:34 5265
they *r* from Ezion-gaber, and ... Num 33:36 5265
they *r* from Kadesh, and pitched in ... Num 33:37 5265
they *r* from Dibon-gad, and ... Num 33:46 5265
they *r* from Almon-diblathaim, and ... Num 33:47 5265
shalt be *r* into all the kingdoms ... Deut 28:25 2189
they *r* from Shittim, and came to ... Josh 3:1 5265
when the people *r* from their ... Josh 3:14 5265
why his hand is not *r* from you ... 1Sa 6:3 5493
Therefore Saul *r* him from him ... 1Sa 18:13 5493
he *r* Amasa out of the highway ... 2Sa 20:12 5437
When he was *r* out of the highway, ... 2Sa 20:13 3014
r all the idols that his fathers ... 1Kin 15:12 5493
even her he *r* from being queen, ... 1Kin 15:13 5493
But the high places were not *r* ... 1Kin 15:14 5493
that the high places were not *r* ... 2Kin 15:4 5493
the high places were not *r* ... 2Kin 15:35 5493
r the laver from off them ... 2Kin 16:17 5493
and *r* them out of his sight ... 2Kin 17:18 5493
Until the LORD *r* Israel out of ... 2Kin 17:23 5493
The nations which thou hast *r* ... 2Kin 17:26 1540
He *r* the high places, and brake ... 2Kin 18:4 5493
of my sight, as I have *r* Israel ... 2Kin 23:27 5493
Geba, and they *r* them to Manahath ... 1Chr 8:6 1540
he *r* them, and begat Uzza, and ... 1Chr 8:7 1540
he *r* her from being queen, ... 2Chr 15:16 5493
they *r* the burnt offerings, that ... 2Chr 35:12 5493
the rock is *r* out of his place ... Job 14:18 6275
the rock be *r* out of his place ... Job 18:4 6275
mine hope hath he *r* like a tree ... Job 19:10 5265
Even so would he have *r* thee out ... Job 36:16 5493
we fear, though the earth be *r* ... Ps 46:2 4171
I *r* his shoulder from the burden ... Ps 81:6 5493
the west, so far hath he *r* our ... Ps 103:12 7368
that it should not be *r* for ever ... Ps 104:5 4131
as mount Zion, which cannot be *r* ... Ps 125:1 4131
The righteous shall never be *r* ... Prov 10:30 4131
And the LORD have *r* men far away ... Is 6:12 7368
I have *r* the bounds of the people ... Is 10:13 5493
Madmenah is *r* ... Is 10:31 5074
fastened in the sure place be *r* ... Is 22:25 4185
shall be *r* like a cottage ... Is 24:20 5110
thou hadst *r* it far unto all the ... Is 26:15 7368
but have *r* their heart far from ... Is 29:13 7368
be *r* into a corner any more ... Is 30:20 3670
stakes thereof shall ever be *r* ... Is 33:20 5265
is *r* from me as a shepherd's tent ... Is 38:12 1556
shall depart, and the hills be *r* ... Is 54:10 4131
the covenant of my peace be *r* ... Is 54:10 4131
I will cause them to be *r* into ... Jer 15:4 2189
I will deliver them to be *r* into ... Jer 24:9 2189
will deliver them to be *r* to all ... Jer 29:18 2189
I will make you to be *r* into all ... Jer 34:17 2189
therefore she is *r* ... Lam 1:8 5206
thou hast *r* my soul far off from ... Lam 3:17 2186
streets, and their gold shall be *r* ... Eze 7:19 5079
them, and will give them to be *r* ... Eze 23:46 2189
as the uncleanness of a *r* woman ... Eze 36:17 5079
stretched themselves shall be *r* ... Amos 6:7 5493
how hath he *r* it from me ... Mic 2:4 4185
day shall the decree be far *r* ... Mic 7:11
say unto this mountain, Be thou *r* ... Mt 21:21 *142*
say unto this mountain, Be thou *r* ... Mk 11:23 *142*
he *r* him into this land, wherein ... Acts 7:4 *3351*
And when he had *r* him, he raised ... Acts 13:22 *3179*
I marvel that ye are so soon *r* ... Gal 1:6 *3346*

REMOVETH {5}
Cursed be he that *r* his ... Deut 27:17 5253
Which *r* the mountains, and they ... Job 9:5 6275
He *r* away the speech of the ... Job 12:20 5493
Whoso *r* stones shall be hurt ... Eccl 10:9 5265
he *r* kings, and setteth up kings ... Dan 2:21 5709

REMOVING {5}
r from thence all the speckled and ... Gen 30:32 5493
a captive, and *r* to and fro ... Is 49:21 5493
of man, prepare thee stuff for *r* ... Eze 12:3 1473
in their sight, as stuff for *r* ... Eze 12:4 1473
signifieth the *r* of those things ... Heb 12:27 *3331*

REMPHAN *(rem'-fan)* {1} *An idol worshipped by Israel.*
Moloch, and the star of your god *R* ... Acts 7:43 *4481*

REND {19}
the hole, that it should not *r* ... Ex 39:23
heads, neither *r* your clothes ... Lev 10:6 6533
then he shall *r* it out of the ... Lev 13:56 7167
his head, nor *r* his clothes ... Lev 21:10 6533
R your clothes, and gird you with ... 2Sa 3:31 7167
I will surely *r* the kingdom from ... 1Kin 11:11 7167
but I will *r* it out of the hand ... 1Kin 11:12 7167
Howbeit I will not *r* away all the ... 1Kin 11:13 7167
I will *r* the kingdom out of the ... 1Kin 11:31 7167
didst *r* thy clothes, and weep ... 2Chr 34:27 7167
A time to *r*, and a time to sew ... Eccl 3:7 7167
that thou wouldest *r* the heavens ... Is 64:1 7167
and a stormy wind shall *r* it ... Eze 13:11 1234
I will even *r* it with a stormy ... Eze 13:13 1234
break, and *r* all their shoulder ... Eze 29:7 1234
will *r* the caul of their heart, ... Hos 13:8 7167
r your heart, and not your ... Joel 2:13 7167
feet, and turn again and *r* you ... Mt 7:6 *4486*
among themselves, Let us not *r* it ... Jn 19:24 *4977*

RENDER {33}
which they shall *r* unto me ... Num 18:9 7725
I will *r* vengeance to mine ... Deut 32:41 7725
and will *r* vengeance to his ... Deut 32:43 7725
did God *r* upon their heads ... Judg 9:57 7725
The LORD *r* to every man his ... 1Sa 26:23 7725
r unto every man according unto ... 2Chr 6:30 5415
for he will *r* unto man his ... Job 33:26 7725
work of a man shall he *r* unto him ... Job 34:11 7999
r to them their desert ... Ps 28:4 7725
They also that *r* evil for good ... Ps 38:20 7999
I will *r* praises unto thee ... Ps 56:12 7999
r unto our neighbours sevenfold ... Ps 79:12 7725
r a reward to the proud ... Ps 94:2 7725
What shall I *r* unto the LORD for ... Ps 116:12 7725
shall not he *r* to every man ... Prov 24:12 7725
I will *r* to the man according to ... Prov 24:29 7725
seven men that can *r* a reason ... Prov 26:16 7725

to *r* his anger with fury, and his Is 66:15 7725
he will *r* unto her a recompence Jer 51:6 7999
I will *r* unto Babylon and to all Jer 51:24 7999
R unto them a recompence, O LORD, Lam 3:64 7725
so will we *r* the calves of our Hos 14:2 7999
will ye *r* me a recompence Joel 3:4 7999
that I will *r* double unto thee Zec 9:12 7725
which shall *r* him the fruits in Mt 21:41 *591*
R therefore unto Caesar the Mt 22:21 *591*
R to Caesar the things that are Mk 12:17 *591*
R therefore unto Caesar the Lk 20:25 *591*
Who will *r* to every man according Rom 2:6 *591*
R therefore to all their dues Rom 13:7 *591*
Let the husband *r* unto the wife 1Cor 7:3 *591*
can we *r* to God again for you 1Th 3:9 *467*
See that none *r* evil for evil 1Th 5:15 *591*

RENDERED {1}
Thus God *r* the wickedness of Judg 9:56 7725
r unto the king of Israel an 2Kin 3:4 7725
But Hezekiah *r* not again 2Chr 32:25 7725
a man's hands shall be *r* unto him Prov 12:14 7725

RENDEREST {1}
for thou *r* to every man according Ps 62:12 7999

RENDERETH {1}
a voice of the LORD that *r* Is 66:6 7999

RENDERING {1}
Not *r* evil for evil, or railing 1Pet 3:9 *591*

RENDING {1}
r it in pieces, while there is Ps 7:2 6561

RENEW {6}
to Gilgal, and *r* the kingdom there 1Sa 11:14 2318
r a right spirit within me Ps 51:10 2318
the LORD shall *r* their strength Is 40:31 2498
let the people *r* their strength Is 41:1 2498
r our days as of old Lam 5:21 2318
to *r* them again unto repentance Heb 6:6 *340*

RENEWED {6}
r the altar of the LORD, that was 2Chr 15:8 2318
in me, and my bow was *r* in my hand Job 29:20 2498
thy youth is *r* like the eagle's Ps 103:5 2318
the inward man is *r* day by day 2Cor 4:16 *341*
be *r* in the spirit of your mind Eph 4:23 *365*
which is *r* in knowledge after the Col 3:10 *341*

RENEWEST {2}
Thou *r* thy witnesses against me, Job 10:17 2318
thou *r* the face of the earth Ps 104:30 2318

RENEWING {2}
transformed by the *r* of your mind Rom 12:2 *342*
and *r* of the Holy Ghost Titus 3:5 *342*

RENOUNCED {1}
But have *r* the hidden things of 2Cor 4:2 *550*

RENOWN {7}
men which were of old, men of *r* Gen 6:4 8034
in the congregation, men of *r* Num 16:2 8034
thy *r* went forth among the Eze 16:14 8034
the harlot because of thy *r* Eze 16:15 8034
raise up for them a plant of *r* Eze 34:29 8034
it shall be to them a *r* the day Eze 39:13 8034
hand, and hast gotten thee *r* Dan 9:15 8034

RENOWNED {4}
These were the *r* of the Num 1:16 7121
of evildoers shall never be *r* Is 14:20 7121
and rulers, great lords and *r* Eze 23:23 7121
the *r* city, which wast strong in Eze 26:17 1984

RENT {68}
and he *r* his clothes Gen 37:29 7167
is without doubt *r* in pieces Gen 37:33 2963
Jacob *r* his clothes, and put Gen 37:34 7167
Then they *r* their clothes, and Gen 44:13 7167
of an habergeon, that it be not *r* Ex 28:32 7167
plague is, his clothes shall be *r* Lev 13:45 6533
the land, *r* their clothes Num 14:6 7167
Joshua *r* his clothes, and fell to Josh 7:6 7167
asses, and wine bottles, old, and *r* Josh 9:4 1234
and, behold, they be *r* Josh 9:13 1234
that he *r* his clothes, and said, Judg 11:35 7167
he *r* him as he would have *r* a Judg 14:6 8156
r him as he would have *r* a kid Judg 14:6 8156
the same day with his clothes *r* 1Sa 4:12 7167
the skirt of his mantle, and it *r* 1Sa 15:27 7167
The LORD hath *r* the kingdom of 1Sa 15:28 7167
for the LORD hath *r* the kingdom 1Sa 28:17 7167
camp from Saul with his clothes *r* 2Sa 1:2 7167
hold on his clothes, and *r* them 2Sa 1:11 7167
r her garment of divers colours 2Sa 13:19 7167
stood by with their clothes *r* 2Sa 13:31 7167
came to meet him with his coat *r* 2Sa 15:32 7167
so that the earth *r* with the 1Kin 1:40 1234
on him, and *r* it in twelve pieces 1Kin 11:30 7167
Behold, the altar shall be *r* 1Kin 13:3 7167
The altar also was *r*, and the 1Kin 13:5 7167
r the kingdom away from the house 1Kin 14:8 7167
strong wind *r* the mountains, and 1Kin 19:11 6561
that he *r* his clothes, and put 1Kin 21:27 7167
clothes, and *r* them in two pieces 2Kin 2:12 7167
that he *r* his clothes, and said, 2Kin 5:7 7167
king of Israel had *r* his clothes 2Kin 5:8 7167
Wherefore hast thou *r* thy clothes 2Kin 5:8 7167
the woman, that he *r* his clothes 2Kin 6:30 7167
Athaliah *r* her clothes, and cried, 2Kin 11:14 7167
For he *r* Israel from the house of 2Kin 17:21 7167
to Hezekiah with their clothes *r* 2Kin 18:37 7167
that he *r* his clothes, and covered 2Kin 19:1 7167
of the law, that he *r* his clothes 2Kin 22:11 7167
hast *r* thy clothes, and wept 2Kin 22:19 7167
Then Athaliah *r* her clothes 2Chr 23:13 7167
of the law, that he *r* his clothes 2Chr 34:19 7167
I *r* my garment and my mantle, and Ezr 9:3 7167
having *r* my garment and my mantle, Ezr 9:5 7167
Mordecai *r* his clothes, and put on Est 4:1 7167
r his mantle, and shaved his head, Job 1:20 7167
they *r* every one his mantle, and Job 2:12 7167
and the cloud is not *r* under them Job 26:8 1234
and instead of a girdle a *r* Is 3:24 5364
to Hezekiah with their clothes *r* Is 36:22 7167
that he *r* his clothes, and covered Is 37:1 7167
nor *r* their garments, neither the Jer 36:24 7167
beards shaven, and their clothes *r* Jer 41:5 7167
pain, and No shall be *r* asunder Eze 30:16 1234
garment, and the *r* is made worse Mt 9:16 *4978*
the high priest *r* his clothes Mt 26:65 *1284*
the veil of the temple was *r* in Mt 27:51 *4977*
earth did quake, and the rocks *r* Mt 27:51 *4977*
the old, and the *r* is made worse Mk 2:21 *4978*
r him sore, and came out of him Mk 9:26 *4682*
the high priest *r* his clothes Mk 14:63 *1284*
the veil of the temple was *r* in Mk 15:38 *4977*
then both the new maketh a *r* Lk 5:36 *4977*
of the temple was *r* in the midst Lk 23:45 *4977*
they *r* their clothes, and ran in Acts 14:14 *1284*
the magistrates *r* off their Acts 16:22 *4048*

RENTEST {1}
though thou *r* thy face with Jer 4:30 7167

REPAID {1}
to the righteous good shall be *r* Prov 13:21 7999

REPAIR {14}
let them *r* the breaches of the 2Kin 12:5 2388
Why *r* ye not the breaches of the 2Kin 12:7 2388
neither to *r* the breaches of the 2Kin 12:8 2388
hewed stone to *r* the breaches of 2Kin 12:12 2388
laid out for the house to *r* it 2Kin 12:12 2393
to *r* the breaches of the house, 2Kin 22:5 2388
and hewn stone to *r* the house 2Kin 22:6 2388
minded to *r* the house of the LORD 2Chr 24:4 2318
gather of all Israel money to *r* 2Chr 24:5 2388
carpenters to *r* the house of the 2Chr 24:12 2318
to *r* the house of the LORD his 2Chr 34:8 2388
in the house of the LORD, to *r* 2Chr 34:10 910
to *r* the desolations thereof, and Ezr 9:9 5975
they shall *r* the waste cities, Is 61:4 2318

REPAIRED {44}
r the cities, and dwelt in them Judg 21:23 1129
r the breaches of the city of 1Kin 11:27 5462
he *r* the altar of the LORD that 1Kin 18:30 7495
not *r* the breaches of the house 2Kin 12:6 2388
r therewith the house of the LORD 2Kin 12:14 2388
Joab *r* the rest of the city 1Chr 11:8 2421
the house of the LORD, and *r* them 2Chr 29:3 2388
r Millo in the city of David, and 2Chr 32:5 2388
he *r* the altar of the LORD, and 2Chr 33:16 1129
next unto them *r* Meremoth the son Neh 3:4 2388
next unto them *r* Meshullam the Neh 3:4 2388
next unto them *r* Zadok the son of Neh 3:4 2388
And next unto them the Tekoites *r* Neh 3:5 2388
Moreover the old gate *r* Jehoiada Neh 3:6 2388
next unto them *r* Melatiah the Neh 3:7 2388
Next unto him *r* Uzziel the son of Neh 3:8 2388
Next unto him also *r* Hananiah the Neh 3:8 2388
next unto them *r* Rephaiah the son Neh 3:9 2388
next unto them *r* Jedaiah the son Neh 3:10 2388
next unto him *r* Hattush the son Neh 3:10 2388
r the other piece, and the tower Neh 3:11 2388
next unto him *r* Shallum the son Neh 3:12 2388
The valley gate *r* Hanun, and the Neh 3:13 2388
But the dung gate *r* Malchiah the Neh 3:14 2388
r Shallun the son of Colhozeh Neh 3:15 2388
After him *r* Nehemiah the son of Neh 3:16 2388
After him *r* the Levites, Rehum Neh 3:17 2388
Next unto him *r* Hashabiah Neh 3:17 2388
After him *r* their brethren, Bavai Neh 3:18 2388
next to him *r* Ezer the son of Neh 3:19 2388
earnestly *r* the other piece Neh 3:20 2388
After him *r* Meremoth the son of Neh 3:21 2388
after him *r* the priests, the men Neh 3:22 2388
After him *r* Benjamin and Hashub Neh 3:23 2388
After him *r* Azariah the son of Neh 3:23 2388
After him *r* Binnui the son of Neh 3:24 2388
them the Tekoites *r* another piece Neh 3:27 2388
the horse gate *r* the priests Neh 3:28 2388
After them *r* Zadok the son of Neh 3:29 2388
After him *r* also Shemaiah the son Neh 3:29 2388
After him *r* Hananiah the son of Neh 3:30 2388
After him *r* Meshullam the son of Neh 3:30 2388
After him *r* Malchiah the Neh 3:31 2388
the sheep gate *r* the goldsmiths Neh 3:32 2388

REPAIRER {1}
The *r* of the breach, The restorer Is 58:12 1443

REPAIRING {1}
the *r* of the house of God, behold 2Chr 24:27 3247

REPAY {8}
he will *r* him to his face Deut 7:10 7999
who shall *r* him what he hath done Job 21:31 7999
prevented me, that I should *r* him Job 41:11 7999
deeds, accordingly he will *r* Is 59:18 7999
the islands he will *r* recompence Is 59:18 7999
when I come again, I will *r* thee Lk 10:35 *591*
I will *r*, saith the Lord Rom 12:19 *457*
with mine own hand, I will *r* it Philem 19 *661*

REPAYETH {1}
r them that hate him to their Deut 7:10 7999

REPEATETH {1}
but he that *r* a matter separateth Prov 17:9 8138

REPENT {46}
the people *r* when they see war Ex 13:17 5162
r of this evil against thy people Ex 32:12 5162
the son of man, that he should *r* Num 23:19 5162
r himself for his servants, when Deut 32:36 5162
of Israel will not lie nor *r* 1Sa 15:29 5162
he is not a man, that he should *r* 1Sa 15:29 5162
they were carried captives, and *r* 1Kin 8:47 7725
myself, and *r* in dust and ashes Job 42:6 5162
let it *r* thee concerning thy Ps 90:13 5162
LORD hath sworn, and will not *r* Ps 110:4 5162
he will *r* himself concerning his Ps 135:14 5162
I have purposed it, and will not *r* Jer 4:28 5162
I will *r* of the evil that I Jer 18:8 5162
voice, then I will *r* of the good Jer 18:10 5162
that I may *r* me of the evil, Jer 26:3 5162
the LORD will *r* him of the evil Jer 26:13 5162
for I *r* me of the evil that I Jer 42:10 5162
R, and turn yourselves from your Eze 14:6 7725
R, and turn yourselves from all Eze 18:30 7725
will I spare, neither will I *r* Eze 24:14 5162
knoweth if he will return and *r* Joel 2:14 5162
can tell if God will turn and *r* Jonah 3:9 5162
And saying, *R* ye Mt 3:2 *3340*
began to preach, and to say, *R* Mt 4:17 *3340*
r ye, and believe the gospel Mk 1:15 *3340*
and preached that men should *r* Mk 6:12 *3340*
but, except ye *r*, ye shall all Lk 13:3 *3340*
but, except ye *r*, ye shall all Lk 13:5 *3340*
them from the dead, they will *r* Lk 16:30 *3340*
and if he *r*, forgive him Lk 17:3 *3340*
turn again to thee, saying, I *r* Lk 17:4 *3340*
Then Peter said unto them, *R* Acts 2:38 *3340*
R ye therefore, and be converted, Acts 3:19 *3340*
R therefore of this thy Acts 8:22 *3340*
all men every where to *r* Acts 17:30 *3340*
the Gentiles, that they should *r* Acts 26:20 *3340*
I do not *r*, though I did *r* 2Cor 7:8 *3338*
him, The Lord sware and will not *r* Heb 7:21 *3338*
from whence thou art fallen, and *r* Rev 2:5 *3340*
out of his place, except thou *r* Rev 2:5 *3340*
R; or else I will Rev 2:16 *3340*
her space to *r* of her fornication Rev 2:21 *3340*
except they *r* of their deeds Rev 2:22 *3340*
and heard, and hold fast, and *r* Rev 3:3 *3340*
be zealous therefore, and *r* Rev 3:19 *3340*

REPENTANCE {26}
r shall be hid from mine eyes Hos 13:14 5164
forth therefore fruits meet for *r* Mt 3:8 *3341*
baptize you with water unto *r* Mt 3:11 *3341*
the righteous, but sinners to *r* Mt 9:13 *3341*
preach the baptism of *r* for the Mk 1:4 *3341*
the righteous, but sinners to *r* Mk 2:17 *3341*
preaching the baptism of *r* for Lk 3:3 *3341*
therefore fruits worthy of *r* Lk 3:8 *3341*
the righteous, but sinners to *r* Lk 5:32 *3341*
just persons, which need no *r* Lk 15:7 *3341*
And that *r* and remission of sins Lk 24:47 *3341*
Saviour, for to give *r* to Israel Acts 5:31 *3341*
the Gentiles granted *r* unto life Acts 11:18 *3341*
his coming the baptism of *r* to Acts 13:24 *3341*
baptized with the baptism of *r* Acts 19:4 *3341*
r toward God, and faith toward our Acts 20:21 *3341*
to God, and do works meet for *r* Acts 26:20 *3341*
goodness of God leadeth thee to *r* Rom 2:4 *3341*
and calling of God are without *r* Rom 11:29 *278*
sorry, but that ye sorrowed to *r* 2Cor 7:9 *3341*
For godly sorrow worketh *r* to 2Cor 7:10 *3341*
r to the acknowledging of the 2Ti 2:25 *3341*
foundation of *r* from dead works Heb 6:1 *3341*
away, to renew them again unto *r* Heb 6:6 *3341*
for he found no place of *r* Heb 12:17 *3341*
but that all should come to *r* 2Pet 3:9 *3341*

REPENTED {32}
it *r* the LORD that he had made Gen 6:6 5162
the LORD *r* of the evil which he Ex 32:14 5162
for it *r* the LORD because of Judg 2:18 5162
the children of Israel *r* them for Judg 21:6 5162
the people *r* them for Benjamin, Judg 21:15 5162
the LORD *r* that he had made Saul 1Sa 15:35 5162
the LORD *r* him of the evil, and 2Sa 24:16 5162
he *r* him of the evil, and said to 1Chr 21:15 5162
r according to the multitude of Ps 106:45 5162
no man *r* him of his wickedness, Jer 8:6 5162
the LORD overthrew, and *r* not Jer 20:16 5162
the LORD *r* him of the evil which Jer 26:19 5162
after that I was turned, I *r* Jer 31:19 5162
The LORD *r* for this Amos 7:3 5162
The LORD *r* for this Amos 7:6 5162
God *r* of the evil, that he had Jonah 3:10 5162
the LORD of hosts, and I *r* not Zec 8:14 5162
were done, because they *r* not Mt 11:20 *3340*
they would have *r* long ago in Mt 11:21 *3340*
because they *r* at the preaching Mt 12:41 *3340*
but afterward he *r*, and went Mt 21:29 *3338*
r not afterward, that ye might Mt 21:32 *3338*
r himself, and brought again the Mt 27:3 *3338*
you, they had a great while ago *r* Lk 10:13 *3340*
for they *r* at the preaching of Lk 11:32 *3340*
to salvation not to be *r* of 2Cor 7:10 *278*
have not *r* of the uncleanness and 2Cor 12:21 *3340*
and she *r* not Rev 2:21 *3340*

R

r not of the works of their hands … Rev 9:20 *3340*
Neither *r* they of their murders, … Rev 9:21 *3340*
they *r* not to give him glory … Rev 16:9 *3340*
sores, and *r* not of their deeds … Rev 16:11 *3340*

REPENTEST {1}
kindness, and *r* thee of the evil … Jonah 4:2 5162

REPENTETH {5}
for it *r* me that I have made them … Gen 6:7 5162
It *r* me that I have set up Saul … 1Sa 15:11 5162
kindness, and *r* him of the evil … Joel 2:13 5162
in heaven over one sinner that *r* … Lk 15:7 *3340*
of God over one sinner that *r* … Lk 15:10 *3340*

REPENTING {1}
I am weary with *r* … Jer 15:6 5162

REPENTINGS {1}
my *r* are kindled together … Hos 11:8 5150

REPETITIONS {1}
But when ye pray, use not vain *r* … Mt 6:7 *945*

REPHAEL *(re'-fa-el)* {1} *A sanctuary servant.*
Othni, and *R*, and Obed, Elzabad, … 1Chr 26:7 7501

REPHAH *(re'-fah)* {1} *A grandson of Ephraim.*
R was his son, also Resheph, and … 1Chr 7:25 7506

REPHAIAH *(ref-a-i'-ah)* {5} See RAPHA, RHESA.
1. Head of a family.
the sons of *R*, the sons of Arnan, … 1Chr 3:21 7509
2. A captain of Simeon.
Pelatiah, and Neariah, and *R* … 1Chr 4:42 7509
3. A son of Tola.
Uzzi, and *R*, and Jeriel, and Jahmai, … 1Chr 7:2 7509
4. Son of Binea.
R his son, Eleasah his son, Azel … 1Chr 9:43 7509
5. A repairer of Jerusalem's wall.
them repaired *R* the son of Hur … Neh 3:9 7509

REPHAIM *(re-fa'-im)* {6} See REPHAIMS. *A valley near Jerusalem.*
themselves in the valley of *R* … 2Sa 5:18 7497
themselves in the valley of *R* … 2Sa 5:22 7497
pitched in the valley of *R* … 2Sa 23:13 7497
encamped in the valley of *R* … 1Chr 11:15 7497
themselves in the valley of *R* … 1Chr 14:9 7497
gathereth ears in the valley of *R* … Is 17:5 7497

REPHAIMS *(re-fa'-ims)* {2} See REPHAIM. *A tribe of Canaanites.*
smote the *R* in Ashteroth Karnaim, … Gen 14:5 7497
and the Perizzites, and the *R* … Gen 15:20 7497

REPHAN See REMPHAN.

REPHIDIM *(ref'-i-dim)* {5} *An Israelite encampment in the wilderness.*
of the LORD, and pitched in *R* … Ex 17:1 7508
and fought with Israel in *R* … Ex 17:8 7508
For they were departed from *R* … Ex 19:2 7508
from Alush, and encamped at *R* … Num 33:14 7508
And they departed from *R*, and … Num 33:15 7508

REPLENISH {2}
r the earth, and subdue it … Gen 1:28 4390
and multiply, and *r* the earth … Gen 9:1 4390

REPLENISHED {5}
because they be *r* from the east … Is 2:6 4390
that pass over the sea, have *r* … Is 23:2 4390
I have *r* every sorrowful soul … Jer 31:25 4390
I shall be *r*, now she is laid … Eze 26:2 4390
and thou wast *r*, and made very … Eze 27:25 4390

REPLIEST {1}
who art thou that *r* against God … Rom 9:20 *470*

REPORT {30}
unto his father their evil *r* … Gen 37:2 1681
Thou shalt not raise a false *r* … Ex 23:1 8088
they brought up an evil *r* of the … Num 13:32 1681
bring up the evil *r* upon the land … Num 14:37 1681
heaven, who shall hear *r* of thee … Deut 2:25 8088
for it is no good *r* that I hear … 1Sa 2:24 8052
It was a true *r* that I heard in … 1Kin 10:6 1697
It was a true *r* which I heard in … 2Chr 9:5 1697
might have matter for an evil *r* … Neh 6:13 8034
a good *r* maketh the bones fat … Prov 15:30 8052
As at the *r* concerning Egypt, so … Is 23:5 8088
be sorely pained at the *r* of Tyre … Is 23:5 8088
vexation only to understand the *r* … Is 28:19 8052
Who hath believed our *r* … Is 53:1 8052
R, say they, and we will *r* it … Jer 20:10 5046
Babylon hath heard the *r* of them … Jer 50:43 8088
Lord, who hath believed our *r* … Jn 12:38 *189*
among you seven men of honest *r* … Acts 6:3 *3140*
of good *r* among all the nation of … Acts 10:22 *3140*
having a good *r* of all the Jews … Acts 22:12 *3140*
Lord, who hath believed our *r* … Rom 10:16 *189*
r that God is in you of a truth … 1Cor 14:25 *518*
By honour and dishonour, by evil *r* … 2Cor 6:8 *1426*
and good *r*: as deceivers … 2Cor 6:8 *2162*
whatsoever things are of good *r* … Phil 4:8 *2163*
good *r* of them which are without … 1Ti 3:7 *3141*
it the elders obtained a good *r* … Heb 11:2 *3140*
obtained a good *r* through faith … Heb 11:39 *3140*
Demetrius hath good *r* of all men … 3Jn 12 *3140*

REPORTED {12}
It is *r* among the heathen, and … Neh 6:6 8085
now shall it be *r* to the king … Neh 6:7 8085
Also they *r* his good deeds before … Neh 6:19 559
in their eyes, when it shall be *r* … Est 1:17 559
r the matter, saying, I have done … Eze 9:11 7725
this saying is commonly *r* among … Mt 28:15 *1310*
r all that the chief priests and … Acts 4:23 *518*
Which was well *r* of by the … Acts 16:2 *3140*
rather, (as we be slanderously *r* … Rom 3:8 *987*
It is *r* commonly that there is … 1Cor 5:1 *191*
Well *r* of for good works … 1Ti 5:10 *3140*
which are now *r* unto you by them … 1Pet 1:12 *312*

REPROACH {88}
and said, God hath taken away my *r* … Gen 30:23 2781
for that were a *r* unto us … Gen 34:14 2781
away the *r* of Egypt from off you … Josh 5:9 2781
among the sheaves, and *r* her not … Ruth 2:15 3637
lay it for a *r* upon all Israel … 1Sa 11:2 2781
and taketh away the *r* from Israel … 1Sa 17:26 2781
of my *r* from the hand of Nabal … 1Sa 25:39 2781
hath sent to *r* the living God … 2Kin 19:4 2778
hath sent him to *r* the living God … 2Kin 19:16 2778
are in great affliction and *r* … Neh 1:3 2781
Jerusalem, that we be no more a *r* … Neh 2:17 2781
turn their *r* upon their own head, … Neh 4:4 2781
the *r* of the heathen our enemies … Neh 5:9 2781
evil report, that they might *r* me … Neh 6:13 2778
me, and plead against me my *r* … Job 19:5 2781
I have heard the check of my *r* … Job 20:3 3639
my heart shall not *r* me so long … Job 27:6 2778
nor taketh up a *r* against his … Ps 15:3 2781
a *r* of men, and despised of the … Ps 22:6 2781
I was a *r* among all mine enemies, … Ps 31:11 2781
make me not the *r* of the foolish … Ps 39:8 2781
in my bones, mine enemies *r* me … Ps 42:10 2778
Thou makest us a *r* to our … Ps 44:13 2781
save me from the *r* of him that … Ps 57:3 2778
for thy sake I have borne *r* … Ps 69:7 2781
with fasting, that was to my *r* … Ps 69:10 2781
Thou hast known my *r*, and my shame … Ps 69:19 2781
R hath broken my heart … Ps 69:20 2781
let them be covered with *r* … Ps 71:13 2781
how long shall the adversary *r* … Ps 74:10 2778
he put them to a perpetual *r* … Ps 78:66 2781
We are become a *r* to our … Ps 79:4 2781
into their bosom their *r*, … Ps 79:12 2781
he is a *r* to his neighbours … Ps 89:41 2781
Lord, the *r* of thy servants … Ps 89:50 2781
the *r* of all the mighty people … Ps 89:50 2781
Mine enemies *r* me all the day … Ps 102:8 2778
I became also a *r* unto them … Ps 109:25 2781
Remove from me *r* and contempt … Ps 119:22 2781
Turn away my *r* which I fear … Ps 119:39 2781
his *r* shall not be wiped away … Prov 6:33 2781
but sin is a *r* to any people … Prov 14:34 2617
also contempt, and with ignominy *r* … Prov 18:3 2781
that causeth shame, and bringeth *r* … Prov 19:26 2659
yea, strife and *r* shall cease … Prov 22:10 7036
by thy name, to take away our *r* … Is 4:1 2781
profit, but a shame, and also a *r* … Is 30:5 2781
hath sent to *r* the living God … Is 37:4 2778
hath sent to *r* the living God … Is 37:17 2778
fear ye not the *r* of men, neither … Is 51:7 2781
shalt not remember the *r* of thy … Is 54:4 2781
word of the LORD is unto them a *r* … Jer 6:10 2781
of the LORD was made a *r* unto me … Jer 20:8 2781
bring an everlasting *r* upon you … Jer 23:40 2781
earth for their hurt, to be a *r* … Jer 24:9 2781
and an hissing, and a *r*, among all … Jer 29:18 2781
I did bear the *r* of my youth … Jer 31:19 2781
astonishment, and a curse, and a *r* … Jer 42:18 2781
a *r* among all the nations of the … Jer 44:8 2781
astonishment, and a curse, and a *r* … Jer 44:12 2781
shall become a desolation, a *r* … Jer 49:13 2781
because we have heard *r* … Jer 51:51 2781
he is filled full with *r* … Lam 3:30 2781
Thou hast heard their *r*, O LORD, … Lam 3:61 2781
consider, and behold our *r* … Lam 5:1 2781
a *r* among the nations that are … Eze 5:14 2781
So it shall be a *r* and a taunt, an … Eze 5:15 2781
as at the time of thy *r* of the … Eze 16:57 2781
Ammonites, and concerning their *r* … Eze 21:28 2781
I made thee a *r* unto the heathen … Eze 22:4 2781
bear the *r* of the people any more … Eze 36:15 2781
r of famine among the heathen … Eze 36:30 2781
thy people are become a *r* to all … Dan 9:16 2781
the *r* offered by him to cease … Dan 11:18 2781
without his own *r* he shall cause … Dan 11:18 2781
his *r* shall his Lord return unto … Hos 12:14 2781
and give not thine heritage to *r* … Joel 2:17 2781
make you a *r* among the heathen … Joel 2:19 2781
ye shall bear the *r* of my people … Mic 6:16 2781
I have heard the *r* of Moab … Zeph 2:8 2781
to whom the *r* of it was a burden … Zeph 3:18 2781
me, to take away my *r* among men … Lk 1:25 *3681*
their company, and shall *r* you … Lk 6:22 *3679*
I speak as concerning *r*, as … 2Cor 11:21 *819*
lest he fall into *r* and the snare … 1Ti 3:7 *3680*
we both labour and suffer *r* … 1Ti 4:10 *3679*
Esteeming the *r* of Christ greater … Heb 11:26 *3680*
without the camp, bearing his *r* … Heb 13:13 *3680*

REPROACHED {15}
Whom hast thou *r* and blasphemed … 2Kin 19:22 2778
messengers thou hast *r* the Lord … 2Kin 19:23 2778
These ten times have ye *r* me … Job 19:3 3637
For it was not an enemy that *r* me … Ps 55:12 2778
that *r* thee are fallen upon me … Ps 69:9 2778
this, that the enemy hath *r* … Ps 74:18 2778
wherewith they have *r* thee … Ps 79:12 2778
Wherewith thine enemies have *r* … Ps 89:51 2778
wherewith they have *r* the … Ps 89:51 2778
Whom hast thou *r* and blasphemed … Is 37:23 2778
thy servants hast thou *r* the Lord … Is 37:24 2778
whereby they have *r* my people … Zeph 2:8 2778
their pride, because they have *r* … Zeph 2:10 2778
of them that *r* thee fell on me … Rom 15:3 *3679*
If ye be *r* for the name of Christ … 1Pet 4:14 *3679*

REPROACHES {5}
the *r* of them that reproached … Ps 69:9 2781
to the curse, and Israel to *r* … Is 43:28 1421
The *r* of them that reproached … Rom 15:3 *3679*
pleasure in infirmities, in *r* … 2Cor 12:10 *5196*
were made a gazingstock both by *r* … Heb 10:33 *3680*

REPROACHEST {1}
thus saying thou *r* us also … Lk 11:45 *5195*

REPROACHETH {7}
a stranger, the same *r* the LORD … Num 15:30 1442
For the voice of him that *r* … Ps 44:16 2778
how the foolish man *r* thee daily … Ps 74:22 2781
wherewith to answer him that *r* me … Ps 119:42 2778
oppresseth the poor *r* his Maker … Prov 14:31 2778
mocketh the poor *r* his Maker … Prov 17:5 2778
that I may answer him that *r* me … Prov 27:11 2778

REPROACHFULLY {2}
have smitten me upon the cheek *r* … Job 16:10 2781
to the adversary to speak *r* … 1Ti 5:14 *5484,3059*

REPROBATE {4}
R silver shall men call them, … Jer 6:30 3988
God gave them over to a *r* mind … Rom 1:28 *96*
minds, *r* concerning the faith … 2Ti 3:8 *96*
and unto every good work *r* … Titus 1:16 *96*

REPROBATES {3}
Christ is in you, except ye be *r* … 2Cor 13:5 *96*
ye shall know that we are not *r* … 2Cor 13:6 *96*
is honest, though we be as *r* … 2Cor 13:7 *96*

REPROOF {15}
and are astonished at his *r* … Job 26:11 1606
Turn you at my *r* … Prov 1:23 8433
my counsel, and would none of my *r* … Prov 1:25 8433
they despised all my *r* … Prov 1:30 8433
and my heart despised *r* … Prov 5:12 8433
but he that refuseth *r* erreth … Prov 10:17 8433
but he that hateth *r* is brutish … Prov 12:1 8433
regardeth *r* shall be honoured … Prov 13:18 8433
he that regardeth *r* is prudent … Prov 15:5 8433
and he that hateth *r* shall die … Prov 15:10 8433
The ear that heareth the *r* of … Prov 15:31 8433
but he that heareth *r* getteth … Prov 15:32 8433
A *r* entereth more into a wise man … Prov 17:10 1606
The rod and *r* give wisdom … Prov 29:15 8433
is profitable for doctrine, for *r* … 2Ti 3:16 *1650*

REPROOFS {2}
not, and in whose mouth are no *r* … Ps 38:14 8433
r of instruction are the way of … Prov 6:23 8433

REPROVE {19}
will *r* the words which the LORD … 2Kin 19:4 3198
but what doth your arguing *r* … Job 6:25 3198
Do ye imagine to *r* words, and the … Job 6:26 3198
He will surely *r* you, if ye do … Job 13:10 3198
Will he *r* thee for fear of thee … Job 22:4 3198
I will not *r* thee for thy … Ps 50:8 3198
but I will *r* thee, and set them in … Ps 50:21 3198
and let him *r* me … Ps 141:5 3198
R not a scorner, lest he hate … Prov 9:8 3198
r one that hath understanding, and … Prov 19:25 3198
unto his words, lest he *r* thee … Prov 30:6 3198
neither *r* after the hearing of … Is 11:3 3198
r with equity for the meek of the … Is 11:4 3198
will *r* the words which the LORD … Is 37:4 3198
and thy backslidings shall *r* thee … Jer 2:19 3198
let no man strive, nor *r* another … Hos 4:4 3198
he will *r* the world of sin, and of … Jn 16:8 *1651*
of darkness, but rather *r* them … Eph 5:11 *1651*
r, rebuke, exhort with all … 2Ti 4:2 *1651*

REPROVED {10}
thus she was *r* … Gen 20:16 3198
Abraham *r* Abimelech because of a … Gen 21:25 3198
he *r* kings for their sakes, … 1Chr 16:21 3198
he *r* kings for their sakes … Ps 105:14 3198
that being often *r* hardeneth his … Prov 29:1 8433
thou not *r* Jeremiah of Anathoth … Jer 29:27 1605
what I shall answer when I am *r* … Hab 2:1 8433
being *r* by him for Herodias his … Lk 3:19 *1651*
light, lest his deeds should be *r* … Jn 3:20 *1651*
But all things that are *r* are … Eph 5:13 *1651*

REPROVER {2}
so is a wise *r* upon an obedient … Prov 25:12 3198
dumb, and shalt not be to them a *r* … Eze 3:26 3198

REPROVETH {4}
he that *r* God, let him answer it … Job 40:2 3198
He that *r* a scorner getteth to … Prov 9:7 3256
scorner loveth not one that *r* him … Prov 15:12 3198
snare for him that *r* in the gate … Is 29:21 3198

REPUTATION {5}
folly him that is in *r* for wisdom … Eccl 10:1 3368
had in *r* among all the people, and … Acts 5:34 *5093*
privately to them which were of *r* … Gal 2:2 *1380*
But made himself of no *r*, and took … Phil 2:7 *2758*
and hold such in *r* … Phil 2:29 *1784*

REPUTED {2}
beasts, and *r* vile in your sight … Job 18:3 2804
of the earth are *r* as nothing … Dan 4:35 2804

REQUEST {19}
them, I would desire a *r* of you … Judg 8:24 7596
perform the *r* of his handmaid … 2Sa 14:15 1697
fulfilled the *r* of his servant … 2Sa 14:22 1697
and the king granted him all his *r* … Ezr 7:6 1246

me, For what dost thou make *r* Neh 2:4 1245
to make *r* before him for her Est 4:8 1245
and what is thy *r* Est 5:3 1246
and what is thy *r* Est 5:6 1246
and said, My petition and my *r* is Est 5:7 1246
my petition, and to perform my *r* Est 5:8 1246
and what is thy *r* Est 7:2 1246
my petition, and my people at my *r* Est 7:3 1246
Haman stood up to make *r* for his Est 7:7 1245
or what is thy *r* further Est 9:12 1246
Oh that I might have my *r* Job 6:8 7596
not withholden the *r* of his lips Ps 21:2 782
And he gave them their *r* Ps 106:15 7596
Making *r*, if by any means now at Rom 1:10 *1189*
for you all making *r* with joy Phil 1:4 *1162*

REQUESTED {5}
earrings that he *r* was a thousand Judg 8:26 7592
he *r* for himself that he might 1Kin 19:4 7592
God granted him that which he *r* 1Chr 4:10 7592
therefore he *r* of the prince of Dan 1:8 1245
Then Daniel *r* of the king Dan 2:49 1156

REQUESTS {1}
let your *r* be made known unto God Phil 4:6 *155*

REQUIRE {29}
your blood of your lives will I *r* Gen 9:5 1875
hand of every beast will I *r* it Gen 9:5 1875
brother will I *r* the life of man Gen 9:5 1875
of my hand didst thou *r* it Gen 31:39 1245
of my hand shalt thou *r* him Gen 43:9 1245
doth the LORD thy God *r* of thee Deut 10:12 7592
in my name, I will *r* it of him Deut 18:19 1875
thy God will surely *r* it of thee Deut 23:21 1875
let the LORD himself *r* it Josh 22:23 1245
Let the LORD even *r* it at the 1Sa 20:16 1245
but one thing I *r* of thee 2Sa 3:13 7592
now *r* his blood of your hand 2Sa 4:11 1245
and whatsoever thou shalt *r* of me 2Sa 19:38 977
all times, as the matter shall *r* 1Kin 8:59 3117
then doth my lord *r* this thing 1Chr 21:3 1245
The LORD look upon it, and *r* it 2Chr 24:22 1875
shall *r* of you, it be done Ezr 7:21 7593
For I was ashamed to *r* of the Ezr 8:22 7592
them, and will *r* nothing of them Neh 5:12 1245
in his heart, Thou wilt not *r* it Ps 10:13 1875
his blood will I *r* at thine hand Eze 3:18 1245
his blood will I *r* at thine hand Eze 3:20 1245
there will I *r* your offerings, and Eze 20:40 1875
but his blood will I *r* at the Eze 33:6 1875
his blood will I *r* at thine hand Eze 33:8 1245
I will *r* my flock at their hand, Eze 34:10 1875
and what doth the LORD *r* of thee Mic 6:8 1875
For the Jews *r* a sign, and the 1Cor 1:22 *154*
flower of her age, and need so *r* 1Cor 7:36 *1096*

REQUIRED {22}
behold, also his blood is *r* Gen 42:22 1875
unto them such things as they *r* Ex 12:36
the king's business *r* haste 1Sa 21:8 1961
and when he *r*, they set bread 2Sa 12:20 7592
as every day's work *r* 1Chr 16:37 3117
as the duty of every day *r* 2Chr 8:14 3117
Why hast thou not *r* of the 2Chr 24:6 1875
as the duty of every day *r* Ezr 3:4 3117
yet for all this *r* not I the Neh 5:18 1245
she *r* nothing but what Hegai the Est 2:15 1245
and sin offering hast thou not *r* Ps 40:6 7592
us away captive *r* of us a song Ps 137:3 7592
they that wasted us *r* of us mirth Ps 137:3
Two things have I *r* of thee Prov 30:7 7592
who hath *r* this at your hand, to Is 1:12 1245
may be *r* of this generation Lk 11:50 *1567*
It shall be *r* of this generation Lk 11:51 *1567*
night thy soul shall be *r* of thee Lk 12:20 *523*
is given, of him shall be much *r* Lk 12:48 *2212*
might have *r* mine own with usury Lk 19:23 *4238*
that it should be as they *r* Lk 23:24 *155*
Moreover it is *r* in stewards 1Cor 4:2 *2212*

REQUIREST {1}
I will do to thee all that thou *r* Ruth 3:11 559

REQUIRETH {2}
and God *r* that which is past Eccl 3:15 1245
is a rare thing that the king *r* Dan 2:11 7593

REQUIRING {1}
r that he might be crucified Lk 23:23 *154*

REQUITE {9}
will certainly *r* us all the evil Gen 50:15 7725
Do ye thus *r* the LORD, O foolish Deut 32:6 1580
I also will *r* you this kindness, 2Sa 2:6 6213
that the LORD will *r* me good for 2Sa 16:12 7725
I will *r* thee in this plat, saith 2Kin 9:26 7999
and spite, to *r* it with thy hand Ps 10:14 5414
and raise me up, that I may *r* them Ps 41:10 7999
God of recompences shall surely *r* Jer 51:56 7999
at home, and to *r* their parents 1Ti 5:4 *287,591*

REQUITED {2}
as I have done, so God hath *r* me Judg 1:7 7999
he hath *r* me evil for good 1Sa 25:21 7725

REQUITING {1}
by *r* the wicked, by recompensing 2Chr 6:23 7725

REREWARD {6}
which was the *r* of all the camps Num 10:25 622
the *r* came after the ark, the Josh 6:9 622
but the *r* came after the ark of Josh 6:13 622
passed on in the *r* with Achish 1Sa 29:2 314

the God of Israel will be your *r* Is 52:12 622
glory of the LORD shall be thy *r* Is 58:8 622

RESCUE {3}
and thou shalt have none to *r* them Deut 28:31 3467
r my soul from their destructions Ps 35:17 7725
take away, and none shall *r* him Hos 5:14 5337

RESCUED {3}
So the people *r* Jonathan, that he 1Sa 14:45 6299
and David *r* his two wives 1Sa 30:18 5337
r him, having understood that he Acts 23:27 *1807*

RESCUETH {1}
He delivereth and *r*, and he worketh Dan 6:27 5338

RESEMBLANCE {1}
This is their *r* through all the Zec 5:6 5869

RESEMBLE {1}
and whereunto shall I *r* it Lk 13:18 *3666*

RESEMBLED {1}
each one *r* the children of a king Judg 8:18 8389

RESEN *(re'-zen)* {1} *A city between Nineveh and Calah.*
R between Nineveh and Calah Gen 10:12 7449

RESERVE {3}
Will he *r* his anger for ever Jer 3:5 5201
for I will pardon them whom I *r* Jer 50:20 7604
to *r* the unjust unto the day of 2Pet 2:9 *5083*

RESERVED {16}
Hast thou not *r* a blessing for me Gen 27:36 680
most holy things, *r* from the fire Num 18:9
because we *r* not to each man his Judg 21:22 3947
she had *r* after she was sufficed Ruth 2:18 3498
but *r* of them for an hundred 2Sa 8:4 3498
but *r* of them an hundred chariots 1Chr 18:4 3498
That the wicked is *r* to the day Job 21:30 2820
Which I have *r* against the time Job 38:23 2820
be *r* unto the hearing of Augustus Acts 25:21 *5083*
I have *r* to myself seven thousand Rom 11:4 *2641*
not away, *r* in heaven for you, 1Pet 1:4 *5083*
darkness, to be *r* unto judgment 2Pet 2:4 *5083*
mist of darkness is *r* for ever 2Pet 2:17 *5083*
r unto fire against the day of 2Pet 3:7 *5083*
he hath *r* in everlasting chains Jude 6 *5083*
to whom is *r* the blackness of Jude 13 *5083*

RESERVETH {2}
he *r* unto us the appointed weeks Jer 5:24 8104
he *r* wrath for his enemies Nah 1:2 5201

RESHEPH *(re'-shef)* {1} *A son of Rephah.*
And Rephah was his son, also *R* 1Chr 7:25 7566

RESIDUE {34}
they shall eat the *r* of that Ex 10:5 3499
the *r* of the families of the sons 1Chr 6:66
the *r* of Israel, of the priests, Neh 11:20 7605
the *r* of the number of archers, Is 21:17 7605
unto the *r* of his people, Is 28:5 7605
am deprived of the *r* of my years Is 38:10 3499
the *r* thereof he maketh a god, Is 44:17 7611
shall I make the *r* thereof an Is 44:19 3499
the *r* of them that remain of this Jer 8:3 7611
the *r* of them will I deliver to Jer 15:9 7611
the *r* of Jerusalem, that remain Jer 24:8 7611
concerning the *r* of the vessels Jer 27:19 3499
the *r* of the elders which were Jer 29:1 3499
with all the *r* of the princes of Jer 39:3 7611
the *r* of the people that were in Jer 41:10 7611
the *r* of the people that remained Jer 52:15 3499
wilt thou destroy all the *r* of Eze 9:8 7611
thy *r* shall be devoured by the Eze 23:25 319
your feet the *r* of your pastures Eze 34:18 3499
ye must foul the *r* with your feet Eze 34:18 3498
unto the *r* of the heathen Eze 36:3 7611
derision to the *r* of the heathen Eze 36:4 7611
against the *r* of the heathen Eze 36:5 7611
the *r* in length over against the Eze 48:18 3498
the *r* shall be for the prince, on Eze 48:21 3498
stamped the *r* with the feet of it Dan 7:7 7606
stamped the *r* with his feet Dan 7:19 7606
the *r* of my people shall spoil Zeph 2:9 7611
to the *r* of the people, saying, Hag 2:2 7611
But now I will not be unto the *r* Zec 8:11 7611
the *r* of the people shall not be Zec 14:2 3499
Yet had he the *r* of the spirit Mal 2:15 7605
they went and told it unto the *r* Mk 16:13 *3062*
That the *r* of men might seek Acts 15:17 *2645*

RESIST {10}
at his right hand to *r* him Zec 3:1 7853
say unto you, That ye *r* not evil Mt 5:39 *436*
not be able to gainsay nor *r* Lk 21:15 *436*
were not able to *r* the wisdom Acts 6:10 *436*
ye do always *r* the Holy Ghost Acts 7:51 *496*
they that *r* shall receive to Rom 13:2 *436*
so do these also *r* the truth 2Ti 3:8 *436*
R the devil, and he will flee from Jas 4:7 *436*
and he doth not *r* you Jas 5:6 *498*
Whom *r* stedfast in the faith, 1Pet 5:9 *436*

RESISTED {2}
For who hath *r* his will Rom 9:19 *436*
Ye have not yet *r* unto blood Heb 12:4 *478*

RESISTETH {4}
Whosoever therefore *r* the power Rom 13:2 *498*
the power, *r* the ordinance of God Rom 13:2 *436*
God *r* the proud, but giveth grace Jas 4:6 *498*
for God *r* the proud, and giveth 1Pet 5:5 *498*

RESOLVED {1}
I am *r* what to do, that, when I Lk 16:4 *1097*

RESORT {4}
the trumpet, *r* ye thither unto us Neh 4:20 6908
whereunto I may continually *r* Ps 71:3 935
the people *r* unto him again Mk 10:1 *4848*
temple, whither the Jews always *r* Jn 18:20 *4905*

RESORTED {5}
r to him out of all their coasts 2Chr 11:13 3320
and all the multitude *r* unto him Mk 2:13 *2064*
many *r* unto him, and said, John Jn 10:41 *2064*
for Jesus ofttimes *r* thither with Jn 18:2 *4863*
unto the women which *r* thither Acts 16:13 *4905*

RESPECT {34}
And the LORD had *r* unto Abel Gen 4:4 8159
and to his offering he had not *r* Gen 4:5 8159
of Israel, and God had *r* unto them Ex 2:25 3045
thou shalt not *r* the person of Lev 19:15 5375
For I will have *r* unto you Lev 26:9 6437
R not thou their offering Num 16:15 6437
Ye shall not *r* persons in Deut 1:17 5234
thou shalt not *r* persons, neither Deut 16:19 6437
neither doth God *r* any person 2Sa 14:14 5375
Yet have thou *r* unto the prayer 1Kin 8:28 6437
had *r* unto them, because of his 2Kin 13:23 6437
Have *r* therefore to the prayer of 2Chr 6:19 6437
nor *r* of persons, nor taking of 2Chr 19:7 4856
Have *r* unto the covenant Ps 74:20 5027
when I have *r* unto all thy Ps 119:6 5027
precepts, and have *r* unto thy ways Ps 119:15 5027
I will have *r* unto thy statutes Ps 119:117 8159
yet hath he *r* unto the lowly Ps 138:6 7200
to have *r* of persons in judgment Prov 24:23 5234
To have *r* of persons is not good Prov 28:21 5234
his eyes shall have *r* to the Holy Is 17:7 7200
neither shall *r* that which his Is 17:8 7200
neither had *r* unto him that Is 22:11 7200
For there is no *r* of persons with Rom 2:11 *4382*
glorious had no glory in this *r* 2Cor 3:10 *3313*
neither is there *r* of persons Eph 6:9 *3382*
Not that I speak in *r* of want Phil 4:11 *2596*
or in *r* of an holyday, or of the Col 2:16 *3313*
and there is no *r* of persons Col 3:25 *4382*
for he had *r* unto the recompence Heb 11:26 *578*
Lord of glory, with *r* of persons Jas 2:1 *4382*
ye have *r* to him that weareth the Jas 2:3 *1914*
But if ye have *r* to persons Jas 2:9 *4380*
who without *r* of persons judgeth 1Pet 1:17 *678*

RESPECTED {1}
they *r* not the persons of the Lam 4:16 5375

RESPECTER {1}
that God is no *r* of persons Acts 10:34 *4381*

RESPECTETH {2}
he *r* not any that are wise of Job 37:24 7200
r not the proud, nor such as turn Ps 40:4 6437

RESPITE {2}
when Pharaoh saw that there was *r* Ex 8:15 7309
unto him, Give us seven days' *r* 1Sa 11:3 7503

REST {275}
But the dove found no *r* for the Gen 8:9 4494
r yourselves under the tree Gen 18:4 8172
Jacob fed the *r* of Laban's flocks Gen 30:36 3498
And he saw that *r* was good Gen 49:15 4496
ye make them *r* from their burdens Ex 5:5 7673
To morrow is the *r* of the holy Ex 16:23 7677
seventh year thou shalt let it *r* Ex 23:11 8058
on the seventh day thou shalt *r* Ex 23:12 7673
that thine ox and thine ass may *r* Ex 23:12 5117
names of the *r* on the other stone Ex 28:10 3498
the seventh is the sabbath of *r* Ex 31:15 7677
with thee, and I will give thee *r* Ex 33:14 5117
on the seventh day thou shalt *r* Ex 34:21 7673
time and in harvest thou shalt *r* Ex 34:21 7673
day, a sabbath of *r* to the LORD Ex 35:2 7677
the *r* of the blood shall be wrung Lev 5:9 7604
of the *r* of the oil that is in Lev 14:17 3499
the *r* of the oil that is in the Lev 14:29 3498
shall be a sabbath of *r* unto you Lev 16:31 7677
seventh day is the sabbath of *r* Lev 23:3 7677
shall be unto you a sabbath of *r* Lev 23:32 7677
be a sabbath of *r* unto the land Lev 25:4 7677
it is a year of *r* unto the land Lev 25:5 7677
even then shall the land *r* Lev 26:34 7673
as it lieth desolate it shall *r* Lev 26:35 7673
it did not *r* in your sabbaths Lev 26:35 7673
beside the *r* of them that were Num 31:8
being the *r* of the prey which the Num 31:32 3499
the *r* of Gilead, and all Bashan, Deut 3:13 3499
have given *r* unto your brethren Deut 3:20 5117
maidservant may *r* as well as thou Deut 5:14 5117
ye are not as yet come to the *r* Deut 12:9 4496
when he giveth you *r* from all Deut 12:10 5117
r from all thine enemies round Deut 25:19 5117
shall the sole of thy foot have *r* Deut 28:65 4494
LORD your God hath given you *r* Josh 1:13 5117
LORD have given your brethren *r* Josh 1:15 5117
shall *r* in the waters of Jordan, Josh 3:13 5117
that the *r* which remained of them Josh 10:20 8300
the *r* of the kingdom of Sihon Josh 13:27 3499
And the land had *r* from war Josh 14:15 8252
There was also a lot for the *r* of Josh 17:2 3498
the *r* of Manasseh's sons had the Josh 17:6 3498
the *r* of the children of Kohath Josh 21:5 3498
the *r* of the Levites, out of the Josh 21:34 3498
the LORD gave them *r* round about Josh 21:44 5117
hath given *r* unto your brethren Josh 22:4 5117
r unto Israel from all their Josh 23:1 5117

R

And the land had *r* forty years ... Judg 3:11 8252
the land had *r* fourscore years ... Judg 3:30 8252
And the land had *r* forty years ... Judg 5:31 8252
but all the *r* of the people bowed ... Judg 7:6 3499
he sent all the *r* of Israel every ... Judg 7:8
LORD grant you that ye may find *r* ... Ruth 1:9 4496
shall I not seek *r* for thee ... Ruth 3:1 4494
for the man will not be in *r* ... Ruth 3:18 8252
the *r* of the people he sent every ... 1Sa 13:2 3499
the *r* we have utterly destroyed ... 1Sa 15:15 3498
Let it *r* on the head of Joab, and ... 2Sa 3:29 2342
the LORD had given him *r* round ... 2Sa 7:1 5117
have caused thee to *r* from all ... 2Sa 7:11 5117
the *r* of the people he delivered ... 2Sa 10:10 3499
the *r* of the people together ... 2Sa 12:28 3499
of the air to *r* on them by day ... 2Sa 21:10 5117
God hath given me *r* on every side ... 1Kin 5:4 5117
that hath given *r* unto his people ... 1Kin 8:56 4496
the *r* of the acts of Solomon, and ... 1Kin 11:41 3499
the *r* of the acts of Jeroboam, ... 1Kin 14:19 3499
Now the *r* of the acts of Rehoboam ... 1Kin 14:29 3499
Now the *r* of the acts of Abijam, ... 1Kin 15:7 3499
The *r* of all the acts of Asa, and ... 1Kin 15:23 3499
Now the *r* of the acts of Nadab, ... 1Kin 15:31 3499
Now the *r* of the acts of Baasha, ... 1Kin 16:5 3499
Now the *r* of the acts of Elah, and ... 1Kin 16:14 3499
Now the *r* of the acts of Zimri, ... 1Kin 16:20 3499
Now the *r* of the acts of Omri ... 1Kin 16:27 3499
But the *r* fled to Aphek, into the ... 1Kin 20:30 3498
Now the *r* of the acts of Ahab, and ... 1Kin 22:39 3499
Now the *r* of the acts of ... 1Kin 22:45 3499
Now the *r* of the acts of Ahaziah ... 2Kin 1:18 3499
spirit of Elijah doth *r* on Elisha ... 2Kin 2:15 5117
thou and thy children of the *r* ... 2Kin 4:7 3498
the *r* of the acts of Joram, and ... 2Kin 8:23 3499
Now the *r* of the acts of Jehu, and ... 2Kin 10:34 3499
the *r* of the acts of Joash, and ... 2Kin 12:19 3499
Now the *r* of the acts of Jehoahaz ... 2Kin 13:8 3499
the *r* of the acts of Joash, and ... 2Kin 13:12 3499
Now the *r* of the acts of Jehoash ... 2Kin 14:15 3499
the *r* of the acts of Amaziah, are ... 2Kin 14:18 3499
Now the *r* of the acts of Jeroboam ... 2Kin 14:28 3499
the *r* of the acts of Azariah, and ... 2Kin 15:6 3499
the *r* of the acts of Zachariah, ... 2Kin 15:11 3499
the *r* of the acts of Shallum, and ... 2Kin 15:15 3499
the *r* of the acts of Menahem, and ... 2Kin 15:21 3499
the *r* of the acts of Pekahiah, and ... 2Kin 15:26 3499
the *r* of the acts of Pekah, and ... 2Kin 15:31 3499
Now the *r* of the acts of Jotham, ... 2Kin 15:36 3499
Now the *r* of the acts of Ahaz ... 2Kin 16:19 3499
the *r* of the acts of Hezekiah, and ... 2Kin 20:20 3499
Now the *r* of the acts of Manasseh ... 2Kin 21:17 3499
Now the *r* of the acts of Amon ... 2Kin 21:25 3499
Now the *r* of the acts of Josiah, ... 2Kin 23:28 3499
Now the *r* of the acts of ... 2Kin 24:5 3499
Now the *r* of the people that were ... 2Kin 25:11 3499
And they smote the *r* of the ... 1Chr 4:43 7611
LORD, after that the ark had *r* ... 1Chr 6:31 4494
Unto the *r* of the children of ... 1Chr 6:77 3498
Joab repaired the *r* of the city ... 1Chr 11:8 7605
all the *r* also of Israel were of ... 1Chr 12:38 7611
the *r* that were chosen, who were ... 1Chr 16:41 7605
the *r* of the people he delivered ... 1Chr 19:11 3499
to thee, who shall be a man of *r* ... 1Chr 22:9 4496
I will give him *r* from all his ... 1Chr 22:9 5117
he not given you *r* on every side ... 1Chr 22:18 3499
hath given *r* unto his people ... 1Chr 23:25 3499
the *r* of the sons of Levi were ... 1Chr 24:20 3498
r for the ark of the covenant of ... 1Chr 28:2 4496
Now the *r* of the acts of Solomon, ... 2Chr 9:29 7605
the *r* of the acts of Abijah, and ... 2Chr 13:22 3499
for the land had *r*, and he had no ... 2Chr 14:6 8252
because the LORD had given him *r* ... 2Chr 14:6 5117
he hath given us *r* on every side ... 2Chr 14:7 5117
for we *r* on thee, and in thy name ... 2Chr 14:11 8172
the LORD gave them *r* round about ... 2Chr 15:15 5117
his God gave him *r* round about ... 2Chr 20:30 5117
Now the *r* of the acts of ... 2Chr 20:34 3499
they brought the *r* of the money ... 2Chr 24:14 7605
Now the *r* of the acts of Amaziah, ... 2Chr 25:26 3499
Now the *r* of the acts of Uzziah, ... 2Chr 26:22 3499
Now the *r* of the acts of Jotham, ... 2Chr 27:7 3499
Now the *r* of his acts and of all ... 2Chr 28:26 3499
Now the *r* of the acts of Hezekiah ... 2Chr 32:32 3499
Now the *r* of the acts of Manasseh ... 2Chr 33:18 3499
Now the *r* of the acts of Josiah, ... 2Chr 35:26 3499
Now the *r* of the acts of ... 2Chr 36:8 3499
the *r* of the chief of the fathers ... Ezr 4:3 7605
the *r* of their companions, unto ... Ezr 4:7 7605
the *r* of their companions ... Ezr 4:9 7606
the *r* of the nations whom the ... Ezr 4:10 7606
the *r* that are on this side the ... Ezr 4:10 7606
to the *r* of their companions that ... Ezr 4:17 7606
unto the *r* beyond the river, ... Ezr 4:17 7606
the *r* of the children of the ... Ezr 6:16 7606
to do with the *r* of the silver ... Ezr 7:18 7606
nor to the *r* that did the work ... Neh 2:16 3499
to the *r* of the people, Be not ye ... Neh 4:14 3499
to the *r* of the people, The work ... Neh 4:19 3499
the *r* of our enemies, heard that ... Neh 6:1 3499
the *r* of the prophets, that would ... Neh 6:14 3499
that which the *r* of the people ... Neh 7:72 7611
But after they had *r*, they did ... Neh 9:28 5117
the *r* of the people, the priests, ... Neh 10:28 7605
the *r* of the people also cast ... Neh 11:1 7605
in the *r* of the king's provinces ... Est 9:12 7605
had *r* from their enemies, and slew ... Est 9:16 5118
then had I been at *r*, ... Job 3:13 5117
and there the weary be at *r* ... Job 3:17 5117
There the prisoners *r* together ... Job 3:18 7599
not in safety, neither had I *r* ... Job 3:26 8252
thou shalt take thy *r* in safety ... Job 11:18 7901
Turn from him, that he may *r* ... Job 14:6 2308
when our *r* together is in the ... Job 17:16 5183
and my sinews take no *r* ... Job 30:17 7901
my flesh also shall *r* in hope ... Ps 16:9 7931
leave the *r* of their substance to ... Ps 17:14 3499
R in the LORD, and wait patiently ... Ps 37:7 1826
neither is there any *r* in my ... Ps 38:3 7965
then would I fly away, and be at *r* ... Ps 55:6 7931
That thou mayest give him *r* from ... Ps 94:13 8252
they should not enter into my *r* ... Ps 95:11 4496
Return unto thy *r*, O my soul ... Ps 116:7 4496
r upon the lot of the righteous ... Ps 125:3 5117
Arise, O LORD, into thy *r* ... Ps 132:8 4496
This is my *r* for ever ... Ps 132:14 4496
neither will he *r* content ... Prov 6:35
he rage or laugh, there is no *r* ... Prov 29:9 5183
thy son, and he shall give thee *r* ... Prov 29:17 5117
heart taketh not *r* in the night ... Eccl 2:23
this hath more *r* than the other ... Eccl 6:5 5183
makest thy flock to *r* at noon ... Song 1:7 7257
shall *r* all of them in the ... Is 7:19 5117
the *r* of the trees of his forest ... Is 10:19 7605
of the LORD shall *r* upon him ... Is 11:2 5117
and his *r* shall be glorious ... Is 11:10 4496
shall give thee *r* from thy sorrow ... Is 14:3 5117
The whole earth is at *r*, and is ... Is 14:7 5117
said unto me, I will take my *r* ... Is 18:4 8252
there also shalt thou have no *r* ... Is 23:12 5117
shall the hand of the LORD *r* ... Is 25:10 5117
This is the *r* wherewith ye may ... Is 28:12 4496
ye may cause the weary to *r* ... Is 28:12 5117
returning and *r* shall ye be saved ... Is 30:15 5183
screech owl also shall *r* there ... Is 34:14 7280
and find for herself a place of *r* ... Is 34:14 4494
to *r* for a light of the people ... Is 51:4 7280
they shall *r* in their beds, each ... Is 57:2 5117
troubled sea, when it cannot *r* ... Is 57:20 8252
for Jerusalem's sake I will not *r* ... Is 62:1 8252
And give him no *r*, till he ... Is 62:7 1824
of the LORD caused him to *r* ... Is 63:14 5117
and where is the place of my *r* ... Is 66:1 4496
ye shall find *r* for your souls ... Jer 6:16 4771
shall return, and shall be in *r* ... Jer 30:10 8252
when I went to cause him to *r* ... Jer 31:2 7280
with the *r* of the people that ... Jer 39:9 3499
in my sighing, and I find no *r* ... Jer 45:3 4496
and Jacob shall return, and be in *r* ... Jer 46:27 8252
up thyself into thy scabbard, *r* ... Jer 47:6 7280
that he may give *r* to the land ... Jer 50:34 7280
and the *r* of the multitude ... Jer 52:15 3499
the heathen, she findeth no *r* ... Lam 1:3 4494
give thyself no *r* ... Lam 2:18 6314
we labour, and have no *r* ... Lam 5:5 5117
will cause my fury to *r* upon them ... Eze 5:13 5117
I make my fury toward thee to *r* ... Eze 16:42 5117
and I will cause my fury to *r* ... Eze 21:17 5117
caused my fury to *r* upon thee ... Eze 24:13 5117
I will go to them that are at *r* ... Eze 38:11 8252
the blessing to *r* in thine house ... Eze 44:30 5117
the *r* of the land shall they give ... Eze 45:8
As for the *r* of the tribes, from ... Eze 48:23 3499
the *r* of the wise men of Babylon ... Dan 2:18 7606
was at *r* in mine house, and ... Dan 4:4 7954
As concerning the *r* of the beasts ... Dan 7:12 7606
for thou shalt *r*, and stand in thy ... Dan 12:13 5117
for this is not your *r* ... Mic 2:10 4496
that I might *r* in the day of ... Hab 3:16 5117
he will *r* in his love, he will ... Zeph 3:17 2790
earth sitteth still, and is at *r* ... Zec 1:11 8252
Damascus shall be the *r* thereof ... Zec 9:1 4496
let the *r* eat every one the flesh ... Zec 11:9 7604
heavy laden, and I will give you *r* ... Mt 11:28 *373*
ye shall find *r* unto your souls ... Mt 11:29 *372*
through dry places, seeking *r* ... Mt 12:43 *372*
Sleep on now, and take your *r* ... Mt 26:45 *373*
The *r* said, Let be, let us see ... Mt 27:49 *3062*
into a desert place, and *r* a while ... Mk 6:31 *373*
Sleep on now, and take your *r* ... Mk 14:41 *373*
there, your peace shall *r* upon it ... Lk 10:6 *1879*
through dry places, seeking *r* ... Lk 11:24 *372*
why take ye thought for the *r* ... Lk 12:26 *3062*
unto the eleven, and to all the *r* ... Lk 24:9 *3062*
spoken of taking of *r* in sleep ... Jn 11:13 *2681*
also my flesh shall *r* in hope ... Acts 2:26 *3062*
to the *r* of the apostles, Men and ... Acts 2:37 *3062*
of the *r* durst no man join ... Acts 5:13 *2663*
or what is the place of my *r* ... Acts 7:49 *1515*
churches *r* throughout all Judaea ... Acts 9:31 *3062*
And the *r*, some on boards, and some ... Acts 27:44 *3062*
it, and the *r* were blinded ... Rom 11:7 *3062*
But to the *r* speak I, not the ... 1Cor 7:12 *3062*
the *r* will I set in order when I ... 1Cor 11:34 *3062*
I had no *r* in my spirit, because ... 2Cor 2:13 *425*
Macedonia, our flesh had no *r* ... 2Cor 7:5 *425*
the power of Christ may *r* upon me ... 2Cor 12:9 *1981*
to you who are troubled *r* with us ... 2Th 1:7 *425*
They shall not enter into my *r* ... Heb 3:11 *2663*
they should not enter into his *r* ... Heb 3:18 *2663*
left us of entering into his *r* ... Heb 4:1 *2663*
have believed do enter into *r* ... Heb 4:3 *2663*
if they shall enter into my *r* ... Heb 4:3 *2663*
God did *r* the seventh day from ... Heb 4:4 *2664*
If they shall enter into my *r* ... Heb 4:5 *2663*
For if Jesus had given them *r* ... Heb 4:8 *2664*
a *r* to the people of God ... Heb 4:9 *4520*
For he that is entered into his *r* ... Heb 4:10 *2663*
therefore to enter into that *r* ... Heb 4:11 *2663*
he no longer should live the *r* of ... 1Pet 4:2 *1954*
unto the *r* in Thyatira, as many ... Rev 2:24 *3062*
they *r* not day and night, saying, ... Rev 4:8 *2192,372*
that they should *r* yet for a ... Rev 6:11 *373*
the *r* of the men which were not ... Rev 9:20 *3062*
they have no *r* day nor night, who ... Rev 14:11 *372*
that they may *r* from their ... Rev 14:13 *373*
But the *r* of the dead lived not ... Rev 20:5 *3062*

RESTED {21}

he *r* on the seventh day from all ... Gen 2:2 7673
because that in it he had *r* from ... Gen 2:3 7673
the ark *r* in the seventh month, ... Gen 8:4 5117
r in all the coasts of Egypt ... Ex 10:14 5117
So the people *r* on the seventh ... Ex 16:30 7673
in them is, and *r* the seventh day ... Ex 20:11 5117
earth, and on the seventh day he *r* ... Ex 31:17 7673
tabernacle they *r* in their tents ... Num 9:18 2583
of the LORD they *r* in the tents ... Num 9:23 2583
the cloud *r* in the wilderness of ... Num 10:12 7931
And when it *r*, he said, Return, O ... Num 10:36 5117
that, when the spirit *r* upon them ... Num 11:25 5117
and the spirit *r* upon them ... Num 11:26 5117
And the land *r* from war ... Josh 11:23 8252
they *r* on the house with timber ... 1Kin 6:10 270
the people *r* themselves upon the ... 2Chr 32:8 5564
fourteenth day of the same *r* they ... Est 9:17 5118
fifteenth day of the same they *r* ... Est 9:18 5118
the Jews *r* from their enemies ... Est 9:22 5117
My bowels boiled, and *r* not ... Job 30:27 1826
r the sabbath day according to ... Lk 23:56 *2270*

RESTEST {1}

r in the law, and makest thy boast ... Rom 2:17 *1879*

RESTETH {4}

him to be in safety, whereon he *r* ... Job 24:23 8172
Wisdom *r* in the heart of him that ... Prov 14:33 5117
for anger *r* in the bosom of fools ... Eccl 7:9 5117
of glory and of God *r* upon you ... 1Pet 4:14 *373*

RESTING {4}

to search out a *r* place for them ... Num 10:33 4496
O LORD God, into thy *r* place ... 2Chr 6:41 5118
spoil not his *r* place ... Prov 24:15 7258
dwellings, and in quiet *r* places ... Is 32:18 4496

RESTINGPLACE {1}

hill, they have forgotten their *r* ... Jer 50:6 7258

RESTITUTION {6}

for he should make full *r* ... Ex 22:3 7999
his own vineyard, shall he make *r* ... Ex 22:5 7999
the fire shall surely make *r* ... Ex 22:6 7999
he shall make *r* unto the owner ... Ex 22:12 7999
to his substance shall the *r* be ... Job 20:18 8545
the times of *r* of all things ... Acts 3:21 *605*

RESTORE {40}

Now therefore *r* the man his wife ... Gen 20:7 7725
and if thou *r* her not, know thou ... Gen 20:7 7725
head, and *r* thee unto thy place ... Gen 40:13 7725
to *r* every man's money into his ... Gen 42:25 7725
he shall *r* five oxen for an ox, ... Ex 22:1 7999
he shall *r* double ... Ex 22:4 7999
that he shall *r* that which he ... Lev 6:4 7725
he shall even *r* it in the ... Lev 6:5 7999
killeth a beast, he shall *r* it ... Lev 24:21 7999
r the overplus unto the man to ... Lev 25:27 7725
if he be not able to *r* it to him ... Lev 25:28 7725
the congregation shall *r* him to ... Num 35:25 7725
thou shalt *r* it to him again ... Deut 22:2 7725
now therefore *r* those lands again ... Judg 11:13 7725
therefore I will *r* it unto thee ... Judg 17:3 7725
and I will *r* it you ... 1Sa 12:3 7725
will *r* thee all the land of Saul ... 2Sa 9:7 7725
he shall *r* the lamb fourfold, ... 2Sa 12:6 7999
r me the kingdom of my father ... 2Sa 16:3 7725
took from thy father, I will *r* ... 1Kin 20:34 7725
R all that was hers, and all the ... 2Kin 8:6 7725
R, I pray you, to them, even this ... Neh 5:11 7725
Then said they, We will *r* them ... Neh 5:12 7725
and his hands shall *r* their goods ... Job 20:10 7725
which he laboured for shall he *r* ... Job 20:18 7725
R unto me the joy of thy ... Ps 51:12 7725
he be found, he shall *r* sevenfold ... Prov 6:31 7999
I will *r* thy judges as at the ... Is 1:26 7725
for a spoil, and none saith, *R* ... Is 42:22 7725
to *r* the preserved of Israel ... Is 49:6 7725
r comforts unto him and to his ... Is 57:18 7999
them up, and *r* them to this place ... Jer 27:22 7725
For I will *r* health unto thee, and ... Jer 30:17 5927
If the wicked *r* the pledge ... Eze 33:15 7725
forth of the commandment to *r* ... Dan 9:25 7725
I will *r* to you the years that ... Joel 2:25 7999
shall first come, and *r* all things ... Mt 17:11 *600*
accusation, I *r* him fourfold ... Lk 19:8 *591*
wilt thou at this time *r* again ... Acts 1:6 *600*
r such an one in the spirit of ... Gal 6:1 *2675*

RESTORED {27}

Abraham, and *r* him Sarah his wife ... Gen 20:14 7725
he *r* the chief butler unto his ... Gen 40:21 7725
me he *r* unto mine office, and him ... Gen 41:13 7725
unto his brethren, My money is *r* ... Gen 42:28 7725
face, and shall not be *r* to thee ... Deut 28:31 7725
when he had *r* the eleven hundred ... Judg 17:3 7725
Yet he *r* the money unto his ... Judg 17:4 7725
from Israel were *r* to Israel ... 1Sa 7:14 7725
that my hand may be *r* me again ... 1Kin 13:6 7725

the king's hand was *r* him again 1Kin 13:6 7725
woman, whose son he had *r* to life.......... 2Kin 8:1 2421
how he had *r* a dead body to life 2Kin 8:5 2421
woman, whose son he had *r* to life.......... 2Kin 8:5 2421
is her son, whom Elisha *r* to life 2Kin 8:5 2421
r it to Judah, after that the 2Kin 14:22 7725
He *r* the coast of Israel from the 2Kin 14:25 7725
which Huram had *r* to Solomon............. 2Chr 8:2 5414
r it to Judah, after that the 2Chr 26:2 7725
and brought unto Babylon, be *r*............. Ezr 6:5 8421
then I *r* that which I took not .... Ps 69:4 7725
but hath *r* to the debtor his.................. Eze 18:7 7725
hath not *r* the pledge, and hath .... Eze 18:12 7725
and it was *r* whole, like as the .... Mt 12:13 *600*
his hand was *r* whole as the other .... Mk 3:5 *600*
and he was *r*, and saw every man........... Mk 8:25 *600*
his hand was *r* whole as the other .... Lk 6:10 *600*
that I may be *r* to you the sooner.......... Heb 13:19 *600*

RESTORER {2}
be unto thee a *r* of thy life..................... Ruth 4:15 7725
The *r* of paths to dwell in...................... Is 58:12 7725

RESTORETH {2}
He *r* my soul .... Ps 23:3 7725
cometh first, and *r* all things.................. Mk 9:12 *600*

RESTRAIN {2}
dost thou *r* wisdom to thyself................. Job 15:8 1639
remainder of wrath shalt thou *r*............... Ps 76:10 2296

RESTRAINED {8}
and the rain from heaven was *r* .... Gen 8:2 3607
now nothing will be *r* from them .... Gen 11:6 1219
the LORD hath *r* me from bearing .... Gen 16:2 6113
the people were *r* from bringing .... Ex 36:6 3607
themselves vile, and he *r* them not.......... 1Sa 3:13 3543
are they *r* .... Is 63:15 662
I *r* the floods thereof, and the .... Eze 31:15 4513
sayings scarce *r* they the people.............. Acts 14:18 *2664*

RESTRAINEST {1}
off fear, and *r* prayer before God .... Job 15:4 1639

RESTRAINT {1}
for there is no *r* to the LORD to 1Sa 14:6 4622

RESTS {1}
he made narrowed *r* round about 1Kin 6:6 4052

RESURRECTION {41}
which say that there is no *r*.................... Mt 22:23 *386*
Therefore in the *r* whose wife .... Mt 22:28 *386*
For in the *r* they neither marry,.............. Mt 22:30 *386*
But as touching the *r* of the dead............ Mt 22:31 *386*
out of the graves after his *r*.................... Mt 27:53 *1454*
which say there is no *r* .... Mk 12:18 *386*
In the *r* therefore, when they................... Mk 12:23 *386*
recompensed at the *r* of the just.............. Lk 14:14 *386*
which deny that there is any *r*................. Lk 20:27 *386*
Therefore in the *r* whose wife of .... Lk 20:33 *386*
the *r* from the dead, neither...................... Lk 20:35 *386*
God, being the children of the *r*.............. Lk 20:36 *386*
done good, unto the *r* of life.................... Jn 5:29 *386*
evil, unto the *r* of damnation .... Jn 5:29 *386*
again in the *r* at the last day.................... Jn 11:24 *386*
Jesus said unto her, I am the *r*................ Jn 11:25 *386*
to be a witness with us of his *r* .... Acts 1:22 *386*
before spake of the *r* of Christ .... Acts 2:31 *386*
through Jesus the *r* from the dead .... Acts 4:2 *386*
of the *r* of the Lord Jesus .... Acts 4:33 *386*
unto them Jesus, and the *r* .... Acts 17:18 *386*
they heard of the *r* of the dead................ Acts 17:32 *386*
r of the dead I am called in...................... Acts 23:6 *386*
Sadducees say that there is no *r*.............. Acts 23:8 *386*
there shall be a *r* of the dead .... Acts 24:15 *386*
Touching the *r* of the dead I am.............. Acts 24:21 *386*
holiness, by the *r* from the dead............... Rom 1:4 *386*
be also in the likeness of his *r*................. Rom 6:5 *386*
that there is no *r* of the dead.................. 1Cor 15:12 *386*
But if there be no *r* of the dead............... 1Cor 15:13 *386*
man came also the *r* of the dead 1Cor 15:21 *386*
So also is the *r* of the dead...................... 1Cor 15:42 *386*
know him, and the power of his *r* .... Phil 3:10 *386*
attain unto the *r* of the dead .... Phil 3:11 *1815*
saying that the *r* is past already.............. 2Ti 2:18 *386*
of *r* of the dead, and of eternal .... Heb 6:2 *386*
that they might obtain a better *r* .... Heb 11:35 *386*
r of Jesus Christ from the dead 1Pet 1:3 *386*
by the *r* of Jesus Christ............................ 1Pet 3:21 *386*
This is the first *r*..................................... Rev 20:5 *386*
he that hath part in the first *r* .... Rev 20:6 *386*

RETAIN {7}
Dost thou still *r* thine integrity............... Job 2:9 2388
me, Let thine heart *r* my words................ Prov 4:4 8551
and strong men *r* riches......................... Prov 11:16 8551
over the spirit to *r* the spirit .... Eccl 8:8 3607
but she shall not *r* the power of............... Dan 11:6 6113
and whose soever sins ye *r*...................... Jn 20:23 *2902*
like to *r* God in their knowledge.............. Rom 1:28 *2192*

RETAINED {6}
r those three hundred men .... Judg 7:8 2388
law, the damsel's father, *r* him................ Judg 19:4 2388
corruption, and I *r* no strength .... Dan 10:8 6113
upon me, and I have *r* no strength .... Dan 10:16 6113
soever sins ye retain, they are *r*.............. Jn 20:23 *2902*
Whom I would have *r* with me .... Philem 13 *2722*

RETAINETH {3}
and happy is every one that *r* her .... Prov 3:18 8551
A gracious woman *r* honour.................... Prov 11:16 8551
he *r* not his anger for ever,.................... Mic 7:18 2388

RETIRE {2}
r ye from him, that he may be................. 2Sa 11:15 7725
r, stay not.. Jer 4:6 5756

RETIRED {2}
the men of Israel *r* in the battle .... Judg 20:39 2015
they *r* from the city, every man 2Sa 20:22 6327

RETURN {263}
till thou *r* unto the ground .... Gen 3:19 7725
art, and unto dust shalt thou *r*................. Gen 3:19 7725
after his *r* from the slaughter of.............. Gen 14:17 7725
R to thy mistress, and submit.................. Gen 16:9 7725
I will certainly *r* unto thee .... Gen 18:10 7725
time appointed I will *r* unto thee............. Gen 18:14 7725
R unto the land of thy fathers,................. Gen 31:3 7725
r unto the land of thy kindred.................. Gen 31:13 7725
R unto thy country, and to thy .... Gen 32:9 7725
r unto my brethren which are in .... Ex 4:18 7725
Moses in Midian, Go, *r* into Egypt........... Ex 4:19 7725
When thou goest to *r* into Egypt .... Ex 4:21 7725
they see war, and they *r* to Egypt............ Ex 13:17 7725
ye shall *r* every man unto his .... Lev 25:10 7725
ye shall *r* every man unto his .... Lev 25:10 7725
year of this jubile ye shall *r* .... Lev 25:13 7725
that he may *r* unto his possession .... Lev 25:27 7725
he shall *r* unto his possession .... Lev 25:28 7725
shall *r* unto his own family, and.............. Lev 25:41 7725
of his fathers shall he *r* .... Lev 25:41 7725
of the jubile the field shall *r* .... Lev 27:24 7725
And when it rested, he said, *R* .... Num 10:36 7725
not better for us to *r* into Egypt.............. Num 14:3 7725
a captain, and let us *r* into Egypt .... Num 14:4 7725
R unto Balak, and thus thou shalt .... Num 23:5 7725
We will not *r* unto our houses, ... Num 32:18 7725
then afterward ye shall *r*........................ Num 32:22 7725
high priest the slayer shall *r* .... Num 35:28 7725
then shall ye *r* every man unto................. Deut 3:20 7725
cause the people to *r* to Egypt................. Deut 17:16 7725
henceforth *r* no more that way................. Deut 17:16 7725
r to his house, lest he die in .... Deut 20:5 7725
r unto his house, lest he die in .... Deut 20:6 7725
r unto his house, lest he die in .... Deut 20:7 7725
r unto his house, lest his......................... Deut 20:8 7725
shalt *r* unto the LORD thy God, and .... Deut 30:2 7725
compassion upon thee, and will *r* .... Deut 30:3 7725
And thou shalt *r* and obey the voice .... Deut 30:8 7725
then ye shall *r* unto the land of................ Josh 1:15 7725
then shall the slayer *r*, and come............. Josh 20:6 7725
therefore now *r* ye, and get you............... Josh 22:4 6437
R with much riches unto your.................. Josh 22:8 7725
is fearful and afraid, let him *r* .... Judg 7:3 7725
when I *r* in peace from the .... Judg 11:31 7725
that she might *r* from the country............ Ruth 1:6 7725
way to *r* unto the land of Judah.............. Ruth 1:7 7725
r each to her mother's house .... Ruth 1:8 7725
Surely we will *r* with thee unto............... Ruth 1:10 7725
r thou after thy sister in law .... Ruth 1:15 7725
or to *r* from following after thee .... Ruth 1:16 7725
but in any wise *r* him a trespass 1Sa 6:3 7725
offering which we shall *r* to him 1Sa 6:4 7725
which ye *r* him for a trespass 1Sa 6:8 7725
If ye do *r* unto the LORD with all 1Sa 7:3 7725
And his *r* was to Ramah 1Sa 7:17 8666
was with him, Come, and let us *r*............. 1Sa 9:5 7725
unto Saul, I will not *r* with thee 1Sa 15:26 7725
r, my son David...................................... 1Sa 26:21 7725
said unto him, Make this fellow *r* 1Sa 29:4 7725
Wherefore now *r*, and go in peace, ... 1Sa 29:7 7725
to *r* into the land of the 1Sa 29:11 7725
ere thou bid the people *r* from 2Sa 2:26 7725
Then said Abner unto him, Go, *r* 2Sa 3:16 7725
your beards be grown, and then *r* 2Sa 10:5 7725
to him, but he shall not *r* to me 2Sa 12:23 7725
r to thy place, and abide with the........... 2Sa 15:19 7725
r thou, and take back thy brethren 2Sa 15:20 7725
r into the city in peace, and your............ 2Sa 15:27 7725
But if thou *r* to the city 2Sa 15:34 7725
R thou, and all thy servants 2Sa 19:14 7725
I shall *r* to him that sent me.................. 2Sa 24:13 7725
the LORD shall *r* his blood upon.............. 1Kin 2:32 7725
therefore *r* upon the head of Joab 1Kin 2:33 7725
therefore the LORD shall *r* thy................. 1Kin 2:44 7725
so *r* unto thee with all their 1Kin 8:48 7725
r every man to his house 1Kin 12:24 7725
kingdom *r* to the house of David.............. 1Kin 12:26 7725
And he said, I may not *r* with thee 1Kin 13:16 7725
r on thy way to the wilderness of............. 1Kin 19:15 7725
for at the *r* of the year the king.............. 1Kin 20:22 8666
came to pass at the *r* of the year............. 1Kin 20:26 8666
let them *r* every man to his house 1Kin 22:17 7725
If thou *r* at all in peace, the 1Kin 22:28 7725
r from me... 2Kin 18:14 7725
and shall *r* to his own land 2Kin 19:7 7725
he came, by the same shall he *r* 2Kin 19:33 7725
but let the shadow *r* backward ten 2Kin 20:10 7725
your beards be grown, and then *r* 1Chr 19:5 7725
and shall *r* and confess thy name,............ 2Chr 6:24 7725
If they *r* to thee with all their 2Chr 6:38 7725
ye me to *r* answer to this people 2Chr 10:6 7725
we may *r* answer to this people............... 2Chr 10:9 7725
r every man to his house 2Chr 11:4 7725
let them *r* therefore every man to............ 2Chr 18:16 7725
of affliction, until I *r* in peace 2Chr 18:26 7725
If thou certainly *r* in peace...................... 2Chr 18:27 7725
he will *r* to the remnant of you, ... 2Chr 30:6 7725
face from you, if ye *r* unto him 2Chr 30:9 7725
and when wilt thou *r*............................... Neh 2:6 7725
r unto us they will be upon you .... Neh 4:12 7725
a captain to *r* to their bondage .... Neh 9:17 7725
bade them *r* Mordecai this answer........... Est 4:15 7725
should *r* upon his own head, and .... Est 9:25 7725
womb, and naked shall I *r* thither............ Job 1:21 7725
R, I pray you, let it not be .... Job 6:29 7725
r again, my righteousness is in............... Job 6:29 7725
He shall *r* no more to his house,.............. Job 7:10 7725
Before I go whence I shall not *r* .... Job 10:21 7725
that he shall *r* out of darkness .... Job 15:22 7725
go the way whence I shall not *r* .... Job 16:22 7725
But as for you all, do ye *r*....................... Job 17:10 7725
If thou *r* to the Almighty, thou............... Job 22:23 7725
he shall *r* to the days of his .... Job 33:25 7725
that they *r* from iniquity .... Job 36:10 7725
they go forth, and *r* not unto them.......... Job 39:4 7725
R, O LORD, deliver my soul..................... Ps 6:4 7725
let them *r* and be ashamed suddenly......... Ps 6:10 7725
sakes therefore *r* thou on high................. Ps 7:7 7725
shall *r* upon his own head .... Ps 7:16 7725
They *r* at evening.................................... Ps 59:6 7725
And at evening let them *r* .... Ps 59:14 7725
Therefore his people *r* hither.................. Ps 73:10 7725
O let not the oppressed *r* ashamed........... Ps 74:21 7725
R, we beseech thee, O God of.................. Ps 80:14 7725
and sayest, *R*, ye children of men........... Ps 90:3 7725
R, O LORD, how long .... Ps 90:13 7725
shall *r* unto righteousness .... Ps 94:15 7725
they die, and *r* to their dust .... Ps 104:29 7725
R unto thy rest, O my soul...................... Ps 116:7 7725
None that go unto her *r* again.................. Prov 2:19 7725
a stone, it will *r* upon him...................... Prov 26:27 7725
rivers come, thither they *r* again .... Eccl 1:7 7725
naked shall he *r* to go as he came .... Eccl 5:15 7725
nor the clouds *r* after the rain................. Eccl 12:2 7725
Then shall the dust *r* to the.................... Eccl 12:7 7725
the spirit shall *r* unto God who............... Eccl 12:7 7725
R, *r*, O Shulamite .... Song 6:13 7725
r, *r*, that we may look upon................... Song 6:13 7725
shall be a tenth, and it shall *r*................. Is 6:13 7725
The remnant shall *r*, even the................. Is 10:21 7725
yet a remnant of them shall *r*.................. Is 10:22 7725
they shall *r* even to the LORD, and .... Is 19:22 7725
enquire ye: *r*, come................................. Is 21:12 7725
the ransomed of the LORD shall *r*............ Is 35:10 7725
a rumour, and *r* to his own land............... Is 37:7 7725
he came, by the same shall he *r* .... Is 37:34 7725
r unto me .... Is 44:22 7725
in righteousness, and shall not *r* .... Is 45:23 7725
the redeemed of the LORD shall *r*............ Is 51:11 7725
let him *r* unto the LORD, and he .... Is 55:7 7725
it shall not *r* unto me void...................... Is 55:11 7725
R for thy servants' sake, the.................. Is 63:17 7725
shall he *r* unto her again .... Jer 3:1 7725
yet *r* again to me, saith the LORD............ Jer 3:1 7725
words toward the north, and say, *R*......... Jer 3:12 7725
R, ye backsliding children, and I............ Jer 3:22 7725
If thou wilt *r*, O Israel, saith.................. Jer 4:1 7725
Israel, saith the LORD, *r* unto me............ Jer 4:1 7725
they have refused to *r*............................. Jer 5:3 7725
shall he turn away, and not *r*.................. Jer 8:4 7725
fast deceit, they refuse to *r*.................... Jer 8:5 7725
I have plucked them out I will *r*.............. Jer 12:15 7725
since they *r* not from their ways .... Jer 15:7 7725
thus saith the LORD, If thou *r*................. Jer 15:19 7725
let them *r* unto thee............................... Jer 15:19 7725
but *r* not thou unto them........................ Jer 15:19 7725
r ye now every one from his evil .... Jer 18:11 7725
for he shall *r* no more, nor see............... Jer 22:10 7725
He shall not *r* thither any more............... Jer 22:11 7725
land whereunto they desire to *r* .... Jer 22:27 7725
thither shall they not *r*........................... Jer 22:27 7725
that none doth *r* from his .... Jer 23:14 7725
The anger of the LORD shall not *r*........... Jer 23:20 7725
for they shall *r* unto me with .... Jer 24:7 7725
in causing you to *r* to this place............. Jer 29:10 7725
I will cause them to *r* to the................... Jer 30:3 7725
and Jacob shall *r*, and shall be in............ Jer 30:10 7725
anger of the LORD shall not *r*.................. Jer 30:24 7725
a great company shall *r* thither............... Jer 31:8 7725
I will cause their captivity to *r*.............. Jer 32:44 7725
and the captivity of Israel to *r* .... Jer 33:7 7725
For I will cause to *r* the......................... Jer 33:11 7725
I will cause their captivity to *r*.............. Jer 33:26 7725
whom they had let go free, to *r*............... Jer 34:11 7725
liberty at their pleasure, to *r*................. Jer 34:16 7725
and cause them to *r* to this city.............. Jer 34:22 7725
R ye now every man from his evil .... Jer 35:15 7725
that they may *r* every man from.............. Jer 36:3 7725
will *r* every one from his evil .... Jer 36:7 7725
shall *r* to Egypt into their own................ Jer 37:7 7725
that thou cause me not to *r* to................. Jer 37:20 7725
cause me to *r* to Jonathan's house.......... Jer 38:26 7725
cause you to *r* to your own land............. Jer 42:12 7725
that they should *r* into the land .... Jer 44:14 7725
have a desire to *r* to dwell there............. Jer 44:14 7725
for none shall *r* but such as.................... Jer 44:14 7725
that escape the sword shall *r* out .... Jer 44:28 7725
and Jacob shall *r*, and be in rest............ Jer 46:27 7725
none shall *r* in vain................................ Jer 50:9 7725
shall not *r* to that which is sold .... Eze 7:13 7725
thereof, which shall not *r* .... Eze 7:13 7725
that he should not *r* from his .... Eze 13:22 7725
shall *r* to their former estate, ... Eze 16:55 7725
her daughters shall *r* to their .... Eze 16:55 7725
thy daughters shall *r* to your................. Eze 16:55 7725
that he should *r* from his ways.............. Eze 18:23 7725
it shall not *r* any more........................... Eze 21:5 7725
I cause it to *r* into his sheath .... Eze 21:30 7725

R

will cause them to *r* into the ... Eze 29:14 7725
and thy cities shall not *r* ... Eze 35:9 3427
he shall not *r* by the way of the ... Eze 46:9 7725
after, it shall *r* to the prince ... Eze 46:17 7725
caused me to *r* to the brink of ... Eze 47:6 7725
now will I *r* to fight with the ... Dan 10:20 7725
shall *r* into his own land ... Dan 11:9 7725
then shall he *r*, and be stirred up ... Dan 11:10 7725
For the king of the north shall *r* ... Dan 11:13 7725
Then shall he *r* into his land ... Dan 11:28 7725
do exploits, and *r* to his own land ... Dan 11:28 7725
At the time appointed he shall *r* ... Dan 11:29 7725
he shall be grieved, and *r* ... Dan 11:30 7725
he shall even *r*, and have ... Dan 11:30 7725
will go and *r* to my first husband ... Hos 2:7 7725
Therefore will I *r*, and take away ... Hos 2:9 7725
shall the children of Israel *r* ... Hos 3:5 7725
go and *r* to my place, till they ... Hos 5:15 7725
Come, and let us *r* unto the LORD ... Hos 6:1 7725
they do not *r* to the LORD their ... Hos 7:10 7725
They *r*, but not to the most High ... Hos 7:16 7725
they shall *r* to Egypt ... Hos 8:13 7725
but Ephraim shall *r* to Egypt ... Hos 9:3 7725
He shall not *r* into the land of ... Hos 11:5 7725
king, because they refused to *r* ... Hos 11:5 7725
I will not *r* to destroy Ephraim ... Hos 11:9 7725
shall his Lord *r* unto him ... Hos 12:14 7725
O Israel, *r* unto the LORD thy God ... Hos 14:1 7725
dwell under his shadow shall *r* ... Hos 14:7 7725
Who knoweth if he will *r* and ... Joel 2:14 7725
speedily will I *r* your recompence ... Joel 3:4 7725
will *r* your recompence upon your ... Joel 3:7 7725
thy reward shall *r* upon thine own ... Obad 15 7725
they shall *r* to the hire of an ... Mic 1:7 7725
r unto the children of Israel ... Mic 5:3 7725
are impoverished, but we will *r* ... Mal 1:4 7725
R unto me, and I will *r* unto ... Mal 3:7 7725
But ye said, Wherein shall we *r* ... Mal 3:7 7725
Then shall ye *r*, and discern ... Mal 3:18 7725
that they should not *r* to Herod ... Mt 2:12 *844*
worthy, let your peace *r* to you ... Mt 10:13 *1994*
I will *r* into my house from ... Mt 12:44 *1994*
field *r* back to take his clothes ... Mt 24:18 *1994*
R to thine own house, and shew how ... Lk 8:39 *5290*
I will *r* unto my house whence I ... Lk 11:24 *5290*
when he will *r* from the wedding ... Lk 12:36 *360*
let him likewise not *r* back ... Lk 17:31 *1994*
for himself a kingdom, and to *r* ... Lk 19:12 *5290*
now no more to *r* to corruption ... Acts 13:34 *5290*
After this I will *r*, and will ... Acts 15:16 *390*
but I will *r* again unto you, if ... Acts 18:21 *344*
Syria, he purposed to *r* through ... Acts 20:3 *5290*

RETURNED {185}
the waters *r* from off the earth ... Gen 8:3 7725
she *r* unto him into the ark, for ... Gen 8:9 7725
which *r* not again unto him any ... Gen 8:12 7725
And they *r*, and came to En-mishpat, ... Gen 14:7 7725
and Abraham *r* unto his place ... Gen 18:33 7725
they *r* into the land of the ... Gen 21:32 7725
So Abraham *r* unto his young men, ... Gen 22:19 7725
departed, and *r* unto his place ... Gen 31:55 7725
And the messengers *r* to Jacob ... Gen 32:6 7725
So Esau *r* that day on his way ... Gen 33:16 7725
And Reuben *r* unto the pit ... Gen 37:29 7725
he *r* unto his brethren, and said, ... Gen 37:30 7725
he *r* to Judah, and said, I cannot ... Gen 38:22 7725
r to them again, and communed with ... Gen 42:24 7725
now we had *r* this second time ... Gen 43:10 7725
Because of the money that was *r* ... Gen 43:18 7725
man his ass, and *r* to the city ... Gen 44:13 7725
Joseph *r* into Egypt, he, and his ... Gen 50:14 7725
r to Jethro his father in law, and ... Ex 4:18 7725
he *r* to the land of Egypt ... Ex 4:20 7725
Moses *r* unto the LORD, and said, ... Ex 5:22 7725
the sea *r* to his strength when ... Ex 14:27 7725
And the waters *r*, and covered the ... Ex 14:28 7725
Moses *r* the words of the people ... Ex 19:8 7725
Moses *r* unto the LORD, and said, ... Ex 32:31 7725
of the congregation *r* unto him ... Ex 34:31 7725
is *r* unto her father's house, as ... Lev 22:13 7725
they *r* from searching of the land ... Num 13:25 7725
sent to search the land, who *r* ... Num 14:36 7725
Aaron *r* unto Moses unto the door ... Num 16:50 7725
he *r* unto him, and, lo, he stood by ... Num 23:6 7725
up, and went and *r* to his place ... Num 24:25 7725
And ye *r* and wept before the LORD ... Deut 1:45 7725
days, until the pursuers be *r* ... Josh 2:16 7725
days, until the pursuers were *r* ... Josh 2:22 7725
So the two men *r*, and descended ... Josh 2:23 7725
of Jordan *r* unto their place ... Josh 4:18 7725
the city once, and *r* into the camp ... Josh 6:14 7725
they *r* to Joshua, and said unto ... Josh 7:3 7725
that all the Israelites *r* unto Ai ... Josh 8:24 7725
And Joshua *r*, and all Israel with ... Josh 10:15 7725
all the people *r* to the camp to ... Josh 10:21 7725
And Joshua *r*, and all Israel with ... Josh 10:38 7725
And Joshua *r*, and all Israel with ... Josh 10:43 7725
and the half tribe of Manasseh *r* ... Josh 22:9 7725
r from the children of Reuben, and ... Josh 22:32 7725
the judge was dead, that they *r* ... Judg 2:19 7725
yea, she *r* answer to herself, ... Judg 5:29 7725
there *r* of the people twenty and ... Judg 7:3 7725
r into the host of Israel, and ... Judg 7:15 7725
Gideon the son of Joash *r* from ... Judg 8:13 7725
that she *r* unto her father, who ... Judg 11:39 7725
And after a time he *r* to take her ... Judg 14:8 7725
r unto their inheritance, and ... Judg 21:23 7725
So Naomi *r*, and Ruth the Moabitess ... Ruth 1:22 7725
which *r* out of the country of ... Ruth 1:22 7725
worshipped before the LORD, and *r* ... 1Sa 1:19 7725
they *r* to Ekron the same day ... 1Sa 6:16 7725
r for a trespass offering unto ... 1Sa 6:17 7725
r from Saul to feed his father's ... 1Sa 17:15 7725
Israel *r* from chasing after the ... 1Sa 17:53 7725
as David *r* from the slaughter of ... 1Sa 17:57 7725
when David was *r* from the ... 1Sa 18:6 7725
Wherefore Saul *r* from pursuing ... 1Sa 23:28 7725
when Saul was *r* from following ... 1Sa 24:1 7725
for the LORD hath *r* the ... 1Sa 25:39 7725
his way, and Saul *r* to his place ... 1Sa 26:25 7725
the camels, and the apparel, and *r* ... 1Sa 27:9 7725
when David was *r* from the ... 2Sa 1:1 7725
and the sword of Saul *r* not empty ... 2Sa 1:22 7725
Joab *r* from following Abner ... 2Sa 2:30 7725
Go, return. And he *r* ... 2Sa 3:16 7725
And when Abner was *r* to Hebron ... 2Sa 3:27 7725
Then David *r* to bless his ... 2Sa 6:20 7725
David gat him a name when he *r* ... 2Sa 8:13 7725
So Joab *r* from the children of ... 2Sa 10:14 7725
and she *r* unto her house ... 2Sa 11:4 7725
all the people *r* unto Jerusalem ... 2Sa 12:31 7725
So Absalom *r* to his own house, and ... 2Sa 14:24 5437
The LORD hath *r* upon thee all the ... 2Sa 16:8 7725
whom thou seekest is as if all *r* ... 2Sa 17:3 7725
find them, they *r* to Jerusalem ... 2Sa 17:20 7725
the people *r* from pursuing after ... 2Sa 18:16 7725
So the king *r*, and came to Jordan ... 2Sa 19:15 7725
and he *r* unto his own place ... 2Sa 19:39 7725
Joab *r* to Jerusalem unto the king ... 2Sa 20:22 7725
the people *r* after him only to ... 2Sa 23:10 7725
r to depart, according to the ... 1Kin 12:24 7725
r not by the way that he came to ... 1Kin 13:10 7725
Jeroboam *r* not from his evil way ... 1Kin 13:33 7725
he *r* back from him, and took a ... 1Kin 19:21 7725
and from thence he *r* to Samaria ... 2Kin 2:25 7725
from him, and *r* to their own land ... 2Kin 3:27 7725
Then he *r*, and walked in the house ... 2Kin 4:35 7725
he *r* to the man of God, he and all ... 2Kin 5:15 7725
And the messengers *r*, and told the ... 2Kin 7:15 7725
that the woman *r* out of the land ... 2Kin 8:3 7725
But king Joram was *r* to be healed ... 2Kin 9:15 7725
and hostages, and *r* to Samaria ... 2Kin 14:14 7725
So Rab-shakeh *r*, and found the ... 2Kin 19:8 7725
of Assyria departed, and went and *r* ... 2Kin 19:36 7725
upon them, and *r* to Jerusalem ... 2Kin 23:20 7725
David *r* to bless his house ... 1Chr 16:43 5437
and all the people *r* to Jerusalem ... 1Chr 20:3 7725
it, that Jeroboam *r* out of Egypt ... 2Chr 10:2 7725
r from going against Jeroboam ... 2Chr 11:4 7725
in abundance, and *r* to Jerusalem ... 2Chr 14:15 7725
Judah *r* to his house in peace to ... 2Chr 19:1 7725
when they *r* to Jerusalem ... 2Chr 19:8 7725
Then they *r*, every man of Judah ... 2Chr 20:27 7725
he *r* to be healed in Jezreel ... 2Chr 22:6 7725
they *r* home in great anger ... 2Chr 25:10 7725
hostages also, and *r* to Samaria ... 2Chr 25:24 7725
then they *r* to Samaria ... 2Chr 28:15 7725
Then all the children of Israel *r* ... 2Chr 31:1 7725
So he *r* with shame of face to his ... 2Chr 32:21 7725
land of Israel, he *r* to Jerusalem ... 2Chr 34:7 7725
and they *r* to Jerusalem ... 2Chr 34:9 7725
then they *r* answer by letter ... Ezr 5:5 8421
And thus they *r* us answer, saying, ... Ezr 5:11 8421
the gate of the valley, and so *r* ... Neh 2:15 7725
that we *r* all of us to the wall, ... Neh 4:15 7725
yet when they *r*, and cried unto ... Neh 9:28 7725
on the morrow she *r* into the ... Est 2:14 7725
Then the king *r* out of the palace ... Est 7:8 7725
my prayer *r* into mine own bosom ... Ps 35:13 7725
and with Aram-zobah, when Joab *r* ... Ps 60:*t* 7725
and they *r* and enquired early after ... Ps 78:34 7725
So I *r*, and considered all the ... Eccl 4:1 7725
Then I *r*, and I saw vanity under ... Eccl 4:7 7725
I *r*, and saw under the sun, that ... Eccl 9:11 7725
So Rabshakeh *r*, and found the king ... Is 37:8 7725
of Assyria departed, and went and *r* ... Is 37:37 7725
So the sun *r* ten degrees, by ... Is 38:8 7725
But she *r* not ... Jer 3:7 7725
they *r* with their vessels empty ... Jer 14:3 7725
Even all the Jews *r* out of all ... Jer 40:12 7725
from Mizpah cast about and *r* ... Jer 41:14 7725
that were *r* from all nations, ... Jer 43:5 7725
r as the appearance of a flash of ... Eze 1:14 7725
have *r* to provoke me to anger ... Eze 8:17 7725
Now when I had *r*, behold, at the ... Eze 47:7 7725
and mine understanding *r* unto me ... Dan 4:34 7725
the same time my reason *r* unto me ... Dan 4:36 7725
honour and brightness *r* unto me ... Dan 4:36 7725
when I *r* the captivity of my ... Hos 6:11 7725
yet have ye not *r* unto me ... Amos 4:6 7725
yet have ye not *r* unto me ... Amos 4:8 7725
yet have ye not *r* unto me ... Amos 4:9 7725
yet have ye not *r* unto me ... Amos 4:10 7725
yet have ye not *r* unto me ... Amos 4:11 7725
and they *r* and said, Like as the ... Zec 1:6 7725
I am *r* to Jerusalem with mercies ... Zec 1:16 7725
that no man passed through nor *r* ... Zec 7:14 7725
I am *r* unto Zion, and will dwell ... Zec 8:3 7725
the morning as he *r* into the city ... Mt 21:18 *1877*
And when he *r*, he found them ... Mk 14:40 *5290*
months, and *r* to her own house ... Lk 1:56 *5290*
And the shepherds *r*, glorifying and ... Lk 2:20 *1994*
they *r* into Galilee, to their own ... Lk 2:39 *5290*
had fulfilled the days, as they *r* ... Lk 2:43 *5290*
of the Holy Ghost *r* from Jordan ... Lk 4:1 *5290*
Jesus *r* in the power of the ... Lk 4:14 *5290*
up into the ship, and *r* back again ... Lk 8:37 *5290*
to pass, that, when Jesus was *r* ... Lk 8:40 *5290*
And the apostles, when they were *r* ... Lk 9:10 *5290*
the seventy *r* again with joy, ... Lk 10:17 *5290*
found that *r* to give glory to God ... Lk 17:18 *5290*
came to pass, that when he was *r* ... Lk 19:15 *1880*
done, smote their breasts, and *r* ... Lk 23:48 *5290*
And they *r*, and prepared spices and ... Lk 23:56 *5290*
r from the sepulchre, and told all ... Lk 24:9 *5290*
r to Jerusalem, and found the ... Lk 24:33 *5290*
r to Jerusalem with great joy ... Lk 24:52 *5290*
Then *r* they unto Jerusalem from ... Acts 1:12 *5290*
them not in the prison, they *r* ... Acts 5:22 *390*
r to Jerusalem, and preached the ... Acts 8:25 *5290*
Saul *r* from Jerusalem, when they ... Acts 12:25 *5290*
from them *r* to Jerusalem ... Acts 13:13 *5290*
they *r* again to Lystra, and to ... Acts 14:21 *5290*
and they *r* home again ... Acts 21:6 *5290*
go with him, and *r* to the castle ... Acts 23:32 *5290*
Arabia, and *r* again unto Damascus ... Gal 1:17 *5290*
have had opportunity to have *r* ... Heb 11:15 *344*
but are now *r* unto the Shepherd ... 1Pet 2:25 *1994*

RETURNETH {7}
goeth forth, he *r* to his earth ... Ps 146:4 7725
As a dog *r* to his vomit ... Prov 26:11 7725
so a fool *r* to his folly ... Prov 26:11 8138
the wind *r* again according to his ... Eccl 1:6 7725
r not thither, but watereth the ... Is 55:10 7725
that passeth out and him that *r* ... Eze 35:7 7725
by, and because of him that *r* ... Zec 9:8 7725

RETURNING {4}
In *r* and rest shall ye be saved ... Is 30:15 7729
r to the house, found the servant ... Lk 7:10 *5290*
Was *r*, and sitting in his chariot ... Acts 8:28 *5290*
who met Abraham *r* from the ... Heb 7:1 *5290*

REU *(re'-u)* {5} See RAGAU. *Son of Peleg.*
lived thirty years, and begat *R* ... Gen 11:18 7466
after he begat *R* two hundred ... Gen 11:19 7466
R lived two and thirty years, and ... Gen 11:20 7466
R lived after he begat Serug two ... Gen 11:21 7466
Eber, Peleg, *R*, ... 1Chr 1:25 7466

REUBEN *(ru'-ben)* {74} See REUBENITE.
1. A son of Jacob and Leah.
a son, and she called his name *R* ... Gen 29:32 7205
R went in the days of wheat ... Gen 30:14 7205
dwelt in that land, that *R* went ... Gen 35:22 7205
R, Jacob's firstborn, and Simeon, ... Gen 35:23 7205
R heard it, and he delivered him ... Gen 37:21 7205
R said unto them, Shed no blood, ... Gen 37:22 7205
And *R* returned unto the pit ... Gen 37:29 7205
R answered them, saying, Spake I ... Gen 42:22 7205
R spake unto his father, saying, ... Gen 42:37 7205
R, Jacob's firstborn ... Gen 46:8 7205
And the sons of *R* ... Gen 46:9 7205
as *R* and Simeon, they shall be ... Gen 48:5 7205
R, thou art my firstborn, my ... Gen 49:3 7205
R, Simeon, Levi, and Judah, ... Ex 1:2 7205
The sons of *R* the firstborn of ... Ex 6:14 7205
these be the families of *R* ... Ex 6:14 7205
And the children of *R*, Israel's ... Num 1:20 7205
On, the son of Peleth, sons of *R* ... Num 16:1 7205
R, the eldest son of Israel ... Num 26:5 7205
the children of *R* ... Num 26:5 7205
the sons of Eliab, the son of *R* ... Deut 11:6 7205
the stone of Bohan the son of *R* ... Josh 15:6 7205
the stone of Bohan the son of *R* ... Josh 18:17 7205
R, Simeon, Levi, and Judah, ... 1Chr 2:1 7205
Now the sons of *R* the firstborn ... 1Chr 5:1 7205
of *R* the firstborn of Israel were ... 1Chr 5:3 7205
2. Descendants of Reuben 1.
of the tribe of *R* ... Num 1:5 7205
of them, even of the tribe of *R* ... Num 1:21 7205
of *R* according to their armies ... Num 2:10 7205
of *R* shall be Elizur the son of ... Num 2:10 7205
of *R* were an hundred thousand ... Num 2:16 7205
prince of the children of *R* ... Num 7:30 7205
the standard of the camp of *R* set ... Num 10:18 7205
of the tribe of *R*, Shammua the ... Num 13:4 7205
Now the children of *R* and the ... Num 32:1 7205
of Gad and the children of *R* came ... Num 32:2 7205
of Gad and to the children of *R* ... Num 32:6 7205
the children of *R* spake unto ... Num 32:25 7205
the children of *R* will pass with ... Num 32:29 7205
Gad and the children of *R* answered ... Num 32:31 7205
of Gad, and to the children of *R* ... Num 32:33 7205
the children of *R* built Heshbon ... Num 32:37 7205
the tribe of the children of *R* ... Num 34:14 7206
R, Gad, and Asher, and Zebulun, Dan ... Deut 27:13 7205
Let *R* live, and not die ... Deut 33:6 7205
And the children of *R*, and the ... Josh 4:12 7205
the tribe of the children of *R* ... Josh 13:15 7205
of the children of *R* was Jordan ... Josh 13:23 7205
of *R* after their families ... Josh 13:23 7205
and Gad, and *R*, and half the tribe ... Josh 18:7 7205
the plain out of the tribe of *R* ... Josh 20:8 7205
had out of the tribe of *R* ... Josh 21:7 7205
And out of the tribe of *R*, Bezer ... Josh 21:36 7205
And the children of *R* and the ... Josh 22:9 7205
land of Canaan, the children of *R* ... Josh 22:10 7205
say, Behold, the children of *R* ... Josh 22:11 7205
sent unto the children of *R* ... Josh 22:13 7205
they came unto the children of *R* ... Josh 22:15 7205
Then the children of *R* and the ... Josh 22:21 7205
us and you, ye children of *R* ... Josh 22:25 7205
the words that the children of *R* ... Josh 22:30 7205

said unto the children of *R* ... Josh 22:31 7205
returned from the children of *R* ... Josh 22:32 7205
land wherein the children of *R* ... Josh 22:33 7205
And the children of *R* and the ... Josh 22:34 7205
For the divisions of *R* there were ... Judg 5:15 7205
For the divisions of *R* there were ... Judg 5:16 7205
The sons of *R*, and the Gadites, and ... 1Chr 5:18 7205
families, out of the tribe of *R* ... 1Chr 6:63 7205
given them out of the tribe of *R* ... 1Chr 6:78 7205
the west side, a portion for *R* ... Eze 48:6 7205
And by the border of *R*, from the ... Eze 48:7 7205
one gate of *R*, one gate of Judah, ... Eze 48:31 7205
Of the tribe of *R* were sealed ... Rev 7:5 *4502*

REUBENITE *(ru'-ben-ite)* {1} See REUBENITES. *A descendant of Reuben.*
Adina the son of Shiza the *R* ... 1Chr 11:42 7206

REUBENITES *(ru'-ben-ites)* {16}
These are the families of the *R* ... Num 26:7 7206
cities thereof, gave I unto the *R* ... Deut 3:12 7206
And unto the *R* and unto the Gadites ... Deut 3:16 7206
in the plain country, of the *R* ... Deut 4:43 7206
it for an inheritance unto the *R* ... Deut 29:8 7206
And to the *R*, and to the Gadites, ... Josh 1:12 7206
it for a possession unto the *R* ... Josh 12:6 7206
With whom the *R* and the Gadites ... Josh 13:8 7206
Then Joshua called the *R*, and the ... Josh 22:1 7206
of Gilead, the Gadites, and the *R* ... 2Kin 10:33 7206
he was prince of the *R* ... 1Chr 5:6 7206
he carried them away, even the *R* ... 1Chr 5:26 7206
the Reubenite, a captain of the *R* ... 1Chr 11:42 7206
other side of Jordan, of the *R* ... 1Chr 12:37 7206
king David made rulers over the *R* ... 1Chr 26:32 7206
the ruler of the *R* was Eliezer ... 1Chr 27:16 7206

REUEL *(re-u'-el)* {10} See DEUEL, JETHRO, RAGUEL.
1. A son of Esau.
and Bashemath bare *R* ... Gen 36:4 7467
R the son of Bashemath the wife ... Gen 36:10 7467
And these are the sons of *R* ... Gen 36:13 7467
are the sons of *R* Esau's son ... Gen 36:17 7467
came of *R* in the land of Edom ... Gen 36:17 7467
Eliphaz, *R*, and Jeush, and Jaalam, ... 1Chr 1:35 7467
The sons of *R* ... 1Chr 1:37 7467
2. Same as Jethro.
when they came to *R* their father ... Ex 2:18 7467
3. Father of Eliasaph.
shall be Eliasaph the son of *R* ... Num 2:14 7467
4. A Benjamite.
son of Shephatiah, the son of *R* ... 1Chr 9:8 7467

REUMAH *(re-u'-mah)* {1} *Concubine of Nahor.*
his concubine, whose name was *R* ... Gen 22:24 7208

REVEAL {7}
The heaven shall *r* his iniquity ... Job 20:27 1540
will *r* unto them the abundance of ... Jer 33:6 1540
seeing thou couldst *r* this secret ... Dan 2:47 1541
to whomsoever the Son will *r* him ... Mt 11:27 *601*
and he to whom the Son will *r* him ... Lk 10:22 *601*
To *r* his Son in me, that I might ... Gal 1:16 *601*
God shall *r* even this unto you ... Phil 3:15 *601*

REVEALED {38}
things which are *r* belong unto us ... Deut 29:29 1540
word of the LORD yet *r* unto him ... 1Sa 3:7 1540
for the LORD *r* himself to Samuel ... 1Sa 3:21 1540
hast *r* to thy servant, saying, I ... 2Sa 7:27 1540
it was *r* in mine ears by the LORD ... Is 22:14 1540
land of Chittim it is *r* to them ... Is 23:1 1540
the glory of the LORD shall be *r* ... Is 40:5 1540
to whom is the arm of the LORD *r* ... Is 53:1 1540
come, and my righteousness to be *r* ... Is 56:1 1540
for unto thee have I *r* my cause ... Jer 11:20 1540
Then was the secret *r* unto Daniel ... Dan 2:19 1541
this secret is not *r* to me for ... Dan 2:30 1541
Persia a thing was *r* unto Daniel ... Dan 10:1 1540
covered, that shall not be *r* ... Mt 10:26 *601*
and hast *r* them unto babes ... Mt 11:25 *601*
and blood hath not *r* it unto thee ... Mt 16:17 *601*
it was *r* unto him by the Holy ... Lk 2:26 *5537*
thoughts of many hearts may be *r* ... Lk 2:35 *601*
and hast *r* them unto babes ... Lk 10:21 *601*
covered, that shall not be *r* ... Lk 12:2 *601*
the day when the Son of man is *r* ... Lk 17:30 *601*
hath the arm of the Lord been *r* ... Jn 12:38 *601*
of God *r* from faith to faith ... Rom 1:17 *601*
God is *r* from heaven against all ... Rom 1:18 *601*
the glory which shall be *r* in us ... Rom 8:18 *601*
But God hath *r* them unto us by ... 1Cor 2:10 *601*
it, because it shall be *r* by fire ... 1Cor 3:13 *601*
If any thing be *r* to another that ... 1Cor 14:30 *601*
which should afterwards be *r* ... Gal 3:23 *601*
as it is now *r* unto his holy ... Eph 3:5 *601*
be *r* from heaven with his mighty ... 2Th 1:7 *602*
first, and that man of sin be *r* ... 2Th 2:3 *601*
that he might be *r* in his time ... 2Th 2:6 *601*
And then shall that Wicked be *r* ... 2Th 2:8 *601*
ready to be *r* in the last time ... 1Pet 1:5 *601*
Unto whom it was *r*, that not unto ... 1Pet 1:12 *601*
that, when his glory shall be *r* ... 1Pet 4:13 *602*
of the glory that shall be *r* ... 1Pet 5:1 *601*

REVEALER {1}
a *r* of secrets, seeing thou ... Dan 2:47 1541

REVEALETH {6}
A talebearer *r* secrets ... Prov 11:13 1540
about as a talebearer *r* secrets ... Prov 20:19 1540
He *r* the deep and secret things ... Dan 2:22 1541
is a God in heaven that *r* secrets ... Dan 2:28 1541
he that *r* secrets maketh known to ... Dan 2:29 1541
but he *r* his secret unto his ... Amos 3:7 1540

REVELATION {10}
r of the righteous judgment of ... Rom 2:5 *602*
according to the *r* of the mystery ... Rom 16:25 *602*
I shall speak to you either by *r* ... 1Cor 14:6 *602*
doctrine, hath a tongue, hath a *r* ... 1Cor 14:26 *602*
but by the *r* of Jesus Christ ... Gal 1:12 *602*
And I went up by *r*, and ... Gal 2:2 *602*
r in the knowledge of him ... Eph 1:17 *602*
How that by *r* he made known unto ... Eph 3:3 *602*
unto you at the *r* of Jesus Christ ... 1Pet 1:13 *602*
The *R* of Jesus Christ, which God ... Rev 1:1 *602*

REVELATIONS {2}
come to visions and *r* of the Lord ... 2Cor 12:1 *602*
through the abundance of the *r* ... 2Cor 12:7 *602*

REVELLINGS {2}
Envyings, murders, drunkenness, *r* ... Gal 5:21 *2970*
lusts, excess of wine, *r* ... 1Pet 4:3 *2970*

REVENGE {5}
me, and *r* me of my persecutors ... Jer 15:15 5358
and we shall take our *r* on him ... Jer 20:10 5360
the Philistines have dealt by *r* ... Eze 25:15 5360
yea, what zeal, yea, what *r* ... 2Cor 7:11 *1557*
a readiness to *r* all disobedience ... 2Cor 10:6 *1556*

REVENGED {1}
offended, and *r* himself upon them ... Eze 25:12 5358

REVENGER {7}
The *r* of blood himself shall slay ... Num 35:19 1350
the *r* of blood shall slay the ... Num 35:21 1350
the *r* of blood according to these ... Num 35:24 1350
out of the hand of the *r* of blood ... Num 35:25 1350
the *r* of blood find him without ... Num 35:27 1350
the *r* of blood kill the slayer ... Num 35:27 1350
a *r* to execute wrath upon him ... Rom 13:4 *1558*

REVENGERS {1}
r of blood to destroy any more ... 2Sa 14:11 1350

REVENGES {1}
the beginning of *r* upon the enemy ... Deut 32:42 6546

REVENGETH {2}
God is jealous, and the LORD *r* ... Nah 1:2 5358
the LORD *r*, and is furious ... Nah 1:2 5358

REVENGING {1}
r of the blood of thy servants ... Ps 79:10 5360

REVENUE {3}
shalt endamage the *r* of the kings ... Ezr 4:13 674
and my *r* than choice silver ... Prov 8:19 8393
harvest of the river, is her *r* ... Is 23:3 8393

REVENUES {3}
but in the *r* of the wicked is ... Prov 15:6 8393
than great *r* without right ... Prov 16:8 8393
they shall be ashamed of your *r* ... Jer 12:13 8393

REVERENCE {13}
my sabbaths, and *r* my sanctuary ... Lev 19:30 3372
my sabbaths, and *r* my sanctuary ... Lev 26:2 7812
he fell on his face, and did *r* ... 2Sa 9:6 7812
did *r* to the king, and said, Let ... 1Kin 1:31 7812
Mordecai bowed not, nor did him *r* ... Est 3:2 7812
Mordecai bowed not, nor did him *r* ... Est 3:5 7812
to be had in *r* of all them that ... Ps 89:7 3372
son, saying, They will *r* my son ... Mt 21:37 *1788*
them, saying, They will *r* my son ... Mk 12:6 *1788*
it may be they will *r* him when ... Lk 20:13 *1788*
wife see that she *r* her husband ... Eph 5:33 *5399*
corrected us, and we gave them *r* ... Heb 12:9 *1788*
may serve God acceptably with *r* ... Heb 12:28 *127*

REVERENCED {1}
king's gate, bowed, and *r* Haman ... Est 3:2 7812

REVEREND {1}
holy and *r* is his name ... Ps 111:9 3372

REVERSE {3}
and I cannot *r* it ... Num 23:20 7725
let it be written to *r* the ... Est 8:5 7725
the king's ring, may no man *r* ... Est 8:8 7725

REVILE {2}
Thou shalt not *r* the gods ... Ex 22:28 7043
are ye, when men shall *r* you ... Mt 5:11 *3679*

REVILED {6}
And they that passed by *r* him ... Mt 27:39 *937*
were crucified with him *r* him ... Mk 15:32 *3679*
Then they *r* him, and said, Thou ... Jn 9:28 *3058*
being *r*, we bless ... 1Cor 4:12 *3058*
when he was *r*, *r* not again ... 1Pet 2:23 *486*

REVILERS {1}
covetous, nor drunkards, nor *r* ... 1Cor 6:10 *3060*

REVILEST {1}
by said, *R* thou God's high priest ... Acts 23:4 *3058*

REVILINGS {2}
neither be ye afraid of their *r* ... Is 51:7 1421
the *r* of the children of Ammon, ... Zeph 2:8 1421

REVIVE {8}
will they *r* the stones out of the ... Neh 4:2 2421
Wilt thou not *r* us again ... Ps 85:6 2421
midst of trouble, thou wilt *r* me ... Ps 138:7 2421
to *r* the spirit of the humble, and ... Is 57:15 2421
to *r* the heart of the contrite ... Is 57:15 2421
After two days will he *r* us ... Hos 6:2 2421
they shall *r* as the corn, and grow ... Hos 14:7 2421
r thy work in the midst of the ... Hab 3:2 2421

REVIVED {6}
spirit of Jacob their father *r* ... Gen 45:27 2421
his spirit came again, and he *r* ... Judg 15:19 2421
came into him again, and he *r* ... 1Kin 17:22 2421
touched the bones of Elisha, he *r* ... 2Kin 13:21 2421
when the commandment came, sin *r* ... Rom 7:9 *326*
Christ both died, and rose, and *r* ... Rom 14:9 *326*

REVIVING {2}
give us a little *r* in our bondage ... Ezr 9:8 4241
kings of Persia, to give us a *r* ... Ezr 9:9 4241

REVOLT {3}
did Libnah *r* from under his hand ... 2Chr 21:10 6586
ye will *r* more and more ... Is 1:5 5627
our God, speaking oppression and *r* ... Is 59:13 5627

REVOLTED {7}
In his days Edom *r* from under the ... 2Kin 8:20 6586
Yet Edom *r* from under the hand of ... 2Kin 8:22 6586
Then Libnah *r* at the same time ... 2Kin 8:22 6586
In his days the Edomites *r* from ... 2Chr 21:8 6586
So the Edomites *r* from under the ... 2Chr 21:10 6586
children of Israel have deeply *r* ... Is 31:6 5627
they are *r* and gone ... Jer 5:23 5498

REVOLTERS {3}
They are all grievous *r*, walking ... Jer 6:28 5637
the *r* are profound to make ... Hos 5:2 7846
all their princes are *r* ... Hos 9:15 5637

REVOLTING {1}
But this people hath a *r* and a ... Jer 5:23 5637

REWARD {80}
shield, and thy exceeding great *r* ... Gen 15:1 7939
for it is your *r* for your service ... Num 18:31 7939
not persons, nor taketh *r* ... Deut 10:17 7810
Cursed be he that taketh *r* to ... Deut 27:25 7810
and will *r* them that hate me ... Deut 32:41 7999
a full *r* be given thee of the ... Ruth 2:12 4909
wherefore the LORD *r* thee good ... 1Sa 24:19 7999
the LORD shall *r* the doer of evil ... 2Sa 3:39 7999
given him a *r* for his tidings ... 2Sa 4:10 1309
recompense it me with such a *r* ... 2Sa 19:36 1578
thyself, and I will give thee a *r* ... 1Kin 13:7 4991
Behold, I say, how they *r* us ... 2Chr 20:11 1580
Give a *r* for me of your substance ... Job 6:22 7809
looketh for the *r* of his work ... Job 7:2
nor taketh *r* against the innocent ... Ps 15:5 7810
keeping of them there is great *r* ... Ps 19:11 6118
Let them be desolate for a *r* of ... Ps 40:15 6118
He shall *r* evil unto mine enemies ... Ps 54:5 7725
there is a *r* for the righteous ... Ps 58:11 6529
for a *r* of their shame that say ... Ps 70:3 6118
behold and see the *r* of the wicked ... Ps 91:8 8011
render a *r* to the proud ... Ps 94:2 1576
Let this be the *r* of mine ... Ps 109:20 6468
and the fruit of the womb is his *r* ... Ps 127:3 7939
righteousness shall be a sure *r* ... Prov 11:18 7938
a *r* in the bosom strong wrath ... Prov 21:14 7810
found it, then there shall be a *r* ... Prov 24:14 319
shall be no *r* to the evil man ... Prov 24:20 319
head, and the LORD shall *r* thee ... Prov 25:22 7999
have a good *r* for their labour ... Eccl 4:9 7999
neither have they any more a *r* ... Eccl 9:5 7999
for the *r* of his hands shall be ... Is 3:11 1576
Which justify the wicked for *r* ... Is 5:23 7810
his *r* is with him, and his work ... Is 40:10 7939
my captives, not for price nor *r* ... Is 45:13 7810
his *r* is with him, and his work ... Is 62:11 7939
guard gave him victuals and a *r* ... Jer 40:5 4864
and in that thou givest a *r* ... Eze 16:34 868
and no *r* is given unto thee, ... Eze 16:34 868
ways, and *r* them their doings ... Hos 4:9 7725
thou hast loved a *r* upon every ... Hos 9:1 868
thy *r* shall return upon thine own ... Obad 15 1576
The heads thereof judge for *r* ... Mic 3:11 7810
and the judge asketh for a *r* ... Mic 7:3 7966
for great is your *r* in heaven ... Mt 5:12 *3408*
which love you, what *r* have ye ... Mt 5:46 *3408*
otherwise ye have no *r* of your ... Mt 6:1 *3408*
I say unto you, They have their *r* ... Mt 6:2 *3408*
himself shall *r* thee openly ... Mt 6:4 *591*
I say unto you, They have their *r* ... Mt 6:5 *3408*
in secret shall *r* thee openly ... Mt 6:6 *591*
I say unto you, They have their *r* ... Mt 6:16 *3408*
in secret, shall *r* thee openly ... Mt 6:18 *591*
shall receive a prophet's *r* ... Mt 10:41 *3408*
shall receive a righteous man's *r* ... Mt 10:41 *3408*
he shall in no wise lose his *r* ... Mt 10:42 *3408*
then he shall *r* every man ... Mt 16:27 *591*
unto you, he shall not lose his *r* ... Mk 9:41 *3408*
your *r* is great in heaven ... Lk 6:23 *3408*
your *r* shall be great, and ye ... Lk 6:35 *3408*
we receive the due *r* of our deeds ... Lk 23:41 *514*
a field with the *r* of iniquity ... Acts 1:18 *3408*
is the *r* not reckoned of grace ... Rom 4:4 *3408*
own *r* according to his own labour ... 1Cor 3:8 *3408*
thereupon, he shall receive a *r* ... 1Cor 3:14 *3408*
this thing willingly, I have a *r* ... 1Cor 9:17 *3408*
What is my *r* then ... 1Cor 9:18 *3408*
of your *r* in a voluntary humility ... Col 2:18 *2603*
receive the *r* of the inheritance ... Col 3:24 *469*
The labourer is worthy of his *r* ... 1Ti 5:18 *3408*
the Lord *r* him according to his ... 2Ti 4:14 *591*
received a just recompence of *r* ... Heb 2:2 *3405*
which hath great recompence of *r* ... Heb 10:35 *3405*
unto the recompence of the *r* ... Heb 11:26 *3405*
And shall receive the *r* of ... 2Pet 2:13 *3408*
but that we receive a full *r* ... 2Jn 8 *3408*
after the error of Balaam for *r* ... Jude 11 *3408*

R

that thou shouldest give r unto Rev 11:18 3408
R her even as she rewarded you, Rev 18:6 591
my r is with me, to give every Rev 22:12 3408

REWARDED {14}
Wherefore have ye r evil for good Gen 44:4 7999
for thou hast r me good, whereas 1Sa 24:17 1580
good, whereas I have r thee evil 1Sa 24:17 1580
The LORD r me according to my 2Sa 22:21 1580
for your work shall be r 2Chr 15:7 7939
If I have r evil unto him that Ps 7:4 1580
The LORD r me according to my Ps 18:20 1580
They r me evil for good to the Ps 35:12 7999
nor r us according to our Ps 103:10 1580
they have r me evil for good, and Ps 109:5 7760
the commandment shall be r Prov 13:13 7999
for they have r evil unto Is 3:9 1580
for thy work shall be r, saith Jer 31:16 7939
Reward her even as she r you Rev 18:6 591

REWARDER {1}
that he is a r of them that Heb 11:6 3406

REWARDETH {6}
he r him, and he shall know it Job 21:19 7999
plentifully r the proud doer Ps 31:23 7999
that r thee as thou hast served Ps 137:8 7999
Whoso r evil for good, evil shall Prov 17:13 7725
formed all things both r the fool Prov 26:10 7936
and r transgressors Prov 26:10 7936

REWARDS {5}
the r of divination in their hand Num 22:7
gifts, and followeth after r Is 1:23 8021
ye shall receive of me gifts and r Dan 2:6 5023
thyself, and give thy r to another Dan 5:17 5023
These are my r that my lovers Hos 2:12 866

REZEPH *(re'-zef)* {2} *A fortress near Haran.*
as Gozan, and Haran, and R, and the 2Kin 19:12 7530
as Gozan, and Haran, and R Is 37:12 7530

REZIA *(re-zi'-ah)* {1} *Son of Ulla.*
Arah, and Haniel, and R 1Chr 7:39 7525

REZIN *(re'-zin)* {10}
1. A king of Syria.
against Judah R the king of Syria 2Kin 15:37 7526
Then R king of Syria and Pekah son 2Kin 16:5 7526
At that time R king of Syria 2Kin 16:6 7526
of it captive to Kir, and slew R 2Kin 16:9 7526
the fierce anger of R with Syria Is 7:4 7526
and the head of Damascus is R Is 7:8 7526
that go softly, and rejoice in R Is 8:6 7526
the adversaries of R against him Is 9:11 7526
2. A family of exiles.
The children of R, the children Ezr 2:48 7526
of Reaiah, the children of R Neh 7:50 7526

REZON *(re'-zon)* {1} *An enemy of Solomon.*
R the son of Eliadah, which fled 1Kin 11:23 7331

RHEGIUM *(re'-je-um)* {1} *A port of southern Italy.*
fetched a compass, and came to R Acts 28:13 4484

RHESA *(re'-sah)* {1} *Son of Zorobabel; an ancestor of Jesus.*
of Joanna, which was the son of R Lk 3:27 4488

RHODA *(ro'-dah)* {1} *A maiden in Mary's house.*
a damsel came to hearken, named R Acts 12:13 4498

RHODES *(rodes)* {1} *A Mediterranean island.*
Coos, and the day following unto R Acts 21:1

RIB {5}
And the r, which the LORD God had Gen 2:22 6763
spear smote him under the fifth r 2Sa 2:23
smote him there under the fifth r 2Sa 3:27
they smote him under the fifth r 2Sa 4:6
him therewith in the fifth r 2Sa 20:10

RIBAI *(rib'-ahee)* {2} *Father of Ittai.*
Ittai the son of R out of Gibeah 2Sa 23:29 7380
Ithai the son of R of Gibeah 1Chr 11:31 7380

RIBBAND {1}
fringe of the borders a r of blue Num 15:38 6616

RIBLAH *(rib'-lah)* {11} *A city on the Orontes River.*
shall go down from Shepham to R Num 34:11 7247
put him in bands at R in the land 2Kin 23:33 7247
up to the king of Babylon to R 2Kin 25:6 7247
them to the king of Babylon to R 2Kin 25:20 7247
slew them at R in the land of 2Kin 25:21 7247
king of Babylon to R in the land Jer 39:5 7247
of Zedekiah in R before his eyes Jer 39:6 7247
to R in the land of Hamath Jer 52:9 7247
all the princes of Judah in R Jer 52:10 7247
them to the king of Babylon to R Jer 52:26 7247
put them to death in R in the Jer 52:27 7247

RIBS {2}
and he took one of his r, and Gen 2:21 6763
it had three r in the mouth of it Dan 7:5 6763

RICH {81}
And Abram was very r in cattle Gen 13:2 3513
say, I have made Abram r Gen 14:23 6238
The r shall not give more, and the Ex 30:15 6223
or stranger wax r by thee Lev 25:47 5381
not young men, whether poor or r Ruth 3:10 6223
The LORD maketh poor, and maketh r 1Sa 2:7 6238
the one r, and the other poor 2Sa 12:1 6223
The r man had exceeding many 2Sa 12:2 6223
came a traveller unto the r man 2Sa 12:4 6223
He shall not be r, neither shall Job 15:29 6238
The r man shall lie down, but he Job 27:19 6223
nor regardeth the r more than the Job 34:19 7771
even the r among the people shall Ps 45:12 6223
Both low and high, r and poor, Ps 49:2 6223
thou afraid when one is made r Ps 49:16 6238
the hand of the diligent maketh r Prov 10:4 6238
The r man's wealth is his strong Prov 10:15 6223
blessing of the LORD, it maketh r Prov 10:22 6238
There is that maketh himself r Prov 13:7 6238
but the r hath many friends Prov 14:20 6223
The r man's wealth is his strong Prov 18:11 6223
but the r answereth roughly Prov 18:23 6223
loveth wine and oil shall not be r Prov 21:17 6238
The r and poor meet together Prov 22:2 6223
The r ruleth over the poor, and Prov 22:7 6223
and he that giveth to the r Prov 22:16 6223
Labour not to be r Prov 23:4 6238
in his ways, though he be r Prov 28:6 6223
The r man is wise in his own Prov 28:11 6223
to be r shall not be innocent Prov 28:20 6238
hasteth to be r hath an evil eye Prov 28:22 1952
but the abundance of the r will Eccl 5:12 6223
and the r sit in low place Eccl 10:6 6223
curse not the r in thy bedchamber Eccl 10:20 6223
and with the r in his death Is 53:9 6223
they are become great, and waxen r Jer 5:27 6238
let not the r man glory in his Jer 9:23 6223
work, and in chests of r apparel Eze 27:24
Ephraim said, Yet I am become r Hos 12:8 6238
For the r men thereof are full of Mic 6:12 6223
for I am r Zec 11:5 6238
That a r man shall hardly enter Mt 19:23 4145
than for a r man to enter into Mt 19:24 4145
there came a r man of Arimathaea, Mt 27:57 4145
than for a r man to enter into Mk 10:25 4145
and many that were r cast in much Mk 12:41 4145
the r he hath sent empty away Lk 1:53 4147
But woe unto you that are r Lk 6:24 4145
The ground of a certain r man Lk 12:16 4145
himself, and is not r toward God Lk 12:21 4147
thy kinsmen, nor thy r neighbours Lk 14:12 4145
There was a certain r man Lk 16:1 4145
There was a certain r man Lk 16:19 4145
which fell from the r man's table Lk 16:21 4145
the r man also died, and was Lk 16:22 4145
for he was very r Lk 18:23 4145
than for a r man to enter into Lk 18:25 4145
among the publicans, and he was r Lk 19:2 4145
saw the r men casting their gifts Lk 21:1 4145
is r unto all that call upon him Rom 10:12 4147
Now ye are full, now ye are r 1Cor 4:8 4147
as poor, yet making many r 2Cor 6:10 4148
Christ, that, though he was r 2Cor 8:9 4145
ye through his poverty might be r 2Cor 8:9 4147
who is r in mercy, for his great Eph 2:4 4145
will be r fall into temptation 1Ti 6:9 4147
them that are r in this world 1Ti 6:17 4145
that they be r in good works, 1Ti 6:18 4147
But the r, in that he is made low Jas 1:10 4145
so also shall the r man fade away Jas 1:11 4145
the poor of this world r in faith Jas 2:5 4145
Do not r men oppress you, and draw Jas 2:6 4145
ye r men, weep and howl for your Jas 5:1 4145
and poverty, (but thou art r) Rev 2:9 4145
Because thou sayest, I am r Rev 3:17 4145
the fire, that thou mayest be r Rev 3:18 4147
and the great men, and the r men Rev 6:15 4145
all, both small and great, r Rev 13:16 4145
of the earth are waxed r through Rev 18:3 4147
things, which were made r by her Rev 18:15 4147
wherein were made r all that had Rev 18:19 4147

RICHER {1}
shall be far r than they all Dan 11:2 6238

RICHES {98}
For all the r which God hath Gen 31:16 6239
For their r were more than that Gen 36:7 7399
with much r unto your tents Josh 22:8 5233
king will enrich him with great r 1Sa 17:25 6239
neither hast asked r for thyself 1Kin 3:11 6239
which thou hast not asked, both r 1Kin 3:13 6239
all the kings of the earth for r 1Kin 10:23 6239
Both r and honour come of thee, and 1Chr 29:12 6239
a good old age, full of days, r 1Chr 29:28 6239
heart, and thou hast not asked r 2Chr 1:11 6239
and I will give thee r, and wealth, 2Chr 1:12 6239
all the kings of the earth in r 2Chr 9:22 6239
and he had r and honour in 2Chr 17:5 6239
Now Jehoshaphat had r and honour 2Chr 18:1 6239
both r with the dead bodies 2Chr 20:25 7399
And Hezekiah had exceeding much r 2Chr 32:27 6239
When he shewed the r of his Est 1:4 6239
told them of the glory of his r Est 5:11 6239
He hath swallowed down r, and he Job 20:15 2428
Will he esteem thy r Job 36:19 7769
better than the r of many wicked Ps 37:16 1995
he heapeth up r, and knoweth not Ps 39:6
in the multitude of their r Ps 49:6 6239
trusted in the abundance of his r Ps 52:7 6239
if r increase, set not your heart Ps 62:10 2428
they increase in r Ps 73:12 2428
the earth is full of thy r Ps 104:24 7075
Wealth and r shall be in his house Ps 112:3 6239
testimonies, as much as in all r Ps 119:14 1952
and in her left hand r and honour Prov 3:16 6239
R and honour are with me Prov 8:18 6239
yea, durable r and righteousness Prov 8:18 1952
R profit not in the day of wrath Prov 11:4 1952
and strong men retain r Prov 11:16 6239
that trusteth in his r shall fall Prov 11:28 6239
himself poor, yet hath great r Prov 13:7 1952
ransom of a man's life are his r Prov 13:8 6239
The crown of the wise is their r Prov 14:24 6239
r are the inheritance of fathers Prov 19:14 1952
rather to be chosen than great r Prov 22:1 6239
and the fear of the LORD are r Prov 22:4 6239
the poor to increase his r Prov 22:16
for r certainly make themselves Prov 23:5
with all precious and pleasant r Prov 24:4 1952
For r are not for ever Prov 27:24 2633
give me neither poverty nor r Prov 30:8 6239
is his eye satisfied with r Eccl 4:8 6239
r kept for the owners thereof to Eccl 5:13 6239
But those r perish by evil Eccl 5:14 6239
man also to whom God hath given r Eccl 5:19 6239
A man to whom God hath given r Eccl 6:2 6239
nor yet r to men of understanding Eccl 9:11 6239
the r of Damascus and the spoil of Is 8:4 2428
as a nest the r of the people Is 10:14 2428
they will carry their r upon the Is 30:6 2428
hidden r of secret places, that Is 45:3 4301
shall eat the r of the Gentiles Is 61:6 2428
not the rich man glory in his r Jer 9:23 6239
so he that getteth r, and not by Jer 17:11 6239
because the r that he hath gotten Jer 48:36 3502
they shall make a spoil of thy r Eze 26:12 2428
of the multitude of all kind of r Eze 27:12 1952
for the multitude of all r Eze 27:18 1952
Thy r, and thy fairs, thy Eze 27:27 1952
earth with the multitude of thy r Eze 27:33 6239
thou hast gotten thee r, and hast Eze 28:4 2428
hast thou increased thy r Eze 28:5 2428
is lifted up because of thy r Eze 28:5 2428
by his strength through his r he Dan 11:2 6239
with a great army and with much r Dan 11:13 7399
them the prey, and spoil, and r Dan 11:24 7399
return into his land with great r Dan 11:28 7399
world, and the deceitfulness of r Mt 13:22 4149
world, and the deceitfulness of r Mk 4:19 4149
r enter into the kingdom of God Mk 10:23 5536
in r to enter into the kingdom of Mk 10:24 5536
and are choked with cares and r Lk 8:14 4149
commit to your trust the true r Lk 16:11
r enter into the kingdom of God Lk 18:24 5536
thou the r of his goodness Rom 2:4 4149
that he might make known the r of Rom 9:23 4149
of them be the r of the world Rom 11:12 4149
of them the r of the Gentiles Rom 11:12 4149
depth of the r both of the wisdom Rom 11:33 4149
unto the r of their liberality 2Cor 8:2 4149
according to the r of his grace Eph 1:7 4149
what the r of the glory of his Eph 1:18 4149
he might shew the exceeding r of Eph 2:7 4149
the unsearchable r of Christ Eph 3:8 4149
according to the r of his glory Eph 3:16 4149
to his r in glory by Christ Jesus Phil 4:19 4149
r of the glory of this mystery Col 1:27 4149
unto all r of the full assurance Col 2:2 4149
nor trust in uncertain r 1Ti 6:17 4149
r than the treasures in Egypt Heb 11:26 4149
Your r are corrupted, and your Jas 5:2 4149
was slain to receive power, and r Rev 5:12 4149
hour so great r is come to nought Rev 18:17 4149

RICHLY {2}
dwell in you r in all wisdom Col 3:16 4146
who giveth us r all things to 1Ti 6:17 4146

RID {6}
that he might r him out of their Gen 37:22 5337
I will r you out of their bondage Ex 6:6 5337
I will r evil beasts out of the Lev 26:6 7673
r them out of the hand of the Ps 82:4 5337
r me, and deliver me out of great Ps 144:7 6475
R me, and deliver me from the hand Ps 144:11 6475

RIDDANCE {2}
thou shalt not make clean r of Lev 23:22 3615
r of all them that dwell in the Zeph 1:18 3617

RIDDEN {1}
upon which thou hast r ever since Num 22:30 7392

RIDDLE {9}
I will now put forth a r unto you Judg 14:12 2420
said unto him, Put forth thy r Judg 14:13 2420
not in three days expound the r Judg 14:14 2420
that he may declare unto us the r Judg 14:15 2420
thou hast put forth a r unto the Judg 14:16 2420
she told the r to the children of Judg 14:17 2420
heifer, ye had not found out my r Judg 14:18 2420
unto them which expounded the r Judg 14:19 2420
Son of man, put forth a r Eze 17:2 2420

RIDE {20}
he made him to r in the second Gen 41:43 7392
He made him r on the high places Deut 32:13 7392
ye that r on white asses, ye that Judg 5:10 7392
for the king's household to r on 2Sa 16:2 7392
me an ass, that I may r thereon 2Sa 19:26 7392
my son to r upon mine own mule 1Kin 1:33 7392
caused Solomon to r upon king 1Kin 1:38 7392
him to r upon the king's mule 1Kin 1:44 7392
So they made him r in his chariot 2Kin 10:16 7392
thou causest me to r upon it Job 30:22 7392
in thy majesty r prosperously Ps 45:4 7392
caused men to r over our heads Ps 66:12 7392
and, We will r upon the swift Is 30:16 7392
I will cause thee to r upon the Is 58:14 7392
they r upon horses, set in array Jer 6:23 7392
they shall r upon horses, every Jer 50:42 7392
I will make Ephraim to r Hos 10:11 7392
we will not r upon horses Hos 14:3 7392

that thou didst *r* upon thine ... Hab 3:8 7392
chariots, and those that *r* in them ... Hag 2:22 7392

RIDER {7}
so that his *r* shall fall backward ... Gen 49:17 7392
his *r* hath he thrown into the sea ... Ex 15:1 7392
his *r* hath he thrown into the sea ... Ex 15:21 7392
she scorneth the horse and his *r* ... Job 39:18 7392
in pieces the horse and his *r* ... Jer 51:21 7392
in pieces the chariot and his *r* ... Jer 51:21 7392
and his *r* with madness ... Zec 12:4 7392

RIDERS {5}
on thy part to set *r* upon them ... 2Kin 18:23 7392
r on mules, camels, and young ... Est 8:10 7392
on thy part to set *r* upon them ... Is 36:8 7392
their *r* shall come down, every ... Hag 2:22 7392
them, and the *r* on horses shall be ... Zec 10:5 7392

RIDETH {7}
what saddle soever he *r* upon that ... Lev 15:9 7392
who *r* upon the heaven in thy help ... Deut 33:26 7392
and the horse that the king *r* upon ... Est 6:8 7392
extol him that *r* upon the heavens ... Ps 68:4 7392
To him that *r* upon the heavens of ... Ps 68:33 7392
the LORD *r* upon a swift cloud, and ... Is 19:1 7392
neither shall he that *r* the horse ... Amos 2:15 7392

RIDGES {1}
Thou waterest the *r* thereof ... Ps 65:10 8525

RIDING {10}
Now he was *r* upon his ass, and his ... Num 22:22 7392
slack not thy *r* for me, except I ... 2Kin 4:24 7392
r in chariots and on horses, they, ... Jer 17:25 7392
r in chariots and on horses, he, ... Jer 22:4 7392
young men, horsemen *r* upon horses ... Eze 23:6 7392
horsemen *r* upon horses, all of ... Eze 23:12 7392
all of them *r* upon horses ... Eze 23:23 7392
thee, all of them *r* upon horses ... Eze 38:15 7392
behold a man *r* upon a red horse, ... Zec 1:8 7392
r upon an ass, and upon a colt the ... Zec 9:9 7392

RIE {2}
wheat and the *r* were not smitten ... Ex 9:32 3698
barley and the *r* in their place ... Is 28:25 3698

RIFLED {1}
shall be taken, and the houses *r* ... Zec 14:2 8155

RIGHT {359}
hand, then I will go to the *r* ... Gen 13:9 3231
or if thou depart to the *r* hand ... Gen 13:9 3225
the Judge of all the earth do *r* ... Gen 18:25 4941
in the *r* way to take my master's ... Gen 24:48 571
that I may turn to the *r* hand ... Gen 24:49 3225
Ephraim in his *r* hand toward ... Gen 48:13 3225
left hand toward Israel's *r* hand ... Gen 48:13 3225
Israel stretched out his *r* hand ... Gen 48:14 3225
saw that his father laid his *r* ... Gen 48:17 3225
put thy *r* hand upon his head ... Gen 48:18 3225
a wall unto them on their *r* hand ... Ex 14:22 3225
a wall unto them on their *r* hand ... Ex 14:29 3225
Thy *r* hand, O LORD, is become ... Ex 15:6 3225
thy *r* hand, O LORD, hath dashed ... Ex 15:6 3225
Thou stretchedst out thy *r* hand ... Ex 15:12 3225
do that which is *r* in his sight ... Ex 15:26 3477
the tip of the *r* ear of Aaron ... Ex 29:20
the tip of the *r* ear of his sons ... Ex 29:20 3233
and upon the thumb of their *r* hand ... Ex 29:20 3233
the great toe of their *r* foot ... Ex 29:20 3233
is upon them, and the *r* shoulder ... Ex 29:22 3233
the *r* shoulder shall ye give unto ... Lev 7:32 3225
shall have the *r* shoulder for his ... Lev 7:33 3225
it upon the tip of Aaron's *r* ear ... Lev 8:23 3233
and upon the thumb of his *r* hand ... Lev 8:23 3233
upon the great toe of his *r* foot ... Lev 8:23 3233
blood upon the tip of their *r* ear ... Lev 8:24 3233
upon the thumbs of their *r* hands ... Lev 8:24 3233
the great toes of their *r* feet ... Lev 8:24 3233
and their fat, and the *r* shoulder ... Lev 8:25 3225
the fat, and upon the *r* shoulder ... Lev 8:26 3225
the *r* shoulder Aaron waved for a ... Lev 9:21 3225
of the *r* ear of him that is to be ... Lev 14:14 3233
and upon the thumb of his *r* hand ... Lev 14:14 3233
upon the great toe of his *r* foot ... Lev 14:14 3233
the priest shall dip his *r* finger ... Lev 14:16 3233
of the *r* ear of him that is to be ... Lev 14:17 3233
and upon the thumb of his *r* hand ... Lev 14:17 3233
upon the great toe of his *r* foot ... Lev 14:17 3233
of the *r* ear of him that is to be ... Lev 14:25 3233
and upon the thumb of his *r* hand ... Lev 14:25 3233
upon the great toe of his *r* foot ... Lev 14:25 3233
r finger some of the oil that is ... Lev 14:27 3233
of the *r* ear of him that is to be ... Lev 14:28 3233
and upon the thumb of his *r* hand ... Lev 14:28 3233
upon the great toe of his *r* foot ... Lev 14:28 3233
as the *r* shoulder are thine ... Num 18:18 3225
to the *r* hand nor to the left ... Num 20:17 3225
to the *r* hand or to the left ... Num 22:26 3225
daughters of Zelophehad speak *r* ... Num 27:7 3651
unto the *r* hand nor to the left ... Deut 2:27 3225
to the *r* hand or to the left ... Deut 5:32 3225
And thou shalt do that which is *r* ... Deut 6:18 3477
whatsoever is *r* in his own eyes ... Deut 12:8 3477
is *r* in the sight of the LORD ... Deut 12:25 3477
r in the sight of the LORD thy ... Deut 12:28 3477
to do that which is *r* in the eyes ... Deut 13:18 3477
shall shew thee, to the *r* hand ... Deut 17:11 3225
the commandment, to the *r* hand ... Deut 17:20 3225
is *r* in the sight of the LORD ... Deut 21:9 3477
the *r* of the firstborn is his ... Deut 21:17 4941
thee this day, to the *r* hand ... Deut 28:14 3225
without iniquity, just and *r* is he ... Deut 32:4 3477
from his *r* hand went a fiery law ... Deut 33:2 3225
it to the *r* hand or to the left ... Josh 1:7 3225
passed over *r* against Jericho ... Josh 3:16
r unto thee to do unto us, do ... Josh 9:25 3477
r hand unto the inhabitants of ... Josh 17:7 3225
to the *r* hand or to the left ... Josh 23:6 3225
his raiment upon his *r* thigh ... Judg 3:16 3225
took the dagger from his *r* thigh ... Judg 3:21 3225
her *r* hand to the workmen's ... Judg 5:26 3225
in their *r* hands to blow withal ... Judg 7:20 3225
could not frame to pronounce it *r* ... Judg 12:6 3651
up, of the one with his *r* hand ... Judg 16:29 3225
that which was *r* in his own eyes ... Judg 17:6 3477
that which was *r* in his own eyes ... Judg 21:25 3477
redeem thou my *r* to thyself ... Ruth 4:6 1353
to the *r* hand or to the left ... 1Sa 6:12 3225
I may thrust out all your *r* eyes ... 1Sa 11:2 3225
teach you the good and the *r* way ... 1Sa 12:23 3477
the *r* hand nor to the left from ... 2Sa 2:19 3225
to thy *r* hand or to thy left ... 2Sa 2:21 3225
none can turn to the *r* hand or to ... 2Sa 14:19 3231
See, thy matters are good and *r* ... 2Sa 15:3 5228
the mighty men were on his *r* hand ... 2Sa 16:6 3225
What *r* therefore have I yet to ... 2Sa 19:28 6666
have also more *r* in David than ye ... 2Sa 19:43 3225
beard with the *r* hand to kiss him ... 2Sa 20:9 3225
on the *r* side of the city that ... 2Sa 24:5 3225
and she sat on his *r* hand ... 1Kin 2:19 3225
was in the *r* side of the house ... 1Kin 6:8 3233
and he set up the *r* pillar ... 1Kin 7:21 3225
bases on the *r* side of the house ... 1Kin 7:39 3225
he set the sea on the *r* side of ... 1Kin 7:39 3233
of pure gold, five on the *r* side ... 1Kin 7:49 3225
do that which is *r* in mine eyes ... 1Kin 11:33 3477
do that is *r* in my sight, to keep ... 1Kin 11:38 3477
only which was *r* in mine eyes ... 1Kin 14:8 3477
was *r* in the eyes of the LORD ... 1Kin 15:5 3477
Asa did that which was *r* in the ... 1Kin 15:11 3477
standing by him on his *r* hand ... 1Kin 22:19 3225
doing that which was *r* in the ... 1Kin 22:43 3477
and said to him, Is thine heart *r* ... 2Kin 10:15 3477
that which is *r* in mine eyes ... 2Kin 10:30 3225
from the *r* corner of the temple ... 2Kin 11:11 3233
Jehoash did that which was *r* in ... 2Kin 12:2 3477
on the *r* side as one cometh into ... 2Kin 12:9 3225
he did that which was *r* in the ... 2Kin 14:3 3477
he did that which was *r* in the ... 2Kin 15:3 3477
he did that which was *r* in the ... 2Kin 15:34 3477
did not that which was *r* in the ... 2Kin 16:2 3477
not *r* against the LORD their God ... 2Kin 17:9 3651
he did that which was *r* in the ... 2Kin 18:3 3477
he did that which was *r* in the ... 2Kin 22:2 3477
to the *r* hand or to the left ... 2Kin 22:2 3225
which were on the *r* hand of the ... 2Kin 23:13 3225
Asaph, who stood on his *r* hand ... 1Chr 6:39 3225
and could use both the *r* hand ... 1Chr 12:2 3231
for the thing was *r* in the eyes ... 1Chr 13:4 3477
the temple, one on the *r* hand ... 2Chr 3:17 3225
name of that on the *r* hand Jachin ... 2Chr 3:17 3227
lavers, and put five on the *r* hand ... 2Chr 4:6 3225
in the temple, five on the *r* hand ... 2Chr 4:7 3225
in the temple, five on the *r* side ... 2Chr 4:8 3225
sea on the *r* side of the east end ... 2Chr 4:10 3233
r in the eyes of the LORD his God ... 2Chr 14:2 3477
of heaven standing on his *r* hand ... 2Chr 18:18 3225
doing that which was *r* in the ... 2Chr 20:32 3477
from the *r* side of the temple to ... 2Chr 23:10 3233
Joash did that which was *r* in the ... 2Chr 24:2 3477
he did that which was *r* in the ... 2Chr 25:2 3477
he did that which was *r* in the ... 2Chr 26:4 3477
he did that which was *r* in the ... 2Chr 27:2 3477
was *r* in the sight of the LORD ... 2Chr 28:1 3477
he did that which was *r* in the ... 2Chr 29:2 3477
wrought that which was good and *r* ... 2Chr 31:20 3477
he did that which was *r* in the ... 2Chr 34:2 3477
and declined neither to the *r* hand ... 2Chr 34:2 3225
to seek of him a *r* way for us ... Ezr 8:21 3477
but ye have no portion, nor *r* ... Neh 2:20 6666
and Maaseiah, on his *r* hand ... Neh 8:4 3225
and gavest them *r* judgments ... Neh 9:13 3477
for thou hast done *r*, but we have ... Neh 9:33 571
whereof one went on the *r* hand ... Neh 12:31 3225
the thing seem *r* before the king, ... Est 8:5 3787
How forcible are *r* words ... Job 6:25 3476
he hideth himself on the *r* hand ... Job 23:9 3225
Upon my *r* hand rise the youth ... Job 30:12 3225
and perverted that which was *r* ... Job 33:27 3477
Should I lie against my *r* ... Job 34:6 4941
even he that hateth *r* govern ... Job 34:17 4941
will not lay upon man more than *r* ... Job 34:23 4941
Thinkest thou this to be *r* ... Job 35:2 4941
but giveth *r* to the poor ... Job 36:6 4941
thine own *r* hand can save thee ... Job 40:14 3225
spoken of me the thing that is *r* ... Job 42:7 3559
spoken of me the thing which is *r* ... Job 42:8 3559
For thou hast maintained my *r* ... Ps 9:4 4941
satest in the throne judging *r* ... Ps 9:4 6664
because he is at my *r* hand ... Ps 16:8 3225
at thy *r* hand there are pleasures ... Ps 16:11 3225
Hear the *r*, O LORD, attend unto ... Ps 17:1 6664
O thou that savest by thy *r* hand ... Ps 17:7 3225
thy *r* hand hath holden me up, and ... Ps 18:35 3225
The statutes of the LORD are *r* ... Ps 19:8 3477
the saving strength of his *r* hand ... Ps 20:6 3225
thy *r* hand shall find out those ... Ps 21:8 3225
their *r* hand is full of bribes ... Ps 26:10 3225
For the word of the LORD is *r* ... Ps 33:4 3477
but thy *r* hand, and thine arm, and ... Ps 44:3 3225
thy *r* hand shall teach thee ... Ps 45:4 3225
of thy kingdom is a *r* sceptre ... Ps 45:6 4334
upon thy *r* hand did stand the ... Ps 45:9 3225
shall help her, and that *r* early ... Ps 46:5 6437
thy *r* hand is full of ... Ps 48:10 3225
renew a *r* spirit within me ... Ps 51:10 3559
save with thy *r* hand, and hear me ... Ps 60:5 3225
thy *r* hand upholdeth me ... Ps 63:8 3225
thou hast holden me by my *r* hand ... Ps 73:23 3225
thou thy hand, even thy *r* hand ... Ps 74:11 3225
of the *r* hand of the most High ... Ps 77:10 3225
their heart was not *r* with him ... Ps 78:37 3559
which his *r* hand had purchased ... Ps 78:54 3225
which thy *r* hand hath planted ... Ps 80:15 3225
be upon the man of thy *r* hand ... Ps 80:17 3225
thy hand, and high is thy *r* hand ... Ps 89:13 3225
sea, and his *r* hand in the rivers ... Ps 89:25 3225
Thou hast set up the *r* hand of ... Ps 89:42 3225
and ten thousand at thy *r* hand ... Ps 91:7 3225
his *r* hand, and his holy arm, hath ... Ps 98:1 3225
And he led them forth by the *r* way ... Ps 107:7 3477
save with thy *r* hand, and answer ... Ps 108:6 3225
and let Satan stand at his *r* hand ... Ps 109:6 3225
stand at the *r* hand of the poor ... Ps 109:31 3225
my Lord, Sit thou at my *r* hand ... Ps 110:1 3225
The LORD at thy *r* hand shall ... Ps 110:5 3225
the *r* hand of the LORD doeth ... Ps 118:15 3225
The *r* hand of the LORD is exalted ... Ps 118:16 3225
the *r* hand of the LORD doeth ... Ps 118:16 3225
O LORD, that thy judgments are *r* ... Ps 119:75 6664
concerning all things to be *r* ... Ps 119:128 3474
LORD is thy shade upon thy *r* hand ... Ps 121:5 3225
let my *r* hand forget her cunning ... Ps 137:5 3225
and thy *r* hand shall save me ... Ps 138:7 3225
me, and thy *r* hand shall hold me ... Ps 139:10 3225
and that my soul knoweth *r* well ... Ps 139:14
afflicted, and the *r* of the poor ... Ps 140:12 4941
I looked on my *r* hand, and beheld, ... Ps 142:4 3225
their *r* hand is a *r* hand of ... Ps 144:8 3225
their *r* hand is a *r* hand of ... Ps 144:11 3225
Length of days is in her *r* hand ... Prov 3:16 3225
I have led thee in *r* paths ... Prov 4:11 3476
Let thine eyes look *r* on, and let ... Prov 4:25 5227
Turn not to the *r* hand nor to the ... Prov 4:27 3225
of my lips shall be *r* things ... Prov 8:6 4339
r to them that find knowledge ... Prov 8:9 3477
passengers who go *r* on their ways ... Prov 9:15 3474
thoughts of the righteous are *r* ... Prov 12:5 4941
of a fool is *r* in his own eyes ... Prov 12:15 3477
a way which seemeth *r* unto a man ... Prov 14:12 3477
than great revenues without *r* ... Prov 16:8 4941
and they love him that speaketh *r* ... Prov 16:13 3477
a way that seemeth *r* unto a man ... Prov 16:25 3477
work be pure, and whether it be *r* ... Prov 20:11 3477
way of a man is *r* in his own eyes ... Prov 21:2 3477
as for the pure, his work is *r* ... Prov 21:8 3477
when thy lips speak *r* things ... Prov 23:16 4339
his lips that giveth a *r* answer ... Prov 24:26 5228
and the ointment of his *r* hand ... Prov 27:16 3225
all travail, and every *r* work ... Eccl 4:4 3788
wise man's heart is at his *r* hand ... Eccl 10:2 3225
his *r* hand doth embrace me ... Song 2:6 3225
his *r* hand should embrace me ... Song 8:3 3225
And he shall snatch on the *r* hand ... Is 9:20 3225
to take away the *r* from the poor ... Is 10:2 4941
Prophesy not unto us *r* things ... Is 30:10 5229
in it, when ye turn to the *r* hand ... Is 30:21 541
even when the needy speaketh *r* ... Is 32:7 4941
the *r* hand of my righteousness ... Is 41:10 3225
LORD thy God will hold thy *r* hand ... Is 41:13 3225
Is there not a lie in my *r* hand ... Is 44:20 3225
whose *r* hand I have holden, to ... Is 45:1 3225
I declare things that are *r* ... Is 45:19 4339
my *r* hand hath spanned the ... Is 48:13 3225
shalt break forth on the *r* hand ... Is 54:3 3225
The LORD hath sworn by his *r* hand ... Is 62:8 3225
That led them by the *r* hand of ... Is 63:12 3225
a noble vine, wholly a *r* seed ... Jer 2:21 571
the *r* of the needy do they not ... Jer 5:28 4941
that getteth riches, and not by *r* ... Jer 17:11 4941
out of my lips was *r* before thee ... Jer 17:16 5227
were the signet upon my *r* hand ... Jer 22:24 3225
is evil, and their force is not *r* ... Jer 23:10
for the *r* of redemption is thine ... Jer 32:7 4941
for the *r* of inheritance is thine ... Jer 32:8 4941
had done *r* in my sight, in ... Jer 34:15 3477
be driven out every man *r* forth ... Jer 49:5 6440
he hath drawn back his *r* hand ... Lam 2:3 3225
he stood with his *r* hand as an ... Lam 2:4 3225
To turn aside the *r* of a man ... Lam 3:35 4941
the face of a lion, on the *r* side ... Eze 1:10 3225
them, lie again on thy *r* side ... Eze 4:6 6227
stood on the *r* side of the house ... Eze 10:3 3225
that dwelleth at thy *r* hand ... Eze 16:46 3225
and do that which is lawful and *r* ... Eze 18:5 6666
done that which is lawful and *r* ... Eze 18:19 6666
and do that which is lawful and *r* ... Eze 18:21 6666
doeth that which is lawful and *r* ... Eze 18:27 6666
or other, either on the *r* hand ... Eze 21:16 3231
At his *r* hand was the divination ... Eze 21:22 3225
more, until he come whose *r* it is ... Eze 21:27 4941
and do that which is lawful and *r* ... Eze 33:14 6666
done that which is lawful and *r* ... Eze 33:16 6666
and do that which is lawful and *r* ... Eze 33:19 6666
arrows to fall out of thy *r* hand ... Eze 39:3 3225
from the *r* side of the house ... Eze 47:1 3233
ran out waters on the *r* side ... Eze 47:2 3233

river, when he held up his *r* hand .... Dan 12:7 3225
for the ways of the LORD are *r* .... Hos 14:9 3477
For they know not to do *r* .... Amos 3:10 5229
the poor in the gate from their *r* .... Amos 5:12
discern between their *r* hand .... Jonah 4:11 3225
the cup of the LORD'S *r* hand .... Hab 2:16 3225
at his *r* hand to resist him .... Zec 3:1 3225
one upon the *r* side of the bowl, ... Zec 4:3 3225
the *r* side of the candlestick .... Zec 4:11 3225
upon his arm, and upon his *r* eye .... Zec 11:17 3225
his *r* eye shall be utterly .... Zec 11:17 3225
people round about, on the *r* hand .... Zec 12:6 3225
aside the stranger from his *r* .... Mal 3:5 3225
if thy *r* eye offend thee, pluck .... Mt 5:29 *1188*
if thy *r* hand offend thee, cut it .... Mt 5:30 *1188*
shall smite thee on thy *r* cheek .... Mt 5:39 *1188*
hand know what thy *r* hand doeth .... Mt 6:3 *1188*
whatsoever is *r* I will give you .... Mt 20:4 *1342*
and whatsoever is *r*, that shall ye .... Mt 20:7 *1342*
may sit, the one on thy *r* hand .... Mt 20:21 *1188*
but to sit on my *r* hand, and on my .... Mt 20:23 *1188*
my Lord, Sit thou on my *r* hand .... Mt 22:44 *1188*
shall set the sheep on his *r* hand .... Mt 25:33 *1188*
King say unto them on his *r* hand .... Mt 25:34 *1188*
sitting on the *r* hand of power .... Mt 26:64 *1188*
his head, and a reed in his *r* hand .... Mt 27:29 *1188*
with him, one on the *r* hand .... Mt 27:38 *1188*
and clothed, and in his *r* mind .... Mk 5:15 *4993*
we may sit, one on thy *r* hand .... Mk 10:37 *1188*
But to sit on my *r* hand and on my .... Mk 10:40 *1188*
to my Lord, Sit thou on my *r* hand .... Mk 12:36 *1188*
sitting on the *r* hand of power .... Mk 14:62 *1188*
the one on his *r* hand, and the .... Mk 15:27 *1188*
a young man sitting on the *r* side .... Mk 16:5 *1188*
and sat on the *r* hand of God .... Mk 16:19 *1188*
of the Lord standing on the *r* .... Lk 1:11 *1188*
a man whose *r* hand was withered .... Lk 6:6 *1188*
Jesus, clothed, and in his *r* mind .... Lk 8:35 *4993*
unto him, Thou hast answered *r* .... Lk 10:28 *3723*
yourselves judge ye not what is *r* .... Lk 12:57 *1342*
my Lord, Sit thou on my *r* hand .... Lk 20:42 *1188*
high priest, and cut off his *r* ear .... Lk 22:50 *1188*
on the *r* hand of the power of God .... Lk 22:69 *1188*
malefactors, one on the *r* hand .... Lk 23:33 *1188*
servant, and cut off his *r* ear .... Jn 18:10 *1188*
the net on the *r* side of the ship .... Jn 21:6 *1188*
my face, for he is on my *r* hand .... Acts 2:25 *1188*
by the *r* hand of God exalted .... Acts 2:33 *1188*
my Lord, Sit thou on my *r* hand .... Acts 2:34 *1188*
And he took him by the *r* hand .... Acts 3:7 *1188*
Whether it be *r* in the sight of .... Acts 4:19 *1342*
with his *r* hand to be a Prince .... Acts 5:31 *1188*
standing on the *r* hand of God .... Acts 7:55 *1188*
man standing on the *r* hand of God .... Acts 7:56 *1188*
is not *r* in the sight of God .... Acts 8:21 *2117*
to pervert the *r* ways of the Lord .... Acts 13:10 *2117*
who is even at the *r* hand of God .... Rom 8:34 *1188*
of righteousness on the *r* hand 2Cor 6:7 *1188*
to me and Barnabas the *r* hands of .... Gal 2:9 *1188*
set him at his own *r* hand in the .... Eph 1:20 *1188*
for this is *r* .... Eph 6:1 *1342*
sitteth on the *r* hand of God .... Col 3:1 *1188*
sat down on the *r* hand of the .... Heb 1:3 *1188*
he at any times, Sit on my *r* hand .... Heb 1:13 *1188*
who is set on the *r* hand of the .... Heb 8:1 *1188*
sat down on the *r* hand of God .... Heb 10:12 *1188*
is set down at the *r* hand of the .... Heb 12:2 *1188*
whereof they have no *r* to eat .... Heb 13:10 *1849*
and is on the *r* hand of God 1Pet 3:22 *1188*
Which have forsaken the *r* way 2Pet 2:15 *2117*
he had in his *r* hand seven stars .... Rev 1:16 *1188*
he laid his *r* hand upon me, ... Rev 1:17 *1188*
which thou sawest in my *r* hand .... Rev 1:20 *1188*
the seven stars in his *r* hand .... Rev 2:1 *1188*
I saw in the *r* hand of him that .... Rev 5:1 *1188*
took the book out of the *r* hand .... Rev 5:7 *1188*
he set his *r* foot upon the sea, ... Rev 10:2 *1188*
to receive a mark in their *r* hand .... Rev 13:16 *1188*
that they may have *r* to the tree .... Rev 22:14 *1849*

RIGHTEOUS {238}

for thee have I seen *r* before me .... Gen 7:1 6662
destroy the *r* with the wicked .... Gen 18:23 6662
there be fifty *r* within the city .... Gen 18:24 6662
for the fifty *r* that are therein .... Gen 18:24 6662
to slay the *r* with the wicked .... Gen 18:25 6662
that the *r* should be as the .... Gen 18:25 6662
in Sodom fifty *r* within the city .... Gen 18:26 6662
shall lack five of the fifty *r* .... Gen 18:28 6662
wilt thou slay also a *r* nation .... Gen 20:4 6662
said, She hath been more *r* than I .... Gen 38:26 6663
the LORD is *r*, and I and my people .... Ex 9:27 6662
the innocent and *r* slay thou not .... Ex 23:7 6662
and perverteth the words of the *r* .... Ex 23:8 6662
Let me die the death of the *r* .... Num 23:10 3477
judgments so *r* as all this law, ... Deut 4:8 6662
and pervert the words of the *r* .... Deut 16:19 6662
then they shall justify the *r* .... Deut 25:1 6662
rehearse the *r* acts of the LORD .... Judg 5:11 6666
even the *r* acts toward the .... Judg 5:11 6666
of all the *r* acts of the LORD 1Sa 12:7 6666
to David, Thou art more *r* than I 1Sa 24:17 6662
a *r* person in his own house upon 2Sa 4:11 6662
who fell upon two men more *r* 1Kin 2:32 6662
and justifying the *r*, to give him 1Kin 8:32 6662
said to all the people, Ye be *r* 2Kin 10:9 6662
and by justifying the *r*, by giving 2Chr 6:23 6662
and they said, The LORD is *r* 2Chr 12:6 6662
O LORD God of Israel, thou art *r* .... Ezr 9:15 6662
for thou art *r* .... Neh 9:8 6662
or where were the *r* cut off .... Job 4:7 6662
Whom, though I were *r*, yet would .... Job 9:15 6663
and if I be *r*, yet will I not lift .... Job 10:15 6662
of a woman, that he should be *r* .... Job 15:14 6662
The *r* also shall hold on his way, ... Job 17:9 6662
to the Almighty, that thou art *r* .... Job 22:3 6663
The *r* see it, and are glad .... Job 22:19 6662
There the *r* might dispute with .... Job 23:7 3477
because he was *r* in his own eyes .... Job 32:1 6662
For Job hath said, I am *r* .... Job 34:5 6663
If thou be *r*, what givest thou .... Job 35:7 6663
not his eyes from the *r* .... Job 36:7 6662
condemn me, that thou mayest be *r* .... Job 40:8 6663
in the congregation of the *r* .... Ps 1:5 6662
the LORD knoweth the way of the *r* .... Ps 1:6 6662
For thou, LORD, wilt bless the *r* .... Ps 5:12 6662
for the *r* God trieth the hearts .... Ps 7:9 6662
God judgeth the *r*, and God is .... Ps 7:11 6662
be destroyed, what can the *r* do .... Ps 11:3 6662
The LORD trieth the *r* .... Ps 11:5 6662
For the *r* LORD loveth .... Ps 11:7 6662
God is in the generation of the *r* .... Ps 14:5 6662
the LORD are true and *r* altogether .... Ps 19:9 6663
and contemptuously against the *r* .... Ps 31:18 6662
in the LORD, and rejoice, ye *r* .... Ps 32:11 6662
Rejoice in the LORD, O ye *r* .... Ps 33:1 6662
eyes of the LORD are upon the *r* .... Ps 34:15 6662
The *r* cry, and the LORD heareth, ... Ps 34:17
Many are the afflictions of the *r* .... Ps 34:19 6662
that hate the *r* shall be desolate .... Ps 34:21 6662
be glad, that favour my *r* cause .... Ps 35:27 6664
A little that a *r* man hath is .... Ps 37:16 6662
but the LORD upholdeth the *r* .... Ps 37:17 6662
but the *r* sheweth mercy, and .... Ps 37:21 6662
have I not seen the *r* forsaken .... Ps 37:25 6662
The *r* shall inherit the land, and .... Ps 37:29 6662
mouth of the *r* speaketh wisdom .... Ps 37:30 6662
The wicked watcheth the *r* .... Ps 37:32 6662
salvation of the *r* is of the LORD .... Ps 37:39 6662
The *r* also shall see, and fear, and .... Ps 52:6 6662
never suffer the *r* to be moved .... Ps 55:22 6662
The *r* shall rejoice when he seeth .... Ps 58:10 6662
there is a reward for the *r* .... Ps 58:11 6662
The *r* shall be glad in the LORD, ... Ps 64:10 6662
But let the *r* be glad .... Ps 68:3 6662
and not be written with the *r* .... Ps 69:28 6662
In his days shall the *r* flourish .... Ps 72:7 6662
horns of the *r* shall be exalted .... Ps 75:10 6662
The *r* shall flourish like the .... Ps 92:12 6662
against the soul of the *r* .... Ps 94:21 6662
Light is sown for the *r*, and .... Ps 97:11 6662
Rejoice in the LORD, ye *r* .... Ps 97:12 6662
The *r* shall see it, and rejoice .... Ps 107:42 3477
and full of compassion, and *r* .... Ps 112:4 6662
the *r* shall be in everlasting .... Ps 112:6 6662
Gracious is the LORD, and *r* .... Ps 116:5 6662
is in the tabernacles of the *r* .... Ps 118:15 6662
into which the *r* shall enter .... Ps 118:20 6662
have learned thy *r* judgments .... Ps 119:7 6664
thee because of thy *r* judgments .... Ps 119:62 6664
that I will keep thy *r* judgments .... Ps 119:106 6664
R art thou, O LORD, and upright .... Ps 119:137 6662
that thou hast commanded are *r* .... Ps 119:138 6664
every one of thy *r* judgments .... Ps 119:160 6664
thee because of thy *r* judgments .... Ps 119:164 6664
not rest upon the lot of the *r* .... Ps 125:3 6662
lest the *r* put forth their hands .... Ps 125:3 6662
The LORD is *r* .... Ps 129:4 6662
Surely the *r* shall give thanks .... Ps 140:13 6662
Let the *r* smite me .... Ps 141:5 6662
the *r* shall compass me about .... Ps 142:7 6662
The LORD is *r* in all his ways, and .... Ps 145:17 6662
the LORD loveth the *r* .... Ps 146:8 6662
layeth up sound wisdom for the *r* .... Prov 2:7 3477
men, and keep the paths of the *r* .... Prov 2:20 6662
but his secret is with the *r* .... Prov 3:32 3477
the soul of the *r* to famish .... Prov 10:3 6662
The mouth of a *r* man is a well of .... Prov 10:11 6662
labour of the *r* tendeth to life .... Prov 10:16 6662
The lips of the *r* feed many .... Prov 10:21 6662
desire of the *r* shall be granted .... Prov 10:24 6662
but the *r* is an everlasting .... Prov 10:25 6662
The hope of the *r* shall be .... Prov 10:28 6662
The *r* shall never be removed .... Prov 10:30 6662
The lips of the *r* know what is .... Prov 10:32 6662
The *r* is delivered out of trouble .... Prov 11:8 6662
When it goeth well with the *r* .... Prov 11:10 6662
seed of the *r* shall be delivered .... Prov 11:21 6662
The desire of the *r* is only good .... Prov 11:23 6662
but the *r* shall flourish as a .... Prov 11:28 6662
The fruit of the *r* is a tree of .... Prov 11:30 6662
the *r* shall be recompensed in the .... Prov 11:31 6662
root of the *r* shall not be moved .... Prov 12:3 6662
The thoughts of the *r* are right .... Prov 12:5 6662
the house of the *r* shall stand .... Prov 12:7 6662
A *r* man regardeth the life of his .... Prov 12:10 6662
the root of the *r* yieldeth fruit .... Prov 12:12 6662
The *r* is more excellent than his .... Prov 12:26 6662
A *r* man hateth lying .... Prov 13:5 6662
The light of the *r* rejoiceth .... Prov 13:9 6662
but to the *r* good shall be repaid .... Prov 13:21 6662
The *r* eateth to the satisfying of .... Prov 13:25 6662
but among the *r* there is favour .... Prov 14:9 3477
the wicked at the gates of the *r* .... Prov 14:19 6662
but the *r* hath hope in his death .... Prov 14:32 6662
house of the *r* is much treasure .... Prov 15:6 6662
the way of the *r* is made plain .... Prov 15:19 3477
The heart of the *r* studieth to .... Prov 15:28 6662
he heareth the prayer of the *r* .... Prov 15:29 6662
R lips are the delight of kings .... Prov 16:13 6664
to overthrow the *r* in judgment .... Prov 18:5 6662
the *r* runneth into it, and is safe .... Prov 18:10 6662
The *r* man wisely considereth the .... Prov 21:12 6662
shall be a ransom for the *r* .... Prov 21:18 6662
but the *r* giveth and spareth not .... Prov 21:26 6662
The father of the *r* shall greatly .... Prov 23:24 6662
against the dwelling of the *r* .... Prov 24:15 6662
saith unto the wicked, Thou art *r* .... Prov 24:24 6662
A *r* man falling down before the .... Prov 25:26 6662
but the *r* are bold as a lion .... Prov 28:1 6662
Whoso causeth the *r* to go astray .... Prov 28:10 3477
When *r* men do rejoice, there is .... Prov 28:12 6662
when they perish, the *r* increase .... Prov 28:28 6662
When the *r* are in authority, the .... Prov 29:2 6662
but the *r* doth sing and rejoice .... Prov 29:6 6662
The *r* considereth the cause of .... Prov 29:7 6662
but the *r* shall see their fall .... Prov 29:16 6662
mine heart, God shall judge the *r* .... Eccl 3:17 6662
Be not *r* over much .... Eccl 7:16 6662
according to the work of the *r* .... Eccl 8:14 6662
to declare all this, that the *r* .... Eccl 9:1 6662
there is one event to the *r* .... Eccl 9:2 6662
Say ye to the *r*, that it shall be .... Is 3:10 6662
righteousness of the *r* from him .... Is 5:23 6662
heard songs, even glory to the *r* .... Is 24:16 6662
that the *r* nation which keepeth .... Is 26:2 6662
raised up the *r* man from the east .... Is 41:2 6664
that we may say, He is *r* .... Is 41:26 6662
shall my *r* servant justify many .... Is 53:11 6662
The *r* perisheth, and no man layeth .... Is 57:1 6662
none considering that the *r* is .... Is 57:1 6662
Thy people also shall be all *r* .... Is 60:21 6662
R art thou, O LORD, when I plead .... Jer 12:1 6662
LORD of hosts, that triest the *r* .... Jer 20:12 6662
will raise unto David a *r* Branch .... Jer 23:5 6662
The LORD is *r* .... Lam 1:18 6662
When a *r* man doth turn from his .... Eze 3:20 6662
if thou warn the *r* man .... Eze 3:21 6662
that the *r* sin not .... Eze 3:21 6662
have made the heart of the *r* sad .... Eze 13:22 6662
they are more *r* than thou .... Eze 16:52 6663
of the *r* shall be upon him .... Eze 18:20 6662
But when the *r* turneth away from .... Eze 18:24 6662
When a *r* man turneth away from .... Eze 18:26 6662
and will cut off from thee the *r* .... Eze 21:3 6662
I will cut off from thee the *r* .... Eze 21:4 6662
And the *r* men, they shall judge .... Eze 23:45 6662
The righteousness of the *r* shall .... Eze 33:12 6662
neither shall the *r* be able to .... Eze 33:12 6662
When I shall say to the *r* .... Eze 33:13 6662
When the *r* turneth from his .... Eze 33:18 6662
for the LORD our God is *r* in all .... Dan 9:14 6662
they sold the *r* for silver .... Amos 2:6 6662
wicked doth compass about the *r* .... Hab 1:4 6662
the man that is more *r* than he .... Hab 1:13 6662
return, and discern between the *r* .... Mal 3:18 6662
for I am not come to call the *r* .... Mt 9:13 *1342*
he that receiveth a *r* man in the .... Mt 10:41 *1342*
a *r* man shall receive a *r* .... Mt 10:41 *1342*
r men have desired to see those .... Mt 13:17 *1342*
Then shall the *r* shine forth as .... Mt 13:43 *1342*
also outwardly appear *r* unto men .... Mt 23:28 *1342*
garnish the sepulchres of the *r* .... Mt 23:29 *1342*
the *r* blood shed upon the earth .... Mt 23:35 *1342*
from the blood of *r* Abel unto the .... Mt 23:35 *1342*
Then shall the *r* answer him .... Mt 25:37 *1342*
but the *r* into life eternal .... Mt 25:46 *1342*
I came not to call the *r*, but .... Mk 2:17 *1342*
And they were both *r* before God .... Lk 1:6 *1342*
I came not to call the *r*, but .... Lk 5:32 *1342*
in themselves that they were *r* .... Lk 18:9 *1342*
Certainly this was a *r* man .... Lk 23:47 *1342*
appearance, but judge *r* judgment .... Jn 7:24 *1342*
O *r* Father, the world hath not .... Jn 17:25 *1342*
of the *r* judgment of God .... Rom 2:5 *1341*
As it is written, There is none *r* .... Rom 3:10 *1342*
scarcely for a *r* man will one die .... Rom 5:7 *1342*
of one shall many be made *r* .... Rom 5:19 *1342*
token of the *r* judgment of God 2Th 1:5 *1342*
Seeing it is a *r* thing with God 2Th 1:6 *1342*
the law is not made for a *r* man 1Ti 1:9 *1342*
the *r* judge, shall give me at 2Ti 4:8 *1342*
he obtained witness that he was *r* .... Heb 11:4 *1342*
prayer of a *r* man availeth much .... Jas 5:16 *1342*
eyes of the Lord are over the *r* 1Pet 3:12 *1342*
if the *r* scarcely be saved, where 1Pet 4:18 *1342*
(For that *r* man dwelling among 2Pet 2:8 *1342*
vexed his *r* soul from day to day 2Pet 2:8 *1342*
the Father, Jesus Christ the *r* 1Jn 2:1 *1342*
If ye know that he is *r*, ye know 1Jn 2:29 *1342*
he that doeth righteousness is *r* 1Jn 3:7 *1342*
even as he is *r* 1Jn 3:7 *1342*
were evil, and his brother's *r* 1Jn 3:12 *1342*
of the waters say, Thou art *r* .... Rev 16:5 *1342*
true and *r* are thy judgments .... Rev 16:7 *1342*
For true and *r* are his judgments .... Rev 19:2 *1342*
is *r*, let him be *r* still .... Rev 22:11 *1343*

RIGHTEOUSLY {8}

judge *r* between every man and his .... Deut 1:16 6664
for thou shalt judge the people *r* .... Ps 67:4 4334
he shall judge the people *r* .... Ps 96:10 4339
Open thy mouth, judge *r*, and plead .... Prov 31:9 6664
He that walketh *r*, and speaketh .... Is 33:15 6666

O LORD of hosts, that judgest *r* ... Jer 11:20 6664
lusts, we should live soberly, *r* ... Titus 2:12 *1346*
himself to him that judgeth *r* ... 1Pet 2:23 *1346*

RIGHTEOUSNESS {303}

and he counted it to him for *r* ... Gen 15:6 6666
So shall my *r* answer for me in ... Gen 30:33 6666
but in *r* shalt thou judge thy ... Lev 19:15 6664
And it shall be our *r*, if we ... Deut 6:25 6666
For my *r* the LORD hath brought me ... Deut 9:4 6666
Not for thy *r*, or for the ... Deut 9:5 6666
good land to possess it for thy *r* ... Deut 9:6 6666
it shall be *r* unto thee before ... Deut 24:13 6666
they shall offer sacrifices of *r* ... Deut 33:19 6664
LORD render to every man his *r* ... 1Sa 26:23 6666
rewarded me according to my *r* ... 2Sa 22:21 6666
recompensed me according to my *r* ... 2Sa 22:25 6666
before thee in truth, and in *r* ... 1Kin 3:6 6666
to give him according to his *r* ... 1Kin 8:32 6666
by giving him according to his *r* ... 2Chr 6:23 6666
yea, return again, my *r* is in it ... Job 6:29 6664
habitation of thy *r* prosperous ... Job 8:6 6664
My *r* I hold fast, and will not let ... Job 27:6 6666
I put on *r*, and it clothed me ... Job 29:14 6664
for he will render unto man his *r* ... Job 33:26 6666
saidst, My *r* is more than God's ... Job 35:2 6664
thy *r* may profit the son of man ... Job 35:8 6666
and will ascribe *r* to my Maker ... Job 36:3 6664
me when I call, O God of my *r* ... Ps 4:1 6664
Offer the sacrifices of *r* ... Ps 4:5 6664
in thy *r* because of mine enemies ... Ps 5:8 6666
me, O LORD, according to my *r* ... Ps 7:8 6664
the LORD according to his *r* ... Ps 7:17 6664
And he shall judge the world in *r* ... Ps 9:8 6664
For the righteous LORD loveth *r* ... Ps 11:7 6666
walketh uprightly, and worketh *r* ... Ps 15:2 6664
me, I will behold thy face in *r* ... Ps 17:15 6664
rewarded me according to my *r* ... Ps 18:20 6664
recompensed me according to my *r* ... Ps 18:24 6664
shall declare his *r* unto a people ... Ps 22:31 6666
paths of *r* for his name's sake ... Ps 23:3 6664
r from the God of his salvation ... Ps 24:5 6666
deliver me in thy *r* ... Ps 31:1 6666
He loveth *r* and judgment ... Ps 33:5 6666
O LORD my God, according to thy *r* ... Ps 35:24 6664
And my tongue shall speak of thy *r* ... Ps 35:28 6664
Thy *r* is like the great mountains ... Ps 36:6 6666
thy *r* to the upright in heart ... Ps 36:10 6666
bring forth thy *r* as the light ... Ps 37:6 6664
I have preached *r* in the great ... Ps 40:9 6664
not hid thy *r* within my heart ... Ps 40:10 6666
because of truth and meekness and *r* ... Ps 45:4 6664
Thou lovest *r*, and hatest ... Ps 45:7 6664
thy right hand is full of *r* ... Ps 48:10 6664
the heavens shall declare his *r* ... Ps 50:6 6664
tongue shall sing aloud of thy *r* ... Ps 51:14 6666
pleased with the sacrifices of *r* ... Ps 51:19 6664
and lying rather than to speak *r* ... Ps 52:3 6664
Do ye indeed speak *r*, O ... Ps 58:1 6664
things in *r* wilt thou answer us ... Ps 65:5 6664
and let them not come into thy *r* ... Ps 69:27 6666
Deliver me in thy *r*, and cause me ... Ps 71:2 6666
My mouth shall shew forth thy *r* ... Ps 71:15 6666
I will make mention of thy *r* ... Ps 71:16 6666
Thy *r* also, O God, is very high ... Ps 71:19 6666
talk of thy *r* all the day long ... Ps 71:24 6666
thy *r* unto the king's son ... Ps 72:1 6666
He shall judge thy people with *r* ... Ps 72:2 6664
people, and the little hills, by *r* ... Ps 72:3 6666
r and peace have kissed each other ... Ps 85:10 6664
r shall look down from heaven ... Ps 85:11 6664
R shall go before him ... Ps 85:13 6664
and thy *r* in the land of ... Ps 88:12 6666
in thy *r* shall they be exalted ... Ps 89:16 6666
But judgment shall return unto *r* ... Ps 94:15 6664
he shall judge the world with *r* ... Ps 96:13 6664
r and judgment are the habitation ... Ps 97:2 6664
The heavens declare his *r* ... Ps 97:6 6664
his *r* hath he openly shewed in ... Ps 98:2 6666
with *r* shall he judge the world ... Ps 98:9 6664
executest judgment and *r* in Jacob ... Ps 99:4 6666
The LORD executeth *r* and judgment ... Ps 103:6 6666
his *r* unto children's children ... Ps 103:17 6666
and he that doeth *r* at all times ... Ps 106:3 6666
for *r* unto all generations for ... Ps 106:31 6666
and his *r* endureth for ever ... Ps 111:3 6666
and his *r* endureth for ever ... Ps 112:3 6666
his *r* endureth for ever ... Ps 112:9 6666
Open to me the gates of *r* ... Ps 118:19 6664
quicken me in thy *r* ... Ps 119:40 6666
and for the word of thy *r* ... Ps 119:123 6664
Thy *r* is an everlasting ... Ps 119:142 6666
r is an everlasting *r* ... Ps 119:142 6664
The *r* of thy testimonies is ... Ps 119:144 6664
for all thy commandments are *r* ... Ps 119:172 6664
Let thy priests be clothed with *r* ... Ps 132:9 6664
answer me, and in thy *r* ... Ps 143:1 6666
goodness, and shall sing of thy *r* ... Ps 145:7 6666
Then shalt thou understand *r* ... Prov 2:9 6664
the words of my mouth are in *r* ... Prov 8:8 6664
yea, durable riches and *r* ... Prov 8:18 6666
I lead in the way of *r*, in the ... Prov 8:20 6666
but *r* delivereth from death ... Prov 10:2 6666
but *r* delivereth from death ... Prov 11:4 6666
The *r* of the perfect shall direct ... Prov 11:5 6666
The *r* of the upright shall ... Prov 11:6 6666
soweth *r* shall be a sure reward ... Prov 11:18 6666
As *r* tendeth to life ... Prov 11:19 6666
speaketh truth sheweth forth *r* ... Prov 12:17 6664
In the way of *r* is life ... Prov 12:28 6666
R keepeth him that is upright in ... Prov 13:6 6666
R exalteth a nation ... Prov 14:34 6666
loveth him that followeth after *r* ... Prov 15:9 6666
Better is a little with *r* than ... Prov 16:8 6666
the throne is established by *r* ... Prov 16:12 6666
if it be found in the way of *r* ... Prov 16:31 6666
He that followeth after *r* ... Prov 21:21 6666
and mercy findeth life, *r*, and ... Prov 21:21 6666
throne shall be established in *r* ... Prov 25:5 6664
and the place of *r*, that iniquity ... Eccl 3:16 6664
just man that perisheth in his *r* ... Eccl 7:15 6664
r lodged in it ... Is 1:21 6664
shalt be called, The city of *r* ... Is 1:26 6664
judgment, and her converts with *r* ... Is 1:27 6666
for *r*, but behold a cry ... Is 5:7 6666
is holy shall be sanctified in *r* ... Is 5:16 6666
take away the *r* of the righteous ... Is 5:23 6666
decreed shall overflow with *r* ... Is 10:22 6666
But with *r* shall he judge the ... Is 11:4 6664
r shall be the girdle of his ... Is 11:5 6664
and seeking judgment, and hasting *r* ... Is 16:5 6664
of the world will learn *r* ... Is 26:9 6664
wicked, yet will he not learn *r* ... Is 26:10 6664
to the line, and *r* to the plummet ... Is 28:17 6666
Behold, a king shall reign in *r* ... Is 32:1 6664
r remain in the fruitful field ... Is 32:16 6666
the work of *r* shall be peace ... Is 32:17 6666
and the effect of *r* quietness ... Is 32:17 6666
filled Zion with judgment and *r* ... Is 33:5 6666
thee with the right hand of my *r* ... Is 41:10 6664
I the LORD have called thee in *r* ... Is 42:6 6664
and let the skies pour down *r* ... Is 45:8 6664
and let *r* spring up together ... Is 45:8 6666
I have raised him up in *r* ... Is 45:13 6664
I the LORD speak *r*, I declare ... Is 45:19 6664
word is gone out of my mouth in *r* ... Is 45:23 6666
one say, in the LORD have I *r* ... Is 45:24 6666
stouthearted, that are far from *r* ... Is 46:12 6666
I bring near my *r* ... Is 46:13 6666
but not in truth, nor in *r* ... Is 48:1 6666
thy *r* as the waves of the sea ... Is 48:18 6666
to me, ye that follow after *r* ... Is 51:1 6664
My *r* is near ... Is 51:5 6664
my *r* shall not be abolished ... Is 51:6 6666
Hearken unto me, ye that know *r* ... Is 51:7 6664
but my *r* shall be for ever, and my ... Is 51:8 6666
In *r* shalt thou be established ... Is 54:14 6666
their *r* is of me, saith the LORD ... Is 54:17 6666
to come, and my *r* to be revealed ... Is 56:1 6666
I will declare thy *r*, and thy ... Is 57:12 6666
my ways, as a nation that did *r* ... Is 58:2 6666
thy *r* shall go before thee ... Is 58:8 6664
and his *r*, it sustained him ... Is 59:16 6666
For he put on *r* as a breastplate ... Is 59:17 6666
peace, and thine exactors *r* ... Is 60:17 6666
they might be called trees of *r* ... Is 61:3 6664
covered me with the robe of *r* ... Is 61:10 6666
so the Lord GOD will cause *r* ... Is 61:11 6666
until the *r* thereof go forth as ... Is 62:1 6664
And the Gentiles shall see thy *r* ... Is 62:2 6664
I that speak in *r*, mighty to save ... Is 63:1 6666
him that rejoiceth and worketh *r* ... Is 64:5 6664
in truth, in judgment, and in *r* ... Jer 4:2 6666
lovingkindness, judgment, and *r* ... Jer 9:24 6666
Execute ye judgment and *r*, and ... Jer 22:3 6666
shall be called, THE LORD OUR *R* ... Jer 23:6 6664
Branch of *r* to grow up unto David ... Jer 33:15 6666
execute judgment and *r* in the land ... Jer 33:15 6666
shall be called, The LORD our *r* ... Jer 33:16 6664
The LORD hath brought forth our *r* ... Jer 51:10 6666
man doth turn from his *r*, and ... Eze 3:20 6664
his *r* which he hath done shall ... Eze 3:20 6666
but their own souls by their *r* ... Eze 14:14 6666
their own souls by their *r* ... Eze 14:20 6666
the *r* of the righteous shall be ... Eze 18:20 6666
in his *r* that he hath done he ... Eze 18:22 6666
righteous turneth away from his *r* ... Eze 18:24 6666
All his *r* that he hath done shall ... Eze 18:24 6666
man turneth away from his *r* ... Eze 18:26 6666
The *r* of the righteous shall not ... Eze 33:12 6666
be able to live for his *r* in the ... Eze 33:12
if he trust to his own *r*, and ... Eze 33:13 6666
the righteous turneth from his *r* ... Eze 33:18 6666
thee, and break off thy sins by *r* ... Dan 4:27 6665
r belongeth unto thee, but unto ... Dan 9:7 6666
O Lord, according to all thy *r* ... Dan 9:16 6666
and to bring in everlasting *r* ... Dan 9:24 6664
many to *r* as the stars for ever ... Dan 12:3 6663
I will betroth thee unto me in *r* ... Hos 2:19 6664
Sow to yourselves in *r*, reap in ... Hos 10:12 6666
till he come and rain *r* upon you ... Hos 10:12 6664
leave off *r* in the earth ... Amos 5:7 6666
waters, and *r* as a mighty stream ... Amos 5:24 6666
and the fruit of *r* into hemlock ... Amos 6:12 6666
ye may know the *r* of the LORD ... Mic 6:5 6666
light, and I shall behold his *r* ... Mic 7:9 6666
seek *r*, seek meekness ... Zeph 2:3 6664
be their God, in truth and in *r* ... Zec 8:8 6666
unto the LORD an offering in *r* ... Mal 3:3 6666
fear my name shall the Sun of *r* ... Mal 4:2 6666
it becometh us to fulfil all *r* ... Mt 3:15 *1343*
which do hunger and thirst after *r* ... Mt 5:6 *1343*
That except your *r* shall exceed ... Mt 5:20 *1343*
shall exceed the *r* of the scribes ... Mt 5:20 *1343*
the kingdom of God, and his *r* ... Mt 6:33 *1343*
came unto you in the way of *r* ... Mt 21:32 *1343*
r before him, all the days of our ... Lk 1:75 *1343*
reprove the world of sin, and of *r* ... Jn 16:8 *1343*
Of *r*, because I go to my Father ... Jn 16:10 *1343*
he that feareth him, and worketh *r* ... Acts 10:35 *1343*
of the devil, thou enemy of all *r* ... Acts 13:10 *1343*
in *r* by that man whom he hath ... Acts 17:31 *1343*
And as he reasoned of *r* ... Acts 24:25 *1343*
For therein is the *r* of God ... Rom 1:17 *1343*
keep the *r* of the law, shall not ... Rom 2:26 *1345*
commend the *r* of God, what shall ... Rom 3:5 *1343*
But now the *r* of God without the ... Rom 3:21 *1343*
Even the *r* of God which is by ... Rom 3:22 *1343*
blood, to declare his *r* for the ... Rom 3:25 *1343*
I say, at this time his *r* ... Rom 3:26 *1343*
and it was counted unto him for *r* ... Rom 4:3 *1343*
his faith is counted for *r* ... Rom 4:5 *1343*
whom God imputeth *r* without works ... Rom 4:6 *1343*
was reckoned to Abraham for *r* ... Rom 4:9 *1343*
a seal of the *r* of the faith ... Rom 4:11 *1343*
that *r* might be imputed unto them ... Rom 4:11 *1343*
law, but through the *r* of faith ... Rom 4:13 *1343*
it was imputed to him for *r* ... Rom 4:22 *1343*
of the gift of *r* shall reign in ... Rom 5:17 *1343*
even so by the *r* of one the free ... Rom 5:18 *1345*
r unto eternal life by Jesus ... Rom 5:21 *1343*
as instruments of *r* unto God ... Rom 6:13 *1343*
death, or of obedience unto *r* ... Rom 6:16 *1343*
sin, ye became the servants of *r* ... Rom 6:18 *1343*
servants to *r* unto holiness ... Rom 6:19 *1343*
of sin, ye were free from *r* ... Rom 6:20 *1343*
That the *r* of the law might be ... Rom 8:4 *1345*
the Spirit is life because of *r* ... Rom 8:10 *1343*
the work, and cut it short in *r* ... Rom 9:28 *1343*
which followed not after *r* ... Rom 9:30 *1343*
have attained to *r* ... Rom 9:30 *1343*
even the *r* which is of faith ... Rom 9:30 *1343*
which followed after the law of *r* ... Rom 9:31 *1343*
hath not attained to the law of *r* ... Rom 9:31 *1343*
they being ignorant of God's *r* ... Rom 10:3 *1343*
about to establish their own *r* ... Rom 10:3 *1343*
themselves unto the *r* of God ... Rom 10:3 *1343*
is the end of the law for *r* to ... Rom 10:4 *1343*
the *r* which is of the law ... Rom 10:5 *1343*
But the *r* which is of faith ... Rom 10:6 *1343*
the heart man believeth unto *r* ... Rom 10:10 *1343*
but *r*, and peace, and joy in the ... Rom 14:17 *1343*
God is made unto us wisdom, and *r* ... 1Cor 1:30 *1343*
Awake to *r*, and sin not ... 1Cor 15:34 *1346*
ministration of *r* exceed in glory ... 2Cor 3:9 *1343*
might be made the *r* of God in him ... 2Cor 5:21 *1343*
by the armour of *r* on the right ... 2Cor 6:7 *1343*
hath *r* with unrighteousness ... 2Cor 6:14 *1343*
his *r* remaineth for ever ... 2Cor 9:9 *1343*
and increase the fruits of your *r* ... 2Cor 9:10 *1343*
transformed as the ministers of *r* ... 2Cor 11:15 *1343*
for if *r* come by the law, then ... Gal 2:21 *1343*
and it was accounted to him for *r* ... Gal 3:6 *1343*
verily *r* should have been by the ... Gal 3:21 *1343*
wait for the hope of *r* by faith ... Gal 5:5 *1343*
which after God is created in *r* ... Eph 4:24 *1343*
Spirit is in all goodness and *r* ... Eph 5:9 *1343*
and having on the breastplate of *r* ... Eph 6:14 *1343*
Being filled with the fruits of *r* ... Phil 1:11 *1343*
touching the *r* which is in the ... Phil 3:6 *1343*
in him, not having mine own *r* ... Phil 3:9 *1343*
the *r* which is of God by faith ... Phil 3:9 *1343*
and follow after *r*, godliness ... 1Ti 6:11 *1343*
but follow *r*, faith, charity ... 2Ti 2:22 *1343*
correction, for instruction in *r* ... 2Ti 3:16 *1343*
is laid up for me a crown of *r* ... 2Ti 4:8 *1343*
Not by works of *r* which we have ... Titus 3:5 *1343*
a sceptre of *r* is the sceptre of ... Heb 1:8 *2118*
Thou hast loved *r*, and hated ... Heb 1:9 *1343*
is unskilful in the word of *r* ... Heb 5:13 *1343*
being by interpretation King of *r* ... Heb 7:2 *1343*
heir of the *r* which is by faith ... Heb 11:7 *1343*
faith subdued kingdoms, wrought *r* ... Heb 11:33 *1343*
r unto them which are exercised ... Heb 12:11 *1343*
of man worketh not the *r* of God ... Jas 1:20 *1343*
and it was imputed unto him for *r* ... Jas 2:23 *1343*
the fruit of *r* is sown in peace ... Jas 3:18 *1343*
dead to sins, should live unto *r* ... 1Pet 2:24 *1343*
with us through the *r* of God ... 2Pet 1:1 *1343*
eighth person, a preacher of *r* ... 2Pet 2:5 *1343*
not to have known the way of *r* ... 2Pet 2:21 *1343*
a new earth, wherein dwelleth *r* ... 2Pet 3:13 *1343*
one that doeth *r* is born of him ... 1Jn 2:29 *1343*
he that doeth *r* is righteous ... 1Jn 3:7 *1343*
doeth not *r* is not of God ... 1Jn 3:10 *1343*
the fine linen is the *r* of saints ... Rev 19:8 *1345*
in *r* he doth judge and make war ... Rev 19:11 *1343*

RIGHTEOUSNESS' {4}

for thy *r* sake bring my soul out ... Ps 143:11 6666
is well pleased for his *r* sake ... Is 42:21 6664
which are persecuted for *r* sake ... Mt 5:10 *1343*
But and if ye suffer for *r* sake ... 1Pet 3:14 *1343*

RIGHTEOUSNESSES {3}

all our *r* are as filthy rags ... Is 64:6 6666
all his *r* shall not be remembered ... Eze 33:13 6666
before thee for our *r*, but for ... Dan 9:18 6666

RIGHTLY {4}

he said, Is not he *r* named Jacob ... Gen 27:36 3588
said unto him, Thou hast *r* judged ... Lk 7:43 *3723*
that thou sayest and teachest *r* ... Lk 20:21 *3723*
r dividing the word of truth ... 2Ti 2:15 *3723*

R

RIGOUR {5}
of Israel to serve with *r* ... Ex 1:13 6531
they made them serve, was with *r* ... Ex 1:14 6531
shalt not rule over him with *r* ... Lev 25:43 6531
not rule one over another with *r* ... Lev 25:46 6531
rule with *r* over him in thy sight ... Lev 25:53 6531

RIMMON *(rim'-mon)* {14}
1. A city in Zebulun.
Lebaoth, and Shilhim, and Ain, and *R* ... Josh 15:32 7417
R with her suburbs, Tabor with ... 1Chr 6:77 7417
from Geba to *R* south of Jerusalem ... Zec 14:10 7417
2. A rock near Gibeah.
the wilderness unto the rock of *R* ... Judg 20:45 7417
to the wilderness unto the rock *R* ... Judg 20:47 7417
abode in the rock *R* four months ... Judg 20:47 7417
Benjamin that were in the rock *R* ... Judg 21:13 7417
3. Father of Baanah and Rechab.
the sons of *R* a Beerothite, of ... 2Sa 4:2 7417
the sons of *R* the Beerothite, ... 2Sa 4:5 7417
the sons of *R* the Beerothite, and ... 2Sa 4:9 7417
4. A Syrian god.
the house of *R* to worship there ... 2Kin 5:18 7417
and I bow myself in the house of *R* ... 2Kin 5:18 7417
bow down myself in the house of *R* ... 2Kin 5:18 7417
5. A city in Simeon.
villages were, Etam, and Ain, *R* ... 1Chr 4:32 7417

RIMMONO See RIMMON.

RIMMON-PAREZ *(rim'-mon-pa'-rez)* {2} *An Israelite encampment in the wilderness.*
from Rithmah, and pitched at *R* ... Num 33:19 7428
And they departed from *R*, and ... Num 33:20 7428

RING {11}
took off his *r* from his hand ... Gen 41:42 2885
above the head of it unto one *r* ... Ex 26:24 2885
at the head thereof, to one *r* ... Ex 36:29 2885
the king took his *r* from his hand ... Est 3:10 2885
and sealed with the king's *r* ... Est 3:12 2885
And the king took off his *r* ... Est 8:2 2885
and seal it with the king's *r* ... Est 8:8 2885
name, and sealed with the king's *r* ... Est 8:8 2885
and sealed it with the king's *r* ... Est 8:10 2885
put a *r* on his hand, and shoes on ... Lk 15:22 *1146*
your assembly a man with a gold *r* ... Jas 2:2 *5554*

RINGLEADER {1}
a *r* of the sect of the Nazarenes ... Acts 24:5 *4414*

RINGS {44}
shalt cast four *r* of gold for it ... Ex 25:12 2885
two *r* shall be in the one side of ... Ex 25:12 2885
two *r* in the other side of it ... Ex 25:12 2885
the *r* by the sides of the ark ... Ex 25:14 2885
shall be in the *r* of the ark ... Ex 25:15 2885
shalt make for it four *r* of gold ... Ex 25:26 2885
put the *r* in the four corners ... Ex 25:26 2885
against the border shall the *r* be ... Ex 25:27 2885
make their *r* of gold for places ... Ex 26:29 2885
r in the four corners thereof ... Ex 27:4 2885
staves shall be put into the *r* ... Ex 27:7 2885
the breastplate two *r* of gold ... Ex 28:23 2885
shalt put the two *r* on the two ... Ex 28:23 2885
chains of gold in the two *r* which ... Ex 28:24 2885
And thou shalt make two *r* of gold ... Ex 28:26 2885
two other *r* of gold thou shalt ... Ex 28:27 2885
bind the breastplate by the *r* ... Ex 28:28 2885
the *r* of the ephod with a lace of ... Ex 28:28 2885
two golden *r* shalt thou make to ... Ex 30:4 2885
bracelets, and earrings, and *r* ... Ex 35:22 2885
made their *r* of gold to be places ... Ex 36:34 2885
And he cast for it four *r* of gold ... Ex 37:3 2885
even two *r* upon the one side of ... Ex 37:3 2885
two *r* upon the other side of it ... Ex 37:3 2885
the *r* by the sides of the ark ... Ex 37:5 2885
And he cast for it four *r* of gold ... Ex 37:13 2885
put the *r* upon the four corners ... Ex 37:13 2885
against the border were the *r* ... Ex 37:14 2885
he made two *r* of gold for it ... Ex 37:27 2885
he cast four *r* for the four ends ... Ex 38:5 2885
the *r* on the sides of the altar ... Ex 38:7 2885
two ouches of gold, and two gold *r* ... Ex 39:16 2885
put the two *r* in the two ends of ... Ex 39:16 2885
chains of gold in the two *r* on ... Ex 39:17 2885
And they made two *r* of gold ... Ex 39:19 2885
And they made two other golden *r* ... Ex 39:20 2885
his *r* unto the *r* of the ephod ... Ex 39:21 2885
of gold, chains, and bracelets, *r* ... Num 31:50 2885
fine linen and purple to silver *r* ... Est 1:6 1550
are as gold *r* set with the beryl ... Song 5:14 1550
The *r*, and nose jewels, ... Is 3:21 2885
As for their *r*, they were so high ... Eze 1:18 1354
their *r* were full of eyes round ... Eze 1:18 1354

RINGSTRAKED {7}
that day the he goats that were *r* ... Gen 30:35 6124
rods, and brought forth cattle *r* ... Gen 30:39 6124
faces of the flocks toward the *r* ... Gen 30:40 6124
thus, The *r* shall be thy hire ... Gen 31:8 6124
then bare all the cattle *r* ... Gen 31:8 6124
leaped upon the cattle were *r* ... Gen 31:10 6124
which leap upon the cattle are *r* ... Gen 31:12 6124

RINNAH *(rin'-nah)* {1} *A descendant of Caleb.*
sons of Shimon were, Amnon, and *R* ... 1Chr 4:20 7441

RINSED {3}
be both scoured, and *r* in water ... Lev 6:28 7857
hath not *r* his hands in water, he ... Lev 15:11 7857
of wood shall be *r* in water ... Lev 15:12 7857

RIOT {3}
not accused of *r* or unruly ... Titus 1:6 *810*
with them to the same excess of *r* ... 1Pet 4:4 *810*
it pleasure to *r* in the daytime ... 2Pet 2:13 *5172*

RIOTING {1}
not in *r* and drunkenness, not in ... Rom 13:13 *2970*

RIOTOUS {3}
among *r* eaters of flesh ... Prov 23:20 2151
of *r* men shameth his father ... Prov 28:7 2151
his substance with *r* living ... Lk 15:13 *811*

RIP {1}
r up their women with child ... 2Kin 8:12 1234

RIPE {7}
thereof brought forth *r* grapes ... Gen 40:10 1310
offer the first of thy *r* fruits ... Ex 22:29
whatsoever is first *r* in the land ... Num 18:13
like the figs that are first *r* ... Jer 24:2
the sickle, for the harvest is *r* ... Joel 3:13 1310
for the harvest of the earth is *r* ... Rev 14:15 *3583*
for her grapes are fully *r* ... Rev 14:18 *187*

RIPENING {1}
the sour grape is *r* in the flower ... Is 18:5 1580

RIPHATH *(ri'-fath)* {2} *A son of Gomer.*
Ashkenaz, and *R*, and Togarmah ... Gen 10:3 7384
Ashchenaz, and *R*, and Togarmah ... 1Chr 1:6 7384

RIPPED {3}
that were with child he *r* up ... 2Kin 15:16 1234
women with child shall be *r* up ... Hos 13:16 1234
because they have *r* up the women ... Amos 1:13 1234

RISE {142}
your feet, and ye shall *r* up early ... Gen 19:2 7925
that I cannot *r* up before thee ... Gen 31:35 6965
R up early in the morning, and ... Ex 8:20 7925
R up early in the morning, and ... Ex 9:13 6965
R up, and get you forth from among ... Ex 12:31 6965
If he *r* again, and walk abroad ... Ex 21:19 6965
Thou shalt *r* up before the hoary ... Lev 19:32 6965
R up, LORD, and let thine enemies ... Num 10:35 6965
call thee, *r* up, and go with them ... Num 22:20 6965
and said, *R* up, Balak, and hear ... Num 23:18 6965
the people shall *r* up as a great ... Num 23:24 6965
a Sceptre shall *r* out of Israel ... Num 24:17 6965
Now *r* up, said I, and get you over ... Deut 2:13 6965
R ye up, take your journey, and ... Deut 2:24 6965
r up against him, and smite him ... Deut 19:11 6965
One witness shall not *r* up ... Deut 19:15 6965
If a false witness *r* up against ... Deut 19:16 6965
r up against thee to be smitten ... Deut 28:7 6965
that shall *r* up after you ... Deut 29:22 6965
and this people will *r* up, and go a ... Deut 31:16 6965
Let them *r* up and help you, and be ... Deut 32:38 6965
loins of them that *r* against him ... Deut 33:11 6965
hate him, that they *r* not again ... Deut 33:11 6965
Then ye shall *r* up from the ... Josh 8:7 6965
I will send them, and they shall *r* ... Josh 18:4 6965
said, *R* thou, and fall upon us ... Judg 8:21 6965
the sun is up, thou shalt *r* early ... Judg 9:33 7925
with smoke *r* up out of the city ... Judg 20:38 5927
him, that he should *r* against me ... 1Sa 22:13 6965
them not to *r* against Saul ... 1Sa 24:7 6965
Wherefore now *r* up early in the ... 1Sa 29:10 7925
the child was dead, thou didst *r* ... 2Sa 12:21 6965
all that *r* against thee to do ... 2Sa 18:32 6965
of Israel, which *r* up against me ... 2Kin 16:7 6965
And they said, Let us *r* up ... Neh 2:18 6965
the earth shall *r* up against him ... Job 20:27 6965
Upon my right hand *r* the youth ... Job 30:12 6965
are they that *r* up against me ... Ps 3:1 6965
from those that *r* up against them ... Ps 17:7 6965
them that they were not able to *r* ... Ps 18:38 6965
above those that *r* up against me ... Ps 18:48 6965
though war should *r* against me ... Ps 27:3 6965
False witnesses did *r* up ... Ps 35:11 6965
down, and shall not be able to *r* ... Ps 36:12 6965
he lieth he shall *r* up no more ... Ps 41:8 6965
them under that *r* up against us ... Ps 44:5 6965
me from them that *r* up against me ... Ps 59:1 6965
the tumult of those that *r* up ... Ps 74:23 6965
the wicked that *r* up against me ... Ps 92:11 6965
Who will *r* up for me against the ... Ps 94:16 6965
At midnight I will *r* to give ... Ps 119:62 6965
It is vain for you to *r* up early ... Ps 127:2 6965
with those that *r* up against thee ... Ps 139:21 8618
pits, that they *r* not up again ... Ps 140:10 6965
their calamity shall *r* suddenly ... Prov 24:22 6965
but when the wicked *r*, a man is ... Prov 28:12 6965
When the wicked *r*, men hide ... Prov 28:28 6965
of the ruler *r* up against thee ... Eccl 10:4 5927
he shall *r* up at the voice of the ... Eccl 12:4 6965
R up, my love, my fair one, and ... Song 2:10 6965
I will *r* now, and go about the ... Song 3:2 6965
Woe unto them that *r* up early in ... Is 5:11 7925
that they do not *r*, nor possess ... Is 14:21 6965
For I will *r* up against them, ... Is 14:22 6965
and it shall fall, and not *r* again ... Is 24:20 6965
are deceased, they shall not *r* ... Is 26:14 6965
For the LORD shall *r* up as in ... Is 28:21 6965
R up, ye women that are at ease ... Is 32:9 6965
Now will I *r*, saith the LORD ... Is 33:10 6965
down together, they shall not *r* ... Is 43:17 6965
every tongue that shall *r* against ... Is 54:17 6965
shall thy light *r* in obscurity ... Is 58:10 2224
r no more, because of the sword ... Jer 25:27 6965
yet should they *r* up every man in ... Jer 37:10 6965
waters *r* up out of the north, and ... Jer 47:2 5927
her, and *r* up to the battle ... Jer 49:14 6965
of them that *r* up against me ... Jer 51:1 6965
shall not *r* from the evil that I ... Jer 51:64 6965
from whom I am not able to *r* up ... Lam 1:14 6965
and another shall *r* after them ... Dan 7:24 6966
she shall no more *r* ... Amos 5:2 6965
I will *r* against the house of ... Amos 7:9 6965
it shall *r* up wholly as a flood ... Amos 8:8 5927
shall fall, and never *r* up again ... Amos 8:14 6965
it shall *r* up wholly like a flood ... Amos 9:5 5927
let us *r* up against her in battle ... Obad 1 6965
shall not *r* up the second time ... Nah 1:9 6965
Shall they not *r* up suddenly that ... Hab 2:7 6965
the day that I *r* up to the prey ... Zeph 3:8 6965
his hand shall *r* up against the ... Zec 14:13 5927
maketh his sun to *r* on the evil ... Mt 5:45 *393*
the children shall *r* up against ... Mt 10:21 *1881*
shall *r* in judgment with this ... Mt 12:41 *450*
r up in the judgment with this ... Mt 12:42 *1453*
and the third day he shall *r* again ... Mt 20:19 *450*
For nation shall *r* against nation ... Mt 24:7 *1453*
And many false prophets shall *r* ... Mt 24:11 *1453*
R, let us be going ... Mt 26:46 *1453*
After three days I will *r* again ... Mt 27:63 *1453*
if Satan *r* up against himself, and ... Mk 3:26 *450*
r night and day, and the seed ... Mk 4:27 *1453*
and after three days *r* again ... Mk 8:31 *450*
killed, he shall *r* the third day ... Mk 9:31 *450*
and the third day he shall *r* again ... Mk 10:34 *450*
unto him, Be of good comfort, *r* ... Mk 10:49 *1453*
therefore, when they shall *r* ... Mk 12:23 *450*
when they shall *r* from the dead ... Mk 12:25 *450*
as touching the dead, that they *r* ... Mk 12:26 *1453*
For nation shall *r* against nation ... Mk 13:8 *1453*
children shall *r* up against their ... Mk 13:12 *1881*
Christs and false prophets shall *r* ... Mk 13:22 *1453*
R up, let us go ... Mk 14:42 *1453*
or to say, *R* up and walk ... Lk 5:23 *1453*
R up, and stand forth in the midst ... Lk 6:8 *1453*
I cannot *r* and give thee ... Lk 11:7 *450*
unto you, Though he will not *r* ... Lk 11:8 *1453*
of his importunity he will *r* ... Lk 11:8 *450*
The queen of the south shall *r* up ... Lk 11:31 *1453*
The men of Nineve shall *r* up in ... Lk 11:32 *450*
ye see a cloud *r* out of the west ... Lk 12:54 *393*
and the third day he shall *r* again ... Lk 18:33 *450*
Nation shall *r* against nation, and ... Lk 21:10 *1453*
r and pray, lest ye enter into ... Lk 22:46 *450*
and the third day *r* again ... Lk 24:7 *450*
to *r* from the dead the third day ... Lk 24:46 *450*
Jesus saith unto him, *R*, take up ... Jn 5:8 *1453*
her, Thy brother shall *r* again ... Jn 11:23 *450*
I know that he shall *r* again in ... Jn 11:24 *450*
that he must *r* again from the ... Jn 20:9 *450*
of Jesus Christ of Nazareth *r* up ... Acts 3:6 *1453*
And there came a voice to him, *R* ... Acts 10:13 *450*
But *r*, and stand upon thy feet ... Acts 26:16 *450*
first that should *r* from the dead ... Acts 26:23 *386*
he that shall *r* to reign over the ... Rom 15:12 *450*
up, if so be that the dead *r* not ... 1Cor 15:15 *1453*
For if the dead *r* not, then is ... 1Cor 15:16 *1453*
dead, if the dead *r* not at all ... 1Cor 15:29 *1453*
it me, if the dead *r* not ... 1Cor 15:32 *1453*
the dead in Christ shall *r* first ... 1Th 4:16 *450*
that another priest should *r* ... Heb 7:11 *450*
and the angel stood, saying, *R* ... Rev 11:1 *1453*
saw a beast *r* up out of the sea, ... Rev 13:1 *305*

RISEN {51}
The sun was *r* upon the earth when ... Gen 19:23 3318
If the sun be *r* upon him, there ... Ex 22:3 2224
ye are *r* up in your fathers' ... Num 32:14 6965
ye are *r* up against my father's ... Judg 9:18 6965
And when she was *r* up to glean ... Ruth 2:15 6965
Yet a man is *r* to pursue thee, and ... 1Sa 25:29 6965
the whole family is *r* against ... 2Sa 14:7 6965
I am *r* up in the room of David my ... 1Kin 8:20 6965
of the man of God was *r* early ... 2Kin 6:15 6965
for I am *r* up in the room of ... 2Chr 6:10 6965
Solomon the son of David, is *r* up ... 2Chr 13:6 6965
Now when Jehoram was *r* up to the ... 2Chr 21:4 6965
but we are *r*, and stand upright ... Ps 20:8 6965
witnesses are *r* up against me ... Ps 27:12 6965
For strangers are *r* up against me ... Ps 54:3 6965
O God, the proud are *r* against me ... Ps 86:14 6965
glory of the LORD is *r* upon thee ... Is 60:1 2224
Violence is *r* up into a rod of ... Eze 7:11 6965
for the waters were *r*, waters to ... Eze 47:5 1342
my people is *r* up as an enemy ... Mic 2:8 6965
born of women there hath not *r* a ... Mt 11:11 *1453*
he is *r* from the dead ... Mt 14:2 *1453*
of man be *r* again from the dead ... Mt 17:9 *450*
But after I am *r* again, I will go ... Mt 26:32 *1453*
the people, He is *r* from the dead ... Mt 27:64 *1453*
for he is *r*, as he said ... Mt 28:6 *1453*
that he is *r* from the dead ... Mt 28:7 *1453*
the Baptist was *r* from the dead ... Mk 6:14 *1453*
he is *r* from the dead ... Mk 6:16 *1453*
Son of man were *r* from the dead ... Mk 9:9 *450*
But after that I am *r*, I will go ... Mk 14:28 *1453*
he is *r* ... Mk 16:6 *1453*
Now when Jesus was *r* early the ... Mk 16:9 *450*
which had seen him after he was *r* ... Mk 16:14 *1453*
a great prophet is *r* up among us ... Lk 7:16 *1453*
that John was *r* from the dead ... Lk 9:7 *1453*
of the old prophets was *r* again ... Lk 9:8 *450*
of the old prophets is *r* again ... Lk 9:19 *450*
the master of the house is *r* up ... Lk 13:25 *1453*

He is not here, but is *r* ... Lk 24:6 *1453*
Saying, The Lord is *r* indeed ... Lk 24:34 *1453*
therefore he was *r* from the dead ... Jn 2:22 *1453*
after that he was *r* from the dead ... Jn 21:14 *1453*
and *r* again from the dead ... Acts 17:3 *450*
died, yea rather, that is *r* again ... Rom 8:34 *1453*
of the dead, then is Christ not *r* ... 1Cor 15:13 *1453*
And if Christ be not *r*, then is ... 1Cor 15:14 *1453*
But now is Christ *r* from the dead ... 1Cor 15:20 *1453*
wherein also ye are *r* with him ... Col 2:12 *4891*
If ye then be *r* with Christ ... Col 3:1 *4891*
no sooner *r* with a burning heat ... Jas 1:11 *393*

RISEST {2}
liest down, and when thou *r* up ... Deut 6:7 6965
liest down, and when thou *r* up ... Deut 11:19 6965

RISETH {14}
for as when a man *r* against his ... Deut 22:26 6965
man before the LORD, that *r* up ... Josh 6:26 6965
of the morning, when the sun *r* ... 2Sa 23:4 2224
commandeth the sun, and it *r* not ... Job 9:7 2224
So man lieth down, and *r* not ... Job 14:12 6965
he *r* up, and no man is sure of ... Job 24:22 6965
he that *r* up against me as the ... Job 27:7 6965
then shall I do when God *r* up ... Job 31:14 6965
seven times, and *r* up again ... Prov 24:16 6965
She *r* also while it is yet night, ... Prov 31:15 6965
shalt not know from whence it *r* ... Is 47:11 7837
Egypt *r* up like a flood, and his ... Jer 46:8 5927
the daughter *r* up against her ... Mic 7:6 6965
He *r* from supper, and laid aside ... Jn 13:4 *1453*

RISING {39}
have in the skin of his flesh a *r* ... Lev 13:2 7613
if the *r* be white in the skin, and ... Lev 13:10 7613
there be quick raw flesh in the *r* ... Lev 13:10 7613
of the boil there be a white *r* ... Lev 13:19 7613
it is a *r* of the burning, and the ... Lev 13:28 7613
if the *r* of the sore be white ... Lev 13:43 7613
And for a *r*, and for a scab, and for ... Lev 14:56 7613
on the east side toward the *r* of ... Num 2:3 4217
Jordan toward the *r* of the sun ... Josh 12:1 4217
r up betimes, and sending ... 2Chr 36:15 7925
r of the morning till the stars ... Neh 4:21 5927
my leanness *r* up in me beareth ... Job 16:8 6965
r betimes for a prey ... Job 24:5 7836
The murderer *r* with the light ... Job 24:14 7925
called the earth from the *r* of ... Ps 50:1 4217
From the *r* of the sun unto the ... Ps 113:3 4217
r early in the morning, it shall ... Prov 27:14 7925
against whom there is no *r* up ... Prov 30:31 510
from the *r* of the sun shall he ... Is 41:25 4217
may know from the *r* of the sun ... Is 45:6 4217
his glory from the *r* of the sun ... Is 59:19 4217
kings to the brightness of thy *r* ... Is 60:3 2225
r up early and speaking, but ye ... Jer 7:13 7925
daily *r* up early and sending them ... Jer 7:25 7925
r early and protesting, saying, ... Jer 11:7 7925
unto you, *r* early and speaking ... Jer 25:3 7925
prophets, *r* early and sending them ... Jer 25:4 7925
both *r* up early, and sending them, ... Jer 26:5 7925
r up early and sending them ... Jer 29:19 7925
r up early and teaching them, yet ... Jer 32:33 7925
unto you, *r* early and speaking ... Jer 35:14 7925
r up early and sending them, ... Jer 35:15 7925
r early and sending them, saying, ... Jer 44:4 7925
their sitting down, and their *r* up ... Lam 3:63 7012
For from the *r* of the sun even ... Mal 1:11 4217
r up a great while before day, he ... Mk 1:35 *450*
the *r* from the dead should mean ... Mk 9:10 *305*
the sepulchre at the *r* of the sun ... Mk 16:2 *393*
r again of many in Israel ... Lk 2:34 *386*

RISSAH *(ris'-sah)* {2} *An Israelite encampment in the wilderness.*
from Libnah, and pitched at *R* ... Num 33:21 7446
And they journeyed from *R*, and ... Num 33:22 7446

RITES {1}
according to all the *r* of it ... Num 9:3 2708

RITHMAH *(rith'-mah)* {2} *An Israelite encampment in the wilderness.*
from Hazeroth, and pitched in *R* ... Num 33:18 7575
And they departed from *R*, and ... Num 33:19 7575

RIVER {176}
a *r* went out of Eden to water the ... Gen 2:10 5104
the name of the second *r* is Gihon ... Gen 2:13 5104
name of the third *r* is Hiddekel ... Gen 2:14 5104
the fourth *r* is Euphrates ... Gen 2:14 5104
from the *r* of Egypt unto the ... Gen 15:18 5104
the great *r*, the *r* Euphrates ... Gen 15:18 5104
he rose up, and passed over the *r* ... Gen 31:21 5104
by the *r* reigned in his stead ... Gen 36:37 5104
and, behold, he stood by the *r* ... Gen 41:1 2975
of the *r* seven well favoured kine ... Gen 41:2 2975
came up after them out of the *r* ... Gen 41:3 2975
kine upon the brink of the *r* ... Gen 41:3 2975
I stood upon the bank of the *r* ... Gen 41:17 2975
came up out of the *r* seven kine ... Gen 41:18 2975
is born ye shall cast into the *r* ... Ex 1:22 2975
down to wash herself at the *r* ... Ex 2:5 2975
shalt take of the water of the *r* ... Ex 4:9 2975
which thou takest out of the *r* ... Ex 4:9 2975
the waters which are in the *r* ... Ex 7:17 2975
fish that is in the *r* shall die ... Ex 7:18 2975
and the *r* shall stink ... Ex 7:18 2975
to drink of the water of the *r* ... Ex 7:18 2975
the waters that were in the *r* ... Ex 7:20 2975
in the *r* were turned to blood ... Ex 7:20 2975
the fish that was in the *r* died ... Ex 7:21 2975
the *r* stank, and the Egyptians ... Ex 7:21 2975
not drink of the water of the *r* ... Ex 7:21 2975
about the *r* for water to drink ... Ex 7:24 2975
not drink of the water of the *r* ... Ex 7:24 2975
that the LORD had smitten the *r* ... Ex 7:25 2975
the *r* shall bring forth frogs ... Ex 8:3 2975
they may remain in the *r* only ... Ex 8:9 2975
they shall remain in the *r* only ... Ex 8:11 2975
rod, wherewith thou smotest the *r* ... Ex 17:5 2975
and from the desert unto the *r* ... Ex 23:31 5104
which is by the *r* of the land of ... Num 22:5 5104
from Azmon unto the *r* of Egypt ... Num 34:5 5158
and unto Lebanon, unto the great *r* ... Deut 1:7 5104
the great *r*, the *r* Euphrates ... Deut 1:7 5104
journey, and pass over the *r* Arnon ... Deut 2:24 5158
is by the brink of the *r* of Arnon ... Deut 2:36 5158
and from the city that is by the *r* ... Deut 2:36 5158
unto any place of the *r* Jabbok ... Deut 2:37 5158
from the *r* of Arnon unto mount ... Deut 3:8 5158
Aroer, which is by the *r* Arnon ... Deut 3:12 5158
unto the *r* Arnon half the valley ... Deut 3:16 5158
the border even unto the *r* Jabbok ... Deut 3:16 5158
is by the bank of the *r* Arnon ... Deut 4:48 5158
wilderness and Lebanon, from the *r* ... Deut 11:24 5104
the *r* Euphrates, even unto the ... Deut 11:24 5104
Lebanon even unto the great *r* ... Josh 1:4 5104
the *r* Euphrates, all the land of ... Josh 1:4 5104
from the *r* Arnon unto mount ... Josh 12:1 5158
is upon the bank of the *r* Arnon ... Josh 12:2 5158
and from the middle of the *r* ... Josh 12:2 5158
Gilead, even unto the *r* Jabbok ... Josh 12:2 5158
is upon the bank of the *r* Arnon ... Josh 13:9 5158
that is in the midst of the *r* ... Josh 13:9 5158
is on the bank of the *r* Arnon ... Josh 13:16 5158
that is in the midst of the *r* ... Josh 13:16 5158
and went out unto the *r* of Egypt ... Josh 15:4 5158
is on the south side of the *r* ... Josh 15:7 5158
her villages, unto the *r* of Egypt ... Josh 15:47 5158
Tappuah westward unto the *r* Kanah ... Josh 16:8 5158
r Kanah, southward of the *r* ... Josh 17:9 5158
was on the north side of the *r* ... Josh 17:9 5158
reached to the *r* that is before ... Josh 19:11 5158
draw unto thee to the *r* Kishon ... Judg 4:7 5158
the Gentiles unto the *r* of Kishon ... Judg 4:13 5158
The *r* of Kishon swept them away, ... Judg 5:21 5158
that ancient *r*, the *r* Kishon ... Judg 5:21 5158
his border at the *r* Euphrates ... 2Sa 8:3 5104
Syrians that were beyond the *r* ... 2Sa 10:16 5104
and we will draw it into the *r* ... 2Sa 17:13 5158
in the midst of the *r* of Gad ... 2Sa 24:5 5158
from the *r* unto the land of the ... 1Kin 4:21 5104
all the region on this side the *r* ... 1Kin 4:24 5104
all the kings on this side the *r* ... 1Kin 4:24 5104
in of Hamath unto the *r* of Egypt ... 1Kin 8:65 5158
shall scatter them beyond the *r* ... 1Kin 14:15 5104
Aroer, which is by the *r* Arnon ... 2Kin 10:33 5158
and in Habor by the *r* of Gozan ... 2Kin 17:6 5104
and in Habor by the *r* of Gozan ... 2Kin 18:11 5104
of Assyria to the *r* Euphrates ... 2Kin 23:29 5104
the *r* of Egypt unto the *r* ... 2Kin 24:7 5158
by the *r* reigned in his stead ... 1Chr 1:48 5104
wilderness from the *r* Euphrates ... 1Chr 5:9 5104
Habor, and Hara, and to the *r* Gozan ... 1Chr 5:26 5104
his dominion by the *r* Euphrates ... 1Chr 18:3 5104
Syrians that were beyond the *r* ... 1Chr 19:16 5104
in of Hamath unto the *r* of Egypt ... 2Chr 7:8 5158
the *r* even unto the land of the ... 2Chr 9:26 5104
rest that are on this side the *r* ... Ezr 4:10 5103
the men on this side the *r* ... Ezr 4:11 5103
no portion on this side the *r* ... Ezr 4:16 5103
and unto the rest beyond the *r* ... Ezr 4:17 5103
over all countries beyond the *r* ... Ezr 4:20 5103
governor on this side the *r* ... Ezr 5:3 5103
governor on this side the *r* ... Ezr 5:6 5103
which were on this side the *r* ... Ezr 5:6 5103
Tatnai, governor beyond the *r* ... Ezr 6:6 5103
which are beyond the *r*, be ye ... Ezr 6:6 5103
even of the tribute beyond the *r* ... Ezr 6:8 5103
governor on this side the *r* ... Ezr 6:13 5103
treasurers which are beyond the *r* ... Ezr 7:21 5103
the people that are beyond the *r* ... Ezr 7:25 5103
to the *r* that runneth to Ahava ... Ezr 8:15 5104
at the *r* of Ahava, that we might ... Ezr 8:21 5104
Then we departed from the *r* of ... Ezr 8:31 5104
the governors on this side the *r* ... Ezr 8:36 5104
me to the governors beyond the *r* ... Neh 2:7 5104
to the governors beyond the *r* ... Neh 2:9 5104
the governor on this side the *r* ... Neh 3:7 5104
Behold, he drinketh up a *r* ... Job 40:23 5104
drink of the *r* of thy pleasures ... Ps 36:8 5158
There is a *r*, the streams whereof ... Ps 46:4 5104
enrichest it with the *r* of God ... Ps 65:9 6388
from the *r* unto the ends of the ... Ps 72:8 5104
sea, and her branches unto the *r* ... Ps 80:11 5104
ran in the dry places like a *r* ... Ps 105:41 5104
namely, by them beyond the *r* ... Is 7:20 5104
up upon them the waters of the *r* ... Is 8:7 5104
he shake his hand over the *r* ... Is 11:15 5104
the *r* shall be wasted and dried up ... Is 19:5 5104
of Sihor, the harvest of the *r* ... Is 23:3 2975
Pass through thy land as a *r* ... Is 23:10 2975
of the *r* unto the stream of Egypt ... Is 27:12 5104
then had thy peace been as a *r* ... Is 48:18 5104
will extend peace to her like a *r* ... Is 66:12 5104
to drink the waters of the *r* ... Jer 2:18 5104
spreadeth out her roots by the *r* ... Jer 17:8 3105
which was by the *r* Euphrates in ... Jer 46:2 5104
the north by the *r* Euphrates ... Jer 46:6 5104
north country by the *r* Euphrates ... Jer 46:10 5104
let tears run down like a *r* day ... Lam 2:18 5158
the captives by the *r* of Chebar ... Eze 1:1 5104
of the Chaldeans by the *r* Chebar ... Eze 1:3 5104
that dwelt by the *r* of Chebar ... Eze 3:15 5104
which I saw by the *r* of Chebar ... Eze 3:23 5104
that I saw by the *r* of Chebar ... Eze 10:15 5104
God of Israel by the *r* of Chebar ... Eze 10:20 5104
which I saw by the *r* of Chebar ... Eze 10:22 5104
My *r* is mine own, and I have made ... Eze 29:3 2975
The *r* is mine, and I have made it ... Eze 29:9 2975
vision that I saw by the *r* Chebar ... Eze 43:3 5104
it was a *r* that I could not pass ... Eze 47:5 5158
a *r* that could not be passed over ... Eze 47:5 5158
to return to the brink of the *r* ... Eze 47:6 5158
at the bank of the *r* were very ... Eze 47:7 5158
shall live whither the *r* cometh ... Eze 47:9 5158
by the *r* upon the bank thereof, ... Eze 47:12 5158
in Kadesh, the *r* to the great sea ... Eze 47:19 5158
to the *r* toward the great sea ... Eze 48:28 5158
vision, and I was by the *r* of Ulai ... Dan 8:2 180
there stood before the *r* a ram ... Dan 8:3 180
I had seen standing before the *r* ... Dan 8:6 180
I was by the side of the great *r* ... Dan 10:4 5104
on this side of the bank of the *r* ... Dan 12:5 2975
on that side of the bank of the *r* ... Dan 12:5 2975
was upon the waters of the *r* ... Dan 12:6 2975
was upon the waters of the *r* ... Dan 12:7 2975
unto the *r* of the wilderness ... Amos 6:14 5158
from the fortress even to the *r* ... Mic 7:12 5104
from the *r* even to the ends of ... Zec 9:10 5104
the deeps of the *r* shall dry up ... Zec 10:11 2975
of him in the *r* of Jordan ... Mk 1:5 *4215*
went out of the city by a *r* side ... Acts 16:13 *4215*
bound in the great *r* Euphrates ... Rev 9:14 *4215*
vial upon the great *r* Euphrates ... Rev 16:12 *4215*
me a pure *r* of water of life ... Rev 22:1 *4215*
of it, and on either side of the *r* ... Rev 22:2 *4215*

RIVER'S {4}
it in the flags by the *r* brink ... Ex 2:3 2975
walked along by the *r* side ... Ex 2:5 2975
by the *r* brink against he come ... Ex 7:15 2975
forth, as gardens by the *r* side ... Num 24:6 5104

RIVERS {77}
upon their streams, upon their *r* ... Ex 7:19 2975
rod over the streams, over the *r* ... Ex 8:5 2975
waters, in the seas, and in the *r* ... Lev 11:9 5158
scales in the seas, and in the *r* ... Lev 11:10 5158
to Jotbath, a land of *r* of waters ... Deut 10:7 5158
r of Damascus, better than all ... 2Kin 5:12 5104
up all the *r* of besieged places ... 2Kin 19:24 2975
He shall not see the *r*, the ... Job 20:17 6390
He cutteth out *r* among the rocks ... Job 28:10 2975
the rock poured me out *r* of oil ... Job 29:6 6388
a tree planted by the *r* of water ... Ps 1:3 6388
thou driedst up mighty *r* ... Ps 74:15 5104
caused waters to run down like *r* ... Ps 78:16 5104
And had turned their *r* into blood ... Ps 78:44 2975
sea, and his right hand in the *r* ... Ps 89:25 5104
He turneth *r* into a wilderness, ... Ps 107:33 5104
R of waters run down mine eyes, ... Ps 119:136 6388
By the *r* of Babylon, there we sat ... Ps 137:1 5104
r of waters in the streets ... Prov 5:16 6388
of the LORD, as the *r* of water ... Prov 21:1 6388
All the *r* run into the sea ... Eccl 1:7 5158
the place from whence the *r* come ... Eccl 1:7 5158
eyes of doves by the *r* of waters ... Song 5:12 650
uttermost part of the *r* of Egypt ... Is 7:18 2975
which is beyond the *r* of Ethiopia ... Is 18:1 5104
whose land the *r* have spoiled ... Is 18:2 5104
whose land the *r* have spoiled ... Is 18:7 5104
And they shall turn the *r* far away ... Is 19:6 5104
and upon every high hill, *r* ... Is 30:25 6388
as *r* of water in a dry place, as ... Is 32:2 6388
be unto us a place of broad *r* ... Is 33:21 5103
all the *r* of the besieged places ... Is 37:25 2975
I will open *r* in high places, and ... Is 41:18 5103
and I will make the *r* islands ... Is 42:15 5103
and through the *r*, they shall not ... Is 43:2 5103
wilderness, and *r* in the desert ... Is 43:19 5103
r in the desert, to give drink to ... Is 43:20 5103
Be dry, and I will dry up thy *r* ... Is 44:27 5103
the thigh, pass over the *r* ... Is 47:2 5103
I make the *r* a wilderness ... Is 50:2 5103
the *r* of waters in a straight way ... Jer 31:9 5158
whose waters are moved as the *r* ... Jer 46:7 5104
his waters are moved like the *r* ... Jer 46:8 5104
Mine eye runneth down with *r* of ... Lam 3:48 6388
and to the hills, to the *r* ... Eze 6:3 650
that lieth in the midst of his *r* ... Eze 29:3 2975
of thy *r* to stick unto thy scales ... Eze 29:4 2975
thee up out of the midst of thy *r* ... Eze 29:4 2975
all the fish of thy *r* shall stick ... Eze 29:4 2975
thee and all the fish of thy *r* ... Eze 29:5 2975
am against thee, and against thy *r* ... Eze 29:10 2975
And I will make the *r* dry, and sell ... Eze 30:12 2975
set him up on high with her *r* ... Eze 31:4 5104
sent out her little *r* unto all ... Eze 31:4 8585
broken by all the *r* of the land ... Eze 31:12 650
and thou camest forth with thy *r* ... Eze 32:2 5104
thy feet, and fouledst their *r* ... Eze 32:2 5104
the *r* shall be full of thee ... Eze 32:6 650
cause their *r* to run like oil, ... Eze 32:14 5104
the mountains of Israel by the *r* ... Eze 34:13 650
in thy valleys, and in all thy *r* ... Eze 35:8 650
and to the hills, to the *r* ... Eze 36:4 650

R

and to the hills, to the *r* Eze 36:6 650
whithersoever the *r* shall come Eze 47:9 5158
for the *r* of waters are dried up, Joel 1:20 650
all the *r* of Judah shall flow Joel 3:18 650
or with ten thousands of *r* of oil Mic 6:7 5158
it dry, and drieth up all the *r* Nah 1:4 5104
gates of the *r* shall be opened Nah 2:6 5104
No, that was situate among the *r* Nah 3:8 2975
the LORD displeased against the *r* Hab 3:8 5104
was thine anger against the *r* Hab 3:8 5104
didst cleave the earth with *r* Hab 3:9 5104
From beyond the *r* of Ethiopia my Zeph 3:10 5104
shall flow *r* of living water Jn 7:38 *4215*
fell upon the third part of the *r* Rev 8:10 *4215*
poured out his vial upon the *r* Rev 16:4 *4215*

RIZIA See REZIA.

RIZPAH *(riz'-pah)* {4} *A concubine of Saul.*
had a concubine, whose name was *R* 2Sa 3:7 7532
sons of *R* the daughter of Aiah 2Sa 21:8 7532
R the daughter of Aiah took 2Sa 21:10 7532
David what *R* the daughter of Aiah 2Sa 21:11 7532

ROAD {1}
Whither have ye made a *r* to day 1Sa 27:10 6584

ROAR {23}
Let the sea *r*, and the fulness 1Chr 16:32 7481
Though the waters thereof *r* Ps 46:3 1993
Thine enemies *r* in the midst of Ps 74:4 7580
let the sea *r*, and the fulness Ps 96:11 7481
Let the sea *r*, and the fulness Ps 98:7 7481
The young lions *r* after their Ps 104:21 7580
they shall *r* like young lions Is 5:29 7580
yea, they shall *r*, and lay hold of Is 5:29 5098
in that day they shall *r* against Is 5:30 5098
he shall cry, yea, *r* Is 42:13 6873
We *r* all like bears, and mourn Is 59:11 1993
though they *r*, yet can they not Jer 5:22 1993
The LORD shall *r* from on high Jer 25:30 7580
he shall mightily *r* upon his Jer 25:30 7580
the sea when the waves thereof *r* Jer 31:35 1993
their voice shall *r* like the sea Jer 50:42 1993
They shall *r* together like lions Jer 51:38 7580
her waves do *r* like great waters Jer 51:55 1993
he shall *r* like a lion Hos 11:10 7580
when he shall *r*, then the Hos 11:10 7580
The LORD also shall *r* out of Zion Joel 3:16 7580
said, The LORD will *r* from Zion Amos 1:2 7580
Will a lion *r* in the forest, when Amos 3:4 7580

ROARED {5}
a young lion *r* against him Judg 14:5 7580
I have *r* by reason of the Ps 38:8 7580
divided the sea, whose waves *r* Is 51:15 1993
The young lions *r* upon him Jer 2:15 7580
The lion hath *r*, who will not Amos 3:8 7580

ROARETH {3}
After it a voice *r* Job 37:4 7580
their voice *r* like the sea Jer 6:23 1993
a loud voice, as when a lion *r* Rev 10:3 *3455*

ROARING {16}
The *r* of the lion, and the voice Job 4:10 7581
me, and from the words of my *r* Ps 22:1 7581
mouths, as a ravening and a *r* lion Ps 22:13 7580
old through my *r* all the day long Ps 32:3 7581
wrath is as the *r* of a lion Prov 19:12 5099
of a king is as the *r* of a lion Prov 20:2 5099
As a *r* lion, and a ranging bear Prov 28:15 5098
Their *r* shall be like a lion, Is 5:29 7581
them like the *r* of the sea Is 5:30 5100
and the young lion *r* on his prey Is 31:4 1897
thereof, by the noise of his *r* Eze 19:7 7581
like a *r* lion ravening the prey Eze 22:25 7580
princes within her are *r* lions Zeph 3:3 7580
a voice of the *r* of young lions Zec 11:3 7581
the sea and the waves *r* Lk 21:25 *2278*
adversary the devil, as a *r* lion 1Pet 5:8 *5612*

ROARINGS {1}
my *r* are poured out like the Job 3:24 7581

ROAST {5}
r with fire, and unleavened bread Ex 12:8 6748
all with water, but *r* with fire Ex 12:9 6748
And thou shalt *r* and eat it in the Deut 16:7 1310
Give flesh to *r* for the priest 1Sa 2:15 6740
he roasteth *r*, and is satisfied Is 44:16 6748

ROASTED {3}
they *r* the passover with fire 2Chr 35:13 1310
I have *r* flesh, and eaten it Is 44:19 6740
the king of Babylon *r* in the fire Jer 29:22 7033

ROASTETH {2}
The slothful man *r* not that which Prov 12:27 2760
he *r* roast, and is satisfied Is 44:16 740

ROB {8}
thy neighbour, neither *r* him Lev 19:13 1497
which shall *r* you of your Lev 26:22 7921
they *r* the threshingfloors 1Sa 23:1 8154
R not the poor, because he is Prov 22:22 1497
that they may *r* the fatherless Is 10:2 962
us, and the lot of them that *r* us Is 17:14 962
r those that robbed them, saith Eze 39:10 962
Will a man *r* God Mal 3:8 6906

ROBBED {13}
they *r* all that came along that Judg 9:25 1497
as a bear *r* of her whelps in the 2Sa 17:8 7909
The bands of the wicked have *r* me Ps 119:61 5749
Let a bear *r* of her whelps meet a Prov 17:12 7909
have *r* their treasures, and I have Is 10:13 8154
But this is a people *r* and spoiled Is 42:22 962
and they shall be *r* Jer 50:37 962
pledge, give again that he had *r* Eze 33:15 5100
them, and rob those that *r* them Eze 39:10 962
Yet ye have *r* me Mal 3:8 6906
ye say, Wherein have we *r* thee Mal 3:8 962
for ye have *r* me, even this whole Mal 3:9 6906
I *r* other churches, taking wages 2Cor 11:8 *4813*

ROBBER {5}
the *r* swalloweth up their Job 5:5 6782
the *r* shall prevail against him Job 18:9 6782
If he beget a son that is a *r* Eze 18:10 6530
way, the same is a thief and a *r* Jn 10:1 *3027*
Now Barabbas was a *r* Jn 18:40 *3027*

ROBBERS {11}
The tabernacles of *r* prosper Job 12:6 7703
for a spoil, and Israel to the *r* Is 42:24 962
become a den of *r* in your eyes Jer 7:11 6530
for the *r* shall enter into it, and Eze 7:22 6530
also the *r* of thy people shall Dan 11:14 6530
as troops of *r* wait for a man, so Hos 6:9 1416
the troop of *r* spoileth without Hos 7:1 1416
if *r* by night, (how art thou cut Obad 5 7703
came before me are thieves and *r* Jn 10:8 *3027*
which are neither *r* of churches Acts 19:37 *2417*
perils of waters, in perils of *r* 2Cor 11:26 *3027*

ROBBERY {7}
and become not vain in *r* Ps 62:10 1498
The *r* of the wicked shall destroy Prov 21:7 7701
I hate *r* for burnt offering Is 61:8 1498
used oppression, and exercised *r* Eze 22:29 1498
up violence and *r* in their palaces Amos 3:10 7701
it is all full of lies and *r* Nah 3:1 6503
thought it not *r* to be equal with Phil 2:6 *725*

ROBBETH {1}
Whoso *r* his father or his mother, Prov 28:24 1497

ROBE {26}
breastplate, and an ephod, and a *r* Ex 28:4 4598
thou shalt make the *r* of the Ex 28:31 4598
upon the hem of the *r* round about Ex 28:34 4598
the *r* of the ephod, and the ephod, Ex 29:5 4598
he made the *r* of the ephod of Ex 39:22 4598
was an hole in the midst of the *r* Ex 39:23 4598
of the *r* pomegranates of blue Ex 39:24 4598
upon the hem of the *r*, round Ex 39:25 4598
the hem of the *r* to minister in Ex 39:26 4598
girdle, and clothed him with the *r* Lev 8:7 4598
of the *r* that was upon him 1Sa 18:4 4598
off the skirt of Saul's *r* privily 1Sa 24:4 4598
see the skirt of thy *r* in my hand 1Sa 24:11 4598
that I cut off the skirt of thy *r* 1Sa 24:11 4598
clothed with a *r* of fine linen 1Chr 15:27 4598
my judgment was as a *r* and a Job 29:14 4598
And I will clothe him with thy *r* Is 22:21 3301
me with the *r* of righteousness Is 61:10 4598
throne, and he laid his *r* from him Jonah 3:6 155
ye pull off the *r* with the Mic 2:8 145
him, and put on him a scarlet *r* Mt 27:28 *5511*
him, they took the *r* off from him Mt 27:31 *5511*
servants, Bring forth the best *r* Lk 15:22 *4749*
and arrayed him in a gorgeous *r* Lk 23:11 *2066*
and they put on him a purple *r* Jn 19:2 *2440*
crown of thorns, and the purple *r* Jn 19:5 *2440*

ROBES {11}
for with such *r* were the king's 2Sa 13:18 4598
his throne, having put on their *r* 1Kin 22:10 899
but put thou on thy *r* 1Kin 22:30 899
on his throne, clothed in their *r* 2Chr 18:9 899
but put thou on thy *r* 2Chr 18:29 899
thrones, and lay away their *r* Eze 26:16 4598
which desire to walk in long *r* Lk 20:46 *4749*
white *r* were given unto every one Rev 6:11 *4749*
the Lamb, clothed with white *r* Rev 7:9 *4749*
which are arrayed in white *r* Rev 7:13 *4749*
and have washed their *r*, and made Rev 7:14 *4749*

ROBOAM *(ro-bo'-am)* {2} See REHOBOAM. *Same as Rehoboam; an ancestor of Jesus.*
And Solomon begat *R* Mt 1:7 *4497*
and *R* begat Abia Mt 1:7 *4497*

ROCK {119}
thee there upon the *r* in Horeb Ex 17:6 6697
and thou shalt smite the *r* Ex 17:6 6697
me, and thou shalt stand upon a *r* Ex 33:21 6697
will put thee in a clift of the *r* Ex 33:22 6697
ye unto the *r* before their eyes Num 20:8 5553
forth to them water out of the *r* Num 20:8 5553
together before the *r*, and he said Num 20:10 5553
we fetch you water out of this *r* Num 20:10 5553
with his rod he smote the *r* twice Num 20:11 5553
and thou puttest thy nest in a *r* Num 24:21 5553
forth water out of the *r* of flint Deut 8:15 6697
He is the *R*, his work is perfect Deut 32:4 6697
him to suck honey out of the *r* Deut 32:13 5553
and oil out of the flinty *r* Deut 32:13 6697
esteemed the *R* of his salvation Deut 32:15 6697
Of the *R* that begat thee thou art Deut 32:18 6697
except their *R* had sold them, and Deut 32:30 6697
For their *r* is not as our *R*, Deut 32:31 6697
their *r* in whom they trusted, Deut 32:37 6697
going up to Akrabbim, from the *r* Judg 1:36 5553
cakes, and lay them upon this *r* Judg 6:20 5553
there rose up fire out of the *r* Judg 6:21 6697
thy God upon the top of this *r* Judg 6:26 4581
and they slew Oreb upon the *r* Oreb Judg 7:25 6697
offered it upon a *r* unto the LORD Judg 13:19 6697
and dwelt in the top of the *r* Etam Judg 15:8 5553
went to the top of the *r* Etam Judg 15:11 5553
and brought him up from the *r* Judg 15:13 5553
wilderness unto the *r* of Rimmon Judg 20:45 5553
the wilderness unto the *r* Rimmon Judg 20:47 5553
abode in the *r* Rimmon four months Judg 20:47 5553
that were in the *r* Rimmon Judg 21:13 5553
is there any *r* like our God 1Sa 2:2 6697
was a sharp *r* on the one side 1Sa 14:4 5553
a sharp *r* on the other side 1Sa 14:4 5553
wherefore he came down into a *r* 1Sa 23:25 5553
and spread it for her upon the *r* 2Sa 21:10 6697
And he said, The LORD is my *r* 2Sa 22:2 5553
The God of my *r* 2Sa 22:3 6697
and who is a *r*, save our God 2Sa 22:32 6697
and blessed be my *r* 2Sa 22:47 6697
the God of the *r* of my salvation 2Sa 22:47 6697
the *R* of Israel spake to me, He 2Sa 23:3 6697
went down to the *r* to David 1Chr 11:15 6697
them unto the top of the *r* 2Chr 25:12 5553
them down from the top of the *r* 2Chr 25:12 5553
out of the *r* for their thirst Neh 9:15 5553
the *r* is removed out of his place Job 14:18 6697
shall the *r* be removed out of his Job 18:4 6697
pen and lead in the *r* for ever Job 19:24 6697
embrace the *r* for want of a Job 24:8 6697
putteth forth his hand upon the *r* Job 28:9 2496
the *r* poured me out rivers of oil Job 29:6 6697
wild goats of the *r* bring forth Job 39:1 5553
She dwelleth and abideth on the *r* Job 39:28 5553
upon the crag of the *r* Job 39:28 5553
The LORD is my *r*, and my fortress, Ps 18:2 5553
or who is a *r* save our God Ps 18:31 6697
and blessed be my *r* Ps 18:46 6697
he shall set me up upon a *r* Ps 27:5 6697
Unto thee will I cry, O LORD my *r* Ps 28:1 6697
be thou my strong *r*, for an house Ps 31:2 6697
For thou art my *r* and my fortress Ps 31:3 5553
clay, and set my feet upon a *r* Ps 40:2 5553
I will say unto God my *r*, Why Ps 42:9 5553
lead me to the *r* that is higher Ps 61:2 6697
He only is my *r* and my salvation Ps 62:2 6697
He only is my *r* and my salvation Ps 62:6 6697
the *r* of my strength, and my Ps 62:7 6697
to save me, for thou art my *r* Ps 71:3 5553
brought streams also out of the *r* Ps 78:16 5553
Behold, he smote the *r*, that the Ps 78:20 6697
remembered that God was their *r* Ps 78:35 6697
with honey out of the *r* should I Ps 81:16 6697
my God, and the *r* of my salvation Ps 89:26 6697
he is my *r*, and there is no Ps 92:15 6697
and my God is the *r* of my refuge Ps 94:22 6697
noise to the *r* of our salvation Ps 95:1 6697
He opened the *r*, and the waters Ps 105:41 6697
Which turned the *r* into a Ps 114:8 6697
the way of a serpent upon a *r* Prov 30:19 6697
that art in the clefts of the *r* Song 2:14 5553
Enter into the *r*, and hide thee in Is 2:10 6697
for a *r* of offence to both the Is 8:14 6697
of Midian at the *r* of Oreb Is 10:26 6697
mindful of the *r* of thy strength Is 17:10 6697
an habitation for himself in a *r* Is 22:16 5553
of a great *r* in a weary land Is 32:2 5553
let the inhabitants of the *r* sing Is 42:11 5553
to flow out of the *r* for them Is 48:21 6697
he clave the *r* also, and the Is 48:21 6697
look unto the *r* whence ye are Is 51:1 6697
made their faces harder than a *r* Jer 5:3 5553
hide it there in a hole of the *r* Jer 13:4 5553
cometh from the *r* of the field Jer 18:14 6697
r of the plain, saith the LORD Jer 21:13 6697
that breaketh the *r* in pieces Jer 23:29 5553
the cities, and dwell in the *r* Jer 48:28 5553
dwellest in the clefts of the *r* Jer 49:16 5553
she set it upon the top of a *r* Eze 24:7 5553
set her blood upon the top of a *r* Eze 24:8 5553
and make her like the top of a *r* Eze 26:4 5553
make thee like the top of a *r* Eze 26:14 5558
Shall horses run upon the *r* Amos 6:12 5558
dwellest in the clefts of the *r* Obad 3 5553
which built his house upon a *r* Mt 7:24 *4073*
for it was founded upon a *r* Mt 7:25 *4073*
upon this *r* I will build my Mt 16:18 *4073*
which he had hewn out in the *r* Mt 27:60 *4073*
which was hewn out of a *r* Mk 15:46 *4073*
and laid the foundation on a *r* Lk 6:48 *4073*
for it was founded upon a *r* Lk 6:48 *4073*
And some fell upon a *r* Lk 8:6 *4073*
They on the *r* are they, which, Lk 8:13 *4073*
a stumblingstone and *r* of offence Rom 9:33 *4073*
spiritual *R* that followed them 1Cor 10:4 *4073*
and that *R* was Christ 1Cor 10:4 *4073*
a *r* of offence, even to them 1Pet 2:8 *4073*

ROCKS {23}
from the top of the *r* I see him Num 23:9 6697
in caves, and in thickets, and in *r* 1Sa 13:6 5553
his men upon the *r* of the wild 1Sa 24:2 6697
in pieces the *r* before the LORD 1Kin 19:11 5553
He cutteth out rivers among the *r* Job 28:10 6697
caves of the earth, and in the *r* Job 30:6 3710
He clave the *r* in the wilderness, Ps 78:15 6697
and the *r* for the conies Ps 104:18 5553
make they their houses in the *r* Prov 30:26 5553
shall go into the holes of the *r* Is 2:19 6697
To go into the clefts of the *r* Is 2:21 6697
and into the tops of the ragged *r* Is 2:21 5553
valleys, and in the holes of the *r* Is 7:19 5553

shall be the munitions of *r* .... Is 33:16 5553
valleys under the clifts of the *r* .... Is 57:5 5553
thickets, and climb up upon the *r* .... Jer 4:29 3710
and out of the holes of the *r* .... Jer 16:16 5553
and roll thee down from the *r* .... Jer 51:25 5553
the *r* are thrown down by him .... Nah 1:6 6697
earth did quake, and the *r* rent .... Mt 27:51 *4073*
lest we should have fallen upon *r* .... Acts 27:29 *5138,5117*
in the *r* of the mountains .... Rev 6:15 *4073*
And said to the mountains and *r* .... Rev 6:16 *4073*

ROD {86}
And he said, A *r* .... Ex 4:2 4294
it, and it became a *r* in his hand .... Ex 4:4 4294
shalt take this *r* in thine hand .... Ex 4:17 4294
Moses took the *r* of God in his .... Ex 4:20 4294
shall say unto Aaron, Take thy *r* .... Ex 7:9 4294
cast down his *r* before Pharaoh .... Ex 7:10 4294
they cast down every man his *r* .... Ex 7:12 4294
but Aaron's *r* swallowed up their .... Ex 7:12 4294
the *r* which was turned to a .... Ex 7:15 4294
I will smite with the *r* that is .... Ex 7:17 4294
Moses, Say unto Aaron, Take thy *r* .... Ex 7:19 4294
and he lifted up the *r*, and smote .... Ex 7:20 4294
hand with thy *r* over the streams .... Ex 8:5 4294
Say unto Aaron, Stretch out thy *r* .... Ex 8:16 4294
stretched out his hand with his *r* .... Ex 8:17 4294
forth his *r* toward heaven .... Ex 9:23 4294
his *r* over the land of Egypt .... Ex 10:13 4294
But lift thou up thy *r*, and .... Ex 14:16 4294
and thy *r*, wherewith thou smotest .... Ex 17:5 4294
with the *r* of God in mine hand .... Ex 17:9 4294
servant, or his maid, with a *r* .... Ex 21:20 7626
of whatsoever passeth under the *r* .... Lev 27:32 7626
take of every one of them a *r* .... Num 17:2 4294
thou every man's name upon his *r* .... Num 17:2 4294
Aaron's name upon the *r* of Levi .... Num 17:3 4294
for one *r* shall be for the head .... Num 17:3 4294
come to pass, that the man's *r* .... Num 17:5 4294
their princes gave him a *r* apiece .... Num 17:6 4294
the *r* of Aaron was among their .... Num 17:6 4294
the *r* of Aaron for the house of .... Num 17:8 4294
looked, and took every man his *r* .... Num 17:9 4294
Bring Aaron's *r* again before the .... Num 17:10 4294
Take the *r*, and gather thou the .... Num 20:8 4294
Moses took the *r* from before the .... Num 20:9 4294
with his *r* he smote the rock .... Num 20:11 4294
end of the *r* that was in his hand 1Sa 14:27 4294
of the *r* that was in mine hand 1Sa 14:43 4294
chasten him with the *r* of men 2Sa 7:14 7626
Let him take his *r* away from me .... Job 9:34 7626
neither is the *r* of God upon them .... Job 21:9 7626
shalt break them with a *r* of iron .... Ps 2:9 7626
thy *r* and thy staff they comfort .... Ps 23:4 7626
the *r* of thine inheritance, which .... Ps 74:2 7626
their transgression with the *r* .... Ps 89:32 7626
The LORD shall send the *r* of thy .... Ps 110:2 4294
For the *r* of the wicked shall not .... Ps 125:3 7626
but a *r* is for the back of him .... Prov 10:13 7626
that spareth his *r* hateth his son .... Prov 13:24 7626
of the foolish is a *r* of pride .... Prov 14:3 2415
the *r* of his anger shall fail .... Prov 22:8 7626
but the *r* of correction shall .... Prov 22:15 7626
if thou beatest him with the *r* .... Prov 23:13 7626
Thou shalt beat him with the *r* .... Prov 23:14 7626
ass, and a *r* for the fool's back .... Prov 26:3 7626
The *r* and reproof give wisdom .... Prov 29:15 7626
the *r* of his oppressor, as in the .... Is 9:4 7626
the *r* of mine anger, and the staff .... Is 10:5 7626
as if the *r* should shake itself .... Is 10:15 7626
he shall smite thee with a *r* .... Is 10:24 7626
as his *r* was upon the sea, so .... Is 10:26 4294
a *r* out of the stem of Jesse .... Is 11:1 2415
the earth with the *r* of his mouth .... Is 11:4 7626
because the *r* of him that smote .... Is 14:29 7626
a staff, and the cummin with a *r* .... Is 28:27 7626
beaten down, which smote with a *r* .... Is 30:31 7626
I see a *r* of an almond tree .... Jer 1:11 4731
and Israel is the *r* of his .... Jer 10:16 7626
staff broken, and the beautiful *r* .... Jer 48:17 4731
and Israel is the *r* of his .... Jer 51:19 7626
affliction by the *r* of his wrath .... Lam 3:1 7626
the *r* hath blossomed, pride hath .... Eze 7:10 4294
risen up into a *r* of wickedness .... Eze 7:11 4294
gone out of a *r* of her branches .... Eze 19:14 4294
strong *r* to be a sceptre to rule .... Eze 19:14 4294
cause you to pass under the *r* .... Eze 20:37 7626
it contemneth the *r* of my son .... Eze 21:10 7626
if the sword contemn even the *r* .... Eze 21:13 7626
of Israel with a *r* upon the cheek .... Mic 5:1 7626
hear ye the *r*, and who hath .... Mic 6:9 4294
Feed thy people with thy *r* .... Mic 7:14 7626
shall I come unto you with a *r* 1Cor 4:21 *4464*
Aaron's *r* that budded, and the .... Heb 9:4 *4464*
shall rule them with a *r* of iron .... Rev 2:27 *4464*
was given me a reed like unto a *r* .... Rev 11:1 *4464*
rule all nations with a *r* of iron .... Rev 12:5 *4464*
shall rule them with a *r* of iron .... Rev 19:15 *4464*

RODANIM See DODANIM.

RODE {15}
they *r* upon the camels, and .... Gen 24:61 7392
sons that *r* on thirty ass colts .... Judg 10:4 7392
that *r* on threescore and ten ass .... Judg 12:14 7392
as she *r* on the ass, that she 1Sa 25:20 7392
r upon an ass, with five damsels 1Sa 25:42 7392
which *r* upon camels, and fled 1Sa 30:17 7392
Absalom *r* upon a mule, and the 2Sa 18:9 7392
he *r* upon a cherub, and did fly 2Sa 22:11 7392
and he *r* thereon, ... 1Kin 13:13 7392
And Ahab *r*, and went to Jezreel 1Kin 18:45 7392
So Jehu *r* in a chariot, and went 2Kin 9:16 7392
thou *r* together after Ahab his 2Kin 9:25 7392
me, save the beast that I *r* upon .... Neh 2:12 7392
So the posts that *r* upon mules .... Est 8:14 7392
he *r* upon a cherub, and did fly .... Ps 18:10 7392

RODS {15}
Jacob took him *r* of green poplar, ... Gen 30:37 4731
white appear which was in the *r* .... Gen 30:37 4731
he set the *r* which he had pilled .... Gen 30:38 4731
the flocks conceived before the *r* .... Gen 30:39 4731
that Jacob laid the *r* before the .... Gen 30:41 4731
they might conceive among the *r* .... Gen 30:41 4731
Aaron's rod swallowed up their *r* .... Ex 7:12 4294
house of their fathers twelve *r* .... Num 17:2 4294
fathers' houses, even twelve *r* .... Num 17:6 4294
rod of Aaron was among their *r* .... Num 17:6 4294
Moses laid up the *r* before the .... Num 17:7 4294
Moses brought out all the *r* from .... Num 17:9 4294
she had strong *r* for the sceptres .... Eze 19:11 4294
her strong *r* were broken and .... Eze 19:12 4294
Thrice was I beaten with *r* 2Cor 11:25 *4463*

ROE {7}
was as light of foot as a wild *r* 2Sa 2:18 6643
as the loving hind and pleasant *r* .... Prov 5:19 3280
Deliver thyself as a *r* from the .... Prov 6:5 6643
is like a *r* or a young hart .... Song 2:9 6643
be thou like a *r* or a young hart .... Song 2:17 6643
be thou like to a *r* or to a young .... Song 8:14 6643
And it shall be as the chased *r* .... Is 13:14 6643

ROEBUCK {4}
may eat thereof, as of the *r* .... Deut 12:15 6643
Even as the *r* and the hart is .... Deut 12:22 6643
The hart, and the *r*, and the fallow .... Deut 14:5 6643
shall eat it alike, as the *r* .... Deut 15:22 6643

ROEBUCKS {1}
hundred sheep, beside harts, and *r* 1Kin 4:23 6643

ROES {5}
swift as the *r* upon the mountains 1Chr 12:8 6643
daughters of Jerusalem, by the *r* .... Song 2:7 6643
daughters of Jerusalem, by the *r* .... Song 3:5 6643
like two young *r* that are twins .... Song 4:5 6646
like two young *r* that are twins .... Song 7:3 6646

ROGELIM *(ro'-ghel-im)* {2} *A city in Gilead.*
and Barzillai the Gileadite of *R* 2Sa 17:27 7274
the Gileadite came down from *R* 2Sa 19:31 7274

ROHGAH *(ro'-gah)* {1} *A son of Shamer.*
Ahi, and *R*, Jehubbah, and Aram 1Chr 7:34 7303

ROLL {28}
till they *r* the stone from the .... Gen 29:8 1556
R great stones upon the mouth of .... Josh 10:18 1556
r a great stone unto me this day 1Sa 14:33 1556
in the province of the Medes, a *r* .... Ezr 6:2 4040
said unto me, Take thee a great *r* .... Is 8:1 1549
Take thee a *r* of a book, and write .... Jer 36:2 4039
unto him, upon a *r* of a book .... Jer 36:4 4039
go thou, and read in the *r* .... Jer 36:6 4039
Take in thine hand the *r* wherein .... Jer 36:14 4039
of Neriah took the *r* in his hand .... Jer 36:14 4039
but they laid up the *r* in the .... Jer 36:20 4039
king sent Jehudi to fetch the *r* .... Jer 36:21 4039
until all the *r* was consumed in .... Jer 36:23 4039
king that he would not burn the *r* .... Jer 36:25 4039
that the king had burned the *r* .... Jer 36:27 4039
Take thee again another *r* .... Jer 36:28 4039
words that were in the first *r* .... Jer 36:28 4039
Thou hast burned this *r*, saying, ... Jer 36:29 4039
Then took Jeremiah another *r* .... Jer 36:32 4039
r thee down from the rocks, and .... Jer 51:25 1556
a *r* of a book was therein .... Eze 2:9 4040
eat this *r*, and go speak unto the .... Eze 3:1 4040
and he caused me to eat that *r* .... Eze 3:2 4040
with this *r* that I give thee .... Eze 3:3 4040
of Aphrah *r* thyself in the dust .... Mic 1:10 6428
and looked, and behold a flying *r* .... Zec 5:1 4040
And I answered, I see a flying *r* .... Zec 5:2 4040
Who shall *r* us away the stone .... Mk 16:3 *617*

ROLLED {12}
they *r* the stone from the well's .... Gen 29:3 1556
r the stone from the well's mouth .... Gen 29:10 1556
This day have I *r* away the .... Josh 5:9 1556
they *r* themselves upon me .... Job 30:14 1556
noise, and garments *r* in blood .... Is 9:5 1556
shall be *r* together as a scroll .... Is 34:4 1556
he *r* a great stone to the door of .... Mt 27:60 *4351*
r back the stone from the door, ... Mt 28:2 *617*
r a stone unto the door of the .... Mk 15:46 *4351*
saw that the stone was *r* away .... Mk 16:4 *617*
they found the stone *r* away from .... Lk 24:2 *617*
as a scroll when it is *r* together .... Rev 6:14 *1507*

ROLLER {1}
to put a *r* to bind it, to make it .... Eze 30:21 2848

ROLLETH {1}
and he that *r* a stone, it will .... Prov 26:27 1556

ROLLING {1}
like a *r* thing before the .... Is 17:13 1534

ROLLS {1}
was made in the house of the *r* .... Ezr 6:1 5609

ROMAMTI-EZER *(romam'-ti-e'-zur)* {2} *A sanctuary servant.*
Hanani, Eliathah, Giddalti, and *R* 1Chr 25:4 7320
The four and twentieth to *R* 1Chr 25:31 7320

ROMAN *(ro'-mun)* {5} See ROMANS. *A citizen of Rome.*
you to scourge a man that is a *R* .... Acts 22:25 *4514*
for this man is a *R* .... Acts 22:26 *4514*
unto him, Tell me, art thou a *R* .... Acts 22:27 *4514*
after he knew that he was a *R* .... Acts 22:29 *4514*
having understood that he was a *R* .... Acts 23:27 *4514*

ROMANS *(ro'-muns)* {7}
the *R* shall come and take away .... Jn 11:48 *4514*
neither to observe, being *R* .... Acts 16:21 *4514*
us openly uncondemned, being *R* .... Acts 16:37 *4514*
when they heard that they were *R* .... Acts 16:38 *4514*
the *R* to deliver any man to die .... Acts 25:16 *4514*
Jerusalem into the hands of the *R* .... Acts 28:17 *4514*
Written to the *R* from Corinthus .... Rom *s* *4514*

ROME *(rome)* {15} See ROMAN. *Administrative center of the Roman Empire.*
about Cyrene, and strangers of *R* .... Acts 2:10 *4516*
all Jews to depart from *R* .... Acts 18:2 *4516*
been there, I must also see *R* .... Acts 19:21 *4516*
must thou bear witness also at *R* .... Acts 23:11 *4516*
and so we went toward *R* .... Acts 28:14 *4516*
And when we came to *R*, the .... Acts 28:16 *4516*
To all that be in *R*, beloved of .... Rom 1:7 *4516*
gospel to you that are at *R* also .... Rom 1:15 *4516*
Unto the Galatians written from *R* .... Gal *s* *4516*
Written from *R* unto the Ephesians .... Eph *s* *4516*
from *R* by Epaphroditus .... Phil *s* *4516*
Written from *R* to the Colossians .... Col *s* *4516*
But, when he was in *R*, he sought 2Ti 1:17 *4516*
the Ephesians, was written from *R* .... 2Ti *s* *4516*
Written from *R* to Philemon .... Philem *s* *4516*

ROMPHA See REMPHAN.

ROOF {20}
they under the shadow of my *r* .... Gen 19:8 6982
shalt make a battlement for thy *r* .... Deut 22:8 1406
them up to the *r* of the house .... Josh 2:6 1406
she had laid in order upon the *r* .... Josh 2:6 1406
she came up unto them upon the *r* .... Josh 2:8 1406
there were upon the *r* about three .... Judg 16:27 1406
walked upon the *r* of the king's 2Sa 11:2 1406
from the *r* he saw a woman washing 2Sa 11:2 1406
the *r* over the gate unto the wall 2Sa 18:24 1406
every one upon the *r* of his house .... Neh 8:16 1406
cleaved to the *r* of their mouth .... Job 29:10 2441
cleave to the *r* of my mouth .... Ps 137:6 2441
the *r* of thy mouth like the best .... Song 7:9 2441
to the *r* of his mouth for thirst .... Lam 4:4 2441
cleave to the *r* of thy mouth .... Eze 3:26 2441
r of one little chamber to the .... Eze 40:13 1406
chamber to the *r* of another .... Eze 40:13 1406
thou shouldest come under my *r* .... Mt 8:8 *4721*
they uncovered the *r* where he was .... Mk 2:4 *4721*
thou shouldest enter under my *r* .... Lk 7:6 *4721*

ROOFS {2}
of all the houses upon whose *r* .... Jer 19:13 1406
upon whose *r* they have offered .... Jer 32:29 1406

ROOM {32}
is there *r* in thy father's house .... Gen 24:23 4725
enough, and *r* to lodge in .... Gen 24:25 4725
the house, and *r* for the camels .... Gen 24:31 4725
now the LORD hath made *r* for us .... Gen 26:22 7337
me continually in the *r* of Joab 2Sa 19:13 8478
Jehoiada in his *r* over the host 1Kin 2:35 8478
the king put in the *r* of Abiathar 1Kin 2:35 8478
him king in the *r* of his father 1Kin 5:1 8478
will set upon thy throne in thy *r* 1Kin 5:5 8478
up in the *r* of David my father 1Kin 8:20 8478
anoint to be prophet in thy *r* 1Kin 19:16 8478
killed him, and reigned in his *r* 2Kin 15:25 8478
in the *r* of Josiah his father 2Kin 23:34 8478
up in the *r* of David my father 2Chr 6:10 8478
made him king in the *r* of his 2Chr 26:1 8478
hast set my feet in a large *r* .... Ps 31:8 4800
Thou preparedst *r* before it .... Ps 80:9
A man's gift maketh *r* for him .... Prov 18:16 7337
not be *r* enough to receive it .... Mal 3:10
in the *r* of his father Herod .... Mt 2:22 *473*
there was no *r* to receive them .... Mk 2:2 *5362*
you a large upper *r* furnished .... Mk 14:15 *508*
was no *r* for them in the inn .... Lk 2:7 *5117*
because I have no *r* where to .... Lk 12:17
sit not down in the highest *r* .... Lk 14:8 *4411*
with shame to take the lowest *r* .... Lk 14:9 *5117*
go and sit down in the lowest *r* .... Lk 14:10 *5117*
hast commanded, and yet there is *r* .... Lk 14:22 *5117*
you a large upper *r* furnished .... Lk 22:12
in, they went up into an upper *r* .... Acts 1:13 *5253*
Porcius Festus came into Felix' *r* .... Acts 24:27 *1240*
r of the unlearned say Amen at 1Cor 14:16 *5117*

ROOMS {7}
r shalt thou make in the ark, and .... Gen 6:14 7064
place, and put captains in their *r* 1Kin 20:24 8478
this day, and dwelt in their *r* 1Chr 4:41 8478
And love the uppermost *r* at feasts .... Mt 23:6 *4411*
and the uppermost *r* at feasts .... Mk 12:39 *4411*
how they chose out the chief *r* .... Lk 14:7 *4411*
and the chief *r* at feasts .... Lk 20:46 *4411*

ROOT {44}
among you a *r* that beareth gall .... Deut 29:18 8328
there a *r* of them against Amalek .... Judg 5:14 8328
he shall *r* up Israel out of this 1Kin 14:15 5428
shall yet again take *r* downward 2Kin 19:30 8328
I have seen the foolish taking *r* .... Job 5:3 8327
Though the *r* thereof wax old in .... Job 14:8 8328
seeing the *r* of the matter is .... Job 19:28 8328

R

My *r* was spread out by the waters .... Job 29:19 8328
would *r* out all mine increase .... Job 31:12 8327
r thee out of the land of the .... Ps 52:5 8327
and didst cause it to take deep *r* .... Ps 80:9 8327
but the *r* of the righteous shall .... Prov 12:3 8328
but the *r* of the righteous .... Prov 12:12 8328
so their *r* shall be as rottenness .... Is 5:24 8328
day there shall be a *r* of Jesse .... Is 11:10 8328
for out of the serpent's *r* shall .... Is 14:29 8328
and I will kill thy *r* with famine .... Is 14:30 8328
them that come of Jacob to take *r* .... Is 27:6 8327
Judah shall again take *r* downward .... Is 37:31 8328
shall not take *r* in the earth .... Is 40:24 8327
as a *r* out of a dry ground .... Is 53:2 8328
to *r* out, and to pull down, and to .... Jer 1:10 5428
them, yea, they have taken *r* .... Jer 12:2 8327
for his *r* was by great waters .... Eze 31:7 8328
their *r* is dried up, they shall .... Hos 9:16 8328
leave them neither *r* nor branch .... Mal 4:1 8328
is laid unto the *r* of the trees .... Mt 3:10 *4491*
and because they had no *r*, they .... Mt 13:6 *4491*
Yet hath he not *r* in himself .... Mt 13:21 *4491*
ye *r* up also the wheat with them .... Mt 13:29 *1610*
and because it had no *r*, it .... Mk 4:6 *4491*
have no *r* in themselves, and so .... Mk 4:17 *4491*
is laid unto the *r* of the trees .... Lk 3:9 *4491*
and these have no *r*, which for a .... Lk 8:13 *4491*
tree, Be thou plucked up by the *r* .... Lk 17:6 *1610*
if the *r* be holy, so are the .... Rom 11:16 *4491*
and with them partakest of the *r* .... Rom 11:17 *4491*
not the *r*, but the *r* thee .... Rom 11:18 *4491*
There shall be a *r* of Jesse .... Rom 15:12 *4491*
of money is the *r* of all evil 1Ti 6:10 *4491*
lest any *r* of bitterness .... Heb 12:15 *4491*
the *R* of David, hath prevailed to .... Rev 5:5 *4491*
I am the *r* and the offspring of .... Rev 22:16 *4491*

ROOTED {8}
the LORD *r* them out of their land .... Deut 29:28 5428
shall be *r* out of his tabernacle .... Job 18:14 5423
yea, let my offspring be *r* out .... Job 31:8 8327
shall be *r* out of it .... Prov 2:22 5255
noonday, and Ekron shall be *r* up .... Zeph 2:4 6131
hath not planted, shall be *r* up .... Mt 15:13 *1610*
that ye, being *r* and grounded in .... Eph 3:17 *4492*
R and built up in him, and .... Col 2:7 *4492*

ROOTS {20}
the *r* out of my land which I have 2Chr 7:20 5428
His *r* are wrapped about the heap, ... Job 8:17 8328
His *r* shall be dried up beneath, ... Job 18:16 8328
the mountains by the *r* .... Job 28:9 8328
and juniper *r* for their meat .... Job 30:4 8328
a Branch shall grow out of his *r* .... Is 11:1 8328
spreadeth out her *r* by the river .... Jer 17:8 8328
the *r* thereof were under him .... Eze 17:6 8328
vine did bend her *r* toward him .... Eze 17:7 8328
he not pull up the *r* thereof .... Eze 17:9 8328
to pluck it up by the *r* thereof .... Eze 17:9 8328
the stump of his *r* in the earth .... Dan 4:15 8330
of the *r* thereof in the earth .... Dan 4:23 8330
to leave the stump of the tree *r* .... Dan 4:26 8330
first horns plucked up by the *r* .... Dan 7:8 6132
her *r* shall one stand up in his .... Dan 11:7 8328
and cast forth his *r* as Lebanon .... Hos 14:5 8328
from above, and his *r* from beneath .... Amos 2:9 8328
the fig tree dried up from the *r* .... Mk 11:20 *4491*
twice dead, plucked up by the *r* .... Jude 12 *1610*

ROPE {1}
and sin as it were with a cart *r* .... Is 5:18 5688

ROPES {6}
new *r* that never were occupied .... Judg 16:11 5688
Delilah therefore took new *r* .... Judg 16:12 5688
all Israel bring *r* to that city 2Sa 17:13 2256
r upon our heads, and go out to 1Kin 20:31 2256
put *r* on their heads, and came to 1Kin 20:32 2256
cut off the *r* of the boat .... Acts 27:32 *4979*

ROSE {131}
that Cain *r* up against Abel his .... Gen 4:8 6965
the men *r* up from thence, and .... Gen 18:16 6965
Lot seeing them *r* up to meet them .... Gen 19:1 6965
Therefore Abimelech *r* early in .... Gen 20:8 7925
Abraham *r* up early in the morning .... Gen 21:14 7925
then Abimelech *r* up, and Phichol .... Gen 21:32 6965
Abraham *r* up early in the morning .... Gen 22:3 7925
r up, and went unto the place of .... Gen 22:3 6965
unto his young men, and they *r* up .... Gen 22:19 6965
they *r* up in the morning, and he .... Gen 24:54 6965
drink, and *r* up, and went his way .... Gen 25:34 6965
they *r* up betimes in the morning, ... Gen 26:31 7925
Jacob *r* up early in the morning, ... Gen 28:18 7925
Then Jacob *r* up, and set his sons .... Gen 31:17 6965
and he *r* up, and passed over the .... Gen 31:21 6965
early in the morning Laban *r* up .... Gen 31:55 7925
he *r* up that night, and took his .... Gen 32:22 6965
over Penuel the sun *r* upon him .... Gen 32:31 2224
his daughters *r* up to comfort him .... Gen 37:35 6965
r up, and went down to Egypt, and .... Gen 43:15 6965
Jacob *r* up from Beer-sheba .... Gen 46:5 6965
neither *r* any from his place for .... Ex 10:23 6965
Pharaoh *r* up in the night, he, and .... Ex 12:30 6965
them that *r* up against thee .... Ex 15:7 6965
r up early in the morning, and .... Ex 24:4 7925
And Moses *r* up, and his minister .... Ex 24:13 6965
they *r* up early on the morrow, and .... Ex 32:6 7925
eat and to drink, and *r* up to play .... Ex 32:6 6965
that all the people *r* up .... Ex 33:8 6965
and all the people *r* up and .... Ex 33:10 6965
Moses *r* up early in the morning, ... Ex 34:4 7925
they *r* up early in the morning, ... Num 14:40 7925
they *r* up before Moses, with .... Num 16:2 6965
And Moses *r* up and went unto .... Num 16:25 6965
Balaam *r* up in the morning, and .... Num 22:13 6965
And the princes of Moab *r* up .... Num 22:14 6965
Balaam *r* up in the morning, and .... Num 22:21 6965
And Balaam *r* up, and went and .... Num 24:25 6965
saw it, he *r* up from among the .... Num 25:7 6965
and *r* up from Seir unto them .... Deut 33:2 2224
Joshua *r* early in the morning .... Josh 3:1 7925
r up upon an heap very far from .... Josh 3:16 6965
Joshua *r* early in the morning, and .... Josh 6:12 7925
that they *r* early about the .... Josh 6:15 7925
So Joshua *r* up early in the .... Josh 7:16 7925
Joshua *r* up early in the morning, ... Josh 8:10 7925
r up early, and the men of the .... Josh 8:14 7925
there *r* up fire out of the rock, ... Judg 6:21 5927
for he *r* up early on the morrow, ... Judg 6:38 7925
r up early, and pitched beside the .... Judg 7:1 7925
And Abimelech *r* up, and all the .... Judg 9:34 6965
and Abimelech *r* up, and the people .... Judg 9:35 6965
he *r* up against them, and smote .... Judg 9:43 6965
morning, that he *r* up to depart .... Judg 19:5 6965
And when the man *r* up to depart .... Judg 19:7 6965
And when the man *r* up to depart .... Judg 19:9 6965
not tarry that night, but he *r* up .... Judg 19:10 6965
her lord *r* up in the morning, and .... Judg 19:27 6965
up upon an ass, and the man *r* up .... Judg 19:28 6965
And the men of Gibeah *r* against me .... Judg 20:5 6965
of Israel *r* up in the morning .... Judg 20:19 6965
of Israel *r* up out of their place .... Judg 20:33 6965
morrow, that the people *r* early .... Judg 21:4 7925
she *r* up before one could know .... Ruth 3:14 6965
So Hannah *r* up after they had 1Sa 1:9 6965
they *r* up in the morning early 1Sa 1:19 7925
when Samuel *r* early to meet Saul 1Sa 15:12 7925
So Samuel *r* up, and went to Ramah 1Sa 16:13 6965
David *r* up early in the morning, ... 1Sa 17:20 7925
But Saul *r* up out of the cave, and 1Sa 24:7 6965
Then they *r* up, and went away that 1Sa 28:25 6965
his men *r* up early to depart in 1Sa 29:11 7925
Absalom *r* up early, and stood 2Sa 15:2 7925
all them that *r* up against thee 2Sa 18:31 6965
them that *r* up against me hast 2Sa 22:40 6965
above them that *r* up against me 2Sa 22:49 6965
r up, and went every man his way 1Kin 1:49 6965
the king *r* up to meet her, and 1Kin 2:19 6965
when I *r* in the morning to give 1Kin 3:21 6965
that Ahab *r* up to go down to the 1Kin 21:16 6965
they *r* up early in the morning, ... 2Kin 3:22 7925
of Israel, the Israelites *r* up 2Kin 3:24 6965
they *r* up in the twilight, to go 2Kin 7:5 6965
he *r* by night, and smote the 2Kin 8:21 6965
they *r* early in the morning, and 2Chr 20:20 7925
he *r* up by night, and smote the 2Chr 21:9 6965
the leprosy even *r* up in his 2Chr 26:19 2224
which were expressed by name *r* up 2Chr 28:15 6965
Then Hezekiah the king *r* early 2Chr 29:20 7925
Then *r* up the chief of the .... Ezr 1:5 6965
Then *r* up Zerubbabel the son of .... Ezr 5:2 6965
Then Ezra *r* up from before the .... Ezr 10:6 6965
priest *r* up with his brethren the .... Neh 3:1 6965
r up, and said unto the nobles, and .... Neh 4:14 6965
r up early in the morning, and .... Job 1:5 7925
me those that *r* up against me .... Ps 18:39 6965
side, when men *r* up against us .... Ps 124:2 6965
I am the *r* of Sharon, and the lily .... Song 2:1 2261
I *r* up to open to my beloved .... Song 5:5 6965
rejoice, and blossom as the *r* .... Is 35:1 2261
Then *r* up certain of the elders .... Jer 26:17 6965
of those that *r* up against me .... Lam 3:62 6965
r up in haste, and spake, and said .... Dan 3:24 6965
afterward I *r* up, and did the .... Dan 8:27 6965
But Jonah *r* up to flee unto .... Jonah 1:3 6965
when the morning *r* the next day .... Jonah 4:7 5927
but they *r* early, and corrupted .... Zeph 3:7 7925
he, casting away his garment, *r* .... Mk 10:50 *450*
r up, and thrust him out of the .... Lk 4:29 *450*
immediately he *r* up before them .... Lk 5:25 *450*
left all, *r* up, and followed him .... Lk 5:28 *450*
though one *r* from the dead .... Lk 16:31 *450*
when he *r* up from prayer, and was .... Lk 22:45 *450*
they *r* up the same hour, and .... Lk 24:33 *450*
that she *r* up hastily and went out .... Jn 11:31 *450*
Then the high priest *r* up .... Acts 5:17 *450*
before these days *r* up Theudas .... Acts 5:36 *450*
After this man *r* up Judas of .... Acts 5:37 *450*
with him after he *r* from the dead .... Acts 10:41 *450*
stood round about him, he *r* up .... Acts 14:20 *450*
But there *r* up certain of the .... Acts 15:5 *1817*
been much disputing, Peter *r* up .... Acts 15:7 *450*
the multitude *r* up together .... Acts 16:22 *4911*
he had thus spoken, the king *r* up .... Acts 26:30 *450*
this end Christ both died, and *r* .... Rom 14:9 *450*
to eat and drink, and *r* up to play 1Cor 10:7 *450*
that he *r* again the third day 1Cor 15:4 *1453*
preached that he *r* from the dead 1Cor 15:12 *1453*
which died for them, and *r* again 2Cor 5:15 *1453*
r again, even so them also which 1Th 4:14 *450*
her smoke *r* up for ever and ever .... Rev 19:3 *305*

ROSH *(rosh)* {1} *A son of Benjamin.*
Gera, and Naaman, Ehi, and *R* .... Gen 46:21 7220

ROT {5}
the LORD doth make thy thigh to *r* .... Num 5:21 5307
belly to swell, and thy thigh to *r* .... Num 5:22 5307
shall swell, and her thigh shall *r* .... Num 5:27 5307
the name of the wicked shall *r* .... Prov 10:7 7537
chooseth a tree that will not *r* .... Is 40:20 7537

ROTTEN {5}
as a *r* thing, consumeth, as a .... Job 13:28 7538
iron as straw, and brass as *r* wood .... Job 41:27 7539
old *r* rags, and let them down by .... Jer 38:11 4418
r rags under thine armholes under .... Jer 38:12 4418
The seed is *r* under their clods, ... Joel 1:17 5685

ROTTENNESS {5}
ashamed is as *r* in his bones .... Prov 12:4 7538
but envy the *r* of the bones .... Prov 14:30 7538
so their root shall be as *r* .... Is 5:24 4716
and to the house of Judah as *r* .... Hos 5:12 7538
r entered into my bones, and I .... Hab 3:16 7538

ROUGH {7}
down the heifer unto a *r* valley .... Deut 21:4 386
he stayeth his *r* wind in the day .... Is 27:8 7186
straight, and the *r* places plain .... Is 40:4 7406
to come up as the *r* caterpillers .... Jer 51:27 5569
the *r* goat is the king of Grecia .... Dan 8:21 8163
they wear a *r* garment to deceive .... Zec 13:4 8181
the *r* ways shall be made smooth .... Lk 3:5 *5138*

ROUGHLY {6}
unto them, and spake *r* unto them .... Gen 42:7 7186
lord of the land, spake *r* to us .... Gen 42:30 7186
what if thy father answer thee *r* 1Sa 20:10 7186
And the king answered the people *r* 1Kin 12:13 7186
And the king answered them *r* 2Chr 10:13 7186
but the rich answereth *r* .... Prov 18:23 5794

ROUND {320}
of Sodom, compassed the house *r* .... Gen 19:4 5921
were in all the borders *r* about .... Gen 23:17 5439
the cities that were *r* about them .... Gen 35:5 5439
your sheaves stood *r* about .... Gen 37:7 5437
which was *r* about every city, ... Gen 41:48 5439
all the Egyptians digged *r* about .... Ex 7:24 5439
the dew lay *r* about the host .... Ex 16:13 5439
there lay a small *r* thing .... Ex 16:14 2636
bounds unto the people *r* about .... Ex 19:12 5439
upon it a crown of gold *r* about .... Ex 25:11 5439
thereto a crown of gold *r* about .... Ex 25:24 5439
border of an hand breadth *r* about .... Ex 25:25 5439
to the border thereof *r* about .... Ex 25:25 5439
All the pillars *r* about the court .... Ex 27:17 5439
woven work *r* about the hole of it .... Ex 28:32 5439
scarlet, *r* about the hem thereof .... Ex 28:33 5439
of gold between them *r* about .... Ex 28:33 5439
upon the hem of the robe *r* about .... Ex 28:34 5439
sprinkle it *r* about upon the .... Ex 29:16 5439
the blood upon the altar *r* about .... Ex 29:20 5439
and the sides thereof *r* about .... Ex 30:3 5439
unto it a crown of gold *r* about .... Ex 30:3 5439
a crown of gold to it *r* about .... Ex 37:2 5439
thereunto a crown of gold *r* about .... Ex 37:11 5439
border of an handbreadth *r* about .... Ex 37:12 5439
for the border thereof *r* about .... Ex 37:12 5439
it, and the sides thereof *r* about .... Ex 37:26 5439
unto it a crown of gold *r* about .... Ex 37:26 5439
All the hangings of the court *r* .... Ex 38:16 5439
and of the court *r* about, were of .... Ex 38:20 5439
the sockets of the court *r* about .... Ex 38:31 5439
all the pins of the court *r* about .... Ex 38:31 5439
with a band *r* about the hole, ... Ex 39:23 5439
r about between the pomegranates .... Ex 39:25 5439
r about the hem of the robe to .... Ex 39:26 5439
shalt set up the court *r* about .... Ex 40:8 5439
the court *r* about the tabernacle .... Ex 40:33 5439
sprinkle the blood *r* about upon .... Lev 1:5 5439
his blood *r* about upon the altar .... Lev 1:11 5439
the blood upon the altar *r* about .... Lev 3:2 5439
thereof *r* about upon the altar .... Lev 3:8 5439
thereof upon the altar *r* about .... Lev 3:13 5439
sprinkle *r* about upon the altar .... Lev 7:2 5439
the altar *r* about with his finger .... Lev 8:15 5439
the blood upon the altar *r* about .... Lev 8:19 5439
the blood upon the altar *r* about .... Lev 8:24 5439
which he sprinkled *r* about upon .... Lev 9:12 5439
sprinkled upon the altar *r* about .... Lev 9:18 5439
to be scraped within *r* about .... Lev 14:41 5439
the horns of the altar *r* about .... Lev 16:18 5439
Ye shall not *r* the corners of .... Lev 19:27 5362
r about them shall be counted as .... Lev 25:31 5439
the heathen that are *r* about you .... Lev 25:44 5439
it, and shall encamp *r* about the .... Num 1:50 5439
pitch *r* about the tabernacle of .... Num 1:53 5439
and by the altar *r* about, and the .... Num 3:26 5439
the pillars of the court *r* about .... Num 3:37 5439
and by the altar *r* about, and their .... Num 4:26 5439
the pillars of the court *r* about .... Num 4:32 5439
set them *r* about the tabernacle .... Num 11:24 5439
r about the camp, and as it were .... Num 11:31 5439
for themselves *r* about the camp .... Num 11:32 5439
all Israel that were *r* about them .... Num 16:34 5439
lick up all that are *r* about us .... Num 22:4 5439
the cities of the country *r* about .... Num 32:33 5439
with the coasts thereof *r* about .... Num 34:12 5439
for the cities *r* about them .... Num 35:2 5439
outward a thousand cubits *r* about .... Num 35:4 5439
the people which are *r* about you .... Deut 6:14 5439
from all your enemies *r* about .... Deut 12:10 5439
the people which are *r* about you .... Deut 13:7 5439
are *r* about him that is slain .... Deut 21:2 5439
from all thine enemies *r* about .... Deut 25:19 5439
war, and go *r* about the city once .... Josh 6:3 5362
hear of it, and shall environ us *r* .... Josh 7:9 5921
Judah *r* about according to their .... Josh 15:12 5439

by the coasts thereof *r* about Josh 18:20 5439
that were *r* about these cities to Josh 19:8 5439
the suburbs thereof *r* about Josh 21:11 5439
with their suburbs *r* about them Josh 21:42 5439
the LORD gave them rest *r* about Josh 21:44 5439
from all their enemies *r* about Josh 23:1 5439
the people that were *r* about them Judg 2:12 5439
hands of their enemies *r* about Judg 2:14 5439
man in his place *r* about the camp Judg 7:21 5439
Belial, beset the house *r* about Judg 19:22 5437
beset the house *r* about upon me Judg 20:5 5437
set liers in wait *r* about Gibeah Judg 20:29 5439
inclosed the Benjamites *r* about Judg 20:43 3803
the camp from the country *r* about 1Sa 14:21 5439
his men *r* about to take them 1Sa 23:26
and the people pitched *r* about him 1Sa 26:5 5439
and the people lay *r* about him 1Sa 26:7 5439
land of the Philistines *r* about 1Sa 31:9 5439
David built *r* about from Millo and 2Sa 5:9 5439
rest *r* about from all his enemies 2Sa 7:1 5439
darkness pavilions *r* about him 2Sa 22:12 5439
and the wall of Jerusalem *r* about 1Kin 3:1 5439
peace on all sides *r* about him 1Kin 4:24 5439
fame was in all nations *r* about 1Kin 4:31 5439
house he built chambers *r* about 1Kin 6:5 5439
the walls of the house *r* about 1Kin 6:5 5439
and he made chambers *r* about 1Kin 6:5 5439
he made narrowed rests *r* about 1Kin 6:6 5439
all the walls of the house *r* 1Kin 6:29 4524
the great court *r* about was with 1Kin 7:12 5439
two rows *r* about upon the one 1Kin 7:18 5439
were two hundred in rows *r* about 1Kin 7:20 5439
it was *r* all about, and his height 1Kin 7:23 5696
cubits did compass it *r* about 1Kin 7:23 5439
under the brim of it *r* about 1Kin 7:24 5439
cubit, compassing the sea *r* about 1Kin 7:24 5439
but the mouth thereof was *r* after 1Kin 7:31 5696
their borders, foursquare, not *r* 1Kin 7:31 5696
a *r* compass of half a cubit high 1Kin 7:35 5696
every one, and additions *r* about 1Kin 7:36 5439
top of the throne was *r* behind 1Kin 10:19 5696
the water ran *r* about the altar 1Kin 18:35 5439
chariots of fire *r* about Elisha 2Kin 6:17 5439
ye shall compass the king *r* about 2Kin 11:8 5439
r about the king, from the right 2Kin 11:11 5439
heathen that were *r* about them 2Kin 17:15 5439
in the places *r* about Jerusalem 2Kin 23:5 4524
built forts against it *r* about 2Kin 25:1 5439
were against the city *r* about 2Kin 25:4 5439
the walls of Jerusalem *r* about 2Kin 25:10 5439
upon the chapiter *r* about 2Kin 25:17 5439
that were *r* about the same cities 1Chr 4:33 5439
and the suburbs thereof *r* about it 1Chr 6:55 5439
they lodged *r* about the house of 1Chr 9:27 5439
land of the Philistines *r* about 1Chr 10:9 5439
And he built the city *r* about 1Chr 11:8 5439
about, even from Millo *r* about 1Chr 11:8 5439
rest from all his enemies *r* about 1Chr 22:9 5439
and of all the chambers *r* about 1Chr 28:12 5439
r in compass, and five cubits the 2Chr 4:2 5696
cubits did compass it *r* about 2Chr 4:2 5439
which did compass it *r* about 2Chr 4:3 5439
cubit, compassing the sea *r* about 2Chr 4:3 5439
all the cities *r* about Gerar 2Chr 14:14 5439
the LORD gave them rest *r* about 2Chr 15:15 5439
the lands that were *r* about Judah 2Chr 17:10 5439
for his God gave him rest *r* about 2Chr 20:30 5439
shall compass the king *r* about 2Chr 23:7 5439
the temple, by the king *r* about 2Chr 23:10 5439
with their mattocks *r* about 2Chr 34:6 5439
plain country *r* about Jerusalem Neh 12:28 5439
them villages *r* about Jerusalem Neh 12:29 5439
and fashioned me together *r* about Job 10:8 5439
His archers compass me *r* about Job 16:13 5437
encamp *r* about my tabernacle Job 19:12 5439
Therefore snares are *r* about thee Job 22:10 5439
it is turned *r* about by his Job 37:12 4524
his teeth are terrible *r* about Job 41:14 5439
set themselves against me *r* about Ps 3:6 5439
his pavilion *r* about him were Ps 18:11 5439
bulls of Bashan have beset me *r* Ps 22:12 3803
up above mine enemies *r* about me Ps 27:6 5439
r about them that fear him Ps 34:7 5439
to them that are *r* about us Ps 44:13 5439
about Zion, and go *r* about her Ps 48:12 5362
be very tempestuous *r* about him Ps 50:3 5439
a dog, and go *r* about the city Ps 59:6 5437
a dog, and go *r* about the city Ps 59:14 5437
let all that be *r* about him bring Ps 76:11 5439
r about their habitations Ps 78:28 5439
shed like water *r* about Jerusalem Ps 79:3 5439
to them that are *r* about us Ps 79:4 5439
They came *r* about me daily like Ps 88:17 5437
to thy faithfulness *r* about thee Ps 89:8 5439
and darkness are *r* about him Ps 97:2 5439
and burneth up his enemies *r* about Ps 97:3 5439
mountains are *r* about Jerusalem Ps 125:2 5439
so the LORD is *r* about his people Ps 125:2 5439
olive plants *r* about thy table Ps 128:3 5439
Thy navel is like a *r* goblet Song 7:2 5469
their *r* tires like the moon, Is 3:18 7720
For the cry is gone *r* about the Is 15:8 5362
I will camp against thee *r* about Is 29:3 1754
it hath set him on fire *r* about Is 42:25 5439
Lift up thine eyes *r* about Is 49:18 5439
Lift up thine eyes *r* about Is 60:4 5439
all the walls thereof *r* about Jer 1:15 5439
are they against her *r* about Jer 4:17 5439
their tents against her *r* about Jer 6:3 5439
the birds *r* about are against her Jer 12:9 5439
devour all things *r* about it Jer 21:14 5439
against all these nations *r* about Jer 25:9 5439
for fear was *r* about, saith the Jer 46:5 5439
sword shall devour *r* about thee Jer 46:14 5439
in array against Babylon *r* about Jer 50:14 5439
Shout against her *r* about Jer 50:15 5439
the bow, camp against it *r* about Jer 50:29 5439
it shall devour all *r* about him Jer 50:32 5439
they shall be against her *r* about Jer 51:2 5439
and built forts against it *r* about Jer 52:4 5439
were by the city *r* about Jer 52:7 5439
the walls of Jerusalem *r* about Jer 52:14 5439
upon the chapiters *r* about Jer 52:22 5439
network were an hundred *r* about Jer 52:23 5439
adversaries should be *r* about him Lam 1:17 5439
fire, which devoureth *r* about Lam 2:3 5439
a solemn day my terrors *r* about Lam 2:22 5439
full of eyes *r* about them four Eze 1:18 5439
of fire *r* about within it Eze 1:27 5439
and it had brightness *r* about Eze 1:27 5439
of the brightness *r* about Eze 1:28 5439
battering rams against it *r* about Eze 4:2 5439
and countries that are *r* about her Eze 5:5 5439
countries that are *r* about her Eze 5:6 5439
the nations that are *r* about you Eze 5:7 5439
the nations that are *r* about you Eze 5:7 5439
fall by the sword *r* about thee Eze 5:12 5439
the nations that are *r* about thee Eze 5:14 5439
the nations that are *r* about thee Eze 5:15 5439
your bones *r* about your altars Eze 6:5 5439
their idols *r* about their altars Eze 6:13 5439
pourtrayed upon the wall *r* about Eze 8:10 5439
wheels, were full of eyes *r* about Eze 10:12 5439
the heathen that are *r* about you Eze 11:12 5439
gather them *r* about against thee Eze 16:37 5439
and all that are *r* about her Eze 16:57 5439
which despise thee *r* about Eze 16:57 5439
and shield and helmet *r* about Eze 23:24 5439
army were upon thy walls *r* about Eze 27:11 5439
shields upon thy walls *r* about Eze 27:11 5439
of all that are *r* about them Eze 28:24 5439
that despise them *r* about them Eze 28:26 5439
rivers running *r* about his plants Eze 31:4 5439
her company is *r* about her grave Eze 32:23 5439
her multitude *r* about her grave Eze 32:24 5439
her graves are *r* about him Eze 32:25 5439
her graves are *r* about him Eze 32:26 5439
the places *r* about my hill a Eze 34:26 5439
of the heathen that are *r* about Eze 36:4 5439
Then the heathen that are left *r* Eze 36:36 5439
caused me to pass by them *r* about Eze 37:2 5439
the outside of the house *r* about Eze 40:5 5439
of the court *r* about the gate Eze 40:14 5439
posts within the gate *r* about Eze 40:16 5439
and windows were *r* about inward Eze 40:16 5439
made for the court *r* about Eze 40:17 5439
and in the arches thereof *r* about Eze 40:25 5439
and in the arches thereof *r* about Eze 40:29 5439
the arches *r* about were five and Eze 40:30 5439
and in the arches thereof *r* about Eze 40:33 5439
and the windows to it *r* about Eze 40:36 5439
an hand broad, fastened *r* about Eze 40:43 5439
r about the house on every side Eze 41:5 5439
for the side chambers *r* about Eze 41:6 5439
still upward *r* about the house Eze 41:7 5439
the height of the house *r* about Eze 41:8 5439
r about the house on every side Eze 41:10 5439
was left was five cubits *r* about Eze 41:11 5439
was five cubits thick *r* about Eze 41:12 5439
the galleries *r* about on their Eze 41:16 5439
door, cieled with wood *r* about Eze 41:16 5439
and by all the wall *r* about within Eze 41:17 5439
through all the house *r* about Eze 41:19 5439
the east, and measured it *r* about Eze 42:15 5439
with the measuring reed *r* about Eze 42:16 5439
with the measuring reed *r* about Eze 42:17 5439
it had a wall *r* about, five Eze 42:20 5439
the whole limit thereof *r* about Eze 43:12 5439
thereof *r* about shall be a span Eze 43:13 5439
and upon the border *r* about Eze 43:20 5439
all the borders thereof *r* about Eze 45:1 5439
in breadth, square *r* about Eze 45:2 5439
fifty cubits *r* about for the Eze 45:2 5439
a row of building *r* about in them Eze 46:23 5439
r about them four, and it was made Eze 46:23 5439
places under the rows *r* about Eze 46:23 5439
It was *r* about eighteen thousand Eze 48:35 5439
yourselves together *r* about Joel 3:11 5439
to judge all the heathen *r* about Joel 3:12 5439
shall be even *r* about the land Amos 3:11 5439
the depth closed me *r* about Jonah 2:5 5437
that had the waters *r* about it Nah 3:8 5439
unto her a wall of fire *r* about Zec 2:5 5439
and the cities thereof *r* about her Zec 7:7 5439
unto all the people *r* about Zec 12:2 5439
devour all the people *r* about Zec 12:6 5439
heathen *r* about shall be gathered Zec 14:14 5439
and all the region *r* about Jordan Mt 3:5 *4066*
out into all that country *r* about Mt 14:35 *4066*
a vineyard, and hedged it *r* about Mt 21:33
all the region *r* about Galilee Mk 1:28 *4066*
when he had looked *r* about on Mk 3:5 *4017*
he looked *r* about on them which Mk 3:34 *2943*
he looked *r* about to see her that Mk 5:32 *4017*
he went *r* about the villages, Mk 6:6 *2943*
may go into the country *r* about Mk 6:36 *2943*
through that whole region *r* about Mk 6:55 *4066*
when they had looked *r* about Mk 9:8 *4017*
And Jesus looked *r* about, and saith Mk 10:23 *4017*
when he had looked *r* about upon Mk 11:11 *4017*
on all that dwelt *r* about them Lk 1:65 *4039*
of the Lord shone *r* about them Lk 2:9 *4034*
through all the region *r* about Lk 4:14 *4066*
place of the country *r* about Lk 4:37 *4066*
looking *r* about upon them all, he Lk 6:10
throughout all the region *r* about Lk 7:17 *4066*
r about besought him to depart Lk 8:37 *4066*
into the towns and country *r* about Lk 9:12 *2943*
about thee, and compass thee *r* Lk 19:43 *4033*
Then came the Jews *r* about him Jn 10:24 *2944*
the cities *r* about unto Jerusalem Acts 5:16 *4038*
suddenly there shined *r* about him Acts 9:3 *4015*
the region that lieth *r* about Acts 14:6 *4066*
the disciples stood *r* about him Acts 14:20 *2944*
heaven a great light *r* about me Acts 22:6 *4015*
down from Jerusalem stood *r* about Acts 25:7 *4026*
shining *r* about me and them which Acts 26:13 *4034*
r about unto Illyricum, I have Rom 15:19 *2943*
overlaid *r* about with gold Heb 9:4 *3840*
was a rainbow *r* about the throne Rev 4:3 *2943*
r about the throne were four and Rev 4:4 *2943*
r about the throne, were four Rev 4:6 *2943*
of many angels *r* about the throne Rev 5:11 *2943*
angels stood *r* about the throne Rev 7:11 *2943*

ROUSE {1}
who shall *r* him up Gen 49:9 6965

ROVERS {1}
David against the band of the *r* 1Chr 12:21

ROW {17}
the first *r* shall be a sardius, a Ex 28:17 2905
this shall be the first *r* Ex 28:17 2905
the second *r* shall be an emerald, Ex 28:18 2905
And the third *r* a ligure, an agate Ex 28:19 2905
And the fourth *r* a beryl, and an Ex 28:20 2905
the first *r* was a sardius, a Ex 39:10 2905
this was the first *r* Ex 39:10 2905
And the second *r*, an emerald, a Ex 39:11 2905
And the third *r*, a ligure, an Ex 39:12 2905
And the fourth *r*, a beryl, an onyx Ex 39:13 2905
set them in two rows, six on a *r* Lev 24:6 4635
put pure frankincense upon each *r* Lev 24:7 4635
stone, and a *r* of cedar beams 1Kin 6:36 2905
five pillars, fifteen in a *r* 1Kin 7:3 2905
a *r* of cedar beams, both for the 1Kin 7:12 2905
stones, and a *r* of new timber Ezr 6:4 5073
there was a *r* of building round Eze 46:23 2905

ROWED {2}
Nevertheless the men *r* hard to Jonah 1:13 2864
So when they had *r* about five Jn 6:19 *1643*

ROWERS {1}
Thy *r* have brought thee into Eze 27:26 7751

ROWING {1}
And he saw them toiling in *r* Mk 6:48 *1643*

ROWS {16}
of stones, even four *r* of stones Ex 28:17 2905
they set in it four *r* of stones Ex 39:10 2905
And thou shalt set them in two *r* Lev 24:6 4634
court with three *r* of hewed stone 1Kin 6:36 2905
upon four *r* of cedar pillars, 1Kin 7:2 2905
And there were windows in three *r* 1Kin 7:4 2905
was with three *r* of hewed stones 1Kin 7:12 2905
two *r* round about upon the one 1Kin 7:18 2905
were two hundred in *r* round about 1Kin 7:20 2905
the knops were cast in two *r* 1Kin 7:24 2905
even two *r* of pomegranates for 1Kin 7:42 2905
Two *r* of oxen were cast, when it 2Chr 4:3 2905
two *r* of pomegranates on each 2Chr 4:13 2905
With three *r* of great stones, and Ezr 6:4 5073
are comely with *r* of jewels Song 1:10 8447
places under the *r* round about Eze 46:23 2918

ROYAL {29}
fat, and he shall yield *r* dainties Gen 49:20 4428
city, as one of the *r* cities Josh 10:2 4467
dwell in the *r* city with thee 1Sa 27:5 4467
of Ammon, and took the *r* city 2Sa 12:26 4410
Solomon gave her of his *r* bounty 1Kin 10:13 4428
arose and destroyed all the seed *r* 2Kin 11:1 4467
son of Elishama, of the seed *r* 2Kin 25:25 4410
bestowed upon him such *r* majesty 1Chr 29:25 4438
the seed *r* of the house of Judah 2Chr 22:10 4467
r wine in abundance, according to Est 1:7 4438
r house which belonged to king Est 1:9 4438
before the king with the crown *r* Est 1:11 4438
let there go a *r* commandment from Est 1:19 4438
let the king give her *r* estate Est 1:19 4438
his house *r* in the tenth month Est 2:16 4438
so that he set the *r* crown upon Est 2:17 4438
that Esther put on her *r* apparel Est 5:1 4438
his *r* throne in the *r* house Est 5:1 4438
Let the *r* apparel be brought Est 6:8 4438
the crown *r* which is set upon his Est 6:8 4438
of the king in *r* apparel of blue Est 8:15 4438
a *r* diadem in the hand of thy God Is 62:3 4410
son of Elishama, of the seed *r* Jer 41:1 4410
spread his *r* pavilion over them Jer 43:10 8237
together to establish a *r* statute Dan 6:7 4430
day Herod, arrayed in *r* apparel Acts 12:21 *937*
If ye fulfil the *r* law according Jas 2:8 *937*
a *r* priesthood, an holy nation, a 1Pet 2:9 *934*

RUBBING {1}
and did eat, *r* them in their hands Lk 6:1 *5597*

RUBBISH {2}
heaps of the *r* which are burned .... Neh 4:2 6083
is decayed, and there is much *r* .... Neh 4:10 6083

RUBIES {6}
the price of wisdom is above *r* .... Job 28:18 6443
She is more precious than *r* .... Prov 3:15 6443
For wisdom is better than *r* .... Prov 8:11 6443
is gold, and a multitude of *r* .... Prov 20:15 6443
for her price is far above *r* .... Prov 31:10 6443
were more ruddy in body than *r* .... Lam 4:7 6443

RUDDER {1}
the sea, and loosed the *r* bands .... Acts 27:40 *4079*

RUDDY {4}
Now he was *r*, and withal of a 1Sa 16:12 132
for he was but a youth, and *r* 1Sa 17:42 132
My beloved is white and *r*, the .... Song 5:10 132
they were more *r* in body than .... Lam 4:7 119

RUDE {1}
But though I be *r* in speech 2Cor 11:6 *2399*

RUDIMENTS {2}
after the *r* of the world, and not .... Col 2:8 *4747*
Christ from the *r* of the world .... Col 2:20 *4747*

RUE {1}
for ye tithe mint and *r* and all .... Lk 11:42 *4076*

RUFUS *(ru'-fus)* {2}
1. Son of Simon the Cyrenian.
the father of Alexander and *R* .... Mk 15:21 *4504*
2. A Christian in Rome.
Salute *R* chosen in the Lord, and .... Rom 16:13 *4504*

RUHAMAH *(ru-ha'-mah)* {1} *A symbolic name of Israel.*
and to your sisters, *R* .... Hos 2:1 7355

RUIN {11}
But they were the *r* of him 2Chr 28:23
brought his strong holds to *r* .... Ps 89:40 4288
and who knoweth the *r* of them both .... Prov 24:22 6365
and a flattering mouth worketh *r* .... Prov 26:28 4072
let this *r* be under thy hand .... Is 3:6 4384
and he brought it to *r* .... Is 23:13 4654
of a defenced city a *r* .... Is 25:2 4654
so iniquity shall not be your *r* .... Eze 18:30 4383
of the seas in the day of thy *r* .... Eze 27:27 4658
Upon his *r* shall all the fowls of .... Eze 31:13 4658
the *r* of that house was great .... Lk 6:49 *4485*

RUINED {3}
For Jerusalem is *r*, and Judah is .... Is 3:8 3782
r cities are become fenced, and .... Eze 36:35 2040
I the LORD build the *r* places .... Eze 36:36 2040

RUINOUS {3}
waste fenced cities into *r* heaps 2Kin 19:25 5327
a city, and it shall be a *r* heap .... Is 17:1 4654
defenced cities into *r* heaps .... Is 37:26 5327

RUINS {3}
faint, and their *r* be multiplied .... Eze 21:15 4383
and I will raise up his *r*, and I .... Amos 9:11 2034
I will build again the *r* thereof .... Acts 15:16 *2679*

RULE {66}
the greater light to *r* the day .... Gen 1:16 4475
the lesser light to *r* the night .... Gen 1:16 4475
to *r* over the day and over the .... Gen 1:18 4910
husband, and he shall *r* over thee .... Gen 3:16 4910
desire, and thou shalt *r* over him .... Gen 4:7 4910
Thou shalt not *r* over him with .... Lev 25:43 7287
ye shall not *r* one over another .... Lev 25:46 7287
the other shall not *r* with rigour .... Lev 25:53 7287
R thou over us, both thou, and thy .... Judg 8:22 4910
unto them, I will not *r* over you .... Judg 8:23 4910
neither shall my son *r* over you .... Judg 8:23 4910
the LORD shall *r* over you .... Judg 8:23 4910
which bare *r* over the people that 1Kin 9:23 7287
that had *r* over his chariots 1Kin 22:31
that bare *r* over the people 2Chr 8:10 7287
servants bare *r* over the people .... Neh 5:15 7980
should bear *r* in his own house .... Est 1:22 8323
that the Jews had *r* over them .... Est 9:1 7980
r thou in the midst of thine .... Ps 110:2 7287
The sun to *r* by day .... Ps 136:8 4475
The moon and stars to *r* by night .... Ps 136:9 4475
By me princes *r*, and nobles, even .... Prov 8:16 8323
hand of the diligent shall bear *r* .... Prov 12:24 4910
A wise servant shall have *r* over .... Prov 17:2 4910
a servant to have *r* over princes .... Prov 19:10 4910
He that hath no *r* over his own .... Prov 25:28 4623
but when the wicked beareth *r* .... Prov 29:2 4910
yet shall he have *r* over all my .... Eccl 2:19 7980
and babes shall *r* over them .... Is 3:4 4910
oppressors, and women *r* over them .... Is 3:12 4910
and they shall *r* over their .... Is 14:2 7287
a fierce king shall *r* over them .... Is 19:4 4910
that *r* this people which is in .... Is 28:14 4910
and princes shall *r* in judgment .... Is 32:1 8323
hand, and his arm shall *r* for him .... Is 40:10 4910
him, and made him *r* over kings .... Is 41:2 7287
carpenter stretcheth out his *r* .... Is 44:13 4910
they that *r* over them make them .... Is 52:5 4910
thou never barest *r* over them .... Is 63:19 4910
the priests bear *r* by their means .... Jer 5:31 7287
the sceptres of them that bare *r* .... Eze 19:11 4910
strong rod to be a sceptre to *r* .... Eze 19:14 4910
poured out, will I *r* over you .... Eze 20:33 4427
shall no more *r* over the nations .... Eze 29:15 7287
which shall bear *r* over all the .... Dan 2:39 7981
have known that the heavens do *r* .... Dan 4:26 7990
that shall *r* with great dominion, ... Dan 11:3 4910
shall cause them to *r* over many .... Dan 11:39 4910
the heathen should *r* over them .... Joel 2:17 4910
and shall sit and *r* upon his throne .... Zec 6:13 4910
that shall *r* my people Israel .... Mt 2:6 *4165*
to *r* over the Gentiles exercise .... Mk 10:42 *757*
when he shall have put down all *r* 1Cor 15:24 *746*
r which God hath distributed to 2Cor 10:13 *2583*
you according to our *r* abundantly 2Cor 10:15 *2583*
many as walk according to this *r* .... Gal 6:16 *2583*
let us walk by the same *r* .... Phil 3:16 *2583*
the peace of God *r* in your hearts .... Col 3:15 *1018*
know not how to *r* his own house 1Ti 3:5 *4291*
Let the elders that *r* well be 1Ti 5:17 *4291*
them which have the *r* over you .... Heb 13:7 *2233*
them that have the *r* over you .... Heb 13:17 *2233*
all them that have the *r* over you .... Heb 13:24 *2233*
he shall *r* them with a rod of .... Rev 2:27 *4165*
who was to *r* all nations with a .... Rev 12:5 *4165*
he shall *r* them with a rod of .... Rev 19:15 *4165*

RULED {13}
that *r* over all that he had, Put, ... Gen 24:2 4910
thy word shall all my people be *r* .... Gen 41:40 5401
r from Aroer, which is upon the .... Josh 12:2 4910
in the days when the judges *r* .... Ruth 1:1 8199
which *r* over the people that 1Kin 5:16 7287
that *r* throughout the house of 1Chr 26:6 4474
which have *r* over all countries .... Ezr 4:20 7990
they that hated them *r* over them .... Ps 106:41 4910
he that *r* the nations in anger, ... Is 14:6 7287
Servants have *r* over us .... Lam 5:8 4910
and with cruelty have ye *r* them .... Eze 34:4 7287
high God *r* in the kingdom of men .... Dan 5:21 7990
to his dominion which he *r* .... Dan 11:4 4910

RULER {84}
he made him *r* over all the land .... Gen 41:43
he said to the *r* of his house .... Gen 43:16 834,5921
a *r* throughout all the land of .... Gen 45:8 4910
nor curse the *r* of thy people .... Ex 22:28 5387
When a *r* hath sinned, and done .... Lev 4:22 5387
a man, every one a *r* among them .... Num 13:2 5387
when Zebul the *r* of the city .... Judg 9:30 8269
have appointed thee *r* over Israel 1Sa 25:30 5057
to appoint me *r* over the people 2Sa 6:21 5057
to be *r* over my people, over 2Sa 7:8 5057
Jairite was a chief *r* about David 2Sa 20:26
appointed him to be *r* over Israel 1Kin 1:35 5057
he made him *r* over all the charge 1Kin 11:28 6485
of Ahikam, the son of Shaphan, *r* 2Kin 25:22 6485
and of him came the chief *r* 1Chr 5:2 5057
the *r* of the house of God 1Chr 9:11 5057
was the *r* over them in time past 1Chr 9:20 5057
thou shalt be *r* over my people 1Chr 11:2 5057
be *r* over my people Israel 1Chr 17:7 5057
of Moses, was *r* of the treasures 1Chr 26:24 5057
his course was Mikloth also the *r* 1Chr 27:4 5057
the *r* of the Reubenites was 1Chr 27:16 5057
he hath chosen Judah to be the *r* 1Chr 28:4 5057
to be a *r* over my people Israel 2Chr 6:5 5057
fail thee a man to be *r* in Israel 2Chr 7:18 4910
to be *r* among his brethren 2Chr 11:22 5057
the *r* of the house of Judah, for 2Chr 19:11 5057
the scribe and Maaseiah the *r* 2Chr 26:11 7860
which Cononiah the Levite was *r* 2Chr 31:12 5057
Azariah the *r* of the house of God 2Chr 31:13 5057
the *r* of the half part of .... Neh 3:9 8269
the *r* of the half part of .... Neh 3:12 8269
the *r* of part of Beth-haccerem .... Neh 3:14 8269
Colhozeh, the *r* of part of Mizpah .... Neh 3:15 8269
the *r* of the half part of .... Neh 3:16 8269
the *r* of the half part of Keilah, ... Neh 3:17 8269
the *r* of the half part of Keilah .... Neh 3:18 8269
the *r* of Mizpah, another piece .... Neh 3:19 8269
Hananiah the *r* of the palace, ... Neh 7:2 8269
was the *r* of the house of God .... Neh 11:11 5057
is little Benjamin with their *r* .... Ps 68:27 7287
even the *r* of the people, and let .... Ps 105:20 4910
house, and *r* of all his substance .... Ps 105:21 4910
having no guide, overseer, or *r* .... Prov 6:7 4910
When thou sittest to eat with a *r* .... Prov 23:1 4910
so is a wicked *r* over the poor .... Prov 28:15 4910
If a *r* hearken to lies, all his .... Prov 29:12 4910
of the *r* rise up against thee .... Eccl 10:4 4910
error which proceedeth from the *r* .... Eccl 10:5 7989
Thou hast clothing, be thou our *r* .... Is 3:6 7101
make me not a *r* of the people .... Is 3:7 7101
Send ye the lamb to the *r* of the .... Is 16:1 4910
in the land, *r* against *r* .... Jer 51:46 4910
there is no king, lord, nor *r* .... Dan 2:10 7990
and hath made thee *r* over them all .... Dan 2:38 7981
made him *r* over the whole .... Dan 2:48 7981
be the third *r* in the kingdom .... Dan 5:7 7981
be the third *r* in the kingdom .... Dan 5:16 7981
be the third *r* in the kingdom .... Dan 5:29 7990
unto me that is to be *r* in Israel .... Mic 5:2 4910
things, that have no *r* over them .... Hab 1:14 4910
behold, there came a certain *r* .... Mt 9:18 *758*
hath made *r* over his household .... Mt 24:45 *2525*
make him *r* over all his goods .... Mt 24:47 *2525*
will make thee *r* over many things .... Mt 25:21 *2525*
will make thee *r* over many things .... Mt 25:23 *2525*
there came from the *r* of the .... Mk 5:35 *752*
saith unto the *r* of the synagogue .... Mk 5:36 *752*
house of the *r* of the synagogue .... Mk 5:38 *752*
he was a *r* of the synagogue .... Lk 8:41 *758*
the *r* of the synagogue's house .... Lk 8:49 *752*
shall make *r* over his household .... Lk 12:42 *2525*
make him *r* over all that he hath .... Lk 12:44 *2525*
the *r* of the synagogue answered .... Lk 13:14 *752*
And a certain *r* asked him, saying, ... Lk 18:18 *758*
When the *r* of the feast had .... Jn 2:9 *755*
named Nicodemus, a *r* of the Jews .... Jn 3:1 *758*
away, saying, Who made thee a *r* .... Acts 7:27 *758*
saying, Who made thee a *r* .... Acts 7:35 *758*
the same did God send to be a *r* .... Acts 7:35 *758*
the chief *r* of the synagogue, ... Acts 18:8 *758*
the chief *r* of the synagogue, and .... Acts 18:17 *752*
speak evil of the *r* of thy people .... Acts 23:5 *758*

RULER'S {2}
Many seek the *r* favour .... Prov 29:26 4910
when Jesus came into the *r* house .... Mt 9:23 *758*

RULERS {80}
then make them *r* over my cattle .... Gen 47:6 8269
all the *r* of the congregation .... Ex 16:22 5387
to be *r* of thousands .... Ex 18:21 8269
r of hundreds, *r* of fifties, ... Ex 18:21 8269
r of fifties, and *r* of tens .... Ex 18:21 8269
r of thousands .... Ex 18:25 8269
r of hundreds, *r* of fifties, ... Ex 18:25 8269
r of fifties, and *r* of tens .... Ex 18:25 8269
all the *r* of the congregation .... Ex 34:31 5387
the *r* brought onyx stones, and .... Ex 35:27 5387
and I will make them *r* over you .... Deut 1:13 7218
the Philistines are *r* over us .... Judg 15:11 4910
and David's sons were chief *r* 2Sa 8:18
r of his chariots, and his 1Kin 9:22 8269
unto the *r* of Jezreel, to the 2Kin 10:1 8269
fetched the *r* over hundreds, with 2Kin 11:4 8269
he took the *r* over hundreds, and 2Kin 11:19 8269
to the *r* of the people, Go, ... 1Chr 21:2 8269
David made *r* over the Reubenites 1Chr 26:32 6485
All these were the *r* of the 1Chr 27:31 8269
with the *r* of the king's work, ... 1Chr 29:6 8269
and gathered the *r* of the city 2Chr 29:20 8269
r of the house of God, gave unto 2Chr 35:8 5057
r hath been chief in this .... Ezr 9:2 5461
Let now our *r* of all the .... Ezr 10:14 8269
the *r* knew not whither I went, or .... Neh 2:16 5461
nor to the nobles, nor to the *r* .... Neh 2:16 5461
said unto the nobles, and to the *r* .... Neh 4:14 5461
the *r* were behind all the house .... Neh 4:16 8269
said unto the nobles, and to the *r* .... Neh 4:19 5461
and I rebuked the nobles, and the *r* .... Neh 5:7 5461
hundred and fifty of the Jews and *r* .... Neh 5:17 5461
together the nobles, and the *r* .... Neh 7:5 5461
the *r* of the people dwelt at .... Neh 11:1 8269
I, and the half of the *r* with me .... Neh 12:40 5461
Then contended I with the *r* .... Neh 13:11 5461
to the *r* of every people of every .... Est 3:12 8269
r of the provinces which are from .... Est 8:9 8269
all the *r* of the provinces, and .... Est 9:3 8269
the *r* take counsel together, ... Ps 2:2 7336
word of the LORD, ye *r* of Sodom .... Is 1:10 7101
wicked, and the sceptre of the *r* .... Is 14:5 4910
All thy *r* are fled together, they .... Is 22:3 7101
the prophets and your *r*, the seers .... Is 29:10 7218
abhorreth, to a servant of *r* .... Is 49:7 4910
to be *r* over the seed of Abraham .... Jer 33:26 4910
I break in pieces captains and *r* .... Jer 51:23 5461
thereof, and all the *r* thereof .... Jer 51:28 5461
wise men, her captains, and her *r* .... Jer 51:57 5461
clothed with blue, captains and *r* .... Eze 23:6 5461
r clothed most gorgeously, ... Eze 23:12 5461
young men, captains and *r*, great .... Eze 23:23 5461
all the *r* of the provinces, to .... Dan 3:2 7984
all the *r* of the provinces, were .... Dan 3:3 7984
her *r* with shame do love, Give ye .... Hos 4:18 4043
one of the *r* of the synagogue .... Mk 5:22 *752*
and ye shall be brought before *r* .... Mk 13:9 *2232*
kings and *r* for my name's sake .... Lk 21:12 *2232*
the chief priests and the *r* .... Lk 23:13 *758*
the *r* also with them derided him, ... Lk 23:35 *758*
our *r* delivered him to be .... Lk 24:20 *758*
Do the *r* know indeed that this is .... Jn 7:26 *758*
Have any of the *r* or of the .... Jn 7:48 *758*
chief *r* also many believed on him .... Jn 12:42 *758*
ye did it, as did also your *r* .... Acts 3:17 *758*
pass on the morrow, that their *r* .... Acts 4:5 *758*
Ye *r* of the people, and elders of .... Acts 4:8 *758*
the *r* were gathered together .... Acts 4:26 *758*
the prophets the *r* of the .... Acts 13:15 *752*
dwell at Jerusalem, and their *r* .... Acts 13:27 *758*
and also of the Jews with their *r* .... Acts 14:5 *758*
into the marketplace unto the *r* .... Acts 16:19 *758*
brethren unto the *r* of the city .... Acts 17:6 *4178*
the *r* of the city, when they .... Acts 17:8 *4178*
For *r* are not a terror to good .... Rom 13:3 *758*
against the *r* of the darkness of .... Eph 6:12 *2888*

RULEST {2}
r not thou over all the kingdoms 2Chr 20:6 4910
Thou *r* the raging of the sea .... Ps 89:9 4910

RULETH {14}
He that *r* over men must be just, ... 2Sa 23:3 4910
let them know that God *r* in Jacob .... Ps 59:13 4910
He *r* by his power for ever .... Ps 66:7 4910
and his kingdom *r* over all .... Ps 103:19 4910
he that *r* his spirit than he that .... Prov 16:32 4910
The rich *r* over the poor, and the .... Prov 22:7 4910
r over another to his own hurt .... Eccl 8:9 7980
the cry of him that *r* among fools .... Eccl 9:17 4910
most High *r* in the kingdom of men .... Dan 4:17 7980
most High *r* in the kingdom of men .... Dan 4:25 7980
most High *r* in the kingdom of men .... Dan 4:32 7980
but Judah yet *r* with God, and is .... Hos 11:12 7300

he that *r*, with diligence … Rom 12:8 *4291*
One that *r* well his own house, … 1Ti 3:4 *4291*

RULING {3}
be just, *r* in the fear of God … 2Sa 23:3 4910
of David, and *r* any more in Judah … Jer 22:30 4910
r their children and their own … 1Ti 3:12 *4291*

RUMAH *(ru'-mah)* {1} See ARUMAH. *Home of Jehoiakim's mother.*
the daughter of Pedaiah of *R* … 2Kin 23:36 7316

RUMBLING {1}
at the *r* of his wheels, the … Jer 47:3 1995

RUMOUR {10}
upon him, and he shall hear a *r* … 2Kin 19:7 8052
upon him, and he shall hear a *r* … Is 37:7 8052
I have heard a *r* from the LORD … Jer 49:14 8052
ye fear for the *r* that shall be … Jer 51:46 8052
a *r* shall both come one year, and … Jer 51:46 8052
in another year shall come a *r* … Jer 51:46 8052
and *r* shall be upon *r* … Eze 7:26 8052
We have heard a *r* from the LORD … Obad 1 8052
And this *r* of him went forth … Lk 7:17 *3056*

RUMOURS {2}
shall hear of wars and *r* of wars … Mt 24:6 *189*
r of wars, be ye not troubled … Mk 13:7 *189*

RUMP {5}
take of the ram the fat and the *r* … Ex 29:22 451
the fat thereof, and the whole *r* … Lev 3:9 451
the *r*, and the fat that covereth … Lev 7:3 451
And he took the fat, and the *r* … Lev 8:25 451
the bullock and of the ram, the *r* … Lev 9:19 451

RUN {71}
whose branches *r* over the wall … Gen 49:22 6805
his flesh *r* with his issue … Lev 15:3 7325
or if it *r* beyond the time of her … Lev 15:25 2100
lest angry fellows *r* upon thee … Judg 18:25 6293
some shall *r* before his chariots … 1Sa 8:11 7323
r to the camp to thy brethren … 1Sa 17:17 7323
he might *r* to Beth-lehem his city … 1Sa 20:6 7323
And he said unto his lad, *R* … 1Sa 20:36 7323
and fifty men to *r* before him … 2Sa 15:1 7323
the son of Zadok, Let me now *r* … 2Sa 18:19 7323
I pray thee, also *r* after Cushi … 2Sa 18:22 7323
Joab said, Wherefore wilt thou *r* … 2Sa 18:22 7323
But howsoever, said he, let me *r* … 2Sa 18:23 7323
And he said unto him, *R* … 2Sa 18:23 7323
by thee I have *r* through a troop … 2Sa 22:30 7323
and fifty men to *r* before him … 1Kin 1:5 7323
that I may *r* to the man of God, … 2Kin 4:22 7323
R now, I pray thee, to meet her, … 2Kin 4:26 7323
I will *r* after him, and take … 2Kin 5:20 7323
For the eyes of the LORD *r* to … 2Chr 16:9 7751
by thee I have *r* through a troop … Ps 18:29 7323
as a strong man to *r* a race … Ps 19:5 7323
as waters which *r* continually … Ps 58:7 1980
They *r* and prepare themselves … Ps 59:4 7323
waters to *r* down like rivers … Ps 78:16 3381
valleys, which *r* among the hills … Ps 104:10 1980
I will *r* the way of thy … Ps 119:32 7323
Rivers of waters *r* down mine eyes … Ps 119:136 3381
For their feet *r* to evil, and make … Prov 1:16 7323
All the rivers *r* into the sea … Eccl 1:7 1980
Draw me, we will *r* after thee … Song 1:4 7323
of locusts shall he *r* upon them … Is 33:4 8264
they shall *r*, and not be weary … Is 40:31 7323
that knew not thee shall *r* unto … Is 55:5 7323
Their feet *r* to evil, and they … Is 59:7 7323
R ye to and fro through the … Jer 5:1 7751
our eyes may *r* down with tears … Jer 9:18 3381
If thou hast *r* with the footmen, … Jer 12:5 7323
r down with tears, because the … Jer 13:17 3381
Let mine eyes *r* down with tears … Jer 14:17 3381
r to and fro by the hedges … Jer 49:3 7751
suddenly make him *r* away from her … Jer 49:19 7323
them suddenly *r* away from her … Jer 50:44 7323
One post shall *r* to meet another, … Jer 51:31 7323
let tears *r* down like a river day … Lam 2:18 3381
neither shall thy tears *r* down … Eze 24:16 935
cause their rivers to *r* like oil … Eze 32:14 3212
many shall *r* to and fro, and … Dan 12:4 7751
and as horsemen, so shall they *r* … Joel 2:4 7323
They shall *r* like mighty men … Joel 2:7 7323
They shall *r* to and fro in the … Joel 2:9 8264
they shall *r* upon the wall, they … Joel 2:9 7323
But let judgment *r* down as waters … Amos 5:24 1556
Shall horses *r* upon the rock … Amos 6:12 7323
even to the east, they shall *r* to … Amos 8:12 7751
they shall *r* like the lightnings … Nah 2:4 7323
that he may *r* that readeth it … Hab 2:2 7323
ye *r* every man unto his own house … Hag 1:9 7323
And said unto him, *R*, speak to … Zec 2:4 7323
the eyes of the LORD, which *r* to … Zec 4:10 7751
did *r* to bring his disciples word … Mt 28:8 *5143*
they which *r* in a race *r* all … 1Cor 9:24 *5143*
So *r*, that ye may obtain … 1Cor 9:24 *5143*
I therefore so *r*, not as … 1Cor 9:26 *5143*
any means I should *r*, or had *r* … Gal 2:2 *5143*
Ye did *r* well … Gal 5:7 *5143*
Christ, that I have not *r* in vain … Phil 2:16 *5143*
let us *r* with patience the race … Heb 12:1 *5143*
ye *r* not with them to the same … 1Pet 4:4 *4936*

RUNNEST {1}
and when thou *r*, thou shalt not … Prov 4:12 7323

RUNNETH {11}
to the river than *r* to Ahava … Ezr 8:15 935
He *r* upon him, even on his neck, … Job 15:26 7323
he *r* upon me like a giant … Job 16:14 7323
my cup *r* over … Ps 23:5 7310
his word *r* very swiftly … Ps 147:15 7323
the righteous *r* into it, and is … Prov 18:10 7323
mine eye *r* down with water, … Lam 1:16 3381
Mine eye *r* down with rivers of … Lam 3:48 3381
bottles break, and the wine *r* out … Mt 9:17 *1632*
Then she *r*, and cometh to Simon … Jn 20:2 *5143*
that willeth, nor of him that *r* … Rom 9:16 *5143*

RUNNING {26}
in an earthen vessel over *r* water … Lev 14:5 2416
that was killed over the *r* water … Lev 14:6 2416
in an earthen vessel over *r* water … Lev 14:50 2416
the slain bird, and in the *r* water … Lev 14:51 2416
of the bird, and with the *r* water … Lev 14:52 2416
When any man hath a *r* issue out … Lev 15:2 2100
and bathe his flesh in *r* water … Lev 15:13 2416
is a leper, or hath a *r* issue … Lev 22:4 2100
r water shall be put thereto in a … Num 19:17 2416
looked, and behold a man *r* alone … 2Sa 18:24 7323
And the watchman saw another man *r* … 2Sa 18:26 7323
said, Behold another man *r* alone … 2Sa 18:26 7323
Me thinketh the *r* of the foremost … 2Sa 18:27 4794
the *r* of Ahimaaz the son of Zadok … 2Sa 18:27 4794
when Naaman saw him *r* after him … 2Kin 5:21 7323
heard the noise of the people *r* … 2Chr 23:12 7323
r waters out of thine own well … Prov 5:15 5140
that be swift in *r* to mischief … Prov 6:18 7323
as the *r* to and fro of locusts … Is 33:4 4944
rivers *r* round about his plants … Eze 31:4 1980
amazed, and *r* to him saluted him … Mk 9:15 *4370*
that the people came *r* together … Mk 9:25 *1998*
into the way, there came one *r* … Mk 10:17 *4370*
r over, shall men give into your … Lk 6:38 *5240*
r under a certain island which is … Acts 27:16 *5295*
of many horses *r* to battle … Rev 9:9 *5143*

RUSH {4}
Can the *r* grow up without mire … Job 8:11 1573
Israel head and tail, branch and *r* … Is 9:14 100
The nations shall *r* like the … Is 17:13 7582
the head or tail, branch or *r* … Is 19:15 100

RUSHED {3}
r forward, and stood in the … Judg 9:44 6584
in wait hasted, and *r* upon Gibeah … Judg 20:37 6584
they *r* with one accord into the … Acts 19:29 *3729*

RUSHES {1}
shall be grass with reeds and *r* … Is 35:7 1573

RUSHETH {1}
as the horse *r* into the battle … Jer 8:6 7857

RUSHING {8}
to the *r* of nations … Is 17:12 7588
that make a *r* like the *r* of … Is 17:12 7582
rush like the *r* of many waters … Is 17:13 7588
at the *r* of his chariots, and at … Jer 47:3 7494
behind me a voice of a great *r* … Eze 3:12 7494
them, and a noise of a great *r* … Eze 3:13 7494
from heaven as of a *r* mighty wind … Acts 2:2 *5342*

RUST {3}
r doth corrupt, and where thieves … Mt 6:19 *1035*
neither moth nor *r* doth corrupt … Mt 6:20 *1035*
the *r* of them shall be a witness … Jas 5:3 *2447*

RUTH *(rooth)* {13} *Wife of Boaz; an ancestor of Jesus.*
Orpah, and the name of the other *R* … Ruth 1:4 7327
but *R* clave unto her … Ruth 1:14 7327
R said, Intreat me not to leave … Ruth 1:16 7327
R the Moabitess, her daughter in … Ruth 1:22 7327
R the Moabitess said unto Naomi, … Ruth 2:2 7327
Then said Boaz unto *R*, Hearest … Ruth 2:8 7327
R the Moabitess said, He said … Ruth 2:21 7327
Naomi said unto *R* her daughter in … Ruth 2:22 7327
answered, I am *R* thine handmaid … Ruth 3:9 7327
buy it also of *R* the Moabitess … Ruth 4:5 7327
Moreover *R* the Moabitess, the … Ruth 4:10 7327
So Boaz took *R*, and she was his … Ruth 4:13 7327
and Booz begat Obed of *R* … Mt 1:5 *4503*

S

SABACHTHANI {2}
voice, saying, Eli, Eli, lama *s* … Mt 27:46 *4518*
voice, saying, Eloi, Eloi, lama *s* … Mk 15:34 *4518*

SABAOTH *(sab'-a-oth)* {2} *Title meaning "Lord of Hosts."*
the Lord of *S* had left us a seed … Rom 9:29 *4519*
into the ears of the Lord of *S* … Jas 5:4 *4519*

SABBATH {137}
rest of the holy *s* unto the LORD … Ex 16:23 7676
for to day is a *s* unto the LORD … Ex 16:25 7676
the seventh day, which is the *s* … Ex 16:26 7676
the LORD hath given you the *s* … Ex 16:29 7676
Remember the *s* day, to keep it … Ex 20:8 7676
day is the *s* of the LORD thy God … Ex 20:10 7676
the LORD blessed the *s* day … Ex 20:11 7676
Ye shall keep the *s* therefore … Ex 31:14 7676
in the seventh is the *s* of rest … Ex 31:15 7676
doeth any work in the *s* day … Ex 31:15 7676
of Israel shall keep the *s* … Ex 31:16 7676
to observe the *s* throughout their … Ex 31:16 7676
holy day, a *s* of rest to the LORD … Ex 35:2 7676
your habitations upon the *s* day … Ex 35:3 7676
It shall be a *s* of rest unto you, … Lev 16:31 7676
the seventh day is the *s* of rest … Lev 23:3 7676
it is the *s* of the LORD in all … Lev 23:3 7676
on the morrow after the *s* the … Lev 23:11 7676
you from the morrow after the *s* … Lev 23:15 7676
s shall ye number fifty days … Lev 23:16 7676
of the month, shall ye have a *s* … Lev 23:24 7677
It shall be unto you a *s* of rest … Lev 23:32 7676
even, shall ye celebrate your *s* … Lev 23:32 7676
on the first day shall be a *s* … Lev 23:39 7677
and on the eighth day shall be a *s* … Lev 23:39 7677
Every *s* he shall set it in order … Lev 24:8 7676
the land keep a *s* unto the LORD … Lev 25:2 7676
be a *s* of rest unto the land … Lev 25:4 7676
unto the land, a *s* for the LORD … Lev 25:4 7676
the *s* of the land shall be meat … Lev 25:6 7676
gathered sticks upon the *s* day … Num 15:32 7676
on the *s* day two lambs of the … Num 28:9 7676
is the burnt offering of every *s* … Num 28:10 7676
Keep the *s* day to sanctify it, as … Deut 5:12 7676
day is the *s* of the LORD thy God … Deut 5:14 7676
commanded thee to keep the *s* day … Deut 5:15 7676
it is neither new moon, nor *s* … 2Kin 4:23 7676
of you that enter in on the *s* … 2Kin 11:5 7676
of all you that go forth on the *s* … 2Kin 11:7 7676
men that were to come in on the *s* … 2Kin 11:9 7676
them that should go out on the *s* … 2Kin 11:9 7676
the covert for the *s* that they … 2Kin 16:18 7676
shewbread, to prepare it every *s* … 1Chr 9:32 7676
part of you entering on the *s* … 2Chr 23:4 7676
men that were to come in on the *s* … 2Chr 23:8 7676
them that were to go out on the *s* … 2Chr 23:8 7676
as she lay desolate she kept *s* … 2Chr 36:21 7673
madest known unto them thy holy *s* … Neh 9:14 7676
any victuals on the *s* day to sell … Neh 10:31 7676
would not buy it of them on the *s* … Neh 10:31 7676
treading winepresses on the *s* … Neh 13:15 7676
into Jerusalem on the *s* day … Neh 13:15 7676
sold on the *s* unto the children … Neh 13:16 7676
that ye do, and profane the *s* day … Neh 13:17 7676
upon Israel by profaning the *s* … Neh 13:18 7676
began to be dark before the *s* … Neh 13:19 7676
not be opened till after the *s* … Neh 13:19 7676
burden be brought in on the *s* day … Neh 13:19 7676
forth came they no more on the *s* … Neh 13:21 7676
the gates, to sanctify the *s* day … Neh 13:22 7676
A Psalm or Song for the *s* day … Ps 92:*t* 7676
that keepeth the *s* from polluting … Is 56:2 7676
keepeth the *s* from polluting it … Is 56:6 7676
turn away thy foot from the *s* … Is 58:13 7676
call the *s* a delight, the holy of … Is 58:13 7676
from one *s* to another, shall all … Is 66:23 7676
and bear no burden on the *s* day … Jer 17:21 7676
out of your houses on the *s* day … Jer 17:22 7676
any work, but hallow ye the *s* day … Jer 17:22 7676
gates of this city on the *s* day … Jer 17:24 7676
but hallow the *s* day … Jer 17:24 7676
unto me to hallow the *s* day … Jer 17:27 7676
gates of Jerusalem on the *s* day … Jer 17:27 7676
but on the *s* it shall be opened, … Eze 46:1 7676
offer unto the LORD in the *s* day … Eze 46:4 7676
offerings, as he did on the *s* day … Eze 46:12 7676
and the *s*, that we may set forth … Amos 8:5 7676
on the *s* day through the corn … Mt 12:1 *4521*
not lawful to do upon the *s* day … Mt 12:2 *4521*
how that on the *s* days the … Mt 12:5 *4521*
in the temple profane the *s* … Mt 12:5 *4521*
of man is Lord even of the *s* day … Mt 12:8 *4521*
it lawful to heal on the *s* days … Mt 12:10 *4521*
it fall into a pit on the *s* day … Mt 12:11 *4521*
lawful to do well on the *s* days … Mt 12:12 *4521*
the winter, neither on the *s* day … Mt 24:20 *4521*
In the end of the *s*, as it began … Mt 28:1 *4521*
straightway on the *s* day he … Mk 1:21 *4521*
the corn fields on the *s* day … Mk 2:23 *4521*
why do they on the *s* day that … Mk 2:24 *4521*
The *s* was made for man … Mk 2:27 *4521*
and not man for the *s* … Mk 2:27 *4521*
Son of man is Lord also of the *s* … Mk 2:28 *4521*
he would heal him on the *s* day … Mk 3:2 *4521*
lawful to do good on the *s* days … Mk 3:4 *4521*
when the *s* day was come, he began … Mk 6:2 *4521*
that is, the day before the *s* … Mk 15:42 *4315*
And when the *s* was past, Mary … Mk 16:1 *4521*
into the synagogue on the *s* day … Lk 4:16 *4521*
and taught them on the *s* days … Lk 4:31 *4521*
on the second *s* after the first … Lk 6:1 *4521*
is not lawful to do on the *s* days … Lk 6:2 *4521*
Son of man is Lord also of the *s* … Lk 6:5 *4521*
it came to pass also on another *s* … Lk 6:6 *4521*
he would heal on the *s* day … Lk 6:7 *4521*

S

lawful on the s days to do good ... Lk 6:9 4521
in one of the synagogues on the s ... Lk 13:10 4521
Jesus had healed on the s day ... Lk 13:14 4521
and be healed, and not on the s day ... Lk 13:14 4521
s loose his ox or his ass from ... Lk 13:15 4521
from this bond on the s day ... Lk 13:16 4521
to eat bread on the s day ... Lk 14:1 4521
Is it lawful to heal on the s day ... Lk 14:3 4521
pull him out on the s day ... Lk 14:5 4521
the preparation, and the s drew on ... Lk 23:54 4521
rested the s day according to the ... Lk 23:56 4521
and on the same day was the s ... Jn 5:9 4521
that was cured, It is the s day ... Jn 5:10 4521
done these things on the s day ... Jn 5:16 4521
he not only had broken the s ... Jn 5:18 4521
ye on the s day circumcise a man ... Jn 7:22 4521
If a man on the s day receive ... Jn 7:23 4521
man every whit whole on the s day ... Jn 7:23 4521
it was the s day when Jesus made ... Jn 9:14 4521
because he keepeth not the s day ... Jn 9:16 4521
upon the cross on the s day ... Jn 19:31 4521
(for that s day was an high day,) ... Jn 19:31 4521
from Jerusalem a s day's journey ... Acts 1:12 4521
into the synagogue on the s day ... Acts 13:14 4521
which are read every s day ... Acts 13:27 4521
be preached to them the next s ... Acts 13:42 4521
the next s day came almost the ... Acts 13:44 4521
in the synagogues every s day ... Acts 15:21 4521
on the s we went out of the city ... Acts 16:13 4521
three s days reasoned with them ... Acts 17:2 4521
reasoned in the synagogue every s ... Acts 18:4 4521
of the new moon, or of the s days ... Col 2:16 4521

SABBATHS {35}
Verily my s ye shall keep ... Ex 31:13 7676
and his father, and keep my s ... Lev 19:3 7676
Ye shall keep my s, and reverence ... Lev 19:30 7676
seven s shall be complete ... Lev 23:15 7676
Beside the s of the LORD, and ... Lev 23:38 7676
number seven s of years unto thee ... Lev 25:8 7676
the space of the seven s of years ... Lev 25:8 7676
Ye shall keep my s, and reverence ... Lev 26:2 7676
Then shall the land enjoy her s ... Lev 26:34 7676
the land rest, and enjoy her s ... Lev 26:34 7676
because it did not rest in your s ... Lev 26:35 7676
of them, and shall enjoy her s ... Lev 26:43 7676
sacrifices unto the LORD in the s ... 1Chr 23:31 7676
morning and evening, on the s ... 2Chr 2:4 7676
commandment of Moses, on the s ... 2Chr 8:13 7676
and the burnt offerings for the s ... 2Chr 31:3 7676
until the land had enjoyed her s ... 2Chr 36:21 7676
burnt offering, of the s, of the ... Neh 10:33 7676
the new moons and s, the calling ... Is 1:13 7676
unto the eunuchs that keep my s ... Is 56:4 7676
saw her, and did mock at her s ... Lam 1:7 4868
s to be forgotten in Zion, and ... Lam 2:6 7676
Moreover also I gave them my s ... Eze 20:12 7676
my s they greatly polluted ... Eze 20:13 7676
in my statutes, but polluted my s ... Eze 20:16 7676
And hallow my s ... Eze 20:20 7676
they polluted my s ... Eze 20:21 7676
my statutes, and had polluted my s ... Eze 20:24 7676
things, and hast profaned my s ... Eze 22:8 7676
and have hid their eyes from my s ... Eze 22:26 7676
same day, and have profaned my s ... Eze 23:38 7676
and they shall hallow my s ... Eze 44:24 7676
and in the new moons, and in the s ... Eze 45:17 7676
gate before the LORD in the s ... Eze 46:3 7676
days, her new moons, and her s ... Hos 2:11 7676

SABEANS *(sab-e'-uns)* {4}
1. Descendants of Sheba.
the S fell upon them, and took ... Job 1:15 7614
and they shall sell them to the S ... Joel 3:8 7615
2. Descendants of Seba.
of Ethiopia and of the S, men of ... Is 45:14 5436
brought S from the wilderness ... Eze 23:42 5433

SABTA *(sab'-tah)* {1} See SABTAH. *A son of Cush.*
Seba, and Havilah, and S, and Raamah ... 1Chr 1:9 5454

SABTAH *(sab'-tah)* {1} See SABTA. *Same as Sabta.*
Seba, and Havilah, and S, and Raamah ... Gen 10:7 5454

SABTECA See SABTECHAH.

SABTECHA *(sab'-te-kah)* {1} See SABTECHAH. *A son of Cush.*
and Sabta, and Raamah, and S ... 1Chr 1:9 5455

SABTECHAH *(sab'-te-kah)* {1} See SABTECHA. *Same as Sabtecha.*
and Sabtah, and Raamah, and S ... Gen 10:7 5455

SACAR *(sa'-kar)* {2} See SHARAR.
1. Father of Ahiham.
Ahiam the son of S the Hararite ... 1Chr 11:35 7940
2. A sanctuary servant.
S the fourth, and Nethaneel the ... 1Chr 26:4 7940

SACHIA See SHACHIA.

SACK {9}
every man's money into his s ... Gen 42:25 8242
as one of them opened his s to ... Gen 42:27 8242
and, lo, it is even in my s ... Gen 42:28 572
bundle of money was in his s ... Gen 42:35 8242
money was in the mouth of his s ... Gen 43:21 572
every man his s to the ground ... Gen 44:11 572
and opened every man his s ... Gen 44:11 572
the cup was found in Benjamin's s ... Gen 44:12 572
wood, or raiment, or skin, or s ... Lev 11:32 8242

SACKBUT {4}
of the cornet, flute, harp, s ... Dan 3:5 5443
of the cornet, flute, harp, s ... Dan 3:7 5443
of the cornet, flute, harp, s ... Dan 3:10 5443
of the cornet, flute, harp, s ... Dan 3:15 5443

SACKCLOTH {46}
put s upon his loins, and mourned ... Gen 37:34 8242
your clothes, and gird you with s ... 2Sa 3:31 8242
the daughter of Aiah took s ... 2Sa 21:10 8242
put s on our loins, and ropes upon ... 1Kin 20:31 8242
So they girded s on their loins ... 1Kin 20:32 8242
put s upon his flesh, and fasted, ... 1Kin 21:27 8242
his flesh, and fasted, and lay in s ... 1Kin 21:27 8242
he had s within upon his flesh ... 2Kin 6:30 8242
and covered himself with s ... 2Kin 19:1 8242
of the priests, covered with s ... 2Kin 19:2 8242
of Israel, who were clothed in s ... 1Chr 21:16 8242
put on s with ashes, and went out ... Est 4:1 8242
the king's gate clothed with s ... Est 4:2 8242
and many lay in s and ashes ... Est 4:3 8242
and to take away his s from him ... Est 4:4 8242
I have sewed s upon my skin ... Job 16:15 8242
thou hast put off my s, and girded ... Ps 30:11 8242
they were sick, my clothing was s ... Ps 35:13 8242
I made s also my garment ... Ps 69:11 8242
of a stomacher a girding of s ... Is 3:24 8242
they shall gird themselves with s ... Is 15:3 8242
loose the s from off thy loins, ... Is 20:2 8242
to baldness, and to girding with s ... Is 22:12 8242
bare, and gird s upon your loins ... Is 32:11
and covered himself with s ... Is 37:1 8242
of the priests covered with s ... Is 37:2 8242
and I make s their covering ... Is 50:3 8242
head as a bulrush, and to spread s ... Is 58:5 8242
For this gird you with s, lament ... Jer 4:8 8242
of my people, gird thee with s ... Jer 6:26 8242
be cuttings, and upon the loins s ... Jer 48:37 8242
of Rabbah, gird you with s ... Jer 49:3 8242
have girded themselves with s ... Lam 2:10 8242
shall also gird themselves with s ... Eze 7:18 8242
for thee, and gird them with s ... Eze 27:31 8242
supplications, with fasting, and s ... Dan 9:3 8242
like a virgin girded with s for ... Joel 1:8 8242
come, lie all night in s, ye ... Joel 1:13 8242
I will bring up s upon all loins ... Amos 8:10 8242
and proclaimed a fast, and put on s ... Jonah 3:5 8242
from him, and covered him with s ... Jonah 3:6 8242
man and beast be covered with s ... Jonah 3:8 8242
would have repented long ago in s ... Mt 11:21 4526
while ago repented, sitting in s ... Lk 10:13 4526
the sun became black as s of hair ... Rev 6:12 4526
and threescore days, clothed in s ... Rev 11:3 4526

SACKCLOTHES {1}
assembled with fasting, and with s ... Neh 9:1 8242

SACK'S {3}
behold, it was in his s mouth ... Gen 42:27 572
every man's money in his s mouth ... Gen 44:1 572
in the s mouth of the youngest, ... Gen 44:2 572

SACKS {9}
to fill their s with corn ... Gen 42:25 3672
to pass as they emptied their s ... Gen 42:35 8242
again in the mouth of your s ... Gen 43:12 572
in our s at the first time are we ... Gen 43:18 572
to the inn, that we opened our s ... Gen 43:21 572
tell who put our money in our s ... Gen 43:22 572
hath given you treasure in your s ... Gen 43:23 572
Fill the men's s with food ... Gen 44:1 572
took old s upon their asses, and ... Josh 9:4 8242

SACKS' {1}
which we found in our s mouths ... Gen 44:8 572

SACRIFICE {218}
Jacob offered s upon the mount ... Gen 31:54 2077
that we may s to the LORD our God ... Ex 3:18 2076
and s unto the LORD our God ... Ex 5:3 2076
saying, Let us go and s to our God ... Ex 5:8 2076
Let us go and do s to the LORD ... Ex 5:17 2076
that they may do s unto the LORD ... Ex 8:8 2076
s to your God in the land ... Ex 8:25 2076
for we shall s the abomination of ... Ex 8:26 2076
shall we s the abomination of the ... Ex 8:26 2076
s to the LORD our God, as he ... Ex 8:27 2076
that ye may s to the LORD your ... Ex 8:28 2076
the people go to s to the LORD ... Ex 8:29 2076
that we may s unto the LORD our ... Ex 10:25 2077
It is the s of the LORD's ... Ex 12:27 2077
therefore I s to the LORD all ... Ex 13:15 2076
shalt s thereon thy burnt ... Ex 20:24 2076
blood of my s with leavened bread ... Ex 23:18 2077
of my s remain until the morning ... Ex 23:18 2282
of the s of their peace offerings ... Ex 29:28 2077
incense thereon, nor burnt s ... Ex 30:9
do s unto their gods, and one call ... Ex 34:15 2076
call thee, and thou eat of his s ... Ex 34:15 2077
the blood of my s with leaven ... Ex 34:25 2077
neither shall the s of the feast ... Ex 34:25 2077
offering be a burnt s of the herd ... Lev 1:3
all on the altar, to be a burnt s ... Lev 1:9
or of the goats, for a burnt s ... Lev 1:10
it is a burnt s, an offering made ... Lev 1:13
if the burnt s for his offering ... Lev 1:14
it is a burnt s, an offering made ... Lev 1:17
oblation be a s of peace offering ... Lev 3:1 2077
he shall offer of the s of the ... Lev 3:3 2077
it on the altar upon the burnt s ... Lev 3:5
if his offering for a s of peace ... Lev 3:6 2077
he shall offer of the s of the ... Lev 3:9 2077
of the s of peace offerings ... Lev 4:10 2077
as the fat of the s of peace ... Lev 4:26 2077
from off the s of peace offerings ... Lev 4:31 2077
from the s of the peace offerings ... Lev 4:35 2077
law of the s of peace offerings ... Lev 7:11 2077
the s of thanksgiving unleavened ... Lev 7:12 2077
leavened bread with the s of ... Lev 7:13 2077
the flesh of the s of his peace ... Lev 7:15 2077
But if the s of his offering be a ... Lev 7:16 2077
same day that he offereth his s ... Lev 7:16 2077
remainder of the flesh of the s ... Lev 7:17 2077
if any of the flesh of the s of ... Lev 7:18 2077
flesh of the s of peace offerings ... Lev 7:20 2077
flesh of the s of peace offerings ... Lev 7:21 2077
He that offereth the s of his ... Lev 7:29 2077
of the s of his peace offerings ... Lev 7:29 2077
of the s of the peace offerings ... Lev 7:37 2077
it was a burnt s for a sweet ... Lev 8:21
offerings, to s before the LORD ... Lev 9:4 2076
beside the burnt s of the morning ... Lev 9:17
and the ram for a s of peace ... Lev 9:18 2077
offereth a burnt offering or s ... Lev 17:8 2077
And if ye offer a s of peace ... Lev 19:5 2077
whosoever offereth a s of peace ... Lev 22:21 2077
when ye will offer a s of ... Lev 22:29 2077
Then ye shall s one kid of the ... Lev 23:19 6213
year for a s of peace offerings ... Lev 23:19 2077
offering, and a meat offering, a s ... Lev 23:37 2077
do not offer a s unto the LORD ... Lev 27:11 7133
a s of peace offerings unto the ... Num 6:17 2077
the s of the peace offerings ... Num 6:18 2077
for a s of peace offerings, two ... Num 7:17 2077
for a s of peace offerings, two ... Num 7:23 2077
for a s of peace offerings, two ... Num 7:29 2077
for a s of peace offerings, two ... Num 7:35 2077
for a s of peace offerings, two ... Num 7:41 2077
for a s of peace offerings, two ... Num 7:47 2077
for a s of peace offerings, two ... Num 7:53 2077
for a s of peace offerings, two ... Num 7:59 2077
for a s of peace offerings, two ... Num 7:65 2077
for a s of peace offerings, two ... Num 7:71 2077
for a s of peace offerings, two ... Num 7:77 2077
for a s of peace offerings, two ... Num 7:83 2077
all the oxen for the s of the ... Num 7:88 2077
or a s in performing a vow, or in ... Num 15:3 2077
with the burnt offering or s ... Num 15:5 2077
or for a s in performing a vow, ... Num 15:8 2077
a s made by fire unto the LORD, ... Num 15:25
and, lo, he stood by his burnt s ... Num 23:6
a s made by fire unto the LORD ... Num 28:6
a s made by fire, of a sweet ... Num 28:8
a s made by fire unto the LORD ... Num 28:13
But ye shall offer a s made by ... Num 28:19
the meat of the s made by fire ... Num 28:24
a s made by fire unto the LORD ... Num 29:6
a s made by fire, of a sweet ... Num 29:13
a s made by fire, of a sweet ... Num 29:36
thou shalt not s it unto the LORD ... Deut 15:21 2076
Thou shalt therefore s the ... Deut 16:2 2076
Thou mayest not s the passover ... Deut 16:5 2076
there thou shalt s the passover ... Deut 16:6 2076
Thou shalt not s unto the LORD ... Deut 17:1 2076
people, from them that offer a s ... Deut 18:3 2077
whole burnt s upon thine altar ... Deut 33:10
not for burnt offering, nor for s ... Josh 22:26 2077
offer a burnt s with the wood of ... Judg 6:26
a great s unto Dagon their god ... Judg 16:23 2077
to s unto the LORD of hosts in ... 1Sa 1:3 2076
offer unto the LORD the yearly s ... 1Sa 1:21 2077
was, that, when any man offered s ... 1Sa 2:13 2077
her husband to offer the yearly s ... 1Sa 2:19 2077
Wherefore kick ye at my s ... 1Sa 2:29 2077
with s nor offering for ever ... 1Sa 3:14 2077
for there is a s of the people to ... 1Sa 9:12 2077
come, because he doth bless the s ... 1Sa 9:13 2077
and to s sacrifices of peace ... 1Sa 10:8 2076
to s unto the LORD thy God ... 1Sa 15:15 2076
to s unto the LORD thy God in ... 1Sa 15:21 2076
Behold, to obey is better than s ... 1Sa 15:22 2077
say, I am come to s to the LORD ... 1Sa 16:2 2076
And call Jesse to the s, and I will ... 1Sa 16:3 2077
I am come to s unto the LORD ... 1Sa 16:5 2076
and come with me to the s ... 1Sa 16:5 2077
his sons, and called them to the s ... 1Sa 16:5 2077
for there is a yearly s there for ... 1Sa 20:6 2077
our family hath a s in the city ... 1Sa 20:29 2077
behold, here be oxen for burnt s ... 2Sa 24:22
king went to Gibeon to s there ... 1Kin 3:4 2076
offered s before the LORD ... 1Kin 8:62 2077
Solomon offered a s of peace ... 1Kin 8:63 2077
If this people go up to do s in ... 1Kin 12:27 2077
of the offering of the evening s ... 1Kin 18:29 4503
water, and pour it on the burnt s ... 1Kin 18:33
of the offering of the evening s ... 1Kin 18:36 4503
fell, and consumed the burnt s ... 1Kin 18:38
offering nor s unto other gods ... 2Kin 5:17 2077
I have a great s to do to Baal ... 2Kin 10:19 2077
as yet the people did s and burnt ... 2Kin 14:4 2076
offering, and the king's burnt s ... 2Kin 16:15
and all the blood of the s ... 2Kin 16:15 2077
nor serve them, nor s to them ... 2Kin 17:35 2076
worship, and to him shall ye do s ... 2Kin 17:36 2076
save only to burn s before him ... 2Chr 2:6
Solomon offered a s of twenty ... 2Chr 7:5 2077
place to myself for an house of s ... 2Chr 7:12 2077
to s unto the LORD God of their ... 2Chr 11:16 2076
them, therefore will I s to them ... 2Chr 28:23 2076
did s still in the high places ... 2Chr 33:17 2076

we do *s* unto him since the days — Ezr 4:2 — 2076
sat astonied until the evening *s* — Ezr 9:4 — 4503
at the evening *s* I arose up from — Ezr 9:5 — 4503
will they *s* — Neh 4:2 — 2076
offerings, and accept thy burnt *s* — Ps 20:3
S and offering thou didst not — Ps 40:6 — 2077
have made a covenant with me by *s* — Ps 50:5 — 2077
For thou desirest not *s* — Ps 51:16 — 2077
I will freely *s* unto thee — Ps 54:6 — 2076
let them *s* the sacrifices of — Ps 107:22 — 2076
to thee the *s* of thanksgiving — Ps 116:17 — 2077
bind the *s* with cords, even unto — Ps 118:27 — 2282
up of my hands as the evening *s* — Ps 141:2 — 4503
The *s* of the wicked is an — Prov 15:8 — 2077
acceptable to the LORD than *s* — Prov 21:3 — 2077
The *s* of the wicked is — Prov 21:27 — 2077
hear, than to give the *s* of fools — Eccl 5:1 — 2077
LORD in that day, and shall do *s* — Is 19:21 — 2077
for the LORD hath a *s* in Bozrah — Is 34:6 — 2077
wentest thou up to offer *s* — Is 57:7 — 2077
of them that shall bring the *s* of — Jer 33:11
offerings, and to do *s* continually — Jer 33:18 — 2077
a *s* in the north country by the — Jer 46:10 — 2077
every side to my *s* — Eze 39:17 — 2077
that I do *s* for you — Eze 39:17 — 2076
even a great *s* upon the mountains — Eze 39:17 — 2077
of my *s* which I have sacrificed — Eze 39:19 — 2076
slew the burnt offering and the *s* — Eze 40:42 — 2077
the *s* for the people, and they — Eze 44:11 — 2077
shall boil the *s* of the people — Eze 46:24 — 2077
by him the daily *s* was taken away — Dan 8:11
s by reason of transgression — Dan 8:12
the vision concerning the daily *s* — Dan 8:13
of the week he shall cause the *s* — Dan 9:27 — 2077
and shall take away the daily *s* — Dan 11:31
the daily *s* shall be taken away — Dan 12:11
without a prince, and without a *s* — Hos 3:4 — 2077
They *s* upon the tops of the — Hos 4:13 — 2076
whores, and they *s* with harlots — Hos 4:14 — 2076
For I desired mercy, and not *s* — Hos 6:6 — 2077
They *s* flesh for the sacrifices — Hos 8:13 — 2076
they *s* bullocks in Gilgal — Hos 12:11 — 2076
the men that *s* kiss the calves — Hos 13:2 — 2076
offer a *s* of thanksgiving with — Amos 4:5
offered a *s* unto the LORD, and — Jonah 1:16 — 2077
But I will *s* unto thee with the — Jonah 2:9 — 2076
Therefore they *s* unto their net — Hab 1:16 — 2076
for the LORD hath prepared a *s* — Zeph 1:7 — 2077
pass in the day of the LORD's *s* — Zeph 1:8 — 2077
and all they that *s* shall come — Zec 14:21 — 2076
And if ye offer the blind for *s* — Mal 1:8 — 2076
I will have mercy, and not *s* — Mt 9:13 — *2378*
I will have mercy, and not *s* — Mt 12:7 — *2378*
every *s* shall be salted with salt — Mk 9:49 — *2378*
to offer a *s* according to that — Lk 2:24 — *2378*
offered *s* unto the idol, and — Acts 7:41 — *2378*
would have done *s* with the people — Acts 14:13 — *2380*
they had not done *s* unto them — Acts 14:18 — *2380*
ye present your bodies a living *s* — Rom 12:1 — *2378*
that are offered in *s* unto idols — 1Cor 8:4 — *1494*
in *s* to idols is any thing — 1Cor 10:19 — *1494*
the things which the Gentiles *s* — 1Cor 10:20 — *2380*
they *s* to devils, and not to God — 1Cor 10:20 — *2380*
This is offered in *s* unto idols — 1Cor 10:28 — *1494*
a *s* to God for a sweetsmelling — Eph 5:2 — *2378*
and if I be offered upon the *s* — Phil 2:17 — *2378*
a *s* acceptable, wellpleasing to — Phil 4:18 — *2378*
those high priests, to offer up *s* — Heb 7:27 — *2378*
put away sin by the *s* of himself — Heb 9:26 — *2378*
into the world, he saith, *S* — Heb 10:5 — *2378*
Above when he said, *S* and offering — Heb 10:8 — *2378*
offered one *s* for sins for ever — Heb 10:12 — *2378*
remaineth no more *s* for sins — Heb 10:26 — *2378*
God a more excellent *s* than Cain — Heb 11:4 — *2378*
s of praise to God continually — Heb 13:15 — *2378*

SACRIFICED {33}
s peace offerings of oxen unto — Ex 24:5 — 2076
have *s* thereunto, and said, These — Ex 32:8 — 2076
They *s* unto devils, not to God — Deut 32:17 — 2076
the LORD, and *s* peace offerings — Josh 8:31 — 2076
they *s* there unto the LORD — Judg 2:5 — 2076
came, and said to the man that *s* — 1Sa 2:15 — 2076
s sacrifices the same day unto — 1Sa 6:15 — 2076
there they *s* sacrifices of peace — 1Sa 11:15 — 2076
six paces, he *s* oxen and fatlings — 2Sa 6:13 — 2076
Only the people *s* in high places — 1Kin 3:2 — 2076
only he *s* and burnt incense in — 1Kin 3:3 — 2076
incense and *s* unto their gods — 1Kin 11:8 — 2076
the people still *s* and burnt — 2Kin 12:3 — 2076
the people *s* and burnt incense — 2Kin 15:4 — 2076
the people *s* and burned incense — 2Kin 15:35 — 2076
And he *s* and burnt incense in the — 2Kin 16:4 — 2076
which *s* for them in the houses of — 2Kin 17:32 — 6213
the Jebusite, then he *s* there — 1Chr 21:28 — 2076
they *s* sacrifices unto the LORD — 1Chr 29:21 — 2076
s sheep and oxen, which could not — 2Chr 5:6 — 2076
He *s* also and burnt incense in the — 2Chr 28:4 — 2076
For he *s* unto the gods of — 2Chr 28:23 — 2076
s thereon peace offerings and — 2Chr 33:16 — 2076
for Amon *s* unto all the carved — 2Chr 33:22 — 2076
of them that had *s* unto them — 2Chr 34:4 — 2076
they *s* their sons and their — Ps 106:37 — 2076
whom they *s* unto the idols of — Ps 106:38 — 2076
these hast thou *s* unto them to be — Eze 16:20 — 2076
sacrifice which I have *s* for you — Eze 39:19 — 2076
they *s* unto Baalim, and burned — Hos 11:2 — 2076
Christ our passover is *s* for us — 1Cor 5:7 — *2380*
to eat things *s* unto idols — Rev 2:14 — *1494*
and to eat things *s* unto idols — Rev 2:20 — *1494*

SACRIFICEDST {1}
which thou *s* the first day at — Deut 16:4 — 2076

SACRIFICES {79}
offered *s* unto the God of his — Gen 46:1 — 2077
said, Thou must give us also *s* — Ex 10:25 — 2077
a burnt offering and *s* for God — Ex 18:12 — 2077
of the *s* of your peace offerings — Lev 7:32 — 2077
the *s* of their peace offerings — Lev 7:34 — 2077
of the *s* of the LORD made by fire — Lev 10:13
the *s* of peace offerings of the — Lev 10:14 — 2077
of Israel may bring their *s* — Lev 17:5 — 2077
no more offer their *s* unto devils — Lev 17:7 — 2077
and over the *s* of your peace — Num 10:10 — 2077
people unto the *s* of their gods — Num 25:2 — 2077
and my bread for my *s* made by fire — Num 28:2
your burnt offerings, and your *s* — Deut 12:6 — 2077
your burnt offerings, and your *s* — Deut 12:11 — 2077
the blood of thy *s* shall be — Deut 12:27 — 2077
Which did eat the fat of their *s* — Deut 32:38 — 2077
shall offer *s* of righteousness — Deut 33:19 — 2077
the *s* of the LORD God of Israel — Josh 13:14
burnt offerings, and with our *s* — Josh 22:27 — 2077
for burnt offerings, nor for *s* — Josh 22:28 — 2077
for meat offerings, or for *s* — Josh 22:29 — 2077
sacrificed *s* the same day unto — 1Sa 6:15 — 2077
to sacrifice *s* of peace offerings — 1Sa 10:8 — 2077
there they sacrificed *s* of peace — 1Sa 11:15 — 2077
delight in burnt offerings and *s* — 1Sa 15:22 — 2077
from Giloh, while he offered *s* — 2Sa 15:12 — 2077
And when they went in to offer *s* — 2Kin 10:24 — 2077
and they offered burnt *s* and peace — 1Chr 16:1
to offer all burnt *s* unto the — 1Chr 23:31
they sacrificed *s* unto the LORD — 1Chr 29:21 — 2077
s in abundance for all Israel — 1Chr 29:21 — 2077
the burnt offering and the *s* — 2Chr 7:1 — 2077
people offered *s* before the LORD — 2Chr 7:4 — 2077
morning and every evening burnt *s* — 2Chr 13:11
the LORD, come near and bring *s* — 2Chr 29:31 — 2077
And the congregation brought in *s* — 2Chr 29:31 — 2077
the place where they offered *s* — Ezr 6:3 — 1685
That they may offer *s* of sweet — Ezr 6:10
that day they offered great *s* — Neh 12:43 — 2077
Offer the *s* of righteousness, and — Ps 4:5 — 2077
offer in his tabernacle *s* of joy — Ps 27:6 — 2077
for thy *s* or thy burnt offerings — Ps 50:8 — 2077
The *s* of God are a broken spirit — Ps 51:17 — 2077
with the *s* of righteousness — Ps 51:19 — 2077
unto thee burnt *s* of fatlings — Ps 66:15
and ate the *s* of the dead — Ps 106:28 — 2077
sacrifice the *s* of thanksgiving — Ps 107:22 — 2077
an house full of *s* with strife — Prov 17:1 — 2077
the multitude of your *s* unto me — Is 1:11 — 2077
let them kill *s* — Is 29:1 — 2282
hast thou honoured me with thy *s* — Is 43:23 — 2077
filled me with the fat of thy *s* — Is 43:24 — 2077
their *s* shall be accepted upon — Is 56:7 — 2077
nor your *s* sweet unto me — Jer 6:20 — 2077
your burnt offerings unto your *s* — Jer 7:21 — 2077
concerning burnt offerings or *s* — Jer 7:22 — 2077
bringing burnt offerings, and *s* — Jer 17:26 — 2077
bringing *s* of praise, unto the — Jer 17:26
and they offered there their *s* — Eze 20:28 — 2077
whereupon they slew their *s* — Eze 40:41
be ashamed because of their *s* — Hos 4:19 — 2077
flesh for the *s* of mine offerings — Hos 8:13 — 2077
their *s* shall be unto them as the — Hos 9:4 — 2077
bring your *s* every morning, and — Amos 4:4 — 2077
Have ye offered unto me *s* — Amos 5:25 — 2077
all whole burnt offerings and *s* — Mk 12:33 — *2378*
Pilate had mingled with their *s* — Lk 13:1 — *2378*
s by the space of forty years in — Acts 7:42 — *2378*
of the *s* partakers of the altar — 1Cor 10:18 — *2378*
offer both gifts and *s* for sins — Heb 5:1 — *2378*
is ordained to offer gifts and *s* — Heb 8:3 — *2378*
were offered both gifts and *s* — Heb 9:9 — *2378*
with better *s* than these — Heb 9:23 — *2378*
can never with those *s* which they — Heb 10:1 — *2378*
But in those *s* there is a — Heb 10:3
s for sin thou hast had no — Heb 10:6
and offering oftentimes the same *s* — Heb 10:11 — *2378*
for with such *s* God is well — Heb 13:16 — *2378*
to offer up spiritual *s* — 1Pet 2:5 — *2378*

SACRIFICETH {7}
He that *s* unto any god, save unto — Ex 22:20 — 2076
to him that *s*, and to him that — Eccl 9:2 — 2076
s, and to him that *s* not — Eccl 9:2 — 2076
that *s* in gardens, and burneth — Is 65:3 — 2076
he that *s* a lamb, as if he cut — Is 66:3 — 2076
s unto the Lord a corrupt thing — Mal 1:14 — 2076

SACRIFICING {2}
s sheep and oxen, that could not — 1Kin 8:5 — 2076
s unto the calves that he had — 1Kin 12:32 — 2076

SACRILEGE {1}
idols, dost thou commit *s* — Rom 2:22 — *2416*

SAD {12}
them, and, behold, they were *s* — Gen 40:6 — 2196
and her countenance was no more *s* — 1Sa 1:18
unto him, Why is thy spirit so *s* — 1Kin 21:5 — 5620
been beforetime *s* in his presence — Neh 2:1 — 7451
unto me, Why is thy countenance *s* — Neh 2:2 — 7451
should not my countenance be *s* — Neh 2:3 — 7489
made the heart of the righteous *s* — Eze 13:22 — 3512
s, whom I have not made *s* — Eze 13:22 — 3510
hypocrites, of a *s* countenance — Mt 6:16 — *4659*
he was *s* at that saying, and went — Mk 10:22 — *4768*
to another, as ye walk, and are *s* — Lk 24:17 — *4659*

SADDLE {4}
what *s* soever he rideth upon that — Lev 15:9 — 4817
I will *s* me an ass, that I may — 2Sa 19:26 — 2280
said unto his sons, *S* me the ass — 1Kin 13:13 — 2280
to his sons, saying, *S* me the ass — 1Kin 13:27 — 2280

SADDLED {10}
s his ass, and took two of his — Gen 22:3 — 2280
s his ass, and went with the — Num 22:21 — 2280
there were with him two asses *s* — Judg 19:10 — 2280
met him, with a couple of asses *s* — 2Sa 16:1 — 2280
he *s* his ass, and arose, and gat — 2Sa 17:23 — 2280
s his ass, and went to Gath to — 1Kin 2:40 — 2280
So they *s* him the ass — 1Kin 13:13 — 2280
that he *s* for him the ass, to wit — 1Kin 13:23 — 2280
And they *s* him — 1Kin 13:27 — 2280
Then she *s* an ass, and said to her — 2Kin 4:24 — 2280

SADDUCEES *(sad'-du-sees)* {14} *Members of a Jewish sect.*
S come to his baptism, he said — Mt 3:7 — *4523*
Pharisees also with the *S* came — Mt 16:1 — *4523*
of the Pharisees and of the *S* — Mt 16:6 — *4523*
of the Pharisees and of the *S* — Mt 16:11 — *4523*
of the Pharisees and of the *S* — Mt 16:12 — *4523*
The same day came to him the *S* — Mt 22:23 — *4523*
that he had put the *S* to silence — Mt 22:34 — *4523*
Then come unto him the *S*, which — Mk 12:18 — *4523*
Then came to him certain of the *S* — Lk 20:27 — *4523*
captain of the temple, and the *S* — Acts 4:1 — *4523*
him, (which is the sect of the *S* — Acts 5:17 — *4523*
that the one part were *S*, and the — Acts 23:6 — *4523*
between the Pharisees and the *S* — Acts 23:7 — *4523*
For the *S* say that there is no — Acts 23:8 — *4523*

SADLY {1}
Wherefore look ye so *s* to day — Gen 40:7 — 7451

SADNESS {1}
for by the *s* of the countenance — Eccl 7:3 — 7455

SADOC *(sa'-dok)* {2} *Father of Achim; an ancestor of Jesus.*
And Azor begat *S* — Mt 1:14 — *4524*
and *S* begat Achim — Mt 1:14

SAFE {13}
on every side, and ye dwelled *s* — 1Sa 12:11 — 983
said, Is the young man Absalom *s* — 2Sa 18:29 — 7965
Cushi, Is the young man Absalom *s* — 2Sa 18:32 — 7965
Their houses are *s* from fear — Job 21:9 — 7965
Hold thou me up, and I shall be *s* — Ps 119:117 — 3467
runneth into it, and is *s* — Prov 18:10 — 7682
his trust in the LORD shall be *s* — Prov 29:25 — 7682
prey, and shall carry it away *s* — Is 5:29 — 6403
and they shall be *s* in their land — Eze 34:27 — 983
because he hath received him *s* — Lk 15:27 — *5198*
bring him *s* unto Felix the — Acts 23:24 — *1295*
that they escaped all *s* to land — Acts 27:44 — *1295*
not grievous, but for you it is *s* — Phil 3:1 — *809*

SAFEGUARD {1}
but with me thou shalt be in *s* — 1Sa 22:23 — 4931

SAFELY {21}
the full, and dwell in your land *s* — Lev 26:5 — 983
And Judah and Israel dwelt *s* — 1Kin 4:25 — 983
And he led them on *s*, so that they — Ps 78:53 — 983
hearkeneth unto me shall dwell *s* — Prov 1:33 — 983
Then shalt thou walk in thy way *s* — Prov 3:23 — 983
her husband doth *s* trust in her — Prov 31:11
He pursued them, and passed *s* — Is 41:3 — 7965
be saved, and Israel shall dwell *s* — Jer 23:6 — 983
and I will cause them to dwell *s* — Jer 32:37 — 983
saved, and Jerusalem shall dwell *s* — Jer 33:16 — 983
And they shall dwell *s* therein — Eze 28:26 — 983
they shall dwell *s* in the — Eze 34:25 — 983
but they shall dwell *s*, and none — Eze 34:28 — 983
and they shall dwell *s* all of them — Eze 38:8 — 983
that are at rest, that dwell *s* — Eze 38:11 — 983
my people of Israel dwelleth *s* — Eze 38:14 — 983
when they dwelt *s* in their land — Eze 39:26 — 983
and will make them to lie down *s* — Hos 2:18 — 983
Jerusalem shall be *s* inhabited — Zec 14:11 — 983
take him, and lead him away *s* — Mk 14:44 — *806*
the jailer to keep them *s* — Acts 16:23 — *806*

SAFETY {19}
ye shall dwell in the land in *s* — Lev 25:18 — 983
your fill, and dwell therein in *s* — Lev 25:19 — 983
about, so that ye dwell in *s* — Deut 12:10 — 983
the LORD shall dwell in *s* by him — Deut 33:12 — 983
then shall dwell in *s* alone — Deut 33:28 — 983
I was not in *s*, neither had I — Job 3:26 — 7951
His children are far from *s* — Job 5:4 — 3468
which mourn may be exalted to *s* — Job 5:11 — 3468
and thou shalt take thy rest in *s* — Job 11:18 — 983
Though it be given him to be in *s* — Job 24:23 — 983
LORD, only makest me dwell in *s* — Ps 4:8 — 983
I will set him in *s* from him that — Ps 12:5 — 3468
An horse is a vain thing for *s* — Ps 33:17 — 8668
of counsellors there is *s* — Prov 11:14 — 8668
but *s* is of the LORD — Prov 21:31 — 8668
of counsellors there is *s* — Prov 24:6 — 8668
and the needy shall lie down in *s* — Is 14:30 — 983
truly found we shut with all *s* — Acts 5:23 — *803*
when they shall say, Peace and *s* — 1Th 5:3 — *803*

SAFFRON {1}
Spikenard and *s* — Song 4:14 — 3750

S

SAID {4003}

And God *s*, Let there be light ... Gen 1:3 559
And God *s*, Let there be a ... Gen 1:6 559
And God *s*, Let the waters under ... Gen 1:9 559
And God *s*, Let the earth bring ... Gen 1:11 559
And God *s*, Let there be lights in ... Gen 1:14 559
And God *s*, Let the waters bring ... Gen 1:20 559
And God *s*, Let the earth bring ... Gen 1:24 559
And God *s*, Let us make man in our ... Gen 1:26 559
God *s* unto them, Be fruitful, and ... Gen 1:28 559
And God *s*, Behold, I have given ... Gen 1:29 559
And the LORD God *s*, It is not good ... Gen 2:18 559
And Adam *s*, This is now bone of my ... Gen 2:23 559
he *s* unto the woman, Yea, hath ... Gen 3:1 559
unto the woman, Yea, hath God *s* ... Gen 3:1 559
the woman *s* unto the serpent, We ... Gen 3:2 559
midst of the garden, God hath *s* ... Gen 3:3 559
the serpent *s* unto the woman, Ye ... Gen 3:4 559
s unto him, Where art thou ... Gen 3:9 559
And he *s*, I heard thy voice in the ... Gen 3:10 559
And he *s*, Who told thee that thou ... Gen 3:11 559
And the man *s*, The woman whom thou ... Gen 3:12 559
the LORD God *s* unto the woman, ... Gen 3:13 559
And the woman *s*, The serpent ... Gen 3:13 559
the LORD God *s* unto the serpent, ... Gen 3:14 559
Unto the woman he *s*, I will ... Gen 3:16 559
And unto Adam he *s*, Because thou ... Gen 3:17 559
And the LORD God *s*, Behold, the ... Gen 3:22 559
she conceived, and bare Cain, and *s* ... Gen 4:1 559
the LORD *s* unto Cain, Why art ... Gen 4:6 559
the LORD *s* unto Cain, Where is ... Gen 4:9 559
And he *s*, I know not ... Gen 4:9 559
And he *s*, What hast thou done ... Gen 4:10 559
And Cain *s* unto the LORD, My ... Gen 4:13 559
And the LORD *s* unto him, Therefore ... Gen 4:15 559
Lamech *s* unto his wives, Adah and ... Gen 4:23 559
s she, hath appointed me another ... Gen 4:25
And the LORD *s*, My spirit shall ... Gen 6:3 559
And the LORD *s*, I will destroy man ... Gen 6:7 559
God *s* unto Noah, The end of all ... Gen 6:13 559
the LORD *s* unto Noah, Come thou ... Gen 7:1 559
the LORD *s* in his heart, I will ... Gen 8:21 559
s unto them, Be fruitful, and ... Gen 9:1 559
And God *s*, This is the token of ... Gen 9:12 559
God *s* unto Noah, This is the ... Gen 9:17 559
And he *s*, Cursed be Canaan ... Gen 9:25 559
And he *s*, Blessed be the LORD God ... Gen 9:26 559
wherefore it is *s*, Even as Nimrod ... Gen 10:9 559
they *s* one to another, Go to, let ... Gen 11:3 559
And they *s*, Go to, let us build us ... Gen 11:4 559
And the LORD *s*, Behold, the people ... Gen 11:6 559
Now the LORD had *s* unto Abram ... Gen 12:1 559
LORD appeared unto Abram, and *s* ... Gen 12:7 559
that he *s* unto Sarai his wife, ... Gen 12:11 559
And Pharaoh called Abram, and *s* ... Gen 12:18 559
Abram *s* unto Lot, Let there be no ... Gen 13:8 559
the LORD *s* unto Abram, after that ... Gen 13:14 559
And he blessed him, and *s*, Blessed ... Gen 14:19 559
And the king of Sodom *s* unto Abram ... Gen 14:21 559
Abram *s* to the king of Sodom, I ... Gen 14:22 559
And Abram *s*, Lord GOD, what wilt ... Gen 15:2 559
And Abram *s*, Behold, to me thou ... Gen 15:3 559
he brought him forth abroad, and *s* ... Gen 15:5 559
he *s* unto him, So shall thy seed ... Gen 15:5 559
he *s* unto him, I am the LORD that ... Gen 15:7 559
And he *s*, Lord GOD, whereby shall ... Gen 15:8 559
he *s* unto him, Take me an heifer ... Gen 15:9 559
he *s* unto Abram, Know of a surety ... Gen 15:13 559
Sarai *s* unto Abram, Behold now, ... Gen 16:2 559
Sarai *s* unto Abram, My wrong be ... Gen 16:5 559
But Abram *s* unto Sarai, Behold, ... Gen 16:6 559
And he *s*, Hagar, Sarai's maid, ... Gen 16:8 559
And she *s*, I flee from the face of ... Gen 16:8 559
the angel of the LORD *s* unto her ... Gen 16:9 559
the angel of the LORD *s* unto her ... Gen 16:10 559
the angel of the LORD *s* unto her ... Gen 16:11 559
for she *s*, Have I also here ... Gen 16:13 559
s unto him, I am the Almighty God ... Gen 17:1 559
God *s* unto Abraham, Thou shalt ... Gen 17:9 559
God *s* unto Abraham, As for Sarai ... Gen 17:15 559
s in his heart, Shall a child be ... Gen 17:17 559
Abraham *s* unto God, O that ... Gen 17:18 559
And God *s*, Sarah thy wife shall ... Gen 17:19 559
day, as God had *s* unto him ... Gen 17:23 1696
And *s*, My Lord, if now I have ... Gen 18:3 559
And they *s*, So do, as thou hast ... Gen 18:5 1696
So do, as thou hast *s* ... Gen 18:5 559
into the tent unto Sarah, and *s* ... Gen 18:6 559
they *s* unto him, Where is Sarah ... Gen 18:9 559
And he *s*, Behold, in the tent ... Gen 18:9 559
And he *s*, I will certainly return ... Gen 18:10 559
And the LORD *s* unto Abraham, ... Gen 18:13 559
And he *s*, Nay ... Gen 18:15 559
And the LORD *s*, Shall I hide from ... Gen 18:17 559
And the LORD *s*, Because the cry of ... Gen 18:20 559
And Abraham drew near, and *s* ... Gen 18:23 559
And the LORD *s*, If I find in Sodom ... Gen 18:26 559
And Abraham answered and *s*, Behold ... Gen 18:27 559
And he *s*, If I find there forty and ... Gen 18:28 559
he spake unto him yet again, and *s* ... Gen 18:29 559
And he *s*, I will not do it for ... Gen 18:29 559
he *s* unto him, Oh let not the ... Gen 18:30 559
And he *s*, I will not do it, if I ... Gen 18:30 559
And he *s*, Behold now, I have taken ... Gen 18:31 559
And he *s*, I will not destroy it ... Gen 18:31 559
And he *s*, Oh let not the Lord be ... Gen 18:32 559
And he *s*, I will not destroy it ... Gen 18:32 559
And he *s*, Behold now, my lords, ... Gen 19:2 559
And they *s*, Nay ... Gen 19:2 559
s unto him, Where are the men ... Gen 19:5 559
And *s*, I pray you, brethren, do ... Gen 19:7 559
And they *s*, Stand back ... Gen 19:9 559
they *s* again, This one fellow ... Gen 19:9 559
the men *s* unto Lot, Hast thou ... Gen 19:12 559
which married his daughters, and *s* ... Gen 19:14 559
them forth abroad, that he *s* ... Gen 19:17 559
Lot *s* unto them, Oh, not so, my ... Gen 19:18 559
he *s* unto him, See, I have ... Gen 19:21 559
the firstborn *s* unto the younger, ... Gen 19:31 559
the firstborn *s* unto the younger ... Gen 19:34 559
Abraham *s* of Sarah his wife, She ... Gen 20:2 559
s to him, Behold, thou art but a ... Gen 20:3 559
and he *s*, Lord, wilt thou slay ... Gen 20:4 559
S he not unto me, She is my ... Gen 20:5 559
and she, even she herself *s* ... Gen 20:5 559
God *s* unto him in a dream, Yea, I ... Gen 20:6 559
s unto him, What hast thou done ... Gen 20:9 559
Abimelech *s* unto Abraham, What ... Gen 20:10 559
And Abraham *s*, Because I thought, ... Gen 20:11 559
that I *s* unto her, This is thy ... Gen 20:13 559
And Abimelech *s*, Behold, my land ... Gen 20:15 559
And unto Sarah he *s*, Behold, I ... Gen 20:16 559
LORD visited Sarah as he had *s* ... Gen 21:1 559
And Sarah *s*, God hath made me to ... Gen 21:6 559
And she *s*, Who would have ... Gen 21:7 559
Who would have *s* unto Abraham ... Gen 21:7 4448
Wherefore she *s* unto Abraham ... Gen 21:10 559
God *s* unto Abraham, Let it not be ... Gen 21:12 559
all that Sarah hath *s* unto thee ... Gen 21:12 559
for she *s*, Let me not see the ... Gen 21:16 559
s unto her, What aileth thee, ... Gen 21:17 559
And Abraham *s*, I will swear ... Gen 21:24 559
And Abimelech *s*, I wot not who ... Gen 21:26 559
Abimelech *s* unto Abraham, What ... Gen 21:29 559
And he *s*, For these seven ewe ... Gen 21:30 559
Abraham, and *s* unto him, Abraham ... Gen 22:1 559
and he *s*, Behold, here I am ... Gen 22:1 559
And he *s*, Take now thy son, thine ... Gen 22:2 559
Abraham *s* unto his young men, ... Gen 22:5 559
unto Abraham his father, and *s* ... Gen 22:7 559
and he *s*, Here am I, my son ... Gen 22:7 559
And he *s*, Behold the fire and the ... Gen 22:7 559
And Abraham *s*, My son, God will ... Gen 22:8 559
unto him out of heaven, and *s* ... Gen 22:11 559
and he *s*, Here am I ... Gen 22:11 559
And he *s*, Lay not thine hand upon ... Gen 22:12 559
as it is *s* to this day, In the ... Gen 22:14 559
And *s*, By myself have I sworn, ... Gen 22:16 559
Abraham *s* unto his eldest servant ... Gen 24:2 559
And the servant *s* unto him ... Gen 24:5 559
Abraham *s* unto him, Beware thou ... Gen 24:6 559
And he *s*, O LORD God of my master ... Gen 24:12 559
the servant ran to meet her, and *s* ... Gen 24:17 559
And she *s*, Drink, my lord ... Gen 24:18 559
had done giving him drink, she *s* ... Gen 24:19 559
And *s*, Whose daughter art thou ... Gen 24:23 559
she *s* unto him, I am the daughter ... Gen 24:24 559
She *s* moreover unto him, We have ... Gen 24:25 559
And he *s*, Blessed be the LORD God ... Gen 24:27 559
And he *s*, Come in, thou blessed of ... Gen 24:31 559
but he *s*, I will not eat, until I ... Gen 24:33 559
And he *s*, Speak on ... Gen 24:33 559
And he *s*, I am Abraham's servant ... Gen 24:34 559
I *s* unto my master, Peradventure ... Gen 24:39 559
he *s* unto me, The LORD, before ... Gen 24:40 559
came this day unto the well, and *s* ... Gen 24:42 559
I *s* unto her, Let me drink, I ... Gen 24:45 559
pitcher from her shoulder, and *s* ... Gen 24:46 559
And I asked her, and *s*, Whose ... Gen 24:47 559
And she *s*, The daughter of Bethuel ... Gen 24:47 559
Laban and Bethuel answered and *s* ... Gen 24:50 559
rose up in the morning, and he *s* ... Gen 24:54 559
And her brother and her mother *s* ... Gen 24:55 559
he *s* unto them, Hinder me not, ... Gen 24:56 559
And they *s*, We will call the ... Gen 24:57 559
s unto her, Wilt thou go with ... Gen 24:58 559
And she *s*, I will go ... Gen 24:58 559
s unto her, Thou art our sister, ... Gen 24:60 559
For she had *s* unto the servant, ... Gen 24:65 559
And the servant had *s*, It is my ... Gen 24:65 559
and she *s*, If it be so, why am I ... Gen 25:22 559
And the LORD *s* unto her, Two ... Gen 25:23 559
Esau *s* to Jacob, Feed me, I pray ... Gen 25:30 559
And Jacob *s*, Sell me this day thy ... Gen 25:31 559
And Esau *s*, Behold, I am at the ... Gen 25:32 559
And Jacob *s*, Swear to me this day ... Gen 25:33 559
the LORD appeared unto him, and *s* ... Gen 26:2 559
and he *s*, She is my sister ... Gen 26:7 559
s he, the men of the place should ... Gen 26:7 559
And Abimelech called Isaac, and *s* ... Gen 26:9 559
Isaac *s* unto him, Because I *s*, ... Gen 26:9 559
And Abimelech *s*, What is this thou ... Gen 26:10 559
Abimelech *s* unto Isaac, Go from ... Gen 26:16 559
and he *s*, For now the LORD hath ... Gen 26:22 559
unto him the same night, and *s* ... Gen 26:24 559
Isaac *s* unto them, Wherefore come ... Gen 26:27 559
And they *s*, We saw certainly that ... Gen 26:28 559
and we *s*, Let there be now an oath ... Gen 26:28 559
s unto him, We have found water ... Gen 26:32 559
eldest son, and *s* unto him, My son ... Gen 27:1 559
he *s* unto him, Behold, here am I ... Gen 27:1 559
And he *s*, Behold now, I am old, I ... Gen 27:2 559
Jacob *s* to Rebekah his mother, ... Gen 27:11 559
And his mother *s* unto him, Upon me ... Gen 27:13 559
And he came unto his father, and *s* ... Gen 27:18 559
and he *s*, Here am I ... Gen 27:18 559
Jacob *s* unto his father, I am ... Gen 27:19 559
Isaac *s* unto his son, How is it ... Gen 27:20 559
And he *s*, Because the LORD thy God ... Gen 27:20 559
Isaac *s* unto Jacob, Come near, I ... Gen 27:21 559
and he felt him, and *s*, The voice ... Gen 27:22 559
And he *s*, Art thou my very son ... Gen 27:24 559
And he *s*, I am ... Gen 27:24 559
And he *s*, Bring it near to me, and ... Gen 27:25 559
And his father Isaac *s* unto him ... Gen 27:26 559
his raiment, and blessed him, and *s* ... Gen 27:27 559
s unto his father, Let my father ... Gen 27:31 559
And Isaac his father *s* unto him ... Gen 27:32 559
And he *s*, I am thy son, thy ... Gen 27:32 559
trembled very exceedingly, and *s* ... Gen 27:33 559
s unto his father, Bless me, even ... Gen 27:34 559
And he *s*, Thy brother came with ... Gen 27:35 559
And he *s*, Is not he rightly named ... Gen 27:36 559
And he *s*, Hast thou not reserved a ... Gen 27:36 559
s unto Esau, Behold, I have made ... Gen 27:37 559
Esau *s* unto his father, Hast thou ... Gen 27:38 559
s unto him, Behold, thy dwelling ... Gen 27:39 559
Esau *s* in his heart, The days of ... Gen 27:41 559
s unto him, Behold, thy brother ... Gen 27:42 559
Rebekah *s* to Isaac, I am weary of ... Gen 27:46 559
s unto him, Thou shalt not take a ... Gen 28:1 559
the LORD stood above it, and *s* ... Gen 28:13 559
awaked out of his sleep, and he *s* ... Gen 28:16 559
And he was afraid, and *s*, How ... Gen 28:17 559
Jacob *s* unto them, My brethren, ... Gen 29:4 559
And they *s*, Of Haran are we ... Gen 29:4 559
he *s* unto them, Know ye Laban the ... Gen 29:5 559
And they *s*, We know him ... Gen 29:5 559
he *s* unto them, Is he well ... Gen 29:6 559
And they *s*, He is well ... Gen 29:6 559
And he *s*, Lo, it is yet high day, ... Gen 29:7 559
And they *s*, We cannot, until all ... Gen 29:8 559
Laban *s* to him, Surely thou art ... Gen 29:14 559
Laban *s* unto Jacob, Because thou ... Gen 29:15 559
and *s*, I will serve thee seven ... Gen 29:18 559
And Laban *s*, It is better that I ... Gen 29:19 559
Jacob *s* unto Laban, Give me my ... Gen 29:21 559
he *s* to Laban, What is this thou ... Gen 29:25 559
And Laban *s*, It must not be so ... Gen 29:26 559
for she *s*, Surely the LORD hath ... Gen 29:32 559
and *s*, Because the LORD hath heard ... Gen 29:33 559
and *s*, Now this time will my ... Gen 29:34 559
and she *s*, Now will I praise the ... Gen 29:35 559
s unto Jacob, Give me children, ... Gen 30:1 559
and he *s*, Am I in God's stead, who ... Gen 30:2 559
And she *s*, Behold my maid Bilhah, ... Gen 30:3 559
And Rachel *s*, God hath judged me, ... Gen 30:6 559
And Rachel *s*, With great ... Gen 30:8 559
And Leah *s*, A troop cometh ... Gen 30:11 559
And Leah *s*, Happy am I, for the ... Gen 30:13 559
Then Rachel *s* to Leah, Give me, I ... Gen 30:14 559
she *s* unto her, Is it a small ... Gen 30:15 559
And Rachel *s*, Therefore he shall ... Gen 30:15 559
Leah went out to meet him, and *s* ... Gen 30:16 559
And Leah *s*, God hath given me my ... Gen 30:18 559
And Leah *s*, God hath endued me ... Gen 30:20 559
and *s*, God hath taken away my ... Gen 30:23 559
and *s*, The LORD shall add to me ... Gen 30:24 559
Joseph, that Jacob *s* unto Laban ... Gen 30:25 559
Laban *s* unto him, I pray thee, if ... Gen 30:27 559
And he *s*, Appoint me thy wages, and ... Gen 30:28 559
he *s* unto him, Thou knowest how I ... Gen 30:29 559
And he *s*, What shall I give thee ... Gen 30:31 559
And Jacob *s*, Thou shalt not give ... Gen 30:31 559
And Laban *s*, Behold, I would it ... Gen 30:34 559
the LORD *s* unto Jacob, Return ... Gen 31:3 559
s unto them, I see your father's ... Gen 31:5 559
If he *s* thus, The speckled shall ... Gen 31:8 559
and if he *s* thus, The ringstraked ... Gen 31:8 559
And I *s*, Here am I ... Gen 31:11 559
And he *s*, Lift up now thine eyes, ... Gen 31:12 559
s unto him, Is there yet any ... Gen 31:14 559
whatsoever God hath *s* unto thee ... Gen 31:16 559
s unto him, Take heed that thou ... Gen 31:24 559
Laban *s* to Jacob, What hast thou ... Gen 31:26 559
s to Laban, Because I was afraid ... Gen 31:31 559
for I *s*, Peradventure thou ... Gen 31:31 559
she *s* to her father, Let it not ... Gen 31:35 559
s to Laban, What is my trespass ... Gen 31:36 559
s unto Jacob, These daughters are ... Gen 31:43 559
Jacob *s* unto his brethren, Gather ... Gen 31:46 559
And Laban *s*, This heap is a ... Gen 31:48 559
for he *s*, The LORD watch between ... Gen 31:49 559
Laban *s* to Jacob, Behold this ... Gen 31:51 559
And when Jacob saw them, he *s* ... Gen 32:2 559
And *s*, If Esau come to the one ... Gen 32:8 559
And Jacob *s*, O God of my father ... Gen 32:9 559
s unto his servants, Pass over ... Gen 32:16 559
For he *s*, I will appease him with ... Gen 32:20 559
And he *s*, Let me go, for the day ... Gen 32:26 559
And he *s*, I will not let thee go, ... Gen 32:26 559
he *s* unto him, What is thy name ... Gen 32:27 559
And he *s*, Jacob ... Gen 32:27 559
And he *s*, Thy name shall be called ... Gen 32:28 559
And Jacob asked him, and *s*, Tell me ... Gen 32:29 559
And he *s*, Wherefore is it that ... Gen 32:29 559
and *s*, Who are those with thee ... Gen 33:5 559
And he *s*, The children which God ... Gen 33:5 559
And he *s*, What meanest thou by all ... Gen 33:8 559
And he *s*, These are to find grace ... Gen 33:8 559
And Esau *s*, I have enough, my ... Gen 33:9 559
And Jacob *s*, Nay, I pray thee, if ... Gen 33:10 559
And he *s*, Let us take our journey, ... Gen 33:12 559
he *s* unto him, My lord knoweth ... Gen 33:13 559

And Esau *s*, Let me now leave with	Gen 33:15	559
And he *s*, What needeth it	Gen 33:15	559
Shechem *s* unto her father and unto	Gen 34:11	559
his father deceitfully, and *s*	Gen 34:13	1696
they *s* unto them, We cannot do	Gen 34:14	559
Jacob *s* to Simeon and Levi, Ye	Gen 34:30	559
And they *s*, Should he deal with	Gen 34:31	559
God *s* unto Jacob, Arise, go up to	Gen 35:1	559
Then Jacob *s* unto his household,	Gen 35:2	559
God *s* unto him, Thy name is Jacob	Gen 35:10	559
God *s* unto him, I am God Almighty	Gen 35:11	559
that the midwife *s* unto her	Gen 35:17	559
he *s* unto them, Hear, I pray you,	Gen 37:6	559
And his brethren *s* to him, Shalt	Gen 37:8	559
and told it his brethren, and *s*	Gen 37:9	559
s unto him, What is this dream	Gen 37:10	559
Israel *s* unto Joseph, Do not thy	Gen 37:13	559
And he *s* to him, Here am I	Gen 37:13	559
he *s* to him, Go, I pray thee, see	Gen 37:14	559
And he *s*, I seek my brethren	Gen 37:16	559
And the man *s*, They are departed	Gen 37:17	559
they *s* one to another, Behold,	Gen 37:19	559
and *s*, Let us not kill him	Gen 37:21	559
Reuben *s* unto them, Shed no blood	Gen 37:22	559
Judah *s* unto his brethren, What	Gen 37:26	559
returned unto his brethren, and *s*	Gen 37:30	559
and *s*, This have we found	Gen 37:32	559
And he knew it, and *s*, It is my	Gen 37:33	559
and he *s*, For I will go down into	Gen 37:35	559
Judah *s* unto Onan, Go in unto thy	Gen 38:8	559
Then *s* Judah to Tamar his	Gen 38:11	559
for he *s*, Lest peradventure he	Gen 38:11	559
turned unto her by the way, and *s*	Gen 38:16	559
And she *s*, What wilt thou give me	Gen 38:16	559
And he *s*, I will send thee a kid	Gen 38:17	559
And she *s*, Wilt thou give me a	Gen 38:17	559
And he *s*, What pledge shall I give	Gen 38:18	559
And she *s*, Thy signet, and thy	Gen 38:18	559
And they *s*, There was no harlot in	Gen 38:21	559
And he returned to Judah, and *s*	Gen 38:22	559
and also the men of the place *s*	Gen 38:22	559
And Judah *s*, Let her take it to	Gen 38:23	559
And Judah *s*, Bring her forth, and	Gen 38:24	559
and she *s*, Discern, I pray thee,	Gen 38:25	559
And Judah acknowledged them, and *s*	Gen 38:26	559
and she *s*, How hast thou broken	Gen 38:29	559
and she *s*, Lie with me	Gen 39:7	559
s unto his master's wife, Behold,	Gen 39:8	559
they *s* unto him, We have dreamed	Gen 40:8	559
Joseph *s* unto them, Do not	Gen 40:8	559
s to him, In my dream, behold, a	Gen 40:9	559
Joseph *s* unto him, This is the	Gen 40:12	559
he *s* unto Joseph, I also was in	Gen 40:16	559
And Joseph answered and *s*, This is	Gen 40:18	559
Pharaoh *s* unto Joseph, I have	Gen 41:15	559
Pharaoh *s* unto Joseph, In my	Gen 41:17	1696
Joseph *s* unto Pharaoh, The dream	Gen 41:25	559
Pharaoh *s* unto his servants, Can	Gen 41:38	559
Pharaoh *s* unto Joseph, Forasmuch	Gen 41:39	559
Pharaoh *s* unto Joseph, See, I	Gen 41:41	559
Pharaoh *s* unto Joseph, I am	Gen 41:44	559
s he, hath made me forget all my	Gen 41:51	559
come, according as Joseph had *s*	Gen 41:54	559
Pharaoh *s* unto all the Egyptians,	Gen 41:55	559
Jacob *s* unto his sons, Why do ye	Gen 42:1	559
And he *s*, Behold, I have heard	Gen 42:2	559
for he *s*, Lest peradventure	Gen 42:4	559
he *s* unto them, Whence come ye	Gen 42:7	559
And they *s*, From the land of	Gen 42:7	559
s unto them, Ye are spies	Gen 42:9	559
they *s* unto him, Nay, my lord,	Gen 42:10	559
he *s* unto them, Nay, but to see	Gen 42:12	559
And they *s*, Thy servants are	Gen 42:13	559
Joseph *s* unto them, That is it	Gen 42:14	559
Joseph *s* unto them the third day,	Gen 42:18	559
they *s* one to another, We are	Gen 42:21	559
he *s* unto his brethren, My money	Gen 42:28	559
we *s* unto him, We are true men	Gen 42:31	559
s unto us, Hereby shall I know	Gen 42:33	559
And Jacob their father *s* unto them	Gen 42:36	559
And he *s*, My son shall not go down	Gen 42:38	559
Egypt, their father *s* unto them	Gen 43:2	559
for the man *s* unto us, Ye shall	Gen 43:5	559
And Israel *s*, Wherefore dealt ye	Gen 43:6	559
And they *s*, The man asked us	Gen 43:7	559
Judah *s* unto Israel his father,	Gen 43:8	559
their father Israel *s* unto them	Gen 43:11	559
he *s* to the ruler of his house,	Gen 43:16	559
and they *s*, Because of the money	Gen 43:18	559
And *s*, O sir, we came indeed down	Gen 43:20	559
And he *s*, Peace be to you, fear	Gen 43:23	559
asked them of their welfare, and *s*	Gen 43:27	559
Benjamin, his mother's son, and *s*	Gen 43:29	559
And he *s*, God be gracious unto	Gen 43:29	559
out, and refrained himself, and *s*	Gen 43:31	559
Joseph *s* unto his steward, Up,	Gen 44:4	559
they *s* unto him, Wherefore saith	Gen 44:7	559
And he *s*, Now also let it be	Gen 44:10	559
Joseph *s* unto them, What deed is	Gen 44:15	559
And Judah *s*, What shall we say	Gen 44:16	559
And he *s*, God forbid that I should	Gen 44:17	559
Judah came near unto him, and *s*	Gen 44:18	559
we *s* unto my lord, We have a	Gen 44:20	559
we *s* unto my lord, The lad cannot	Gen 44:22	559
And our father *s*, Go again, and buy	Gen 44:25	559
And we *s*, We cannot go down	Gen 44:26	559
thy servant my father *s* unto us	Gen 44:27	559
the one went out from me, and I *s*	Gen 44:28	559
Joseph *s* unto his brethren, I am	Gen 45:3	559
Joseph *s* unto his brethren, Come	Gen 45:4	559
And he *s*, I am Joseph your brother	Gen 45:4	559
Pharaoh *s* unto Joseph, Say unto	Gen 45:17	559
he *s* unto them, See that ye fall	Gen 45:24	559
Joseph, which he had *s* unto them	Gen 45:27	1697
And Israel *s*, It is enough	Gen 45:28	559
in the visions of the night, and *s*	Gen 46:2	559
And he *s*, Here am I	Gen 46:2	559
And he *s*, I am God, the God of thy	Gen 46:3	559
Israel *s* unto Joseph, Now let me	Gen 46:30	559
Joseph *s* unto his brethren, and	Gen 46:31	559
Joseph came and told Pharaoh, and *s*	Gen 47:1	559
Pharaoh *s* unto his brethren, What	Gen 47:3	559
they *s* unto Pharaoh, Thy servants	Gen 47:3	559
They *s* moreover unto Pharaoh, For	Gen 47:4	559
Pharaoh *s* unto Jacob, How old art	Gen 47:8	559
Jacob *s* unto Pharaoh, The days of	Gen 47:9	559
Egyptians came unto Joseph, and *s*	Gen 47:15	559
And Joseph *s*, Give your cattle	Gen 47:16	559
s unto him, We will not hide it	Gen 47:18	559
Then Joseph *s* unto the people,	Gen 47:23	559
And they *s*, Thou hast saved our	Gen 47:25	559
s unto him, If now I have found	Gen 47:29	559
And he *s*, I will do as thou hast	Gen 47:30	559
I will do as thou hast *s*	Gen 47:30	1697
And he *s*, Swear unto me	Gen 47:31	559
And one told Jacob, and *s*, Behold,	Gen 48:2	559
Jacob *s* unto Joseph, God Almighty	Gen 48:3	559
s unto me, Behold, I will make	Gen 48:4	559
Israel beheld Joseph's sons, and *s*	Gen 48:8	559
Joseph *s* unto his father, They	Gen 48:9	559
And he *s*, Bring them, I pray thee,	Gen 48:9	559
Israel *s* unto Joseph, I had not	Gen 48:11	559
And he blessed Joseph, and *s*	Gen 48:15	559
Joseph *s* unto his father, Not so,	Gen 48:18	559
And his father refused, and *s*	Gen 48:19	559
Israel *s* unto Joseph, Behold, I	Gen 48:21	559
Jacob called unto his sons, and *s*	Gen 49:1	559
s unto them, I am to be gathered	Gen 49:29	559
And Pharaoh *s*, Go up, and bury thy	Gen 50:6	559
in the floor of Atad, they *s*	Gen 50:11	559
their father was dead, they *s*	Gen 50:15	559
and they *s*, Behold, we be thy	Gen 50:18	559
Joseph *s* unto them, Fear not	Gen 50:19	559
Joseph *s* unto his brethren, I die	Gen 50:24	559
he *s* unto his people, Behold, the	Ex 1:9	559
And he *s*, When ye do the office of	Ex 1:16	559
s unto them, Why have ye done	Ex 1:18	559
And the midwives *s* unto Pharaoh	Ex 1:19	559
she had compassion on him, and *s*	Ex 2:6	559
Then *s* his sister to Pharaoh's	Ex 2:7	559
And Pharaoh's daughter *s* to her	Ex 2:8	559
And Pharaoh's daughter *s* unto her	Ex 2:9	559
and she *s*, Because I drew him out	Ex 2:10	559
he *s* to him that did the wrong,	Ex 2:13	559
And he *s*, Who made thee a prince	Ex 2:14	559
And Moses feared, and *s*, Surely	Ex 2:14	559
came to Reuel their father, he *s*	Ex 2:18	559
And they *s*, An Egyptian delivered	Ex 2:19	559
he *s* unto his daughters, And where	Ex 2:20	559
for he *s*, I have been a stranger	Ex 2:22	559
And Moses *s*, I will now turn aside	Ex 3:3	559
of the midst of the bush, and *s*	Ex 3:4	559
And he *s*, Here am I	Ex 3:4	559
And he *s*, Draw not nigh hither	Ex 3:5	559
Moreover he *s*, I am the God of	Ex 3:6	559
And the LORD *s*, I have surely seen	Ex 3:7	559
Moses *s* unto God, Who am I, that	Ex 3:11	559
And he *s*, Certainly I will be with	Ex 3:12	559
Moses *s* unto God, Behold, when I	Ex 3:13	559
God *s* unto Moses, I AM THAT I AM	Ex 3:14	559
and he *s*, Thus shalt thou say unto	Ex 3:14	559
God *s* moreover unto Moses, Thus	Ex 3:15	559
And I have *s*, I will bring you up	Ex 3:17	559
And Moses answered and *s*, But,	Ex 4:1	559
And the LORD *s* unto him, What is	Ex 4:2	559
And he *s*, A rod	Ex 4:2	559
And he *s*, Cast it on the ground	Ex 4:3	559
the LORD *s* unto Moses, Put forth	Ex 4:4	559
the LORD *s* furthermore unto him,	Ex 4:6	559
And he *s*, Put thine hand into thy	Ex 4:7	559
Moses *s* unto the LORD, O my Lord,	Ex 4:10	559
And the LORD *s* unto him, Who hath	Ex 4:11	559
And he *s*, O my Lord, send, I pray	Ex 4:13	559
kindled against Moses, and he *s*	Ex 4:14	559
s unto him, Let me go, I pray	Ex 4:18	559
Jethro *s* to Moses, Go in peace	Ex 4:18	559
the LORD *s* unto Moses in Midian,	Ex 4:19	559
the LORD *s* unto Moses, When thou	Ex 4:21	559
son, and cast it at his feet, and *s*	Ex 4:25	559
then she *s*, A bloody husband thou	Ex 4:26	559
And the LORD *s* to Aaron, Go into	Ex 4:27	559
And Pharaoh *s*, Who is the LORD,	Ex 5:2	559
And they *s*, The God of the Hebrews	Ex 5:3	559
And the king of Egypt *s* unto them	Ex 5:4	559
And Pharaoh *s*, Behold, the people	Ex 5:5	559
But he *s*, Ye are idle, ye are	Ex 5:17	559
were in evil case, after it was *s*	Ex 5:19	559
they *s* unto them, The LORD look	Ex 5:21	559
returned unto the LORD, and *s*	Ex 5:22	559
Then the LORD *s* unto Moses	Ex 6:1	559
s unto him, I am the LORD	Ex 6:2	559
and Moses, to whom the LORD *s*	Ex 6:26	559
Moses *s* before the LORD, Behold,	Ex 6:30	559
the LORD *s* unto Moses, See, I	Ex 7:1	559
as the LORD had *s*	Ex 7:13	1696
the LORD *s* unto Moses, Pharaoh's	Ex 7:14	559
as the LORD had *s*	Ex 7:22	1696
called for Moses and Aaron, and *s*	Ex 8:8	559
Moses *s* unto Pharaoh, Glory over	Ex 8:9	559
And he *s*, To morrow	Ex 8:10	559
And he *s*, Be it according to thy	Ex 8:10	559
as the LORD had *s*	Ex 8:15	1696
the LORD *s* unto Moses, Say unto	Ex 8:16	559
Then the magicians *s* unto Pharaoh	Ex 8:19	1696
as the LORD had *s*	Ex 8:19	1696
the LORD *s* unto Moses, Rise up	Ex 8:20	559
for Moses and for Aaron, and *s*	Ex 8:25	559
And Moses *s*, It is not meet so to	Ex 8:26	559
And Pharaoh *s*, I will let you go,	Ex 8:28	559
And Moses *s*, Behold, I go out from	Ex 8:29	559
Then the LORD *s* unto Moses	Ex 9:1	559
the LORD *s* unto Moses and unto	Ex 9:8	559
the LORD *s* unto Moses, Rise up	Ex 9:13	559
the LORD *s* unto Moses, Stretch	Ex 9:22	559
s unto them, I have sinned this	Ex 9:27	559
Moses *s* unto him, As soon as I am	Ex 9:29	559
the LORD *s* unto Moses, Go in unto	Ex 10:1	559
s unto him, Thus saith the LORD	Ex 10:3	559
And Pharaoh's servants *s* unto him	Ex 10:7	559
he *s* unto them, Go, serve the	Ex 10:8	559
And Moses *s*, We will go with our	Ex 10:9	559
he *s* unto them, Let the LORD be	Ex 10:10	559
the LORD *s* unto Moses, Stretch	Ex 10:12	559
and he *s*, I have sinned against	Ex 10:16	559
the LORD *s* unto Moses, Stretch	Ex 10:21	559
Pharaoh called unto Moses, and *s*	Ex 10:24	559
And Moses *s*, Thou must give us	Ex 10:25	559
Pharaoh *s* unto him, Get thee from	Ex 10:28	559
And Moses *s*, Thou hast spoken well	Ex 10:29	559
the LORD *s* unto Moses, Yet will I	Ex 11:1	559
And Moses *s*, Thus saith the LORD,	Ex 11:4	559
the LORD *s* unto Moses, Pharaoh	Ex 11:9	559
s unto them, Draw out and take you	Ex 12:21	559
for Moses and Aaron by night, and *s*	Ex 12:31	559
go, serve the LORD, as ye have *s*	Ex 12:31	1696
and your herds, as ye have *s*	Ex 12:32	1696
for they *s*, We be all dead men	Ex 12:33	559
the LORD *s* unto Moses and Aaron,	Ex 12:43	559
Moses *s* unto the people, Remember	Ex 13:3	559
for God *s*, Lest peradventure the	Ex 13:17	559
against the people, and they *s*	Ex 14:5	559
they *s* unto Moses, Because there	Ex 14:11	559
Moses *s* unto the people, Fear ye	Ex 14:13	559
the LORD *s* unto Moses, Wherefore	Ex 14:15	559
so that the Egyptians *s*, Let us	Ex 14:25	559
the LORD *s* unto Moses, Stretch	Ex 14:26	559
The enemy *s*, I will pursue, I	Ex 15:9	559
And *s*, If thou wilt diligently	Ex 15:26	559
children of Israel *s* unto them	Ex 16:3	559
Then *s* the LORD unto Moses,	Ex 16:4	559
Aaron *s* unto all the children of	Ex 16:6	559
And Moses *s*, This shall be, when	Ex 16:8	559
they *s* one to another, It is	Ex 16:15	559
Moses *s* unto them, This is the	Ex 16:15	559
And Moses *s*, Let no man leave of	Ex 16:19	559
he *s* unto them, This is that	Ex 16:23	559
is that which the LORD hath *s*	Ex 16:23	1696
And Moses *s*, Eat that to day	Ex 16:25	559
the LORD *s* unto Moses, How long	Ex 16:28	559
And Moses *s*, This is the thing	Ex 16:32	559
Moses *s* unto Aaron, Take a pot,	Ex 16:33	559
people did chide with Moses, and *s*	Ex 17:2	559
Moses *s* unto them, Why chide ye	Ex 17:2	559
murmured against Moses, and *s*	Ex 17:3	559
the LORD *s* unto Moses, Go on	Ex 17:5	559
Moses *s* unto Joshua, Choose us	Ex 17:9	559
Joshua did as Moses had *s* to him	Ex 17:10	559
the LORD *s* unto Moses, Write this	Ex 17:14	559
For he *s*, Because the LORD hath	Ex 17:16	559
for he *s*, I have been an alien in	Ex 18:3	559
s he, was mine help, and delivered	Ex 18:4	
he *s* unto Moses, I thy father in	Ex 18:6	559
And Jethro *s*, Blessed be the LORD,	Ex 18:10	559
that he did to the people, he *s*	Ex 18:14	559
Moses *s* unto his father in law,	Ex 18:15	559
Moses' father in law *s* unto him	Ex 18:17	559
in law, and did all that he had *s*	Ex 18:24	559
people answered together, and *s*	Ex 19:8	559
the LORD *s* unto Moses, Lo, I come	Ex 19:9	559
the LORD *s* unto Moses, Go unto	Ex 19:10	559
he *s* unto the people, Be ready	Ex 19:15	559
the LORD *s* unto Moses, Go down,	Ex 19:21	559
Moses *s* unto the LORD, The people	Ex 19:23	559
And the LORD *s* unto him, Away, get	Ex 19:24	559
they *s* unto Moses, Speak thou	Ex 20:19	559
Moses *s* unto the people, Fear not	Ex 20:20	559
the LORD *s* unto Moses, Thus thou	Ex 20:22	559
I have *s* unto you be circumspect	Ex 23:13	559
he *s* unto Moses, Come up unto the	Ex 24:1	559
answered with one voice, and *s*	Ex 24:3	559
which the LORD hath *s* will we do	Ex 24:3	1696
and they *s*, All that the LORD hath	Ex 24:7	559
that the LORD hath *s* will we do	Ex 24:7	1696
sprinkled it on the people, and *s*	Ex 24:8	559
the LORD *s* unto Moses, Come up to	Ex 24:12	559
he *s* unto the elders, Tarry ye	Ex 24:14	559
the LORD *s* unto Moses, Take unto	Ex 30:34	559
s unto him, Up, make us gods,	Ex 32:1	559
Aaron *s* unto them, Break off the	Ex 32:2	559
and they *s*, These be thy gods, O	Ex 32:4	559
and Aaron made proclamation, and *s*	Ex 32:5	559
the LORD *s* unto Moses, Go, get	Ex 32:7	1696
have sacrificed thereunto, and *s*	Ex 32:8	559
the LORD *s* unto Moses, I have	Ex 32:9	559

besought the LORD his God, and s Ex 32:11 559
he s unto Moses, There is a noise Ex 32:17 559
And he s, It is not the voice of Ex 32:18 559
Moses s unto Aaron, What did this Ex 32:21 559
And Aaron s, Let not the anger of Ex 32:22 559
For they s unto me, Make us gods, Ex 32:23 559
I s unto them, Whosoever hath any Ex 32:24 559
in the gate of the camp, and s Ex 32:26 559
he s unto them, Thus saith the Ex 32:27 559
For Moses had s, Consecrate Ex 32:29 559
that Moses s unto the people, Ye Ex 32:30 559
returned unto the LORD, and s Ex 32:31 559
the LORD s unto Moses, Whosoever Ex 32:33 559
the LORD s unto Moses, Depart, and Ex 33:1 1696
For the LORD had s unto Moses Ex 33:5 559
Moses s unto the LORD, See, thou Ex 33:12 559
Yet thou hast s, I know thee by Ex 33:12 559
And he s, My presence shall go Ex 33:14 559
he s unto him, If thy presence go Ex 33:15 559
the LORD s unto Moses, I will do Ex 33:17 559
And he s, I beseech thee, shew me Ex 33:18 559
And he s, I will make all my Ex 33:19 559
And he s, Thou canst not see my Ex 33:20 559
And the LORD s, Behold, there is a Ex 33:21 559
the LORD s unto Moses, Hew thee Ex 34:1 559
And he s, If now I have found Ex 34:9 559
And he s, Behold, I make a Ex 34:10 559
the LORD s unto Moses, Write thou Ex 34:27 559
s unto them, These are the words Ex 35:1 559
Moses s unto the children of Ex 35:30 559
Moses s unto the congregation, Lev 8:5 559
Moses s unto Aaron and to his sons Lev 8:31 559
he s unto Aaron, Take thee a Lev 9:2 559
And Moses s, This is the thing Lev 9:6 559
Moses s unto Aaron, Go unto the Lev 9:7 559
Then Moses s unto Aaron, This is Lev 10:3 559
s unto them, Come near, carry Lev 10:4 559
as Moses had s Lev 10:5 1696
Moses s unto Aaron, and unto Lev 10:6 559
Aaron s unto Moses, Behold, this Lev 10:19 1696
the LORD s unto Moses, Speak unto Lev 16:2 559
Therefore I s unto the children Lev 17:12 559
therefore I s unto the children Lev 17:14 559
But I have s unto you, Ye shall Lev 20:24 559
the LORD s unto Moses, Speak unto Lev 21:1 559
the LORD s unto Moses, Number all Num 3:40 559
the LORD s unto Moses, They shall Num 7:11 559
And those men s unto him, We are Num 9:7 559
Moses s unto them, Stand still, Num 9:8 559
Moses s unto Hobab, the son of Num 10:29 559
the place of which the LORD s Num 10:29 559
he s unto him, I will not go Num 10:30 559
And he s, Leave us not, I pray Num 10:31 559
the ark set forward, that Moses s Num 10:35 559
And when it rested, he s, Return, Num 10:36 559
of Israel also wept again, and s Num 11:4 559
Moses s unto the LORD, Wherefore Num 11:11 559
the LORD s unto Moses, Gather Num 11:16 559
And Moses s, The people, among Num 11:21 559
and thou hast s, I will give them Num 11:21 559
the LORD s unto Moses, Is the Num 11:23 559
a young man, and told Moses, and s Num 11:27 559
of his young men, answered and s Num 11:28 559
Moses s unto him, Enviest thou Num 11:29 559
And they s, Hath the LORD indeed Num 12:2 559
And he s, Hear now my words Num 12:6 559
Aaron s unto Moses, Alas, my lord Num 12:11 559
the LORD s unto Moses, If her Num 12:14 559
s unto them, Get you up this way Num 13:17 559
And they told him, and s, We came Num 13:27 559
the people before Moses, and s Num 13:30 559
the men that went up with him s Num 13:31 559
whole congregation s unto them Num 14:2 559
they s one to another, Let us Num 14:4 559
the LORD s unto Moses, How long Num 14:11 559
Moses s unto the LORD, Then the Num 14:13 559
And the LORD s, I have pardoned Num 14:20 559
which ye s should be a prey, them Num 14:31 559
I the LORD have s, I will surely Num 14:35 1696
And Moses s, Wherefore now do ye Num 14:41 559
the LORD s unto Moses, The man Num 15:35 559
s unto them, Ye take too much Num 16:3 559
Moses s unto Korah, Hear, I pray Num 16:8 559
which s, We will not come up Num 16:12 559
s unto the LORD, Respect not thou Num 16:15 559
Moses s unto Korah, Be thou and Num 16:16 559
they fell upon their faces, and s Num 16:22 559
And Moses s, Hereby ye shall know Num 16:28 559
for they s, Lest the earth Num 16:34 559
as the LORD s to him by the hand Num 16:40 1696
Moses s unto Aaron, Take a censer Num 16:46 559
the LORD s unto Moses, Bring Num 17:10 559
the LORD s unto Aaron, Thou and Num 18:1 559
therefore I have s unto them Num 18:24 559
he s unto them, Hear now, ye Num 20:10 559
Edom s unto him, Thou shalt not Num 20:18 559
the children of Israel s unto him Num 20:19 559
And he s, Thou shalt not go Num 20:20 559
vowed a vow unto the LORD, and s Num 21:2 559
the people came to Moses, and s Num 21:7 559
the LORD s unto Moses, Make thee Num 21:8 559
Wherefore it is s in the book of Num 21:14 559
the LORD s unto Moses, Fear him Num 21:34 559
Moab s unto the elders of Midian, Num 22:4 559
he s unto them, Lodge here this Num 22:8 559
And God came unto Balaam, and s Num 22:9 559
Balaam s unto God, Balak the son Num 22:10 559
God s unto Balaam, Thou shalt not Num 22:12 559
s unto the princes of Balak, Get Num 22:13 559
up, and they went unto Balak, and s Num 22:14 559
s to him, Thus saith Balak the Num 22:16 559
s unto the servants of Balak, If Num 22:18 559
s unto him, If the men come to Num 22:20 559
she s unto Balaam, What have I Num 22:28 559
Balaam s unto the ass, Because Num 22:29 559
the ass s unto Balaam, Am not I Num 22:30 559
And he s, Nay Num 22:30 559
the angel of the LORD s unto him Num 22:32 559
Balaam s unto the angel of the Num 22:34 559
angel of the LORD s unto Balaam Num 22:35 559
Balak s unto Balaam, Did I not Num 22:37 559
Balaam s unto Balak, Lo, I am Num 22:38 559
Balaam s unto Balak, Build me Num 23:1 559
Balaam s unto Balak, Stand by thy Num 23:3 559
he s unto him, I have prepared Num 23:4 559
a word in Balaam's mouth, and s Num 23:5 559
And he took up his parable, and s Num 23:7 559
Balak s unto Balaam, What hast Num 23:11 559
And he answered and s, Must I not Num 23:12 559
Balak s unto him, Come, I pray Num 23:13 559
he s unto Balak, Stand here by Num 23:15 559
and put a word in his mouth, and s Num 23:16 559
Balak s unto him, What hath the Num 23:17 559
And he took up his parable, and s Num 23:18 559
hath he s, and shall he not do it Num 23:19 559
this time it shall be s of Jacob Num 23:23 559
Balak s unto Balaam, Neither Num 23:25 559
s unto Balak, Told not I thee, Num 23:26 559
Balak s unto Balaam, Come, I pray Num 23:27 559
Balaam s unto Balak, Build me Num 23:29 559
And Balak did as Balaam had s Num 23:30 559
And he took up his parable, and s Num 24:3 559
Balaam the son of Beor hath s Num 24:3 5002
man whose eyes are open hath s Num 24:3 5002
He hath s, which heard the words Num 24:4 5002
Balak s unto Balaam, I called Num 24:10 559
Balaam s unto Balak, Spake I not Num 24:12 559
And he took up his parable, and s Num 24:15 559
Balaam the son of Beor hath s Num 24:15 5002
man whose eyes are open hath s Num 24:15 5002
He hath s, which heard the words Num 24:16 5002
he took up his parable, and s Num 24:20 559
and took up his parable, and s Num 24:21 559
And he took up his parable, and s Num 24:23 559
the LORD s unto Moses, Take all Num 25:4 559
Moses s unto the judges of Israel Num 25:5 559
For the LORD had s of them Num 26:65 559
the LORD s unto Moses, Get thee Num 27:12 559
the LORD s unto Moses, Take thee Num 27:18 559
Moses s unto them, Have ye saved Num 31:15 559
Eleazar the priest s unto the men Num 31:21 559
they s unto Moses, Thy servants Num 31:49 559
s they, if we have found grace in Num 32:5 559
Moses s unto the children of Gad Num 32:6 559
And they came near unto him, and s Num 32:16 559
Moses s unto them, If ye will do Num 32:20 559
Moses s unto them, If the Num 32:29 559
As the LORD hath s unto thy Num 32:31 1696
And they s, The LORD commanded my Num 36:2 559
of the sons of Joseph hath s well Num 36:5 1696
And ye answered me, and s, The Deut 1:14 559
I s unto you, Ye are come unto Deut 1:20 559
of thy fathers hath s unto thee Deut 1:21 1696
unto me every one of you, and s Deut 1:22 559
and brought us word again, and s Deut 1:25 559
ye murmured in your tents, and s Deut 1:27 559
Then I s unto you, Dread not, Deut 1:29 559
which ye s should be a prey, and Deut 1:39 559
s unto me, We have sinned against Deut 1:41 559
And the LORD s unto me, Say unto Deut 1:42 559
And the LORD s unto me, Distress Deut 2:9 559
s I, and get you over the brook Deut 2:13 559
And the LORD s unto me, Behold, I Deut 2:31 559
And the LORD s unto me, Fear him Deut 3:2 559
and the LORD s unto me, Let it Deut 3:26 559
in Horeb, when the LORD s unto me Deut 4:10 559
s unto them, Hear, O Israel, the Deut 5:1 559
And ye s, Behold, the LORD our God Deut 5:24 559
and the LORD s unto me, I have Deut 5:28 559
they have well s all that they Deut 5:28 559
as the LORD hath s unto thee Deut 9:3 1696
And the LORD s unto me, Arise, get Deut 9:12 559
LORD had s he would destroy you Deut 9:25 559
therefore unto the LORD, and s Deut 9:26 559
At that time the LORD s unto me Deut 10:1 559
And the LORD s unto me, Arise, Deut 10:11 559
tread upon, as he hath s unto you Deut 11:25 1696
as the LORD hath s unto you Deut 17:16 559
as he hath s unto them Deut 18:2 1696
And the LORD s unto me, They have Deut 18:17 559
s unto them, Ye have seen all Deut 29:2 559
a God, as he hath s unto thee Deut 29:13 1696
he s unto them, I am an hundred Deut 31:2 559
also the LORD hath s unto me Deut 31:2 559
before thee, as the LORD hath s Deut 31:3 1696
s unto him in the sight of all Deut 31:7 559
the LORD s unto Moses, Behold, Deut 31:14 559
the LORD s unto Moses, Behold, Deut 31:16 559
the son of Nun a charge, and s Deut 31:23 559
And he s, I will hide my face from Deut 32:20 559
I s, I would scatter them into Deut 32:26 559
he s unto them, Set your hearts Deut 32:46 559
And he s, The LORD came from Sinai Deut 33:2 559
and he s, Hear, LORD, the voice of Deut 33:7 559
And of Levi he s, Let thy Thummim Deut 33:8 559
Who s unto his father and to his Deut 33:9 559
And of Benjamin he s, The beloved Deut 33:12 559
And of Joseph he s, Blessed of the Deut 33:13 559
And of Zebulun he s, Rejoice, Deut 33:18 559
And of Gad he s, Blessed be he Deut 33:20 559
And of Dan he s, Dan is a lion's Deut 33:22 559
And of Naphtali he s, O Naphtali, Deut 33:23 559
And of Asher he s, Let Asher be Deut 33:24 559
And the LORD s unto him, This is Deut 34:4 559
given unto you, as I s unto Moses Josh 1:3 1696
s thus, There came men unto me, Josh 2:4 559
she s unto the men, I know that Josh 2:9 559
she s unto them, Get you to the Josh 2:16 559
the men s unto her, We will be Josh 2:17 559
And she s, According unto your Josh 2:21 559
they s unto Joshua, Truly the Josh 2:24 559
Joshua s unto the people, Josh 3:5 559
the LORD s unto Joshua, This day Josh 3:7 559
Joshua s unto the children of Josh 3:9 559
And Joshua s, Hereby ye shall know Josh 3:10 559
Joshua s unto them, Pass over Josh 4:5 559
that time the LORD s unto Joshua Josh 5:2 559
the LORD s unto Joshua, This day Josh 5:9 559
s unto him, Art thou for us, or Josh 5:13 559
And he s, Nay Josh 5:14 559
s unto him, What saith my lord Josh 5:14 559
of the LORD's host s unto Joshua Josh 5:15 559
the LORD s unto Joshua, See, I Josh 6:2 559
s unto them, Take up the ark of Josh 6:6 559
he s unto the people, Pass on, and Josh 6:7 559
Joshua s unto the people, Shout Josh 6:16 559
But Joshua had s unto the two men Josh 6:22 559
s unto him, Let not all the Josh 7:3 559
And Joshua s, Alas, O Lord GOD, Josh 7:7 559
the LORD s unto Joshua, Get thee Josh 7:10 559
Joshua s unto Achan, My son, give Josh 7:19 559
And Achan answered Joshua, and s Josh 7:20 559
And Joshua s, Why hast thou Josh 7:25 559
the LORD s unto Joshua, Fear not, Josh 8:1 559
the LORD s unto Joshua, Stretch Josh 8:18 559
s unto him, and to the men of Josh 9:6 559
men of Israel s unto the Hivites Josh 9:7 559
they s unto Joshua, We are thy Josh 9:8 559
Joshua s unto them, Who are ye Josh 9:8 559
they s unto him, From a very far Josh 9:9 559
But all the princes s unto all Josh 9:19 559
And the princes s unto them Josh 9:21 559
And they answered Joshua, and s Josh 9:24 559
the LORD s unto Joshua, Fear them Josh 10:8 559
he s in the sight of Israel, Sun, Josh 10:12 559
And Joshua s, Roll great stones Josh 10:18 559
Then s Joshua, Open the mouth of Josh 10:22 559
s unto the captains of the men of Josh 10:24 559
Joshua s unto them, Fear not, nor Josh 10:25 559
the LORD s unto Joshua, Be not Josh 11:6 559
to all that the LORD s unto Moses Josh 11:23 1696
and the LORD s unto him, Thou art Josh 13:1 559
inheritance, as he s unto them Josh 13:14 1696
inheritance, as he s unto them Josh 13:33 1696
Jephunneh the Kenezite s unto him Josh 14:6 559
LORD s unto Moses the man of God Josh 14:6 1696
LORD hath kept me alive, as he s Josh 14:10 1696
to drive them out, as the LORD s Josh 14:12 1696
And Caleb s, He that smiteth Josh 15:16 559
Caleb s unto her, What wouldest Josh 15:18 559
And the children of Joseph s Josh 17:16 559
Joshua s unto the children of Josh 18:3 559
s unto them, Ye have kept all Josh 22:2 559
s unto the heads of the thousands Josh 22:21 1696
Therefore we s, Let us now Josh 22:26 559
Therefore s we, that it shall be, Josh 22:28 559
s unto the children of Reuben Josh 22:31 559
s unto them, I am old and stricken Josh 23:2 559
Joshua s unto all the people, Josh 24:2 559
And the people answered and s Josh 24:16 559
Joshua s unto the people, Ye Josh 24:19 559
the people s unto Joshua, Nay Josh 24:21 559
Joshua s unto the people, Ye are Josh 24:22 559
And they s, We are witnesses Josh 24:22 559
s he, the strange gods which are Josh 24:23 559
the people s unto Joshua, The Josh 24:24 559
Joshua s unto all the people, Josh 24:27 559
And the LORD s, Judah shall go up Judg 1:2 559
Judah s unto Simeon his brother, Judg 1:3 559
And Adoni-bezek s, Threescore and Judg 1:7 559
And Caleb s, He that smiteth Judg 1:12 559
Caleb s unto her, What wilt thou Judg 1:14 559
she s unto him, Give me a Judg 1:15 559
Hebron unto Caleb, as Moses s Judg 1:20 1696
they s unto him, Shew us, we pray Judg 1:24 559
up from Gilgal to Bochim, and s Judg 2:1 559
and I s, I will never break my Judg 2:1 559
Wherefore I also s, I will not Judg 2:3 559
them for evil, as the LORD had s Judg 2:15 1696
and he s, Because that this people Judg 2:20 559
that were by Gilgal, and s Judg 3:19 559
who s, Keep silence Judg 3:19 559
And Ehud s, I have a message from Judg 3:20 559
the parlour were locked, they s Judg 3:24 559
he s unto them, Follow after me Judg 3:28 559
s unto him, Hath not the LORD God Judg 4:6 559
Barak s unto her, If thou wilt go Judg 4:8 559
And she s, I will surely go with Judg 4:9 559
And Deborah s unto Barak, Up Judg 4:14 559
s unto him, Turn in, my lord, Judg 4:18 559
he s unto her, Give me, I pray Judg 4:19 559
Again he s unto her, Stand in the Judg 4:20 559
s unto him, Come, and I will shew Judg 4:22 559
s the angel of the LORD, curse ye Judg 5:23 559

which *s* unto them, Thus saith the	Judg 6:8	559
I *s* unto you, I am the LORD your	Judg 6:10	559
s unto him, The LORD is with thee	Judg 6:12	559
Gideon *s* unto him, Oh my Lord, if	Judg 6:13	559
And the LORD looked upon him, and *s*	Judg 6:14	559
he *s* unto him, Oh my Lord,	Judg 6:15	559
And the LORD *s* unto him, Surely I	Judg 6:16	559
he *s* unto him, If now I have	Judg 6:17	559
And he *s*, I will tarry until thou	Judg 6:18	559
And the angel of God *s* unto him	Judg 6:20	559
an angel of the LORD, Gideon *s*	Judg 6:22	559
And the LORD *s* unto him, Peace be	Judg 6:23	559
night, that the LORD *s* unto him	Judg 6:25	559
and did as the LORD had *s* unto him	Judg 6:27	1696
they *s* one to another, Who hath	Judg 6:29	559
they enquired and asked, they *s*	Judg 6:29	559
the men of the city *s* unto Joash	Judg 6:30	559
Joash *s* unto all that stood	Judg 6:31	559
Gideon *s* unto God, If thou wilt	Judg 6:36	559
by mine hand, as thou hast *s*	Judg 6:36	1696
by mine hand, as thou hast *s*	Judg 6:37	1696
Gideon *s* unto God, Let not thine	Judg 6:39	559
the LORD *s* unto Gideon, The	Judg 7:2	559
the LORD *s* unto Gideon, The	Judg 7:4	559
the LORD *s* unto Gideon, Every one	Judg 7:5	559
the LORD *s* unto Gideon, By the	Judg 7:7	559
night, that the LORD *s* unto him	Judg 7:9	559
a dream unto his fellow, and *s*	Judg 7:13	559
And his fellow answered and *s*	Judg 7:14	559
into the host of Israel, and *s*	Judg 7:15	559
he *s* unto them, Look on me, and do	Judg 7:17	559
And the men of Ephraim *s* unto him	Judg 8:1	559
he *s* unto them, What have I done	Judg 8:2	559
toward him, when he had *s* that	Judg 8:3	1696
he *s* unto the men of Succoth,	Judg 8:5	559
And the princes of Succoth *s*	Judg 8:6	559
And Gideon *s*, Therefore when the	Judg 8:7	559
unto the men of Succoth, and *s*	Judg 8:15	559
Then *s* he unto Zebah and Zalmunna,	Judg 8:18	559
And he *s*, They were my brethren,	Judg 8:19	559
he *s* unto Jether his firstborn,	Judg 8:20	559
Then Zebah and Zalmunna *s*, Rise	Judg 8:21	559
the men of Israel *s* unto Gideon	Judg 8:22	559
Gideon *s* unto them, I will not	Judg 8:23	559
Gideon *s* unto them, I would	Judg 8:24	559
for they *s*, He is our brother	Judg 9:3	559
s unto them, Hearken unto me, ye	Judg 9:7	559
they *s* unto the olive tree, Reign	Judg 9:8	559
But the olive tree *s* unto them	Judg 9:9	559
the trees *s* to the fig tree, Come	Judg 9:10	559
But the fig tree *s* unto them	Judg 9:11	559
Then *s* the trees unto the vine,	Judg 9:12	559
the vine *s* unto them, Should I	Judg 9:13	559
Then *s* all the trees unto the	Judg 9:14	559
the bramble *s* unto the trees, If	Judg 9:15	559
And Gaal the son of Ebed *s*	Judg 9:28	559
he *s* to Abimelech, Increase thine	Judg 9:29	559
he *s* to Zebul, Behold, there come	Judg 9:36	559
Zebul *s* unto him, Thou seest the	Judg 9:36	559
And Gaal spake again and *s*, See	Judg 9:37	559
Then *s* Zebul unto him, Where is	Judg 9:38	559
s unto the people that were with	Judg 9:48	559
s unto him, Draw thy sword, and	Judg 9:54	559
the LORD *s* unto the children of	Judg 10:11	559
of Israel *s* unto the LORD	Judg 10:15	559
of Gilead *s* one to another	Judg 10:18	559
s unto him, Thou shalt not	Judg 11:2	559
they *s* unto Jephthah, Come, and be	Judg 11:6	559
Jephthah *s* unto the elders of	Judg 11:7	559
elders of Gilead *s* unto Jephthah	Judg 11:8	559
Jephthah *s* unto the elders of	Judg 11:9	559
elders of Gilead *s* unto Jephthah	Judg 11:10	559
s unto him, Thus saith Jephthah,	Judg 11:15	559
Israel *s* unto him, Let us pass,	Judg 11:19	559
vowed a vow unto the LORD, and *s*	Judg 11:30	559
that he rent his clothes, and *s*	Judg 11:35	559
she *s* unto him, My father, if	Judg 11:36	559
she *s* unto her father, Let this	Judg 11:37	559
And he *s*, Go	Judg 11:38	559
s unto Jephthah, Wherefore	Judg 12:1	559
Jephthah *s* unto them, I and my	Judg 12:2	559
smote Ephraim, because they *s*	Judg 12:4	559
Ephraimites which were escaped *s*	Judg 12:5	559
that the men of Gilead *s* unto him	Judg 12:5	559
If he *s*, Nay	Judg 12:5	559
Then *s* they unto him, Say now	Judg 12:6	559
and he *s* Sibboleth	Judg 12:6	559
s unto her, Behold now, thou art	Judg 13:3	559
But he *s* unto me, Behold, thou	Judg 13:7	559
Manoah intreated the LORD, and *s*	Judg 13:8	559
s unto him, Behold, the man hath	Judg 13:10	559
s unto him, Art thou the man that	Judg 13:11	559
And he *s*, I am	Judg 13:11	559
And Manoah *s*, Now let thy words	Judg 13:12	559
angel of the LORD *s* unto Manoah	Judg 13:13	559
Of all that I *s* unto the woman	Judg 13:13	559
Manoah *s* unto the angel of the	Judg 13:15	559
angel of the LORD *s* unto Manoah	Judg 13:16	559
Manoah *s* unto the angel of the	Judg 13:17	559
the angel of the LORD *s* unto him	Judg 13:18	559
Manoah *s* unto his wife, We shall	Judg 13:22	559
But his wife *s* unto him, If the	Judg 13:23	559
his father and his mother, and *s*	Judg 14:2	559
father and his mother *s* unto him	Judg 14:3	559
Samson *s* unto his father, Get her	Judg 14:3	559
Samson *s* unto them, I will now	Judg 14:12	559
they *s* unto him, Put forth thy	Judg 14:13	559
he *s* unto them, Out of the eater	Judg 14:14	559
that they *s* unto Samson's wife,	Judg 14:15	559
wife wept before him, and *s*	Judg 14:16	559
he *s* unto her, Behold, I have not	Judg 14:16	559
the men of the city *s* unto him on	Judg 14:18	559
he *s* unto them, If ye had not	Judg 14:18	559
and he *s*, I will go in to my wife	Judg 15:1	559
And her father *s*, I verily thought	Judg 15:2	559
Samson *s* concerning them, Now	Judg 15:3	559
Then the Philistines *s*, Who hath	Judg 15:6	559
Samson *s* unto them, Though ye	Judg 15:7	559
And the men of Judah *s*, Why are ye	Judg 15:10	559
s to Samson, Knowest thou not	Judg 15:11	559
he *s* unto them, As they did unto	Judg 15:11	559
they *s* unto him, We are come down	Judg 15:12	559
Samson *s* unto them, Swear unto me	Judg 15:12	559
And Samson *s*, With the jawbone of	Judg 15:16	559
and called on the LORD, and *s*	Judg 15:18	559
s unto her, Entice him, and see	Judg 16:5	559
Delilah *s* to Samson, Tell me, I	Judg 16:6	559
Samson *s* unto her, If they bind	Judg 16:7	559
she *s* unto him, The Philistines	Judg 16:9	559
Delilah *s* unto Samson, Behold,	Judg 16:10	559
he *s* unto her, If they bind me	Judg 16:11	559
s unto him, The Philistines be	Judg 16:12	559
Delilah *s* unto Samson, Hitherto	Judg 16:13	559
he *s* unto her, If thou weavest	Judg 16:13	559
s unto him, The Philistines be	Judg 16:14	559
she *s* unto him, How canst thou	Judg 16:15	559
s unto her, There hath not come a	Judg 16:17	559
And she *s*, The Philistines be upon	Judg 16:20	559
he awoke out of his sleep, and *s*	Judg 16:20	559
for they *s*, Our god hath	Judg 16:23	559
for they *s*, Our god hath	Judg 16:24	559
hearts were merry, that they *s*	Judg 16:25	559
Samson *s* unto the lad that held	Judg 16:26	559
Samson called unto the LORD, and *s*	Judg 16:28	559
And Samson *s*, Let me die with the	Judg 16:30	559
he *s* unto his mother, The eleven	Judg 17:2	559
And his mother *s*, Blessed be thou	Judg 17:2	559
to his mother, his mother *s*	Judg 17:3	559
Micah *s* unto him, Whence comest	Judg 17:9	559
he *s* unto him, I am a Levite of	Judg 17:9	559
Micah *s* unto him, Dwell with me,	Judg 17:10	559
Then *s* Micah, Now know I that the	Judg 17:13	559
they *s* unto them, Go, search the	Judg 18:2	559
s unto him, Who brought thee	Judg 18:3	559
he *s* unto them, Thus and thus	Judg 18:4	559
they *s* unto him, Ask counsel, we	Judg 18:5	559
And the priest *s* unto them	Judg 18:6	559
and their brethren *s* unto them	Judg 18:8	559
And they *s*, Arise, that we may go	Judg 18:9	559
s unto their brethren, Do ye know	Judg 18:14	559
Then *s* the priest unto them, What	Judg 18:18	559
they *s* unto him, Hold thy peace,	Judg 18:19	559
s unto Micah, What aileth thee,	Judg 18:23	559
And he *s*, Ye have taken away my	Judg 18:24	559
And the children of Dan *s* unto him	Judg 18:25	559
father *s* unto his son in law	Judg 19:5	559
father had *s* unto the man	Judg 19:6	559
and the damsel's father *s*, Comfort	Judg 19:8	559
s unto him, Behold, now the day	Judg 19:9	559
the servant *s* unto his master,	Judg 19:11	559
And his master *s* unto him, We will	Judg 19:12	559
he *s* unto his servant, Come, and	Judg 19:13	559
and the old man *s*, Whither goest	Judg 19:17	559
he *s* unto him, We are passing	Judg 19:18	559
And the old man *s*, Peace be with	Judg 19:20	559
s unto them, Nay, my brethren,	Judg 19:23	559
he *s* unto her, Up, and let us be	Judg 19:28	559
it was so, that all that saw it *s*	Judg 19:30	559
Then *s* the children of Israel	Judg 20:3	559
that was slain, answered and *s*	Judg 20:4	559
and asked counsel of God, and *s*	Judg 20:18	559
And the LORD *s*, Judah shall go up	Judg 20:18	559
And the LORD *s*, Go up against him	Judg 20:23	559
And the LORD *s*, Go up	Judg 20:28	559
And the children of Benjamin *s*	Judg 20:32	559
But the children of Israel *s*	Judg 20:32	559
for they *s*, Surely they are	Judg 20:39	559
And *s*, O LORD God of Israel, why	Judg 21:3	559
And the children of Israel *s*	Judg 21:5	559
for Benjamin their brother, and *s*	Judg 21:6	559
And they *s*, What one is there of	Judg 21:8	559
the elders of the congregation *s*	Judg 21:16	559
And they *s*, There must be an	Judg 21:17	559
Then they *s*, Behold, there is a	Judg 21:19	559
Naomi *s* unto her two daughters in	Ruth 1:8	559
they *s* unto her, Surely we will	Ruth 1:10	559
And Naomi *s*, Turn again, my	Ruth 1:11	559
And she *s*, Behold, thy sister in	Ruth 1:15	559
And Ruth *s*, Intreat me not to	Ruth 1:16	559
was moved about them, and they *s*	Ruth 1:19	559
she *s* unto them, Call me not	Ruth 1:20	559
Ruth the Moabitess *s* unto Naomi	Ruth 2:2	559
she *s* unto her, Go, my daughter	Ruth 2:2	559
s unto the reapers, The LORD be	Ruth 2:4	559
Then *s* Boaz unto his servant that	Ruth 2:5	559
over the reapers answered and *s*	Ruth 2:6	559
And she *s*, I pray you, let me	Ruth 2:7	559
Then *s* Boaz unto Ruth, Hearest	Ruth 2:8	559
s unto him, Why have I found	Ruth 2:10	559
s unto her, It hath fully been	Ruth 2:11	559
Then she *s*, Let me find favour in	Ruth 2:13	559
Boaz *s* unto her, At mealtime come	Ruth 2:14	559
And her mother in law *s* unto her	Ruth 2:19	559
with whom she had wrought, and *s*	Ruth 2:19	559
Naomi *s* unto her daughter in law,	Ruth 2:20	559
Naomi *s* unto her, The man is near	Ruth 2:20	559
And Ruth the Moabitess *s*, He *s*	Ruth 2:21	559
Naomi *s* unto Ruth her daughter in	Ruth 2:22	559
her mother in law *s* unto her	Ruth 3:1	559
she *s* unto her, All that thou	Ruth 3:5	559
And he *s*, Who art thou	Ruth 3:9	559
And he *s*, Blessed be thou of the	Ruth 3:10	559
And he *s*, Let it not be known that	Ruth 3:14	559
Also he *s*, Bring the vail that	Ruth 3:15	559
came to her mother in law, she *s*	Ruth 3:16	559
And she *s*, These six measures of	Ruth 3:17	559
for he *s* to me, Go not empty unto	Ruth 3:17	559
Then *s* she, Sit still, my	Ruth 3:18	559
unto whom he *s*, Ho, such a one	Ruth 4:1	559
of the elders of the city, and *s*	Ruth 4:2	559
he *s* unto the kinsman, Naomi,	Ruth 4:3	559
And he *s*, I will redeem it	Ruth 4:4	559
Then *s* Boaz, What day thou buyest	Ruth 4:5	559
And the kinsman *s*, I cannot redeem	Ruth 4:6	559
Therefore the kinsman *s* unto Boaz	Ruth 4:8	559
Boaz *s* unto the elders, and unto	Ruth 4:9	559
in the gate, and the elders, *s*	Ruth 4:11	559
the women *s* unto Naomi, Blessed	Ruth 4:14	559
Then *s* Elkanah her husband to her	1Sa 1:8	559
And she vowed a vow, and *s*, O LORD	1Sa 1:11	559
Eli *s* unto her, How long wilt	1Sa 1:14	559
And Hannah answered and *s*, No, my	1Sa 1:15	559
Then Eli answered and *s*, Go in	1Sa 1:17	559
And she *s*, Let thine handmaid find	1Sa 1:18	559
for she *s* unto her husband, I	1Sa 1:22	559
And Elkanah her husband *s* unto her	1Sa 1:23	559
And she *s*, Oh my lord, as thy soul	1Sa 1:26	559
And Hannah prayed, and *s*, My heart	1Sa 2:1	559
s to the man that sacrificed,	1Sa 2:15	559
And if any man *s* unto him, Let	1Sa 2:16	559
blessed Elkanah and his wife, and *s*	1Sa 2:20	559
he *s* unto them, Why do ye such	1Sa 2:23	559
s unto him, Thus saith the LORD,	1Sa 2:27	559
I *s* indeed that thy house, and the	1Sa 2:30	559
And he ran unto Eli, and *s*, Here am	1Sa 3:5	559
And he *s*, I called not	1Sa 3:5	559
Samuel arose and went to Eli, and *s*	1Sa 3:6	559
And he arose and went to Eli, and *s*	1Sa 3:8	559
Therefore Eli *s* unto Samuel	1Sa 3:9	559
the LORD *s* to Samuel, Behold, I	1Sa 3:11	559
Then Eli called Samuel, and *s*	1Sa 3:16	559
And he *s*, What is the thing that	1Sa 3:17	559
that the LORD hath *s* unto thee	1Sa 3:17	1696
the things that he *s* unto thee	1Sa 3:17	1696
And he *s*, It is the LORD	1Sa 3:18	559
the camp, the elders of Israel *s*	1Sa 4:3	559
the noise of the shout, they *s*	1Sa 4:6	559
were afraid, for they *s*, God is	1Sa 4:7	559
And they *s*, Woe unto us	1Sa 4:7	559
the noise of the crying, he *s*	1Sa 4:14	559
the man *s* unto Eli, I am he that	1Sa 4:16	559
And he *s*, What is there done, my	1Sa 4:16	559
And the messenger answered and *s*	1Sa 4:17	559
that stood by her *s* unto her	1Sa 4:20	1696
And she *s*, The glory is departed	1Sa 4:22	559
Ashdod saw that it was so, they *s*	1Sa 5:7	559
the Philistines unto them, and *s*	1Sa 5:8	559
lords of the Philistines, and *s*	1Sa 5:11	559
And they *s*, If ye send away the	1Sa 6:3	559
Then *s* they, What shall be the	1Sa 6:4	559
And the men of Beth-shemesh *s*	1Sa 6:20	559
And Samuel *s*, Gather all Israel to	1Sa 7:5	559
s there, We have sinned against	1Sa 7:6	559
children of Israel *s* to Samuel	1Sa 7:8	559
s unto him, Behold, thou art old,	1Sa 8:5	559
displeased Samuel, when they *s*	1Sa 8:6	559
the LORD *s* unto Samuel, Hearken	1Sa 8:7	559
And he *s*, This will be the manner	1Sa 8:11	559
and they *s*, Nay	1Sa 8:19	559
the LORD *s* to Samuel, Hearken	1Sa 8:22	559
Samuel *s* unto the men of Israel,	1Sa 8:22	559
Kish *s* to Saul his son, Take now	1Sa 9:3	559
Saul *s* to his servant that was	1Sa 9:5	559
he *s* unto him, Behold now, there	1Sa 9:6	559
Then *s* Saul to his servant, But,	1Sa 9:7	559
servant answered Saul again, and *s*	1Sa 9:8	559
Then *s* Saul to his servant, Well	1Sa 9:10	1697
Saul to his servant, Well *s*	1Sa 9:10	559
s unto them, Is the seer here	1Sa 9:11	559
And they answered them, and *s*	1Sa 9:12	559
saw Saul, the LORD *s* unto him	1Sa 9:17	6030
near to Samuel in the gate, and *s*	1Sa 9:18	559
And Samuel answered Saul, and *s*	1Sa 9:19	559
And Saul answered and *s*, Am not I a	1Sa 9:21	559
Samuel *s* unto the cook, Bring the	1Sa 9:23	559
gave thee, of which I *s* unto thee	1Sa 9:23	559
And Samuel *s*, Behold that which is	1Sa 9:24	559
it been kept for thee since I *s*	1Sa 9:24	559
Samuel *s* to Saul, Bid the servant	1Sa 9:27	559
his head, and kissed him, and *s*	1Sa 10:1	559
then the people *s* one to another	1Sa 10:11	559
of the same place answered and *s*	1Sa 10:12	559
And Saul's uncle *s* unto him	1Sa 10:14	559
And he *s*, To seek the asses	1Sa 10:14	559
And Saul's uncle *s*, Tell me, I	1Sa 10:15	559
pray thee, what Samuel *s* unto you	1Sa 10:15	559
Saul *s* unto his uncle, He told us	1Sa 10:16	559
s unto the children of Israel,	1Sa 10:18	559
ye have *s* unto him, Nay, but set	1Sa 10:19	559
Samuel *s* to all the people, See	1Sa 10:24	559
And all the people shouted, and *s*	1Sa 10:24	559
But the children of Belial *s*	1Sa 10:27	559
the men of Jabesh *s* unto Nahash	1Sa 11:1	559
the elders of Jabesh *s* unto him	1Sa 11:3	559

and Saul *s*, What aileth the people	1Sa 11:5	559
they *s* unto the messengers that	1Sa 11:9	559
Therefore the men of Jabesh *s*	1Sa 11:10	559
the people *s* unto Samuel, Who is	1Sa 11:12	559
unto Samuel, Who is he that *s*	1Sa 11:12	559
And Saul *s*, There shall not a man	1Sa 11:13	559
Then *s* Samuel to the people, Come	1Sa 11:14	559
Samuel *s* unto all Israel, Behold,	1Sa 12:1	559
voice in all that ye *s* unto me	1Sa 12:1	559
And they *s*, Thou hast not	1Sa 12:4	559
he *s* unto them, The LORD is	1Sa 12:5	559
Samuel *s* unto the people, It is	1Sa 12:6	559
And they cried unto the LORD, and *s*	1Sa 12:10	559
against you, ye *s* unto me, Nay	1Sa 12:12	559
And all the people *s* unto Samuel	1Sa 12:19	559
Samuel *s* unto the people, Fear	1Sa 12:20	559
And Saul *s*, Bring hither a burnt	1Sa 13:9	559
And Samuel *s*, What hast thou done	1Sa 13:11	559
And Saul *s*, Because I saw that the	1Sa 13:11	559
Therefore *s* I, The Philistines	1Sa 13:12	559
Samuel *s* to Saul, Thou hast done	1Sa 13:13	559
for the Philistines *s*, Lest the	1Sa 13:19	559
s unto the young man that bare	1Sa 14:1	559
Jonathan *s* to the young man that	1Sa 14:6	559
And his armourbearer *s* unto him	1Sa 14:7	559
Then *s* Jonathan, Behold, we will	1Sa 14:8	559
and the Philistines *s*, Behold, the	1Sa 14:11	559
and his armourbearer, and *s*	1Sa 14:12	559
Jonathan *s* unto his armourbearer,	1Sa 14:12	559
Then *s* Saul unto the people that	1Sa 14:17	559
Saul *s* unto Ahiah, Bring hither	1Sa 14:18	559
Saul *s* unto the priest, Withdraw	1Sa 14:19	559
answered one of the people, and *s*	1Sa 14:28	559
Then *s* Jonathan, My father hath	1Sa 14:29	559
And he *s*, Ye have transgressed	1Sa 14:33	559
And Saul *s*, Disperse yourselves	1Sa 14:34	559
And Saul *s*, Let us go down after	1Sa 14:36	559
And they *s*, Do whatsoever seemeth	1Sa 14:36	559
Then *s* the priest, Let us draw	1Sa 14:36	559
And Saul *s*, Draw ye near hither,	1Sa 14:38	559
Then *s* he unto all Israel, Be ye	1Sa 14:40	559
And the people *s* unto Saul	1Sa 14:40	559
Therefore Saul *s* unto the LORD	1Sa 14:41	559
And Saul *s*, Cast lots between me	1Sa 14:42	559
Then Saul *s* to Jonathan, Tell me	1Sa 14:43	559
And Jonathan told him, and *s*	1Sa 14:43	559
And the people *s* unto Saul	1Sa 14:45	559
Samuel also *s* unto Saul, The LORD	1Sa 15:1	559
Saul *s* unto the Kenites, Go,	1Sa 15:6	559
Saul *s* unto him, Blessed be thou	1Sa 15:13	559
And Samuel *s*, What meaneth then	1Sa 15:14	559
And Saul *s*, They have brought them	1Sa 15:15	559
Then Samuel *s* unto Saul, Stay, and	1Sa 15:16	559
the LORD hath *s* to me this night	1Sa 15:16	1696
And he *s* unto him, Say on	1Sa 15:16	559
And Samuel *s*, When thou wast	1Sa 15:17	559
LORD sent thee on a journey, and *s*	1Sa 15:18	559
Saul *s* unto Samuel, Yea, I have	1Sa 15:20	559
And Samuel *s*, Hath the LORD as	1Sa 15:22	559
Saul *s* unto Samuel, I have sinned	1Sa 15:24	559
Samuel *s* unto Saul, I will not	1Sa 15:26	559
Samuel *s* unto him, The LORD hath	1Sa 15:28	559
Then he *s*, I have sinned	1Sa 15:30	559
Then *s* Samuel, Bring ye hither to	1Sa 15:32	559
And Agag *s*, Surely the bitterness	1Sa 15:32	559
And Samuel *s*, As thy sword hath	1Sa 15:33	559
the LORD *s* unto Samuel, How long	1Sa 16:1	559
And Samuel *s*, How can I go	1Sa 16:2	559
And the LORD *s*, Take an heifer	1Sa 16:2	559
town trembled at his coming, and *s*	1Sa 16:4	559
And he *s*, Peaceably	1Sa 16:5	559
that he looked on Eliab, and *s*	1Sa 16:6	559
But the LORD *s* unto Samuel	1Sa 16:7	559
And he *s*, Neither hath the LORD	1Sa 16:8	559
And he *s*, Neither hath the LORD	1Sa 16:9	559
Samuel *s* unto Jesse, The LORD	1Sa 16:10	559
Samuel *s* unto Jesse, Are here all	1Sa 16:11	559
And he *s*, There remaineth yet the	1Sa 16:11	559
Samuel *s* unto Jesse, Send and	1Sa 16:11	559
And the LORD *s*, Arise, anoint him	1Sa 16:12	559
And Saul's servants *s* unto him	1Sa 16:15	559
Saul *s* unto his servants, Provide	1Sa 16:17	559
one of the servants, and *s*	1Sa 16:18	559
sent messengers unto Jesse, and *s*	1Sa 16:19	559
s unto them, Why are ye come out	1Sa 17:8	559
And the Philistine *s*, I defy the	1Sa 17:10	559
Jesse *s* unto David his son, Take	1Sa 17:17	559
And the men of Israel *s*, Have ye	1Sa 17:25	559
kindled against David, and he *s*	1Sa 17:28	559
And David *s*, What have I now done	1Sa 17:29	559
David *s* to Saul, Let no man's	1Sa 17:32	559
Saul *s* to David, Thou art not	1Sa 17:33	559
David *s* unto Saul, Thy servant	1Sa 17:34	559
David *s* moreover, The LORD that	1Sa 17:37	559
Saul *s* unto David, Go, and the	1Sa 17:37	559
David *s* unto Saul, I cannot go	1Sa 17:39	559
And the Philistine *s* unto David	1Sa 17:43	559
And the Philistine *s* to David	1Sa 17:44	559
Then *s* David to the Philistine,	1Sa 17:45	559
he *s* unto Abner, the captain of	1Sa 17:55	559
And Abner *s*, As thy soul liveth, O	1Sa 17:55	559
And the king *s*, Enquire thou whose	1Sa 17:56	559
Saul *s* to him, Whose son art thou	1Sa 17:58	559
one another as they played, and *s*	1Sa 18:7	559
and he *s*, They have ascribed unto	1Sa 18:8	559
for he *s*, I will smite David even	1Sa 18:11	559
Saul *s* to David, Behold my elder	1Sa 18:17	559
For Saul *s*, Let not mine hand be	1Sa 18:17	559
David *s* unto Saul, Who am I	1Sa 18:18	559
And Saul *s*, I will give him her,	1Sa 18:21	559
Wherefore Saul *s* to David	1Sa 18:21	559
And David *s*, Seemeth it to you a	1Sa 18:23	559
And Saul *s*, Thus shall ye say to	1Sa 18:25	559
s unto him, Let not the king sin	1Sa 19:4	559
messengers to take David, she *s*	1Sa 19:14	559
Saul *s* unto Michal, Why hast thou	1Sa 19:17	559
Saul, He *s* unto me, Let me go	1Sa 19:17	559
and he asked and *s*, Where are	1Sa 19:22	559
And one *s*, Behold, they be at	1Sa 19:22	559
s before Jonathan, What have I	1Sa 20:1	559
he *s* unto him, God forbid	1Sa 20:2	559
And David sware moreover, and *s*	1Sa 20:3	559
Then *s* Jonathan unto David,	1Sa 20:4	559
David *s* unto Jonathan, Behold, to	1Sa 20:5	559
And Jonathan *s*, Far be it from	1Sa 20:9	559
Then *s* David to Jonathan, Who	1Sa 20:10	559
Jonathan *s* unto David, Come, and	1Sa 20:11	559
Jonathan *s* unto David, O LORD God	1Sa 20:12	559
Then Jonathan *s* to David, To	1Sa 20:18	559
Saul *s* unto Jonathan his son,	1Sa 20:27	559
And he *s*, Let me go, I pray thee	1Sa 20:29	559
he *s* unto him, Thou son of the	1Sa 20:30	559
s unto him, Wherefore shall he be	1Sa 20:32	559
he *s* unto his lad, Run, find out	1Sa 20:36	559
cried after the lad, and *s*	1Sa 20:37	559
s unto him, Go, carry them to the	1Sa 20:40	559
And Jonathan *s* to David, Go in	1Sa 20:42	559
s unto him, Why art thou alone,	1Sa 21:1	559
David *s* unto Ahimelech the priest	1Sa 21:2	559
hath *s* unto me, Let no man know	1Sa 21:2	559
the priest answered David, and *s*	1Sa 21:4	559
s unto him, Of a truth women have	1Sa 21:5	559
David *s* unto Ahimelech, And is	1Sa 21:8	559
And the priest *s*, The sword of	1Sa 21:9	559
And David *s*, There is none like	1Sa 21:9	559
the servants of Achish *s* unto him	1Sa 21:11	559
Then *s* Achish unto his servants,	1Sa 21:14	559
he *s* unto the king of Moab, Let	1Sa 22:3	559
And the prophet Gad *s* unto David	1Sa 22:5	559
Then Saul *s* unto his servants	1Sa 22:7	559
over the servants of Saul, and *s*	1Sa 22:9	559
And Saul *s*, Hear now, thou son of	1Sa 22:12	559
Saul *s* unto him, Why have ye	1Sa 22:13	559
Ahimelech answered the king, and *s*	1Sa 22:14	559
And the king *s*, Thou shalt surely	1Sa 22:16	559
the king *s* unto the footmen that	1Sa 22:17	559
And the king *s* to Doeg, Turn thou,	1Sa 22:18	559
David *s* unto Abiathar, I knew it	1Sa 22:22	559
the LORD *s* unto David, Go, and	1Sa 23:2	559
And David's men *s* unto him	1Sa 23:3	559
And the LORD answered him and *s*	1Sa 23:4	559
And Saul *s*, God hath delivered him	1Sa 23:7	559
he *s* to Abiathar the priest,	1Sa 23:9	559
Then *s* David, O LORD God of	1Sa 23:10	559
And the LORD *s*, He will come down	1Sa 23:11	559
Then *s* David, Will the men of	1Sa 23:12	559
And the LORD *s*, They will deliver	1Sa 23:12	559
And he *s* unto him, Fear not	1Sa 23:17	559
And Saul *s*, Blessed be ye of the	1Sa 23:21	559
And the men of David *s* unto him	1Sa 24:4	559
day of which the LORD *s* unto thee	1Sa 24:4	559
he *s* unto his men, The LORD	1Sa 24:6	559
David *s* to Saul, Wherefore	1Sa 24:9	559
and I *s*, I will not put forth mine	1Sa 24:10	559
words unto Saul, that Saul *s*	1Sa 24:16	559
he *s* to David, Thou art more	1Sa 24:17	559
David *s* unto the young men, Get	1Sa 25:5	559
answered David's servants, and *s*	1Sa 25:10	559
David *s* unto his men, Gird ye on	1Sa 25:13	559
she *s* unto her servants, Go on	1Sa 25:19	559
Now David had *s*, Surely in vain	1Sa 25:21	559
And fell at his feet, and *s*	1Sa 25:24	559
David *s* to Abigail, Blessed be	1Sa 25:32	559
s unto her, Go up in peace to	1Sa 25:35	559
heard that Nabal was dead, he *s*	1Sa 25:39	559
on her face to the earth, and *s*	1Sa 25:41	559
s to Ahimelech the Hittite, and to	1Sa 26:6	559
And Abishai *s*, I will go down with	1Sa 26:6	559
Then *s* Abishai to David, God hath	1Sa 26:8	559
David *s* to Abishai, Destroy him	1Sa 26:9	559
David *s* furthermore, As the LORD	1Sa 26:10	559
Then Abner answered and *s*, Who art	1Sa 26:14	559
David *s* to Abner, Art not thou a	1Sa 26:15	559
And Saul knew David's voice, and *s*	1Sa 26:17	559
And David *s*, It is my voice, my	1Sa 26:17	559
And he *s*, Wherefore doth my lord	1Sa 26:18	559
Then *s* Saul, I have sinned	1Sa 26:21	559
And David answered and *s*, Behold	1Sa 26:22	559
Then Saul *s* to David, Blessed be	1Sa 26:25	559
David *s* in his heart, I shall now	1Sa 27:1	559
David *s* unto Achish, If I have	1Sa 27:5	559
And Achish *s*, Whither have ye made	1Sa 27:10	559
And David *s*, Against the south of	1Sa 27:10	559
Achish *s* unto David, Know thou	1Sa 28:1	559
David *s* to Achish, Surely thou	1Sa 28:2	559
Achish *s* to David, Therefore will	1Sa 28:2	559
Then *s* Saul unto his servants,	1Sa 28:7	559
And his servants *s* to him, Behold,	1Sa 28:7	559
and he *s*, I pray thee, divine unto	1Sa 28:8	559
And the woman *s* unto him, Behold,	1Sa 28:9	559
Then *s* the woman, Whom shall I	1Sa 28:11	559
And he *s*, Bring me up Samuel	1Sa 28:11	559
And the king *s* unto her, Be not	1Sa 28:13	559
And the woman *s* unto Saul, I saw	1Sa 28:13	559
he *s* unto her, What form is he of	1Sa 28:14	559
And she *s*, An old man cometh up	1Sa 28:14	559
Samuel *s* to Saul, Why hast thou	1Sa 28:15	559
Then *s* Samuel, Wherefore then	1Sa 28:16	559
s unto him, Behold, thine	1Sa 28:21	559
But he refused, and *s*, I will not	1Sa 28:23	559
Then *s* the princes of the	1Sa 29:3	559
Achish *s* unto the princes of the	1Sa 29:3	559
of the Philistines *s* unto him	1Sa 29:4	559
s unto him, Surely, as the LORD	1Sa 29:6	559
David *s* unto Achish, But what	1Sa 29:8	559
s to David, I know that thou art	1Sa 29:9	559
princes of the Philistines have *s*	1Sa 29:9	559
David *s* to Abiathar the priest,	1Sa 30:7	559
David *s* unto him, To whom	1Sa 30:13	559
And he *s*, I am a young man of	1Sa 30:13	559
David *s* to him, Canst thou bring	1Sa 30:15	559
And he *s*, Swear unto me by God,	1Sa 30:15	559
before those other cattle, and *s*	1Sa 30:20	559
those that went with David, and *s*	1Sa 30:22	559
Then *s* David, Ye shall not do so,	1Sa 30:23	559
Then *s* Saul unto his armourbearer	1Sa 31:4	559
David *s* unto him, From whence	2Sa 1:3	559
he *s* unto him, Out of the camp of	2Sa 1:3	559
David *s* unto him, How went the	2Sa 1:4	559
David *s* unto the young man that	2Sa 1:5	559
And the young man that told him *s*	2Sa 1:6	559
he *s* unto me, Who art thou	2Sa 1:8	559
He *s* unto me again, Stand, I pray	2Sa 1:9	559
David *s* unto the young man that	2Sa 1:13	559
David *s* unto him, How wast thou	2Sa 1:14	559
called one of the young men, and *s*	2Sa 1:15	559
David *s* unto him, Thy blood be	2Sa 1:16	559
And the LORD *s* unto him, Go up	2Sa 2:1	559
And David *s*, Whither shall I go up	2Sa 2:1	559
And he *s*, Unto Hebron	2Sa 2:1	559
s unto them, Blessed be ye of the	2Sa 2:5	559
Abner *s* to Joab, Let the young	2Sa 2:14	559
And Joab *s*, Let them arise	2Sa 2:14	559
Abner looked behind him, and *s*	2Sa 2:20	559
Abner *s* to him, Turn thee aside	2Sa 2:21	559
Abner *s* again to Asahel, Turn	2Sa 2:22	559
Then Abner called to Joab, and *s*	2Sa 2:26	559
And Joab *s*, As God liveth, unless	2Sa 2:27	559
and Ish-bosheth *s* to Abner	2Sa 3:7	559
the words of Ish-bosheth, and *s*	2Sa 3:8	559
And he *s*, Well	2Sa 3:13	559
Then *s* Abner unto him, Go, return	2Sa 3:16	559
Abner *s* unto David, I will arise	2Sa 3:21	559
Then Joab came to the king, and *s*	2Sa 3:24	559
when David heard it, he *s*	2Sa 3:28	559
David *s* to Joab, and to all the	2Sa 3:31	559
king lamented over Abner, and *s*	2Sa 3:33	559
the king *s* unto his servants,	2Sa 3:38	559
s to the king, Behold the head of	2Sa 4:8	559
s unto them, As the LORD liveth,	2Sa 4:9	559
and the LORD *s* to thee, Thou shalt	2Sa 5:2	559
David *s* on that day, Whosoever	2Sa 5:8	559
Wherefore they *s*, The blind and	2Sa 5:8	559
the LORD *s* unto David, Go up	2Sa 5:19	559
and David smote them there, and *s*	2Sa 5:20	559
David enquired of the LORD, he *s*	2Sa 5:23	559
afraid of the LORD that day, and *s*	2Sa 6:9	559
Saul came out to meet David, and *s*	2Sa 6:20	559
David *s* unto Michal, It was	2Sa 6:21	559
That the king *s* unto Nathan the	2Sa 7:2	559
Nathan *s* to the king, Go, do all	2Sa 7:3	559
and sat before the LORD, and he *s*	2Sa 7:18	559
it for ever, and do as thou hast *s*	2Sa 7:25	1696
And David *s*, Is there yet any that	2Sa 9:1	559
unto David, the king *s* unto him	2Sa 9:2	559
And he *s*, Thy servant is he	2Sa 9:2	559
And the king *s*, is there not yet	2Sa 9:3	559
Ziba *s* unto the king, Jonathan	2Sa 9:3	559
And the king *s* unto him, Where is	2Sa 9:4	559
Ziba *s* unto the king, Behold, he	2Sa 9:4	559
And David *s*, Mephibosheth	2Sa 9:6	559
David *s* unto him, Fear not	2Sa 9:7	559
And he bowed himself, and *s*	2Sa 9:8	559
s unto him, I have given unto thy	2Sa 9:9	559
Then *s* Ziba unto the king,	2Sa 9:11	559
s the king, he shall eat at my	2Sa 9:11	
Then *s* David, I will shew	2Sa 10:2	559
of Ammon *s* unto Hanun their lord	2Sa 10:3	559
and the king *s*, Tarry at Jericho	2Sa 10:5	559
And he *s*, If the Syrians be too	2Sa 10:11	559
And one *s*, Is not this Bath-sheba,	2Sa 11:3	559
and sent and told David, and *s*	2Sa 11:5	559
David *s* to Uriah, Go down to thy	2Sa 11:8	559
David *s* unto Uriah, Camest thou	2Sa 11:10	559
Uriah *s* unto David, The ark, and	2Sa 11:11	559
David *s* to Uriah, Tarry here to	2Sa 11:12	559
And the messenger *s* unto David	2Sa 11:23	559
Then David *s* unto the messenger,	2Sa 11:25	559
s unto him, There were two men in	2Sa 12:1	559
he *s* to Nathan, As the LORD	2Sa 12:5	559
Nathan *s* to David, Thou art the	2Sa 12:7	559
David *s* unto Nathan, I have	2Sa 12:13	559
Nathan *s* unto David, The LORD	2Sa 12:13	559
for they *s*, Behold, while the	2Sa 12:18	559
therefore David *s* unto his	2Sa 12:19	559
And they *s*, He is dead	2Sa 12:19	559
Then *s* his servants unto him,	2Sa 12:21	559
And he *s*, While the child was yet	2Sa 12:22	559
for I *s*, Who can tell whether GOD	2Sa 12:22	559
sent messengers to David, and *s*	2Sa 12:27	559
he *s* unto him, Why art thou,	2Sa 13:4	559
Amnon *s* unto him, I love Tamar,	2Sa 13:4	559
Jonadab *s* unto him, Lay thee down	2Sa 13:5	559
Amnon *s* unto the king, I pray	2Sa 13:6	559

And Amnon *s*, Have out all men from 2Sa 13:9 559
Amnon *s* unto Tamar, Bring the 2Sa 13:10 559
s unto her, Come lie with me, my 2Sa 13:11 559
Amnon *s* unto her, Arise, be gone 2Sa 13:15 559
she *s* unto him, There is no cause 2Sa 13:16 559
that ministered unto him, and *s* 2Sa 13:17 559
And Absalom her brother *s* unto her 2Sa 13:20 559
And Absalom came to the king, and *s* 2Sa 13:24 559
the king *s* to Absalom, Nay, my 2Sa 13:25 559
Then *s* Absalom, If not, I pray 2Sa 13:26 559
And the king *s* unto him, Why 2Sa 13:26 559
David's brother, answered and *s* 2Sa 13:32 559
Jonadab *s* unto the king, Behold, 2Sa 13:35 559
as thy servant *s*, so it is 2Sa 13:35 1697
s unto her, I pray thee, feign 2Sa 14:2 559
ground, and did obeisance, and *s* 2Sa 14:4 559
And the king *s* unto her, What 2Sa 14:5 559
against thine handmaid, and they *s* 2Sa 14:7 559
the king *s* unto the woman, Go to 2Sa 14:8 559
woman of Tekoah *s* unto the king 2Sa 14:9 559
And the king *s*, Whosoever saith 2Sa 14:10 559
Then *s* she, I pray thee, let the 2Sa 14:11 559
And he *s*, As the LORD liveth, 2Sa 14:11 559
Then the woman *s*, Let thine 2Sa 14:12 559
And he *s*, Say on 2Sa 14:12 559
And the woman *s*, Wherefore then 2Sa 14:13 559
and thy handmaid *s*, I will now 2Sa 14:15 559
Then thine handmaid *s*, The word 2Sa 14:17 559
s unto the woman, Hide not from 2Sa 14:18 559
And the woman *s*, Let my lord the 2Sa 14:18 559
And the king *s*, Is not the hand of 2Sa 14:19 559
And the woman answered and *s* 2Sa 14:19 559
the king *s* unto Joab, Behold now, 2Sa 14:21 559
and Joab *s*, Today thy servant 2Sa 14:22 559
And the king *s*, Let him turn to 2Sa 14:24 559
Therefore he *s* unto his servants, 2Sa 14:30 559
s unto him, Wherefore have thy 2Sa 14:31 559
Absalom called unto him, and *s* 2Sa 15:2 559
And he *s*, Thy servant is of one of 2Sa 15:2 559
Absalom *s* unto him, See, thy 2Sa 15:3 559
Absalom *s* moreover, Oh that I 2Sa 15:4 559
that Absalom *s* unto the king, I 2Sa 15:7 559
And the king *s* unto him, Go in 2Sa 15:9 559
David *s* unto all his servants 2Sa 15:14 559
king's servants *s* unto the king 2Sa 15:15 559
Then *s* the king to Ittai the 2Sa 15:19 559
And Ittai answered the king, and *s* 2Sa 15:21 559
David *s* to Ittai, Go and pass over 2Sa 15:22 559
the king *s* unto Zadok, Carry back 2Sa 15:25 559
The king *s* also unto Zadok the 2Sa 15:27 559
And David *s*, O LORD, I pray thee, 2Sa 15:31 559
Unto whom David *s*, If thou 2Sa 15:33 559
the king *s* unto Ziba, What 2Sa 16:2 559
And Ziba *s*, The asses be for the 2Sa 16:2 559
And the king *s*, And where is thy 2Sa 16:3 559
Ziba *s* unto the king, Behold, he 2Sa 16:3 559
for he *s*, Today shall the house 2Sa 16:3 559
Then *s* the king to Ziba, Behold, 2Sa 16:4 559
And Ziba *s*, I humbly beseech thee 2Sa 16:4 559
thus *s* Shimei when he cursed, 2Sa 16:7 559
Then *s* Abishai the son of Zeruiah 2Sa 16:9 559
And the king *s*, What have I to do 2Sa 16:10 559
because the LORD hath *s* unto him 2Sa 16:10 559
David *s* to Abishai, and to all his 2Sa 16:11 559
that Hushai *s* unto Absalom, God 2Sa 16:16 559
Absalom *s* to Hushai, Is this thy 2Sa 16:17 559
Hushai *s* unto Absalom, Nay 2Sa 16:18 559
Then *s* Absalom to Ahithophel, 2Sa 16:20 559
Ahithophel *s* unto Absalom, Go in 2Sa 16:21 559
Ahithophel *s* unto Absalom 2Sa 17:1 559
Then *s* Absalom, Call now Hushai 2Sa 17:5 559
Hushai *s* unto Absalom, The 2Sa 17:7 559
s Hushai, thou knowest thy father 2Sa 17:8 559
and all the men of Israel *s* 2Sa 17:14 559
Then *s* Hushai unto Zadok and to 2Sa 17:15 559
to the woman to the house, they *s* 2Sa 17:20 559
And the woman *s* unto them, They be 2Sa 17:20 559
s unto David, Arise, and pass 2Sa 17:21 559
for they *s*, The people is hungry, 2Sa 17:29 559
the king *s* unto the people, I 2Sa 18:2 559
the king *s* unto them, What 2Sa 18:4 559
man saw it, and told Joab, and *s* 2Sa 18:10 559
Joab *s* unto the man that told him 2Sa 18:11 559
the man *s* unto Joab, Though I 2Sa 18:12 559
Then *s* Joab, I may not tarry thus 2Sa 18:14 559
for he *s*, I have no son to keep 2Sa 18:18 559
Then *s* Ahimaaz the son of Zadok, 2Sa 18:19 559
Joab *s* unto him, Thou shalt not 2Sa 18:20 559
Then *s* Joab to Cushi, Go tell the 2Sa 18:21 559
Then *s* Ahimaaz the son of Zadok 2Sa 18:22 559
And Joab *s*, Wherefore wilt thou 2Sa 18:22 559
But howsoever, *s* he, let me run 2Sa 18:23
And he *s* unto him, Run 2Sa 18:23 559
And the king *s*, If he be alone, 2Sa 18:25 559
called unto the porter, and *s* 2Sa 18:26 559
And the king *s*, He also bringeth 2Sa 18:26 559
And the watchman *s*, Me thinketh 2Sa 18:27 559
And the king *s*, He is a good man, 2Sa 18:27 559
s unto the king, All is well 2Sa 18:28 559
his face before the king, and *s* 2Sa 18:28 559
And the king *s*, Is the young man 2Sa 18:29 559
And the king *s* unto him, Turn 2Sa 18:30 559
and Cushi *s*, Tidings, my lord the 2Sa 18:31 559
the king *s* unto Cushi, Is the 2Sa 18:32 559
and as he went, thus he *s*, O my 2Sa 18:33 559
s Thou hast shamed this day the 2Sa 19:5 559
s unto the king, Let not my lord 2Sa 19:19 559
the son of Zeruiah answered and *s* 2Sa 19:21 559

And David *s*, What have I to do 2Sa 19:22 559
Therefore the king *s* unto Shimei 2Sa 19:23 559
king, that the king *s* unto him 2Sa 19:25 559
for thy servant *s*, I will saddle 2Sa 19:26 559
And the king *s* unto him, Why 2Sa 19:29 559
I have *s*, Thou and Ziba divide the 2Sa 19:29 559
Mephibosheth *s* unto the king, Yea 2Sa 19:30 559
the king *s* unto Barzillai, Come 2Sa 19:33 559
Barzillai *s* unto the king, How 2Sa 19:34 559
s unto the king, Why have our 2Sa 19:41 559
answered the men of Judah, and *s* 2Sa 19:43 559
and he blew a trumpet, and *s* 2Sa 20:1 559
Then *s* the king to Amasa, 2Sa 20:4 559
David *s* to Abishai, Now shall 2Sa 20:6 559
Joab *s* to Amasa, Art thou in 2Sa 20:9 559
of Joab's men stood by him, and *s* 2Sa 20:11 559
come near unto her, the woman *s* 2Sa 20:17 559
Then she *s* unto him, Hear the 2Sa 20:17 559
And Joab answered and *s*, Far be it, 2Sa 20:20 559
And the woman *s* unto Joab, Behold, 2Sa 20:21 559
the Gibeonites, and *s* unto them 2Sa 21:2 559
Wherefore David *s* unto the 2Sa 21:3 559
And the Gibeonites *s* unto him 2Sa 21:4 559
And he *s*, What ye shall say, that 2Sa 21:4 559
And the king *s*, I will give them 2Sa 21:6 559
And he *s*, The LORD is my rock, and 2Sa 22:2 559
David the son of Jesse *s*, and the 2Sa 23:1 5002
the sweet psalmist of Israel, *s* 2Sa 23:1 5002
The God of Israel *s*, the Rock of 2Sa 23:3 559
And David longed, and *s*, Oh that 2Sa 23:15 559
And he *s*, Be it far from me, O 2Sa 23:17 559
For the king *s* to Joab the 2Sa 24:2 559
Joab *s* unto the king, Now the 2Sa 24:3 559
David *s* unto the LORD, I have 2Sa 24:10 559
s unto him, Shall seven years of 2Sa 24:13 559
David *s* unto Gad, I am in a great 2Sa 24:14 559
s to the angel that destroyed the 2Sa 24:16 559
angel that smote the people, and *s* 2Sa 24:17 559
s unto him, Go up, rear an altar 2Sa 24:18 559
And Araunah *s*, Wherefore is my 2Sa 24:21 559
And David *s*, To buy the 2Sa 24:21 559
Araunah *s* unto David, Let my lord 2Sa 24:22 559
Araunah *s* unto the king, The LORD 2Sa 24:23 559
the king *s* unto Araunah, Nay 2Sa 24:24 559
Wherefore his servants *s* unto him 1Kin 1:2 559
And the king *s*, What wouldest thou 1Kin 1:16 559
she *s* unto him, My lord, thou 1Kin 1:17 559
And Nathan *s*, My lord, O king, 1Kin 1:24 559
My lord, O king, hast thou *s* 1Kin 1:24 559
Then king David answered and *s* 1Kin 1:28 559
And the king sware, and *s*, As the 1Kin 1:29 559
did reverence to the king, and *s* 1Kin 1:31 559
And king David *s*, Call me Zadok 1Kin 1:32 559
The king also *s* unto them 1Kin 1:33 559
Jehoiada answered the king, and *s* 1Kin 1:36 559
and all the people *s*, God save 1Kin 1:39 559
the sound of the trumpet, he *s* 1Kin 1:41 559
and Adonijah *s* unto him, Come in 1Kin 1:42 559
s to Adonijah, Verily our lord 1Kin 1:43 559
And also thus *s* the king, Blessed 1Kin 1:48 559
And Solomon *s*, If he will shew 1Kin 1:52 559
Solomon *s* unto him, Go to thine 1Kin 1:53 559
(*s* he) a man on the throne of 1Kin 2:4 559
And she *s*, Comest thou peaceably 1Kin 2:13 559
And he *s*, Peaceably 1Kin 2:13 559
He *s* moreover, I have somewhat to 1Kin 2:14 559
And she *s*, Say on 1Kin 2:14 559
And he *s*, Thou knowest that the 1Kin 2:15 559
And she *s* unto him, Say on 1Kin 2:16 559
And he *s*, Speak, I pray thee, unto 1Kin 2:17 559
And Bath-sheba *s*, Well 1Kin 2:18 559
Then she *s*, I desire one small 1Kin 2:20 559
And the king *s* unto her, Ask on, 1Kin 2:20 559
And she *s*, Let Abishag the 1Kin 2:21 559
s unto his mother, And why dost 1Kin 2:22 559
Abiathar the priest *s* the king 1Kin 2:26 559
s unto him, Thus saith the king, 1Kin 2:30 559
And he *s*, Nay 1Kin 2:30 559
word again, saying, Thus *s* Joab 1Kin 2:30 1696
And the king *s* unto him, Do as he 1Kin 2:31 559
Do as he hath *s* 1Kin 2:31 1696
s unto him, Build thee an house 1Kin 2:36 559
Shimei *s* unto the king, The 1Kin 2:38 559
as my lord the king hath *s* 1Kin 2:38 1696
s unto him, Did I not make thee 1Kin 2:42 559
The king *s* moreover to Shimei 1Kin 2:44 559
and God *s*, Ask what I shall give 1Kin 3:5 559
And Solomon *s*, Thou hast shewed 1Kin 3:6 559
God *s* unto him, Because thou hast 1Kin 3:11 559
And the one woman *s*, O my lord, I 1Kin 3:17 559
And the other woman *s*, Nay 1Kin 3:22 559
And this *s*, No 1Kin 3:22 559
Then *s* the king, The one saith, 1Kin 3:23 559
And the king *s*, Bring me a sword 1Kin 3:24 559
And the king *s*, Divide the living 1Kin 3:25 559
yearned upon her son, and she *s* 1Kin 3:26 559
But the other *s*, Let it be 1Kin 3:26 559
Then the king answered and *s* 1Kin 3:27 559
that he rejoiced greatly, and *s* 1Kin 5:7 559
The LORD *s* that he would dwell in 1Kin 8:12 559
And he *s*, Blessed be the LORD God 1Kin 8:15 559
the LORD *s* unto David my father, 1Kin 8:18 559
And he *s*, LORD God of Israel, 1Kin 8:23 559
the place of which thou hast *s* 1Kin 8:29 559
And the LORD *s* unto him, I have 1Kin 9:3 559
And he *s*, What cities are these 1Kin 9:13 559
she *s* to the king, It was a true 1Kin 10:6 559
concerning which the LORD *s* unto 1Kin 11:2 559

Wherefore the LORD *s* unto Solomon 1Kin 11:11 559
Hadad *s* to Pharaoh, Let me depart 1Kin 11:21 559
Then Pharaoh *s* unto him, But what 1Kin 11:22 559
he *s* to Jeroboam, Take thee ten 1Kin 11:31 559
he *s* unto them, Depart yet for 1Kin 12:5 559
father while he yet lived, and *s* 1Kin 12:6 559
he *s* unto them, What counsel give 1Kin 12:9 559
Jeroboam *s* in his heart, Now 1Kin 12:26 559
s unto them, It is too much for 1Kin 12:28 559
in the word of the LORD, and *s* 1Kin 13:2 559
s unto the man of God, Intreat 1Kin 13:6 559
the king *s* unto the man of God, 1Kin 13:7 1696
And the man of God *s* unto the king 1Kin 13:8 559
And their father *s* unto them 1Kin 13:12 1696
he *s* unto his sons, Saddle me the 1Kin 13:13 559
he *s* unto him, Art thou the man 1Kin 13:14 559
And he *s*, I am 1Kin 13:14 559
Then he *s* unto him, Come home 1Kin 13:15 559
And he *s*, I may not return with 1Kin 13:16 559
For it was *s* to me by the word of 1Kin 13:17 1697
He *s* unto him, I am a prophet 1Kin 13:18 559
from the way heard thereof, he *s* 1Kin 13:26 559
Jeroboam *s* to his wife, Arise, I 1Kin 14:2 559
the LORD *s* unto Ahijah, Behold, 1Kin 14:5 559
came in at the door, that he *s* 1Kin 14:6 559
s unto Ahab, As the LORD God of 1Kin 17:1 559
and he called to her, and *s* 1Kin 17:10 559
fetch it, he called to her, and *s* 1Kin 17:11 559
And she *s*, As the LORD thy God 1Kin 17:12 559
Elijah *s* unto her, Fear not 1Kin 17:13 559
go and do as thou hast *s* 1Kin 17:13 559
she *s* unto Elijah, What have I to 1Kin 17:18 559
he *s* unto her, Give me thy son 1Kin 17:19 559
And he cried unto the LORD, and *s* 1Kin 17:20 559
and cried unto the LORD, and *s* 1Kin 17:21 559
and Elijah *s*, See, thy son liveth 1Kin 17:23 559
And the woman *s* to Elijah, Now by 1Kin 17:24 559
Ahab *s* unto Obadiah, Go into the 1Kin 18:5 559
him, and fell on his face, and *s* 1Kin 18:7 559
And he *s*, What have I sinned, that 1Kin 18:9 559
and when they *s*, He is not there 1Kin 18:10 559
And Elijah *s*, As the LORD of hosts 1Kin 18:15 559
saw Elijah, that Ahab *s* unto him 1Kin 18:17 559
came unto all the people, and *s* 1Kin 18:21 559
Then *s* Elijah unto the people, I, 1Kin 18:22 559
And all the people answered and *s* 1Kin 18:24 559
Elijah *s* unto the prophets of 1Kin 18:25 559
that Elijah mocked them, and *s* 1Kin 18:27 559
Elijah *s* unto all the people, 1Kin 18:30 559
and laid him on the wood, and *s* 1Kin 18:33 559
And he *s*, Do it the second time 1Kin 18:34 559
And he *s*, Do it the third time 1Kin 18:34 559
the prophet came near, and *s* 1Kin 18:36 559
and they *s*, The LORD, he is the 1Kin 18:39 559
Elijah *s* unto them, Take the 1Kin 18:40 559
Elijah *s* unto Ahab, Get thee up, 1Kin 18:41 559
s to his servant, Go up now, look 1Kin 18:43 559
And he went up, and looked, and *s* 1Kin 18:43 559
And he *s*, Go again seven times 1Kin 18:43 559
at the seventh time, that he *s* 1Kin 18:44 559
And he *s*, Go up, say unto Ahab, 1Kin 18:44 559
and *s*, It is enough 1Kin 19:4 559
him, and *s* unto him, Arise and eat 1Kin 19:5 559
second time, and touched him, and *s* 1Kin 19:7 559
he *s* unto him, What dost thou 1Kin 19:9 559
And he *s*, I have been very jealous 1Kin 19:10 559
And he *s*, Go forth, and stand upon 1Kin 19:11 559
there came a voice unto him, and *s* 1Kin 19:13 559
And he *s*, I have been very jealous 1Kin 19:14 559
And the LORD *s* unto him, Go, 1Kin 19:15 559
oxen, and ran after Elijah, and *s* 1Kin 19:20 559
he *s* unto him, Go back again 1Kin 19:20 559
s unto him, Thus saith Ben-hadad, 1Kin 20:2 559
the king of Israel answered and *s* 1Kin 20:4 559
the messengers came again, and *s* 1Kin 20:5 559
all the elders of the land, and *s* 1Kin 20:7 559
and all the people *s* unto him 1Kin 20:8 559
Wherefore he *s* unto the 1Kin 20:9 559
And Ben-hadad sent unto him, and *s* 1Kin 20:10 559
the king of Israel answered and *s* 1Kin 20:11 559
that he *s* unto his servants, Set 1Kin 20:12 559
And Ahab *s*, By whom 1Kin 20:14 559
And he *s*, Thus saith the LORD, 1Kin 20:14 559
Then he *s*, Who shall order the 1Kin 20:14 559
And he *s*, Whether they be come out 1Kin 20:18 559
s unto him, Go, strengthen 1Kin 20:22 559
of the king of Syria *s* unto him 1Kin 20:23 559
unto the king of Israel, and *s* 1Kin 20:28 559
LORD, Because the Syrians have *s* 1Kin 20:28 559
And his servants *s* unto him 1Kin 20:31 559
came to the king of Israel, and *s* 1Kin 20:32 559
And he *s*, Is he yet alive 1Kin 20:32 559
and they *s*, Thy brother Ben-hadad 1Kin 20:33 559
Then he *s*, Go ye, bring him 1Kin 20:33 559
And Ben-hadad *s* unto him, The 1Kin 20:34 559
Then *s* Ahab, I will send thee 1Kin 20:34
s unto his neighbour in the word 1Kin 20:35 559
Then *s* he unto him, Because thou 1Kin 20:36 559
Then he found another man, and *s* 1Kin 20:37 559
and he *s*, Thy servant went out 1Kin 20:39 559
and brought a man unto me, and *s* 1Kin 20:39 559
And the king of Israel *s* unto him 1Kin 20:40 559
he *s* unto him, Thus saith the 1Kin 20:42 559
Naboth *s* to Ahab, The LORD forbid 1Kin 21:3 559
for he had *s*, I will not give 1Kin 21:4 559
s unto him, Why is thy spirit so 1Kin 21:5 1696
he *s* unto her, Because I spake 1Kin 21:6 1696
s unto him, Give me thy vineyard 1Kin 21:6 559

And Jezebel his wife *s* unto him 1Kin 21:7 559
was dead, that Jezebel *s* to Ahab 1Kin 21:15 559
Ahab *s* to Elijah, Hast thou found 1Kin 21:20 559
of Israel *s* unto his servants 1Kin 22:3 559
he *s* unto Jehoshaphat, Wilt thou 1Kin 22:4 559
Jehoshaphat *s* to the king of 1Kin 22:4 559
Jehoshaphat *s* unto the king of 1Kin 22:5 559
s unto them, Shall I go against 1Kin 22:6 559
And they *s*, Go up 1Kin 22:6 559
And Jehoshaphat *s*, Is there not 1Kin 22:7 559
king of Israel *s* unto Jehoshaphat 1Kin 22:8 559
And Jehoshaphat *s*, Let not the 1Kin 22:8 559
of Israel called an officer, and *s* 1Kin 22:9 559
and he *s*, Thus saith the LORD, 1Kin 22:11 559
And Micaiah *s*, As the LORD liveth, 1Kin 22:14 559
And the king *s* unto him, Micaiah, 1Kin 22:15 559
And the king *s* unto him, How many 1Kin 22:16 559
And he *s*, I saw all Israel 1Kin 22:17 559
and the LORD *s*, These have no 1Kin 22:17 559
king of Israel *s* unto Jehoshaphat 1Kin 22:18 559
And he *s*, Hear thou therefore the 1Kin 22:19 559
And the LORD *s*, Who shall persuade 1Kin 22:20 559
one *s* on this manner, and another 1Kin 22:20 559
and another *s* on that manner 1Kin 22:20 559
and stood before the LORD, and *s* 1Kin 22:21 559
And the LORD *s* unto him, Wherewith 1Kin 22:22 559
And he *s*, I will go forth, and I 1Kin 22:22 559
And he *s*, Thou shalt persuade him, 1Kin 22:22 559
smote Micaiah on the cheek, and *s* 1Kin 22:24 559
And Micaiah *s*, Behold, thou shalt 1Kin 22:25 559
And the king of Israel *s*, Take 1Kin 22:26 559
And Micaiah *s*, If thou return at 1Kin 22:28 559
And he *s*, Hearken, O people, every 1Kin 22:28 559
king of Israel *s* unto Jehoshaphat 1Kin 22:30 559
saw Jehoshaphat, that they *s* 1Kin 22:32 559
wherefore he *s* unto the driver of 1Kin 22:34 559
Then *s* Ahaziah the son of Ahab 1Kin 22:49 559
s unto them, Go, enquire of 2Kin 1:2 559
the LORD *s* to Elijah the Tishbite 2Kin 1:3 1696
he *s* unto them, Why are ye now 2Kin 1:5 559
they *s* unto him, There came a man 2Kin 1:6 559
s unto us, Go, turn again unto 2Kin 1:6 559
he *s* unto them, What manner of 2Kin 1:7 1696
And he *s*, It is Elijah the 2Kin 1:8 559
Thou man of God, the king hath *s* 2Kin 1:9 1696
s to the captain of fifty, If I 2Kin 1:10 1696
s unto him, O man of God, thus 2Kin 1:11 1696
man of God, thus hath the king *s* 2Kin 1:11 559
s unto them, If I be a man of God 2Kin 1:12 1696
s unto him, O man of God, I pray 2Kin 1:13 1696
angel of the LORD *s* unto Elijah 2Kin 1:15 1696
he *s* unto him, Thus saith the 2Kin 1:16 1696
Elijah *s* unto Elisha, Tarry here, 2Kin 2:2 559
Elisha *s* unto him, As the LORD 2Kin 2:2 559
s unto him, Knowest thou that the 2Kin 2:3 559
And he *s*, Yea, I know it 2Kin 2:3 559
Elijah *s* unto him, Elisha, tarry 2Kin 2:4 559
And he *s*, As the LORD liveth, and 2Kin 2:4 559
s unto him, Knowest thou that the 2Kin 2:5 559
Elijah *s* unto him, Tarry, I pray 2Kin 2:6 559
And he *s*, As the LORD liveth, and 2Kin 2:6 559
over, that Elijah *s* unto Elisha 2Kin 2:9 559
And Elisha *s*, I pray thee, let a 2Kin 2:9 559
And he *s*, Thou hast asked a hard 2Kin 2:10 559
him, and smote the waters, and *s* 2Kin 2:14 559
view at Jericho saw him, they *s* 2Kin 2:15 559
they *s* unto him, Behold now, 2Kin 2:16 559
And he *s*, Ye shall not send 2Kin 2:16 559
him till he was ashamed, he *s* 2Kin 2:17 559
he *s* unto them, Did I not say 2Kin 2:18 559
the men of the city *s* unto Elisha 2Kin 2:19 559
And he *s*, Bring me a new cruse, and 2Kin 2:20 559
and cast the salt in there, and *s* 2Kin 2:21 559
s unto him, Go up, thou bald head 2Kin 2:23 559
And he *s*, I will go up 2Kin 3:7 559
And he *s*, Which way shall we go up 2Kin 3:8 559
And the king of Israel *s*, Alas 2Kin 3:10 559
But Jehoshaphat *s*, Is there not 2Kin 3:11 559
Israel's servants answered and *s* 2Kin 3:11 559
And Jehoshaphat *s*, The word of the 2Kin 3:12 559
Elisha *s* unto the king of Israel, 2Kin 3:13 559
And the king of Israel *s* unto him 2Kin 3:13 559
And Elisha *s*, As the LORD of hosts 2Kin 3:14 559
And he *s*, Thus saith the LORD, 2Kin 3:16 559
And they *s*, This is blood 2Kin 3:23 559
Elisha *s* unto her, What shall I 2Kin 4:2 559
And she *s*, Thine handmaid hath not 2Kin 4:2 559
Then he *s*, Go, borrow thee 2Kin 4:3 559
that she *s* unto her son, Bring me 2Kin 4:6 559
he *s* unto her, There is not a 2Kin 4:6 559
And he *s*, Go, sell the oil, and pay 2Kin 4:7 559
she *s* unto her husband, Behold 2Kin 4:9 559
he *s* to Gehazi his servant, Call 2Kin 4:12 559
he *s* unto him, Say now unto her, 2Kin 4:13 559
And he *s*, What then is to be done 2Kin 4:14 559
And he *s*, Call her 2Kin 4:15 559
And he *s*, About this season, 2Kin 4:16 559
And she *s*, Nay, my lord, thou man 2Kin 4:16 559
season that Elisha had *s* unto her 2Kin 4:17 1696
he *s* unto his father, My head, my 2Kin 4:19 559
he *s* to a lad, Carry him to his 2Kin 4:19 559
she called unto her husband, and *s* 2Kin 4:22 559
And he *s*, Wherefore wilt thou go 2Kin 4:23 559
And she *s*, It shall be well 2Kin 4:23 559
s to her servant, Drive, and go 2Kin 4:24 559
that he *s* to Gehazi his servant, 2Kin 4:25 559
And the man of God *s*, Let her 2Kin 4:27 559
Then she *s*, Did I desire a son of 2Kin 4:28 559
Then he *s* to Gehazi, Gird up thy 2Kin 4:29 559
And the mother of the child *s* 2Kin 4:30 559
And he called Gehazi, and *s* 2Kin 4:36 559
she was come in unto him, he *s* 2Kin 4:36 559
he *s* unto his servant, Set on the 2Kin 4:38 559
that they cried out, and *s* 2Kin 4:40 559
But he *s*, Then bring meal 2Kin 4:41 559
and he *s*, Pour out for the people, 2Kin 4:41 559
And he *s*, Give unto the people, 2Kin 4:42 559
And his servitor *s*, What, should I 2Kin 4:43 559
He *s* again, Give the people, that 2Kin 4:43 559
she *s* unto her mistress, Would 2Kin 5:3 559
thus *s* the maid that is of the 2Kin 5:4 1696
And the king of Syria *s*, Go to, go 2Kin 5:5 559
that he rent his clothes, and *s* 2Kin 5:7 559
was wroth, and went away, and *s* 2Kin 5:11 559
near, and spake unto him, and *s* 2Kin 5:13 559
and he *s*, Behold, now I know that 2Kin 5:15 559
But he *s*, As the LORD liveth, 2Kin 5:16 559
And Naaman *s*, Shall there not then 2Kin 5:17 559
he *s* unto him, Go in peace 2Kin 5:19 559
of Elisha the man of God, *s* 2Kin 5:20 559
the chariot to meet him, and *s* 2Kin 5:21 559
And he *s*, All is well 2Kin 5:22 559
And Naaman *s*, Be content, take two 2Kin 5:23 559
Elisha *s* unto him, Whence comest 2Kin 5:25 559
And he *s*, Thy servant went no 2Kin 5:25 559
he *s* unto him, Went not mine 2Kin 5:26 559
of the prophets *s* unto Elisha 2Kin 6:1 559
And one *s*, Be content, I pray thee 2Kin 6:3 559
and he cried, and *s*, Alas, master 2Kin 6:5 559
And the man of God *s*, Where fell 2Kin 6:6 559
Therefore *s* he, Take it up to 2Kin 6:7 559
s unto them, Will ye not shew me 2Kin 6:11 559
And one of his servants *s*, None, 2Kin 6:12 559
And he *s*, Go and spy where he is, 2Kin 6:13 559
And his servant *s* unto him 2Kin 6:15 559
And Elisha prayed, and *s*, LORD, I 2Kin 6:17 559
Elisha prayed unto the LORD, and *s* 2Kin 6:18 559
Elisha *s* unto them, This is not 2Kin 6:19 559
come into Samaria, that Elisha *s* 2Kin 6:20 559
the king of Israel *s* unto Elisha 2Kin 6:21 559
And he *s*, If the LORD do not help 2Kin 6:27 559
And the king *s* unto her, What 2Kin 6:28 559
answered, This woman *s* unto me 2Kin 6:28 559
I *s* unto her on the next day, 2Kin 6:29 559
Then he *s*, God do so and more also 2Kin 6:31 559
he *s* to the elders, See ye how 2Kin 6:32 559
and he *s*, Behold, this evil is of 2Kin 6:33 559
Then Elisha *s*, Hear ye the word 2Kin 7:1 559
answered the man of God, and *s* 2Kin 7:2 559
And he *s*, Behold, thou shalt see 2Kin 7:2 559
they *s* one to another, Why sit we 2Kin 7:3 559
they *s* one to another, Lo, the 2Kin 7:6 559
Then they *s* one to another, We do 2Kin 7:9 559
s unto his servants, I will now 2Kin 7:12 559
one of his servants answered and *s* 2Kin 7:13 559
he died, as the man of God had *s* 2Kin 7:17 1696
answered the man of God, and *s* 2Kin 7:19 559
And he *s*, Behold, thou shalt see 2Kin 7:19 559
And Gehazi *s*, My lord, O king, 2Kin 8:5 559
the king *s* unto Hazael, Take a 2Kin 8:8 559
and came and stood before him, and *s* 2Kin 8:9 559
Elisha *s* unto him, Go, say unto 2Kin 8:10 559
And Hazael *s*, Why weepeth my lord 2Kin 8:12 559
And Hazael *s*, But what, is thy 2Kin 8:13 559
who *s* to him, What *s* Elisha to 2Kin 8:14 559
s unto him, Gird up thy loins, and 2Kin 9:1 559
and he *s*, I have an errand to thee 2Kin 9:5 559
And Jehu *s*, Unto which of all us 2Kin 9:5 559
And he *s*, To thee, O captain 2Kin 9:5 559
s unto him, Thus saith the LORD 2Kin 9:6 559
one *s* unto him, Is all well 2Kin 9:11 559
he *s* unto them, Ye know the man, 2Kin 9:11 559
And they *s*, It is false 2Kin 9:12 559
And he *s*, Thus and thus spake he to 2Kin 9:12 559
And Jehu *s*, If it be your minds 2Kin 9:15 559
company of Jehu as he came, and *s* 2Kin 9:17 559
And Joram *s*, Take an horseman, and 2Kin 9:17 559
on horseback to meet him, and *s* 2Kin 9:18 559
And Jehu *s*, What hast thou to do 2Kin 9:18 559
which came to them, and *s* 2Kin 9:19 559
And Joram *s*, Make ready 2Kin 9:21 559
when Joram saw Jehu, that he *s* 2Kin 9:22 559
s to Ahaziah, There is treachery, 2Kin 9:23 559
Then *s* Jehu to Bidkar his captain 2Kin 9:25 559
And Jehu followed after him, and *s* 2Kin 9:27 559
entered in at the gate, she *s* 2Kin 9:31 559
up his face to the window, and *s* 2Kin 9:32 559
And he *s*, Throw her down 2Kin 9:33 559
in, he did eat and drink, and *s* 2Kin 9:34 559
And he *s*, This is the word of the 2Kin 9:36 559
were exceedingly afraid, and *s* 2Kin 10:4 559
And he *s*, Lay ye them in two heaps 2Kin 10:8 559
s to all the people, Ye be 2Kin 10:9 559
of Ahaziah king of Judah, and *s* 2Kin 10:13 559
And he *s*, Take them alive 2Kin 10:14 559
s to him, Is thine heart right, 2Kin 10:15 559
And he *s*, Come with me, and see my 2Kin 10:16 559
s unto them, Ahab served Baal a 2Kin 10:18 559
And Jehu *s*, Proclaim a solemn 2Kin 10:20 559
he *s* unto him that was over the 2Kin 10:22 559
s unto the worshippers of Baal, 2Kin 10:23 559
fourscore men without, and *s* 2Kin 10:24 559
that Jehu *s* to the guard and to 2Kin 10:25 559
the LORD *s* unto Jehu, Because 2Kin 10:30 559
and they clapped their hands, and *s* 2Kin 11:12 559
s unto them, Have her forth 2Kin 11:15 559
For the priest had *s*, Let her not 2Kin 11:15 559
Jehoash *s* to the priests, All the 2Kin 12:4 559
s unto them, Why repair ye not 2Kin 12:7 559
him, and wept over his face, and *s* 2Kin 13:14 559
Elisha *s* unto him, Take bow and 2Kin 13:15 559
he *s* to the king of Israel, Put 2Kin 13:16 559
And he *s*, Open the window eastward 2Kin 13:17 559
Then Elisha *s*, Shoot 2Kin 13:17 559
And he *s*, The arrow of the LORD's 2Kin 13:17 559
And he *s*, Take the arrows 2Kin 13:18 559
he *s* unto the king of Israel, 2Kin 13:18 559
of God was wroth with him, and *s* 2Kin 13:19 559
the LORD *s* not that he would blot 2Kin 14:27 1696
whereof the LORD had *s* unto them 2Kin 17:12 559
as he had *s* by all his servants 2Kin 17:23 1696
And Rab-shakeh *s* unto them 2Kin 18:19 559
hath *s* to Judah and Jerusalem, Ye 2Kin 18:22 559
The LORD *s* to me, Go up against 2Kin 18:25 559
Then *s* Eliakim the son of Hilkiah 2Kin 18:26 559
But Rab-shakeh *s* unto them 2Kin 18:27 559
they *s* unto him, Thus saith 2Kin 19:3 559
Isaiah *s* unto them, Thus shall ye 2Kin 19:6 559
prayed before the LORD, and *s* 2Kin 19:15 559
reproached the Lord, and hast *s* 2Kin 19:23 559
s unto him, Thus saith the LORD, 2Kin 20:1 559
And Isaiah *s*, Take a lump of figs 2Kin 20:7 559
Hezekiah *s* unto Isaiah, What 2Kin 20:8 559
And Isaiah *s*, This sign shalt thou 2Kin 20:9 559
s unto him, What *s* these men 2Kin 20:14 559
And Hezekiah *s*, They are come from 2Kin 20:14 559
And he *s*, What have they seen in 2Kin 20:15 559
Isaiah *s* unto Hezekiah, Hear the 2Kin 20:16 559
Then *s* Hezekiah unto Isaiah, Good 2Kin 20:19 559
And he *s*, Is it not good, if peace 2Kin 20:19 559
of the LORD, of which the LORD *s* 2Kin 21:4 559
of which the LORD *s* to David 2Kin 21:7 559
priest *s* unto Shaphan the scribe 2Kin 22:8 559
brought the king word again, and *s* 2Kin 22:9 559
she *s* unto them, Thus saith the 2Kin 22:15 559
Then he *s*, What title is that 2Kin 23:17 559
And he *s*, Let him alone 2Kin 23:18 559
And the LORD *s*, I will remove 2Kin 23:27 559
chosen, and the house of which I *s* 2Kin 23:27 559
of the LORD, as the LORD had *s* 2Kin 24:13 1696
s unto them, Fear not to be the 2Kin 25:24 559
Then *s* Saul to his armourbearer, 1Chr 10:4 559
and the LORD thy God *s* unto thee 1Chr 11:2 559
inhabitants of Jebus *s* to David 1Chr 11:5 559
And David *s*, Whosoever smiteth the 1Chr 11:6 559
And David longed, and *s*, Oh that 1Chr 11:17 559
And *s*, My God forbid it me, that I 1Chr 11:19 559
s unto them, If ye be come 1Chr 12:17 559
chief of the captains, and he *s* 1Chr 12:18
David *s* unto all the congregation 1Chr 13:2 559
all the congregation *s* that they 1Chr 13:4
And the LORD *s* unto him, Go up 1Chr 14:10 559
Then David *s*, God hath broken in 1Chr 14:11 559
God *s* unto him, Go not up after 1Chr 14:14 559
Then David *s*, None ought to carry 1Chr 15:2 559
s unto them, Ye are the chief of 1Chr 15:12 559
And all the people *s*, Amen, and 1Chr 16:36 559
that David *s* to Nathan the 1Chr 17:1 559
Then Nathan *s* unto David, Do all 1Chr 17:2 559
came and sat before the LORD, and *s* 1Chr 17:16 559
for ever, and do as thou hast *s* 1Chr 17:23 1696
And David *s*, I will shew kindness 1Chr 19:2 559
the children of Ammon *s* to Hanun 1Chr 19:3 559
And the king *s*, Tarry at Jericho 1Chr 19:5 559
And he *s*, If the Syrians be too 1Chr 19:12 559
David *s* to Joab and to the rulers 1Chr 21:2 559
David *s* unto God, I have sinned 1Chr 21:8 559
s unto him, Thus saith the LORD, 1Chr 21:11 559
David *s* unto Gad, I am in a great 1Chr 21:13 559
s to the angel that destroyed, It 1Chr 21:15 559
David *s* unto God, Is it not I 1Chr 21:17 559
Then David *s* to Ornan, Grant me 1Chr 21:22 559
Ornan *s* unto David, Take it to 1Chr 21:23 559
And king David *s* to Ornan, Nay 1Chr 21:24 559
Then David *s*, This is the house 1Chr 22:1 559
And David *s*, Solomon my son is 1Chr 22:5 559
David *s* to Solomon, My son, as 1Chr 22:7 559
thy God, as he hath *s* of thee 1Chr 22:11 1696
s David, to praise therewith 1Chr 23:5
For David *s*, The LORD God of 1Chr 23:25 559
because the LORD had *s* he would 1Chr 27:23 559
king stood up upon his feet, and *s* 1Chr 28:2 559
But God *s* unto me, Thou shalt not 1Chr 28:3 559
he *s* unto me, Solomon thy son, he 1Chr 28:6 559
s David, the LORD made me 1Chr 28:19
David *s* to Solomon his son, Be 1Chr 28:20 559
king *s* unto all the congregation 1Chr 29:1 559
and David *s*, Blessed be thou, LORD 1Chr 29:10 559
David *s* to all the congregation, 1Chr 29:20 559
s unto him, Ask what I shall give 2Chr 1:7 559
Solomon *s* unto God, Thou hast 2Chr 1:8 559
God *s* to Solomon, Because this 2Chr 1:11 559
Huram *s* moreover, Blessed be the 2Chr 2:12 559
Then *s* Solomon, The LORD hath 2Chr 6:1 559
The LORD hath *s* that he would 2Chr 6:1 559
And he *s*, Blessed be the LORD God 2Chr 6:4 559
But the LORD *s* to David my father 2Chr 6:8 559
And *s*, O LORD God of Israel, there 2Chr 6:14 559
the place whereof thou hast *s* 2Chr 6:20 559
s unto him, I have heard thy 2Chr 7:12 559
for he *s*, My wife shall not dwell 2Chr 8:11 559
she *s* to the king, It was a true 2Chr 9:5 559
he *s* unto them, Come again unto 2Chr 10:5 559
he *s* unto them, What advice give 2Chr 10:9 559

s unto them, Thus saith the LORD, 2Chr 12:5 559
and they *s*, The LORD is righteous 2Chr 12:6 559
which is in mount Ephraim, and *s* 2Chr 13:4 559
Therefore he *s* unto Judah 2Chr 14:7 559
cried unto the LORD his God, and *s* 2Chr 14:11 559
s unto him, Hear ye me, Asa, and 2Chr 15:2 559
s unto him, Because thou hast 2Chr 16:7 559
Ahab king of Israel *s* unto 2Chr 18:3 559
Jehoshaphat *s* unto the king of 2Chr 18:4 559
s unto them, Shall we go to 2Chr 18:5 559
And they *s*, Go up 2Chr 18:5 559
But Jehoshaphat *s*, Is there not 2Chr 18:6 559
king of Israel *s* unto Jehoshaphat 2Chr 18:7 559
And Jehoshaphat *s*, Let not the 2Chr 18:7 559
for one of his officers, and *s* 2Chr 18:8 559
had made him horns of iron, and *s* 2Chr 18:10 559
And Micaiah *s*, As the LORD liveth, 2Chr 18:13 559
to the king, the king *s* unto him 2Chr 18:14 559
And he *s*, Go ye up, and prosper, and 2Chr 18:14 559
And the king *s* to him, How many 2Chr 18:15 559
Then he *s*, I did see all Israel 2Chr 18:16 559
and the LORD *s*, These have no 2Chr 18:16 559
king of Israel *s* to Jehoshaphat 2Chr 18:17 559
Again he *s*, Therefore hear the 2Chr 18:18 559
And the LORD *s*, Who shall entice 2Chr 18:19 559
and stood before the LORD, and *s* 2Chr 18:20 559
And the LORD *s* unto him, Wherewith 2Chr 18:20 559
And he *s*, I will go out, and be a 2Chr 18:21 559
And the LORD *s*, Thou shalt entice 2Chr 18:21 559
Micaiah upon the cheek, and *s* 2Chr 18:23 559
And Micaiah *s*, Behold, thou shalt 2Chr 18:24 559
Then the king of Israel *s* 2Chr 18:25 559
And Micaiah *s*, If thou certainly 2Chr 18:27 559
And he *s*, Hearken, all ye people 2Chr 18:27 559
king of Israel *s* unto Jehoshaphat 2Chr 18:29 559
saw Jehoshaphat, that they *s* 2Chr 18:31 559
therefore he *s* to his chariot man 2Chr 18:33 559
s to king Jehoshaphat, Shouldest 2Chr 19:2 559
s to the judges, Take heed what 2Chr 19:6 559
And *s*, O LORD God of our fathers, 2Chr 20:6 559
And he *s*, Hearken ye, all Judah, 2Chr 20:15 559
forth, Jehoshaphat stood and *s* 2Chr 20:20 559
Because, *s* they, he is the son of 2Chr 22:9 559
he *s* unto them, Behold, the 2Chr 23:3 559
as the LORD hath *s* of the sons of 2Chr 23:3 1696
and his sons anointed him, and *s* 2Chr 23:11 559
Athaliah rent her clothes, and *s* 2Chr 23:13 559
s unto them, Have her forth of 2Chr 23:14 559
For the priest *s*, Slay her not in 2Chr 23:14 559
s to them, Go out unto the cities 2Chr 24:5 559
s unto him, Why hast thou not 2Chr 24:6 559
s unto them, Thus saith God, Why 2Chr 24:20 559
And when he died, he *s*, The LORD 2Chr 24:22 559
Amaziah *s* to the man of God, But 2Chr 25:9 559
which *s* unto him, Why hast thou 2Chr 25:15 559
him, that the king *s* unto him 2Chr 25:16 559
Then the prophet forbare, and *s* 2Chr 25:16 559
s unto him, It appertaineth not 2Chr 26:18 559
for they *s*, He is a leper 2Chr 26:23 559
s unto them, Behold, because the 2Chr 28:9 559
s unto them, Ye shall not bring 2Chr 28:13 559
and he *s*, Because the gods of the 2Chr 28:23 559
s unto them, Hear me, ye Levites, 2Chr 29:5 559
in to Hezekiah the king, and *s* 2Chr 29:18 559
Then Hezekiah answered and *s* 2Chr 29:31 559
house of Zadok answered him, and *s* 2Chr 31:10 559
the LORD, whereof the LORD had *s* 2Chr 33:4 559
God, of which God had *s* to David 2Chr 33:7 559
s to Shaphan the scribe, I have 2Chr 34:15 559
s unto the Levites that taught 2Chr 35:3 559
the king *s* to his servants, Have 2Chr 35:23 559
And the Tirshatha *s* unto them Ezr 2:63 559
s unto them, Let us build with Ezr 4:2 559
s unto them, Ye have nothing to Ezr 4:3 559
s thus unto them, Who hath Ezr 5:3 560
Then *s* we unto them after this Ezr 5:4 560
s unto them thus, Who commanded Ezr 5:9 560
s unto him, Take these vessels, Ezr 5:15 560
I *s* unto them, Ye are holy unto Ezr 8:28 559
And *s*, O my God, I am ashamed and Ezr 9:6 559
s unto Ezra, We have trespassed Ezr 10:2 559
s unto them, Ye have transgressed Ezr 10:10 559
s with a loud voice, As thou hast Ezr 10:12 559
with a loud voice, As thou hast *s* Ezr 10:12 1697
they *s* unto me, The remnant that Neh 1:3 559
And *s*, I beseech thee, O LORD God Neh 1:5 559
Wherefore the king *s* unto me Neh 2:2 559
s unto the king, Let the king Neh 2:3 559
Then the king *s* unto me, For what Neh 2:4 559
I *s* unto the king, If it please Neh 2:5 559
And the king *s* unto me, (the queen Neh 2:6 559
Moreover I *s* unto the king, If it Neh 2:7 559
Then *s* I unto them, Ye see the Neh 2:17 559
And they *s*, Let us rise up and Neh 2:18 559
us to scorn, and despised us, and *s* Neh 2:19 559
s unto them, The God of heaven, Neh 2:20 559
and the army of Samaria, and *s* Neh 4:2 559
the Ammonite was by him, and he *s* Neh 4:3 559
And Judah *s*, The strength of the Neh 4:10 559
And our adversaries *s*, They shall Neh 4:11 559
they *s* unto us ten times, From Neh 4:12 559
s unto the nobles, and to the Neh 4:14 559
I *s* unto the nobles, and to the Neh 4:19 559
the same time *s* I unto the people Neh 4:22 559
For there were that *s*, We, our Neh 5:2 559
Some also there were that *s* Neh 5:3 559
There were also that *s*, We have Neh 5:4 559
s unto them, Ye exact usury, Neh 5:7 559

I *s* unto them, We after our Neh 5:8 559
Also I *s*, It is not good that ye Neh 5:9 559
Then *s* they, We will restore them Neh 5:12 559
Also I shook my lap, and *s* Neh 5:13 559
And all the congregation *s* Neh 5:13 559
and he *s*, Let us meet together in Neh 6:10 559
And I *s*, Should such a man as I Neh 6:11 559
I *s* unto them, Let not the gates Neh 7:3 559
And the Tirshatha *s* unto them Neh 7:65 559
s unto all the people, This day Neh 8:9 559
Then he *s* unto them, Go your way, Neh 8:10 559
Shebaniah, and Pethahiah, *s* Neh 9:5 559
had made them a molten calf, and *s* Neh 9:18 559
contended I with the rulers, and *s* Neh 13:11 559
s unto them, What evil thing is Neh 13:17 559
s unto them, Why lodge ye about Neh 13:21 559
Then the king *s* to the wise men, Est 1:13 559
Then *s* the king's servants that Est 2:2 559
king's gate, *s* unto Mordecai, Why Est 3:3 559
Haman *s* unto king Ahasuerus, Est 3:8 559
the king *s* unto Haman, The silver Est 3:11 559
Then *s* the king unto her, What Est 5:3 559
Then the king *s*, Cause Haman to Est 5:5 559
that he may do as Esther hath *s* Est 5:5 1697
the king *s* unto Esther at the Est 5:6 559
Then answered Esther, and *s* Est 5:7 559
do to morrow as the king hath *s* Est 5:8 1697
Haman *s* moreover, Yea, Esther the Est 5:12 559
Then *s* Zeresh his wife and all his Est 5:14 559
And the king *s*, What honour and Est 6:3 559
Then *s* the king's servants that Est 6:3 559
And the king *s*, Who is in the Est 6:4 559
And the king's servants *s* unto him Est 6:5 559
And the king *s*, Let him come in Est 6:5 559
And the king *s* unto him, What Est 6:6 559
Then the king *s* to Haman, Make Est 6:10 559
and the horse, as thou hast *s* Est 6:10 1696
Then *s* his wise men and Zeresh his Est 6:13 559
the king *s* again unto Esther on Est 7:2 559
Esther the queen answered and *s* Est 7:3 559
s unto Esther the queen, Who is Est 7:5 559
And Esther *s*, The adversary and Est 7:6 559
Then *s* the king, Will he force Est 7:8 559
s before the king, Behold also, Est 7:9 559
Then the king *s*, Hang him thereon Est 7:9 559
And *s*, If it please the king, and Est 8:5 559
Ahasuerus *s* unto Esther the queen Est 8:7 559
the king *s* unto Esther the queen, Est 9:12 559
Then *s* Esther, If it please the Est 9:13 559
for Job *s*, It may be that my sons Job 1:5 559
the LORD *s* unto Satan, Whence Job 1:7 559
Satan answered the LORD, and *s* Job 1:7 559
the LORD *s* unto Satan, Hast thou Job 1:8 559
Satan answered the LORD, and *s* Job 1:9 559
the LORD *s* unto Satan, Behold, Job 1:12 559
came a messenger unto Job, and *s* Job 1:14 559
there came also another, and *s* Job 1:16 559
there came also another, and *s* Job 1:17 559
there came also another, and *s* Job 1:18 559
And *s*, Naked came I out of my Job 1:21 559
the LORD *s* unto Satan, From Job 2:2 559
And Satan answered the LORD, and *s* Job 2:2 559
the LORD *s* unto Satan, Hast thou Job 2:3 559
And Satan answered the LORD, and *s* Job 2:4 559
the LORD *s* unto Satan, Behold, he Job 2:6 559
Then *s* his wife unto him, Dost Job 2:9 559
But he *s* unto her, Thou speakest Job 2:10 559
And Job spake, and *s*, Job 3:2 559
and the night in which it was *s* Job 3:3 559
the Temanite answered and *s* Job 4:1 559
But Job answered and *s*, Job 6:1 559
answered Bildad the Shuhite, and *s* Job 8:1 559
Then Job answered and *s*, Job 9:1 559
is one thing, therefore I *s* it Job 9:22 559
Zophar the Naamathite, and *s* Job 11:1 559
For thou hast *s*, My doctrine is Job 11:4 559
And Job answered and *s*, Job 12:1 559
Eliphaz the Temanite, and *s* Job 15:1 559
Then Job answered and *s*, Job 16:1 559
I have *s* to corruption, Thou art Job 17:14 7121
answered Bildad the Shuhite, and *s* Job 18:1 559
Then Job answered and *s*, Job 19:1 559
Zophar the Naamathite, and *s* Job 20:1 559
But Job answered and *s*, Job 21:1 559
the Temanite answered and *s* Job 22:1 559
Which *s* unto God, Depart from us Job 22:17 559
Then Job answered and *s*, Job 23:1 559
answered Bildad the Shuhite, and *s* Job 25:1 559
But Job answered and *s*, Job 26:1 559
Job continued his parable, and *s* Job 27:1 559
And unto man he *s*, Behold, the Job 28:28 559
Job continued his parable, and *s* Job 29:1 559
Then I *s*, I shall die in my nest, Job 29:18 559
or have *s* to the fine gold, Thou Job 31:24 559
If the men of my tabernacle *s* not Job 31:31 559
Barachel the Buzite answered and *s* Job 32:6 559
I *s*, Days should speak, and Job 32:7 559
Therefore I *s*, Hearken to me Job 32:10 559
I *s*, I will answer also my part, Job 32:17 559
Furthermore Elihu answered and *s* Job 34:1 559
For Job hath *s*, I am righteous Job 34:5 559
For he hath *s*, It profiteth a man Job 34:9 559
it is meet to be *s* unto God Job 34:31 559
Elihu spake moreover, and *s* Job 35:1 559
Elihu also proceeded, and *s* Job 36:1 559
Job out of the whirlwind, and *s* Job 38:1 559
And *s*, Hitherto shalt thou come, Job 38:11 559
the LORD answered Job, and *s* Job 40:1 559

Then Job answered the LORD, and *s* Job 40:3 559
Job out of the whirlwind, and *s* Job 40:6 559
Then Job answered the LORD, and *s* Job 42:1 559
the LORD *s* to Eliphaz the Job 42:7 559
The LORD hath *s* unto me, Thou art Ps 2:7 559
He hath *s* in his heart, I shall Ps 10:6 559
He hath *s* in his heart, God hath Ps 10:11 559
he hath *s* in his heart, Thou wilt Ps 10:13 559
Who have *s*, With our tongue will Ps 12:4 559
The fool hath *s* in his heart Ps 14:1 559
thou hast *s* unto the LORD, Thou Ps 16:2 559
hand of Saul: And he *s* Ps 18:t 559
my heart *s* unto thee, Thy face, Ps 27:8 559
And in my prosperity I *s*, I shall Ps 30:6 559
I *s*, Thou art my God Ps 31:14 559
For I *s* in my haste, I am cut off Ps 31:22 559
I *s*, I will confess my Ps 32:5 559
their mouth wide against me, and *s* Ps 35:21 559
For I *s*, Hear me, lest otherwise Ps 38:16 559
I *s*, I will take heed to my ways, Ps 39:1 559
Then *s* I, Lo, I come Ps 40:7 559
I *s*, LORD, be merciful unto me Ps 41:4 559
s unto him, David is come to the Ps 52:t 559
The fool hath *s* in his heart Ps 53:1 559
s to Saul, Doth not David hide Ps 54:t 559
And I *s*, Oh that I had wings like Ps 55:6 559
The Lord *s*, I will bring again Ps 68:22 559
They *s* in their hearts, Let us Ps 74:8 559
I *s* unto the fools, Deal not Ps 75:4 559
And I *s*, This is my infirmity Ps 77:10 559
they *s*, Can God furnish a table Ps 78:19 559
I have *s*, Ye are gods Ps 82:6 559
They have *s*, Come, and let us cut Ps 83:4 559
Who *s*, Let us take to ourselves Ps 83:12 559
And of Zion it shall be *s*, This and Ps 87:5 559
For I have *s*, Mercy shall be Ps 89:2 559
When I *s*, My foot slippeth Ps 94:18 559
with this generation, and *s* Ps 95:10 559
I *s*, O my God, take me not away Ps 102:24 559
Therefore he *s* that he would Ps 106:23 559
The LORD *s* unto my Lord, Sit thou Ps 110:1 5002
I *s* in my haste, All men are Ps 116:11 559
I have *s* that I would keep thy Ps 119:57 559
I was glad when they *s* unto me Ps 122:1 559
then *s* they among the heathen, Ps 126:2 559
who *s*, Rase it, rase it, even to Ps 137:7 559
I *s* unto the LORD, Thou art my Ps 140:6 559
I *s*, Thou art my refuge and my Ps 142:5 559
s unto me, Let thine heart retain Prov 4:4 559
with an impudent face *s* unto him Prov 7:13 559
it is that it be *s* unto thee Prov 25:7 559
any thing whereof it may be *s* Eccl 1:10 559
I *s* in mine heart, Go to now, I Eccl 2:1 559
I *s* of laughter, It is mad Eccl 2:2 559
Then *s* I in my heart, As it Eccl 2:15 559
Then I *s* in my heart, that this Eccl 2:15 1696
I *s* in mine heart, God shall Eccl 3:17 559
I *s* in mine heart concerning the Eccl 3:18 559
I *s*, I will be wise Eccl 7:23 559
I *s* that this also is vanity Eccl 8:14 559
Then *s* I, Wisdom is better than Eccl 9:16 559
s unto me, Rise up, my love, my Song 2:10 559
to whom I *s*, Saw ye him whom my Song 3:3
I *s*, I will go up to the palm Song 7:8 559
In mine ears *s* the LORD of hosts, Is 5:9
And one cried unto another, and *s* Is 6:3 559
Then *s* I, Woe is me Is 6:5 559
And he laid it upon my mouth, and *s* Is 6:7 559
Then *s* I, Here am I Is 6:8 559
And he *s*, Go, and tell this people, Is 6:9 559
Then *s* I, Lord, how long Is 6:11 559
Then *s* the LORD unto Isaiah, Go Is 7:3 559
But Ahaz *s*, I will not ask, Is 7:12 559
And he *s*, Hear ye now, O house of Is 7:13 559
Moreover the LORD *s* unto me Is 8:1 559
Then *s* the LORD to me, Call his Is 8:3 559
For thou hast *s* in thine heart, I Is 14:13 559
For so the LORD *s* unto me Is 18:4 559
And the LORD *s*, Like as my servant Is 20:3 559
For thus hath the Lord *s* unto me Is 21:6 559
And he answered and *s*, Babylon is Is 21:9 559
The watchman *s*, The morning Is 21:12 559
For thus hath the Lord *s* unto me Is 21:16 559
Therefore *s* I, Look away from me Is 22:4 559
And he *s*, Thou shalt no more Is 23:12 559
But I *s*, My leanness, my leanness Is 24:16 559
And it shall be *s* in that day Is 25:9 559
To whom he *s*, This is the rest Is 28:12 559
Because ye have *s*, We have made a Is 28:15 559
Wherefore the Lord *s*, Forasmuch Is 29:13 559
But ye *s*, No Is 30:16 559
nor the churl *s* to be bountiful Is 32:5 559
And Rabshakeh *s* unto them, Say ye Is 36:4 559
s to Judah and to Jerusalem, Ye Is 36:7 559
the LORD *s* unto me, Go up against Is 36:10 559
Then *s* Eliakim and Shebna and Joah Is 36:11 559
But Rabshakeh *s*, Hath my master Is 36:12 559
voice in the Jews' language, and *s* Is 36:13 559
they *s* unto him, Thus saith Is 37:3 559
Isaiah *s* unto them, Thus shall ye Is 37:6 559
reproached the Lord, and hast *s* Is 37:24 559
s unto him, Thus saith the LORD, Is 38:1 559
And *s*, Remember now, O LORD, I Is 38:3 559
I *s* in the cutting off of my days Is 38:10 559
I *s*, I shall not see the LORD, Is 38:11 559
For Isaiah had *s*, Let them take a Is 38:21 559
Hezekiah also had *s*, What is the Is 38:22 559
s unto him, What *s* these men Is 39:3 559

And Hezekiah *s*, They are come from	Is 39:3	559
Then *s* he, What have they seen in	Is 39:4	559
Then *s* Isaiah to Hezekiah, Hear	Is 39:5	559
Then *s* Hezekiah to Isaiah, Good	Is 39:8	559
He *s* moreover, For there shall be	Is 39:8	559
The voice *s*, Cry	Is 40:6	559
And he *s*, What shall I cry	Is 40:6	559
every one *s* to his brother, Be of	Is 41:6	559
s unto thee, Thou art my servant	Is 41:9	559
I *s* not unto the seed of Jacob,	Is 45:19	559
thou hast *s*, None seeth me	Is 47:10	559
thou hast *s* in thine heart, I am,	Is 47:10	559
s unto me, Thou art my servant, O	Is 49:3	559
Then I *s*, I have laboured in vain	Is 49:4	559
And he *s*, It is a light thing that	Is 49:6	559
But Zion *s*, The LORD hath	Is 49:14	559
which have *s* to thy soul, Bow	Is 51:23	559
For he *s*, Surely they are my	Is 63:8	559
I *s*, Behold me, behold me, unto a	Is 65:1	559
you out for my name's sake, *s*	Is 66:5	559
Then *s* I, Ah, Lord GOD	Jer 1:6	559
But the LORD *s* unto me, Say not,	Jer 1:7	559
And the LORD *s* unto me, Behold, I	Jer 1:9	559
And I *s*, I see a rod of an almond	Jer 1:11	559
Then *s* the LORD unto me, Thou	Jer 1:12	559
and I *s*, I see a seething pot	Jer 1:13	559
Then the LORD *s* unto me, Out of	Jer 1:14	559
Neither *s* they, Where is the LORD	Jer 2:6	559
The priests *s* not, Where is the	Jer 2:8	559
The LORD *s* also unto me in the	Jer 3:6	559
I *s* after she had done all these	Jer 3:7	559
And the LORD *s* unto me, The	Jer 3:11	559
But I *s*, How shall I put thee	Jer 3:19	559
and I *s*, Thou shalt call me, My	Jer 3:19	559
Then *s* I, Ah, Lord GOD	Jer 4:10	559
time shall it be *s* to this people	Jer 4:11	559
For thus hath the LORD *s*, The	Jer 4:27	559
Therefore I *s*, Surely these are	Jer 5:4	559
They have belied the LORD, and *s*	Jer 5:12	559
For thus hath the LORD of hosts *s*	Jer 6:6	559
But they *s*, We will not walk	Jer 6:16	559
But they *s*, We will not hearken	Jer 6:17	559
but I *s*, Truly this is a grief,	Jer 10:19	559
Then answered I, and *s*, So be it,	Jer 11:5	559
Then the LORD *s* unto me, Proclaim	Jer 11:6	559
And the LORD *s* unto me, A	Jer 11:9	559
because they *s*, He shall not see	Jer 12:4	559
days, that the LORD *s* unto me	Jer 13:6	559
Then *s* the LORD unto me, Pray not	Jer 14:11	559
Then *s* I, Ah, Lord GOD	Jer 14:13	559
Then the LORD *s* unto me, The	Jer 14:14	559
Then *s* the LORD unto me, Though	Jer 15:1	559
The LORD *s*, Verily it shall be	Jer 15:11	559
LORD, that it shall no more be *s*	Jer 16:14	559
Thus *s* the LORD unto me	Jer 17:19	559
wherewith I *s* I would benefit	Jer 18:10	559
And they *s*, There is no hope	Jer 18:12	559
Then *s* they, Come, and let us	Jer 18:18	559
and *s* to all the people,	Jer 19:14	559
Then *s* Jeremiah unto him, The	Jer 20:3	559
Then I *s*, I will not make mention	Jer 20:9	559
Then *s* Jeremiah unto them, Thus	Jer 21:3	559
that despise me, The LORD hath *s*	Jer 23:17	1696
I have heard what the prophets *s*	Jer 23:25	559
Then *s* the LORD unto me, What	Jer 24:3	559
And I *s*, Figs	Jer 24:3	559
They *s*, Turn ye again now every	Jer 25:5	559
Then *s* the princes and all the	Jer 26:16	559
Then the prophet Jeremiah *s* unto	Jer 28:5	559
Even the prophet Jeremiah *s*	Jer 28:6	559
Then *s* the prophet Jeremiah unto	Jer 28:15	559
Because ye have *s*, The LORD hath	Jer 29:15	559
And Jeremiah *s*, The word of the	Jer 32:6	559
s unto me, Buy my field, I pray	Jer 32:8	559
And thou hast *s* unto me, O Lord	Jer 32:25	559
I *s* unto them, Drink ye wine	Jer 35:5	559
But they *s*, We will drink no wine	Jer 35:6	559
came up into the land, that we *s*	Jer 35:11	559
Jeremiah *s* unto the house of the	Jer 35:18	559
they *s* unto him, Sit down now, and	Jer 36:15	559
s unto Baruch, We will surely	Jer 36:16	559
Then *s* the princes unto Baruch,	Jer 36:19	559
Then *s* Jeremiah, It is false	Jer 37:14	559
him secretly in his house, and *s*	Jer 37:17	559
And Jeremiah *s*, There is	Jer 37:17	559
s he, thou shalt be delivered	Jer 37:17	559
Moreover Jeremiah *s* unto king	Jer 37:18	559
the princes *s* unto the king	Jer 38:4	559
Then Zedekiah the king *s*, Behold,	Jer 38:5	559
the Ethiopian *s* unto Jeremiah	Jer 38:12	559
the king *s* unto Jeremiah, I will	Jer 38:14	559
Then Jeremiah *s* unto Zedekiah	Jer 38:15	559
Then *s* Jeremiah unto Zedekiah,	Jer 38:17	559
Zedekiah the king *s* unto Jeremiah	Jer 38:19	559
But Jeremiah *s*, They shall not	Jer 38:20	559
Then *s* Zedekiah unto Jeremiah,	Jer 38:24	559
what thou hast *s* unto the king	Jer 38:25	1696
also what the king *s* unto thee	Jer 38:25	1696
s unto him, The LORD thy God hath	Jer 40:2	559
and done according as he hath *s*	Jer 40:3	1696
he was not yet gone back, he *s*	Jer 40:5	
s unto him, Dost thou certainly	Jer 40:14	559
s unto Johanan the son of Kareah	Jer 40:16	559
he *s* unto them, Come to Gedaliah	Jer 41:6	559
among them that *s* unto Ishmael	Jer 41:8	559
s unto Jeremiah the prophet, Let,	Jer 42:2	559
Jeremiah the prophet *s* unto them	Jer 42:4	559
Then they *s* to Jeremiah, The LORD	Jer 42:5	559
s unto them, Thus saith the LORD,	Jer 42:9	559
The LORD hath *s* concerning you, O	Jer 42:19	1696
Then Jeremiah *s* unto all the	Jer 44:20	559
Moreover Jeremiah *s* unto all the	Jer 44:24	559
and they *s*, Arise, and let us go	Jer 46:16	559
and their adversaries *s*, We offend	Jer 50:7	559
Jeremiah *s* to Seraiah, When thou	Jer 51:61	559
And I *s*, My strength and my hope is	Lam 3:18	559
then I *s*, I am cut off	Lam 3:54	559
they *s* among the heathen, They	Lam 4:15	559
taken in their pits, of whom we *s*	Lam 4:20	559
he *s* unto me, Son of man, stand	Eze 2:1	559
he *s* unto me, Son of man, I send	Eze 2:3	559
Moreover he *s* unto me, Son of man	Eze 3:1	559
he *s* unto me, Son of man, cause	Eze 3:3	559
he *s* unto me, Son of man, go, get	Eze 3:4	559
Moreover he *s* unto me, Son of man	Eze 3:10	559
he *s* unto me, Arise, go forth	Eze 3:22	559
s unto me, Go, shut thyself	Eze 3:24	559
And the LORD *s*, Even thus shall	Eze 4:13	559
Then *s* I, Ah Lord GOD	Eze 4:14	559
Then he *s* unto me, Lo, I have	Eze 4:15	559
Moreover he *s* unto me, Son of man	Eze 4:16	559
that I have not *s* in vain that I	Eze 6:10	1696
Then *s* he unto me, Son of man,	Eze 8:5	559
He *s* furthermore unto me, Son of	Eze 8:6	559
Then *s* he unto me, Son of man,	Eze 8:8	559
he *s* unto me, Go in, and behold	Eze 8:9	559
Then *s* he unto me, Son of man,	Eze 8:12	559
He *s* also unto me, Turn thee yet	Eze 8:13	559
Then *s* he unto me, Hast thou seen	Eze 8:15	559
Then he *s* unto me, Hast thou seen	Eze 8:17	559
And the LORD *s* unto him, Go	Eze 9:4	559
the others he *s* in mine hearing	Eze 9:5	559
he *s* unto them, Defile the house,	Eze 9:7	559
fell upon my face, and cried, and *s*	Eze 9:8	559
Then *s* he unto me, The iniquity	Eze 9:9	559
the man clothed with linen, and *s*	Eze 10:2	559
Then *s* he unto me, Son of man,	Eze 11:2	559
fell upon me, and *s* unto me, Speak	Eze 11:5	559
Thus have ye *s*, O house of Israel	Eze 11:5	559
and cried with a loud voice, and *s*	Eze 11:13	559
inhabitants of Jerusalem have *s*	Eze 11:15	559
s unto thee, What doest thou	Eze 12:9	559
shall it not be *s* unto you	Eze 13:12	559
I *s* unto thee when thou wast in	Eze 16:6	559
I *s* unto thee when thou wast in	Eze 16:6	559
Then *s* I unto them, Cast ye away	Eze 20:7	559
then I *s*, I will pour out my fury	Eze 20:8	559
then I *s*, I would pour out my	Eze 20:13	559
But I *s* unto their children in	Eze 20:18	559
then I *s*, I would pour out my	Eze 20:21	559
Then I *s* unto them, What is the	Eze 20:29	559
Then *s* I, Ah Lord GOD	Eze 20:49	559
I the LORD have *s* it	Eze 21:17	1696
The LORD *s* moreover unto me	Eze 23:36	559
Then *s* I unto her that was old in	Eze 23:43	559
And the people *s* unto me, Wilt	Eze 24:19	559
Tyrus hath *s* against Jerusalem	Eze 26:2	559
O Tyrus, thou hast *s*, I am of	Eze 27:3	559
is lifted up, and thou hast *s*	Eze 28:2	559
midst of his rivers, which hath *s*	Eze 29:3	559
because he hath *s*, The river is	Eze 29:9	559
Because thou hast *s*, These two	Eze 35:10	559
the enemy hath *s* against you	Eze 36:2	559
my holy name, when they *s* to them	Eze 36:20	559
he *s* unto me, Son of man, can	Eze 37:3	559
Again he *s* unto me, Prophesy upon	Eze 37:4	559
Then *s* he unto me, Prophesy unto	Eze 37:9	559
Then he *s* unto me, Son of man,	Eze 37:11	559
And the man *s* unto me, Son of man,	Eze 40:4	1696
he *s* unto me, This chamber, whose	Eze 40:45	1696
he *s* unto me, This is the most	Eze 41:4	559
he *s* unto me, This is the table	Eze 41:22	1696
Then *s* he unto me, The north	Eze 42:13	559
he *s* unto me, Son of man, the	Eze 43:7	559
he *s* unto me, Son of man, thus	Eze 43:18	559
Then *s* the LORD unto me	Eze 44:2	559
And the LORD *s* unto me, Son of man	Eze 44:5	559
Then *s* he unto me, This is the	Eze 46:20	559
Then *s* he unto me, These are the	Eze 46:24	559
he *s* unto me, Son of man, hast	Eze 47:6	559
Then *s* he unto me, These waters	Eze 47:8	559
of the eunuchs *s* unto Daniel	Dan 1:10	559
Then *s* Daniel to Melzar, whom the	Dan 1:11	559
had *s* he should bring them in	Dan 1:18	559
the king *s* unto them, I have	Dan 2:3	559
s to the Chaldeans, The thing is	Dan 2:5	560
They answered again and *s*, Let the	Dan 2:7	560
The king answered and *s*, I know of	Dan 2:8	560
answered before the king, and *s*	Dan 2:10	560
s to Arioch the king's captain,	Dan 2:15	560
Daniel answered and *s*, Blessed be	Dan 2:20	560
he went and *s* thus unto him	Dan 2:24	560
s thus unto him, I have found a	Dan 2:25	560
s to Daniel, whose name was	Dan 2:26	560
in the presence of the king, and *s*	Dan 2:27	560
king answered unto Daniel, and *s*	Dan 2:47	560
s to the king Nebuchadnezzar, O	Dan 3:9	560
s unto them, Is it true, O	Dan 3:14	560
s to the king, O Nebuchadnezzar,	Dan 3:16	560
s unto his counsellors, Did not	Dan 3:24	560
s unto the king, True, O king	Dan 3:24	560
He answered and *s*, Lo, I see four	Dan 3:25	560
fiery furnace, and spake, and *s*	Dan 3:26	560
Then Nebuchadnezzar spake, and *s*	Dan 3:28	560
s thus, Hew down the tree, and cut	Dan 4:14	560
The king spake, and *s*,	Dan 4:19	560
Belteshazzar answered and *s*	Dan 4:19	560
The king spake, and *s*, Is not this	Dan 4:30	560
s to the wise men of Babylon,	Dan 5:7	560
and the queen spake and *s*, O king,	Dan 5:10	560
s unto Daniel, Art thou that	Dan 5:13	560
s before the king, Let thy gifts	Dan 5:17	560
Then *s* these men, We shall not	Dan 6:5	560
s thus unto him, King Darius,	Dan 6:6	560
The king answered and *s*, The thing	Dan 6:12	560
s before the king, That Daniel,	Dan 6:13	560
s unto the king, Know, O king,	Dan 6:15	560
s unto Daniel, Thy God whom thou	Dan 6:16	560
s to Daniel, O Daniel, servant of	Dan 6:20	560
Then *s* Daniel unto the king, O	Dan 6:21	4449
Daniel spake and *s*, I saw in my	Dan 7:2	560
they *s* thus unto it, Arise,	Dan 7:5	560
Thus he *s*, The fourth beast shall	Dan 7:23	560
another saint *s* unto that certain	Dan 8:13	559
he *s* unto me, Unto two thousand	Dan 8:14	559
banks of Ulai, which called, and *s*	Dan 8:16	559
but he *s* unto me, Understand, O	Dan 8:17	559
And he *s*, Behold, I will make thee	Dan 8:19	559
God, and made my confession, and *s*	Dan 9:4	559
me, and talked with me, and *s*	Dan 9:22	559
he *s* unto me, O Daniel, a man	Dan 10:11	559
Then *s* he unto me, Fear not,	Dan 10:12	559
s unto him that stood before me,	Dan 10:16	559
And *s*, O man greatly beloved, fear	Dan 10:19	559
unto me, I was strengthened, and *s*	Dan 10:19	559
Then *s* he, Knowest thou wherefore	Dan 10:20	559
one *s* to the man clothed in linen	Dan 12:6	559
then *s* I, O my Lord, what shall	Dan 12:8	559
And he *s*, Go thy way, Daniel	Dan 12:9	559
And the LORD *s* to Hosea, Go, take	Hos 1:2	559
And the LORD *s* unto him, Call his	Hos 1:4	559
God *s* unto him, Call her name	Hos 1:6	559
Then *s* God, Call his name Lo-ammi	Hos 1:9	559
place where it was *s* unto them	Hos 1:10	559
there it shall be *s* unto them	Hos 1:10	559
for she *s*, I will go after my	Hos 2:5	559
her fig trees, whereof she hath *s*	Hos 2:12	559
Then *s* the LORD unto me, Go yet,	Hos 3:1	559
I *s* unto her, Thou shalt abide	Hos 3:3	559
And Ephraim *s*, Yet I am become	Hos 12:8	559
deliverance, as the LORD hath *s*	Joel 2:32	559
And he *s*, The LORD will roar from	Amos 1:2	559
the grass of the land, then I *s*	Amos 7:2	559
Then *s* I, O Lord GOD, cease, I	Amos 7:5	559
And the LORD *s* unto me, Amos, what	Amos 7:8	559
And I *s*, A plumbline	Amos 7:8	559
Then *s* the Lord, Behold, I will	Amos 7:8	559
Also Amaziah *s* unto Amos, O thou	Amos 7:12	559
s to Amaziah, I was no prophet,	Amos 7:14	559
the flock, and the LORD *s* unto me	Amos 7:15	559
And he *s*, Amos, what seest thou	Amos 8:2	559
And I *s*, A basket of summer fruit	Amos 8:2	559
Then *s* the LORD unto me, The end	Amos 8:2	559
and he *s*, Smite the lintel of the	Amos 9:1	559
s unto him, What meanest thou, O	Jonah 1:6	559
they *s* every one to his fellow,	Jonah 1:7	559
Then *s* they unto him, Tell us, we	Jonah 1:8	559
he *s* unto them, I am an Hebrew	Jonah 1:9	559
s unto him, Why hast thou done	Jonah 1:10	559
Then *s* they unto him, What shall	Jonah 1:11	559
he *s* unto them, Take me up, and	Jonah 1:12	559
they cried unto the LORD, and *s*	Jonah 1:14	559
And *s*, I cried by reason of mine	Jonah 2:2	559
Then I *s*, I am cast out of thy	Jonah 2:4	559
day's journey, and he cried, and *s*	Jonah 3:4	559
that he had *s* that he would do	Jonah 3:10	1696
And he prayed unto the LORD, and *s*	Jonah 4:2	559
Then *s* the LORD, Doest thou well	Jonah 4:4	559
and wished in himself to die, and *s*	Jonah 4:8	559
God *s* to Jonah, Doest thou well	Jonah 4:9	559
And he *s*, I do well to be angry,	Jonah 4:9	559
Then *s* the LORD, Thou hast had	Jonah 4:10	559
And I *s*, Hear, I pray you, O heads	Mic 3:1	559
shall cover her which *s* unto me	Mic 7:10	559
And the LORD answered me, and *s*	Hab 2:2	559
that *s* in her heart, I am, and	Zeph 2:15	559
I *s*, Surely thou wilt fear me,	Zeph 3:7	559
day it shall be *s* to Jerusalem	Zeph 3:16	559
And the priests answered and *s*	Hag 2:12	559
Then *s* Haggai, If one that is	Hag 2:13	559
And the priests answered and *s*	Hag 2:13	559
Then answered Haggai, and *s*	Hag 2:14	559
and they returned and *s*, Like as	Zec 1:6	559
Then *s* I, O my lord, what are	Zec 1:9	559
that talked with me *s* unto me	Zec 1:9	559
the myrtle trees answered and *s*	Zec 1:10	559
among the myrtle trees, and *s*	Zec 1:11	559
angel of the LORD answered and *s*	Zec 1:12	559
that communed with me *s* unto me	Zec 1:14	559
I *s* unto the angel that talked	Zec 1:19	559
Then *s* I, What come these to do	Zec 1:21	559
Then *s* I, Whither goest thou	Zec 2:2	559
And he *s* unto me, To measure	Zec 2:2	559
s unto him, Run, speak to this	Zec 2:4	559
the LORD *s* unto Satan, The LORD	Zec 3:2	559
And unto him he *s*, Behold, I have	Zec 3:4	559
And I *s*, Let them set a fair mitre	Zec 3:5	559
s unto me, What seest thou	Zec 4:2	559
And I *s*, I have looked, and behold	Zec 4:2	559
s unto me, Knowest thou not what	Zec 4:5	559
And I *s*, No, my lord	Zec 4:5	559
s unto him, What are these two	Zec 4:11	559
s unto him, What be these two	Zec 4:12	559
And he answered me and *s*, Knowest	Zec 4:13	559

And I *s*, No, my lord	Zec 4:13	559
Then *s* he, These are the two	Zec 4:14	559
he *s* unto me, What seest thou	Zec 5:2	559
Then *s* he unto me, This is the	Zec 5:3	559
s unto me, Lift up now thine eyes	Zec 5:5	559
And I *s*, What is it	Zec 5:6	559
And he *s*, This is an ephah that	Zec 5:6	559
He *s* moreover, This is their	Zec 5:6	559
And he *s*, This is wickedness	Zec 5:8	559
Then *s* I to the angel that talked	Zec 5:10	559
he *s* unto me, To build it an	Zec 5:11	559
s unto the angel that talked with	Zec 6:4	559
s unto me, These are the four	Zec 6:5	559
and he *s*, Get you hence, walk to	Zec 6:7	559
Then *s* I, I will not feed you	Zec 11:9	559
I *s* unto them, If ye think good,	Zec 11:12	559
And the LORD *s* unto me, Cast it	Zec 11:13	559
And the LORD *s* unto me, Take unto	Zec 11:15	559
Ye *s* also, Behold, what a	Mal 1:13	559
But ye *s*, Wherein shall we return	Mal 3:7	559
Ye have *s*, It is vain to serve	Mal 3:14	559
they *s* unto him, In Bethlehem of	Mt 2:5	2036
he sent them to Bethlehem, and *s*	Mt 2:8	2036
he *s* unto them, O generation of	Mt 3:7	2036
And Jesus answering *s* unto him	Mt 3:15	2036
the tempter came to him, he *s*	Mt 4:3	2036
But he answered and *s*, It is	Mt 4:4	2036
Jesus *s* unto him, It is written	Mt 4:7	5346
that it was *s* by them of old time	Mt 5:21	2046
that it was *s* by them of old time	Mt 5:27	2046
It hath been *s*, Whosoever shall	Mt 5:31	2046
hath been *s* by them of old time	Mt 5:33	2046
Ye have heard that it hath been *s*	Mt 5:38	2046
Ye have heard that it hath been *s*	Mt 5:43	2046
The centurion answered and *s*	Mt 8:8	5346
s to them that followed, Verily I	Mt 8:10	4483
Jesus *s* unto the centurion, Go	Mt 8:13	4483
s unto him, Master, I will follow	Mt 8:19	4483
of his disciples *s* unto him	Mt 8:21	4483
But Jesus *s* unto him, Follow me	Mt 8:22	4483
And he *s* unto them, Go	Mt 8:32	4483
Jesus seeing their faith *s* unto	Mt 9:2	4483
the scribes *s* within themselves	Mt 9:3	4483
And Jesus knowing their thoughts *s*	Mt 9:4	4483
they *s* unto his disciples, Why	Mt 9:11	4483
he *s* unto them, They that be	Mt 9:12	4483
Jesus *s* unto them, Can the	Mt 9:15	4483
For she *s* within herself, If I	Mt 9:21	3004
about, and when he saw her, he *s*	Mt 9:22	2036
He *s* unto them, Give place	Mt 9:24	3004
They *s* unto him, Yea, Lord	Mt 9:28	3004
But the Pharisees *s*, He casteth	Mt 9:34	3004
s unto him, Art thou he that	Mt 11:3	2036
s unto them, Go and shew John	Mt 11:4	2036
At that time Jesus answered and *s*	Mt 11:25	2036
they *s* unto him, Behold, thy	Mt 12:2	2036
But he *s* unto them, Have ye not	Mt 12:3	2036
he *s* unto them, What man shall	Mt 12:11	2036
all the people were amazed, and *s*	Mt 12:23	3004
the Pharisees heard it, they *s*	Mt 12:24	2036
s unto them, Every kingdom	Mt 12:25	2036
and *s* unto them, An evil and	Mt 12:39	2036
Then one *s* unto him, Behold, thy	Mt 12:47	2036
s unto him that told him, Who is	Mt 12:48	2036
hand toward his disciples, and *s*	Mt 12:49	2036
s unto him, Why speakest thou	Mt 13:10	2036
s unto them, Because it is given	Mt 13:11	2063
s unto him, Sir, didst not thou	Mt 13:27	2063
He *s* unto them, An enemy hath	Mt 13:28	2063
The servants *s* unto him, Wilt	Mt 13:28	5346
But he *s*, Nay	Mt 13:29	5346
s unto them, He that soweth the	Mt 13:37	2036
Then *s* he unto them, Therefore	Mt 13:52	2036
that they were astonished, and *s*	Mt 13:54	3004
But Jesus *s* unto them, A prophet	Mt 13:57	2036
s unto his servants, This is John	Mt 14:2	2036
For John *s* unto him, It is not	Mt 14:4	3004
instructed of her mother, *s*	Mt 14:8	5346
But Jesus *s* unto them, They need	Mt 14:16	2036
He *s*, Bring them hither to me	Mt 14:18	2036
And Peter answered him and *s*	Mt 14:28	2036
And he *s*, Come	Mt 14:29	2036
s unto him, O thou of little	Mt 14:31	3004
s unto them, Why do ye also	Mt 15:3	2036
s unto them, Hear, and understand	Mt 15:10	2036
s unto him, Knowest thou that the	Mt 15:12	2036
But he answered and *s*, Every plant	Mt 15:13	2036
s unto him, Declare unto us this	Mt 15:15	2036
And Jesus *s*, Are ye also yet	Mt 15:16	2036
But he answered and *s*, I am not	Mt 15:24	2036
But he answered and *s*, It is not	Mt 15:26	2036
And she *s*, Truth, Lord	Mt 15:27	2036
s unto her, O woman, great is thy	Mt 15:28	2036
his disciples unto him, and *s*	Mt 15:32	2036
And they *s*, Seven, and a few little	Mt 15:34	2036
s unto them, When it is evening,	Mt 16:2	2036
Then Jesus *s* unto them, Take heed	Mt 16:6	2036
he *s* unto them, O ye of little	Mt 16:8	2036
And they *s*, Some say that thou art	Mt 16:14	2036
And Simon Peter answered and *s*	Mt 16:16	2036
s unto him, Blessed art thou,	Mt 16:17	2036
s unto Peter, Get thee behind me,	Mt 16:23	2036
Then *s* Jesus unto his disciples,	Mt 16:24	2036
s unto Jesus, Lord, it is good	Mt 17:4	2036
a voice out of the cloud, which *s*	Mt 17:5	3004
Jesus came and touched them, and *s*	Mt 17:7	2036
s unto them, Elias truly shall	Mt 17:11	2036
Then Jesus answered and *s*, O	Mt 17:17	2036
disciples to Jesus apart, and *s*	Mt 17:19	2036
Jesus *s* unto them, Because of	Mt 17:20	2036
Jesus *s* unto them, The Son of man	Mt 17:22	2036
tribute money came to Peter, and *s*	Mt 17:24	2036
And *s*, Verily I say unto you,	Mt 18:3	2036
Then came Peter to him, and *s*	Mt 18:21	2036
s unto him, O thou wicked servant	Mt 18:32	3004
s unto them, Have ye not read,	Mt 19:4	2036
And *s*, For this cause shall a man	Mt 19:5	2036
But he *s* unto them, All men	Mt 19:11	2036
But Jesus *s*, Suffer little	Mt 19:14	2036
s unto him, Good Master, what	Mt 19:16	2036
he *s* unto him, Why callest thou	Mt 19:17	2036
Jesus *s*, Thou shalt do no murder,	Mt 19:18	2036
Jesus *s* unto him, If thou wilt be	Mt 19:21	5346
Then *s* Jesus unto his disciples,	Mt 19:23	2036
s unto them, With men this is	Mt 19:26	2036
s unto him, Behold, we have	Mt 19:27	2036
Jesus *s* unto them, Verily I say	Mt 19:28	2036
s unto them; Go ye also	Mt 20:4	2036
But he answered one of them, and *s*	Mt 20:13	2036
apart in the way, and *s* unto them,	Mt 20:17	2036
he *s* unto her, What wilt thou	Mt 20:21	2036
But Jesus answered and *s*, Ye know	Mt 20:22	2036
Jesus called them unto him, and *s*	Mt 20:25	2036
stood still, and called them, and *s*	Mt 20:32	2036
And the multitude *s*, This is Jesus	Mt 21:11	3004
s unto them, It is written, My	Mt 21:13	3004
s unto him, Hearest thou what	Mt 21:16	2036
s unto it, Let no fruit grow on	Mt 21:19	3004
s unto them, Verily I say unto	Mt 21:21	2036
unto him as he was teaching, and *s*	Mt 21:23	3004
s unto them, I also will ask you	Mt 21:24	2036
And they answered Jesus, and *s*	Mt 21:27	2036
he *s* unto them, Neither tell I	Mt 21:27	5346
and he came to the first, and *s*	Mt 21:28	2036
He answered and *s*, I will not	Mt 21:29	2036
came to the second, and *s* likewise	Mt 21:30	2036
And he answered and *s*, I go sir	Mt 21:30	2036
they *s* among themselves, This is	Mt 21:38	2036
unto them again by parables, and *s*	Mt 22:1	3004
Then *s* the king to the servants,	Mt 22:13	2036
perceived their wickedness, and *s*	Mt 22:18	2036
Saying, Master, Moses *s*, If a man	Mt 22:24	2036
s unto them, Ye do err, not	Mt 22:29	2036
Jesus *s* unto him, Thou shalt love	Mt 22:37	2036
The LORD *s* unto my Lord, Sit thou	Mt 22:44	2036
Jesus *s* unto them, See ye not all	Mt 24:2	2036
s unto them, Take heed that no	Mt 24:4	2036
the foolish *s* unto the wise, Give	Mt 25:8	2036
But he answered and *s*, Verily I	Mt 25:12	2036
His lord *s* unto him, Well done,	Mt 25:21	5346
received two talents came and *s*	Mt 25:22	2036
His lord *s* unto him, Well done,	Mt 25:23	5346
received the one talent came and *s*	Mt 25:24	2036
s unto him, Thou wicked and	Mt 25:26	2036
sayings, he *s* unto his disciples,	Mt 26:1	2036
But they *s*, Not on the feast day,	Mt 26:5	3004
he *s* unto them, Why trouble ye	Mt 26:10	2036
s unto them, What will ye give me	Mt 26:15	2036
And he *s*, Go into the city to such	Mt 26:18	2036
And as they did eat, he *s*, Verily	Mt 26:21	2036
And he answered and *s*, He that	Mt 26:23	2036
which betrayed him, answered and *s*	Mt 26:25	2036
He *s* unto him, Thou hast	Mt 26:25	3004
unto him, Thou hast *s*	Mt 26:25	2036
and gave it to the disciples, and *s*	Mt 26:26	2036
s unto him, Though all men shall	Mt 26:33	2036
Jesus *s* unto him, Verily I say	Mt 26:34	5346
Peter *s* unto him, Though I should	Mt 26:35	3004
Likewise also *s* all the disciples	Mt 26:35	2036
forthwith he came to Jesus, and *s*	Mt 26:49	2036
Jesus *s* unto him, Friend,	Mt 26:50	2036
Then *s* Jesus unto him, Put up	Mt 26:52	3004
In that same hour *s* Jesus to the	Mt 26:55	2036
And *s*, This fellow	Mt 26:61	2036
This fellow *s*, I am	Mt 26:61	5346
s unto him, Answerest thou	Mt 26:62	2036
s unto him, I adjure thee by the	Mt 26:63	2036
Jesus saith unto him, Thou hast *s*	Mt 26:64	2036
They answered and *s*, He is guilty	Mt 26:66	2036
s unto them that were there, This	Mt 26:71	3004
s to Peter, Surely thou also art	Mt 26:73	2036
which *s* unto him, Before the cock	Mt 26:75	2046
And they *s*, What is that to us	Mt 27:4	2036
took the silver pieces, and *s*	Mt 27:6	2036
Jesus *s* unto him, Thou sayest	Mt 27:11	5346
Then *s* Pilate unto him, Hearest	Mt 27:13	3004
Pilate *s* unto them, Whom will ye	Mt 27:17	2036
s unto them, Whether of the twain	Mt 27:21	2036
They *s*, Barabbas	Mt 27:21	2036
And the governor *s*, Why, what evil	Mt 27:23	5346
answered all the people, and *s*	Mt 27:25	2036
with the scribes and elders, *s*	Mt 27:41	3004
for he *s*, I am the Son of God	Mt 27:43	2036
there, when they heard that, *s*	Mt 27:47	3004
The rest *s*, Let be, let us see	Mt 27:49	3004
we remember that that deceiver *s*	Mt 27:63	2036
Pilate *s* unto them, Ye have a	Mt 27:65	5346
s unto the women, Fear not ye	Mt 28:5	2036
for he is risen, as he *s*	Mt 28:6	2036
Then *s* Jesus unto them, Be not	Mt 28:10	3004
Jesus *s* unto them, Come ye after	Mk 1:17	2036
they *s* unto him, All men seek for	Mk 1:37	3004
he *s* unto them, Let us go into	Mk 1:38	3004
he *s* unto the sick of the palsy,	Mk 2:5	3004
he *s* unto them, Why reason ye	Mk 2:8	2036
custom, and *s* unto him, Follow me	Mk 2:14	3004
they *s* unto his disciples, How is	Mk 2:16	3004
Jesus *s* unto them, Can the	Mk 2:19	2036
And the Pharisees *s* unto him	Mk 2:24	3004
he *s* unto them, Have ye never	Mk 2:25	3004
he *s* unto them, The sabbath was	Mk 2:27	3004
for they *s*, He is beside himself	Mk 3:21	3004
which came down from Jerusalem *s*	Mk 3:22	3004
s unto them in parables, How can	Mk 3:23	3004
Because they *s*, He hath an	Mk 3:30	3004
they *s* unto him, Behold, thy	Mk 3:32	2036
on them which sat about him, and *s*	Mk 3:34	3004
s unto them in his doctrine,	Mk 4:2	3004
he *s* unto them, He that hath ears	Mk 4:9	3004
he *s* unto them, Unto you it is	Mk 4:11	3004
he *s* unto them, Know ye not this	Mk 4:13	3004
he *s* unto them, Is a candle	Mk 4:21	3004
he *s* unto them, Take heed what ye	Mk 4:24	3004
And he *s*, So is the kingdom of God	Mk 4:26	3004
And he *s*, Whereunto shall we liken	Mk 4:30	3004
s unto the sea, Peace, be still	Mk 4:39	2036
he *s* unto them, Why are ye so	Mk 4:40	2036
s one to another, What manner of	Mk 4:41	3004
And cried with a loud voice, and *s*	Mk 5:7	2036
For he *s* unto him, Come out of	Mk 5:8	3004
For she *s*, If I may touch but his	Mk 5:28	3004
him about in the press, and *s*	Mk 5:30	3004
And his disciples *s* unto him	Mk 5:31	3004
he *s* unto her, Daughter, thy	Mk 5:34	2036
synagogue's house certain which *s*	Mk 5:35	3004
hand, and *s* unto her, Talitha cumi	Mk 5:41	3004
But Jesus *s* unto them, A prophet	Mk 6:4	3004
he *s* unto them, In what place	Mk 6:10	3004
and he *s*, That John the Baptist	Mk 6:14	3004
Others *s*, That it is Elias	Mk 6:15	3004
And others *s*, That it is a prophet	Mk 6:15	3004
when Herod heard thereof, he *s*	Mk 6:16	2036
For John had *s* unto Herod	Mk 6:18	3004
of the *s* Herodias came in	Mk 6:22	846
the king *s* unto the damsel, Ask	Mk 6:22	2036
s unto her mother, What shall I	Mk 6:24	2036
And she *s*, The head of John the	Mk 6:24	2036
And he *s* unto them, Come ye	Mk 6:31	2036
his disciples came unto him, and *s*	Mk 6:35	3004
s unto them, Give ye them to eat	Mk 6:37	2036
s unto them, Well hath Esaias	Mk 7:6	2036
he *s* unto them, Full well ye	Mk 7:9	3004
For Moses *s*, Honour thy father and	Mk 7:10	2036
he *s* unto them, Hearken unto me	Mk 7:14	3004
And he *s*, That which cometh out of	Mk 7:20	3004
But Jesus *s* unto her, Let the	Mk 7:27	2036
answered and *s* unto him, Yes, Lord	Mk 7:28	3004
he *s* unto her, For this saying go	Mk 7:29	2036
And they *s*, Seven	Mk 8:5	2036
And they *s*, Seven	Mk 8:20	2036
he *s* unto them, How is it that ye	Mk 8:21	3004
And he looked up, and *s*, I see men	Mk 8:24	3004
he *s* unto them, Whosoever will	Mk 8:34	2036
he *s* unto them, Verily I say unto	Mk 9:1	3004
s to Jesus, Master, it is good	Mk 9:5	3004
of the multitude answered and *s*	Mk 9:17	2036
And he *s*, Of a child	Mk 9:21	2036
Jesus *s* unto him, If thou canst	Mk 9:23	2036
s with tears, Lord, I believe	Mk 9:24	3004
insomuch that many *s*, He is dead	Mk 9:26	3004
he *s* unto them, This kind can	Mk 9:29	2036
s unto them, The Son of man is	Mk 9:31	3004
him in his arms, he *s* unto them,	Mk 9:36	2036
But Jesus *s*, Forbid him not	Mk 9:39	2036
s unto them, What did Moses	Mk 10:3	2036
And they *s*, Moses suffered to	Mk 10:4	2036
s unto them, For the hardness of	Mk 10:5	2036
s unto them, Suffer the little	Mk 10:14	2036
Jesus *s* unto him, Why callest	Mk 10:18	2036
s unto him, Master, all these	Mk 10:20	2036
s unto him, One thing thou	Mk 10:21	2036
And Jesus answered and *s*, Verily I	Mk 10:29	2036
he *s* unto them, What would ye	Mk 10:36	2036
They *s* unto him, Grant unto us	Mk 10:37	2036
But Jesus *s* unto them, Ye know	Mk 10:38	2036
And they *s* unto him, We can	Mk 10:39	2036
Jesus *s* unto them, Ye shall	Mk 10:39	2036
s unto him, What wilt thou that I	Mk 10:51	3004
The blind man *s* unto him, Lord,	Mk 10:51	2036
Jesus *s* unto him, Go thy way	Mk 10:52	2036
them that stood there *s* unto them	Mk 11:5	3004
they *s* unto them even as Jesus	Mk 11:6	2036
s unto it, No man eat fruit of	Mk 11:14	2036
s unto them, I will also ask of	Mk 11:29	2036
s unto Jesus, We cannot tell	Mk 11:33	3004
husbandmen *s* among themselves	Mk 12:7	2036
s unto them, Why tempt ye me	Mk 12:15	2036
they *s* unto him, Caesar's	Mk 12:16	2036
And Jesus answering *s* unto them	Mk 12:17	2036
And Jesus answering *s* unto them	Mk 12:24	2036
And the scribe *s* unto him, Well,	Mk 12:32	2036
Master, thou hast *s* the truth	Mk 12:32	2036
he *s* unto him, Thou art not far	Mk 12:34	2036
And Jesus answered and *s*, while he	Mk 12:35	3004
David himself *s* by the Holy Ghost	Mk 12:36	2036
The Lord *s* to my Lord, Sit thou	Mk 12:36	2036
he *s* unto them in his doctrine,	Mk 12:38	3004
And Jesus answering *s* unto him	Mk 13:2	2036
But they *s*, Not on the feast day,	Mk 14:2	3004
within themselves, and *s*, Why was	Mk 14:4	3004
And Jesus *s*, Let her alone	Mk 14:6	2036
his disciples *s* unto him	Mk 14:12	3004
and found as he had *s* unto them	Mk 14:16	2036
as they sat and did eat, Jesus *s*	Mk 14:18	2036

S

and another *s*, Is it I	Mk 14:19	
s unto them, It is one of the	Mk 14:20	2036
and brake it and gave to them, and *s*	Mk 14:22	2036
he *s* unto them, This is my blood	Mk 14:24	2036
But Peter *s* unto him, Although	Mk 14:29	5346
Likewise also *s* they all	Mk 14:31	3004
And he *s*, Abba, Father, all things	Mk 14:36	3004
s unto them, Are ye come out, as	Mk 14:48	2036
s unto him, Art thou the Christ,	Mk 14:61	3004
And Jesus *s*, I am	Mk 14:62	2036
she looked upon him, and *s*	Mk 14:67	3004
that stood by *s* again to Peter	Mk 14:70	3004
the word that Jesus *s* unto him	Mk 14:72	2036
And he answering *s* unto him	Mk 15:2	2036
s again unto them, What will ye	Mk 15:12	2036
Then Pilate *s* unto them, Why,	Mk 15:14	3004
s among themselves with the	Mk 15:31	3004
stood by, when they heard it *s*	Mk 15:35	3004
out, and gave up the ghost, he *s*	Mk 15:39	2036
they *s* among themselves, Who	Mk 16:3	3004
ye see him, as he *s* unto you	Mk 16:7	2036
neither *s* they any thing to any	Mk 16:8	2036
he *s* unto them, Go ye into all	Mk 16:15	2036
But the angel *s* unto him, Fear	Lk 1:13	2036
Zacharias *s* unto the angel,	Lk 1:18	2036
And the angel answering *s* unto him	Lk 1:19	2036
the angel came in unto her, and *s*	Lk 1:28	2036
And the angel *s* unto her, Fear not	Lk 1:30	2036
Then *s* Mary unto the angel, How	Lk 1:34	2036
s unto her, The Holy Ghost shall	Lk 1:35	2036
And Mary *s*, Behold the handmaid of	Lk 1:38	2036
spake out with a loud voice, and *s*	Lk 1:42	2036
And Mary *s*, My soul doth magnify	Lk 1:46	2036
And his mother answered and *s*	Lk 1:60	2036
they *s* unto her, There is none of	Lk 1:61	2036
And the angel *s* unto them, Fear	Lk 2:10	2036
the shepherds *s* one to another,	Lk 2:15	2036
which is *s* in the law of the Lord	Lk 2:24	2046
in his arms, and blessed God, and *s*	Lk 2:28	2036
s unto Mary his mother, Behold,	Lk 2:34	2036
and his mother *s* unto him, Son,	Lk 2:48	2036
he *s* unto them, How is it that ye	Lk 2:49	2036
Then *s* he to the multitude that	Lk 3:7	3004
s unto him, Master, what shall we	Lk 3:12	2036
he *s* unto them, Exact no more	Lk 3:13	2036
he *s* unto them, Do violence to no	Lk 3:14	2036
a voice came from heaven, which *s*	Lk 3:22	3004
And the devil *s* unto him, If thou	Lk 4:3	2036
And the devil *s* unto him, All this	Lk 4:6	2036
s unto him, Get thee behind me,	Lk 4:8	2036
s unto him, If thou be the Son of	Lk 4:9	2036
And Jesus answering *s* unto him	Lk 4:12	2036
unto him, It is *s*	Lk 4:12	2046
And they *s*, Is not this Joseph's	Lk 4:22	3004
he *s* unto them, Ye will surely	Lk 4:23	2036
And he *s*, Verily I say unto you,	Lk 4:24	2036
he *s* unto them, I must preach the	Lk 4:43	2036
he *s* unto Simon, Launch out into	Lk 5:4	2036
And Simon answering *s* unto him	Lk 5:5	2036
Jesus *s* unto Simon, Fear not	Lk 5:10	2036
he *s* unto him, Man, thy sins are	Lk 5:20	2036
he answering *s* unto them	Lk 5:22	2036
(he *s* unto the sick of the palsy,	Lk 5:24	2036
and he *s* unto him, Follow me	Lk 5:27	2036
And Jesus answering *s* unto them	Lk 5:31	2036
they *s* unto him, Why do the	Lk 5:33	2036
he *s* unto them, Can ye make the	Lk 5:34	2036
of the Pharisees *s* unto them	Lk 6:2	2036
And Jesus answering them *s*	Lk 6:3	2036
he *s* unto them, That the Son of	Lk 6:5	3004
s to the man which had the	Lk 6:8	2036
Then *s* Jesus unto them, I will	Lk 6:9	2036
he *s* unto the man, Stretch forth	Lk 6:10	2036
his eyes on his disciples, and *s*	Lk 6:20	3004
s unto the people that followed	Lk 7:9	2036
on her, and *s* unto her, Weep not	Lk 7:13	2036
And he *s*, Young man, I say unto	Lk 7:14	2036
men were come unto him, they *s*	Lk 7:20	2036
Then Jesus answering *s* unto them	Lk 7:22	2036
And the Lord *s*, Whereunto then	Lk 7:31	2036
And Jesus answering *s* unto him	Lk 7:40	2036
Simon answered and *s*, I suppose	Lk 7:43	2036
he *s* unto him, Thou hast rightly	Lk 7:43	2036
s unto Simon, Seest thou this	Lk 7:44	5346
he *s* unto her, Thy sins are	Lk 7:48	2036
he *s* to the woman, Thy faith hath	Lk 7:50	2036
when he had *s* these things, he	Lk 8:8	3004
And he *s*, Unto you it is given to	Lk 8:10	2036
was told him by certain which *s*	Lk 8:20	3004
s unto them, My mother and my	Lk 8:21	2036
he *s* unto them, Let us go over	Lk 8:22	2036
he *s* unto them, Where is your	Lk 8:25	2036
him, and with a loud voice *s*	Lk 8:28	2036
And he *s*, Legion	Lk 8:30	2036
And Jesus *s*, Who touched me	Lk 8:45	2036
and they that were with him *s*	Lk 8:45	2036
And Jesus *s*, Somebody hath touched	Lk 8:46	2036
he *s* unto her, Daughter, be of	Lk 8:48	2036
but he *s*, Weep not	Lk 8:52	2036
he *s* unto them, Take nothing for	Lk 9:3	2036
because that it was *s* of some	Lk 9:7	3004
And Herod *s*, John have I beheaded	Lk 9:9	2036
s unto him, Send the multitude	Lk 9:12	2036
But he *s* unto them, Give ye them	Lk 9:13	2036
And they *s*, We have no more but	Lk 9:13	2036
he *s* to his disciples, Make them	Lk 9:14	2036
They answering *s*, John the	Lk 9:19	2036
He *s* unto them, But whom say ye	Lk 9:20	2036

Peter answering *s*, The Christ of	Lk 9:20	2036
he *s* to them all, If any man will	Lk 9:23	3004
Peter *s* unto Jesus, Master, it is	Lk 9:33	2036
not knowing what he *s*	Lk 9:33	3004
And Jesus answering *s*, O faithless	Lk 9:41	2036
did, he *s* unto his disciples,	Lk 9:43	2036
s unto them, Whosoever shall	Lk 9:48	2036
And John answered and *s*, Master, we	Lk 9:49	2036
Jesus *s* unto him, Forbid him not	Lk 9:50	2036
James and John saw this, they *s*	Lk 9:54	2036
he turned, and rebuked them, and *s*	Lk 9:55	2036
the way, a certain man *s* unto him	Lk 9:57	2036
Jesus *s* unto him, Foxes have	Lk 9:58	2036
he *s* unto another, Follow me	Lk 9:59	2036
But he *s*, Lord, suffer me first	Lk 9:59	2036
Jesus *s* unto him, Let the dead	Lk 9:60	2036
And another also *s*, Lord, I will	Lk 9:61	2036
Jesus *s* unto him, No man, having	Lk 9:62	2036
Therefore *s* he unto them, The	Lk 10:2	3004
he *s* unto them, I beheld Satan as	Lk 10:18	2036
Jesus rejoiced in spirit, and *s*	Lk 10:21	2036
s privately, Blessed are the eyes	Lk 10:23	2036
He *s* unto him, What is written in	Lk 10:26	2036
And he answering *s*, Thou shalt	Lk 10:27	2036
he *s* unto him, Thou hast answered	Lk 10:28	2036
s unto Jesus, And who is my	Lk 10:29	2036
And Jesus answering *s*, A certain	Lk 10:30	2036
s unto him, Take care of him	Lk 10:35	2036
And he *s*, He that shewed mercy on	Lk 10:37	2036
Then *s* Jesus unto him, Go, and do	Lk 10:37	2036
serving, and came to him, and *s*	Lk 10:40	2036
s unto her, Martha, Martha, thou	Lk 10:41	2036
one of his disciples *s* unto him	Lk 11:1	2036
he *s* unto them, When ye pray, say	Lk 11:2	2036
he *s* unto them, Which of you	Lk 11:5	2036
But some of them *s*, He casteth	Lk 11:15	2036
s unto them, Every kingdom	Lk 11:17	2036
s unto him, Blessed is the womb	Lk 11:27	2036
But he *s*, Yea rather, blessed are	Lk 11:28	2036
And the Lord *s* unto him, Now do ye	Lk 11:39	2036
s unto him, Master, thus saying	Lk 11:45	3004
And he *s*, Woe unto you also, ye	Lk 11:46	2036
Therefore also *s* the wisdom of	Lk 11:49	2036
as he *s* these things unto them,	Lk 11:53	3004
And one of the company *s* unto him	Lk 12:13	2036
he *s* unto him, Man, who made me a	Lk 12:14	2036
he *s* unto them, Take heed, and	Lk 12:15	2036
And he *s*, This will I do	Lk 12:18	2036
But God *s* unto him, Thou fool,	Lk 12:20	2036
And he *s* unto his disciples,	Lk 12:22	2036
Then Peter *s* unto him, Lord,	Lk 12:41	2036
And the Lord *s*, Who then is that	Lk 12:42	2036
he *s* also to the people, When ye	Lk 12:54	3004
And Jesus answering *s* unto them	Lk 13:2	2036
Then *s* he unto the dresser of his	Lk 13:7	2036
And he answering *s* unto him	Lk 13:8	3004
s unto her, Woman, thou art	Lk 13:12	2036
s unto the people, There are six	Lk 13:14	3004
The Lord then answered him, and *s*	Lk 13:15	2036
when he had *s* these things, all	Lk 13:17	3004
Then *s* he, Unto what is the	Lk 13:18	3004
And again he *s*, Whereunto shall I	Lk 13:20	2036
Then *s* one unto him, Lord, are	Lk 13:23	2036
And he *s* unto them,	Lk 13:23	2036
he *s* unto them, Go ye, and tell	Lk 13:32	2036
Then *s* he also to him that bade	Lk 14:12	3004
he *s* unto him, Blessed is he that	Lk 14:15	2036
Then *s* he unto him, A certain man	Lk 14:16	2036
The first *s* unto him, I have	Lk 14:18	2036
And another *s*, I have bought five	Lk 14:19	2036
And another *s*, I have married a	Lk 14:20	2036
being angry *s* to his servant	Lk 14:21	2036
And the servant *s*, Lord, it is	Lk 14:22	2036
the lord *s* unto the servant, Go	Lk 14:23	2036
and he turned, and *s* unto them,	Lk 14:25	2036
And he *s*, A certain man had two	Lk 15:11	2036
younger of them *s* to his father	Lk 15:12	2036
And when he came to himself, he *s*	Lk 15:17	2036
the son *s* unto him, Father, I	Lk 15:21	2036
But the father *s* to his servants,	Lk 15:22	2036
he *s* unto him, Thy brother is	Lk 15:27	2036
he answering *s* to his father, Lo,	Lk 15:29	2036
he *s* unto him, Son, thou art ever	Lk 15:31	2036
he *s* also unto his disciples,	Lk 16:1	3004
s unto him, How is it that I hear	Lk 16:2	2036
Then the steward *s* within himself	Lk 16:3	2036
s unto the first, How much owest	Lk 16:5	3004
And he *s*, An hundred measures of	Lk 16:6	2036
he *s* unto him, Take thy bill, and	Lk 16:6	2036
Then *s* he to another, And how much	Lk 16:7	2036
And he *s*, An hundred measures of	Lk 16:7	2036
he *s* unto him, Take thy bill, and	Lk 16:7	3004
he *s* unto them, Ye are they which	Lk 16:15	2036
And he cried and *s*, Father Abraham,	Lk 16:24	2036
But Abraham *s*, Son, remember that	Lk 16:25	2036
Then he *s*, I pray thee therefore,	Lk 16:27	2036
And he *s*, Nay, father Abraham	Lk 16:30	2036
he *s* unto him, If they hear not	Lk 16:31	2036
Then *s* he unto the disciples, It	Lk 17:1	2036
the apostles *s* unto the Lord,	Lk 17:5	2036
And the Lord *s*, If ye had faith as	Lk 17:6	2036
they lifted up their voices, and *s*	Lk 17:13	3004
saw them, he *s* unto them, Go shew	Lk 17:14	2036
And Jesus answering *s*, Were there	Lk 17:17	2036
he *s* unto him, Arise, go thy way	Lk 17:19	2036
come, he answered them and *s*	Lk 17:20	2036
he *s* unto the disciples, The days	Lk 17:22	2036
and *s* unto him, Where, Lord	Lk 17:37	3004

he *s* unto them, Wheresoever the	Lk 17:37	2036
but afterward he *s* within himself	Lk 18:4	2036
And the Lord *s*, Hear what the	Lk 18:6	2036
Jesus called them unto him, and *s*	Lk 18:16	2036
Jesus *s* unto him, Why callest	Lk 18:19	2036
And he *s*, All these have I kept	Lk 18:21	2036
he *s* unto him, Yet lackest thou	Lk 18:22	2036
that he was very sorrowful, he *s*	Lk 18:24	2036
And they that heard it *s*, Who then	Lk 18:26	2036
And he *s*, The things which are	Lk 18:27	2036
Then Peter *s*, Lo, we have left	Lk 18:28	2036
he *s* unto them, Verily I say unto	Lk 18:29	2036
s unto them, Behold, we go up to	Lk 18:31	2036
And he *s*, Lord, that I may receive	Lk 18:41	2036
Jesus *s* unto him, Receive thy	Lk 18:42	2036
s unto him, Zacchaeus, make haste	Lk 19:5	2036
stood, and *s* unto the Lord	Lk 19:8	2036
Jesus *s* unto him, This day is	Lk 19:9	2036
He *s* therefore, A certain	Lk 19:12	2036
s unto them, Occupy till I come	Lk 19:13	2036
he *s* unto him, Well, thou good	Lk 19:17	2036
he *s* likewise to him, Be thou	Lk 19:19	2036
he *s* unto them that stood by,	Lk 19:24	2036
they *s* unto him, Lord, he hath	Lk 19:25	2036
found even as he had *s* unto them	Lk 19:32	2036
the owners thereof *s* unto them	Lk 19:33	2036
And they *s*, The Lord hath need of	Lk 19:34	2036
among the multitude *s* unto him	Lk 19:39	2036
s unto them, I tell you that, if	Lk 19:40	2036
s unto them, I will also ask you	Lk 20:3	2036
Jesus *s* unto them, Neither tell I	Lk 20:8	2036
Then *s* the lord of the vineyard,	Lk 20:13	2036
And when they heard it, they *s*	Lk 20:16	2036
And he beheld them, and *s*, What is	Lk 20:17	2036
s unto them, Why tempt ye me	Lk 20:23	2036
They answered and *s*, Caesar's	Lk 20:24	2036
he *s* unto them, Render therefore	Lk 20:25	2036
And Jesus answering *s* unto them	Lk 20:34	2036
of the scribes answering *s*	Lk 20:39	2036
Master, thou hast well *s*	Lk 20:39	2036
he *s* unto them, How say they that	Lk 20:41	2036
The Lord *s* unto my Lord, Sit thou	Lk 20:42	2036
people he *s* unto his disciples	Lk 20:45	2036
And he *s*, Of a truth I say unto	Lk 21:3	2036
with goodly stones and gifts, he *s*	Lk 21:5	2036
And he *s*, Take heed that ye be not	Lk 21:8	2036
Then *s* he unto them, Nation shall	Lk 21:10	3004
they *s* unto him, Where wilt thou	Lk 22:9	2036
he *s* unto them, Behold, when ye	Lk 22:10	2036
and found as he had *s* unto them	Lk 22:13	2046
he *s* unto them, With desire I	Lk 22:15	2036
the cup, and gave thanks, and *s*	Lk 22:17	2036
he *s* unto them, The kings of the	Lk 22:25	2036
And the Lord *s*, Simon, Simon,	Lk 22:31	2036
he *s* unto him, Lord, I am ready	Lk 22:33	2036
And he *s*, I tell thee, Peter, the	Lk 22:34	3004
he *s* unto them, When I sent you	Lk 22:35	2036
And they *s*, Nothing	Lk 22:35	2036
Then *s* he unto them, But now, he	Lk 22:36	2036
And they *s*, Lord, behold, here are	Lk 22:38	2036
he *s* unto them, It is enough	Lk 22:38	2036
he *s* unto them, Pray that ye	Lk 22:40	2036
s unto them, Why sleep ye	Lk 22:46	2036
But Jesus *s* unto him, Judas,	Lk 22:48	2036
they *s* unto him, Lord, shall we	Lk 22:49	2036
And Jesus answered and *s*, Suffer ye	Lk 22:51	2036
Then Jesus *s* unto the chief	Lk 22:52	2036
earnestly looked upon him, and *s*	Lk 22:56	2036
while another saw him, and *s*	Lk 22:58	5346
And Peter *s*, Man, I am not	Lk 22:58	2036
And Peter *s*, Man, I know not what	Lk 22:60	2036
the Lord, how he had *s* unto him	Lk 22:61	2036
he *s* unto them, If I tell you, ye	Lk 22:67	2036
Then *s* they all, Art thou then	Lk 22:70	5346
he *s* unto them, Ye say that I am	Lk 22:70	2036
And they *s*, What need we any	Lk 22:71	2036
And he answered him and *s*, Thou	Lk 23:3	5346
Then *s* Pilate to the chief	Lk 23:4	2036
S unto them, Ye have brought this	Lk 23:14	2036
he *s* unto them the third time,	Lk 23:22	2036
But Jesus turning unto them *s*	Lk 23:28	2036
Then *s* Jesus, Father, forgive	Lk 23:34	3004
he *s* unto Jesus, Lord, remember	Lk 23:42	3004
Jesus *s* unto him, Verily I say	Lk 23:43	2036
had cried with a loud voice, he *s*	Lk 23:46	2036
and having *s* thus, he gave up the	Lk 23:46	2036
they *s* unto them, Why seek ye the	Lk 24:5	2036
he *s* unto them, What manner of	Lk 24:17	2036
was Cleopas, answering *s* unto him	Lk 24:18	2036
he *s* unto them, What things	Lk 24:19	2036
they *s* unto him, Concerning Jesus	Lk 24:19	2036
which *s* that he was alive	Lk 24:23	3004
it even so as the women had *s*	Lk 24:24	2036
Then he *s* unto them, O fools, and	Lk 24:25	2036
they *s* one to another, Did not	Lk 24:32	2036
he *s* unto them, Why are ye	Lk 24:38	2036
he *s* unto them, Have ye here any	Lk 24:41	2036
he *s* unto them, These are the	Lk 24:44	2036
s unto them, Thus it is written,	Lk 24:46	2036
Then *s* they unto him, Who art	Jn 1:22	2036
He *s*, I am the voice of one	Jn 1:23	5346
the Lord, as *s* the prophet Esaias	Jn 1:23	2036
s unto him, Why baptizest thou	Jn 1:25	2036
This is he of whom I *s*, After me	Jn 1:30	2036
with water, the same *s* unto me	Jn 1:33	2036
They *s* unto him, Rabbi, (which is	Jn 1:38	2036
And when Jesus beheld him, he *s*	Jn 1:42	2036
And Nathanael *s* unto him, Can	Jn 1:46	2036

s unto him, Before that Philip	Jn 1:48	2036
s unto him, Because I *s* unto	Jn 1:50	2036
s unto them that sold doves, Take	Jn 2:16	2036
s unto him, What sign shewest	Jn 2:18	2036
s unto them, Destroy this temple,	Jn 2:19	2036
Then *s* the Jews, Forty and six	Jn 2:20	2036
that he had *s* this unto them	Jn 2:22	3004
and the word which Jesus had *s*	Jn 2:22	2036
s unto him, Rabbi, we know that	Jn 3:2	2036
s unto him, Verily, verily, I say	Jn 3:3	2036
Marvel not that I *s* unto thee	Jn 3:7	2036
s unto him, How can these things	Jn 3:9	2036
s unto him, Art thou a master of	Jn 3:10	2036
s unto him, Rabbi, he that was	Jn 3:26	2036
John answered and *s*, A man can	Jn 3:27	2036
bear me witness, that I *s*	Jn 3:28	2036
s unto her, If thou knewest the	Jn 4:10	2036
s unto her, Whosoever drinketh of	Jn 4:13	2036
The woman answered and *s*, I have	Jn 4:17	2036
Jesus *s* unto her, Thou hast well	Jn 4:17	3004
unto her, Thou hast well *s*	Jn 4:17	2036
yet no man *s*, What seekest thou	Jn 4:27	2036
But he *s* unto them, I have meat	Jn 4:32	2036
Therefore *s* the disciples one to	Jn 4:33	3004
s unto the woman, Now we believe,	Jn 4:42	3004
Then *s* Jesus unto him, Except ye	Jn 4:48	2036
they *s* unto him, Yesterday at the	Jn 4:52	2036
in the which Jesus *s* unto him	Jn 4:53	2036
The Jews therefore *s* unto him	Jn 5:10	3004
made me whole, the same *s* unto me	Jn 5:11	2036
man is that which *s* unto thee	Jn 5:12	2036
s unto him, Behold, thou art made	Jn 5:14	2036
but *s* also that God was his	Jn 5:18	3004
s unto them, Verily, verily, I	Jn 5:19	2036
And this he *s* to prove him	Jn 6:6	3004
And Jesus *s*, Make the men sit down	Jn 6:10	2036
he *s* unto his disciples, Gather	Jn 6:12	3004
the miracle that Jesus did, *s*	Jn 6:14	3004
they *s* unto him, Rabbi, when	Jn 6:25	2036
Jesus answered them and *s*, Verily,	Jn 6:26	2036
Then *s* they unto him, What shall	Jn 6:28	2036
s unto them, This is the work of	Jn 6:29	2036
They *s* therefore unto him, What	Jn 6:30	2036
Then Jesus *s* unto them, Verily,	Jn 6:32	2036
Then *s* they unto him, Lord,	Jn 6:34	2036
Jesus *s* unto them, I am the bread	Jn 6:35	2036
But I *s* unto you, That ye also	Jn 6:36	2036
murmured at him, because he *s*	Jn 6:41	2036
And they *s*, Is not this Jesus, the	Jn 6:42	3004
s unto them, Murmur not among	Jn 6:43	2036
Then Jesus *s* unto them, Verily,	Jn 6:53	2036
These things *s* he in the	Jn 6:59	2036
when they had heard this, *s*	Jn 6:60	2036
he *s* unto them, Doth this offend	Jn 6:61	2036
And he *s*, Therefore *s* I unto	Jn 6:65	3004
Therefore *s* I unto you, that no	Jn 6:65	2046
Then *s* Jesus unto the twelve,	Jn 6:67	2036
His brethren therefore *s* unto him	Jn 7:3	2036
Then Jesus *s* unto them, My time	Jn 7:6	3004
When he had *s* these words unto	Jn 7:9	2036
sought him at the feast, and *s*	Jn 7:11	3004
for some *s*, He is a good man	Jn 7:12	3004
others *s*, Nay	Jn 7:12	3004
Jesus answered them, and *s*	Jn 7:16	2036
The people answered and *s*, Thou	Jn 7:20	2036
s unto them, I have done one work	Jn 7:21	2036
Then *s* some of them of Jerusalem,	Jn 7:25	3004
the people believed on him, and *s*	Jn 7:31	3004
Then *s* Jesus unto them, Yet a	Jn 7:33	2036
Then *s* the Jews among themselves,	Jn 7:35	2036
of saying is this that he *s*	Jn 7:36	2036
on me, as the scripture hath *s*	Jn 7:38	2036
when they heard this saying, *s*	Jn 7:40	3004
Others *s*, This is the Christ	Jn 7:41	3004
But some *s*, Shall Christ come out	Jn 7:41	3004
Hath not the scripture *s*, That	Jn 7:42	2036
they *s* unto them, Why have ye not	Jn 7:45	2036
s unto him, Art thou also of	Jn 7:52	2036
This they *s*, tempting him, that	Jn 8:6	3004
s unto them, He that is without	Jn 8:7	2036
he *s* unto him, Woman, where are	Jn 8:10	2036
She *s*, No man, Lord	Jn 8:11	2036
Jesus *s* unto her, Neither do I	Jn 8:11	2036
Pharisees therefore *s* unto him	Jn 8:13	2036
s unto them, Though I bear record	Jn 8:14	2036
Then *s* they unto him, Where is	Jn 8:19	3004
Then *s* Jesus again unto them, I	Jn 8:21	2036
Then *s* the Jews, Will he kill	Jn 8:22	3004
he *s* unto them, Ye are from	Jn 8:23	2036
I *s* therefore unto you, that ye	Jn 8:24	2036
Then *s* they unto him, Who art	Jn 8:25	3004
Even the same that I *s* unto you	Jn 8:25	2980
Then *s* Jesus unto them, When ye	Jn 8:28	2036
Then *s* Jesus to those Jews which	Jn 8:31	3004
s unto him, Abraham is our father	Jn 8:39	2036
Then *s* they to him, We be not	Jn 8:41	2036
Jesus *s* unto them, If God were	Jn 8:42	2036
s unto him, Say we not well that	Jn 8:48	2036
Then *s* the Jews unto him, Now we	Jn 8:52	2036
Then *s* the Jews unto him, Thou	Jn 8:57	2036
Jesus *s* unto them, Verily, verily	Jn 8:58	2036
s unto him, Go, wash in the pool	Jn 9:7	2036
had seen him that he was blind, *s*	Jn 9:8	3004
Some *s*, This is he	Jn 9:9	3004
others *s*, He is like him	Jn 9:9	
but he *s*, I am he	Jn 9:9	3004
Therefore *s* they unto him, How	Jn 9:10	3004
He answered and *s*, A man that is	Jn 9:11	2036
s unto me, Go to the pool of	Jn 9:11	2036
Then *s* they unto him, Where is he	Jn 9:12	2036
He *s*, I know not	Jn 9:12	3004
He *s* unto them, He put clay upon	Jn 9:15	2036
Therefore *s* some of the Pharisees	Jn 9:16	3004
Others *s*, How can a man that is a	Jn 9:16	3004
He *s*, He is a prophet	Jn 9:17	2036
His parents answered them and *s*	Jn 9:20	2036
Therefore *s* his parents, He is of	Jn 9:23	2036
s unto him, Give God the praise	Jn 9:24	2036
He answered and *s*, Whether he be a	Jn 9:25	2036
Then *s* they to him again, What	Jn 9:26	2036
Then they reviled him, and *s*	Jn 9:28	2036
s unto them, Why herein is a	Jn 9:30	2036
s unto him, Thou wast altogether	Jn 9:34	2036
he *s* unto him, Dost thou believe	Jn 9:35	2036
He answered and *s*, Who is he, Lord	Jn 9:36	2036
Jesus *s* unto him, Thou hast both	Jn 9:37	2036
And he *s*, Lord, I believe	Jn 9:38	5346
And Jesus *s*, For judgment I am	Jn 9:39	2036
s unto him, Are we blind also	Jn 9:40	2036
Jesus *s* unto them, If ye were	Jn 9:41	2036
Then *s* Jesus unto them again,	Jn 10:7	2036
And many of them *s*, He hath a	Jn 10:20	3004
Others *s*, These are not the words	Jn 10:21	3004
s unto him, How long dost thou	Jn 10:24	3004
not of my sheep, as I *s* unto you	Jn 10:26	2036
it not written in your law, I *s*	Jn 10:34	2036
because I *s*, I am the Son of God	Jn 10:36	2036
And many resorted unto him, and *s*	Jn 10:41	3004
When Jesus heard that, he *s*	Jn 11:4	2036
These things *s* he	Jn 11:11	2036
Then *s* his disciples, Lord, if he	Jn 11:12	2036
Then *s* Jesus unto them plainly,	Jn 11:14	2036
Then *s* Thomas, which is called	Jn 11:16	2036
Then *s* Martha unto Jesus, Lord,	Jn 11:21	2036
Jesus *s* unto her, I am the	Jn 11:25	2036
And when she had so *s*, she went	Jn 11:28	2036
And *s*, Where have ye laid him	Jn 11:34	2036
They *s* unto him, Lord, come and	Jn 11:34	3004
Then *s* the Jews, Behold how he	Jn 11:36	3004
And some of them *s*, Could not this	Jn 11:37	2036
Jesus *s*, Take ye away the stone	Jn 11:39	3004
S I not unto thee, that, if thou	Jn 11:40	2036
And Jesus lifted up his eyes, and *s*	Jn 11:41	2036
the people which stand by I *s* it	Jn 11:42	2036
and the Pharisees a council, and *s*	Jn 11:47	3004
s unto them, Ye know nothing at	Jn 11:49	2036
This he *s*, not that he cared for	Jn 12:6	2036
Then *s* Jesus, Let her alone	Jn 12:7	2036
therefore *s* among themselves	Jn 12:19	2036
and heard it, *s* that it thundered	Jn 12:29	3004
others *s*, An angel spake to him	Jn 12:29	3004
Jesus answered and *s*, This voice	Jn 12:30	2036
This he *s*, signifying what death	Jn 12:33	3004
Then Jesus *s* unto them, Yet a	Jn 12:35	2036
because that Esaias *s* again	Jn 12:39	2036
These things *s* Esaias, when he	Jn 12:41	2036
Jesus cried and *s*, He that	Jn 12:44	2036
even as the Father *s* unto me	Jn 12:50	2046
s unto him, What I do thou	Jn 13:7	2036
therefore *s* he, Ye are not all	Jn 13:11	2036
he *s* unto them, Know ye what I	Jn 13:12	2036
When Jesus had thus *s*, he was	Jn 13:21	2036
in spirit, and testified, and *s*	Jn 13:21	2036
Then *s* Jesus unto him, That thou	Jn 13:27	3004
bag, that Jesus had *s* unto him	Jn 13:29	3004
when he was gone out, Jesus *s*	Jn 13:31	3004
as I *s* unto the Jews, Whither I	Jn 13:33	2036
Simon Peter *s* unto him, Lord,	Jn 13:36	3004
Peter *s* unto him, Lord, why	Jn 13:37	3004
s unto him, If a man love me, he	Jn 14:23	2036
whatsoever I have *s* unto you	Jn 14:26	2036
Ye have heard how I *s* unto you	Jn 14:28	2036
me, ye would rejoice, because I *s*	Jn 14:28	2036
the word that I *s* unto you	Jn 15:20	2036
these things I *s* not unto you at	Jn 16:4	2036
But because I have *s* these things	Jn 16:6	2980
therefore *s* I, that he shall take	Jn 16:15	2036
Then *s* some of his disciples	Jn 16:17	2036
They *s* therefore, What is this	Jn 16:18	3004
s unto them, Do ye enquire among	Jn 16:19	2036
among yourselves of that I *s*	Jn 16:19	2036
His disciples *s* unto him, Lo, now	Jn 16:29	3004
up his eyes to heaven, and *s*	Jn 17:1	2036
s unto them, Whom seek ye	Jn 18:4	2036
soon then as he had *s* unto them	Jn 18:6	2036
And they *s*, Jesus of Nazareth	Jn 18:7	2036
Then *s* Jesus unto Peter, Put up	Jn 18:11	2036
and in secret have I *s* nothing	Jn 18:20	2980
heard me, what I have *s* unto them	Jn 18:21	2980
behold, they know what I *s*	Jn 18:21	2036
They *s* therefore unto him, Art	Jn 18:25	2036
He denied it, and *s*, I am not	Jn 18:25	2036
then went out unto them, and *s*	Jn 18:29	2036
s unto him, If he were not a	Jn 18:30	2036
Then *s* Pilate unto them, Take ye	Jn 18:31	2036
The Jews therefore *s* unto him	Jn 18:31	2036
s unto him, Art thou the King of	Jn 18:33	2036
Pilate therefore *s* unto him	Jn 18:37	2036
And when he had *s* this, he went	Jn 18:38	2036
And *s*, Hail, King of the Jews	Jn 19:3	3004
Then *s* the chief priests of the	Jn 19:21	3004
but that he *s*, I am King of the	Jn 19:21	2036
They *s* therefore among themselves	Jn 19:24	2036
had received the vinegar, he *s*	Jn 19:30	2036
And when she had thus *s*, she	Jn 20:14	2036
And when he had so *s*, he shewed	Jn 20:20	2036
Then *s* Jesus to them again, Peace	Jn 20:21	2036
And when he had *s* this, he	Jn 20:22	2036
disciples therefore *s* unto him	Jn 20:25	3004
But he *s* unto them, Except I	Jn 20:25	2036
shut, and stood in the midst, and *s*	Jn 20:26	2036
s unto him, My Lord and my God	Jn 20:28	2036
he *s* unto them, Cast the net on	Jn 21:6	2036
he *s* unto him the third time	Jn 21:17	2036
he *s* unto him, Lord, thou knowest	Jn 21:17	2036
on his breast at supper, and *s*	Jn 21:20	2036
yet Jesus *s* not unto him, He	Jn 21:23	2036
he *s* unto them, It is not for you	Acts 1:7	2036
Which also *s*, Ye men of Galilee,	Acts 1:11	2036
the midst of the disciples, and *s*	Acts 1:15	2036
And they prayed, and *s*, Thou, Lord,	Acts 1:24	2036
Others mocking *s*, These men are	Acts 2:13	3004
s unto them, Ye men of Judaea, and	Acts 2:14	669
The Lord *s* unto my Lord, Sit thou	Acts 2:34	2036
s unto Peter and to the rest of	Acts 2:37	2036
Then Peter *s* unto them, Repent,	Acts 2:38	5346
his eyes upon him with John, *s*	Acts 3:4	2036
Then Peter *s*, Silver and gold have	Acts 3:6	2036
For Moses truly *s* unto the	Acts 3:22	2036
s unto them, Ye rulers of the	Acts 4:8	2036
s unto them, Whether it be right	Acts 4:19	2036
priests and elders had *s* unto them	Acts 4:23	2036
to God with one accord, and *s*	Acts 4:24	2036
mouth of thy servant David hast *s*	Acts 4:25	2036
neither *s* any of them that ought	Acts 4:32	3004
But Peter *s*, Ananias, why hath	Acts 5:3	2036
And she *s*, Yea, for so much	Acts 5:8	2036
Then Peter *s* unto her, How is it	Acts 5:9	2036
and brought them forth, and *s*	Acts 5:19	2036
the other apostles answered and *s*	Acts 5:29	2036
s unto them, Ye men of Israel,	Acts 5:35	2036
of the disciples unto them, and *s*	Acts 6:2	2036
Then they suborned men, which *s*	Acts 6:11	3004
set up false witnesses, which *s*	Acts 6:13	3004
Then *s* the high priest, Are these	Acts 7:1	2036
And he *s*, Men, brethren, and	Acts 7:2	5346
s unto him, Get thee out of thy	Acts 7:3	2036
be in bondage will I judge, *s* God	Acts 7:7	2036
Then *s* the Lord to him, Put off	Acts 7:33	2036
which *s* unto the children of	Acts 7:37	2036
And *s*, Behold, I see the heavens	Acts 7:56	2036
And when he had *s* this, he fell	Acts 7:60	2036
But Peter *s* unto him, Thy money	Acts 8:20	2036
Then answered Simon, and *s*	Acts 8:24	2036
Then the Spirit *s* unto Philip	Acts 8:29	2036
him read the prophet Esaias, and *s*	Acts 8:30	2036
And he *s*, How can I, except some	Acts 8:31	2036
the eunuch answered Philip, and *s*	Acts 8:34	2036
and the eunuch *s*, See, here is	Acts 8:36	5346
And Philip *s*, If thou believest	Acts 8:37	2036
And he answered and *s*, I believe	Acts 8:37	2036
And he *s*, Who art thou, Lord	Acts 9:5	2036
And the Lord *s*, I am Jesus whom	Acts 9:5	2036
And he trembling and astonished *s*	Acts 9:6	2036
And the Lord *s* unto him, Arise, and	Acts 9:6	
to him *s* the Lord in a vision,	Acts 9:10	2036
And he *s*, Behold, I am here, Lord	Acts 9:10	2036
And the Lord *s* unto him, Arise, and	Acts 9:11	
But the Lord *s* unto him, Go thy	Acts 9:15	2036
and putting his hands on him *s*	Acts 9:17	2036
that heard him were amazed, and *s*	Acts 9:21	3004
Peter *s* unto him, Aeneas, Jesus	Acts 9:34	2036
and turning him to the body *s*	Acts 9:40	2036
on him, he was afraid, and *s*	Acts 10:4	2036
he *s* unto him, Thy prayers and	Acts 10:4	2036
But Peter *s*, Not so, Lord	Acts 10:14	2036
the vision, the Spirit *s* unto him	Acts 10:19	2036
and *s*, Behold, I am he whom ye	Acts 10:21	2036
And they *s*, Cornelius the	Acts 10:22	2036
he *s* unto them, Ye know how that	Acts 10:28	5346
And Cornelius *s*, Four days ago I	Acts 10:30	5346
And *s*, Cornelius, thy prayer is	Acts 10:31	5346
Then Peter opened his mouth, and *s*	Acts 10:34	2036
But I *s*, Not so, Lord	Acts 11:8	2036
s unto him, Send men to Joppa, and	Acts 11:13	2036
word of the Lord, how that he *s*	Acts 11:16	3004
And the angel *s* unto him, Gird	Acts 12:8	2036
Peter was come to himself, he *s*	Acts 12:11	2036
they *s* unto her, Thou art mad	Acts 12:15	2036
Then *s* they, It is his angel	Acts 12:15	3004
And he *s*, Go shew these things	Acts 12:17	2036
Lord, and fasted, the Holy Ghost *s*	Acts 13:2	2036
And *s*, O full of all subtilty and	Acts 13:10	2036
up, and beckoning with his hand *s*	Acts 13:16	2036
whom also he gave testimony, and *s*	Acts 13:22	2036
John fulfilled his course, he *s*	Acts 13:25	3004
he *s* on this wise, I will give	Acts 13:34	5346
Paul and Barnabas waxed bold, and *s*	Acts 13:46	2036
S with a loud voice, Stand	Acts 14:10	2036
Judaea taught the brethren, and *s*	Acts 15:1	
s unto them, Men and brethren, ye	Acts 15:7	2036
days after Paul *s* unto Barnabas	Acts 15:36	2036
s to the spirit, I command thee	Acts 16:18	2036
And brought them out, and *s*	Acts 16:30	5346
And they *s*, Believe on the Lord	Acts 16:31	2036
But Paul *s* unto them, They have	Acts 16:37	5346
And some *s*, What will this babbler	Acts 17:18	3004
in the midst of Mars' hill, and *s*	Acts 17:22	5346
also of your own poets have *s*	Acts 17:28	2046
and others *s*, We will hear thee	Acts 17:32	2036
s unto them, Your blood be upon	Acts 18:6	2036
Gallio *s* unto the Jews, If it	Acts 18:14	2036
He *s* unto them, Have ye received	Acts 19:2	2036
they *s* unto him, We have not so	Acts 19:2	2036

he s unto them, Unto what then ... Acts 19:3 2036
And they s, Unto John's baptism ... Acts 19:3 2036
Then s Paul, John verily baptized ... Acts 19:4 2036
And the evil spirit answered and s ... Acts 19:15 2036
workmen of like occupation, and s ... Acts 19:25 2036
had appeased the people, he s ... Acts 19:35 5346
fell on him, and embracing him s ... Acts 20:10 2036
he s unto them, Ye know, from the ... Acts 20:18 2036
words of the Lord Jesus, how he s ... Acts 20:35 2036
who s to Paul through the Spirit, ... Acts 21:4 3004
bound his own hands and feet, and s ... Acts 21:11 2036
s unto him, Thou seest, brother, ... Acts 21:20 2036
he s unto the chief captain, May ... Acts 21:37 3004
Who s, Canst thou speak Greek ... Acts 21:37 5346
But Paul s, I am a man which am a ... Acts 21:39 2036
he s unto me, I am Jesus of ... Acts 22:8 2036
And I s, What shall I do, Lord ... Acts 22:10 2036
And the Lord s unto me, Arise, and ... Acts 22:10 2036
s unto me, Brother Saul, receive ... Acts 22:13 2036
And he s, The God of our fathers ... Acts 22:14 2036
And I s, Lord, they know that I ... Acts 22:19 2036
And he s unto me, Depart ... Acts 22:21 2036
then lifted up their voices, and s ... Acts 22:22 3004
Paul s unto the centurion that ... Acts 22:25 2036
s unto him, Tell me, art thou a ... Acts 22:27 2036
He s, Yea ... Acts 22:27 5346
And Paul s, But I was free born ... Acts 22:28 5346
beholding the council, s, Men and ... Acts 23:1 2036
Then s Paul unto him, God shall ... Acts 23:3 2036
And they that stood by s, Revilest ... Acts 23:4 2036
Then s Paul, I wist not, brethren ... Acts 23:5 5346
And when he had so s, there arose ... Acts 23:7 2980
the Lord stood by him, and s ... Acts 23:11 2036
the chief priests and elders, and s ... Acts 23:14 2036
of the centurions unto him, and s ... Acts 23:17 5346
him to the chief captain, and s ... Acts 23:18 5346
And he s, The Jews have agreed to ... Acts 23:20 2036
s he, when thine accusers are ... Acts 23:35 5346
that way, he deferred them, and s ... Acts 24:22 2036
s he, which among you are able, ... Acts 25:5 5346
a pleasure, answered Paul, and s ... Acts 25:9 2036
Then s Paul, I stand at Caesar's ... Acts 25:10 2036
Then Agrippa s unto Festus ... Acts 25:22 5346
s he, thou shalt hear him ... Acts 25:22 5346
And Festus s, King Agrippa, and all ... Acts 25:24 5346
Then Agrippa s unto Paul, Thou ... Acts 26:1 5346
And I s, Who art thou, Lord ... Acts 26:15 2036
And he s, I am Jesus whom thou ... Acts 26:15 2036
Festus s with a loud voice, Paul, ... Acts 26:24 5346
But he s, I am not mad, most ... Acts 26:25 5346
Then Agrippa s unto Paul, Almost ... Acts 26:28 5346
And Paul s, I would to God, that ... Acts 26:29 2036
Then s Agrippa unto Festus, This ... Acts 26:32 5346
s unto them, Sirs, I perceive ... Acts 27:10 3004
forth in the midst of them, and s ... Acts 27:21 2036
Paul s to the centurion and to the ... Acts 27:31 2036
they s among themselves, No doubt ... Acts 28:4 3004
minds, and s that he was a god ... Acts 28:6 3004
he s unto them, Men and brethren, ... Acts 28:17 3004
they s unto him, We neither ... Acts 28:21 2036
And when he had s these words ... Acts 28:29 2036
known lust, except the law had s ... Rom 7:7 3004
It was s unto her, The elder ... Rom 9:12 4483
place where it was s unto them ... Rom 9:26 4483
And as Esaias s before, Except the ... Rom 9:29 4280
given thanks, he brake it, and s ... 1Cor 11:24 2036
as God hath s, I will dwell in ... 2Cor 6:16 2036
for I have s before, that ye are ... 2Cor 7:3 4280
that, as I s, ye may be ready ... 2Cor 9:3 3004
he s unto me, My grace is ... 2Cor 12:9 2046
As we s before, so say I now ... Gal 1:9 4280
I s unto Peter before them all, ... Gal 2:14 2036
even a prophet of their own, s ... Titus 1:12 2036
of the angels s he at any time ... Heb 1:5 2036
of the angels s he at any times ... Heb 1:13 2046
with that generation, and s ... Heb 3:10 2036
While it is s, To day if ye will ... Heb 3:15 3004
do enter into rest, as he s ... Heb 4:3 2046
as it is s, To day if ye will ... Heb 4:7 2046
but he that s unto him, Thou art ... Heb 5:5 2980
an oath by him that s unto him ... Heb 7:21 3004
Then s I, Lo, I come (in the ... Heb 10:7 2036
Above when he s, Sacrifice and ... Heb 10:8 3004
Then s he, Lo, I come to do thy ... Heb 10:9 2046
for after that he had s before ... Heb 10:15 4280
For we know him that hath s ... Heb 10:30 2036
Of whom it was s, That in Isaac ... Heb 11:18 2980
was the sight, that Moses s ... Heb 12:21 2036
for he hath s, I will never leave ... Heb 13:5 2046
For he that s, Do not commit ... Jas 2:11 2036
adultery, s also, Do not kill ... Jas 2:11 2036
him a railing accusation, but s ... Jude 9 2036
which s, Come up hither, and I ... Rev 4:1 3004
And the four beasts s, Amen ... Rev 5:14 3004
it was s unto them, that they ... Rev 6:11 4483
s to the mountains and rocks, Fall ... Rev 6:16 3004
I s unto him, Sir, thou knowest ... Rev 7:14 2046
he s to me, These are they which ... Rev 7:14 2036
heaven spake unto me again, and s ... Rev 10:8 3004
s unto him, Give me the little ... Rev 10:9 3004
he s unto me, Take it, and eat it ... Rev 10:9 3004
he s unto me, Thou must prophesy ... Rev 10:11 3004
And the angel s unto me, Wherefore ... Rev 17:7 2036
And again they s, Alleluia ... Rev 19:3 2046
he s unto me, See thou do it not ... Rev 19:10 3004
And he that sat upon the throne s ... Rev 21:5 2036
And he s unto me, Write ... Rev 21:5 3004
And he s unto me, It is done ... Rev 21:6 2036
he s unto me, These sayings are ... Rev 22:6 2036

SAIDST {22}

Why s thou, She is my sister ... Gen 12:19 559
how s thou, She is my sister ... Gen 26:9 559
Isaac, the LORD which s unto me ... Gen 32:9 559
And thou s, I will surely do thee ... Gen 32:12 559
thou s unto thy servants, Bring ... Gen 44:21 559
thou s unto thy servants, Except ... Gen 44:23 559
s unto them, I will multiply your ... Ex 32:13 1696
now thy mouth, wherewith thou s ... Judg 9:38 559
thou s unto me, The word that I ... 1Kin 2:42 559
this to be right, that thou s ... Job 35:2 559
For thou s, What advantage will ... Job 35:3 559
When thou s, Seek ye my face ... Ps 27:8 559
in vision to thy holy one, and s ... Ps 89:19 559
And thou s, I shall be a lady for ... Is 47:7 559
yet s thou not, There is no hope ... Is 57:10 559
and thou s, I will not transgress ... Jer 2:20 559
but thou s, There is no hope ... Jer 2:25 559
but thou s, I will not hear ... Jer 22:21 559
thou s, Fear not ... Lam 3:57 559
Because thou s, Aha, against my ... Eze 25:3 559
and thy judges of whom thou s ... Hos 13:10 559
in that s thou truly ... Jn 4:18 2046

SAIL {8}

mast, they could not spread the s ... Is 33:23 5251
thou spreadest forth to be thy s ... Eze 27:7 5251
as he was about to s into Syria ... Acts 20:3 321
had determined to s by Ephesus ... Acts 20:16 3896
that we should s into Italy ... Acts 27:1 636
meaning to s by the coasts of ... Acts 27:2 4126
into the quicksands, strake s ... Acts 27:17 4632
thee all them that s with thee ... Acts 27:24 4126

SAILED {15}

But as they s he fell asleep ... Lk 8:23 4126
and from thence they s to Cyprus ... Acts 13:4 636
thence s to Antioch, from whence ... Acts 14:26 636
took Mark, and s unto Cyprus ... Acts 15:39 1602
s thence into Syria, and with him ... Acts 18:18 1602
And he s from Ephesus ... Acts 18:21 321
we s away from Philippi after the ... Acts 20:6 1602
s unto Assos, there intending to ... Acts 20:13 321
we s thence, and came the next day ... Acts 20:15 636
s into Syria, and landed at Tyre ... Acts 21:3 4126
we s under Cyprus, because the ... Acts 27:4 5284
when we had s over the sea of ... Acts 27:5 1277
when we had s slowly many days, ... Acts 27:7 1020
we s under Crete, over against ... Acts 27:7 5284
thence, they s close by Crete ... Acts 27:13 3881

SAILING {3}

finding a ship s over unto ... Acts 21:2 1276
a ship of Alexandria s into Italy ... Acts 27:6 4126
when s was now dangerous, because ... Acts 27:9 4144

SAILORS {1}

and all the company in ships, and s ... Rev 18:17 3492

SAINT {5}

camp, and Aaron the s of the LORD ... Ps 106:16 6918
Then I heard one s speaking ... Dan 8:13 6918
another s said unto that certain ... Dan 8:13 6918
unto that certain s which spake ... Dan 8:13
Salute every s in Christ Jesus ... Phil 4:21 40

SAINTS {95}

he came with ten thousands of s ... Deut 33:2 6944
all his s are in thy hand ... Deut 33:3 6918
He will keep the feet of his s ... 1Sa 2:9 2623
let thy s rejoice in goodness ... 2Chr 6:41 2623
to which of the s wilt thou turn ... Job 5:1 6918
he putteth no trust in his s ... Job 15:15 6918
But to the s that are in the ... Ps 16:3 6918
O ye s of his, and give thanks at ... Ps 30:4 2623
O love the LORD, all ye his s ... Ps 31:23 2623
O fear the LORD, ye his s ... Ps 34:9 6918
judgment, and forsaketh not his s ... Ps 37:28 2623
Gather my s together unto me ... Ps 50:5 2623
for it is good before thy s ... Ps 52:9 2623
the flesh of thy s unto the ... Ps 79:2 2623
unto his people, and to his s ... Ps 85:8 2623
also in the congregation of the s ... Ps 89:5 6918
feared in the assembly of the s ... Ps 89:7 6918
he preserveth the souls of his s ... Ps 97:10 2623
of the LORD is the death of his s ... Ps 116:15 2623
and let thy s shout for joy ... Ps 132:9 2623
her s shall shout aloud for joy ... Ps 132:16 2623
and thy s shall bless thee ... Ps 145:10 2623
people, the praise of all his s ... Ps 148:14 2623
praise in the congregation of s ... Ps 149:1 2623
Let the s be joyful in glory ... Ps 149:5 2623
this honour have all his s ... Ps 149:9 2623
and preserveth the way of his s ... Prov 2:8 2623
But the s of the most High shall ... Dan 7:18 6922
the same horn made war with the s ... Dan 7:21 6922
given to the s of the most High ... Dan 7:22 6922
that the s possessed the kingdom ... Dan 7:22 6922
wear out the s of the most High ... Dan 7:25 6922
people of the s of the most High ... Dan 7:27 6922
God, and is faithful with the s ... Hos 11:12 6918
come, and all the s with thee ... Zec 14:5 6918
bodies of the s which slept arose ... Mt 27:52 40
hath done to thy s at Jerusalem ... Acts 9:13 40
to the s which dwelt at Lydda ... Acts 9:32 40
up, and when he had called the s ... Acts 9:41 40
many of the s did I shut up in ... Acts 26:10 40
beloved of God, called to be s ... Rom 1:7 40
s according to the will of God ... Rom 8:27 40
to the necessity of s ... Rom 12:13 40
Jerusalem to minister unto the s ... Rom 15:25 40
the poor s which are at Jerusalem ... Rom 15:26 40
may be accepted of the s ... Rom 15:31 40
her in the Lord, as becometh s ... Rom 16:2 40
all the s which are with them ... Rom 16:15 40
in Christ Jesus, called to be s ... 1Cor 1:2 40
the unjust, and not before the s ... 1Cor 6:1 40
that the s shall judge the world ... 1Cor 6:2 40
as in all churches of the s ... 1Cor 14:33 40
the collection for the s, as I ... 1Cor 16:1 40
to the ministry of the s,) ... 1Cor 16:15 40
with all the s which are in all ... 2Cor 1:1 40
of the ministering to the s ... 2Cor 8:4 40
touching the ministering to the s ... 2Cor 9:1 40
only supplieth the want of the s ... 2Cor 9:12 40
All the s salute you ... 2Cor 13:13 40
to the s which are at Ephesus, and ... Eph 1:1 40
Jesus, and love unto all the s ... Eph 1:15 40
glory of his inheritance in the s ... Eph 1:18 40
but fellowcitizens with the s ... Eph 2:19 40
am less than the least of all s ... Eph 3:8 40
with all s what is the breadth ... Eph 3:18 40
For the perfecting of the s ... Eph 4:12 40
named among you, as becometh s ... Eph 5:3 40
and supplication for all s ... Eph 6:18 40
to all the s in Christ Jesus ... Phil 1:1 40
All the s salute you, chiefly ... Phil 4:22 40
To the s and faithful brethren in ... Col 1:2 40
love which ye have to all the s ... Col 1:4 40
the inheritance of the s in light ... Col 1:12 40
but now is made manifest to his s ... Col 1:26 40
Lord Jesus Christ with all his s ... 1Th 3:13 40
come to be glorified in his s ... 2Th 1:10 40
the Lord Jesus, and toward all s ... Philem 5 40
of the s are refreshed by thee ... Philem 7 40
that ye have ministered to the s ... Heb 6:10 40
the rule over you, and all the s ... Heb 13:24 40
was once delivered unto the s ... Jude 3 40
with ten thousands of his s ... Jude 14 40
which are the prayers of s ... Rev 5:8 40
it with the prayers of all s upon ... Rev 8:3 40
came with the prayers of the s ... Rev 8:4 40
the prophets, and to the s ... Rev 11:18 40
unto him to make war with the s ... Rev 13:7 40
patience and the faith of the s ... Rev 13:10 40
Here is the patience of the s ... Rev 14:12 40
true are thy ways, thou King of s ... Rev 15:3 40
For they have shed the blood of s ... Rev 16:6 40
drunken with the blood of the s ... Rev 17:6 40
the blood of prophets, and of s ... Rev 18:24 40
linen is the righteousness of s ... Rev 19:8 40
compassed the camp of the s about ... Rev 20:9 40

SAINTS' {1}

if she have washed the s feet ... 1Ti 5:10 40

SAITH {1262}

s the LORD, for because thou hast ... Gen 22:16 5002
Thy servant Jacob s thus, I have ... Gen 32:4 559
what he s to you, do ... Gen 41:55 559
Wherefore s my lord these words ... Gen 44:7 1696
Thus s thy son Joseph, God hath ... Gen 45:9 559
Thus s the LORD, Israel is my son ... Ex 4:22 559
Thus s the LORD God of Israel, ... Ex 5:1 559
Thus s Pharaoh, I will not give ... Ex 5:10 559
Thus s the LORD, In this thou ... Ex 7:17 559
Thus s the LORD, Let my people go ... Ex 8:1 559
Thus s the LORD, Let my people go ... Ex 8:20 559
Thus s the LORD God of the ... Ex 9:1 559
Thus s the LORD God of the ... Ex 9:13 559
Thus s the LORD God of the ... Ex 10:3 559
Thus s the LORD, About midnight ... Ex 11:4 559
Thus s the LORD God of Israel, ... Ex 32:27 559
s the LORD, as ye have spoken in ... Num 14:28 559
Thus s thy brother Israel, Thou ... Num 20:14 559
Thus s Balak the son of Zippor, ... Num 22:16 559
but what the LORD s, that will I ... Num 24:13 1696
the LORD to battle, as my lord s ... Num 32:27 1696
What s my lord unto his servant ... Josh 5:14 1696
for thus s the LORD God of Israel ... Josh 7:13 559
Thus s the whole congregation of ... Josh 22:16 559
Thus s the LORD God of Israel, ... Josh 24:2 559
Thus s the LORD God of Israel, I ... Judg 6:8 559
Thus s Jephthah, Israel took not ... Judg 11:15 559
Thus s the LORD, Did I plainly ... 1Sa 2:27 559
the LORD God of Israel s, I said ... 1Sa 2:30 5002
but now the LORD s, Be it far ... 1Sa 2:30 5002
all that he s cometh surely to ... 1Sa 9:6 1696
Thus s the LORD God of Israel, I ... 1Sa 10:18 559
Thus s the LORD of hosts, I ... 1Sa 15:2 559
and he s, Let not Jonathan know ... 1Sa 20:3 559
As s the proverb of the ancients, ... 1Sa 24:13 559
Thus s the LORD, Shalt thou build ... 2Sa 7:5 559
Thus s the LORD of hosts, I took ... 2Sa 7:8 559
Thus s the LORD God of Israel, I ... 2Sa 12:7 559
Thus s the LORD, Behold, I will ... 2Sa 12:11 559
Whosoever s ought unto thee, ... 2Sa 14:10 1696
and let us hear likewise what he s ... 2Sa 17:5 6310
Thus s the LORD, I offer thee ... 2Sa 24:12 1696
Thus s the king, Come forth ... 1Kin 2:30 559
Then said the king, The one s ... 1Kin 3:23 559
and the other s, Nay ... 1Kin 3:23 559
for thus s the LORD, the God of ... 1Kin 11:31 559
Thus s the LORD, Ye shall not go ... 1Kin 12:24 559
O altar, altar, thus s the LORD ... 1Kin 13:2 559
Thus s the LORD, Forasmuch as ... 1Kin 13:21 559
Thus s the LORD God of Israel, ... 1Kin 14:7 559
For thus s the LORD God of Israel ... 1Kin 17:14 559
said unto him, Thus s Ben-hadad, ... 1Kin 20:2 559

Thus *s* the LORD, Hast thou seen	1Kin 20:13	559
Thus *s* the LORD, Even by the	1Kin 20:14	559
Thus *s* the LORD, Because the	1Kin 20:28	559
and said, Thy servant Ben-hadad *s*	1Kin 20:32	559
Thus *s* the LORD, Because thou	1Kin 20:42	559
Thus *s* the LORD, Hast thou killed	1Kin 21:19	559
Thus *s* the LORD, In the place	1Kin 21:19	559
Thus *s* the LORD, With these shalt	1Kin 22:11	559
liveth, what the LORD *s* unto me	1Kin 22:14	559
Thus *s* the king, Put this fellow	1Kin 22:27	559
Now therefore thus *s* the LORD	2Kin 1:4	559
Thus *s* the LORD, Is it not	2Kin 1:6	559
Thus *s* the LORD, Forasmuch as	2Kin 1:16	559
Thus *s* the LORD, I have healed	2Kin 2:21	559
Thus *s* the LORD, Make this valley	2Kin 3:16	559
For thus *s* the LORD, Ye shall not	2Kin 3:17	559
for thus *s* the LORD, They shall	2Kin 4:43	559
rather then, when he *s* to thee	2Kin 5:13	559
Thus *s* the LORD, To morrow about	2Kin 7:1	559
Thus *s* the LORD, I have anointed	2Kin 9:3	559
Thus *s* the LORD God of Israel, I	2Kin 9:6	559
Thus *s* the LORD, I have anointed	2Kin 9:12	559
Thus *s* the king, Is it peace	2Kin 9:18	559
Thus *s* the king, Is it peace	2Kin 9:19	559
the blood of his sons, *s* the LORD	2Kin 9:26	559
thee in this plat, *s* the LORD	2Kin 9:26	5002
Thus *s* the great king, the king	2Kin 18:19	559
Thus *s* the king, Let not Hezekiah	2Kin 18:29	559
for thus *s* the king of Assyria,	2Kin 18:31	559
Thus *s* Hezekiah, This day is a	2Kin 19:3	559
Thus *s* the LORD, Be not afraid of	2Kin 19:6	559
Thus *s* the LORD God of Israel,	2Kin 19:20	559
Therefore thus *s* the LORD	2Kin 19:32	559
come into this city, *s* the LORD	2Kin 19:33	5002
Thus *s* the LORD, Set thine house	2Kin 20:1	559
Thus *s* the LORD, the God of David	2Kin 20:5	559
nothing shall be left, *s* the LORD	2Kin 20:17	559
Therefore thus *s* the LORD God of	2Kin 21:12	559
Thus *s* the LORD God of Israel,	2Kin 22:15	559
Thus *s* the LORD, Behold, I will	2Kin 22:16	559
Thus *s* the LORD God of Israel, As	2Kin 22:18	559
also have heard thee, *s* the LORD	2Kin 22:19	5002
Thus *s* the LORD, Thou shalt not	1Chr 17:4	559
Thus *s* the LORD of hosts, I took	1Chr 17:7	559
Thus *s* the LORD, I offer thee	1Chr 21:10	559
Thus *s* the LORD, Choose thee	1Chr 21:11	559
Thus *s* the LORD, Ye shall not go	2Chr 11:4	559
Thus *s* the LORD, Ye have forsaken	2Chr 12:5	559
Thus *s* the LORD, With these thou	2Chr 18:10	559
LORD liveth, even what my God *s*	2Chr 18:13	559
Thus *s* the king, Put this fellow	2Chr 18:26	559
Thus *s* the LORD unto you, Be not	2Chr 20:15	559
Thus *s* the LORD God of David thy	2Chr 21:12	559
and said unto them, Thus *s* God	2Chr 24:20	559
Thus *s* Sennacherib king of	2Chr 32:10	559
Thus *s* the LORD God of Israel,	2Chr 34:23	559
Thus *s* the LORD, Behold, I will	2Chr 34:24	559
Thus *s* the LORD God of Israel	2Chr 34:26	559
even heard thee also, *s* the LORD	2Chr 34:27	5002
Thus *s* Cyrus king of Persia, All	2Chr 36:23	559
Thus *s* Cyrus king of Persia, The	Ezr 1:2	559
among the heathen, and Gashmu *s* it	Neh 6:6	559
The depth *s*, It is not in me	Job 28:14	559
and the sea *s*, It is not with me	Job 28:14	559
he is gracious unto him, and *s*	Job 33:24	559
But none *s*, Where is God my maker	Job 35:10	559
For he *s* to the snow, Be thou on	Job 37:6	559
He *s* among the trumpets, Ha, ha	Job 39:25	559
now will I arise, *s* the LORD	Ps 12:5	559
of the wicked *s* within my heart	Ps 36:1	5002
But unto the wicked God *s*	Ps 50:16	559
understanding, she *s* to him,	Prov 9:4	559
understanding, she *s* to him,	Prov 9:16	559
naught, it is naught, *s* the buyer	Prov 20:14	559
The slothful man *s*, There is a	Prov 22:13	559
Eat and drink, *s* he to thee	Prov 23:7	559
He that *s* unto the wicked, Thou	Prov 24:24	559
The slothful man *s*, There is a	Prov 26:13	559
deceiveth his neighbour, and *s*	Prov 26:19	559
his father or his mother, and *s*	Prov 28:24	559
and the fire that *s* not, It is	Prov 30:16	559
eateth, and wipeth her mouth, and *s*	Prov 30:20	559
s the Preacher, vanity of	Eccl 1:2	559
neither *s* he, For whom do I	Eccl 4:8	
s the preacher, counting one by	Eccl 7:27	559
he *s* to every one that he is a	Eccl 10:3	559
of vanities, *s* the preacher	Eccl 12:8	559
s the LORD	Is 1:11	559
us reason together, *s* the LORD	Is 1:18	559
Therefore *s* the Lord, the LORD of	Is 1:24	5002
s the Lord GOD of hosts	Is 3:15	5002
Moreover the LORD *s*, Because the	Is 3:16	559
Thus *s* the Lord GOD, It shall not	Is 7:7	559
For he *s*, Are not my princes	Is 10:8	559
For he *s*, By the strength of my	Is 10:13	559
Therefore thus *s* the Lord GOD of	Is 10:24	559
s the LORD of hosts, and cut off	Is 14:22	5002
and son, and nephew, *s* the LORD	Is 14:22	5002
destruction, *s* the LORD of hosts	Is 14:23	5002
of Israel, *s* the LORD of hosts	Is 17:3	5002
thereof, *s* the LORD God of Israel	Is 17:6	5002
s the Lord, the LORD of hosts	Is 19:4	5002
ye die, *s* the Lord GOD of hosts	Is 22:14	559
Thus *s* the Lord GOD of hosts, Go,	Is 22:15	559
s the LORD of hosts, shall the	Is 22:25	5002
Therefore thus *s* the Lord GOD	Is 28:16	559
and he *s*, I cannot	Is 29:11	559
and he *s*, I am not learned	Is 29:12	559
Therefore thus *s* the LORD	Is 29:22	559
s the LORD, that take counsel,	Is 30:1	5002
Wherefore thus *s* the Holy One of	Is 30:12	559
For thus *s* the Lord GOD, the Holy	Is 30:15	559
s the LORD, whose fire is in Zion	Is 31:9	5002
Now will I rise, *s* the LORD	Is 33:10	559
Thus *s* the great king, the king	Is 36:4	559
Thus *s* the king, Let not Hezekiah	Is 36:14	559
for thus *s* the king of Assyria,	Is 36:16	559
Thus *s* Hezekiah, This day is a	Is 37:3	559
Thus *s* the LORD, Be not afraid of	Is 37:6	559
Thus *s* the LORD God of Israel,	Is 37:21	559
Therefore thus *s* the LORD	Is 37:33	559
come into this city, *s* the LORD	Is 37:34	5002
Thus *s* the LORD, Set thine house	Is 38:1	559
Thus *s* the LORD, the God of David	Is 38:5	559
nothing shall be left, *s* the LORD	Is 39:6	559
comfort ye my people, *s* your God	Is 40:1	559
s the Holy One	Is 40:25	559
s the LORD, and thy redeemer, the	Is 41:14	5002
Produce your cause, *s* the LORD	Is 41:21	559
reasons, *s* the King of Jacob	Is 41:21	559
Thus *s* God the LORD, he that	Is 42:5	559
for a spoil, and none *s*, Restore	Is 42:22	559
But now thus *s* the LORD that	Is 43:1	559
s the LORD, and my servant whom I	Is 43:10	5002
s the LORD, that I am God	Is 43:12	5002
Thus *s* the LORD, your redeemer,	Is 43:14	559
Thus *s* the LORD, which maketh a	Is 43:16	559
Thus *s* the LORD that made thee,	Is 44:2	559
Thus *s* the LORD the King of	Is 44:6	559
yea, he warmeth himself, and *s*	Is 44:16	559
it, and prayeth unto it, and *s*	Is 44:17	559
Thus *s* the LORD, thy redeemer, and	Is 44:24	559
that *s* to Jerusalem, Thou shalt	Is 44:26	559
That *s* to the deep, Be dry, and I	Is 44:27	559
That *s* of Cyrus, He is my	Is 44:28	559
Thus *s* the LORD to his anointed,	Is 45:1	559
unto him that *s* unto his father	Is 45:10	559
Thus *s* the LORD, the Holy One of	Is 45:11	559
nor reward, *s* the LORD of hosts	Is 45:13	559
Thus *s* the LORD, The labour of	Is 45:14	559
For thus *s* the LORD that created	Is 45:18	559
Thus *s* the LORD, thy Redeemer,	Is 48:17	559
s the LORD, unto the wicked	Is 48:22	559
s the LORD that formed me from	Is 49:5	559
Thus *s* the LORD, the Redeemer of	Is 49:7	559
Thus *s* the LORD, In an acceptable	Is 49:8	559
s the LORD, thou shalt surely	Is 49:18	5002
Thus *s* the Lord GOD, Behold, I	Is 49:22	559
But thus *s* the LORD, Even the	Is 49:25	559
Thus *s* the LORD, Where is the	Is 50:1	559
Thus *s* thy Lord the LORD, and thy	Is 51:22	559
For thus *s* the LORD, Ye have sold	Is 52:3	559
For thus *s* the Lord GOD, My	Is 52:4	559
s the LORD, that my people is	Is 52:5	5002
make them to howl, *s* the LORD	Is 52:5	5002
that *s* unto Zion, Thy God	Is 52:7	559
of the married wife, *s* the LORD	Is 54:1	559
when thou wast refused, *s* thy God	Is 54:6	559
on thee, *s* the LORD thy Redeemer	Is 54:8	559
s the LORD that hath mercy on	Is 54:10	559
is of me, *s* the LORD	Is 54:17	5002
are your ways my ways, *s* the LORD	Is 55:8	5002
Thus *s* the LORD, Keep ye judgment	Is 56:1	559
For thus *s* the LORD unto the	Is 56:4	559
the outcasts of Israel *s*, Yet	Is 56:8	5002
For thus *s* the high and lofty One	Is 57:15	559
to him that is near, *s* the LORD	Is 57:19	559
no peace, *s* my God, to the wicked	Is 57:21	559
in Jacob, *s* the LORD	Is 59:20	5002
my covenant with them, *s* the LORD	Is 59:21	559
s the LORD, from henceforth and	Is 59:21	559
s the LORD, which have burned	Is 65:7	559
Thus *s* the LORD, As the new wine	Is 65:8	559
is found in the cluster, and one *s*	Is 65:8	559
Therefore thus *s* the Lord GOD	Is 65:13	559
all my holy mountain, *s* the LORD	Is 65:25	559
Thus *s* the LORD, The heaven is my	Is 66:1	559
things have been, *s* the LORD	Is 66:2	5002
s the LORD	Is 66:9	559
s thy God	Is 66:9	559
For thus *s* the LORD, Behold, I	Is 66:12	559
be consumed together, *s* the LORD	Is 66:17	5002
s the LORD, as the children of	Is 66:20	559
and for Levites, *s* the LORD	Is 66:21	559
s the LORD, so shall your seed and	Is 66:22	5002
to worship before me, *s* the LORD	Is 66:23	559
thee to deliver thee, *s* the LORD	Jer 1:8	5002
kingdoms of the north, *s* the LORD	Jer 1:15	5002
s the LORD, to deliver thee	Jer 1:19	5002
saying, Thus *s* the LORD	Jer 2:2	559
shall come upon them, *s* the LORD	Jer 2:3	5002
Thus *s* the LORD, What iniquity	Jer 2:5	559
you, *s* the LORD, and with your	Jer 2:9	5002
be ye very desolate, *s* the LORD	Jer 2:12	5002
in thee, *s* the Lord GOD of hosts	Jer 2:19	5002
marked before me, *s* the Lord GOD	Jer 2:22	5002
against me, *s* the LORD	Jer 2:29	5002
return again to me, *s* the LORD	Jer 3:1	5002
heart, but feignedly, *s* the LORD	Jer 3:10	5002
backsliding Israel, *s* the LORD	Jer 3:12	5002
s the LORD, and I will not keep	Jer 3:12	5002
not obeyed my voice, *s* the LORD	Jer 3:13	5002
backsliding children, *s* the LORD	Jer 3:14	5002
s the LORD, they shall say no	Jer 3:16	5002
me, O house of Israel, *s* the LORD	Jer 3:20	5002
s the LORD, return unto me	Jer 4:1	5002
For thus *s* the LORD to the men of	Jer 4:3	559
s the LORD, that the heart of the	Jer 4:9	5002
rebellious against me, *s* the LORD	Jer 4:17	5002
s the LORD	Jer 5:9	5002
against me, *s* the LORD	Jer 5:11	5002
Wherefore thus *s* the LORD God of	Jer 5:14	559
O house of Israel, *s* the LORD	Jer 5:15	5002
s the LORD, I will not make a	Jer 5:18	5002
s the LORD	Jer 5:22	5002
s the LORD	Jer 5:29	5002
Thus *s* the LORD of hosts, They	Jer 6:9	559
of the land, *s* the LORD	Jer 6:12	5002
shall be cast down, *s* the LORD	Jer 6:15	559
Thus *s* the LORD, Stand ye in the	Jer 6:16	559
Therefore thus *s* the LORD	Jer 6:21	559
Thus *s* the LORD, Behold, a people	Jer 6:22	559
Thus *s* the LORD of hosts, the God	Jer 7:3	559
even I have seen it, *s* the LORD	Jer 7:11	5002
s the LORD, and I spake unto you,	Jer 7:13	5002
s the LORD	Jer 7:19	5002
Therefore thus *s* the Lord GOD	Jer 7:20	559
Thus *s* the LORD of hosts, the God	Jer 7:21	559
done evil in my sight, *s* the LORD	Jer 7:30	5002
s the LORD, that it shall no more	Jer 7:32	5002
s the LORD, they shall bring out	Jer 8:1	5002
driven them, *s* the LORD of hosts	Jer 8:3	5002
say unto them, Thus *s* the LORD	Jer 8:4	559
shall be cast down, *s* the LORD	Jer 8:12	559
surely consume them, *s* the LORD	Jer 8:13	5002
they shall bite you, *s* the LORD	Jer 8:17	5002
and they know not me, *s* the LORD	Jer 9:3	5002
refuse to know me, *s* the LORD	Jer 9:6	5002
Therefore thus *s* the LORD of	Jer 9:7	559
s the LORD	Jer 9:9	5002
And the LORD *s*, Because they have	Jer 9:13	559
Therefore thus *s* the LORD of	Jer 9:15	559
Thus *s* the LORD of hosts,	Jer 9:17	559
Thus *s* the LORD, Even the	Jer 9:22	5002
Thus *s* the LORD, Let not the wise	Jer 9:23	559
things I delight, *s* the LORD	Jer 9:24	5002
s the LORD, that I will punish	Jer 9:25	5002
Thus *s* the LORD, Learn not the	Jer 10:2	559
For thus *s* the LORD, Behold, I	Jer 10:18	559
Thus *s* the LORD God of Israel	Jer 11:3	559
Therefore thus *s* the LORD	Jer 11:11	559
Therefore thus *s* the LORD of the	Jer 11:21	559
Therefore thus *s* the LORD of	Jer 11:22	559
Thus *s* the LORD against all mine	Jer 12:14	559
destroy that nation, *s* the LORD	Jer 12:17	5002
Thus *s* the LORD unto me, Go and	Jer 13:1	559
Thus *s* the LORD, After this	Jer 13:9	559
whole house of Judah, *s* the LORD	Jer 13:11	5002
Thus *s* the LORD God of Israel,	Jer 13:12	559
Thus *s* the LORD, Behold, I will	Jer 13:13	559
and the sons together, *s* the LORD	Jer 13:14	5002
thy measures from me, *s* the LORD	Jer 13:25	5002
Thus *s* the LORD unto this people,	Jer 14:10	559
Therefore thus *s* the LORD	Jer 14:15	559
shalt tell them, Thus *s* the LORD	Jer 15:2	559
over them four kinds, *s* the LORD	Jer 15:3	5002
s the LORD, thou art gone	Jer 15:6	5002
before their enemies, *s* the LORD	Jer 15:9	5002
Therefore thus *s* the LORD	Jer 15:19	559
and to deliver thee, *s* the LORD	Jer 15:20	5002
For thus *s* the LORD concerning	Jer 16:3	559
For thus *s* the LORD, Enter not	Jer 16:5	559
s the LORD, even lovingkindness	Jer 16:5	5002
For thus *s* the LORD of hosts, the	Jer 16:9	559
s the LORD, and have walked after	Jer 16:11	5002
s the LORD, that it shall no more	Jer 16:14	5002
s the LORD, and they shall fish	Jer 16:16	5002
Thus *s* the LORD	Jer 17:5	559
Thus *s* the LORD	Jer 17:21	559
s the LORD, to bring in no burden	Jer 17:24	5002
s the LORD	Jer 18:6	5002
saying, Thus *s* the LORD	Jer 18:11	559
Therefore thus *s* the LORD	Jer 18:13	559
Thus *s* the LORD, Go and get a	Jer 19:1	559
Thus *s* the LORD of hosts, the God	Jer 19:3	559
s the LORD, that this place shall	Jer 19:6	5002
them, Thus *s* the LORD of hosts	Jer 19:11	559
s the LORD, and to the inhabitants	Jer 19:12	5002
Thus *s* the LORD of hosts, the God	Jer 19:15	559
For thus *s* the LORD, Behold, I	Jer 20:4	559
Thus *s* the LORD God of Israel	Jer 21:4	559
s the LORD, I will deliver	Jer 21:7	5002
thou shalt say, Thus *s* the LORD	Jer 21:8	559
evil, and not for good, *s* the LORD	Jer 21:10	5002
O house of David, thus *s* the LORD	Jer 21:12	559
and rock of the plain, *s* the LORD	Jer 21:13	5002
fruit of your doings, *s* the LORD	Jer 21:14	5002
Thus *s* the LORD	Jer 22:1	559
Thus *s* the LORD	Jer 22:3	559
s the LORD, that this house shall	Jer 22:5	5002
For thus *s* the LORD unto the	Jer 22:6	559
For thus *s* the LORD touching	Jer 22:11	559
That *s*, I will build me a wide	Jer 22:14	559
s the LORD	Jer 22:16	5002
Therefore thus *s* the LORD	Jer 22:18	559
s the LORD, though Coniah the son	Jer 22:24	5002
Thus *s* the LORD, Write ye this	Jer 22:30	559
s the LORD	Jer 23:1	5002
Therefore thus *s* the LORD God of	Jer 23:2	559
evil of your doings, *s* the LORD	Jer 23:2	5002
shall they be lacking, *s* the LORD	Jer 23:4	5002
s the LORD, that I will raise	Jer 23:5	5002
s the LORD, that they shall no	Jer 23:7	5002
their wickedness, *s* the LORD	Jer 23:11	5002

of their visitation, *s* the LORD ... Jer 23:12 5002
Therefore thus *s* the LORD of ... Jer 23:15 559
Thus *s* the LORD of hosts, Hearken ... Jer 23:16 559
s the LORD, and not a God afar off ... Jer 23:23 5002
s the LORD ... Jer 23:24 5002
s the LORD ... Jer 23:24 5002
s the LORD ... Jer 23:28 5002
s the LORD ... Jer 23:29 5002
s the LORD, that steal my words ... Jer 23:30 5002
s the LORD, that use their ... Jer 23:31 5002
use their tongues, and say, He *s* ... Jer 23:31 5002
s the LORD, and do tell them, and ... Jer 23:32 5002
this people at all, *s* the LORD ... Jer 23:32 5002
will even forsake you, *s* the LORD ... Jer 23:33 5002
therefore thus *s* the LORD ... Jer 23:38 559
Thus *s* the LORD, the God of ... Jer 24:5 559
surely thus *s* the LORD, So will I ... Jer 24:8 559
not hearkened unto me, *s* the LORD ... Jer 25:7 5002
Therefore thus *s* the LORD of ... Jer 25:8 559
s the LORD, and Nebuchadrezzar the ... Jer 25:9 5002
s the LORD, for their iniquity, ... Jer 25:12 5002
For thus *s* the LORD God of Israel ... Jer 25:15 559
Thus *s* the LORD of hosts, the God ... Jer 25:27 559
them, Thus *s* the LORD of hosts ... Jer 25:28 559
of the earth, *s* the LORD of hosts ... Jer 25:29 5002
wicked to the sword, *s* the LORD ... Jer 25:31 5002
Thus *s* the LORD of hosts, Behold, ... Jer 25:32 559
Thus *s* the LORD ... Jer 26:2 559
say unto them, Thus *s* the LORD ... Jer 26:4 559
saying, Thus *s* the LORD of hosts ... Jer 26:18 559
Thus *s* the LORD to me ... Jer 27:2 559
Thus *s* the LORD of hosts, the God ... Jer 27:4 559
s the LORD, with the sword, and ... Jer 27:8 5002
in their own land, *s* the LORD ... Jer 27:11 5002
s the LORD, yet they prophesy a ... Jer 27:15 5002
people, saying, Thus *s* the LORD ... Jer 27:16 559
For thus *s* the LORD of hosts ... Jer 27:19 559
thus *s* the LORD of hosts, the God ... Jer 27:21 559
day that I visit them, *s* the LORD ... Jer 27:22 5002
went into Babylon, *s* the LORD ... Jer 28:4 5002
people, saying, Thus *s* the LORD ... Jer 28:11 559
Hananiah, saying, Thus *s* the LORD ... Jer 28:13 559
For thus *s* the LORD of hosts, the ... Jer 28:14 559
Therefore thus *s* the LORD ... Jer 28:16 559
Thus *s* the LORD of hosts, the God ... Jer 29:4 559
For thus *s* the LORD of hosts, the ... Jer 29:8 559
I have not sent them, *s* the LORD ... Jer 29:9 5002
For thus *s* the LORD, That after ... Jer 29:10 559
s the LORD, thoughts of peace, and ... Jer 29:11 5002
will be found of you, *s* the LORD ... Jer 29:14 5002
I have driven you, *s* the LORD ... Jer 29:14 5002
Know that thus *s* the LORD of the ... Jer 29:16 559
Thus *s* the LORD of hosts ... Jer 29:17 559
s the LORD, which I sent unto ... Jer 29:19 5002
but ye would not hear, *s* the LORD ... Jer 29:19 5002
Thus *s* the LORD of hosts, the God ... Jer 29:21 559
know, and am a witness, *s* the LORD ... Jer 29:23 5002
Thus *s* the LORD concerning ... Jer 29:31 559
Therefore thus *s* the LORD ... Jer 29:32 559
will do for my people, *s* the LORD ... Jer 29:32 5002
s the LORD, that I will bring ... Jer 30:3 5002
Israel and Judah, *s* the LORD ... Jer 30:3 559
For thus *s* the LORD ... Jer 30:5 559
s the LORD of hosts, that I will ... Jer 30:8 5002
O my servant Jacob, *s* the LORD ... Jer 30:10 5002
thee, *s* the LORD, to save thee ... Jer 30:11 5002
For thus *s* the LORD, Thy bruise ... Jer 30:12 559
thee of thy wounds, *s* the LORD ... Jer 30:17 5002
Thus *s* the LORD ... Jer 30:18 559
s the LORD ... Jer 30:21 5002
s the LORD, will I be the God of ... Jer 31:1 5002
Thus *s* the LORD, The people which ... Jer 31:2 559
For thus *s* the LORD ... Jer 31:7 559
with my goodness, *s* the LORD ... Jer 31:14 5002
Thus *s* the LORD ... Jer 31:15 559
Thus *s* the LORD ... Jer 31:16 559
shall be rewarded, *s* the LORD ... Jer 31:16 5002
s the LORD, that thy children ... Jer 31:17 5002
have mercy upon him, *s* the LORD ... Jer 31:20 5002
Thus *s* the LORD of hosts, the God ... Jer 31:23 559
s the LORD, that I will sow the ... Jer 31:27 5002
to build, and to plant, *s* the LORD ... Jer 31:28 5002
s the LORD, that I will make a ... Jer 31:31 5002
an husband unto them, *s* the LORD ... Jer 31:32 5002
s the LORD, I will put my law in ... Jer 31:33 5002
the greatest of them, *s* the LORD ... Jer 31:34 5002
Thus *s* the LORD, which giveth the ... Jer 31:35 559
s the LORD, then the seed of ... Jer 31:36 5002
Thus *s* the LORD ... Jer 31:37 559
that they have done, *s* the LORD ... Jer 31:37 5002
s the LORD, that the city shall ... Jer 31:38 5002
Thus *s* the LORD, Behold, I will ... Jer 32:3 559
be until I visit him, *s* the LORD ... Jer 32:5 5002
Thus *s* the LORD of hosts, the God ... Jer 32:14 559
For thus *s* the LORD of hosts, the ... Jer 32:15 559
Therefore thus *s* the LORD ... Jer 32:28 559
work of their hands, *s* the LORD ... Jer 32:30 5002
And now therefore thus *s* the LORD ... Jer 32:36 559
For thus *s* the LORD ... Jer 32:42 559
captivity to return, *s* the LORD ... Jer 32:44 5002
Thus *s* the LORD the maker thereof ... Jer 33:2 559
For thus *s* the LORD, the God of ... Jer 33:4 559
Thus *s* the LORD ... Jer 33:10 559
land, as at the first, *s* the LORD ... Jer 33:11 559
Thus *s* the LORD of hosts ... Jer 33:12 559
him that telleth them, *s* the LORD ... Jer 33:13 559
s the LORD, that I will perform ... Jer 33:14 5002
For thus *s* the LORD ... Jer 33:17 559

Thus *s* the LORD ... Jer 33:20 559
Thus *s* the LORD ... Jer 33:25 559
Thus *s* the LORD, the God of ... Jer 34:2 559
and tell him, Thus *s* the LORD ... Jer 34:2 559
Thus *s* the LORD of thee, Thou ... Jer 34:4 559
pronounced the word, *s* the LORD ... Jer 34:5 5002
Thus *s* the LORD, the God of ... Jer 34:13 559
Therefore thus *s* the LORD ... Jer 34:17 559
s the LORD, to the sword, to the ... Jer 34:17 5002
s the LORD, and cause them to ... Jer 34:22 5002
Thus *s* the LORD of hosts, the God ... Jer 35:13 559
s the LORD ... Jer 35:13 5002
Therefore thus *s* the LORD God of ... Jer 35:17 559
Thus *s* the LORD of hosts, the God ... Jer 35:18 559
Therefore thus *s* the LORD of ... Jer 35:19 559
king of Judah, Thus *s* the LORD ... Jer 36:29 559
Therefore thus *s* the LORD of ... Jer 36:30 559
Thus *s* the LORD, the God of ... Jer 37:7 559
Thus *s* the LORD ... Jer 37:9 559
Thus *s* the LORD, He that ... Jer 38:2 559
Thus *s* the LORD, This city shall ... Jer 38:3 559
Thus *s* the LORD, the God of hosts ... Jer 38:17 559
Thus *s* the LORD of hosts, the God ... Jer 39:16 559
thee in that day, *s* the LORD ... Jer 39:17 5002
put thy trust in me, *s* the LORD ... Jer 39:18 5002
Thus *s* the LORD, the God of ... Jer 42:9 559
be not afraid of him, *s* the LORD ... Jer 42:11 5002
Thus *s* the LORD of hosts, the God ... Jer 42:15 559
For thus *s* the LORD of hosts, the ... Jer 42:18 559
Thus *s* the LORD of hosts, the God ... Jer 43:10 559
Thus *s* the LORD of hosts, the God ... Jer 44:2 559
Therefore now thus *s* the LORD ... Jer 44:7 559
Therefore thus *s* the LORD of ... Jer 44:11 559
Thus *s* the LORD of hosts, the God ... Jer 44:25 559
s the LORD, that my name shall no ... Jer 44:26 559
s the LORD, that I will punish ... Jer 44:29 5002
Thus *s* the LORD ... Jer 44:30 559
Thus *s* the LORD, the God of ... Jer 45:2 559
say unto him, The LORD *s* thus ... Jer 45:4 559
evil upon all flesh, *s* the LORD ... Jer 45:5 5002
fear was round about, *s* the LORD ... Jer 46:5 5002
and he *s*, I will go up, and will ... Jer 46:8 559
s the King, whose name is the ... Jer 46:18 5002
s the LORD, though it cannot be ... Jer 46:23 5002
of hosts, the God of Israel, *s* ... Jer 46:25 559
as in the days of old, *s* the LORD ... Jer 46:26 5002
O Jacob my servant, *s* the LORD ... Jer 46:28 5002
Thus *s* the LORD ... Jer 47:2 559
Moab thus *s* the LORD of hosts ... Jer 48:1 559
s the LORD, that I will send unto ... Jer 48:12 5002
s the King, whose name is the ... Jer 48:15 5002
and his arm is broken, *s* the LORD ... Jer 48:25 5002
I know his wrath, *s* the LORD ... Jer 48:30 5002
s the LORD, him that offereth in ... Jer 48:35 5002
is no pleasure, *s* the LORD ... Jer 48:38 5002
For thus *s* the LORD ... Jer 48:40 559
O inhabitant of Moab, *s* the LORD ... Jer 48:43 5002
of their visitation, *s* the LORD ... Jer 48:44 5002
in the latter days, *s* the LORD ... Jer 48:47 5002
The Ammonites, thus *s* the LORD ... Jer 49:1 559
s the LORD, that I will cause an ... Jer 49:2 5002
that were his heirs, *s* the LORD ... Jer 49:2 559
s the Lord GOD of hosts, from all ... Jer 49:5 5002
the children of Ammon, *s* the LORD ... Jer 49:6 5002
Edom, thus *s* the LORD of hosts ... Jer 49:7 559
For thus *s* the LORD ... Jer 49:12 559
s the LORD, that Bozrah shall ... Jer 49:13 5002
thee down from thence, *s* the LORD ... Jer 49:16 5002
s the LORD, no man shall abide ... Jer 49:18 559
in that day, *s* the LORD of hosts ... Jer 49:26 5002
shall smite, thus *s* the LORD ... Jer 49:28 559
inhabitants of Hazor, *s* the LORD ... Jer 49:30 5002
s the LORD, which have neither ... Jer 49:31 5002
all sides thereof, *s* the LORD ... Jer 49:32 5002
Thus *s* the LORD of hosts ... Jer 49:35 559
even my fierce anger, *s* the LORD ... Jer 49:37 5002
king and the princes, *s* the LORD ... Jer 49:38 5002
the captivity of Elam, *s* the LORD ... Jer 49:39 5002
s the LORD, the children of ... Jer 50:4 5002
shall be satisfied, *s* the LORD ... Jer 50:10 5002
Therefore thus *s* the LORD of ... Jer 50:18 559
s the LORD, the iniquity of ... Jer 50:20 5002
s the LORD, and do according to ... Jer 50:21 5002
cut off in that day, *s* the LORD ... Jer 50:30 5002
proud, *s* the Lord GOD of hosts ... Jer 50:31 5002
Thus *s* the LORD of hosts ... Jer 50:33 559
s the LORD, and upon the ... Jer 50:35 5002
cities thereof, *s* the LORD ... Jer 50:40 5002
Thus *s* the LORD ... Jer 51:1 559
in Zion in your sight, *s* the LORD ... Jer 51:24 5002
s the LORD, which destroyest all ... Jer 51:25 5002
be desolate for ever, *s* the LORD ... Jer 51:26 5002
For thus *s* the LORD of hosts, the ... Jer 51:33 559
Therefore thus *s* the LORD ... Jer 51:36 559
sleep, and not wake, *s* the LORD ... Jer 51:39 5002
her from the north, *s* the LORD ... Jer 51:48 5002
s the LORD, that I will do ... Jer 51:52 5002
come unto her, *s* the LORD ... Jer 51:53 5002
s the King, whose name is the ... Jer 51:57 5002
Thus *s* the LORD of hosts ... Jer 51:58 559
The LORD is my portion, *s* my soul ... Lam 3:24 559
Who is he that *s*, and it cometh to ... Lam 3:37 559
unto them, Thus *s* the Lord GOD ... Eze 2:4 559
and tell them, Thus *s* the Lord GOD ... Eze 3:11 559
unto them, Thus *s* the Lord GOD ... Eze 3:27 559
Thus *s* the Lord GOD ... Eze 5:5 559
Therefore thus *s* the Lord GOD ... Eze 5:7 559
Therefore thus *s* the Lord GOD ... Eze 5:8 559

as I live, *s* the Lord GOD ... Eze 5:11 5002
Thus *s* the Lord GOD to the ... Eze 6:3 559
Thus *s* the Lord GOD ... Eze 6:11 559
thus *s* the Lord GOD unto the land ... Eze 7:2 559
Thus *s* the Lord GOD ... Eze 7:5 559
Thus *s* the LORD ... Eze 11:5 559
Therefore thus *s* the Lord GOD ... Eze 11:7 559
a sword upon you, *s* the Lord GOD ... Eze 11:8 5002
say, Thus *s* the Lord GOD ... Eze 11:16 559
say, Thus *s* the Lord GOD ... Eze 11:17 559
their own heads, *s* the Lord GOD ... Eze 11:21 5002
unto them, Thus *s* the Lord GOD ... Eze 12:10 559
Thus *s* the Lord GOD of the ... Eze 12:19 559
therefore, Thus *s* the Lord GOD ... Eze 12:23 559
will perform it, *s* the Lord GOD ... Eze 12:25 5002
unto them, Thus *s* the Lord GOD ... Eze 12:28 559
shall be done, *s* the Lord GOD ... Eze 12:28 5002
Thus *s* the Lord GOD ... Eze 13:3 559
divination, saying, The LORD *s* ... Eze 13:6 5002
whereas ye say, The LORD *s* it ... Eze 13:7 5002
Therefore thus *s* the Lord GOD ... Eze 13:8 559
I am against you, *s* the Lord GOD ... Eze 13:8 5002
Therefore thus *s* the Lord GOD ... Eze 13:13 559
there is no peace, *s* the Lord GOD ... Eze 13:16 5002
And say, Thus *s* the Lord GOD ... Eze 13:18 559
Wherefore thus *s* the Lord GOD ... Eze 13:20 559
unto them, Thus *s* the Lord GOD ... Eze 14:4 559
of Israel, Thus *s* the Lord GOD ... Eze 14:6 559
may be their God, *s* the Lord GOD ... Eze 14:11 5002
righteousness, *s* the Lord GOD ... Eze 14:14 5002
s the Lord GOD, they shall ... Eze 14:16 5002
s the Lord GOD, they shall ... Eze 14:18 5002
s the Lord GOD, they shall ... Eze 14:20 5002
For thus *s* the Lord GOD ... Eze 14:21 559
I have done in it, *s* the Lord GOD ... Eze 14:23 5002
Therefore thus *s* the Lord GOD ... Eze 15:6 559
a trespass, *s* the Lord GOD ... Eze 15:8 5002
And say, Thus *s* the Lord GOD unto ... Eze 16:3 559
s the Lord GOD, and thou becamest ... Eze 16:8 5002
had put upon thee, *s* the Lord GOD ... Eze 16:14 5002
and thus it was, *s* the Lord GOD ... Eze 16:19 5002
s the Lord GOD ... Eze 16:23 5002
s the Lord GOD, seeing thou doest ... Eze 16:30 5002
Thus *s* the Lord GOD ... Eze 16:36 559
upon thine head, *s* the Lord GOD ... Eze 16:43 5002
s the Lord GOD, Sodom thy sister ... Eze 16:48 5002
and thine abominations, *s* the LORD ... Eze 16:58 5002
For thus *s* the Lord GOD ... Eze 16:59 559
thou hast done, *s* the Lord GOD ... Eze 16:63 5002
And say, Thus *s* the Lord GOD ... Eze 17:3 559
Say thou, Thus *s* the Lord GOD ... Eze 17:9 559
s the Lord GOD, surely in the ... Eze 17:16 5002
Therefore thus *s* the Lord GOD ... Eze 17:19 559
Thus *s* the Lord GOD ... Eze 17:22 559
s the Lord GOD, ye shall not have ... Eze 18:3 5002
shall surely live, *s* the Lord GOD ... Eze 18:9 5002
s the Lord GOD ... Eze 18:23 5002
Yet *s* the house of Israel, The ... Eze 18:29 559
to his ways, *s* the Lord GOD ... Eze 18:30 5002
of him that dieth, *s* the Lord GOD ... Eze 18:32 5002
unto them, Thus *s* the Lord GOD ... Eze 20:3 559
s the Lord GOD, I will not be ... Eze 20:3 5002
unto them, Thus *s* the Lord GOD ... Eze 20:5 559
unto them, Thus *s* the Lord GOD ... Eze 20:27 559
of Israel, Thus *s* the Lord GOD ... Eze 20:30 559
s the Lord GOD, I will not be ... Eze 20:31 5002
s the Lord GOD, surely with a ... Eze 20:33 5002
I plead with you, *s* the Lord GOD ... Eze 20:36 5002
of Israel, thus *s* the Lord GOD ... Eze 20:39 559
s the Lord GOD, there shall all ... Eze 20:40 5002
house of Israel, *s* the Lord GOD ... Eze 20:44 5002
Thus *s* the Lord GOD ... Eze 20:47 559
land of Israel, Thus *s* the LORD ... Eze 21:3 559
brought to pass, *s* the Lord GOD ... Eze 21:7 5002
prophesy, and say, Thus *s* the LORD ... Eze 21:9 559
shall be no more, *s* the Lord GOD ... Eze 21:13 5002
Therefore thus *s* the Lord GOD ... Eze 21:24 559
Thus *s* the Lord GOD ... Eze 21:26 559
Thus *s* the Lord GOD concerning ... Eze 21:28 559
Thus *s* the Lord GOD, The city ... Eze 22:3 559
hast forgotten me, *s* the Lord GOD ... Eze 22:12 5002
Therefore thus *s* the Lord GOD ... Eze 22:19 559
Thus *s* the Lord GOD, when the ... Eze 22:28 559
upon their heads, *s* the Lord GOD ... Eze 22:31 5002
O Aholibah, thus *s* the Lord GOD ... Eze 23:22 559
For thus *s* the Lord GOD ... Eze 23:28 559
Thus *s* the Lord GOD ... Eze 23:32 559
I have spoken it, *s* the Lord GOD ... Eze 23:34 559
Therefore thus *s* the Lord GOD ... Eze 23:35 559
For thus *s* the Lord GOD ... Eze 23:46 559
unto them, Thus *s* the Lord GOD ... Eze 24:3 559
Wherefore thus *s* the Lord GOD ... Eze 24:6 559
Therefore thus *s* the Lord GOD ... Eze 24:9 559
they judge thee, *s* the Lord GOD ... Eze 24:14 5002
of Israel, Thus *s* the Lord GOD ... Eze 24:21 559
Thus *s* the Lord GOD ... Eze 25:3 559
For thus *s* the Lord GOD ... Eze 25:6 559
Thus *s* the Lord GOD ... Eze 25:8 559
Thus *s* the Lord GOD ... Eze 25:12 559
Therefore thus *s* the Lord GOD ... Eze 25:13 559
know my vengeance, *s* the Lord GOD ... Eze 25:14 5002
Thus *s* the Lord GOD ... Eze 25:15 559
Therefore thus *s* the Lord GOD ... Eze 25:16 559
Therefore thus *s* the Lord GOD ... Eze 26:3 559
I have spoken it, *s* the Lord GOD ... Eze 26:5 5002
For thus *s* the Lord GOD ... Eze 26:7 559
have spoken it, *s* the Lord GOD ... Eze 26:14 5002
Thus *s* the Lord GOD to Tyrus ... Eze 26:15 559

For thus *s* the Lord GOD	Eze 26:19	559
be found again, *s* the Lord GOD	Eze 26:21	5001
many isles, Thus *s* the Lord GOD	Eze 27:3	559
of Tyrus, Thus *s* the Lord GOD	Eze 28:2	559
Therefore thus *s* the Lord GOD	Eze 28:6	559
I have spoken it, *s* the Lord GOD	Eze 28:10	5002
say unto him, Thus *s* the Lord GOD	Eze 28:12	559
And say, Thus *s* the Lord GOD	Eze 28:22	559
Thus *s* the Lord GOD	Eze 28:25	559
and say, Thus *s* the Lord GOD	Eze 29:3	559
Therefore thus *s* the Lord GOD	Eze 29:8	559
Yet thus *s* the Lord GOD	Eze 29:13	559
Therefore thus *s* the Lord GOD	Eze 29:19	559
wrought for me, *s* the Lord GOD	Eze 29:20	5002
and say, Thus *s* the Lord GOD	Eze 30:2	559
Thus *s* the LORD	Eze 30:6	559
it by the sword, *s* the Lord GOD	Eze 30:6	5002
Thus *s* the Lord GOD	Eze 30:10	559
Thus *s* the Lord GOD	Eze 30:13	559
Therefore thus *s* the Lord GOD	Eze 30:22	559
Therefore thus *s* the Lord GOD	Eze 31:10	559
Thus *s* the Lord GOD	Eze 31:15	559
all his multitude, *s* the Lord GOD	Eze 31:18	5002
Thus *s* the Lord GOD	Eze 32:3	559
upon thy land, *s* the Lord GOD	Eze 32:8	5002
For thus *s* the Lord GOD	Eze 32:11	559
to run like oil, *s* the Lord GOD	Eze 32:14	5002
all her multitude, *s* the Lord GOD	Eze 32:16	5002
by the sword, *s* the Lord GOD	Eze 32:31	5002
all his multitude, *s* the Lord GOD	Eze 32:32	5002
s the Lord GOD, I have no	Eze 33:11	5002
unto them, Thus *s* the Lord GOD	Eze 33:25	559
unto them, Thus *s* the Lord GOD	Eze 33:27	559
Thus *s* the Lord GOD unto the	Eze 34:2	559
As I live *s* the Lord GOD, surely	Eze 34:8	5002
Thus *s* the Lord GOD	Eze 34:10	559
For thus *s* the Lord GOD	Eze 34:11	559
them to lie down, *s* the Lord GOD	Eze 34:15	5002
O my flock, thus *s* the Lord GOD	Eze 34:17	559
Therefore thus *s* the Lord GOD	Eze 34:20	559
are my people, *s* the Lord GOD	Eze 34:30	5002
and I am your God, *s* the Lord GOD	Eze 34:31	5002
say unto it, Thus *s* the Lord GOD	Eze 35:3	559
s the Lord GOD, I will prepare	Eze 35:6	5002
s the Lord GOD, I will even do	Eze 35:11	5002
Thus *s* the Lord GOD	Eze 35:14	559
Thus *s* the Lord GOD	Eze 36:2	559
and say, Thus *s* the Lord GOD	Eze 36:3	559
Thus *s* the Lord GOD to the	Eze 36:4	559
Therefore thus *s* the Lord GOD	Eze 36:5	559
the valleys, Thus *s* the Lord GOD	Eze 36:6	559
Therefore thus *s* the Lord GOD	Eze 36:7	559
Thus *s* the Lord GOD	Eze 36:13	559
nations any more, *s* the Lord GOD	Eze 36:14	5002
to fall any more, *s* the Lord GOD	Eze 36:15	5002
of Israel, Thus *s* the Lord GOD	Eze 36:22	559
s the Lord GOD, when I shall be	Eze 36:23	5002
s the Lord GOD, be it known unto	Eze 36:32	5002
Thus *s* the Lord GOD	Eze 36:33	559
Thus *s* the Lord GOD	Eze 36:37	559
Thus *s* the Lord GOD unto these	Eze 37:5	559
to the wind, Thus *s* the Lord GOD	Eze 37:9	559
unto them, Thus *s* the Lord GOD	Eze 37:12	559
it, and performed it, *s* the LORD	Eze 37:14	5002
unto them, Thus *s* the Lord GOD	Eze 37:19	559
unto them, Thus *s* the Lord GOD	Eze 37:21	559
And say, Thus *s* the Lord GOD	Eze 38:3	559
Thus *s* the Lord GOD	Eze 38:10	559
say unto Gog, Thus *s* the Lord GOD	Eze 38:14	559
Thus *s* the Lord GOD	Eze 38:17	559
s the Lord GOD, that my fury	Eze 38:18	5002
all my mountains, *s* the Lord GOD	Eze 38:21	5002
Gog, and say, Thus *s* the Lord GOD	Eze 39:1	559
I have spoken it, *s* the Lord GOD	Eze 39:5	5002
and it is done, *s* the Lord GOD	Eze 39:8	5002
that robbed them, *s* the Lord GOD	Eze 39:10	5002
be glorified, *s* the Lord GOD	Eze 39:13	5002
son of man, thus *s* the Lord GOD	Eze 39:17	559
all men of war, *s* the Lord GOD	Eze 39:20	5002
Therefore thus *s* the Lord GOD	Eze 39:25	559
house of Israel, *s* the Lord GOD	Eze 39:29	5002
Son of man, thus *s* the Lord GOD	Eze 43:18	559
s the Lord GOD, a young bullock	Eze 43:19	5002
I will accept you, *s* the Lord GOD	Eze 43:27	5002
of Israel, Thus *s* the Lord GOD	Eze 44:6	559
Thus *s* the Lord GOD	Eze 44:9	559
s the Lord GOD, and they shall	Eze 44:12	5002
fat and the blood, *s* the Lord GOD	Eze 44:15	5002
his sin offering, *s* the Lord GOD	Eze 44:27	5002
Thus *s* the Lord GOD	Eze 45:9	559
from my people, *s* the Lord GOD	Eze 45:9	559
for them, *s* the Lord GOD	Eze 45:15	5002
Thus *s* the Lord GOD	Eze 45:18	559
Thus *s* the Lord GOD	Eze 46:1	559
Thus *s* the Lord GOD	Eze 46:16	559
Thus *s* the Lord GOD	Eze 47:13	559
his inheritance, *s* the Lord GOD	Eze 47:23	5002
their portions, *s* the Lord GOD	Eze 48:29	5002
lovers, and forgat me, *s* the LORD	Hos 2:13	5002
s the LORD, that thou shalt call	Hos 2:16	5002
s the LORD, I will hear the	Hos 2:21	5002
them in their houses, *s* the LORD	Hos 11:11	5002
s the LORD, turn ye even to me	Joel 2:12	5002
Thus *s* the LORD	Amos 1:3	559
captivity unto Kir, *s* the LORD	Amos 1:5	559
Thus *s* the LORD	Amos 1:6	559
shall perish, *s* the Lord GOD	Amos 1:8	559
Thus *s* the LORD	Amos 1:9	559
Thus *s* the LORD	Amos 1:11	559
Thus *s* the LORD	Amos 1:13	559
his princes together, *s* the LORD	Amos 1:15	559
Thus *s* the LORD	Amos 2:1	559
thereof with him, *s* the LORD	Amos 2:3	559
Thus *s* the LORD	Amos 2:4	559
Thus *s* the LORD	Amos 2:6	559
s the LORD	Amos 2:11	5002
naked in that day, *s* the LORD	Amos 2:16	5002
s the LORD, who store up violence	Amos 3:10	5002
Therefore thus *s* the Lord GOD	Amos 3:11	559
Thus *s* the LORD	Amos 3:12	559
s the Lord GOD, the God of hosts,	Amos 3:13	5001
shall have an end, *s* the LORD	Amos 3:15	5001
them into the palace, *s* the LORD	Amos 4:3	5001
of Israel, *s* the Lord GOD	Amos 4:5	5001
not returned unto me, *s* the LORD	Amos 4:6	5001
not returned unto me, *s* the LORD	Amos 4:8	5001
not returned unto me, *s* the LORD	Amos 4:9	5001
not returned unto me, *s* the LORD	Amos 4:10	5001
not returned unto me, *s* the LORD	Amos 4:11	5001
For thus *s* the Lord GOD	Amos 5:3	559
For thus *s* the LORD unto the	Amos 5:4	559
God of hosts, the Lord, *s* thus	Amos 5:16	559
pass through thee, *s* the LORD	Amos 5:17	559
s the LORD, whose name is The God	Amos 5:27	559
s the LORD the God of hosts, I	Amos 6:8	5002
s the LORD the God of hosts	Amos 6:14	5002
It shall not be, *s* the LORD	Amos 7:3	559
also shall not be, *s* the Lord GOD	Amos 7:6	559
For thus Amos *s*, Jeroboam shall	Amos 7:11	559
Therefore thus *s* the LORD	Amos 7:17	559
in that day, *s* the Lord GOD	Amos 8:3	5002
s the Lord GOD, that I will cause	Amos 8:9	5002
s the Lord GOD, that I will send	Amos 8:11	5002
s the LORD	Amos 9:7	5002
the house of Jacob, *s* the LORD	Amos 9:8	5002
s the LORD that doeth this	Amos 9:12	5002
s the LORD, that the plowman	Amos 9:13	5002
given them, *s* the LORD thy God	Amos 9:15	559
Thus *s* the Lord GOD concerning	Obad 1	559
that *s* in his heart, Who shall	Obad 3	559
I bring thee down, *s* the LORD	Obad 4	5002
s the LORD, even destroy the wise	Obad 8	5002
Therefore thus *s* the LORD	Mic 2:3	559
Thus *s* the LORD concerning the	Mic 3:5	559
s the LORD, will I assemble her	Mic 4:6	5002
s the LORD, that I will cut off	Mic 5:10	5002
Hear ye now what the LORD *s*	Mic 6:1	559
Thus *s* the LORD	Nah 1:12	559
s the LORD of hosts, and I will	Nah 2:13	5002
against thee, *s* the LORD of hosts	Nah 3:5	5002
Woe unto him that *s* to the wood	Hab 2:19	559
from off the land, *s* the LORD	Zeph 1:2	5002
man from off the land, *s* the LORD	Zeph 1:3	5002
s the LORD, that there shall be	Zeph 1:10	5002
s the LORD of hosts, the God of	Zeph 2:9	5002
s the LORD, until the day that I	Zeph 3:8	5002
before your eyes, *s* the LORD	Zeph 3:20	559
thus *s* the LORD of hosts	Hag 1:5	559
Thus *s* the LORD of hosts	Hag 1:7	559
I will be glorified, *s* the LORD	Hag 1:8	559
s the LORD of hosts	Hag 1:9	5002
saying, I am with you, *s* the LORD	Hag 1:13	5002
strong, O Zerubbabel, *s* the LORD	Hag 2:4	5002
of the land, *s* the LORD, and work	Hag 2:4	5002
am with you, *s* the LORD of hosts	Hag 2:4	5002
For thus *s* the LORD of hosts	Hag 2:6	559
with glory, *s* the LORD of hosts	Hag 2:7	559
gold is mine, *s* the LORD of hosts	Hag 2:8	5002
the former, *s* the LORD of hosts	Hag 2:9	5002
I give peace, *s* the LORD of hosts	Hag 2:9	559
Thus *s* the LORD of hosts	Hag 2:11	559
this nation before me, *s* the LORD	Hag 2:14	5002
ye turned not to me, *s* the LORD	Hag 2:17	5002
s the LORD of hosts, will I take	Hag 2:23	5002
s the LORD, and will make thee as	Hag 2:23	5002
chosen thee, *s* the LORD of hosts	Hag 2:23	5002
them, Thus *s* the LORD of hosts	Zec 1:3	559
s the LORD of hosts, and I will	Zec 1:3	5002
unto you, *s* the LORD of hosts	Zec 1:3	559
saying, Thus *s* the LORD of hosts	Zec 1:4	559
nor hearken unto me, *s* the LORD	Zec 1:4	5002
saying, Thus *s* the LORD of hosts	Zec 1:14	559
Therefore thus *s* the LORD	Zec 1:16	559
s the LORD of hosts, and a line	Zec 1:16	5002
saying, Thus *s* the LORD of hosts	Zec 1:17	559
s the LORD, will be unto her a	Zec 2:5	5002
the land of the north, *s* the LORD	Zec 2:6	5002
winds of the heaven, *s* the LORD	Zec 2:6	5002
For thus *s* the LORD of hosts	Zec 2:8	559
in the midst of thee, *s* the LORD	Zec 2:10	5002
Thus *s* the LORD of hosts	Zec 3:7	559
s the LORD of hosts, and I will	Zec 3:9	5002
s the LORD of hosts, shall ye	Zec 3:10	5002
by my spirit, *s* the LORD of hosts	Zec 4:6	559
s the LORD of hosts, and it shall	Zec 5:4	5002
not hear, *s* the LORD of hosts	Zec 7:13	559
Thus *s* the LORD of hosts	Zec 8:2	559
Thus *s* the LORD	Zec 8:3	559
Thus *s* the LORD of hosts	Zec 8:4	559
Thus *s* the LORD of hosts	Zec 8:6	559
s the LORD of hosts	Zec 8:6	5002
Thus *s* the LORD of hosts	Zec 8:7	559
Thus *s* the LORD of hosts	Zec 8:9	559
former days, *s* the LORD of hosts	Zec 8:11	5002
For thus *s* the LORD of hosts	Zec 8:14	559
s the LORD of hosts, and I	Zec 8:14	559
things that I hate, *s* the LORD	Zec 8:17	5002
Thus *s* the LORD of hosts	Zec 8:19	559
Thus *s* the LORD of hosts	Zec 8:20	559
Thus *s* the LORD of hosts	Zec 8:23	559
and down in his name, *s* the LORD	Zec 10:12	5002
Thus *s* the LORD my God	Zec 11:4	559
of the land, *s* the LORD	Zec 11:6	5002
s the LORD, which stretcheth	Zec 12:1	5002
s the LORD, I will smite every	Zec 12:4	5002
s the LORD of hosts, that I will	Zec 13:2	5002
is my fellow, *s* the LORD of hosts	Zec 13:7	5002
s the LORD, two parts therein	Zec 13:8	5002
I have loved you, *s* the LORD	Mal 1:2	5002
s the LORD	Mal 1:2	559
Whereas Edom *s*, We are	Mal 1:4	559
thus *s* the LORD of hosts, They	Mal 1:4	559
s the LORD of hosts unto you, O	Mal 1:6	559
s the LORD of hosts	Mal 1:8	559
s the LORD of hosts	Mal 1:9	559
s the LORD of hosts, neither will	Mal 1:10	559
the heathen, *s* the LORD of hosts	Mal 1:11	559
at it, *s* the LORD of hosts	Mal 1:13	559
s the LORD	Mal 1:13	559
s the LORD of hosts, and my name	Mal 1:14	559
s the LORD of hosts, I will even	Mal 2:2	559
be with Levi, *s* the LORD of hosts	Mal 2:4	559
of Levi, *s* the LORD of hosts	Mal 2:8	559
s that he hateth putting away	Mal 2:16	559
his garment, *s* the LORD of hosts	Mal 2:16	559
shall come, *s* the LORD of hosts	Mal 3:1	559
fear not me, *s* the LORD of hosts	Mal 3:5	559
unto you, *s* the LORD of hosts	Mal 3:7	559
s the LORD of hosts, if I will	Mal 3:10	559
in the field, *s* the LORD of hosts	Mal 3:11	559
land, *s* the LORD of hosts	Mal 3:12	559
been stout against me, *s* the LORD	Mal 3:13	559
s the LORD of hosts, in that day	Mal 3:17	559
s the LORD of hosts, that it	Mal 4:1	559
do this, *s* the LORD of hosts	Mal 4:3	559
s unto him, If thou be the Son of	Mt 4:6	*3004*
s unto him, All these things will	Mt 4:9	*3004*
Then *s* Jesus unto him, Get thee	Mt 4:10	*3004*
he *s* unto them, Follow me, and I	Mt 4:19	*3004*
Not every one that *s* unto me	Mt 7:21	*3004*
Jesus *s* unto him, See thou tell	Mt 8:4	*3004*
Jesus *s* unto him, I will come and	Mt 8:7	*3004*
Jesus *s* unto him, The foxes have	Mt 8:20	*3004*
he *s* unto them, Why are ye	Mt 8:26	*3004*
(then *s* he to the sick of the	Mt 9:6	*3004*
and he *s* unto him, Follow me	Mt 9:9	*3004*
Jesus *s* unto them, Believe ye	Mt 9:28	*3004*
Then *s* he unto his disciples, The	Mt 9:37	*3004*
Then *s* he to the man, Stretch	Mt 12:13	*3004*
Then he *s*, I will return into my	Mt 12:44	*3004*
the prophecy of Esaias, which *s*	Mt 13:14	*3004*
Jesus *s* unto them, Have ye	Mt 13:51	*3004*
Jesus *s* unto them, How many	Mt 15:34	*3004*
He *s* unto them, But whom say ye	Mt 16:15	*3004*
He *s*, Yes	Mt 17:25	*3004*
Peter *s* unto him, Of strangers	Mt 17:26	*3004*
Jesus *s* unto him, Then are the	Mt 17:26	*5346*
Jesus *s* unto him, I say not unto	Mt 18:22	*3004*
He *s* unto them, Moses because of	Mt 19:8	*3004*
He *s* unto him, Which	Mt 19:18	*3004*
The young man *s* unto him, All	Mt 19:20	*3004*
s unto them, Why stand ye here	Mt 20:6	*3004*
He *s* unto them, Go ye also into	Mt 20:7	*3004*
the vineyard *s* unto his steward	Mt 20:8	*3004*
She *s* unto him, Grant that these	Mt 20:21	*3004*
he *s* unto them, Ye shall drink	Mt 20:23	*3004*
And Jesus *s* unto them, Yea	Mt 21:16	*3004*
Jesus *s* unto them, Verily I say	Mt 21:31	*3004*
Jesus *s* unto them, Did ye never	Mt 21:42	*3004*
Then *s* he to his servants, The	Mt 22:8	*3004*
he *s* unto him, Friend, how camest	Mt 22:12	*3004*
he *s* unto them, Whose is this	Mt 22:20	*3004*
Then *s* he unto them, Render	Mt 22:21	*3004*
He *s* unto them, How then doth	Mt 22:43	*3004*
and say unto him, The Master *s*	Mt 26:18	*3004*
Then *s* Jesus unto them, All ye	Mt 26:31	*3004*
s unto the disciples, Sit ye here	Mt 26:36	*3004*
Then *s* he unto them, My soul is	Mt 26:38	*3004*
s unto Peter, What, could ye not	Mt 26:40	*3004*
s unto them, Sleep on now, and	Mt 26:45	*3004*
Jesus *s* unto him, Thou hast said	Mt 20.04	*3004*
Pilate *s* unto them, What shall I	Mt 27:22	*3004*
him, and *s* unto him, I will	Mk 1:41	*3004*
s unto him, See thou say nothing	Mk 1:44	*3004*
(he *s* to the sick of the palsy,)	Mk 2:10	*3004*
he *s* unto them, They that are	Mk 2:17	*3004*
he *s* unto the man which had the	Mk 3:3	*3004*
he *s* unto them, Is it lawful to	Mk 3:4	*3004*
he *s* unto the man, Stretch forth	Mk 3:5	*3004*
he *s* unto them, Let us pass over	Mk 4:35	*3004*
but *s* unto him, Go home to thy	Mk 5:19	*3004*
he *s* unto the ruler of the	Mk 5:36	*3004*
he *s* unto them, Why make ye this	Mk 5:39	*3004*
He *s* unto them, How many loaves	Mk 6:38	*3004*
s unto them, Be of good cheer	Mk 6:50	*3004*
he *s* unto them, Are ye so without	Mk 7:18	*3004*
s unto him, Ephphatha, that is,	Mk 7:34	*3004*
unto him, and *s* unto them,	Mk 8:1	*3004*
sighed deeply in his spirit, and *s*	Mk 8:12	*3004*
he *s* unto them, Why reason ye,	Mk 8:17	*3004*
he *s* unto them, But whom say ye	Mk 8:29	*3004*
s unto him, Thou art the Christ	Mk 8:29	*3004*
He answereth him, and *s*, O	Mk 9:19	*3004*
s unto them, If any man desire to	Mk 9:35	*3004*

he *s* unto them, Whosoever shall Mk 10:11 *3004*
s unto his disciples, How hardly Mk 10:23 *3004*
s unto them, Children, how hard Mk 10:24 *3004*
And Jesus looking upon them *s* Mk 10:27 *3004*
s unto them, Ye know that they Mk 10:42 *3004*
s unto them, Go your way into the Mk 11:2 *3004*
calling to remembrance *s* unto him Mk 11:21 *3004*
And Jesus answering *s* unto them Mk 11:22 *3004*
which he *s* shall come to pass Mk 11:23 *3004*
he shall have whatsoever he *s* Mk 11:23 *3004*
And Jesus answering *s* unto them Mk 11:33 *3004*
he *s* unto them, Whose is this Mk 12:16 *3004*
s unto them, Verily I say unto Mk 12:43 *3004*
one of his disciples *s* unto him Mk 13:1 *3004*
s unto them, Go ye into the city, Mk 14:13 *3004*
of the house, The Master *s* Mk 14:14 *3004*
Jesus *s* unto them, All ye shall Mk 14:27 *3004*
Jesus *s* unto him, Verily I say Mk 14:30 *3004*
he *s* to his disciples, Sit ye Mk 14:32 *3004*
s unto them, My soul is exceeding Mk 14:34 *3004*
s unto Peter, Simon, sleepest Mk 14:37 *3004*
s unto them, Sleep on now, and Mk 14:41 *3004*
he goeth straightway to him, and *s* Mk 14:45 *3004*
priest rent his clothes, and *s* Mk 14:63 *3004*
scripture was fulfilled, which *s* Mk 15:28 *3004*
he *s* unto them, Be not affrighted Mk 16:6 *3004*
s unto them, He that hath two Lk 3:11 *3004*
for he *s*, The old is better Lk 5:39 *3004*
And he *s*, Master, say on Lk 7:40 *5346*
and finding none, he *s*, I will Lk 11:24 *3004*
Abraham *s* unto him, They have Lk 16:29 *3004*
Hear what the unjust judge *s* Lk 18:6 *3004*
he *s* unto him, Out of thine own Lk 19:22 *3004*
David himself *s* in the book of Lk 20:42 *3004*
the house, The Master *s* unto thee Lk 22:11 *3004*
s unto them, Peace be unto you Lk 24:36 *3004*
And he *s*, I am not Jn 1:21 *3004*
seeth Jesus coming unto him, and *s* Jn 1:29 *3004*
upon Jesus as he walked, he *s* Jn 1:36 *3004*
s unto them, What seek ye Jn 1:38 *3004*
He *s* unto them, Come and see Jn 1:39 *3004*
s unto him, We have found the Jn 1:41 *3004*
Philip, and *s* unto him, Follow me Jn 1:43 *3004*
s unto him, We have found him, of Jn 1:45 *3004*
Philip *s* unto him, Come and see Jn 1:46 *3004*
s of him, Behold an Israelite Jn 1:47 *3004*
Nathanael *s* unto him, Whence Jn 1:48 *3004*
s unto him, Rabbi, thou art the Jn 1:49 *3004*
he *s* unto him, Verily, verily, I Jn 1:51 *3004*
the mother of Jesus *s* unto him Jn 2:3 *3004*
Jesus *s* unto her, Woman, what Jn 2:4 *3004*
His mother *s* unto the servants, Jn 2:5 *3004*
Whatsoever he *s* unto you Jn 2:5 *3004*
Jesus *s* unto them, Fill the Jn 2:7 *3004*
he *s* unto them, Draw out now, and Jn 2:8 *3004*
s unto him, Every man at the Jn 2:10 *3004*
Nicodemus *s* unto him, How can a Jn 3:4 *3004*
Jesus *s* unto her, Give me to Jn 4:7 *3004*
Then *s* the woman of Samaria unto Jn 4:9 *3004*
God, and who it is that *s* to thee Jn 4:10 *3004*
The woman *s* unto him, Sir, thou Jn 4:11 *3004*
The woman *s* unto him, Sir, give Jn 4:15 *3004*
Jesus *s* unto her, Go, call thy Jn 4:16 *3004*
The woman *s* unto him, Sir, I Jn 4:19 *3004*
Jesus *s* unto her, Woman, believe Jn 4:21 *3004*
The woman *s* unto him, I know that Jn 4:25 *3004*
Jesus *s* unto her, I that speak Jn 4:26 *3004*
into the city, and *s* to the men, Jn 4:28 *3004*
Jesus *s* unto them, My meat is to Jn 4:34 *3004*
The nobleman *s* unto him, Sir, Jn 4:49 *3004*
Jesus *s* unto him, Go thy way Jn 4:50 *3004*
he *s* unto him, Wilt thou be made Jn 5:6 *3004*
Jesus *s* unto him, Rise, take up Jn 5:8 *3004*
he *s* unto Philip, Whence shall we Jn 6:5 *3004*
Peter's brother, *s* unto him, Jn 6:8 *3004*
But he *s* unto them, It is I Jn 6:20 *3004*
how is it then that he *s*, I came Jn 6:42 *3004*
Nicodemus *s* unto them, (he that Jn 7:50 *3004*
because he *s*, Whither I go, ye Jn 8:22 *3004*
Jesus *s* unto them, Even the same Jn 8:25 *3004*
Jesus *s* unto them, If ye were Jn 8:39 *3004*
Then after that *s* he to his Jn 11:7 *3004*
and after that he *s* unto them Jn 11:11 *3004*
Jesus *s* unto her, Thy brother Jn 11:23 *3004*
Martha *s* unto him, I know that he Jn 11:24 *3004*
She *s* unto him, Yea, Lord Jn 11:27 *3004*
s unto him, Lord, by this time he Jn 11:39 *3004*
Jesus *s* unto her, Said I not unto Jn 11:40 *3004*
Jesus *s* unto them, Loose him, and Jn 11:44 *3004*
Then *s* one of his disciples, Jn 12:4 *3004*
Peter *s* unto him, Lord, dost thou Jn 13:6 *3004*
Peter *s* unto him, Thou shalt Jn 13:8 *3004*
Simon Peter *s* unto him, Lord, not Jn 13:9 *3004*
Jesus *s* to him, He that is washed Jn 13:10 *3004*
lying on Jesus' breast *s* unto him Jn 13:25 *3004*
Thomas *s* unto him, Lord, we know Jn 14:5 *3004*
Jesus *s* unto him, I am the way, Jn 14:6 *3004*
Philip *s* unto him, Lord, shew us Jn 14:8 *3004*
Jesus *s* unto him, Have I been so Jn 14:9 *3004*
Judas *s* unto him, not Iscariot, Jn 14:22 *3004*
What is this that he *s* unto us Jn 16:17 *3004*
therefore, What is this that he *s* Jn 16:18 *3004*
we cannot tell what he *s* Jn 16:18 *2980*
Jesus *s* unto them, I am he Jn 18:5 *3004*
Then *s* the damsel that kept the Jn 18:17 *3004*
He *s*, I am not Jn 18:17 *3004*
whose ear Peter cut off, *s* Jn 18:26 *3004*
Pilate *s* unto him, What is truth Jn 18:38 *3004*
s unto them, I find in him no Jn 18:38 *3004*
s unto them, Behold, I bring him Jn 19:4 *3004*
Pilate *s* unto them, Behold the Jn 19:5 *3004*
Pilate *s* unto them, Take ye him, Jn 19:6 *3004*
s unto Jesus, Whence art thou Jn 19:9 *3004*
Then *s* Pilate unto him, Speakest Jn 19:10 *3004*
he *s* unto the Jews, Behold your Jn 19:14 *3004*
Pilate *s* unto them, Shall I Jn 19:15 *3004*
might be fulfilled, which *s* Jn 19:24 *3004*
he *s* unto his mother, Woman, Jn 19:26 *3004*
Then *s* he to the disciple, Behold Jn 19:27 *3004*
scripture might be fulfilled, *s* Jn 19:28 *3004*
and he knoweth that he *s* true Jn 19:35 *3004*
And again another scripture *s* Jn 19:37 *3004*
s unto them, They have taken away Jn 20:2 *3004*
She *s* unto them, Because they Jn 20:13 *3004*
Jesus *s* unto her, Woman, why Jn 20:15 *3004*
s unto him, Sir, if thou have Jn 20:15 *3004*
Jesus *s* unto her, Mary Jn 20:16 *3004*
herself, and *s* unto him, Rabboni Jn 20:16 *3004*
Jesus *s* unto her, Touch me not Jn 20:17 *3004*
s unto them, Peace be unto you Jn 20:19 *3004*
s unto them, Receive ye the Holy Jn 20:22 *3004*
Then *s* he to Thomas, Reach hither Jn 20:27 *3004*
Jesus *s* unto him, Thomas, because Jn 20:29 *3004*
Simon Peter *s* unto them, I go a Jn 21:3 *3004*
Then Jesus *s* unto them, Children, Jn 21:5 *3004*
whom Jesus loved *s* unto Peter Jn 21:7 *3004*
Jesus *s* unto them, Bring of the Jn 21:10 *3004*
Jesus *s* unto them, Come and dine Jn 21:12 *3004*
Jesus *s* to Simon Peter, Simon, Jn 21:15 *3004*
He *s* unto him, Yea, Lord Jn 21:15 *3004*
He *s* unto him, Feed my lambs Jn 21:15 *3004*
He *s* to him again the second time Jn 21:16 *3004*
He *s* unto him, Yea, Lord Jn 21:16 *3004*
He *s* unto him, Feed my sheep Jn 21:16 *3004*
He *s* unto him the third time, Jn 21:17 *3004*
Jesus *s* unto him, Feed my sheep Jn 21:17 *3004*
this, he *s* unto him, Follow me Jn 21:19 *3004*
Peter seeing him *s* to Jesus Jn 21:21 *3004*
Jesus *s* unto him, If I will that Jn 21:22 *3004*
s he, ye have heard of me Acts 1:4
s God, I will pour out of my Acts 2:17 *3004*
but he *s* himself, The Lord said Acts 2:34 *3004*
as *s* the prophet, Acts 7:48 *3004*
s the Lord Acts 7:49 *3004*
he *s* unto him, Cast thy garment Acts 12:8 *3004*
Wherefore he *s* also in another Acts 13:35 *3004*
s the Lord, who doeth all these Acts 15:17 *3004*
Thus *s* the Holy Ghost, So shall Acts 21:11 *3004*
and he *s*,) Acts 22:2 *5346*
that what things soever the law *s* Rom 3:19 *3004*
it *s* to them who are under the Rom 3:19 *2980*
For what *s* the scripture Rom 4:3 *3004*
For he *s* to Moses, I will have Rom 9:15 *3004*
For the scripture *s* unto Pharaoh Rom 9:17 *3004*
As he *s* also in Osee, I will call Rom 9:25 *3004*
But what *s* it Rom 10:8 *3004*
For the scripture *s*, Whosoever Rom 10:11 *3004*
For Esaias *s*, Lord, who hath Rom 10:16 *3004*
First Moses *s*, I will provoke you Rom 10:19 *3004*
But Esaias is very bold, and *s* Rom 10:20 *3004*
But to Israel he *s*, All day long Rom 10:21 *3004*
not what the scripture *s* of Elias Rom 11:2 *3004*
But what *s* the answer of God unto Rom 11:4 *3004*
And David *s*, Let their table be Rom 11:9 *3004*
I will repay, *s* the Lord Rom 12:19 *3004*
s the Lord, every knee shall bow Rom 14:11 *3004*
And again he *s*, Rejoice, ye Rom 15:10 *3004*
And again, Esaias *s*, There shall Rom 15:12 *3004*
I say, that every one of you *s* 1Cor 1:12 *3004*
For while one *s*, I am of Paul 1Cor 3:4 *3004*
for two, *s* he, shall be one flesh 1Cor 6:16 *5346*
or *s* not the law the same also 1Cor 9:8 *3004*
Or *s* he it altogether for our 1Cor 9:10 *3004*
will they not hear me, *s* the Lord 1Cor 14:21 *3004*
obedience, as also *s* the law 1Cor 14:34 *3004*
But when he *s* all things are put 1Cor 15:27 *2036*
(For he *s*, I have heard thee in a 2Cor 6:2 *3004*
s the Lord, and touch not the 2Cor 6:17 *3004*
and daughters, *s* the Lord Almighty 2Cor 6:18 *3004*
He *s* not, And to seeds, as of many Gal 3:16 *3004*
Nevertheless what *s* the scripture Gal 4:30 *3004*
Wherefore he *s*, When he ascended Eph 4:8 *3004*
Wherefore he *s*, Awake thou that Eph 5:14 *3004*
For the scripture *s*, Thou shalt 1Ti 5:18 *3004*
into the world, he *s*, And let all Heb 1:6 *3004*
And of the angels he *s*, Who maketh Heb 1:7 *3004*
But unto the Son he *s*, Thy throne Heb 1:8
Wherefore (as the Holy Ghost *s* Heb 3:7 *3004*
As he *s* also in another place, Heb 5:6 *3004*
s he, that thou make all things Heb 8:5 *5346*
For finding fault with them, he *s* Heb 8:8 *3004*
s the Lord, when I will make a Heb 8:8 *3004*
I regarded them not, *s* the Lord Heb 8:9 *3004*
after those days, *s* the Lord Heb 8:10 *3004*
In that he *s*, A new covenant, he Heb 8:13 *3004*
he cometh into the world, he *s* Heb 10:5 *3004*
s the Lord, I will put my laws Heb 10:16 *3004*
me, I will recompense, *s* the Lord Heb 10:30 *3004*
scripture was fulfilled which *s* Jas 2:23 *3004*
that the scripture *s* in vain Jas 4:5 *3004*
Wherefore he *s*, God resisteth the Jas 4:6 *3004*
He that *s*, I know him, and keepeth 1Jn 2:4 *3004*
He that *s* he abideth in him ought 1Jn 2:6 *3004*
He that *s* he is in the light, and 1Jn 2:9 *3004*
s the Lord, which is, and which Rev 1:8 *3004*
These things *s* he that holdeth Rev 2:1 *3004*
the Spirit *s* unto the churches Rev 2:7 *3004*
These things *s* the first and the Rev 2:8 *3004*
the Spirit *s* unto the churches Rev 2:11 *3004*
These things *s* he which hath the Rev 2:12 *3004*
the Spirit *s* unto the churches Rev 2:17 *3004*
These things *s* the Son of God, Rev 2:18 *3004*
the Spirit *s* unto the churches Rev 2:29 *3004*
These things *s* he that hath the Rev 3:1 *3004*
the Spirit *s* unto the churches Rev 3:6 *3004*
These things *s* he that is holy, Rev 3:7 *3004*
the Spirit *s* unto the churches Rev 3:13 *3004*
These things *s* the Amen, the Rev 3:14 *3004*
the Spirit *s* unto the churches Rev 3:22 *3004*
And one of the elders *s* unto me Rev 5:5 *3004*
s the Spirit, that they may rest Rev 14:13 *3004*
he *s* unto me, The waters which Rev 17:15 *3004*
for she *s* in her heart, I sit a Rev 18:7 *3004*
he *s* unto me, Write, Blessed are Rev 19:9 *3004*
he *s* unto me, These are the true Rev 19:9 *3004*
Then *s* he unto me, See thou do it Rev 22:9 *3004*
he *s* unto me, Seal not the Rev 22:10 *3004*
which testifieth these things *s* Rev 22:20 *3004*

SAKE {146}
cursed is the ground for thy *s* Gen 3:17 5668
the ground any more for man's *s* Gen 8:21 5668
it may be well with me for thy *s* Gen 12:13 5668
he entreated Abram well for her *s* Gen 12:16 5668
I will not do it for forty's *s* Gen 18:29 5668
not destroy it for twenty's *s* Gen 18:31 5668
I will not destroy it for ten's *s* Gen 18:32 5668
they will slay me for my wife's *s* Gen 20:11 1697
seed for my servant Abraham's *s* Gen 26:24 5668
LORD hath blessed me for thy *s* Gen 30:27 1558
Egyptian's house for Joseph's *s* Gen 39:5 1558
to the Egyptians for Israel's *s* Ex 18:8 182
let him go free for his eye's *s* Ex 21:26 8478
let him go free for his tooth's *s* Ex 21:27 8478
unto him, Enviest thou for my *s* Num 11:29
was zealous for my *s* among them Num 25:11 7068
day of the plague for Peor's *s* Num 25:18 1697
his people for his great name's *s* 1Sa 12:22 5668
to destroy the city for my *s* 1Sa 23:10 5668
kingdom for his people Israel's *s* 2Sa 5:12 5668
For thy word's *s*, and according to 2Sa 7:21 5668
him kindness for Jonathan's *s* 2Sa 9:1 5668
for Jonathan thy father's *s* 2Sa 9:7 5668
for my *s* with the young man 2Sa 18:5
of a far country for thy name's *s* 1Kin 8:41 4616
do it for David thy father's *s* 1Kin 11:12 4616
thy son for David my servant's *s* 1Kin 11:13 4616
for Jerusalem's *s* which I have 1Kin 11:13 4616
tribe for my servant David's *s* 1Kin 11:32 4616
and for Jerusalem's *s* 1Kin 11:32 4616
his life for David my servant's *s* 1Kin 11:34 4616
Nevertheless for David's *s* did 1Kin 15:4 4616
Judah for David his servant's *s* 2Kin 8:19 4616
city, to save it, for mine own *s* 2Kin 19:34 4616
s, and for my servant David's *s* 2Kin 19:34 4616
defend this city for mine own *s* 2Kin 20:6 4616
and for my servant David's *s* 2Kin 20:6 4616
O LORD, for thy servant's *s* 1Chr 17:19 4616
country for thy great name's *s* 2Chr 6:32 4616
for thy great mercies' *s* thou Neh 9:31
the children's *s* of mine own body Job 19:17
oh save me for thy mercies' *s* Ps 6:4 4616
of righteousness for his name's *s* Ps 23:3 4616
thou me for thy goodness' *s* Ps 25:7 4616
For thy name's *s*, O LORD, pardon Ps 25:11 4616
for thy name's *s* lead me, and Ps 31:3 4616
save me for thy mercies' *s* Ps 31:16
for thy *s* are we killed all the Ps 44:22
and redeem us for thy mercies' *s* Ps 44:26 4616
GOD of hosts, be ashamed for my *s* Ps 69:6
seek thee be confounded for my *s* Ps 69:6
Because for thy *s* I have borne Ps 69:7 4616
away our sins, for thy name's *s* Ps 79:9 4616
he saved them for his name's *s* Ps 106:8 4616
O GOD the Lord, for thy name's *s* Ps 109:21 4616
thy mercy, and for thy truth's *s* Ps 115:1
For thy servant David's *s* turn Ps 132:10 5668
me, O LORD, for thy name's *s* Ps 143:11
for thy righteousness' *s* bring my Ps 143:11
city to save it for mine own *s* Is 37:35
and for my servant David's *s* Is 37:35 4616
pleased for his righteousness' *s* Is 42:21 4616
For your *s* I have sent to Babylon Is 43:14 4616
thy transgressions for mine own *s* Is 43:25 4616
For Jacob my servant's *s*, and Is 45:4 4616
For my name's *s* will I defer mine Is 48:9 4616
own *s*, even for mine own *s* Is 48:11 4616
against thee shall fall for thy *s* Is 54:15 4616
For Zion's *s* will I not hold my Is 62:1 4616
for Jerusalem's *s* I will not rest Is 62:1 4616
Return for thy servants' *s* Is 63:17 4616
that cast you out for my name's *s* Is 66:5 4616
us, do thou it for thy name's *s* Jer 14:7 4616
Do not abhor us, for thy name's *s* Jer 14:21 4616
know that for thy *s* I have Jer 15:15
But I wrought for my name's *s* Eze 20:9 4616
But I wrought for my name's *s* Eze 20:14 4616
hand, and wrought for my name's *s* Eze 20:22 4616
wrought with you for my name's *s* Eze 20:44 4616
but for mine holy name's *s* Eze 36:22
is desolate, for the Lord's *s* Dan 9:17 4616
defer not, for thine own *s* Dan 9:19 4616
for I know that for my *s* this Jonah 1:12 7945
for your *s* be plowed as a field Mic 3:12 1558

persecuted for righteousness' *s*... Mt 5:10 *1752*
against you falsely, for my *s*... Mt 5:11 *1752*
governors and kings for my *s*... Mt 10:18 *1752*
hated of all men for my name's *s*... Mt 10:22
his life for my *s* shall find it,... Mt 10:39 *1752*
put him in prison for Herodias' *s*... Mt 14:3
nevertheless for the oath's *s*... Mt 14:9
his life for my *s* shall find it,... Mt 16:25 *1752*
for the kingdom of heaven's *s*,... Mt 19:12
or lands, for my name's *s*,... Mt 19:29 *1752*
of all nations for my name's *s*... Mt 24:9
but for the elect's *s* those days... Mt 24:22
ariseth for the word's *s*,... Mk 4:17
him in prison for Herodias' *s*... Mk 6:17
yet for his oath's *s*, and for... Mk 6:26
shall lose his life for my *s*,... Mk 8:35 *1752*
or children, or lands, for my *s*,... Mk 10:29 *1752*
before rulers and kings for my *s*... Mk 13:9 *1752*
hated of all men for my name's *s*... Mk 13:13
but for the elect's *s*, whom he... Mk 13:20
as evil, for the Son of man's *s*... Lk 6:22 *1752*
will lose his life for my *s*,... Lk 9:24 *1752*
for the kingdom of God's *s*,... Lk 18:29 *1752*
kings and rulers for my name's *s*,... Lk 21:12 *1752*
hated of all men for my name's *s*... Lk 21:17
they came not for Jesus' *s* only... Jn 12:9
I will lay down my life for thy *s*... Jn 13:37
thou lay down thy life for my *s*... Jn 13:38
believe me for the very works' *s*... Jn 14:11
they do unto you for my name's *s*,... Jn 15:21
he must suffer for my name's *s*... Acts 9:16
For which hope's *s*, king Agrippa,... Acts 26:7
was not written for his *s* alone... Rom 4:23
For thy *s* we are killed all the... Rom 8:36 *1752*
wrath, but also for conscience *s*... Rom 13:5
for the Lord Jesus Christ's *s*... Rom 15:30
We are fools for Christ's *s*... 1Cor 4:10
And this I do for the gospel's *s*,... 1Cor 9:23
no question for conscience *s*... 1Cor 10:25
no question for conscience *s*... 1Cor 10:27
eat not for his *s* that shewed it... 1Cor 10:28
shewed it, and for conscience *s*... 1Cor 10:28
your servants for Jesus' *s*... 2Cor 4:5
delivered unto death for Jesus' *s*... 2Cor 4:11
in distresses for Christ's *s*... 2Cor 12:10
for Christ's *s* hath forgiven you... Eph 4:32 *1722*
him, but also to suffer for his *s*... Phil 1:29
in my flesh for his body's *s*... Col 1:24
For which things' *s* the wrath of... Col 3:6
men we were among you for your *s*... 1Th 1:5
highly in love for their work's *s*... 1Th 5:13
a little wine for thy stomach's *s*... 1Ti 5:23
ought not, for filthy lucre's *s*... Titus 1:11
Yet for love's *s* I rather beseech... Philem 9
ordinance of man for the Lord's *s*... 1Pet 2:13
if ye suffer for righteousness' *s*... 1Pet 3:14
are forgiven you for his name's *s*... 1Jn 2:12
For the truth's *s*, which dwelleth... 2Jn 2
for his name's *s* they went forth... 3Jn 7
and for my name's *s* hast laboured... Rev 2:3

SAKES {31}
spare all the place for their *s*... Gen 18:26 5668
But I will for their *s* remember... Lev 26:45
LORD was angry with me for your *s*... Deut 1:37 1558
LORD was wroth with me for your *s*... Deut 3:26 6616
LORD was angry with me for your *s*... Deut 4:21 1697
Be favourable unto them for our *s*... Judg 21:22
s that the hand of the LORD is... Ruth 1:13
he reproved kings for their *s*... 1Chr 16:21 5921
for their *s* therefore return thou... Ps 7:7 5921
he reproved kings for their *s*... Ps 105:14 5921
went ill with Moses for their *s*... Ps 106:32 6616
For my brethren and companions' *s*... Ps 122:8 6616
so will I do for my servants' *s*... Is 65:8 6616
I do not this for your *s*, O house... Eze 36:22 6616
Not for your *s* do I this, saith... Eze 36:32 6616
but for their *s* that shall make... Dan 2:30 1701
rebuke the devourer for your *s*... Mal 3:11
for their *s* which sat with him,... Mk 6:26
I am glad for your *s* that I was... Jn 11:15
not because of me, but for your *s*... Jn 12:30
for their *s* I sanctify myself,... Jn 17:19
they are enemies for your *s*... Rom 11:28
are beloved for the fathers' *s*... Rom 11:28
myself and to Apollos for your *s*... 1Cor 4:6
saith he it altogether for our *s*... 1Cor 9:10
For our *s*, no doubt, this is... 1Cor 9:10
for your *s* forgave I it in the... 2Cor 2:10
For all things are for your *s*... 2Cor 4:15
yet for your *s* he became poor,... 2Cor 8:9
we joy for your *s* before our God... 1Th 3:9
all things for the elect's *s*... 2Ti 2:10

SAKIA See SHACHIA.

SALA *(sa'-lah)* {1} See SALAH. *Father of Heber; an ancestor of Jesus.*
of Heber, which was the son of *S*... Lk 3:35 *4527*

SALAH *(sa'-lah)* {6} See SALA. *Son of Arphaxad.*
And Arphaxad begat *S*... Gen 10:24 7974
and *S* begat Eber... Gen 10:24 7974
five and thirty years, and begat *S*... Gen 11:12 7974
after he begat *S* four hundred... Gen 11:13 7974
S lived thirty years, and begat... Gen 11:14 7974
S lived after he begat Eber four... Gen 11:15 7974

SALAMIS *(sal'-a-mis)* {1} *A city on Cyprus.*
And when they were at *S*, they... Acts 13:5 *4529*

SALATHIEL *(sa-la'-the-el)* {4} See SHEALTIEL. *Descendant of Jehoiakim; an ancestor of Jesus.*
Assir, *S* his son,... 1Chr 3:17 7597
to Babylon, Jechonias begat *S*... Mt 1:12 *4528*
and *S* begat Zorobabel... Mt 1:12 *4528*
Zorobabel, which was the son of *S*... Lk 3:27 *4528*

SALCAH *(sal'-kah)* {2} See SALCHAH. *A city in Gad.*
reigned in mount Hermon, and in *S*... Josh 12:5 5548
Hermon, and all Bashan unto *S*... Josh 13:11 5548

SALCHAH *(sal'-kah)* {2} See SALCAH. *Same as Salcah.*
all Gilead, and all Bashan, unto *S*... Deut 3:10 5548
in the land of Bashan unto *S*... 1Chr 5:11 5548

SALE {3}
count the years of the *s* thereof... Lev 25:27 4465
the price of his *s* shall be... Lev 25:50 4465
cometh of the *s* of his patrimony... Deut 18:8 4465

SALECAH See SALCHAH.

SALEM *(sa'-lem)* {4} See JERUSALEM. *The city of Melchizedek.*
king of *S* brought forth bread... Gen 14:18 8004
In *S* also is his tabernacle, and... Ps 76:2 8004
For this Melchisedec, king of *S*... Heb 7:1 *4532*
and after that also King of *S*... Heb 7:2 *4532*

SALIM *(sa'-lim)* {1} *A city near Aenon.*
was baptizing in Aenon near to *S*... Jn 3:23 *4530*

SALLAI *(sal'-lahee)* {2} See SALLU.
1. An exile.
And after him Gabbai, *S*, nine... Neh 11:8 5543
2. A priest with Zerubbabel.
Of *S*, Kallai... Neh 12:20 5543

SALLU *(sal'-lu)* {3} See SALLAI. *A priest with Zerubbabel.*
S, Amok, Hilkiah, Jedaiah... Neh 12:7 5543
S the son of Meshullam, the son... 1Chr 9:7 5543
S the son of Meshullam, the son... Neh 11:7 5543

SALMA *(sal'-mah)* {5} See SALMON, ZALMA.
1. Father of Boaz.
And Nahshon begat *S*, and *S*... 1Chr 2:11 8007
2. A son of Caleb.
begat Salma, and *S* begat Boaz,... 1Chr 2:11 8007
S the father of Beth-lehem,... 1Chr 2:51 8007
The sons of *S*... 1Chr 2:54 8007

SALMI See SALMA.

SALMON *(sal'-mon)* {6} See SALMA.
1. Father of Boaz.
begat Nahshon, and Nahshon begat *S*... Ruth 4:20 8009
S begat Boaz, and Boaz begat Obed,... Ruth 4:21 8012
and Naasson begat *S*... Mt 1:4 *4533*
And *S* begat Booz of Rachab... Mt 1:5 *4533*
of Booz, which was the son of *S*... Lk 3:32 *4533*
2. A mountain near Shechem.
in it, it was white as snow in *S*... Ps 68:14 6756

SALMONE *(sal-mo'-ne)* {1} *A promontory on Crete.*
under Crete, over against *S*... Acts 27:7 *4534*

SALOME *(sa-lo'-me)* {2} *A female follower of Jesus.*
James the less and of Joses, and *S*... Mk 15:40 *4539*
and Mary the mother of James, and *S*... Mk 16:1 *4539*

SALT {41}
of Siddim, which is the *S* Sea... Gen 14:3 4417
him, and she became a pillar of *s*... Gen 19:26 4417
offering shalt thou season with *s*... Lev 2:13 4417
s of the covenant of thy God to... Lev 2:13 4417
offerings thou shalt offer *s*... Lev 2:13 4417
it is a covenant of *s* for ever... Num 18:19 4417
coast of the *s* sea eastward... Num 34:3 4417
out of it shall be at the *s* sea... Num 34:12 4417
sea of the plain, even the *s* sea... Deut 3:17 4417
land thereof is brimstone, and *s*... Deut 29:23 4417
sea of the plain, even the *s* sea... Josh 3:16 4417
even the *s* sea on the east, the... Josh 12:3 4417
was from the shore of the *s* sea... Josh 15:2 4417
And the east border was the *s* sea... Josh 15:5 4417
And Nibshan, and the city of *S*... Josh 15:62 5898
were at the north bay of the *s*... Josh 18:19 4417
down the city, and sowed it with *s*... Judg 9:45 4417
of the Syrians in the valley of *s*... 2Sa 8:13 4417
me a new cruse, and put *s* therein... 2Kin 2:20 4417
waters, and cast the *s* in there... 2Kin 2:21 4417
in the valley of *s* ten thousand... 2Kin 14:7 4417
the valley of *s* eighteen thousand... 1Chr 18:12 4417
and to his sons by a covenant of *s*... 2Chr 13:5 4417
and went to the valley of *s*... 2Chr 25:11 4417
of the God of heaven, wheat, *s*... Ezr 6:9 4416
s without prescribing how much... Ezr 7:22 4416
is unsavoury be eaten without *s*... Job 6:6 4417
the valley of *s* twelve thousand... Ps 60:*t* 4417
in the wilderness, in a *s* land... Jer 17:6 4420
priests shall cast *s* upon them... Eze 43:24 4417
they shall be given to *s*... Eze 47:11 4417
Ye are the *s* of the earth... Mt 5:13 *217*
but if the *s* have lost his savour... Mt 5:13 *217*
sacrifice shall be salted with *s*... Mk 9:49 *251*
S is good... Mk 9:50 *217*
but if the *s* have lost his... Mk 9:50 *217*
Have *s* in yourselves, and have... Mk 9:50 *217*
S is good... Lk 14:34 *217*
but if the *s* have lost his savour... Lk 14:34 *217*
alway with grace, seasoned with *s*... Col 4:6 *217*
no fountain both yield *s* water... Jas 3:12 *252*

SALTED {4}
thou wast not *s* at all, nor... Eze 16:4 4414
savour, wherewith shall it be *s*... Mt 5:13 *233*
every one shall be *s* with fire... Mk 9:49 *233*
sacrifice shall be *s* with salt... Mk 9:49 *233*

SALTNESS {1}
but if the salt have lost his *s*... Mk 9:50 *1096,358*

SALTPITS {1}
the breeding of nettles, and *s*... Zeph 2:9 4417

SALU *(sa'-lu)* {1} *Father of Zimri.*
woman, was Zimri, the son of *S*... Num 25:14 5543

SALUTATION {6}
what manner of *s* this should be... Lk 1:29 *783*
Elisabeth heard the *s* of Mary... Lk 1:41 *783*
of thy *s* sounded in mine ears... Lk 1:44 *783*
The *s* of me Paul with mine own... 1Cor 16:21 *783*
The *s* by the hand of me Paul... Col 4:18 *783*
The *s* of Paul with mine own hand,... 2Th 3:17 *783*

SALUTATIONS {1}
love *s* in the marketplaces,... Mk 12:38 *783*

SALUTE {39}
And they will *s* thee, and give thee... 1Sa 10:4 7965
to meet him, that he might *s* him... 1Sa 13:10 1288
of the wilderness to *s* our master... 1Sa 25:14 1288
to *s* him, and to bless him,... 2Sa 8:10 7592,7965
if thou meet any man, *s* him not... 2Kin 4:29 1288
and if any *s* thee, answer him not... 2Kin 4:29 1288
we go down to *s* the children of... 2Kin 10:13 7965
if ye *s* your brethren only, what... Mt 5:47 *782*
when ye come into an house, *s* it... Mt 10:12 *782*
And began to *s* him, Hail, King of... Mk 15:18 *782*
and *s* no man by the way... Lk 10:4 *782*
came unto Caesarea to *s* Festus... Acts 25:13 *782*
S my wellbeloved Epaenetus, who... Rom 16:5 *782*
S Andronicus and Junia, my kinsmen... Rom 16:7 *782*
S Urbane, our helper in Christ,... Rom 16:9 *782*
S Apelles approved in Christ... Rom 16:10 *782*
S them which are of Aristobulus'... Rom 16:10 *782*
S Herodion my kinsman... Rom 16:11 *782*
S Tryphena and Tryphosa, who... Rom 16:12 *782*
S the beloved Persis, which... Rom 16:12 *782*
S Rufus chosen in the Lord, and... Rom 16:13 *782*
S Asyncritus, Phlegon, Hermas,... Rom 16:14 *782*
S Philologus, and Julia, Nereus,... Rom 16:15 *782*
S one another with an holy kiss... Rom 16:16 *782*
The churches of Christ *s* you... Rom 16:16 *782*
and Sosipater, my kinsmen, *s* you... Rom 16:21 *782*
this epistle, *s* you in the Lord... Rom 16:22 *782*
The churches of Asia *s* you... 1Cor 16:19 *782*
Priscilla *s* you much in the Lord,... 1Cor 16:19 *782*
All the saints *s* you... 2Cor 13:13 *782*
S every saint in Christ Jesus... Phil 4:21 *782*
All the saints *s* you, chiefly... Phil 4:22 *782*
S the brethren which are in... Col 4:15 *782*
S Prisca and Aquila, and the... 2Ti 4:19 *782*
All that are with me *s* thee... Titus 3:15 *782*
There *s* thee Epaphras, my... Philem 23 *782*
S all them that have the rule... Heb 13:24 *782*
They of Italy *s* you... Heb 13:24 *782*
Our friends *s* thee... 3Jn 14 *782*

SALUTED {9}
the house of Micah, and *s* him... Judg 18:15 7592,7965
and came and *s* his brethren... 1Sa 17:22 7592,7965
near to the people, he *s* them... 1Sa 30:21 7592,7965
he *s* him, and said to him, Is... 2Kin 10:15 1288
amazed, and running to him *s* him... Mk 9:15 *782*
of Zacharias, and *s* Elisabeth... Lk 1:40 *782*
s the church, he went down to... Acts 18:22 *782*
s the brethren, and abode with... Acts 21:7 *782*
And when he had *s* them, he... Acts 21:19 *782*

SALUTETH {5}
and of the whole church, *s* you... Rom 16:23 *782*
the chamberlain of the city *s* you... Rom 16:23 *782*
my fellowprisoner *s* you, and... Col 4:10 *782*
s you, always labouring fervently... Col 4:12 *782*
elected together with you, *s* you... 1Pet 5:13 *782*

SALVATION {164}
I have waited for thy *s*, O LORD... Gen 49:18 3444
see the *s* of the LORD, which he... Ex 14:13 3444
and song, and he is become my *s*... Ex 15:2 3444
esteemed the Rock of his *s*... Deut 32:15 3444
because I rejoice in thy *s*... 1Sa 2:1 3444
the LORD hath wrought *s* in Israel... 1Sa 11:13 8668
wrought this great *s* in Israel... 1Sa 14:45 3444
wrought a great *s* for all Israel... 1Sa 19:5 8668
is my shield, and the horn of my *s*... 2Sa 22:3 3468
also given me the shield of thy *s*... 2Sa 22:36 3468
be the God of the rock of my *s*... 2Sa 22:47 3468
He is the tower of *s* for his king... 2Sa 22:51 3444
for this is all my *s*, and all my... 2Sa 23:5 3468
shew forth from day to day his *s*... 1Chr 16:23 3444
say ye, Save us, O God of our *s*... 1Chr 16:35 3468
O LORD God, be clothed with *s*... 2Chr 6:41 8668
see the *s* of the LORD with you, O... 2Chr 20:17 3444
He also shall be my *s*... Job 13:16 3444
S belongeth unto the LORD... Ps 3:8 3444
I will rejoice in thy *s*... Ps 9:14 3444
my heart shall rejoice in thy *s*... Ps 13:5 3444
Oh that the *s* of Israel were come... Ps 14:7 3444
my buckler, and the horn of my *s*... Ps 18:2 3468
also given me the shield of thy *s*... Ps 18:35 3468
and let the God of my *s* be exalted... Ps 18:46 3468
We will rejoice in thy *s*, and in... Ps 20:5 3444
in thy *s* how greatly shall he... Ps 21:1 3444
His glory is great in thy *s*... Ps 21:5 3444
from the God of his *s*... Ps 24:5 3468
for thou art the God of my *s*... Ps 25:5 3468
The LORD is my light and my *s*... Ps 27:1 3468

S

neither forsake me, O God of my *s* ... Ps 27:9 3468
say unto my soul, I am thy *s* ... Ps 35:3 3444
it shall rejoice in his *s* ... Ps 35:9 3444
But the *s* of the righteous is of ... Ps 37:39 8668
haste to help me, O Lord my *s* ... Ps 38:22 8668
thy faithfulness and thy *s* ... Ps 40:10 8668
as love thy *s* say continually ... Ps 40:16 8668
aright will I shew the *s* of God ... Ps 50:23 3468
Restore unto me the joy of thy *s* ... Ps 51:12 3468
O God, thou God of my *s* ... Ps 51:14 8668
Oh that the *s* of Israel were come ... Ps 53:6 3444
from him cometh my *s* ... Ps 62:1 3444
He only is my rock and my *s* ... Ps 62:2 3444
He only is my rock and my *s* ... Ps 62:6 3444
In God is my *s* and my glory ... Ps 62:7 3468
thou answer us, O God of our *s* ... Ps 65:5 3468
benefits, even the God of our *s* ... Ps 68:19 3444
that is our God is the God of *s* ... Ps 68:20 4190
hear me, in the truth of thy *s* ... Ps 69:13 3468
let thy *s*, O God, set me up on ... Ps 69:29 3444
as love thy *s* say continually ... Ps 70:4 3444
and thy *s* all the day ... Ps 71:15 8668
working *s* in the midst of the ... Ps 74:12 3444
in God, and trusted not in his *s* ... Ps 78:22 3444
Help us, O God of our *s*, for the ... Ps 79:9 3468
Turn us, O God of our *s*, and cause ... Ps 85:4 3468
mercy, O LORD, and grant us thy *s* ... Ps 85:7 3468
Surely his *s* is nigh them that ... Ps 85:9 3468
O lord God of my *s*, I have cried ... Ps 88:1 3444
my God, and the rock of my *s* ... Ps 89:26 3444
I satisfy him, and shew him my *s* ... Ps 91:16 3444
joyful noise to the rock of our *s* ... Ps 95:1 3468
shew forth his *s* from day to day ... Ps 96:2 3444
The LORD hath made known his *s* ... Ps 98:2 3444
earth have seen the *s* of our God ... Ps 98:3 3444
O visit me with thy *s* ... Ps 106:4 3444
I will take the cup of *s*, and call ... Ps 116:13 3444
and song, and is become my *s* ... Ps 118:14 3444
s is in the tabernacles of the ... Ps 118:15 3444
hast heard me, and art become my *s* ... Ps 118:21 3444
also unto me, O LORD, even thy *s* ... Ps 119:41 8668
My soul fainteth for thy *s* ... Ps 119:81 8668
Mine eyes fail for thy *s*, and for ... Ps 119:123 3444
S is far from the wicked ... Ps 119:155 3444
LORD, I have hoped for thy *s* ... Ps 119:166 3444
I have longed for thy *s*, O LORD ... Ps 119:174 3444
also clothe her priests with *s* ... Ps 132:16 3468
the Lord, the strength of my *s* ... Ps 140:7 3444
It is he that giveth *s* unto kings ... Ps 144:10 8668
he will beautify the meek with *s* ... Ps 149:4 3444
Behold, God is my *s* ... Is 12:2 3444
he also is become my *s* ... Is 12:2 3444
draw water out of the wells of *s* ... Is 12:3 3444
hast forgotten the God of thy *s* ... Is 17:10 3468
will be glad and rejoice in his *s* ... Is 25:9 3444
s will God appoint for walls and ... Is 26:1 3444
our *s* also in the time of trouble ... Is 33:2 3444
of thy times, and strength of *s* ... Is 33:6 3444
open, and let them bring forth *s* ... Is 45:8 3468
in the LORD with an everlasting *s* ... Is 45:17 8668
far off, and my *s* shall not tarry ... Is 46:13 8668
I will place *s* in Zion for Israel ... Is 46:13 8668
that thou mayest be my *s* unto the ... Is 49:6 3444
in a day of *s* have I helped thee ... Is 49:8 3444
my *s* is gone forth, and mine arms ... Is 51:5 3468
but my *s* shall be for ever, and my ... Is 51:6 3444
ever, and my *s* from generation to ... Is 51:8 3444
of good, that publisheth *s* ... Is 52:7 3444
earth shall see the *s* of our God ... Is 52:10 3444
for my *s* is near to come, and my ... Is 56:1 3444
for *s*, but it is far off from us ... Is 59:11 3444
his arm brought *s* unto him ... Is 59:16 3467
an helmet of *s* upon his head ... Is 59:17 3444
but thou shalt call thy walls *S* ... Is 60:18 3444
clothed me with the garments of *s* ... Is 61:10 3468
the *s* thereof as a lamp that ... Is 62:1 3444
of Zion, Behold, thy *s* cometh ... Is 62:11 3468
mine own arm brought *s* unto me ... Is 63:5 3467
Truly in vain is *s* hoped for from ... Jer 3:23
LORD our God is the *s* of Israel ... Jer 3:23 8668
wait for the *s* of the LORD ... Lam 3:26 8668
S is of the LORD ... Jonah 2:9 3444
I will wait for the God of my *s* ... Mic 7:7 3468
thine horses and thy chariots of *s* ... Hab 3:8 3444
forth for the *s* of thy people ... Hab 3:13 3468
even for *s* with thine anointed ... Hab 3:13 3468
I will joy in the God of my *s* ... Hab 3:18 3468
he is just, and having *s* ... Zec 9:9 3467
hath raised up an horn of *s* for ... Lk 1:69 *4991*
To give knowledge of *s* unto his ... Lk 1:77 *4991*
For mine eyes have seen thy *s* ... Lk 2:30 *4992*
all flesh shall see the *s* of God ... Lk 3:6 *4992*
This day is *s* come to this house, ... Lk 19:9 *4991*
for *s* is of the Jews ... Jn 4:22 *4991*
Neither is there *s* in any other ... Acts 4:12 *4991*
to you is the word of this *s* sent ... Acts 13:26 *4991*
for *s* unto the ends of the earth ... Acts 13:47 *4991*
which shew unto us the way of *s* ... Acts 16:17 *4991*
that the *s* of God is sent unto ... Acts 28:28 *4992*
s to every one that believeth ... Rom 1:16 *4991*
mouth confession is made unto *s* ... Rom 10:10 *4991*
fall *s* is come unto the Gentiles ... Rom 11:11 *4991*
for now is our *s* nearer than when ... Rom 13:11 *4991*
it is for your consolation and *s* ... 2Cor 1:6 *4991*
it is for your consolation and *s* ... 2Cor 1:6 *4991*
in the day of *s* have I succoured ... 2Cor 6:2 *4991*
behold, now is the day of *s* ... 2Cor 6:2 *4991*
to *s* not to be repented of ... 2Cor 7:10 *4991*
of truth, the gospel of your *s* ... Eph 1:13 *4991*
And take the helmet of *s*, and the ... Eph 6:17 *4992*
turn to my *s* through your prayer ... Phil 1:19 *4991*
of perdition, but to you of *s* ... Phil 1:28 *4991*
work out your own *s* with fear ... Phil 2:12 *4991*
and for an helmet, the hope of *s* ... 1Th 5:8 *4991*
but to obtain *s* by our Lord Jesus ... 1Th 5:9 *4991*
the beginning chosen you to *s* ... 2Th 2:13 *4991*
s which is in Christ Jesus with ... 2Ti 2:10 *4991*
unto *s* through faith which is in ... 2Ti 3:15 *4991*
s hath appeared to all men ... Titus 2:11 *4992*
for them who shall be heirs of *s* ... Heb 1:14 *4991*
escape, if we neglect so great *s* ... Heb 2:3 *4991*
s perfect through sufferings ... Heb 2:10 *4991*
s unto all them that obey him ... Heb 5:9 *4991*
you, and things that accompany *s* ... Heb 6:9 *4991*
second time without sin unto *s* ... Heb 9:28 *4991*
s ready to be revealed in the ... 1Pet 1:5 *4991*
faith, even the *s* of your souls ... 1Pet 1:9 *4991*
Of which *s* the prophets have ... 1Pet 1:10 *4991*
longsuffering of our Lord is *s* ... 2Pet 3:15 *4991*
to write unto you of the common *s* ... Jude 3 *4991*
S to our God which sitteth upon ... Rev 7:10 *4991*
saying in heaven, Now is come *s* ... Rev 12:10 *4991*
S, and glory, and honour, and power, ... Rev 19:1 *4991*

SAMARIA *(sa-ma'-re-ah)* {124} See SAMARITAN.
1. A city in Ephraim.
he bought the hill *S* of Shemer ... 1Kin 16:24 8111
of Shemer, owner of the hill, *S* ... 1Kin 16:24 8111
his fathers, and was buried in *S* ... 1Kin 16:28 8111
reigned over Israel in *S* twenty ... 1Kin 16:29 8111
of Baal, which he had built in *S* ... 1Kin 16:32 8111
And there was a sore famine in *S* ... 1Kin 18:2 8111
and he went up and besieged *S* ... 1Kin 20:1 8111
if the dust of *S* shall suffice ... 1Kin 20:10 8111
There are men come out of *S* ... 1Kin 20:17 8111
Damascus, as my father made in *S* ... 1Kin 20:34 8111
heavy and displeased, and came to *S* ... 1Kin 20:43 8111
king of Israel, which is in *S* ... 1Kin 21:18 8111
in the entrance of the gate of *S* ... 1Kin 22:10 8111
king died, and was brought to *S* ... 1Kin 22:37 8111
and they buried the king in *S* ... 1Kin 22:37 8111
the chariot in the pool of *S* ... 1Kin 22:38 8111
in *S* the seventeenth year of ... 1Kin 22:51 8111
his upper chamber that was in *S* ... 2Kin 1:2 8111
and from thence he returned to *S* ... 2Kin 2:25 8111
in *S* the eighteenth year of ... 2Kin 3:1 8111
went out of *S* the same time ... 2Kin 3:6 8111
with the prophet that is in *S* ... 2Kin 5:3 8111
But he led them to *S* ... 2Kin 6:19 8111
pass, when they were come into *S* ... 2Kin 6:20 8111
they were in the midst of *S* ... 2Kin 6:20 8111
host, and went up, and besieged *S* ... 2Kin 6:24 8111
And there was a great famine in *S* ... 2Kin 6:25 8111
for a shekel, in the gate of *S* ... 2Kin 7:1 8111
about this time in the gate of *S* ... 2Kin 7:18 8111
And Ahab had seventy sons in *S* ... 2Kin 10:1 8111
Jehu wrote letters, and sent to *S* ... 2Kin 10:1 8111
arose and departed, and came to *S* ... 2Kin 10:12 8111
And when he came to *S*, he slew all ... 2Kin 10:17 8111
all that remained unto Ahab in *S* ... 2Kin 10:17 8111
and they buried him in *S* ... 2Kin 10:35 8111
over Israel in *S* was twenty ... 2Kin 10:36 8111
began to reign over Israel in *S* ... 2Kin 13:1 8111
remained the grove also in *S* ... 2Kin 13:6 8111
and they buried him in *S* ... 2Kin 13:9 8111
to reign over Israel in *S* ... 2Kin 13:10 8111
Joash was buried in *S* with the ... 2Kin 13:13 8111
and hostages, and returned to *S* ... 2Kin 14:14 8111
was buried in *S* with the kings of ... 2Kin 14:16 8111
of Israel began to reign in *S* ... 2Kin 14:23 8111
reign over Israel in *S* six months ... 2Kin 15:8 8111
and he reigned a full month in *S* ... 2Kin 15:13 8111
went up from Tirzah, and came to *S* ... 2Kin 15:14 8111
Shallum the son of Jabesh in *S* ... 2Kin 15:14 8111
Israel, and reigned ten years in *S* ... 2Kin 15:17 8111
began to reign over Israel in *S* ... 2Kin 15:23 8111
against him, and smote him in *S* ... 2Kin 15:25 8111
began to reign over Israel in *S* ... 2Kin 15:27 8111
reign in *S* over Israel nine years ... 2Kin 17:1 8111
all the land, and went up to *S* ... 2Kin 17:5 8111
Hoshea the king of Assyria took *S* ... 2Kin 17:6 8111
king of Assyria came up against *S* ... 2Kin 18:9 8111
king of Israel, *S* was taken ... 2Kin 18:10 8111
they delivered *S* out of mine hand ... 2Kin 18:34 8111
over Jerusalem the line of *S* ... 2Kin 21:13 8111
the entering in of the gate of *S* ... 2Chr 18:9 8111
caught him, (for he was hid in *S* ... 2Chr 22:9 8111
from *S* even unto Beth-horon, and ... 2Chr 25:13 8111
hostages also, and returned to *S* ... 2Chr 25:24 8111
them, and brought the spoil to *S* ... 2Chr 28:8 8111
before the host that came to *S* ... 2Chr 28:9 8111
then they returned to *S* ... 2Chr 28:15 8111
And the head of Ephraim is *S* ... Is 7:9 8111
the head of *S* is Remaliah's son ... Is 7:9 8111
the spoil of *S* shall be taken ... Is 8:4 8111
Ephraim and the inhabitant of *S* ... Is 9:9 8111
is not *S* as Damascus ... Is 10:9 8111
excel them of Jerusalem and of *S* ... Is 10:10 8111
I not, as I have done unto *S* ... Is 10:11 8111
And thine elder sister is *S* ... Eze 16:46 8111
Neither hath *S* committed half of ... Eze 16:51 8111
daughters, and the captivity of *S* ... Eze 16:53 8111
to their former estate, and *S* ... Eze 16:55 8111
S is Aholah, and Jerusalem ... Eze 23:4 8111
with the cup of thy sister *S* ... Eze 23:33 8111
S shall become desolate ... Hos 13:16 8111
dwell in *S* in the corner of a bed ... Amos 3:12 8111
Judah, which he saw concerning *S* ... Mic 1:1 8111
is it not *S* ... Mic 1:5 8111
Therefore I will make *S* as an ... Mic 1:6 8111
Philip went down to the city of *S* ... Acts 8:5 *4540*
and bewitched the people of *S* ... Acts 8:9 *4540*
S had received the word of God ... Acts 8:14 *4540*
2. Territory of the northern tribes.
which are in the cities of *S* ... 1Kin 13:32 8111
by the palace of Ahab king of *S* ... 1Kin 21:1 8111
the messengers of the king of *S* ... 2Kin 1:3 8111
of *S* instead of the children of ... 2Kin 17:24 8111
and they possessed *S*, and dwelt in ... 2Kin 17:24 8111
and placed in the cities of *S* ... 2Kin 17:26 8111
they had carried away from *S* came ... 2Kin 17:28 8111
of the prophet that came out of *S* ... 2Kin 23:18 8111
that were in the cities of *S* ... 2Kin 23:19 8111
years he went down to Ahab to *S* ... 2Chr 18:2 8111
over, and set in the cities of *S* ... Ezr 4:10 8115
their companions that dwell in *S* ... Ezr 4:17 8115
his brethren and the army of *S* ... Neh 4:2 8111
they delivered *S* out of my hand ... Is 36:19 8111
seen folly in the prophets of *S* ... Jer 23:13 8111
vines upon the mountains of *S* ... Jer 31:5 8111
Shechem, from Shiloh, and from *S* ... Jer 41:5 8111
and the wickedness of *S* ... Hos 7:1 8111
Thy calf, O *S*, hath cast thee off ... Hos 8:5 8111
but the calf of *S* shall be broken ... Hos 8:6 8111
The inhabitants of *S* shall fear ... Hos 10:5 8111
As for *S*, her king is cut off as ... Hos 10:7 8111
upon the mountains of *S*, and ... Amos 3:9 8111
that are in the mountain of *S* ... Amos 4:1 8111
and trust in the mountain of *S* ... Amos 6:1 8111
They that swear by the sin of *S* ... Amos 8:14 8111
of Ephraim, and the fields of *S* ... Obad 19 8111
3. District north of Judah.
he passed through the midst of *S* ... Lk 17:11 *4540*
And he must needs go through *S* ... Jn 4:4 *4540*
Then cometh he to a city of *S* ... Jn 4:5 *4540*
cometh a woman of *S* to draw water ... Jn 4:7 *4540*
saith the woman of *S* unto him ... Jn 4:9 *4540*
of me, which am a woman of *S* ... Jn 4:9 *4540*
and in all Judaea, and in *S* ... Acts 1:8 *4540*
the regions of Judaea and *S* ... Acts 8:1 *4540*
all Judaea and Galilee and *S* ... Acts 9:31 *4540*
they passed through Phenice and *S* ... Acts 15:3 *4540*

SAMARITAN *(sa-mar'-i-tun)* {3} See SAMARITANS. *An inhabitant of Samaria.*
But a certain *S*, as he journeyed, ... Lk 10:33 *4541*
and he was a *S* ... Lk 17:16 *4541*
Say we not well that thou art a *S* ... Jn 8:48 *4541*

SAMARITANS *(sa-mar'-i-tuns)* {7}
high places which the *S* had made ... 2Kin 17:29 8118
any city of the *S* enter ye not ... Mt 10:5 *4541*
entered into a village of the *S* ... Lk 9:52 *4541*
Jews have no dealings with the *S* ... Jn 4:9 *4541*
many of the *S* of that city ... Jn 4:39 *4541*
So when the *S* were come unto him, ... Jn 4:40 *4541*
gospel in many villages of the *S* ... Acts 8:25 *4541*

SAME {333}
the *s* is it that compasseth the ... Gen 2:13 1931
saying, This *s* shall comfort us ... Gen 5:29
the *s* became mighty men which ... Gen 6:4 1992
the *s* day were all the fountains ... Gen 7:11 2088
the *s* is a great city ... Gen 10:12 1931
the king of Bela (the *s* is Zoar ... Gen 14:8 1931
In the *s* day the LORD made a ... Gen 15:18 1931
the *s* is the father of the ... Gen 19:37 1931
the *s* is the father of the ... Gen 19:38 1931
the *s* day that Isaac was weaned ... Gen 21:8
the *s* is Hebron in the land of ... Gen 23:2 1931
the *s* is Hebron in the land of ... Gen 23:19 1931
let the *s* be she that thou hast ... Gen 24:14 1931
let the *s* be the woman whom the ... Gen 24:44 1931
thee, with that *s* red pottage ... Gen 25:30 2088
received in the *s* year an ... Gen 26:12 1931
appeared unto him the *s* night ... Gen 26:24 1931
And it came to pass the *s* day ... Gen 26:32 1931
And he lodged there that *s* night ... Gen 32:13 1931
every city, laid he up in the *s* ... Gen 41:48
he spake unto them these *s* words ... Gen 44:6
the *s* is Beth-lehem ... Gen 48:7 1931
Pharaoh commanded the *s* day the ... Ex 5:6 1931
the fourteenth day of the *s* month ... Ex 12:6 2088
the *s* day came they into the ... Ex 19:1 1931
and his flowers, shall be of the *s* ... Ex 25:31
knop under two branches of the *s* ... Ex 25:35
knop under two branches of the *s* ... Ex 25:35
knop under two branches of the *s* ... Ex 25:35
their branches shall be of the *s* ... Ex 25:36
his horns shall be of the *s* ... Ex 27:2 1931
is upon it, shall be of the *s* ... Ex 28:8
horns thereof shall be of the *s* ... Ex 30:2
and his flowers, were of the *s* ... Ex 37:17
knop under two branches of the *s* ... Ex 37:21
knop under two branches of the *s* ... Ex 37:21
knop under two branches of the *s* ... Ex 37:21
and their branches were of the *s* ... Ex 37:22
the horns thereof were of the *s* ... Ex 37:25
the horns thereof were of the *s* ... Ex 38:2
that was upon it, was of the *s* ... Ex 39:5
the *s* day that it is offered ... Lev 7:15
it shall be eaten the *s* day that ... Lev 7:16
be eaten the *s* day ye offer it ... Lev 19:6
On the *s* day it shall be eaten up ... Lev 22:30 1931
of the *s* month is the feast of ... Lev 23:6 2088
ye shall do no work in that *s* day ... Lev 23:28 6106

not be afflicted in that *s* day	Lev 23:29	6106
that doeth any work in that *s* day	Lev 23:30	6106
the *s* soul will I destroy from	Lev 23:30	6106
cover the *s* with a covering of	Num 4:8	1931
shall hallow his head that *s* day	Num 6:11	1931
even the *s* soul shall be cut off	Num 9:13	1931
the *s* will we do unto thee	Num 10:32	
the *s* reproacheth the LORD	Num 15:30	1931
anger was kindled the *s* time	Num 32:10	1931
prayed for Aaron also the *s* time	Deut 9:20	1931
of thine increase the *s* year	Deut 14:28	1931
charged the people the *s* day	Deut 27:11	1931
wrote this song the *s* day	Deut 31:22	1931
after the *s* manner seven times	Josh 6:15	2088
of Israel, and the valley of the *s*	Josh 11:16	
the *s* is Jerusalem	Josh 15:8	1931
And it came to pass the *s* night	Judg 6:25	1931
thee, the *s* shall go with thee	Judg 7:4	1931
go with thee, the *s* shall not go	Judg 7:4	1931
And it came to pass the *s* night	Judg 7:9	1931
came to Shiloh the *s* day with his	1Sa 4:12	1931
the *s* day unto the LORD	1Sa 6:15	1931
they returned to Ekron the *s* day	1Sa 6:16	1931
this *s* shall reign over my people	1Sa 9:17	2088
one of the *s* place answered and	1Sa 10:12	
the *s* was the first altar that he	1Sa 14:35	
and spake according to the *s* words	1Sa 17:23	428
and spake after the *s* manner	1Sa 17:30	2088
all his men, that *s* day together	1Sa 31:6	1931
there, and died in the *s* place	2Sa 2:23	8478
the *s* is the city of David	2Sa 5:7	1931
burned with fire in the *s* place	2Sa 23:7	
the *s* was Adino the Eznite	2Sa 23:8	1931
the borders thereof were of the *s*	1Kin 7:35	
The *s* day did the king hallow the	1Kin 8:64	1931
And he gave a sign the *s* day	1Kin 13:3	1931
by the *s* way that thou camest	1Kin 13:9	
went out of Samaria the *s* time	2Kin 3:6	1931
Libnah revolted at the *s* time	2Kin 8:22	1931
that which springeth of the *s*	2Kin 19:29	
by the *s* shall he return, and	2Kin 19:33	
the *s* is Abraham	1Chr 1:27	1931
were round about the *s* cities	1Chr 4:33	
the *s* to Jacob for a law, and to	1Chr 16:17	
And it came to pass the *s* night	1Chr 17:3	1931
Also at the *s* time Solomon kept	2Chr 7:8	1931
the *s* may be a priest of them	2Chr 13:9	
offered unto the LORD the *s* time	2Chr 15:11	1931
some of the people the *s* time	2Chr 16:10	1931
the *s* is Micaiah the son of Imla	2Chr 18:7	1931
name of the *s* place was called	2Chr 20:26	1931
The *s* time also did Libnah revolt	2Chr 21:10	1931
the *s* year an hundred talents of	2Chr 27:5	1931
Hath not the *s* Hezekiah taken	2Chr 32:12	1931
This *s* Hezekiah also stopped the	2Chr 32:30	1931
and upon the inhabitants of the *s*	2Chr 34:28	
the LORD was prepared the *s* day	2Chr 35:16	1931
sedition within the *s* of old time	Ezr 4:15	1459
At the *s* time came to them Tatnai	Ezr 5:3	
the *s* king Cyrus made a decree to	Ezr 5:13	
Then came the *s* Sheshbazzar	Ezr 5:16	1791
year of Cyrus the king the *s*	Ezr 6:3	
(the *s* is Kelita,) Pethahiah,	Ezr 10:23	1933
Likewise at the *s* time said I	Neh 4:22	1931
answered them after the *s* manner	Neh 6:4	2088
that the *s* Levites might have the	Neh 10:37	1992
on the thirteenth day of the *s*	Est 9:1	
day of the *s* rested they, and made	Est 9:17	
day of the *s* they rested, and made	Est 9:18	
and the fifteenth day of the *s*	Est 9:21	
and sow wickedness, reap the *s*	Job 4:8	
ye know, the *s* do I know also	Job 13:2	
the tongue of thy dogs in the *s*	Ps 68:23	
and he poureth out of the *s*	Ps 75:8	2088
But thou art the *s*, and thy years	Ps 102:27	1931
confirmed the *s* unto Jacob for a	Ps 105:10	
of the *s* the LORD's name is to be	Ps 113:3	
the *s* is the companion of a	Prov 28:24	1931
no man remembered that *s* poor man	Eccl 9:15	1931
In the *s* day shall the Lord shave	Is 7:20	1931
At the *s* time spake the LORD by	Is 20:2	1931
that which springeth of the *s*	Is 37:30	
by the *s* shall he return, and	Is 37:34	
which will not serve the *s*	Jer 27:8	
And it came to pass the *s* year	Jer 28:1	1931
the *s* year in the seventh month	Jer 28:17	1931
At the *s* time, saith the LORD,	Jer 31:1	1931
vineyards and fields at the *s* time	Jer 39:10	1931
the *s* wicked man shall die in his	Eze 3:18	1931
the *s* wheels also turned not from	Eze 10:16	1992
s faces which I saw by the river	Eze 10:22	1992
this shall not be the *s*	Eze 21:26	2063
defiled my sanctuary in the *s* day	Eze 23:38	1931
then they came the *s* day into my	Eze 23:39	1931
of the day, even of this *s* day	Eze 24:2	6106
against Jerusalem this *s* day	Eze 24:2	6106
that at the *s* time shall things	Eze 38:10	1931
at the *s* time when Gog shall come	Eze 38:18	1931
shall go out by the way of the *s*	Eze 44:3	
worshippeth shall the *s* hour be	Dan 3:6	
ye shall be cast the *s* hour into	Dan 3:15	
The *s* hour was the thing	Dan 4:33	
At the *s* time my reason returned	Dan 4:36	
In the *s* hour came forth fingers	Dan 5:5	
were found in the *s* Daniel	Dan 5:12	
the *s* horn made war with the	Dan 7:21	1797
was a nation even to that *s* time	Dan 12:1	1931
father will go in unto the *s* maid	Amos 2:7	
In the *s* day also will I punish	Zeph 1:9	1931
Babylon, and come thou the *s* day	Zec 6:10	1931
s my name shall be great among	Mal 1:11	
the *s* John had his raiment of	Mt 3:4	*846*
the *s* shall be called great in	Mt 5:19	*3778*
do not even the publicans the *s*	Mt 5:46	*846*
that *s* hour what ye shall speak	Mt 10:19	*1565*
the *s* is my brother, and sister,	Mt 12:50	*846*
The *s* day went Jesus out of the	Mt 13:1	*1565*
the *s* is he that heareth the word	Mt 13:20	*3778*
Canaan came out of the *s* coasts	Mt 15:22	*1565*
At the *s* time came the disciples	Mt 18:1	*1565*
the *s* is greatest in the kingdom	Mt 18:4	*3778*
But the *s* servant went out, and	Mt 18:28	*1565*
the *s* is become the head of the	Mt 21:42	*3778*
The *s* day came to him the	Mt 22:23	*1565*
the end, the *s* shall be saved	Mt 24:13	*3778*
talents went and traded with the *s*	Mt 25:16	*846*
the dish, the *s* shall betray me	Mt 26:23	*3778*
third time, saying the *s* words	Mt 26:44	*846*
I shall kiss, that *s* is he	Mt 26:48	*846*
In that *s* hour said Jesus to the	Mt 26:55	*1565*
with him, cast the *s* in his teeth	Mt 27:44	*846*
the *s* is my brother, and my sister	Mk 3:35	*3778*
And the *s* day, when the even was	Mk 4:35	*1565*
the gospel's, the *s* shall save it	Mk 8:35	*3778*
the *s* shall be last of all, and	Mk 9:35	
asked him again of the *s* matter	Mk 10:10	*846*
the end, the *s* shall be saved	Mk 13:13	*3778*
and prayed, and spake the *s* words	Mk 14:39	*846*
I shall kiss, that *s* is he	Mk 14:44	*846*
there were in the *s* country	Lk 2:8	*846*
the *s* man was just and devout,	Lk 2:25	*3778*
for sinners also do even the *s*	Lk 6:33	*846*
For with the *s* measure that ye	Lk 6:38	*846*
in that *s* hour he cured many of	Lk 7:21	*846*
is forgiven, the *s* loveth little	Lk 7:47	
for my sake, the *s* shall save it	Lk 9:24	*3778*
you all, the *s* shall be great	Lk 9:48	*3778*
in the *s* house remain, eating and	Lk 10:7	*846*
out into the streets of the *s*	Lk 10:10	*846*
the *s* hour what ye ought to say	Lk 12:12	*846*
The *s* day there came certain of	Lk 13:31	*846*
the *s* was accused unto him that	Lk 16:1	*3778*
But the *s* day that Lot went out	Lk 17:29	
the *s* is become the head of the	Lk 20:17	*3778*
the scribes the *s* hour sought to	Lk 20:19	*846*
the *s* shall receive greater	Lk 20:47	*3778*
the *s* day Pilate and Herod were	Lk 23:12	*846*
thou art in the *s* condemnation	Lk 23:40	*846*
(The *s* had not consented to the	Lk 23:51	*3778*
two of them went that *s* day to a	Lk 24:13	*846*
And they rose up the *s* hour	Lk 24:33	*846*
The *s* was in the beginning with	Jn 1:2	*3778*
The *s* came for a witness, to bear	Jn 1:7	*3778*
the *s* said unto me, Upon whom	Jn 1:33	*1565*
the *s* is he which baptizeth with	Jn 1:33	*3778*
The *s* came to Jesus by night, and	Jn 3:2	*3778*
the *s* baptizeth, and all men come	Jn 3:26	*3778*
knew that it was at the *s* hour	Jn 4:53	*1565*
on the *s* day it was the sabbath	Jn 5:9	*1565*
the *s* said unto me, Take up thy	Jn 5:11	*1565*
the *s* works that I do, bear	Jn 5:36	*846*
sent him, the *s* is true, and no	Jn 7:18	*3778*
Even the *s* that I said unto you	Jn 8:25	*3748*
the *s* is a thief and a robber	Jn 10:1	*1565*
still in the *s* place where he was	Jn 11:6	
being the high priest that *s* year	Jn 11:49	*1565*
The *s* came therefore to Philip,	Jn 12:21	*3778*
the *s* shall judge him in the last	Jn 12:48	*1565*
the *s* bringeth forth much fruit	Jn 15:5	*3778*
was the high priest that *s* year	Jn 18:13	*1565*
Then the *s* day at evening, being	Jn 20:19	*1565*
this *s* Jesus, which is taken up	Acts 1:11	*3778*
unto that *s* day that he was taken	Acts 1:22	
that God hath made that *s* Jesus	Acts 2:36	*5126*
the *s* day there were added unto	Acts 2:41	*1565*
The *s* dealt subtilly with our	Acts 7:19	*3778*
the *s* did God send to be a ruler	Acts 7:35	*5126*
in the *s* city used sorcery	Acts 8:9	
and began at the *s* scripture	Acts 8:35	*5026*
the *s* night Peter was sleeping	Acts 12:6	*1565*
the *s* unto us their children	Acts 13:33	*5026*
The *s* heard Paul speak	Acts 14:9	*3778*
tell you the *s* things by mouth	Acts 15:27	*846*
The *s* followed Paul and us, and	Acts 16:17	*3778*
And he came out the *s* hour	Acts 16:18	*846*
he took them the *s* hour of the	Acts 16:33	*1565*
And because he was of the *s* craft	Acts 18:3	*3673*
the *s* time there arose no small	Acts 19:23	*1565*
the *s* man had four daughters,	Acts 21:9	*5129*
the *s* hour I looked up upon him	Acts 22:13	*846*
Or else let these *s* here say	Acts 24:20	*3778*
In the *s* quarters were	Acts 28:7	*1565*
of death, not only do the *s*	Rom 1:32	*846*
that judgest doest the *s* things	Rom 2:1	*846*
do such things, and doest the *s*	Rom 2:3	*846*
who hath subjected the *s* in hope	Rom 8:20	
Even for this *s* purpose have I	Rom 9:17	*846*
of the *s* lump to make one vessel	Rom 9:21	*846*
for the *s* Lord over all is rich	Rom 10:12	*846*
all members have not the *s* office	Rom 12:4	*846*
Be of the *s* mind one toward	Rom 12:16	*846*
thou shalt have praise of the *s*	Rom 13:3	*846*
that ye all speak the *s* thing	1Cor 1:10	*846*
joined together in the *s* mind	1Cor 1:10	*846*
s mind and in the *s* judgment	1Cor 1:10	*846*
Let every man abide in the *s*	1Cor 7:20	*5026*
love God, the *s* is known of him	1Cor 8:3	*3778*
or saith not the law the *s* also	1Cor 9:8	*5023*
did all eat the *s* spiritual meat	1Cor 10:3	*846*
all drink the *s* spiritual drink	1Cor 10:4	*846*
That the Lord Jesus the *s* night	1Cor 11:23	*846*
After the *s* manner also he took	1Cor 11:25	*5615*
of gifts, but the *s* Spirit	1Cor 12:4	*846*
administrations, but the *s* Lord	1Cor 12:5	*846*
but it is the *s* God which worketh	1Cor 12:6	*846*
word of knowledge by the *s* Spirit	1Cor 12:8	*846*
To another faith by the *s* Spirit	1Cor 12:9	*846*
gifts of healing by the *s* Spirit	1Cor 12:9	*846*
have the *s* care one for another	1Cor 12:25	*846*
All flesh is not the *s* flesh	1Cor 15:39	*846*
in the enduring of the *s*	2Cor 1:6	*846*
but the *s* which is made sorry by	2Cor 2:2	
And I wrote this *s* unto you	2Cor 2:3	*846*
the *s* vail untaken away in the	2Cor 3:14	*846*
are changed into the *s* image from	2Cor 3:18	*846*
We having the *s* spirit of faith,	2Cor 4:13	*846*
Now for a recompence in the *s*	2Cor 6:13	*846*
for I perceive that the *s* epistle	2Cor 7:8	*1565*
finish in you the *s* grace also	2Cor 8:6	*846*
which put the *s* earnest care into	2Cor 8:16	*846*
by us to the glory of the *s* Lord	2Cor 8:19	*3778*
in this *s* confident boasting	2Cor 9:4	*5026*
that the *s* might be ready, as a	2Cor 9:5	*5026*
walked we not in the *s* spirit	2Cor 12:18	*846*
walked we not in the *s* steps	2Cor 12:18	*846*
the *s* was mighty in me toward the	Gal 2:8	*2532*
the *s* which I also was forward to	Gal 2:10	
the *s* are the children of Abraham	Gal 3:7	*3778*
be fellowheirs, and of the *s* body	Eph 3:6	*4954*
He that descended is the *s* also	Eph 4:10	*846*
the *s* shall he receive of the	Eph 6:8	*3778*
do the *s* things unto them,	Eph 6:9	*846*
sent unto you for the *s* purpose	Eph 6:22	*846*
Having the *s* conflict which ye	Phil 1:30	*846*
be likeminded, having the *s* love	Phil 2:2	*846*
For the *s* cause also do ye joy,	Phil 2:18	*846*
To write the *s* things to you, to	Phil 3:1	*846*
let us walk by the *s* rule	Phil 3:16	*846*
let us mind the *s* thing	Phil 3:16	*846*
they be of the *s* mind in the Lord	Phil 4:2	*846*
watch in the *s* with thanksgiving	Col 4:2	*846*
sent unto you for the *s* purpose	Col 4:8	*846*
the *s* commit thou to faithful men	2Ti 2:2	*5023*
but thou art the *s*, and thy years	Heb 1:12	*846*
likewise took part of the *s*	Heb 2:14	*846*
after the *s* example of unbelief	Heb 4:11	*846*
every one of you do shew the *s*	Heb 6:11	*846*
oftentimes the *s* sacrifices	Heb 10:11	*846*
heirs with him of the *s* promise	Heb 11:9	*846*
Jesus Christ the *s* yesterday	Heb 13:8	*846*
the *s* is a perfect man, and able	Jas 3:2	*3778*
Out of the *s* mouth proceedeth	Jas 3:10	*846*
forth at the *s* place sweet water	Jas 3:11	*846*
the *s* is made the head of the	1Pet 2:7	*3778*
likewise with the *s* mind	1Pet 4:1	*846*
with them to the *s* excess of riot	1Pet 4:4	*846*
so minister the *s* one to another	1Pet 4:10	*846*
knowing that the *s* afflictions	1Pet 5:9	*846*
of the *s* is he brought in bondage	2Pet 2:19	*3778*
by the *s* word are kept in store,	2Pet 3:7	*846*
the *s* hath not the Father	1Jn 2:23	3761
but as the *s* anointing teacheth	1Jn 2:27	*846*
the *s* shall be clothed in white	Rev 3:5	*3778*
the *s* hour was there a great	Rev 11:13	*1565*
The *s* shall drink of the wine of	Rev 14:10	*846*

SAMGAR-NEBO *(sam'-gar-ne'-bo)* {1} *A prince of Babylon.*

gate, even Nergal-sharezer, *S*	Jer 39:3	5562

SAMLAH *(sam'-lah)* {4} *A king of Edom.*

S of Masrekah reigned in his	Gen 36:36	8072
S died, and Saul of Rehoboth by	Gen 36:37	8072
S of Masrekah reigned in his	1Chr 1:47	8072
when *S* was dead, Shaul of	1Chr 1:48	8072

SAMOS *(sa'-mos)* {1} *An island in the Aegean Sea.*

and the next day we arrived at *S*	Acts 20:15	*4544*

SAMOTHRACE See SAMOTHRACIA.

SAMOTHRACIA *(sam-o-thra'-she-ah)* {1} *An island in the Aegean Sea.*

came with a straight course to *S*	Acts 16:11	*4543*

SAMSON *(sam'-sun)* {36} See SAMSON'S. *A judge of Israel.*

bare a son, and called his name *S*	Judg 13:24	8123
S went down to Timnath, and saw a	Judg 14:1	8123
S said unto his father, Get her	Judg 14:3	8123
Then went *S* down, and his father	Judg 14:5	8123
and she pleased *S* well	Judg 14:7	8123
and *S* made there a feast	Judg 14:10	8123
S said unto them, I will now put	Judg 14:12	8123
that *S* visited his wife with a	Judg 15:1	8123
S said concerning them, Now shall	Judg 15:3	8123
S went and caught three hundred	Judg 15:4	8123
And they answered, *S*, the son in	Judg 15:6	8123
S said unto them, Though ye have	Judg 15:7	8123
To bind *S* are we come up, to do	Judg 15:10	8123
of the rock Etam, and said to *S*	Judg 15:11	8123
S said unto them, Swear unto me,	Judg 15:12	8123
S said, With the jawbone of an	Judg 15:16	8123
Then went *S* to Gaza, and saw there	Judg 16:1	8123
Gazites, saying, *S* is come hither	Judg 16:2	8123
S lay till midnight, and arose at	Judg 16:3	8123
And Delilah said to *S*, Tell me, I	Judg 16:6	8123
S said unto her, If they bind me	Judg 16:7	8123

S

The Philistines be upon thee, *S*. Judg 16:9 8123
And Delilah said unto *S*, Behold, Judg 16:10 8123
The Philistines be upon thee, *S*. Judg 16:12 8123
And Delilah said unto *S*, Hitherto Judg 16:13 8123
The Philistines be upon thee, *S*. Judg 16:14 8123
The Philistines be upon thee, *S*. Judg 16:20 8123
Our god hath delivered *S* our Judg 16:23 8123
merry, that they said, Call for *S*. Judg 16:25 8123
they called for *S* out of the Judg 16:25 8123
S said unto the lad that held him Judg 16:26 8123
that beheld while *S* made sport Judg 16:27 8123
S called unto the LORD, and said, Judg 16:28 8123
S took hold of the two middle Judg 16:29 8123
S said, Let me die with the Judg 16:30 8123
of Gedeon, and of Barak, and of *S*. Heb 11:32 *4546*

SAMSON'S *(sam'-suns)* {3}
day, that they said unto *S* wife Judg 14:15 8123
S wife wept before him, and said, Judg 14:16 8123
But *S* wife was given to his Judg 14:20 8123

SAMUEL *(sam'-u-el)* {142} See SHEMUEL. *A priest and judge of Israel.*
bare a son, and called his name *S* 1Sa 1:20 8050
But *S* ministered before the LORD, 1Sa 2:18 8050
the child *S* grew before the LORD 1Sa 2:21 8050
And the child *S* grew on, and was in 1Sa 2:26 8050
the child *S* ministered unto the 1Sa 3:1 8050
was, and *S* was laid down to sleep 1Sa 3:3 8050
That the LORD called *S* 1Sa 3:4 8050
And the LORD called yet again, *S* 1Sa 3:6 8050
S arose and went to Eli, and said, 1Sa 3:6 8050
Now *S* did not yet know the LORD, 1Sa 3:7 8050
the LORD called *S* again the third 1Sa 3:8 8050
Therefore Eli said unto *S* 1Sa 3:9 8050
So *S* went and lay down in his 1Sa 3:9 8050
as at other times, *S*, *S* 1Sa 3:10 8050
Then *S* answered, Speak 1Sa 3:10 8050
And the LORD said to *S*, Behold, I 1Sa 3:11 8050
S lay until the morning, and 1Sa 3:15 8050
S feared to shew Eli the vision 1Sa 3:15 8050
Eli called *S*, and said, *S* 1Sa 3:16 8050
S told him every whit, and hid 1Sa 3:18 8050
S grew, and the LORD was with him, 1Sa 3:19 8050
even to Beer-sheba knew that *S* 1Sa 3:20 8050
to *S* in Shiloh by the word of the 1Sa 3:21 8050
the word of *S* came to all Israel 1Sa 4:1 8050
S spake unto all the house of 1Sa 7:3 8050
S said, Gather all Israel to 1Sa 7:5 8050
S judged the children of Israel 1Sa 7:6 8050
the children of Israel said to *S* 1Sa 7:8 8050
S took a sucking lamb, and offered 1Sa 7:9 8050
S cried unto the LORD for Israel 1Sa 7:9 8050
as *S* was offering up the burnt 1Sa 7:10 8050
Then *S* took a stone, and set it 1Sa 7:12 8050
the Philistines all the days of *S* 1Sa 7:13 8050
S judged Israel all the days of 1Sa 7:15 8050
when *S* was old, that he made his 1Sa 8:1 8050
and came to *S* unto Ramah, 1Sa 8:4 8050
But the thing displeased *S* 1Sa 8:6 8050
And *S* prayed unto the LORD 1Sa 8:6 8050
And the LORD said unto *S*, Hearken 1Sa 8:7 8050
S told all the words of the LORD 1Sa 8:10 8050
refused to obey the voice of *S* 1Sa 8:19 8050
S heard all the words of the 1Sa 8:21 8050
And the LORD said to *S*, Hearken 1Sa 8:22 8050
S said unto the men of Israel, Go 1Sa 8:22 8050
S came out against them, for to 1Sa 9:14 8050
Now the LORD had told *S* in his 1Sa 9:15 8050
when *S* saw Saul, the LORD said 1Sa 9:17 8050
Saul drew near to *S* in the gate 1Sa 9:18 8050
S answered Saul, and said, I am 1Sa 9:19 8050
S took Saul and his servant, and 1Sa 9:22 8050
S said unto the cook, Bring the 1Sa 9:23 8050
S said, Behold that which is left 1Sa 9:24
So Saul did eat with *S* that day 1Sa 9:24 8050
S communed with Saul upon the top 1Sa 9:25
that *S* called Saul to the top of 1Sa 9:26 8050
went out both of them, he and *S* 1Sa 9:26 8050
S said to Saul, Bid the servant 1Sa 9:27 8050
Then *S* took a vial of oil, and 1Sa 10:1 8050
had turned his back to go from *S* 1Sa 10:9 8050
they were no where, we came to *S* 1Sa 10:14 8050
I pray thee, what *S* said unto you 1Sa 10:15 8050
of the kingdom, whereof *S* spake 1Sa 10:16 8050
S called the people together unto 1Sa 10:17 8050
when *S* had caused all the tribes 1Sa 10:20 8050
S said to all the people, See ye 1Sa 10:24 8050
Then *S* told the people the manner 1Sa 10:25 8050
S sent all the people away, every 1Sa 10:25 8050
not forth after Saul and after *S* 1Sa 11:7 8050
And the people said unto *S* 1Sa 11:12 8050
Then said *S* to the people, Come, 1Sa 11:14 8050
S said unto all Israel, Behold, I 1Sa 12:1 8050
S said unto the people, It is the 1Sa 12:6 8050
and Bedan, and Jephthah, and *S* 1Sa 12:11 8050
So *S* called unto the LORD 1Sa 12:18 8050
greatly feared the LORD and *S* 1Sa 12:18 8050
And all the people said unto *S* 1Sa 12:19 8050
S said unto the people, Fear not 1Sa 12:20 8050
the set time that *S* had appointed 1Sa 13:8 8050
but *S* came not to Gilgal 1Sa 13:8 8050
burnt offering, behold, *S* came 1Sa 13:10 8050
S said, What hast thou done 1Sa 13:11 8050
S said to Saul, Thou hast done 1Sa 13:13 8050
S arose, and gat him up from 1Sa 13:15 8050
S also said unto Saul, The LORD 1Sa 15:1 8050
came the word of the LORD unto *S* 1Sa 15:10 8050
And it grieved *S* 1Sa 15:11 8050
when *S* rose early to meet Saul in 1Sa 15:12 8050
in the morning, it was told *S* 1Sa 15:12 8050
And *S* came to Saul 1Sa 15:13 8050
S said, What meaneth then this 1Sa 15:14 8050
Then *S* said unto Saul, Stay, and I 1Sa 15:16 8050
S said, When thou wast little in 1Sa 15:17 8050
And Saul said unto *S*, Yea, I have 1Sa 15:20 8050
S said, Hath the LORD as great 1Sa 15:22 8050
And Saul said unto *S*, I have 1Sa 15:24 8050
S said unto Saul, I will not 1Sa 15:26 8050
as *S* turned about to go away, he 1Sa 15:27 8050
S said unto him, The LORD hath 1Sa 15:28 8050
So *S* turned again after Saul 1Sa 15:31 8050
Then said *S*, Bring ye hither to 1Sa 15:32 8050
S said, As thy sword hath made 1Sa 15:33 8050
S hewed Agag in pieces before the 1Sa 15:33 8050
Then *S* went to Ramah 1Sa 15:34 8050
S came no more to see Saul until 1Sa 15:35 8050
nevertheless *S* mourned for Saul 1Sa 15:35 8050
And the LORD said unto *S*, How long 1Sa 16:1 8050
And *S* said, How can I go 1Sa 16:2 8050
S did that which the LORD spake, 1Sa 16:4 8050
But the LORD said unto *S*, Look 1Sa 16:7 8050
and made him pass before *S* 1Sa 16:8 8050
of his sons to pass before *S* 1Sa 16:10 8050
S said unto Jesse, The LORD hath 1Sa 16:10 8050
S said unto Jesse, Are here all 1Sa 16:11 8050
S said unto Jesse, Send and fetch 1Sa 16:11 8050
Then *S* took the horn of oil, and 1Sa 16:13 8050
So *S* rose up, and went to Ramah 1Sa 16:13 8050
came to *S* to Ramah, and told him 1Sa 19:18 8050
S went and dwelt in Naioth 1Sa 19:18 8050
S standing as appointed over them 1Sa 19:20 8050
and he asked and said, Where are *S* 1Sa 19:22 8050
before *S* in like manner, and lay 1Sa 19:24 8050
And *S* died 1Sa 25:1 8050
Now *S* was dead, and all Israel had 1Sa 28:3 8050
And he said, Bring me up *S* 1Sa 28:11 8050
And when the woman saw *S*, she 1Sa 28:12 8050
And Saul perceived that it was *S* 1Sa 28:14 8050
S said to Saul, Why hast thou 1Sa 28:15 8050
Then said *S*, Wherefore then dost 1Sa 28:16 8050
afraid, because of the words of *S* 1Sa 28:20 8050
And the sons of *S* 1Chr 6:28 8050
S the seer did ordain in their 1Chr 9:22 8050
to the word of the LORD by *S* 1Chr 11:3 8050
And all that *S* the seer, and Saul 1Chr 26:28 8050
written in the book of *S* the seer 1Chr 29:29 8050
from the days of *S* the prophet 2Chr 35:18 8050
S among them that call upon his Ps 99:6 8050
S stood before me, yet my mind Jer 15:1 8050
Yea, and all the prophets from *S* Acts 3:24 *4545*
fifty years, until *S* the prophet Acts 13:20 *4545*
of David also, and *S*, and of the Heb 11:32 *4545*

SANBALLAT *(san-bal'-lat)* {10} *An opponent of Nehemiah.*
When *S* the Horonite, and Tobiah Neh 2:10 5571
But when *S* the Horonite, and Neh 2:19 5571
that when *S* heard that we builded Neh 4:1 5571
But it came to pass, that when *S* Neh 4:7 5571
Now it came to pass, when *S* Neh 6:1 5571
That *S* and Geshem sent unto me, Neh 6:2 5571
Then sent *S* his servant unto me Neh 6:5 5571
for Tobiah and *S* had hired him Neh 6:12 5571
S according to these their works, Neh 6:14 5571
was son in law to *S* the Horonite Neh 13:28 5571

SANCTIFICATION {5}
us wisdom, and righteousness, and *s* 1Cor 1:30 *38*
is the will of God, even your *s* 1Th 4:3 *38*
how to possess his vessel in *s* 1Th 4:4 *38*
salvation through *s* of the Spirit 2Th 2:13 *38*
through *s* of the Spirit, unto 1Pet 1:2 *38*

SANCTIFIED {62}
blessed the seventh day, and *s* it Gen 2:3 6942
unto the people, and *s* the people Ex 19:14 6942
tabernacle shall be *s* by my glory Ex 29:43 6942
all that was therein, and *s* them Lev 8:10 6942
s it, to make reconciliation upon Lev 8:15 6942
s Aaron, and his garments, and his Lev 8:30 6942
I will be *s* in them that come Lev 10:3 6942
if he that *s* it will redeem his Lev 27:15 6942
if he that *s* the field will in Lev 27:19 6942
s it, and all the instruments Num 7:1 6942
and had anointed them, and *s* them Num 7:1 6942
land of Egypt I *s* them for myself Num 8:17 6942
the LORD, and he was *s* in them Num 20:13 6942
because ye *s* me not in the midst Deut 32:51 6942
s Eleazar his son to keep the ark 1Sa 7:1 6942
he *s* Jesse and his sons, and called 1Sa 16:5 6942
though it were *s* this day in the 1Sa 21:5 6942
the Levites *s* themselves to bring 1Chr 15:14 6942
priests that were present were *s* 2Chr 5:11 6942
s this house, that my name may be 2Chr 7:16 6942
house, which I have *s* for my name 2Chr 7:20 6942
s themselves, and came, according 2Chr 29:15 6942
so they *s* the house of the LORD 2Chr 29:17 6942
have we prepared and *s*, and, 2Chr 29:19 6942
other priests had *s* themselves 2Chr 29:34 6942
had not *s* themselves sufficiently 2Chr 30:3 6942
which he hath *s* for ever 2Chr 30:8 6942
s themselves, and brought in the 2Chr 30:15 6942
the congregation that were not *s* 2Chr 30:17 6942
number of priests *s* themselves 2Chr 30:24 6942
they *s* themselves in holiness 2Chr 31:18 6942
they *s* it, and set up the doors of Neh 3:1 6942
unto the tower of Meah they *s* it Neh 3:1 6942
they *s* holy things unto the Neh 12:47 6942
the Levites *s* them unto the Neh 12:47 6942
s them, and rose up early in the Job 1:5 6942
holy shall be *s* in righteousness Is 5:16 6942
I have commanded my *s* ones Is 13:3 6942
forth out of the womb I *s* thee Jer 1:5 6942
I will be *s* in you before the Eze 20:41 6942
in her, and shall be *s* in her Eze 28:22 6942
shall be *s* in them in the sight Eze 28:25 6942
when I shall be *s* in you before Eze 36:23 6942
me, when I shall be *s* in thee Eze 38:16 6942
am *s* in them in the sight of many Eze 39:27 6942
that are *s* of the sons of Zadok Eze 48:11 6942
ye of him, whom the Father hath *s* Jn 10:36 *37*
also might be *s* through the truth Jn 17:19 *37*
among all them which are *s* Acts 20:32 *37*
among them which are *s* by faith Acts 26:18 *37*
being *s* by the Holy Ghost Rom 15:16 *37*
them that are *s* in Christ Jesus 1Cor 1:2 *37*
but ye are washed, but ye are *s* 1Cor 6:11 *37*
husband is *s* by the wife, and the 1Cor 7:14 *37*
wife is *s* by the husband 1Cor 7:14 *37*
For it is *s* by the word of God and 1Ti 4:5 *37*
shall be a vessel unto honour, *s* 2Ti 2:21 *37*
they who are *s* are all of one Heb 2:11 *37*
By the which will we are *s* Heb 10:10 *37*
for ever them that are *s* Heb 10:14 *37*
the covenant, wherewith he was *s* Heb 10:29 *37*
to them that are *s* by God the Jude 1 *37*

SANCTIFIETH {4}
or the temple that *s* the gold Mt 23:17 *37*
or the altar that *s* the gift Mt 23:19 *37*
For both he that *s* and they who Heb 2:11 *37*
s to the purifying of the flesh Heb 9:13 *37*

SANCTIFY {70}
S unto me all the firstborn, Ex 13:2 6942
s them to day and to morrow, and Ex 19:10 6942
s themselves, lest the LORD break Ex 19:22 6942
bounds about the mount, and *s* it Ex 19:23 6942
s them, that they may minister Ex 28:41 6942
thou shalt *s* the breast of the Ex 29:27 6942
made, to consecrate and to *s* them Ex 29:33 6942
and thou shalt anoint it, to *s* it Ex 29:36 6942
atonement for the altar, and *s* it Ex 29:37 6942
I will *s* the tabernacle of the Ex 29:44 6942
I will *s* also both Aaron and his Ex 29:44 6942
And thou shalt *s* them, that they Ex 30:29 6942
I am the LORD that doth *s* you Ex 31:13 6942
all his vessels, and *s* the altar Ex 40:10 6942
the laver and his foot, and *s* it Ex 40:11 6942
garments, and anoint him, and *s* him Ex 40:13 6942
the laver and his foot, to *s* them Lev 8:11 6942
head, and anointed him, to *s* him Lev 8:12 6942
ye shall therefore *s* yourselves Lev 11:44 6942
S yourselves therefore, and be ye Lev 20:7 6942
I am the LORD which *s* you Lev 20:8 6942
Thou shalt *s* him therefore Lev 21:8 6942
for I the LORD, which *s* you Lev 21:8 6942
for I the LORD do *s* him Lev 21:15 6942
for I the LORD do *s* them Lev 21:23 6942
I the LORD do *s* them Lev 22:9 6942
for I the LORD do *s* them Lev 22:16 6942
when a man shall *s* his house to Lev 27:14 6942
if a man shall *s* unto the LORD Lev 27:16 6942
If he *s* his field from the year Lev 27:17 6942
But if he *s* his field after the Lev 27:18 6942
if a man *s* unto the LORD a field Lev 27:22 6942
firstling, no man shall *s* it Lev 27:26 6942
S yourselves against to morrow, Num 11:18 6942
to *s* me in the eyes of the Num 20:12 6942
to *s* me at the water before their Num 27:14 6942
Keep the sabbath day to *s* it Deut 5:12 6942
shalt *s* unto the LORD thy God Deut 15:19 6942
unto the people, *S* yourselves Josh 3:5 6942
s the people, and say, *S* Josh 7:13 6942
s yourselves, and come with me to 1Sa 16:5 6942
s yourselves, both ye and your 1Chr 15:12 6942
that he should *s* the most holy 1Chr 23:13 6942
s now yourselves 2Chr 29:5 6942
s the house of the LORD God of 2Chr 29:5 6942
first day of the first month to *s* 2Chr 29:17 6942
to *s* themselves than the priests 2Chr 29:34 6942
clean, to *s* them unto the LORD 2Chr 30:17 6942
s yourselves, and prepare your 2Chr 35:6 6942
the gates, to *s* the sabbath day Neh 13:22 6942
S the LORD of hosts himself Is 8:13 6942
of him, they shall *s* my name Is 29:23 6942
s the Holy One of Jacob, and shall Is 29:23 6942
They that *s* themselves, and purify Is 66:17 6942
that I am the LORD that *s* them Eze 20:12 6942
I will *s* my great name, which was Eze 36:23 6942
know that I the LORD do *s* Israel Eze 37:28 6942
I magnify myself, and *s* myself Eze 38:23 6942
they shall not *s* the people with Eze 44:19 6942
the utter court, to *s* the people Eze 46:20 6942
S ye a fast, call a solemn Joel 1:14 6942
s a fast, call a solemn assembly Joel 2:15 6942
s the congregation, assemble the Joel 2:16 6942
S them through thy truth Jn 17:17 *37*
And for their sakes I *s* myself Jn 17:19 *37*
That he might *s* and cleanse it Eph 5:26 *37*
very God of peace *s* you wholly 1Th 5:23 *37*
that he might *s* the people with Heb 13:12 *37*
But *s* the Lord God in your hearts 1Pet 3:15 *37*

SANCTUARIES {5}
that he profane not my *s* Lev 21:23 4720
bring your *s* unto desolation, and Lev 26:31 4720
into the *s* of the LORD's house Jer 51:51 4720

Thou hast defiled thy *s* by the Eze 28:18 4720
the *s* of Israel shall be laid Amos 7:9 4720

SANCTUARY {137}
for thee to dwell in, in the *S* Ex 15:17 4720
And let them make me a *s* Ex 25:8 4720
shekel after the shekel of the *s* Ex 30:13 6944
after the shekel of the *s* Ex 30:24 6944
of work for the service of the *s* Ex 36:1 6944
the work of the service of the *s* Ex 36:3 6944
wrought all the work of the *s* Ex 36:4 6944
work for the offering of the *s* Ex 36:6 6944
after the shekel of the *s* Ex 38:24 6944
after the shekel of the *s* Ex 38:25 6944
shekel, after the shekel of the *s* Ex 38:26 6944
were cast the sockets of the *s* Ex 38:27 6944
LORD, before the vail of the *s* Lev 4:6 6944
silver, after the shekel of the *s* Lev 5:15 6944
from before the *s* out of the camp Lev 10:4 6944
thing, nor come into the *s* Lev 12:4 4720
make an atonement for the holy *s* Lev 16:33 4720
my sabbaths, and reverence my *s* Lev 19:30 4720
seed unto Molech, to defile my *s* Lev 20:3 4720
Neither shall he go out of the *s* Lev 21:12 4720
nor profane the *s* of his God Lev 21:12 4720
my sabbaths, and reverence my *s* Lev 26:2 4720
silver, after the shekel of the *s* Lev 27:3 6944
according to the shekel of the *s* Lev 27:25 6944
keeping the charge of the *s* Num 3:28 6944
the vessels of the *s* wherewith Num 3:31 6944
that keep the charge of the *s* Num 3:32 6944
keeping the charge of the *s* for Num 3:38 4720
of the *s* shalt thou take them Num 3:47 6944
after the shekel of the *s* Num 3:50 6944
wherewith they minister in the *s* Num 4:12 6944
made an end of covering the *s* Num 4:15 6944
and all the vessels of the *s* Num 4:15 6944
of all that therein is, in the *s* Num 4:16 6944
because the service of the *s* Num 7:9 6944
after the shekel of the *s* Num 7:13 6944
after the shekel of the *s* Num 7:19 6944
after the shekel of the *s* Num 7:25 6944
after the shekel of the *s* Num 7:31 6944
after the shekel of the *s* Num 7:37 6944
after the shekel of the *s* Num 7:43 6944
after the shekel of the *s* Num 7:49 6944
after the shekel of the *s* Num 7:55 6944
after the shekel of the *s* Num 7:61 6944
after the shekel of the *s* Num 7:67 6944
after the shekel of the *s* Num 7:73 6944
after the shekel of the *s* Num 7:79 6944
after the shekel of the *s* Num 7:85 6944
apiece, after the shekel of the *s* Num 7:86 6944
of Israel come nigh unto the *s* Num 8:19 6944
set forward, bearing the *s* Num 10:21 4720
shall bear the iniquity of the *s* Num 18:1 4720
come nigh the vessels of the *s* Num 18:3 6944
ye shall keep the charge of the *s* Num 18:5 6944
after the shekel of the *s* Num 18:16 6944
he hath defiled the *s* of the LORD Num 19:20 4720
that was by the *s* of the LORD Josh 24:26 4720
and all the instruments of the *s* 1Chr 9:29 6944
build ye the *s* of the LORD God, 1Chr 22:19 4720
for the governors of the *s* 1Chr 24:5 6944
thee to build an house for the *s* 1Chr 28:10 4720
have built thee a *s* therein for 2Chr 20:8 4720
go out of the *s* 2Chr 26:18 4720
for the kingdom, and for the *s* 2Chr 29:21 4720
the LORD, and enter into his *s* 2Chr 30:8 4720
to the purification of the *s* 2Chr 30:19 6944
the sword in the house of their *s* 2Chr 36:17 4720
where are the vessels of the *s* Neh 10:39 4720
Send thee help from the *s* Ps 20:2 6944
so as I have seen thee in the *s* Ps 63:2 6944
of my God, my King, in the *s* Ps 68:24 6944
Until I went into the *s* of God Ps 73:17 4720
enemy hath done wickedly in the *s* Ps 74:3 6944
They have cast fire into thy *s* Ps 74:7 4720
Thy way, O God, is in the *s* Ps 77:13 6944
them to the border of his *s* Ps 78:54 6944
he built his *s* like high palaces, Ps 78:69 4720
strength and beauty are in his *s* Ps 96:6 4720
down from the height of his *s* Ps 102:19 6944
Judah was his *s*, and Israel his Ps 114:2 6944
Lift up your hands in the *s* Ps 134:2 6944
Praise God in his *s* Ps 150:1 6944
And he shall be for a *s* Is 8:14 4720
he shall come to his *s* to pray Is 16:12 4720
profaned the princes of the *s* Is 43:28 6944
to beautify the place of my *s* Is 60:13 4720
have trodden down thy *s* Is 63:18 4720
beginning is the place of our *s* Jer 17:12 4720
the heathen entered into her *s* Lam 1:10 4720
his altar, he hath abhorred his *s* Lam 2:7 4720
be slain in the *s* of the Lord Lam 2:20 4720
the stones of the *s* are poured Lam 4:1 6944
because thou hast defiled my *s* Eze 5:11 4720
I should go far off from my *s* Eze 8:6 4720
and begin at my *s* Eze 9:6 4720
s in the countries where they Eze 11:16 4720
have defiled my *s* in the same day Eze 23:38 4720
same day into my *s* to profane it Eze 23:39 4720
Behold, I will profane my *s* Eze 24:21 4720
thou saidst, Aha, against my *s* Eze 25:3 4720
will set my *s* in the midst of Eze 37:26 4720
when my *s* shall be in the midst Eze 37:28 4720
squared, and the face of the *s* Eze 41:21 6944
the temple and the *s* had two doors Eze 41:23 6944
make a separation between the *s* Eze 42:20 6944
place of the house, without the *s* Eze 43:21 4720
s which looketh toward the east Eze 44:1 4720
with every going forth of the *s* Eze 44:5 4720
have brought into my *s* strangers Eze 44:7
in flesh, to be in my *s*, to Eze 44:7 4720
my charge in my *s* for yourselves Eze 44:8 4720
in flesh, shall enter into my *s* Eze 44:9 4720
they shall be ministers in my *s* Eze 44:11 4720
that kept the charge of my *s* when Eze 44:15 4720
They shall enter into my *s* Eze 44:16 4720
the day that he goeth into the *s* Eze 44:27 6944
inner court, to minister in the *s* Eze 44:27 6944
for the *s* five hundred in length Eze 45:2 6944
and in it shall be the *s* and the Eze 45:3 4720
priests the ministers of the *s* Eze 45:4 4720
and an holy place for the *s* Eze 45:4 4720
without blemish, and cleanse the *s* Eze 45:18 4720
they they issued out of the *s* Eze 47:12 4720
the *s* shall be in the midst of it Eze 48:8 4720
the *s* of the LORD shall be in the Eze 48:10 4720
the *s* of the house shall be in Eze 48:21 4720
the place of his *s* was cast down Dan 8:11 4720
of desolation, to give both the *s* Dan 8:13 6944
then shall the *s* be cleansed Dan 8:14 6944
shine upon thy *s* that is desolate Dan 9:17 4720
shall destroy the city and the *s* Dan 9:26 6944
shall pollute the *s* of strength Dan 11:31 4720
her priests have polluted the *s* Zeph 3:4 6944
A minister of the *s*, and of the Heb 8:2 *39*
of divine service, and a worldly *s* Heb 9:1 *39*
which is called the *s* Heb 9:2 *39*
the *s* by the high priest for sin Heb 13:11 *39*

SAND {28}
as the *s* which is upon the sea Gen 22:17 2344
make thy seed as the *s* of the sea Gen 32:12 2344
gathered corn as the *s* of the sea Gen 41:49 2344
the Egyptian, and hid him in the *s* Ex 2:12 2344
and of treasures hid in the *s* Deut 33:19 2344
even as the *s* that is upon the Josh 11:4 2344
as the *s* by the sea side for Judg 7:12 2344
people as the *s* which is on the 1Sa 13:5 2344
as the *s* that is by the sea for 2Sa 17:11 2344
as the *s* which is by the sea in 1Kin 4:20 2344
even as the *s* that is on the 1Kin 4:29 2344
be heavier than the *s* of the sea Job 6:3 2344
I shall multiply my days as the *s* Job 29:18 2344
fowls like as the *s* of the sea Ps 78:27 2344
are more in number than the *s* Ps 139:18 2344
stone is heavy, and the *s* weighty Prov 27:3 2344
Israel be as the *s* of the sea Is 10:22 2344
Thy seed also had been as the *s* Is 48:19 2344
which have placed the *s* for the Jer 5:22 2344
to me above the *s* of the seas Jer 15:8 2344
neither the *s* of the sea measured Jer 33:22 2344
shall be as the *s* of the sea Hos 1:10 2344
gather the captivity as the *s* Hab 1:9 2344
which built his house upon the *s* Mt 7:26 *285*
of Israel be as the *s* of the sea Rom 9:27 *285*
as the *s* which is by the sea Heb 11:12 *285*
And I stood upon the *s* of the sea Rev 13:1 *285*
of whom is as the *s* of the sea Rev 20:8 *285*

SANDALS {2}
But be shod with *s* Mk 6:9 *4547*
Gird thyself, and bind on thy *s* Acts 12:8 *4547*

SANG {12}
Then *s* Moses and the children of Ex 15:1 7891
Then Israel *s* this song, Spring Num 21:17 7891
Then *s* Deborah and Barak the son Judg 5:1 7891
of whom they *s* one to another in 1Sa 29:5 6030
worshipped, and the singers *s* 2Chr 29:28 7891
they *s* praises with gladness, and 2Chr 29:30
they *s* together by course in Ezr 3:11 6030
And the singers *s* loud, with Neh 12:42 7891
When the morning stars *s* together Job 38:7 7442
which he *s* unto the LORD, Ps 7:t 7891
they *s* his praise Ps 106:12 7891
prayed, and *s* praises unto God Acts 16:25 *5214*

SANK {2}
they *s* into the bottom as a stone Ex 15:5 3381
they *s* as lead in the mighty Ex 15:10 6749

SANSANNAH *(san-san'-nah)* {1} *A city in Judah.*
And Ziklag, and Madmannah, and *S* Josh 15:31 5578

SAP {1}
trees of the LORD are full of *s* Ps 104:16

SAPH *(saf)* {1} See SIPHAI. *A descendant of Rapha.*
Sibbechai the Hushathite slew *S* 2Sa 21:18 5593

SAPHIR *(sa'-fur)* {1} *A city in Ephraim.*
ye away, thou inhabitant of *S* Mic 1:11 8208

SAPPHIRA *(saf-fi'-rah)* {1} *Wife of Ananias.*
Ananias, with *S* his wife, sold a Acts 5:1 *4551*

SAPPHIRE {9}
it were a paved work of a *s* stone Ex 24:10 5601
row shall be an emerald, a *s* Ex 28:18 5601
the second row, an emerald, a *s* Ex 39:11 5601
with the precious onyx, or the *s* Job 28:16 5601
rubies, their polishing was of *s* Lam 4:7 5601
as the appearance of a *s* stone Eze 1:26 5601
over them as it were a *s* stone Eze 10:1 5601
the onyx, and the jasper, the *s* Eze 28:13 5601
the second, *s* Rev 21:19 *4552*

SAPPHIRES {3}
stones of it are the place of *s* Job 28:6 5601
as bright ivory overlaid with *s* Song 5:14 5601
and lay thy foundations with *s* Is 54:11 5601

SARA *(sa'-rah)* {1} See SARAH. *Greek form of Sarah 1.*
Through faith also *S* herself Heb 11:11 *4564*

SARAH *(sa'-rah)* {39} See SARA, SARAH'S, SARAI, SERAH.
1. Wife of Abraham.
Sarai, but *S* shall her name be Gen 17:15 8283
and shall *S*, that is ninety years Gen 17:17 8283
S thy wife shall bear thee a son Gen 17:19 8283
which *S* shall bear unto thee at Gen 17:21 8283
hastened into the tent unto *S* Gen 18:6 8283
unto him, Where is *S* thy wife Gen 18:9 8283
S thy wife shall have a son Gen 18:10 8283
S heard it in the tent door, Gen 18:10 8283
S were old and well stricken in Gen 18:11 8283
it ceased to be with *S* after the Gen 18:11 8283
Therefore *S* laughed within Gen 18:12 8283
Abraham, Wherefore did *S* laugh Gen 18:13 8283
of life, and *S* shall have a son Gen 18:14 8283
Then *S* denied, saying, I laughed Gen 18:15 8283
And Abraham said of *S* his wife Gen 20:2 8283
king of Gerar sent, and took *S* Gen 20:2 8283
and restored him *S* his wife Gen 20:14 8283
unto *S* he said, Behold, I have Gen 20:16 8283
because of *S* Abraham's wife Gen 20:18 8283
the LORD visited *S* as he had said Gen 21:1 8283
LORD did unto *S* as he had spoken Gen 21:1 8283
For *S* conceived, and bare Abraham Gen 21:2 8283
whom *S* bare to him, Isaac Gen 21:3 8283
S said, God hath made me to laugh Gen 21:6 8283
that *S* should have given children Gen 21:7 8283
S saw the son of Hagar the Gen 21:9 8283
in all that *S* hath said unto thee Gen 21:12 8283
S was an hundred and seven and Gen 23:1 8283
were the years of the life of *S* Gen 23:1 8283
And *S* died in Kirjath-arba Gen 23:2 8283
and Abraham came to mourn for *S* Gen 23:2 8283
Abraham buried *S* his wife in the Gen 23:19 8283
S my master's wife bare a son to Gen 24:36 8283
was Abraham buried, and *S* his wife Gen 25:10 8283
they buried Abraham and *S* his wife Gen 49:31 8283
father, and unto *S* that bare you Is 51:2 8283
I come, and *S* shall have a son Rom 9:9 *4564*
Even as *S* obeyed Abraham, calling 1Pet 3:6 *4564*
2. A daughter of Asher.
of the daughter of Asher was *S* Num 26:46 8294

SARAH'S *(sa'-rahs)* {3}
her into his mother *S* tent Gen 24:67 8283
S handmaid, bare unto Abraham Gen 25:12 8283
yet the deadness of *S* womb Rom 4:19 *4564*

SARAI *(sa'-rahee)* {16} See SARAH, SARAI'S. *The original name of Sarah.*
the name of Abram's wife was *S* Gen 11:29 8297
But *S* was barren Gen 11:30 8297
S his daughter in law, his son Gen 11:31 8297
And Abram took *S* his wife, and Lot Gen 12:5 8297
that he said unto *S* his wife Gen 12:11 8297
plagues because of *S* Abram's wife Gen 12:17 8297
Now *S* Abram's wife bare him no Gen 16:1 8297
S said unto Abram, Behold now, Gen 16:2 8297
Abram hearkened to the voice of *S* Gen 16:2 8297
S Abram's wife took Hagar her Gen 16:3 8297
S said unto Abram, My wrong be Gen 16:5 8297
But Abram said unto *S*, Behold, Gen 16:6 8297
when *S* dealt hardly with her, she Gen 16:6 8297
from the face of my mistress *S* Gen 16:8 8297
As for *S* thy wife, thou shalt not Gen 17:15 8297
thou shalt not call her name *S* Gen 17:15 8297

SARAI'S *(sa'-rahees)* {1}
S maid, whence camest thou Gen 16:8 8297

SARAPH *(sa'-raf)* {1} *A descendant of Shelah.*
men of Chozeba, and Joash, and *S* 1Chr 4:22 8315

SARDINE {1}
upon like a jasper and a *s* stone Rev 4:3 *4555*

SARDIS *(sar'-dis)* {3} *A city in Lydia in Asia Minor.*
and unto Thyatira, and unto *S* Rev 1:11 *4554*
angel of the church in *S* write Rev 3:1 *4554*
in *S* which have not defiled their Rev 3:4 *4554*

SARDITES *(sar'-dites)* {1} *Descendants of Sered.*
of Sered, the family of the *S* Num 26:26 5625

SARDIUS {4}
the first row shall be a *s* Ex 28:17 124
the first row was a *s*, a topaz, Ex 39:10 124
stone was thy covering, the *s* Eze 28:13 124
the sixth, *s* Rev 21:20 *4556*

SARDONYX {1}
The fifth, *s* Rev 21:20 *4557*

SAREPTA *(sa-rep'-tah)* {1} See ZAREPHATH. *A city near Sidon.*
them was Elias sent, save unto *S* Lk 4:26 *4558*

SARGON *(sar'-gon)* {1} *An Assyrian king.*
(when *S* the king of Assyria sent Is 20:1 5623

SARID *(sa'-rid)* {2} *A city in Zebulun.*
of their inheritance was unto *S* Josh 19:10 8301
turned from *S* eastward toward the Josh 19:12 8301

SARON *(sa'-ron)* {1} See SHARON. *The area between Joppa and Caesarea.*
S saw him, and turned to the Lord Acts 9:35 *4565*

SARSECHIM *(sar'-se-kim)* {1} *A prince of Babylon.*
Nergal-sharezer, Samgar-nebo, *S* Jer 39:3 8310

SAR-SEKIM See SARSECHIM.

SARUCH *(sa'-ruk)* {1} See SERUG. *Father of Nahor; an ancestor of Jesus.*
Which was the son of *S*, which was Lk 3:35 *4562*

SAT {194}
he *s* in the tent door in the heat Gen 18:1 3427
Lot *s* in the gate of Sodom Gen 19:1 3427
s her down over against him a Gen 21:16 3427
she *s* over against him, and lift Gen 21:16 3427
camel's furniture, and *s* upon them Gen 31:34 3427
And they *s* down to eat bread Gen 37:25 3427
s in an open place, which is by Gen 38:14 3427
they *s* before him, the firstborn Gen 43:33 3427
himself, and *s* upon the bed Gen 48:2 3427
and he *s* down by a well Ex 2:15 3427
that *s* on his throne unto the Ex 12:29 3427
when we *s* by the flesh pots, and Ex 16:3 3427
put it under him, and he *s* thereon Ex 17:12 3427
that Moses *s* to judge the people Ex 18:13 3427
the people *s* down to eat and to Ex 32:6 3427
s that hath the issue shall wash Lev 15:6 3427
she *s* upon shall wash his clothes Lev 15:22 3427
and they *s* down at thy feet Deut 33:3 8497
s under an oak which was in Judg 6:11 3427
the woman as she *s* in the field Judg 13:9 3427
And they *s* down, and did eat and Judg 19:6 3427
he *s* him down in a street of the Judg 19:15 3427
s there before the LORD, and Judg 20:26 3427
And she *s* beside the reapers Ruth 2:14 3427
to the gate, and *s* him down there Ruth 4:1 3427
And he turned aside, and *s* down Ruth 4:1 3427
And they *s* down Ruth 4:2 3427
Now Eli the priest *s* upon a seat 1Sa 1:9 3427
Eli *s* upon a seat by the wayside 1Sa 4:13 3427
as he *s* in his house with his 1Sa 19:9 3427
the king *s* him down to eat meat 1Sa 20:24 3427
the king *s* upon his seat, as at 1Sa 20:25 3427
Abner *s* by Saul's side, and 1Sa 20:25 3427
from the earth, and *s* upon the bed 1Sa 28:23 3427
and they *s* down, the one on the 2Sa 2:13 3427
when the king *s* in his house 2Sa 7:1 3427
s before the LORD, and he said, 2Sa 7:18 3427
David *s* between the two gates 2Sa 18:24 3427
the king arose, and *s* in the gate 2Sa 19:8 3427
The Tachmonite that *s* in the seat 2Sa 23:8 3427
Then *s* Solomon upon the throne of 1Kin 2:12 3427
s down on his throne, and caused a 1Kin 2:19 3427
and she *s* on his right hand 1Kin 2:19 3427
as they *s* at the table, that the 1Kin 13:20 3427
as soon as he *s* on his throne 1Kin 16:11 3427
s down under a juniper tree 1Kin 19:4 3427
of Belial, and *s* before him 1Kin 21:13 3427
of Judah *s* each on his throne 1Kin 22:10 3427
he *s* on the top of an hill 2Kin 1:9 3427
he *s* on her knees till noon, and 2Kin 4:20 3427
But Elisha *s* in his house, and the 2Kin 6:32 3427
house, and the elders *s* with him 2Kin 6:32 3427
he *s* on the throne of the kings 2Kin 11:19 3427
Jeroboam *s* upon his throne 2Kin 13:13 3427
as David *s* in his house, that 1Chr 17:1 3427
s before the LORD, and said, Who 1Chr 17:16 3427
Then Solomon *s* on the throne of 1Chr 29:23 3427
Jehoshaphat king of Judah *s* 2Chr 18:9 3427
they *s* in a void place at the 2Chr 18:9 3427
of my beard, and *s* down astonied Ezr 9:3 3427
I *s* astonied until the evening Ezr 9:4 3427
all the people *s* in the street of Ezr 10:9 3427
s down in the first day of the Ezr 10:16 3427
heard these words, that I *s* down Neh 1:4 3427
booths, and *s* under the booths Neh 8:17 3427
when the king Ahasuerus *s* on the Est 1:2 3427
which *s* the first in the kingdom Est 1:14 3427
then Mordecai *s* in the king's Est 2:19 3427
while Mordecai *s* in the king's Est 2:21 3427
the king and Haman *s* down to drink Est 3:15 3427
the king *s* upon his royal throne Est 5:1 3427
he *s* down among the ashes Job 2:8 3427
So they *s* down with him upon the Job 2:13 3427
s chief, and dwelt as a king in Job 29:25 3427
I have not *s* with vain persons, Ps 26:4 3427
of Babylon, there we *s* down Ps 137:1 3427
I *s* down under his shadow with Song 2:3 3427
In the ways hast thou *s* for them Jer 3:2 3427
I *s* not in the assembly of the Jer 15:17 3427
I *s* alone because of thy hand Jer 15:17 3427
s down in the entry of the new Jer 26:10 3427
before all the Jews that *s* in the Jer 32:12 3427
and, lo, all the princes *s* there Jer 36:12 3427
Now the king *s* in the winterhouse Jer 36:22 3427
s in the middle gate, even Jer 39:3 3427
I *s* where they *s*, and remained Eze 3:15 3427
of Chebar, and I *s* where they *s* Eze 3:15 3427
as I *s* in mine house, and the Eze 8:1 3427
the elders of Judah *s* before me Eze 8:1 3427
there *s* women weeping for Tammuz Eze 8:14 3427
of Israel unto me, and *s* before me Eze 14:1 3427
of the LORD, and *s* before me Eze 20:1 3427
but Daniel *s* in the gate of the Dan 2:49
him with sackcloth, and *s* in ashes Jonah 3:6 3427
s on the east side of the city, Jonah 4:5 3427
s under it in the shadow, till he Jonah 4:5 3427
The people which *s* in darkness Mt 4:16 *2521*
and to them which *s* in the region Mt 4:16 *2521*
as Jesus *s* at meat in the house, Mt 9:10 *345*
s down with him and his disciples Mt 9:10 *4873*
the house, and *s* by the sea side Mt 13:1 *2521*
so that he went into a ship, and *s* Mt 13:2 *2521*
s down, and gathered the good into Mt 13:48 *2523*
them which *s* with him at meat, he Mt 14:9 *4873*
into a mountain, and *s* down there Mt 15:29 *2521*
as he *s* upon the mount of Olives, Mt 24:3 *2521*
it on his head, as he *s* at meat Mt 26:7 *345*
he *s* down with the twelve Mt 26:20 *345*
I *s* daily with you teaching in Mt 26:55 *2516*
s with the servants, to see the Mt 26:58 *2521*
Now Peter *s* without in the palace Mt 26:69 *2521*
stone from the door, and *s* upon it Mt 28:2 *2521*
as Jesus *s* at meat in his house, Mk 2:15 *2621*
sinners *s* also together with Mk 2:15 *4873*
And the multitude *s* about him Mk 3:32 *2521*
about on them which *s* about him Mk 3:34 *2521*
into a ship, and *s* in the sea Mk 4:1 *2521*
Herod and them that *s* with him Mk 6:22 *4873*
for their sakes which *s* with him Mk 6:26 *4873*
they *s* down in ranks, by hundreds Mk 6:40 *377*
he *s* down, and called the twelve, Mk 9:35 *2523*
s by the highway side begging Mk 10:46 *2521*
a colt tied, whereon never man *s* Mk 11:2 *2523*
and he *s* upon him Mk 11:7 *2523*
Jesus *s* over against the treasury Mk 12:41 *2523*
as he *s* upon the mount of Olives Mk 13:3 *2521*
as he *s* at meat, there came a Mk 14:3 *2621*
And as they *s* and did eat, Jesus Mk 14:18 *345*
he *s* with the servants, and warmed Mk 14:54 *4775*
unto the eleven as they *s* at meat Mk 16:14 *345*
s on the right hand of God Mk 16:19 *2523*
again to the minister, and *s* down Lk 4:20 *2523*
he *s* down, and taught the people Lk 5:3 *2523*
of others that *s* down with them Lk 5:29 *2621*
And he that was dead *s* up, and Lk 7:15 *339*
house, and *s* down to meat Lk 7:36 *347*
when she knew that Jesus *s* at Lk 7:37 *345*
they that *s* at meat with him Lk 7:49 *4873*
which also *s* at Jesus' feet, and Lk 10:39 *3869*
and he went in, and *s* down to meat Lk 11:37 *377*
when one of them that *s* at meat Lk 14:15 *4873*
a certain blind man *s* by the way Lk 18:35 *2521*
tied, whereon yet never man *s* Lk 19:30 *2523*
he *s* down, and the twelve apostles Lk 22:14 *377*
together, Peter *s* down among them Lk 22:55 *2521*
beheld him as he *s* by the fire Lk 22:56 *2521*
as he *s* at meat with them, he Lk 24:30 *2625*
his journey, *s* thus on the well Jn 4:6 *2516*
there he *s* with his disciples Jn 6:3 *2521*
So the men *s* down, in number Jn 6:10 *377*
he *s* down, and taught them Jn 8:2 *2523*
said, Is not this he that *s* Jn 9:8 *2521*
but Mary *s* still in the house Jn 11:20 *2516*
them that *s* at the table with him Jn 12:2 *4873*
had found a young ass, *s* thereon Jn 12:14 *2523*
s down in the judgment seat in a Jn 19:13 *2523*
fire, and it *s* upon each of them Acts 2:3 *2523*
s for alms at the Beautiful gate Acts 3:10 *2521*
all that *s* in the council, Acts 6:15 *2516*
and when she saw Peter, she *s* up Acts 9:40 *339*
s upon his throne, and made an Acts 12:21 *2523*
on the sabbath day, and *s* down Acts 13:14 *2523*
there *s* a certain man at Lystra, Acts 14:8 *2521*
we *s* down, and spake unto the Acts 16:13 *2523*
there *s* in a window a certain Acts 20:9 *2521*
morrow I *s* on the judgment seat Acts 25:17 *2523*
Bernice, and they that *s* with them Acts 26:30 *4775*
The people *s* down to eat and drink 1Cor 10:7 *2523*
s down on the right hand of the Heb 1:3 *2523*
s down on the right hand of God Heb 10:12 *2523*
in heaven, and one *s* on the throne Rev 4:2 *2521*
he that *s* was to look upon like a Rev 4:3 *2521*
to him that *s* on the throne Rev 4:9 *2521*
before him that *s* on the throne Rev 4:10 *2521*
s on the throne a book written Rev 5:1 *2521*
of him that *s* upon the throne Rev 5:7 *2521*
he that *s* on him had a bow Rev 6:2 *2521*
power was given to him that *s* Rev 6:4 *2521*
he that *s* on him had a pair of Rev 6:5 *2521*
his name that *s* on him was Death, Rev 6:8 *2521*
vision, and them that *s* on them Rev 9:17 *2521*
which *s* before God on their seats Rev 11:16 *2521*
upon the cloud one *s* like unto Rev 14:14 *2521*
voice to him that *s* on the cloud Rev 14:15 *2521*
he that *s* on the cloud thrust in Rev 14:16 *2521*
God that *s* on the throne, saying, Rev 19:4 *2521*
he that *s* upon him was called Rev 19:11 *2521*
against him that *s* on the horse Rev 19:19 *2521*
of him that *s* upon the horse Rev 19:21 *2521*
they *s* upon them, and judgment was Rev 20:4 *2523*
white throne, and him that *s* on it Rev 20:11 *2521*
he that *s* upon the throne said, Rev 21:5 *2521*

SATAN *(sa'-tun)* {55} *The adversary.*
S stood up against Israel, and 1Chr 21:1 7854
LORD, and *S* came also among them Job 1:6 7854
And the LORD said unto *S*, Whence Job 1:7 7854
Then *S* answered the LORD, and said Job 1:7 7854
And the LORD said unto *S*, Hast Job 1:8 7854
Then *S* answered the LORD, and said Job 1:9 7854
And the LORD said unto *S*, Behold, Job 1:12 7854
So *S* went forth from the presence Job 1:12 7854
S came also among them to present Job 2:1 7854
And the LORD said unto *S*, From Job 2:2 7854
S answered the LORD, and said, Job 2:2 7854
And the LORD said unto *S*, Hast Job 2:3 7854
S answered the LORD, and said, Job 2:4 7854
And the LORD said unto *S*, Behold, Job 2:6 7854
So went *S* forth from the presence Job 2:7 7854
let *S* stand at his right hand Ps 109:6 7854
S standing at his right hand to Zec 3:1 7854
S, The LORD rebuke thee, O *S* Zec 3:2 7854
Jesus unto him, Get thee hence, *S* Mt 4:10 *4567*
And if *S* cast out *S*, he is Mt 12:26 *4567*
unto Peter, Get thee behind me, *S* Mt 16:23 *4567*
forty days, tempted of *S* Mk 1:13 *4567*
How can *S* cast out *S* Mk 3:23 *4567*
if *S* rise up against himself, and Mk 3:26 *4567*
S cometh immediately, and taketh Mk 4:15 *4567*
saying, Get thee behind me, *S* Mk 8:33 *4567*
unto him, Get thee behind me, *S* Lk 4:8 *4567*
I beheld *S* as lightning fall from Lk 10:18 *4567*
If *S* also be divided against Lk 11:18 *4567*
whom *S* hath bound, lo, these Lk 13:16 *4567*
Then entered *S* into Judas Lk 22:3 *4567*
S hath desired to have you, that Lk 22:31 *4567*
after the sop *S* entered into him Jn 13:27 *4567*
why hath *S* filled thine heart to Acts 5:3 *4567*
and from the power of *S* unto God Acts 26:18 *4567*
bruise *S* under your feet shortly Rom 16:20 *4567*
unto *S* for the destruction of the 1Cor 5:5 *4567*
that *S* tempt you not for your 1Cor 7:5 *4567*
Lest *S* should get an advantage of 2Cor 2:11 *4567*
for *S* himself is transformed into 2Cor 11:14 *4567*
the messenger of *S* to buffet me 2Cor 12:7 *4567*
but *S* hindered us 1Th 2:18 *4567*
the working of *S* with all power 2Th 2:9 *4567*
whom I have delivered unto *S* 1Ti 1:20 *4567*
are already turned aside after *S* 1Ti 5:15 *4567*
not, but are the synagogue of *S* Rev 2:9 *4567*
slain among you, where *S* dwelleth Rev 2:13 *4567*
have not known the depths of *S* Rev 2:24 *4567*
make them of the synagogue of *S* Rev 3:9 *4567*
serpent, called the Devil, and *S* Rev 12:9 *4567*
serpent, which is the Devil, and *S* Rev 20:2 *4567*
S shall be loosed out of his Rev 20:7 *4567*

SATAN'S *(sa'-tuns)* {1}
dwellest, even where *S* seat is Rev 2:13 *4567*

SATEST {2}
thou *s* in the throne judging Ps 9:4 3427
s upon a stately bed, and a table Eze 23:41 3427

SATIATE {2}
I will *s* the soul of the priests Jer 31:14 7301
shall devour, and it shall be *s* Jer 46:10 7646

SATIATED {1}
For I have *s* the weary soul, and I Jer 31:25 7301

SATISFACTION {2}
Moreover ye shall take no *s* for Num 35:31 3724
ye shall take no *s* for him that Num 35:32 3724

SATISFIED {42}
my lust shall be *s* upon them Ex 15:9 4390
and ye shall eat, and not be *s* Lev 26:26 7646
shall come, and shall eat and be *s* Deut 14:29 7646
s with favour, and full with the Deut 33:23 7649
God, and are not *s* with my flesh Job 19:22 7646
shall not be *s* with bread Job 27:14 7646
we cannot be *s* Job 31:31 7646
I shall be *s*, when I awake, with Ps 17:15 7646
The meek shall eat and be *s* Ps 22:26 7646
They shall be abundantly *s* with Ps 36:8 7301
days of famine they shall be *s* Ps 37:19 7646
meat, and grudge if they be not *s* Ps 59:15 7646
My soul shall be *s* as with marrow Ps 63:5 7646
we shall be *s* with the goodness Ps 65:4 7646
of the rock should I have *s* thee Ps 81:16 7649
the earth is *s* with the fruit of Ps 104:13 7646
his land shall be *s* with bread Prov 12:11 7646
A man shall be *s* with good by the Prov 12:14 7646
good man shall be *s* from himself Prov 14:14
A man's belly shall be *s* with the Prov 18:20 7646
and he that hath it shall abide *s* Prov 19:23 7649
and thou shalt be *s* with bread Prov 20:13 7646
so the eyes of man are never *s* Prov 27:20 7646
are three things that are never *s* Prov 30:15 7646
the eye is not *s* with seeing Eccl 1:8 7646
neither is his eye *s* with riches Eccl 4:8 7646
silver shall not be *s* with silver Eccl 5:10 7646
left hand, and they shall not be *s* Is 9:20 7646
he roasteth roast, and is *s* Is 44:16 7646
of his soul, and shall be *s* Is 53:11 7646
be *s* with the breasts of her Is 66:11 7646
shall be *s* with my goodness Jer 31:14 7646
all that spoil her shall be *s* Jer 50:10 7646
his soul shall be *s* upon mount Jer 50:19 7646
the Assyrians, to be *s* with bread Lam 5:6 7646
them, and yet couldest not be *s* Eze 16:28 7646
and yet thou wast not *s* herewith Eze 16:29 7646
oil, and ye shall be *s* therewith Joel 2:19 7646
ye shall eat in plenty, and be *s* Joel 2:26 7646
but they were not *s* Amos 4:8 7646
Thou shalt eat, but not be *s* Mic 6:14 7646
and is as death, and cannot be *s* Hab 2:5 7646

SATISFIEST {1}
s the desire of every living Ps 145:16 7646

SATISFIETH {3}
Who *s* thy mouth with good things Ps 103:5 7646
For he *s* the longing soul, and Ps 107:9 7646
your labour for that which *s* not Is 55:2 7654

SATISFY {10}
To *s* the desolate and waste ground Job 38:27 7646
O *s* us early with thy mercy Ps 90:14 7646
With long life will I *s* him Ps 91:16 7646
I will *s* her poor with bread Ps 132:15 7646
let her breasts *s* thee at all Prov 5:19 7301
if he steal to *s* his soul when he Prov 6:30 4390

hungry, and *s* the afflicted soul Is 58:10 7646
s thy soul in drought, and make Is 58:11 7646
they shall not *s* their souls Eze 7:19 7646
From whence can a man *s* these men Mk 8:4 *5526*

SATISFYING {2}
eateth to the *s* of his soul Prov 13:25 7648
any honour to the *s* of the flesh Col 2:23 *4140*

SATISIFED {1}
s them with the bread of heaven Ps 105:40 7649

SATYR {1}
the *s* shall cry to his fellow Is 34:14 8163

SATYRS {1}
there, and *s* shall dance there Is 13:21 8163

SAUL *(sawl)* {391} See PAUL, SAUL'S, SHAUL.
1. The first king of Israel.
And he had a son, whose name was *S* 1Sa 9:2 7586
And Kish said to *S* his son 1Sa 9:3 7586
S said to his servant that was 1Sa 9:5 7586
Then said *S* to his servant, But, 1Sa 9:7 7586
And the servant answered *S* again 1Sa 9:8 7586
Then said *S* to his servant, Well 1Sa 9:10 7586
in his ear a day before *S* came 1Sa 9:15 7586
And when Samuel saw *S*, the LORD 1Sa 9:17 7586
Then *S* drew near to Samuel in the 1Sa 9:18 7586
And Samuel answered *S*, and said, I 1Sa 9:19 7586
S answered and said, Am not I a 1Sa 9:21 7586
And Samuel took *S* and his servant, 1Sa 9:22 7586
was upon it, and set it before *S* 1Sa 9:24 7586
So *S* did eat with Samuel that day 1Sa 9:24 7586
Samuel communed with *S* upon the 1Sa 9:25 7586
that Samuel called *S* to the top 1Sa 9:26 7586
S arose, and they went out both of 1Sa 9:26 7586
end of the city, Samuel said to *S* 1Sa 9:27 7586
Is *S* also among the prophets 1Sa 10:11 7586
Is *S* also among the prophets 1Sa 10:12 7586
S said unto his uncle, He told us 1Sa 10:16 7586
S the son of Kish was taken 1Sa 10:21 7586
S also went home to Gibeah 1Sa 10:26 7586
the messengers to Gibeah of *S* 1Sa 11:4 7586
S came after the herd out of the 1Sa 11:5 7586
S said, What aileth the people 1Sa 11:5 7586
S when he heard those tidings 1Sa 11:6 7586
cometh not forth after *S* and after 1Sa 11:7 7586
that *S* put the people in three 1Sa 11:11 7586
that said, Shall *S* reign over us 1Sa 11:12 7586
S said, There shall not a man be 1Sa 11:13 7586
there they made *S* king before the 1Sa 11:15 7586
and there *S* and all the men of 1Sa 11:15 7586
S reigned one year 1Sa 13:1 7586
S chose him three thousand men of 1Sa 13:2 7586
thousand were with *S* in Michmash 1Sa 13:2 7586
S blew the trumpet throughout all 1Sa 13:3 7586
all Israel heard say that *S* had 1Sa 13:4 7586
called together after *S* to Gilgal 1Sa 13:4 7586
As for *S*, he was yet in Gilgal, 1Sa 13:7 7586
S said, Bring hither a burnt 1Sa 13:9 7586
S went out to meet him, that he 1Sa 13:10 7586
S said, Because I saw that the 1Sa 13:11 7586
And Samuel said to *S*, Thou hast 1Sa 13:13 7586
S numbered the people that were 1Sa 13:15 7586
And *S*, and Jonathan his son, and the 1Sa 13:16 7586
of the people that were with *S* 1Sa 13:22 7586
but with *S* and with Jonathan his 1Sa 13:22 7586
that Jonathan the son of *S* said 1Sa 14:1 7586
S tarried in the uttermost part 1Sa 14:2 7586
the watchmen of *S* in Gibeah of 1Sa 14:16 7586
Then said *S* unto the people that 1Sa 14:17 7586
S said unto Ahiah, Bring hither 1Sa 14:18 7586
while *S* talked unto the priest, 1Sa 14:19 7586
S said unto the priest, Withdraw 1Sa 14:19 7586
And *S* and all the people that were 1Sa 14:20 7586
the Israelites that were with *S* 1Sa 14:21 7586
for *S* had adjured the people, 1Sa 14:24 7586
Then they told *S*, saying, Behold, 1Sa 14:33 7586
S said, Disperse yourselves among 1Sa 14:34 7586
S built an altar unto the LORD 1Sa 14:35 7586
S said, Let us go down after the 1Sa 14:36 7586
S asked counsel of God, Shall I 1Sa 14:37 7586
S said, Draw ye near hither, all 1Sa 14:38 7586
And the people said unto *S* 1Sa 14:40 7586
Therefore *S* said unto the LORD 1Sa 14:41 7586
And *S* and Jonathan were taken 1Sa 14:41 7586
S said, Cast lots between me and 1Sa 14:42 7586
Then *S* said to Jonathan, Tell me 1Sa 14:43 7586
S answered, God do so and more 1Sa 14:44 7586
And the people said unto *S* 1Sa 14:45 7586
Then *S* went up from following the 1Sa 14:46 7586
So *S* took the kingdom over Israel 1Sa 14:47 7586
Now the sons of *S* were Jonathan 1Sa 14:49 7586
And Kish was the father of *S* 1Sa 14:51 7586
the Philistines all the days of *S* 1Sa 14:52 7586
when *S* saw any strong man, or any 1Sa 14:52 7586
Samuel also said unto *S*, The LORD 1Sa 15:1 7586
S gathered the people together, 1Sa 15:4 7586
S came to a city of Amalek, and 1Sa 15:5 7586
S said unto the Kenites, Go, 1Sa 15:6 7586
S smote the Amalekites from 1Sa 15:7 7586
But *S* and the people spared Agag, 1Sa 15:9 7586
that I have set up *S* to be king 1Sa 15:11 7586
early to meet *S* in the morning 1Sa 15:12 7586
S came to Carmel, and, behold, he 1Sa 15:12 7586
And Samuel came to *S* 1Sa 15:13 7586
S said unto him, Blessed be thou 1Sa 15:13 7586
S said, They have brought them 1Sa 15:15 7586
Then Samuel said unto *S*, Stay, and 1Sa 15:16 7586
S said unto Samuel, Yea, I have 1Sa 15:20 7586
S said unto Samuel, I have sinned 1Sa 15:24 7586
And Samuel said unto *S*, I will not 1Sa 15:26 7586
So Samuel turned again after *S* 1Sa 15:31 7586
and *S* worshipped the LORD 1Sa 15:31 7586
S went up to his house to Gibeah 1Sa 15:34 7586
up to his house to Gibeah of *S* 1Sa 15:34 7586
see *S* until the day of his death 1Sa 15:35 7586
nevertheless Samuel mourned for *S* 1Sa 15:35 7586
he had made *S* king over Israel 1Sa 15:35 7586
How long wilt thou mourn for *S* 1Sa 16:1 7586
if *S* hear it, he will kill me 1Sa 16:2 7586
of the LORD departed from *S* 1Sa 16:14 7586
S said unto his servants, Provide 1Sa 16:17 7586
Wherefore *S* sent messengers unto 1Sa 16:19 7586
sent them by David his son unto *S* 1Sa 16:20 7586
And David came to *S*, and stood 1Sa 16:21 7586
S sent to Jesse, saying, Let 1Sa 16:22 7586
evil spirit from God was upon *S* 1Sa 16:23 7586
so *S* was refreshed, and was well, 1Sa 16:23 7586
And *S* and the men of Israel were 1Sa 17:2 7586
a Philistine, and ye servants to *S* 1Sa 17:8 7586
When *S* and all Israel heard those 1Sa 17:11 7586
for an old man in the days of *S* 1Sa 17:12 7586
went and followed *S* to the battle 1Sa 17:13 7586
and the three eldest followed *S* 1Sa 17:14 7586
returned from *S* to feed his 1Sa 17:15 7586
Now *S*, and they, and all the men of 1Sa 17:19 7586
they rehearsed them before *S* 1Sa 17:31 7586
And David said to *S*, Let no man's 1Sa 17:32 7586
S said to David, Thou art not 1Sa 17:33 7586
And David said unto *S*, Thy servant 1Sa 17:34 7586
S said unto David, Go, and the 1Sa 17:37 7586
S armed David with his armour, and 1Sa 17:38 7586
And David said unto *S*, I cannot go 1Sa 17:39 7586
when *S* saw David go forth against 1Sa 17:55 7586
brought him before *S* with the 1Sa 17:57 7586
S said to him, Whose son art thou 1Sa 17:58 7586
made an end of speaking unto *S* 1Sa 18:1 7586
S took him that day, and would let 1Sa 18:2 7586
went out whithersoever *S* sent him 1Sa 18:5 7586
S set him over the men of war, and 1Sa 18:5 7586
and dancing, to meet king *S* 1Sa 18:6 7586
S hath slain his thousands, and 1Sa 18:7 7586
S was very wroth, and the saying 1Sa 18:8 7586
S eyed David from that day and 1Sa 18:9 7586
evil spirit from God came upon *S* 1Sa 18:10 7586
And *S* cast the javelin 1Sa 18:11 7586
S was afraid of David, because 1Sa 18:12 7586
with him, and was departed from *S* 1Sa 18:12 7586
Therefore *S* removed him from him, 1Sa 18:13 7586
Wherefore when *S* saw that he 1Sa 18:15 7586
S said to David, Behold my elder 1Sa 18:17 7586
For *S* said, Let not mine hand be 1Sa 18:17 7586
And David said unto *S*, Who am I 1Sa 18:18 7586
and they told *S*, and the thing 1Sa 18:20 7586
S said, I will give him her, that 1Sa 18:21 7586
Wherefore *S* said to David, Thou 1Sa 18:21 7586
S commanded his servants, saying, 1Sa 18:22 7586
And the servants of *S* told him 1Sa 18:24 7586
S said, Thus shall ye say to 1Sa 18:25 7586
But *S* thought to make David fall 1Sa 18:25 7586
S gave him Michal his daughter to 1Sa 18:27 7586
S saw and knew that the LORD was 1Sa 18:28 7586
S was yet the more afraid of 1Sa 18:29 7586
and *S* became David's enemy 1Sa 18:29 7586
wisely than all the servants of *S* 1Sa 18:30 7586
S spake to Jonathan his son, and 1Sa 19:1 7586
S my father seeketh to kill thee 1Sa 19:2 7586
good of David unto *S* his father 1Sa 19:4 7586
S hearkened unto the voice of 1Sa 19:6 7586
S sware, As the LORD liveth, he 1Sa 19:6 7586
And Jonathan brought David to *S* 1Sa 19:7 7586
spirit from the LORD was upon *S* 1Sa 19:9 7586
S sought to smite David even to 1Sa 19:10 7586
S also sent messengers unto 1Sa 19:11 7586
when *S* sent messengers to take 1Sa 19:14 7586
S sent the messengers again to 1Sa 19:15 7586
S said unto Michal, Why hast thou 1Sa 19:17 7586
And Michal answered *S*, He said 1Sa 19:17 7586
him all that *S* had done to him 1Sa 19:18 7586
And it was told *S*, saying, Behold, 1Sa 19:19 7586
S sent messengers to take David 1Sa 19:20 7586
God was upon the messengers of *S* 1Sa 19:20 7586
And when it was told *S*, he sent 1Sa 19:21 7586
S sent messengers again the third 1Sa 19:21 7586
Is *S* also among the prophets 1Sa 19:24 7586
Nevertheless *S* spake not any 1Sa 20:26 7586
S said unto Jonathan his son, 1Sa 20:27 7586
And Jonathan answered *S*, David 1Sa 20:28 7586
And Jonathan answered *S* his father 1Sa 20:32 7586
S cast a javelin at him to smite 1Sa 20:33 7586
servants of *S* was there that day 1Sa 21:7 7586
of the herdmen that belonged to *S* 1Sa 21:7 7586
and fled that day for fear of *S* 1Sa 21:10 7586
S hath slain his thousands, and 1Sa 21:11 7586
When *S* heard that David was 1Sa 22:6 7586
(now *S* abode in Gibeah under a 1Sa 22:6 7586
Then *S* said unto his servants 1Sa 22:7 7586
was set over the servants of *S* 1Sa 22:9 7586
S said, Hear now, thou son of 1Sa 22:12 7586
S said unto him, Why have ye 1Sa 22:13 7586
Abiathar shewed David that *S* had 1Sa 22:21 7586
that he would surely tell *S* 1Sa 22:22 7586
it was told *S* that David was come 1Sa 23:7 7586
S said, God hath delivered him 1Sa 23:7 7586
S called all the people together 1Sa 23:8 7586
David knew that *S* secretly 1Sa 23:9 7586
that *S* seeketh to come to Keilah 1Sa 23:10 7586
will *S* come down, as thy servant 1Sa 23:11 7586
me and my men into the hand of *S* 1Sa 23:12 7586
it was told *S* that David was 1Sa 23:13 7586
S sought him every day, but God 1Sa 23:14 7586
David saw that *S* was come out to 1Sa 23:15 7586
for the hand of *S* my father shall 1Sa 23:17 7586
that also *S* my father knoweth 1Sa 23:17 7586
up the Ziphites to *S* to Gibeah 1Sa 23:19 7586
S said, Blessed be ye of the LORD 1Sa 23:21 7586
arose, and went to Ziph before *S* 1Sa 23:24 7586
S also and his men went to seek 1Sa 23:25 7586
when *S* heard that, he pursued 1Sa 23:25 7586
S went on this side of the 1Sa 23:26 7586
haste to get away for fear of *S* 1Sa 23:26 7586
for *S* and his men compassed David 1Sa 23:26 7586
But there came a messenger unto *S* 1Sa 23:27 7586
Wherefore *S* returned from 1Sa 23:28 7586
to pass, when *S* was returned from 1Sa 24:1 7586
Then *S* took three thousand chosen 1Sa 24:2 7586
S went in to cover his feet 1Sa 24:3 7586
them not to rise against *S* 1Sa 24:7 7586
But *S* rose up out of the cave, and 1Sa 24:7 7586
out of the cave, and cried after *S* 1Sa 24:8 7586
when *S* looked behind him, David 1Sa 24:8 7586
And David said to *S*, Wherefore 1Sa 24:9 7586
words unto *S*, that *S* said 1Sa 24:16 7586
S lifted up his voice, and wept 1Sa 24:16 7586
And David sware unto *S* 1Sa 24:22 7586
And *S* went home 1Sa 24:22 7586
But *S* had given Michal his 1Sa 25:44 7586
Ziphites came unto *S* to Gibeah 1Sa 26:1 7586
Then *S* arose, and went down to the 1Sa 26:2 7586
S pitched in the hill of Hachilah 1Sa 26:3 7586
he saw that *S* came after him into 1Sa 26:3 7586
understood that *S* was come in 1Sa 26:4 7586
to the place where *S* had pitched 1Sa 26:5 7586
beheld the place where *S* lay 1Sa 26:5 7586
S lay in the trench, and the 1Sa 26:5 7586
go down with me to *S* to the camp 1Sa 26:6 7586
S lay sleeping within the trench, 1Sa 26:7 7586
S knew David's voice, and said, Is 1Sa 26:17 7586
Then said *S*, I have sinned 1Sa 26:21 7586
Then *S* said to David, Blessed be 1Sa 26:25 7586
way, and *S* returned to his place 1Sa 26:25 7586
perish one day by the hand of *S* 1Sa 27:1 7586
S shall despair of me, to seek me 1Sa 27:1 7586
it was told *S* that David was fled 1Sa 27:4 7586
S had put away those that had 1Sa 28:3 7586
S gathered all Israel together, 1Sa 28:4 7586
when *S* saw the host of the 1Sa 28:5 7586
when *S* enquired of the LORD, the 1Sa 28:6 7586
Then said *S* unto his servants, 1Sa 28:7 7586
S disguised himself, and put on 1Sa 28:8 7586
thou knowest what *S* hath done 1Sa 28:9 7586
S sware to her by the LORD, 1Sa 28:10 7586
and the woman spake to *S*, saying, 1Sa 28:12 7586
for thou art *S* 1Sa 28:12 7586
And the woman said unto *S*, I saw 1Sa 28:13 7586
S perceived that it was Samuel, 1Sa 28:14 7586
And Samuel said to *S*, Why hast 1Sa 28:15 7586
S answered, I am sore distressed 1Sa 28:15 7586
Then *S* fell straightway all along 1Sa 28:20 7586
And the woman came unto *S*, and saw 1Sa 28:21 7586
And she brought it before *S* 1Sa 28:25 7586
the servant of *S* the king of 1Sa 29:3 7586
S slew his thousands, and David 1Sa 29:5 7586
Philistines followed hard upon *S* 1Sa 31:2 7586
And the battle went sore against *S* 1Sa 31:3 7586
Then said *S* unto his armourbearer 1Sa 31:4 7586
Therefore *S* took a sword, and fell 1Sa 31:4 7586
armourbearer saw that *S* was dead 1Sa 31:5 7586
So *S* died, and his three sons, and 1Sa 31:6 7586
the men of Israel fled, and that *S* 1Sa 31:7 7586
the slain, that they found *S* 1Sa 31:8 7586
the Philistines had done to *S* 1Sa 31:11 7586
all night, and took the body of *S* 1Sa 31:12 7586
came to pass after the death of *S* 2Sa 1:1 7586
camp from *S* with his clothes rent 2Sa 1:2 7586
and *S* and Jonathan his son are dead 2Sa 1:4 7586
told him, How knowest thou that *S* 2Sa 1:5 7586
behold, *S* leaned upon his spear 2Sa 1:6 7586
wept, and fasted until even, for *S* 2Sa 1:12 7586
with this lamentation over *S* 2Sa 1:17 7586
vilely cast away, the shield of *S* 2Sa 1:21 7586
the sword of *S* returned not empty 2Sa 1:22 7586
S and Jonathan were lovely and 2Sa 1:23 7586
daughters of Israel, weep over *S* 2Sa 1:24 7586
were they that buried *S* 2Sa 2:4 7586
unto your lord, even unto *S* 2Sa 2:5 7586
for your master *S* is dead 2Sa 2:7 7586
took Ish-bosheth the son of *S* 2Sa 2:8 7586
of Ish-bosheth the son of *S* 2Sa 2:12 7586
to Ish-bosheth the son of *S* 2Sa 2:15 7586
long war between the house of *S* 2Sa 3:1 7586
and the house of *S* waxed weaker 2Sa 3:1 7586
was war between the house of *S* 2Sa 3:6 7586
himself strong for the house of *S* 2Sa 3:6 7586
S had a concubine, whose name was 2Sa 3:7 7586
unto the house of *S* thy father 2Sa 3:8 7586
the kingdom from the house of *S* 2Sa 3:10 7586
old when the tidings came of *S* 2Sa 4:4 7586
the son of *S* thine enemy, which 2Sa 4:8 7586
my lord the king this day of *S* 2Sa 4:8 7586
S is dead, thinking to have 2Sa 4:10 7586
when *S* was king over us, thou 2Sa 5:2 7586
of *S* came out to meet David 2Sa 6:20 7586
Michal the daughter of *S* had no 2Sa 6:23 7586
from him, as I took it from *S* 2Sa 7:15 7586

that is left of the house of S ... 2Sa 9:1 7586
there was of the house of S a ... 2Sa 9:2 7586
not yet any of the house of S ... 2Sa 9:3 7586
the son of Jonathan, the son of S ... 2Sa 9:6 7586
thee all the land of S thy father ... 2Sa 9:7 7586
son all that pertained to S ... 2Sa 9:9 7586
thee out of the hand of S ... 2Sa 12:7 7586
of the family of the house of S ... 2Sa 16:5 7586
all the blood of the house of S ... 2Sa 16:8 7586
the servant of the house of S ... 2Sa 19:17 7586
Mephibosheth the son of S came ... 2Sa 19:24 7586
And the LORD answered, It is for S ... 2Sa 21:1 7586
S sought to slay them in his zeal ... 2Sa 21:2 7586
will have no silver nor gold of S ... 2Sa 21:4 7586
up unto the LORD in Gibeah of S ... 2Sa 21:6 7586
the son of Jonathan the son of S ... 2Sa 21:7 7586
David and Jonathan the son of S ... 2Sa 21:7 7586
of Aiah, whom she bare unto S ... 2Sa 21:8 7586
sons of Michal the daughter of S ... 2Sa 21:8 7586
of Aiah, the concubine of S ... 2Sa 21:11 7586
David went and took the bones of S ... 2Sa 21:12 7586
Philistines had slain S in Gilboa ... 2Sa 21:12 7586
up from thence the bones of S ... 2Sa 21:13 7586
And the bones of S and Jonathan his ... 2Sa 21:14 7586
enemies, and out of the hand of S ... 2Sa 22:1 7586
in the days of S they made war ... 1Chr 5:10 7586
Ner begat Kish, and Kish begat S ... 1Chr 8:33 7586
S begat Jonathan, and Malchi-shua, ... 1Chr 8:33 7586
and Kish begat S ... 1Chr 9:39 7586
S begat Jonathan, and Malchi-shua, ... 1Chr 9:39 7586
Philistines followed hard after S ... 1Chr 10:2 7586
and Malchi-shua, the sons of S ... 1Chr 10:2 7586
And the battle went sore against S ... 1Chr 10:3 7586
Then said S to his armourbearer, ... 1Chr 10:4 7586
So S took a sword, and fell upon ... 1Chr 10:4 7586
armourbearer saw that S was dead ... 1Chr 10:5 7586
So S died, and his three sons, and ... 1Chr 10:6 7586
saw that they fled, and that S ... 1Chr 10:7 7586
the slain, that they found S ... 1Chr 10:8 7586
the Philistines had done to S ... 1Chr 10:11 7586
men, and took away the body of S ... 1Chr 10:12 7586
So S died for his transgression ... 1Chr 10:13 7586
time past, even when S was king ... 1Chr 11:2 7586
because of S the son of Kish ... 1Chr 12:1 7586
Philistines against S to battle ... 1Chr 12:19 7586
He will fall to his master S to ... 1Chr 12:19 7586
to turn the kingdom of S to him ... 1Chr 12:23 7586
of Benjamin, the kindred of S ... 1Chr 12:29 7586
kept the ward of the house of S ... 1Chr 12:29 7586
not at it in the days of S ... 1Chr 13:3 7586
of S looking out at a window saw ... 1Chr 15:29 7586
S the son of Kish, and Abner the ... 1Chr 26:28 7586
enemies, and from the hand of S ... Ps 18:t 7586
Doeg the Edomite came and told S ... Ps 52:t 7586
the Ziphims came and said to S ... Ps 54:t 7586
when he fled from S in the cave ... Ps 57:t 7586
when S sent, and they watched the ... Ps 59:t 7586
Gibeah of S is fled ... Is 10:29 7586
gave unto them S the son of Cis ... Acts 13:21 *4569*

2. An Edomite king.

S of Rehoboth by the river ... Gen 36:37 7586
S died, and Baal-hanan the son of ... Gen 36:38 7586

3. Original name of Paul.

man's feet, whose name was S ... Acts 7:58 *4569*
S was consenting unto his death ... Acts 8:1 *4569*
As for S, he made havock of the ... Acts 8:3 *4569*
And S, yet breathing out ... Acts 9:1 *4569*
a voice saying unto him, Saul, S ... Acts 9:4 *4569*
And S arose from the earth ... Acts 9:8 *4569*
house of Judas for one called S ... Acts 9:11 *4569*
his hands on him said, Brother S ... Acts 9:17 *4569*
Then was S certain days with the ... Acts 9:19 *4569*
But S increased the more in ... Acts 9:22 *4569*
their laying await was known of S ... Acts 9:24 *4569*
when S was come to Jerusalem, he ... Acts 9:26 *4569*
Barnabas to Tarsus, for to seek S ... Acts 11:25 *4569*
by the hands of Barnabas and S ... Acts 11:30 *4569*
S returned from Jerusalem, when ... Acts 12:25 *4569*
up with Herod the tetrarch, and S ... Acts 13:1 *4569*
S for the work whereunto I have ... Acts 13:2 *4569*
who called for Barnabas and S ... Acts 13:7 *4569*
Then S, (who also is called Paul, ... Acts 13:9 *4569*
a voice saying unto me, Saul, S ... Acts 22:7 *4569*
stood, and said unto me, Brother S ... Acts 22:13 *4569*
in the Hebrew tongue, Saul, S ... Acts 26:14 *4569*

SAUL'S {31} *Refers to Saul 1.*

asses of Kish S father were lost ... 1Sa 9:3 7586
S uncle said unto him and to his ... 1Sa 10:14 7586
S uncle said, Tell me, I pray ... 1Sa 10:15 7586
the name of S wife was Ahinoam, ... 1Sa 14:50 7586
Abner, the son of Ner, S uncle ... 1Sa 14:50 7586
S servants said unto him, Behold ... 1Sa 16:15 7586
also in the sight of S servants ... 1Sa 18:5 7586
and there was a javelin in S hand ... 1Sa 18:10 7586
to pass at the time when Merab S ... 1Sa 18:19 7586
Michal S daughter loved David ... 1Sa 18:20 7586
S servants spake those words in ... 1Sa 18:23 7586
that Michal S daughter loved him ... 1Sa 18:28 7586
But Jonathan S son delighted much ... 1Sa 19:2 7586
he slipped away out of S presence ... 1Sa 19:10 7586
arose, and Abner sat by S side ... 1Sa 20:25 7586
Then S anger was kindled against ... 1Sa 20:30 7586
Jonathan S son arose, and went to ... 1Sa 23:16 7586
off the skirt of S robe privily ... 1Sa 24:4 7586
because he had cut off S skirt ... 1Sa 24:5 7586
the cruse of water from S bolster ... 1Sa 26:12 7586
Abinadab, and Melchi-shua, S sons ... 1Sa 31:2 7586
the son of Ner, captain of S host ... 2Sa 2:8 7586
Ish-bosheth S son was forty years ... 2Sa 2:10 7586
first bring Michal S daughter ... 2Sa 3:13 7586
messengers to Ish-bosheth S son ... 2Sa 3:14 7586
when S son heard that Abner was ... 2Sa 4:1 7586
S son had two men that were ... 2Sa 4:2 7586
S son, had a son that was lame of ... 2Sa 4:4 7586
Michal S daughter looked through ... 2Sa 6:16 7586
S servant, and said unto him, I ... 2Sa 9:9 7586
even of S brethren of Benjamin ... 1Chr 12:2 7586

SAVE {235}

me, but they will s thee alive ... Gen 12:12 2421
S only that which the young men ... Gen 14:24 1107
s the bread which he did eat ... Gen 39:6 3588,518
to s your lives by a great ... Gen 45:7 2421
this day, to s much people alive ... Gen 50:20 2421
every daughter ye shall s alive ... Ex 1:22 2421
s that which every man must eat, ... Ex 12:16 389
s unto the LORD only, he shall be ... Ex 22:20 1115
s Caleb the son of Jephunneh, and ... Num 14:30 3588,518
s Caleb the son of Jephunneh, and ... Num 26:65 3588,518
S Caleb the son of Jephunneh the ... Num 32:12 3588,518
S Caleb the son of Jephunneh ... Deut 1:36 2108
S when there shall be no poor ... Deut 15:4 657
against your enemies, to s you ... Deut 20:4 3467
thou shalt s alive nothing that ... Deut 20:16 2421
cried, and there was none to s her ... Deut 22:27 3467
evermore, and no man shall s thee ... Deut 28:29 3467
that ye will s alive my father, ... Josh 2:13 2421
us quickly, and s us, and help us ... Josh 10:6 3467
burned none of them, s Hazor only ... Josh 11:13 2108
s the Hivites the inhabitants of ... Josh 11:19 1115
s cities to dwell in, with their ... Josh 14:4 3588,518
the LORD, (s us not this day,) ... Josh 22:22 3467
thou shalt s Israel from the hand ... Judg 6:14 3467
Lord, wherewith shall I s Israel ... Judg 6:15 3467
will ye s him ... Judg 6:31 3467
If thou wilt s Israel by mine ... Judg 6:36 3467
thou wilt s Israel by mine hand ... Judg 6:37 3467
men that lapped will I s you ... Judg 7:7 3467
This is nothing else s the sword ... Judg 7:14 1115,518
it may s us out of the hand of ... 1Sa 4:3 3467
that he will s us out of the hand ... 1Sa 7:8 3467
that he may s my people out of ... 1Sa 9:16 3467
shouted, and said, God s the king ... 1Sa 10:24 2421
said, How shall this man s us ... 1Sa 10:27 3467
then, if there be no man to s us ... 1Sa 11:3 3467
the LORD to s by many or by few ... 1Sa 14:6 3467
If thou s not thy to night, to ... 1Sa 19:11 4422
for there is no other s that here ... 1Sa 21:9 2108
the Philistines, and s Keilah ... 1Sa 23:2 3467
s four hundred young men, which ... 1Sa 30:17 3588,518
s to every man his wife and his ... 1Sa 30:22 3588,518
s my people Israel out of the ... 2Sa 3:18 3467
s one little ewe lamb, which he ... 2Sa 12:3 3588,518
God s the king, God s the king ... 2Sa 16:16 2421
God s the king, God s the king ... 2Sa 16:16 2421
the afflicted people thou wilt s ... 2Sa 22:28 3467
For who is God, s the LORD ... 2Sa 22:32 1107
and who is a rock, s our God ... 2Sa 22:32 1107
looked, but there was none to s ... 2Sa 22:42 3467
that thou mayest s thine own life ... 1Kin 1:12 4422
him, and say, God s king Adonijah ... 1Kin 1:25 2421
and say, God s king Solomon ... 1Kin 1:34 2421
people said, God s king Solomon ... 1Kin 1:39 2421
the house, s we two in the house ... 1Kin 3:18 2108
the ark s the two tables of stone ... 1Kin 8:9 7535
s only in the matter of Uriah the ... 1Kin 15:5
we may find grass to s the horses ... 1Kin 18:5 2421
peradventure he will s thy life ... 1Kin 20:31 2421
s only with the king of Israel ... 1Kin 22:31 3588,518
in the house, s a pot of oil ... 2Kin 4:2 3467
if they s us alive, we shall live ... 2Kin 7:4 2421
hands, and said, God s the king ... 2Kin 11:12 2421
S that the high places were not ... 2Kin 15:4 7535
s me out of the hand of the king ... 2Kin 16:7 3467
s thou us out of his hand, that ... 2Kin 19:19 3467
I will defend this city, to s it ... 2Kin 19:34 3467
s the poorest sort of the people ... 2Kin 24:14 2108
S us, O God of our salvation, and ... 1Chr 16:35 3467
s only to burn sacrifice before ... 2Chr 2:6 518
There was nothing in the ark s ... 2Chr 5:10 7535
s only with the king of Israel ... 2Chr 18:30 3588,518
s Jehoahaz, the youngest of his ... 2Chr 21:17 3467
s the priests, and they that ... 2Chr 23:6 3588,518
him, and said, God s the king ... 2Chr 23:11 2421
s the beast that I rode upon ... Neh 2:12 3588,518
go into the temple to s his life ... Neh 6:11 2425
but s his life ... Job 2:6 8104
he shall not s of that which he ... Job 20:20 4422
he shall s the humble person ... Job 22:29 3467
thine own right hand can s thee ... Job 40:14 3467
s me, O my God ... Ps 3:7 3467
oh s me for thy mercies' sake ... Ps 6:4 3467
s me from all them that persecute ... Ps 7:1 3467
For thou wilt s the afflicted ... Ps 18:27 3467
For who is God s the LORD ... Ps 18:31 1107
or who is a rock s our God ... Ps 18:31 2108
but there was none to s them ... Ps 18:41 3467
S, LORD ... Ps 20:9 3467
S me from the lion's mouth ... Ps 22:21 3467
S thy people, and bless thine ... Ps 28:9 3467
for an house of defence to s me ... Ps 31:2 3467
s me for thy mercies' sake ... Ps 31:16 3467
s them, because they trust in him ... Ps 37:40 3467
neither did their own arm s them ... Ps 44:3 3467
bow, neither shall my sword s me ... Ps 44:6 3467
S me, O God, by thy name, and ... Ps 54:1 3467
and the LORD shall s me ... Ps 55:16 3467
s me from the reproach of him ... Ps 57:3 3467
iniquity, and s me from bloody men ... Ps 59:2 3467
s with thy right hand, and hear me ... Ps 60:5 3467
S me, O God ... Ps 69:1 3467
For God will s Zion, and will ... Ps 69:35 3467
thine ear unto me, and s me ... Ps 71:2 3467
hast given commandment to s me ... Ps 71:3 3467
he shall s the children of the ... Ps 72:4 3467
shall s the souls of the needy ... Ps 72:13 3467
to s all the meek of the earth ... Ps 76:9 3467
up thy strength, and come and s us ... Ps 80:2 3444
s thy servant that trusteth in ... Ps 86:2 3467
s the son of thine handmaid ... Ps 86:16 3467
S us, O LORD our God, and gather ... Ps 106:47 3467
s with thy right hand, and answer ... Ps 108:6 3467
O s me according to thy mercy ... Ps 109:26 3467
to s him from those that condemn ... Ps 109:31 3467
S now, I beseech thee, O LORD ... Ps 118:25 3467
I am thine, s me ... Ps 119:94 3467
s me, and I shall keep thy ... Ps 119:146 3467
and thy right hand shall s me ... Ps 138:7 3467
hear their cry, and will s them ... Ps 145:19 3467
on the LORD, and he shall s thee ... Prov 20:22 3467
waited for him, and he will s us ... Is 25:9 3467
he will s us ... Is 33:22 3467
he will come and s you ... Is 35:4 3467
s us from his hand, that all the ... Is 37:20 3467
city to s it for mine own sake ... Is 37:35 3467
The LORD was ready to s me ... Is 38:20 3467
and pray unto a god that cannot s ... Is 45:20 3467
nor s him out of his trouble ... Is 46:7 3467
s thee from these things that ... Is 47:13 3467
none shall s thee ... Is 47:15 3467
thee, and I will s thy children ... Is 49:25 3467
not shortened, that it cannot s ... Is 59:1 3467
in righteousness, mighty to s ... Is 63:1 3467
they will say, Arise, and s us ... Jer 2:27 3467
if they can s thee in the time of ... Jer 2:28 3467
but they shall not s them at all ... Jer 11:12 3467
as a mighty man that cannot s ... Jer 14:9 3467
for I am with thee to s thee ... Jer 15:20 3467
s me, and I shall be saved ... Jer 17:14 3467
I will s thee from afar, and thy ... Jer 30:10 3467
thee, saith the LORD, to s thee ... Jer 30:11 3467
s thy people, the remnant of ... Jer 31:7 3467
for I am with you to s you ... Jer 42:11 3467
I will s thee from afar off, and ... Jer 46:27 3467
s your lives, and be like the ... Jer 48:6 4422
for a nation that could not s us ... Lam 4:17 3467
his wicked way, to s his life ... Eze 3:18 2421
will ye s the souls alive that ... Eze 13:18 2421
to s the souls alive that should ... Eze 13:19 2421
he shall s his soul alive ... Eze 18:27 2421
Therefore will I s my flock ... Eze 34:22 3467
I will also s you from all your ... Eze 36:29 3467
but I will s them out of all ... Eze 37:23 3467
s of thee, O king, he shall be ... Dan 6:7 3861
s of thee, O king, shall be cast ... Dan 6:12 3861
will s them by the LORD their God ... Hos 1:7 3467
will not s them by bow, nor by ... Hos 1:7 3467
that may s thee in all thy cities ... Hos 13:10 3467
Asshur shall not s us ... Hos 14:3 3467
of violence, and thou wilt not s ... Hab 1:2 3467
he will s, he will rejoice over ... Zeph 3:17 3467
I will s her that halteth, and ... Zeph 3:19 3467
I will s my people from the east ... Zec 8:7 3467
so will I s you, and ye shall be a ... Zec 8:13 3467
the LORD their God shall s them ... Zec 9:16 3467
I will s the house of Joseph, and ... Zec 10:6 3467
The LORD also shall s the tents ... Zec 12:7 3467
for he shall s his people from ... Mt 1:21 *4982*
and awoke him, saying, Lord, s us ... Mt 8:25 *4982*
s the Son, and he to whomsoever ... Mt 11:27 *1508*
s in his own country, and in his ... Mt 13:57 *1508*
he cried, saying, Lord, s me ... Mt 14:30 *4982*
For whosoever will s his life ... Mt 16:25 *4982*
they saw no man, s Jesus only ... Mt 17:8 *1508*
is come to s that which was lost ... Mt 18:11 *4982*
s they to whom it is given ... Mt 19:11 *235*
it in three days, s thyself ... Mt 27:40 *4982*
himself he cannot s ... Mt 27:42 *4982*
whether Elias will come to s him ... Mt 27:49 *4982*
to s life, or to kill ... Mk 3:4 *4982*
s Peter, and James, and John the ... Mk 5:37 *1508*
s that he laid his hands upon a ... Mk 6:5 *1508*
for their journey, s a staff only ... Mk 6:8 *1508*
For whosoever will s his life ... Mk 8:35 *4982*
the gospel's, the same shall s it ... Mk 8:35 *4982*
s Jesus only with themselves ... Mk 9:8 *235*
S thyself, and come down from the ... Mk 15:30 *4982*
himself he cannot s ... Mk 15:31 *4982*
s unto Sarepta, a city of Sidon, ... Lk 4:26 *1508*
to s life, or to destroy it ... Lk 6:9 *4982*
s Peter, and James, and John, and ... Lk 8:51 *1508*
For whosoever will s his life ... Lk 9:24 *4982*
for my sake, the same shall s it ... Lk 9:24 *4982*
men's lives, but to s them ... Lk 9:56 *4982*
glory to God, s this stranger ... Lk 17:18 *1508*
seek to s his life shall lose it ... Lk 17:33 *4982*
none is good, s one, that is, God ... Lk 18:19 *1508*
seek and to s that which was lost ... Lk 19:10 *4982*
let him s himself, if he be ... Lk 23:35 *4982*
the king of the Jews, s thyself ... Lk 23:37 *4982*
thou be Christ, s thyself and us ... Lk 23:39 *4982*
there, s that one whereinto his ... Jn 6:22 *1508*
s he which is of God, he hath ... Jn 6:46 *1508*

Father, *s* me from this hour .... Jn 12:27 4982
the world, but to *s* the world .... Jn 12:47 4982
needeth not *s* to wash his feet .... Jn 13:10 2228
S yourselves from this untoward .... Acts 2:40 4982
S that the Holy Ghost witnesseth .... Acts 20:23 4133
s only that they keep themselves .... Acts 21:25 1508
the centurion, willing to *s* Paul .... Acts 27:43 1295
my flesh, and might *s* some of them .... Rom 11:14 4982
preaching to *s* them that believe 1Cor 1:21 4982
s Jesus Christ, and him crucified 1Cor 2:2 1508
s the spirit of man which is in 1Cor 2:11 1508
whether thou shalt *s* thy husband 1Cor 7:16 4982
whether thou shalt *s* thy wife 1Cor 7:16 4982
that I might by all means *s* some 1Cor 9:22 4982
received I forty stripes *s* one 2Cor 11:24 3844
s James the Lord's brother .... Gal 1:19 1508
s in the cross of our Lord Jesus .... Gal 6:14 1508
came into the world to *s* sinners 1Ti 1:15 4982
this thou shalt both *s* thyself 1Ti 4:16 4982
that was able to *s* him from death .... Heb 5:7 4982
Wherefore he is able also to *s* .... Heb 7:25 4982
which is able to *s* your souls .... Jas 1:21 4982
can faith *s* him .... Jas 2:14 4982
is one lawgiver, who is able to *s* .... Jas 4:12 4982
prayer of faith shall *s* the sick .... Jas 5:15 4982
his way shall *s* a soul from death .... Jas 5:20 4982
even baptism doth also now *s* us 1Pet 3:21 4982
others *s* with fear, pulling them .... Jude 23 4982
s he that had the mark, or the .... Rev 13:17 1508

SAVED {104}
they said, Thou hast *s* our lives .... Gen 47:25
but *s* the men children alive .... Ex 1:17 2421
have *s* the men children alive .... Ex 1:18 2421
Thus the LORD *s* Israel that day .... Ex 14:30 3467
ye shall be *s* from your enemies .... Num 10:9 3467
I had slain thee, and *s* her alive .... Num 22:33 2421
Have ye *s* all the women alive .... Num 31:15 2421
O people *s* by the LORD, the .... Deut 33:29 3467
Joshua *s* Rahab the harlot alive, ... Josh 6:25 2421
saying, Mine own hand hath *s* me .... Judg 7:2 3467
if ye had *s* them alive, I would .... Judg 8:19 2421
they had *s* alive of the women of .... Judg 21:14 2421
who himself *s* you out of all your 1Sa 10:19 3467
So the LORD *s* Israel that day 1Sa 14:23 3467
So David *s* the inhabitants of 1Sa 23:5 3467
David *s* neither man nor woman 1Sa 27:11 2421
which this day have *s* thy life 2Sa 19:5 4422
The king *s* us out of the hand of 2Sa 19:9 5337
so shall I be *s* from mine enemies 2Sa 22:4 3467
s himself there, not once nor 2Kin 6:10 8104
but he *s* them by the hand of 2Kin 14:27 3467
the LORD *s* them by a great 1Chr 11:14 3467
Thus the LORD *s* Hezekiah and the 2Chr 32:22 3467
who *s* them out of the hand of .... Neh 9:27 3467
so shall I be *s* from mine enemies .... Ps 18:3 3467
There is no king *s* by the .... Ps 33:16 3467
s him out of all his troubles .... Ps 34:6 3467
But thou hast *s* us from our .... Ps 44:7 3467
and we shall be *s* .... Ps 80:3 3467
and we shall be *s* .... Ps 80:7 3467
and we shall be *s* .... Ps 80:19 3467
Nevertheless he *s* them for his .... Ps 106:8 3467
he *s* them from the hand of him .... Ps 106:10 3467
he *s* them out of their distresses .... Ps 107:13 3467
walketh uprightly shall be *s* .... Prov 28:18 3467
returning and rest shall ye be *s* .... Is 30:15 3467
I have declared, and have *s* .... Is 43:12 3467
But Israel shall be *s* in the LORD .... Is 45:17 3467
Look unto me, and be ye *s*, all the .... Is 45:22 3467
the angel of his presence *s* them .... Is 63:9 3467
is continuance, and we shall be *s* .... Is 64:5 3467
wickedness, that thou mayest be *s* .... Jer 4:14 3467
summer is ended, and we are not *s* .... Jer 8:20 3467
save me, and I shall be *s* .... Jer 17:14 3467
In his days Judah shall be *s* .... Jer 23:6 3467
but he shall be *s* out of it .... Jer 30:7 3467
In those days shall Judah be *s* .... Jer 33:16 3467
endureth to the end shall be *s* .... Mt 10:22 4982
amazed, saying, Who then can be *s* .... Mt 19:25 4982
unto the end, the same shall be *s* .... Mt 24:13 4982
there should no flesh be *s* .... Mt 24:22 4982
He *s* others; himself he .... Mt 27:42 4982
themselves, Who then can be *s* .... Mk 10:26 4982
unto the end, the same shall be *s* .... Mk 13:13 4982
those days, no flesh should be *s* .... Mk 13:20 4982
with the scribes, He *s* others .... Mk 15:31 4982
and is baptized shall be *s* .... Mk 16:16 4982
we should be *s* from our enemies .... Lk 1:71 4991
the woman, Thy faith hath *s* thee .... Lk 7:50 4982
lest they should believe and be *s* .... Lk 8:12 4982
Lord, are there few that be *s* .... Lk 13:23 4982
heard it said, Who then can be *s* .... Lk 18:26 4982
thy faith hath *s* thee .... Lk 18:42 4982
derided him, saying, He *s* others .... Lk 23:35 4982
the world through him might be *s* .... Jn 3:17 4982
things I say, that ye might be *s* .... Jn 5:34 4982
any man enter in, he shall be *s* .... Jn 10:9 4982
the name of the Lord shall be *s* .... Acts 2:21 4982
church daily such as should be *s* .... Acts 2:47 4982
among men, whereby we must be *s* .... Acts 4:12 4982
thou and all thy house shall be *s* .... Acts 11:14 4982
manner of Moses, ye cannot be *s* .... Acts 15:1 4982
Lord Jesus Christ we shall be *s* .... Acts 15:11 4982
Sirs, what must I do to be *s* .... Acts 16:30 4982
Jesus Christ, and thou shalt be *s* .... Acts 16:31 4982
should be *s* was then taken away .... Acts 27:20 4982
abide in the ship, ye cannot be *s* .... Acts 27:31 4982
we shall be *s* from wrath through .... Rom 5:9 4982
we shall be *s* by his life .... Rom 5:10 4982
For we are *s* by hope .... Rom 8:24 4982
of the sea, a remnant shall be *s* .... Rom 9:27 4982
Israel is, that they might be *s* .... Rom 10:1 4991
from the dead, thou shalt be *s* .... Rom 10:9 4982
the name of the Lord shall be *s* .... Rom 10:13 4982
And so all Israel shall be *s* .... Rom 11:26 4982
but unto us which are *s* it is the 1Cor 1:18 4982
but he himself shall be *s* 1Cor 3:15 4982
that the spirit may be *s* in the 1Cor 5:5 4982
of many, that they may be *s* 1Cor 10:33 4982
By which also ye are *s*, if ye 1Cor 15:2 4982
of Christ, in them that are *s* 2Cor 2:15 4982
with Christ, (by grace ye are *s* .... Eph 2:5 4982
by grace are ye *s* through faith .... Eph 2:8 4982
the Gentiles that they might be *s* 1Th 2:16 4982
the truth, that they might be *s* 2Th 2:10 4982
Who will have all men to be *s* 1Ti 2:4 4982
she shall be *s* in childbearing 1Ti 2:15 4982
Who hath *s* us, and called us with 2Ti 1:9 4982
according to his mercy he *s* us .... Titus 3:5 4982
is, eight souls were *s* by water 1Pet 3:20 1295
And if the righteous scarcely be *s* 1Pet 4:18 4982
but *s* Noah the eighth person, a 2Pet 2:5 5442
having *s* the people out of the .... Jude 5 4982
s shall walk in the light of it .... Rev 21:24 4982

SAVEST {3}
thou *s* me from violence 2Sa 22:3 3467
how *s* thou the arm that hath no .... Job 26:2 3467
O thou that *s* by thy right hand .... Ps 17:7 3467

SAVETH {7}
which *s* Israel, though it be in 1Sa 14:39 3467
that the LORD *s* not with sword 1Sa 17:47 3467
But he *s* the poor from the sword .... Job 5:15 3467
which *s* the upright in heart .... Ps 7:10 3467
I that the LORD *s* his anointed .... Ps 20:6 3467
s such as be of a contrite spirit .... Ps 34:18 3467
he *s* them out of their distresses .... Ps 107:19 3467

SAVING {12}
hast shewed unto me in *s* my life .... Gen 19:19 2421
s that every one put them off for .... Neh 4:23
the *s* strength of his right hand .... Ps 20:6 3468
he is the *s* strength of his .... Ps 28:8 3444
thy *s* health among all nations .... Ps 67:2 3444
s the beholding of them with .... Eccl 5:11 518
s that I will not utterly destroy .... Amos 9:8 657
s for the cause of fornication, ... Mt 5:32 3924
was cleansed, *s* Naaman the Syrian .... Lk 4:27 1508
that believe to the *s* of the soul .... Heb 10:39 4047
an ark to the *s* of his house .... Heb 11:7 4991
knoweth *s* he that receiveth it .... Rev 2:17 1508

SAVIOUR {37}
my high tower, and my refuge, my *s* 2Sa 22:3 3467
(And the LORD gave Israel a *s* 2Kin 13:5 3467
They forgat God their *s*, which .... Ps 106:21 3467
and he shall send them a *s* .... Is 19:20 3467
the Holy One of Israel, thy *S* .... Is 43:3 3467
and beside me there is no *s* .... Is 43:11 3467
thyself, O God of Israel, the *S* .... Is 45:15 3467
a just God and a *S* .... Is 45:21 3467
know that I the LORD am thy *S* .... Is 49:26 3467
know that I the LORD am thy *S* .... Is 60:16 3467
so he was their *S* .... Is 63:8 3467
the *s* thereof in time of trouble, ... Jer 14:8 3467
for there is no *s* beside me .... Hos 13:4 3467
spirit hath rejoiced in God my *S* .... Lk 1:47 4990
this day in the city of David a *S* .... Lk 2:11 4990
the Christ, the *S* of the world .... Jn 4:42 4990
right hand to be a Prince and a *S* .... Acts 5:31 4990
promise raised unto Israel a *S* .... Acts 13:23 4990
and he is the *s* of the body .... Eph 5:23 4990
whence also we look for the *S* .... Phil 3:20 4990
by the commandment of God our *S* 1Ti 1:1 4990
in the sight of God our *S* 1Ti 2:3 4990
God, who is the *S* of all men 1Ti 4:10 4990
appearing of our *S* Jesus Christ 2Ti 1:10 4990
to the commandment of God our *S* .... Titus 1:3 4990
and the Lord Jesus Christ our *S* .... Titus 1:4 4990
of God our *S* in all things .... Titus 2:10 4990
great God and our *S* Jesus Christ .... Titus 2:13 4990
love of God our *S* toward man .... Titus 3:4 4990
through Jesus Christ our *S* .... Titus 3:6 4990
of God and our *S* Jesus Christ 2Pet 1:1 4990
of our Lord and *S* Jesus Christ 2Pet 1:11 4990
S Jesus Christ, they are again 2Pet 2:20 4990
us the apostles of the Lord and *S* 2Pet 3:2 4990
of our Lord and *S* Jesus Christ 2Pet 3:18 4990
the Son to be the *S* of the world 1Jn 4:14 4990
To the only wise God our *S* .... Jude 25 4990

SAVIOURS {2}
mercies thou gavest them *s* .... Neh 9:27 3467
s shall come up on mount Zion to .... Obad 21 3467

SAVOUR {54}
And the LORD smelled a sweet *s* .... Gen 8:21 7381
because ye have made our *s* to be .... Ex 5:21 7381
it is a sweet *s*, an offering made .... Ex 29:18 7381
for a sweet *s* before the LORD .... Ex 29:25 7381
offering thereof, for a sweet *s* .... Ex 29:41 7381
of a sweet *s* unto the LORD .... Lev 1:9 7381
of a sweet *s* unto the LORD .... Lev 1:13 7381
of a sweet *s* unto the LORD .... Lev 1:17 7381
of a sweet *s* unto the LORD .... Lev 2:2 7381
of a sweet *s* unto the LORD .... Lev 2:9 7381
burnt on the altar for a sweet *s* .... Lev 2:12 7381
of a sweet *s* unto the LORD .... Lev 3:5 7381
made by fire for a sweet *s* .... Lev 3:16 7381
altar for a sweet *s* unto the LORD .... Lev 4:31 7381
it upon the altar for a sweet *s* .... Lev 6:15 7381
offer for a sweet *s* unto the LORD .... Lev 6:21 7381
a burnt sacrifice for a sweet *s* .... Lev 8:21 7381
were consecrations for a sweet *s* .... Lev 8:28 7381
fat for a sweet *s* unto the LORD .... Lev 17:6 7381
fire unto the LORD for a sweet *s* .... Lev 23:13 7381
by fire, of sweet *s* unto the LORD .... Lev 23:18 7381
smell the *s* of your sweet odours .... Lev 26:31 7381
to make a sweet *s* unto the LORD .... Num 15:3 7381
for a sweet *s* unto the LORD .... Num 15:7 7381
of a sweet *s* unto the LORD .... Num 15:10 7381
of a sweet *s* unto the LORD .... Num 15:13 7381
of a sweet *s* unto the LORD .... Num 15:14 7381
for a sweet *s* unto the LORD, with .... Num 15:24 7381
for a sweet *s* unto the LORD .... Num 18:17 7381
by fire, for a sweet *s* unto me .... Num 28:2 7381
in mount Sinai for a sweet *s* .... Num 28:6 7381
of a sweet *s* unto the LORD .... Num 28:8 7381
for a burnt offering of a sweet *s* .... Num 28:13 7381
of a sweet *s* unto the LORD .... Num 28:24 7381
for a sweet *s* unto the LORD .... Num 28:27 7381
for a sweet *s* unto the LORD .... Num 29:2 7381
unto their manner, for a sweet *s* .... Num 29:6 7381
unto the LORD for a sweet *s* .... Num 29:8 7381
of a sweet *s* unto the LORD .... Num 29:13 7381
of a sweet *s* unto the LORD .... Num 29:36 7381
to send forth a stinking *s* .... Eccl 10:1 7381
Because of the *s* of thy good .... Song 1:3 7381
offer sweet *s* to all their idols .... Eze 6:13 7381
set it before them for a sweet *s* .... Eze 16:19 7381
also they made their sweet *s* .... Eze 20:28 7381
will accept you with your sweet *s* .... Eze 20:41 7381
his ill *s* shall come up, because .... Joel 2:20 6709
but if the salt have lost his *s* .... Mt 5:13 3471
but if the salt have lost his *s* .... Lk 14:34 3471
maketh manifest the *s* of his 2Cor 2:14 3744
are unto God a sweet *s* of Christ 2Cor 2:15 2175
we are the *s* of death unto death 2Cor 2:16 3744
to the other the *s* of life unto 2Cor 2:16 3744
to God for a sweetsmelling *s* .... Eph 5:2 3744

SAVOUREST {2}
for thou *s* not the things that be .... Mt 16:23 5426
for thou *s* not the things that be .... Mk 8:33 5426

SAVOURS {1}
of sweet *s* unto the God of heaven .... Ezr 6:10 5208

SAVOURY {6}
And make me *s* meat, such as I love .... Gen 27:4 4303
me venison, and make me *s* meat .... Gen 27:7 4303
I will make them *s* meat for thy .... Gen 27:9 4303
and his mother made *s* meat .... Gen 27:14 4303
And she gave the *s* meat and the .... Gen 27:17 4303
And he also had made *s* meat .... Gen 27:31 4303

SAW {548}
God *s* the light, that it was good .... Gen 1:4 7200
and God *s* that it was good .... Gen 1:10 7200
and God *s* that it was good .... Gen 1:12 7200
and God *s* that it was good .... Gen 1:18 7200
and God *s* that it was good .... Gen 1:21 7200
and God *s* that it was good .... Gen 1:25 7200
God *s* every thing that he had .... Gen 1:31 7200
when the woman *s* that the tree .... Gen 3:6 7200
That the sons of God *s* the .... Gen 6:2 7200
God *s* that the wickedness of man .... Gen 6:5 7200
s the nakedness of his father, and .... Gen 9:22 7200
they *s* not their father's .... Gen 9:23 7200
The princes also of Pharaoh *s* her .... Gen 12:15 7200
when she *s* that she had conceived .... Gen 16:4 7200
when she *s* that she had conceived .... Gen 16:5 7200
and when he *s* them, he ran to meet .... Gen 18:2 7200
Sarah *s* the son of Hagar the .... Gen 21:9 7200
eyes, and she *s* a well of water .... Gen 21:19 7200
his eyes, and *s* the place afar off .... Gen 22:4 7200
to pass, when he *s* the earring and .... Gen 24:30 7200
and he lifted up his eyes, and *s* .... Gen 24:63 7200
up her eyes, and when she *s* Isaac .... Gen 24:64 7200
looked out at a window, and *s* .... Gen 26:8 7200
We *s* certainly that the LORD was .... Gen 26:28 7200
When Esau *s* that Isaac had .... Gen 28:6 7200
when Jacob *s* Rachel the daughter .... Gen 29:10 7200
when the LORD *s* that Leah was .... Gen 29:31 7200
when Rachel *s* that she bare Jacob .... Gen 30:1 7200
When Leah *s* that she had left .... Gen 30:9 7200
s in a dream, and, behold, the .... Gen 31:10 7200
And when Jacob *s* them, he said, ... Gen 32:2 7200
when he *s* that he prevailed not .... Gen 32:25 7200
s the women and the children .... Gen 33:5 7200
s her, he took her, and lay with .... Gen 34:2 7200
when his brethren *s* that their .... Gen 37:4 7200
when they *s* him afar off, even .... Gen 37:18 7200
Judah *s* there a daughter of a .... Gen 38:2 7200
for she *s* that Shelah was grown, ... Gen 38:14 7200
When Judah *s* her, he thought her .... Gen 38:15 7200
his master *s* that the LORD was .... Gen 39:3 7200
when she *s* that he had left his .... Gen 39:13 7200
When the chief baker *s* that the .... Gen 40:16 7200
such as I never *s* in all the land .... Gen 41:19 7200
I *s* in my dream, and, behold, ... Gen 41:22 7200
Now when Jacob *s* that there was .... Gen 42:1 7200
Joseph *s* his brethren, and he knew .... Gen 42:7 7200
in that we *s* the anguish of his .... Gen 42:21 7200
their father *s* the bundles of .... Gen 42:35 7200
when Joseph *s* Benjamin with them, ... Gen 43:16 7200
s his brother Benjamin, his .... Gen 43:29 7200
and I *s* him not since .... Gen 44:28 7200

S

when he *s* the wagons which Joseph ... Gen 45:27 7200
when Joseph *s* that his father ... Gen 48:17 7200
he *s* that rest was good, and the ... Gen 49:15 7200
s the mourning in the floor of ... Gen 50:11 7200
when Joseph's brethren *s* that ... Gen 50:15 7200
Joseph *s* Ephraim's children of ... Gen 50:23 7200
when she *s* him that he was a ... Ex 2:2 7200
when she *s* the ark among the ... Ex 2:5 7200
had opened it, she *s* the child ... Ex 2:6 7200
when he *s* that there was no man, ... Ex 2:12 7200
when the LORD *s* that he turned ... Ex 3:4 7200
But when Pharaoh *s* that there was ... Ex 8:15 7200
when Pharaoh *s* that the rain and ... Ex 9:34 7200
They *s* not one another, neither ... Ex 10:23 7200
Israel *s* the Egyptians dead upon ... Ex 14:30 7200
Israel *s* that great work which ... Ex 14:31 7200
when the children of Israel *s* it ... Ex 16:15 7200
when Moses' father in law *s* all ... Ex 18:14 7200
all the people *s* the thunderings, ... Ex 20:18 7200
and when the people *s* it, they ... Ex 20:18 7200
And they *s* the God of Israel ... Ex 24:10 7200
also they *s* God, and did eat and ... Ex 24:11 2372
when the people *s* that Moses ... Ex 32:1 7200
And when Aaron *s* it, he built an ... Ex 32:5 7200
that he *s* the calf, and the ... Ex 32:19 7200
when Moses *s* that the people were ... Ex 32:25 7200
all the people *s* the cloudy ... Ex 33:10 7200
the children of Israel *s* Moses ... Ex 34:30 7200
of Israel *s* the face of Moses ... Ex 34:35 7200
which when all the people *s* ... Lev 9:24 7200
moreover we *s* the children of ... Num 13:28 7200
all the people that we *s* in it ... Num 13:32 7200
there we *s* the giants, the sons ... Num 13:33 7200
s that Aaron was dead, they ... Num 20:29 7200
Balak the son of Zippor *s* all ... Num 22:2 7200
the ass *s* the angel of the LORD ... Num 22:23 7200
when the ass *s* the angel of the ... Num 22:25 7200
when the ass *s* the angel of the ... Num 22:27 7200
he *s* the angel of the LORD ... Num 22:31 7200
And the ass *s* me, and turned from ... Num 22:33 7200
when Balaam *s* that it pleased the ... Num 24:1 7200
he *s* Israel abiding in his tents ... Num 24:2 7200
which *s* the vision of the ... Num 24:4 2372
which *s* the vision of the ... Num 24:16 2372
s it, he rose up from among the ... Num 25:7 7200
when they *s* the land of Jazer, and ... Num 32:1 7200
s the land, they discouraged the ... Num 32:9 7200
which ye *s* by the way of the ... Deut 1:19 7200
of the words, but *s* no similitude ... Deut 4:12 7200
for ye *s* no manner of similitude ... Deut 4:15 7200
temptations which thine eyes *s* ... Deut 7:19 7200
And when the LORD *s* it, he ... Deut 32:19 7200
When I *s* among the spoils a ... Josh 7:21 7200
to pass, when the king of Ai *s* it ... Josh 8:14 7200
of Ai looked behind them, they *s* ... Josh 8:20 7200
all Israel *s* that the ambush had ... Josh 8:21 7200
the spies *s* a man come forth out ... Judg 1:24 7200
and when they *s* that, behold, the ... Judg 3:24 7200
when Gaal *s* the people, he said ... Judg 9:36 7200
when the men of Israel *s* that ... Judg 9:55 7200
And it came to pass, when he *s* her ... Judg 11:35 7200
when I *s* that ye delivered me not ... Judg 12:3 7200
s a woman in Timnath of the ... Judg 14:1 7200
it came to pass, when they *s* him ... Judg 14:11 7200
s there an harlot, and went in ... Judg 16:1 7200
when Delilah *s* that he had told ... Judg 16:18 7200
And when the people *s* him, they ... Judg 16:24 7200
s the people that were therein, ... Judg 18:7 7200
when Micah *s* that they were too ... Judg 18:26 7200
the father of the damsel *s* him ... Judg 19:3 7200
he *s* a wayfaring man in the ... Judg 19:17 7200
was so, that all that *s* it said ... Judg 19:30 7200
Benjamin *s* that they were smitten ... Judg 20:36 7200
for they *s* that evil was come ... Judg 20:41 7200
When she *s* that she was ... Ruth 1:18 7200
her mother in law *s* what she had ... Ruth 2:18 7200
men of Ashdod *s* that it was so ... 1Sa 5:7 7200
s the ark, and rejoiced to see it ... 1Sa 6:13 7200
And when Samuel *s* Saul, the LORD ... 1Sa 9:17 7200
that knew him beforetime *s* that ... 1Sa 10:11 7200
when we *s* that they were no where ... 1Sa 10:14 7200
when ye *s* that Nahash the king of ... 1Sa 12:12 7200
When the men of Israel *s* that ... 1Sa 13:6 7200
Because I *s* that the people were ... 1Sa 13:11 7200
when Saul *s* any strong man, or ... 1Sa 14:52 7200
of Israel, when they *s* the man ... 1Sa 17:24 7200
s David, he disdained him ... 1Sa 17:42 7200
when the Philistines *s* their ... 1Sa 17:51 7200
when Saul *s* David go forth ... 1Sa 17:55 7200
Wherefore when Saul *s* that he ... 1Sa 18:15 7200
And Saul *s* and knew that the LORD ... 1Sa 18:28 7200
when they *s* the company of the ... 1Sa 19:20 7200
I *s* the son of Jesse coming to ... 1Sa 22:9 7200
David *s* that Saul was come out to ... 1Sa 23:15 7200
And when Abigail *s* David, she ... 1Sa 25:23 7200
but I thine handmaid *s* not the ... 1Sa 25:25 7200
he *s* that Saul came after him ... 1Sa 26:3 7200
gat them away, and no man *s* it ... 1Sa 26:12 7200
when Saul *s* the host of the ... 1Sa 28:5 7200
And when the woman *s* Samuel ... 1Sa 28:12 7200
I *s* gods ascending out of the ... 1Sa 28:13 7200
s that he was sore troubled, and ... 1Sa 28:21 7200
armourbearer *s* that Saul was dead ... 1Sa 31:5 7200
s that the men of Israel fled, and ... 1Sa 31:7 7200
he looked behind him, he *s* me ... 2Sa 1:7 7200
s king David leaping and dancing ... 2Sa 6:16 7200
when the children of Ammon *s* that ... 2Sa 10:6 7200
When Joab *s* that the front of the ... 2Sa 10:9 7200

s that the Syrians were fled ... 2Sa 10:14 7200
when the Syrians *s* that they were ... 2Sa 10:15 7200
s that they were smitten before ... 2Sa 10:19 7200
from the roof he *s* a woman ... 2Sa 11:2 7200
But when David *s* that his ... 2Sa 12:19 7200
house, and *s* not the king's face ... 2Sa 14:24 7200
and *s* not the king's face ... 2Sa 14:28 7200
Nevertheless a lad *s* them ... 2Sa 17:18 7200
when Ahithophel *s* that his ... 2Sa 17:23 7200
And a certain man *s* it, and told ... 2Sa 18:10 7200
I *s* Absalom hanged in an oak ... 2Sa 18:10 7200
the watchman *s* another man ... 2Sa 18:26 7200
I *s* a great tumult, but I knew ... 2Sa 18:29 7200
when the man *s* that all the ... 2Sa 20:12 7200
when he *s* that every one that ... 2Sa 20:12 7200
spake unto the LORD when he *s* the ... 2Sa 24:17 7200
s the king and his servants coming ... 2Sa 24:20 7200
for they *s* that the wisdom of God ... 1Kin 3:28 7200
So when all Israel *s* that the ... 1Kin 12:16 7200
s the carcase cast in the way, and ... 1Kin 13:25 7200
when Zimri *s* that the city was ... 1Kin 16:18 7200
came to pass, when Ahab *s* Elijah ... 1Kin 18:17 7200
And when all the people *s* it ... 1Kin 18:39 7200
And when he *s* that, he arose, and ... 1Kin 19:3 7200
I *s* all Israel scattered upon the ... 1Kin 22:17 7200
I *s* the LORD sitting on his ... 1Kin 22:19 7200
of the chariots *s* Jehoshaphat ... 1Kin 22:32 7200
And Elisha *s* it, and he cried, My ... 2Kin 2:12 7200
And he *s* him no more ... 2Kin 2:12 7200
were to view at Jericho *s* him ... 2Kin 2:15 7200
the Moabites *s* the water on the ... 2Kin 3:22 7200
when the king of Moab *s* that the ... 2Kin 3:26 7200
the man of God *s* her afar off ... 2Kin 4:25 7200
when Naaman *s* him running after ... 2Kin 5:21 7200
and he *s*: and ... 2Kin 6:17 7200
LORD opened their eyes, and they *s* ... 2Kin 6:20 7200
said unto Elisha, when he *s* them ... 2Kin 6:21 7200
came to pass, when Joram *s* Jehu ... 2Kin 9:22 7200
Ahaziah the king of Judah *s* this ... 2Kin 9:27 7200
Ahaziah *s* that her son was dead ... 2Kin 11:1 7200
when they *s* that there was much ... 2Kin 12:10 7200
for he *s* the oppression of Israel ... 2Kin 13:4 7200
For the LORD *s* the affliction of ... 2Kin 14:26 7200
s an altar that was at Damascus ... 2Kin 16:10 7200
Damascus, the king *s* the altar ... 2Kin 16:12 7200
armourbearer *s* that Saul was dead ... 1Chr 10:5 7200
in the valley *s* that they fled ... 1Chr 10:7 7200
at a window *s* king David dancing ... 1Chr 15:29 7200
when the children of Ammon *s* that ... 1Chr 19:6 7200
Now when Joab *s* that the battle ... 1Chr 19:10 7200
s that the Syrians were fled ... 1Chr 19:15 7200
when the Syrians *s* that they were ... 1Chr 19:16 7200
when the servants of Hadarezer *s* ... 1Chr 19:19 7200
s the angel of the LORD stand ... 1Chr 21:16 7200
Ornan turned back, and *s* the angel ... 1Chr 21:20 7200
s David, and went out of the ... 1Chr 21:21 7200
At that time when David *s* that ... 1Chr 21:28 7200
Israel *s* how the fire came down ... 2Chr 7:3 7200
when all Israel *s* that the king ... 2Chr 10:16 7200
when the LORD *s* that they humbled ... 2Chr 12:7 7200
when they *s* that the LORD his God ... 2Chr 15:9 7200
I *s* the LORD sitting upon his ... 2Chr 18:18 7200
of the chariots *s* Jehoshaphat ... 2Chr 18:31 7200
Ahaziah *s* that her son was dead ... 2Chr 22:10 7200
when they *s* that there was much ... 2Chr 24:11 7200
they *s* one another in the face, ... 2Chr 25:21 7200
s the heaps, they blessed the ... 2Chr 31:8 7200
when Hezekiah *s* that Sennacherib ... 2Chr 32:2 7200
that were about us *s* these things ... Neh 6:16 7200
In those days *s* I in Judah some ... Neh 13:15 7200
In those days also *s* I Jews that ... Neh 13:23 7200
which *s* the king's face, and which ... Est 1:14 7200
when Haman *s* that Mordecai bowed ... Est 3:5 7200
when the king *s* Esther the queen ... Est 5:2 7200
but when Haman *s* Mordecai in the ... Est 5:9 7200
for he *s* that there was evil ... Est 7:7 7200
for they *s* that his grief was ... Job 2:13 7200
as infants which never *s* light ... Job 3:16 7200
The eye also which *s* him shall ... Job 20:9 7805
The young men *s* me, and hid ... Job 29:8 7200
and when the eye *s* me, it gave ... Job 29:11 7200
when I *s* my help in the gate ... Job 31:21 7200
When Elihu *s* that there was no ... Job 32:5 7200
s his sons, and his sons' sons, ... Job 42:16 7200
They *s* it, and so they marvelled ... Ps 48:5 7200
when I *s* the prosperity of the ... Ps 73:3 7200
The waters *s* thee, O God, the ... Ps 77:16 7200
thee, O God, the waters *s* thee ... Ps 77:16 7200
me, proved me, and *s* my work ... Ps 95:9 7200
the earth *s*, and trembled ... Ps 97:4 7200
The sea *s* it, and fled ... Ps 114:3 7200
Then I *s*, and considered it well ... Prov 24:32 2372
Then I *s* that wisdom excelleth ... Eccl 2:13 7200
This also I *s*, that it was from ... Eccl 2:24 7200
moreover I *s* under the sun the ... Eccl 3:16 7200
and I *s* vanity under the sun ... Eccl 4:7 7200
so I *s* the wicked buried, who had ... Eccl 8:10 7200
s under the sun, that the race is ... Eccl 9:11 7200
S ye him whom my soul loveth ... Song 3:3 7200
The daughters *s* her, and blessed ... Song 6:9 7200
which he *s* concerning Judah and ... Is 1:1 2372
son of Amoz *s* concerning Judah ... Is 2:1 2372
I *s* also the Lord sitting upon a ... Is 6:1 7200
or shall the *s* magnify itself ... Is 10:15 4883
he *s* a chariot with a couple of ... Is 21:7 7200
The isles *s* it, and feared ... Is 41:5 7200
and the LORD *s* it, and it ... Is 59:15 7200
he *s* that there was no man, and ... Is 59:16 7200

her treacherous sister Judah *s* it ... Jer 3:7 7200
And I *s*, when for all the causes ... Jer 3:8 7200
Zedekiah the king of Judah *s* them ... Jer 39:4 7200
s Johanan the son of Kareah ... Jer 41:13 7200
and were well, and *s* no evil ... Jer 44:17 7200
the adversaries *s* her, and did ... Lam 1:7 7200
opened, and I *s* visions of God ... Eze 1:1 7200
I *s* as the colour of amber, as ... Eze 1:27 7200
I *s* as it were the appearance of ... Eze 1:27 7200
And when I *s* it, I fell upon my ... Eze 1:28 7200
as the glory which I *s* by the ... Eze 3:23 7200
the vision that I *s* in the plain ... Eze 8:4 7200
So I went in and *s* ... Eze 8:10 7200
that I *s* by the river of Chebar ... Eze 10:15 7200
is the living creature that I *s* ... Eze 10:20 7200
which I *s* by the river of Chebar ... Eze 10:22 7200
among whom I *s* Jaazaniah the son ... Eze 11:1 7200
s thee polluted in thine own ... Eze 16:6 7200
I took them away as I *s* good ... Eze 16:50 7200
Now when she *s* that she had ... Eze 19:5 7200
then they *s* every high hill, and ... Eze 20:28 7200
when her sister Aholibah *s* this ... Eze 23:11 7200
Then I *s* that she was defiled, ... Eze 23:13 7200
for when she *s* men pourtrayed ... Eze 23:14 7200
as soon as she *s* them with her ... Eze 23:16
I *s* also the height of the house ... Eze 41:8 7200
of the vision which I *s*, even ... Eze 43:3 7200
according to the vision that I *s* ... Eze 43:3 7200
that I *s* by the river Chebar ... Eze 43:3 7200
s these men, upon whose bodies ... Dan 3:27 2370
I *s* a dream which made me afraid, ... Dan 4:5 2370
I *s*, and behold a tree in the ... Dan 4:10 2370
I *s* in the visions of my head ... Dan 4:13 2370
And whereas the king *s* a watcher ... Dan 4:23 2370
the king *s* the part of the hand ... Dan 5:5 2370
I *s* in my vision by night, and, ... Dan 7:2 2370
After this I *s* in the night ... Dan 7:7 2370
I *s* in the night visions, and, ... Dan 7:13 2370
And I *s* in a vision ... Dan 8:2 7200
and it came to pass, when I *s* ... Dan 8:2 7200
I *s* in a vision, and I was by the ... Dan 8:2 7200
Then I lifted up mine eyes, and *s* ... Dan 8:3 7200
I *s* the ram pushing westward, and ... Dan 8:4 7200
I *s* him come close unto the ram, ... Dan 8:7 7200
And I Daniel alone *s* the vision ... Dan 10:7 7200
were with me *s* not the vision ... Dan 10:7 7200
s this great vision, and there ... Dan 10:8 7200
When Ephraim *s* his sickness ... Hos 5:13 7200
Judah *s* his wound, then went ... Hos 5:13
I *s* your fathers as the firstripe ... Hos 9:10 7200
as I *s* Tyrus, is planted in a ... Hos 9:13 7200
which he *s* concerning Israel in ... Amos 1:1 2372
I *s* the Lord standing upon the ... Amos 9:1 7200
God *s* their works, that they ... Jonah 3:10 7200
which he *s* concerning Samaria and ... Mic 1:1 2372
I *s* the tents of Cushan in ... Hab 3:7 7200
The mountains *s* thee, and they ... Hab 3:10 7200
Who is left among you that *s* this ... Hag 2:3 7200
I *s* by night, and behold a man ... Zec 1:8 7200
Then lifted I up mine eyes, and *s* ... Zec 1:18 7200
which they *s* in the east, went ... Mt 2:9 *1492*
When they *s* the star, they ... Mt 2:10 *1492*
they *s* the young child with Mary ... Mt 2:11 *2147*
when he *s* that he was mocked of ... Mt 2:16 *1492*
But when he *s* many of the ... Mt 3:7 *1492*
he *s* the Spirit of God descending ... Mt 3:16 *1492*
sat in darkness *s* great light ... Mt 4:16 *1492*
s two brethren, Simon called ... Mt 4:18 *1492*
he *s* other two brethren, James ... Mt 4:21 *1492*
he *s* his wife's mother laid, and ... Mt 8:14 *1492*
Now when Jesus *s* great multitudes ... Mt 8:18 *1492*
and when they *s* him, they besought ... Mt 8:34 *1492*
But when the multitudes *s* it ... Mt 9:8 *1492*
he *s* a man, named Matthew, ... Mt 9:9 *1492*
And when the Pharisees *s* it ... Mt 9:11 *1492*
him about, and when he *s* her ... Mt 9:22 *1492*
s the minstrels and the people ... Mt 9:23 *1492*
But when he *s* the multitudes, he ... Mt 9:36 *1492*
But when the Pharisees *s* it ... Mt 12:2 *1492*
the blind and dumb both spake and *s* ... Mt 12:22 *991*
s a great multitude, and was moved ... Mt 14:14 *1492*
when the disciples *s* him walking ... Mt 14:26 *1492*
But when he *s* the wind boisterous ... Mt 14:30 *991*
they *s* the dumb to speak, ... Mt 15:31 *991*
they *s* no man, save Jesus only ... Mt 17:8 *1492*
fellowservants *s* what was done ... Mt 18:31 *1492*
s others standing idle in the ... Mt 20:3 *1492*
scribes *s* the wonderful things ... Mt 21:15 *1492*
when he *s* a fig tree in the way, ... Mt 21:19 *1492*
And when the disciples *s* it ... Mt 21:20 *1492*
But when the husbandmen *s* the son ... Mt 21:38 *1492*
he *s* there a man which had not on ... Mt 22:11 *1492*
when *s* we thee an hungred, and fed ... Mt 25:37 *1492*
When *s* we thee a stranger, and ... Mt 25:38 *1492*
Or when *s* we thee sick, or in ... Mt 25:39 *1492*
when *s* we thee an hungred, or ... Mt 25:44 *1492*
But when his disciples *s* it ... Mt 26:8 *1492*
the porch, another maid *s* him ... Mt 26:71 *1492*
when he *s* that he was condemned, ... Mt 27:3 *1492*
When Pilate *s* that he could ... Mt 27:24 *1492*
s the earthquake, and those things ... Mt 27:54 *1492*
And when they *s* him, they ... Mt 28:17 *1492*
he *s* the heavens opened, and the ... Mk 1:10 *1492*
he *s* Simon and Andrew his brother ... Mk 1:16 *1492*
he *s* James the son of Zebedee, and ... Mk 1:19 *1492*
When Jesus *s* their faith, he said ... Mk 2:5 *1492*
We never *s* it on this fashion ... Mk 2:12 *1492*
he *s* Levi the son of Alphaeus ... Mk 2:14 *1492*

and Pharisees *s* him eat with ... Mk 2:16 *1492*
unclean spirits, when they *s* him ... Mk 3:11 *2334*
But when he *s* Jesus afar off, he ... Mk 5:6 *1492*
they that *s* it told them how it ... Mk 5:16 *1492*
and when he *s* him, he fell at his ... Mk 5:22 *1492*
the people *s* them departing, and ... Mk 6:33 *1492*
s much people, and was moved with ... Mk 6:34 *1492*
he *s* them toiling in rowing ... Mk 6:48 *1492*
But when they *s* him walking upon ... Mk 6:49 *1492*
For they all *s* him, and were ... Mk 6:50 *1492*
when they *s* some of his disciples ... Mk 7:2 *1492*
him, he asked him if he *s* ought ... Mk 8:23 *991*
restored, and *s* every man clearly ... Mk 8:25 *1689*
they *s* no man any more, save ... Mk 9:8 *1492*
he *s* a great multitude about them ... Mk 9:14 *1492*
and when he *s* him, straightway the ... Mk 9:20 *1492*
When Jesus *s* that the people came ... Mk 9:25 *1492*
we *s* one casting out devils in ... Mk 9:38 *1492*
But when Jesus *s* it, he was much ... Mk 10:14 *1492*
they *s* the fig tree dried up from ... Mk 11:20 *1492*
when Jesus *s* that he answered ... Mk 12:34 *1492*
when she *s* Peter warming himself, ... Mk 14:67 *1492*
a maid *s* him again, and began to ... Mk 14:69 *1492*
s that he so cried out, and gave ... Mk 15:39 *1492*
they *s* that the stone was rolled ... Mk 16:4 *2334*
they *s* a young man sitting on the ... Mk 16:5 *1492*
And when Zacharias *s* him, he was ... Lk 1:12 *1492*
And when she *s* him, she was ... Lk 1:29 *1492*
And when they *s* him, they were ... Lk 2:48 *1492*
s two ships standing by the lake ... Lk 5:2 *1492*
When Simon Peter *s* it, he fell ... Lk 5:8 *1492*
when he *s* their faith, he said ... Lk 5:20 *1492*
s a publican, named Levi, sitting ... Lk 5:27 *2300*
And when the Lord *s* her, he had ... Lk 7:13 *1492*
which had bidden him *s* it ... Lk 7:39 *1492*
When he *s* Jesus, he cried out, and ... Lk 8:28 *1492*
that fed them *s* what was done ... Lk 8:34 *1492*
They also which *s* it told them by ... Lk 8:36 *1492*
when the woman *s* that she was not ... Lk 8:47 *1492*
they *s* his glory, and the two men ... Lk 9:32 *1492*
we *s* one casting out devils in ... Lk 9:49 *1492*
disciples James and John *s* this ... Lk 9:54 *1492*
and when he *s* him, he passed by on ... Lk 10:31 *1492*
and when he *s* him, he had ... Lk 10:33 *1492*
And when the Pharisee *s* it ... Lk 11:38 *1492*
And when Jesus *s* her, he called ... Lk 13:12 *1492*
a great way off, his father *s* him ... Lk 15:20 *1492*
And when he *s* them, he said unto ... Lk 17:14 *1492*
when he *s* that he was healed, ... Lk 17:15 *1492*
but when his disciples *s* it ... Lk 18:15 *1492*
when Jesus *s* that he was very ... Lk 18:24 *1492*
and all the people, when they *s* it ... Lk 18:43 *1492*
up, and *s* him, and said unto him, ... Lk 19:5 *1492*
And when they *s* it, they all ... Lk 19:7 *1492*
But when the husbandmen *s* him ... Lk 20:14 *1492*
s the rich men casting their ... Lk 21:1 *1492*
he *s* also a certain poor widow ... Lk 21:2 *1492*
about him *s* what would follow ... Lk 22:49 *1492*
a little while another *s* him ... Lk 22:58 *1492*
And when Herod *s* Jesus, he was ... Lk 23:8 *1492*
the centurion *s* what was done ... Lk 23:47 *1492*
but him they *s* not ... Lk 24:24 *1492*
I *s* the Spirit descending from ... Jn 1:32 *2300*
And I *s*, and bare record that this ... Jn 1:34 *3708*
s them following, and saith unto ... Jn 1:38 *2300*
s where he dwelt, and abode with ... Jn 1:39 *1492*
Jesus *s* Nathanael coming to him, ... Jn 1:47 *1492*
wast under the fig tree, I *s* thee ... Jn 1:48 *1492*
I *s* thee under the fig tree, ... Jn 1:50 *1492*
when they *s* the miracles which he ... Jn 2:23 *2334*
When Jesus *s* him lie, and knew ... Jn 5:6 *1492*
because they *s* his miracles which ... Jn 6:2 *3708*
s a great company come unto him, ... Jn 6:5 *2300*
on the other side of the sea *s* ... Jn 6:22 *1492*
s that Jesus was not there ... Jn 6:24 *1492*
me, not because ye *s* the miracles ... Jn 6:26 *1492*
s none but the woman, he said ... Jn 8:10 *2300*
and he *s* it, and was glad ... Jn 8:56 *1492*
he *s* a man which was blind from ... Jn 9:1 *1492*
comforted her, when they *s* Mary ... Jn 11:31 *1492*
s him, she fell down at his feet, ... Jn 11:32 *1492*
Jesus therefore *s* her weeping ... Jn 11:33 *1492*
when he *s* his glory, and spake of ... Jn 12:41 *1492*
therefore and officers *s* him ... Jn 19:6 *1492*
When Jesus therefore *s* his mother ... Jn 19:26 *1492*
s that he was dead already, they ... Jn 19:33 *1492*
he that *s* it bare record, and his ... Jn 19:35 *3708*
s the linen clothes lying ... Jn 20:5 *991*
first to the sepulchre, and he *s* ... Jn 20:8 *1492*
s Jesus standing, and knew not ... Jn 20:14 *2334*
glad, when they *s* the Lord ... Jn 20:20 *1492*
they *s* a fire of coals there, and ... Jn 21:9 *991*
And all the people *s* him walking ... Acts 3:9 *1492*
And when Peter *s* it, he answered ... Acts 3:12 *1492*
Now when they *s* the boldness of ... Acts 4:13 *2334*
s his face as it had been the ... Acts 6:15 *1492*
When Moses *s* it, he wondered at ... Acts 7:31 *1492*
s the glory of God, and Jesus ... Acts 7:55 *1492*
when Simon *s* that through laying ... Acts 8:18 *2300*
that the eunuch *s* him no more ... Acts 8:39 *1492*
his eyes were opened, he *s* no man ... Acts 9:8 *991*
dwelt at Lydda and Saron *s* him ... Acts 9:35 *1492*
and when she *s* Peter, she sat up ... Acts 9:40 *1492*
He *s* in a vision evidently about ... Acts 10:3 *1492*
s heaven opened, and a certain ... Acts 10:11 *2334*
and in a trance I *s* a vision ... Acts 11:5 *1492*
s fourfooted beasts of the earth, ... Acts 11:6 *1492*
because he *s* it pleased the Jews, ... Acts 12:3 *1492*
but thought he *s* a vision ... Acts 12:9 *991*
s him, they were astonished ... Acts 12:16 *1492*
when he *s* what was done, believed ... Acts 13:12 *1492*
unto his fathers, and *s* corruption ... Acts 13:36 *1492*
God raised again, *s* no corruption ... Acts 13:37 *1492*
when the Jews *s* the multitudes ... Acts 13:45 *1492*
when the people *s* what Paul had ... Acts 14:11 *1492*
when her masters *s* that the hope ... Acts 16:19 *1492*
when he *s* the city wholly given ... Acts 17:16 *2334*
when they *s* him in the temple, ... Acts 21:27 *2300*
when they *s* the chief captain and ... Acts 21:32 *1492*
were with me *s* indeed the light ... Acts 22:9 *2300*
s him saying unto me, Make haste, ... Acts 22:18 *1492*
I *s* in the way a light from ... Acts 26:13 *1492*
when the barbarians *s* the ... Acts 28:4 *1492*
s no harm come to him, they ... Acts 28:6 *2334*
whom when Paul *s*, he thanked God, ... Acts 28:15 *1492*
other of the apostles *s* I none ... Gal 1:19 *1492*
when they *s* that the gospel of ... Gal 2:7 *1492*
But when I *s* that they walked not ... Gal 2:14 *1492*
same conflict which ye *s* in me ... Phil 1:30 *1492*
me, and *s* my works forty years ... Heb 3:9 *1492*
because they *s* he was a proper ... Heb 11:23 *1492*
and of all things that he *s* ... Rev 1:2 *1492*
I *s* seven golden candlesticks ... Rev 1:12 *1492*
And when I *s* him, I fell at his ... Rev 1:17 *1492*
and upon the seats I *s* four ... Rev 4:4 *1492*
I *s* in the right hand of him that ... Rev 5:1 *1492*
I *s* a strong angel proclaiming ... Rev 5:2 *1492*
I *s* when the Lamb opened one of ... Rev 6:1 *1492*
And I *s*, and behold a white horse ... Rev 6:2 *1492*
I *s* under the altar the souls of ... Rev 6:9 *1492*
after these things I *s* four ... Rev 7:1 *1492*
I *s* another angel ascending from ... Rev 7:2 *1492*
I *s* the seven angels which stood ... Rev 8:2 *1492*
I *s* a star fall from heaven unto ... Rev 9:1 *1492*
thus I *s* the horses in the vision ... Rev 9:17 *1492*
I *s* another mighty angel come ... Rev 10:1 *1492*
the angel which I *s* stand upon ... Rev 10:5 *1492*
fear fell upon them which *s* them ... Rev 11:11 *2334*
when the dragon *s* that he was ... Rev 12:13 *1492*
s a beast rise up out of the sea, ... Rev 13:1 *1492*
the beast which I *s* was like unto ... Rev 13:2 *1492*
I *s* one of his heads as it were ... Rev 13:3 *1492*
I *s* another angel fly in the ... Rev 14:6 *1492*
I *s* another sign in heaven, great ... Rev 15:1 *1492*
I *s* as it were a sea of glass ... Rev 15:2 *1492*
I *s* three unclean spirits like ... Rev 16:13 *1492*
I *s* a woman sit upon a scarlet ... Rev 17:3 *1492*
I *s* the woman drunken with the ... Rev 17:6 *1492*
and when I *s* her, I wondered with ... Rev 17:6 *1492*
after these things I *s* another ... Rev 18:1 *1492*
cried when they *s* the smoke of ... Rev 18:18 *3708*
I *s* heaven opened, and behold a ... Rev 19:11 *1492*
I *s* an angel standing in the sun ... Rev 19:17 *1492*
I *s* the beast, and the kings of ... Rev 19:19 *1492*
I *s* an angel come down from ... Rev 20:1 *1492*
I *s* thrones, and they sat upon ... Rev 20:4 *1492*
I *s* the souls of them that were ... Rev 20:4
I *s* a great white throne, and him ... Rev 20:11 *1492*
I *s* the dead, small and great, ... Rev 20:12 *1492*
I *s* a new heaven and a new earth ... Rev 21:1 *1492*
I John *s* the holy city, new ... Rev 21:2 *1492*
And I *s* no temple therein ... Rev 21:22 *1492*
I John *s* these things, and heard ... Rev 22:8 *991*

SAWED {1}

s with saws, within and without, ... 1Kin 7:9 1641

SAWEST {21}

said unto Abraham, What *s* thou ... Gen 20:10 7200
thou *s* it, and didst rejoice ... 1Sa 19:5 7200
for what *s* thou ... 1Sa 28:13 7200
told him, And, behold, thou *s* him ... 2Sa 18:11 7200
When thou *s* a thief, then thou ... Ps 50:18 7200
lovedst their bed where thou *s* it ... Is 57:8 2372
Thou, O king, *s*, and behold a ... Dan 2:31 2370
Thou *s* till that a stone was cut ... Dan 2:34 2370
And whereas thou *s* the feet ... Dan 2:41 2370
forasmuch as thou *s* the iron ... Dan 2:41 2370
whereas thou *s* iron mixed with ... Dan 2:43 2370
Forasmuch as thou *s* that the ... Dan 2:45 2370
The tree that thou *s*, which grew, ... Dan 4:20 2370
The ram which thou *s* having two ... Dan 8:20 7200
which thou *s* in my right hand ... Rev 1:20 *1492*
thou *s* are the seven churches ... Rev 1:20 *1492*
The beast that thou *s* was ... Rev 17:8 *1492*
horns which thou *s* are ten kings ... Rev 17:12 *1492*
unto me, The waters which thou *s* ... Rev 17:15 *1492*
horns which thou *s* upon the beast ... Rev 17:16 1492
which thou *s* is that great city ... Rev 17:18 1492

SAWN {1}

were stoned, they were *s* asunder ... Heb 11:37 *4249*

SAWS {3}

were therein, and put them under *s* ... 2Sa 12:31 4050
of hewed stones, sawed with *s* ... 1Kin 7:9 4050
were in it, and cut them with *s* ... 1Chr 20:3 4050

SAY {1056}

shall see thee, that they shall *s* ... Gen 12:12 559
S, I pray thee, thou art my ... Gen 12:13 559
is thine, lest thou shouldest *s* ... Gen 14:23 559
s of me, He is my brother ... Gen 20:13 559
that the damsel to whom I shall *s* ... Gen 24:14 559
and she shall *s*, Drink, and I will ... Gen 24:14 559
I *s* to her, Give me, I pray thee, ... Gen 24:43 559
she *s* to me, Both drink thou, and ... Gen 24:44 559
for he feared to *s*, She is my ... Gen 26:7 559
Then thou shalt *s*, They be thy ... Gen 32:18 559
s ye moreover, Behold, thy ... Gen 32:20 559
what ye shall *s* unto me I will ... Gen 34:11 559
according as ye shall *s* unto me ... Gen 34:12 559
for I heard them *s*, Let us go to ... Gen 37:17 559
him into some pit, and we will *s* ... Gen 37:20 559
and I have heard *s* of thee ... Gen 41:15 559
we certainly know that he would *s* ... Gen 43:7 559
s unto them, Wherefore have ye ... Gen 44:4 559
What shall we *s* unto my lord ... Gen 44:16 559
s unto him, Thus saith thy son ... Gen 45:9 559
S unto thy brethren, This do ye ... Gen 45:17 559
s unto him, My brethren, and my ... Gen 46:31 559
shall call you, and shall *s* ... Gen 46:33 559
That ye shall *s*, Thy servants' ... Gen 46:34 559
So shall ye *s* unto Joseph ... Gen 50:17 559
shall *s* unto them, The God of ... Ex 3:13 559
and they shall *s* to me, What is ... Ex 3:13 559
what shall I *s* unto them ... Ex 3:13 559
Thus shalt thou *s* unto the ... Ex 3:14 559
Thus shalt thou *s* unto the ... Ex 3:15 559
s unto them, The LORD God of your ... Ex 3:16 559
of Egypt, and ye shall *s* unto him ... Ex 3:18 559
for they will *s*, The LORD hath ... Ex 4:1 559
and teach thee what thou shalt *s* ... Ex 4:12 1696
thou shalt *s* unto Pharaoh, Thus ... Ex 4:22 559
I *s* unto thee, Let my son go, ... Ex 4:23 559
and they *s* to us, Make brick ... Ex 5:16 559
therefore ye *s*, Let us go and do ... Ex 5:17 559
Wherefore *s* unto the children of ... Ex 6:6 559
of Egypt all that I *s* unto thee ... Ex 6:29 1696
then thou shalt *s* unto Aaron ... Ex 7:9 559
And thou shalt *s* unto him, The ... Ex 7:16 559
S unto Aaron, Take thy rod, and ... Ex 7:19 559
s unto him, Thus saith the LORD, ... Ex 8:1 559
S unto Aaron, Stretch forth thine ... Ex 8:5 559
S unto Aaron, Stretch out thy rod ... Ex 8:16 559
s unto him, Thus saith the LORD, ... Ex 8:20 559
s unto him, Thus saith the LORD ... Ex 9:13 559
your children shall *s* unto you ... Ex 12:26 559
That ye shall *s*, It is the ... Ex 12:27 559
that thou shalt *s* unto him ... Ex 13:14 559
For Pharaoh will *s* of the ... Ex 14:3 559
S unto all the congregation of ... Ex 16:9 559
Thus shalt thou *s* to the house of ... Ex 19:3 559
Thus thou shalt *s* unto the ... Ex 20:22 559
And if the servant shall plainly *s* ... Ex 21:5 559
should the Egyptians speak, and *s* ... Ex 32:12 559
S unto the children of Israel, Ye ... Ex 33:5 559
s unto them, If any man of you ... Lev 1:2 559
s unto them, When any man hath a ... Lev 15:2 559
of Israel, and *s* unto them ... Lev 17:2 559
And thou shalt *s* unto them ... Lev 17:8 559
s unto them, I am the LORD your ... Lev 18:2 559
s unto them, Ye shall be holy ... Lev 19:2 559
thou shalt *s* to the children of ... Lev 20:2 559
s unto them, There shall none be ... Lev 21:1 559
S unto them, Whosoever he be of ... Lev 22:3 559
s unto them, Whatsoever he be of ... Lev 22:18 559
s unto them, Concerning the ... Lev 23:2 559
s unto them, When ye be come into ... Lev 23:10 559
s unto them, When ye come into ... Lev 25:2 559
And if ye shall *s*, What shall we ... Lev 25:20 559
s unto them, When a man shall ... Lev 27:2 559
s unto them, If any man's wife go ... Num 5:12 559
s unto the woman, If no man have ... Num 5:19 559
the priest shall *s* unto the woman ... Num 5:21 559
And the woman shall *s*, Amen, amen ... Num 5:22 559
s unto them, When either man or ... Num 6:2 559
s unto him, When thou lightest ... Num 8:2 559
that thou shouldest *s* unto me ... Num 11:12 559
s thou unto the people, Sanctify ... Num 11:18 559
S unto them, As truly as I live, ... Num 14:28 559
s unto them, When ye be come into ... Num 15:2 559
s unto them, When ye come into ... Num 15:18 559
s unto them, When ye take of the ... Num 18:26 559
Therefore thou shalt *s* unto them ... Num 18:30 559
they that speak in proverbs *s* ... Num 21:27 559
what the LORD will *s* unto me more ... Num 22:19 1696
word which I shall *s* unto thee ... Num 22:20 1696
any power at all to *s* any thing ... Num 22:38 1696
Go again unto Balak, and *s* thus ... Num 23:16 1696
Wherefore *s*, Behold, I give unto ... Num 25:12 559
s unto them, My offering, and my ... Num 28:2 559
And thou shalt *s* unto them ... Num 28:3 559
s unto them, When ye are passed ... Num 33:51 559
s unto them, When ye come into ... Num 34:2 559
s unto them, When ye be come over ... Num 35:10 559
S unto them, Go not up, neither ... Deut 1:42 559
hear all these statutes, and *s* ... Deut 4:6 559
all that the LORD our God shall *s* ... Deut 5:27 559
Go *s* to them, Get you into your ... Deut 5:30 559
Then thou shalt *s* unto thy son ... Deut 6:21 559
If thou shalt *s* in thine heart, ... Deut 7:17 559
thou *s* in thine heart, My power ... Deut 8:17 559
and of whom thou hast heard *s* ... Deut 9:2
whence thou broughtest us out *s* ... Deut 9:28 559
promised thee, and thou shalt *s* ... Deut 12:20 559
If thou shalt hear *s* in one of ... Deut 13:12
if he *s* unto thee, I will not go ... Deut 15:16 559
shalt dwell therein, and shalt *s* ... Deut 17:14 559
if thou *s* in thine heart, How ... Deut 18:21 559
shall *s* unto them, Hear, O Israel ... Deut 20:3 559
unto the people, and they shall *s* ... Deut 20:8 559
And they shall answer and *s* ... Deut 21:7 559
they shall *s* unto the elders of ... Deut 21:20 559
up an evil name upon her, and *s* ... Deut 22:14 559
father shall *s* unto the elders ... Deut 22:16 559
to the gate unto the elders, and *s* ... Deut 25:7 559

S

and if he stand to it, and *s* Deut 25:8 559
in his face, and shall answer and *s* Deut 25:9 559
s unto him, I profess this day Deut 26:3 559
s before the LORD thy God, A Deut 26:5 559
Then thou shalt *s* before the LORD Deut 26:13 559
s unto all the men of Israel with Deut 27:14 559
all the people shall answer and *s* Deut 27:15 559
and all the people shall *s* Deut 27:16 559
And all the people shall *s* Deut 27:17 559
And all the people shall *s* Deut 27:18 559
And all the people shall *s* Deut 27:19 559
And all the people shall *s* Deut 27:20 559
And all the people shall *s* Deut 27:21 559
And all the people shall *s* Deut 27:22 559
And all the people shall *s* Deut 27:23 559
And all the people shall *s* Deut 27:24 559
And all the people shall *s* Deut 27:25 559
And all the people shall *s* Deut 27:26 559
In the morning thou shalt *s* Deut 28:67 559
and at even thou shalt *s*, Would Deut 28:67 559
come from a far land, shall *s* Deut 29:22 559
Even all nations shall *s*, Deut 29:24 559
Then men shall *s*, Because they Deut 29:25 559
in heaven, that thou shouldest *s* Deut 30:12 559
the sea, that thou shouldest *s* Deut 30:13 559
so that they will *s* in that day Deut 31:17 559
strangely, and lest they should *s* Deut 32:27 559
And he shall *s*, Where are their Deut 32:37 559
I lift up my hand to heaven, and *s* Deut 32:40 559
and shall *s*, Destroy them Deut 33:27 559
O Lord, what shall I *s*, when Josh 7:8 559
Up, sanctify the people, and *s* Josh 7:13 559
for they will *s*, They flee before Josh 8:6 559
s unto them, We are your servants Josh 9:11 559
And the children of Israel heard *s* Josh 22:11 559
that your children may not *s* to Josh 22:27 559
when they should so *s* to us or to Josh 22:28 559
time to come, that we may *s* again Josh 22:28 559
come and enquire of thee, and *s* Judg 4:20 559
that thou shalt *s*, No Judg 4:20 559
be, that of whom I *s* unto thee Judg 7:4 559
and of whomsoever I *s* unto thee Judg 7:4 559
And thou shalt hear what they *s* Judg 7:11 1696
every side of all the camp, and *s* Judg 7:18 559
that men *s* not of me, A woman Judg 9:54 559
they unto him, *S* now Shibboleth Judg 12:6 559
said unto him, How canst thou *s* Judg 16:15 559
said unto them, What *s* ye Judg 18:8 559
and what is this that ye *s* unto me Judg 18:24 559
that we will *s* unto them Judg 21:22 559
If I should *s*, I have hope, if I Ruth 1:12 559
and a morsel of bread, and shall *s* 1Sa 2:36 559
he call thee, that thou shalt *s* 1Sa 3:9 559
in all that they *s* unto thee 1Sa 8:7 559
and they will *s* unto thee, The 1Sa 10:2 559
Thus shall ye *s* unto the men of 1Sa 11:9 559
all Israel heard *s* that Saul had 1Sa 13:4 559
If they *s* thus unto us, Tarry 1Sa 14:9 559
But if they *s* thus, Come up unto 1Sa 14:10 559
s unto them, Bring me hither 1Sa 14:34 559
And he said unto him, *S* on 1Sa 15:16 1696
Take an heifer with thee, and *s* 1Sa 16:2 559
Commune with David secretly, and *s* 1Sa 18:22 559
said, Thus shall ye *s* to David 1Sa 18:25 559
Wherefore they *s*, Is Saul also 1Sa 19:24 559
thy father at all miss me, then *s* 1Sa 20:6 559
If he *s* thus, It is well 1Sa 20:7 559
If I expressly *s* unto the lad 1Sa 20:21 559
But if I *s* thus unto the young 1Sa 20:22 559
thus shall ye *s* to him that 1Sa 25:6 559
thou *s* unto my servant David 2Sa 7:8 559
what can David *s* more unto thee 2Sa 7:20 1696
he *s* unto thee, Wherefore 2Sa 11:20 559
then *s* thou, Thy servant Uriah 2Sa 11:21 559
Thus shalt thou *s* unto Joab 2Sa 11:25 559
s unto him, I pray thee, let my 2Sa 13:5 559
when I *s* unto you, Smite Amnon 2Sa 13:28 559
And he said, *S* on 2Sa 14:12 1696
I may send thee to the king, to *s* 2Sa 14:32 559
of the trumpet, then ye shall *s* 2Sa 15:10 559
But if he thus *s*, I have no 2Sa 15:26 559
s unto Absalom, I will be thy 2Sa 15:34 559
Who shall then *s*, Wherefore hast 2Sa 16:10 559
that whosoever heareth it will *s* 2Sa 17:9 559
for the people heard *s* that day 2Sa 19:2 559
s ye to Amasa, Art thou not of my 2Sa 19:13 559
s, I pray you, unto Joab, Come 2Sa 20:16 559
And he said, What ye shall *s* 2Sa 21:4 559
he moved David against them to *s* 2Sa 24:1 559
s unto David, Thus saith the LORD 2Sa 24:12 559
s unto him, Didst not thou, my 1Kin 1:13 559
eat and drink before him, and *s* 1Kin 1:25 559
and blow ye with the trumpet, and *s* 1Kin 1:34 559
God of my lord the king *s* so too 1Kin 1:36 559
I have somewhat to *s* unto thee 1Kin 2:14 1697
And she said, *S* on 1Kin 2:14 1696
And she said unto him, *S* on 1Kin 2:16 1696
king, (for he will not *s* thee nay 1Kin 2:17 559
I pray thee, *s* me not nay 1Kin 2:20 559
for I will not *s* thee nay 1Kin 2:20 559
and they shall *s*, Why hath the 1Kin 9:8 559
thus shalt thou *s* unto them 1Kin 12:10 559
the which the LORD did *s* to thee 1Kin 13:22 1696
and thus shalt thou *s* unto her 1Kin 14:5 1696
people that were encamped heard *s* 1Kin 16:16 559
s unto Ahab, Prepare thy chariot, 1Kin 18:44 559
said, Let not the king *s* so 1Kin 22:8 559
And *s*, Thus saith the king, Put 1Kin 22:27 559

s unto them, Is it not because 2Kin 1:3 1696
s unto him, Thus saith the LORD, 2Kin 1:6 1696
unto them, Did I not *s* unto you 2Kin 2:18 559
S now unto her, Behold, thou hast 2Kin 4:13 559
s unto her, Is it well with thee 2Kin 4:26 559
did I not *s*, Do not deceive me 2Kin 4:28 559
If we *s*, We will enter into the 2Kin 7:4 559
behold, I *s*, they are even as all 2Kin 7:13
s unto him, Thou mayest certainly 2Kin 8:10 559
oil, and pour it on his head, and *s* 2Kin 9:3 559
send to meet them, and let him *s* 2Kin 9:17 559
so that they shall not *s*, This is 2Kin 9:37 559
But if ye *s* unto me, We trust in 2Kin 18:22 559
Thus shall ye *s* to your master, 2Kin 19:6 559
when he heard *s* of Tirhakah king 2Kin 19:9 559
the LORD, thus shall ye *s* to him 2Kin 22:18 559
The sons, I *s*, of Reuben the 1Chr 5:3
let men *s* among the nations, The 1Chr 16:31 559
s ye, Save us, O God of our 1Chr 16:35 559
thou *s* unto my servant David 1Chr 17:7 559
LORD commanded Gad to *s* to David 1Chr 21:18 559
so that he shall *s*, Why hath the 2Chr 7:21 559
thus shalt thou *s* unto them 2Chr 10:10 559
said, Let not the king *s* so 2Chr 18:7 559
shall I adjure thee that thou *s* 2Chr 18:15 559
And *s*, Thus saith the king, Put 2Chr 18:26 559
Behold, I *s*, how they reward us, 2Chr 20:11
went out before the army, and to *s* 2Chr 20:21 559
the LORD, so shall ye *s* unto him 2Chr 34:26 559
them what they should *s* unto Iddo Ezr 8:17 1696
God, what shall we *s* after this Ezr 9:10 559
The number, I *s*, of the men of Neh 7:7
the Girgashites, to give it, I *s* Neh 9:8
Media *s* this day unto all the Est 1:18 559
Did I *s*, Bring unto me Job 6:22 559
When I lie down, I *s*, When shall Job 7:4 559
When I *s*, My bed shall comfort me Job 7:13 559
who will *s* unto him, What doest Job 9:12 559
if I *s*, I am perfect, it shall Job 9:20
If I *s*, I will forget my Job 9:27 559
I will *s* unto God, Do not condemn Job 10:2 559
But ye should *s*, Why persecute we Job 19:28 559
they which have seen him shall *s* Job 20:7 559
Therefore they *s* unto God Job 21:14 559
For ye *s*, Where is the house of Job 21:28 559
are cast down, then thou shalt *s* Job 22:29 559
what he would *s* unto me Job 23:5 559
Destruction and death *s*, We have Job 28:22 559
whilst ye searched out what to *s* Job 32:11 4405
Lest ye should *s*, We have found Job 32:13 559
He looketh upon men, and if any *s* Job 33:27 559
If thou hast any thing to *s* Job 33:32 4405
Is it fit to *s* to a king, Thou Job 34:18 559
or who can *s*, Thou hast wrought Job 36:23 559
Teach us what we shall *s* unto him Job 37:19 559
go, and *s* unto thee, Here we are Job 38:35 559
Many there be which *s* of my soul Ps 3:2 559
There be many that *s*, Who will Ps 4:6 559
how *s* ye to my soul, Flee as a Ps 11:1 559
Lest mine enemy *s*, I have Ps 13:4 559
wait, I *s*, on the LORD Ps 27:14
s unto my soul, I am thy Ps 35:3 559
All my bones shall *s*, LORD, who Ps 35:10 559
Let them not *s* in their hearts, Ps 35:25 559
let them not *s*, We have swallowed Ps 35:25 559
let them *s* continually, Let the Ps 35:27 559
of their shame that *s* unto me Ps 40:15 559
love thy salvation *s* continually Ps 40:16 559
s they, cleaveth fast unto him Ps 41:8
while they continually *s* unto me Ps 42:3 559
I will *s* unto God my rock, Why Ps 42:9 559
while they *s* daily unto me, Where Ps 42:10 559
So that a man shall *s*, Verily Ps 58:11 559
for who, *s* they, doth hear Ps 59:7
they *s*, Who shall see them Ps 64:5 559
S unto God, How terrible art thou Ps 66:3 559
a reward of their shame that *s* Ps 70:3 559
love thy salvation *s* continually Ps 70:4 559
And they *s*, How doth God know Ps 73:11 559
If I *s*, I will speak thus Ps 73:15 559
Wherefore should the heathen *s* Ps 79:10 559
I will *s* of the LORD, He is my Ps 91:2 559
Yet they *s*, The LORD shall not Ps 94:7 559
S among the heathen that the LORD Ps 96:10 559
and let all the people *s*, Amen Ps 106:48 559
Let the redeemed of the LORD *s* so Ps 107:2 559
Wherefore should the heathen *s* Ps 115:2 559
Let Israel now *s*, that his mercy Ps 118:2 559
Let the house of Aaron now *s* Ps 118:3 559
Let them now that fear the LORD *s* Ps 118:4 559
companions' sakes, I will now *s* Ps 122:8 1696
was on our side, now may Israel *s* Ps 124:1 559
from my youth, may Israel now *s* Ps 129:1 559
Neither do they which go by *s* Ps 129:8 559
I *s*, more than they that watch Ps 130:6
If I *s*, Surely the darkness shall Ps 139:11 559
If they *s*, Come with us, let us Prov 1:11 559
S not unto thy neighbour, Go, and Prov 3:28 559
And *s*, How have I hated Prov 5:12 559
S unto wisdom, Thou art my sister Prov 7:4 559
Who can *s*, I have made my heart Prov 20:9 559
S not thou, I will recompense Prov 20:22 559
have stricken me, shalt thou *s* Prov 23:35 559
S not, I will do so to him as he Prov 24:29 559
I be full, and deny thee, and *s* Prov 30:9 559
satisfied, yea, four things *s* not Prov 30:15 559
neither *s* thou before the angel, Eccl 5:6 559
I *s*, that an untimely birth is Eccl 6:3 559

S not thou, What is the cause Eccl 7:10 559
who may *s* unto him, What doest Eccl 8:4 559
draw nigh, when thou shalt *s* Eccl 12:1 559
And many people shall go and *s* Is 2:3 559
S ye to the righteous, that it Is 3:10 559
That *s*, Let him make speed, and Is 5:19 559
s unto him, Take heed, and be Is 7:4 559
S ye not, A confederacy, to all Is 8:12 559
them to whom this people shall *s* Is 8:12 559
And when they shall *s* unto you Is 8:19 559
that *s* in the pride and stoutness Is 9:9 559
And in that day thou shalt *s* Is 12:1 559
And in that day shall ye *s* Is 12:4 559
against the king of Babylon, and *s* Is 14:4 559
s unto thee, Art thou also become Is 14:10 559
how *s* ye unto Pharaoh, I am the Is 19:11 559
of this isle shall *s* in that day Is 20:6 559
which is over the house, and *s* Is 22:15 559
works are in the dark, and they *s* Is 29:15 559
for shall the work *s* of him that Is 29:16 559
framed *s* of him that framed it Is 29:16 559
Which *s* to the seers, See not Is 30:10 559
thou shalt *s* unto it, Get thee Is 30:22 559
And the inhabitant shall not *s* Is 33:24 559
S to them that are of a fearful Is 35:4 559
S ye now to Hezekiah, Thus saith Is 36:4 559
I *s*, sayest thou, (but they are Is 36:5 559
But if thou *s* to me, We trust in Is 36:7 559
Thus shall ye *s* unto your master, Is 37:6 559
he heard *s* concerning Tirhakah Is 37:9 559
s to Hezekiah, Thus saith the Is 38:5 559
What shall I *s* Is 38:15 1696
s unto the cities of Judah, Is 40:9 559
and beforetime, that we may *s* Is 41:26 559
The first shall *s* to Zion Is 41:27
that *s* to the molten images, Ye Is 42:17 559
I will *s* to the north, Give up Is 43:6 559
or let them hear, and *s*, It is Is 43:9 559
One shall *s*, I am the LORD's Is 44:5 559
knowledge nor understanding to *s* Is 44:19 559
he cannot deliver his soul, nor *s* Is 44:20 559
Shall the clay *s* to him that Is 45:9 559
Surely, shall one *s*, in the LORD Is 45:24 559
lest thou shouldest *s*, Mine idol Is 48:5 559
lest thou shouldest *s*, Behold, I Is 48:7 559
s ye, The LORD hath redeemed his Is 48:20 559
thou mayest *s* to the prisoners Is 49:9 559
shall *s* again in thine ears, The Is 49:20 559
Then shalt thou *s* in thine heart Is 49:21 559
s unto Zion, Thou art my people Is 51:16 559
neither let the eunuch *s*, Behold, Is 56:3 559
s they, I will fetch wine, and we Is 56:12
And shall *s*, Cast ye up, cast ye Is 57:14 559
s they, and thou seest not Is 58:3
thou shalt cry, and he shall *s* Is 58:9 559
S ye to the daughter of Zion, Is 62:11 559
Which *s*, Stand by thyself, come Is 65:5 559
said unto me, *S* not, I am a child Jer 1:7 559
How canst thou *s*, I am not Jer 2:23 559
time of their trouble they will *s* Jer 2:27 559
wherefore *s* my people, We are Jer 2:31 559
They *s*, If a man put away his Jer 3:1 559
words toward the north, and *s* Jer 3:12 559
the LORD, they shall *s* no more Jer 3:16 559
and *s*, Blow ye the trumpet in the Jer 4:5 559
cry, gather together, and *s* Jer 4:5 559
And though they *s*, The LORD liveth Jer 5:2 559
neither understandest what they *s* Jer 5:15 1696
come to pass, when ye shall *s* Jer 5:19 559
Neither *s* they in their heart, Jer 5:24 559
and proclaim there this word, and *s* Jer 7:2 559
which is called by my name, and *s* Jer 7:10 559
But thou shalt *s* unto them Jer 7:28 559
Moreover thou shalt *s* unto them Jer 8:4 559
How do ye *s*, We are wise, and the Jer 8:8 559
Thus shall ye *s* unto them Jer 10:11 560
s thou unto them, Thus saith the Jer 11:3 559
and they shall *s* unto thee Jer 13:12 559
Then shalt thou *s* unto them Jer 13:13 559
S unto the king and to the queen, Jer 13:18 559
What wilt thou *s* when he shall Jer 13:21 559
if thou *s* in thine heart, Jer 13:22 559
behold, the prophets *s* unto them Jer 14:13 559
and I sent them not, yet they *s* Jer 14:15 559
thou shalt *s* this word unto them Jer 14:17 559
if they *s* unto thee, Whither Jer 15:2 559
words, and they shall *s* unto thee Jer 16:10 559
Then shalt thou *s* unto them Jer 16:11 559
the ends of the earth, and shall *s* Jer 16:19 559
they *s* unto me, Where is the word Jer 17:15 559
s unto them, Hear ye the word of Jer 17:20 559
And *s*, Hear ye the word of the Jer 19:3 559
shalt *s* unto them, Thus saith the Jer 19:11 559
s they, and we will report it Jer 20:10
them, Thus shall ye *s* to Zedekiah Jer 21:3 559
And unto this people thou shalt *s* Jer 21:8 559
the house of the king of Judah, *s* Jer 21:11
which *s*, Who shall come down Jer 21:13 559
And *s*, Hear the word of the LORD, Jer 22:2 559
they shall *s* every man to his Jer 22:8 559
LORD, that they shall no more *s* Jer 23:7 559
They *s* still unto them that Jer 23:17 559
they *s* unto every one that Jer 23:17 559
that use their tongues, and *s* Jer 23:31 559
thou shalt then *s* unto them Jer 23:33 559
and the people, that shall *s* Jer 23:34 559
Thus shall ye *s* every one to his Jer 23:35 559
Thus shalt thou *s* to the prophet Jer 23:37 559

But since ye *s*, The burden of the .... Jer 23:38 559
Because ye *s* this word, The .... Jer 23:38 559
unto you, saying, Ye shall not *s* .... Jer 23:38 559
Therefore thou shalt *s* unto them .... Jer 25:27 559
then shalt thou *s* unto them .... Jer 25:28 559
s unto them, The LORD shall roar .... Jer 25:30 559
And thou shalt *s* unto them .... Jer 26:4 559
command them to *s* unto their .... Jer 27:4 559
Thus shall ye *s* unto your masters .... Jer 27:4 559
publish ye, praise ye, and *s* .... Jer 31:7 559
it in the isles afar off, and *s* .... Jer 31:10 559
those days they shall *s* no more .... Jer 31:29 559
dost thou prophesy, and *s*, Thus .... Jer 32:3 559
this city, whereof ye *s*, It shall .... Jer 32:36 559
bought in this land, whereof ye *s* .... Jer 32:43 559
which ye *s* shall be desolate .... Jer 33:10 559
the voice of them that shall *s* .... Jer 33:11 559
thou shalt *s* to Jehoiakim king of .... Jer 36:29 559
Thus shall ye *s* to the king of .... Jer 37:7 559
princes, and those women shall *s* .... Jer 38:22 559
s unto thee, Declare unto us now .... Jer 38:25 559
Then thou shalt *s* unto them .... Jer 38:26 559
him even as he shall *s* unto thee .... Jer 39:12 1696
But if ye *s*, We will not dwell in .... Jer 42:13 559
all that the LORD our God shall *s* .... Jer 42:20 559
our God hath not sent thee to *s* .... Jer 43:2 559
s unto them, Thus saith the LORD .... Jer 43:10 559
Thou didst *s*, Woe is me now .... Jer 45:3 559
Thus shalt thou *s* unto him .... Jer 45:4 559
s ye, Stand fast, and prepare thee .... Jer 46:14 559
How *s* ye, We are mighty and strong .... Jer 48:14 559
and all ye that know his name, *s* .... Jer 48:17 559
and her that escapeth, and *s* .... Jer 48:19 559
s, Babylon is taken, Bel is .... Jer 50:2 559
shall the inhabitant of Zion *s* .... Jer 51:35 559
of Chaldea, shall Jerusalem *s* .... Jer 51:35 559
Then shalt thou *s*, O LORD, thou .... Jer 51:62 559
And thou shalt *s*, Thus shall .... Jer 51:64 559
They *s* to their mothers, Where is .... Lam 2:12 559
they *s*, We have swallowed her up .... Lam 2:16 559
and thou shalt *s* unto them .... Eze 2:4 559
of man, hear what I *s* unto thee .... Eze 2:8 1696
When I *s* unto the wicked, Thou .... Eze 3:18 559
mouth, and thou shalt *s* unto them .... Eze 3:27 559
And *s*, Ye mountains of Israel, ... Eze 6:3 559
and stamp with thy foot, and *s* .... Eze 6:11 559
for they *s*, The LORD seeth us not .... Eze 8:12 559
for they *s*, The LORD hath .... Eze 9:9 559
Which *s*, It is not near .... Eze 11:3 559
Therefore *s*, Thus saith the Lord .... Eze 11:16 559
Therefore *s*, Thus saith the Lord .... Eze 11:17 559
S thou unto them, Thus saith the .... Eze 12:10 559
S, I am your sign .... Eze 12:11 559
s unto the people of the land, ... Eze 12:19 559
but *s* unto them, The days are at .... Eze 12:23 1696
will I *s* the word, and will .... Eze 12:25 1696
they of the house of Israel *s* .... Eze 12:27 559
Therefore *s* unto them, Thus saith .... Eze 12:28 559
s thou unto them that prophesy .... Eze 13:2 559
a lying divination, whereas ye *s* .... Eze 13:7 559
S unto them which daub it with .... Eze 13:11 559
will *s* unto you, The wall is no .... Eze 13:15 559
And *s*, Thus saith the Lord GOD .... Eze 13:18 559
s unto them, Thus saith the Lord .... Eze 14:4 559
Therefore *s* unto the house of .... Eze 14:6 559
a sword upon that land, and *s* .... Eze 14:17 559
And *s*, Thus saith the Lord GOD .... Eze 16:3 559
And *s*, Thus saith the Lord GOD .... Eze 17:3 559
S thou, Thus saith the Lord GOD .... Eze 17:9 559
S now to the rebellious house, ... Eze 17:12 559
Yet *s* ye, Why .... Eze 18:19 559
Yet ye *s*, The way of the Lord is .... Eze 18:25 559
And *s*, What is thy mother .... Eze 19:2 559
s unto them, Thus saith the Lord .... Eze 20:3 559
s unto them, Thus saith the Lord .... Eze 20:5 559
s unto them, Thus saith the Lord .... Eze 20:27 559
Wherefore *s* unto the house of .... Eze 20:30 559
shall not be at all, that ye *s* .... Eze 20:32 559
s to the forest of the south, ... Eze 20:47 559
they *s* of me, Doth he not speak .... Eze 20:49 559
s to the land of Israel, Thus .... Eze 21:3 559
shall be, when they *s* unto thee .... Eze 21:7 559
Son of man, prophesy, and *s* .... Eze 21:9 559
S, A sword, a sword is sharpened, ... Eze 21:9 559
because, I *s*, that ye are come to .... Eze 21:24
thou, son of man, prophesy and *s* .... Eze 21:28 559
even *s* thou, The sword, the sword .... Eze 21:28 559
Then *s* thou, Thus saith the Lord .... Eze 22:3 559
s unto her, Thou art the land .... Eze 22:24 559
s unto them, Thus saith the Lord .... Eze 24:3 559
s unto the Ammonites, Hear the .... Eze 25:3 559
Because that Moab and Seir do *s* .... Eze 25:8 559
s to thee, How art thou destroyed .... Eze 26:17 559
s unto Tyrus, O thou that art .... Eze 27:3 559
s unto the prince of Tyrus, Thus .... Eze 28:2 559
Wilt thou yet *s* before him that .... Eze 28:9 559
s unto him, Thus saith the Lord .... Eze 28:12 559
And *s*, Thus saith the Lord GOD .... Eze 28:22 559
Speak, and *s*, Thus saith the Lord .... Eze 29:3 559
Son of man, prophesy and *s* .... Eze 30:2 559
s unto him, Thou art like a young .... Eze 32:2 559
s unto them, When I bring the .... Eze 33:2 559
When I *s* unto the wicked, O .... Eze 33:8 559
S unto them, As I live, saith the .... Eze 33:11 559
s unto the children of thy people .... Eze 33:12 559
When I shall *s* to the righteous, ... Eze 33:13 559
when I *s* unto the wicked, Thou .... Eze 33:14 559
Yet the children of thy people *s* .... Eze 33:17 559
Yet ye *s*, The way of the Lord is .... Eze 33:20 559
Wherefore *s* unto them, Thus saith .... Eze 33:25 559
S thou thus unto them, Thus saith .... Eze 33:27 559
s unto them, Thus saith the Lord .... Eze 34:2 559
s unto it, Thus saith the Lord .... Eze 35:3 559
the mountains of Israel, and *s* .... Eze 36:1 559
Therefore prophesy and *s*, Thus .... Eze 36:3 559
s unto the mountains, and to the .... Eze 36:6 559
Because they *s* unto you, Thou .... Eze 36:13 559
Therefore *s* unto the house of .... Eze 36:22 559
And they shall *s*, This land that .... Eze 36:35 559
s unto them, O ye dry bones, hear .... Eze 37:4 559
s to the wind, Thus saith the .... Eze 37:9 559
behold, they *s*, Our bones are .... Eze 37:11 559
s unto them, Thus saith the Lord .... Eze 37:12 559
S unto them, Thus saith the Lord .... Eze 37:19 1696
s unto them, Thus saith the Lord .... Eze 37:21 1696
And *s*, Thus saith the Lord GOD .... Eze 38:3 559
And thou shalt *s*, I will go up to .... Eze 38:11 559
shall *s* unto thee, Art thou come .... Eze 38:13 559
s unto Gog, Thus saith the Lord .... Eze 38:14 559
man, prophesy against Gog, and *s* .... Eze 39:1 559
I *s* unto thee concerning all the .... Eze 44:5 1696
thou shalt *s* to the rebellious, ... Eze 44:6 559
or *s* unto him, What doest thou .... Dan 4:35 560
thy father, the king, I *s* .... Dan 5:11
S ye unto your brethren, Ammi .... Hos 2:1 559
then shall she *s*, I will go and .... Hos 2:7 559
I will *s* to them which were not .... Hos 2:23 559
and they shall *s*, Thou art my God .... Hos 2:23 559
For now they shall *s*, We have no .... Hos 10:3 559
they shall *s* to the mountains, ... Hos 10:8 559
they *s* of them, Let the men that .... Hos 13:2 559
s unto him, Take away all .... Hos 14:2 559
neither will we *s* any more to the .... Hos 14:3 559
Ephraim shall *s*, What have I to .... Hos 14:8
porch and the altar, and let them *s* .... Joel 2:17 559
should they *s* among the people .... Joel 2:17 559
s unto his people, Behold, I will .... Joel 2:19 559
let the weak *s*, I am strong .... Joel 3:10 559
in the land of Egypt, and *s* .... Amos 3:9 559
which *s* to their masters, Bring, ... Amos 4:1 559
they shall *s* in all the highways, ... Amos 5:16 559
shall *s* unto him that is by the .... Amos 6:10 559
and he shall *s*, No .... Amos 6:10 559
Then shall he *s*, Hold thy tongue .... Amos 6:10 559
in a thing of nought, which *s* .... Amos 6:13 559
swear by the sin of Samaria, and *s* .... Amos 8:14 559
shall die by the sword, which *s* .... Amos 9:10 559
with a doleful lamentation, and *s* .... Mic 2:4 559
s they to them that prophesy .... Mic 2:6
they lean upon the LORD, and *s* .... Mic 3:11 559
And many nations shall come, and *s* .... Mic 4:2 559
are gathered against thee, that *s* .... Mic 4:11 559
thee shall flee from thee, and *s* .... Nah 3:7 559
to see what he will *s* unto me .... Hab 2:1 1696
proverb against him, and *s* .... Hab 2:6 559
that *s* in their heart, The LORD .... Zeph 1:12 559
of hosts, saying, This people *s* .... Hag 1:2 559
Therefore *s* thou unto them, Thus .... Zec 1:3 559
and they that sell them *s*, Blessed .... Zec 11:5 559
of Judah shall *s* in their heart .... Zec 12:5 559
that begat him shall *s* unto him .... Zec 13:3 559
But he shall *s*, I am no prophet, ... Zec 13:5 559
And one shall *s* unto him, What are .... Zec 13:6 559
I will *s*, It is my people .... Zec 13:9 559
and they shall *s*, The LORD is my .... Zec 13:9 559
Yet ye *s*, Wherein hast thou loved .... Mal 1:2 559
eyes shall see, and ye shall *s* .... Mal 1:5 559
And ye *s*, Wherein have we despised .... Mal 1:6 559
and ye *s*, Wherein have we polluted .... Mal 1:7 559
In that ye *s*, The table of the .... Mal 1:7 559
ye have profaned it, in that ye *s* .... Mal 1:12 559
Yet ye *s*, Wherefore .... Mal 2:14 559
Yet ye *s*, Wherein have we wearied .... Mal 2:17 559
When ye *s*, Every one that doeth .... Mal 2:17 559
But ye *s*, Wherein have we robbed .... Mal 3:8 559
Yet ye *s*, What have we spoken so .... Mal 3:13 559
think not to *s* within yourselves, ... Mt 3:9 *3004*
for I *s* unto you, that God is .... Mt 3:9 *3004*
Jesus began to preach, and to *s* .... Mt 4:17 *3004*
shall *s* all manner of evil .... Mt 5:11 *2036*
For verily I *s* unto you, Till .... Mt 5:18 *3004*
For I *s* unto you, That except .... Mt 5:20 *3004*
But I *s* unto you, That whosoever .... Mt 5:22 *3004*
whosoever shall *s* to his brother .... Mt 5:22 *2036*
but whosoever shall *s*, Thou fool, ... Mt 5:22 *2036*
Verily I *s* unto thee, Thou shalt .... Mt 5:26 *3004*
But I *s* unto you, That whosoever .... Mt 5:28 *3004*
But I *s* unto you, That whosoever .... Mt 5:32 *3004*
But I *s* unto you, Swear not at .... Mt 5:34 *3004*
But I *s* unto you, That ye resist .... Mt 5:39 *3004*
But I *s* unto you, Love your .... Mt 5:44 *3004*
Verily I *s* unto you, They have .... Mt 6:2 *3004*
Verily I *s* unto you, They have .... Mt 6:5 *3004*
Verily I *s* unto you, They have .... Mt 6:16 *3004*
Therefore I *s* unto you, Take no .... Mt 6:25 *3004*
yet I *s* unto you, That even .... Mt 6:29 *3004*
Or how wilt thou *s* to thy brother .... Mt 7:4 *3004*
Many will *s* to me in that day, ... Mt 7:22 *3004*
I *s* to this man, Go, and he goeth .... Mt 8:9 *3004*
followed, Verily I *s* unto you .... Mt 8:10 *3004*
I *s* unto you, That many shall .... Mt 8:11 *3004*
For whether is easier, to *s* .... Mt 9:5 *3004*
or to *s*, Arise, and walk .... Mt 9:5 *3004*
Verily I *s* unto you, It shall be .... Mt 10:15 *3004*
for verily I *s* unto you, Ye shall .... Mt 10:23 *3004*
a disciple, verily I *s* unto you .... Mt 10:42 *3004*
Jesus began to *s* unto the .... Mt 11:7 *3004*
I *s* unto you, and more than a .... Mt 11:9 *3004*
Verily I *s* unto you, Among them .... Mt 11:11 *3004*
eating nor drinking, and they *s* .... Mt 11:18 *3004*
eating and drinking, and they *s* .... Mt 11:19 *3004*
But I *s* unto you, It shall be .... Mt 11:22 *3004*
But I *s* unto you, That it shall .... Mt 11:24 *3004*
But I *s* unto you, That in this .... Mt 12:6 *3004*
Wherefore I *s* unto you, All .... Mt 12:31 *3004*
But I *s* unto you, That every idle .... Mt 12:36 *3004*
For verily I *s* unto you, That .... Mt 13:17 *3004*
harvest I will *s* to the reapers .... Mt 13:30 *2046*
They *s* unto him, Yea, Lord .... Mt 13:51 *3004*
they *s* unto him, We have here but .... Mt 14:17 *3004*
But ye *s*, Whosoever shall .... Mt 15:5 *3004*
Whosoever shall *s* to his father .... Mt 15:5 *2036*
And his disciples *s* unto him .... Mt 15:33 *3004*
them, When it is evening, ye *s* .... Mt 16:2 *3004*
Whom do men *s* that I the Son of .... Mt 16:13 *3004*
Some *s* that thou art John the .... Mt 16:14 *3004*
them, But whom *s* ye that I am .... Mt 16:15 *3004*
I *s* also unto thee, That thou art .... Mt 16:18 *3004*
Verily I *s* unto you, There be .... Mt 16:28 *3004*
Why then *s* the scribes that Elias .... Mt 17:10 *3004*
But I *s* unto you, That Elias is .... Mt 17:12 *3004*
for verily I *s* unto you, If ye .... Mt 17:20 *3004*
ye shall *s* unto this mountain, ... Mt 17:20 *2046*
And said, Verily I *s* unto you .... Mt 18:3 *3004*
for I *s* unto you, That in heaven .... Mt 18:10 *3004*
he find it, verily I *s* unto you .... Mt 18:13 *3004*
Verily I *s* unto you, Whatsoever .... Mt 18:18 *3004*
Again I *s* unto you, That if two .... Mt 18:19 *3004*
I *s* not unto thee, Until seven .... Mt 18:22 *3004*
They *s* unto him, Why did Moses .... Mt 19:7 *3004*
I *s* unto you, Whosoever shall put .... Mt 19:9 *3004*
His disciples *s* unto him, If the .... Mt 19:10 *3004*
disciples, Verily I *s* unto you .... Mt 19:23 *3004*
again I *s* unto you, It is easier .... Mt 19:24 *3004*
unto them, Verily I *s* unto you .... Mt 19:28 *3004*
They *s* unto him, Because no man .... Mt 20:7 *3004*
They *s* unto him, We are able .... Mt 20:22 *3004*
They *s* unto him, Lord, that our .... Mt 20:33 *3004*
if any man *s* ought unto you, ye .... Mt 21:3 *2036*
ought unto you, ye shall *s* .... Mt 21:3 *2046*
him, Hearest thou what these *s* .... Mt 21:16 *3004*
unto them, Verily I *s* unto you .... Mt 21:21 *3004*
if ye shall *s* unto this mountain .... Mt 21:21 *2036*
themselves, saying, If we shall *s* .... Mt 21:25 *2036*
he will *s* unto us, Why did ye not .... Mt 21:25 *2046*
But if we shall *s*, Of men .... Mt 21:26 *2036*
They *s* unto him, The first .... Mt 21:31 *3004*
unto them, Verily I *s* unto you .... Mt 21:31 *3004*
They *s* unto him, He will .... Mt 21:41 *3004*
Therefore *s* I unto you, The .... Mt 21:43 *3004*
They *s* unto him, Caesar's .... Mt 22:21 *3004*
which *s* that there is no .... Mt 22:23 *3004*
They *s* unto him, The son of David .... Mt 22:42 *3004*
for they *s*, and do not .... Mt 23:3 *3004*
you, ye blind guides, which *s* .... Mt 23:16 *3004*
And *s*, If we had been in the days .... Mt 23:30 *3004*
Verily I *s* unto you, All these .... Mt 23:36 *3004*
For I *s* unto you, Ye shall not .... Mt 23:39 *3004*
me henceforth, till ye shall *s* .... Mt 23:39 *2036*
verily I *s* unto you, There shall .... Mt 24:2 *3004*
Then if any man shall *s* unto you .... Mt 24:23 *2036*
if they shall *s* unto you, Behold, ... Mt 24:26 *2036*
Verily I *s* unto you, This .... Mt 24:34 *3004*
Verily I *s* unto you, That he .... Mt 24:47 *3004*
evil servant shall *s* in his heart .... Mt 24:48 *2036*
and said, Verily I *s* unto you .... Mt 25:12 *3004*
Then shall the King *s* unto them .... Mt 25:34 *2046*
s unto them, Verily I .... Mt 25:40 *2046*
unto them, Verily I *s* unto you .... Mt 25:40 *3004*
Then shall he *s* also unto them on .... Mt 25:41 *2046*
them, saying, Verily I *s* unto you .... Mt 25:45 *3004*
Verily I *s* unto you, Wheresoever .... Mt 26:13 *3004*
s unto him, The Master saith, My .... Mt 26:18 *2036*
eat, he said, Verily I *s* unto you .... Mt 26:21 *3004*
every one of them to *s* unto him .... Mt 26:22 *3004*
But I *s* unto you, I will not .... Mt 26:29 *3004*
Verily I *s* unto thee, That this .... Mt 26:34 *5346*
nevertheless I *s* unto you .... Mt 26:64 *3004*
They all *s* unto him, Let him be .... Mt 27:22 *3004*
called Golgotha, that is to *s* .... Mt 27:33 *3004*
that is to *s*, My God, my God, why .... Mt 27:46
s unto the people, He is risen .... Mt 27:64 *2036*
S ye, His disciples came by night .... Mt 28:13 *2036*
See thou *s* nothing to any man .... Mk 1:44 *2036*
Whether is it easier to *s* to the .... Mk 2:9 *2036*
or to *s*, Arise, and take up thy .... Mk 2:9 *2036*
I *s* unto thee, Arise, and take up .... Mk 2:11 *3004*
s unto him, Why do the disciples .... Mk 2:18 *3004*
Verily I *s* unto you, All sins .... Mk 3:28 *3004*
s unto him, Master, carest thou .... Mk 4:38 *3004*
Damsel, I *s* unto thee, arise .... Mk 5:41 *3004*
Verily I *s* unto you, It shall be .... Mk 6:11 *3004*
they *s* unto him, Shall we go and .... Mk 6:37 *3004*
And when they knew, they *s* .... Mk 6:38 *3004*
bread with defiled, that is to *s* .... Mk 7:2 *3004*
But ye *s*, If a man shall .... Mk 7:11 *3004*
If a man shall *s* to his father or .... Mk 7:11 *2036*
It is Corban, that is to *s* .... Mk 7:11
verily I *s* unto you, There shall .... Mk 8:12 *3004*
They *s* unto him, Twelve .... Mk 8:19 *3004*
them, Whom do men *s* that I am .... Mk 8:27 *3004*
but some *s*, Elias .... Mk 8:28
them, But whom *s* ye that I am .... Mk 8:29 *3004*
unto them, Verily I *s* unto you .... Mk 9:1 *3004*

S

For he wist not what to *s* Mk 9:6 2980
Why *s* the scribes that Elias must Mk 9:11 3004
But I *s* unto you, That Elias is Mk 9:13 3004
to Christ, verily I *s* unto you Mk 9:41 3004
Verily I *s* unto you, Whosoever Mk 10:15 3004
Then Peter began to *s* unto him Mk 10:28 3004
and said, Verily I *s* unto you Mk 10:29 3004
he began to cry out, and *s* Mk 10:47 3004
And if any man *s* unto you, Why do Mk 11:3 2036
s ye that the Lord hath need of Mk 11:3 2036
For verily I *s* unto you, That Mk 11:23 3004
shall *s* unto this mountain Mk 11:23 2036
Therefore I *s* unto you, What Mk 11:24 3004
s unto him, By what authority Mk 11:28 3004
themselves, saying, If we shall *s* Mk 11:31 2036
he will *s*, Why then did ye not Mk 11:31 2046
But if we shall *s*, Of men Mk 11:32 2036
they *s* unto him, Master, we know Mk 12:14 3004
which *s* there is no resurrection Mk 12:18 3004
How *s* the scribes that Christ is Mk 12:35 3004
unto them, Verily I *s* unto you Mk 12:43 3004
Jesus answering them began to *s* Mk 13:5 3004
And then if any man shall *s* to you Mk 13:21 2036
Verily I *s* unto you, that this Mk 13:30 3004
what I *s* unto you I *s* unto all Mk 13:37 3004
Verily I *s* unto you, Wheresoever Mk 14:9 3004
s ye to the goodman of the house, Mk 14:14 2036
Jesus said, Verily I *s* unto you Mk 14:18 3004
to *s* unto him one by one, Is it I Mk 14:19 3004
Verily I *s* unto you, I will drink Mk 14:25 3004
Verily I *s* unto thee, That this Mk 14:30 3004
We heard him *s*, I will destroy Mk 14:58 3004
him, and to *s* unto him, Prophesy Mk 14:65 3004
began to *s* to them that stood by, Mk 14:69 3004
begin not to *s* within yourselves, Lk 3:8 3004
for I *s* unto you, That God is Lk 3:8 3004
And he began to *s* unto them Lk 4:21 3004
Ye will surely *s* unto me this Lk 4:23 2046
And he said, Verily I *s* unto you Lk 4:24 3004
Whether is easier, to *s*, Thy sins Lk 5:23 2036
or to *s*, Rise up and walk Lk 5:23 2036
I *s* unto thee, Arise, and take up Lk 5:24 3004
But I *s* unto you which hear, Love Lk 6:27 3004
how canst thou *s* to thy brother Lk 6:42 3004
and do not the things which I *s* Lk 6:46 3004
but *s* in a word, and my servant Lk 7:7 2036
I *s* unto one, Go, and he goeth Lk 7:8 3004
I *s* unto you, I have not found so Lk 7:9 3004
Young man, I *s* unto thee, Arise Lk 7:14 3004
I *s* unto you, and much more than a Lk 7:26 3004
For I *s* unto you, Among those Lk 7:28 3004
and ye *s*, He hath a devil Lk 7:33 3004
and ye *s*, Behold a gluttonous man, Lk 7:34 3004
I have somewhat to *s* unto thee Lk 7:40 2036
And he saith, Master, *s* on Lk 7:40 2036
Wherefore I *s* unto thee, Her sins Lk 7:47 3004
him began to *s* within themselves Lk 7:49 3004
Whom *s* the people that I am Lk 9:18 3004
but some *s* Elias Lk 9:19 2036
and others *s*, that one of the old Lk 9:19
them, But whom *s* ye that I am Lk 9:20 3004
house ye enter, first *s*, Peace be Lk 10:5 3004
s unto them, The kingdom of God Lk 10:9 3004
the streets of the same, and *s* Lk 10:10 2036
But I *s* unto you, that it shall Lk 10:12 3004
said unto them, When ye pray, *s* Lk 11:2 3004
s unto him, Friend, lend me three Lk 11:5 2036
he from within shall answer and *s* Lk 11:7 2036
I *s* unto you, Though he will not Lk 11:8 3004
I *s* unto you, Ask, and it shall be Lk 11:9 3004
because ye *s* that I cast out Lk 11:18 3004
thick together, he began to *s* Lk 11:29 3004
verily I *s* unto you, It shall be Lk 11:51 3004
he began to *s* unto his disciples Lk 12:1 3004
I *s* unto you my friends, Be not Lk 12:4 3004
yea, I *s* unto you, Fear him Lk 12:5 3004
Also I *s* unto you, Whosoever Lk 12:8 3004
shall answer, or what ye shall *s* Lk 12:11 2036
the same hour what ye ought to *s* Lk 12:12 2036
I will *s* to my soul, Soul, thou Lk 12:19 2046
disciples, Therefore I *s* unto you Lk 12:22 3004
yet I *s* unto you, that Solomon in Lk 12:27 3004
verily I *s* unto you, that he Lk 12:37 3004
Of a truth I *s* unto you, that he Lk 12:44 3004
and if that servant *s* in his heart Lk 12:45 2036
out of the west, straightway ye *s* Lk 12:54 3004
ye see the south wind blow, ye *s* Lk 12:55 3004
I *s* unto you, will seek to enter Lk 13:24 3004
s unto you, I know you not whence Lk 13:25 2046
Then shall ye begin to *s*, We have Lk 13:26 3004
But he shall *s*, I tell you, I Lk 13:27 2046
and verily I *s* unto you, Ye shall Lk 13:35 3004
the time come when ye shall *s* Lk 13:35 2036
s to thee, Give this man place Lk 14:9 2046
he may *s* unto thee, Friend, go up Lk 14:10 2036
to *s* to them that were bidden Lk 14:17 2036
For I *s* unto you, That none of Lk 14:24 3004
I *s* unto you, that likewise joy Lk 15:7 3004
I *s* unto you, there is joy in the Lk 15:10 3004
will *s* unto him, Father, I have Lk 15:18 2046
I *s* unto you, Make to yourselves Lk 16:9 3004
ye might *s* unto this sycamine Lk 17:6 3004
will *s* unto him by and by, when he Lk 17:7 2046
And will not rather *s* unto him Lk 17:8 2046
things which are commanded you, *s* Lk 17:10 3004
Neither shall they *s*, Lo here Lk 17:21 2046
And they shall *s* to you, See here Lk 17:23 2046
Verily I *s* unto you, Whosoever Lk 18:17 3004
unto them, Verily I *s* unto you Lk 18:29 3004
For I *s* unto you, That unto every Lk 19:26 3004
thus shall ye *s* unto him, Because Lk 19:31 2046
themselves, saying, If we shall *s* Lk 20:5 2036
he will *s*, Why then believed ye Lk 20:5 2046
But and if we *s*, Of men Lk 20:6 2036
How *s* they that Christ is David's Lk 20:41 2036
he said, Of a truth I *s* unto you Lk 21:3 3004
Verily I *s* unto you, This Lk 21:32 3004
ye shall *s* unto the goodman of Lk 22:11 2046
For I *s* unto you, I will not any Lk 22:16 3004
For I *s* unto you, I will not Lk 22:18 3004
For I *s* unto you, that this that Lk 22:37 3004
he said unto them, Ye *s* that I am Lk 22:70 3004
coming, in the which they shall *s* Lk 23:29 2046
they begin to *s* to the mountains Lk 23:30 3004
Verily I *s* unto thee, To day Lk 23:43 3004
unto him, Rabbi, (which is to *s* Jn 1:38 3004
I *s* unto you, Hereafter ye shall Jn 1:51 3004
I *s* unto thee, Except a man be Jn 3:3 3004
I *s* unto thee, Except a man be Jn 3:5 3004
I *s* unto thee, We speak that we Jn 3:11 3004
and ye *s*, that in Jerusalem is the Jn 4:20 3004
S not ye, There are yet four Jn 4:35 3004
I *s* unto you, Lift up your eyes, Jn 4:35 3004
I *s* unto you, The Son can do Jn 5:19 3004
I *s* unto you, He that heareth my Jn 5:24 3004
I *s* unto you, The hour is coming, Jn 5:25 3004
but these things I *s*, that ye Jn 5:34 3004
I *s* unto you, Ye seek me, not Jn 6:26 3004
I *s* unto you, Moses gave you not Jn 6:32 3004
I *s* unto you, He that believeth Jn 6:47 3004
I *s* unto you, Except ye eat the Jn 6:53 3004
and they *s* nothing unto him Jn 7:26 3004
They *s* unto him, Master, this Jn 8:4 3004
I have many things to *s* and to Jn 8:26 2980
verily, I *s* unto you, Whosoever Jn 8:34 3004
if I *s* the truth, why do ye not Jn 8:46 3004
S we not well that thou art a Jn 8:48 3004
I *s* unto you, If a man keep my Jn 8:51 3004
of whom ye *s*, that he is your God Jn 8:54 3004
and if I should *s*, I know him not, Jn 8:55 3004
I *s* unto you, Before Abraham was, Jn 8:58 3004
They *s* unto the blind man again, Jn 9:17 3004
your son, who ye *s* was born blind Jn 9:19 3004
but now ye *s*, We see Jn 9:41 3004
I *s* unto you, He that entereth Jn 10:1 3004
I *s* unto you, I am the door of Jn 10:7 3004
S ye of him, whom the Father hath Jn 10:36 3004
His disciples *s* unto him, Master, Jn 11:8 3004
I *s* unto you, Except a corn of Jn 12:24 3004
and what shall I *s* Jn 12:27 2036
me a commandment, what I should *s* Jn 12:49 2036
and ye *s* well Jn 13:13 3004
I *s* unto you, The servant is not Jn 13:16 3004
I *s* unto you, He that receiveth Jn 13:20 3004
I *s* unto you, that one of you Jn 13:21 3004
so now I *s* to you Jn 13:33 3004
I *s* unto thee, The cock shall not Jn 13:38 3004
I *s* unto you, He that believeth Jn 14:12 3004
yet many things to *s* unto you Jn 16:12 3004
I *s* unto you, That ye shall weep Jn 16:20 3004
I *s* unto you, Whatsoever ye shall Jn 16:23 3004
I *s* not unto you, that I will Jn 16:26 3004
they *s* unto her, Woman, why Jn 20:13 3004
which is to *s*, Master, Jn 20:16 3004
s unto them, I ascend unto my Jn 20:17 2036
They *s* unto him, We also go with Jn 21:3 3004
I *s* unto thee, When thou wast Jn 21:18 3004
tongue, Aceldama, that is to *s* Acts 1:19
whatsoever he shall *s* unto you Acts 3:22 2980
they could *s* nothing against it Acts 4:14 471
now I *s* unto you, Refrain from Acts 5:38 3004
For we have heard him *s*, that Acts 6:14 3004
That word, I *s*, ye know, which Acts 10:37 3004
exhortation for the people, *s* on Acts 13:15 3004
said, What will this babbler *s* Acts 17:18 3004
therefore this that we *s* to thee Acts 21:23 3004
For the Sadducees *s* that there is Acts 23:8 3004
who hath something to *s* unto thee Acts 23:18 2980
to his accusers also to *s* before Acts 23:30 3004
Or else let these same here *s* Acts 24:20 2036
and Moses did *s* should come Acts 26:22 2980
Saying, Go unto this people, and *s* Acts 28:26 2036
of God, what shall we *s* Rom 3:5 2046
and as some affirm that we *s* Rom 3:8 3004
To declare, I *s*, at this time his Rom 3:26
What shall we *s* then that Abraham Rom 4:1 2046
for we *s* that faith was reckoned Rom 4:9 3004
What shall we *s* then Rom 6:1 2046
What shall we *s* then Rom 7:7 2046
shall we then *s* to these things Rom 8:31 2046
I *s* the truth in Christ, I lie Rom 9:1 3004
What shall we *s* then Rom 9:14 2046
Thou wilt *s* then unto me, Why Rom 9:19 2046
formed *s* to him that formed it Rom 9:20 2046
What shall we *s* then Rom 9:30 2046
S not in thine heart, Who shall Rom 10:6 2036
But I *s*, Have they not heard Rom 10:18 3004
But I *s*, Did not Israel know Rom 10:19 3004
I *s* then, Hath God cast away his Rom 11:1 2046
I *s* then, Have they stumbled that Rom 11:11 2046
Thou wilt *s* then, The branches Rom 11:19 2046
For I *s*, through the grace given Rom 12:3 3004
Now I *s* that Jesus Christ was a Rom 15:8 3004
Now this I *s*, that every one of 1Cor 1:12 3004
Lest any should *s* that I had 1Cor 1:15 2036
I *s* therefore to the unmarried and 1Cor 7:8 3004
for the present distress, I *s* 1Cor 7:26
But this I *s*, brethren, the time 1Cor 7:29 5346
S I these things as a man 1Cor 9:8 2980
judge ye what I *s* 1Cor 10:15 5346
What *s* I then 1Cor 10:19 5346
But I *s*, that the things which 1Cor 10:20
But if any man *s* unto you 1Cor 10:28 2036
Conscience, I *s*, not thine own, 1Cor 10:29 3004
What shall I *s* to you 1Cor 11:22 2036
that no man can *s* that Jesus is 1Cor 12:3 2036
If the foot shall *s*, Because I am 1Cor 12:15 2036
And if the ear shall *s*, Because I 1Cor 12:16 2036
And the eye cannot *s* unto the hand 1Cor 12:21 2036
the room of the unlearned *s* Amen 1Cor 14:16 2046
will they not *s* that ye are mad 1Cor 14:23 2046
how *s* some among you that there 1Cor 15:12 3004
But some man will *s*, How are the 1Cor 15:35 2046
Now this I *s*, brethren, that 1Cor 15:50 5346
We are confident, I *s*, and willing 2Cor 5:8
you unprepared, we (that we *s* not 2Cor 9:4 3004
But this I *s*, He which soweth 2Cor 9:6
s they, are weighty and powerful 2Cor 10:10 5346
I *s* again, Let no man think me a 2Cor 11:16 3004
for I will *s* the truth 2Cor 12:6 2046
so *s* I now again, If any man Gal 1:9 3004
And this I *s*, that the covenant, Gal 3:17 3004
Now I *s*, That the heir, as long Gal 4:1 3004
I Paul *s* unto you, that if ye be Gal 5:2 3004
This I *s* then, Walk in the Spirit Gal 5:16 3004
This I *s* therefore, and testify in Eph 4:17 3004
and again I *s*, Rejoice Phil 4:4 2046
by him, I *s*, whether they be Col 1:20
And this I *s*, lest any man should Col 2:4 3004
s to Archippus, Take heed to the Col 4:17 2036
For this we *s* unto you by the 1Th 4:15 3004
For when they shall *s*, Peace and 1Th 5:3 3004
understanding neither what they *s* 1Ti 1:7 3004
Consider what I *s* 2Ti 2:7 3004
having no evil thing to *s* of you Titus 2:8 3004
albeit I do not *s* to thee how Philem 19 3004
thou wilt also do more than I *s* Philem 21 3004
Of whom we have many things to *s* Heb 5:11 3056
And as I may so *s*, Levi also, who Heb 7:9 2036
not made with hands, that is to *s* Heb 9:11
through the veil, that is to *s* Heb 10:20
For they that *s* such things Heb 11:14 3004
And what shall I more *s* Heb 11:32 3004
So that we may boldly *s*, The Lord Heb 13:6 3004
Let no man *s* when he is tempted, Jas 1:13 3004
s unto him, Sit thou here in a Jas 2:3 2036
s to the poor, Stand thou there, Jas 2:3 2036
though a man *s* he hath faith, and Jas 2:14 3004
And one of you *s* unto them Jas 2:16 2036
Yea, a man may *s*, Thou hast faith Jas 2:18 2046
Go to now, ye that *s*, To day or Jas 4:13 3004
For that ye ought to *s*, If the Jas 4:15 3004
If we *s* that we have fellowship 1Jn 1:6 2036
If we *s* that we have no sin, we 1Jn 1:8 2036
If we *s* that we have not sinned, 1Jn 1:10 2036
If a man *s*, I love God, and hateth 1Jn 4:20 2036
I do not *s* that he shall pray for 1Jn 5:16 3004
them which *s* they are apostles Rev 2:2 5335
of them which *s* they are Jews Rev 2:9 3004
But unto you I *s*, and unto the Rev 2:24 3004
which *s* they are Jews, and are not Rev 3:9 3004
seal, I heard the second beast *s* Rev 6:3 3004
seal, I heard the third beast *s* Rev 6:5 3004
in the midst of the four beasts *s* Rev 6:6 3004
the voice of the fourth beast *s* Rev 6:7 3004
I heard the angel of the waters *s* Rev 16:5 3004
heard another out of the altar *s* Rev 16:7 3004
And the Spirit and the bride *s* Rev 22:17 3004
And let him that heareth *s* Rev 22:17 2036

SAYEST {40}
thou *s* unto me, Bring up this Ex 33:12 559
will do whatsoever thou *s* unto me Num 22:17 559
All that thou *s* unto me I will do Ruth 3:5 559
And now thou *s*, Go, tell thy lord, 1Kin 18:11 559
And now thou *s*, Go, tell thy lord, 1Kin 18:14 559
Thou *s*, (but they are but vain 2Kin 18:20 559
Thou *s*, Lo, thou hast smitten the 2Chr 25:19 559
so will we do as thou *s* Neh 5:12 559
are no such things done as thou *s* Neh 6:8 559
And thou *s*, How doth God know Job 22:13 559
Although thou *s* thou shalt not Job 35:14 559
and *s*, Return, ye children of men Ps 90:3 559
If thou *s*, Behold, we knew it not Prov 24:12 559
s thou, (but they are but vain Is 36:5
Why *s* thou, O Jacob, and speakest, Is 40:27 559
that *s* in thine heart, I am, and Is 47:8 559
Yet thou *s*, Because I am innocent Jer 2:35 559
plead with thee, because thou *s* Jer 2:35 559
Thou *s*, Prophesy not against Amos 7:16 559
saying, I know not what thou *s* Mt 26:70 3004
And Jesus said unto him, Thou *s* Mt 27:11 3004
thee, and *s* thou, Who touched me Mk 5:31 3004
neither understand I what thou *s* Mk 14:68 3004
said unto him, Thou *s* it Mk 15:2 3004
thee, and *s* thou, Who touched me Lk 8:45 2036
Master, we know that thou *s* Lk 20:21 3004
said, Man, I know not what thou *s* Lk 22:60 3004
answered him and said, Thou *s* it Lk 23:3 3004
What *s* thou of thyself Jn 1:22 3004
but what *s* thou Jn 8:5 3004
how *s* thou, Ye shall be made free Jn 8:33 3004
and thou *s*, If a man keep my Jn 8:52 3004
What *s* thou of him, that he hath Jn 9:17 3004

how *s* thou, The Son of man must .... Jn 12:34 3004
how *s* thou then, Shew us the .... Jn 14:9 3004
S thou this thing of thyself, or .... Jn 18:34 3004
answered, Thou *s* that I am a king .... Jn 18:37 3004
Thou that *s* a man should not .... Rom 2:22 3004
he understandeth not what thou *s* 1Cor 14:16 3004
Because thou *s*, I am rich, and .... Rev 3:17 3004

SAYING {1446}

And God blessed them, *s*, Be .... Gen 1:22 559
the LORD God commanded the man, *s* .... Gen 2:16 559
of which I commanded thee, *s* .... Gen 3:17 559
And he called his name Noah, *s* .... Gen 5:29 559
And God spake unto Noah, *s* .... Gen 8:15 559
Noah, and to his sons with him, *s* .... Gen 9:8 559
came unto Abram in a vision, *s* .... Gen 15:1 559
word of the LORD came unto him, *s* .... Gen 15:4 559
made a covenant with Abram, *s* .... Gen 15:18 559
and God talked with him, *s* .... Gen 17:3 559
Sarah laughed within herself, *s* .... Gen 18:12 559
Wherefore did Sarah laugh, *s* .... Gen 18:13 559
Then Sarah denied, *s*, I laughed .... Gen 18:15 559
then the angels hastened Lot, *s* .... Gen 19:15 559
of his host spake unto Abraham, *s* .... Gen 21:22 559
that it was told Abraham, *s* .... Gen 22:20 559
and spake unto the sons of Heth, *s* .... Gen 23:3 559
answered Abraham, *s* unto him .... Gen 23:5 559
And he communed with them, *s* .... Gen 23:8 559
in at the gate of his city, *s* .... Gen 23:10 559
of the people of the land, *s* .... Gen 23:13 559
answered Abraham, *s* unto him .... Gen 23:14 559
unto me, and that sware unto me, *s* .... Gen 24:7 559
words of Rebekah his sister, *s* .... Gen 24:30 559
And my master made me swear, *s* .... Gen 24:37 559
charged all his people, *s* .... Gen 26:11 559
strive with Isaac's herdmen, *s* .... Gen 26:20 559
spake unto Jacob her son, *s* .... Gen 27:6 559
speak unto Esau thy brother, *s* .... Gen 27:6 559
him he gave him a charge, *s* .... Gen 28:6 559
And Jacob vowed a vow, *s*, If God .... Gen 28:20 559
the words of Laban's sons, *s* .... Gen 31:1 559
God spake unto me in a dream, *s* .... Gen 31:11
spake unto me yesternight, *s* .... Gen 31:29 559
And he commanded them, *s*, Thus .... Gen 32:4 559
messengers returned to Jacob, *s* .... Gen 32:6 559
And he commanded the foremost, *s* .... Gen 32:17 559
meeteth thee, and asketh thee, *s* .... Gen 32:17 559
all that followed the droves, *s* .... Gen 32:19 559
spake unto his father Hamor, *s* .... Gen 34:4 559
And Hamor communed with them, *s* .... Gen 34:8 559
with the men of their city, *s* .... Gen 34:20 559
but his father observed the *s* .... Gen 37:11 1697
and the man asked him, *s*, What .... Gen 37:15 559
And it was told Tamar, *s*, Behold .... Gen 38:13 559
he asked the men of that place, *s* .... Gen 38:21 559
after, that it was told Judah, *s* .... Gen 38:24 559
she sent to her father in law, *s* .... Gen 38:25 559
upon his hand a scarlet thread, *s* .... Gen 38:28 559
she caught him by his garment, *s* .... Gen 39:12 559
her house, and spake unto them, *s* .... Gen 39:14 559
him according to these words, *s* .... Gen 39:17 559
wife, which she spake unto him, *s* .... Gen 39:19 559
the ward of his lord's house, *s* .... Gen 40:7 559
the chief butler unto Pharaoh, *s* .... Gen 41:9 559
And Joseph answered Pharaoh, *s* .... Gen 41:16 559
is it that I spake unto you, *s* .... Gen 42:14 559
And Reuben answered them, *s* .... Gen 42:22 559
s, Spake I not unto you, *s* .... Gen 42:22 559
s one to another, What is this .... Gen 42:28 559
that befell unto them; *s* .... Gen 42:29 559
Reuben spake unto his father, *s* .... Gen 42:37 559
And Judah spake unto him, *s* .... Gen 43:3 559
did solemnly protest unto us, *s* .... Gen 43:3 559
our state, and of our kindred, *s* .... Gen 43:7 559
the steward of his house, *s* .... Gen 44:1 559
My lord asked his servants, *s* .... Gen 44:19 559
for the lad unto my father, *s* .... Gen 44:32 559
was heard in Pharaoh's house, *s* .... Gen 45:16 559
And told him, *s*, Joseph is yet .... Gen 45:26 559
And Pharaoh spake unto Joseph, *s* .... Gen 47:5 559
And he blessed them that day, *s* .... Gen 48:20 559
In thee shall Israel bless, *s* .... Gen 48:20 559
unto the house of Pharaoh, *s* .... Gen 50:4 559
you, in the ears of Pharaoh, *s* .... Gen 50:4 559
My father made me swear, *s* .... Gen 50:5 559
sent a messenger unto Joseph, *s* .... Gen 50:16 559
did command before he died, *s* .... Gen 50:16 559
oath of the children of Israel, *s* .... Gen 50:25 559
Pharaoh charged all his people, *s* .... Ex 1:22 559
and of Jacob, appeared unto me, *s* .... Ex 3:16 559
the people, and their officers, *s* .... Ex 5:6 559
therefore they cry, *s*, Let us go .... Ex 5:8 559
and they spake to the people, *s* .... Ex 5:10 559
And the taskmasters hasted them, *s* .... Ex 5:13 559
came and cried unto Pharaoh, *s* .... Ex 5:15 559
And the LORD spake unto Moses, *s* .... Ex 6:10 559
And Moses spake before the LORD, *s* .... Ex 6:12 559
That the LORD spake unto Moses, *s* .... Ex 6:29 559
spake unto Moses and unto Aaron, *s* .... Ex 7:8 559
Pharaoh shall speak unto you, *s* .... Ex 7:9 559
Hebrews hath sent me unto thee, *s* .... Ex 7:16 559
the LORD appointed a set time, *s* .... Ex 9:5 559
and bow down themselves unto me, *s* .... Ex 11:8 559
and Aaron in the land of Egypt, *s* .... Ex 12:1 559
all the congregation of Israel, *s* .... Ex 12:3 559
And the LORD spake unto Moses, *s* .... Ex 13:1 559
shalt shew thy son in that day, *s* .... Ex 13:8 559
asketh thee in time to come, *s* .... Ex 13:14 559
sworn the children of Israel, *s* .... Ex 13:19 559
And the LORD spake unto Moses, *s* .... Ex 14:1 559
that we did tell thee in Egypt, *s* .... Ex 14:12 559
song unto the LORD, and spake, *s* .... Ex 15:1 559
people murmured against Moses, *s* .... Ex 15:24 559
And the LORD spake unto Moses, *s* .... Ex 16:11 559
speak unto them, *s*, At even ye .... Ex 16:12 559
And Moses cried unto the LORD, *s* .... Ex 17:4 559
because they tempted the LORD, *s* .... Ex 17:7 559
unto him out of the mountain, *s* .... Ex 19:3 559
unto the people round about, *s* .... Ex 19:12 559
for thou chargedst us, *s*, Set .... Ex 19:23 559
And God spake all these words, *s* .... Ex 20:1 559
And the LORD spake unto Moses, *s* .... Ex 25:1 559
And the LORD spake unto Moses, *s* .... Ex 30:11 559
And the LORD spake unto Moses, *s* .... Ex 30:17 559
the LORD spake unto Moses, *s* .... Ex 30:22 559
unto the children of Israel, *s* .... Ex 30:31 559
And the LORD spake unto Moses, *s* .... Ex 31:1 559
And the LORD spake unto Moses, *s* .... Ex 31:12 559
unto the children of Israel, *s* .... Ex 31:13 559
Abraham, to Isaac, and to Jacob, *s* .... Ex 33:1 559
of the children of Israel, *s* .... Ex 35:4 559
thing which the LORD commanded, *s* .... Ex 35:4 559
And they spake unto Moses, *s* .... Ex 36:5 559
proclaimed throughout the camp, *s* .... Ex 36:6 559
And the LORD spake unto Moses, *s* .... Ex 40:1 559
tabernacle of the congregation, *s* .... Lev 1:1 559
And the LORD spake unto Moses, *s* .... Lev 4:1 559
unto the children of Israel, *s* .... Lev 4:2 559
And the LORD spake unto Moses, *s* .... Lev 5:14 559
And the LORD spake unto Moses, *s* .... Lev 6:1 559
And the LORD spake unto Moses, *s* .... Lev 6:8 559
Command Aaron and his sons, *s* .... Lev 6:9 559
And the LORD spake unto Moses, *s* .... Lev 6:19 559
And the LORD spake unto Moses, *s* .... Lev 6:24 559
unto Aaron and to his sons, *s* .... Lev 6:25 559
And the LORD spake unto Moses, *s* .... Lev 7:22 559
unto the children of Israel, *s* .... Lev 7:23 559
And the LORD spake unto Moses, *s* .... Lev 7:28 559
unto the children of Israel, *s* .... Lev 7:29 559
And the LORD spake unto Moses, *s* .... Lev 8:1 559
consecrations, as I commanded, *s* .... Lev 8:31 559
of Israel thou shalt speak, *s* .... Lev 9:3 559
This is it that the LORD spake, *s* .... Lev 10:3 559
And the LORD spake unto Aaron, *s* .... Lev 10:8 559
of Aaron which were left alive, *s* .... Lev 10:16 559
Moses and to Aaron, *s* unto them .... Lev 11:1 559
unto the children of Israel, *s* .... Lev 11:2 559
And the LORD spake unto Moses, *s* .... Lev 12:1 559
unto the children of Israel, *s* .... Lev 12:2 559
LORD spake unto Moses and Aaron, *s* .... Lev 13:1 559
And the LORD spake unto Moses, *s* .... Lev 14:1 559
spake unto Moses and unto Aaron, *s* .... Lev 14:33 559
shall come and tell the priest, *s* .... Lev 14:35 559
spake unto Moses and to Aaron, *s* .... Lev 15:1 559
And the LORD spake unto Moses, *s* .... Lev 17:1 559
which the LORD hath commanded, *s* .... Lev 17:2 559
And the LORD spake unto Moses, *s* .... Lev 18:1 559
And the LORD spake unto Moses, *s* .... Lev 19:1 559
And the LORD spake unto Moses, *s* .... Lev 20:1 559
And the LORD spake unto Moses, *s* .... Lev 21:16 559
Speak unto Aaron, *s*, Whosoever he .... Lev 21:17 559
And the LORD spake unto Moses, *s* .... Lev 22:1 559
And the LORD spake unto Moses, *s* .... Lev 22:17 559
And the LORD spake unto Moses, *s* .... Lev 22:26 559
And the LORD spake unto Moses, *s* .... Lev 23:1 559
And the LORD spake unto Moses, *s* .... Lev 23:9 559
And the LORD spake unto Moses, *s* .... Lev 23:23 559
unto the children of Israel, *s* .... Lev 23:24 559
And the LORD spake unto Moses, *s* .... Lev 23:26 559
And the LORD spake unto Moses, *s* .... Lev 23:33 559
unto the children of Israel, *s* .... Lev 23:34 559
And the LORD spake unto Moses, *s* .... Lev 24:1 559
And the LORD spake unto Moses, *s* .... Lev 24:13 559
unto the children of Israel, *s* .... Lev 24:15 559
unto Moses in mount Sinai, *s* .... Lev 25:1 559
And the LORD spake unto Moses, *s* .... Lev 27:1 559
come out of the land of Egypt, *s* .... Num 1:1 559
the LORD had spoken unto Moses, *s* .... Num 1:48 559
spake unto Moses and unto Aaron, *s* .... Num 2:1 559
And the LORD spake unto Moses, *s* .... Num 3:5 559
And the LORD spake unto Moses, *s* .... Num 3:11 559
in the wilderness of Sinai, *s* .... Num 3:14 559
And the LORD spake unto Moses, *s* .... Num 3:44 559
spake unto Moses and unto Aaron, *s* .... Num 4:1 559
spake unto Moses and unto Aaron, *s* .... Num 4:17 559
And the LORD spake unto Moses, *s* .... Num 4:21 559
And the LORD spake unto Moses, *s* .... Num 5:1 559
And the LORD spake unto Moses, *s* .... Num 5:5 559
And the LORD spake unto Moses, *s* .... Num 5:11 559
And the LORD spake unto Moses, *s* .... Num 6:1 559
And the LORD spake unto Moses, *s* .... Num 6:22 559
unto Aaron and unto his sons, *s* .... Num 6:23 559
children of Israel, *s* unto them .... Num 6:23 559
And the LORD spake unto Moses, *s* .... Num 7:4 559
And the LORD spake unto Moses, *s* .... Num 8:1 559
And the LORD spake unto Moses, *s* .... Num 8:5 559
And the LORD spake unto Moses, *s* .... Num 8:23 559
come out of the land of Egypt, *s* .... Num 9:1 559
And the LORD spake unto Moses, *s* .... Num 9:9 559
unto the children of Israel, *s* .... Num 9:10 559
And the LORD spake unto Moses, *s* .... Num 10:1 559
for they weep unto me, *s*, Give us .... Num 11:13 559
wept in the ears of the LORD, *s* .... Num 11:18 559
you, and have wept before him, *s* .... Num 11:20 559
And Moses cried unto the LORD, *s* .... Num 12:13 559
And the LORD spake unto Moses, *s* .... Num 13:1 559
unto the children of Israel, *s* .... Num 13:32 559
of the children of Israel, *s* .... Num 14:7 559
the fame of thee will speak, *s* .... Num 14:15 559
according as thou hast spoken, *s* .... Num 14:17 559
spake unto Moses and unto Aaron, *s* .... Num 14:26 559
into the top of the mountain, *s* .... Num 14:40 559
And the LORD spake unto Moses, *s* .... Num 15:1 559
And the LORD spake unto Moses, *s* .... Num 15:17 559
And the LORD spake unto Moses, *s* .... Num 15:37 559
Korah and unto all his company, *s* .... Num 16:5 559
spake unto Moses and unto Aaron, *s* .... Num 16:20 559
And the LORD spake unto Moses, *s* .... Num 16:23 559
Speak unto the congregation, *s* .... Num 16:24 559
he spake unto the congregation, *s* .... Num 16:26 559
And the LORD spake unto Moses, *s* .... Num 16:36 559
against Moses and against Aaron, *s* .... Num 16:41 559
And the LORD spake unto Moses, *s* .... Num 16:44 559
And the LORD spake unto Moses, *s* .... Num 17:1 559
of Israel spake unto Moses, *s* .... Num 17:12 559
And the LORD spake unto Moses, *s* .... Num 18:25 559
spake unto Moses and unto Aaron, *s* .... Num 19:1 559
which the LORD hath commanded, *s* .... Num 19:2 559
chode with Moses, and spake, *s* .... Num 20:3 559
And the LORD spake unto Moses, *s* .... Num 20:7 559
the coast of the land of Edom, *s* .... Num 20:23 559
Sihon king of the Amorites, *s* .... Num 21:21 559
of his people, to call him, *s* .... Num 22:5 559
of Moab, hath sent unto me, *s* .... Num 22:10
of the mountains of the east, *s* .... Num 23:7
unto Balak, Told not I thee, *s* .... Num 23:26 559
which thou sentest unto me, *s* .... Num 24:12 559
And the LORD spake unto Moses, *s* .... Num 25:10 559
And the LORD spake unto Moses, *s* .... Num 25:16 559
the son of Aaron the priest, *s* .... Num 26:1 559
of Moab by Jordan near Jericho, *s* .... Num 26:3 559
And the LORD spake unto Moses, *s* .... Num 26:52 559
tabernacle of the congregation, *s* .... Num 27:2 559
And the LORD spake unto Moses, *s* .... Num 27:6 559
unto the children of Israel, *s* .... Num 27:8 559
And Moses spake unto the LORD, *s* .... Num 27:15 559
And the LORD spake unto Moses, *s* .... Num 28:1 559
the children of Israel, *s* .... Num 30:1 559
And the LORD spake unto Moses, *s* .... Num 31:1 559
And Moses spake unto the people, *s* .... Num 31:3 559
And the LORD spake unto Moses, *s* .... Num 31:25 559
princes of the congregation, *s* .... Num 32:2 559
the same time, and he sware, *s* .... Num 32:10 559
of Reuben spake unto Moses, *s* .... Num 32:25 559
children of Reuben answered, *s* .... Num 32:31 559
Moab by Jordan, near Jericho, *s* .... Num 33:50 559
And the LORD spake unto Moses, *s* .... Num 34:1 559
the children of Israel, *s* .... Num 34:13 559
And the LORD spake unto Moses, *s* .... Num 34:16 559
of Moab by Jordan near Jericho, *s* .... Num 35:1 559
And the LORD spake unto Moses, *s* .... Num 35:9 559
to the word of the LORD, *s* .... Num 36:5 559
the daughters of Zelophehad, *s* .... Num 36:6 559
Moses to declare this law, *s* .... Deut 1:5 559
our God spake unto us in Horeb, *s* .... Deut 1:6 559
I spake unto you at that time, *s* .... Deut 1:9 559
your judges at that time, *s* .... Deut 1:16 559
And the *s* pleased me well .... Deut 1:23 1697
have discouraged our heart, *s* .... Deut 1:28 559
words, and was wroth, and sware, *s* .... Deut 1:34 559
angry with me for your sakes, *s* .... Deut 1:37 559
And the LORD spake unto me, *s* .... Deut 2:2 559
And command thou the people, *s* .... Deut 2:4 559
That the LORD spake unto me, *s* .... Deut 2:17 559
of Heshbon with words of peace, *s* .... Deut 2:26 559
I commanded you at that time, *s* .... Deut 3:18 559
commanded Joshua at that time, *s* .... Deut 3:21 559
besought the LORD at that time, *s* .... Deut 3:23 559
up into the mount;) *s* .... Deut 5:5 559
asketh thee in time to come, *s* .... Deut 6:20 559
cast them out from before thee, *s* .... Deut 9:4 559
the LORD spake unto me, *s* .... Deut 9:13 559
sent you from Kadesh-barnea, *s* .... Deut 9:23 559
enquire not after their gods, *s* .... Deut 12:30 559
whereof he spake unto thee, *s* .... Deut 13:2 559
own soul, entice thee secretly, *s* .... Deut 13:6 559
hath given thee to dwell there, *s* .... Deut 13:12 559
the inhabitants of their city, *s* .... Deut 13:13 559
a thought in thy wicked heart, *s* .... Deut 15:9 559
therefore I command thee, *s* .... Deut 15:11 559
in the day of the assembly, *s* .... Deut 18:16 559
Wherefore I command thee, *s* .... Deut 19:7 559
shall speak unto the people, *s* .... Deut 20:5 559
of speech against her, *s*, I found .... Deut 22:17 559
of Israel commanded the people, *s* .... Deut 27:1 559
Levites spake unto all Israel, *s* .... Deut 27:9 559
the people the same day, *s* .... Deut 27:11 559
he bless himself in his heart, *s* .... Deut 29:19 559
And Moses commanded them, *s* .... Deut 31:10 559
of the covenant of the LORD, *s* .... Deut 31:25 559
unto Moses that selfsame day, *s* .... Deut 32:48 559
unto Isaac, and unto Jacob, *s* .... Deut 34:4 559
son of Nun, Moses' minister, *s* .... Josh 1:1 559
the officers of the people, *s* .... Josh 1:10 559
host, and command the people, *s* .... Josh 1:11 559
of Manasseh, spake Joshua, *s* .... Josh 1:12 559
of the LORD commanded you, *s* .... Josh 1:13 559
And they answered Joshua, *s* .... Josh 1:16 559
two men to spy secretly, *s* .... Josh 2:1 559
was told the king of Jericho, *s* .... Josh 2:2 559
of Jericho sent unto Rahab, *s* .... Josh 2:3 559
And they commanded the people, *s* .... Josh 3:3 559
Joshua spake unto the priests, *s* .... Josh 3:6 559
bear the ark of the covenant, *s* .... Josh 3:8 559

the LORD spake unto Joshua, *s* Josh 4:1 559
And command ye them, *s*, Take you Josh 4:3 559
their fathers in time to come, *s* Josh 4:6 559
And the LORD spake unto Joshua, *s* Josh 4:15 559
commanded the priests, *s*, Come ye Josh 4:17 559
unto the children of Israel, *s* Josh 4:21 559
their fathers in time to come, *s* Josh 4:21 559
shall let your children know, *s* Josh 4:22 559
had commanded the people, *s* Josh 6:10 559
adjured them at that time, *s* Josh 6:26 559
of Beth-el, and spake unto them, *s* Josh 7:2 559
And he commanded them, *s*, Behold, Josh 8:4 559
of our country spake to us, *s* Josh 9:11 559
them, and he spake unto them, *s* Josh 9:22 559
Wherefore have ye beguiled us, *s* Josh 9:22 559
and unto Debir king of Eglon, *s* Josh 10:3 559
Joshua to the camp to Gilgal, *s* Josh 10:6 559
And it was told Joshua, *s*, The Josh 10:17 559
And Moses sware on that day, *s* Josh 14:9 559
of Nun, and before the princes, *s* Josh 17:4 559
of Joseph spake unto Joshua, *s* Josh 17:14 559
even to Ephraim and to Manasseh, *s* Josh 17:17 559
that went to describe the land, *s* Josh 18:8 559
LORD also spake unto Joshua, *s* Josh 20:1 559
to the children of Israel, *s* Josh 20:2 559
Shiloh in the land of Canaan, *s* Josh 21:2 559
And he spake unto them, *s*, Return Josh 22:8 559
and they spake with them, *s* Josh 22:15 559
done it for fear of this thing, *s* Josh 22:24 559
might speak unto our children, *s* Josh 22:24 559
of Israel asked the LORD, *s* Judg 1:1 559
LORD God of Israel commanded, *s* Judg 4:6
the son of Abinoam on that day, *s* Judg 5:1 559
which our fathers told us of, *s* Judg 6:13 559
day he called him Jerubbaal, *s* Judg 6:32 559
vaunt themselves against me, *s* Judg 7:2 559
in the ears of the people, *s* Judg 7:3 559
throughout all mount Ephraim, *s* Judg 7:24 559
also unto the men of Penuel, *s* Judg 8:9 559
with whom ye did upbraid me, *s* Judg 8:15 559
house of his mother's father, *s* Judg 9:1 559
unto Abimelech privily, *s* Judg 9:31 559
of Israel cried unto the LORD, *s* Judg 10:10 559
king of the children of Ammon, *s* Judg 11:12 559
unto the king of Edom, *s*, Let me, Judg 11:17 559
woman came and told her husband, *s* Judg 13:6 559
And they spake unto him, *s* Judg 15:13 559
And it was told the Gazites, *s* Judg 16:2 559
and were quiet all the night, *s* Judg 16:2 559
the lords of the Philistines, *s* Judg 16:18 559
of the house, the old man, *s* Judg 19:22 559
the people arose as one man, *s* Judg 20:8 559
all the tribe of Benjamin, *s* Judg 20:12 559
and asked counsel of the LORD, *s* Judg 20:23 559
stood before it in those days,) *s* Judg 20:28 559
of Israel had sworn in Mizpeh, *s* Judg 21:1 559
not up to the LORD to Mizpeh, *s* Judg 21:5 559
valiantest, and commanded them, *s* Judg 21:10 559
children of Israel have sworn, *s* Judg 21:18 559
the children of Benjamin, *s* Judg 21:20 559
Boaz commanded his young men, *s* Ruth 2:15 559
And I thought to advertise thee, *s* Ruth 4:4 559
her neighbours gave it a name, *s* Ruth 4:17 559
son, and called his name Samuel, *s* 1Sa 1:20
she named the child I-chabod, *s* 1Sa 4:21 559
that the Ekronites cried out, *s* 1Sa 5:10 559
the priests and the diviners, *s* 1Sa 6:2 559
inhabitants of Kirjath-jearim, *s* 1Sa 6:21 559
unto all the house of Israel, *s* 1Sa 7:3 559
the name of it Eben-ezer, *s* 1Sa 7:12 559
his ear a day before Saul came, *s* 1Sa 9:15 559
Saul to the top of the house, *s* 1Sa 9:26 559
asses, and sorroweth for you, *s* 1Sa 10:2 559
by the hands of messengers, *s* 1Sa 11:7 559
throughout all the land, *s* 1Sa 13:3 559
Saul had adjured the people, *s* 1Sa 14:24 559
the people with an oath, *s* 1Sa 14:28 559
Then they told Saul, *s*, Behold, 1Sa 14:33 559
word of the LORD unto Samuel, *s* 1Sa 15:10 559
morning, it was told Samuel, *s* 1Sa 15:12 559
And Saul sent to Jesse, *s*, Let 1Sa 16:22 559
to the men that stood by him, *s* 1Sa 17:26 559
answered him after this manner, *s* 1Sa 17:27 559
wroth, and the *s* displeased him 1Sa 18:8 1697
And Saul commanded his servants, *s* 1Sa 18:22
the servants of Saul told him, *s* 1Sa 18:24 559
and Jonathan told David, *s* 1Sa 19:2 559
Michal David's wife told him, *s* 1Sa 19:11 559
messengers again to see David, *s* 1Sa 19:15 559
And it was told Saul, *s*, Behold, 1Sa 19:19 559
with the house of David, *s* 1Sa 20:16
And, behold, I will send a lad, *s* 1Sa 20:21
of us in the name of the LORD, *s* 1Sa 20:42 559
to another of him in dances, *s* 1Sa 21:11 559
Then they told David, *s*, Behold, 1Sa 23:1 559
David enquired of the LORD, *s* 1Sa 23:2 559
the Ziphites to Saul to Gibeah, *s* 1Sa 23:19 559
came a messenger unto Saul, *s* 1Sa 23:27 559
that it was told him, *s*, Behold, 1Sa 24:1 559
the cave, and cried after Saul, *s* 1Sa 24:8 559
hearest thou men's words, *s* 1Sa 24:9 559
men told Abigail, Nabal's wife, *s* 1Sa 25:14 559
to Carmel, they spake unto her, *s* 1Sa 25:40 559
came unto Saul to Gibeah, *s* 1Sa 26:1 559
of Zeruiah, brother to Joab, *s* 1Sa 26:6 559
and to Abner the son of Ner, *s* 1Sa 26:14 559
in the inheritance of the LORD, *s* 1Sa 26:19 559
to bring tidings to Gath, *s* 1Sa 27:11 559

Lest they should tell on us, *s* 1Sa 27:11 559
And Achish believed David, *s* 1Sa 27:12 559
Saul sware to her by the LORD, *s* 1Sa 28:10 559
and the woman spake to Saul, *s* 1Sa 28:12 559
sang one to another in dances, *s* 1Sa 29:5 559
And David enquired at the LORD, *s* 1Sa 30:8 559
of Judah, even to his friends, *s* 1Sa 30:26 559
hath testified against thee, *s* 2Sa 1:16 559
David enquired of the LORD, *s* 2Sa 2:1 559
And they told David, *s*, That the 2Sa 2:4 559
to David on his behalf, *s* 2Sa 3:12 559
s also, Make thy league with me, 2Sa 3:12 559
to Ish-bosheth Saul's son, *s* 2Sa 3:14 559
with the elders of Israel, *s* 2Sa 3:17 559
the LORD hath spoken of David, *s* 2Sa 3:18 559
him were come, they told Joab, *s* 2Sa 3:23 559
it was yet day, David sware, *s* 2Sa 3:35 559
When one told me, *s*, Behold, Saul 2Sa 4:10 559
to David unto Hebron, and spake, *s* 2Sa 5:1 559
which spake unto David, *s* 2Sa 5:6 559
And David enquired of the LORD, *s* 2Sa 5:19 559
And it was told king David, *s* 2Sa 6:12 559
of the LORD came unto Nathan, *s* 2Sa 7:4 559
to feed my people Israel, *s* 2Sa 7:7 559
thy name be magnified for ever, *s* 2Sa 7:26 559
hast revealed to thy servant, *s* 2Sa 7:27 559
And David sent to Joab, *s*, Send me 2Sa 11:6 559
And when they had told David, *s* 2Sa 11:10 559
And he wrote in the letter, *s* 2Sa 11:15 559
And charged the messenger, *s* 2Sa 11:19 559
Then David sent home to Tamar, *s* 2Sa 13:7 559
had commanded his servants, *s* 2Sa 13:28 559
that tidings came to David, *s* 2Sa 13:30 559
Joab, Behold, I sent unto thee, *s* 2Sa 14:32 559
I abode at Geshur in Syria, *s* 2Sa 15:8 559
all the tribes of Israel, *s* 2Sa 15:10 559
came a messenger to David, *s* 2Sa 15:13 559
And one told David, *s*, Ahithophel 2Sa 15:31 559
the *s* pleased Absalom well, and 2Sa 17:4 1697
Absalom spake unto him, *s* 2Sa 17:6 559
shall we do after his *s* 2Sa 17:6 1697
send quickly, and tell David, *s* 2Sa 17:16 559
Joab and Abishai and Ittai, *s* 2Sa 18:5 559
thee and Abishai and Ittai, *s* 2Sa 18:12 559
they told unto all the people, *s* 2Sa 19:8 559
all the tribes of Israel, *s* 2Sa 19:9 559
and to Abiathar the priests, *s* 2Sa 19:11 559
Speak unto the elders of Judah, *s* 2Sa 19:11 559
Then she spake, *s*, They were wont 2Sa 20:18 559
were wont to speak in old time, *s* 2Sa 20:18 559
men of David sware unto him, *s* 2Sa 21:17 559
the prophet Gad, David's seer, *s* 2Sa 24:11 559
David, according to the *s* of Gad 2Sa 24:19 1697
son of Haggith exalted himself, *s* 1Kin 1:5 559
displeased him at any time in *s* 1Kin 1:6 559
the mother of Solomon, *s*, Hast 1Kin 1:11 559
swear unto thine handmaid, *s* 1Kin 1:13 559
thy God unto thine handmaid, *s* 1Kin 1:17
And they told the king, *s*, Behold 1Kin 1:23 559
thee by the LORD God of Israel, *s* 1Kin 1:30 559
to bless our lord king David, *s* 1Kin 1:47 559
And it was told Solomon, *s* 1Kin 1:51 559
hold on the horns of the altar, *s* 1Kin 1:51 559
and he charged Solomon his son, *s* 1Kin 2:1 559
which he spake concerning me, *s* 1Kin 2:4 559
and I sware to him by the LORD, *s* 1Kin 2:8 559
king Solomon sware by the LORD, *s* 1Kin 2:23 559
Benaiah the son of Jehoiada, *s* 1Kin 2:29 559
brought the king word again, *s* 1Kin 2:30 559
said unto the king, The *s* is good 1Kin 2:38 1697
And they told Shimei, *s*, Behold, 1Kin 2:39 559
LORD, and protested unto thee, *s* 1Kin 2:42 559
And Solomon sent to Hiram, *s* 1Kin 5:2 559
spake unto David my father, *s* 1Kin 5:5 559
And Hiram sent to Solomon, *s* 1Kin 5:8 559
of the LORD came to Solomon, *s* 1Kin 6:11 559
with his hand fulfilled it, *s* 1Kin 8:15 559
that thou promisedst him, *s* 1Kin 8:25 559
that carried them captives, *s* 1Kin 8:47 559
of Israel with a loud voice, *s* 1Kin 8:55 559
I promised to David thy father, *s* 1Kin 9:5 559
came, and spake unto Rehoboam, *s* 1Kin 12:3 559
And they spake unto him, *s* 1Kin 12:7 559
people, who have spoken to me, *s* 1Kin 12:9 559
up with him spake unto him, *s* 1Kin 12:10 559
people that spake unto thee, *s* 1Kin 12:10 559
day, as the king had appointed, *s* 1Kin 12:12 559
the counsel of the young men, *s* 1Kin 12:14 559
LORD, that he might perform his *s* 1Kin 12:15 1697
the people answered the king, *s* 1Kin 12:16 559
unto Shemaiah the man of God, *s* 1Kin 12:22 559
to the remnant of the people, *s* 1Kin 12:23 559
And he gave a sign the same day, *s* 1Kin 13:3 559
heard the *s* of the man of God 1Kin 13:4 1697
forth his hand from the altar, *s* 1Kin 13:4 559
me by the word of the LORD, *s* 1Kin 13:9 559
me by the word of the LORD, *s* 1Kin 13:18 559
of God that came from Judah, *s* 1Kin 13:21 559
And he spake to his sons, *s* 1Kin 13:27 559
And they mourned over him, *s* 1Kin 13:30
him, that he spake to his sons, *s* 1Kin 13:31 559
For the *s* which he cried by the 1Kin 13:32 1697
Syria, that dwelt at Damascus, *s* 1Kin 15:18 559
according unto the *s* of the LORD 1Kin 15:29 1697
son of Hanani against Baasha, *s* 1Kin 16:1 559
word of the LORD came unto him, *s* 1Kin 17:2 559
word of the LORD came unto him, *s* 1Kin 17:8 559
did according to the *s* of Elijah 1Kin 17:15 1697

to Elijah in the third year, *s* 1Kin 18:1 559
from morning even until noon, *s* 1Kin 18:26 559
whom the word of the LORD came, *s* 1Kin 18:31 559
sent a messenger unto Elijah, *s* 1Kin 19:2 559
lord, O king, according to thy *s* 1Kin 20:4 1697
said, Thus speaketh Ben-hadad, *s* 1Kin 20:5 559
Although I have sent unto thee, *s* 1Kin 20:5 559
unto Ahab king of Israel, *s* 1Kin 20:13 559
sent out, and they told him, *s* 1Kin 20:17 559
And Ahab spake unto Naboth, *s* 1Kin 21:2 559
And she wrote in the letters, *s* 1Kin 21:9 559
to bear witness against him, *s* 1Kin 21:10 559
in the presence of the people, *s* 1Kin 21:13 559
Then they sent to Jezebel, *s* 1Kin 21:14 559
came to Elijah the Tishbite, *s* 1Kin 21:17 559
And thou shalt speak unto him, *s* 1Kin 21:19 559
And thou shalt speak unto him, *s* 1Kin 21:19 559
of Jezebel also spake the LORD, *s* 1Kin 21:23 559
came to Elijah the Tishbite, *s* 1Kin 21:28 559
all the prophets prophesied so, *s* 1Kin 22:12 559
to call Micaiah spake unto him, *s* 1Kin 22:13 559
had rule over his chariots, *s* 1Kin 22:31 559
the going down of the sun, *s* 1Kin 22:36 559
according to the *s* of Elisha 2Kin 2:22 1697
Jehoshaphat the king of Judah, *s* 2Kin 3:7 559
of the prophets unto Elisha, *s* 2Kin 4:1 559
again to meet him, and told him, *s* 2Kin 4:31 559
one went in, and told his lord, *s* 2Kin 5:4 559
letter to the king of Israel, *s* 2Kin 5:6 559
that he sent to the king, *s* 2Kin 5:8 559
sent a messenger unto him, *s* 2Kin 5:10 559
according to the *s* of the man of 2Kin 5:14 1697
My master hath sent me, *s* 2Kin 5:22 559
took counsel with his servants, *s* 2Kin 6:8 559
sent unto the king of Israel, *s* 2Kin 6:9 559
And it was told him, *s*, Behold, he 2Kin 6:13 559
there cried a woman unto him, *s* 2Kin 6:26 559
and they told them, *s*, We came to 2Kin 7:10 559
hide themselves in the field, *s* 2Kin 7:12 559
after the host of the Syrians, *s* 2Kin 7:14 559
of God had spoken to the king, *s* 2Kin 7:18 559
son he had restored to life, *s* 2Kin 8:1 559
did after the *s* of the man of God 2Kin 8:2 1697
the servant of the man of God, *s* 2Kin 8:4 559
unto her a certain officer, *s* 2Kin 8:6 559
and it was told him, *s*, The man of 2Kin 8:7 559
and enquire of the LORD by him, *s* 2Kin 8:8 559
of Syria hath sent me to thee, *s* 2Kin 8:9 559
Thus and thus spake he to me, *s* 2Kin 9:12 559
stairs, and blew with trumpets, *s* 2Kin 9:13 559
And the watchman told, *s*, The 2Kin 9:18 559
And the watchman told, *s*, He came 2Kin 9:20 559
servant Elijah the Tishbite, *s* 2Kin 9:36 559
brought up Ahab's children, *s* 2Kin 10:1 559
of the children, sent to Jehu, *s* 2Kin 10:5 559
letter the second time to them, *s* 2Kin 10:6 559
came a messenger, and told him, *s* 2Kin 10:8 559
according to the *s* of the LORD 2Kin 10:17 1697
And he commanded them, *s*, This is 2Kin 11:5 559
wherein the LORD commanded, *s* 2Kin 14:6 559
son of Jehu, king of Israel, *s* 2Kin 14:8 559
sent to Amaziah king of Judah, *s* 2Kin 14:9 559
the cedar that was in Lebanon, *s* 2Kin 14:9 559
LORD which he spake unto Jehu, *s* 2Kin 15:12 559
king of Assyria, *s*, I am thy 2Kin 16:7 559
commanded Urijah the priest, *s* 2Kin 16:15 559
prophets, and by all the seers, *s* 2Kin 17:13 559
spake to the king of Assyria, *s* 2Kin 17:26 559
the king of Assyria commanded, *s* 2Kin 17:27 559
a covenant, and charged them, *s* 2Kin 17:35 559
the king of Assyria to Lachish, *s* 2Kin 18:14 559
the Jews' language, and spake, *s* 2Kin 18:28 559
make you trust in the LORD, *s* 2Kin 18:30 559
when he persuadeth you, *s* 2Kin 18:32 559
for the king's commandment was, *s* 2Kin 18:36 559
messengers again unto Hezekiah, *s* 2Kin 19:9 559
to Hezekiah king of Judah, *s* 2Kin 19:10 559
thou trustest deceive thee, *s* 2Kin 19:10 559
son of Amoz sent to Hezekiah, *s* 2Kin 19:20 559
wall, and prayed unto the LORD, *s* 2Kin 20:2 559
word of the LORD came to him, *s* 2Kin 20:4 559
by his servants the prophets, *s* 2Kin 21:10 559
to the house of the LORD, *s* 2Kin 22:3 559
the scribe shewed the king, *s* 2Kin 22:10 559
a servant of the king's, *s* 2Kin 22:12 559
king commanded all the people, *s* 2Kin 23:21 559
mother called his name Jabez, *s* 1Chr 4:9 559
called on the God of Israel, *s* 1Chr 4:10 559
to David unto Hebron, *s*, Behold, 1Chr 11:1 559
upon advisement sent him away, *s* 1Chr 12:19 559
was afraid of God that day, *s* 1Chr 13:12 559
And David enquired of God, *s* 1Chr 14:10 559
S, Unto thee will I give the land 1Chr 16:18 559
S, Touch not mine anointed, and do 1Chr 16:22
the word of God came to Nathan, *s* 1Chr 17:3 559
I commanded to feed my people, *s* 1Chr 17:6 559
name may be magnified for ever, *s* 1Chr 17:24 559
spake unto Gad, David's seer, *s* 1Chr 21:9 559
Go and tell David, *s*, Thus saith 1Chr 21:10 559
And David went up at the *s* of Gad 1Chr 21:19 1697
word of the LORD came to me, *s* 1Chr 22:8 559
Israel to help Solomon his son, *s* 1Chr 22:17
sent to Huram the king of Tyre, *s* 2Chr 2:3 559
of musick, and praised the LORD, *s* 2Chr 5:13
his mouth to my father David, *s* 2Chr 6:4 559
which thou hast promised him, *s* 2Chr 6:16 559
in the land of their captivity, *s* 2Chr 6:37 559
and praised the LORD, *s*, For he 2Chr 7:3

with David thy father, *s*, There ... 2Chr 7:18 559
came and spake to Rehoboam, *s* ... 2Chr 10:3 559
his father while he yet lived, *s* ... 2Chr 10:6 559
And they spake unto him, *s* ... 2Chr 10:7 559
which have spoken to me, *s* ... 2Chr 10:9 559
up with him spake unto him, *s* ... 2Chr 10:10 559
people that spake unto thee, *s* ... 2Chr 10:10 559
third day, as the king bade, *s* ... 2Chr 10:12 559
the advice of the young men, *s* ... 2Chr 10:14 559
the people answered the king, *s* ... 2Chr 10:16 559
to Shemaiah the man of God, *s* ... 2Chr 11:2 559
Israel in Judah and Benjamin, *s* ... 2Chr 11:3 559
of the LORD came to Shemaiah, *s* ... 2Chr 12:7 559
Syria, that dwelt at Damascus, *s* ... 2Chr 16:2 559
all the prophets prophesied so, *s* ... 2Chr 18:11 559
to call Micaiah spake to him, *s* ... 2Chr 18:12 559
one spake *s* after this manner, and ... 2Chr 18:19 559
another *s* after that manner ... 2Chr 18:19 559
chariots that were with him, *s* ... 2Chr 18:30 559
And he charged them, *s*, Thus shall ... 2Chr 19:9 559
some that told Jehoshaphat, *s* ... 2Chr 20:2 559
sanctuary therein for thy name, *s* ... 2Chr 20:8 559
prophesied against Jehoshaphat, *s* ... 2Chr 20:37 559
to him from Elijah the prophet, *s* ... 2Chr 21:12 559
where the LORD commanded, *s* ... 2Chr 25:4 559
there came a man of God to him, *s* ... 2Chr 25:7 559
son of Jehu, king of Israel, *s* ... 2Chr 25:17 559
sent to Amaziah king of Judah, *s* ... 2Chr 25:18 559
the cedar that was in Lebanon, *s* ... 2Chr 25:18 559
to the commandment of the king, *s* ... 2Chr 30:6 559
But Hezekiah prayed for them, *s* ... 2Chr 30:18 559
through the midst of the land, *s* ... 2Chr 32:4 559
and spake comfortably to them, *s* ... 2Chr 32:6 559
Judah that were at Jerusalem, *s* ... 2Chr 32:9 559
to die by famine and by thirst, *s* ... 2Chr 32:11 559
commanded Judah and Jerusalem, *s* ... 2Chr 32:12 559
and to speak against him, *s* ... 2Chr 32:17 559
the king word back again, *s* ... 2Chr 34:16 559
the scribe told the king, *s* ... 2Chr 34:18 559
Asaiah a servant of the king's, *s* ... 2Chr 34:20 559
But he sent ambassadors to him, *s* ... 2Chr 35:21 559
and put it also in writing, *s* ... 2Chr 36:22 559
and put it also in writing, *s* ... Ezr 1:1 559
thus they returned us answer, *s* ... Ezr 5:11 560
we had spoken unto the king, *s* ... Ezr 8:22 559
done, the princes came to me, *s* ... Ezr 9:1 559
by thy servants the prophets, *s* ... Ezr 9:11 559
commandedst thy servant Moses, *s* ... Neh 1:8 559
and Geshem sent unto me, *s* ... Neh 6:2 559
And I sent messengers unto them, *s* ... Neh 6:3 559
to preach of thee at Jerusalem, *s* ... Neh 6:7 559
Then I sent unto him, *s*, There ... Neh 6:8 559
For they all made us afraid, *s* ... Neh 6:9 559
Levites stilled all the people, *s* ... Neh 8:11 559
their cities, and in Jerusalem, *s* ... Neh 8:15 559
and made them swear by God, *s* ... Neh 13:25 559
the *s* pleased the king and the ... Est 1:21 1697
silence, and I heard a voice, *s* ... Job 4:16 559
place, then it shall deny him, *s* ... Job 8:18 559
He wandereth abroad for bread, *s* ... Job 15:23 559
waiteth for the twilight, *s* ... Job 24:15 559
heard the voice of thy words, *s* ... Job 33:8 559
LORD, and against his anointed, *s* ... Ps 2:2 559
the lip, they shake the head, *s* ... Ps 22:7 559
will open my dark *s* upon the harp ... Ps 49:4 2420
S, God hath forsaken him ... Ps 71:11 559
S, Unto thee will I give the land ... Ps 105:11 559
S, Touch not mine anointed, and do ... Ps 105:15
Mine eyes fail for thy word, *s* ... Ps 119:82 559
wasted us required of us mirth, *s* ... Ps 137:3
city she uttereth her words, *s* ... Prov 1:21
I communed with mine own heart, *s* ... Eccl 1:16 559
of my beloved that knocketh, *s* ... Song 5:2
of the house of his father, *s* ... Is 3:6
In that day shall he swear, *s* ... Is 3:7 559
shall take hold of one man, *s* ... Is 4:1 559
I heard the voice of the Lord, *s* ... Is 6:8 559
it was told the house of David, *s* ... Is 7:2 559
evil counsel against thee, *s* ... Is 7:5 559
the LORD spake again unto Ahaz, *s* ... Is 7:10 559
LORD spake also unto me again, *s* ... Is 8:5 559
walk in the way of this people, *s* ... Is 8:11 559
thee, and the cedars of Lebanon, *s* ... Is 14:8
upon thee, and consider thee, *s* ... Is 14:16 559
The LORD of hosts hath sworn, *s* ... Is 14:24 559
But now the LORD hath spoken, *s* ... Is 16:14 559
of bulrushes upon the waters, *s* ... Is 18:2
the LORD of hosts shall bless, *s* ... Is 19:25 559
LORD by Isaiah the son of Amoz, *s* ... Is 20:2 559
even the strength of the sea, *s* ... Is 23:4 559
deliver to one that is learned, *s* ... Is 29:11 559
to him that is not learned, *s* ... Is 29:12 559
shall hear a word behind thee, *s* ... Is 30:21 559
make you trust in the LORD, *s* ... Is 36:15 559
lest Hezekiah persuade you, *s* ... Is 36:18 559
for the king's commandment was, *s* ... Is 36:21 559
he sent messengers to Hezekiah, *s* ... Is 37:9 559
to Hezekiah king of Judah, *s* ... Is 37:10 559
thou trustest, deceive thee, *s* ... Is 37:10 559
Hezekiah prayed unto the LORD, *s* ... Is 37:15 559
son of Amoz sent unto Hezekiah, *s* ... Is 37:21 559
the word of the LORD to Isaiah, *s* ... Is 38:4 559
him that smote the anvil, *s* ... Is 41:7 559
right hand, *s* unto thee, Fear not ... Is 41:13 559
even *s* to Jerusalem, Thou shalt ... Is 44:28 559
make supplication unto thee, *s* ... Is 45:14
things that are not yet done, *s* ... Is 46:10 559
himself to the LORD, speak, *s* ... Is 56:3 559
of old, Moses, and his people, *s* ... Is 63:11
word of the LORD came unto me, *s* ... Jer 1:4 559
word of the LORD came unto me, *s* ... Jer 1:11 559
came unto me the second time, *s* ... Jer 1:13 559
word of the LORD came to me, *s* ... Jer 2:1 559
cry in the ears of Jerusalem, *s* ... Jer 2:2 559
S to a stock, Thou art my father ... Jer 2:27 559
this people and Jerusalem, *s* ... Jer 4:10 559
that spreadeth her hands, *s* ... Jer 4:31
Jacob, and publish it in Judah, *s* ... Jer 5:20 559
daughter of my people slightly, *s* ... Jer 6:14 559
Also I set watchmen over you, *s* ... Jer 6:17
came to Jeremiah from the LORD, *s* ... Jer 7:1 559
Trust ye not in lying words, *s* ... Jer 7:4 559
this thing commanded I them, *s* ... Jer 7:23 559
repented him of his wickedness, *s* ... Jer 8:6 559
daughter of my people slightly, *s* ... Jer 8:11 559
came to Jeremiah from the LORD, *s* ... Jer 11:1 559
Egypt, from the iron furnace, *s* ... Jer 11:4 559
and in the streets of Jerusalem, *s* ... Jer 11:6 559
rising early and protesting, *s* ... Jer 11:7 559
had devised devices against me, *s* ... Jer 11:19
Anathoth, that seek thy life, *s* ... Jer 11:21 559
came unto me the second time, *s* ... Jer 13:3 559
word of the LORD came unto me, *s* ... Jer 13:8 559
of the LORD came also unto me, *s* ... Jer 16:1 559
came to Jeremiah from the LORD, *s* ... Jer 18:1 559
word of the LORD came to me, *s* ... Jer 18:5 559
the inhabitants of Jerusalem, *s* ... Jer 18:11 559
watched for my halting, *s* ... Jer 20:10
brought tidings to my father, *s* ... Jer 20:15 559
the son of Maaseiah the priest, *s* ... Jer 21:1 559
They shall not lament for him, *s* ... Jer 22:18 559
they shall not lament for him, *s* ... Jer 22:18
that prophesy lies in my name, *s* ... Jer 23:25 559
or a priest, shall ask thee, *s* ... Jer 23:33 559
LORD, and I have sent unto you, *s* ... Jer 23:38 559
word of the LORD came unto me, *s* ... Jer 24:4 559
the inhabitants of Jerusalem, *s* ... Jer 25:2 559
came this word from the LORD, *s* ... Jer 26:1 559
and all the people took him, *s* ... Jer 26:8 559
in the name of the LORD, *s* ... Jer 26:9 559
princes and to all the people, *s* ... Jer 26:11 559
princes and to all the people, *s* ... Jer 26:12 559
all the assembly of the people, *s* ... Jer 26:17 559
to all the people of Judah, *s* ... Jer 26:18 559
unto Jeremiah from the LORD, *s* ... Jer 27:1 559
which speak unto you, *s*, Ye ... Jer 27:9 559
according to all these words, *s* ... Jer 27:12 559
prophets that speak unto you, *s* ... Jer 27:14 559
priests and to all this people, *s* ... Jer 27:16 559
that prophesy unto you, *s* ... Jer 27:16 559
priests and of all the people, *s* ... Jer 28:1 559
of hosts, the God of Israel, *s* ... Jer 28:2 559
the presence of all the people, *s* ... Jer 28:11 559
neck of the prophet Jeremiah, *s* ... Jer 28:12 559
Go and tell Hananiah, *s*, Thus ... Jer 28:13 559
Nebuchadnezzar king of Babylon) *s* ... Jer 29:3 559
of Judah which are in Babylon, *s* ... Jer 29:22 559
to Shemaiah the Nehelamite, *s* ... Jer 29:24 559
of hosts, the God of Israel, *s* ... Jer 29:25 559
priest, and to all the priests, *s* ... Jer 29:25 559
he sent unto us in Babylon, *s* ... Jer 29:28 559
word of the LORD unto Jeremiah, *s* ... Jer 29:30 559
to all them of the captivity, *s* ... Jer 29:31 559
came to Jeremiah from the LORD, *s* ... Jer 30:1 559
the LORD God of Israel, *s* ... Jer 30:2 559
they called thee an Outcast, *s* ... Jer 30:17 559
hath appeared of old unto me, *s* ... Jer 31:3
and every man his brother, *s* ... Jer 31:34 559
king of Judah had shut him up, *s* ... Jer 32:3 559
word of the LORD came unto me, *s* ... Jer 32:6 559
uncle shall come unto thee, *s* ... Jer 32:7 559
I charged Baruch before them, *s* ... Jer 32:13 559
Neriah, I prayed unto the LORD, *s* ... Jer 32:16 559
word of the LORD unto Jeremiah, *s* ... Jer 32:26 559
up in the court of the prison, *s* ... Jer 33:1 559
of the LORD came unto Jeremiah, *s* ... Jer 33:19 559
of the LORD came to Jeremiah, *s* ... Jer 33:23 559
what this people have spoken, *s* ... Jer 33:24 559
against all the cities thereof, *s* ... Jer 34:1 559
and they will lament thee, *s* ... Jer 34:5
came to Jeremiah from the LORD, *s* ... Jer 34:12 559
out of the house of bondmen, *s* ... Jer 34:13 559
son of Josiah king of Judah, *s* ... Jer 35:1 559
Rechab our father commanded us, *s* ... Jer 35:6 559
word of the LORD unto Jeremiah, *s* ... Jer 35:12 559
up early and sending them, *s* ... Jer 35:15 559
unto Jeremiah from the LORD, *s* ... Jer 36:1 559
And Jeremiah commanded Baruch, *s* ... Jer 36:5 559
the son of Cushi, unto Baruch, *s* ... Jer 36:14 559
And they asked Baruch, *s*, Tell us ... Jer 36:17 559
wrote at the mouth of Jeremiah, *s* ... Jer 36:27 559
Thou hast burned this roll, *s* ... Jer 36:29 559
Why hast thou written therein, *s* ... Jer 36:29 559
priest to the prophet Jeremiah, *s* ... Jer 37:3 559
LORD unto the prophet Jeremiah, *s* ... Jer 37:6 559
Deceive not yourselves, *s* ... Jer 37:9 559
he took Jeremiah the prophet, *s* ... Jer 37:13 559
which prophesied unto you, *s* ... Jer 37:19 559
had spoken unto all the people, *s* ... Jer 38:1 559
house, and spake to the king, *s* ... Jer 38:8 559
Ebed-melech the Ethiopian, *s* ... Jer 38:10 559
sware secretly unto Jeremiah, *s* ... Jer 38:16 559
the captain of the guard, *s* ... Jer 39:11 559
up in the court of the prison, *s* ... Jer 39:15 559
to Ebed-melech the Ethiopian, *s* ... Jer 39:16 559
unto them and to their men, *s* ... Jer 40:9 559
to Gedaliah in Mizpah secretly, *s* ... Jer 40:15 559
S, No; but we will ... Jer 42:14 559
sent me unto the LORD your God, *s* ... Jer 42:20 559
s unto Jeremiah, Thou speakest ... Jer 43:2 559
unto Jeremiah in Tahpanhes, *s* ... Jer 43:8 559
and in the country of Pathros, *s* ... Jer 44:1 559
rising early and sending them, *s* ... Jer 44:4 559
in Pathros, answered Jeremiah, *s* ... Jer 44:15 559
had given him that answer, *s* ... Jer 44:20 559
of hosts, the God of Israel, *s* ... Jer 44:25 559
and fulfilled with your hand, *s* ... Jer 44:25 559
Judah in all the land of Egypt, *s* ... Jer 44:26 559
son of Josiah king of Judah, *s* ... Jer 45:1 559
They shall howl, *s*, How is it ... Jer 48:39
that trusted in her treasures, *s* ... Jer 49:4
is sent unto the heathen, *s* ... Jer 49:14
of Zedekiah king of Judah, *s* ... Jer 49:34 559
with their faces thitherward, *s* ... Jer 50:5
of hosts hath sworn by himself, *s* ... Jer 51:14
at the daughter of Jerusalem, *s* ... Lam 2:15
me a voice of a great rushing, *s* ... Eze 3:12
word of the LORD came unto me, *s* ... Eze 3:16 559
word of the LORD came unto me, *s* ... Eze 6:1 559
word of the LORD came unto me, *s* ... Eze 7:1 559
in mine ears with a loud voice, *s* ... Eze 9:1 559
his side, reported the matter, *s* ... Eze 9:11 559
the man clothed with linen, *s* ... Eze 10:6 559
word of the LORD came unto me, *s* ... Eze 11:14 559
of the LORD also came unto me, *s* ... Eze 12:1 559
the word of the LORD unto me, *s* ... Eze 12:8 559
word of the LORD came to me, *s* ... Eze 12:17 559
word of the LORD came unto me, *s* ... Eze 12:21 559
ye have in the land of Israel, *s* ... Eze 12:22 559
word of the LORD came to me, *s* ... Eze 12:26 559
word of the LORD came unto me, *s* ... Eze 13:1 559
vanity and lying divination, *s* ... Eze 13:6 559
they have seduced my people, *s* ... Eze 13:10 559
word of the LORD came unto me, *s* ... Eze 14:2 559
of the LORD came again to me, *s* ... Eze 14:12 559
word of the LORD came unto me, *s* ... Eze 15:1 559
word of the LORD came unto me, *s* ... Eze 16:1 559
use this proverb against thee, *s* ... Eze 16:44 559
word of the LORD came unto me, *s* ... Eze 17:1 559
word of the LORD came unto me, *s* ... Eze 17:11 559
of the LORD came unto me again, *s* ... Eze 18:1 559
concerning the land of Israel, *s* ... Eze 18:2 559
the word of the LORD unto me, *s* ... Eze 20:2 559
lifted up mine hand unto them, *s* ... Eze 20:5 559
word of the LORD came unto me, *s* ... Eze 20:45 559
word of the LORD came unto me, *s* ... Eze 21:1 559
word of the LORD came unto me, *s* ... Eze 21:8 559
of the LORD came unto me again, *s* ... Eze 21:18 559
word of the LORD came unto me, *s* ... Eze 22:1 559
word of the LORD came unto me, *s* ... Eze 22:17 559
word of the LORD came unto me, *s* ... Eze 22:23 559
and divining lies unto them, *s* ... Eze 22:28 559
of the LORD came again unto me, *s* ... Eze 23:1 559
word of the LORD came unto me, *s* ... Eze 24:1 559
word of the LORD came unto me, *s* ... Eze 24:15 559
word of the LORD came unto me, *s* ... Eze 24:20 559
of the LORD came again unto me, *s* ... Eze 25:1 559
word of the LORD came unto me, *s* ... Eze 26:1 559
of the LORD came again unto me, *s* ... Eze 27:1 559
for thee, and lament over thee, *s* ... Eze 27:32
of the LORD came again unto me, *s* ... Eze 28:1 559
word of the LORD came unto me, *s* ... Eze 28:11 559
word of the LORD came unto me, *s* ... Eze 28:20 559
word of the LORD came unto me, *s* ... Eze 29:1 559
word of the LORD came unto me, *s* ... Eze 29:17 559
of the LORD came again unto me, *s* ... Eze 30:1 559
word of the LORD came unto me, *s* ... Eze 30:20 559
word of the LORD came unto me, *s* ... Eze 31:1 559
word of the LORD came unto me, *s* ... Eze 32:1 559
word of the LORD came unto me, *s* ... Eze 32:17 559
word of the LORD came unto me, *s* ... Eze 33:1 559
Thus ye speak, *s*, If our ... Eze 33:10 559
out of Jerusalem came unto me, *s* ... Eze 33:21 559
word of the LORD came unto me, *s* ... Eze 33:23 559
of the land of Israel speak, *s* ... Eze 33:24 559
every one to his brother, *s* ... Eze 33:30 559
word of the Lord came unto me, *s* ... Eze 34:1 559
word of the LORD came unto me, *s* ... Eze 35:1 559
the mountains of Israel, *s* ... Eze 35:12 559
word of the LORD came unto me, *s* ... Eze 36:16 559
of the LORD came again unto me, *s* ... Eze 37:15 559
people shall speak unto thee, *s* ... Eze 37:18 559
word of the LORD came unto me, *s* ... Eze 38:1 559
and before him I told the dream, *s* ... Dan 4:8
one coming down from heaven, and *s* ... Dan 4:23 560
there fell a voice from heaven, *s* ... Dan 4:31
and commanded the prophets, *s* ... Amos 2:12 559
up from the land of Egypt, *s* ... Amos 3:1 559
to Jeroboam king of Israel, *s* ... Amos 7:10 559
S, When will the new moon be gone ... Amos 8:5 559
unto Jonah the son of Amittai, *s* ... Jonah 1:1 559
unto Jonah the second time, *s* ... Jonah 3:1 559
of the king and his nobles, *s* ... Jonah 3:7 559
thee, O LORD, was not this my *s* ... Jonah 4:2 1697
the spirit and falsehood do lie, *s* ... Mic 2:11
of Josedech, the high priest, *s* ... Hag 1:1 559
speaketh the LORD of hosts, *s* ... Hag 1:2 559
the LORD by Haggai the prophet, *s* ... Hag 1:3 559
LORD's message unto the people, *s* ... Hag 1:13 559
the LORD by the prophet Haggai, *s* ... Hag 2:1 559
to the residue of the people, *s* ... Hag 2:2 559
the LORD by Haggai the prophet, *s* ... Hag 2:10 559
the priests concerning the law, *s* ... Hag 2:11 559
and twentieth day of the month, *s* ... Hag 2:20 559

Zerubbabel, governor of Judah, s .... Hag 2:21 559
the son of Iddo the prophet, s .... Zec 1:1 559
the former prophets have cried, s.............. Zec 1:4 559
the son of Iddo the prophet, s .... Zec 1:7 559
with me said unto me, Cry thou, s .... Zec 1:14 559
Cry yet, s, Thus saith the LORD .... Zec 1:17 559
And he spake, s, These are the .... Zec 1:21 559
Run, speak to this young man, s .... Zec 2:4 559
those that stood before him, s .... Zec 3:4 559
the LORD protested unto Joshua, s .... Zec 3:6 559
the angel that talked with me, s............... Zec 4:4 559
he answered and spake unto me, s .... Zec 4:6 559
of the LORD unto Zerubbabel, s .... Zec 4:6 559
word of the LORD came unto me, s.............. Zec 4:8 559
he upon me, and spake unto me, s .... Zec 6:8 559
word of the LORD came unto me, s.............. Zec 6:9 559
And speak unto him, s, Thus.................... Zec 6:12 559
speaketh the LORD of hosts, s .... Zec 6:12 559
of hosts, and to the prophets, s .... Zec 7:3 559
of the LORD of hosts unto me, s................. Zec 7:4 559
of the land, and to the priests, s .... Zec 7:5 559
the LORD came unto Zechariah, s .... Zec 7:8 559
speaketh the LORD of hosts, s................... Zec 7:9 559
the LORD of hosts came to me, s................ Zec 8:1 559
the LORD of hosts came unto me, s .... Zec 8:18 559
one city shall go to another, s................. Zec 8:21 559
the skirt of him that is a Jew, s .... Zec 8:23 559
appeared unto him in a dream, s............... Mt 1:20 3004
of the Lord by the prophet, s .... Mt 1:22 3004
S, Where is he that is born King............... Mt 2:2 3004
appeareth to Joseph in a dream, s............. Mt 2:13 3004
of the Lord by the prophet, s .... Mt 2:15 3004
spoken by Jeremy the prophet, s .... Mt 2:17 3004
S, Arise, and take the young child .... Mt 2:20 3004
And s, Repent ye .... Mt 3:2 3004
of by the prophet Esaias, s .... Mt 3:3 3004
But John forbad him, s, I have .... Mt 3:14 3004
And lo a voice from heaven, s .... Mt 3:17 3004
spoken by Esaias the prophet, s .... Mt 4:14 3004
his mouth, and taught them, s .... Mt 5:2 3004
Therefore take no thought, s .... Mt 6:31 3004
came a leper and worshipped him, s.......... Mt 8:2 3004
forth his hand, and touched him, s .... Mt 8:3 3004
And s, Lord, my servant lieth at .... Mt 8:6 3004
spoken by Esaias the prophet, s .... Mt 8:17 3004
came to him, and awoke him, s .... Mt 8:25 3004
But the men marvelled, s, What................ Mt 8:27 3004
And, behold, they cried out, s .... Mt 8:29 3004
So the devils besought him, s................... Mt 8:31 3004
to him the disciples of John, s .... Mt 9:14 3004
ruler, and worshipped him, s.................... Mt 9:18 3004
men followed him, crying, and s .... Mt 9:27 3004
Then touched he their eyes, s .... Mt 9:29 3004
and Jesus straitly charged them, s............ Mt 9:30 3004
and the multitudes marvelled, s................ Mt 9:33 3004
sent forth, and commanded them, s .... Mt 10:5 3004
And as ye go, preach, s, The .... Mt 10:7 3004
And s, We have piped unto you, and .... Mt 11:17 3004
And they asked him, s, Is it..................... Mt 12:10 3004
spoken by Esaias the prophet, s .... Mt 12:17 3004
and of the Pharisees answered, s.............. Mt 12:38 3004
things unto them in parables, s................ Mt 13:3 3004
parable put he forth unto them, s .... Mt 13:24 3004
parable put he forth unto them, s .... Mt 13:31 3004
was spoken by the prophet, s .... Mt 13:35 3004
and his disciples came unto him, s............ Mt 13:36 3004
his disciples came to him, s .... Mt 14:15 3004
on the sea, they were troubled, s.............. Mt 14:26 3004
Jesus spake unto them, s, Be of .... Mt 14:27 3004
and beginning to sink, he cried, s .... Mt 14:30 3004
ship came and worshipped him, s .... Mt 14:33 3004
which were of Jerusalem, s...................... Mt 15:1 3004
For God commanded, s, Honour thy .... Mt 15:4 3004
did Esaias prophesy of you, s .... Mt 15:7 3004
offended, after they heard this s .... Mt 15:12 3058
same coasts, and cried unto him, s............ Mt 15:22 3004
disciples came and besought him, s .... Mt 15:23 3004
came she and worshipped him, s............... Mt 15:25 3004
they reasoned among themselves, s........... Mt 16:7 3004
he asked his disciples, s.......................... Mt 16:13 3004
him, and began to rebuke him, s .... Mt 16:22 3004
mountain, Jesus charged them, s............... Mt 17:9 3004
And his disciples asked him, s.................. Mt 17:10 3004
man, kneeling down to him, and s .... Mt 17:14 3004
the house, Jesus prevented him, s............. Mt 17:25 3004
came the disciples unto Jesus, s .... Mt 18:1 3004
fell down, and worshipped him, s .... Mt 18:26 3004
him, and took him by the throat, s............. Mt 18:28 3004
at his feet, and besought him, s .... Mt 18:29 3004
s unto him, Is it lawful for a .... Mt 19:3 3004
All men cannot receive this s .... Mt 19:11 3056
when the young man heard that s.............. Mt 19:22 3056
they were exceedingly amazed, s............... Mt 19:25 3004
S, These last have wrought but .... Mt 20:12 3004
Jesus passed by, cried out, s .... Mt 20:30 3004
but they cried the more, s........................ Mt 20:31 3004
S unto them, Go into the village .... Mt 21:2 3004
was spoken by the prophet, s .... Mt 21:4 3004
and that followed, cried, s....................... Mt 21:9 3004
all the city was moved, s .... Mt 21:10 3004
crying in the temple, and s...................... Mt 21:15 3004
saw it, they marvelled, s .... Mt 21:20 3004
they reasoned with themselves, s .... Mt 21:25 3004
all he sent unto them his son, s .... Mt 21:37 3004
he sent forth other servants, s .... Mt 22:4 3004
disciples with the Herodians, s .... Mt 22:16 3004
S, Master, Moses said, If a man................ Mt 22:24 3004
was spoken unto you by God, s .... Mt 22:31 3004
a question, tempting him, and s .... Mt 22:35 3004
S, What think ye of Christ .... Mt 22:42 3004
David in spirit call him Lord, s .... Mt 22:43 3004
S, The scribes and the Pharisees .... Mt 23:2 3004
came unto him privately, s....................... Mt 24:3 3004
For many shall come in my name, s .... Mt 24:5 3004
But the wise answered, s, Not so .... Mt 25:9 3004
came also the other virgins, s .... Mt 25:11 3004
and brought other five talents, s .... Mt 25:20 3004
shall the righteous answer him, s.............. Mt 25:37 3004
shall they also answer him, s .... Mt 25:44 3004
Then shall he answer them, s .... Mt 25:45 3004
saw it, they had indignation, s .... Mt 26:8 3004
s unto him, Where wilt thou that............... Mt 26:17 3004
thanks, and gave it to them, s .... Mt 26:27 3004
and fell on his face, and prayed, s............ Mt 26:39 3004
the second time, and prayed, s .... Mt 26:42 3004
the third time, s the same words.............. Mt 26:44 2036
betrayed him gave them a sign, s .... Mt 26:48 3004
high priest rent his clothes, s .... Mt 26:65 3004
S, Prophesy unto us, thou Christ, ... Mt 26:68 3004
and a damsel came unto him, s .... Mt 26:69 3004
But he denied before them all, s .... Mt 26:70 3004
began he to curse and to swear, s............ Mt 26:74
S, I have sinned in that I have.................. Mt 27:4 3004
spoken by Jeremy the prophet, s .... Mt 27:9 3004
and the governor asked him, s .... Mt 27:11 3004
seat, his wife sent unto him, s .... Mt 27:19 3004
But they cried out the more, s.................. Mt 27:23 3004
his hands before the multitude, s............. Mt 27:24 3004
knee before him, and mocked him, s......... Mt 27:29 3004
And s, Thou that destroyest the .... Mt 27:40 3004
Jesus cried with a loud voice, s .... Mt 27:46 3004
were done, they feared greatly, s .... Mt 27:54 3004
S, Sir, we remember that that.................. Mt 27:63 3004
behold, Jesus met them, s .... Mt 28:9 3004
S, Say ye, His disciples came by .... Mt 28:13 3004
this s is commonly reported among.......... Mt 28:15 3056
Jesus came and spake unto them, s.......... Mt 28:18 3004
And preached, s, There cometh one .... Mk 1:7 3004
there came a voice from heaven, s............ Mk 1:11
And s, The time is fulfilled, and .... Mk 1:15 3004
S, Let us alone... Mk 1:24 3004
And Jesus rebuked him, s, Hold thy .... Mk 1:25 3004
questioned among themselves, s............... Mk 1:27 3004
s unto him, If thou wilt, thou.................... Mk 1:40 3004
all amazed, and glorified God, s .... Mk 2:12 3004
fell down before him, and cried, s............ Mk 3:11 3004
And he answered them, s, Who is my ...... Mk 3:33 3004
And he answered, s, My name is .... Mk 5:9 3004
And all the devils besought him, s .... Mk 5:12 3004
And besought him greatly, s .... Mk 5:23 3004
hearing him were astonished, s .... Mk 6:2 3004
haste unto the king, and asked, s............ Mk 6:25 3004
unto her, For this s go thy way .... Mk 7:29 3056
were beyond measure astonished, s......... Mk 7:37 3004
And he charged them, s, Take heed, ... Mk 8:15 3004
they reasoned among themselves, s .... Mk 8:16 3004
he sent him away to his house, s .... Mk 8:26 3004
s unto them, Whom do men say that....... Mk 8:27 3004
And he spake that s openly .... Mk 8:32 3056
disciples, he rebuked Peter, s.................. Mk 8:33 3004
a voice came out of the cloud, s .... Mk 9:7 3004
they kept that s with themselves,............ Mk 9:10 3056
And they asked him, s, Why say the .... Mk 9:11 3004
s unto him, Thou dumb and deaf .... Mk 9:25 3004
But they understood not that s .... Mk 9:32 4487
And John answered him, s, Master,......... Mk 9:38 3004
And he was sad at that s, and went .... Mk 10:22 3056
s among themselves, Who then can......... Mk 10:26 3004
S, Behold, we go up to Jerusalem .... Mk 10:33
sons of Zebedee, come unto him, s.......... Mk 10:35 3004
s unto him, Be of good comfort,.............. Mk 10:49 3004
and they that followed, cried, s.............. Mk 11:9 3004
s unto them, Is it not written, ... Mk 11:17 3004
they reasoned with themselves, s .... Mk 11:31 3004
sent him also last unto them, s................ Mk 12:6 3004
and they asked him, s,............................. Mk 12:18 3004
in the bush God spake unto him, s.......... Mk 12:26 3004
For many shall come in my name, s .... Mk 13:6 3004
him had given them a token, s .... Mk 14:44 3004
bare false witness against him, s............ Mk 14:57 3004
in the midst, and asked Jesus, s .... Mk 14:60 3004
But he denied, s, I know not, ... Mk 14:68 3004
he began to curse and to swear, s........... Mk 14:71
And Pilate asked him again, s................. Mk 15:4 3004
But Pilate answered them, s................... Mk 15:9 3004
on him, wagging their heads, and s......... Mk 15:29 3004
Jesus cried with a loud voice, s .... Mk 15:34 3004
a reed, and gave him to drink, s .... Mk 15:36 3004
and hid herself five months, s .... Lk 1:24 3004
him, she was troubled at his s................ Lk 1:29 3056
for a writing table, and wrote, s .... Lk 1:63 3004
laid them up in their hearts, s................ Lk 1:66 3004
the Holy Ghost, and prophesied, s .... Lk 1:67 3004
heavenly host praising God, and s .... Lk 2:13 3004
they made known abroad the s .... Lk 2:17 4487
they understood not the s which .... Lk 2:50 4487
words of Esaias the prophet, s .... Lk 3:4 3004
And the people asked him, s .... Lk 3:10 3004
likewise demanded of him, s .... Lk 3:14 3004
s unto them all, I indeed baptize............ Lk 3:16 3004
And Jesus answered him, s, It is .... Lk 4:4 3004
S, Let us alone....................................... Lk 4:34 3004
And Jesus rebuked him, s, Hold thy .... Lk 4:35 3004
and spake among themselves, s.............. Lk 4:36 3004
out of many, crying out, and s................ Lk 4:41 3004
he fell down at Jesus' knees, s................ Lk 5:8 3004
on his face, and besought him, s .... Lk 5:12 3004
forth his hand, and touched him, s .... Lk 5:13 2036
the Pharisees began to reason, s.............. Lk 5:21 3004
God, and were filled with fear, s .... Lk 5:26 3004
murmured against his disciples, s .... Lk 5:30 3004
they besought him instantly, s................. Lk 7:4 3004
s unto him, Lord, trouble not .... Lk 7:6 3004
and they glorified God, s, That a .... Lk 7:16 3004
disciples sent them to Jesus, s .... Lk 7:19 3004
Baptist hath sent us unto thee, s............. Lk 7:20 3004
and calling one to another, and s .... Lk 7:32 3004
it, he spake within himself, s .... Lk 7:39 3004
And his disciples asked him, s .... Lk 8:9 3004
they came to him, and awoke him, s .... Lk 8:24 3004
s one to another, What manner of........... Lk 8:25 3004
And Jesus asked him, s, What is .... Lk 8:30 3004
but Jesus sent him away, s..................... Lk 8:38 3004
s to him, Thy daughter is dead............... Lk 8:49 3004
heard it, he answered him, s.................. Lk 8:50 3004
her by the hand, and called, s .... Lk 8:54 3004
and he asked them, s, Whom say the ...... Lk 9:18 3004
S, The Son of man must suffer .... Lk 9:22 2036
came a voice out of the cloud, s .... Lk 9:35 3004
a man of the company cried out, s .... Lk 9:38 3004
But they understood not this s .... Lk 9:45 4487
they feared to ask him of that s .... Lk 9:45 4487
returned again with joy, s...................... Lk 10:17 3004
stood up, and tempted him, s .... Lk 10:25 3004
thus s thou reproachest us also .... Lk 11:45 3004
he spake a parable unto them, s.............. Lk 12:16 3004
And he thought within himself, s .... Lk 12:17 3004
and to knock at the door, s..................... Lk 13:25 3004
s unto him, Get thee out, and................. Lk 13:31 3004
unto the lawyers and Pharisees, s .... Lk 14:3 3004
And answered them, s, Which of you ...... Lk 14:5 2036
chief rooms; s unto them .... Lk 14:7 3004
S, This man began to build, and .... Lk 14:30 3004
Pharisees and scribes murmured, s .... Lk 15:2 3004
spake this parable unto them, s .... Lk 15:3 3004
s unto them, Rejoice with me .... Lk 15:6 3004
and her neighbours together, s .... Lk 15:9 3004
in a day turn again to thee, s .... Lk 17:4 3004
S, There was in a city a judge, ... Lk 18:2 3004
and she came unto him, s, Avenge .... Lk 18:3 3004
but smote upon his breast, s .... Lk 18:13 3004
And a certain ruler asked him, s............. Lk 18:18 3004
this s was hid from them, neither .... Lk 18:34 4487
And he cried, s, Jesus, thou son .... Lk 18:38 3004
S, What wilt thou that I shall do .... Lk 18:41 3004
they saw it, they all murmured, s............ Lk 19:7 3004
and sent a message after him, s............. Lk 19:14 3004
Then came the first, s, Lord, thy .... Lk 19:16 3004
And the second came, s, Lord, thy .... Lk 19:18 3004
And another came, s, Lord, behold, ... Lk 19:20 3004
S, Go ye into the village over .... Lk 19:30 2036
S, Blessed be the King that.................... Lk 19:38 3004
S, If thou hadst known, even thou .... Lk 19:42 3004
S unto them, It is written, My................. Lk 19:46 3004
And spake unto him, s, Tell us, by .... Lk 20:2 3004
they reasoned with themselves, s .... Lk 20:5 3004
they reasoned among themselves, s.......... Lk 20:14 3004
And they asked him, s, Master, we.......... Lk 20:21 3004
S, Master, Moses wrote unto us,............. Lk 20:28 3004
And they asked him, s, Master, but......... Lk 21:7 3004
for many shall come in my name, s .... Lk 21:8 3004
And he sent Peter and John, s .... Lk 22:8 2036
and brake it, and gave unto them, s........ Lk 22:19 3004
also the cup after supper, s................... Lk 22:20 3004
S, Father, if thou be willing,.................. Lk 22:42 3004
And he denied him, s, Woman, I .... Lk 22:57 3004
another confidently affirmed, s .... Lk 22:59 3004
him on the face, and asked him, s .... Lk 22:64 3004
and led him into their council, s .... Lk 22:66 3004
And they began to accuse him, s............. Lk 23:2 3004
s that he himself is Christ a .... Lk 23:2 3004
And Pilate asked him, s, Art thou........... Lk 23:3 3004
And they were the more fierce, s .... Lk 23:5 3004
And they cried out all at once, s .... Lk 23:18 3004
But they cried, s, Crucify him, ... Lk 23:21 3004
also with them derided him, s................ Lk 23:35 3004
And s, If thou be the king of the............. Lk 23:37 3004
were hanged railed on him, s .... Lk 23:39 3004
other answering rebuked him, s.............. Lk 23:40 3004
was done, he glorified God, s .... Lk 23:47 3004
S, The Son of man must be .... Lk 24:7 3004
found not his body, they came, s .... Lk 24:23 3004
But they constrained him, s .... Lk 24:29 3004
S, The Lord is risen indeed, and .... Lk 24:34 3004
bare witness of him, and cried, s .... Jn 1:15 3004
John answered them, s, I baptize .... Jn 1:26 3004
And John bare record, s, I saw the.......... Jn 1:32 3004
while his disciples prayed him, s .... Jn 4:31 3004
And herein is that s true, One .... Jn 4:37 3056
on him for the s of the woman .... Jn 4:39 3056
we believe, not because of thy s .... Jn 4:42 2981
servants met him, and told him, s .... Jn 4:51 3004
strove among themselves, s .... Jn 6:52 3004
this, said, This is an hard s .... Jn 6:60 3056
And the Jews marvelled, s, How .... Jn 7:15 3004
in the temple as he taught, s................. Jn 7:28 3004
What manner of s is this that he............ Jn 7:36 3056
feast, Jesus stood and cried, s .... Jn 7:37 3004
therefore, when they heard this s........... Jn 7:40 3056
spake Jesus again unto them, s .... Jn 8:12 3004
say unto you, If a man keep my s .... Jn 8:51 3056
thou sayest, If a man keep my s .... Jn 8:52 3056
but I know him, and keep his s .... Jn 8:55 3056
And his disciples asked him, s .... Jn 9:2 3004

And they asked them, *s*, Is this Jn 9:19 3004
The Jews answered him, *s*, For a Jn 10:33 3004
his sisters sent unto him, *s* Jn 11:3 3004
Mary her sister secretly, *s* Jn 11:28 2036
and went out, followed her, *s* Jn 11:31 3004
s unto him, Lord, if thou hadst Jn 11:32 3004
of Galilee, and desired him, *s* Jn 12:21 3004
And Jesus answered them, *s* Jn 12:23 3004
came there a voice from heaven, *s* Jn 12:28
That the *s* of Esaias the prophet Jn 12:38 3056
if they have kept my *s*, they will Jn 15:20 3056
That the *s* might be fulfilled, Jn 18:9 3056
with the palm of his hand, *s* Jn 18:22 2036
That the *s* of Jesus might be Jn 18:32 3056
Then cried they all again, *s* Jn 18:40 3004
saw him, they cried out, *s* Jn 19:6 3004
Pilate therefore heard that *s* Jn 19:8 3056
but the Jews cried out, *s* Jn 19:12 3004
Pilate therefore heard that *s* Jn 19:13 3056
Then went this *s* abroad among the Jn 21:23 3056
together, they asked of him, *s* Acts 1:6 3004
s one to another, Behold, are not Acts 2:7 3004
s one to another, What meaneth Acts 2:12 3004
words did he testify and exhort, *s* Acts 2:40 3004
s unto Abraham, And in thy seed Acts 3:25 3004
S, What shall we do to these men Acts 4:16 3004
S, The prison truly found we shut Acts 5:23 3004
Then came one and told them, *s* Acts 5:25 3004
S, Did not we straitly command Acts 5:28 3004
the *s* pleased the whole multitude Acts 6:5 3056
have set them at one again, *s* Acts 7:26 2036
wrong thrust him away, *s*, Who Acts 7:27 2036
Then fled Moses at this *s* Acts 7:29 3056
S, I am the God of thy fathers, Acts 7:32
This Moses whom they refused, *s* Acts 7:35 2036
S unto Aaron, Make us gods to go Acts 7:40 2036
Stephen, calling upon God, and *s* Acts 7:59 3007
from the least to the greatest, *s* Acts 8:10 3007
S, Give me also this power, that Acts 8:19 3007
of the Lord spake unto Philip, *s* Acts 8:26 3007
and heard a voice *s* unto him Acts 9:4 3007
to him, and *s* unto him, Cornelius Acts 10:3 2036
But Peter took him up, *s*, Stand Acts 10:26 3004
S, Thou wentest in to men Acts 11:3 3004
it by order unto them, *s* Acts 11:4 3004
And I heard a voice *s* unto me Acts 11:7 3004
their peace, and glorified God, *s* Acts 11:18 3004
on the side, and raised him up, *s* Acts 12:7 3004
And the people gave a shout, *s* Acts 12:22
the synagogue sent unto them, *s* Acts 13:15 3004
so hath the Lord commanded us, *s* Acts 13:47
s in the speech of Lycaonia, The Acts 14:11 3004
And *s*, Sirs, why do ye these Acts 14:15 3004
the Pharisees which believed, *s* Acts 15:5 3004
their peace, James answered, *s* Acts 15:13 3004
words, subverting your souls, *s* Acts 15:24 3004
of Macedonia, and prayed him, *s* Acts 16:9 3004
her household, she besought us, *s* Acts 16:15 3004
followed Paul and us, and cried, *s* Acts 16:17 3004
them to the magistrates, *s* Acts 16:20 2036
Paul cried with a loud voice, *s* Acts 16:28 3004
magistrates sent the serjeants, *s* Acts 16:35 3004
of the prison told this *s* to Paul Acts 16:36 3056
s that there is another king, one Acts 17:7 3004
and brought him unto Areopagus, *s* Acts 17:19 3004
S, This fellow persuadeth men to Acts 18:13 3004
But bade them farewell, *s* Acts 18:21 2036
s unto the people, that they Acts 19:4 3004
the name of the Lord Jesus, *s* Acts 19:13 3004
and Achaia, to go to Jerusalem, *s* Acts 19:21 2036
s that they be no gods, which are Acts 19:26 3004
full of wrath, and cried out, *s* Acts 19:28 3004
s that bonds and afflictions abide Acts 20:23 3004
not be persuaded, we ceased, *s* Acts 21:14 2036
Moses, *s* that they ought not to Acts 21:21 3004
unto them in the Hebrew tongue, *s* Acts 21:40 3004
and heard a voice *s* unto me Acts 22:7 3004
And saw him *s* unto me, Make haste, Acts 22:18 3004
went and told the chief captain, *s* Acts 22:26 3004
part arose, and strove, *s*, We find Acts 23:9 3004
s that they would neither eat nor Acts 23:12 3004
called unto him two centurions, *s* Acts 23:23 2036
Tertullus began to accuse him, *s* Acts 24:2 3004
s that these things were so Acts 24:9 5335
Paul's cause unto the king, *s* Acts 25:14 3004
s in the Hebrew tongue, Saul, Acts 26:14 3004
s none other things than those Acts 26:22 3004
they talked between themselves, *s* Acts 26:31 3004
S, Fear not, Paul Acts 27:24 3004
besought them all to take meat, *s* Acts 27:33 3004
S, Go unto this people, and say, Acts 28:26 3004
S, Blessed are they whose Rom 4:7
to God against Israel, *s* Rom 11:2 3004
is briefly comprehended in this *s* Rom 13:9 3056
the cup, when he had supped, *s* 1Cor 11:25 3004
to pass the *s* that is written 1Cor 15:54 3056
before the gospel unto Abraham, *s* Gal 3:8
This is a faithful *s*, and worthy 1Ti 1:15 3056
This is a true *s*, If a man desire 1Ti 3:1 3056
This is a faithful *s* and worthy of 1Ti 4:9 3056
It is a faithful *s* 2Ti 2:11 3056
s that the resurrection is past 2Ti 2:18 3004
This is a faithful *s*, and these Titus 3:8 3056
in a certain place testified, *s* Heb 2:6 3004
S, I will declare thy name unto Heb 2:12 3004
s in David, To day, after so long Heb 4:7 3004
S, Surely blessing I will bless Heb 6:14 3004
and every man his brother, *s* Heb 8:11 3004
S, This is the blood of the Heb 9:20 3004
but now he hath promised, *s* Heb 12:26 3004
And *s*, Where is the promise of his 2Pet 3:4 3004
from Adam, prophesied of these, *s* Jude 14 3004
S, I am Alpha and Omega, the first Rev 1:11 3004
hand upon me, *s* unto me, Fear not Rev 1:17 3004
and they rest not day and night, *s* Rev 4:8 3004
their crowns before the throne, *s* Rev 4:10 3004
And they sung a new song, *s* Rev 5:9 3004
S with a loud voice, Worthy is Rev 5:12 3004
all that are in them, heard I *s* Rev 5:13 3004
thunder, one of the four beasts *s* Rev 6:1 3004
they cried with a loud voice, *s* Rev 6:10 3004
S, Hurt not the earth, neither Rev 7:3 3004
And cried with a loud voice, *s* Rev 7:10 3004
S, Amen Rev 7:12 3004
s unto me, What are these which Rev 7:13 3004
s with a loud voice, Woe, woe, Rev 8:13 3004
S to the sixth angel which had Rev 9:14 3004
a voice from heaven *s* unto me Rev 10:4 3004
and the angel stood, *s*, Rise, and Rev 11:1 3004
voice from heaven *s* unto them Rev 11:12 3004
were great voices in heaven, *s* Rev 11:15 3004
S, We give thee thanks, O Lord Rev 11:17 3004
I heard a loud voice *s* in heaven Rev 12:10 3004
and they worshipped the beast, *s* Rev 13:4 3004
s to them that dwell on the earth Rev 13:14 3004
S with a loud voice, Fear God, and Rev 14:7 3004
there followed another angel, *s* Rev 14:8 3004
s with a loud voice, If any man Rev 14:9 3004
a voice from heaven *s* unto me Rev 14:13 3004
him that had the sharp sickle, *s* Rev 14:18 3004
God, and the song of the Lamb, *s* Rev 15:3 3004
the temple *s* to the seven angels Rev 16:1 3004
of heaven, from the throne, *s* Rev 16:17 3004
with me, *s* unto me, Come hither Rev 17:1 3004
mightily with a strong voice, *s* Rev 18:2 3004
another voice from heaven, *s* Rev 18:4 3004
for the fear of her torment, *s* Rev 18:10 3004
And *s*, Alas, alas that great city, Rev 18:16 3004
saw the smoke of her burning, *s* Rev 18:18 3004
and cried, weeping and wailing, *s* Rev 18:19 3004
and cast it into the sea, *s* Rev 18:21 3004
voice of much people in heaven, *s* Rev 19:1 3004
God that sat on the throne, *s* Rev 19:4 3004
a voice came out of the throne, *s* Rev 19:5 3004
voice of mighty thunderings, *s* Rev 19:6 3004
s to all the fowls that fly in Rev 19:17 3004
a great voice out of heaven *s* Rev 21:3 3004
plagues, and talked with me, *s* Rev 21:9 3004

SAYINGS {31}
Moses told these *s* unto all the Num 14:39 1697
that when thy *s* come to pass we Judg 13:17 1697
and came and told him all those *s* 1Sa 25:12 1697
of Abijah, and his ways, and his *s* 2Chr 13:22 1697
written among the *s* of the seers 2Chr 33:19 1697
their posterity approve their *s* Ps 49:13 6310
I will utter dark *s* of old Ps 78:2 2420
of the wise, and their dark *s* Prov 1:6 2420
Hear, O my son, and receive my *s* Prov 4:10 561
incline thine ear unto my *s* Prov 4:20 561
whosoever heareth these *s* of mine Mt 7:24 3056
one that heareth these *s* of mine Mt 7:26 3056
when Jesus had ended these *s* Mt 7:28 3056
when Jesus had finished these *s* Mt 19:1 3056
Jesus had finished all these *s* Mt 26:1 3056
all these *s* were noised abroad Lk 1:65 4487
kept all these *s* in her heart Lk 2:51 4487
cometh to me, and heareth my *s* Lk 6:47 3056
s in the audience of the people Lk 7:1 4487
about an eight days after these *s* Lk 9:28 3056
Let these *s* sink down into your Lk 9:44 3056
again among the Jews for these *s* Jn 10:19 3056
loveth me not keepeth not my *s* Jn 14:24 3056
with these *s* scarce restrained Acts 14:18 3004
And when they heard these *s* Acts 19:28
mightest be justified in thy *s* Rom 3:4 3056
me, These are the true *s* of God Rev 19:9 3056
These *s* are faithful and true Rev 22:6 3056
s of the prophecy of this book Rev 22:7 3056
which keep the *s* of this book Rev 22:9 3056
Seal not the *s* of the prophecy of Rev 22:10 3056

SCAB {7}
skin of his flesh a rising, a *s* Lev 13:2 5597
it is but a *s* Lev 13:6 4556
But if the *s* spread much abroad Lev 13:7 4556
the *s* spreadeth in the skin, then Lev 13:8 4556
And for a rising, and for a *s* Lev 14:56 5597
with the emerods, and with the *s* Deut 28:27 1618
the Lord will smite with a *s* the Is 3:17 5597

SCABBARD {1}
put up thyself into thy *s* Jer 47:6 8593

SCABBED {2}
in his eye, or be scurvy, or *s* Lev 21:20 3217
or having a wen, or scurvy, or *s* Lev 22:22 3217

SCAFFOLD {1}
For Solomon had made a brasen *s* 2Chr 6:13 3595

SCALES {10}
s in the waters, in the seas, and Lev 11:9 7193
s in the seas, and in the rivers, Lev 11:10 7193
hath no fins nor *s* in the waters Lev 11:12 7193
that have fins and *s* shall ye eat Deut 14:9 7193
hath not fins and *s* ye may not eat Deut 14:10 7193
His *s* are his pride, shut up Job 41:15 650,4043
and weighed the mountains in *s* Is 40:12 6425
of thy rivers to stick unto thy *s* Eze 29:4 7193
thy rivers shall stick unto thy *s* Eze 29:4 7193
from his eyes as it had been *s* Acts 9:18 3013

SCALETH {1}
A wise man *s* the city of the Prov 21:22 5927

SCALL {14}
it is a dry *s*, even a leprosy Lev 13:30 5424
look on the plague of the *s* Lev 13:31 5424
the plague of the *s* seven days Lev 13:31 5424
if the *s* spread not, and there be Lev 13:32 5424
the *s* be not in sight deeper than Lev 13:32 5424
but the *s* shall he not shave Lev 13:33 5424
that hath the *s* seven days more Lev 13:33 5424
the priest shall look on the *s* Lev 13:34 5424
if the *s* be not spread in the Lev 13:34 5424
But if the *s* spread much in the Lev 13:35 5424
if the *s* be spread in the skin, Lev 13:36 5424
But if the *s* be in his sight at a Lev 13:37 5424
the *s* is healed, he is clean Lev 13:37 5424
manner of plague of leprosy, and *s* Lev 14:54 5424

SCALP {1}
the hairy *s* of such an one as Ps 68:21 6936

SCANT {1}
the *s* measure that is abominable Mic 6:10 7332

SCAPEGOAT {4}
LORD, and the other lot for the *s* Lev 16:8 5799
on which the lot fell to be the *s* Lev 16:10 5799
go for a *s* into the wilderness Lev 16:10 5799
for the *s* shall wash his clothes Lev 16:26 5799

SCARCE {3}
Jacob was yet *s* gone out from the Gen 27:30
with these sayings *s* restrained Acts 14:18 3433
s were come over against Cnidus, Acts 27:7 3433

SCARCELY {2}
For *s* for a righteous man will Rom 5:7 3433
And if the righteous *s* be saved 1Pet 4:18 3433

SCARCENESS {1}
thou shalt eat bread without *s* Deut 8:9 4544

SCAREST {1}
Then thou *s* me with dreams, and Job 7:14 2865

SCARLET {52}
and bound upon his hand a *s* thread Gen 38:28 8144
that had the *s* thread upon his Gen 38:30 8144
blue, and purple, and *s*, and fine Ex 25:4 8144,8438
linen, and blue, and purple, and *s* Ex 26:1 8144,8438
a vail of blue, and purple, and *s* Ex 26:31 8144,8438
tent, of blue, and purple, and *s* Ex 26:36 8144,8438
cubits, of blue, and purple, and *s* Ex 27:16 8144,8438
gold, and blue, and purple, and *s* Ex 28:5 8144,8438
gold, of blue, and of purple, of *s* Ex 28:6 8144,8438
of gold, of blue, and purple, and *s* Ex 28:8 8144,8438
of blue, and of purple, and of *s* Ex 28:15 8144,8438
of blue, and of purple, and of *s* Ex 28:33 8144,8438
blue, and purple, and *s*, and fine Ex 35:6 8144,8438
was found blue, and purple, and *s* Ex 35:23 8144,8438
of blue, and of purple, and of *s* Ex 35:25 8144,8438
in blue, and in purple, in *s* Ex 35:35 8144,8438
linen, and blue, and purple, and *s* Ex 36:8 8144,8438
a vail of blue, and purple, and *s* Ex 36:35 8144,8438
door of blue, and purple, and *s* Ex 36:37 8144,8438
of blue, and purple, and *s* Ex 38:18 8144,8438
in blue, and in purple, and in *s* Ex 38:23 8144,8438
And of the blue, and purple, and *s* Ex 39:1 8144,8438
of gold, blue, and purple, and *s* Ex 39:2 8144,8438
and in the purple, and in the *s* Ex 39:3 8144,8438
of gold, blue, and purple, and *s* Ex 39:5 8144,8438
of gold, blue, and purple, and *s* Ex 39:8 8144,8438
of blue, and purple, and *s*, and Ex 39:24 8144,8438
linen, and blue, and purple, and *s* Ex 39:29 8144,8438
and clean, and cedar wood, and *s* Lev 14:4 8144,8438
it, and the cedar wood, and the *s* Lev 14:6 8144,8438
two birds, and cedar wood, and *s* Lev 14:49 8144,8438
wood, and the hyssop, and the *s* Lev 14:51 8144,8438
with the hyssop, and with the *s* Lev 14:52 8144,8438
spread upon them a cloth of *s* Num 4:8 8144,8438
cedar wood, and hyssop, and *s* Num 19:6 8144,8438
thou shalt bind this line of *s* Josh 2:18 8144
she bound the *s* line in the Josh 2:21 8144
over Saul, who clothed you in *s* 2Sa 1:24 8144
her household are clothed with *s* Prov 31:21 8144
Thy lips are like a thread of *s* Song 4:3 8144
though your sins be as *s*, they Is 1:18 8144
brought up in *s* embrace dunghills Lam 4:5 8144
thereof, shall be clothed with *s* Dan 5:7 711
thou shalt be clothed with *s* Dan 5:16 711
and they clothed Daniel with *s* Dan 5:29 711
red, the valiant men are in *s* Nah 2:3 8529
him, and put on him a *s* robe Mt 27:28 2847
s wool, and hyssop, and sprinkled Heb 9:19 2847
woman sit upon a *s* coloured beast Rev 17:3 2847
s colour, and decked with gold and Rev 17:4 2847
linen, and purple, and silk, and *s* Rev 18:12 2847
in fine linen, and purple, and *s* Rev 18:16 2847

SCATTER {38}
from thence did the LORD *s* them Gen 11:9 6327
in Jacob, and *s* them in Israel Gen 49:7 6327
I will *s* you among the heathen, Lev 26:33 2210
and *s* thou the fire yonder Num 16:37 2219
the LORD shall *s* you among the Deut 4:27 6327
the LORD shall *s* thee among all Deut 28:64 6327
I would *s* them into corners, I Deut 32:26 6284
shall *s* them beyond the river, 1Kin 14:15 2219
I will *s* you abroad among the Neh 1:8 6327
s them by thy power Ps 59:11 5128
s thou the people that delight in Ps 68:30 967

S

and to *s* them in the lands ... Ps 106:27 2219
Cast forth lightning, and *s* them ... Ps 144:6 6327
s the cummin, and cast in the ... Is 28:25 2236
and the whirlwind shall *s* them ... Is 41:16 6327
I will *s* them also among the ... Jer 9:16 6327
Therefore will I *s* them as the ... Jer 13:24 6327
I will *s* them as with an east ... Jer 18:17 6327
s the sheep of my pasture ... Jer 23:1 6327
I will *s* into all winds them that ... Jer 49:32 2219
will *s* them toward all those ... Jer 49:36 2219
part thou shalt *s* in the wind ... Eze 5:2 2219
thee will I *s* into all the winds ... Eze 5:10 2219
I will *s* a third part into all ... Eze 5:12 2219
I will *s* your bones round about ... Eze 6:5 2219
and *s* them over the city ... Eze 10:2 2236
I will *s* toward every wind all ... Eze 12:14 2219
when I shall *s* them among the ... Eze 12:15 6327
that I would *s* them among the ... Eze 20:23 6327
I will *s* thee among the heathen, ... Eze 22:15 6327
I will *s* the Egyptians among the ... Eze 29:12 6327
I will *s* the Egyptians among the ... Eze 30:23 6327
I will *s* the Egyptians among the ... Eze 30:26 6327
off his leaves, and *s* his fruit ... Dan 4:14 921
he shall *s* among them the prey, ... Dan 11:24 967
to *s* the power of the holy people ... Dan 12:7 5310
came out as a whirlwind to *s* me ... Hab 3:14 6327
over the land of Judah to *s* it ... Zec 1:21 2219

SCATTERED {71}
lest we be *s* abroad upon the face ... Gen 11:4 6327
So the LORD *s* them abroad from ... Gen 11:8 6327
So the people were *s* abroad ... Ex 5:12 6327
LORD, and let thine enemies be *s* ... Num 10:35 6327
the LORD thy God hath *s* thee ... Deut 30:3 6327
that they which remained were *s* ... 1Sa 11:11 6327
and the people were *s* from him ... 1Sa 13:8 6327
that the people were *s* from me ... 1Sa 13:11 5310
there *s* over the face of all the ... 2Sa 18:8 6327
And he sent out arrows, and *s* them ... 2Sa 22:15 6327
I saw all Israel *s* upon the hills ... 1Kin 22:17 6327
and all his army were *s* from him ... 2Kin 25:5 6327
all Israel *s* upon the mountains ... 2Chr 18:16 6327
is a certain people *s* abroad ... Est 3:8 6340
stout lion's whelps are *s* abroad ... Job 4:11 6504
brimstone shall be *s* upon his ... Job 18:15 2219
he sent out his arrows, and *s* them ... Ps 18:14 6327
hast *s* us among the heathen ... Ps 44:11 2219
for God hath *s* the bones of him ... Ps 53:5 6340
hast cast us off, thou hast *s* us ... Ps 60:1 6555
God arise, let his enemies be *s* ... Ps 68:1 6327
When the Almighty *s* kings in it ... Ps 68:14 6566
thou hast *s* thine enemies with ... Ps 89:10 6340
workers of iniquity shall be *s* ... Ps 92:9 6504
Our bones are *s* at the grave's ... Ps 141:7 6340
swift messengers, to a nation *s* ... Is 18:2 4900
the LORD of hosts of a people *s* ... Is 18:7 4900
up of thyself the nations were *s* ... Is 33:3 5310
hast *s* thy ways to the strangers ... Jer 3:13 6340
and all their flocks shall be *s* ... Jer 10:21 6327
Ye have *s* my flock, and driven ... Jer 23:2 6327
all nations whither I have *s* thee ... Jer 30:11 6327
He that *s* Israel will gather him, ... Jer 31:10 2219
gathered unto thee should be *s* ... Jer 40:15 6327
Israel is a *s* sheep ... Jer 50:17 6340
and all his army was *s* from him ... Jer 52:8 6327
when ye shall be *s* through the ... Eze 6:8 2219
although I have *s* them among the ... Eze 11:16 6327
countries where ye have been *s* ... Eze 11:17 6327
shall be *s* toward all winds ... Eze 17:21 6566
of the countries wherein ye are *s* ... Eze 20:34 6327
countries wherein ye have been *s* ... Eze 20:41 6327
the people among whom they are *s* ... Eze 28:25 6327
the people whither they were *s* ... Eze 29:13 6327
And they were *s*, because there is ... Eze 34:5 6327
of the field, when they were *s* ... Eze 34:5 6327
my flock was *s* upon all the face ... Eze 34:6 6327
he is among his sheep that are *s* ... Eze 34:12 6566
they have been *s* in the cloudy ... Eze 34:12 6327
horns, till ye have *s* them abroad ... Eze 34:21 6327
I *s* them among the heathen, and ... Eze 36:19 6327
that my people be not *s* every man ... Eze 46:18 6327
whom they have *s* among the ... Joel 3:2 6327
thy people is *s* upon the ... Nah 3:18 6340
the everlasting mountains were *s* ... Hab 3:6 6327
are the horns which have *s* Judah ... Zec 1:19 2219
are the horns which have *s* Judah ... Zec 1:21 2219
But I *s* them with a whirlwind ... Zec 7:14
shepherd, and the sheep shall be *s* ... Zec 13:7 6327
were *s* abroad, as sheep having no ... Mt 9:36 *4496*
of the flock shall be *s* abroad ... Mt 26:31 *1287*
shepherd, and the sheep shall be *s* ... Mk 14:27 *1287*
he hath *s* the proud in the ... Lk 1:51 *1287*
of God that were *s* abroad ... Jn 11:52 *1287*
is now come, that ye shall be *s* ... Jn 16:32 *4650*
as many as obeyed him, were *s* ... Acts 5:36 *1262*
they were all *s* abroad throughout ... Acts 8:1 *1289*
were *s* abroad went every where ... Acts 8:4 *1289*
Now they which were *s* abroad upon ... Acts 11:19 *1289*
twelve tribes which are *s* abroad ... Jas 1:1 *1290*
to the strangers *s* throughout ... 1Pet 1:1 *1290*

SCATTERETH {10}
he *s* his bright cloud ... Job 37:11 6327
which *s* the east wind upon the ... Job 38:24 6327
he *s* the hoar frost like ashes ... Ps 147:16 6340
There is that *s*, and yet ... Prov 11:24 6340
in the throne of judgment *s* away ... Prov 20:8 2219
A wise king *s* the wicked, and ... Prov 20:26 2219
s abroad the inhabitants thereof ... Is 24:1 6327
gathereth not with me *s* abroad ... Mt 12:30 *4650*
he that gathereth not with me *s* ... Lk 11:23 *4650*
catcheth them, and *s* the sheep ... Jn 10:12 *4650*

SCATTERING {1}
flame of a devouring fire, with *s* ... Is 30:30 5311

SCENT {3}
Yet through the *s* of water it ... Job 14:9 7381
in him, and his *s* is not changed ... Jer 48:11 7381
the *s* thereof shall be as the ... Hos 14:7 2143

SCEPTRE {15}
The *s* shall not depart from Judah ... Gen 49:10 7626
a *S* shall rise out of Israel, and ... Num 24:17 7626
king shall hold out the golden *s* ... Est 4:11 8275
the golden *s* that was in his hand ... Est 5:2 8275
near, and touched the top of the *s* ... Est 5:2 8275
out the golden *s* toward Esther ... Est 8:4 8275
the *s* of thy kingdom is a right ... Ps 45:6 7626
of thy kingdom is a right *s* ... Ps 45:6 7626
wicked, and the *s* of the rulers ... Is 14:5 7626
no strong rod to be a *s* to rule ... Eze 19:14 7626
him that holdeth the *s* from the ... Amos 1:5 7626
that holdeth the *s* from Ashkelon ... Amos 1:8 7626
the *s* of Egypt shall depart away ... Zec 10:11 7626
a *s* of righteousness is the ... Heb 1:8 *4464*
is the *s* of thy kingdom ... Heb 1:8 *4464*

SCEPTRES {1}
for the *s* of them that bare rule ... Eze 19:11 7626

SCEVA *(see'-vah)* {1} *A Jewish priest at Ephesus.*
And there were seven sons of one *S* ... Acts 19:14 *4630*

SCHISM {1}
there should be no *s* in the body ... 1Cor 12:25 *4978*

SCHOLAR {2}
the great, the teacher as the *s* ... 1Chr 25:8 8527
doeth this, the master and the *s* ... Mal 2:12 6030

SCHOOL {1}
daily in the *s* of one Tyrannus ... Acts 19:9 *4981*

SCHOOLMASTER {2}
was our *s* to bring us unto Christ ... Gal 3:24 *3807*
come, we are no longer under a *s* ... Gal 3:25 *3807*

SCIENCE {2}
in knowledge, and understanding *s* ... Dan 1:4 4093
oppositions of *s* falsely so ... 1Ti 6:20 *1108*

SCOFF {1}
they shall *s* at the kings, and the ... Hab 1:10 7046

SCOFFERS {1}
shall come in the last days *s* ... 2Pet 3:3 *1703*

SCORCH {1}
given unto him to *s* men with fire ... Rev 16:8 *2739*

SCORCHED {3}
when the sun was up, they were *s* ... Mt 13:6 *2739*
But when the sun was up, it was *s* ... Mk 4:6 *2739*
men were *s* with great heat, and ... Rev 16:9 *2739*

SCORN {16}
thee, and laughed thee to *s* ... 2Kin 19:21
but they laughed them to *s* ... 2Chr 30:10
heard it, they laughed us to *s* ... Neh 2:19
he thought *s* to lay hands on ... Est 3:6 959
just upright man is laughed to *s* ... Job 12:4
My friends *s* me ... Job 16:20 3887
and the innocent laugh them to *s* ... Job 22:19
they that see me laugh me to *s* ... Ps 22:7
a reproach to our neighbours, a *s* ... Ps 44:13 3933
a reproach to our neighbours, a *s* ... Ps 79:4 3933
thee, and laughed thee to *s* ... Is 37:22
thou shalt be laughed to *s* ... Eze 23:32
princes shall be a *s* unto them ... Hab 1:10 4890
And they laughed him to *s* ... Mt 9:24 *2606*
And they laughed him to *s* ... Mk 5:40 *2606*
And they laughed him to *s*, knowing ... Lk 8:53 *2606*

SCORNER {11}
He that reproveth a *s* getteth to ... Prov 9:7 3887
Reprove not a *s*, lest he hate ... Prov 9:8 3887
but a *s* heareth not rebuke ... Prov 13:1 3887
A *s* seeketh wisdom, and findeth it ... Prov 14:6 3887
A *s* loveth not one that reproveth ... Prov 15:12 3887
Smite a *s*, and the simple will ... Prov 19:25 3887
When the *s* is punished, the ... Prov 21:11 3887
haughty *s* is his name, who ... Prov 21:24 3887
Cast out the *s*, and contention ... Prov 22:10 3887
the *s* is an abomination to men ... Prov 24:9 3887
the *s* is consumed, and all that ... Is 29:20 3887

SCORNERS {4}
the *s* delight in their scorning, ... Prov 1:22 3887
Surely he scorneth the *s* ... Prov 3:34 3887
Judgments are prepared for *s* ... Prov 19:29 3887
he stretched out his hand with *s* ... Hos 7:5 3945

SCORNEST {2}
but if thou *s*, thou alone shalt ... Prov 9:12 3887
as an harlot, in that thou *s* hire ... Eze 16:31 7046

SCORNETH {4}
He *s* the multitude of the city, ... Job 39:7 7832
she *s* the horse and his rider ... Job 39:18 7832
Surely he *s* the scorners ... Prov 3:34 3887
An ungodly witness *s* judgment ... Prov 19:28 3887

SCORNFUL {3}
nor sitteth in the seat of the *s* ... Ps 1:1 3887
S men bring a city into a snare ... Prov 29:8 3944
ye *s* men, that rule this people ... Is 28:14 3944

SCORNING {3}
Job, who drinketh up *s* like water ... Job 34:7 3933
the *s* of those that are at ease ... Ps 123:4 3933
the scorners delight in their *s* ... Prov 1:22 3944

SCORPION {2}
ask an egg, will he offer him a *s* ... Lk 11:12 *4651*
torment was as the torment of a *s* ... Rev 9:5 *4651*

SCORPION PASS See MAALEH-ACRABBIM.

SCORPIONS {9}
wherein were fiery serpents, and *s* ... Deut 8:15 6137
but I will chastise you with *s* ... 1Kin 12:11 6137
but I will chastise you with *s* ... 1Kin 12:14 6137
but I will chastise you with *s* ... 2Chr 10:11 6137
but I will chastise you with *s* ... 2Chr 10:14 6137
thee, and thou dost dwell among *s* ... Eze 2:6 6137
power to tread on serpents and *s* ... Lk 10:19 *4651*
as the *s* of the earth have power ... Rev 9:3 *4651*
And they had tails like unto *s* ... Rev 9:10 *4651*

SCOURED {1}
a brasen pot, it shall be both *s* ... Lev 6:28 4838

SCOURGE {12}
be hid from the *s* of the tongue ... Job 5:21 7752
If the *s* slay suddenly, he will ... Job 9:23 7752
up a *s* for him according to the ... Is 10:26 7752
overflowing *s* shall pass through ... Is 28:15 7885
overflowing *s* shall pass through ... Is 28:18 7752
and they will *s* you in their ... Mt 10:17 *3164*
to the Gentiles to mock, and to *s* ... Mt 20:19 *3164*
shall ye *s* in your synagogues ... Mt 23:34 *3164*
shall mock him, and shall *s* him ... Mk 10:34 *3164*
And they shall *s* him, and put him ... Lk 18:33 *3164*
he had made a *s* of small cords ... Jn 2:15 *5416*
you to *s* a man that is a Roman ... Acts 22:25 *3147*

SCOURGED {4}
she shall be *s* ... Lev 19:20 1244
and when he had *s* Jesus, he ... Mt 27:26 *5417*
Jesus, when he had *s* him, to be ... Mk 15:15 *5417*
therefore took Jesus, and *s* him ... Jn 19:1 *3146*

SCOURGES {1}
s in your sides, and thorns in ... Josh 23:13 7850

SCOURGETH {1}
s every son whom he receiveth ... Heb 12:6 *3146*

SCOURGING {1}
that he should be examined by *s* ... Acts 22:24 *3148*

SCOURGINGS {1}
had trial of cruel mockings and *s* ... Heb 11:36 *3148*

SCRABBLED {1}
s on the doors of the gate, and ... 1Sa 21:13 8427

SCRAPE {3}
pour out the dust that they *s* off ... Lev 14:41 7096
a potsherd to *s* himself withal ... Job 2:8 1623
I will also *s* her dust from her, ... Eze 26:4 5500

SCRAPED {2}
house to be *s* within round about ... Lev 14:41 7106
and after he hath *s* the house ... Lev 14:43 7096

SCREECH {1}
the *s* owl also shall rest there, ... Is 34:14 3917

SCRIBE {52}
and Seraiah was the *s* ... 2Sa 8:17 5608
And Sheva was *s* ... 2Sa 20:25 5608
in the chest, that the king's *s* ... 2Kin 12:10 5608
the household, and Shebna the *s* ... 2Kin 18:18 5608
the household, and Shebna the *s* ... 2Kin 18:37 5608
the household, and Shebna the *s* ... 2Kin 19:2 5608
the son of Meshullam, the *s* ... 2Kin 22:3 5608
priest said unto Shaphan the *s* ... 2Kin 22:8 5608
Shaphan the *s* came to the king, ... 2Kin 22:9 5608
Shaphan the *s* shewed the king, ... 2Kin 22:10 5608
son of Michaiah, and Shaphan the *s* ... 2Kin 22:12 5608
and the principal *s* of the host ... 2Kin 25:19 5608
and Shavsha was *s* ... 1Chr 18:16 5608
the son of Nethaneel the *s* ... 1Chr 24:6 5608
a counsellor, a wise man, and a *s* ... 1Chr 27:32 5608
was much money, the king's *s* ... 2Chr 24:11 5608
by the hand of Jeiel the *s* ... 2Chr 26:11 5608
answered and said to Shaphan the *s* ... 2Chr 34:15 5608
Then Shaphan the *s* told the king ... 2Chr 34:18 5608
son of Micah, and Shaphan the *s* ... 2Chr 34:20 5608
Shimshai the *s* wrote a letter ... Ezr 4:8 5613
the chancellor, and Shimshai the *s* ... Ezr 4:9 5613
chancellor, and to Shimshai the *s* ... Ezr 4:17 5613
before Rehum, and Shimshai the *s* ... Ezr 4:23 5613
he was a ready *s* in the law of ... Ezr 7:6 5608
gave unto Ezra the priest, the *s* ... Ezr 7:11 5608
even a *s* of the words of the ... Ezr 7:11 5608
a *s* of the law of the God of ... Ezr 7:12 5613
the *s* of the law of the God of ... Ezr 7:21 5613
they spake unto Ezra the *s* to ... Neh 8:1 5608
Ezra the *s* stood upon a pulpit of ... Neh 8:4 5608
and Ezra the priest the *s* ... Neh 8:9 5608
and the Levites, unto Ezra the *s* ... Neh 8:13 5608
and of Ezra the priest, the *s* ... Neh 12:26 5608
of God, and Ezra the *s* before them ... Neh 12:36 5608
the priest, and Zadok the *s* ... Neh 13:13 5608
Where is the *s* ... Is 33:18 5608
over the house, and Shebna the *s* ... Is 36:3 5608
the household, and Shebna the *s* ... Is 36:22 5608
the household, and Shebna the *s* ... Is 37:2 5608
Gemariah the son of Shaphan the *s* ... Jer 36:10 5608
sat there, even Elishama the *s* ... Jer 36:12 5608
in the chamber of Elishama the *s* ... Jer 36:20 5608
of Abdeel, to take Baruch the *s* ... Jer 36:26 5608
roll, and gave it to Baruch the *s* ... Jer 36:32 5608

in the house of Jonathan the *s* ... Jer 37:15 5608
to the house of Jonathan the *s* ... Jer 37:20 5608
and the principal *s* of the host ... Jer 52:25 5608
And a certain *s* came, and said unto ... Mt 8:19 *1122*
Therefore every *s* which is ... Mt 13:52 *1122*
the *s* said unto him, Well, Master ... Mk 12:32 *1122*
where is the *s* ... 1Cor 1:20 *1122*

SCRIBE'S {2}
king's house, into the *s* chamber ... Jer 36:12 5608
it out of Elishama the *s* chamber ... Jer 36:21 5608

SCRIBES {68}
and Ahiah, the sons of Shisha, *s* ... 1Kin 4:3 5608
the families of the *s* which dwelt ... 1Chr 2:55 5608
and of the Levites there were *s* ... 2Chr 34:13 5608
Then were the king's *s* called on ... Est 3:12 5608
Then were the king's *s* called at ... Est 8:9 5608
the pen of the *s* is in vain ... Jer 8:8 5608
s of the people together, he ... Mt 2:4 *1122*
exceed the righteousness of the *s* ... Mt 5:20 *1122*
having authority, and not as the *s* ... Mt 7:29 *1122*
certain of the *s* said within ... Mt 9:3 *1122*
Then certain of the *s* and of the ... Mt 12:38 *1122*
Then came to Jesus *s* and Pharisees ... Mt 15:1 *1122*
the elders and chief priests and *s* ... Mt 16:21 *1122*
Why then say the *s* that Elias ... Mt 17:10 *1122*
the chief priests and unto the *s* ... Mt 20:18 *1122*
s saw the wonderful things that ... Mt 21:15 *1122*
Saying, The *s* and the Pharisees ... Mt 23:2 *1122*
But woe unto you, *s* and Pharisees, ... Mt 23:13 *1122*
Woe unto you, *s* and Pharisees, ... Mt 23:14 *1122*
Woe unto you, *s* and Pharisees, ... Mt 23:15 *1122*
Woe unto you, *s* and Pharisees, ... Mt 23:23 *1122*
Woe unto you, *s* and Pharisees, ... Mt 23:25 *1122*
Woe unto you, *s* and Pharisees, ... Mt 23:27 *1122*
Woe unto you, *s* and Pharisees, ... Mt 23:29 *1122*
you prophets, and wise men, and *s* ... Mt 23:34 *1122*
the chief priests, and the *s* ... Mt 26:3 *1122*
the high priest, where the *s* ... Mt 26:57 *1122*
priests mocking him, with the *s* ... Mt 27:41 *1122*
had authority, and not as the *s* ... Mk 1:22 *1122*
certain of the *s* sitting there ... Mk 2:6 *1122*
And when the *s* and Pharisees saw ... Mk 2:16 *1122*
the *s* which came down from ... Mk 3:22 *1122*
Pharisees, and certain of the *s* ... Mk 7:1 *1122*
s asked him, Why walk not thy ... Mk 7:5 *1122*
and of the chief priests, and *s* ... Mk 8:31 *1122*
Why say the *s* that Elias must ... Mk 9:11 *1122*
the *s* questioning with them ... Mk 9:14 *1122*
And he asked the *s*, What question ... Mk 9:16 *1122*
the chief priests, and unto the *s* ... Mk 10:33 *1122*
And the *s* and chief priests heard ... Mk 11:18 *1122*
him the chief priests, and the *s* ... Mk 11:27 *1122*
And one of the *s* came, and having ... Mk 12:28 *1122*
How say the *s* that Christ is the ... Mk 12:35 *1122*
in his doctrine, Beware of the *s* ... Mk 12:38 *1122*
the *s* sought how they might take ... Mk 14:1 *1122*
from the chief priest and the *s* ... Mk 14:43 *1122*
priests and the elders and the *s* ... Mk 14:53 *1122*
consultation with the elders and *s* ... Mk 15:1 *1122*
said among themselves with the *s* ... Mk 15:31 *1122*
And the *s* and the Pharisees began ... Lk 5:21 *1122*
But their *s* and Pharisees murmured ... Lk 5:30 *1122*
And the *s* and Pharisees watched him ... Lk 6:7 *1122*
the elders and chief priests and *s* ... Lk 9:22 *1122*
Woe unto you, *s* and Pharisees, ... Lk 11:44 *1122*
these things unto them, the *s* ... Lk 11:53 *1122*
s murmured, saying, This man ... Lk 15:2 *1122*
But the chief priests and the *s* ... Lk 19:47 *1122*
the *s* came upon him with the ... Lk 20:1 *1122*
the *s* the same hour sought to lay ... Lk 20:19 *1122*
certain of the *s* answering said ... Lk 20:39 *1122*
Beware of the *s*, which desire to ... Lk 20:46 *1122*
s sought how they might kill him ... Lk 22:2 *1122*
the *s* came together, and led him ... Lk 22:66 *1122*
s stood and vehemently accused him ... Lk 23:10 *1122*
And the *s* and Pharisees brought ... Jn 8:3 *1122*
their rulers, and elders, and *s* ... Acts 4:5 *1122*
people, and the elders, and the *s* ... Acts 6:12 *1122*
the *s* that were of the Pharisees' ... Acts 23:9 *1122*

SCRIP {7}
bag which he had, even in a *s* ... 1Sa 17:40 3219
Nor *s* for your journey, neither ... Mt 10:10 *4082*
no *s*, no bread, no money in their ... Mk 6:8 *4082*
journey, neither staves, nor *s* ... Lk 9:3 *4082*
Carry neither purse, nor *s* ... Lk 10:4 *4082*
I sent you without purse, and *s* ... Lk 22:35 *4082*
him take it, and likewise his *s* ... Lk 22:36 *4082*

SCRIPTURE {32}
which is noted in the *s* of truth ... Dan 10:21 3791
And have ye not read this *s* ... Mk 12:10 *1124*
the *s* was fulfilled, which saith, ... Mk 15:28 *1124*
This day is this *s* fulfilled in ... Lk 4:21 *1124*
and they believed the *s*, and the ... Jn 2:22 *1124*
as the *s* hath said, out of his ... Jn 7:38 *1124*
Hath not the *s* said, That Christ ... Jn 7:42 *1124*
came, and the *s* cannot be broken ... Jn 10:35 *1124*
but that the *s* may be fulfilled, ... Jn 13:18 *1124*
that the *s* might be fulfilled ... Jn 17:12 *1124*
that the *s* might be fulfilled, ... Jn 19:24 *1124*
that the *s* might be fulfilled, ... Jn 19:28 *1124*
that the *s* should be fulfilled, A ... Jn 19:36 *1124*
And again another *s* saith, They ... Jn 19:37 *1124*
For as yet they knew not the *s* ... Jn 20:9 *1124*
this *s* must needs have been ... Acts 1:16 *1124*
The place of the *s* which he read ... Acts 8:32 *1124*
his mouth, and began at the same *s* ... Acts 8:35 *1124*
For what saith the *s* ... Rom 4:3 *1124*
For the *s* saith unto Pharaoh, ... Rom 9:17 *1124*
For the *s* saith, Whosoever ... Rom 10:11 *1124*
ye not what the *s* saith of Elias ... Rom 11:2 *1124*
And the *s*, foreseeing that God ... Gal 3:8 *1124*
But the *s* hath concluded all ... Gal 3:22 *1124*
Nevertheless what saith the *s* ... Gal 4:30 *1124*
For the *s* saith, Thou shalt not ... 1Ti 5:18 *1124*
All *s* is given by inspiration of ... 2Ti 3:16 *1124*
the royal law according to the *s* ... Jas 2:8 *1124*
the *s* was fulfilled which saith, ... Jas 2:23 *1124*
ye think that the *s* saith in vain ... Jas 4:5 *1124*
also it is contained in the *s* ... 1Pet 2:6 *1124*
of the *s* is of any private ... 2Pet 1:20 *1124*

SCRIPTURES {21}
them, Did ye never read in the *s* ... Mt 21:42 *1124*
Ye do err, not knowing the *s* ... Mt 22:29 *1124*
how then shall the *s* be fulfilled ... Mt 26:54 *1124*
that the *s* of the prophets might ... Mt 26:56 *1124*
err, because ye know not the *s* ... Mk 12:24 *1124*
but the *s* must be fulfilled ... Mk 14:49 *1124*
s the things concerning himself ... Lk 24:27 *1124*
and while he opened to us the *s* ... Lk 24:32 *1124*
that they might understand the *s* ... Lk 24:45 *1124*
Search the *s* ... Jn 5:39 *1124*
reasoned with them out of the *s* ... Acts 17:2 *1124*
of mind, and searched the *s* daily ... Acts 17:11 *1124*
eloquent man, and mighty in the *s* ... Acts 18:24 *1124*
shewing by the *s* that Jesus was ... Acts 18:28 *1124*
by his prophets in the holy *s* ... Rom 1:2 *1124*
comfort of the *s* might have hope ... Rom 15:4 *1124*
by the *s* of the prophets, ... Rom 16:26 *1124*
for our sins according to the *s* ... 1Cor 15:3 *1124*
the third day according to the *s* ... 1Cor 15:4 *1124*
child thou hast known the holy *s* ... 2Ti 3:15 *1121*
as they do also the other *s* ... 2Pet 3:16 *1124*

SCROLL {2}
shall be rolled together as a *s* ... Is 34:4 5612
the heaven departed as a *s* when ... Rev 6:14 *975*

SCUM {5}
to the pot whose *s* is therein ... Eze 24:6 2457
whose *s* is not gone out of it ... Eze 24:6 2457
that the *s* of it may be consumed ... Eze 24:11 2457
her great *s* went not forth out of ... Eze 24:12 2457
her *s* shall be in the fire ... Eze 24:12 2457

SCURVY {2}
a blemish in his eye, or be *s* ... Lev 21:20 1618
or maimed, or having a wen, or *s* ... Lev 22:22 1618

SCYTHIAN *(sith'-e-un)* {1} *A barbarous people north of the Black Sea.*
nor uncircumcision, Barbarian, *S* ... Col 3:11 *4658*

SEA {401}
dominion over the fish of the *s* ... Gen 1:26 3220
dominion over the fish of the *s* ... Gen 1:28 3220
and upon all the fishes of the *s* ... Gen 9:2 3220
of Siddim, which is the Salt *S* ... Gen 14:3 3220
sand which is upon the *s* shore ... Gen 22:17 3220
thy seed as the sand of the *s* ... Gen 32:12 3220
corn as the sand of the *s* ... Gen 41:49 3220
shall dwell at the haven of the *s* ... Gen 49:13 3220
and cast them into the Red *s* ... Ex 10:19 3220
of the wilderness of the Red *s* ... Ex 13:18 3220
between Migdol and the *s*, over ... Ex 14:2 3220
it shall ye encamp by the *s* ... Ex 14:2 3220
overtook them encamping by the *s* ... Ex 14:9 3220
stretch out thine hand over the *s* ... Ex 14:16 3220
ground through the midst of the *s* ... Ex 14:16 3220
stretched out his hand over the *s* ... Ex 14:21 3220
the LORD caused the *s* to go back ... Ex 14:21 3220
night, and made the *s* dry land ... Ex 14:21 3220
of the *s* upon the dry ground ... Ex 14:22 3220
after them to the midst of the *s* ... Ex 14:23 3220
Stretch out thine hand over the *s* ... Ex 14:26 3220
forth his hand over the *s* ... Ex 14:27 3220
the *s* returned to his strength ... Ex 14:27 3220
Egyptians in the midst of the *s* ... Ex 14:27 3220
that came into the *s* after them ... Ex 14:28 3220
dry land in the midst of the *s* ... Ex 14:29 3220
Egyptians dead upon the *s* shore ... Ex 14:30 3220
rider hath he thrown into the *s* ... Ex 15:1 3220
his host hath he cast into the *s* ... Ex 15:4 3220
also are drowned in the Red *s* ... Ex 15:4 3220
congealed in the heart of the *s* ... Ex 15:8 3220
with thy wind, the *s* covered them ... Ex 15:10 3220
and with his horsemen into the *s* ... Ex 15:19 3220
the waters of the *s* upon them ... Ex 15:19 3220
on dry land in the midst of the *s* ... Ex 15:19 3220
rider hath he thrown into the *s* ... Ex 15:21 3220
brought Israel from the Red *s* ... Ex 15:22 3220
LORD made heaven and earth, the *s* ... Ex 20:11 3220
Red *s* even unto the *s* of the ... Ex 23:31 3220
or shall all the fish of the *s* be ... Num 11:22 3220
and brought quails from the *s* ... Num 11:31 3220
and the Canaanites dwell by the *s* ... Num 13:29 3220
by the way of the Red *s* ... Num 14:25 3220
mount Hor by the way of the Red *s* ... Num 21:4 3220
LORD, What he did in the Red *s* ... Num 21:14 3220
of the *s* into the wilderness ... Num 33:8 3220
Elim, and encamped by the Red *s* ... Num 33:10 3220
And they removed from the Red *s* ... Num 33:11 3220
coast of the salt *s* eastward ... Num 34:3 3220
out of it shall be at the *s* ... Num 34:5 3220
have the great *s* for a border ... Num 34:6 3220
from the great *s* ye shall point ... Num 34:7 3220
of the *s* of Chinnereth eastward ... Num 34:11 3220
out of it shall be at the salt *s* ... Num 34:12 3220
the plain over against the Red *s* ... Deut 1:1 3220
and in the south, and by the *s* side ... Deut 1:7 3220
by the way of the Red *s* ... Deut 1:40 3220
by the way of the Red *s*, as the ... Deut 2:1 3220
s of the plain, even the salt *s* ... Deut 3:17 3220
even unto the *s* of the plain ... Deut 4:49 3220
Red *s* to overflow them as they ... Deut 11:4 3220
uttermost *s* shall your coast be ... Deut 11:24 3220
Neither is it beyond the *s* ... Deut 30:13 3220
Who shall go over the *s* for us ... Deut 30:13 3220
land of Judah, unto the utmost *s* ... Deut 34:2 3220
unto the great *s* toward the going ... Josh 1:4 3220
up the water of the Red *s* for you ... Josh 2:10 3220
s of the plain, even the salt *s* ... Josh 3:16 3220
LORD your God did to the Red *s* ... Josh 4:23 3220
Canaanites, which were by the *s* ... Josh 5:1 3220
the great *s* over against Lebanon ... Josh 9:1 3220
is upon the *s* shore in multitude ... Josh 11:4 3220
from the plain to the *s* of ... Josh 12:3 3220
unto the *s* of the plain ... Josh 12:3 3220
even the salt *s* on the east ... Josh 12:3 3220
even unto the edge of the *s* of ... Josh 13:27 3220
was from the shore of the salt *s* ... Josh 15:2 3220
out of that coast were at the *s* ... Josh 15:4 3220
And the east border was the salt *s* ... Josh 15:5 3220
s at the uttermost part of Jordan ... Josh 15:5 3220
out of the border were at the *s* ... Josh 15:11 3220
west border was to the great *s* ... Josh 15:12 3220
From Ekron even unto the *s* ... Josh 15:46 3220
river of Egypt, and the great *s* ... Josh 15:47 3220
goings out thereof are at the *s* ... Josh 16:3 3220
the border went out toward the *s* ... Josh 16:6 3220
goings out thereof were at the *s* ... Josh 16:8 3220
the outgoings of it were at the *s* ... Josh 17:9 3220
and the *s* is his border ... Josh 17:10 3220
the corner of the *s* southward ... Josh 18:14 3220
salt *s* at the south end of Jordan ... Josh 18:19 3220
their border went up toward the *s* ... Josh 19:11 3220
at the *s* from the coast to Achzib ... Josh 19:29 3220
even unto the great *s* westward ... Josh 23:4 3220
and ye came unto the *s* ... Josh 24:6 3220
and horsemen unto the Red *s* ... Josh 24:6 3220
and brought the *s* upon them ... Josh 24:7 3220
Asher continued on the *s* shore ... Judg 5:17 3220
sand by the *s* side for multitude ... Judg 7:12 3220
the wilderness unto the Red *s* ... Judg 11:16 3220
is on the *s* shore in multitude ... 1Sa 13:5 3220
that is by the *s* for multitude ... 2Sa 17:11 3220
And the channels of the *s* appeared ... 2Sa 22:16 3220
which is by the *s* in multitude ... 1Kin 4:20 3220
the sand that is on the *s* shore ... 1Kin 4:29 3220
them down from Lebanon unto the *s* ... 1Kin 5:9 3220
I will convey them by *s* in floats ... 1Kin 5:9 3220
And he made a molten *s*, ten cubits ... 1Kin 7:23 3220
compassing the *s* round about ... 1Kin 7:24 3220
the *s* was set above upon them, and ... 1Kin 7:25 3220
he set the *s* on the right side of ... 1Kin 7:39 3220
And one *s*, and twelve oxen under ... 1Kin 7:44 3220
s, and twelve oxen under the *s* ... 1Kin 7:44 3220
Eloth, on the shore of the Red *s* ... 1Kin 9:26 3220
that had knowledge of the *s* ... 1Kin 9:27 3220
For the king had at *s* a navy of ... 1Kin 10:22 3220
Go up now, look toward the *s* ... 1Kin 18:43 3220
a little cloud out of the *s* ... 1Kin 18:44 3220
of Hamath unto the *s* of the plain ... 2Kin 14:25 3220
took down the *s* from off the ... 2Kin 16:17 3220
the brasen *s* that was in the ... 2Kin 25:13 3220
The two pillars, one *s*, and the ... 2Kin 25:16 3220
Let the *s* roar, and the fulness ... 1Chr 16:32 3220
Solomon made the brasen *s* ... 1Chr 18:8 3220
to thee in flotes by *s* to Joppa ... 2Chr 2:16 3220
Also he made a molten *s* of ten ... 2Chr 4:2 3220
compassing the *s* round about ... 2Chr 4:3 3220
the *s* was set above upon them, and ... 2Chr 4:4 3220
but the *s* was for the priests to ... 2Chr 4:6 3220
he set the *s* on the right side of ... 2Chr 4:10 3220
One *s*, and twelve oxen under it ... 2Chr 4:15 3220
at the *s* side in the land of Edom ... 2Chr 8:17 3220
that had knowledge of the *s* ... 2Chr 8:18 3220
beyond the *s* on this side Syria ... 2Chr 20:2 3220
from Lebanon to the *s* of Joppa ... Ezr 3:7 3220
heardest their cry by the Red *s* ... Neh 9:9 3220
didst divide the *s* before them ... Neh 9:11 3220
midst of the *s* on the dry land ... Neh 9:11 3220
land, and upon the isles of the *s* ... Est 10:1 3220
be heavier than the sand of the *s* ... Job 6:3 3220
Am I a *s*, or a whale, that thou ... Job 7:12 3220
treadeth upon the waves of the *s* ... Job 9:8 3220
the earth, and broader than the *s* ... Job 11:9 3220
the fishes of the *s* shall declare ... Job 12:8 3220
As the waters fail from the *s* ... Job 14:11 3220
He divideth the *s* with his power ... Job 26:12 3220
the *s* saith, It is not with me ... Job 28:14 3220
and covereth the bottom of the *s* ... Job 36:30 3220
Or who shut up the *s* with doors ... Job 38:8 3220
entered into the springs of the *s* ... Job 38:16 3220
he maketh the *s* like a pot of ... Job 41:31 3220
of the air, and the fish of the *s* ... Ps 8:8 3220
of the *s* together as an heap ... Ps 33:7 3220
carried into the midst of the *s* ... Ps 46:2 3220
them that are afar off upon the *s* ... Ps 65:5 3220
He turned the *s* into dry land ... Ps 66:6 3220
again from the depths of the *s* ... Ps 68:22 3220
have dominion also from *s* to *s* ... Ps 72:8 3220
divide the *s* by thy strength ... Ps 74:13 3220
Thy way is in the *s*, and thy path ... Ps 77:19 3220
He divided the *s*, and caused them ... Ps 78:13 3220
fowls like as the sand of the *s* ... Ps 78:27 3220

but the *s* overwhelmed their	Ps 78:53	3220
sent out her boughs unto the *s*	Ps 80:11	3220
Thou rulest the raging of the *s*	Ps 89:9	3220
I will set his hand also in the *s*	Ps 89:25	3220
than the mighty waves of the *s*	Ps 93:4	3220
The *s* is his, and he made it	Ps 95:5	3220
let the *s* roar, and the fulness	Ps 96:11	3220
Let the *s* roar, and the fulness	Ps 98:7	3220
So is this great and wide *s*	Ps 104:25	3220
him at the *s*, even at the Red *s*	Ps 106:7	3220
He rebuked the Red *s* also	Ps 106:9	3220
and terrible things by the Red *s*	Ps 106:22	3220
that go down to the *s* in ships	Ps 107:23	3220
The *s* saw it, and fled	Ps 114:3	3220
What ailed thee, O thou *s*	Ps 114:5	3220
divided the Red *s* into parts	Ps 136:13	3220
Pharaoh and his host in the Red *s*	Ps 136:15	3220
in the uttermost parts of the *s*	Ps 139:9	3220
made heaven, and earth, the *s*	Ps 146:6	3220
When he gave to the *s* his decree	Prov 8:29	3220
lieth down in the midst of the *s*	Prov 23:34	3220
of a ship in the midst of the *s*	Prov 30:19	3220
All the rivers run into the *s*	Eccl 1:7	3220
yet the *s* is not full	Eccl 1:7	3220
them like the roaring of the *s*	Is 5:30	3220
afflict her by the way of the *s*	Is 9:1	3220
Israel be as the sand of the *s*	Is 10:22	3220
and as his rod was upon the *s*	Is 10:26	3220
LORD, as the waters cover the *s*	Is 11:9	3220
and from the islands of the *s*	Is 11:11	3220
the tongue of the Egyptian *s*	Is 11:15	3220
out, they are gone over the *s*	Is 16:8	3220
That sendeth ambassadors by the *s*	Is 18:2	3220
the waters shall fail from the *s*	Is 19:5	3220
The burden of the desert of the *s*	Is 21:1	3220
of Zidon, that pass over the *s*	Is 23:2	3220
for the *s* hath spoken, even the	Is 23:4	3220
even the strength of the *s*	Is 23:4	3220
stretched out his hand over the *s*	Is 23:11	3220
they shall cry aloud from the *s*	Is 24:14	3220
of Israel in the isles of the *s*	Is 24:15	3220
slay the dragon that is in the *s*	Is 27:1	3220
earth, ye that go down to the *s*	Is 42:10	3220
LORD, which maketh a way in the *s*	Is 43:16	3220
as the waves of the *s*	Is 48:18	3220
at my rebuke I dry up the *s*	Is 50:2	3220
not it which hath dried the *s*	Is 51:10	3220
hath made the depths of the *s*	Is 51:10	3220
LORD thy God, that divided the *s*	Is 51:15	3220
wicked are like the troubled *s*	Is 57:20	3220
s shall be converted unto thee	Is 60:5	3220
s with the shepherd of his flock	Is 63:11	3220
of the *s* by a perpetual decree	Jer 5:22	3220
their voice roareth like the *s*	Jer 6:23	3220
the isles which are beyond the *s*	Jer 25:22	3220
the pillars, and concerning the *s*	Jer 27:19	3220
which divideth the *s* when the	Jer 31:35	3220
the sand of the *s* measured	Jer 33:22	3220
mountains, and as Carmel by the *s*	Jer 46:18	3220
Ashkelon, and against the *s* shore	Jer 47:7	3220
thy plants are gone over the *s*	Jer 48:32	3220
they reach even to the *s* of Jazer	Jer 48:32	3220
thereof was heard in the Red *s*	Jer 49:21	3220
there is sorrow on the *s*	Jer 49:23	3220
their voice shall roar like the *s*	Jer 50:42	3220
and I will dry up her *s*, and make	Jer 51:36	3220
The *s* is come up upon Babylon	Jer 51:42	3220
the brasen *s* that was in the	Jer 52:17	3220
The two pillars, one *s*, and twelve	Jer 52:20	3220
thy breach is great like the *s*	Lam 2:13	3220
Even the *s* monsters draw out the	Lam 4:3	
the remnant of the *s* coast	Eze 25:16	3220
as the *s* causeth his waves to	Eze 26:3	3220
of nets in the midst of the *s*	Eze 26:5	3220
the *s* shall come down from their	Eze 26:16	3220
city, which wast strong in the *s*	Eze 26:17	3220
in the *s* shall be troubled at thy	Eze 26:18	3220
art situate at the entry of the *s*	Eze 27:3	3220
all the ships of the *s* with their	Eze 27:9	3220
and all the pilots of the *s*	Eze 27:29	3220
destroyed in the midst of the *s*	Eze 27:32	3220
So that the fishes of the *s*	Eze 38:20	3220
passengers on the east of the *s*	Eze 39:11	3220
into the desert, and go into the *s*	Eze 47:8	3220
being brought forth into the *s*	Eze 47:8	3220
kinds, as the fish of the great *s*	Eze 47:10	3220
the north side, from the great *s*	Eze 47:15	3220
from the *s* shall be Hazar-enan	Eze 47:17	3220
from the border unto the east *s*	Eze 47:18	3220
Kadesh, the river to the great *s*	Eze 47:19	3220
be the great *s* from the border	Eze 47:20	3220
to the river toward the great *s*	Eze 48:28	3220
heaven strove upon the great *s*	Dan 7:2	3221
great beasts came up from the *s*	Dan 7:3	3221
shall be as the sand of the *s*	Hos 1:10	3220
the fishes of the *s* also shall be	Hos 4:3	3220
with his face toward the east *s*	Joel 2:20	3220
hinder part toward the utmost *s*	Joel 2:20	3220
calleth for the waters of the *s*	Amos 5:8	3220
they shall wander from *s* to *s*	Amos 8:12	3220
my sight in the bottom of the *s*	Amos 9:3	3220
calleth for the waters of the *s*	Amos 9:6	3220
sent out a great wind into the *s*	Jonah 1:4	3220
was a mighty tempest in the *s*	Jonah 1:4	3220
that were in the ship into the *s*	Jonah 1:5	3220
of heaven, which hath made the *s*	Jonah 1:9	3220
that the *s* may be calm unto us	Jonah 1:11	3220
for the *s* wrought, and was	Jonah 1:11	3220
up, and cast me forth into the *s*	Jonah 1:12	3220
so shall the *s* be calm unto you	Jonah 1:12	3220
for the *s* wrought, and was	Jonah 1:13	3220
and cast him forth into the *s*	Jonah 1:15	3220
the *s* ceased from her raging	Jonah 1:15	3220
from *s* to *s*, and from mountain	Mic 7:12	3220
sins into the depths of the *s*	Mic 7:19	3220
He rebuketh the *s*, and maketh it	Nah 1:4	3220
about it, whose rampart was the *s*	Nah 3:8	3220
and her wall was from the *s*	Nah 3:8	3220
makest men as the fishes of the *s*	Hab 1:14	3220
LORD, as the waters cover the *s*	Hab 2:14	3220
was thy wrath against the *s*	Hab 3:8	3220
through the *s* with thine horses	Hab 3:15	3220
heaven, and the fishes of the *s*	Zeph 1:3	3220
the inhabitants of the *s* coast	Zeph 2:5	3220
the *s* coast shall be dwellings and	Zeph 2:6	3220
heavens, and the earth, and the *s*	Hag 2:6	3220
he will smite her power in the *s*	Zec 9:4	3220
shall be from *s* even to *s*	Zec 9:10	3220
through the *s* with affliction	Zec 10:11	3220
and shall smite the waves in the *s*	Zec 10:11	3220
half of them toward the former *s*	Zec 14:8	3220
half of them toward the hinder *s*	Zec 14:8	3220
which is upon the *s* coast	Mt 4:13	*3864*
Nephthalim, by the way of the *s*	Mt 4:15	*2281*
walking by the *s* of Galilee	Mt 4:18	*2281*
brother, casting a net into the *s*	Mt 4:18	*2281*
arose a great tempest in the *s*	Mt 8:24	*2281*
and rebuked the winds and the *s*	Mt 8:26	*2281*
even the winds and the *s* obey him	Mt 8:27	*2281*
down a steep place into the *s*	Mt 8:32	*2281*
the house, and sat by the *s* side	Mt 13:1	*2281*
a net, that was cast into the *s*	Mt 13:47	*2281*
was now in the midst of the *s*	Mt 14:24	*2281*
went unto them, walking on the *s*	Mt 14:25	*2281*
saw him walking on the *s*, they	Mt 14:26	*2281*
came nigh unto the *s* of Galilee	Mt 15:29	*2281*
offend them, go thou to the *s*	Mt 17:27	*2281*
drowned in the depth of the *s*	Mt 18:6	*2281*
and be thou cast into the *s*	Mt 21:21	*2281*
for ye compass *s* and land to make	Mt 23:15	*2281*
as he walked by the *s* of Galilee	Mk 1:16	*2281*
brother casting a net into the *s*	Mk 1:16	*2281*
he went forth again by the *s* side	Mk 2:13	*2281*
with his disciples to the *s*	Mk 3:7	*2281*
again to teach by the *s* side	Mk 4:1	*2281*
into a ship, and sat in the *s*	Mk 4:1	*2281*
was by the *s* on the land	Mk 4:1	*2281*
the wind, and said unto the *s*	Mk 4:39	*2281*
even the wind and the *s* obey him	Mk 4:41	*2281*
over unto the other side of the *s*	Mk 5:1	*2281*
down a steep place into the *s*	Mk 5:13	*2281*
and were choked in the *s*	Mk 5:13	*2281*
and he was nigh unto the *s*	Mk 5:21	*2281*
ship was in the midst of the *s*	Mk 6:47	*2281*
unto them, walking upon the *s*	Mk 6:48	*2281*
they saw him walking upon the *s*	Mk 6:49	*2281*
he came unto the *s* of Galilee	Mk 7:31	*2281*
neck, and he were cast into the *s*	Mk 9:42	*2281*
and be thou cast into the *s*	Mk 11:23	*2281*
from the *s* coast of Tyre and Sidon	Lk 6:17	*3882*
his neck, and he cast into the *s*	Lk 17:2	*2281*
root, and be thou planted in the *s*	Lk 17:6	*2281*
the *s* and the waves roaring	Lk 21:25	*2281*
Jesus went over the *s* of Galilee	Jn 6:1	*2281*
which is the *s* of Tiberias	Jn 6:1	*2281*
disciples went down unto the *s*	Jn 6:16	*2281*
went over the *s* toward Capernaum	Jn 6:17	*2281*
the *s* arose by reason of a great	Jn 6:18	*2281*
they see Jesus walking on the *s*	Jn 6:19	*2281*
s saw that there was none other	Jn 6:22	*2281*
him on the other side of the *s*	Jn 6:25	*2281*
disciples at the *s* of Tiberias	Jn 21:1	*2281*
and did cast himself into the *s*	Jn 21:7	*2281*
made heaven, and earth, and the *s*	Acts 4:24	*2281*
land of Egypt, and in the Red *s*	Acts 7:36	*2281*
whose house is by the *s* side	Acts 10:6	*2281*
one Simon a tanner by the *s* side	Acts 10:32	*2281*
made heaven, and earth, and the *s*	Acts 14:15	*2281*
Paul to go as it were to the *s*	Acts 17:14	*2281*
had sailed over the *s* of Cilicia	Acts 27:5	*3989*
had let down the boat into the *s*	Acts 27:30	*2281*
and cast out the wheat into the *s*	Acts 27:38	*2281*
committed themselves unto the *s*	Acts 27:40	*2281*
cast themselves first into the *s*	Acts 27:43	
though he hath escaped the *s*	Acts 28:4	*2281*
of Israel be as the sand of the *s*	Rom 9:27	*2281*
and all passed through the *s*	1Cor 10:1	*2281*
Moses in the cloud and in the *s*	1Cor 10:2	*2281*
wilderness, in perils in the *s*	2Cor 11:26	*2281*
is by the *s* shore innumerable	Heb 11:12	*2281*
through the Red *s* as by dry land	Heb 11:29	*2281*
of the *s* driven with the wind	Jas 1:6	*2281*
serpents, and of things in the *s*	Jas 3:7	*1724*
Raging waves of the *s*, foaming	Jude 13	*2281*
a *s* of glass like unto crystal	Rev 4:6	*2281*
earth, and such as are in the *s*	Rev 5:13	*2281*
blow on the earth, nor on the *s*	Rev 7:1	*2281*
given to hurt the earth and the *s*	Rev 7:2	*2281*
Hurt not the earth, neither the *s*	Rev 7:3	*2281*
with fire was cast into the *s*	Rev 8:8	*2281*
third part of the *s* became blood	Rev 8:8	*2281*
the creatures which were in the *s*	Rev 8:9	*2281*
he set his right foot upon the *s*	Rev 10:2	*2281*
which I saw stand upon the *s*	Rev 10:5	*2281*
things that therein are, and the *s*	Rev 10:6	*2281*
angel which standeth upon the *s*	Rev 10:8	*2281*
of the earth and of the *s*	Rev 12:12	*2281*
And I stood upon the sand of the *s*	Rev 13:1	*2281*
saw a beast rise up out of the *s*	Rev 13:1	*2281*
made heaven, and earth, and the *s*	Rev 14:7	*2281*
I saw as it were a *s* of glass	Rev 15:2	*2281*
his name, stand on the *s* of glass	Rev 15:2	*2281*
poured out his vial upon the *s*	Rev 16:3	*2281*
every living soul died in the *s*	Rev 16:3	*2281*
sailors, and as many as trade by *s*	Rev 18:17	*2281*
the *s* by reason of her costliness	Rev 18:19	*2281*
millstone, and cast it into the *s*	Rev 18:21	*2281*
of whom is as the sand of the *s*	Rev 20:8	*2281*
the *s* gave up the dead which were	Rev 20:13	*2281*
and there was no more *s*	Rev 21:1	*2281*

SEAFARING {1}

that wast inhabited of *s* men	Eze 26:17	3220

SEAL {26}

name, and sealed them with his *s*	1Kin 21:8	2368
Levites, and priests, *s* unto it	Neh 9:38	2856
s it with the king's ring	Est 8:8	2856
It is turned as clay to the *s*	Job 38:14	2368
up together as with a close *s*	Job 41:15	2368
Set me as a *s* upon thine heart,	Song 8:6	2368
heart, as a *s* upon thine arm	Song 8:6	2368
s the law among my disciples	Is 8:16	2856
s them, and take witnesses in the	Jer 32:44	2856
to *s* up the vision and prophecy,	Dan 9:24	2856
s the book, even to the time of	Dan 12:4	2856
set to his *s* that God is true	Jn 3:33	*4972*
a *s* of the righteousness of the	Rom 4:11	*4973*
for the *s* of mine apostleship are	1Cor 9:2	*4973*
God standeth sure, having this *s*	2Ti 2:19	*4973*
when he had opened the second *s*	Rev 6:3	*4973*
And when he had opened the third *s*	Rev 6:5	*4973*
when he had opened the fourth *s*	Rev 6:7	*4973*
And when he had opened the fifth *s*	Rev 6:9	*4973*
when he had opened the sixth *s*	Rev 6:12	*4973*
having the *s* of the living God	Rev 7:2	*4973*
when he had opened the seventh *s*	Rev 8:1	*4973*
the *s* of God in their foreheads	Rev 9:4	*4973*
S up those things which the seven	Rev 10:4	*4972*
set a *s* upon him, that he should	Rev 20:3	*4972*
S not the sayings of the prophecy	Rev 22:10	*4972*

SEALED {36}

me, and *s* up among my treasures	Deut 32:34	2856
s them with his seal, and sent the	1Kin 21:8	2856
Now those that *s* were, Nehemiah,	Neh 10:1	2856
and *s* with the king's ring	Est 3:12	2856
s with the king's ring, may no	Est 8:8	2856
s it with the king's ring, and	Est 8:10	2856
My transgression is *s* up in a bag	Job 14:17	2856
a spring shut up, a fountain *s*	Song 4:12	2856
as the words of a book that is *s*	Is 29:11	2856
for it is *s*	Is 29:11	2856
s it, and took witnesses, and	Jer 32:10	2856
both that which was *s* according	Jer 32:11	2856
of the purchase, both which is *s*	Jer 32:14	2856
the king *s* it with his own signet	Dan 6:17	2857
s till the time of the end	Dan 12:9	2856
for him hath God the Father *s*	Jn 6:27	*4972*
have *s* to them this fruit, I will	Rom 15:28	*4972*
Who hath also *s* us, and given the	2Cor 1:22	*4972*
ye were *s* with that holy Spirit	Eph 1:13	*4972*
whereby ye are *s* unto the day of	Eph 4:30	*4972*
the backside, *s* with seven seals	Rev 5:1	*2696*
till we have *s* the servants of	Rev 7:3	*4972*
the number of them which were *s*	Rev 7:4	*4972*
and there were *s* an hundred	Rev 7:4	*4972*
of Juda were *s* twelve thousand	Rev 7:5	*4972*
of Reuben were *s* twelve thousand	Rev 7:5	*4972*
of Gad were *s* twelve thousand	Rev 7:5	*4972*
of Aser were *s* twelve thousand	Rev 7:6	*4972*
Nepthalim were *s* twelve thousand	Rev 7:6	*4972*
Manasses were *s* twelve thousand	Rev 7:6	*4972*
of Simeon were *s* twelve thousand	Rev 7:7	*4972*
of Levi were *s* twelve thousand	Rev 7:7	*4972*
Issachar were *s* twelve thousand	Rev 7:7	*4972*
of Zabulon were *s* twelve thousand	Rev 7:8	*4972*
of Joseph were *s* twelve thousand	Rev 7:8	*4972*
Benjamin were *s* twelve thousand	Rev 7:8	*4972*

SEALEST {1}

Thou *s* up the sum, full of wisdom	Eze 28:12	2856

SEALETH {3}

and *s* up the stars	Job 9:7	2856
of men, and *s* their instruction,	Job 33:16	2856
He *s* up the hand of every man	Job 37:7	2856

SEALING {1}

s the stone, and setting a watch	Mt 27:66	*4972*

SEALS {5}

the backside, sealed with seven *s*	Rev 5:1	*4973*
book, and to loose the *s* thereof	Rev 5:2	*4973*
and to loose the seven *s* thereof	Rev 5:5	*4973*
book, and to open the *s* thereof	Rev 5:9	*4973*
when the Lamb opened one of the *s*	Rev 6:1	*4973*

SEAM {1}

now the coat was without *s*	Jn 19:23	*729*

SEARCH {48}

He shall not *s* whether it be good	Lev 27:33	1239
to *s* out a resting place for them	Num 10:33	8446
that they may *s* the land of	Num 13:2	8446
which we have gone to *s* it	Num 13:32	8446
which we passed through to *s* it	Num 14:7	8446
which Moses sent to *s* the land	Num 14:36	8446
the men that went to *s* the land	Num 14:38	8446
they shall *s* us out the land, and	Deut 1:22	2658

to *s* you out a place to pitch ... Deut 1:33 8446
shalt thou enquire, and make *s* ... Deut 13:14 2713
of Israel to *s* out the country ... Josh 2:2 2658
be come to *s* out all the country ... Josh 2:3 2658
to spy out the land, and to *s* it ... Judg 18:2 2713
said unto them, Go, *s* the land ... Judg 18:2 2713
that I will *s* him out throughout ... 1Sa 23:23 2664
to *s* the city, and to spy it out, ... 2Sa 10:3 2713
they shall *s* thine house, and the ... 1Kin 20:6 2664
unto the worshippers of Baal, *S* ... 2Kin 10:23 2664
servants come unto thee for to *s* ... 1Chr 19:3 2713
That *s* may be made in the book of ... Ezr 4:15 1240
s hath been made, and it is found ... Ezr 4:19 1240
let there be *s* made in the king's ... Ezr 5:17 1240
s was made in the house of the ... Ezr 6:1 1240
thyself to the *s* of their fathers ... Job 8:8 2714
it good that he should *s* you out ... Job 13:9 2713
thou walked in the *s* of the depth ... Job 38:16 2714
Shall not God *s* this out ... Ps 44:21 2713
They *s* out iniquities ... Ps 64:6 2664
they accomplish a diligent *s* ... Ps 64:6 2665
and my spirit made diligent *s* ... Ps 77:6 2664
S me, O God, and know my heart ... Ps 139:23 2713
of kings is to *s* out a matter ... Prov 25:2 2713
so for men to *s* their own glory ... Prov 25:27 2714
s out by wisdom concerning all ... Eccl 1:13 8446
mine heart to know, and to *s* ... Eccl 7:25 8446
I have not found it by secret *s* ... Jer 2:34 4290
I the LORD *s* the heart, I try the ... Jer 17:10 2713
when ye shall *s* for me with all ... Jer 29:13 1875
Let us *s* and try our ways, and turn ... Lam 3:40 2664
none did *s* or seek after them ... Eze 34:6 1875
did my shepherds *s* for my flock ... Eze 34:8 1875
I, even I, will both *s* my sheep ... Eze 34:11 1875
end of seven months shall they *s* ... Eze 39:14 2713
in the top of Carmel, I will *s* ... Amos 9:3 2664
that I will *s* Jerusalem with ... Zeph 1:12 2664
s diligently for the young child ... Mt 2:8 *1833*
S the scriptures ... Jn 5:39 *2045*
S, and look ... Jn 7:52 *2045*

SEARCHED {20}
Laban *s* all the tent, but found ... Gen 31:34 4959
And he *s*, but found not the images ... Gen 31:35 2664
Whereas thou hast *s* all my stuff ... Gen 31:37 4959
And he *s*, and began at the eldest, ... Gen 44:12 2664
s the land from the wilderness of ... Num 13:21 8446
of the land which they had *s* unto ... Num 13:32 8446
were of them that *s* the land ... Num 14:6 8446
the days in which ye *s* the land ... Num 14:34 8446
the valley of Eshcol, and *s* it out ... Deut 1:24 7270
Lo this, we have *s* it, so it is ... Job 5:27 2713
he prepared it, yea, and *s* it out ... Job 28:27 2713
cause which I knew not I *s* out ... Job 29:16 2713
whilst ye *s* out what to say ... Job 32:11 2713
the number of his years be *s* out ... Job 36:26 2714
O lord, thou hast *s* me, and known ... Ps 139:1 2713
of the earth *s* out beneath ... Jer 31:37 2713
the LORD, though it cannot be *s* ... Jer 46:23 2713
How are the things of Esau *s* out ... Obad 6 2664
s the scriptures daily, whether ... Acts 17:11 *350*
s diligently, who prophesied of ... 1Pet 1:10 *1830*

SEARCHEST {2}
mine iniquity, and *s* after my sin ... Job 10:6 1875
s for her as for hid treasures ... Prov 2:4 2664

SEARCHETH {8}
for the LORD *s* all hearts ... 1Chr 28:9 1875
darkness, and *s* out all perfection ... Job 28:3 2713
he *s* after every green thing ... Job 39:8 1875
but his neighbour cometh and *s* him ... Prov 18:17 2713
that hath understanding *s* him out ... Prov 28:11 2713
he that *s* the hearts knoweth what ... Rom 8:27 *2045*
for the Spirit *s* all things ... 1Cor 2:10 *2045*
that I am he which *s* the reins ... Rev 2:23 *2045*

SEARCHING {5}
they returned from *s* of the land ... Num 13:25 8446
Canst thou by *s* find out God ... Job 11:7 2714
s all the inward parts of the ... Prov 20:27 2664
there is no *s* of his ... Is 40:28 2714
S what, or what manner of time ... 1Pet 1:11 *2045*

SEARCHINGS {1}
there were great *s* of heart ... Judg 5:16 2714

SEARED {1}
conscience *s* with a hot iron ... 1Ti 4:2 *2743*

SEAS {25}
of the waters called he *S* ... Gen 1:10 3220
and fill the waters in the *s* ... Gen 1:22 3220
and scales in the waters, in the *s* ... Lev 11:9 3220
have not fins and scales in the *s* ... Lev 11:10 3220
suck of the abundance of the *s* ... Deut 33:19 3220
things that are therein, the *s* ... Neh 9:6 3220
through the paths of the *s* ... Ps 8:8 3220
For he hath founded it upon the *s* ... Ps 24:2 3220
Which stilleth the noise of the *s* ... Ps 65:7 3220
heaven and earth praise him, the *s* ... Ps 69:34 3220
in heaven, and in earth, in the *s* ... Ps 135:6 3220
a noise like the noise of the *s* ... Is 17:12 3220
to me above the sand of the *s* ... Jer 15:8 3220
borders are in the midst of the *s* ... Eze 27:4 3220
glorious in the midst of the *s* ... Eze 27:25 3220
broken thee in the midst of the *s* ... Eze 27:26 3220
of the *s* in the day of thy ruin ... Eze 27:27 3220
thy wares went forth out of the *s* ... Eze 27:33 3220
thou shalt be broken by the *s* in ... Eze 27:34 3220
of God, in the midst of the *s* ... Eze 28:2 3220
are slain in the midst of the *s* ... Eze 28:8 3220
and thou art as a whale in the *s* ... Eze 32:2 3220
of his palace between the *s* in ... Dan 11:45 3220
the deep, in the midst of the *s* ... Jonah 2:3 3220
into a place where two *s* met ... Acts 27:41 *1337*

SEASON {56}
and they continued a *s* in ward ... Gen 40:4 3117
in his *s* from year to year ... Ex 13:10 4150
offering shalt thou *s* with salt ... Lev 2:13 4414
I will give you rain in due *s* ... Lev 26:4 6256
the passover at his appointed *s* ... Num 9:2 4150
shall keep it in his appointed *s* ... Num 9:3 4150
s among the children of Israel ... Num 9:7 4150
of the LORD in his appointed *s* ... Num 9:13 4150
to offer unto me in their due *s* ... Num 28:2 4150
rain of your land in his due *s* ... Deut 11:14 6256
at the *s* that thou camest forth ... Deut 16:6 4150
the rain unto thy land in his *s* ... Deut 28:12 6256
dwelt in the wilderness a long *s* ... Josh 24:7 3117
And he said, About this *s*, ... 2Kin 4:16 4150
bare a son at that *s* that Elisha ... 2Kin 4:17 4150
were at that *s* in the high place ... 1Chr 21:29 6256
Now for a long *s* Israel hath been ... 2Chr 15:3 3117
shock of corn cometh in in his *s* ... Job 5:26 6256
are pierced in me in the night *s* ... Job 30:17
bring forth Mazzaroth in his *s* ... Job 38:32 6256
bringeth forth his fruit in his *s* ... Ps 1:3 6256
and in the night *s*, and am not ... Ps 22:2
give them their meat in due *s* ... Ps 104:27 6256
givest them their meat in due *s* ... Ps 145:15 6256
and a word spoken in due *s* ... Prov 15:23 6256
To every thing there is a *s* ... Eccl 3:1 2165
and thy princes eat in due *s* ... Eccl 10:17 6256
a word in *s* to him that is weary ... Is 50:4
former and the latter, in his *s* ... Jer 5:24 6256
not be day and night in their *s* ... Jer 33:20 6256
the shower to come down in his *s* ... Eze 34:26 6256
lives were prolonged for a *s* ... Dan 7:12 2166
and my wine in the *s* thereof ... Hos 2:9 4150
to give them meat in due *s* ... Mt 24:45 *2540*
saltness, wherewith will ye *s* it ... Mk 9:50 *741*
And at the *s* he sent to the ... Mk 12:2 *2540*
shall be fulfilled in their *s* ... Lk 1:20 *2540*
he departed from him for a *s* ... Lk 4:13 *2540*
their portion of meat in due *s* ... Lk 12:42 *2540*
that *s* some that told him of the ... Lk 13:1 *2540*
at the *s* he sent a servant to the ... Lk 20:10 *2540*
desirous to see him of a long *s* ... Lk 23:8
down at a certain *s* into the pool ... Jn 5:4 *2540*
ye were willing for a *s* to ... Jn 5:35 *5610*
blind, not seeing the sun for a *s* ... Acts 13:11 *2540*
he himself stayed in Asia for a *s* ... Acts 19:22 *5550*
when I have a convenient *s* ... Acts 24:25 *2540*
sorry, though it were but for a *s* ... 2Cor 7:8 *5610*
for in due *s* we shall reap, if we ... Gal 6:9 *2540*
be instant in *s* ... 2Ti 4:2 *2121*
out of *s*; reprove ... 2Ti 4:2 *171*
he therefore departed for a *s* ... Philem 15 *5610*
the pleasures of sin for a *s* ... Heb 11:25 *4340*
rejoice, though now for a *s* ... 1Pet 1:6 *3641*
should rest yet for a little *s* ... Rev 6:11 *5550*
that he must be loosed a little *s* ... Rev 20:3 *5550*

SEASONED {2}
savour, wherewith shall it be *s* ... Lk 14:34 *741*
s with salt, that ye may know how ... Col 4:6 *741*

SEASONS {12}
let them be for signs, and for *s* ... Gen 1:14 4150
them judge the people at all *s* ... Ex 18:22 6256
they judged the people at all *s* ... Ex 18:26 6256
ye shall proclaim in their *s* ... Lev 23:4 4150
also instruct me in the night *s* ... Ps 16:7
He appointed the moon for *s* ... Ps 104:19 4150
And he changeth the times and the *s* ... Dan 2:21 2166
render him the fruits in their *s* ... Mt 21:41 *2540*
you to know the times or the *s* ... Acts 1:7 *2540*
rain from heaven, and fruitful *s* ... Acts 14:17 *2540*
I have been with you at all *s* ... Acts 20:18 *5550*
But of the times and the *s* ... 1Th 5:1 *2540*

SEAT {58}
shalt make a mercy *s* of pure gold ... Ex 25:17
in the two ends of the mercy *s* ... Ex 25:18
even of the mercy *s* shall ye make ... Ex 25:19
the mercy *s* with their wings ... Ex 25:20
toward the mercy *s* shall the ... Ex 25:20
the mercy *s* above upon the ark ... Ex 25:21
with thee from above the mercy *s* ... Ex 25:22
thou shalt put the mercy *s* upon ... Ex 26:34
before the mercy *s* that is over ... Ex 30:6
the mercy *s* that is thereupon, and ... Ex 31:7
staves thereof, with the mercy *s* ... Ex 35:12
he made the mercy *s* of pure gold ... Ex 37:6
on the two ends of the mercy *s* ... Ex 37:7
out of the mercy *s* made he the ... Ex 37:8
with their wings over the mercy *s* ... Ex 37:9
staves thereof, and the mercy *s* ... Ex 39:35
put the mercy *s* above upon the ... Ex 40:20
the vail before the mercy *s* ... Lev 16:2
in the cloud upon the mercy *s* ... Lev 16:2
s that is upon the testimony ... Lev 16:13
finger upon the mercy *s* eastward ... Lev 16:14
before the mercy *s* shall he ... Lev 16:14
and sprinkle it upon the mercy *s* ... Lev 16:15
and before the mercy *s* ... Lev 16:15
mercy *s* that was upon the ark of ... Num 7:89
And he arose out of his *s* ... Judg 3:20 3678
Now Eli the priest sat upon a *s* ... 1Sa 1:9 3678
Eli sat upon a *s* by the wayside ... 1Sa 4:13 3678
that he fell from off the *s* ... 1Sa 4:18 3678
because thy *s* will be empty ... 1Sa 20:18 4186
And the king sat upon his *s* ... 1Sa 20:25 4186
times, even upon a *s* by the wall ... 1Sa 20:25 4186
The Tachmonite that sat in the *s* ... 2Sa 23:8 7674
caused a *s* to be set for the ... 1Kin 2:19 3678
either side on the place of the *s* ... 1Kin 10:19 7675
and of the place of the mercy *s* ... 1Chr 28:11
set his *s* above all the princes ... Est 3:1 3678
that I might come even to his *s* ... Job 23:3 8499
I prepared my *s* in the street ... Job 29:7 4186
sitteth in the *s* of the scornful ... Ps 1:1 4186
on a *s* in the high places of the ... Prov 9:14 3678
where was the *s* of the image of ... Eze 8:3 4186
I am a God, I sit in the *s* of God ... Eze 28:2 4186
cause the *s* of violence to come ... Amos 6:3 7675
and the Pharisees sit in Moses' *s* ... Mt 23:2 *2515*
he was set down on the judgment *s* ... Mt 27:19 *968*
sat down in the judgment *s* in a ... Jn 19:13 *968*
and brought him to the judgment *s* ... Acts 18:12 *968*
he drave them from the judgment *s* ... Acts 18:16 *968*
and beat him before the judgment *s* ... Acts 18:17 *968*
day sitting on the judgment *s* ... Acts 25:6 *968*
I stand at Caesar's judgment *s* ... Acts 25:10 *968*
morrow I sat on the judgment *s* ... Acts 25:17 *968*
before the judgment *s* of Christ ... Rom 14:10 *968*
before the judgment *s* of Christ ... 2Cor 5:10 *968*
dwellest, even where Satan's *s* is ... Rev 2:13 *2362*
gave him his power, and his *s* ... Rev 13:2 *2362*
his vial upon the *s* of the beast ... Rev 16:10 *2362*

SEATED {1}
portion of the lawgiver, was he *s* ... Deut 33:21 5603

SEATS {11}
the *s* of them that sold doves, ... Mt 21:12 *2515*
the chief *s* in the synagogues, ... Mt 23:6 *4410*
the *s* of them that sold doves ... Mk 11:15 *2515*
the chief *s* in the synagogues, and ... Mk 12:39 *4410*
put down the mighty from their *s* ... Lk 1:52 *2362*
the uppermost *s* in the synagogues ... Lk 11:43 *4410*
the highest *s* in the synagogues, ... Lk 20:46 *4410*
and draw you before the judgment *s* ... Jas 2:6
the throne were four and twenty *s* ... Rev 4:4 *2362*
upon the *s* I saw four and twenty ... Rev 4:4 *2362*
which sat before God on their *s* ... Rev 11:16 *2362*

SEATWARD {1}
even to the mercy *s* were the ... Ex 37:9

SEBA *(se'-bah)* {4} See SABEANS, SHEBA.
1. A son of Cush.
S, and Havilah, and Sabtah, and ... Gen 10:7 5434
S, and Havilah, and Sabta, and ... 1Chr 1:9 5434
2. The land.
of Sheba and *S* shall offer gifts ... Ps 72:10 5434
ransom, Ethiopia and *S* for thee ... Is 43:3 5434

SEBAM See SHEBAM.

SEBAT *(se'-bat)* {1} *The eleventh month of the Hebrew year.*
month, which is the month *S* ... Zec 1:7 7627

SECACAH *(se-ca'-cah)* {1} *A village in Judah.*
Beth-arabah, Middin, and *S* ... Josh 15:61 5527

SECHU *(se'-ku)* {1} *A city in Benjamin.*
came to a great well that is in *S* ... 1Sa 19:22 7906

SECOND {173}
and the morning were the *s* day ... Gen 1:8 8145
the name of the *s* river is Gihon ... Gen 2:13 8145
with lower, *s*, and third stories ... Gen 6:16 8145
of Noah's life, in the *s* month ... Gen 7:11 8145
And in the *s* month, on the seven ... Gen 8:14 8145
Abraham out of heaven the *s* time ... Gen 22:15 8145
again, and bare Jacob a *s* son ... Gen 30:7 8145
Leah's maid bare Jacob a *s* son ... Gen 30:12 8145
And so commanded he the *s*, and the ... Gen 32:19 8145
And he slept and dreamed the *s* time ... Gen 41:5 8145
in the *s* chariot which he had ... Gen 41:43 4932
the name of the *s* called he ... Gen 41:52 8145
now we had returned this *s* time ... Gen 43:10
they came unto him the *s* year ... Gen 47:18 8145
And when he went out the *s* day ... Ex 2:13 8145
on the fifteenth day of the *s* ... Ex 16:1 8145
curtain, in the coupling of the *s* ... Ex 26:4 8145
that is in the coupling of the *s* ... Ex 26:5 8145
the curtain which coupleth the *s* ... Ex 26:10 8145
for the *s* side of the tabernacle ... Ex 26:20 8145
the *s* row shall be an emerald, a ... Ex 28:18 8145
curtain, in the coupling of the *s* ... Ex 36:11 8145
was in the coupling of the *s* ... Ex 36:12 8145
the curtain which coupleth the *s* ... Ex 36:17 8145
And the *s* row, an emerald, a ... Ex 39:11 8145
in the first month in the *s* year ... Ex 40:17 8145
he shall offer the *s* for a burnt ... Lev 5:10 8145
it shall be washed the *s* time ... Lev 13:58 8145
on the first day of the *s* month ... Num 1:1 8145
in the *s* year after they were ... Num 1:1 8145
on the first day of the *s* month ... Num 1:18 8145
shall set forth in the *s* rank ... Num 2:16 8145
On the *s* day Nethaneel the son of ... Num 7:18 8145
in the first month of the *s* year ... Num 9:1 8145
The fourteenth day of the *s* month ... Num 9:11 8145
When ye blow an alarm the *s* time ... Num 10:6 8145
the *s* month, in the *s* year ... Num 10:11 8145
on the *s* day ye shall offer ... Num 29:17 8145
the children of Israel the *s* time ... Josh 5:2 8145
the *s* day they compassed the city ... Josh 6:14 8145
which took it on the *s* day ... Josh 10:32 8145
the *s* lot came forth to Simeon, ... Josh 19:1 8145
even the *s* bullock of seven years ... Judg 6:25 8145

S

place, and take the *s* bullock ... Judg 6:26 8145
the *s* bullock was offered upon ... Judg 6:28 8145
children of Benjamin the *s* day ... Judg 20:24 8145
them out of Gibeah the *s* day ... Judg 20:25 8145
and the name of his *s*, Abiah ... 1Sa 8:2 4932
which was the *s* day of the month, ... 1Sa 20:27 8145
no meat the *s* day of the month ... 1Sa 20:34 8145
I will not smite him the *s* time ... 1Sa 26:8 8138
And his *s*, Chileab, of Abigail the ... 2Sa 3:3 4932
and when he sent again the *s* time ... 2Sa 14:29 8145
month Zif, which is the *s* month ... 1Kin 6:1 8145
appeared to Solomon the *s* time ... 1Kin 9:2 8145
the *s* year of Asa king of Judah ... 1Kin 15:25 8147
And he said, Do it the *s* time ... 1Kin 18:34 8138
And they did it the *s* time ... 1Kin 18:34 8138
of the LORD came again the *s* time ... 1Kin 19:7 8145
the *s* year of Jehoram the son of ... 2Kin 1:17 8147
Then he sent out a *s* on horseback ... 2Kin 9:19 8145
wrote a letter the *s* time to them ... 2Kin 10:6 8145
In the *s* year of Joash son of ... 2Kin 14:1 8147
In the *s* year of Pekah the son of ... 2Kin 15:32 8147
and in the *s* year that which ... 2Kin 19:29 8145
and the priests of the *s* order ... 2Kin 23:4 4932
like unto these had the *s* pillar ... 2Kin 25:17 8145
priest, and Zephaniah the *s* priest ... 2Kin 25:18 4932
Eliab, and Abinadab the *s*, and ... 1Chr 2:13 8145
the *s* Daniel, of Abigail the ... 1Chr 3:1 8145
the *s* Jehoiakim, the third ... 1Chr 3:15 8145
the name of the *s* was Zelophehad ... 1Chr 7:15 8145
Bela his firstborn, Ashbel the *s* ... 1Chr 8:1 8145
Ulam his firstborn, Jehush the *s* ... 1Chr 8:39 8145
Ezer the first, Obadiah the *s* ... 1Chr 12:9 8145
their brethren of the *s* degree ... 1Chr 15:18 4932
was the chief, and Zizah the *s* ... 1Chr 23:11 8145
Jeriah the first, Amariah the *s* ... 1Chr 23:19 8145
Micah the first, and Jesiah the *s* ... 1Chr 23:20 8145
to Jehoiarib, the *s* to Jedaiah, ... 1Chr 24:7 8145
Jeriah the first, Amariah the *s* ... 1Chr 24:23 8145
the *s* to Gedaliah, who with his ... 1Chr 25:9 8145
the firstborn, Jediael the *s* ... 1Chr 26:2 8145
the firstborn, Jehozabad the *s* ... 1Chr 26:4 8145
Hilkiah the *s*, Tebaliah the third ... 1Chr 26:11 8145
over the course of the *s* month ... 1Chr 27:4 8145
the son of David king the *s* time ... 1Chr 29:22 8145
in the *s* day of the month ... 2Chr 3:2 8145
pay unto him, both the *s* year ... 2Chr 27:5 8145
keep the passover in the *s* month ... 2Chr 30:2 8145
unleavened bread in the *s* month ... 2Chr 30:13 8145
the fourteenth day of the *s* month ... 2Chr 30:15 8145
put him in the *s* chariot that he ... 2Chr 35:24 4932
basons of a *s* sort four hundred ... Ezr 1:10 4932
Now in the *s* year of their coming ... Ezr 3:8 8145
God at Jerusalem, in the *s* month ... Ezr 3:8 8145
So it ceased unto the *s* year of ... Ezr 4:24 8648
on the *s* day were gathered ... Neh 8:13 8145
son of Senuah was *s* over the city ... Neh 11:9 4932
Bakbukiah the *s* among his ... Neh 11:17 4932
into the *s* house of the women ... Est 2:14 8145
were gathered together the *s* time ... Est 2:19 8145
the *s* day at the banquet of wine ... Est 7:2 8145
to confirm this *s* letter of Purim ... Est 9:29 8145
and the name of the *s*, Kezia ... Job 42:14 8145
is one alone, and there is not a *s* ... Eccl 4:8 8145
with the *s* child that shall stand ... Eccl 4:15 8145
shall set his hand again the *s* ... Is 11:11 8145
the *s* year that which springeth ... Is 37:30 8145
the LORD came unto me the *s* time ... Jer 1:13 8145
the LORD came unto me the *s* time ... Jer 13:3 8145
came unto Jeremiah the *s* time ... Jer 33:1 8145
it came to pass the *s* day after ... Jer 41:4 8145
The *s* pillar also and the ... Jer 52:22 8145
priest, and Zephaniah the *s* priest ... Jer 52:24 4932
the *s* face was the face of a man, ... Eze 10:14 8145
on the *s* day thou shalt offer a ... Eze 43:22 8145
in the *s* year of the reign of ... Dan 2:1 8147
And behold another beast, a *s* ... Dan 7:5 8578
LORD came unto Jonah the *s* time ... Jonah 3:1 8145
shall not rise up the *s* time ... Nah 1:9
gate, and an howling from the *s* ... Zeph 1:10 4932
In the *s* year of Darius the king, ... Hag 1:1 8147
in the *s* year of Darius the king ... Hag 1:15 8147
in the *s* year of Darius, came the ... Hag 2:10 8147
in the *s* year of Darius, came the ... Zec 1:1 8147
in the *s* year of Darius, came the ... Zec 1:7 8147
in the *s* chariot black horses ... Zec 6:2 8145
And he came to the *s*, and said ... Mt 21:30 *1208*
Likewise the *s* also, and the third ... Mt 22:26 *1208*
the *s* is like unto it, Thou shalt ... Mt 22:39 *1208*
He went away again the *s* time ... Mt 26:42 *1208*
the *s* took her, and died, neither ... Mk 12:21 *1208*
the *s* is like, namely this, Thou ... Mk 12:31 *1208*
And the *s* time the cock crew ... Mk 14:72 *1208*
it came to pass on the *s* sabbath ... Lk 6:1 *1207*
if he shall come in the *s* watch ... Lk 12:38 *1208*
the *s* came, saying, Lord, thy ... Lk 19:18 *1208*
the *s* took her to wife, and he ... Lk 20:30 *1208*
can he enter the *s* time into his ... Jn 3:4 *1208*
This is again the *s* miracle that ... Jn 4:54 *1208*
He saith to him again the *s* time ... Jn 21:16 *1208*
at the *s* time Joseph was made ... Acts 7:13 *1208*
spake unto him again the *s* time ... Acts 10:15 *1208*
the *s* ward, they came unto the ... Acts 12:10 *1208*
it is also written in the *s* psalm ... Acts 13:33 *1208*
the *s* man is the Lord from heaven ... 1Cor 15:47 *1208*
that ye might have a *s* benefit ... 2Cor 1:15 *1208*
as if I were present, the *s* time ... 2Cor 13:2 *1208*
The *s* epistle to the Corinthians ... 2Cor *s* *1208*
The *s* epistle to the ... 2Th *s* *1208*
The *s* epistle unto Timotheus, ... 2Ti *s* *1208*
brought before Nero the *s* time ... 2Ti *s* *1208*
the first and *s* admonition reject ... Titus 3:10 *1208*
place have been sought for the *s* ... Heb 8:7 *1208*
And after the *s* veil, the ... Heb 9:3 *1208*
But into the *s* went the high ... Heb 9:7 *1208*
for him shall he appear the *s* ... Heb 9:28 *1208*
that he may establish the *s* ... Heb 10:9 *1208*
This *s* epistle, beloved, I now ... 2Pet 3:1 *1208*
shall not be hurt of the *s* death ... Rev 2:11 *1208*
the *s* beast like a calf, and the ... Rev 4:7 *1208*
And when he had opened the *s* seal ... Rev 6:3 *1208*
I heard the *s* beast say ... Rev 6:3 *1208*
the *s* angel sounded, and as it ... Rev 8:8 *1208*
The *s* woe is past ... Rev 11:14 *1208*
the *s* angel poured out his vial ... Rev 16:3 *1208*
on such the *s* death hath no power ... Rev 20:6 *1208*
This is the *s* death ... Rev 20:14 *1208*
which is the *s* death ... Rev 21:8 *1208*
the *s*, sapphire ... Rev 21:19 *1208*

SECONDARILY {1}
s prophets, thirdly teachers, ... 1Cor 12:28 *1208*

SECRET {68}
soul, come not thou into their *s* ... Gen 49:6 5475
and putteth it in a *s* place ... Deut 27:15 5643
The *s* things belong unto the LORD ... Deut 29:29 5641
I have a *s* errand unto thee, O ... Judg 3:19 5643
after my name, seeing it is *s* ... Judg 13:18 6383
they had emerods in their *s* parts ... 1Sa 5:9 8368
morning, and abide in a *s* place ... 1Sa 19:2 5643
that thou wouldest keep me *s* ... Job 14:13 5641
Hast thou heard the *s* of God ... Job 15:8 5475
is there any *s* thing with thee ... Job 15:11 328
shall be hid in his *s* places ... Job 20:26 6845
when the *s* of God was upon my ... Job 29:4 5475
and bind their faces in *s* ... Job 40:13 2934
in the *s* places doth he murder ... Ps 10:8 4565
a young lion lurking in *s* places ... Ps 17:12 4565
He made darkness his *s* place ... Ps 18:11 5643
cleanse thou me from *s* faults ... Ps 19:12 5641
The *s* of the LORD is with them ... Ps 25:14 5475
in the *s* of his tabernacle shall ... Ps 27:5 5643
Thou shalt hide them in the *s* of ... Ps 31:20 5643
Hide me from the *s* counsel of the ... Ps 64:2 5475
may shoot in *s* at the perfect ... Ps 64:4 4565
thee in the *s* place of thunder ... Ps 81:7 5643
our *s* sins in the light of thy ... Ps 90:8 5956
He that dwelleth in the *s* place ... Ps 91:1 5643
from thee, when I was made in *s* ... Ps 139:15 5643
but his *s* is with the righteous ... Prov 3:32 5475
and bread eaten in *s* is pleasant ... Prov 9:17 5643
A gift in *s* pacifieth anger ... Prov 21:14 5643
and discover not a *s* to another ... Prov 25:9 5475
Open rebuke is better than *s* love ... Prov 27:5 5641
into judgment, with every *s* thing ... Eccl 12:14 5956
in the *s* places of the stairs, ... Song 2:14 5643
LORD will discover their *s* parts ... Is 3:17 6596
and hidden riches of *s* places ... Is 45:3 4565
I have not spoken in *s*, in a dark ... Is 45:19 5643
spoken in *s* from the beginning ... Is 48:16 5643
I have not found it by *s* search ... Jer 2:34 5643
weep in *s* places for your pride ... Jer 13:17 4565
Can any hide himself in *s* places ... Jer 23:24 4565
I have uncovered his *s* places ... Jer 49:10 4565
in wait, and as a lion in *s* places ... Lam 3:10 4565
and they shall pollute my *s* place ... Eze 7:22 6845
there is no *s* that they can hide ... Eze 28:3 5640
God of heaven concerning this *s* ... Dan 2:18 7328
Then was the *s* revealed unto ... Dan 2:19 7328
He revealeth the deep and *s* things ... Dan 2:22 5642
The *s* which the king hath ... Dan 2:27 7328
this *s* is not revealed to me for ... Dan 2:30 7328
seeing thou couldest reveal this *s* ... Dan 2:47 7328
no *s* troubleth thee, tell me the ... Dan 4:9 7328
but he revealeth his *s* unto his ... Amos 3:7 5475
That thine alms may be in *s* ... Mt 6:4 *2927*
in *s* himself shall reward thee ... Mt 6:4 *2927*
pray to thy Father which is in *s* ... Mt 6:6 *2927*
in *s* shall reward thee openly ... Mt 6:6 *2927*
but unto thy Father which is in *s* ... Mt 6:18 *2927*
and thy Father, which seeth in *s* ... Mt 6:18 *2927*
kept *s* from the foundation of the ... Mt 13:35 *2928*
behold, he is in the *s* chambers ... Mt 24:26 *5009*
neither was any thing kept *s* ... Mk 4:22 *614*
For nothing is *s*, that shall not ... Lk 8:17 *2927*
a candle, putteth it in a *s* place ... Lk 11:33 *2926*
no man that doeth any thing in *s* ... Jn 7:4 *2927*
not openly, but as it were in *s* ... Jn 7:10 *2927*
and in *s* have I said nothing ... Jn 18:20 *2927*
which was kept *s* since the world ... Rom 16:25 *4601*
which are done of them in *s* ... Eph 5:12 *2931*

SECRETLY {20}
Wherefore didst thou flee away *s* ... Gen 31:27 2244
as thine own soul, entice thee *s* ... Deut 13:6 5643
he that smiteth his neighbour *s* ... Deut 27:24 5643
want of all things *s* in the siege ... Deut 28:57 5643
out of Shittim two men to spy *s* ... Josh 2:1 2791
saying, Commune with David *s* ... 1Sa 18:22 3909
David knew that Saul *s* practised ... 1Sa 23:9 2790
For thou didst it *s* ... 2Sa 12:12 5643
did *s* those things that were not ... 2Kin 17:9 2644
Now a thing was *s* brought to me ... Job 4:12 1589
if ye do *s* accept persons ... Job 13:10 5643
And my heart hath been *s* enticed ... Job 31:27 5643
He lieth in wait *s* as a lion in ... Ps 10:9 4565
thou shalt keep them *s* in a ... Ps 31:20 6845
the king asked him *s* in his house ... Jer 37:17 5643
the king sware *s* unto Jeremiah ... Jer 38:16 5643
spake to Gedaliah in Mizpah *s* ... Jer 40:15 5643
was as to devour the poor *s* ... Hab 3:14 4565
way, and called Mary her sister *s* ... Jn 11:28 *2977*
but *s* for fear of the Jews, ... Jn 19:38 *2928*

SECRETS {10}
her hand, and taketh him by the *s* ... Deut 25:11 4016
would shew thee the *s* of wisdom ... Job 11:6 8587
for he knoweth the *s* of the heart ... Ps 44:21 8587
A talebearer revealeth *s* ... Prov 11:13 5475
about as a talebearer revealeth *s* ... Prov 20:19 5475
a God in heaven that revealeth *s* ... Dan 2:28 7328
he that revealeth *s* maketh known ... Dan 2:29 7328
LORD of kings, and a revealer of *s* ... Dan 2:47 7328
the *s* of men by Jesus Christ ... Rom 2:16 *2927*
thus are the *s* of his heart made ... 1Cor 14:25 *2927*

SECT {5}
(which is the *s* of the Sadducees, ... Acts 5:17 *139*
there rose up certain of the *s* of ... Acts 15:5 *139*
of the *s* of the Nazarenes ... Acts 24:5 *139*
s of our religion I lived a ... Acts 26:5 *139*
for as concerning this *s*, we know ... Acts 28:22 *139*

SECU See SECHU.

SECUNDUS *(se-cun'-dus)* {1} *A Christian in Thessalonica.*
Thessalonians, Aristarchus and *S* ... Acts 20:4 *4580*

SECURE {7}
for the host was *s* ... Judg 8:11 983
of the Zidonians, quiet and *s* ... Judg 18:7 982
go, ye shall come unto a people *s* ... Judg 18:10 982
a people that were at quiet and *s* ... Judg 18:27 982
And thou shalt be *s*, because there ... Job 11:18 982
and they that provoke God are *s* ... Job 12:6 987
we will persuade him, and *s* you ... Mt 28:14 4160,275

SECURELY {2}
seeing he dwelleth *s* by thee ... Prov 3:29 983
pass by *s* as men averse from war ... Mic 2:8 983

SECURITY {1}
And when they had taken *s* of Jason ... Acts 17:9 *2425*

SEDITION {5}
that they have moved *s* within the ... Ezr 4:15 849
and *s* have been made therein ... Ezr 4:19 849
for a certain *s* made in the city ... Lk 23:19 *4714*
released unto them him that for *s* ... Lk 23:25 *4714*
a mover of *s* among all the Jews ... Acts 24:5 *4714*

SEDITIONS {1}
emulations, wrath, strife, *s* ... Gal 5:20 *1370*

SEDUCE {3}
shall shew signs and wonders, to *s* ... Mk 13:22 *635*
you concerning them that *s* you ... 1Jn 2:26 *4105*
to *s* my servants to commit ... Rev 2:20 *4105*

SEDUCED {3}
Manasseh *s* them to do more evil ... 2Kin 21:9 8582
they have also *s* Egypt, even they ... Is 19:13 8582
because they have *s* my people ... Eze 13:10 2937

SEDUCERS {1}
s shall wax worse and worse, ... 2Ti 3:13 *1114*

SEDUCETH {1}
but the way of the wicked *s* them ... Prov 12:26 8582

SEDUCING {1}
faith, giving heed to *s* spirits ... 1Ti 4:1 *4108*

SEE {597}
Adam to *s* what he would call them ... Gen 2:19 7200
to *s* if the waters were abated ... Gen 8:8 7200
the LORD came down to *s* the city ... Gen 11:5 7200
when the Egyptians shall *s* thee ... Gen 12:12 7200
now, and *s* whether they have done ... Gen 18:21 7200
And he said unto him, *S*, I have ... Gen 19:21 2009
Let me not *s* the death of the ... Gen 21:16 7200
were dim, so that he could not *s* ... Gen 27:1 7200
and blessed him, and said, *S* ... Gen 27:27 7200
I *s* your father's countenance, ... Gen 31:5 7200
Lift up now thine eyes, and *s* ... Gen 31:12 7200
s, God is witness betwixt me and ... Gen 31:50 7200
and afterward I will *s* his face ... Gen 32:20 7200
went out to *s* the daughters of ... Gen 34:1 7200
s whether it be well with thy ... Gen 37:14 7200
we shall *s* what will become of ... Gen 37:20 7200
and spake unto them, saying, *S* ... Gen 39:14 7200
And Pharaoh said unto Joseph, *S* ... Gen 41:41 7200
to *s* the nakedness of the land ye ... Gen 42:9 7200
but to *s* the nakedness of the ... Gen 42:12 7200
saying, Ye shall not *s* my face ... Gen 43:3 7200
unto us, Ye shall not *s* my face ... Gen 43:5 7200
ye shall *s* my face no more ... Gen 44:23 7200
for we may not *s* the man's face ... Gen 44:26 7200
lest peradventure I *s* the evil ... Gen 44:34 7200
And, behold, your eyes *s*, and the ... Gen 45:12 7200
S that ye fall not out by the way ... Gen 45:24
I will go and *s* him before I die ... Gen 45:28 7200
for age, so that he could not *s* ... Gen 48:10 7200
I had not thought to *s* thy face ... Gen 48:11 7200
women, and *s* them upon the stools ... Ex 1:16 7200
s this great sight, why the bush ... Ex 3:3 7200
saw that he turned aside to *s* ... Ex 3:4 7200
s whether they be yet alive ... Ex 4:18 7200
s that thou do all those wonders ... Ex 4:21 7200
did *s* that they were in evil case ... Ex 5:19 7200
Now shalt thou *s* what I will do ... Ex 6:1 7200
And the LORD said unto Moses, *S* ... Ex 7:1 7200
one cannot be able to *s* the earth ... Ex 10:5 7200
to thyself, *s* my face no more ... Ex 10:28 7200
I will *s* thy face again no more ... Ex 10:29 7200

when I *s* the blood, I will pass ... Ex 12:13 7200
the people repent when they *s* war ... Ex 13:17 7200
s the salvation of the LORD, ... Ex 14:13 7200
ye shall *s* them again no more for ... Ex 14:13 7200
then ye shall *s* the glory of the ... Ex 16:7 7200
S, for that the LORD hath given ... Ex 16:29 7200
that they may *s* the bread ... Ex 16:32 7200
to *s* whether he have put his hand ... Ex 22:8
If thou *s* the ass of him that ... Ex 23:5 7200
S, I have called by name Bezaleel ... Ex 31:2 7200
And Moses said unto the LORD, *S* ... Ex 33:12 7200
he said, Thou canst not *s* my face ... Ex 33:20 7200
for there shall no man *s* me ... Ex 33:20 7200
thou shalt *s* my back parts ... Ex 33:23 7200
art shall *s* the work of the LORD ... Ex 34:10 7200
unto the children of Israel, *S* ... Ex 35:30 7200
And if the priest *s* that, behold, ... Lev 13:8 7200
And the priest shall *s* him ... Lev 13:10 7200
the priest shall *s* the raw flesh ... Lev 13:15 7200
And the priest shall *s* him ... Lev 13:17 7200
the priest shall *s* the plague ... Lev 13:30 7200
priest go into it to *s* the plague ... Lev 14:36 7200
priest shall go in to *s* the house ... Lev 14:36 7200
s her nakedness, and she *s* his ... Lev 20:17 7200
in to *s* when the holy things are ... Num 4:20 7200
let me not *s* my wretchedness ... Num 11:15 7200
thou shalt *s* now whether my word ... Num 11:23 7200
And *s* the land, what it is ... Num 13:18 7200
Surely they shall not *s* the land ... Num 14:23 7200
any of them that provoked me *s* it ... Num 14:23 7200
that thence he might *s* the utmost ... Num 22:41 7200
from the top of the rocks I *s* him ... Num 23:9 7200
from whence thou mayest *s* them ... Num 23:13 7200
thou shalt *s* but the utmost part ... Num 23:13 7200
of them, and shalt not *s* them all ... Num 23:13 7200
I shall *s* him, but not now ... Num 24:17 7200
s the land which I have given ... Num 27:12 7200
from Kadesh-barnea to *s* the land ... Num 32:8 7200
shall *s* the land which I sware ... Num 32:11 7200
evil generation *s* that good land ... Deut 1:35 7200
he shall *s* it, and to him will I ... Deut 1:36 7200
s the good land that is beyond ... Deut 3:25 7200
the land which thou shalt *s* ... Deut 3:28 7200
wood and stone, which neither *s* ... Deut 4:28 7200
neither let me *s* this great fire ... Deut 18:16 7200
Thou shalt not *s* thy brother's ox ... Deut 22:1 7200
Thou shalt not *s* thy brother's ... Deut 22:4 7200
that he *s* no unclean thing in ... Deut 23:14 7200
s that thou art called by the ... Deut 28:10 7200
of thine eyes which thou shalt *s* ... Deut 28:34 7200
of thine eyes which thou shalt *s* ... Deut 28:67 7200
Thou shalt *s* it no more again ... Deut 28:68 7200
heart to perceive, and eyes to *s* ... Deut 29:4 7200
when they *s* the plagues of that ... Deut 29:22 7200
S, I have set before thee this ... Deut 30:15 7200
I will *s* what their end shall be ... Deut 32:20 7200
S now that I, even I, am he, and ... Deut 32:39 7200
Yet thou shalt *s* the land before ... Deut 32:52 7200
thee to *s* it with thine eyes ... Deut 34:4 7200
When ye *s* the ark of the covenant ... Josh 3:3 7200
And the LORD said unto Joshua, *S* ... Josh 6:2 7200
s, I have given into thy hand the ... Josh 8:1 7200
S, I have commanded you ... Josh 8:8 7200
by Jordan, a great altar to *s* to ... Josh 22:10 4758
S there come people down by the ... Judg 9:37 2009
he turned aside to *s* the carcase ... Judg 14:8 7200
s wherein his great strength ... Judg 16:5 7200
And *s*, and, behold, if the ... Judg 21:21 7200
thou shalt *s* an enemy in my ... 1Sa 2:32 5027
to wax dim, that he could not *s* ... 1Sa 3:2 7200
were dim, that he could not *s* ... 1Sa 4:15 7200
And *s*, if it goeth up by the way ... 1Sa 6:9 7200
saw the ark, and rejoiced to *s* it ... 1Sa 6:13 7200
S ye him whom the LORD hath ... 1Sa 10:24 7200
s this great thing, which the ... 1Sa 12:16 7200
s that your wickedness is great, ... 1Sa 12:17 7200
now, and *s* who is gone from us ... 1Sa 14:17 7200
s, I pray you, how mine eyes have ... 1Sa 14:29 7200
s wherein this sin hath been this ... 1Sa 14:38 7200
Samuel came no more to *s* Saul ... 1Sa 15:35 7200
that thou mightest *s* the battle ... 1Sa 17:28 7200
and what I *s*, that I will tell ... 1Sa 19:3 7200
the messengers again to *s* David ... 1Sa 19:15 7200
I pray thee, and *s* my brethren ... 1Sa 20:29 7200
servants, Lo, ye *s* the man is mad ... 1Sa 21:14 7200
s his place where his haunt is, ... 1Sa 23:22 7200
S therefore, and take knowledge of ... 1Sa 23:23 7200
Moreover, my father, *s*, yea, *s* ... 1Sa 24:11 7200
s that there is neither evil nor ... 1Sa 24:11 7200
and judge between me and thee, and *s* ... 1Sa 24:15 7200
s, I have hearkened to thy voice, ... 1Sa 25:35 7200
now *s* where the king's spear is, ... 1Sa 26:16 7200
that is, Thou shalt not *s* my face ... 2Sa 3:13 7200
when thou comest to *s* my face ... 2Sa 3:13 7200
S now, I dwell in an house of ... 2Sa 7:2 7200
when thy father cometh to *s* thee ... 2Sa 13:5 7200
meat in my sight, that I may *s* it ... 2Sa 13:5 7200
when the king was come to *s* him ... 2Sa 13:6 7200
house, and let him not *s* my face ... 2Sa 14:24 7200
he said unto his servants, *S* ... 2Sa 14:30 7200
let me *s* the king's face ... 2Sa 14:32 7200
And Absalom said unto him, *S* ... 2Sa 15:3 7200
S, I will tarry in the plain of ... 2Sa 15:28 7200
eyes of my lord the king may *s* it ... 2Sa 24:3 7200
s what answer I shall return to ... 2Sa 24:13 7200
Hiram came out from Tyre to *s* the ... 1Kin 9:12 7200
now *s* to thine own house, David ... 1Kin 12:16 7200
But Ahijah could not *s* ... 1Kin 14:4 7200
and Elijah said, *S*, thy son liveth ... 1Kin 17:23 7200
s how this man seeketh mischief ... 1Kin 20:7 7200
and mark, and *s* what thou doest ... 1Kin 20:22 7200
thou shalt *s* in that day, when ... 1Kin 22:25 7200
if thou *s* me when I am taken from ... 2Kin 2:10 7200
not look toward thee, nor *s* thee ... 2Kin 3:14 7200
s wind, neither shall ye *s* rain ... 2Kin 3:17 7200
s how he seeketh a quarrel ... 2Kin 5:7 7200
open his eyes, that he may *s* ... 2Kin 6:17 7200
of these men, that they may *s* ... 2Kin 6:20 7200
S ye how this son of a murderer ... 2Kin 6:32 7200
thou shalt *s* it with thine eyes, ... 2Kin 7:2 7200
) and let us send and *s* ... 2Kin 7:13 7200
of the Syrians, saying, Go and *s* ... 2Kin 7:14 7200
thou shalt *s* it with thine eyes, ... 2Kin 7:19 7200
to *s* Joram the son of Ahab in ... 2Kin 8:29 7200
of Judah was come down to *s* Joram ... 2Kin 9:16 7200
he came, and said, I *s* a company ... 2Kin 9:17 7200
s now this cursed woman, and bury ... 2Kin 9:34 6485
me, and *s* my zeal for the LORD ... 2Kin 10:16 7200
open, LORD, thine eyes, and *s* ... 2Kin 19:16 7200
thine eyes shall not *s* all the ... 2Kin 22:20 7200
said, What title is that that I *s* ... 2Kin 23:17 7200
now, David, *s* to thine own house ... 2Chr 10:16 7200
I did *s* all Israel scattered upon ... 2Chr 18:16 7200
thou shalt *s* on that day when ... 2Chr 18:24 7200
s the salvation of the LORD with ... 2Chr 20:17 7200
to *s* Jehoram the son of Ahab at ... 2Chr 22:6 7200
s that ye hasten the matter ... 2Chr 24:5
let us *s* one another in the face ... 2Chr 25:17 7200
hissing, as ye *s* with your eyes ... 2Chr 29:8 7200
them up to desolation, as ye *s* ... 2Chr 30:7 7200
neither shall thine eyes *s* all ... 2Chr 34:28 7200
for us to *s* the king's dishonour ... Ezr 4:14 2370
Ye *s* the distress that we are in, ... Neh 2:17 7200
They shall not know, neither *s* ... Neh 4:11 7200
didst *s* the affliction of our ... Neh 9:9 7200
to *s* whether Mordecai's matters ... Est 3:4 7200
so long as I *s* Mordecai the Jew ... Est 5:13 7200
For how can I endure to *s* the ... Est 8:6 7200
or how can I endure to *s* the ... Est 8:6 7200
neither let it *s* the dawning of ... Job 3:9 7200
ye *s* my casting down, and are ... Job 6:21 7200
mine eye shall no more *s* good ... Job 7:7 7200
hath seen me shall *s* me no more ... Job 7:8 7789
he goeth by me, and I *s* him not ... Job 9:11 7200
they flee away, they *s* no good ... Job 9:25 7200
therefore *s* thou mine affliction ... Job 10:15 7200
as for my hope, who shall *s* it ... Job 17:15 7789
yet in my flesh shall I *s* God ... Job 19:26 2372
Whom I shall *s* for myself ... Job 19:27 2372
which saw him shall *s* him no more ... Job 20:9
He shall not *s* the rivers ... Job 20:17 7200
His eyes shall *s* his destruction, ... Job 21:20 7200
darkness, that thou canst not *s* ... Job 22:11 7200
The righteous *s* it, and are glad ... Job 22:19 7200
right hand, that I cannot *s* him ... Job 23:9 7200
they that know him not *s* his days ... Job 24:1 2372
saying, No eye shall *s* me ... Job 24:15 7789
Then did he *s* it, and declare it ... Job 28:27 7200
Doth not he *s* my ways, and count ... Job 31:4 7200
he shall *s* his face with joy ... Job 33:26 7200
and his life shall *s* the light ... Job 33:28 7200
That which I *s* not teach thou me ... Job 34:32 2372
Look unto the heavens, and *s* ... Job 35:5 7200
thou sayest thou shalt not *s* him ... Job 35:14 7789
Every man may *s* it ... Job 36:25 2372
now men *s* not the bright light ... Job 37:21 7200
he will never *s* it ... Ps 10:11 7200
to *s* if there were any that did ... Ps 14:2 7200
thine Holy One to *s* corruption ... Ps 16:10 7200
All they that *s* me laugh me to ... Ps 22:7 7200
unless I had believed to *s* the ... Ps 27:13 7200
they that did *s* me without fled ... Ps 31:11 7200
taste and *s* that the LORD is good ... Ps 34:8 7200
many days, that he may *s* good ... Ps 34:12 7200
in thy light shall we *s* light ... Ps 36:9 7200
are cut off, thou shalt *s* it ... Ps 37:34 7200
many shall *s* it, and fear, and ... Ps 40:3 7200
And if he come to *s* me, he ... Ps 41:6 7200
for ever, and not *s* corruption ... Ps 49:9 7200
they shall never *s* light ... Ps 49:19 7200
The righteous also shall *s* ... Ps 52:6 7200
to *s* if there were any that did ... Ps 53:2 7200
that they may not *s* the sun ... Ps 58:8 2372
God shall let me *s* my desire upon ... Ps 59:10 7200
To *s* thy power and thy glory, so ... Ps 63:2 7200
they say, Who shall *s* them ... Ps 64:5 7200
all that *s* them shall flee away ... Ps 64:8 7200
Come and *s* the works of God ... Ps 66:5 7200
eyes be darkened, that they *s* not ... Ps 69:23 7200
The humble shall *s* this, and be ... Ps 69:32 7200
We *s* not our signs ... Ps 74:9 7200
that they which hate me may *s* it ... Ps 86:17 7200
that liveth, and shall not *s* death ... Ps 89:48 7200
s the reward of the wicked ... Ps 91:8 7200
Mine eye also shall *s* my desire ... Ps 92:11 5027
they say, The LORD shall not *s* ... Ps 94:7 7200
formed the eye, shall he not *s* ... Ps 94:9 5027
and all the people *s* his glory ... Ps 97:6 7200
That I may *s* the good of thy ... Ps 106:5 7200
These *s* the works of the LORD, and ... Ps 107:24 7200
The righteous shall *s* it, and ... Ps 107:42 7200
until he *s* his desire upon his ... Ps 112:8 7200
The wicked shall *s* it, and be ... Ps 112:10 7200
eyes have they, but they *s* not ... Ps 115:5 7200
therefore shall I *s* my desire ... Ps 118:7 7200
thee will be glad when they *s* me ... Ps 119:74 7200
and thou shalt *s* the good of ... Ps 128:5 7200
thou shalt *s* thy children's ... Ps 128:6 7200
eyes have they, but they *s* not ... Ps 135:16 7200
Thine eyes did *s* my substance ... Ps 139:16 7200
s if there be any wicked way in ... Ps 139:24 7200
Lest the LORD *s* it, and it ... Prov 24:18 7200
the righteous shall *s* their fall ... Prov 29:16 7200
thing whereof it may be said, *S* ... Eccl 1:10 7200
till I might *s* what was that good ... Eccl 2:3 7200
that they might *s* that they ... Eccl 3:18 7200
him to *s* what shall be after him ... Eccl 3:22 7200
is profit to them that *s* the sun ... Eccl 7:11 7200
to *s* the business that is done ... Eccl 8:16 7200
let me *s* thy countenance, let me ... Song 2:14 7200
to *s* the fruits of the valley ... Song 6:11 7200
to *s* whether the vine flourished, ... Song 6:11 7200
What will ye *s* in the Shulamite ... Song 6:13 2372
let us *s* if the vine flourish, ... Song 7:12 7200
hasten his work, that we may *s* it ... Is 5:19 7200
s ye indeed, but perceive not ... Is 6:9 7200
lest they *s* with their eyes, and ... Is 6:10 7200
Isaiah the son of Amoz did *s* ... Is 13:1 2372
They that *s* thee shall narrowly ... Is 14:16 7200
s ye, when he lifteth up an ... Is 18:3 7200
is lifted up, they will not *s* ... Is 26:11 2372
but they shall *s*, and be ashamed ... Is 26:11 2372
blind shall *s* out of obscurity ... Is 29:18 7200
Which say to the seers, *S* not ... Is 30:10 7200
thine eyes shall *s* thy teachers ... Is 30:20 7200
of them that *s* shall not be dim ... Is 32:3 7200
Thine eyes shall *s* the king in ... Is 33:17 2372
Thou shalt not *s* a fierce people, ... Is 33:19 7200
thine eyes shall *s* Jerusalem a ... Is 33:20 7200
they shall *s* the glory of the ... Is 35:2 7200
open thine eyes, O LORD, and *s* ... Is 37:17 7200
I said, I shall not *s* the LORD ... Is 38:11 7200
and all flesh shall *s* it together ... Is 40:5 7200
That they may *s*, and know, and ... Is 41:20 7200
and look, ye blind, that ye may *s* ... Is 42:18 7200
they *s* not, nor know ... Is 44:9 7200
their eyes, that they cannot *s* ... Is 44:18 7200
Thou hast heard, *s* all this ... Is 48:6 2372
servant of rulers, Kings shall *s* ... Is 49:7 7200
for they shall *s* eye to eye ... Is 52:8 7200
shall *s* the salvation of our God ... Is 52:10 7200
not been told them shall they *s* ... Is 52:15 7200
and when we shall *s* him, there is ... Is 53:2 7200
for sin, he shall *s* his seed ... Is 53:10 7200
He shall *s* of the travail of his ... Is 53:11 7200
up thine eyes round about, and *s* ... Is 60:4 7200
Then thou shalt *s*, and flow ... Is 60:5 7200
all that *s* them shall acknowledge ... Is 61:9 7200
shall *s* thy righteousness ... Is 62:2 7200
behold, *s*, we beseech thee, we ... Is 64:9 5027
And when ye *s* this, your heart ... Is 66:14 7200
and they shall come, and *s* my glory ... Is 66:18 7200
S, I have this day set thee over ... Jer 1:10 7200
I *s* a rod of an almond tree ... Jer 1:11 7200
and I said, I *s* a seething pot ... Jer 1:13 7200
over the isles of Chittim, and *s* ... Jer 2:10 7200
s if there be such a thing ... Jer 2:10 7200
s that it is an evil thing and ... Jer 2:19 7200
s thy way in the valley, know ... Jer 2:23 7200
s ye the word of the LORD ... Jer 2:31 7200
s where thou hast not been lien ... Jer 3:2 7200
How long shall I *s* the standard ... Jer 4:21 7200
s now, and know, and seek in the ... Jer 5:1 7200
shall we *s* sword nor famine ... Jer 5:12 7200
which have eyes, and *s* not ... Jer 5:21 7200
LORD, Stand ye in the ways, and *s* ... Jer 6:16 7200
s what I did to it for the ... Jer 7:12 7200
let me *s* thy vengeance on them ... Jer 11:20 7200
said, He shall not *s* our last end ... Jer 12:4 7200
them, Ye shall not *s* the sword ... Jer 14:13 7200
shall not *s* when good cometh ... Jer 17:6 7200
shall not *s* when heat cometh, but ... Jer 17:8 7200
let me *s* thy vengeance on them ... Jer 20:12 7200
forth out of the womb to *s* labour ... Jer 20:18 7200
no more, nor *s* his native country ... Jer 22:10 7200
shall *s* this land no more ... Jer 22:12 7200
places that I shall not *s* him ... Jer 23:24 7200
s whether a man doth travail with ... Jer 30:6 7200
wherefore do I *s* every man with ... Jer 30:6 7200
of Egypt, where we shall *s* no war ... Jer 42:14 7200
ye shall *s* this place no more ... Jer 42:18 7200
comest to Babylon, and shalt *s* ... Jer 51:61 7200
s, O LORD, and consider ... Lam 1:11 7200
s if there be any sorrow like ... Lam 1:12 7200
thou shalt *s* greater abominations ... Eze 8:6 7200
thou shalt *s* greater abominations ... Eze 8:13 7200
thou shalt *s* greater abominations ... Eze 8:15 7200
which have eyes to *s*, and *s* not ... Eze 12:2 7200
that thou *s* not the ground ... Eze 12:6 7200
that he *s* not the ground with his ... Eze 12:12 7200
yet shall he not *s* it, though he ... Eze 12:13 7200
upon the prophets that *s* vanity ... Eze 13:9 2374
which *s* visions of peace for her, ... Eze 13:16 2374
ye shall *s* no more vanity ... Eze 13:23 2372
ye shall *s* their way and their ... Eze 14:22 7200
when ye *s* their ways and their ... Eze 14:23 7200
that they may *s* all thy nakedness ... Eze 16:37 7200
all flesh shall *s* that I the LORD ... Eze 20:48 7200
Whiles they *s* vanity unto thee, ... Eze 21:29 2372
Pharaoh shall *s* them, and shall be ... Eze 32:31 7200
if the watchman *s* the sword come ... Eze 33:6 7200
all the heathen shall *s* my ... Eze 39:21 7200
for why should he *s* your faces ... Dan 1:10 7200
because ye *s* the thing is gone ... Dan 2:8 2370

I *s* four men loose, walking in ... Dan 3:25 2370
iron, wood, and stone, which *s* not ... Dan 5:23 2370
your young men shall *s* visions ... Joel 2:28 7200
Pass ye unto Calneh, and *s* ... Amos 6:2 7200
till he might *s* what would become ... Jonah 4:5 7200
man of wisdom shall *s* thy name ... Mic 6:9 7200
she that is mine enemy shall *s* it ... Mic 7:10 7200
The nations shall *s* and be ... Mic 7:16 7200
which Habakkuk the prophet did *s* ... Hab 1:1 2372
will watch to *s* what he will say ... Hab 2:1 7200
thou shalt not *s* evil any more ... Zeph 3:15 7200
and how do ye *s* it now ... Hag 2:3 7200
to *s* what is the breadth thereof, ... Zec 2:2 7200
shall *s* the plummet in the hand ... Zec 4:10 7200
And I answered, I *s* a flying roll ... Zec 5:2 7200
s what is this that goeth forth ... Zec 5:5 7200
Ashkelon shall *s* it, and fear ... Zec 9:5 7200
Gaza also shall *s* it, and be very ... Zec 9:5
yea, their children shall *s* it ... Zec 10:7 7200
And your eyes shall *s*, and ye shall ... Mal 1:5 7200
for they shall *s* God ... Mt 5:8 3700
that they may *s* your good works, ... Mt 5:16 1492
then shalt thou *s* clearly to cast ... Mt 7:5 1227
unto him, *S* thou tell no man ... Mt 8:4 3708
saying, *S* that no man know it ... Mt 9:30 3708
things which ye do hear and *s* ... Mt 11:4 991
ye out into the wilderness to *s* ... Mt 11:7 2300
But what went ye out for to *s* ... Mt 11:8 1492
But what went ye out for to *s* ... Mt 11:9 1492
we would *s* a sign from thee ... Mt 12:38 1492
because they seeing *s* not ... Mt 13:13 991
and seeing ye shall *s*, and shall ... Mt 13:14 991
they should *s* with their eyes ... Mt 13:15 1492
blessed are your eyes, for they *s* ... Mt 13:16 991
to *s* those things which ye ... Mt 13:17 1492
those things which ye *s* ... Mt 13:17 991
lame to walk, and the blind to *s* ... Mt 15:31 991
till they *s* the Son of man coming ... Mt 16:28 1492
the king came in to *s* the guests ... Mt 22:11 2300
Ye shall not *s* me henceforth, ... Mt 23:39 1492
S ye not all these things ... Mt 24:2 991
s that ye be not troubled ... Mt 24:6 3708
When ye therefore shall *s* the ... Mt 24:15 1492
they shall *s* the Son of man ... Mt 24:30 3700
when ye shall *s* all these things, ... Mt 24:33 1492
with the servants, to *s* the end ... Mt 26:58 1492
Hereafter shall ye *s* the Son of ... Mt 26:64 3700
s thou to that ... Mt 27:4 3700
s ye to it ... Mt 27:24 3700
let us *s* whether Elias will come ... Mt 27:49 1492
the other Mary to *s* the sepulchre ... Mt 28:1 2334
s the place where the Lord lay ... Mt 28:6 1492
there shall ye *s* him ... Mt 28:7 3700
Galilee, and there shall they *s* me ... Mt 28:10 3700
S thou say nothing to any man ... Mk 1:44 3708
That seeing they may *s*, and not ... Mk 4:12 991
they went out to *s* what it was ... Mk 5:14 1492
s him that was possessed with the ... Mk 5:15 2334
he looked round about to *s* her ... Mk 5:32 1492
go and *s* ... Mk 6:38 1492
Having eyes, *s* ye not ... Mk 8:18 991
I *s* men as trees, walking ... Mk 8:24 991
bring me a penny, that I may *s* it ... Mk 12:15 1492
s what manner of stones and what ... Mk 13:1 2396
But when ye shall *s* the ... Mk 13:14 1492
then shall they *s* the Son of man ... Mk 13:26 3700
when ye shall *s* these things come ... Mk 13:29 1492
ye shall *s* the Son of man sitting ... Mk 14:62 3700
now from the cross, that we may *s* ... Mk 15:32 1492
let us *s* whether Elias will come ... Mk 15:36 1492
there shall ye *s* him, as he said ... Mk 16:7 3700
s this thing which is come to ... Lk 2:15 1492
Ghost, that he should not *s* death ... Lk 2:26 1492
all flesh shall *s* the salvation ... Lk 3:6 3700
then shalt thou *s* clearly to pull ... Lk 6:42 1227
how that the blind *s*, the lame ... Lk 7:22 308
out into the wilderness for to *s* ... Lk 7:24 2300
But what went ye out for to *s* ... Lk 7:25 1492
But what went ye out for to *s* ... Lk 7:26 1492
that seeing they might not *s* ... Lk 8:10 991
which enter in may *s* the light ... Lk 8:16 991
stand without, desiring to *s* thee ... Lk 8:20 1492
they went out to *s* what was done ... Lk 8:35 1492
And he desired to *s* him ... Lk 9:9 1492
till they *s* the kingdom of God ... Lk 9:27 1492
which *s* the things that ye *s* ... Lk 10:23 991
kings have desired to *s* those ... Lk 10:24 1492
those things which ye *s* ... Lk 10:24 991
which come in may *s* the light ... Lk 11:33 991
When ye *s* a cloud rise out of the ... Lk 12:54 1492
when ye *s* the south wind blow, ye ... Lk 12:55
of teeth, when ye shall *s* Abraham ... Lk 13:28 3700
I say unto you, Ye shall not *s* me ... Lk 13:35 1492
and I must needs go and *s* it ... Lk 14:18 1492
when ye shall desire to *s* one of ... Lk 17:22 1492
Son of man, and ye shall not *s* it ... Lk 17:22 3700
And they shall say to you, *S* here ... Lk 17:23 2400
or, *s* there ... Lk 17:23 2400
he sought to *s* Jesus who he was ... Lk 19:3 1492
up into a sycomore tree to *s* him ... Lk 19:4 1492
reverence him when they *s* him ... Lk 20:13 1492
when ye shall *s* Jerusalem ... Lk 21:20 1492
then shall they *s* the Son of man ... Lk 21:27 3700
When they now shoot forth, ye *s* ... Lk 21:30 991
when ye *s* these things come to ... Lk 21:31 1492
to *s* him of a long season ... Lk 23:8 1492
handle me, and *s* ... Lk 24:39 1492
flesh and bones, as ye *s* me have ... Lk 24:39 2334
Upon whom thou shalt *s* the Spirit ... Jn 1:33 1492
He saith unto them, Come and *s* ... Jn 1:39 1492
Philip saith unto him, Come and *s* ... Jn 1:46 1492
thou shalt *s* greater things than ... Jn 1:50 3700
Hereafter ye shall *s* heaven open ... Jn 1:51 3700
he cannot *s* the kingdom of God ... Jn 3:3 1492
not the Son shall not *s* life ... Jn 3:36 3700
s a man, which told me all things ... Jn 4:29 1492
Jesus unto him, Except ye *s* signs ... Jn 4:48 1492
they *s* Jesus walking on the sea, ... Jn 6:19 2334
shewest thou then, that we may *s* ... Jn 6:30 1492
if ye shall *s* the Son of man ... Jn 6:62 2334
may *s* the works that thou doest ... Jn 7:3 2334
my saying, he shall never *s* death ... Jn 8:51 2334
Abraham rejoiced to *s* my day ... Jn 8:56 1492
mine eyes, and I washed, and do *s* ... Jn 9:15 991
how then doth he now *s* ... Jn 9:19 991
whereas I was blind, now I *s* ... Jn 9:25 991
that they which *s* not might *s* ... Jn 9:39 991
that they which *s* might be made ... Jn 9:39 991
but now ye say, We *s* ... Jn 9:41 991
said unto him, Lord, come and *s* ... Jn 11:34 1492
thou shouldest *s* the glory of God ... Jn 11:40 3700
that they might *s* Lazarus also ... Jn 12:9 1492
saying, Sir, we would *s* Jesus ... Jn 12:21 1492
they should not *s* with their eyes ... Jn 12:40 1492
but ye *s* me ... Jn 14:19 2334
to my Father, and ye *s* me no more ... Jn 16:10 2334
while, and ye shall not *s* me ... Jn 16:16 2334
a little while, and ye shall *s* me ... Jn 16:16 3700
while, and ye shall not *s* me ... Jn 16:17 2334
a little while, and ye shall *s* me ... Jn 16:17 3700
while, and ye shall not *s* me ... Jn 16:19 2334
a little while, and ye shall *s* me ... Jn 16:19 3700
but I will *s* you again, and your ... Jn 16:22 3700
Did not I *s* thee in the garden ... Jn 18:26 1492
Except I shall *s* in his hands the ... Jn 20:25 1492
and your young men shall *s* visions ... Acts 2:17 3070
thine Holy One to *s* corruption ... Acts 2:27 1492
his flesh did *s* corruption ... Acts 2:31 1492
shed forth this, which ye now *s* ... Acts 2:33 991
made this man strong, whom ye *s* ... Acts 3:16 2334
I *s* the heavens opened, and the ... Acts 7:56 2334
and the eunuch said, *S*, here is ... Acts 8:36 2400
thine Holy One to *s* corruption ... Acts 13:35 1492
of the Lord, and *s* how they do ... Acts 15:36
been there, I must also *s* Rome ... Acts 19:21 1492
Moreover ye *s* and hear, that not ... Acts 19:26 2334
of God, shall *s* my face no more ... Acts 20:25 3700
they should *s* his face no more ... Acts 20:38 2334
when I could not *s* for the glory ... Acts 22:11 1689
s that Just One, and shouldest ... Acts 22:14 1492
S thou tell no man that thou hast ... Acts 23:22
ye *s* this man, about whom all the ... Acts 25:24 2334
to *s* you, and to speak with you ... Acts 28:20 1492
and seeing ye shall *s*, and not ... Acts 28:26 991
they should *s* with their eyes ... Acts 28:27 1492
For I long to *s* you, that I may ... Rom 1:11 1492
But I *s* another law in my members ... Rom 7:23 991
But if we hope for that we *s* not ... Rom 8:25 991
eyes that they should not *s* ... Rom 11:8 991
be darkened, that they may not *s* ... Rom 11:10 991
was not spoken of, they shall *s* ... Rom 15:21 3700
for I trust to *s* you in my ... Rom 15:24 2300
For ye *s* your calling, brethren, ... 1Cor 1:26 991
For if any man *s* thee which hast ... 1Cor 8:10 1492
For now we *s* through a glass, ... 1Cor 13:12 991
For I will not *s* you now by the ... 1Cor 16:7 1492
s that he may be with you without ... 1Cor 16:10 991
s that ye abound in this grace ... 2Cor 8:7
I went up to Jerusalem to *s* Peter ... Gal 1:18 2477
Ye *s* how large a letter I have ... Gal 6:11 1492
to make all men *s* what is the ... Eph 3:9 5461
S then that ye walk circumspectly ... Eph 5:15 991
the wife *s* that she reverence her ... Eph 5:33 1492
s you, or else be absent, I may ... Phil 1:27 1492
so soon as I shall *s* how it will ... Phil 2:23 542
when ye *s* him again, ye may ... Phil 2:28 1492
the more abundantly to *s* your ... 1Th 2:17 1492
always, desiring greatly to *s* us ... 1Th 3:6 1492
as we also to *s* you ... 1Th 3:6
that we might *s* your face ... 1Th 3:10 1492
S that none render evil for evil ... 1Th 5:15 3708
whom no man hath seen, nor can *s* ... 1Ti 6:16 1492
Greatly desiring to *s* thee ... 2Ti 1:4 1492
But now we *s* not yet all things ... Heb 2:8 3708
But we *s* Jesus, who was made a ... Heb 2:9 991
So we *s* that they could not enter ... Heb 3:19 991
for, *S*, saith he, that thou make ... Heb 8:5 3708
as ye *s* the day approaching ... Heb 10:25 991
that he should not *s* death ... Heb 11:5 1492
which no man shall *s* the Lord ... Heb 12:14 3700
S that ye refuse not him that ... Heb 12:25 991
if he come shortly, I will *s* you ... Heb 13:23 3700
Ye *s* then how that by works a man ... Jas 2:24 3708
in whom, though now ye *s* him not ... 1Pet 1:8 3708
s that ye love one another with a ... 1Pet 1:22
s good days, let him refrain his ... 1Pet 3:10 1492
cannot *s* afar off, and hath ... 2Pet 1:9 3467
for we shall *s* him as he is ... 1Jn 3:2 3700
If any man *s* his brother sin a ... 1Jn 5:16 1492
I trust I shall shortly *s* thee ... 3Jn 14 1492
and every eye shall *s* him, and they ... Rev 1:7 3700
I turned to *s* the voice that ... Rev 1:12 991
with eyesalve, that thou mayest *s* ... Rev 3:18 991
the four beasts saying, Come and *s* ... Rev 6:1 991
the second beast say, Come and *s* ... Rev 6:3 991
the third beast say, Come and *s* ... Rev 6:5 991
s thou hurt not the oil and the ... Rev 6:6
the fourth beast say, Come and *s* ... Rev 6:7 991
which neither can *s*, nor hear, ... Rev 9:20 991
nations shall *s* their dead bodies ... Rev 11:9 991
walk naked, and they *s* his shame ... Rev 16:15 991
am no widow, and shall *s* no sorrow ... Rev 18:7 1492
when they shall *s* the smoke of ... Rev 18:9 991
he said unto me, *S* thou do it not ... Rev 19:10 3700
And they shall *s* his face ... Rev 22:4 3708
he unto me, *S* thou do it not ... Rev 22:9 3708

SEED (280)

forth grass, the herb yielding *s* ... Gen 1:11 2233
whose *s* is in itself, upon the ... Gen 1:11 2233
herb yielding *s* after his kind, ... Gen 1:12 2233
whose *s* was in itself, after his ... Gen 1:12 2233
given you every herb bearing *s* ... Gen 1:29 2233
is the fruit of a tree yielding *s* ... Gen 1:29 2233
and between thy *s* and her *s* ... Gen 3:15 2233
me another *s* instead of Abel ... Gen 4:25 2233
to keep *s* alive upon the face of ... Gen 7:3 2233
you, and with your *s* after you ... Gen 9:9 2233
Unto thy *s* will I give this land ... Gen 12:7 2233
I give it, and to thy *s* for ever ... Gen 13:15 2233
I will make thy *s* as the dust of ... Gen 13:16 2233
then shall thy *s* also be numbered ... Gen 13:16 2233
to me thou hast given no *s* ... Gen 15:3 2233
said unto him, So shall thy *s* be ... Gen 15:5 2233
Know of a surety that thy *s* shall ... Gen 15:13 2233
Unto thy *s* have I given this land ... Gen 15:18 2233
I will multiply thy *s* exceedingly ... Gen 16:10 2233
thy *s* after thee in their ... Gen 17:7 2233
unto thee, and to thy *s* after thee ... Gen 17:7 2233
to thy *s* after thee, the land ... Gen 17:8 2233
thy *s* after thee in their ... Gen 17:9 2233
me and you and thy *s* after thee ... Gen 17:10 2233
stranger, which is not of thy *s* ... Gen 17:12 2233
covenant, and with his *s* after him ... Gen 17:19 2233
we may preserve *s* of our father ... Gen 19:32 2233
we may preserve *s* of our father ... Gen 19:34 2233
in Isaac shall thy *s* be called ... Gen 21:12 2233
a nation, because he is thy *s* ... Gen 21:13 2233
thy *s* as the stars of the heaven ... Gen 22:17 2233
thy *s* shall possess the gate of ... Gen 22:17 2233
in thy *s* shall all the nations of ... Gen 22:18 2233
Unto thy *s* will I give this land ... Gen 24:7 2233
let thy *s* possess the gate of ... Gen 24:60 2233
for unto thee, and unto thy *s* ... Gen 26:3 2233
I will make thy *s* to multiply as ... Gen 26:4 2233
will give unto thy *s* all these ... Gen 26:4 2233
in thy *s* shall all the nations of ... Gen 26:4 2233
multiply thy *s* for my servant ... Gen 26:24 2233
to thee, and to thy *s* with thee ... Gen 28:4 2233
thee will I give it, and to thy *s* ... Gen 28:13 2233
thy *s* shall be as the dust of the ... Gen 28:14 2233
in thy *s* shall all the families ... Gen 28:14 2233
make thy *s* as the sand of the sea ... Gen 32:12 2233
to thy *s* after thee will I give ... Gen 35:12 2233
raise up *s* to thy brother ... Gen 38:8 2233
knew that the *s* should not be his ... Gen 38:9 2233
he should give *s* to his brother ... Gen 38:9 2233
Jacob, and all his *s* with him ... Gen 46:6 2233
all his *s* brought he with him ... Gen 46:7 2233
and give us *s*, that we may live, ... Gen 47:19 2233
lo, here is *s* for you, and ye ... Gen 47:23 2233
for *s* of the field, and for your ... Gen 47:24 2233
will give this land to thy *s* ... Gen 48:4 2233
lo, God hath shewed me also thy *s* ... Gen 48:11 2233
his *s* shall become a multitude of ... Gen 48:19 2233
and it was like coriander *s* ... Ex 16:31 2233
ever unto him and his *s* after him ... Ex 28:43 2233
to his *s* throughout their ... Ex 30:21 2233
I will multiply your *s* as the ... Ex 32:13 2233
spoken of will I give unto your *s* ... Ex 32:13 2233
Unto thy *s* will I give it ... Ex 33:1 2233
any sowing *s* which is to be sown ... Lev 11:37 2233
if any water be put upon the *s* ... Lev 11:38 2233
If a woman have conceived *s* ... Lev 12:2 2233
if any man's *s* of copulation go ... Lev 15:16 2233
whereon is the *s* of copulation ... Lev 15:17 2233
shall lie with *s* of copulation ... Lev 15:18 2233
of him whose *s* goeth from him, and ... Lev 15:32 2233
thou shalt not let any of thy *s* ... Lev 18:21 2233
not sow thy field with mingled *s* ... Lev 19:19
giveth any of his *s* unto Molech ... Lev 20:2 2233
hath given of his *s* unto Molech ... Lev 20:3 2233
he giveth of his *s* unto Molech ... Lev 20:4 2233
he profane his *s* among his people ... Lev 21:15 2233
Whosoever he be of thy *s* in their ... Lev 21:17 2233
s of Aaron the priest shall come ... Lev 21:21 2233
all your *s* among your generations ... Lev 22:3 2233
of the *s* of Aaron is a leper ... Lev 22:4 2233
or a man whose *s* goeth from him ... Lev 22:4
and ye shall sow your *s* in vain ... Lev 26:16 2233
be according to the *s* thereof ... Lev 27:16 2233
a homer of barley *s* shall be ... Lev 27:16 2233
whether of the *s* of the land ... Lev 27:30 2233
be free, and shall conceive *s* ... Num 5:28 2233
And the manna was as coriander *s* ... Num 11:7 2233
and his *s* shall possess it ... Num 14:24 2233
which is not of the *s* of Aaron ... Num 16:40 2233
unto thee and to thy *s* with thee ... Num 18:19 2233
it is no place of *s*, or of figs, ... Num 20:5 2233
his *s* shall be in many waters, and ... Num 24:7 2233
his *s* after him, even the ... Num 25:13 2233
them and to their *s* after them ... Deut 1:8 2233
he chose their *s* after them ... Deut 4:37 2233
and he chose their *s* after them ... Deut 10:15 2233

to give unto them and to their *s* ... Deut 11:9 2233
out, where thou sowedst thy *s* ... Deut 11:10 2233
tithe all the increase of thy *s* ... Deut 14:22 2233
of thy *s* which thou hast sown ... Deut 22:9 2233
carry much *s* out into the field ... Deut 28:38 2233
a wonder, and upon thy *s* for ever ... Deut 28:46 2233
and the plagues of thy *s*, even ... Deut 28:59 2233
heart, and the heart of thy *s* ... Deut 30:6 2233
that both thou and thy *s* may live ... Deut 30:19 2233
out of the mouths of their *s* ... Deut 31:21 2233
saying, I will give it unto thy *s* ... Deut 34:4 2233
of Canaan, and multiplied his *s* ... Josh 24:3 2233
of the *s* which the LORD shall ... Ruth 4:12 2233
The LORD give thee *s* of this ... 1Sa 2:20 2233
he will take the tenth of your *s* ... 1Sa 8:15 2233
between my *s* and thy *s* for ever ... 1Sa 20:42 2233
will not cut off my *s* after me ... 1Sa 24:21 2233
this day of Saul, and of his *s* ... 2Sa 4:8 2233
I will set up thy *s* after thee ... 2Sa 7:12 2233
David, and to his *s* for evermore ... 2Sa 22:51 2233
upon the head of his *s* for ever ... 1Kin 2:33 2233
but upon David, and upon his *s* ... 1Kin 2:33 2233
he was of the king's *s* in Edom ... 1Kin 11:14 2233
for this afflict the *s* of David ... 1Kin 11:39 2233
would contain two measures of *s* ... 1Kin 18:32 2233
unto thee, and unto thy *s* for ever ... 2Kin 5:27 2233
and destroyed all the *s* royal ... 2Kin 11:1 2233
LORD rejected all the *s* of Israel ... 2Kin 17:20 2233
son of Elishama, of the *s* royal ... 2Kin 25:25 2233
O ye *s* of Israel his servant, ye ... 1Chr 16:13 2233
I will raise up thy *s* after thee ... 1Chr 17:11 2233
gavest it to the *s* of Abraham thy ... 2Chr 20:7 2233
destroyed all the *s* royal of the ... 2Chr 22:10 2233
their father's house, and their *s* ... Ezr 2:59 2233
so that the holy *s* have mingled ... Ezr 9:2 2233
their father's house, nor their *s* ... Neh 7:61 2233
the *s* of Israel separated ... Neh 9:2 2233
to give it, I say, to his *s* ... Neh 9:8 2233
Mordecai be of the *s* of the Jews ... Est 6:13 2233
took upon them, and upon their *s* ... Est 9:27 2233
of them perish from their *s* ... Est 9:28 2233
for themselves and for their *s* ... Est 9:31 2233
and speaking peace to all his *s* ... Est 10:3 2233
also that thy *s* shall be great ... Job 5:25 2233
Their *s* is established in their ... Job 21:8 2233
that he will bring home thy *s* ... Job 39:12 2233
David, and to his *s* for evermore ... Ps 18:50 2233
their *s* from among the children ... Ps 21:10 2233
all ye the *s* of Jacob, glorify ... Ps 22:23 2233
fear him, all ye the *s* of Israel ... Ps 22:23 2233
A *s* shall serve him ... Ps 22:30 2233
his *s* shall inherit the earth ... Ps 25:13 2233
forsaken, nor his *s* begging bread ... Ps 37:25 2233
and his *s* is blessed ... Ps 37:26 2233
but the *s* of the wicked shall be ... Ps 37:28 2233
The *s* also of his servants shall ... Ps 69:36 2233
Thy *s* will I establish for ever, ... Ps 89:4 2233
His *s* also will I make to endure ... Ps 89:29 2233
His *s* shall endure for ever, and ... Ps 89:36 2233
their *s* shall be established ... Ps 102:28 2233
O ye *s* of Abraham his servant, ye ... Ps 105:6 2233
To overthrow their *s* also among ... Ps 106:27 2233
His *s* shall be mighty upon earth ... Ps 112:2 2233
and weepeth, bearing precious *s* ... Ps 126:6 2233
but the *s* of the righteous shall ... Prov 11:21 2233
In the morning sow thy *s*, and in ... Eccl 11:6 2233
a *s* of evildoers, children that ... Is 1:4 2233
the *s* of an homer shall yield an ... Is 5:10 2233
so the holy *s* shall be the ... Is 6:13 2233
the *s* of evildoers shall never be ... Is 14:20 2233
shalt thou make thy *s* to flourish ... Is 17:11 2233
And by great waters the *s* of Sihor ... Is 23:3 2233
shall he give the rain of thy *s* ... Is 30:23 2233
the *s* of Abraham my friend ... Is 41:8 2233
I will bring thy *s* from the east ... Is 43:5 2233
I will pour my spirit upon thy *s* ... Is 44:3 2233
I said not unto the *s* of Jacob ... Is 45:19 2233
all the *s* of Israel be justified ... Is 45:25 2233
Thy *s* also had been as the sand, ... Is 48:19 2233
for sin, he shall see his *s* ... Is 53:10 2233
thy *s* shall inherit the Gentiles, ... Is 54:3 2233
that it may give *s* to the sower ... Is 55:10 2233
the *s* of the adulterer and the ... Is 57:3 2233
transgression, a *s* of falsehood, ... Is 57:4 2233
nor out of the mouth of thy *s* ... Is 59:21 2233
out of the mouth of thy seed's *s* ... Is 59:21 2233
their *s* shall be known among the ... Is 61:9 2233
that they are the *s* which the ... Is 61:9 2233
will bring forth a *s* out of Jacob ... Is 65:9 2233
for they are the *s* of the blessed ... Is 65:23 2233
saith the LORD, so shall your *s* ... Is 66:22 2233
a noble vine, wholly a right *s* ... Jer 2:21 2233
even the whole *s* of Ephraim ... Jer 7:15 2233
are they cast out, he and his *s* ... Jer 22:28 2233
for no man of his *s* shall prosper ... Jer 22:30 2233
which led the *s* of the house of ... Jer 23:8 2233
Shemaiah the Nehelamite, and his *s* ... Jer 29:32 2233
thy *s* from the land of their ... Jer 30:10 2233
house of Judah with the *s* of man ... Jer 31:27 2233
of man, and with the *s* of beast ... Jer 31:27 2233
then the *s* of Israel also shall ... Jer 31:36 2233
the *s* of Israel for all that they ... Jer 31:37 2233
the *s* of David my servant ... Jer 33:22 2233
will I cast away the *s* of Jacob ... Jer 33:26 2233
s to be rulers over the *s* of ... Jer 33:26 2233
be rulers over the *s* of Abraham ... Jer 33:26 2233
shall ye build house, nor sow *s* ... Jer 35:7 2233
we vineyard, nor field, nor *s* ... Jer 35:9 2233
And I will punish him and his *s* ... Jer 36:31 2233
son of Elishama, of the *s* royal ... Jer 41:1 2233
thy *s* from the land of their ... Jer 46:27 2233
his *s* is spoiled, and his brethren ... Jer 49:10 2233
He took also of the *s* of the land ... Eze 17:5 2233
And hath taken of the king's *s* ... Eze 17:13 2233
unto the *s* of the house of Jacob ... Eze 20:5 2233
Levites that be of the *s* of Zadok ... Eze 43:19 2233
of the *s* of the house of Israel ... Eze 44:22 2233
of Israel, and of the king's *s* ... Dan 1:3 2233
themselves with the *s* of men ... Dan 2:43 2234
of the *s* of the Medes, which was ... Dan 9:1 2233
The *s* is rotten under their clods ... Joel 1:17 6507
of grapes him that soweth *s* ... Amos 9:13 2233
Is the *s* yet in the barn ... Hag 2:19 2233
For the *s* shall be prosperous ... Zec 8:12 2233
Behold, I will corrupt your *s* ... Mal 2:3 2233
That he might seek a godly *s* ... Mal 2:15 2233
which received *s* by the way side ... Mt 13:19 *4687*
received the *s* into stony places ... Mt 13:20 *4687*
He also that received *s* among the ... Mt 13:22 *4687*
But he that received *s* into the ... Mt 13:23 *4687*
which sowed good *s* in his field ... Mt 13:24 *4690*
not thou sow good *s* in thy field ... Mt 13:27 *4690*
is like to a grain of mustard *s* ... Mt 13:31
the good *s* is the Son of man ... Mt 13:37 *4690*
the good *s* are the children of ... Mt 13:38 *4690*
faith as a grain of mustard *s* ... Mt 17:20
raise up *s* unto his brother ... Mt 22:24 *4690*
man should cast *s* into the ground ... Mk 4:26 *4703*
the *s* should spring and grow up, ... Mk 4:27 *4703*
It is like a grain of mustard *s* ... Mk 4:31 *4690*
raise up *s* unto his brother ... Mk 12:19 *4690*
took a wife, and dying left no *s* ... Mk 12:20 *4690*
and died, neither left he any *s* ... Mk 12:21 *4690*
the seven had her, and left no *s* ... Mk 12:22 *4690*
to Abraham, and to his *s* for ever ... Lk 1:55 *4690*
A sower went out to sow his *s* ... Lk 8:5 *4703*
The *s* is the word of God ... Lk 8:11 *4703*
It is like a grain of mustard *s* ... Lk 13:19
had faith as a grain of mustard *s* ... Lk 17:6
raise up *s* unto his brother ... Lk 20:28 *4690*
Christ cometh of the *s* of David ... Jn 7:42 *4690*
answered him, We be Abraham's *s* ... Jn 8:33 *4690*
I know that ye are Abraham's *s* ... Jn 8:37 *4690*
in thy *s* shall all the kindreds ... Acts 3:25 *4690*
to his *s* after him, when as yet ... Acts 7:5 *4690*
That his *s* should sojourn in a ... Acts 7:6 *4690*
Of this man's *s* hath God ... Acts 13:23 *4690*
which was made of the *s* of David ... Rom 1:3 *4690*
was not to Abraham, or to his *s* ... Rom 4:13 *4690*
might be sure to all the *s* ... Rom 4:16 *4690*
was spoken, So shall thy *s* be ... Rom 4:18 *4690*
because they are the *s* of Abraham ... Rom 9:7 *4690*
In Isaac shall thy *s* be called ... Rom 9:7 *4690*
the promise are counted for the *s* ... Rom 9:8 *4690*
Lord of Sabaoth had left us a *s* ... Rom 9:29 *4690*
of the *s* of Abraham, of the tribe ... Rom 11:1 *4690*
him, and to every *s* his own body ... 1Cor 15:38 *4690*
Now he that ministereth *s* to the ... 2Cor 9:10 *4690*
food, and multiply your *s* sown ... 2Cor 9:10 *4703*
Are they the *s* of Abraham ... 2Cor 11:22 *4690*
his *s* were the promises made ... Gal 3:16 *4690*
but as of one, And to thy *s* ... Gal 3:16 *4690*
till the *s* should come to whom ... Gal 3:19 *4690*
Christ's, then are ye Abraham's *s* ... Gal 3:29 *4690*
that Jesus Christ of the *s* of ... 2Ti 2:8 *4690*
he took on him the *s* of Abraham ... Heb 2:16 *4690*
received strength to conceive *s* ... Heb 11:11 *4690*
in Isaac shall thy *s* be called ... Heb 11:18 *4690*
born again, not of corruptible *s* ... 1Pet 1:23 *4701*
for his *s* remaineth in him ... 1Jn 3:9 *4690*
war with the remnant of her *s* ... Rev 12:17 *4690*

SEED'S {1}
out of the mouth of thy *s* seed ... Is 59:21 2233

SEEDS {5}
sow thy vineyard with divers *s* ... Deut 22:9
some *s* fell by the way side, and ... Mt 13:4
indeed is the least of all *s* ... Mt 13:32 *4690*
all the *s* that be in the earth ... Mk 4:31 *4690*
He saith not, And to *s*, as of many ... Gal 3:16 *4690*

SEEDTIME {1}
While the earth remaineth, *s* ... Gen 8:22 2233

SEEING {116}
s I go childless, and the steward ... Gen 15:2
S that Abraham shall surely ... Gen 18:18
Lot *s* them rose up to meet them ... Gen 19:1 7200
s thou hast not withheld thy son, ... Gen 22:12 7200
s the LORD hath prospered my way ... Gen 24:56
s ye hate me, and have sent me ... Gen 26:27 7200
Esau *s* that the daughters of ... Gen 28:8 7200
s that his life is bound up in ... Gen 44:30
the dumb, or deaf, or the *s* ... Ex 4:11 6493
s he hath dealt deceitfully with ... Ex 21:8
hurt, or driven away, no man *s* it ... Ex 22:10 7200
s ye were strangers in the land ... Ex 23:9 3588
s it is most holy, and God hath ... Lev 10:17 3588
s all the people were in ... Num 15:26 3588
s all the congregation are holy, ... Num 16:3 3588
s him not, and cast it upon him, ... Num 35:23 7200
s I am a great people, forasmuch ... Josh 17:14
s ye rebel to day against the ... Josh 22:18
after my name, *s* it is secret ... Judg 13:18
s I have a Levite to my priest ... Judg 17:13 3588
s that this man is come into mine ... Judg 19:23 310
s we have sworn by the LORD that ... Judg 21:7 7200
s the women are destroyed out of ... Judg 21:16 3588
s the LORD hath testified against ... Ruth 1:21
of me, *s* I am a stranger ... Ruth 2:10
s I have rejected him from ... 1Sa 16:1
s he hath defied the armies of ... 1Sa 17:36 3588
s that I am a poor man, and ... 1Sa 18:23
s he is the anointed of the LORD ... 1Sa 24:6 3588
s the LORD hath withholden thee ... 1Sa 25:26 834
s the LORD is departed from thee, ... 1Sa 28:16
concerning Amnon, *s* he was dead ... 2Sa 13:39 3588
s I go whither I may, return thou ... 2Sa 15:20
s that thou hast no tidings ready ... 2Sa 18:22
s the speech of all Israel is ... 2Sa 19:11
this day, mine eyes even *s* it ... 1Kin 1:48 7200
Solomon *s* the young man that he ... 1Kin 11:28 7200
s your master's sons are with you ... 2Kin 10:2
s there is no wrong in mine hands ... 1Chr 12:17
s the heaven and heaven of heavens ... 2Chr 2:6 3588
s that thou our God hast punished ... Ezr 9:13 3588
sad, *s* thou art not sick ... Neh 2:2
S his days are determined, the ... Job 14:5 518
s the root of the matter is found ... Job 19:28
s he judgeth those that are high ... Job 21:22
s in your answers there remaineth ... Job 21:34
s times are not hidden from the ... Job 24:1 7200
S it is hid from the eyes of all ... Job 28:21
him, *s* he delighted in him ... Ps 22:8 3588
S thou hatest instruction, and ... Ps 50:17
s he dwelleth securely by thee ... Prov 3:29 7200
wisdom, *s* he hath no heart to it ... Prov 17:16
The hearing ear, and the *s* eye ... Prov 20:12 7200
the eye is not satisfied with *s* ... Eccl 1:8 7200
s that which now is in the days ... Eccl 2:16
S there be many things that ... Eccl 6:11 3588
I was dismayed at the *s* of it ... Is 21:3 7200
and shutteth his eyes from *s* evil ... Is 33:15 7200
S many things, but thou observest ... Is 42:20 7200
s I have lost my children, and am ... Is 49:21
s she hath wrought lewdness with ... Jer 11:15
s the LORD hath given it a charge ... Jer 47:7
s thou doest all these things, ... Eze 16:30
S he despised the oath by ... Eze 17:18
S then that I will cut off from ... Eze 21:4 3282
s vanity, and divining lies unto ... Eze 22:28
s thou couldest reveal this secret ... Dan 2:47 1768
s thou hast forgotten the law of ... Hos 4:6
s the multitudes, he went up into ... Mt 5:1 *1492*
Jesus *s* their faith said unto the ... Mt 9:2 *1492*
because they *s* see not ... Mt 13:13 *991*
s ye shall see, and shall not ... Mt 13:14 *991*
That *s* they may see, and not ... Mk 4:12 *991*
s a fig tree afar off having ... Mk 11:13 *1492*
shall this be, *s* I know not a man ... Lk 1:34 *1893*
who *s* Jesus fell on his face, and ... Lk 5:12 *1492*
that *s* they might not see, and ... Lk 8:10 *991*
fear God, *s* thou art in the same ... Lk 23:40 *3754*
s that thou doest these things ... Jn 2:18 *3754*
therefore, and washed, and came *s* ... Jn 9:7 *991*
Peter *s* him saith to Jesus, Lord, ... Jn 21:21 *1492*
s it is but the third hour of the ... Acts 2:15 *1063*
He *s* this before spake of the ... Acts 2:31 *4275*
Who *s* Peter and John about to go ... Acts 3:3 *1492*
s one of them suffer wrong, he ... Acts 7:24 *1492*
s the miracles which he did ... Acts 8:6 *991*
hearing a voice, but *s* no man ... Acts 9:7 *2334*
not *s* the sun for a season ... Acts 13:11 *991*
but *s* ye put it from you, and ... Acts 13:46 *1894*
s the prison doors open, he drew ... Acts 16:27 *1492*
s that he is Lord of heaven and ... Acts 17:24
s he giveth to all life, and ... Acts 17:25
S then that these things cannot ... Acts 19:36
S that by thee we enjoy great ... Acts 24:2
s ye shall see, and not perceive ... Acts 28:26 *991*
S it is one God, which shall ... Rom 3:30 *1897*
s he understandeth not what thou ... 1Cor 14:16 *1894*
S then that we have such hope, we ... 2Cor 3:12
s we have this ministry, as we ... 2Cor 4:1
S that many glory after the flesh ... 2Cor 11:18 *1893*
gladly, *s* ye yourselves are wise ... 2Cor 11:19
s that ye have put off the old ... Col 3:9
S it is a righteous thing with ... 2Th 1:6 *1512*
S therefore it remaineth that ... Heb 4:6 *1893*
S then that we have a great high ... Heb 4:14
uttered, *s* ye are dull of hearing ... Heb 5:11 *1893*
s they crucify to themselves the ... Heb 6:6
by him, *s* he ever liveth to make ... Heb 7:25
s that there are priests that ... Heb 8:4
as *s* him who is invisible ... Heb 11:27 *3708*
Wherefore *s* we also are compassed ... Heb 12:1
S ye have purified your souls in ... 1Pet 1:22
man dwelling among them, in *s* ... 2Pet 2:8 *990*
S then that all these things ... 2Pet 3:11
s that ye look for such things, ... 2Pet 3:14
s ye know these things before, ... 2Pet 3:17

SEEK {244}
And he said, I *s* my brethren ... Gen 37:16 1245
that he may *s* occasion against us ... Gen 43:18 1556
shall not *s* for yellow hair ... Lev 13:36 1239
neither *s* after wizards, to be ... Lev 19:31 1245
that ye *s* not after your own ... Num 15:39 8446
and *s* ye the priesthood also ... Num 16:10 1245
to *s* for enchantments, but he set ... Num 24:1 7125
thou shalt *s* the LORD thy God ... Deut 4:29 1245
if thou *s* him with all thy heart ... Deut 4:29 1875
unto his habitation shall ye *s* ... Deut 12:5 1875
thee until thy brother *s* after it ... Deut 22:2 1875
Thou shalt not *s* their peace nor ... Deut 23:6 1875

shall I not *s* rest for thee, that ... Ruth 3:1 1245
thee, and arise, go *s* the asses ... 1Sa 9:3 1245
which thou wentest to *s* are found ... 1Sa 10:2 1245
And he said, To *s* the asses ... 1Sa 10:14 1245
to *s* out a man, who is a cunning ... 1Sa 16:16 1245
Saul was come out to *s* his life ... 1Sa 23:15 1245
also and his men went to *s* him ... 1Sa 23:25 1245
of all Israel, and went to *s* David ... 1Sa 24:2 1245
they that *s* evil to my lord, be ... 1Sa 25:26 1245
to pursue thee, and to *s* thy soul ... 1Sa 25:29 1245
to *s* David in the wilderness of ... 1Sa 26:2 1245
of Israel is come out to *s* a flea ... 1Sa 26:20 1245
to *s* me any more in any coast of ... 1Sa 27:1 1245
S me a woman that hath a familiar ... 1Sa 28:7 1245
Philistines came up to *s* David ... 2Sa 5:17 1245
Gath to Achish to *s* his servants ... 1Kin 2:40 1245
my lord hath not sent to *s* thee ... 1Kin 18:10 1245
they *s* my life, to take it away ... 1Kin 19:10 1245
they *s* my life, to take it away ... 1Kin 19:14 1245
go, we pray thee, and *s* thy master ... 2Kin 2:16 1245
bring you to the man whom ye *s* ... 2Kin 6:19 1245
to *s* pasture for their flocks ... 1Chr 4:39 1245
Philistines went up to *s* David ... 1Chr 14:8 1245
of them rejoice that *s* the LORD ... 1Chr 16:10 1245
S the LORD and his strength ... 1Chr 16:11 1875
s his face continually ... 1Chr 16:11 1245
your soul to *s* the LORD your God ... 1Chr 22:19 1875
s for all the commandments of the ... 1Chr 28:8 1875
if thou *s* him, he will be found ... 1Chr 28:9 1875
s my face, and turn from their ... 2Chr 7:14 1245
such as set their hearts to *s* the ... 2Chr 11:16 1245
not his heart to *s* the LORD ... 2Chr 12:14 1875
commanded Judah to *s* the LORD God ... 2Chr 14:4 1875
and if ye *s* him, he will be found ... 2Chr 15:2 1875
s the LORD God of their fathers ... 2Chr 15:12 1875
That whosoever would not *s* the ... 2Chr 15:13 1875
prepared thine heart to *s* God ... 2Chr 19:3 1875
and set himself to *s* the LORD ... 2Chr 20:3 1875
of Judah they came to *s* the LORD ... 2Chr 20:4 1245
That prepareth his heart to *s* God ... 2Chr 30:19 1875
to *s* his God, he did it with all ... 2Chr 31:21 1875
he began to *s* after the God of ... 2Chr 34:3 1875
for we *s* your God, as ye do ... Ezr 4:2 1875
to *s* the LORD God of Israel, did ... Ezr 6:21 1875
heart to *s* the law of the LORD ... Ezr 7:10 1875
to *s* of him a right way for us ... Ezr 8:21 1245
upon all them for good that *s* him ... Ezr 8:22 1245
nor *s* their peace or their wealth ... Ezr 9:12 1875
that there was come a man to *s* ... Neh 2:10 1245
I would *s* unto God, and unto God ... Job 5:8 1875
thou shalt *s* me in the morning ... Job 7:21 7836
thou wouldest *s* unto God betimes ... Job 8:5 7836
shall *s* to please the poor ... Job 20:10
love vanity, and *s* after leasing ... Ps 4:2 1245
not forsaken them that *s* thee ... Ps 9:10 1875
countenance, will not *s* after God ... Ps 10:4 1875
s out his wickedness till thou ... Ps 10:15 1875
any that did understand, and *s* God ... Ps 14:2 1875
shall praise the LORD that *s* him ... Ps 22:26 1875
the generation of them that *s* him ... Ps 24:6 1875
him, that *s* thy face, O Jacob ... Ps 24:6 1245
of the LORD, that will I *s* after ... Ps 27:4 1245
When thou saidst, *S* ye my face ... Ps 27:8 1245
thee, Thy face, LORD, will I *s* ... Ps 27:8 1245
but they that *s* the LORD shall ... Ps 34:10 1875
s peace, and pursue it ... Ps 34:14 1245
put to shame that *s* after my soul ... Ps 35:4 1245
They also that *s* after my life ... Ps 38:12 1245
they that *s* my hurt speak ... Ps 38:12 1875
confounded together that *s* after ... Ps 40:14 1245
Let all those that *s* thee rejoice ... Ps 40:16 1245
did understand, that did *s* God ... Ps 53:2 1875
oppressors *s* after my soul ... Ps 54:3 1245
early will I *s* thee ... Ps 63:1 7836
But those that *s* my soul, to ... Ps 63:9 1245
let not those that *s* thee be ... Ps 69:6 1245
your heart shall live that *s* God ... Ps 69:32 1875
confounded that *s* after my soul ... Ps 70:2 1245
Let all those that *s* thee rejoice ... Ps 70:4 1245
and dishonour that *s* my hurt ... Ps 71:13 1245
unto shame, that *s* my hurt ... Ps 71:24 1245
that they may *s* thy name, O LORD ... Ps 83:16 1245
prey, and *s* their meat from God ... Ps 104:21 1245
of them rejoice that *s* the LORD ... Ps 105:3 1245
S the LORD, and his strength ... Ps 105:4 1875
s his face evermore ... Ps 105:4 1245
let them *s* their bread also out ... Ps 109:10 1875
that *s* him with the whole heart ... Ps 119:2 1875
for I *s* thy precepts ... Ps 119:45 1875
for they *s* not thy statutes ... Ps 119:155 1875
s thy servant ... Ps 119:176 1245
LORD our God I will *s* thy good ... Ps 122:9 1245
they shall *s* me early, but they ... Prov 1:28 7836
thee, diligently to *s* thy face ... Prov 7:15 7836
those that *s* me early shall find ... Prov 8:17 7836
to and fro of them that *s* death ... Prov 21:6 1245
they that go to *s* mixed wine ... Prov 23:30 2713
I will *s* it yet again ... Prov 23:35 1245
but they that *s* the LORD ... Prov 28:5 1245
but the just *s* his soul ... Prov 29:10 1245
Many *s* the ruler's favour ... Prov 29:26 1245
And I gave my heart to *s* and search ... Eccl 1:13 1875
to *s* out wisdom, and the reason of ... Eccl 7:25 1245
though a man labour to *s* it out ... Eccl 8:17 1245
I will *s* him whom my soul loveth ... Song 3:2 1245
that we may *s* him with thee ... Song 6:1 1245
s judgment, relieve the oppressed ... Is 1:17 1875
S unto them that have familiar ... Is 8:19 1875
not a people *s* unto their God ... Is 8:19 1875
neither do they *s* the LORD of ... Is 9:13 1875
to it shall the Gentiles *s* ... Is 11:10 1875
they shall *s* to the idols, and to ... Is 19:3 1875
within me will I *s* thee early ... Is 26:9 7836
Woe unto them that *s* deep to hide ... Is 29:15
One of Israel, neither *s* the LORD ... Is 31:1 1875
S ye out of the book of the LORD, ... Is 34:16 1875
Thou shalt *s* them, and shalt not ... Is 41:12 1245
When the poor and needy *s* water ... Is 41:17 1245
seed of Jacob, *S* ye me in vain ... Is 45:19 1245
righteousness, ye that *s* the LORD ... Is 51:1 1245
S ye the LORD while he may be ... Is 55:6 1875
Yet they *s* me daily, and delight ... Is 58:2 1875
all they that *s* her will not ... Jer 2:24 1245
trimmest thou thy way to *s* love ... Jer 2:33 1245
thee, they will *s* thy life ... Jer 4:30 1245
s in the broad places thereof, if ... Jer 5:1 1245
that *s* thy life, saying, Prophesy ... Jer 11:21 1245
hands of them that *s* their lives ... Jer 19:7 1245
they that *s* their lives, shall ... Jer 19:9 1245
hand of those that *s* their life ... Jer 21:7 1245
the hand of them that *s* thy life ... Jer 22:25 1245
s the peace of the city whither I ... Jer 29:7 1875
And ye shall *s* me, and find me, ... Jer 29:13 1245
they *s* thee not ... Jer 30:14 1875
hand of them that *s* their life ... Jer 34:20 1245
hand of them that *s* their life ... Jer 34:21 1245
hand of these men that *s* thy life ... Jer 38:16 1245
the hand of them that *s* his life ... Jer 44:30 1245
s them not ... Jer 45:5 1245
hand of those that *s* their lives ... Jer 46:26 1245
and before them that *s* their life ... Jer 49:37 1245
shall go, and *s* the LORD their God ... Jer 50:4 1245
All her people sigh, they *s* bread ... Lam 1:11 1245
and they shall *s* peace, and there ... Eze 7:25 1245
then shall they *s* a vision of the ... Eze 7:26 1245
none did search or *s* after them ... Eze 34:6 1245
search my sheep, and *s* them out ... Eze 34:11 1239
so will I *s* out my sheep, and will ... Eze 34:12 1239
I will *s* that which was lost, and ... Eze 34:16 1245
to *s* by prayer and supplications, ... Dan 9:3 1245
and she shall *s* them, but shall ... Hos 2:7 1245
s the LORD their God, and David ... Hos 3:5 1245
and with their herds to *s* the LORD ... Hos 5:6 1245
their offence, and *s* my face ... Hos 5:15 1245
affliction they will *s* me early ... Hos 5:15 7836
their God, nor *s* him for all this ... Hos 7:10 1245
for it is time to *s* the LORD ... Hos 10:12 1875
S ye me, and ye shall live ... Amos 5:4 1875
But *s* not Beth-el, nor enter into ... Amos 5:5 1875
S the LORD, and ye shall live ... Amos 5:6 1875
S him that maketh the seven stars ... Amos 5:8
S good, and not evil, that ye may ... Amos 5:14 1875
fro to *s* the word of the LORD, and ... Amos 8:12 1245
whence shall I *s* comforters for ... Nah 3:7 1245
thou also shalt *s* strength ... Nah 3:11 1245
S ye the LORD, all ye meek of the ... Zeph 2:3 1245
s righteousness, *s* meekness ... Zeph 2:3 1245
LORD, and to *s* the LORD of hosts ... Zec 8:21 1245
strong nations shall come to *s* ... Zec 8:22 1245
neither shall *s* the young one ... Zec 11:16 1245
that I will *s* to destroy all the ... Zec 12:9 1245
they should *s* the law at his ... Mal 2:7 1245
That he might *s* a godly seed ... Mal 2:15 1245
and the Lord, whom ye *s*, shall ... Mal 3:1 1245
for Herod will *s* the young child ... Mt 2:13 *2212*
these things do the Gentiles *s* ... Mt 6:32 *1934*
But *s* ye first the kingdom of God ... Mt 6:33 *2212*
s, and ye shall find ... Mt 7:7 *2212*
for I know that ye *s* Jesus ... Mt 28:5 *2212*
said unto him, All men *s* for thee ... Mk 1:37 *2212*
thy brethren without *s* for thee ... Mk 3:32 *2212*
this generation *s* after a sign ... Mk 8:12 *1934*
Ye *s* Jesus of Nazareth, which was ... Mk 16:6 *2212*
s, and ye shall find ... Lk 11:9 *2212*
they *s* a sign ... Lk 11:29 *1934*
s not ye what ye shall eat, or ... Lk 12:29 *2212*
the nations of the world *s* after ... Lk 12:30 *1934*
But rather *s* ye the kingdom of ... Lk 12:31 *2212*
will *s* to enter in, and shall not ... Lk 13:24 *2212*
s diligently till she find it ... Lk 15:8 *2212*
Whosoever shall *s* to save his ... Lk 17:33 *2212*
For the Son of man is come to *s* ... Lk 19:10 *2212*
Why *s* ye the living among the ... Lk 24:5 *2212*
and saith unto them, What *s* ye ... Jn 1:38 *2212*
because I *s* not mine own will ... Jn 5:30 *2212*
s not the honour that cometh from ... Jn 5:44 *2212*
verily, I say unto you, Ye *s* me ... Jn 6:26 *2212*
not this he, whom they *s* to kill ... Jn 7:25 *2212*
Ye shall *s* me, and shall not find ... Jn 7:34 *2212*
this that he said, Ye shall *s* me ... Jn 7:36 *2212*
I go my way, and ye shall *s* me ... Jn 8:21 *2212*
but ye *s* to kill me, because my ... Jn 8:37 *2212*
But now ye *s* to kill me, a man ... Jn 8:40 *2212*
And I *s* not mine own glory ... Jn 8:50 *2212*
Ye shall *s* me ... Jn 13:33 *2212*
and said unto them, Whom *s* ye ... Jn 18:4 *2212*
asked he them again, Whom *s* ye ... Jn 18:7 *2212*
if therefore ye *s* me, let these ... Jn 18:8 *2212*
him, Behold, three men *s* thee ... Acts 10:19 *2212*
said, Behold, I am he whom ye *s* ... Acts 10:21 *2212*
Barnabas to Tarsus, for to *s* Saul ... Acts 11:25 *327*
of men might *s* after the Lord ... Acts 15:17 *1567*
That they should *s* the Lord ... Acts 17:27 *2212*
in well doing *s* for glory ... Rom 2:7 *2212*
am left alone, and they *s* my life ... Rom 11:3 *2212*
the Greeks *s* after wisdom ... 1Cor 1:22 *2212*
s not to be loosed ... 1Cor 7:27 *2212*
s not a wife ... 1Cor 7:27 *2212*
Let no man *s* his own, but every ... 1Cor 10:24 *2212*
s that ye may excel to the ... 1Cor 14:12 *2212*
for I *s* not yours, but you ... 2Cor 12:14 *2212*
Since ye *s* a proof of Christ ... 2Cor 13:3 *2212*
or do I *s* to please men ... Gal 1:10 *2212*
while we *s* to be justified by ... Gal 2:17 *2212*
For all *s* their own, not the ... Phil 2:21 *2212*
s those things which are above, ... Col 3:1 *2212*
of them that diligently *s* him ... Heb 11:6 *1567*
plainly that they *s* a country ... Heb 11:14 *1934*
city, but we *s* one to come ... Heb 13:14 *1934*
let him *s* peace, and ensue it ... 1Pet 3:11 *2212*
in those days shall men *s* death ... Rev 9:6 *2212*

SEEKEST {9}

asked him, saying, What *s* thou ... Gen 37:15 1245
shew thee the man whom thou *s* ... Judg 4:22 1245
the man whom thou *s* is as if all ... 2Sa 17:3 1245
thou *s* to destroy a city and a ... 2Sa 20:19 1245
thou *s* to go to thine own country ... 1Kin 11:22 1245
If thou *s* her as silver, and ... Prov 2:4 1245
s thou great things for thyself ... Jer 45:5 1245
yet no man said, What *s* thou ... Jn 4:27 *2212*
whom *s* thou ... Jn 20:15 *2212*

SEEKETH {44}

Saul my father *s* to kill thee ... 1Sa 19:2 1245
thy father, that he *s* my life ... 1Sa 20:1 1245
for he that *s* my life *s* thy ... 1Sa 22:23 1245
that *s* my life *s* thy life ... 1Sa 22:23 1245
that Saul *s* to come to Keilah ... 1Sa 23:10 1245
saying, Behold, David *s* thy hurt ... 1Sa 24:9 1245
forth of my bowels, *s* my life ... 2Sa 16:11 1245
and see how this man *s* mischief ... 1Kin 20:7 1245
see how he *s* a quarrel against me ... 2Kin 5:7 579
From thence she *s* the prey ... Job 39:29 2658
the righteous, and *s* to slay him ... Ps 37:32 1245
He that diligently *s* good ... Prov 11:27 7836
but he that *s* mischief, it shall ... Prov 11:27 1875
A scorner *s* wisdom, and findeth it ... Prov 14:6 1245
hath understanding *s* knowledge ... Prov 15:14 1245
covereth a transgression *s* love ... Prov 17:9 1245
An evil man *s* only rebellion ... Prov 17:11 1245
exalteth his gate *s* destruction ... Prov 17:19 1245
man, having separated himself, *s* ... Prov 18:1 1245
the ear of the wise *s* knowledge ... Prov 18:15 1245
She *s* wool, and flax, and worketh ... Prov 31:13 1875
Which yet my soul *s*, but I find ... Eccl 7:28 1245
he *s* unto him a cunning workman ... Is 40:20 1245
judgment, that *s* the truth ... Jer 5:1 1245
This is Zion, whom no man *s* after ... Jer 30:17 1875
for this man *s* not the welfare of ... Jer 38:4 1875
for him, to the soul that *s* him ... Lam 3:25 1875
punishment of him that *s* unto him ... Eze 14:10 1875
As a shepherd *s* out his flock in ... Eze 34:12 1243
and he that *s* findeth ... Mt 7:8 *2212*
generation *s* after a sign ... Mt 12:39 *1934*
generation *s* after a sign ... Mt 16:4 *1934*
s that which is gone astray ... Mt 18:12 *2212*
and he that *s* findeth ... Lk 11:10 *2212*
for the Father *s* such to worship ... Jn 4:23 *2212*
he himself *s* to be known openly ... Jn 7:4 *2212*
of himself *s* his own glory ... Jn 7:18 *2212*
but he that *s* his glory that sent ... Jn 7:18 *2212*
there is one that *s* and judgeth ... Jn 8:50 *2212*
there is none that *s* after God ... Rom 3:11 *1567*
not obtained that which he *s* for ... Rom 11:7 *1934*
s not her own, is not easily ... 1Cor 13:5 *2212*

SEEKING {14}

s the wealth of his people, and ... Est 10:3 1875
and *s* judgment, and hasting ... Is 16:5 1875
places, *s* rest, and findeth none ... Mt 12:43 *2212*
a merchant man, *s* goodly pearls ... Mt 13:45 *2212*
s of him a sign from heaven, ... Mk 8:11 *2212*
back again to Jerusalem, *s* him ... Lk 2:45 *2212*
through dry places, *s* rest ... Lk 11:24 *2212*
s to catch something out of his ... Lk 11:54 *2212*
I come *s* fruit on this fig tree ... Lk 13:7 *2212*
and came to Capernaum, *s* for Jesus ... Jn 6:24 *2212*
s to turn away the deputy from ... Acts 13:8 *2212*
he went about *s* some to lead him ... Acts 13:11 *2212*
not *s* mine own profit, but the ... 1Cor 10:33 *2212*
about, *s* whom he may devour ... 1Pet 5:8 *2212*

SEEM {22}

I shall *s* to him as a deceiver ... Gen 27:12 1961
It shall not *s* hard unto thee, ... Deut 15:18 7185
brother should *s* vile unto thee ... Deut 25:3 7034
if it *s* evil unto you to serve ... Josh 24:15
him as it shall *s* good unto thee ... 1Sa 24:4
him what shall *s* good unto thee ... 2Sa 19:37
that which shall *s* good unto thee ... 2Sa 19:38
if it *s* good to thee, I will give ... 1Kin 21:2
If it *s* good unto you, and that it ... 1Chr 13:2
if it *s* good to the king, let ... Ezr 5:17
whatsoever shall *s* good to thee ... Ezr 7:18 3191
the trouble *s* little before thee ... Neh 9:32 4591
If it *s* good unto the king, let ... Est 5:4
the thing *s* right before the king ... Est 8:5
If it *s* good unto thee to come ... Jer 40:4 5869
but if it *s* ill unto thee to come ... Jer 40:4 5869
they shall *s* like torches, they ... Nah 2:4 4758
But if any man *s* to be ... 1Cor 11:16 *1380*
which *s* to be more feeble, are ... 1Cor 12:22 *1380*
That I may not *s* as if I would ... 2Cor 10:9 *1380*
any of you should *s* to come short ... Heb 4:1 *1380*
man among you *s* to be religious ... Jas 1:26 *1380*

SEEMED See APPENDIX.

SEEMETH {28}

It *s* to me there is as it were a .... Lev 14:35 7200
S it but a small thing unto you, ... Num 16:9
as it *s* good and right unto thee .... Josh 9:25 5869
us whatsoever *s* good unto thee .... Judg 10:15 5869
do with them what *s* good unto you........ Judg 19:24 5869
unto her, Do what *s* thee good........ 1Sa 1:23 5869
let him do what *s* him good........ 1Sa 3:18 5869
with us all that *s* good unto you 1Sa 11:10 5869
Do whatsoever *s* good unto thee 1Sa 14:36 5869
Saul, Do what *s* good unto thee 1Sa 14:40 5869
S it to you a light thing to be a........ 1Sa 18:23 5869
the LORD do that which *s* him good........ 2Sa 10:12 5869
him do to me as *s* good unto him 2Sa 15:26 5869
What *s* you best I will do 2Sa 18:4 5869
and offer up what *s* good unto him........ 2Sa 24:22 5869
do with them as it *s* good to thee........ Est 3:11 5869
is a way which *s* right unto a man .... Prov 14:12 6440
is a way that *s* right unto a man .... Prov 16:25 6440
is first in his own cause *s* just........ Prov 18:17
do with me as *s* good and meet unto........ Jer 26:14 5869
whither it *s* good and convenient........ Jer 40:4 5869
or go wheresoever it *s* convenient .... Jer 40:5 5869
S it a small thing unto you to .... Eze 34:18 5869
even that which he *s* to have........ Lk 8:18 *1380*
He *s* to be a setter forth of .... Acts 17:18 *1380*
For it *s* to me unreasonable to........ Acts 25:27 *1380*
If any man among you *s* to be wise........ 1Cor 3:18 *1380*
for the present *s* to be joyous .... Heb 12:11 *1380*

SEEMLY See APPENDIX.

SEEN {277}

for thee have I *s* righteous........ Gen 7:1 7200
were the tops of the mountains *s*........ Gen 8:5 7200
the bow shall be *s* in the cloud........ Gen 9:14 7200
mount of the LORD it shall be *s*........ Gen 22:14 7200
for I have *s* all that Laban doeth........ Gen 31:12 7200
God hath *s* mine affliction and the .... Gen 31:42 7200
for I have *s* God face to face, and .... Gen 32:30 7200
for therefore I have *s* thy face .... Gen 33:10 7200
as though I had *s* the face of God .... Gen 33:10 7200
Egypt, and of all that ye have *s*........ Gen 45:13 7200
me die, since I have *s* thy face........ Gen 46:30 7200
I have surely *s* the affliction of........ Ex 3:7 7200
I have also *s* the oppression........ Ex 3:9 7200
s that which is done to you in........ Ex 3:16
nor thy fathers' fathers have *s*........ Ex 10:6 7200
no leavened bread be *s* with thee........ Ex 13:7 7200
s with thee in all thy quarters........ Ex 13:7 7200
Egyptians whom ye have *s* to day .... Ex 14:13 7200
Ye have *s* what I did unto the........ Ex 19:4 7200
Ye have *s* that I have talked with........ Ex 20:22 7200
I have *s* this people, and, behold,........ Ex 32:9 7200
but my face shall not be *s*........ Ex 33:23 7200
thee, neither let any man be *s*........ Ex 34:3 7200
whether he hath *s* or known of it........ Lev 5:1 7200
after that he hath been *s* of the........ Lev 13:7 7200
he shall be *s* of the priest again .... Lev 13:7 7200
that thou LORD art *s* face to face .... Num 14:14 7200
those men which have *s* my glory........ Num 14:22 7200
neither hath he *s* perverseness in........ Num 23:21 7200
And when thou hast *s* it, thou also .... Num 27:13 7200
moreover we have *s* the sons of........ Deut 1:28 7200
where thou hast *s* how that the........ Deut 1:31 7200
Thine eyes have *s* all that the........ Deut 3:21 7200
Your eyes have *s* what the LORD........ Deut 4:3 7200
things which thine eyes have *s*........ Deut 4:9 7200
we have *s* this day that God doth........ Deut 5:24 7200
I have *s* this people, and, behold,........ Deut 9:13 7200
things, which thine eyes have *s*........ Deut 10:21 7200
which have not *s* the chastisement........ Deut 11:2 7200
But your eyes have *s* all the........ Deut 11:7 7200
s with thee in all thy coast .... Deut 16:4 7200
blood, neither have our eyes *s* it........ Deut 21:7 7200
Ye have *s* all that the LORD did........ Deut 29:2 7200
which thine eyes have *s*, the........ Deut 29:3 7200
ye have *s* their abominations, and........ Deut 29:17 7200
to his mother, I have not *s* him........ Deut 33:9 7200
ye have *s* all that the LORD your .... Josh 23:3 7200
your eyes have *s* what I have done .... Josh 24:7 7200
who had *s* all the great works of........ Judg 2:7 7200
was there a shield or spear *s*........ Judg 5:8 7200
for because I have *s* an angel of........ Judg 6:22 7200
with him, What ye have *s* me do .... Judg 9:48 7200
surely die, because we have *s* God .... Judg 13:22 7200
I have *s* a woman in Timnath of........ Judg 14:2 7200
for we have *s* the land, and,........ Judg 18:9 7200
s from the day that the children........ Judg 19:30 7200
lords of the Philistines had *s* it 1Sa 6:16 7200
I have *s* a son of Jesse the........ 1Sa 16:18 7200
Have ye *s* this man that is come........ 1Sa 17:25 7200
haunt is, and who hath *s* him there 1Sa 23:22 7200
this day thine eyes have *s* how 1Sa 24:10 7200
not be *s* to come into the city........ 2Sa 17:17 7200
Go tell the king what thou hast *s*........ 2Sa 18:21 7200
he was *s* upon the wings of the 2Sa 22:11 7200
there was no stone *s* 1Kin 6:18 7200
the ends of the staves were *s* out........ 1Kin 8:8 7200
and they were not *s* without........ 1Kin 8:8 7200
Sheba had *s* all Solomon's wisdom 1Kin 10:4 7200
I came, and mine eyes had *s* it 1Kin 10:7 7200
trees, nor were *s* unto this day 1Kin 10:12 7200
For his sons had *s* what way the 1Kin 13:12 7200
Hast thou *s* all this great........ 1Kin 20:13 7200
Surely I have *s* yesterday the........ 2Kin 9:26 7200
thy prayer, I have *s* thy tears 2Kin 20:5 7200
What have they *s* in thine house 2Kin 20:15 7200
are in mine house have they *s* 2Kin 20:15 7200
him at Megiddo, when he had *s* him........ 2Kin 23:29 7200
now have I *s* with joy thy people,........ 1Chr 29:17 7200
the ends of the staves were *s*........ 2Chr 5:9 7200
but they were not *s* without 2Chr 5:9 7200
Sheba had *s* the wisdom of Solomon 2Chr 9:3 7200
I came, and mine eyes had *s* it 2Chr 9:6 7200
there were none such *s* before in........ 2Chr 9:11 7200
that had *s* the first house, when........ Ezr 3:12 7200
they had *s* concerning this matter........ Est 9:26 7200
Even as I have *s*, they that plow .... Job 4:8 7200
I have *s* the foolish taking root........ Job 5:3 7200
hath *s* me shall see me no more........ Job 7:8 7210
him, saying, I have not *s* thee........ Job 8:18 7200
up the ghost, and no eye had *s* me .... Job 10:18 7200
Lo, mine eye hath *s* all this .... Job 13:1 7200
which I have *s* I will declare .... Job 15:17 2372
they which have *s* him shall say........ Job 20:7 7200
all ye yourselves have *s* it........ Job 27:12 2372
the vulture's eye hath not *s* .... Job 28:7 7805
If I have *s* any perish for want .... Job 31:19 7200
away, that it cannot be *s*........ Job 33:21 7210
bones that were not *s* stick out .... Job 33:21 7200
or hast thou *s* the doors of the .... Job 38:17 7200
or hast thou *s* the treasures of........ Job 38:22 7200
Thou hast *s* it........ Ps 10:14 7200
the channels of waters were *s* .... Ps 18:15 7200
said, Aha, aha, our eye hath *s* it........ Ps 35:21 7200
This thou hast *s*, O LORD........ Ps 35:22 7200
yet have I not *s* the righteous .... Ps 37:25 7200
I have *s* the wicked in great .... Ps 37:35 7200
so have we *s* in the city of the........ Ps 48:8 7200
mine eye hath *s* his desire upon .... Ps 54:7 7200
for I have *s* violence and strife........ Ps 55:9 7200
so as I have *s* thee in the .... Ps 63:2 2372
They have *s* thy goings, O God........ Ps 68:24 7200
the years wherein we have *s* evil........ Ps 90:15 7200
have *s* the salvation of our God........ Ps 98:3 7200
I have *s* an end of all perfection........ Ps 119:96 7200
the prince whom thine eyes have *s*........ Prov 25:7 7200
I have *s* all the works that are........ Eccl 1:14 7200
I have *s* the travail, which God .... Eccl 3:10 7200
who hath not *s* the evil work that........ Eccl 4:3 7200
evil which I have *s* under the sun........ Eccl 5:13 7200
Behold that which I have *s*........ Eccl 5:18 7200
evil which I have *s* under the sun........ Eccl 6:1 7200
Moreover he hath not *s* the sun .... Eccl 6:5 7200
twice told, yet hath he *s* no good .... Eccl 6:6 7200
All things have I *s* in the days........ Eccl 7:15 7200
All this have I *s*, and applied my........ Eccl 8:9 7200
have I *s* also under the sun........ Eccl 9:13 7200
evil which I have *s* under the sun........ Eccl 10:5 7200
I have *s* servants upon horses, and........ Eccl 10:7 7200
for mine eyes have *s* the King .... Is 6:5 7200
in darkness have *s* a great light........ Is 9:2 7200
when it is *s* that Moab is weary .... Is 16:12 7200
Ye have *s* also the breaches of........ Is 22:9 7200
thy prayer, I have *s* thy tears .... Is 38:5 7200
What have they *s* in thine house .... Is 39:4 7200
that is in mine house have they *s* .... Is 39:4 7200
Aha, I am warm, I have *s* the fire........ Is 44:16 7200
yea, thy shame shall be *s* .... Is 47:3 7200
I have *s* his ways, and will heal........ Is 57:18 7200
and his glory shall be *s* upon thee........ Is 60:2 7200
the ear, neither hath the eye *s* .... Is 64:4 7200
who hath *s* such things........ Is 66:8 7200
my fame, neither have *s* my glory........ Is 66:19 7200
LORD unto me, Thou hast well *s*........ Jer 1:12 7200
the king, Hast thou *s* that which........ Jer 3:6 7200
Behold, even I have *s* it, saith........ Jer 7:11 7200
thou hast *s* me, and tried mine........ Jer 12:3 7200
I have *s* thine adulteries, and thy........ Jer 13:27 7200
I have *s* folly in the prophets of........ Jer 23:13 7200
I have *s* also in the prophets of .... Jer 23:14 7200
Ye have *s* all the evil that I........ Jer 44:2 7200
Wherefore have I *s* them dismayed........ Jer 46:5 7200
because they have *s* her nakedness .... Lam 1:8 7200
for she hath *s* that the heathen .... Lam 1:10 7200
Thy prophets have *s* vain and........ Lam 2:14 2372
but have *s* for thee false burdens .... Lam 2:14 2372
we have found, we have *s* it........ Lam 2:16 7200
I am the man that hath *s*........ Lam 3:1 7200
O LORD, thou hast *s* my wrong........ Lam 3:59 7200
Thou hast *s* all their vengeance........ Lam 3:60 7200
hast thou *s* what the ancients of .... Eze 8:12 7200
said he unto me, Hast thou *s* this........ Eze 8:15 7200
he said unto me, Hast thou *s* this........ Eze 8:17 7200
that I had *s* went up from me........ Eze 11:24 7200
own spirit, and have *s* nothing........ Eze 13:3 7200
They have *s* vanity and lying........ Eze 13:6 2372
Have ye not *s* a vain vision, and........ Eze 13:7 2372
s lies, therefore, behold, I am .... Eze 13:8 2372
me, Son of man, hast thou *s* this........ Eze 47:6 7200
unto me the dream which I have *s*........ Dan 2:26 2370
visions of my dream that I have *s* .... Dan 4:9 2370
I king Nebuchadnezzar have *s*........ Dan 4:18 2370
which I had *s* standing before the........ Dan 8:6 7200
had *s* the vision, and sought for........ Dan 8:15 7200
whom I had *s* in the vision at the........ Dan 9:21 7200
I have *s* an horrible thing in the........ Hos 6:10 7200
for now have I *s* with mine eyes........ Zec 9:8 7200
And the LORD shall be *s* over them........ Zec 9:14 7200
and the diviners have *s* a lie........ Zec 10:2 2372
for we have *s* his star in the .... Mt 2:2 *1492*
alms before men, to be *s* of them .... Mt 6:1 *2300*
that they may be *s* of men........ Mt 6:5 *5316*
It was never so *s* in Israel........ Mt 9:33 *5316*
which ye see, and have not *s* them........ Mt 13:17 *1492*
and ye, when ye had *s* it, repented........ Mt 21:32 *1492*
works they do for to be *s* of men........ Mt 23:5 *2300*
till they have *s* the kingdom of........ Mk 9:1 *1492*
no man what things they had *s* .... Mk 9:9 *1492*
was alive, and had been *s* of her .... Mk 16:11 *2300*
had *s* him after he was risen .... Mk 16:14 *2300*
he had *s* a vision in the temple .... Lk 1:22 *3708*
And when they had *s* it, they made........ Lk 2:17 *1492*
things that they had heard and *s* .... Lk 2:20 *1492*
before he had *s* the Lord's Christ .... Lk 2:26 *1492*
mine eyes have *s* thy salvation .... Lk 2:30 *1492*
We have *s* strange things to day .... Lk 5:26 *1492*
tell John what things ye have *s* .... Lk 7:22 *1492*
of those things which they had *s*........ Lk 9:36 *3708*
which ye see, and have not *s* them........ Lk 10:24 *1492*
the mighty works that they had *s* .... Lk 19:37 *1492*
he hoped to have *s* some miracle........ Lk 23:8 *1492*
had also *s* a vision of angels........ Lk 24:23 *3708*
supposed that they had *s* a spirit .... Lk 24:37 *2334*
No man hath *s* God at any time .... Jn 1:18 *3708*
know, and testify that we have *s* .... Jn 3:11 *3708*
And what he hath *s* and heard, that .... Jn 3:32 *3708*
having *s* all the things that he........ Jn 4:45 *3708*
at any time, nor *s* his shape........ Jn 5:37 *3708*
when they had *s* the miracle that........ Jn 6:14 *1492*
unto you, That ye also have *s* me .... Jn 6:36 *3708*
that any man hath *s* the Father........ Jn 6:46 *3708*
is of God, he hath *s* the Father........ Jn 6:46 *3708*
which I have *s* with my Father........ Jn 8:38 *3708*
which ye have *s* with your father........ Jn 8:38 *3708*
years old, and hast thou *s* Abraham .... Jn 8:57 *3708*
had *s* him that he was blind........ Jn 9:8 *2334*
unto him, Thou hast both *s* him........ Jn 9:37 *3708*
had *s* the things which Jesus did,........ Jn 11:45 *2300*
ye know him, and have *s* him........ Jn 14:7 *3708*
hath *s* me hath *s* the Father........ Jn 14:9 *3708*
but now have they both *s* and hated........ Jn 15:24 *3708*
disciples that she had *s* the Lord .... Jn 20:18 *3708*
said unto him, We have *s* the Lord........ Jn 20:25 *3708*
Thomas, because thou hast *s* me........ Jn 20:29 *3708*
blessed are they that have not *s*........ Jn 20:29 *1492*
being *s* of them forty days, and........ Acts 1:3 *3700*
as ye have *s* him go into heaven .... Acts 1:11 *2300*
speak the things which we have *s* .... Acts 4:20 *1492*
I have *s*, I have *s* the........ Acts 7:34 *1492*
to the fashion that he had *s* .... Acts 7:44 *3708*
hath *s* in a vision a man named .... Acts 9:12 *1492*
how he had *s* the Lord in the way........ Acts 9:27 *1492*
vision which he had *s* should mean........ Acts 10:17 *1492*
he had *s* an angel in his house .... Acts 11:13 *1492*
had *s* the grace of God, was glad,........ Acts 11:23 *1492*
he was *s* many days of them which........ Acts 13:31 *3700*
And after he had *s* the vision........ Acts 16:10 *1492*
and when they had *s* the brethren .... Acts 16:40 *1492*
(For they had *s* before with him........ Acts 21:29 *4308*
unto all men of what thou hast *s* .... Acts 22:15 *3708*
of these things which thou hast *s*........ Acts 26:16 *1492*
of the world are clearly *s*........ Rom 1:20 *2529*
but hope that is *s* is not hope........ Rom 8:24 *991*
as it is written, Eye hath not *s* 1Cor 2:9 *1492*
have I not *s* Jesus Christ our 1Cor 9:1 *3708*
And that he was *s* of Cephas........ 1Cor 15:5 *3700*
he was *s* of above five hundred 1Cor 15:6 *3700*
After that, he was *s* of James 1Cor 15:7 *3700*
last of all he was *s* of me also 1Cor 15:8 *3700*
not at the things which are *s*........ 2Cor 4:18 *991*
but at the things which are not *s* 2Cor 4:18 *991*
things which are *s* are temporal........ 2Cor 4:18 *991*
which are not *s* are eternal........ 2Cor 4:18 *991*
and heard, and *s* in me, do .... Phil 4:9 *1492*
have not *s* my face in the flesh........ Col 2:1 *3708*
those things which he hath not *s* .... Col 2:18 *3708*
s of angels, preached unto the........ 1Ti 3:16 *3700*
whom no man hath *s*, nor can see........ 1Ti 6:16 *1492*
for, the evidence of things not *s* .... Heb 11:1 *991*
so that things which are *s* were........ Heb 11:3 *991*
of God of things not *s* as yet .... Heb 11:7 *991*
but having *s* them afar off, and........ Heb 11:13 *1492*
have *s* the end of the Lord........ Jas 5:11 *1492*
Whom having not *s*, ye love........ 1Pet 1:8 *1492*
which we have *s* with our eyes........ 1Jn 1:1 *3708*
was manifested, and we have *s* it........ 1Jn 1:2 *3708*
That which we have *s* and heard........ 1Jn 1:3 *3708*
whosoever sinneth hath not *s* him........ 1Jn 3:6 *3708*
No man hath *s* God at any time........ 1Jn 4:12 *2300*
And we have *s* and do testify that........ 1Jn 4:14 *2300*
not his brother whom he hath *s* 1Jn 4:20 *3708*
he love God whom he hath not *s*........ 1Jn 4:20 *3708*
he that doeth evil hath not *s* God 3Jn 11 *3780*
the things which thou hast *s* .... Rev 1:19 *1492*
there was *s* in his temple the ark .... Rev 11:19 *3700*
And when I had heard and *s*, I fell .... Rev 22:8 *991*

SEER {21}

Come, and let us go to the *s* 1Sa 9:9 7200
Prophet was beforetime called a *S*........ 1Sa 9:9 7200
and said unto them, Is the *s* here 1Sa 9:11 7200
Saul, and said, I am the *s* 1Sa 9:19 7200
the priest, Art not thou a *s* 2Sa 15:27 7200
unto the prophet Gad, David's *s* 2Sa 24:11 2374
Samuel the *s* did ordain in their 1Chr 9:22 7200
LORD spake unto Gad, David's *s* 1Chr 21:9 2374
the king's *s* in the words of God........ 1Chr 25:5 2374
And all that Samuel the *s*, and Saul........ 1Chr 26:28 7200
in the book of Samuel the *s* 1Chr 29:29 7200
and in the book of Gad the *s*........ 1Chr 29:29 2374
in the visions of Iddo the *s*........ 2Chr 9:29 2374
and of Iddo the *s* concerning........ 2Chr 12:15 2374

S

at that time Hanani the *s* came to 2Chr 16:7 7200
Then Asa was wroth with the *s* 2Chr 16:10 7200
Hanani the *s* went out to meet him 2Chr 19:2 2374
of David, and of Gad the king's *s* 2Chr 29:25 2374
words of David, and of Asaph the *s* 2Chr 29:30 2374
Heman, and Jeduthun the king's *s* 2Chr 35:15 2374
Amaziah said unto Amos, O thou *s* Amos 7:12 2374

SEER'S {1}
I pray thee, where the *s* house is 1Sa 9:18 7200

SEERS {6}
all the prophets, and by all the *s* 2Kin 17:13 2374
the words of the *s* that spake to 2Chr 33:18 2374
among the sayings of the *s* 2Chr 33:19 2374
rulers, the *s* hath he covered Is 29:10 2374
Which say to the *s*, See not Is 30:10 7200
Then shall the *s* be ashamed Mic 3:7 2374

SEEST {36}
For all the land which thou *s* Gen 13:15 7200
spake unto her, Thou God *s* me Gen 16:13 7210
and all that thou *s* is mine Gen 31:43 7200
for in that day thou *s* my face Ex 10:28 7200
heaven, and when thou *s* the sun Deut 4:19 7200
in every place that thou *s* Deut 12:13 7200
s horses, and chariots, and a Deut 20:1 7200
s among the captives a beautiful Deut 21:11 7200
him, Thou *s* the shadow of the Judg 9:36 7200
S thou how Ahab humbleth himself 1Kin 21:29 7200
or *s* thou as man seeth Job 10:4 7200
S thou a man diligent in his Prov 22:29 2372
S thou a man wise in his own Prov 26:12 7200
S thou a man that is hasty in his Prov 29:20 2372
If thou *s* the oppression of the Eccl 5:8 7200
fasted, say they, and thou *s* not Is 58:3 7200
when thou *s* the naked, that thou Is 58:7 7200
me, saying, Jeremiah, what *s* thou Jer 1:11 7200
second time, saying, What *s* thou Jer 1:13 7200
S thou not what they do in the Jer 7:17 7200
s the reins and the heart, let me Jer 20:12 7200
the LORD unto me, What *s* thou Jer 24:3 7200
and, behold, thou *s* it Jer 32:24 7200
Son of man, *s* thou what they do Eze 8:6 7200
declare all that thou *s* to the Eze 40:4 7200
and as thou *s*, deal with thy Dan 1:13 7200
said unto me, Amos, what *s* thou Amos 7:8 7200
And he said, Amos, what *s* thou Amos 8:2 7200
And said unto me, What *s* thou Zec 4:2 7200
And he said unto me, What *s* thou Zec 5:2 7200
Thou *s* the multitude thronging Mk 5:31 *991*
S thou these great buildings Mk 13:2 *991*
unto Simon, *S* thou this woman Lk 7:44 *991*
Lord, and said unto him, Thou *s* Acts 21:20 *2334*
S thou how faith wrought with his Jas 2:22 *991*
and, What thou *s*, write in a book, Rev 1:11 *991*

SEETH {54}
here looked after him that *s* me Gen 16:13 7210
when he *s* that the lad is not Gen 44:31 7200
and when he *s* thee, he will be Ex 4:14 7200
when he *s* the blood upon the Ex 12:23 7200
And if, when the priest *s* it Lev 13:20 7200
when he *s* that their power is Deut 32:36 7200
for the LORD *s* not as man *s* 1Sa 16:7 7200
city is pleasant, as my lord *s* 2Kin 2:19 7200
heap, and *s* the place of stones Job 8:17 2372
or seest thou as man *s* Job 10:4 7200
he *s* wickedness also Job 11:11 7200
a covering to him, that he *s* not Job 22:14 7200
his eye *s* every precious thing Job 28:10 7200
and *s* under the whole heaven Job 28:24 7200
of man, and he *s* all his goings Job 34:21 7200
but now mine eye *s* thee Job 42:5 7200
for he *s* that his day is coming Ps 37:13 7200
For he *s* that wise men die, Ps 49:10 7200
rejoice when he *s* the vengeance Ps 58:10 2372
nor night *s* sleep with his eyes Eccl 8:16 7200
let him declare what he *s* Is 21:6 7200
when he that looketh upon it *s* Is 28:4 7200
the dark, and they say, Who *s* us Is 29:15 7200
But when he *s* his children, the Is 29:23 7200
thou hast said, None *s* me Is 47:10 7200
for they say, The LORD *s* us not Eze 8:12 7200
the earth, and the LORD *s* not Eze 9:9 7200
The vision that he *s* is for many Eze 12:27 2372
that *s* all his father's sins Eze 18:14 7200
If when he *s* the sword come upon Eze 33:3 7200
when any *s* a man's bone, then Eze 39:15 7200
thy Father which *s* in secret Mt 6:4 *991*
thy Father which *s* in secret Mt 6:6 *991*
which *s* in secret, shall reward Mt 6:18 *991*
s the tumult, and them that wept Mk 5:38 *2334*
s Abraham afar off, and Lazarus in Lk 16:23 *3708*
The next day John *s* Jesus coming Jn 1:29 *991*
but what he *s* the Father do Jn 5:19 *991*
that every one which *s* the Son Jn 6:40 *2334*
But by what means he now *s* Jn 9:21 *991*
s the wolf coming, and leaveth the Jn 10:12 *2334*
because he *s* the light of this Jn 11:9 *991*
that *s* me *s* him that sent me Jn 12:45 *2334*
receive, because it *s* him not Jn 14:17 *2334*
while, and the world *s* me no more Jn 14:19 *2334*
s the stone taken away from the Jn 20:1 *991*
and *s* the linen clothes lie, Jn 20:6 *2334*
s two angels in white sitting, Jn 20:12 *2334*
s the disciple whom Jesus loved Jn 21:20 *991*
for what a man *s*, why doth he yet Rom 8:24 *991*
me above that which he *s* me to be 2Cor 12:6 *991*
s his brother have need, and 1Jn 3:17 *2334*

SEETHE {9}
to day, and *s* that ye will *s* Ex 16:23 1310
Thou shalt not *s* a kid in his Ex 23:19 1310
s his flesh in the holy place Ex 29:31 1310
Thou shalt not *s* a kid in his Ex 34:26 1310
Thou shalt not *s* a kid in his Deut 14:21 1310
s pottage for the sons of the 2Kin 4:38 1310
let them *s* the bones of it Eze 24:5 1310
and take of them, and *s* therein Zec 14:21 1310

SEETHING {3}
came, while the flesh was in *s* 1Sa 2:13 1310
as out of a *s* pot or caldron Job 41:20 5301
and I said, I see a *s* pot Jer 1:13 5301

SEGUB *(se'-gub)* {3}
1. A son of Hiel.
thereof in his youngest son *S* 1Kin 16:34 7687
2. A son of Hezron.
and she bare him *S* 1Chr 2:21 7687
S begat Jair, who had three and 1Chr 2:22 7687

SEIR *(se'-ur)* {39}
1. A region south of the Dead Sea.
And the Horites in their mount *S* Gen 14:6 8165
his brother unto the land of *S* Gen 32:3 8165
until I come unto my lord unto *S* Gen 33:14 8165
that day on his way unto *S* Gen 33:16 8165
Thus dwelt Esau in mount *S* Gen 36:8 8165
father of the Edomites in mount *S* Gen 36:9 8165
the children of *S* in the land of Gen 36:21 8165
their dukes in the land of *S* Gen 36:30 8165
S also shall be a possession for Num 24:18 8165
way of mount *S* unto Kadesh-barnea Deut 1:2 8165
as bees do, and destroyed you in *S* Deut 1:44 8165
we compassed mount *S* many days Deut 2:1 8165
of Esau, which dwell in *S* Deut 2:4 8165
S unto Esau for a possession Deut 2:5 8165
of Esau, which dwelt in *S* Deut 2:8 8165
Horims also dwelt in *S* beforetime Deut 2:12 8165
of Esau, which dwelt in *S* Deut 2:22 8165
children of Esau which dwell in *S* Deut 2:29 8165
and rose up from *S* unto them Deut 33:2 8165
mount Halak, that goeth up to *S* Josh 11:17 8165
mount Halak, that goeth up to *S* Josh 12:7 8165
from Baalah westward unto mount *S* Josh 15:10 8165
and I gave unto Esau mount *S* Josh 24:4 8165
LORD, when thou wentest out of *S* Judg 5:4 8165
five hundred men, went to mount *S* 1Chr 4:42 8165
of Ammon and Moab and mount *S* 2Chr 20:10 8165
of Ammon, Moab, and mount *S* 2Chr 20:22 8165
the inhabitants of mount *S* 2Chr 20:23 8165
an end of the inhabitants of *S* 2Chr 20:23 8165
of the children of *S* ten thousand 2Chr 25:11 8165
the gods of the children of *S* 2Chr 25:14 8165
He calleth to me out of *S* Is 21:11 8165
S do say, Behold, the house of Eze 25:8 8165
man, set thy face against mount *S* Eze 35:2 8165
Behold, O mount *S*, I am against Eze 35:3 8165
will I make mount *S* most desolate Eze 35:7 8165
thou shalt be desolate, O mount *S* Eze 35:15 8165
2. Grandfather of Hori.
are the sons of *S* the Horite Gen 36:20 8165
And the sons of *S* 1Chr 1:38 8165

SEIRAH See SEIRATH.

SEIRATH *(se'-ur-ath)* {1} *A city in Ephraim.*
the quarries, and escaped unto *S* Judg 3:26 8167

SEIZE {4}
the ambush, and *s* upon the city Josh 8:7 3423
night, let darkness *s* upon it Job 3:6 3947
Let death *s* upon them, and let Ps 55:15 3451
let us *s* on his inheritance Mt 21:38 *2722*

SEIZED {1}
to flee, and fear hath *s* on her Jer 49:24 2388

SELA *(se'-lah)* {1} See SELAH. *Same as Selah 1.*
the land from *S* to the wilderness Is 16:1 5554

SELAH *(se'-lah)* {75} See JOKTHEEL, SELA.
1. Capital of Edom.
took *S* by war, and called the name 2Kin 14:7 5554
2. A musical notation.
no help for him in God. *S* Ps 3:2 5542
me out of his holy hill. *S* Ps 3:4 5542
blessing is upon thy people. *S* Ps 3:8 5542
vanity, and seek after leasing? *S* Ps 4:2 5542
your bed, and be still. *S* Ps 4:4 5542
mine honour in the dust. *S* Ps 7:5 5542
his own hands. Higgaion. *S* Ps 9:16 5542
themselves to be but men. *S* Ps 9:20 5542
accept thy burnt sacrifice; *S* Ps 20:3 5542
the request of his lips. *S* Ps 21:2 5542
thy face, O Jacob. *S* Ps 24:6 5542
he is the King of glory. *S* Ps 24:10 5542
the drought of summer. *S* Ps 32:4 5542
the iniquity of my sin. *S* Ps 32:5 5542
songs of deliverance. *S* Ps 32:7 5542
state is altogether vanity. *S* Ps 39:5 5542
every man is vanity. *S* Ps 39:11 5542
thy name for ever. *S* Ps 44:8 5542
with the swelling thereof. *S* Ps 46:3 5542
Jacob is our refuge. *S* Ps 46:7 5542
Jacob is our refuge. *S* Ps 46:11 5542
Jacob whom he loved. *S* Ps 47:4 5542
establish it for ever. *S* Ps 48:8 5542
approve their sayings. *S* Ps 49:13 5542
he shall receive me. *S* Ps 49:15 5542
God is judge himself. *S* Ps 50:6 5542
to speak righteousness. *S* Ps 52:3 5542
land of the living. *S* Ps 52:5 5542
set God before them. *S* Ps 54:3 5542
remain in the wilderness. *S* Ps 55:7 5542
that abideth of old. *S* Ps 55:19 5542
swallow me up. *S* Ps 57:3 5542
are fallen themselves. *S* Ps 57:6 5542
wicked transgressors. *S* Ps 59:5 5542
ends of the earth. *S* Ps 59:13 5542
because of the truth. *S* Ps 60:4 5542
the covert of thy wings. *S* Ps 61:4 5542
but they curse inwardly. *S* Ps 62:4 5542
is a refuge for us. *S* Ps 62:8 5542
sing to thy name. *S* Ps 66:4 5542
exalt themselves. *S* Ps 66:7 5542
offer bullocks with goats. *S* Ps 66:15 5542
face to shine upon us; *S* Ps 67:1 5542
the nations upon earth. *S* Ps 67:4 5542
through the wilderness; *S* Ps 68:7 5542
the God of our salvation. *S* Ps 68:19 5542
praises unto the Lord. *S* Ps 68:32 5542
up the pillars of it. *S* Ps 75:3 5542
sword, and the battle. *S* Ps 76:3 5542
the meek of the earth. *S* Ps 76:9 5542
was overwhelmed. *S* Ps 77:3 5542
up his tender mercies? *S* Ps 77:9 5542
of Jacob and Joseph. *S* Ps 77:15 5542
the waters of Meribah. *S* Ps 81:7 5542
persons of the wicked? *S* Ps 82:2 5542
the children of Lot. *S* Ps 83:8 5542
be still praising thee. *S* Ps 84:4 5542
O God of Jacob. *S* Ps 84:8 5542
covered all their sin. *S* Ps 85:2 5542
O city of God. *S* Ps 87:3 5542
man was born there. *S* Ps 87:6 5542
me with all thy waves. *S* Ps 88:7 5542
dead arise and praise thee? *S* Ps 88:10 5542
throne to all generations. *S* Ps 89:4 5542
witness in heaven. *S* Ps 89:37 5542
him with shame. *S* Ps 89:45 5542
hand of the grave? *S* Ps 89:48 5542
is under their lips. *S* Ps 140:3 5542
have set gins for me. *S* Ps 140:5 5542
they exalt themselves. *S* Ps 140:8 5542
as a thirsty land. *S* Ps 143:6 5542
from mount Paran. *S* Hab 3:3 5542
even thy word. *S* Hab 3:9 5542
foundation unto the neck. *S* Hab 3:13 5542

SELA-HAMMAHLEKOTH *(se'-lah-ham-mah'-le-koth)* {1} *A hill in the wilderness of Maon.*
they called that place *S* 1Sa 23:28 5555

SELED *(se'-led)* {2} *A descendant of Jerahmeel.*
S, and Appaim: but *S* died 1Chr 2:30 5540

SELEUCIA *(sel-u-si'-ah)* {1} *A city in Syria.*
the Holy Ghost, departed unto *S* Acts 13:4 *4581*

SELF See APPENDIX.

SELFSAME {15}
In the *s* day entered Noah, and Gen 7:13 2088,6106
of their foreskin in the *s* day Gen 17:23 2088,6106
In the *s* day was Abraham Gen 17:26 2088,6106
for in this *s* day have I brought Ex 12:17 2088,6106
even the *s* day it came to pass, Ex 12:41 2088,6106
And it came to pass the *s* day Ex 12:51 2088,6106
until the *s* day that ye have Lev 23:14 2088,6106
And ye shall proclaim on the *s* day Lev 23:21 2088,6106
LORD spake unto Moses that *s* day Deut 32:48 2088,6106
and parched corn in the *s* day Josh 5:11 2088,6106
in the *s* day the hand of the LORD Eze 40:1 2088,6106
servant was healed in the *s* hour Mt 8:13 *1565*
the *s* Spirit, dividing to every 1Cor 12:11 *846*
wrought us for the *s* thing is God 2Cor 5:5 *846,5124*
For behold this *s* thing, that ye 2Cor 7:11 *846*

SELFWILL {1}
in their *s* they digged down a Gen 49:6 7522

SELFWILLED {2}
not *s*, not soon angry, not given Titus 1:7 *829*
Presumptuous are they, *s*, they 2Pet 2:10 *829*

SELL {35}
S me this day thy birthright Gen 25:31 4376
let us *s* him to the Ishmeelites, Gen 37:27 4376
if a man *s* his daughter to be a Ex 21:7 4376
to *s* her unto a strange nation he Ex 21:8 4376
then they shall *s* the live ox Ex 21:35 4376
or a sheep, and kill it, or *s* it Ex 22:1 4376
And if thou *s* ought unto thy Lev 25:14 4376
the fruits he shall *s* unto thee Lev 25:15 4376
of the fruits doth he *s* unto thee Lev 25:16 4376
if a man *s* a dwelling house in a Lev 25:29 4376
s himself unto the stranger or Lev 25:47 4376
Thou shalt *s* me meat for money, Deut 2:28 7666
or thou mayest *s* it unto an alien Deut 14:21 4376
but thou shalt not *s* her at all Deut 21:14 4376
for the LORD shall *s* Sisera into Judg 4:9 4376
which did *s* himself to work 1Kin 21:25 4376
s the oil, and pay thy debt, and 2Kin 4:7 4376
will ye even *s* your brethren Neh 5:8 4376
victuals on the sabbath day to *s* Neh 10:31 4376
Buy the truth, and *s* it not Prov 23:23 4376
s the land into the hand of the Eze 30:12 4376
And they shall not *s* of it Eze 48:14 4376
I will *s* your sons and your Joel 3:8 4376
they shall *s* them to the Sabeans, Joel 3:8 4376
moon be gone, that we may *s* corn Amos 8:5 7666
s the refuse of the wheat Amos 8:6 7666
and they that *s* them say, Blessed Zec 11:5 4376
s that thou hast, and give to the Mt 19:21 *4453*
but go ye rather to them that *s* Mt 25:9 *4453*

s whatsoever thou hast, and give ... Mk 10:21 4453
S that ye have, and give alms ... Lk 12:33 4453
s all that thou hast, and ... Lk 18:22 4453
let him s his garment, and buy one ... Lk 22:36 4453
there a year, and buy and s ... Jas 4:13 1710
And that no man might buy or s ... Rev 13:17 4453

SELLER {4}
as with the buyer, so with the s ... Is 24:2 4376
buyer rejoice, nor the s mourn ... Eze 7:12 4376
For the s shall not return to ... Eze 7:13 4376
a s of purple, of the city of ... Acts 16:14 4211

SELLERS {1}
s of all kind of ware lodged ... Neh 13:20 4376

SELLEST {1}
Thou s thy people for nought, and ... Ps 44:12 4376

SELLETH {7}
s him, or if he be found in his ... Ex 21:16 4376
merchandise of him, or s him ... Deut 24:7 4376
s a parcel of land, which was our ... Ruth 4:3 4376
be upon the head of him that s it ... Prov 11:26 7666
She maketh fine linen, and s it ... Prov 31:24 4376
that s nations through her ... Nah 3:4 4376
s all that he hath, and buyeth ... Mt 13:44 4453

SELVEDGE {2}
from the s in the coupling ... Ex 26:4 7098
from the s in the coupling ... Ex 36:11 7098

SELVES {7}
know of your own s that summer is ... Lk 21:30 1438
of your own s shall men arise ... Acts 20:30 846
gave their own s to the Lord ... 2Cor 8:5 1438
prove your own s ... 2Cor 13:5 1438
Know ye not your own s, how that ... 2Cor 13:5 1438
shall be lovers of their own s ... 2Ti 3:2 5367
only, deceiving your own s ... Jas 1:22 846

SEM *(sem)* {1} See SHEM. *Greek form of Shem.*
Arphaxad, which was the son of S ... Lk 3:36 4590

SEMACHIAH *(sem-a-ki'-ah)* {1} *A sanctuary servant.*
were strong men, Elihu, and S ... 1Chr 26:7 5565

SEMEI *(sem'-e-i)* {1} See SHEMAIAH. *A son of Joseph; an ancestor of Jesus.*
which was the son of S, which ... Lk 3:26 4584

SEMEIN See SEMEI.

SENAAH *(sen'-a-ah)* {2} See HASSENAAH. *A city in Judah.*
The children of S, three thousand ... Ezr 2:35 5570
The children of S, three thousand ... Neh 7:38 5570

SENATE {1}
all the s of the children of ... Acts 5:21 1087

SENATORS {1}
and teach his s wisdom ... Ps 105:22 2205

SEND {234}
he shall s his angel before thee, ... Gen 24:7 7971
s me good speed this day, and shew ... Gen 24:12 7136
will s his angel with thee, and ... Gen 24:40 7971
he said, S me away unto my master ... Gen 24:54 7971
s me away that I may go to my ... Gen 24:56 7971
then I will s, and fetch thee from ... Gen 27:45 7971
S me away, that I may go unto ... Gen 30:25 7971
come, and I will s thee unto them ... Gen 37:13 7971
I will s thee a kid from the ... Gen 38:17 7971
give me a pledge, till thou s it ... Gen 38:17 7971
S one of you, and let him fetch ... Gen 42:16 7971
If thou wilt s our brother with ... Gen 43:4 7971
But if thou wilt not s him ... Gen 43:5 7971
S the lad with me, and we will ... Gen 43:8 7971
that he may s away your other ... Gen 43:14 7971
for God did s me before you to ... Gen 45:5 7971
I will s thee unto Pharaoh, that ... Ex 3:10 7971
And he said, O my Lord, s, I pray ... Ex 4:13 7971
the hand of him whom thou wilt s ... Ex 4:13 7971
that he s the children of Israel ... Ex 7:2 7971
I will s swarms of flies upon ... Ex 8:21 7971
For I will at this time s all my ... Ex 9:14 7971
S therefore now, and gather thy ... Ex 9:19 7971
that they might s them out of the ... Ex 12:33 7971
I s an Angel before thee, to keep ... Ex 23:20 7971
I will s my fear before thee, and ... Ex 23:27 7971
I will s hornets before thee, ... Ex 23:28 7971
I will s an angel before thee ... Ex 33:2 7971
me know whom thou wilt s with me ... Ex 33:12 7971
shall s him away by the hand of a ... Lev 16:21 7971
I will also s wild beasts among ... Lev 26:22 7971
I will s the pestilence among you ... Lev 26:25 7971
are left alive of you I will s a ... Lev 26:36 935
S thou men, that they may search ... Num 13:2 7971
of their fathers shall ye s a man ... Num 13:2 7971
Did I not earnestly s unto thee ... Num 22:37 7971
of Israel, shall ye s to the war ... Num 31:4 7971
We will s men before us, and they ... Deut 1:22 7971
God will s the hornet among them ... Deut 7:20 7971
I will s grass in thy fields for ... Deut 11:15 5414
the elders of his city shall s ... Deut 19:12 7971
hand, and s her out of his house ... Deut 24:1 7971
The LORD shall s upon thee ... Deut 28:20 7971
the LORD shall s against thee ... Deut 28:48 7971
I will also s the teeth of beasts ... Deut 32:24 7971
and I will s them, and they shall ... Josh 18:4 7971
thou didst s come again unto us ... Judg 13:8 7971
S away the ark of the God of ... 1Sa 5:11 7971
we shall s it to his place ... 1Sa 6:2 7971
If ye s away the ark of the God ... 1Sa 6:3 7971
the God of Israel, s it not empty ... 1Sa 6:3 7971
s it away, that it may go ... 1Sa 6:8 7971
s thee a man out of the land of ... 1Sa 9:16 7971
Up, that I may s thee away ... 1Sa 9:26 7971
that we may s messengers unto all ... 1Sa 11:3 7971
the LORD, and he shall s thunder ... 1Sa 12:17 5414
I will s thee to Jesse the ... 1Sa 16:1 7971
And Samuel said unto Jesse, S ... 1Sa 16:11 7971
S me David thy son, which is with ... 1Sa 16:19 7971
I then s not unto thee, and shew ... 1Sa 20:12 7971
s thee away, that thou mayest go ... 1Sa 20:13 7971
And, behold, I will s a lad ... 1Sa 20:21 7971
Wherefore now s and fetch him unto ... 1Sa 20:31 7971
the business whereabout I s thee ... 1Sa 21:2 7971
men of my lord, whom thou didst s ... 1Sa 25:25 7971
saying, S me Uriah the Hittite ... 2Sa 11:6 7971
that I may s thee to the king, to ... 2Sa 14:32 7971
by them ye shall s unto me every ... 2Sa 15:36 7971
Now therefore s quickly, and tell ... 2Sa 17:16 7971
whithersoever thou shalt s them ... 1Kin 8:44 7971
I will s rain upon the earth ... 1Kin 18:1 5414
Now therefore s, and gather to me ... 1Kin 18:19 7971
Yet I will s my servants unto ... 1Kin 20:6 7971
All that thou didst s for to thy ... 1Kin 20:9 7971
I will s thee away with this ... 1Kin 20:34 7971
And he said, Ye shall not s ... 2Kin 2:16 7971
till he was ashamed, he said, S ... 2Kin 2:17 7971
S me, I pray thee, one of the ... 2Kin 4:22 7971
I will s a letter unto the king ... 2Kin 5:5 7971
that this man doth s unto me to ... 2Kin 5:7 7971
and spy where he is, that I may s ... 2Kin 6:13 7971
and let us s and see ... 2Kin 7:13 7971
s to meet them, and let him say, ... 2Kin 9:17 7971
s against Judah Rezin the king of ... 2Kin 15:37 7971
I will s a blast upon him, and he ... 2Kin 19:7 5414
let us s abroad unto our brethren ... 1Chr 13:2 7971
didst s him cedars to build him ... 2Chr 2:3 7971
S me now therefore a man cunning ... 2Chr 2:7 7971
S me also cedar trees, fir trees, ... 2Chr 2:8 7971
let him s unto his servants ... 2Chr 2:15 7971
s rain upon thy land, which thou ... 2Chr 6:27 5414
by the way that thou shalt s them ... 2Chr 6:34 7971
or if I s pestilence among my ... 2Chr 7:13 7971
At that time did king Ahaz s unto ... 2Chr 28:16 7971
s his servants to Jerusalem ... 2Chr 32:9 7971
let the king s his pleasure to us ... Ezr 5:17 7972
thou wouldest s me unto Judah ... Neh 2:5 7971
So it pleased the king to s me ... Neh 2:6 7971
s portions unto them for whom ... Neh 8:10 7971
to s portions, and to make great ... Neh 8:12 7971
They s forth their little ones ... Job 21:11 7971
Canst thou s lightnings, that ... Job 38:35 7971
S thee help from the sanctuary, ... Ps 20:2 7971
O s out thy light and thy truth ... Ps 43:3 7971
He shall s from heaven, and save ... Ps 57:3 7971
God shall s forth his mercy and ... Ps 57:3 7971
didst s a plentiful rain, whereby ... Ps 68:9 5130
he doth s out his voice, and that ... Ps 68:33 5414
The LORD shall s the rod of thy ... Ps 110:2 7971
I beseech thee, s now prosperity ... Ps 118:25
S thine hand from above ... Ps 144:7 7971
the sluggard to them that s him ... Prov 10:26 7971
of truth to them that s unto thee ... Prov 22:21 7971
messenger to them that s him ... Prov 25:13 7971
to s forth a stinking savour ... Eccl 10:1 5042
the Lord, saying, Whom shall I s ... Is 6:8 7971
Here am I; s me ... Is 6:8 7971
I will s him against an ... Is 10:6 7971
s among his fat ones leanness ... Is 10:16 7971
S ye the lamb to the ruler of the ... Is 16:1 7971
he shall s them a saviour, and a ... Is 19:20 7971
that s forth thither the feet of ... Is 32:20 7971
I will s a blast upon him, and he ... Is 37:7 7971
didst s thy messengers far off, ... Is 57:9 7971
I will s those that escape of ... Is 66:19 7971
go to all that I shall s thee ... Jer 1:7 7971
s unto Kedar, and consider ... Jer 2:10 7971
I will s serpents, cockatrices, ... Jer 8:17 7971
I will s a sword after them, till ... Jer 9:16 7971
s for cunning women, that they ... Jer 9:17 7971
I will s for many fishers, saith ... Jer 16:16 7971
after will I s for many hunters, ... Jer 16:16 7971
I will s the sword, the famine, ... Jer 24:10 7971
Behold, I will s and take all the ... Jer 25:9 7971
all the nations, to whom I s thee ... Jer 25:15 7971
sword that I will s among them ... Jer 25:16 7971
sword which I will s among you ... Jer 25:27 7971
s them to the king of Edom, and to ... Jer 27:3 7971
I will s upon them the sword, the ... Jer 29:17 7971
S to all them of the captivity, ... Jer 29:31 7971
LORD thy God shall s thee to us ... Jer 42:5 7971
LORD our God, to whom we s thee ... Jer 42:6 7971
Behold, I will s and take ... Jer 43:10 7971
that I will s unto him wanderers, ... Jer 48:12 7971
I will s the sword after them, ... Jer 49:37 7971
will s unto Babylon fanners, that ... Jer 51:2 7971
I s thee to the children of ... Eze 2:3 7971
I do s thee unto them ... Eze 2:4 7971
When I shall s upon them the evil ... Eze 5:16 7971
which I will s to destroy you ... Eze 5:16 7971
So will I s upon you famine and ... Eze 5:17 7971
I will s mine anger upon thee, and ... Eze 7:3 7971
will s famine upon it, and will ... Eze 14:13 7971
Or if I s a pestilence into that ... Eze 14:19 7971
How much more when I s my four ... Eze 14:21 7971
For I will s into her pestilence, ... Eze 28:23 7971
I will s a fire on Magog, and ... Eze 39:6 7971
but I will s a fire upon his ... Hos 8:14 7971
I will s you corn, and wine, and ... Joel 2:19 7971
But I will s a fire into the ... Amos 1:4 7971
But I will s a fire on the wall ... Amos 1:7 7971
But I will s a fire on the wall ... Amos 1:10 7971
But I will s a fire upon Teman, ... Amos 1:12 7971
But I will s a fire upon Moab, and ... Amos 2:2 7971
But I will s a fire upon Judah, ... Amos 2:5 7971
that I will s a famine in the ... Amos 8:11 7971
I will even s a curse upon you, ... Mal 2:2 7971
I will s my messenger, and he ... Mal 3:1 7971
I will s you Elijah the prophet ... Mal 4:5 7971
that he will s forth labourers ... Mt 9:38 1544
I s you forth as sheep in the ... Mt 10:16 649
I am come to s peace on earth ... Mt 10:34 906
I came not to s peace, but a ... Mt 10:34 906
I s my messenger before thy face, ... Mt 11:10 649
till he s forth judgment unto ... Mt 12:20 1544
of man shall s forth his angels ... Mt 13:41 649
s the multitude away, that they ... Mt 14:15 630
besought him, saying, S her away ... Mt 15:23 630
I will not s them away fasting, ... Mt 15:32 630
and straightway he will s them ... Mt 21:3 649
I s unto you prophets, and wise ... Mt 23:34 649
he shall s his angels with a ... Mt 24:31 649
I s my messenger before thy face, ... Mk 1:2 649
that he might s them forth to ... Mk 3:14 649
him much that he would not s them ... Mk 5:10 649
S us into the swine, that we may ... Mk 5:12 3992
began to s them forth by two and ... Mk 6:7 649
S them away, that they may go ... Mk 6:36 630
if I s them away fasting to their ... Mk 8:3 630
straightway he will s him hither ... Mk 11:3 649
they s unto him certain of the ... Mk 12:13 649
And then shall he s his angels ... Mk 13:27 649
I s my messenger before thy face, ... Lk 7:27 649
S the multitude away, that they ... Lk 9:12 630
that he would s forth labourers ... Lk 10:2 1544
I s you forth as lambs among ... Lk 10:3 649
I will s them prophets and ... Lk 11:49 649
I am come to s fire on the earth ... Lk 12:49 906
s Lazarus, that he may dip the ... Lk 16:24 3992
that thou wouldest s him to my ... Lk 16:27 3992
I will s my beloved son ... Lk 20:13 3992
I s the promise of my Father upon ... Lk 24:49 649
whomsoever I s receiveth me ... Jn 13:20 3992
whom the Father will s in my name ... Jn 14:26 3992
whom I will s unto you from the ... Jn 15:26 3992
I depart, I will s him unto you ... Jn 16:7 3992
believed that thou didst s me ... Jn 17:8 649
hath sent me, even so s I you ... Jn 20:21 3992
he shall s Jesus Christ, which ... Acts 3:20 649
come, I will s thee into Egypt ... Acts 7:34 649
the same did God s to be a ruler ... Acts 7:35 649
now s men to Joppa, and call for ... Acts 10:5 3992
to s for thee into his house ... Acts 10:22 3343
S therefore to Joppa, and call ... Acts 10:32 3992
S men to Joppa, and call for Simon ... Acts 11:13 649
determined to s relief unto the ... Acts 11:29 3992
to s chosen men of their own ... Acts 15:22 3992
brethren s greeting unto the ... Acts 15:23
to s chosen men unto you with our ... Acts 15:25 3992
for I will s thee far hence unto ... Acts 22:21 1821
that he would s for him to ... Acts 25:3 3343
kept till I might s him to Caesar ... Acts 25:21 3992
I have determined to s him ... Acts 25:25 3992
me unreasonable to s a prisoner ... Acts 25:27 3992
Gentiles, unto whom now I s thee ... Acts 26:17 649
them will I s to bring your ... 1Cor 16:3 3992
to s Timotheus shortly unto you ... Phil 2:19 3992
therefore I hope to s presently ... Phil 2:23 3992
to s to you Epaphroditus, my ... Phil 2:25 3992
God shall s them strong delusion ... 2Th 2:11 3992
When I shall s Artemas unto thee, ... Titus 3:12 3992
Doth a fountain s forth at the ... Jas 3:11 1032
s it unto the seven churches ... Rev 1:11 3992
shall s gifts one to another ... Rev 11:10 3992

SENDEST {6}
when thou s him out free from ... Deut 15:13 7971
when thou s him away free from ... Deut 15:18 7971
do, and whithersoever thou s us ... Josh 1:16 7971
that thou s to enquire of ... 2Kin 1:6 7971
his countenance, and s him away ... Job 14:20 7971
Thou s forth thy spirit, they are ... Ps 104:30 7971

SENDETH {15}
hand, and s her out of his house ... Deut 24:3 7971
the LORD s rain upon the earth ... 1Kin 17:14 5414
and s waters upon the fields ... Job 5:10 7971
also he s them out, and they ... Job 12:15 7971
He s the springs into the valleys ... Ps 104:10 7971
He s forth his commandment upon ... Ps 147:15 7971
He s out his word, and melteth ... Ps 147:18 7971
He that s a message by the hand ... Prov 26:6 7971
my spikenard s forth the smell ... Song 1:12 5414
That s ambassadors by the sea, ... Is 18:2 7971
s rain on the just and on the ... Mt 5:45 1026
he s forth two of his disciples, ... Mk 11:1 649
he s forth two of his disciples, ... Mk 14:13 649
he s an ambassage, and desireth ... Lk 14:32 649
governor Felix s greeting ... Acts 23:26 649

SENDING {14}
this evil in s me away is greater ... 2Sa 13:16 7971
rising up betimes, and s ... 2Chr 36:15 7971
of s portions one to another ... Est 9:19 4916
of s portions one to another, and ... Est 9:22 4916
by s evil angels among them ... Ps 78:49 4917
shall be for the s forth of oxen ... Is 7:25 4916
daily rising up early and s them ... Jer 7:25 7971
prophets, rising early and s them ... Jer 25:4 7971
s them, but ye have not hearkened ... Jer 26:5 7971

rising up early and *s* them .... Jer 29:19 7971
s them, saying, Return ye now .... Jer 35:15 7971
s them, saying, Oh, do not this .... Jer 44:4 7971
in *s* his ambassadors into Egypt .... Eze 17:15 7971
God *s* his own Son in the likeness .... Rom 8:3 *3992*

SENEH *(se'-neh)* {1} *A rock in Benjamin.*
Bozez, and the name of the other *S* 1Sa 14:4 5573

SENIR *(se'-nur)* {2} See SHENIR. *A mountain between Amana and Hermon.*
from Bashan unto Baal-hermon and *S* ... 1Chr 5:23 8149
thy ship boards of fir trees of *S* .... Eze 27:5 8149

SENNACHERIB *(sen-nak'-er-ib)* {13} *An Assyrian king.*
year of king Hezekiah did *S* king 2Kin 18:13 5576
and hear the words of *S*, which 2Kin 19:16 5576
S king of Assyria I have heard 2Kin 19:20 5576
So *S* king of Assyria departed, and 2Kin 19:36 5576
S king of Assyria came, and 2Chr 32:1 5576
when Hezekiah saw that *S* was come 2Chr 32:2 5576
After this did *S* king of Assyria 2Chr 32:9 5576
Thus saith *S* king of Assyria, ... 2Chr 32:10 5576
the hand of *S* the king of Assyria 2Chr 32:22 5576
that *S* king of Assyria came up .... Is 36:1 5576
and hear all the words of *S* .... Is 37:17 5576
to me against *S* king of Assyria .... Is 37:21 5576
So *S* king of Assyria departed, and .... Is 37:37 5576

SENSE {1}
of God distinctly, and gave the *s* .... Neh 8:8 7922

SENSES {1}
s exercised to discern both good .... Heb 5:14 *145*

SENSUAL {2}
not from above, but is earthly, *s* .... Jas 3:15 *5591*
they who separate themselves, *s* .... Jude 19 *5591*

SENT {687}
Therefore the LORD God *s* him .... Gen 3:23 7971
he *s* forth a raven, which went .... Gen 8:7 7971
Also he *s* forth a dove from him, ... Gen 8:8 7971
again he *s* forth the dove out of .... Gen 8:10 7971
and *s* forth the dove .... Gen 8:12 7971
they *s* him away, and his wife, and .... Gen 12:20 7971
the LORD hath *s* us to destroy it .... Gen 19:13 7971
s Lot out of the midst of the .... Gen 19:29 7971
and Abimelech king of Gerar *s* .... Gen 20:2 7971
and the child, and *s* her away .... Gen 21:14 7971
they *s* away Rebekah their sister, ... Gen 24:59 7971
s them away from Isaac his son, ... Gen 25:6 7971
me, and have *s* me away from you .... Gen 26:27 7971
have *s* thee away in peace .... Gen 26:29 7971
Isaac *s* them away, and they .... Gen 26:31 7971
and she *s* and called Jacob her .... Gen 27:42 7971
And Isaac *s* away Jacob .... Gen 28:5 7971
s him away to Padan-aram, to take .... Gen 28:6 7971
And Jacob *s* and called Rachel and .... Gen 31:4 7971
that I might have *s* thee away .... Gen 31:27 7971
thou hadst *s* me away now empty .... Gen 31:42 7971
Jacob *s* messengers before him to .... Gen 32:3 7971
I have *s* to tell my lord, that I .... Gen 32:5 7971
it is a present *s* unto my lord .... Gen 32:18 7971
s them over the brook .... Gen 32:23 5674
and *s* over that he had .... Gen 32:23 5674
So he *s* him out of the vale of .... Gen 37:14 7971
they *s* the coat of many colours, ... Gen 37:32 7971
Judah *s* the kid by the hand of .... Gen 38:20 7971
I *s* this kid, and thou hast not .... Gen 38:23 7971
she *s* to her father in law, ... Gen 38:25 7971
and he *s* and called for all the .... Gen 41:8 7971
Then Pharaoh *s* and called Joseph, ... Gen 41:14 7971
Jacob *s* not with his brethren .... Gen 42:4 7971
s messes unto them from before .... Gen 43:34 7971
was light, the men were *s* away .... Gen 44:3 7971
God *s* me before you to preserve .... Gen 45:7 7971
it was not you that *s* me hither .... Gen 45:8 7971
to his father he *s* after this .... Gen 45:23 7971
So he *s* his brethren away, and .... Gen 45:24 7971
which Joseph had *s* to carry him .... Gen 45:27 7971
which Pharaoh had *s* to carry him .... Gen 46:5 7971
he *s* Judah before him unto Joseph .... Gen 46:28 7971
they *s* a messenger unto Joseph, ... Gen 50:16 6680
she *s* her maid to fetch it .... Ex 2:5 7971
unto thee, that I have *s* thee .... Ex 3:12 7971
your fathers hath *s* me unto you .... Ex 3:13 7971
Israel, I AM hath *s* me unto you .... Ex 3:14 7971
God of Jacob, hath *s* me unto you .... Ex 3:15 7971
words of the LORD who had *s* him .... Ex 4:28 7971
why is it that thou hast *s* me .... Ex 5:22 7971
the Hebrews hath *s* me unto thee .... Ex 7:16 7971
And Pharaoh *s*, and, behold, there .... Ex 9:7 7971
and the LORD *s* thunder and hail, and ... Ex 9:23 5414
And Pharaoh *s*, and called for Moses .... Ex 9:27 7971
wife, after he had *s* her back .... Ex 18:2 7964
he *s* young men of the children of .... Ex 24:5 7971
s them from the wilderness of .... Num 13:3 7971
which Moses *s* to spy out the land .... Num 13:16 7971
Moses *s* them to spy out the land .... Num 13:17 7971
which Moses *s* to search the land, ... Num 14:36 7971
Moses *s* to call Dathan and Abiram, ... Num 16:12 7971
hath *s* me to do all these works .... Num 16:28 7971
then the LORD hath not *s* me .... Num 16:29 7971
Moses *s* messengers from Kadesh .... Num 20:14 7971
s an angel, and hath brought us .... Num 20:16 7971
the LORD *s* fiery serpents among .... Num 21:6 7971
Israel *s* messengers unto Sihon .... Num 21:21 7971
Moses *s* to spy out Jaazer, and .... Num 21:32 7971
He *s* messengers therefore unto .... Num 22:5 7971
of Moab, hath *s* unto me, saying, ... Num 22:10 7971
Balak *s* yet again princes, more, ... Num 22:15 7971
s to Balaam, and to the princes .... Num 22:40 7971
Moses *s* them to the war, a .... Num 31:6 7971
when I *s* them from Kadesh-barnea .... Num 32:8 7971
I *s* messengers out of the .... Deut 2:26 7971
the LORD *s* you from Kadesh-barnea ..... Deut 9:23 7971
which *s* her away, may not take .... Deut 24:4 7971
which the LORD *s* him to do in the .... Deut 34:11 7971
Joshua the son of Nun *s* out of .... Josh 2:1 7971
the king of Jericho *s* unto Rahab .... Josh 2:3 7971
she *s* them away, and they departed .... Josh 2:21 7971
she hid the messengers that we *s* .... Josh 6:17 7971
which Joshua *s* to spy out Jericho .... Josh 6:25 7971
Joshua *s* men from Jericho to Ai, ... Josh 7:2 7971
So Joshua *s* messengers, and they .... Josh 7:22 7971
valour, and *s* them away by night .... Josh 8:3 7971
Joshua therefore *s* them forth .... Josh 8:9 7971
s unto Hoham king of Hebron .... Josh 10:3 7971
the men of Gibeon *s* unto Joshua .... Josh 10:6 7971
that he *s* to Jobab king of Madon, ... Josh 11:1 7971
s me from Kadesh-barnea to espy .... Josh 14:7 7971
I was in the day that Moses *s* me .... Josh 14:11 7971
blessed them, and *s* them away .... Josh 22:6 7971
when Joshua *s* them away also unto .... Josh 22:7 7971
the children of Israel *s* unto the .... Josh 22:13 7971
I *s* Moses also and Aaron, and I .... Josh 24:5 7971
and warred against Israel, and *s* .... Josh 24:9 7971
I *s* the hornet before you, which .... Josh 24:12 7971
of Joseph *s* to descry Beth-el .... Judg 1:23
s a present unto Eglon the king .... Judg 3:15 7971
he *s* away the people that bare .... Judg 3:18 7971
And she *s* and called Barak the son .... Judg 4:6 7971
he was *s* on foot into the valley .... Judg 5:15 7971
That the LORD *s* a prophet unto .... Judg 6:8 7971
have not I *s* thee .... Judg 6:14 7971
he *s* messengers throughout all .... Judg 6:35 7971
he *s* messengers unto Asher, and .... Judg 6:35 7971
he *s* all the rest of Israel every .... Judg 7:8 7971
Gideon *s* messengers throughout .... Judg 7:24 7971
Then God *s* an evil spirit between .... Judg 9:23 7971
he *s* messengers unto Abimelech .... Judg 9:31 7971
Jephthah *s* messengers unto the .... Judg 11:12 7971
Jephthah *s* messengers again unto .... Judg 11:14 7971
Then Israel *s* messengers unto the .... Judg 11:17 7971
in like manner they *s* unto the .... Judg 11:17 7971
Israel *s* messengers unto Sihon .... Judg 11:19 7971
words of Jephthah which he *s* him .... Judg 11:28 7971
he *s* her away for two months .... Judg 11:38 7971
daughters, whom he *s* abroad .... Judg 12:9 7971
had told her all his heart, she *s* .... Judg 16:18 7971
the children of Dan *s* of their .... Judg 18:2 7971
s her into all the coasts of .... Judg 19:29 7971
s her throughout all the country .... Judg 20:6 7971
the tribes of Israel *s* men .... Judg 20:12 7971
the congregation *s* thither twelve .... Judg 21:10 7971
the whole congregation *s* some to .... Judg 21:13 7971
So the people *s* to Shiloh 1Sa 4:4 7971
They *s* therefore and gathered all 1Sa 5:8 7971
Therefore they *s* the ark of God 1Sa 5:10 7971
So they *s* and gathered together 1Sa 5:11 7971
And they *s* messengers to the 1Sa 6:21 7971
Samuel *s* all the people away, ... 1Sa 10:25 7971
s them throughout all the coasts 1Sa 11:7 7971
the LORD, then the LORD *s* Moses 1Sa 12:8 7971
the LORD *s* Jerubbaal, and Bedan, ... 1Sa 12:11 7971
and the LORD *s* thunder and rain 1Sa 12:18 5414
people he *s* every man to his tent 1Sa 13:2 7971
The LORD *s* me to anoint thee to 1Sa 15:1 7971
the LORD *s* thee on a journey, and 1Sa 15:18 7971
gone the way which the LORD *s* me 1Sa 15:20 7971
And he *s*, and brought him in 1Sa 16:12 7971
Wherefore Saul *s* messengers unto 1Sa 16:19 7971
s them by David his son unto Saul 1Sa 16:20 7971
Saul *s* to Jesse, saying, Let 1Sa 16:22 7971
and he *s* for him 1Sa 17:31 3947
went out whithersoever Saul *s* him 1Sa 18:5 7971
Saul also *s* messengers unto 1Sa 19:11 7971
when Saul *s* messengers to take 1Sa 19:14 7971
Saul *s* the messengers again to 1Sa 19:15 7971
s away mine enemy, that he is 1Sa 19:17 7971
Saul *s* messengers to take David 1Sa 19:20 7971
he *s* other messengers, and they 1Sa 19:21 7971
Saul *s* messengers again the third 1Sa 19:21 7971
for the LORD hath *s* thee away 1Sa 20:22 7971
Then the king *s* to call Ahimelech 1Sa 22:11 7971
David *s* out ten young men, and 1Sa 25:5 7971
David *s* messengers out of the 1Sa 25:14 7971
which *s* thee this day to meet me 1Sa 25:32 7971
And David *s* and communed with 1Sa 25:39 7971
David *s* us unto thee, to take 1Sa 25:40 7971
David therefore *s* out spies 1Sa 26:4 7971
he *s* of the spoil unto the elders 1Sa 30:26 7971
armour, and *s* into the land of the 1Sa 31:9 7971
David *s* messengers unto the men 2Sa 2:5 7971
Abner *s* messengers to David on 2Sa 3:12 7971
David *s* messengers to Ish-bosheth 2Sa 3:14 7971
And Ish-bosheth *s*, and took her 2Sa 3:15 7971
And David *s* Abner away 2Sa 3:21 7971
for he had *s* him away, and he was 2Sa 3:22 7971
he hath *s* him away, and he is gone 2Sa 3:23 7971
is it that thou hast *s* him away 2Sa 3:24 7971
he *s* messengers after Abner, ... 2Sa 3:26 7971
Hiram king of Tyre *s* messengers 2Sa 5:11 7971
Then Toi *s* Joram his son unto 2Sa 8:10 7971
Then king David *s*, and fetched him 2Sa 9:5 7971
David *s* to comfort him by the 2Sa 10:2 7971
that he hath *s* comforters unto 2Sa 10:3 7971
hath not David rather *s* his 2Sa 10:3 7971
to their buttocks, and *s* them away 2Sa 10:4 7971
he *s* to meet them, because the 2Sa 10:5 7971
David, the children of Ammon *s* 2Sa 10:6 7971
he *s* Joab, and all the host of the 2Sa 10:7 7971
And Hadarezer *s*, and brought out 2Sa 10:16 7971
to battle, that David *s* Joab 2Sa 11:1 7971
And David *s* and enquired after the 2Sa 11:3 7971
David *s* messengers, and took her 2Sa 11:4 7971
And the woman conceived, and *s* 2Sa 11:5 7971
David *s* to Joab, saying, Send me 2Sa 11:6 7971
And Joab *s* Uriah to David 2Sa 11:6 7971
s it by the hand of Uriah 2Sa 11:14 7971
Then Joab *s* and told David all the 2Sa 11:18 7971
David all that Joab had *s* him for 2Sa 11:22 7971
the mourning was past, David *s* 2Sa 11:27 7971
the LORD *s* Nathan unto David 2Sa 12:1 7971
he *s* by the hand of Nathan the 2Sa 12:25 7971
Joab *s* messengers to David, and 2Sa 12:27 7971
Then David *s* home to Tamar, ... 2Sa 13:7 7971
Joab *s* to Tekoah, and fetched 2Sa 14:2 7971
Therefore Absalom *s* for Joab 2Sa 14:29 7971
to have *s* him to the king 2Sa 14:29 7971
when he *s* again the second time, ... 2Sa 14:29 7971
I *s* unto thee, saying, Come 2Sa 14:32 7971
But Absalom *s* spies throughout 2Sa 15:10 7971
Absalom *s* for Ahithophel the 2Sa 15:12 7971
David *s* forth a third part of the 2Sa 18:2 7971
When Joab *s* the king's servant, ... 2Sa 18:29 7971
And king David *s* to Zadok and to 2Sa 19:11 7971
so that they *s* this word unto the 2Sa 19:14 7971
he *s* out arrows, and scattered 2Sa 22:15 7971
He *s* from above, he took me 2Sa 22:17 7971
I shall return to him that *s* me 2Sa 24:13 7971
So the LORD *s* a pestilence upon 2Sa 24:15 5414
the king hath *s* with him Zadok 1Kin 1:44 7971
So king Solomon *s*, and they 1Kin 1:53 7971
king Solomon *s* by the hand of 1Kin 2:25 7971
Then Solomon *s* Benaiah the son of 1Kin 2:29 7971
And the king *s* and called for 1Kin 2:36 7971
And the king *s* and called for 1Kin 2:42 7971
Hiram king of Tyre *s* his servants 1Kin 5:1 7971
Solomon *s* to Hiram, saying, ... 1Kin 5:2 7971
Hiram *s* to Solomon, saying, I 1Kin 5:8 7971
he *s* them to Lebanon, ten 1Kin 5:14 7971
And king Solomon *s* and fetched 1Kin 7:13 7971
eighth day he *s* the people away 1Kin 8:66 7971
Hiram *s* to the king sixscore 1Kin 9:14 7971
Hiram *s* in the navy his servants, ... 1Kin 9:27 7971
That they *s* and called him 1Kin 12:3 7971
Then king Rehoboam *s* Adoram 1Kin 12:18 7971
was come again, that they *s* 1Kin 12:20 7971
for I am *s* to thee with heavy 1Kin 14:6 7971
king Asa *s* them to Ben-hadad, the 1Kin 15:18 7971
I have *s* unto thee a present of 1Kin 15:19 7971
s the captains of the hosts which 1Kin 15:20 7971
my lord hath not *s* to seek thee 1Kin 18:10 7971
So Ahab *s* unto all the children 1Kin 18:20 7971
Then Jezebel *s* a messenger unto 1Kin 19:2 7971
he *s* messengers to Ahab king of 1Kin 20:2 7971
Although I have *s* unto thee 1Kin 20:5 7971
for he *s* unto me for my wives, and 1Kin 20:7 7971
And Ben-hadad *s* unto him, and said, ... 1Kin 20:10 7971
and Ben-hadad *s* out, and they told 1Kin 20:17 7971
covenant with him, and *s* him away 1Kin 20:34 7971
s the letters unto the elders and 1Kin 21:8 7971
did as Jezebel had *s* unto them 1Kin 21:11 7971
letters which she had *s* unto them 1Kin 21:11 7971
Then they *s* to Jezebel, saying, ... 1Kin 21:14 7971
he *s* messengers, and said unto 2Kin 1:2 7971
again unto the king that *s* you 2Kin 1:6 7971
Then the king *s* unto him a 2Kin 1:9 7971
Again also he *s* unto him another 2Kin 1:11 7971
he *s* again a captain of the third 2Kin 1:13 7971
LORD, Forasmuch as thou hast *s* 2Kin 1:16 7971
for the LORD hath *s* me to Beth-el 2Kin 2:2 7971
for the LORD hath *s* me to Jericho 2Kin 2:4 7971
for the LORD hath *s* me to Jordan 2Kin 2:6 7971
They *s* therefore fifty men 2Kin 2:17 7971
s to Jehoshaphat the king of 2Kin 3:7 7971
I have therewith *s* Naaman my 2Kin 5:6 7971
that he *s* to the king, saying, ... 2Kin 5:8 7971
Elisha *s* a messenger unto him, ... 2Kin 5:10 7971
My master hath *s* me, saying, ... 2Kin 5:22 7971
the man of God *s* unto the king of 2Kin 6:9 7971
the king of Israel *s* to the place 2Kin 6:10 7971
Therefore *s* he thither horses, and 2Kin 6:14 7971
he *s* them away, and they went to 2Kin 6:23 7971
the king *s* a man from before him 2Kin 6:32 7971
hath *s* to take away mine head 2Kin 6:32 7971
the king *s* after the host of the 2Kin 7:14 7971
king of Syria hath *s* me to thee 2Kin 8:9 7971
Then he *s* out a second on 2Kin 9:19 7971
s to Samaria, unto the rulers of 2Kin 10:1 7971
s to Jehu, saying, We are thy 2Kin 10:5 7971
baskets, and *s* him them to Jezreel 2Kin 10:7 7971
Jehu *s* through all Israel 2Kin 10:21 7971
And the seventh year Jehoiada *s* 2Kin 11:4 7971
s it to Hazael king of Syria 2Kin 12:18 7971
Then Amaziah *s* messengers to 2Kin 14:8 7971
Israel *s* to Amaziah king of Judah 2Kin 14:9 7971
s to the cedar that was in 2Kin 14:9 7971
but they *s* after him to Lachish, ... 2Kin 14:19 7971
So Ahaz *s* messengers to 2Kin 16:7 7971
s it for a present to the king of 2Kin 16:8 7971
king Ahaz *s* to Urijah the priest 2Kin 16:10 7971
king Ahaz had *s* from Damascus 2Kin 16:11 7971
for he had *s* messengers to So 2Kin 17:4 7971
which I *s* to you by my servants 2Kin 17:13 7971

the LORD *s* lions among them 2Kin 17:25 7971
he hath *s* lions among them 2Kin 17:26 7971
Hezekiah king of Judah *s* to the 2Kin 18:14 7971
And the king of Assyria *s* Tartan 2Kin 18:17 7971
Hath my master *s* me to thy master 2Kin 18:27 7971
hath he not *s* me to the men which 2Kin 18:27
he *s* Eliakim, which was over the 2Kin 19:2 7971
hath *s* to reproach the living God 2Kin 19:4 7971
he *s* messengers again unto 2Kin 19:9 7971
which hath *s* him to reproach the 2Kin 19:16 7971
the son of Amoz *s* to Hezekiah 2Kin 19:20 7971
s letters and a present unto 2Kin 20:12 7971
that the king *s* Shaphan the son 2Kin 22:3 7971
Tell the man that *s* you to me 2Kin 22:15 7971
s you to enquire of the LORD 2Kin 22:18 7971
And the king *s*, and they gathered 2Kin 23:1 7971
were there in the mount, and *s* 2Kin 23:16 7971
the LORD *s* against him bands of 2Kin 24:2 7971
s them against Judah to destroy 2Kin 24:2 7971
of Moab, after he had *s* them away 1Chr 8:8 7971
armour, and *s* into the land of the 1Chr 10:9 7971
upon advisement *s* him away 1Chr 12:19 7971
of Tyre *s* messengers to David 1Chr 14:1 7971
He *s* Hadoram his son to king 1Chr 18:10 7971
David *s* messengers to comfort him 1Chr 19:2 7971
that he hath *s* comforters unto 1Chr 19:3 7971
by their buttocks, and *s* them away 1Chr 19:4 7971
And he *s* to meet them 1Chr 19:5 7971
the children of Ammon *s* a 1Chr 19:6 7971
he *s* Joab, and all the host of the 1Chr 19:8 7971
they *s* messengers, and drew forth 1Chr 19:16 7971
bring again to him that *s* me 1Chr 21:12 7971
So the LORD *s* pestilence upon 1Chr 21:14 5414
God *s* an angel unto Jerusalem to 1Chr 21:15 7971
Solomon *s* to Huram the king of 2Chr 2:3 7971
which he *s* to Solomon, Because 2Chr 2:11 7971
now I have *s* a cunning man, 2Chr 2:13 7971
he *s* the people away into their 2Chr 7:10 7971
Huram *s* him by the hands of his 2Chr 8:18 7971
And they *s* and called him 2Chr 10:3 7971
Then king Rehoboam *s* Hadoram that 2Chr 10:18 7971
s to Ben-hadad king of Syria, 2Chr 16:2 7971
I have *s* thee silver and gold 2Chr 16:3 7971
s the captains of his armies 2Chr 16:4 7971
of his reign he *s* to his princes 2Chr 17:7 7971
And with them he *s* Levites 2Chr 17:8
Yet he *s* prophets to them, to 2Chr 24:19 7971
s all the spoil of them unto the 2Chr 24:23 7971
of the army which Amaziah *s* back 2Chr 25:13 7725
he *s* unto him a prophet, which 2Chr 25:15 7971
s to Joash, the son of Jehoahaz, 2Chr 25:17 7971
Joash king of Israel *s* to Amaziah 2Chr 25:18 7971
s to the cedar that was in 2Chr 25:18 7971
but they *s* to Lachish after him, 2Chr 25:27 7971
Hezekiah *s* to all Israel and Judah 2Chr 30:1 7971
And the LORD *s* an angel, which cut 2Chr 32:21 7971
who *s* unto him to enquire of the 2Chr 32:31 7971
he *s* Shaphan the son of Azaliah, 2Chr 34:8 7971
Tell ye the man that *s* you to me 2Chr 34:23 7971
who *s* you to enquire of the LORD, 2Chr 34:26 7971
Then the king *s* and gathered 2Chr 34:29 7971
But he *s* ambassadors to him, 2Chr 35:21 7971
expired, king Nebuchadnezzar *s* 2Chr 36:10 7971
s to them by his messengers 2Chr 36:15 7971
the letter that they *s* unto him Ezr 4:11 7972
dishonour, therefore have we *s* Ezr 4:14 7972
Then *s* the king an answer unto Ezr 4:17 7972
The letter which ye *s* unto us Ezr 4:18 7972
the river, *s* unto Darius the king Ezr 5:6 7972
They *s* a letter unto him, wherein Ezr 5:7 7972
that which Darius the king had *s* Ezr 6:13 7972
as thou art *s* of the king Ezr 7:14 7972
Then *s* I for Eliezer, for Ariel, Ezr 8:16 7971
I *s* them with commandment unto Ezr 8:17 6680
Now the king had *s* captains of Neh 2:9 7971
Geshem *s* unto me, saying, Come, Neh 6:2 7971
I *s* messengers unto them, saying, Neh 6:3 7971
Yet they *s* unto me four times Neh 6:4 7971
Then *s* Sanballat his servant unto Neh 6:5 7971
Then I *s* unto him, saying, There Neh 6:8 7971
perceived that God had not *s* him Neh 6:12 7971
Judah *s* many letters unto Tobiah Neh 6:17 1980
Tobiah *s* letters to put me in Neh 6:19 7971
For he *s* letters into all the Est 1:22 7971
the letters were *s* by posts into Est 3:13 7971
she *s* raiment to clothe Mordecai, Est 4:4 7971
and when he came home, he *s* Est 5:10 7971
s letters by posts on horseback, Est 8:10 7971
s letters unto all the Jews that Est 9:20 7971
he *s* the letters unto all the Est 9:30 7971
and *s* and called for their three Job 1:4 7971
were gone about, that Job *s* Job 1:5 7971
Thou hast *s* widows away empty, and Job 22:9 7971
Who hath *s* out the wild ass free Job 39:5 7971
he *s* out his arrows, and scattered Ps 18:14 7971
He *s* from above, he took me, he Ps 18:16 7971
when Saul *s*, and they watched the Ps 59:*t* 7971
the skies *s* out a sound Ps 77:17 5414
he *s* them meat to the full Ps 78:25 7971
He *s* divers sorts of flies among Ps 78:45 7971
She *s* out her boughs unto the sea Ps 80:11 7971
He *s* a man before them, even Ps 105:17 7971
The king *s* and loosed him Ps 105:20 7971
He *s* Moses his servant Ps 105:26 7971
He *s* darkness, and made it dark Ps 105:28 7971
but *s* leanness into their soul Ps 106:15 7971
He *s* his word, and healed them, and Ps 107:20 7971
He *s* redemption unto his people Ps 111:9 7971

Who *s* tokens and wonders into the Ps 135:9 7971
She hath *s* forth her maidens Prov 9:3 7971
messenger shall be *s* against him Prov 17:11 7971
The Lord *s* a word into Jacob, and Is 9:8 7971
Sargon the king of Assyria *s* him Is 20:1 7971
the king of Assyria *s* Rabshakeh Is 36:2 7971
Hath my master *s* me to thy master Is 36:12 7971
hath he not *s* me to the men that Is 36:12
he *s* Eliakim, who was over the Is 37:2 7971
hath *s* to reproach the living God Is 37:4 7971
he *s* messengers to Hezekiah, Is 37:9 7971
which hath *s* to reproach the Is 37:17 7971
the son of Amoz *s* unto Hezekiah Is 37:21 7971
s letters and a present to Is 39:1 7971
or deaf, as my messenger that I *s* Is 42:19 7971
For your sake I have *s* to Babylon Is 43:14 7971
GOD, and his Spirit, hath *s* me Is 48:16 7971
in the thing whereto I *s* it Is 55:11 7971
he hath *s* me to bind up the Is 61:1 7971
s unto you all my servants the Jer 7:25 7971
their nobles have *s* their little Jer 14:3 7971
I *s* them not, neither have I Jer 14:14 7971
I *s* them not, yet they say, Sword Jer 14:15 7971
the LORD had *s* him to prophesy Jer 19:14 7971
when king Zedekiah *s* unto him Jer 21:1 7971
I have not *s* these prophets, yet Jer 23:21 7971
yet I *s* them not, nor commanded Jer 23:32 7971
I have *s* unto you, saying, Ye Jer 23:38 7971
whom I have *s* out of this place Jer 24:5 7971
the LORD hath *s* unto you all his Jer 25:4 7971
unto whom the LORD had *s* me Jer 25:17 7971
whom I *s* unto you, both rising up Jer 26:5 7971
The LORD *s* me to prophesy against Jer 26:12 7971
for of a truth the LORD hath *s* me Jer 26:15 7971
the king *s* men into Egypt Jer 26:22 7971
For I have not *s* them, saith the Jer 27:15 7971
that the LORD hath truly *s* him Jer 28:9 7971
The LORD hath not *s* thee Jer 28:15 7971
that Jeremiah the prophet *s* from Jer 29:1 7971
(whom Zedekiah king of Judah *s* Jer 29:3 7971
I have not *s* them, saith the LORD Jer 29:9 7971
which I *s* unto them by my Jer 29:19 7971
whom I have *s* from Jerusalem to Jer 29:20 7971
Because thou hast *s* letters in Jer 29:25 7971
For therefore he *s* unto us in Jer 29:28 7971
I *s* him not, and he caused you to Jer 29:31 7971
I have *s* also unto you all my Jer 35:15 7971
Therefore all the princes *s* Jer 36:14 7971
So the king *s* Jehudi to fetch the Jer 36:21 7971
Zedekiah the king *s* Jehucal the Jer 37:3 7971
that *s* you unto me to enquire of Jer 37:7 7971
Then Zedekiah the king *s*, and took Jer 37:17 7971
Then Zedekiah the king *s*, and took Jer 38:14 7971
the captain of the guard *s* Jer 39:13 7971
Even they *s*, and took Jeremiah out Jer 39:14 7971
the king of the Ammonites hath *s* Jer 40:14 7971
unto whom ye *s* me to present your Jer 42:9 7971
when ye *s* me unto the LORD your Jer 42:20 7971
the which he hath *s* me unto you Jer 42:21 7971
LORD their God had *s* him to them Jer 43:1 7971
our God hath not *s* thee to say Jer 43:2 7971
Howbeit I *s* unto you all my Jer 44:4 7971
ambassador is *s* unto the heathen Jer 49:14 7971
hath he *s* fire into my bones Lam 1:13 7971
behold, an hand was *s* unto me Eze 2:9 7971
For thou art not *s* to a people of Eze 3:5 7971
had I *s* thee to them, they would Eze 3:6 7971
and the LORD hath not *s* them Eze 13:6 7971
s messengers unto them into Eze 23:16 7971
that ye have *s* for men to come Eze 23:40 7971
far, unto whom a messenger was *s* Eze 23:40 7971
s out her little rivers unto all Eze 31:4 7971
Then Nebuchadnezzar the king *s* to Dan 3:2 7972
who hath *s* his angel, and Dan 3:28 7972
the part of the hand *s* from him Dan 5:24 7972
My God hath *s* his angel, and hath Dan 6:22 7972
for unto thee am I now *s* Dan 10:11 7971
the Assyrian, and *s* to king Jareb Hos 5:13 7971
my great army which I *s* among you Joel 2:25 7971
I have *s* among you the pestilence Amos 4:10 7971
s to Jeroboam king of Israel Amos 7:10 7971
an ambassador is *s* among the Obad 1 7971
But the LORD *s* out a great wind Jonah 1:4 2904
I *s* before thee Moses, Aaron, and Mic 6:4 7971
as the LORD their God had *s* him Hag 1:12 7971
whom the LORD hath *s* to walk to Zec 1:10 7971
After the glory hath he *s* me unto Zec 2:8 7971
that the LORD of hosts hath *s* me Zec 2:9 7971
LORD of hosts hath *s* me unto thee Zec 2:11 7971
LORD of hosts hath *s* me unto you Zec 4:9 7971
LORD of hosts hath *s* me unto you Zec 6:15 7971
When they had *s* unto the house of Zec 7:2 7971
s in his spirit by the former Zec 7:12 7971
blood of thy covenant I have *s* Zec 9:11 7971
have *s* this commandment unto you Mal 2:4 7971
he *s* them to Bethlehem, and said, Mt 2:8 3992
s forth, and slew all the children Mt 2:16 649
These twelve Jesus *s* forth Mt 10:5 649
me receiveth him that *s* me Mt 10:40 649
he *s* two of his disciples, Mt 11:2 3992
Then Jesus *s* the multitude away, Mt 13:36 863
And he *s*, and beheaded John in the Mt 14:10 3992
while he *s* the multitudes away Mt 14:22 630
when he had *s* the multitudes away Mt 14:23 630
they *s* out into all that country Mt 14:35 649
I am not *s* but unto the lost Mt 15:24 649
he *s* away the multitude, and took Mt 15:39 630
he *s* them into his vineyard Mt 20:2 649

then *s* Jesus two disciples, Mt 21:1 649
near, he *s* his servants to the Mt 21:34 649
he *s* other servants more than the Mt 21:36 649
of all he *s* unto them his son Mt 21:37 649
s forth his servants to call them Mt 22:3 649
he *s* forth other servants, saying Mt 22:4 649
he *s* forth his armies, and Mt 22:7 3992
they *s* out unto him their Mt 22:16 649
them which are *s* unto thee Mt 23:37 649
seat, his wife *s* unto him, Mt 27:19 649
him, and forthwith *s* him away Mk 1:43 1544
without, *s* unto him, calling him Mk 3:31 649
And when they had *s* away the Mk 4:36 863
For Herod himself had *s* forth Mk 6:17 649
the king *s* an executioner Mk 6:27 649
while he *s* away the people Mk 6:45 628
And when he had *s* them away Mk 6:46 657
and he *s* them away Mk 8:9 630
he *s* him away to his house, Mk 8:26 649
not me, but him that *s* me Mk 9:37 649
at the season he *s* to the Mk 12:2 649
and beat him, and *s* him away empty Mk 12:3 649
again he *s* unto them another Mk 12:4 649
s him away shamefully handled Mk 12:4 649
And again he *s* another Mk 12:5 649
he *s* him also last unto them, Mk 12:6 649
am *s* to speak unto thee, and to Lk 1:19 649
month the angel Gabriel was *s* Lk 1:26 649
and the rich he hath *s* empty away Lk 1:53 1821
he hath *s* me to heal the Lk 4:18 649
But unto none of them was Elias *s* Lk 4:26 3992
for therefore am I *s* Lk 4:43 649
he *s* unto him the elders of the Lk 7:3 649
the centurion *s* friends to him, Lk 7:6 3992
And they that were *s*, returning to Lk 7:10 3992
of his disciples *s* them to Jesus Lk 7:19 3992
John Baptist hath *s* us unto thee Lk 7:20 649
but Jesus *s* him away, saying, Lk 8:38 630
he *s* them to preach the kingdom Lk 9:2 649
me receiveth him that *s* me Lk 9:48 649
s messengers before his face Lk 9:52 649
s them two and two before his face Lk 10:1 649
me despiseth him that *s* me Lk 10:16 649
stonest them that are *s* unto thee Lk 13:34 649
s his servant at supper time to Lk 14:17 649
he *s* him into his fields to feed Lk 15:15 3992
s a message after him, saying, We Lk 19:14 649
he *s* two of his disciples, Lk 19:29 649
they that were *s* went their way Lk 19:32 649
at the season he *s* a servant to Lk 20:10 640
beat him, and *s* him away empty Lk 20:10 1821
again he *s* another servant Lk 20:11 3992
shamefully, and *s* him away empty Lk 20:11 1821
And again he *s* a third Lk 20:12 3992
s forth spies, which should feign Lk 20:20 649
he *s* Peter and John, saying, Go and Lk 22:8 649
When I *s* you without purse, and Lk 22:35 649
he *s* him to Herod, who himself Lk 23:7 375
robe, and *s* him again to Pilate Lk 23:11 375
for I *s* you to him Lk 23:15 375
There was a man *s* from God Jn 1:6 649
but was *s* to bear witness of that Jn 1:8
of John, when the Jews *s* priests Jn 1:19 649
give an answer to them that *s* us Jn 1:22 3992
they which were *s* were of the Jn 1:24 649
but he that *s* me to baptize with Jn 1:33 3992
For God *s* not his Son into the Jn 3:17 649
but that I am *s* before him Jn 3:28 649
For he whom God hath *s* speaketh Jn 3:34 649
to do the will of him that *s* me Jn 4:34 3992
I *s* you to reap that whereon ye Jn 4:38 649
not the Father which hath *s* him Jn 5:23 3992
and believeth on him that *s* me Jn 5:24 3992
of the Father which hath *s* me Jn 5:30 3992
Ye *s* unto John, and he bare Jn 5:33 649
of me, that the Father hath *s* me Jn 5:36 649
Father himself, which hath *s* me Jn 5:37 3992
for whom he hath *s*, him ye Jn 5:38 649
ye believe on him whom he hath *s* Jn 6:29 649
but the will of him that *s* me Jn 6:38 3992
the Father's will which hath *s* me Jn 6:39 3992
this is the will of him that *s* me Jn 6:40 3992
Father which hath *s* me draw him Jn 6:44 3992
As the living Father hath *s* me Jn 6:57 649
is not mine, but his that *s* me Jn 7:16 3992
that seeketh his glory that *s* him Jn 7:18 3992
myself, but he that *s* me is true Jn 7:28 3992
I am from him, and he hath *s* me Jn 7:29 649
the chief priests *s* officers to Jn 7:32 649
and then I go unto him that *s* me Jn 7:33 3992
but I and the Father that *s* me Jn 8:16 3992
the Father that *s* me beareth Jn 8:18 3992
but he that *s* me is true Jn 8:26 3992
And he that *s* me is with me Jn 8:29 3992
came I of myself, but he *s* me Jn 8:42 649
work the works of him that *s* me Jn 9:4 3992
(which is by interpretation, S Jn 9:7 649
and *s* into the world, Thou Jn 10:36 649
Therefore his sisters *s* unto him Jn 11:3 649
may believe that thou hast *s* me Jn 11:42 649
not on me, but on him that *s* me Jn 12:44 3992
that seeth me seeth him that *s* me Jn 12:45 3992
but the Father which *s* me Jn 12:49 3992
neither he that is *s* greater than Jn 13:16 652
greater than he that *s* him Jn 13:16 652
me receiveth him that *s* me Jn 13:20 3992
mine, but the Father's which *s* me Jn 14:24 3992
they know not him that *s* me Jn 15:21 3992

now I go my way to him that *s* me ... Jn 16:5 *3992*
and Jesus Christ, whom thou hast *s* ... Jn 17:3 *649*
As thou hast *s* me into the world, ... Jn 17:18 *649*
have I also *s* them into the world ... Jn 17:18 *649*
may believe that thou hast *s* me ... Jn 17:21 *649*
may know that thou hast *s* me ... Jn 17:23 *649*
have known that thou hast *s* me ... Jn 17:25 *649*
Now Annas had *s* him bound unto ... Jn 18:24 *649*
as my Father hath *s* me, even so ... Jn 20:21 *649*
s him to bless you, in turning ... Acts 3:26 *649*
s to the prison to have them ... Acts 5:21 *649*
he *s* out our fathers first ... Acts 7:12 *1821*
Then *s* Joseph, and called his ... Acts 7:14 *649*
they *s* unto them Peter and John ... Acts 8:14 *649*
the way as thou camest, hath *s* me ... Acts 9:17 *649*
and *s* him forth to Tarsus ... Acts 9:30 *1821*
they *s* unto him two men, desiring ... Acts 9:38 *649*
unto them, he *s* them to Joppa ... Acts 10:8 *649*
the men which were *s* from ... Acts 10:17 *649*
for I have *s* them ... Acts 10:20 *649*
were *s* unto him from Cornelius ... Acts 10:21 *649*
as soon as I was *s* for ... Acts 10:29 *3343*
for what intent ye have *s* for me ... Acts 10:29 *3343*
Immediately therefore I *s* to thee ... Acts 10:33 *3992*
The word which God *s* unto the ... Acts 10:36 *649*
I was, *s* from Caesarea unto me ... Acts 11:11 *649*
they *s* forth Barnabas, that he ... Acts 11:22 *1821*
s it to the elders by the hands ... Acts 11:30 *649*
that the Lord hath *s* his angel ... Acts 12:11 *1821*
hands on them, they *s* them away ... Acts 13:3 *630*
being *s* forth by the Holy Ghost, ... Acts 13:4 *1599*
of the synagogue *s* unto them ... Acts 13:15 *649*
is the word of this salvation *s* ... Acts 13:26 *649*
We have *s* therefore Judas and ... Acts 15:27 *649*
the magistrates *s* the serjeants ... Acts 16:35 *649*
magistrates have *s* to let you go ... Acts 16:36 *649*
brethren immediately *s* away Paul ... Acts 17:10 *1599*
s away Paul to go as it were to ... Acts 17:14 *1821*
So he *s* into Macedonia two of ... Acts 19:22 *649*
s unto him, desiring him that he ... Acts 19:31 *3992*
And from Miletus he *s* to Ephesus ... Acts 20:17 *3992*
I *s* straightway to thee, and gave ... Acts 23:30 *3992*
he *s* for Paul, and heard him ... Acts 24:24 *3343*
wherefore he *s* for him the ... Acts 24:26 *3343*
of God is *s* unto the Gentiles ... Acts 28:28 *649*
they preach, except they be *s* ... Rom 10:15 *649*
s by Phebe servant of the church ... Rom *s*
For Christ *s* me not to baptize, ... 1Cor 1:17 *649*
cause have I *s* unto you Timotheus ... 1Cor 4:17 *3992*
we have *s* with him the brother, ... 2Cor 8:18 *4842*
we have *s* with them our brother, ... 2Cor 8:22 *4842*
Yet have I *s* the brethren, lest ... 2Cor 9:3 *3992*
by any of them whom I *s* unto you ... 2Cor 12:17 *649*
Titus, and with him I *s* a brother ... 2Cor 12:18 *4882*
God *s* forth his Son, made of a ... Gal 4:4 *1821*
God hath *s* forth the Spirit of ... Gal 4:6 *1821*
Whom I have *s* unto you for the ... Eph 6:22 *3992*
I *s* him therefore the more ... Phil 2:28 *3992*
even in Thessalonica ye *s* once ... Phil 4:16 *3992*
the things which were *s* from you ... Phil 4:18
Whom I have *s* unto you for the ... Col 4:8 *3992*
s Timotheus, our brother, and ... 1Th 3:2 *3992*
I *s* to know your faith, lest by ... 1Th 3:5 *375*
And Tychicus have I *s* to Ephesus ... 2Ti 4:12 *649*
Whom I have *s* again ... Philem 12 *628*
s forth to minister for them who ... Heb 1:14 *649*
had *s* them out another way ... Jas 2:25 *1524*
the Holy Ghost *s* down from heaven ... 1Pet 1:12 *649*
as unto them that are *s* by him ... 1Pet 2:14 *3992*
because that God *s* his only ... 1Jn 4:9 *649*
s his Son to be the propitiation ... 1Jn 4:10 *649*
do testify that the Father *s* the ... 1Jn 4:14 *649*
and he *s* and signified it by his ... Rev 1:1 *649*
of God *s* forth into all the earth ... Rev 5:6 *649*
s his angel to shew unto his ... Rev 22:6 *649*
I Jesus have *s* mine angel to ... Rev 22:16 *3992*

SENTENCE {11}
shall shew thee the *s* of judgment ... Deut 17:9 1697
thou shalt do according to the *s* ... Deut 17:10 1697
According to the *s* of the law ... Deut 17:11 6310
the *s* which they shall shew thee ... Deut 17:11 1697
Let my *s* come forth from thy ... Ps 17:2 4941
A divine *s* is in the lips of the ... Prov 16:10 7081
Because *s* against an evil work is ... Eccl 8:11 6599
also will I give *s* against them ... Jer 4:12 4941
Pilate gave *s* that it should be ... Lk 23:24 *1948*
Wherefore my *s* is, that we ... Acts 15:19 *2919*
But we had the *s* of death in ... 2Cor 1:9 *610*

SENTENCES {2}
of dreams, and shewing of hard *s* ... Dan 5:12 280
and understanding dark *s*, shall ... Dan 8:23 2420

SENTEST {4}
thou *s* forth thy wrath, which ... Ex 15:7 7971
unto the land whither thou *s* us ... Num 13:27 7971
messengers which thou *s* unto me ... Num 24:12 7971
the things which thou *s* to me for ... 1Kin 5:8 7971

SENUAH *(sen'-u-ah)* {1} See HASSENUAH. *Father of Judah.*
Judah the son of *S* was second ... Neh 11:9 5574

SEORIM *(se-o'-rim)* {1} *A sanctuary servant.*
third to Harim, the fourth to *S* ... 1Chr 24:8 8188

SEPARATE {32}
s thyself, I pray thee, from me ... Gen 13:9 6504
And Jacob did *s* the lambs, and set ... Gen 30:40 6504
him that was *s* from his brethren ... Gen 49:26 5139
Thus shall ye *s* the children of ... Lev 15:31 5144
that they *s* themselves from the ... Lev 22:2 5144
s themselves to vow a vow of a ... Num 6:2 6381
to *s* themselves unto the LORD ... Num 6:2 5144
He shall *s* himself from wine and ... Num 6:3 5144
Thus shalt thou *s* the Levites ... Num 8:14 914
S yourselves from among this ... Num 16:21 914
Thou shalt *s* three cities for ... Deut 19:2 914
Thou shalt *s* three cities for ... Deut 19:7 914
the LORD shall *s* him unto evil ... Deut 29:21 914
the *s* cities for the children of ... Josh 16:9 3995
For thou didst *s* them from among ... 1Kin 8:53 914
s yourselves from the people of ... Ezr 10:11 914
to *s* himself thence in the midst ... Jer 37:12 2505
the *s* place at the end toward the ... Eze 41:12 1508
the *s* place, and the building, ... Eze 41:13 1508
of the *s* place toward the east, ... Eze 41:14 1508
the *s* place which was behind it ... Eze 41:15 1508
that was over against the *s* place ... Eze 42:1 1508
east, over against the *s* place ... Eze 42:10 1508
which are before the *s* place ... Eze 42:13 1508
he shall *s* them one from another, ... Mt 25:32 *873*
when they shall *s* you from their ... Lk 6:22 *873*
S me Barnabas and Saul for the ... Acts 13:2 *873*
Who shall *s* us from the love of ... Rom 8:35 *5562*
shall be able to *s* us from the ... Rom 8:39 *5562*
out from among them, and be ye *s* ... 2Cor 6:17 *873*
s from sinners, and made higher ... Heb 7:26 *5562*
These be they who *s* themselves ... Jude 19 *873*

SEPARATED {33}
they *s* themselves the one from ... Gen 13:11 6504
after that Lot was *s* from him ... Gen 13:14 6504
people shall be *s* from thy bowels ... Gen 25:23 6504
so shall we be *s*, I and thy people ... Ex 33:16 6395
which have *s* you from other ... Lev 20:24 914
which I have *s* from you as ... Lev 20:25 914
that the God of Israel hath *s* you ... Num 16:9 914
time the LORD *s* the tribe of Levi ... Deut 10:8 914
when he *s* the sons of Adam, he ... Deut 32:8 6504
him that was *s* from his brethren ... Deut 33:16 5139
of the Gadites there *s* themselves ... 1Chr 12:8 914
and Aaron was *s*, that he should ... 1Chr 23:13 914
the captains of the host *s* to the ... 1Chr 25:1 914
Then Amaziah *s* them, to wit, the ... 2Chr 25:10 914
all such as had *s* themselves unto ... Ezr 6:21 6395
Then I *s* twelve of the chief of ... Ezr 8:24 914
have not *s* themselves from the ... Ezr 9:1 914
himself *s* from the congregation ... Ezr 10:8 914
of them by their names, were *s* ... Ezr 10:16 914
we are *s* upon the wall, one far ... Neh 4:19 6504
the seed of Israel *s* themselves ... Neh 9:2 914
all they that had *s* themselves ... Neh 10:28 914
that they *s* from Israel all the ... Neh 13:3 914
having *s* himself, seeketh and ... Prov 18:1 6504
but the poor is *s* from his ... Prov 19:4 6504
hath utterly *s* me from his people ... Is 56:3 914
iniquities have *s* between you ... Is 59:2 914
for themselves are *s* with whores ... Hos 4:14 6504
s themselves unto that shame ... Hos 9:10 5144
s the disciples, disputing daily ... Acts 19:9 *873*
s unto the gospel of God, ... Rom 1:1 *873*
who *s* me from my mother's womb, ... Gal 1:15 *873*
s himself, fearing them which ... Gal 2:12 *873*

SEPARATETH {5}
in the which he *s* himself unto ... Num 6:5 5144
All the days that he *s* himself ... Num 6:6 5144
a whisperer *s* chief friends ... Prov 16:28 6504
repeateth a matter *s* very friends ... Prov 17:9 6504
which *s* himself from me, and ... Eze 14:7 5144

SEPARATING {1}
s myself, as I have done these so ... Zec 7:3 5144

SEPARATION {26}
according to the days of the *s* ... Lev 12:2 5079
be unclean two weeks, as in her *s* ... Lev 12:5 5079
upon in her *s* shall be unclean ... Lev 15:20 5079
days out of the time of her *s* ... Lev 15:25 5079
it run beyond the time of her *s* ... Lev 15:25 5079
shall be as the days of her *s* ... Lev 15:25 5079
be unto her as the bed of her *s* ... Lev 15:26 5079
as the uncleanness of her *s* ... Lev 15:26 5079
All the days of his *s* shall he ... Num 6:4 5145
s there shall no razor come upon ... Num 6:5 5145
All the days of his *s* he is holy ... Num 6:8 5145
unto the LORD the days of his *s* ... Num 6:12 5145
lost, because his *s* was defiled ... Num 6:12 5145
the days of his *s* are fulfilled ... Num 6:13 5145
shall shave the head of his *s* at ... Num 6:18 5145
the hair of the head of his *s* ... Num 6:18 5145
after the hair of his *s* is shaven ... Num 6:19 5145
offering unto the LORD for his *s* ... Num 6:21 5145
he must do after the law of his *s* ... Num 6:21 5145
of Israel for a water of *s* ... Num 19:9 5079
because the water of *s* was not ... Num 19:13 5079
the water of *s* hath not been ... Num 19:20 5079
water of *s* shall wash his clothes ... Num 19:21 5079
of *s* shall be unclean until even ... Num 19:21 5079
be purified with the water of *s* ... Num 31:23 5079
to make a *s* between the sanctuary ... Eze 42:20 914

SEPHAR *(se'-far)* {1} *A mountain in Arabia.*
as thou goest unto *S* a mount of ... Gen 10:30 5611

SEPHARAD *(sef'-a-rad)* {1} *A city in Media.*
of Jerusalem, which is in *S* ... Obad 20 5614

SEPHARVAIM *(sef-ar-va'-im)* {6} See SEPHARVITES. *A city in Mesopotamia.*
Ava, and from Hamath, and from *S* ... 2Kin 17:24 5617
and Anammelech, the gods of *S* ... 2Kin 17:31 5617
where are the gods of *S*, Hena, and ... 2Kin 18:34 5617
and the king of the city of *S* ... 2Kin 19:13 5617
where are the gods of *S* ... Is 36:19 5617
and the king of the city of *S* ... Is 37:13 5617

SEPHARVITES *(sef-ar-vites)* {1} *Inhabitants of Sepharvaim.*
the *S* burnt their children in ... 2Kin 17:31 5616

SEPULCHRE {54}
us shall withhold from thee his *s* ... Gen 23:6 6913
knoweth of his *s* unto this day ... Deut 34:6 6900
was buried in the *s* of Joash his ... Judg 8:32 6913
s in the border of Benjamin at ... 1Sa 10:2 6900
buried him in the *s* of his father ... 2Sa 2:32 6913
buried it in the *s* of Abner in ... 2Sa 4:12 6913
was buried in the *s* of his father ... 2Sa 17:23 6913
in the *s* of Kish his father ... 2Sa 21:14 6913
come unto the *s* of thy fathers ... 1Kin 13:22 6913
then bury me in the *s* wherein the ... 1Kin 13:31 6913
buried him in his *s* with his ... 2Kin 9:28 6900
cast the man into the *s* of Elisha ... 2Kin 13:21 6913
he was buried in his *s* in the ... 2Kin 21:26 6900
It is the *s* of the man of God, ... 2Kin 23:17 6913
and buried him in his own *s* ... 2Kin 23:30 6900
their throat is an open *s* ... Ps 5:9 6913
thou hast hewed thee out a *s* here ... Is 22:16 6913
that heweth him out an *s* on high ... Is 22:16 6913
Their quiver is as an open *s* ... Jer 5:16 6913
great stone to the door of the *s* ... Mt 27:60 *3419*
Mary, sitting over against the *s* ... Mt 27:61 *5028*
Command therefore that the *s* be ... Mt 27:64 *5028*
So they went, and made the *s* sure ... Mt 27:66 *5028*
and the other Mary to see the *s* ... Mt 28:1 *5028*
quickly from the *s* with fear ... Mt 28:8 *3419*
laid him in a *s* which was hewn ... Mk 15:46 *3419*
a stone unto the door of the *s* ... Mk 15:46 *3419*
they came unto the *s* at the ... Mk 16:2 *3419*
the stone from the door of the *s* ... Mk 16:3 *3419*
And entering into the *s*, they saw ... Mk 16:5 *3419*
out quickly, and fled from the *s* ... Mk 16:8 *3419*
laid it in a *s* that was hewn in ... Lk 23:53 *3418*
followed after, and beheld the *s* ... Lk 23:55 *3419*
the morning, they came unto the *s* ... Lk 24:1 *3418*
the stone rolled away from the *s* ... Lk 24:2 *3419*
And returned from the *s*, and told ... Lk 24:9 *3419*
arose Peter, and ran unto the *s* ... Lk 24:12 *3419*
which were early at the *s* ... Lk 24:22 *3419*
which were with us went to the *s* ... Lk 24:24 *3419*
and in the garden a new *s*, wherein ... Jn 19:41 *3419*
for the *s* was nigh at hand ... Jn 19:42 *3419*
when it was yet dark, unto the *s* ... Jn 20:1 *3419*
the stone taken away from the *s* ... Jn 20:1 *3419*
taken away the Lord out of the *s* ... Jn 20:2 *3419*
other disciple, and came to the *s* ... Jn 20:3 *3419*
Peter, and came first to the *s* ... Jn 20:4 *3419*
following him, and went into the *s* ... Jn 20:6 *3419*
which came first to the *s* ... Jn 20:8 *3419*
stood without at the *s* weeping ... Jn 20:11 *3419*
down, and looked into the *s* ... Jn 20:11 *3419*
his *s* is with us unto this day ... Acts 2:29 *3418*
laid in the *s* that Abraham bought ... Acts 7:16 *3418*
from the tree, and laid him in a *s* ... Acts 13:29 *3419*
Their throat is an open *s* ... Rom 3:13 *5028*

SEPULCHRES {16}
the choice of our *s* bury thy dead ... Gen 23:6 6913
he spied the *s* that were there in ... 2Kin 23:16 6913
and took the bones out of the *s* ... 2Kin 23:16 6913
And they buried him in his own *s* ... 2Chr 16:14 6913
but not in the *s* of the kings ... 2Chr 21:20 6913
him not in the *s* of the kings ... 2Chr 24:25 6913
into the *s* of the kings of Israel ... 2Chr 28:27 6913
of the *s* of the sons of David ... 2Chr 32:33 6913
in one of the *s* of his fathers ... 2Chr 35:24 6913
city, the place of my fathers' *s* ... Neh 2:3 6913
unto the city of my fathers' *s* ... Neh 2:5 6913
place over against the *s* of David ... Neh 3:16 6913
for ye are like unto whited *s* ... Mt 23:27 *5028*
garnish the *s* of the righteous, ... Mt 23:29 *3419*
ye build the *s* of the prophets ... Lk 11:47 *3419*
killed them, and ye build their *s* ... Lk 11:48 *3419*

SERAH *(se'-rah)* {2} See SARAH. *A daughter of Asher.*
and Beriah, and *S* their sister ... Gen 46:17 8294
and Beriah, and *S* their sister ... 1Chr 7:30 8294

SERAIAH *(se-ra-i'-ah)* {20} See SHAVSHA.
1. David's scribe.
and *S* was the scribe ... 2Sa 8:17 8304
2. High priest in Zedekiah's time.
the guard took *S* the chief priest ... 2Kin 25:18 8304
And Azariah begat *S*, and Seraiah ... 1Chr 6:14 8304
Seraiah, and *S* begat Jehozadak, ... 1Chr 6:14 8304
king of Persia, Ezra the son of *S* ... Ezr 7:1 8304
the guard took *S* the chief priest ... Jer 52:24 8304
3. Son of Tanhumeth.
S the son of Tanhumeth the ... 2Kin 25:23 8304
S the son of Tanhumeth, and the ... Jer 40:8 8304
4. A son of Kenaz.
Othniel, and *S* ... 1Chr 4:13 8304
S begat Joab, the father of the ... 1Chr 4:14 8304
5. Son of Asiel.
the son of Josibiah, the son of *S* ... 1Chr 4:35 8304
6. A priest with Zerubbabel.
Jeshua, Nehemiah, *S*, Reelaiah, ... Ezr 2:2 8304
S, Azariah, Jeremiah, ... Neh 10:2 8304
S, Jeremiah, Ezra, ... Neh 12:1 8304
of *S*, Meraiah ... Neh 12:12 8304
7. An exile.
S the son of Hilkiah, the son of ... Neh 11:11 8304

8. Son of Azriel.
S the son of Azriel, and Shelemiah Jer 36:26 8304
9. Son of Neriah.
commanded *S* the son of Neriah Jer 51:59 8304
this *S* was a quiet prince Jer 51:59 8304
And Jeremiah said to *S*, When thou Jer 51:61 8304

SERAPHIMS {2}
Above it stood the *s* Is 6:2 8314
Then flew one of the *s* unto me Is 6:6 8314

SERED *(se'-red)* {2} See SARDITES. *A son of Zebulun.*
S, and Elon, and Jahleel Gen 46:14 5624
of *S*, the family of the Sardites Num 26:26 5624

SEREDITES See SARDITES.

SERGIUS *(sur'-je-us)* {1} *Roman governor of Cyprus.*
country, *S* Paulus, a prudent man Acts 13:7 *4588*

SERJEANTS {2}
day, the magistrates sent the *s* Acts 16:35 *4465*
the *s* told these words unto the Acts 16:38 *4465*

SERPENT {38}
Now the *s* was more subtil than Gen 3:1 5175
And the woman said unto the *s* Gen 3:2 5175
the *s* said unto the woman, Ye Gen 3:4 5175
The *s* beguiled me, and I did eat Gen 3:13 5175
And the LORD God said unto the *s* Gen 3:14 5175
Dan shall be a *s* by the way Gen 49:17 5175
on the ground, and it became a *s* Ex 4:3 5175
Pharaoh, and it shall become a *s* Ex 7:9 8577
his servants, and it became a *s* Ex 7:10 8577
a *s* shalt thou take in thine hand Ex 7:15 5175
unto Moses, Make thee a fiery *s* Num 21:8 8314
And Moses made a *s* of brass Num 21:9 5175
that if a *s* had bitten any man, Num 21:9 5175
when he beheld the *s* of brass Num 21:9 5175
the brasen *s* that Moses had made 2Kin 18:4 5175
hand hath formed the crooked *s* Job 26:13 5175
poison is like the poison of a *s* Ps 58:4 5175
sharpened their tongues like a *s* Ps 140:3 5175
At the last it biteth like a *s* Prov 23:32 5175
the way of a *s* upon a rock Prov 30:19 5175
an hedge, a *s* shall bite him Eccl 10:8 5175
Surely the *s* will bite without Eccl 10:11 5175
fruit shall be a fiery flying *s* Is 14:29 8314
punish leviathan the piercing *s* Is 27:1 5175
even leviathan that crooked *s* Is 27:1 5175
lion, the viper and fiery flying *s* Is 30:6 8314
voice thereof shall go like a *s* Jer 46:22 5175
hand on the wall, and a *s* bit him Amos 5:19 5175
sea, thence will I command the *s* Amos 9:3 5175
They shall lick the dust like a *s* Mic 7:17 5175
ask a fish, will he give him a *s* Mt 7:10 *3789*
will he for a fish give him a *s* Lk 11:11 *3789*
lifted up the *s* in the wilderness Jn 3:14 *3789*
as the *s* beguiled Eve through his 2Cor 11:3 *3789*
dragon was cast out, that old *s* Rev 12:9 *3789*
a time, from the face of the *s* Rev 12:14 *3789*
the *s* cast out of his mouth water Rev 12:15 *3789*
hold on the dragon, that old *s* Rev 20:2 *3789*

SERPENT'S {2}
for out of the *s* root shall come Is 14:29 5175
and dust shall be the *s* meat Is 65:25 5175

SERPENTS {13}
man his rod, and they became *s* Ex 7:12 8577
sent fiery *s* among the people Num 21:6 5175
that he take away the *s* from us Num 21:7 5175
wilderness, wherein were fiery *s* Deut 8:15 5175
with the poison of *s* of the dust Deut 32:24 2119
For, behold, I will send *s* Jer 8:17 5175
be ye therefore wise as *s* Mt 10:16 *3789*
Ye *s*, ye generation of vipers, Mt 23:33 *3789*
They shall take up *s* Mk 16:18 *3789*
give unto you power to tread on *s* Lk 10:19 *3789*
tempted, and were destroyed of *s* 1Cor 10:9 *3789*
of beasts, and of birds, and of *s* Jas 3:7 *2062*
for their tails were like unto *s* Rev 9:19 *3789*

SERUG *(se'-rug)* {5} See SARUCH. *Father of Nahor.*
two and thirty years, and begat *S* Gen 11:20 8286
after he begat *S* two hundred Gen 11:21 8286
S lived thirty years, and begat Gen 11:22 8286
S lived after he begat Nahor two Gen 11:23 8286
S, Nahor, Terah, 1Chr 1:26 8286

SERVANT {494}
a *s* of servants shall he be unto Gen 9:25 5650
and Canaan shall be his *s* Gen 9:26 5650
and Canaan shall be his *s* Gen 9:27 5650
not away, I pray thee, from thy *s* Gen 18:3 5650
therefore are ye come to your *s* Gen 18:5 5650
thy *s* hath found grace in thy Gen 19:19 5650
unto his eldest *s* of his house Gen 24:2 5650
the *s* said unto him, Peradventure Gen 24:5 5650
the *s* put his hand under the Gen 24:9 5650
the *s* took ten camels of the Gen 24:10 5650
hast appointed for thy *s* Isaac Gen 24:14 5650
the *s* ran to meet her, and said, Gen 24:17 5650
And he said, I am Abraham's *s* Gen 24:34 5650
when Abraham's *s* heard their Gen 24:52 5650
the *s* brought forth jewels of Gen 24:53 5650
and her nurse, and Abraham's *s* Gen 24:59 5650
the *s* took Rebekah, and went his Gen 24:61 5650
For she had said unto the *s* Gen 24:65 5650
the *s* had said, It is my master Gen 24:65 5650
the *s* told Isaac all things that Gen 24:66 5650
thy seed for my *s* Abraham's sake Gen 26:24 5650
Thy *s* Jacob saith thus, I have Gen 32:4 5650
which thou hast shewed unto thy *s* Gen 32:10 5650
shalt say, They be thy *s* Jacob's Gen 32:18 5650
Behold, thy *s* Jacob is behind us Gen 32:20 5650
God hath graciously given thy *s* Gen 33:5 5650
pray thee, pass over before his *s* Gen 33:14 5650
these words, saying, The Hebrew *s* Gen 39:17 5650
After this manner did thy *s* to me Gen 39:19 5650
s to the captain of the guard Gen 41:12 5650
Thy *s* our father is in good Gen 43:28 5650
whom it is found shall be my *s* Gen 44:10 5650
cup is found, he shall be my *s* Gen 44:17 5650
and said, Oh my lord, let thy *s* Gen 44:18 5650
thine anger burn against thy *s* Gen 44:18 5650
we came up unto thy *s* my father Gen 44:24 5650
thy *s* my father said unto us, Ye Gen 44:27 5650
when I come to thy *s* my father Gen 44:30 5650
down the gray hairs of thy *s* our Gen 44:31 5650
For thy *s* became surety for the Gen 44:32 5650
let thy *s* abide instead of the Gen 44:33 5650
bear, and became a *s* unto tribute Gen 49:15 5647
since thou hast spoken unto thy *s* Ex 4:10 5650
But every man's *s* that is bought Ex 12:44 5650
an hired *s* shall not eat thereof Ex 12:45 7916
believed the LORD, and his *s* Moses Ex 14:31 5650
If thou buy an Hebrew *s*, six Ex 21:2 5650
if the *s* shall plainly say, I Ex 21:5 5650
And if a man smite his *s*, or his Ex 21:20 5650
if a man smite the eye of his *s* Ex 21:26 5650
but his *s* Joshua, the son of Nun, Ex 33:11 8334
of the priest, or an hired *s* Lev 22:10 7916
for thee, and for thy *s*, and for Lev 25:6 5650
for thy maid, and for thy hired *s* Lev 25:6 7916
But as an hired *s*, and as a Lev 25:40 7916
an hired *s* shall it be with him Lev 25:50 7916
as a yearly hired *s* shall he be Lev 25:53 7916
hast thou afflicted thy *s* Num 11:11 5650
the *s* of Moses, one of his young Num 11:28 8334
My *s* Moses is not so, who is Num 12:7 5650
to speak against my *s* Moses Num 12:8 5650
But my *s* Caleb, because he had Num 14:24 5650
begun to shew thy *s* thy greatness Deut 3:24 5650
wast a *s* in the land of Egypt Deut 5:15 5650
and he shall be thy *s* for ever Deut 15:17 5650
worth a double hired *s* to thee Deut 15:18 7916
the *s* which is escaped from his Deut 23:15 5650
oppress an hired *s* that is poor Deut 24:14 7916
So Moses the *s* of the LORD died Deut 34:5 5650
the *s* of the LORD it came to pass Josh 1:1 5650
Moses my *s* is dead Josh 1:2 5650
which Moses my *s* commanded thee Josh 1:7 5650
the word which Moses the *s* of the Josh 1:13 5650
which Moses the LORD's *s* gave you Josh 1:15 5650
What saith my lord unto his *s* Josh 5:14 5650
As Moses the *s* of the LORD Josh 8:31 5650
as Moses the *s* of the LORD had Josh 8:33 5650
s Moses to give you all the land Josh 9:24 5650
as Moses the *s* of the LORD Josh 11:12 5650
As the LORD commanded Moses his *s* Josh 11:15 5650
Them did Moses the *s* of the LORD Josh 12:6 5650
Moses the *s* of the LORD gave it Josh 12:6 5650
even as Moses the *s* of the LORD Josh 13:8 5650
the *s* of the LORD sent me from Josh 14:7 5650
which Moses the *s* of the LORD Josh 18:7 5650
the *s* of the LORD commanded you Josh 22:2 5650
which Moses the *s* of the LORD Josh 22:4 5650
which Moses the *s* of the LORD Josh 22:5 5650
the *s* of the LORD, died, being an Josh 24:29 5650
the *s* of the LORD, died, being an Judg 2:8 5650
Phurah thy *s* down to the host Judg 7:10 5288
went he down with Phurah his *s* Judg 7:11 5288
into the hand of thy *s* Judg 15:18 5650
her again, having his *s* with him Judg 19:3 5288
he, and his concubine, and his *s* Judg 19:9 5288
the *s* said unto his master, Come, Judg 19:11 5288
And he said unto his *s*, Come, and Judg 19:13 5288
Then said Boaz unto his *s* that Ruth 2:5 5288
the *s* that was set over the Ruth 2:6 5288
sacrifice, the priest's *s* came 1Sa 2:13 5288
the fat, the priest's *s* came 1Sa 2:15 5288
for thy *s* heareth 1Sa 3:9 5650
for thy *s* heareth 1Sa 3:10 5650
Saul said to his *s* that was with 1Sa 9:5 5288
Then said Saul to his *s*, But, 1Sa 9:7 5288
the *s* answered Saul again, and 1Sa 9:8 5288
Then said Saul to his *s*, Well 1Sa 9:10 5288
And Samuel took Saul and his *s* 1Sa 9:22 5288
Did the *s* pass on before us, (and 1Sa 9:27 5288
uncle said unto him and to his *s* 1Sa 10:14 5288
thy *s* will go and fight with this 1Sa 17:32 5650
Thy *s* kept his father's sheep, and 1Sa 17:34 5650
Thy *s* slew both the lion and the 1Sa 17:36 5650
I am the son of thy *s* Jesse the 1Sa 17:58 5650
not the king sin against his *s* 1Sa 19:4 5650
thy *s* shall have peace 1Sa 20:7 5650
thou shalt deal kindly with thy *s* 1Sa 20:8 5650
for thou hast brought thy *s* into 1Sa 20:8 5650
hath stirred up my *s* against me 1Sa 22:8 5650
king impute any thing unto his *s* 1Sa 22:15 5650
for thy *s* knew nothing of all 1Sa 22:15 5650
thy *s* hath certainly heard that 1Sa 23:10 5650
come down, as thy *s* hath heard 1Sa 23:11 5650
I beseech thee, tell thy *s* 1Sa 23:11 5650
and hath kept his *s* from evil 1Sa 25:39 5650
be a *s* to wash the feet of the 1Sa 25:41 5650
my lord thus pursue after his *s* 1Sa 26:18 5650
the king hear the words of his *s* 1Sa 26:19 5650
for why should thy *s* dwell in the 1Sa 27:5 5650
he shall be my *s* for ever 1Sa 27:12 5650
thou shalt know what thy *s* can do 1Sa 28:2 5650
the *s* of Saul the king of Israel, 1Sa 29:3 5650
thy *s* so long as I have been with 1Sa 29:8 5650
man of Egypt, *s* to an Amalekite 1Sa 30:13 5650
By the hand of my *s* David I will 2Sa 3:18 5650
Go and tell my *s* David, Thus saith 2Sa 7:5 5650
so shalt thou say unto my *s* David 2Sa 7:8 5650
for thou, Lord GOD, knowest thy *s* 2Sa 7:20 5650
things, to make thy *s* know them 2Sa 7:21 5650
thou hast spoken concerning thy *s* 2Sa 7:25 5650
let the house of thy *s* David be 2Sa 7:26 5650
of Israel, hast revealed to thy *s* 2Sa 7:27 5650
therefore hath thy *s* found in his 2Sa 7:27 5650
promised this goodness unto thy *s* 2Sa 7:28 5650
thee to bless the house of thy *s* 2Sa 7:29 5650
of thy *s* be blessed for ever 2Sa 7:29 5650
of Saul a *s* whose name was Ziba 2Sa 9:2 5650
And he said, Thy *s* is he 2Sa 9:2 5650
And he answered, Behold thy *s* 2Sa 9:6 5650
himself, and said, What is thy *s* 2Sa 9:8 5650
the king called to Ziba, Saul's *s* 2Sa 9:9 5288
his *s*, so shall thy *s* do 2Sa 9:11 5650
Thy *s* Uriah the Hittite is dead 2Sa 11:21 5650
thy *s* Uriah the Hittite is dead 2Sa 11:24 5650
Then he called his *s* that 2Sa 13:17 5288
Then his *s* brought her out, and 2Sa 13:18 8334
now, thy *s* hath sheepshearers 2Sa 13:24 5650
and his servants go with thy *s* 2Sa 13:24 5650
as thy *s* said, so it is 2Sa 13:35 5650
for thy *s* Joab, he bade me, and he 2Sa 14:19 5650
hath thy *s* Joab done this thing 2Sa 14:20 5650
Today thy *s* knoweth that I have 2Sa 14:22 5650
fulfilled the request of his *s* 2Sa 14:22 5650
Thy *s* is of one of the tribes of 2Sa 15:2 5650
For thy *s* vowed a vow while I 2Sa 15:8 5650
even there also will thy *s* be 2Sa 15:21 5650
say unto Absalom, I will be thy *s* 2Sa 15:34 5650
have been thy father's *s* hitherto 2Sa 15:34 5650
so will I now also be thy *s* 2Sa 15:34 5650
Ziba the *s* of Mephibosheth met 2Sa 16:1 5288
the king's *s*, and me thy *s* 2Sa 18:29 5650
Ziba the *s* of the house of Saul, 2Sa 19:17 5288
s did perversely the day that my 2Sa 19:19 5650
For thy *s* doth know that I have 2Sa 19:20 5650
My lord, O king, my *s* deceived me 2Sa 19:26 5650
for thy *s* said, I will saddle me 2Sa 19:26 5650
because thy *s* is lame 2Sa 19:26 5650
thy *s* unto my lord the king 2Sa 19:27 5650
yet didst thou set thy *s* among 2Sa 19:28 5650
can thy *s* taste what I eat or 2Sa 19:35 5650
wherefore then should thy *s* be 2Sa 19:35 5650
Thy *s* will go a little way over 2Sa 19:36 5650
Let thy *s*, I pray thee, turn back 2Sa 19:37 5650
But behold thy *s* Chimham 2Sa 19:37 5650
take away the iniquity of thy *s* 2Sa 24:10 5650
is my lord the king come to his *s* 2Sa 24:21 5650
but Solomon thy *s* hath he not 1Kin 1:19 5650
But me, even me thy *s*, and Zadok 1Kin 1:26 5650
thy *s* Solomon, hath he not called 1Kin 1:26 5650
hast not shewed it unto thy *s* 1Kin 1:27 5650
not slay his *s* with the sword 1Kin 1:51 5650
king hath said, so will thy *s* do 1Kin 2:38 5650
Thou hast shewed unto thy *s* David 1Kin 3:6 5650
thou hast made thy *s* king instead 1Kin 3:7 5650
thy *s* is in the midst of thy 1Kin 3:8 5650
Give therefore thy *s* an 1Kin 3:9 5650
Who hast kept with thy *s* David my 1Kin 8:24 5650
keep with thy *s* David my father 1Kin 8:25 5650
unto thy *s* David my father 1Kin 8:26 5650
respect unto the prayer of thy *s* 1Kin 8:28 5650
which thy *s* prayeth before thee 1Kin 8:28 5650
unto the prayer which thy *s* shall 1Kin 8:29 5650
thou to the supplication of thy *s* 1Kin 8:30 5650
unto the supplication of thy *s* 1Kin 8:52 5650
by the hand of Moses thy *s* 1Kin 8:53 5650
by the hand of Moses his *s* 1Kin 8:56 5650
he maintain the cause of his *s* 1Kin 8:59 5650
the LORD had done for David his *s* 1Kin 8:66 5650
thee, and will give it to thy *s* 1Kin 11:11 5650
Ephrathite of Zereda, Solomon's *s* 1Kin 11:26 5650
one tribe for my *s* David's sake 1Kin 11:32 5650
that David my *s* may have a light 1Kin 11:36 5650
commandments, as David my *s* did 1Kin 11:38 5650
If thou wilt be a *s* unto this 1Kin 12:7 5650
thou hast not been as my *s* David 1Kin 14:8 5650
hand of his *s* Ahijah the prophet 1Kin 14:18 5650
by his *s* Ahijah the Shilonite 1Kin 15:29 5650
his *s* Zimri, captain of half his 1Kin 16:9 5650
thy *s* into the hand of Ahab 1Kin 18:9 5650
but I thy *s* fear the LORD from my 1Kin 18:12 5650
God in Israel, and that I am thy *s* 1Kin 18:36 5650
And said to his *s*, Go up now, look 1Kin 18:43 5288
to Judah, and left his *s* there 1Kin 19:3 5288
to thy *s* at the first I will do 1Kin 20:9 5650
Thy *s* Ben-hadad saith, I pray 1Kin 20:32 5650
Thy *s* went out into the midst of 1Kin 20:39 5650
as thy *s* was busy here and there, 1Kin 20:40 5650
saying, Thy *s* my husband is dead 2Kin 4:1 5650
that thy *s* did fear the LORD 2Kin 4:1 5650
And he said to Gehazi his *s* 2Kin 4:12 5288
saddled an ass, and said to her *s* 2Kin 4:24 5288
off, that he said to Gehazi his *s* 2Kin 4:25 5288
and he said unto his *s*, Set on the 2Kin 4:38 5288
sent Naaman my *s* to thee, that 2Kin 5:6 5650
thee, take a blessing of thy *s* 2Kin 5:15 5650
be given to thy *s* two mules' 2Kin 5:17 5650
for thy *s* will henceforth offer 2Kin 5:17 5650
this thing the LORD pardon thy *s* 2Kin 5:18 5650
LORD pardon thy *s* in this thing 2Kin 5:18 5650

S

the *s* of Elisha the man of God, 2Kin 5:20 5288
And he said, Thy *s* went no whither 2Kin 5:25 5650
when the *s* of the man of God was 2Kin 6:15 8334
his *s* said unto him, Alas, my 2Kin 6:15 5288
Gehazi the *s* of the man of God 2Kin 8:4 5288
said, But what, is thy *s* a dog 2Kin 8:13 5650
by his *s* Elijah the Tishbite 2Kin 9:36 5650
which he spake by his *s* Elijah 2Kin 10:10 5650
spake by the hand of his *s* Jonah 2Kin 14:25 5650
of Assyria, saying, I am thy *s* 2Kin 16:7 5650
and Hoshea became his *s*, and gave 2Kin 17:3 5650
all that Moses the *s* of the LORD 2Kin 18:12 5650
sake, and for my *s* David's sake 2Kin 19:34 5650
sake, and for my *s* David's sake 2Kin 20:6 5650
that my *s* Moses commanded them 2Kin 21:8 5650
Asahiah a *s* of the king's, saying 2Kin 22:12 5650
became his *s* three years 2Kin 24:1 5650
a *s* of the king of Babylon, unto 2Kin 25:8 5650
And Sheshan had a *s*, an Egyptian, 1Chr 2:34 5650
daughter to Jarha his *s* to wife 1Chr 2:35 5650
Moses the *s* of God had commanded 1Chr 6:49 5650
O ye seed of Israel his *s* 1Chr 16:13 5650
Go and tell David my *s*, Thus saith 1Chr 17:4 5650
shalt thou say unto my *s* David 1Chr 17:7 5650
to thee for the honour of thy *s* 1Chr 17:18 5650
for thou knowest thy *s* 1Chr 17:18 5650
thou hast spoken concerning thy *s* 1Chr 17:23 5650
thy *s* be established before thee 1Chr 17:24 5650
hast told thy *s* that thou wilt 1Chr 17:25 5650
therefore thy *s* hath found in his 1Chr 17:25 5650
promised this goodness unto thy *s* 1Chr 17:26 5650
thee to bless the house of thy *s* 1Chr 17:27 5650
do away the iniquity of thy *s* 1Chr 21:8 5650
which Moses the *s* of the LORD had 2Chr 1:3 5650
Thou which hast kept with thy *s* 2Chr 6:15 5650
keep with thy *s* David my father 2Chr 6:16 5650
thou hast spoken unto thy *s* David 2Chr 6:17 5650
therefore to the prayer of thy *s* 2Chr 6:19 5650
which thy *s* prayeth before thee 2Chr 6:19 5650
thy *s* prayeth toward this place 2Chr 6:20 5650
unto the supplications of thy *s* 2Chr 6:21 5650
the mercies of David thy *s* 2Chr 6:42 5650
the *s* of Solomon the son of David 2Chr 13:6 5650
of Moses the *s* of the LORD 2Chr 24:6 5650
the collection that Moses the *s* 2Chr 24:9 5650
God, and against his *s* Hezekiah 2Chr 32:16 5650
Asaiah a *s* of the king's, saying, 2Chr 34:20 5650
mayest hear the prayer of thy *s* Neh 1:6 5650
thou commandedst thy *s* Moses Neh 1:7 5650
that thou commandedst thy *s* Moses Neh 1:8 5650
attentive to the prayer of thy *s* Neh 1:11 5650
thy *s* this day, and grant him Neh 1:11 5650
if thy *s* have found favour in thy Neh 2:5 5650
the Horonite, and Tobiah the *s* Neh 2:10 5650
the Horonite, and Tobiah the *s* Neh 2:19 5650
with his *s* lodge within Jerusalem Neh 4:22 5650
Then sent Sanballat his *s* unto me Neh 6:5 5650
laws, by the hand of Moses thy *s* Neh 9:14 5650
was given by Moses the *s* of God Neh 10:29 5650
Hast thou considered my *s* Job Job 1:8 5650
Hast thou considered my *s* Job Job 2:3 5650
the *s* is free from his master Job 3:19 5650
As a *s* earnestly desireth the Job 7:2 5650
I called my *s*, and he gave me no Job 19:16 5650
thou take him for a *s* for ever Job 41:4 5650
that is right, as my *s* Job hath Job 42:7 5650
and seven rams, and go to my *s* Job Job 42:8 5650
my *s* Job shall pray for you Job 42:8 5650
which is right, like my *s* Job Job 42:8 5650
the *s* of the LORD, who spake unto Ps 18:*t* 5650
Moreover by them is thy *s* warned Ps 19:11 5650
Keep back thy *s* also from Ps 19:13 5650
put not thy *s* away in anger Ps 27:9 5650
Make thy face to shine upon thy *s* Ps 31:16 5650
in the prosperity of his *s* Ps 35:27 5650
Psalm of David, the *s* of the LORD Ps 36:*t* 5650
And hide not thy face from thy *s* Ps 69:17 5650
He chose David also his *s* Ps 78:70 5650
save thy *s* that trusteth in thee Ps 86:2 5650
Rejoice the soul of thy *s* Ps 86:4 5650
give thy strength unto thy *s* Ps 86:16 5650
I have sworn unto David my *s* Ps 89:3 5650
I have found David my *s* Ps 89:20 5650
made void the covenant of thy *s* Ps 89:39 5650
O ye seed of Abraham his *s* Ps 105:6 5650
even Joseph, who was sold for a *s* Ps 105:17 5650
He sent Moses his *s* Ps 105:26 5650
holy promise, and Abraham his *s* Ps 105:42 5650
but let thy *s* rejoice Ps 109:28 5650
O LORD, truly I am thy *s* Ps 116:16 5650
I am thy *s*, and the son of thine Ps 116:16 5650
Deal bountifully with thy *s* Ps 119:17 5650
but thy *s* did meditate in thy Ps 119:23 5650
Stablish thy word unto thy *s* Ps 119:38 5650
Remember the word unto thy *s* Ps 119:49 5650
Thou hast dealt well with thy *s* Ps 119:65 5650
according to thy word unto thy *s* Ps 119:76 5650
How many are the days of thy *s* Ps 119:84 5650
Be surety for thy *s* for good Ps 119:122 5650
Deal with thy *s* according unto Ps 119:124 5650
I am thy *s* Ps 119:125 5650
Make thy face to shine upon thy *s* Ps 119:135 5650
therefore thy *s* loveth it Ps 119:140 5650
seek thy *s* Ps 119:176 5650
For thy *s* David's sake turn not Ps 132:10 5650
an heritage unto Israel his *s* Ps 136:22 5650
not into judgment with thy *s* Ps 143:2 5650
for I am thy *s* Ps 143:12 5650
his *s* from the hurtful sword Ps 144:10 5650
the fool shall be *s* to the wise Prov 11:29 5650
He that is despised, and hath a *s* Prov 12:9 5650
king's favour is toward a wise *s* Prov 14:35 5650
A wise *s* shall have rule over a Prov 17:2 5650
much less for a *s* to have rule Prov 19:10 5650
the borrower is *s* to the lender Prov 22:7 5650
A *s* will not be corrected by Prov 29:19 5650
his *s* from a child shall have him Prov 29:21 5650
Accuse not a *s* unto his master, Prov 30:10 5650
For a *s* when he reigneth Prov 30:22 5650
lest thou hear thy *s* curse thee Eccl 7:21 5650
Like as my *s* Isaiah hath walked Is 20:3 5650
that I will call my *s* Eliakim the Is 22:20 5650
as with the *s*, so with his master Is 24:2 5650
sake, and for my *s* David's sake Is 37:35 5650
But thou, Israel, art my *s* Is 41:8 5650
and said unto thee, Thou art my *s* Is 41:9 5650
Behold my *s*, whom I uphold Is 42:1 5650
Who is blind, but my *s* Is 42:19 5650
perfect, and blind as the LORD's *s* Is 42:19 5650
LORD, and my *s* whom I have chosen Is 43:10 5650
Yet now hear, O Jacob my *s* Is 44:1 5650
Fear not, O Jacob, my *s* Is 44:2 5650
for thou art my *s* Is 44:21 5650
thou art my *s* Is 44:21 5650
That confirmeth the word of his *s* Is 44:26 5650
LORD hath redeemed his *s* Jacob Is 48:20 5650
And said unto me, Thou art my *s* Is 49:3 5650
me from the womb to be his *s* Is 49:5 5650
s to raise up the tribes of Jacob Is 49:6 5650
to a *s* of rulers, Kings shall see Is 49:7 5650
that obeyeth the voice of his *s* Is 50:10 5650
my *s* shall deal prudently, he Is 52:13 5650
shall my righteous *s* justify many Is 53:11 5650
Is Israel a *s* Jer 2:14 5650
the king of Babylon, my *s* Jer 25:9 5650
the king of Babylon, my *s* Jer 27:6 5650
O my *s* Jacob, saith the LORD Jer 30:10 5650
be broken with David my *s* Jer 33:21 5650
I multiply the seed of David my *s* Jer 33:22 5650
the seed of Jacob, and David my *s* Jer 33:26 5650
name, and caused every man his *s* Jer 34:16 5650
the king of Babylon, my *s* Jer 43:10 5650
O my *s* Jacob, and be not dismayed, Jer 46:27 5650
Fear thou not, O Jacob my *s* Jer 46:28 5650
that I have given to my *s* Jacob Eze 28:25 5650
shall feed them, even my *s* David Eze 34:23 5650
my *s* David a prince among them Eze 34:24 5650
David my *s* shall be king over Eze 37:24 5650
that I have given unto Jacob my *s* Eze 37:25 5650
my *s* David shall be their prince Eze 37:25 5650
s of the living God, is thy God, Dan 6:20 5649
in the law of Moses the *s* of God Dan 9:11 5650
our God, hear the prayer of thy *s* Dan 9:17 5650
For how can the *s* of this my lord Dan 10:17 5650
I take thee, O Zerubbabel, my *s* Hag 2:23 5650
will bring forth my *s* the BRANCH Zec 3:8 5650
his father, and a *s* his master Mal 1:6 5650
Remember ye the law of Moses my *s* Mal 4:4 5650
my *s* lieth at home sick of the Mt 8:6 *3816*
only, and my *s* shall be healed Mt 8:8 *3816*
and to my *s*, Do this, and he doeth Mt 8:9 *1401*
his *s* was healed in the selfsame Mt 8:13 *3816*
master, nor the *s* above his lord Mt 10:24 *1401*
his master, and the *s* as his lord Mt 10:25 *1401*
Behold my *s*, whom I have chosen Mt 12:18 *3816*
The *s* therefore fell down, and Mt 18:26 *1401*
Then the lord of that *s* was moved Mt 18:27 *1401*
But the same *s* went out, and found Mt 18:28 *1401*
said unto him, O thou wicked *s* Mt 18:32 *1401*
among you, let him be your *s* Mt 20:27 *1401*
among you shall be your *s* Mt 23:11 *1249*
Who then is a faithful and wise *s* Mt 24:45 *1401*
Blessed is that *s*, whom his lord Mt 24:46 *1401*
if that evil *s* shall say in his Mt 24:48 *1401*
The lord of that *s* shall come in Mt 24:50 *1401*
done, thou good and faithful *s* Mt 25:21 *1401*
Well done, good and faithful *s* Mt 25:23 *1401*
him, Thou wicked and slothful *s* Mt 25:26 *1401*
s into outer darkness Mt 25:30 *1401*
struck a *s* of the high priest's, Mt 26:51 *1401*
shall be last of all, and *s* of all Mk 9:35 *1249*
the chiefest, shall be *s* of all Mk 10:44 *1401*
he sent to the husbandmen a *s* Mk 12:2 *1401*
again he sent unto them another *s* Mk 12:4 *1401*
smote a *s* of the high priest, and Mk 14:47 *1401*
He hath holpen his *s* Israel Lk 1:54 *3816*
us in the house of his *s* David Lk 1:69 *3816*
thou thy *s* depart in peace Lk 2:29 *1401*
And a certain centurion's *s* Lk 7:2 *1401*
that he would come and heal his *s* Lk 7:3 *1401*
a word, and my *s* shall be healed Lk 7:7 *3816*
and to my *s*, Do this, and he doeth Lk 7:8 *1401*
found the *s* whole that had been Lk 7:10 *1401*
Blessed is that *s*, whom his lord Lk 12:43 *1401*
if that *s* say in his heart, My Lk 12:45 *1401*
The lord of that *s* will come in a Lk 12:46 *1401*
And that *s*, which knew his lord's Lk 12:47 *1401*
sent his *s* at supper time to say Lk 14:17 *1401*
So that *s* came, and shewed his Lk 14:21 *1401*
house being angry said to his *s* Lk 14:21 *1401*
the *s* said, Lord, it is done as Lk 14:22 *1401*
And the lord said unto the *s* Lk 14:23 *1401*
No *s* can serve two masters Lk 16:13 *3610*
having a *s* plowing or feeding Lk 17:7 *1401*
Doth he thank that *s* because he Lk 17:9 *1401*
said unto him, Well, thou good *s* Lk 19:17 *1401*
will I judge thee, thou wicked *s* Lk 19:22 *1401*
he sent a *s* to the husbandmen Lk 20:10 *1401*
And again he sent another *s* Lk 20:11 *1401*
smote the *s* of the high priest Lk 22:50 *1401*
committeth sin is the *s* of sin Jn 8:34 *1401*
the *s* abideth not in the house Jn 8:35 *1401*
I am, there shall also my *s* be Jn 12:26 *1249*
The *s* is not greater than his Jn 13:16 *1401*
for the *s* knoweth not what his Jn 15:15 *1401*
The *s* is not greater than his Jn 15:20 *1401*
it, and smote the high priest's *s* Jn 18:10 *1401*
mouth of thy *s* David hast said Acts 4:25 *3816*
a *s* of Jesus Christ, called to be Rom 1:1 *1401*
thou that judgest another man's *s* Rom 14:4 *3610*
which is a *s* of the church which Rom 16:1 *1248*
sent by Phebe *s* of the church at Rom *s* *1248*
Art thou called being a *s* 1Cor 7:21 *1401*
is called in the Lord, being a *s* 1Cor 7:22 *1401*
called, being free, is Christ's *s* 1Cor 7:22 *1401*
yet have I made myself *s* unto all 1Cor 9:19 *1402*
I should not be the *s* of Christ Gal 1:10 *1401*
child, differeth nothing from a *s* Gal 4:1 *1401*
Wherefore thou art no more a *s* Gal 4:7 *1401*
and took upon him the form of a *s* Phil 2:7 *1401*
a *s* of Christ, saluteth you, Col 4:12 *1401*
the *s* of the Lord must not strive 2Ti 2:24 *1401*
a *s* of God, and an apostle of Titus 1:1 *1401*
Not now as a *s*, but above a Philem 16 *1401*
now as a *s*, but above a *s* Philem 16 *1401*
to Philemon, by Onesimus, a *s* Philem *s* *3610*
faithful in all his house, as a *s* Heb 3:5 *2324*
a *s* of God and of the Lord Jesus Jas 1:1 *1401*
Simon Peter, a *s* and an apostle of 2Pet 1:1 *1401*
the *s* of Jesus Christ, and brother Jude 1 *1401*
it by his angel unto his *s* John Rev 1:1 *1401*
the song of Moses the *s* of God Rev 15:3 *1401*

SERVANT'S {9}

in, I pray you, into your *s* house Gen 19:2 5650
thou hast spoken also of thy *s* 2Sa 7:19 5650
to thy son for David my *s* sake 1Kin 11:13 5650
of his life for David my *s* sake 1Kin 11:34 5650
Judah for David his *s* sake 2Kin 8:19 5650
thou hast also spoken of thy *s* 1Chr 17:17 5650
O LORD, for thy *s* sake, and 1Chr 17:19 5650
For Jacob my *s* sake, and Israel Is 45:4 5650
The *s* name was Malchus Jn 18:10 *1401*

SERVANTS {476}

a servant of *s* shall he be unto Gen 9:25 5650
captive, he armed his trained *s* Gen 14:14
himself against them, he and his *s* Gen 14:15 5650
the morning, and called all his *s* Gen 20:8 5650
which Abimelech's *s* had violently Gen 21:25 5650
of herds, and great store of *s* Gen 26:14 5657
s had digged in the days of Gen 26:15 5650
Isaac's *s* digged in the valley, Gen 26:19 5650
and there Isaac's *s* digged a well Gen 26:25 5650
the same day, that Isaac's *s* came Gen 26:32 5650
have I given to him for *s* Gen 27:37 5650
them into the hand of his *s* Gen 32:16 5650
and said unto his *s*, Pass over Gen 32:16 5650
he made a feast unto all his *s* Gen 40:20 5650
and of the chief baker among his *s* Gen 40:20 5650
Pharaoh was wroth with his *s* Gen 41:10 5650
and in the eyes of all his *s* Gen 41:37 5650
And Pharaoh said unto his *s* Gen 41:38 5650
but to buy food are thy *s* come Gen 42:10 5650
are true men, thy *s* are no spies Gen 42:11 5650
Thy *s* are twelve brethren, the Gen 42:13 5650
God forbid that thy *s* should do Gen 44:7 5650
whomsoever of thy *s* it be found Gen 44:9 5650
found out the iniquity of thy *s* Gen 44:16 5650
behold, we are my lord's *s* Gen 44:16 5650
My lord asked his *s*, saying, Have Gen 44:19 5650
And thou saidst unto thy *s* Gen 44:21 5650
And thou saidst unto thy *s* Gen 44:23 5650
thy *s* shall bring down the gray Gen 44:31 5650
it pleased Pharaoh well, and his *s* Gen 45:16 5650
Thy *s* are shepherds, both we, and Gen 47:3 5650
for thy *s* have no pasture for Gen 47:4 5650
let thy *s* dwell in the land of Gen 47:4 5650
our land will be *s* unto Pharaoh Gen 47:19 5650
lord, and we will be Pharaoh's *s* Gen 47:25 5650
Joseph commanded his *s* the Gen 50:2 5650
him went up all the *s* of Pharaoh Gen 50:7 5650
of the *s* of the God of thy father Gen 50:17 5650
and they said, Behold, we be thy *s* Gen 50:18 5650
dealest thou thus with thy *s* Ex 5:15 5650
is no straw given unto thy *s* Ex 5:16 5650
and, behold, thy *s* are beaten Ex 5:16 5650
Pharaoh, and in the eyes of his *s* Ex 5:21 5650
before Pharaoh, and before his *s* Ex 7:10 5650
Pharaoh, and in the sight of his *s* Ex 7:20 5650
bed, and into the house of thy *s* Ex 8:3 5650
thy people, and upon all thy *s* Ex 8:4 5650
I intreat for thee, and for thy *s* Ex 8:9 5650
and from thy houses, and from thy *s* Ex 8:11 5650
of flies upon thee, and upon thy *s* Ex 8:21 5650
depart from Pharaoh, from his *s* Ex 8:29 5650
of flies from Pharaoh, from his *s* Ex 8:31 5650
upon thine heart, and upon thy *s* Ex 9:14 5650
s of Pharaoh made his *s* Ex 9:20 5650
the word of the LORD left his *s* Ex 9:21 5650
But as for thee and thy *s*, I know Ex 9:30 5650
hardened his heart, he and his *s* Ex 9:34 5650
his heart, and the heart of his *s* Ex 10:1 5650
and the houses of all thy *s* Ex 10:6 5650
Pharaoh's *s* said unto him, How Ex 10:7 5650

in the sight of Pharaoh's *s*	Ex 11:3	5650
all these thy *s* shall come down	Ex 11:8	5650
up in the night, he, and all his *s*	Ex 12:30	5650
of his *s* was turned against the	Ex 14:5	5650
Abraham, Isaac, and Israel, thy *s*	Ex 32:13	5650
For they are my *s*, which I	Lev 25:42	5650
me the children of Israel are *s*	Lev 25:55	5650
they are my *s* whom I brought	Lev 25:55	5650
and said unto the *s* of Balak	Num 22:18	5650
ass, and his two *s* were with him	Num 22:22	5288
Thy *s* have taken the sum of the	Num 31:49	5650
for cattle, and thy *s* have cattle	Num 32:4	5650
given unto thy *s* for a possession	Num 32:5	5650
saying, Thy *s* will do as my lord	Num 32:25	5650
But thy *s* will pass over, every	Num 32:27	5650
As the LORD hath said unto thy *s*	Num 32:31	5650
Remember thy *s*, Abraham, Isaac,	Deut 9:27	5650
unto Pharaoh, and unto all his *s*	Deut 29:2	5650
and repent himself for his *s*	Deut 32:36	5650
he will avenge the blood of his *s*	Deut 32:43	5650
Egypt to Pharaoh, and to all his *s*	Deut 34:11	5650
said unto Joshua, We are thy *s*	Josh 9:8	5650
From a very far country thy *s* are	Josh 9:9	5650
and say unto them, We are your *s*	Josh 9:11	5650
it was certainly told thy *s*	Josh 9:24	5650
Slack not thy hand from thy *s*	Josh 10:6	5650
When he was gone out, his *s* came	Judg 3:24	5650
Then Gideon took ten men of his *s*	Judg 6:27	5650
the young man which is with thy *s*	Judg 19:19	5650
that ye be not *s* unto the Hebrews	1Sa 4:9	5647
of them, and give them to his *s*	1Sa 8:14	5650
give to his officers, and to his *s*	1Sa 8:15	5650
and ye shall be his *s*	1Sa 8:17	5650
Take now one of the *s* with thee	1Sa 9:3	5650
Pray for thy *s* unto the LORD thy	1Sa 12:19	5650
Saul's *s* said unto him, Behold	1Sa 16:15	5650
Let our lord now command thy *s*	1Sa 16:16	5650
And Saul said unto his *s*, Provide	1Sa 16:17	5650
Then answered one of the *s*	1Sa 16:18	5288
I a Philistine, and ye *s* to Saul	1Sa 17:8	5650
kill me, then will we be your *s*	1Sa 17:9	5650
kill him, then shall ye be our *s*	1Sa 17:9	5650
and also in the sight of Saul's *s*	1Sa 18:5	5650
And Saul commanded his *s*, saying,	1Sa 18:22	5650
in thee, and all his *s* love thee	1Sa 18:22	5650
Saul's *s* spake those words in the	1Sa 18:23	5650
the *s* of Saul told him, saying,	1Sa 18:24	5650
when his *s* told David these words	1Sa 18:26	5650
wisely than all the *s* of Saul	1Sa 18:30	5650
Jonathan his son, and to all his *s*	1Sa 19:1	5650
and I have appointed my *s* to such	1Sa 21:2	5288
Now a certain man of the *s* of	1Sa 21:7	5650
the *s* of Achish said unto him, Is	1Sa 21:11	5650
Then said Achish unto his *s*	1Sa 21:14	5650
all his *s* were standing about him	1Sa 22:6	5650
unto his *s* that stood about him	1Sa 22:7	5650
which was set over the *s* of Saul	1Sa 22:9	5650
faithful among all thy *s* as David	1Sa 22:14	5650
But the *s* of the king would not	1Sa 22:17	5650
stayed his *s* with these words	1Sa 24:7	582
cometh to thine hand unto thy *s*	1Sa 25:8	5650
And Nabal answered David's *s*	1Sa 25:10	5650
there be many *s* now a days that	1Sa 25:10	5650
And she said unto her *s*, Go on	1Sa 25:19	5288
when the *s* of David were come to	1Sa 25:40	5650
wash the feet of the *s* of my lord	1Sa 25:41	5650
Then said Saul unto his *s*	1Sa 28:7	5650
his *s* said to him, Behold, there	1Sa 28:7	5650
But his *s*, together with the	1Sa 28:23	5650
it before Saul, and before his *s*	1Sa 28:25	5650
s that are come with thee	1Sa 29:10	5650
the *s* of Ish-bosheth the son of	2Sa 2:12	5650
the *s* of David, went out, and met	2Sa 2:13	5650
Saul, and twelve of the *s* of David	2Sa 2:15	5650
of Israel, before the *s* of David	2Sa 2:17	5650
lacked of David's *s* nineteen men	2Sa 2:30	5650
But the *s* of David had smitten of	2Sa 2:31	5650
the *s* of David and Joab came from	2Sa 3:22	5650
And the king said unto his *s*	2Sa 3:38	5650
eyes of the handmaids of his *s*	2Sa 6:20	5650
so the Moabites became David's *s*	2Sa 8:2	5650
and the Syrians became *s* to David	2Sa 8:6	5650
that were on the *s* of Hadadezer	2Sa 8:7	5650
all they of Edom became David's *s*	2Sa 8:14	5650
therefore, and thy sons, and thy *s*	2Sa 9:10	5650
Ziba had fifteen sons and twenty *s*	2Sa 9:10	5650
of Ziba were *s* unto Mephibosheth	2Sa 9:12	5650
the hand of his *s* for his father	2Sa 10:2	5650
David's *s* came into the land of	2Sa 10:2	5650
David rather sent his *s* unto thee	2Sa 10:3	5650
Wherefore Hanun took David's *s*	2Sa 10:4	5650
when all the kings that were *s* to	2Sa 10:19	5650
his *s* with him, and all Israel	2Sa 11:1	5650
house with all the *s* of his lord	2Sa 11:9	5650
the *s* of my lord, are encamped in	2Sa 11:11	5650
on his bed with the *s* of his lord	2Sa 11:13	5650
of the people of the *s* of David	2Sa 11:17	5650
shot from off the wall upon thy *s*	2Sa 11:24	5650
and some of the king's *s* be dead	2Sa 11:24	5650
the *s* of David feared to tell him	2Sa 12:18	5650
David saw that his *s* whispered	2Sa 12:19	5650
therefore David said unto his *s*	2Sa 12:19	5650
Then said his *s* unto him, What	2Sa 12:21	5650
his *s* go with thy servant	2Sa 13:24	5650
Now Absalom had commanded his *s*	2Sa 13:28	5288
the *s* of Absalom did unto Amnon	2Sa 13:29	5288
all his *s* stood by with their	2Sa 13:31	5650
also and all his *s* wept very sore	2Sa 13:36	5650
Therefore he said unto his *s*	2Sa 14:30	5650
Absalom's *s* set the field on fire	2Sa 14:30	5650
Wherefore have thy *s* set my field	2Sa 14:31	5650
David said unto all his *s* that	2Sa 15:14	5650
the king's *s* said unto the king,	2Sa 15:15	5650
thy *s* are ready to do whatsoever	2Sa 15:15	5650
all his *s* passed on beside him	2Sa 15:18	5650
at all the *s* of king David	2Sa 16:6	5650
said to Abishai, and to all his *s*	2Sa 16:11	5650
when Absalom's *s* came to the	2Sa 17:20	5650
were slain before the *s* of David	2Sa 18:7	5650
And Absalom met the *s* of David	2Sa 18:9	5650
this day the faces of all thy *s*	2Sa 19:5	5650
regardest neither princes nor *s*	2Sa 19:6	5650
and speak comfortably unto thy *s*	2Sa 19:7	5650
king, Return thou, and all thy *s*	2Sa 19:14	5650
sons and his twenty *s* with him	2Sa 19:17	5650
take thou thy lord's *s*, and pursue	2Sa 20:6	5650
his *s* with him, and fought against	2Sa 21:15	5650
of David, and by the hand of his *s*	2Sa 21:22	5650
his *s* coming on toward him	2Sa 24:20	5650
Wherefore his *s* said unto him	1Kin 1:2	5650
all the men of Judah the king's *s*	1Kin 1:9	5650
Take with you the *s* of your lord	1Kin 1:33	5650
moreover the king's *s* came to	1Kin 1:47	5650
that two of the *s* of Shimei ran	1Kin 2:39	5650
saying, Behold, thy *s* be in Gath	1Kin 2:39	5650
to Gath to Achish to seek his *s*	1Kin 2:40	5650
went, and brought his *s* from Gath	1Kin 2:40	5650
and made a feast to all his *s*	1Kin 3:15	5650
of Tyre sent his *s* unto Solomon	1Kin 5:1	5650
my *s* shall be with thy *s*	1Kin 5:6	5650
thy *s* according to all that thou	1Kin 5:6	5650
My *s* shall bring them down from	1Kin 5:9	5650
mercy with thy *s* that walk before	1Kin 8:23	5650
in heaven, and do, and judge thy *s*	1Kin 8:32	5650
and forgive the sin of thy *s*	1Kin 8:36	5650
they were men of war, and his *s*	1Kin 9:22	5650
And Hiram sent in the navy his *s*	1Kin 9:27	5650
of the sea, with the *s* of Solomon	1Kin 9:27	5650
table, and the sitting of his *s*	1Kin 10:5	5650
thy men, happy are these thy *s*	1Kin 10:8	5650
to her own country, she and her *s*	1Kin 10:13	5650
of his father's *s* with him	1Kin 11:17	5650
then they will be thy *s* for ever	1Kin 12:7	5650
them into the hand of his *s*	1Kin 15:18	5650
Yet I will send my *s* unto thee to	1Kin 20:6	5650
house, and the houses of thy *s*	1Kin 20:6	5650
that he said unto his *s*, Set	1Kin 20:12	5650
the *s* of the king of Syria said	1Kin 20:23	5650
his *s* said unto him, Behold now,	1Kin 20:31	5650
king of Israel said unto his *s*	1Kin 22:3	5650
Let my *s* go with thy *s* in	1Kin 22:49	5650
and the life of these fifty thy *s*	2Kin 1:13	5650
be with thy *s* fifty strong men	2Kin 2:16	5650
the king of Israel's *s* answered	2Kin 3:11	5650
his *s* came near, and spake unto	2Kin 5:13	5650
and laid them upon two of his *s*	2Kin 5:23	5288
I pray thee, and go with thy *s*	2Kin 6:3	5650
and took counsel with his *s*	2Kin 6:8	5650
and he called his *s*, and said unto	2Kin 6:11	5650
And one of his *s* said, None, my	2Kin 6:12	5650
in the night, and said unto his *s*	2Kin 7:12	5650
And one of his *s* answered and said,	2Kin 7:13	5650
the blood of my *s* the prophets	2Kin 9:7	5650
blood of all the *s* of the LORD	2Kin 9:7	5650
came forth to the *s* of his lord	2Kin 9:11	5650
his *s* carried him in a chariot to	2Kin 9:28	5650
to Jehu, saying, We are thy *s*	2Kin 10:5	5650
the prophets of Baal, all his *s*	2Kin 10:19	5647
you none of the *s* of the LORD	2Kin 10:23	5650
his *s* arose, and made a conspiracy	2Kin 12:20	5650
the son of Shomer, his *s*, smote	2Kin 12:21	5650
that he slew his *s* which had	2Kin 14:5	5650
sent to you by my *s* the prophets	2Kin 17:13	5650
said by all his *s* the prophets	2Kin 17:23	5650
of the least of my master's *s*	2Kin 18:24	5650
to thy *s* in the Syrian language	2Kin 18:26	5650
So the *s* of king Hezekiah came to	2Kin 19:5	5650
with which the *s* of the king of	2Kin 19:6	5288
LORD spake by his *s* the prophets	2Kin 21:10	5650
the *s* of Amon conspired against	2Kin 21:23	5650
Thy *s* have gathered the money	2Kin 22:9	5650
his *s* carried him in a chariot	2Kin 23:30	5650
he spake by his *s* the prophets	2Kin 24:2	5650
At that time the *s* of	2Kin 24:10	5650
the city, and his *s* did besiege it	2Kin 24:11	5650
he, and his mother, and his *s*	2Kin 24:12	5650
not to be the *s* of the Chaldees	2Kin 25:24	5650
and the Moabites became David's *s*	1Chr 18:2	5650
and the Syrians became David's *s*	1Chr 18:6	5650
that were on the *s* of Hadarezer	1Chr 18:7	5650
all the Edomites became David's *s*	1Chr 18:13	5650
So the *s* of David came into the	1Chr 19:2	5650
are not his *s* come unto thee for	1Chr 19:3	5650
Wherefore Hanun took David's *s*	1Chr 19:4	5650
when the *s* of Hadarezer saw that	1Chr 19:19	5650
peace with David, and became his *s*	1Chr 19:19	5647
of David, and by the hand of his *s*	1Chr 20:8	5650
are they not all my lord's *s*	1Chr 21:3	5650
for I know that thy *s* can skill	2Chr 2:8	5650
my *s* shall be with thy *s*,	2Chr 2:8	5650
And, behold, I will give to thy *s*	2Chr 2:10	5650
of, let him send unto his *s*	2Chr 2:15	5650
and shewest mercy unto thy *s*	2Chr 6:14	5650
heaven, and do, and judge thy *s*	2Chr 6:23	5650
and forgive the sin of thy *s*	2Chr 6:27	5650
Solomon make no *s* for his work	2Chr 8:9	5650
him by the hands of his *s* ships	2Chr 8:18	5650
s that had knowledge of the sea	2Chr 8:18	5650
they went with the *s* of Solomon	2Chr 8:18	5650
table, and the sitting of his *s*	2Chr 9:4	5650
thy men, and happy are these thy *s*	2Chr 9:7	5650
the *s* also of Huram, and the	2Chr 9:10	5650
the *s* of Solomon, which brought	2Chr 9:10	5650
to her own land, she and her *s*	2Chr 9:12	5650
to Tarshish with the *s* of Huram	2Chr 9:21	5650
them, they will be thy *s* for ever	2Chr 10:7	5650
Nevertheless they shall be his *s*	2Chr 12:8	5650
his own *s* conspired against him	2Chr 24:25	5650
that he slew his *s* that had	2Chr 25:3	5650
Assyria send his *s* to Jerusalem	2Chr 32:9	5650
his *s* spake yet more against the	2Chr 32:16	5650
his *s* conspired against him, and	2Chr 33:24	5650
All that was committed to thy *s*	2Chr 34:16	5650
and the king said to his *s*	2Chr 35:23	5650
His *s* therefore took him out of	2Chr 35:24	5650
where they were *s* to him and his	2Chr 36:20	5650
The children of Solomon's *s*	Ezr 2:55	5650
and the children of Solomon's *s*	Ezr 2:58	5650
Beside their *s* and their maids, of	Ezr 2:65	5650
Thy *s* the men on this side the	Ezr 4:11	5649
We are the *s* of the God of heaven	Ezr 5:11	5649
commanded by thy *s* the prophets	Ezr 9:11	5650
for the children of Israel thy *s*	Neh 1:6	5650
Now these are thy *s* and thy people	Neh 1:10	5650
and to the prayer of thy *s*	Neh 1:11	5650
therefore we his *s* will arise	Neh 2:20	5650
half of my *s* wrought in the work	Neh 4:16	5288
I, nor my brethren, nor my *s*	Neh 4:23	5288
our sons and our daughters to be *s*	Neh 5:5	5650
likewise, and my brethren, and my *s*	Neh 5:10	5288
even their *s* bare rule over the	Neh 5:15	5288
all my *s* were gathered thither	Neh 5:16	5288
The children of Solomon's *s*	Neh 7:57	5650
and the children of Solomon's *s*	Neh 7:60	5650
upon Pharaoh, and on all his *s*	Neh 9:10	5650
we are *s* this day, and for the	Neh 9:36	5650
thereof, behold, we are *s* in it	Neh 9:36	5650
and the children of Solomon's *s*	Neh 11:3	5650
some of my *s* set I at the gates,	Neh 13:19	5288
unto all his princes and his *s*	Est 1:3	5650
Then said the king's *s* that	Est 2:2	5288
unto all his princes and his *s*	Est 2:18	5650
And all the king's *s*, that were in	Est 3:2	5650
Then the king's *s*, which were in	Est 3:3	5650
All the king's *s*, and the people	Est 4:11	5650
the princes and *s* of the king	Est 5:11	5650
Then said the king's *s* that	Est 6:3	5288
the king's *s* said unto him,	Est 6:5	5288
they have slain the *s* with the	Job 1:15	5288
burned up the sheep, and the *s*	Job 1:16	5288
slain the *s* with the edge of the	Job 1:17	5288
Behold, he put no trust in his *s*	Job 4:18	5650
LORD redeemeth the soul of his *s*	Ps 34:22	5650
also of his *s* shall inherit it	Ps 69:36	5650
The dead bodies of thy *s* have	Ps 79:2	5650
the blood of thy *s* which is shed	Ps 79:10	5650
Lord, the reproach of thy *s*	Ps 89:50	5650
it repent thee concerning thy *s*	Ps 90:13	5650
Let thy work appear unto thy *s*	Ps 90:16	5650
For thy *s* take pleasure in her	Ps 102:14	5650
children of thy *s* shall continue	Ps 102:28	5650
to deal subtilly with his *s*	Ps 105:25	5650
O ye *s* of the LORD, praise the	Ps 113:1	5650
for all are thy *s*	Ps 119:91	5650
as the eyes of *s* look unto the	Ps 123:2	5650
all ye *s* of the LORD, which by	Ps 134:1	5650
praise him, O ye *s* of the LORD	Ps 135:1	5650
upon Pharaoh, and upon all his *s*	Ps 135:9	5650
repent himself concerning his *s*	Ps 135:14	5650
to lies, all his *s* are wicked	Prov 29:12	8334
I got me *s* and maidens, and had	Eccl 2:7	5650
and had *s* born in my house	Eccl 2:7	
I have seen *s* upon horses	Eccl 10:7	5650
walking as *s* upon the earth	Eccl 10:7	5650
in the land of the LORD for *s*	Is 14:2	5650
of the least of my master's *s*	Is 36:9	5650
unto thy *s* in the Syrian language	Is 36:11	5650
So the *s* of king Hezekiah came to	Is 37:5	5650
wherewith the *s* of the king of	Is 37:6	5288
By thy *s* hast thou reproached the	Is 37:24	5650
the heritage of the *s* of the LORD	Is 54:17	5650
the name of the LORD, to be his *s*	Is 56:6	5650
it, and my *s* shall dwell there	Is 65:9	5650
my *s* shall eat, but ye shall be	Is 65:13	5650
my *s* shall drink, but ye shall be	Is 65:13	5650
my *s* shall rejoice, but ye shall	Is 65:13	5650
my *s* shall sing for joy of heart,	Is 65:14	5650
call his *s* by another name	Is 65:15	5650
LORD shall be known toward his *s*	Is 66:14	5650
unto you all my *s* the prophets	Jer 7:25	5650
Zedekiah king of Judah, and his *s*	Jer 21:7	5650
throne of David, thou, and thy *s*	Jer 22:2	5650
and on horses, he, and his *s*	Jer 22:4	5650
unto you all his *s* the prophets	Jer 25:4	5650
Pharaoh king of Egypt, and his *s*	Jer 25:19	5650
to the words of my *s* the prophets	Jer 26:5	5650
unto them by my *s* the prophets	Jer 29:19	5650
they turned, and caused the *s*	Jer 34:11	5650
them into subjection for *s*	Jer 34:11	5650
subjection, to be unto you for *s*	Jer 34:16	5650
unto you all my *s* the prophets	Jer 35:15	5650
nor any of his *s* that heard all	Jer 36:24	5650
seed and his *s* for their iniquity	Jer 36:31	5650
But neither he, nor his *s*	Jer 37:2	5650

against thee, or against thy *s* Jer 37:18 5650
unto you all my *s* the prophets Jer 44:4 5650
and into the hand of his *s* Jer 46:26 5650
S have ruled over us Lam 5:8 5650
by my *s* the prophets of Israel Eze 38:17 5650
his inheritance to one of his *s* Eze 46:17 5650
Prove thy *s*, I beseech thee, ten Dan 1:12 5650
and as thou seest, deal with thy *s* Dan 1:13 5650
tell thy *s* the dream, and we will Dan 2:4 5649
Let the king tell his *s* the dream Dan 2:7 5649
ye *s* of the most high God, come Dan 3:26 5649
delivered his *s* that trusted in Dan 3:28 5649
hearkened unto thy *s* the prophets Dan 9:6 5650
before us by his *s* the prophets Dan 9:10 5650
And also upon the *s* and upon the Joel 2:29 5650
secret unto his *s* the prophets Amos 3:7 5650
thee out of the house of *s* Mic 6:4 5650
I commanded my *s* the prophets Zec 1:6 5650
they shall be a spoil to their *s* Zec 2:9 5647
So the *s* of the householder came Mt 13:27 *1401*
The *s* said unto him, Wilt thou Mt 13:28 *1401*
And said unto his *s*, This is John Mt 14:2 *1401*
which would take account of his *s* Mt 18:23 *1401*
he sent his *s* to the husbandmen, Mt 21:34 *1401*
And the husbandmen took his *s* Mt 21:35 *1401*
he sent other *s* more than the Mt 21:36 *1401*
sent forth his *s* to call them Mt 22:3 *1401*
Again, he sent forth other *s* Mt 22:4 *1401*
And the remnant took his *s* Mt 22:6 *1401*
Then saith he to his *s*, The Mt 22:8 *1401*
So those *s* went out into the Mt 22:10 *1401*
Then said the king to the *s* Mt 22:13 *1401*
far country, who called his own *s* Mt 25:14 *1401*
time the lord of those *s* cometh Mt 25:19 *1401*
and went in, and sat with the *s* Mt 26:58 *5257*
in the ship with the hired *s* Mk 1:20 *341*
house, and gave authority to his *s* Mk 13:34 *1401*
and he sat with the *s*, and warmed Mk 14:54 *5257*
the *s* did strike him with the Mk 14:65 *5257*
Blessed are those *s*, whom the Lk 12:37 *1401*
find them so, blessed are those *s* Lk 12:38 *1401*
How many hired *s* of my father's Lk 15:17 *3407*
make me as one of thy hired *s* Lk 15:19 *3407*
But the father said to his *s* Lk 15:22 *1401*
And he called one of the *s* Lk 15:26 *3816*
you, say, We are unprofitable *s* Lk 17:10 *1401*
And he called his ten *s*, and Lk 19:13 *1401*
these *s* to be called unto him Lk 19:15 *1401*
His mother saith unto the *s* Jn 2:5 *1249*
(but the *s* which drew the water Jn 2:9 *1249*
his *s* met him, and told him, Jn 4:51 *1401*
Henceforth I call you not *s* Jn 15:15 *1401*
And the *s* and officers stood there, Jn 18:18 *1401*
One of the *s* of the high priest Jn 18:26 *1401*
this world, then would my *s* fight Jn 18:36 *5257*
And on my *s* and on my handmaidens Acts 2:18 *1401*
and grant unto thy *s*, that with Acts 4:29 *1401*
he called two of his household *s* Acts 10:7
These men are the *s* of the most Acts 16:17 *1401*
ye yield yourselves *s* to obey Rom 6:16 *1401*
his *s* ye are to whom ye obey Rom 6:16 *1401*
that ye were the *s* of sin Rom 6:17 *1401*
ye became the *s* of righteousness Rom 6:18 *1402*
your members *s* to uncleanness Rom 6:19 *1401*
s to righteousness unto holiness Rom 6:19 *1401*
For when ye were the *s* of sin Rom 6:20 *1401*
free from sin, and become *s* to God Rom 6:22 *1402*
be not ye the *s* of men 1Cor 7:23 *1401*
ourselves your *s* for Jesus' sake 2Cor 4:5 *1401*
S, be obedient to them that are Eph 6:5 *1401*
but as the *s* of Christ, doing the Eph 6:6 *1401*
the *s* of Jesus Christ, to all the Phil 1:1 *1401*
S, obey in all things your Col 3:22 *1401*
give unto your *s* that which is Col 4:1 *1401*
Let as many *s* as are under the 1Ti 6:1 *1401*
Exhort *s* to be obedient unto Titus 2:9 *1401*
but as the *s* of God 1Pet 2:16 *1401*
S, be subject to your masters 1Pet 2:18 *3610*
are the *s* of corruption 2Pet 2:19 *1401*
to shew unto his *s* things which Rev 1:1 *1401*
teach and to seduce my *s* to commit Rev 2:20 *1401*
till we have sealed the *s* of our Rev 7:3 *1401*
declared to his *s* the prophets Rev 10:7 *1401*
reward unto thy *s* the prophets Rev 11:18 *1401*
the blood of his *s* at her hand Rev 19:2 *1401*
Praise our God, all ye his *s* Rev 19:5 *1401*
and his *s* shall serve him Rev 22:3 *1401*
s the things which must shortly Rev 22:6 *1401*

SERVANTS' {4}

Thy *s* trade hath been about Gen 46:34 5650
of Pharaoh, and into his *s* houses Ex 8:24 5650
Return for thy *s* sake, the tribes Is 63:17 5650
so will I do for my *s* sakes Is 65:8 5650

SERVE {209}

is not theirs, and shall *s* them Gen 15:13 5647
that nation, whom they shall *s* Gen 15:14 5647
and the elder shall *s* the younger Gen 25:23 5647
Let people *s* thee, and nations bow Gen 27:29 5647
thou live, and shalt *s* thy brother Gen 27:40 5647
thou therefore *s* me for nought Gen 29:15 5647
I will *s* thee seven years for Gen 29:18 5647
did not I *s* with thee for Rachel Gen 29:25 5647
the service which thou shalt *s* Gen 29:27 5647
of Israel to *s* with rigour Ex 1:13 5647
service, wherein they made them *s* Ex 1:14 5647
ye shall *s* God upon this mountain Ex 3:12 5647
Let my son go, that he may *s* me Ex 4:23 5647
that they may *s* me in the Ex 7:16 5647
my people go, that they may *s* me Ex 8:1 5647
my people go, that they may *s* me Ex 8:20 5647
my people go, that they may *s* me Ex 9:1 5647
my people go, that they may *s* me Ex 9:13 5647
my people go, that they may *s* me Ex 10:3 5647
that they may *s* the LORD their Ex 10:7 5647
them, Go, *s* the LORD your God Ex 10:8 5647
ye that are men, and *s* the LORD Ex 10:11 5647
Moses, and said, Go ye, *s* the LORD Ex 10:24 5647
we take to *s* the LORD our God Ex 10:26 5647
not with what we must *s* the LORD Ex 10:26 5647
s the LORD, as ye have said Ex 12:31 5647
that we may *s* the Egyptians Ex 14:12 5647
better for us to *s* the Egyptians Ex 14:12 5647
down thyself to them, nor *s* them Ex 20:5 5647
servant, six years he shall *s* Ex 21:2 5647
and he shall *s* him for ever Ex 21:6 5647
nor *s* them, nor do after their Ex 23:24 5647
ye shall *s* the LORD your God, and Ex 23:25 5647
for if thou *s* their gods, it will Ex 23:33 5647
compel him to *s* as a bondservant Lev 25:39 5656
shall *s* thee unto the year of Lev 25:40 5647
families of the Gershonites, to *s* Num 4:24 5647
so shall they *s* Num 4:26 5647
thereof, and shall *s* no more Num 8:25 5647
and ye shall *s* Num 18:7 5647
for their service which they *s* Num 18:21 5647
s them, which the LORD thy God Deut 4:19 5647
And there ye shall *s* gods, the Deut 4:28 5647
thyself unto them, nor *s* them Deut 5:9 5647
s him, and shalt swear by his name Deut 6:13 5647
me, that they may *s* other gods Deut 7:4 5647
neither shalt thou *s* their gods Deut 7:16 5647
s them, and worship them, I Deut 8:19 5647
to *s* the LORD thy God with all Deut 10:12 5647
him shalt thou *s*, and to him shalt Deut 10:20 5647
to *s* him with all your heart and Deut 11:13 5647
s other gods, and worship them Deut 11:16 5647
did these nations *s* their gods Deut 12:30 5647
hast not known, and let us *s* them Deut 13:2 5647
obey his voice, and ye shall *s* him Deut 13:4 5647
s other gods, which thou hast not Deut 13:6 5647
s other gods, which ye have not Deut 13:13 5647
unto thee, and *s* thee six years Deut 15:12 5647
unto thee, and they shall *s* thee Deut 20:11 5647
to go after other gods to *s* them Deut 28:14 5647
and there shalt thou *s* other gods Deut 28:36 5647
Therefore shalt thou *s* thine Deut 28:48 5647
and there thou shalt *s* other gods Deut 28:64 5647
s the gods of these nations Deut 29:18 5647
and worship other gods, and *s* them Deut 30:17 5647
s them, and provoke me, and break Deut 31:20 5647
unto this day, and *s* under tribute Josh 16:10 5647
to *s* him with all your heart and Josh 22:5 5647
to swear by them, neither *s* them Josh 23:7 5647
s him in sincerity and in truth Josh 24:14 5647
and *s* ye the LORD Josh 24:14 5647
seem evil unto you to *s* the LORD Josh 24:15 5647
you this day whom ye will *s* Josh 24:15 5647
and my house, we will *s* the LORD Josh 24:15 5647
forsake the LORD, to *s* other gods Josh 24:16 5647
therefore will we also *s* the LORD Josh 24:18 5647
the people, Ye cannot *s* the LORD Josh 24:19 5647
s strange gods, then he will turn Josh 24:20 5647
but we will *s* the LORD Josh 24:21 5647
chosen you the LORD, to *s* him Josh 24:22 5647
The LORD our God will we *s* Josh 24:24 5647
in following other gods to *s* them Judg 2:19 5647
is Shechem, that we should *s* him Judg 9:28 5647
s the men of Hamor the father of Judg 9:28 5647
for why should we *s* him Judg 9:28 5647
Abimelech, that we should *s* him Judg 9:38 5647
unto the LORD, and *s* him only 1Sa 7:3 5647
that thou do as occasion *s* thee 1Sa 10:7 5647
with us, and we will *s* thee 1Sa 11:1 5647
of our enemies, and we will *s* thee 1Sa 12:10 5647
s him, and obey his voice, and not 1Sa 12:14 5647
but *s* the LORD with all your 1Sa 12:20 5647
s him in truth with all your 1Sa 12:24 5647
shall ye be our servants, and *s* us 1Sa 17:9 5647
LORD, saying, Go, *s* other gods 1Sa 26:19 5647
Jerusalem, then I will *s* the LORD 2Sa 15:8 5647
And again, whom should I *s* 2Sa 16:19 5647
should I not *s* in the presence of 2Sa 16:19 5647
which I knew not shall *s* me 2Sa 22:44 5647
s other gods, and worship them 1Kin 9:6 5647
us, lighter, and we will *s* thee 1Kin 12:4 5647
people this day, and wilt *s* them 1Kin 12:7 5647
but Jehu shall *s* him much 2Kin 10:18 5647
nor *s* them, nor sacrifice to them 2Kin 17:35 5647
land, and *s* the king of Babylon 2Kin 25:24 5647
s him with a perfect heart and 1Chr 28:9 5647
s other gods, and worship them 2Chr 7:19 5647
he put upon us, and we will *s* thee 2Chr 10:4 5647
to *s* him, and that ye should 2Chr 29:11 8334
s the LORD your God, that the 2Chr 30:8 5647
commanded Judah to *s* the LORD God 2Chr 33:16 5647
that were present in Israel to *s* 2Chr 34:33 5647
even to *s* the LORD their God 2Chr 34:33 5647
s now the LORD your God, and his 2Chr 35:3 5647
Almighty, that we should *s* him Job 21:15 5647
s him, they shall spend their Job 36:11 5647
the unicorn be willing to *s* thee Job 39:9 5647
S the LORD with fear, and rejoice Ps 2:11 5647
whom I have not known shall *s* me Ps 18:43 5647
A seed shall *s* him Ps 22:30 5647
all nations shall *s* him Ps 72:11 5647
be all they that *s* graven images Ps 97:7 5647
S the LORD with gladness Ps 100:2 5647
in a perfect way, he shall *s* me Ps 101:6 8334
and the kingdoms, to *s* the LORD Ps 102:22 5647
wherein thou wast made to *s* Is 14:3 5647
shall *s* with the Assyrians Is 19:23 5647
caused thee to *s* with an offering Is 43:23 5647
hast made me to *s* with thy sins Is 43:24 5647
to *s* him, and to love the name of Is 56:6 8334
that will not *s* thee shall perish Is 60:12 5647
so shall ye *s* strangers in a land Jer 5:19 5647
went after other gods to *s* them Jer 11:10 5647
to *s* them, and to worship them, Jer 13:10 5647
there shall ye *s* other gods day Jer 16:13 5647
I will cause thee to *s* thine Jer 17:4 5647
go not after other gods to *s* them Jer 25:6 5647
these nations shall *s* the king of Jer 25:11 5647
great kings shall *s* themselves of Jer 25:14 5647
field have I given also to *s* him Jer 27:6 5647
And all nations shall *s* him Jer 27:7 5647
kings shall *s* themselves of him Jer 27:7 5647
kingdom which will not *s* the same Jer 27:8 5647
Ye shall not *s* the king of Jer 27:9 5647
s him, those will I let remain Jer 27:11 5647
s him and his people, and live Jer 27:12 5647
will not *s* the king of Babylon Jer 27:13 5647
Ye shall not *s* the king of Jer 27:14 5647
s the king of Babylon, and live Jer 27:17 5647
that they may *s* Nebuchadnezzar Jer 28:14 5647
and they shall *s* him Jer 28:14 5647
shall no more *s* themselves of him Jer 30:8 5647
But they shall *s* the LORD their Jer 30:9 5647
none should *s* himself of them Jer 34:9 5647
that none should *s* themselves of Jer 34:10 5647
go not after other gods to *s* them Jer 35:15 5647
Fear not to *s* the Chaldeans Jer 40:9 5647
s the king of Babylon, and it Jer 40:9 5647
at Mizpah to *s* the Chaldeans Jer 40:10 5975,6440
to *s* other gods, whom they knew Jer 44:3 5647
the countries, to *s* wood and stone Eze 20:32 8334
s ye every one his idols, and Eze 20:39 5647
all of them in the land, *s* me Eze 20:40 5647
s a great service against Tyrus Eze 29:18 5647
food unto them that *s* the city Eze 48:18 5647
they that *s* the city shall *s* Eze 48:19 5647
they *s* not thy gods, nor worship Dan 3:12 6399
and Abed-nego, do not ye *s* my gods Dan 3:14 6399
our God whom we *s* is able to Dan 3:17 6399
king, that we will not *s* thy gods Dan 3:18 6399
might not *s* nor worship any god Dan 3:28 6399
and languages, should *s* him Dan 7:14 6399
kingdom, and all dominions shall *s* Dan 7:27 6399
to *s* him with one consent Zeph 3:9 5647
Ye have said, It is vain to *s* God Mal 3:14 5647
thy God, and him only shalt thou *s* Mt 4:10 *3000*
No man can *s* two masters Mt 6:24 *1398*
Ye cannot *s* God and mammon Mt 6:24 *1398*
enemies might *s* him without fear Lk 1:74 *3000*
thy God, and him only shalt thou *s* Lk 4:8 *3000*
my sister hath left me to *s* alone Lk 10:40 *1247*
and will come forth and *s* them Lk 12:37 *1247*
Lo, these many years do I *s* thee Lk 15:29 *1398*
No servant can *s* two masters Lk 16:13 *1398*
Ye cannot *s* God and mammon Lk 16:13 *1398*
s me, till I have eaten and Lk 17:8 *1247*
that is chief, as he that doth *s* Lk 22:26 *1247*
If any man *s* me, let him follow Jn 12:26 *1247*
if any man *s* me, him will my Jn 12:26 *1247*
the word of God, and *s* tables Acts 6:2 *1247*
come forth, and *s* me in this place Acts 7:7 *3000*
of God, whose I am, and whom I *s* Acts 27:23 *3000*
whom I *s* with my spirit in the Rom 1:9 *3000*
henceforth we should not *s* sin Rom 6:6 *1398*
that we should *s* in newness of Rom 7:6 *1398*
mind I myself *s* the law of God Rom 7:25 *1398*
The elder shall *s* the younger Rom 9:12 *1398*
For they that are such *s* not our Rom 16:18 *1398*
flesh, but by love *s* one another Gal 5:13 *1398*
for ye *s* the Lord Christ Col 3:24 *1398*
to God from idols to *s* the living 1Th 1:9 *1398*
whom I *s* from my forefathers with 2Ti 1:3 *3000*
Who *s* unto the example and shadow Heb 8:5 *3000*
dead works to *s* the living God Heb 9:14 *3000*
whereby we may *s* God acceptably Heb 12:28 *3000*
to eat which *s* the tabernacle Heb 13:10 *3000*
s him day and night in his temple Rev 7:15 *3000*
and his servants shall *s* him Rev 22:3 *3000*

SERVED {74}

Twelve years they *s* Chedorlaomer Gen 14:4 5647
Jacob *s* seven years for Rachel Gen 29:20 5647
s with him yet seven other years Gen 29:30 5647
children, for whom I have *s* thee Gen 30:26 5647
Thou knowest how I have *s* thee Gen 30:29 5647
all my power I have *s* your father Gen 31:6 5647
I *s* thee fourteen years for thy Gen 31:41 5647
grace in his sight, and he *s* him Gen 39:4 8334
Joseph with them, and he *s* them Gen 40:4 8334
ye shall possess *s* their gods Deut 12:2 5647
s other gods, and worshipped them, Deut 17:3 5647
s other gods, and worshipped them, Deut 29:26 5647
s other gods, and bowed yourselves Josh 23:16 5647
and they *s* other gods Josh 24:2 5647
the gods which your fathers *s* on Josh 24:14 5647
the gods which your fathers *s* Josh 24:15 5647
Israel *s* the LORD all the days of Josh 24:31 5647
the people *s* the LORD all the Judg 2:7 5647
sight of the LORD, and *s* Baalim Judg 2:11 5647

the LORD, and *s* Baal and Ashtaroth...... Judg 2:13 5647
to their sons, and *s* their gods .... Judg 3:6 5647
God, and *s* Baalim and the groves........ Judg 3:7 5647
and the children of Israel *s* .... Judg 3:8 5647
So the children of Israel *s* Eglon........ Judg 3:14 5647
unto him, Why hast thou *s* us thus........ Judg 8:1 6213
s Baalim, and Ashtaroth, and the .... Judg 10:6 5647
and forsook the LORD, and *s* not him..... Judg 10:6 5647
our God, and also *s* Baalim .... Judg 10:10 5647
have forsaken me, and *s* other gods ...... Judg 10:13 5647
from among them, and *s* the LORD.......... Judg 10:16 5647
and Ashtaroth, and *s* the LORD only 1Sa 7:4 5647
s other gods, so do they also............. 1Sa 8:8 5647
have *s* Baalim and Ashtaroth 1Sa 12:10 5647
made peace with Israel, and *s* them....... 2Sa 10:19 5647
as I have *s* in thy father's................ 2Sa 16:19 5647
s Solomon all the days of his.............. 1Kin 4:21 5647
have worshipped them, and *s* them......... 1Kin 9:9 5647
s Baal, and worshipped him................ 1Kin 16:31 5647
For he *s* Baal, and worshipped him,........ 1Kin 22:53 5647
unto them, Ahab *s* Baal a little 2Kin 10:18 5647
For they *s* idols, whereof the 2Kin 17:12 5647
all the host of heaven, and *s* Baal 2Kin 17:16 5647
s their own gods, after the................. 2Kin 17:33 5647
s their graven images, both their......... 2Kin 17:41 5647
the king of Assyria, and *s* him not 2Kin 18:7 5647
all the host of heaven, and *s* them........ 2Kin 21:3 5647
s the idols that his father 2Kin 21:21 5647
the idols that his father *s* 2Kin 21:21 5647
and told David how the men were *s*........ 1Chr 19:5
their officers that *s* the king in 1Chr 27:1 8334
and worshipped them, and *s* them 2Chr 7:22 5647
fathers, and *s* groves and idols............ 2Chr 24:18 5647
all the host of heaven, and *s* them........ 2Chr 33:3 5647
his father had made, and *s* them.......... 2Chr 33:22 5647
For they have not *s* thee in their .... Neh 9:35 5647
the seven chamberlains that *s* in........... Est 1:10 8334
And they *s* their idols...................... Ps 106:36 5647
rewardeth thee as thou hast *s* us.......... Ps 137:8 1580
king himself is *s* by the field .... Eccl 5:9 5647
s strange gods in your land, so............. Jer 5:19 5647
have loved, and whom they have *s* .... Jer 8:2 5647
after other gods, and have *s* them .... Jer 16:11 5647
worshipped other gods, and *s* them .... Jer 22:9 5647
when he hath *s* thee six years.............. Jer 34:14 5647
which *s* the king of Babylon, into ... Jer 52:12 5975,6440
service that he had *s* against it .... Eze 29:18 5647
labour wherewith he *s* against it........... Eze 29:20 5647
those that *s* themselves of them .... Eze 34:27 5647
Israel *s* for a wife, and for a............... Hos 12:12 5647
but *s* God with fastings and................. Lk 2:37 *3000*
and Martha *s* .... Jn 12:2 *1247*
after he had *s* his own generation.......... Acts 13:36 *5256*
s the creature more than the .... Rom 1:25 *3000*
he hath *s* with me in the gospel .... Phil 2:22 *1398*

SERVEDST {1}
Because thou *s* not the LORD thy .... Deut 28:47 5647

SERVEST {2}
Thy God whom thou *s* continually.......... Dan 6:16 6399
whom thou *s* continually, able to .... Dan 6:20 6399

SERVETH {9}
thereof, and all that *s* thereto............. Num 3:36 5656
spareth his own son that *s* him .... Mal 3:17 5647
s God and him that *s* him not .... Mal 3:18 5647
sitteth at meat, or he that *s* .... Lk 22:27 *1247*
but I am among you as he that *s* .... Lk 22:27 *1247*
s Christ is acceptable to God .... Rom 14:18 *1398*
but prophesying *s* not for them............. 1Cor 14:22
Wherefore then *s* the law..................... Gal 3:19

SERVICE {133}
give thee this also for the *s*.................. Gen 29:27 5656
for thou knowest my *s* which I............... Gen 30:26 5656
in all manner of *s* in the field............... Ex 1:14 5656
all their *s*, wherein they made................ Ex 1:14 5656
that ye shall keep this *s*...................... Ex 12:25 5656
unto you, What mean ye by this *s* .... Ex 12:26 5656
shalt keep this *s* in this month .... Ex 13:5 5656
tabernacle in all the *s* thereof .... Ex 27:19 5656
the *s* of the tabernacle of the .... Ex 30:16 5656
And the cloths of *s*, and the holy .... Ex 31:10 8278
The cloths of *s*, to do *s* in .... Ex 35:19 8278
to do *s* in the holy place, the.................. Ex 35:19 8334
congregation, and for all his *s*................ Ex 35:21 5656
wood for any work of the *s*.................... Ex 35:24 5656
work for the *s* of the sanctuary .... Ex 36:1 5656
work of the *s* of the sanctuary .... Ex 36:3 5656
than enough for the *s* of the work.......... Ex 36:5 5656
for the *s* of the Levites, by the .... Ex 38:21 5656
and scarlet, they made cloths of *s*.......... Ex 39:1 8278
to do *s* in the holy place, and .... Ex 39:1 8334
of the *s* of the tabernacle..................... Ex 39:40 5656
The cloths of *s* to do.......................... Ex 39:41 8278
to do *s* in the holy place .... Ex 39:41 8334
to do the *s* of the tabernacle.................. Num 3:7 5656
to do the *s* of the tabernacle.................. Num 3:8 5656
cords of it for all the *s* thereof .... Num 3:26 5656
the hanging, and all the *s* thereof .... Num 3:31 5656
This shall be the *s* of the sons .... Num 4:4 5656
appoint them every one to his *s* .... Num 4:19 5656
that enter in to perform the *s*................. Num 4:23 5656
This is the *s* of the families of .... Num 4:24 5656
and all the instruments of their *s*........... Num 4:26 5656
his sons shall be all the *s* of .... Num 4:27 5656
their burdens, and in all their *s* .... Num 4:27 5656
This is the *s* of the families of .... Num 4:28 5656
one that entereth into the *s* .... Num 4:30 6635
according to all their *s* in the................ Num 4:31 5656
instruments, and with all their *s*............ Num 4:32 5656
This is the *s* of the families of .... Num 4:33 5656
Merari, according to all their *s* .... Num 4:33 5656
one that entereth into the *s* .... Num 4:35 6635
all that might do *s* in the...................... Num 4:37 5647
one that entereth into the *s* .... Num 4:39 6635
of all that might do *s* in the .... Num 4:41 5647
one that entereth into the *s* .... Num 4:43 6635
came to do the *s* of the ministry............. Num 4:47 5656
the *s* of the burden in the..................... Num 4:47 5656
every one according to his *s* .... Num 4:49 5656
do the *s* of the tabernacle of the .... Num 7:5 5656
to every man according to his *s*............... Num 7:5 5656
of Gershon, according to their *s* .... Num 7:7 5656
of Merari, according unto their *s* .... Num 7:8 5656
because the *s* of the sanctuary .... Num 7:9 5656
may execute the *s* of the LORD .... Num 8:11 5656
do the *s* of the tabernacle of the .... Num 8:15 5647
to do the *s* of the children of................. Num 8:19 5656
their *s* in the tabernacle of the............... Num 8:22 5656
the *s* of the tabernacle of the .... Num 8:24 5656
cease waiting upon the *s* thereof............. Num 8:25 5656
keep the charge, and shall do no *s* .... Num 8:26 5656
s of the tabernacle of the LORD .... Num 16:9 5656
for all the *s* of the tabernacle................. Num 18:4 5656
to do the *s* of the tabernacle of .... Num 18:6 5656
office unto you as a *s* of gift.................. Num 18:7 5656
for their *s* which they serve,.................. Num 18:21 5656
even the *s* of the tabernacle of .... Num 18:21 5656
do the *s* of the tabernacle of the .... Num 18:23 5656
your *s* in the tabernacle of the .... Num 18:31 5656
that we might do the *s* of the .... Josh 22:27 5656
thou the grievous *s* of thy father 1Kin 12:4 5656
the *s* of song in the house of the 1Chr 6:31 3027
appointed unto all manner of *s* of............ 1Chr 6:48 5656
work of the *s* of the house of God........... 1Chr 9:13 5656
were over the work of the *s*.................... 1Chr 9:19 5656
the *s* of the house of the LORD 1Chr 23:24 5656
vessels of it for the *s* thereof 1Chr 23:26 5656
the *s* of the house of the LORD 1Chr 23:28 5656
the work of the *s* of the house of............ 1Chr 23:28 5656
in the *s* of the house of the LORD 1Chr 23:32 5656
to their offices in their *s*..................... 1Chr 24:3 5656
s to come into the house of the 1Chr 24:19 5656
to the *s* of the sons of Asaph 1Chr 25:1 5656
workmen according to their *s* was 1Chr 25:1 5656
for the *s* of the house of God,................ 1Chr 25:6 5656
able men for strength for the *s*............... 1Chr 26:8 5656
the LORD, and in the *s* of the king........... 1Chr 26:30 5656
for all the work of the *s* of the 1Chr 28:13 5656
for all the vessels of *s* in the................. 1Chr 28:13 5656
instruments of all manner of *s* 1Chr 28:14 5656
instruments of every kind of *s*................ 1Chr 28:14 5656
the *s* of the house of the LORD 1Chr 28:20 5656
for all the *s* of the house of God............. 1Chr 28:21 5656
skilful man, for any manner of *s*............. 1Chr 28:21 5656
his *s* this day unto the LORD 1Chr 29:5 3027
gave for the *s* of the house of 1Chr 29:7 5656
courses of the priests to their *s* 2Chr 8:14 5656
that they may know my *s*, and the 2Chr 12:8 5656
the *s* of the kingdoms of the................... 2Chr 12:8 5656
of the *s* of the house of the LORD 2Chr 24:12 5656
So the *s* of the house of the LORD 2Chr 29:35 5656
every man according to his *s* 2Chr 31:2 5656
his daily portion for their *s* in............... 2Chr 31:16 5656
in the *s* of the house of God.................. 2Chr 31:21 5656
the work in any manner of *s* 2Chr 34:13 5656
encouraged them to the *s* of the 2Chr 35:2 5656
So the *s* was prepared, and the 2Chr 35:10 5656
might not depart from their *s*................. 2Chr 35:15 5656
So all the *s* of the LORD was 2Chr 35:16 5656
their courses, for the *s* of God............... Ezr 6:18 5673
for the *s* of the house of thy God........... Ezr 7:19 6402
for the *s* of the Levites, two .... Ezr 8:20 5656
for the *s* of the house of our God .... Neh 10:32 5656
cattle, and herb for the *s* of man............. Ps 104:14 5656
his neighbour's *s* without wages.............. Jer 22:13 5647
to serve a great *s* against Tyrus .... Eze 29:18 5656
for the *s* that he had served................... Eze 29:20 5656
the house, for all the *s* thereof .... Eze 44:14 5656
will think that he doeth God *s* .... Jn 16:2 *2999*
the *s* of God, and the promises................ Rom 9:4 *2999*
God, which is your reasonable *s* .... Rom 12:1 *3000*
that my *s* which I have for..................... Rom 15:31 *1248*
s not only supplieth the want of.............. 2Cor 9:12 *3009*
taking wages of them, to do you *s*........... 2Cor 11:8 *1248*
ye did *s* unto them which by .... Gal 4:8 *1398*
With good will doing *s*, as to the............. Eph 6:7 *1398*
s of your faith, I joy, and .... Phil 2:17 *3009*
supply your lack of *s* toward me .... Phil 2:30 *3009*
but rather do them *s*, because 1Ti 6:2 *1398*
had also ordinances of divine *s* .... Heb 9:1 *2999*
accomplishing the *s* of God.................... Heb 9:6 *2999*
make him that did the *s* perfect.............. Heb 9:9 *3000*
know thy works, and charity, and *s* .... Rev 2:19 *1248*

SERVILE {12}
ye shall do no *s* work therein .... Lev 23:7 5656
ye shall do no *s* work therein .... Lev 23:8 5656
ye shall do no *s* work therein .... Lev 23:21 5656
Ye shall do no *s* work therein .... Lev 23:25 5656
ye shall do no *s* work therein .... Lev 23:35 5656
and ye shall do no *s* work therein .... Lev 23:36 5656
do no manner of *s* work therein .... Num 28:18 5656
ye shall do no *s* work.......................... Num 28:25 5656
ye shall do no *s* work.......................... Num 28:26 5656
ye shall do no *s* work.......................... Num 29:1 5656
ye shall do no *s* work, and ye .... Num 29:12 5656
ye shall do no *s* work therein .... Num 29:35 5656

SERVING {7}
we have let Israel go from *s* us............... Ex 14:5 5647
to thee, in *s* thee six years..................... Deut 15:18 5647
Martha was cumbered about much *s* .... Lk 10:40 *1248*
S the Lord with all humility of................ Acts 20:19 *1398*
tribes, instantly *s* God day .... Acts 26:7 *3000*
fervent in spirit; *s* the Lord .... Rom 12:11 *1398*
s divers lusts and pleasures,.................... Titus 3:3 *1398*

SERVITOR {1}
his *s* said, What, should I set................. 2Kin 4:43 8334

SERVITUDE {2}
the grievous *s* of thy father 2Chr 10:4 5656
affliction, and because of great *s* .... Lam 1:3 5656

SET {695}
God *s* them in the firmament of............... Gen 1:17 5414
the LORD *s* a mark upon Cain, lest........... Gen 4:15 7760
shalt thou *s* in the side thereof............... Gen 6:16 7760
I do *s* my bow in the cloud, and it .... Gen 9:13 5414
at this *s* time in the next year .... Gen 17:21 4150
had dressed, and *s* it before them .... Gen 18:8 5414
forth, and *s* him without the city .... Gen 19:16 3240
at the *s* time of which God had................ Gen 21:2 4150
Abraham *s* seven ewe lambs of the .... Gen 21:28 5324
which thou hast *s* by themselves.............. Gen 21:29 5324
there was *s* meat before him to .... Gen 24:33 7760
all night, because the sun was *s*.............. Gen 28:11 935
behold a ladder *s* up on the earth .... Gen 28:12 5324
s it up for a pillar, and poured .... Gen 28:18 7760
which I have *s* for a pillar .... Gen 28:22 7760
he *s* three days' journey betwixt .... Gen 30:36 7760
he *s* the rods which he had pilled .... Gen 30:38 3322
s the faces of the flocks toward................ Gen 30:40 5414
s his sons and his wives upon.................. Gen 31:17 5375
s his face toward the mount..................... Gen 31:21 7760
s it here before my brethren and.............. Gen 31:37 7760
a stone, and *s* it up for a pillar................ Gen 31:45 7311
Jacob *s* up a pillar in the place .... Gen 35:14 5324
Jacob *s* a pillar upon her grave .... Gen 35:20 5324
s him over the land of Egypt................... Gen 41:33 7896
I have *s* thee over all the land .... Gen 41:41 5414
s him before thee, then let me .... Gen 43:9 3322
himself, and said, *S* on bread.................. Gen 43:31 7760
they *s* on for him by himself, and............ Gen 43:32 7760
that I may *s* mine eyes upon him .... Gen 44:21 7760
father, and *s* him before Pharaoh............. Gen 47:7 5975
he *s* Ephraim before Manasseh .... Gen 48:20 7760
Therefore they did *s* over them .... Ex 1:11 7760
s them upon an ass, and he .... Ex 4:20 7392
taskmasters had *s* over them .... Ex 5:14 7760
neither did he *s* his heart to .... Ex 7:23 7896
And the LORD appointed a *s* time.............. Ex 9:5 4150
That thou shalt *s* apart unto the .... Ex 13:12
thou shalt *s* bounds unto the................... Ex 19:12
S bounds about the mount, and................ Ex 19:23
which thou shalt *s* before them .... Ex 21:1 7760
I will *s* thy bounds from the Red.............. Ex 23:31 7896
and stones to be *s* in the ephod............... Ex 25:7 4394
thou shalt *s* upon the table..................... Ex 25:30 5414
s in order one against another................. Ex 26:17 7947
thou shalt *s* the table without .... Ex 26:35 7760
them to be *s* in ouches of gold................. Ex 28:11 4142
thou shalt *s* in it settings of .... Ex 28:17 4390
they shall be *s* in gold in their .... Ex 28:20 7660
to *s* them, and in carving of .... Ex 31:5 4390
that they are *s* on mischief .... Ex 32:22
stones to be *s* for the ephod, and............. Ex 35:9 4394
onyx stones, and stones to be *s* .... Ex 35:27 4394
to *s* them, and in carving of wood,........... Ex 35:33 4390
to be *s* by the four corners of it.............. Ex 37:3
they *s* in it four rows of stones................ Ex 39:10 4390
with the lamps to be *s* in order .... Ex 39:37
s up the tabernacle of the tent .... Ex 40:2 6965
s in order the things that are to .... Ex 40:4
that are to be *s* in order upon it............... Ex 40:4
thou shalt *s* the altar of gold................... Ex 40:5 5414
thou shalt *s* the altar of the.................... Ex 40:6 5414
thou shalt *s* the laver between................. Ex 40:7 5414
thou shalt *s* up the court round............... Ex 40:8 7760
s up the boards thereof, and put .... Ex 40:18 7760
s the staves on the ark, and put .... Ex 40:20 7760
s up the vail of the covering, and............ Ex 40:21 7760
he *s* the bread in order upon it................ Ex 40:23 6186
he *s* up the hanging at the door .... Ex 40:28 7760
he *s* the laver between the tent .... Ex 40:30 7760
s up the hanging of the court .... Ex 40:33 5414
I will even *s* my face against .... Lev 17:10 5414
I will *s* my face against that man............ Lev 20:3 5414
Then I will *s* my face against .... Lev 20:5 7760
I will even *s* my face against .... Lev 20:6 5414
thou shalt *s* them in two rows,................ Lev 24:6 7760
Every sabbath he shall *s* it in.................. Lev 24:8
neither shall ye *s* up any image............... Lev 26:1 5414
I will *s* my tabernacle among you .... Lev 26:11 5414
I will *s* my face against you, and............. Lev 26:17 5414
the Levites shall *s* it up .... Num 1:51 6965
These shall first *s* forth .... Num 2:9 5265
they shall *s* forth in the second .... Num 2:16 5265
of the congregation shall *s* .... Num 2:17 5265
encamp, so shall they *s* forward .... Num 2:17 5265
standards, and so they *s* forward .... Num 2:34 5265
as the camp is to *s* forward .... Num 4:15 5265
near, and *s* her before the LORD .... Num 5:16 5975
the priest shall *s* the woman .... Num 5:18 5975
shall *s* the woman before the LORD.......... Num 5:30 5975

had fully *s* up the tabernacle ... Num 7:1 6965
thou shalt *s* the Levites before ... Num 8:13 5975
and the sons of Merari *s* forward ... Num 10:17 5265
s forward according to their ... Num 10:18 5265
And the Kohathites *s* forward ... Num 10:21 5265
the other did *s* up the tabernacle ... Num 10:21 6965
s forward according to their ... Num 10:22 5265
of the children of Dan *s* forward ... Num 10:25 5265
their armies, when they *s* forward ... Num 10:28 5265
to pass, when the ark *s* forward ... Num 10:35 5265
s them round about the tabernacle ... Num 11:24 5975
serpent, and *s* it upon a pole ... Num 21:8 7760
the children of Israel *s* forward ... Num 21:10 5265
the children of Israel *s* forward ... Num 22:1 5265
but he *s* his face toward the ... Num 24:1 7896
s a man over the congregation, ... Num 27:16 6485
s him before Eleazar the priest, ... Num 27:19 5975
s him before Eleazar the priest, ... Num 27:22 5975
do unto the LORD in your *s* feasts ... Num 29:39 4150
I have *s* the land before you ... Deut 1:8 5414
God hath *s* the land before thee ... Deut 1:21 5414
which I *s* before you this day ... Deut 4:8 5414
this is the law which Moses *s* ... Deut 4:44 7760
The LORD did not *s* his love upon ... Deut 7:7
I *s* before you this day a ... Deut 11:26 5414
judgments which I *s* before you ... Deut 11:32 5414
shall choose to *s* his name there ... Deut 14:24 7760
shalt thou *s* thee up any image ... Deut 16:22 6965
I will *s* a king over me, like as ... Deut 17:14 7760
in any wise *s* him king over thee ... Deut 17:15 7760
shalt thou *s* king over thee ... Deut 17:15 7760
thou mayest not *s* a stranger over ... Deut 17:15 5414
time have *s* in thine inheritance ... Deut 19:14 1379
s it down before the altar of the ... Deut 26:4 3240
thou shalt *s* it before the LORD ... Deut 26:10 3240
that thou shalt *s* thee up great ... Deut 27:2 6965
that ye shall *s* up these stones, ... Deut 27:4 6965
that the LORD thy God will *s* thee ... Deut 28:1 5414
king which thou shalt *s* over thee ... Deut 28:36 6965
which would not adventure to *s* ... Deut 28:56 3322
curse, which I have *s* before thee ... Deut 30:1 5414
I have *s* before thee this day ... Deut 30:15 5414
that I have *s* before you life and ... Deut 30:19 5414
he *s* the bounds of the people ... Deut 32:8 5324
s on fire the foundations of the ... Deut 32:22
S your hearts unto all the words ... Deut 32:46 7760
Joshua *s* up twelve stones in the ... Josh 4:9 6965
son shall he *s* up the gates of it ... Josh 6:26 5324
that ye shall *s* the city on fire ... Josh 8:8 3341
s them to lie in ambush between ... Josh 8:12 7760
And when they had *s* the people ... Josh 8:13 7760
and hasted and *s* the city on fire ... Josh 8:19
s men by it for to keep them ... Josh 10:18 6485
s up the tabernacle of the ... Josh 18:1 7931
s them a statute and an ordinance ... Josh 24:25 7760
s it up there under an oak, that ... Josh 24:26 6965
the sword, and *s* the city on fire ... Judg 1:8 7971
my present, and *s* it before thee ... Judg 6:18 3240
him shalt thou *s* by himself ... Judg 7:5 3322
and they had but newly *s* the watch ... Judg 7:19 6965
the LORD *s* every man's sword ... Judg 7:22 7760
the men of Shechem *s* liers in ... Judg 9:25 7760
rise early, and *s* upon the city ... Judg 9:33 6584
s the hold on fire upon them ... Judg 9:49
when he had *s* the brands on fire, ... Judg 15:5
they *s* him between the pillars ... Judg 16:25 5975
of Dan *s* up the graven image ... Judg 18:30 6965
they *s* them up Micah's graven ... Judg 18:31 7760
s their battle again in array in ... Judg 20:22
Israel *s* liers in wait round ... Judg 20:29 7760
which they had *s* beside Gibeah ... Judg 20:36 7760
also they *s* on fire all the ... Judg 20:48 7971
that was *s* over the reapers ... Ruth 2:5 5324
the servant that was *s* over the ... Ruth 2:6 5324
to *s* them among princes, and to ... 1Sa 2:8 3427
he hath *s* the world upon them ... 1Sa 2:8 7896
house of Dagon, and *s* it by Dagon ... 1Sa 5:2 3322
and *s* him in his place again ... 1Sa 5:3 7725
whereon they *s* down the ark of ... 1Sa 6:18 3240
s it between Mizpeh and Shen, and ... 1Sa 7:12 7760
will *s* them to ear his ground, and ... 1Sa 8:12
days ago, *s* not thy mind on them ... 1Sa 9:20 7760
I said unto thee, *S* it by thee ... 1Sa 9:23 7760
was upon it, and *s* it before Saul ... 1Sa 9:24 7760
s it before thee, and eat ... 1Sa 9:24 7760
him, Nay, but *s* a king over us ... 1Sa 10:19 7760
the LORD hath *s* a king over you ... 1Sa 12:13 5414
according to the *s* time that ... 1Sa 13:8 4150
that I have *s* up Saul to be king ... 1Sa 15:11 4427
he *s* him up a place, and is gone ... 1Sa 15:12 5324
s the battle in array against the ... 1Sa 17:2
out to *s* your battle in array ... 1Sa 17:8
Saul *s* him over the men of war, ... 1Sa 18:5 7760
so that his name was much *s* by ... 1Sa 18:30 3335
which was *s* over the servants of ... 1Sa 22:9 5324
as thy life was much *s* by this ... 1Sa 26:24 1431
so let my life be much *s* by in ... 1Sa 26:24 1431
let me *s* a morsel of bread before ... 1Sa 28:22 7760
to *s* up the throne of David over ... 2Sa 3:10 6965
they *s* the ark of God upon a new ... 2Sa 6:3 7392
s it in his place, in the midst ... 2Sa 6:17 3322
I will *s* up thy seed after thee, ... 2Sa 7:12 6965
the Syrians *s* themselves in array ... 2Sa 10:17
S ye Uriah in the forefront of ... 2Sa 11:15 3051
they *s* bread before him, and he ... 2Sa 12:20 7760
and it was *s* on David's head ... 2Sa 12:30
go and *s* it on fire ... 2Sa 14:30
servants *s* the field on fire ... 2Sa 14:30
thy servants *s* my field on fire ... 2Sa 14:31
they *s* down the ark of God ... 2Sa 15:24 3332
s captains of thousands and ... 2Sa 18:1 7760
have *s* thyself against me ... 2Sa 18:13 3320
yet didst thou *s* thy servant ... 2Sa 19:28 7896
but he tarried longer than the *s* ... 2Sa 20:5 4150
David *s* him over his guard ... 2Sa 23:23 7760
that all Israel *s* their faces on ... 1Kin 2:15 7760
caused a seat to be *s* for the ... 1Kin 2:19 7760
s me on the throne of David my ... 1Kin 2:24 3427
whom I will *s* upon thy throne in ... 1Kin 5:5 5414
to *s* there the ark of the ... 1Kin 6:19 5414
he *s* the cherubims within the ... 1Kin 6:27 5414
to *s* upon the tops of the pillars ... 1Kin 7:16 5414
he *s* up the pillars in the porch ... 1Kin 7:21 6965
he *s* up the right pillar, and ... 1Kin 7:21 6965
he *s* up the left pillar, and ... 1Kin 7:21 6965
the sea was *s* above upon them, and ... 1Kin 7:25
he *s* the sea on the right side of ... 1Kin 7:39 5414
I have *s* there a place for the ... 1Kin 8:21 7760
which I have *s* before you ... 1Kin 9:6 5414
to *s* thee on the throne of Israel ... 1Kin 10:9 5414
he *s* the one in Beth-el, and the ... 1Kin 12:29 7760
for his eyes were *s* by reason of ... 1Kin 14:4 6965
to *s* up his son after him, and to ... 1Kin 15:4 6965
s up the gates thereof in his ... 1Kin 16:34 5324
servants, *S* yourselves in array ... 1Kin 20:12 7760
they *s* themselves in array ... 1Kin 20:12 7760
s Naboth on high among the people ... 1Kin 21:9 3427
s two men, sons of Belial, before ... 1Kin 21:10 3427
s Naboth on high among the people ... 1Kin 21:12 3427
thou shalt *s* aside that which is ... 2Kin 4:4 5265
let us *s* for him there a bed, and ... 2Kin 4:10 7760
S on the great pot, and seethe ... 2Kin 4:38 8239
should I *s* this before an hundred ... 2Kin 4:43 5414
So he *s* it before them, and they ... 2Kin 4:44 5414
s bread and water before them, ... 2Kin 6:22 7760
strong holds wilt thou *s* on fire ... 2Kin 8:12 7971
s him on his father's throne, and ... 2Kin 10:3 7760
the money that every man is *s* at ... 2Kin 12:4 6187
s it beside the altar, on the ... 2Kin 12:9 5414
Hazael *s* his face to go up to ... 2Kin 12:17 7760
they *s* them up images and groves ... 2Kin 17:10 5324
on thy part to *s* riders upon them ... 2Kin 18:23 5414
the LORD, *S* thine house in order ... 2Kin 20:1
he *s* a graven image of the grove ... 2Kin 21:7 7760
that was *s* over the men of war ... 2Kin 25:19 6496
s his throne above the throne of ... 2Kin 25:28 5414
these are they whom David *s* over ... 1Chr 6:31 5975
seer did ordain in their *s* office ... 1Chr 9:22 530
porters, were in their *s* office ... 1Chr 9:26 530
had the *s* office over the things ... 1Chr 9:31 530
they *s* themselves in the midst of ... 1Chr 11:14 3320
David *s* him over his guard ... 1Chr 11:25 7760
s it in the midst of the tent ... 1Chr 16:1 3322
battle was *s* against him before ... 1Chr 19:10
they *s* themselves in array ... 1Chr 19:11
s the battle in array against ... 1Chr 19:17
it was *s* upon David's head ... 1Chr 20:2
s up an altar unto the LORD in ... 1Chr 21:18 6965
he *s* masons to hew wrought stones ... 1Chr 22:2 5975
Now *s* your heart and your soul to ... 1Chr 22:19 5414
four thousand were to *s* forward ... 1Chr 23:4 5329
the new moons, and on the *s* feasts ... 1Chr 23:31 4150
onyx stones, and stones to be *s* ... 1Chr 29:2 4394
because I have *s* my affection to ... 1Chr 29:3 7521
he *s* threescore and ten thousand ... 2Chr 2:18 6213
overseers to *s* the people a work ... 2Chr 2:18
s thereon palm trees and chains ... 2Chr 3:5 5927
the sea was *s* above upon them, and ... 2Chr 4:4
s them in the temple, five on the ... 2Chr 4:7 5414
he *s* the sea on the right side of ... 2Chr 4:10 5414
whereon the shewbread was *s* ... 2Chr 4:19
am *s* on the throne of Israel, as ... 2Chr 6:10 3427
had *s* it in the midst of the ... 2Chr 6:13 5414
which I have *s* before you ... 2Chr 7:19 5414
in thee to *s* thee on his throne ... 2Chr 9:8 5414
the tribes of Israel such as *s* ... 2Chr 11:16 5414
Abijah *s* the battle in array with ... 2Chr 13:3 631
Jeroboam also *s* the battle in ... 2Chr 13:3
the shewbread also *s* they in ... 2Chr 13:11
they *s* the battle in array in the ... 2Chr 14:10
s garrisons in the land of Judah, ... 2Chr 17:2 5414
And he *s* judges in the land ... 2Chr 19:5 5975
did Jehoshaphat *s* of the Levites ... 2Chr 19:8 5975
s himself to seek the LORD, and ... 2Chr 20:3 5414
s yourselves, stand ye still, and ... 2Chr 20:17 3320
the LORD *s* ambushments against ... 2Chr 20:22 5414
he *s* all the people, every man ... 2Chr 23:10 5975
that were *s* over the host ... 2Chr 23:14 6485
he *s* the porters at the gates of ... 2Chr 23:19 5975
s the king upon the throne of the ... 2Chr 23:20 3427
s it without at the gate of the ... 2Chr 24:8 5414
they *s* the house of God in his ... 2Chr 24:13 5975
s them up to be his gods, and ... 2Chr 25:14 5975
he *s* the Levites in the house of ... 2Chr 29:25 5975
house of the LORD was *s* in order ... 2Chr 29:35 3559
new moons, and for the *s* feasts ... 2Chr 31:3 4150
of the priests, in their *s* office ... 2Chr 31:15 530
for in their *s* office they ... 2Chr 31:18 530
he *s* captains of war over the ... 2Chr 32:6 5414
he *s* a carved image, the idol ... 2Chr 33:7 7760
s up groves and graven images, ... 2Chr 33:19 5975
the Kohathites, to *s* it forward ... 2Chr 34:12 5329
he *s* the priests in their charges ... 2Chr 35:2 5975
of God to *s* it up in his place ... Ezr 2:68 5975
they *s* the altar upon his bases ... Ezr 3:3 3559
of all the *s* feasts of the LORD ... Ezr 3:5 4150
to *s* forward the work of the ... Ezr 3:8 5329
to *s* forward the workmen in the ... Ezr 3:9 5329
they *s* the priests in their ... Ezr 3:10 5975
s in the cities of Samaria, and ... Ezr 4:10 3488
have *s* up the walls thereof, and ... Ezr 4:12 3635
builded, and the walls *s* up again ... Ezr 4:13 3635
again, and the walls thereof *s* up ... Ezr 4:16 3635
king of Israel builded and *s* up ... Ezr 5:11 3635
from his house, and being *s* up ... Ezr 6:11 2211
they *s* the priests in their ... Ezr 6:18 6966
s magistrates and judges, which ... Ezr 7:25 4483
to *s* up the house of our God, and ... Ezr 9:9 7311
I have chosen to *s* my name there ... Neh 1:9 7931
and I *s* him a time ... Neh 2:6 5414
it, and *s* up the doors of it ... Neh 3:1 5975
s up the doors thereof, the locks ... Neh 3:3 5975
s up the doors thereof, and the ... Neh 3:6 5975
s up the doors thereof, the locks ... Neh 3:13 5975
s up the doors thereof, the locks ... Neh 3:14 5975
s up the doors thereof, the locks ... Neh 3:15 5975
s a watch against them day and ... Neh 4:9 5975
Therefore *s* I in the lower places ... Neh 4:13 5975
I even *s* the people after their ... Neh 4:13 5975
I *s* a great assembly against them ... Neh 5:7 5414
not *s* up the doors upon the gates ... Neh 6:1 5975
I had *s* up the doors, and the ... Neh 7:1 5975
s over us because of our sins ... Neh 9:37 5414
the new moons, for the *s* feasts ... Neh 10:33 4150
and *s* them in their place ... Neh 13:11 5975
of my servants *s* I at the gates ... Neh 13:19 5975
so that he *s* the royal crown upon ... Est 2:17 7760
s his seat above all the princes ... Est 3:1 7760
royal which is *s* upon his head ... Est 6:8 5414
Esther *s* Mordecai over the house ... Est 8:2 7760
To *s* up on high those that be low ... Job 5:11 7760
the terrors of God do *s* ... Job 6:4
that thou shouldest *s* thine heart ... Job 7:17 7896
why hast thou *s* me as a mark ... Job 7:20 7760
who shall *s* me a time to plead ... Job 9:19 3259
thou wouldest appoint me a *s* time ... Job 14:13 2706
pieces, and *s* me up for his mark ... Job 16:12 6965
he hath *s* darkness in my paths ... Job 19:8 7760
have *s* with the dogs of my flock ... Job 30:1 7896
they *s* forward my calamity, they ... Job 30:13 3276
s thy words in order before me, ... Job 33:5
If he *s* his heart upon man, if he ... Job 34:14 7760
and *s* others in their stead ... Job 34:24 5975
that which should be *s* on thy ... Job 36:16 5183
place, and *s* bars and doors, ... Job 38:10 7760
canst thou *s* the dominion thereof ... Job 38:33 7760
kings of the earth *s* themselves ... Ps 2:2 3320
Yet have I *s* my king upon my holy ... Ps 2:6 5258
that have *s* themselves against me ... Ps 3:6 7896
s apart him that is godly for ... Ps 4:3 6395
who hast *s* thy glory above the ... Ps 8:1 5414
are privily *s* against the poor ... Ps 10:8 6845
I will *s* him in safety from him ... Ps 12:5 7896
I have *s* the LORD always before ... Ps 16:8 7737
they have *s* their eyes bowing ... Ps 17:11 7896
In them hath he *s* a tabernacle ... Ps 19:4 7760
our God we will *s* up our banners ... Ps 20:5 1713
he shall *s* me up upon a rock ... Ps 27:5 7311
thou hast *s* my feet in a large ... Ps 31:8 5975
s my feet upon a rock, and ... Ps 40:2 6965
s them in order before thine eyes ... Ps 50:21
they have not *s* God before them ... Ps 54:3 7760
among them that are *s* on fire ... Ps 57:4
s not your heart upon them ... Ps 62:10 7896
salvation, O God, *s* me up on high ... Ps 69:29
They *s* their mouth against the ... Ps 73:9 8371
Surely thou didst *s* them in ... Ps 73:18 7896
they *s* up their ensigns for signs ... Ps 74:4 7760
Thou hast *s* all the borders of ... Ps 74:17 5324
That they might *s* their hope in ... Ps 78:7 7760
a generation that *s* not their ... Ps 78:8 3559
shall *s* us in the way of his ... Ps 85:13 7760
have not *s* thee before them ... Ps 86:14 7760
I will *s* his hand also in the sea ... Ps 89:25 7760
Thou hast *s* up the right hand of ... Ps 89:42 7311
Thou hast *s* our iniquities before ... Ps 90:8 7896
Because he hath *s* his love upon ... Ps 91:14
I will *s* him on high, because he ... Ps 91:14
I will *s* no wicked thing before ... Ps 101:3 7896
her, yea, the *s* time, is come ... Ps 102:13 4150
Thou hast *s* a bound that they may ... Ps 104:9 7760
S thou a wicked man over him ... Ps 109:6 6485
That he may *s* him with princes, ... Ps 113:8 3427
me, and *s* me in a large place ... Ps 118:5
For there are *s* thrones of ... Ps 122:5 3427
thy body will I *s* upon thy throne ... Ps 132:11 7896
they have *s* gins for me ... Ps 140:5 7896
Let my prayer be *s* forth before ... Ps 141:2 3559
S a watch, O LORD, before my ... Ps 141:3 7896
But ye have *s* at nought all my ... Prov 1:25 6544
I was *s* up from everlasting, from ... Prov 8:23 5258
when he *s* a compass upon the face ... Prov 8:27 2710
which thy fathers have *s* ... Prov 22:28 6213
Wilt thou *s* thine eyes upon that ... Prov 23:5 5774
also he hath *s* the world in their ... Eccl 3:11 5414
God also hath *s* the one over ... Eccl 7:14 6213
men is fully *s* in them to do evil ... Eccl 8:11
Folly is *s* in great dignity, and ... Eccl 10:6 5414
out, and *s* in order many proverbs ... Eccl 12:9
washed with milk, and fitly *s* ... Song 5:12 3427
as gold rings *s* with the beryl ... Song 5:14 4390
s upon sockets of fine gold ... Song 5:15 3245
heap of wheat *s* about with lilies ... Song 7:2 5473
S me as a seal upon thine heart, ... Song 8:6 7760

instead of well *s* hair baldness .... Is 3:24 4748
s a king in the midst of it, even .... Is 7:6
Therefore the LORD shall *s* up the .... Is 9:11 7682
that the Lord shall *s* his hand .... Is 11:11 3254
he shall *s* up an ensign for the .... Is 11:12 5375
and *s* them in their own land .... Is 14:1 3240
shalt *s* it with strange slips .... Is 17:10 2232
I will *s* the Egyptians against .... Is 19:2 5526
s a watchman, let him declare .... Is 21:6 5975
I am *s* in my ward whole nights .... Is 21:8 5324
the horsemen shall *s* themselves .... Is 22:7 7896
they *s* up the towers thereof, ... Is 23:13 6965
who would *s* the briers and thorns .... Is 27:4 5414
the women come, and *s* them on fire .... Is 27:11
on thy part to *s* riders upon them .... Is 36:8 5414
the LORD, *S* thine house in order .... Is 38:1
I will *s* in the desert the fir .... Is 41:19 7760
till he have *s* judgment in the .... Is 42:4 7760
it hath *s* him on fire round about .... Is 42:25 7760
s it in order for me, since I .... Is 44:7
s up the wood of their graven .... Is 45:20 5375
s him in his place, and he .... Is 46:7 3240
s up my standard to the people .... Is 49:22 7311
therefore have I *s* my face like a .... Is 50:7 7760
high mountain hast thou *s* thy bed .... Is 57:7 7760
hast thou *s* up thy remembrance .... Is 57:8 7760
I have *s* watchmen upon thy walls, ... Is 62:6 6485
I will *s* a sign among them, and I .... Is 66:19 7760
I have this day *s* thee over the .... Jer 1:10 6485
they shall *s* every one his throne .... Jer 1:15 5414
S up the standard toward Zion .... Jer 4:6 5375
they *s* a trap, they catch men .... Jer 5:26 5324
Tekoa, and *s* up a sign of fire in .... Jer 6:1 5375
Also I *s* watchmen over you, ... Jer 6:17 6965
s in array as men for war against .... Jer 6:23
I have *s* thee for a tower and a .... Jer 6:27 5414
where I *s* my name at the first, ... Jer 7:12 7931
they have *s* their abominations in .... Jer 7:30 7760
my law which I *s* before them .... Jer 9:13 5414
any more, and to *s* up my curtains .... Jer 10:20 6965
ye *s* up altars to that shameful .... Jer 11:13 7760
I *s* before you the way of life, ... Jer 21:8 5414
For I have *s* my face against this .... Jer 21:10 7760
I will *s* up shepherds over them .... Jer 23:4 6965
two baskets of figs were *s* before .... Jer 24:1 3259
For I will *s* mine eyes upon them .... Jer 24:6 7760
my law, which I have *s* before you .... Jer 26:4 5414
S thee up waymarks, make thee .... Jer 31:21 5324
s thine heart toward the highway, ... Jer 31:21 7896
children's teeth are *s* on edge .... Jer 31:29 6949
his teeth shall be *s* on edge .... Jer 31:30 6949
Which hast *s* signs and wonders in .... Jer 32:20 7760
s fire on this city, and burn it .... Jer 32:29 3341
But they *s* their abominations in .... Jer 32:34 7760
whom he had *s* at liberty at their .... Jer 34:16 7971
I *s* before the sons of the house .... Jer 35:5 5414
say, Thy friends have *s* thee on .... Jer 38:22 5496
that he had *s* over them Gedaliah .... Jer 40:11 6485
If ye wholly *s* your faces to .... Jer 42:15 7760
it be with all the men that *s* .... Jer 42:17 7760
will *s* his throne upon these .... Jer 43:10 7760
that I *s* before you and before .... Jer 44:10 5414
I will *s* my face against you for .... Jer 44:11 7760
that have *s* their faces to go .... Jer 44:12 7760
I will *s* my throne in Elam, and .... Jer 49:38 7760
and publish, and *s* up a standard .... Jer 50:2 5375
they shall *s* themselves in array .... Jer 50:9
S up the standard upon the walls .... Jer 51:12 5375
s up the watchmen, prepare the .... Jer 51:12 6965
S ye up a standard in the land, ... Jer 51:27 5375
s his throne above the throne of .... Jer 52:32 5414
he hath *s* up the horn of thine .... Lam 2:17 7311
He hath *s* me in dark places, as .... Lam 3:6 3427
s me as a mark for the arrow .... Lam 3:12 5324
s me upon my feet, that I heard .... Eze 2:2 5975
s me upon my feet, and spake with .... Eze 3:24 5975
s the camp also against it, and .... Eze 4:2 5414
s battering rams against it round .... Eze 4:2 7760
s it for a wall of iron between .... Eze 4:3 5414
s thy face against it, and it .... Eze 4:3 3559
Therefore thou shalt *s* thy face .... Eze 4:7 3559
I have *s* it in the midst of the .... Eze 5:5 7760
s thy face toward the mountains .... Eze 6:2 7760
his ornament, he *s* it in majesty .... Eze 7:20 7760
have I *s* it far from them .... Eze 7:20 5414
s a mark upon the foreheads of .... Eze 9:4 8427
for I have *s* thee for a sign unto .... Eze 12:6 5414
s thy face against the daughters .... Eze 13:17 7760
these men have *s* up their idols .... Eze 14:3 5927
I will *s* my face against that man .... Eze 14:8 5414
I will *s* my face against them .... Eze 15:7 5414
when I *s* my face against them .... Eze 15:7 7760
and thou hast *s* mine oil and mine .... Eze 16:18 5414
thou hast even *s* it before them .... Eze 16:19 5414
he *s* it in a city of merchants .... Eze 17:4 7760
waters, and *s* it as a willow tree .... Eze 17:5 7760
of the high cedar, and will *s* it .... Eze 17:22 5414
children's teeth are *s* on edge .... Eze 18:2 6949
Then the nations *s* against him on .... Eze 19:8 5414
s thy face toward the south, and .... Eze 20:46 7760
s thy face toward Jerusalem, and .... Eze 21:2 7760
I have *s* the point of the sword .... Eze 21:15 5414
left, whithersoever thy face is *s* .... Eze 21:16 3259
thee have they *s* light by father .... Eze 22:7
that was *s* apart for pollution .... Eze 22:10 5079
which shall *s* against thee .... Eze 23:24 7760
I will *s* judgment before them, and .... Eze 23:24 5414
I will *s* my jealousy against thee .... Eze 23:25 5414

thou hast *s* mine incense and mine .... Eze 23:41 7760
the king of Babylon *s* himself .... Eze 24:2 5564
S on a pot, *s* it on, and also .... Eze 24:3 8239
she *s* it upon the top of a rock .... Eze 24:7 7760
I have *s* her blood upon the top .... Eze 24:8 5414
Then *s* it empty upon the coals .... Eze 24:11 5975
that whereupon they *s* their minds .... Eze 24:25 4853
s thy face against the Ammonites, ... Eze 25:2 7760
they shall *s* their palaces in .... Eze 25:4 3427
he shall *s* engines of war against .... Eze 26:9 5414
shall *s* thee in the low parts of .... Eze 26:20 3427
I shall *s* glory in the land of .... Eze 26:20 5414
they *s* forth thy comeliness .... Eze 27:10 5414
though thou *s* thine heart as the .... Eze 28:2 5414
Because thou hast *s* thine heart .... Eze 28:6 5414
and I have *s* thee so .... Eze 28:14 5414
s thy face against Zidon, and .... Eze 28:21 7760
s thy face against Pharaoh king .... Eze 29:2 7760
when I have *s* a fire in Egypt, and .... Eze 30:8 5414
will *s* fire in Zoan, and will .... Eze 30:14 5414
And I will *s* fire in Egypt .... Eze 30:16 5414
the deep *s* him up on high with .... Eze 31:4 7311
s darkness upon thy land, saith .... Eze 32:8 5414
Whose graves are *s* in the sides .... Eze 32:23 5414
They have *s* her a bed in the .... Eze 32:25 5414
and *s* him for their watchman .... Eze 33:2 5414
I have *s* thee a watchman unto the .... Eze 33:7 5414
I will *s* up one shepherd over .... Eze 34:23 6965
s thy face against mount Seir, and .... Eze 35:2 7760
s me down in the midst of the .... Eze 37:1 5117
will *s* my sanctuary in the midst .... Eze 37:26 5414
s thy face against Gog, the land .... Eze 38:2 7760
shall *s* on fire and burn the .... Eze 39:9 1197
then shall he *s* up a sign by it, ... Eze 39:15 1129
I will *s* my glory among the .... Eze 39:21 5414
s me upon a very high mountain, ... Eze 40:2 5117
s thine heart upon all that I .... Eze 40:4 7760
but ye have *s* keepers of my .... Eze 44:8 7760
of the eunuchs had *s* over Daniel .... Dan 1:11 4487
the God of heaven *s* up a kingdom .... Dan 2:44 6966
he *s* Shadrach, Meshach, and .... Dan 2:49 4483
he *s* it up in the plain of Dura, ... Dan 3:1 6966
Nebuchadnezzar the king had *s* up .... Dan 3:2 6966
Nebuchadnezzar the king had *s* up .... Dan 3:3 6966
that Nebuchadnezzar had *s* up .... Dan 3:3 6966
Nebuchadnezzar the king hath *s* up .... Dan 3:5 6966
Nebuchadnezzar the king had *s* up .... Dan 3:7 6966
hast *s* over the affairs of the .... Dan 3:12 4483
golden image which thou hast *s* up .... Dan 3:12 6966
golden image which I have *s* up .... Dan 3:14 6966
golden image which thou hast *s* up .... Dan 3:18 6966
and whom he would he *s* up .... Dan 5:19 7313
It pleased Darius to *s* over the .... Dan 6:1 3966
the king thought to *s* him over .... Dan 6:3 3966
s his heart on Daniel to deliver .... Dan 6:14 7761
the judgment was *s*, and the books .... Dan 7:10 3488
he touched me, and *s* me upright .... Dan 8:18 5975
I *s* my face unto the Lord God, to .... Dan 9:3 5414
which he *s* before us by his .... Dan 9:10 5414
which *s* me upon my knees and upon .... Dan 10:10 5128
didst *s* thine heart to understand .... Dan 10:12 5414
I *s* my face toward the ground, and .... Dan 10:15 5414
and he shall *s* forth a great .... Dan 11:11 5975
shall *s* forth a multitude greater .... Dan 11:13 5975
He shall also *s* his face to enter .... Dan 11:17 7760
that maketh desolate *s* up .... Dan 12:11 5414
s her as in the day that she was .... Hos 2:3 3322
s her like a dry land, and slay .... Hos 2:3 7896
they *s* their heart on their .... Hos 4:8 5375
he hath *s* an harvest for thee, ... Hos 6:11 7896
S the trumpet to thy mouth .... Hos 8:1
They have *s* up kings, but not by .... Hos 8:4
how shall I *s* thee as Zeboim .... Hos 11:8 7761
a strong people *s* in battle array .... Joel 2:5
I will *s* a plumbline in the midst .... Amos 7:8 7760
that we may *s* forth wheat .... Amos 8:5 6605
I will *s* mine eyes upon them for .... Amos 9:4 7760
though thou *s* thy nest among the .... Obad 4 7760
will *s* thee as a gazingstock .... Nah 3:6 7760
be *s* wide open unto thine enemies .... Nah 3:13
s me upon the tower, and will .... Hab 2:1 3320
that he may *s* his nest on high, ... Hab 2:9 7760
Let them *s* a fair mitre upon his .... Zec 3:5 7760
So they *s* a fair mitre upon his .... Zec 3:5 7760
s there upon her own base .... Zec 5:11 3240
s them upon the head of Joshua .... Zec 6:11 7760
for I *s* all men every one against .... Zec 8:10 7971
that work wickedness are *s* up .... Mal 3:15 1129
and when he was *s*, his disciples .... Mt 5:1 2523
A city that is *s* on an hill .... Mt 5:14 2749
For I am come to *s* a man at .... Mt 10:35 1369
s him in the midst of them, ... Mt 18:2 2476
clothes, and they *s* him thereon .... Mt 21:7 1940
he shall *s* the sheep on his right .... Mt 25:33 2476
When he was *s* down on the .... Mt 27:19 2521
s up over his head his accusation .... Mt 27:37 2007
And at even, when the sun did *s* .... Mk 1:32 1416
not to be *s* on a candlestick .... Mk 4:21 2007
to his disciples to *s* before them .... Mk 6:41 3908
to his disciples to *s* before them .... Mk 8:6 3908
they did *s* them before the people .... Mk 8:6 3908
commanded to *s* them also before .... Mk 8:7 3908
many things, and be *s* at nought .... Mk 9:12 1847
s him in the midst of them .... Mk 9:36 2476
s an hedge about it, and digged a .... Mk 12:1 4060
as many have taken in hand to *s* .... Lk 1:1 392
this child is *s* for the fall .... Lk 2:34 2749
s him on a pinnacle of the temple .... Lk 4:9 2476

to *s* at liberty them that are .... Lk 4:18 649
I also am a man *s* under authority .... Lk 7:8 5021
to *s* before the multitude .... Lk 9:16 3908
took a child, and *s* him by him, ... Lk 9:47 2476
he stedfastly *s* his face to go to .... Lk 9:51 4741
such things as are *s* before you .... Lk 10:8 3908
s him on his own beast, and .... Lk 10:34 1913
and I have nothing to *s* before him .... Lk 11:6 3908
the colt, and they *s* Jesus thereon .... Lk 19:35 1913
were *s* down together, Peter sat .... Lk 22:55 4776
his men of war *s* him at nought .... Lk 23:11 1848
there were *s* there six waterpots .... Jn 2:6 2749
beginning doth *s* forth good wine .... Jn 2:10 5087
received his testimony hath *s* to .... Jn 3:33 4972
to them that were *s* down .... Jn 6:11 345
when they had *s* her in the midst, ... Jn 8:3 2476
was *s* down again, he said unto .... Jn 13:12 377
Now there was *s* a vessel full of .... Jn 19:29 2749
when they had *s* them in the midst .... Acts 4:7 2476
was *s* at nought of you builders .... Acts 4:11 1848
they *s* them before the council .... Acts 5:27 2476
Whom they *s* before the apostles .... Acts 6:6 2476
s up false witnesses, which said, ... Acts 6:13 2476
not so much as to *s* his foot on .... Acts 7:5 968
would have *s* them at one again, ... Acts 7:26 4900
upon a *s* day Herod, arrayed in .... Acts 12:21 5002
Holy Ghost, *s* his eyes on him, ... Acts 13:9 816
I have *s* thee to be a light of .... Acts 13:47 5087
ruins thereof, and I will *s* it up .... Acts 15:16 461
he *s* meat before them, and .... Acts 16:34 3908
s all the city on an uproar, and .... Acts 17:5 2350
no man shall *s* on thee to hurt .... Acts 18:10 2007
is in danger to be *s* at nought .... Acts 19:27 2064
we went aboard, and *s* forth .... Acts 21:2 321
Paul down, and *s* him before them .... Acts 22:30 2476
beasts, that they may *s* Paul on .... Acts 23:24 1913
man might have been *s* at liberty .... Acts 26:32 630
Whom God hath *s* forth to be a .... Rom 3:25 4388
or why dost thou *s* at nought thy .... Rom 14:10 1848
For I think that God hath *s* forth 1Cor 4:9 584
s them to judge who are least 1Cor 6:4 2523
whatsoever is *s* before you 1Cor 10:27 3908
the rest will I *s* in order when I 1Cor 11:34 1299
But now hath God *s* the members 1Cor 12:18 5087
God hath *s* some in the church, ... 1Cor 12:28 5087
hath been evidently *s* forth .... Gal 3:1 4270
s him at his own right hand in .... Eph 1:20 2523
knowing that I am *s* for the .... Phil 1:17 2749
S your affection on things above, ... Col 3:2 5426
that thou shouldest *s* in order .... Titus 1:5 1930
didst *s* him over the works of thy .... Heb 2:7 2525
hold upon the hope *s* before us .... Heb 6:18 4295
who is *s* on the right hand of the .... Heb 8:1 2523
the race that is *s* before us .... Heb 12:1 4295
who for the joy that was *s* before .... Heb 12:2 4295
is *s* down at the right hand of .... Heb 12:2 2523
brother Timothy is *s* at liberty .... Heb 13:23 630
and it is *s* on fire of hell .... Jas 3:6 5394
are *s* forth for an example, ... Jude 7 4295
I have *s* before thee an open door .... Rev 3:8 1325
am *s* down with my Father in his .... Rev 3:21 2523
behold, a throne was *s* in heaven .... Rev 4:2 2749
he *s* his right foot upon the sea, ... Rev 10:2 5087
s a seal upon him, that he should .... Rev 20:3 4972

SETH *(seth)* {8} See SHETH. *A son of Adam and Eve.*
bare a son, and called his name *S* .... Gen 4:25 8352
And to *S*, to him also there was .... Gen 4:26 8352
and called his name *S* .... Gen 5:3 8352
S were eight hundred years .... Gen 5:4 8352
S lived an hundred and five years, ... Gen 5:6 8352
S lived after he begat Enos eight .... Gen 5:7 8352
all the days of *S* were nine .... Gen 5:8 8352
of Enos, which was the son of *S* .... Lk 3:38 4589

SETHUR *(se'-thur)* {1} *A spy sent to the Promised Land.*
of Asher, *S* the son of Michael .... Num 13:13 5639

SETTER {1}
He seemeth to be a *s* forth of .... Acts 17:18 2604

SETTEST {7}
thou *s* thine hand to in the land .... Deut 23:20 4916
all that thou *s* thine hand unto .... Deut 28:8 4916
in all that thou *s* thine hand .... Deut 28:20 4916
that thou *s* a watch over me .... Job 7:12 7760
thou *s* a print upon the heels of .... Job 13:27
thou *s* a crown of pure gold on .... Ps 21:3 7896
s me before thy face for ever .... Ps 41:12 5324

SETTETH {22}
And when the tabernacle *s* forward .... Num 1:51 5265
And when the camp *s* forward .... Num 4:5 5265
is poor, and *s* his heart upon it .... Deut 24:15 5375
Cursed be he that *s* light by his .... Deut 27:16 7034
and *s* me upon my high places 2Sa 22:34 5975
He *s* an end to darkness, and .... Job 28:3 7760
feet, and *s* me upon my high places .... Ps 18:33 5975
he *s* himself in a way that is not .... Ps 36:4 3320
his strength *s* fast the mountains .... Ps 65:6 3559
God *s* the solitary in families .... Ps 68:6 3427
putteth down one, and *s* up another .... Ps 75:7 7311
as the flame *s* the mountains on .... Ps 83:14 3857
Yet *s* he the poor on high from .... Ps 107:41
lay wait, as he that *s* snares .... Jer 5:26 7918
of Neriah *s* thee on against us .... Jer 43:3 5496
that *s* up his idols in his heart .... Eze 14:4 5927
s up his idols in his heart, and .... Eze 14:7 5927
he removeth kings, and *s* up kings .... Dan 2:21 6966
s up over it the basest of men .... Dan 4:17 6966
s him on a pinnacle of the temple .... Mt 4:5 2476

but *s* it on a candlestick, that ... Lk 8:16 *2007*
s on fire the course of nature ... Jas 3:6 *5394*

SETTING {3}
In their *s* of their threshold by ... Eze 43:8 5414
sealing the stone, and *s* a watch ... Mt 27:66 *3326*
Now when the sun was *s*, all they ... Lk 4:40 *1416*

SETTINGS {1}
thou shalt set in it *s* of stones ... Ex 28:17 4396

SETTLE {10}
But I will *s* him in mine house and ... 1Chr 17:14 5975
I will *s* you after your old ... Eze 36:11 3427
the lower *s* shall be two cubits ... Eze 43:14 5835
from the lesser *s* even to the ... Eze 43:14 5835
greater *s* shall be four cubits ... Eze 43:14 5835
the *s* shall be fourteen cubits ... Eze 43:17 5835
and on the four corners of the *s* ... Eze 43:20 5835
corners of the *s* of the altar ... Eze 45:19 5835
S it therefore in your hearts, ... Lk 21:14 *5087*
stablish, strengthen, *s* you ... 1Pet 5:10 *2311*

SETTLED {7}
a *s* place for thee to abide in ... 1Kin 8:13 4349
he *s* his countenance stedfastly, ... 2Kin 8:11 5975
O LORD, thy word is *s* in heaven ... Ps 119:89 5324
Before the mountains were *s* ... Prov 8:25 2883
he hath *s* on his lees, and hath ... Jer 48:11 8252
the men that are *s* on their lees ... Zeph 1:12 7087
in the faith grounded and *s* ... Col 1:23 *1476*

SETTLEST {1}
thou *s* the furrows thereof ... Ps 65:10 5181

SEVEN {465}
s years, and begat sons and ... Gen 5:7 7651
and *s* years, and begat Lamech ... Gen 5:25 7651
he begat Lamech *s* hundred eighty ... Gen 5:26 7651
s hundred seventy and *s* years ... Gen 5:31 7651
For yet *s* days, and I will cause ... Gen 7:4 7651
And it came to pass after *s* days ... Gen 7:10 7651
And he stayed yet other *s* days ... Gen 8:10 7651
And he stayed yet other *s* days ... Gen 8:12 7651
And in the second month, on the *s* ... Gen 8:14 7651
s years, and begat sons and ... Gen 11:21 7651
Abraham set *s* ewe lambs of the ... Gen 21:28 7651
What mean these *s* ewe lambs which ... Gen 21:29 7651
For these *s* ewe lambs shalt thou ... Gen 21:30 7651
And Sarah was an hundred and *s* ... Gen 23:1 7651
an hundred and thirty and *s* years ... Gen 25:17 7651
I will serve thee *s* years for ... Gen 29:18 7651
Jacob served *s* years for Rachel ... Gen 29:20 7651
serve with me yet *s* other years ... Gen 29:27 7651
served with him yet *s* other years ... Gen 29:30 7651
pursued after him *s* days' journey ... Gen 31:23 7651
himself to the ground *s* times ... Gen 33:3 7651
of the river *s* well favoured kine ... Gen 41:2 7651
s other kine came up after them ... Gen 41:3 7651
did eat up the *s* well favoured ... Gen 41:4 7651
s ears of corn came up upon one ... Gen 41:5 7651
s thin ears and blasted with the ... Gen 41:6 7651
the *s* thin ears devoured the ... Gen 41:7
thin ears devoured the *s* rank ... Gen 41:7 7651
came up out of the river *s* kine ... Gen 41:18 7651
s other kine came up after them, ... Gen 41:19 7651
did eat up the first *s* fat kine ... Gen 41:20 7651
s ears came up in one stalk, full ... Gen 41:22 7651
s ears, withered, thin, and ... Gen 41:23 7651
ears devoured the *s* good ears ... Gen 41:24 7651
The *s* good kine are *s* years ... Gen 41:26 7651
the *s* good ears are *s* years ... Gen 41:26 7651
the *s* thin and ill favoured kine ... Gen 41:27 7651
came up after them are *s* years ... Gen 41:27 7651
the *s* empty ears blasted with the ... Gen 41:27 7651
wind shall be *s* years of famine ... Gen 41:27 7651
there come *s* years of great ... Gen 41:29 7651
after them *s* years of famine ... Gen 41:30 7651
of Egypt in the *s* plenteous years ... Gen 41:34 7651
against the *s* years of famine ... Gen 41:36 7651
in the *s* plenteous years the ... Gen 41:47 7651
up all the food of the *s* years ... Gen 41:48 7651
the *s* years of plenteousness, ... Gen 41:53 7651
the *s* years of dearth began to ... Gen 41:54 7651
all the souls were *s* ... Gen 46:25 7651
was an hundred forty and *s* years ... Gen 47:28 7651
a mourning for his father *s* days ... Gen 50:10 7651
priest of Midian had *s* daughters ... Ex 2:16 7651
were an hundred thirty and *s* years ... Ex 6:16 7651
an hundred and thirty and *s* years ... Ex 6:20 7651
s days were fulfilled, after that ... Ex 7:25 7651
S days shall ye eat unleavened ... Ex 12:15 7651
S days shall there be no leaven ... Ex 12:19 7651
S days thou shalt eat unleavened ... Ex 13:6 7651
bread shall be eaten *s* days ... Ex 13:7 7651
s days it shall be with his dam ... Ex 22:30 7651
shalt eat unleavened bread *s* days ... Ex 23:15 7651
shalt make the *s* lamps thereof ... Ex 25:37 7651
stead shall put them on *s* days ... Ex 29:30 7651
s days shalt thou consecrate them ... Ex 29:35 7651
S days thou shalt make an ... Ex 29:37 7651
S days thou shalt eat unleavened ... Ex 34:18 7651
And he made his *s* lamps, and his ... Ex 37:23 7651
s hundred and thirty shekels, ... Ex 38:24 7651
talents, and a thousand *s* hundred ... Ex 38:25 7651
of the thousand *s* hundred seventy ... Ex 38:28 7651
the blood *s* times before the LORD ... Lev 4:6 7651
sprinkle it *s* times before the ... Lev 4:17 7651
thereof upon the altar *s* times ... Lev 8:11 7651
of the congregation in *s* days ... Lev 8:33 7651
for *s* days shall he consecrate ... Lev 8:33 7651
congregation day and night *s* days ... Lev 8:35 7651

then she shall be unclean *s* days ... Lev 12:2 7651
him that hath the plague *s* days ... Lev 13:4 7651
shall shut him up *s* days more ... Lev 13:5 7651
priest shall shut him up *s* days ... Lev 13:21 7651
priest shall shut him up *s* days ... Lev 13:26 7651
the plague of the scall *s* days ... Lev 13:31 7651
that hath the scall *s* days more ... Lev 13:33 7651
up it that hath the plague *s* days ... Lev 13:50 7651
he shall shut it up *s* days more ... Lev 13:54 7651
cleansed from the leprosy *s* times ... Lev 14:7 7651
abroad out of his tent *s* days ... Lev 14:8 7651
finger *s* times before the LORD ... Lev 14:16 7651
left hand *s* times before the LORD ... Lev 14:27 7651
and shut up the house *s* days ... Lev 14:38 7651
and sprinkle the house *s* times ... Lev 14:51 7651
himself *s* days for his cleansing ... Lev 15:13 7651
she shall be put apart *s* days ... Lev 15:19 7651
him, he shall be unclean *s* days ... Lev 15:24 7651
shall number to herself *s* days ... Lev 15:28 7651
the blood with his finger *s* times ... Lev 16:14 7651
upon it with his finger *s* times ... Lev 16:19 7651
then it shall be *s* days under the ... Lev 22:27 7651
s days ye must eat unleavened ... Lev 23:6 7651
made by fire unto the LORD *s* days ... Lev 23:8 7651
s sabbaths shall be complete ... Lev 23:15 7651
s lambs without blemish of the ... Lev 23:18 7651
for *s* days unto the LORD ... Lev 23:34 7651
S days ye shall offer an offering ... Lev 23:36 7651
keep a feast unto the LORD *s* days ... Lev 23:39 7651
before the LORD your God *s* days ... Lev 23:40 7651
unto the LORD *s* days in the year ... Lev 23:41 7651
Ye shall dwell in booths *s* days ... Lev 23:42 7651
thou shalt number *s* sabbaths of ... Lev 25:8 7651
unto thee, *s* times *s* years ... Lev 25:8 7651
the space of the *s* sabbaths of ... Lev 25:8 7651
then I will punish you *s* times ... Lev 26:18 7651
I will bring *s* times more plagues ... Lev 26:21 7651
you yet *s* times for your sins ... Lev 26:24 7651
will chastise you *s* times for ... Lev 26:28 7651
s thousand and four hundred ... Num 1:31 7651
and two thousand and *s* hundred ... Num 1:39 7651
s thousand and four hundred ... Num 2:8 7651
and two thousand and *s* hundred ... Num 2:26 7651
s thousand and six hundred ... Num 2:31 7651
numbered of them were *s* thousand ... Num 3:22 7651
were two thousand *s* hundred ... Num 4:36 7651
the *s* lamps shall give light over ... Num 8:2 7651
should she not be ashamed *s* days ... Num 12:14 7651
be shut out from the camp *s* days ... Num 12:14 7651
was shut out from the camp *s* days ... Num 12:15 7651
(Now Hebron was built *s* years ... Num 13:22 7651
s hundred, beside them that died ... Num 16:49 7651
of the congregation *s* times ... Num 19:4 7651
any man shall be unclean *s* days ... Num 19:11 7651
the tent, shall be unclean *s* days ... Num 19:14 7651
a grave, shall be unclean *s* days ... Num 19:16 7651
Balak, Build me here *s* altars ... Num 23:1 7651
me here *s* oxen and *s* rams ... Num 23:1 7651
him, I have prepared *s* altars ... Num 23:4 7651
built *s* altars, and offered a ... Num 23:14 7651
Balak, Build me here *s* altars ... Num 23:29 7651
me here *s* bullocks and *s* rams ... Num 23:29 7651
thousand and *s* hundred and thirty ... Num 26:7 7651
and two thousand and *s* hundred ... Num 26:34 7651
thousand and a thousand *s* hundred ... Num 26:51 7651
s lambs of the first year without ... Num 28:11 7651
s days shall unleavened bread be ... Num 28:17 7651
s lambs of the first year ... Num 28:19 7651
lamb, throughout the *s* lambs ... Num 28:21 7651
daily, throughout the *s* days ... Num 28:24 7651
s lambs of the first year ... Num 28:27 7651
one lamb, throughout the *s* lambs ... Num 28:29 7651
s lambs of the first year without ... Num 29:2 7651
one lamb, throughout the *s* lambs ... Num 29:4 7651
s lambs of the first year ... Num 29:8 7651
one lamb, throughout the *s* lambs ... Num 29:10 7651
keep a feast unto the LORD *s* days ... Num 29:12 7651
And on the seventh day *s* bullocks ... Num 29:32 7651
s lambs of the first year without ... Num 29:36 7651
ye abide without the camp *s* days ... Num 31:19 7651
three hundred thousand and *s* ... Num 31:36 7651
s thousand and five hundred sheep, ... Num 31:43 7651
was sixteen thousand *s* hundred ... Num 31:52 7651
s nations greater and mightier ... Deut 7:1 7651
At the end of every *s* years thou ... Deut 15:1 7651
s days shalt thou eat unleavened ... Deut 16:3 7651
with thee in all thy coast *s* days ... Deut 16:4 7651
S weeks shalt thou number unto ... Deut 16:9 7651
begin to number the *s* weeks from ... Deut 16:9 7651
the feast of tabernacles *s* days ... Deut 16:13 7651
S days shalt thou keep a solemn ... Deut 16:15 7651
way, and flee before thee *s* ways ... Deut 28:7 7651
them, and flee *s* ways before them ... Deut 28:25 7651
At the end of every *s* years ... Deut 31:10 7651
s priests shall bear before the ... Josh 6:4 7651
the ark *s* trumpets of rams' horns ... Josh 6:4 7651
ye shall compass the city *s* times ... Josh 6:4 7651
let *s* priests bear *s* trumpets ... Josh 6:6 7651
the *s* priests bearing the *s* ... Josh 6:8 7651
s priests bearing *s* trumpets ... Josh 6:13 7651
after the same manner *s* times ... Josh 6:15 7651
they compassed the city *s* times ... Josh 6:15 7651
the children of Israel *s* tribes ... Josh 18:2 7651
they shall divide it into *s* parts ... Josh 18:5 7651
describe the land into *s* parts ... Josh 18:6 7651
by cities into *s* parts in a book ... Josh 18:9 7651
into the hand of Midian *s* years ... Judg 6:1 7651
the second bullock of *s* years old ... Judg 6:25 7651

s hundred shekels of gold ... Judg 8:26 7651
And he judged Israel *s* years ... Judg 12:9 7651
me within the *s* days of the feast ... Judg 14:12 7651
And she wept before him the *s* days ... Judg 14:17 7651
If they bind me with *s* green ... Judg 16:7 7651
Philistines brought up to her *s* ... Judg 16:8 7651
If thou weavest the *s* locks of my ... Judg 16:13 7651
shave off the *s* locks of his head ... Judg 16:19 7651
numbered *s* hundred chosen men ... Judg 20:15 7651
all this people there were *s* ... Judg 20:16 7651
is better to thee than *s* sons ... Ruth 4:15 7651
so that the barren hath born *s* ... 1Sa 2:5 7651
of the Philistines *s* months ... 1Sa 6:1 7651
s days shalt thou tarry, till I ... 1Sa 10:8 7651
Give us *s* days' respite, that we ... 1Sa 11:3 7651
And he tarried *s* days, according ... 1Sa 13:8 7651
Jesse made *s* of his sons to pass ... 1Sa 16:10 7651
tree at Jabesh, and fasted *s* days ... 1Sa 31:13 7651
the house of Judah was *s* years ... 2Sa 2:11 7651
he reigned over Judah *s* years ... 2Sa 5:5 7651
s hundred horsemen, and twenty ... 2Sa 8:4 7651
David slew the men of *s* hundred ... 2Sa 10:18 7651
Let *s* men of his sons be ... 2Sa 21:6 7651
and they fell all *s* together ... 2Sa 21:9 7651
thirty and *s* in all ... 2Sa 23:39 7651
Shall *s* years of famine come unto ... 2Sa 24:13 7651
s years reigned he in Hebron, and ... 1Kin 2:11 7651
and the third was *s* cubits broad ... 1Kin 6:6 7651
So was he *s* years in building it ... 1Kin 6:38 7651
s for the one chapiter ... 1Kin 7:17 7651
and *s* for the other chapiter ... 1Kin 7:17 7651
s days and *s* days, even ... 1Kin 8:65 7651
And he had *s* hundred wives, ... 1Kin 11:3 7651
did Zimri reign *s* days in Tirzah ... 1Kin 16:15 7651
And he said, Go again *s* times ... 1Kin 18:43 7651
have left me *s* thousand in Israel ... 1Kin 19:18 7651
of Israel, being *s* thousand ... 1Kin 20:15 7651
one over against the other *s* days ... 1Kin 20:29 7651
s thousand of the men that were ... 1Kin 20:30 7651
a compass of *s* days' journey ... 2Kin 3:9 7651
he took with him *s* hundred men ... 2Kin 3:26 7651
and the child sneezed *s* times ... 2Kin 4:35 7651
Go and wash in Jordan *s* times ... 2Kin 5:10 7651
dipped himself *s* times in Jordan, ... 2Kin 5:14 7651
also come upon the land *s* years ... 2Kin 8:1 7651
land of the Philistines *s* years ... 2Kin 8:2 7651
came to pass at the *s* years' end ... 2Kin 8:3 7651
S years old was Jehoash when he ... 2Kin 11:21 7651
even *s* thousand, and craftsmen and ... 2Kin 24:16 7651
And it came to pass in the *s* ... 2Kin 25:27 7651
in the twelfth month, on the *s* ... 2Kin 25:27 7651
and there he reigned *s* years ... 1Chr 3:4 7651
Johanan, and Dalaiah, and Anani, *s* ... 1Chr 3:24 7651
and Jachan, and Zia, and Heber, *s* ... 1Chr 5:13 7651
four and forty thousand *s* hundred ... 1Chr 5:18 7651
fourscore and *s* thousand ... 1Chr 7:5 7651
and *s* hundred and threescore ... 1Chr 9:13 7651
were to come after *s* days from ... 1Chr 9:25 7651
oak in Jabesh, and fasted *s* days ... 1Chr 10:12 7651
s thousand and one hundred ... 1Chr 12:25 7651
were three thousand and *s* hundred ... 1Chr 12:27 7651
and spear thirty and *s* thousand ... 1Chr 12:34 7651
offered *s* bullocks and *s* rams ... 1Chr 15:26 7651
s thousand horsemen, and twenty ... 1Chr 18:4 7651
David slew of the Syrians *s* ... 1Chr 19:18 7651
s hundred, were officers among ... 1Chr 26:30 7651
s hundred chief fathers, whom ... 1Chr 26:32 7651
s thousand talents of refined ... 1Chr 29:4 7651
s years reigned he in Hebron, and ... 1Chr 29:27 7651
Solomon kept the feast *s* days ... 2Chr 7:8 7651
dedication of the altar *s* days ... 2Chr 7:9 7651
s days, and the feast *s* days ... 2Chr 7:9 7651
s rams, the same may be a priest ... 2Chr 13:9 7651
s hundred oxen and *s* thousand ... 2Chr 15:11 7651
s thousand and *s* hundred rams, ... 2Chr 17:11 7651
s thousand and *s* hundred he ... 2Chr 17:11 7651
Joash was *s* years old when he ... 2Chr 24:1 7651
s thousand and five hundred, that ... 2Chr 26:13 7651
And they brought *s* bullocks ... 2Chr 29:21 7651
s rams, and *s* lambs ... 2Chr 29:21 7651
s he goats, for a sin offering ... 2Chr 29:21 7651
bread *s* days with great gladness ... 2Chr 30:21 7651
eat throughout the feast *s* days ... 2Chr 30:22 7651
took counsel to keep other *s* days ... 2Chr 30:23 7651
they kept other *s* days with ... 2Chr 30:23 7651
bullocks and *s* thousand sheep ... 2Chr 30:24 7651
feast of unleavened bread *s* days ... 2Chr 35:17 7651
s hundred seventy and five ... Ezr 2:5 7651
Zaccai, *s* hundred and threescore ... Ezr 2:9 7651
s hundred and forty and three ... Ezr 2:25 7651
and Ono, *s* hundred twenty and five ... Ezr 2:33 7651
a thousand two hundred forty and *s* ... Ezr 2:38 7651
of whom there were *s* thousand ... Ezr 2:65 7651
three hundred thirty and *s* ... Ezr 2:65 7651
horses were *s* hundred thirty ... Ezr 2:66 7651
asses, six thousand *s* hundred ... Ezr 2:67 7651
unleavened bread *s* days with joy ... Ezr 6:22 7651
of his *s* counsellors, to enquire ... Ezr 7:14 7655
s lambs, twelve he goats for a ... Ezr 8:35 7651
Zaccai, *s* hundred and threescore ... Neh 7:14 7651
six hundred threescore and *s* ... Neh 7:18 7651
two thousand threescore and *s* ... Neh 7:19 7651
Beeroth, *s* hundred forty and three ... Neh 7:29 7651
and Ono, *s* hundred twenty and one ... Neh 7:37 7651
a thousand two hundred forty and *s* ... Neh 7:41 7651
of whom there were *s* thousand ... Neh 7:67 7651
three hundred thirty and *s* ... Neh 7:67 7651
horses, *s* hundred thirty and six ... Neh 7:68 7651

six thousand *s* hundred and twenty ... Neh 7:69 7651
threescore and *s* priests' garments ... Neh 7:72 7651
And they kept the feast *s* days ... Neh 8:18 7651
Ethiopia, over an hundred and *s* ... Est 1:1 7651
s days, in the court of the ... Est 1:5 7651
the *s* chamberlains that served in ... Est 1:10 7651
the *s* princes of Persia and Media, ... Est 1:14 7651
s maidens, which were meet to be ... Est 2:9 7651
s provinces, unto every province ... Est 8:9 7651
s provinces of the kingdom of ... Est 9:30 7651
there were born unto him *s* sons ... Job 1:2 7651
also was *s* thousand sheep ... Job 1:3 7651
with him upon the ground *s* days ... Job 2:13 7651
s nights, and none spake a word ... Job 2:13 7651
in *s* there shall no evil touch ... Job 5:19 7651
take unto you now *s* bullocks ... Job 42:8 7651
s rams, and go to my servant Job, ... Job 42:8 7651
He had also *s* sons and three ... Job 42:13 7658
of earth, purified *s* times ... Ps 12:6 7659
S times a day do I praise thee ... Ps 119:164 7651
s are an abomination unto him ... Prov 6:16 7651
she hath hewn out her *s* pillars ... Prov 9:1 7651
For a just man falleth *s* times ... Prov 24:16 7651
s men that can render a reason ... Prov 26:16 7651
for there are *s* abominations in ... Prov 26:25 7651
Give a portion to *s*, and also to ... Eccl 11:2 7651
in that day *s* women shall take ... Is 4:1 7651
shall smite it in the *s* streams ... Is 11:15 7651
sevenfold, as the light of *s* days ... Is 30:26 7651
She that hath borne *s* languisheth ... Jer 15:9 7651
At the end of *s* years let ye go ... Jer 34:14 7651
s men of them that were near the ... Jer 52:25 7651
of the Jews *s* hundred forty ... Jer 52:30 7651
And it came to pass in the *s* ... Jer 52:31 7651
astonished among them *s* days ... Eze 3:15 7651
came to pass at the end of *s* days ... Eze 3:16 7651
And it came to pass in the *s* ... Eze 29:17 7651
shall burn them with fire *s* years ... Eze 39:9 7651
s months shall the house of ... Eze 39:12 7651
after the end of *s* months shall ... Eze 39:14 7651
they went up unto it by *s* steps ... Eze 40:22 7651
there were *s* steps to go up to it ... Eze 40:26 7651
the breadth of the door, *s* cubits ... Eze 41:3 7651
S days shalt thou prepare every ... Eze 43:25 7651
S days shall they purge the altar ... Eze 43:26 7651
they shall reckon unto him *s* days ... Eze 44:26 7651
the passover, a feast of *s* days ... Eze 45:21 7651
s days of the feast he shall ... Eze 45:23 7651
s bullocks and *s* rams without ... Eze 45:23 7651
s rams without blemish daily the ... Eze 45:23 7651
without blemish daily the *s* days ... Eze 45:23 7651
like in the feast of the *s* days ... Eze 45:25 7651
should heat the furnace one *s* ... Dan 3:19 7655
let *s* times pass over him ... Dan 4:16 7655
till *s* times pass over him ... Dan 4:23 7655
s times shall pass over thee, ... Dan 4:25 7655
s times shall pass over thee, ... Dan 4:32 7655
the Prince shall be *s* weeks ... Dan 9:25 7651
Seek him that maketh the *s* stars ... Amos 5:8 3598
we raise against him *s* shepherds ... Mic 5:5 7651
upon one stone shall be *s* eyes ... Zec 3:9 7651
his *s* lamps thereon ... Zec 4:2 7651
and *s* pipes to the *s* lamps ... Zec 4:2 7651
hand of Zerubbabel with those *s* ... Zec 4:10 7651
taketh with himself *s* other ... Mt 12:45 *2033*
And they said, *S*, and a few little ... Mt 15:34 *2033*
And he took the *s* loaves and the ... Mt 15:36 *2033*
meat that was left *s* baskets full ... Mt 15:37 *2033*
Neither the *s* loaves of the four ... Mt 16:10 *2033*
till *s* times ... Mt 18:21 *2034*
say not unto thee, Until *s* times ... Mt 18:22 *2034*
but, Until seventy times *s* ... Mt 18:22 *2033*
Now there were with us *s* brethren ... Mt 22:25 *2033*
whose wife shall she be of the *s* ... Mt 22:28 *2033*
And they said, *S* ... Mk 8:5 *2033*
and he took the *s* loaves, and gave ... Mk 8:6 *2033*
meat that was left *s* baskets ... Mk 8:8 *2033*
when the *s* among four thousand, ... Mk 8:20 *2033*
And they said, *S* ... Mk 8:20 *2033*
Now there were *s* brethren ... Mk 12:20 *2033*
the *s* had her, and left no seed ... Mk 12:22 *2033*
for the *s* had her to wife ... Mk 12:23 *2033*
out of whom he had cast *s* devils ... Mk 16:9 *2033*
s years from her virginity ... Lk 2:36 *2033*
out of whom went *s* devils ... Lk 8:2 *2033*
taketh to him *s* other spirits ... Lk 11:26 *2033*
against thee *s* times in a day ... Lk 17:4 *2034*
s times in a day turn again to ... Lk 17:4 *2034*
There were therefore *s* brethren ... Lk 20:29 *2033*
and in like manner the *s* also ... Lk 20:31 *2033*
for *s* had her to wife ... Lk 20:33 *2033*
among you *s* men of honest report ... Acts 6:3 *2033*
when he had destroyed *s* nations ... Acts 13:19 *2033*
there were *s* sons of one Sceva, a ... Acts 19:14 *2033*
where we abode *s* days ... Acts 20:6 *2033*
we tarried there *s* days ... Acts 21:4 *2033*
which was one of the *s* ... Acts 21:8 *2033*
when the *s* days were almost ended ... Acts 21:27 *2033*
desired to tarry with them *s* days ... Acts 28:14 *2033*
reserved to myself *s* thousand men ... Rom 11:4 *2035*
they were compassed about *s* days ... Heb 11:30 *2033*
John to the *s* churches which are ... Rev 1:4 *2033*
from the *s* Spirits which are ... Rev 1:4 *2033*
send it unto the *s* churches which ... Rev 1:11 *2033*
I saw *s* golden candlesticks ... Rev 1:12 *2033*
And in the midst of the *s* ... Rev 1:13 *2033*
he had in his right hand *s* stars ... Rev 1:16 *2033*
The mystery of the *s* stars which ... Rev 1:20 *2033*
the *s* golden candlesticks ... Rev 1:20 *2033*
The *s* stars are the angels of the ... Rev 1:20 *2033*
are the angels of the *s* churches ... Rev 1:20 *2033*
the *s* candlesticks which thou ... Rev 1:20 *2033*
thou sawest are the *s* churches ... Rev 1:20 *2033*
the *s* stars in his right hand ... Rev 2:1 *2033*
of the *s* golden candlesticks ... Rev 2:1 *2033*
he that hath the *s* Spirits of God ... Rev 3:1 *2033*
Spirits of God, and the *s* stars ... Rev 3:1 *2033*
there were *s* lamps of fire ... Rev 4:5 *2033*
which are the *s* Spirits of God ... Rev 4:5 *2033*
the backside, sealed with *s* seals ... Rev 5:1 *2033*
to loose the *s* seals thereof ... Rev 5:5 *2033*
it had been slain, having *s* horns ... Rev 5:6 *2033*
horns and *s* eyes, which are ... Rev 5:6 *2033*
which are the *s* Spirits of God ... Rev 5:6 *2033*
I saw the *s* angels which stood ... Rev 8:2 *2033*
and to them were given *s* trumpets ... Rev 8:2 *2033*
the *s* angels which had the *s* ... Rev 8:6 *2033*
s thunders uttered their voices ... Rev 10:3 *2033*
when the *s* thunders had uttered ... Rev 10:4 *2033*
which the *s* thunders uttered ... Rev 10:4 *2033*
were slain of men *s* thousand ... Rev 11:13 *2033*
great red dragon, having *s* heads ... Rev 12:3 *2033*
horns, and *s* crowns upon his heads ... Rev 12:3 *2033*
up out of the sea, having *s* heads ... Rev 13:1 *2033*
s angels having the *s* last ... Rev 15:1 *2033*
the *s* angels came out of the ... Rev 15:6 *2033*
the temple, having the *s* plagues ... Rev 15:6 *2033*
gave unto the *s* angels *s* ... Rev 15:7 *2033*
till the *s* plagues of the *s* ... Rev 15:8 *2033*
the temple saying to the *s* angels ... Rev 16:1 *2033*
there came one of the *s* angels ... Rev 17:1 *2033*
angels which had the *s* vials ... Rev 17:1 *2033*
of blasphemy, having *s* heads ... Rev 17:3 *2033*
her, which hath the *s* heads ... Rev 17:7 *2033*
The *s* heads are *s* mountains, ... Rev 17:9 *2033*
And there are *s* kings ... Rev 17:10 *2033*
he is the eighth, and is of the *s* ... Rev 17:11 *2033*
the *s* angels which had the ... Rev 21:9 *2033*
s vials full of the *s* last ... Rev 21:9 *2033*

SEVENFOLD {6}

vengeance shall be taken on him *s* ... Gen 4:15 7659
If Cain shall be avenged *s* ... Gen 4:24 7659
truly Lamech seventy and *s* ... Gen 4:24 7659
render unto our neighbours *s* into ... Ps 79:12 7659
he be found, he shall restore *s* ... Prov 6:31 7659
the light of the sun shall be *s* ... Is 30:26 7659

SEVENS {2}

thou shalt take to thee by *s* ... Gen 7:2 7651
Of fowls also of the air by *s* ... Gen 7:3 7651

SEVENTEEN {10}

being *s* years old, was feeding ... Gen 37:2 7651,6240
in the land of Egypt *s* years ... Gen 47:28 7651,6240
thereof, even threescore and *s* men . Judg 8:14 7657,7651
he reigned *s* years in Jerusalem, ... 1Kin 14:21 7651,6240
in Samaria, and reigned *s* years ... 2Kin 13:1 7651,6240
were *s* thousand and two hundred .. 1Chr 7:11 7651,6240
he reigned *s* years in Jerusalem, ... 2Chr 12:13 7651,6240
of Harim, a thousand and *s* ... Ezr 2:39 7651,6240
of Harim, a thousand and *s* ... Neh 7:42 7651,6240
money, even *s* shekels of silver ... Jer 32:9 7651,6240

SEVENTEENTH {6}

the *s* day of the month, the same ... Gen 7:11 7651,6240
on the *s* day of the month, upon ... Gen 8:4 7651,6240
over Israel in Samaria the *s* year ... 1Kin 22:51 7651,6240
In the *s* year of Pekah the son of ... 2Kin 16:1 7651,6240
The *s* to Hezir, the eighteenth to ... 1Chr 24:15 7651,6240
The *s* to Joshbekashah, he, his ... 1Chr 25:24 7651,6240

SEVENTH {120}

on the *s* day God ended his work ... Gen 2:2 7637
he rested on the *s* day from all ... Gen 2:2 7637
And God blessed the *s* day, and ... Gen 2:3 7637
And the ark rested in the *s* month ... Gen 8:4 7637
the first day until the *s* day ... Ex 12:15 7637
in the *s* day there shall be an ... Ex 12:16 7637
in the *s* day shall be a feast to ... Ex 13:6 7637
but on the *s* day, which is the ... Ex 16:26 7637
people on the *s* day for to gather ... Ex 16:27 7637
go out of his place on the *s* day ... Ex 16:29 7637
So the people rested on the *s* day ... Ex 16:30 7637
But the *s* day is the sabbath of ... Ex 20:10 7637
in them is, and rested the *s* day ... Ex 20:11 7637
in the *s* he shall go out free for ... Ex 21:2 7637
But the *s* year thou shalt let it ... Ex 23:11 7637
on the *s* day thou shalt rest ... Ex 23:12 7637
the *s* day he called unto Moses ... Ex 24:16 7637
but in the *s* is the sabbath of ... Ex 31:15 7637
on the *s* day he rested, and was ... Ex 31:17 7637
but on the *s* day thou shalt rest ... Ex 34:21 7637
but on the *s* day there shall be ... Ex 35:2 7637
shall look on him the *s* day ... Lev 13:5 7637
shall look on him again the *s* day ... Lev 13:6 7637
shall look upon him the *s* day ... Lev 13:27 7637
in the *s* day the priest shall ... Lev 13:32 7637
in the *s* day the priest shall ... Lev 13:34 7637
look on the plague on the *s* day ... Lev 13:51 7637
But it shall be on the *s* day ... Lev 14:9 7637
priest shall come again the *s* day ... Lev 14:39 7637
that in the *s* month, on the tenth ... Lev 16:29 7637
but the *s* day is the sabbath of ... Lev 23:3 7637
in the *s* day is an holy ... Lev 23:8 7637
s sabbath shall ye number fifty ... Lev 23:16 7637
of Israel, saying, In the *s* month ... Lev 23:24 7637
s month there shall be a day of ... Lev 23:27 7637
The fifteenth day of this *s* month ... Lev 23:34 7637
the fifteenth day of the *s* month ... Lev 23:39 7637
shall celebrate it in the *s* month ... Lev 23:41 7637
But in the *s* year shall be a ... Lev 25:4 7637
on the tenth day of the *s* month ... Lev 25:9 7637
say, What shall we eat the *s* year ... Lev 25:20 7637
on the *s* day shall he shave it ... Num 6:9 7637
On the *s* day Elishama the son of ... Num 7:48 7637
on the *s* day he shall be clean ... Num 19:12 7637
then the *s* day he shall not be ... Num 19:12 7637
on the third day, and on the *s* day ... Num 19:19 7637
on the *s* day he shall purify ... Num 19:19 7637
on the *s* day ye shall have an ... Num 28:25 7637
And in the *s* month, on the first ... Num 29:1 7637
this *s* month an holy convocation ... Num 29:7 7637
the *s* month ye shall have an holy ... Num 29:12 7637
on the *s* day seven bullocks, two ... Num 29:32 7637
on the third day, and on the *s* day ... Num 31:19 7637
wash your clothes on the *s* day ... Num 31:24 7637
But the *s* day is the sabbath of ... Deut 5:14 7637
The *s* year, the year of release, ... Deut 15:9 7637
then in the *s* year thou shalt let ... Deut 15:12 7637
on the *s* day shall be a solemn ... Deut 16:8 7637
the *s* day ye shall compass the ... Josh 6:4 7637
And it came to pass on the *s* day ... Josh 6:15 7637
And it came to pass at the *s* time ... Josh 6:16 7637
the *s* lot came out for the tribe ... Josh 19:40 7637
And it came to pass on the *s* day ... Judg 14:15 7637
and it came to pass on the *s* day ... Judg 14:17 7637
s day before the sun went down ... Judg 14:18 7637
And it came to pass on the *s* day ... 2Sa 12:18 7637
Ethanim, which is the *s* month ... 1Kin 8:2 7637
s year of Asa king of Judah, and ... 1Kin 16:10 7651
s year of Asa king of Judah did ... 1Kin 16:15 7651
And it came to pass at the *s* time ... 1Kin 18:44 7637
that in the *s* day the battle was ... 1Kin 20:29 7637
the *s* year Jehoiada sent and ... 2Kin 11:4 7637
In the *s* year of Jehu Jehoash ... 2Kin 12:1 7651
s year of Joash king of Judah ... 2Kin 13:10 7651
s year of Jeroboam king of Israel ... 2Kin 15:1 7651
which was the *s* year of Hoshea ... 2Kin 18:9 7651
on the *s* day of the month, which ... 2Kin 25:8 7651
it came to pass in the *s* month ... 2Kin 25:25 7637
Ozem the sixth, David the *s* ... 1Chr 2:15 7637
Attai the sixth, Eliel the *s* ... 1Chr 12:11 7637
The *s* to Hakkoz, the eighth to ... 1Chr 24:10 7637
The *s* to Jesharelah, he, his sons ... 1Chr 25:14 7637
the sixth, Elioenai the *s* ... 1Chr 26:3 7637
Ammiel the sixth, Issachar the *s* ... 1Chr 26:5 7637
The *s* captain for the *s* ... 1Chr 27:10 7637
feast which was in the *s* month ... 2Chr 5:3 7637
twentieth day of the *s* month he ... 2Chr 7:10 7637
And in the *s* year Jehoiada ... 2Chr 23:1 7637
and finished them in the *s* month ... 2Chr 31:7 7637
when the *s* month was come, and the ... Ezr 3:1 7637
From the first day of the *s* month ... Ezr 3:6 7637
in the *s* year of Artaxerxes the ... Ezr 7:7 7651
was in the *s* year of the king ... Ezr 7:8 7637
when the *s* month came, the ... Neh 7:73 7637
upon the first day of the *s* month ... Neh 8:2 7637
in the feast of the *s* month ... Neh 8:14 7637
and that we would leave the *s* year ... Neh 10:31 7637
On the *s* day, when the heart of ... Est 1:10 7637
in the *s* year of his reign ... Est 2:16 7651
died the same year in the *s* month ... Jer 28:17 7637
it came to pass in the *s* month ... Jer 41:1 7637
in the *s* year three thousand Jews ... Jer 52:28 7651
And it came to pass in the *s* year ... Eze 20:1 7637
in the *s* day of the month, that ... Eze 30:20 7651
so thou shalt do the *s* day of the ... Eze 45:20 7651
In the *s* month, in the fifteenth ... Eze 45:25 7651
In the *s* month, in the one and ... Hag 2:1 7637
s month, even those seventy years ... Zec 7:5 7637
the fifth, and the fast of the *s* ... Zec 8:19 7637
also, and the third, unto the *s* ... Mt 22:26 *2035*
Yesterday at the *s* hour the fever ... Jn 4:52 *1442*
place of the *s* day on this wise ... Heb 4:4 *1442*
God did rest the *s* day from all ... Heb 4:4 *1442*
the *s* from Adam, prophesied of ... Jude 14 *1442*
And when he had opened the *s* seal ... Rev 8:1 *1442*
days of the voice of the *s* angel ... Rev 10:7 *1442*
And the *s* angel sounded ... Rev 11:15 *1442*
the *s* angel poured out his vial ... Rev 16:17 *1442*
the *s*, chrysolite ... Rev 21:20 *1442*

SEVENTY {61}

avenged sevenfold, truly Lamech *s* ... Gen 4:24 7657
And Cainan lived *s* years, and begat ... Gen 5:12 7657
of Lamech were seven hundred *s* ... Gen 5:31 7657
And Terah lived *s* years, and begat ... Gen 11:26 7657
and Abram was *s* and five years old ... Gen 12:4 7657
the loins of Jacob were *s* souls ... Ex 1:5 7657
s of the elders of Israel ... Ex 24:1 7657
s of the elders of Israel ... Ex 24:9 7657
of the thousand seven hundred *s* ... Ex 38:28 7657
of the offering was *s* talents ... Ex 38:29 7657
one silver bowl of *s* shekels ... Num 7:13 7657
one silver bowl of *s* shekels ... Num 7:19 7657
one silver bowl of *s* shekels ... Num 7:25 7657
one silver bowl of *s* shekels ... Num 7:31 7657
one silver bowl of *s* shekels ... Num 7:37 7657
a silver bowl of *s* shekels ... Num 7:43 7657
one silver bowl of *s* shekels ... Num 7:49 7657
one silver bowl of *s* shekels ... Num 7:55 7657
one silver bowl of *s* shekels ... Num 7:61 7657
one silver bowl of *s* shekels ... Num 7:67 7657
one silver bowl of *s* shekels ... Num 7:73 7657
one silver bowl of *s* shekels ... Num 7:79 7657
and thirty shekels, each bowl *s* ... Num 7:85 7657

Gather unto me *s* men of the Num 11:16 7657
gathered the *s* men of the elders Num 11:24 7657
him, and gave it unto the *s* elders Num 11:25 7657
s thousand and five thousand sheep Num 31:32 7657
father, in slaying his *s* brethren Judg 9:56 7657
even to Beer-sheba *s* thousand men 2Sa 24:15 7657
Ahab had *s* sons in Samaria 2Kin 10:1 7657
being *s* persons, were with the 2Kin 10:6 7657
slew *s* persons, and put their 2Kin 10:7 7657
fell of Israel *s* thousand men 1Chr 21:14 7657
Parosh, two thousand an hundred *s* Ezr 2:3 7657
of Shephatiah, three hundred *s* Ezr 2:4 7657
children of Arah, seven hundred *s* Ezr 2:5 7657
house of Jeshua, nine hundred *s* Ezr 2:36 7657
of the children of Hodaviah, *s* Ezr 2:40 7657
of Athaliah, and with him *s* males Ezr 8:7 7657
and Zabbud, and with them *s* males Ezr 8:14 7657
all Israel, ninety and six rams, *s* Ezr 8:35 7657
Parosh, two thousand an hundred *s* Neh 7:8 7657
of Shephatiah, three hundred *s* Neh 7:9 7657
house of Jeshua, nine hundred *s* Neh 7:39 7657
and of the children of Hodevah, *s* Neh 7:43 7657
kept the gates, were an hundred *s* Neh 11:19 7657
enemies, and slew of their foes *s* Est 9:16 7657
Tyre shall be forgotten *s* years Is 23:15 7657
after the end of *s* years shall Is 23:15 7657
to pass after the end of *s* years Is 23:17 7657
serve the king of Babylon *s* years Jer 25:11 7657
when *s* years are accomplished, Jer 25:12 7657
the LORD, That after *s* years be Jer 29:10 7657
there stood before them *s* men of Eze 8:11 7657
the west was *s* cubits broad Eze 41:12 7657
that he would accomplish *s* years Dan 9:2 7657
S weeks are determined upon thy Dan 9:24 7657
seventh month, even those *s* years Zec 7:5 7657
but, Until *s* times seven Mt 18:22 *1441*
the Lord appointed other *s* also Lk 10:1 *1440*
the *s* returned again with joy, Lk 10:17 *1440*

SEVER {4}
I will *s* in that day the land of Ex 8:22 6395
the LORD shall *s* between the Ex 9:4 6395
they shall *s* out men of continual Eze 39:14 914
s the wicked from among the just, Mt 13:49 *873*

SEVERAL See APPENDIX.

SEVERALLY {1}
to every man *s* as he will 1Cor 12:11 *2398*

SEVERED {3}
have *s* you from other people, Lev 20:26 914
Then Moses *s* three cities on this Deut 4:41 914
had *s* himself from the Kenites, Judg 4:11 6504

SEVERITY {2}
the goodness and *s* of God Rom 11:22 *663*
on them which fell, *s* Rom 11:22 *663*

SEW {2}
A time to rend, and a time to *s* Eccl 3:7 8609
Woe to the women that *s* pillows Eze 13:18 8609

SEWED {2}
they *s* fig leaves together, and Gen 3:7 8609
I have *s* sackcloth upon my skin, Job 16:15 8609

SEWEST {1}
a bag, and thou *s* up mine iniquity Job 14:17 2950

SEWETH {1}
No man also *s* a piece of new Mk 2:21 *1976*

SHAALABBIN *(sha-al-ab'-bin)* {1} See SHAALBIM. *A city in Dan.*
And *S*, and Ajalon, and Jethlah, Josh 19:42 8169

SHAALBIM *(sha-al'-bim)* {2} See SHAALABBIN, SHAALBONITE. *Same as Shaalabbin.*
mount Heres in Aijalon, and in *S* Judg 1:35 8169
son of Dekar, in Makaz, and in *S* 1Kin 4:9 8169

SHAALBON See SHAALBONITE.

SHAALBONITE *(sha-al'-bo-nite)* {2} *A native of Shaalabbin.*
Eliahba the *S*, of the sons of 2Sa 23:32 8170
the Baharumite, Eliahba the *S* 1Chr 11:33 8170

SHAALIM See SHALIM.

SHAAPH *(sha'-af)* {2} *A son of Jahdai.*
Gesham, and Pelet, and Ephah, and *S* 1Chr 2:47 8174
She bare also *S* the father of 1Chr 2:49 8174

SHAARAIM *(sha-a-ra'-im)* {2} See SHARAIM, SHARUHEN. *A city in Judah.*
fell down by the way to *S* 1Sa 17:52 8189
and at Beth-birei, and at *S* 1Chr 4:31 8189

SHAASHGAZ *(sha-ash'-gaz)* {1} *A servant of King Ahasuerus.*
of the women, to the custody of *S* Est 2:14 8190

SHABBETHAI *(shab'-be-thahee)* {3}
1. A Levite who dealt with the foreign wife problem.
and *S* the Levite helped them Ezr 10:15 7678
2. A Levite who aided Ezra.
and Sherebiah, Jamin, Akkub, *S* Neh 8:7 7678
3. A family of exiles.
And *S* and Jozabad, of the chief of Neh 11:16 7678

SHACHIA *(sha-ki'-ah)* {1} *A son of Shaharaim.*
And Jeuz, and *S*, and Mirma 1Chr 8:10 7634

SHADE {1}
the LORD is thy *s* upon thy right Ps 121:5 6783

SHADOW {73}
came they under the *s* of my roof Gen 19:8 6738
come and put your trust in my *s* Judg 9:15 6738
Thou seest the *s* of the mountains Judg 9:36 6738
shall the *s* go forward ten 2Kin 20:9 6738
for the *s* to go down ten degrees 2Kin 20:10 6738
but let the *s* return backward ten 2Kin 20:10 6738
he brought the *s* ten degrees 2Kin 20:11 6738
our days on the earth are as a *s* 1Chr 29:15 6738
and the *s* of death stain it Job 3:5 6757
servant earnestly desireth the *s* Job 7:2 6738
our days upon earth are a *s* Job 8:9 6738
of darkness and the *s* of death Job 10:21 6757
of the *s* of death, without any Job 10:22 6738
out to light the *s* of death Job 12:22 6757
he fleeth also as a *s*, and Job 14:2 6738
on my eyelids is the *s* of death Job 16:16 6757
and all my members are as a *s* Job 17:7 6738
is to them even as the *s* of death Job 24:17 6757
in the terrors of the *s* of death Job 24:17 6757
of darkness, and the *s* of death Job 28:3 6757
nor *s* of death, where the workers Job 34:22 6757
seen the doors of the *s* of death Job 38:17 6757
trees cover him with their *s* Job 40:22 6752
hide me under the *s* of thy wings Ps 17:8 6738
the valley of the *s* of death Ps 23:4 6757
trust under the *s* of thy wings Ps 36:7 6738
and covered us with the *s* of death Ps 44:19 6757
in the *s* of thy wings will I make Ps 57:1 6738
therefore in the *s* of thy wings Ps 63:7 6738
were covered with the *s* of it Ps 80:10 6738
abide under the *s* of the Almighty Ps 91:1 6738
days are like a *s* that declineth Ps 102:11 6738
in the *s* of death, being bound in Ps 107:10 6757
the *s* of death, and brake their Ps 107:14 6738
gone like the *s* when it declineth Ps 109:23 6738
days are as a *s* that passeth away Ps 144:4 6738
life which he spendeth as a *s* Eccl 6:12 6738
his days, which are as a *s* Eccl 8:13 6738
under his *s* with great delight Song 2:3 6738
shall be a tabernacle for a *s* in Is 4:6 6738
in the land of the *s* of death Is 9:2 6757
make thy *s* as the night in the Is 16:3 6738
a *s* from the heat, when the blast Is 25:4 6738
the heat with the *s* of a cloud Is 25:5 6738
and to trust in the *s* of Egypt Is 30:2 6738
the trust in the *s* of Egypt your Is 30:3 6738
as the *s* of a great rock in a Is 32:2 6738
and hatch, and gather under her *s* Is 34:15 6738
bring again the *s* of the degrees Is 38:8 6738
in the *s* of his hand hath he hid Is 49:2 6738
thee in the *s* of mine hand Is 51:16 6738
of the *s* of death, through a land Jer 2:6 6757
he turn it into the *s* of death Jer 13:16 6757
They that fled stood under the *s* Jer 48:45 6738
Under his *s* we shall live among Lam 4:20 6738
in the *s* of the branches thereof Eze 17:23 6738
under his *s* dwelt all great Eze 31:6 6738
earth are gone down from his *s* Eze 31:12 6738
that dwelt under his *s* in the Eze 31:17 6738
of the field had *s* under it Dan 4:12 2927
because the *s* thereof is good Hos 4:13 6738
dwell under his *s* shall return Hos 14:7 6738
turneth the *s* of death into the Amos 5:8 6757
a booth, and sat under it in the *s* Jonah 4:5 6738
it might be a *s* over his head Jonah 4:6 6738
s of death light is sprung up Mt 4:16 *4639*
air may lodge under the *s* of it Mk 4:32 *4639*
in the *s* of death, to guide our Lk 1:79 *4639*
that at the least the *s* of Peter Acts 5:15 *4639*
Which are a *s* of things to come Col 2:17 *4639*
s of heavenly things, as Moses Heb 8:5 *4639*
For the law having a *s* of good Heb 10:1 *4639*
neither *s* of turning Jas 1:17 *644*

SHADOWING {3}
Woe to the land *s* with wings Is 18:1 6767
fair branches, and with a *s* shroud Eze 31:3 6751
of glory *s* the mercyseat Heb 9:5 *2683*

SHADOWS {3}
the *s* flee away, turn, my beloved Song 2:17 6752
the *s* flee away, I will get me to Song 4:6 6752
for the *s* of the evening are Jer 6:4 6752

SHADRACH *(sha'-drak)* {15} See HANANIAH. *A companion of Daniel.*
and to Hananiah, of *S* Dan 1:7 7714
of the king, and he set *S*, Meshach Dan 2:49 7715
of the province of Babylon, *S* Dan 3:12 7715
rage and fury commanded to bring *S* Dan 3:13 7715
said unto them, Is it true, O *S* Dan 3:14 7715
S, Meshach, and Abed-nego, Dan 3:16 7715
his visage was changed against *S* Dan 3:19 7715
that were in his army to bind *S* Dan 3:20 7715
slew those men that took up *S* Dan 3:22 7715
And these three men, *S*, Meshach, Dan 3:23 7715
furnace, and spake, and said, *S* Dan 3:26 7715
Then *S*, Meshach, and Abed-nego, Dan 3:26 7715
and said, Blessed be the God of *S* Dan 3:28 7715
thing amiss against the God of *S* Dan 3:29 7715
Then the king promoted *S*, Meshach Dan 3:30 7715

SHADY {2}
He lieth under the *s* trees Job 40:21 6628
The *s* trees cover him with their Job 40:22 6628

SHAFT {4}
his *s*, and his branches, his bowls Ex 25:31 3409
his *s*, and his branch, his bowls, Ex 37:17 3409
beaten gold, unto the *s* thereof Num 8:4 3409
hid me, and made me a polished *s* Is 49:2 2671

SHAGE *(sha'-ghe)* {1} *A "mighty man" of David.*
the son of *S* the Hararite 1Chr 11:34 7681

SHAGEE See SHAGE.

SHAGEH See SHAGE.

SHAHAR *(sha'-har)* {1} *A musical notation.*
chief Musician upon Aijeleth *S* Ps 22:*t* 7837

SHAHARAIM *(sha-ha-ra'-im)* {1} *A Benjamite from Moab.*
S begat children in the country 1Chr 8:8 7842

SHAHAZIMAH *(sha-haz'-i-mah)* {1} *A city in Issachar.*
the coast reacheth to Tabor, and *S* Josh 19:22 7831

SHAHAZUMAH See SHAHAZIMAH.

SHAKE {39}
other times before, and *s* myself Judg 16:20 5287
So God *s* out every man from his Neh 5:13 5287
which made all my bones to *s* Job 4:14 6342
He shall *s* off his unripe grape Job 15:33 2554
you, and *s* mine head at you Job 16:4 5128
the lip, they *s* the head, saying, Ps 22:7 5128
though the mountains *s* with the Ps 46:3 7493
make their loins continually to *s* Ps 69:23 4571
thereof shall *s* like Lebanon Ps 72:16 7493
ariseth to *s* terribly the earth Is 2:19 6206
ariseth to *s* terribly the earth Is 2:21 6206
as if the rod should *s* itself Is 10:15 5130
he shall *s* his hand against the Is 10:32 5130
he *s* his hand over the river Is 11:15 5130
s the hand, that they may go into Is 13:2 5130
Therefore I will *s* the heavens Is 13:13 7264
to tremble, that did *s* kingdoms Is 14:16 7493
the foundations of the earth do *s* Is 24:18 7493
Carmel *s* off their fruits Is 33:9 5287
S thyself from the dust Is 52:2 5287
all my bones *s* Jer 23:9 7363
thy walls shall *s* at the noise of Eze 26:10 7493
Shall not the isles *s* at the Eze 26:15 7493
The suburbs shall *s* at the sound Eze 27:28 7493
I made the nations to *s* at the Eze 31:16 7493
shall *s* at my presence, and the Eze 38:20 7493
s off his leaves, and scatter his Dan 4:14 5426
the heavens and the earth shall *s* Joel 3:16 7493
of the door, that the posts may *s* Amos 9:1 7493
I will *s* the heavens, and the Hag 2:6 7493
I will *s* all nations, and the Hag 2:7 7493
I will *s* the heavens and the earth Hag 2:21 7493
I will *s* mine hand upon them, and Zec 2:9 5130
s off the dust of your feet Mt 10:14 *1621*
for fear of him the keepers did *s* Mt 28:4 *4579*
s off the dust under your feet Mk 6:11 *1621*
that house, and could not *s* it Lk 6:48 *4531*
s off the very dust from your Lk 9:5 *660*
Yet once more I *s* not the earth Heb 12:26 *4579*

SHAKED {1}
looked upon me they *s* their heads Ps 109:25 5128

SHAKEN {22}
the sound of a *s* leaf shall chase Lev 26:36 5086
as a reed is *s* in the water 1Kin 14:15 5110
Jerusalem hath *s* her head at thee 2Kin 19:21 5128
promise, even thus be he *s* out Neh 5:13 5287
s me to pieces, and set me up for Job 16:12 6327
the wicked might be *s* out of it Job 38:13 5287
also of the hills moved and were *s* Ps 18:7 1607
Jerusalem hath *s* her head at thee Is 37:22 5128
the fir trees shall be terribly *s* Nah 2:3 7477
if they be *s*, they shall even Nah 3:12 5128
A reed *s* with the wind Mt 11:7 *4531*
powers of the heavens shall be *s* Mt 24:29 *4531*
that are in heaven shall be *s* Mk 13:25 *4531*
s together, and running over, Lk 6:38 *4531*
A reed *s* with the wind Lk 7:24 *4531*
the powers of heaven shall be *s* Lk 21:26 *4531*
the place was *s* where they were Acts 4:31 *4531*
foundations of the prison were *s* Acts 16:26 *4531*
That ye be not soon *s* in mind 2Th 2:2 *4531*
of those things that are *s* Heb 12:27 *4531*
which cannot be *s* may remain Heb 12:27 *4531*
when she is *s* of a mighty wind Rev 6:13 *4579*

SHAKETH {7}
Which *s* the earth out of her Job 9:6 7264
of the LORD *s* the wilderness Ps 29:8 2342
the LORD *s* the wilderness of Ps 29:8 2342
thereof; for it *s* Ps 60:2 4131
itself against him that *s* it Is 10:15 5130
LORD of hosts, which he *s* over it Is 19:16 5130
that *s* his hands from holding of Is 33:15 5287

SHAKING {8}
he laugheth at the *s* of a spear Job 41:29 7494
a *s* of the head among the people Ps 44:14 4493
as the *s* of an olive tree, two or Is 17:6 5363
fear because of the *s* of the hand Is 19:16 8573
be as the *s* of an olive tree Is 24:13 5363
in battles of *s* will he fight Is 30:32 8573
there was a noise, and behold a *s* Eze 37:7 7494
a great *s* in the land of Israel Eze 38:19 7494

SHALEM *(sha'-lem)* {1} *A city in Ephraim.*
And Jacob came to *S*, a city of Gen 33:18 8003

SHALIM *(sha'-lim)* {1} *A district in Dan.*
they passed through the land of *S* 1Sa 9:4 8171

SHALISHA *(shal'-i-shah)* {1} *A district in Ephraim.*
and passed through the land of *S* 1Sa 9:4 8031

SHALISHAH See SHALISHA.

SHALL See APPENDIX.

SHALLECHETH *(shal'-le-keth)* {1} *A gate of the First Temple.*
forth westward, with the gate *S* 1Chr 26:16 7996

SHALLIM See Shalim.

SHALLUM *(shal'-lum)* {27} See Jehoahaz, Meshelemiah, Shillem.
1. A king of Israel.
S the son of Jabesh conspired 2Kin 15:10 7967
S the son of Jabesh began to 2Kin 15:13 7967
smote *S* the son of Jabesh in 2Kin 15:14 7967
And the rest of the acts of *S* 2Kin 15:15 7967
2. Husband of Huldah.
the wife of *S* the son of Tikvah, 2Kin 22:14 7967
the wife of *S* the son of Tikvath, 2Chr 34:22 7967
3. A descendant of Jerahmeel.
begat Sisamai, and Sisamai begat *S* 1Chr 2:40 7967
S begat Jekamiah, and Jekamiah 1Chr 2:41 7967
4. A son of King Josiah.
the third Zedekiah, the fourth *S* 1Chr 3:15 7967
thus saith the Lord touching *S* Jer 22:11 7967
5. Grandson of Simeon.
S his son, Mibsam his son, Mishma 1Chr 4:25 7967
6. Father of Hilkiah.
begat Zadok, and Zadok begat *S* 1Chr 6:12 7967
S begat Hilkiah, and Hilkiah begat 1Chr 6:13 7967
The son of *S*, the son of Zadok, Ezr 7:2 7967
7. Son of Naphtali.
Jahziel, and Guni, and Jezer, and *S* 1Chr 7:13 7967
8. A family of exiles.
And the porters were, *S*, and Akkub, 1Chr 9:17 7967
S was the chief 1Chr 9:17 7967
S the son of Kore, the son of 1Chr 9:19 7967
the firstborn of *S* the Korahite 1Chr 9:31 7967
the children of *S*, the children Ezr 2:42 7967
the children of *S*, the children Neh 7:45 7967
9. Father of Jehizkiah.
and Jehizkiah the son of *S* 2Chr 28:12 7967
10. A gatekeeper who married a foreigner.
S, and Telem, and Uri Ezr 10:24 7967
11. A son of Bani who married a foreigner.
S, Amariah, and Joseph Ezr 10:42 7967
12. A rebuilder of Jerusalem's wall.
repaired *S* the son of Halohesh Neh 3:12 7967
13. Father of Hanameel.
Hanameel the son of *S* thine uncle Jer 32:7 7967
14. Father of Maaseiah.
chamber of Maaseiah the son of *S* Jer 35:4 7967

SHALLUN *(shal'-lun)* {1} *A rebuilder of Jerusalem's wall.*
repaired *S* the son of Colhozeh Neh 3:15 7968

SHALMAI *(shal'-mahee)* {2} *A family of exiles.*
of Hagab, the children of *S* Ezr 2:46 8073
of Hagaba, the children of *S* Neh 7:48 8014

SHALMAN *(shal'-man)* {1} See Shalmaneser. *A king of Assyria.*
as *S* spoiled Beth-arbel in the Hos 10:14 8020

SHALMANESER *(shal-man-e'-zer)* {2} See Shalman. *A king of Assyria.*
him came up *S* king of Assyria 2Kin 17:3 8022
that *S* king of Assyria came up 2Kin 18:9 8022

SHALT See APPENDIX.

SHAMA *(sha'-mah)* {1} *A "mighty man" of David.*
Uzzia the Ashterathite, *S* 1Chr 11:44 8091

SHAMARIAH {1} *Son of Rehoboam.*
Jeush, and *S*, and Zaham 2Chr 11:19

SHAMBLES {1}
Whatsoever is sold in the *s* 1Cor 10:25 *3111*

SHAME {100}
unto their *s* among their enemies Ex 32:25 8103
might put them to *s* in any thing Judg 18:7 3637
because his father had done him *s* 1Sa 20:34 3637
whither shall I cause my *s* to go 2Sa 13:13 2781
So he returned with *s* of face to 2Chr 32:21 1322
hate thee shall be clothed with *s* Job 8:22 1322
long will ye turn my glory into *s* Ps 4:2 3639
put to *s* that seek after my soul Ps 35:4 3637
let them be clothed with *s* Ps 35:26 1322
put to *s* that wish me evil Ps 40:14 3637
of their *s* that say unto me Ps 40:15 1322
hast put them to *s* that hated us Ps 44:7 954
hast cast off, and put us to *s* Ps 44:9 3637
the *s* of my face hath covered me, Ps 44:15 1322
thou hast put them to *s*, because Ps 53:5 954
s hath covered my face Ps 69:7 3639
hast known my reproach, and my *s* Ps 69:19 1322
for a reward of their *s* that say Ps 70:3 1322
for they are brought unto *s* Ps 71:24 2659
Fill their faces with *s* Ps 83:16 7036
yea, let them be put to *s* Ps 83:17 2659
thou hast covered him with *s* Ps 89:45 955
adversaries be clothed with *s* Ps 109:29 3639
O Lord, put me not to *s* Ps 119:31 954
His enemies will I clothe with *s* Ps 132:18 1322
but *s* shall be the promotion of Prov 3:35 7036
a scorner getteth to himself *s* Prov 9:7 7036
harvest is a son that causeth *s* Prov 10:5 954
When pride cometh, then cometh *s* Prov 11:2 7036
but a prudent man covereth *s* Prov 12:16 7036
man is loathsome, and cometh to *s* Prov 13:5 2659
s shall be to him that refuseth Prov 13:18 7036
is against him that causeth *s* Prov 14:35 954
rule over a son that causeth *s* Prov 17:2 954
it, it is folly and *s* unto him Prov 18:13 3639
mother, is a son that causeth *s* Prov 19:26 954
thy neighbour hath put thee to *s* Prov 25:8 3637
he that heareth it put thee to *s* Prov 25:10 2616
himself bringeth his mother to *s* Prov 29:15 954
uncovered, to the *s* of Egypt Is 20:4 6172
be the *s* of thy lord's house Is 22:18 7036
the strength of Pharaoh be your *s* Is 30:3 1322
be an help nor profit, but a *s* Is 30:5 1322
yea, thy *s* shall be seen Is 47:3 2781
I hid not my face from *s* and Is 50:6 3639
for thou shalt not be put to *s* Is 54:4 2659
shalt forget the *s* of thy youth Is 54:4 1322
For your *s* ye shall have double Is 61:7 1322
For *s* hath devoured the labour of Jer 3:24 1322
We lie down in our *s*, and our Jer 3:25 1322
thy face, that thy *s* may appear Jer 13:26 7036
my days should be consumed with *s* Jer 20:18 1322
upon you, and a perpetual *s* Jer 23:40 3640
The nations have heard of thy *s* Jer 46:12 7036
hath Moab turned the back with *s* Jer 48:39 954
s hath covered our faces Jer 51:51 3639
s shall be upon all faces, and Eze 7:18 955
bear thine own *s* for thy sins Eze 16:52 3639
confounded also, and bear thy *s* Eze 16:52 3639
That thou mayest bear thine own *s* Eze 16:54 3639
mouth any more because of thy *s* Eze 16:63 3639
yet have they borne their *s* with Eze 32:24 3639
yet have they borne their *s* with Eze 32:25 3639
bear their *s* with them that go Eze 32:30 3639
neither bear the *s* of the heathen Eze 34:29 3639
have borne the *s* of the heathen Eze 36:6 3639
you, they shall bear their *s* Eze 36:7 3639
the *s* of the heathen any more Eze 36:15 3639
that they have borne their *s* Eze 39:26 3639
but they shall bear their *s* Eze 44:13 3639
to everlasting life, and some to *s* Dan 12:2 2781
will I change their glory into *s* Hos 4:7 7036
her rulers with *s* do love Hos 4:18 7036
separated themselves unto that *s* Hos 9:10 1322
Ephraim shall receive *s*, and Hos 10:6 1317
brother Jacob *s* shall cover thee Obad 10 955
of Saphir, having thy *s* naked Mic 1:11 1322
them, that they shall not take *s* Mic 2:6 3639
s shall cover her which said unto Mic 7:10 955
nakedness, and the kingdoms thy *s* Nah 3:5 7036
Thou hast consulted *s* to thy Hab 2:10 1322
Thou art filled with *s* for glory Hab 2:16 7036
but the unjust knoweth no *s* Zeph 3:5 1322
where they have been put to *s* Zeph 3:19 1322
thou begin with *s* to take the Lk 14:9 *152*
worthy to suffer *s* for his name Acts 5:41 *818*
I write not these things to *s* you 1Cor 4:14 *1788*
I speak to your *s* 1Cor 6:5 *1791*
but if it be a *s* for a woman to 1Cor 11:6 *149*
long hair, it is a *s* unto him 1Cor 11:14 *819*
of God, and *s* them that have not 1Cor 11:22 *2617*
for it is a *s* for women to speak 1Cor 14:35 *149*
I speak this to your *s* 1Cor 15:34 *1791*
For it is a *s* even to speak of Eph 5:12 *149*
and whose glory is in their *s* Phil 3:19 *152*
afresh, and put him to an open *s* Heb 6:6 *3856*
the cross, despising the *s* Heb 12:2 *152*
the sea, foaming out their own *s* Jude 13 *152*
that the *s* of thy nakedness do Rev 3:18 *152*
he walk naked, and they see his *s* Rev 16:15 *808*

SHAMED *(sha'-med)* {4} *A son of Elpaal.*
her take it to her, lest we be *s* Gen 38:23 937
said Thou hast *s* this day the 2Sa 19:5 3001
Eber, and Misham, and *S*, who built 1Chr 8:12 8106
Ye have *s* the counsel of the poor Ps 14:6 954

SHAMEFACEDNESS {1}
in modest apparel, with *s* 1Ti 2:9 *127*

SHAMEFUL {2}
ye set up altars to that *s* thing Jer 11:13 1322
s spewing shall be on thy glory Hab 2:16 7022

SHAMEFULLY {4}
that conceived them hath done *s* Hos 2:5 3001
head, and sent him away *s* handled Mk 12:4 *821*
beat him also, and entreated him *s* Lk 20:11 *818*
were *s* entreated, as ye know, at 1Th 2:2 *5195*

SHAMELESSLY {1}
vain fellows *s* uncovereth himself 2Sa 6:20 1540

SHAMER *(sha'-mur)* {2} See Shomer.
1. Son of Mahli.
the son of Bani, the son of *S* 1Chr 6:46 8106
2. Son of Heber.
And the sons of *S* 1Chr 7:34 8106

SHAMETH {1}
of riotous men *s* his father Prov 28:7 3637

SHAMGAR *(sham'-gar)* {2} *A judge of Israel.*
after him was *S* the son of Anath, Judg 3:31 8044
In the days of *S* the son of Anath Judg 5:6 8044

SHAMHUTH *(sham'-huth)* {1} See Shammoth. *A captain in David's army.*
fifth month was *S* the Izrahite 1Chr 27:8 8049

SHAMIR *(sha'-mur)* {4}
1. A city in Judah.
And in the mountains, *S*, and Jattir Josh 15:48 8069
2. A city near Mt. Ephraim.
he dwelt in *S* in mount Ephraim Judg 10:1 8069
and died, and was buried in *S* Judg 10:2 8069
3. Son of Micah the Levite.
the sons of Michah; *S* 1Chr 24:24 8053

SHAMLAI See Samlah.

SHAMMA *(sham'-mah)* {1} See Shammah. *A son of Zophah.*
Bezer, and Hod, and *S*, and Shilshah, 1Chr 7:37 8037

SHAMMAH *(sham'-mah)* {8} See Shamma, Shammoth, Shimea, Shimma.
1. A son of Reuel.
Nahath, and Zerah, *S*, and Mizzah Gen 36:13 8048
duke Nahath, duke Zerah, duke *S* Gen 36:17 8048
Nahath, Zerah, *S*, and Mizzah 1Chr 1:37 8048
2. A son of Jesse.
Then Jesse made *S* to pass by 1Sa 16:9 8048
unto him Abinadab, and the third *S* 1Sa 17:13 8048
3. A "mighty man" of David.
after him was *S* the son of Agee 2Sa 23:11 8048
4. A Hararite "mighty man" of David.
S the Hararite, Ahiam the son of 2Sa 23:33 8048
5. A Harodite "mighty man" of David.
S the Harodite, Elika the 2Sa 23:25 8048

SHAMMAI *(sham'-mahee)* {6}
1. A son of Onan.
And the sons of Onam were, *S* 1Chr 2:28 8060
And the sons of *S* 1Chr 2:28 8060
the sons of Jada the brother of *S* 1Chr 2:32 8060
2. Father of Maon.
and Rekem begat *S* 1Chr 2:44 8060
And the son of *S* was Maon 1Chr 2:45 8060
3. A descendant of Caleb.
and she bare Miriam, and *S*, and 1Chr 4:17 8060

SHAMMOTH *(sham'-moth)* {1} See Shammah, Shamhuth. *A "mighty man" of David.*
S the Harorite, Helez the 1Chr 11:27 8054

SHAMMUA *(sham-mu'-ah)* {4} See Shammuah, Shemaiah, Shimea.
1. A spy sent to the Promised Land.
of Reuben, *S* the son of Zaccur Num 13:4 8051
2. A son of David.
S, and Shobab, Nathan, and Solomon, 1Chr 14:4 8051
3. A family of exiles.
brethren, and Abda the son of *S* Neh 11:17 8051
4. A priest with Zerubbabel.
Of Bilgah, *S* Neh 12:18 8051

SHAMMUAH *(sham-mu'-ah)* {1} See Shammua. *Same as Shammua 2.*
S, and Shobab, and Nathan, and 2Sa 5:14 8051

SHAMSHERAI *(sham'-she-rahee)* {1} *A son of Jeroham.*
And *S*, and Sheharíah, and Athaliah, 1Chr 8:26 8125

SHAPE {2}
a bodily *s* like a dove upon him Lk 3:22 *1491*
voice at any time, nor seen his *s* Jn 5:37 *1491*

SHAPEN {1}
Behold, I was *s* in iniquity Ps 51:5 2342

SHAPES {1}
the *s* of the locusts were like Rev 9:7 *3667*

SHAPHAM *(sha'-fam)* {1} *A Gadite chief.*
S the next, and Jaanai, and Shaphat 1Chr 5:12 8223

SHAPHAN *(sha'-fan)* {30}
1. A scribe in Josiah's time.
king sent *S* the son of Azaliah 2Kin 22:3 8227
priest said unto *S* the scribe 2Kin 22:8 8227
And Hilkiah gave the book to *S* 2Kin 22:8 8227
S the scribe came to the king, and 2Kin 22:9 8227
S the scribe shewed the king, 2Kin 22:10 8227
S read it before the king 2Kin 22:10 8227
S the scribe, and Asahiah a 2Kin 22:12 8227
and Ahikam, and Achbor, and *S* 2Kin 22:14 8227
he sent *S* the son of Azaliah, and 2Chr 34:8 8227
said to *S* the scribe, I have 2Chr 34:15 8227
Hilkiah delivered the book to *S* 2Chr 34:15 8227
S carried the book to the king, 2Chr 34:16 8227
Then *S* the scribe told the king, 2Chr 34:18 8227
S read it before the king 2Chr 34:18 8227
S the scribe, and Asaiah a servant 2Chr 34:20 8227
Gemariah the son of *S* the scribe Jer 36:10 8227
the son of Gemariah, the son of *S* Jer 36:11 8227
Achbor, and Gemariah the son of *S* Jer 36:12 8227
2. Father of Ahikam.
priest, and Ahikam the son of *S* 2Kin 22:12 8227
the son of Ahikam, the son of *S* 2Kin 25:22 8227
Hilkiah, and Ahikam the son of *S* 2Chr 34:20 8227
the son of *S* was with Jeremiah Jer 26:24 8227
the son of Ahikam the son of *S* Jer 39:14 8227
the son of Ahikam the son of *S* Jer 40:5 8227
the son of *S* sware unto them Jer 40:9 8227
the son of Ahikam the son of *S* Jer 40:11 8227
the son of *S* with the sword Jer 41:2 8227
the son of Ahikam the son of *S* Jer 43:6 8227
3. Messenger for Jeremiah.
the hand of Elasah the son of *S* Jer 29:3 8227
4. Father of Jaazaniah.
them stood Jaazaniah the son of *S* Eze 8:11 8227

SHAPHAT *(sha'-fat)* {8}
1. A spy sent to the Promised Land.
of Simeon, *S* the son of Hori Num 13:5 8202
2. Father of Elisha the prophet.
and Elisha the son of *S* of 1Kin 19:16 8202
and found Elisha the son of *S* 1Kin 19:19 8202
said, Here is Elisha the son of *S* 2Kin 3:11 8202
of *S* shall stand on him this day 2Kin 6:31 8202
3. A grandson of Shechaniah.
and Bariah, and Neariah, and *S* 1Chr 3:22 8202
4. A chief Gadite.
next, and Jaanai, and *S* in Bashan 1Chr 5:12 8202
5. A shepherd of David's herds.
valleys was *S* the son of Adlai 1Chr 27:29 8202

SHAPHER *(sha'-fur)* {2} *An Israelite encampment in the wilderness.*
Kehelathah, and pitched in mount *S* ...... Num 33:23 8234
And they removed from mount *S* .... Num 33:24 8234

SHAPHIR See SHAPHER.

SHARAI *(sha'-rahee)* {1} *Married a foreigner in exile.*
Machnadebai, Shashai, *S*, ... Ezr 10:40 8298

SHARAIM *(sha-ra'-im)* {1} See SHAARAIM. *Same as Shaaraim.*
And *S*, and Adithaim, and Gederah, and Josh 15:36 8189

SHARAR *(sha'-rar)* {1} See SARAR. *A "mighty man" of David.*
Ahiam the son of *S* the Hararite 2Sa 23:33 8325

SHARE {1}
to sharpen every man his *s* 1Sa 13:20 4282

SHAREZER *(sha-re'-zur)* {2} See SHEREZER. *Son of Sennacherib.*
S his sons smote him with the................ 2Kin 19:37 8272
S his sons smote him with the................ Is 37:38 8272

SHARON *(sha'-run)* {6} See SARON, SHARONITE.
1. A plain of Ephraim.
in *S* was Shitrai the Sharonite................ 1Chr 27:29 8289
I am the rose of *S*, and the lily .... Song 2:1 8289
S is like a wilderness............................. Is 33:9 8289
it, the excellency of Carmel and *S* .... Is 35:2 8289
S shall be a fold of flocks, and.............. Is 65:10 8289
2. A plain or city in Gad.
towns, and in all the suburbs of *S* 1Chr 5:16 8289

SHARONITE *(sha'-run-ite)* {1} *An inhabitant of Sharon 1.*
fed in Sharon was Shitrai the *S*............. 1Chr 27:29 8290

SHARP {25}
Then Zipporah took a *s* stone .... Ex 4:25 6864
unto Joshua, Make thee *s* knives .... Josh 5:2 6697
And Joshua made him *s* knives .... Josh 5:3 6697
there was a *s* rock on the one 1Sa 14:4 8127
a *s* rock on the other side 1Sa 14:4 8127
S stones are under him........................... Job 41:30 2303
he spreadeth *s* pointed things .... Job 41:30 2742
Thine arrows are *s* in the heart .... Ps 45:5 8150
like a *s* rasor, working .... Ps 52:2 3913
arrows, and their tongue a *s* sword .... Ps 57:4 2299
S arrows of the mighty, with.................. Ps 120:4 8150
wormwood, *s* as a twoedged sword .... Prov 5:4 2299
a maul, and a sword, and a *s* arrow .... Prov 25:18 8150
Whose arrows are *s*, and all their............ Is 5:28 8150
Behold, I will make thee a new *s* .... Is 41:15 2742
hath made my mouth like a *s* sword .... Is 49:2 2299
son of man, take thee a *s* knife................ Eze 5:1 2299
contention was so *s* between them .... Acts 15:39
his mouth went a *s* twoedged sword .... Rev 1:16 *3691*
hath the *s* sword with two edges.............. Rev 2:12 *3691*
crown, and in his hand a *s* sickle .... Rev 14:14 *3691*
heaven, he also having a *s* sickle .... Rev 14:17 *3691*
cry to him that had the *s* sickle............... Rev 14:18 *3691*
saying, Thrust in thy *s* sickle.................. Rev 14:18 *3691*
out of his mouth goeth a *s* sword .... Rev 19:15 *3691*

SHARPEN {2}
to *s* every man his share, and his 1Sa 13:20 3913
for the axes, and to *s* the goads.............. 1Sa 13:21 5324

SHARPENED {4}
They have *s* their tongues like a............. Ps 140:3 8150
Say, A sword, a sword is *s* .... Eze 21:9 2300
It is *s* to make a sore slaughter .... Eze 21:10 2300
this sword is *s*, and it is......................... Eze 21:11 2300

SHARPENETH {3}
mine enemy *s* his eyes upon me............... Job 16:9 3913
Iron *s* iron .... Prov 27:17 2300
so a man *s* the countenance of his........... Prov 27:17 2300

SHARPER {2}
upright is *s* than a thorn hedge .... Mic 7:4
s than any twoedged sword, ... Heb 4:12 *5114*

SHARPLY {2}
And they did chide with him *s*................. Judg 8:1 2394
Wherefore rebuke them *s*, that................ Titus 1:13 *664*

SHARPNESS {1}
lest being present I should use *s* 2Cor 13:10 *664*

SHARUHEN *(sha-ru'-hen)* {1} See SHAARAIM, SHILHIM. *A city in Simeon.*
And Beth-lebaoth, and *S*......................... Josh 19:6 8287

SHASHAI *(sha'-shahee)* {1} *Married a foreigner in exile.*
Machnadebai, *S*, Sharai, ... Ezr 10:40 8343

SHASHAK *(sha'-shak)* {2} *A son of Elpaal.*
And Ahio, *S*, and Jeremoth, ... 1Chr 8:14 8349
and Penuel, the sons of *S* 1Chr 8:25 8349

SHAUL *(sha'-ul)* {7} See SAUL, SHAULITES.
1. A son of Simeon.
S the son of a Canaanitish woman.......... Gen 46:10 7586
S the son of a Canaanitish woman.......... Ex 6:15 7586
of *S*, the family of the Shaulites .... Num 26:13 7586
and Jamin, Jarib, Zerah, and *S* 1Chr 4:24 7586
2. A king of Edom.
S of Rehoboth by the river 1Chr 1:48 7586
when *S* was dead, Baal-hanan the 1Chr 1:49 7586
3. Son of Kohath.
son, Uzziah his son, and *S* his son 1Chr 6:24 7586

SHAULITES *(sha'-ul-ites)* {1} *Decendants of Shaul 1.*
of Shaul, the family of the *S* .... Num 26:13 7587

SHAVE {14}
but the scall shall he not *s* .... Lev 13:33 1548
s off all his hair, and wash .... Lev 14:8 1548
that he shall *s* all his hair off .... Lev 14:9 1548
even all his hair he shall *s* off .... Lev 14:9 1548
neither shall they *s* off the .... Lev 21:5 1548
then he shall *s* his head in the................ Num 6:9 1548
on the seventh day shall he *s* it .... Num 6:9 1548
the Nazarite shall *s* the head of .... Num 6:18 1548
let them *s* all their flesh, and .... Num 8:7 5674,8593
and she shall *s* her head, and pare .... Deut 21:12 1548
she caused him to *s* off the seven .... Judg 16:19 1548
Lord *s* with a razor that is hired............. Is 7:20 1548
Neither shall they *s* their heads .... Eze 44:20 1548
them, that they may *s* their heads........... Acts 21:24 *3587*

SHAVED {4}
he *s* himself, and changed his .... Gen 41:14 1548
s off the one half of their......................... 2Sa 10:4 1548
s them, and cut off their garments.......... 1Chr 19:4 1548
s his head, and fell down upon the .... Job 1:20 1494

SHAVEH *(sha'-veh)* {2} *A valley near Aenon.*
Ham, and the Emims in *S* Kiriathaim .... Gen 14:5 7741
were with him, at the valley of *S*............ Gen 14:17 7740

SHAVEN {7}
He shall be *s*, but the scall .... Lev 13:33 1548
the hair of his separation is *s* .... Num 6:19 1548
if I be *s*, then my strength will .... Judg 16:17 1548
to grow again after he was *s* .... Judg 16:22 1548
men, having their beards *s* .... Jer 41:5 1548
is even all one as if she were *s* 1Cor 11:5 *3587*
for a woman to be shorn or *s* 1Cor 11:6 *3587*

SHAVSHA *(shav'-shah)* {1} See SERAIAH, SHEVA, SHISHA. *David's scribe.*
and *S* was scribe.................................... 1Chr 18:16 7798

SHE See APPENDIX.

SHEAF {9}
my *s* arose, and also stood upright.......... Gen 37:7 485
about, and made obeisance to my *s*.......... Gen 37:7 485
then ye shall bring a *s* of the.................. Lev 23:10 6016
shall wave the *s* before the LORD .... Lev 23:11 6016
s an he lamb without blemish of.............. Lev 23:12 6016
the *s* of the wave offering .... Lev 23:15 6016
and hast forgot a *s* in the field .... Deut 24:19 6016
take away the *s* from the hungry............ Job 24:10 6016
and like a torch of fire in a *s*.................. Zec 12:6 5995

SHEAL *(she'-al)* {1} *Married a foreigner in exile.*
Malluch, and Adaiah, Jashub, and *S*....... Ezr 10:29 7594

SHEALTIEL *(she-al'-te-el)* {9} See SALATHIEL. *Father of Zerubbabel.*
and Zerubbabel the son of *S* .... Ezr 3:2 7597
began Zerubbabel the son of *S* .... Ezr 3:8 7597
rose up Zerubbabel the son of *S* .... Ezr 5:2 7597
up with Zerubbabel the son of *S* .... Neh 12:1 7597
unto Zerubbabel the son of *S*.................. Hag 1:1 7597
Then Zerubbabel the son of *S*................. Hag 1:12 7597
spirit of Zerubbabel the son of *S* .... Hag 1:14 7597
now to Zerubbabel the son of *S* .... Hag 2:2 7597
my servant, the son of *S* .... Hag 2:23 7597

SHEAR {4}
And Laban went to *s* his sheep .... Gen 31:19 1494
up to Timnath to *s* his sheep .... Gen 38:13 1494
nor *s* the firstling of thy sheep .... Deut 15:19 1494
that Nabal did *s* his sheep....................... 1Sa 25:4 1494

SHEARER {1}
and like a lamb dumb before his *s* .... Acts 8:32 *2751*

SHEARERS {3}
now I have heard that thou hast *s*........... 1Sa 25:7 1494
flesh that I have killed for my *s* 1Sa 25:11 1494
as a sheep before her *s* is dumb .... Is 53:7 1494

SHEARIAH *(she-a-ri'-ah)* {2} *Son of Azel.*
Bocheru, and Ishmael, and *S*.................. 1Chr 8:38 8187
Bocheru, and Ishmael, and *S*.................. 1Chr 9:44 8187

SHEARING {3}
he was *s* his sheep in Carmel 1Sa 25:2 1494
he was at the *s* house in the way..... 2Kin 10:12 1044,7462
them at the pit of the *s* house................. 2Kin 10:14 1044

SHEAR-JASHUB *(she'-ar-ja'-shub)* {1} *Symbolic name of a son of Isaiah.*
S thy son, at the end of the .... Is 7:3 7610

SHEATH {8}
and drew it out of the *s* thereof 1Sa 17:51 8593
upon his loins in the *s* thereof................. 2Sa 20:8 8593
sword again into the *s* thereof................. 1Chr 21:27 5084
draw forth my sword out of his *s* .... Eze 21:3 8593
his *s* against all flesh from the .... Eze 21:4 8593
drawn forth my sword out of his *s* .... Eze 21:5 8593
I cause it to return into his *s* .... Eze 21:30 8593
Put up thy sword into the *s*..................... Jn 18:11 *2336*

SHEAVES {9}
we were binding *s* in the field .... Gen 37:7 485
your *s* stood round about, and made....... Gen 37:7 485
after the reapers among the *s*................. Ruth 2:7 6016
Let her glean even among the *s*.............. Ruth 2:15 6016
on the sabbath, and bringing in *s* .... Neh 13:15 6194
bringing his *s* with him .... Ps 126:6 485
nor he that bindeth *s* his bosom............. Ps 129:7
cart is pressed that is full of *s* .... Amos 2:13 5995
them as the *s* into the floor .... Mic 4:12 5995

SHEBA *(she'-bah)* {32} See BATH-SHEBA, BEERSHEBA, SHEBAH.
1. Son of Raamah.
Raamah; *S*, and Dedan............................ Gen 10:7 7614
Raamah; *S*, and Dedan............................ 1Chr 1:9 7614
2. Son of Yoktan.
And Obal, and Abimael, and *S* .... Gen 10:28 7614
And Ebal, and Abimael, and *S*................. 1Chr 1:22 7614
3. Son of Yokshan.
And Jokshan begat *S*, and Dedan .... Gen 25:3 7614
Jokshan; *S*, and Dedan 1Chr 1:32 7614
4. A region in southwestern Arabia.
when the queen of *S* heard of the 1Kin 10:1 7614
when the queen of *S* had seen all............ 1Kin 10:4 7614
queen of *S* gave to king Solomon............ 1Kin 10:10 7614
the queen of *S* all her desire 1Kin 10:13 7614
when the queen of *S* heard of the 2Chr 9:1 7614
when the queen of *S* had seen the............ 2Chr 9:3 7614
the queen of *S* gave king Solomon 2Chr 9:9 7614
to the queen of *S* all her desire 2Chr 9:12 7614
companies of *S* waited for them.............. Job 6:19 7614
the kings of *S* and Seba shall.................. Ps 72:10 7614
shall be given of the gold of *S*................. Ps 72:15 7614
all they from *S* shall come....................... Is 60:6 7614
cometh there to me incense from *S* .... Jer 6:20 7614
The merchants of *S* and Raamah, ... Eze 27:22 7614
and Eden, the merchants of *S* .... Eze 27:23 7614
S, and Dedan, and the merchants of....... Eze 38:13 7614
5. A city in Simeon.
inheritance Beer-sheba, or *S* .... Josh 19:2 7652
6. A son of Bichri.
a man of Belial, whose name was *S* 2Sa 20:1 7652
followed *S* the son of Bichri 2Sa 20:2 7652
Now shall *S* the son of Bichri do 2Sa 20:6 7652
to pursue after *S* the son of..................... 2Sa 20:7 7652
pursued after *S* the son of Bichri 2Sa 20:10 7652
to pursue after *S* the son of..................... 2Sa 20:13 7652
S the son of Bichri by name, hath........... 2Sa 20:21 7652
the head of *S* the son of Bichri................ 2Sa 20:22 7652
7. A chief Gadite.
were, Michael, and Meshullam, and *S* 1Chr 5:13 7652

SHEBAH *(she'-bah)* {1} See SHEBA. *A well at Beer-sheba.*
And he called it *S*.................................... Gen 26:33 7656

SHEBAM *(she'-bam)* {1} See SHIBMAH. *A city in Reuben.*
and Heshbon, and Elealeh, and *S* .... Num 32:3 7643

SHEBANIAH *(sheb-a-ni'-ah)* {7} See SHECHANIAH.
1. A priest who moved the Ark.
And *S*, and Jehoshaphat, and.................. 1Chr 15:24 7645
2. A Levite who aided Ezra.
Jeshua, and Bani, Kadmiel, *S*.................. Neh 9:4 7645
Hashabniah, Sherebiah, Hodijah, *S* .... Neh 9:5 7645
And their brethren, *S*, Hodijah, ... Neh 10:10 7645
3. A priest who renewed the covenant.
Hattush, *S*, Malluch,............................... Neh 10:4 7645
of *S*, Joseph... Neh 12:14 7645
4. A Levite who renewed the covenant.
Zaccur, Sherebiah, *S*, ... Neh 10:12 7645

SHEBARIM *(sheb'-a-rim)* {1} *A place near Jericho.*
from before the gate even unto *S*............ Josh 7:5 7671

SHEBAT See SEBAT.

SHEBER *(she'-bur)* {1} *A son of Caleb.*
Caleb's concubine, bare *S*........................ 1Chr 2:48 7669

SHEBNA *(sheb'-nah)* {9}
1. King Hezekiah's scribe.
S the scribe, and Joah the son of 2Kin 18:18 7644
Eliakim the son of Hilkiah, and *S*........... 2Kin 18:26 7644
S the scribe, and Joah the son of 2Kin 18:37 7644
S the scribe, and the elders of................. 2Kin 19:2 7644
S the scribe, and Joah, Asaph's............... Is 36:3 7644
Then said Eliakim and *S* and Joah .... Is 36:11 7644
S the scribe, and Joah, the son of............ Is 36:22 7644
S the scribe, and the elders of................. Is 37:2 7644
2. An unspecified treasurer.
unto this treasurer, even unto *S* .... Is 22:15 7644

SHEBNAH See SHEBNA.

SHEBUEL *(she-bu'-el)* {3} See SHUBAEL.
1. A son of Gershom.
sons of Gershom, *S* was the chief........... 1Chr 23:16 7619
S the son of Gershom, the son of 1Chr 26:24 7619
2. A son of Haman.
Bukkiah, Mattaniah, Uzziel, *S*................. 1Chr 25:4 7619

SHECANIAH *(shek-a-ni'-ah)* {2} See SHEBANIAH, SHECHANIAH.
1. A priest in David's time.
ninth to Jeshua, the tenth to *S* 1Chr 24:11 7935
2. A priest in Hezekiah's time.
and Shemaiah, Amariah, and *S* 2Chr 31:15 7935

SHECHANIAH *(shek-a-ni'-ah)* {8} See SHEBANIAH, SHECANIAH.
1. Head of a Davidic family.
sons of Obadiah, the sons of *S* 1Chr 3:21 7935
And the sons of *S* 1Chr 3:22 7935
2. A family of exiles.
Of the sons of *S*, of the sons of................ Ezr 8:3 7935
3. Another family of exiles.
Of the sons of *S* .... Ezr 8:5 7935
4. Married a foreigner in exile.
S the son of Jehiel, one of the .... Ezr 10:2 7935
5. Father of Shemaiah.
also Shemaiah the son of *S*..................... Neh 3:29 7935
6. Son of Arah.
son in law of *S* the son of Arah .... Neh 6:18 7935
7. A priest with Zerubbabel.
S, Rehum, Meremoth, ... Neh 12:3 7935

SHECHEM (*she'-kem*) {62} See SHECHEMITES, SHECHEM'S, SICHEM, SYCHEM.
1. *A Levitical city near Mt. Ephraim.*
Jacob came to Shalem, a city of *S* ... Gen 33:18 7927
them under the oak which was by *S* ... Gen 35:4 7927
to feed their father's flock in *S* ... Gen 37:12 7927
thy brethren feed the flock in *S* ... Gen 37:13 7927
vale of Hebron, and he came to *S* ... Gen 37:14 7927
Michmethah, that lieth before *S* ... Josh 17:7 7927
and *S* in mount Ephraim, and ... Josh 20:7 7927
For they gave them *S* with her ... Josh 21:21 7927
all the tribes of Israel to *S* ... Josh 24:1 7927
a statute and an ordinance in *S* ... Josh 24:25 7927
And his concubine that was in *S* ... Judg 8:31 7927
to *S* unto his mother's brethren ... Judg 9:1 7927
in the ears of all the men of *S* ... Judg 9:2 7927
all the men of *S* all these words ... Judg 9:3 7927
all the men of *S* gathered ... Judg 9:6 7927
plain of the pillar that was in *S* ... Judg 9:6 7927
Hearken unto me, ye men of *S* ... Judg 9:7 7927
king over the men of *S*, because ... Judg 9:18 7927
Abimelech, and devour the men of *S* ... Judg 9:20 7927
fire come out from the men of *S* ... Judg 9:20 7927
between Abimelech and the men of *S* ... Judg 9:23 7927
the men of *S* dealt treacherously ... Judg 9:23 7927
and upon the men of *S*, which aided ... Judg 9:24 7927
the men of *S* set liers in wait ... Judg 9:25 7927
his brethren, and went over to *S* ... Judg 9:26 7927
the men of *S* put their confidence ... Judg 9:26 7927
Ebed and his brethren be come to *S* ... Judg 9:31 7927
wait against *S* in four companies ... Judg 9:34 7927
Gaal went out before the men of *S* ... Judg 9:39 7927
that they should not dwell in *S* ... Judg 9:41 7927
men of the tower of *S* heard that ... Judg 9:46 7927
tower of *S* were gathered together ... Judg 9:47 7927
men of the tower of *S* died also ... Judg 9:49 7927
all the evil of the men of *S* did ... Judg 9:57 7927
that goeth up from Beth-el to *S* ... Judg 21:19 7927
And Rehoboam went to *S* ... 1Kin 12:1 7927
were come to *S* to make him king ... 1Kin 12:1 7927
Jeroboam built *S* in mount Ephraim ... 1Kin 12:25 7927
S in mount Ephraim with her ... 1Chr 6:67 7927
S also and the towns thereof, unto ... 1Chr 7:28 7927
And Rehoboam went to *S* ... 2Chr 10:1 7927
for to *S* were all Israel come to ... 2Chr 10:1 7927
I will rejoice, I will divide *S* ... Ps 60:6 7927
I will rejoice, I will divide *S* ... Ps 108:7 7927
That there came certain from *S* ... Jer 41:5 7927
2. *Son of Hamor.*
when *S* the son of Hamor the ... Gen 34:2 7928
S spake unto his father Hamor ... Gen 34:4 7928
Hamor the father of *S* went out ... Gen 34:6 7928
The soul of my son *S* longeth for ... Gen 34:8 7928
S said unto her father and unto ... Gen 34:11 7928
And the sons of Jacob answered *S* ... Gen 34:13 7928
pleased Hamor, and *S* Hamor's son ... Gen 34:18 7928
S his son came unto the gate of ... Gen 34:20 7928
unto *S* his son hearkened all that ... Gen 34:24 7928
S his son with the edge of the ... Gen 34:26 7928
up out of Egypt, buried they in *S* ... Josh 24:32 7928
S for an hundred pieces of silver ... Josh 24:32 7928
Who is Abimelech, and who is *S* ... Judg 9:28 7928
the men of Hamor the father of *S* ... Judg 9:28 7928
3. *Son of Gilead.*
and of *S*, the family of the ... Num 26:31 7928
Asriel, and for the children of *S* ... Josh 17:2 7928
4. *A son of Shemidah.*
of Shemidah were, Ahian, and *S* ... 1Chr 7:19 7928

SHECHEMITES (*she'-kem-ites*) {1} *Descendants of Shechem.*
of Shechem, the family of the *S* ... Num 26:31 7930

SHECHEM'S (*she'-kems*) {2} *Refers to Shechem 2.*
S father, for an hundred pieces ... Gen 33:19 7927
and took Dinah out of *S* house ... Gen 34:26 7927

SHED {52}
by man shall his blood be *s* ... Gen 9:6 8210
S no blood, but cast him into ... Gen 37:22 8210
there shall no blood be *s* for him ... Ex 22:2
there shall be blood *s* for him ... Ex 22:3
he hath *s* blood ... Lev 17:4 8210
of the blood that is *s* therein ... Num 35:33 8210
but by the blood of him that *s* it ... Num 35:33 8210
blood be not *s* in thy land ... Deut 19:10 8210
Our hands have not *s* this blood ... Deut 21:7 8210
thee from coming to *s* blood ... 1Sa 25:26
that thou hast *s* blood causeless ... 1Sa 25:31 8210
this day from coming to *s* blood ... 1Sa 25:33
s out his bowels to the ground ... 2Sa 20:10 8210
s the blood of war in peace, and ... 1Kin 2:5 7760
the innocent blood, which Joab *s* ... 1Kin 2:31 8210
Moreover Manasseh *s* innocent ... 2Kin 21:16 8210
for the innocent blood that he *s* ... 2Kin 24:4 8210
Thou hast *s* blood abundantly, and ... 1Chr 22:8 8210
because thou hast *s* much blood ... 1Chr 22:8 8210
a man of war, and hast *s* blood ... 1Chr 28:3 8210
Their blood have they *s* like ... Ps 79:3 8210
blood of thy servants which is *s* ... Ps 79:10 8210
s innocent blood, even the blood ... Ps 106:38 8210
to evil, and make haste to *s* blood ... Prov 1:16 8210
hands that *s* innocent blood ... Prov 6:17 8210
make haste to *s* innocent blood ... Is 59:7 8210
s not innocent blood in this ... Jer 7:6 8210
neither *s* innocent blood in this ... Jer 22:3 8210
for to *s* innocent blood, and for ... Jer 22:17 8210
that have *s* the blood of the just ... Lam 4:13 8210
wedlock and *s* blood are judged ... Eze 16:38 8210
in thy blood that thou hast *s* ... Eze 22:4 8210
in thee to their power to *s* blood ... Eze 22:6 8210
men that carry tales to *s* blood ... Eze 22:9 8210
have they taken gifts to *s* blood ... Eze 22:12 8210
to *s* blood, and to destroy souls ... Eze 22:27 8210
the manner of women that *s* blood ... Eze 23:45 8210
toward your idols, and *s* blood ... Eze 33:25 8210
hast *s* the blood of the children ... Eze 35:5 5064
that they had *s* upon the land ... Eze 36:18 8210
because they have *s* innocent ... Joel 3:19 8210
righteous blood *s* upon the earth ... Mt 23:35 1632
which is *s* for many for the ... Mt 26:28 1632
testament, which is *s* for many ... Mk 14:24 1632
which was *s* from the foundation ... Lk 11:50 1632
in my blood, which is *s* for you ... Lk 22:20 1632
he hath *s* forth this, which ye ... Acts 2:33 1632
blood of thy martyr Stephen was *s* ... Acts 22:20 1632
Their feet are swift to *s* blood ... Rom 3:15 1632
because the love of God is *s* ... Rom 5:5 1632
Which he *s* on us abundantly ... Titus 3:6 1632
For they have *s* the blood of ... Rev 16:6 1632

SHEDDER {1}
a *s* of blood, and that doeth the ... Eze 18:10 8210

SHEDDETH {2}
Whoso *s* man's blood, by man shall ... Gen 9:6 8210
The city *s* blood in the midst of ... Eze 22:3 8210

SHEDDING {1}
and without *s* of blood is no ... Heb 9:22 130

SHEDEUR (*shed'-e-ur*) {5} *A Reubenite who counted the people.*
Elizur the son of *S* ... Num 1:5 7707
shall be Elizur the son of *S* ... Num 2:10 7707
fourth day Elizur the son of *S* ... Num 7:30 7707
offering of Elizur the son of *S* ... Num 7:35 7707
his host was Elizur the son of *S* ... Num 10:18 7707

SHEEP {187}
And Abel was a keeper of *s* ... Gen 4:2 6629
and he had *s*, and oxen, and he asses ... Gen 12:16 6629
And Abimelech took *s*, and oxen, and ... Gen 20:14 6629
And Abraham took *s* and oxen, and ... Gen 21:27 6629
three flocks of *s* lying by it ... Gen 29:2 6629
well's mouth, and watered the *s* ... Gen 29:3 6629
his daughter cometh with the *s* ... Gen 29:6 6629
water ye the *s*, and go and feed ... Gen 29:7 6629
then we water the *s* ... Gen 29:8 6629
Rachel came with her father's *s* ... Gen 29:9 6629
the *s* of Laban his mother's ... Gen 29:10 6629
all the brown cattle among the *s* ... Gen 30:32 3775
the goats, and brown among the *s* ... Gen 30:33 3775
it, and all the brown among the *s* ... Gen 30:35 3775
And Laban went to shear his *s* ... Gen 31:19 6629
They took their *s*, and their oxen ... Gen 34:28 6629
up to Timnath to shear his *s* ... Gen 38:13 6629
upon the oxen, and upon the *s* ... Ex 9:3 6629
ye shall take it out from the *s* ... Ex 12:5 3532
and thy peace offerings, thy *s* ... Ex 20:24 6629
a man shall steal an ox, or a *s* ... Ex 22:1 7716
for an ox, and four *s* for a *s* ... Ex 22:1 6629
whether it be ox, or ass, or *s* ... Ex 22:4 7716
it be for ox, for ass, for *s* ... Ex 22:9 7716
an ass, or an ox, or a *s*, or any ... Ex 22:10 7716
do with thine oxen, and with thy *s* ... Ex 22:30 6629
among thy cattle, whether ox or *s* ... Ex 34:19 7716
of the flocks, namely, of the *s* ... Lev 1:10 3775
no manner of fat, of ox, or of *s* ... Lev 7:23 3775
blemish, of the beeves, of the *s* ... Lev 22:19 3775
freewill offering in beeves or *s* ... Lev 22:21 6629
When a bullock, or a *s*, or a goat ... Lev 22:27 3775
whether it be ox, or *s* ... Lev 27:26 7716
of a cow, or the firstling of a *s* ... Num 18:17 3775
And Balak offered oxen and *s* ... Num 22:40 6629
of the LORD be not as *s* which ... Num 27:17 6629
and of the asses, and of the *s* ... Num 31:28 6629
thousand and five thousand *s* ... Num 31:32 6629
thirty thousand and five hundred *s* ... Num 31:36 6629
tribute of the *s* was six hundred ... Num 31:37 6629
seven thousand and five hundred *s* ... Num 31:43 6629
little ones, and folds for your *s* ... Num 32:24 6792
and folds of *s* ... Num 32:36 6629
thy kine, and the flocks of thy *s* ... Deut 7:13 6629
the ox, the *s*, and the goat ... Deut 14:4 3775
lusteth after, for oxen, or for *s* ... Deut 14:26 6629
nor shear the firstling of thy *s* ... Deut 15:19 6629
LORD thy God any bullock, or *s* ... Deut 17:1 7716
sacrifice, whether it be ox or *s* ... Deut 18:3 7716
the first of the fleece of thy *s* ... Deut 18:4 6629
brother's ox or his *s* go astray ... Deut 22:1 7716
thy kine, and the flocks of thy *s* ... Deut 28:4 6629
thy kine, and the flocks of thy *s* ... Deut 28:18 6629
thy *s* shall be given unto thine ... Deut 28:31 6629
of thy kine, or flocks of thy *s* ... Deut 28:51 6629
Butter of kine, and milk of *s* ... Deut 32:14 6629
woman, young and old, and ox, and *s* ... Josh 6:21 7716
his oxen, and his asses, and his *s* ... Josh 7:24 6629
sustenance for Israel, neither *s* ... Judg 6:4 7716
He will take the tenth of your *s* ... 1Sa 8:17 6629
flew upon the spoil, and took *s* ... 1Sa 14:32 6629
man his ox, and every man his *s* ... 1Sa 14:34 7716
infant and suckling, ox and *s* ... 1Sa 15:3 7716
spared Agag, and the best of the *s* ... 1Sa 15:9 6629
bleating of the *s* in mine ears ... 1Sa 15:14 6629
people spared the best of the *s* ... 1Sa 15:15 6629
the people took of the spoil, *s* ... 1Sa 15:21 6629
and, behold, he keepeth the *s* ... 1Sa 16:11 6629
thy son, which is with the *s* ... 1Sa 16:19 6629
feed his father's *s* at Beth-lehem ... 1Sa 17:15 6629
left the *s* with a keeper, and took ... 1Sa 17:20 6629
those few *s* in the wilderness ... 1Sa 17:28 6629
Thy servant kept his father's *s* ... 1Sa 17:34 6629
and oxen, and asses, and *s*, with ... 1Sa 22:19 7716
great, and he had three thousand *s* ... 1Sa 25:2 6629
he was shearing his *s* in Carmel ... 1Sa 25:2 6629
that Nabal did shear his *s* ... 1Sa 25:4 6629
we were with them keeping the *s* ... 1Sa 25:16 6629
five *s* ready dressed, and five ... 1Sa 25:18 6629
woman alive, and took away the *s* ... 1Sa 27:9 6629
sheepcote, from following the *s* ... 2Sa 7:8 6629
And honey, and butter, and *s* ... 2Sa 17:29 6629
but these *s*, what have they done ... 2Sa 24:17 6629
And Adonijah slew *s* and oxen and fat ... 1Kin 1:9 6629
s in abundance, and hath called ... 1Kin 1:19 6629
s in abundance, and hath called ... 1Kin 1:25 6629
of the pastures, and an hundred *s* ... 1Kin 4:23 6629
him before the ark, sacrificing *s* ... 1Kin 8:5 6629
an hundred and twenty thousand *s* ... 1Kin 8:63 6629
as *s* that have not a shepherd ... 1Kin 22:17 6629
and oliveyards, and vineyards, and *s* ... 2Kin 5:26 6629
of *s* two hundred and fifty ... 1Chr 5:21 6629
and oil, and oxen, and *s* abundantly ... 1Chr 12:40 6629
even from following the *s* ... 1Chr 17:7 6629
but as for these *s*, what have ... 1Chr 21:17 6629
him before the ark, sacrificed *s* ... 2Chr 5:6 6629
an hundred and twenty thousand *s* ... 2Chr 7:5 6629
of cattle, and carried away *s* ... 2Chr 14:15 6629
hundred oxen and seven thousand *s* ... 2Chr 15:11 6629
And Ahab killed *s* and oxen for him ... 2Chr 18:2 6629
as *s* that have no shepherd ... 2Chr 18:16 6629
hundred oxen and three thousand *s* ... 2Chr 29:33 6629
bullocks and seven thousand *s* ... 2Chr 30:24 6629
bullocks and ten thousand *s* ... 2Chr 30:24 6629
brought in the tithe of oxen and *s* ... 2Chr 31:6 6629
and they builded the *s* gate ... Neh 3:1 6629
s gate repaired the goldsmiths ... Neh 3:32 6629
daily was one ox and six choice *s* ... Neh 5:18 6629
of Meah, even unto the *s* gate ... Neh 12:39 6629
also was seven thousand *s* ... Job 1:3 6629
heaven, and hath burned up the *s* ... Job 1:16 6629
warmed with the fleece of my *s* ... Job 31:20 3532
for he had fourteen thousand *s* ... Job 42:12 6629
All *s* and oxen, yea, and the beasts ... Ps 8:7 6792
us like *s* appointed for meat ... Ps 44:11 6629
counted as *s* for the slaughter ... Ps 44:22 6629
Like *s* they are laid in the grave ... Ps 49:14 6629
against the *s* of thy pasture ... Ps 74:1 6629
his own people to go forth like *s* ... Ps 78:52 6629
s of thy pasture will give thee ... Ps 79:13 6629
his pasture, and the *s* of his hand ... Ps 95:7 6629
people, and the *s* of his pasture ... Ps 100:3 6629
I have gone astray like a lost *s* ... Ps 119:176 7716
that our *s* may bring forth ... Ps 144:13 6629
a flock of *s* that are even shorn ... Song 4:2
Thy teeth are as a flock of *s* ... Song 6:6 7353
nourish a young cow, and two *s* ... Is 7:21 6629
as a *s* that no man taketh up ... Is 13:14 6629
slaying oxen, and killing *s* ... Is 22:13 6629
All we like *s* have gone astray ... Is 53:6 6629
as a *s* before her shearers is ... Is 53:7 7353
them out like *s* for the slaughter ... Jer 12:3 6629
scatter the *s* of my pasture ... Jer 23:1 6629
My people hath been lost *s* ... Jer 50:6 6629
Israel is a scattered *s* ... Jer 50:17 7716
My *s* wandered through all the ... Eze 34:6 6629
I, even I, will both search my *s* ... Eze 34:11 6629
is among his *s* that are scattered ... Eze 34:12 6629
so will I seek out my *s*, and will ... Eze 34:12 6629
a wife, and for a wife he kept *s* ... Hos 12:12
the flocks of *s* are made desolate ... Joel 1:18 6629
them together as the *s* of Bozrah ... Mic 2:12 6629
young lion among the flocks of *s* ... Mic 5:8 6629
and the *s* shall be scattered ... Zec 13:7 6629
abroad, as *s* having no shepherd ... Mt 9:36 4263
the lost *s* of the house of Israel ... Mt 10:6 4263
I send you forth as *s* in the ... Mt 10:16 4263
among you, that shall have one *s* ... Mt 12:11 4263
then is a man better than a *s* ... Mt 12:12 4263
the lost *s* of the house of Israel ... Mt 15:24 4263
if a man have an hundred *s* ... Mt 18:12 4263
you, he rejoiceth more of that *s* ... Mt 18:13
divideth his *s* from the goats ... Mt 25:32 4263
he shall set the *s* on his right ... Mt 25:33 4263
the *s* of the flock shall be ... Mt 26:31 4263
because they were as *s* not having ... Mk 6:34 4263
and the *s* shall be scattered ... Mk 14:27 4263
man of you, having an hundred *s* ... Lk 15:4 4263
I have found my *s* which was lost ... Lk 15:6 4263
temple those that sold oxen and *s* ... Jn 2:14 4263
all out of the temple, and the *s* ... Jn 2:15 4263
Jerusalem by the *s* market a pool ... Jn 5:2 4262
the door is the shepherd of the *s* ... Jn 10:2 4263
and the *s* hear his voice ... Jn 10:3 4263
and he calleth his own *s* by name ... Jn 10:3 4263
when he putteth forth his own *s* ... Jn 10:4 4263
before them, and the *s* follow him ... Jn 10:4 4263
unto you, I am the door of the *s* ... Jn 10:7 4263
but the *s* did not hear them ... Jn 10:8 4263
giveth his life for the *s* ... Jn 10:11 4263
shepherd, whose own the *s* are not ... Jn 10:12 4263
the wolf coming, and leaveth the *s* ... Jn 10:12 4263
them, and scattereth the *s* ... Jn 10:12 4263
hireling, and careth not for the *s* ... Jn 10:13 4263
the good shepherd, and know my *s* ... Jn 10:14
and I lay down my life for the *s* ... Jn 10:15 4263
other *s* I have, which are not of ... Jn 10:16 4263
not, because ye are not of my *s* ... Jn 10:26 4263
My *s* hear my voice, and I know ... Jn 10:27 4263

He saith unto him, Feed my *s* ... Jn 21:16 *4263*
Jesus saith unto him, Feed my *s* ... Jn 21:17 *4263*
this, He was led as a *s* to the ... Acts 8:32 *4263*
accounted as *s* for the slaughter ... Rom 8:36 *4263*
that great shepherd of the *s* ... Heb 13:20 *4263*
For ye were as *s* going astray ... 1Pet 2:25 *4263*
flour, and wheat, and beasts, and *s* ... Rev 18:13 *4263*

SHEEPCOTE {2}
of hosts, I took thee from the *s* ... 2Sa 7:8 5116
of hosts, I took thee from the *s* ... 1Chr 17:7 5116

SHEEPCOTES {1}
And he came to the *s* by the way ... 1Sa 24:3 1448,6629

SHEEPFOLD {1}
not by the door into the *s* ... Jn 10:1 *833,4263*

SHEEPFOLDS {3}
We will build *s* here for our ... Num 32:16 1488,6629
Why abodest thou among the *s* ... Judg 5:16 4942
servant, and took him from the *s* ... Ps 78:70 4356,6629

SHEEPMASTER {1}
And Mesha king of Moab was a *s* ... 2Kin 3:4 5349

SHEEP'S {1}
which come to you in *s* clothing ... Mt 7:15 *4263*

SHEEPSHEARERS {3}
and went up unto his *s* to Timnath ... Gen 38:12 1494,6629
that Absalom had *s* in Baal-hazor ... 2Sa 13:23 1494
Behold now, thy servant hath *s* ... 2Sa 13:24 1494

SHEEPSKINS {1}
they wandered about in *s* and ... Heb 11:37 *3374*

SHEERAH See SHERAH.

SHEET {2}
as it had been a great *s* knit at ... Acts 10:11 *3607*
descend, as it had been a great *s* ... Acts 11:5 *3607*

SHEETS {2}
then I will give you thirty *s* ... Judg 14:12 5466
then shall ye give me thirty *s* ... Judg 14:13 5466

SHEHARIAH *(she-ha-ri'-ah)* {1} *A son of Jeroham.*
And Shamsherai, and *S*, and Athaliah, ... 1Chr 8:26 7841

SHEKEL {43}
golden earring of half a *s* weight ... Gen 24:22 1235
half a *s* after the *s* of the ... Ex 30:13 8255
(a *s* is twenty gerahs ... Ex 30:13 8255
an half *s* shall be the offering ... Ex 30:13 8255
shall not give less than half a *s* ... Ex 30:15 8255
after the *s* of the sanctuary, and ... Ex 30:24 8255
after the *s* of the sanctuary ... Ex 38:24 8255
after the *s* of the sanctuary ... Ex 38:25 8255
for every man, that is, half a *s* ... Ex 38:26 8255
after the *s* of the sanctuary, for ... Ex 38:26 8255
after the *s* of the sanctuary, for ... Lev 5:15 8255
after the *s* of the sanctuary ... Lev 27:3 8255
to the *s* of the sanctuary ... Lev 27:25 8255
twenty gerahs shall be the *s* ... Lev 27:25 8255
after the *s* of the sanctuary ... Num 3:47 8255
(the *s* is twenty gerahs ... Num 3:47 8255
after the *s* of the sanctuary ... Num 3:50 8255
after the *s* of the sanctuary ... Num 7:13 8255
after the *s* of the sanctuary ... Num 7:19 8255
after the *s* of the sanctuary ... Num 7:25 8255
after the *s* of the sanctuary ... Num 7:31 8255
after the *s* of the sanctuary ... Num 7:37 8255
after the *s* of the sanctuary ... Num 7:43 8255
after the *s* of the sanctuary ... Num 7:49 8255
after the *s* of the sanctuary ... Num 7:55 8255
after the *s* of the sanctuary ... Num 7:61 8255
after the *s* of the sanctuary ... Num 7:67 8255
after the *s* of the sanctuary ... Num 7:73 8255
after the *s* of the sanctuary ... Num 7:79 8255
after the *s* of the sanctuary ... Num 7:85 8255
after the *s* of the sanctuary ... Num 7:86 8255
after the *s* of the sanctuary, ... Num 18:16 8255
the fourth part of a *s* of silver ... 1Sa 9:8 8255
of fine flour be sold for a *s* ... 2Kin 7:1 8255
and two measures of barley for a *s* ... 2Kin 7:1 8255
of fine flour was sold for a *s* ... 2Kin 7:16 8255
and two measures of barley for a *s* ... 2Kin 7:16 8255
Two measures of barley for a *s* ... 2Kin 7:18 8255
a measure of fine flour for a *s* ... 2Kin 7:18 8255
s for the service of the house of ... Neh 10:32 8255
the *s* shall be twenty gerahs ... Eze 45:12 8255
the *s* great, and falsifying the ... Amos 8:5 8255

SHEKELS {96}
is worth four hundred *s* of silver ... Gen 23:15 8255
of Heth, four hundred *s* of silver ... Gen 23:16 8255
her hands of ten *s* weight of gold ... Gen 24:22 8255
their master thirty *s* of silver ... Ex 21:32 8255
of pure myrrh five hundred *s* ... Ex 30:23
much, even two hundred and fifty *s* ... Ex 30:23
calamus two hundred and fifty *s* ... Ex 30:23
And of cassia five hundred *s* ... Ex 30:24
and seven hundred and thirty *s* ... Ex 38:24 8255
and threescore and fifteen *s* ... Ex 38:25 8255
five *s* he made hooks for the ... Ex 38:28
and two thousand and four hundred *s* ... Ex 38:29 8255
thy estimation by *s* of silver ... Lev 5:15 8255
shall be fifty *s* of silver ... Lev 27:3 8255
thy estimation shall be thirty *s* ... Lev 27:4 8255
shall be of the male twenty *s* ... Lev 27:5 8255
and for the female ten *s* ... Lev 27:5 8255
be of the male five *s* of silver ... Lev 27:6 8255
shall be three *s* of silver ... Lev 27:6 8255
thy estimation shall be fifteen *s* ... Lev 27:7 8255
and for the female ten *s* ... Lev 27:7 8255
be valued at fifty *s* of silver ... Lev 27:16 8255
take five *s* apiece by the poll ... Num 3:47 8255
hundred and threescore and five *s* ... Num 3:50
was an hundred and thirty *s* ... Num 7:13
one silver bowl of seventy *s* ... Num 7:13
One spoon of ten *s* of gold ... Num 7:14
was an hundred and thirty *s* ... Num 7:19
one silver bowl of seventy *s* ... Num 7:19 8255
One spoon of gold of ten *s* ... Num 7:20
was an hundred and thirty *s* ... Num 7:25
one silver bowl of seventy *s* ... Num 7:25 8255
One golden spoon of ten *s* ... Num 7:26
weight of an hundred and thirty *s* ... Num 7:31
one silver bowl of seventy *s* ... Num 7:31 8255
One golden spoon of ten *s* ... Num 7:32
was an hundred and thirty *s* ... Num 7:37
one silver bowl of seventy *s* ... Num 7:37 8255
One golden spoon of ten *s* ... Num 7:38
weight of an hundred and thirty *s* ... Num 7:43
a silver bowl of seventy *s* ... Num 7:43 8255
One golden spoon of ten *s* ... Num 7:44
was an hundred and thirty *s* ... Num 7:49
one silver bowl of seventy *s* ... Num 7:49 8255
One golden spoon of ten *s* ... Num 7:50
weight of an hundred and thirty *s* ... Num 7:55
one silver bowl of seventy *s* ... Num 7:55 8255
One golden spoon of ten *s* ... Num 7:56
was an hundred and thirty *s* ... Num 7:61
one silver bowl of seventy *s* ... Num 7:61 8255
One golden spoon of ten *s* ... Num 7:62
was an hundred and thirty *s* ... Num 7:67
one silver bowl of seventy *s* ... Num 7:67 8255
One golden spoon of ten *s* ... Num 7:68
was an hundred and thirty *s* ... Num 7:73
one silver bowl of seventy *s* ... Num 7:73 8255
One golden spoon of ten *s* ... Num 7:74
was an hundred and thirty *s* ... Num 7:79
one silver bowl of seventy *s* ... Num 7:79 8255
One golden spoon of ten *s* ... Num 7:80
weighing an hundred and thirty *s* ... Num 7:85
two thousand and four hundred *s* ... Num 7:85
of incense, weighing ten *s* apiece ... Num 7:86
spoons was an hundred and twenty *s* ... Num 7:86
for the money of five *s*, after ... Num 18:16 8255
thousand seven hundred and fifty *s* ... Num 31:52 8255
him in an hundred *s* of silver ... Deut 22:19
damsel's father fifty *s* of silver ... Deut 22:29
and two hundred *s* of silver ... Josh 7:21 8255
a wedge of gold of fifty *s* weight ... Josh 7:21 8255
and seven hundred *s* of gold ... Judg 8:26
The eleven hundred *s* of silver ... Judg 17:2
hundred *s* of silver to his mother ... Judg 17:3
took two hundred *s* of silver ... Judg 17:4
I will give thee ten *s* of silver ... Judg 17:10
coat was five thousand *s* of brass ... 1Sa 17:5 8255
weighed six hundred *s* of iron ... 1Sa 17:7 8255
hundred *s* after the king's weight ... 2Sa 14:26 8255
have given thee ten *s* of silver ... 2Sa 18:11
thousand *s* of silver in mine hand ... 2Sa 18:12
hundred *s* of brass in weight ... 2Sa 21:16
and the oxen for fifty *s* of silver ... 2Sa 24:24 8255
six hundred *s* of gold went to one ... 1Kin 10:16
Egypt for six hundred *s* of silver ... 1Kin 10:29
of each man fifty *s* of silver ... 2Kin 15:20 8255
six hundred *s* of gold by weight ... 1Chr 21:25 8255
for six hundred *s* of silver ... 2Chr 1:17
of the nails was fifty *s* of gold ... 2Chr 3:9 8255
six hundred *s* of beaten gold went ... 2Chr 9:15
three hundred *s* of gold went to ... 2Chr 9:16
and wine, beside forty *s* of silver ... Neh 5:15 8255
money, even seventeen *s* of silver ... Jer 32:9 8255
be by weight, twenty *s* a day ... Eze 4:10 8255
twenty *s*, five and twenty ... Eze 45:12 8255
five and twenty *s*, fifteen *s* ... Eze 45:12 8255

SHELAH *(she'-lah)* {11} See SALAH, SHELANITES.
1. Son of Judah.
and called his name *S* ... Gen 38:5 7956
house, till *S* my son be grown ... Gen 38:11 7956
for she saw that *S* was grown ... Gen 38:14 7956
that I gave her not to *S* my son ... Gen 38:26 7956
Er, and Onan, and *S*, and Pharez, and ... Gen 46:12 7956
of *S*, the family of the ... Num 26:20 7956
Er, and Onan, and *S* ... 1Chr 2:3 7956
The sons of *S* the son of Judah ... 1Chr 4:21 7956
2. Son of Arphaxad.
And Arphaxad begat *S*, and Shelah ... 1Chr 1:18 7974
begat Shelah, and *S* begat Eber ... 1Chr 1:18 7956
Shem, Arphaxad, *S*, ... 1Chr 1:24 7956

SHELANITE See SHELANITES.

SHELANITES *(she'-lan-ites)* {1} *Descendants of Shelah.*
of Shelah, the family of the *S* ... Num 26:20 8024

SHELEMIAH *(shel-e-mi'-ah)* {10} See MESHELEMIAH, SHALLUM.
1. A sanctuary servant.
And the lot eastward fell to *S* ... 1Chr 26:14 8018
2. A son of Bani who married a foreigner.
And *S*, and Nathan, and Adaiah, ... Ezr 10:39 8018
3. Another son of Bani.
Azareel, and *S*, Shemariah, ... Ezr 10:41 8018
4. Father of Hananiah.
repaired Hananiah the son of *S* ... Neh 3:30 8018
5. A treasury sevant.
S the priest, and Zadok the scribe ... Neh 13:13 8018
6. Son of Cushi.
son of Nethaniah, the son of *S* ... Jer 36:14 8018
7. Son of Abdeel.
S the son of Abdeel, to take ... Jer 36:26 8018
8. Father of Jehucal.
king sent Jehucal the son of *S* ... Jer 37:3 8018
of Pashur, and Jucal the son of *S* ... Jer 38:1 8018
9. Father of Irijah.
name was Irijah, the son of *S* ... Jer 37:13 8018

SHELEPH *(she'-lef)* {2} *A son of Joktan.*
And Joktan begat Almodad, and *S* ... Gen 10:26 8026
And Joktan begat Almodad, and *S* ... 1Chr 1:20 8026

SHELESH *(she'-lesh)* {1} *A son of Helem.*
Zophah, and Imna, and *S*, and Amal ... 1Chr 7:35 8028

SHELOMI *(shel'-o-mi)* {1} *Father of Ahihud.*
of Asher, Ahihud the son of *S* ... Num 34:27 8015

SHELOMITH *(shel'-o-mith)* {9}
1. Daughter of Debri.
(and his mother's name was *S* ... Lev 24:11 8019
2. Daughter of Zerubbabel.
and Hananiah, and *S* their sister ... 1Chr 3:19 8019
3. A son of Shimei.
S, and Haziel, and Haran, three ... 1Chr 23:9 8013
4. A son of Izhar.
S the chief ... 1Chr 23:18 8013
5. A descendant of Eliezer.
and Zichri his son, and *S* his son ... 1Chr 26:25 8013
Which *S* and his brethren were over ... 1Chr 26:26 8013
thing, it was under the hand of *S* ... 1Chr 26:28 8019
6. A child of King Rehoboam.
Abijah, and Attai, and Ziza, and *S* ... 2Chr 11:20 8019
7. A family of exiles.
And of the sons of *S* ... Ezr 8:10 8019

SHELOMOTH *(shel'-o-moth)* {2} See SHELOMITH. *A descendant of Izhar.*
S: of the sons of *S* ... 1Chr 24:22 8013

SHELTER {2}
embrace the rock for want of a *s* ... Job 24:8 4268
For thou hast been a *s* for me ... Ps 61:3 4268

SHELUMIEL {5}
S the son of Zurishaddai ... Num 1:6 8017
shall be *S* the son of Zurishaddai ... Num 2:12 8017
On the fifth day *S* the son of ... Num 7:36 8017
of *S* the son of Zurishaddai ... Num 7:41 8017
was *S* the son of Zurishaddai ... Num 10:19 8017

SHEM *(shem)* {17} See SEM. *A son of Noah.*
and Noah begat *S*, Ham, and Japheth ... Gen 5:32 8035
And Noah begat three sons, *S*, ... Gen 6:10 8035
selfsame day entered Noah, and *S* ... Gen 7:13 8035
went forth of the ark, were *S* ... Gen 9:18 8035
And *S* and Japheth took a garment, ... Gen 9:23 8035
Blessed be the LORD God of *S* ... Gen 9:26 8035
he shall dwell in the tents of *S* ... Gen 9:27 8035
of the sons of Noah, *S*, Ham, and ... Gen 10:1 8035
Unto *S* also, the father of all ... Gen 10:21 8035
The children of *S* ... Gen 10:22 8035
These are the sons of *S*, after ... Gen 10:31 8035
These are the generations of *S* ... Gen 11:10 8035
S was an hundred years old, and ... Gen 11:10 8035
S lived after he begat Arphaxad ... Gen 11:11 8035
Noah, *S*, Ham, and Japheth ... 1Chr 1:4 8035
The sons of *S* ... 1Chr 1:17 8035
S, Arphaxad, Shelah, ... 1Chr 1:24 8035

SHEMA *(she'-mah)* {6} See SHEMAIAH, SHIMHI.
1. A city in Judah.
Amam, and *S*, and Moladah, ... Josh 15:26 8087
2. A son of Hebron.
Korah, and Tappuah, and Rekem, and *S* 1Chr 2:43 8087
S begat Raham, the father of ... 1Chr 2:44 8087
3. Father of Azaz.
the son of Azaz, the son of *S* ... 1Chr 5:8 8087
4. A Benjamite Chief.
Beriah also, and *S*, who were heads ... 1Chr 8:13 8087
5. A priest who aided Ezra.
beside him stood Mattithiah, and *S* ... Neh 8:4 8087

SHEMAAH *(shem'-a-ah)* {1} *Father of two warriors in David's army.*
the sons of *S* the Gibeathite ... 1Chr 12:3 8094

SHEMAIAH *(shem-a-i'-ah)* {40} See SHAMMUA, SHEMA, SHIMEI, SIMEI.
1. A prophet in King Rehoboam's time.
of God came unto *S* the man of God ... 1Kin 12:22 8098
the LORD came to *S* the man of God ... 2Chr 11:2 8098
Then came *S* the prophet to ... 2Chr 12:5 8098
the word of the LORD came to *S* ... 2Chr 12:7 8098
in the book of *S* the prophet ... 2Chr 12:15 8098
2. Son of Shechaniah.
S: and the sons of Shemaiah ... 1Chr 3:22 8098
3. Father of Shimri.
the son of Shimri, the son of *S* ... 1Chr 4:37 8098
4. Son of Joel.
S his son, Gog his son, Shimei ... 1Chr 5:4 8098
5. Son of Hasshub.
S the son of Hasshub, the son of ... 1Chr 9:14 8098
S the son of Hashub, the son of ... Neh 11:15 8098
6. Father of Obadiah.
And Obadiah the son of *S*, the son ... 1Chr 9:16 8098
7. A priest who moved the Ark.
S the chief, and his brethren two ... 1Chr 15:8 8098
for Uriel, Asaiah, and Joel, *S* ... 1Chr 15:11 8098
8. Son of Nathaneel.
S the son of Nethaneel the scribe ... 1Chr 24:6 8098
9. A sanctuary servant.
S the firstborn, Jehozabad the ... 1Chr 26:4 8098
Also unto *S* his son were sons ... 1Chr 26:6 8098
The sons of *S* ... 1Chr 26:7 8098

10. A Levite teacher of the people.
with them he sent Levites, even S.......... 2Chr 17:8 8098
11. A Levite who cleansed the temple.
S, and Uzziel 2Chr 29:14 8098
12. A Levite in Hezekiah's time.
and Miniamin, and Jeshua, and S.......... 2Chr 31:15 8098
13. A Levite in Josiah's time.
Conaniah also, and S and Nethaneel, ... 2Chr 35:9 8098
14. A family of exiles.
are these, Eliphelet, Jeiel, and S .... Ezr 8:13 8098
15. A messenger of Ezra.
I for Eliezer, for Ariel, for S .... Ezr 8:16 8098
16. A priest who married a foreigner.
Maaseiah, and Elijah, and S .... Ezr 10:21 8098
17. A son of Harim.
Eliezer, Ishijah, Malchiah, S.................... Ezr 10:31 8098
18. A rebuilder of Jerusalem's wall.
also S the son of Shechaniah.................... Neh 3:29 8098
19. Son of Delaiah.
I came unto the house of S the................ Neh 6:10 8098
20. A priest who renewed the covenant.
Maaziah, Bilgai, S .... Neh 10:8 8098
S, and Joiarib, Jedaiah, ... Neh 12:6 8098
of S, Jehonathan..................................... Neh 12:18 8098
Judah, and Benjamin, and S, and .... Neh 12:34 8098
the son of Jonathan, the son of S........... Neh 12:35 8098
21. A priest who dedicated the wall.
And his brethren, S, and Azarael,.......... Neh 12:36 8098
22. A priest who gave thanks at the wall.
And Maaseiah, and S, and Eleazar, and . Neh 12:42 8098
23. Father of Urijah.
the son of S of Kirjath-jearim................ Jer 26:20 8098
24. A false prophet.
also speak to S the Nehelamite.............. Jer 29:24 8098
LORD concerning S the Nehelamite........ Jer 29:31 8098
Because that S hath prophesied.............. Jer 29:31 8098
I will punish S the Nehelamite, ... Jer 29:32 8098
25. Father of Delaiah.
scribe, and Delaiah the son of S .... Jer 36:12 8098

SHEMARIAH *(shem-a-ri'-ah)* {3}
1. A warrior in David's army.
and Jerimoth, and Bealiah, and S.......... 1Chr 12:5 8114
2. Married a foreigner in exile.
Benjamin, Malluch, and S...................... Ezr 10:32 8114
3. Married a foreigner in exile
Azareel, and Shelemiah, S, ... Ezr 10:41 8114

SHEMEBER *(shem-e'-ber)* {1} *King of Zeboim.*
S king of Zeboiim, and the king of........ Gen 14:2 8038

SHEMED See SHAMED.

SHEMER *(she'-mur)* {2} *Owner of a hill, later the site of Samaria.*
of S for two talents of silver.................. 1Kin 16:24 8106
he built, after the name of S.................. 1Kin 16:24 8106

SHEMIDA *(shem-i'-dah)* {2} See SHEMIDAH. *Son of Gilead.*
And of S, the family of the..................... Num 26:32 8061
Hepher, and for the children of S............ Josh 17:2 8061

SHEMIDAH *(shem-i'-dah)* {1} See SHEMIDA, SHEMIDAITES. *Same as Shemida.*
And the sons of S were, Ahian, and........ 1Chr 7:19 8061

SHEMIDAITES *(shem'-i-dah-ites)* {1} *Descendants of Shemida.*
of Shemida, the family of the S .... Num 26:32 8062

SHEMINITH *(shem'-i-nith)* {3} *A musical notation.*
with harps on the S to excel.................... 1Chr 15:21 8067
chief Musician on Neginoth upon S........ Ps 6:t 8067
To the chief Musician upon S................. Ps 12:t 8067

SHEMIRAMOTH *(she-mir'-a-moth)* {4}
1. A priest who moved the Ark.
Zechariah, Ben, and Jaaziel, and S......... 1Chr 15:18 8070
And Zechariah, and Aziel, and S............ 1Chr 15:20 8070
to him Zechariah, Jeiel, and S................ 1Chr 16:5 8070
2. A Levite in Jehoshaphat's time.
and Zebadiah, and Asahel, and S........... 2Chr 17:8 8070

SHEMUEL *(shem-u'-el)* {3} See SAMUEL.
1. A Simeonite prince.
of Simeon, S the son of Ammihud .... Num 34:20 8050
2. Another name for Samuel the prophet.
the son of Joel, the son of S................... 1Chr 6:33 8050
3. Head of a family in Issachar.
and Jahmai, and Jibsam, and S............... 1Chr 7:2 8050

SHEN *(shen)* {1} *A place in Benjamin.*
and set it between Mizpeh and S............ 1Sa 7:12 8129

SHENAZAR *(she-na'-zar)* {1} *Descendant of King Jehoiakim.*
Malchiram also, and Pedaiah, and S....... 1Chr 3:18 8137

SHENAZZAR See SHENAZAR.

SHENIR *(she'-nur)* {2} See SENIR, SION. *A mountain between Amana and Hermon.*
and the Amorites call it S .... Deut 3:9 8149
top of Amana, from the top of S............. Song 4:8 8149

SHEOL See HELL.

SHEPHAM *(she'-fam)* {2} See SHIPMITE. *A place east of the Sea of Cinneroth.*
east border from Hazar-enan to S........... Num 34:10 8221
shall go down from S to Riblah .... Num 34:11 8221

SHEPHATIAH *(shef-a-ti'-ah)* {13}
1. A son of David.
and the fifth, S the son of Abital 2Sa 3:4 8203
The fifth, S of Abital 1Chr 3:3 8203
Michri, and Meshullam the son of S 1Chr 9:8 8203
2. A warrior in David's army.
and Shemariah, and S the Haruphite, ... 1Chr 12:5 8203
3. A Simeonite prince.
Simeonites, S the son of Maachah 1Chr 27:16 8203
4. A son of King Jehoshaphat.
and Azariah, and Michael, and S............ 2Chr 21:2 8203
5. A family of exiles with Zerubbabel.
The children of S, three hundred .... Ezr 2:4 8203
The children of S, three hundred .... Neh 7:9 8203
6. Descendants of a servant of Solomon.
The children of S, the children............... Ezr 2:57 8203
The children of S, the children............... Neh 7:59 8203
7. A family of exiles with Ezra.
And of the sons of S .... Ezr 8:8 8203
8. A family of exiles who resettled in Jerusalem.
the son of Amariah, the son of S............ Neh 11:4 8203
9. A prince of Judah.
Then S the son of Mattan, and................ Jer 38:1 8203

SHEPHELAH See PLAIN.

SHEPHER See SHAPHER.

SHEPHERD {43}
for every s is an abomination.......... Gen 46:34 7462,6629
(from thence is the s, the stone .... Gen 49:24 7462
be not as sheep which have no s .... Num 27:17 7462
hills, as sheep that have not a s............. 1Kin 22:17 7462
as sheep that have no s.......................... 2Chr 18:16 7462
The LORD is my s .... Ps 23:1 7462
O S of Israel, thou that leadest .... Ps 80:1 7462
which are given from one s.................... Eccl 12:11 7462
He shall feed his flock like a s .... Is 40:11 7462
That saith of Cyrus, He is my s.............. Is 44:28 7462
the sea with the s of his flock .... Is 63:11 7462
keep him, as a s doth his flock .... Jer 31:10 7462
as a s putteth on his garment................. Jer 43:12 7462
who is that s that will stand .... Jer 49:19 7462
who is that s that will stand .... Jer 50:44 7462
break in pieces with thee the s.............. Jer 51:23 7462
scattered, because there is no s .... Eze 34:5 7462
the field, because there was no s............ Eze 34:8 7462
As a s seeketh out his flock in................ Eze 34:12 7462
And I will set up one s over them .... Eze 34:23 7462
feed them, and he shall be their s .... Eze 34:23 7462
and they all shall have one s .... Eze 37:24 7462
As the s taketh out of the mouth............ Amos 3:12 7462
troubled, because there was no s............ Zec 10:2 7462
the instruments of a foolish s .... Zec 11:15 7462
I will raise up a s in the land .... Zec 11:16 7462
Woe to the idol s that leaveth................. Zec 11:17 7473
Awake, O sword, against my s................. Zec 13:7 7462
smite the s, and the sheep shall .... Zec 13:7 7462
abroad, as sheep having no s.................. Mt 9:36 4166
as a s divideth his sheep from .... Mt 25:32 4166
it is written, I will smite the s .... Mt 26:31 4166
they were as sheep not having a s.......... Mk 6:34 4166
it is written, I will smite the s .... Mk 14:27 4166
by the door is the s of the sheep............ Jn 10:2 4166
I am the good s .... Jn 10:11 4166
the good s giveth his life for .... Jn 10:11 4166
that is an hireling, and not the s .... Jn 10:12 4166
I am the good s, and know my sheep ...... Jn 10:14 4166
there shall be one fold, and one s .... Jn 10:16 4166
that great s of the sheep,....................... Heb 13:20 4166
but are now returned unto the S............. 1Pet 2:25 4166
And when the chief S shall appear 1Pet 5:4 750

SHEPHERD'S {2}
put them in a s bag which he had,.......... 1Sa 17:40 7462
and is removed from me as a s tent........ Is 38:12 7473

SHEPHERDS {37}
And the men are s, for their trade... Gen 46:32 7462,6629
unto Pharaoh, Thy servants are s.... Gen 47:3 7462,6629
the s came and drove them away .... Ex 2:17 7462
us out of the hand of the s .... Ex 2:19 7462
now thy s which were with us, we 1Sa 25:7 7462
neither shall the s make their .... Is 13:20 7462
when a multitude of s is called .... Is 31:4 7462
they are s that cannot understand .... Is 56:11 7462
The s with their flocks shall................... Jer 6:3 7462
I will set up s over them which.............. Jer 23:4 7462
Howl, ye s, and cry................................. Jer 25:34 7462
the s shall have no way to flee, ... Jer 25:35 7462
A voice of the cry of the s .... Jer 25:36 7462
shall be an habitation of s...................... Jer 33:12 7462
their s have caused them to go............... Jer 50:6 7462
prophesy against the s of Israel .... Eze 34:2 7462
saith the Lord GOD unto the s................. Eze 34:2 7462
Woe be to the s of Israel that do .... Eze 34:2 7462
should not the s feed the flocks.............. Eze 34:2 7462
Therefore, ye s, hear the word of............ Eze 34:7 7462
neither did my s search for my .... Eze 34:8 7462
but the s fed themselves, and fed .... Eze 34:8 7462
Therefore, O ye s, hear the word .... Eze 34:9 7462
Behold, I am against the s .... Eze 34:10 7462
neither shall the s feed .... Eze 34:10 7462
habitations of the s shall mourn .... Amos 1:2 7462
we raise against him seven s .... Mic 5:5 7462
Thy s slumber, O king of Assyria .... Nah 3:18 7462
be dwellings and cottages for s .... Zeph 2:6 7462
anger was kindled against the s............. Zec 10:3 7462
a voice of the howling of the s .... Zec 11:3 7462
their own s pity them not........................ Zec 11:5 7462
Three s also I cut off in one.................... Zec 11:8 7462
country s abiding in the field.................. Lk 2:8 4166
the s said one to another, Let us .... Lk 2:15 4166
which were told them by the s .... Lk 2:18 4166
the s returned, glorifying and .... Lk 2:20 4166

SHEPHERDS' {1}
feed thy kids beside the s tents .... Song 1:8 7462

SHEPHI *(she'-fi)* {1} See SHEPHO. *A son of Shobal.*
Alian, and Manahath, and Ebal, S........... 1Chr 1:40 8195

SHEPHO *(she'-fo)* {1} See SHEPHI. *Same as Shephi.*
Alvan, and Manahath, and Ebal, S .... Gen 36:23 8195

SHEPHUPHAM See SHUPHAM.

SHEPHUPHAN *(shef'-u-fan)* {1} See SHUPHAM, SHUPPIM. *A son of Bela.*
And Gera, and S, and Huram 1Chr 8:5 8197

SHERAH *(she'-rah)* {1} *Daughter of Beriah.*
(And his daughter was S, who built......... 1Chr 7:24 7609

SHERD {1}
a s to take fire from the hearth .... Is 30:14 2789

SHERDS {1}
and thou shalt break the s thereof .... Eze 23:34 2789

SHEREBIAH *(sher-e-bi'-ah)* {8}
1. A family of exiles.
and S, with his sons and his.................... Ezr 8:18 8274
of the chief of the priests, S .... Ezr 8:24 8274
Also Jeshua, and Bani, and S .... Neh 8:7 8274
Kadmiel, Shebaniah, Bunni, S .... Neh 9:4 8274
and Kadmiel, Bani, Hashabniah, S.......... Neh 9:5 8274
2. A Levite who renewed the covenant.
Zaccur, S, Shebaniah,.............................. Neh 10:12 8274
Jeshua, Binnui, Kadmiel, S .... Neh 12:8 8274
Hashabiah, S, and Jeshua the son............ Neh 12:24 8274

SHERESH *(she'-resh)* {1} *Son of Machir.*
and the name of his brother was S 1Chr 7:16 8329

SHEREZER *(she-re'-zur)* {1} See SHAREZER. *A messenger in Zechariah's time.*
had sent unto the house of God S............ Zec 7:2 8272

SHERIFFS {2}
the counsellors, the s, and all.................. Dan 3:2 8614
the counsellors, the s, and all.................. Dan 3:3 8614

SHESHACH *(she'-shak)* {2} See BABYLON. *Another name for Babylon.*
the king of S shall drink after.................. Jer 25:26 8347
How is S taken .... Jer 51:41 8347

SHESHAI *(she'-shahee)* {3} *A son of Anak.*
where Ahiman, S, and Talmai, the.......... Num 13:22 8344
thence the three sons of Anak, S............ Josh 15:14 8344
and they slew S, and Ahiman, and .... Judg 1:10 8344

SHESHAK See SHESHACH.

SHESHAN *(she'-shan)* {5} *A descendant of Jerahmeel.*
S. And the children of S.......................... 1Chr 2:31 8348
Now S had no sons, but daughters 1Chr 2:34 8348
S had a servant, an Egyptian, ... 1Chr 2:34 8348
S gave his daughter to Jarha his 1Chr 2:35 8348

SHESHBAZZAR *(shesh-baz'-zur)* {4} See ZERUBBABEL. *Same as Zerubbabel.*
and numbered them unto S, the............... Ezr 1:8 8339
All these did S bring up with.................. Ezr 1:11 8339
unto one, whose name was S.................... Ezr 5:14 8339
Then came the same S, and laid the .... Ezr 5:16 8339

SHETH *(sheth)* {2} See SETH.
1. A Moabite chief.
and destroy all the children of S............. Num 24:17 8352
2. Same as Seth.
Adam, S, Enosh, ... 1Chr 1:1 8352

SHETHAR *(she'-thar)* {1} *A prince of Media and Persia.*
the next unto him was Carshena, S .... Est 1:14 8369

SHETHAR-BOZENAI See SHETHAR-BOZNAI.

SHETHAR-BOZNAI *(she'-thar-boz'-nahee)* {4} *A Persian official.*
on this side the river, and S.................... Ezr 5:3 8370
on this side the river, and S.................... Ezr 5:6 8370
governor beyond the river, S .... Ezr 6:6 8370
on this side the river, S.......................... Ezr 6:13 8370

SHETHER BAZNAI See SHETHAR BOZNAI.

SHEVA *(she'-vah)* {2} See SHAVSHA.
1. David's scribe.
And S was scribe..................................... 2Sa 20:25 7724
2. Son of Maachah.
S the father of Machbenah, and the........ 1Chr 2:49 7724

SHEW {228}
unto a land that I will s thee.................. Gen 12:1 7200
which thou shalt s unto me .... Gen 20:13 6213
s kindness unto my master Abraham...... Gen 24:12 6213
s kindness, I pray thee, unto me,............ Gen 40:14 6213
s Pharaoh, and say unto him, My........... Gen 46:31 5046
you, saying, S a miracle for you.............. Ex 7:9 5414
for to s in thee my power........................ Ex 9:16 7200
that I might s these my signs.................. Ex 10:1 7896
thou shalt s thy son in that day,.............. Ex 13:8 5046
which he will s to you to day .... Ex 14:13 6213
shalt s them the way wherein they.......... Ex 18:20 3045
According to all that I s thee .... Ex 25:9 7200
s me now thy way, that I may know .... Ex 33:13 3045
I beseech thee, s me thy glory................ Ex 33:18 7200
s mercy on whom I will s mercy.............. Ex 33:19
the LORD will s who are his.................... Num 16:5 3045
to s you by what way ye should go.......... Deut 1:33 7200
thou hast begun to s thy servant............ Deut 3:24 7200
to s you the word of the LORD .... Deut 5:5 5046
with them, nor s mercy unto them .... Deut 7:2
s thee mercy, and have compassion .... Deut 13:17 5414
they shall s thee the sentence of............. Deut 17:9 5046
LORD shall choose shall s thee................ Deut 17:10 5046
sentence which they shall s thee .... Deut 17:11 5046

nor *s* favour to the young	Deut 28:50	
ask thy father, and he will *s* thee	Deut 32:7	5046
that ye will also *s* kindness unto	Josh 2:12	6213
that he would not *s* them the land	Josh 5:6	7200
S us, we pray thee, the entrance	Judg 1:24	7200
the city, and we will *s* thee mercy	Judg 1:24	6213
I will *s* thee the man whom thou	Judg 4:22	7200
then *s* me a sign that thou	Judg 6:17	6213
Samuel feared to *s* Eli the vision	1Sa 3:15	5046
s them the manner of the king	1Sa 8:9	5046
peradventure he can *s* us our way	1Sa 9:6	5046
that I may *s* thee the word of God	1Sa 9:27	8085
s thee what thou shalt do	1Sa 10:8	3045
to us, and we will *s* you a thing	1Sa 14:12	3045
I will *s* thee what thou shalt do	1Sa 16:3	3045
small, but that he will *s* it me	1Sa 20:2	1540
send not unto thee, and *s* it thee	1Sa 20:12	1540
thee evil, then I will *s* it thee	1Sa 20:13	1540
s me the kindness of the LORD	1Sa 20:14	6213
he fled, and did not *s* it to me	1Sa 22:17	1540
young men, and they will *s* thee	1Sa 25:8	5046
And now the LORD *s* kindness	2Sa 2:6	6213
which against Judah do *s* kindness	2Sa 3:8	6213
that I may *s* him kindness for	2Sa 9:1	6213
that I may *s* the kindness of God	2Sa 9:3	6213
for I will surely *s* thee kindness	2Sa 9:7	6213
I will *s* kindness unto Hanun the	2Sa 10:2	6213
s me both it, and his habitation	2Sa 15:25	7200
thou wilt *s* thyself merciful	2Sa 22:26	
man thou wilt *s* thyself upright	2Sa 22:26	
the pure thou wilt *s* thyself pure	2Sa 22:27	
thou wilt *s* thyself unsavoury	2Sa 22:27	
If he will *s* himself a worthy man	1Kin 1:52	
therefore, and *s* thyself a man	1Kin 2:2	
But *s* kindness unto the sons of	1Kin 2:7	6213
saying, Go, *s* thyself unto Ahab	1Kin 18:1	7200
Elijah went to *s* himself unto	1Kin 18:2	7200
I will surely *s* myself unto him	1Kin 18:15	7200
Will ye not *s* me which of us is	2Kin 6:11	5046
I will now *s* you what the Syrians	2Kin 7:12	5046
s forth from day to day his	1Chr 16:23	1319
I will *s* kindness unto Hanun the	1Chr 19:2	6213
to *s* himself strong in the behalf	2Chr 16:9	
but they could not *s* their	Ezr 2:59	5046
but they could not *s* their	Neh 7:61	5046
to *s* them light, and the way	Neh 9:19	
to *s* the people and the princes	Est 1:11	7200
her that she should not *s* it	Est 2:10	5046
to *s* it unto Esther, and to	Est 4:8	7200
s me wherefore thou contendest	Job 10:2	3045
that he would *s* thee the secrets	Job 11:6	5046
I will *s* thee, hear me	Job 15:17	2331
durst not *s* you mine opinion	Job 32:6	2331
I also will *s* mine opinion	Job 32:10	2331
I also will *s* mine opinion	Job 32:17	2331
to *s* unto man his uprightness	Job 33:23	5046
I will *s* thee that I have yet to	Job 36:2	2331
that say, Who will *s* us any good	Ps 4:6	7200
I will *s* forth all thy marvellous	Ps 9:1	5608
That I may *s* forth all thy praise	Ps 9:14	5608
Thou wilt *s* me the path of life	Ps 16:11	3045
S thy marvellous lovingkindness,	Ps 17:7	
thou wilt *s* thyself merciful	Ps 18:25	
man thou wilt *s* thyself upright	Ps 18:25	
the pure thou wilt *s* thyself pure	Ps 18:26	
thou wilt *s* thyself froward	Ps 18:26	
S me thy ways, O LORD	Ps 25:4	3045
he will *s* them his covenant	Ps 25:14	3045
every man walketh in a vain *s*	Ps 39:6	6754
will I *s* the salvation of God	Ps 50:23	7200
my mouth shall *s* forth thy praise	Ps 51:15	5046
My mouth shall *s* forth thy	Ps 71:15	5608
we will *s* forth thy praise to all	Ps 79:13	5608
S us thy mercy, O LORD, and grant	Ps 85:7	7200
S me a token for good	Ps 86:17	6213
Wilt thou *s* wonders to the dead	Ps 88:10	6213
him, and *s* him my salvation	Ps 91:16	7200
To *s* forth thy lovingkindness in	Ps 92:2	5046
To *s* that the LORD is upright	Ps 92:15	5046
vengeance belongeth, *s* thyself	Ps 94:1	3313
s forth his salvation from day to	Ps 96:2	1319
who can *s* forth all his praise	Ps 106:2	8085
that he remembered not to *s* mercy	Ps 109:16	6213
friends must *s* himself friendly	Prov 18:24	
The *s* of their countenance doth	Is 3:9	1971
formed them will *s* them no favour	Is 27:11	
shall *s* the lighting down of his	Is 30:30	7200
forth, and *s* us what shall happen	Is 41:22	5046
let them *s* the former things,	Is 41:22	5046
S the things that are to come	Is 41:23	5046
this, and *s* us former things	Is 43:9	8085
they shall *s* forth my praise	Is 43:21	5608
shall come, let them *s* unto them	Is 44:7	5046
this, and *s* yourselves men	Is 46:8	
thou didst *s* them no mercy	Is 47:6	7760
are in darkness, *S* yourselves	Is 49:9	1540
s my people their transgression,	Is 58:1	5046
they shall *s* forth the praises of	Is 60:6	1319
when thou shalt *s* this people all	Jer 16:10	5046
where I will not *s* you favour	Jer 16:13	5414
I will *s* them the back, and not	Jer 18:17	7200
s thee great and mighty things,	Jer 33:3	5046
That the LORD thy God may *s* us	Jer 42:3	5046
I will *s* mercies unto you, that	Jer 42:12	5414
are cruel, and will not *s* mercy	Jer 50:42	
to *s* the king of Babylon that his	Jer 51:31	5046
yea, thou shalt *s* her all her	Eze 22:2	3045
with their mouth they *s* much love	Eze 33:31	6213
Wilt thou not *s* us what thou	Eze 37:18	5046
upon all that I shall *s* thee	Eze 40:4	7200
for to the intent that I might *s*	Eze 40:4	7200
s the house to the house of	Eze 43:10	5046
s them the form of the house, and	Eze 43:11	3045
for to *s* the king his dreams	Dan 2:2	5046
we will *s* the interpretation	Dan 2:4	2324
But if ye *s* the dream, and the	Dan 2:6	2324
therefore *s* me the dream, and the	Dan 2:6	2324
we will *s* the interpretation of	Dan 2:7	2324
I shall know that ye can *s* me the	Dan 2:9	2324
that can *s* the king's matter	Dan 2:10	2324
that can *s* it before the king	Dan 2:11	2324
that he would *s* the king the	Dan 2:16	2324
I will *s* unto the king the	Dan 2:24	2324
the soothsayers, *s* unto the king	Dan 2:27	2324
I thought it good to *s* the signs	Dan 4:2	2324
s me the interpretation thereof,	Dan 5:7	2324
he will *s* the interpretation	Dan 5:12	5046
but they could not *s* the	Dan 5:15	2324
forth, and I am come to *s* thee	Dan 9:23	5046
But I will *s* thee that which is	Dan 10:21	5046
now will I *s* thee the truth	Dan 11:2	5046
I will *s* wonders in the heavens	Joel 2:30	5414
I *s* unto him marvellous things	Mic 7:15	7200
face, and I will *s* the nations thy	Nah 3:5	7200
Why dost thou *s* me iniquity	Hab 1:3	7200
I will *s* thee what these be	Zec 1:9	7200
s mercy and compassions every man	Zec 7:9	6213
s thyself to the priest, and offer	Mt 8:4	*1166*
s John again those things which	Mt 11:4	*518*
he shall *s* judgment to the	Mt 12:18	*518*
do *s* forth themselves in him	Mt 14:2	*1754*
would *s* them a sign from heaven	Mt 16:1	*1925*
Jesus to *s* unto his disciples	Mt 16:21	*1166*
S me the tribute money	Mt 22:19	*1925*
disciples came to him for to *s*	Mt 24:1	*1925*
shall *s* great signs and wonders	Mt 24:24	*1325*
s thyself to the priest, and offer	Mk 1:44	*1166*
do *s* forth themselves in him	Mk 6:14	*1754*
shall rise, and shall *s* signs	Mk 13:22	*1325*
he will *s* you a large upper room	Mk 14:15	*1166*
to *s* thee these glad tidings	Lk 1:19	*2097*
s thyself to the priest, and offer	Lk 5:14	*1166*
I will *s* you to whom he is like	Lk 6:47	*5263*
s how great things God hath done	Lk 8:39	*1334*
Go *s* yourselves unto the priests	Lk 17:14	*1925*
S me a penny	Lk 20:24	*1925*
for a *s* make long prayers	Lk 20:47	*4392*
he shall *s* you a large upper room	Lk 22:12	*1166*
he will *s* him greater works than	Jn 5:20	*1166*
things, *s* thyself to the world	Jn 7:4	*5319*
where he were, he should *s* it	Jn 11:57	*3377*
s us the Father, and it sufficeth	Jn 14:8	*1166*
sayest thou then, *S* us the Father	Jn 14:9	*1166*
he will *s* you things to come	Jn 16:13	*312*
of mine, and shall *s* it unto you	Jn 16:14	*312*
of mine, and shall *s* it unto you	Jn 16:15	*312*
but I shall *s* you plainly of the	Jn 16:25	*312*
s whether of these two thou hast	Acts 1:24	*322*
I will *s* wonders in heaven above,	Acts 2:19	*1325*
the land which I shall *s* thee	Acts 7:3	*1166*
For I will *s* him how great things	Acts 9:16	*5263*
Go *s* these things unto James, and	Acts 12:17	*518*
which *s* unto us the way of	Acts 16:17	*2605*
willing to *s* the Jews a pleasure,	Acts 24:27	*2698*
should *s* light unto the people,	Acts 26:23	*2605*
Which *s* the work of the law	Rom 2:15	*1731*
that I might *s* my power in thee,	Rom 9:17	*1731*
if God, willing to *s* his wrath	Rom 9:22	*1731*
ye do *s* the Lord's death till he	1Cor 11:26	*2605*
yet *s* I unto you a more excellent	1Cor 12:31	*1166*
Behold, I *s* you a mystery	1Cor 15:51	*3004*
Wherefore *s* ye to them, and before	2Cor 8:24	*1731*
to make a fair *s* in the flesh	Gal 6:12	*2146*
s the exceeding riches of his	Eph 2:7	*1731*
he made a *s* of them openly,	Col 2:15	*1165*
a *s* of wisdom in will worship	Col 2:23	*3056*
For they themselves *s* of us what	1Th 1:9	*518*
might *s* forth all longsuffering	1Ti 1:16	*1731*
learn first to *s* piety at home	1Ti 5:4	*2151*
Which in his times he shall *s*	1Ti 6:15	*1166*
Study to *s* thyself approved unto	2Ti 2:15	*3936*
s the same diligence to the full	Heb 6:11	*1731*
willing more abundantly to *s* unto	Heb 6:17	*1925*
s me thy faith without thy works,	Jas 2:18	*1166*
I will *s* thee my faith by my	Jas 2:18	*1166*
let him *s* out of a good	Jas 3:13	*1166*
that ye should *s* forth the	1Pet 2:9	*1804*
s unto you that eternal life,	1Jn 1:2	*518*
to *s* unto his servants things	Rev 1:1	*1166*
I will *s* thee things which must	Rev 4:1	*1166*
I will *s* unto thee the judgment	Rev 17:1	*1166*
I will *s* thee the bride, the	Rev 21:9	*1166*
to *s* unto his servants the things	Rev 22:6	*1166*

SHEWBREAD {18}

upon the table *s* before me alway	Ex 25:30	3899,6440
and all his vessels, and the *s*	Ex 35:13	3899,6440
all the vessels thereof, and the *s*	Ex 39:36	3899,6440
upon the table of *s* they shall	Num 4:7	6440
was no bread there but the *s*	1Sa 21:6	3899,6440
of gold, whereupon the *s* was	1Kin 7:48	3899,6440
the Kohathites, were over the *s*	1Chr 9:32	3899,4635
Both for the *s*, and for the fine	1Chr 23:29	3899,4635
he gave gold for the tables of *s*	1Chr 28:16	4635
incense, and for the continual *s*	2Chr 2:4	4635
the tables whereon the *s* was set	2Chr 4:19	3899,6440
the *s* also set they in order upon	2Chr 13:11	3899,4635
the *s* table, with all the vessels	2Chr 29:18	4635
For the *s*, and for the continual	Neh 10:33	3899,4635
house of God, and did eat the *s*	Mt 12:4	*740,4286*
the high priest, and did eat the *s*	Mk 2:26	*740,4286*
of God, and did take and eat the *s*	Lk 6:4	*740,4286*
and the table, and the *s*	Heb 9:2	*4286,740*

SHEWED {135}

which thou hast *s* unto me in	Gen 19:19	6213
hast *s* kindness unto my master	Gen 24:14	6213
which thou hast *s* unto thy	Gen 32:10	6213
s him mercy, and gave him favour	Gen 39:21	5186
God hath *s* Pharaoh what he is	Gen 41:25	5046
as God hath *s* thee all this	Gen 41:39	3045
God hath *s* me also thy seed	Gen 48:11	7200
the LORD *s* him a tree, which when	Ex 15:25	3384
which was *s* thee in the mount	Ex 25:40	7200
which was *s* thee in the mount	Ex 26:30	7200
as it was *s* thee in the mount, so	Ex 27:8	7200
reddish, and it be *s* to the priest	Lev 13:19	7200
shall be *s* unto the priest	Lev 13:49	7200
mind of the LORD might be *s* them	Lev 24:12	6567
which the LORD had *s* Moses	Num 8:4	7200
s them the fruit of the land	Num 13:26	7200
signs which I have *s* among them	Num 14:11	6213
Unto thee it was *s*, that thou	Deut 4:35	7200
upon earth he *s* thee his great	Deut 4:36	7200
LORD our God hath *s* us his glory	Deut 5:24	7200
And the LORD *s* signs and wonders,	Deut 6:22	5414
the LORD *s* him all the land of	Deut 34:1	7200
s in the sight of all Israel	Deut 34:12	6213
LORD, since I have *s* you kindness	Josh 2:12	6213
when he *s* them the entrance into	Judg 1:25	7200
they *s* Sisera that Barak the son	Judg 4:12	5046
Neither *s* they kindness to the	Judg 8:35	6213
which he had *s* unto Israel	Judg 8:35	6213
s her husband, and said unto him,	Judg 13:10	5046
he have *s* us all these things	Judg 13:23	7200
for he hath *s* me all his heart	Judg 16:18	5046
unto her, It hath fully been *s* me	Ruth 2:11	5046
she *s* her mother in law with whom	Ruth 2:19	5046
for thou hast *s* more kindness in	Ruth 3:10	3190
s it to the men of Jabesh	1Sa 11:9	5046
for ye *s* kindness to all the	1Sa 15:6	6213
Jonathan *s* him all those things	1Sa 19:7	5046
Abiathar *s* David that Saul had	1Sa 22:21	5046
thou hast *s* this day how that	1Sa 24:18	5046
that ye have *s* this kindness unto	2Sa 2:5	6213
as his father *s* kindness unto me	2Sa 10:2	6213
s David all that Joab had sent	2Sa 11:22	5046
thou hast not *s* it unto thy	1Kin 1:27	3045
Thou hast *s* unto thy servant	1Kin 3:6	6213
he did, and his might that he *s*	1Kin 16:27	6213
and his might that he *s*, and how	1Kin 22:45	6213
And he *s* him the place	2Kin 6:6	7200
howbeit the LORD hath *s* me that	2Kin 8:10	7200
The LORD hath *s* me that thou	2Kin 8:13	7200
LORD, and *s* them the king's son	2Kin 11:4	7200
s them all the house of his	2Kin 20:13	7200
that Hezekiah *s* them not	2Kin 20:13	7200
treasures that I have not *s* them	2Kin 20:15	7200
And Shaphan the scribe *s* the king	2Kin 22:10	7200
his father *s* kindness to me	1Chr 19:2	6213
Thou hast *s* great mercy unto	2Chr 1:8	6213
that the LORD had *s* unto David	2Chr 7:10	6213
hath been *s* from the LORD our God	Ezr 9:8	
When he *s* the riches of his	Est 1:4	7200
Esther had not *s* her people nor	Est 2:10	5046
Esther had not yet *s* her kindred	Est 2:20	5046
for they had *s* him the people of	Est 3:6	5046
pity should be *s* from his friend	Job 6:14	
for he hath *s* me his marvellous	Ps 31:21	
Thou hast *s* thy people hard	Ps 60:3	
until I have *s* thy strength unto	Ps 71:18	5046
Thou, which hast *s* me great	Ps 71:20	7200
and his wonders that he had *s* them	Ps 78:11	7200
s in the sight of the heathen	Ps 98:2	1540
They *s* his signs among them, and	Ps 105:27	7760
He hath *s* his people the power of	Ps 111:6	5046
the LORD, which hath *s* us light	Ps 118:27	
I *s* before him my trouble	Ps 142:2	5046
his wickedness shall be *s* before	Prov 26:26	1540
wherein I have *s* myself wise	Eccl 2:19	
Let favour be *s* to the wicked	Is 26:10	
s them the house of his precious	Is 39:2	7200
that Hezekiah *s* them not	Is 39:2	7200
treasures that I have not *s* them	Is 39:4	7200
s to him the way of understanding	Is 40:14	3045
and have saved, and I have *s*	Is 43:12	8085
out of my mouth, and I *s* them	Is 48:3	8085
it came to pass I *s* it thee	Is 48:5	8085
I have *s* thee new things from	Is 48:6	8085
The LORD *s* me, and, behold, two	Jer 24:1	7200
the word that the LORD hath *s* me	Jer 38:21	7200
the things that the LORD had *s* me	Eze 11:25	7200
s them my judgments, which if a	Eze 20:11	3045
neither have they *s* difference	Eze 22:26	3045
Thus hath the Lord GOD *s* unto me	Amos 7:1	7200
Thus hath the Lord GOD *s* unto me	Amos 7:4	7200
Thus he *s* me	Amos 7:7	7200
Thus hath the Lord GOD *s* unto me	Amos 8:1	7200
He hath *s* thee, O man, what is	Mic 6:8	5046
the LORD *s* me four carpenters	Zec 1:20	7200
he *s* me Joshua the high priest	Zec 3:1	7200
s unto the chief priests all the	Mt 28:11	*518*
He hath *s* strength with his arm	Lk 1:51	*4160*
Lord had *s* great mercy upon her	Lk 1:58	*3170*

s unto him all the kingdoms of ... Lk 4:5 1166
the disciples of John *s* him of ... Lk 7:18 518
he said, He that *s* mercy on him ... Lk 10:37 4160
came, and *s* his lord these things ... Lk 14:21 518
even Moses *s* at the bush, when he ... Lk 20:37 3377
he *s* them his hands and his feet ... Lk 24:40 1925
works have I *s* you from my Father ... Jn 10:32 1166
he *s* unto them his hands and his ... Jn 20:20 1166
After these things Jesus *s* ... Jn 21:1 5319
and on this wise *s* he himself ... Jn 21:1 5319
Jesus *s* himself to his disciples ... Jn 21:14 5319
To whom also he *s* himself alive ... Acts 1:3 3936
which God before had *s* by the ... Acts 3:18 4293
this miracle of healing was *s* ... Acts 4:22 1096
the next day he *s* himself unto ... Acts 7:26 3700
out, after that he had *s* wonders ... Acts 7:36 4160
they have slain them which *s* ... Acts 7:52 4293
but God hath *s* me that I should ... Acts 10:28 1166
up the third day, and *s* him ... Acts 10:40 1325,1717,1096
he *s* us how he had seen an angel ... Acts 11:13 518
and confessed, and *s* their deeds ... Acts 19:18 312
unto you, but have *s* you, and have ... Acts 20:20 312
I have *s* you all things, how that ... Acts 20:35 5268
thou hast *s* these things to me ... Acts 23:22 1718
But *s* first unto them of Damascus ... Acts 26:20 518
the barbarous people *s* us no ... Acts 28:2 3930
came *s* or spake any harm of thee ... Acts 28:21 518
for God hath *s* it unto them ... Rom 1:19 5319
eat not for his sake that *s* it ... 1Cor 10:28 3377
which ye have *s* toward his name, ... Heb 6:10 1731
pattern *s* to thee in the mount ... Heb 8:5 1166
mercy, that hath *s* no mercy ... Jas 2:13 4160
our Lord Jesus Christ hath *s* me ... 2Pet 1:14 1213
s me that great city, the holy ... Rev 21:10 1166
he *s* me a pure river of water of ... Rev 22:1 1166
the angel which *s* me these things ... Rev 22:8 1166

SHEWEDST {2}
s signs and wonders upon Pharaoh, ... Neh 9:10 5414
then thou *s* me their doings ... Jer 11:18 7200

SHEWEST {5}
s mercy unto thy servants, that ... 2Chr 6:14
again thou *s* thyself marvellous ... Job 10:16
Thou *s* lovingkindness unto ... Jer 32:18 6213
What sign *s* thou unto us, seeing ... Jn 2:18 1166
unto him, What sign *s* thou then ... Jn 6:30 4160

SHEWETH {20}
is about to do he *s* unto Pharaoh ... Gen 41:28 7200
whatsoever he *s* me I will tell ... Num 23:3 7200
there is none that *s* me that my ... 1Sa 22:8 1540,241
or *s* unto me that my son hath ... 1Sa 22:8 1540,241
s mercy to his anointed, unto ... 2Sa 22:51 6213
Then he *s* them their work, and ... Job 36:9 5046
The noise thereof *s* concerning it ... Job 36:33 5046
s mercy to his anointed, to David ... Ps 18:50 6213
and the firmament *s* his handywork ... Ps 19:1 5046
and night unto night *s* knowledge ... Ps 19:2 2331
but the righteous *s* mercy ... Ps 37:21
A good man *s* favour, and lendeth ... Ps 112:5
He *s* his word unto Jacob, his ... Ps 147:19 5046
truth *s* forth righteousness ... Prov 12:17 5046
and the tender grass *s* itself ... Prov 27:25 7200
yea, there is none that *s* ... Is 41:26 5046
s him all the kingdoms of the ... Mt 4:8 1166
s him all things that himself ... Jn 5:20 1166
runneth, but of God that *s* mercy ... Rom 9:16 1658
he that *s* mercy, with ... Rom 12:8 1658

SHEWING {15}
s mercy unto thousands of them ... Ex 20:6 6213
s mercy unto thousands of them ... Deut 5:10 6213
s to the generation to come the ... Ps 78:4 5608
s himself through the lattice ... Song 2:9 6692
iniquities by *s* mercy to the poor ... Dan 4:27
and *s* of hard sentences, and ... Dan 5:12 263
till the day of his *s* unto Israel ... Lk 1:80 323
s the glad tidings of the kingdom ... Lk 8:1
s the coats and garments which ... Acts 9:39 1925
s by the scriptures that Jesus ... Acts 18:28 1925
of God, *s* himself that he is God ... 2Th 2:4 584
In all things *s* thyself a pattern ... Titus 2:7 3930
in doctrine *s* uncorruptness, ... Titus 2:7
but *s* all good fidelity ... Titus 2:10 1731
s all meekness unto all men ... Titus 3:2 1731

SHIBAH See SHEBAH.

SHIBBOLETH *(shib'-bo-leth)* {1} See SIDDOLETH. *Password that distinguished Gileadites from Ephraimites.*
said they unto him, Say now *S* ... Judg 12:6 7641

SHIBMAH *(shib'-mah)* {1} See SHEBAM, SIBMAH. *A city in Reuben.*
(their names being changed,) and *S* ... Num 32:38 7643

SHICRON *(shi'-cron)* {1} *A city in Judah.*
and the border was drawn to *S* ... Josh 15:11 7942

SHIELD {45}
I am thy *s*, and thy exceeding ... Gen 15:1 4043
the *s* of thy help, and who is the ... Deut 33:29 4043
was there a *s* or spear seen among ... Judg 5:8 4043
one bearing a *s* went before him ... 1Sa 17:7 6793
that bare the *s* went before him ... 1Sa 17:41 6793
and with a spear, and with a *s* ... 1Sa 17:45 3591
for there the *s* of the mighty is ... 2Sa 1:21 4043
the *s* of Saul, as though he had ... 2Sa 1:21 4043
he is my *s*, and the horn of my ... 2Sa 22:3 4043
given me the *s* of thy salvation ... 2Sa 22:36 4043
three pound of gold went to one *s* ... 1Kin 10:17 4043
there, nor come before it with *s* ... 2Kin 19:32 4043
the battle, that could handle *s* ... 1Chr 12:8 6793
The children of Judah that bare *s* ... 1Chr 12:24 6793
captains, and with them with *s* ... 1Chr 12:34 6793
shekels of gold went to one *s* ... 2Chr 9:16 4043
bow and *s* two hundred thousand ... 2Chr 17:17 4043
war, that could handle spear and *s* ... 2Chr 25:5 6793
the glittering spear and the *s* ... Job 39:23 3591
But thou, O LORD, art a *s* for me ... Ps 3:3 4043
wilt thou compass him as with a *s* ... Ps 5:12 6793
given me the *s* of thy salvation ... Ps 18:35 4043
The LORD is my strength and my *s* ... Ps 28:7 4043
he is our help and our *s* ... Ps 33:20 4043
Take hold of *s* and buckler, and ... Ps 35:2 4043
and bring them down, O Lord our *s* ... Ps 59:11 4043
he the arrows of the bow, the *s* ... Ps 76:3 4043
Behold, O God our *s*, and look upon ... Ps 84:9 4043
For the LORD God is a sun and *s* ... Ps 84:11 4043
his truth shall be thy *s* and ... Ps 91:4 6793
he is their help and their *s* ... Ps 115:9 4043
he is their help and their *s* ... Ps 115:10 4043
he is their help and their *s* ... Ps 115:11 4043
Thou art my hiding place and my *s* ... Ps 119:114 4043
my *s*, and he in whom I trust ... Ps 144:2 4043
he is a *s* unto them that put ... Prov 30:5 4043
ye princes, and anoint the *s* ... Is 21:5 4043
horsemen, and Kir uncovered the *s* ... Is 22:6 4043
Order ye the buckler and *s* ... Jer 46:3 6793
and the Libyans, that handle the *s* ... Jer 46:9 4043
set against thee buckler and *s* ... Eze 23:24 4043
they hanged the *s* and helmet in ... Eze 27:10 4043
all of them with *s* and helmet ... Eze 38:5 4043
The *s* of his mighty men is made ... Nah 2:3 4043
Above all, taking the *s* of faith ... Eph 6:16 2375

SHIELDS {23}
David took the *s* of gold that ... 2Sa 8:7 7982
three hundred *s* of beaten gold ... 1Kin 10:17 4043
he took away all the *s* of gold ... 1Kin 14:26 4043
made in their stead brasen *s* ... 1Kin 14:27 4043
give king David's spears and *s* ... 2Kin 11:10 7982
David took the *s* of gold that ... 1Chr 18:7 7982
three hundred *s* made he of beaten ... 2Chr 9:16 4043
And in every several city he put *s* ... 2Chr 11:12 6793
he carried away also the *s* of ... 2Chr 12:9 4043
king Rehoboam made *s* of brass ... 2Chr 12:10 4043
and out of Benjamin, that bare *s* ... 2Chr 14:8 4043
spears, and bucklers, and *s* ... 2Chr 23:9 7982
them throughout all the host *s* ... 2Chr 26:14 4043
and made darts and *s* in abundance ... 2Chr 32:5 4043
stones, and for spices, and for *s* ... 2Chr 32:27 4043
them held both the spears, the *s* ... Neh 4:16 4043
for the *s* of the earth belong ... Ps 47:9 4043
bucklers, all *s* of mighty men ... Song 4:4 7982
there, nor come before it with *s* ... Is 37:33 4043
gather the *s* ... Jer 51:11 7982
they hanged their *s* upon thy ... Eze 27:11 7982
great company with bucklers and *s* ... Eze 38:4 4043
and burn the weapons, both the *s* ... Eze 39:9 4043

SHIGGAION *(shig-gah'-yon)* {1} See SHIGIONOTH. *A musical notation.*
S of David, which he sang unto ... Ps 7:t 7692

SHIGIONOTH *(shig-i'-o-noth)* {1} See SHIGGAION. *A musical notation.*
of Habakkuk the prophet upon *S* ... Hab 3:1 7692

SHIHON *(shi'-hon)* {1} *A city in Issachar.*
Haphraim, and *S*, and Anaharath, ... Josh 19:19 7866

SHIHOR *(shi'-hor)* {1} See SHIHOR-LIBNATH. *Same as Sihor.*
from *S* of Egypt even unto the ... 1Chr 13:5 7883

SHIHOR-LIBNATH *(shi'-hor-lib'-nath)* {1} *A small river in Asher.*
to Carmel westward, and to *S* ... Josh 19:26 7884

SHIKKERON See SHICRON.

SHILHI *(shil'-hi)* {2} *Father of Azubah.*
name was Azubah the daughter of *S* ... 1Kin 22:42 7977
name was Azubah the daughter of *S* ... 2Chr 20:31 7977

SHILHIM *(shil'-him)* {1} See SHAARAIM, SHARUHEN. *A city in Judah.*
And Lebaoth, and *S*, and Ain, and ... Josh 15:32 7978

SHILLEM *(shil'-lem)* {2} See SHALLUM, SHILLEMITES. *A son of Naphtali.*
Jahzeel, and Guni, and Jezer, and *S* ... Gen 46:24 8006
of *S*, the family of the ... Num 26:49 8006

SHILLEMITES *(shil'-lem-ites)* {1} *Descendants of Shillem.*
of Shillem, the family of the *S* ... Num 26:49 8016

SHILOAH *(shi-lo'-ah)* {1} See SILOAH, SILOAM. *A fountain in Jerusalem.*
the waters of *S* that go softly ... Is 8:6 7975

SHILOH *(shi'-loh)* {33} See SHILONITE.
1. Symbolic name for the Ruler from Judah.
between his feet, until *S* come ... Gen 49:10 7886
2. A city in Ephraim.
of Israel assembled together at *S* ... Josh 18:1 7887
lots for you before the LORD in *S* ... Josh 18:8 7887
again to Joshua to the host at *S* ... Josh 18:9 7887
for them in *S* before the LORD ... Josh 18:10 7887
by lot in *S* before the LORD ... Josh 19:51 7887
them at *S* in the land of Canaan ... Josh 21:2 7887
the children of Israel out of *S* ... Josh 22:9 7887
gathered themselves together at *S* ... Josh 22:12 7887
that the house of God was in *S* ... Judg 18:31 7887
brought them unto the camp to *S* ... Judg 21:12 7887
S yearly in a place which is on ... Judg 21:19 7887
if the daughters of *S* come out to ... Judg 21:21 7887
his wife of the daughters of *S* ... Judg 21:21 7887
unto the LORD of hosts in *S* ... 1Sa 1:3 7887
rose up after they had eaten in *S* ... 1Sa 1:9 7887
unto the house of the LORD in *S* ... 1Sa 1:24 7887
So they did in *S* unto all the ... 1Sa 2:14 7887
And the LORD appeared again in *S* ... 1Sa 3:21 7887
in *S* by the word of the LORD ... 1Sa 3:21 7887
of the LORD out of *S* unto us ... 1Sa 4:3 7887
So the people sent to *S*, that ... 1Sa 4:4 7887
came to *S* the same day with his ... 1Sa 4:12 7887
of Eli, the LORD's priest in *S* ... 1Sa 14:3 7887
concerning the house of Eli in *S* ... 1Kin 2:27 7887
and get thee to *S* ... 1Kin 14:2 7887
did so, and arose, and went to *S* ... 1Kin 14:4 7887
he forsook the tabernacle of *S* ... Ps 78:60 7887
now unto my place which was in *S* ... Jer 7:12 7887
your fathers, as I have done to *S* ... Jer 7:14 7887
will I make this house like *S* ... Jer 26:6 7887
This house shall be like *S* ... Jer 26:9 7887
came certain from Shechem, from *S* ... Jer 41:5 7887

SHILONI *(shi-lo'-ni)* {1} See SHILONITE. *Father of Zechariah.*
son of Zechariah, the son of *S* ... Neh 11:5 8023

SHILONITE *(shi'-lon-ite)* {5} See SHILONI, SHILONITES. *An inhabitant of Shiloh.*
Ahijah the *S* found him in the way ... 1Kin 11:29 7888
the LORD spake by Ahijah the *S* ... 1Kin 12:15 7888
spake by his servant Ahijah the *S* ... 1Kin 15:29 7888
in the prophecy of Ahijah the *S* ... 2Chr 9:29 7888
S to Jeroboam the son of Nebat ... 2Chr 10:15 7888

SHILONITES *(shi'-lon-ites)* {1}
And of the *S* ... 1Chr 9:5 7888

SHILSHAH *(shil'-shah)* {1} *Son of Zophah.*
Bezer, and Hod, and Shamma, and *S* ... 1Chr 7:37 8030

SHIMEA *(shim'-e-ah)* {4} See SHAMMAH, SHAMMUA, SHAMMUAH, SHIMEAH, SHIMEATHITES, SHIMMA.
1. David's brother.
Jonathan the son of *S* David's ... 1Chr 20:7 8092
2. A son of David.
S, and Shobab, and Nathan, and ... 1Chr 3:5 8092
3. Father of Haggiah.
S his son, Haggiah his son, ... 1Chr 6:30 8092
4. Father of Berachiah.
son of Berachiah, the son of *S* ... 1Chr 6:39 8092

SHIMEAH *(shim'-e-ah)* {4} See SHIMEA, SHIMEAM.
1. Same as Shimea 1.
the son of *S* David's brother ... 2Sa 13:3 8093
the son of *S* David's brother, ... 2Sa 13:32 8093
Jonathan the son of *S* the brother ... 2Sa 21:21 8092
2. A relative of King Saul.
And Mikloth begat *S* ... 1Chr 8:32 8039

SHIMEAM *(shim'-e-am)* {1} See SHIMEA. *Son of Mikloth.*
And Mikloth begat *S* ... 1Chr 9:38 8043

SHIMEATH *(shim'-e-ath)* {2} *Mother of Jozachar.*
For Jozachar the son of *S* ... 2Kin 12:21 8100
Zabad the son of *S* an Ammonitess ... 2Chr 24:26 8100

SHIMEATHITES *(shim'-e-ath-ites)* {1} *A family of scribes.*
the Tirathites, the *S*, and ... 1Chr 2:55 8101

SHIMEI *(shim'-e-i)* {42} See SHEMAIAH, SHIMHI, SHIMI, SHIMITES.
1. A son of Gershon.
families; Libni, and *S* ... Num 3:18 8096
Gershom; Libni, and *S* ... 1Chr 6:17 8096
the son of Zimmah, the son of *S* ... 1Chr 6:42 8096
Gershonites were, Laadan, and *S* ... 1Chr 23:7 8096
And the sons of *S* were, Jahath, ... 1Chr 23:10 8096
These four were the sons of *S* ... 1Chr 23:10 8096
2. A son of Gera.
house of Saul, whose name was *S* ... 2Sa 16:5 8096
thus said *S* when he cursed, Come ... 2Sa 16:7 8096
S went along on the hill's side ... 2Sa 16:13 8096
S the son of Gera, a Benjamite, ... 2Sa 19:16 8096
S the son of Gera fell down ... 2Sa 19:18 8096
Shall not *S* be put to death for ... 2Sa 19:21 8096
Therefore the king said unto *S* ... 2Sa 19:23 8096
hast with thee *S* the son of Gera ... 1Kin 2:8 8096
And the king sent and called for *S* ... 1Kin 2:36 8096
S said unto the king, The saying ... 1Kin 2:38 8096
S dwelt in Jerusalem many days ... 1Kin 2:38 8096
of *S* ran away unto Achish son of ... 1Kin 2:39 8096
And they told *S*, saying, Behold, ... 1Kin 2:39 8096
S arose, and saddled his ass, and ... 1Kin 2:40 8096
S went, and brought his servants ... 1Kin 2:40 8096
it was told Solomon that *S* had ... 1Kin 2:41 8096
And the king sent and called for *S* ... 1Kin 2:42 8096
The king said moreover to *S* ... 1Kin 2:44 8096
3. An officer of David.
and Nathan the prophet, and *S* ... 1Kin 1:8 8096
4. An officer of Solomon.
S the son of Elah, in Benjamin ... 1Kin 4:18 8096
5. A descendant of King Jehoiakim.
of Pedaiah were, Zerubbabel, and *S* ... 1Chr 3:19 8096
6. Son of Zacchur.
son, Zacchur his son, *S* his son ... 1Chr 4:26 8096
S had sixteen sons and six ... 1Chr 4:27 8096
7. Son of Gog.
his son, Gog his son, *S* his son, ... 1Chr 5:4 8096
8. Son of Libni.
his son, *S* his son, Uzza his son, ... 1Chr 6:29 8096
9. A Levite of the Laadan family.
The sons of *S* ... 1Chr 23:9 8096
10. A sanctuary servant.
The tenth to *S*, he, his sons, and ... 1Chr 25:17 8096

11. A vineyard keeper.
the vineyards was *S* the Ramathite ... 1Chr 27:27 8096
12. A Levite who cleansed the Temple.
Jehiel, and *S* ... 2Chr 29:14 8096
13. A Temple servant in Hezekiah's time.
S his brother was the next ... 2Chr 31:12 8096
S his brother, at the commandment ... 2Chr 31:13 8096
14. A Levite who married a foreigner.
Jozabad, and *S*, and Kelaiah, (the ... Ezr 10:23 8096
15. A Hashumite who married a foreigner.
Jeremai, Manasseh, and *S* ... Ezr 10:33 8096
16. A Banite who married a foreigner.
And Bani, and Binnui, *S*, ... Ezr 10:38 8096
17. Grandfather of Mordecai.
the son of Jair, the son of *S* ... Est 2:5 8096
18. A representative of the Gershonites.
the family of *S* apart, and their ... Zec 12:13 8097

SHIMEITES See SHIMITES.

SHIMEON *(shim'-e-on)* {1} See SIMEON. *A member of the Harim family.*
Ishijah, Malchiah, Shemaiah, *S* ... Ezr 10:31 8095

SHIMHI *(shim'-hi)* {1} See SHEMA, SHIMEI. *Father of a chief family in Judah.*
and Shimrath, the sons of *S* ... 1Chr 8:21 8096

SHIMI *(shi'-mi)* {1} See SHIMEI, SHIMITES. *Same as Shimei 1.*
Libni, and *S*, according to their ... Ex 6:17 8096

SHIMITES *(shi'-mites)* {1} *Descendants of Shimei 1.*
Libnites, and the family of the *S* ... Num 3:21 8097

SHIMMA *(shim'-mah)* {1} See SHAMMAH. *Same as Shamma.*
the second, and *S* the third, ... 1Chr 2:13 8092

SHIMON *(shi'-mon)* {1} *A descendant of Caleb.*
And the sons of *S* were, Amnon, and ... 1Chr 4:20 7889

SHIMRATH *(shim'-rath)* {1} *A son of Shimri.*
And Adaiah, and Beraiah, and *S* ... 1Chr 8:21 8119

SHIMRI *(shim'-ri)* {3} See SIMRI.
1. Head of a family in Simeon.
the son of Jedaiah, the son of *S* ... 1Chr 4:37 8113
2. Father of Jedaiah.
Jediael the son of *S*, and Joha his ... 1Chr 11:45 8113
3. A Levite who cleansed the Temple.
S, and Jeiel ... 2Chr 29:13 8113

SHIMRITH *(shim'-rith)* {1} See SHOMER. *Mother of Jehozabad.*
the son of *S* a Moabitess ... 2Chr 24:26 8116

SHIMROM *(shim'-rom)* {1} See SHIMRON. *A son of Issachar.*
were, Tola, and Puah, Jashub, and *S* ... 1Chr 7:1 8110

SHIMRON *(shim'-ron)* {4} See SHIMROM, SHIMRONITES. *Same as Shimron.*
Tola, and Phuvah, and Job, and *S* ... Gen 46:13 8110
of *S*, the family of the ... Num 26:24 8110
of Madon, and to the king of *S* ... Josh 11:1 8110
And Kattath, and Nahallal, and *S* ... Josh 19:15 8110

SHIMRONITE See SHIMRONITES.

SHIMRONITES *(shim'-ron-ites)* {1} *Descendants of Shimrom.*
of Shimron, the family of the *S* ... Num 26:24 8117

SHIMRON-MERON *(shim'-ron-me'-ron)* {1} *A city in Galilee.*
The king of *S*, one ... Josh 12:20 8112

SHIMSHAI *(shim'-shahee)* {4} *An opponent of Nehemiah.*
S the scribe wrote a letter ... Ezr 4:8 8124
S the scribe, and the rest of ... Ezr 4:9 8124
to *S* the scribe, and to the rest ... Ezr 4:17 8124
S the scribe, and their companions ... Ezr 4:23 8124

SHINAB *(shi'-nab)* {1} *King of Admah.*
S king of Admah, and Shemeber king ... Gen 14:2 8134

SHINAR *(shi'-nar)* {7} *A nation in Babylonia.*
and Calneh, in the land of *S* ... Gen 10:10 8152
found a plain in the land of *S* ... Gen 11:2 8152
in the days of Amraphel king of *S* ... Gen 14:1 8152
of nations, and Amraphel king of *S* ... Gen 14:9 8152
Cush, and from Elam, and from *S* ... Is 11:11 8152
land of *S* to the house of his god ... Dan 1:2 8152
it an house in the land of *S* ... Zec 5:11 8152

SHINE {32}
LORD make his face *s* upon thee ... Num 6:25 215
neither let the light *s* upon it ... Job 3:4 3313
s upon the counsel of the wicked ... Job 10:3 3313
thou shalt *s* forth, thou shalt be ... Job 11:17 5774
the spark of his fire shall not *s* ... Job 18:5 5050
the light shall *s* upon thy ways ... Job 22:28 5050
commandeth it not to *s* by the ... Job 36:32
the light of his cloud to *s* ... Job 37:15 3313
By his neesings a light doth *s* ... Job 41:18 1984
He maketh a path to *s* after him ... Job 41:32 215
thy face to *s* upon thy servant ... Ps 31:16 215
and cause his face to *s* upon us ... Ps 67:1 215
between the cherubims, *s* forth ... Ps 80:1 3313
O God, and cause thy face to *s* ... Ps 80:3 215
of hosts, and cause thy face to *s* ... Ps 80:7 215
God of hosts, cause thy face to *s* ... Ps 80:19 215
man, and oil to make his face to *s* ... Ps 104:15 6670
thy face to *s* upon thy servant ... Ps 119:135 215
man's wisdom maketh his face to *s* ... Eccl 8:1 215
shall not cause her light to *s* ... Is 13:10 5050
Arise, *s*; for thy light ... Is 60:1 215
They are waxen fat, they *s* ... Jer 5:28 6245
cause thy face to *s* upon thy ... Dan 9:17 215
they that be wise shall *s* as the ... Dan 12:3 2094
Let your light so *s* before men ... Mt 5:16 *2989*
Then shall the righteous *s* forth ... Mt 13:43 *1584*
and his face did *s* as the sun ... Mt 17:2 *2989*
image of God, should *s* unto them ... 2Cor 4:4 *826*
the light to *s* out of darkness ... 2Cor 4:6 *2989*
among whom ye *s* as lights in the ... Phil 2:15 *5316*
shall *s* no more at all in thee ... Rev 18:23 *5316*
neither of the moon, to *s* in it ... Rev 21:23 *5316*

SHINED {9}
he *s* forth from mount Paran, and ... Deut 33:2 3313
When his candle *s* upon my head ... Job 29:3 1984
If I beheld the sun when it *s* ... Job 31:26 1984
perfection of beauty, God hath *s* ... Ps 50:2 3313
death, upon them hath the light *s* ... Is 9:2 5050
the earth *s* with his glory ... Eze 43:2 215
suddenly there *s* round about him ... Acts 9:3 *4015*
him, and a light *s* in the prison ... Acts 12:7 *2989*
hath *s* in our hearts, to give the ... 2Cor 4:6 *2989*

SHINETH {9}
even to the moon, and it *s* not ... Job 25:5 166
but the night *s* as the day ... Ps 139:12 215
as the shining light, that *s* more ... Prov 4:18 215
the east, and *s* even unto the west ... Mt 24:27 *5316*
s unto the other part under ... Lk 17:24 *2989*
And the light *s* in darkness ... Jn 1:5 *5316*
a light that *s* in a dark place ... 2Pet 1:19 *5316*
is past, and the true light now *s* ... 1Jn 2:8 *5316*
was as the sun *s* in his strength ... Rev 1:16 *5316*

SHINING {11}
the earth by clear *s* after rain ... 2Sa 23:4 5051
of the just is as the *s* light ... Prov 4:18 5051
the *s* of a flaming fire by night ... Is 4:5 5051
the stars shall withdraw their *s* ... Joel 2:10 5051
the stars shall withdraw their *s* ... Joel 3:15 5051
at the *s* of thy glittering spear ... Hab 3:11 5051
And his raiment became *s*, ... Mk 9:3 *4744*
as when the bright *s* of a candle ... Lk 11:36 *796*
men stood by them in *s* garments ... Lk 24:4 *797*
He was a burning and a *s* light ... Jn 5:35 *5316*
s round about me and them which ... Acts 26:13 *4034*

SHION See SHIHON.

SHIP {71}
the way of a *s* in the midst of ... Prov 30:19 591
shall gallant *s* pass thereby ... Is 33:21 6716
They have made all thy *s* boards ... Eze 27:5
he found a *s* going to Tarshish ... Jonah 1:3 591
so that the *s* was like to be ... Jonah 1:4 591
that were in the *s* into the sea ... Jonah 1:5 591
gone down into the sides of the *s* ... Jonah 1:5 5600
in a *s* with Zebedee their father, ... Mt 4:21 *4143*
And they immediately left the *s* ... Mt 4:22 *4143*
And when he was entered into a *s* ... Mt 8:23 *4143*
insomuch that the *s* was covered ... Mt 8:24 *4143*
And he entered into a *s*, and passed ... Mt 9:1 *4143*
him, so that he went into a *s* ... Mt 13:2 *4143*
he departed thence by *s* into a ... Mt 14:13 *4143*
his disciples to get into a *s* ... Mt 14:22 *4143*
But the *s* was now in the midst of ... Mt 14:24 *4143*
Peter was come down out of the *s* ... Mt 14:29 *4143*
And when they were come into the *s* ... Mt 14:32 *4143*
Then they that were in the *s* came ... Mt 14:33 *4143*
away the multitude, and took *s* ... Mt 15:39 *4143*
were in the *s* mending their nets ... Mk 1:19 *4143*
in the *s* with the hired servants ... Mk 1:20 *4143*
that a small *s* should wait on him ... Mk 3:9 *4142*
so that he entered into a *s* ... Mk 4:1 *4143*
took him even as he was in the *s* ... Mk 4:36 *4143*
and the waves beat into the *s* ... Mk 4:37 *4143*
was in the hinder part of the *s* ... Mk 4:38
And when he was come out of the *s* ... Mk 5:2 *4143*
And when he was come into the *s* ... Mk 5:18 *4143*
again by *s* unto the other side ... Mk 5:21 *4143*
a desert place by *s* privately ... Mk 6:32 *4143*
his disciples to get into the *s* ... Mk 6:45 *4143*
the *s* was in the midst of the sea ... Mk 6:47 *4143*
he went up unto them into the *s* ... Mk 6:51 *4143*
when they were come out of the *s* ... Mk 6:54 *4143*
into a *s* with his disciples ... Mk 8:10 *4143*
entering into the *s* again ... Mk 8:13 *4143*
neither had they in the *s* with ... Mk 8:14 *4143*
and taught the people out of the *s* ... Lk 5:3 *4143*
which were in the other *s* ... Lk 5:7 *4143*
went into a *s* with his disciples ... Lk 8:22 *4143*
and he went up into the *s*, and ... Lk 8:37 *4143*
And entered into a *s*, and went over ... Jn 6:17 *4143*
sea, and drawing nigh unto the *s* ... Jn 6:19 *4143*
willingly received him into the *s* ... Jn 6:21 *4143*
immediately the *s* was at the land ... Jn 6:21 *4143*
and entered into a *s* immediately ... Jn 21:3 *4143*
net on the right side of the *s* ... Jn 21:6 *4143*
disciples came in a little *s* ... Jn 21:8 *4142*
And we went before to *s*, and sailed ... Acts 20:13 *4143*
they accompanied him unto the *s* ... Acts 20:38 *4143*
finding a *s* sailing over unto ... Acts 21:2 *4143*
for there the *s* was to unlade her ... Acts 21:3 *4143*
leave one of another, we took *s* ... Acts 21:6 *4143*
entering into a *s* of Adramyttium ... Acts 27:2 *4143*
a *s* of Alexandria sailing into ... Acts 27:6 *4143*
not only of the lading and *s* ... Acts 27:10 *4143*
the master and the owner of the *s* ... Acts 27:11 *3490*
when the *s* was caught, and could ... Acts 27:15 *4143*
used helps, undergirding the *s* ... Acts 27:17 *4143*
the next day they lightened the *s* ... Acts 27:18
own hands the tackling of the *s* ... Acts 27:19 *4143*
life among you, but of the *s* ... Acts 27:22 *4143*
were about to flee out of the *s* ... Acts 27:30 *4143*
Except these abide in the *s* ... Acts 27:31 *4143*
we were in all in the *s* two ... Acts 27:37 *4143*
enough, they lightened the *s* ... Acts 27:38 *4143*
were possible, to thrust in the *s* ... Acts 27:39 *4143*
seas met, they ran the *s* aground ... Acts 27:41 *3491*
and some on broken pieces of the *s* ... Acts 27:44 *4143*
we departed in a *s* of Alexandria ... Acts 28:11 *4143*

SHIPHI *(shi'-fi)* {1} *Father of Ziza.*
And Ziza the son of *S*, the son of ... 1Chr 4:37 8230

SHIPHMITE *(shif'-mite)* {1} *Family name of Zabdi.*
the wine cellars was Zabdi the *S* ... 1Chr 27:27 8225

SHIPHRAH *(shif'-rah)* {1} *A Hebrew midwife in Egypt.*
which the name of the one was *S* ... Ex 1:15 8236

SHIPHTAN *(shif'-tan)* {1} *Father of Kemuel.*
of Ephraim, Kemuel the son of *S* ... Num 34:24 8204

SHIPMASTER {2}
So the *s* came to him, and said ... Jonah 1:6 7227,2259
And every *s*, and all the company in ... Rev 18:17 *2942*

SHIPMEN {3}
s that had knowledge of the sea, ... 1Kin 9:27 582,591
about midnight the *s* deemed that ... Acts 27:27 *3492*
as the *s* were about to flee out ... Acts 27:30 *3492*

SHIPPING {1}
his disciples, they also took *s* ... Jn 6:24 *4143*

SHIPS {39}
and he shall be for an haven of *s* ... Gen 49:13 591
s shall come come from the coast ... Num 24:24 6716
thee into Egypt again with *s* ... Deut 28:68 591
and why did Dan remain in *s* ... Judg 5:17 591
made a navy of *s* in Ezion-geber ... 1Kin 9:26
Jehoshaphat made *s* of Tharshish ... 1Kin 22:48 591
for the *s* were broken at ... 1Kin 22:48 591
go with thy servants in the *s* ... 1Kin 22:49 591
by the hands of his servants *s* ... 2Chr 8:18 591
For the king's *s* went to Tarshish ... 2Chr 9:21 591
the *s* of Tarshish bringing gold ... 2Chr 9:21 591
him to make *s* to go to Tarshish ... 2Chr 20:36 591
they made the *s* in Ezion-gaber ... 2Chr 20:36 591
the *s* were broken, that they were ... 2Chr 20:37 591
are passed away as the swift *s* ... Job 9:26 591
Thou breakest the *s* of Tarshish ... Ps 48:7 591
There go the *s* ... Ps 104:26 591
They that go down to the sea in *s* ... Ps 107:23 591
She is like the merchants' *s* ... Prov 31:14 591
And upon all the *s* of Tarshish ... Is 2:16 591
Howl, ye *s* of Tarshish ... Is 23:1 591
Howl, ye *s* of Tarshish ... Is 23:14 591
Chaldeans, whose cry is in the *s* ... Is 43:14 591
the *s* of Tarshish first, to bring ... Is 60:9 591
all the *s* of the sea with their ... Eze 27:9 591
The *s* of Tarshish did sing of ... Eze 27:25 591
sea, shall come down from their *s* ... Eze 27:29 591
messengers go forth from me in *s* ... Eze 30:9 6716
For the *s* of Chittim shall come ... Dan 11:30 6716
and with horsemen, and with many *s* ... Dan 11:40 591
were also with him other little *s* ... Mk 4:36 *4142*
saw two *s* standing by the lake ... Lk 5:2 *4143*
And he entered into one of the *s* ... Lk 5:3 *4143*
they came, and filled both the *s* ... Lk 5:7 *4143*
they had brought their *s* to land ... Lk 5:11 *4143*
Behold also the *s*, which though ... Jas 3:4 *4143*
part of the *s* were destroyed ... Rev 8:9 *4143*
and all the company in *s*, and ... Rev 18:17 *4143*
had *s* in the sea by reason of her ... Rev 18:19 *4143*

SHIPWRECK {2}
was I stoned, thrice I suffered *s* ... 2Cor 11:25 *3489*
away concerning faith have made *s* ... 1Ti 1:19 *3489*

SHISHA *(shi'-shah)* {1} See SHAVSHA. *Father of Elihoreph and Ahiah.*
Elihoreph and Ahiah, the sons of *S* ... 1Kin 4:3 7894

SHISHAK *(shi'-shak)* {7} *A king of Egypt.*
unto *S* king of Egypt, and was in ... 1Kin 11:40 7895
that *S* king of Egypt came up ... 1Kin 14:25 7895
S king of Egypt came up against ... 2Chr 12:2 7895
to Jerusalem because of *S* ... 2Chr 12:5 7895
I also left you in the hand of *S* ... 2Chr 12:5 7895
upon Jerusalem by the hand of *S* ... 2Chr 12:7 7895
So *S* king of Egypt came up ... 2Chr 12:9 7895

SHITRAI *(shit'-ra-i)* {1} *A herdsman in David's court.*
fed in Sharon was *S* the Sharonite ... 1Chr 27:29 7861

SHITTAH {1}
the *s* tree, and the myrtle, and the ... Is 41:19 7848

SHITTIM *(shit'-tim)* {32} *A place in Moab.*
and badgers' skins, and *s* wood, ... Ex 25:5 7848
they shall make an ark of *s* wood ... Ex 25:10 7848
thou shalt make staves of *s* wood ... Ex 25:13 7848
shalt also make a table of *s* wood ... Ex 25:23 7848
shalt make the staves of *s* wood ... Ex 25:28 7848
tabernacle of *s* wood standing up ... Ex 26:15 7848
And thou shalt make bars of *s* wood ... Ex 26:26 7848
of *s* wood overlaid with gold ... Ex 26:32 7848
hanging five pillars of *s* wood ... Ex 26:37 7848
shalt make an altar of *s* wood ... Ex 27:1 7848
for the altar, staves of *s* wood ... Ex 27:6 7848
of *s* wood shalt thou make it ... Ex 30:1 7848
shalt make the staves of *s* wood ... Ex 30:5 7848
and badgers' skins, and *s* wood, ... Ex 35:7 7848
with whom was found *s* wood for ... Ex 35:24 7848
for the tabernacle of *s* wood ... Ex 36:20 7848
And he made bars of *s* wood ... Ex 36:31 7848
thereunto four pillars of *s* wood ... Ex 36:36 7848
Bezaleel made the ark of *s* wood ... Ex 37:1 7848

And he made staves of *s* wood .... Ex 37:4 7848
And he made the table of *s* wood .... Ex 37:10 7848
And he made the staves of *s* wood .... Ex 37:15 7848
made the incense altar of *s* wood .... Ex 37:25 7848
And he made the staves of *s* wood .... Ex 37:28 7848
altar of burnt offering of *s* wood .... Ex 38:1 7848
And he made the staves of *s* wood .... Ex 38:6 7848
And Israel abode in *S*, and the............... Num 25:1 7851
And I made an ark of *s* wood .... Deut 10:3 7848
out of *S* two men to spy secretly .... Josh 2:1 7851
and they removed from *S*, and came .... Josh 3:1 7851
and shall water the valley of *S*............... Joel 3:18 7851
answered him from *S* unto Gilgal .... Mic 6:5 7851

SHIVERS {1}
potter shall they be broken to *s* .... Rev 2:27 *4937*

SHIZA *(shi'-zah)* {1} *A "mighty man" of David.*
Adina the son of *S* the Reubenite 1Chr 11:42 7877

SHOA *(sho'-ah)* {1} *A tribal enemy of Israel.*
and all the Chaldeans, Pekod, and *S*...... Eze 23:23 7772

SHOBAB *(sho'-bab)* {4}
1. A son of David.
Shammuah, and *S*, and Nathan, and 2Sa 5:14 7727
Shimea, and *S*, and Nathan, and 1Chr 3:5 7727
and *S*, Nathan, and Solomon 1Chr 14:4 7727
2. A son of Caleb.
Jesher, and *S*, and Ardon....................... 1Chr 2:18 7727

SHOBACH *(sho'-bak)* {2} See SHOPHACH. *A Syrian defeated by David.*
S the captain of the host of.................... 2Sa 10:16 7731
smote *S* the captain of their host 2Sa 10:18 7731

SHOBAI *(sho'-bahee)* {2} *A family of exiles.*
of Hatita, the children of *S* .... Ezr 2:42 7630
of Hatita, the children of *S* .... Neh 7:45 7630

SHOBAL *(sho'-bal)* {9}
1. A son of Seir.
Lotan, and *S*, and Zibeon, and Anah,..... Gen 36:20 7732
And the children of *S* were these .... Gen 36:23 7732
duke Lotan, duke *S*, duke Zibeon,.......... Gen 36:29 7732
Lotan, and *S*, and Zibeon, and Anah,..... 1Chr 1:38 7732
The sons of *S* 1Chr 1:40 7732
2. A son of Caleb.
S the father of Kirjath-jearim,.............. 1Chr 2:50 7732
S the father of Kirjath-jearim............... 1Chr 2:52 7732
3. A son of Judah.
Hezron, and Carmi, and Hur, and *S*......... 1Chr 4:1 7732
Reaiah the son of *S* begat Jahath......... 1Chr 4:2 7732

SHOBEK *(sho'-bek)* {1} *A clan leader who renewed the covenant.*
Hallohesh, Pileha, *S*, ... Neh 10:24 7733

SHOBI *(sho'-bi)* {1} *A son of Nahash.*
that *S* the son of Nahash of 2Sa 17:27 7629

SHOCHO *(sho'-ko)* {1} See CHOCHO. *A city in Judah.*
S with the villages thereof, and 2Chr 28:18 7755

SHOCHOH *(sho'-ko)* {2} See SHOCHO, SHOCO, SOCHOH, SOCO, SOCOH. *Same as Shocho.*
and were gathered together at *S* 1Sa 17:1 7755
to Judah, and pitched between *S* 1Sa 17:1 7755

SHOCK {1}
like as a *s* of corn cometh in in .... Job 5:26 1430

SHOCKS {1}
and burnt up both the *s*, and also .... Judg 15:5 1430

SHOCO *(sho'-ko)* {1} See SHOCHOH. *Same as Shocho.*
And Beth-zur, and *S*, and Adullam,........ 2Chr 11:7 7755

SHOD {4}
s them, and gave them to eat and to 2Chr 28:15 5274
s thee with badgers' skin, and I .... Eze 16:10 5274
But be *s* with sandals .... Mk 6:9 *5265*
your feet *s* with the preparation .... Eph 6:15 *5265*

SHOE {9}
loose his *s* from off his foot, and .... Deut 25:9 5275
of him that hath his *s* loosed................. Deut 25:10 5275
thy *s* is not waxen old upon thy .... Deut 29:5 5275
Loose thy *s* from off thy foot................. Josh 5:15 5275
a man plucked off his *s*, and gave .... Ruth 4:7 5275
So he drew off his *s* .... Ruth 4:8 5275
over Edom will I cast out my *s*................ Ps 60:8 5275
over Edom will I cast out my *s*................ Ps 108:9 5275
put off thy *s* from thy foot .... Is 20:2 5275

SHOELATCHET {1}
take from a thread even to a *s*......... Gen 14:23 8288,5275

SHOE'S {1}
whose *s* latchet I am not worthy .... Jn 1:27 *5266*

SHOES {21}
put off thy *s* from off thy feet,................ Ex 3:5 5275
your *s* on your feet, and your .... Ex 12:11 5275
Thy *s* shall be iron and brass .... Deut 33:25 4515
And old *s* and clouted upon their .... Josh 9:5 5275
our *s* are become old by reason of.......... Josh 9:13 5275
in his *s* that were on his feet 1Kin 2:5 5275
How beautiful are thy feet with *s* .... Song 7:1 5275
the latchet of their *s* be broken .... Is 5:27 5275
put on thy *s* upon thy feet, and .... Eze 24:17 5275
heads, and your *s* upon your feet .... Eze 24:23 5275
and the poor for a pair of *s* .... Amos 2:6 5275
and the needy for a pair of *s* .... Amos 8:6 5275
whose *s* I am not worthy to bear........... Mt 3:11 *5266*
neither two coats, neither *s* .... Mt 10:10 *5266*
the latchet of whose *s* I am not .... Mk 1:7 *5266*
the latchet of whose *s* I am not .... Lk 3:16 *5266*
neither purse, nor scrip, nor *s* .... Lk 10:4 *5266*
on his hand, and *s* on his feet .... Lk 15:22 *5266*
you without purse, and scrip, and *s* .... Lk 22:35 *5266*

Put off thy *s* from thy feet...................... Acts 7:33 *5266*
whose *s* of his feet I am not.................... Acts 13:25 *5266*

SHOHAM *(sho'-ham)* {1} *A Merarite.*
Beno, and *S*, and Zaccur, and Ibri 1Chr 24:27 7719

SHOMER *(sho'-mur)* {2} See SHAMER, SHIMRITH.
1. Same as Shimrith.
and Jehozabad the son of *S*................... 2Kin 12:21 7763
2. Son of Heber.
And Heber begat Japhlet, and *S* 1Chr 7:32 7763

SHONE {7}
face *s* while he talked with him .... Ex 34:29 7160
behold, the skin of his face *s*................... Ex 34:30 7160
that the skin of Moses' face *s* .... Ex 34:35 7160
the sun *s* upon the water, and the 2Kin 3:22 2224
of the Lord *s* round about them .... Lk 2:9 *4034*
suddenly there *s* from heaven a.............. Acts 22:6 *4015*
the day *s* not for a third part of .... Rev 8:12 *5316*

SHOOK {12}
for the oxen *s* it 2Sa 6:6 8058
Then the earth *s* and trembled 2Sa 22:8 1607
foundations of heaven moved and *s* 2Sa 22:8 1607
Also I *s* my lap, and said, So God .... Neh 5:13 5287
Then the earth *s* and trembled .... Ps 18:7 1607
The earth *s*, the heavens also................ Ps 68:8 7493
the earth trembled and *s* .... Ps 77:18 7493
over the sea, he *s* the kingdoms............. Is 23:11 7264
But they *s* off the dust of their.............. Acts 13:51 *1621*
he *s* his raiment, and said unto .... Acts 18:6 *1621*
he *s* off the beast into the fire, ... Acts 28:5 *660*
Whose voice then *s* the earth,................ Heb 12:26 *4531*

SHOOT {21}
he made the middle bar to *s*.................... Ex 36:33 1272
I will *s* three arrows on the side............. 1Sa 20:20 3384
find out now the arrows which I *s* 1Sa 20:36 3384
that they would *s* from the wall.............. 2Sa 11:20 3384
Then Elisha said, *S*.............................. 2Kin 13:17 3384
nor *s* an arrow there, nor come 2Kin 19:32 3384
to *s* with bow, and skilful in war,............ 1Chr 5:18 1869
to *s* arrows and great stones.................. 2Chr 26:15 3384
that they may privily *s* at the .... Ps 11:2 3384
they *s* out the lip, they shake .... Ps 22:7 6362
bendeth his bow to *s* his arrows............. Ps 58:7
bend their bows to *s* their arrows .... Ps 64:3
That they may *s* in secret at the .... Ps 64:4 3384
suddenly do they *s* at him .... Ps 64:4 3384
But God shall *s* at them with an .... Ps 64:7 3384
s out thine arrows, and destroy.............. Ps 144:6 7971
nor *s* an arrow there, nor come .... Is 37:33
s at her, spare no arrows .... Jer 50:14 3034
neither *s* up their top among the............ Eze 31:14 5414
ye shall *s* forth your branches,.............. Eze 36:8 5414
When they now *s* forth, ye see and .... Lk 21:30 *4261*

SHOOTERS {1}
the *s* shot from off the wall upon 2Sa 11:24 3384

SHOOTETH {3}
his branch *s* forth in his garden .... Job 8:16 3318
In measure, when it *s* forth .... Is 27:8 7971
herbs, and *s* out great branches .... Mk 4:32 *4160*

SHOOTING {2}
s arrows out of a bow, even of................ 1Chr 12:2
of the *s* up of the latter growth.............. Amos 7:1 5927

SHOPHACH *(sho'-fak)* {2} See SHOBACH. *Same as Shoback.*
S the captain of the host of.................... 1Chr 19:16 7780
killed *S* the captain of the host.............. 1Chr 19:18 7780

SHOPHAN *(sho'-fan)* {1} See ZAPHON. *A city in Gad.*
And Atroth, *S*, and Jaazer, and............. Num 32:35 5855

SHORE {17}
the sand which is upon the sea *s*............ Gen 22:17 8193
the Egyptians dead upon the sea *s*.......... Ex 14:30 8193
is upon the sea *s* in multitude .... Josh 11:4 8193
was from the *s* of the salt sea................ Josh 15:2 7097
Asher continued on the sea *s*.................. Judg 5:17 2348
is on the sea *s* in multitude 1Sa 13:5 8193
as the sand that is on the sea *s*.............. 1Kin 4:29 8193
on the *s* of the Red sea, in the 1Kin 9:26 8193
Ashkelon, and against the sea *s* .... Jer 47:7 2348
whole multitude stood on the *s* .... Mt 13:2 *123*
when it was full, they drew to *s* .... Mt 13:48 *123*
of Gennesaret, and drew to the *s* .... Mk 6:53 *4358*
now come, Jesus stood on the *s*.............. Jn 21:4 *123*
and we kneeled down on the *s* .... Acts 21:5 *123*
a certain creek with a *s*, into .... Acts 27:39 *123*
to the wind, and made toward *s*.............. Acts 27:40 *123*
which is by the sea *s* innumerable .... Heb 11:12 *5491*

SHORN {4}
a flock of sheep that are even *s*.............. Song 4:2 7094
having *s* his head in Cenchrea .... Acts 18:18 *2751*
be not covered, let her also be *s* 1Cor 11:6 *2751*
for a woman to be *s* or shaven................. 1Cor 11:6 *2751*

SHORT {13}
Moses, Is the LORD's hand waxed *s*........ Num 11:23 7114
the LORD began to cut Israel *s* 2Kin 10:32
the light is *s* because of......................... Job 17:12 7138
the triumphing of the wicked is *s* .... Job 20:5 7138
Remember how *s* my time is................... Ps 89:47 2465
come *s* of the glory of God .... Rom 3:23 *5302*
cut it *s* in righteousness......................... Rom 9:28 *4932*
because a *s* work will the Lord .... Rom 9:28 *4932*
I say, brethren, the time is *s* 1Cor 7:29 *4958*
from you for a *s* time in presence............ 1Th 2:17 *5610*
you should seem to come *s* of it.............. Heb 4:1 *5302*
knoweth that he hath but a *s* time............ Rev 12:12 *3641*
he must continue a *s* space.................... Rev 17:10 *3641*

SHORTENED {9}
The days of his youth hast thou *s*............ Ps 89:45 7114
he *s* my days .... Ps 102:23 7114
years of the wicked shall be *s* .... Prov 10:27 7114
Is my hand *s* at all, that it...................... Is 50:2 7114
Behold, the LORD's hand is not *s* .... Is 59:1 7114
And except those days should be *s* .... Mt 24:22 *2856*
sake those days shall be *s* .... Mt 24:22 *2856*
that the Lord had *s* those days .... Mk 13:20 *2856*
hath chosen, he hath *s* the days .... Mk 13:20 *2856*

SHORTER {2}
For the bed is *s* than that a man .... Is 28:20 7114
Now the upper chambers were *s* .... Eze 42:5 7114

SHORTLY {15}
God will *s* bring it to pass...................... Gen 41:32 4116
s be brought again from Babylon............. Jer 27:16 4120
Now will I *s* pour out my fury.................. Eze 7:8 7138
he himself would depart *s* thither ... Acts 25:4 *1722,5034*
bruise Satan under your feet *s* .... Rom 16:20 *1722,5034*
But I will come to you *s*, if the................ 1Cor 4:19 *5030*
to send Timotheus *s* unto you.................. Phil 2:19 *5030*
that I also myself shall come *s* .... Phil 2:24 *5030*
thee, hoping to come unto thee *s*............. 1Ti 3:14 *5032*
thy diligence to come *s* unto me.............. 2Ti 4:9 *5030*
with whom, if he come *s*, I will................ Heb 13:23 *5032*
Knowing that *s* I must put off.................. 2Pet 1:14 *5031*
But I trust I shall *s* see thee 3Jn 14 *2112*
things which must *s* come to pass ... Rev 1:1 *1722,5034*
the things which must *s* be done..... Rev 22:6 *1722,5034*

SHOSHANNIM *(sho-shan'-nim)* {2} *A musical notation.*
To the chief Musician upon *S*................. Ps 45:*t* 7799
To the chief Musician upon *S*................. Ps 69:*t* 7799

SHOSHANNIM-EDUTH *(sho-shan'-nim-e'-duth)* {1} *A musical notation.*
To the chief Musician upon *S*................. Ps 80:*t* 7802

SHOT {16}
budded, and her blossoms *s* forth .... Gen 40:10 5927
him, and *s* at him, and hated him .... Gen 49:23 7232
surely be stoned, or *s* through .... Ex 19:13 3384
We have *s* at them................................. Num 21:30 3384
thereof, as though I *s* at a mark 1Sa 20:20 7971
lad ran, he *s* an arrow beyond him 1Sa 20:36 3384
of the arrow which Jonathan had *s*.......... 1Sa 20:37 3384
the shooters *s* from off the wall............... 2Sa 11:24 3384
said, Shoot. And he *s*............................ 2Kin 13:17 3384
the archers *s* at king Josiah.................... 2Chr 35:23 3384
and he *s* out lightnings, and.................... Ps 18:14 7232
Their tongue is as an arrow *s* out............. Jer 9:8 7819
forth branches, and *s* forth sprigs .... Eze 17:6 7971
s forth her branches toward him,............. Eze 17:7 7971
of waters, when he *s* forth...................... Eze 31:5 7971
he hath *s* up his top among the............... Eze 31:10 7971

SHOULD {783}
not good that the man *s* be alone........... Gen 2:18
lest any finding him *s* kill him .... Gen 4:15
the righteous *s* be as the wicked .... Gen 18:25
that Sarah *s* have given children............. Gen 21:7
If it be your mind that I *s* bury................ Gen 23:8
the place *s* kill me for Rebekah............... Gen 26:7
why *s* I be deprived also of you.............. Gen 27:45
the cattle *s* be gathered together .... Gen 29:7
than that I *s* give her to another .... Gen 29:19
that they *s* conceive when they .... Gen 30:38
if men *s* overdrive them one day,............ Gen 33:13
S he deal with our sister as with .... Gen 34:31
knew that the seed *s* not be his............... Gen 38:9
lest that he *s* give seed to his................. Gen 38:9
they *s* put me into the dungeon.............. Gen 40:15
heard that they *s* eat bread there .... Gen 43:25
s do according to this thing.................... Gen 44:7
how then *s* we steal out of thy .... Gen 44:8
said, God forbid that I *s* do so .... Gen 44:17
for if he *s* leave his father, his .... Gen 44:22
for why *s* we die in thy presence .... Gen 47:15
that Pharaoh *s* have the fifth .... Gen 47:26
that I *s* go unto Pharaoh .... Ex 3:11
that I *s* bring forth the children .... Ex 3:11
that I *s* obey his voice to let .... Ex 5:2
than that we *s* die in the .... Ex 14:12
for he *s* make full restitution................... Ex 22:3
Wherefore *s* the Egyptians speak, ... Ex 32:12
hath commanded, that ye *s* do them .... Ex 35:1
that they *s* be stones for a .... Ex 39:7
the hole, that it *s* not rend...................... Ex 39:23
things which *s* not be done..................... Lev 4:13
things which *s* not be done..................... Lev 4:22
the LORD commanded that ye *s* do.......... Lev 9:6
ye *s* indeed have eaten it in the .... Lev 10:18
s it have been accepted in the .... Lev 10:19
that ye *s* be defiled thereby .... Lev 11:43
other people, that ye *s* be mine .... Lev 20:26
that they *s* bring forth him that .... Lev 24:23
that ye *s* not be their bondmen .... Lev 26:13
which *s* be the LORD's firstling,.............. Lev 27:26
unto them was that they *s* bear............... Num 7:9
that they *s* keep the passover .... Num 9:4
Whence *s* I have flesh to give .... Num 11:13
s she not be ashamed seven days............ Num 12:14
wives and our children *s* be a prey.......... Num 14:3
ones, which ye said *s* be a prey .... Num 14:31
declared what *s* be done to him .... Num 15:34
that we and our cattle *s* die there .... Num 20:4
God is not a man, that he *s* lie .... Num 23:19
the son of man, that he *s* repent.............. Num 23:19
Why *s* the name of our father be............. Num 27:4
that they *s* not go into the land............... Num 32:9

S

Because he *s* have remained in the .... Num 35:28
that he *s* come again to dwell in .... Num 35:32
time all the things which ye *s* do .... Deut 1:18
to shew you by what way ye *s* go .... Deut 1:33
ones, which ye said *s* be a prey .... Deut 1:39
that ye *s* do so in the land .... Deut 4:5
sware that I *s* not go over Jordan .... Deut 4:21
that I *s* not go in unto that good .... Deut 4:21
which *s* kill his neighbour .... Deut 4:42
Now therefore why *s* we die .... Deut 5:25
the end that he *s* multiply horses .... Deut 17:16
so *s* ye sin against the LORD your .... Deut 20:18
if he *s* exceed, and beat him above .... Deut 25:3
then thy brother *s* seem vile unto .... Deut 25:3
Lest there *s* be among you man, or .... Deut 29:18
lest there *s* be among you a root .... Deut 29:18
lest their adversaries *s* behave .... Deut 32:27
strangely, and lest they *s* say .... Deut 32:27
How *s* one chase a thousand, and .... Deut 32:30
Joshua commanded that they *s* take .... Josh 8:29
that they *s* bless the people of .... Josh 8:33
in the place which he *s* choose .... Josh 9:27
that they *s* come against Israel .... Josh 11:20
when they *s* so say to us or to .... Josh 22:28
God forbid that we *s* rebel .... Josh 22:29
forbid that we *s* forsake the LORD .... Josh 24:16
that we *s* give bread unto thine .... Judg 8:6
that we *s* give bread unto thy men .... Judg 8:15
S I leave my fatness, wherewith .... Judg 9:9
S I forsake my sweetness, and my .... Judg 9:11
S I leave my wine, which cheereth .... Judg 9:13
is Shechem, that we *s* serve him .... Judg 9:28
for why *s* we serve him .... Judg 9:28
is Abimelech, that we *s* serve him .... Judg 9:38
that they *s* not dwell in Shechem .... Judg 9:41
that they *s* make a great flame .... Judg 20:38
that there *s* be to day one tribe .... Judg 21:3
at this time, that ye *s* be guilty .... Judg 21:22
If I *s* say, I have hope .... Ruth 1:12
if I *s* have an husband also to .... Ruth 1:12
to night, and *s* also bear sons .... Ruth 1:12
s walk before me for ever 1Sa 2:30
that I *s* not reign over them 1Sa 8:7
can shew us our way that we *s* go 1Sa 9:6
if the man *s* yet come thither 1Sa 10:22
for then *s* ye go after vain 1Sa 12:21
God forbid that I *s* sin against 1Sa 12:23
s have been utterly destroyed 1Sa 15:21
he is not a man, that he *s* repent 1Sa 15:29
that he *s* defy the armies of the 1Sa 17:26
that I *s* be son in law to the 1Sa 18:18
s have been given to David 1Sa 18:19
servants, that they *s* kill David 1Sa 19:1
why *s* I kill thee 1Sa 19:17
why *s* my father hide this thing 1Sa 20:2
I *s* not fail to sit with the king 1Sa 20:5
that he *s* rise against me, to lie 1Sa 22:13
The LORD forbid that I *s* do this 1Sa 24:6
The LORD forbid that I *s* stretch 1Sa 26:11
better for me than that I *s* 1Sa 27:1
for why *s* thy servant dwell in 1Sa 27:5
Lest they *s* tell on us, saying, ... 1Sa 27:11
for wherewith *s* he reconcile 1Sa 29:4
s it not be with the heads of 1Sa 29:4
wherefore *s* I smite thee to the 2Sa 2:22
how then *s* I hold up my face to 2Sa 2:22
he is dead, wherefore *s* I fast 2Sa 12:23
unto him, Why *s* he go with thee 2Sa 13:26
s I this day make thee go up and 2Sa 15:20
Why *s* this dead dog curse my lord 2Sa 16:9
And again, whom *s* I serve 2Sa 16:19
s I not serve in the presence of 2Sa 16:19
Though I *s* receive a thousand 2Sa 18:12
Otherwise I *s* have wrought 2Sa 18:13
that the king *s* take it to his 2Sa 19:19
that ye *s* this day be adversaries 2Sa 19:22
that I *s* go up with the king unto 2Sa 19:34
wherefore then *s* thy servant be 2Sa 19:35
why *s* the king recompense it me 2Sa 19:36
that our advice *s* not be first 2Sa 19:43
that I *s* swallow up or destroy 2Sa 20:20
s be destroyed from remaining in 2Sa 21:5
from me, O LORD, that I *s* do this 2Sa 23:17
who *s* sit on the throne of my 1Kin 1:27
of David drew nigh that he *s* die 1Kin 2:1
their faces on me, that I *s* reign 1Kin 2:15
that the beams *s* not be fastened 1Kin 6:6
the good way wherein they *s* walk 1Kin 8:36
that he *s* not go after other gods 1Kin 11:10
which told me that I *s* be king 1Kin 14:2
that I *s* give the inheritance of 1Kin 21:3
that *s* have reigned in his stead 2Kin 3:27
s I set this before an hundred 2Kin 4:43
what *s* I wait for the LORD any 2Kin 6:33
if the LORD *s* make windows in 2Kin 7:19
that he *s* do this great thing 2Kin 8:13
with them that *s* go out on the 2Kin 11:9
that they *s* be the LORD's people 2Kin 11:17
that they *s* not do like them 2Kin 17:15
them how they *s* fear the LORD 2Kin 17:28
that the LORD *s* deliver Jerusalem 2Kin 18:35
that they *s* become a desolation 2Kin 22:19
that they *s* bring them in and out 1Chr 9:28
it me, that I *s* do this thing 1Chr 11:19
for those that *s* make a sound 1Chr 16:42
people, that they *s* be plagued 1Chr 21:17
say to David, that David *s* go up 1Chr 21:18
that he *s* sanctify the most holy 1Chr 23:13

that they *s* keep the charge of 1Chr 23:32
who *s* prophesy with harps, with 1Chr 25:1
that we *s* be able to offer so 1Chr 29:14
that I *s* build him an house, save 2Chr 2:6
that they *s* burn after the manner 2Chr 4:20
the good way, wherein they *s* walk 2Chr 6:27
God of Israel *s* be put to death 2Chr 15:13
that *s* praise the beauty of 2Chr 20:21
that they *s* be the LORD's people 2Chr 23:16
unclean in any thing *s* enter in 2Chr 23:19
that they *s* not go with him to 2Chr 25:13
that ye *s* minister unto him, and 2Chr 29:11
the sin offering *s* be made for 2Chr 29:24
that they *s* come to the house of 2Chr 30:1
that they *s* come to keep the 2Chr 30:5
Why *s* the kings of Assyria come, ... 2Chr 32:4
that your God *s* be able to 2Chr 32:14
that they *s* not eat of the most .... Ezr 2:63
why *s* damage grow to the hurt of .... Ezr 4:22
for why *s* there be wrath against .... Ezr 7:23
them what they *s* say unto Iddo .... Ezr 8:17
that they *s* bring unto us .... Ezr 8:17
S we again break thy commandments .... Ezr 9:14
so that there *s* be no remnant nor .... Ezr 9:14
to swear that they *s* do according .... Ezr 10:5
that they *s* gather themselves .... Ezr 10:7
all his substance *s* be forfeited .... Ezr 10:8
why *s* not my countenance be sad, ... Neh 2:3
that they *s* do according to this .... Neh 5:12
why *s* the work cease, whilst I .... Neh 6:3
And I said, *S* such a man as I flee .... Neh 6:11
that I *s* be afraid, and do so, and .... Neh 6:13
that they *s* not eat of the most .... Neh 7:65
that the children of Israel *s* .... Neh 8:14
And that they *s* publish and .... Neh 8:15
in the way wherein they *s* go .... Neh 9:12
promisedst them that they *s* go in .... Neh 9:15
and the way wherein they *s* go .... Neh 9:19
that they *s* go in to possess it .... Neh 9:23
that we *s* bring the firstfruits .... Neh 10:37
portion *s* be for the singers .... Neh 11:23
the Moabite *s* not come into the .... Neh 13:1
them, that he *s* curse them .... Neh 13:2
that the gates *s* be shut, and .... Neh 13:19
charged that they *s* not be opened .... Neh 13:19
that there *s* no burden be brought .... Neh 13:19
that they *s* cleanse themselves .... Neh 13:22
and that they *s* come .... Neh 13:22
that they *s* do according to every .... Est 1:8
that every man *s* bear rule in his .... Est 1:22
that it *s* be published according .... Est 1:22
her that she *s* not shew it .... Est 2:10
did, and what *s* become of her .... Est 2:11
that they *s* be ready against that .... Est 3:14
that she *s* go in unto the king .... Est 4:8
that the Jews *s* be ready against .... Est 8:13
that they *s* keep the fourteenth .... Est 9:21
that they *s* make them days of .... Est 9:22
s return upon his own head, and .... Est 9:25
his sons *s* be hanged on the .... Est 9:25
unto them, so as it *s* not fail .... Est 9:27
that these days *s* be remembered .... Est 9:28
that these days of Purim *s* not .... Est 9:28
or why the breasts that I *s* suck .... Job 3:12
For now *s* I have lain still and .... Job 3:13
and been quiet, I *s* have slept .... Job 3:13
Then *s* I yet have comfort .... Job 6:10
is my strength, that I *s* hope .... Job 6:11
end, that I *s* prolong my life .... Job 6:11
pity *s* be shewed from his friend .... Job 6:14
thy latter end *s* greatly increase .... Job 8:7
but how *s* man be just with God .... Job 9:2
that I *s* answer him .... Job 9:32
we *s* come together in judgment .... Job 9:32
I *s* have been as though I had not .... Job 10:19
I *s* have been carried from the .... Job 10:19
S not the multitude of words be .... Job 11:2
s a man full of talk be justified .... Job 11:2
S thy lies make men hold their .... Job 11:3
and it *s* be your wisdom .... Job 13:5
it good that he *s* search you out .... Job 13:9
S a wise man utter vain knowledge .... Job 15:2
S he reason with unprofitable .... Job 15:3
What is man, that he *s* be clean .... Job 15:14
a woman, that he *s* be righteous .... Job 15:14
of my lips *s* asswage your grief .... Job 16:5
But ye *s* say, Why persecute we .... Job 19:28
why *s* not my spirit be troubled .... Job 21:4
the Almighty, that we *s* serve him .... Job 21:15
and what profit *s* we have, if we .... Job 21:15
so *s* I be delivered for ever from .... Job 23:7
God forbid that I *s* justify you .... Job 27:5
why then *s* I think upon a maid .... Job 31:1
for I *s* have denied the God that .... Job 31:28
Days *s* speak, and multitude of .... Job 32:7
multitude of years *s* teach wisdom .... Job 32:7
Lest ye *s* say, We have found out .... Job 32:13
S I lie against my right .... Job 34:6
he *s* delight himself with God .... Job 34:9
from God, that he *s* do wickedness .... Job 34:10
that he *s* commit iniquity .... Job 34:10
that he *s* enter into judgment .... Job 34:23
S it be according to thy mind .... Job 34:33
that which *s* be set on thy table .... Job 36:16
on thy table *s* be full of fatness .... Job 36:16
prevented me, that I *s* repay him .... Job 41:11
Though an host *s* encamp against .... Ps 27:3
though war *s* rise against me, in .... Ps 27:3

that I *s* not go down to the pit .... Ps 30:3
otherwise they *s* rejoice over me .... Ps 38:16
Wherefore *s* I fear in the days of .... Ps 49:5
That he *s* still live for ever, and .... Ps 49:9
that which *s* have been for their .... Ps 69:22
I *s* offend against the generation .... Ps 73:15
that they *s* make them known to .... Ps 78:5
even the children which *s* be born .... Ps 78:6
who *s* arise and declare them to .... Ps 78:6
Wherefore *s* the heathen say, ... Ps 79:10
I *s* soon have subdued their .... Ps 81:14
The haters of the LORD *s* have .... Ps 81:15
but their time *s* have endured for .... Ps 81:15
He *s* have fed them also with the .... Ps 81:16
the rock *s* I have satisfied thee .... Ps 81:16
they *s* not enter into my rest .... Ps 95:11
that it *s* not be removed for ever .... Ps 104:5
his wrath, lest he *s* destroy them .... Ps 106:23
Wherefore *s* the heathen say, ... Ps 115:2
I *s* then have perished in mine .... Ps 119:92
If I *s* count them, they are more .... Ps 139:18
to know the way wherein I *s* walk .... Ps 143:8
that the waters *s* not pass his .... Prov 8:29
up a child in the way he *s* go .... Prov 22:6
why *s* he take away thy bed from .... Prov 22:27
which they *s* do under the heaven .... Eccl 2:3
because I *s* leave it unto the man .... Eccl 2:18
for a man, than that he *s* eat .... Eccl 2:24
that he *s* make his soul enjoy .... Eccl 2:24
And also that every man *s* eat .... Eccl 3:13
that men *s* fear before him .... Eccl 3:14
than that a man *s* rejoice in his .... Eccl 3:22
wherefore *s* God be angry at thy .... Eccl 5:6
to the end that man *s* find .... Eccl 7:14
for why *s* I be as one that .... Song 1:7
when I *s* find thee without, I .... Song 8:1
yea, I *s* not be despised .... Song 8:1
His left hand *s* be under my head, ... Song 8:3
and his right hand *s* embrace me .... Song 8:3
Why *s* ye be stricken any more .... Is 1:5
we *s* have been as Sodom .... Is 1:9
we *s* have been like unto Gomorrah .... Is 1:9
he looked that it *s* bring forth .... Is 5:2
that it *s* bring forth grapes .... Is 5:4
instructed me that I *s* not walk .... Is 8:11
s not a people seek unto their .... Is 8:19
as if the rod *s* shake itself .... Is 10:15
as if the staff *s* lift up itself .... Is 10:15
that the LORD *s* deliver Jerusalem .... Is 36:20
nails, that it *s* not be moved .... Is 41:7
for how *s* my name be polluted .... Is 48:11
his name *s* not have been cut off .... Is 48:19
that she *s* not have compassion on .... Is 49:15
that I *s* know how to speak a word .... Is 50:4
that he *s* not die in the pit .... Is 51:14
nor that his bread *s* fail .... Is 51:14
is no beauty that we *s* desire him .... Is 53:2
Noah *s* no more go over the earth .... Is 54:9
S I receive comfort in these .... Is 57:6
for the spirit *s* fail before me .... Is 57:16
that they *s* not stumble .... Is 63:13
thy sons and thy daughters *s* eat .... Jer 5:17
that my days *s* be consumed with .... Jer 20:18
then they *s* have turned them from .... Jer 23:22
s ye be utterly unpunished .... Jer 25:29
that they *s* not give him into the .... Jer 26:24
that I *s* drive you out .... Jer 27:10
drive you out, and ye *s* perish .... Jer 27:10
wherefore *s* this city be laid .... Jer 27:17
that ye *s* be officers in the .... Jer 29:26
that I *s* remove it from before my .... Jer 32:31
that they *s* do this abomination, ... Jer 32:35
night, and that there *s* not be day .... Jer 33:20
that he *s* not have a son to reign .... Jer 33:21
that they *s* be no more a nation .... Jer 33:24
That every man *s* let his .... Jer 34:9
that none *s* serve himself of them .... Jer 34:9
every one *s* let his manservant .... Jer 34:10
that none *s* serve themselves of .... Jer 34:10
yet *s* they rise up every man in .... Jer 37:10
the king commanded that they *s* .... Jer 37:21
that they *s* give him daily a .... Jer 37:21
Shaphan, that he *s* carry him home .... Jer 39:14
wherefore *s* he slay thee, that .... Jer 40:15
gathered unto thee *s* be scattered .... Jer 40:15
that they *s* return into the land .... Jer 44:14
king of Babylon *s* come and smite .... Jer 46:13
Though Babylon *s* mount up to .... Jer 51:53
though she *s* fortify the height .... Jer 51:53
the evil that *s* come upon Babylon .... Jer 51:60
thou didst command that they *s* .... Lam 1:10
because the comforter that *s* .... Lam 1:16
adversaries *s* be round about him .... Lam 1:17
It is good that a man *s* both hope .... Lam 3:26
that our prayer *s* not pass .... Lam 3:44
the enemy *s* have entered into the .... Lam 4:12
that I *s* go far off from my .... Eze 8:6
to slay the souls that *s* not die .... Eze 13:19
the souls alive that *s* not live .... Eze 13:19
that he *s* not return from his .... Eze 13:22
s I be enquired of at all by them .... Eze 14:3
they *s* deliver but their own .... Eze 14:14
at all that the wicked *s* die .... Eze 18:23
not that he *s* return from his .... Eze 18:23
that his voice *s* no more be heard .... Eze 19:9
that it *s* not be polluted before .... Eze 20:9
that it *s* not be polluted before .... Eze 20:14
that it *s* not be polluted in the .... Eze 20:22

judgments whereby they *s* not live	Eze 20:25	
s we then make mirth	Eze 21:10	
that *s* make up the hedge, and	Eze 22:30	
the land, that I *s* not destroy it	Eze 22:30	
a rock, that it *s* not be covered	Eze 24:8	
away in them, how *s* we then live	Eze 33:10	
s not the shepherds feed the	Eze 34:2	
that he *s* bring certain of the	Dan 1:3	
for why *s* he see your faces worse	Dan 1:10	
and the wine that they *s* drink	Dan 1:16	
king had said he *s* bring them in	Dan 1:18	
that the wise men *s* be slain	Dan 2:13	
his fellows *s* not perish with the	Dan 2:18	
what *s* come to pass hereafter	Dan 2:29	
that they *s* offer an oblation	Dan 2:46	
that he *s* be cast into the midst	Dan 3:11	
commanded that they *s* heat the	Dan 3:19	
that they *s* read this writing, and	Dan 5:15	
that he *s* be the third ruler in	Dan 5:29	
which *s* be over the whole kingdom	Dan 6:1	
the king *s* have no damage	Dan 6:2	
commanded that they *s* take Daniel	Dan 6:23	
and languages, *s* serve him	Dan 7:14	
what then *s* a king do to us	Hos 10:3	
my desire that I *s* chastise them	Hos 10:10	
for he *s* not stay long in the	Hos 13:13	
that the heathen *s* rule over them	Joel 2:17	
wherefore *s* they say among the	Joel 2:17	
s not I spare Nineveh, that great	Jonah 4:11	
that I *s* make thee a desolation,	Mic 6:16	
their dwelling *s* not be cut off	Zeph 3:7	
that the LORD's house *s* be built	Hag 1:2	
S I weep in the fifth month,	Zec 7:3	
S ye not hear the words which the	Zec 7:7	
their ears, that they *s* not hear	Zec 7:11	
lest they *s* hear the law, and the	Zec 7:12	
s it also be marvellous in mine	Zec 8:6	
s I accept this of your hand	Mal 1:13	
priest's lips *s* keep knowledge	Mal 2:7	
they *s* seek the law at his mouth	Mal 2:7	
of them where Christ *s* be born	Mt 2:4	
that they *s* not return to Herod	Mt 2:12	
that one of thy members *s* perish	Mt 5:29	
whole body *s* be cast into hell	Mt 5:29	
that one of thy members *s* perish	Mt 5:30	
whole body *s* be cast into hell	Mt 5:30	
ye would that men *s* do to you	Mt 7:12	
unto him, Art thou he that *s* come	Mt 11:3	
that they *s* not make him known	Mt 12:16	
time they *s* see with their eyes	Mt 13:15	
s understand with their heart, and	Mt 13:15	
s be converted, and I *s* heal	Mt 13:15	
Whence *s* we have so much bread in	Mt 15:33	
that ye *s* beware of the leaven of	Mt 16:11	
he his disciples that they *s* tell	Mt 16:20	
lest we *s* offend them, go thou to	Mt 17:27	
one of these little ones *s* perish	Mt 18:14	
prison, till he *s* pay the debt	Mt 18:30	
till he *s* pay all that was due	Mt 18:34	
that he *s* put his hands on them,	Mt 19:13	
that they *s* have received more	Mt 20:10	
because they *s* hold their peace	Mt 20:31	
except those days *s* be shortened	Mt 24:22	
there *s* no flesh be saved	Mt 24:22	
then at my coming I *s* have	Mt 25:27	
Though I *s* die with thee, yet	Mt 26:35	1163
that they *s* ask Barabbas, and	Mt 27:20	
that a small ship *s* wait on him	Mk 3:9	
multitude, lest they *s* throng him	Mk 3:9	
that they *s* not make him known	Mk 3:12	
that they *s* be with him, and that	Mk 3:14	
at any time they *s* be converted	Mk 4:12	
their sins *s* be forgiven them	Mk 4:12	
secret, but that it *s* come abroad	Mk 4:22	
as if a man *s* cast seed into the	Mk 4:26	
s sleep, and rise night and day	Mk 4:27	
and the seed *s* spring	Mk 4:27	
straitly that no man *s* know it	Mk 5:43	
something *s* be given her to eat	Mk 5:43	
commanded them that they *s* take	Mk 6:8	
and preached that men *s* repent	Mk 6:12	
them that they *s* tell no man	Mk 7:36	
that they *s* tell no man of him	Mk 8:30	
he charged them that they *s* tell	Mk 9:9	
the rising from the dead *s* mean	Mk 9:10	
that they *s* cast him out	Mk 9:18	
would not that any man *s* know it	Mk 9:30	
themselves, who *s* be the greatest	Mk 9:34	
to him, that he *s* touch them	Mk 10:13	
what things *s* happen unto him	Mk 10:32	3195
What would ye that I *s* do for you	Mk 10:36	
him that he *s* hold his peace	Mk 10:48	
wilt thou that I *s* do unto thee	Mk 10:51	
s carry any vessel through the	Mk 11:16	
that his brother *s* take his wife	Mk 12:19	
those days, no flesh *s* be saved	Mk 13:20	
If I *s* die with thee, I will not	Mk 14:31	1163
that he *s* rather release Barabbas	Mk 15:11	
upon them, what every man *s* take	Mk 15:24	
manner of salutation this *s* be	Lk 1:29	
mother of my Lord *s* come to me	Lk 1:43	
time came that she *s* be delivered	Lk 1:57	
That we *s* be saved from our	Lk 1:71	
that all the world *s* be taxed	Lk 2:1	
that she *s* be delivered	Lk 2:6	
that he *s* not see death, before	Lk 2:26	
that he *s* not depart from them	Lk 4:42	
the other ship, that they *s* come	Lk 5:7	
as ye would that men *s* do to you	Lk 6:31	
was worthy for whom he *s* do this	Lk 7:4	
saying, Art thou he that *s* come	Lk 7:19	
saying, Art thou he that *s* come	Lk 7:20	
their hearts, lest they *s* believe	Lk 8:12	
they *s* tell no man what was done	Lk 8:56	
except we *s* go and buy meat for	Lk 9:13	
he *s* accomplish at Jerusalem	Lk 9:31	3195
them, which of them *s* be greatest	Lk 9:46	
was come that he *s* be received up	Lk 9:51	
It was meet that we *s* make merry	Lk 15:32	
than that he *s* offend one of	Lk 17:2	
and it *s* obey you	Lk 17:6	
when the kingdom of God *s* come	Lk 17:20	
him, that he *s* hold his peace	Lk 18:39	
of God *s* immediately appear	Lk 19:11	3195
not that I *s* reign over them	Lk 19:27	
if these *s* hold their peace, the	Lk 19:40	
that they *s* give him of the fruit	Lk 20:10	
which *s* feign themselves just men	Lk 20:20	
that his brother *s* take his wife	Lk 20:28	
them it was that *s* do this thing	Lk 22:23	3195
which of them *s* be accounted the	Lk 22:24	
that it *s* be as they required	Lk 23:24	
holden that they *s* not know him	Lk 24:16	
he which *s* have redeemed Israel	Lk 24:21	3195
remission of sins *s* be preached	Lk 24:47	
but that he *s* be made manifest to	Jn 1:31	
not that any *s* testify of man	Jn 2:25	
believeth in him *s* not perish	Jn 3:15	
believeth in him *s* not perish	Jn 3:16	
lest his deeds *s* be reproved	Jn 3:20	
That all men *s* honour the Son,	Jn 5:23	
that *s* come into the world	Jn 6:14	
he hath given me I *s* lose nothing	Jn 6:39	
but *s* raise it up again at the	Jn 6:39	
believed not, and who *s* betray him	Jn 6:64	
for he it was that *s* betray him	Jn 6:71	3195
the law of Moses *s* not be broken	Jn 7:23	
that believe on him *s* receive	Jn 7:39	3195
us, that such *s* be stoned	Jn 8:5	
ye *s* have known my Father also	Jn 8:19	
and if I *s* say, I know him not, I	Jn 8:55	
of God *s* be made manifest in him	Jn 9:3	
he *s* be put out of the synagogue	Jn 9:22	
ye were blind, ye *s* have no sin	Jn 9:41	
which *s* come into the world	Jn 11:27	
even this man *s* not have died	Jn 11:37	
that one man *s* die for the people	Jn 11:50	
that Jesus *s* die for that nation	Jn 11:51	3195
but that also he *s* gather	Jn 11:52	
he *s* shew it, that they might	Jn 11:57	
Simon's son, which *s* betray him,	Jn 12:4	3195
the Son of man *s* be glorified	Jn 12:23	
signifying what death he *s* die	Jn 12:33	3195
that they *s* not see with their	Jn 12:40	
and be converted, and I *s* heal them	Jn 12:40	
lest they *s* be put out of the	Jn 12:42	
on me *s* not abide in darkness	Jn 12:46	
I *s* say, and what I *s* speak	Jn 12:49	
s depart out of this world unto	Jn 13:1	
For he knew who *s* betray him	Jn 13:11	
that ye *s* do as I have done to	Jn 13:15	
that he *s* ask who it *s* be of	Jn 13:24	
that he *s* give something to the	Jn 13:29	
ye *s* have known my Father also	Jn 14:7	
and ordained you, that ye *s* go	Jn 15:16	
and that your fruit *s* remain	Jn 15:16	
that ye *s* not be offended	Jn 16:1	
not that any man *s* ask thee	Jn 16:30	
that he *s* give eternal life to as	Jn 17:2	
all things that *s* come upon him	Jn 18:4	
that one man *s* die for the people	Jn 18:14	
hall, lest they *s* be defiled	Jn 18:28	
signifying what death he *s* die	Jn 18:32	3195
that I *s* not be delivered to the	Jn 18:36	
that I *s* bear witness unto the	Jn 18:37	
that I *s* release unto you one at	Jn 18:39	
that the bodies *s* not remain upon	Jn 19:31	
that the scripture *s* be fulfilled	Jn 19:36	
by what death he *s* glorify God	Jn 21:19	
that that disciple *s* not die	Jn 21:23	
if they *s* be written every one, I	Jn 21:25	
the books that *s* be written	Jn 21:25	
commanded them that they *s* not	Acts 1:4	
that he *s* be holden of it	Acts 2:24	
right hand, that I *s* not be moved	Acts 2:25	
church daily such as *s* be saved	Acts 2:47	
prophets, that Christ *s* suffer	Acts 3:18	
lest they *s* have been stoned	Acts 5:26	
that ye *s* not teach in this name	Acts 5:28	
they commanded that they *s* not	Acts 5:40	
that we *s* leave the word of God	Acts 6:2	
That his seed *s* sojourn in a	Acts 7:6	
that they *s* bring them into	Acts 7:6	
that he *s* make it according to	Acts 7:44	
can I, except some man *s* guide me	Acts 8:31	
vision which he had seen *s* mean	Acts 10:17	
I *s* not call any man common or	Acts 10:28	
that these *s* not be baptized,	Acts 10:47	
that he *s* go as far as Antioch	Acts 11:22	
by the Spirit that there *s* be	Acts 11:28	3195
that they *s* be put to death	Acts 12:19	
they Pilate that he *s* be slain	Acts 13:28	
s first have been spoken to you	Acts 13:46	
preach unto you that ye *s* turn	Acts 14:15	
s go up to Jerusalem unto the	Acts 15:2	
s hear the word of the gospel	Acts 15:7	
That they *s* seek the Lord, if	Acts 17:27	
would that I *s* bear with you	Acts 18:14	
that they *s* believe on him which	Acts 19:4	
on him which *s* come after him	Acts 19:4	
great goddess Diana *s* be despised	Acts 19:27	
her magnificence *s* be destroyed	Acts 19:27	3195
that they *s* see his face no more	Acts 20:38	3195
that he *s* not go up to Jerusalem	Acts 21:4	
disciple, with whom we *s* lodge	Acts 21:16	
until that an offering *s* be	Acts 21:26	
for it is not fit that he *s* live	Acts 22:22	
bade that he *s* be examined by	Acts 22:24	
him which *s* have examined him	Acts 22:29	3195
fearing lest Paul *s* have been	Acts 23:10	
s have been killed of them	Acts 23:27	3195
that he *s* forbid none of his	Acts 24:23	
He hoped also that money *s* have	Acts 24:26	
that Paul *s* be kept at Caesarea,	Acts 25:4	
Why *s* it be thought a thing	Acts 26:8	
that God *s* raise the dead	Acts 26:8	
the Gentiles, that they *s* repent	Acts 26:20	
prophets and Moses did say *s* come	Acts 26:22	3195
That Christ *s* suffer, and that he	Acts 26:23	
that he *s* be the first that	Acts 26:23	
first that *s* rise from the dead	Acts 26:23	
s shew light unto the people, and	Acts 26:23	3195
that we *s* sail into Italy	Acts 27:1	
fearing lest they *s* fall into the	Acts 27:17	
all hope that we *s* be saved was	Acts 27:20	
ye *s* have hearkened unto me, and	Acts 27:21	1163
Then fearing lest we *s* have	Acts 27:29	
lest any of them *s* swim out	Acts 27:42	
that they which could swim *s* cast	Acts 27:43	
looked when he *s* have swollen	Acts 28:6	3195
lest they *s* see with their eyes,	Acts 28:27	
s be converted, and I *s* heal	Acts 28:27	
that preachest a man *s* not steal	Rom 2:21	
a man *s* not commit adultery	Rom 2:22	
that he *s* be the heir of the	Rom 4:13	
even so we also *s* walk in newness	Rom 6:4	
henceforth we *s* not serve sin	Rom 6:6	
that ye *s* obey it in the lusts	Rom 6:12	
that ye *s* be married to another,	Rom 7:4	
that we *s* bring forth fruit unto	Rom 7:4	
that we *s* serve in newness of	Rom 7:6	
what we *s* pray for as we ought	Rom 8:26	
slumber, eyes that they *s* not see	Rom 11:8	
and ears that they *s* not hear	Rom 11:8	
they stumbled that they *s* fall	Rom 11:11	
that ye *s* be ignorant of this	Rom 11:25	
lest ye *s* be wise in your own	Rom 11:25	
That I *s* be the minister of Jesus	Rom 15:16	
lest I *s* build upon another man's	Rom 15:20	
Lest any *s* say that I had	1Cor 1:15	
Christ *s* be made of none effect	1Cor 1:17	
That no flesh *s* glory in his	1Cor 1:29	
That your faith *s* not stand in	1Cor 2:5	
thing that I *s* be judged of you	1Cor 4:3	
that one *s* have his father's wife	1Cor 5:1	
he that ploweth *s* plow in hope	1Cor 9:10	3784
in hope *s* be partaker of his hope	1Cor 9:10	
lest we *s* hinder the gospel of	1Cor 9:12	
the gospel *s* live of the gospel	1Cor 9:14	
that it *s* be so done unto me	1Cor 9:15	
than that any man *s* make my	1Cor 9:15	
others, I myself *s* be a castaway	1Cor 9:27	
I would not that ye *s* be ignorant	1Cor 10:1	
to the intent we *s* not lust after	1Cor 10:6	
I would not that ye *s* have	1Cor 10:20	
ourselves, we *s* not be judged	1Cor 11:31	
that we *s* not be condemned with	1Cor 11:32	
That there *s* be no schism in the	1Cor 12:25	
but that the members *s* have the	1Cor 12:25	
that we *s* not trust in ourselves,	2Cor 1:9	
that with me there *s* be yea yea	2Cor 1:17	
I *s* have sorrow from them of whom	2Cor 2:3	
not that ye *s* be grieved, but	2Cor 2:4	
lest perhaps such a one *s* be	2Cor 2:7	
Lest Satan *s* get an advantage of	2Cor 2:11	
image of God, *s* shine unto them	2Cor 4:4	
that they which live *s* not	2Cor 5:15	
that no man *s* blame us in this	2Cor 8:20	
lest our boasting of you *s* be in	2Cor 9:3	
ye) *s* be ashamed in this same	2Cor 9:4	
For though I *s* boast somewhat	2Cor 10:8	
destruction, I *s* not be ashamed	2Cor 10:8	
so your minds *s* be corrupted from	2Cor 11:3	
lest any man *s* think of me above	2Cor 12:6	
lest I *s* be exalted above measure	2Cor 12:7	
lest I *s* be exalted above measure	2Cor 12:7	
not that we *s* appear approved,	2Cor 13:7	
but that ye *s* do that which is	2Cor 13:7	
being present I *s* use sharpness	2Cor 13:10	
I *s* not be the servant of Christ	Gal 1:10	
lest by any means I *s* run	Gal 2:2	
that we *s* go unto the heathen, and	Gal 2:9	
would that we *s* remember the poor	Gal 2:10	
that ye *s* not obey the truth,	Gal 3:1	
that it *s* make the promise of	Gal 3:17	
till the seed *s* come to whom the	Gal 3:19	
s have been by the law	Gal 3:21	
which *s* afterwards be revealed	Gal 3:23	3195
you that ye *s* not obey the truth	Gal 5:7	
only lest they *s* suffer	Gal 6:12	
But God forbid that I *s* glory	Gal 6:14	
of the world, that we *s* be holy	Eph 1:4	
That we *s* be to the praise of his	Eph 1:12	
of works, lest any man *s* boast	Eph 2:9	

ordained that we *s* walk in them Eph 2:10
the Gentiles *s* be fellowheirs Eph 3:6
that I *s* preach among the Eph 3:8
but that it *s* be holy and without Eph 5:27
But I would ye *s* understand Phil 1:12
name of Jesus every knee *s* bow Phil 2:10
that every tongue *s* confess that Phil 2:11
lest I *s* have sorrow upon sorrow Phil 2:27
that in him *s* all fulness dwell Col 1:19
lest any man *s* beguile you with Col 2:4
That no man *s* be moved by these 1Th 3:3
that we *s* suffer tribulation 1Th 3:4 *3195*
that ye *s* abstain from 1Th 4:3
That every one of you *s* know how 1Th 4:4
that that day *s* overtake you as a 1Th 5:4
we *s* live together with him 1Th 5:10
that they *s* believe a lie 2Th 2:11
would not work, neither *s* he eat 2Th 3:10
s hereafter believe on him to 1Ti 1:16 *3195*
we *s* live soberly, righteously, Titus 2:12
we *s* be made heirs according to Titus 3:7
that thy benefit *s* not be as it Philem 14
at any time we *s* let them slip Heb 2:1
God *s* taste death for every man Heb 2:9
they *s* not enter into his rest Heb 3:18
any of you *s* seem to come short Heb 4:1
priest *s* rise after the order of Heb 7:11
he *s* not be a priest, seeing that Heb 8:4
then *s* no place have been sought Heb 8:7
heavens *s* be purified with these Heb 9:23
Nor yet that he *s* offer himself Heb 9:25
the worshippers once purged *s* Heb 10:2
of goats *s* take away sins Heb 10:4
that he *s* not see death Heb 11:5
which he *s* after receive for an Heb 11:8 *3195*
the firstborn *s* touch them Heb 11:28
without us *s* not be made perfect Heb 11:40
heard intreated that the word *s* Heb 12:19
of truth, that we *s* be a kind of Jas 1:18
of the grace that *s* come unto you 1Pet 1:10
and the glory that *s* follow 1Pet 1:11
that ye *s* shew forth the praises 1Pet 2:9
that ye *s* follow his steps 1Pet 2:21
s live unto righteousness 1Pet 2:24
that ye *s* inherit a blessing 1Pet 3:9
That he no longer *s* live the rest 1Pet 4:2
those that after *s* live ungodly 2Pet 2:6 *3195*
not willing that any *s* perish 2Pet 3:9
but that all *s* come to repentance 2Pet 3:9
that we *s* be called the sons of 1Jn 3:1
that we *s* love one another 1Jn 3:11
That we *s* believe on the name of 1Jn 3:23
ye have heard that it *s* come 1Jn 4:3
the beginning, ye *s* walk in it 2Jn 6
exhort you that ye *s* earnestly Jude 3
s be mockers in the last time Jude 18
who *s* walk after their own Jude 18
that they *s* kill one another Rev 6:4
that they *s* rest yet for a little Rev 6:11
that *s* be killed as they were, Rev 6:11 *3195*
as they were, *s* be fulfilled Rev 6:11
that the wind *s* not blow on the Rev 7:1
that he *s* offer it with the Rev 8:3
s not hurt the grass of the earth Rev 9:4
given that they *s* not kill them Rev 9:5
but that they *s* be tormented five Rev 9:5
that they *s* not worship devils, Rev 9:20
that there *s* be time no longer Rev 10:6
the mystery of God *s* be finished Rev 10:7
the dead, that they *s* be judged Rev 11:18
that they *s* feed her there a Rev 12:6
that they *s* make an image to the Rev 13:14
image of the beast *s* both speak Rev 13:15
image of the beast *s* be killed Rev 13:15
she *s* be arrayed in fine linen Rev 19:8
that with it he *s* smite the Rev 19:15
that he *s* deceive the nations no Rev 20:3
the thousand years *s* be fulfilled Rev 20:3

SHOULDER {38}
unto Hagar, putting it on her *s* Gen 21:14 7926
with her pitcher upon her *s* Gen 24:15 7926
forth with her pitcher on her *s* Gen 24:45 7926
let down her pitcher from her *s* Gen 24:46
and bowed his *s* to bear, and became Gen 49:15 7926
that is upon them, and the right *s* Ex 29:22 7785
the *s* of the heave offering, Ex 29:27 7785
the right *s* shall ye give unto Lev 7:32 7785
have the right *s* for his part Lev 7:33 7785
the heave *s* have I taken of the Lev 7:34 7785
and their fat, and the right *s* Lev 8:25 7785
on the fat, and upon the right *s* Lev 8:26 7785
the right *s* Aaron waved for a Lev 9:21 7785
heave *s* shall ye eat in a clean Lev 10:14 7785
The heave *s* and the wave breast Lev 10:15 7785
take the sodden *s* of the ram Num 6:19 2220
with the wave breast and heave *s* Num 6:20 7785
and as the right *s* are thine Num 18:18 7785
shall give unto the priest the *s* Deut 18:3 2220
man of you a stone upon his *s* Josh 4:5 7926
and took it, and laid it on his *s* Judg 9:48 7926
And the cook took up the *s* 1Sa 9:24 7785
and withdrew the *s*, and hardened Neh 9:29 3802
let mine arm fall from my *s* blade Job 31:22 7929
Surely I would take it upon my *s* Job 31:36 7926
I removed his *s* from the burden Ps 81:6 7926
his burden, and the staff of his *s* Is 9:4 7926
government shall be upon his *s* Is 9:6 7926
be taken away from off thy *s* Is 10:27 7926
of David will I lay upon his *s* Is 22:22 7926
They bear him upon the *s*, they Is 46:7 3802
bare it upon my *s* in their sight Eze 12:7 3802
bear upon his *s* in the twilight Eze 12:12 3802
good piece, the thigh, and the *s* Eze 24:4 3802
didst break, and rend all their *s* Eze 29:7 3802
made bald, and every *s* was peeled Eze 29:18 3802
have thrust with side and with *s* Eze 34:21 3802
to hearken, and pulled away the *s* Zec 7:11 3802

SHOULDERPIECES {4}
It shall have the two *s* thereof Ex 28:7 3802
put them on the *s* of the ephod Ex 28:25 3802
They made *s* for it, to couple it Ex 39:4 3802
and put them on the *s* of the ephod Ex 39:18 3802

SHOULDERS {20}
and laid it upon both their *s* Gen 9:23 7926
up in their clothes upon their *s* Ex 12:34 7926
the *s* of the ephod for stones of Ex 28:12 3802
upon his two *s* for a memorial Ex 28:12 3802
he put them on the *s* of the ephod Ex 39:7 3802
they should bear upon their *s* Num 7:9 3802
and he shall dwell between his *s* Deut 33:12 3802
and all, and put them upon his *s* Judg 16:3 3802
from his *s* and upward he was 1Sa 9:2 7926
than any of the people from his *s* 1Sa 10:23 7926
a target of brass between his *s* 1Sa 17:6 3802
their *s* with the staves thereon 1Chr 15:15 3802
shall not be a burden upon your *s* 2Chr 35:3 3802
But they shall fly upon the *s* of Is 11:14 3802
burden depart from off their *s* Is 14:25 7926
riches upon the *s* of young asses Is 30:6 3802
shall be carried upon their *s* Is 49:22 3802
shalt thou bear it upon thy *s* Eze 12:6 3802
be borne, and lay them on men's *s* Mt 23:4 *5606*
found it, he layeth it on his *s* Lk 15:5 *5606*

SHOULDEST {73}
thee that thou *s* not eat Gen 3:11
that is thine, lest thou *s* say Gen 14:23
thou *s* have brought guiltiness Gen 26:10
s thou therefore serve me for Gen 29:15
that thou *s* say unto me, Carry Num 11:12
s be driven to worship them, and Deut 4:19
thee, and that thou *s* keep all his Deut 26:18
That thou *s* enter into covenant Deut 29:12
is not in heaven, that thou *s* say Deut 30:12
beyond the sea, that thou *s* say Deut 30:13
Israel, and *s* thou possess it Judg 11:23
that thou *s* take knowledge of me, Ruth 2:10
for why *s* thou bring me to thy 1Sa 20:8
that thou *s* look upon such a dead 2Sa 9:8
that thou *s* tell them who shall 1Kin 1:20
me that thou *s* surely recover 2Kin 8:14
Thou *s* have smitten five or six 2Kin 13:19
for why *s* thou meddle to thy hurt 2Kin 14:10
to thy hurt, that thou *s* fall 2Kin 14:10
that thou *s* be to lay waste 2Kin 19:25
that thou *s* be ruler over my 1Chr 17:7
S thou help the ungodly, and love 2Chr 19:2
why *s* thou be smitten 2Chr 25:16
why *s* thou meddle to thine hurt, 2Chr 25:19
to thine hurt, that thou *s* fall 2Chr 25:19
is man, that thou *s* magnify him Job 7:17
that thou *s* set thine heart upon Job 7:17
that thou *s* visit him every Job 7:18
unto thee that thou *s* oppress Job 10:3
that thou *s* despise the work of Job 10:3
That thou *s* take it to the bound Job 38:20
that thou *s* know the paths to the Job 38:20
or that thou *s* take my covenant Ps 50:16
s mark iniquities, O Lord, who Ps 130:3
Lest thou *s* ponder the path of Prov 5:6
than that thou *s* be put lower in Prov 25:7
Though thou *s* bray a fool in a Prov 27:22
Better is it that thou *s* not vow Eccl 5:5
than that thou *s* vow Eccl 5:5
why *s* thou destroy thyself Eccl 7:16
why *s* thou die before thy time Eccl 7:17
that thou *s* take hold of this Eccl 7:18
that thou *s* be to lay waste Is 37:26
lest thou *s* say, Mine idol hath Is 48:5
lest thou *s* say, Behold, I knew Is 48:7
thee by the way that thou *s* go Is 48:17
s be my servant to raise up the Is 49:6
that thou *s* be afraid of a man Is 51:12
why *s* thou be as a stranger in Jer 14:8
Why *s* thou be as a man astonied, Jer 14:9
that thou *s* put him in prison, and Jer 29:26
though thou *s* make thy nest as Jer 49:16
But thou *s* not have looked on the Obad 12
neither *s* thou have rejoiced over Obad 12
neither *s* thou have spoken Obad 12
Thou *s* not have entered into the Obad 13
thou *s* not have looked on their Obad 13
Neither *s* thou have stood in the Obad 14
neither *s* thou have delivered up Obad 14
that thou *s* come under my roof Mt 8:8
S not thou also have had Mt 18:33
we would that thou *s* do for us Mk 10:35
that thou *s* enter under my roof Lk 7:6
thou *s* see the glory of God Jn 11:40
I pray not that thou *s* take them Jn 17:15
but that thou *s* keep them from Jn 17:15
that thou *s* be for salvation unto Acts 13:47
that thou *s* know his will, and see Acts 22:14
s hear the voice of his mouth Acts 22:14
that thou *s* set in order the Titus 1:5
that thou *s* receive him for ever Philem 15
that thou *s* give reward unto thy Rev 11:18
s destroy them which destroy the Rev 11:18

SHOUT {38}
voice of them that *s* for mastery Ex 32:18 6030
the *s* of a king is among them Num 23:21 8643
people shall *s* with a great *s* Josh 6:5 7321
people shall *s* with a great *s* Josh 6:5 8643
people, saying, Ye shall not *s* Josh 6:10 7321
mouth, until the day I bid you *s* Josh 6:10 7321
then shall ye *s* Josh 6:10 7321
Joshua said unto the people, *S* Josh 6:16 7321
the people shouted with a great *s* Josh 6:20 8643
all Israel shouted with a great *s* 1Sa 4:5 8643
heard the noise of the *s*, they 1Sa 4:6 8643
s in the camp of the Hebrews 1Sa 4:6
Then the men of Judah gave a *s* 2Chr 13:15 7321
the people shouted with a great *s* Ezr 3:11 8643
s of joy from the noise of the Ezr 3:13 8643
the people shouted with a loud *s* Ezr 3:13 8643
let them ever *s* for joy, because Ps 5:11 7442
s for joy, all ye that are Ps 32:11 7442
Let them *s* for joy, and be glad, Ps 35:27 7442
s unto God with the voice of Ps 47:1 7321
God is gone up with a *s*, the LORD Ps 47:5 8643
they *s* for joy, they also sing Ps 65:13 7321
and let thy saints *s* for joy Ps 132:9 7442
her saints shall *s* aloud for joy Ps 132:16 7442
Cry out and *s*, thou inhabitant of Is 12:6 7442
let them *s* from the top of the Is 42:11 6681
s, ye lower parts of the earth Is 44:23 7321
he shall give a *s*, as they that Jer 25:30
s among the chief of the nations Jer 31:7 6670
S against her round about Jer 50:15 7321
shall lift up a *s* against thee Jer 51:14 1959
Also when I cry and *s*, he shutteth Lam 3:8 7768
s, O Israel Zeph 3:14 7321
s, O daughter of Jerusalem Zec 9:9 7321
And the people gave a *s*, saying, Acts 12:22 *2019*
descend from heaven with a *s* 1Th 4:16 *2752*

SHOUTED {14}
the noise of the people as they *s* Ex 32:17 7452
when all the people saw, they *s* Lev 9:24 7442
So the people *s* when the priests Josh 6:20 7321
the people *s* with a great shout, Josh 6:20 7321
the Philistines *s* against him Judg 15:14 7321
all Israel *s* with a great shout, 1Sa 4:5 7321
And all the people *s*, and said, God 1Sa 10:24 7321
to the fight, and *s* for the battle 1Sa 17:20 7321
of Israel and of Judah arose, and *s* 1Sa 17:52 7321
and as the men of Judah *s*, it came 2Chr 13:15 7321
all the people *s* with a great Ezr 3:11 7321
and many *s* aloud for joy Ezr 3:12 8643
for the people *s* with a loud Ezr 3:13 7321
and all the sons of God *s* for joy Job 38:7 7321

SHOUTETH {1}
man that *s* by reason of wine Ps 78:65 7442

SHOUTING {15}
up the ark of the LORD with *s* 2Sa 6:15 8643
the covenant of the LORD with *s* 1Chr 15:28 8643
LORD with a loud voice, and with *s* 2Chr 15:14 8643
thunder of the captains, and the *s* Job 39:25 8643
the wicked perish, there is *s* Prov 11:10 7440
for the *s* for thy summer fruits Is 16:9 1959
singing, neither shall there be *s* Is 16:10 7321
made their vintage *s* to cease Is 16:10 1959
the morning, and the *s* at noontide Jer 20:16 8643
none shall tread with *s* Jer 48:33 1959
their *s* shall be no *s* Jer 48:33 1959
to lift up the voice with *s* Eze 21:22 8643
with *s* in the day of battle, with Amos 1:14 8643
shall die with tumult, with *s* Amos 2:2 8643

SHOUTINGS {1}
the headstone thereof with *s* Zec 4:7 8663

SHOVEL {1}
hath been winnowed with the *s* Is 30:24 7371

SHOVELS {9}
to receive his ashes, and his *s* Ex 27:3 3257
of the altar, the pots, and the *s* Ex 38:3 3257
censers, the fleshhooks, and the *s* Num 4:14 3257
Hiram made the lavers, and the *s* 1Kin 7:40 3257
And the pots, and the *s*, and the 1Kin 7:45 3257
And the pots, and the *s*, and the 2Kin 25:14 3257
And Huram made the pots, and the *s* 2Chr 4:11 3257
The pots also, and the *s*, and the 2Chr 4:16 3257
The caldrons also, and the *s* Jer 52:18 3257

SHOWER {4}
there shall be an overflowing *s* Eze 13:11 1653
be an overflowing *s* in mine anger Eze 13:13 1653
I will cause the *s* to come down Eze 34:26 1653
ye say, There cometh a *s* Lk 12:54 *3655*

SHOWERS {9}
herb, and as the *s* upon the grass Deut 32:2 7241
wet with the *s* of the mountains Job 24:8 2230
thou makest it soft with *s* Ps 65:10 7241
as *s* that water the earth Ps 72:6 7241
Therefore the *s* have been Jer 3:3 7241
or can the heavens give *s* Jer 14:22 7241
there shall be *s* of blessing Eze 34:26 1653
as the *s* upon the grass, that Mic 5:7 7241
clouds, and give them *s* of rain Zec 10:1 1653

SHRANK {2}
eat not of the sinew which *s* Gen 32:32 5384
Jacob's thigh in the sinew that *s* Gen 32:32 5384

SHRED {1}
s them into the pot of pottage ... 2Kin 4:39 6398
SHRINES {1}
which made silver s for Diana ... Acts 19:24 *3485*
SHROUD {1}
branches, and with a shadowing s ... Eze 31:3 2793
SHRUBS {1}
cast the child under one of the s ... Gen 21:15 7880
SHUA *(shu'-ah)* {2} See SHUAH.
1. Daughter of Judah.
the daughter of S the Canaanitess ... 1Chr 2:3 7770
2. Daughter of Heber.
and Hotham, and S their sister ... 1Chr 7:32 7774
SHUAH *(shu'-ah)* {5}
1. A son of Abraham.
and Midian, and Ishbak, and S ... Gen 25:2 7744
and Midian, and Ishbak, and S ... 1Chr 1:32 7744
2. Same as Shua 1.
Canaanite, whose name was S ... Gen 38:2 7770
daughter of S Judah's wife died ... Gen 38:12 7770
3. A descendant of Caleb.
the brother of S begat Mehir ... 1Chr 4:11 7746
SHUAL *(shu'-al)* {2}
1. A district in Benjamin.
to Ophrah, unto the land of S ... 1Sa 13:17 7777
2. Son of Zophah.
Suah, and Harnepher, and S, and Beri ... 1Chr 7:36 7777
SHUBAEL *(shu'-ba-el)* {3} See SHEBUEL.
1. Son of Amram.
sons of Amram; S ... 1Chr 24:20 2619
of the sons of S ... 1Chr 24:20 2619
2. A sanctuary servant.
The thirteenth to S, he, his sons ... 1Chr 25:20 2619
SHUHAH See SHUAH.
SHUHAM *(shu'-ham)* {1} See HUSHIM, SHUHAMITES.
A son of Dan.
of S, the family of the ... Num 26:42 7748
SHUHAMITES *(shu'-ham-ites)* {2} *Descendants of Shuham.*
of Shuham, the family of the S ... Num 26:42 7749
All the families of the S ... Num 26:43 7749
SHUHITE *(shu'-hite)* {5} *A descendant of Shuah.*
the Temanite, and Bildad the S ... Job 2:11 7747
Then answered Bildad the S ... Job 8:1 7747
Then answered Bildad the S ... Job 18:1 7747
Then answered Bildad the S ... Job 25:1 7747
the Temanite and Bildad the S ... Job 42:9 7747
SHULAMITE *(shu'-lam-ite)* {2} *An inhabitant of Shulam.*
Return, return, O S ... Song 6:13 7759
What will ye see in the S ... Song 6:13 7759
SHULAMMITE See SHULAMITE.
SHUMATHITES *(shu'-math-ites)* {1} *Descendants of Shobal.*
and the Puhites, and the S ... 1Chr 2:53 8126
SHUN {1}
But s profane and vain babblings ... 2Ti 2:16 *4026*
SHUNAMMITE *(shu'-nam-mite)* {8} *An inhabitant of Shunem.*
of Israel, and found Abishag a S ... 1Kin 1:3 7767
Abishag the S ministered unto the ... 1Kin 1:15 7767
he give me Abishag the S to wife ... 1Kin 2:17 7767
Let Abishag the S be given to ... 1Kin 2:21 7767
ask Abishag the S for Adonijah ... 1Kin 2:22 7767
Gehazi his servant, Call this S ... 2Kin 4:12 7767
servant, Behold, yonder is that S ... 2Kin 4:25 7767
Gehazi, and said, Call this S ... 2Kin 4:36 7767
SHUNEM *(shu'-nem)* {3} See SHUNAMMITE. *A city in Issachar.*
Jezreel, and Chesulloth, and S ... Josh 19:18 7766
together, and came and pitched in S ... 1Sa 28:4 7766
on a day, that Elisha passed to S ... 2Kin 4:8 7766
SHUNI *(shu'-ni)* {2} See SHUNITES. *A son of Gad.*
Ziphion, and Haggi, S, and Ezbon, ... Gen 46:16 7764
of S, the family of the Shunites ... Num 26:15 7764
SHUNITES *(shu'-nites)* {1} *Descendants of Shuni.*
of Shuni, the family of the S ... Num 26:15 7765
SHUNNED {1}
For I have not s to declare unto ... Acts 20:27 *5288*
SHUPHAM *(shu'-fam)* {1} See SHEPHUPHAN, SHUPHAMITES. *A son of Benjamin.*
Of S, the family of the ... Num 26:39 8197
SHUPHAMITES *(shu'-fam-ites)* {1} *Descendants of Shupham.*
Of Shupham, the family of the S ... Num 26:39 7781
SHUPPIM *(shup'-pim)* {3} See MUPPIM, SHEPHUPHAN.
1. A Benjamite.
S also, and Huppim, the children ... 1Chr 7:12 8206
to wife the sister of Huppim and S ... 1Chr 7:15 8206
2. A Levite gatekeeper.
To S and Hosah the lot came forth ... 1Chr 26:16 8206
SHUR *(shur)* {6} *A wilderness east of Egypt.*
by the fountain in the way to S ... Gen 16:7 7793
and dwelled between Kadesh and S ... Gen 20:1 7793
And they dwelt from Havilah unto S ... Gen 25:18 7793
went out into the wilderness of S ... Ex 15:22 7793
Havilah until thou comest to S ... 1Sa 15:7 7793
of the land, as thou goest to S ... 1Sa 27:8 7793
SHUSHAN *(shu'-shan)* {21} See SHOSHANNIM. *Capital of Persia.*
year, as I was in S the palace ... Neh 1:1 7800
which was in S the palace ... Est 1:2 7800
that were present in S the palace ... Est 1:5 7800
young virgins unto S the palace ... Est 2:3 7800
Now in S the palace there was a ... Est 2:5 7800
together unto S the palace ... Est 2:8 7800
decree was given in S the palace ... Est 3:15 7800
but the city S was perplexed ... Est 3:15 7800
was given at S to destroy them ... Est 4:8 7800
the Jews that are present in S ... Est 4:16 7800
decree was given at S the palace ... Est 8:14 7800
and the city of S rejoiced ... Est 8:15 7800
in S the palace the Jews slew and ... Est 9:6 7800
of those that were slain in S the ... Est 9:11 7800
five hundred men in S the palace ... Est 9:12 7800
to the Jews which are in S to do ... Est 9:13 7800
and the decree was given at S ... Est 9:14 7800
For the Jews that were in S ... Est 9:15 7800
and slew three hundred men at S ... Est 9:15 7800
at S assembled together on the ... Est 9:18 7800
that I was at S in the palace ... Dan 8:2 7800
SHUSHAN-EDUTH *(shu'-shan-e'-duth)* {1}
To the chief Musician upon S ... Ps 60:*t* 7802
SHUT {105}
and the LORD s him in ... Gen 7:16 5462
them, and s the door after him, ... Gen 19:6 5462
house to them, and s to the door ... Gen 19:10 5462
the wilderness hath s them in ... Ex 14:3 5462
then the priest shall s up him ... Lev 13:4 5462
then the priest shall s him up ... Lev 13:5 5462
unclean, and shall not s him up ... Lev 13:11 5462
priest shall s him up seven days ... Lev 13:21 5462
priest shall s him up seven days ... Lev 13:26 5462
then the priest shall s up him ... Lev 13:31 5462
the priest shall s up him that ... Lev 13:33 5462
s up it that hath the plague ... Lev 13:50 5462
he shall s it up seven days more ... Lev 13:54 5462
s up the house seven days ... Lev 14:38 5462
s up shall be unclean until the ... Lev 14:46 5462
let her be s out from the camp ... Num 12:14 5462
Miriam was s out from the camp ... Num 12:15 5462
he s up the heaven, that there be ... Deut 11:17 6113
nor s thine hand from thy poor ... Deut 15:7 7092
them, and the LORD had s them up ... Deut 32:30 5462
is gone, and there is none s up ... Deut 32:36 6113
were gone out, they s the gate ... Josh 2:7 5462
Now Jericho was straitly s up ... Josh 6:1 5462
s the doors of the parlour upon ... Judg 3:23 5462
s it to them, and gat them up to ... Judg 9:51 5462
but the LORD had s up her womb ... 1Sa 1:5 5462
the LORD had s up her womb ... 1Sa 1:6 5462
s up their calves at home ... 1Sa 6:10 3607
for he is s in, by entering into ... 1Sa 23:7 5462
So they were s up unto the day of ... 2Sa 20:3 6887
When heaven is s up, and there is ... 1Kin 8:35 6113
the wall, and him that is s up ... 1Kin 14:10 6113
the wall, and him that is s up ... 1Kin 21:21 6113
thou shalt s the door upon thee ... 2Kin 4:4 5462
s the door upon her and upon her ... 2Kin 4:5 5462
s the door upon him, and went out ... 2Kin 4:21 5462
s the door upon them twain, and ... 2Kin 4:33 5462
s the door, and hold him fast at ... 2Kin 6:32 5462
the wall, and him that is s up ... 2Kin 9:8 6113
for there was not any s up ... 2Kin 14:26 6113
the king of Assyria s him up ... 2Kin 17:4 6113
When the heaven is s up, and there ... 2Chr 6:26 6113
If I s up heaven that there be no ... 2Chr 7:13 6113
s up the doors of the house of ... 2Chr 28:24 5462
Also they have s up the doors of ... 2Chr 29:7 5462
son of Mehetabeel, who was s up ... Neh 6:10 6113
let us s the doors of the temple ... Neh 6:10 5462
let them s the doors, and bar them ... Neh 7:3 1479
that the gates should be s ... Neh 13:19 5462
Because it s not up the doors of ... Job 3:10 5462
s up, or gather together, then ... Job 11:10 5462
Or who s up the sea with doors, ... Job 38:8 5526
s up together as with a close ... Job 41:15 5462
hast not s me up into the hand of ... Ps 31:8 5462
let not the pit s her mouth upon ... Ps 69:15 332
hath he in anger s up his tender ... Ps 77:9 7092
I am s up, and I cannot come forth ... Ps 88:8 3607
doors shall be s in the streets ... Eccl 12:4 5462
a spring s up, a fountain sealed ... Song 4:12 5274
their ears heavy, and s their eyes ... Is 6:10 8173
so he shall open, and none shall s ... Is 22:22 5462
and he shall s, and none shall open ... Is 22:22 5462
every house is s up, that no man ... Is 24:10 5462
shall be s up in the prison, and ... Is 24:22 5462
and s thy doors about thee ... Is 26:20 5462
for he hath s their eyes, that ... Is 44:18 2902
and the gates shall not be s ... Is 45:1 5462
the kings shall s their mouths at ... Is 52:15 7092
they shall not be s day nor night ... Is 60:11 5462
to bring forth, and s the womb ... Is 66:9 6113
cities of the south shall be s up ... Jer 13:19 5462
a burning fire s up in my bones ... Jer 20:9 6113
Jeremiah the prophet was s up in ... Jer 32:2 3607
king of Judah had s him up ... Jer 32:3 3607
while he was yet s up in the ... Jer 33:1 6113
Baruch, saying, I am s up ... Jer 36:5 6113
while he was s up in the court of ... Jer 39:15 6113
s thyself within thine house ... Eze 3:24 5462
and it was s ... Eze 44:1 5462
This gate shall be s, it shall ... Eze 44:2 5462
in by it, therefore it shall be s ... Eze 44:2 5462
shall be s the six working days ... Eze 46:1 5462
shall not be s until the evening ... Eze 46:2 5462
going forth one shall s the gate ... Eze 46:12 5462
hath s the lions' mouths, that ... Dan 6:22 5463
wherefore s thou up the vision ... Dan 8:26 5640
s up the words, and seal the book, ... Dan 12:4 5640
that would s the doors for nought ... Mal 1:10 5462
and when thou hast s thy door ... Mt 6:6 *2808*
for ye s up the kingdom of heaven ... Mt 23:13 *2808*
and the door was s ... Mt 25:10 *2808*
that he s up John in prison ... Lk 3:20 *2623*
the heaven was s up three years ... Lk 4:25 *2808*
the door is now s, and my children ... Lk 11:7 *2808*
hath s to the door, and ye begin ... Lk 13:25 *608*
when the doors were s where the ... Jn 20:19 *2808*
came Jesus, the doors being s ... Jn 20:26 *2808*
truly found we s with all safety ... Acts 5:23 *2808*
and forthwith the doors were s ... Acts 21:30 *2808*
the saints did I s up in prison ... Acts 26:10 *2623*
s up unto the faith which should ... Gal 3:23 *4788*
an open door, and no man can s it ... Rev 3:8 *2808*
These have power to s heaven ... Rev 11:6 *2808*
s him up, and set a seal upon him, ... Rev 20:3 *2808*
it shall not be s at all by day ... Rev 21:25 *2808*
SHUTHALHITES *(shu'-thal-hites)* {1} *Descendants of Shuthelah.*
of Shuthelah, the family of the S ... Num 26:35 8364
SHUTHELAH *(shu'-the-lah)* {4} See SHUTHALHITES.
1. A son of Ephraim.
of S, the family of the ... Num 26:35 7803
And these are the sons of S ... Num 26:36 7803
S, and Bered his son, and Tahath ... 1Chr 7:20 7803
2. Son of Zabad.
S his son, and Ezer, and Elead, ... 1Chr 7:21 7803
SHUTHELAHITES See SHUTHALHITES.
SHUTTETH {8}
he s up a man, and there can be no ... Job 12:14 5462
He s his eyes to devise froward ... Prov 16:30 6095
he that s his lips is esteemed a ... Prov 17:28 331
s his eyes from seeing evil ... Is 33:15 6105
cry and shout, he s out my prayer ... Lam 3:8 5640
s up his bowels of compassion ... 1Jn 3:17 *2808*
he that openeth, and no man s ... Rev 3:7 *2808*
and s, and no man openeth ... Rev 3:7 *2808*
SHUTTING {1}
about the time of s of the gate ... Josh 2:5 5462
SHUTTLE {1}
are swifter than a weaver's s ... Job 7:6 708
SIA *(si'-ah)* {1} See SIAHA. *A family of exiles.*
of Keros, the children of S ... Neh 7:47 5517
SIAHA *(si'-a-hah)* {1} See SIA. *Same as Sia.*
of Keros, the children of S ... Ezr 2:44 5517
SIBBECAI *(sib'-be-cahee)* {2} See SIBBECHAI. *A "mighty man" of David.*
S the Hushathite, Ilai the ... 1Chr 11:29 5444
eighth month was S the Hushathite ... 1Chr 27:11 5444
SIBBECHAI *(sib'-be-kahee)* {2} See SIBBECAI. *Same as Sibbecai.*
then S the Hushathite slew Saph, ... 2Sa 21:18 5444
at which time S the Hushathite ... 1Chr 20:4 5444
SIBBOLETH *(sib'-bo-leth)* {1} See SHIBBOLETH. *The Ephraimite pronunciation of Shibboleth.*
and he said S ... Judg 12:6 5451
SIBMAH *(sib'-mah)* {4} *A city in Reuben.*
And Kirjathaim, and S, and ... Josh 13:19 7643
languish, and the vine of S ... Is 16:8 7643
weeping of Jazer the vine of S ... Is 16:9 7643
O vine of S, I will weep for thee ... Jer 48:32 7643
SIBRAIM *(sib'-ra-im)* {1} *A city in Syria between Damascus and Hamath.*
Hamath, Berothah, S, which is ... Eze 47:16 5453
SICHEM *(si'-kem)* {1} See SHECHEM, SYCHEM. *A place on the plain of Moreh.*
the land unto the place of S ... Gen 12:6 7927
SICK {88}
Joseph, Behold, thy father is s ... Gen 48:1 2470
of her that is s of her flowers ... Lev 15:33 1739
to take David, she said, He is s ... 1Sa 19:14 2470
because three days agone I fell s ... 1Sa 30:13 2470
bare unto David, and it was very s ... 2Sa 12:15 605
that he fell s for his sister ... 2Sa 13:2 2470
on thy bed, and make thyself s ... 2Sa 13:5 2470
Amnon lay down, and made himself s ... 2Sa 13:6 2470
Abijah the son of Jeroboam fell s ... 1Kin 14:1 2470
for he is s ... 1Kin 14:5 2470
the mistress of the house, fell s ... 1Kin 17:17 2470
that was in Samaria, and was s ... 2Kin 1:2 2470
Ben-hadad the king of Syria was s ... 2Kin 8:7 2470
Ahab in Jezreel, because he was s ... 2Kin 8:29 2470
Now Elisha was fallen s of his ... 2Kin 13:14 2470
days was Hezekiah s unto death ... 2Kin 20:1 2470
heard that Hezekiah had been s ... 2Kin 20:12 2470
Ahab at Jezreel, because he was s ... 2Chr 22:6 2470
days Hezekiah was s to the death ... 2Chr 32:24 2470
sad, seeing thou art not s ... Neh 2:2 2470
But as for me, when they were s ... Ps 35:13 2470
Hope deferred maketh the heart s ... Prov 13:12 2470
shalt thou say, and I was not s ... Prov 23:35 2470
for I am s of love ... Song 2:5 2470
ye tell him, that I am s of love ... Song 5:8 2470
the whole head is s, and the whole ... Is 1:5 2483
inhabitant shall not say, I am s ... Is 33:24 2470
days was Hezekiah s unto death ... Is 38:1 2470

S

king of Judah, when he had been *s* — Is 38:9 — 2470
he had heard that he had been *s* — Is 39:1 — 2470
them that are *s* with famine — Jer 14:18 — 8463
have ye healed that which was *s* — Eze 34:4 — 2470
will strengthen that which was *s* — Eze 34:16 — 2470
fainted, and was *s* certain days — Dan 8:27 — 2470
made him *s* with bottles of wine — Hos 7:5 — 2470
I make thee *s* in smiting thee — Mic 6:13 — 2470
and if ye offer the lame and *s* — Mal 1:8 — 2470
was torn, and the lame, and the *s* — Mal 1:13 — 2470
they brought unto him all *s* — Mt 4:24 — *2192,2560*
lieth at home *s* of the palsy — Mt 8:6 — *3885*
mother laid, and *s* of a fever — Mt 8:14 — *4445*
word, and healed all that were *s* — Mt 8:16 — *2192,2560*
to him a man *s* of the palsy — Mt 9:2 — *3885*
said unto the *s* of the palsy — Mt 9:2 — *3885*
saith he to the *s* of the palsy — Mt 9:6 — *3885*
a physician, but they that are *s* — Mt 9:12 — *2192,2560*
Heal the *s*, cleanse the lepers, — Mt 10:8 — *770*
toward them, and he healed their *s* — Mt 14:14 — *732*
I was *s*, and ye visited me — Mt 25:36 — *770*
Or when saw we thee *s*, or in — Mt 25:39 — *772*
s, and in prison, and ye visited me — Mt 25:43 — *772*
or a stranger, or naked, or *s* — Mt 25:44 — *772*
wife's mother lay *s* of a fever — Mk 1:30 — *4445*
that were *s* of divers diseases — Mk 1:34 — *2192,2560*
him, bringing one *s* of the palsy — Mk 2:3 — *3885*
wherein the *s* of the palsy lay — Mk 2:4 — *3885*
he said unto the *s* of the palsy — Mk 2:5 — *3885*
to say to the *s* of the palsy — Mk 2:9 — *3885*
(he saith to the *s* of the palsy — Mk 2:10 — *3885*
physician, but they that are *s* — Mk 2:17 — *2192,2560*
laid his hands upon a few *s* folk — Mk 6:5 — *732*
with oil many that were *s* — Mk 6:13 — *732*
about in beds those that were *s* — Mk 6:55 — *2192,2560*
they laid the *s* in the streets, — Mk 6:56 — *770*
they shall lay hands on the *s* — Mk 16:18 — *732*
all they that had any *s* with — Lk 4:40 — *770*
(he said unto the *s* of the palsy — Lk 5:24 — *3885*
but they that are *s* — Lk 5:31 — *2192,2560*
who was dear unto him, was *s* — Lk 7:2 — *2192,2560*
the servant whole that had been *s* — Lk 7:10 — *770*
kingdom of God, and to heal the *s* — Lk 9:2 — *770*
heal the *s* that are therein, and — Lk 10:9 — *772*
whose son was *s* at Capernaum — Jn 4:46 — *770*
Now a certain man was *s*, named — Jn 11:1 — *770*
hair, whose brother Lazarus was *s* — Jn 11:2 — *770*
behold, he whom thou lovest is *s* — Jn 11:3 — *770*
had heard therefore that he was *s* — Jn 11:6 — *770*
forth the *s* into the streets — Acts 5:15 — *772*
unto Jerusalem, bringing *s* folks — Acts 5:16 — *772*
years, and was *s* of the palsy — Acts 9:33 — *3885*
in those days, that she was *s* — Acts 9:37 — *770*
the *s* handkerchiefs or aprons — Acts 19:12 — *770*
of Publius lay *s* of a fever — Acts 28:8
ye had heard that he had been *s* — Phil 2:26 — *770*
indeed he was *s* nigh unto death — Phil 2:27 — *770*
have I left at Miletum *s* — 2Ti 4:20 — *770*
Is any *s* among you — Jas 5:14 — *770*
prayer of faith shall save the *s* — Jas 5:15 — *2577*

SICKLE {12}
to put the *s* to the corn — Deut 16:9 — 2770
but thou shalt not move a *s* unto — Deut 23:25 — 2770
him that handleth the *s* in the — Jer 50:16 — 4038
Put ye in the *s*, for the harvest — Joel 3:13 — 4038
immediately he putteth in the *s* — Mk 4:29 — *1407*
crown, and in his hand a sharp *s* — Rev 14:14 — *1407*
sat on the cloud, Thrust in thy *s* — Rev 14:15 — *1407*
thrust in his *s* on the earth — Rev 14:16 — *1407*
heaven, he also having a sharp *s* — Rev 14:17 — *1407*
cry to him that had the sharp *s* — Rev 14:18 — *1407*
saying, Thrust in thy sharp *s* — Rev 14:18 — *1407*
thrust in his *s* into the earth — Rev 14:19 — *1407*

SICKLY {1}
s among you, and many sleep — 1Cor 11:30 — *732*

SICKNESS {20}
I will take *s* away from the midst — Ex 23:25 — 4245
lie with a woman having her *s* — Lev 20:18 — 1739
will take away from thee all *s* — Deut 7:15 — 2483
Also every *s*, and every plague, — Deut 28:61 — 2483
plague, whatsoever *s* there be — 1Kin 8:37 — 4245
his *s* was so sore, that there was — 1Kin 17:17 — 2483
sick of his *s* whereof he died — 2Kin 13:14 — 2483
sore or whatsoever *s* there be — 2Chr 6:28 — 4245
thou shalt have great *s* by — 2Chr 21:15 — 2483
out by reason of the *s* day by day — 2Chr 21:15 — 2483
fell out by reason of his *s* — 2Chr 21:19 — 2483
wilt make all his bed in his *s* — Ps 41:3 — 2483
much sorrow and wrath with his *s* — Eccl 5:17 — 2483
sick, and was recovered of his *s* — Is 38:9 — 2483
he will cut me off with pining *s* — Is 38:12
When Ephraim saw his *s*, and Judah — Hos 5:13 — 2483
and healing all manner of *s* — Mt 4:23 — *3554*
the kingdom, and healing every *s* — Mt 9:35 — *3554*
out, and to heal all manner of *s* — Mt 10:1 — *3554*
This *s* is not unto death, but for — Jn 11:4 — *769*

SICKNESSES {4}
and of long continuance, and sore *s* — Deut 28:59 — 2483
the *s* which the LORD hath laid — Deut 29:22 — 8463
our infirmities, and bare our *s* — Mt 8:17 — *3554*
And to have power to heal *s* — Mk 3:15 — *3554*

SIDDIM *(sid'-dim)* {3} *Area of Sodom and Gomorrah.*
joined together in the vale of *S* — Gen 14:3 — 7708
battle with them in the vale of *S* — Gen 14:8 — 7708
the vale of *S* was full of — Gen 14:10 — 7708

SIDE {443}
shalt thou set in the *s* thereof — Gen 6:16 — 6654
that was openly by the way *s* — Gen 38:21
walked along by the river's *s* — Ex 2:5 — 3027
and strike it on the two *s* posts — Ex 12:7
the two *s* posts with the blood — Ex 12:22
the lintel, and on the two *s* posts — Ex 12:23
his hands, the one on the one *s* — Ex 17:12
and the other on the other *s* — Ex 17:12
rings shall be in the one *s* of it — Ex 25:12 — 6753
and two rings in the other *s* of it — Ex 25:12 — 6753
the candlestick out of the one *s* — Ex 25:32 — 6654
candlestick out of the other *s* — Ex 25:32 — 6654
And a cubit on the one *s* — Ex 26:13
a cubit on the other *s* of that — Ex 26:13
on this *s* and on that *s* — Ex 26:13
boards on the south *s* southward — Ex 26:18 — 6285
And for the second *s* of the — Ex 26:20 — 6763
s there shall be twenty boards — Ex 26:20 — 6285
of the one *s* of the tabernacle — Ex 26:26 — 6763
of the other *s* of the tabernacle — Ex 26:27 — 6763
boards of the *s* of the tabernacle — Ex 26:27 — 6763
s of the tabernacle toward the — Ex 26:35 — 6763
put the table on the north *s* — Ex 26:35 — 6763
for the south *s* southward there — Ex 27:9 — 6285
an hundred cubits long for one *s* — Ex 27:9
likewise for the north *s* in — Ex 27:11 — 6285
of the court on the west *s* shall — Ex 27:12 — 6285
of the court on the east *s* — Ex 27:13 — 6285
The hangings of one *s* of the gate — Ex 27:14 — 3802
on the other *s* shall be hangings — Ex 27:15 — 3802
which is in the *s* of the ephod — Ex 28:26 — 5676
on the one *s* and on the other were — Ex 32:15
and said, Who is on the LORD's *s* — Ex 32:26
Put every man his sword by his *s* — Ex 32:27 — 3409
uttermost *s* of another curtain — Ex 36:11 — 8193
boards for the south *s* southward — Ex 36:23 — 6285
for the other *s* of the tabernacle — Ex 36:25 — 6763
of the one *s* of the tabernacle — Ex 36:31 — 6763
of the other *s* of the tabernacle — Ex 36:32 — 6763
two rings upon the one *s* of it — Ex 37:3 — 6763
two rings upon the other *s* of it — Ex 37:3 — 6763
One cherub on the end on this *s* — Ex 37:8
cherub on the other end on that *s* — Ex 37:8
out of the one *s* thereof, and — Ex 37:18 — 6654
out of the other *s* thereof — Ex 37:18 — 6654
on the south *s* southward the — Ex 38:9 — 6285
for the north *s* the hangings were — Ex 38:11 — 6285
for the west *s* were hangings of — Ex 38:12 — 6285
for the east *s* eastward fifty — Ex 38:13 — 6285
The hangings of the one *s* of the — Ex 38:14 — 3802
for the other *s* of the court gate — Ex 38:15 — 3802
which was on the *s* of the ephod — Ex 39:19 — 5676
upon the *s* of the tabernacle — Ex 40:22 — 3409
on the *s* of the tabernacle — Ex 40:24 — 3409
he shall kill it on the *s* of the — Lev 1:11 — 3409
wrung out at the *s* of the altar — Lev 1:15 — 7023
offering upon the *s* of the altar — Lev 5:9 — 7023
on the east *s* toward the rising — Num 2:3 — 6924
On the south *s* shall be the — Num 2:10
On the west *s* shall be the — Num 2:18
be on the north *s* by their armies — Num 2:25
the *s* of the tabernacle southward — Num 3:29 — 3409
these shall pitch on the *s* of the — Num 3:35 — 3409
south *s* shall take their journey — Num 10:6
it were a day's journey on this *s* — Num 11:31 — 3541
a day's journey on the other *s* — Num 11:31 — 3541
Dathan, and Abiram, on every *s* — Num 16:27 — 5439
pitched on the other *s* of Arnon — Num 21:13 — 5676
Moab on this *s* Jordan by Jericho — Num 22:1 — 5676
on this *s*, and a wall on that *s* — Num 22:24
as gardens by the river's *s* — Num 24:6
with them on yonder *s* Jordan — Num 32:19 — 5676
to us on this *s* Jordan eastward — Num 32:19 — 5676
on this *s* Jordan may be ours — Num 32:32 — 5676
to Riblah, on the east *s* of Ain — Num 34:11 — 6924
shall reach unto the *s* of the sea — Num 34:11 — 3802
their inheritance on this *s* — Num 34:15 — 5676
on the east *s* two thousand cubits — Num 35:5 — 6285
on the south *s* two thousand — Num 35:5 — 6285
on the west *s* two thousand cubits — Num 35:5 — 6285
on the north *s* two thousand — Num 35:5 — 6285
three cities on this *s* Jordan — Num 35:14 — 5676
this *s* Jordan in the wilderness — Deut 1:1 — 5676
On this *s* Jordan, in the land of — Deut 1:5 — 5676
and in the south, and by the sea *s* — Deut 1:7 — 2348
land that was on this *s* Jordan — Deut 3:8 — 5676
ask from the one *s* of heaven unto — Deut 4:32 — 7097
s Jordan toward the sunrising — Deut 4:41 — 5676
On this *s* Jordan, in the valley — Deut 4:46 — 5676
which were on this *s* Jordan — Deut 4:47 — 5676
plain on this *s* Jordan eastward — Deut 4:49 — 5676
they not on the other *s* Jordan — Deut 11:30 — 5676
put it in the *s* of the ark of the — Deut 31:26 — 6654
Moses gave you on this *s* Jordan — Josh 1:14 — 5676
s Jordan toward the sunrising — Josh 1:15 — 5676
that were on the other *s* Jordan — Josh 2:10 — 5676
which were on the *s* of Jordan — Josh 5:1 — 5676
on the east *s* of Beth-el — Josh 7:2
and dwelt on the other *s* Jordan — Josh 7:7 — 5676
and Ai, on the west *s* of Ai — Josh 8:9
and pitched on the north *s* of Ai — Josh 8:11
and Ai, on the west *s* of the city — Josh 8:12
on this *s*, and some on that *s* — Josh 8:22
judges, stood on this *s* the ark — Josh 8:33
on that *s* before the priests the — Josh 8:33
kings which were on this *s* Jordan — Josh 9:1 — 5676
their land on the other *s* Jordan — Josh 12:1 — 5676
on this *s* Jordan on the west — Josh 12:7 — 5676
on the other *s* Jordan eastward — Josh 13:27 — 5676
of Moab, on the other *s* Jordan — Josh 13:32 — 5676
half tribe on the other *s* Jordan — Josh 14:3 — 5676
to the south *s* to Maaleh-acrabbim — Josh 15:3
on the south *s* unto Kadesh-barnea — Josh 15:3
is on the south *s* of the river — Josh 15:7
unto the south *s* of the Jebusite — Josh 15:8 — 3802
along unto the *s* of mount Jearim — Josh 15:10 — 3802
which is Chesalon, on the north *s* — Josh 15:10
out unto the *s* of Ekron northward — Josh 15:11 — 3802
on the east *s* was Ataroth-addar — Josh 16:5
sea to Michmethah on the north *s* — Josh 16:6
which were on the other *s* Jordan — Josh 17:5 — 5676
was on the north *s* of the river — Josh 17:9
on the north *s* was from Jordan — Josh 18:12 — 6285
the border went up to the *s* of — Josh 18:12 — 3802
of Jericho on the north *s* — Josh 18:12
toward Luz, to the *s* of Luz — Josh 18:13 — 3802
south *s* of the nether Beth-horon — Josh 18:13
to the *s* of Jebusi on the south, — Josh 18:16 — 3802
passed along toward the *s* over — Josh 18:18 — 3802
to the *s* of Beth-hoglah northward — Josh 18:19 — 3802
the border of it on the east *s* — Josh 18:20 — 6285
it on the north *s* to Hannathon — Josh 19:14
toward the north *s* of Beth-emek — Josh 19:27
to Zebulun on the south *s* — Josh 19:34
reacheth to Asher on the west *s* — Josh 19:34
on the other *s* Jordan by Jericho — Josh 20:8 — 5676
gave you on the other *s* Jordan — Josh 22:4 — 5676
on this *s* Jordan westward — Josh 22:7 — 5676
other *s* of the flood in old time — Josh 24:2 — 5676
from the other *s* of the flood — Josh 24:3 — 5676
which dwelt on the other *s* Jordan — Josh 24:8 — 5676
on the other *s* of the flood — Josh 24:14 — 5676
were on the other *s* of the flood — Josh 24:15 — 5676
on the north *s* of the hill of — Josh 24:30
on the north *s* of the hill Gaash — Judg 2:9
were on the north *s* of them — Judg 7:1
sand by the sea *s* for multitude — Judg 7:12 — 8193
also on every *s* of all the camp — Judg 7:18 — 5439
to Gideon on the other *s* Jordan — Judg 7:25 — 5676
of all their enemies on every *s* — Judg 8:34 — 5439
other *s* Jordan in the land of the — Judg 10:8 — 5676
came by the east *s* of the land of — Judg 11:18
pitched on the other *s* of Arnon — Judg 11:18 — 5676
on the *s* of mount Ephraim — Judg 19:1 — 3411
toward the *s* of mount Ephraim — Judg 19:18 — 3411
is on the north *s* of Beth-el — Judg 21:19
on the east *s* of the highway that — Judg 21:19
backward by the *s* of the gate — 1Sa 4:18 — 3027
in a coffer by the *s* thereof — 1Sa 6:8 — 6654
hand of your enemies on every *s* — 1Sa 12:11 — 5439
garrison, that is on the other *s* — 1Sa 14:1 — 5676
was a sharp rock on the one *s* — 1Sa 14:4 — 5676
and a sharp rock on the other *s* — 1Sa 14:4 — 5676
unto all Israel, Be ye on one *s* — 1Sa 14:40 — 5676
my son will be on the other *s* — 1Sa 14:40 — 5676
all his enemies on every *s* — 1Sa 14:47 — 5439
stood on a mountain on the one *s* — 1Sa 17:3
on a mountain on the other *s* — 1Sa 17:3
three arrows on the *s* thereof — 1Sa 20:20 — 6654
the arrows are on this *s* of thee — 1Sa 20:21
arose, and Abner sat by Saul's *s* — 1Sa 20:25 — 6654
went on this *s* of the mountain — 1Sa 23:26 — 6654
his men on that *s* of the mountain — 1Sa 23:26 — 6654
David went over to the other *s* — 1Sa 26:13 — 5676
were on the other *s* of the valley — 1Sa 31:7 — 5676
that were on the other *s* Jordan — 1Sa 31:7 — 5676
the one on the one *s* of the pool — 2Sa 2:13
other on the other *s* of the pool — 2Sa 2:13
his sword in his fellow's *s* — 2Sa 2:16 — 6654
the way of the hill *s* behind him — 2Sa 13:34 — 6654
on the hill's *s* over against him — 2Sa 16:13 — 6763
And the king stood by the gate *s* — 2Sa 18:4 — 3027
on the right *s* of the city that — 2Sa 24:5 — 3225
the region on this *s* the river — 1Kin 4:24 — 5676
all the kings on this *s* the river — 1Kin 4:24 — 5676
which were about him on every *s* — 1Kin 5:3
God hath given me rest on every *s* — 1Kin 5:4 — 5439
was in the right *s* of the house — 1Kin 6:8 — 3802
s posts were a fifth part of the — 1Kin 6:31
one *s* of the floor to the other — 1Kin 7:7
at the *s* of every addition — 1Kin 7:30 — 5676
bases on the right *s* of the house — 1Kin 7:39 — 3802
five on the left *s* of the house — 1Kin 7:39 — 3802
s of the house eastward over — 1Kin 7:39 — 3802
of pure gold, five on the right *s* — 1Kin 7:49
either *s* on the place of the seat — 1Kin 10:19
lions stood there on the one *s* — 1Kin 10:20
on the other *s* as red as blood — 2Kin 3:22 — 5048
window, and said, Who is on my *s* — 2Kin 9:32
on the right *s* as one cometh into — 2Kin 12:9 — 3225
it on the north *s* of the altar — 2Kin 16:14 — 3409
unto the east *s* of the valley — 1Chr 4:39 — 4217
on the other *s* Jordan by Jericho, — 1Chr 6:78 — 5676
on the east *s* of Jordan — 1Chr 6:78 — 4217
Thine are we, David, and on thy *s* — 1Chr 12:18
And on the other *s* of Jordan — 1Chr 12:37 — 5676
he not given you rest on every *s* — 1Chr 22:18 — 5439
this *s* Jordan westward in all the — 1Chr 26:30 — 5676
the temple, five on the right *s* — 2Chr 4:8
on the right *s* of the east end — 2Chr 4:10 — 3802
at the sea *s* in the land of Edom — 2Chr 8:17 — 8193
stays on each *s* of the sitting — 2Chr 9:18
lions stood there on the one *s* — 2Chr 9:19
having Judah and Benjamin on his *s* — 2Chr 11:12
he hath given us rest on every *s* — 2Chr 14:7 — 5439

beyond the sea on this *s* Syria 2Chr 20:2
from the right *s* of the temple to 2Chr 23:10 3802
to the left *s* of the temple 2Chr 23:10 3802
other, and guided them on every *s* 2Chr 32:22 5439
the west *s* of the city of David 2Chr 32:30
of David, on the west *s* of Gihon 2Chr 33:14
rest that are on this *s* the river Ezr 4:10 5675
the men on this *s* the river Ezr 4:11 5675
no portion on this *s* the river Ezr 4:16 5675
governor on this *s* the river Ezr 5:3 5675
governor on this *s* the river Ezr 5:6 5675
which were on this *s* the river Ezr 5:6 5675
governor on this *s* the river Ezr 6:13 5675
the governors on this *s* the river Ezr 8:36 5676
the governor on this *s* the river Neh 3:7 5676
one had his sword girded by his *s* Neh 4:18 4975
about all that he hath on every *s* Job 1:10 5439
shall make him afraid on every *s* Job 18:11 5439
shall be ready at his *s* Job 18:12 6763
He hath destroyed me on every *s* Job 19:10 5439
The wicked walk on every *s* Ps 12:8 5439
fear was on every *s* Ps 31:13 5439
little hills rejoice on every *s* Ps 65:12 2296
and comfort me on every *s* Ps 71:21 5437
A thousand shall fall at thy *s* Ps 91:7 6654
The LORD is on my *s* Ps 118:6
been the LORD who was on our *s* Ps 124:1
been the LORD who was on our *s* Ps 124:2
on the *s* of their oppressors Eccl 4:1 3027
shall be nursed at thy *s* Is 60:4 6654
the enemy and fear is on every *s* Jer 6:25 5439
defaming of many, fear on every *s* Jer 20:10 5439
cry unto them, Fear is on every *s* Jer 49:29 5439
ninety and six pomegranates on a *s* Jer 52:23 7307
face of a lion, on the right *s* Eze 1:10 3225
the face of an ox on the left *s* Eze 1:10 8040
had two, which covered on this *s* Eze 1:23
had two, which covered on that *s* Eze 1:23
Lie thou also upon thy left *s* Eze 4:4 6654
them, lie again on thy right *s* Eze 4:6 6654
turn thee from one *s* to another Eze 4:8 6654
that thou shalt lie upon thy *s* Eze 4:9 6654
with a writer's inkhorn by his *s* Eze 9:2 4975
had the writer's inkhorn by his *s* Eze 9:3 4975
which had the inkhorn by his *s* Eze 9:11 4975
stood on the right *s* of the house Eze 10:3 3225
is on the east *s* of the city Eze 11:23 6954
thee on every *s* for thy whoredom Eze 16:33 5439
him on every *s* from the provinces Eze 19:8 5439
them against thee on every *s* Eze 23:22 5439
I will open the *s* of Moab from Eze 25:9 3802
by the sword upon her on every *s* Eze 28:23 5439
Because ye have thrust with *s* Eze 34:21 6654
and swallowed you up on every *s* Eze 36:3 5439
and will gather them on every *s* Eze 37:21 5439
every *s* to my sacrifice that I do Eze 39:17 5439
on this *s*, and three on that *s* Eze 40:10 6311
measure on this *s* and on that *s* Eze 40:10
chambers was one cubit on this *s* Eze 40:12
the space was one cubit on that *s* Eze 40:12
were six cubits on this *s* Eze 40:12
and six cubits on that *s* Eze 40:12
the pavement by the *s* of the Eze 40:18 3802
on this *s* and three on that *s* Eze 40:21
this *s*, and another on that *s* Eze 40:26
on this *s*, and on that *s* Eze 40:34
on this *s*, and on that *s* Eze 40:37
gate were two tables on this *s* Eze 40:39
and two tables on that *s* Eze 40:39
at the *s* without, as one goeth up Eze 40:40 3802
and on the other *s*, which was at Eze 40:40 3802
Four tables were on this *s* Eze 40:41 3802
that *s*, by the *s* of the gate Eze 40:41 3802
which was at the *s* of the north Eze 40:44 3802
one at the *s* of the east gate Eze 40:44 3802
the porch, five cubits on this *s* Eze 40:48
and five cubits on that *s* Eze 40:48
gate was three cubits on this *s* Eze 40:48
and three cubits on that *s* Eze 40:48
this *s*, and another on that *s* Eze 40:49
six cubits broad on the one *s* Eze 41:1 6311
six cubits broad on the other *s* Eze 41:1
were five cubits on the one *s* Eze 41:2
and five cubits on the other *s* Eze 41:2
and the breadth of every *s* chamber Eze 41:5 6763
round about the house on every *s* Eze 41:5 5439
the *s* chambers were three, one Eze 41:6 6763
for the *s* chambers round about Eze 41:6 6763
still upward to the *s* chambers Eze 41:7 6763
the foundations of the *s* chambers Eze 41:8 6763
was for the *s* chamber without Eze 41:9 6763
the *s* chambers that were within Eze 41:9 6763
round about the house on every *s* Eze 41:10 5439
the doors of the *s* chambers were Eze 41:11 6763
on the one *s* and on the other *s* Eze 41:15
toward the palm tree on the one *s* Eze 41:19
the palm tree on the other *s* Eze 41:19
on the one *s* and on the other *s* Eze 41:26
upon the *s* chambers of the house, Eze 41:26 6763
was the entry on the east *s* Eze 42:9 6921
He measured the east *s* with the Eze 42:16 7307
He measured the north *s*, five Eze 42:17 7307
He measured the south *s*, five Eze 42:18 7307
He turned about to the west *s* Eze 42:19 7307
be for the prince on the one *s* Eze 45:7
on the other *s* of the oblation of Eze 45:7
city, from the west *s* westward Eze 45:7 6285
and from the east *s* eastward Eze 45:7 6285
which was at the *s* of the gate Eze 46:19
from the right *s* of the house Eze 47:1
at the south *s* of the altar Eze 47:1
ran out waters on the right *s* Eze 47:2 3802
were very many trees on the one *s* Eze 47:7
on this *s* and on that *s* Eze 47:12
of the land toward the north *s* Eze 47:15 6285
And this is the north *s* Eze 47:17 6285
the east *s* ye shall measure from Eze 47:18 6285
And this is the east *s* Eze 47:18 6285
And the south *s* southward, from Eze 47:19 6285
And this is the south *s* southward Eze 47:19 6285
The west *s* also shall be the Eze 47:20 6285
This is the west *s* Eze 47:20 6285
the east *s* unto the west *s* Eze 48:2 6285
east *s* even unto the west *s* Eze 48:3 6285
the east *s* unto the west *s* Eze 48:4 6285
the east *s* unto the west *s* Eze 48:5 6285
east *s* even unto the west *s* Eze 48:6 6285
the east *s* unto the west *s* Eze 48:7 6285
the east *s* unto the west *s* Eze 48:8 6285
the east *s* unto the west *s* Eze 48:8 6285
the north *s* four thousand and five Eze 48:16 6285
the south *s* four thousand and five Eze 48:16 6285
on the east *s* four thousand and Eze 48:16 6285
the west *s* four thousand and five Eze 48:16 6285
be for the prince, on the one *s* Eze 48:21 6285
the east *s* unto the west *s* Eze 48:23 6285
the east *s* unto the west *s* Eze 48:24 6285
the east *s* unto the west *s* Eze 48:25 6285
the east *s* unto the west *s* Eze 48:26 6285
the east *s* unto the west *s* Eze 48:27 6285
of Gad, at the south *s* southward Eze 48:28 6285
out of the city on the north *s* Eze 48:30 6285
at the east *s* four thousand and Eze 48:32 6285
at the south *s* four thousand and Eze 48:33 6285
At the west *s* four thousand and Eze 48:34 6285
and it raised up itself on one *s* Dan 7:5 7859
as I was by the *s* of the great Dan 10:4 3027
but she shall not stand on his *s* Dan 11:17
the one on this *s* of the bank of Dan 12:5
the other on that *s* of the bank Dan 12:5
that thou stoodest on the other *s* Obad 11 5048
and sat on the east *s* of the city Jonah 4:5 6924
one upon the right *s* of the bowl Zec 4:3
the other upon the left *s* thereof Zec 4:3
the right *s* of the candlestick Zec 4:11
and upon the left *s* thereof Zec 4:11
off as on this *s* according to it Zec 5:3
off as on that *s* according to it Zec 5:3
to depart unto the other *s* Mt 8:18 *4008*
other *s* into the country of the Mt 8:28 *4008*
of the house, and sat by the sea *s* Mt 13:1 *3844*
some seeds fell by the way *s* Mt 13:4 *3844*
which received seed by the way *s* Mt 13:19 *3844*
to go before him unto the other *s* Mt 14:22 *4008*
were come to the other *s*, they Mt 16:5 *4008*
blind men sitting by the way *s* Mt 20:30 *3844*
he went forth again by the sea *s* Mk 2:13 *3844*
began again to teach by the sea *s* Mk 4:1 *3844*
he sowed, some fell by the way *s* Mk 4:4 *3844*
And these are they by the way *s* Mk 4:15 *3844*
Let us pass over unto the other *s* Mk 4:35 *4008*
over unto the other *s* of the sea Mk 5:1 *4008*
again by ship unto the other *s* Mk 5:21 *4008*
to go to the other *s* before unto Mk 6:45 *4008*
again departed to the other *s* Mk 8:13 *4008*
Judaea by the farther *s* of Jordan Mk 10:1 *4008*
sat by the highway *s* begging Mk 10:46 *3844*
young man sitting on the right *s* Mk 16:5 *1188*
right *s* of the altar of incense Lk 1:11 *1188*
he sowed, some fell by the way *s* Lk 8:5 *3844*
Those by the way *s* are they that Lk 8:12 *3844*
over unto the other *s* of the lake Lk 8:22 *4008*
him, he passed by on the other *s* Lk 10:31 *492*
him, and passed by on the other *s* Lk 10:32 *492*
man sat by the way *s* begging Lk 18:35 *3844*
round, and keep thee in on every *s* Lk 19:43 *3840*
s of the sea saw that there was Jn 6:22 *4008*
him on the other *s* of the sea Jn 6:25 *4008*
others with him, on either *s* one Jn 19:18 *1782*
with a spear pierced his *s* Jn 19:34 *4125*
unto them his hands and his *s* Jn 20:20 *4125*
and thrust my hand into his *s* Jn 20:25 *4125*
thy hand, and thrust it into my *s* Jn 20:27 *4125*
net on the right *s* of the ship Jn 21:6 *3313*
whose house is by the sea *s* Acts 10:6 *3844*
one Simon a tanner by the sea *s* Acts 10:32 *3844*
and he smote Peter on the *s* Acts 12:7 *4125*
went out of the city by a river *s* Acts 16:13 *3844*
We are troubled on every *s* 2Cor 4:8
but we were troubled on every *s* 2Cor 7:5
on either *s* of the river, was Rev 22:2 *1782*

SIDES {48}
the rings by the *s* of the ark Ex 25:14 6763
shall come out of the *s* of it Ex 25:32 6654
it shall hang over the *s* of the Ex 26:13 6654
for the *s* of the tabernacle Ex 26:22 3411
of the tabernacle in the two *s* Ex 26:23 3411
for the two *s* westward Ex 26:27 3411
be upon the two *s* of the altar Ex 27:7 6763
the two *s* of the ephod underneath Ex 28:27 3802
the *s* thereof round about, and the Ex 30:3 7023
upon the two *s* of it shalt thou Ex 30:4 6654
were written on both their *s* Ex 32:15 5676
for the *s* of the tabernacle Ex 36:27 3411
of the tabernacle in the two *s* Ex 36:28 3411
the tabernacle for the *s* westward Ex 36:32 3411
the rings by the *s* of the ark Ex 37:5 6763
going out of the *s* thereof Ex 37:18 6654
the *s* thereof round about, and the Ex 37:26 7023
of it, upon the two *s* thereof Ex 37:27 6654
the rings on the *s* of the altar Ex 38:7 6763
put them on the two *s* of the Ex 39:20 3802
in your eyes, and thorns in your *s* Num 33:55 6654
unto you, and scourges in your *s* Josh 23:13 6654
they shall be as thorns in your *s* Judg 2:3 6654
colours of needlework on both *s* Judg 5:30
men remained in the *s* of the cave 1Sa 24:3 3411
peace on all *s* round about him 1Kin 4:24 5676
cubits on the *s* of the house 1Kin 6:16 3411
to the *s* of Lebanon, and will cut 2Kin 19:23 3411
on the *s* of the north, the city Ps 48:2 3411
vine by the *s* of thine house Ps 128:3 3411
in the *s* of the north Is 14:13 3411
down to hell, to the *s* of the pit Is 14:15 3411
mountains, to the *s* of Lebanon Is 37:24 3411
ye shall be borne upon her *s* Is 66:12 6654
be raised from the *s* of the earth Jer 6:22 3411
nest in the *s* of the hole's mouth Jer 48:28 5676
their calamity from all *s* thereof Jer 49:32 5676
under their wings on their four *s* Eze 1:8 7253
went, they went upon their four *s* Eze 1:17 7253
went, they went upon their four *s* Eze 10:11 7253
are set in the *s* of the pit Eze 32:23 3411
the *s* of the door were five Eze 41:2 3802
on the *s* of the porch, and upon Eze 41:26 3802
He measured it by the four *s* Eze 42:20 7307
was a place on the two *s* westward Eze 46:19 3411
for these are his *s* east and west Eze 48:1 6285
him that is by the *s* of the house Amos 6:10 3411
gone down into the *s* of the ship Jonah 1:5 3411

SIDON *(si'-don)* {14} See SIDONIANS, ZIDON.
1. Son of Canaan.
Canaan begat *S* his firstborn, and Gen 10:15 6721
2. Phoenician city north of Tyre.
of the Canaanites was from *S* Gen 10:19 6721
you, had been done in Tyre and *S* Mt 11:21 *4605*
S at the day of judgment, than Mt 11:22 *4605*
into the coasts of Tyre and *S* Mt 15:21 *4605*
and they about Tyre and *S*, a great Mk 3:8 *4605*
into the borders of Tyre and *S* Mk 7:24 *4605*
from the coasts of Tyre and *S* Mk 7:31 *4605*
save unto Sarepta, a city of *S* Lk 4:26 *4605*
from the sea coast of Tyre and *S* Lk 6:17 *4605*
works had been done in Tyre and *S* Lk 10:13 *4605*
S at the judgment, than for you Lk 10:14 *4605*
displeased with them of Tyre and *S* Acts 12:20 *4605*
And the next day we touched at *S* Acts 27:3 *4605*

SIDONIANS *(si-do'-ne-uns)* {5} See ZIDONIANS. *Inhabitants of Sidon.*
(Which Hermon the *S* call Sirion Deut 3:9 6722
and Mearah that is beside the *S* Josh 13:4 6722
Misrephoth-maim, and all the *S* Josh 13:6 6722
and all the Canaanites, and the *S* Judg 3:3 6722
to hew timber like unto the *S* 1Kin 5:6 6722

SIEGE {17}
life) to employ them in the *s* Deut 20:19 4692
thy God hath given thee, in the *s* Deut 28:53 4692
he hath nothing left him in the *s* Deut 28:55 4692
of all things secretly in the *s* Deut 28:57 4692
and all Israel laid *s* to Gibbethon 1Kin 15:27 6696
he himself laid *s* against Lachish 2Chr 32:9
ye abide in the *s* in Jerusalem 2Chr 32:10 4692
will lay *s* against thee with a Is 29:3 6696
the flesh of his friend in the *s* Jer 19:9 4692
lay *s* against it, and build a fort Eze 4:2 4692
and thou shalt lay *s* against it Eze 4:3 6696
face toward the *s* of Jerusalem Eze 4:7 4692
thou hast ended the days of thy *s* Eze 4:8 4692
the days of the *s* are fulfilled Eze 5:2 4692
he hath laid *s* against us Mic 5:1 4692
Draw thee waters for the *s* Nah 3:14 4692
be in the *s* both against Judah Zec 12:2 4692

SIEVE {2}
the nations with the *s* of vanity Is 30:28 5299
like as corn is sifted in a *s* Amos 9:9 3531

SIFT {3}
to *s* the nations with the sieve Is 30:28 5130
I will *s* the house of Israel Amos 9:9 5128
that he may *s* you as wheat Lk 22:31 *4617*

SIFTED {1}
like as corn is *s* in a sieve Amos 9:9 5128

SIGH {7}
all the merryhearted do *s* Is 24:7 584
her priests *s*, her virgins are Lam 1:4 584
All her people *s*, they seek bread Lam 1:11 584
They have heard that I *s* Lam 1:21 584
the foreheads of the men that *s* Eze 9:4 584
S therefore, thou son of man, Eze 21:6 584
with bitterness *s* before their Eze 21:6 584

SIGHED {3}
the children of Israel *s* by Ex 2:23 584
And looking up to heaven, he *s* Mk 7:34 *4727*
he *s* deeply in his spirit, and Mk 8:12 *389*

SIGHEST {1}
say unto thee, Wherefore *s* thou Eze 21:7 584

SIGHETH {1}
yea, she *s*, and turneth backward Lam 1:8 584

SIGHING {7}

For my *s* cometh before I eat, and	Job 3:24	585
for the *s* of the needy, now will	Ps 12:5	603
with grief, and my years with *s*	Ps 31:10	585
Let the *s* of the prisoner come	Ps 79:11	603
all the *s* thereof have I made to	Is 21:2	585
and sorrow and *s* shall flee away	Is 35:10	585
I fainted in my *s*, and I find no	Jer 45:3	585

SIGHS {1}

for my *s* are many, and my heart is	Lam 1:22	585

SIGHT {333}

tree that is pleasant to the *s*	Gen 2:9	4758
now I have found favour in thy *s*	Gen 18:3	5869
servant hath found grace in thy *s*	Gen 19:19	5869
in Abraham's *s* because of his son	Gen 21:11	5869
in thy *s* because of the lad	Gen 21:12	5869
I may bury my dead out of my *s*	Gen 23:4	6440
I should bury my dead out of my *s*	Gen 23:8	6440
that I may find grace in thy *s*	Gen 32:5	5869
to find grace in the *s* of my lord	Gen 33:8	5869
now I have found grace in thy *s*	Gen 33:10	5869
me find grace in the *s* of my lord	Gen 33:15	5869
was wicked in the *s* of the LORD	Gen 38:7	5869
And Joseph found grace in his *s*	Gen 39:4	5869
gave him favour in the *s* of the	Gen 39:21	5869
ought left in the *s* of my lord	Gen 47:18	6440
us find grace in the *s* of my lord	Gen 47:25	5869
now I have found grace in thy *s*	Gen 47:29	5869
turn aside, and see this great *s*	Ex 3:3	4758
favour in the *s* of the Egyptians	Ex 3:21	5869
the signs in the *s* of the people	Ex 4:30	5869
in the *s* of Pharaoh, and in the	Ex 7:20	5869
and in the *s* of his servants	Ex 7:20	5869
the heaven in the *s* of Pharaoh	Ex 9:8	5869
favour in the *s* of the Egyptians	Ex 11:3	5869
in the *s* of Pharaoh's servants,	Ex 11:3	5869
and in the *s* of the people	Ex 11:3	5869
favour in the *s* of the Egyptians	Ex 12:36	5869
do that which is right in his *s*	Ex 15:26	5869
Moses did so in the *s* of the	Ex 17:6	5869
s of all the people upon mount	Ex 19:11	5869
the *s* of the glory of the LORD	Ex 24:17	4758
hast also found grace in my *s*	Ex 33:12	5869
if I have found grace in thy *s*	Ex 33:13	5869
that I may find grace in thy *s*	Ex 33:13	5869
people have found grace in thy *s*	Ex 33:16	5869
for thou hast found grace in my *s*	Ex 33:17	5869
now I have found grace in thy *s*	Ex 34:9	5869
in the *s* of all the house of	Ex 40:38	5869
accepted in the *s* of the LORD	Lev 10:19	5869
the plague in *s* be deeper than	Lev 13:3	4758
in *s* be not deeper than the skin,	Lev 13:4	4758
the plague in his *s* be at a stay	Lev 13:5	5869
it be in *s* lower than the skin,	Lev 13:20	4758
it be in *s* deeper than the skin	Lev 13:25	4758
if it be in *s* deeper than the	Lev 13:30	4758
it be not in *s* deeper than the	Lev 13:31	4758
the scall be not in *s* deeper than	Lev 13:32	4758
nor be in *s* deeper than the skin	Lev 13:34	4758
the scall be in his *s* at a stay	Lev 13:37	5869
which in *s* are lower than the	Lev 14:37	4758
cut off in the *s* of their people	Lev 20:17	5869
with rigour over him in thy *s*	Lev 25:53	5869
of Egypt in the *s* of the heathen	Lev 26:45	5869
in the *s* of Aaron their father	Num 3:4	6440
have I not found favour in thy *s*	Num 11:11	5869
if I have found favour in thy *s*	Num 11:15	5869
were in our own *s* as grasshoppers	Num 13:33	5869
and so we were in their *s*	Num 13:33	5869
shall burn the heifer in his *s*	Num 19:5	5869
in the *s* of all the congregation	Num 20:27	5869
woman in the *s* of Moses, and in	Num 25:6	5869
in the *s* of all the congregation	Num 25:6	5869
and give him a charge in their *s*	Num 27:19	5869
if we have found grace in thy *s*	Num 32:5	5869
done evil in the *s* of the LORD	Num 32:13	5869
in the *s* of all the Egyptians	Num 33:3	5869
in the *s* of the nations, which	Deut 4:6	5869
evil in the *s* of the LORD thy God	Deut 4:25	5869
brought thee out in his *s* with	Deut 4:37	6440
and good in the *s* of the LORD	Deut 6:18	5869
wickedly in the *s* of the LORD	Deut 9:18	5869
is right in the *s* of the LORD	Deut 12:25	5869
right in the *s* of the LORD thy	Deut 12:28	5869
in the *s* of the LORD thy God	Deut 17:2	5869
is right in the *s* of the LORD	Deut 21:9	5869
s of thine eyes which thou shalt	Deut 28:34	4758
for the *s* of thine eyes which	Deut 28:67	4758
unto him in the *s* of all Israel	Deut 31:7	5869
will do evil in the *s* of the LORD	Deut 31:29	5869
shewed in the *s* of all Israel	Deut 34:12	5869
thee in the *s* of all Israel	Josh 3:7	5869
Joshua in the *s* of all Israel	Josh 4:14	5869
and he said in the *s* of Israel	Josh 10:12	5869
and drive them from out of your *s*	Josh 23:5	6440
did those great signs in our *s*	Josh 24:17	5869
did evil in the *s* of the LORD	Judg 2:11	5869
did evil in the *s* of the LORD	Judg 3:7	5869
evil again in the *s* of the LORD	Judg 3:12	5869
done evil in the *s* of the LORD	Judg 3:12	5869
did evil in the *s* of the LORD	Judg 4:1	5869
did evil in the *s* of the LORD	Judg 6:1	5869
now I have found grace in thy *s*	Judg 6:17	5869
of the LORD departed out of his *s*	Judg 6:21	5869
evil again in the *s* of the LORD	Judg 10:6	5869
evil again in the *s* of the LORD	Judg 13:1	5869
him in whose *s* I shall find grace	Ruth 2:2	5869
said, Let me find favour in thy *s*	Ruth 2:13	5869
handmaid find grace in thy *s*	1Sa 1:18	5869
ye have done in the *s* of the LORD	1Sa 12:17	5869
thou wast little in thine own *s*	1Sa 15:17	5869
didst evil in the *s* of the LORD	1Sa 15:19	5869
for he hath found favour in my *s*	1Sa 16:22	5869
in the *s* of all the people	1Sa 18:5	5869
also in the *s* of Saul's servants	1Sa 18:5	5869
me in the host is good in my *s*	1Sa 29:6	5869
I know that thou art good in my *s*	1Sa 29:9	5869
and will be base in mine own *s*	2Sa 6:22	5869
all thine enemies out of thy *s*	2Sa 7:9	6440
was yet a small thing in thy *s*	2Sa 7:19	5869
of the LORD, to do evil in his *s*	2Sa 12:9	5869
thy wives in the *s* of this sun	2Sa 12:11	5869
meat, and dress the meat in my *s*	2Sa 13:5	5869
make me a couple of cakes in my *s*	2Sa 13:6	5869
it, and made cakes in his *s*	2Sa 13:8	5869
that I have found grace in thy *s*	2Sa 14:22	5869
that I may find grace in thy *s*	2Sa 16:4	5869
concubines in the *s* of all Israel	2Sa 16:22	5869
to my cleanness in his eye *s*	2Sa 22:25	5869
s to sit on the throne of Israel	1Kin 8:25	6440
my name, will I cast out of my *s*	1Kin 9:7	6440
did evil in the *s* of the LORD	1Kin 11:6	5869
great favour in the *s* of Pharaoh	1Kin 11:19	5869
ways, and do that is right in my *s*	1Kin 11:38	5869
did evil in the *s* of the LORD	1Kin 14:22	5869
he did evil in the *s* of the LORD	1Kin 15:26	5869
he did evil in the *s* of the LORD	1Kin 15:34	5869
that he did in the *s* of the LORD	1Kin 16:7	5869
doing evil in the *s* of the LORD	1Kin 16:19	5869
s of the LORD above all that were	1Kin 16:30	5869
to work evil in the *s* of the LORD	1Kin 21:20	5869
wickedness in the *s* of the LORD	1Kin 21:25	5869
he did evil in the *s* of the LORD	1Kin 22:52	5869
servants, be precious in thy *s*	2Kin 1:13	5869
my life now be precious in thy *s*	2Kin 1:14	5869
wrought evil in the *s* of the LORD	2Kin 3:2	5869
light thing in the *s* of the LORD	2Kin 3:18	5869
he did evil in the *s* of the LORD	2Kin 8:18	5869
and did evil in the *s* of the LORD	2Kin 8:27	5869
in the *s* of the LORD all his days	2Kin 12:2	5869
was evil in the *s* of the LORD	2Kin 13:2	5869
was evil in the *s* of the LORD	2Kin 13:11	5869
was right in the *s* of the LORD	2Kin 14:3	5869
was evil in the *s* of the LORD	2Kin 14:24	5869
was right in the *s* of the LORD	2Kin 15:3	5869
was evil in the *s* of the LORD	2Kin 15:9	5869
was evil in the *s* of the LORD	2Kin 15:18	5869
was evil in the *s* of the LORD	2Kin 15:24	5869
was evil in the *s* of the LORD	2Kin 15:28	5869
was right in the *s* of the LORD	2Kin 15:34	5869
in the *s* of the LORD his God	2Kin 16:2	5869
was evil in the *s* of the LORD	2Kin 17:2	5869
to do evil in the *s* of the LORD	2Kin 17:17	5869
and removed them out of his *s*	2Kin 17:18	6440
he had cast them out of his *s*	2Kin 17:20	6440
LORD removed Israel out of his *s*	2Kin 17:23	6440
was right in the *s* of the LORD	2Kin 18:3	5869
done that which is good in thy *s*	2Kin 20:3	5869
was evil in the *s* of the LORD	2Kin 21:2	5869
wickedness in the *s* of the LORD	2Kin 21:6	5869
done that which was evil in my *s*	2Kin 21:15	5869
was evil in the *s* of the LORD	2Kin 21:16	5869
was evil in the *s* of the LORD	2Kin 21:20	5869
was right in the *s* of the LORD	2Kin 22:2	5869
remove Judah also out of my *s*	2Kin 23:27	6440
was evil in the *s* of the LORD	2Kin 23:32	5869
was evil in the *s* of the LORD	2Kin 23:37	5869
to remove them out of his *s*	2Kin 24:3	6440
was evil in the *s* of the LORD	2Kin 24:9	5869
was evil in the *s* of the LORD	2Kin 24:19	5869
was evil in the *s* of the LORD	1Chr 2:3	5869
do that which is good in his *s*	1Chr 19:13	5869
much blood upon the earth in my *s*	1Chr 22:8	6440
in the *s* of all Israel the	1Chr 28:8	5869
in the *s* of all Israel, and	1Chr 29:25	5869
in my *s* to sit upon the throne of	2Chr 6:16	6440
my name, will I cast out of my *s*	2Chr 7:20	6440
was right in the *s* of the LORD	2Chr 20:32	5869
Wherefore he did evil in the *s* of	2Chr 22:4	5869
the *s* of the LORD all the days of	2Chr 24:2	5869
was right in the *s* of the LORD	2Chr 25:2	5869
was right in the *s* of the LORD	2Chr 26:4	5869
was right in the *s* of the LORD	2Chr 27:2	5869
was right in the *s* of the LORD	2Chr 28:1	5869
was right in the *s* of the LORD	2Chr 29:2	5869
s of all nations from thenceforth	2Chr 32:23	5869
was evil in the *s* of the LORD	2Chr 33:2	5869
much evil in the *s* of the LORD	2Chr 33:6	5869
was evil in the *s* of the LORD	2Chr 33:22	5869
was right in the *s* of the LORD	2Chr 34:2	5869
evil in the *s* of the LORD his God	2Chr 36:5	5869
was evil in the *s* of the LORD	2Chr 36:9	5869
evil in the *s* of the LORD his God	2Chr 36:12	5869
in the *s* of the kings of Persia	Ezr 9:9	6440
him mercy in the *s* of this man	Neh 1:11	6440
have found favour in thy *s*	Neh 2:5	6440
the book in the *s* of all people	Neh 8:5	5869
s of all them that looked upon	Est 2:15	5869
favour in his *s* more than all the	Est 2:17	6440
that she obtained favour in his *s*	Est 5:2	5869
found favour in the *s* of the king	Est 5:8	5869
If I have found favour in thy *s*	Est 7:3	5869
if I have found favour in his *s*	Est 8:5	5869
heavens are not clean in his *s*	Job 15:15	5869
beasts, and reputed vile in your *s*	Job 18:3	5869
I am an alien in their *s*	Job 19:15	5869
established in their *s* with them	Job 21:8	6440
the stars are not pure in his *s*	Job 25:5	5869
men in the open *s* of others	Job 34:26	7200
be cast down even at the *s* of him	Job 41:9	4758
foolish shall not stand in thy *s*	Ps 5:5	5869
the heathen be judged in thy *s*	Ps 9:19	6440
are far above out of his *s*	Ps 10:5	5048
my heart, be acceptable in thy *s*	Ps 19:14	6440
and done this evil in thy *s*	Ps 51:4	5869
shall their blood be in his *s*	Ps 72:14	5869
who may stand in thy *s* when once	Ps 76:7	6440
did he in the *s* of their fathers	Ps 78:12	5048
s by the revenging of the blood	Ps 79:10	5869
For a thousand years in thy *s* are	Ps 90:4	5869
shewed in the *s* of the heathen	Ps 98:2	5869
lies shall not tarry in my *s*	Ps 101:7	5869
Precious in the *s* of the LORD is	Ps 116:15	5869
for in thy *s* shall no man living	Ps 143:2	6440
is spread in the *s* of any bird	Prov 1:17	5869
understanding in the *s* of God	Prov 3:4	5869
beloved in the *s* of my mother	Prov 4:3	6440
man that is good in his *s* wisdom	Eccl 2:26	6440
Better is the *s* of the eyes than	Eccl 6:9	4758
Be not hasty to go out of his *s*	Eccl 8:3	6440
heart, and in the *s* of thine eyes	Eccl 11:9	4758
eyes, and prudent in their own *s*	Is 5:21	6440
not judge after the *s* of his eyes	Is 11:3	4758
so have we been in thy *s*, O LORD	Is 26:17	6440
done that which is good in thy *s*	Is 38:3	5869
Since thou wast precious in my *s*	Is 43:4	5869
thine abominations out of my *s*	Jer 4:1	6440
And I will cast you out of my *s*	Jer 7:15	6440
of Judah have done evil in my *s*	Jer 7:30	5869
cast them out of my *s*, and let	Jer 15:1	6440
If it do evil in my *s*, that it	Jer 18:10	5869
blot out their sin from thy *s*	Jer 18:23	6440
s of the men that go with thee	Jer 19:10	5869
in the *s* of Hanameel mine uncle's	Jer 32:12	5869
turned, and had done right in my *s*	Jer 34:15	5869
in the *s* of the men of Judah	Jer 43:9	5869
they have done in Zion in your *s*	Jer 51:24	5869
cometh out of man, in their *s*	Eze 4:12	5869
of thee in the *s* of the nations	Eze 5:8	5869
in the *s* of all that pass by	Eze 5:14	5869
And he went in in my *s*	Eze 10:2	5869
mounted up from the earth in my *s*	Eze 10:19	5869
and remove by day in their *s*	Eze 12:3	5869
place to another place in their *s*	Eze 12:3	5869
forth thy stuff by day in their *s*	Eze 12:4	5869
shalt go forth at even in their *s*	Eze 12:4	5869
thou through the wall in their *s*	Eze 12:5	5869
In their *s* shalt thou bear it	Eze 12:6	5869
it upon my shoulder in their *s*	Eze 12:7	5869
upon thee in the *s* of many women	Eze 16:41	5869
in whose *s* I made myself known	Eze 20:9	5869
in whose *s* I brought them out	Eze 20:14	5869
polluted in the *s* of the heathen	Eze 20:22	5869
in whose *s* I brought them forth	Eze 20:22	5869
lothe yourselves in your own *s*	Eze 20:43	6440
as a false divination in their *s*	Eze 21:23	5869
thyself in the *s* of the heathen	Eze 22:16	5869
s of all them that behold thee	Eze 28:18	5869
in them in the *s* of the heathen	Eze 28:25	5869
in your own *s* for your iniquities	Eze 36:31	6440
in the *s* of all that passed by	Eze 36:34	5869
in them in the *s* of many nations	Eze 39:27	5869
and write it in their *s*, that they	Eze 43:11	5869
the *s* thereof to the end of all	Dan 4:11	2379
the *s* thereof to all the earth	Dan 4:20	2379
away her whoredoms out of her *s*	Hos 2:2	6440
lewdness in the *s* of her lovers	Hos 2:10	5869
us up, and we shall live in his *s*	Hos 6:2	6440
my *s* in the bottom of the sea	Amos 9:3	5869
I said, I am cast out of thy *s*	Jonah 2:4	5869
evil is good in the *s* of the LORD	Mal 2:17	5869
The blind receive their *s*	Mt 11:5	*308*
for so it seemed good in thy *s*	Mt 11:26	*1715*
immediately their eyes received *s*	Mt 20:34	*308*
Lord, that I might receive my *s*	Mk 10:51	*308*
And immediately he received his *s*	Mk 10:52	*308*
be great in the *s* of the Lord	Lk 1:15	*1799*
and recovering of *s* to the blind	Lk 4:18	*309*
many that were blind he gave *s*	Lk 7:21	*991*
for so it seemed good in thy *s*	Lk 10:21	*1715*
against heaven, and in thy *s*	Lk 15:21	*1799*
is abomination in the *s* of God	Lk 16:15	*1799*
Lord, that I may receive my *s*	Lk 18:41	*308*
said unto him, Receive thy *s*	Lk 18:42	*308*
And immediately he received his *s*	Lk 18:43	*308*
that came together to that *s*	Lk 23:48	*2335*
and he vanished out of their *s*	Lk 24:31	
I went and washed, and I received *s*	Jn 9:11	*308*
him how he had received his *s*	Jn 9:15	*308*
had been blind, and received his *s*	Jn 9:18	*308*
of him that had received his *s*	Jn 9:18	*308*
cloud received him out of their *s*	Acts 1:9	*3788*
Whether it be right in the *s* of	Acts 4:19	*1799*
wisdom in the *s* of Pharaoh king	Acts 7:10	*1726*
saw it, he wondered at the *s*	Acts 7:31	*3705*
is not right in the *s* of God	Acts 8:21	*1799*
And he was three days without *s*	Acts 9:9	*991*
him, that he might receive his *s*	Acts 9:12	*308*
that thou mightest receive thy *s*	Acts 9:17	*308*
and he received *s* forthwith	Acts 9:18	*308*
in remembrance in the *s* of God	Acts 10:31	*1799*
me, Brother Saul, receive thy *s*	Acts 22:13	*308*
no flesh be justified in his *s*	Rom 3:20	*1799*

things honest in the *s* of all men ... Rom 12:17 *1799*
in the *s* of God speak we in ... 2Cor 2:17 *2714*
man's conscience in the *s* of God ... 2Cor 4:2 *1799*
(For we walk by faith, not by *s* ... 2Cor 5:7 *1491*
s of God might appear unto you ... 2Cor 7:12 *1799*
not only in the *s* of the Lord ... 2Cor 8:21 *1799*
but also in the *s* of men ... 2Cor 8:21 *1799*
by the law in the *s* of God ... Gal 3:11 *3844*
and unreproveable in his *s* ... Col 1:22 *2714*
Jesus Christ, in the *s* of God ... 1Th 1:3 *1715*
acceptable in the *s* of God our ... 1Ti 2:3 *1799*
give thee charge in the *s* of God ... 1Ti 6:13 *1799*
that is not manifest in his *s* ... Heb 4:13 *1799*
And so terrible was the *s*, that ... Heb 12:21 *5324*
which is wellpleasing in his *s* ... Heb 13:21 *1799*
yourselves in the *s* of the Lord ... Jas 4:10 *1799*
which is in the *s* of God of great ... 1Pet 3:4 *1799*
things that are pleasing in his *s* ... 1Jn 3:22 *1799*
in *s* like unto an emerald ... Rev 4:3 *3706*
on the earth in the *s* of men ... Rev 13:13 *1799*
power to do in the *s* of the beast ... Rev 13:14 *1799*

SIGHTS {1}
and fearful *s* and great signs shall ... Lk 21:11 *5400*

SIGN {76}
to the voice of the first *s* ... Ex 4:8 226
believe the voice of the latter *s* ... Ex 4:8 226
to morrow shall this *s* be ... Ex 8:23 226
it shall be for a *s* unto thee ... Ex 13:9 226
for it is a *s* between me and you ... Ex 31:13 226
It is a *s* between me and the ... Ex 31:17 226
they shall be a *s* unto the ... Num 16:38 226
and they became a *s* ... Num 26:10 5251
bind them for a *s* upon thine hand ... Deut 6:8 226
bind them for a *s* upon your hand ... Deut 11:18 226
and giveth thee a *s* or a wonder ... Deut 13:1 226
the *s* or the wonder come to pass, ... Deut 13:2 226
they shall be upon thee for a *s* ... Deut 28:46 226
That this may be a *s* among you ... Josh 4:6 226
then shew me a *s* that thou ... Judg 6:17 226
s between the men of Israel ... Judg 20:38
And this shall be a *s* unto thee ... 1Sa 2:34 226
and this shall be a *s* unto us ... 1Sa 14:10 226
he gave a *s* the same day, saying, ... 1Kin 13:3 4159
This is the *s* which the LORD hath ... 1Kin 13:3 4159
according to the *s* which the man ... 1Kin 13:5 4159
And this shall be a *s* unto thee ... 2Kin 19:29 226
What shall be the *s* that the LORD ... 2Kin 20:8 226
This *s* shalt thou have of the ... 2Kin 20:9 226
unto him, and he gave him a *s* ... 2Chr 32:24 4159
Ask thee a *s* of the LORD thy God ... Is 7:11 226
Lord himself shall give you a *s* ... Is 7:14 226
And it shall be for a *s* and for a ... Is 19:20 226
and barefoot three years for a *s* ... Is 20:3 226
And this shall be a *s* unto thee ... Is 37:30 226
this shall be a *s* unto thee from ... Is 38:7 226
What is the *s* that I shall go up ... Is 38:22 226
for an everlasting *s* that shall ... Is 55:13 226
And I will set a *s* among them ... Is 66:19 226
Tekoa, and set up a *s* of fire in ... Jer 6:1 4864
And this shall be a *s* unto you ... Jer 44:29 226
This shall be a *s* to the house of ... Eze 4:3 226
for a *s* unto the house of Israel ... Eze 12:6 4159
Say, I am your *s* ... Eze 12:11 4159
that man, and will make him a *s* ... Eze 14:8 226
to be a *s* between me and them, ... Eze 20:12 226
and they shall be a *s* between me ... Eze 20:20 226
Thus Ezekiel is unto you a *s* ... Eze 24:24 4159
and thou shalt be a *s* unto them ... Eze 24:27 4159
then shall he set up a *s* by it ... Eze 39:15 6725
s the writing, that it be not ... Dan 6:8 7560
we would see a *s* from thee ... Mt 12:38 *4592*
generation seeketh after a *s* ... Mt 12:39 *4592*
there shall no *s* be given to it ... Mt 12:39 *4592*
but the *s* of the prophet Jonas ... Mt 12:39 *4592*
would shew them a *s* from heaven ... Mt 16:1 *4592*
generation seeketh after a *s* ... Mt 16:4 *4592*
there shall no *s* be given unto it ... Mt 16:4 *4592*
but the *s* of the prophet Jonas ... Mt 16:4 *4592*
what shall be the *s* of thy coming ... Mt 24:3 *4592*
then shall appear the *s* of the ... Mt 24:30 *4592*
that betrayed him gave them a *s* ... Mt 26:48 *4592*
seeking of him a *s* from heaven ... Mk 8:11 *4592*
this generation seek after a *s* ... Mk 8:12 *4592*
There shall no *s* be given unto ... Mk 8:12 *4592*
what shall be the *s* when all ... Mk 13:4 *4592*
And this shall be a *s* unto you ... Lk 2:12 *4592*
for a *s* which shall be spoken ... Lk 2:34 *4592*
sought of him a *s* from heaven ... Lk 11:16 *4592*
they seek a *s* ... Lk 11:29 *4592*
and there shall no *s* be given it ... Lk 11:29 *4592*
but the *s* of Jonas the prophet ... Lk 11:29 *4592*
Jonas was a *s* unto the Ninevites ... Lk 11:30 *4592*
what *s* will there be when these ... Lk 21:7 *4592*
What *s* shewest thou unto us, ... Jn 2:18 *4592*
What *s* shewest thou then, that we ... Jn 6:30 *4592*
whose *s* was Castor and Pollux ... Acts 28:11 *3902*
he received the *s* of circumcision ... Rom 4:11 *4592*
For the Jews require a *s*, and the ... 1Cor 1:22 *4592*
Wherefore tongues are for a *s* ... 1Cor 14:22 *4592*
And I saw another *s* in heaven ... Rev 15:1 *4592*

SIGNED {4}
king Darius *s* the writing ... Dan 6:9 7560
knew that the writing was *s* ... Dan 6:10 7560
Hast thou not *s* a decree, that ... Dan 6:12 7560
nor the decree that thou hast *s* ... Dan 6:13 7560

SIGNET {11}
And she said, Thy *s*, and thy ... Gen 38:18 2368
pray thee, whose are these, the *s* ... Gen 38:25 2858
stone, like the engravings of a *s* ... Ex 28:11 2368
names, like the engravings of a *s* ... Ex 28:21 2368
it, like the engravings of a *s* ... Ex 28:36 2368
names, like the engravings of a *s* ... Ex 39:14 2368
like to the engravings of a *s* ... Ex 39:30 2368
were the *s* upon my right hand ... Jer 22:24 2368
the king sealed it with his own *s* ... Dan 6:17 5824
and with the *s* of his lords ... Dan 6:17 5824
LORD, and will make thee as a *s* ... Hag 2:23 2368

SIGNETS {1}
as *s* are graven, with the names ... Ex 39:6 2368

SIGNIFICATION {1}
and none of them is without *s* ... 1Cor 14:10 *880*

SIGNIFIED {2}
s by the Spirit that there should ... Acts 11:28 *4591*
s it by his angel unto his ... Rev 1:1 *4591*

SIGNIFIETH {1}
s the removing of those things ... Heb 12:27 *1213*

SIGNIFY {4}
to *s* the accomplishment of the ... Acts 21:26 *1229*
s to the chief captain that he ... Acts 23:15 *1718*
not withal to *s* the crimes laid ... Acts 25:27 *4591*
of Christ which was in them did *s* ... 1Pet 1:11 *1213*

SIGNIFYING {4}
s what death he should die ... Jn 12:33 *4591*
s what death he should die ... Jn 18:32 *4591*
s by what death he should glorify ... Jn 21:19 *4591*
The Holy Ghost this *s*, that the ... Heb 9:8 *1213*

SIGNS {53}
and let them be for *s*, and for ... Gen 1:14 226
will not believe also these two *s* ... Ex 4:9 226
hand, wherewith thou shalt do *s* ... Ex 4:17 226
all the *s* which he had commanded ... Ex 4:28 226
did the *s* in the sight of the ... Ex 4:30 226
Pharaoh's heart, and multiply my *s* ... Ex 7:3 226
might shew these my *s* before him ... Ex 10:1 226
my *s* which I have done among them ... Ex 10:2 226
for all the *s* which I have shewed ... Num 14:11 226
nation, by temptations, by *s* ... Deut 4:34 226
And the LORD shewed *s* and wonders, ... Deut 6:22 226
which thine eyes saw, and the *s* ... Deut 7:19 226
great terribleness, and with *s* ... Deut 26:8 226
which thine eyes have seen, the *s* ... Deut 29:3 226
In all the *s* and the wonders, ... Deut 34:11 226
did those great *s* in our sight ... Josh 24:17 226
when these *s* are come unto thee, ... 1Sa 10:7 226
all those *s* came to pass that day ... 1Sa 10:9 226
And shewedst *s* and wonders upon ... Neh 9:10 226
they set up their ensigns for *s* ... Ps 74:4 226
We see not our *s* ... Ps 74:9 226
How he had wrought his *s* in Egypt ... Ps 78:43 226
They shewed his *s* among them ... Ps 105:27 226
the LORD hath given me are for *s* ... Is 8:18 226
not dismayed at the *s* of heaven ... Jer 10:2 226
Which hast set *s* and wonders in ... Jer 32:20 226
out of the land of Egypt with *s* ... Jer 32:21 226
I thought it good to shew the *s* ... Dan 4:2 852
How great are his *s* ... Dan 4:3 852
and rescueth, and he worketh *s* ... Dan 6:27 852
ye not discern the *s* of the times ... Mt 16:3 *4592*
prophets, and shall shew great *s* ... Mt 24:24 *4592*
shall rise, and shall shew *s* ... Mk 13:22 *4592*
these *s* shall follow them that ... Mk 16:17 *4592*
the word with *s* following ... Mk 16:20 *4592*
they made *s* to his father, how he ... Lk 1:62 *1770*
great *s* shall there be from ... Lk 21:11 *4591*
And there shall be *s* in the sun ... Lk 21:25 *4591*
Jesus unto him, Except ye see *s* ... Jn 4:48 *4591*
many other *s* truly did Jesus in ... Jn 20:30 *4591*
above, and *s* in the earth beneath ... Acts 2:19 *4591*
you by miracles and wonders and *s* ... Acts 2:22 *4591*
s were done by the apostles ... Acts 2:43 *4591*
and that *s* and wonders may be done ... Acts 4:30 *4591*
hands of the apostles were many *s* ... Acts 5:12 *4591*
s in the land of Egypt, and in the ... Acts 7:36 *4591*
the miracles and *s* which were done ... Acts 8:13 *4591*
word of his grace, and granted *s* ... Acts 14:3 *4591*
Through mighty *s* and wonders, by ... Rom 15:19 *4591*
Truly the *s* of an apostle were ... 2Cor 12:12 *4591*
among you in all patience, in *s* ... 2Cor 12:12 *4591*
of Satan with all power and *s* ... 2Th 2:9 *4591*
bearing them witness, both with *s* ... Heb 2:4 *4591*

SIHON *(si'-hon)* {37} *An Amorite king.*
unto *S* king of the Amorites ... Num 21:21 5511
S would not suffer Israel to pass ... Num 21:23 5511
but *S* gathered all his people ... Num 21:23 5511
of *S* the king of the Amorites ... Num 21:26 5511
let the city of *S* be built ... Num 21:27 5511
a flame from the city of *S* ... Num 21:28 5511
into captivity unto *S* king of the ... Num 21:29 5511
didst unto *S* king of the Amorites ... Num 21:34 5511
the kingdom of *S* king of the ... Num 32:33 5511
After he had slain *S* the king of ... Deut 1:4 5511
into thine hand *S* the Amorite ... Deut 2:24 5511
S king of Heshbon with words of ... Deut 2:26 5511
But *S* king of Heshbon would not ... Deut 2:30 5511
Behold, I have begun to give *S* ... Deut 2:31 5511
Then *S* came out against us, he and ... Deut 2:32 5511
didst unto *S* king of the Amorites ... Deut 3:2 5511
as we did unto *S* king of Heshbon, ... Deut 3:6 5511
in the land of *S* king of the ... Deut 4:46 5511
S the king of Heshbon, and Og the ... Deut 29:7 5511
shall do unto them as he did to *S* ... Deut 31:4 5511
were on the other side Jordan, *S* ... Josh 2:10 5511
to *S* king of Heshbon, and to Og ... Josh 9:10 5511
S king of the Amorites, who dwelt ... Josh 12:2 5511
the border of *S* king of Heshbon ... Josh 12:5 5511
all the cities of *S* king of the ... Josh 13:10 5511
all the kingdom of *S* king of the ... Josh 13:21 5511
and Reba, which were dukes of *S* ... Josh 13:21 5511
the kingdom of *S* king of Heshbon ... Josh 13:27 5511
unto *S* king of the Amorites ... Judg 11:19 5511
But *S* trusted not Israel to pass ... Judg 11:20 5511
but *S* gathered all his people ... Judg 11:20 5511
LORD God of Israel delivered *S* ... Judg 11:21 5511
in the country of *S* king of the ... 1Kin 4:19 5511
so they possessed the land of *S* ... Neh 9:22 5511
S king of the Amorites, and Og ... Ps 135:11 5511
S king of the Amorites ... Ps 136:19 5511
and a flame from the midst of *S* ... Jer 48:45 5511

SIHOR *(si'-hor)* {3} See SHIHOR. *A river in southern Canaan.*
From *S*, which is before Egypt, ... Josh 13:3 7883
And by great waters the seed of *S* ... Is 23:3 7883
Egypt, to drink the waters of *S* ... Jer 2:18 7883

SIKKUTH See MOLOCH.

SILAS *(si'-las)* {13} See SILVANUS. *A co-worker with Paul.*
Judas surnamed Barsabas, and *S* ... Acts 15:22 *4609*
We have sent therefore Judas and *S* ... Acts 15:27 *4609*
And Judas and *S*, being prophets ... Acts 15:32 *4609*
it pleased *S* to abide there still ... Acts 15:34 *4609*
And Paul chose *S*, and departed, ... Acts 15:40 *4609*
was gone, they caught Paul and *S* ... Acts 16:19 *4609*
S prayed, and sang praises unto ... Acts 16:25 *4609*
and fell down before Paul and *S* ... Acts 16:29 *4609*
and consorted with Paul and *S* ... Acts 17:4 *4609*
Paul and *S* by night unto Berea ... Acts 17:10 *4609*
but *S* and Timotheus abode there ... Acts 17:14 *4609*
and receiving a commandment unto *S* ... Acts 17:15 *4609*
And when *S* and Timotheus were come ... Acts 18:5 *4609*

SILENCE {35}
who said, Keep *s* ... Judg 3:19 2013
was before mine eyes, there was *s* ... Job 4:16 1827
waited, and kept *s* at my counsel ... Job 29:21 1826
terrify me, that I kept *s* ... Job 31:34 1826
Let the lying lips be put to *s* ... Ps 31:18 481
When I kept *s*, my bones waxed old ... Ps 32:3 2790
keep not *s* ... Ps 35:22 2790
I was dumb with *s*, I held my ... Ps 39:2 1747
shall come, and shall not keep *s* ... Ps 50:3 2790
hast thou done, and I kept *s* ... Ps 50:21 2790
Keep not thou *s*, O God ... Ps 83:1 1824
my soul had almost dwelt in *s* ... Ps 94:17 1745
neither any that go down into *s* ... Ps 115:17 1745
a time to keep *s*, and a time to ... Eccl 3:7 2814
is laid waste, and brought to *s* ... Is 15:1 1820
is laid waste, and brought to *s* ... Is 15:1
Keep *s* before me, O islands ... Is 41:1 2790
mention of the LORD, keep not *s* ... Is 62:6 1824
I will not keep *s*, but will ... Is 65:6 2814
the LORD our God hath put us to *s* ... Jer 8:14 1826
sit upon the ground, and keep *s* ... Lam 2:10 1826
He sitteth alone and keepeth *s* ... Lam 3:28 1826
prudent shall keep *s* in that time ... Amos 5:13 1826
they shall cast them forth with *s* ... Amos 8:3 2013
all the earth keep *s* before him ... Hab 2:20 2013
he had put the Sadducees to *s* ... Mt 22:34 *5392*
Then all the multitude kept *s* ... Acts 15:12 *4601*
And when there was made a great *s* ... Acts 21:40 *4602*
to them, they kept the more *s* ... Acts 22:2 *2271*
let him keep *s* in the church ... 1Cor 14:28 *4601*
your women keep *s* in the churches ... 1Cor 14:34 *4601*
learn in *s* with all subjection ... 1Ti 2:11 *2271*
over the man, but to be in *s* ... 1Ti 2:12 *2271*
to *s* the ignorance of foolish men ... 1Pet 2:15 *5392*
there was *s* in heaven about the ... Rev 8:1 *4602*

SILENT {9}
the wicked shall be *s* in darkness ... 1Sa 2:9 1826
in the night season, and am not *s* ... Ps 22:2 1947
be not *s* to me ... Ps 28:1 2790
lest, if thou be *s* to me, I ... Ps 28:1 2790
sing praise to thee, and not be *s* ... Ps 30:12 1826
let them be *s* in the grave ... Ps 31:17 1826
Sit thou *s*, and get thee into ... Is 47:5 1748
cities, and let us be *s* there ... Jer 8:14 1826
Be *s*, O all flesh, before the ... Zec 2:13 2013

SILK {4}
her clothing is *s* and purple ... Prov 31:22 8336
linen, and I covered thee with *s* ... Eze 16:10 4897
raiment was of fine linen, and *s* ... Eze 16:13 4897
and fine linen, and purple, and *s* ... Rev 18:12 *2596*

SILLA *(sil'-lah)* {1} *A place near Jerusalem.*
of Millo, which goeth down to *S* ... 2Kin 12:20 5538

SILLY {3}
man, and envy slayeth the *s* one ... Job 5:2 6601
is like a *s* dove without heart ... Hos 7:11 6601
lead captive *s* women laden with ... 2Ti 3:6 *1133*

SILOAH *(si-lo'-ah)* {1} See SHILOAH, SILOAM. *Same as Siloam.*
pool of *S* by the king's garden ... Neh 3:15 7975

SILOAM *(si'-lo-am)* {3} See SILOAH. *A pool south of Jerusalem.*
upon whom the tower in *S* fell ... Lk 13:4 *4611*
him, Go, wash in the pool of *S* ... Jn 9:7 *4611*
said unto me, Go to the pool of *S* ... Jn 9:11 *4611*

SILVANUS *(sil-va'-nus)* {4} See SILAS.
1. A co-worker with Paul.
among you by us, even by me and *S* 2Cor 1:19 *4610*
Paul, and *S*, and Timotheus, unto 1Th 1:1 *4610*
Paul, and *S*, and Timotheus, unto 2Th 1:1 *4610*
2. A messenger for Peter.
By *S*, a faithful brother unto you............ 1Pet 5:12 *4610*

SILVER {319}
was very rich in cattle, in *s* .... Gen 13:2 3701
brother a thousand pieces of *s* .... Gen 20:16 3701
worth four hundred shekels of *s*............. Gen 23:15 3701
Abraham weighed to Ephron the *s* .... Gen 23:16 3701
Heth, four hundred shekels of *s* .... Gen 23:16 3701
given him flocks, and herds, and *s* .... Gen 24:35 3701
servant brought forth jewels of *s*............ Gen 24:53 3701
for twenty pieces of *s* .... Gen 37:28 3701
And put my cup, the *s* cup, in the .... Gen 44:2 3701
out of thy lord's house *s* or gold .... Gen 44:8 3701
he gave three hundred pieces of *s* .... Gen 45:22 3701
in her house, jewels of *s* .... Ex 3:22 3701
of her neighbour, jewels of *s*.................... Ex 11:2 3701
of the Egyptians jewels of *s* .... Ex 12:35 3701
shall not make with me gods of *s*............. Ex 20:23 3701
their master thirty shekels of *s* .... Ex 21:32 3701
gold, and *s*, and brass,............................. Ex 25:3 3701
of *s* under the twenty boards .... Ex 26:19 3701
And their forty sockets of *s*..................... Ex 26:21 3701
boards, and their sockets of *s*.................. Ex 26:25 3701
gold, upon the four sockets of *s* .... Ex 26:32 3701
and their fillets shall be of *s* .... Ex 27:10 3701
the pillars and their fillets of *s* .... Ex 27:11 3701
court shall be filleted with *s* .... Ex 27:17 3701
their hooks shall be of *s* .... Ex 27:17 3701
works, to work in gold, and in *s*............... Ex 31:4 3701
gold, and *s*, and brass,............................. Ex 35:5 3701
that did offer an offering of *s* .... Ex 35:24 3701
works, to work in gold, and in *s*............... Ex 35:32 3701
forty sockets of *s* he made under............. Ex 36:24 3701
And their forty sockets of *s* .... Ex 36:26 3701
sockets were sixteen sockets of *s*............. Ex 36:30 3701
cast for them four sockets of *s* .... Ex 36:36 3701
and their fillets were of *s* .... Ex 38:10 3701
the pillars and their fillets of *s* .... Ex 38:11 3701
the pillars and their fillets of *s* .... Ex 38:12 3701
the pillars and their fillets of *s* .... Ex 38:17 3701
of their chapiters of *s* .... Ex 38:17 3701
of the court were filleted with *s*.............. Ex 38:17 3701
their hooks of *s*, and the.......................... Ex 38:19 3701
chapiters and their fillets of *s* .... Ex 38:19 3701
the *s* of them that were numbered .... Ex 38:25 3701
of the hundred talents of *s* were.............. Ex 38:27 3701
thy estimation by shekels of *s* .... Lev 5:15 3701
shall be fifty shekels of *s*........................ Lev 27:3 3701
be of the male five shekels of *s*............... Lev 27:6 3701
shall be three shekels of *s*....................... Lev 27:6 3701
be valued at fifty shekels of *s* .... Lev 27:16 3701
And his offering was one *s* charger......... Num 7:13 3701
one *s* bowl of seventy shekels,................. Num 7:13 3701
for his offering one *s* charger .... Num 7:19 3701
one *s* bowl of seventy shekels,................. Num 7:19 3701
His offering was one *s* charger .... Num 7:25 3701
one *s* bowl of seventy shekels,................. Num 7:25 3701
His offering was one *s* charger of........... Num 7:31 3701
one *s* bowl of seventy shekels,................. Num 7:31 3701
His offering was one *s* charger .... Num 7:37 3701
one *s* bowl of seventy shekels,................. Num 7:37 3701
His offering was one *s* charger of........... Num 7:43 3701
a *s* bowl of seventy shekels,..................... Num 7:43 3701
His offering was one *s* charger .... Num 7:49 3701
one *s* bowl of seventy shekels,................. Num 7:49 3701
His offering was one *s* charger of........... Num 7:55 3701
one *s* bowl of seventy shekels,................. Num 7:55 3701
His offering was one *s* charger .... Num 7:61 3701
one *s* bowl of seventy shekels,................. Num 7:61 3701
His offering was one *s* charger .... Num 7:67 3701
one *s* bowl of seventy shekels,................. Num 7:67 3701
His offering was one *s* charger .... Num 7:73 3701
one *s* bowl of seventy shekels,................. Num 7:73 3701
His offering was one *s* charger .... Num 7:79 3701
one *s* bowl of seventy shekels,................. Num 7:79 3701
of *s*, twelve *s* bowls................................. Num 7:84 3701
Each charger of *s* weighing an .... Num 7:85 3701
all the *s* vessels weighed two................... Num 7:85 3701
Make thee two trumpets of *s*.................... Num 10:2 3701
would give me his house full of *s* .... Num 22:18 3701
would give me his house full of *s* .... Num 24:13 3701
Only the gold, and the *s*, the .... Num 31:22 3701
the *s* or gold that is on them .... Deut 7:25 3701
and thy flocks multiply, and thy *s*........... Deut 8:13 3701
he greatly multiply to himself *s* .... Deut 17:17 3701
him in an hundred shekels of *s* .... Deut 22:19 3701
father fifty shekels of *s*.......................... Deut 22:29 3701
and their idols, wood and stone, *s*........... Deut 29:17 3701
But all the *s*, and gold, and...................... Josh 6:19 3701
only the *s*, and the gold, and the............. Josh 6:24 3701
and two hundred shekels of *s*.................. Josh 7:21 3701
of my tent, and the *s* under it.................. Josh 7:21 3701
in his tent, and the *s* under it.................. Josh 7:22 3701
Achan the son of Zerah, and the *s* .... Josh 7:24 3701
and with very much cattle, with *s*............ Josh 22:8 3701
for an hundred pieces of *s*...................... Josh 24:32 7192
ten pieces of *s* out of the house .... Judg 9:4 3701
of us eleven hundred pieces of *s*............. Judg 16:5 3701
of *s* that were taken from thee .... Judg 17:2 3701
ears, behold, the *s* is with me.................. Judg 17:2 3701
shekels of *s* to his mother........................ Judg 17:3 3701
I had wholly dedicated the *s* unto............ Judg 17:3 3701
took two hundred shekels of *s*................. Judg 17:4 3701
thee ten shekels of *s* by the year .... Judg 17:10 3701
and crouch to him for a piece of *s*........... 1Sa 2:36 3701
the fourth part of a shekel of *s*............... 1Sa 9:8 3701
brought with him vessels of *s*.................. 2Sa 8:10 3701
unto the LORD, with the *s*........................ 2Sa 8:11 3701
have given thee ten shekels of *s* 2Sa 18:11 3701
shekels of *s* in mine hand 2Sa 18:12 3701
We will have no *s* nor gold of.................... 2Sa 21:4 3701
the oxen for fifty shekels of *s*.................. 2Sa 24:24 3701
even the *s*, and the gold, and the............. 1Kin 7:51 3701
none were of *s*... 1Kin 10:21 3701
of Tharshish, bringing gold, and *s* 1Kin 10:22 3701
man his present, vessels of *s*.................. 1Kin 10:25 3701
And the king made *s* to be in 1Kin 10:27 3701
for six hundred shekels of *s* 1Kin 10:29 3701
into the house of the LORD, *s*.................. 1Kin 15:15 3701
Then Asa took all the *s* and the 1Kin 15:18 3701
sent unto thee a present of *s* 1Kin 15:19 3701
of Shemer for two talents of *s*................. 1Kin 16:24 3701
Thy *s* and thy gold is mine 1Kin 20:3 3701
Thou shalt deliver me thy *s* 1Kin 20:5 3701
and for my children, and for my *s*........... 1Kin 20:7 3701
else thou shalt pay a talent of *s* 1Kin 20:39 3701
and took with him ten talents of *s*........... 2Kin 5:5 3701
them, I pray thee, a talent of *s* 2Kin 5:22 3701
two talents of *s* in two bags 2Kin 5:23 3701
sold for fourscore pieces of *s*.................. 2Kin 6:25 3701
dove's dung for five pieces of *s* 2Kin 6:25 3701
eat and drink, and carried thence *s* 2Kin 7:8 3701
the house of the LORD bowls of *s*............ 2Kin 12:13 3701
vessels of gold, or vessels of *s*................ 2Kin 12:13 3701
And he took all the gold and *s*................. 2Kin 14:14 3701
gave Pul a thousand talents of *s*............. 2Kin 15:19 3701
of each man fifty shekels of *s*.................. 2Kin 15:20 3701
And Ahaz took the *s* and gold that......... 2Kin 16:8 3701
Judah three hundred talents of *s*............ 2Kin 18:14 3701
Hezekiah gave him all the *s* that............ 2Kin 18:15 3701
of his precious things, the *s* 2Kin 20:13 3701
that he may sum the *s* which is 2Kin 22:4 3701
of an hundred talents of *s* 2Kin 23:33 3701
And Jehoiakim gave the *s* and the 2Kin 23:35 3701
he exacted the *s* and the gold of 2Kin 23:35 3701
gold, in gold, and of *s*, in *s* 2Kin 25:15 3701
manner of vessels of gold and *s*............... 1Chr 18:10 3701
unto the LORD, with the *s*....................... 1Chr 18:11 3701
of *s* to hire them chariots 1Chr 19:6 3701
a thousand thousand talents of *s* 1Chr 22:14 3701
Of the gold, the *s*, and the brass, ... 1Chr 22:16 3701
s also for all instruments of..................... 1Chr 28:14
all instruments of *s* by weight.................. 1Chr 28:14 3701
the candlesticks of *s* by weight 1Chr 28:15 3701
s for the tables of *s*.................................. 1Chr 28:16 3701
likewise *s* by weight for every.................. 1Chr 28:17
by weight for every bason of *s*................. 1Chr 28:17 3701
the *s* for things of *s*, and........................ 1Chr 29:2 3701
own proper good, of gold and *s*............... 1Chr 29:3 3701
thousand talents of refined *s*................... 1Chr 29:4 3701
and the *s* for things of *s*.......................... 1Chr 29:5 3701
of *s* ten thousand talents, and of............. 1Chr 29:7 3701
And the king made *s* and gold at 2Chr 1:15 3701
for six hundred shekels of *s* 2Chr 1:17 3701
cunning to work in gold, and in *s* 2Chr 2:7 3701
skilful to work in gold, and in *s* 2Chr 2:14 3701
and the *s*, and the gold, and all the......... 2Chr 5:1 3701
brought gold and *s* to Solomon................ 2Chr 9:14 3701
none were of *s*... 2Chr 9:20 3701
of Tarshish bringing gold, and *s*.............. 2Chr 9:21 3701
man his present, vessels of *s*.................. 2Chr 9:24 3701
the king made *s* in Jerusalem as.............. 2Chr 9:27 3701
that he himself had dedicated, *s* 2Chr 15:18 3701
Then Asa brought out *s* and gold 2Chr 16:2 3701
behold, I have sent thee *s* 2Chr 16:3 3701
presents, and tribute *s*............................ 2Chr 17:11 3701
father gave them great gifts of *s* 2Chr 21:3 3701
spoons, and vessels of gold and *s* 2Chr 24:14 3701
for an hundred talents of *s* 2Chr 25:6 3701
same year an hundred talents of *s* 2Chr 27:5 3701
he made himself treasuries for *s* 2Chr 32:27 3701
land in an hundred talents of *s* 2Chr 36:3 3701
men of his place help him with *s* .... Ezr 1:4 3701
their hands with vessels of *s* .... Ezr 1:6 3701
of gold, a thousand chargers of *s* .... Ezr 1:9 3701
s basons of a second sort four .... Ezr 1:10 3701
of *s* were five thousand and four............. Ezr 1:11 3701
gold, and five thousand pound of *s*.......... Ezr 2:69 3701
s of the house of God, which.................... Ezr 5:14 3702
s vessels of the house of God,.................. Ezr 6:5 3702
And to carry the *s* and gold, which......... Ezr 7:15 3702
And all the *s* and gold that thou............. Ezr 7:16 3702
to do with the rest of the *s* .... Ezr 7:18 3702
Unto an hundred talents of *s* .... Ezr 7:22 3702
And weighed unto them the *s* .... Ezr 8:25 3701
six hundred and fifty talents of *s*............ Ezr 8:26 3701
s vessels an hundred talents, and............ Ezr 8:26 3701
and the *s* and the gold are a..................... Ezr 8:28 3701
the Levites the weight of the *s* .... Ezr 8:30 3701
Now on the fourth day was the *s* .... Ezr 8:33 3701
wine, beside forty shekels of *s*................ Neh 5:15 3701
and two hundred pounds of *s*................... Neh 7:71 3701
gold, and two thousand pounds of *s* .... Neh 7:72 3701
fine linen and purple to *s* rings................ Est 1:6 3701
the beds were of gold and *s*..................... Est 1:6 3701
pay ten thousand talents of *s* to.............. Est 3:9 3701
The *s* is given to thee, the........................ Est 3:11 3701
who filled their houses with *s*.................. Job 3:15 3701
and thou shalt have plenty of *s* .... Job 22:25 3701
Though he heap up *s* as the dust............. Job 27:16 3701
the innocent shall divide the *s* .... Job 27:17 3701
Surely there is a vein for the *s* .... Job 28:1 3701
neither shall *s* be weighed for.................. Job 28:15 3701
as *s* tried in a furnace of earth,................ Ps 12:6 3701
thou hast tried us, as *s* is tried................ Ps 66:10 3701
wings of a dove covered with *s*................. Ps 68:13 3701
submit himself with pieces of *s* .... Ps 68:30 3701
He brought them forth also with *s* .... Ps 105:37 3701
Their idols are *s* and gold, the................. Ps 115:4 3701
me than thousands of gold and *s* .... Ps 119:72 3701
The idols of the heathen are *s* .... Ps 135:15 3701
If thou seekest her as *s*, and .... Prov 2:4 3701
better than the merchandise of *s*............. Prov 3:14 3701
Receive my instruction, and not *s* .... Prov 8:10 3701
and my revenue than choice *s* .... Prov 8:19 3701
tongue of the just is as choice *s*.............. Prov 10:20 3701
rather to be chosen than *s*!..................... Prov 16:16 3701
The fining pot is for *s*, and the................. Prov 17:3 3701
and loving favour rather than *s* .... Prov 22:1 3701
Take away the dross from the *s*................ Prov 25:4 3701
apples of gold in pictures of *s* .... Prov 25:11 3701
a potsherd covered with *s* dross .... Prov 26:23 3701
As the fining pot for *s*, and the................ Prov 27:21 3701
I gathered me also *s* and gold, and.......... Eccl 2:8 3701
He that loveth *s* shall not be .... Eccl 5:10 3701
shall not be satisfied with *s* .... Eccl 5:10 3701
Or ever the *s* cord be loosed, or............... Eccl 12:6 3701
borders of gold with studs of *s*................ Song 1:11 3701
He made the pillars thereof of *s*.............. Song 3:10 3701
will build upon her a palace of *s* .... Song 8:9 3701
to bring a thousand pieces of *s* .... Song 8:11 3701
Thy *s* is become dross, thy wine.............. Is 1:22 3701
Their land also is full of *s* .... Is 2:7 3701
a man shall cast his idols of *s* .... Is 2:20 3701
them, which shall not regard *s* .... Is 13:17 3701
of thy graven images of *s*........................ Is 30:22 3701
shall cast away his idols of *s*.................... Is 31:7 3701
of his precious things, the *s*.................... Is 39:2 3701
with gold, and casteth *s* chains .... Is 40:19 3701
weigh *s* in the balance, and hire a........... Is 46:6 3701
have refined thee, but not with *s* .... Is 48:10 3701
bring thy sons from far, their *s*............... Is 60:9 3701
gold, and for iron I will bring *s*............... Is 60:17 3701
Reprobate *s* shall men call them, ... Jer 6:30 3701
They deck it with *s* and with gold .... Jer 10:4 3701
S spread into plates is brought .... Jer 10:9 3701
even seventeen shekels of *s* .... Jer 32:9 3701
and that which was of *s* in *s*.................... Jer 52:19 3701
shall cast their *s* in the streets .... Eze 7:19 3701
their *s* and their gold shall not................ Eze 7:19 3701
wast thou decked with gold and *s*............ Eze 16:13 3701
fair jewels of my gold and of my *s* .... Eze 16:17 3701
they are even the dross of *s* .... Eze 22:18 3701
As they gather *s*, and brass, and .... Eze 22:20 3701
As *s* is melted in the midst of.................. Eze 22:22 3701
with *s*, iron, tin, and lead, they .... Eze 27:12 3701
gold and *s* into thy treasures.................. Eze 28:4 3701
to carry away *s* and gold, to take .... Eze 38:13 3701
gold, his breast and his arms of *s*........... Dan 2:32 3702
iron, the clay, the brass, the *s* .... Dan 2:35 3702
iron, the brass, the clay, the *s*................. Dan 2:45 3702
s vessels which his father .... Dan 5:2 3702
praised the gods of gold, and of *s* .... Dan 5:4 3702
thou hast praised the gods of *s* .... Dan 5:23 3702
with their precious vessels of *s* .... Dan 11:8 3701
shall he honour with gold, and *s*............. Dan 11:38 3701
the treasures of gold and of *s* .... Dan 11:43 3701
wine, and oil, and multiplied her *s* .... Hos 2:8 3701
her to me for fifteen pieces of *s*.............. Hos 3:2 3701
of their *s* and their gold have .... Hos 8:4 3701
the pleasant places for their *s* .... Hos 9:6 3701
them molten images of their *s*.................. Hos 13:2 3701
Because ye have taken my *s* .... Joel 3:5 3701
they sold the righteous for *s*.................... Amos 2:6 3701
That we may buy the poor for *s* .... Amos 8:6 3701
Take ye the spoil of *s*, take the................ Nah 2:9 3701
it is laid over with gold and *s* .... Hab 2:19 3701
all they that bear *s* are cut off................ Zeph 1:11 3701
Neither their *s* nor their gold................... Zeph 1:18 3701
The *s* is mine, and the gold is.................. Hag 2:8 3701
Then take *s* and gold, and make .... Zec 6:11 3701
heaped up *s* as the dust, and fine............ Zec 9:3 3701
for my price thirty pieces of *s* .... Zec 11:12 3701
And I took the thirty pieces of *s* .... Zec 11:13 3701
will refine them as *s* is refined................ Zec 13:9 3701
be gathered together, gold, and *s* .... Zec 14:14 3701
sit as a refiner and purifier of *s* .... Mal 3:3 3701
Levi, and purge them as gold and *s* .... Mal 3:3 3701
Provide neither gold, nor *s* .... Mt 10:9 *696*
with him for thirty pieces of *s*................. Mt 26:15 *694*
pieces of *s* to the chief priests .... Mt 27:3 *694*
the pieces of *s* in the temple.................... Mt 27:5 *694*
chief priests took the *s* pieces .... Mt 27:6 *694*
they took the thirty pieces of *s*................ Mt 27:9 *694*
what woman having ten pieces of *s* .... Lk 15:8 *1406*
Then Peter said, *S* and gold have I........... Acts 3:6 *694*
Godhead is like unto gold, or *s* .... Acts 17:29 *696*
it fifty thousand pieces of *s*..................... Acts 19:19 *694*
which made *s* shrines for Diana,.............. Acts 19:24 *693*
I have coveted no man's *s* .... Acts 20:33 *694*
upon this foundation gold, *s* 1Cor 3:12 *696*
not only vessels of gold and of *s*............... 2Ti 2:20 *693*
Your gold and *s* is cankered .... Jas 5:3 *696*
with corruptible things, as *s* 1Pet 1:18 *694*
devils, and idols of gold, and *s*................ Rev 9:20 *693*
The merchandise of gold, and *s*............... Rev 18:12 *696*

SILVERLINGS {1}
a thousand vines at a thousand *s* .... Is 7:23 3701

SILVERSMITH {1}
certain man named Demetrius, a *s* .... Acts 19:24 *695*

SIMEON *(sim'-e-un)* {50} See SHIMEON, SIMEONITES, SIMON.
1. A son of Jacob.
and she called his name *S* .... Gen 29:33 8095
that two of the sons of Jacob, *S* .... Gen 34:25 8095
And Jacob said to *S* and Levi, Ye.......... Gen 34:30 8095
Reuben, Jacob's firstborn, and *S* .... Gen 35:23 8095
with them, and took from them *S* .... Gen 42:24 8095
S is not, and ye will take...................... Gen 42:36 8095
he brought *S* out unto them .... Gen 43:23 8095
And the sons of *S* .... Gen 46:10 8095
as Reuben and *S*, they shall be .... Gen 48:5 8095
S and Levi are brethren .... Gen 49:5 8095
Reuben, *S*, Levi, and Judah,.................... Ex 1:2 8095
And the sons of *S* .... Ex 6:15 8095
these are the families of *S* .... Ex 6:15 8095
2. Descendants of Simeon 1 and their land.
Of *S* .... Num 1:6 8095
Of the children of *S*, by their .... Num 1:22 8095
of them, even of the tribe of *S* .... Num 1:23 8095
by him shall be the tribe of *S* .... Num 2:12 8095
S shall be Shelumiel the son of.............. Num 2:12 8095
prince of the children of *S* .... Num 7:36 8095
of *S* was Shelumiel the son of................ Num 10:19 8095
Of the tribe of *S*, Shaphat the................ Num 13:5 8095
The sons of *S* after their........................ Num 26:12 8095
of the tribe of the children of *S* .... Num 34:20 8095
S, and Levi, and Judah, and Issachar ..... Deut 27:12 8095
And the second lot came forth to *S*......... Josh 19:1 8095
of *S* according to their families.............. Josh 19:1 8095
of *S* according to their families.............. Josh 19:8 8095
inheritance of the children of *S* .... Josh 19:9 8095
therefore the children of *S* had .... Josh 19:9 8095
Judah, and out of the tribe of *S* .... Josh 21:4 8099
of the tribe of the children of *S* .... Josh 21:9 8095
And Judah said unto *S* his brother .... Judg 1:3 8095
So *S* went with him................................ Judg 1:3 8095
And Judah went with *S* his brother .... Judg 1:17 8095
Reuben, *S*, Levi, and Judah,................... 1Chr 2:1 8095
The sons of *S* were, Nemuel, and 1Chr 4:24 8095
of them, even of the sons of *S* 1Chr 4:42 8095
of the tribe of the children of *S* 1Chr 6:65 8095
Of the children of *S*, mighty men........... 1Chr 12:25 8095
Ephraim and Manasseh, and out of *S*...... 2Chr 15:9 8095
of Manasseh, and Ephraim, and *S* 2Chr 34:6 8095
west side, *S* shall have a portion .... Eze 48:24 8095
And by the border of *S*, from the............ Eze 48:25 8095
one gate of *S*, one gate of....................... Eze 48:33 8095
Of the tribe of *S* were sealed.................. Rev 7:7 *4826*
3. A devout man who blessed Jesus.
in Jerusalem, whose name was *S* .... Lk 2:25 *4826*
S blessed them, and said unto Mary .... Lk 2:34 *4826*
4. Father of Levi; an ancestor of Jesus.
Which was the son of *S*, which was .... Lk 3:30 *4826*
5. A prophet of Antioch.
S that was called Niger, and .... Acts 13:1 *4826*
6. Same as Simon Peter.
S hath declared how God at the .... Acts 15:14 *4826*

SIMEONITES *(sim'-e-un-ites)* {3} *Descendants of Simeon 1.*
of a chief house among the *S* .... Num 25:14 8099
These are the families of the *S* .... Num 26:14 8099
of the *S*, Shephatiah the son of.............. 1Chr 27:16 8099

SIMILITUDE {11}
the *s* of the LORD shall he behold........... Num 12:8 8544
voice of the words, but saw no *s* .... Deut 4:12 8544
for ye saw no manner of *s* on the .... Deut 4:15 8544
the *s* of any figure, the likeness.............. Deut 4:16 8544
And under it was the *s* of oxen 2Chr 4:3 1823
the *s* of an ox that eateth grass............... Ps 106:20 8403
polished after the *s* of a palace .... Ps 144:12 8403
one like the *s* of the sons of men............ Dan 10:16 1823
the *s* of Adam's transgression.................. Rom 5:14 *3667*
for that after the *s* of............................. Heb 7:15 *3665*
which are made after the *s* of God.......... Jas 3:9 *3669*

SIMILITUDES {1}
multiplied visions, and used *s* .... Hos 12:10 1819

SIMON *(si'mun)* {69} See BAR JONA, NIGER, PETER, SIMEON, SIMON'S, ZELOTES.
1. Same as Peter.
S called Peter, and Andrew his .... Mt 4:18 *4613*
The first, *S*, who is called Peter .... Mt 10:2 *4613*
S Peter answered and said, Thou .... Mt 16:16 *4613*
him, Blessed art thou, *S* Bar-jona .... Mt 16:17 *4613*
saying, What thinkest thou, *S* .... Mt 17:25 *4613*
by the sea of Galilee, he saw *S*.............. Mk 1:16 *4613*
they entered into the house of *S* .... Mk 1:29 *4613*
And *S* and they that were with him........ Mk 1:36 *4613*
And *S* he surnamed Peter....................... Mk 3:16 *4613*
sleeping, and saith unto Peter, *S*........... Mk 14:37 *4613*
had left speaking, he said unto *S*........... Lk 5:4 *4613*
S answering said unto him, Master......... Lk 5:5 *4613*
When *S* Peter saw it, he fell down .... Lk 5:8 *4613*
which were partners with *S* .... Lk 5:10 *4613*
And Jesus said unto *S*, Fear not .... Lk 5:10 *4613*
S, (whom he also named Peter,) and .... Lk 6:14 *4613*
And the Lord said, *S*, *S*,......................... Lk 22:31 *4613*
indeed, and hath appeared to *S* .... Lk 24:34 *4613*
was Andrew, *S* Peter's brother .... Jn 1:40 *4613*
first findeth his own brother *S* .... Jn 1:41 *4613*
Thou art *S* the son of Jona .... Jn 1:42 *4613*
S Peter's brother, saith unto him............ Jn 6:8 *4613*
Then *S* Peter answered him, Lord,.......... Jn 6:68 *4613*
Then cometh he to *S* Peter .... Jn 13:6 *4613*
S Peter saith unto him, Lord, not .... Jn 13:9 *4613*
S Peter therefore beckoned to him .... Jn 13:24 *4613*
S Peter said unto him, Lord,................... Jn 13:36 *4613*
Then *S* Peter having a sword drew .... Jn 18:10 *4613*
S Peter followed Jesus, and so did .... Jn 18:15 *4613*
S Peter stood and warmed himself........... Jn 18:25 *4613*
she runneth, and cometh to *S* Peter .... Jn 20:2 *4613*
Then cometh *S* Peter following him .... Jn 20:6 *4613*
There were together *S* Peter .... Jn 21:2 *4613*
S Peter saith unto them, I go a............... Jn 21:3 *4613*
Now when *S* Peter heard that it.............. Jn 21:7 *4613*
S Peter went up, and drew the net.......... Jn 21:11 *4613*
Jesus saith to *S* Peter, *S*......................... Jn 21:15 *4613*
to him again the second time, *S* .... Jn 21:16 *4613*
saith unto him the third time, *S*............... Jn 21:17 *4613*
men to Joppa, and call for one *S*............. Acts 10:5 *4613*
And called, and asked whether *S*............ Acts 10:18 *4613*
to Joppa, and call hither *S* .... Acts 10:32 *4613*
Send men to Joppa, and call for *S* .... Acts 11:13 *4613*
S Peter, a servant and an apostle 2Pet 1:1 *4613*
2. A Canaanite disciple of Jesus.
S the Canaanite, and Judas..................... Mt 10:4 *4613*
and Thaddaeus, and *S* the Canaanite, ... Mk 3:18 *4613*
of Alphaeus, and *S* called Zelotes,.......... Lk 6:15 *4613*
S Zelotes, and Judas the brother............. Acts 1:13 *4613*
3. A brother of Jesus.
brethren, James, and Joses, and *S* .... Mt 13:55 *4613*
James, and Joses, and of Juda, and *S*...... Mk 6:3 *4613*
4. A leper in Bethany.
in the house of *S* the leper .... Mt 26:6 *4613*
in the house of *S* the leper .... Mk 14:3 *4613*
5. A Cyrenian who bore Jesus' cross.
found a man of Cyrene, *S* by name.......... Mt 27:32 *4613*
And they compel one *S* a Cyrenian......... Mk 15:21 *4613*
away, they laid hold upon one *S* .... Lk 23:26 *4613*
6. A Pharisee.
Jesus answering said unto him, *S*........... Lk 7:40 *4613*
S answered and said, I suppose.............. Lk 7:43 *4613*
to the woman, and said unto *S* .... Lk 7:44 *4613*
7. Father of Judas Iscariot.
of Judas Iscariot the son of *S*................. Jn 6:71 *4613*
to Judas Iscariot, the son of *S* .... Jn 13:26 *4613*
8. A Samaritan sorcerer.
there was a certain man, called *S* .... Acts 8:9 *4613*
Then *S* himself believed also.................. Acts 8:13 *4613*
when *S* saw that through laying on .... Acts 8:18 *4613*
Then answered *S*, and said, Pray ye........ Acts 8:24 *4613*
9. A tanner at Joppa.
days in Joppa with one *S* a tanner .... Acts 9:43 *4613*
He lodgeth with one *S* a tanner .... Acts 10:6 *4613*
of one *S* a tanner by the sea side .... Acts 10:32 *4613*

SIMON'S *(si'-muns)* {7}
1. Refers to Simon 1.
But *S* wife's mother lay sick of a .... Mk 1:30 *4613*
and entered into *S* house......................... Lk 4:38 *4613*
S wife's mother was taken with a .... Lk 4:38 *4613*
one of the ships, which was *S* .... Lk 5:3 *4613*
2. Refers to Simon 7.
S son, which should betray him,............ Jn 12:4 *4613*
Iscariot, *S* son, to betray him .... Jn 13:2 *4613*
3. Refers to Simon 9.
had made enquiry for *S* house .... Acts 10:17 *4613*

SIMPLE {20}
LORD is sure, making wise the *s*............ Ps 19:7 6612
The LORD preserveth the *s*...................... Ps 116:6 6612
giveth understanding unto the *s*............. Ps 119:130 6612
To give subtilty to the *s* .... Prov 1:4 6612
How long, ye *s* ones, will ye love............. Prov 1:22 6612
away of the *s* shall slay them .... Prov 1:32 6612
And beheld among the *s* ones.................. Prov 7:7 6612
O ye *s*, understand wisdom .... Prov 8:5 6612
Whoso is *s*, let him turn in..................... Prov 9:4 6612
she is *s*, and knoweth nothing................ Prov 9:13 6615
Whoso is *s*, let him turn in..................... Prov 9:16 6612
The *s* believeth every word..................... Prov 14:15 6612
The *s* inherit folly .... Prov 14:18 6612
a scorner, and the *s* will beware.............. Prov 19:25 6612
is punished, the *s* is made wise .... Prov 21:11 6612
but the *s* pass on, and are....................... Prov 22:3 6612
but the *s* pass on, and are....................... Prov 27:12 6612
that erreth, and for him that is *s*............ Eze 45:20 6612
deceive the hearts of the *s* .... Rom 16:18 *172*
is good, and *s* concerning evil .... Rom 16:19 *185*

SIMPLICITY {5}
and they went in their *s*, and they 2Sa 15:11 8537
ye simple ones, will ye love *s*................. Prov 1:22 6612
that giveth, let him do it with *s*.............. Rom 12:8 *572*
of our conscience, that in *s*..................... 2Cor 1:12 *572*
from the *s* that is in Christ..................... 2Cor 11:3 *572*

SIMRI *(sim'-ri)* {1} See SHIMRI. *A sanctuary servant.*
S the chief, (for though he was 1Chr 26:10 8113

SIN *(sin)* {448}
1. A transgression.
not well, *s* lieth at the door .... Gen 4:7 2403
because their *s* is very grievous.............. Gen 18:20 2403
on me and on my kingdom a great *s* .... Gen 20:9 2401
what is my *s*, that thou hast so .... Gen 31:36 2403
wickedness, and *s* against God................ Gen 39:9 2398
Do not *s* against the child .... Gen 42:22 2398
of thy brethren, and their *s* .... Gen 50:17 2403
my *s* only this once, and intreat .... Ex 10:17 2403
before your faces, that ye *s* not .... Ex 20:20 2398
lest they make thee *s* against me............. Ex 23:33 2398
it is a *s* offering.. Ex 29:14 2403
for a *s* offering for atonement .... Ex 29:36 2403
of the *s* offering of atonements................ Ex 30:10 2403
brought so great a *s* upon them............... Ex 32:21 2401
people, Ye have sinned a great *s*............... Ex 32:30 2401
make an atonement for your *s*................. Ex 32:30 2403
this people have sinned a great *s* .... Ex 32:31 2401
now, if thou wilt forgive their *s* .... Ex 32:32 2403
I will visit their *s* upon them.................. Ex 32:34 2403
iniquity and transgression and *s*............. Ex 34:7 2402
and pardon our iniquity and our *s*.......... Ex 34:9 2403
If a soul shall *s* through.......................... Lev 4:2 2398
do *s* according to the .... Lev 4:3 2398
according to the *s* of the people .... Lev 4:3 819
then let him bring for his *s* .... Lev 4:3 2403
unto the LORD for a *s* offering................. Lev 4:3 2403
of the bullock for the *s* offering .... Lev 4:8 2403
of Israel *s* through ignorance .... Lev 4:13 7686
When the *s*, which they have................... Lev 4:14 2403
offer a young bullock for the *s* .... Lev 4:14 2403
with the bullock for a *s* offering .... Lev 4:20 2403
it is a *s* offering for the........................... Lev 4:21 2403
Or if his *s*, wherein he hath.................... Lev 4:23 2403
it is a *s* offering.. Lev 4:24 2403
of the *s* offering with his finger .... Lev 4:25 2403
for him as concerning his *s* .... Lev 4:26 2403
common people *s* through ignorance....... Lev 4:27 2398
Or if his *s*, which he hath sinned .... Lev 4:28 2403
for his *s* which he hath sinned .... Lev 4:28 2403
upon the head of the *s* offering .... Lev 4:29 2403
slay the *s* offering in the place .... Lev 4:29 2403
he bring a lamb for a *s* offering .... Lev 4:32 2403
upon the head of the *s* offering .... Lev 4:33 2403
slay it for a *s* offering in the.................. Lev 4:33 2403
of the *s* offering with his finger .... Lev 4:34 2403
for his *s* that he hath committed .... Lev 4:35 2403
And if a soul *s*, and hear the voice......... Lev 5:1 2398
for his *s* which he hath sinned .... Lev 5:6 2403
of the goats, for a *s* offering .... Lev 5:6 2403
for him concerning his *s*......................... Lev 5:6 2403
one for a *s* offering, and the .... Lev 5:7 2403
which is for the *s* offering first................ Lev 5:8 2403
sprinkle of the blood of the *s* .... Lev 5:9 2403
it is a *s* offering.. Lev 5:9 2403
for his *s* which he hath sinned .... Lev 5:10 2403
of fine flour for a *s* offering.................... Lev 5:11 2403
for it is a *s* offering.................................. Lev 5:11 2403
it is a *s* offering.. Lev 5:12 2403
for him as touching his *s* that he............ Lev 5:13 2403
s through ignorance, in the holy .... Lev 5:15 2398
And if a soul *s*, and commit any of .... Lev 5:17 2398
If a soul *s*, and commit a trespass .... Lev 6:2 2398
most holy, as is the *s* offering .... Lev 6:17 2403
This is the law of the *s* offering.............. Lev 6:25 2403
offering is killed shall the *s*................... Lev 6:25 2403
offereth it for *s* shall eat it .... Lev 6:26 2398
no *s* offering, whereof any of the............ Lev 6:30 2403
As the *s* offering is, so is the .... Lev 7:7 2403
of the *s* offering, and of the.................... Lev 7:37 2403
and a bullock for the *s* offering.............. Lev 8:2 2403
the bullock for the *s* offering.................. Lev 8:14 2403
of the bullock for the *s* offering .... Lev 8:14 2403
a young calf for a *s* offering .... Lev 9:2 2403
kid of the goats for a *s* offering.............. Lev 9:3 2403
altar, and offer thy *s* offering .... Lev 9:7 2403
slew the calf of the *s* offering................. Lev 9:8 2403
above the liver of the *s* offering.............. Lev 9:10 2403
which was the *s* offering for the.............. Lev 9:15 2403
and slew it, and offered it for *s* .... Lev 9:15 2403
from offering of the *s* offering................ Lev 9:22 2403
sought the goat of the *s* offering .... Lev 10:16 2403
the *s* offering in the holy place................ Lev 10:17 2403
they offered their *s* offering................... Lev 10:19 2403
I had eaten the *s* offering to day .... Lev 10:19 2403
for a *s* offering, unto the door .... Lev 12:6 2403
and the other for a *s* offering .... Lev 12:8 2403
he shall kill the *s* offering .... Lev 14:13 2403
for as the *s* offering is the...................... Lev 14:13 2403
priest shall offer the *s* offering............... Lev 14:19 2403
and the one shall be a *s* offering .... Lev 14:22 2403
to get, the one for a *s* offering................ Lev 14:31 2403
them, the one for a *s* offering.................. Lev 15:15 2403
offer the one for a *s* offering................... Lev 15:30 2403
a young bullock for a *s* offering .... Lev 16:3 2403
of the goats for a *s* offering .... Lev 16:5 2403
his bullock of the *s* offering .... Lev 16:6 2403
and offer him for a *s* offering................. Lev 16:9 2403
the bullock of the *s* offering.................... Lev 16:11 2403
s offering which is for himself.................. Lev 16:11 2403
kill the goat of the *s* offering.................. Lev 16:15 2403
the fat of the *s* offering shall.................. Lev 16:25 2403
And the bullock for the *s* offering........... Lev 16:27 2403
and the goat for the *s* offering................ Lev 16:27 2403
and not suffer *s* upon him .... Lev 19:17 2399
LORD for his *s* which he hath done .... Lev 19:22 2403
the *s* which he hath done shall be........... Lev 19:22 2403
they shall bear their *s*............................ Lev 20:20 2399
lest they bear *s* for it, and die .... Lev 22:9 2399
kid of the goats for a *s* offering.............. Lev 23:19 2403
curseth his God shall bear his *s* .... Lev 24:15 2399
commit any *s* that men commit............... Num 5:6 2403
their *s* which they have done................... Num 5:7 2403
offer the one for a *s* offering................... Num 6:11 2403
without blemish for a *s* offering.............. Num 6:14 2403
and shall offer his *s* offering .... Num 6:16 2403
kid of the goats for a *s* offering.............. Num 7:16 2403
kid of the goats for a *s* offering.............. Num 7:22 2403
kid of the goats for a *s* offering.............. Num 7:28 2403
kid of the goats for a *s* offering.............. Num 7:34 2403

S

kid of the goats for a *s* offering Num 7:40 2403
kid of the goats for a *s* offering Num 7:46 2403
kid of the goats for a *s* offering Num 7:52 2403
kid of the goats for a *s* offering Num 7:58 2403
kid of the goats for a *s* offering Num 7:64 2403
kid of the goats for a *s* offering Num 7:70 2403
kid of the goats for a *s* offering Num 7:76 2403
kid of the goats for a *s* offering Num 7:82 2403
the goats for *s* offering twelve Num 7:87 2403
shalt thou take for a *s* offering Num 8:8 2403
offer the one for a *s* offering Num 8:12 2403
season, that man shall bear his *s* Num 9:13 2399
thee, lay not the *s* upon us Num 12:11 2403
kid of the goats for a *s* offering Num 15:24 2403
their *s* offering before the LORD, Num 15:25 2403
if any soul *s* through ignorance, Num 15:27 2398
the first year for a *s* offering Num 15:27 2403
of all flesh, shall one man *s* Num 16:22 2398
every *s* offering of theirs, and Num 18:9 2403
congregation, lest they bear *s* Num 18:22 2399
shall bear no *s* by reason of it Num 18:32 2399
it is a purification for *s* Num 19:9 2403
heifer of purification for *s* Num 19:17 2403
but died in his own *s*, and had no Num 27:3 2399
one kid of the goats for a *s* Num 28:15 2403
And one goat for a *s* offering Num 28:22 2403
kid of the goats for a *s* offering Num 29:5 2403
kid of the goats for a *s* offering Num 29:11 2403
beside the *s* offering of Num 29:11 2403
kid of the goats for a *s* offering Num 29:16 2403
kid of the goats for a *s* offering Num 29:19 2403
And one goat for a *s* offering Num 29:22 2403
kid of the goats for a *s* offering Num 29:25 2403
And one goat for a *s* offering Num 29:28 2403
And one goat for a *s* offering Num 29:31 2403
And one goat for a *s* offering Num 29:34 2403
And one goat for a *s* offering Num 29:38 2403
be sure your *s* will find you out Num 32:23 2403
And I took your *s*, the calf which Deut 9:21 2403
their wickedness, nor to their *s* Deut 9:27 2403
thee, and it be *s* unto thee Deut 15:9 2399
for any iniquity, or for any *s* Deut 19:15 2403
in any *s* that he sinneth Deut 19:15 2399
so should ye *s* against the LORD Deut 20:18 2398
committed a *s* worthy of death Deut 21:22 2399
the damsel no *s* worthy of death Deut 22:26 2399
and it would be *s* in thee Deut 23:21 2399
to vow, it shall be no *s* in thee Deut 23:22 2399
shalt not cause the land to *s* Deut 24:4 2398
the LORD, and it be *s* unto thee Deut 24:15 2399
be put to death for his own *s* Deut 24:16 2399
Wherefore the *s* of the young men 1Sa 2:17 2403
If one man *s* against another, the 1Sa 2:25 2398
but if a man *s* against the LORD, 1Sa 2:25 2398
God forbid that I should *s* 1Sa 12:23 2398
the people *s* against the LORD, in 1Sa 14:33 2398
s not against the LORD in eating 1Sa 14:34 2398
see wherein this *s* hath been this 1Sa 14:38 2403
is as the *s* of witchcraft 1Sa 15:23 2403
I pray thee, pardon my *s* 1Sa 15:25 2403
Let not the king *s* against his 1Sa 19:4 2398
thou *s* against innocent blood 1Sa 19:5 2398
what is my *s* before thy father, 1Sa 20:1 2403
The LORD also hath put away thy *s* 2Sa 12:13 2403
forgive the *s* of thy people 1Kin 8:34 2403
thy name, and turn from their *s* 1Kin 8:35 2403
forgive the *s* of thy servants, and 1Kin 8:36 2403
If they *s* against thee, (for 1Kin 8:46 2398
And this thing became a *s* 1Kin 12:30 2403
this thing became *s* unto the 1Kin 13:34 2403
the sins of Jeroboam, who did *s* 1Kin 14:16 2398
and who made Israel to *s* 1Kin 14:16 2398
in his *s* wherewith he made Israel 1Kin 15:26 2403
wherewith he made Israel to *s* 1Kin 15:26 2398
sinned, and which he made Israel *s* 1Kin 15:30 2398
in his *s* wherewith he made Israel 1Kin 15:34 2403
wherewith he made Israel to *s* 1Kin 15:34 2398
hast made my people Israel to *s* 1Kin 16:2 2398
and by which they made Israel to *s* 1Kin 16:13 2398
in his *s* which he did, to make 1Kin 16:19 2403
which he did, to make Israel to *s* 1Kin 16:19 2398
in his *s* wherewith he made Israel 1Kin 16:26 2403
wherewith he made Israel to *s* 1Kin 16:26 2398
me to call my *s* to remembrance 1Kin 17:18 5771
me to anger, and made Israel to *s* 1Kin 21:22 2398
of Nebat, who made Israel to *s* 1Kin 22:52 2398
of Nebat, which made Israel to *s* 2Kin 3:3 2398
of Nebat, who made Israel to *s* 2Kin 10:29 2398
Jeroboam, which made Israel to *s* 2Kin 10:31 2398
s money was not brought into the 2Kin 12:16 2403
of Nebat, which made Israel to *s* 2Kin 13:2 2398
of Jeroboam, who made Israel *s* 2Kin 13:6 2398
son of Nebat, who made Israel *s* 2Kin 13:11 2398
be put to death for his own *s* 2Kin 14:6 2399
of Nebat, who made Israel to *s* 2Kin 14:24 2398
of Nebat, who made Israel to *s* 2Kin 15:9 2398
of Nebat, who made Israel to *s* 2Kin 15:18 2398
of Nebat, who made Israel to *s* 2Kin 15:24 2398
of Nebat, who made Israel to *s* 2Kin 15:28 2398
LORD, and made them *s* 2Kin 17:21 2398
a great *s* 2Kin 17:21 2401
Judah also to *s* with his idols 2Kin 21:11 2398
beside his *s* wherewith he made 2Kin 21:16 2403
wherewith he made Judah to *s* 2Kin 21:16 2398
his *s* that he sinned, are they 2Kin 21:17 2403
of Nebat, who made Israel to *s* 2Kin 23:15 2398
If a man *s* against his neighbour, 2Chr 6:22 2398
forgive the *s* of thy people 2Chr 6:25 2403
thy name, and turn from their *s* 2Chr 6:26 2403
forgive the *s* of thy servants, and 2Chr 6:27 2403
If they *s* against thee, (for 2Chr 6:36 2398
heaven, and will forgive their *s* 2Chr 7:14 2403
every man shall die for his own *s* 2Chr 25:4 2399
for a *s* offering for the kingdom, 2Chr 29:21 2403
the *s* offering before the king 2Chr 29:23 2403
the *s* offering should be made for 2Chr 29:24 2403
intreated of him, and all his *s* 2Chr 33:19
for a *s* offering for all Israel, Ezr 6:17 2409
twelve he goats for a *s* offering Ezr 8:35 2403
let not their *s* be blotted out Neh 4:5 2403
should be afraid, and do so, and *s* Neh 6:13 2398
for the *s* offerings to make an Neh 10:33 2403
king of Israel *s* by these things Neh 13:26 2398
did outlandish women cause to *s* Neh 13:26 2398
this did not Job *s* with his lips Job 2:10 2398
thy habitation, and shalt not *s* Job 5:24 2398
iniquity, and searchest after my *s* Job 10:6 2403
If I *s*, then thou markest me, and Job 10:14 2398
to know my transgression and my *s* Job 13:23 2403
dost thou not watch over my *s* Job 14:16 2403
are full of the *s* of his youth Job 20:11
have I suffered my mouth to *s* by Job 31:30 2398
he addeth rebellion unto his *s* Job 34:37 2403
have, if I be cleansed from my *s* Job 35:3 2403
Stand in awe, and *s* not Ps 4:4 2398
is forgiven, whose *s* is covered Ps 32:1 2401
I acknowledged my *s* unto thee Ps 32:5 2403
forgavest the iniquity of my *s* Ps 32:5 2403
rest in my bones because of my *s* Ps 38:3 2403
I will be sorry for my *s* Ps 38:18 2403
that I *s* not with my tongue Ps 39:1 2398
s offering hast thou not required Ps 40:6 2401
iniquity, and cleanse me from my *s* Ps 51:2 2403
and my *s* is ever before me Ps 51:3 2403
in *s* did my mother conceive me Ps 51:5 2399
my transgression, nor for my *s* Ps 59:3 2403
For the *s* of their mouth and the Ps 59:12 2403
thou hast covered all their *s* Ps 85:2 2403
and let his prayer become *s* Ps 109:7 2401
let not the *s* of his mother be Ps 109:14 2403
that I might not *s* against thee Ps 119:11 2398
the fruit of the wicked to *s* Prov 10:16 2403
of words there wanteth not *s* Prov 10:19 6588
Fools make a mock at *s* Prov 14:9 817
but *s* is a reproach to any people Prov 14:34 2403
heart clean, I am pure from my *s* Prov 20:9 2403
the plowing of the wicked, is *s* Prov 21:4 2403
The thought of foolishness is *s* Prov 24:9 2403
thy mouth to cause thy flesh to *s* Eccl 5:6 2398
and they declare their *s* as Sodom Is 3:9 2403
s as it were with a cart rope Is 5:18 2402
is taken away, and thy *s* purged Is 6:7 2403
all the fruit to take away his *s* Is 27:9 2403
that they may add *s* to *s* Is 30:1 2403
hands have made unto you for a *s* Is 31:7 2399
make his soul an offering for *s* Is 53:10 817
and he bare the *s* of many, and made Is 53:12 2399
or what is our *s* that we have Jer 16:10 2403
their iniquity and their *s* double Jer 16:18 2403
The *s* of Judah is written with a Jer 17:1 2403
spoil, and thy high places for *s* Jer 17:3 2403
blot out their *s* from thy sight Jer 18:23 2403
I will remember their *s* no more Jer 31:34 2403
abomination, to cause Judah to *s* Jer 32:35 2398
forgive their iniquity and their *s* Jer 36:3 2403
their land was filled with *s* Jer 51:5 817
the punishment of the *s* of Sodom Lam 4:6
warning, he shall die in his *s* Eze 3:20 2403
s not, and he doth not *s* Eze 3:21 2398
in his *s* that he hath sinned, in Eze 18:24 2403
if he turn from his *s*, and do that Eze 33:14 2403
the *s* offering and the trespass Eze 40:39 2403
the *s* offering, and the trespass Eze 42:13 2403
a young bullock for a *s* offering Eze 43:19 2403
bullock also of the *s* offering Eze 43:21 2403
without blemish for a *s* offering Eze 43:22 2403
every day a goat for a *s* offering Eze 43:25 2403
he shall offer his *s* offering Eze 44:27 2403
the *s* offering, and the trespass Eze 44:29 2403
he shall prepare the *s* offering Eze 45:17 2403
of the blood of the *s* offering Eze 45:19 2403
land a bullock for a *s* offering Eze 45:22 2403
the goats daily for a *s* offering Eze 45:23 2403
days, according to the *s* offering Eze 45:25 2403
the *s* offering, where they shall Eze 46:20 2403
and praying, and confessing my *s* Dan 9:20 2403
the *s* of my people Israel, and Dan 9:20 2403
They eat up the *s* of my people Hos 4:8 2403
hath made many altars to *s* Hos 8:11 2398
altars shall be unto him to *s* Hos 8:11 2398
the *s* of Israel, shall be Hos 10:8 2403
none iniquity in me that were *s* Hos 12:8 2399
And now they *s* more and more, and Hos 13:2 2398
his *s* is hid Hos 13:12 2403
that swear by the *s* of Samaria Amos 8:14 819
of the *s* to the daughter of Zion Mic 1:13 2403
transgression, and to Israel his *s* Mic 3:8 2403
of my body for the *s* of my soul Mic 6:7 2403
inhabitants of Jerusalem for *s* Zec 13:1 2403
I say unto you, All manner of *s* Mt 12:31 *266*
oft shall my brother *s* against me Mt 18:21 *264*
taketh away the *s* of the world Jn 1:29 *266*
s no more, lest a worse thing Jn 5:14 *264*
He that is without *s* among you Jn 8:7 *361*
go, and *s* no more Jn 8:11 *264*
Whosoever committeth *s* is the Jn 8:34 *266*
is the servant of *s* Jn 8:34 *266*
Which of you convinceth me of *s* Jn 8:46 *266*
him, saying, Master, who did *s* Jn 9:2 *264*
were blind, ye should have no *s* Jn 9:41 *266*
therefore your *s* remaineth Jn 9:41 *266*
unto them, they had not had *s* Jn 15:22 *266*
they have no cloke for their *s* Jn 15:22 *266*
other man did, they had not had *s* Jn 15:24 *266*
he will reprove the world of *s* Jn 16:8 *266*
Of *s*, because they believe not on Jn 16:9 *266*
me unto thee hath the greater *s* Jn 19:11 *266*
lay not this *s* to their charge Acts 7:60 *266*
that they are all under *s* Rom 3:9 *266*
by the law is the knowledge of *s* Rom 3:20 *266*
whom the Lord will not impute *s* Rom 4:8 *266*
as by one man *s* entered into the Rom 5:12 *266*
into the world, and death by *s* Rom 5:12 *266*
until the law *s* was in the world Rom 5:13 *266*
but *s* is not imputed when there Rom 5:13 *266*
But where *s* abounded, grace did Rom 5:20 *266*
That as *s* hath reigned unto death Rom 5:21 *266*
Shall we continue in *s*, that Rom 6:1 *266*
How shall we, that are dead to *s* Rom 6:2 *266*
that the body of *s* might be Rom 6:6 *266*
henceforth we should not serve *s* Rom 6:6 *266*
he that is dead is freed from *s* Rom 6:7 *266*
that he died, he died unto *s* once Rom 6:10 *266*
to be dead indeed unto *s*, but Rom 6:11 *266*
Let not *s* therefore reign in your Rom 6:12 *266*
of unrighteousness unto *s* Rom 6:13 *266*
For *s* shall not have dominion Rom 6:14 *266*
shall we *s*, because we are not Rom 6:15 *264*
whether of *s* unto death, or of Rom 6:16 *266*
that ye were the servants of *s* Rom 6:17 *266*
Being then made free from *s* Rom 6:18 *266*
when ye were the servants of *s* Rom 6:20 *266*
But now being made free from *s* Rom 6:22 *266*
For the wages of *s* is death Rom 6:23 *266*
Is the law *s* Rom 7:7 *266*
Nay, I had not known *s*, but by Rom 7:7 *266*
But *s*, taking occasion by the Rom 7:8 *266*
For without the law *s* was dead Rom 7:8 *266*
came, *s* revived, and I died Rom 7:9 *266*
For *s*, taking occasion by the Rom 7:11 *266*
But *s*, that it might appear *s*, Rom 7:13 *266*
that *s* by the commandment might Rom 7:13 *266*
but I am carnal, sold under *s* Rom 7:14 *266*
but *s* that dwelleth in me Rom 7:17 *266*
but *s* that dwelleth in me Rom 7:20 *266*
law of *s* which is in my members Rom 7:23 *266*
but with the flesh the law of *s* Rom 7:25 *266*
made me free from the law of *s* Rom 8:2 *266*
for *s*, condemned *s* in the flesh Rom 8:3 *266*
the body is dead because of *s* Rom 8:10 *266*
whatsoever is not of faith is *s* Rom 14:23 *266*
Every *s* that a man doeth is 1Cor 6:18 *265*
But when ye so against the 1Cor 8:12 *264*
conscience, ye *s* against Christ 1Cor 8:12 *264*
Awake to righteousness, and *s* not 1Cor 15:34 *264*
The sting of death is *s* 1Cor 15:56 *266*
and the strength of *s* is the law 1Cor 15:56 *266*
to be *s* for us, who knew no *s* 2Cor 5:21 *266*
Christ the minister of *s* Gal 2:17 *266*
hath concluded all under *s* Gal 3:22 *266*
Be ye angry, and *s* not Eph 4:26 *264*
and that man of *s* be revealed 2Th 2:3 *266*
Them that *s* rebuke before all, 1Ti 5:20 *264*
through the deceitfulness of *s* Heb 3:13 *266*
like as we are, yet without *s* Heb 4:15 *266*
s by the sacrifice of himself Heb 9:26 *266*
time without *s* unto salvation Heb 9:28 *266*
sacrifices for *s* thou hast had no Heb 10:6 *266*
offering for *s* thou wouldest not, Heb 10:8 *266*
there is no more offering for *s* Heb 10:18 *266*
For if we *s* wilfully after that Heb 10:26 *264*
the pleasures of *s* for a season Heb 11:25 *266*
the *s* which doth so easily beset Heb 12:1 *266*
unto blood, striving against *s* Heb 12:4 *266*
by the high priest for *s*, are Heb 13:11 *266*
conceived, it bringeth forth *s* Jas 1:15 *266*
and *s*, when it is finished, Jas 1:15 *266*
respect to persons, ye commit *s* Jas 2:9 *266*
and doeth it not, to him it is *s* Jas 4:17 *266*
Who did no *s*, neither was guile 1Pet 2:22 *266*
in the flesh hath ceased from *s* 1Pet 4:1 *266*
and that cannot cease from *s* 2Pet 2:14 *266*
his Son cleanseth us from all *s* 1Jn 1:7 *266*
If we say that we have no *s* 1Jn 1:8 *266*
write I unto you, that ye *s* not 1Jn 2:1 *264*
And if any man *s*, we have an 1Jn 2:1 *264*
Whosoever committeth *s* 1Jn 3:4 *266*
for *s* is the transgression of the 1Jn 3:4 *266*
and in him is no *s* 1Jn 3:5 *266*
that committeth *s* is of the devil 1Jn 3:8 *266*
is born of God doth not commit *s* 1Jn 3:9 *266*
and he cannot *s*, because he is 1Jn 3:9 *264*
s a *s* which is not unto death 1Jn 5:16 *264*
for them that *s* not unto death 1Jn 5:16 *264*
There is a *s* unto death 1Jn 5:16 *266*
All unrighteousness is *s* 1Jn 5:17 *266*
there is a *s* not unto death 1Jn 5:17 *266*

2. Eastern border of Egypt.

And I will pour my fury upon *S* Eze 30:15 5512
S shall have great pain, and No Eze 30:16 5512

3. Desert between Elim and Sinai.

came unto the wilderness of *S* Ex 16:1 5512
from the wilderness of *S*, after Ex 17:1 5512

encamped in the wilderness of S ... Num 33:11 5512
out of the wilderness of S ... Num 33:12 5512

SINA *(si'-nah)* {2} See SINAI. *Greek form of Sinai.*
him in the wilderness of mount S ... Acts 7:30 4614
which spake to him in the mount S ... Acts 7:38 4614

SINAI *(si'-nahee)* {37} See HOREB, SINA. *Mountainous district in the southern Sinai peninsula.*
Sin, which is between Elim and S ... Ex 16:1 5514
they into the wilderness of S ... Ex 19:1 5514
and were come to the desert of S ... Ex 19:2 5514
of all the people upon mount S ... Ex 19:11 5514
mount S was altogether on a smoke ... Ex 19:18 5514
the LORD came down upon mount S ... Ex 19:20 5514
people cannot come up to mount S ... Ex 19:23 5514
of the LORD abode upon mount S ... Ex 24:16 5514
communing with him upon mount S ... Ex 31:18 5514
up in the morning unto mount S ... Ex 34:2 5514
morning, and went up unto mount S ... Ex 34:4 5514
mount S with the two tables of ... Ex 34:29 5514
had spoken with him in mount S ... Ex 34:32 5514
LORD commanded Moses in mount S ... Lev 7:38 5514
the LORD, in the wilderness of S ... Lev 7:38 5514
LORD spake unto Moses in mount S ... Lev 25:1 5514
in mount S by the hand of Moses ... Lev 26:46 5514
the children of Israel in mount S ... Lev 27:34 5514
unto Moses in the wilderness of S ... Num 1:1 5514
them in the wilderness of S ... Num 1:19 5514
LORD spake with Moses in mount S ... Num 3:1 5514
the LORD, in the wilderness of S ... Num 3:4 5514
unto Moses in the wilderness of S ... Num 3:14 5514
unto Moses in the wilderness of S ... Num 9:1 5514
at even in the wilderness of S ... Num 9:5 5514
out of the wilderness of S ... Num 10:12 5514
of Israel in the wilderness of S ... Num 26:64 5514
in mount S for a sweet savour ... Num 28:6 5514
and pitched in the wilderness of S ... Num 33:15 5514
they removed from the desert of S ... Num 33:16 5514
And he said, The LORD came from S ... Deut 33:2 5514
even that S from before the LORD ... Judg 5:5 5514
camest down also upon mount S ... Neh 9:13 5514
even S itself was moved at the ... Ps 68:8 5514
the Lord is among them, as in S ... Ps 68:17 5514
the one from the mount S, which ... Gal 4:24 4614
this Agar is mount S in Arabia ... Gal 4:25 4614

SINCE {70}
hath blessed thee s my coming ... Gen 30:30
and I saw him not s ... Gen 44:28 2008
s I have seen thy face, because ... Gen 46:30 310
nor s thou hast spoken unto thy ... Ex 4:10 227
For s I came to Pharaoh to speak ... Ex 5:23 4480
s the foundation thereof even ... Ex 9:18 4480
of Egypt s it became a nation ... Ex 9:24 4480
s the day that they were upon the ... Ex 10:6 4480
ever s I was thine unto this day ... Num 22:30 5750
s the day that God created man ... Deut 4:32 4480
s in Israel like unto Moses ... Deut 34:10 5750
s I have shewed you kindness ... Josh 2:12 3588
even s the LORD spake this word ... Josh 14:10 227
law s the death of thine husband ... Ruth 2:11 310
s the day that I brought them up ... 1Sa 8:8
it been kept for thee s I said ... 1Sa 9:24
s I came out, and the vessels of ... 1Sa 21:5
I have found no fault in him s he ... 1Sa 29:3
s the day of thy coming unto me ... 1Sa 29:6
I have not dwelt in any house s ... 2Sa 7:6
as s the time that I commanded ... 2Sa 7:11 4480
S the day that I brought forth my ... 1Kin 8:16 4480
all the fruits of the field s the ... 2Kin 8:6
s the day their fathers came ... 2Kin 21:15 4480
house s the day that I brought up ... 1Chr 17:5 4480
s the time that I commanded ... 1Chr 17:10
S the day that I brought forth my ... 2Chr 6:5 4480
for s the time of Solomon the son ... 2Chr 30:26
S the people began to bring the ... 2Chr 31:10
we do sacrifice unto him s the ... Ezr 4:2
s that time even until now hath ... Ezr 5:16 4481
S the days of our fathers have we ... Ezr 9:7
for s the days of Jeshua the son ... Neh 8:17
s the time of the kings of ... Neh 9:32
s man was placed upon earth ... Job 20:4 4480
commanded the morning s thy days ... Job 38:12
S thou art laid down, no feller ... Is 14:8 227
concerning Moab s that time ... Is 16:13
S thou wast precious in my sight ... Is 43:4
s I appointed the ancient people ... Is 44:7
For s the beginning of the world ... Is 64:4
S the day that your fathers came ... Jer 7:25 4480
s they return not from their ways ... Jer 15:7
For s I spake, I cried out, I ... Jer 20:8 1767
But s ye say, The burden of the ... Jer 23:38 518
for s I spake against him, I do ... Jer 31:20 1767
But s we left off to burn incense ... Jer 44:18 4480,227
for s thou spakest of him, thou ... Jer 48:27 1767
such as never was s there was a ... Dan 12:1
S those days were, when one came ... Hag 2:16
such as was not s the beginning ... Mt 24:21 575
is it ago s this came unto him ... Mk 9:21 5613
which have been s the world began ... Lk 1:70 575
but this woman s the time I came ... Lk 7:45 575
s that time the kingdom of God is ... Lk 16:16 575
day s these things were done ... Lk 24:21 575
S the world began was it not ... Jn 9:32 1537
holy prophets s the world began ... Acts 3:21 575
the Holy Ghost s ye believed ... Acts 19:2
s I went up to Jerusalem for to ... Acts 24:11 575,3739
was kept secret s the world began ... Rom 16:25
For s by man came death, by man ... 1Cor 15:21 1894
S ye seek a proof of Christ ... 2Cor 13:3 1893
S we heard of your faith in ... Col 1:4
s the day ye heard of it, and knew ... Col 1:6 575
s the day we heard it, do not ... Col 1:9 575
of the oath, which was s the law ... Heb 7:28 3326
s the foundation of the world ... Heb 9:26 575
for s the fathers fell asleep ... 2Pet 3:4 575,3739
such as was not s men were upon ... Rev 16:18 575,3739

SINCERE {2}
that ye may be s and without ... Phil 1:10 1506
desire the s milk of the word ... 1Pet 2:2 97

SINCERELY {3}
if ye have done truly and s ... Judg 9:16 8549
s with Jerubbaal and with his ... Judg 9:19 8549
Christ of contention, not s ... Phil 1:16 55

SINCERITY {7}
fear the LORD, and serve him in s ... Josh 24:14 8549
with the unleavened bread of s ... 1Cor 5:8 1505
that in simplicity and godly s ... 2Cor 1:12 1505
but as of s, but as of God, in ... 2Cor 2:17 1505
and to prove the s of your love ... 2Cor 8:8 1103
love our Lord Jesus Christ in s ... Eph 6:24 861
shewing uncorruptness, gravity, s ... Titus 2:7 861

SINEW {3}
eat not of the s which shrank ... Gen 32:32 1517
thigh in the s that shrank ... Gen 32:32 1517
and thy neck is an iron s ... Is 48:4 1517

SINEWS {5}
and hast fenced me with bones and s ... Job 10:11 1517
and my s take no rest ... Job 30:17 6207
the s of his stones are wrapped ... Job 40:17 1517
And I will lay s upon you, and will ... Eze 37:6 1517
And when I beheld, lo, the s ... Eze 37:8 1517

SINFUL {8}
stead, an increase of s men ... Num 32:14 2400
Ah s nation, a people laden with ... Is 1:4 2398
Lord GOD are upon the s kingdom ... Amos 9:8 2401
this adulterous and s generation ... Mk 8:38 268
for I am a s man, O Lord ... Lk 5:8 268
delivered into the hands of s men ... Lk 24:7 268
might become exceeding s ... Rom 7:13 268
Son in the likeness of s flesh ... Rom 8:3 266

SING {110}
I will s unto the LORD, for he ... Ex 15:1 7891
S ye to the LORD, for he hath ... Ex 15:21 7891
noise of them that s do I hear ... Ex 32:18 6031
s ye unto it ... Num 21:17 6030
I, even I, will s unto the LORD ... Judg 5:3 7891
I will s praise to the LORD God ... Judg 5:3 2167
did they not s one to another of ... 1Sa 21:11 6030
S unto him, s psalms unto him ... 1Chr 16:9 7891
S unto the LORD, all the earth ... 1Chr 16:23 7891
shall the trees of the wood s out ... 1Chr 16:33 7442
And when they began to s and to ... 2Chr 20:22 7440
and such as taught to s praise ... 2Chr 23:13 1984
commanded the Levites to s praise ... 2Chr 29:30 1984
the widow's heart to s for joy ... Job 29:13 7442
will s praise to the name of the ... Ps 7:17
I will s praise to thy name, O ... Ps 9:2
S praises to the LORD, which ... Ps 9:11
I will s unto the LORD, because ... Ps 13:6 7891
and s praises unto thy name ... Ps 18:49
so will we s and praise thy power ... Ps 21:13 7891
I will s, yea ... Ps 27:6 7891
I will s praises unto the LORD ... Ps 27:6 2167
S unto the LORD, O ye saints of ... Ps 30:4 2167
my glory may s praise to thee ... Ps 30:12 2167
s unto him with the psaltery and ... Ps 33:2 2167
S unto him a new song ... Ps 33:3 7891
S praises to God, s praises ... Ps 47:6 2167
s praises unto our King, s ... Ps 47:6 2167
s ye praises with understanding ... Ps 47:7 2167
my tongue shall s aloud of thy ... Ps 51:14 7442
I will s and give praise ... Ps 57:7 7891
I will s unto thee among the ... Ps 57:9 2167
But I will s of thy power ... Ps 59:16 7891
I will s aloud of thy mercy in ... Ps 59:16 7442
thee, O my strength, will I s ... Ps 59:17 2167
So will I s praise unto thy name ... Ps 61:8 2167
they shout for joy, they also s ... Ps 65:13 7891
S forth the honour of his name ... Ps 66:2 2167
thee, and shall s unto thee ... Ps 66:4 2167
they shall s to thy name ... Ps 66:4 2167
the nations be glad and s for joy ... Ps 67:4 7442
S unto God ... Ps 68:4 7891
s praises to his name ... Ps 68:4 2167
S unto God, ye kingdoms of the ... Ps 68:32 7891
O s praises unto the Lord ... Ps 68:32 2167
unto thee will I s with the harp ... Ps 71:22 2167
rejoice when I s unto thee ... Ps 71:23 2167
I will s praises to the God of ... Ps 75:9
S aloud unto God our strength ... Ps 81:1 7442
I will s of the mercies of the ... Ps 89:1 7891
to s praises unto thy name, O ... Ps 92:1 2167
O come, let us s unto the LORD ... Ps 95:1 7442
O s unto the LORD a new song ... Ps 96:1 7891
s unto the LORD, all the earth ... Ps 96:1 7891
S unto the LORD, bless his name ... Ps 96:2 7891
O s unto the LORD a new song ... Ps 98:1 7891
noise, and rejoice, and s praise ... Ps 98:4 2167
S unto the LORD with the harp ... Ps 98:5 2167
I will s of mercy and judgment ... Ps 101:1 7891
unto thee, O LORD, will I s ... Ps 101:1 2167
which s among the branches ... Ps 104:12 5414,6963
I will s unto the LORD as long as ... Ps 104:33 7891
I will s praise to my God while I ... Ps 104:33 2167
S unto him ... Ps 105:2 7891
s psalms unto him ... Ps 105:2 2167
I will s and give praise, even ... Ps 108:1 7891
I will s praises unto thee among ... Ps 108:3 2167
s praises unto his name ... Ps 135:3 2167
S us one of the songs of Zion ... Ps 137:3 7891
How shall we s the LORD's song in ... Ps 137:4 7891
gods will I s praise unto thee ... Ps 138:1 2167
they shall s in the ways of the ... Ps 138:5 7891
I will s a new song unto thee, O ... Ps 144:9 7891
will I s praises unto thee ... Ps 144:9 2167
shall s of thy righteousness ... Ps 145:7 7442
I will s praises unto my God ... Ps 146:2 2167
for it is good to s praises unto ... Ps 147:1 2167
S unto the LORD with thanksgiving ... Ps 147:7 6030
s praise upon the harp unto our ... Ps 147:7 2167
S unto the LORD a new song, and ... Ps 149:1 7891
let them s praises unto him with ... Ps 149:3 2167
let them s aloud upon their beds ... Ps 149:5 7442
but the righteous doth s and ... Prov 29:6 7442
Now will I s to my wellbeloved a ... Is 5:1 7891
S unto the LORD ... Is 12:5 2167
years shall Tyre s as an harlot ... Is 23:15 7892
s many songs, that thou mayest be ... Is 23:16
they shall s for the majesty of ... Is 24:14 7442
Awake and s, ye that dwell in dust ... Is 26:19 7442
In that day s ye unto her ... Is 27:2 6031
hart, and the tongue of the dumb s ... Is 35:6 7442
therefore we will s my songs to ... Is 38:20
S unto the LORD a new song, and ... Is 42:10 7891
let the inhabitants of the rock s ... Is 42:11 7442
S, O ye heavens ... Is 44:23 7442
S, O heavens ... Is 49:13 7442
the voice together shall they s ... Is 52:8 7442
s together, ye waste places of ... Is 52:9 7442
S, O barren, thou that didst not ... Is 54:1 7442
servants shall s for joy of heart ... Is 65:14 7442
S unto the LORD, praise ye the ... Jer 20:13 7891
S with gladness for Jacob, and ... Jer 31:7 7442
s in the height of Zion, and shall ... Jer 31:12 7442
is therein, shall s for Babylon ... Jer 51:48 7442
did s of thee in thy market ... Eze 27:25 7788
and she shall s there, as in the ... Hos 2:15 6030
voice shall s in the windows ... Zeph 2:14 7891
S, O daughter of Zion ... Zeph 3:14 7442
S and rejoice, O daughter of Zion ... Zec 2:10 7442
the Gentiles, and s unto thy name ... Rom 15:9 5567
I will s with the spirit ... 1Cor 14:15 5567
I will s with the understanding ... 1Cor 14:15 5567
church will I s praise unto thee ... Heb 2:12 5214
let him s psalms ... Jas 5:13 5567
they s the song of Moses the ... Rev 15:3 103

SINGED {1}
nor was an hair of their head s ... Dan 3:27 2761

SINGER {2}
Heman a s, the son of Joel, the ... 1Chr 6:33 7891
To the chief s on my stringed ... Hab 3:19 5329

SINGERS {38}
harps also and psalteries for s ... 1Kin 10:12 7891
And these are the s, chief of the ... 1Chr 9:33 7891
their brethren to be the s with ... 1Chr 15:16 7891
So the s, Heman, Asaph, and Ethan ... 1Chr 15:19 7891
that bare the ark, and the s ... 1Chr 15:27 7891
the master of the song with the s ... 1Chr 15:27 7891
Also the Levites which were the s ... 2Chr 5:12 7891
s were as one, to make one sound ... 2Chr 5:13 7891
and harps and psalteries for s ... 2Chr 9:11 7891
he appointed s unto the LORD, and ... 2Chr 20:21 7891
also the s with instruments of ... 2Chr 23:13 7891
the s sang, and the trumpeters ... 2Chr 29:28 7892
the s the sons of Asaph were in ... 2Chr 35:15 7891
The s: the children of Asaph ... Ezr 2:41 7891
and some of the people, and the s ... Ezr 2:70 7891
priests, and the Levites, and the s ... Ezr 7:7 7891
any of the priests and Levites, s ... Ezr 7:24 2171
Of the s also ... Ezr 10:24 7891
doors, and the porters and the s ... Neh 7:1 7891
The s: the children of Asaph ... Neh 7:44 7891
Levites, and the porters, and the s ... Neh 7:73 7891
the Levites, the porters, the s ... Neh 10:28 7891
and the porters, and the s ... Neh 10:39 7891
the s were over the business of ... Neh 11:22 7891
portion should be for the s ... Neh 11:23 7891
the sons of the s gathered ... Neh 12:28 7891
for the s had builded them ... Neh 12:29 7891
the s sang loud, with Jezrahiah ... Neh 12:42 7891
And both the s and the porters kept ... Neh 12:45 7891
of old there were chief of the s ... Neh 12:46 7891
gave the portions of the s ... Neh 12:47 7891
be given to the Levites, and the s ... Neh 13:5 7891
for the Levites and the s, that ... Neh 13:10 7891
The s went before, the players on ... Ps 68:25 7891
As well the s as the players on ... Ps 87:7 7891
I gat me men s and women s ... Eccl 2:8 7891
of the s in the inner court ... Eze 40:44 7891

SINGETH {1}
so is he that s songs to an heavy ... Prov 25:20 7891

SINGING {29}
out of all cities of Israel, s ... 1Sa 18:6 7891
voice of s men and s women ... 2Sa 19:35 7891
of the congregation with s ... 1Chr 6:32 7892
with all their might, and with s ... 1Chr 13:8 7892
Moses, with rejoicing and with s ... 2Chr 23:18 7892
s with loud instruments unto the ... 2Chr 30:21
and all the s men and the s ... 2Chr 35:25 7891

S

hundred *s* men and *s* women ... Ezr 2:65 7891
and five *s* men and *s* women ... Neh 7:67 7891
with thanksgivings, and with *s* ... Neh 12:27 7892
come before his presence with *s* ... Ps 100:2 7445
laughter, and our tongue with *s* ... Ps 126:2 7440
the time of the *s* of birds is ... Song 2:12 2158
they break forth into *s* ... Is 14:7 7440
the vineyards there shall be no *s* ... Is 16:10 7442
and rejoice even with joy and *s* ... Is 35:2 7442
break forth into *s*, ye mountains, ... Is 44:23 7440
with a voice of *s* declare ye ... Is 48:20 7440
and break forth into *s*, O ... Is 49:13 7440
return, and come with *s* unto Zion ... Is 51:11 7440
break forth into *s*, and cry aloud, ... Is 54:1 7440
break forth before you into *s* ... Is 55:12 7440
he will joy over thee with *s* ... Zeph 3:17 7440
and hymns and spiritual songs, *s* ... Eph 5:19 *103*
s with grace in your hearts to ... Col 3:16 *103*

SINGLE {2}
if therefore thine eye be *s* ... Mt 6:22 *573*
therefore when thine eye is *s* ... Lk 11:34 *573*

SINGLENESS {3}
meat with gladness and *s* of heart, ... Acts 2:46 *858*
in *s* of your heart, as unto ... Eph 6:5 *572*
but in *s* of heart, fearing God ... Col 3:22 *572*

SINGULAR {1}
When a man shall make a *s* vow ... Lev 27:2 6381

SINIM *(si'-nim)* {1} *An unspecified people.*
and these from the land of *S* ... Is 49:12 5515

SINITE *(si'-nite)* {2} *A tribe of Canaanites.*
Hivite, and the Arkite, and the *S* ... Gen 10:17 5513
Hivite, and the Arkite, and the *S* ... 1Chr 1:15 5513

SINK {6}
I *s* in deep mire, where there is ... Ps 69:2 2883
out of the mire, and let me not *s* ... Ps 69:14 2883
shalt say, Thus shall Babylon *s* ... Jer 51:64 8257
and beginning to *s*, he cried, ... Mt 14:30 *2670*
ships, so that they began to *s* ... Lk 5:7 *1036*
Let these sayings *s* down into ... Lk 9:44 *5087*

SINNED {119}
unto them, I have *s* this time ... Ex 9:27 2398
he *s* yet more, and hardened his ... Ex 9:34 2398
I have *s* against the LORD your ... Ex 10:16 2398
the people, Ye have *s* a great sin ... Ex 32:30 2398
this people have *s* a great sin ... Ex 32:31 2398
Whosoever hath *s* against me ... Ex 32:33 2398
for his sin, which he hath *s* ... Lev 4:3 2398
sin, which they have *s* against it ... Lev 4:14 2398
When a ruler hath *s*, and done ... Lev 4:22 2398
Or if his sin, wherein he hath *s* ... Lev 4:23 2398
Or if his sin, which he hath *s* ... Lev 4:28 2398
for his sin which he hath *s* ... Lev 4:28 2398
that he hath *s* in that thing ... Lev 5:5 2398
LORD for his sin which he hath *s* ... Lev 5:6 2398
him for his sin which he hath *s* ... Lev 5:10 2398
then he that *s* shall bring for ... Lev 5:11 2398
that he hath *s* in one of these ... Lev 5:13 2398
it shall be, because he hath *s* ... Lev 6:4 2398
him, for that he *s* by the dead ... Num 6:11 2398
foolishly, and wherein we have *s* ... Num 12:11 2398
for we have *s* ... Num 14:40 2398
came to Moses, and said, We have *s* ... Num 21:7 2398
the angel of the LORD, I have *s* ... Num 22:34 2398
ye have *s* against the LORD ... Num 32:23 2398
We have *s* against the LORD, we ... Deut 1:41 2398
ye had *s* against the LORD your ... Deut 9:16 2398
of all your sins which ye *s* ... Deut 9:18 2398
Israel hath *s*, and they have also ... Josh 7:11 2398
Indeed I have *s* against the LORD ... Josh 7:20 2398
We have *s* against thee, both ... Judg 10:10 2398
said unto the LORD, We have *s* ... Judg 10:15 2398
I have not *s* against thee ... Judg 11:27 2398
We have *s* against the LORD ... 1Sa 7:6 2398
unto the LORD, and said, We have *s* ... 1Sa 12:10 2398
Saul said unto Samuel, I have *s* ... 1Sa 15:24 2398
Then he said, I have *s* ... 1Sa 15:30 2398
he hath not *s* against thee ... 1Sa 19:4 2398
I have not *s* against thee ... 1Sa 24:11 2398
Then said Saul, I have *s* ... 1Sa 26:21 2398
I have *s* against the LORD ... 2Sa 12:13 2398
servant doth know that I have *s* ... 2Sa 19:20 2398
I have *s* greatly in that I have ... 2Sa 24:10 2398
the people, and said, Lo, I have *s* ... 2Sa 24:17 2398
because they have *s* against thee ... 1Kin 8:33 2398
because they have *s* against thee ... 1Kin 8:35 2398
them captives, saying, We have *s* ... 1Kin 8:47 2398
people that have *s* against thee ... 1Kin 8:50 2398
the sins of Jeroboam which he *s* ... 1Kin 15:30 2398
of Elah his son, by which they *s* ... 1Kin 16:13 2398
For his sins which he *s* in doing ... 1Kin 16:19 2398
And he said, What have I *s* ... 1Kin 18:9 2398
had *s* against the LORD their God ... 2Kin 17:7 2398
that he did, and his sin that he *s* ... 2Kin 21:17 2398
I have *s* greatly, because I have ... 1Chr 21:8 2398
even I it is that have *s* and done ... 1Chr 21:17 2398
because they have *s* against thee ... 2Chr 6:24 2398
because they have *s* against thee ... 2Chr 6:26 2398
captivity, saying, We have *s* ... 2Chr 6:37 2398
people which have *s* against thee ... 2Chr 6:39 2398
which we have *s* against thee ... Neh 1:6 2398
I and my father's house have *s* ... Neh 1:6 2398
but *s* against thy judgments, ... Neh 9:29 2398
It may be that my sons have *s* ... Job 1:5 2398
In all this Job *s* not, nor ... Job 1:22 2398
I have *s* ... Job 7:20 2398
thy children have *s* against him ... Job 8:4 2398
doth the grave those which have *s* ... Job 24:19 2398
upon men, and if any say, I have *s* ... Job 33:27 2398
for I have *s* against thee ... Ps 41:4 2398
Against thee, thee only, have I *s* ... Ps 51:4 2398
they *s* yet more against him by ... Ps 78:17 2398
For all this they *s* still ... Ps 78:32 2398
We have *s* with our fathers, we ... Ps 106:6 2398
LORD, he against whom we have *s* ... Is 42:24 2398
Thy first father hath *s*, and thy ... Is 43:27 2398
for we have *s* ... Is 64:5 2398
because thou sayest, I have not *s* ... Jer 2:35 2398
for we have *s* against the LORD ... Jer 3:25 2398
because we have *s* against the ... Jer 8:14 2398
we have *s* against thee ... Jer 14:7 2398
for we have *s* against thee ... Jer 14:20 2398
whereby they have *s* against me ... Jer 33:8 2398
iniquities, whereby they have *s* ... Jer 33:8 2398
because ye have *s* against the ... Jer 40:3 2398
because ye have *s* against the ... Jer 44:23 2398
they have *s* against the LORD ... Jer 50:7 2398
for she hath *s* against the LORD ... Jer 50:14 2398
Jerusalem hath grievously *s* ... Lam 1:8 2398
Our fathers have *s*, and are not ... Lam 5:7 2398
woe unto us, that we have *s* ... Lam 5:16 2398
and in his sin that he hath *s* ... Eze 18:24 2398
with violence, and thou hast *s* ... Eze 28:16 2398
wherein they have *s*, and will ... Eze 37:23 2398
We have *s*, and have committed ... Dan 9:5 2398
because we have *s* against thee ... Dan 9:8 2398
because we have *s* against him ... Dan 9:11 2398
we have *s*, we have done wickedly ... Dan 9:15 2398
increased, so they *s* against me ... Hos 4:7 2398
thou hast *s* from the days of ... Hos 10:9 2398
because I have *s* against him ... Mic 7:9 2398
and hast *s* against thy soul ... Hab 2:10 2398
they have *s* against the LORD ... Zeph 1:17 2398
I have *s* in that I have betrayed ... Mt 27:4 *264*
I have *s* against heaven, and ... Lk 15:18 *264*
I have *s* against heaven, and in ... Lk 15:21 *264*
answered, Neither hath this man *s* ... Jn 9:3 *264*
For as many as have *s* without law ... Rom 2:12 *264*
as many as have *s* in the law ... Rom 2:12 *264*
For all have *s*, and come short of ... Rom 3:23 *264*
upon all men, for that all have *s* ... Rom 5:12 *264*
even over them that had not *s* ... Rom 5:14 *264*
And not as it was by one that *s* ... Rom 5:16 *264*
and if thou marry, thou hast not *s* ... 1Cor 7:28 *264*
if a virgin marry, she hath not *s* ... 1Cor 7:28 *264*
bewail many which have *s* already ... 2Cor 12:21 *4258*
to them which heretofore have *s* ... 2Cor 13:2 *4258*
was it not with them that had *s* ... Heb 3:17 *264*
God spared not the angels that *s* ... 2Pet 2:4 *264*
If we say that we have not *s* ... 1Jn 1:10 *264*

SINNER {21}
much more the wicked and the *s* ... Prov 11:31 2398
but wickedness overthroweth the *s* ... Prov 13:6 2403
the wealth of the *s* is laid up ... Prov 13:22 2398
but to the *s* he giveth travail, ... Eccl 2:26 2398
but the *s* shall be taken by her ... Eccl 7:26 2398
Though a *s* do evil an hundred ... Eccl 8:12 2398
as is the good, so is the *s* ... Eccl 9:2 2398
but one *s* destroyeth much good ... Eccl 9:18 2398
but the *s* being an hundred years ... Is 65:20 2398
woman in the city, which was a *s* ... Lk 7:37 *268*
for she is a *s* ... Lk 7:39 *268*
heaven over one *s* that repenteth ... Lk 15:7 *268*
of God over one *s* that repenteth ... Lk 15:10 *268*
saying, God be merciful to me a *s* ... Lk 18:13 *268*
be guest with a man that is a *s* ... Lk 19:7 *268*
man that is a *s* do such miracles ... Jn 9:16 *268*
we know that this man is a *s* ... Jn 9:24 *268*
and said, Whether he be a *s* or no ... Jn 9:25 *268*
why yet am I also judged as a *s* ... Rom 3:7 *268*
that he which converteth the *s* ... Jas 5:20 *268*
shall the ungodly and the *s* appear ... 1Pet 4:18 *268*

SINNERS {48}
s before the LORD exceedingly ... Gen 13:13 2400
The censers of these *s* against ... Num 16:38 2400
destroy the *s* the Amalekites ... 1Sa 15:18 2400
nor standeth in the way of *s* ... Ps 1:1 2400
nor *s* in the congregation of the ... Ps 1:5 2400
will he teach *s* in the way ... Ps 25:8 2400
Gather not my soul with *s* ... Ps 26:9 2400
s shall be converted unto thee ... Ps 51:13 2400
Let the *s* be consumed out of the ... Ps 104:35 2400
if *s* entice thee, consent thou ... Prov 1:10 2400
Evil pursueth *s* ... Prov 13:21 2400
Let not thine heart envy *s* ... Prov 23:17 2400
of the *s* shall be together, and ... Is 1:28 2400
destroy the *s* thereof out of it ... Is 13:9 2400
The *s* in Zion are afraid ... Is 33:14 2400
All the *s* of my people shall die ... Amos 9:10 2400
s came and sat down with him and ... Mt 9:10 *268*
your Master with publicans and *s* ... Mt 9:11 *268*
righteous, but *s* to repentance ... Mt 9:13 *268*
a friend of publicans and *s* ... Mt 11:19 *268*
is betrayed into the hands of *s* ... Mt 26:45 *268*
s sat also together with Jesus and ... Mk 2:15 *268*
saw him eat with publicans and *s* ... Mk 2:16 *268*
and drinketh with publicans and *s* ... Mk 2:16 *268*
righteous, but *s* to repentance ... Mk 2:17 *268*
is betrayed into the hands of *s* ... Mk 14:41 *268*
eat and drink with publicans and *s* ... Lk 5:30 *268*
righteous, but *s* to repentance ... Lk 5:32 *268*
for *s* also love those that love ... Lk 6:32 *268*
for *s* also do even the same ... Lk 6:33 *268*
for *s* also lend to *s* ... Lk 6:34 *268*
a friend of publicans and *s* ... Lk 7:34 *268*
were *s* above all the Galilaeans ... Lk 13:2 *268*
think ye that they were *s* above ... Lk 13:4 *3781*
publicans and *s* for to hear him ... Lk 15:1 *268*
saying, This man receiveth *s* ... Lk 15:2 *268*
we know that God heareth not *s* ... Jn 9:31 *268*
us, in that, while we were yet *s* ... Rom 5:8 *268*
disobedience many were made *s* ... Rom 5:19 *268*
nature, and not *s* of the Gentiles, ... Gal 2:15 *268*
we ourselves also are found *s* ... Gal 2:17 *268*
for the ungodly and for *s* ... 1Ti 1:9 *268*
came into the world to save *s* ... 1Ti 1:15 *268*
undefiled, separate from *s* ... Heb 7:26 *268*
of *s* against himself, lest ye be ... Heb 12:3 *268*
Cleanse your hands, ye *s* ... Jas 4:8 *268*
ungodly *s* have spoken against him ... Jude 15 *268*

SINNEST {1}
If thou *s*, what doest thou ... Job 35:6 2398

SINNETH {22}
for the soul that *s* ignorantly ... Num 15:28 7683
when he *s* by ignorance before the ... Num 15:28 2398
for him that *s* through ignorance ... Num 15:29 6213
for any sin, in any sin that he *s* ... Deut 19:15 2398
(for there is no man that *s* not ... 1Kin 8:46 2398
(for there is no man which *s* not ... 2Chr 6:36 2398
But he that *s* against me wrongeth ... Prov 8:36 2398
He that despiseth his neighbour *s* ... Prov 14:21 2398
he that hasteth with his feet *s* ... Prov 19:2 2398
to anger *s* against his own soul ... Prov 20:2 2398
earth, that doeth good, and *s* not ... Eccl 7:20 2398
when the land *s* against me by ... Eze 14:13 2398
the soul that *s*, it shall die ... Eze 18:4 2398
The soul that *s*, it shall die ... Eze 18:20 2398
in the day that he *s* ... Eze 33:12 2398
s against his own body ... 1Cor 6:18 *264*
let him do what he will, he *s* not ... 1Cor 7:36 *264*
that is such is subverted, and *s* ... Titus 3:11 *264*
Whosoever abideth in him *s* not ... 1Jn 3:6 *264*
whosoever *s* hath not seen him, ... 1Jn 3:6 *264*
for the devil *s* from the ... 1Jn 3:8 *264*
whosoever is born of God *s* not ... 1Jn 5:18 *264*

SINNING {2}
withheld thee from *s* against me ... Gen 20:6 2398
these that a man doeth, *s* therein ... Lev 6:3 2398

SINS {172}
transgressions in all their *s* ... Lev 16:16 2403
transgressions in all their *s* ... Lev 16:21 2403
from all your *s* before the LORD ... Lev 16:30 2403
for all their *s* once a year ... Lev 16:34 2403
you seven times more for your *s* ... Lev 26:18 2403
upon you according to your *s* ... Lev 26:21 2403
you yet seven times for your *s* ... Lev 26:24 2403
you seven times for your *s* ... Lev 26:28 2403
ye be consumed in all their *s* ... Num 16:26 2403
of all your *s* which ye sinned ... Deut 9:18 2403
your transgressions nor your *s* ... Josh 24:19 2403
added unto all our *s* this evil ... 1Sa 12:19 2403
up because of the *s* of Jeroboam ... 1Kin 14:16 2403
their *s* which they had committed ... 1Kin 14:22 2403
walked in all the *s* of his father ... 1Kin 15:3 2403
Because of the *s* of Jeroboam ... 1Kin 15:30 2403
provoke me to anger with their *s* ... 1Kin 16:2 2403
For all the *s* of Baasha, and the ... 1Kin 16:13 2403
the *s* of Elah his son, by which ... 1Kin 16:13 2403
For his *s* which he sinned in ... 1Kin 16:19 2403
s of Jeroboam the son of Nebat ... 1Kin 16:31 2403
he cleaved unto the *s* of Jeroboam ... 2Kin 3:3 2403
Howbeit from the *s* of Jeroboam ... 2Kin 10:29 2399
not from the *s* of Jeroboam ... 2Kin 10:31 2403
followed the *s* of Jeroboam the ... 2Kin 13:2 2403
the *s* of the house of Jeroboam ... 2Kin 13:6 2403
s of Jeroboam the son of Nebat ... 2Kin 13:11 2403
s of Jeroboam the son of Nebat ... 2Kin 14:24 2403
he departed not from the *s* of ... 2Kin 15:9 2403
not all his days from the *s* of ... 2Kin 15:18 2403
he departed not from the *s* of ... 2Kin 15:24 2403
he departed not from the *s* of ... 2Kin 15:28 2403
the *s* of Jeroboam which he did ... 2Kin 17:22 2403
for the *s* of Manasseh, according ... 2Kin 24:3 2403
s against the LORD your God ... 2Chr 28:10 819
ye intend to add more to our *s* ... 2Chr 28:13 2403
confess the *s* of the children of ... Neh 1:6 2403
and stood and confessed their *s* ... Neh 9:2 2403
hast set over us because of our *s* ... Neh 9:37 2403
How many are mine iniquities and *s* ... Job 13:23 2403
servant also from presumptuous *s* ... Ps 19:13
Remember not the *s* of my youth ... Ps 25:7 2403
and forgive all my *s* ... Ps 25:18 2403
Hide thy face from my *s*, and blot ... Ps 51:9 2399
my *s* are not hid from thee ... Ps 69:5 819
deliver us, and purge away our *s* ... Ps 79:9 2403
our secret *s* in the light of thy ... Ps 90:8
not dealt with us after our *s* ... Ps 103:10 2399
be holden with the cords of his *s* ... Prov 5:22 2403
but love covereth all *s* ... Prov 10:12 6588
covereth his *s* shall not prosper ... Prov 28:13 6588
though your *s* be as scarlet, they ... Is 1:18 2399
cast all my *s* behind thy back ... Is 38:17 2399
LORD's hand double for all her *s* ... Is 40:2 2403
hast made me to serve with thy *s* ... Is 43:24 2403
sake, and will not remember thy *s* ... Is 43:25 2403
and, as a cloud, thy *s* ... Is 44:22 2403
and the house of Jacob their *s* ... Is 58:1 2403
your *s* have hid his face from you ... Is 59:2 2403
thee, and our *s* testify against us ... Is 59:12 2403

your *s* have withholden good Jer 5:25 2403
their iniquity, and visit their *s* Jer 14:10 2403
price, and that for all thy *s* Jer 15:13 2403
because thy *s* were increased Jer 30:14 2403
because thy *s* were increased, I Jer 30:15 2403
the *s* of Judah, and they shall not Jer 50:20 2403
a man for the punishment of his *s* Lam 3:39 2399
For the *s* of her prophets, and the Lam 4:13 2403
he will discover thy *s* Lam 4:22 2403
Samaria committed half of thy *s* Eze 16:51 2403
bear thine own shame for thy *s* Eze 16:52 2403
his father's *s* which he hath done Eze 18:14 2403
all his *s* that he hath committed Eze 18:21 2403
all your doings your *s* do appear Eze 21:24 2403
ye shall bear the *s* of your idols Eze 23:49 2399
our *s* be upon us, and we pine away Eze 33:10 2403
None of his *s* that he hath Eze 33:16 2403
break off thy *s* by righteousness, Dan 4:27 2408
because for our *s*, and for the Dan 9:16 2399
and to make an end of *s*, and to Dan 9:24 2403
their iniquity, and visit their *s* Hos 8:13 2403
iniquity, he will visit their *s* Hos 9:9 2403
transgressions and your mighty *s* Amos 5:12 2403
for the *s* of the house of Israel Mic 1:5 2403
thee desolate because of thy *s* Mic 6:13 2403
thou wilt cast all their *s* into Mic 7:19 2403
save his people from their *s* Mt 1:21 *266*
him in Jordan, confessing their *s* Mt 3:6 *266*
thy *s* be forgiven thee Mt 9:2 *266*
to say, Thy *s* be forgiven thee Mt 9:5 *266*
hath power on earth to forgive *s* Mt 9:6 *266*
for many for the remission of *s* Mt 26:28 *266*
repentance for the remission of *s* Mk 1:4 *266*
of Jordan, confessing their *s* Mk 1:5 *266*
Son, thy *s* be forgiven thee Mk 2:5 *266*
who can forgive *s* but God only Mk 2:7 *266*
the palsy, Thy *s* be forgiven thee Mk 2:9 *266*
hath power on earth to forgive *s* Mk 2:10 *266*
All *s* shall be forgiven unto the Mk 3:28 *265*
their *s* should be forgiven them Mk 4:12 *265*
by the remission of their *s* Lk 1:77 *266*
repentance for the remission of *s* Lk 3:3 *266*
him, Man, thy *s* are forgiven thee Lk 5:20 *266*
Who can forgive *s*, but God alone Lk 5:21 *266*
to say, Thy *s* be forgiven thee Lk 5:23 *266*
power upon earth to forgive *s* Lk 5:24 *266*
Wherefore I say unto thee, Her *s* Lk 7:47 *266*
said unto her, Thy *s* are forgiven Lk 7:48 *266*
Who is this that forgiveth *s* also Lk 7:49 *266*
And forgive us our *s* Lk 11:4 *266*
remission of *s* should be preached Lk 24:47 *266*
seek me, and shall die in your *s* Jn 8:21 *266*
you, that ye shall die in your *s* Jn 8:24 *266*
I am he, ye shall die in your *s* Jn 8:24 *266*
Thou wast altogether born in *s* Jn 9:34 *266*
Whose soever *s* ye remit, they are Jn 20:23 *266*
and whose soever *s* ye retain Jn 20:23
Christ for the remission of *s* Acts 2:38 *266*
that your *s* may be blotted out, Acts 3:19 *266*
to Israel, and forgiveness of *s* Acts 5:31 *266*
him shall receive remission of *s* Acts 10:43 *266*
unto you the forgiveness of *s* Acts 13:38 *266*
be baptized, and wash away thy *s* Acts 22:16 *266*
they may receive forgiveness of *s* Acts 26:18 *266*
the remission of *s* that are past Rom 3:25 *265*
forgiven, and whose *s* are covered Rom 4:7 *266*
in the flesh, the motions of *s* Rom 7:5 *266*
when I shall take away their *s* Rom 11:27 *266*
our *s* according to the scriptures 1Cor 15:3 *266*
ye are yet in your *s* 1Cor 15:17 *266*
Who gave himself for our *s* Gal 1:4 *266*
his blood, the forgiveness of *s* Eph 1:7 *3900*
who were dead in trespasses and *s* Eph 2:1 *266*
Even when we were dead in *s* Eph 2:5 *3900*
blood, even the forgiveness of *s* Col 1:14 *266*
body of the *s* of the flesh by the Col 2:11 *266*
And you, being dead in your *s* Col 2:13 *3900*
saved, to fill up their *s* alway 1Th 2:16 *266*
be partaker of other men's *s* 1Ti 5:22 *266*
Some men's *s* are open beforehand, 1Ti 5:24 *266*
captive silly women laden with *s* 2Ti 3:6 *266*
he had by himself purged our *s* Heb 1:3 *266*
for the *s* of the people Heb 2:17 *266*
both gifts and sacrifices for *s* Heb 5:1 *266*
also for himself, to offer for *s* Heb 5:3 *266*
up sacrifice, first for his own *s* Heb 7:27 *266*
their unrighteousness, and their *s* Heb 8:12 *266*
offered to bear the *s* of many Heb 9:28 *266*
have had no more conscience of *s* Heb 10:2 *266*
again made of *s* every year Heb 10:3 *266*
and of goats should take away *s* Heb 10:4 *266*
which can never take away *s* Heb 10:11 *266*
one sacrifice for *s* for ever Heb 10:12 *266*
And their *s* and iniquities will I Heb 10:17 *266*
remaineth no more sacrifice for *s* Heb 10:26 *266*
and if he have committed *s* Jas 5:15 *266*
and shall hide a multitude of *s* Jas 5:20 *266*
Who his own self bare our *s* in 1Pet 2:24 *266*
tree, that we, being dead to *s* 1Pet 2:24 *266*
also hath once suffered for *s* 1Pet 3:18 *266*
shall cover the multitude of *s* 1Pet 4:8 *266*
that he was purged from his old *s* 2Pet 1:9 *266*
If we confess our *s*, he is 1Jn 1:9 *266*
and just to forgive us our *s* 1Jn 1:9 *266*
he is the propitiation for our *s* 1Jn 2:2 *266*
but also for the *s* of the whole 1Jn 2:2
because your *s* are forgiven you 1Jn 2:12 *266*
was manifested to take away our *s* 1Jn 3:5 *266*
to be the propitiation for our *s* 1Jn 4:10 *266*
us from our *s* in his own blood Rev 1:5 *266*
that ye be not partakers of her *s* Rev 18:4 *266*
For her *s* have reached unto Rev 18:5 *266*

SION *(si'-on)* {9} See SHENIR, SIRION, ZION.
1. The peak of Mount Hermon.
even unto mount *S* which is Hermon Deut 4:48 7865
2. A district of Jerusalem.
waiteth for thee, O God in *S* Ps 65:1 6726
Tell ye the daughter of *S* Mt 21:5 *4622*
Fear not, daughter of *S* Jn 12:15 *4622*
I lay in *S* a stumblingstone and Rom 9:33 *4622*
shall come out of *S* the Deliverer Rom 11:26 *4622*
But ye are come unto mount *S* Heb 12:22 *4622*
I lay in *S* a chief corner stone, 1Pet 2:6 *4622*
lo, a Lamb stood on the mount *S* Rev 14:1 *4622*

SIPHMOTH *(sif'-moth)* {1} *A city in Judah.*
Aroer, and to them which were in *S* 1Sa 30:28 8224

SIPPAI *(sip'-pahee)* {1} See SAPH. *Son of Rapha.*
Sibbechai the Hushathite slew *S* 1Chr 20:4 5598

SIR {12}
And said, O *s*, we came indeed down Gen 43:20 113
came and said unto him, *S*, didst Mt 13:27 *2962*
And he answered and said, I go *s* Mt 21:30 *2962*
Saying, *S*, we remember that that Mt 27:63 *2962*
The woman saith unto him, *S* Jn 4:11 *2962*
The woman saith unto him, *S* Jn 4:15 *2962*
The woman saith unto him, *S* Jn 4:19 *2962*
The nobleman saith unto him, *S* Jn 4:49 *2962*
The impotent man answered him, *S* Jn 5:7 *2962*
and desired him, saying, *S* Jn 12:21 *2962*
the gardener, saith unto him, *S* Jn 20:15 *2962*
And I said unto him, *S*, thou Rev 7:14 *2962*

SIRAH *(si'-rah)* {1} *A well near Hebron.*
him again from the well of *S* 2Sa 3:26 5626

SIRION *(sir'-e-on)* {2} See HERMON. *A Sidonian name for Mount Hermon.*
Which Hermon the Sidonians call *S* Deut 3:9 8304
Lebanon and *S* like a young unicorn Ps 29:6 8304

SIRS {7}
set them at one again, saying, *S* Acts 7:26 *435*
And saying, *S*, why do ye these Acts 14:15 *435*
And brought them out, and said, *S* Acts 16:30 *2962*
of like occupation, and said, *S* Acts 19:25 *435*
And said unto them, *S*, I perceive Acts 27:10 *435*
in the midst of them, and said, *S* Acts 27:21 *435*
Wherefore, *s*, be of good cheer Acts 27:25 *435*

SISAMAI *(sis'-a-mahee)* {2} *Son of Eleasah.*
And Eleasah begat *S* 1Chr 2:40 5581
and *S* begat Shallum 1Chr 2:40 5581

SISERA *(sis'-e-rah)* {21}
1. A captain in the Canaanite army.
the captain of whose host was *S* Judg 4:2 5516
unto thee to the river Kishon, *S* Judg 4:7 5516
for the LORD shall sell *S* into Judg 4:9 5516
they shewed *S* that Barak the son Judg 4:12 5516
S gathered together all his Judg 4:13 5516
hath delivered *S* into thine hand Judg 4:14 5516
And the LORD discomfited *S* Judg 4:15 5516
so that *S* lighted down off his Judg 4:15 5516
all the host of *S* fell upon the Judg 4:16 5516
Howbeit *S* fled away on his feet Judg 4:17 5516
And Jael went out to meet *S* Judg 4:18 5516
And, behold, as Barak pursued *S* Judg 4:22 5516
S lay dead, and the nail was in Judg 4:22 5516
in their courses fought against *S* Judg 5:20 5516
and with the hammer she smote *S* Judg 5:26 5516
The mother of *S* looked out at a Judg 5:28 5516
to *S* a prey of divers colours, a Judg 5:30 5516
he sold them into the hand of *S* 1Sa 12:9 5516
as to *S*, as to Jabin, at the Ps 83:9 5516
2. A family of exiles.
of Barkos, the children of *S* Ezr 2:53 5516
of Barkos, the children of *S* Neh 7:55 5516

SISMAI See SISAMAI.

SISTER {109}
the *s* of Tubal-cain was Naamah Gen 4:22 269
Say, I pray thee, thou art my *s* Gen 12:13 269
Why saidst thou, She is my *s* Gen 12:19 269
of Sarah his wife, She is my *s* Gen 20:2 269
Said he not unto me, She is my *s* Gen 20:5 269
And yet indeed she is my *s* Gen 20:12 269
heard the words of Rebekah his *s* Gen 24:30 269
And they sent away Rebekah their *s* Gen 24:59 269
and said unto her, Thou art our *s* Gen 24:60 269
the *s* to Laban the Syrian Gen 25:20 269
and he said, She is my *s* Gen 26:7 269
and how saidst thou, She is my *s* Gen 26:9 269
the *s* of Nebajoth, to be his wife Gen 28:9 269
no children, Rachel envied her *s* Gen 30:1 269
have I wrestled with my *s* Gen 30:8 269
he had defiled Dinah their *s* Gen 34:13 269
to give our *s* to one that is Gen 34:14 269
because they had defiled their *s* Gen 34:27 269
deal with our *s* as with an harlot Gen 34:31 269
Ishmael's daughter, *s* of Nebajoth Gen 36:3 269
and Lotan's *s* was Timna Gen 36:22 269
Isui, and Beriah, and Serah their *s* Gen 46:17 269
his *s* stood afar off, to wit what Ex 2:4 269
Then said his *s* to Pharaoh's Ex 2:7 269
Jochebed his father's *s* to wife Ex 6:20 1733
Amminadab, *s* of Naashon, to wife Ex 6:23 269
the *s* of Aaron, took a timbrel in Ex 15:20 269
The nakedness of thy *s*, the Lev 18:9 269
of thy father, she is thy *s* Lev 18:11 269
the nakedness of thy father's *s* Lev 18:12 269
the nakedness of thy mother's *s* Lev 18:13 269
shalt thou take a wife to her *s* Lev 18:18 269
And if a man shall take his *s* Lev 20:17 269
the nakedness of thy mother's *s* Lev 20:19 269
nor of thy father's *s* Lev 20:19 269
for his *s* a virgin, that is nigh Lev 21:3 269
for his brother, or for his *s* Num 6:7 269
of a prince of Midian, their *s* Num 25:18 269
Aaron and Moses, and Miriam their *s* Num 26:59 269
be he that lieth with his *s* Deut 27:22 269
not her younger *s* fairer than she Judg 15:2 269
thy *s* in law is gone back unto Ruth 1:15 2994
return thou after thy *s* in law Ruth 1:15 2994
the son of David had a fair *s* 2Sa 13:1 269
that he fell sick for his *s* Tamar 2Sa 13:2 269
Tamar, my brother Absalom's *s* 2Sa 13:4 269
let my *s* Tamar come, and give me 2Sa 13:5 269
I pray thee, let Tamar my *s* come 2Sa 13:6 269
unto her, Come lie with me, my *s* 2Sa 13:11 269
but hold now thy peace, my *s* 2Sa 13:20 269
because he had forced his *s* Tamar 2Sa 13:22 269
day that he forced his *s* Tamar 2Sa 13:32 269
s to Zeruiah Joab's mother 2Sa 17:25 269
him to wife the *s* of his own wife 1Kin 11:19 269
the *s* of Tahpenes the queen 1Kin 11:19 269
the *s* of Tahpenes bare him 1Kin 11:20 269
s of Ahaziah, took Joash the son 2Kin 11:2 269
and Timna was Lotan's *s* 1Chr 1:39 269
the concubines, and Tamar their *s* 1Chr 3:9 269
and Hananiah, and Shelomith their *s* 1Chr 3:19 269
name of their *s* was Hazelelponi 1Chr 4:3 269
of his wife Hodiah the *s* of Naham 1Chr 4:19 269
took to wife the *s* of Huppim 1Chr 7:15 269
his *s* Hammoleketh bare Ishod, and 1Chr 7:18 269
and Beriah, and Serah their *s* 1Chr 7:30 269
and Hotham, and Shua their *s* 1Chr 7:32 269
(for she was the *s* of Ahaziah 2Chr 22:11 269
worm, Thou art my mother, and my *s* Job 17:14 269
Say unto wisdom, Thou art my *s* Prov 7:4 269
Thou hast ravished my heart, my *s* Song 4:9 269
How fair is thy love, my *s* Song 4:10 269
A garden inclosed is my *s* Song 4:12 269
I am come into my garden, my *s* Song 5:1 269
saying, Open to me, my *s* Song 5:2 269
We have a little *s*, and she hath Song 8:8 269
what shall we do for our *s* in the Song 8:8 269
And her treacherous *s* Judah saw it Jer 3:7 269
treacherous *s* Judah feared not Jer 3:8 269
for all this her treacherous *s* Jer 3:10 269
my brother! or, Ah *s*! Jer 22:18 269
thou art the *s* of thy sisters, Eze 16:45 269
And thine elder *s* is Samaria Eze 16:46 269
and thy younger *s*, that dwelleth Eze 16:46 269
Sodom thy *s* hath not done, she Eze 16:48 269
was the iniquity of thy *s* Sodom Eze 16:49 269
For thy *s* Sodom was not mentioned Eze 16:56 269
in thee hath humbled his *s* Eze 22:11 269
the elder, and Aholibah her *s* Eze 23:4 269
when her *s* Aholibah saw this, she Eze 23:11 269
more than her *s* in her whoredoms Eze 23:11 269
my mind was alienated from her *s* Eze 23:18 269
hast walked in the way of thy *s* Eze 23:31 269
with the cup of thy *s* Samaria Eze 23:33 269
or for *s* that hath had no husband Eze 44:25 269
the same is my brother, and *s* Mt 12:50 *79*
the same is my brother, and my *s* Mk 3:35 *79*
she had a *s* called Mary, which Lk 10:39 *79*
dost thou not care that my *s* hath Lk 10:40 *79*
the town of Mary and her *s* Martha Jn 11:1 *79*
Now Jesus loved Martha, and her *s* Jn 11:5 *79*
and called Mary her *s* secretly Jn 11:28 *79*
the *s* of him that was dead, saith Jn 11:39 *79*
his mother, and his mother's *s* Jn 19:25 *79*
I commend unto you Phebe our *s* Rom 16:1 *79*
and Julia, Nereus, and his *s* Rom 16:15 *79*
A brother or a *s* is not under 1Cor 7:15 *79*
we not power to lead about a *s* 1Cor 9:5 *79*
If a brother or *s* be naked Jas 2:15 *79*
of thy elect *s* greet thee 2Jn 13 *79*

SISTER'S {7}
and bracelets upon his *s* hands Gen 24:30 269
the tidings of Jacob his *s* son Gen 29:13 269
he hath uncovered his *s* nakedness Lev 20:17 269
Shuppim, whose *s* name was Maachah 1Chr 7:15 269
shalt drink of thy *s* cup deep Eze 23:32 269
when Paul's *s* son heard of their Acts 23:16 *79*
s son to Barnabas, (touching whom Col 4:10 *431*

SISTERS {19}
mother, and my brethren, and my *s* Josh 2:13 269
Whose *s* were Zeruiah, and Abigail 1Chr 2:16 269
called for their three *s* to eat Job 1:4 269
all his brethren, and all his *s* Job 42:11 269
and thou art the sister of thy *s* Eze 16:45 269
hast justified thy *s* in all thine Eze 16:51 269
also, which hast judged thy *s* Eze 16:52 269
in that thou hast justified thy *s* Eze 16:52 269
When thy *s*, Sodom and her Eze 16:55 269
when thou shalt receive thy *s* Eze 16:61 269
and to your *s*, Ruhamah Hos 2:1 269
And his *s*, are they not all with Mt 13:56 *79*
houses, or brethren, or *s* Mt 19:29 *79*
are not his *s* here with us Mk 6:3 *79*
left house, or brethren, or *s* Mk 10:29 *79*
time, houses, and brethren, and *s* Mk 10:30 *79*
and children, and brethren, and *s* Lk 14:26 *79*

Therefore his *s* sent unto him	Jn 11:3	*79*
the younger as *s*, with all purity	1Ti 5:2	*79*

SIT {113}

arise, I pray thee, *s* and eat of	Gen 27:19	3427
go to war, and shall ye *s* here	Num 32:6	3427
ye that *s* in judgment, and walk by	Judg 5:10	3427
S still, my daughter, until thou	Ruth 3:18	3427
turn aside, *s* down here	Ruth 4:1	3427
the city, and said, *S* ye down here	Ruth 4:2	3427
made them *s* in the chiefest place	1Sa 9:22	5414
for we will not *s* down till he	1Sa 16:11	5437
I should not fail to *s* with the	1Sa 20:5	3427
the king doth *s* in the gate	2Sa 19:8	3427
he shall *s* upon my throne	1Kin 1:13	3427
he shall *s* upon my throne	1Kin 1:17	3427
s on the throne of my lord the	1Kin 1:20	3427
he shall *s* upon my throne	1Kin 1:24	3427
who should *s* on the throne of my	1Kin 1:27	3427
he shall *s* upon my throne in my	1Kin 1:30	3427
he may come and *s* upon my throne	1Kin 1:35	3427
one to *s* on my throne this day	1Kin 1:48	3427
him a son to *s* on his throne	1Kin 3:6	3427
s on the throne of Israel, as the	1Kin 8:20	3427
to *s* on the throne of Israel	1Kin 8:25	3427
Why *s* we here until we die	2Kin 7:3	3427
if we *s* still here, we die also	2Kin 7:4	3427
shall *s* on the throne of Israel	2Kin 10:30	3427
Thy sons shall *s* on the throne of	2Kin 15:12	3427
me to the men which *s* on the wall	2Kin 18:27	3427
hath chosen Solomon my son to *s*	1Chr 28:5	3427
to *s* upon the throne of Israel	2Chr 6:16	3427
will not *s* with the wicked	Ps 26:5	3427
They that *s* in the gate speak	Ps 69:12	3427
Such as *s* in darkness and in the	Ps 107:10	3427
S thou at my right hand, until I	Ps 110:1	3427
Princes also did *s* and speak	Ps 119:23	3427
to *s* up late, to eat the bread of	Ps 127:2	3427
their children shall also *s* upon	Ps 132:12	3427
and the rich *s* in low place	Eccl 10:6	3427
desolate shall *s* upon the ground	Is 3:26	3427
I will *s* also upon the mount of	Is 14:13	3427
he shall *s* upon it in truth in	Is 16:5	3427
Their strength is to *s* still	Is 30:7	7674
to the men that *s* upon the wall	Is 36:12	3427
them that *s* in darkness out of	Is 42:7	3427
s in the dust, O virgin daughter	Is 47:1	3427
of Babylon, *s* on the ground	Is 47:1	3427
S thou silent, and get thee into	Is 47:5	3427
I shall not *s* as a widow, neither	Is 47:8	3427
warm at, nor fire to *s* before it	Is 47:14	3427
arise, and *s* down, O Jerusalem	Is 52:2	3427
Why do we *s* still	Jer 8:14	3427
kings that *s* upon David's throne	Jer 13:13	3427
queen, Humble yourselves, *s* down	Jer 13:18	3427
to *s* with them to eat and to drink	Jer 16:8	3427
s upon the throne of the house of	Jer 33:17	3427
S down now, and read it in our	Jer 36:15	3427
He shall have none to *s* upon the	Jer 36:30	3427
from thy glory, and *s* in thirst	Jer 48:18	3427
How doth the city *s* solitary	Lam 1:1	3427
of Zion *s* upon the ground	Lam 2:10	3427
they shall *s* upon the ground, and	Eze 26:16	3427
I *s* in the seat of God, in the	Eze 28:2	3427
they *s* before thee as my people,	Eze 33:31	3427
he shall *s* in it to eat bread	Eze 44:3	3427
and the Ancient of days did *s*	Dan 7:9	3488
But the judgment shall *s*, and they	Dan 7:26	3488
for there will I *s* to judge all	Joel 3:12	3427
But they shall *s* every man under	Mic 4:4	3427
when I *s* in darkness, the LORD	Mic 7:8	3427
and thy fellows that *s* before thee	Zec 3:8	3427
shall bear the glory, and shall *s*	Zec 6:13	3427
he shall *s* as a refiner and	Mal 3:3	3427
shall *s* down with Abraham, and	Mt 8:11	*347*
multitude to *s* down on the grass	Mt 14:19	*347*
multitude to *s* down on the ground	Mt 15:35	*377*
when the Son of man shall *s* in	Mt 19:28	*2523*
ye also shall *s* upon twelve	Mt 19:28	*2523*
that these my two sons may *s*	Mt 20:21	*2523*
but to *s* on my right hand, and on	Mt 20:23	*2523*
S thou on my right hand, till I	Mt 22:44	*2521*
the Pharisees *s* in Moses' seat	Mt 23:2	*2523*
then shall he *s* upon the throne	Mt 25:31	*2523*
S ye here, while I go and pray	Mt 26:36	*2523*
all *s* down by companies upon the	Mk 6:39	*347*
people to *s* down on the ground	Mk 8:6	*377*
him, Grant unto us that we may *s*	Mk 10:37	*2523*
But to *s* on my right hand and on	Mk 10:40	*2523*
S thou on my right hand, till I	Mk 12:36	*2521*
S ye here, while I shall pray	Mk 14:32	*2523*
light to them that *s* in darkness	Lk 1:79	*2521*
Make them *s* down by fifties in a	Lk 9:14	*2625*
did so, and made them all *s* down	Lk 9:15	*347*
and make them to *s* down to meat	Lk 12:37	*347*
shall *s* down in the kingdom of	Lk 13:29	*347*
s not down in the highest room	Lk 14:8	*2625*
s down in the lowest room	Lk 14:10	*377*
of them that *s* at meat with thee	Lk 14:10	*4873*
s down quickly, and write fifty	Lk 16:6	*2523*
the field, Go and *s* down to meat	Lk 17:7	*377*
my Lord, *S* thou on my right hand,	Lk 20:42	*2521*
s on thrones judging the twelve	Lk 22:30	*2523*
s on the right hand of the power	Lk 22:69	*2521*
Jesus said, Make the men *s* down	Jn 6:10	*377*
up Christ to *s* on his throne	Acts 2:30	*2523*
my Lord, *S* thou on my right hand,	Acts 2:34	*2521*
he would come up and *s* with him	Acts 8:31	*2523*
s at meat in the idol's temple	1Cor 8:10	*2621*
made us *s* together in heavenly	Eph 2:6	*4776*
S on my right hand, until I make	Heb 1:13	*2521*
S thou here in a good place	Jas 2:3	*2521*
or *s* here under my footstool	Jas 2:3	*2521*
I grant to *s* with me in my throne	Rev 3:21	*2523*
I saw a woman *s* upon a scarlet	Rev 17:3	*2521*
I *s* a queen, and am no widow, and	Rev 18:7	*2521*
horses, and of them that *s* on them	Rev 19:18	*2521*

SITH {1} *See also* SINCE.

s thou hast not hated blood, even	Eze 35:6	518

SITHRI See ZITHRI.

SITNAH *(sit'-nah)* {1} *A well near Gerar.*

and he called the name of it *S*	Gen 26:21	7856

SITTEST {7}

why *s* thou thyself alone, and all	Ex 18:14	3427
them when thou *s* in thine house	Deut 6:7	3427
them when thou *s* in thine house	Deut 11:19	3427
Thou *s* and speakest against thy	Ps 50:20	3427
When thou *s* to eat with a ruler,	Prov 23:1	3427
that *s* upon the throne of David,	Jer 22:2	3427
for *s* thou to judge me after the	Acts 23:3	*2521*

SITTETH {42}

of Pharaoh that *s* upon his throne	Ex 11:5	3427
and every thing, whereon he *s*	Lev 15:4	3427
he that *s* on any thing whereon he	Lev 15:6	3427
that she *s* upon shall be unclean	Lev 15:20	3427
or on any thing whereon she *s*	Lev 15:23	3427
whatsoever she *s* upon shall be	Lev 15:26	3427
when he *s* upon the throne of his	Deut 17:18	3427
also Solomon *s* on the throne of	1Kin 1:46	3427
that *s* at the king's gate	Est 6:10	3427
nor *s* in the seat of the scornful	Ps 1:1	3427
He that *s* in the heavens shall	Ps 2:4	3427
He *s* in the lurking places of the	Ps 10:8	3427
The LORD *s* upon the flood	Ps 29:10	3427
yea, the LORD *s* King for ever	Ps 29:10	3427
God *s* upon the throne of his	Ps 47:8	3427
he *s* between the cherubims	Ps 99:1	3427
For she *s* at the door of her	Prov 9:14	3427
A king that *s* in the throne of	Prov 20:8	3427
when he *s* among the elders of the	Prov 31:23	3427
While the king *s* at his table	Song 1:12	
to him that *s* in judgment	Is 28:6	3427
It is he that *s* upon the circle	Is 40:22	3427
As the partridge *s* on eggs	Jer 17:11	1716
that *s* upon the throne of David	Jer 29:16	3427
He *s* alone and keepeth silence,	Lam 3:28	3427
and, behold, all the earth *s* still	Zec 1:11	3427
this is a woman that *s* in the	Zec 5:7	3427
of God, and by him that *s* thereon	Mt 23:22	*2521*
s not down first, and counteth the	Lk 14:28	*2523*
s not down first, and consulteth	Lk 14:31	*2523*
is greater, he that *s* at meat	Lk 22:27	*345*
is not he that *s* at meat	Lk 22:27	*345*
be revealed to another that *s* by	1Cor 14:30	*2521*
where Christ *s* on the right hand	Col 3:1	*2521*
so that he as God *s* in the temple	2Th 2:4	*2523*
unto him that *s* upon the throne	Rev 5:13	*2521*
face of him that *s* on the throne	Rev 6:16	*2521*
our God which *s* upon the throne	Rev 7:10	*2521*
he that *s* on the throne shall	Rev 7:15	*2521*
whore that *s* upon many waters	Rev 17:1	*2521*
mountains, on which the woman *s*	Rev 17:9	*2521*
thou sawest, where the whore *s*	Rev 17:15	*2521*

SITTING {43}

the dam *s* upon the young, or upon	Deut 22:6	7257
he was *s* in a summer parlour,	Judg 3:20	3427
the *s* of his servants, and the	1Kin 10:5	4186
God, and found him *s* under an oak	1Kin 13:14	3427
I saw the LORD *s* on his throne	1Kin 22:19	3427
of the prophets were *s* before him	2Kin 4:38	3427
the captains of the host were *s*	2Kin 9:5	3427
the *s* of his servants, and the	2Chr 9:4	4186
stays on each side of the *s* place	2Chr 9:18	3427
I saw the LORD *s* upon his throne,	2Chr 18:18	3427
unto me, (the queen also *s* by him	Neh 2:6	3427
the Jew *s* at the king's gate	Est 5:13	3427
saw also the Lord *s* upon a throne	Is 6:1	3427
princes *s* upon the throne of	Jer 17:25	3427
kings *s* upon the throne of David	Jer 22:4	3427
s upon the throne of David, and	Jer 22:30	3427
the king then *s* in the gate of	Jer 38:7	3427
Behold their *s* down, and their	Lam 3:63	3427
s at the receipt of custom	Mt 9:9	*2521*
unto children *s* in the markets	Mt 11:16	*2521*
two blind men *s* by the way side,	Mt 20:30	*2521*
s upon an ass, and a colt the foal	Mt 21:5	*1910*
man *s* on the right hand of power	Mt 26:64	*2521*
s down they watched him there	Mt 27:36	*2521*
s over against the sepulchre	Mt 27:61	*2521*
certain of the scribes *s* there	Mk 2:6	*2521*
s at the receipt of custom	Mk 2:14	*2521*
the devil, and had the legion, *s*	Mk 5:15	*2521*
man *s* on the right hand of power	Mk 14:62	*2521*
a young man *s* on the right side	Mk 16:5	*2521*
s in the midst of the doctors,	Lk 2:46	*2516*
and doctors of the law *s* by	Lk 5:17	*2521*
s at the receipt of custom	Lk 5:27	*2521*
children *s* in the marketplace	Lk 7:32	*2521*
s at the feet of Jesus, clothed,	Lk 8:35	*2521*
repented, *s* in sackcloth and ashes	Lk 10:13	*2521*
doves, and the changers of money *s*	Jn 2:14	*2521*
King cometh, *s* on an ass's colt	Jn 12:15	*2521*
And seeth two angels in white *s*	Jn 20:12	*2516*
all the house where they were *s*	Acts 2:2	*2521*
s in his chariot read Esaias the	Acts 8:28	*2521*
the next day *s* on the judgment	Acts 25:6	*2523*
I saw four and twenty elders *s*	Rev 4:4	*2521*

SITUATE {3}

The forefront of the one was *s*	1Sa 14:5	4690
O thou that art *s* at the entry of	Eze 27:3	3427
that was *s* among the rivers, that	Nah 3:8	3427

SITUATION {2}

the *s* of this city is pleasant,	2Kin 2:19	4186
Beautiful for *s*, the joy of the	Ps 48:2	5131

SIVAN *(si'-van)* {1} *Third month of the Hebrew year.*

third month, that is, the month *S*	Est 8:9	5510

SIX {202}

Noah was *s* hundred years old when	Gen 7:6	8337
In the *s* hundredth year of Noah's	Gen 7:11	8337
came to pass in the *s* hundredth	Gen 8:13	8337
s years old, when Hagar bare	Gen 16:16	8337
because I have born him *s* sons	Gen 30:20	8337
and *s* years for thy cattle	Gen 31:41	8337
the souls were threescore and *s*	Gen 46:26	8337
about *s* hundred thousand on foot	Ex 12:37	8337
he took *s* hundred chosen chariots	Ex 14:7	8337
S days ye shall gather it	Ex 16:26	8337
S days shalt thou labour, and do	Ex 20:9	8337
For in *s* days the LORD made	Ex 20:11	8337
servant, *s* years he shall serve	Ex 21:2	8337
s years thou shalt sow thy land,	Ex 23:10	8337
S days thou shalt do thy work, and	Ex 23:12	8337
and the cloud covered it *s* days	Ex 24:16	8337
s branches shall come out of the	Ex 25:32	8337
so in the *s* branches that come	Ex 25:33	8337
according to the *s* branches that	Ex 25:35	8337
s curtains by themselves, and	Ex 26:9	8337
westward thou shalt make *s* boards	Ex 26:22	8337
S of their names on one stone, and	Ex 28:10	8337
the other *s* names of the rest on	Ex 28:10	8337
S days may work be done	Ex 31:15	8337
for in *s* days the LORD made	Ex 31:17	8337
S days thou shalt work, but on	Ex 34:21	8337
S days shall work be done, but on	Ex 35:2	8337
and *s* curtains by themselves	Ex 36:16	8337
westward he made *s* boards	Ex 36:27	8337
s branches going out of the sides	Ex 37:18	8337
so throughout the *s* branches	Ex 37:19	8337
according to the *s* branches going	Ex 37:21	8337
for *s* hundred thousand and three	Ex 38:26	8337
purifying threescore and *s* days	Lev 12:5	8337
S days shall work be done	Lev 23:3	8337
s on a row, upon the pure table	Lev 24:6	8337
S years thou shalt sow thy field,	Lev 25:3	8337
s years thou shalt prune thy	Lev 25:3	8337
s thousand and five hundred	Num 1:21	8337
forty and five thousand and *s* hundred	Num 1:25	8337
and fourteen thousand and *s* hundred	Num 1:27	8337
numbered were *s* hundred thousand	Num 1:46	8337
and fourteen thousand and *s* hundred	Num 2:4	8337
s thousand and four hundred,	Num 2:9	8337
s thousand and five hundred	Num 2:11	8337
thousand and *s* hundred and fifty	Num 2:15	8337
and seven thousand and *s* hundred	Num 2:31	8337
hosts were *s* hundred thousand	Num 2:32	8337
s hundred, keeping the charge of	Num 3:28	8337
were *s* thousand and two hundred	Num 3:34	8337
thousand and *s* hundred and thirty	Num 4:40	8337
s covered wagons, and twelve oxen	Num 7:3	8337
are *s* hundred thousand footmen	Num 11:21	8337
and five thousand and *s* hundred	Num 26:41	8337
s hundred thousand and a thousand	Num 26:51	8337
was *s* hundred thousand and seventy	Num 31:32	8337
of the sheep was *s* hundred	Num 31:37	8337
beeves were thirty and *s* thousand	Num 31:38	8337
And thirty and *s* thousand beeves,	Num 31:44	8337
shall be *s* cities for refuge	Num 35:6	8337
cities which ye shall give *s*	Num 35:13	8337
These *s* cities shall be a refuge,	Num 35:15	8337
S days thou shalt labour, and do	Deut 5:13	8337
unto thee, and serve thee *s* years	Deut 15:12	8337
to thee, in serving thee *s* years	Deut 15:18	8337
S days thou shalt eat unleavened	Deut 16:8	8337
Thus shalt thou do *s* days	Josh 6:3	8337
so they did *s* days	Josh 6:14	8337
of them about thirty and *s* men	Josh 7:5	8337
s cities with their villages	Josh 15:59	8337
s cities with their villages	Josh 15:62	8337
s hundred men with an ox goad	Judg 3:31	8337
And Jephthah judged Israel *s* years	Judg 12:7	8337
s hundred men appointed with	Judg 18:11	8337
the *s* hundred men appointed with	Judg 18:16	8337
entering of the gate with the *s*	Judg 18:17	8337
s thousand men that drew sword,	Judg 20:15	8337
But *s* hundred men turned and fled	Judg 20:47	8337
he measured *s* measures of barley,	Ruth 3:15	8337
These *s* measures of barley gave	Ruth 3:17	8337
s thousand horsemen, and people as	1Sa 13:5	8337
with him, about *s* hundred men	1Sa 13:15	8337
with him were about *s* hundred men	1Sa 14:2	8337
Gath, whose height was *s* cubits	1Sa 17:4	8337
weighed *s* hundred shekels of iron	1Sa 17:7	8337
men, which were about *s* hundred	1Sa 23:13	8337
he passed over with the *s* hundred	1Sa 27:2	8337
the *s* hundred men that were with	1Sa 30:9	8337
Judah was seven years and *s* months	2Sa 2:11	8337
Judah seven years and *s* months	2Sa 5:5	8337
ark of the LORD had gone *s* paces	2Sa 6:13	8337
s hundred men which came after	2Sa 15:18	8337
that had on every hand *s* fingers	2Sa 21:20	8337

fingers, and on every foot *s* toes ... 2Sa 21:20 8337
and the middle was *s* cubits broad ... 1Kin 6:6 8337
one year was *s* hundred threescore ... 1Kin 10:14 8337
threescore and *s* talents of gold, ... 1Kin 10:14 8337
s hundred shekels of gold went to ... 1Kin 10:16 8337
The throne had *s* steps, and the ... 1Kin 10:19 8337
and on the other upon the *s* steps ... 1Kin 10:20 8337
went out of Egypt for *s* hundred ... 1Kin 10:29 8337
(For *s* months did Joab remain ... 1Kin 11:16 8337
s years reigned he in Tirzah ... 1Kin 16:23 8337
s thousand pieces of gold, and ten ... 2Kin 5:5 8337
in the house of the LORD *s* years ... 2Kin 11:3 8337
have smitten five or *s* times ... 2Kin 13:19 8337
over Israel in Samaria *s* months ... 2Kin 15:8 8337
These *s* were born unto him in ... 1Chr 3:4 8337
reigned seven years and *s* months ... 1Chr 3:4 8337
Bariah, and Neariah, and Shaphat, *s* ... 1Chr 3:22 8337
had sixteen sons and *s* daughters ... 1Chr 4:27 8337
and twenty thousand and *s* hundred ... 1Chr 7:2 8337
were bands of soldiers for war, *s* ... 1Chr 7:4 8337
was twenty and *s* thousand men ... 1Chr 7:40 8337
And Azel had *s* sons, whose names ... 1Chr 8:38 8337
brethren, *s* hundred and ninety ... 1Chr 9:6 8337
nine hundred and fifty and *s* ... 1Chr 9:9 8337
And Azel had *s* sons, whose names ... 1Chr 9:44 8337
shield and spear were *s* thousand ... 1Chr 12:24 8337
Levi four thousand and *s* hundred ... 1Chr 12:26 8337
and eight thousand and *s* hundred ... 1Chr 12:35 8337
s on each hand, and *s* on each ... 1Chr 20:6 8337
s hundred shekels of gold by ... 1Chr 21:25 8337
s thousand were officers and ... 1Chr 23:4 8337
Hashabiah, and Mattithiah, *s* ... 1Chr 25:3 8337
Eastward were *s* Levites, ... 1Chr 26:17 8337
for *s* hundred shekels of silver ... 2Chr 1:17 8337
s hundred to oversee them ... 2Chr 2:2 8337
and three thousand and *s* hundred ... 2Chr 2:17 8337
s hundred overseers to set the ... 2Chr 2:18 8337
amounting to *s* hundred talents ... 2Chr 3:8 8337
Solomon in one year was *s* hundred ... 2Chr 9:13 8337
threescore and *s* talents of gold ... 2Chr 9:13 8337
s hundred shekels of beaten gold ... 2Chr 9:15 8337
there were *s* steps to the throne, ... 2Chr 9:18 8337
and on the other upon the *s* steps ... 2Chr 9:19 8337
In the *s* and thirtieth year of the ... 2Chr 16:1 8337
hid in the house of God *s* years ... 2Chr 22:12 8337
were two thousand and *s* hundred ... 2Chr 26:12 8337
things were *s* hundred oxen ... 2Chr 29:33 8337
s hundred small cattle, and three ... 2Chr 35:8 8337
of Bani, *s* hundred forty and two ... Ezr 2:10 8337
s hundred twenty and three ... Ezr 2:11 8337
Adonikam, *s* hundred sixty and *s* ... Ezr 2:13 8337
Bigvai, two thousand fifty and *s* ... Ezr 2:14 8337
The men of Netophah, fifty and *s* ... Ezr 2:22 8337
and Gaba, *s* hundred twenty and one ... Ezr 2:26 8337
of Magbish, an hundred fifty and *s* ... Ezr 2:30 8337
thousand and *s* hundred and thirty ... Ezr 2:35 8337
of Nekoda, *s* hundred fifty and two ... Ezr 2:60 8337
were seven hundred thirty and *s* ... Ezr 2:66 8337
s thousand seven hundred and ... Ezr 2:67 8337
weighed unto their hand *s* hundred ... Ezr 8:26 8337
s rams, seventy and seven lambs, ... Ezr 8:35 8337
was one ox and *s* choice sheep ... Neh 5:18 8337
of Arah, *s* hundred fifty and two ... Neh 7:10 8337
Binnui, *s* hundred forty and eight ... Neh 7:15 8337
s hundred twenty and eight ... Neh 7:16 8337
s hundred threescore and seven ... Neh 7:18 8337
of Adin, *s* hundred fifty and five ... Neh 7:20 8337
and Gaba, *s* hundred twenty and one ... Neh 7:30 8337
of Nekoda, *s* hundred forty and two ... Neh 7:62 8337
horses, seven hundred thirty and *s* ... Neh 7:68 8337
s thousand seven hundred and ... Neh 7:69 8337
s months with oil of myrrh, and ... Est 2:12 8337
s months with sweet odours, and ... Est 2:12 8337
shall deliver thee in *s* troubles ... Job 5:19 8337
s thousand camels, and a thousand ... Job 42:12 8337
These *s* things doth the LORD hate ... Prov 6:16 8337
each one had *s* wings ... Is 6:2 8337
when he hath served thee *s* years ... Jer 34:14 8337
and *s* pomegranates on a side ... Jer 52:23 8337
were four thousand and *s* hundred ... Jer 52:30 8337
s men came from the way of the ... Eze 9:2 8337
of *s* cubits long by the cubit ... Eze 40:5 8337
were *s* cubits on this side ... Eze 40:12 8337
and *s* cubits on that side ... Eze 40:12 8337
s cubits broad on the one side, ... Eze 41:1 8337
s cubits broad on the other side, ... Eze 41:1 8337
and the door, *s* cubits ... Eze 41:3 8337
the wall of the house, *s* cubits ... Eze 41:5 8337
a full reed of *s* great cubits ... Eze 41:8 8337
shall be shut the *s* working days ... Eze 46:1 8337
shall be *s* lambs without blemish ... Eze 46:4 8337
blemish, and *s* lambs, and a ram ... Eze 46:6 8337
and the breadth thereof *s* cubits ... Dan 3:1 8353
after *s* days Jesus taketh Peter, ... Mt 17:1 *1803*
after *s* days Jesus taketh with ... Mk 9:2 *1803*
s months, when great famine was ... Lk 4:25 *1803*
There are *s* days in which men ... Lk 13:14 *1803*
set there *s* waterpots of stone ... Jn 2:6 *1803*
s years was this temple in ... Jn 2:20 *1803*
Then Jesus *s* days before the ... Jn 12:1 *1803*
Moreover these *s* brethren ... Acts 11:12 *1803*
s months, teaching the word of ... Acts 18:11 *1803*
space of three years and *s* months ... Jas 5:17 *1803*
each of them *s* wings about him ... Rev 4:8 *1803*
is *s* hundred threescore and *s* ... Rev 13:18 *5516*
a thousand and *s* hundred furlongs ... Rev 14:20 *1812*

SIXSCORE {2}
to the king *s* talents of gold ... 1Kin 9:14 3967,6242
are more than *s* thousand ... Jonah 4:11 8147,6240,7239

SIXTEEN {23}
she bare unto Jacob, even *s* souls ... Gen 46:18 8337,6240
sockets of silver, *s* sockets ... Ex 26:25 8337,6240
sockets were *s* sockets of silver ... Ex 36:30 8337,6240
s thousand and five hundred ... Num 26:22 8337,6240
And the persons were *s* thousand ... Num 31:40 8337,6240
And *s* thousand persons ... Num 31:46 8337,6240
was *s* thousand seven hundred ... Num 31:52 8337,6240
s cities with their villages ... Josh 15:41 8337,6240
s cities with their villages ... Josh 19:22 8337,6240
in Samaria, and reigned *s* years ... 2Kin 13:10 8337,6240
Azariah, which was *s* years old ... 2Kin 14:21 8337,6240
S years old was he when he began ... 2Kin 15:2 8337,6240
he reigned *s* years in Jerusalem ... 2Kin 15:33 8337,6240
reigned *s* years in Jerusalem, and ... 2Kin 16:2 8337,6240
And Shimei had *s* sons and six ... 1Chr 4:27 8337,6240
the sons of Eleazar there were *s* ... 1Chr 24:4 8337,6240
and two sons, and *s* daughters ... 2Chr 13:21 8337,6240
was *s* years old, and made him ... 2Chr 26:1 8337,6240
S years old was Uzziah when he ... 2Chr 26:3 8337,6240
he reigned *s* years in Jerusalem ... 2Chr 27:1 8337,6240
reigned *s* years in Jerusalem ... 2Chr 27:8 8337,6240
he reigned *s* years in Jerusalem ... 2Chr 28:1 8337,6240
two hundred threescore and *s* ... Acts 27:37 *1440,1803*

SIXTEENTH {3}
to Bilgah, the *s* to Immer, ... 1Chr 24:14 8337,6240
The *s* to Hananiah, he, his sons, ... 1Chr 25:23 8337,6240
in the *s* day of the first month ... 2Chr 29:17 8337,6240

SIXTH {47}
and the morning were the *s* day ... Gen 1:31 8345
again, and bare Jacob the *s* son ... Gen 30:19 8345
that on the *s* day they shall ... Ex 16:5 8345
that on the *s* day they gathered ... Ex 16:22 8345
the *s* day the bread of two days ... Ex 16:29 8345
shalt double the *s* curtain in the ... Ex 26:9 8345
blessing upon you in the *s* year ... Lev 25:21 8345
On the *s* day Eliasaph the son of ... Num 7:42 8345
on the *s* day eight bullocks, two ... Num 29:29 8345
The *s* lot came out to the ... Josh 19:32 8345
And the *s*, Ithream, by Eglah ... 2Sa 3:5 8345
s year of Asa king of Judah began ... 1Kin 16:8 8337
even in the *s* year of Hezekiah, ... 2Kin 18:10 8337
Ozem the *s*, David the seventh ... 1Chr 2:15 8345
the *s*, Ithream by Eglah his wife ... 1Chr 3:3 8345
Attai the *s*, Eliel the seventh, ... 1Chr 12:11 8345
to Malchijah, the *s* to Mijamin, ... 1Chr 24:9 8345
The *s* to Bukkiah, he, his sons, ... 1Chr 25:13 8345
Elam the fifth, Jehohanan the *s* ... 1Chr 26:3 8345
Ammiel the *s*, Issachar the ... 1Chr 26:5 8345
The *s* captain for the *s* month ... 1Chr 27:9 8345
which was in the *s* year of the ... Ezr 6:15 8353
Hanun the *s* son of Zalaph, ... Neh 3:30 8345
by measure, the *s* part of an hin ... Eze 4:11 8345
in the *s* year, in the *s* month ... Eze 8:1 8345
and leave but the *s* part of thee ... Eze 39:2 8338
the *s* part of an ephah of an ... Eze 45:13 8345
ye shall give the *s* part of an ... Eze 45:13 8341
the *s* part of an ephah, and the ... Eze 46:14 8345
Darius the king, in the *s* month ... Hag 1:1 8345
and twentieth day of the *s* month ... Hag 1:15 8345
Again he went out about the *s* ... Mt 20:5 *1623*
Now from the *s* hour there was ... Mt 27:45 *1623*
when the *s* hour was come, there ... Mk 15:33 *1623*
in the *s* month the angel Gabriel ... Lk 1:26 *1623*
this is the *s* month with her, who ... Lk 1:36 *1623*
And it was about the *s* hour ... Lk 23:44 *1623*
and it was about the *s* hour ... Jn 4:6 *1623*
the passover, and about the *s* hour ... Jn 19:14 *1623*
housetop to pray about the *s* hour ... Acts 10:9 *1623*
when he had opened the *s* seal ... Rev 6:12 *1623*
the *s* angel sounded, and I heard a ... Rev 9:13 *1623*
Saying to the *s* angel which had ... Rev 9:14 *1623*
the *s* angel poured out his vial ... Rev 16:12 *1623*
the *s*, sardius ... Rev 21:20 *1623*

SIXTY {15}
And Mahalaleel lived *s* and five ... Gen 5:15 8346
And Jared lived an hundred *s* ... Gen 5:18 8346
days of Jared were nine hundred *s* ... Gen 5:20 8346
And Enoch lived *s* and five years, ... Gen 5:21 8346
of Enoch were three hundred *s* ... Gen 5:23 8346
of Methuselah were nine hundred *s* ... Gen 5:27 8346
years old even unto *s* years old ... Lev 27:3 8346
And if it be from *s* years old ... Lev 27:7 8346
the rams *s*, the he goats *s* ... Num 7:88 8346
the lambs of the first year *s* ... Num 7:88 8346
of Adonikam, six hundred *s* ... Ezr 2:13 8346
some an hundredfold, some *s* ... Mt 13:23 *1835*
forth, some thirty, and some *s* ... Mk 4:8 *1835*
fruit, some thirtyfold, some *s* ... Mk 4:20 *1835*

SIXTYFOLD {1}
some an hundredfold, some *s* ... Mt 13:8 *1835*

SIYON See SION.

SIZE {5}
the curtains were all of one *s* ... Ex 36:9 4060
the eleven curtains were of one *s* ... Ex 36:15 4060
were of one measure and one *s* ... 1Kin 6:25 7095
casting, one measure, and one *s* ... 1Kin 7:37 7095
and for all manner of measure and *s* ... 1Chr 23:29 4060

SKIES {5}
waters, and thick clouds of the *s* ... 2Sa 22:12 7834
waters and thick clouds of the *s* ... Ps 18:11 7834
the *s* sent out a sound ... Ps 77:17 7834
let the *s* pour down righteousness ... Is 45:8 7834
and is lifted up even to the *s* ... Jer 51:9 7834

SKILFUL {7}
s in war, were four and forty ... 1Chr 5:18 3925
about the song, because he was *s* ... 1Chr 15:22 995
workmanship every willing *s* man ... 1Chr 28:21 2451
s to work in gold, and in silver, ... 2Chr 2:14 3045
of brutish men, and *s* to destroy ... Eze 21:31 2796
s in all wisdom, and cunning in ... Dan 1:4 7919
such as are *s* of lamentation to ... Amos 5:16 3045

SKILFULLY {1}
play *s* with a loud noise ... Ps 33:3 3190

SKILFULNESS {1}
guided them by the *s* of his hands ... Ps 78:72 8394

SKILL {7}
can *s* to hew timber like unto the ... 1Kin 5:6 3045
that can *s* to grave with the ... 2Chr 2:7 3045
can *s* to cut timber in Lebanon ... 2Chr 2:8 3045
all that could *s* of instruments ... 2Chr 34:12 995
nor yet favour to men of *s* ... Eccl 9:11 3045
s in all learning and wisdom ... Dan 1:17 7919
am now come forth to give thee *s* ... Dan 9:22 7919

SKIN {77}
only, it is his raiment for his *s* ... Ex 22:27 5785
flesh of the bullock, and his *s* ... Ex 29:14 5785
the *s* of his face shone while he ... Ex 34:29 5785
behold, the *s* of his face shone ... Ex 34:30 5785
that the *s* of Moses' face shone ... Ex 34:35 5785
the *s* of the bullock, and all his ... Lev 4:11 5785
shall have to himself the *s* of ... Lev 7:8 5785
vessel of wood, or raiment, or *s* ... Lev 11:32 5785
in the *s* of his flesh a rising ... Lev 13:2 5785
it be in the *s* of his flesh like ... Lev 13:2 5785
the plague in the *s* of the flesh ... Lev 13:3 5785
be deeper than the *s* of his flesh ... Lev 13:3 5785
be white in the *s* of his flesh ... Lev 13:4 5785
in sight be not deeper than the *s* ... Lev 13:4 5785
and the plague spread not in the *s* ... Lev 13:5 5785
and the plague spread not in the *s* ... Lev 13:6 5785
scab spread much abroad in the *s* ... Lev 13:7 5785
the scab spreadeth in the *s* ... Lev 13:8 5785
if the rising be white in the *s* ... Lev 13:10 5785
old leprosy in the *s* of his flesh ... Lev 13:11 5785
leprosy break out abroad in the *s* ... Lev 13:12 5785
the leprosy cover all the *s* of ... Lev 13:12 5785
in which, even in the *s* thereof ... Lev 13:18 5785
it be in sight lower than the *s* ... Lev 13:20 5785
and if it be not lower than the *s* ... Lev 13:21 5785
if it spread much abroad in the *s* ... Lev 13:22 5785
in the *s* whereof there is a hot ... Lev 13:24 5785
it be in sight deeper than the *s* ... Lev 13:25 5785
it be no lower than the other *s* ... Lev 13:26 5785
it be spread much abroad in the *s* ... Lev 13:27 5785
his place, and spread not in the *s* ... Lev 13:28 5785
it be in sight deeper than the *s* ... Lev 13:30 5785
be not in sight deeper than the *s* ... Lev 13:31 5785
be not in sight deeper than the *s* ... Lev 13:32 5785
the scall be not spread in the *s* ... Lev 13:34 5785
nor be in sight deeper than the *s* ... Lev 13:34 5785
much in the *s* after his cleansing ... Lev 13:35 5785
if the scall be spread in the *s* ... Lev 13:36 5785
the *s* of their flesh bright spots ... Lev 13:38 5785
if the bright spots in the *s* of ... Lev 13:39 5785
spot that groweth in the *s* ... Lev 13:39 5785
appeareth in the *s* of the flesh ... Lev 13:43 5785
a *s*, or in any thing made of *s* ... Lev 13:48 5785
in the garment, or in the *s* ... Lev 13:49 5785
in the woof, or in any thing of *s* ... Lev 13:49 5785
warp, or in the woof, or in a *s* ... Lev 13:51 5785
or in any work that is made of *s* ... Lev 13:51 5785
or in linen, or any thing of *s* ... Lev 13:52 5785
in the woof, or in any thing of *s* ... Lev 13:53 5785
of the garment, or out of the *s* ... Lev 13:56 5785
in the woof, or in any thing of *s* ... Lev 13:57 5785
or whatsoever thing of *s* it be ... Lev 13:58 5785
And every garment, and every *s* ... Lev 15:17 5785
her *s*, and her flesh, and her blood ... Num 19:5 5785
S for *s*, yea, all that a man ... Job 2:4 5785
my *s* is broken, and become ... Job 7:5 5785
Thou hast clothed me with *s* ... Job 10:11 5785
I have sewed sackcloth upon my *s* ... Job 16:15 1539
devour the strength of his *s* ... Job 18:13 5785
My bone cleaveth to my *s* and to my ... Job 19:20 5785
am escaped with the *s* of my teeth ... Job 19:20 5785
though after my *s* worms destroy ... Job 19:26 5785
My *s* is black upon me, and my ... Job 30:30 5785
thou fill his *s* with barbed irons ... Job 41:7 5785
groaning my bones cleave to my *s* ... Ps 102:5 1320
Can the Ethiopian change his *s* ... Jer 13:23 5785
My flesh and my *s* hath he made old ... Lam 3:4 5785
their *s* cleaveth to their bones ... Lam 4:8 5785
Our *s* was black like an oven ... Lam 5:10 5785
and shod thee with badgers' *s* ... Eze 16:10
upon you, and cover you with *s* ... Eze 37:6 5785
them, and the *s* covered them above ... Eze 37:8 5785
pluck off their *s* from off them ... Mic 3:2 5785
flay their *s* from off them ... Mic 3:3 5785
a girdle of a *s* about his loins ... Mk 1:6 *1193*

SKINS {24}
did the LORD God make coats of *s* ... Gen 3:21 5785
she put the *s* of the kids of the ... Gen 27:16 5785
s dyed red, and badgers' *s* ... Ex 25:5 5785
for the tent of rams' *s* dyed red ... Ex 26:14 5785
and a covering above of badgers' *s* ... Ex 26:14 5785
s dyed red, and badgers' *s* ... Ex 35:7 5785
red *s* of rams, and badgers' *s* ... Ex 35:23 5785

S

for the tent of rams' *s* dyed red ... Ex 36:19 5785
covering of badgers' *s* above that ... Ex 36:19 5785
the covering of rams' *s* dyed red ... Ex 39:34 5785
and the covering of badgers' *s* ... Ex 39:34 5785
warp, or woof, or any thing of *s* ... Lev 13:59 5785
shall burn in the fire their *s* ... Lev 16:27 5785
the covering of badgers' *s* ... Num 4:6 5785
with a covering of badgers' *s* ... Num 4:8 5785
within a covering of badgers' *s* ... Num 4:10 5785
it with a covering of badgers' *s* ... Num 4:11 5785
with a covering of badgers' *s* ... Num 4:12 5785
upon it a covering of badgers' *s* ... Num 4:14 5785
badgers' *s* that is above upon it ... Num 4:25
raiment, and all that is made of *s* ... Num 31:20 5785

SKIP {1}
maketh them also to *s* like a calf ... Ps 29:6 7540

SKIPPED {2}
The mountains *s* like rams ... Ps 114:4 7540
Ye mountains, that ye *s* like rams ... Ps 114:6 7540

SKIPPEDST {1}
spakest of him, thou *s* for joy ... Jer 48:27 5110

SKIPPING {1}
the mountains, *s* upon the hills ... Song 2:8 7092

SKIRT {12}
wife, nor discover his father's *s* ... Deut 22:30 3671
he uncovereth his father's *s* ... Deut 27:20 3671
thy *s* over thine handmaid ... Ruth 3:9 3671
hold upon the *s* of his mantle ... 1Sa 15:27 3671
cut off the *s* of Saul's robe ... 1Sa 24:4 3671
because he had cut off Saul's *s* ... 1Sa 24:5 3671
see the *s* of thy robe in my hand ... 1Sa 24:11 3671
that I cut off the *s* of thy robe ... 1Sa 24:11 3671
and I spread my *s* over thee ... Eze 16:8 3671
flesh in the *s* of his garment ... Hag 2:12 3671
with his *s* do touch bread, or ... Hag 2:12 3671
of the *s* of him that is a Jew ... Zec 8:23 3671

SKIRTS {7}
down to the *s* of his garments ... Ps 133:2 6310
Also in thy *s* is found the blood ... Jer 2:34 3671
iniquity are thy *s* discovered ... Jer 13:22 7757
I discover thy *s* upon thy face ... Jer 13:26 7757
Her filthiness is in her *s* ... Lam 1:9 7757
in number, and bind them in thy *s* ... Eze 5:3 3671
will discover thy *s* upon thy face ... Nah 3:5 7757

SKULL {5}
head, and all to brake his *s* ... Judg 9:53 1538
found no more of her than the *s* ... 2Kin 9:35 1538
that is to say, a place of a *s* ... Mt 27:33 *2898*
interpreted, The place of a *s* ... Mk 15:22 *2898*
a place called the place of a *s* ... Jn 19:17 *2898*

SKY {7}
and in his excellency on the *s* ... Deut 33:26 7834
thou with him spread out the *s* ... Job 37:18 7834
for the *s* is red ... Mt 16:2 *3772*
for the *s* is red and lowring ... Mt 16:3 *3772*
ye can discern the face of the *s* ... Mt 16:3 *3772*
ye can discern the face of the *s* ... Lk 12:56 *3772*
the stars of the *s* in multitude ... Heb 11:12 *3772*

SLACK {8}
he will not be *s* to him that ... Deut 7:10 309
God, thou shalt not *s* to pay it ... Deut 23:21 309
S not thy hand from thy servants ... Josh 10:6 7503
How long are ye *s* to go to ... Josh 18:3 7503
s not thy riding for me, except I ... 2Kin 4:24 6113
poor that dealeth with a *s* hand ... Prov 10:4 7423
to Zion, Let not thine hands be *s* ... Zeph 3:16 7503
The Lord is not *s* concerning his ... 2Pet 3:9 *1019*

SLACKED {1}
Therefore the law is *s*, and ... Hab 1:4 6313

SLACKNESS {1}
his promise, as some men count *s* ... 2Pet 3:9 *1022*

SLAIN {183}
for I have *s* a man to my wounding ... Gen 4:23 2026
The sons of Jacob came upon the *s* ... Gen 34:27 2491
them in the blood of the *s* bird ... Lev 14:51 7819
ye shall be *s* before your enemies ... Lev 26:17 5062
flocks and the herds be *s* for them ... Num 11:22 7819
therefore he hath *s* them in the ... Num 14:16 7819
whosoever toucheth one that is *s* ... Num 19:16 2491
him that touched a bone, or one *s* ... Num 19:18 2491
me, surely now also I had *s* thee ... Num 22:33 2026
prey, and drink the blood of the *s* ... Num 23:24 2491
name of the Israelite that was *s* ... Num 25:14 5221
even that was *s* with the ... Num 25:14 5221
woman that was *s* was Cozbi ... Num 25:15 5221
which was *s* in the day of the ... Num 25:18 5221
the rest of them that were *s* ... Num 31:8 2491
and whosoever hath touched any *s* ... Num 31:19 2491
After he had *s* Sihon the king of ... Deut 1:4 5221
If one be found *s* in the land ... Deut 21:1 2491
and it be not known who hath *s* him ... Deut 21:1 2491
are round about him that is *s* ... Deut 21:2 2491
city which is next unto the *s* man ... Deut 21:3 2491
that are next unto the *s* man ... Deut 21:6 2491
ox shall be *s* before thine eyes ... Deut 28:31 2873
and that with the blood of the *s* ... Deut 32:42 2491
them up all *s* before Israel ... Josh 11:6 2491
among them that were *s* by them ... Josh 13:22 2491
have *s* his sons, threescore and ... Judg 9:18 2026
of an ass have I *s* a thousand men ... Judg 15:16 5221
husband of the woman that was *s* ... Judg 20:4 7523
by night, and thought to have *s* me ... Judg 20:5 2026
Eli, Hophni and Phinehas, were *s* ... 1Sa 4:11 4191
Saul hath *s* his thousands, and ... 1Sa 18:7 5221
LORD liveth, he shall not be *s* ... 1Sa 19:6 4191
night, to morrow thou shalt be *s* ... 1Sa 19:11 4191
unto him, Wherefore shall he be *s* ... 1Sa 20:32 4191
Saul hath *s* his thousands, and ... 1Sa 21:11 5221
Saul had *s* the LORD's priests ... 1Sa 22:21 2026
fell down *s* in mount Gilboa ... 1Sa 31:1 2491
Philistines came to strip the *s* ... 1Sa 31:8 2491
I have *s* the LORD's anointed ... 2Sa 1:16 4191
Israel is *s* upon thy high places ... 2Sa 1:19 2491
From the blood of the *s*, from the ... 2Sa 1:22 2491
thou wast *s* in thine high places ... 2Sa 1:25 2491
because he had *s* their brother ... 2Sa 3:30 4191
more, when wicked men have *s* a ... 2Sa 4:11 2026
hast *s* him with the sword of the ... 2Sa 12:9 2026
Absalom hath *s* all the king's ... 2Sa 13:30 5221
s all the young men the king's ... 2Sa 13:32 4191
s before the servants of David ... 2Sa 18:7 5062
Philistines had *s* Saul in Gilboa ... 2Sa 21:12 5221
sword, thought to have *s* David ... 2Sa 21:16 5221
And he hath *s* oxen and fat cattle ... 1Kin 1:19 2076
down this day, and hath *s* oxen ... 1Kin 1:25 2076
s the Canaanites that dwelt in ... 1Kin 9:16 2026
host was gone up to bury the *s* ... 1Kin 11:15 2491
s him, according to the word of ... 1Kin 13:26 4191
and hath also *s* the king ... 1Kin 16:16 5221
withal how he had *s* all the ... 1Kin 19:1 2026
s thy prophets with the sword ... 1Kin 19:10 2026
s thy prophets with the sword ... 1Kin 19:14 2026
the kings are surely *s*, and they ... 2Kin 3:23 2717
the king's sons which were *s* ... 2Kin 11:2 4191
Athaliah, so that he was not *s* ... 2Kin 11:2 4191
within the ranges, let him be *s* ... 2Kin 11:8 4191
Let her not be *s* in the house of ... 2Kin 11:15 4191
and there was she *s* ... 2Kin 11:16 4191
which had *s* the king his father ... 2Kin 14:5 5221
For there fell down many *s* ... 1Chr 5:22 2491
fell down *s* in mount Gilboa ... 1Chr 10:1 2491
Philistines came to strip the *s* ... 1Chr 10:8 2491
hundred *s* by him at one time ... 1Chr 11:11 2491
so there fell down *s* of Israel ... 2Chr 13:17 2491
also hast *s* thy brethren of thy ... 2Chr 21:13 2026
to the camp had *s* all the eldest ... 2Chr 22:1 2026
and when they had *s* him, they ... 2Chr 22:9 4191
among the king's sons that were *s* ... 2Chr 22:11 4191
let him be *s* with the sword ... 2Chr 23:14 4191
after that they had *s* Athaliah ... 2Chr 23:21 4191
ye have *s* them in a rage that ... 2Chr 28:9 2026
people, to be destroyed, to be *s* ... Est 7:4 2026
were *s* in Shushan the palace was ... Est 9:11 2026
Esther the queen, The Jews have *s* ... Est 9:12 2026
they have *s* the servants with the ... Job 1:15 5221
s the servants with the edge of ... Job 1:17 5221
and where the *s* are, there is she ... Job 39:30 2491
ye shall be *s* all of you ... Ps 62:3 7523
like the *s* that lie in the grave, ... Ps 88:5 2491
Rahab in pieces, as one that is *s* ... Ps 89:10 2491
strong men have been *s* by her ... Prov 7:26 2026
I shall be *s* in the streets ... Prov 22:13 7523
and those that are ready to be *s* ... Prov 24:11 2027
and they shall fall under the *s* ... Is 10:4 2026
the raiment of those that are *s* ... Is 14:19 2026
thy land, and *s* thy people ... Is 14:20 2026
thy *s* men are not *s* with the ... Is 22:2 2491
and shall no more cover her *s* ... Is 26:21 2026
or is he *s* according to the ... Is 27:7 2026
of them that are *s* by him ... Is 27:7 2026
Their *s* also shall be cast out, ... Is 34:3 2491
the *s* of the LORD shall be many ... Is 66:16 2491
night for the *s* of the daughter ... Jer 9:1 2491
then behold the *s* with the sword ... Jer 14:18 2491
men be *s* by the sword in battle ... Jer 18:21 5221
the *s* of the LORD shall be at ... Jer 25:33 2491
whom I have *s* in mine anger and in ... Jer 33:5 5221
day after he had *s* Gedaliah ... Jer 41:4 4191
whom he had *s* because of Gedaliah ... Jer 41:9 5221
filled it with them that were *s* ... Jer 41:9 2491
after that he had *s* Gedaliah the ... Jer 41:16 5221
the son of Nethaniah had *s* ... Jer 41:18 5221
Thus the *s* shall fall in the land ... Jer 51:4 2491
all her *s* shall fall in the midst ... Jer 51:47 2491
caused the *s* of Israel to fall ... Jer 51:49 2491
shall fall the *s* of all the earth ... Jer 51:49 2491
the prophet be *s* in the sanctuary ... Lam 2:20 2026
thou hast *s* them in the day of ... Lam 2:21 2026
thou hast *s*, thou hast not pitied ... Lam 3:43 2026
They that be *s* with the sword are ... Lam 4:9 2491
than they that be *s* with hunger ... Lam 4:9 2491
down your *s* men before your idols ... Eze 6:4 2491
the *s* shall fall in the midst of ... Eze 6:7 2491
when their *s* men shall be among ... Eze 6:13 2491
and fill the courts with the *s* ... Eze 9:7 2491
multiplied your *s* in this city ... Eze 11:6 2491
the streets thereof with the *s* ... Eze 11:6 2491
Your *s* whom ye have laid in the ... Eze 11:7 2491
That thou hast *s* my children ... Eze 16:21 7819
third time, the sword of the *s* ... Eze 21:14 2491
sword of the great men that are *s* ... Eze 21:14 2491
upon the necks of them that are *s* ... Eze 21:29 2491
For when they had *s* their ... Eze 23:39 7819
the field shall be *s* by the sword ... Eze 26:6 2026
are *s* in the midst of the seas ... Eze 28:8 2491
when the *s* shall fall in Egypt, ... Eze 30:4 2491
and fill the land with the *s* ... Eze 30:11 2491
them that be *s* with the sword ... Eze 31:17 2491
with them that be *s* by the sword ... Eze 31:18 2491
of them that are *s* by the sword ... Eze 32:20 2491
lie uncircumcised, *s* by the sword ... Eze 32:21 2491
all of them *s*, fallen by the ... Eze 32:22 2491
all of them *s*, fallen by the ... Eze 32:23 2491
about her grave, all of them *s* ... Eze 32:24 2491
of the *s* with all her multitude ... Eze 32:25 2491
uncircumcised, *s* by the sword ... Eze 32:25 2491
in the midst of them that be *s* ... Eze 32:25 2491
s by the sword, though they ... Eze 32:26 2490
them that are *s* with the sword ... Eze 32:28 2491
by them that were *s* by the sword ... Eze 32:29 2491
which are gone down with the *s* ... Eze 32:30 2491
with them that be *s* by the sword ... Eze 32:30 2491
and all his army *s* by the sword ... Eze 32:31 2491
them that are *s* with the sword ... Eze 32:32 2491
fill his mountains with his *s* men ... Eze 35:8 2491
fall that are *s* with the sword ... Eze 35:8 2491
O breath, and breathe upon these *s* ... Eze 37:9 2026
that the wise men should be *s* ... Dan 2:13 6992
Daniel and his fellows to be *s* ... Dan 2:13 6992
the king of the Chaldeans was *s* ... Dan 5:30 6992
beheld even till the beast was *s* ... Dan 7:11 6992
and many shall fall down *s* ... Dan 11:26 2491
I have *s* them by the words of my ... Hos 6:5 2026
young men have I *s* with the sword ... Amos 4:10 2026
and there is a multitude of *s* ... Nah 3:3 2491
also, ye shall be *s* by my sword ... Zeph 2:12 2491
chief priests and scribes, and be *s* ... Lk 9:22 *615*
wicked hands have crucified and *s* ... Acts 2:23 *337*
who was *s*; and all ... Acts 5:36 *337*
have ye offered to me *s* beasts ... Acts 7:42 *4968*
they have *s* them which shewed ... Acts 7:52 *615*
they Pilate that he should be *s* ... Acts 13:28 *337*
eat nothing until we have *s* Paul ... Acts 23:14 *615*
having *s* the enmity thereby ... Eph 2:16 *615*
were *s* with the sword ... Heb 11:37 *1722,5408,599*
who was *s* among you, where Satan ... Rev 2:13 *615*
stood a Lamb as it had been *s* ... Rev 5:6 *4969*
for thou wast *s*, and hast redeemed ... Rev 5:9 *4969*
Lamb that was *s* to receive power ... Rev 5:12 *4969*
that were *s* for the word of God ... Rev 6:9 *4969*
were *s* of men seven thousand ... Rev 11:13 *615*
Lamb *s* from the foundation of the ... Rev 13:8 *4969*
of all that were *s* upon the earth ... Rev 18:24 *4969*
the remnant were *s* with the sword ... Rev 19:21 *615*

SLANDER {3}
by bringing up a *s* upon the land ... Num 14:36 1681
For I have heard the *s* of many ... Ps 31:13 1681
lips, and he that uttereth a *s* ... Prov 10:18 1681

SLANDERED {1}
he hath *s* thy servant unto my ... 2Sa 19:27 7270

SLANDERERS {1}
must their wives be grave, not *s* ... 1Ti 3:11 *1228*

SLANDEREST {1}
thou *s* thine own mother's son ... Ps 50:20 5414,1848

SLANDERETH {1}
Whoso privily *s* his neighbour ... Ps 101:5 3960

SLANDEROUSLY {1}
not rather, (as we be *s* reported ... Rom 3:8 *987*

SLANDERS {2}
revolters, walking with *s* ... Jer 6:28 7400
every neighbour will walk with *s* ... Jer 9:4 7400

SLANG {1}
s it, and smote the Philistine in ... 1Sa 17:49 7049

SLAUGHTER {56}
return from the *s* of Chedorlaomer ... Gen 14:17 5221
them with a great *s* at Gibeon ... Josh 10:10 4347
slaying them with a very great *s* ... Josh 10:20 4347
vineyards, with a very great *s* ... Judg 11:33 4347
them hip and thigh with a great *s* ... Judg 15:8 4347
and there was a very great *s* ... 1Sa 4:10 4347
also a great *s* among the people ... 1Sa 4:17 4046
many of the people with a great *s* ... 1Sa 6:19 4347
And that first *s*, which Jonathan ... 1Sa 14:14 4347
greater *s* among the Philistines ... 1Sa 14:30 4347
from the *s* of the Philistine ... 1Sa 17:57 5221
from the *s* of the Philistine ... 1Sa 18:6 5221
and slew them with a great *s* ... 1Sa 19:8 4347
and smote them with a great *s* ... 1Sa 23:5 4347
from the *s* of the Amalekites ... 2Sa 1:1 5221
There is a *s* among the people ... 2Sa 17:9 4046
there was a great *s* that ... 2Sa 18:7 4046
slew the Syrians with a great *s* ... 1Kin 20:21 4347
people slew them with a great *s* ... 2Chr 13:17 4347
come from the *s* of the Edomites ... 2Chr 25:14 5221
who smote him with a great *s* ... 2Chr 28:5 4347
the stroke of the sword, and *s* ... Est 9:5 2027
we are counted as sheep for the *s* ... Ps 44:22 2878
as an ox goeth to the *s*, or as a ... Prov 7:22 2875
for him according to the *s* of ... Is 10:26 4347
Prepare *s* for his children for ... Is 14:21 4293
s of them that are slain by him ... Is 27:7 2027
waters in the day of the great *s* ... Is 30:25 2027
he hath delivered them to the *s* ... Is 34:2 2875
a great *s* in the land of Idumea ... Is 34:6 2875
he is brought as a lamb to the *s* ... Is 53:7 2875
and ye shall all bow down to the *s* ... Is 65:12 2875
of Hinnom, but the valley of *s* ... Jer 7:32 2028
or an ox that is brought to the *s* ... Jer 11:19 2873
them out like sheep for the *s* ... Jer 12:3 2873
and prepare them for the day of *s* ... Jer 12:3 2028
of Hinnom, but The valley of *s* ... Jer 19:6 2028
for the days of your *s* and of your ... Jer 25:34 2873
young men are gone down to the *s* ... Jer 48:15 2875
let them go down to the *s* ... Jer 50:27 2875
them down like lambs to the *s* ... Jer 51:40 2873
every man a *s* weapon in his hand ... Eze 9:2 4660
It is sharpened to make a sore *s* ... Eze 21:10 2873

it is wrapped up for the *s*	Eze 21:15	2875
to open the mouth in the *s*	Eze 21:22	7524
for the *s* it is furbished, to	Eze 21:28	2875
when the *s* is made in the midst	Eze 26:15	2027
revolters are profound to make *s*	Hos 5:2	7819
mount of Esau may be cut off by *s*	Obad 9	6993
Feed the flock of the *s*	Zec 11:4	2028
And I will feed the flock of *s*	Zec 11:7	2028
He was led as a sheep to the *s*	Acts 8:32	4967
s against the disciples of the	Acts 9:1	5408
are accounted as sheep for the *s*	Rom 8:36	4967
returning from the *s* of the kings	Heb 7:1	2871
your hearts, as in a day of *s*	Jas 5:5	4967

SLAVE {1}

is he a homeborn *s*	Jer 2:14	

SLAVES {1}

and horses, and chariots, and *s*	Rev 18:13	4983

SLAY {117}

one that findeth me shall *s* me	Gen 4:14	2026
to *s* the righteous with the	Gen 18:25	4191
wilt thou *s* also a righteous	Gen 20:4	2026
they will *s* me for my wife's sake	Gen 20:11	2026
and took the knife to *s* his son	Gen 22:10	7819
then will I *s* my brother Jacob	Gen 27:41	2026
together against me, and *s* me	Gen 34:30	5221
conspired against him to *s* him	Gen 37:18	4191
now therefore, and let us *s* him	Gen 37:20	2026
profit is it if we *s* our brother	Gen 37:26	2026
S my two sons, if I bring him not	Gen 42:37	4191
house, Bring these men home, and *s*	Gen 43:16	2875
this thing, he sought to *s* Moses	Ex 2:15	2026
I will *s* thy son, even thy	Ex 4:23	2026
put a sword in their hand to *s* us	Ex 5:21	2026
neighbour, to *s* him with guile	Ex 21:14	2026
innocent and righteous *s* thou not	Ex 23:7	2026
And thou shalt *s* the ram, and thou	Ex 29:16	7819
to *s* them in the mountains, and to	Ex 32:12	2026
s every man his brother, and every	Ex 32:27	2026
s the sin offering in the place	Lev 4:29	7819
s it for a sin offering in the	Lev 4:33	7819
he shall *s* the lamb in the place	Lev 14:13	7819
and ye shall *s* the beast	Lev 20:15	2026
one shall *s* her before his face	Num 19:3	7819
S ye every one his men that were	Num 25:5	2026
himself shall *s* the murderer	Num 35:19	4191
he meeteth him, he shall *s* him	Num 35:19	4191
of blood shall *s* the murderer	Num 35:21	4191
out to *s* them in the wilderness	Deut 9:28	4191
because the way is long, and *s* him	Deut 19:6	5221
reward to *s* an innocent person	Deut 27:25	5221
did the children of Israel *s* with	Josh 13:22	2026
them alive, I would not *s* you	Judg 8:19	2026
his firstborn, Up, and *s* them	Judg 8:20	2026
s me, that men say not of me, A	Judg 9:54	4191
because the LORD would *s* them	1Sa 2:25	4191
the God of Israel to us, to *s* us	1Sa 5:10	4191
his own place, that it *s* us not	1Sa 5:11	4191
his sheep, and *s* them here, and eat	1Sa 14:34	7819
but *s* both man and woman, infant	1Sa 15:3	4191
to *s* David without a cause	1Sa 19:5	4191
him, and to *s* him in the morning	1Sa 19:11	4191
me in the bed, that I may *s* him	1Sa 19:15	4191
be in me iniquity, *s* me thyself	1Sa 20:8	4191
of his father to *s* David	1Sa 20:33	4191
s the priests of the LORD	1Sa 22:17	4191
I pray thee, upon me, and *s* me	2Sa 1:9	4191
king to *s* Abner the son of Ner	2Sa 3:37	4191
Saul sought to *s* them in his zeal	2Sa 21:2	5221
not *s* his servant with the sword	1Kin 1:51	4191
living child, and in no wise *s* it	1Kin 3:26	4191
living child, and in no wise *s* it	1Kin 3:27	4191
king of Judah did Baasha *s* him	1Kin 15:28	4191
to remembrance, and to *s* my son	1Kin 17:18	4191
into the hand of Ahab, to *s* me	1Kin 18:9	4191
cannot find thee, he shall *s* me	1Kin 18:12	2026
and he shall *s* me	1Kin 18:14	2026
the sword of Hazael shall Jehu *s*	1Kin 19:17	4191
the sword of Jehu shall Elisha *s*	1Kin 19:17	4191
from me, a lion shall *s* thee	1Kin 20:36	5221
men wilt thou *s* with the sword	2Kin 8:12	2026
to the captains, Go in, and *s* them	2Kin 10:25	5221
them, and, behold, they *s* them	2Kin 17:26	4191
of mount Seir, utterly to *s*	2Chr 20:23	2763
S her not in the house of the	2Chr 23:14	4191
s them, and cause the work to	Neh 4:11	2026
for they will come to *s* thee	Neh 6:10	2026
night will they come to *s* thee	Neh 6:10	2026
for their life, to destroy, to *s*	Est 8:11	2026
If the scourge *s* suddenly	Job 9:23	4191
Though he *s* me, yet will I trust	Job 13:15	6991
the viper's tongue shall *s* him	Job 20:16	2026
Evil shall *s* the wicked	Ps 34:21	4191
to *s* such as be of upright	Ps 37:14	2873
righteous, and seeketh to *s* him	Ps 37:32	4191
S them not, lest my people forget	Ps 59:11	2026
They *s* the widow and the stranger,	Ps 94:6	2026
that he might even *s* the broken	Ps 109:16	4191
Surely thou wilt *s* the wicked	Ps 139:19	6991
away of the simple shall *s* them	Prov 1:32	2026
of his lips shall he *s* the wicked	Is 11:4	4191
famine, and he shall *s* thy remnant	Is 14:30	2026
he shall *s* the dragon that is in	Is 27:1	2026
for the Lord GOD shall *s* thee	Is 65:15	4191
out of the forest shall *s* them	Jer 5:6	5221
the sword to *s*, and the dogs to	Jer 15:3	2026
their counsel against me to *s* me	Jer 18:23	1194
shall *s* them with the sword	Jer 20:4	5221
he shall *s* them before your eyes	Jer 29:21	5221
the son of Nethaniah to *s* thee	Jer 40:14	5221,5315
I will *s* Ishmael the son of	Jer 40:15	5221
wherefore should he *s* thee	Jer 40:15	5221
that said unto Ishmael, *S* us not	Jer 41:8	4191
S all her bullocks	Jer 50:27	2717
S utterly old and young, both	Eze 9:6	2026
to *s* the souls that should not	Eze 13:19	4191
they shall *s* their sons and their	Eze 23:47	4191
He shall *s* with the sword thy	Eze 26:8	4191
he shall *s* thy people by the	Eze 26:11	4191
to *s* thereon the burnt offering	Eze 40:39	7819
they shall *s* the burnt offering	Eze 44:11	7819
to *s* the wise men of Babylon	Dan 2:14	6992
a dry land, and *s* her with thirst	Hos 2:3	4191
yet will I *s* even the beloved	Hos 9:16	4191
will *s* all the princes thereof	Amos 2:3	2026
I will *s* the last of them with	Amos 9:1	2026
the sword, and it shall *s* them	Amos 9:4	2026
continually to *s* the nations	Hab 1:17	2026
Whose possessors *s* them, and hold	Zec 11:5	2026
and some of them they shall *s*	Lk 11:49	615
bring hither, and *s* them before me	Lk 19:27	2695
Jesus, and sought to *s* him	Jn 5:16	615
heart, and took counsel to *s* them	Acts 5:33	337
but they went about to *s* him	Acts 9:29	337
s and eat	Acts 11:7	2380
for to *s* the third part of men	Rev 9:15	615

SLAYER {19}

that the *s* may flee thither,	Num 35:11	7523
shall judge between the *s*	Num 35:24	5221
congregation shall deliver the *s*	Num 35:25	7523
But if the *s* shall at any time	Num 35:26	7523
the revenger of blood kill the *s*	Num 35:27	7523
death of the high priest the *s*	Num 35:28	7523
That the *s* might flee thither,	Deut 4:42	7523
that every *s* may flee thither	Deut 19:3	7523
And this is the case of the *s*	Deut 19:4	7523
avenger of the blood pursue the *s*	Deut 19:6	7523
That the *s* that killeth any	Josh 20:3	7523
deliver the *s* up into his hand	Josh 20:5	7523
then shall the *s* return, and come	Josh 20:6	7523
to be a city of refuge for the *s*	Josh 21:13	7523
to be a city of refuge for the *s*	Josh 21:21	7523
to be a city of refuge for the *s*	Josh 21:27	7523
to be a city of refuge for the *s*	Josh 21:32	7523
to be a city of refuge for the *s*	Josh 21:38	7523
to give it into the hand of the *s*	Eze 21:11	2026

SLAYETH {5}

him, Therefore whosoever *s* Cain	Gen 4:15	2026
s him, even so is this matter	Deut 22:26	7523,5315
man, and envy *s* the silly one	Job 5:2	4191
yet say before him that *s* thee	Eze 28:9	2026
in the hand of him that *s* thee	Eze 28:9	2490

SLAYING {7}

of *s* all the inhabitants of Ai in	Josh 8:24	2026
end of *s* them with a very great	Josh 10:20	5221
in *s* his seventy brethren	Judg 9:56	2026
with whom I sojourn, by *s* her son	1Kin 17:20	4191
s oxen, and killing sheep, eating	Is 22:13	2026
s the children in the valleys	Is 57:5	7819
to pass, while they were *s* them	Eze 9:8	5221

SLEEP {84}

caused a deep *s* to fall upon Adam	Gen 2:21	3462
down, a deep *s* fell upon Abram	Gen 15:12	8639
and lay down in that place to *s*	Gen 28:11	7901
And Jacob awaked out of his *s*	Gen 28:16	8142
my *s* departed from mine eyes	Gen 31:40	8142
wherein shall he *s*	Ex 22:27	7901
thou shalt not *s* with his pledge	Deut 24:12	7901
that he may *s* in his own raiment,	Deut 24:13	7901
thou shalt *s* with thy fathers	Deut 31:16	7901
And he awaked out of his *s*	Judg 16:14	8142
she made him *s* upon her knees	Judg 16:19	3462
And he awoke out of his *s*, and said	Judg 16:20	8142
was, and Samuel was laid down to *s*	1Sa 3:3	
because a deep *s* from the LORD	1Sa 26:12	8639
thou shalt *s* with thy fathers, I	2Sa 7:12	7901
the king shall *s* with his fathers	1Kin 1:21	7901
that night could not the king *s*	Est 6:1	8142
when deep *s* falleth on men,	Job 4:13	8639
for now shall I *s* in the dust	Job 7:21	7901
nor be raised out of their *s*	Job 14:12	8142
when deep *s* falleth upon men, in	Job 33:15	
both lay me down in peace, and *s*	Ps 4:8	3462
lest I *s* the *s* of death	Ps 13:3	3462
spoiled, they have slept their *s*	Ps 76:5	8142
and horse are cast into a dead *s*	Ps 76:6	7290
the Lord awaked as one out of *s*	Ps 78:65	3463
they are as a *s*	Ps 90:5	8142
shall neither slumber nor *s*	Ps 121:4	3462
for so he giveth his beloved *s*	Ps 127:2	8142
I will not give *s* to mine eyes	Ps 132:4	8142
lie down, and thy *s* shall be sweet	Prov 3:24	8142
For they *s* not, except they have	Prov 4:16	3462
their *s* is taken away, unless	Prov 4:16	8142
Give not *s* to thine eyes, nor	Prov 6:4	8142
How long wilt thou *s*, O sluggard	Prov 6:9	7901
when wilt thou arise out of thy *s*	Prov 6:9	8142
Yet a little *s*, a little slumber,	Prov 6:10	8142
little folding of the hands to *s*	Prov 6:10	7901
casteth into a deep *s*	Prov 19:15	8639
Love not *s*, lest thou come to	Prov 20:13	8142
Yet a little *s*, a little slumber,	Prov 24:33	8142
little folding of the hands to *s*	Prov 24:33	7901
The *s* of a labouring man is sweet	Eccl 5:12	8142
the rich will not suffer him to *s*	Eccl 5:12	3462
nor night seeth *s* with his eyes	Eccl 8:16	8142
I *s*, but my heart waketh	Song 5:2	3463
none shall slumber nor *s*	Is 5:27	3463
out upon you the spirit of deep *s*	Is 29:10	8639
and my *s* was sweet unto me	Jer 31:26	8142
they may rejoice, and *s*	Jer 51:39	3462
a perpetual *s*, and not wake	Jer 51:39	8142
they shall *s* a perpetual *s*,	Jer 51:57	3462
and they shall *s* a perpetual *s*	Jer 51:57	8142
the wilderness, and *s* in the woods	Eze 34:25	3462
troubled, and his *s* brake from him	Dan 2:1	8142
and his *s* went from him	Dan 6:18	8139
I was in a deep *s* on my face	Dan 8:18	7290
then was I in a deep *s* on my face	Dan 10:9	7290
many of them that *s* in the dust	Dan 12:2	3463
man that is wakened out of his *s*	Zec 4:1	8142
s did as the angel of the Lord	Mt 1:24	5258
S on now, and take your rest	Mt 26:45	2518
And should *s*, and rise night and day	Mk 4:27	2518
S on now, and take your rest	Mk 14:41	2518
were with him were heavy with *s*	Lk 9:32	5258
And said unto them, Why *s* ye	Lk 22:46	2518
go, that I may awake him out of *s*	Jn 11:11	1852
said his disciples, Lord, if he *s*	Jn 11:12	2837
had spoken of taking of rest in *s*	Jn 11:13	5258
by the will of God, fell on *s*	Acts 13:36	2837
the prison awaking out of his *s*	Acts 16:27	1853
being fallen into a deep *s*	Acts 20:9	5258
preaching, he sunk down with *s*	Acts 20:9	5258
it is high time to awake out of *s*	Rom 13:11	5258
and sickly among you, and many *s*	1Cor 11:30	2837
We shall not all *s*, but we shall	1Cor 15:51	2837
even so them also which *s* in	1Th 4:14	2837
Therefore let us not *s*, as do	1Th 5:6	2518
they that *s* *s* in the night	1Th 5:7	2518
us, that, whether we wake or *s*	1Th 5:10	2518

SLEEPER {1}

unto him, What meanest thou, O *s*	Jonah 1:6	7290

SLEEPEST {4}

Awake, why *s* thou, O Lord	Ps 44:23	3462
when thou *s*, it shall keep thee	Prov 6:22	7901
saith unto Peter, Simon, *s* thou	Mk 14:37	2518
he saith, Awake thou that *s*	Eph 5:14	2518

SLEEPETH {7}

a journey, or peradventure he *s*	1Kin 18:27	3463
but he that *s* in harvest is a son	Prov 10:5	7290
their baker *s* all the night	Hos 7:6	3463
for the maid is not dead, but *s*	Mt 9:24	2518
the damsel is not dead, but *s*	Mk 5:39	2518
she is not dead, but *s*	Lk 8:52	2518
unto them, Our friend Lazarus *s*	Jn 11:11	2837

SLEEPING {6}

Saul lay *s* within the trench, and	1Sa 26:7	3463
s, lying down, loving to slumber	Is 56:10	1957
coming suddenly he find you *s*	Mk 13:36	2518
And he cometh, and findeth them *s*	Mk 14:37	2518
he found them *s* for sorrow	Lk 22:45	2837
Peter was *s* between two soldiers	Acts 12:6	2837

SLEIGHT {1}

wind of doctrine, by the *s* of men	Eph 4:14	2940

SLEPT {49}

sleep to fall upon Adam, and he *s*	Gen 2:21	3462
And he *s* and dreamed the second	Gen 41:5	3462
But Uriah *s* at the door of the	2Sa 11:9	7901
So David *s* with his fathers, and	1Kin 2:10	7901
beside me, while thine handmaid *s*	1Kin 3:20	3463
that David *s* with his fathers	1Kin 11:21	7901
Solomon *s* with his fathers, and	1Kin 11:43	7901
he *s* with his fathers, and Nadab	1Kin 14:20	7901
Rehoboam *s* with his fathers, and	1Kin 14:31	7901
Abijam *s* with his fathers	1Kin 15:8	7901
Asa *s* with his fathers, and was	1Kin 15:24	7901
So Baasha *s* with his fathers, and	1Kin 16:6	7901
So Omri *s* with his fathers, and	1Kin 16:28	7901
s under a juniper tree, behold,	1Kin 19:5	3462
So Ahab *s* with his fathers	1Kin 22:40	7901
Jehoshaphat *s* with his fathers,	1Kin 22:50	7901
Joram *s* with his fathers, and was	2Kin 8:24	7901
And Jehu *s* with his fathers	2Kin 10:35	7901
Jehoahaz *s* with his fathers	2Kin 13:9	7901
And Joash *s* with his fathers	2Kin 13:13	7901
Jehoash *s* with his fathers, and	2Kin 14:16	7901
that the king *s* with his fathers	2Kin 14:22	7901
Jeroboam *s* with his fathers, even	2Kin 14:29	7901
So Azariah *s* with his fathers	2Kin 15:7	7901
Menahem *s* with his fathers	2Kin 15:22	7901
Jotham *s* with his fathers, and was	2Kin 15:38	7901
Ahaz *s* with his fathers, and was	2Kin 16:20	7901
Hezekiah *s* with his fathers	2Kin 20:21	7901
Manasseh *s* with his fathers, and	2Kin 21:18	7901
So Jehoiakim *s* with his fathers	2Kin 24:6	7901
Solomon *s* with his fathers, and he	2Chr 9:31	7901
Rehoboam *s* with his fathers, and	2Chr 12:16	7901
So Abijah *s* with his fathers, and	2Chr 14:1	7901
Asa *s* with his fathers, and died	2Chr 16:13	7901
Now Jehoshaphat *s* with his	2Chr 21:1	7901
that the king *s* with his fathers	2Chr 26:2	7901
So Uzziah *s* with his fathers, and	2Chr 26:23	7901
Jotham *s* with his fathers, and	2Chr 27:9	7901
Ahaz *s* with his fathers, and they	2Chr 28:27	7901
Hezekiah *s* with his fathers, and	2Chr 32:33	7901
So Manasseh *s* with his fathers,	2Chr 33:20	7901
and been quiet, I should have *s*	Job 3:13	3462
I laid me down and *s*	Ps 3:5	3462
spoiled, they have *s* their sleep	Ps 76:5	5123

But while men *s*, his enemy came .... Mt 13:25 *2518*
tarried, they all slumbered and *s* .... Mt 25:5 *2518*
of the saints which *s* arose .... Mt 27:52 *2837*
and stole him away while we *s* .... Mt 28:13 *2837*
the firstfruits of them that *s* 1Cor 15:20 *2837*

SLEW {196}
Abel his brother, and *s* him .... Gen 4:8 2026
seed instead of Abel, whom Cain *s* .... Gen 4:25 2026
city boldly, and *s* all the males .... Gen 34:25 2026
they *s* Hamor and Shechem his son .... Gen 34:26 2026
and the LORD *s* him .... Gen 38:7 4191
wherefore he *s* him also .... Gen 38:10 4191
for in their anger they *s* a man .... Gen 49:6 2026
he *s* the Egyptian, and hid him in .... Ex 2:12 5221
that the LORD *s* all the firstborn .... Ex 13:15 2026
And he *s* it .... Lev 8:15 7819
And he *s* it .... Lev 8:23 7819
s the calf of the sin offering, ... Lev 9:8 7819
And he *s* the burnt offering .... Lev 9:12 7819
s it, and offered it for sin, as .... Lev 9:15 7819
He *s* also the bullock and the ram .... Lev 9:18 7819
and they *s* all the males .... Num 31:7 2026
they *s* the kings of Midian, ... Num 31:8 2026
son of Beor they *s* with the sword .... Num 31:8 2026
turned again, and *s* the men of Ai .... Josh 8:21 5221
of Israel, that they *s* them not .... Josh 9:26 2026
s them with a great slaughter at .... Josh 10:10 5221
of Israel *s* with the sword .... Josh 10:11 2026
s them, and hanged them on five .... Josh 10:26 4191
he took, and smote them, and *s* them .... Josh 11:17 4191
they *s* of them in Bezek ten .... Judg 1:4 5221
they *s* the Canaanites and the .... Judg 1:5 5221
they *s* Sheshai, and Ahiman, and .... Judg 1:10 5221
they *s* the Canaanites that .... Judg 1:17 5221
they *s* of Moab at that time about .... Judg 3:29 5221
which *s* of the Philistines six .... Judg 3:31 5221
they *s* Oreb upon the rock Oreb, ... Judg 7:25 2026
Zeeb they *s* at the winepress of .... Judg 7:25 2026
Penuel, and *s* the men of the city .... Judg 8:17 2026
men were they whom ye *s* at Tabor .... Judg 8:18 2026
s Zebah and Zalmunna, ... Judg 8:21 2026
s his brethren the sons of .... Judg 9:5 2026
their brother, which *s* them .... Judg 9:24 2026
were in the fields, and *s* them .... Judg 9:44 5221
s the people that was therein, and .... Judg 9:45 2026
men say not of me, A woman *s* him .... Judg 9:54 2026
s him at the passages of Jordan .... Judg 12:6 7819
s thirty men of them, and took .... Judg 14:19 5221
s a thousand men therewith .... Judg 15:15 5221
our country, which *s* many of us .... Judg 16:24 2491
So the dead which he *s* at his .... Judg 16:30 4191
than they which he *s* in his life .... Judg 16:30 4191
s two thousand men of them .... Judg 20:45 5221
they *s* a bullock, and brought the 1Sa 1:25 7819
they *s* of the army in the field 1Sa 4:2 5221
s the Ammonites until the heat of 1Sa 11:11 5221
and his armourbearer *s* after him 1Sa 14:13 4191
calves, and *s* them on the ground 1Sa 14:32 7819
him that night, and *s* them there 1Sa 14:34 7819
his beard, and smote him, and *s* him 1Sa 17:35 4191
Thy servant *s* both the lion and 1Sa 17:36 5221
and smote the Philistine, and *s* him 1Sa 17:50 4191
s him, and cut off his head 1Sa 17:51 4191
s of the Philistines two hundred 1Sa 18:27 5221
s the Philistine, and the LORD 1Sa 19:5 5221
s them with a great slaughter 1Sa 19:8 5221
s on that day fourscore and five 1Sa 22:18 4191
Saul *s* his thousands, and David 1Sa 29:5 5221
they *s* not any, either great or 1Sa 30:2 4191
and the Philistines *s* Jonathan 1Sa 31:2 5221
s him, because I was sure that he 2Sa 1:10 4191
and Abishai his brother *s* Abner 2Sa 3:30 2026
s him, and beheaded him, and took 2Sa 4:7 4191
s him in Ziklag, who thought that 2Sa 4:10 2026
his young men, and they *s* them 2Sa 4:12 2026
David *s* of the Syrians two and 2Sa 8:5 5221
David *s* the men of seven hundred 2Sa 10:18 2126
the one smote the other, and *s* him 2Sa 14:6 4191
the life of his brother whom he *s* 2Sa 14:7 2026
about and smote Absalom, and *s* him 2Sa 18:15 4191
because he *s* the Gibeonites 2Sa 21:1 4191
Sibbechai the Hushathite *s* Saph 2Sa 21:18 5221
s the brother of Goliath the 2Sa 21:19 5221
the brother of David *s* him 2Sa 21:21 5221
hundred, whom he *s* at one time 2Sa 23:8 2491
defended it, and *s* the Philistines 2Sa 23:12 5221
s them, and had the name among 2Sa 23:18 2491
he *s* two lionlike men of Moab 2Sa 23:20 5221
s a lion in the midst of a pit in 2Sa 23:20 5221
he *s* an Egyptian, a goodly man 2Sa 23:21 2026
hand, and *s* him with his own spear 2Sa 23:21 5221
And Adonijah *s* sheep and oxen and 1Kin 1:9 2076
the son of Jether, whom he *s* 1Kin 2:5 2026
s them with the sword, my father 1Kin 2:32 2026
up, and fell upon him, and *s* him 1Kin 2:34 4191
when David *s* them of Zobah 1Kin 11:24 2026
lion met him by the way, and *s* him 1Kin 13:24 4191
that he *s* all the house of Baasha 1Kin 16:11 5221
s the prophets of the LORD 1Kin 18:13 2026
the brook Kishon, and *s* them there 1Kin 18:40 7819
s them, and boiled their flesh 1Kin 19:21 2076
And they *s* every one his man 1Kin 20:20 5221
s the Syrians with a great 1Kin 20:21 5221
the children of Israel *s* of the 1Kin 20:29 5221
him, a lion found him, and *s* him 1Kin 20:36 5221
Had Zimri peace, who *s* his master 2Kin 9:31 2026
s seventy persons, and put their 2Kin 10:7 7819
against my master, and *s* him 2Kin 10:9 2026
but who *s* all these 2Kin 10:9 5221
So Jehu *s* all that remained of 2Kin 10:11 5221
s them at the pit of the shearing 2Kin 10:14 7819
he *s* all that remained unto Ahab 2Kin 10:17 5221
s Mattan the priest of Baal 2Kin 11:18 2026
they *s* Athaliah with the sword 2Kin 11:20 4191
s Joash in the house of Millo, ... 2Kin 12:20 5221
that he *s* his servants which had 2Kin 14:5 5221
of the murderers he *s* not 2Kin 14:6 4191
He *s* of Edom in the valley of 2Kin 14:7 5221
him to Lachish, and *s* him there 2Kin 14:19 4191
s him, and reigned in his stead 2Kin 15:10 4191
s him, and reigned in his stead 2Kin 15:14 4191
s him, and reigned in his stead, ... 2Kin 15:30 4191
of it captive to Kir, and *s* Rezin 2Kin 16:9 4191
among them, which *s* some of them 2Kin 17:25 2026
s the king in his own house 2Kin 21:23 4191
the people of the land *s* all them 2Kin 21:24 5221
he *s* all the priests of the high 2Kin 23:20 2076
he *s* him at Megiddo, when he had 2Kin 23:29 4191
they *s* the sons of Zedekiah 2Kin 25:7 7819
s them at Riblah in the land of 2Kin 25:21 4191
and he *s* him 1Chr 2:3 4191
that were born in that land *s* 1Chr 7:21 2026
and the Philistines *s* Jonathan 1Chr 10:2 5221
therefore he *s* him, and turned the 1Chr 10:14 4191
it, and *s* the Philistines 1Chr 11:14 5221
he *s* them, and had a name among 1Chr 11:20 2490
he *s* two lionlike men of Moab 1Chr 11:22 5221
s a lion in a pit in a snowy day 1Chr 11:22 5221
he *s* an Egyptian, a man of great 1Chr 11:23 5221
hand, and *s* him with his own spear 1Chr 11:23 2026
David *s* of the Syrians two and 1Chr 18:5 5221
Abishai the son Zeruiah *s* of the 1Chr 18:12 5221
David *s* of the Syrians seven 1Chr 19:18 2026
Sibbechai the Hushathite *s* Sippai 1Chr 20:4 5221
Elhanan the son of Jair *s* Lahmi 1Chr 20:5 5221
of Shimea David's brother *s* him 1Chr 20:7 5221
his people *s* them with a great 2Chr 13:17 5221
s all his brethren with the sword 2Chr 21:4 2026
ministered to Ahaziah, he *s* them 2Chr 22:8 2026
Athaliah, so that she *s* him not 2Chr 22:11 4191
king's house, they *s* her there 2Chr 23:15 4191
s Mattan the priest of Baal 2Chr 23:17 2026
had done to him, but *s* his son 2Chr 24:22 2026
s him on his bed, and he died 2Chr 24:25 2026
that he *s* his servants that had 2Chr 25:3 2026
But he *s* not their children, but 2Chr 25:4 4191
Lachish after him, and *s* him there 2Chr 25:27 4191
of Remaliah *s* in Judah an hundred 2Chr 28:6 2026
s Maaseiah the king's son, and 2Chr 28:7 2026
bowels *s* him there with the sword 2Chr 32:21 5307
him, and *s* him in his own house 2Chr 33:24 4191
But the people of the land *s* all 2Chr 33:25 5221
who *s* their young men with the 2Chr 36:17 2026
s thy prophets which testified .... Neh 9:26 2026
in Shushan the palace the Jews *s* .... Est 9:6 2026
the enemy of the Jews, *s* they .... Est 9:10 2026
s three hundred men at Shushan .... Est 9:15 2026
s of their foes seventy and five .... Est 9:16 2026
s the fattest of them, and smote .... Ps 78:31 2026
When he *s* them, then they sought .... Ps 78:34 2026
into blood, and *s* their fish .... Ps 105:29 4191
great nations, and *s* mighty kings .... Ps 135:10 2026
And *s* famous kings .... Ps 136:18 2026
killeth an ox is as if he *s* a man .... Is 66:3 5221
Because he *s* me not from the womb .... Jer 20:17 4191
who *s* him with the sword, and cast .... Jer 26:23 5221
Then the king of Babylon *s* the .... Jer 39:6 7819
Babylon *s* all the nobles of Judah .... Jer 39:6 7819
s him, whom the king of Babylon .... Jer 41:2 4191
Ishmael also *s* all the Jews that .... Jer 41:3 5221
the son of Nethaniah *s* them .... Jer 41:7 7819
s them not among their brethren .... Jer 41:8 4191
the king of Babylon *s* the sons of .... Jer 52:10 7819
he *s* also all the princes of .... Jer 52:10 7819
s all that were pleasant to the .... Lam 2:4 2026
they went forth, and *s* in the city .... Eze 9:7 5221
and *s* her with the sword .... Eze 23:10
whereupon they *s* their sacrifices .... Eze 40:41 7819
they *s* the burnt offering .... Eze 40:42 7819
the flame of the fire *s* those men .... Dan 3:22 6992
whom he would he *s* .... Dan 5:19 6992
s all the children that were in .... Mt 2:16 *337*
him out of the vineyard, and *s* him .... Mt 21:39 *615*
them spitefully, and *s* them .... Mt 22:6 *615*
whom ye *s* between the temple and .... Mt 23:35 *5407*
s them, think ye that they were .... Lk 13:4 *615*
raised up Jesus, whom ye *s* .... Acts 5:30 *1315*
whom they *s* and hanged on a tree .... Acts 10:39 *337*
the raiment of them that *s* him .... Acts 22:20 *337*
deceived me, and by it *s* me .... Rom 7:11 *615*
that wicked one, and *s* his brother 1Jn 3:12 *4969*
And wherefore *s* he him 1Jn 3:12 *4969*

SLEWEST {1}
whom thou *s* in the valley of Elah 1Sa 21:9 5221

SLIDDEN {1}
is this people of Jerusalem *s* .... Jer 8:5 7725

SLIDE {3}
their foot shall *s* in due time .... Deut 32:35 4131
therefore I shall not *s* .... Ps 26:1 4571
none of his steps shall *s* .... Ps 37:31 4571

SLIDETH {1}
For Israel *s* back as a .... Hos 4:16 5637

SLIGHTLY {2}
of the daughter of my people *s* .... Jer 6:14 7043
of the daughter of my people *s* .... Jer 8:11 7043

SLIME {2}
stone, and *s* had they for morter .... Gen 11:3 2564
of bulrushes, and daubed it with *s* .... Ex 2:3 2564

SLIMEPITS {1}
the vale of Siddim was full of *s* .... Gen 14:10 2564

SLING {8}
every one could *s* stones at an .... Judg 20:16 7049
and his *s* was in his hand 1Sa 17:40 7050
over the Philistine with a *s* 1Sa 17:50 7050
enemies, them shall he *s* out 1Sa 25:29 7049
as out of the middle of a *s* 1Sa 25:29 7050
As he that bindeth a stone in a *s* .... Prov 26:8 4773
I will *s* out the inhabitants of .... Jer 10:18 7049
devour, and subdue with *s* stones .... Zec 9:15 7050

SLINGERS {1}
howbeit the *s* went about it, and 2Kin 3:25 7051

SLINGS {1}
and bows, and *s* to cast stones 2Chr 26:14 7050

SLINGSTONES {1}
s are turned with him into .... Job 41:28 68,7050

SLIP {5}
so that my feet did not *s* 2Sa 22:37 4571
He that is ready to *s* with his .... Job 12:5 4571
paths, that my footsteps *s* not .... Ps 17:5 4131
under me, that my feet did not *s* .... Ps 18:36 4571
at any time we should let them *s* .... Heb 2:1 *3901*

SLIPPED {2}
but he *s* away out of Saul's 1Sa 19:10 6362
my steps had well nigh *s* .... Ps 73:2 8210

SLIPPERY {3}
Let their way be dark and *s* .... Ps 35:6 2519
thou didst set them in *s* places .... Ps 73:18 2513
them as *s* ways in the darkness .... Jer 23:12 2519

SLIPPETH {3}
the head *s* from the helve, and .... Deut 19:5 5394
when my foot *s*, they magnify .... Ps 38:16 4131
When I said, My foot *s* .... Ps 94:18 4131

SLIPS {1}
and shalt set it with strange *s* .... Is 17:10 2156

SLIVER {1}
And he took all the gold and the *s* 2Chr 25:24

SLOTHFUL {15}
be not *s* to go, and to enter to .... Judg 18:9 6101
but the *s* shall be under tribute .... Prov 12:24 7423
The *s* man roasteth not that which .... Prov 12:27 7423
The way of the *s* man is as an .... Prov 15:19 6102
He also that is *s* in his work is .... Prov 18:9 7503
A *s* man hideth his hand in his .... Prov 19:24 6102
The desire of the *s* killeth him .... Prov 21:25 6102
The *s* man saith, There is a lion .... Prov 22:13 6102
I went by the field of the *s* .... Prov 24:30 6102
The *s* man saith, There is a lion .... Prov 26:13 6102
so doth the *s* upon his bed .... Prov 26:14 6102
The *s* hideth his hand in his .... Prov 26:15 6102
s servant, thou knewest that I .... Mt 25:26 *3636*
Not *s* in business .... Rom 12:11 *3636*
That ye be not *s*, but followers .... Heb 6:12 *3576*

SLOTHFULNESS {2}
S casteth into a deep sleep .... Prov 19:15 6103
By much *s* the building decayeth .... Eccl 10:18 6103

SLOW {15}
but I am *s* of speech .... Ex 4:10 3515
and of a *s* tongue .... Ex 4:10 750
s to anger, and of great kindness, ... Neh 9:17 750
s to anger, and plenteous in mercy .... Ps 103:8 750
s to anger, and of great mercy .... Ps 145:8 750
He that is *s* to wrath is of great .... Prov 14:29 750
but he that is *s* to anger .... Prov 15:18 750
He that is *s* to anger is better .... Prov 16:32 750
s to anger, and of great kindness, ... Joel 2:13 750
s to anger, and of great kindness, ... Jonah 4:2 750
The LORD is *s* to anger, and great .... Nah 1:3 750
s of heart to believe all that .... Lk 24:25 *1021*
liars, evil beasts, *s* bellies .... Titus 1:12 *692*
s to speak, *s* to wrath .... Jas 1:19 *1021*

SLOWLY {1}
And when we had sailed *s* many days .... Acts 27:7 *1020*

SLUGGARD {6}
Go to the ant, thou *s* .... Prov 6:6 6102
How long wilt thou sleep, O *s* .... Prov 6:9 6102
so is the *s* to them that send him .... Prov 10:26 6102
The soul of the *s* desireth .... Prov 13:4 6102
The *s* will not plow by reason of .... Prov 20:4 6102
The *s* is wiser in his own conceit .... Prov 26:16 6102

SLUICES {1}
purposes thereof, all that make *s* .... Is 19:10 7938

SLUMBER {10}
he that keepeth thee will not *s* .... Ps 121:3 5123
Israel shall neither *s* nor sleep .... Ps 121:4 5123
mine eyes, or *s* to mine eyelids, ... Ps 132:4 8572
eyes, nor *s* to thine eyelids .... Prov 6:4 8572
Yet a little sleep, a little *s* .... Prov 6:10 8572
Yet a little sleep, a little *s* .... Prov 24:33 8572
none shall *s* nor sleep .... Is 5:27 5123
sleeping, lying down, loving to *s* .... Is 56:10 5123
Thy shepherds *s*, O king of .... Nah 3:18 5123
hath given them the spirit of *s* .... Rom 11:8 *2659*

SLUMBERED {1}
bridegroom tarried, they all *s* Mt 25:5 *3573*

SLUMBERETH {1}
not, and their damnation *s* not 2Pet 2:3 *3573*

SLUMBERINGS {1}
upon men, in *s* upon the bed Job 33:15 8572

SMALL {97}
the house with blindness, both *s* Gen 19:11 6996
Is it a *s* matter that thou hast Gen 30:15 4592
it shall become *s* dust in all the Ex 9:9
there lay a *s* round thing Ex 16:14 1851
as *s* as the hoar frost on the Ex 16:14 1851
but every *s* matter they shall Ex 18:22 6996
but every *s* matter they judged Ex 18:26 6996
thou shalt beat some of it very *s* Ex 30:36 1854
full of sweet incense beaten *s* Lev 16:12 1851
Seemeth it but a *s* thing unto you Num 16:9 4592
Is it a *s* thing that thou hast Num 16:13 4592
took the *s* towns thereof, and Num 32:41
hear the *s* as well as the great Deut 1:17 6996
stamped it, and ground it very *s* Deut 9:21 3190
even until it was as *s* as dust Deut 9:21 1854
divers weights, a great and a *s* Deut 25:13 6996
divers measures, a great and a *s* Deut 25:14 6996
as the *s* rain upon the tender Deut 32:2
smote the men of the city, both *s* 1Sa 5:9 6996
will do nothing either great or *s* 1Sa 20:2 6996
slew not any, either great or *s* 1Sa 30:2 6996
neither *s* nor great, neither sons 1Sa 30:19 6996
this was yet a *s* thing in thy 2Sa 7:19 6994
be not one *s* stone found there 2Sa 17:13 1571
Then did I beat them as *s* as the 2Sa 22:43
I desire one *s* petition of thee 1Kin 2:20 6996
and after the fire a still *s* voice 1Kin 19:12 1851
Fight neither with *s* nor great 1Kin 22:31 6996
their inhabitants were of *s* power 2Kin 19:26 7116
and all the people, both *s* 2Kin 23:2 6996
Kidron, and stamped it *s* to powder 2Kin 23:6 1854
place, and stamped it *s* to powder 2Kin 23:15 1854
And all the people, both *s* 2Kin 25:26 6996
yet this was a *s* thing in thine 1Chr 17:17 6994
as well the *s* as the great, the 1Chr 25:8 6996
as well the *s* as the great, 1Chr 26:13 6996
whether *s* or great, whether man 2Chr 15:13 6996
Fight ye not with *s* or great 2Chr 18:30 6996
came with a *s* company of men 2Chr 24:24 4705
as well to the great as to the *s* 2Chr 31:15 6996
and all the people, great and *s* 2Chr 34:30 6996
thousand and six hundred *s* cattle 2Chr 35:8
offerings five thousand *s* cattle 2Chr 35:9
of the house of God, great and *s* 2Chr 36:18 6996
the palace, both unto great and *s* Est 1:5 6996
honour, both to great and *s* Est 1:20 6996
The *s* and great are there Job 3:19 6996
Though thy beginning was *s* Job 8:7 4705
consolations of God *s* with thee Job 15:11 4592
For he maketh *s* the drops of Job 36:27 1639
likewise to the *s* rain, and to the Job 37:6
Then did I beat them *s* as the Ps 18:42
creeping innumerable, both *s* Ps 104:25 6996
them that fear the LORD, both *s* Ps 115:13 6996
I am *s* and despised Ps 119:141 6810
of adversity, thy strength is *s* Prov 24:10 6862
s cattle above all that were in Eccl 2:7
had left unto us a very *s* remnant Is 1:9 4592
Is it a *s* thing for you to weary Is 7:13 4592
and the remnant shall be very *s* Is 16:14 4213
issue, all vessels of *s* quantity Is 22:24 6996
strangers shall be like *s* dust Is 29:5 1851
their inhabitants were of *s* power Is 37:27 7116
are counted as the *s* dust of the Is 40:15
the mountains, and beat them *s* Is 41:15 1854
Thou hast not brought me the *s* Is 43:23
For a *s* moment have I forsaken Is 54:7 6996
and a *s* one a strong nation Is 60:22 6810
the *s* shall die in this land Jer 16:6 6996
them, and they shall not be *s* Jer 30:19 6819
Yet a *s* number that escape the Jer 44:28 4962
I will make thee *s* among the Jer 49:15 6996
this of thy whoredoms a *s* matter Eze 16:20 4592
Seemeth it a *s* thing unto you to Eze 34:18 4592
become strong with a *s* people Dan 11:23 4592
for he is *s* Amos 7:2 6996
for he is *s* Amos 7:5 6996
forth wheat, making the ephah *s* Amos 8:5 6694
I have made thee *s* among the Obad 2 6996
hath despised the day of *s* things Zec 4:10 6996
that a *s* ship should wait on him Mk 3:9 *4142*
And they had a few *s* fishes Mk 8:7 *2485*
he had made a scourge of *s* cords Jn 2:15 *4979*
barley loaves, and two *s* fishes Jn 6:9 *3795*
there was no *s* stir among the Acts 12:18 *3641*
and Barnabas had no *s* dissension Acts 15:2 *3641*
arose no *s* stir about that way Acts 19:23 *3641*
brought no *s* gain unto the Acts 19:24 *3641*
this day, witnessing both to *s* Acts 26:22 *3398*
no *s* tempest lay on us, all hope Acts 27:20 *3641*
But with me it is a very *s* thing 1Cor 4:3 *1646*
turned about with a very *s* helm Jas 3:4 *1646*
and them that fear thy name, *s* Rev 11:18 *3398*
And he causeth all, both *s* Rev 13:16 *3398*
and ye that fear him, both *s* Rev 19:5 *3398*
men, both free and bond, both *s* Rev 19:18 *3398*
And I saw the dead, *s* and great, Rev 20:12 *3398*

SMALLEST {2}
of the *s* of the tribes of Israel 1Sa 9:21 6996
unworthy to judge the *s* matters 1Cor 6:2 *1646*

SMART {1}
for a stranger shall *s* for it Prov 11:15 7321,7451

SMELL {20}
he smelled the *s* of his raiment Gen 27:27 7381
the *s* of my son is as the *s* Gen 27:27 7381
to *s* thereto, shall even be cut Ex 30:38 7306
I will not *s* the savour of your Lev 26:31 7306
see, nor hear, nor eat, nor *s* Deut 4:28 7306
All thy garments *s* of myrrh Ps 45:8
noses have they, but they *s* not Ps 115:6 7306
sendeth forth the *s* thereof Song 1:12 7381
the tender grape give a good *s* Song 2:13 7381
the *s* of thine ointments than all Song 4:10 7381
the *s* of thy garments is like the Song 4:11 7381
garments is like the *s* of Lebanon Song 4:11 7381
the *s* of thy nose like apples Song 7:8 7381
The mandrakes give a *s*, and at our Song 7:13 7381
of sweet *s* there shall be stink Is 3:24 1314
nor the *s* of fire had passed on Dan 3:27 7382
olive tree, and his *s* as Lebanon Hos 14:6 7381
I will not *s* in your solemn Amos 5:21 7306
from you, an odour of a sweet *s* Phil 4:18 *2175*

SMELLED {2}
the LORD *s* a sweet savour Gen 8:21 7306
he *s* the smell of his raiment, and Gen 27:27 7306

SMELLETH {1}
he *s* the battle afar off, the Job 39:25 7306

SMELLING {3}
and my fingers with sweet *s* myrrh Song 5:5 5674
lilies, dropping sweet *s* myrrh Song 5:13 5674
were hearing, where were the *s* 1Cor 12:17 *3750*

SMITE {125}
neither will I again *s* any more Gen 8:21 5221
s it, then the other company Gen 32:8 5221
s me, and the mother with the Gen 32:11 5221
s Egypt with all my wonders which Ex 3:20 5221
I will *s* with the rod that is in Ex 7:17 5221
I will *s* all thy borders with Ex 8:2 5062
s the dust of the land, that it Ex 8:16 5221
out my hand, that I may *s* thee Ex 9:15 5221
will *s* all the firstborn in the Ex 12:12 5221
when I *s* the land of Egypt Ex 12:13 5221
pass through to *s* the Egyptians Ex 12:23 5062
come in unto your houses to *s* you Ex 12:23 5062
and thou shalt *s* the rock, and Ex 17:6 5221
one *s* another with a stone, or Ex 21:18 5221
if a man *s* his servant, or his Ex 21:20 5221
if a man *s* the eye of his servant Ex 21:26 5221
if he *s* out his manservant's Ex 21:27 5307
I will *s* them with the pestilence Num 14:12 5221
shall prevail, that we may *s* them Num 22:6 5221
shall *s* the corners of Moab, and Num 24:17 4272
Vex the Midianites, and *s* them Num 25:17 5221
if he *s* him with an instrument of Num 35:16 5221
if he *s* him with throwing a stone Num 35:17 5221
Or if he *s* him with an hand Num 35:18 5221
Or in enmity *s* him with his hand, Num 35:21 5221
thou shalt *s* them, and utterly Deut 7:2 5221
Thou shalt surely *s* the Deut 13:15 5221
s him mortally that he die, and Deut 19:11 5221
thou shalt *s* every male thereof Deut 20:13 5221
The LORD shall *s* thee with a Deut 28:22 5221
The LORD will *s* thee with the Deut 28:27 5221
The LORD shall *s* thee with Deut 28:28 5221
The LORD shall *s* thee in the Deut 28:35 5221
s through the loins of them that Deut 33:11 4272
three thousand men go up and *s* Ai Josh 7:3 6221
and help me, that we may *s* Gibeon Josh 10:4 6221
and *s* the hindmost of them Josh 10:19
LORD and the children of Israel *s* Josh 12:6 5221
for these did Moses *s*, and cast Josh 13:12 5221
thou shalt *s* the Midianites as Judg 6:16 5221
and they began to *s* of the people Judg 20:31 5221
the battle, Benjamin began to *s* Judg 20:39 5221
Go and *s* the inhabitants of Judg 21:10 5221
s Amalek, and utterly destroy all 1Sa 15:3 5221
and I will *s* thee, and take thine 1Sa 17:46 5221
I will *s* David even to the wall 1Sa 18:11 5221
Saul sought to *s* David even to 1Sa 19:10 5221
cast a javelin at him to *s* him 1Sa 20:33 5221
Shall I go and *s* these Philistines 1Sa 23:2 5221
s the Philistines, and save Keilah 1Sa 23:2 5221
now therefore let me *s* him 1Sa 26:8 5221
I will not *s* him the second time 1Sa 26:8
LORD liveth, the LORD shall *s* him 1Sa 26:10 5062
should I *s* thee to the ground 2Sa 2:22 5221
to *s* the host of the Philistines 2Sa 5:24 5221
and when I say unto you, *S* Amnon 2Sa 13:28 5221
s the city with the edge of the 2Sa 15:14 5221
and I will *s* the king only 2Sa 17:2 5221
why didst thou not *s* him there to 2Sa 18:11 5221
For the LORD shall *s* Israel 1Kin 14:15 5221
of the LORD, *S* me, I pray thee 1Kin 20:35 5221
And the man refused to *s* him 1Kin 20:35 5221
man, and said, *S* me, I pray thee 1Kin 20:37 5221
ye shall *s* every fenced city, and 2Kin 3:19 5221
S this people, I pray thee, with 2Kin 6:18 5221
them, My father, shall I *s* them 2Kin 6:21 5221
shall I *s* them 2Kin 6:21 5221
answered, Thou shalt not *s* them 2Kin 6:22 5221
wouldest thou *s* those whom thou 2Kin 6:22 5221
thou shalt *s* the house of Ahab 2Kin 9:7 5221
S him also in the chariot 2Kin 9:27 5221
for thou shalt *s* the Syrians in 2Kin 13:17 5221
king of Israel, *S* upon the ground 2Kin 13:18 5221
now thou shalt *s* Syria but thrice 2Kin 13:19 5221
to *s* the host of the Philistines 1Chr 14:15 5221
plague will the LORD *s* thy people 2Chr 21:14 5062
The sun shall not *s* thee by day Ps 121:6 5221
Let the righteous *s* me Ps 141:5 1986
S a scorner, and the simple will Prov 19:25 5221
Therefore the Lord will *s* with a Is 3:17 5596
he shall *s* thee with a rod, and Is 10:24 5221
he shall *s* the earth with the rod Is 11:4 5221
shall *s* it in the seven streams, Is 11:15 5221
And the LORD shall *s* Egypt Is 19:22 5062
he shall *s* and heal it Is 19:22 5062
shall the heat nor sun *s* them Is 49:10 5221
to *s* with the fist of wickedness Is 58:4 5221
let us *s* him with the tongue, and Jer 18:18 5221
I will *s* the inhabitants of this Jer 21:6 5221
he shall *s* them with the edge of Jer 21:7 5221
he shall *s* the land of Egypt, and Jer 43:11 5221
come and *s* the land of Egypt Jer 46:13 5221
king of Babylon shall *s*, thus Jer 49:28 5221
part, and *s* about it with a knife Eze 5:2 5221
S with thine hand, and stamp with Eze 6:11 5221
after him through the city, and *s* Eze 9:5 5221
s therefore upon thy thigh Eze 21:12 5606
s thine hands together, and let Eze 21:14 5221
I will also *s* mine hands together Eze 21:17 5221
when I shall *s* all them that Eze 32:15 5221
I will *s* thy bow out of thy left Eze 39:3 5221
I will *s* the winter house with Amos 3:15 5221
he will *s* the great house with Amos 6:11 5221
S the lintel of the door, that Amos 9:1 5221
they shall *s* the judge of Israel Mic 5:1 5221
melteth, and the knees *s* together Nah 2:10 6375
he will *s* her power in the sea Zec 9:4 5221
shall *s* the waves in the sea, and Zec 10:11 5221
and they shall *s* the land, and out Zec 11:6 3807
I will *s* every horse with Zec 12:4 5221
will *s* every horse of the people Zec 12:4 5221
s the shepherd, and the sheep Zec 13:7 5221
plague wherewith the LORD will *s* Zec 14:12 5062
wherewith the LORD will *s* the Zec 14:18 5062
come and *s* the earth with a curse Mal 4:6 5221
but whosoever shall *s* thee on thy Mt 5:39 *4474*
And shall begin to *s* his Mt 24:49 *5180*
I will *s* the shepherd, and the Mt 26:31 *3960*
I will *s* the shepherd, and the Mk 14:27 *3960*
shall we *s* with the sword Lk 22:49 *3960*
by him to *s* him on the mouth Acts 23:2 *5180*
Paul unto him, God shall *s* thee Acts 23:3 *5180*
if a man *s* you on the face 2Cor 11:20 *1194*
to *s* the earth with all plagues, Rev 11:6 *3960*
with it he should *s* the nations Rev 19:15 *3960*

SMITERS {1}
I gave my back to the *s*, and my Is 50:6 5221

SMITEST {2}
Wherefore *s* thou thy fellow Ex 2:13 5221
but if well, why *s* thou me Jn 18:23 *1194*

SMITETH {13}
He that *s* a man, so that he die, Ex 21:12 5221
he that *s* his father, or his Ex 21:15 5221
out of the hand of him that *s* him Deut 25:11 5221
Cursed be he that *s* his neighbour Deut 27:24 5221
He that *s* Kirjath-sepher, and Josh 15:16 5221
He that *s* Kirjath-sepher, and Judg 1:12 5221
s the Jebusites, and the lame and 2Sa 5:8 5221
Whosoever *s* the Jebusites first 1Chr 11:6 5221
he *s* through the proud Job 26:12 4272
turneth not unto him that *s* them Is 9:13 5221
his cheek to him that *s* him Lam 3:30 5221
know that I am the LORD that *s* Eze 7:9 5221
unto him that *s* thee on the one Lk 6:29 *5180*

SMITH {3}
Now there was no *s* found 1Sa 13:19 2796
The *s* with the tongs both worketh Is 44:12 2796,1270
I have created the *s* that bloweth Is 54:16 2796

SMITHS {4}
and all the craftsmen and *s* 2Kin 24:14 4525
s a thousand, all that were 2Kin 24:16 4525
Judah, with the carpenters and *s* Jer 24:1 4525
and the carpenters, and the *s* Jer 29:2 4525

SMITING {5}
he spied an Egyptian *s* an Hebrew Ex 2:11 5221
a name when he returned from *s* of 2Sa 8:13 5221
so that in *s* he wounded him 1Kin 20:37 5221
they went forward *s* the Moabites 2Kin 3:24 5221
will I make thee sick in *s* thee Mic 6:13 5221

SMITTEN {63}
that the LORD had *s* the river Ex 7:25 5221
And the flax and the barley was *s* Ex 9:31 5221
the wheat and the rie were not *s* Ex 9:32 5221
be *s* that he die, there shall no Ex 22:2 5221
that ye be not *s* before your Num 14:42 5062
that thou hast *s* me these three Num 22:28 5221
Wherefore hast thou *s* thine ass Num 22:32 5221
which the LORD had *s* among them Num 33:4 5221
lest ye be *s* before your enemies Deut 1:42 5062
thee to be *s* before thy face Deut 28:7 5062
thee to be *s* before thine enemies Deut 28:25 5062
s it with the edge of the sword, Judg 1:8 5221
They are *s* down before us, as at Judg 20:32 5062
of Benjamin saw that they were *s* Judg 20:36 5062
Surely they are *s* down before us Judg 20:39 5062
battle, Israel was *s* before the 1Sa 4:2 5062

S

the LORD *s* us to day before the	1Sa 4:3	5062
fought, and Israel was *s*, and they	1Sa 4:10	5062
died not were *s* with the emerods	1Sa 5:12	5221
because the LORD had *s* many of	1Sa 6:19	5221
they were *s* before Israel	1Sa 7:10	5062
s a garrison of the Philistines	1Sa 13:4	5221
s Ziklag, and burned it with fire	1Sa 30:1	5221
of David had *s* of Benjamin	2Sa 2:31	5221
had *s* all the host of Hadadezer	2Sa 8:9	5221
against Hadadezer, and *s* him	2Sa 8:10	5221
that they were *s* before Israel	2Sa 10:15	5062
that they were *s* before Israel	2Sa 10:19	5062
ye from him, that he may be *s*	2Sa 11:15	5221
Israel be *s* down before the enemy	1Kin 8:33	5062
after he had *s* every male in Edom	1Kin 11:15	5221
and when he also had *s* the waters	2Kin 2:14	5221
slain, and they have *s* one another	2Kin 3:23	5221
have *s* five or six times	2Kin 13:19	5221
then hadst thou *s* Syria till thou	2Kin 13:19	5221
Thou hast indeed *s* Edom, and thine	2Kin 14:10	5221
of Hamath heard how David had *s*	1Chr 18:9	5221
against Hadarezer, and *s* him	1Chr 18:10	5221
and they were *s*	2Chr 20:22	5062
why shouldest thou be *s*	2Chr 25:16	5221
Lo, thou hast *s* the Edomites	2Chr 25:19	5221
out, because the LORD had *s* him	2Chr 26:20	5060
s Judah, and carried away captives	2Chr 28:17	5221
they have *s* me upon the cheek	Job 16:10	5221
for thou hast *s* all mine enemies	Ps 3:7	5221
persecute him whom thou hast *s*	Ps 69:26	5221
My heart is *s*, and withered like	Ps 102:4	5221
he hath *s* my life down to the	Ps 143:3	1792
hand against them, and hath *s* them	Is 5:25	5221
the gate is *s* with destruction	Is 24:12	3807
Hath he *s* him, as he smote those	Is 27:7	5221
stricken, *s* of God, and afflicted	Is 53:4	5221
In vain have I *s* your children	Jer 2:30	5221
why hast thou *s* us, and there is	Jer 14:19	5221
For though ye had *s* the whole	Jer 37:10	5221
therefore I have *s* mine hand at	Eze 22:13	5221
unto me, saying, The city is *s*	Eze 33:21	5221
year after that the city was *s*	Eze 40:1	5221
he hath *s*, and he will bind us up	Hos 6:1	5221
Ephraim is *s*, their root is dried	Hos 9:16	5221
I have *s* you with blasting and	Amos 4:9	5221
me to be *s* contrary to the law	Acts 23:3	*5180*
the third part of the sun was *s*	Rev 8:12	*4141*

SMOKE {45}

the *s* of the country went up as	Gen 19:28	7008
went up as the *s* of a furnace	Gen 19:28	7008
mount Sinai was altogether on a *s*	Ex 19:18	6225
the *s* thereof ascended as the	Ex 19:18	6227
ascended as the *s* of a furnace	Ex 19:18	6227
jealousy shall *s* against that man	Deut 29:20	6225
the *s* of the city ascended up to	Josh 8:20	6227
that the *s* of the city ascended,	Josh 8:21	6227
with *s* rise up out of the city	Judg 20:38	6227
of the city with a pillar of *s*	Judg 20:40	6227
There went up a *s* out of his	2Sa 22:9	6227
Out of his nostrils goeth *s*	Job 41:20	6227
There went up a *s* out of his	Ps 18:8	6227
into *s* shall they consume away	Ps 37:20	6227
As *s* is driven away, so drive	Ps 68:2	6227
why doth thine anger *s* against	Ps 74:1	6225
For my days are consumed like *s*	Ps 102:3	6227
he toucheth the hills, and they *s*	Ps 104:32	6225
am become like a bottle in the *s*	Ps 119:83	7008
the mountains, and they shall *s*	Ps 144:5	6225
as *s* to the eyes, so is the	Prov 10:26	6227
the wilderness like pillars of *s*	Song 3:6	6227
s by day, and the shining of a	Is 4:5	6227
and the house was filled with *s*	Is 6:4	6227
mount up like the lifting up of *s*	Is 9:18	6227
shall come from the north a *s*	Is 14:31	6227
the *s* thereof shall go up for	Is 34:10	6227
heavens shall vanish away like *s*	Is 51:6	6227
These are a *s* in my nose, a fire	Is 65:5	6227
as the *s* out of the chimney	Hos 13:3	6227
blood, and fire, and pillars of *s*	Joel 2:30	6227
I will burn her chariots in the *s*	Nah 2:13	6227
blood, and fire, and vapour of *s*	Acts 2:19	*2586*
the *s* of the incense, which came	Rev 8:4	*2586*
there arose a *s* out of the pit,	Rev 9:2	*2586*
as the *s* of a great furnace	Rev 9:2	*2586*
by reason of the *s* of the pit	Rev 9:2	*2586*
there came out of the *s* locusts	Rev 9:3	*2586*
of their mouths issued fire and *s*	Rev 9:17	*2586*
killed, by the fire, and by the *s*	Rev 9:18	*2586*
the *s* of their torment ascendeth	Rev 14:11	*2586*
with *s* from the glory of God	Rev 15:8	*2586*
shall see the *s* of her burning	Rev 18:9	*2586*
they saw the *s* of her burning	Rev 18:18	*2586*
her *s* rose up for ever and ever	Rev 19:3	*2586*

SMOKING {5}

it was dark, behold a *s* furnace	Gen 15:17	6227
of the trumpet, and the mountain *s*	Ex 20:18	6226
two tails of these *s* firebrands	Is 7:4	6226
the *s* flax shall he not quench	Is 42:3	3544
s flax shall he not quench, till	Mt 12:20	*5187*

SMOOTH {6}

is a hairy man, and I am a *s* man	Gen 27:11	2509
hands, and upon the *s* of his neck	Gen 27:16	2513
chose him five *s* stones out of	1Sa 17:40	2512
things, speak unto us *s* things	Is 30:10	2513
Among the *s* stones of the stream	Is 57:6	2511
and the rough ways shall be made *s*	Lk 3:5	*3006*

SMOOTHER {2}

of his mouth were *s* than butter	Ps 55:21	2505
and her mouth is *s* than oil	Prov 5:3	2513

SMOOTHETH {1}

he that *s* with the hammer him	Is 41:7	2505

SMOTE {230}

s the Rephaims in Ashteroth	Gen 14:5	5221
and *s* all the country of the	Gen 14:7	5221
s them, and pursued them unto	Gen 14:15	5221
they *s* the men that were at the	Gen 19:11	5221
who *s* Midian in the field of Moab	Gen 36:35	5221
s the waters that were in the	Ex 7:20	5221
s the dust of the earth, and it	Ex 8:17	5221
the hail *s* throughout all the	Ex 9:25	5221
the hail *s* every herb of the	Ex 9:25	5221
when he *s* the Egyptians, and	Ex 12:27	5062
that at midnight the LORD *s* all	Ex 12:29	5221
then shall he that *s* him be quit	Ex 21:19	5221
for on the day that I *s* all the	Num 3:13	5221
on the day that I *s* every	Num 8:17	5221
the LORD *s* the people with a very	Num 11:33	5221
s them, and discomfited them, even	Num 14:45	5221
with his rod he *s* the rock twice	Num 20:11	5221
Israel *s* him with the edge of the	Num 21:24	5221
So they *s* him, and his sons, and	Num 21:35	5221
Balaam *s* the ass, to turn her	Num 22:23	5221
and he *s* her again	Num 22:25	5221
he *s* the ass with a staff	Num 22:27	5221
and he *s* his hands together	Num 24:10	5606
LORD *s* before the congregation of	Num 32:4	5221
he that *s* him shall surely be put	Num 35:21	5221
we *s* him, and his sons, and all his	Deut 2:33	5221
we *s* him until none was left to	Deut 3:3	5221
Moses and the children of Israel *s*	Deut 4:46	5221
s the hindmost of thee, even all	Deut 25:18	
us unto battle, and we *s* them	Deut 29:7	5221
the men of Ai *s* of them about	Josh 7:5	5221
and *s* them in the going down	Josh 7:5	5221
and they *s* them, so that they let	Josh 8:22	5221
s it with the edge of the sword	Josh 8:24	5221
the children of Israel *s* them not	Josh 9:18	5221
s them to Azekah, and unto	Josh 10:10	5221
And afterward Joshua *s* them	Josh 10:26	5221
s it with the edge of the sword,	Josh 10:28	5221
he *s* it with the edge of the	Josh 10:30	5221
s it with the edge of the sword,	Josh 10:32	5221
and Joshua *s* him and his people,	Josh 10:33	5221
s it with the edge of the sword,	Josh 10:35	5221
s it with the edge of the sword,	Josh 10:37	5221
they *s* them with the edge of the	Josh 10:39	5221
So Joshua *s* all the country of	Josh 10:40	5221
Joshua *s* them from Kadesh-barnea	Josh 10:41	5221
who *s* them, and chased them unto	Josh 11:8	5221
and they *s* them, until they left	Josh 11:8	5221
s the king thereof with the sword	Josh 11:10	5221
they *s* all the souls that were	Josh 11:11	5221
s them with the edge of the sword	Josh 11:12	5221
but every man they *s* with the	Josh 11:14	5221
he took, and *s* them, and slew them	Josh 11:17	5221
which the children of Israel *s*	Josh 12:1	5221
the children of Israel *s* on this	Josh 12:7	5221
whom Moses *s* with the princes of	Josh 13:21	5221
s it with the edge of the sword,	Josh 19:47	5221
because he *s* his neighbour	Josh 20:5	5221
they *s* the city with the edge of	Judg 1:25	5221
s Israel, and possessed the city	Judg 3:13	5221
s the nail into his temples, and	Judg 4:21	8628
and with the hammer she *s* Sisera	Judg 5:26	1986
she *s* off his head, when she had	Judg 5:26	4277
s it that it fell, and overturned	Judg 7:13	5221
Nobah and Jogbehah, and *s* the host	Judg 8:11	5221
rose up against them, and *s* them	Judg 9:43	5221
hand of Israel, and they *s* them	Judg 11:21	5221
he *s* them from Aroer, even till	Judg 11:33	5221
and the men of Gilead *s* Ephraim	Judg 12:4	5221
he *s* them hip and thigh with a	Judg 15:8	5221
they *s* them with the edge of the	Judg 18:27	5221
the LORD *s* Benjamin before Israel	Judg 20:35	5062
s all the city with the edge of	Judg 20:37	5221
s them with the edge of the sword	Judg 20:48	5221
these are the Gods that *s* the	1Sa 4:8	5221
s them with emerods, even Ashdod	1Sa 5:6	5221
he *s* the men of the city, both	1Sa 5:9	5221
that it is not his hand that *s* us	1Sa 6:9	5060
he *s* the men of Beth-shemesh,	1Sa 6:19	5221
even he *s* of the people fifty	1Sa 6:19	5221
s them, until they came under	1Sa 7:11	5221
Jonathan *s* the garrison of the	1Sa 13:3	5221
they *s* the Philistines that day	1Sa 14:31	5221
s the Amalekites, and delivered	1Sa 14:48	5221
Saul *s* the Amalekites from	1Sa 15:7	5221
s him, and delivered it out of his	1Sa 17:35	5221
his beard, and *s* him, and slew him	1Sa 17:35	5221
s the Philistine in his forehead,	1Sa 17:49	5221
s the Philistine, and slew him	1Sa 17:50	5221
he *s* the javelin into the wall	1Sa 19:10	5221
s he with the edge of the sword,	1Sa 22:19	5221
s them with a great slaughter	1Sa 23:5	5221
that David's heart *s* him	1Sa 24:5	5221
days after, that the LORD *s* Nabal	1Sa 25:38	5062
David *s* the land, and left neither	1Sa 27:9	5221
David *s* them from the twilight	1Sa 30:17	5221
And he *s* him that he died	2Sa 1:15	5221
spear *s* him under the fifth rib	2Sa 2:23	5221
s him there under the fifth rib,	2Sa 3:27	5221
they *s* him under the fifth rib	2Sa 4:6	5221
in his bedchamber, and they *s* him	2Sa 4:7	5221
David *s* them there, and said, The	2Sa 5:20	5221
s the Philistines from Geba until	2Sa 5:25	5221
God *s* him there for his error	2Sa 6:7	5221
that David *s* the Philistines, and	2Sa 8:1	5221
he *s* Moab, and measured them with	2Sa 8:2	5221
David *s* also Hadadezer, the son	2Sa 8:3	5221
s Shobach the captain of their	2Sa 10:18	5221
Who *s* Abimelech the son of	2Sa 11:21	5221
them, but the one *s* the other	2Sa 14:6	5221
Deliver him that *s* his brother	2Sa 14:7	5221
about and *s* Absalom, and slew him	2Sa 18:15	5221
so he *s* him therewith in the	2Sa 20:10	5221
s the Philistine, and killed him	2Sa 21:17	5221
s the Philistines until his hand	2Sa 23:10	5221
David's heart *s* him after that he	2Sa 24:10	5221
saw the angel that *s* the people	2Sa 24:17	5221
of Israel, and *s* Ijon, and Dan, and	1Kin 15:20	5221
Baasha *s* him at Gibbethon, which	1Kin 15:27	5221
that he *s* all the house of	1Kin 15:29	5221
s him, and killed him, in the	1Kin 16:10	5221
s the horses and chariots, and slew	1Kin 20:21	5221
And the man *s* him, so that in	1Kin 20:37	5221
s Micaiah on the cheek, and said,	1Kin 22:24	5221
s the king of Israel between the	1Kin 22:34	5221
s the waters, and they were	2Kin 2:8	5221
s the waters, and said, Where is	2Kin 2:14	5221
s the Moabites, so that they fled	2Kin 3:24	5221
slingers went about it, and *s* it	2Kin 3:25	5221
And he *s* them with blindness	2Kin 6:18	5221
s the Edomites which compassed	2Kin 8:21	5221
s Jehoram between his arms, and	2Kin 9:24	5221
they *s* them with the edge of the	2Kin 10:25	5221
Hazael *s* them in all the coasts	2Kin 10:32	5221
his servants, *s* him, and he died	2Kin 12:21	5221
And he *s* thrice, and stayed	2Kin 13:18	5221
And the LORD *s* the king, so that	2Kin 15:5	5221
s him before the people, and slew	2Kin 15:10	5221
s Shallum the son of Jabesh in	2Kin 15:14	5221
Then Menahem *s* Tiphsah, and all	2Kin 15:16	5221
not to him, therefore he *s* it	2Kin 15:16	5221
s him in Samaria, in the palace	2Kin 15:25	5221
s him, and slew him, and reigned in	2Kin 15:30	5221
He *s* the Philistines, even unto	2Kin 18:8	5221
s in the camp of the Assyrians an	2Kin 19:35	5221
Sharezer his sons *s* him with the	2Kin 19:37	5221
And the king of Babylon *s* them	2Kin 25:21	5221
s Gedaliah, that he died, and the	2Kin 25:25	5221
which *s* Midian in the field of	1Chr 1:46	5221
s their tents, and the habitations	1Chr 4:41	5221
they *s* the rest of the Amalekites	1Chr 4:43	5221
he *s* him, because he put his hand	1Chr 13:10	5221
and David *s* them there	1Chr 14:11	5221
and they *s* the host of the	1Chr 14:16	5221
that David *s* the Philistines, and	1Chr 18:1	5221
And he *s* Moab	1Chr 18:2	5221
David *s* Hadarezer king of Zobah	1Chr 18:3	5221
Joab *s* Rabbah, and destroyed it	1Chr 20:1	5221
therefore he *s* Israel	1Chr 21:7	5221
came to pass, that God *s* Jeroboam	2Chr 13:15	5062
So the LORD *s* the Ethiopians	2Chr 14:12	5062
they *s* all the cities round about	2Chr 14:14	5221
They *s* also the tents of cattle,	2Chr 14:15	5221
and they *s* Ijon, and Dan, and	2Chr 16:4	5221
s Micaiah upon the cheek, and said	2Chr 18:23	5221
s the king of Israel between the	2Chr 18:33	5221
s the Edomites which compassed	2Chr 21:9	5221
after all this the LORD *s* him in	2Chr 21:18	5062
and the Syrians *s* Joram	2Chr 22:5	5221
s of the children of Seir ten	2Chr 25:11	5221
s three thousand of them, and took	2Chr 25:13	5221
and they *s* him, and carried away a	2Chr 28:5	5221
who *s* him with a great slaughter	2Chr 28:5	5221
the gods of Damascus, which *s* him	2Chr 28:23	5221
s certain of them, and plucked off	Neh 13:25	5221
Thus the Jews *s* all their enemies	Est 9:5	5221
s the four corners of the house,	Job 1:19	5060
s Job with sore boils from the	Job 2:7	5221
s of Edom in the valley of salt	Ps 60:*t*	5221
he *s* the rock, that the waters	Ps 78:20	5221
s down the chosen men of Israel	Ps 78:31	3766
s all the firstborn in Egypt	Ps 78:51	5221
he *s* his enemies in the hinder	Ps 78:66	5221
He *s* their vines also and their	Ps 105:33	5221
He *s* also all the firstborn in	Ps 105:36	5221
Who *s* the firstborn of Egypt,	Ps 135:8	5221
Who *s* great nations, and slew	Ps 135:10	5221
To him that *s* Egypt in their	Ps 136:10	5221
To him which *s* great kings	Ps 136:17	5221
the city found me, they *s* me	Song 5:7	5221
again stay upon him that *s* them	Is 10:20	5221
He who *s* the people in wrath with	Is 14:6	5221
rod of him that *s* thee is broken	Is 14:29	5221
as he *s* those that	Is 27:7	4347
those that *s* him	Is 27:7	5221
beaten down, which *s* with a rod	Is 30:31	5221
s in the camp of the Assyrians an	Is 37:36	5221
Sharezer his sons *s* him with the	Is 37:38	5221
the hammer him that *s* the anvil	Is 41:7	1986
was I wroth, and *s* him	Is 57:17	5221
for in my wrath I *s* thee, but in	Is 60:10	5221
Then Pashur *s* Jeremiah the	Jer 20:2	5221
was instructed, I *s* upon my thigh	Jer 31:19	5606
s him, and put him in prison in	Jer 37:15	5221
s Gedaliah the son of Ahikam the	Jer 41:2	5221
Nebuchadrezzar king of Babylon *s*	Jer 46:2	5221
before that Pharaoh *s* Gaza	Jer 47:1	5221
And the king of Babylon *s* them	Jer 52:27	5221
which *s* the image upon his feet	Dan 2:34	4223

the stone that *s* the image became ... Dan 2:35 4223
his knees *s* one against another ... Dan 5:6 5368
s the ram, and brake his two horns ... Dan 8:7 5221
it *s* the gourd that it withered ... Jonah 4:7 5221
I *s* you with blasting and with ... Hag 2:17 5221
high priest's, and *s* off his ear ... Mt 26:51 *851*
others *s* him with the palms of ... Mt 26:67 *4474*
Christ, Who is he that *s* thee ... Mt 26:68 *3817*
the reed, and *s* him on the head ... Mt 27:30 *5180*
s a servant of the high priest, ... Mk 14:47 *3817*
they *s* him on the head with a ... Mk 15:19 *5180*
but *s* upon his breast, saying, ... Lk 18:13 *5180*
one of them *s* the servant of the ... Lk 22:50 *3960*
held Jesus mocked him, and *s* him ... Lk 22:63 *1194*
Prophesy, who is it that *s* thee ... Lk 22:64 *3817*
s their breasts, and returned ... Lk 23:48 *5180*
s the high priest's servant, and ... Jn 18:10 *3817*
they *s* him with their hands ... Jn 19:3 *1325,4475*
was oppressed, and *s* the Egyptian ... Acts 7:24 *3960*
he *s* Peter on the side, and raised ... Acts 12:7 *3960*
the angel of the Lord *s* him ... Acts 12:23 *3960*

SMOTEST {1}
rod, wherewith thou *s* the river ... Ex 17:5 5221

SMYRNA *(smir'-na)* {2} *A city of Ionia in Asia Minor.*
unto Ephesus, and unto *S*, and unto ... Rev 1:11 *4667*
angel of the church in *S* write ... Rev 2:8 *4668*

SNAIL {2}
and the lizard, and the *s*, and the ... Lev 11:30 2546
As a *s* which melteth, let every ... Ps 58:8 7642

SNARE {46}
shall this man be a *s* unto us ... Ex 10:7 4170
it will surely be a *s* unto thee ... Ex 23:33 4170
lest it be for a *s* in the midst ... Ex 34:12 4170
for that will be a *s* unto thee ... Deut 7:16 4170
their gods shall be a *s* unto you ... Judg 2:3 4170
thing became a *s* unto Gideon ... Judg 8:27 4170
her, that she may be a *s* to him ... 1Sa 18:21 4170
then layest thou a *s* for my life ... 1Sa 28:9 5367
own feet, and he walketh upon a *s* ... Job 18:8 7639
The *s* is laid for him in the ... Job 18:10 2256
table become a *s* before them ... Ps 69:22 6341
thee from the *s* of the fowler ... Ps 91:3 6341
which were a *s* unto them ... Ps 106:36 4170
The wicked have laid a *s* for me ... Ps 119:110 6341
bird out of the *s* of the fowlers ... Ps 124:7 6341
the *s* is broken, and we are ... Ps 124:7 6341
The proud have hid a *s* for me ... Ps 140:5 6341
have they privily laid a *s* for me ... Ps 142:3 6341
as a bird hasteth to the *s* ... Prov 7:23 6341
and his lips are the *s* of his soul ... Prov 18:7 4170
It is a *s* to the man who ... Prov 20:25 4170
his ways, and get a *s* to thy soul ... Prov 22:25 4170
of an evil man there is a *s* ... Prov 29:6 4170
men bring a city into a *s* ... Prov 29:8 6315
The fear of man bringeth a *s* ... Prov 29:25 4170
birds that are caught in the *s* ... Eccl 9:12 6341
for a *s* to the inhabitants of ... Is 8:14 4170
Fear, and the pit, and the *s* ... Is 24:17 6341
the pit shall be taken in the *s* ... Is 24:18 6341
lay a *s* for him that reproveth in ... Is 29:21 6983
Fear, and the pit, and the *s* ... Jer 48:43 6341
the pit shall be taken in the *s* ... Jer 48:44 6341
I have laid a *s* for thee, and thou ... Jer 50:24 3369
a *s* is come upon us, desolation ... Lam 3:47 6354
him, and he shall be taken in my *s* ... Eze 12:13 4686
him, and he shall be taken in my *s* ... Eze 17:20 4686
ye have been a *s* on Mizpah ... Hos 5:1 6341
but the prophet is a *s* of a ... Hos 9:8 6341
a bird fall in a *s* upon the earth ... Amos 3:5 6341
one take up a *s* from the earth ... Amos 3:5 6341
For as a *s* shall it come on all ... Lk 21:35 *3803*
Let their table be made a *s* ... Rom 11:9 *3803*
not that I may cast a *s* upon you ... 1Cor 7:35 *1029*
reproach and the *s* of the devil ... 1Ti 3:7 *3803*
rich fall into temptation and a *s* ... 1Ti 6:9 *3803*
out of the *s* of the devil ... 2Ti 2:26 *3803*

SNARED {9}
unto thee, lest thou be *s* therein ... Deut 7:25 3369
thou be not *s* by following them ... Deut 12:30 5367
the wicked is *s* in the work of ... Ps 9:16 5367
Thou art *s* with the words of thy ... Prov 6:2 3369
The wicked is *s* by the ... Prov 12:13 4170
the sons of men *s* in an evil time ... Eccl 9:12 3369
and fall, and be broken, and be *s* ... Is 8:15 3369
fall backward, and be broken, and *s* ... Is 28:13 3369
they are all of them *s* in holes ... Is 42:22 6351

SNARES {15}
but they shall be *s* and traps unto ... Josh 23:13 6341
the *s* of death prevented me ... 2Sa 22:6 4170
Therefore *s* are round about thee, ... Job 22:10 6341
his nose pierceth through *s* ... Job 40:24 4170
Upon the wicked he shall rain *s* ... Ps 11:6 6341
the *s* of death prevented me ... Ps 18:5 4170
seek after my life lay *s* for me ... Ps 38:12 5367
they commune of laying *s* privily ... Ps 64:5 4170
Keep me from the *s* which they ... Ps 141:9 6341
to depart from the *s* of death ... Prov 13:14 4170
to depart from the *s* of death ... Prov 14:27 4170
s are in the way of the froward ... Prov 22:5 6341
death the woman, whose heart is *s* ... Eccl 7:26 4685
lay wait, as he that setteth *s* ... Jer 5:26 3353
to take me, and hid *s* for my feet ... Jer 18:22 6341

SNATCH {1}
he shall *s* on the right hand, and ... Is 9:20 1504

SNEEZED {1}
the child *s* seven times, and the ... 2Kin 4:35 2237

SNORTING {1}
The *s* of his horses was heard ... Jer 8:16 5170

SNOUT {1}
As a jewel of gold in a swine's *s* ... Prov 11:22 639

SNOW {24}
behold, his hand was leprous as *s* ... Ex 4:6 7950
Miriam became leprous, white as *s* ... Num 12:10 7950
the midst of a pit in time of *s* ... 2Sa 23:20 7950
presence a leper as white as *s* ... 2Kin 5:27 7950
the ice, and wherein the *s* is hid ... Job 6:16 7950
If I wash myself with *s* water ... Job 9:30 7950
and heat consume the *s* waters ... Job 24:19 7950
For he saith to the *s*, Be thou on ... Job 37:6 7950
into the treasures of the *s* ... Job 38:22 7950
me, and I shall be whiter than *s* ... Ps 51:7 7950
it, it was white as *s* in Salmon ... Ps 68:14 7949
He giveth *s* like wool ... Ps 147:16 7950
Fire, and hail; *s*, and vapours ... Ps 148:8 7950
As the cold of *s* in the time of ... Prov 25:13 7950
As *s* in summer, and as rain in ... Prov 26:1 7950
afraid of the *s* for her household ... Prov 31:21 7950
they shall be as white as *s* ... Is 1:18 7950
the *s* from heaven, and returneth ... Is 55:10 7950
Will a man leave the *s* of Lebanon ... Jer 18:14 7950
Her Nazarites were purer than *s* ... Lam 4:7 7950
sit, whose garment was white as *s* ... Dan 7:9 8517
and his raiment white as *s* ... Mt 28:3 *5510*
shining, exceeding white as *s* ... Mk 9:3 *5510*
white like wool, as white as *s* ... Rev 1:14 *5510*

SNOWY {1}
slew a lion in a pit in a *s* day ... 1Chr 11:22 7950

SNUFFDISHES {3}
the *s* thereof, shall be of pure ... Ex 25:38 4289
lamps, and his snuffers, and his *s* ... Ex 37:23 4289
his lamps, and his tongs, and his *s* ... Num 4:9 4289

SNUFFED {2}
they *s* up the wind like dragons ... Jer 14:6 7602
and ye have *s* at it, saith the ... Mal 1:13 5301

SNUFFERS {6}
he made his seven lamps, and his *s* ... Ex 37:23 4457
And the bowls, and the *s*, and the ... 1Kin 7:50 4212
of the LORD bowls of silver, *s* ... 2Kin 12:13 4212
pots, and the shovels, and the *s* ... 2Kin 25:14 4212
And the *s*, and the basons, and the ... 2Chr 4:22 4212
also, and the shovels, and the *s* ... Jer 52:18 4212

SNUFFETH {1}
that *s* up the wind at her ... Jer 2:24 7602

SO so *Also see* APPENDIX.
A king of Egypt.
messengers to *S* king of Egypt ... 2Kin 17:4 5471

SOAKED {1}
their land shall be *s* with blood ... Is 34:7 7301

SOBER {12}
or whether we be *s*, it is for ... 2Cor 5:13 *4993*
but let us watch and be *s* ... 1Th 5:6 *3525*
let us, who are of the day, be *s* ... 1Th 5:8 *3525*
husband of one wife, vigilant, *s* ... 1Ti 3:2 *4998*
wives be grave, not slanderers, *s* ... 1Ti 3:11 *3524*
a lover of good men, *s*, just, ... Titus 1:8 *4998*
That the aged men be *s*, grave, ... Titus 2:2 *3524*
may teach the young women to be *s* ... Titus 2:4 *4994*
likewise exhort to be *s* minded ... Titus 2:6 *4993*
up the loins of your mind, be *s* ... 1Pet 1:13 *3525*
be ye therefore *s*, and watch unto ... 1Pet 4:7 *4993*
Be *s*, be vigilant ... 1Pet 5:8 *3525*

SOBERLY {2}
but to think *s*, according as God ... Rom 12:3 *1519,4993*
worldly lusts, we should live *s* ... Titus 2:12 *4996*

SOBERNESS {1}
forth the words of truth and *s* ... Acts 26:25 *4997*

SOBRIETY {2}
apparel, with shamefacedness and *s* ... 1Ti 2:9 *4997*
and charity and holiness with *s* ... 1Ti 2:15 *4997*

SOCHO *(so'-ko)* {1} See SOCHOH. *A son of Heber.*
Gedor, and Heber the father of *S* ... 1Chr 4:18 7755

SOCHOH *(so'-ko)* {1} See SHOCHOH, SOCHO, SOCOH. *A city in Judah near Adullam.*
to him pertained *S*, and all the ... 1Kin 4:10 7755

SOCKET {1}
hundred talents, a talent for a *s* ... Ex 38:27 134

SOCKETS {54}
thou shalt make forty *s* of silver ... Ex 26:19 134
two *s* under one board for his two ... Ex 26:19 134
two *s* under another board for his ... Ex 26:19 134
And their forty *s* of silver ... Ex 26:21 134
two *s* under one board ... Ex 26:21 134
two *s* under another board ... Ex 26:21 134
s of silver, sixteen *s* ... Ex 26:25 134
two *s* under one board ... Ex 26:25 134
two *s* under another board ... Ex 26:25 134
gold, upon the four *s* of silver ... Ex 26:32 134
cast five *s* of brass for them ... Ex 26:37 134
their twenty *s* shall be of brass ... Ex 27:10 134
and their twenty *s* of brass ... Ex 27:11 134
their pillars ten, and their *s* ten ... Ex 27:12 134
pillars three, and their *s* three ... Ex 27:14 134
pillars three, and their *s* three ... Ex 27:15 134
shall be four, and their *s* four ... Ex 27:16 134
be of silver, and their *s* of brass ... Ex 27:17 134
twined linen, and their *s* of brass ... Ex 27:18 134
his bars, his pillars, and his *s* ... Ex 35:11 134
court, his pillars, and their *s* ... Ex 35:17 134
forty *s* of silver he made under ... Ex 36:24 134
two *s* under one board for his two ... Ex 36:24 134
two *s* under another board for his ... Ex 36:24 134
And their forty *s* of silver ... Ex 36:26 134
two *s* under one board ... Ex 36:26 134
two *s* under another board ... Ex 36:26 134
s were sixteen *s* of silver ... Ex 36:30 134
under every board two *s* ... Ex 36:30 134
he cast for them four *s* of silver ... Ex 36:36 134
but their five *s* were of brass ... Ex 36:38 134
twenty, and their brasen *s* twenty ... Ex 38:10 134
and their brasen *s* twenty ... Ex 38:11 134
their pillars ten, and their *s* ten ... Ex 38:12 134
pillars three, and their *s* three ... Ex 38:14 134
pillars three, and their *s* three ... Ex 38:15 134
the *s* for the pillars were of ... Ex 38:17 134
four, and their *s* of brass four ... Ex 38:19 134
were cast the *s* of the sanctuary ... Ex 38:27 134
and the *s* of the vail ... Ex 38:27 134
an hundred *s* of the hundred ... Ex 38:27 134
therewith he made the *s* to the ... Ex 38:30 134
the *s* of the court round about, ... Ex 38:31 134
the *s* of the court gate, and all ... Ex 38:31 134
bars, and his pillars, and his *s* ... Ex 39:33 134
the court, his pillars, and his *s* ... Ex 39:40 134
the tabernacle, and fastened his *s* ... Ex 40:18 134
the *s* thereof, and all the vessels ... Num 3:36 134
the court round about, and their *s* ... Num 3:37 134
pillars thereof, and *s* thereof, ... Num 4:31 134
the court round about, and their *s* ... Num 4:32 134
marble, set upon *s* of fine gold ... Song 5:15 134

SOCOH *(so'-ko)* {2} See SOCHOH.
1. Same as Sochoh.
Jarmuth, and Adullam, *S*, and Azekah ... Josh 15:35 7755
2. A city in the hill country of Judah.
Shamir, and Jattir, and *S*, ... Josh 15:48 7755

SOD {2}
And Jacob *s* pottage ... Gen 25:29 2102
holy offerings *s* they in pots ... 2Chr 35:13 1310

SODDEN {6}
nor *s* at all with water, but ... Ex 12:9 1310
wherein it is *s* shall be broken ... Lev 6:28 1310
if it be *s* in a brasen pot, it ... Lev 6:28 1310
take the *s* shoulder of the ram ... Num 6:19 1311
he will not have *s* flesh of thee ... 1Sa 2:15 1310
women have *s* their own children ... Lam 4:10 1310

SODERING {1}
saying, It is ready for the *s* ... Is 41:7 1694

SODI *(so'-di)* {1} *A spy sent to the Promised Land.*
of Zebulun, Gaddiel the son of *S* ... Num 13:10 5476

SODOM *(sod'-om)* {48} See SODOMA, SODOMITE. *A city on the Salt Sea.*
as thou goest, unto *S*, and ... Gen 10:19 5467
before the LORD destroyed *S* ... Gen 13:10 5467
and pitched his tent toward *S* ... Gen 13:12 5467
But the men of *S* were wicked ... Gen 13:13 5467
made war with Bera king of *S* ... Gen 14:2 5467
And there went out the king of *S* ... Gen 14:8 5467
and the kings of *S* and Gomorrah ... Gen 14:10 5467
And they took all the goods of *S* ... Gen 14:11 5467
brother's son, who dwelt in *S* ... Gen 14:12 5467
the king of *S* went out to meet ... Gen 14:17 5467
the king of *S* said unto Abram, ... Gen 14:21 5467
And Abram said to the king of *S* ... Gen 14:22 5467
from thence, and looked toward *S* ... Gen 18:16 5467
LORD said, Because the cry of *S* ... Gen 18:20 5467
from thence, and went toward *S* ... Gen 18:22 5467
If I find in *S* fifty righteous ... Gen 18:26 5467
came two angels to *S* at even ... Gen 19:1 5467
and Lot sat in the gate of *S* ... Gen 19:1 5467
of the city, even the men of *S* ... Gen 19:4 5467
Then the LORD rained upon *S* ... Gen 19:24 5467
he looked toward *S* and Gomorrah ... Gen 19:28 5467
therein, like the overthrow of *S* ... Deut 29:23 5467
their vine is of the vine of *S* ... Deut 32:32 5467
remnant, we should have been as *S* ... Is 1:9 5467
word of the LORD, ye rulers of *S* ... Is 1:10 5467
and they declare their sin as *S* ... Is 3:9 5467
shall be as when God overthrew *S* ... Is 13:19 5467
they are all of them unto me as *S* ... Jer 23:14 5467
As in the overthrow of *S* and ... Jer 49:18 5467
As God overthrew *S* and Gomorrah ... Jer 50:40 5467
the punishment of the sin of *S* ... Lam 4:6 5467
dwelleth at thy right hand, is *S* ... Eze 16:46 5467
S thy sister hath not done, she ... Eze 16:48 5467
was the iniquity of thy sister *S* ... Eze 16:49 5467
captivity, the captivity of *S* ... Eze 16:53 5467
When thy sisters, *S* and her ... Eze 16:55 5467
For thy sister *S* was not ... Eze 16:56 5467
some of you, as God overthrew *S* ... Amos 4:11 5467
Israel, Surely Moab shall be as *S* ... Zeph 2:9 5467
more tolerable for the land of *S* ... Mt 10:15 *4670*
done in thee, had been done in *S* ... Mt 11:23 *4670*
land of *S* in the day of judgment ... Mt 11:24 *4670*
It shall be more tolerable for *S* ... Mk 6:11 *4670*
more tolerable in that day for *S* ... Lk 10:12 *4670*
Lot went out of *S* it rained fire ... Lk 17:29 *4670*
And turning the cities of *S* ... 2Pet 2:6 *4670*
Even as *S* and Gomorrha, and the ... Jude 7 *4670*
which spiritually is called *S* ... Rev 11:8 *4670*

SODOMA *(sod'-o-mah)* {1} See SODOM. *Greek form of Sodom.*
left us a seed, we had been as *S* ... Rom 9:29 *4670*

SODOMITE {1}
nor a *s* of the sons of Israel ... Deut 23:17 6945

SODOMITES {3}
And there were also *s* in the land ... 1Kin 14:24 6945
took away the *s* out of the land ... 1Kin 15:12 6945
And the remnant of the *s*, which ... 1Kin 22:46 6945

SOEVER {16}
what saddle *s* he rideth upon that ... Lev 15:9 834
What man *s* there be of the house ... Lev 17:3
What man *s* of the seed of Aaron ... Lev 22:4
What thing *s* I command you, ... Deut 12:32 834
that what thing *s* thou shalt hear ... 2Sa 15:35 834
the people, how many *s* they be ... 2Sa 24:3
supplication *s* be made by any man ... 1Kin 8:38 834
s shall be made of any man ... 2Chr 6:29 834
what cause *s* shall come to you of ... 2Chr 19:10
wherewith *s* they shall blaspheme .. Mk 3:28 *3745,302*
In what place *s* ye enter into a ... Mk 6:10 *1437*
unto you, What things *s* ye desire ... Mk 11:24 *3745,302*
for what things *s* he doeth ... Jn 5:19 *302*
Whose *s* sins ye remit, they are ... Jn 20:23 *302*
whose *s* sins ye retain, they are ... Jn 20:23 *302*
that what things *s* the law saith ... Rom 3:19 *1437*

SOFT {8}
For God maketh my heart *s* ... Job 23:16 7401
will he speak *s* words unto thee ... Job 41:3 7390
thou makest it *s* with showers ... Ps 65:10 4127
A *s* answer turneth away wrath ... Prov 15:1 7390
a *s* tongue breaketh the bone ... Prov 25:15 7390
A man clothed in *s* raiment ... Mt 11:8 *3120*
they that wear *s* clothing are in ... Mt 11:8 *3120*
A man clothed in *s* raiment ... Lk 7:25 *3120*

SOFTER {1}
his words were *s* than oil ... Ps 55:21 7401

SOFTLY {7}
and I will lead on *s*, according as ... Gen 33:14 328
went *s* unto him, and smote the ... Judg 4:21 3814
and she came *s*, and uncovered his ... Ruth 3:7 3909
and lay in sackcloth, and went *s* ... 1Kin 21:27 328
the waters of Shiloah that go *s* ... Is 8:6 328
I shall go *s* all my years in the ... Is 38:15
And when the south wind blew *s* ... Acts 27:13 *5285*

SOIL {1}
in a good *s* by great waters ... Eze 17:8 7704

SOJOURN {33}
went down into Egypt to *s* there ... Gen 12:10 1481
This one fellow came in to *s* ... Gen 19:9 1481
S in this land, and I will be with ... Gen 26:3 1481
For to *s* in the land are we come ... Gen 47:4 1481
when a stranger shall *s* with thee ... Ex 12:48 1481
the strangers which *s* among you ... Lev 17:8 1481
of the strangers that *s* among you ... Lev 17:10 1481
of the strangers that *s* among you ... Lev 17:13 1481
if a stranger *s* with thee in your ... Lev 19:33 1481
of the strangers that *s* in Israel ... Lev 20:2 1481
the strangers that do *s* among you ... Lev 25:45 1481
if a stranger shall *s* among you ... Num 9:14 1481
And if a stranger *s* with you ... Num 15:14 1481
to *s* where he could find a place ... Judg 17:8 1481
I go to *s* where I may find a ... Judg 17:9 1481
went to *s* in the country of Moab ... Ruth 1:1 1481
evil upon the widow with whom I *s* ... 1Kin 17:20 1481
s wheresoever thou canst *s* ... 2Kin 8:1 1481
that I *s* in Mesech, that I dwell ... Ps 120:5 1481
shall carry her afar off to *s* ... Is 23:7 1481
aforetime into Egypt to *s* there ... Is 52:4 1481
into Egypt, and go to *s* there ... Jer 42:15 1481
faces to go into Egypt to *s* there ... Jer 42:17 1481
whither ye desire to go and to *s* ... Jer 42:22 1481
say, Go not into Egypt to *s* there ... Jer 43:2 1481
into the land of Egypt to *s* there ... Jer 44:12 1481
into the land of Egypt to *s* there ... Jer 44:14 1481
into the land of Egypt to *s* there ... Jer 44:28 1481
They shall no more *s* there ... Lam 4:15 1481
out of the country where they *s* ... Eze 20:38 4033
to the strangers that *s* among you ... Eze 47:22 1481
seed should *s* in a strange land ... Acts 7:6 *1510,3941*

SOJOURNED {12}
Kadesh and Shur, and *s* in Gerar ... Gen 20:1 1481
to the land wherein thou hast *s* ... Gen 21:23 1481
Abraham *s* in the Philistines' ... Gen 21:34 1481
I have *s* with Laban, and stayed ... Gen 32:4 1481
Hebron, where Abraham and Isaac *s* ... Gen 35:27 1481
out of all Israel, where he *s* ... Deut 18:6 1481
s there with a few, and became ... Deut 26:5 1481
who was a Levite, and he *s* there ... Judg 17:7 1481
and he *s* in Gibeah ... Judg 19:16 1481
s in the land of the Philistines ... 2Kin 8:2 1481
Jacob *s* in the land of Ham ... Ps 105:23 1481
By faith he *s* in the land of ... Heb 11:9 *3939*

SOJOURNER {8}
I am a stranger and a *s* with you ... Gen 23:4 8453
a *s* of the priest, or an hired ... Lev 22:10 8453
though he be a stranger, or a *s* ... Lev 25:35 8453
as an hired servant, and as a *s* ... Lev 25:40 8453
if a *s* or stranger wax rich by ... Lev 25:47 1616
unto the stranger or *s* by thee ... Lev 25:47 8453
stranger, and for the *s* among them ... Num 35:15 8453
I am a stranger with thee, and a *s* ... Ps 39:12 8453

SOJOURNERS {3}
for ye are strangers and *s* with me ... Lev 25:23 8453
were *s* there until this day ... 2Sa 4:3 1481
are strangers before thee, and *s* ... 1Chr 29:15 8453

SOJOURNETH {15}
of her that *s* in her house, ... Ex 3:22 1481
the stranger that *s* among you ... Ex 12:49 1481
or a stranger that *s* among you ... Lev 16:29 1481
that *s* among you eat blood ... Lev 17:12 1481
nor any stranger that *s* among you ... Lev 18:26 1481
for thy stranger that *s* with thee ... Lev 25:6 1481
for the stranger that *s* with you ... Num 15:15 1481
for the stranger that *s* with you ... Num 15:16 1481
and the stranger that *s* among them ... Num 15:26 1481
the stranger that *s* among them ... Num 15:29 1481
the stranger that *s* among them ... Num 19:10 1481
the stranger that *s* among them ... Josh 20:9 1481
remaineth in any place where he *s* ... Ezr 1:4 1481
of the stranger that *s* in Israel ... Eze 14:7 1481
that in what tribe the stranger *s* ... Eze 47:23 1481

SOJOURNING {3}
Now the *s* of the children of ... Ex 12:40 4186
s on the side of mount Ephraim ... Judg 19:1 1481
the time of your *s* here in fear ... 1Pet 1:17 *3940*

SOLACE {1}
let us *s* ourselves with loves ... Prov 7:18 5965

SOLD {82}
he *s* his birthright unto Jacob ... Gen 25:33 4376
for he hath *s* us, and hath quite ... Gen 31:15 4376
s Joseph to the Ishmeelites for ... Gen 37:28 4376
the Midianites *s* him into Egypt ... Gen 37:36 4376
and *s* unto the Egyptians ... Gen 41:56 7666
he it was that *s* to all the ... Gen 42:6 7666
brother, whom ye *s* into Egypt ... Gen 45:4 4376
yourselves, that ye *s* me hither ... Gen 45:5 4376
for the Egyptians *s* every man his ... Gen 47:20 4376
wherefore they *s* not their lands ... Gen 47:22 4376
then he shall be *s* for his theft ... Ex 22:3 4376
The land shall not be *s* for ever ... Lev 25:23 4376
poor, and hath *s* away some of his ... Lev 25:25 4376
redeem that which his brother *s* ... Lev 25:25 4465
unto the man to whom he *s* it ... Lev 25:27 4376
then that which is *s* shall remain ... Lev 25:28 4465
within a whole year after it is *s* ... Lev 25:29 4465
then the house that was *s* ... Lev 25:33 4465
of their cities may not be *s* ... Lev 25:34 4376
be waxen poor, and be *s* unto thee ... Lev 25:39 4376
they shall not be *s* as bondmen ... Lev 25:42 4376
After that he is *s* he may be ... Lev 25:48 4376
him from the year that he was *s* ... Lev 25:50 4376
or if he have *s* the field to ... Lev 27:20 4376
then it shall be *s* according to ... Lev 27:27 4376
shall be *s* or redeemed ... Lev 27:28 4376
be *s* unto thee, and serve thee six ... Deut 15:12 4376
there ye shall be *s* unto your ... Deut 28:68 4376
except their Rock had *s* them ... Deut 32:30 4376
he *s* them into the hands of their ... Judg 2:14 4376
he *s* them into the hand of ... Judg 3:8 4376
the LORD *s* them into the hand of ... Judg 4:2 4376
he *s* them into the hands of the ... Judg 10:7 4376
he *s* them into the hand of Sisera ... 1Sa 12:9 4376
because thou hast *s* thyself to ... 1Kin 21:20 4376
until an ass's head was *s* for ... 2Kin 6:25
of fine flour be *s* for a shekel ... 2Kin 7:1
of fine flour was *s* for a shekel ... 2Kin 7:16
s themselves to do evil in the ... 2Kin 17:17 4376
which were *s* unto the heathen ... Neh 5:8 4376
or shall they be *s* unto us ... Neh 5:8 4376
the day wherein they *s* victuals ... Neh 13:15 4376
s on the sabbath unto the ... Neh 13:16 4376
For we are *s*, I and my people, to ... Est 7:4 4376
But if we had been *s* for bondmen ... Est 7:4 4376
Joseph, who was *s* for a servant ... Ps 105:17 4376
is it to whom I have *s* you ... Is 50:1 4376
iniquities have ye *s* yourselves ... Is 50:1 4376
Ye have *s* yourselves for nought ... Is 52:3 4376
which hath been *s* unto thee ... Jer 34:14 4376
our wood is *s* unto us ... Lam 5:4 935,4242
not return to that which is *s* ... Eze 7:13 4465
s a girl for wine, that they ... Joel 3:3 4376
have ye *s* unto the Grecians ... Joel 3:6 4376
the place whither ye have *s* them ... Joel 3:7 4376
because they *s* the righteous for ... Amos 2:6 4376
not two sparrows *s* for a farthing ... Mt 10:29 *4453*
s all that he had, and bought it ... Mt 13:46 *4097*
his lord commanded him to be *s* ... Mt 18:25 *4097*
God, and cast out all them that *s* ... Mt 21:12 *4453*
and the seats of them that *s* doves ... Mt 21:12 *4453*
might have been *s* for much ... Mt 26:9 *4097*
and began to cast out them that *s* ... Mk 11:15 *4453*
and the seats of them that *s* doves ... Mk 11:15 *4453*
For it might have been *s* for more ... Mk 14:5 *4097*
five sparrows *s* for two farthings ... Lk 12:6 *4453*
they drank, they bought, they *s* ... Lk 17:28 *4453*
to cast out them that *s* therein ... Lk 19:45 *4453*
in the temple those that *s* oxen ... Jn 2:14 *4453*
And said unto them that *s* doves ... Jn 2:16 *4453*
s for three hundred pence ... Jn 12:5 *4097*
s their possessions and goods, and ... Acts 2:45 *4097*
of lands or houses *s* them ... Acts 4:34 *4453*
prices of the things that were *s* ... Acts 4:34 *4097*
s it, and brought the money, and ... Acts 4:37 *4453*
his wife, *s* a possession, ... Acts 5:1 *4453*
and after it was *s*, was it not in ... Acts 5:4 *4097*
Tell me whether ye *s* the land for ... Acts 5:8 *591*
with envy, *s* Joseph into Egypt ... Acts 7:9 *591*
but I am carnal, *s* under sin ... Rom 7:14 *4097*
Whatsoever is *s* in the shambles, ... 1Cor 10:25 *4453*
morsel of meat *s* his birthright ... Heb 12:16 *591*

SOLDIER {6}
four parts, to every *s* a part ... Jn 19:23 *4757*
a devout *s* of them that waited on ... Acts 10:7 *4757*
by himself with a *s* that kept him ... Acts 28:16 *4757*
companion in labour, and fellow *s* ... Phil 2:25
as a good *s* of Jesus Christ ... 2Ti 2:3 *4757*
him who hath chosen him to be a *s* ... 2Ti 2:4 *4758*

SOLDIERS {29}
fathers, were bands of *s* for war ... 1Chr 7:4 6635
thousand and two hundred *s* ... 1Chr 7:11
But the *s* of the army which ... 2Chr 25:13 1121
require of the king a band of *s* ... Ezr 8:22 2428
therefore the armed *s* of Moab ... Is 15:4 2502
authority, having *s* under me ... Mt 8:9 *4757*
Then the *s* of the governor took ... Mt 27:27 *4757*
unto him the whole band of *s* ... Mt 27:27
they gave large money unto the *s* ... Mt 28:12 *4757*
the *s* led him away into the hall, ... Mk 15:16 *4757*
the *s* likewise demanded of him, ... Lk 3:14 *4754*
authority, having under me *s* ... Lk 7:8 *4757*
the *s* also mocked him, coming to ... Lk 23:36 *4757*
the *s* platted a crown of thorns, ... Jn 19:2 *4757*
Then the *s*, when they had ... Jn 19:23 *4757*
These things therefore the *s* did ... Jn 19:24 *4757*
Then came the *s*, and brake the ... Jn 19:32 *4757*
But one of the *s* with a spear ... Jn 19:34 *4757*
four quaternions of *s* to keep him ... Acts 12:4 *4757*
Peter was sleeping between two *s* ... Acts 12:6 *4757*
was no small stir among the *s* ... Acts 12:18 *4757*
Who immediately took *s* and ... Acts 21:32 *4757*
saw the chief captain and the *s* ... Acts 21:32 *4757*
that he was borne of the *s* for ... Acts 21:35 *4757*
them, commanded the *s* to go down ... Acts 23:10 *4753*
two hundred *s* to go to Caesarea ... Acts 23:23 *4757*
Then the *s*, as it was commanded ... Acts 23:31 *4757*
said to the centurion and to the *s* ... Acts 27:31 *4757*
Then the *s* cut off the ropes of ... Acts 27:32 *4757*

SOLDIERS' {1}
the *s* counsel was to kill the ... Acts 27:42 *4757*

SOLE {12}
no rest for the *s* of her foot ... Gen 8:9 3709
from the *s* of thy foot unto the ... Deut 28:35 3709
would not adventure to set the *s* ... Deut 28:56 3709
neither shall the *s* of thy foot ... Deut 28:65 3709
Every place that the *s* of your ... Josh 1:3 3709
from the *s* of his foot even to ... 2Sa 14:25 3709
with the *s* of my feet have I ... 2Kin 19:24 3709
the *s* of his foot unto his crown ... Job 2:7 3709
From the *s* of the foot even unto ... Is 1:6 3709
with the *s* of my feet have I ... Is 37:25 3709
the *s* of their feet was like the ... Eze 1:7 3709
was like the *s* of a calf's foot ... Eze 1:7 3709

SOLEMN {29}
it is a *s* assembly ... Lev 23:36 6116
your gladness, and in your *s* days ... Num 10:10 4150
offering, or in your *s* feasts ... Num 15:3 4150
day ye shall have a *s* assembly ... Num 29:35 6116
a *s* assembly to the LORD thy God ... Deut 16:8 6116
Seven days shalt thou keep a *s* ... Deut 16:15 2287
Proclaim a *s* assembly for Baal ... 2Kin 10:20 6116
on the *s* feasts of the LORD our ... 2Chr 2:4 4150
eighth day they made a *s* assembly ... 2Chr 7:9 6116
the new moons, and on the *s* feasts ... 2Chr 8:13 4150
the eighth day was a *s* assembly ... Neh 8:18 6116
appointed, on our *s* feast day ... Ps 81:3 2282
upon the harp with a *s* sound ... Ps 92:3
is iniquity, even the *s* meeting ... Is 1:13 6116
because none come to the *s* feasts ... Lam 1:4 4150
the LORD hath caused the *s* feasts ... Lam 2:6 4150
LORD, as in the day of a *s* feast ... Lam 2:7 4150
Thou hast called as in a *s* day my ... Lam 2:22 4150
of Jerusalem in her *s* feasts ... Eze 36:38 4150
before the LORD in the *s* feasts ... Eze 46:9 4150
her sabbaths, and all her *s* feasts ... Hos 2:11 4150
What will ye do in the *s* day ... Hos 9:5 4150
as in the days of the *s* feast ... Hos 12:9 4150
call a *s* assembly, gather the ... Joel 1:14 6116
a fast, call a *s* assembly ... Joel 2:15 6116
not smell in your *s* assemblies ... Amos 5:21 6116
O Judah, keep thy *s* feasts ... Nah 1:15 2282
are sorrowful for the *s* assembly ... Zeph 3:18 4150
even the dung of your *s* feasts ... Mal 2:3 2282

SOLEMNITIES {3}
Look upon Zion, the city of our *s* ... Is 33:20 4150
in all *s* of the house of Israel ... Eze 45:17 4150
in the *s* the meat offering shall ... Eze 46:11 4150

SOLEMNITY {2}
in the *s* of the year of release, ... Deut 31:10 4150
the night when a holy *s* is kept ... Is 30:29 2282

SOLEMNLY {2}
The man did *s* protest unto us, ... Gen 43:3 5749
howbeit yet protest *s* unto them ... 1Sa 8:9 5749

SOLES {7}
Every place whereon the *s* of your ... Deut 11:24 3709
as soon as the *s* of the feet of ... Josh 3:13 3709
the *s* of the priests' feet were ... Josh 4:18 3709
put them under the *s* of his feet ... 1Kin 5:3 3709
down at the *s* of thy feet ... Is 60:14 3709
and the place of the *s* of my feet ... Eze 43:7 3709
they shall be ashes under the *s* ... Mal 4:3 3709

SOLITARILY {1}
which dwell *s* in the wood ... Mic 7:14 910

SOLITARY {7}

Lo, let that night be *s*	Job 3:7	1565
For want and famine they were *s*	Job 30:3	1565
God setteth the *s* in families	Ps 68:6	3173
in the wilderness in a *s* way	Ps 107:4	3452
the *s* place shall be glad for	Is 35:1	6723
How doth the city sit *s*, that was	Lam 1:1	910
out, and departed into a *s* place	Mk 1:35	*2048*

SOLOMON *(sol'-o-mun)* {281} See JEDIDIAH, SOLOMON'S. *Son of David; king of Israel.*

and Shobab, and Nathan, and *S*	2Sa 5:14	8010
a son, and he called his name *S*	2Sa 12:24	8010
S his brother, he called not	1Kin 1:10	8010
unto Bath-sheba the mother of *S*	1Kin 1:11	8010
life, and the life of thy son *S*	1Kin 1:12	8010
Assuredly *S* thy son shall reign	1Kin 1:13	8010
Assuredly *S* thy son shall reign	1Kin 1:17	8010
but *S* thy servant hath he not	1Kin 1:19	8010
my son *S* shall be counted	1Kin 1:21	8010
son of Jehoiada, and thy servant *S*	1Kin 1:26	8010
Assuredly *S* thy son shall reign	1Kin 1:30	8010
cause *S* my son to ride upon mine	1Kin 1:33	8010
trumpet, and say, God save king *S*	1Kin 1:34	8010
the king, even so be he with *S*	1Kin 1:37	8010
caused *S* to ride upon king	1Kin 1:38	8010
of the tabernacle, and anointed *S*	1Kin 1:39	8010
the people said, God save king *S*	1Kin 1:39	8010
lord king David hath made *S* king	1Kin 1:43	8010
also *S* sitteth on the throne of	1Kin 1:46	8010
name of *S* better than thy name	1Kin 1:47	8010
And Adonijah feared because of *S*	1Kin 1:50	8010
And it was told *S*, saying, Behold,	1Kin 1:51	8010
Behold, Adonijah feareth king *S*	1Kin 1:51	8010
Let king *S* swear unto me to day	1Kin 1:51	8010
S said, If he will shew himself a	1Kin 1:52	8010
So king *S* sent, and they brought	1Kin 1:53	8010
came and bowed himself to king *S*	1Kin 1:53	8010
S said unto him, Go to thine	1Kin 1:53	8010
and he charged *S* his son, saying,	1Kin 2:1	8010
Then sat *S* upon the throne of	1Kin 2:12	8010
to Bath-sheba the mother of *S*	1Kin 2:13	8010
unto *S* the king, (for he will not	1Kin 2:17	8010
therefore went unto king *S*	1Kin 2:19	8010
king *S* answered and said unto his	1Kin 2:22	8010
Then king *S* sware by the LORD,	1Kin 2:23	8010
king *S* sent by the hand of	1Kin 2:25	8010
So *S* thrust out Abiathar from	1Kin 2:27	8010
it was told king *S* that Joab was	1Kin 2:29	8010
Then *S* sent Benaiah the son of	1Kin 2:29	8010
it was told *S* that Shimei had	1Kin 2:41	8010
king *S* shall be blessed, and the	1Kin 2:45	8010
was established in the hand of *S*	1Kin 2:46	8010
S made affinity with Pharaoh king	1Kin 3:1	8010
S loved the LORD, walking in the	1Kin 3:3	8010
did *S* offer upon that altar	1Kin 3:4	8010
appeared to *S* in a dream by night	1Kin 3:5	8010
S said, Thou hast shewed unto thy	1Kin 3:6	8010
that *S* had asked this thing	1Kin 3:10	8010
And *S* awoke	1Kin 3:15	8010
So king *S* was king over all	1Kin 4:1	8010
S had twelve officers over all	1Kin 4:7	8010
Taphath the daughter of *S* to wife	1Kin 4:11	8010
Basmath the daughter of *S* to wife	1Kin 4:15	8010
S reigned over all kingdoms from	1Kin 4:21	8010
served *S* all the days of his life	1Kin 4:21	8010
to Beer-sheba, all the days of *S*	1Kin 4:25	8010
S had forty thousand stalls of	1Kin 4:26	8010
provided victual for king *S*	1Kin 4:27	8010
And God gave *S* wisdom and	1Kin 4:29	8010
people to hear the wisdom of *S*	1Kin 4:34	8010
of Tyre sent his servants unto *S*	1Kin 5:1	8010
And *S* sent to Hiram, saying,	1Kin 5:2	8010
when Hiram heard the words of *S*	1Kin 5:7	8010
And Hiram sent to *S*, saying, I	1Kin 5:8	8010
So Hiram gave *S* cedar trees	1Kin 5:10	8010
S gave Hiram twenty thousand	1Kin 5:11	8010
thus gave *S* to Hiram year by year	1Kin 5:11	8010
And the LORD gave *S* wisdom	1Kin 5:12	8010
was peace between Hiram and *S*	1Kin 5:12	8010
king *S* raised a levy out of all	1Kin 5:13	8010
S had threescore and ten thousand	1Kin 5:15	8010
which king *S* built for the LORD	1Kin 6:2	8010
And the word of the LORD came to *S*	1Kin 6:11	8010
So *S* built the house, and finished	1Kin 6:14	8010
So *S* overlaid the house within	1Kin 6:21	8010
But *S* was building his own house	1Kin 7:1	8010
S made also an house for	1Kin 7:8	8010
And king *S* sent and fetched Hiram	1Kin 7:13	8010
And he came to king *S*, and wrought	1Kin 7:14	8010
king *S* for the house of the LORD	1Kin 7:40	8010
which Hiram made to king *S* for	1Kin 7:45	8010
S left all the vessels unweighed,	1Kin 7:47	8010
S made all the vessels that	1Kin 7:48	8010
ended all the work that king *S*	1Kin 7:51	8010
S brought in the things which	1Kin 7:51	8010
Then *S* assembled the elders of	1Kin 8:1	8010
unto king *S* in Jerusalem, that	1Kin 8:1	8010
king *S* at the feast in the month	1Kin 8:2	8010
And king *S*, and all the	1Kin 8:5	8010
Then spake *S*, The LORD said that	1Kin 8:12	8010
S stood before the altar of the	1Kin 8:22	8010
that when *S* had made an end of	1Kin 8:54	8010
S offered a sacrifice of peace	1Kin 8:63	8010
And at that time *S* held a feast	1Kin 8:65	8010
when *S* had finished the building	1Kin 9:1	8010
appeared to *S* the second time	1Kin 9:2	8010
when *S* had built the two houses,	1Kin 9:10	8010
had furnished *S* with cedar trees	1Kin 9:11	8010
that then king *S* gave Hiram	1Kin 9:11	8010
the cities which *S* had given him	1Kin 9:12	8010
of the levy which king *S* raised	1Kin 9:15	8010
S built Gezer, and Beth-horon the	1Kin 9:17	8010
the cities of store that *S* had	1Kin 9:19	8010
that which *S* desired to build in	1Kin 9:19	8010
upon those did *S* levy a tribute	1Kin 9:21	8010
of Israel did *S* make no bondmen	1Kin 9:22	8010
house which *S* had built for her	1Kin 9:24	
year did *S* offer burnt offerings	1Kin 9:25	8010
king *S* made a navy of ships in	1Kin 9:26	8010
the sea, with the servants of *S*	1Kin 9:27	8010
talents, and brought it to king *S*	1Kin 9:28	8010
of Sheba heard of the fame of *S*	1Kin 10:1	8010
and when she was come to *S*	1Kin 10:2	8010
S told her all her questions	1Kin 10:3	8010
the queen of Sheba gave to king *S*	1Kin 10:10	8010
king *S* gave unto the queen of	1Kin 10:13	8010
beside that which *S* gave her of	1Kin 10:13	8010
to *S* in one year was six hundred	1Kin 10:14	8010
king *S* made two hundred targets	1Kin 10:16	8010
accounted of in the days of *S*	1Kin 10:21	8010
So king *S* exceeded all the kings	1Kin 10:23	8010
And all the earth sought to *S*	1Kin 10:24	8010
S gathered together chariots and	1Kin 10:26	8010
S had horses brought out of Egypt	1Kin 10:28	8010
But king *S* loved many strange	1Kin 11:1	8010
S clave unto these in love	1Kin 11:2	8010
when *S* was old, that his wives	1Kin 11:4	8010
For *S* went after Ashtoreth the	1Kin 11:5	8010
S did evil in the sight of the	1Kin 11:6	8010
Then did *S* build an high place	1Kin 11:7	8010
And the LORD was angry with *S*	1Kin 11:9	8010
Wherefore the LORD said unto *S*	1Kin 11:11	8010
stirred up an adversary unto *S*	1Kin 11:14	8010
to Israel all the days of *S*	1Kin 11:25	8010
S built Millo, and repaired the	1Kin 11:27	8010
S seeing the young man that he	1Kin 11:28	8010
the kingdom out of the hand of *S*	1Kin 11:31	8010
S sought therefore to kill	1Kin 11:40	8010
was in Egypt until the death of *S*	1Kin 11:40	8010
And the rest of the acts of *S*	1Kin 11:41	8010
in the book of the acts of *S*	1Kin 11:41	8010
the time that *S* reigned in	1Kin 11:42	8010
S slept with his fathers, and was	1Kin 11:43	8010
fled from the presence of king *S*	1Kin 12:2	8010
that stood before *S* his father	1Kin 12:6	8010
again to Rehoboam the son of *S*	1Kin 12:21	8010
Speak unto Rehoboam, the son of *S*	1Kin 12:23	8010
the son of *S* reigned in Judah	1Kin 14:21	8010
shields of gold which *S* had made	1Kin 14:26	8010
to *S* his son, In this house, and	2Kin 21:7	8010
which *S* the king of Israel had	2Kin 23:13	8010
all the vessels of gold which *S*	2Kin 24:13	8010
the bases which *S* had made for	2Kin 25:16	8010
and Shobab, and Nathan, and *S*	1Chr 3:5	8010
temple that *S* built in Jerusalem	1Chr 6:10	8010
until *S* had built the house of	1Chr 6:32	8010
and Shobab, Nathan, and *S*	1Chr 14:4	8010
wherewith *S* made the brasen sea,	1Chr 18:8	8010
S my son is young and tender, and	1Chr 22:5	8010
Then he called for *S* his son	1Chr 22:6	8010
And David said to *S*, My son, as	1Chr 22:7	8010
for his name shall be *S*, and I	1Chr 22:9	8010
of Israel to help *S* his son	1Chr 22:17	8010
he made *S* his son king over	1Chr 23:1	8010
he hath chosen *S* my son to sit	1Chr 28:5	8010
S thy son, he shall build my	1Chr 28:6	8010
S my son, know thou the God of	1Chr 28:9	8010
Then David gave to *S* his son the	1Chr 28:11	8010
And David said to *S* his son	1Chr 28:20	8010
S my son, whom alone God hath	1Chr 29:1	8010
give unto *S* my son a perfect	1Chr 29:19	8010
they made *S* the son of David king	1Chr 29:22	8010
Then *S* sat on the throne of the	1Chr 29:23	8010
themselves unto *S* the king	1Chr 29:24	8010
the LORD magnified *S* exceedingly	1Chr 29:25	8010
S his son reigned in his stead	1Chr 29:28	8010
And *S* the son of David was	2Chr 1:1	8010
Then *S* spake unto all Israel, to	2Chr 1:2	8010
So *S*, and all the congregation	2Chr 1:3	8010
and *S* and the congregation sought	2Chr 1:5	8010
S went up thither to the brasen	2Chr 1:6	8010
that night did God appear unto *S*	2Chr 1:7	8010
S said unto God, Thou hast shewed	2Chr 1:8	8010
And God said to *S*, Because this	2Chr 1:11	8010
Then *S* came from his journey to	2Chr 1:13	8010
S gathered chariots and horsemen	2Chr 1:14	8010
S had horses brought out of Egypt	2Chr 1:16	8010
S determined to build an house	2Chr 2:1	8010
S told out threescore and ten	2Chr 2:2	8010
S sent to Huram the king of Tyre,	2Chr 2:3	8010
in writing, which he sent to *S*	2Chr 2:11	8010
S numbered all the strangers that	2Chr 2:17	8010
Then *S* began to build the house	2Chr 3:1	8010
these are the things wherein *S*	2Chr 3:3	8010
for king *S* for the house of God	2Chr 4:11	8010
S for the house of the LORD of	2Chr 4:16	8010
Thus *S* made all these vessels in	2Chr 4:18	8010
S made all the vessels that were	2Chr 4:19	8010
Thus all the work that *S* made for	2Chr 5:1	8010
S brought in all the things that	2Chr 5:1	8010
Then *S* assembled the elders of	2Chr 5:2	8010
Also king *S*, and all the	2Chr 5:6	8010
Then said *S*, The LORD hath said	2Chr 6:1	8010
For *S* had made a brasen scaffold,	2Chr 6:13	8010
Now when *S* had made an end of	2Chr 7:1	8010
king *S* offered a sacrifice of	2Chr 7:5	8010
Moreover *S* hallowed the middle of	2Chr 7:7	8010
which *S* had made was not able to	2Chr 7:7	8010
Also at the same time *S* kept the	2Chr 7:8	8010
had shewed unto David, and to *S*	2Chr 7:10	8010
Thus *S* finished the house of the	2Chr 7:11	8010
the LORD appeared to *S* by night	2Chr 7:12	8010
wherein *S* had built the house of	2Chr 8:1	8010
which Huram had restored to *S*	2Chr 8:2	8010
S built them, and caused the	2Chr 8:2	8010
S went to Hamath-zobah, and	2Chr 8:3	8010
all the store cities that *S* had	2Chr 8:6	8010
all that *S* desired to build in	2Chr 8:6	8010
them did *S* make to pay tribute	2Chr 8:8	8010
S make no servants for his work	2Chr 8:9	8010
S brought up the daughter of	2Chr 8:11	8010
Then *S* offered burnt offerings	2Chr 8:12	8010
Now all the work of *S* was	2Chr 8:16	8010
Then went *S* to Ezion-geber, and to	2Chr 8:17	8010
with the servants of *S* to Ophir	2Chr 8:18	8010
gold, and brought them to king *S*	2Chr 8:18	8010
of Sheba heard of the fame of *S*	2Chr 9:1	8010
she came to prove *S* with hard	2Chr 9:1	8010
and when she was come to *S*	2Chr 9:1	8010
S told her all her questions	2Chr 9:2	8010
hid from *S* which he told her not	2Chr 9:2	8010
of Sheba had seen the wisdom of *S*	2Chr 9:3	8010
as the queen of Sheba gave king *S*	2Chr 9:9	8010
of Huram, and the servants of *S*	2Chr 9:10	8010
king *S* gave to the queen of Sheba	2Chr 9:12	8010
to *S* in one year was six hundred	2Chr 9:13	8010
brought gold and silver to *S*	2Chr 9:14	8010
king *S* made two hundred targets	2Chr 9:15	8010
vessels of king *S* were of gold	2Chr 9:20	8010
accounted of in the days of *S*	2Chr 9:20	8010
king *S* passed all the kings of	2Chr 9:22	8010
earth sought the presence of *S*	2Chr 9:23	8010
S had four thousand stalls for	2Chr 9:25	8010
they brought unto *S* horses out of	2Chr 9:28	8010
Now the rest of the acts of *S*	2Chr 9:29	8010
S reigned in Jerusalem over all	2Chr 9:30	8010
S slept with his fathers, and he	2Chr 9:31	8010
from the presence of *S* the king	2Chr 10:2	8010
S his father while he yet lived	2Chr 10:6	8010
Speak unto Rehoboam the son of *S*	2Chr 11:3	8010
made Rehoboam the son of *S* strong	2Chr 11:17	8010
walked in the way of David and *S*	2Chr 11:17	8010
shields of gold which *S* had made	2Chr 12:9	8010
the servant of *S* the son of David	2Chr 13:6	8010
against Rehoboam the son of *S*	2Chr 13:7	8010
for since the time of *S* the son	2Chr 30:26	8010
to *S* his son, In this house, and	2Chr 33:7	8010
S the son of David king of Israel	2Chr 35:3	8010
to the writing of *S* his son	2Chr 35:4	8010
of David, and of *S* his son	Neh 12:45	8010
Did not *S* king of Israel sin by	Neh 13:26	8010
A Psalm for *S*	Ps 72:*t*	8010
A Song of degrees for *S*	Ps 127:*t*	8010
The Proverbs of *S* the son of	Prov 1:1	8010
The proverbs of *S*	Prov 10:1	8010
These are also proverbs of *S*	Prov 25:1	8010
of Kedar, as the curtains of *S*	Song 1:5	8010
King *S* made himself a chariot of	Song 3:9	8010
behold king *S* with the crown	Song 3:11	8010
S had a vineyard at Baal-hamon	Song 8:11	8010
thou, O *S*, must have a thousand,	Song 8:12	8010
which king *S* had made in the	Jer 52:20	8010
David the king begat *S* of her	Mt 1:6	*4672*
And *S* begat Roboam	Mt 1:7	*4672*
That even *S* in all his glory was	Mt 6:29	*4672*
the earth to hear the wisdom of *S*	Mt 12:42	*4672*
behold, a greater than *S* is here	Mt 12:42	*4672*
the earth to hear the wisdom of *S*	Lk 11:31	*4672*
behold, a greater than *S* is here	Lk 11:31	*4672*
that *S* in all his glory was not	Lk 12:27	*4672*
But *S* built him an house	Acts 7:47	*4672*

SOLOMON'S *(sol'-o-muns)* {25}

S provision for one day was	1Kin 4:22	8010
all that came unto king *S* table	1Kin 4:27	8010
S wisdom excelled the wisdom of	1Kin 4:30	8010
Beside the chief of *S* officers	1Kin 5:16	8010
S builders and Hiram's builders	1Kin 5:18	8010
year of *S* reign over Israel	1Kin 6:1	8010
all *S* desire which he was pleased	1Kin 9:1	8010
present unto his daughter, *S* wife	1Kin 9:16	8010
officers that were over *S* work	1Kin 9:23	8010
of Sheba had seen all *S* wisdom	1Kin 10:4	8010
all king *S* drinking vessels were	1Kin 10:21	8010
S servant, whose mother's name	1Kin 11:26	8010
S son was Rehoboam, Abia his son,	1Chr 3:10	8010
all that came into *S* heart to	2Chr 7:11	8010
were the chief of king *S* officers	2Chr 8:10	8010
The children of *S* servants	Ezr 2:55	8010
and the children of *S* servants	Ezr 2:58	8010
The children of *S* servants	Neh 7:57	8010
and the children of *S* servants	Neh 7:60	8010
and the children of *S* servants	Neh 11:3	8010
The song of songs, which is *S*	Song 1:1	8010
Behold his bed, which is *S*	Song 3:7	8010
walked in the temple in *S* porch	Jn 10:23	*4672*
in the porch that is called *S*	Acts 3:11	*4672*
all with one accord in *S* porch	Acts 5:12	*4672*

SOME See APPENDIX.

SOMEBODY See APPENDIX.

SOMETHING See APPENDIX.

SOMETIME See APPENDIX.

S

SOMETIMES {3}
s were far off are made nigh by ... Eph 2:13 *4218*
For ye were *s* darkness, but now ... Eph 5:8 *4218*
we ourselves also were *s* foolish ... Titus 3:3 *4218*

SOMEWHAT See APPENDIX.

SON {2381}
the city, after the name of his *s* ... Gen 4:17 1121
and she bare a *s*, and called his ... Gen 4:25 1121
to him also there was born a *s* ... Gen 4:26 1121
begat a *s* in his own likeness, ... Gen 5:3
eighty and two years, and begat a *s* ... Gen 5:28 1121
his younger *s* had done unto him ... Gen 9:24 1121
And Terah took Abram his *s* ... Gen 11:31 1121
Lot the *s* of Haran his son's *s*, ... Gen 11:31
in law, his *s* Abram's wife ... Gen 11:31
his wife, and Lot his brother's *s* ... Gen 12:5 1121
took Lot, Abram's brother's *s* ... Gen 14:12 1121
art with child, and shalt bear a *s* ... Gen 16:11 1121
And Hagar bare Abram a *s* ... Gen 16:15 1121
her, and give thee a *s* also of her ... Gen 17:16 1121
wife shall bear thee a *s* indeed ... Gen 17:19 1121
And Abraham took Ishmael his *s* ... Gen 17:23 1121
Ishmael his *s* was thirteen years ... Gen 17:25 1121
circumcised, and Ishmael his *s* ... Gen 17:26 1121
lo, Sarah thy wife shall have a *s* ... Gen 18:10 1121
of life, and Sarah shall have a *s* ... Gen 18:14 1121
s in law, and thy sons, and thy ... Gen 19:12 1121
And the firstborn bare a *s* ... Gen 19:37 1121
And the younger, she also bare a *s* ... Gen 19:38 1121
bare Abraham a *s* in his old age ... Gen 21:2 1121
of his *s* that was born unto him ... Gen 21:3 1121
Abraham circumcised his *s* Isaac ... Gen 21:4 1121
when his *s* Isaac was born unto ... Gen 21:5 1121
have born him a *s* in his old age ... Gen 21:7 1121
Sarah saw the *s* of Hagar the ... Gen 21:9 1121
Cast out this bondwoman and her *s* ... Gen 21:10 1121
for the *s* of this bondwoman shall ... Gen 21:10 1121
shall not be heir with my *s* ... Gen 21:10
Abraham's sight because of his *s* ... Gen 21:11 1121
also of the *s* of the bondwoman ... Gen 21:13 1121
with my *s*, nor with my son's *s* ... Gen 21:23 5220
And he said, Take now thy *s* ... Gen 22:2 1121
thine only *s* Isaac ... Gen 22:2
men with him, and Isaac his *s* ... Gen 22:3 1121
and laid it upon Isaac his *s* ... Gen 22:6 1121
and he said, Here am I, my *s* ... Gen 22:7 1121
And Abraham said, My *s*, God will ... Gen 22:8 1121
in order, and bound Isaac his *s* ... Gen 22:9 1121
and took the knife to slay his *s* ... Gen 22:10 1121
thou hast not withheld thy *s* ... Gen 22:12 1121
thine only *s* from me ... Gen 22:12
offering in the stead of his *s* ... Gen 22:13 1121
thing, and hast not withheld thy *s* ... Gen 22:16 1121
thine only *s* ... Gen 22:16
for me to Ephron the *s* of Zohar ... Gen 23:8 1121
unto my *s* of the daughters of the ... Gen 24:3 1121
and take a wife unto my *s* Isaac ... Gen 24:4 1121
must I needs bring thy *s* again ... Gen 24:5 1121
thou bring not my *s* thither again ... Gen 24:6 1121
take a wife unto my *s* from thence ... Gen 24:7 1121
only bring not my *s* thither again ... Gen 24:8 1121
s of Milcah, the wife of Nahor, ... Gen 24:15 1121
of Bethuel the *s* of Milcah ... Gen 24:24 1121
a *s* to my master when she was old ... Gen 24:36 1121
to my *s* of the daughters of the ... Gen 24:37 1121
kindred, and take a wife unto my *s* ... Gen 24:38 1121
a wife for my *s* of my kindred ... Gen 24:40 1121
appointed out for my master's *s* ... Gen 24:44 1121
daughter of Bethuel, Nahor's *s* ... Gen 24:47 1121
brother's daughter unto his *s* ... Gen 24:48 1121
sent them away from Isaac his *s* ... Gen 25:6 1121
Ephron the *s* of Zohar the Hittite ... Gen 25:9 1121
that God blessed his *s* Isaac ... Gen 25:11 1121
of Ishmael, Abraham's *s*, whom ... Gen 25:12 1121
generations of Isaac, Abraham's *s* ... Gen 25:19 1121
see, he called Esau his eldest *s* ... Gen 27:1 1121
and said unto him, My *s* ... Gen 27:1 1121
when Isaac spake to Esau his *s* ... Gen 27:5 1121
And Rebekah spake unto Jacob her *s* ... Gen 27:6 1121
Now therefore, my *s*, obey my ... Gen 27:8 1121
him, Upon me be thy curse, my *s* ... Gen 27:13 1121
raiment of her eldest *s* Esau ... Gen 27:15 1121
put them upon Jacob her younger *s* ... Gen 27:15 1121
into the hand of her *s* Jacob ... Gen 27:17 1121
who art thou, my *s* ... Gen 27:18 1121
And Isaac said unto his *s*, How is ... Gen 27:20 1121
hast found it so quickly, my *s* ... Gen 27:20 1121
thee, that I may feel thee, my *s* ... Gen 27:21 1121
thou be my very *s* Esau or not ... Gen 27:21 1121
he said, Art thou my very *s* Esau ... Gen 27:24 1121
Come near now, and kiss me, my *s* ... Gen 27:26 1121
the smell of my *s* is as the smell ... Gen 27:27 1121
And he said, I am thy *s*, thy ... Gen 27:32 1121
shall I do now unto thee, my *s* ... Gen 27:37 1121
her elder *s* were told to Rebekah ... Gen 27:42 1121
and called Jacob her younger *s* ... Gen 27:42 1121
Now therefore, my *s*, obey my ... Gen 27:43 1121
s of Bethuel the Syrian, the ... Gen 28:5 1121
daughter of Ishmael Abraham's *s* ... Gen 28:9 1121
Know ye Laban the *s* of Nahor ... Gen 29:5 1121
and that he was Rebekah's *s* ... Gen 29:12 1121
tidings of Jacob his sister's *s* ... Gen 29:13 1121
And Leah conceived, and bare a *s* ... Gen 29:32 1121
she conceived again, and bare a *s* ... Gen 29:33 1121
therefore given me this *s* also ... Gen 29:33
she conceived again, and bare a *s* ... Gen 29:34 1121
she conceived again, and bare a *s* ... Gen 29:35 1121
conceived, and bare Jacob a *s* ... Gen 30:5 1121
my voice, and hath given me a *s* ... Gen 30:6 1121
again, and bare Jacob a second *s* ... Gen 30:7 1121
Zilpah Leah's maid bare Jacob a *s* ... Gen 30:10 1121
Leah's maid bare Jacob a second *s* ... Gen 30:12 1121
and bare Jacob the fifth *s* ... Gen 30:17 1121
again, and bare Jacob the sixth *s* ... Gen 30:19 1121
And she conceived, and bare a *s* ... Gen 30:23 1121
LORD shall add to me another *s* ... Gen 30:24 1121
when Shechem the *s* of Hamor the ... Gen 34:2 1121
The soul of my *s* Shechem longeth ... Gen 34:8 1121
Hamor, and Shechem Hamor's *s* ... Gen 34:18 1121
Shechem his *s* came unto the gate ... Gen 34:20 1121
unto Shechem his *s* hearkened all ... Gen 34:24 1121
Shechem his *s* with the edge of ... Gen 34:26 1121
thou shalt have this *s* also ... Gen 35:17 1121
Eliphaz the *s* of Adah the wife of ... Gen 36:10 1121
Reuel the *s* of Bashemath the wife ... Gen 36:10 1121
was concubine to Eliphaz Esau's *s* ... Gen 36:12 1121
Eliphaz the firstborn *s* of Esau ... Gen 36:15 1121
are the sons of Reuel Esau's *s* ... Gen 36:17 1121
Bela the *s* of Beor reigned in ... Gen 36:32 1121
Jobab the *s* of Zerah of Bozrah ... Gen 36:33 1121
died, and Hadad the *s* of Bedad ... Gen 36:35 1121
Baal-hanan the *s* of Achbor ... Gen 36:38 1121
Baal-hanan the *s* of Achbor died ... Gen 36:39 1121
he was the *s* of his old age ... Gen 37:3 1121
and mourned for his *s* many days ... Gen 37:34 1121
into the grave unto my *s* mourning ... Gen 37:35 1121
And she conceived, and bare a *s* ... Gen 38:3 1121
she conceived again, and bare a *s* ... Gen 38:4 1121
yet again conceived, and bare a *s* ... Gen 38:5 1121
house, till Shelah my *s* be grown ... Gen 38:11 1121
I gave her not to Shelah my *s* ... Gen 38:26 1121
My *s* shall not go down with you ... Gen 42:38 1121
brother Benjamin, his mother's *s* ... Gen 43:29 1121
God be gracious unto thee, my *s* ... Gen 43:29 1121
unto him, Thus saith thy *s* Joseph ... Gen 45:9 1121
Joseph my *s* is yet alive ... Gen 45:28 1121
Shaul the *s* of a Canaanitish ... Gen 46:10 1121
and he called his *s* Joseph ... Gen 47:29 1121
thy *s* Joseph cometh unto thee ... Gen 48:2 1121
refused, and said, I know it, my *s* ... Gen 48:19 1121
from the prey, my *s*, thou art ... Gen 49:9 1121
the *s* of Manasseh were brought up ... Gen 50:23 1121
if it be a *s*, then ye shall kill ... Ex 1:16 1121
Every *s* that is born ye shall ... Ex 1:22 1121
the woman conceived, and bare a *s* ... Ex 2:2 1121
daughter, and he became her *s* ... Ex 2:10 1121
And she bare him a *s*, and he called ... Ex 2:22 1121
saith the LORD, Israel is my *s* ... Ex 4:22 1121
And I say unto thee, Let my *s* go ... Ex 4:23 1121
him go, behold, I will slay thy *s* ... Ex 4:23 1121
and cut off the foreskin of her *s* ... Ex 4:25 1121
Shaul the *s* of a Canaanitish ... Ex 6:15 1121
Eleazar Aaron's *s* took him one of ... Ex 6:25 1121
of thy *s*, and of thy son's *s* ... Ex 10:2 1121
thou shalt shew thy *s* in that day ... Ex 13:8 1121
it shall be when thy *s* asketh ... Ex 13:14 1121
not do any work, thou, nor thy *s* ... Ex 20:10 1121
he have betrothed her unto his *s* ... Ex 21:9 1121
Whether he have gored a *s* ... Ex 21:31 1121
the *s* of thy handmaid, and the ... Ex 23:12 1121
that *s* that is priest in his ... Ex 29:30 1121
by name Bezaleel the *s* of Uri ... Ex 31:2 1121
the *s* of Hur, of the tribe of ... Ex 31:2 1121
the *s* of Ahisamach, of the tribe ... Ex 31:6 1121
LORD, even every man upon his *s* ... Ex 32:29 1121
the *s* of Nun, a young man, ... Ex 33:11 1121
by name Bezaleel the *s* of Uri ... Ex 35:30 1121
the *s* of Hur, of the tribe of ... Ex 35:30 1121
the *s* of Ahisamach, of the tribe ... Ex 35:34 1121
of Ithamar, *s* to Aaron the priest ... Ex 38:21 1121
And Bezaleel the *s* of Uri ... Ex 38:22 1121
the *s* of Hur, of the tribe of ... Ex 38:22 1121
s of Ahisamach, of the tribe of ... Ex 38:23 1121
purifying are fulfilled, for a *s* ... Lev 12:6 1121
and for his father, and for his *s* ... Lev 21:2 1121
the *s* of an Israelitish woman, ... Lev 24:10 1121
this *s* of the Israelitish woman ... Lev 24:10 1121
the Israelitish woman's *s* ... Lev 24:11 1121
his uncle, or his uncle's *s* ... Lev 25:49 1121
Elizur the *s* of Shedeur ... Num 1:5 1121
Shelumiel the *s* of Zurishaddai ... Num 1:6 1121
Nahshon the *s* of Amminadab ... Num 1:7 1121
Nethaneel the *s* of Zuar ... Num 1:8 1121
Eliab the *s* of Helon ... Num 1:9 1121
Elishama the *s* of Ammihud ... Num 1:10 1121
Gamaliel the *s* of Pedahzur ... Num 1:10 1121
Abidan the *s* of Gideoni ... Num 1:11 1121
Ahiezer the *s* of Ammishaddai ... Num 1:12 1121
Pagiel the *s* of Ocran ... Num 1:13 1121
Eliasaph the *s* of Deuel ... Num 1:14 1121
Ahira the *s* of Enan ... Num 1:15 1121
of Reuben, Israel's eldest *s* ... Num 1:20 1121
Nahshon the *s* of Amminadab shall ... Num 2:3 1121
Nethaneel the *s* of Zuar shall be ... Num 2:5 1121
Eliab the *s* of Helon shall be ... Num 2:7 1121
shall be Elizur the *s* of Shedeur ... Num 2:10 1121
be Shelumiel the *s* of Zurishaddai ... Num 2:12 1121
shall be Eliasaph the *s* of Reuel ... Num 2:14 1121
be Elishama the *s* of Ammihud ... Num 2:18 1121
be Gamaliel the *s* of Pedahzur ... Num 2:20 1121
shall be Abidan the *s* of Gideoni ... Num 2:22 1121
be Ahiezer the *s* of Ammishaddai ... Num 2:25 1121
shall be Pagiel the *s* of Ocran ... Num 2:27 1121
shall be Ahira the *s* of Enan ... Num 2:29 1121
shall be Eliasaph the *s* of Lael ... Num 3:24 1121
be Elizaphan the *s* of Uzziel ... Num 3:30 1121
Eleazar the *s* of Aaron the priest ... Num 3:32 1121
was Zuriel the *s* of Abihail ... Num 3:35 1121
to the office of Eleazar the *s* of ... Num 4:16 1121
Ithamar the *s* of Aaron the priest ... Num 4:28 1121
Ithamar the *s* of Aaron the priest ... Num 4:33 1121
Ithamar the *s* of Aaron the priest ... Num 7:8 1121
was Nahshon the *s* of Amminadab ... Num 7:12 1121
of Nahshon the *s* of Amminadab ... Num 7:17 1121
day Nethaneel the *s* of Zuar ... Num 7:18 1121
of Nethaneel the *s* of Zuar ... Num 7:23 1121
third day Eliab the *s* of Helon ... Num 7:24 1121
offering of Eliab the *s* of Helon ... Num 7:29 1121
day Elizur the *s* of Shedeur ... Num 7:30 1121
of Elizur the *s* of Shedeur ... Num 7:35 1121
Shelumiel the *s* of Zurishaddai ... Num 7:36 1121
of Shelumiel the *s* of Zurishaddai ... Num 7:41 1121
sixth day Eliasaph the *s* of Deuel ... Num 7:42 1121
of Eliasaph the *s* of Deuel ... Num 7:47 1121
day Elishama the *s* of Ammihud ... Num 7:48 1121
of Elishama the *s* of Ammihud ... Num 7:53 1121
Gamaliel the *s* of Pedahzur ... Num 7:54 1121
of Gamaliel the *s* of Pedahzur ... Num 7:59 1121
ninth day Abidan the *s* of Gideoni ... Num 7:60 1121
of Abidan the *s* of Gideoni ... Num 7:65 1121
day Ahiezer the *s* of Ammishaddai ... Num 7:66 1121
of Ahiezer the *s* of Ammishaddai ... Num 7:71 1121
day Pagiel the *s* of Ocran ... Num 7:72 1121
offering of Pagiel the *s* of Ocran ... Num 7:77 1121
twelfth day Ahira the *s* of Enan ... Num 7:78 1121
offering of Ahira the *s* of Enan ... Num 7:83 1121
was Nahshon the *s* of Amminadab ... Num 10:14 1121
was Nethaneel the *s* of Zuar ... Num 10:15 1121
Zebulun was Eliab the *s* of Helon ... Num 10:16 1121
host was Elizur the *s* of Shedeur ... Num 10:18 1121
Shelumiel the *s* of Zurishaddai ... Num 10:19 1121
Gad was Eliasaph the *s* of Deuel ... Num 10:20 1121
was Elishama the *s* of Ammihud ... Num 10:22 1121
was Gamaliel the *s* of Pedahzur ... Num 10:23 1121
was Abidan the *s* of Gideoni ... Num 10:24 1121
was Ahiezer the *s* of Ammishaddai ... Num 10:25 1121
Asher was Pagiel the *s* of Ocran ... Num 10:26 1121
Naphtali was Ahira the *s* of Enan ... Num 10:27 1121
the *s* of Raguel the Midianite, ... Num 10:29 1121
And Joshua the *s* of Nun, the ... Num 11:28 1121
Reuben, Shammua the *s* of Zaccur ... Num 13:4 1121
of Simeon, Shaphat the *s* of Hori ... Num 13:5 1121
Judah, Caleb the *s* of Jephunneh ... Num 13:6 1121
of Issachar, Igal the *s* of Joseph ... Num 13:7 1121
of Ephraim, Oshea the *s* of Nun ... Num 13:8 1121
of Benjamin, Palti the *s* of Raphu ... Num 13:9 1121
of Zebulun, Gaddiel the *s* of Sodi ... Num 13:10 1121
of Manasseh, Gaddi the *s* of Susi ... Num 13:11 1121
of Dan, Ammiel the *s* of Gemalli ... Num 13:12 1121
of Asher, Sethur the *s* of Michael ... Num 13:13 1121
Naphtali, Nahbi the *s* of Vophsi ... Num 13:14 1121
of Gad, Geuel the *s* of Machi ... Num 13:15 1121
Oshea the *s* of Nun Jehoshua ... Num 13:16 1121
And Joshua the *s* of Nun, and Caleb ... Num 14:6 1121
Caleb the *s* of Jephunneh, which ... Num 14:6 1121
save Caleb the *s* of Jephunneh ... Num 14:30 1121
Jephunneh, and Joshua the *s* of Nun ... Num 14:30 1121
But Joshua the *s* of Nun, and Caleb ... Num 14:38 1121
Caleb the *s* of Jephunneh, which ... Num 14:38 1121
the *s* of Izhar, the *s* of Kohath ... Num 16:1 1121
the *s* of Levi, and Dathan and ... Num 16:1 1121
the *s* of Peleth, sons of Reuben, ... Num 16:1 1121
Eleazar the *s* of Aaron the priest ... Num 16:37 1121
Take Aaron and Eleazar his *s* ... Num 20:25 1121
and put them upon Eleazar his *s* ... Num 20:26 1121
and put them upon Eleazar his *s* ... Num 20:28 1121
Balak the *s* of Zippor saw all ... Num 22:2 1121
Balak the *s* of Zippor was king of ... Num 22:4 1121
Balaam the *s* of Beor to Pethor ... Num 22:5 1121
unto God, Balak the *s* of Zippor ... Num 22:10 1121
Thus saith Balak the *s* of Zippor ... Num 22:16 1121
hearken unto me, thou *s* of Zippor ... Num 23:18 1121
neither the *s* of man, that he ... Num 23:19 1121
Balaam the *s* of Beor hath said, ... Num 24:3 1121
Balaam the *s* of Beor hath said, ... Num 24:15 1121
the *s* of Eleazar ... Num 25:7 1121
the *s* of Aaron the priest, saw it ... Num 25:7 1121
the *s* of Eleazar ... Num 25:11 1121
the *s* of Aaron the priest, hath ... Num 25:11 1121
the *s* of Salu, a prince of a ... Num 25:14 1121
unto Eleazar the *s* of Aaron the ... Num 26:1 1121
Reuben, the eldest *s* of Israel ... Num 26:5
Zelophehad the *s* of Hepher had no ... Num 26:33 1121
save Caleb the *s* of Jephunneh ... Num 26:65 1121
Jephunneh, and Joshua the *s* of Nun ... Num 26:65 1121
the *s* of Hepher ... Num 27:1 1121
the *s* of Gilead ... Num 27:1 1121
the *s* of Machir ... Num 27:1 1121
the *s* of Manasseh, of the ... Num 27:1 1121
of Manasseh the *s* of Joseph ... Num 27:1 1121
his family, because he hath no *s* ... Num 27:4 1121
If a man die, and have no *s* ... Num 27:8 1121
Take thee Joshua the *s* of Nun ... Num 27:18 1121
Phinehas the *s* of Eleazar the ... Num 31:6 1121
Balaam also the *s* of Beor they ... Num 31:8 1121
Save Caleb the *s* of Jephunneh the ... Num 32:12 1121
Kenezite, and Joshua the *s* of Nun ... Num 32:12 1121
priest, and Joshua the *s* of Nun ... Num 32:28 1121
tribe of Manasseh the *s* of Joseph ... Num 32:33 1121
the *s* of Manasseh went to Gilead ... Num 32:39 1121
unto Machir the *s* of Manasseh ... Num 32:40 1121
Jair the *s* of Manasseh went and ... Num 32:41 1121
priest, and Joshua the *s* of Nun ... Num 34:17 1121

Judah, Caleb the *s* of Jephunneh	Num 34:19	1121
Simeon, Shemuel the *s* of Ammihud	Num 34:20	1121
Benjamin, Elidad the *s* of Chislon	Num 34:21	1121
of Dan, Bukki the *s* of Jogli	Num 34:22	1121
Manasseh, Hanniel the *s* of Ephod	Num 34:23	1121
Ephraim, Kemuel the *s* of Shiphtan	Num 34:24	1121
Elizaphan the *s* of Parnach	Num 34:25	1121
Issachar, Paltiel the *s* of Azzan	Num 34:26	1121
of Asher, Ahihud the *s* of Shelomi	Num 34:27	1121
Pedahel the *s* of Ammihud	Num 34:28	1121
the *s* of Machir	Num 36:1	1121
the *s* of Manasseh, of the	Num 36:1	1121
sons of Manasseh the *s* of Joseph	Num 36:12	1121
thee, as a man doth bear his *s*	Deut 1:31	1121
Save Caleb the *s* of Jephunneh	Deut 1:36	1121
But Joshua the *s* of Nun, which	Deut 1:38	1121
Jair the *s* of Manasseh took all	Deut 3:14	1121
not do any work, thou, nor thy *s*	Deut 5:14	1121
thou, and thy *s*, and thy son's *s*	Deut 6:2	1121
when thy *s* asketh thee in time to	Deut 6:20	1121
Then thou shalt say unto thy *s*	Deut 6:21	1121
thou shalt not give unto his *s*	Deut 7:3	1121
shalt thou take unto thy *s*	Deut 7:3	1121
turn away thy *s* from following me	Deut 7:4	1121
that, as a man chasteneth his *s*	Deut 8:5	1121
Eleazar his *s* ministered in the	Deut 10:6	1121
sons of Eliab, the *s* of Reuben	Deut 11:6	1121
God shall choose, thou, and thy *s*	Deut 12:18	1121
the *s* of thy mother, or thy *s*,	Deut 13:6	1121
the LORD thy God, thou, and thy *s*	Deut 16:11	1121
in thy feast, thou, and thy *s*	Deut 16:14	1121
you any one that maketh his *s* or	Deut 18:10	1121
if the firstborn *s* be hers that	Deut 21:15	1121
that he may not make the *s* of the	Deut 21:16	1121
before the *s* of the hated	Deut 21:16	1121
But he shall acknowledge the *s* of	Deut 21:17	1121
have a stubborn and rebellious *s*	Deut 21:18	1121
This our *s* is stubborn and	Deut 21:20	1121
Balaam the *s* of Beor of Pethor of	Deut 23:4	1121
of her bosom, and toward her *s*	Deut 28:56	1121
gave Joshua the *s* of Nun a charge	Deut 31:23	1121
he, and Hoshea the *s* of Nun	Deut 32:44	1121
Joshua the *s* of Nun was full of	Deut 34:9	1121
spake unto Joshua the *s* of Nun	Josh 1:1	1121
Joshua the *s* of Nun sent out of	Josh 2:1	1121
and came to Joshua the *s* of Nun	Josh 2:23	1121
Joshua the *s* of Nun called the	Josh 6:6	1121
in his youngest *s* shall he set up	Josh 6:26	
the *s* of Carmi, the *s* of Zabdi,	Josh 7:1	1121
the *s* of Zerah, of the tribe of	Josh 7:1	1121
the *s* of Carmi, the *s* of Zabdi,	Josh 7:18	1121
the *s* of Zabdi, the *s* of Zerah,	Josh 7:18	1121
the *s* of Zerah, of the tribe of	Josh 7:18	1121
And Joshua said unto Achan, My *s*	Josh 7:19	1121
him, took Achan the *s* of Zerah	Josh 7:24	1121
Balaam also the *s* of Beor	Josh 13:22	1121
of Machir the *s* of Manasseh	Josh 13:31	1121
priest, and Joshua the *s* of Nun	Josh 14:1	1121
Caleb the *s* of Jephunneh the	Josh 14:6	1121
him, and gave unto Caleb the *s* of	Josh 14:13	1121
the inheritance of Caleb the *s* of	Josh 14:14	1121
stone of Bohan the *s* of Reuben	Josh 15:6	1121
went up by the valley of the *s* of	Josh 15:8	1121
unto Caleb the *s* of Jephunneh he	Josh 15:13	1121
And Othniel the *s* of Kenaz	Josh 15:17	1121
the *s* of Joseph by their families	Josh 17:2	1121
the *s* of Hepher	Josh 17:3	1121
the *s* of Gilead	Josh 17:3	1121
the *s* of Machir	Josh 17:3	1121
the *s* of Manasseh, had no sons,	Josh 17:3	1121
and before Joshua the *s* of Nun	Josh 17:4	1121
the valley of the *s* of Hinnom	Josh 18:16	1121
stone of Bohan the *s* of Reuben	Josh 18:17	1121
to Joshua the *s* of Nun among them	Josh 19:49	1121
priest, and Joshua the *s* of Nun	Josh 19:51	1121
and unto Joshua the *s* of Nun	Josh 21:1	1121
gave they to Caleb the *s* of	Josh 21:12	1121
Phinehas the *s* of Eleazar the	Josh 22:13	1121
Did not Achan the *s* of Zerah	Josh 22:20	1121
Phinehas the *s* of Eleazar the	Josh 22:31	1121
Phinehas the *s* of Eleazar the	Josh 22:32	1121
Then Balak the *s* of Zippor	Josh 24:9	1121
called Balaam the *s* of Beor to	Josh 24:9	1121
things, that Joshua the *s* of Nun	Josh 24:29	1121
Eleazar the *s* of Aaron died	Josh 24:33	1121
that pertained to Phinehas his *s*	Josh 24:33	1121
And Othniel the *s* of Kenaz	Judg 1:13	1121
And Joshua the *s* of Nun, the	Judg 2:8	1121
them, even Othniel the *s* of Kenaz	Judg 3:9	1121
Othniel the *s* of Kenaz died	Judg 3:11	1121
a deliverer, Ehud the *s* of Gera	Judg 3:15	1121
him was Shamgar the *s* of Anath	Judg 3:31	1121
called Barak the *s* of Abinoam out	Judg 4:6	1121
shewed Sisera that Barak the *s* of	Judg 4:12	1121
Barak the *s* of Abinoam on that	Judg 5:1	1121
days of Shamgar the *s* of Anath	Judg 5:6	1121
captive, thou *s* of Abinoam	Judg 5:12	1121
his *s* Gideon threshed wheat by	Judg 6:11	1121
Gideon the *s* of Joash hath done	Judg 6:29	1121
said unto Joash, Bring out thy *s*	Judg 6:30	1121
sword of Gideon the *s* of Joash	Judg 7:14	1121
Gideon the *s* of Joash returned	Judg 8:13	1121
and thy *s*, and thy son's *s* also	Judg 8:22	1121
neither shall my *s* rule over you	Judg 8:23	1121
And Jerubbaal the *s* of Joash went	Judg 8:29	1121
in Shechem, she also bare him a *s*	Judg 8:31	1121
Gideon the *s* of Joash died in a	Judg 8:32	1121
Abimelech the *s* of Jerubbaal went	Judg 9:1	1121
youngest *s* of Jerubbaal was left	Judg 9:5	1121
the *s* of his maidservant, king	Judg 9:18	1121
Gaal the *s* of Ebed came with his	Judg 9:26	1121
Gaal the *s* of Ebed said, Who is	Judg 9:28	1121
is not he the *s* of Jerubbaal	Judg 9:28	1121
the words of Gaal the *s* of Ebed	Judg 9:30	1121
Behold, Gaal the *s* of Ebed	Judg 9:31	1121
Gaal the *s* of Ebed went out, and	Judg 9:35	1121
of Jotham the *s* of Jerubbaal	Judg 9:57	1121
defend Israel Tola the *s* of Puah	Judg 10:1	1121
the *s* of Dodo, a man of Issachar	Judg 10:1	1121
he was the *s* of an harlot	Judg 11:1	1121
for thou art the *s* of a strange	Judg 11:2	1121
better than Balak the *s* of Zippor	Judg 11:25	1121
her he had neither *s* nor daughter	Judg 11:34	1121
after him Abdon the *s* of Hillel	Judg 12:13	1121
Abdon the *s* of Hillel the	Judg 12:15	1121
thou shalt conceive, and bear a *s*	Judg 13:3	1121
thou shalt conceive, and bear a *s*	Judg 13:5	1121
thou shalt conceive, and bear a *s*	Judg 13:7	1121
And the woman bare a *s*, and called	Judg 13:24	1121
the *s* in law of the Timnite,	Judg 15:6	2860
Blessed be thou of the LORD, my *s*	Judg 17:2	1121
the LORD from my hand for my *s*	Judg 17:3	1121
the *s* of Gershom	Judg 18:30	1121
the *s* of Manasseh, he and his sons	Judg 18:30	1121
father said unto his *s* in law	Judg 19:5	2860
the *s* of Eleazar	Judg 20:28	1121
the *s* of Aaron, stood before it	Judg 20:28	1121
her conception, and she bare a *s*	Ruth 4:13	1121
There is a *s* born to Naomi	Ruth 4:17	1121
the *s* of Jeroham	1Sa 1:1	1121
the *s* of Elihu, the *s* of Tohu,	1Sa 1:1	1121
the *s* of Zuph, an Ephrathite	1Sa 1:1	1121
had conceived, that she bare a *s*	1Sa 1:20	1121
gave her *s* suck until she weaned	1Sa 1:23	1121
he answered, I called not, my *s*	1Sa 3:6	1121
Samuel, and said, Samuel, my *s*	1Sa 3:16	1121
he said, What is there done, my *s*	1Sa 4:16	1121
for thou hast born a *s*	1Sa 4:20	1121
sanctified Eleazar his *s* to keep	1Sa 7:1	1121
the *s* of Abiel, the *s* of Zeror,	1Sa 9:1	1121
the *s* of Bechorath	1Sa 9:1	1121
the *s* of Aphiah, a Benjamite, a	1Sa 9:1	1121
And he had a *s*, whose name was	1Sa 9:2	1121
And Kish said to Saul his *s*	1Sa 9:3	1121
saying, What shall I do for my *s*	1Sa 10:2	1121
that is come unto the *s* of Kish	1Sa 10:11	1121
Saul the *s* of Kish was taken	1Sa 10:21	1121
And Saul, and Jonathan his *s*	1Sa 13:16	1121
Jonathan his *s* was there found	1Sa 13:22	1121
that Jonathan the *s* of Saul said	1Sa 14:1	1121
the *s* of Ahitub, I-chabod's	1Sa 14:3	1121
the *s* of Phinehas, the *s* of Eli	1Sa 14:3	1121
though it be in Jonathan my *s*	1Sa 14:39	1121
Jonathan my *s* will be on the	1Sa 14:40	1121
lots between me and Jonathan my *s*	1Sa 14:42	1121
the *s* of Ner, Saul's uncle	1Sa 14:50	1121
of Abner was the *s* of Abiel	1Sa 14:51	1121
I have seen a *s* of Jesse the	1Sa 16:18	1121
and said, Send me David thy *s*	1Sa 16:19	1121
them by David his *s* unto Saul	1Sa 16:20	1121
Now David was the *s* of that	1Sa 17:12	1121
And Jesse said unto David his *s*	1Sa 17:17	1121
Abner, whose *s* is this youth	1Sa 17:55	1121
thou whose *s* the stripling is	1Sa 17:56	1121
Whose *s* art thou, thou young man	1Sa 17:58	1121
I am the *s* of thy servant Jesse	1Sa 17:58	1121
that I should be *s* in law to the	1Sa 18:18	2860
Thou shalt this day be my *s* in	1Sa 18:21	2859
therefore be the king's *s* in law	1Sa 18:22	2859
thing to be a king's *s* in law	1Sa 18:23	2859
well to be the king's *s* in law	1Sa 18:26	2859
he might be the king's *s* in law	1Sa 18:27	2859
And Saul spake to Jonathan his *s*	1Sa 19:1	1121
But Jonathan Saul's *s* delighted	1Sa 19:2	1121
and Saul said unto Jonathan his *s*	1Sa 20:27	1121
cometh not the *s* of Jesse to meat	1Sa 20:27	1121
Thou *s* of the perverse rebellious	1Sa 20:30	1121
know that thou hast chosen the *s*	1Sa 20:30	1121
For as long as the *s* of Jesse	1Sa 20:31	1121
will the *s* of Jesse give every	1Sa 22:7	1121
s hath made a league with the *s*	1Sa 22:8	1121
my *s* hath stirred up my servant	1Sa 22:8	1121
I saw the *s* of Jesse coming to	1Sa 22:9	1121
Nob, to Ahimelech the *s* of Ahitub	1Sa 22:9	1121
the *s* of Ahitub, and all his	1Sa 22:11	1121
said, Hear now, thou *s* of Ahitub	1Sa 22:12	1121
the *s* of Jesse, in that thou hast	1Sa 22:13	1121
which is the king's *s* in law	1Sa 22:14	2860
sons of Ahimelech the *s* of Ahitub	1Sa 22:20	1121
when Abiathar the *s* of Ahimelech	1Sa 23:6	1121
And Jonathan Saul's *s* arose	1Sa 23:16	1121
Is this thy voice, my *s* David	1Sa 24:16	1121
thy servants, and to thy *s* David	1Sa 25:8	1121
and who is the *s* of Jesse	1Sa 25:10	1121
for he is such a *s* of Belial	1Sa 25:17	1121
wife, to Phalti the *s* of Laish	1Sa 25:44	1121
Saul lay, and Abner the *s* of Ner	1Sa 26:5	1121
and to Abishai the *s* of Zeruiah	1Sa 26:6	1121
people, and to Abner the *s* of Ner	1Sa 26:14	1121
Is this thy voice, my *s* David	1Sa 26:17	1121
return, my *s* David	1Sa 26:21	1121
Blessed be thou, my *s* David	1Sa 26:25	1121
the *s* of Maoch, king of Gath	1Sa 27:2	1121
the priest, Ahimelech's *s*	1Sa 30:7	1121
Jonathan his *s* are dead also	2Sa 1:4	1121
Saul and Jonathan his *s* be dead	2Sa 1:5	1121
for Saul, and for Jonathan his *s*	2Sa 1:12	1121
I am the *s* of a stranger, an	2Sa 1:13	1121
over Saul and over Jonathan his *s*	2Sa 1:17	1121
But Abner the *s* of Ner, captain	2Sa 2:8	1121
took Ish-bosheth the *s* of Saul	2Sa 2:8	1121
Ish-bosheth Saul's *s* was forty	2Sa 2:10	1121
And Abner the *s* of Ner, and the	2Sa 2:12	1121
of Ish-bosheth the *s* of Saul	2Sa 2:12	1121
Joab the *s* of Zeruiah, and the	2Sa 2:13	1121
to Ish-bosheth the *s* of Saul	2Sa 2:15	1121
Absalom the *s* of Maacah the	2Sa 3:3	1121
fourth, Adonijah the *s* of Haggith	2Sa 3:4	1121
fifth, Shephatiah the *s* of Abital	2Sa 3:4	1121
to Ish-bosheth Saul's *s*, saying,	2Sa 3:14	1121
even from Phaltiel the *s* of Laish	2Sa 3:15	1121
Abner the *s* of Ner came to the	2Sa 3:23	1121
Thou knowest Abner the *s* of Ner	2Sa 3:25	1121
the blood of Abner the *s* of Ner	2Sa 3:28	1121
king to slay Abner the *s* of Ner	2Sa 3:37	1121
when Saul's *s* heard that Abner	2Sa 4:1	1121
Saul's *s* had two men that were	2Sa 4:2	1121
And Jonathan, Saul's *s*, had a *s*	2Sa 4:4	1121
the *s* of Saul thine enemy	2Sa 4:8	1121
his father, and he shall be my *s*	2Sa 7:14	1121
the *s* of Rehob, king of Zobah, as	2Sa 8:3	1121
sent Joram his *s* unto king David	2Sa 8:10	1121
s of Rehob, king of Zobah	2Sa 8:12	1121
Joab the *s* of Zeruiah was over	2Sa 8:16	1121
Jehoshaphat the *s* of Ahilud was	2Sa 8:16	1121
And Zadok the *s* of Ahitub, and	2Sa 8:17	1121
and Ahimelech the *s* of Abiathar	2Sa 8:17	1121
Benaiah the *s* of Jehoiada was	2Sa 8:18	1121
the king, Jonathan hath yet a *s*	2Sa 9:3	1121
the *s* of Ammiel, in Lo-debar	2Sa 9:4	1121
the *s* of Ammiel, from Lo-debar	2Sa 9:5	1121
the *s* of Jonathan	2Sa 9:6	1121
the *s* of Saul, was come unto	2Sa 9:6	1121
s all that pertained to Saul	2Sa 9:9	1121
that thy master's *s* may have food	2Sa 9:10	1121
s shall eat bread alway at my	2Sa 9:10	1121
And Mephibosheth had a young *s*	2Sa 9:12	1121
Hanun his *s* reigned in his stead	2Sa 10:1	1121
unto Hanun the *s* of Nahash	2Sa 10:2	1121
Abimelech the *s* of Jerubbesheth	2Sa 11:21	1121
became his wife, and bare him a *s*	2Sa 11:27	1121
and she bare a *s*, and he called his	2Sa 12:24	1121
that Absalom the *s* of David had a	2Sa 13:1	1121
Amnon the *s* of David loved her	2Sa 13:1	1121
the *s* of Shimeah David's brother	2Sa 13:3	1121
Why art thou, being the king's *s*	2Sa 13:4	1121
king said to Absalom, Nay, my *s*	2Sa 13:25	1121
the *s* of Shimeah David's brother,	2Sa 13:32	1121
the *s* of Ammihud, king of Geshur	2Sa 13:37	1121
David mourned for his *s* every day	2Sa 13:37	1121
Now Joab the *s* of Zeruiah	2Sa 14:1	1121
any more, lest they destroy my *s*	2Sa 14:11	1121
hair of thy *s* fall to the earth	2Sa 14:11	1121
me and my *s* together out of the	2Sa 14:16	1121
two sons with you, Ahimaaz thy *s*	2Sa 15:27	1121
and Jonathan the *s* of Abiathar	2Sa 15:27	1121
their two sons, Ahimaaz Zadok's *s*	2Sa 15:36	
and Jonathan Abiathar's *s*	2Sa 15:36	
said, And where is thy master's *s*	2Sa 16:3	1121
name was Shimei, the *s* of Gera	2Sa 16:5	1121
into the hand of Absalom thy *s*	2Sa 16:8	1121
Then said Abishai the *s* of	2Sa 16:9	1121
to all his servants, Behold, my *s*	2Sa 16:11	1121
serve in the presence of his *s*	2Sa 16:19	1121
which Amasa was a man's *s*	2Sa 17:25	1121
that Shobi the *s* of Nahash of	2Sa 17:27	1121
Machir the *s* of Ammiel of	2Sa 17:27	1121
hand of Abishai the *s* of Zeruiah	2Sa 18:2	1121
mine hand against the king's *s*	2Sa 18:12	1121
I have no *s* to keep my name in	2Sa 18:18	1121
Then said Ahimaaz the *s* of Zadok	2Sa 18:19	1121
because the king's *s* is dead	2Sa 18:20	1121
Then said Ahimaaz the *s* of Zadok	2Sa 18:22	1121
Wherefore wilt thou run, my *s*	2Sa 18:22	1121
running of Ahimaaz the *s* of Zadok	2Sa 18:27	1121
O my *s* Absalom, my *s*, my *s*	2Sa 18:33	1121
for thee, O Absalom, my *s*, my *s*	2Sa 18:33	1121
the king was grieved for his *s*	2Sa 19:2	1121
O my *s* Absalom	2Sa 19:4	1121
O Absalom, my *s*, my *s*	2Sa 19:4	1121
And Shimei the *s* of Gera, a	2Sa 19:16	1121
Shimei the *s* of Gera fell down	2Sa 19:18	1121
But Abishai the *s* of Zeruiah	2Sa 19:21	1121
Mephibosheth the *s* of Saul came	2Sa 19:24	1121
the *s* of Bichri, a Benjamite	2Sa 20:1	1121
we inheritance in the *s* of Jesse	2Sa 20:1	1121
and followed Sheba the *s* of Bichri	2Sa 20:2	1121
Now shall Sheba the *s* of Bichri	2Sa 20:6	1121
after Sheba the *s* of Bichri	2Sa 20:7	1121
after Sheba the *s* of Bichri	2Sa 20:10	1121
after Sheba the *s* of Bichri	2Sa 20:13	1121
Sheba the *s* of Bichri by name,	2Sa 20:21	1121
the head of Sheba the *s* of Bichri	2Sa 20:22	1121
Benaiah the *s* of Jehoiada was	2Sa 20:23	1121
Jehoshaphat the *s* of Ahilud was	2Sa 20:24	1121
the *s* of Jonathan the *s* of Saul	2Sa 21:7	1121
David and Jonathan the *s* of Saul	2Sa 21:7	1121
s of Barzillai the Meholathite	2Sa 21:8	1121
the bones of Jonathan his *s* from	2Sa 21:12	1121
and the bones of Jonathan his *s*	2Sa 21:13	1121
Jonathan his *s* buried they in the	2Sa 21:14	1121
But Abishai the *s* of Zeruiah	2Sa 21:17	1121
Elhanan the *s* of Jaare-oregim	2Sa 21:19	1121
Jonathan the *s* of Shimeah the	2Sa 21:21	1121

S

David the *s* of Jesse said, and the	2Sa 23:1	1121
Eleazar the *s* of Dodo the Ahohite	2Sa 23:9	1121
the *s* of Agee the Hararite	2Sa 23:11	1121
the *s* of Zeruiah, was chief among	2Sa 23:18	1121
And Benaiah the *s* of Jehoiada	2Sa 23:20	1121
the *s* of a valiant man, of	2Sa 23:20	1121
did Benaiah the *s* of Jehoiada	2Sa 23:22	1121
Elhanan the *s* of Dodo of	2Sa 23:24	1121
Ira the *s* of Ikkesh the Tekoite,	2Sa 23:26	1121
Heleb the *s* of Baanah, a	2Sa 23:29	1121
Ittai the *s* of Ribai out of	2Sa 23:29	1121
Ahiam the *s* of Sharar the	2Sa 23:33	1121
Eliphelet the *s* of Ahasbai	2Sa 23:34	1121
the *s* of the Maachathite, Eliam	2Sa 23:34	1121
Eliam the *s* of Ahithophel the	2Sa 23:34	1121
Igal the *s* of Nathan of Zobah,	2Sa 23:36	1121
to Joab the *s* of Zeruiah,	2Sa 23:37	1121
Then Adonijah the *s* of Haggith	1Kin 1:5	1121
with Joab the *s* of Zeruiah	1Kin 1:7	1121
and Benaiah the *s* of Jehoiada	1Kin 1:8	1121
the *s* of Haggith doth reign	1Kin 1:11	1121
and the life of thy *s* Solomon	1Kin 1:12	1121
thy *s* shall reign after me	1Kin 1:13	1121
thy *s* shall reign after me	1Kin 1:17	1121
my *s* Solomon shall be counted	1Kin 1:21	1121
and Benaiah the *s* of Jehoiada	1Kin 1:26	1121
thy *s* shall reign after me	1Kin 1:30	1121
and Benaiah the *s* of Jehoiada	1Kin 1:32	1121
cause Solomon my *s* to ride upon	1Kin 1:33	1121
Benaiah the *s* of Jehoiada	1Kin 1:36	1121
and Benaiah the *s* of Jehoiada	1Kin 1:38	1121
Jonathan the *s* of Abiathar the	1Kin 1:42	1121
and Benaiah the *s* of Jehoiada	1Kin 1:44	1121
and he charged Solomon his *s*	1Kin 2:1	1121
Joab the *s* of Zeruiah did to me	1Kin 2:5	1121
Israel, unto Abner the *s* of Ner	1Kin 2:5	1121
and unto Amasa the *s* of Jether	1Kin 2:5	1121
with thee Shimei the *s* of Gera	1Kin 2:8	1121
Adonijah the *s* of Haggith came to	1Kin 2:13	1121
and for Joab the *s* of Zeruiah	1Kin 2:22	1121
hand of Benaiah the *s* of Jehoiada	1Kin 2:25	1121
sent Benaiah the *s* of Jehoiada	1Kin 2:29	1121
to wit, Abner the *s* of Ner	1Kin 2:32	1121
Israel, and Amasa the *s* of Jether	1Kin 2:32	1121
So Benaiah the *s* of Jehoiada went	1Kin 2:34	1121
the king put Benaiah the *s* of	1Kin 2:35	1121
Achish *s* of Maachah king of Gath	1Kin 2:39	1121
Benaiah the *s* of Jehoiada	1Kin 2:46	1121
him a *s* to sit on his throne	1Kin 3:6	1121
took my *s* from beside me, while	1Kin 3:20	1121
morning, behold, it was not my *s*	1Kin 3:21	1121
is my *s*, and the dead is thy *s*	1Kin 3:22	1121
is thy *s*, and the living is my *s*	1Kin 3:22	1121
This is my *s* that liveth, and thy	1Kin 3:23	1121
that liveth, and thy *s* is the dead	1Kin 3:23	1121
but thy *s* is the dead, and my *s*	1Kin 3:23	1121
for her bowels yearned upon her *s*	1Kin 3:26	1121
Azariah the *s* of Zadok the priest	1Kin 4:2	1121
Jehoshaphat the *s* of Ahilud	1Kin 4:3	1121
Benaiah the *s* of Jehoiada was	1Kin 4:4	1121
Azariah the *s* of Nathan was over	1Kin 4:5	1121
Zabud the *s* of Nathan was	1Kin 4:5	1121
Adoniram the *s* of Abda was over	1Kin 4:6	1121
The *s* of Hur, in mount Ephraim	1Kin 4:8	1133
The *s* of Dekar, in Makaz, and in	1Kin 4:9	1128
The *s* of Hesed, in Aruboth	1Kin 4:10	1136
The *s* of Abinadab, in all the	1Kin 4:11	1125
Baana the *s* of Ahilud	1Kin 4:12	1121
The *s* of Geber, in Ramoth-gilead	1Kin 4:13	1127
towns of Jair the *s* of Manasseh	1Kin 4:13	1121
Ahinadab the *s* of Iddo had	1Kin 4:14	1121
Baanah the *s* of Hushai was in	1Kin 4:16	1121
Jehoshaphat the *s* of Paruah	1Kin 4:17	1121
Shimei the *s* of Elah, in Benjamin	1Kin 4:18	1121
Geber the *s* of Uri was in the	1Kin 4:19	1121
David my father, saying, Thy *s*	1Kin 5:5	1121
a wise *s* over this great people	1Kin 5:7	1121
He was a widow's *s* of the tribe	1Kin 7:14	1121
but thy *s* that shall come forth	1Kin 8:19	1121
rend it out of the hand of thy *s*	1Kin 11:12	1121
thy *s* for David my servant's sake	1Kin 11:13	1121
Tahpenes bare him Genubath his *s*	1Kin 11:20	1121
Rezon the *s* of Eliadah, which	1Kin 11:23	1121
And Jeroboam the *s* of Nebat	1Kin 11:26	1121
unto his *s* will I give one tribe,	1Kin 11:36	1121
Rehoboam his *s* reigned in his	1Kin 11:43	1121
when Jeroboam the *s* of Nebat	1Kin 12:2	1121
unto Jeroboam the *s* of Nebat	1Kin 12:15	1121
we inheritance in the *s* of Jesse	1Kin 12:16	1121
to Rehoboam the *s* of Solomon	1Kin 12:21	1121
the *s* of Solomon, king of Judah,	1Kin 12:23	1121
the *s* of Jeroboam fell sick	1Kin 14:1	1121
to ask a thing of thee for her *s*	1Kin 14:5	1121
Nadab his *s* reigned in his stead	1Kin 14:20	1121
Rehoboam the *s* of Solomon reigned	1Kin 14:21	1121
Abijam his *s* reigned in his stead	1Kin 14:31	1121
year of king Jeroboam the *s* of	1Kin 15:1	1121
to set up his *s* after him	1Kin 15:4	1121
Asa his *s* reigned in his stead	1Kin 15:8	1121
the *s* of Tabrimon	1Kin 15:18	1121
the *s* of Hezion, king of Syria,	1Kin 15:18	1121
Jehoshaphat his *s* reigned in his	1Kin 15:24	1121
Nadab the *s* of Jeroboam began to	1Kin 15:25	1121
And Baasha the *s* of Ahijah	1Kin 15:27	1121
the *s* of Ahijah to reign over all	1Kin 15:33	1121
the *s* of Hanani against Baasha	1Kin 16:1	1121
house of Jeroboam the *s* of Nebat	1Kin 16:3	1121
Elah his *s* reigned in his stead	1Kin 16:6	1121
hand of the prophet Jehu the *s* of	1Kin 16:7	1121
king of Judah began Elah the *s* of	1Kin 16:8	1121
Baasha, and the sins of Elah his *s*	1Kin 16:13	1121
followed Tibni the *s* of Ginath	1Kin 16:21	1121
followed Tibni the *s* of Ginath	1Kin 16:22	1121
way of Jeroboam the *s* of Nebat	1Kin 16:26	1121
Ahab his *s* reigned in his stead	1Kin 16:28	1121
s of Omri to reign over Israel	1Kin 16:29	1121
Ahab the *s* of Omri reigned over	1Kin 16:29	1121
Ahab the *s* of Omri did evil in	1Kin 16:30	1121
sins of Jeroboam the *s* of Nebat	1Kin 16:31	1121
thereof in his youngest *s* Segub	1Kin 16:34	
he spake by Joshua the *s* of Nun	1Kin 16:34	1121
go in and dress it for me and my *s*	1Kin 17:12	1121
after make for thee and for thy *s*	1Kin 17:13	1121
that the *s* of the woman, the	1Kin 17:17	1121
to remembrance, and to slay my *s*	1Kin 17:18	1121
he said unto her, Give me thy *s*	1Kin 17:19	1121
whom I sojourn, by slaying her *s*	1Kin 17:20	1121
and Elijah said, See, thy *s* liveth	1Kin 17:23	1121
Jehu the *s* of Nimshi shalt thou	1Kin 19:16	1121
Elisha the *s* of Shaphat of	1Kin 19:16	1121
and found Elisha the *s* of Shaphat	1Kin 19:19	1121
house of Jeroboam the *s* of Nebat	1Kin 21:22	1121
house of Baasha the *s* of Ahijah	1Kin 21:22	1121
one man, Micaiah the *s* of Imlah	1Kin 22:8	1121
hither Micaiah the *s* of Imlah	1Kin 22:9	1121
Zedekiah the *s* of Chenaanah made	1Kin 22:11	1121
But Zedekiah the *s* of Chenaanah	1Kin 22:24	1121
city, and to Joash the king's *s*	1Kin 22:26	1121
Ahaziah his *s* reigned in his	1Kin 22:40	1121
Jehoshaphat the *s* of Asa began to	1Kin 22:41	1121
Then said Ahaziah the *s* of Ahab	1Kin 22:49	1121
Jehoram his *s* reigned in his	1Kin 22:50	1121
Ahaziah the *s* of Ahab began to	1Kin 22:51	1121
way of Jeroboam the *s* of Nebat	1Kin 22:52	1121
s of Jehoshaphat king of Judah	2Kin 1:17	1121
because he had no *s*	2Kin 1:17	1121
Now Jehoram the *s* of Ahab began	2Kin 3:1	1121
sins of Jeroboam the *s* of Nebat	2Kin 3:3	1121
Here is Elisha the *s* of Shaphat	2Kin 3:11	1121
Then he took his eldest *s* that	2Kin 3:27	1121
full, that she said unto her *s*	2Kin 4:6	1121
of life, thou shalt embrace a *s*	2Kin 4:16	1121
bare a *s* at that season that	2Kin 4:17	1121
said, Did I desire a *s* of my lord	2Kin 4:28	1121
unto him, he said, Take up thy *s*	2Kin 4:36	1121
to the ground, and took up her *s*	2Kin 4:37	1121
woman said unto me, Give thy *s*	2Kin 6:28	1121
and we will eat my *s* to morrow	2Kin 6:28	1121
So we boiled my *s*, and did eat him	2Kin 6:29	1121
her on the next day, Give thy *s*	2Kin 6:29	1121
and she hath hid her *s*	2Kin 6:29	1121
if the head of Elisha the *s* of	2Kin 6:31	1121
See ye how this *s* of a murderer	2Kin 6:32	1121
whose *s* he had restored to life,	2Kin 8:1	1121
whose *s* he had restored to life,	2Kin 8:5	1121
is the woman, and this is her *s*	2Kin 8:5	1121
Thy *s* Ben-hadad king of Syria	2Kin 8:9	1121
the *s* of Ahab king of Israel	2Kin 8:16	1121
Jehoram the *s* of Jehoshaphat king	2Kin 8:16	1121
Ahaziah his *s* reigned in his	2Kin 8:24	1121
the *s* of Ahab king of Israel did	2Kin 8:25	1121
s of Jehoram king of Judah begin	2Kin 8:25	1121
for he was the *s* in law of the	2Kin 8:27	2860
he went with Joram the *s* of Ahab	2Kin 8:28	1121
Ahaziah the *s* of Jehoram king of	2Kin 8:29	1121
Joram the *s* of Ahab in Jezreel	2Kin 8:29	1121
Jehu the *s* of Jehoshaphat	2Kin 9:2	1121
Jehoshaphat the *s* of Nimshi	2Kin 9:2	1121
house of Jeroboam the *s* of Nebat	2Kin 9:9	1121
house of Baasha the *s* of Ahijah	2Kin 9:9	1121
So Jehu the *s* of Jehoshaphat the	2Kin 9:14	1121
the *s* of Nimshi conspired against	2Kin 9:14	1121
driving of Jehu the *s* of Nimshi	2Kin 9:20	1121
s of Ahab began Ahaziah to reign	2Kin 9:29	1121
he lighted on Jehonadab the *s* of	2Kin 10:15	1121
and Jehonadab the *s* of Rechab	2Kin 10:23	1121
sins of Jeroboam the *s* of Nebat	2Kin 10:29	1121
Jehoahaz his *s* reigned in his	2Kin 10:35	1121
Ahaziah saw that her *s* was dead	2Kin 11:1	1121
took Joash the *s* of Ahaziah	2Kin 11:2	1121
LORD, and shewed them the king's *s*	2Kin 11:4	1121
And he brought forth the king's *s*	2Kin 11:12	1121
For Jozachar the *s* of Shimeath	2Kin 12:21	1121
and Jehozabad the *s* of Shomer	2Kin 12:21	1121
Amaziah his *s* reigned in his	2Kin 12:21	1121
the *s* of Ahaziah king of Judah	2Kin 13:1	1121
king of Judah Jehoahaz the *s* of	2Kin 13:1	1121
sins of Jeroboam the *s* of Nebat	2Kin 13:2	1121
hand of Ben-hadad the *s* of Hazael	2Kin 13:3	1121
Joash his *s* reigned in his stead	2Kin 13:9	1121
the *s* of Jehoahaz to reign over	2Kin 13:10	1121
sins of Jeroboam the *s* of Nebat	2Kin 13:11	1121
Ben-hadad his *s* reigned in his	2Kin 13:24	1121
Jehoash the *s* of Jehoahaz took	2Kin 13:25	1121
the *s* of Hazael the cities	2Kin 13:25	1121
s of Jehoahaz king of Israel	2Kin 14:1	1121
the *s* of Joash king of Judah	2Kin 14:1	1121
the *s* of Jehoahaz *s* of Jehu,	2Kin 14:8	1121
Give thy daughter to my *s* to wife	2Kin 14:9	1121
s of Jehoash the *s* of Ahaziah	2Kin 14:13	1121
Jeroboam his *s* reigned in his	2Kin 14:16	1121
Amaziah the *s* of Joash king of	2Kin 14:17	1121
s of Jehoahaz king of Israel	2Kin 14:17	1121
fifteenth year of Amaziah the *s*	2Kin 14:23	1121
king of Judah Jeroboam the *s* of	2Kin 14:23	1121
sins of Jeroboam the *s* of Nebat	2Kin 14:24	1121
the *s* of Amittai, the prophet,	2Kin 14:25	1121
hand of Jeroboam the *s* of Joash	2Kin 14:27	1121
Zachariah his *s* reigned in his	2Kin 14:29	1121
s of Amaziah king of Judah to	2Kin 15:1	1121
Jotham the king's *s* was over the	2Kin 15:5	1121
Jotham his *s* reigned in his stead	2Kin 15:7	1121
s of Jeroboam reign over Israel	2Kin 15:8	1121
sins of Jeroboam the *s* of Nebat	2Kin 15:9	1121
Shallum the *s* of Jabesh conspired	2Kin 15:10	1121
Shallum the *s* of Jabesh began to	2Kin 15:13	1121
For Menahem the *s* of Gadi went up	2Kin 15:14	1121
smote Shallum the *s* of Jabesh in	2Kin 15:14	1121
s of Gadi to reign over Israel	2Kin 15:17	1121
sins of Jeroboam the *s* of Nebat	2Kin 15:18	1121
Pekahiah his *s* reigned in his	2Kin 15:22	1121
king of Judah Pekahiah the *s* of	2Kin 15:23	1121
sins of Jeroboam the *s* of Nebat	2Kin 15:24	1121
But Pekah the *s* of Remaliah	2Kin 15:25	1121
s of Remaliah began to reign over	2Kin 15:27	1121
sins of Jeroboam the *s* of Nebat	2Kin 15:28	1121
Hoshea the *s* of Elah made a	2Kin 15:30	1121
against Pekah the *s* of Remaliah	2Kin 15:30	1121
year of Jotham the *s* of Uzziah	2Kin 15:30	1121
the *s* of Remaliah king of Israel	2Kin 15:32	1121
the *s* of Uzziah king of Judah to	2Kin 15:32	1121
Syria, and Pekah the *s* of Remaliah	2Kin 15:37	1121
Ahaz his *s* reigned in his stead	2Kin 15:38	1121
the *s* of Remaliah	2Kin 16:1	1121
Ahaz the *s* of Jotham	2Kin 16:1	1121
made his *s* to pass through the	2Kin 16:3	1121
Pekah *s* of Remaliah king of	2Kin 16:5	1121
saying, I am thy servant and thy *s*	2Kin 16:7	1121
Hezekiah his *s* reigned in his	2Kin 16:20	1121
the *s* of Elah to reign in Samaria	2Kin 17:1	1121
made Jeroboam the *s* of Nebat king	2Kin 17:21	1121
Hoshea *s* of Elah king of Israel	2Kin 18:1	1121
that Hezekiah the *s* of Ahaz king	2Kin 18:1	1121
Hoshea *s* of Elah king of Israel	2Kin 18:9	1121
to them Eliakim the *s* of Hilkiah	2Kin 18:18	1121
Joah the *s* of Asaph the recorder	2Kin 18:18	1121
said Eliakim the *s* of Hilkiah	2Kin 18:26	1121
came Eliakim the *s* of Hilkiah	2Kin 18:37	1121
Joah the *s* of Asaph the recorder,	2Kin 18:37	1121
Isaiah the prophet the *s* of Amoz	2Kin 19:2	1121
Then Isaiah the *s* of Amoz sent to	2Kin 19:20	1121
Esar-haddon his *s* reigned in his	2Kin 19:37	1121
Isaiah the *s* of Amoz came to him	2Kin 20:1	1121
the *s* of Baladan, king of Babylon	2Kin 20:12	1121
Manasseh his *s* reigned in his	2Kin 20:21	1121
he made his *s* pass through the	2Kin 21:6	1121
to David, and to Solomon his *s*	2Kin 21:7	1121
Amon his *s* reigned in his stead	2Kin 21:18	1121
Josiah his *s* king in his stead	2Kin 21:24	1121
Josiah his *s* reigned in his stead	2Kin 21:26	1121
sent Shaphan the *s* of Azaliah	2Kin 22:3	1121
the *s* of Meshullam, the scribe,	2Kin 22:3	1121
and Ahikam the *s* of Shaphan	2Kin 22:12	1121
Achbor the *s* of Michaiah, and	2Kin 22:12	1121
wife of Shallum the *s* of Tikvah	2Kin 22:14	1121
the *s* of Harhas, keeper of the	2Kin 22:14	1121
that no man might make his *s* or	2Kin 23:10	1121
which Jeroboam the *s* of Nebat	2Kin 23:15	1121
took Jehoahaz the *s* of Josiah	2Kin 23:30	1121
s of Josiah king in the room of	2Kin 23:34	1121
Jehoiachin his *s* reigned in his	2Kin 24:6	1121
he made Gedaliah the *s* of Ahikam	2Kin 25:22	1121
Ahikam, the *s* of Shaphan, ruler	2Kin 25:22	1121
even Ishmael the *s* of Nethaniah	2Kin 25:23	1121
and Johanan the *s* of Careah	2Kin 25:23	1121
Seraiah the *s* of Tanhumeth the	2Kin 25:23	1121
Jaazaniah the *s* of a Maachathite,	2Kin 25:23	1121
that Ishmael the *s* of Nethaniah,	2Kin 25:25	1121
the *s* of Elishama, of the seed	2Kin 25:25	1121
Bela the *s* of Beor	1Chr 1:43	1121
Jobab the *s* of Zerah of Bozrah	1Chr 1:44	1121
was dead, Hadad the *s* of Bedad	1Chr 1:46	1121
Baal-hanan the *s* of Achbor	1Chr 1:49	1121
Caleb the *s* of Hezron begat	1Chr 2:18	1121
the *s* of Shammai was Maon	1Chr 2:45	1121
the sons of Caleb the *s* of Hur	1Chr 2:50	1121
Absalom the *s* of Maachah the	1Chr 3:2	1121
fourth, Adonijah the *s* of Haggith	1Chr 3:2	1121
s was Rehoboam, Abia his *s*	1Chr 3:10	1121
Asa his *s*, Jehoshaphat his *s*	1Chr 3:10	1121
Joram his *s*, Ahaziah his *s*	1Chr 3:11	1121
Joash his *s*	1Chr 3:11	1121
Amaziah his *s*	1Chr 3:12	1121
Azariah his *s*	1Chr 3:12	1121
Jotham his *s*	1Chr 3:12	1121
Ahaz his *s*	1Chr 3:13	1121
Hezekiah his *s*	1Chr 3:13	1121
Manasseh his *s*	1Chr 3:13	1121
Amon his *s*, Josiah his *s*	1Chr 3:14	1121
Jeconiah his *s*, Zedekiah his *s*	1Chr 3:16	1121
Assir, Salathiel his *s*,	1Chr 3:17	1121
Reaiah the *s* of Shobal begat	1Chr 4:2	1121
of Aharhel the *s* of Harum	1Chr 4:8	1121
sons of Caleb the *s* of Jephunneh	1Chr 4:15	1121
of Shelah the *s* of Judah were	1Chr 4:21	1121
Shallum his *s*, Mibsam his *s*,	1Chr 4:25	1121
Mishma his *s*	1Chr 4:25	1121
Hamuel his *s*, Zacchur his *s*	1Chr 4:26	1121
Shimei his *s*	1Chr 4:26	1121
and Joshah the *s* of Amaziah	1Chr 4:34	1121
Jehu the *s* of Josibiah	1Chr 4:35	1121
s of Seraiah, the *s* of Asiel,	1Chr 4:35	1121
Ziza the *s* of Shiphi	1Chr 4:37	1121
the *s* of Allon	1Chr 4:37	1121

the *s* of Jedaiah 1Chr 4:37 1121
s of Shimri, the *s* of Shemaiah 1Chr 4:37 1121
sons of Joseph the *s* of Israel 1Chr 5:1 1121
Shemaiah his *s*, Gog his *s*, 1Chr 5:4 1121
Shimei his *s* 1Chr 5:4 1121
Micah his *s*, Reaia his *s* 1Chr 5:5 1121
Baal his *s* 1Chr 5:5 1121
Beerah his *s*, whom 1Chr 5:6 1121
And Bela the *s* of Azaz 1Chr 5:8 1121
the *s* of Shema, the *s* of Joel, 1Chr 5:8 1121
children of Abihail the *s* of Huri 1Chr 5:14 1121
the *s* of Jaroah 1Chr 5:14 1121
the *s* of Gilead 1Chr 5:14 1121
the *s* of Michael 1Chr 5:14 1121
the *s* of Jeshishai 1Chr 5:14 1121
the *s* of Jahdo, the *s* of Buz 1Chr 5:14 1121
Ahi the *s* of Abdiel 1Chr 5:15 1121
the *s* of Guni, chief of the house 1Chr 5:15 1121
Libni his *s*, Jahath his *s* 1Chr 6:20 1121
Zimmah his *s* 1Chr 6:20 1121
Joah his *s*, Iddo his *s*, Zerah 1Chr 6:21 1121
Zerah his *s*, Jeaterai his *s* 1Chr 6:21 1121
Amminadab his *s*, Korah his *s* 1Chr 6:22 1121
Assir his *s* 1Chr 6:22 1121
Elkanah his *s* 1Chr 6:23 1121
Ebiasaph his *s*, and Assir his *s* 1Chr 6:23 1121
Tahath his *s*, Uriel his *s* 1Chr 6:24 1121
Uzziah his *s*, and Shaul his *s* 1Chr 6:24 1121
Zophai his *s*, and Nahath his *s*, 1Chr 6:26 1121
Eliab his *s*, Jeroham his *s* 1Chr 6:27 1121
Elkanah his *s* 1Chr 6:27 1121
Mahli, Libni his *s*, Shimei his 1Chr 6:29 1121
s, Shimei his *s*, Uzza his *s* 1Chr 6:29 1121
Shimea his *s*, Haggiah his *s* 1Chr 6:30 1121
Asaiah his *s* 1Chr 6:30 1121
the *s* of Joel, the *s* of Shemuel 1Chr 6:33 1121
The *s* of Elkanah 1Chr 6:34 1121
the *s* of Jeroham 1Chr 6:34 1121
the *s* of Eliel, the *s* of Toah, 1Chr 6:34 1121
The *s* of Zuph, the *s* of Elkanah 1Chr 6:35 1121
s of Mahath, the *s* of Amasai, 1Chr 6:35 1121
The *s* of Elkanah, the *s* of Joel 1Chr 6:36 1121
of Azariah, the *s* of Zephaniah, 1Chr 6:36 1121
The *s* of Tahath, the *s* of Assir 1Chr 6:37 1121
s of Ebiasaph, the *s* of Korah, 1Chr 6:37 1121
The *s* of Izhar, the *s* of Kohath 1Chr 6:38 1121
the *s* of Levi, the *s* of Israel 1Chr 6:38 1121
even Asaph the *s* of Berachiah 1Chr 6:39 1121
of Berachiah, the *s* of Shimea, 1Chr 6:39 1121
The *s* of Michael 1Chr 6:40 1121
the *s* of Baaseiah 1Chr 6:40 1121
the *s* of Malchiah 1Chr 6:40 1121
The *s* of Ethni, the *s* of Zerah, 1Chr 6:41 1121
the *s* of Adaiah 1Chr 6:41 1121
The *s* of Ethan, the *s* of Zimmah 1Chr 6:42 1121
the *s* of Shimei 1Chr 6:42 1121
The *s* of Jahath 1Chr 6:43 1121
the *s* of Gershom, the *s* of Levi 1Chr 6:43 1121
Ethan the *s* of Kishi 1Chr 6:44 1121
the *s* of Abdi, the *s* of Malluch 1Chr 6:44 1121
The *s* of Hashabiah 1Chr 6:45 1121
s of Amaziah, the *s* of Hilkiah, 1Chr 6:45 1121
The *s* of Amzi, the *s* of Bani, 1Chr 6:46 1121
the *s* of Shamer 1Chr 6:46 1121
The *s* of Mahli, the *s* of Mushi, 1Chr 6:47 1121
the *s* of Merari, the *s* of Levi 1Chr 6:47 1121
Eleazar his *s*, Phinehas his *s* 1Chr 6:50 1121
Abishua his *s* 1Chr 6:50 1121
Bukki his *s*, Uzzi his *s* 1Chr 6:51 1121
Zerahiah his *s* 1Chr 6:51 1121
Meraioth his *s*, Amariah his *s* 1Chr 6:52 1121
Ahitub his *s* 1Chr 6:52 1121
Zadok his *s*, Ahimaaz his *s* 1Chr 6:53 1121
gave to Caleb the *s* of Jephunneh 1Chr 6:56 1121
the wife of Machir bare a *s* 1Chr 7:16 1121
s of Machir, the *s* of Manasseh 1Chr 7:17 1121
and Bered his *s*, and Tahath his *s* 1Chr 7:20 1121
Eladah his *s*, and Tahath his *s* 1Chr 7:20 1121
Zabad his *s*, and Shuthelah his *s* 1Chr 7:21 1121
wife, she conceived, and bare a *s* 1Chr 7:23 1121
And Rephah was his *s*, also Resheph 1Chr 7:25 1121
and Telah his *s*, and Tahan his *s* 1Chr 7:25 1121
Laadan his *s*, Ammihud his *s*, 1Chr 7:26 1121
Laadan his *s*, Ammihud his *s* 1Chr 7:26 1121
Elishama his *s* 1Chr 7:26 1121
Non his *s*, Jehoshuah his *s* 1Chr 7:27 1121
of Joseph the *s* of Israel 1Chr 7:29 1121
And his firstborn *s* Abdon, and Zur, 1Chr 8:30 1121
the *s* of Jonathan was Merib-baal 1Chr 8:34 1121
Rapha was his *s*, Eleasah his *s*, 1Chr 8:37 1121
Azel his *s* 1Chr 8:37 1121
Uthai the *s* of Ammihud 1Chr 9:4 1121
the *s* of Omri, the *s* of Imri, 1Chr 9:4 1121
the *s* of Bani, of the children of 1Chr 9:4 1121
children of Pharez the *s* of Judah 1Chr 9:4 1121
Sallu the *s* of Meshullam 1Chr 9:7 1121
the *s* of Hodaviah 1Chr 9:7 1121
of Hodaviah, the *s* of Hasenuah, 1Chr 9:7 1121
And Ibneiah the *s* of Jeroham 1Chr 9:8 1121
of Jeroham, and Elah the *s* of Uzzi 1Chr 9:8 1121
the *s* of Michri, and Meshullam the 1Chr 9:8 1121
and Meshullam the *s* of Shephatiah 1Chr 9:8 1121
s of Reuel, the *s* of Ibnijah 1Chr 9:8 1121
And Azariah the *s* of Hilkiah 1Chr 9:11 1121
the *s* of Meshullam 1Chr 9:11 1121
the *s* of Zadok 1Chr 9:11 1121
the *s* of Meraioth 1Chr 9:11 1121
the *s* of Ahitub, the ruler of the 1Chr 9:11 1121
And Adaiah the *s* of Jeroham 1Chr 9:12 1121
the *s* of Pashur 1Chr 9:12 1121
the *s* of Malchijah 1Chr 9:12 1121
and Maasiai the *s* of Adiel 1Chr 9:12 1121
the *s* of Jahzerah 1Chr 9:12 1121
the *s* of Meshullam 1Chr 9:12 1121
the *s* of Meshillemith 1Chr 9:12 1121
of Meshillemith, the *s* of Immer 1Chr 9:12 1121
Shemaiah the *s* of Hasshub 1Chr 9:14 1121
the *s* of Azrikam 1Chr 9:14 1121
the *s* of Hashabiah, of the sons 1Chr 9:14 1121
and Mattaniah the *s* of Micah 1Chr 9:15 1121
the *s* of Zichri, the *s* of Asaph 1Chr 9:15 1121
And Obadiah the *s* of Shemaiah 1Chr 9:16 1121
the *s* of Galal 1Chr 9:16 1121
the *s* of Jeduthun, and Berechiah 1Chr 9:16 1121
and Berechiah the *s* of Asa 1Chr 9:16 1121
the *s* of Elkanah, that dwelt in 1Chr 9:16 1121
And Shallum the *s* of Kore 1Chr 9:19 1121
the *s* of Ebiasaph 1Chr 9:19 1121
the *s* of Korah, and his brethren, 1Chr 9:19 1121
Phinehas the *s* of Eleazar was the 1Chr 9:20 1121
Zechariah the *s* of Meshelemiah 1Chr 9:21 1121
And his firstborn *s* Abdon, then 1Chr 9:36 1121
the *s* of Jonathan was Merib-baal 1Chr 9:40 1121
Rephaiah his *s*, Eleasah his *s* 1Chr 9:43 1121
Azel his *s* 1Chr 9:43 1121
kingdom unto David the *s* of Jesse 1Chr 10:14 1121
So Joab the *s* of Zeruiah went 1Chr 11:6 1121
him was Eleazar the *s* of Dodo 1Chr 11:12 1121
Benaiah the *s* of Jehoiada 1Chr 11:22 1121
the *s* of a valiant man of Kabzeel 1Chr 11:22 1121
did Benaiah the *s* of Jehoiada 1Chr 11:24 1121
of Joab, Elhanan the *s* of Dodo of 1Chr 11:26 1121
Ira the *s* of Ikkesh the Tekoite, 1Chr 11:28 1121
Heled the *s* of Baanah the 1Chr 11:30 1121
Ithai the *s* of Ribai of Gibeah, 1Chr 11:31 1121
Jonathan the *s* of Shage the 1Chr 11:34 1121
Ahiam the *s* of Sacar the Hararite 1Chr 11:35 1121
the Hararite, Eliphal the *s* of Ur 1Chr 11:35 1121
Carmelite, Naarai the *s* of Ezbai 1Chr 11:37 1121
Nathan, Mibhar the *s* of Haggeri 1Chr 11:38 1121
of Joab the *s* of Zeruiah, 1Chr 11:39 1121
the Hittite, Zabad the *s* of Ahlai 1Chr 11:41 1121
Adina the *s* of Shiza the 1Chr 11:42 1121
Hanan the *s* of Maachah, and 1Chr 11:43 1121
Jediael the *s* of Shimri, and Joha 1Chr 11:45 1121
because of Saul the *s* of Kish 1Chr 12:1 1121
and on thy side, thou *s* of Jesse 1Chr 12:18 1121
appointed Heman the *s* of Joel 1Chr 15:17 1121
Asaph the *s* of Berechiah 1Chr 15:17 1121
brethren, Ethan the *s* of Kushaiah 1Chr 15:17 1121
Obed-edom also the *s* of Jeduthun 1Chr 16:38 1121
his father, and he shall be my *s* 1Chr 17:13 1121
sent Hadoram his *s* to king David 1Chr 18:10 1121
Abishai the *s* Zeruiah slew of the 1Chr 18:12 1121
Joab the *s* of Zeruiah was over 1Chr 18:15 1121
and Jehoshaphat the *s* of Ahilud 1Chr 18:15 1121
And Zadok the *s* of Ahitub, and 1Chr 18:16 1121
and Abimelech the *s* of Abiathar 1Chr 18:16 1121
Benaiah the *s* of Jehoiada was 1Chr 18:17 1121
his *s* reigned in his stead 1Chr 19:1 1121
unto Hanun the *s* of Nahash 1Chr 19:2 1121
Elhanan the *s* of Jair slew Lahmi 1Chr 20:5 1121
and he also was the *s* of the giant 1Chr 20:6 3025
Jonathan the *s* of Shimea David's 1Chr 20:7 1121
David said, Solomon my *s* is young 1Chr 22:5 1121
Then he called for Solomon his *s* 1Chr 22:6 1121
And David said to Solomon, My *s* 1Chr 22:7 1121
a *s* shall be born to thee, who 1Chr 22:9 1121
and he shall be my *s*, and I will be 1Chr 22:10 1121
Now, my *s*, the LORD be with thee 1Chr 22:11 1121
of Israel to help Solomon his *s* 1Chr 22:17 1121
Solomon his *s* king over Israel 1Chr 23:1 1121
Shemaiah the *s* of Nethaneel the 1Chr 24:6 1121
and Ahimelech the *s* of Abiathar 1Chr 24:6 1121
the *s* of Kish was Jerahmeel 1Chr 24:29 1121
was Meshelemiah the *s* of Kore 1Chr 26:1 1121
Shemaiah his *s* were sons born 1Chr 26:6 1121
Then for Zechariah his *s*, a wise 1Chr 26:14 1121
And Shebuel the *s* of Gershom 1Chr 26:24 1121
the *s* of Moses, was ruler of the 1Chr 26:24 1121
Rehabiah his *s* 1Chr 26:25 1121
and Jeshaiah his *s* 1Chr 26:25 1121
and Joram his *s*, and Zichri his *s* 1Chr 26:25 1121
and Shelomith his *s* 1Chr 26:25 1121
the seer, and Saul the *s* of Kish 1Chr 26:28 1121
of Kish, and Abner the *s* of Ner 1Chr 26:28 1121
Joab the *s* of Zeruiah, had 1Chr 26:28 1121
was Jashobeam the *s* of Zabdiel 1Chr 27:2 1121
was Benaiah the *s* of Jehoiada 1Chr 27:5 1121
in his course was Ammizabad his *s* 1Chr 27:6 1121
Joab, and Zebadiah his *s* after him 1Chr 27:7 1121
Ira the *s* of Ikkesh the Tekoite 1Chr 27:9 1121
was Eliezer the *s* of Zichri 1Chr 27:16 1121
Shephatiah the *s* of Maachah 1Chr 27:16 1121
Hashabiah the *s* of Kemuel 1Chr 27:17 1121
Issachar, Omri the *s* of Michael 1Chr 27:18 1121
Ishmaiah the *s* of Obadiah 1Chr 27:19 1121
Jerimoth the *s* of Azriel 1Chr 27:19 1121
Ephraim, Hoshea the *s* of Azaziah 1Chr 27:20 1121
Manasseh, Joel the *s* of Pedaiah 1Chr 27:20 1121
Gilead, Iddo the *s* of Zechariah 1Chr 27:21 1121
Benjamin, Jaasiel the *s* of Abner 1Chr 27:21 1121
Of Dan, Azareel the *s* of Jeroham 1Chr 27:22 1121
Joab the *s* of Zeruiah began to 1Chr 27:24 1121
was Azmaveth the *s* of Adiel 1Chr 27:25 1121
was Jehonathan the *s* of Uzziah 1Chr 27:25 1121
ground was Ezri the *s* of Chelub 1Chr 27:26 1121
was Shaphat the *s* of Adlai 1Chr 27:29 1121
Jehiel the *s* of Hachmoni was with 1Chr 27:32 1121
was Jehoiada the *s* of Benaiah 1Chr 27:34 1121
he hath chosen Solomon my *s* to 1Chr 28:5 1121
And he said unto me, Solomon thy *s* 1Chr 28:6 1121
for I have chosen him to be my *s* 1Chr 28:6 1121
And thou, Solomon my *s*, know thou 1Chr 28:9 1121
his *s* the pattern of the porch 1Chr 28:11 1121
And David said to Solomon his *s* 1Chr 28:20 1121
the congregation, Solomon my *s* 1Chr 29:1 1121
unto Solomon my *s* a perfect heart 1Chr 29:19 1121
they made Solomon the *s* of David 1Chr 29:22 1121
Thus David the *s* of Jesse reigned 1Chr 29:26 1121
Solomon his *s* reigned in his 1Chr 29:28 1121
Solomon the *s* of David was 2Chr 1:1 1121
altar, that Bezaleel the *s* of Uri 2Chr 1:5 1121
the *s* of Hur, had made, he put 2Chr 1:5 1121
given to David the king a wise *s* 2Chr 2:12 1121
The *s* of a woman of the daughters 2Chr 2:14 1121
but thy *s* which shall come forth 2Chr 6:9 1121
against Jeroboam the *s* of Nebat 2Chr 9:29 1121
Rehoboam his *s* reigned in his 2Chr 9:31 1121
when Jeroboam the *s* of Nebat 2Chr 10:2 1121
to Jeroboam the *s* of Nebat 2Chr 10:15 1121
inheritance in the *s* of Jesse 2Chr 10:16 1121
unto Rehoboam the *s* of Solomon 2Chr 11:3 1121
Rehoboam the *s* of Solomon strong 2Chr 11:17 1121
Jerimoth the *s* of David to wife 2Chr 11:18 1121
daughter of Eliab the *s* of Jesse 2Chr 11:18 1121
Abijah the *s* of Maachah the chief 2Chr 11:22 1121
Abijah his *s* reigned in his stead 2Chr 12:16 1121
Yet Jeroboam the *s* of Nebat 2Chr 13:6 1121
servant of Solomon the *s* of David 2Chr 13:6 1121
against Rehoboam the *s* of Solomon 2Chr 13:7 1121
Asa his *s* reigned in his stead 2Chr 14:1 1121
came upon Azariah the *s* of Oded 2Chr 15:1 1121
Jehoshaphat his *s* reigned in his 2Chr 17:1 1121
him was Amasiah the *s* of Zichri 2Chr 17:16 1121
the same is Micaiah the *s* of Imla 2Chr 18:7 1121
quickly Micaiah the *s* of Imla 2Chr 18:8 1121
Zedekiah the *s* of Chenaanah had 2Chr 18:10 1121
Then Zedekiah the *s* of Chenaanah 2Chr 18:23 1121
city, and to Joash the king's *s* 2Chr 18:25 1121
Jehu the *s* of Hanani the seer 2Chr 19:2 1121
and Zebadiah the *s* of Ishmael 2Chr 19:11 1121
upon Jahaziel the *s* of Zechariah 2Chr 20:14 1121
the *s* of Benaiah 2Chr 20:14 1121
the *s* of Jeiel 2Chr 20:14 1121
the *s* of Mattaniah 2Chr 20:14 1121
the book of Jehu the *s* of Hanani 2Chr 20:34 1121
Then Eliezer the *s* of Dodavah of 2Chr 20:37 1121
Jehoram his *s* reigned in his 2Chr 21:1 1121
that there was never a *s* left him 2Chr 21:17 1121
his youngest *s* king in his stead 2Chr 22:1 1121
So Ahaziah the *s* of Jehoram king 2Chr 22:1 1121
went with Jehoram the *s* of Ahab 2Chr 22:5 1121
Azariah the *s* of Jehoram king of 2Chr 22:6 1121
Jehoram the *s* of Ahab at Jezreel 2Chr 22:6 1121
against Jehu the *s* of Nimshi 2Chr 22:7 1121
he is the *s* of Jehoshaphat, who 2Chr 22:9 1121
Ahaziah saw that her *s* was dead 2Chr 22:10 1121
king, took Joash the *s* of Ahaziah 2Chr 22:11 1121
Azariah the *s* of Jeroham 2Chr 23:1 1121
Ishmael the *s* of Jehohanan 2Chr 23:1 1121
and Azariah the *s* of Obed 2Chr 23:1 1121
Obed, and Maaseiah the *s* of Adaiah 2Chr 23:1 1121
and Elishaphat the *s* of Zichri 2Chr 23:1 1121
the king's *s* shall reign, as the 2Chr 23:3 1121
they brought out the king's *s* 2Chr 23:11 1121
the *s* of Jehoiada the priest 2Chr 24:20 1121
had done to him, but slew his *s* 2Chr 24:22 1121
Zabad the *s* of Shimeath an 2Chr 24:26 1121
Jehozabad the *s* of Shimrith a 2Chr 24:26 1121
Amaziah his *s* reigned in his 2Chr 24:27 1121
the *s* of Jehoahaz 2Chr 25:17 1121
the *s* of Jehu, king of Israel, 2Chr 25:17 1121
Give thy daughter to my *s* to wife 2Chr 25:18 1121
the *s* of Joash 2Chr 25:23 1121
the *s* of Jehoahaz 2Chr 25:23 1121
Amaziah the *s* of Joash king of 2Chr 25:25 1121
s of Jehoahaz king of Israel 2Chr 25:25 1121
Jotham his *s* was over the king's 2Chr 26:21 1121
the prophet, the *s* of Amoz, write 2Chr 26:22 1121
Jotham his *s* reigned in his stead 2Chr 26:23 1121
Ahaz his *s* reigned in his stead 2Chr 27:9 1121
in the valley of the *s* of Hinnom 2Chr 28:3 1121
For Pekah the *s* of Remaliah slew 2Chr 28:6 1121
slew Maaseiah the king's *s* 2Chr 28:7 1121
Ephraim, Azariah the *s* of Johanan 2Chr 28:12 1121
Berechiah the *s* of Meshillemoth, 2Chr 28:12 1121
and Jehizkiah the *s* of Shallum 2Chr 28:12 1121
Shallum, and Amasa the *s* of Hadlai 2Chr 28:12 1121
Hezekiah his *s* reigned in his 2Chr 28:27 1121
arose, Mahath the *s* of Amasai 2Chr 29:12 1121
Joel the *s* of Azariah, of the 2Chr 29:12 1121
of Merari, Kish the *s* of Abdi 2Chr 29:12 1121
Azariah the *s* of Jehalelel 2Chr 29:12 1121
Joah the *s* of Zimmah, and Eden the 2Chr 29:12 1121
of Zimmah, and Eden the *s* of Joah 2Chr 29:12 1121
s of David king of Israel there 2Chr 30:26 1121
Kore the *s* of Imnah the Levite, 2Chr 31:14 1121
the prophet Isaiah the *s* of Amoz 2Chr 32:20 1121
the *s* of Amoz, and in the book of 2Chr 32:32 1121
Manasseh his *s* reigned in his 2Chr 32:33 1121
in the valley of the *s* of Hinnom 2Chr 33:6 1121
said to David and to Solomon his *s* 2Chr 33:7 1121
Amon his *s* reigned in his stead 2Chr 33:20 1121

Josiah his *s* king in his stead	2Chr 33:25	1121
he sent Shaphan the *s* of Azaliah	2Chr 34:8	1121
Joah the *s* of Joahaz the recorder	2Chr 34:8	1121
and Ahikam the *s* of Shaphan	2Chr 34:20	1121
Shaphan, and Abdon the *s* of Micah	2Chr 34:20	1121
wife of Shallum the *s* of Tikvath	2Chr 34:22	1121
the *s* of Hasrah, keeper of the	2Chr 34:22	1121
the *s* of David king of Israel did	2Chr 35:3	1121
to the writing of Solomon his *s*	2Chr 35:4	1121
took Jehoahaz the *s* of Josiah	2Chr 36:1	1121
Jehoiachin his *s* reigned in his	2Chr 36:8	1121
stood up Jeshua the *s* of Jozadak	Ezr 3:2	1121
and Zerubbabel the *s* of Shealtiel	Ezr 3:2	1121
Zerubbabel the *s* of Shealtiel	Ezr 3:8	1121
and Jeshua the *s* of Jozadak	Ezr 3:8	1121
and Zechariah the *s* of Iddo	Ezr 5:1	1247
up Zerubbabel the *s* of Shealtiel	Ezr 5:2	1247
and Jeshua the *s* of Jozadak	Ezr 5:2	1247
and Zechariah the *s* of Iddo	Ezr 6:14	1247
Ezra the *s* of Seraiah	Ezr 7:1	1121
s of Azariah, the *s* of Hilkiah,	Ezr 7:1	1121
The *s* of Shallum	Ezr 7:2	1121
the *s* of Zadok, the *s* of Ahitub	Ezr 7:2	1121
The *s* of Amariah	Ezr 7:3	1121
the *s* of Azariah	Ezr 7:3	1121
the *s* of Meraioth	Ezr 7:3	1121
The *s* of Zerahiah	Ezr 7:4	1121
the *s* of Uzzi, the *s* of Bukki,	Ezr 7:4	1121
The *s* of Abishua	Ezr 7:5	1121
the *s* of Phinehas	Ezr 7:5	1121
the *s* of Eleazar	Ezr 7:5	1121
the *s* of Aaron the chief priest	Ezr 7:5	1121
Elihoenai the *s* of Zerahiah	Ezr 8:4	1121
the *s* of Jahaziel, and with him	Ezr 8:5	1121
Ebed the *s* of Jonathan, and with	Ezr 8:6	1121
Jeshaiah the *s* of Athaliah	Ezr 8:7	1121
Zebadiah the *s* of Michael	Ezr 8:8	1121
Obadiah the *s* of Jehiel, and with	Ezr 8:9	1121
the *s* of Josiphiah, and with him	Ezr 8:10	1121
Zechariah the *s* of Bebai, and with	Ezr 8:11	1121
Johanan the *s* of Hakkatan	Ezr 8:12	1121
the *s* of Levi, the *s* of Israel	Ezr 8:18	1121
the *s* of Uriah the priest	Ezr 8:33	1121
him was Eleazar the *s* of Phinehas	Ezr 8:33	1121
them was Jozabad the *s* of Jeshua	Ezr 8:33	1121
and Noadiah the *s* of Binnui	Ezr 8:33	1121
And Shechaniah the *s* of Jehiel	Ezr 10:2	1121
of Johanan the *s* of Eliashib	Ezr 10:6	1121
Only Jonathan the *s* of Asahel	Ezr 10:15	1121
Jahaziah the *s* of Tikvah were	Ezr 10:15	1121
sons of Jeshua the *s* of Jozadak	Ezr 10:18	1121
of Nehemiah the *s* of Hachaliah	Neh 1:1	1121
them builded Zaccur the *s* of Imri	Neh 3:2	1121
the *s* of Urijah, the *s* of Koz	Neh 3:4	1121
Meshullam the *s* of Berechiah	Neh 3:4	1121
Berechiah, the *s* of Meshezabeel	Neh 3:4	1121
repaired Zadok the *s* of Baana	Neh 3:4	1121
repaired Jehoiada the *s* of Paseah	Neh 3:6	1121
and Meshullam the *s* of Besodeiah	Neh 3:6	1121
repaired Uzziel the *s* of Harhaiah	Neh 3:8	1121
the *s* of one of the apothecaries	Neh 3:8	1121
repaired Rephaiah the *s* of Hur	Neh 3:9	1121
Jedaiah the *s* of Harumaph	Neh 3:10	1121
Hattush the *s* of Hashabniah	Neh 3:10	1121
Malchijah the *s* of Harim, and	Neh 3:11	1121
Hashub the *s* of Pahath-moab,	Neh 3:11	1121
Shallum the *s* of Halohesh	Neh 3:12	1121
repaired Malchiah the *s* of Rechab	Neh 3:14	1121
Shallun the *s* of Colhozeh	Neh 3:15	1121
repaired Nehemiah the *s* of Azbuk	Neh 3:16	1121
the Levites, Rehum the *s* of Bani	Neh 3:17	1121
Bavai the *s* of Henadad, the ruler	Neh 3:18	1121
him repaired Ezer the *s* of Jeshua	Neh 3:19	1121
After him Baruch the *s* of Zabbai	Neh 3:20	1121
the *s* of Urijah the *s* of Koz	Neh 3:21	1121
s of Maaseiah the *s* of Ananiah	Neh 3:23	1121
the *s* of Henadad another piece	Neh 3:24	1121
Palal the *s* of Uzai, over against	Neh 3:25	1121
After him Pedaiah the *s* of Parosh	Neh 3:25	1121
After them repaired Zadok the *s*	Neh 3:29	1121
also Shemaiah the *s* of Shechaniah	Neh 3:29	1121
Hananiah the *s* of Shelemiah	Neh 3:30	1121
and Hanun the sixth *s* of Zalaph	Neh 3:30	1121
him repaired Meshullam the *s* of	Neh 3:30	1121
Malchiah the goldsmith's *s* unto	Neh 3:31	1121
the *s* of Delaiah	Neh 6:10	1121
of Delaiah the *s* of Mehetabeel	Neh 6:10	1121
because he was the *s* in law of	Neh 6:18	2860
law of Shechaniah the *s* of Arah	Neh 6:18	1121
his *s* Johanan had taken the	Neh 6:18	1121
of Meshullam the *s* of Berechiah	Neh 6:18	1121
s of Nun unto that day had not	Neh 8:17	1121
the *s* of Hachaliah, and Zidkijah,	Neh 10:1	1121
both Jeshua the *s* of Azaniah	Neh 10:9	1121
the priest the *s* of Aaron shall	Neh 10:38	1121
Athaiah the *s* of Uzziah	Neh 11:4	1121
the *s* of Zechariah	Neh 11:4	1121
the *s* of Amariah	Neh 11:4	1121
the *s* of Shephatiah	Neh 11:4	1121
the *s* of Mahalaleel, of the	Neh 11:4	1121
And Maaseiah the *s* of Baruch	Neh 11:5	1121
the *s* of Colhozeh	Neh 11:5	1121
the *s* of Hazaiah	Neh 11:5	1121
the *s* of Adaiah	Neh 11:5	1121
the *s* of Joiarib	Neh 11:5	1121
the *s* of Zechariah	Neh 11:5	1121
of Zechariah, the *s* of Shiloni	Neh 11:5	1121
Sallu the *s* of Meshullam	Neh 11:7	1121
the *s* of Joed, the *s* of Pedaiah	Neh 11:7	1121
the *s* of Pedaiah, the *s* of	Neh 11:7	1121
the *s* of Kolaiah	Neh 11:7	1121
the *s* of Maaseiah	Neh 11:7	1121
the *s* of Ithiel, the *s* of	Neh 11:7	1121
s of Ithiel, the *s* of Jesaiah	Neh 11:7	1121
Joel the *s* of Zichri was their	Neh 11:9	1121
Judah the *s* of Senuah was second	Neh 11:9	1121
Jedaiah the *s* of Joiarib, Jachin	Neh 11:10	1121
Seraiah the *s* of Hilkiah	Neh 11:11	1121
the *s* of Meshullam	Neh 11:11	1121
the *s* of Zadok	Neh 11:11	1121
the *s* of Meraioth	Neh 11:11	1121
the *s* of Ahitub, was the ruler of	Neh 11:11	1121
and Adaiah the *s* of Jeroham	Neh 11:12	1121
the *s* of Pelaliah	Neh 11:12	1121
the *s* of Amzi	Neh 11:12	1121
the *s* of Zechariah	Neh 11:12	1121
s of Pashur, the *s* of Malchiah,	Neh 11:12	1121
and Amashai the *s* of Azareel	Neh 11:13	1121
the *s* of Ahasai	Neh 11:13	1121
the *s* of Meshillemoth	Neh 11:13	1121
the *s* of Immer	Neh 11:13	1121
the *s* of one of the great men	Neh 11:14	1121
Shemaiah the *s* of Hashub	Neh 11:15	1121
the *s* of Azrikam	Neh 11:15	1121
the *s* of Hashabiah	Neh 11:15	1121
the *s* of Bunni	Neh 11:15	1121
And Mattaniah the *s* of Micha	Neh 11:17	1121
the *s* of Zabdi, the *s* of Asaph,	Neh 11:17	1121
Abda the *s* of Shammua	Neh 11:17	1121
the *s* of Galal, the *s* of	Neh 11:17	1121
s of Galal, the *s* of Jeduthun	Neh 11:17	1121
Jerusalem was Uzzi the *s* of Bani	Neh 11:22	1121
the *s* of Hashabiah	Neh 11:22	1121
s of Mattaniah, the *s* of Micha	Neh 11:22	1121
Pethahiah the *s* of Meshezabeel,	Neh 11:24	1121
children of Zerah the *s* of Judah	Neh 11:24	1121
Zerubbabel the *s* of Shealtiel	Neh 12:1	1121
days of Johanan the *s* of Eliashib	Neh 12:23	1121
and Jeshua the *s* of Kadmiel	Neh 12:24	1121
days of Joiakim the *s* of Jeshua	Neh 12:26	1121
the *s* of Jozadak, and in the days	Neh 12:26	1121
Zechariah the *s* of Jonathan	Neh 12:35	1121
the *s* of Shemaiah	Neh 12:35	1121
the *s* of Mattaniah	Neh 12:35	1121
the *s* of Michaiah	Neh 12:35	1121
the *s* of Zaccur, the *s* of Asaph	Neh 12:35	1121
of David, and of Solomon his *s*	Neh 12:45	1121
s of Zaccur, the *s* of Mattaniah	Neh 13:13	1121
the *s* of Eliashib the high priest	Neh 13:28	1121
was *s* in law to Sanballat the	Neh 13:28	2860
the *s* of Jair, the *s* of Shimei,	Est 2:5	1121
the *s* of Kish, a Benjamite	Est 2:5	1121
the *s* of Hammedatha the Agagite	Est 3:1	1121
gave it unto Haman the *s* of	Est 3:10	1121
the *s* of Hammedatha the Agagite	Est 8:5	1121
sons of Haman the *s* of Hammedatha	Est 9:10	1121
Because Haman the *s* of Hammedatha	Est 9:24	1121
He shall neither have *s* nor	Job 18:19	5209
the *s* of man, which is a worm	Job 25:6	1121
the *s* of Barachel the Buzite	Job 32:2	1121
Elihu the *s* of Barachel the	Job 32:6	1121
may profit the *s* of man	Job 35:8	1121
hath said unto me, Thou art my *S*	Ps 2:7	1121
Kiss the *S*, lest he be angry, and	Ps 2:12	1248
when he fled from Absalom his *s*	Ps 3:*t*	1121
the *s* of man, that thou visitest	Ps 8:4	1121
slanderest thine own mother's *s*	Ps 50:20	1121
righteousness unto the king's *s*	Ps 72:1	1121
of David the *s* of Jesse are ended	Ps 72:20	1121
upon the *s* of man whom thou	Ps 80:17	1121
save the *s* of thine handmaid	Ps 86:16	1121
nor the *s* of wickedness afflict	Ps 89:22	1121
and the *s* of thine handmaid	Ps 116:16	1121
or the *s* of man, that thou makest	Ps 144:3	1121
in princes, nor in the *s* of man	Ps 146:3	1121
of Solomon the *s* of David	Prov 1:1	1121
My *s*, hear the instruction of thy	Prov 1:8	1121
My *s*, if sinners entice thee,	Prov 1:10	1121
My *s*, walk not thou in the way	Prov 1:15	1121
My *s*, if thou wilt receive my	Prov 2:1	1121
My *s*, forget not my law	Prov 3:1	1121
My *s*, despise not the chastening	Prov 3:11	1121
even as a father the *s* in whom he	Prov 3:12	1121
My *s*, let not them depart from	Prov 3:21	1121
For I was my father's *s*, tender	Prov 4:3	1121
Hear, O my *s*, and receive my	Prov 4:10	1121
My *s*, attend to my words	Prov 4:20	1121
My *s*, attend unto my wisdom, and	Prov 5:1	1121
And why wilt thou, my *s*, be	Prov 5:20	1121
My *s*, if thou be surety for thy	Prov 6:1	1121
Do this now, my *s*, and deliver	Prov 6:3	1121
My *s*, keep thy father's	Prov 6:20	1121
My *s*, keep my words, and lay up my	Prov 7:1	1121
A wise *s* maketh a glad father	Prov 10:1	1121
but a foolish *s* is the heaviness	Prov 10:1	1121
gathereth in summer is a wise *s*	Prov 10:5	1121
harvest is a *s* that causeth shame	Prov 10:5	1121
A wise *s* heareth his father's	Prov 13:1	1121
that spareth his rod hateth his *s*	Prov 13:24	1121
A wise *s* maketh a glad father	Prov 15:20	1121
rule over a *s* that causeth shame	Prov 17:2	1121
A foolish *s* is a grief to his	Prov 17:25	1121
A foolish *s* is the calamity of	Prov 19:13	1121
Chasten thy *s* while there is hope	Prov 19:18	1121
is a *s* that causeth shame, and	Prov 19:26	1121
Cease, my *s*, to hear the	Prov 19:27	1121
My *s*, if thine heart be wise, my	Prov 23:15	1121
Hear thou, my *s*, and be wise, and	Prov 23:19	1121
My *s*, give me thine heart, and let	Prov 23:26	1121
My *s*, eat thou honey, because it	Prov 24:13	1121
My *s*, fear thou the LORD and the	Prov 24:21	1121
My *s*, be wise, and make my heart	Prov 27:11	1121
Whoso keepeth the law is a wise *s*	Prov 28:7	1121
Correct thy *s*, and he shall give	Prov 29:17	1121
him become his *s* at the length	Prov 29:21	4497
The words of Agur the *s* of Jakeh	Prov 30:1	1121
What, my *s*	Prov 31:2	1248
and what, the *s* of my womb	Prov 31:2	1248
and what, the *s* of my vows	Prov 31:2	1248
the *s* of David, king in Jerusalem	Eccl 1:1	1121
and he begetteth a *s*, and there is	Eccl 5:14	1121
when thy king is the *s* of nobles	Eccl 10:17	1121
And further, by these, my *s*	Eccl 12:12	1121
vision of Isaiah the *s* of Amoz	Is 1:1	1121
The word that Isaiah the *s* of	Is 2:1	1121
the days of Ahaz the *s* of Jotham	Is 7:1	1121
the *s* of Uzziah, king of Judah,	Is 7:1	1121
Pekah the *s* of Remaliah, king of	Is 7:1	1121
Ahaz, thou, and Shear-jashub thy *s*	Is 7:3	1121
Syria, and of the *s* of Remaliah	Is 7:4	1121
the *s* of Remaliah, have taken	Is 7:5	1121
midst of it, even the *s* of Tabeal	Is 7:6	1121
head of Samaria is Remaliah's *s*	Is 7:9	1121
shall conceive, and bear a *s*	Is 7:14	1121
Zechariah the *s* of Jeberechiah	Is 8:2	1121
and she conceived, and bare a *s*	Is 8:3	1121
rejoice in Rezin and Remaliah's *s*	Is 8:6	1121
is born, unto us a *s* is given	Is 9:6	1121
Isaiah the *s* of Amoz did see	Is 13:1	1121
O Lucifer, *s* of the morning	Is 14:12	1121
the name, and remnant, and *s*	Is 14:22	5209
I am the *s* of the wise	Is 19:11	1121
the wise, the *s* of ancient kings	Is 19:11	1121
the LORD by Isaiah the *s* of Amoz	Is 20:2	1121
servant Eliakim the *s* of Hilkiah	Is 22:20	1121
unto him Eliakim, Hilkiah's *s*	Is 36:3	1121
the scribe, and Joah, Asaph's *s*	Is 36:3	1121
the *s* of Hilkiah, that was over	Is 36:22	1121
the *s* of Asaph, the recorder, to	Is 36:22	1121
Isaiah the prophet the *s* of Amoz	Is 37:2	1121
Then Isaiah the *s* of Amoz sent	Is 37:21	1121
Esar-haddon his *s* reigned in his	Is 37:38	1121
the *s* of Amoz came unto him	Is 38:1	1121
the *s* of Baladan, king of Babylon	Is 39:1	1121
compassion on the *s* of her womb	Is 49:15	1121
of the *s* of man which shall be	Is 51:12	1121
the *s* of man that layeth hold on	Is 56:2	1121
Neither let the *s* of the stranger	Is 56:3	1121
of Jeremiah the *s* of Hilkiah	Jer 1:1	1121
the *s* of Amon king of Judah	Jer 1:2	1121
the *s* of Josiah king of Judah	Jer 1:3	1121
the *s* of Josiah king of Judah	Jer 1:3	1121
thee mourning, as for an only *s*	Jer 6:26	3173
in the valley of the *s* of Hinnom	Jer 7:31	1121
nor the valley of the *s* of Hinnom	Jer 7:32	1121
because of Manasseh the *s* of	Jer 15:4	1121
the valley of the *s* of Hinnom	Jer 19:2	1121
nor The valley of the *s* of Hinnom	Jer 19:6	1121
Now Pashur the *s* of Immer the	Jer 20:1	1121
unto him Pashur the *s* of Melchiah	Jer 21:1	1121
Zephaniah the *s* of Maaseiah the	Jer 21:1	1121
the *s* of Josiah king of Judah	Jer 22:11	1121
the *s* of Josiah king of Judah	Jer 22:18	1121
though Coniah the *s* of Jehoiakim	Jer 22:24	1121
away captive Jeconiah the *s* of	Jer 24:1	1121
the *s* of Josiah king of Judah	Jer 25:1	1121
the *s* of Amon king of Judah	Jer 25:3	1121
s of Josiah king of Judah came	Jer 26:1	1121
Urijah the *s* of Shemaiah of	Jer 26:20	1121
namely, Elnathan the *s* of Achbor	Jer 26:22	1121
the hand of Ahikam the *s* of	Jer 26:24	1121
s of Josiah king of Judah came	Jer 27:1	1121
him, and his *s*, and his son's *s*	Jer 27:7	1121
away captive Jeconiah the *s* of	Jer 27:20	1121
that Hananiah the *s* of Azur the	Jer 28:1	1121
the *s* of Jehoiakim king of Judah	Jer 28:4	1121
hand of Elasah the *s* of Shaphan	Jer 29:3	1121
and Gemariah the *s* of Hilkiah	Jer 29:3	1121
Israel, of Ahab the *s* of Kolaiah	Jer 29:21	1121
and of Zedekiah the *s* of Maaseiah	Jer 29:21	1121
to Zephaniah the *s* of Maaseiah	Jer 29:25	1121
Is Ephraim my dear *s*	Jer 31:20	1121
Hanameel the *s* of Shallum thine	Jer 32:7	1121
So Hanameel mine uncle's *s* came	Jer 32:8	1121
field of Hanameel my uncle's *s*	Jer 32:9	1121
unto Baruch the *s* of Neriah	Jer 32:12	1121
the *s* of Maaseiah, in the sight	Jer 32:12	1121
sight of Hanameel mine uncle's *s*	Jer 32:12	
unto Baruch the *s* of Neriah	Jer 32:16	1121
in the valley of the *s* of Hinnom	Jer 32:35	1121
have a *s* to reign upon his throne	Jer 33:21	1121
the *s* of Josiah king of Judah	Jer 35:1	1121
took Jaazaniah the *s* of Jeremiah	Jer 35:3	1121
the *s* of Habaziniah, and his	Jer 35:3	1121
the *s* of Igdaliah, a man of God,	Jer 35:4	1121
of Maaseiah the *s* of Shallum	Jer 35:4	1121
for Jonadab the *s* of Rechab our	Jer 35:6	1121
the *s* of Rechab our father in all	Jer 35:8	1121
words of Jonadab the *s* of Rechab	Jer 35:14	1121
s of Rechab have performed the	Jer 35:16	1121
Jonadab the *s* of Rechab shall not	Jer 35:19	1121
the *s* of Josiah king of Judah	Jer 36:1	1121
called Baruch the *s* of Neriah	Jer 36:4	1121
Baruch the *s* of Neriah did	Jer 36:8	1121

the *s* of Josiah king of Judah	Jer 36:9	1121
the *s* of Shaphan the scribe	Jer 36:10	1121
When Michaiah the *s* of Gemariah	Jer 36:11	1121
the *s* of Shaphan, had heard out	Jer 36:11	1121
and Delaiah the *s* of Shemaiah	Jer 36:12	1121
and Elnathan the *s* of Achbor	Jer 36:12	1121
and Gemariah the *s* of Shaphan	Jer 36:12	1121
and Zedekiah the *s* of Hananiah	Jer 36:12	1121
sent Jehudi the *s* of Nethaniah	Jer 36:14	1121
the *s* of Shelemiah	Jer 36:14	1121
the *s* of Cushi, unto Baruch,	Jer 36:14	1121
So Baruch the *s* of Neriah took	Jer 36:14	1121
Jerahmeel the *s* of Hammelech	Jer 36:26	1121
and Seraiah the *s* of Azriel	Jer 36:26	1121
and Shelemiah the *s* of Abdeel	Jer 36:26	1121
the scribe, the *s* of Neriah	Jer 36:32	1121
king Zedekiah the *s* of Josiah	Jer 37:1	1121
of Coniah the *s* of Jehoiakim	Jer 37:1	1121
sent Jehucal the *s* of Shelemiah	Jer 37:3	1121
Zephaniah the *s* of Maaseiah the	Jer 37:3	1121
the *s* of Shelemiah	Jer 37:13	1121
the *s* of Hananiah	Jer 37:13	1121
Then Shephatiah the *s* of Mattan	Jer 38:1	1121
and Gedaliah the *s* of Pashur	Jer 38:1	1121
Jucal the *s* of Shelemiah, and	Jer 38:1	1121
Pashur the *s* of Malchiah, heard	Jer 38:1	1121
of Malchiah the *s* of Hammelech	Jer 38:6	1121
s of Ahikam the *s* of Shaphan	Jer 39:14	1121
s of Ahikam the *s* of Shaphan	Jer 40:5	1121
the *s* of Ahikam to Mizpah	Jer 40:6	1121
Babylon had made Gedaliah the *s*	Jer 40:7	1121
even Ishmael the *s* of Nethaniah	Jer 40:8	1121
Seraiah the *s* of Tanhumeth, and	Jer 40:8	1121
Jezaniah the *s* of a Maachathite,	Jer 40:8	1121
Gedaliah the *s* of Ahikam	Jer 40:9	1121
the *s* of Shaphan sware unto them	Jer 40:9	1121
s of Ahikam the *s* of Shaphan	Jer 40:11	1121
Moreover Johanan the *s* of Kareah	Jer 40:13	1121
the *s* of Nethaniah to slay thee	Jer 40:14	1121
But Gedaliah the *s* of Ahikam	Jer 40:14	1121
Then Johanan the *s* of Kareah	Jer 40:15	1121
slay Ishmael the *s* of Nethaniah	Jer 40:15	1121
But Gedaliah the *s* of Ahikam said	Jer 40:16	1121
said unto Johanan the *s* of Kareah	Jer 40:16	1121
that Ishmael the *s* of Nethaniah	Jer 41:1	1121
of Nethaniah the *s* of Elishama	Jer 41:1	1121
the *s* of Ahikam to Mizpah	Jer 41:1	1121
arose Ishmael the *s* of Nethaniah	Jer 41:2	1121
smote Gedaliah the *s* of Ahikam	Jer 41:2	1121
the *s* of Shaphan with the sword	Jer 41:2	1121
Ishmael the *s* of Nethaniah went	Jer 41:6	1121
Come to Gedaliah the *s* of Ahikam	Jer 41:6	1121
that Ishmael the *s* of Nethaniah	Jer 41:7	1121
Ishmael the *s* of Nethaniah filled	Jer 41:9	1121
to Gedaliah the *s* of Ahikam	Jer 41:10	1121
Ishmael the *s* of Nethaniah	Jer 41:10	1121
But when Johanan the *s* of Kareah	Jer 41:11	1121
the *s* of Nethaniah had done	Jer 41:11	1121
with Ishmael the *s* of Nethaniah	Jer 41:12	1121
saw Johanan the *s* of Kareah	Jer 41:13	1121
went unto Johanan the *s* of Kareah	Jer 41:14	1121
But Ishmael the *s* of Nethaniah	Jer 41:15	1121
Then took Johanan the *s* of Kareah	Jer 41:16	1121
from Ishmael the *s* of Nethaniah	Jer 41:16	1121
slain Gedaliah the *s* of Ahikam	Jer 41:16	1121
of them, because Ishmael the *s* of	Jer 41:18	1121
slain Gedaliah the *s* of Ahikam	Jer 41:18	1121
and Johanan the *s* of Kareah	Jer 42:1	1121
and Jezaniah the *s* of Hoshaiah	Jer 42:1	1121
called he Johanan the *s* of Kareah	Jer 42:8	1121
spake Azariah the *s* of Hoshaiah	Jer 43:2	1121
and Johanan the *s* of Kareah	Jer 43:2	1121
But Baruch the *s* of Neriah	Jer 43:3	1121
So Johanan the *s* of Kareah	Jer 43:4	1121
But Johanan the *s* of Kareah	Jer 43:5	1121
s of Ahikam the *s* of Shaphan	Jer 43:6	1121
and Baruch the *s* of Neriah	Jer 43:6	1121
spake unto Baruch the *s* of Neriah	Jer 45:1	1121
the *s* of Josiah king of Judah	Jer 45:1	1121
the *s* of Josiah king of Judah	Jer 46:2	1121
neither shall a *s* of man dwell in	Jer 49:18	1121
nor any *s* of man dwell in it	Jer 49:33	1121
neither shall any *s* of man dwell	Jer 50:40	1121
neither doth any *s* of man pass	Jer 51:43	1121
commanded Seraiah the *s* of Neriah	Jer 51:59	1121
the *s* of Maaseiah, when he went	Jer 51:59	1121
the *s* of Buzi, in the land of the	Eze 1:3	1121
S of man, stand upon thy feet, and	Eze 2:1	1121
S of man, I send thee to the	Eze 2:3	1121
s of man, be not afraid of them,	Eze 2:6	1121
s of man, hear what I say unto	Eze 2:8	1121
S of man, eat that thou findest	Eze 3:1	1121
S of man, cause thy belly to eat,	Eze 3:3	1121
S of man, go, get thee unto the	Eze 3:4	1121
S of man, all my words that I	Eze 3:10	1121
S of man, I have made thee a	Eze 3:17	1121
O *s* of man, behold, they shall	Eze 3:25	1121
s of man, take thee a tile, and	Eze 4:1	1121
S of man, behold, I will break	Eze 4:16	1121
s of man, take thee a sharp knife	Eze 5:1	1121
S of man, set thy face toward the	Eze 6:2	1121
thou *s* of man, thus saith the	Eze 7:2	1121
S of man, lift up thine eyes now	Eze 8:5	1121
S of man, seest thou what they do	Eze 8:6	1121
S of man, dig now in the wall	Eze 8:8	1121
stood Jaazaniah the *s* of Shaphan	Eze 8:11	1121
S of man, hast thou seen what the	Eze 8:12	1121
Hast thou seen this, O *s* of man	Eze 8:15	1121
Hast thou seen this, O *s* of man	Eze 8:17	1121
I saw Jaazaniah the *s* of Azur	Eze 11:1	1121
and Pelatiah the *s* of Benaiah	Eze 11:1	1121
S of man, these are the men that	Eze 11:2	1121
them, prophesy, O *s* of man	Eze 11:4	1121
Pelatiah the *s* of Benaiah died	Eze 11:13	1121
S of man, thy brethren, even thy	Eze 11:15	1121
S of man, thou dwellest in the	Eze 12:2	1121
thou *s* of man, prepare thee stuff	Eze 12:3	1121
S of man, hath not the house of	Eze 12:9	1121
S of man, eat thy bread with	Eze 12:18	1121
S of man, what is that proverb	Eze 12:22	1121
S of man, behold, they of the	Eze 12:27	1121
S of man, prophesy against the	Eze 13:2	1121
thou *s* of man, set thy face	Eze 13:17	1121
S of man, these men have set up	Eze 14:3	1121
S of man, when the land sinneth	Eze 14:13	1121
deliver neither *s* nor daughter	Eze 14:20	1121
S of man, What is the vine tree	Eze 15:2	1121
S of man, cause Jerusalem to know	Eze 16:2	1121
S of man, put forth a riddle, and	Eze 17:2	1121
so also the soul of the *s* is mine	Eze 18:4	1121
If he beget a *s* that is a robber,	Eze 18:10	1121
Now, lo, if he beget a *s*, that	Eze 18:14	1121
doth not the *s* bear the iniquity	Eze 18:19	1121
When the *s* hath done that which	Eze 18:19	1121
The *s* shall not bear the iniquity	Eze 18:20	1121
father bear the iniquity of the *s*	Eze 18:20	1121
S of man, speak unto the elders	Eze 20:3	1121
s of man, wilt thou judge them	Eze 20:4	1121
s of man, speak unto the house of	Eze 20:27	1121
S of man, set thy face toward the	Eze 20:46	1121
S of man, set thy face toward	Eze 21:2	1121
thou *s* of man, with the breaking	Eze 21:6	1121
S of man, prophesy, and say, Thus	Eze 21:9	1121
it contemneth the rod of my *s*	Eze 21:10	1121
Cry and howl, *s* of man	Eze 21:12	1121
s of man, prophesy, and smite	Eze 21:14	1121
thou *s* of man, appoint thee two	Eze 21:19	1121
s of man, prophesy and say, Thus	Eze 21:28	1121
thou *s* of man, wilt thou judge,	Eze 22:2	1121
S of man, the house of Israel is	Eze 22:18	1121
S of man, say unto her, Thou art	Eze 22:24	1121
S of man, there were two women,	Eze 23:2	1121
S of man, wilt thou judge Aholah	Eze 23:36	1121
S of man, write thee the name of	Eze 24:2	1121
S of man, behold, I take away	Eze 24:16	1121
thou *s* of man, shall it not be in	Eze 24:25	1121
S of man, set thy face against	Eze 25:2	1121
S of man, because that Tyrus hath	Eze 26:2	1121
Now, thou *s* of man, take up a	Eze 27:2	1121
S of man, say unto the prince of	Eze 28:2	1121
S of man, take up a lamentation	Eze 28:12	1121
S of man, set thy face against	Eze 28:21	1121
S of man, set thy face against	Eze 29:2	1121
S of man, Nebuchadrezzar king of	Eze 29:18	1121
S of man, prophesy and say, Thus	Eze 30:2	1121
S of man, I have broken the arm	Eze 30:21	1121
S of man, speak unto Pharaoh king	Eze 31:2	1121
S of man, take up a lamentation	Eze 32:2	1121
S of man, wail for the multitude	Eze 32:18	1121
S of man, speak to the children	Eze 33:2	1121
O *s* of man, I have set thee a	Eze 33:7	1121
Therefore, O thou *s* of man	Eze 33:10	1121
thou *s* of man, say unto the	Eze 33:12	1121
S of man, they that inhabit those	Eze 33:24	1121
thou *s* of man, the children of	Eze 33:30	1121
S of man, prophesy against the	Eze 34:2	1121
S of man, set thy face against	Eze 35:2	1121
thou *s* of man, prophesy unto the	Eze 36:1	1121
S of man, when the house of	Eze 36:17	1121
S of man, can these bones live	Eze 37:3	1121
s of man, and say to the wind,	Eze 37:9	1121
S of man, these bones are the	Eze 37:11	1121
thou *s* of man, take thee one	Eze 37:16	1121
S of man, set thy face against	Eze 38:2	1121
s of man, prophesy and say unto	Eze 38:14	1121
thou *s* of man, prophesy against	Eze 39:1	1121
thou *s* of man, thus saith the	Eze 39:17	1121
S of man, behold with thine eyes,	Eze 40:4	1121
S of man, the place of my throne,	Eze 43:7	1121
Thou *s* of man, shew the house to	Eze 43:10	1121
S of man, thus saith the Lord GOD	Eze 43:18	1121
S of man, mark well, and behold	Eze 44:5	1121
father, or for mother, or for *s*	Eze 44:25	1121
S of man, hast thou seen this	Eze 47:6	1121
the fourth is like the *S* of God	Dan 3:25	1247
And thou his *s*, O Belshazzar, hast	Dan 5:22	1247
one like the *S* of man came with	Dan 7:13	1247
unto me, Understand, O *s* of man	Dan 8:17	1121
year of Darius the *s* of Ahasuerus	Dan 9:1	1121
the *s* of Beeri, in the days of	Hos 1:1	1121
days of Jeroboam the *s* of Joash	Hos 1:1	1121
which conceived, and bare him a *s*	Hos 1:3	1121
she conceived, and bare a *s*	Hos 1:8	1121
him, and called my *s* out of Egypt	Hos 11:1	1121
he is an unwise *s*	Hos 13:13	1121
came to Joel the *s* of Pethuel	Joel 1:1	1121
the *s* of Joash king of Israel	Amos 1:1	1121
neither was I an prophet's *s*	Amos 7:14	1121
it as the mourning of an only *s*	Amos 8:10	
came unto Jonah the *s* of Amittai	Jonah 1:1	1121
what Balaam the *s* of Beor	Mic 6:5	1121
For the *s* dishonoureth the father	Mic 7:6	1121
unto Zephaniah the *s* of Cushi	Zeph 1:1	1121
the *s* of Gedaliah	Zeph 1:1	1121
the *s* of Amariah	Zeph 1:1	1121
the *s* of Hizkiah	Zeph 1:1	1121
the days of Josiah the *s* of Amon	Zeph 1:1	1121
Zerubbabel the *s* of Shealtiel	Hag 1:1	1121
and to Joshua the *s* of Josedech	Hag 1:1	1121
Zerubbabel the *s* of Shealtiel	Hag 1:12	1121
Joshua the *s* of Josedech, the	Hag 1:12	1121
of Zerubbabel the *s* of Shealtiel	Hag 1:14	1121
of Joshua the *s* of Josedech	Hag 1:14	1121
to Zerubbabel the *s* of Shealtiel	Hag 2:2	1121
and to Joshua the *s* of Josedech	Hag 2:2	1121
s of Josedech, the high priest	Hag 2:4	1121
the *s* of Shealtiel, saith the	Hag 2:23	1121
the *s* of Berechiah	Zec 1:1	1121
the *s* of Iddo the prophet, saying	Zec 1:1	1121
the *s* of Berechiah	Zec 1:7	1121
the *s* of Iddo the prophet, saying	Zec 1:7	1121
of Josiah the *s* of Zephaniah	Zec 6:10	1121
head of Joshua the *s* of Josedech	Zec 6:11	1121
to Hen the *s* of Zephaniah, for a	Zec 6:14	1121
as one mourneth for his only *s*	Zec 12:10	
A *s* honoureth his father, and a	Mal 1:6	1121
his own *s* that serveth him	Mal 3:17	1121
s of David, the *s* of Abraham	Mt 1:1	5207
thou *s* of David, fear not to take	Mt 1:20	5207
And she shall bring forth a *s*	Mt 1:21	5207
child, and shall bring forth a *s*	Mt 1:23	5207
had brought forth her firstborn *s*	Mt 1:25	5207
Out of Egypt have I called my *s*	Mt 2:15	5207
saying, This is my beloved *S*	Mt 3:17	5207
he said, If thou be the *S* of God	Mt 4:3	5207
unto him, If thou be the *S* of God	Mt 4:6	5207
James the *s* of Zebedee, and John	Mt 4:21	
of you, whom if his *s* ask bread	Mt 7:9	5207
but the *S* of man hath not where	Mt 8:20	5207
with thee, Jesus, thou *S* of God	Mt 8:29	5207
S, be of good cheer	Mt 9:2	5048
S of man hath power on earth to	Mt 9:6	5207
Thou *s* of David, have mercy on us	Mt 9:27	5207
James the *s* of Zebedee, and John	Mt 10:2	
James the *s* of Alphaeus, and	Mt 10:3	
till the *S* of man be come	Mt 10:23	5207
he that loveth *s* or daughter more	Mt 10:37	5207
The *S* of man came eating and	Mt 11:19	5207
and no man knoweth the *S*, but the	Mt 11:27	5207
any man the Father, save the *S*	Mt 11:27	5207
whomsoever the *S* will reveal him	Mt 11:27	5207
For the *S* of man is Lord even of	Mt 12:8	5207
said, Is not this the *s* of David	Mt 12:23	5207
a word against the *S* of man	Mt 12:32	5207
so shall the *S* of man be three	Mt 12:40	5207
the good seed is the *S* of man	Mt 13:37	5207
The *S* of man shall send forth his	Mt 13:41	5207
Is not this the carpenter's *s*	Mt 13:55	5207
Of a truth thou art the *S* of God	Mt 14:33	5207
on me, O Lord, thou *s* of David	Mt 15:22	5207
do men say that I the *S* of man am	Mt 16:13	5207
Christ, the *S* of the living God	Mt 16:16	5207
For the *S* of man shall come in	Mt 16:27	5207
till they see the *S* of man coming	Mt 16:28	5207
which said, This is my beloved *S*	Mt 17:5	5207
until the *S* of man be risen again	Mt 17:9	5207
also the *S* of man suffer of them	Mt 17:12	5207
Lord, have mercy on my *s*	Mt 17:15	5207
The *S* of man shall be betrayed	Mt 17:22	5207
For the *S* of man is come to save	Mt 18:11	5207
in the regeneration when the *S* of	Mt 19:28	5207
the *S* of man shall be betrayed	Mt 20:18	5207
Even as the *S* of man came not to	Mt 20:28	5207
on us, O Lord, thou *s* of David	Mt 20:30	5207
on us, O Lord, thou *s* of David	Mt 20:31	5207
saying, Hosanna to the *s* of David	Mt 21:9	5207
saying, Hosanna to the *s* of David	Mt 21:15	5207
he came to the first, and said, *S*	Mt 21:28	5043
of all he sent unto them his *s*	Mt 21:37	5207
saying, They will reverence my *s*	Mt 21:37	5207
But when the husbandmen saw the *s*	Mt 21:38	5207
which made a marriage for his *s*	Mt 22:2	5207
whose *s* is he	Mt 22:42	5207
They say unto him, The *s* of David	Mt 22:42	
how is he his *s*	Mt 22:45	5207
blood of Zacharias *s* of Barachias	Mt 23:35	5207
the coming of the *S* of man be	Mt 24:27	5207
sign of the *S* of man in heaven	Mt 24:30	5207
they shall see the *S* of man	Mt 24:30	5207
the coming of the *S* of man be	Mt 24:37	5207
the coming of the *S* of man be	Mt 24:39	5207
ye think not the *S* of man cometh	Mt 24:44	5207
hour wherein the *S* of man cometh	Mt 25:13	5207
When the *S* of man shall come in	Mt 25:31	5207
the *S* of man is betrayed to be	Mt 26:2	5207
The *S* of man goeth as it is	Mt 26:24	5207
by whom the *S* of man is betrayed	Mt 26:24	5207
the *S* of man is betrayed into the	Mt 26:45	5207
thou be the Christ, the *S* of God	Mt 26:63	5207
Hereafter shall ye see the *S* of	Mt 26:64	5207
If thou be the *S* of God, come	Mt 27:40	5207
for he said, I am the *S* of God	Mt 27:43	5207
Truly this was the *S* of God	Mt 27:54	5207
name of the Father, and of the *S*	Mt 28:19	5207
of Jesus Christ, the *S* of God	Mk 1:1	5207
saying, Thou art my beloved *S*	Mk 1:11	5207
he saw James the *s* of Zebedee	Mk 1:19	
unto the sick of the palsy, *S*	Mk 2:5	5043
S of man hath power on earth to	Mk 2:10	5207
he saw Levi the *s* of Alphaeus	Mk 2:14	
Therefore the *S* of man is Lord	Mk 2:28	5207
saying, Thou art the *S* of God	Mk 3:11	5207
James the *s* of Zebedee, and John	Mk 3:17	
James the *s* of Alphaeus, and	Mk 3:18	

thou *S* of the most high God	Mk 5:7	*5207*
the *s* of Mary, the brother of	Mk 6:3	*5207*
that the *S* of man must suffer	Mk 8:31	*5207*
shall the *S* of man be ashamed	Mk 8:38	*5207*
saying, This is my beloved *S*	Mk 9:7	*5207*
till the *S* of man were risen from	Mk 9:9	*5207*
how it is written of the *S* of man	Mk 9:12	*5207*
I have brought unto thee my *s*	Mk 9:17	*5207*
The *S* of man is delivered into	Mk 9:31	*5207*
the *S* of man shall be delivered	Mk 10:33	*5207*
For even the *S* of man came not to	Mk 10:45	*5207*
the *s* of Timaeus, sat by the	Mk 10:46	*5207*
thou *s* of David, have mercy on me	Mk 10:47	*5207*
Thou *s* of David, have mercy on me	Mk 10:48	*5207*
Having yet therefore one *s*	Mk 12:6	*5207*
saying, They will reverence my *s*	Mk 12:6	*5207*
that Christ is the *s* of David	Mk 12:35	*5207*
and whence is he then his *s*	Mk 12:37	*5207*
to death, and the father the *s*	Mk 13:12	*5043*
then shall they see the *S* of man	Mk 13:26	*5207*
are in heaven, neither the *S*	Mk 13:32	*5207*
For the *S* of man is as a man	Mk 13:34	
The *S* of man indeed goeth, as it	Mk 14:21	*5207*
by whom the *S* of man is betrayed	Mk 14:21	*5207*
the *S* of man is betrayed into the	Mk 14:41	*5207*
the Christ, the *S* of the Blessed	Mk 14:61	*5207*
ye shall see the *S* of man sitting	Mk 14:62	*5207*
Truly this man was the *S* of God	Mk 15:39	*5207*
Elisabeth shall bear thee a *s*	Lk 1:13	*5207*
in thy womb, and bring forth a *s*	Lk 1:31	*5207*
be called the *S* of the Highest	Lk 1:32	*5207*
thee shall be called the *S* of God	Lk 1:35	*5207*
also conceived a *s* in her old age	Lk 1:36	*5207*
and she brought forth a *s*	Lk 1:57	*5207*
she brought forth her firstborn *s*	Lk 2:7	*5207*
and his mother said unto him, *S*	Lk 2:48	*5043*
s of Zacharias in the wilderness	Lk 3:2	*5207*
which said, Thou art my beloved *S*	Lk 3:22	*5207*
(as was supposed) the *s* of Joseph	Lk 3:23	*5207*
Joseph, which was the *s* of Heli	Lk 3:23	
Which was the *s* of Matthat	Lk 3:24	
Matthat, which was the *s* of Levi	Lk 3:24	
Levi, which was the *s* of Melchi	Lk 3:24	
Melchi, which was the *s* of Janna	Lk 3:24	
Janna, which was the *s* of Joseph	Lk 3:24	
Which was the *s* of Mattathias	Lk 3:25	
which was the *s* of Amos, which	Lk 3:25	
of Amos, which was the *s* of Naum	Lk 3:25	
of Naum, which was the *s* of Esli	Lk 3:25	
of Esli, which was the *s* of Nagge	Lk 3:25	
Which was the *s* of Maath, which	Lk 3:26	
which was the *s* of Mattathias	Lk 3:26	
which was the *s* of Semei	Lk 3:26	
Semei, which was the *s* of Joseph	Lk 3:26	
Joseph, which was the *s* of Juda	Lk 3:26	
Which was the *s* of Joanna	Lk 3:27	
Joanna, which was the *s* of Rhesa	Lk 3:27	
which was the *s* of Zorobabel	Lk 3:27	
which was the *s* of Salathiel	Lk 3:27	
which was the *s* of Neri,	Lk 3:27	
Which was the *s* of Melchi	Lk 3:28	
Melchi, which was the *s* of Addi	Lk 3:28	
of Addi, which was the *s* of Cosam	Lk 3:28	
Cosam, which was the *s* of Elmodam	Lk 3:28	
of Elmodam, which was the *s* of Er	Lk 3:28	
Which was the *s* of Jose, which	Lk 3:29	
Jose, which was the *s* of Eliezer	Lk 3:29	
Eliezer, which was the *s* of Jorim	Lk 3:29	
Jorim, which was the *s* of Matthat	Lk 3:29	
Matthat, which was the *s* of Levi	Lk 3:29	
Which was the *s* of Simeon	Lk 3:30	
Simeon, which was the *s* of Juda	Lk 3:30	
Juda, which was the *s* of Joseph	Lk 3:30	
Joseph, which was the *s* of Jonan	Lk 3:30	
Jonan, which was the *s* of Eliakim	Lk 3:30	
Which was the *s* of Melea, which	Lk 3:31	
Melea, which was the *s* of Menan	Lk 3:31	
which was the *s* of Mattatha	Lk 3:31	
which was the *s* of Nathan	Lk 3:31	
Nathan, which was the *s* of David	Lk 3:31	
Which was the *s* of Jesse, which	Lk 3:32	
of Jesse, which was the *s* of Obed	Lk 3:32	
of Obed, which was the *s* of Booz	Lk 3:32	
Booz, which was the *s* of Salmon	Lk 3:32	
which was the *s* of Naasson	Lk 3:32	
Which was the *s* of Aminadab	Lk 3:33	
Aminadab, which was the *s* of Aram	Lk 3:33	
of Aram, which was the *s* of Esrom	Lk 3:33	
Esrom, which was the *s* of Phares	Lk 3:33	
Phares, which was the *s* of Juda	Lk 3:33	
Which was the *s* of Jacob, which	Lk 3:34	
Jacob, which was the *s* of Isaac	Lk 3:34	
Isaac, which was the *s* of Abraham	Lk 3:34	
Abraham, which was the *s* of Thara	Lk 3:34	
Thara, which was the *s* of Nachor	Lk 3:34	
Which was the *s* of Saruch	Lk 3:35	
Saruch, which was the *s* of Ragau	Lk 3:35	
Ragau, which was the *s* of Phalec	Lk 3:35	
Phalec, which was the *s* of Heber	Lk 3:35	
of Heber, which was the *s* of Sala	Lk 3:35	
Which was the *s* of Cainan	Lk 3:36	
which was the *s* of Arphaxad	Lk 3:36	
Arphaxad, which was the *s* of Sem	Lk 3:36	
of Sem, which was the *s* of Noe	Lk 3:36	
of Noe, which was the *s* of Lamech	Lk 3:36	
Which was the *s* of Mathusala	Lk 3:37	
which was the *s* of Enoch	Lk 3:37	
Enoch, which was the *s* of Jared	Lk 3:37	
which was the *s* of Maleleel	Lk 3:37	
which was the *s* of Cainan	Lk 3:37	
Which was the *s* of Enos, which	Lk 3:38	
of Enos, which was the *s* of Seth	Lk 3:38	
of Seth, which was the *s* of Adam	Lk 3:38	
of Adam, which was the *s* of God	Lk 3:38	
unto him, If thou be the *S* of God	Lk 4:3	*5207*
unto him, If thou be the *S* of God	Lk 4:9	*5207*
they said, Is not this Joseph's *s*	Lk 4:22	*5207*
Thou art Christ the *S* of God	Lk 4:41	*5207*
But that ye may know that the *S*	Lk 5:24	*5207*
That the *S* of man is Lord also of	Lk 6:5	*5207*
James the *s* of Alphaeus, and Simon	Lk 6:15	
as evil, for the *S* of man's sake	Lk 6:22	*5207*
the only *s* of his mother, and she	Lk 7:12	*5207*
The *S* of man is come eating and	Lk 7:34	*5207*
Jesus, thou *S* of God most high	Lk 8:28	*5207*
The *S* of man must suffer many	Lk 9:22	*5207*
of him shall the *S* of man be	Lk 9:26	*5207*
saying, This is my beloved *S*	Lk 9:35	*5207*
I beseech thee, look upon my *s*	Lk 9:38	*5207*
Bring thy *s* hither	Lk 9:41	*5207*
for the *S* of man shall be	Lk 9:44	*5207*
For the *S* of man is not come to	Lk 9:56	*5207*
but the *S* of man hath not where	Lk 9:58	*5207*
if the *s* of peace be there, your	Lk 10:6	*5207*
and no man knoweth who the *S* is	Lk 10:22	*5207*
and who the Father is, but the *S*	Lk 10:22	*5207*
he to whom the *S* will reveal him	Lk 10:22	*5207*
If a *s* shall ask bread of any of	Lk 11:11	*5207*
so shall also the *S* of man be to	Lk 11:30	*5207*
him shall the *S* of man also	Lk 12:8	*5207*
speak a word against the *S* of man	Lk 12:10	*5207*
for the *S* of man cometh at an	Lk 12:40	*5207*
shall be divided against the *s*	Lk 12:53	*5207*
and the *s* against the father	Lk 12:53	*5207*
younger *s* gathered all together	Lk 15:13	*5207*
no more worthy to be called thy *s*	Lk 15:19	*5207*
the *s* said unto him, Father, I	Lk 15:21	*5207*
no more worthy to be called thy *s*	Lk 15:21	*5207*
For this my *s* was dead, and is	Lk 15:24	*5207*
Now his elder *s* was in the field	Lk 15:25	*5207*
as soon as this thy *s* was come	Lk 15:30	*5207*
And he said unto him, *S*, thou art	Lk 15:31	*5043*
But Abraham said, *S*, remember	Lk 16:25	*5043*
one of the days of the *S* of man	Lk 17:22	*5207*
so shall also the *S* of man be in	Lk 17:24	*5207*
also in the days of the *S* of man	Lk 17:26	*5207*
day when the *S* of man is revealed	Lk 17:30	*5207*
when the *S* of man cometh, shall	Lk 18:8	*5207*
S of man shall be accomplished	Lk 18:31	*5207*
thou *s* of David, have mercy on me	Lk 18:38	*5207*
Thou *s* of David, have mercy on me	Lk 18:39	*5207*
as he also is a *s* of Abraham	Lk 19:9	*5207*
For the *S* of man is come to seek	Lk 19:10	*5207*
I will send my beloved *s*	Lk 20:13	*5207*
say they that Christ is David's *s*	Lk 20:41	*5207*
him Lord, how is he then his *s*	Lk 20:44	*5207*
then shall they see the *S* of man	Lk 21:27	*5207*
and to stand before the *S* of man	Lk 21:36	*5207*
truly the *S* of man goeth, as it	Lk 22:22	*5207*
thou the *S* of man with a kiss	Lk 22:48	*5207*
Hereafter shall the *S* of man sit	Lk 22:69	*5207*
all, Art thou then the *S* of God	Lk 22:70	*5207*
The *S* of man must be delivered	Lk 24:7	*5207*
the only begotten *S*, which is in	Jn 1:18	*5207*
record that this is the *S* of God	Jn 1:34	*5207*
Thou art Simon the *s* of Jona	Jn 1:42	*5207*
of Nazareth, the *s* of Joseph	Jn 1:45	*5207*
him, Rabbi, thou art the *S* of God	Jn 1:49	*5207*
and descending upon the *S* of man	Jn 1:51	*5207*
even the *S* of man which is in	Jn 3:13	*5207*
even so must the *S* of man be	Jn 3:14	*5207*
that he gave his only begotten *S*	Jn 3:16	*5207*
For God sent not his *S* into the	Jn 3:17	*5207*
of the only begotten *S* of God	Jn 3:18	*5207*
The Father loveth the *S*, and hath	Jn 3:35	*5207*
on the *S* hath everlasting life	Jn 3:36	*5207*
not the *S* shall not see life	Jn 3:36	*5207*
that Jacob gave to his *s* Joseph	Jn 4:5	*5207*
whose *s* was sick at Capernaum	Jn 4:46	*5207*
he would come down, and heal his *s*	Jn 4:47	*5207*
thy *s* liveth	Jn 4:50	*5207*
and told him, saying, Thy *s* liveth	Jn 4:51	*3816*
Jesus said unto him, Thy *s* liveth	Jn 4:53	*5207*
The *S* can do nothing of himself,	Jn 5:19	*5207*
these also doeth the *S* likewise	Jn 5:19	*5207*
For the Father loveth the *S*	Jn 5:20	*5207*
even so the *S* quickeneth whom he	Jn 5:21	*5207*
committed all judgment unto the *S*	Jn 5:22	*5207*
That all men should honour the *S*	Jn 5:23	*5207*
He that honoureth not the *S*	Jn 5:23	*5207*
hear the voice of the *S* of God	Jn 5:25	*5207*
to the *S* to have life in himself	Jn 5:26	*5207*
also, because he is the *S* of man	Jn 5:27	*5207*
which the *S* of man shall give	Jn 6:27	*5207*
that every one which seeth the *S*	Jn 6:40	*5207*
the *s* of Joseph, whose father and	Jn 6:42	*5207*
ye eat the flesh of the *S* of man	Jn 6:53	*5207*
if ye shall see the *S* of man	Jn 6:62	*5207*
Christ, the *S* of the living God	Jn 6:69	*5207*
of Judas Iscariot the *s* of Simon	Jn 6:71	
ye have lifted up the *S* of man	Jn 8:28	*5207*
but the *S* abideth ever	Jn 8:35	*5207*
If the *S* therefore shall make you	Jn 8:36	*5207*
them, saying, Is this your *s*	Jn 9:19	*5207*
said, We know that this is our *s*	Jn 9:20	*5207*
Dost thou believe on the *S* of God	Jn 9:35	*5207*
because I said, I am the *S* of God	Jn 10:36	*5207*
that the *S* of God might be	Jn 11:4	*5207*
the *S* of God, which should come	Jn 11:27	*5207*
Judas Iscariot, Simon's *s*	Jn 12:4	
that the *S* of man should be	Jn 12:23	*5207*
The *S* of man must be lifted up	Jn 12:34	*5207*
who is this *S* of man	Jn 12:34	*5207*
of Judas Iscariot, Simon's *s*	Jn 13:2	
to Judas Iscariot, the *s* of Simon	Jn 13:26	
Now is the *S* of man glorified, and	Jn 13:31	*5207*
Father may be glorified in the *S*	Jn 14:13	*5207*
glorify thy *S*, that thy *S* also	Jn 17:1	*5207*
is lost, but the *s* of perdition	Jn 17:12	*5207*
he made himself the *S* of God	Jn 19:7	*5207*
his mother, Woman, behold thy *s*	Jn 19:26	*5207*
Jesus is the Christ, the *S* of God	Jn 20:31	*5207*
s of Jonas, lovest thou me more	Jn 21:15	
s of Jonas, lovest thou me	Jn 21:16	
s of Jonas, lovest thou me	Jn 21:17	
James the *s* of Alphaeus, and Simon	Acts 1:13	
hath glorified his *S* Jesus	Acts 3:13	*3816*
God, having raised up his *S* Jesus	Acts 3:26	*3816*
The *s* of consolation,) a Levite,	Acts 4:36	*5207*
and nourished him for her own *s*	Acts 7:21	*5207*
the *S* of man standing on the	Acts 7:56	*5207*
that Jesus Christ is the *S* of God	Acts 8:37	*5207*
that he is the *S* of God	Acts 9:20	*5207*
gave unto them Saul the *s* of Cis	Acts 13:21	*5207*
I have found David the *s* of Jesse	Acts 13:22	
the second psalm, Thou art my *S*	Acts 13:33	*5207*
the *s* of a certain woman, which	Acts 16:1	*5207*
a Pharisee, the *s* of a Pharisee	Acts 23:6	*5207*
when Paul's sister's *s* heard of	Acts 23:16	*5207*
Concerning his *S* Jesus Christ our	Rom 1:3	*5207*
to be the *S* of God with power	Rom 1:4	*5207*
my spirit in the gospel of his *S*	Rom 1:9	*5207*
to God by the death of his *S*	Rom 5:10	*5207*
God sending his own *S* in the	Rom 8:3	*5207*
conformed to the image of his *S*	Rom 8:29	*5207*
He that spared not his own *S*	Rom 8:32	*5207*
I come, and Sarah shall have a *s*	Rom 9:9	*5207*
of his *S* Jesus Christ our Lord	1Cor 1:9	*5207*
Timotheus, who is my beloved *s*	1Cor 4:17	*5043*
then shall the *S* also himself be	1Cor 15:28	*5207*
For the *S* of God, Jesus Christ,	2Cor 1:19	*5207*
To reveal his *S* in me, that I	Gal 1:16	*5207*
live by the faith of the *S* of God	Gal 2:20	*5207*
was come, God sent forth his *S*	Gal 4:4	*5207*
Spirit of his *S* into your hearts	Gal 4:6	*5207*
art no more a servant, but a *s*	Gal 4:7	*5207*
and if a *s*, then an heir of God	Gal 4:7	*5207*
Cast out the bondwoman and her *s*	Gal 4:30	*5207*
for the *s* of the bondwoman shall	Gal 4:30	*5207*
heir with the *s* of the free woman	Gal 4:30	*5207*
of the knowledge of the *S* of God	Eph 4:13	*5207*
as a *s* with the father, he hath	Phil 2:22	*5043*
us into the kingdom of his dear *S*	Col 1:13	*5207*
sister's *s* to Barnabas, (touching	Col 4:10	*431*
And to wait for his *S* from heaven	1Th 1:10	*5207*
be revealed, the *s* of perdition	2Th 2:3	*5207*
Timothy, my own *s* in the faith	1Ti 1:2	*5043*
s Timothy, according to the	1Ti 1:18	*5043*
To Timothy, my dearly beloved *s*	2Ti 1:2	*5043*
Thou therefore, my *s*, be strong	2Ti 2:1	*5043*
mine own *s* after the common faith	Titus 1:4	*5043*
I beseech thee for my *s* Onesimus	Philem 10	*5043*
last days spoken unto us by his *S*	Heb 1:2	*5207*
he at any time, Thou art my *S*	Heb 1:5	*5207*
Father, and he shall be to me a *S*	Heb 1:5	*5207*
But unto the *S* he saith, Thy	Heb 1:8	*5207*
or the *s* of man, that thou	Heb 2:6	*5207*
But Christ as a *s* over his own	Heb 3:6	*5207*
the heavens, Jesus the *S* of God	Heb 4:14	*5207*
that said unto him, Thou art my *S*	Heb 5:5	*5207*
Though he were a *S*, yet learned	Heb 5:8	*5207*
to themselves the *S* of God afresh	Heb 6:6	*5207*
but made like unto the *S* of God	Heb 7:3	*5207*
was since the law, maketh the *S*	Heb 7:28	*5207*
trodden under foot the *S* of God	Heb 10:29	*5207*
offered up his only begotten *s*	Heb 11:17	
the *s* of Pharaoh's daughter	Heb 11:24	*5207*
unto you as unto children, My *s*	Heb 12:5	*5207*
scourgeth every *s* whom he	Heb 12:6	*5207*
for what *s* is he whom the father	Heb 12:7	*5207*
Isaac his *s* upon the altar	Jas 2:21	*5207*
and so doth Marcus my *s*	1Pet 5:13	*5207*
glory, This is my beloved *S*	2Pet 1:17	*5207*
the way of Balaam the *s* of Bosor	2Pet 2:15	
and with his *S* Jesus Christ	1Jn 1:3	*5207*
his *S* cleanseth us from all sin	1Jn 1:7	*5207*
that denieth the Father and the *S*	1Jn 2:22	*5207*
Whosoever denieth the *S*, the same	1Jn 2:23	*5207*
the *S* hath the Father also	1Jn 2:23	
ye also shall continue in the *S*	1Jn 2:24	*5207*
For this purpose the *S* of God was	1Jn 3:8	*5207*
on the name of his *S* Jesus Christ	1Jn 3:23	*5207*
only begotten *S* into the world	1Jn 4:9	*5207*
sent his *S* to be the propitiation	1Jn 4:10	*5207*
that the Father sent the *S* to be	1Jn 4:14	*5207*
that Jesus is the *S* of God	1Jn 4:15	*5207*
that Jesus is the *S* of God	1Jn 5:5	*5207*
which he hath testified of his *S*	1Jn 5:9	*5207*
He that believeth on the *S* of God	1Jn 5:10	*5207*
the record that God gave of his *S*	1Jn 5:10	*5207*
life, and this life is in his *S*	1Jn 5:11	*5207*
He that hath the *S* hath life	1Jn 5:12	*5207*
not the *S* of God hath not life	1Jn 5:12	*5207*
on the name of the *S* of God	1Jn 5:13	*5207*

on the name of the *S* of God	1Jn 5:13	*5207*
we know that the *S* of God is come	1Jn 5:20	*5207*
even in his *S* Jesus Christ	1Jn 5:20	*5207*
the *S* of the Father, in truth and	2Jn 3	*5207*
he hath both the Father and the *S*	2Jn 9	*5207*
one like unto the *S* of man	Rev 1:13	*5207*
These things saith the *S* of God	Rev 2:18	*5207*
one sat like unto the *S* of man	Rev 14:14	*5207*
be his God, and he shall be my *s*	Rev 21:7	*5207*

SONG {78}

of Israel this *s* unto the LORD	Ex 15:1	7892
The LORD is my strength and *s*	Ex 15:2	2176
Then Israel sang this *s*, Spring	Num 21:17	7892
therefore write ye this *s* for you	Deut 31:19	7892
that this *s* may be a witness for	Deut 31:19	7892
that this *s* shall testify against	Deut 31:21	7892
wrote this *s* the same day	Deut 31:22	7892
of Israel the words of this *s*	Deut 31:30	7892
this *s* in the ears of the people	Deut 32:44	7892
awake, awake, utter a *s*	Judg 5:12	7892
unto the LORD the words of this *s*	2Sa 22:1	7892
of *s* in the house of the LORD	1Chr 6:31	7892
chief of the Levites, was for *s*	1Chr 15:22	4853
he instructed about the *s*	1Chr 15:22	4853
master of the *s* with the singers	1Chr 15:27	4853
for *s* in the house of the LORD	1Chr 25:6	7892
the *s* of the LORD began also with	2Chr 29:27	7892
And now am I their *s*, yea, I am	Job 30:9	5058
this *s* in the day that the LORD	Ps 18:*t*	7892
with my *s* will I praise him	Ps 28:7	7892
S at the dedication of the house	Ps 30:*t*	7892
Sing unto him a new *s*	Ps 33:3	7892
he hath put a new *s* in my mouth	Ps 40:3	7892
the night his *s* shall be with me	Ps 42:8	7892
of Korah, A Maschil, A *S* of loves	Ps 45:*t*	7892
sons of Korah, A *S* upon Alamoth	Ps 46:*t*	7892
A *S* and Psalm for the sons of	Ps 48:*t*	7892
Musician, A Psalm and *S* of David	Ps 65:*t*	7892
the chief Musician, A *S* or Psalm	Ps 66:*t*	7892
on Neginoth, A Psalm or *S*	Ps 67:*t*	7892
Musician, A Psalm or *S* of David	Ps 68:*t*	7892
I was the *s* of the drunkards	Ps 69:12	5058
praise the name of God with a *s*	Ps 69:30	7892
Altaschith, A Psalm or *S* of Asaph	Ps 75:*t*	7892
Neginoth, A Psalm or *S* of Asaph	Ps 76:*t*	7892
to remembrance my *s* in the night	Ps 77:6	5058
A *S* or Psalm of Asaph	Ps 83:*t*	7892
A Psalm or *S* for the sons of	Ps 87:*t*	7892
A *S* or Psalm for the sons of	Ps 88:*t*	7892
A Psalm or *S* for the sabbath day	Ps 92:*t*	7892
O sing unto the LORD a new *s*	Ps 96:1	7892
O sing unto the LORD a new *s*	Ps 98:1	7892
A *S* or Psalm of David	Ps 108:*t*	7892
The LORD is my strength and *s*	Ps 118:14	2176
A *S* of degrees	Ps 120:*t*	7892
A *S* of degrees	Ps 121:*t*	7892
A *S* of degrees of David	Ps 122:*t*	7892
A *S* of degrees	Ps 123:*t*	7892
A *S* of degrees of David	Ps 124:*t*	7892
A *S* of degrees	Ps 125:*t*	7892
A *S* of degrees	Ps 126:*t*	7892
A *S* of degrees for Solomon	Ps 127:*t*	7892
A *S* of degrees	Ps 128:*t*	7892
A *S* of degrees	Ps 129:*t*	7892
A *S* of degrees	Ps 130:*t*	7892
A *S* of degrees of David	Ps 131:*t*	7892
A *S* of degrees	Ps 132:*t*	7892
A *S* of degrees of David	Ps 133:*t*	7892
A *S* of degrees	Ps 134:*t*	7892
away captive required of us a *s*	Ps 137:3	
the LORD's *s* in a strange land	Ps 137:4	7892
I will sing a new *s* unto thee	Ps 144:9	7892
Sing unto the LORD a new *s*	Ps 149:1	7892
for a man to hear the *s* of fools	Eccl 7:5	7892
The *s* of songs, which is	Song 1:1	7892
a *s* of my beloved touching his	Is 5:1	7892
JEHOVAH is my strength and my *s*	Is 12:2	2176
shall not drink wine with a *s*	Is 24:9	7892
In that day shall this *s* be sung	Is 26:1	7892
Ye shall have a *s*, as in the	Is 30:29	7892
Sing unto the LORD a new *s*	Is 42:10	7892
and their *s* all the day	Lam 3:14	5058
s of one that hath a pleasant	Eze 33:32	7892
And they sung a new *s*, saying,	Rev 5:9	*5603*
it were a new *s* before the throne	Rev 14:3	*5603*
learn that *s* but the hundred	Rev 14:3	*5603*
they sing the *s* of Moses the	Rev 15:3	*5603*
the *s* of the Lamb, saying, Great	Rev 15:3	*5603*

SONGS {20}

thee away with mirth, and with *s*	Gen 31:27	7892
his *s* were a thousand and five	1Kin 4:32	7892
instructed in the *s* of the LORD	1Chr 25:7	7892
s of praise and thanksgiving unto	Neh 12:46	7892
who giveth *s* in the night	Job 35:10	2158
me about with *s* of deliverance	Ps 32:7	7438
Thy statutes have been my *s* in	Ps 119:54	2158
Sing us one of the *s* of Zion	Ps 137:3	7892
that singeth *s* to an heavy heart	Prov 25:20	7892
The song of *s*, which is Solomon's	Song 1:1	7892
make sweet melody, sing many *s*	Is 23:16	7892
part of the earth have we heard *s*	Is 24:16	2158
return, and come to Zion with *s*	Is 35:10	7440
therefore we will sing my *s* to	Is 38:20	5058
cause the noise of thy *s* to cease	Eze 26:13	7892
away from me the noise of thy *s*	Amos 5:23	7892
the *s* of the temple shall be	Amos 8:3	7892
all your *s* into lamentation	Amos 8:10	7892
in psalms and hymns and spiritual *s*	Eph 5:19	*5603*
in psalms and hymns and spiritual *s*	Col 3:16	*5603*

SON'S {22}

and Lot the son of Haran his *s* son	Gen 11:31	1121
and Abram called his *s* name	Gen 16:15	1121
with my son, nor with my *s* son	Gen 21:23	5220
and let her be thy master's *s* wife	Gen 24:51	1121
me, and I will eat of my *s* venison	Gen 27:25	1121
arise, and eat of his *s* venison	Gen 27:31	1121
I pray thee, of thy *s* mandrakes	Gen 30:14	1121
take away my *s* mandrakes also	Gen 30:15	1121
thee to night for thy *s* mandrakes	Gen 30:15	1121
hired thee with my *s* mandrakes	Gen 30:16	1121
whether it be thy *s* coat or no	Gen 37:32	1121
knew it, and said, It is my *s* coat	Gen 37:33	1121
ears of thy son, and of thy *s* son	Ex 10:2	1121
The nakedness of thy *s* daughter	Lev 18:10	1121
she is thy *s* wife	Lev 18:15	1121
shalt thou take her *s* daughter	Lev 18:17	1121
thou, and thy son, and thy *s* son	Deut 6:2	1121
and thy son, and thy *s* son also	Judg 8:22	1121
the kingdom out of his *s* hand	1Kin 11:35	1121
but in his *s* days will I bring	1Kin 21:29	1121
his name, and what is his *s* name	Prov 30:4	1121
him, and his son, and his *s* son	Jer 27:7	1121

SONS {1080}

and he begat *s* and daughters	Gen 5:4	1121
and seven years, and begat *s*	Gen 5:7	1121
and fifteen years, and begat *s*	Gen 5:10	1121
and forty years, and begat *s*	Gen 5:13	1121
and thirty years, and begat *s*	Gen 5:16	1121
eight hundred years, and begat *s*	Gen 5:19	1121
three hundred years, and begat *s*	Gen 5:22	1121
eighty and two years, and begat *s*	Gen 5:26	1121
ninety and five years, and begat *s*	Gen 5:30	1121
That the *s* of God saw the	Gen 6:2	1121
when the *s* of God came in unto	Gen 6:4	1121
And Noah begat three *s*, Shem, Ham,	Gen 6:10	1121
come into the ark, thou, and thy *s*	Gen 6:18	1121
And Noah went in, and his *s*	Gen 7:7	1121
the *s* of Noah, and Noah's wife, and	Gen 7:13	1121
three wives of his *s* with them	Gen 7:13	1121
ark, thou, and thy wife, and thy *s*	Gen 8:16	1121
And Noah went forth, and his *s*	Gen 8:18	1121
And God blessed Noah and his *s*	Gen 9:1	1121
to his *s* with him, saying,	Gen 9:8	1121
the *s* of Noah, that went forth of	Gen 9:18	1121
These are the three *s* of Noah	Gen 9:19	1121
the generations of the *s* of Noah	Gen 10:1	1121
unto them were *s* born after the	Gen 10:1	1121
The *s* of Japheth	Gen 10:2	1121
And the *s* of Gomer	Gen 10:3	1121
And the *s* of Javan	Gen 10:4	1121
And the *s* of Ham	Gen 10:6	1121
And the *s* of Cush	Gen 10:7	1121
and the *s* of Raamah	Gen 10:7	1121
These are the *s* of Ham, after	Gen 10:20	1121
And unto Eber were born two *s*	Gen 10:25	1121
all these were the *s* of Joktan	Gen 10:29	1121
These are the *s* of Shem, after	Gen 10:31	1121
are the families of the *s* of Noah	Gen 10:32	1121
five hundred years, and begat *s*	Gen 11:11	1121
and three years, and begat *s*	Gen 11:13	1121
and three years, and begat *s*	Gen 11:15	1121
and thirty years, and begat *s*	Gen 11:17	1121
hundred and nine years, and begat *s*	Gen 11:19	1121
and seven years, and begat *s*	Gen 11:21	1121
two hundred years, and begat *s*	Gen 11:23	1121
and nineteen years, and begat *s*	Gen 11:25	1121
son in law, and thy *s*, and thy	Gen 19:12	1121
out, and spake unto his *s* in law	Gen 19:14	2860
one that mocked unto his *s* in law	Gen 19:14	2860
dead, and spake unto the *s* of Heth	Gen 23:3	1121
in the presence of the *s* of my	Gen 23:11	1121
in the audience of the *s* of Heth	Gen 23:16	1121
a buryingplace by the *s* of Heth	Gen 23:20	1121
the *s* of Dedan were Asshurim, and	Gen 25:3	1121
And the *s* of Midian	Gen 25:4	1121
But unto the *s* of the concubines,	Gen 25:6	1121
his *s* Isaac and Ishmael buried him	Gen 25:9	1121
purchased of the *s* of Heth	Gen 25:10	1121
are the names of the *s* of Ishmael	Gen 25:13	1121
These are the *s* of Ishmael	Gen 25:16	1121
thy mother's *s* bow down to thee	Gen 27:29	1121
because I have born him three *s*	Gen 29:34	1121
me, because I have born him six *s*	Gen 30:20	1121
gave them into the hand of his *s*	Gen 30:35	1121
he heard the words of Laban's *s*	Gen 31:1	1121
Then Jacob rose up, and set his *s*	Gen 31:17	1121
hast not suffered me to kiss my *s*	Gen 31:28	1121
Laban rose up, and kissed his *s*	Gen 31:55	1121
womenservants, and his eleven *s*	Gen 32:22	3206
now his *s* were with his cattle in	Gen 34:5	1121
the *s* of Jacob came out of the	Gen 34:7	1121
the *s* of Jacob answered Shechem	Gen 34:13	1121
sore, that two of the *s* of Jacob	Gen 34:25	1121
The *s* of Jacob came upon the	Gen 34:27	1121
not pursue after the *s* of Jacob	Gen 35:5	1121
Now the *s* of Jacob were twelve	Gen 35:22	1121
The *s* of Leah	Gen 35:23	1121
The *s* of Rachel	Gen 35:24	1121
the *s* of Bilhah, Rachel's	Gen 35:25	1121
the *s* of Zilpah, Leah's handmaid	Gen 35:26	1121
these are the *s* of Jacob, which	Gen 35:26	1121
his *s* Esau and Jacob buried him	Gen 35:29	1121
these are the *s* of Esau, which	Gen 36:5	1121
And Esau took his wives, and his *s*	Gen 36:6	1121
These are the names of Esau's *s*	Gen 36:10	1121
the *s* of Eliphaz were Teman, Omar	Gen 36:11	1121
these were the *s* of Adah Esau's	Gen 36:12	1121
And these are the *s* of Reuel	Gen 36:13	1121
these were the *s* of Bashemath	Gen 36:13	1121
And these were the *s* of Aholibamah	Gen 36:14	1121
These were dukes of the *s* of Esau	Gen 36:15	1121
the *s* of Eliphaz the firstborn	Gen 36:15	1121
these were the *s* of Adah	Gen 36:16	1121
these are the *s* of Reuel Esau's	Gen 36:17	1121
these are the *s* of Bashemath	Gen 36:17	1121
these are the *s* of Aholibamah	Gen 36:18	1121
These are the *s* of Esau, who is	Gen 36:19	1121
These are the *s* of Seir the	Gen 36:20	1121
the lad was with the *s* of Bilhah	Gen 37:2	1121
with the *s* of Zilpah, his	Gen 37:2	1121
And all his *s* and all his daughters	Gen 37:35	1121
unto Joseph were born two *s*	Gen 41:50	1121
in Egypt, Jacob said unto his *s*	Gen 42:1	1121
the *s* of Israel came to buy corn	Gen 42:5	1121
We are all one man's *s*	Gen 42:11	1121
the *s* of one man in the land of	Gen 42:13	1121
twelve brethren, *s* of our father	Gen 42:32	1121
his father, saying, Slay my two *s*	Gen 42:37	1121
know that my wife bare me two *s*	Gen 44:27	
the *s* of Israel carried Jacob	Gen 46:5	1121
His *s*, and his sons' *s* with him	Gen 46:7	1121
came into Egypt, Jacob and his *s*	Gen 46:8	1121
And the *s* of Reuben	Gen 46:9	1121
And the *s* of Simeon	Gen 46:10	1121
And the *s* of Levi	Gen 46:11	1121
And the *s* of Judah	Gen 46:12	1121
the *s* of Pharez were Hezron and	Gen 46:12	1121
And the *s* of Issachar	Gen 46:13	1121
And the *s* of Zebulun	Gen 46:14	1121
These be the *s* of Leah, which she	Gen 46:15	1121
all the souls of his *s* and his	Gen 46:15	1121
And the *s* of Gad	Gen 46:16	1121
And the *s* of Asher	Gen 46:17	1121
and the *s* of Beriah	Gen 46:17	1121
These are the *s* of Zilpah	Gen 46:18	1121
The *s* of Rachel Jacob's wife	Gen 46:19	1121
the *s* of Benjamin were Belah, and	Gen 46:21	1121
These are the *s* of Rachel	Gen 46:22	1121
And the *s* of Dan	Gen 46:23	1121
And the *s* of Naphtali	Gen 46:24	1121
These are the *s* of Bilhah	Gen 46:25	1121
the *s* of Joseph, which were born	Gen 46:27	1121
and he took with him his two *s*	Gen 48:1	1121
And now thy two *s*, Ephraim and	Gen 48:5	1121
And Israel beheld Joseph's *s*	Gen 48:8	1121
unto his father, They are my *s*	Gen 48:9	1121
And Jacob called unto his *s*	Gen 49:1	1121
together, and hear, ye *s* of Jacob	Gen 49:2	1121
made an end of commanding his *s*	Gen 49:33	1121
his *s* did unto him according as	Gen 50:12	1121
For his *s* carried him into the	Gen 50:13	1121
and ye shall put them upon your *s*	Ex 3:22	1121
And Moses took his wife and his *s*	Ex 4:20	1121
The *s* of Reuben the firstborn of	Ex 6:14	1121
And the *s* of Simeon	Ex 6:15	1121
the *s* of Levi according to their	Ex 6:16	1121
The *s* of Gershon	Ex 6:17	1121
And the *s* of Kohath	Ex 6:18	1121
And the *s* of Merari	Ex 6:19	1121
And the *s* of Izhar	Ex 6:21	1121
And the *s* of Uzziel	Ex 6:22	1121
And the *s* of Korah	Ex 6:24	1121
young and with our old, with our *s*	Ex 10:9	1121
to thee and to thy *s* for ever	Ex 12:24	1121
And her two *s*; of which	Ex 18:3	1121
father in law, came with his *s*	Ex 18:5	1121
thy wife, and her two *s* with her	Ex 18:6	1121
she have born him *s* or daughters	Ex 21:4	1121
the firstborn of thy *s* shalt thou	Ex 22:29	1121
his *s* shall order it from evening	Ex 27:21	1121
his *s* with him, from among the	Ex 28:1	1121
Eleazar and Ithamar, Aaron's *s*	Ex 28:1	1121
for Aaron thy brother, and his *s*	Ex 28:4	1121
for Aaron's *s* thou shalt make	Ex 28:40	1121
thy brother, and his *s* with him	Ex 28:41	1121
be upon Aaron, and upon his *s*	Ex 28:43	1121
his *s* thou shalt bring unto the	Ex 29:4	1121
And thou shalt bring his *s*	Ex 29:8	1121
them with girdles, Aaron and his *s*	Ex 29:9	1121
shalt consecrate Aaron and his *s*	Ex 29:9	1121
his *s* shall put their hands upon	Ex 29:10	1121
his *s* shall put their hands upon	Ex 29:15	1121
his *s* shall put their hands upon	Ex 29:19	1121
the tip of the right ear of his *s*	Ex 29:20	1121
upon his garments, and upon his *s*	Ex 29:21	1121
the garments of his *s* with him	Ex 29:21	1121
and his garments, and his *s*	Ex 29:21	1121
Aaron, and in the hands of his *s*	Ex 29:24	1121
and of that which is for his *s*	Ex 29:27	1121
his *s* shall eat the flesh of the	Ex 29:32	1121
thou do unto Aaron, and to his *s*	Ex 29:35	1121
sanctify also both Aaron and his *s*	Ex 29:44	1121
his *s* shall wash their hands and	Ex 30:19	1121
thou shalt anoint Aaron and his *s*	Ex 30:30	1121
priest, and the garments of his *s*	Ex 31:10	1121
the ears of your wives, of your *s*	Ex 32:2	1121
all the *s* of Levi gathered	Ex 32:26	1121
of their daughters unto thy *s*	Ex 34:16	1121
make thy *s* go a whoring after	Ex 34:16	1121
of thy *s* thou shalt redeem	Ex 34:20	1121
priest, and the garments of his *s*	Ex 35:19	1121
work for Aaron, and for his *s*	Ex 39:27	1121

S

Context	Reference	Strong's
his *s* unto the door of the	Ex 40:12	1121
And thou shalt bring his *s*	Ex 40:14	1121
his *s* washed their hands and their	Ex 40:31	1121
and the priests, Aaron's *s*	Lev 1:5	1121
the *s* of Aaron the priest shall	Lev 1:7	1121
And the priests, Aaron's *s*	Lev 1:8	1121
and the priests, Aaron's *s*	Lev 1:11	1121
bring it to Aaron's *s* the priests	Lev 2:2	1121
Aaron's *s* the priests shall	Lev 3:2	1121
Aaron's *s* shall burn it on the	Lev 3:5	1121
Aaron's *s* shall sprinkle the	Lev 3:8	1121
the *s* of Aaron shall sprinkle the	Lev 3:13	1121
Command Aaron and his *s*, saying,	Lev 6:9	1121
the *s* of Aaron shall offer it	Lev 6:14	1121
thereof shall Aaron and his *s* eat	Lev 6:16	1121
the offering of Aaron and of his *s*	Lev 6:20	1121
the priest of his *s* that is	Lev 6:22	1121
Speak unto Aaron and to his *s*	Lev 6:25	1121
shall all the *s* of Aaron have	Lev 7:10	1121
He among the *s* of Aaron, that	Lev 7:33	1121
unto his *s* by a statute for ever	Lev 7:34	1121
and of the anointing of his *s*	Lev 7:35	1121
his *s* with him, and the garments,	Lev 8:2	1121
And Moses brought Aaron and his *s*	Lev 8:6	1121
And Moses brought Aaron's *s*	Lev 8:13	1121
his *s* laid their hands upon the	Lev 8:14	1121
his *s* laid their hands upon the	Lev 8:18	1121
his *s* laid their hands upon the	Lev 8:22	1121
And he brought Aaron's *s*, and Moses	Lev 8:24	1121
upon his garments, and upon his *s*	Lev 8:30	1121
Aaron, and his garments, and his *s*	Lev 8:30	1121
Moses said unto Aaron and to his *s*	Lev 8:31	1121
Aaron and his *s* shall eat it	Lev 8:31	1121
his *s* did all things which the	Lev 8:36	1121
that Moses called Aaron and his *s*	Lev 9:1	1121
the *s* of Aaron brought the blood	Lev 9:9	1121
Aaron's *s* presented unto him the	Lev 9:12	1121
Aaron's *s* presented unto him the	Lev 9:18	1121
the *s* of Aaron, took either of	Lev 10:1	1121
the *s* of Uzziel the uncle of	Lev 10:4	1121
Eleazar and unto Ithamar, his *s*	Lev 10:6	1121
nor thy *s* with thee, when ye go	Lev 10:9	1121
his *s* that were left, Take the	Lev 10:12	1121
thou, and thy *s*, and thy daughters	Lev 10:14	1121
the *s* of Aaron which were left	Lev 10:16	1121
or unto one of his *s* the priests	Lev 13:2	1121
the death of the two *s* of Aaron	Lev 16:1	1121
Speak unto Aaron, and unto his *s*	Lev 17:2	1121
unto the priests the *s* of Aaron	Lev 21:1	1121
told it unto Aaron, and to his *s*	Lev 21:24	1121
Speak unto Aaron and to his *s*	Lev 22:2	1121
Speak unto Aaron, and to his *s*	Lev 22:18	1121
ye shall eat the flesh of your *s*	Lev 26:29	1121
the captain of the *s* of Gad shall	Num 2:14	1121
the captain of the *s* of Ephraim	Num 2:18	1121
the captain of the *s* of Benjamin	Num 2:22	1121
are the names of the *s* of Aaron	Num 3:2	1121
are the names of the *s* of Aaron	Num 3:3	1121
Levites unto Aaron and to his *s*	Num 3:9	1121
thou shalt appoint Aaron and his *s*	Num 3:10	1121
these were the *s* of Levi by their	Num 3:17	1121
these are the names of the *s* of	Num 3:18	1121
the *s* of Kohath by their families	Num 3:19	1121
the *s* of Merari by their families	Num 3:20	1121
the charge of the *s* of Gershon in	Num 3:25	1121
The families of the *s* of Kohath	Num 3:29	1121
charge of the *s* of Merari shall	Num 3:36	1121
shall be Moses, and Aaron and his *s*	Num 3:38	1121
redeemed, unto Aaron and to his *s*	Num 3:48	1121
redeemed unto Aaron and to his *s*	Num 3:51	1121
Take the sum of the *s* of Kohath	Num 4:2	1121
Kohath from among the *s* of Levi	Num 4:2	1121
shall be the service of the *s* of	Num 4:4	1121
Aaron shall come, and his *s*	Num 4:5	1121
his *s* have made an end of	Num 4:15	1121
the *s* of Kohath shall come to	Num 4:15	1121
things are the burden of the *s* of	Num 4:15	1121
his *s* shall go in, and appoint	Num 4:19	1121
also the sum of the *s* of Gershon	Num 4:22	1121
his *s* shall be all the service of	Num 4:27	1121
of the *s* of the Gershonites	Num 4:27	1121
service of the families of the *s*	Num 4:28	1121
As for the *s* of Merari, thou	Num 4:29	1121
the families of the *s* of Merari	Num 4:33	1121
s of the Kohathites after their	Num 4:34	1121
were numbered of the *s* of Gershon	Num 4:38	1121
the families of the *s* of Gershon	Num 4:41	1121
the families of the *s* of Merari	Num 4:42	1121
the families of the *s* of Merari	Num 4:45	1121
Speak unto Aaron and unto his *s*	Num 6:23	1121
he gave unto the *s* of Gershon	Num 7:7	1121
oxen he gave unto the *s* of Merari	Num 7:8	1121
But unto the *s* of Kohath he gave	Num 7:9	1121
before Aaron, and before his *s*	Num 8:13	1121
to his *s* from among the children	Num 8:19	1121
before Aaron, and before his *s*	Num 8:22	1121
the *s* of Aaron, the priests,	Num 10:8	1121
the *s* of Gershon and the	Num 10:17	1121
the *s* of Merari set forward,	Num 10:17	1121
the *s* of Anak, which come of the	Num 13:33	1121
the *s* of Eliab, and On, the son of	Num 16:1	1121
of Peleth, *s* of Reuben, took men	Num 16:1	1121
too much upon you, ye *s* of Levi	Num 16:7	1121
Hear, I pray you, ye *s* of Levi	Num 16:8	1121
brethren the *s* of Levi with thee	Num 16:10	1121
Dathan and Abiram, the *s* of Eliab	Num 16:12	1121
tents, and their wives, and their *s*	Num 16:27	1121
said unto Aaron, Thou and thy *s*	Num 18:1	1121
thy *s* with thee shall bear the	Num 18:1	1121
thy *s* with thee shall minister	Num 18:2	1121
thy *s* with thee shall keep your	Num 18:7	1121
of the anointing, and to thy *s*	Num 18:8	1121
most holy for thee and for thy *s*	Num 18:9	1121
given them unto thee, and to thy *s*	Num 18:11	1121
LORD, have I given thee, and thy *s*	Num 18:19	1121
he hath given his *s* that escaped	Num 21:29	1121
So they smote him, and his *s*	Num 21:35	1121
And the *s* of Pallu	Num 26:8	1121
And the *s* of Eliab	Num 26:9	1121
The *s* of Simeon after their	Num 26:12	1121
The *s* of Judah were Er and Onan	Num 26:19	1121
the *s* of Judah after their	Num 26:20	1121
And the *s* of Pharez were	Num 26:21	1121
Of the *s* of Issachar after their	Num 26:23	1121
Of the *s* of Zebulun after their	Num 26:26	1121
The *s* of Joseph after their	Num 26:28	1121
Of the *s* of Manasseh	Num 26:29	1121
These are the *s* of Gilead	Num 26:30	1121
the son of Hepher had no *s*	Num 26:33	1121
These are the *s* of Ephraim after	Num 26:35	1121
And these are the *s* of Shuthelah	Num 26:36	1121
s of Ephraim according to those	Num 26:37	1121
These are the *s* of Joseph after	Num 26:37	1121
The *s* of Benjamin after their	Num 26:38	1121
the *s* of Bela were Ard and Naaman	Num 26:40	1121
These are the *s* of Benjamin after	Num 26:41	1121
These are the *s* of Dan after	Num 26:42	1121
Of the *s* of Beriah	Num 26:45	1121
the *s* of Asher according to those	Num 26:47	1121
Of the *s* of Naphtali after their	Num 26:48	1121
died in his own sin, and had no *s*	Num 27:3	1121
the families of the *s* of Joseph	Num 36:1	1121
the *s* of the other tribes of the	Num 36:3	1121
The tribe of the *s* of Joseph hath	Num 36:5	1121
unto their father's brothers' *s*	Num 36:11	1121
into the families of the *s* of	Num 36:12	1121
seen the *s* of the Anakims there	Deut 1:28	1121
and we smote him, and his *s*	Deut 2:33	1121
them thy *s*, and thy sons' *s*	Deut 4:9	1121
the *s* of Eliab, the son of Reuben	Deut 11:6	1121
the LORD your God, ye, and your *s*	Deut 12:12	1121
for even their *s* and their	Deut 12:31	1121
the LORD, him and his *s* for ever	Deut 18:5	1121
the priests the *s* of Levi shall	Deut 21:5	1121
when he maketh his *s* to inherit	Deut 21:16	1121
nor a sodomite of the *s* of Israel	Deut 23:17	1121
Thy *s* and thy daughters shall be	Deut 28:32	1121
Thou shalt beget *s* and daughters,	Deut 28:41	1121
own body, the flesh of thy *s*	Deut 28:53	1121
it unto the priests the *s* of Levi	Deut 31:9	1121
when he separated the *s* of Adam	Deut 32:8	1121
because of the provoking of his *s*	Deut 32:19	1121
and the wedge of gold, and his *s*	Josh 7:24	1121
drove thence the three *s* of Anak	Josh 15:14	1121
the son of Manasseh, had no *s*	Josh 17:3	1121
had an inheritance among his *s*	Josh 17:6	1121
s had the land of Gilead	Josh 17:6	1121
which Jacob bought of the *s* of	Josh 24:32	1121
thence the three *s* of Anak	Judg 1:20	1121
gave their daughters to their *s*	Judg 3:6	1121
brethren, even the *s* of my mother	Judg 8:19	1121
ten *s* of his body begotten	Judg 8:30	1121
that all the *s* of Jerubbaal	Judg 9:2	1121
his brethren the *s* of Jerubbaal	Judg 9:5	1121
this day, and have slain his *s*	Judg 9:18	1121
ten *s* of Jerubbaal might come, and	Judg 9:24	1121
he had thirty *s* that rode on	Judg 10:4	1121
And Gilead's wife bare him *s*	Judg 11:2	1121
and his wife's *s* grew up, and they	Judg 11:2	1121
And he had thirty *s*, and thirty	Judg 12:9	1121
daughters from abroad for his *s*	Judg 12:9	1121
And he had forty *s* and thirty	Judg 12:14	1121
and consecrated one of his *s*	Judg 17:5	1121
man was unto him as one of his *s*	Judg 17:11	1121
his *s* were priests to the tribe	Judg 18:30	1121
certain *s* of Belial, beset the	Judg 19:22	1121
he, and his wife, and his two *s*	Ruth 1:1	1121
and the name of his two *s* Mahlon	Ruth 1:2	1121
and she was left, and her two *s*	Ruth 1:3	1121
the woman was left of her two *s*	Ruth 1:5	3206
there yet any more *s* in my womb	Ruth 1:11	1121
to night, and should also bear *s*	Ruth 1:12	1121
is better to thee than seven *s*	Ruth 4:15	1121
And the two *s* of Eli, Hophni and	1Sa 1:3	1121
his wife, and to all her *s*	1Sa 1:4	1121
not I better to thee than ten *s*	1Sa 1:8	1121
the *s* of Eli were *s* of Belial	1Sa 2:12	1121
she conceived, and bare three *s*	1Sa 2:21	1121
heard all that his *s* did unto all	1Sa 2:22	1121
Nay, my *s*	1Sa 2:24	1121
and honourest thy *s* above me	1Sa 2:29	1121
that shall come upon thy two *s*	1Sa 2:34	1121
because his *s* made themselves	1Sa 3:13	1121
and the two *s* of Eli, Hophni and	1Sa 4:4	1121
and the two *s* of Eli, Hophni and	1Sa 4:11	1121
the people, and thy two *s* also	1Sa 4:17	1121
that he made his *s* judges over	1Sa 8:1	1121
his *s* walked not in his ways, but	1Sa 8:3	1121
thy *s* walk not in thy ways	1Sa 8:5	1121
He will take your *s*, and appoint	1Sa 8:11	1121
and, behold, my *s* are with you	1Sa 12:2	1121
Now the *s* of Saul were Jonathan,	1Sa 14:49	1121
provided me a king among his *s*	1Sa 16:1	1121
And he sanctified Jesse and his *s*	1Sa 16:5	1121
of his *s* to pass before Samuel	1Sa 16:10	1121
and he had eight *s*	1Sa 17:12	1121
the three eldest *s* of Jesse went	1Sa 17:13	1121
the names of his three *s* that	1Sa 17:13	1121
one of the *s* of Ahimelech the son	1Sa 22:20	1121
shalt thou and thy *s* be with me	1Sa 28:19	1121
and their wives, and their *s*	1Sa 30:3	1121
was grieved, every man for his *s*	1Sa 30:6	1121
neither *s* nor daughters, neither	1Sa 30:19	1121
hard upon Saul and upon his *s*	1Sa 31:2	1121
and Melchi-shua, Saul's *s*	1Sa 31:2	1121
So Saul died, and his three *s*	1Sa 31:6	1121
his *s* were dead, they forsook the	1Sa 31:7	1121
his three *s* fallen in mount	1Sa 31:8	1121
the bodies of his *s* from the wall	1Sa 31:12	1121
were three *s* of Zeruiah there	2Sa 2:18	1121
unto David were *s* born in Hebron	2Sa 3:2	1121
these men the *s* of Zeruiah be too	2Sa 3:39	1121
the *s* of Rimmon a Beerothite, of	2Sa 4:2	1121
the *s* of Rimmon the Beerothite,	2Sa 4:5	1121
the *s* of Rimmon the Beerothite,	2Sa 4:9	1121
and there were yet *s* and daughters	2Sa 5:13	1121
the *s* of Abinadab, drave the new	2Sa 6:3	1121
David's *s* were chief rulers	2Sa 8:18	1121
Thou therefore, and thy *s*, and thy	2Sa 9:10	1121
Now Ziba had fifteen *s* and twenty	2Sa 9:10	1121
my table, as one of the king's *s*	2Sa 9:11	1121
Absalom invited all the king's *s*	2Sa 13:23	1121
and all the king's *s* go with him	2Sa 13:27	1121
Then all the king's *s* arose	2Sa 13:29	1121
hath slain all the king's *s*	2Sa 13:30	1121
all the young men the king's *s*	2Sa 13:32	1121
that all the king's *s* are dead	2Sa 13:33	1121
king, Behold, the king's *s* come	2Sa 13:35	1121
that, behold, the king's *s* came	2Sa 13:36	1121
And thy handmaid had two *s*	2Sa 14:6	1121
Absalom there were born three *s*	2Sa 14:27	1121
in peace, and your two *s* with you	2Sa 15:27	1121
have there with them their two *s*	2Sa 15:36	1121
I to do with you, ye *s* of Zeruiah	2Sa 16:10	1121
thy life, and the lives of thy *s*	2Sa 19:5	1121
house of Saul, and his fifteen *s*	2Sa 19:17	1121
ye *s* of Zeruiah, that ye should	2Sa 19:22	1121
men of his *s* be delivered unto us	2Sa 21:6	1121
But the king took the two *s* of	2Sa 21:8	1121
the five *s* of Michal the daughter	2Sa 21:8	1121
which was of the *s* of the giant	2Sa 21:16	3211
which was of the *s* of the giant	2Sa 21:18	3211
But the *s* of Belial shall be all	2Sa 23:6	
of the *s* of Jashen, Jonathan,	2Sa 23:32	1121
all his brethren the king's *s*	1Kin 1:9	1121
hath called all the *s* of the king	1Kin 1:19	1121
and hath called all the king's *s*	1Kin 1:25	1121
the *s* of Barzillai the Gileadite	1Kin 2:7	1121
Ahiah, the *s* of Shisha, scribes	1Kin 4:3	1121
Chalcol, and Darda, the *s* of Mahol	1Kin 4:31	1121
household among the *s* of Pharaoh	1Kin 11:20	1121
which were not of the *s* of Levi	1Kin 12:31	1121
his *s* came and told him all the	1Kin 13:11	1121
For his *s* had seen what way the	1Kin 13:12	1121
And he said unto his *s*, Saddle me	1Kin 13:13	1121
And he spake to his *s*, saying,	1Kin 13:27	1121
him, that he spake to his *s*	1Kin 13:31	1121
of the tribes of the *s* of Jacob	1Kin 18:31	1121
a certain man of the *s* of the	1Kin 20:35	1121
s of Belial, before him, to bear	1Kin 21:10	1121
the *s* of the prophets that were	2Kin 2:3	1121
the *s* of the prophets that were	2Kin 2:5	1121
fifty men of the *s* of the	2Kin 2:7	1121
when the *s* of the prophets which	2Kin 2:15	1121
woman of the wives of the *s* of	2Kin 4:1	1121
unto him my two *s* to be bondmen	2Kin 4:1	3206
the door upon thee and upon thy *s*	2Kin 4:4	1121
the door upon her and upon her *s*	2Kin 4:5	1121
the *s* of the prophets were	2Kin 4:38	1121
pottage for the *s* of the prophets	2Kin 4:38	1121
men of the *s* of the prophets	2Kin 5:22	1121
the *s* of the prophets said unto	2Kin 6:1	1121
of Naboth, and the blood of his *s*	2Kin 9:26	1121
And Ahab had seventy *s* in Samaria	2Kin 10:1	1121
your master's *s* are with you	2Kin 10:2	1121
and meetest of your master's *s*	2Kin 10:3	1121
heads of the men your master's *s*	2Kin 10:6	1121
Now the king's *s*, being seventy	2Kin 10:6	1121
them, that they took the king's *s*	2Kin 10:7	1121
brought the heads of the king's *s*	2Kin 10:8	1121
the king's *s* which were slain	2Kin 11:2	1121
Thy *s* shall sit on the throne of	2Kin 15:12	1121
And they caused their *s* and their	2Kin 17:17	1121
Sharezer his *s* smote him with the	2Kin 19:37	1121
of thy *s* that shall issue from	2Kin 20:18	1121
they slew the *s* of Zedekiah	2Kin 25:7	1121
The *s* of Japheth	1Chr 1:5	1121
And the *s* of Gomer	1Chr 1:6	1121
And the *s* of Javan	1Chr 1:7	1121
The *s* of Ham	1Chr 1:8	1121
And the *s* of Cush	1Chr 1:9	1121
And the *s* of Raamah	1Chr 1:9	1121
The *s* of Shem	1Chr 1:17	1121
And unto Eber were born two *s*	1Chr 1:19	1121
All these were the *s* of Joktan	1Chr 1:23	1121
The *s* of Abraham	1Chr 1:28	1121
These are the *s* of Ishmael	1Chr 1:31	1121
Now the *s* of Keturah, Abraham's	1Chr 1:32	1121
And the *s* of Jokshan	1Chr 1:32	1121
And the *s* of Midian	1Chr 1:33	1121
All these are the *s* of Keturah	1Chr 1:33	1121
The *s* of Isaac	1Chr 1:34	1121
The *s* of Esau	1Chr 1:35	1121
The *s* of Eliphaz	1Chr 1:36	1121

The *s* of Reuel 1Chr 1:37 1121
And the *s* of Seir 1Chr 1:38 1121
And the *s* of Lotan 1Chr 1:39 1121
The *s* of Shobal 1Chr 1:40 1121
And the *s* of Zibeon 1Chr 1:40 1121
The *s* of Anah 1Chr 1:41 1121
And the *s* of Dishon 1Chr 1:41 1121
The *s* of Ezer 1Chr 1:42 1121
The *s* of Dishan 1Chr 1:42 1121
These are the *s* of Israel 1Chr 2:1 1121
The *s* of Judah 1Chr 2:3 1121
All the *s* of Judah were five 1Chr 2:4 1121
The *s* of Pharez 1Chr 2:5 1121
And the *s* of Zerah 1Chr 2:6 1121
And the *s* of Carmi 1Chr 2:7 1121
And the *s* of Ethan 1Chr 2:8 1121
The *s* also of Hezron, that were 1Chr 2:9 1121
And the *s* of Zeruiah 1Chr 2:16 1121
of Jerioth: her *s* are these 1Chr 2:18 1121
All these belonged to the *s* of 1Chr 2:23 1121
the *s* of Jerahmeel the firstborn 1Chr 2:25 1121
the *s* of Ram the firstborn of 1Chr 2:27 1121
the *s* of Onam were, Shammai, and 1Chr 2:28 1121
And the *s* of Shammai 1Chr 2:28 1121
And the *s* of Nadab 1Chr 2:30 1121
And the *s* of Appaim 1Chr 2:31 1121
And the *s* of Ishi 1Chr 2:31 1121
the *s* of Jada the brother of 1Chr 2:32 1121
And the *s* of Jonathan 1Chr 2:33 1121
These were the *s* of Jerahmeel 1Chr 2:33 1121
Now Sheshan had no *s*, but 1Chr 2:34 1121
Now the *s* of Caleb the brother of 1Chr 2:42 1121
the *s* of Mareshah the father of 1Chr 2:42 1121
And the *s* of Hebron 1Chr 2:43 1121
And the *s* of Jahdai 1Chr 2:47 1121
These were the *s* of Caleb the son 1Chr 2:50 1121
father of Kirjath-jearim had *s* 1Chr 2:52 1121
The *s* of Salma 1Chr 2:54 1121
Now these were the *s* of David 1Chr 3:1 1121
These were all the *s* of David 1Chr 3:9 1121
beside the *s* of the concubines, 1Chr 3:9 1121
the *s* of Josiah were, the 1Chr 3:15 1121
And the *s* of Jehoiakim 1Chr 3:16 1121
And the *s* of Jeconiah 1Chr 3:17 1121
the *s* of Pedaiah were, Zerubbabel 1Chr 3:19 1121
and the *s* of Zerubbabel 1Chr 3:19 1121
And the *s* of Hananiah 1Chr 3:21 1121
the *s* of Rephaiah 1Chr 3:21 1121
the *s* of Arnan 1Chr 3:21 1121
the *s* of Obadiah 1Chr 3:21 1121
the *s* of Shechaniah 1Chr 3:21 1121
And the *s* of Shechaniah 1Chr 3:22 1121
and the *s* of Shemaiah 1Chr 3:22 1121
And the *s* of Neariah 1Chr 3:23 1121
the *s* of Elioenai were, Hodaiah, 1Chr 3:24 1121
The *s* of Judah 1Chr 4:1 1121
These are the *s* of Hur, the 1Chr 4:4 1121
These were the *s* of Naarah 1Chr 4:6 1121
the *s* of Helah were, Zereth, and 1Chr 4:7 1121
And the *s* of Kenaz 1Chr 4:13 1121
and the *s* of Othniel 1Chr 4:13 1121
the *s* of Caleb the son of 1Chr 4:15 1121
the *s* of Elah, even Kenaz 1Chr 4:15 1121
And the *s* of Jehaleleel 1Chr 4:16 1121
the *s* of Ezra were, Jether, and 1Chr 4:17 1121
these are the *s* of Bithiah the 1Chr 4:18 1121
the *s* of his wife Hodiah the 1Chr 4:19 1121
the *s* of Shimon were, Amnon, and 1Chr 4:20 1121
the *s* of Ishi were, Zoheth, and 1Chr 4:20 1121
The *s* of Shelah the son of Judah 1Chr 4:21 1121
The *s* of Simeon were, Nemuel, and 1Chr 4:24 1121
And the *s* of Mishma 1Chr 4:26 1121
And Shimei had sixteen *s* and six 1Chr 4:27 1121
of them, even of the *s* of Simeon 1Chr 4:42 1121
and Uzziel, the *s* of Ishi 1Chr 4:42 1121
Now the *s* of Reuben the firstborn 1Chr 5:1 1121
the *s* of Joseph the son of Israel 1Chr 5:1 1121
The *s*, I say, of Reuben the 1Chr 5:3 1121
The *s* of Joel 1Chr 5:4 1121
The *s* of Reuben, and the Gadites, 1Chr 5:18 1121
The *s* of Levi 1Chr 6:1 1121
And the *s* of Kohath 1Chr 6:2 1121
The *s* also of Aaron 1Chr 6:3 1121
The *s* of Levi 1Chr 6:16 1121
be the names of the *s* of Gershom 1Chr 6:17 1121
the *s* of Kohath were, Amram, and 1Chr 6:18 1121
The *s* of Merari 1Chr 6:19 1121
The *s* of Kohath 1Chr 6:22 1121
And the *s* of Elkanah 1Chr 6:25 1121
the *s* of Elkanah 1Chr 6:26 1121
And the *s* of Samuel 1Chr 6:28 1121
The *s* of Merari 1Chr 6:29 1121
Of the *s* of the Kohathites 1Chr 6:33 1121
their brethren the *s* of Merari 1Chr 6:44 1121
his *s* offered upon the altar of 1Chr 6:49 1121
And these are the *s* of Aaron 1Chr 6:50 1121
of the *s* of Aaron, of the 1Chr 6:54 1121
to the *s* of Aaron they gave the 1Chr 6:57 1121
unto the *s* of Kohath, which were 1Chr 6:61 1121
to the *s* of Gershom throughout 1Chr 6:62 1121
Unto the *s* of Merari were given 1Chr 6:63 1121
s of Kohath had cities of their 1Chr 6:66 1121
of the remnant of the *s* of Kohath 1Chr 6:70 1121
Unto the *s* of Gershom were given 1Chr 6:71 1121
Now the *s* of Issachar were, Tola, 1Chr 7:1 1121
And the *s* of Tola 1Chr 7:2 1121
And the *s* of Uzzi 1Chr 7:3 1121
and the *s* of Izrahiah 1Chr 7:3 1121
for they had many wives and *s* 1Chr 7:4 1121
The *s* of Benjamin 1Chr 7:6 1121
And the *s* of Bela 1Chr 7:7 1121
And the *s* of Becher 1Chr 7:8 1121
All these are the *s* of Becher 1Chr 7:8 1121
The *s* also of Jediael 1Chr 7:10 1121
and the *s* of Bilhan 1Chr 7:10 1121
All these the *s* of Jediael 1Chr 7:11 1121
of Ir, and Hushim, the *s* of Aher 1Chr 7:12 1121
The *s* of Naphtali 1Chr 7:13 1121
and Shallum, the *s* of Bilhah 1Chr 7:13 1121
The *s* of Manasseh 1Chr 7:14 1121
and his *s* were Ulam and Rakem 1Chr 7:16 1121
And the *s* of Ulam 1Chr 7:17 1121
These were the *s* of Gilead 1Chr 7:17 1121
the *s* of Shemidah were, Ahian, and 1Chr 7:19 1121
And the *s* of Ephraim 1Chr 7:20 1121
The *s* of Asher 1Chr 7:30 1121
And the *s* of Beriah 1Chr 7:31 1121
And the *s* of Japhlet 1Chr 7:33 1121
And the *s* of Shamer 1Chr 7:34 1121
the *s* of his brother Helem 1Chr 7:35 1121
The *s* of Zophah 1Chr 7:36 1121
And the *s* of Jether 1Chr 7:38 1121
And the *s* of Ulla 1Chr 7:39 1121
the *s* of Bela were, Addar, and 1Chr 8:3 1121
And these are the *s* of Ehud 1Chr 8:6 1121
These were his *s*, heads of the 1Chr 8:10 1121
The *s* of Elpaal 1Chr 8:12 1121
Ispah, and Joha, the *s* of Beriah 1Chr 8:16 1121
and Jobab, the *s* of Elpaal 1Chr 8:18 1121
and Shimrath, the *s* of Shimhi 1Chr 8:21 1121
and Penuel, the *s* of Shashak 1Chr 8:25 1121
and Zichri, the *s* of Jeroham 1Chr 8:27 1121
the *s* of Micah were, Pithon, and 1Chr 8:35 1121
And Azel had six *s*, whose names 1Chr 8:38 1121
All these were the *s* of Azel 1Chr 8:38 1121
the *s* of Eshek his brother were, 1Chr 8:39 1121
the *s* of Ulam were mighty men of 1Chr 8:40 1121
of valour, archers, and had many *s* 1Chr 8:40 1121
and had many *s*, and sons' *s* 1Chr 8:40 1121
these are of the *s* of Benjamin 1Chr 8:40 1121
Asaiah the firstborn, and his *s* 1Chr 9:5 1121
And of the *s* of Zerah 1Chr 9:6 1121
And of the *s* of Benjamin 1Chr 9:7 1121
of Hashabiah, of the *s* of Merari 1Chr 9:14 1121
some of the *s* of the priests made 1Chr 9:30 1121
of the *s* of the Kohathites, were 1Chr 9:32 1121
the *s* of Micah were, Pithon, and 1Chr 9:41 1121
And Azel had six *s*, whose names 1Chr 9:44 1121
these were the *s* of Azel 1Chr 9:44 1121
hard after Saul, and after his *s* 1Chr 10:2 1121
and Malchi-shua, the *s* of Saul 1Chr 10:2 1121
So Saul died, and his three *s* 1Chr 10:6 1121
his *s* were dead, then they 1Chr 10:7 1121
his *s* fallen in mount Gilboa 1Chr 10:8 1121
of Saul, and the bodies of his *s* 1Chr 10:12 1121
The *s* of Hashem the Gizonite, 1Chr 11:34 1121
Jehiel the *s* of Hothan the 1Chr 11:44 1121
the *s* of Elnaam, and Ithmah the 1Chr 11:46 1121
the *s* of Shemaah the Gibeathite 1Chr 12:3 1121
and Pelet, the *s* of Azmaveth 1Chr 12:3 1121
the *s* of Jeroham of Gedor 1Chr 12:7 1121
These were of the *s* of Gad 1Chr 12:14 1121
and David begat more *s* and 1Chr 14:3 1121
Of the *s* of Kohath 1Chr 15:5 1121
Of the *s* of Merari 1Chr 15:6 1121
Of the *s* of Gershom 1Chr 15:7 1121
Of the *s* of Elizaphan 1Chr 15:8 1121
Of the *s* of Hebron 1Chr 15:9 1121
Of the *s* of Uzziel 1Chr 15:10 1121
of the *s* of Merari their brethren 1Chr 15:17 1121
the *s* of Jeduthun were porters 1Chr 16:42 1121
thee, which shall be of thy *s* 1Chr 17:11 1121
the *s* of David were chief about 1Chr 18:17 1121
and his four *s* with him hid 1Chr 21:20 1121
into courses among the *s* of Levi 1Chr 23:6 1121
The *s* of Laadan 1Chr 23:8 1121
The *s* of Shimei 1Chr 23:9 1121
the *s* of Shimei were, Jahath, 1Chr 23:10 1121
These four were the *s* of Shimei 1Chr 23:10 1121
Jeush and Beriah had not many *s* 1Chr 23:11 1121
The *s* of Kohath 1Chr 23:12 1121
The *s* of Amram 1Chr 23:13 1121
his *s* for ever, to burn incense 1Chr 23:13 1121
his *s* were named of the tribe of 1Chr 23:14 1121
The *s* of Moses were, Gershom, and 1Chr 23:15 1121
Of the *s* of Gershom, Shebuel was 1Chr 23:16 1121
the *s* of Eliezer were, Rehabiah 1Chr 23:17 1121
And Eliezer had none other *s* 1Chr 23:17 1121
but the *s* of Rehabiah were very 1Chr 23:17 1121
Of the *s* of Izhar 1Chr 23:18 1121
Of the *s* of Hebron 1Chr 23:19 1121
Of the *s* of Uzziel 1Chr 23:20 1121
The *s* of Merari 1Chr 23:21 1121
The *s* of Mahli 1Chr 23:21 1121
And Eleazar died, and had no *s* 1Chr 23:22 1121
brethren the *s* of Kish took them 1Chr 23:22 1121
The *s* of Mushi 1Chr 23:23 1121
These were the *s* of Levi after 1Chr 23:24 1121
s of Aaron for the service of the 1Chr 23:28 1121
the charge of the *s* of Aaron 1Chr 23:32 1121
the divisions of the *s* of Aaron 1Chr 24:1 1121
The *s* of Aaron 1Chr 24:1 1121
both Zadok of the *s* of Eleazar 1Chr 24:3 1121
and Ahimelech of the *s* of Ithamar 1Chr 24:3 1121
more chief men found of the *s* of 1Chr 24:4 1121
Eleazar than of the *s* of Ithamar 1Chr 24:4 1121
Among the *s* of Eleazar there were 1Chr 24:4 1121
eight among the *s* of Ithamar 1Chr 24:4 1121
of God, were of the *s* of Eleazar 1Chr 24:5 1121
Eleazar, and of the *s* of Ithamar 1Chr 24:5 1121
the rest of the *s* of Levi were 1Chr 24:20 1121
Of the *s* of Amram 1Chr 24:20 1121
of the *s* of Shubael 1Chr 24:20 1121
of the *s* of Rehabiah, the first 1Chr 24:21 1121
of the *s* of Shelomoth 1Chr 24:22 1121
And the *s* of Hebron 1Chr 24:23 1121
Of the *s* of Uzziel 1Chr 24:24 1121
of the *s* of Michah 1Chr 24:24 1121
of the *s* of Isshiah 1Chr 24:25 1121
The *s* of Merari were Mahli and 1Chr 24:26 1121
the *s* of Jaaziah 1Chr 24:26 1121
The *s* of Merari by Jaaziah 1Chr 24:27 1121
Mahli came Eleazar, who had no *s* 1Chr 24:28 1121
The *s* also of Mushi 1Chr 24:30 1121
These were the *s* of the Levites 1Chr 24:30 1121
the *s* of Aaron in the presence of 1Chr 24:31 1121
to the service of the *s* of Asaph 1Chr 25:1 1121
Of the *s* of Asaph 1Chr 25:2 1121
the *s* of Asaph under the hands of 1Chr 25:2 1121
the *s* of Jeduthun 1Chr 25:3 1121
the *s* of Heman 1Chr 25:4 1121
All these were the *s* of Heman the 1Chr 25:5 1121
And God gave to Heman fourteen *s* 1Chr 25:5 1121
his brethren and *s* were twelve 1Chr 25:9 1121
The third to Zaccur, he, his *s* 1Chr 25:10 1121
The fourth to Izri, he, his *s* 1Chr 25:11 1121
The fifth to Nethaniah, he, his *s* 1Chr 25:12 1121
The sixth to Bukkiah, he, his *s* 1Chr 25:13 1121
seventh to Jesharelah, he, his *s* 1Chr 25:14 1121
The eighth to Jeshaiah, he, his *s* 1Chr 25:15 1121
The ninth to Mattaniah, he, his *s* 1Chr 25:16 1121
The tenth to Shimei, he, his *s* 1Chr 25:17 1121
eleventh to Azareel, he, his *s* 1Chr 25:18 1121
twelfth to Hashabiah, he, his *s* 1Chr 25:19 1121
thirteenth to Shubael, he, his *s* 1Chr 25:20 1121
to Mattithiah, he, his *s*, and his 1Chr 25:21 1121
fifteenth to Jeremoth, he, his *s* 1Chr 25:22 1121
sixteenth to Hananiah, he, his *s* 1Chr 25:23 1121
to Joshbekashah, he, his *s* 1Chr 25:24 1121
eighteenth to Hanani, he, his *s* 1Chr 25:25 1121
nineteenth to Mallothi, he, his *s* 1Chr 25:26 1121
twentieth to Eliathah, he, his *s* 1Chr 25:27 1121
and twentieth to Hothir, he, his *s* 1Chr 25:28 1121
twentieth to Giddalti, he, his *s* 1Chr 25:29 1121
twentieth to Mahazioth, he, his *s* 1Chr 25:30 1121
to Romamti-ezer, he, his *s* 1Chr 25:31 1121
son of Kore, of the *s* of Asaph 1Chr 26:1 1121
the *s* of Meshelemiah were, 1Chr 26:2 1121
Moreover the *s* of Obed-edom were, 1Chr 26:4 1121
unto Shemaiah his son were *s* born 1Chr 26:6 1121
The *s* of Shemaiah 1Chr 26:7 1121
All these of the *s* of Obed-edom 1Chr 26:8 1121
they and their *s* and their brethren 1Chr 26:8 1121
And Meshelemiah had *s* and brethren, 1Chr 26:9 1121
of the children of Merari, had *s* 1Chr 26:10 1121
all the *s* and brethren of Hosah 1Chr 26:11 1121
to his *s* the house of Asuppim 1Chr 26:15 1121
the porters among the *s* of Kore 1Chr 26:19 1121
of Kore, and among the *s* of Merari 1Chr 26:19 1121
As concerning the *s* of Laadan 1Chr 26:21 1121
the *s* of the Gershonite Laadan, 1Chr 26:21 1121
The *s* of Jehieli 1Chr 26:22 1121
his *s* were for the outward 1Chr 26:29 1121
of Hachmoni was with the king's *s* 1Chr 27:32 1121
of the king, and of his *s*, with 1Chr 28:1 1121
among the *s* of my father he liked 1Chr 28:4 1121
And of all my *s*, (for the LORD 1Chr 28:5 1121
for the LORD hath given me many *s* 1Chr 28:5 1121
all the *s* likewise of king David, 1Chr 29:24 1121
Heman, of Jeduthun, with their *s* 2Chr 5:12 1121
his *s* had cast them off from 2Chr 11:14 1121
and begat twenty and eight *s* 2Chr 11:21 1121
to his *s* by a covenant of salt 2Chr 13:5 1121
in the hand of the *s* of David 2Chr 13:8 1121
the *s* of Aaron, and the Levites, 2Chr 13:9 1121
are the *s* of Aaron, and the 2Chr 13:10 1121
wives, and begat twenty and two *s* 2Chr 13:21 1121
a Levite of the *s* of Asaph 2Chr 20:14 1121
had brethren the *s* of Jehoshaphat 2Chr 21:2 1121
all these were the *s* of 2Chr 21:2 1121
light to him and to his *s* for ever 2Chr 21:7 1121
and his *s* also, and his wives 2Chr 21:17 1121
Jehoahaz, the youngest of his *s* 2Chr 21:17 1121
the *s* of the brethren of Ahaziah, 2Chr 22:8 1121
the king's *s* that were slain 2Chr 22:11 1121
LORD hath said of the *s* of David 2Chr 23:3 1121
his *s* anointed him, and said, God 2Chr 23:11 1121
and he begat *s* and daughters 2Chr 24:3 1121
For the *s* of Athaliah, that 2Chr 24:7 1121
of the *s* of Jehoiada the priest 2Chr 24:25 1121
Now concerning his *s*, and the 2Chr 24:27 1121
but to the priests the *s* of Aaron 2Chr 26:18 1121
two hundred thousand, women, *s* 2Chr 28:8 1121
fallen by the sword, and our *s* 2Chr 29:9 1121
My *s*, be not now negligent 2Chr 29:11 1121
of the *s* of the Kohathites 2Chr 29:12 1121
of the *s* of Merari, Kish the son 2Chr 29:12 1121
And of the *s* of Elizaphan 2Chr 29:13 1121
and of the *s* of Asaph 2Chr 29:13 1121
And of the *s* of Heman 2Chr 29:14 1121
and of the *s* of Jeduthun 2Chr 29:14 1121
he commanded the priests the *s* of 2Chr 29:21 1121
ones, their wives, and their *s* 2Chr 31:18 1121
Also of the *s* of Aaron the 2Chr 31:19 1121

S

the sepulchres of the *s* of David 2Chr 32:33 1121
the Levites, of the *s* of Merari 2Chr 34:12 1121
of the *s* of the Kohathites, to 2Chr 34:12 1121
the *s* of Aaron were busied in 2Chr 35:14 1121
and for the priests the *s* of Aaron 2Chr 35:14 1121
the singers the *s* of Asaph were 2Chr 35:15 1121
his *s* until the reign of the 2Chr 36:20 1121
Then stood Jeshua with his *s* Ezr 3:9 1121
and his brethren, Kadmiel and his *s* Ezr 3:9 1121
the *s* of Judah, together, to set Ezr 3:9 1121
the *s* of Henadad, with their *s* Ezr 3:9 1121
the Levites the *s* of Asaph with Ezr 3:10 1121
the life of the king, and of his *s* Ezr 6:10 1123
the realm of the king and his *s* Ezr 7:23 1123
Of the *s* of Phinehas Ezr 8:2 1121
of the *s* of Ithamar Ezr 8:2 1121
of the *s* of David Ezr 8:2 1121
Of the *s* of Shechaniah, of the Ezr 8:3 1121
Shechaniah, of the *s* of Pharosh Ezr 8:3 1121
Of the *s* of Pahath-moab Ezr 8:4 1121
Of the *s* of Shechaniah Ezr 8:5 1121
Of the *s* also of Adin Ezr 8:6 1121
And of the *s* of Elam Ezr 8:7 1121
And of the *s* of Shephatiah Ezr 8:8 1121
Of the *s* of Joab Ezr 8:9 1121
And of the *s* of Shelomith Ezr 8:10 1121
And of the *s* of Bebai Ezr 8:11 1121
And of the *s* of Azgad Ezr 8:12 1121
And of the last *s* of Adonikam Ezr 8:13 1121
Of the *s* also of Bigvai Ezr 8:14 1121
found there none of the *s* of Levi Ezr 8:15 1121
of the *s* of Mahli, the son of Ezr 8:18 1121
and Sherebiah, with his *s* and his Ezr 8:18 1121
him Jeshaiah of the *s* of Merari Ezr 8:19 1121
his brethren and their *s* Ezr 8:19 1121
for themselves, and for their *s* Ezr 9:2 1121
not your daughters unto their *s* Ezr 9:12 1121
take their daughters unto your *s* Ezr 9:12 1121
of Jehiel, one of the *s* of Elam Ezr 10:2 1121
among the *s* of the priests there Ezr 10:18 1121
of the *s* of Jeshua the son of Ezr 10:18 1121
And of the *s* of Immer Ezr 10:20 1121
And of the *s* of Harim Ezr 10:21 1121
And of the *s* of Pashur Ezr 10:22 1121
of the *s* of Parosh Ezr 10:25 1121
And of the *s* of Elam Ezr 10:26 1121
And of the *s* of Zattu Ezr 10:27 1121
Of the *s* also of Bebai Ezr 10:28 1121
And of the *s* of Bani Ezr 10:29 1121
And of the *s* of Pahath-moab Ezr 10:30 1121
And of the *s* of Harim Ezr 10:31 1121
Of the *s* of Hashum Ezr 10:33 1121
Of the *s* of Bani Ezr 10:34 1121
Of the *s* of Nebo Ezr 10:43 1121
gate did the *s* of Hassenaah build Neh 3:3 1121
fight for your brethren, your *s* Neh 4:14 1121
there were that said, We, our *s* Neh 5:2 1121
lo, we bring into bondage our *s* Neh 5:5 1121
Binnui of the *s* of Henadad Neh 10:9 1121
law of God, their wives, their *s* Neh 10:28 1121
take their daughters for our *s* Neh 10:30 1121
Also the firstborn of our *s* Neh 10:36 1121
All the *s* of Perez that dwelt at Neh 11:6 1121
And these are the *s* of Benjamin Neh 11:7 1121
Of the *s* of Asaph, the singers Neh 11:22 1121
The *s* of Levi, the chief of the Neh 12:23 1121
the *s* of the singers gathered Neh 12:28 1121
of the priests' *s* with trumpets Neh 12:35 1121
give your daughters unto their *s* Neh 13:25 1121
take their daughters unto your *s* Neh 13:25 1121
And one of the *s* of Joiada Neh 13:28 1121
The ten *s* of Haman the son of Est 9:10 1121
the palace, and the ten *s* of Haman Est 9:12 1121
let Haman's ten *s* be hanged upon Est 9:13 1121
and they hanged Haman's ten *s* Est 9:14 1121
his *s* should be hanged on the Est 9:25 1121
there were born unto him seven *s* Job 1:2 1121
his *s* went and feasted in their Job 1:4 1121
It may be that my *s* have sinned Job 1:5 1121
when the *s* of God came to present Job 1:6 1121
And there was a day when his *s* Job 1:13 1121
came also another, and said, Thy *s* Job 1:18 1121
when the *s* of God came to present Job 2:1 1121
His *s* come to honour, and he Job 14:21 1121
all the *s* of God shouted for joy Job 38:7 1121
thou guide Arcturus with his *s* Job 38:32 1121
He had also seven *s* and three Job 42:13 1121
and saw his *s*, and his sons' *s* Job 42:16 1121
O ye *s* of men, how long will ye Ps 4:2 1121
trust in thee before the *s* of men Ps 31:19 1121
he beholdeth all the *s* of men Ps 33:13 1121
Maschil, for the *s* of Korah Ps 42:*t* 1121
chief Musician for the *s* of Korah Ps 44:*t* 1121
for the *s* of Korah, A Maschil, A Ps 45:*t* 1121
chief Musician for the *s* of Korah Ps 46:*t* 1121
A Psalm for the *s* of Korah Ps 47:*t* 1121
Song and Psalm for the *s* of Korah Ps 48:*t* 1121
A Psalm for the *s* of Korah Ps 49:*t* 1121
set on fire, even the *s* of men Ps 57:4 1121
ye judge uprightly, O ye *s* of men Ps 58:1 1121
people, the *s* of Jacob and Joseph Ps 77:15 1121
A Psalm for the *s* of Korah Ps 84:*t* 1121
A Psalm for the *s* of Korah Ps 85:*t* 1121
Psalm or Song for the *s* of Korah Ps 87:*t* 1121
A Song or Psalm for the *s* of Ps 88:*t* 1121
who among the *s* of the mighty can Ps 89:6 1121
Yea, they sacrificed their *s* Ps 106:37 1121
blood, even the blood of their *s* Ps 106:38 1121

That our *s* may be as plants grown Ps 144:12 1121
To make known to the *s* of men his Ps 145:12 1121
and my voice is to the *s* of man Prov 8:4 1121
delights were with the *s* of men Prov 8:31 1121
to the *s* of man to be exercised Eccl 1:13 1121
was that good for the *s* of men Eccl 2:3 1121
and the delights of the *s* of men Eccl 2:8 1121
which God hath given to the *s* of Eccl 3:10 1121
the estate of the *s* of men Eccl 3:18 1121
the *s* of men befalleth beasts Eccl 3:19 1121
therefore the heart of the *s* of Eccl 8:11 1121
also the heart of the *s* of men is Eccl 9:3 1121
so are the *s* of men snared in an Eccl 9:12 1121
so is my beloved among the *s* Song 2:3 1121
Sharezer his *s* smote him with the Is 37:38 1121
of thy *s* that shall issue from Is 39:7 1121
bring my *s* from far, and my Is 43:6 1121
of things to come concerning my *s* Is 45:11 1121
shall bring thy *s* in their arms Is 49:22 1121
the *s* whom she hath brought forth Is 51:18 1121
the *s* that she hath brought up Is 51:18 1121
Thy *s* have fainted, they lie at Is 51:20 1121
his form more than the *s* of men Is 52:14 1121
place and a name better than of *s* Is 56:5 1121
Also the *s* of the stranger, that Is 56:6 1121
ye *s* of the sorceress, the seed Is 57:3 1121
thy *s* shall come from far, and thy Is 60:4 1121
first, to bring thy *s* from far Is 60:9 1121
the *s* of strangers shall build up Is 60:10 1121
The *s* also of them that afflicted Is 60:14 1121
the *s* of the alien shall be your Is 61:5 1121
virgin, so shall thy *s* marry thee Is 62:5 1121
the *s* of the stranger shall not Is 62:8 1121
flocks and their herds, their *s* Jer 3:24 1121
and thy bread, which thy *s* Jer 5:17 1121
the *s* together shall fall upon Jer 6:21 1121
son of Hinnom, to burn their *s* Jer 7:31 1121
their *s* and their daughters shall Jer 11:22 1121
the *s* together, saith the LORD Jer 13:14 1121
them, their wives, nor their *s* Jer 14:16 1121
neither shalt thou have *s* or Jer 16:2 1121
saith the LORD concerning the *s* Jer 16:3 1121
to burn their *s* with fire for Jer 19:5 1121
them to eat the flesh of their *s* Jer 19:9 1121
Take ye wives, and beget *s* Jer 29:6 1121
and take wives for your *s*, and give Jer 29:6 1121
to husbands, that they may bear *s* Jer 29:6 1121
upon all the ways of the *s* of men Jer 32:19 1121
son of Hinnom, to cause their *s* Jer 32:35 1121
and his brethren, and all his *s* Jer 35:3 1121
the chamber of the *s* of Hanan Jer 35:4 1121
I set before the *s* of the house Jer 35:5 1121
neither ye, nor your *s* for ever Jer 35:6 1121
our days, we, our wives, our *s* Jer 35:8 1121
commanded his *s* not to drink wine Jer 35:14 1121
Because the *s* of Jonadab the son Jer 35:16 1121
s of Zedekiah in Riblah before Jer 39:6 1121
and Jonathan the *s* of Kareah Jer 40:8 1121
the *s* of Ephai the Netophathite, Jer 40:8 1121
for thy *s* are taken captives, and Jer 48:46 1121
Hath Israel no *s* Jer 49:1 1121
the *s* of Zedekiah before his eyes Jer 52:10 1121
The precious *s* of Zion, Lam 4:2 1121
eat the *s* in the midst of thee Eze 5:10 1121
the *s* shall eat their fathers Eze 5:10 1121
deliver neither *s* nor daughters Eze 14:16 1121
deliver neither *s* nor daughters Eze 14:18 1121
shall be brought forth, both *s* Eze 14:22 1121
Moreover thou hast taken thy *s* Eze 16:20 1121
when ye make your *s* to pass Eze 20:31 1121
and they were mine, and they bare *s* Eze 23:4 1121
they took her *s* and her daughters, Eze 23:10 1121
they shall take thy *s* and thy Eze 23:25 1121
and have also caused their *s* Eze 23:37 1121
they shall slay their *s* and their Eze 23:47 1121
and your *s* and your daughters whom Eze 24:21 1121
they set their minds, their *s* Eze 24:25 1121
s of Zadok among the *s* of Levi Eze 40:46 1121
the *s* of Zadok, that kept the Eze 44:15 1121
give a gift unto any of his *s* Eze 46:16 1121
but he shall give his *s* Eze 46:18 1121
are sanctified of the *s* of Zadok Eze 48:11 1121
he was driven from the *s* of men Dan 5:21 1123
of the *s* of men touched my lips Dan 10:16 1121
But his *s* shall be stirred up, and Dan 11:10 1121
Ye are the *s* of the living God Hos 1:10 1121
withered away from the *s* of men Joel 1:12 1121
and your *s* and your daughters shall Joel 2:28 1121
And I will sell your *s* and your Joel 3:8 1121
raised up of your *s* for prophets Amos 2:11 1121
an harlot in the city, and thy *s* Amos 7:17 1121
man, nor waiteth for the *s* of men Mic 5:7 1121
thy *s*, O Zion, against thy *s* Zec 9:13 1121
and he shall purify the *s* of Levi Mal 3:3 1121
therefore ye *s* of Jacob are not Mal 3:6 1121
of Zebedee's children with her *s* Mt 20:20 *5207*
Grant that these my two *s* may sit Mt 20:21 *5207*
A certain man had two *s* Mt 21:28 *5043*
the two *s* of Zebedee, and began to Mt 26:37 *5207*
which is, The *s* of thunder Mk 3:17 *5207*
be forgiven unto the *s* of men Mk 3:28 *5207*
the *s* of Zebedee, come unto him, Mk 10:35 *5207*
the *s* of Zebedee, which were Lk 5:10 *5207*
by whom do your *s* cast them out Lk 11:19 *5207*
he said, A certain man had two *s* Lk 15:11 *5207*
he power to become the *s* of God Jn 1:12 *5043*
the *s* of Zebedee, and two other of Jn 21:2
and your *s* and your daughters shall Acts 2:17 *5207*

for a sum of money of the *s* of Acts 7:16 *5207*
of Madian, where he begat two *s* Acts 7:29 *5207*
there were seven *s* of one Sceva Acts 19:14 *5207*
of God, they are the *s* of God Rom 8:14 *5207*
the manifestation of the *s* of God Rom 8:19 *5207*
but as my beloved *s* I warn you 1Cor 4:14 *5043*
unto you, and ye shall be my *s* 2Cor 6:18 *5207*
might receive the adoption of *s* Gal 4:5 *5206*
And because ye are *s*, God hath Gal 4:6 *5207*
written, that Abraham had two *s* Gal 4:22 *5207*
not made known unto the *s* of men Eph 3:5 *5207*
the *s* of God, without rebuke, in Phil 2:15 *5043*
in bringing many *s* unto glory Heb 2:10 *5207*
they that are of the *s* of Levi Heb 7:5 *5207*
blessed both the *s* of Joseph Heb 11:21 *5207*
God dealeth with you as with *s* Heb 12:7 *5207*
then are ye bastards, and not *s* Heb 12:8 *5207*
we should be called the *s* of God 1Jn 3:1 *5043*
Beloved, now are we the *s* of God 1Jn 3:2 *5043*

SONS' {26}

wife, and thy *s* wives with thee Gen 6:18 1121
his *s* wives with him, into the Gen 7:7 1121
sons, and thy *s* wives with thee Gen 8:16 1121
his wife, and his *s* wives with him Gen 8:18 1121
sons, and his *s* sons with him, his Gen 46:7 1121
his *s* daughters, and all his seed Gen 46:7 1121
loins, besides Jacob's *s* wives Gen 46:26 1121
sons, and his *s* garments with him Ex 29:21 1121
his *s* by a statute for ever from Ex 29:28 1121
of Aaron shall be his *s* after him Ex 29:29 1121
his *s* garments, to minister in Ex 39:41 1121
shall be Aaron's and his *s* Lev 2:3 1121
shall be Aaron's and his *s* Lev 2:10 1121
breast shall be Aaron's and his *s* Lev 7:31 1121
hands, and upon his *s* hands Lev 8:27 1121
upon his *s* garments with him Lev 8:30 1121
sons, and his *s* garments with him Lev 8:30 1121
it is thy due, and thy *s* due Lev 10:13 1121
for they be thy due, and thy *s* due Lev 10:14 1121
thy *s* with thee, by a statute for Lev 10:15 1121
And it shall be Aaron's and his *s* Lev 24:9 1121
them thy sons, and thy *s* sons Deut 4:9 1121
s sons, an hundred and fifty 1Chr 8:40 1121
his *s* sons, even four generations Job 42:16 1121
thereof shall be his *s* Eze 46:16 1121
shall be his *s* for them Eze 46:17 1121

SOON {65}

as *s* as he had left communing Gen 18:33 834
as *s* as Isaac had made an end of Gen 27:30 834
As *s* as the morning was light, Gen 44:3
it that ye are come so *s* to day Ex 2:18 4116
As *s* as I am gone out of the city Ex 9:29
as *s* as he came nigh unto the Ex 32:19 834
that ye shall *s* utterly perish Deut 4:26 4116
as *s* as they which pursued after Josh 2:7 834
as *s* as we had heard these things Josh 2:11
as *s* as the soles of the feet of Josh 3:13
they ran as *s* as he had stretched Josh 8:19
as *s* as the sun was down, Joshua Josh 8:29
as *s* as Gideon was dead, that the Judg 8:33 834
as *s* as the sun is up, thou shalt Judg 9:33
As *s* as ye be come into the city, 1Sa 9:13
that as *s* as he had made an end 1Sa 13:10
as *s* as the lad was gone, David 1Sa 20:41
as *s* as ye be up early in the 1Sa 29:10
as *s* as David had made an end of 2Sa 6:18
as *s* as he had made an end of 2Sa 13:36
As *s* as ye hear the sound of the 2Sa 15:10
as *s* as they hear, they shall be 2Sa 22:45
as *s* as he sat on his throne, 1Kin 16:11
as *s* as I am gone from thee, that 1Kin 18:12
as *s* as thou art departed from me 1Kin 20:36
as *s* as he was departed from him, 1Kin 20:36
Now as *s* as this letter cometh to 2Kin 10:2
as *s* as he had made an end of 2Kin 10:25
as *s* as the kingdom was confirmed 2Kin 14:5 834
as *s* as the commandment came 2Chr 31:5
my maker would *s* take me away Job 32:22 4592
As *s* as they hear of me, they Ps 18:44
For they shall *s* be cut down like Ps 37:2 4120
go astray as *s* as they be born Ps 58:3
Ethiopia shall *s* stretch out her Ps 68:31 7323
I should *s* have subdued their Ps 81:14 4592
for it is *s* cut off, and we fly Ps 90:10 2440
They *s* forgat his works Ps 106:13 4116
He that is *s* angry dealeth Prov 14:17 7116
for as *s* as Zion travailed, she Is 66:8 1571
as *s* as she saw them with her Eze 23:16 4758
How *s* is the fig tree withered Mt 21:20 *3916*
And as *s* as he had spoken, Mk 1:42
As *s* as Jesus heard the word that Mk 5:36 *2112*
as *s* as ye be entered into it, ye Mk 11:2 *2112*
as *s* as he was come, he goeth Mk 14:45
that, as *s* as the days of his Lk 1:23
For, lo, as *s* as the voice of thy Lk 1:44
as *s* as it was sprung up, it Lk 8:6
But as *s* as this thy son was come Lk 15:30 *3753*
as *s* as it was day, the elders of Lk 22:66
as *s* as he knew that he belonged Lk 23:7
as *s* as she heard that Jesus was Jn 11:20
As *s* as she heard that, she arose Jn 11:29
but as *s* as she is delivered of Jn 16:21 *3752*
As *s* then as he had said unto Jn 18:6
As *s* then as they were come to Jn 21:9
as *s* as I was sent for Acts 10:29
Now as *s* as it was day, there was Acts 12:18 *1096*
I marvel that ye are so *s* removed Gal 1:6 *5030*

so *s* as I shall see how it will ... Phil 2:23
That ye be not *s* shaken in mind ... 2Th 2:2 *5030*
not *s* angry, not given to wine, ... Titus 1:7 *3711*
as *s* as I had eaten it, my belly ... Rev 10:10 *3753*
her child as *s* as it was born ... Rev 12:4 *3752*

SOONER {2}
I may be restored to you the *s* ... Heb 13:19 *5032*
For the sun is no *s* risen with a ... Jas 1:11

SOOTHSAYER {1}
also the son of Beor, the *s* ... Josh 13:22 7080

SOOTHSAYERS {6}
are *s* like the Philistines, and ... Is 2:6 6049
astrologers, the magicians, the *s* ... Dan 2:27 1505
the Chaldeans, and the *s* ... Dan 4:7 1505
the Chaldeans, and the *s* ... Dan 5:7 1505
astrologers, Chaldeans, and *s* ... Dan 5:11 1505
and thou shalt have no more *s* ... Mic 5:12 6049

SOOTHSAYING {1}
her masters much gain by *s* ... Acts 16:16 *3132*

SOP {4}
it is, to whom I shall give a *s* ... Jn 13:26 *5596*
And when he had dipped the *s* ... Jn 13:26 *5596*
after the *s* Satan entered into ... Jn 13:27 *5596*
the *s* went immediately out ... Jn 13:30 *5596*

SOPATER *(so'-pa-ter)* {1} See SOSIPATER. *A Christian from Berea.*
him into Asia *S* of Berea ... Acts 20:4 *4986*

SOPE {2}
with nitre, and take thee much *s* ... Jer 2:22 1287
fire, and like fullers' *s* ... Mal 3:2 1287

SOPHERETH *(so-fe'-reth)* {2} *A family of exiles.*
of Sotai, the children of *S* ... Ezr 2:55 5618
of Sotai, the children of *S* ... Neh 7:57 5618

SORCERER {2}
Paphos, they found a certain *s* ... Acts 13:6 *3097*
But Elymas the *s* (for so is his ... Acts 13:8 *3097*

SORCERERS {6}
also called the wise men and the *s* ... Ex 7:11 3784
to your enchanters, nor to your *s* ... Jer 27:9 3786
and the astrologers, and the *s* ... Dan 2:2 3784
be a swift witness against the *s* ... Mal 3:5 3784
murderers, and whoremongers, and *s* ... Rev 21:8 *5332*
For without are dogs, and *s* ... Rev 22:15 *5333*

SORCERESS {1}
near hither, ye sons of the *s* ... Is 57:3 6049

SORCERIES {5}
for the multitude of thy *s* ... Is 47:9 3785
and with the multitude of thy *s* ... Is 47:12 3785
time he had bewitched them with *s* ... Acts 8:11 *3095*
of their murders, nor of their *s* ... Rev 9:21 *5331*
for by thy *s* were all nations ... Rev 18:23 *5331*

SORCERY {1}
in the same city used *s*, and ... Acts 8:9 *3096*

SORE {98}
And they pressed *s* upon the man ... Gen 19:9 3966
and the men were *s* afraid ... Gen 20:8 3966
because thou *s* longedst after thy ... Gen 31:30
the third day, when they were *s* ... Gen 34:25 3510
the famine waxed *s* in the land of ... Gen 41:56 2388
the famine was so *s* in all lands ... Gen 41:57 2388
And the famine was *s* in the land ... Gen 43:1 3515
for the famine is *s* in the land ... Gen 47:4 3515
for the famine was very *s* ... Gen 47:13 3515
a great and very *s* lamentation ... Gen 50:10 3515
and they were *s* afraid ... Ex 14:10 3966
bald forehead, a white reddish *s* ... Lev 13:42 5061
if the rising of the *s* be white ... Lev 13:43 5061
Moab was *s* afraid of the people, ... Num 22:3 3966
signs and wonders, great and *s* ... Deut 6:22 7451
with a *s* botch that cannot be ... Deut 28:35 7451
and *s* sicknesses, and of long ... Deut 28:59 7451
therefore we were *s* afraid of our ... Josh 9:24 3966
so that Israel was *s* distressed ... Judg 10:9 3966
her, because she lay *s* upon him ... Judg 14:17
he was *s* athirst, and called on ... Judg 15:18 3966
all Israel, and the battle was *s* ... Judg 20:34 3513
lifted up their voices, and wept *s* ... Judg 21:2
her adversary also provoked her *s* ... 1Sa 1:6 3708
prayed unto the LORD, and wept *s* ... 1Sa 1:10
for his hand is *s* upon us ... 1Sa 5:7 7185
there was *s* war against the ... 1Sa 14:52 2389
fled from him, and were *s* afraid ... 1Sa 17:24 3966
was *s* afraid of Achish the king ... 1Sa 21:12 3966
Saul answered, I am *s* distressed ... 1Sa 28:15 3966
was *s* afraid, because of the ... 1Sa 28:20 3966
and saw that he was *s* troubled ... 1Sa 28:21 3966
And the battle went *s* against Saul ... 1Sa 31:3 3513
he was *s* wounded of the archers ... 1Sa 31:3 3966
for he was *s* afraid ... 1Sa 31:4 3966
was a very *s* battle that day ... 2Sa 2:17 7188
and all his servants wept very *s* ... 2Sa 13:36 1419
and his sickness was so *s*, that ... 1Kin 17:17 2389
there was a *s* famine in Samaria ... 1Kin 18:2 2389
that the battle was too *s* for him ... 2Kin 3:26 2388
was *s* troubled for this thing ... 2Kin 6:11
And Hezekiah wept *s* ... 2Kin 20:3 1419
And the battle went *s* against Saul ... 1Chr 10:3 3513
for he was *s* afraid ... 1Chr 10:4 3966
whatsoever *s* or whatsoever ... 2Chr 6:28 5061
every one shall know his own *s* ... 2Chr 6:29 5061
so he died of *s* diseases ... 2Chr 21:19 7451
transgressed *s* against the LORD ... 2Chr 28:19
for I am *s* wounded ... 2Chr 35:23 3966
for the people wept very *s* ... Ezr 10:1
Then I was very *s* afraid, ... Neh 2:2 7235
And it grieved me *s* ... Neh 13:8 3966
smote Job with *s* boils from the ... Job 2:7 7451
For he maketh *s*, and bindeth up ... Job 5:18 3510
and vex them in his *s* displeasure ... Ps 2:5
My soul is also *s* vexed ... Ps 6:3 3966
enemies be ashamed and *s* vexed ... Ps 6:10 3966
in me, and thy hand presseth me *s* .. Ps 38:2 5704,3966
I am feeble and *s* broken ... Ps 38:8
my friends stand aloof from my *s* ... Ps 38:11 5061
Though thou hast *s* broken us in ... Ps 44:19
My heart is *s* pained within me ... Ps 55:4
s troubles, shalt quicken me ... Ps 71:20 7451
my *s* ran in the night, and ceased ... Ps 77:2 3027
Thou hast thrust *s* at me that I ... Ps 118:13
The LORD hath chastened me *s* ... Ps 118:18
this *s* travail hath God given to ... Eccl 1:13 7451
vanity, yea, it is a *s* travail ... Eccl 4:8 7451
There is a *s* evil which I have ... Eccl 5:13 2470
And this also is a *s* evil, that in ... Eccl 5:16 2470
In that day the LORD with his *s* ... Is 27:1 7186
And Hezekiah wept *s* ... Is 38:3 1419
like bears, and mourn *s* like doves ... Is 59:11
Be not wroth very *s*, O LORD, ... Is 64:9 3966
thy peace, and afflict us very *s* ... Is 64:12 3966
and mine eye shall weep *s*, and run ... Jer 13:17
but weep *s* for him that goeth ... Jer 22:10
Your mother shall be *s* confounded ... Jer 50:12 3966
the famine was *s* in the city ... Jer 52:6 2388
She weepeth *s* in the night, and ... Lam 1:2
Mine enemies chased me *s*, like a ... Lam 3:52
four *s* judgments upon Jerusalem ... Eze 14:21 7451
sharpened to make a *s* slaughter ... Eze 21:10
and their kings shall be *s* afraid ... Eze 27:35 8178
was *s* displeased with himself, and ... Dan 6:14 7690
you, even with a *s* destruction ... Mic 2:10 4834
The LORD hath been *s* displeased ... Zec 1:2
I am very *s* displeased with the ... Zec 1:15
on their face, and were *s* afraid ... Mt 17:6 *4970*
for he is lunatick, and *s* vexed ... Mt 17:15 *2560*
they were *s* displeased, ... Mt 21:15 *23*
they were *s* amazed in themselves ... Mk 6:51 *3029*
for they were *s* afraid ... Mk 9:6 *1630*
the spirit cried, and rent him *s* ... Mk 9:26 *4183*
and John, and began to be *s* amazed ... Mk 14:33 *1568*
and they were *s* afraid ... Lk 2:9 *3173*
And they all wept *s*, and fell on ... Acts 20:37 *2425*
grievous *s* upon the men which had ... Rev 16:2 *1668*

SOREK *(so'-rek)* {1} *A valley between Ashkelon and Gaza.*
loved a woman in the valley of *S* ... Judg 16:4 7796

SORELY {2}
The archers have *s* grieved him ... Gen 49:23 4843
so shall they be *s* pained at the ... Is 23:5

SORER {1}
Of how much *s* punishment, suppose ... Heb 10:29 *5501*

SORES {4}
and bruises, and putrifying *s* ... Is 1:6 4347
was laid at his gate, full of *s* ... Lk 16:20 *1669*
the dogs came and licked his *s* ... Lk 16:21 *1668*
because of their pains and their *s* ... Rev 16:11 *1668*

SORROW {70}
I will greatly multiply thy *s* ... Gen 3:16 6093
in *s* thou shalt bring forth ... Gen 3:16 6089
in *s* shalt thou eat of it all the ... Gen 3:17 6093
my gray hairs with *s* to the grave ... Gen 42:38 3015
my gray hairs with *s* to the grave ... Gen 44:29 7451
our father with *s* to the grave ... Gen 44:31 3015
s shall take hold on the ... Ex 15:14 2427
the eyes, and cause *s* of heart ... Lev 26:16 1727
and failing of eyes, and *s* of mind ... Deut 28:65 1671
saying, Because I bare him with *s* ... 1Chr 4:9 6090
is nothing else but *s* of heart ... Neh 2:2 7455
turned unto them from *s* to joy ... Est 9:22 3015
womb, nor hid *s* from mine eyes ... Job 3:10 5999
yea, I would harden myself in *s* ... Job 6:10 2427
eye also is dim by reason of *s* ... Job 17:7 3708
s is turned into joy before him ... Job 41:22 1670
having *s* in my heart daily ... Ps 13:2 3015
my *s* is continually before me ... Ps 38:17 4341
and my *s* was stirred ... Ps 39:2 3511
also and *s* are in the midst of it ... Ps 55:10 5999
yet is their strength labour and *s* ... Ps 90:10 205
oppression, affliction, and *s* ... Ps 107:39 3015
I found trouble and *s* ... Ps 116:3 3015
winketh with the eye causeth *s* ... Prov 10:10 6094
rich, and he addeth no *s* with it ... Prov 10:22 6089
but by *s* of the heart the spirit ... Prov 15:13 6094
a fool doeth it to his *s* ... Prov 17:21 8424
who hath *s* ... Prov 23:29 17
increaseth knowledge increaseth *s* ... Eccl 1:18 4341
in darkness, and he hath much *s* ... Eccl 5:17 3708
S is better than laughter ... Eccl 7:3 3708
Therefore remove *s* from thy heart ... Eccl 11:10 3708
the land, behold darkness and *s* ... Is 5:30 6862
shall give thee rest from thy *s* ... Is 14:3 6090
day of grief and of desperate *s* ... Is 17:11 3511
and there shall be heaviness and *s* ... Is 29:2 592
obtain joy and gladness, and *s* ... Is 35:10 3015
ye shall lie down in *s* ... Is 50:11 4620
and *s* and mourning shall flee away ... Is 51:11 3015
but ye shall cry for *s* of heart ... Is 65:14 3511
I would comfort myself against *s* ... Jer 8:18 3015
of the womb to see labour and *s* ... Jer 20:18 3015
thy *s* is incurable for the ... Jer 30:15 4341
they shall not *s* any more at all ... Jer 31:12 1669
and make them rejoice from their *s* ... Jer 31:13 3015
the LORD hath added grief to my *s* ... Jer 45:3 4341
there is *s* on the sea ... Jer 49:23 1674
And the land shall tremble and *s* ... Jer 51:29 2342
be any *s* like unto my *s* ... Lam 1:12 4341
you, all people, and behold my *s* ... Lam 1:18 4341
Give them *s* of heart, thy curse ... Lam 3:65 4044
be filled with drunkenness and *s* ... Eze 23:33 3015
they shall *s* a little for the ... Hos 8:10 2490
he found them sleeping for *s* ... Lk 22:45 *3077*
you, *s* hath filled your heart ... Jn 16:6 *3077*
but your *s* shall be turned into ... Jn 16:20 *3077*
when she is in travail hath *s* ... Jn 16:21 *3077*
And ye now therefore have *s* ... Jn 16:22 *3077*
and continual *s* in my heart ... Rom 9:2 *3601*
I should have *s* from them of whom ... 2Cor 2:3 *3077*
be swallowed up with overmuch *s* ... 2Cor 2:7 *3077*
For godly *s* worketh repentance to ... 2Cor 7:10 *3077*
but the *s* of the world worketh ... 2Cor 7:10 *3077*
lest I should have *s* upon *s* ... Phil 2:27 *3077*
which are asleep, that ye *s* not ... 1Th 4:13 *3076*
so much torment and *s* give her ... Rev 18:7 *3997*
and am no widow, and shall see no *s* ... Rev 18:7 *3997*
shall be no more death, neither *s* ... Rev 21:4 *3997*

SORROWED {2}
but that ye *s* to repentance ... 2Cor 7:9 *3076*
that ye *s* after a godly sort, ... 2Cor 7:11 *3076*

SORROWETH {1}
s for you, saying, What shall I ... 1Sa 10:2 1672

SORROWFUL {18}
lord, I am a woman of a *s* spirit ... 1Sa 1:15 7186
refused to touch are as my *s* meat ... Job 6:7 1741
But I am poor and *s* ... Ps 69:29 3510
Even in laughter the heart is *s* ... Prov 14:13 3510
I have replenished every *s* soul ... Jer 31:25 1669
are *s* for the solemn assembly ... Zeph 3:18 3013
also shall see it, and be very *s* ... Zec 9:5 2342
heard that saying, he went away *s* ... Mt 19:22 *3076*
And they were exceeding *s*, and ... Mt 26:22 *3076*
sons of Zebedee, and began to be *s* ... Mt 26:37 *3076*
unto them, My soul is exceeding *s* ... Mt 26:38 *4036*
And they began to be *s*, and to say ... Mk 14:19 *3076*
My soul is exceeding *s* unto death ... Mk 14:34 *4036*
when he heard this, he was very *s* ... Lk 18:23 *4036*
when Jesus saw that he was very *s* ... Lk 18:24 *4036*
and ye shall be *s*, but your sorrow ... Jn 16:20 *3076*
As *s*, yet alway rejoicing ... 2Cor 6:10 *3076*
and that I may be the less *s* ... Phil 2:28 *253*

SORROWING {2}
father and I have sought thee *s* ... Lk 2:48 *3600*
S most of all for the words which ... Acts 20:38 *3600*

SORROWS {22}
for I know their *s* ... Ex 3:7 4341
The *s* of hell compassed me about ... 2Sa 22:6 2256
I am afraid of all my *s*, I know ... Job 9:28 6094
God distributeth *s* in his anger ... Job 21:17 2256
young ones, they cast out their *s* ... Job 39:3 2256
Their *s* shall be multiplied that ... Ps 16:4 6094
The *s* of death compassed me, and ... Ps 18:4 2256
The *s* of hell compassed me about ... Ps 18:5 2256
Many *s* shall be to the wicked ... Ps 32:10 4341
The *s* of death compassed me, and ... Ps 116:3 2256
up late, to eat the bread of *s* ... Ps 127:2 6089
For all his days are *s*, and his ... Eccl 2:23 4341
s shall take hold of them ... Is 13:8 2256
a man of *s*, and acquainted with ... Is 53:3 4341
our griefs, and carried our *s* ... Is 53:4 4341
shall not *s* take thee, as a woman ... Jer 13:21 2256
s have taken her, as a woman in ... Jer 49:24 2256
by the vision my *s* are turned ... Dan 10:16 6735
The *s* of a travailing woman shall ... Hos 13:13 2256
All these are the beginning of *s* ... Mt 24:8 *5604*
these are the beginnings of *s* ... Mk 13:8 *5604*
themselves through with many *s* ... 1Ti 6:10 *3601*

SORRY {14}
is none of you that is *s* for me ... 1Sa 22:8 2470
neither be ye *s* ... Neh 8:10 6087
I will be *s* for my sin ... Ps 38:18 1672
who shall be *s* for thee ... Is 51:19 5110
And the king was *s* ... Mt 14:9 *3076*
And they were exceeding *s* ... Mt 17:23 *3076*
what was done, they were very *s* ... Mt 18:31 *3076*
And the king was exceeding *s* ... Mk 6:26 *4036*
For if I make you *s*, who is he ... 2Cor 2:2 *3076*
the same which is made *s* by me ... 2Cor 2:2 *3076*
though I made you *s* with a letter ... 2Cor 7:8 *3076*
the same epistle hath made you *s* ... 2Cor 7:8 *3076*
rejoice, not that ye were made *s* ... 2Cor 7:9 *3076*
for ye were made *s* after a godly ... 2Cor 7:9 *3076*

SORT {21}
two of every *s* shalt thou bring ... Gen 6:19
two of every *s* shall come unto ... Gen 6:20
his kind, every bird of every *s* ... Gen 7:14 3671
save the poorest *s* of the people ... 2Kin 24:14
by lot, one *s* with another ... 1Chr 24:5
offer so willingly after this *s* ... 1Chr 29:14
time in such *s* as it was written ... 2Chr 30:5
basons of a second *s* four hundred ... Ezr 1:10
to Artaxerxes the king in this *s* ... Ezr 4:8 3660
unto me four times after this *s* ... Neh 6:4 1697
with the men of the common *s* were ... Eze 23:42
the ravenous birds of every *s* ... Eze 39:4 3671
of every *s* of your oblations, ... Eze 44:30
the children which are of your *s* ... Dan 1:10 1524

God that can deliver after this *s* ... Dan 3:29
lewd fellows of the baser *s* ... Acts 17:5
more boldly unto you in some *s* ... Rom 15:15 *3313*
every man's work of what *s* it is ... 1Cor 3:13 *3697*
that ye sorrowed after a godly *s* ... 2Cor 7:11
For of this *s* are they which ... 2Ti 3:6
on their journey after a godly *s* ... 3Jn 6 *516*

SORTS {7}
not wear a garment of divers *s* ... Deut 22:11
ten days store of all *s* of wine ... Neh 5:18
He sent divers *s* of flies among ... Ps 78:45
and there came divers *s* of flies ... Ps 105:31
instruments, and that of all *s* ... Eccl 2:8
thy merchants in all *s* of things ... Eze 27:24 4360
them clothed with all *s* of armour ... Eze 38:4 4358

SOSIPATER *(so-sip'-a-tur)* {1} See SOPATER. *A relative of Paul.*
and Lucius, and Jason, and *S* ... Rom 16:21 *4989*

SOSTHENES *(sos'-the-neze)* {2}
1. Chief ruler of a synagogue in Corinth.
Then all the Greeks took *S* ... Acts 18:17 *4988*
2. A co-worker with Paul.
will of God, and *S* our brother, ... 1Cor 1:1 *4988*

SOTAI *(so'-tahee)* {2} *A family of Temple servants.*
the children of *S*, the children ... Ezr 2:55 5479
the children of *S*, the children ... Neh 7:57 5479

SOTTISH {1}
they are *s* children, and they have ... Jer 4:22 5530

SOUGHT {126}
and he *s* where to weep ... Gen 43:30 1245
this thing, he *s* to slay Moses ... Ex 2:15 1245
the men are dead which *s* thy life ... Ex 4:19 1245
LORD met him, and *s* to kill him ... Ex 4:24 1245
that every one which *s* the LORD ... Ex 33:7 1245
Moses diligently *s* the goat of ... Lev 10:16 1875
not his enemy, neither *s* his harm ... Num 35:23 1245
because he hath *s* to thrust thee ... Deut 13:10 1245
the pursuers *s* them throughout ... Josh 2:22 1245
that he *s* an occasion against the ... Judg 14:4 1245
days the tribe of the Danites *s* ... Judg 18:1 1245
and when they *s* him, he could not ... 1Sa 10:21 1245
the LORD hath *s* him a man after ... 1Sa 13:14 1245
by which Jonathan *s* to go over ... 1Sa 14:4 1245
Saul *s* to smite David even to the ... 1Sa 19:10 1245
Saul *s* him every day, but God ... 1Sa 23:14 1245
he *s* no more again for him ... 1Sa 27:4 1245
Ye *s* for David in times past to ... 2Sa 3:17 1245
thine enemy, which *s* thy life ... 2Sa 4:8 1245
And when they had *s* and could not ... 2Sa 17:20 1245
Saul *s* to slay them in his zeal ... 2Sa 21:2 1245
Let there be *s* for my lord the ... 1Kin 1:2 1245
So they *s* for a fair damsel ... 1Kin 1:3 1245
And all the earth *s* to Solomon ... 1Kin 10:24 1245
Solomon *s* therefore to kill ... 1Kin 11:40 1245
they *s* three days, but found him ... 2Kin 2:17 1245
for that we *s* him not after the ... 1Chr 15:13 1875
reign of David they were *s* for ... 1Chr 26:31 1875
and the congregation *s* unto it ... 2Chr 1:5 1875
earth *s* the presence of Solomon ... 2Chr 9:23 1245
because we have *s* the LORD our ... 2Chr 14:7 1875
the LORD our God, we have *s* him ... 2Chr 14:7 1875
s him, he was found of them ... 2Chr 15:4 1245
s him with their whole desire ... 2Chr 15:15 1245
his disease he *s* not to the LORD ... 2Chr 16:12 1875
David, and *s* not unto Baalim ... 2Chr 17:3 1875
But *s* to the LORD God of his ... 2Chr 17:4 1875
they are *s* children, and they have ... Jer 4:22 5530
And he *s* Ahaziah ... 2Chr 22:9 1245
who *s* the LORD with all his heart ... 2Chr 22:9 1875
Why hast thou *s* after the gods of ... 2Chr 25:15 1875
because they *s* after the gods of ... 2Chr 25:20 1875
he *s* God in the days of Zechariah ... 2Chr 26:5 1875
and as long as he *s* the LORD ... 2Chr 26:5 1875
These *s* their register among ... Ezr 2:62 1245
These *s* their register among ... Neh 7:64 1245
s the Levites out of all their ... Neh 12:27 1245
fair young virgins *s* for the king ... Est 2:2 1245
s to lay hand on the king ... Est 2:21 1245
wherefore Haman *s* to destroy all ... Est 3:6 1245
who *s* to lay hand on the king ... Est 6:2 1245
lay hand on such as *s* their hurt ... Est 9:2 1245
I *s* the LORD, and he heard me, and ... Ps 34:4 1875
I *s* him, but he could not be ... Ps 37:36 1245
day of my trouble I *s* the Lord ... Ps 77:2 1875
he slew them, then they *s* him ... Ps 78:34 1875
violent men have *s* after my soul ... Ps 86:14 1245
s out of all them that have ... Ps 111:2 1875
With my whole heart have I *s* thee ... Ps 119:10 1875
for I have *s* thy precepts ... Ps 119:94 1875
I *s* in mine heart to give myself ... Eccl 2:3 8446
but they have *s* out many ... Eccl 7:29 1245
s out, and set in order many ... Eccl 12:9 2713
The preacher *s* to find out ... Eccl 12:10 1245
By night on my bed I *s* him whom ... Song 3:1 1245
I *s* him, but I found him not ... Song 3:1 1245
I *s* him, but I found him not ... Song 3:2 1245
I *s* him, but I could not find him ... Song 5:6 1245
S out, A city not forsaken ... Is 62:12 1875
I am *s* of them that asked not for ... Is 65:1 1875
I am found of them that *s* me not ... Is 65:1 1245
in, for my people that have *s* me ... Is 65:10 1875
have walked, and whom they have *s* ... Jer 8:2 1875
brutish, and have not *s* the LORD ... Jer 10:21 1875
the king *s* to put him to death ... Jer 26:21 1245
his enemy, and that *s* his life ... Jer 44:30 1245
iniquity of Israel shall be *s* for ... Jer 50:20 1245
while they *s* their meat to ... Lam 1:19 1245
I *s* for a man among them, that ... Eze 22:30 1245
though thou be *s* for, yet shalt ... Eze 26:21 1245
neither have ye *s* that which was ... Eze 34:4 1245
they *s* Daniel and his fellows to ... Dan 2:13 1158
counsellors and my lords *s* unto me ... Dan 4:36 1158
princes *s* to find occasion ... Dan 6:4 1158
s for the meaning, then, behold, ... Dan 8:15 1245
how are his hidden things *s* up ... Obad 6 1156
and those that have not *s* the LORD ... Zeph 1:6 1245
s to go that they might walk to ... Zec 6:7 1245
which *s* the young child's life ... Mt 2:20 *2212*
But when they *s* to lay hands on ... Mt 21:46 *2212*
from that time he *s* opportunity ... Mt 26:16 *2212*
s false witness against Jesus, to ... Mt 26:59 *2212*
s how they might destroy him ... Mk 11:18 *2212*
they *s* to lay hold on him, but ... Mk 12:12 *2212*
the scribes *s* how they might take ... Mk 14:1 *2212*
he *s* how he might conveniently ... Mk 14:11 *2212*
all the council *s* for witness ... Mk 14:55 *2212*
they *s* him among their kinsfolk ... Lk 2:44 *327*
father and I have *s* thee sorrowing ... Lk 2:48 *2212*
unto them, How is it that ye *s* me ... Lk 2:49 *2212*
and the people *s* him, and came unto ... Lk 4:42 *2212*
they *s* means to bring him in, and ... Lk 5:18 *2212*
whole multitude *s* to touch him ... Lk 6:19 *2212*
s of him a sign from heaven ... Lk 11:16 *2212*
s fruit thereon, and found none ... Lk 13:6 *2212*
he *s* to see Jesus who he was ... Lk 19:3 *2212*
of the people *s* to destroy him ... Lk 19:47 *2212*
same hour *s* to lay hands on him ... Lk 20:19 *2212*
scribes *s* how they might kill him ... Lk 22:2 *2212*
s opportunity to betray him unto ... Lk 22:6 *2212*
s to slay him, because he had ... Jn 5:16 *2212*
Therefore the Jews *s* the more to ... Jn 5:18 *2212*
because the Jews *s* to kill him ... Jn 7:1 *2212*
Then the Jews *s* him at the feast, ... Jn 7:11 *2212*
Then they *s* to take him ... Jn 7:30 *2212*
Therefore they *s* again to take ... Jn 10:39 *2212*
the Jews of late *s* to stone thee ... Jn 11:8 *2212*
Then *s* they for Jesus, and spake ... Jn 11:56 *2212*
Pilate *s* to release him ... Jn 19:12 *2212*
And when Herod had *s* for him ... Acts 12:19 *1934*
s to bring them out to the people ... Acts 17:5 *2212*
Because they *s* it not by faith, ... Rom 9:32 *2212*
I was found of them that *s* me not ... Rom 10:20 *2212*
Nor of men *s* we glory, neither of ... 1Th 2:6 *2212*
he *s* me out very diligently, and ... 2Ti 1:17 *2212*
place have been *s* for the second ... Heb 8:7 *2212*
though he *s* it carefully with ... Heb 12:17 *1567*

SOUL {460}
and man became a living *s* ... Gen 2:7 5315
my *s* shall live because of thee ... Gen 12:13 5315
that *s* shall be cut off from his ... Gen 17:14 5315
and my *s* shall live ... Gen 19:20 5315
that my *s* may bless thee before I ... Gen 27:4 5315
venison, that thy *s* may bless me ... Gen 27:19 5315
venison, that my *s* may bless thee ... Gen 27:25 5315
venison, that thy *s* may bless me ... Gen 27:31 5315
his *s* clave unto Dinah the ... Gen 34:3 5315
The *s* of my son Shechem longeth ... Gen 34:8 5315
as her *s* was in departing, (for ... Gen 35:18 5315
that we saw the anguish of his *s* ... Gen 42:21 5315
O my *s*, come not thou into their ... Gen 49:6 5315
that *s* shall be cut off from ... Ex 12:15 5315
even that *s* shall be cut off from ... Ex 12:19 5315
a ransom for his *s* unto the LORD ... Ex 30:12 5315
that *s* shall be cut off from ... Ex 31:14 5315
saying, If a *s* shall sin through ... Lev 4:2 5315
And if a *s* sin, and hear the voice ... Lev 5:1 5315
Or if a *s* touch any unclean thing ... Lev 5:2 5315
Or if a *s* swear, pronouncing with ... Lev 5:4 5315
If a *s* commit a trespass, and sin ... Lev 5:15 5315
And if a *s* sin, and commit any of ... Lev 5:17 5315
If a *s* sin, and commit a trespass ... Lev 6:2 5315
the *s* that eateth of it shall ... Lev 7:18 5315
But the *s* that eateth of the ... Lev 7:20 5315
even that *s* shall be cut off from ... Lev 7:20 5315
Moreover the *s* that shall touch ... Lev 7:21 5315
even that *s* shall be cut off from ... Lev 7:21 5315
even the *s* that eateth it shall ... Lev 7:25 5315
Whatsoever *s* it be that eateth ... Lev 7:27 5315
even that *s* shall be cut off from ... Lev 7:27 5315
against that *s* that eateth blood ... Lev 17:10 5315
maketh an atonement for the *s* ... Lev 17:11 5315
No *s* of you shall eat blood, ... Lev 17:12 5315
every *s* that eateth that which ... Lev 17:15 5315
that *s* shall be cut off from ... Lev 19:8 5315
the *s* that turneth after such as ... Lev 20:6 5315
even set my face against that *s* ... Lev 20:6 5315
that *s* shall be cut off from my ... Lev 22:3 5315
The *s* which hath touched any such ... Lev 22:6 5315
priest buy any *s* with his money ... Lev 22:11 5315
For whatsoever *s* it be that shall ... Lev 23:29 5315
whatsoever *s* it be that doeth any ... Lev 23:30 5315
the same *s* will I destroy from ... Lev 23:30 5315
and my *s* shall not abhor you ... Lev 26:11 5315
or if your *s* abhor my judgments, ... Lev 26:15 5315
idols, and my *s* shall abhor you ... Lev 26:30 5315
because their *s* abhorred my ... Lev 26:43 5315
even the same *s* shall be cut off ... Num 9:13 5315
But now our *s* is dried away ... Num 11:6 5315
if any *s* sin through ignorance, ... Num 15:27 5315
for the *s* that sinneth ignorantly ... Num 15:28 5315
But the *s* that doeth ought ... Num 15:30 5315
that *s* shall be cut off from ... Num 15:30 5315
that *s* shall utterly be cut off ... Num 15:31 5315
that *s* shall be cut off from ... Num 19:13 5315
that *s* shall be cut off from ... Num 19:20 5315
the *s* that toucheth it shall be ... Num 19:22 5315
the *s* of the people was much ... Num 21:4 5315
our *s* loatheth this light bread ... Num 21:5 5315
an oath to bind his *s* with a bond ... Num 30:2 5315
wherewith she hath bound her *s* ... Num 30:4 5315
she hath bound her *s* shall stand ... Num 30:4 5315
wherewith she hath bound her *s* ... Num 30:5 5315
lips, wherewith she bound her *s* ... Num 30:6 5315
she bound her *s* shall stand ... Num 30:7 5315
lips, wherewith she bound her *s* ... Num 30:8 5315
or bound her *s* by a bond with an ... Num 30:10 5315
she bound her *s* shall stand ... Num 30:11 5315
or concerning the bond of her *s* ... Num 30:12 5315
binding oath to afflict the *s* ... Num 30:13 5315
one *s* of five hundred, both of ... Num 31:28 5315
keep thy *s* diligently, lest thou ... Deut 4:9 5315
all thy heart and with all thy *s* ... Deut 4:29 5315
thine heart, and with all thy *s* ... Deut 6:5 5315
all thy heart and with all thy *s* ... Deut 10:12 5315
all your heart and with all your *s* ... Deut 11:13 5315
words in your heart and in your *s* ... Deut 11:18 5315
whatsoever thy *s* lusteth after ... Deut 12:15 5315
because thy *s* longeth to eat ... Deut 12:20 5315
whatsoever thy *s* lusteth after ... Deut 12:20 5315
whatsoever thy *s* lusteth after ... Deut 12:21 5315
all your heart and with all your *s* ... Deut 13:3 5315
friend, which is as thine own *s* ... Deut 13:6 5315
whatsoever thy *s* lusteth after ... Deut 14:26 5315
or for whatsoever thy *s* desireth ... Deut 14:26 5315
thine heart, and with all thy *s* ... Deut 26:16 5315
thine heart, and with all thy *s* ... Deut 30:2 5315
thine heart, and with all thy *s* ... Deut 30:6 5315
thine heart, and with all thy *s* ... Deut 30:10 5315
all your heart and with all your *s* ... Josh 22:5 5315
O my *s*, thou hast trodden down ... Judg 5:21 5315
his *s* was grieved for the misery ... Judg 10:16 5315
so that his *s* was vexed unto ... Judg 16:16 5315
And she was in bitterness of *s* ... 1Sa 1:10 5315
poured out my *s* before the LORD ... 1Sa 1:15 5315
said, Oh my lord, as thy *s* liveth ... 1Sa 1:26 5315
take as much as thy *s* desireth ... 1Sa 2:16 5315
And Abner said, As thy *s* liveth ... 1Sa 17:55 5315
that the *s* of Jonathan was knit ... 1Sa 18:1 5315
was knit with the *s* of David ... 1Sa 18:1 5315
Jonathan loved him as his own *s* ... 1Sa 18:1 5315
because he loved him as his own *s* ... 1Sa 18:3 5315
LORD liveth, and as thy *s* liveth ... 1Sa 20:3 5315
David, Whatsoever thy *s* desireth ... 1Sa 20:4 5315
loved him as he loved his own *s* ... 1Sa 20:17 5315
the desire of thy *s* to come down ... 1Sa 23:20 5315
yet thou huntest my *s* to take it ... 1Sa 24:11 5315
LORD liveth, and as thy *s* liveth ... 1Sa 25:26 5315
to pursue thee, and to seek thy *s* ... 1Sa 25:29 5315
but the *s* of my lord shall be ... 1Sa 25:29 5315
because my *s* was precious in ... 1Sa 26:21 5315
because the *s* of all the people ... 1Sa 30:6 5315
my *s* out of all adversity ... 2Sa 4:9 5315
that are hated of David's *s* ... 2Sa 5:8 5315
thou livest, and as thy *s* liveth ... 2Sa 11:11 5315
the *s* of king David longed to go ... 2Sa 13:39
answered and said, As thy *s* liveth ... 2Sa 14:19 5315
redeemed my *s* out of all distress ... 1Kin 1:29 5315
their heart and with all their *s* ... 1Kin 2:4 5315
their heart, and with all their *s* ... 1Kin 8:48 5315
to all that thy *s* desireth ... 1Kin 11:37 5315
let this child's *s* come into him ... 1Kin 17:21 5315
the *s* of the child came into him ... 1Kin 17:22 5315
LORD liveth, and as thy *s* liveth ... 2Kin 2:2 5315
LORD liveth, and as thy *s* liveth ... 2Kin 2:4 5315
LORD liveth, and as thy *s* liveth ... 2Kin 2:6 5315
for her *s* is vexed within her ... 2Kin 4:27 5315
LORD liveth, and as thy *s* liveth ... 2Kin 4:30 5315
all their heart and all their *s* ... 2Kin 23:3 5315
all his heart, and with all his *s* ... 2Kin 23:25 5315
your *s* to seek the LORD your God ... 1Chr 22:19 5315
with all their *s* in the land of ... 2Chr 6:38 5315
their heart and with all their *s* ... 2Chr 15:12 5315
all his heart, and with all his *s* ... 2Chr 34:31 5315
and life unto the bitter in *s* ... Job 3:20 5315
The things that my *s* refused to ... Job 6:7 5315
in the bitterness of my *s* ... Job 7:11 5315
So that my *s* chooseth strangling, ... Job 7:15 5315
yet would I not know my *s* ... Job 9:21 5315
My *s* is weary of my life ... Job 10:1 5315
speak in the bitterness of my *s* ... Job 10:1 5315
In whose hand is the *s* of every ... Job 12:10 5315
his *s* within him shall mourn ... Job 14:22 5315
if your *s* were in my soul's stead ... Job 16:4 5315
How long will ye vex my *s* ... Job 19:2 5315
dieth in the bitterness of his *s* ... Job 21:25 5315
And what his *s* desireth, even that ... Job 23:13 5315
the *s* of the wounded crieth out ... Job 24:12 5315
the Almighty, who hath vexed my *s* ... Job 27:2 5315
when God taketh away his *s* ... Job 27:8 5315
they pursue my *s* as the wind ... Job 30:15 5082
now my *s* is poured out upon me ... Job 30:16 5315
was not my *s* grieved for the poor ... Job 30:25 5315
sin by wishing a curse to his *s* ... Job 31:30 5315
keepeth back his *s* from the pit ... Job 33:18 5315
bread, and his *s* dainty meat ... Job 33:20 5315
his *s* draweth near unto the grave ... Job 33:22 5315
He will deliver his *s* from going ... Job 33:28 5315
To bring back his *s* from the pit ... Job 33:30 5315
Many there be which say of my *s* ... Ps 3:2 5315
My *s* is also sore vexed ... Ps 6:3 5315
Return, O LORD, deliver my *s* ... Ps 6:4 5315

Lest he tear my *s* like a lion ... Ps 7:2 5315
Let the enemy persecute my *s* ... Ps 7:5 5315
how say ye to my *s*, Flee as a ... Ps 11:1 5315
that loveth violence his *s* hateth ... Ps 11:5 5315
long shall I take counsel in my *s* ... Ps 13:2 5315
O my *s*, thou hast said unto the ... Ps 16:2
thou wilt not leave my *s* in hell ... Ps 16:10 5315
deliver my *s* from the wicked, ... Ps 17:13 5315
LORD is perfect, converting the *s* ... Ps 19:7 5315
Deliver my *s* from the sword ... Ps 22:20 5315
and none can keep alive his own *s* ... Ps 22:29 5315
He restoreth my *s* ... Ps 23:3 5315
not lifted up his *s* unto vanity ... Ps 24:4 5315
thee, O LORD, do I lift up my *s* ... Ps 25:1 5315
His *s* shall dwell at ease ... Ps 25:13 5315
O keep my *s*, and deliver me ... Ps 25:20 5315
Gather not my *s* with sinners ... Ps 26:9 5315
brought up my *s* from the grave ... Ps 30:3 5315
hast known my *s* in adversities ... Ps 31:7 5315
is consumed with grief, yea, my *s* ... Ps 31:9 5315
To deliver their *s* from death ... Ps 33:19 5315
Our *s* waiteth for the LORD ... Ps 33:20 5315
My *s* shall make her boast in the ... Ps 34:2 5315
redeemeth the *s* of his servants ... Ps 34:22 5315
say unto my *s*, I am thy salvation ... Ps 35:3 5315
put to shame that seek after my *s* ... Ps 35:4 5315
cause they have digged for my *s* ... Ps 35:7 5315
my *s* shall be joyful in the LORD ... Ps 35:9 5315
for good to the spoiling of my *s* ... Ps 35:12 5315
I humbled my *s* with fasting ... Ps 35:13 5315
rescue my *s* from their ... Ps 35:17 5315
seek after my *s* to destroy it ... Ps 40:14 5315
heal my *s* ... Ps 41:4 5315
so panteth my *s* after thee ... Ps 42:1 5315
My *s* thirsteth for God, for the ... Ps 42:2 5315
things, I pour out my *s* in me ... Ps 42:4 5315
Why art thou cast down, O my *s* ... Ps 42:5 5315
my *s* is cast down within me ... Ps 42:6 5315
Why art thou cast down, O my *s* ... Ps 42:11 5315
Why art thou cast down, O my *s* ... Ps 43:5 5315
For our *s* is bowed down to the ... Ps 44:25 5315
redemption of their *s* is precious ... Ps 49:8 5315
But God will redeem my *s* from the ... Ps 49:15 5315
while he lived he blessed his *s* ... Ps 49:18 5315
me, and oppressors seek after my *s* ... Ps 54:3 5315
is with them that uphold my *s* ... Ps 54:4 5315
He hath delivered my *s* in peace ... Ps 55:18 5315
my steps, when they wait for my *s* ... Ps 56:6 5315
hast delivered my *s* from death ... Ps 56:13 5315
for my *s* trusteth in thee ... Ps 57:1 5315
My *s* is among lions ... Ps 57:4 5315
my *s* is bowed down ... Ps 57:6 5315
lo, they lie in wait for my *s* ... Ps 59:3 5315
Truly my *s* waiteth upon God ... Ps 62:1 5315
My *s*, wait thou only upon God ... Ps 62:5 5315
my *s* thirsteth for thee, my flesh ... Ps 63:1 5315
My *s* shall be satisfied as with ... Ps 63:5 5315
My *s* followeth hard after thee ... Ps 63:8 5315
But those that seek my *s*, to ... Ps 63:9 5315
Which holdeth our *s* in life ... Ps 66:9 5315
what he hath done for my *s* ... Ps 66:16 5315
the waters are come in unto my *s* ... Ps 69:1 5315
and chastened my *s* with fasting ... Ps 69:10 5315
Draw nigh unto my *s*, and redeem it ... Ps 69:18 5315
confounded that seek after my *s* ... Ps 70:2 5315
for my *s* take counsel together ... Ps 71:10 5315
that are adversaries to my *s* ... Ps 71:13 5315
and my *s*, which thou hast redeemed ... Ps 71:23 5315
shall redeem their *s* from deceit ... Ps 72:14 5315
O deliver not the *s* of thy ... Ps 74:19 5315
my *s* refused to be comforted ... Ps 77:2 5315
he spared not their *s* from death ... Ps 78:50 5315
My *s* longeth, yea, even fainteth ... Ps 84:2 5315
Preserve my *s* ... Ps 86:2 5315
Rejoice the *s* of thy servant ... Ps 86:4 5315
thee, O Lord, do I lift up my *s* ... Ps 86:4 5315
my *s* from the lowest hell ... Ps 86:13 5315
men have sought after my *s* ... Ps 86:14 5315
For my *s* is full of troubles ... Ps 88:3 5315
LORD, why castest thou off my *s* ... Ps 88:14 5315
shall he deliver his *s* from the ... Ps 89:48 5315
my *s* had almost dwelt in silence ... Ps 94:17 5315
me thy comforts delight my *s* ... Ps 94:19 5315
against the *s* of the righteous ... Ps 94:21 5315
Bless the LORD, O my *s* ... Ps 103:1 5315
Bless the LORD, O my *s*, and forget ... Ps 103:2 5315
bless the LORD, O my *s* ... Ps 103:22 5315
Bless the LORD, O my *s* ... Ps 104:1 5315
Bless thou the LORD, O my *s* ... Ps 104:35 5315
but sent leanness into their *s* ... Ps 106:15 5315
thirsty, their *s* fainted in them ... Ps 107:5 5315
For he satisfieth the longing *s* ... Ps 107:9 5315
the hungry *s* with goodness ... Ps 107:9 5315
Their *s* abhorreth all manner of ... Ps 107:18 5315
their *s* is melted because of ... Ps 107:26 5315
them that speak evil against my *s* ... Ps 109:20 5315
him from those that condemn his *s* ... Ps 109:31 5315
I beseech thee, deliver my *s* ... Ps 116:4 5315
Return unto thy rest, O my *s* ... Ps 116:7 5315
hast delivered my *s* from death ... Ps 116:8 5315
My *s* breaketh for the longing ... Ps 119:20 5315
My *s* cleaveth unto the dust ... Ps 119:25 5315
My *s* melteth for heaviness ... Ps 119:28 5315
My *s* fainteth for thy salvation ... Ps 119:81 5315
My *s* is continually in my hand ... Ps 119:109 5315
therefore doth my *s* keep them ... Ps 119:129 5315
My *s* hath kept thy testimonies ... Ps 119:167 5315
Let my *s* live, and it shall praise ... Ps 119:175 5315
Deliver my *s*, O LORD, from lying ... Ps 120:2 5315
My *s* hath long dwelt with him ... Ps 120:6 5315
he shall preserve thy *s* ... Ps 121:7 5315
Our *s* is exceedingly filled with ... Ps 123:4 5315
the stream had gone over our *s* ... Ps 124:4 5315
proud waters had gone over our *s* ... Ps 124:5 5315
Our *s* is escaped as a bird out of ... Ps 124:7 5315
my *s* doth wait, and in his word do ... Ps 130:5 5315
My *s* waiteth for the Lord more ... Ps 130:6 5315
my *s* is even as a weaned child ... Ps 131:2 5315
me with strength in my *s* ... Ps 138:3 5315
that my *s* knoweth right well ... Ps 139:14 5315
leave not my *s* destitute ... Ps 141:8 5315
no man cared for my *s* ... Ps 142:4 5315
Bring my *s* out of prison, that I ... Ps 142:7 5315
the enemy hath persecuted my *s* ... Ps 143:3 5315
my *s* thirsteth after thee, as a ... Ps 143:6 5315
for I lift up my *s* unto thee ... Ps 143:8 5315
sake bring my *s* out of trouble ... Ps 143:11 5315
all them that afflict my *s* ... Ps 143:12 5315
Praise the LORD, O my *s* ... Ps 146:1 5315
knowledge is pleasant unto thy *s* ... Prov 2:10 5315
So shall they be life unto thy *s* ... Prov 3:22 5315
satisfy his *s* when he is hungry ... Prov 6:30 5315
doeth it destroyeth his own *s* ... Prov 6:32 5315
against me wrongeth his own *s* ... Prov 8:36 5315
the *s* of the righteous to famish ... Prov 10:3 5315
man doeth good to his own *s* ... Prov 11:17 5315
The liberal *s* shall be made fat ... Prov 11:25 5315
but the *s* of the transgressors ... Prov 13:2 5315
The *s* of the sluggard desireth, ... Prov 13:4 5315
but the *s* of the diligent shall ... Prov 13:4 5315
accomplished is sweet to the *s* ... Prov 13:19 5315
eateth to the satisfying of his *s* ... Prov 13:25 5315
instruction despiseth his own *s* ... Prov 15:32 5315
keepeth his way preserveth his *s* ... Prov 16:17 5315
as an honeycomb, sweet to the *s* ... Prov 16:24 5315
his lips are the snare of his *s* ... Prov 18:7 5315
that the *s* be without knowledge, ... Prov 19:2 5315
getteth wisdom loveth his own *s* ... Prov 19:8 5315
an idle *s* shall suffer hunger ... Prov 19:15 5315
the commandment keepeth his own *s* ... Prov 19:16 5315
let not thy *s* spare for his ... Prov 19:18 5315
anger sinneth against his own *s* ... Prov 20:2 5315
The *s* of the wicked desireth evil ... Prov 21:10 5315
keepeth his *s* from troubles ... Prov 21:23 5315
he that doth keep his *s* shall be ... Prov 22:5 5315
spoil the *s* of those that spoiled ... Prov 22:23 5315
his ways, and get a snare to thy *s* ... Prov 22:25 5315
and shalt deliver his *s* from hell ... Prov 23:14 5315
and he that keepeth thy *s*, doth ... Prov 24:12 5315
knowledge of wisdom be unto thy *s* ... Prov 24:14 5315
refresheth the *s* of his masters ... Prov 25:13 5315
As cold waters to a thirsty *s* ... Prov 25:25 5315
The full *s* loatheth an honeycomb ... Prov 27:7 5315
but to the hungry *s* every bitter ... Prov 27:7 5315
but the just seek his *s* ... Prov 29:10 5315
he shall give delight unto thy *s* ... Prov 29:17 5315
with a thief hateth his own *s* ... Prov 29:24 5315
that he should make his *s* enjoy ... Eccl 2:24 5315
I labour, and bereave my *s* of good ... Eccl 4:8 5315
for his *s* of all that he desireth ... Eccl 6:2 5315
his *s* be not filled with good, and ... Eccl 6:3 5315
Which yet my *s* seeketh, but I ... Eccl 7:28 5315
Tell me, O thou whom my *s* loveth ... Song 1:7 5315
bed I sought him whom my *s* loveth ... Song 3:1 5315
I will seek him whom my *s* loveth ... Song 3:2 5315
said, Saw ye him whom my *s* loveth ... Song 3:3 5315
but I found him whom my *s* loveth ... Song 3:4 5315
my *s* failed when he spake ... Song 5:6 5315
my *s* made me like the chariots of ... Song 6:12 5315
your appointed feasts my *s* hateth ... Is 1:14 5315
Woe unto their *s* ... Is 3:9 5315
and of his fruitful field, both *s* ... Is 10:18 5315
desire of our *s* is to thy name ... Is 26:8 5315
With my *s* have I desired thee in ... Is 26:9 5315
but he awaketh, and his *s* is empty ... Is 29:8 5315
is faint, and his *s* hath appetite ... Is 29:8 5315
to make empty the *s* of the hungry ... Is 32:6 5315
years in the bitterness of my *s* ... Is 38:15 5315
but thou hast in love to my *s* ... Is 38:17 5315
elect, in whom my *s* delighteth ... Is 42:1 5315
that he cannot deliver his *s* ... Is 44:20 5315
which have said to thy *s*, Bow ... Is 51:23 5315
make his *s* an offering for sin ... Is 53:10 5315
shall see of the travail of his *s* ... Is 53:11 5315
hath poured out his *s* unto death ... Is 53:12 5315
let your *s* delight itself in ... Is 55:2 5315
hear, and your *s* shall live ... Is 55:3 5315
wherefore have we afflicted our *s* ... Is 58:3 5315
a day for a man to afflict his *s* ... Is 58:5 5315
thou draw out thy *s* to the hungry ... Is 58:10 5315
and satisfy the afflicted *s* ... Is 58:10 5315
and satisfy thy *s* in drought ... Is 58:11 5315
my *s* shall be joyful in my God ... Is 61:10 5315
their *s* delighteth in their ... Is 66:3 5315
the sword reacheth unto the *s* ... Jer 4:10 5315
because thou hast heard, O my *s* ... Jer 4:19 5315
for my *s* is wearied because of ... Jer 4:31 5315
shall not my *s* be avenged on such ... Jer 5:9 5315
shall not my *s* be avenged on such ... Jer 5:29 5315
lest my *s* depart from thee ... Jer 6:8 5315
shall not my *s* be avenged on such ... Jer 9:9 5315
my *s* into the hand of her enemies ... Jer 12:7 5315
my *s* shall weep in secret places ... Jer 13:17 5315
hath thy *s* lothed Zion ... Jer 14:19 5315
they have digged a pit for my *s* ... Jer 18:20 5315
for he hath delivered the *s* of ... Jer 20:13 5315
their *s* shall be as a watered ... Jer 31:12 5315
I will satiate the *s* of the ... Jer 31:14 5315
For I have satiated the weary *s* ... Jer 31:25 5315
replenished every sorrowful *s* ... Jer 31:25 5315
my whole heart and with my whole *s* ... Jer 32:41 5315
LORD liveth, that made us this *s* ... Jer 38:16 5315
then thy *s* shall live, and this ... Jer 38:17 5315
unto thee, and thy *s* shall live ... Jer 38:20 5315
his *s* shall be satisfied upon ... Jer 50:19 5315
and deliver every man his *s* ... Jer 51:6 5315
deliver ye every man his *s* from ... Jer 51:45 5315
things for meat to relieve the *s* ... Lam 1:11 5315
relieve my *s* is far from me ... Lam 1:16 5315
when their *s* was poured out into ... Lam 2:12 5315
removed my *s* far off from peace ... Lam 3:17 5315
My *s* hath them still in ... Lam 3:20 5315
LORD is my portion, saith my *s* ... Lam 3:24 5315
to the *s* that seeketh him ... Lam 3:25 5315
hast pleaded the causes of my *s* ... Lam 3:58 5315
but thou hast delivered thy *s* ... Eze 3:19 5315
also thou hast delivered thy *s* ... Eze 3:21 5315
my *s* hath not been polluted ... Eze 4:14 5315
as the *s* of the father, so also ... Eze 18:4 5315
so also the *s* of the son is mine ... Eze 18:4 5315
the *s* that sinneth, it shall die ... Eze 18:4 5315
The *s* that sinneth, it shall die ... Eze 18:20 5315
right, he shall save his *s* alive ... Eze 18:27 5315
and that which your *s* pitieth ... Eze 24:21 5315
warning shall deliver his *s* ... Eze 33:5 5315
but thou hast delivered thy *s* ... Eze 33:9 5315
for their bread for their *s* shall ... Hos 9:4 5315
compassed me about, even to the *s* ... Jonah 2:5 5315
When my *s* fainted within me I ... Jonah 2:7 5315
of my body for the sin of my *s* ... Mic 6:7 5315
my *s* desired the firstripe fruit ... Mic 7:1 5315
his *s* which is lifted up is not ... Hab 2:4 5315
and hast sinned against thy *s* ... Hab 2:10 5315
my *s* lothed them ... Zec 11:8 5315
and their *s* also abhorred me ... Zec 11:8 5315
but are not able to kill the *s* ... Mt 10:28 5590
which is able to destroy both *s* ... Mt 10:28 5590
in whom my *s* is well pleased ... Mt 12:18 5590
whole world, and lose his own *s* ... Mt 16:26 5590
a man give in exchange for his *s* ... Mt 16:26 5590
all thy heart, and with all thy *s* ... Mt 22:37 5590
My *s* is exceeding sorrowful, even ... Mt 26:38 5590
whole world, and lose his own *s* ... Mk 8:36 5590
a man give in exchange for his *s* ... Mk 8:37 5590
all thy heart, and with all thy *s* ... Mk 12:30 5590
understanding, and with all the *s* ... Mk 12:33 5590
My *s* is exceeding sorrowful unto ... Mk 14:34 5590
My *s* doth magnify the Lord, ... Lk 1:46 5590
pierce through thy own *s* also ... Lk 2:35 5590
all thy heart, and with all thy *s* ... Lk 10:27 5590
And I will say to my *s*, *S*, thou ... Lk 12:19 5590
And I will say to my *s*, *S* ... Lk 12:19 5590
this night thy *s* shall be ... Lk 12:20 5590
Now is my *s* troubled ... Jn 12:27 5590
thou wilt not leave my *s* in hell ... Acts 2:27 5590
that his *s* was not left in hell, ... Acts 2:31 5590
And fear came upon every *s* ... Acts 2:43 5590
shall come to pass, that every *s* ... Acts 3:23 5590
were of one heart and of one *s* ... Acts 4:32 5590
upon every *s* of man that doeth ... Rom 2:9 5590
Let every *s* be subject unto the ... Rom 13:1 5590
man Adam was made a living *s* ... 1Cor 15:45 5590
I call God for a record upon my *s* ... 2Cor 1:23 5590
I pray God your whole spirit and *s* ... 1Th 5:23 5590
even to the dividing asunder of *s* ... Heb 4:12 5590
we have as an anchor of the *s* ... Heb 6:19 5590
my *s* shall have no pleasure in ... Heb 10:38 5590
believe to the saving of the *s* ... Heb 10:39 5590
his way shall save a *s* from death ... Jas 5:20 5590
lusts, which war against the *s* ... 1Pet 2:11 5590
vexed his righteous *s* from day to ... 2Pet 2:8 5590
health, even as thy *s* prospereth ... 3Jn 2 5590
every living *s* died in the sea ... Rev 16:3 5590
the fruits that thy *s* lusted ... Rev 18:14 5590

SOUL'S {1}

if your soul were in my *s* stead ... Job 16:4 5315

SOULS {78}

the *s* that they had gotten in ... Gen 12:5 5315
all the *s* of his sons and his ... Gen 46:15 5315
bare unto Jacob, even sixteen *s* ... Gen 46:18 5315
all the *s* were fourteen ... Gen 46:22 5315
all the *s* were seven ... Gen 46:25 5315
All the *s* that came with Jacob ... Gen 46:26 5315
all the *s* were threescore and six ... Gen 46:26 5315
born him in Egypt, were two *s* ... Gen 46:27 5315
all the *s* of the house of Jacob, ... Gen 46:27 5315
all the *s* that came out of the ... Ex 1:5 5315
the loins of Jacob were seventy *s* ... Ex 1:5 5315
according to the number of the *s* ... Ex 12:4 5315
to make an atonement for your *s* ... Ex 30:15 5315
to make an atonement for your *s* ... Ex 30:16 5315
month, ye shall afflict your *s* ... Lev 16:29 5315
you, and ye shall afflict your *s* ... Lev 16:31 5315
to make an atonement for your *s* ... Lev 17:11 5315
even the *s* that commit them shall ... Lev 18:29 5315
make your *s* abominable by beast ... Lev 20:25 5315
and ye shall afflict your *s* ... Lev 23:27 5315
rest, and ye shall afflict your *s* ... Lev 23:32 5315
these sinners against their own *s* ... Num 16:38 5315
and ye shall afflict your *s* ... Num 29:7 5315
wherewith they have bound their *s* ... Num 30:9 5315
for our *s* before the LORD ... Num 31:50 5315
all the *s* that were therein ... Josh 10:28 5315

S

all the *s* that were therein ... Josh 10:30 5315
all the *s* that were therein, ... Josh 10:32 5315
all the *s* that were therein he ... Josh 10:35 5315
all the *s* that were therein ... Josh 10:37 5315
all the *s* that were therein ... Josh 10:37 5315
all the *s* that were therein ... Josh 10:39 5315
they smote all the *s* that were ... Josh 11:11 5315
all your hearts and in all your *s* ... Josh 23:14 5315
the *s* of thine enemies, them ... 1Sa 25:29 5315
and shall save the *s* of the needy ... Ps 72:13 5315
he preserveth the *s* of his saints ... Ps 97:10 5315
and he that winneth *s* is wise ... Prov 11:30 5315
A true witness delivereth *s* ... Prov 14:25 5315
me, and the *s* which I have made ... Is 57:16 5397
of the *s* of the poor innocents ... Jer 2:34 5315
and ye shall find rest for your *s* ... Jer 6:16 5315
procure great evil against our *s* ... Jer 26:19 5315
ye this great evil against your *s* ... Jer 44:7 5315
their meat to relieve their *s* ... Lam 1:19 5315
they shall not satisfy their *s* ... Eze 7:19 5315
head of every stature to hunt *s* ... Eze 13:18 5315
Will ye hunt the *s* of my people ... Eze 13:18 5315
will ye save the *s* alive that ... Eze 13:18 5315
to slay the *s* that should not die ... Eze 13:19 5315
to save the *s* alive that should ... Eze 13:19 5315
there hunt the *s* to make them fly ... Eze 13:20 5315
your arms, and will let the *s* go ... Eze 13:20 5315
even the *s* that ye hunt to make ... Eze 13:20 5315
own *s* by their righteousness ... Eze 14:14 5315
own *s* by their righteousness ... Eze 14:20 5315
Behold, all *s* are mine ... Eze 18:4 5315
they have devoured *s* ... Eze 22:25 5315
to shed blood, and to destroy *s* ... Eze 22:27 5315
and ye shall find rest unto your *s* ... Mt 11:29 *5590*
your patience possess ye your *s* ... Lk 21:19 *5590*
unto them about three thousand *s* ... Acts 2:41 *5590*
kindred, threescore and fifteen *s* ... Acts 7:14 *5590*
Confirming the *s* of the disciples ... Acts 14:22 *5590*
you with words, subverting your *s* ... Acts 15:24 *5590*
hundred threescore and sixteen *s* ... Acts 27:37 *5590*
of God only, but also our own *s* ... 1Th 2:8 *5590*
for they watch for your *s* ... Heb 13:17 *5590*
which is able to save your *s* ... Jas 1:21 *5590*
even the salvation of your *s* ... 1Pet 1:9 *5590*
s in obeying the truth through ... 1Pet 1:22 *5590*
the Shepherd and Bishop of your *s* ... 1Pet 2:25 *5590*
eight *s* were saved by water ... 1Pet 3:20 *5590*
of their *s* to him in well doing ... 1Pet 4:19 *5590*
beguiling unstable *s* ... 2Pet 2:14 *5590*
I saw under the altar the *s* of ... Rev 6:9 *5590*
chariots, and slaves, and *s* of men ... Rev 18:13 *5590*
I saw the *s* of them that were ... Rev 20:4 *5590*

SOUND {89}

his *s* shall be heard when he ... Ex 28:35 6963
the trumpet of the jubile to *s* on ... Lev 25:9 5674
s throughout all your land ... Lev 25:9 5674
the *s* of a shaken leaf shall ... Lev 26:36 6963
blow, but ye shall not *s* an alarm ... Num 10:7 7321
when ye hear the *s* of the trumpet ... Josh 6:5 6963
people heard the *s* of the trumpet ... Josh 6:20 6963
when thou hearest the *s* of a ... 2Sa 5:24 6963
with the *s* of the trumpet ... 2Sa 6:15 6963
as ye hear the *s* of the trumpet ... 2Sa 15:10 6963
the earth rent with the *s* of them ... 1Kin 1:40 6963
Joab heard the *s* of the trumpet ... 1Kin 1:41 6963
Ahijah heard the *s* of her feet ... 1Kin 14:6 6963
for there is a *s* of abundance of ... 1Kin 18:41 6963
is not the *s* of his master's feet ... 2Kin 6:32 6963
when thou shalt hear a *s* of going ... 1Chr 14:15 6963
were appointed to *s* with cymbals ... 1Chr 15:19 8085
with *s* of the cornet, and with ... 1Chr 15:28 6963
but Asaph made a *s* with cymbals ... 1Chr 16:5 8085
for those that should make a *s* ... 1Chr 16:42 8085
to make one *s* to be heard in ... 2Chr 5:13 6963
ye hear the *s* of the trumpet ... Neh 4:20 6963
A dreadful *s* is in his ears ... Job 15:21 6963
and rejoice at the *s* of the organ ... Job 21:12 6963
the *s* that goeth out of his mouth ... Job 37:2 1899
that it is the *s* of the trumpet ... Job 39:24 6963
the LORD with the *s* of a trumpet ... Ps 47:5 6963
the skies sent out a *s* ... Ps 77:17 6963
the people that know the joyful *s* ... Ps 89:15 8643
upon the harp with a solemn *s* ... Ps 92:3 1902
s of cornet make a joyful noise ... Ps 98:6 6963
Let my heart be *s* in thy statutes ... Ps 119:80 8549
him with the *s* of the trumpet ... Ps 150:3 8629
He layeth up *s* wisdom for the ... Prov 2:7 8454
keep *s* wisdom and discretion ... Prov 3:21 8454
Counsel is mine, and *s* wisdom ... Prov 8:14 8454
A *s* heart is the life of the ... Prov 14:30 4832
when the *s* of the grinding is low ... Eccl 12:4 6963
shall *s* like an harp for Moab ... Is 16:11 1993
the *s* of the trumpet, the alarm ... Jer 4:19 6963
hear the *s* of the trumpet ... Jer 4:21 6963
Hearken to the *s* of the trumpet ... Jer 6:17 6963
s of the neighing of his strong ... Jer 8:16 6963
the *s* of the millstones, and the ... Jer 25:10 6963
nor hear the *s* of the trumpet, ... Jer 42:14 6963
heart shall *s* for Moab like pipes ... Jer 48:36 1993
mine heart shall *s* like pipes for ... Jer 48:36 1993
A *s* of battle is in the land, and ... Jer 50:22 6963
A *s* of a cry cometh from Babylon, ... Jer 51:54 6963
the *s* of the cherubims' wings was ... Eze 10:5 6963
the *s* of thy harps shall be no ... Eze 26:13 6963
isles shake at the *s* of thy fall ... Eze 26:15 6963
at the *s* of the cry of thy pilots ... Eze 27:28 6963
to shake at the *s* of his fall ... Eze 31:16 6963
heareth the *s* of the trumpet ... Eze 33:4 6963
He heard the *s* of the trumpet, and ... Eze 33:5 6963
time ye hear the *s* of the cornet ... Dan 3:5 7032
people heard the *s* of the cornet ... Dan 3:7 7032
shall hear the *s* of the cornet ... Dan 3:10 7032
time ye hear the *s* of the cornet ... Dan 3:15 7032
s an alarm in my holy mountain ... Joel 2:1 7321
with the *s* of the trumpet ... Amos 2:2 6963
That chant to the *s* of the viol ... Amos 6:5 6310
do not *s* a trumpet before thee, ... Mt 6:2 *4537*
with a great *s* of a trumpet ... Mt 24:31 *5456*
he hath received him safe and *s* ... Lk 15:27 *5198*
and thou hearest the *s* thereof ... Jn 3:8 *5456*
suddenly there came a *s* from ... Acts 2:2 *2279*
their *s* went into all the earth, ... Rom 10:18 *5353*
even things without life giving *s* ... 1Cor 14:7 *5456*
the trumpet give an uncertain *s* ... 1Cor 14:8 *5456*
for the trumpet shall *s*, and the ... 1Cor 15:52 *4537*
that is contrary to *s* doctrine ... 1Ti 1:10 *5198*
power, and of love, and of a *s* mind ... 2Ti 1:7 *4995*
Hold fast the form of *s* words ... 2Ti 1:13 *5198*
they will not endure *s* doctrine ... 2Ti 4:3 *5198*
that he may be able by *s* doctrine ... Titus 1:9 *5198*
that they may be *s* in the faith ... Titus 1:13 *5198*
things which become *s* doctrine ... Titus 2:1 *5198*
s in faith, in charity, in ... Titus 2:2 *5198*
S speech, that cannot be ... Titus 2:8 *5199*
the *s* of a trumpet, and the voice ... Heb 12:19 *2279*
his voice as the *s* of many waters ... Rev 1:15 *5456*
trumpets prepared themselves to *s* ... Rev 8:6 *4537*
three angels, which are yet to *s* ... Rev 8:13 *4537*
the *s* of their wings was as the ... Rev 9:9 *5456*
the *s* of chariots of many horses ... Rev 9:9 *5456*
angel, when he shall begin to *s* ... Rev 10:7 *4537*
the *s* of a millstone shall be ... Rev 18:22 *5456*

SOUNDED {18}

the voice of the trumpet *s* long ... Ex 19:19
when I have *s* my father about to ... 1Sa 20:12 2713
the priests *s* trumpets before ... 2Chr 7:6 2690
the priests *s* with the trumpets ... 2Chr 13:14 2690
s with trumpets, also the singers ... 2Chr 23:13 8628
singers sang, and the trumpeters *s* ... 2Chr 29:28 2690
he that *s* the trumpet was by me ... Neh 4:18 8628
of thy salutation *s* in mine ears ... Lk 1:44 *1096*
And *s*, and found it twenty fathoms ... Acts 27:28 *1001*
they *s* again, and found it fifteen ... Acts 27:28 *1001*
For from you *s* out the word of ... 1Th 1:8 *1837*
The first angel *s*, and there ... Rev 8:7 *4537*
And the second angel *s*, and as it ... Rev 8:8 *4537*
And the third angel *s*, and there ... Rev 8:10 *4537*
And the fourth angel *s*, and the ... Rev 8:12 *4537*
And the fifth angel *s*, and I saw a ... Rev 9:1 *4537*
And the sixth angel *s*, and I heard ... Rev 9:13 *4537*
And the seventh angel *s* ... Rev 11:15 *4537*

SOUNDETH {1}

when the trumpet *s* long, they ... Ex 19:13

SOUNDING {7}

psalteries and harps and cymbals, *s* ... 1Chr 15:16 8085
and twenty priests *s* with trumpets ... 2Chr 5:12 2690
his priests with *s* trumpets to ... 2Chr 13:12 8643
him upon the high *s* cymbals ... Ps 150:5 8643
the *s* of thy bowels and of thy ... Is 63:15 1995
not the *s* again of the mountains ... Eze 7:7 1906
charity, I am become as *s* brass ... 1Cor 13:1 *2278*

SOUNDNESS {4}

There is no *s* in my flesh because ... Ps 38:3 4974
and there is no *s* in my flesh ... Ps 38:7 4974
unto the head there is no *s* in it ... Is 1:6 4974
s in the presence of you all ... Acts 3:16 *3647*

SOUNDS {1}

they give a distinction in the *s* ... 1Cor 14:7 *5353*

SOUR {5}

the *s* grape is ripening in the ... Is 18:5 1155
The fathers have eaten a *s* grape ... Jer 31:29 1155
every man that eateth the *s* grape ... Jer 31:30 1155
The fathers have eaten *s* grapes ... Eze 18:2 1155
Their drink is *s* ... Hos 4:18 5493

SOUTH {143}

going on still toward the *s* ... Gen 12:9 5045
had, and Lot with him, into the *s* ... Gen 13:1 5045
from the *s* even to Beth-el ... Gen 13:3 5045
from thence toward the *s* country ... Gen 20:1 5045
for he dwelt in the *s* country ... Gen 24:62 5045
and to the north, and to the *s* ... Gen 28:14 5045
boards on the *s* side southward ... Ex 26:18 5045
of the tabernacle toward the *s* ... Ex 26:35 8486
for the *s* side southward there ... Ex 27:9 5045
boards for the *s* side southward ... Ex 36:23 5045
on the *s* side southward the ... Ex 38:9 5045
On the *s* side shall be the ... Num 2:10 8486
s side shall take their journey ... Num 10:6 8486
And they ascended by the *s* ... Num 13:22 5045
dwell in the land of the *s* ... Num 13:29 5045
Canaanite, which dwelt in the *s* ... Num 21:1 5045
which dwelt in the *s* in the land ... Num 33:40 5045
Then your *s* quarter shall be from ... Num 34:3 5045
your *s* border shall be the ... Num 34:3 5045
the *s* to the ascent of Akrabbim ... Num 34:4 5045
be from the *s* to Kadesh-barnea ... Num 34:4 5045
on the *s* side two thousand cubits ... Num 35:5 5045
and in the vale, and in the *s* ... Deut 1:7 5045
possess thou the west and the *s* ... Deut 33:23 1864
And the *s*, and the plain of the ... Deut 34:3 5045
country of the hills, and of the *s* ... Josh 10:40 5045
and of the plains *s* of Chinneroth ... Josh 11:2 5045
the hills, and all the *s* country ... Josh 11:16 5045
and from the *s*, under ... Josh 12:3 8486
wilderness, and in the *s* country ... Josh 12:8 5045
From the *s*, all the land of the ... Josh 13:4 8486
the uttermost part of the *s* coast ... Josh 15:1 5045
their *s* border was from the shore ... Josh 15:2 5045
it went out to the *s* side to ... Josh 15:3 5045
ascended up on the *s* side unto ... Josh 15:3 5045
this shall be your *s* coast ... Josh 15:4 5045
which is on the *s* side of the ... Josh 15:7 5045
unto the *s* side of the Jebusite ... Josh 15:8 5045
for thou hast given me a *s* land ... Josh 15:19 5045
abide in their coast on the *s* ... Josh 18:5 5045
s side of the nether Beth-horon ... Josh 18:13 5045
the *s* quarter was from the end of ... Josh 18:15 5045
to the side of Jebusi on the *s* ... Josh 18:16 5045
salt sea at the *s* end of Jordan ... Josh 18:19 5045
this was the *s* coast ... Josh 18:19 5045
to Baalath-beer, Ramath of the *s* ... Josh 19:8 5045
reacheth to Zebulun on the *s* side ... Josh 19:34 5045
in the mountain, and in the *s* ... Judg 1:9 5045
for thou hast given me a *s* land ... Judg 1:15 5045
which lieth in the *s* of Arad ... Judg 1:16 5045
Shechem, and on the *s* of Lebonah ... Judg 21:19 5045
arose out of a place toward the *s* ... 1Sa 20:41 5045
which is on the *s* of Jeshimon ... 1Sa 23:19 3225
in the plain on the *s* of Jeshimon ... 1Sa 23:24 3225
said, Against the *s* of Judah ... 1Sa 27:10 5045
of Judah, and against the *s* of the ... 1Sa 27:10 5045
against the *s* of the Kenites ... 1Sa 27:10 5045
the Amalekites had invaded the *s* ... 1Sa 30:1 5045
upon the *s* of the Cherethites ... 1Sa 30:14 5045
to Judah, and upon the *s* of Caleb ... 1Sa 30:14 5045
and to them which were in *s* Ramoth ... 1Sa 30:27 5045
they went out to the *s* of Judah ... 2Sa 24:7 5045
and three looking toward the *s* ... 1Kin 7:25 5045
house eastward over against the *s* ... 1Kin 7:39 5045
the east, west, north, and *s* ... 1Chr 9:24 5045
and three looking toward the *s* ... 2Chr 4:4 5045
the east end, over against the *s* ... 2Chr 4:10 5045
of the *s* of Judah, and had taken ... 2Chr 28:18 5045
and the chambers of the *s* ... Job 9:9 8486
Out of the *s* cometh the whirlwind ... Job 37:9 2315
quieteth the earth by the *s* wind ... Job 37:17 1864
and stretch her wings toward the *s* ... Job 39:26 8486
nor from the west, nor from the *s* ... Ps 75:6 4057
power he brought in the *s* wind ... Ps 78:26 8486
the *s* thou hast created them ... Ps 89:12 3225
from the north, and from the *s* ... Ps 107:3 3220
O LORD, as the streams in the *s* ... Ps 126:4 5045
The wind goeth toward the *s* ... Eccl 1:6 1864
and if the tree fall toward the *s* ... Eccl 11:3 1864
and come, thou *s* ... Song 4:16 8486
whirlwinds in the *s* pass through ... Is 21:1 5045
The burden of the beasts of the *s* ... Is 30:6 5045
and to the *s*, Keep not back ... Is 43:6 8486
cities of the *s* shall be shut up ... Jer 13:19 5045
from the mountains, and from the *s* ... Jer 17:26 5045
valley, and in the cities of the *s* ... Jer 32:44 5045
vale, and in the cities of the *s* ... Jer 33:13 5045
of man, set thy face toward the *s* ... Eze 20:46 8486
and drop thy word toward the *s* ... Eze 20:46 1864
against the forest of the *s* field ... Eze 20:46 5045
And say to the forest of the *s* ... Eze 20:47 5045
all faces from the *s* to the north ... Eze 20:47 5045
all flesh from the *s* to the north ... Eze 21:4 5045
as the frame of a city on the *s* ... Eze 40:2 5045
that he brought me toward the *s* ... Eze 40:24 1864
and behold a gate toward the *s* ... Eze 40:24 1864
in the inner court toward the *s* ... Eze 40:27 1864
toward the *s* an hundred cubits ... Eze 40:27 1864
to the inner court by the *s* gate ... Eze 40:28 1864
he measured the *s* gate according ... Eze 40:28 1864
their prospect was toward the *s* ... Eze 40:44 1864
whose prospect is toward the *s* ... Eze 40:45 1864
and another door toward the *s* ... Eze 41:11 1864
s was a door in the head of the ... Eze 42:12 1864
the *s* chambers, which are before ... Eze 42:13 1864
He measured the *s* side, five ... Eze 42:18 1864
go out by the way of the *s* gate ... Eze 46:9 5045
s gate shall go forth by the way ... Eze 46:9 5045
at the *s* side of the altar ... Eze 47:1 5045
the *s* side southward, from Tamar ... Eze 47:19 5045
this is the *s* side southward ... Eze 47:19 8486
in breadth, and toward the *s* five ... Eze 48:10 5045
the *s* side four thousand and five ... Eze 48:16 5045
toward the *s* two hundred and fifty ... Eze 48:17 5045
at the *s* side southward, the ... Eze 48:28 5045
at the *s* side four thousand and ... Eze 48:33 5045
exceeding great, toward the *s* ... Dan 8:9 5045
the king of the *s* shall be strong ... Dan 11:5 5045
s shall come to the king of the ... Dan 11:6 5045
So the king of the *s* shall come ... Dan 11:9 5045
the king of the *s* shall be moved ... Dan 11:11 5045
up against the king of the *s* ... Dan 11:14 5045
the arms of the *s* shall not ... Dan 11:15 5045
king of the *s* with a great army ... Dan 11:25 5045
the king of the *s* shall be ... Dan 11:25 5045
return, and come toward the *s* ... Dan 11:29 5045
the king of the *s* push at him ... Dan 11:40 5045
they of the *s* shall possess the ... Obad 19 5045
shall possess the cities of the *s* ... Obad 20 5045
go forth toward the *s* country ... Zec 6:6 8486
her, when men inhabited the *s* ... Zec 7:7 5045
shall go with whirlwinds of the *s* ... Zec 9:14 8486
north, and half of it toward the *s* ... Zec 14:4 5045
Geba to Rimmon *s* of Jerusalem ... Zec 14:10 5045
The queen of the *s* shall rise up ... Mt 12:42 *3558*

The queen of the *s* shall rise up ... Lk 11:31 *3558*
And when ye see the *s* wind blow ... Lk 12:55 *3558*
and from the north, and from the *s* ... Lk 13:29 *3558*
go toward the *s* unto the way that ... Acts 8:26 *3314*
Crete, and lieth toward the *s* west ... Acts 27:12 *3047*
when the *s* wind blew softly, ... Acts 27:13 *3558*
and after one day the *s* wind blew ... Acts 28:13 *3558*
on the *s* three gates ... Rev 21:13 *3558*

SOUTHWARD {24}
where thou art northward, and *s* ... Gen 13:14 5045
twenty boards on the south side *s* ... Ex 26:18 8486
for the south side *s* there shall ... Ex 27:9 8486
boards for the south side *s* ... Ex 36:23 8486
on the south side *s* the hangings ... Ex 38:9 8486
on the side of the tabernacle *s* ... Ex 40:24 5045
on the side of the tabernacle *s* ... Num 3:29 8486
unto them, Get you up this way *s* ... Num 13:17 5045
eyes westward, and northward, and *s* ... Deut 3:27 8486
s was the uttermost part of the ... Josh 15:1 8486
sea, from the bay that looketh *s* ... Josh 15:2 5045
the coast of Edom *s* were Kabzeel ... Josh 15:21 5045
the river Kanah, *s* of the river ... Josh 17:9 5045
S it was Ephraim's, and northward ... Josh 17:10 5045
side of Luz, which is Beth-el, *s* ... Josh 18:13 5045
compassed the corner of the sea *s* ... Josh 18:14 5045
that lieth before Beth-horon *s* ... Josh 18:14 5045
the other *s* over against Gibeah ... 1Sa 14:5 5045
To Obed-edom *s* ... 1Chr 26:15 5045
s four a day, and toward Asuppim ... 1Chr 26:17 5045
And the south side *s*, from Tamar ... Eze 47:19 5045
And this is the south side *s* ... Eze 47:19 5045
of Gad, at the south side *s* ... Eze 48:28 5045
westward, and northward, and *s* ... Dan 8:4 5045

SOW {37}
for you, and ye shall *s* the land ... Gen 47:23 2232
six years thou shalt *s* thy land ... Ex 23:10 2232
thou shalt not *s* thy field with ... Lev 19:19 2232
Six years thou shalt *s* thy field ... Lev 25:3 2232
thou shalt neither *s* thy field ... Lev 25:4 2232
ye shall not *s*, neither reap that ... Lev 25:11 2232
behold, we shall not *s*, nor ... Lev 25:20 2232
ye shall *s* the eighth year, and ... Lev 25:22 2232
ye shall *s* your seed in vain, for ... Lev 26:16 2232
Thou shalt not *s* thy vineyard ... Deut 22:9 2232
and in the third year *s* ye ... 2Kin 19:29 2232
s wickedness, reap the same ... Job 4:8 2232
Then let me *s*, and let another eat ... Job 31:8 2232
s the fields, and plant vineyards, ... Ps 107:37 2232
They that *s* in tears shall reap ... Ps 126:5 2232
observeth the wind shall not *s* ... Eccl 11:4 2232
In the morning *s* thy seed ... Eccl 11:6 2232
the plowman plow all day to *s* ... Is 28:24 2232
that thou shalt *s* the ground ... Is 30:23 2232
are ye that *s* beside all waters ... Is 32:20 2232
and in the third year *s* ye ... Is 37:30 2232
ground, and *s* not among thorns ... Jer 4:3 2232
that I will *s* the house of Israel ... Jer 31:27 2232
nor *s* seed, nor plant vineyard, ... Jer 35:7 2232
I will *s* her unto me in the earth ... Hos 2:23 2232
S to yourselves in righteousness, ... Hos 10:12 2232
Thou shalt *s*, but thou shalt not ... Mic 6:15 2232
I will *s* them among the people ... Zec 10:9 2232
for they *s* not, neither do they ... Mt 6:26 *4687*
Behold, a sower went forth to *s* ... Mt 13:3 *4687*
didst not thou *s* good seed in thy ... Mt 13:27 *4687*
there went out a sower to *s* ... Mk 4:3 *4687*
A sower went out to *s* his seed ... Lk 8:5 *4687*
for they neither *s* nor reap ... Lk 12:24 *4687*
and reapest that thou didst not *s* ... Lk 19:21 *4687*
down, and reaping that I did not *s* ... Lk 19:22 *4687*
the *s* that was washed to her ... 2Pet 2:22 *5300*

SOWED {10}
Then Isaac *s* in that land, and ... Gen 26:12 2232
down the city, and *s* it with salt ... Judg 9:45 2232
And when he *s*, some seeds fell by ... Mt 13:4 *4687*
which *s* good seed in his field ... Mt 13:24 *4687*
s tares among the wheat, and went ... Mt 13:25 *4687*
a man took, and *s* in his field ... Mt 13:31 *4687*
The enemy that *s* them is the ... Mt 13:39 *4687*
knewest that I reap where I *s* not ... Mt 25:26 *4687*
And it came to pass, as he *s* ... Mk 4:4 *4687*
and as he *s*, some fell by the way ... Lk 8:5 *4687*

SOWEDST {1}
came out, where thou *s* thy seed ... Deut 11:10 2232

SOWER {8}
that it may give seed to the *s* ... Is 55:10 2232
Cut off the *s* from Babylon, and ... Jer 50:16 2232
Behold, a *s* went forth to sow ... Mt 13:3 *4687*
ye therefore the parable of the *s* ... Mt 13:18 *4687*
Behold, there went out a *s* to sow ... Mk 4:3 *4687*
The *s* soweth the word ... Mk 4:14 *4687*
A *s* went out to sow his seed ... Lk 8:5 *4687*
s both minister bread for your ... 2Cor 9:10 *4687*

SOWEST {3}
fool, that which thou *s* is not ... 1Cor 15:36 *4687*
And that which thou *s* ... 1Cor 15:37 *4687*
thou *s* not that body that shall ... 1Cor 15:37 *4687*

SOWETH {15}
he *s* discord ... Prov 6:14 7971
he that *s* discord among brethren ... Prov 6:19 7971
but to him that *s* righteousness ... Prov 11:18 2232
A froward man *s* strife ... Prov 16:28 7971
He that *s* iniquity shall reap ... Prov 22:8 2232
treader of grapes him that *s* seed ... Amos 9:13 4900
He that *s* the good seed is the ... Mt 13:37 *4687*
The sower *s* the word ... Mk 4:14 *4687*
that both he that *s* and he that ... Jn 4:36 *4687*
herein is that saying true, One *s* ... Jn 4:37 *4687*
He which *s* sparingly shall reap ... 2Cor 9:6 *4687*
he which *s* bountifully shall reap ... 2Cor 9:6 *4687*
for whatsoever a man *s*, that ... Gal 6:7 *4687*
For he that *s* to his flesh shall ... Gal 6:8 *4687*
but he that *s* to the Spirit shall ... Gal 6:8 *4687*

SOWING {2}
any *s* seed which is to be sown ... Lev 11:37 2221
shall reach unto the *s* time ... Lev 26:5 2233

SOWN {32}
which thou hast *s* in the field ... Ex 23:16 2232
any sowing seed which is to be *s* ... Lev 11:37 2232
which is neither eared nor *s* ... Deut 21:4 2232
of thy seed which thou hast *s* ... Deut 22:9 2232
and burning, that it is not *s* ... Deut 29:23 2232
And so it was, when Israel had *s* ... Judg 6:3 2232
Light is *s* for the righteous, and ... Ps 97:11 2232
every thing *s* by the brooks, ... Is 19:7 4218
yea, they shall not be *s* ... Is 40:24 2232
that are *s* in it to spring forth ... Is 61:11 2221
in a land that was not *s* ... Jer 2:2 2232
They have *s* wheat, but shall reap ... Jer 12:13 2232
you, and ye shall be tilled and *s* ... Eze 36:9 2232
For they have *s* the wind, and they ... Hos 8:7 2232
that no more of thy name be *s* ... Nah 1:14 2232
Ye have *s* much, and bring in ... Hag 1:6 2232
that which was *s* in his heart ... Mt 13:19 *4687*
reaping where thou hast not *s* ... Mt 25:24 *4687*
the way side, where the word is *s* ... Mk 4:15 *4687*
word that was *s* in their hearts ... Mk 4:15 *4687*
which are *s* on stony ground ... Mk 4:16 *4687*
are they which are *s* among thorns ... Mk 4:18 *4687*
they which are *s* on good ground ... Mk 4:20 *4687*
when it is *s* in the earth, is ... Mk 4:31 *4687*
But when it is *s*, it groweth up, ... Mk 4:32 *4687*
If we have *s* unto you spiritual ... 1Cor 9:11 *4687*
It is *s* in corruption ... 1Cor 15:42 *4687*
It is *s* in dishonour ... 1Cor 15:43 *4687*
it is *s* in weakness ... 1Cor 15:43 *4687*
It is *s* a natural body ... 1Cor 15:44 *4687*
food, and multiply your seed *s* ... 2Cor 9:10
is *s* in peace of them that make ... Jas 3:18 *4687*

SPACE {27}
abode with him the *s* of a month ... Gen 29:14 3117
put a *s* betwixt drove and drove ... Gen 32:16 7305
the *s* of the seven sabbaths of ... Lev 25:8 3117
within the *s* of a full year ... Lev 25:30 4390
the *s* in which we came from ... Deut 2:14 3117
there shall be a *s* between you ... Josh 3:4 7350
a great *s* being between them ... 1Sa 26:13 4725
now for a little *s* grace hath ... Ezr 9:8 7281
within the *s* of two full years ... Jer 28:11 5750
The *s* also before the little ... Eze 40:12 1366
the *s* was one cubit on that side ... Eze 40:12 1366
about the *s* of one hour after ... Lk 22:59 *1339*
it was about the *s* of three hours ... Acts 5:7 *1292*
put the apostles forth a little *s* ... Acts 5:34 *1024*
sacrifices by the *s* of forty ... Acts 7:42
about the *s* of four hundred ... Acts 13:20
Benjamin, by the *s* of forty years ... Acts 13:21
after they had tarried there a *s* ... Acts 15:33 *5550*
boldly for the *s* of three months ... Acts 19:8 *1909*
continued by the *s* of two years ... Acts 19:10 *1909*
the *s* of two hours cried out ... Acts 19:34 *1909*
that by the *s* of three years I ... Acts 20:31 *4158*
the earth by the *s* of three years ... Jas 5:17
I gave her *s* to repent of her ... Rev 2:21 *5550*
about the *s* of half an hour ... Rev 8:1
by the *s* of a thousand and six ... Rev 14:20 *575*
he must continue a short *s* ... Rev 17:10

SPAIN *(spane)* {2} *Land at the western extremity of the Mediterranean Sea.*
I take my journey into *S*, I will ... Rom 15:24 *4681*
fruit, I will come by you into *S* ... Rom 15:28 *4681*

SPAKE {588}
And God *s* unto Noah, saying, ... Gen 8:15 1696
God *s* unto Noah, and to his sons ... Gen 9:8 559
name of the LORD that *s* unto her ... Gen 16:13 1696
he *s* unto him yet again, and said, ... Gen 18:29 1696
s unto his sons in law, which ... Gen 19:14 1696
of his host *s* unto Abraham ... Gen 21:22 559
Isaac *s* unto Abraham his father, ... Gen 22:7 559
s unto the sons of Heth, saying, ... Gen 23:3 1696
he *s* unto Ephron in the audience ... Gen 23:13 1696
which *s* unto me, and that sware ... Gen 24:7 1696
saying, Thus *s* the man unto me ... Gen 24:30 1696
when Isaac *s* to Esau his son ... Gen 27:5 1696
Rebekah *s* unto Jacob her son, ... Gen 27:6 559
And while he yet *s* with them ... Gen 29:9 1696
the angel of God *s* unto me in a ... Gen 31:11 559
your father *s* unto me yesternight ... Gen 31:29 559
and *s* kindly unto the damsel ... Gen 34:3 1696
Shechem *s* unto his father Hamor, ... Gen 34:4 559
of the place where God *s* with him ... Gen 35:15 1696
as she *s* to Joseph day by day, ... Gen 39:10 1696
s unto them, saying, See, he hath ... Gen 39:14 559
she *s* unto him according to these ... Gen 39:17 1696
of his wife, which she *s* unto him ... Gen 39:19 1696
Then *s* the chief butler unto ... Gen 41:9 1696
unto them, and *s* roughly unto them ... Gen 42:7 1696
That is it that I *s* unto you ... Gen 42:14 1696
S I not unto you, saying, Do not ... Gen 42:22 559
for he *s* unto them by an ... Gen 42:23
s roughly to us, and took us for ... Gen 42:30 1696
Reuben *s* unto his father, saying, ... Gen 42:37 559
Judah *s* unto him, saying, The man ... Gen 43:3 559
well, the old man of whom ye *s* ... Gen 43:27 559
brother, of whom ye *s* unto me ... Gen 43:29 559
he *s* unto them these same words ... Gen 44:6 1696
God *s* unto Israel in the visions ... Gen 46:2 559
Pharaoh *s* unto Joseph, saying, ... Gen 47:5 559
it that their father *s* unto them ... Gen 49:28 1696
Joseph *s* unto the house of ... Gen 50:4 1696
Joseph wept when they *s* unto him ... Gen 50:17 1696
them, and *s* kindly unto them ... Gen 50:21 1696
the king of Egypt *s* to the Hebrew ... Ex 1:15 559
Aaron *s* all the words which the ... Ex 4:30 1696
they *s* to the people, saying, ... Ex 5:10 559
God *s* unto Moses, and said unto ... Ex 6:2 1696
Moses *s* so unto the children of ... Ex 6:9 1696
the LORD *s* unto Moses, saying, ... Ex 6:10 1696
Moses *s* before the LORD, saying, ... Ex 6:12 1696
the LORD *s* unto Moses and unto ... Ex 6:13 1696
These are they which *s* to Pharaoh ... Ex 6:27 1696
pass on the day when the LORD *s* ... Ex 6:28 1696
That the LORD *s* unto Moses ... Ex 6:29 1696
old, when they *s* unto Pharaoh ... Ex 7:7 1696
the LORD *s* unto Moses and unto ... Ex 7:8 559
the LORD *s* unto Moses, Say unto ... Ex 7:19 559
the LORD *s* unto Moses, Go unto ... Ex 8:1 559
the LORD *s* unto Moses, Say unto ... Ex 8:5 559
the LORD *s* unto Moses and Aaron in ... Ex 12:1 559
the LORD *s* unto Moses, saying, ... Ex 13:1 1696
the LORD *s* unto Moses, saying, ... Ex 14:1 1696
this song unto the LORD, and *s* ... Ex 15:1 559
Moses *s* unto Aaron, Say unto all ... Ex 16:9 559
as Aaron *s* unto the whole ... Ex 16:10 1696
the LORD *s* unto Moses, saying, ... Ex 16:11 1696
waxed louder and louder, Moses *s* ... Ex 19:19 1696
unto the people, and *s* unto them ... Ex 19:25 559
God *s* all these words, saying, ... Ex 20:1 1696
the LORD *s* unto Moses, saying, ... Ex 25:1 1696
the LORD *s* unto Moses, saying, ... Ex 30:11 1696
the LORD *s* unto Moses, saying, ... Ex 30:17 1696
Moreover the LORD *s* unto Moses ... Ex 30:22 1696
the LORD *s* unto Moses, saying, ... Ex 31:1 1696
the LORD *s* unto Moses, saying, ... Ex 31:12 559
the LORD *s* unto Moses face to ... Ex 33:11 1696
s unto the children of Israel ... Ex 34:34 1696
Moses *s* unto all the congregation ... Ex 35:4 559
they *s* unto Moses, saying, The ... Ex 36:5 559
the LORD *s* unto Moses, saying, ... Ex 40:1 1696
s unto him out of the tabernacle ... Lev 1:1 1696
the LORD *s* unto Moses, saying, ... Lev 4:1 1696
the LORD *s* unto Moses, saying, ... Lev 5:14 1696
the LORD *s* unto Moses, saying, ... Lev 6:1 1696
the LORD *s* unto Moses, saying, ... Lev 6:8 1696
the LORD *s* unto Moses, saying, ... Lev 6:19 1696
the LORD *s* unto Moses, saying, ... Lev 6:24 1696
the LORD *s* unto Moses, saying, ... Lev 7:22 1696
the LORD *s* unto Moses, saying, ... Lev 7:28 1696
the LORD *s* unto Moses, saying, ... Lev 8:1 1696
Aaron, This is it that the LORD *s* ... Lev 10:3 1696
the LORD *s* unto Aaron, saying, ... Lev 10:8 1696
Moses *s* unto Aaron, and unto ... Lev 10:12 1696
the LORD *s* unto Moses and to Aaron ... Lev 11:1 1696
the LORD *s* unto Moses, saying, ... Lev 12:1 1696
the LORD *s* unto Moses and Aaron, ... Lev 13:1 1696
the LORD *s* unto Moses, saying, ... Lev 14:1 1696
the LORD *s* unto Moses and unto ... Lev 14:33 1696
the LORD *s* unto Moses and to Aaron ... Lev 15:1 1696
the LORD *s* unto Moses after the ... Lev 16:1 1696
the LORD *s* unto Moses, saying, ... Lev 17:1 1696
the LORD *s* unto Moses, saying, ... Lev 18:1 1696
the LORD *s* unto Moses, saying, ... Lev 19:1 1696
the LORD *s* unto Moses, saying, ... Lev 20:1 1696
the LORD *s* unto Moses, saying, ... Lev 21:16 1696
the LORD *s* unto Moses, saying, ... Lev 22:1 1696
the LORD *s* unto Moses, saying, ... Lev 22:17 1696
the LORD *s* unto Moses, saying, ... Lev 22:26 1696
the LORD *s* unto Moses, saying, ... Lev 23:1 1696
the LORD *s* unto Moses, saying, ... Lev 23:9 1696
the LORD *s* unto Moses, saying, ... Lev 23:23 1696
the LORD *s* unto Moses, saying, ... Lev 23:26 1696
the LORD *s* unto Moses, saying, ... Lev 23:33 1696
the LORD *s* unto Moses, saying, ... Lev 24:1 1696
the LORD *s* unto Moses, saying, ... Lev 24:13 1696
Moses *s* to the children of Israel ... Lev 24:23 1696
the LORD *s* unto Moses in mount ... Lev 25:1 1696
the LORD *s* unto Moses, saying, ... Lev 27:1 1696
the LORD *s* unto Moses in the ... Num 1:1 1696
the LORD *s* unto Moses and unto ... Num 2:1 1696
LORD *s* with Moses in mount Sinai ... Num 3:1 1696
the LORD *s* unto Moses, saying, ... Num 3:5 1696
the LORD *s* unto Moses, saying, ... Num 3:11 1696
the LORD *s* unto Moses in the ... Num 3:14 1696
the LORD *s* unto Moses, saying, ... Num 3:44 1696
the LORD *s* unto Moses and unto ... Num 4:1 1696
the LORD *s* unto Moses and unto ... Num 4:17 1696
the LORD *s* unto Moses, saying, ... Num 4:21 1696
the LORD *s* unto Moses, saying, ... Num 5:1 1696
as the LORD *s* unto Moses, so did ... Num 5:4 1696
the LORD *s* unto Moses, saying, ... Num 5:5 1696
the LORD *s* unto Moses, saying, ... Num 5:11 1696
the LORD *s* unto Moses, saying, ... Num 6:1 1696
the LORD *s* unto Moses, saying, ... Num 6:22 1696
the LORD *s* unto Moses, saying, ... Num 7:4 559
and he *s* unto him ... Num 7:89 1696
the LORD *s* unto Moses, saying, ... Num 8:1 1696
the LORD *s* unto Moses, saying, ... Num 8:5 1696
the LORD *s* unto Moses, saying, ... Num 8:23 1696
the LORD *s* unto Moses in the ... Num 9:1 1696

Moses *s* unto the children of ... Num 9:4 1696
the LORD *s* unto Moses, saying, ... Num 9:9 1696
the LORD *s* unto Moses, saying, ... Num 10:1 1696
s unto him, and took of the spirit ... Num 11:25 1696
Aaron *s* against Moses because of ... Num 12:1 1696
the LORD *s* suddenly unto Moses, ... Num 12:4 559
the LORD *s* unto Moses, saying, ... Num 13:1 1696
they *s* unto all the company of ... Num 14:7 559
the LORD *s* unto Moses and unto ... Num 14:26 1696
the LORD *s* unto Moses, saying, ... Num 15:1 1696
the LORD *s* unto Moses, saying, ... Num 15:17 1696
the LORD *s* unto Moses, saying, ... Num 15:37 559
he *s* unto Korah and unto all his ... Num 16:5 1696
the LORD *s* unto Moses and unto ... Num 16:20 1696
the LORD *s* unto Moses, saying, ... Num 16:23 1696
he *s* unto the congregation, ... Num 16:26 1696
the LORD *s* unto Moses, saying, ... Num 16:36 1696
the LORD *s* unto Moses, saying, ... Num 16:44 1696
the LORD *s* unto Moses, saying, ... Num 17:1 1696
Moses *s* unto the children of ... Num 17:6 1696
children of Israel *s* unto Moses ... Num 17:12 559
the LORD *s* unto Aaron, Behold, I ... Num 18:8 1696
the LORD *s* unto Aaron, Thou shalt ... Num 18:20 559
the LORD *s* unto Moses, saying, ... Num 18:25 1696
the LORD *s* unto Moses and unto ... Num 19:1 1696
the people chode with Moses, and *s* ... Num 20:3 559
the LORD *s* unto Moses, saying, ... Num 20:7 1696
the LORD *s* unto Moses and Aaron, ... Num 20:12 559
the LORD *s* unto Moses and Aaron in ... Num 20:23 559
the people *s* against God, and ... Num 21:5 1696
whereof the LORD *s* unto Moses ... Num 21:16 559
s unto him the words of Balak ... Num 22:7 1696
S I not also to thy messengers ... Num 24:12 1696
the LORD *s* unto Moses, saying, ... Num 25:10 1696
the LORD *s* unto Moses, saying, ... Num 25:16 1696
that the LORD *s* unto Moses ... Num 26:1 559
Eleazar the priest *s* with them in ... Num 26:3 1696
the LORD *s* unto Moses, saying, ... Num 26:52 1696
the LORD *s* unto Moses, saying, ... Num 27:6 559
Moses *s* unto the LORD, saying, ... Num 27:15 1696
the LORD *s* unto Moses, saying, ... Num 28:1 1696
Moses *s* unto the heads of the ... Num 30:1 1696
the LORD *s* unto Moses, saying, ... Num 31:1 1696
Moses *s* unto the people, saying, ... Num 31:3 1696
the LORD *s* unto Moses, saying, ... Num 31:25 559
s unto Moses, and to Eleazar the ... Num 32:2 559
children of Reuben *s* unto Moses ... Num 32:25 559
the LORD *s* unto Moses in the ... Num 33:50 1696
the LORD *s* unto Moses, saying, ... Num 34:1 1696
the LORD *s* unto Moses, saying, ... Num 34:16 1696
the LORD *s* unto Moses in the ... Num 35:1 1696
the LORD *s* unto Moses, saying, ... Num 35:9 1696
s before Moses, and before the ... Num 36:1 1696
s unto all Israel on this side ... Deut 1:1 1696
that Moses *s* unto the children of ... Deut 1:3 1696
LORD our God *s* unto us in Horeb ... Deut 1:6 1696
I *s* unto you at that time, saying ... Deut 1:9 559
So I *s* unto you ... Deut 1:43 1696
Red sea, as the LORD *s* unto me ... Deut 2:1 1696
And the LORD *s* unto me, saying, ... Deut 2:2 559
That the LORD *s* unto me, saying, ... Deut 2:17 1696
the LORD *s* unto you out of the ... Deut 4:12 1696
on the day that the LORD *s* unto ... Deut 4:15 1696
which Moses *s* unto the children ... Deut 4:45 1696
These words the LORD *s* unto all ... Deut 5:22 1696
of your words, when ye *s* unto me ... Deut 5:28 1696
which the LORD *s* with you in the ... Deut 9:10 1696
Furthermore the LORD *s* unto me ... Deut 9:13 559
which the LORD *s* unto you in the ... Deut 10:4 1696
to pass, whereof he *s* unto thee ... Deut 13:2 1696
the Levites *s* unto all Israel ... Deut 27:9 1696
by the way whereof I *s* unto thee ... Deut 28:68 559
s these words unto all Israel ... Deut 31:1 1696
Moses *s* in the ears of all the ... Deut 31:30 1696
s all the words of this song in ... Deut 32:44 1696
the LORD *s* unto Moses that ... Deut 32:48 1696
that the LORD *s* unto Joshua the ... Josh 1:1 559
of Manasseh, *s* Joshua, saying, ... Josh 1:12 559
Joshua *s* unto the priests, saying ... Josh 3:6 559
that the LORD *s* unto Joshua ... Josh 4:1 559
Jordan, as the LORD *s* unto Joshua ... Josh 4:8 1696
of Israel, as Moses *s* unto them ... Josh 4:12 1696
the LORD *s* unto Joshua, saying, ... Josh 4:15 559
he *s* unto the children of Israel, ... Josh 4:21 559
s unto them, saying, Go up and ... Josh 7:2 559
of our country *s* to us, saying, ... Josh 9:11 559
he *s* unto them, saying, Wherefore ... Josh 9:22 1696
Then *s* Joshua to the LORD in the ... Josh 10:12 1696
even since the LORD *s* this word ... Josh 14:10 1696
whereof the LORD *s* in that day ... Josh 14:12 1696
children of Joseph *s* unto Joshua ... Josh 17:14 1696
Joshua *s* unto the house of Joseph ... Josh 17:17 559
The LORD also *s* unto Joshua ... Josh 20:1 1696
whereof I *s* unto you by the hand ... Josh 20:2 1696
they *s* unto them at Shiloh in the ... Josh 21:2 1696
he *s* unto them, saying, Return ... Josh 22:8 559
they *s* with them, saying, ... Josh 22:15 1696
Gad and the children of Manasseh *s* ... Josh 22:30 1696
LORD your God *s* concerning you ... Josh 23:14 1696
of the LORD which he *s* unto us ... Josh 24:27 1696
LORD *s* these words unto all the ... Judg 2:4 1696
Penuel, and *s* unto them likewise ... Judg 8:8 1696
he *s* also unto the men of Penuel, ... Judg 8:9 559
his mother's brethren *s* of him in ... Judg 9:3 1696
Gaal *s* again and said, See there ... Judg 9:37 1696
they *s* unto him, saying, No ... Judg 15:13 559
s to the master of the house, the ... Judg 19:22 559
kinsman of whom Boaz *s* came by ... Ruth 4:1 1696

Now Hannah, she *s* in her heart ... 1Sa 1:13 1696
Samuel *s* unto all the house of ... 1Sa 7:3 559
went to enquire of God, thus he *s* ... 1Sa 9:9 559
the man whom I *s* to thee of ... 1Sa 9:17 559
of the kingdom, whereof Samuel *s* ... 1Sa 10:16 559
Samuel did that which the LORD *s* ... 1Sa 16:4 1696
s according to the same words ... 1Sa 17:23 1696
David *s* to the men that stood by ... 1Sa 17:26 559
heard when he *s* unto the men ... 1Sa 17:28 1696
and *s* after the same manner ... 1Sa 17:30 559
words were heard which David *s* ... 1Sa 17:31 1696
Saul's servants *s* those words in ... 1Sa 18:23 1696
saying, On this manner *s* David ... 1Sa 18:24 1696
Saul *s* to Jonathan his son, and to ... 1Sa 19:1 1696
Jonathan *s* good of David unto ... 1Sa 19:4 1696
Nevertheless Saul *s* not any thing ... 1Sa 20:26 1696
they *s* to Nabal according to all ... 1Sa 25:9 1696
they *s* unto her, saying, David ... 1Sa 25:40 1696
and the woman *s* to Saul, saying, ... 1Sa 28:12 559
hath done to him, as he *s* by me ... 1Sa 28:17 1696
for the people *s* of stoning him ... 1Sa 30:6 559
Abner also *s* in the ears of ... 2Sa 3:19 1696
Israel to David unto Hebron, and *s* ... 2Sa 5:1 559
which *s* unto David, saying, ... 2Sa 5:6 559
s I a word with any of the tribes ... 2Sa 7:7 1696
we *s* unto him, and he would not ... 2Sa 12:18 1696
Absalom *s* unto his brother Amnon ... 2Sa 13:22 1696
the woman of Tekoah *s* to the king ... 2Sa 14:4 559
Absalom *s* unto him, saying, ... 2Sa 17:6 559
Then she *s*, saying, They were ... 2Sa 20:18 559
David *s* unto the LORD the words ... 2Sa 22:1 1696
The Spirit of the LORD *s* by me ... 2Sa 23:2 1696
said, the Rock of Israel *s* to me ... 2Sa 23:3 1696
David *s* unto the LORD when he saw ... 2Sa 24:17 559
Wherefore Nathan *s* unto ... 1Kin 1:11 559
And while he yet *s*, behold, ... 1Kin 1:42 1696
his word which he *s* concerning me ... 1Kin 2:4 1696
which he *s* concerning the house ... 1Kin 2:27 1696
Thus they *s* before the king ... 1Kin 3:22 1696
Then *s* the woman whose the living ... 1Kin 3:26 559
he *s* three thousand proverbs ... 1Kin 4:32 1696
he *s* of trees, from the cedar ... 1Kin 4:33 1696
he *s* also of beasts, and of fowl, ... 1Kin 4:33 1696
as the LORD *s* unto David my ... 1Kin 5:5 1696
which I *s* unto David thy father ... 1Kin 6:12 1696
Then *s* Solomon, The LORD said ... 1Kin 8:12 559
which *s* with his mouth unto David ... 1Kin 8:15 1696
hath performed his word that he *s* ... 1Kin 8:20 1696
came, and *s* unto Rehoboam, saying, ... 1Kin 12:3 1696
they *s* unto him, saying, If thou ... 1Kin 12:7 1696
were grown up with him *s* unto him ... 1Kin 12:10 1696
unto this people that *s* unto thee ... 1Kin 12:10 1696
s to them after the counsel of ... 1Kin 12:14 1696
which the LORD *s* by Ahijah the ... 1Kin 12:15 1696
an angel *s* unto me by the word of ... 1Kin 13:18 1696
of the LORD, which he *s* unto him ... 1Kin 13:26 1696
he *s* to his sons, saying, Saddle ... 1Kin 13:27 1696
that he *s* to his sons, saying, ... 1Kin 13:31 559
which he *s* by the hand of his ... 1Kin 14:18 1696
which he *s* by his servant Ahijah ... 1Kin 15:29 1696
which he *s* against Baasha by Jehu ... 1Kin 16:12 1696
which he *s* by Joshua the son of ... 1Kin 16:34 1696
of the LORD, which he *s* by Elijah ... 1Kin 17:16 1696
s unto the king of Israel, and ... 1Kin 20:28 559
Ahab *s* unto Naboth, saying, Give ... 1Kin 21:2 1696
Because I *s* unto Naboth the ... 1Kin 21:6 1696
And of Jezebel also *s* the LORD ... 1Kin 21:23 1696
gone to call Micaiah *s* unto him ... 1Kin 22:13 1696
the word of the LORD which he *s* ... 1Kin 22:38 1696
he *s* unto him, Thou man of God, ... 2Kin 1:9 1696
the saying of Elisha which he *s* ... 2Kin 2:22 1696
s unto him, and said, My father, ... 2Kin 5:13 1696
who *s* when the king came down to ... 2Kin 7:17 1696
Then *s* Elisha unto the woman, ... 2Kin 8:1 1696
thus *s* he to me, saying, Thus ... 2Kin 9:12 559
which he *s* by his servant Elijah ... 2Kin 9:36 1696
which the LORD *s* concerning the ... 2Kin 10:10 1696
which he *s* by his servant Elijah ... 2Kin 10:10 1696
of the LORD, which he *s* to Elijah ... 2Kin 10:17 1696
which he *s* by the hand of his ... 2Kin 14:25 1696
of the LORD which he *s* unto Jehu ... 2Kin 15:12 1696
Wherefore they *s* to the king of ... 2Kin 17:26 559
voice in the Jews' language, and *s* ... 2Kin 18:28 1696
the LORD *s* by his servants the ... 2Kin 21:10 1696
what I *s* against this place ... 2Kin 22:19 1696
which he *s* by his servants the ... 2Kin 24:2 1696
he *s* kindly to him, and set his ... 2Kin 25:28 1696
David *s* to the chief of the ... 1Chr 15:16 559
s I a word to any of the judges ... 1Chr 17:6 1696
And the LORD *s* unto Gad, David's ... 1Chr 21:9 1696
which he *s* in the name of the ... 1Chr 21:19 1696
Then Solomon *s* unto all Israel, ... 2Chr 1:2 559
he *s* with his mouth to my father ... 2Chr 6:4 1696
came and *s* to Rehoboam, saying, ... 2Chr 10:3 1696
they *s* unto him, saying, If thou ... 2Chr 10:7 1696
brought up with him *s* unto him ... 2Chr 10:10 1696
the people that *s* unto thee ... 2Chr 10:10 1696
which he *s* by the hand of Ahijah ... 2Chr 10:15 1696
went to call Micaiah *s* to him ... 2Chr 18:12 1696
one *s* saying after this manner, ... 2Chr 18:19 559
Hezekiah *s* comfortably unto all ... 2Chr 30:22 1696
s comfortably to them, saying, ... 2Chr 32:6 1696
his servants *s* yet more against ... 2Chr 32:16 1696
they *s* against the God of ... 2Chr 32:19 1696
he *s* unto him, and he gave him a ... 2Chr 32:24 559
the LORD *s* to Manasseh, and to his ... 2Chr 33:10 1696
the words of the seers that *s* to ... 2Chr 33:18 1696
they *s* to her to that effect ... 2Chr 34:22 1696

the singing women *s* of Josiah in ... 2Chr 35:25 559
he *s* before his brethren and the ... Neh 4:2 559
they *s* unto Ezra the scribe to ... Neh 8:1 559
their children *s* half in the ... Neh 13:24 1696
when they *s* daily unto him, and he ... Est 3:4 559
Again Esther *s* unto Hatach ... Est 4:10 559
Esther *s* yet again before the ... Est 8:3 1696
nights, and none *s* a word unto him ... Job 2:13 1696
And Job *s*, and said, ... Job 3:2 6030
I arose, and they *s* against me ... Job 19:18 1696
After my words they *s* not again ... Job 29:22
I had waited, (for they *s* not ... Job 32:16 1696
Elihu *s* moreover, and said, ... Job 35:1 6030
who *s* unto the LORD the words of ... Ps 18:*t* 1696
For he *s*, and it was done ... Ps 33:9 559
then *s* I with my tongue, ... Ps 39:3 1696
Yea, they *s* against God ... Ps 78:19 1696
He *s* unto them in the cloudy ... Ps 99:7 1696
He *s*, and there came divers sorts ... Ps 105:31 559
He *s*, and the locusts came, and ... Ps 105:34 559
so that he *s* unadvisedly with his ... Ps 106:33 981
the man *s* unto Ithiel, even unto ... Prov 30:1 5002
My beloved *s*, and said unto me, ... Song 2:10 6030
my soul failed when he *s* ... Song 5:6 1696
the LORD *s* again unto Ahaz ... Is 7:10 1696
The LORD *s* also unto me again, ... Is 8:5 1696
For the LORD *s* thus to me with a ... Is 8:11 559
At the same time *s* the LORD by ... Is 20:2 1696
when I *s*, ye did not hear ... Is 65:12 1696
when I *s*, they did not hear ... Is 66:4 1696
I *s* unto you, rising up early and ... Jer 7:13 1696
For I *s* not unto your fathers, ... Jer 7:22 1696
and heard, but they *s* not aright ... Jer 8:6 1696
them, neither *s* unto them ... Jer 14:14 1696
which I commanded not, nor *s* it ... Jer 19:5 1696
For since I *s*, I cried out, I ... Jer 20:8 1696
I *s* unto thee in thy prosperity ... Jer 22:21 1696
s unto all the people of Judah ... Jer 25:2 1696
Then *s* the priests and the ... Jer 26:11 559
Then *s* Jeremiah unto all the ... Jer 26:12 559
s to all the assembly of the ... Jer 26:17 559
s to all the people of Judah, ... Jer 26:18 559
I *s* also to Zedekiah king of ... Jer 27:12 1696
Also I *s* to the priests and to all ... Jer 27:16 1696
s unto me in the house of the ... Jer 28:1 559
Hananiah *s* in the presence of all ... Jer 28:11 559
that the LORD *s* concerning Israel ... Jer 30:4 1696
for since I *s* against him ... Jer 31:20 1696
Then Jeremiah the prophet *s* all ... Jer 34:6 1696
from the day I *s* unto thee ... Jer 36:2 1696
which he *s* by the prophet ... Jer 37:2 1696
house, and *s* to the king, saying, ... Jer 38:8 1696
s to Gedaliah in Mizpah secretly ... Jer 40:15 559
Then *s* Azariah the son of ... Jer 43:2 559
s unto Baruch the son of Neriah ... Jer 45:1 1696
The word that the LORD *s* to ... Jer 46:13 1696
that the LORD *s* against Babylon ... Jer 50:1 1696
done that which he *s* against the ... Jer 51:12 1696
s kindly unto him, and set his ... Jer 52:32 1696
and I heard a voice of one that *s* ... Eze 1:28 1696
entered into me when he *s* unto me ... Eze 2:2 1696
that I heard him that *s* unto me ... Eze 2:2 1696
s with me, and said unto me, Go, ... Eze 3:24 1696
he *s* unto the man clothed with ... Eze 10:2 559
Then I *s* unto them of the ... Eze 11:25 1696
So I *s* unto the people in the ... Eze 24:18 1696
the king *s* unto Ashpenaz the ... Dan 1:3 559
Then *s* the Chaldeans to the king ... Dan 2:4 1696
They *s* and said to the king ... Dan 3:9 6032
Nebuchadnezzar *s* and said unto ... Dan 3:14 6032
therefore he *s*, and commanded that ... Dan 3:19 6032
and rose up in haste, and *s* ... Dan 3:24 6032
the burning fiery furnace, and *s* ... Dan 3:26 6032
Then Nebuchadnezzar *s*, and said, ... Dan 3:28 6032
The king *s*, and said, Belteshazzar ... Dan 4:19 6032
The king *s*, and said, Is not this ... Dan 4:30 6032
And the king *s*, and said to the ... Dan 5:7 6032
and the queen *s* and said, O king, ... Dan 5:10 6032
And the king *s* and said unto Daniel ... Dan 5:13 6032
s before the king concerning the ... Dan 6:12 560
Now the king *s* and said unto ... Dan 6:16 6032
and the king *s* and said to Daniel, ... Dan 6:20 6032
Daniel *s* and said, I saw in my ... Dan 7:2 6032
the great words which the horn *s* ... Dan 7:11 4449
a mouth that *s* very great things, ... Dan 7:20 4449
unto that certain saint which *s* ... Dan 8:13 1696
which *s* in thy name to our kings, ... Dan 9:6 1696
which he *s* against us, and against ... Dan 9:12 1696
then I opened my mouth, and *s* ... Dan 10:16 1696
in Beth-el, and there he *s* with us ... Hos 12:4 1696
When Ephraim *s* trembling, he ... Hos 13:1 1696
the LORD *s* unto the fish, and it ... Jonah 2:10 559
Then *s* Haggai the LORD's ... Hag 1:13 559
And he *s*, saying, These are the ... Zec 1:21 559
s unto those that stood before ... Zec 3:4 559
s to the angel that talked with ... Zec 4:4 559
s unto me, saying, This is the ... Zec 4:6 559
s unto me, saying, Behold, these ... Zec 6:8 1696
the LORD *s* often one to another ... Mal 3:16 1696
While he *s* these things unto them ... Mt 9:18 *2980*
devil was cast out, the dumb *s* ... Mt 9:33 *2980*
that the blind and dumb both *s* ... Mt 12:22 *2980*
he *s* many things unto them in ... Mt 13:3 *2980*
Another parable *s* he unto them ... Mt 13:33 *2980*
All these things *s* Jesus unto the ... Mt 13:34 *2980*
a parable *s* he not unto them ... Mt 13:34 *2980*
But straightway Jesus *s* unto them ... Mt 14:27 *2980*
ye do not understand that I *s* it ... Mt 16:11 *2036*

While he yet s, behold, a bright Mt 17:5 2980
disciples understood that he s Mt 17:13 2036
they perceived that he s of them Mt 21:45 3004
s unto them again by parables, and Mt 22:1 2036
Then s Jesus to the multitude, and Mt 23:1 2980
And while he yet s, lo, Judas, one Mt 26:47 2980
s unto them, saying, All power is Mt 28:18 2980
he s to his disciples, that a Mk 3:9 2036
parables s he the word unto them Mk 4:33 2980
a parable s he not unto them Mk 4:34 2980
While he yet s, there came from Mk 5:35 2980
tongue was loosed, and he s plain Mk 7:35 2980
And he s that saying openly Mk 8:32 2980
I s to thy disciples that they Mk 9:18 2036
how in the bush God s unto him Mk 12:26 2036
But he s the more vehemently, If Mk 14:31 3004
and prayed, and s the same words Mk 14:39 2036
And immediately, while he yet s Mk 14:43 2980
she s out with a loud voice, and Lk 1:42 400
As he s to our fathers, to Lk 1:55 2980
and his tongue loosed, and he s Lk 1:64 2980
As he s by the mouth of his holy Lk 1:70 2980
s of him to all them that looked Lk 2:38 2980
the saying which he s unto them Lk 2:50 2980
s among themselves, saying, What Lk 4:36 4814
he s also a parable unto them Lk 5:36 3004
he s a parable unto them, Can the Lk 6:39 2036
he s within himself, saying, This Lk 7:39 2036
of every city, he s by a parable Lk 8:4 2036
While he yet s, there cometh one Lk 8:49 2980
s unto them of the kingdom of God Lk 9:11 2980
s of his decease which he should Lk 9:31 3004
While he thus s, there came a Lk 9:34 3004
devil was gone out, the dumb s Lk 11:14 2980
as he s these things, a certain Lk 11:27 3004
And as he s, a certain Pharisee Lk 11:37 2980
he s a parable unto them, saying, Lk 12:16 2036
He s also this parable Lk 13:6 3004
Jesus answering s unto the Lk 14:3 2036
he s this parable unto them, Lk 15:3 2036
he s a parable unto them to this Lk 18:1 3004
he s this parable unto certain Lk 18:9 2036
s a parable, because he was nigh Lk 19:11 2036
s unto him, saying, Tell us, by Lk 20:2 2036
as some s of the temple, how it Lk 21:5 3004
And he s to them a parable Lk 21:29 2036
And while he yet s, behold a Lk 22:47 2980
And immediately, while he yet s Lk 22:60 2980
blasphemously s they against him Lk 22:65 3004
to release Jesus, s again to them Lk 23:20 4377
remember how he s unto you when Lk 24:6 2980
And as they thus s, Jesus himself Lk 24:36 2980
are the words which I s unto you Lk 24:44 2980
saying, This was he of whom I s Jn 1:15 2036
But he s of the temple of his Jn 2:21 3004
He s of Judas Iscariot the son of Jn 6:71 3004
Howbeit no man s openly of him Jn 7:13 2980
(But this s he of the Spirit, Jn 7:39 2036
Never man s like this man Jn 7:46 2980
Then s Jesus again unto them, Jn 8:12 2980
These words s Jesus in the Jn 8:20 2980
that he s to them of the Father Jn 8:27 3004
As he s these words, many Jn 8:30 2980
These words s his parents Jn 9:22 2036
We know that God s unto Moses Jn 9:29 2980
This parable s Jesus unto them Jn 10:6 2036
they were which he s unto them Jn 10:6 2980
that John s of this man were true Jn 10:41 2036
Howbeit Jesus s of his death Jn 11:13 2046
And this s he not of himself Jn 11:51 2036
s among themselves, as they stood Jn 11:56 3004
others said, An angel s to him Jn 12:29 2980
These things s Jesus, and departed Jn 12:36 2980
might be fulfilled, which he s Jn 12:38 2036
he saw his glory, and s of him Jn 12:41 2980
on another, doubting of whom he s Jn 13:22 3004
ask who it should be of whom he s Jn 13:24 3004
what intent he s this unto him Jn 13:28 2036
These words s Jesus, and lifted up Jn 17:1 2980
might be fulfilled, which he s Jn 18:9 2036
s unto her that kept the door, and Jn 18:16 2036
him, I s openly to the world Jn 18:20 2980
might be fulfilled, which he s Jn 18:32 2036
This s he, signifying by what Jn 21:19 2036
David s before concerning Judas Acts 1:16 4227
He seeing this before s of the Acts 2:31 2980
as they s unto the people, the Acts 4:1 2980
they s the word of God with Acts 4:31 2980
and the spirit by which he s Acts 6:10 2980
God s on this wise, That his seed Acts 7:6 2980
which s to him in the mount Sina Acts 7:38 2980
unto those things which Philip s Acts 8:6 3004
angel of the Lord s unto Philip Acts 8:26 2980
he s boldly in the name of the Acts 9:29 2980
when the angel which s unto Acts 10:7 2980
the voice s unto him again the Acts 10:15
While Peter yet s these words Acts 10:44 2980
s unto the Grecians, preaching Acts 11:20 2980
s against those things which were Acts 13:45 483
synagogue of the Jews, and so s Acts 14:1 2980
s unto the women which resorted Acts 16:13 2980
they s unto him the word of the Acts 16:32 2980
Then s the Lord to Paul in the Acts 18:9 2036
being fervent in the spirit, he s Acts 18:25 2980
and they s with tongues, and Acts 19:6 2980
s boldly for the space of three Acts 19:8 3955
but s evil of that way before the Acts 19:9 2551
of all for the words which he s Acts 20:38 2046
he s unto them in the Hebrew Acts 21:40 4377
when they heard that he s in the Acts 22:2 4377
not the voice of him that s to me Acts 22:9 2980
as he thus s for himself, Festus Acts 26:24 626
But when the Jews s against it Acts 28:19 483
came shewed or s any harm of thee Acts 28:21 2980
Well s the Holy Ghost by Esaias Acts 28:25 2980
I s as a child, I understood as a 1Cor 13:11 2980
would that ye all s with tongues 1Cor 14:5 2980
but as we s all things to you in 2Cor 7:14 2980
is then the blessedness ye s of Gal 4:15
in divers manners s in time past Heb 1:1 2980
For he s in a certain place of Heb 4:4 2046
of which tribe Moses s nothing Heb 7:14 2980
who refused him that s on earth Heb 12:25 5537
but holy men of God s as they 2Pet 1:21 2980
to see the voice that s with me Rev 1:12 2980
heard from heaven s unto me again Rev 10:8 2980
like a lamb, and he s as a dragon Rev 13:11 2980

SPAKEST {10}
the man that s unto the woman Judg 13:11 1696
s of also in mine ears, behold, Judg 17:2 559
thy words which thou s unto me 1Sa 28:21 1696
thou s also with thy mouth, and 1Kin 8:24 1696
which thou s unto thy servant 1Kin 8:26 1696
as thou s by the hand of Moses 1Kin 8:53 1696
s with thy mouth, and hast 2Chr 6:15 1696
s with them from heaven, and Neh 9:13 1696
Then thou s in vision to thy holy Ps 89:19 1696
for since thou s of him, thou Jer 48:27 1697

SPAN {8}
a s shall be the length thereof, Ex 28:16 2239
a s shall be the breadth thereof Ex 28:16 2239
a s was the length thereof, and a Ex 39:9 2239
a s the breadth thereof, being Ex 39:9 2239
height was six cubits and a s 1Sa 17:4 2239
and meted out heaven with the s Is 40:12 2239
fruit, and children of a s long Lam 2:20 2949
thereof round about shall be a s Eze 43:13 2239

SPANNED {1}
my right hand hath s the heavens Is 48:13 2946

SPARE {40}
not s the place for the fifty Gen 18:24 5375
then I will s all the place for Gen 18:26 5375
pity him, neither shalt thou s Deut 13:8 2550
The LORD will not s him, but then Deut 29:20 5545
all that they have, and s them not 1Sa 15:3 2550
s me according to the greatness Neh 13:22 2347
let him not s Job 6:10 2550
my reins asunder, and doth not s Job 16:13 2550
Though he s it, and forsake it not Job 20:13 2550
God shall cast upon him, and not s Job 27:22 2550
me, and s not to spit in my face Job 30:10 2820
O s me, that I may recover Ps 39:13 8159
He shall s the poor and needy, and Ps 72:13 2347
therefore he will not s in the Prov 6:34 2550
let not thy soul s for his crying Prov 19:18 5375
no man shall s his brother Is 9:19 2550
their eye shall not s children Is 13:18 2347
he shall not s Is 30:14 2550
s not, lengthen thy cords, and Is 54:2 2820
s not, lift up thy voice like a Is 58:1 2820
I will not pity, nor s, nor have Jer 13:14 2347
he shall not s them, neither have Jer 21:7 2347
bow, shoot at her, s no arrows Jer 50:14 2550
and s ye not her young men Jer 51:3 2550
neither shall mine eye s, neither Eze 5:11 2347
And mine eye shall not s thee Eze 7:4 2347
And mine eye shall not s, neither Eze 7:9 2347
mine eye shall not s, neither Eze 8:18 2347
let not your eye s, neither have Eze 9:5 2347
for me also, mine eye shall not s Eze 9:10 2347
not go back, neither will I s Eze 24:14 2347
S thy people, O LORD, and give not Joel 2:17 2347
And should not I s Nineveh Jonah 4:11 2347
not s continually to slay the Hab 1:17 2550
and I will s them, as a man Mal 3:17 2550
have bread enough and to s Lk 15:17 4052
take heed lest he also s not thee Rom 11:21 5339
but I s you 1Cor 7:28 5339
that to s you I came not as yet 2Cor 1:23 5339
if I come again, I will not s 2Cor 13:2 5339

SPARED {12}
But Saul and the people s Agag 1Sa 15:9 2550
for the people s the best of the 1Sa 15:15 2550
but mine eye s thee 1Sa 24:10 2347
he s to take of his own flock and 2Sa 12:4 2550
But the king s Mephibosheth 2Sa 21:7 2550
my master hath s Naaman this 2Kin 5:20 2820
he s not their soul from death, Ps 78:50 2820
Nevertheless mine eye s them from Eze 20:17 2347
He that s not his own Son, but Rom 8:32 5339
For if God s not the natural Rom 11:21 5339
For if God s not the angels that 2Pet 2:4 5339
s not the old world, but saved 2Pet 2:5 5339

SPARETH {4}
He that s his rod hateth his son Prov 13:24 2820
that hath knowledge s his words Prov 17:27 2820
but the righteous giveth and s not Prov 21:26 2820
as a man s his own son that Mal 3:17 2550

SPARING {1}
in among you, not s the flock Acts 20:29 5339

SPARINGLY {2}
He which soweth s shall reap also 2Cor 9:6 5340
shall reap also s 2Cor 9:6 5340

SPARK {2}
the s of his fire shall not shine Job 18:5 7632
as tow, and the maker of it as a s Is 1:31 5213

SPARKLED {1}
they s like the colour of Eze 1:7 5340

SPARKS {4}
unto trouble, as the s fly upward Job 5:7 1121,7565
lamps, and s of fire leap out Job 41:19 3590
compass yourselves about with s Is 50:11 2131
in the s that ye have kindled Is 50:11 2131

SPARROW {2}
the s hath found an house, and the Ps 84:3 6833
am as a s alone upon the house Ps 102:7 6833

SPARROWS {4}
Are not two s sold for a farthing Mt 10:29 4765
ye are of more value than many s Mt 10:31 4765
Are not five s sold for two Lk 12:6 4765
ye are of more value than many s Lk 12:7 4765

SPAT {1}
he s on the ground, and made clay Jn 9:6 4429

SPEAK {513}
taken upon me to s unto the Lord Gen 18:27 1696
the LORD be angry, and I will s Gen 18:30 1696
taken upon me to s unto the Lord Gen 18:31 1696
I will s yet but this once Gen 18:32 1696
And he said, S on Gen 24:33 1696
we cannot s unto thee bad or good Gen 24:50 1696
I heard thy father s unto Esau Gen 27:6 1696
Take heed that thou s not to Gen 31:24 1696
Take thou heed that thou s not to Gen 31:29 1696
Thus shall ye s unto my lord Esau Gen 32:4 559
this manner shall ye s unto Esau Gen 32:19 1696
could not s peaceably unto him Gen 37:4 1696
what shall we s Gen 44:16 1696
s a word in my lord's ears, and Gen 44:18 1696
have found grace in your eyes, s Gen 50:4 1696
I know that he can s well Ex 4:14 1696
And thou shalt s unto him, and put Ex 4:15 1696
came to Pharaoh to s in thy name Ex 5:23 1696
s unto Pharaoh king of Egypt, Ex 6:11 1696
s thou unto Pharaoh king of Egypt Ex 6:29 1696
Thou shalt s all that I command Ex 7:2 1696
thy brother shall s unto Pharaoh Ex 7:2 1696
When Pharaoh shall s unto you Ex 7:9 1696
S now in the ears of the people, Ex 11:2 1696
S ye unto all the congregation of Ex 12:3 1696
S unto the children of Israel, Ex 14:2 1696
s unto the children of Israel, Ex 14:15 1696
s unto them, saying, At even ye Ex 16:12 1696
s unto the children of Israel Ex 19:6 1696
may hear when I s with thee Ex 19:9 1696
S thou with us, and we will hear Ex 20:19 1696
but let not God s with us Ex 20:19 1696
neither shalt thou s in a cause Ex 23:2 6030
his voice, and do all that I s Ex 23:22 1696
S unto the children of Israel, Ex 25:2 1696
thou shalt s unto all that are Ex 28:3 1696
meet you, to s there unto thee Ex 29:42 1696
thou shalt s unto the children of Ex 30:31 1696
S thou also unto the children of Ex 31:13 1696
Wherefore should the Egyptians s Ex 32:12 559
in before the LORD to s with him Ex 34:34 1696
until he went in to s with him Ex 34:35 1696
S unto the children of Israel, and Lev 1:2 1696
S unto the children of Israel, Lev 4:2 1696
S unto Aaron and to his sons, Lev 6:25 1696
S unto the children of Israel, Lev 7:23 1696
S unto the children of Israel, Lev 7:29 1696
children of Israel thou shalt s Lev 9:3 1696
S unto the children of Israel, Lev 11:2 1696
S unto the children of Israel, Lev 12:2 1696
S unto the children of Israel, and Lev 15:2 1696
S unto Aaron thy brother, that he Lev 16:2 1696
S unto Aaron, and unto his sons, Lev 17:2 1696
S unto the children of Israel, and Lev 18:2 1696
S unto all the congregation of Lev 19:2 1696
S unto the priests the sons of Lev 21:1 559
S unto Aaron, saying, Whosoever Lev 21:17 1696
S unto Aaron and to his sons, that Lev 22:2 1696
S unto Aaron, and to his sons, and Lev 22:18 1696
S unto the children of Israel, and Lev 23:2 1696
S unto the children of Israel, and Lev 23:10 1696
S unto the children of Israel, Lev 23:24 1696
S unto the children of Israel, Lev 23:34 1696
thou shalt s unto the children of Lev 24:15 1696
S unto the children of Israel, and Lev 25:2 1696
S unto the children of Israel, and Lev 27:2 1696
S unto the children of Israel, Num 5:6 1696
S unto the children of Israel, and Num 5:12 1696
S unto the children of Israel, and Num 6:2 1696
S unto Aaron and unto his sons, Num 6:23 1696
of the congregation to s with him Num 7:89 1696
S unto Aaron, and say unto him, Num 8:2 1696
S unto the children of Israel, Num 9:10 1696
will s unto him in a dream Num 12:6 1696
With him will I s mouth to mouth Num 12:8 1696
to s against my servant Moses Num 12:8 1696
heard the fame of thee will s Num 14:15 559
S unto the children of Israel, and Num 15:2 1696
S unto the children of Israel, and Num 15:18 1696
S unto the children of Israel, and Num 15:38 1696
S unto the congregation, saying, Num 16:24 1696
S unto Eleazar the son of Aaron Num 16:37 559
S unto the children of Israel, and Num 17:2 1696
Thus s unto the Levites, and say Num 18:26 1696
S unto the children of Israel, Num 19:2 1696

s ye unto the rock before their ... Num 20:8 1696
they that *s* in proverbs say ... Num 21:27
as the LORD shall *s* unto me ... Num 22:8 1696
the word that I shalt *s* unto thee ... Num 22:35 1696
unto thee, that thou shall *s* ... Num 22:35 1696
in my mouth, that shall I *s* ... Num 22:38 1696
unto Balak, and thus thou shalt *s* ... Num 23:5 1696
Must I not take heed to *s* that ... Num 23:12 1696
the LORD saith, that will I *s* ... Num 24:13 1696
daughters of Zelophehad *s* right ... Num 27:7 1696
thou shalt *s* unto the children of ... Num 27:8 1696
S unto the children of Israel, and ... Num 33:51 1696
S unto the children of Israel, and ... Num 35:10 1696
s no more unto me of this matter ... Deut 3:26 1696
judgments which I *s* in your ears ... Deut 5:1 1696
s thou unto us all that the LORD ... Deut 5:27 1696
LORD our God shall *s* unto thee ... Deut 5:27 1696
I will *s* unto thee all the ... Deut 5:31 1696
S not thou in thine heart, after ... Deut 9:4 559
for I *s* not with your children ... Deut 11:2
he shall *s* unto them all that I ... Deut 18:18 1696
words which he shall *s* in my name ... Deut 18:19 1696
presume to *s* a word in my name ... Deut 18:20 1696
I have not commanded him to *s* ... Deut 18:20 1696
or that shall *s* in the name of ... Deut 18:20 1696
approach and *s* unto the people, ... Deut 20:2 1696
officers shall *s* unto the people ... Deut 20:5 1696
the officers shall *s* further unto ... Deut 20:8 1696
shall call him, and *s* unto him ... Deut 25:8 1696
And thou shalt *s* and say before the ... Deut 26:5 6030
And the Levites shall *s*, and say ... Deut 27:14 6030
that I may *s* these words in their ... Deut 31:28 1696
ear, O ye heavens, and I will *s* ... Deut 32:1 1696
Joshua to *s* unto the people ... Josh 4:10 1696
S to the children of Israel, ... Josh 20:2 1696
might *s* unto our children ... Josh 22:24 559
S, ye that ride on white asses, ... Judg 5:10 7878
me, and I will *s* but this once ... Judg 6:39 1696
S, I pray you, in the ears of all ... Judg 9:2 1696
to *s* friendly unto her, and to ... Judg 19:3 1696
it, take advice, and *s* your minds ... Judg 19:30 1696
to *s* to the children of Benjamin ... Judg 21:13 1696
call thee, that thou shalt say, *S* ... 1Sa 3:9 1696
Then Samuel answered, *S* ... 1Sa 3:10 1696
that a man cannot *s* to him ... 1Sa 25:17 1696
s in thine audience, and hear the ... 1Sa 25:24 1696
Abner went also to *s* in the ears ... 2Sa 3:19 1696
in the gate to *s* with him quietly ... 2Sa 3:27 1696
so did Nathan *s* unto David ... 2Sa 7:17 1696
I pray thee, *s* unto the king ... 2Sa 13:13 1696
s on this manner unto him ... 2Sa 14:3 1696
s one word unto my lord the king ... 2Sa 14:12 1696
for the king doth *s* this thing as ... 2Sa 14:13 1696
s of this thing unto my lord the ... 2Sa 14:15 1696
I will now *s* unto the king ... 2Sa 14:15 1696
said, Let my lord the king now *s* ... 2Sa 14:18 1696
if not; *s* thou ... 2Sa 17:6 1696
s comfortably unto thy servants ... 2Sa 19:7 1696
Now therefore why *s* ye not a word ... 2Sa 19:10 2790
S unto the elders of Judah, ... 2Sa 19:11 1696
hither, that I may *s* with thee ... 2Sa 20:16 1696
They were wont to *s* in old time ... 2Sa 20:18 1696
And he said, *S*, I pray thee, unto ... 1Kin 2:17 559
I will *s* for thee unto the king ... 1Kin 2:18 1696
to *s* unto him for Adonijah ... 1Kin 2:19 1696
s good words to them, then they ... 1Kin 12:7 1696
Thus shalt thou *s* unto this ... 1Kin 12:10 559
S unto Rehoboam, the son of ... 1Kin 12:23 559
And thou shalt *s* unto him, saying, ... 1Kin 21:19 1696
And thou shalt *s* unto him, saying, ... 1Kin 21:19 1696
of them, and *s* that which is good ... 1Kin 22:13 1696
LORD saith unto me, that will I *s* ... 1Kin 22:14 1696
the LORD from me to *s* unto thee ... 1Kin 22:24 1696
S ye now to Hezekiah, Thus saith ... 2Kin 18:19 559
and Joah, unto Rab-shakeh, *S* ... 2Kin 18:26 1696
and to thee, to *s* these words ... 2Kin 18:27 1696
Thus shall ye *s* to Hezekiah king ... 2Kin 19:10 559
so did Nathan *s* unto David ... 1Chr 17:15 1696
What can David *s* more to thee for ... 1Chr 17:18
s good words to them, they will ... 2Chr 10:7 1696
S unto Rehoboam the son of ... 2Chr 11:3 559
one of theirs, and *s* thou good ... 2Chr 18:12 1696
what my God saith, that will I *s* ... 2Chr 18:13 1696
the LORD from me to *s* unto thee ... 2Chr 18:23 1696
to *s* against him, saying, As the ... 2Chr 32:17 559
could not *s* in the Jews' language ... Neh 13:24 1696
to morrow *s* thou unto the king ... Est 5:14 559
to *s* unto the king to hang ... Est 6:4 559
I will *s* in the anguish of my ... Job 7:11 1696
How long wilt thou *s* these things ... Job 8:2 4448
If I *s* of strength, lo, he is ... Job 9:19
Then would I *s*, and not fear him ... Job 9:35 1696
I will *s* in the bitterness of my ... Job 10:1 1696
But oh that God would *s*, and open ... Job 11:5 1696
Or *s* to the earth, and it shall ... Job 12:8 7878
Surely I would *s* to the Almighty, ... Job 13:3 1696
Will ye *s* wickedly for God ... Job 13:7 1696
peace, let me alone, that I may *s* ... Job 13:13 1696
or let me *s*, and answer thou me ... Job 13:22 1696
I also could *s* as ye do ... Job 16:4 1696
Though I *s*, my grief is not ... Job 16:6 1696
mark, and afterwards we will *s* ... Job 18:2 1696
Suffer me that I may *s* ... Job 21:3 1696
My lips shall not *s* wickedness ... Job 27:4 1696
I said, Days should *s*, and ... Job 32:7 1696
I will *s*, that I may be refreshed ... Job 32:20 1696
hold thy peace, and I will *s* ... Job 33:31 1696
s, for I desire to justify thee ... Job 33:32 1696

therefore *s* what thou knowest ... Job 34:33 1696
I have yet to *s* on God's behalf ... Job 36:2 4405
Shall it be told him that I *s* ... Job 37:20 1696
If a man *s*, surely he shall be ... Job 37:20 559
will he *s* soft words unto thee ... Job 41:3 1696
Hear, I beseech thee, and I will *s* ... Job 42:4 1696
Then shall he *s* unto them in his ... Ps 2:5 1696
shalt destroy them that *s* leasing ... Ps 5:6 1696
They *s* vanity every one with his ... Ps 12:2 1696
and with a double heart do they *s* ... Ps 12:2 1696
with their mouth they *s* proudly ... Ps 17:10 1696
which *s* peace to their neighbours ... Ps 28:3 1696
doth every one *s* of his glory ... Ps 29:9 559
which *s* grievous things proudly ... Ps 31:18 1696
For they *s* not peace ... Ps 35:20 1696
And my tongue shall *s* of thy ... Ps 35:28 1897
seek my hurt *s* mischievous things ... Ps 38:12 1696
s of them, they are more than can ... Ps 40:5 1696
Mine enemies *s* evil of me ... Ps 41:5 559
I *s* of the things which I have ... Ps 45:1 559
My mouth shall *s* of wisdom ... Ps 49:3 1696
Hear, O my people, and I will *s* ... Ps 50:7 1696
rather than to *s* righteousness ... Ps 52:3 1696
Do ye indeed *s* righteousness, O ... Ps 58:1 1696
for cursing and lying which they *s* ... Ps 59:12 5608
them that *s* lies shall be stopped ... Ps 63:11 1696
that sit in the gate *s* against me ... Ps 69:12 7878
For mine enemies *s* against me ... Ps 71:10 559
s wickedly concerning oppression ... Ps 73:8 1696
they *s* loftily ... Ps 73:8 1696
If I say, I will *s* thus ... Ps 73:15 5608
s not with a stiff neck ... Ps 75:5 1696
I am so troubled that I cannot *s* ... Ps 77:4 1696
hear what God the LORD will *s* ... Ps 85:8 1696
for he will *s* peace unto his ... Ps 85:8 1696
shall they utter and *s* hard things ... Ps 94:4 1696
of them that *s* evil against my ... Ps 109:20 1696
They have mouths, but they *s* not ... Ps 115:5 1696
neither *s* they through their ... Ps 115:7 1897
also did sit and *s* against me ... Ps 119:23 1696
I will *s* of thy testimonies also ... Ps 119:46 1696
My tongue shall *s* of thy word ... Ps 119:172 6030
but when I *s*, they are for war ... Ps 120:7 1696
but they shall *s* with the enemies ... Ps 127:5 1696
They have mouths, but they *s* not ... Ps 135:16 1696
For they *s* against thee wickedly, ... Ps 139:20 559
I will *s* of the glorious honour ... Ps 145:5 7878
men shall *s* of the might of thy ... Ps 145:6 559
They shall *s* of the glory of thy ... Ps 145:11 559
My mouth shall *s* the praise of ... Ps 145:21 1696
for I will *s* of excellent things ... Prov 8:6 1696
For my mouth shall *s* truth ... Prov 8:7 1897
S not in the ears of a fool ... Prov 23:9 1696
when thy lips *s* right things ... Prov 23:16 1696
to keep silence, and a time to *s* ... Eccl 3:7 1696
of those that are asleep to *s* ... Song 7:9 1680
s the word, and it shall not stand ... Is 8:10 1696
if they *s* not according to this ... Is 8:20 559
All they shall *s* and say unto thee ... Is 14:10 6030
of Egypt *s* the language of Canaan ... Is 19:18 1696
tongue will he *s* to this people ... Is 28:11 1696
shalt *s* out of the ground, and thy ... Is 29:4 1696
s unto us smooth things, prophesy ... Is 30:10 1696
shall be ready to *s* plainly ... Is 32:4 1696
the vile person will *s* villany ... Is 32:6 1696
Shebna and Joah unto Rabshakeh, *S* ... Is 36:11 1696
s not to us in the Jews' language ... Is 36:11 1696
and to thee to *s* these words ... Is 36:12 1696
Thus shall ye *s* to Hezekiah king ... Is 37:10 559
S ye comfortably to Jerusalem, and ... Is 40:2 1696
then let them *s* ... Is 41:1 1696
I the LORD *s* righteousness, I ... Is 45:19 1696
that I should know how to *s* a ... Is 50:4 5790
that day that I am he that doth *s* ... Is 52:6 1696
joined himself to the LORD, *s* ... Is 56:3 559
they trust in vanity, and *s* lies ... Is 59:4 1696
I that *s* in righteousness, mighty ... Is 63:1 1696
behold, I cannot *s* ... Jer 1:6 1696
I command thee thou shalt *s* ... Jer 1:7 1696
s unto them all that I command ... Jer 1:17 1696
great men, and will *s* unto them ... Jer 5:5 1696
of hosts, Because ye *s* this word ... Jer 5:14 1696
To whom shall I *s*, and give ... Jer 6:10 1696
Therefore thou shalt *s* all these ... Jer 7:27 1696
and will not *s* the truth ... Jer 9:5 1696
taught their tongue to *s* lies ... Jer 9:5 1696
S, Thus saith the LORD, Even the ... Jer 9:22 1696
as the palm tree, but *s* not ... Jer 10:5 1696
s unto the men of Judah, and to ... Jer 11:2 1696
though they *s* fair words unto ... Jer 12:6 1696
thou shalt *s* unto them this word ... Jer 13:12 559
I shall *s* concerning a nation ... Jer 18:7 1696
I shall *s* concerning a nation ... Jer 18:9 1696
s to the men of Judah, and to the ... Jer 18:11 559
before thee to *s* good for them ... Jer 18:20 1696
nor *s* any more in his name ... Jer 20:9 1696
of Judah, and *s* there this word, ... Jer 22:1 1696
they *s* a vision of their own ... Jer 23:16 1696
let him *s* my word faithfully ... Jer 23:28 1696
s unto all the cities of Judah, ... Jer 26:2 1696
I command thee to *s* unto them ... Jer 26:2 1696
him to *s* unto all the people ... Jer 26:8 1696
to *s* all these words in your ears ... Jer 26:15 1696
which *s* unto you, saying, Ye ... Jer 27:9 559
of the prophets that *s* unto you ... Jer 27:14 559
this word that I *s* in thine ears ... Jer 28:7 1696
Thus shalt thou also *s* to ... Jer 29:24 559
shall *s* with him mouth to mouth, ... Jer 32:4 1696

s to Zedekiah king of Judah, and ... Jer 34:2 559
he shall *s* with thee mouth to ... Jer 34:3 1696
s unto them, and bring them into ... Jer 35:2 1696
of the LORD, which I *s* unto thee ... Jer 38:20 1696
s to Ebed-melech the Ethiopian, ... Jer 39:16 559
thy feet, and I will *s* unto thee ... Eze 2:1 1696
thou shalt *s* my words unto them, ... Eze 2:7 1696
go *s* unto the house of Israel ... Eze 3:1 1696
s with my words unto them ... Eze 3:4 1696
all my words that I shall *s* unto ... Eze 3:10 1696
s unto them, and tell them, Thus ... Eze 3:11 1696
But when I *s* with thee, I will ... Eze 3:27 1696
fell upon me, and said unto me, *S* ... Eze 11:5 559
I will *s*, and the word that I ... Eze 12:25 1696
that I shall *s* shall come to pass ... Eze 12:25 1696
Therefore *s* unto them, and say ... Eze 14:4 1696
s a parable unto the house of ... Eze 17:2 4911
s unto the elders of Israel, and ... Eze 20:3 1696
s unto the house of Israel, and ... Eze 20:27 1696
say of me, Doth he not *s* parables ... Eze 20:49 4911
S unto the house of Israel, Thus ... Eze 24:21 559
which is escaped, and thou shalt *s* ... Eze 24:27 1696
S, and say, Thus saith the Lord ... Eze 29:3 1696
s unto Pharaoh king of Egypt, and ... Eze 31:2 559
strong among the mighty shall *s* ... Eze 32:21 1696
s to the children of thy people, ... Eze 33:2 1696
if thou dost not *s* to warn the ... Eze 33:8 1696
s unto the house of Israel ... Eze 33:10 559
Thus ye *s*, saying, If our ... Eze 33:10 559
wastes of the land of Israel *s* ... Eze 33:24 559
s one to another, every one to ... Eze 33:30 1696
of thy people shall *s* unto thee ... Eze 37:18 559
S unto every feathered fowl, and ... Eze 39:17 559
and corrupt words to *s* before me ... Dan 2:9 560
which *s* any thing amiss against ... Dan 3:29 560
he shall *s* great words against ... Dan 7:25 4449
the words that I *s* unto thee ... Dan 10:11 1696
and said, Let my lord *s* ... Dan 10:19 1696
they shall *s* lies at one table ... Dan 11:27 1696
shall *s* marvellous things against ... Dan 11:36 1696
and *s* comfortably unto her ... Hos 2:14 1696
time, but at the end it shall *s* ... Hab 2:3 6315
shall not do iniquity, nor *s* lies ... Zeph 3:13 1696
S now to Zerubbabel the son of ... Hag 2:2 559
S to Zerubbabel, governor of ... Hag 2:21 559
s to this young man, saying, ... Zec 2:4 1696
s unto him, saying, Thus speaketh ... Zec 6:12 559
to *s* unto the priests which were ... Zec 7:3 559
S unto all the people of the land ... Zec 7:5 559
S ye every man the truth to his ... Zec 8:16 1696
he shall *s* peace unto the heathen ... Zec 9:10 1696
but *s* the word only, and my ... Mt 8:8 *2036*
no thought how or what ye shall *s* ... Mt 10:19 *2980*
in that same hour what ye shall *s* ... Mt 10:19 *2980*
For it is not ye that *s*, but the ... Mt 10:20 *2980*
in darkness, that *s* ye in light ... Mt 10:27 *2036*
can ye, being evil, *s* good things ... Mt 12:34 *2980*
every idle word that men shall *s* ... Mt 12:36 *2980*
without, desiring to *s* with him ... Mt 12:46 *2980*
without, desiring to *s* with thee ... Mt 12:47 *2980*
Therefore *s* I to them in parables ... Mt 13:13 *2980*
when they saw the dumb to *s* ... Mt 15:31 *2980*
and suffered not the devils to *s* ... Mk 1:34 *2980*
doth this man thus *s* blasphemies ... Mk 2:7 *2980*
deaf to hear, and the dumb to *s* ... Mk 7:37 *2980*
that can lightly *s* evil of me ... Mk 9:39 *2551*
he began to *s* unto them by ... Mk 12:1 *3004*
beforehand what ye shall *s* ... Mk 13:11 *2980*
given you in that hour, that *s* ye ... Mk 13:11 *2980*
for it is not ye that *s*, but the ... Mk 13:11 *2980*
I know not this man of whom ye *s* ... Mk 14:71 *3004*
they shall *s* with new tongues ... Mk 16:17 *2980*
and am sent to *s* unto thee ... Lk 1:19 *2980*
shalt be dumb, and not able to *s* ... Lk 1:20 *2980*
out, he could not *s* unto them ... Lk 1:22 *2980*
them suffered them not to *s* ... Lk 4:41 *2980*
when all men shall *s* well of you ... Lk 6:26 *2036*
was dead sat up, and began to *s* ... Lk 7:15 *2980*
he began to *s* unto the people ... Lk 7:24 *3004*
provoke him to *s* of many things ... Lk 11:53 *653*
whosoever shall *s* a word against ... Lk 12:10 *2046*
s to my brother, that he divide ... Lk 12:13 *2036*
Then began he to *s* to the people ... Lk 20:9 *3004*
And the two disciples heard him *s* ... Jn 1:37 *2980*
One of the two which heard John *s* ... Jn 1:40
We *s* that we do know, and testify ... Jn 3:11 *2980*
her, I that *s* unto thee am he ... Jn 4:26 *2980*
the words that I *s* unto you ... Jn 6:63 *2980*
of God, or whether I *s* of myself ... Jn 7:17 *2980*
I *s* to the world those things ... Jn 8:26 *3004*
hath taught me, I *s* these things ... Jn 8:28 *2980*
I *s* that which I have seen with ... Jn 8:38 *2980*
he shall *s* for himself ... Jn 9:21 *2980*
I should say, and what I should *s* ... Jn 12:49 *2980*
whatsoever I *s* therefore, even as ... Jn 12:50 *2980*
the Father said unto me, so I *s* ... Jn 12:50 *2980*
I *s* not of you all ... Jn 13:18 *3004*
s unto you I *s* not of myself ... Jn 14:10 *2980*
for he shall not *s* of himself ... Jn 16:13 *2980*
he shall hear, that shall he *s* ... Jn 16:13 *2980*
no more *s* unto you in proverbs ... Jn 16:25 *2980*
and these things I *s* in the world ... Jn 17:13 *2980*
began to *s* with other tongues, as ... Acts 2:4 *2980*
heard them *s* in his own language ... Acts 2:6 *2980*
not all these which *s* Galilaeans ... Acts 2:7 *2980*
we do hear them *s* in our tongues ... Acts 2:11 *2980*
let me freely *s* unto you of the ... Acts 2:29 *2036*
that they *s* henceforth to no man ... Acts 4:17 *2980*

commanded them not to s at all ... Acts 4:18 5350
For we cannot but s the things ... Acts 4:20 2980
all boldness they may s thy word ... Acts 4:29 2980
s in the temple to the people all ... Acts 5:20 2980
should not s in the name of Jesus ... Acts 5:40 2980
We have heard him s blasphemous ... Acts 6:11 2980
This man ceaseth not to s ... Acts 6:13 2980
when he cometh, shall s unto thee ... Acts 10:32 2980
they heard them s with tongues ... Acts 10:46 2980
And as I began to s, the Holy ... Acts 11:15 2980
The same heard Paul s ... Acts 14:9 2980
by a vision, Be not afraid, but s ... Acts 18:9 2980
he began to s boldly in the ... Acts 18:26 3955
chief captain, May I s unto thee ... Acts 21:37 2036
Who said, Canst thou s Greek ... Acts 21:37 1097
suffer me to s unto the people ... Acts 21:39 2980
Thou shalt not s evil of the ... Acts 23:5 2046
had beckoned unto him to s ... Acts 24:10 3004
art permitted to s for thyself ... Acts 26:1 3004
but s forth the words of truth and ... Acts 26:25 669
before whom also I s freely ... Acts 26:26 2980
you, to see you, and to s with you ... Acts 28:20 4354
(I s as a man) ... Rom 3:5 3004
I s after the manner of men ... Rom 6:19 3004
(for I s to them that know the ... Rom 7:1 2980
For I s to you Gentiles, inasmuch ... Rom 11:13 3004
For I will not dare to s of any ... Rom 15:18 2980
that ye all s the same thing, and ... 1Cor 1:10 3004
Howbeit we s wisdom among them ... 1Cor 2:6 2980
But we s the wisdom of God in a ... 1Cor 2:7 2980
Which things also we s, not in ... 1Cor 2:13 2980
could not s unto you as unto ... 1Cor 3:1 2980
I s to your shame ... 1Cor 6:5 3004
But I s this by permission, and ... 1Cor 7:6 3004
But to the rest s I, not the Lord ... 1Cor 7:12 3004
this I s for your own profit ... 1Cor 7:35 3004
I s as to wise men ... 1Cor 10:15 3004
do all s with tongues ... 1Cor 12:30 2980
Though I s with the tongues of ... 1Cor 13:1 2980
except I shall s to you either by ... 1Cor 14:6 2980
for ye shall s into the air ... 1Cor 14:9 2980
I s with tongues more than ye all ... 1Cor 14:18 2980
I had rather s five words with my ... 1Cor 14:19 2980
lips will I s unto this people ... 1Cor 14:21 2980
all s with tongues, and there come ... 1Cor 14:23 2980
If any man s in an unknown tongue ... 1Cor 14:27 2980
let him s to himself, and to God ... 1Cor 14:28 2980
Let the prophets s two or three ... 1Cor 14:29 2980
is not permitted unto them to s ... 1Cor 14:34 2980
for women to s in the church ... 1Cor 14:35 2980
and forbid not to s with tongues ... 1Cor 14:39 2980
I s this to your shame ... 1Cor 15:34 3004
the sight of God s we in Christ ... 2Cor 2:17 2980
we also believe, and therefore s ... 2Cor 4:13 2980
(I s as unto my children,) be ye ... 2Cor 6:13 3004
I s not this to condemn you ... 2Cor 7:3 3004
I s not by commandment, but by ... 2Cor 8:8 3004
That which I s, I s it not ... 2Cor 11:17 2980
I s as concerning reproach, as ... 2Cor 11:21 3004
(I s foolishly,) I am bold also ... 2Cor 11:21 3004
(I s as a fool) I am more ... 2Cor 11:23 2980
we s before God in Christ ... 2Cor 12:19 2980
I s after the manner of men ... Gal 3:15 3004
s every man truth with his ... Eph 4:25 2980
For it is a shame even to s of ... Eph 5:12 3004
but I s concerning Christ and the ... Eph 5:32 3004
that therein I may s boldly ... Eph 6:20 3955
as I ought to s ... Eph 6:20 2980
bold to s the word without fear ... Phil 1:14 2980
Not that I s in respect of want ... Phil 4:11 3004
to s the mystery of Christ, for ... Col 4:3 2980
make it manifest, as I ought to s ... Col 4:4 2980
that we need not to s any thing ... 1Th 1:8 2980
we were bold in our God to s unto ... 1Th 2:2 2980
with the gospel, even so we s ... 1Th 2:4 2980
Forbidding us to s to the ... 1Th 2:16 2980
(I s the truth in Christ, and lie ... 1Ti 2:7 3004
the adversary to s reproachfully ... 1Ti 5:14
But s thou the things which ... Titus 2:1 2980
These things s, and exhort, and ... Titus 2:15 2980
To s evil of no man, to be no ... Titus 3:2 987
the world to come, whereof we s ... Heb 2:5 2980
salvation, though we thus s ... Heb 6:9 2980
we cannot now s particularly ... Heb 9:5 3004
man be swift to hear, slow to s ... Jas 1:19 2980
So s ye, and so do, as they that ... Jas 2:12 2980
S not evil one of another, ... Jas 4:11 2635
whereas they s against you as ... 1Pet 2:12 2635
and his lips that they s no guile ... 1Pet 3:10 2980
that, whereas they s evil of you ... 1Pet 3:16 2635
If any man s, let him s as ... 1Pet 4:11 2980
not afraid to s evil of dignities ... 2Pet 2:10 987
s evil of the things that they ... 2Pet 2:12 987
For when they s great swelling ... 2Pet 2:18 5350
therefore s they of the world, and ... 1Jn 4:5 2980
s face to face, that our joy may ... 2Jn 12 2980
thee, and we shall s face to face ... 3Jn 14 2980
dominion, and s evil of dignities ... Jude 8 987
But these s evil of those things ... Jude 10 987
the depths of Satan, as they s ... Rev 2:24 3004
image of the beast should both s ... Rev 13:15 2980

SPEAKER {2}
Let not an evil s be established ... Ps 140:11 376,3956
because he was the chief s ... Acts 14:12 3056

SPEAKEST {17}
wherefore then s thou so to me ... 1Sa 9:21 1696
Why s thou any more of thy ... 2Sa 19:29 1696
that thou s in thy bedchamber ... 2Kin 6:12 1696
Thou s as one of the foolish ... Job 2:10 1696
sittest and s against thy brother ... Ps 50:20 1696
mightest be justified when thou s ... Ps 51:4 1696
Why sayest thou, O Jacob, and s ... Is 40:27 1696
for thou s falsely of Ishmael ... Jer 40:16 1696
unto Jeremiah, Thou s falsely ... Jer 43:2 1696
nor s to warn the wicked from his ... Eze 3:18 1696
for thou s lies in the name of ... Zec 13:3 1696
Why s thou unto them in parables ... Mt 13:10 2980
s thou this parable unto us, or ... Lk 12:41 3004
now s thou plainly ... Jn 16:29 2980
thou plainly, and s no proverb ... Jn 16:29 3004
unto him, S thou not unto me ... Jn 19:10 2980
this new doctrine, whereof thou s ... Acts 17:19 2980

SPEAKETH {74}
it is my mouth that s unto you ... Gen 45:12 1696
as a man s unto his friend ... Ex 33:11 1696
thee, saying, All that the LORD s ... Num 23:26 1696
When a prophet s in the name of ... Deut 18:22 1696
Thus s Ben-hadad, saying, ... 1Kin 20:5 559
as one of the foolish women s ... Job 2:10 1696
He that s flattery to his friends ... Job 17:5 5046
For God s once, yea twice, yet ... Job 33:14 1696
and the tongue that s proud things ... Ps 12:3 1696
and s the truth in his heart ... Ps 15:2 1696
mouth of the righteous s wisdom ... Ps 37:30 1897
if he come to see me, he s vanity ... Ps 41:6 1696
Whose mouth s vanity, and their ... Ps 144:8 1696
children, whose mouth s vanity ... Ps 144:11 1696
the man that s froward things ... Prov 2:12 1696
he s with his feet, he teacheth ... Prov 6:13 4448
A false witness that s lies ... Prov 6:19 6315
mouth of the wicked s frowardness ... Prov 10:32
He that s truth sheweth forth ... Prov 12:17 6315
There is that s like the ... Prov 12:18 981
but a deceitful witness s lies ... Prov 14:25 6315
and they love him that s right ... Prov 16:13 1696
he that s lies shall not escape ... Prov 19:5 6315
he that s lies shall perish ... Prov 19:9 6315
the man that heareth s constantly ... Prov 21:28 1696
When he s fair, believe him not ... Prov 26:25 6963
evildoer, and every mouth s folly ... Is 9:17 1696
even when the needy s right ... Is 32:7 1696
righteously, and s uprightly ... Is 33:15 1696
it s deceit ... Jer 9:8 1696
one s peaceably to his neighbour ... Jer 9:8 1696
word which the LORD s unto you ... Jer 10:1 1696
Thus s the LORD of hosts, the God ... Jer 28:2 559
Thus s the LORD of hosts, the God ... Jer 29:25 559
Thus s the LORD God of Israel, ... Jer 30:2 559
of the Almighty God when he s ... Eze 10:5 1696
they abhor him that s uprightly ... Amos 5:10 1696
Thus s the LORD of hosts, saying, ... Hag 1:2 559
Thus s the LORD of hosts, saying, ... Zec 6:12 559
Thus s the LORD of hosts, saying, ... Zec 7:9 559
of your Father which s in you ... Mt 10:20 2036
but whosoever s against the Holy ... Mt 12:32 2036
of the heart the mouth s ... Mt 12:34 2980
Who is this which s blasphemies ... Lk 5:21 2980
of the heart his mouth s ... Lk 6:45 2980
is earthly, and s of the earth ... Jn 3:31 2980
God hath sent s the words of God ... Jn 3:34 2980
He that s of himself seeketh his ... Jn 7:18 2980
he s boldly, and they say nothing ... Jn 7:26 2980
s a lie, he s of his own ... Jn 8:44 2980
himself a king s against Caesar ... Jn 19:12 483
For David s concerning him, I ... Acts 2:25 3004
of whom s the prophet this ... Acts 8:34 3004
which is of faith s on this wise ... Rom 10:6 3004
For he that s in an unknown ... 1Cor 14:2 2980
an unknown tongue s not unto men ... 1Cor 14:2 2980
in the spirit he s mysteries ... 1Cor 14:2 2980
s unto men to edification ... 1Cor 14:3 2980
He that s in an unknown tongue ... 1Cor 14:4 2980
than he that s with tongues ... 1Cor 14:5 2980
be unto him that s a barbarian ... 1Cor 14:11 2980
he that s shall be a barbarian ... 1Cor 14:11 2980
Wherefore let him that s in an ... 1Cor 14:13 2980
Now the Spirit s expressly ... 1Ti 4:1 3004
and by it he being dead yet s ... Heb 11:4 2980
which s unto you as unto children ... Heb 12:5 1256
that s better things than that of ... Heb 12:24 2980
See that ye refuse not him that s ... Heb 12:25 2980
away from him that s from heaven ... Heb 12:25
He that s evil of his brother, and ... Jas 4:11 2635
s evil of the law, and judgeth the ... Jas 4:11 2635
their mouth s great swelling ... Jude 16 2980

SPEAKING {62}
to pass, before he had done s ... Gen 24:15 1696
before I had done s in mine heart ... Gen 24:45 1696
till Moses had done s with them ... Ex 34:33 1696
one s unto him from off the mercy ... Num 7:89 1696
made an end of s all these words ... Num 16:31 1696
s out of the midst of the fire ... Deut 4:33 1696
the voice of the living God s out ... Deut 5:26 1696
s of them when thou sittest in ... Deut 11:19 1696
made an end of s unto the people ... Deut 20:9 1696
Moses made an end of s all these ... Deut 32:45 1696
when he had made an end of s ... Judg 15:17 1696
her, then she left s unto her ... Ruth 1:18 1696
he had made an end of s unto Saul ... 1Sa 18:1 1696
an end of s these words unto Saul ... 1Sa 24:16 1696
soon as he had made an end of s ... 2Sa 13:36 1696
s from the mouth of the LORD ... 2Chr 36:12
and s peace to all his seed ... Est 10:3 1696
While he was yet s, there came ... Job 1:16 1696
While he was yet s, there came ... Job 1:17 1696
While he was yet s, there came ... Job 1:18 1696
who can withhold himself from s ... Job 4:2 4405
they left off s ... Job 32:15 4405
evil, and thy lips from s guile ... Ps 34:13 1696
as soon as they be born, s lies ... Ps 58:3 1696
forth of the finger, and s vanity ... Is 58:9 1696
pleasure, nor s thine own words ... Is 58:13 1696
our God, s oppression and revolt, ... Is 59:13 1696
and while they are yet s, I will ... Is 65:24 1696
unto you, rising up early and s ... Jer 7:13 1696
unto you, rising early and s ... Jer 25:3 1696
all the people heard Jeremiah s ... Jer 26:7 1696
Jeremiah had made an end of s all ... Jer 26:8 1696
unto you, rising early and s ... Jer 35:14 1696
in s such words unto them ... Jer 38:4 1696
So they left off s with him ... Jer 38:27 2790
of s unto all the people all the ... Jer 43:1 1696
I heard him s unto me out of the ... Eze 43:6 1696
of man, and a mouth s great things ... Dan 7:8 4449
Then I heard one saint s, and ... Dan 8:13 1696
Now as he was s with me, I was in ... Dan 8:18 1696
And whiles I was s, and praying, and ... Dan 9:20 1696
Yea, whiles I was s in prayer ... Dan 9:21 1696
shall be heard for their much s ... Mt 6:7 4180
Now when he had left s, he said ... Lk 5:4 2980
s of the things pertaining to the ... Acts 1:3 3004
s unto Moses, that he should make ... Acts 7:44 2980
s to them, persuaded them to ... Acts 13:43 4354
abode they s boldly in the Lord ... Acts 14:3 3955
s perverse things, to draw away ... Acts 20:30 2980
earth, I heard a voice s unto me ... Acts 26:14 2980
that no man s by the Spirit of ... 1Cor 12:3 2980
if I come unto you s with tongues ... 1Cor 14:6 2980
ye seek a proof of Christ s in me ... 2Cor 13:3 2980
But s the truth in love, may grow ... Eph 4:15 226
and anger, and clamour, and evil s ... Eph 4:31 988
S to yourselves in psalms and ... Eph 5:19 2980
S lies in hypocrisy ... 1Ti 4:2 5573
s things which they ought not ... 1Ti 5:13 2980
excess of riot, s evil of you ... 1Pet 4:4 987
the dumb ass s with man's voice ... 2Pet 2:16 5350
s in them of these things ... 2Pet 3:16 2980
unto him a mouth s great things ... Rev 13:5 2980

SPEAKINGS {1}
and envies, and all evil s ... 1Pet 2:1 2636

SPEAR {45}
Stretch out the s that is in thy ... Josh 8:18 3591
Joshua stretched out the s that ... Josh 8:18 3591
wherewith he stretched out the s ... Josh 8:26 3591
was there a shield or s seen ... Judg 5:8 7420
there was neither sword nor s ... 1Sa 13:22 2595
the staff of his s was like a ... 1Sa 17:7 2595
to me with a sword, and with a s ... 1Sa 17:45 2595
LORD saveth not with sword and s ... 1Sa 17:47 2595
here under thine hand s or sword ... 1Sa 21:8 2595
having his s in his hand, and all ... 1Sa 22:6 2595
his s stuck in the ground at his ... 1Sa 26:7 2595
with the s even to the earth at ... 1Sa 26:8 2595
take thou now the s that is at ... 1Sa 26:11 2595
So David took the s and the cruse ... 1Sa 26:12 2595
And now see where the king's s is ... 1Sa 26:16 2595
and said, Behold the king's s ... 1Sa 26:22 2595
behold, Saul leaned upon his s ... 2Sa 1:6 2595
with the hinder end of the s ... 2Sa 2:23 2595
that the s came out behind him ... 2Sa 2:23 2595
the weight of whose s weighed ... 2Sa 21:16 7013
the staff of whose s was like a ... 2Sa 21:19 2595
with iron and the staff of a s ... 2Sa 23:7 2595
he lift up his s against eight ... 2Sa 23:8
he lifted up his s against three ... 2Sa 23:18 2595
the Egyptian had a s in his hand ... 2Sa 23:21 2595
and plucked the s out of the ... 2Sa 23:21 2595
hand, and slew him with his own s ... 2Sa 23:21 2595
he lifted up his s against three ... 1Chr 11:11 2595
for lifting up his s against ... 1Chr 11:20 2595
hand was a s like a weaver's beam ... 1Chr 11:23 2595
and plucked the s out of the ... 1Chr 11:23 2595
hand, and slew him with his own s ... 1Chr 11:23 2595
s were six thousand and eight ... 1Chr 12:24 7420
s thirty and seven thousand ... 1Chr 12:34 2595
whose s staff was like a weaver's ... 1Chr 20:5 2595
forth to war, that could handle s ... 2Chr 25:5 7420
against him, the glittering s ... Job 39:23 2595
the s, the dart, nor the ... Job 41:26 2595
he laugheth at the shaking of a s ... Job 41:29 3591
Draw out also the s, and stop the ... Ps 35:3 2595
bow, and cutteth the s in sunder ... Ps 46:9 2595
They shall lay hold on bow and s ... Jer 6:23 3591
bright sword and the glittering s ... Nah 3:3 2595
the shining of thy glittering s ... Hab 3:11 2595
with a s pierced his side ... Jn 19:34 3057

SPEARMEN {2}
Rebuke the company of s, the ... Ps 68:30 7070
s two hundred, at the third hour ... Acts 23:23 1187

SPEAR'S {1}
his s head weighed six hundred ... 1Sa 17:7 2595

SPEARS {16}
the Hebrews make them swords or s ... 1Sa 13:19 2595
the priest give king David's s ... 2Kin 11:10 2595
several city he put shields and s ... 2Chr 11:12 7420
of men that bare targets and s ... 2Chr 14:8 7420
to the captains of hundreds s ... 2Chr 23:9 2595
all the host shields, and s ... 2Chr 26:14 7420
with their swords, their s ... Neh 4:13 7420

half of them held both the *s* Neh 4:16 7420
half of them held the *s* from the Neh 4:21 7420
or his head with fish *s* Job 41:7 6767
sons of men, whose teeth are *s* Ps 57:4 2595
their *s* into pruninghooks Is 2:4 2595
furbish the *s*, and put on the Jer 46:4 7420
and the handstaves, and the *s* Eze 39:9 7420
and your pruninghooks into *s* Joel 3:10 7420
their *s* into pruninghooks Mic 4:3 2595

SPECIAL {2}
to be a *s* people unto himself Deut 7:6 5459
God wrought *s* miracles by the Acts 19:11 *3756,3858,5177*

SPECIALLY {6}
S the day that thou stoodest Deut 4:10
s before thee, O king Agrippa, Acts 25:26 *3122*
all men, *s* of those that believe 1Ti 4:10 *3122*
s for those of his own house, he 1Ti 5:8 *3122*
s they of the circumcision Titus 1:10 *3122*
s to me, but how much more unto Philem 16 *3122*

SPECKLED {11}
removing from thence all the *s* Gen 30:32 5348
the spotted and *s* among the goats Gen 30:32 5348
every one that is not *s* and Gen 30:33 5348
and all the she goats that were *s* Gen 30:35 5348
forth cattle ringstraked, *s* Gen 30:39 5348
thus, The *s* shall be thy wages Gen 31:8 5348
then all the cattle bare *s* Gen 31:8 5348
the cattle were ringstraked, *s* Gen 31:10 5348
the cattle are ringstraked, *s* Gen 31:12 5348
heritage is unto me as a *s* bird Jer 12:9 6641
him were there red horses, *s* Zec 1:8 8320

SPECTACLE {1}
we are made a *s* unto the world 1Cor 4:9 *2302*

SPED {1}
Have they not *s* Judg 5:30 4672

SPEECH {49}
of Lamech, hearken unto my *s* Gen 4:23 565
was of one language, and of one *s* Gen 11:1 1697
not understand one another's *s* Gen 11:7 8193
but I am slow of *s*, and of a slow Ex 4:10 6310
give occasions of *s* against her Deut 22:14 1697
given occasions of *s* against her Deut 22:17 1697
my *s* shall distil as the dew, as Deut 32:2 565
To fetch about this form of *s* 2Sa 14:20 1697
seeing the *s* of all Israel is 2Sa 19:11 1697
the *s* pleased the Lord, that 1Kin 3:10 1697
s unto the people of Jerusalem 2Chr 32:18 3066
spake half in the *s* of Ashdod Neh 13:24 3066
removeth away the *s* of the trusty Job 12:20 8193
Hear diligently my *s*, and my Job 13:17 4405
Hear diligently my *s*, and let this Job 21:2 4405
liar, and make my *s* nothing worth Job 24:25 4405
and my *s* dropped upon them Job 29:22 4405
order our *s* by reason of darkness Job 37:19
thine ear unto me, and hear my *s* Ps 17:6 565
Day unto day uttereth *s*, and night Ps 19:2 562
There is no *s* nor language, where Ps 19:3 562
With her much fair *s* she caused Prov 7:21 3948
Excellent *s* becometh not a fool Prov 17:7 8193
of scarlet, and thy *s* is comely Song 4:3 4057
hearken, and hear my *s* Is 28:23 565
thy *s* shall be low out of the Is 29:4 565
thy *s* shall whisper out of the Is 29:4 565
give ear unto my *s* Is 32:9 565
a people of a deeper *s* than thou Is 33:19 8193
use this *s* in the land of Judah Jer 31:23 1697
of the Almighty, the voice of *s* Eze 1:24 1999
sent to a people of a strange *s* Eze 3:5 8193
Not to many people of a strange *s* Eze 3:6 8193
O LORD, I have heard thy *s* Hab 3:2 8088
for thy *s* bewrayeth thee Mt 26:73 *2981*
and had an impediment in his *s* Mk 7:32 *3424*
and thy *s* agreeth thereto Mk 14:70 *2981*
Why do ye not understand my *s* Jn 8:43 *2981*
saying in the *s* of Lycaonia Acts 14:11 *3072*
continued his *s* until midnight Acts 20:7 *3056*
with excellency of *s* or of wisdom 1Cor 2:1 *3056*
And my *s* and my preaching was not 1Cor 2:4 *3056*
not the *s* of them which are 1Cor 4:19 *3056*
hope, we use great plainness of *s* 2Cor 3:12
is my boldness of *s* toward you 2Cor 7:4
is weak, and his *s* contemptible 2Cor 10:10 *3056*
But though I be rude in *s* 2Cor 11:6 *3056*
Let your *s* be alway with grace, Col 4:6 *3056*
Sound *s*, that cannot be condemned Titus 2:8 *3056*

SPEECHES {7}
even apparently, and not in dark *s* Num 12:8 2420
the *s* of one that is desperate, Job 6:26 561
or with *s* wherewith he can do no Job 15:3 4405
will I answer him with your *s* Job 32:14 561
Job, I pray thee, hear my *s* Job 33:1 4405
fair *s* deceive the hearts of the Rom 16:18 *2129*
of all their hard *s* which ungodly Jude 15

SPEECHLESS {3}
And he was *s* Mt 22:12 *5392*
beckoned unto them, and remained *s* Lk 1:22 *2974*
which journeyed with him stood *s* Acts 9:7 *1769*

SPEED {11}
thee, send me good *s* this day Gen 24:12 7136
cried after the lad, Make *s* 1Sa 20:38 4120
make *s* to depart, lest he 2Sa 15:14 4116
s to get him up to his chariot 1Kin 12:18 553
But king Rehoboam made *s* to get 2Chr 10:18 553
let it be done with *s* Ezr 6:12 629
That say, Let him make *s*, and Is 5:19 4116
they shall come with *s* swiftly Is 5:26 4120
for to come to him with all *s* Acts 17:15 *5613,5033*
your house, neither bid him God *s* 2Jn 10 *5463*
For he that biddeth him God *s* is 2Jn 11 *5463*

SPEEDILY {19}
Then they *s* took down every man Gen 44:11 4116
for me than that I should *s* 1Sa 27:1 4422
the wilderness, but *s* pass over 2Sa 17:16 5674
divided them *s* among all the 2Chr 35:13
the king had sent, so they did *s* Ezr 6:13 629
That thou mayest buy *s* with this Ezr 7:17 629
require of you, it be done *s* Ezr 7:21 629
judgment be executed *s* upon him Ezr 7:26 629
he *s* gave her her things for Est 2:9 926
deliver me *s* Ps 31:2 4120
hear me *s* Ps 69:17 4118
thy tender mercies *s* prevent us Ps 79:8 4118
the day when I call answer me *s* Ps 102:2 4118
Hear me *s*, O LORD Ps 143:7 4118
an evil work is not executed *s* Eccl 8:11 4120
thine health shall spring forth *s* Is 58:8 4120
s will I return your recompence Joel 3:4 4120
Let us go *s* to pray before the Zec 8:21 1980
you that he will avenge them *s* Lk 18:8 *1722,5034*

SPEEDY {1}
for he shall make even a *s* Zeph 1:18 926

SPEND {7}
I will *s* mine arrows upon them Deut 32:23 3615
They *s* their days in wealth, and Job 21:13 3615
they shall *s* their days in Job 36:11 3615
we *s* our years as a tale that is Ps 90:9 3615
Wherefore do ye *s* money for that Is 55:2 8254
he would not *s* the time in Asia Acts 20:16 *5551*
And I will very gladly *s* and be 2Cor 12:15 *1159*

SPENDEST {1}
and whatsoever thou *s* more Lk 10:35 *4325*

SPENDETH {3}
but a foolish man *s* it up Prov 21:20 1104
with harlots *s* his substance Prov 29:3 6
vain life which he *s* as a shadow Eccl 6:12 6213

SPENT {19}
And the water was *s* in the bottle Gen 21:15 3615
my lord, how that our money is *s* Gen 47:18 8552
your strength shall be *s* in vain Lev 26:20 8552
were by Jebus, the day was far *s* Judg 19:11 7286
for the bread is *s* in our vessels 1Sa 9:7 235
shuttle, and are *s* without hope Job 7:6 3615
For my life is *s* with grief Ps 31:10 3615
I have *s* my strength for nought, Is 49:4 3615
all the bread in the city were *s* Jer 37:21 8552
had *s* all that she had, and was Mk 5:26 *1159*
And when the day was now far *s* Mk 6:35
which had *s* all her living upon Lk 8:43 *4321*
And when he had *s* all, there arose Lk 15:14 *1159*
evening, and the day is far *s* Lk 24:29 *2827*
s their time in nothing else Acts 17:21 *2119*
after he had *s* some time there, Acts 18:23 *4160*
Now when much time was *s*, and when Acts 27:9 *1230*
The night is far *s*, the day is at Rom 13:12 *4298*
very gladly spend and be *s* for you 2Cor 12:15 *1550*

SPEWING {1}
shameful *s* shall be on thy glory Hab 2:16 7022

SPICE {5}
And *s*, and oil for the light, and Ex 35:28 1314
the traffick of the *s* merchants 1Kin 10:15 7402
neither was there any such *s* as 2Chr 9:9 1314
have gathered my myrrh with my *s* Song 5:1 1313
s it well, and let the bones be Eze 24:10 7543

SPICED {1}
of *s* wine of the juice of my Song 8:2 7544

SPICERY {1}
with their camels bearing *s* Gen 37:25 5219

SPICES {31}
little balm, and a little honey, *s* Gen 43:11 5219
s for anointing oil, and for sweet Ex 25:6 1314
s of pure myrrh five hundred Ex 30:23 1314
Moses, Take unto thee sweet *s* Ex 30:34 5561
these sweet *s* with pure Ex 30:34 5561
s for anointing oil, and for the Ex 35:8 1314
and the pure incense of sweet *s* Ex 37:29 5561
train, with camels that bare *s* 1Kin 10:2 1314
of *s* very great store, and 1Kin 10:10 1314
of *s* as these which the queen of 1Kin 10:10 1314
and garments, and armour, and *s* 1Kin 10:25 1314
the silver, and the gold, and the *s* 2Kin 20:13 1314
and the frankincense, and the *s* 1Chr 9:29 1314
made the ointment of the *s* 1Chr 9:30 1314
company, and camels that bare *s* 2Chr 9:1 1314
of *s* great abundance, and precious 2Chr 9:9 1314
gold, and raiment, harness, and *s* 2Chr 9:24 1314
divers kinds of *s* prepared by the 2Chr 16:14
and for precious stones, and for *s* 2Chr 32:27 1314
of thine ointments than all *s* Song 4:10 1314
and aloes, with all the chief *s* Song 4:14 1314
that the *s* thereof may flow out Song 4:16 1314
His cheeks are as a bed of *s* Song 5:13 1314
into his garden, to the beds of *s* Song 6:2 1314
hart upon the mountains of *s* Song 8:14 1314
the silver, and the gold, and the *s* Is 39:2 1314
in thy fairs with chief of all *s* Eze 27:22 1314
and Salome, had bought sweet *s* Mk 16:1 *759*
And they returned, and prepared *s* Lk 23:56 *759*
bringing the *s* which they had Lk 24:1 *759*
it in linen clothes with the *s* Jn 19:40 *759*

SPIDER {1}
The *s* taketh hold with her hands, Prov 30:28 8079

SPIDER'S {2}
and whose trust shall be a *s* web Job 8:14 5908
eggs, and weave the *s* web Is 59:5 5908

SPIED {6}
he *s* an Egyptian smiting an Ex 2:11 7200
men that had *s* out the country Josh 6:22 7270
he *s* the company of Jehu as he 2Kin 9:17 7200
behold, they *s* a band of men 2Kin 13:21 7200
he *s* the sepulchres that were 2Kin 23:16 7200
that were *s* in the land of Judah 2Kin 23:24 7200

SPIES {14}
them, and said unto them, Ye are *s* Gen 42:9 7270
true men, thy servants are no *s* Gen 42:11 7270
spake unto you, saying, Ye are *s* Gen 42:14 7270
life of Pharaoh surely ye are *s* Gen 42:16 7270
took us for *s* of the country Gen 42:30 7270
we are no *s* Gen 42:31 7270
shall I know that ye are no *s* Gen 42:34 7270
Israel came by the way of the *s* Num 21:1 871
the young men that were *s* went in Josh 6:23 7270
the *s* saw a man come forth out of Judg 1:24 8104
David therefore sent out *s* 1Sa 26:4 7270
But Absalom sent *s* throughout all 2Sa 15:10 7270
they watched him, and sent forth *s* Lk 20:20 *1455*
she had received the *s* with peace Heb 11:31 *2685*

SPIKENARD {5}
my *s* sendeth forth the smell Song 1:12 5373
camphire, with *s*, Song 4:13 5373
S and saffron Song 4:14 5373
of ointment of *s* very precious Mk 14:3 *3487,4101*
Mary a pound of ointment of *s* Jn 12:3 *3487,4101*

SPILLED {3}
that he *s* it on the ground, lest Gen 38:9 7843
the bottles, and the wine is *s* Mk 2:22 *1632*
will burst the bottles, and be *s* Lk 5:37 *1632*

SPILT {1}
are as water *s* on the ground, 2Sa 14:14 5064

SPIN {3}
hearted did *s* with their hands Ex 35:25 2901
they toil not, neither do they *s* Mt 6:28 *3514*
they toil not, they *s* not Lk 12:27 *3514*

SPINDLE {1}
She layeth her hands to the *s* Prov 31:19 3601

SPIRIT {505}
the *S* of God moved upon the face Gen 1:2 7307
My *s* shall not always strive with Gen 6:3 7307
morning that his *s* was troubled Gen 41:8 7307
is, a man in whom the *S* of God is Gen 41:38 7307
the *s* of Jacob their father Gen 45:27 7307
not unto Moses for anguish of *s* Ex 6:9 7307
have filled with the *s* of wisdom Ex 28:3 7307
have filled him with the *s* of God Ex 31:3 7307
every one whom his *s* made willing Ex 35:21 7307
hath filled him with the *s* of God Ex 35:31 7307
or woman that hath a familiar *s* Lev 20:27 178
the *s* of jealousy come upon him, Num 5:14 7307
or if the *s* of jealousy come upon Num 5:14 7307
Or when the *s* of jealousy cometh Num 5:30 7307
take of the *s* which is upon thee Num 11:17 7307
took of the *s* that was upon him, Num 11:25 7307
when the *s* rested upon them, they Num 11:25 7307
and the *s* rested upon them Num 11:26 7307
LORD would put his *s* upon them Num 11:29 7307
because he had another *s* with him Num 14:24 7307
the *s* of God came upon him Num 24:2 7307
of Nun, a man in whom is the *s* Num 27:18 7307
the LORD thy God hardened his *s* Deut 2:30 7307
Nun was full of the *s* of wisdom Deut 34:9 7307
was there *s* in them any more Josh 5:1 7307
the *S* of the LORD came upon him, Judg 3:10 7307
But the *S* of the LORD came upon Judg 6:34 7307
sent an evil *s* between Abimelech Judg 9:23 7307
Then the *S* of the LORD came upon Judg 11:29 7307
the *S* of the LORD began to move Judg 13:25 7307
the *S* of the LORD came mightily Judg 14:6 7307
the *S* of the LORD came upon him, Judg 14:19 7307
the *S* of the LORD came mightily Judg 15:14 7307
his *s* came again, and he revived Judg 15:19 7307
I am a woman of a sorrowful *s* 1Sa 1:15 7307
the *S* of the LORD will come upon 1Sa 10:6 7307
the *S* of God came upon him, and he 1Sa 10:10 7307
the *S* of God came upon Saul when 1Sa 11:6 7307
the *S* of the LORD came upon David 1Sa 16:13 7307
But the *S* of the LORD departed 1Sa 16:14 7307
an evil *s* from the LORD troubled 1Sa 16:14 7307
an evil *s* from God troubleth thee 1Sa 16:15 7307
when the evil *s* from God is upon 1Sa 16:16 7307
when the evil *s* from God was upon 1Sa 16:23 7307
the evil *s* departed from him 1Sa 16:23 7307
that the evil *s* from God came 1Sa 18:10 7307
the evil *s* from the LORD was upon 1Sa 19:9 7307
the *S* of God was upon the 1Sa 19:20 7307
the *S* of God was upon him also, 1Sa 19:23 7307
me a woman that hath a familiar *s* 1Sa 28:7 178
that hath a familiar *s* at En-dor 1Sa 28:7 178
divine unto me by the familiar *s* 1Sa 28:8 178
eaten, his *s* came again to him 1Sa 30:12 7307
The *S* of the LORD spake by me, and 2Sa 23:2 7307
there was no more *s* in her 1Kin 10:5 7307
that the *S* of the LORD shall 1Kin 18:12 7307
unto him, Why is thy *s* so sad 1Kin 21:5 7307
And there came forth a *s*, and stood 1Kin 22:21 7307
I will be a lying *s* in the mouth 1Kin 22:22 7307

the LORD hath put a lying *s* in 1Kin 22:23 7307
Which way went the *S* of the LORD 1Kin 22:24 7307
portion of thy *s* be upon me 2Kin 2:9 7307
The *s* of Elijah doth rest on 2Kin 2:15 7307
lest peradventure the *S* of the 2Kin 2:16 7307
up the *s* of Pul king of Assyria 1Chr 5:26 7307
the *s* of Tilgath-pilneser king of 1Chr 5:26 7307
of one that had a familiar *s* 1Chr 10:13 178
Then the *s* came upon Amasai, who 1Chr 12:18 7307
of all that he had by the *s* 1Chr 28:12 7307
there was no more *s* in her 2Chr 9:4 7307
the *S* of God came upon Azariah 2Chr 15:1 7307
Then there came out a *s*, and stood 2Chr 18:20 7307
be a lying *s* in the mouth of all 2Chr 18:21 7307
lying *s* in the mouth of these thy 2Chr 18:22 7307
Which way went the *S* of the LORD 2Chr 18:23 7307
came the *S* of the LORD in the 2Chr 20:14 7307
Jehoram the *s* of the Philistines 2Chr 21:16 7307
the *S* of God came upon Zechariah 2Chr 24:20 7307
and dealt with a familiar *s* 2Chr 33:6 178
up the *s* of Cyrus king of Persia 2Chr 36:22 7307
up the *s* of Cyrus king of Persia Ezr 1:1 7307
all them whose *s* God had raised Ezr 1:5 7307
also thy good *s* to instruct them Neh 9:20 7307
them by thy *s* in thy prophets Neh 9:30 7307
Then a *s* passed before my face Job 4:15 7307
poison whereof drinketh up my *s* Job 6:4 7307
will speak in the anguish of my *s* Job 7:11 7307
visitation hath preserved my *s* Job 10:12 7307
thou turnest thy *s* against God Job 15:13 7307
the *s* of my understanding causeth Job 20:3 7307
why should not my *s* be troubled Job 21:4 7307
and whose *s* came from thee Job 26:4 5397
By his *s* he hath garnished the Job 26:13 7307
the *s* of God is in my nostrils Job 27:3 7307
But there is a *s* in man Job 32:8 7307
the *s* within me constraineth me Job 32:18 7307
The *s* of God hath made me, and the Job 33:4 7307
if he gather unto himself his *s* Job 34:14 7307
Into thine hand I commit my *s* Ps 31:5 7307
in whose *s* there is no guile Ps 32:2 7307
saveth such as be of a contrite *s* Ps 34:18 7307
and renew a right *s* within me Ps 51:10 7307
and take not thy holy *s* from me Ps 51:11 7307
and uphold me with thy free *s* Ps 51:12 7307
sacrifices of God are a broken *s* Ps 51:17 7307
He shall cut off the *s* of princes Ps 76:12 7307
and my *s* was overwhelmed Ps 77:3 7307
my *s* made diligent search Ps 77:6 7307
whose *s* was not stedfast with God Ps 78:8 7307
Thou sendest forth thy *s*, they Ps 104:30 7307
Because they provoked his *s* Ps 106:33 7307
Whither shall I go from thy *s* Ps 139:7 7307
When my *s* was overwhelmed within Ps 142:3 7307
Therefore is my *s* overwhelmed Ps 143:4 7307
my *s* faileth Ps 143:7 7307
thy *s* is good Ps 143:10 7307
I will pour out my *s* unto you Prov 1:23 7307
faithful *s* concealeth the matter Prov 11:13 7307
that is hasty of *s* exalteth folly Prov 14:29 7307
therein is a breach in the *s* Prov 15:4 7307
of the heart the *s* is broken Prov 15:13 7307
an haughty *s* before a fall Prov 16:18 7307
be of an humble *s* with the lowly Prov 16:19 7307
he that ruleth his *s* than he that Prov 16:32 7307
but a broken *s* drieth the bones Prov 17:22 7307
is of an excellent *s* Prov 17:27 7307
The *s* of a man will sustain his Prov 18:14 7307
but a wounded *s* who can bear Prov 18:14 7307
The *s* of man is the candle of the Prov 20:27 5397
s is like a city that is broken Prov 25:28 7307
shall uphold the humble in *s* Prov 29:23 7307
all is vanity and vexation of *s* Eccl 1:14 7307
that this also is vexation of *s* Eccl 1:17 7307
all was vanity and vexation of *s* Eccl 2:11 7307
all is vanity and vexation of *s* Eccl 2:17 7307
also is vanity and vexation of *s* Eccl 2:26 7307
Who knoweth the *s* of man that Eccl 3:21 7307
the *s* of the beast that goeth Eccl 3:21 7307
is also vanity and vexation of *s* Eccl 4:4 7307
with travail and vexation of *s* Eccl 4:6 7307
also is vanity and vexation of *s* Eccl 4:16 7307
is also vanity and vexation of *s* Eccl 6:9 7307
the patient in *s* is better than Eccl 7:8 7307
is better than the proud in *s* Eccl 7:8 7307
Be not hasty in thy *s* to be angry Eccl 7:9 7307
over the *s* to retain the *s* Eccl 8:8 7307
If the *s* of the ruler rise up Eccl 10:4 7307
not what is the way of the *s* Eccl 11:5 7307
the *s* shall return unto God who Eccl 12:7 7307
thereof by the *s* of judgment Is 4:4 7307
and by the *s* of burning Is 4:4 7307
the *s* of the LORD shall rest upon Is 11:2 7307
the *s* of wisdom and understanding, Is 11:2 7307
the *s* of counsel and might Is 11:2 7307
the *s* of knowledge and of the fear Is 11:2 7307
the *s* of Egypt shall fail in the Is 19:3 7307
a perverse *s* in the midst thereof Is 19:14 7307
with my *s* within me will I seek Is 26:9 7307
for a *s* of judgment to him that Is 28:6 7307
as of one that hath a familiar *s* Is 29:4 178
out upon you the *s* of deep sleep Is 29:10 7307
They also that erred in *s* shall Is 29:24 7307
with a covering, but not of my *s* Is 30:1 7307
and their horses flesh, and not *s* Is 31:3 7307
Until the *s* be poured upon us Is 32:15 7307
his *s* it hath gathered them Is 34:16 7307
these things is the life of my *s* Is 38:16 7307
because the *s* of the LORD bloweth Is 40:7 7307
hath directed the *S* of the LORD Is 40:13 7307
I have put my *s* upon him Is 42:1 7307
s to them that walk therein Is 42:5 7307
I will pour my *s* upon thy seed Is 44:3 7307
and now the Lord GOD, and his *S* Is 48:16 7307
a woman forsaken and grieved in *s* Is 54:6 7307
that is of a contrite and humble *s* Is 57:15 7307
to revive the *s* of the humble Is 57:15 7307
for the *s* should fail before me, Is 57:16 7307
the *S* of the LORD shall lift up a Is 59:19 7307
My *s* that is upon thee, and my Is 59:21 7307
The *S* of the Lord GOD is upon me Is 61:1 7307
of praise for the *s* of heaviness Is 61:3 7307
rebelled, and vexed his holy *S* Is 63:10 7307
he that put his holy *S* within him Is 63:11 7307
the *S* of the LORD caused him to Is 63:14 7307
and shall howl for vexation of *s* Is 65:14 7307
that is poor and of a contrite *s* Is 66:2 7307
the *s* of the kings of the Medes Jer 51:11 7307
whither the *s* was to go, they Eze 1:12 7307
Whithersoever the *s* was to go Eze 1:20 7307
went, thither was their *s* to go Eze 1:20 7307
for the *s* of the living creature Eze 1:20 7307
for the *s* of the living creature Eze 1:21 7307
the *s* entered into me when he Eze 2:2 7307
Then the *s* took me up, and I heard Eze 3:12 7307
So the *s* lifted me up, and took me Eze 3:14 7307
bitterness, in the heat of my *s* Eze 3:14 7307
Then the *s* entered into me, and Eze 3:24 7307
the *s* lifted me up between the Eze 8:3 7307
for the *s* of the living creature Eze 10:17 7307
Moreover the *s* lifted me up Eze 11:1 7307
the *S* of the LORD fell upon me, Eze 11:5 7307
and I will put a new *s* within you Eze 11:19 7307
Afterwards the *s* took me up Eze 11:24 7307
by the *S* of God into Chaldea Eze 11:24 7307
prophets, that follow their own *s* Eze 13:3 7307
make you a new heart and a new *s* Eze 18:31 7307
every *s* shall faint, and all knees Eze 21:7 7307
a new *s* will I put within you Eze 36:26 7307
And I will put my *s* within you Eze 36:27 7307
me out in the *s* of the LORD Eze 37:1 7307
And shall put my *s* in you, and ye Eze 37:14 7307
out my *s* upon the house of Israel Eze 39:29 7307
So the *s* took me up, and brought Eze 43:5 7307
wherewith his *s* was troubled Dan 2:1 7307
my *s* was troubled to know the Dan 2:3 7307
in whom is the *s* of the holy gods Dan 4:8 7308
because I know that the *s* of the Dan 4:9 7308
for the *s* of the holy gods is in Dan 4:18 7308
in whom is the *s* of the holy gods Dan 5:11 7308
Forasmuch as an excellent *s* Dan 5:12 7308
that the *s* of the gods is in thee Dan 5:14 7308
because an excellent *s* was in him Dan 6:3 7308
in my *s* in the midst of my body Dan 7:15 7308
for the *s* of whoredoms hath Hos 4:12 7307
for the *s* of whoredoms is in the Hos 5:4 7307
will pour out my *s* upon all flesh Joel 2:28 7307
those days will I pour out my *s* Joel 2:29 7307
is the *s* of the LORD straitened Mic 2:7 7307
If a man walking in the *s* Mic 2:11 7307
of power by the *s* of the LORD Mic 3:8 7307
the LORD stirred up the *s* of Hag 1:14 7307
the *s* of Joshua the son of Hag 1:14 7307
the *s* of all the remnant of the Hag 1:14 7307
so my *s* remaineth among you Hag 2:5 7307
might, nor by power, but by my *s* Zec 4:6 7307
quieted my *s* in the north country Zec 6:8 7307
in his *s* by the former prophets Zec 7:12 7307
formeth the *s* of man within him Zec 12:1 7307
Jerusalem, the *s* of grace and of Zec 12:10 7307
the unclean *s* to pass out of the Zec 13:2 7307
Yet had he the residue of the *s* Mal 2:15 7307
Therefore take heed to your *s* Mal 2:15 7307
therefore take heed to your *s* Mal 2:16 7307
he saw the *S* of God descending Mt 3:16 4151
the *s* into the wilderness to be Mt 4:1 4151
Blessed are the poor in *s* Mt 5:3 4151
but the *S* of your Father which Mt 10:20 4151
I will put my *S* upon him, and he Mt 12:18 4151
I cast out devils by the *S* of God Mt 12:28 4151
When the unclean *s* is gone out of Mt 12:43 4151
were troubled, saying, It is a *s* Mt 14:26 5326
doth David in *s* call him Lord Mt 22:43 4151
the *s* indeed is willing, but the Mt 26:41 4151
the *S* like a dove descending upon Mk 1:10 4151
immediately the *s* driveth him Mk 1:12 4151
synagogue a man with an unclean *s* Mk 1:23 4151
when the unclean *s* had torn him Mk 1:26 4151
when Jesus perceived in his *s* Mk 2:8 4151
they said, He hath an unclean *s* Mk 3:30 4151
the tombs a man with an unclean *s* Mk 5:2 4151
out of the man, thou unclean *s* Mk 5:8 4151
they supposed it had been a *s* Mk 6:49 5326
young daughter had an unclean *s* Mk 7:25 4151
And he sighed deeply in his *s* Mk 8:12 4151
thee my son, which hath a dumb *s* Mk 9:17 4151
him, straightway the *s* tare him Mk 9:20 4151
together, he rebuked the foul *s* Mk 9:25 4151
unto him, Thou dumb and deaf *s* Mk 9:25 4151
the *s* cried, and rent him sore, and Mk 9:26 4151
The *s* truly is ready, but the Mk 14:38 4151
he shall go before him in the *s* Lk 1:17 4151
my *s* hath rejoiced in God my Lk 1:47 4151
child grew, and waxed strong in *s* Lk 1:80 4151
he came by the *S* into the temple Lk 2:27 4151
child grew, and waxed strong in *s* Lk 2:40 4151
was led by the *S* into the Lk 4:1 4151
the power of the *S* into Galilee Lk 4:14 4151
The *S* of the Lord is upon me, Lk 4:18 4151
which had a *s* of an unclean devil Lk 4:33 4151
unclean *s* to come out of the man Lk 8:29 4151
her *s* came again, and she arose Lk 8:55 4151
a *s* taketh him, and he suddenly Lk 9:39 4151
And Jesus rebuked the unclean *s* Lk 9:42 4151
not what manner of *s* ye are of Lk 9:55 4151
In that hour Jesus rejoiced in *s* Lk 10:21 4151
the Holy *S* to them that ask him Lk 11:13 4151
When the unclean *s* is gone out of Lk 11:24 4151
a *s* of infirmity eighteen years Lk 13:11 4151
into thy hands I commend my *s* Lk 23:46 4151
supposed that they had seen a *s* Lk 24:37 4151
for a *s* hath not flesh and bones, Lk 24:39 4151
I saw the *S* descending from Jn 1:32 4151
thou shalt see the *S* descending Jn 1:33 4151
man be born of water and of the *S* Jn 3:5 4151
which is born of the *S* is *s* Jn 3:6 4151
every one that is born of the *S* Jn 3:8 4151
not the *S* by measure unto him Jn 3:34 4151
shall worship the Father in *s* Jn 4:23 4151
God is a *S* Jn 4:24 4151
worship him must worship him in *s* Jn 4:24 4151
It is the *s* that quickeneth Jn 6:63 4151
that I speak unto you, they are *s* Jn 6:63 4151
(But this spake he of the *S* Jn 7:39 4151
with her, he groaned in the *s* Jn 11:33 4151
thus said, he was troubled in *s* Jn 13:21 4151
Even the *S* of truth Jn 14:17 4151
the Father, even the *S* of truth Jn 15:26 4151
the *S* of truth, is come, he will Jn 16:13 4151
as the *S* gave them utterance Acts 2:4 4151
pour out of my *S* upon all flesh Acts 2:17 4151
pour out in those days of my *S* Acts 2:18 4151
to tempt the *S* of the Lord Acts 5:9 4151
wisdom and the *s* by which he spake Acts 6:10 4151
saying, Lord Jesus, receive my *s* Acts 7:59 4151
Then the *S* said unto Philip, Go Acts 8:29 4151
the *S* of the Lord caught away Acts 8:39 4151
the *S* said unto him, Behold, Acts 10:19 4151
the *S* bade me go with them, Acts 11:12 4151
signified by the *S* that there Acts 11:28 4151
but the *S* suffered them not Acts 16:7 4151
with a *s* of divination met us Acts 16:16 4151
grieved, turned and said to the *s* Acts 16:18 4151
his *s* was stirred in him, when he Acts 17:16 4151
Paul was pressed in the *s* Acts 18:5 4151
and being fervent in the *s* Acts 18:25 4151
And the evil *s* answered and said, Acts 19:15 4151
the evil *s* was leaped on them Acts 19:16 4151
ended, Paul purposed in the *s* Acts 19:21 4151
go bound in the *s* unto Jerusalem Acts 20:22 4151
who said to Paul through the *S* Acts 21:4 4151
neither angel, nor *s* Acts 23:8 4151
but if a *s* or an angel hath Acts 23:9 4151
according to the *s* of holiness Rom 1:4 4151
whom I serve with my *s* in the Rom 1:9 4151
is that of the heart, in the *s* Rom 2:29 4151
we should serve in newness of *s* Rom 7:6 4151
after the flesh, but after the *S* Rom 8:1 4151
For the law of the the *S* of life Rom 8:2 4151
after the flesh, but after the *S* Rom 8:4 4151
the *S* the things of the *S* Rom 8:5 4151
not in the flesh, but in the *S* Rom 8:9 4151
if so be that the *S* of God dwell Rom 8:9 4151
any man have not the *S* of Christ Rom 8:9 4151
but the *S* is life because of Rom 8:10 4151
But if the *S* of him that raised Rom 8:11 4151
by his *S* that dwelleth in you Rom 8:11 4151
but if ye through the *S* do Rom 8:13 4151
many as are led by the *S* of God Rom 8:14 4151
the *s* of bondage again to fear Rom 8:15 4151
have received the *S* of adoption Rom 8:15 4151
The *S* itself beareth witness with Rom 8:16 4151
itself beareth witness with our *s* Rom 8:16 4151
have the firstfruits of the *S* Rom 8:23 4151
Likewise the *S* also helpeth our Rom 8:26 4151
but the *S* itself maketh Rom 8:26 4151
knoweth what is the mind of the *S* Rom 8:27 4151
hath given them the *s* of slumber Rom 11:8 4151
fervent in *s* Rom 12:11 4151
by the power of the *S* of God Rom 15:19 4151
sake, and for the love of the *S* Rom 15:30 4151
but in demonstration of the *S* 1Cor 2:4 4151
revealed them unto us by his *S* 1Cor 2:10 4151
for the *S* searcheth all things, 1Cor 2:10 4151
save the *s* of man which is in him 1Cor 2:11 4151
knoweth no man, but the *S* of God 1Cor 2:11 4151
not the *s* of the world 1Cor 2:12 4151
but the *s* which is of God 1Cor 2:12 4151
not the things of the *S* of God 1Cor 2:14 4151
that the *S* of God dwelleth in you 1Cor 3:16 4151
in love, and in the *s* of meekness 1Cor 4:21 4151
absent in body, but present in *s* 1Cor 5:3 4151
ye are gathered together, and my *s* 1Cor 5:4 4151
that the *s* may be saved in the 1Cor 5:5 4151
Jesus, and by the *S* of our God 1Cor 6:11 4151
is joined unto the Lord is one *s* 1Cor 6:17 4151
God in your body, and in your *s* 1Cor 6:20 4151
may be holy both in body and in *s* 1Cor 7:34 4151
also that I have the *S* of God 1Cor 7:40 4151
that no man speaking by the *S* of 1Cor 12:3 4151
of gifts, but the same *S* 1Cor 12:4 4151
But the manifestation of the *S* is 1Cor 12:7 4151
given by the *S* the word of wisdom 1Cor 12:8 4151
word of knowledge by the same *S* 1Cor 12:8 4151

To another faith by the same S 1Cor 12:9 4151
gifts of healing by the same S 1Cor 12:9 4151
that one and the selfsame S 1Cor 12:11 4151
For by one S are we all baptized 1Cor 12:13 4151
been all made to drink into one S 1Cor 12:13 4151
howbeit in the s he speaketh 1Cor 14:2 4151
tongue, my s prayeth, but my 1Cor 14:14 4151
I will pray with the s, and I will 1Cor 14:15 4151
I will sing with the s, and I will 1Cor 14:15 4151
when thou shalt bless with the s 1Cor 14:16 4151
last Adam was made a quickening s 1Cor 15:45 4151
For they have refreshed my s 1Cor 16:18 4151
earnest of the S in our hearts 2Cor 1:22 4151
I had no rest in my s, because I 2Cor 2:13 4151
but with the S of the living God 2Cor 3:3 4151
not of the letter, but of the s 2Cor 3:6 4151
killeth, but the s giveth life 2Cor 3:6 4151
of the s be rather glorious 2Cor 3:8 4151
Now the Lord is that S 2Cor 3:17 4151
where the S of the Lord is, there 2Cor 3:17 4151
even as by the S of the Lord 2Cor 3:18 4151
We having the same s of faith 2Cor 4:13 4151
unto us the earnest of the S 2Cor 5:5 4151
all filthiness of the flesh and s 2Cor 7:1 4151
because his s was refreshed by 2Cor 7:13 4151
or if ye receive another s 2Cor 11:4 4151
walked we not in the same s 2Cor 12:18 4151
Received ye the S by the works of Gal 3:2 4151
having begun in the S, are ye now Gal 3:3 4151
that ministereth to you the S Gal 3:5 4151
promise of the S through faith Gal 3:14 4151
God hath sent forth the S of his Gal 4:6 4151
him that was born after the S Gal 4:29 4151
For we through the S wait for the Gal 5:5 4151
This I say then, Walk in the S Gal 5:16 4151
the flesh lusteth against the S Gal 5:17 4151
and the S against the flesh Gal 5:17 4151
But if ye be led of the S Gal 5:18 4151
But the fruit of the S is love Gal 5:22 4151
If we live in the S, let us also Gal 5:25 4151
let us also walk in the S Gal 5:25 4151
such an one in the s of meekness Gal 6:1 4151
but he that soweth to the S shall Gal 6:8 4151
of the S reap life everlasting Gal 6:8 4151
Lord Jesus Christ be with your s Gal 6:18 4151
with that holy S of promise Eph 1:13 4151
may give unto you the s of wisdom Eph 1:17 4151
the s that now worketh in the Eph 2:2 4151
access by one S unto the Father Eph 2:18 4151
habitation of God through the S Eph 2:22 4151
apostles and prophets by the S Eph 3:5 4151
might by his S in the inner man Eph 3:16 4151
of the S in the bond of peace Eph 4:3 4151
There is one body, and one S Eph 4:4 4151
be renewed in the s of your mind Eph 4:23 4151
And grieve not the holy S of God Eph 4:30 4151
fruit of the S is in all goodness Eph 5:9 4151
but be filled with the S Eph 5:18 4151
salvation, and the sword of the S Eph 6:17 4151
prayer and supplication in the S Eph 6:18 4151
supply of the S of Jesus Christ Phil 1:19 4151
that ye stand fast in one s Phil 1:27 4151
love, if any fellowship of the S Phil 2:1 4151
which worship God in the s Phil 3:3 4151
unto us your love in the S Col 1:8 4151
flesh, yet am I with you in the s Col 2:5 4151
also given unto us his holy S 1Th 4:8 4151
Quench not the S 1Th 5:19 4151
and I pray God your whole s 1Th 5:23 4151
or be troubled, neither by s 2Th 2:2 4151
consume with the s of his mouth 2Th 2:8 4151
through sanctification of the S 2Th 2:13 4151
in the flesh, justified in the S 1Ti 3:16 4151
Now the S speaketh expressly, 1Ti 4:1 4151
in conversation, in charity, in s 1Ti 4:12 4151
hath not given us the s of fear 2Ti 1:7 4151
Lord Jesus Christ be with thy s 2Ti 4:22 4151
Lord Jesus Christ be with your s Philem 25 4151
the dividing asunder of soul and s Heb 4:12 4151
who through the eternal S offered Heb 9:14 4151
done despite unto the S of grace Heb 10:29 4151
as the body without the s is dead Jas 2:26 4151
The s that dwelleth in us lusteth Jas 4:5 4151
through sanctification of the S 1Pet 1:2 4151
or what manner of time the S of 1Pet 1:11 4151
the S unto unfeigned love of the 1Pet 1:22 4151
the ornament of a meek and quiet s 1Pet 3:4 4151
the flesh, but quickened by the S 1Pet 3:18 4151
live according to God in the s 1Pet 4:6 4151
for the s of glory and of God 1Pet 4:14 4151
by the S which he hath given us 1Jn 3:24 4151
Beloved, believe not every s 1Jn 4:1 4151
Hereby know ye the S of God 1Jn 4:2 4151
Every s that confesseth that 1Jn 4:2 4151
every s that confesseth not that 1Jn 4:3 4151
this is that s of antichrist, 1Jn 4:3
Hereby know we the s of truth 1Jn 4:6 4151
of truth, and the s of error 1Jn 4:6 4151
because he hath given us of his S 1Jn 4:13 4151
it is the S that beareth witness, 1Jn 5:6 4151
witness, because the S is truth 1Jn 5:6 4151
that bear witness in earth, the s 1Jn 5:8 4151
sensual, having not the S Jude 19 4151
I was in the S on the Lord's day, Rev 1:10 4151
let him hear what the S saith Rev 2:7 4151
let him hear what the S saith Rev 2:11 4151
let him hear what the S saith Rev 2:17 4151
let him hear what the S saith Rev 2:29 4151
let him hear what the S saith Rev 3:6 4151
let him hear what the S saith Rev 3:13 4151
let him hear what the S saith Rev 3:22 4151
And immediately I was in the s Rev 4:2 4151
an half the S of life from God Rev 11:11 4151
Yea, saith the S, that they may Rev 14:13 4151
away in the s into the wilderness Rev 17:3 4151
and the hold of every foul s Rev 18:2 4151
of Jesus is the s of prophecy Rev 19:10 4151
me away in the s to a great Rev 21:10 4151
And the S and the bride say, Come Rev 22:17 4151

SPIRITS {46}

not them that have familiar s Lev 19:31 178
after such as have familiar s Lev 20:6 178
the God of the s of all flesh Num 16:22 7307
the God of the s of all flesh Num 27:16 7307
or a consulter with familiar s Deut 18:11 178
away those that had familiar s 1Sa 28:3 178
off those that have familiar s 1Sa 28:9 178
and dealt with familiar s 2Kin 21:6 178
the workers with familiar s 2Kin 23:24 178
Who maketh his angels s Ps 104:4 7307
but the LORD weigheth the s Prov 16:2 7307
unto them that have familiar s Is 8:19 178
and to them that have familiar s Is 19:3 178
are the four s of the heavens Zec 6:5 7307
he cast out the s with his word Mt 8:16 4151
gave them power against unclean s Mt 10:1 4151
other s more wicked than himself Mt 12:45 4151
commandeth he even the unclean s Mk 1:27 4151
And unclean s, when they saw him, Mk 3:11 4151
And the unclean s went out Mk 5:13 4151
and gave them power over unclean s Mk 6:7 4151
power he commandeth the unclean s Lk 4:36 4151
that were vexed with unclean s Lk 6:18 4151
and plagues, and of evil s Lk 7:21 4151
which had been healed of evil s Lk 8:2 4151
that the s are subject unto you Lk 10:20 4151
other s more wicked than himself Lk 11:26 4151
which were vexed with unclean s Acts 5:16 4151
For unclean s, crying with loud Acts 8:7 4151
the evil s went out of them Acts 19:12 4151
evil s the name of the Lord Jesus Acts 19:13 4151
to another discerning of s 1Cor 12:10 4151
the s of the prophets are subject 1Cor 14:32 4151
faith, giving heed to seducing s 1Ti 4:1 4151
he saith, Who maketh his angels s Heb 1:7 4151
Are they not all ministering s Heb 1:14 4151
subjection unto the Father of s Heb 12:9 4151
to the s of just men made perfect Heb 12:23 4151
and preached unto the s in prison 1Pet 3:19 4151
but try the s whether they are of 1Jn 4:1 4151
from the seven S which are before Rev 1:4 4151
he that hath the seven S of God Rev 3:1 4151
which are the seven S of God Rev 4:5 4151
which are the seven S of God sent Rev 5:6 4151
I saw three unclean s like frogs Rev 16:13 4151
For they are the s of devils Rev 16:14 4151

SPIRITUAL {28}

the s man is mad, for the Hos 9:7 7307
I may impart unto you some s gift Rom 1:11 4152
For we know that the law is s Rom 7:14 4152
made partakers of their s things Rom 15:27 4152
comparing s things with s 1Cor 2:13 4152
But he that is s judgeth all 1Cor 2:15 4152
not speak unto you as unto s 1Cor 3:1 4152
If we have sown unto you s things 1Cor 9:11 4152
And did all eat the same s meat 1Cor 10:3 4152
And did all drink the same s drink 1Cor 10:4 4152
for they drank of that s Rock 1Cor 10:4 4152
Now concerning s gifts, brethren, 1Cor 12:1 4152
after charity, and desire s gifts 1Cor 14:1 4152
as ye are zealous of s gifts 1Cor 14:12 4151
himself to be a prophet, or s 1Cor 14:37 4152
it is raised a s body 1Cor 15:44 4152
body, and there is a s body 1Cor 15:44 4152
that was not first which is s 1Cor 15:46 4152
and afterward that which is s 1Cor 15:46 4152
in a fault, ye which are s Gal 6:1 4152
who hath blessed us with all s Eph 1:3 4152
s songs, singing and making melody Eph 5:19 4152
against s wickedness in high Eph 6:12 4152
in all wisdom and s understanding Col 1:9 4152
s songs, singing with grace in Col 3:16 4152
stones, are built up a s house 1Pet 2:5 4152
to offer up s sacrifices 1Pet 2:5 4152

SPIRITUALLY {3}

but to be s minded is life and Rom 8:6 3588,4151
because they are s discerned 1Cor 2:14 4153
which s is called Sodom and Egypt, Rev 11:8 4153

SPIT {11}

issue s upon him that is clean Lev 15:8 7556
her father had but s in her face Num 12:14 3417
s in his face, and shall answer and Deut 25:9 3417
me, and spare not to s in my face Job 30:10 7536
Then did they s in his face Mt 26:67 1716
they s upon him, and took the reed Mt 27:30 1716
fingers into his ears, and he s Mk 7:33 4429
and when he had s on his eyes Mk 8:23 4429
shall s upon him, and shall kill Mk 10:34 1716
And some began to s on him Mk 14:65 1716
did s upon him, and bowing their Mk 15:19 1716

SPITE {1}

for thou beholdest mischief and s Ps 10:14 3708

SPITEFULLY {2}

his servants, and entreated them s Mt 22:6 5195
s entreated, and spitted on Lk 18:32 5195

SPITTED {1}

and spitefully entreated, and s on Lk 18:32 1716

SPITTING {1}

I hid not my face from shame and s Is 50:6 7536

SPITTLE {3}

let his s fall down upon his 1Sa 21:13 7388
me alone till I swallow down my s Job 7:19 7536
the ground, and made clay of the s Jn 9:6 4427

SPOIL {118}

and at night he shall divide the s Gen 49:27 7998
and ye shall s the Egyptians Ex 3:22 5337
overtake, I will divide the s Ex 15:9 7998
took the s of all their cattle, Num 31:9 962
And they took all the s, and all Num 31:11 7998
captives, and the prey, and the s Num 31:12 7998
(For the men of war had taken s Num 31:53 962
the s of the cities which we took Deut 2:35 7998
the s of the cities, we took for Deut 3:7 7998
thou shalt gather all the s of it Deut 13:16 7998
all the s thereof every whit, for Deut 13:16 7998
the city, even all the s thereof Deut 20:14 7998
shalt eat the s of thine enemies Deut 20:14 7998
only the s thereof, and the cattle Josh 8:2 7998
the s of that city Israel took Josh 8:27 7998
all the s of these cities, and the Josh 11:14 7998
divide the s of your enemies with Josh 22:8 7998
the necks of them that take the s Judg 5:30 7998
men of them, and took their s Judg 14:19 2488
the s of their enemies which they 1Sa 14:30 7998
And the people flew upon the s 1Sa 14:32 7998
s them until the morning light, 1Sa 14:36 962
LORD, but didst fly upon the s 1Sa 15:19 7998
But the people took of the s 1Sa 15:21 7998
because of all the great s that 1Sa 30:16 7998
sons nor daughters, neither s 1Sa 30:19 7998
and said, This is David's s 1Sa 30:20 7998
of the s that we have recovered 1Sa 30:22 7998
he sent of the s unto the elders 1Sa 30:26 7998
the s of the enemies of the LORD 1Sa 30:26 7998
and brought in a great s with them 2Sa 3:22 7998
of the s of Hadadezer, son of 2Sa 8:12 7998
he brought forth the s of the 2Sa 12:30 7998
returned after him only to s 2Sa 23:10 6584
now therefore, Moab, to the s 2Kin 3:23 7998
prey and a s to all their enemies 2Kin 21:14 4933
exceeding much s out of the city 1Chr 20:2 7998
and they carried away very much s 2Chr 14:13 7998
was exceeding much s in them 2Chr 14:14 961
of the s which they had brought, 2Chr 15:11 7998
came to take away the s of them 2Chr 20:25 7998
three days in gathering of the s 2Chr 20:25 7998
sent all the s of them unto the 2Chr 24:23 7998
thousand of them, and took much s 2Chr 25:13 961
took also away much s from them 2Chr 28:8 7998
and brought the s to Samaria 2Chr 28:8 7998
the s before the princes and all 2Chr 28:14 961
with the s clothed all that were 2Chr 28:15 7998
sword, to captivity, and to a s Ezr 9:7 961
to take the s of them for a prey Est 3:13 7998
to take the s of them for a prey, Est 8:11 7998
but on the s laid they not their Est 9:10 961
plucked the s out of his teeth Job 29:17 2964
which hate us s for themselves Ps 44:10 8154
tarried at home divided the s Ps 68:12 7998
All that pass by the way s him Ps 89:41 8155
and let the strangers s his labour Ps 109:11 962
word, as one that findeth great s Ps 119:162 7998
we shall fill our houses with s Prov 1:13 7998
to divide the s with the proud Prov 16:19 7998
s the soul of those that spoiled Prov 22:23 6906
s not his resting place Prov 24:15 7703
that he shall have no need of s Prov 31:11 7998
little foxes, that s the vines Song 2:15 2254
the s of the poor is in your Is 3:14 1500
the s of Samaria shall be taken Is 8:4 7998
rejoice when they divide the s Is 9:3 7998
give him a charge, to take the s Is 10:6 7998
they shall s them of the east Is 11:14 962
is the portion of them that s us Is 17:14 8154
when thou shalt cease to s Is 33:1 7703
your s shall be gathered like the Is 33:4 7998
is the prey of a great s divided Is 33:23 7998
for a s, and none saith, Restore Is 42:22 4933
Who gave Jacob for a s, and Israel Is 42:24 4882
divide the s with the strong Is 53:12 7998
wolf of the evenings shall s them Jer 5:6 7703
violence and s is heard in her Jer 6:7 7701
I give to the s without price Jer 15:13 957
and all thy treasures to the s Jer 17:3 957
their enemies, which shall s them Jer 20:5 962
cried out, I cried violence and s Jer 20:8 7701
they that s thee shall be a Jer 30:16 7701
thee shall be a s Jer 30:16 4933
cometh to s all the Philistines Jer 47:4 7703
the LORD will s the Philistines Jer 47:4 7703
Kedar, and s the men of the east Jer 49:28 7703
the multitude of their cattle a s Jer 49:32 7998
And Chaldea shall be a s Jer 50:10 7998
all that s her shall be satisfied Jer 50:10 7998
the wicked of the earth for a s Eze 7:21 7998
through the land, and they s it Eze 14:15 7921
thee for a s to the heathen Eze 25:7 957
shall become a s to the nations Eze 26:5 957

they shall make a *s* of thy riches ... Eze 26:12 7997
take her multitude, and take her *s* ... Eze 29:19 7997
they shall *s* the pomp of Egypt, ... Eze 32:12 7703
To take a *s*, and to take a prey ... Eze 38:12 7998
thee, Art thou come to take a *s* ... Eze 38:13 7998
and goods, to take a great *s* ... Eze 38:13 7998
they shall *s* those that spoiled ... Eze 39:10 7997
remove violence and *s*, and execute ... Eze 45:9 7701
scatter among them the prey, and *s* ... Dan 11:24 7998
by flame, by captivity, and by *s* ... Dan 11:33 961
altars, he shall *s* their images ... Hos 10:2 7703
he shall *s* the treasure of all ... Hos 13:15 8154
Take ye the *s* of silver, take the ... Nah 2:9 962
of silver, take the *s* of gold ... Nah 2:9 7997
of the people shall *s* thee ... Hab 2:8 7701
the *s* of beasts, which made them ... Hab 2:17 962
residue of my people shall *s* them ... Zeph 2:9 7998
they shall be a *s* to their ... Zec 2:9 7998
thy *s* shall be divided in the ... Zec 14:1 7998
s his goods, except he first bind ... Mt 12:29 *1283*
and then he will *s* his house ... Mt 12:29 *1283*
s his goods, except he will first ... Mk 3:27 *1283*
and then he will *s* his house ... Mk 3:27 *1283*
Beware lest any man *s* you through ... Col 2:8 *4812*

SPOILED {55}
s the city, because they had ... Gen 34:27 962
s even all that was in the house ... Gen 34:29 962
And they *s* the Egyptians ... Ex 12:36 5337
s evermore, and no man shall save ... Deut 28:29 1497
the hands of spoilers that *s* them ... Judg 2:14 8155
of the hand of those that *s* them ... Judg 2:16 8154
of the hands of them that *s* them ... 1Sa 14:48 8154
and they *s* their tents ... 1Sa 17:53 8155
s the tents of the Syrians ... 2Kin 7:16 962
and they *s* all the cities ... 2Chr 14:14 962
He leadeth counsellors away *s* ... Job 12:17 7758
He leadeth princes away *s* ... Job 12:19 7758
The stouthearted are *s*, they have ... Ps 76:5 7997
the soul of those that *s* them ... Prov 22:23 6906
their houses shall be *s*, and their ... Is 13:16 8155
whose land the rivers have *s* ... Is 18:2 958
whose land the rivers have *s* ... Is 18:7 958
be utterly emptied, and utterly *s* ... Is 24:3 962
that spoilest, and thou wast not *s* ... Is 33:1 7703
cease to spoil, thou shalt be *s* ... Is 33:1 7703
But this is a people robbed and *s* ... Is 42:22 8154
why is he *s* ... Jer 2:14 957
for we are *s* ... Jer 4:13 7703
for the whole land is *s* ... Jer 4:20 7703
suddenly are my tents *s*, and my ... Jer 4:20 7703
And when thou art *s*, what wilt ... Jer 4:30 7703
heard out of Zion, How are we *s* ... Jer 9:19 7703
My tabernacle is *s*, and all my ... Jer 10:20 7703
deliver him that is *s* out of the ... Jer 21:12 1497
deliver the *s* out of the hand of ... Jer 22:3 1497
for the LORD hath *s* their pasture ... Jer 25:36 7703
for it is *s* ... Jer 48:1 7703
Moab is *s*, and gone up out of her ... Jer 48:15 7703
ye it in Arnon, that Moab is *s* ... Jer 48:20 7703
Howl, O Heshbon, for Ai is *s* ... Jer 49:3 7703
his seed is *s*, and his brethren, ... Jer 49:10 7703
Because the LORD hath *s* Babylon ... Jer 51:55 7703
hath *s* none by violence, hath ... Eze 18:7 1497
hath *s* by violence, hath not ... Eze 18:12 1497
neither hath *s* by violence ... Eze 18:16 1497
s his brother by violence, and did ... Eze 18:18 1497
will give them to be removed and *s* ... Eze 23:46 957
shall spoil those that *s* them ... Eze 39:10 7997
and all thy fortresses shall be *s* ... Hos 10:14 7703
as Shalman *s* Beth-arbel in the ... Hos 10:14 7701
thee, and thy palaces shall be *s* ... Amos 3:11 962
the *s* against the strong, so that ... Amos 5:9 7701
so that the *s* shall come against ... Amos 5:9 7701
and say, We be utterly *s* ... Mic 2:4 7703
Because thou hast *s* many nations ... Hab 2:8 7997
me unto the nations which *s* you ... Zec 2:8 7997
because the mighty are *s* ... Zec 11:2 7703
for their glory is *s* ... Zec 11:3 7703
for the pride of Jordan is *s* ... Zec 11:3 7703
having *s* principalities and powers ... Col 2:15 *554*

SPOILER {9}
to them from the face of the *s* ... Is 16:4 7703
the *s* ceaseth, the oppressors are ... Is 16:4 7701
treacherously, and the *s* spoileth ... Is 21:2 7703
for the *s* shall suddenly come ... Jer 6:26 7703
of the young men a *s* at noonday ... Jer 15:8 7703
the *s* shall come upon every city, ... Jer 48:8 7703
for the *s* of Moab shall come upon ... Jer 48:18 7703
the *s* is fallen upon thy summer ... Jer 48:32 7703
Because the *s* is come upon her, ... Jer 51:56 7703

SPOILERS {7}
the hands of *s* that spoiled them ... Judg 2:14 8154
the *s* came out of the camp of the ... 1Sa 13:17 7843
the garrison, and the *s*, they also ... 1Sa 14:15 7843
delivered them into the hand of *s* ... 2Kin 17:20 8154
The *s* are come upon all high ... Jer 12:12 7703
for the *s* shall come unto her ... Jer 51:48 7703
yet from me shall *s* come unto her ... Jer 51:53 7703

SPOILEST {1}
Woe to thee that *s*, and thou wast ... Is 33:1 7703

SPOILETH {4}
and the needy from him that *s* him ... Ps 35:10 1497
treacherously, and the spoiler *s* ... Is 21:2 7703
and the troop of robbers *s* without ... Hos 7:1 6584
the cankerworm *s*, and fleeth away ... Nah 3:16 6584

SPOILING {5}
evil for good to the *s* of my soul ... Ps 35:12 7908
because of the *s* of the daughter ... Is 22:4 7701
crying shall be from Horonaim, *s* ... Jer 48:3 7701
for *s* and violence are before me ... Hab 1:3 7701
took joyfully the *s* of your goods ... Heb 10:34 *724*

SPOILS {5}
When I saw among the *s* a goodly ... Josh 7:21 7998
Out of the *s* won in battles did ... 1Chr 26:27 7998
with the *s* of their hands ... Is 25:11 698
he trusted, and divideth his *s* ... Lk 11:22 *4661*
Abraham gave the tenth of the *s* ... Heb 7:4 *205*

SPOKEN {286}
as the LORD had *s* unto him ... Gen 12:4 1696
that which he hath *s* of him ... Gen 18:19 1696
city, for the which thou hast *s* ... Gen 19:21 1696
LORD did unto Sarah as he had *s* ... Gen 21:1 1696
time of which God had *s* to him ... Gen 21:2 1696
son's wife, as the LORD hath *s* ... Gen 24:51 1696
that which I have *s* to thee of ... Gen 28:15 1696
thing which I have *s* unto Pharaoh ... Gen 41:28 1696
to the word that Joseph had *s* ... Gen 44:2 1696
thou hast *s* unto thy servant ... Ex 4:10 1696
which the LORD had *s* unto Moses ... Ex 4:30 1696
as the LORD had *s* unto Moses ... Ex 9:12 1696
as the LORD had *s* by Moses ... Ex 9:35 1696
And Moses said, Thou hast *s* well ... Ex 10:29 1696
that the LORD hath *s* we will do ... Ex 19:8 1696
all this land that I have *s* of ... Ex 32:13 559
place of which I have *s* unto thee ... Ex 32:34 1696
this thing also that thou hast *s* ... Ex 33:17 1696
all that the LORD had *s* with him ... Ex 34:32 1696
statutes which the LORD hath *s* ... Lev 10:11 1696
For the LORD had *s* unto Moses ... Num 1:48 1696
for the LORD hath *s* good ... Num 10:29 1696
the LORD indeed *s* only by Moses ... Num 12:2 1696
hath he not *s* also by us ... Num 12:2 1696
great, according as thou hast *s* ... Num 14:17 1696
as ye have *s* in mine ears, so ... Num 14:28 1696
which the LORD hath *s* unto Moses ... Num 15:22 1696
for we have *s* against the LORD, ... Num 21:7 1696
And Balak did as Balaam had *s* ... Num 23:2 1696
unto him, What hath the LORD *s* ... Num 23:17 1696
thou hast *s* is good for us to do ... Deut 1:14 1696
which they have *s* unto thee ... Deut 5:28 1696
well said all that they have *s* ... Deut 5:28 1696
before thee, as the LORD hath *s* ... Deut 6:19 1696
because he hath *s* to turn you ... Deut 13:5 1696
They have well *s* that which they ... Deut 18:17 1696
that which they have *s* ... Deut 18:17
word which the LORD hath not *s* ... Deut 18:21 1696
thing which the LORD hath not *s* ... Deut 18:22 1696
prophet hath *s* it presumptuously ... Deut 18:22 1696
the LORD thy God, as he hath *s* ... Deut 26:19 1696
when Joshua had *s* unto the people ... Josh 6:8 559
had *s* unto the house of Israel ... Josh 21:45 1696
for that thou hast *s* friendly ... Ruth 2:13 1696
and grief have I *s* hitherto ... 1Sa 1:16 1696
I have *s* concerning his house ... 1Sa 3:12 1696
matter which thou and I have *s* of ... 1Sa 20:23 1696
that he hath *s* concerning thee ... 1Sa 25:30 1696
God liveth, unless thou hadst *s* ... 2Sa 2:27 1696
for the LORD hath *s* of David ... 2Sa 3:18 559
maidservants which thou hast *s* of ... 2Sa 6:22 559
but thou hast *s* also of thy ... 2Sa 7:19 1696
hast *s* concerning thy servant ... 2Sa 7:25 1696
for thou, O Lord GOD, hast *s* it ... 2Sa 7:29 1696
that my lord the king hath *s* ... 2Sa 14:19 1696
Ahithophel hath *s* after this ... 2Sa 17:6 1696
if Adonijah have not *s* this word ... 1Kin 2:23 1696
this people, who have *s* to me ... 1Kin 12:9 1696
is the sign which the LORD hath *s* ... 1Kin 13:3 1696
which he had *s* unto the king ... 1Kin 13:11 1696
for the LORD hath *s* it ... 1Kin 14:11 1696
answered and said, It is well *s* ... 1Kin 18:24 1697
the Jezreelite had *s* to him ... 1Kin 21:4 1696
the LORD hath *s* evil concerning ... 1Kin 22:23 1696
peace, the LORD hath not *s* by me ... 1Kin 22:28 1696
of the LORD which Elijah had *s* ... 2Kin 1:17 1696
thou be *s* for to the king ... 2Kin 4:13 1696
the man of God had *s* to the king ... 2Kin 7:18 1696
the LORD hath *s* concerning him ... 2Kin 19:21 1696
will do the thing that he hath *s* ... 2Kin 20:9 1696
of the LORD which thou hast *s* ... 2Kin 20:19 1696
for thou hast also *s* of thy ... 1Chr 17:17 1696
hast *s* concerning thy servant ... 1Chr 17:23 1696
the wine, which my lord hath *s* of ... 2Chr 2:15 559
performed his word that he hath *s* ... 2Chr 6:10 1696
which thou hast *s* unto thy ... 2Chr 6:17 1696
this people, which have *s* to me ... 2Chr 10:9 1696
the LORD hath *s* evil against thee ... 2Chr 18:22 1696
then hath not the LORD *s* by me ... 2Chr 18:27 1696
that the word of the LORD *s* by ... 2Chr 36:22 1696
because we had *s* unto the king ... Ezr 8:22 559
words that he had *s* unto me ... Neh 2:18 559
fail of all that thou hast *s* ... Est 6:10 1696
who had *s* good for the king, ... Est 7:9 1696
and after that I have *s*, mock on ... Job 21:3 1696
Elihu had waited till Job had *s* ... Job 32:4 1697
my tongue hath *s* in my mouth ... Job 33:2 1696
thou hast *s* in mine hearing ... Job 33:8 559
Job hath *s* without knowledge, and ... Job 34:35 1696
Once have I *s* ... Job 40:5 1696
LORD had *s* these words unto Job ... Job 42:7 1696
for ye have not *s* of me the thing ... Job 42:7 1696
in that ye have not *s* of me the ... Job 42:8 1696
mighty God, even the LORD, hath *s* ... Ps 50:1 1696
God hath *s* in his holiness ... Ps 60:6 1696
God hath *s* once ... Ps 62:11 1696
have uttered, and my mouth hath *s* ... Ps 66:14 1696
Glorious things are *s* of thee ... Ps 87:3 1696
God hath *s* in his holiness ... Ps 108:7 1696
they have *s* against me with a ... Ps 109:2 1696
I believed, therefore have I *s* ... Ps 116:10 1696
a word *s* in due season, how good ... Prov 15:23
A word fitly *s* is like apples of ... Prov 25:11 1696
no heed unto all words that are *s* ... Eccl 7:21 1696
the day when she shall be *s* for ... Song 8:8 1696
for the LORD hath *s*, I have ... Is 1:2 1696
the mouth of the LORD hath *s* it ... Is 1:20 1696
is the word that the LORD hath *s* ... Is 16:13 1696
But now the LORD hath *s*, saying, ... Is 16:14 1696
the LORD God of Israel hath *s* it ... Is 21:17 1696
for the LORD hath *s* it ... Is 22:25 1696
for the sea hath *s*, even the ... Is 23:4 559
for the LORD hath *s* this word ... Is 24:3 1696
for the LORD hath *s* it ... Is 25:8 1696
For thus hath the LORD *s* unto me ... Is 31:4 559
the LORD hath *s* concerning him ... Is 37:22 1696
will do this thing that he hath *s* ... Is 38:7 1696
He hath both *s* unto me, and ... Is 38:15 559
of the LORD which thou hast *s* ... Is 39:8 1696
the mouth of the LORD hath *s* it ... Is 40:5 1696
I have not *s* in secret, in a dark ... Is 45:19 1696
yea, I have *s* it, I will also ... Is 46:11 1696
I, even I, have *s* ... Is 48:15 1696
I have not *s* in secret from the ... Is 48:16 1696
the mouth of the LORD hath *s* it ... Is 58:14 1696
your lips have *s* lies, your ... Is 59:3 1696
Behold, thou hast *s* and done evil ... Jer 3:5 1696
because I have *s* it, I have ... Jer 4:28 1696
whom the mouth of the LORD hath *s* ... Jer 9:12 1696
for the LORD hath *s* ... Jer 13:15 1696
I have not *s* to them, yet they ... Jer 23:21 1696
and, What hath the LORD *s* ... Jer 23:35 1696
and, What hath the LORD *s* ... Jer 23:37 1696
I have *s* unto you, rising early ... Jer 25:3 1696
for he hath *s* to us in the name ... Jer 26:16 1696
as the LORD hath *s* against the ... Jer 27:13 1696
have *s* lying words in my name, ... Jer 29:23 1696
that I have *s* unto thee in a book ... Jer 30:2 1696
what thou hast *s* is come to pass ... Jer 32:24 1696
thou not what this people have *s* ... Jer 33:24 1696
notwithstanding I have *s* unto you ... Jer 35:14 1696
because I have *s* unto them ... Jer 35:17 1696
I have *s* unto thee against Israel ... Jer 36:2 1696
the LORD, which he had *s* unto him ... Jer 36:4 1696
had *s* unto all the people ... Jer 38:1 1696
As for the word that thou hast *s* ... Jer 44:16 1696
have both *s* with your mouths ... Jer 44:25 1696
be destroyed, as the LORD hath *s* ... Jer 48:8 559
thou hast *s* against this place, ... Jer 51:62 1696
I the LORD have *s* it in my zeal ... Eze 5:13 1696
I the LORD have *s* it ... Eze 5:15 1696
I the LORD have *s* it ... Eze 5:17 1696
word which I have *s* shall be done ... Eze 12:28 1696
have ye not *s* a lying divination, ... Eze 13:7 1696
albeit I have not *s* ... Eze 13:7 559
Because ye have *s* vanity, and seen ... Eze 13:8 1696
deceived when he hath *s* a thing ... Eze 14:9 1696
know that I the LORD have *s* it ... Eze 17:21 1696
I the LORD have *s* and have done it ... Eze 17:24 1696
for I the LORD have *s* it ... Eze 21:32 1696
I the LORD have *s* it, and will do ... Eze 22:14 1696
GOD, when the LORD hath not *s* ... Eze 22:28 1696
for I have *s* it, saith the Lord ... Eze 23:34 1696
I the LORD have *s* it ... Eze 24:14 1696
for I have *s* it, saith the Lord ... Eze 26:5 1696
for I the LORD have *s* it, saith ... Eze 26:14 1696
for I have *s* it, saith the Lord ... Eze 28:10 1696
I the LORD have *s* it ... Eze 30:12 1696
I the LORD have *s* it ... Eze 34:24 1696
s against the mountains of Israel ... Eze 35:12 559
I *s* against the residue of the ... Eze 36:5 1696
I have *s* in my jealousy and in my ... Eze 36:6 1696
I the LORD have *s* it, and I will ... Eze 36:36 1696
ye know that I the LORD have *s* it ... Eze 37:14 1696
Art thou he of whom I have *s* in ... Eze 38:17 1696
in the fire of my wrath have I *s* ... Eze 38:19 1696
for I have *s* it, saith the Lord ... Eze 39:5 1696
this is the day whereof I have *s* ... Eze 39:8 1696
Nebuchadnezzar, to thee it is *s* ... Dan 4:31 560
when he had *s* this word unto me, ... Dan 10:11 1696
when he had *s* such words unto me, ... Dan 10:15 1696
And when he had *s* unto me, I was ... Dan 10:19 1696
yet they have *s* lies against me ... Hos 7:13 1696
They have *s* words, swearing ... Hos 10:4 1696
I have also *s* by the prophets, and ... Hos 12:10 1696
for the LORD hath *s* it ... Joel 3:8 1696
that the LORD hath *s* against you ... Amos 3:1 1696
the Lord GOD hath *s*, who can but ... Amos 3:8 1696
shall be with you, as ye have *s* ... Amos 5:14 559
neither shouldest thou have *s* ... Obad 12 6310
for the LORD hath *s* it ... Obad 18 1696
of the LORD of hosts hath *s* it ... Mic 4:4 1696
inhabitants thereof have *s* lies ... Mic 6:12 1696
For the idols have *s* vanity ... Zec 10:2 1696
What have we *s* so much against ... Mal 3:13 1696
was *s* of the Lord by the prophet ... Mt 1:22 *4483*
was *s* of the Lord by the prophet ... Mt 2:15 *4483*
which was *s* by Jeremy the prophet ... Mt 2:17 *4483*
which was *s* by the prophets ... Mt 2:23 *4483*
For this is he that was *s* of by ... Mt 3:3 *4483*
which was *s* by Esaias the prophet ... Mt 4:14 *4483*
which was *s* by Esaias the prophet ... Mt 8:17 *4483*

which was *s* by Esaias the prophet Mt 12:17 *4483*
which was *s* by the prophet Mt 13:35 *4483*
which was *s* by the prophet Mt 21:4 *4483*
that which was *s* unto you by God Mt 22:31 *4483*
s of by Daniel the prophet, stand Mt 24:15 *4483*
saying, He hath *s* blasphemy Mt 26:65 *987*
which was *s* by Jeremy the prophet Mt 27:9 *4483*
which was *s* by the prophet Mt 27:35 *4483*
And as soon as he had *s*, Mk 1:42 *2036*
Jesus heard the word that was *s* Mk 5:36 *2980*
he had *s* the parable against them Mk 12:12 *2036*
s of by Daniel the prophet, Mk 13:14 *4483*
be *s* of for a memorial of her Mk 14:9 *2980*
after the Lord had *s* unto them Mk 16:19 *2980*
those things which were *s* of him Lk 2:33 *2980*
a sign which shall be *s* against Lk 2:34 *483*
Therefore whatsoever ye have *s* in Lk 12:3 *2036*
that which ye have *s* in the ear Lk 12:3 *2980*
knew they the things which were *s* Lk 18:34 *3004*
And when he had thus *s*, he went Lk 19:28 *2036*
had *s* this parable against them Lk 20:19 *2036*
all that the prophets have *s* Lk 24:25 *2980*
And when he had thus *s*, he shewed Lk 24:40 *2036*
word that Jesus had *s* unto him Jn 4:50 *2036*
When he had thus *s*, he spat on Jn 9:6 *2036*
had *s* of taking of rest in sleep Jn 11:13 *3004*
And when he thus had *s*, he cried Jn 11:43 *2036*
the word that I have *s*, the same Jn 12:48 *2980*
For I have not *s* of myself Jn 12:49 *2980*
These things have I *s* unto you Jn 14:25 *2980*
the word which I have *s* unto you Jn 15:3 *2980*
These things have I *s* unto you Jn 15:11 *2980*
s unto them, they had not had sin Jn 15:22 *2980*
These things have I *s* unto you Jn 16:1 *2980*
These things have I *s* unto you in Jn 16:25 *2980*
These things I have *s* unto you Jn 16:33 *2980*
When Jesus had *s* these words Jn 18:1 *2036*
And when he had thus *s*, one of the Jn 18:22 *2036*
answered him, If I have *s* evil Jn 18:23 *2980*
that he had *s* these things unto Jn 20:18 *2036*
And when he had *s* this, he saith Jn 21:19 *2036*
when he had *s* these things, while Acts 1:9 *2036*
which was *s* by the prophet Joel Acts 2:16 *2046*
which God hath *s* by the mouth of Acts 3:21 *2980*
follow after, as many as have *s* Acts 3:24 *2980*
which ye have *s* come upon me Acts 8:24 *2046*
the way, and that he had *s* to him Acts 9:27 *2980*
which is *s* of in the prophets Acts 13:40 *2046*
those things which were *s* by Paul Acts 13:45 *3004*
should first have been *s* to you Acts 13:46 *2980*
the things which were *s* of Paul Acts 16:14 *2980*
these things cannot be *s* against Acts 19:36 *369*
And when he had thus *s*, he Acts 19:41 *2036*
And when he had thus *s*, he kneeled Acts 20:36 *2036*
spirit or an angel hath *s* to him Acts 23:9 *2980*
And when he had thus *s*, the king Acts 26:30 *2036*
those things which were *s* by Paul Acts 27:11 *3004*
And when he had thus *s*, he took Acts 27:35 *2036*
that every where it is *s* against Acts 28:22 *483*
believed the things which were *s* Acts 28:24 *3004*
after that Paul had *s* one word Acts 28:25 *2036*
you all, that your faith is *s* of Rom 1:8 *2605*
according to that which was *s* Rom 4:18 *2046*
not then your good be evil *s* of Rom 14:16 *987*
written, To whom he was not *s* of Rom 15:21 *312*
why am I evil *s* of for that for 1Cor 10:30 *987*
how shall it be known what is *s* 1Cor 14:9 *2980*
I believed, and therefore have I *s* 2Cor 4:13 *2980*
last days *s* unto us by his Son Heb 1:2 *2980*
For if the word *s* by angels was Heb 2:2 *2980*
first began to be *s* by the Lord Heb 2:3 *2980*
things which were to be *s* after Heb 3:5 *2980*
afterward have *s* of another day Heb 4:8 *2980*
are *s* pertaineth to another tribe Heb 7:13 *3004*
which we have *s* this is the sum Heb 8:1 *3004*
For when Moses had *s* every Heb 9:19 *2980*
should not be *s* to them any more Heb 12:19 *4369*
who have *s* unto you the word of Heb 13:7 *2980*
who have *s* in the name of the Jas 5:10 *2980*
on their part he is evil *s* of 1Pet 4:14 *987*
way of truth shall be evil *s* of 2Pet 2:2 *987*
s before by the holy prophets 2Pet 3:2 *4280*
sinners have *s* against him Jude 15 *2980*
ye the words which were *s* before Jude 17 *4280*

SPOKES {1}
and their felloes, and their *s* 1Kin 7:33 2840

SPOKESMAN {1}
he shall be thy *s* unto the people Ex 4:16 1696

SPOON {12}
One *s* of ten shekels of gold, Num 7:14 3709
One *s* of gold of ten shekels, Num 7:20 3709
One golden *s* of ten shekels, full Num 7:26 3709
One golden *s* of ten shekels, full Num 7:32 3709
One golden *s* of ten shekels, full Num 7:38 3709
One golden *s* of ten shekels, full Num 7:44 3709
One golden *s* of ten shekels, full Num 7:50 3709
One golden *s* of ten shekels, full Num 7:56 3709
One golden *s* of ten shekels, full Num 7:62 3709
One golden *s* of ten shekels, full Num 7:68 3709
One golden *s* of ten shekels, full Num 7:74 3709
One golden *s* of ten shekels, full Num 7:80 3709

SPOONS {12}
s thereof, and covers thereof, and Ex 25:29 3709
the table, his dishes, and his *s* Ex 37:16 3709
put thereon the dishes, and the *s* Num 4:7 3709
silver bowls, twelve *s* of gold Num 7:84 3709
The golden *s* were twelve, full of Num 7:86 3709
the gold of the *s* was an hundred Num 7:86 3709
snuffers, and the basons, and the *s* 1Kin 7:50 3709
and the snuffers, and the *s* 2Kin 25:14 3709
snuffers, and the basons, and the *s* 2Chr 4:22 3709
and to offer withal, and *s* 2Chr 24:14 3709
snuffers, and the bowls, and the *s* Jer 52:18 3709
and the candlesticks, and the *s* Jer 52:19 3709

SPORT {6}
for Samson, that he may make us *s* Judg 16:25 7832
and he made them *s* Judg 16:25 6711
that beheld while Samson made *s* Judg 16:27 7832
It is as *s* to a fool to do Prov 10:23 7814
and saith, Am not I in *s* Prov 26:19 7832
Against whom do ye *s* yourselves Is 57:4 6026

SPORTING {2}
Isaac was *s* with Rebekah his wife Gen 26:8 6711
s themselves with their own 2Pet 2:13 *1792*

SPOT {26}
a rising, a scab, or bright *s* Lev 13:2 934
If the bright *s* be white in the Lev 13:4 934
be a white rising, or a bright *s* Lev 13:19 934
if the bright *s* stay in his place Lev 13:23 934
burneth have a white bright *s* Lev 13:24 934
in the bright *s* be turned white Lev 13:25 934
be no white hair in the bright *s* Lev 13:26 934
if the bright *s* stay in his place Lev 13:28 934
it is a freckled *s* that groweth Lev 13:39 933
and for a scab, and for a bright *s* Lev 14:56 934
bring thee a red heifer without *s* Num 19:2 8549
first year without *s* day by day Num 28:3 8549
lambs of the first year without *s* Num 28:9 8549
lambs of the first year without *s* Num 28:11 8549
lambs of the first year without *s* Num 29:17 8549
lambs of the first year without *s* Num 29:26 8549
their *s* is not the *s* of his Deut 32:5 3971
is not the *s* of his children Deut 32:5
thou lift up thy face without *s* Job 11:15 3971
there is no *s* in thee Song 4:7 3971
a glorious church, not having *s* Eph 5:27 *4696*
keep this commandment without *s* 1Ti 6:14 *784*
offered himself without *s* to God Heb 9:14 *299*
lamb without blemish and without *s* 1Pet 1:19 *784*
found of him in peace, without *s* 2Pet 3:14 *784*

SPOTS {6}
bright *s*, even white bright *s* Lev 13:38 934
if the bright *s* in the skin of Lev 13:39 934
his skin, or the leopard his *s* Jer 13:23 2272
S they are and blemishes, sporting 2Pet 2:13 *4696*
These are *s* in your feasts of Jude 12 *4694*

SPOTTED {7}
s cattle, and all the brown cattle Gen 30:32 2921
cattle among the sheep, and the *s* Gen 30:32 2921
s among the goats, and brown among Gen 30:33 2921
goats that were ringstraked and *s* Gen 30:35 2921
she goats that were speckled and *s* Gen 30:35 2921
ringstraked, speckled, and *s* Gen 30:39 2921
even the garment *s* by the flesh Jude 23 *4695*

SPOUSE {6}
Come with me from Lebanon, my *s* Song 4:8 3618
my heart, my sister, my *s* Song 4:9 3618
fair is thy love, my sister, my *s* Song 4:10 3618
Thy lips, O my *s*, drop as the Song 4:11 3618
inclosed is my sister, my *s* Song 4:12 3618
into my garden, my sister, my *s* Song 5:1 3618

SPOUSES {2}
your *s* shall commit adultery Hos 4:13 3618
nor your *s* when they commit Hos 4:14 3618

SPRANG {7}
and immediately it *s* up, because Mk 4:5 *1816*
and did yield fruit that *s* up Mk 4:8 *305*
and the thorns *s* up with it Lk 8:7 *4855*
ground, and *s* up, and bare fruit an Lk 8:8 *5453*
s in, and came trembling, and fell Acts 16:29 *1530*
that our Lord *s* out of Juda Heb 7:14 *393*
Therefore *s* there even of one, and Heb 11:12 *1080*

SPREAD {109}
of the Canaanites *s* abroad Gen 10:18 6327
thou shalt *s* abroad to the west, Gen 28:14 6555
a field, where he had *s* his tent Gen 33:19 5186
s his tent beyond the tower of Gen 35:21 5186
I will *s* abroad my hands unto the Ex 9:29 6566
s abroad his hands unto the LORD Ex 9:33 6566
the cherubims *s* out their wings Ex 37:9 6566
he *s* abroad the tent over the Ex 40:19 6566
the plague *s* not in the skin Lev 13:5 6581
the plague *s* not in the skin, the Lev 13:6 6581
But if the scab *s* much abroad in Lev 13:7 6581
if it *s* much abroad in the skin, Lev 13:22 6581
s not, it is a burning boil Lev 13:23 6581
if it be *s* much abroad in the Lev 13:27 6581
s not in the skin, but it be Lev 13:28 6581
and, behold, if the scall *s* not Lev 13:32 6581
if the scall be not *s* in the skin Lev 13:34 6581
But if the scall *s* much in the Lev 13:35 6581
if the scall be *s* in the skin Lev 13:36 6581
if the plague be *s* in the garment Lev 13:51 6581
plague be not *s* in the garment Lev 13:53 6581
colour, and the plague be not *s* Lev 13:55 6581
if the plague be *s* in the walls Lev 14:39 6581
if the plague be *s* in the house Lev 14:44 6581
plague hath not *s* in the house Lev 14:48 6581
shall *s* over it a cloth wholly of Num 4:6 6566
they shall *s* a cloth of blue Num 4:7 6566
they shall *s* upon them a cloth of Num 4:8 6566
they shall *s* a cloth of blue Num 4:11 6566
and *s* a purple cloth thereon Num 4:13 6566
they shall *s* upon it a covering Num 4:14 6566
they *s* them all abroad for Num 11:32 7849
As the valleys are they *s* forth Num 24:6 5186
they shall *s* the cloth before the Deut 22:17 6566
they *s* a garment, and did cast Judg 8:25 6566
in Judah, and *s* themselves in Lehi Judg 15:9 5203
s therefore thy skirt over thine Ruth 3:9 6566
they were *s* abroad upon all the 1Sa 30:16 5203
s themselves in the valley of 2Sa 5:18 5203
s themselves in the valley of 2Sa 5:22 5203
So they *s* Absalom a tent upon the 2Sa 16:22 5186
s a covering over the well's 2Sa 17:19 6566
mouth, and *s* ground corn thereon 2Sa 17:19 7849
s it for her upon the rock, from 2Sa 21:10 5186
the street, and did *s* them abroad 2Sa 22:43 7554
s gold upon the cherubims, and 1Kin 6:32 7286
For the cherubims *s* forth their 1Kin 8:7 6566
s forth his hands toward heaven 1Kin 8:22 6566
s forth his hands toward this 1Kin 8:38 6566
with his hands *s* up to heaven 1Kin 8:54 6566
s it on his face, so that he died 2Kin 8:15 6566
the LORD, and *s* it before the LORD 2Kin 19:14 6566
s themselves in the valley of 1Chr 14:9 6584
the Philistines yet again *s* 1Chr 14:13 6584
that *s* out their wings, and 1Chr 28:18 6566
The wings of these cherubims *s* 2Chr 3:13 6566
For the cherubims *s* forth their 2Chr 5:8 6566
of Israel, and *s* forth his hands 2Chr 6:12 6566
s forth his hands toward heaven, 2Chr 6:13 6566
shall *s* forth his hands in this 2Chr 6:29 6566
his name *s* abroad even to the 2Chr 26:8 3212
And his name *s* far abroad 2Chr 26:15 3318
s out my hands unto the LORD my Ezr 9:5 6566
My root was *s* out by the waters, Job 29:19 6605
Hast thou with him *s* out the sky Job 37:18 7554
He *s* a cloud for a covering Ps 105:39 6566
they have *s* a net by the wayside Ps 140:5 6566
net is *s* in the sight of any bird Prov 1:17 2219
when ye *s* forth your hands, I Is 1:15 6566
the worm is *s* under thee, and the Is 14:11 3331
they that *s* nets upon the waters Is 19:8 6566
vail that is *s* over all nations Is 25:7 5259
he shall *s* forth his hands in the Is 25:11 6566
mast, they could not *s* the sail Is 33:23 6566
the LORD, and *s* it before the LORD Is 37:14 6566
he that *s* forth the earth, and Is 42:5 7554
to *s* sackcloth and ashes under him Is 58:5 3331
I have *s* out my hands all the day Is 65:2 6566
they shall *s* them before the sun, Jer 8:2 7849
Silver *s* into plates is brought Jer 10:9 7554
he shall *s* his royal pavilion Jer 43:10 5186
shall *s* his wings over Moab Jer 48:40 6566
eagle, and *s* his wings over Bozrah Jer 49:22 6566
The adversary hath *s* out his hand Lam 1:10 6566
he hath *s* a net for my feet, he Lam 1:13 6566
And he *s* it before me Eze 2:10 6566
My net also will I *s* upon him Eze 12:13 6566
I *s* my skirt over thee, and Eze 16:8 6566
I will *s* my net upon him, and he Eze 17:20 6566
and *s* their net over him Eze 19:8 6566
shalt be a place to *s* nets upon Eze 26:14 4894
I will therefore *s* out my net Eze 32:3 6566
shall be a place to *s* forth nets Eze 47:10 4894
on Mizpah, and a net *s* upon Tabor Hos 5:1 6566
I will *s* my net upon them Hos 7:12 6566
His branches shall *s*, and his Hos 14:6 3212
as the morning *s* upon the Joel 2:2 6566
their horsemen shall *s* themselves Hab 1:8 6335
prosperity shall yet be *s* abroad Zec 1:17 6327
for I have *s* you abroad as the Zec 2:6 6566
s dung upon your faces, even the Mal 2:3 2219
s abroad his fame in all that Mt 9:31 *1310*
a very great multitude *s* their Mt 21:8 *4766*
immediately his fame *s* abroad Mk 1:28 *1831*
(for his name was *s* abroad Mk 6:14 *4766*
many *s* their garments in the way Mk 11:8 *4766*
they *s* their clothes in the way Lk 19:36 *5291*
But that it *s* no further among Acts 4:17 *1268*
faith to God-ward is *s* abroad 1Th 1:8 *1831*

SPREADEST {1}
which thou *s* forth to be thy sail Eze 27:7 4666

SPREADETH {14}
the scab *s* in the skin, then the Lev 13:8 6581
s abroad her wings, taketh them, Deut 32:11 6566
Which alone *s* out the heavens, and Job 9:8 5186
throne, and *s* his cloud upon it Job 26:9 6576
he *s* his light upon it, and Job 36:30 6566
he *s* sharp pointed things upon Job 41:30 7502
neighbour *s* a net for his feet Prov 29:5 6566
as he that swimmeth *s* forth his Is 25:11 6566
the goldsmith *s* it over with gold Is 40:19 7554
s them out as a tent to dwell in Is 40:22 4969
that *s* abroad the earth by myself Is 44:24 7554
that *s* her hands, saying, Woe is Jer 4:31 6566
that *s* out her roots by the river Jer 17:8 7971
Zion *s* forth her hands, and there Lam 1:17 6566

SPREADING {4}
it is a *s* plague Lev 13:57 6524
s himself like a green bay tree Ps 37:35 6168
became a *s* vine of low stature, Eze 17:6 5628
It shall be a place for the *s* of Eze 26:5 4894

SPREADINGS {1}
understand the *s* of the clouds Job 36:29 4666

SPRIGS {2}
cut off the *s* with pruninghooks ... Is 18:5 2150
forth branches, and shot forth *s* ... Eze 17:6 6288

SPRING {23}
sang this song, *S* up, O well ... Num 21:17 5927
depths that *s* out of valleys and ... Deut 8:7 3318
and when the day began to *s* ... Judg 19:25 5927
to pass about the *s* of the day ... 1Sa 9:26 5927
forth unto the *s* of the waters ... 2Kin 2:21 4161
doth trouble *s* out of the ground ... Job 5:6 6779
bud of the tender herb to *s* forth ... Job 38:27 6779
Truth shall *s* out of the earth ... Ps 85:11 6779
When the wicked *s* as the grass ... Ps 92:7 6524
troubled fountain, and a corrupt *s* ... Prov 25:26 4726
a *s* shut up, a fountain sealed ... Song 4:12 1530
before they *s* forth I tell you of ... Is 42:9 6779
now it shall *s* forth ... Is 43:19 6779
they shall *s* up as among the ... Is 44:4 6779
let righteousness *s* up together ... Is 45:8 6779
health shall *s* forth speedily ... Is 58:8 6779
like a *s* of water, whose waters ... Is 58:11 4161
that are sown in it to *s* forth ... Is 61:11 6779
praise to *s* forth before all the ... Is 61:11 6779
wither in all the leaves of her *s* ... Eze 17:9 6780
his *s* shall become dry, and his ... Hos 13:15 4726
pastures of the wilderness do *s* ... Joel 2:22 1876
and day, and the seed should *s* ... Mk 4:27 *985*

SPRINGETH {4}
the hyssop that *s* out of the wall ... 1Kin 4:33 3318
year that which *s* of the same ... 2Kin 19:29 7823
year that which *s* of the same ... Is 37:30 7823
thus judgment *s* up as hemlock in ... Hos 10:4 6524

SPRINGING {5}
and found there a well of *s* water ... Gen 26:19 2416
as the tender grass *s* out of the ... 2Sa 23:4
thou blessest the *s* thereof ... Ps 65:10 6780
water *s* up into everlasting life ... Jn 4:14 *242*
of bitterness *s* up trouble you ... Heb 12:15 *5453*

SPRINGS {16}
the plain, under the *s* of Pisgah ... Deut 4:49 794
and of the vale, and of the *s* ... Josh 10:40 794
and in the plains, and in the *s* ... Josh 12:8 794
give me also *s* of water ... Josh 15:19 1543
upper *s*, and the nether *s* ... Josh 15:19 1543
give me also *s* of water ... Judg 1:15 1543
the upper *s* and the nether *s* ... Judg 1:15 1543
entered into the *s* of the sea ... Job 38:16 5033
all my *s* are in thee ... Ps 87:7 4599
He sendeth the *s* into the valleys ... Ps 104:10 4599
and the thirsty land *s* of water ... Is 35:7 4002
water, and the dry land *s* of water ... Is 41:18 4161
even by the *s* of water shall he ... Is 49:10 4002
dry up her sea, and make her *s* dry ... Jer 51:36 4726

SPRINKLE {31}
let Moses *s* it toward the heaven ... Ex 9:8 2236
s it round about upon the altar ... Ex 29:16 2236
s the blood upon the altar round ... Ex 29:20 2236
s it upon Aaron, and upon his ... Ex 29:21 5137
s the blood round about upon the ... Lev 1:5 2236
shall *s* his blood round about ... Lev 1:11 2236
s the blood upon the altar round ... Lev 3:2 2236
Aaron's sons shall *s* the blood ... Lev 3:8 2236
the sons of Aaron shall *s* the ... Lev 3:13 2236
s of the blood seven times before ... Lev 4:6 5137
s it seven times before the LORD ... Lev 4:17 5137
he shall *s* of the blood of the ... Lev 5:9 5137
he *s* round about upon the altar ... Lev 7:2 2236
he shall *s* upon him that is to be ... Lev 14:7 5137
shall *s* of the oil with his ... Lev 14:16 5137
the priest shall *s* with his right ... Lev 14:27 5137
water, and *s* the house seven times ... Lev 14:51 5137
s it with his finger upon the ... Lev 16:14 5137
he *s* of the blood with his finger ... Lev 16:14 5137
s it upon the mercy seat, and ... Lev 16:15 5137
he shall *s* of the blood upon it ... Lev 16:19 5137
the priest shall *s* the blood upon ... Lev 17:6 2236
S water of purifying upon them ... Num 8:7 5137
thou shalt *s* their blood upon the ... Num 18:17 2236
s of her blood directly before ... Num 19:4 5137
s it upon the tent, and upon all ... Num 19:18 5137
the clean person shall *s* upon the ... Num 19:19 5137
s upon it all the blood of the ... 2Kin 16:15 2236
So shall he *s* many nations ... Is 52:15 5137
Then will I *s* clean water upon ... Eze 36:25 2236
thereon, and to *s* blood thereon ... Eze 43:18 2236

SPRINKLED {25}
Moses *s* it up toward heaven ... Ex 9:10 2236
of the blood he *s* on the altar ... Ex 24:6 2236
s it on the people, and said ... Ex 24:8 2236
when there is *s* of the blood ... Lev 6:27 5137
it was *s* in the holy place ... Lev 6:27 5137
he *s* thereof upon the altar seven ... Lev 8:11 5137
Moses *s* the blood upon the altar ... Lev 8:19 2236
Moses *s* the blood upon the altar ... Lev 8:24 2236
s it upon Aaron, and upon his ... Lev 8:30 5137
which he *s* round about upon the ... Lev 9:12 2236
which he *s* upon the altar round ... Lev 9:18 2236
of separation was not *s* upon him ... Num 19:13 2236
hath not been *s* upon him ... Num 19:20 2236
of her blood was *s* on the wall ... 2Kin 9:33 5137
and *s* the blood of his peace ... 2Kin 16:13 2236
the blood, and *s* it on the altar ... 2Chr 29:22 2236
they *s* the blood upon the altar ... 2Chr 29:22 2236
they *s* the blood upon the altar ... 2Chr 29:22 2236
the priests *s* the blood, which ... 2Chr 30:16 2236
the priests *s* the blood from ... 2Chr 35:11 2236
s dust upon their heads toward ... Job 2:12 2236
blood shall be *s* upon my garments ... Is 63:3 5137
s both the book, and all the ... Heb 9:19 *4472*
Moreover he *s* with blood both the ... Heb 9:21 *4472*
having our hearts *s* from an evil ... Heb 10:22 *4472*

SPRINKLETH {2}
that *s* the blood of the peace ... Lev 7:14 2236
that he that *s* the water of ... Num 19:21 5137

SPRINKLING {4}
ashes of an heifer *s* the unclean ... Heb 9:13 *4472*
the *s* of blood, lest he that ... Heb 11:28 *4378*
covenant, and to the blood of *s* ... Heb 12:24 *4473*
s of the blood of Jesus Christ ... 1Pet 1:2 *4473*

SPROUT {1}
be cut down, that it will *s* again ... Job 14:7 2498

SPRUNG {6}
the east wind *s* up after them ... Gen 41:6 6779
the east wind, *s* up after them ... Gen 41:23 6779
it is a leprosy *s* up in his bald ... Lev 13:42 6524
and shadow of death light is *s* up ... Mt 4:16 *393*
and forthwith they *s* up, because ... Mt 13:5 *1816*
and the thorns *s* up, and choked ... Mt 13:7 *305*
But when the blade was *s* up ... Mt 13:26 *985*
and as soon as it was *s* up ... Lk 8:6 *5453*

SPUE {4}
That the land *s* not you out also ... Lev 18:28 6958
to dwell therein, *s* you not out ... Lev 20:22 6958
Drink ye, and be drunken, and *s* ... Jer 25:27 7006
I will *s* thee out of my mouth ... Rev 3:16 *1692*

SPUED {1}
as it *s* out the nations that were ... Lev 18:28 6958

SPUN {2}
and brought that which they had *s* ... Ex 35:25 4299
them up in wisdom *s* goats' hair ... Ex 35:26 2901

SPUNGE {3}
one of them ran, and took a *s* ... Mt 27:48 *4699*
filled a *s* full of vinegar, and ... Mk 15:36 *4699*
and they filled a *s* with vinegar ... Jn 19:29 *4699*

SPY {12}
Moses sent to *s* out the land ... Num 13:16 8446
Moses sent them to *s* out the land ... Num 13:17 8446
And Moses sent to *s* out Jaazer ... Num 21:32 7270
of Shittim two men to *s* secretly ... Josh 2:1 7270
Joshua sent to *s* out Jericho ... Josh 6:25 7270
to *s* out the land, and to search ... Judg 18:2 7270
to *s* out the country of Laish ... Judg 18:14 7270
went to *s* out the land went up ... Judg 18:17 7270
to *s* it out, and to overthrow it ... 2Sa 10:3 7270
s where he is, that I may send and ... 2Kin 6:13 7200
overthrow, and to *s* out the land ... 1Chr 19:3 7200
who came in privily to *s* out our ... Gal 2:4 *2684*

SQUARE {3}
And all the doors and posts were *s* ... 1Kin 7:5 7251
s in the four squares thereof ... Eze 43:16 7251
hundred in breadth, *s* round about ... Eze 45:2 7251

SQUARED {1}
The posts of the temple were *s* ... Eze 41:21 7251

SQUARES {2}
square in the four *s* thereof ... Eze 43:16 7253
broad in the four *s* thereof ... Eze 43:17 7253

STABILITY {1}
shall be the *s* of thy times ... Is 33:6 530

STABLE {2}
the world also shall be *s* ... 1Chr 16:30 3559
I will make Rabbah a *s* for camels ... Eze 25:5 5116

STABLISH {12}
I will *s* the throne of his ... 2Sa 7:13 3559
I will *s* his throne for ever ... 1Chr 17:12 3559
as he went to *s* his dominion by ... 1Chr 18:3 5324
Then will I *s* the throne of thy ... 2Chr 7:18 6965
To *s* this among them, that they ... Est 9:21 6965
S thy word unto thy servant, who ... Ps 119:38 6965
to *s* you according to my gospel ... Rom 16:25 *4741*
To the end he may *s* your hearts ... 1Th 3:13 *4741*
s you in every good word and work ... 2Th 2:17 *4741*
Lord is faithful, who shall *s* you ... 2Th 3:3 *4741*
s your hearts ... Jas 5:8 *4741*
a while, make you perfect, *s* ... 1Pet 5:10 *4741*

STABLISHED {4}
Therefore the LORD *s* the kingdom ... 2Chr 17:5 3559
the world also is *s*, that it ... Ps 93:1 3559
He hath also *s* them for ever and ... Ps 148:6 5975
s in the faith, as ye have been ... Col 2:7 *950*

STABLISHETH {2}
blood, and *s* a city by iniquity ... Hab 2:12 3559
Now he which *s* us with you in ... 2Cor 1:21 *950*

STACHYS (*sta'-kis*) {1} *A Christian in Rome.*
helper in Christ, and *S* my beloved ... Rom 16:9 *4720*

STACKS {1}
in thorns, so that the *s* of corn ... Ex 22:6 1430

STACTE {1}
Take unto thee sweet spices, *s* ... Ex 30:34 5198

STAFF {43}
for with my *s* I passed over this ... Gen 32:10 4731
thy *s* that is in thine hand ... Gen 38:18 4294
the signet, and bracelets, and *s* ... Gen 38:25 4294
your feet, and your *s* in your hand ... Ex 12:11 4731
again, and walk abroad upon his *s* ... Ex 21:19 4938
I have broken the *s* of your bread ... Lev 26:26 4294
they bare it between two upon a *s* ... Num 13:23 4132
and he smote the ass with a *s* ... Num 22:27 4731
end of the *s* that was in his hand ... Judg 6:21 4938
the *s* of his spear was like a ... 1Sa 17:7 2671
And he took his *s* in his hand ... 1Sa 17:40 4731
a leper, or that leaneth on a *s* ... 2Sa 3:29 6418
the *s* of whose spear was like a ... 2Sa 21:19 6086
with iron and the *s* of a spear ... 2Sa 23:7 6086
but he went down to him with a *s* ... 2Sa 23:21 7626
take my *s* in thine hand, and go ... 2Kin 4:29 4938
lay my *s* upon the face of the ... 2Kin 4:29 4938
laid the *s* upon the face of the ... 2Kin 4:31 4938
upon the *s* of this bruised reed ... 2Kin 18:21 4938
and he went down to him with a *s* ... 1Chr 11:23 7626
whose spear *s* was like a weaver's ... 1Chr 20:5 6086
thy rod and thy *s* they comfort me ... Ps 23:4 4938
he brake the whole *s* of bread ... Ps 105:16 4294
and from Judah the stay and the *s* ... Is 3:1 4938
the *s* of his shoulder, the rod of ... Is 9:4 4294
the *s* in their hand is mine ... Is 10:5 4294
or as if the *s* should lift up ... Is 10:15 4294
shall lift up his *s* against thee ... Is 10:24 4294
hath broken the *s* of the wicked ... Is 14:5 4294
fitches are beaten out with a *s* ... Is 28:27 4294
where the grounded *s* shall pass ... Is 30:32 4294
in the *s* of this broken reed ... Is 36:6 4938
say, How is the strong *s* broken ... Jer 48:17 4294
I will break the *s* of bread in ... Eze 4:16 4294
and will break your *s* of bread ... Eze 5:16 4294
will break the *s* of the bread ... Eze 14:13 4294
because they have been a *s* of ... Eze 29:6 4938
their *s* declareth unto them ... Hos 4:12 4731
every man with his *s* in his hand ... Zec 8:4 4938
And I took my *s*, even Beauty, and ... Zec 11:10 4731
Then I cut asunder mine other *s* ... Zec 11:14 4731
for their journey, save a *s* only ... Mk 6:8 *4464*
leaning upon the top of his *s* ... Heb 11:21 *4464*

STAGGER {3}
he maketh them to *s* like a ... Job 12:25 8582
s like a drunken man, and are at ... Ps 107:27 5128
they *s*, but not with strong drink ... Is 29:9 5128

STAGGERED {1}
He *s* not at the promise of God ... Rom 4:20 *1252*

STAGGERETH {1}
as a drunken man *s* in his vomit ... Is 19:14 8582

STAIN {3}
and the shadow of death *s* it ... Job 3:5 1350
to *s* the pride of all glory, and ... Is 23:9 2490
and I will *s* all my raiment ... Is 63:3 1351

STAIRS {10}
winding *s* into the middle chamber ... 1Kin 6:8 3883
it under him on the top of the *s* ... 2Kin 9:13 4609
unto the *s* that go down from the ... Neh 3:15 4609
Then stood up upon the *s*, of the ... Neh 9:4 4608
they went up by the *s* of the city ... Neh 12:37 4609
in the secret places of the *s* ... Song 2:14 4095
east, and went up the *s* thereof ... Eze 40:6 4609
his *s* shall look toward the east ... Eze 43:17 4609
And when he came upon the *s* ... Acts 21:35 *304*
him licence, Paul stood on the *s* ... Acts 21:40 *304*

STAKES {2}
not one of the *s* thereof shall ... Is 33:20 3489
thy cords, and strengthen thy *s* ... Is 54:2 3489

STALK {3}
ears of corn came up upon one *s* ... Gen 41:5 7070
seven ears came up in one *s* ... Gen 41:22 7070
it hath no *s* ... Hos 8:7 7054

STALKS {1}
and hid them with the *s* of flax ... Josh 2:6 6086

STALL {3}
calves out of the midst of the *s* ... Amos 6:4 4770
and grow up as calves of the *s* ... Mal 4:2 4770
his ox or his ass from the *s* ... Lk 13:15 *5336*

STALLED {1}
herbs where love is, than a *s* ox ... Prov 15:17 75

STALLS {4}
s of horses for his chariots ... 1Kin 4:26 723
had four thousand *s* for horses ... 2Chr 9:25 723
s for all manner of beasts, and ... 2Chr 32:28 723
there shall be no herd in the *s* ... Hab 3:17 7517

STAMMERERS {1}
the tongue of the *s* shall be ... Is 32:4 5926

STAMMERING {2}
For with *s* lips and another tongue ... Is 28:11 3934
of a *s* tongue, that thou canst ... Is 33:19 3932

STAMP {2}
I did *s* them as the mire of the ... 2Sa 22:43 1854
s with thy foot, and say, Alas for ... Eze 6:11 7554

STAMPED {9}
s it, and ground it very small ... Deut 9:21 3807
s it small to powder, and cast the ... 2Kin 23:6 1854
s it small to powder, and burned ... 2Kin 23:15 1854
s it, and burnt it at the brook ... 2Chr 15:16 1854
s with the feet, and rejoiced in ... Eze 25:6 7554
s the residue with the feet of it ... Dan 7:7 7512
s the residue with his feet ... Dan 7:19 7512
down to the ground, and *s* upon him ... Dan 8:7 7429
to the ground, and *s* upon them ... Dan 8:10 7429

STAMPING {1}
At the noise of the *s* of the ... Jer 47:3 8161

STANCHED {1}
immediately her issue of blood *s* ... Lk 8:44 *2476*

S

STAND {274}

And they said, *S* back ... Gen 19:9 5066
I *s* here by the well of water ... Gen 24:13 5324
Behold, I *s* by the well of water ... Gen 24:43 5324
thou shalt *s* by the river's brink ... Ex 7:15 5324
the morning, and *s* before Pharaoh ... Ex 8:20 3320
the magicians could not *s* before ... Ex 9:11 5975
s before Pharaoh, and say unto him ... Ex 9:13 3320
s still, and see the salvation of ... Ex 14:13 3320
I will *s* before thee there upon ... Ex 17:6 5975
to morrow I will *s* on the top of ... Ex 17:9 5324
all the people *s* by thee from ... Ex 18:14 5324
pillar *s* at the tabernacle door ... Ex 33:10 5975
me, and thou shalt *s* upon a rock ... Ex 33:21 5324
neither shall any woman *s* before ... Lev 18:23 5975
neither shalt thou *s* against the ... Lev 19:16 5975
no power to *s* before your enemies ... Lev 26:37 8617
shall estimate it, so shall it *s* ... Lev 27:14 6965
to thy estimation it shall *s* ... Lev 27:17 6965
of the men that shall *s* with you ... Num 1:5 5975
S still, and I will hear what the ... Num 9:8 5975
that they may *s* there with thee ... Num 11:16 3320
to *s* before the congregation to ... Num 16:9 5975
S by thy burnt offering, and I ... Num 23:3 3320
S here by thy burnt offering, ... Num 23:15 3320
he shall *s* before Eleazar the ... Num 27:21 5975
then all her vows shall *s* ... Num 30:4 6965
she hath bound her soul shall *s* ... Num 30:4 6965
she hath bound her soul, shall *s* ... Num 30:5 6965
then her vows shall *s*, and her ... Num 30:7 6965
she bound her soul shall *s* ... Num 30:7 6965
their souls, shall *s* against her ... Num 30:9 6965
then all her vows shall *s* ... Num 30:11 6965
she bound her soul shall *s* ... Num 30:11 6965
the bond of her soul, shall not *s* ... Num 30:12 6965
die not, until he *s* before the ... Num 35:12 5975
s thou here by me, and I will ... Deut 5:31 5975
no man be able to *s* before thee ... Deut 7:24 3320
Who can *s* before the children of ... Deut 9:2 3320
to *s* before the LORD to minister ... Deut 10:8 5975
no man be able to *s* before you ... Deut 11:25 3320
to *s* to minister in the name of ... Deut 18:5 5975
which *s* there before the LORD ... Deut 18:7 5975
shall *s* before the LORD, before ... Deut 19:17 5975
Thou shalt *s* abroad, and the man ... Deut 24:11 5975
and if he *s* to it, and say, I like ... Deut 25:8 5975
These shall *s* upon mount Gerizim ... Deut 27:12 5975
these shall *s* upon mount Ebal to ... Deut 27:13 5975
Ye *s* this day all of you before ... Deut 29:10 5324
shall not any man be able to *s* ... Josh 1:5 3320
ye shall *s* still in Jordan ... Josh 3:8 5975
they shall *s* upon an heap ... Josh 3:13 5975
could not *s* before their enemies ... Josh 7:12 6965
thou canst not *s* before thine ... Josh 7:13 6965
not a man of them *s* before thee ... Josh 10:8 5975
Sun, *s* thou still upon Gibeon ... Josh 10:12 1826
s at the entering of the gate of ... Josh 20:4 5975
that city, until he *s* before the ... Josh 20:6 5975
to *s* before you unto this day ... Josh 23:9 5975
any longer *s* before their enemies ... Judg 2:14 5975
S in the door of the tent, and it ... Judg 4:20 5975
Who is able to *s* before this holy ... 1Sa 6:20 5975
but *s* thou still a while, that I ... 1Sa 9:27 5975
Now therefore *s* still, that I may ... 1Sa 12:7 3320
Now therefore *s* and see this great ... 1Sa 12:16 3320
then we will *s* still in our place ... 1Sa 14:9 5975
David, I pray thee, *s* before me ... 1Sa 16:22 5975
s beside my father in the field ... 1Sa 19:3 5975
He said unto me again, *S*, I pray ... 2Sa 1:9 5975
unto him, Turn aside, and *s* here ... 2Sa 18:30 3320
let her *s* before the king, and let ... 1Kin 1:2 5975
not *s* to minister because of the ... 1Kin 8:11 5975
which *s* continually before thee, ... 1Kin 10:8 5975
of Israel liveth, before whom I *s* ... 1Kin 17:1 5975
of hosts liveth, before whom I *s* ... 1Kin 18:15 5975
s upon the mount before the LORD ... 1Kin 19:11 5975
of hosts liveth, before whom I *s* ... 2Kin 3:14 5975
will surely come out to me, and *s* ... 2Kin 5:11 5975
the LORD liveth, before whom I *s* ... 2Kin 5:16 5975
Shaphat shall *s* on him this day ... 2Kin 6:31 5975
how then shall we *s* ... 2Kin 10:4 5975
of the LORD *s* between the earth ... 1Chr 21:16 5975
to *s* every morning to thank and ... 1Chr 23:30 5975
s to minister by reason of the ... 2Chr 5:14 5975
which *s* continually before thee, ... 2Chr 9:7 5975
we *s* before this house, and in thy ... 2Chr 20:9 5975
s ye still, and see the salvation ... 2Chr 20:17 5975
hath chosen you to *s* before him ... 2Chr 29:11 5975
Jerusalem and Benjamin to *s* to it ... 2Chr 34:32 5975
s in the holy place according to ... 2Chr 35:5 5975
for we cannot *s* before thee ... Ezr 9:15 5975
and we are not able to *s* without ... Ezr 10:13 5975
rulers of all the congregation *s* ... Ezr 10:14 5975
and while they *s* by, let them shut ... Neh 7:3 5975
S up and bless the LORD your God ... Neh 9:5 6965
Mordecai's matters would *s* ... Est 3:4 5975
to *s* for their life, to destroy, ... Est 8:11 5975
his house, but it shall not *s* ... Job 8:15 5975
that he shall *s* at the latter day ... Job 19:25 6965
I *s* up, and thou regardest me not ... Job 30:20 5975
words in order before me, *s* up ... Job 33:5 3320
s still, and consider the wondrous ... Job 37:14 5975
and they *s* as a garment ... Job 38:14 3320
who then is able to *s* before me ... Job 41:10 3320
shall not *s* in the judgment ... Ps 1:5 6965
S in awe, and sin not ... Ps 4:4
foolish shall not *s* in thy sight ... Ps 5:5 3320
but we are risen, and *s* upright ... Ps 20:8 5749
or who shall *s* in his holy place ... Ps 24:3 6965
hast made my mountain to *s* strong ... Ps 30:7 5975
of the world *s* in awe of him ... Ps 33:8 1481
and buckler, and *s* up for mine help ... Ps 35:2 6965
my friends *s* aloof from my sore ... Ps 38:11 5975
and my kinsmen *s* afar off ... Ps 38:11 5975
upon thy right hand did *s* the ... Ps 45:9 5324
Their eyes *s* out with fatness ... Ps 73:7 3318
who may *s* in thy sight when once ... Ps 76:7 5975
made the waters to *s* as an heap ... Ps 78:13 5324
my covenant shall *s* fast with him ... Ps 89:28 539
not made him to *s* in the battle ... Ps 89:43 6965
or who will *s* up for me against ... Ps 94:16 3320
let Satan *s* at his right hand ... Ps 109:6 5975
For he shall *s* at the right hand ... Ps 109:31 5975
They *s* fast for ever and ever, and ... Ps 111:8 5564
Our feet shall *s* within thy gates ... Ps 122:2 5975
iniquities, O Lord, who shall *s* ... Ps 130:3 5975
which by night *s* in the house of ... Ps 134:1 5975
Ye that *s* in the house of the ... Ps 135:2 5975
who can *s* before his cold ... Ps 147:17 5975
house of the righteous shall *s* ... Prov 12:7 5975
counsel of the LORD, that shall *s* ... Prov 19:21 6965
he shall *s* before kings ... Prov 22:29 3320
he shall not *s* before mean men ... Prov 22:29 3320
s not in the place of great men ... Prov 25:6 5975
but who is able to *s* before envy ... Prov 27:4 5975
that shall *s* up in his stead ... Eccl 4:15 5975
s not in an evil thing ... Eccl 8:3 5975
the Lord GOD, It shall not *s* ... Is 7:7 6965
speak the word, and it shall not *s* ... Is 8:10 6965
which shall *s* for an ensign of ... Is 11:10 5975
as I have purposed, so shall it *s* ... Is 14:24 6965
My lord, I *s* continually upon the ... Is 21:8 5975
groves and images shall not *s* up ... Is 27:9 6965
agreement with hell shall not *s* ... Is 28:18 6965
and by liberal things shall he *s* ... Is 32:8 6965
word of our God shall *s* for ever ... Is 40:8 6965
gathered together, let them *s* up ... Is 44:11 5975
done, saying, My counsel shall *s* ... Is 46:10 6965
S now with thine enchantments, and ... Is 47:12 5975
s up, and save thee from these ... Is 47:13 5975
unto them, they *s* up together ... Is 48:13 5975
let us *s* together ... Is 50:8 5975
s up, O Jerusalem, which hast ... Is 51:17 6965
And strangers shall *s* and feed your ... Is 61:5 5975
S by thyself, come not near to me ... Is 65:5 7126
S ye in the ways, and see, and ask ... Jer 6:16 5975
S in the gate of the LORD's house ... Jer 7:2 5975
s before me in this house, which ... Jer 7:10 5975
asses did *s* in the high places ... Jer 14:6 5975
again, and thou shalt *s* before me ... Jer 15:19 5975
s in the gate of the children of ... Jer 17:19 5975
S in the court of the LORD's ... Jer 26:2 5975
a man to *s* before me for ever ... Jer 35:19 5975
shall know whose words shall *s* ... Jer 44:28 6965
surely *s* against you for evil ... Jer 44:29 6965
s forth with your helmets ... Jer 46:4 3320
say ye, *S* fast, and prepare thee ... Jer 46:14 3320
they did not *s*, because the day ... Jer 46:21 5975
of Aroer, *s* by the way, and espy ... Jer 48:19 5975
shepherd that will *s* before me ... Jer 49:19 5975
shepherd that will *s* before me ... Jer 50:44 5975
the sword, go away, *s* not still ... Jer 51:50 5975
s upon thy feet, and I will speak ... Eze 2:1 5975
for the house of Israel to *s* in ... Eze 13:5 5975
of his covenant it might *s* ... Eze 17:14 5975
s in the gap before me for the ... Eze 22:30 5975
they shall *s* upon the land ... Eze 27:29 5975
all their loins to be at a *s* ... Eze 29:7 5976
their trees *s* up in their height ... Eze 31:14 5975
Ye *s* upon your sword, ye work ... Eze 33:26 5975
they shall *s* before them to ... Eze 44:11 5975
they shall *s* before me to offer ... Eze 44:15 5975
they shall *s* in judgment ... Eze 44:24 5975
shall *s* by the post of the gate, ... Eze 46:2 5975
that the fishers shall *s* upon it ... Eze 47:10 5975
in them to *s* in the king's palace ... Dan 1:4 5975
they might *s* before the king ... Dan 1:5 5975
kingdoms, and it shall *s* for ever ... Dan 2:44 6966
made *s* upon the feet as a man, and ... Dan 7:4 6966
that no beasts might *s* before him ... Dan 8:4 5975
power in the ram to *s* before him ... Dan 8:7 5975
four kingdoms shall *s* up out of ... Dan 8:22 5975
dark sentences, shall *s* up ... Dan 8:23 5975
he shall also *s* up against the ... Dan 8:25 5975
I speak unto thee, and *s* upright ... Dan 10:11 5975
there shall *s* up yet three kings ... Dan 11:2 5975
And a mighty king shall *s* up ... Dan 11:3 5975
And when he shall *s* up, his ... Dan 11:4 5975
neither shall he *s*, nor his arm ... Dan 11:6 5975
shall one *s* up in his estate ... Dan 11:7 5975
many *s* up against the king of the ... Dan 11:14 5975
will, and none shall *s* before him ... Dan 11:16 5975
he shall *s* in the glorious land, ... Dan 11:16 5975
but she shall not *s* on his side ... Dan 11:17 5975
Then shall *s* up in his estate a ... Dan 11:20 5975
estate shall *s* up a vile person ... Dan 11:21 5975
but he shall not *s* ... Dan 11:25 5975
arms shall *s* on his part, and they ... Dan 11:31 5975
at that time shall Michael *s* up ... Dan 12:1 5975
s in thy lot at the end of the ... Dan 12:13 5975
Neither shall he *s* that handleth ... Amos 2:15 5975
And he shall *s* and feed in the ... Mic 5:4 5975
Who can *s* before his indignation ... Nah 1:6 5975
S, *s*, shall they cry ... Nah 2:8 5975
I will *s* upon my watch, and set me ... Hab 2:1 5975
to walk among these that *s* by ... Zec 3:7 5975
that *s* by the Lord of the whole ... Zec 4:14 5975
his feet shall *s* in that day upon ... Zec 14:4 5975
away while they *s* upon their feet ... Zec 14:12 5975
who shall *s* when he appeareth ... Mal 3:2 5975
against itself shall not *s* ... Mt 12:25 *2476*
how shall then his kingdom *s* ... Mt 12:26 *2476*
mother and thy brethren *s* without ... Mt 12:47 *2476*
Why *s* ye here all the day idle ... Mt 20:6 *2476*
s in the holy place, (whoso ... Mt 24:15 *2476*
had the withered hand, *S* forth ... Mk 3:3 *1453*
itself, that kingdom cannot *s* ... Mk 3:24 *2476*
itself, that house cannot *s* ... Mk 3:25 *2476*
and be divided, he cannot *s* ... Mk 3:26 *2476*
there be some of them that *s* here ... Mk 9:1 *2476*
And when ye *s* praying, forgive, if ... Mk 11:25 *4739*
that *s* in the presence of God ... Lk 1:19 *3936*
Rise up, and *s* forth in the midst ... Lk 6:8 *2476*
mother and thy brethren *s* without ... Lk 8:20 *2476*
himself, how shall his kingdom *s* ... Lk 11:18 *2476*
door, and ye begin to *s* without ... Lk 13:25 *2476*
to *s* before the Son of man ... Lk 21:36 *2476*
the people which *s* by I said it ... Jn 11:42 *4026*
why *s* ye gazing up into heaven ... Acts 1:11 *2476*
this man *s* here before you whole ... Acts 4:10 *3936*
Go, *s* and speak in the temple to ... Acts 5:20 *2476*
commanded the chariot to *s* still ... Acts 8:38 *2476*
Peter took him up, saying, *S* up ... Acts 10:26 *450*
loud voice, *S* upright on thy feet ... Acts 14:10 *450*
I *s* at Caesar's judgment seat, ... Acts 25:10 *2476*
And now I *s* and am judged for the ... Acts 26:6 *2476*
But rise, and *s* upon thy feet ... Acts 26:16 *2476*
into this grace wherein we *s* ... Rom 5:2 *2476*
God according to election might *s* ... Rom 9:11 *3306*
for God is able to make him *s* ... Rom 14:4 *2476*
for we shall all *s* before the ... Rom 14:10 *3936*
should not *s* in the wisdom of men ... 1Cor 2:5 *1510*
ye have received, and wherein ye *s* ... 1Cor 15:1 *2476*
why *s* we in jeopardy every hour ... 1Cor 15:30
s fast in the faith, quit you ... 1Cor 16:13 *4739*
for by faith ye *s* ... 2Cor 1:24 *2476*
for I *s* in doubt of you ... Gal 4:20 *639*
S fast therefore in the liberty ... Gal 5:1 *4739*
that ye may be able to *s* against ... Eph 6:11 *2476*
day, and having done all, to *s* ... Eph 6:13 *2476*
S therefore, having your loins ... Eph 6:14 *2476*
that ye *s* fast in one spirit, ... Phil 1:27 *4739*
so *s* fast in the Lord, my dearly ... Phil 4:1 *4739*
in prayers, that ye may *s* perfect ... Col 4:12 *2476*
we live, if ye *s* fast in the Lord ... 1Th 3:8 *4739*
s fast, and hold the traditions ... 2Th 2:15 *4739*
S thou there, or sit here under ... Jas 2:3 *2476*
true grace of God wherein ye *s* ... 1Pet 5:12 *2476*
I *s* at the door, and knock ... Rev 3:20 *2476*
and who shall be able to *s* ... Rev 6:17 *2476*
angel which I saw *s* upon the sea ... Rev 10:5 *2476*
s on the sea of glass, having the ... Rev 15:2 *2476*
shall *s* afar off for the fear of ... Rev 18:15 *2476*
small and great, *s* before God ... Rev 20:12 *2476*

STANDARD {18}

camp, and every man by his own *s* ... Num 1:52 1714
Israel shall pitch by his own *s* ... Num 2:2 1714
the *s* of the camp of Judah pitch ... Num 2:3 1714
On the south side shall be the *s* ... Num 2:10 1714
be the *s* of the camp of Ephraim ... Num 2:18 1714
The *s* of the camp of Dan shall be ... Num 2:25 1714
In the first place went the *s* of ... Num 10:14 1714
the *s* of the camp of Reuben set ... Num 10:18 1714
the *s* of the camp of the children ... Num 10:22 1714
the *s* of the camp of the children ... Num 10:25 1714
set up my *s* to the people ... Is 49:22 5251
shall lift up a *s* against him ... Is 59:19 5127
lift up a *s* for the people ... Is 62:10 5251
Set up the *s* toward Zion ... Jer 4:6 5251
How long shall I see the *s* ... Jer 4:21 5251
and publish, and set up a *s* ... Jer 50:2 5251
Set up the *s* upon the walls of ... Jer 51:12 5251
Set ye up a *s* in the land ... Jer 51:27 5251

STANDARD-BEARER {1}

shall be as when a *s* fainteth ... Is 10:18 5264

STANDARDS {3}

every man in his place by their *s* ... Num 2:17 1714
shall go hindmost with their *s* ... Num 2:31 1714
so they pitched by their *s* ... Num 2:34 1714

STANDEST {6}

wherefore *s* thou without ... Gen 24:31 5975
whereon thou *s* is holy ground ... Ex 3:5 5975
the place whereon thou *s* is holy ... Josh 5:15 5975
Why *s* thou afar off, O LORD ... Ps 10:1 5975
place where thou *s* is holy ground ... Acts 7:33 *2476*
broken off, and thou *s* by faith ... Rom 11:20 *2476*

STANDETH {30}

and that thy cloud *s* over them ... Num 14:14 5975
which *s* before thee, he shall go ... Deut 1:38 5975
s to minister there before the ... Deut 17:12 5975
But with him that *s* here with us ... Deut 29:15 5975
the pillars whereupon the house *s* ... Judg 16:26 3559
him, Behold, Haman *s* in the court ... Est 6:5 5975
the king, *s* in the house of Haman ... Est 7:9 5975
nor *s* in the way of sinners, nor ... Ps 1:1 5975
My foot *s* in an even place ... Ps 26:12 5975
counsel of the LORD *s* for ever ... Ps 33:11 5975
God *s* in the congregation of the ... Ps 82:1 5324
but my heart *s* in awe of thy word ... Ps 119:161
She *s* in the top of high places, ... Prov 8:2 5324
he *s* behind our wall, he looketh ... Song 2:9 5975
The LORD *s* up to plead ... Is 3:13 5324

and *s* to judge the people .... Is 3:13 5975
and set him in his place, and he *s* .... Is 46:7 5975
backward, and justice *s* afar off .... Is 59:14 5975
the great prince which *s* for the .... Dan 12:1 5975
nor feed that that *s* still .... Zec 11:16 5324
but there *s* one among you, whom .... Jn 1:26 *2476*
friend of the bridegroom, which *s* .... Jn 3:29 *2476*
to his own master he *s* or falleth .... Rom 14:4 *4739*
Nevertheless he that *s* stedfast 1Cor 7:37 *2476*
eat no flesh while the world *s* 1Cor 8:13
he *s* take heed lest he fall 1Cor 10:12 *2476*
the foundation of God *s* sure 2Ti 2:19 *2476*
every priest *s* daily ministering .... Heb 10:11 *2476*
the judge *s* before the door .... Jas 5:9 *2476*
of the angel which *s* upon the sea .... Rev 10:8 *2476*

STANDING {55}
the stacks of corn, or the *s* corn .... Ex 22:6 7054
tabernacle of shittim wood *s* up .... Ex 26:15 5975
tabernacle of shittim wood, *s* up .... Ex 36:20 5975
neither rear you up a *s* image .... Lev 26:1 4676
angel of the LORD *s* in the way .... Num 22:23 5324
angel of the LORD *s* in the way .... Num 22:31 5324
into the *s* corn of thy neighbour .... Deut 23:25 7054
unto thy neighbour's *s* corn .... Deut 23:25 7054
the *s* corn of the Philistines .... Judg 15:5 7054
the shocks, and also the *s* corn .... Judg 15:5 7054
Samuel *s* as appointed over them, ... 1Sa 19:20 5975
all his servants were *s* about him 1Sa 22:6 5324
the lion *s* by the carcase 1Kin 13:25 5975
the lion *s* by the carcase 1Kin 13:28 5975
all the host of heaven *s* by him 1Kin 22:19 5975
and two lions *s* by the stays 2Chr 9:18 5975
of heaven *s* on his right hand 2Chr 18:18 5975
Esther the queen *s* in the court .... Est 5:2 5975
in deep mire, where there is no *s* .... Ps 69:2 4613
the wilderness into a *s* water .... Ps 107:35 98
turned the rock into a *s* water .... Ps 114:8 98
I had seen *s* before the river .... Dan 8:6 5975
I saw the Lord *s* upon the altar .... Amos 9:1 5324
he shall receive of you his *s* .... Mic 1:11 5979
thy *s* images out of the midst of .... Mic 5:13 4676
me Joshua the high priest *s* .... Zec 3:1 5975
Satan *s* at his right hand to .... Zec 3:1 5975
which go forth from *s* before the .... Zec 6:5 3320
love to pray *s* in the synagogues .... Mt 6:5 *2476*
unto you, There be some *s* here .... Mt 16:28 *2476*
hour, and saw others *s* idle in the .... Mt 20:3 *2476*
went out, and found others *s* idle .... Mt 20:6 *2476*
s without, sent unto him, calling .... Mk 3:31 *2476*
s where it ought not, (let him .... Mk 13:14 *2476*
unto him an angel of the Lord *s* .... Lk 1:11 *2476*
And saw two ships *s* by the lake .... Lk 5:2 *2476*
of a truth, there be some *s* here .... Lk 9:27 *2476*
s afar off, would not lift up so .... Lk 18:13 *2476*
and the woman *s* in the midst .... Jn 8:9 *2476*
his mother, and the disciple *s* by .... Jn 19:26 *3936*
herself back, and saw Jesus *s* .... Jn 20:14 *2476*
s up with the eleven, lifted up .... Acts 2:14 *2476*
man which was healed *s* with them .... Acts 4:14 *2476*
the keepers *s* without before the .... Acts 5:23 *2476*
put in prison are *s* in the temple .... Acts 5:25 *2476*
Jesus *s* on the right hand of God, ... Acts 7:55 *2476*
the Son of man *s* on the right .... Acts 7:56 *2476*
Stephen was shed, I also was *s* by .... Acts 22:20 *2186*
voice, that I cried *s* among them .... Acts 24:21 *2476*
as the first tabernacle was yet *s* ...... Heb 9:8 *2192,4174*
the earth *s* out of the water and 2Pet 3:5 *4921*
s on the four corners of the .... Rev 7:1 *2476*
the two candlesticks *s* before the .... Rev 11:4 *2476*
S afar off for the fear of her .... Rev 18:10 *2476*
And I saw an angel *s* in the sun .... Rev 19:17 *2476*

STANK {4}
and the river *s*, and the Egyptians .... Ex 7:21 887
and the land *s* .... Ex 8:14 887
morning, and it bred worms, and *s* .... Ex 16:20 887
saw that they *s* before David 2Sa 10:6 887

STAR {15}
there shall come a *S* out of Jacob .... Num 24:17 3556
the *s* of your god, which ye made .... Amos 5:26 3556
we have seen his *s* in the east .... Mt 2:2 *792*
what time the *s* appeared .... Mt 2:7 *792*
and, lo, the *s*, which they saw in .... Mt 2:9 *792*
When they saw the *s*, they .... Mt 2:10 *792*
the *s* of your god Remphan, ... Acts 7:43 *798*
for one *s* differeth from another 1Cor 15:41 *792*
differeth from another *s* in glory 1Cor 15:41 *792*
the day *s* arise in your hearts 2Pet 1:19 *5459*
And I will give him the morning *s* .... Rev 2:28 *792*
there fell a great *s* from heaven .... Rev 8:10 *792*
the name of the *s* is called .... Rev 8:11 *792*
I saw a *s* fall from heaven unto .... Rev 9:1 *792*
David, and the bright and morning *s* .... Rev 22:16 *792*

STARE {1}
they look and *s* upon me .... Ps 22:17 7200

STARGAZERS {1}
Let now the astrologers, the *s* .... Is 47:13 2374,3556

STARS {51}
he made the *s* also .... Gen 1:16 3556
now toward heaven, and tell the *s* .... Gen 15:5 3556
thy seed as the *s* of the heaven .... Gen 22:17 3556
to multiply as the *s* of heaven .... Gen 26:4 3556
the eleven *s* made obeisance to me .... Gen 37:9 3556
your seed as the *s* of heaven .... Ex 32:13 3556
ye are this day as the *s* of .... Deut 1:10 3556
the sun, and the moon, and the *s* .... Deut 4:19 3556
as the *s* of heaven for multitude .... Deut 10:22 3556
whereas ye were as the *s* of .... Deut 28:62 3556
the *s* in their courses fought .... Judg 5:20 3556
like to the *s* of the heavens 1Chr 27:23 3556
the morning till the *s* appeared .... Neh 4:21 3556
thou as the *s* of heaven, and .... Neh 9:23 3556
Let the *s* of the twilight thereof .... Job 3:9 3556
and sealeth up the *s* .... Job 9:7 3556
and behold the height of the *s* .... Job 22:12 3556
the *s* are not pure in his sight .... Job 25:5 3556
When the morning *s* sang together .... Job 38:7 3556
of thy fingers, the moon and the *s* .... Ps 8:3 3556
The moon and *s* to rule by night .... Ps 136:9 3556
He telleth the number of the *s* .... Ps 147:4 3556
praise him, all ye *s* of light .... Ps 148:3 3556
the light, or the moon, or the *s* .... Eccl 12:2 3556
For the *s* of heaven and the .... Is 13:10 3556
my throne above the *s* of God .... Is 14:13 3556
of the *s* for a light by night, ... Jer 31:35 3556
and make the *s* thereof dark .... Eze 32:7 3556
of the *s* to the ground, and .... Dan 8:10 3556
righteousness as the *s* for ever .... Dan 12:3 3556
the *s* shall withdraw their .... Joel 2:10 3556
the *s* shall withdraw their .... Joel 3:15 3556
Seek him that maketh the seven *s* .... Amos 5:8 3598
thou set thy nest among the *s* .... Obad 4 3556
merchants above the *s* of heaven .... Nah 3:16 3556
the *s* shall fall from heaven, and .... Mt 24:29 *792*
the *s* of heaven shall fall, and .... Mk 13:25 *792*
sun, and in the moon, and in the *s* .... Lk 21:25 *798*
when neither sun nor *s* in many .... Acts 27:20 *798*
moon, and another glory of the *s* 1Cor 15:41 *792*
so many as the *s* of the sky in .... Heb 11:12 *798*
wandering *s*, to whom is reserved .... Jude 13 *792*
he had in his right hand seven *s* .... Rev 1:16 *792*
The mystery of the seven *s* which .... Rev 1:20 *792*
The seven *s* are the angels of the .... Rev 1:20 *792*
the seven *s* in his right hand .... Rev 2:1 *792*
Spirits of God, and the seven *s* .... Rev 3:1 *792*
the *s* of heaven fell unto the .... Rev 6:13 *792*
moon, and the third part of the *s* .... Rev 8:12 *792*
upon her head a crown of twelve *s* .... Rev 12:1 *792*
the third part of the *s* of heaven .... Rev 12:4 *792*

STATE {14}
man asked us straitly of our *s* .... Gen 43:7
set the house of God in his *s* 2Chr 24:13 4971
according to the *s* of the king .... Est 1:7 3027
according to the *s* of the king .... Est 2:18 3027
his best *s* is altogether vanity .... Ps 39:5 5324
to know the *s* of thy flocks .... Prov 27:23 6440
knowledge the *s* thereof shall be .... Prov 28:2 3651
from thy *s* shall he pull thee .... Is 22:19 4612
the last *s* of that man is worse .... Mt 12:45
the last *s* of that man is worse .... Lk 11:26
good comfort, when I know your *s* .. Phil 2:19 *3588,4012*
will naturally care for your *s* .... Phil 2:20 *3588,4012*
learned, in whatsoever *s* I am .... Phil 4:11
All my *s* shall Tychicus declare .... Col 4:7 *3588,2596*

STATELY {1}
And satest upon a *s* bed, and a .... Eze 23:41 3520

STATION {1}
And I will drive thee from thy *s* .... Is 22:19 4673

STATURE {17}
we saw in it are men of a great *s* .... Num 13:32 4060
or on the height of his *s* 1Sa 16:7 6967
Gath, where was a man of great *s* 2Sa 21:20 4055
an Egyptian, a man of great *s* 1Chr 11:23 4060
Gath, where was a man of great *s* 1Chr 20:6 4060
This thy *s* is like to a palm tree .... Song 7:7 6967
the high ones of *s* shall be hewn .... Is 10:33 6967
and of the Sabeans, men of *s* .... Is 45:14 4060
the head of every *s* to hunt souls .... Eze 13:18 6967
became a spreading vine of low *s* .... Eze 17:6 6967
her *s* was exalted among the thick .... Eze 19:11 6967
shadowing shroud, and of an high *s* .... Eze 31:3 6967
can add one cubit unto his *s* .... Mt 6:27 *2244*
And Jesus increased in wisdom and *s* .... Lk 2:52 *2244*
can add to his *s* one cubit .... Lk 12:25 *2244*
press, because he was little of *s* .... Lk 19:3 *2244*
unto the measure of the *s* of the .... Eph 4:13 *2244*

STATUTE {35}
there he made for them a *s* .... Ex 15:25 2706
it shall be a *s* for ever unto .... Ex 27:21 2708
it shall be a *s* for ever unto him .... Ex 28:43 2708
shall be theirs for a perpetual *s* .... Ex 29:9 2708
his sons' by a *s* for ever from .... Ex 29:28 2706
it shall be a *s* for ever to them, ... Ex 30:21 2706
It shall be a perpetual *s* for .... Lev 3:17 2708
It shall be a *s* for ever in your .... Lev 6:18 2706
it is a *s* for ever unto the LORD .... Lev 6:22 2706
unto his sons by a *s* for ever .... Lev 7:34 2706
by a *s* for ever throughout their .... Lev 7:36 2708
it shall be a *s* for ever .... Lev 10:9 2708
sons' with thee, by a *s* for ever .... Lev 10:15 2706
this shall be a *s* for ever unto .... Lev 16:29 2708
your souls, by a *s* for ever .... Lev 16:31 2708
be an everlasting *s* unto you .... Lev 16:34 2708
This shall be a *s* for ever unto .... Lev 17:7 2708
it shall be a *s* for ever .... Lev 23:14 2708
it shall be a *s* for ever in all .... Lev 23:21 2708
it shall be a *s* for ever .... Lev 23:31 2708
It shall be a *s* for ever in your .... Lev 23:41 2708
it shall be a *s* for ever in your .... Lev 24:3 2708
made by fire by a perpetual *s* .... Lev 24:9 2706
with thee, by a *s* for ever .... Num 18:11 2706
with thee, by a *s* for ever .... Num 18:19 2706
it shall be a *s* for ever .... Num 18:23 2708
among them, for a *s* for ever .... Num 19:10 2708
shall be a perpetual *s* unto them .... Num 19:21 2708
of Israel a *s* of judgment .... Num 27:11 2708
So these things shall be for a *s* .... Num 35:29 2708
people that day, and set them a *s* .... Josh 24:25 2706
day forward, that he made it a *s* 1Sa 30:25 2706
For this was a *s* for Israel .... Ps 81:4 2706
together to establish a royal *s* .... Dan 6:7 7010
That no decree nor *s* which the .... Dan 6:15 7010

STATUTES {132}
my charge, my commandments, my *s* .... Gen 26:5 2708
commandments, and keep all his *s* .... Ex 15:26 2706
I do make them know the *s* of God .... Ex 18:16 2706
the children of Israel all the *s* .... Lev 10:11 2706
Ye shall therefore keep my *s* .... Lev 18:5 2708
Ye shall therefore keep my *s* .... Lev 18:26 2708
Ye shall keep my *s* .... Lev 19:19 2708
shall ye observe all my *s* .... Lev 19:37 2708
And ye shall keep my *s*, and do them .... Lev 20:8 2708
Ye shall therefore keep all my *s* .... Lev 20:22 2708
Wherefore ye shall do my *s* .... Lev 25:18 2708
If ye walk in my *s*, and keep my .... Lev 26:3 2708
And if ye shall despise my *s* .... Lev 26:15 2708
because their soul abhorred my *s* .... Lev 26:43 2708
These are the *s* and judgments and .... Lev 26:46 2706
These are the *s*, which the LORD .... Num 30:16 2706
hearken, O Israel, unto the *s* .... Deut 4:1 2706
Behold, I have taught you *s* .... Deut 4:5 2706
which shall hear all these *s* .... Deut 4:6 2706
is there so great, that hath *s* .... Deut 4:8 2706
me at that time to teach you *s* .... Deut 4:14 2706
Thou shalt keep therefore his *s* .... Deut 4:40 2706
are the testimonies, and the *s* .... Deut 4:45 2706
unto them, Hear, O Israel, the *s* .... Deut 5:1 2706
all the commandments, and the *s* .... Deut 5:31 2706
these are the commandments, the *s* .... Deut 6:1 2706
LORD thy God, to keep all his *s* .... Deut 6:2 2708
God, and his testimonies, and his *s* .... Deut 6:17 2706
mean the testimonies, and the *s* .... Deut 6:20 2706
commanded us to do all these *s* .... Deut 6:24 2706
keep the commandments, and the *s* .... Deut 7:11 2706
and his judgments, and his *s* .... Deut 8:11 2708
of the LORD, and his *s*, which I .... Deut 10:13 2708
God, and keep his charge, and his *s* .... Deut 11:1 2708
ye shall observe to do all the *s* .... Deut 11:32 2706
These are the *s* and judgments, ... Deut 12:1 2706
thou shalt observe and do these *s* .... Deut 16:12 2706
the words of this law and these *s* .... Deut 17:19 2706
hath commanded thee to do these *s* .... Deut 26:16 2706
in his ways, and to keep his *s* .... Deut 26:17 2706
and do his commandments and his *s* .... Deut 27:10 2706
his *s* which I command thee this .... Deut 28:15 2708
his *s* which he commanded thee .... Deut 28:45 2708
his *s* which are written in this .... Deut 30:10 2708
to keep his commandments and his *s* .... Deut 30:16 2708
and as for his *s*, I did not depart 2Sa 22:23 2708
walk in his ways, to keep his *s* 1Kin 2:3 2708
walking in the *s* of David his 1Kin 3:3 2708
walk in my ways, to keep my *s* 1Kin 3:14 2706
if thou wilt walk in my *s* 1Kin 6:12 2708
keep his commandments, and his *s* 1Kin 8:58 2706
LORD our God, to walk in his *s* 1Kin 8:61 2706
commanded thee, and wilt keep my *s* 1Kin 9:4 2706
my *s* which I have set before you, ... 1Kin 9:6 2708
hast not kept my covenant and my *s* 1Kin 11:11 2708
in mine eyes, and to keep my *s* 1Kin 11:33 2708
he kept my commandments and my *s* 1Kin 11:34 2708
right in my sight, to keep my *s* 1Kin 11:38 2708
walked in the *s* of the heathen, ... 2Kin 17:8 2708
keep my commandments and my *s* 2Kin 17:13 2708
And they rejected his *s*, and his 2Kin 17:15 2706
but walked in the *s* of Israel 2Kin 17:19 2708
neither do they after their *s* 2Kin 17:34 2708
And the *s*, and the ordinances, and 2Kin 17:37 2706
his *s* with all their heart and all 2Kin 23:3 2708
thou takest heed to fulfil the *s* 1Chr 22:13 2706
thy testimonies, and thy *s* 1Chr 29:19 2706
thee, and shalt observe my *s* 2Chr 7:17 2706
if ye turn away, and forsake my *s* 2Chr 7:19 2708
between law and commandment, *s* 2Chr 19:10 2706
to the whole law and the *s* 2Chr 33:8 2706
and his testimonies, and his *s* 2Chr 34:31 2706
to do it, and to teach in Israel *s* .... Ezr 7:10 2706
the LORD, and of his *s* to Israel .... Ezr 7:11 2706
kept the commandments, nor the *s* .... Neh 1:7 2706
judgments, and true laws, good *s* .... Neh 9:13 2706
and commandedst them precepts, *s* .... Neh 9:14 2706
Lord, and his judgments and his *s* .... Neh 10:29 2706
I did not put away his *s* from me .... Ps 18:22 2708
The *s* of the LORD are right, ... Ps 19:8 6490
hast thou to do to declare my *s* .... Ps 50:16 2706
If they break my *s*, and keep not .... Ps 89:31 2708
That they might observe his *s* .... Ps 105:45 2706
ways were directed to keep thy *s* .... Ps 119:5 2706
I will keep thy *s* .... Ps 119:8 2706
teach me thy *s* .... Ps 119:12 2706
I will delight myself in thy *s* .... Ps 119:16 2708
thy servant did meditate in thy *s* .... Ps 119:23 2706
teach me thy *s* .... Ps 119:26 2706
me, O LORD, the way of thy *s* .... Ps 119:33 2706
and I will meditate in thy *s* .... Ps 119:48 2706
Thy *s* have been my songs in the .... Ps 119:54 2706
teach me thy *s* .... Ps 119:64 2706
teach me thy *s* .... Ps 119:68 2706
that I might learn thy *s* .... Ps 119:71 2706
Let my heart be sound in thy *s* .... Ps 119:80 2706
yet do I not forget thy *s* .... Ps 119:83 2706

mine heart to perform thy *s* alway .... Ps 119:112 2706
respect unto thy *s* continually .... Ps 119:117 2706
down all them that err from thy *s* .... Ps 119:118 2706
unto thy mercy, and teach me thy *s* .... Ps 119:124 2706
and teach me thy *s* .... Ps 119:135 2706
I will keep thy *s* .... Ps 119:145 2706
for they seek not thy *s* .... Ps 119:155 2706
when thou hast taught me thy *s* .... Ps 119:171 2706
his word unto Jacob, his *s* .... Ps 147:19 2706
nor walked in my law, nor in my *s* .... Jer 44:10 2708
walked in his law, nor in his *s* .... Jer 44:23 2708
my *s* more than the countries that .... Eze 5:6 2708
have refused my judgments and my *s* .... Eze 5:6 2708
you, and have not walked in my *s* .... Eze 5:7 2708
for ye have not walked in my *s* .... Eze 11:12 2706
That they may walk in my *s* .... Eze 11:20 2708
Hath walked in my *s*, and hath kept .... Eze 18:9 2708
my judgments, hath walked in my *s* .... Eze 18:17 2708
and right, and hath kept all my *s* .... Eze 18:19 2708
hath committed, and keep all my *s* .... Eze 18:21 2708
And I gave them my *s*, and shewed .... Eze 20:11 2708
they walked not in my *s*, and they .... Eze 20:13 2708
judgments, and walked not in my *s* .... Eze 20:16 2708
ye not in the *s* of your fathers .... Eze 20:18 2706
walk in my *s*, and keep my .... Eze 20:19 2708
they walked not in my *s*, neither .... Eze 20:21 2708
judgments, but had despised my *s* .... Eze 20:24 2708
them also *s* that were not good .... Eze 20:25 2706
had robbed, walk in the *s* of life .... Eze 33:15 2708
you, and cause you to walk in my *s* .... Eze 36:27 2706
in my judgments, and observe my *s* .... Eze 37:24 2708
my *s* in all mine assemblies .... Eze 44:24 2708
For the *s* of Omri are kept, and .... Mic 6:16 2708
But my words and my *s*, which I .... Zec 1:6 2706
Horeb for all Israel, with the *s* .... Mal 4:4 2706

STAVES {49}

thou shalt make *s* of shittim wood .... Ex 25:13 905
thou shalt put the *s* into the .... Ex 25:14 905
The *s* shall be in the rings of .... Ex 25:15 905
places of the *s* to bear the table .... Ex 25:27 905
shalt make the *s* of shittim wood .... Ex 25:28 905
thou shalt make *s* for the altar .... Ex 27:6 905
s of shittim wood, and overlay .... Ex 27:6 905
the *s* shall be put into the rings .... Ex 27:7 905
the *s* shall be upon the two sides .... Ex 27:7 905
for the *s* to bear it withal .... Ex 30:4 905
shalt make the *s* of shittim wood .... Ex 30:5 905
the *s* thereof, with the mercy .... Ex 35:12 905
The table, and his *s*, and all his .... Ex 35:13 905
And the incense altar, and his *s* .... Ex 35:15 905
with his brasen grate, his *s* .... Ex 35:16 905
he made *s* of shittim wood, and .... Ex 37:4 905
he put the *s* into the rings by .... Ex 37:5 905
for the *s* to bear the table .... Ex 37:14 905
he made the *s* of shittim wood, and .... Ex 37:15 905
for the *s* to bear it withal .... Ex 37:27 905
he made the *s* of shittim wood, and .... Ex 37:28 905
of brass, to be places for the *s* .... Ex 38:5 905
he made the *s* of shittim wood, and .... Ex 38:6 905
he put the *s* into the rings on .... Ex 38:7 905
the *s* thereof, and the mercy seat, ... Ex 39:35 905
and his grate of brass, his *s* .... Ex 39:39 905
set the *s* on the ark, and put the .... Ex 40:20 905
and shall put in the *s* thereof .... Num 4:6 905
and shall put in the *s* thereof .... Num 4:8 905
and shall put to the *s* thereof .... Num 4:11 905
skins, and put to the *s* of it .... Num 4:14 905
of the lawgiver, with their *s* .... Num 21:18 4938
that thou comest to me with *s* 1Sa 17:43 4731
the ark and the *s* thereof above 1Kin 8:7 905
And they drew out the *s*, that the 1Kin 8:8 905
that the ends of the *s* were seen 1Kin 8:8 905
shoulders with the *s* thereon 1Chr 15:15 4133
the ark and the *s* thereof above 2Chr 5:8 905
And they drew out the *s* of the ark 2Chr 5:9 905
that the ends of the *s* were seen 2Chr 5:9 905
his *s* the head of his villages .... Hab 3:14 4294
And I took unto me two *s* .... Zec 11:7 4731
coats, neither shoes, nor yet *s* .... Mt 10:10 *4464*
great multitude with swords and *s* .... Mt 26:47 *3586*
with swords and *s* for to take me .... Mt 26:55 *3586*
great multitude with swords and *s* .... Mk 14:43 *3586*
with swords and with *s* to take me .... Mk 14:48 *3586*
for your journey, neither *s* .... Lk 9:3 *4464*
against a thief, with swords and *s* .... Lk 22:52 *3586*

STAY See APPENDIX.

STAYED See APPENDIX.

STAYETH {1}

he *s* his rough wind in the day of .... Is 27:8 1898

STAYS {4}

there were *s* on either side on 1Kin 10:19 3027
and two lions stood beside the *s* 1Kin 10:19 3027
s on each side of the sitting 2Chr 9:18 3027
and two lions standing by the *s* 2Chr 9:18 3027

STEAD See APPENDIX.

STEADS {1}

in their *s* until the captivity 1Chr 5:22 8478

STEADY {1}

his hands were *s* until the going .... Ex 17:12 530

STEAL {22}

away secretly, and *s* away from me .... Gen 31:27 1589
how then should we *s* out of thy .... Gen 44:8 1589
Thou shalt not *s* .... Ex 20:15 1589
If a man shall *s* an ox, or a .... Ex 22:1 1589
Ye shall not *s*, neither deal .... Lev 19:11 1589
Neither shalt thou *s* .... Deut 5:19 1589
as people being ashamed *s* away 2Sa 19:3 1589
if he *s* to satisfy his soul when .... Prov 6:30 1589
or lest I be poor, and *s*, and take .... Prov 30:9 1589
Will ye *s*, murder, and commit .... Jer 7:9 1589
that *s* my words every one from .... Jer 23:30 1589
where thieves break through and *s* .... Mt 6:19 *2813*
do not break through nor *s* .... Mt 6:20 *2813*
commit adultery, Thou shalt not *s* .... Mt 19:18 *2813*
s him away, and say unto the .... Mt 27:64 *2813*
adultery, Do not kill, Do not *s* .... Mk 10:19 *2813*
adultery, Do not kill, Do not *s* .... Lk 18:20 *2813*
thief cometh not, but for to *s* .... Jn 10:10 *2813*
man should not *s*, dost thou *s* .... Rom 2:21 *2813*
shalt not kill, Thou shalt not *s* .... Rom 13:9 *2813*
Let him that stole *s* no more .... Eph 4:28 *2813*

STEALETH {3}

And he that *s* a man, and selleth .... Ex 21:16 1589
a tempest *s* him away in the night .... Job 27:20 1589
for every one that *s* shall be cut .... Zec 5:3 1589

STEALING {2}

If a man be found *s* any of his .... Deut 24:7 1589
and lying, and killing, and *s* .... Hos 4:2 1589

STEALTH {1}

them by *s* that day into the city 2Sa 19:3 1589

STEDFAST {11}

yea, thou shalt be *s*, and shalt .... Job 11:15 3332
whose spirit was not *s* with God .... Ps 78:8 539
were they *s* in his covenant .... Ps 78:37 539
s for ever, and his kingdom that .... Dan 6:26 7011
he that standeth *s* in his heart 1Cor 7:37 *1476*
my beloved brethren, be ye *s* 1Cor 15:58 *1476*
And our hope of you is *s*, knowing, ... 2Cor 1:7 *949*
the word spoken by angels was *s* .... Heb 2:2 *949*
of our confidence *s* unto the end .... Heb 3:14 *949*
of the soul, both sure and *s* .... Heb 6:19 *949*
Whom resist *s* in the faith, ... 1Pet 5:9 *4731*

STEDFASTLY {10}

she was *s* minded to go with her .... Ruth 1:18 553
And he settled his countenance *s* 2Kin 8:11 7760
he *s* set his face to go to .... Lk 9:51 *4741*
while they looked *s* toward heaven .... Acts 1:10 *816*
they continued *s* in the apostles' .... Acts 2:42 *4342*
in the council, looking *s* on him .... Acts 6:15 *816*
looked up *s* into heaven, and saw .... Acts 7:55 *816*
who *s* beholding him, and .... Acts 14:9 *816*
s behold the face of Moses for 2Cor 3:7 *816*
children of Israel could not *s* 2Cor 3:13 *816*

STEDFASTNESS {2}

the *s* of your faith in Christ .... Col 2:5 *4733*
the wicked, fall from your own *s* 2Pet 3:17 *4740*

STEEL {4}

so that a bow of *s* is broken by 2Sa 22:35 5154
the bow of *s* shall strike him .... Job 20:24 5154
so that a bow of *s* is broken by .... Ps 18:34 5154
break the northern iron and the *s* .... Jer 15:12 5178

STEEP {5}

the *s* places shall fall, and every .... Eze 38:20 4095
that are poured down a *s* place .... Mic 1:4 4174
down a *s* place into the sea .... Mt 8:32 *2911*
down a *s* place into the sea .... Mk 5:13 *2911*
down a *s* place into the lake .... Lk 8:33 *2911*

STEM {1}

forth a rod out of the *s* of Jesse .... Is 11:1 1503

STEP {2}

there is but a *s* between me 1Sa 20:3 6587
If my *s* hath turned out of the .... Job 31:7 838

STEPHANAS *(stef'-a-nas)* {3} *A convert of Paul from Achaia.*

baptized also the household of *S* 1Cor 1:16 *4734*
brethren, (ye know the house of *S* 1Cor 16:15 *4734*
I am glad of the coming of *S* 1Cor 16:17 *4734*

STEPHANUS {1}

was written from Philippi by *S* .... 1Cor *s* *4734*

STEPHEN *(ste'-ven)* {7} *A leader of the Jerusalem church.*

and they chose *S*, a man full of .... Acts 6:5 *4736*
And *S*, full of faith and power, did .... Acts 6:8 *4736*
and of Asia, disputing with *S* .... Acts 6:9 *4736*
And they stoned *S*, calling upon .... Acts 7:59 *4736*
men carried *S* to his burial .... Acts 8:2 *4736*
S travelled as far as Phenice .... Acts 11:19 *4736*
blood of thy martyr *S* was shed .... Acts 22:20 *4736*

STEPPED {1}

the troubling of the water *s* in .... Jn 5:4 *1684*

STEPPETH {1}

coming, another *s* down before me .... Jn 5:7 *2597*

STEPS {38}

thou go up by *s* unto mine altar .... Ex 20:26 4609
Thou hast enlarged my *s* under me 2Sa 22:37 6806
The throne had six *s*, and the top 1Kin 10:19 4609
and on the other upon the six *s* 1Kin 10:20 4609
And there were six *s* to the throne 2Chr 9:18 4609
and on the other upon the six *s* 2Chr 9:19 4609
For now thou numberest my *s* .... Job 14:16 6806
The *s* of his strength shall be .... Job 18:7 6806
My foot hath held his *s*, his way .... Job 23:11 838
When I washed my *s* with butter .... Job 29:6 1978
he see my ways, and count all my *s* .... Job 31:4 6806
unto him the number of my *s* .... Job 31:37 6806
have now compassed us in our *s* .... Ps 17:11 838
Thou hast enlarged my *s* under me .... Ps 18:36 6806
The *s* of a good man are ordered .... Ps 37:23 4703
none of his *s* shall slide .... Ps 37:31 838
neither have our *s* declined from .... Ps 44:18 838
hide themselves, they mark my *s* .... Ps 56:6 6119
They have prepared a net for my *s* .... Ps 57:6 6471
my *s* had well nigh slipped .... Ps 73:2 838
shall set us in the way of his *s* .... Ps 85:13 6471
Order my *s* in thy word .... Ps 119:133 6471
thy *s* shall not be straitened .... Prov 4:12 6806
her *s* take hold on hell .... Prov 5:5 6806
but the LORD directeth his *s* .... Prov 16:9 6806
the poor, and the *s* of the needy .... Is 26:6 6471
man that walketh to direct his *s* .... Jer 10:23 6806
They hunt our *s*, that we cannot .... Lam 4:18 6806
they went up unto it by seven *s* .... Eze 40:22 4609
there were seven *s* to go up to it .... Eze 40:26 4609
and the going up to it had eight *s* .... Eze 40:31 4609
and the going up to it had eight *s* .... Eze 40:34 4609
and the going up to it had eight *s* .... Eze 40:37 4609
he brought me by the *s* whereby .... Eze 40:49 4609
the Ethiopians shall be at his *s* .... Dan 11:43 4703
but who also walk in the *s* of .... Rom 4:12 *2487*
walked we not in the same *s* 2Cor 12:18 *2487*
that ye should follow his *s* 1Pet 2:21 *2487*

STERN {1}

cast four anchors out of the *s* .... Acts 27:29 *4403*

STEWARD {13}

the *s* of my house is this Eliezer .... Gen 15:2 1121,4943
near to the *s* of Joseph's house .... Gen 43:19 376,834,5921
he commanded the *s* of his house .... Gen 44:1 834,5921
far off, Joseph said unto his *s* .... Gen 44:4 834,5921
of Arza *s* of his house in Tirzah 1Kin 16:9 834,5921
of the vineyard saith unto his *s* .... Mt 20:8 *2012*
the wife of Chuza Herod's *s* .... Lk 8:3 *2012*
then is that faithful and wise *s* .... Lk 12:42 *3623*
a certain rich man, which had a *s* .... Lk 16:1 *3623*
for thou mayest be no longer *s* .... Lk 16:2 *3621*
Then the *s* said within himself, ... Lk 16:3 *3622*
the lord commended the unjust *s* .... Lk 16:8 *3622*
be blameless, as the *s* of God .... Titus 1:7 *3622*

STEWARDS {4}

the *s* over all the substance and 1Chr 28:1 8269
s of the mysteries of God 1Cor 4:1 *3623*
Moreover it is required in *s* 1Cor 4:2 *3623*
as good *s* of the manifold grace 1Pet 4:10 *3623*

STEWARDSHIP {3}

give an account of thy *s* .... Lk 16:2 *3622*
my lord taketh away from me the *s* .... Lk 16:3 *3622*
that, when I am put out of the *s* .... Lk 16:4 *3622*

STICK {14}

And he cut down a *s*, and cast it in 2Kin 6:6 6086
bones that were not seen *s* out .... Job 33:21 8205
they *s* together, that they cannot .... Job 41:17 3920
For thine arrows *s* fast in me .... Ps 38:2 5181
withered, it is become like a *s* .... Lam 4:8 6086
thy rivers to *s* unto thy scales .... Eze 29:4 1692
rivers shall *s* unto thy scales .... Eze 29:4 1692
thou son of man, take thee one *s* .... Eze 37:16 6086
then take another *s*, and write .... Eze 37:16 6086
the *s* of Ephraim, and for all the .... Eze 37:16 6086
them one to another into one *s* .... Eze 37:17 6086
I will take the *s* of Joseph .... Eze 37:19 6086
him, even with the *s* of Judah .... Eze 37:19 6086
of Judah, and make them one *s* .... Eze 37:19 6086

STICKETH {1}

that *s* closer than a brother .... Prov 18:24 1695

STICKS {6}

gathered *s* upon the sabbath day .... Num 15:32 6086
s brought him unto Moses and Aaron .... Num 15:33 6086
woman was there gathering of *s* 1Kin 17:10 6086
and, behold, I am gathering two *s* 1Kin 17:12 6086
the *s* whereon thou writest shall .... Eze 37:20 6086
Paul had gathered a bundle of *s* .... Acts 28:3 *5484*

STIFF {3}

know thy rebellion, and thy *s* neck .... Deut 31:27 7186
speak not with a *s* neck .... Ps 75:5 6277
their ear, but made their neck *s* .... Jer 17:23 7185

STIFFENED {1}

but he *s* his neck, and hardened 2Chr 36:13 7185

STIFFHEARTED {1}

they are impudent children and *s* .... Eze 2:4 2389,3820

STIFFNECKED {9}

and, behold, it is a *s* people .... Ex 32:9 7186,6203
for thou art a *s* people .... Ex 33:3 7186,6203
of Israel, Ye are a *s* people .... Ex 33:5 7186,6203
for it is a *s* people .... Ex 34:9 7186,6203
for thou art a *s* people .... Deut 9:6 7186,6203
and, behold, it is a *s* people .... Deut 9:13 7186,6203
of your heart, and be no more *s* .... Deut 10:16 7185,6203
Now be ye not *s*, as your fathers 2Chr 30:8 7185,6203
Ye *s* and uncircumcised in heart and .... Acts 7:51 *4644*

STILL {1}

going on *s* toward the south .... Gen 12:9 5265
but they were *s* ill favoured .... Gen 41:21
let them go, and wilt hold them *s* .... Ex 9:2
the people, Fear ye not, stand *s* .... Ex 14:13
arm they shall be as *s* as a stone .... Ex 15:16 1826
thou shalt let it rest and lie *s* .... Ex 23:11
if it appear *s* in the garment, ... Lev 13:57 5750
And Moses said unto them, Stand *s* .... Num 9:8
went to search the land, lived *s* .... Num 14:38
ye shall stand *s* in Jordan .... Josh 3:8
Sun, stand thou *s* upon Gibeon .... Josh 10:12 1826
And the sun stood *s*, and the moon .... Josh 10:13 1826
So the sun stood *s* in the midst .... Josh 10:13

that stood *s* in their strength ... Josh 11:13
therefore he blessed you *s* ... Josh 24:10
and are ye *s* ... Judg 18:9 2814
Then said she, Sit *s*, my daughter ... Ruth 3:18
on,) but stand thou *s* a while ... 1Sa 9:27
Now therefore stand *s*, that I may ... 1Sa 12:7
But if ye shall *s* do wickedly ... 1Sa 12:25
then we will stand *s* in our place ... 1Sa 14:9
things, and also shalt *s* prevail ... 1Sa 26:25
Asahel fell down and died stood *s* ... 2Sa 2:23
and all the people stood *s* ... 2Sa 2:28
But David tarried *s* at Jerusalem ... 2Sa 11:1
good for me to have been there *s* ... 2Sa 14:32
forth, and cursed *s* as he came ... 2Sa 16:5
And he turned aside, and stood *s* ... 2Sa 18:30
saw that all the people stood *s* ... 2Sa 20:12
one that came by him stood *s* ... 2Sa 20:12
and after the fire a *s* small voice ... 1Kin 19:12 1827
in Gilead is ours, and we be *s* ... 1Kin 22:3
came to pass, as they *s* went on ... 2Kin 2:11
and if we sit *s* here, we die also ... 2Kin 7:4
the people *s* sacrificed and burnt ... 2Kin 12:3 5750
burnt incense *s* on the high ... 2Kin 15:4 5750
burned incense *s* in the high ... 2Kin 15:35 5750
set yourselves, stand ye *s* ... 2Chr 20:17
no power to keep *s* the kingdom ... 2Chr 22:9
sacrifice *s* in the high places ... 2Chr 33:17 5750
they stood *s* in the prison gate ... Neh 12:39
s he holdeth fast his integrity ... Job 2:3 5750
him, Dost thou *s* retain thine ... Job 2:9 5750
For now should I have lain *s* ... Job 3:13
It stood *s*, but I could not ... Job 4:16
but keep it *s* within his mouth ... Job 20:13
(for they spake not, but stood *s* ... Job 32:16 5975
stand *s*, and consider the wondrous ... Job 37:14 5975
own heart upon your bed, and be *s* ... Ps 4:4 1826
that thou mightest *s* the enemy ... Ps 8:2 7673
he leadeth me beside the *s* waters ... Ps 23:2 4496
Be *s*, and know that I am God ... Ps 46:10 7503
That he should *s* live for ever ... Ps 49:9 5750
as goeth on *s* in his trespasses ... Ps 68:21
the earth feared, and was *s* ... Ps 76:8 8252
For all this they sinned *s* ... Ps 78:32 5750
hold not thy peace, and be not *s* ... Ps 83:1 8252
they will be *s* praising thee ... Ps 84:4 5750
They shall *s* bring forth fruit in ... Ps 92:14 5750
so that the waves thereof are *s* ... Ps 107:29 2814
when I awake, I am *s* with thee ... Ps 139:18 5750
he *s* taught the people knowledge ... Eccl 12:9 5750
but his hand is stretched out *s* ... Is 5:25 5750
but his hand is stretched out *s* ... Is 9:12 5750
but his hand is stretched out *s* ... Is 9:17 5750
but his hand is stretched out *s* ... Is 9:21 5750
but his hand is stretched out *s* ... Is 10:4 5750
Be *s*, ye inhabitants of the isle ... Is 23:2 1826
this, Their strength is to sit *s* ... Is 30:7 7673
I have been *s*, and refrained ... Is 42:14 2790
Why do we sit *s* ... Jer 8:14
They say *s* unto them that despise ... Jer 23:17
I let remain *s* in their own land ... Jer 27:11
I do earnestly remember him *s* ... Jer 31:20 5750
If ye will *s* abide in this land ... Jer 42:10
into thy scabbard, rest, and be *s* ... Jer 47:6 1826
the sword, go away, stand not *s* ... Jer 51:50 5975
soul hath them *s* in remembrance ... Lam 3:20
the children of thy people *s* are ... Eze 33:30
a winding about *s* upward to the ... Eze 41:7
s upward round about the house ... Eze 41:7
breadth of the house was *s* upward ... Eze 41:7
moon stood *s* in their habitation ... Hab 3:11
behold, all the earth sitteth *s* ... Zec 1:11
nor feed that that standeth *s* ... Zec 11:16
And Jesus stood *s*, and called them ... Mt 20:32 *2476*
and said unto the sea, Peace, be *s* ... Mk 4:39 *5392*
And Jesus stood *s*, and commanded ... Mk 10:49 *2476*
and they that bare him stood *s* ... Lk 7:14 *2476*
unto them, he abode *s* in Galilee ... Jn 7:9
he abode two days *s* in the same ... Jn 11:6
but Mary sat *s* in the house ... Jn 11:20
commanded the chariot to stand *s* ... Acts 8:38 *2476*
it pleased Silas to abide there *s* ... Acts 15:34
Silas and Timotheus abode there *s* ... Acts 17:14
if they abide not *s* in unbelief ... Rom 11:23
thee to abide *s* at Ephesus ... 1Ti 1:3 *4357*
is unjust, let him be unjust *s* ... Rev 22:11 *2089*
is filthy, let him be filthy *s* ... Rev 22:11 *2089*
righteous, let him be righteous *s* ... Rev 22:11 *2089*
that is holy, let him be holy *s* ... Rev 22:11 *2089*

STILLED {2}
Caleb *s* the people before Moses ... Num 13:30 2013
So the Levites *s* all the people ... Neh 8:11 2814

STILLEST {1}
waves thereof arise, thou *s* them ... Ps 89:9 7623

STILLETH {1}
Which *s* the noise of the seas ... Ps 65:7 7623

STING {2}
O death, where is thy *s* ... 1Cor 15:55 *2759*
The *s* of death is sin ... 1Cor 15:56 *2759*

STINGETH {1}
a serpent, and *s* like an adder ... Prov 23:32 6567

STINGS {1}
there were *s* in their tails ... Rev 9:10 *2759*

STINK {8}
to *s* among the inhabitants of the ... Gen 34:30 887
shall die, and the river shall *s* ... Ex 7:18 887
and it did not *s*, neither was ... Ex 16:24 887
My wounds *s* and are corrupt ... Ps 38:5 887
of sweet smell there shall be *s* ... Is 3:24 4716
their *s* shall come up out of ... Is 34:3 889
his *s* shall come up, and his ill ... Joel 2:20 889
I have made the *s* of your camps ... Amos 4:10 889

STINKETH {2}
their fish *s*, because there is no ... Is 50:2 887
unto him, Lord, by this time he *s* ... Jn 11:39 *3605*

STINKING {1}
to send forth a *s* savour ... Eccl 10:1 887

STIR {20}
who shall *s* him up ... Num 24:9 6965
the innocent shall *s* up himself ... Job 17:8 5782
is so fierce that dare *s* him up ... Job 41:10 5782
S up thyself, and awake to my ... Ps 35:23 5782
did not *s* up all his wrath ... Ps 78:38 5782
Manasseh *s* up thy strength, and ... Ps 80:2 5782
but grievous words *s* up anger ... Prov 15:1 5927
of the field, that ye *s* not up ... Song 2:7 5782
of the field, that ye *s* not up ... Song 3:5 5782
of Jerusalem, that ye *s* not up ... Song 8:4 5782
the LORD of hosts shall *s* up a ... Is 10:26 5782
I will *s* up the Medes against ... Is 13:17 5782
he shall *s* up jealousy like a man ... Is 42:13 5782
s up all against the realm of ... Dan 11:2 5782
he shall *s* up his power and his ... Dan 11:25 5782
was no small *s* among the soldiers ... Acts 12:18 *5017*
arose no small *s* about that way ... Acts 19:23 *5017*
that thou *s* up the gift of God ... 2Ti 1:6 *329*
to *s* you up by putting you in ... 2Pet 1:13 *1326*
in both which I *s* up your pure ... 2Pet 3:1 *1326*

STIRRED {23}
every one whose heart *s* him up ... Ex 35:21 5375
all the women whose heart *s* them ... Ex 35:26 5375
even every one whose heart *s* him ... Ex 36:2 5375
hath *s* up my servant against me ... 1Sa 22:8 6965
If the LORD have *s* thee up ... 1Sa 26:19 5496
the LORD *s* up an adversary unto ... 1Kin 11:14 6965
God *s* him up another adversary ... 1Kin 11:23 6965
LORD, whom Jezebel his wife *s* up ... 1Kin 21:25 5496
the God of Israel *s* up the spirit ... 1Chr 5:26 5782
Moreover the LORD *s* up against ... 2Chr 21:16 5782
the LORD *s* up the spirit of Cyrus ... 2Chr 36:22 5782
the LORD *s* up the spirit of Cyrus ... Ezr 1:1 5782
and my sorrow was *s* ... Ps 39:2 5916
But his sons shall be *s* up ... Dan 11:10 1624
then shall he return, and be *s* up ... Dan 11:10 1624
s up to battle with a very great ... Dan 11:25 1624
the LORD *s* up the spirit of ... Hag 1:14 5782
they *s* up the people, and the ... Acts 6:12 *4787*
But the Jews *s* up the devout and ... Acts 13:50 *3951*
Jews *s* up the Gentiles, and made ... Acts 14:2 *1892*
thither also, and *s* up the people ... Acts 17:13 *4531*
Athens, his spirit was *s* in him ... Acts 17:16 *3947*
s up all the people, and laid ... Acts 21:27 *4797*

STIRRETH {8}
As an eagle *s* up her nest ... Deut 32:11 5782
Hatred *s* up strifes ... Prov 10:12 5782
A wrathful man *s* up strife ... Prov 15:18 1624
is of a proud heart *s* up strife ... Prov 28:25 1624
An angry man *s* up strife, and a ... Prov 29:22 1624
it *s* up the dead for thee, even ... Is 14:9 5782
that *s* up himself to take hold of ... Is 64:7 5782
He *s* up the people, teaching ... Lk 23:5 *383*

STIRS {1}
Thou that art full of *s*, a ... Is 22:2 8663

STOCK {8}
or to the *s* of the stranger's ... Lev 25:47 6133
the *s* thereof die in the ground ... Job 14:8 1503
their *s* shall not take root in ... Is 40:24 1503
I fall down to the *s* of a tree ... Is 44:19 944
Saying to a *s*, Thou art my father ... Jer 2:27 6086
the *s* is a doctrine of vanities ... Jer 10:8 6086
children of the *s* of Abraham ... Acts 13:26 *1085*
of the *s* of Israel, of the tribe ... Phil 3:5 *1085*

STOCKS {9}
puttest my feet also in the *s* ... Job 13:27 5465
He putteth my feet in the *s* ... Job 33:11 5465
a fool to the correction of the *s* ... Prov 7:22 5914
adultery with stones and with *s* ... Jer 3:9 6086
put him in the *s* that were in the ... Jer 20:2 4115
forth Jeremiah out of the *s* ... Jer 20:3 4115
put him in prison, and in the *s* ... Jer 29:26 6729
My people ask counsel at their *s* ... Hos 4:12 6086
and made their feet fast in the *s* ... Acts 16:24 *3586*

STOIC See STOICKS.

STOICKS (*sto'-ics*) {1} *A sect of Greek philosophers.*
of the Epicureans, and of the *S* ... Acts 17:18 *4770*

STOLE {6}
Jacob *s* away unawares to Laban ... Gen 31:20 1589
so Absalom *s* the hearts of the ... 2Sa 15:6 1589
s him from among the king's sons ... 2Kin 11:2 1589
s him from among the king's sons ... 2Chr 22:11 1589
s him away while we slept ... Mt 28:13 *2813*
Let him that *s* steal no more ... Eph 4:28 *2813*

STOLEN {15}
that shall be counted *s* with me ... Gen 30:33 1589
Rachel had *s* the images that were ... Gen 31:19 1589
that thou hast *s* away unawares to ... Gen 31:26 1589
yet wherefore hast thou *s* my gods ... Gen 31:30 1589
knew not that Rachel had *s* them ... Gen 31:32 1589
s by day, or *s* by night ... Gen 31:39 1589
For indeed I was *s* away out of ... Gen 40:15 1589
it be *s* out of the man's house ... Ex 22:7 1589
And if it be *s* from him, he shall ... Ex 22:12 1589
accursed thing, and have also *s* ... Josh 7:11 1589
the men of Judah *s* thee away ... 2Sa 19:41 1589
which had *s* them from the street ... 2Sa 21:12 1589
S waters are sweet, and bread ... Prov 9:17 1589
not have *s* till they had enough ... Obad 5 1589

STOMACHER {1}
instead of a *s* a girding of ... Is 3:24 6614

STOMACH'S {1}
use a little wine for thy *s* sake ... 1Ti 5:23 *4751*

STONE {191}
there is bdellium and the onyx *s* ... Gen 2:12 68
And they had brick for *s*, and slime ... Gen 11:3 68
took the *s* that he had put for ... Gen 28:18 68
And this *s*, which I have set for a ... Gen 28:22 68
a great *s* was upon the well's ... Gen 29:2 68
they rolled the *s* from the well's ... Gen 29:3 68
put the *s* again upon the well's ... Gen 29:3 68
till they roll the *s* from the ... Gen 29:8 68
rolled the *s* from the well's ... Gen 29:10 68
And Jacob took a *s*, and set it up ... Gen 31:45 68
with him, even a pillar of *s* ... Gen 35:14 68
is the shepherd, the *s* of Israel ... Gen 49:24 68
Then Zipporah took a sharp *s* ... Ex 4:25 6697
of wood, and in vessels of *s* ... Ex 7:19 68
their eyes, and will they not *s* us ... Ex 8:26 5619
they sank into the bottom as a *s* ... Ex 15:5 68
arm they shall be as still as a *s* ... Ex 15:16 68
they be almost ready to *s* me ... Ex 17:4 5619
and they took a *s*, and put it under ... Ex 17:12 68
thou wilt make me an altar of *s* ... Ex 20:25 68
thou shalt not build it of hewn *s* ... Ex 20:25
and one smite another with a *s* ... Ex 21:18 68
were a paved work of a sapphire *s* ... Ex 24:10
and I will give thee tables of *s* ... Ex 24:12 68
Six of their names on one *s* ... Ex 28:10 68
names of the rest on the other *s* ... Ex 28:10 68
With the work of an engraver in *s* ... Ex 28:11 68
tables of testimony, tables of *s* ... Ex 31:18 68
tables of *s* like unto the first ... Ex 34:1 68
tables of *s* like unto the first ... Ex 34:4 68
in his hand the two tables of *s* ... Ex 34:4 68
the land shall *s* him with stones ... Lev 20:2 7275
they shall *s* them with stones ... Lev 20:27 7275
and let all the congregation *s* him ... Lev 24:14 7275
shall certainly *s* him ... Lev 24:16 7275
of the camp, and *s* him with stones ... Lev 24:23 7275
up any image of *s* in your land ... Lev 26:1 68
bade *s* them with stones ... Num 14:10 7275
all the congregation shall *s* him ... Num 15:35 7275
if he smite him with throwing a *s* ... Num 35:17 68
Or with any *s*, wherewith a man ... Num 35:23 68
wrote them upon two tables of *s* ... Deut 4:13 68
work of men's hands, wood and *s* ... Deut 4:28 68
he wrote them in two tables of *s* ... Deut 5:22 68
mount to receive the tables of *s* ... Deut 9:9 68
s written with the finger of God ... Deut 9:10 68
LORD gave me the two tables of *s* ... Deut 9:11 68
tables of *s* like unto the first ... Deut 10:1 68
tables of *s* like unto the first ... Deut 10:3 68
thou shalt *s* him with stones ... Deut 13:10 5619
shalt *s* them with stones, till ... Deut 17:5 5619
his city shall *s* him with stones ... Deut 21:21 7275
the men of her city shall *s* her ... Deut 22:21 5619
ye shall *s* them with stones that ... Deut 22:24 5619
thou serve other gods, wood and *s* ... Deut 28:36 68
have known, even wood and *s* ... Deut 28:64 68
and their idols, wood and *s* ... Deut 29:17 68
man of you a *s* upon his shoulder ... Josh 4:5 68
the border went up to the *s* of ... Josh 15:6 68
descended to the *s* of Bohan the ... Josh 18:17 68
the law of God, and took a great *s* ... Josh 24:26 68
this *s* shall be a witness unto us ... Josh 24:27 68
and ten persons, upon one *s* ... Judg 9:5 68
and ten persons, upon one *s* ... Judg 9:18 68
there, where there was a great *s* ... 1Sa 6:14 68
were, and put them on the great *s* ... 1Sa 6:15 68
even unto the great *s* of Abel ... 1Sa 6:18
which *s* remaineth unto this day ... 1Sa 6:18
Then Samuel took a *s*, and set it ... 1Sa 7:12 68
roll a great *s* unto me this day ... 1Sa 14:33 68
in his bag, and took thence a *s* ... 1Sa 17:49 68
that the *s* sunk into his forehead ... 1Sa 17:49 68
with a sling and with a *s*, and ... 1Sa 17:50 68
and shalt remain by the *s* Ezel ... 1Sa 20:19 68
within him, and he became as a *s* ... 1Sa 25:37 68
be not one small *s* found there ... 2Sa 17:13 6872
at the great *s* which is in Gibeon ... 2Sa 20:8 68
fat cattle by the *s* of Zoheleth ... 1Kin 1:9 68
was built of *s* made ready before ... 1Kin 6:7 68
there was no *s* seen ... 1Kin 6:18 68
court with three rows of hewed *s* ... 1Kin 6:36 1496
the ark save the two tables of *s* ... 1Kin 8:9 68
out, and *s* him, that he may die ... 1Kin 21:10 5619
of land cast every man his *s* ... 2Kin 3:25 68
And to masons, and hewers of *s* ... 2Kin 12:12 68
hewed *s* to repair the breaches of ... 2Kin 12:12 68
work of men's hands, wood and *s* ... 2Kin 19:18 68
hewn *s* to repair the house ... 2Kin 22:6 68
timber also and *s* have I prepared ... 1Chr 22:14 68
abundance, hewers and workers of *s* ... 1Chr 22:15 68
silver, in brass, in iron, in *s* ... 2Chr 2:14 68
gave they it, to buy hewn *s* ... 2Chr 34:11 68
even break down their *s* wall ... Neh 4:3 68
as a *s* into the mighty waters ... Neh 9:11 68
and brass is molten out of the *s* ... Job 28:2 68

or who laid the corner *s* thereof ... Job 38:6 68
The waters are hid as with a *s* ... Job 38:30 68
His heart is as firm as a *s* ... Job 41:24 68
thou dash thy foot against a *s* ... Ps 91:12 68
The *s* which the builders refused ... Ps 118:22 68
become the head *s* of the corner ... Ps 118:22
A gift is as a precious *s* in the ... Prov 17:8 68
the *s* wall thereof was broken ... Prov 24:31 68
As he that bindeth a *s* in a sling ... Prov 26:8 68
and he that rolleth a *s*, it will ... Prov 26:27 68
A *s* is heavy, and the sand weighty ... Prov 27:3 68
but for a *s* of stumbling and for a ... Is 8:14 68
a foundation a *s*, a tried *s* ... Is 28:16 68
a precious corner *s* ... Is 28:16
work of men's hands, wood and *s* ... Is 37:19 68
and to a *s*, Thou hast brought me ... Jer 2:27 68
not take of thee a *s* for a corner ... Jer 51:26 68
a corner, nor a *s* for foundations ... Jer 51:26 68
that thou shalt bind a *s* to it ... Jer 51:63 68
hath inclosed my ways with hewn *s* ... Lam 3:9 1496
the dungeon, and cast a *s* upon me ... Lam 3:53 68
as the appearance of a sapphire *s* ... Eze 1:26 68
over them as it were a sapphire *s* ... Eze 10:1 68
was as the colour of a beryl *s* ... Eze 10:9 68
they shall *s* thee with stones, and ... Eze 16:40 7275
the countries, to serve wood and *s* ... Eze 20:32 68
company shall *s* them with stones ... Eze 23:47 7275
every precious *s* was thy covering ... Eze 28:13 68
of hewn *s* for the burnt offering ... Eze 40:42 68
Thou sawest till that a *s* was cut ... Dan 2:34 69
the *s* that smote the image became ... Dan 2:35 69
as thou sawest that the *s* was cut ... Dan 2:45 69
brass, of iron, of wood, and of *s* ... Dan 5:4 69
gold, of brass, iron, wood, and *s* ... Dan 5:23 69
a *s* was brought, and laid upon the ... Dan 6:17 69
ye have built houses of hewn *s* ... Amos 5:11 1496
For the *s* shall cry out of the ... Hab 2:11 68
to the dumb *s*, Arise, it shall ... Hab 2:19 68
from before a *s* was laid upon a ... Hag 2:15 68
a *s* in the temple of the LORD ... Hag 2:15 68
For behold the *s* that I have laid ... Zec 3:9 68
upon one *s* shall be seven eyes ... Zec 3:9 68
made their hearts as an adamant *s* ... Zec 7:12 8068
a burdensome *s* for all people ... Zec 12:3 68
thou dash thy foot against a *s* ... Mt 4:6 *3037*
ask bread, will he give him a *s* ... Mt 7:9 *3037*
The *s* which the builders rejected ... Mt 21:42 *3037*
fall on this *s* shall be broken ... Mt 21:44 *3037*
be left here one *s* upon another ... Mt 24:2 *3037*
he rolled a great *s* to the door ... Mt 27:60 *3037*
the sepulchre sure, sealing the *s* ... Mt 27:66 *3037*
rolled back the *s* from the door ... Mt 28:2 *3037*
The *s* which the builders rejected ... Mk 12:10 *3037*
not be left one *s* upon another ... Mk 13:2 *3037*
rolled a *s* unto the door of the ... Mk 15:46 *3037*
Who shall roll us away the *s* from ... Mk 16:3 *3037*
saw that the *s* was rolled away ... Mk 16:4 *3037*
command this *s* that it be made ... Lk 4:3 *3037*
thou dash thy foot against a *s* ... Lk 4:11 *3037*
is a father, will he give him a *s* ... Lk 11:11 *3037*
leave in thee one *s* upon another ... Lk 19:44 *3037*
all the people will *s* us ... Lk 20:6 *2642*
The *s* which the builders rejected ... Lk 20:17 *3037*
fall upon that *s* shall be broken ... Lk 20:18 *3037*
not be left one *s* upon another ... Lk 21:6 *3037*
in a sepulchre that was hewn in *s* ... Lk 23:53 *2991*
they found the *s* rolled away from ... Lk 24:2 *3037*
which is by interpretation, A *s* ... Jn 1:42 *4074*
were set there six waterpots of *s* ... Jn 2:6 *3035*
let him first cast a *s* at her ... Jn 8:7 *3037*
took up stones again to *s* him ... Jn 10:31 *3034*
which of those works do ye *s* me ... Jn 10:32 *3034*
For a good work we *s* thee not ... Jn 10:33 *3034*
the Jews of late sought to *s* thee ... Jn 11:8 *3034*
It was a cave, and a *s* lay upon it ... Jn 11:38 *3037*
Jesus said, Take ye away the *s* ... Jn 11:39 *3037*
Then they took away the *s* from ... Jn 11:41 *3037*
seeth the *s* taken away from the ... Jn 20:1 *3037*
This is the *s* which was set at ... Acts 4:11 *3037*
them despitefully, and to *s* them, ... Acts 14:5 *3036*
like unto gold, or silver, or *s* ... Acts 17:29 *3037*
not in tables of *s*, but in ... 2Cor 3:3 *3035*
himself being the chief corner *s* ... Eph 2:20
whom coming, as unto a living *s* ... 1Pet 2:4 *3037*
I lay in Sion a chief corner *s* ... 1Pet 2:6 *3037*
the *s* which the builders ... 1Pet 2:7 *3037*
a *s* of stumbling, and a rock of ... 1Pet 2:8 *3037*
manna, and will give him a white *s* ... Rev 2:17 *5586*
in the *s* a new name written, ... Rev 2:17 *5586*
upon like a jasper and a sardine *s* ... Rev 4:3 *3037*
gold, and silver, and brass, and *s* ... Rev 9:20 *3035*
every *s* about the weight of a ... Rev 16:21
up a *s* like a great millstone ... Rev 18:21 *3037*
was like unto a *s* most precious ... Rev 21:11 *3037*
precious, even like a jasper *s* ... Rev 21:11 *3037*

STONED {22}

it, but he shall surely be *s* ... Ex 19:13 5619
then the ox shall be surely *s* ... Ex 21:28 5619
the ox shall be *s*, and his owner ... Ex 21:29 5619
of silver, and the ox shall be *s* ... Ex 21:32 5619
s him with stones, and he died ... Num 15:36 7275
all Israel *s* him with stones, and ... Josh 7:25 5619
after they had *s* them with stones ... Josh 7:25 7275
all Israel *s* him with stones, ... 1Kin 12:18 7275
s him with stones, that he died ... 1Kin 21:13 5619
to Jezebel, saying, Naboth is *s* ... 1Kin 21:14 5619
Jezebel heard that Naboth was *s* ... 1Kin 21:15 5619
of Israel *s* him with stones ... 2Chr 10:18 7275
him, and *s* him with stones at the ... 2Chr 24:21 7275
and killed another, and *s* another ... Mt 21:35 *3036*
us, that such should be *s* ... Jn 8:5 *3036*
lest they should have been *s* ... Acts 5:26 *3034*
him out of the city, and *s* him ... Acts 7:58 *3036*
they *s* Stephen, calling upon God, ... Acts 7:59 *3036*
the people, and, having *s* Paul ... Acts 14:19 *3034*
I beaten with rods, once was I *s* ... 2Cor 11:25 *3034*
They were *s*, they were sawn ... Heb 11:37 *3034*
touch the mountain, it shall be *s* ... Heb 12:20 *3036*

STONE'S {1}

from them about a *s* cast, and ... Lk 22:41 *3037*

STONES {179}

and he took of the *s* of that place ... Gen 28:11 68
said unto his brethren, Gather *s* ... Gen 31:46 68
and they took *s*, and made an heap ... Gen 31:46 68
Onyx *s*, and *s* to be set in ... Ex 25:7 68
And thou shalt take two onyx *s* ... Ex 28:9 68
shalt thou engrave the two *s* with ... Ex 28:11 68
thou shalt put the two *s* upon the ... Ex 28:12 68
s of memorial unto the children ... Ex 28:12 68
shalt set in it settings of *s* ... Ex 28:17 68
even four rows of *s* ... Ex 28:17 68
the *s* shall be with the names of ... Ex 28:21 68
And in cutting of *s*, to set them, ... Ex 31:5 68
And onyx *s*, and *s* to be set ... Ex 35:9 68
And the rulers brought onyx *s* ... Ex 35:27 68
s to be set, for the ephod, and ... Ex 35:27 68
And in the cutting of *s*, to set ... Ex 35:33 68
they wrought onyx *s* inclosed in ... Ex 39:6 68
that they should be *s* for a ... Ex 39:7 68
And they set in it four rows of *s* ... Ex 39:10 68
the *s* were according to the names ... Ex 39:14 68
away the *s* in which the plague is ... Lev 14:40 68
And they shall take other *s* ... Lev 14:42 68
put them in the place of those *s* ... Lev 14:42 68
that he hath taken away the *s* ... Lev 14:43 68
the *s* of it, and the timber ... Lev 14:45 68
the land shall stone him with *s* ... Lev 20:2 68
they shall stone them with *s* ... Lev 20:27 68
or scabbed, or hath his *s* broken ... Lev 21:20 810
of the camp, and stone him with *s* ... Lev 24:23 68
bade stone them with *s* ... Num 14:10 68
stone him with *s* without the camp ... Num 15:35 68
the camp, and stoned him with *s* ... Num 15:36 68
a land whose *s* are iron, and out ... Deut 8:9 68
And thou shalt stone him with *s* ... Deut 13:10 68
woman, and shalt stone them with *s* ... Deut 17:5 68
his city shall stone him with *s* ... Deut 21:21 68
stone her with *s* that she die ... Deut 22:21 68
stone them with *s* that they die ... Deut 22:24 68
He that is wounded in the *s* ... Deut 23:1
thou shalt set thee up great *s* ... Deut 27:2 68
that ye shall set up these *s* ... Deut 27:4 68
the LORD thy God, an altar of *s* ... Deut 27:5 68
of the LORD thy God of whole *s* ... Deut 27:6 68
thou shalt write upon the *s* all ... Deut 27:8 68
feet stood firm, twelve *s* ... Josh 4:3 68
saying, What mean ye by these *s* ... Josh 4:6 68
these *s* shall be for a memorial ... Josh 4:7 68
took up twelve *s* out of the midst ... Josh 4:8 68
Joshua set up twelve *s* in the ... Josh 4:9 68
And those twelve *s*, which they ... Josh 4:20 68
come, saying, What mean these *s* ... Josh 4:21 68
And all Israel stoned him with *s* ... Josh 7:25 68
after they had stoned them with *s* ... Josh 7:25 68
a great heap of *s* unto this day ... Josh 7:26 68
raise thereon a great heap of *s* ... Josh 8:29 68
law of Moses, an altar of whole *s* ... Josh 8:31 68
he wrote there upon the *s* a copy ... Josh 8:32 68
s from heaven upon them unto ... Josh 10:11 68
Roll great *s* upon the mouth of ... Josh 10:18 68
laid great *s* in the cave's mouth, ... Josh 10:27 68
could sling *s* at an hair breadth ... Judg 20:16 68
five smooth *s* out of the brook ... 1Sa 17:40 68
of gold with the precious *s* ... 2Sa 12:30 68
he cast *s* at David, and at all the ... 2Sa 16:6 68
threw *s* at him, and cast dust ... 2Sa 16:13 68
a very great heap of *s* upon him ... 2Sa 18:17 68
s, costly *s*, and hewed *s* ... 1Kin 5:17 68
timber and *s* to build the house ... 1Kin 5:18 68
All these were of costly *s* ... 1Kin 7:9 68
to the measures of hewed *s* ... 1Kin 7:9 1496
of costly *s*, even great *s* ... 1Kin 7:10 68
s of ten cubits, and *s* of ... 1Kin 7:10 68
And above were costly *s*, after the ... 1Kin 7:11 68
after the measures of hewed *s* ... 1Kin 7:11 1496
was with three rows of hewed *s* ... 1Kin 7:12 1496
and very much gold, and precious *s* ... 1Kin 10:2 68
very great store, and precious *s* ... 1Kin 10:10 68
of almug trees, and precious *s* ... 1Kin 10:11 68
silver to be in Jerusalem as *s* ... 1Kin 10:27 68
and all Israel stoned him with *s* ... 1Kin 12:18 68
and they took away the *s* of Ramah ... 1Kin 15:22 68
And Elijah took twelve *s*, ... 1Kin 18:31 68
with the *s* he built an altar in ... 1Kin 18:32 68
sacrifice, and the wood, and the *s* ... 1Kin 18:38 68
of the city, and stoned him with *s* ... 1Kin 21:13 68
every good piece of land with *s* ... 2Kin 3:19 68
left they the *s* thereof ... 2Kin 3:25 68
and put it upon a pavement of *s* ... 2Kin 16:17 68
hand and the left in hurling *s* ... 1Chr 12:2 68
and there were precious *s* in it ... 1Chr 20:2 68
s to build the house of God ... 1Chr 22:2 68
onyx *s*, and *s* to be set, ... 1Chr 29:2 68
to be set, glistering *s* ... 1Chr 29:2 68
and all manner of precious *s* ... 1Chr 29:2 68
s, and marble *s* in abundance ... 1Chr 29:2 68
they with whom precious *s* were ... 1Chr 29:8 68
at Jerusalem as plenteous as *s* ... 2Chr 1:15 68
house with precious *s* for beauty ... 2Chr 3:6 68
gold in abundance, and precious *s* ... 2Chr 9:1 68
great abundance, and precious *s* ... 2Chr 9:9 68
brought algum trees and precious *s* ... 2Chr 9:10 68
made silver in Jerusalem as *s* ... 2Chr 9:27 68
of Israel stoned him with *s* ... 2Chr 10:18 68
they carried away the *s* of Ramah ... 2Chr 16:6 68
him, and stoned him with *s* at the ... 2Chr 24:21 68
and bows, and slings to cast *s* ... 2Chr 26:14 68
to shoot arrows and great *s* withal ... 2Chr 26:15 68
and for gold, and for precious *s* ... 2Chr 32:27 68
which is builded with great *s* ... Ezr 5:8 69
With three rows of great *s* ... Ezr 6:4 69
will they revive the *s* out of the ... Neh 4:2 68
in league with the *s* of the field ... Job 5:23 68
Is my strength the strength of *s* ... Job 6:12 68
the heap, and seeth the place of *s* ... Job 8:17 68
The waters wear the *s* ... Job 14:19 68
of Ophir as the *s* of the brooks ... Job 22:24 6697
the *s* of darkness, and the shadow ... Job 28:3 68
The *s* of it are the place of ... Job 28:6 68
the sinews of his *s* are wrapped ... Job 40:17 6344
Sharp *s* are under him ... Job 41:30 2789
his thick clouds passed, hail *s* ... Ps 18:12
hail *s* and coals of fire ... Ps 18:13
servants take pleasure in her *s* ... Ps 102:14 68
thy little ones against the *s* ... Ps 137:9 5553
our daughters may be as corner *s* ... Ps 144:12 2106
A time to cast away *s*, and a time ... Eccl 3:5 68
and a time to gather *s* together ... Eccl 3:5 68
Whoso removeth *s* shall be hurt ... Eccl 10:9 68
it, and gathered out the *s* thereof ... Is 5:2 5619
but we will build with hewn *s* ... Is 9:10 1496
that go down to the *s* of the pit ... Is 14:19 68
when he maketh all the *s* of the ... Is 27:9 68
confusion, and the *s* of emptiness ... Is 34:11 68
I will lay thy *s* with fair colors ... Is 54:11 68
and all thy borders of pleasant *s* ... Is 54:12 68
Among the smooth *s* of the stream ... Is 57:6
and for wood brass, and for *s* iron ... Is 60:17 68
gather out the *s* ... Is 62:10 68
and committed adultery with *s* ... Jer 3:9 68
Take great *s* in thine hand, and ... Jer 43:9 68
upon these *s* that I have hid ... Jer 43:10 68
broken my teeth with gravel *s* ... Lam 3:16 2687
the *s* of the sanctuary are poured ... Lam 4:1 68
and they shall stone thee with *s* ... Eze 16:40 68
company shall stone them with *s* ... Eze 23:47 68
and they shall lay thy *s* and thy ... Eze 26:12 68
spices, and with all precious *s* ... Eze 27:22 68
in the midst of the *s* of fire ... Eze 28:14 68
from the midst of the *s* of fire ... Eze 28:16 68
and silver, and with precious *s* ... Dan 11:38 68
I will pour down the *s* thereof ... Mic 1:6 68
timber thereof and the *s* thereof ... Zec 5:4 68
devour, and subdue with sling *s* ... Zec 9:15 68
they shall be as the *s* of a crown ... Zec 9:16 68
these *s* to raise up children unto ... Mt 3:9 *3037*
that these *s* be made bread ... Mt 4:3 *3037*
crying, and cutting himself with *s* ... Mk 5:5 *3037*
and at him they cast *s*, and wounded ... Mk 12:4 *3036*
him, Master, see what manner of *s* ... Mk 13:1 *3037*
these *s* to raise up children unto ... Lk 3:8 *3037*
the *s* would immediately cry out ... Lk 19:40 *3037*
how it was adorned with goodly *s* ... Lk 21:5 *3037*
took they up *s* to cast at him ... Jn 8:59 *3037*
Jews took up *s* again to stone him ... Jn 10:31 *3037*
gold, silver, precious *s*, wood, ... 1Cor 3:12 *3037*
death, written and engraven in *s* ... 2Cor 3:7 *3037*
Ye also, as lively *s*, are built ... 1Pet 2:5 *3037*
and decked with gold and precious *s* ... Rev 17:4 *3037*
of gold, and silver, and precious *s* ... Rev 18:12 *3037*
decked with gold, and precious *s* ... Rev 18:16 *3037*
with all manner of precious *s* ... Rev 21:19 *3037*

STONESQUARERS {1}

builders did hew them, and the *s* ... 1Kin 5:18 1382

STONEST {2}

s them which are sent unto thee, ... Mt 23:37 *3036*
s them that are sent unto thee ... Lk 13:34 *3036*

STONING {1}

for the people spake of *s* him ... 1Sa 30:6 5619

STONY {7}

judges are overthrown in *s* places ... Ps 141:6 5553
I will take the *s* heart out of ... Eze 11:19 68
I will take away the *s* heart out ... Eze 36:26 68
Some fell upon *s* places, where ... Mt 13:5 *4075*
received the seed into *s* places ... Mt 13:20 *4075*
And some fell on *s* ground, where ... Mk 4:5 *4075*
which are sown on *s* ground ... Mk 4:16 *4075*

STOOD {339}

and, lo, three men *s* by him ... Gen 18:2 5324
he *s* by them under the tree, and ... Gen 18:8 5975
but Abraham *s* yet before the LORD ... Gen 18:22 5975
place where he *s* before the LORD ... Gen 19:27 5975
Abraham *s* up from before his dead ... Gen 23:3 6965
Abraham *s* up, and bowed himself ... Gen 23:7 6965
he *s* by the camels at the well ... Gen 24:30 5975
And, behold, the LORD *s* above it ... Gen 28:13 5324
my sheaf arose, and also *s* upright ... Gen 37:7 5324
your sheaves *s* round about ... Gen 37:7
and, behold, he *s* by the river ... Gen 41:1 5975
s by the other kine upon the ... Gen 41:3 5975

I *s* upon the bank of the river Gen 41:17 5975
he *s* before Pharaoh king of Egypt Gen 41:46 5975
down to Egypt, and *s* before Joseph Gen 43:15 5975
before all them that *s* by him Gen 45:1 5324
there *s* no man with him, while Gen 45:1 5975
And his sister *s* afar off, to wit Ex 2:4 3320
but Moses *s* up and helped them, and Ex 2:17 6965
who *s* in the way, as they came Ex 5:20 5324
the furnace, and *s* before Pharaoh Ex 9:10 5975
their face, and *s* behind them Ex 14:19 5975
the floods *s* upright as an heap, Ex 15:8 5324
the people *s* by Moses from the Ex 18:13 5975
they *s* at the nether part of the Ex 19:17 3320
it, they removed, and *s* afar off Ex 20:18 5975
And the people *s* afar off, and Ex 20:21 5975
Then Moses *s* in the gate of the Ex 32:26 5975
s every man at his tent door, and Ex 33:8 5324
s at the door of the tabernacle, Ex 33:9 5975
s with him there, and proclaimed Ex 34:5 3320
drew near and *s* before the LORD Lev 9:5 5975
the people *s* up all that day, and Num 11:32 6965
s in the door of the tabernacle, Num 12:5 5975
s in the door of the tabernacle Num 16:18 5975
s in the door of their tents, and Num 16:27 5324
he *s* between the dead and the Num 16:48 5975
the angel of the LORD *s* in the Num 22:22 3320
But the angel of the LORD *s* in a Num 22:24 5975
s in a narrow place, where was no Num 22:26 5975
he *s* by his burnt sacrifice, he, Num 23:6 5324
he *s* by his burnt offering, and Num 23:17 5324
they *s* before Moses, and before Num 27:2 5975
came near and *s* under the mountain Deut 4:11 5975
(I *s* between the LORD and you at Deut 5:5 5975
the pillar of the cloud *s* over Deut 31:15 5975
which came down from above *s* Josh 3:16 5975
s firm on dry ground in the midst Josh 3:17 5975
where the priests' feet *s* firm Josh 4:3 4673
bare the ark of the covenant *s* Josh 4:9 4673
the ark *s* in the midst of Jordan Josh 4:10 5975
there *s* a man over against him Josh 5:13 5975
s on this side the ark and on that Josh 8:33 5975
And the sun *s* still, and the moon Josh 10:13 1826
So the sun *s* still in the midst Josh 10:13 5975
that *s* still in their strength Josh 11:13 5975
of blood, until he *s* before the Josh 20:9 5975
there *s* not a man of all their Josh 21:44 5975
all that *s* by him went out from Judg 3:19 5975
said unto all that *s* against him Judg 6:31 5975
they *s* every man in his place Judg 7:21 5975
s in the top of mount Gerizim, and Judg 9:7 5975
s in the entering of the gate of Judg 9:35 5975
s in the entering of the gate of Judg 9:44 5975
pillars upon which the house *s* Judg 16:29 3559
s by the entering of the gate Judg 18:16 5324
the priest *s* in the entering of Judg 18:17 5324
s before it in those days,) Judg 20:28 5975
am the woman that *s* by thee here 1Sa 1:26 5324
And the LORD came, and *s*, and called 1Sa 3:10 3320
women that *s* by her said unto her 1Sa 4:20 5324
s there, where there was a great 1Sa 6:14 5975
when he *s* among the people, he 1Sa 10:23 3320
came to Saul, and *s* before him 1Sa 16:21 5975
the Philistines *s* on a mountain 1Sa 17:3 5975
Israel *s* on a mountain on the 1Sa 17:3 5975
And he *s* and cried unto the armies 1Sa 17:8 5975
spake to the men that *s* by him 1Sa 17:26 5975
s upon the Philistine, and took 1Sa 17:51 5975
his servants that *s* about him 1Sa 22:7 5324
unto the footmen that *s* about him 1Sa 22:17 5324
s on the top of an hill afar off 1Sa 26:13 5975
So I *s* upon him, and slew him, 2Sa 1:10 5975
Asahel fell down and died *s* still 2Sa 2:23 5975
troop, and *s* on the top of an hill 2Sa 2:25 5975
and all the people *s* still 2Sa 2:28 5975
all his servants *s* by with their 2Sa 13:31 5324
s beside the way of the gate 2Sa 15:2 5975
the king *s* by the gate side, and 2Sa 18:4 5975
And he turned aside, and *s* still 2Sa 18:30 5975
And one of Joab's men *s* by him 2Sa 20:11 5975
saw that all the people *s* still 2Sa 20:12 5975
one that came by him *s* still 2Sa 20:12 5975
the city, and it *s* in the trench 2Sa 20:15 5975
But he *s* in the midst of the 2Sa 23:12 3320
presence, and *s* before the king 1Kin 1:28 5975
s before the ark of the covenant 1Kin 3:15 5975
unto the king, and *s* before him 1Kin 3:16 5975
It *s* upon twelve oxen, three 1Kin 7:25 5975
all the congregation of Israel *s* 1Kin 8:14 5975
Solomon *s* before the altar of the 1Kin 8:22 5975
And he *s*, and blessed all the 1Kin 8:55 5975
two lions *s* beside the stays 1Kin 10:19 5975
twelve lions *s* there on the one 1Kin 10:20 5975
that *s* before Solomon his father 1Kin 12:6 5975
with him, and which *s* before him 1Kin 12:8 5975
Jeroboam *s* by the altar to burn 1Kin 13:1 5975
in the way, and the ass *s* by it 1Kin 13:24 5975
the lion also *s* by the carcase 1Kin 13:24 5975
s in the entering in of the cave 1Kin 19:13 5975
s before the LORD, and said, I 1Kin 22:21 5975
went, and *s* to view afar off 2Kin 2:7 5975
and they two *s* by Jordan 2Kin 2:7 5975
back, and *s* by the bank of Jordan 2Kin 2:13 5975
and upward, and *s* in the border 2Kin 3:21 5975
had called her, she *s* before him 2Kin 4:12 5975
had called her, she *s* in the door 2Kin 4:15 5975
s at the door of the house of 2Kin 5:9 5975
company, and came, and *s* before him 2Kin 5:15 5975
went in, and *s* before his master 2Kin 5:25 5975

s before him, and said, Thy son 2Kin 8:9 5975
there *s* a watchman on the tower 2Kin 9:17 5975
two kings *s* not before him 2Kin 10:4 5975
morning, that he went out, and *s* 2Kin 10:9 5975
And the guard *s*, every man with 2Kin 11:11 5975
the king *s* by a pillar, as the 2Kin 11:14 5975
he revived, and *s* up on his feet 2Kin 13:21 6965
s by the conduit of the upper 2Kin 18:17 5975
Then Rab-shakeh *s* and cried with a 2Kin 18:28 5975
the king *s* by a pillar, and made a 2Kin 23:3 5975
all the people *s* to the covenant 2Kin 23:3 5975
who *s* on his right hand, even 1Chr 6:39 5975
sons of Merari *s* on the left hand 1Chr 6:44
Satan *s* up against Israel, and 1Chr 21:1 5975
the angel of the LORD *s* by the 1Chr 21:15 5975
David the king *s* up upon his feet 1Chr 28:2 6965
they *s* on their feet, and their 2Chr 3:13 5975
It *s* upon twelve oxen, three 2Chr 4:4 5975
s at the east end of the altar, 2Chr 5:12 5975
all the congregation of Israel *s* 2Chr 6:3 5975
he *s* before the altar of the LORD 2Chr 6:12 5975
and upon it he *s*, and kneeled down 2Chr 6:13 5975
before them, and all Israel *s* 2Chr 7:6 5975
twelve lions *s* there on the one 2Chr 9:19 5975
with the old men that had *s* 2Chr 10:6 5975
up with him, that *s* before him 2Chr 10:8 5975
Abijah *s* up upon mount Zemaraim, 2Chr 13:4 6965
s before the LORD, and said, I 2Chr 18:20 5975
Jehoshaphat *s* in the congregation 2Chr 20:5 5975
all Judah *s* before the LORD, with 2Chr 20:13 5975
s up to praise the LORD God of 2Chr 20:19 6965
as they went forth, Jehoshaphat *s* 2Chr 20:20 5975
Moab *s* up against the inhabitants 2Chr 20:23 5975
the king *s* at his pillar at the 2Chr 23:13 5975
which *s* above the people, and said 2Chr 24:20 5975
s up against them that came from 2Chr 28:12 6965
And the Levites *s* with the 2Chr 29:26 5975
they *s* in their place after their 2Chr 30:16 5975
the king *s* in his place, and made 2Chr 34:31 5975
the priests *s* in their place, and 2Chr 35:10 5975
till there *s* up a priest with Ezr 2:63 5975
Then *s* up Jeshua the son of Ezr 3:2 6965
Then *s* Jeshua with his sons and Ezr 3:9 5975
And Ezra the priest *s* up, and said Ezr 10:10 6965
till there *s* up a priest with Neh 7:65 5975
Ezra the scribe *s* upon a pulpit Neh 8:4 5975
and beside him *s* Mattithiah Neh 8:4
he opened it, all the people *s* up Neh 8:5 5975
the people *s* in their place Neh 8:7
from all strangers, and *s* and Neh 9:2 5975
they *s* up in their place, and read Neh 9:3 6965
Then *s* up upon the stairs, of the Neh 9:4 6965
they *s* still in the prison gate Neh 12:39 5975
So *s* the two companies of them Neh 12:40 5975
s in the inner court of the Est 5:1 5975
the king's gate, that he *s* not up Est 5:9 6965
Haman *s* up to make request for Est 7:7 5975
arose, and *s* before the king, Est 8:4 5975
s for their lives, and had rest Est 9:16 5975
the hair of my flesh *s* up Job 4:15 5568
It *s* still, but I could not Job 4:16 5975
and the aged arose, and *s* up Job 29:8 5975
I *s* up, and I cried in the Job 30:28 6965
but *s* still, and answered no more Job 32:16 5975
he commanded, and it *s* fast Ps 33:9 5975
the waters *s* above the mountains Ps 104:6 5975
chosen *s* before him in the breach Ps 106:23 5975
Then *s* up Phinehas, and executed Ps 106:30 5975
Above it *s* the seraphims Is 6:2 5975
he *s* by the conduit of the upper Is 36:2 5975
Then Rabshakeh *s*, and cried with a Is 36:13 5975
Samuel *s* before me, yet my mind Jer 15:1 5975
Remember that I *s* before thee to Jer 18:20 5975
he *s* in the court of the LORD's Jer 19:14 5975
For who hath *s* in the counsel of Jer 23:18 5975
But if they had *s* in my counsel Jer 23:22 5975
that *s* in the house of the LORD Jer 28:5 5975
princes which *s* beside the king Jer 36:21 5975
gods, and all the women that *s* by Jer 44:15 5975
they *s* not, because the LORD did Jer 46:15 5975
They that fled *s* under the shadow Jer 48:45 5975
he *s* with his right hand as an Lam 2:4 5324
and when those *s*, these *s* Eze 1:21 5975
when they *s*, they let down their Eze 1:24 5975
was over their heads, when they *s* Eze 1:25 5975
the glory of the LORD *s* there Eze 3:23 5975
there *s* before them seventy men Eze 8:11 5975
in the midst of them *s* Jaazaniah Eze 8:11 5975
s beside the brasen altar Eze 9:2 5975
Now the cherubims *s* on the right Eze 10:3 5975
s over the threshold of the house Eze 10:4
went in, and *s* beside the wheels Eze 10:6 5975
When they *s*, these *s* Eze 10:17 5975
house, and *s* over the cherubims Eze 10:18 5975
every one *s* at the door of the Eze 10:19 5975
s upon the mountain which is on Eze 11:23 5975
For the king of Babylon *s* at the Eze 21:21 5975
and *s* up upon their feet, an Eze 37:10 5975
and he *s* in the gate Eze 40:3 5975
and the man *s* by me Eze 43:6 5975
of the house *s* toward the east Eze 47:1
therefore *s* they before the king Dan 1:19 5975
So they came and *s* before the king Dan 2:2 5975
was excellent, *s* before thee Dan 2:31 6966
they *s* before the image that Dan 3:3 6966
times ten thousand *s* before him Dan 7:10 6966
near unto one of them that *s* by Dan 7:16 6966
there *s* before the river a ram Dan 8:3 5975

behold, there *s* before me as the Dan 8:15 5975
So he came near where I *s* Dan 8:17 5977
broken, whereas four *s* up for it Dan 8:22 5975
this word unto me, I *s* trembling Dan 10:11 5975
and said unto him that *s* before me Dan 10:16 5975
s to confirm and to strengthen him Dan 11:1 5975
there *s* other two, the one on Dan 12:5 5975
there they *s* Hos 10:9 5975
the Lord *s* upon a wall made by a Amos 7:7 5324
thou have *s* in the crossway Obad 14 5975
He *s*, and measured the earth Hab 3:6 5975
moon *s* still in their habitation Hab 3:11 5975
he *s* among the myrtle trees that Zec 1:8 5975
the man that *s* among the myrtle Zec 1:10 5975
that *s* among the myrtle trees Zec 1:11 5975
garments, and *s* before the angel Zec 3:3 5975
unto those that *s* before him Zec 3:4 5975
And the angel of the LORD *s* by Zec 3:5 5975
s over where the young child was Mt 2:9 *2476*
mother and his brethren *s* without Mt 12:46 *2476*
whole multitude *s* on the shore Mt 13:2 *2476*
And Jesus *s* still, and called them, Mt 20:32 *2476*
came unto him they that *s* by Mt 26:73 *2476*
Jesus *s* before the governor Mt 27:11 *2476*
Some of them that *s* there Mt 27:47 *2476*
And Jesus *s* still, and commanded Mk 10:49 *2476*
them that *s* there said unto them Mk 11:5 *2476*
of them that *s* by drew a sword Mk 14:47 *3936*
the high priest *s* up in the midst Mk 14:60 *450*
and began to say to them that *s* by Mk 14:69 *3936*
they that *s* by said again to Mk 14:70 *3936*
And some of them that *s* by Mk 15:35 *3936*
which *s* over against him, saw Mk 15:39 *3936*
sabbath day, and *s* up for to read Lk 4:16 *450*
he *s* over her, and rebuked the Lk 4:39 *2186*
he *s* by the lake of Gennesaret, Lk 5:1 *2476*
And he arose and *s* forth Lk 6:8 *2476*
s in the plain, and the company of Lk 6:17 *2476*
and they that bare him *s* still Lk 7:14 *2476*
s at his feet behind him weeping, Lk 7:38 *2476*
and the two men that *s* with him Lk 9:32 *4921*
And, behold, a certain lawyer *s* up Lk 10:25 *450*
were lepers, which *s* afar off Lk 17:12 *2476*
The Pharisee *s* and prayed thus Lk 18:11 *2476*
And Jesus *s*, and commanded him to Lk 18:40 *2476*
And Zacchaeus *s*, and said unto the Lk 19:8 *2476*
And he said unto them that *s* by Lk 19:24 *3936*
And the chief priests and scribes *s* Lk 23:10 *2476*
And the people *s* beholding Lk 23:35 *2476*
s afar off, beholding these Lk 23:49 *2476*
two men *s* by them in shining Lk 24:4 *2186*
Jesus himself *s* in the midst of Lk 24:36 *2476*
Again the next day after John *s* Jn 1:35 *2476*
when the people which *s* on the Jn 6:22 *2476*
great day of the feast, Jesus *s* Jn 7:37 *2476*
as they *s* in the temple, What Jn 11:56 *2476*
The people therefore, that *s* by Jn 12:29 *2476*
which betrayed him, *s* with them Jn 18:5 *2476*
But Peter *s* at the door without Jn 18:16 *2476*
the servants and officers *s* there Jn 18:18 *2476*
Peter *s* with them, and warmed Jn 18:18 *2476*
one of the officers which *s* by Jn 18:22 *3936*
And Simon Peter *s* and warmed Jn 18:25 *2476*
Now there *s* by the cross of Jesus Jn 19:25 *2476*
But Mary *s* without at the Jn 20:11 *2476*
s in the midst, and saith unto Jn 20:19 *2476*
s in the midst, and said, Peace be Jn 20:26 *2476*
now come, Jesus *s* on the shore Jn 21:4 *2476*
two men *s* by them in white Acts 1:10 *3936*
in those days Peter *s* up in the Acts 1:15 *450*
And he leaping up *s*, and walked, and Acts 3:8 *2476*
The kings of the earth *s* up Acts 4:26 *3936*
Then *s* there up one in the Acts 5:34 *450*
journeyed with him *s* speechless Acts 9:7 *2476*
all the widows *s* by him weeping Acts 9:39 *3936*
house, and *s* before the gate, Acts 10:17 *2186*
a man *s* before me in bright Acts 10:30 *2476*
an angel in his house, which *s* Acts 11:13 *2476*
there *s* up one of them named Acts 11:28 *450*
told how Peter *s* before the gate Acts 12:14 *2476*
Then Paul *s* up, and beckoning with Acts 13:16 *450*
the disciples *s* round about him Acts 14:20 *2944*
There *s* a man of Macedonia, and Acts 16:9 *2476*
Then Paul *s* in the midst of Mars' Acts 17:22 *2476*
Paul *s* on the stairs, and beckoned Acts 21:40 *2476*
Came unto me, and *s*, and said unto Acts 22:13 *2186*
said unto the centurion that *s* by Acts 22:25 *2476*
that *s* by him to smite him on the Acts 23:2 *3936*
And they that *s* by said, Revilest Acts 23:4 *3936*
night following the Lord *s* by him Acts 23:11 *2186*
while I *s* before the council, Acts 24:20 *2476*
down from Jerusalem *s* round about Acts 25:7 *4026*
whom when the accusers *s* up Acts 25:18 *2476*
Paul *s* forth in the midst of them Acts 27:21 *2476*
For there *s* by me this night the Acts 27:23 *3936*
my first answer no man *s* with me 2Ti 4:16 *4836*
the Lord *s* with me, and 2Ti 4:17 *3936*
Which *s* only in meats and drinks, Heb 9:10
s a Lamb as it had been slain, Rev 5:6 *2476*
s before the throne, and before Rev 7:9 *2476*
all the angels *s* round about the Rev 7:11 *2476*
seven angels which *s* before God Rev 8:2 *2476*
s at the altar, having a golden Rev 8:3 *2476*
and the angel *s*, saying, Rise, and Rev 11:1 *2476*
them, and they *s* upon their feet Rev 11:11 *2476*
the dragon *s* before the woman Rev 12:4 *2476*
I *s* upon the sand of the sea, and Rev 13:1 *2476*

S

a Lamb *s* on the mount Sion, and ... Rev 14:1 *2476*
many as trade by sea, *s* afar off, ... Rev 18:17 *2476*

STOODEST {3}
that thou *s* in the way against me ... Num 22:34 5324
thou *s* before the LORD thy God in ... Deut 4:10 5975
day that thou *s* on the other side ... Obad 11 5975

STOOL {1}
there a bed, and a table, and a *s* ... 2Kin 4:10 3678

STOOLS {1}
women, and see them upon the *s* ... Ex 1:16 70

STOOP {4}
the proud helpers do *s* under him ... Job 9:13 7817
in the heart of man maketh it *s* ... Prov 12:25 7812
They *s*, they bow down together ... Is 46:2 7164
shoes I am not worthy to *s* down ... Mk 1:7 *2955*

STOOPED {7}
he *s* down, he couched as a lion, ... Gen 49:9 3766
David *s* with his face to the ... 1Sa 24:8 6915
he *s* with his face to the ground, ... 1Sa 28:14 6915
old man, or him that *s* for age ... 2Chr 36:17 3486
But Jesus *s* down, and with his ... Jn 8:6 *2955*
And again he *s* down, and wrote on ... Jn 8:8 *2955*
she *s* down, and looked into the ... Jn 20:11 *3879*

STOOPETH {1}
Bel boweth down, Nebo *s*, their ... Is 46:1 7164

STOOPING {2}
s down, he beheld the linen ... Lk 24:12 *3879*
he *s* down, and looking in, saw the ... Jn 20:5 *3879*

STOP {7}
down, that the rain *s* thee not ... 1Kin 18:44 6113
s all wells of water, and mar ... 2Kin 3:19 5640
his mighty men to *s* the waters of ... 2Chr 32:3 5640
s the way against them that ... Ps 35:3 5462
and all iniquity shall *s* her mouth ... Ps 107:42 7092
it shall *s* the noses of the ... Eze 39:11 2629
no man shall *s* me of this ... 2Cor 11:10 *5420*

STOPPED {15}
and the windows of heaven were *s* ... Gen 8:2 5534
the Philistines had *s* them ... Gen 26:15 5640
for the Philistines had *s* them ... Gen 26:18 5640
or his flesh be *s* from his issue ... Lev 15:3 2856
they *s* all the wells of water, and ... 2Kin 3:25 5640
who *s* all the fountains, and the ... 2Chr 32:4 5640
This same Hezekiah also *s* the ... 2Chr 32:30 5640
that the breaches began to be *s* ... Neh 4:7 5640
them that speak lies shall be *s* ... Ps 63:11 5534
And that the passages are *s* ... Jer 51:32 8610
s their ears, that they should ... Zec 7:11 3513
s their ears, and ran upon him ... Acts 7:57 *4912*
that every mouth may be *s* ... Rom 3:19 *5420*
Whose mouths must be *s*, who ... Titus 1:11 *1998*
promises, *s* the mouths of lions, ... Heb 11:33 *5420*

STOPPETH {4}
hope, and iniquity *s* her mouth ... Job 5:16 7092
the deaf adder that *s* her ear ... Ps 58:4 331
Whoso *s* his ears at the cry of ... Prov 21:13 331
that *s* his ears from hearing of ... Is 33:15 331

STORE {25}
of herds, and great *s* of servants ... Gen 26:14
that food shall be for *s* to the ... Gen 41:36 6487
come in ye shall eat of the old *s* ... Lev 25:22
And ye shall eat old *s*, and bring ... Lev 26:10 3462
shall be thy basket and thy *s* ... Deut 28:5 4863
shall be thy basket and thy *s* ... Deut 28:17 4863
Is not this laid up in *s* with me ... Deut 32:34
the cities of *s* that Solomon had ... 1Kin 9:19 4543
gold, and of spices very great *s* ... 1Kin 10:10
have laid up in *s* unto this day ... 2Kin 20:17 686
all this *s* that we have prepared ... 1Chr 29:16 1995
wilderness, and all the *s* cities ... 2Chr 8:4 4543
all the *s* cities that Solomon had ... 2Chr 8:6 4543
s of victual, and of oil and wine ... 2Chr 11:11 214
all the *s* cities of Naphtali ... 2Chr 16:4 4543
in Judah castles, and cities of *s* ... 2Chr 17:12 4543
which is left is this great *s* ... 2Chr 31:10 1995
once in ten days *s* of all sorts ... Neh 5:18 7235
full, affording all manner of *s* ... Ps 144:13
have laid up in *s* until this day ... Is 39:6 686
who *s* up violence and robbery in ... Amos 3:10 686
for there is none end of the *s* ... Nah 2:9 8498
every one of you lay by him in *s* ... 1Cor 16:2 *2343*
Laying up in *s* for themselves a ... 1Ti 6:19 *597*
by the same word are kept in *s* ... 2Pet 3:7 *2343*

STOREHOUSE {2}
ye all the tithes into the *s* ... Mal 3:10 214
which neither have *s* nor barn ... Lk 12:24 *5009*

STOREHOUSES {6}
And Joseph opened all the *s* ... Gen 41:56 834
the blessing upon thee in thy *s* ... Deut 28:8 618
over the *s* in the fields, in the ... 1Chr 27:25 214
S also for the increase of corn, ... 2Chr 32:28 4543
he layeth up the depth in *s* ... Ps 33:7 214
the utmost border, open her *s* ... Jer 50:26 3965

STORIES {5}
third *s* shalt thou make it ... Gen 6:16
round about on their three *s* ... Eze 41:16
against gallery in three *s* ... Eze 42:3
For they were in three *s*, but had ... Eze 42:6
that buildeth his *s* in the heaven ... Amos 9:6 4609

STORK {5}
And the *s*, the heron after her ... Lev 11:19 2624
And the *s*, and the heron after her ... Deut 14:18 2624
as for the *s*, the fir trees are ... Ps 104:17 2624
the *s* in the heaven knoweth her ... Jer 8:7 2624
had wings like the wings of a *s* ... Zec 5:9 2624

STORM {14}
as chaff that the *s* carrieth away ... Job 21:18 5492
as a *s* hurleth him out of his ... Job 27:21
hasten my escape from the windy *s* ... Ps 55:8 5584
and make them afraid with thy *s* ... Ps 83:15 5492
He maketh the *s* a calm, so that ... Ps 107:29 5591
of refuge, and for a covert from *s* ... Is 4:6 2230
his distress, a refuge from the *s* ... Is 25:4 2230
ones is as a *s* against the wall ... Is 25:4 2230
tempest of hail and a destroying *s* ... Is 28:2 8178
and great noise, with *s* and ... Is 29:6 5492
shalt ascend and come like a *s* ... Eze 38:9 7722
way in the whirlwind and in the *s* ... Nah 1:3 8183
And there arose a great *s* of wind ... Mk 4:37 *2978*
there came down a *s* of wind on ... Lk 8:23 *2978*

STORMY {4}
commandeth, and raiseth the *s* wind ... Ps 107:25 5591
s wind fulfilling his word ... Ps 148:8 5591
and a *s* wind shall rend it ... Eze 13:11 5591
rend it with a *s* wind in my fury ... Eze 13:13 5591

STORY {2}
are written in the *s* of the ... 2Chr 13:22 4097
they are written in the *s* of the ... 2Chr 24:27 4097

STOUT {4}
the *s* lion's whelps are scattered ... Job 4:11
s heart of the king of Assyria ... Is 10:12 1433
look was more *s* than his fellows ... Dan 7:20 7229
Your words have been *s* against me ... Mal 3:13 2388

STOUTHEARTED {2}
The *s* are spoiled, they have ... Ps 76:5 47,3820
Hearken unto me, ye *s*, that are ... Is 46:12 47,3820

STOUTNESS {1}
say in the pride and *s* of heart, ... Is 9:9 1433

STRAIGHT {28}
ascend up every man *s* before him ... Josh 6:5
every man *s* before him, and they ... Josh 6:20
the kine took the *s* way to the ... 1Sa 6:12 3474
brought it *s* down to the west ... 2Chr 32:30 3474
make thy way *s* before my face ... Ps 5:8 3474
thine eyelids look *s* before thee ... Prov 4:25 3474
which is crooked cannot be made *s* ... Eccl 1:15 8626
for who can make that *s*, which he ... Eccl 7:13 8626
make *s* in the desert a highway ... Is 40:3 3474
and the crooked shall be made *s* ... Is 40:4 4334
before them, and crooked things *s* ... Is 42:16 4334
and make the crooked places *s* ... Is 45:2 3474
the rivers of waters in a *s* way ... Jer 31:9 3474
And their feet were *s* feet ... Eze 1:7 3474
they went every one *s* forward ... Eze 1:9 5676
And they went every one *s* forward ... Eze 1:12 5676
the firmament were their wings *s* ... Eze 1:23 3474
they went every one *s* forward ... Eze 10:22 5676
way of the Lord, make his paths *s* ... Mt 3:3 *2117*
way of the Lord, make his paths *s* ... Mk 1:3 *2117*
way of the Lord, make his paths *s* ... Lk 3:4 *2117*
and the crooked shall be made *s* ... Lk 3:5 *2117*
and immediately she was made *s* ... Lk 13:13 *461*
Make *s* the way of the Lord, as ... Jn 1:23 *2116*
into the street which is called *S* ... Acts 9:11 *2117*
we came with a *s* course to ... Acts 16:11 *2113*
we came with a *s* course unto Coos ... Acts 21:1 *2113*
make *s* paths for your feet, lest ... Heb 12:13 *3717*

STRAIGHTWAY {42}
the city, ye shall *s* find him ... 1Sa 9:13 3651
Then Saul fell *s* all along on the ... 1Sa 28:20 4116
He goeth after her *s*, as an ox ... Prov 7:22 6597
s there remained no strength in ... Dan 10:17 6258
went up *s* out of the water ... Mt 3:16 *2117*
they *s* left their nets, and ... Mt 4:20 *2112*
And *s* Jesus constrained his ... Mt 14:22 *2112*
But *s* Jesus spake unto them, ... Mt 14:27 *2112*
s ye shall find an ass tied, and a ... Mt 21:2 *2112*
and *s* he will send them ... Mt 21:3 *2112*
and *s* took his journey ... Mt 25:15 *2112*
s one of them ran, and took a ... Mt 27:48 *2112*
s coming up out of the water, he ... Mk 1:10 *2112*
s they forsook their nets, and ... Mk 1:18 *2112*
And *s* he called them ... Mk 1:20 *2112*
s on the sabbath day he entered ... Mk 1:21 *2112*
s many were gathered together, ... Mk 2:2 *2112*
s took counsel with the Herodians ... Mk 3:6 *2112*
s the fountain of her blood was ... Mk 5:29 *2112*
s the damsel arose, and walked ... Mk 5:42 *2112*
she came in *s* with haste unto the ... Mk 6:25 *2112*
s he constrained his disciples to ... Mk 6:45 *2112*
out of the ship, *s* they knew him, ... Mk 6:54 *2112*
s his ears were opened, and the ... Mk 7:35 *2112*
s he entered into a ship with his ... Mk 8:10 *2112*
s all the people, when they ... Mk 9:15 *2112*
he saw him, *s* the spirit tare him ... Mk 9:20 *2112*
s the father of the child cried ... Mk 9:24 *2112*
s he will send him hither ... Mk 11:3 *2112*
as he was come, he goeth *s* to him ... Mk 14:45 *2112*
s in the morning the chief ... Mk 15:1 *2112*
drunk old wine *s* desireth new ... Lk 5:39 *2112*
spirit came again, and she arose *s* ... Lk 8:55 *3916*
s ye say, There cometh a shower ... Lk 12:54 *2112*
will not *s* pull him out on the ... Lk 14:5 *2112*
himself, and shall *s* glorify him ... Jn 13:32 *2117*
Then fell she down *s* at his feet ... Acts 5:10 *3916*
s he preached Christ in the ... Acts 9:20 *2112*
and was baptized, he and all his, *s* ... Acts 16:33 *3916*
Then *s* they departed from him ... Acts 22:29 *2112*
I sent *s* to thee, and gave ... Acts 23:30 *1824*
s forgetteth what manner of man ... Jas 1:24 *2112*

STRAIN {1}
which *s* at a gnat, and swallow a ... Mt 23:24 *1368*

STRAIT {10}
Israel saw that they were in a *s* ... 1Sa 13:6 6887
said unto Gad, I am in a great *s* ... 2Sa 24:14 6887
dwell with thee is too *s* for us ... 2Kin 6:1 6862
said unto Gad, I am in a great *s* ... 1Chr 21:13 6887
out of the *s* into a broad place ... Job 36:16 6862
ears, The place is too *s* for me ... Is 49:20 6862
Enter ye in at the *s* gate ... Mt 7:13 *4728*
Because *s* is the gate, and narrow ... Mt 7:14 *4728*
Strive to enter in at the *s* gate ... Lk 13:24 *4728*
For I am in a *s* betwixt two ... Phil 1:23 *4912*

STRAITEN {1}
seek their lives, shall *s* them ... Jer 19:9 6693

STRAITENED {8}
steps of his strength shall be *s* ... Job 18:7 3334
and the breadth of the waters is *s* ... Job 37:10 4164
goest, thy steps shall not be *s* ... Prov 4:12 3334
was *s* more than the lowest ... Eze 42:6 680
is the spirit of the LORD *s* ... Mic 2:7 7114
and how am I *s* till it be ... Lk 12:50 *4912*
Ye are not *s* in us, but ye are ... 2Cor 6:12 *4729*
but ye are *s* in your own bowels ... 2Cor 6:12 *4729*

STRAITENETH {1}
the nations, and *s* them again ... Job 12:23 5148

STRAITEST {1}
that after the most *s* sect of our ... Acts 26:5 *196*

STRAITLY {11}
The man asked us *s* of our state ... Gen 43:7
for he had *s* sworn the children ... Ex 13:19
Now Jericho was *s* shut up because ... Josh 6:1
Thy father *s* charged the people ... 1Sa 14:28
Jesus *s* charged them, saying, See ... Mt 9:30
he *s* charged him, and forthwith ... Mk 1:43
he *s* charged them that they ... Mk 3:12 *4183*
he charged them *s* that no man ... Mk 5:43 *4183*
he *s* charged them, and commanded ... Lk 9:21
let us *s* threaten them, that they ... Acts 4:17 *547*
Did not we *s* command you that ye ... Acts 5:28

STRAITNESS {5}
thee, in the siege, and in the *s* ... Deut 28:53 4689
him in the siege, and in the *s* ... Deut 28:55 4689
things secretly in the siege and *s* ... Deut 28:57 4689
broad place, where there is no *s* ... Job 36:16 4164
of his friend in the siege and *s* ... Jer 19:9 4689

STRAITS {2}
his sufficiency he shall be in *s* ... Job 20:22 3334
overtook her between the *s* ... Lam 1:3 4712

STRAKE {1}
s sail, and so were driven ... Acts 27:17 *5465*

STRAKES {2}
and pilled white *s* in them ... Gen 30:37 6479
walls of the house with hollow *s* ... Lev 14:37 8258

STRANGE {76}
Put away the *s* gods that are ... Gen 35:2 5236
they gave unto Jacob all the *s* ... Gen 35:4 5236
but made himself *s* unto them ... Gen 42:7 5234
have been a stranger in a *s* land ... Ex 2:22 5237
I have been an alien in a *s* land ... Ex 18:3 5237
to sell her unto a *s* nation he ... Ex 21:8 5237
shall offer no *s* incense thereon ... Ex 30:9 2114
offered *s* fire before the LORD, ... Lev 10:1 2114
when they offered *s* fire before ... Num 3:4 2114
when they offered *s* fire before ... Num 26:61 2114
and there was no *s* god with him ... Deut 32:12 5236
him to jealousy with *s* gods ... Deut 32:16 2114
forsake the LORD, and serve *s* gods ... Josh 24:20 5236
the *s* gods which are among you, ... Josh 24:23 5236
they put away the *s* gods from ... Judg 10:16 5236
for thou art the son of a *s* woman ... Judg 11:2 312
hearts, then put away the *s* gods ... 1Sa 7:3 5236
king Solomon loved many *s* women ... 1Kin 11:1 5237
did he for all his *s* wives ... 1Kin 11:8 5237
drunk *s* waters, and with the sole ... 2Kin 19:24 2114
away the altars of the *s* gods ... 2Chr 14:3 5236
And he took away the *s* gods ... 2Chr 33:15 5236
have taken *s* wives of the people ... Ezr 10:2 5237
and have taken *s* wives, to ... Ezr 10:10 5237
of the land, and from the *s* wives ... Ezr 10:11 5237
s wives in our cities come at ... Ezr 10:14 5237
s wives by the first day of the ... Ezr 10:17 5237
were found that had taken *s* wives ... Ezr 10:18 5237
All these had taken *s* wives ... Ezr 10:44 5237
our God in marrying *s* wives ... Neh 13:27 5237
that ye make yourselves *s* to me ... Job 19:3 1970
My breath is *s* to my wife ... Job 19:17 2114
a *s* punishment to the workers of ... Job 31:3 5235
out our hands to a *s* god ... Ps 44:20 2114
There shall no *s* god be in thee ... Ps 81:9 2114
shalt thou worship any *s* god ... Ps 81:9 5236
Jacob from a people of *s* language ... Ps 114:1 3937
sing the LORD's song in a *s* land ... Ps 137:4 5236
from the hand of *s* children ... Ps 144:7 5236
me from the hand of *s* children ... Ps 144:11 2114
To deliver thee from the *s* woman ... Prov 2:16 2114
For the lips of a *s* woman drop as ... Prov 5:3 2114
son, be ravished with a *s* woman ... Prov 5:20 2114
of the tongue of a *s* woman ... Prov 6:24 5237
may keep thee from the *s* woman ... Prov 7:5 2114
a pledge of him for a *s* woman ... Prov 20:16 5237
The way of man is froward and *s* ... Prov 21:8 2114

The mouth of *s* women is a deep ... Prov 22:14 2114
a *s* woman is a narrow pit ... Prov 23:27 5237
Thine eyes shall behold *s* women ... Prov 23:33 2114
a pledge of him for a *s* woman ... Prov 27:13 5237
and shalt set it with *s* slips ... Is 17:10 2114
he may do his work, his *s* work ... Is 28:21 2114
bring to pass his act, his *s* act ... Is 28:21 5237
when there was no *s* god among you ... Is 43:12 2114
plant of a *s* vine unto me ... Jer 2:21 5237
served *s* gods in your land, so ... Jer 5:19 5236
graven images, and with *s* vanities ... Jer 8:19 5236
sent to a people of a *s* speech ... Eze 3:5 6012
Not to many people of a *s* speech ... Eze 3:6 6012
most strong holds with a *s* god ... Dan 11:39 5236
for they have begotten *s* children ... Hos 5:7 2114
they were counted as a *s* thing ... Hos 8:12 2114
as are clothed with *s* apparel ... Zeph 1:8 5237
married the daughter of a *s* god ... Mal 2:11 5236
We have seen *s* things to day ... Lk 5:26 *3861*
seed should sojourn in a *s* land ... Acts 7:6 *245*
to be a setter forth of *s* gods ... Acts 17:18 *3581*
certain *s* things to our ears ... Acts 17:20 *3579*
them even unto *s* cities ... Acts 26:11 *1854*
of promise, as in a *s* country ... Heb 11:9 *245*
about with divers and *s* doctrines ... Heb 13:9 *3581*
Wherein they think it *s* that ye ... 1Pet 4:4 *3579*
think it not *s* concerning the ... 1Pet 4:12 *3579*
as though some *s* thing happened ... 1Pet 4:12 *3581*
and going after *s* flesh, are set ... Jude 7 *2087*

STRANGELY {1}
should behave themselves *s* ... Deut 32:27 5234

STRANGER {129}
a *s* in a land that is not theirs ... Gen 15:13 1616
the land wherein thou art a *s* ... Gen 17:8 4033
or bought with money of any *s* ... Gen 17:12 1121,5235
and bought with money of the *s* ... Gen 17:27 1121,5235
I am a *s* and a sojourner with you ... Gen 23:4 1616
the land wherein thou art a *s* ... Gen 28:4 4033
land wherein his father was a *s* ... Gen 37:1 4033
I have been a *s* in a strange land ... Ex 2:22 1616
of Israel, whether he be a *s* ... Ex 12:19 1616
There shall no *s* eat thereof ... Ex 12:43 1121,5235
when a *s* shall sojourn with thee, ... Ex 12:48 1616
unto the *s* that sojourneth among ... Ex 12:49 1616
nor thy *s* that is within thy ... Ex 20:10 1616
Thou shalt neither vex a *s* ... Ex 22:21 1616
Also thou shalt not oppress a *s* ... Ex 23:9 1616
for ye know the heart of a *s* ... Ex 23:9 1616
the son of thy handmaid, and the *s* ... Ex 23:12 1616
but a *s* shall not eat thereof, ... Ex 29:33 2114
putteth any of it upon a *s* ... Ex 30:33 2114
or a *s* that sojourneth among you ... Lev 16:29 1616
blood, neither shall any *s* that ... Lev 17:12 1616
one of your own country, or a *s* ... Lev 17:15 1616
nor any *s* that sojourneth among ... Lev 18:26 1616
leave them for the poor and *s* ... Lev 19:10 1616
if a *s* sojourn with thee in your ... Lev 19:33 1616
But the *s* that dwelleth with you ... Lev 19:34 1616
There shall no *s* eat of the holy ... Lev 22:10 2114
daughter also be married unto a *s* .. Lev 22:12 376,2114
but there shall no *s* eat thereof ... Lev 22:13 2114
them unto the poor, and to the *s* ... Lev 23:22 1616
as well the *s*, as he that is born ... Lev 24:16 1616
manner of law, as well for the *s* ... Lev 24:22 1616
for thy *s* that sojourneth with ... Lev 25:6 8453
yea, though he be a *s*, or a ... Lev 25:35 1616
a sojourner or *s* wax rich by thee ... Lev 25:47 8453
unto the *s* or sojourner by thee ... Lev 25:47 1616
the *s* that cometh nigh shall be ... Num 1:51 2114
the *s* that cometh nigh shall be ... Num 3:10 2114
the *s* that cometh nigh shall be ... Num 3:38 2114
if a *s* shall sojourn among you, ... Num 9:14 1616
one ordinance, both for the *s* ... Num 9:14 1616
if a *s* sojourn with you, or ... Num 15:14 1616
also for the *s* that sojourneth ... Num 15:15 1616
so shall the *s* be before the LORD ... Num 15:15 1616
for the *s* that sojourneth with ... Num 15:16 1616
the *s* that sojourneth among them ... Num 15:26 1616
for the *s* that sojourneth among ... Num 15:29 1616
he be born in the land, or a *s* ... Num 15:30 1616
the children of Israel, that no *s* ... Num 16:40 376,2114
a *s* shall not come nigh unto you ... Num 18:4 2114
the *s* that cometh nigh shall be ... Num 18:7 2114
unto the *s* that sojourneth among ... Num 19:10 1616
children of Israel, and for the *s* ... Num 35:15 1616
and the *s* that is with him ... Deut 1:16 1616
nor thy *s* that is within thy ... Deut 5:14 1616
and widow, and loveth the *s* ... Deut 10:18 1616
Love ye therefore the *s* ... Deut 10:19 1616
unto the *s* that is in thy gates ... Deut 14:21 1616
inheritance with thee,) and the *s* ... Deut 14:29 1616
is within thy gates, and the *s* ... Deut 16:11 1616
maidservant, and the Levite, the *s* ... Deut 16:14 1616
thou mayest not set a *s* over thee .... Deut 17:15 376,5237
because thou wast a *s* in his land ... Deut 23:7 1616
Unto a *s* thou mayest lend upon ... Deut 23:20 5237
not pervert the judgment of the *s* ... Deut 24:17 1616
it shall be for the *s*, for the ... Deut 24:19 1616
it shall be for the *s*, for the ... Deut 24:20 1616
it shall be for the *s*, for the ... Deut 24:21 1616
shall not marry without unto a *s* ... Deut 25:5 376,2114
and the *s* that is among you ... Deut 26:11 1616
given it unto the Levite, the *s* ... Deut 26:12 1616
unto the Levite, and unto the *s* ... Deut 26:13 1616
perverteth the judgment of the *s* ... Deut 27:19 1616
The *s* that is within thee shall ... Deut 28:43 1616
thy *s* that is in thy camp, from ... Deut 29:11 1616
the *s* that shall come from a far ... Deut 29:22 5237
thy *s* that is within thy gates, ... Deut 31:12 1616
of the LORD, as well the *s* ... Josh 8:33 1616
for the *s* that sojourneth among ... Josh 20:9 1616
aside hither into the city of a *s* ... Judg 19:12 5237
knowledge of me, seeing I am a *s* ... Ruth 2:10 5237
he answered, I am the son of a *s* 2Sa 1:13 376,1616
for thou art a *s*, and also an ... 2Sa 15:19 5237
there was no *s* with us in the ... 1Kin 3:18 2114
Moreover concerning a *s*, that is ... 1Kin 8:41 5237
that the *s* calleth to thee for ... 1Kin 8:43 5237
Moreover concerning the *s* ... 2Chr 6:32 5237
that the *s* calleth to thee for ... 2Chr 6:33 5237
given, and no *s* passed among them ... Job 15:19 2114
and my maids, count me for a *s* ... Job 19:15 2114
The *s* did not lodge in the street ... Job 31:32 1616
for I am a *s* with thee, and a ... Ps 39:12 1616
I am become a *s* unto my brethren, ... Ps 69:8 2114
They slay the widow and the *s* ... Ps 94:6 1616
I am a *s* in the earth ... Ps 119:19 1616
even from the *s* which flattereth ... Prov 2:16 5237
labours be in the house of a *s* ... Prov 5:10 5237
and embrace the bosom of a *s* ... Prov 5:20 5237
hast stricken thy hand with a *s* ... Prov 6:1 2114
from the *s* which flattereth with ... Prov 7:5 5237
surety for a *s* shall smart for it ... Prov 11:15 2114
a *s* doth not intermeddle with his ... Prov 14:10 2114
garment that is surety for a *s* ... Prov 20:16 2114
a *s*, and not thine own lips ... Prov 27:2 5237
garment that is surety for a *s* ... Prov 27:13 2114
to eat thereof, but a *s* eateth it ... Eccl 6:2 376,5237
Neither let the son of the *s* ... Is 56:3 5236
Also the sons of the *s*, that join ... Is 56:6 5236
the sons of the *s* shall not drink ... Is 62:8 5236
If ye oppress not the *s*, the ... Jer 7:6 1616
thou be as a *s* in the land ... Jer 14:8 1616
no wrong, do no violence to the *s* ... Jer 22:3 1616
or of the *s* that sojourneth in ... Eze 14:7 1616
dealt by oppression with the *s* ... Eze 22:7 1616
have oppressed the *s* wrongfully ... Eze 22:29 1616
No *s*, uncircumcised in heart, nor ... Eze 44:9 1121,5236
of any *s* that is among the ... Eze 44:9 1121,5236
in what tribe the *s* sojourneth ... Eze 47:23 1616
in the day that he became a *s* ... Obad 12 5235
widow, nor the fatherless, the *s* ... Zec 7:10 1616
turn aside the *s* from his right ... Mal 3:5 1616
I was a *s*, and ye took me in ... Mt 25:35 *3581*
When saw we thee a *s*, and took ... Mt 25:38 *3581*
I was a *s*, and ye took me not in ... Mt 25:43 *3581*
an hungred, or athirst, or a *s* ... Mt 25:44 *3581*
to give glory to God, save this *s* ... Lk 17:18 *241*
Art thou only a *s* in Jerusalem ... Lk 24:18 *3939*
a *s* will they not follow, but ... Jn 10:5 *245*
was a *s* in the land of Madian, ... Acts 7:29 *3941*

STRANGER'S {2}
Neither from a *s* hand shall ye ... Lev 22:25 1121,5236
or to the stock of the *s* family ... Lev 25:47 1616

STRANGERS {79}
Are we not counted of him *s* ... Gen 31:15 5237
the land wherein they were *s* ... Gen 36:7 4033
pilgrimage, wherein they were *s* ... Ex 6:4 1481
for ye were *s* in the land of ... Ex 22:21 1616
seeing ye were *s* in the land of ... Ex 23:9 1616
or of the *s* which sojourn among ... Lev 17:8 1616
or of the *s* that sojourn among ... Lev 17:10 1616
or of the *s* that sojourn among ... Lev 17:13 1616
for ye were *s* in the land of ... Lev 19:34 1616
or of the *s* that sojourn in ... Lev 20:2 1616
of Israel, or of the *s* in Israel ... Lev 22:18 1616
for ye are *s* and sojourners with ... Lev 25:23 1616
the *s* that do sojourn among you ... Lev 25:45 8453
for ye were *s* in the land of ... Deut 10:19 1616
or of thy *s* that are in thy land ... Deut 24:14 1616
the gods of the *s* of the land ... Deut 31:16 5236
the *s* that were conversant among ... Josh 8:35 1616
S shall submit themselves unto me . 2Sa 22:45 1121,5236
S shall fade away, and they shall 2Sa 22:46 1121,5236
but few, even a few, and *s* in it ... 1Chr 16:19 1481
to gather together the *s* that ... 1Chr 22:2 1616
For we are *s* before thee, and ... 1Chr 29:15 1616
Solomon numbered all the *s* that 2Chr 2:17 582,1616
the *s* with them out of Ephraim and ... 2Chr 15:9 1481
the *s* that came out of the land ... 2Chr 30:25 1616
separated themselves from all *s* ...... Neh 9:2 1121,5236
Thus cleansed I them from all *s* ... Neh 13:30 5236
the *s* shall submit themselves ... Ps 18:44 1121,5236
The *s* shall fade away, and be ... Ps 18:45 1121,5236
For *s* are risen up against me, and ... Ps 54:3 2114
yea, very few, and *s* in it ... Ps 105:12 1481
let the *s* spoil his labour ... Ps 109:11 2114
The LORD preserveth the *s* ... Ps 146:9 1616
Lest *s* be filled with thy wealth ... Prov 5:10 2114
s devour it in your presence, and ... Is 1:7 2114
is desolate, as overthrown by *s* ... Is 1:7 2114
themselves in the children of *s* ... Is 2:6 5237
of the fat ones shall *s* eat ... Is 5:17 1481
the *s* shall be joined with them, ... Is 14:1 1616
a palace of *s* to be no city ... Is 25:2 2114
shalt bring down the noise of *s* ... Is 25:5 2114
of thy *s* shall be like small dust ... Is 29:5 2114
the sons of *s* shall build up thy ... Is 60:10 5236
s shall stand and feed your flocks ... Is 61:5 2114
for I have loved *s*, and after them ... Jer 2:25 2114
to the *s* under every green tree ... Jer 3:13 2114
so shall ye serve *s* in a land ... Jer 5:19 2114
s shall no more serve themselves ... Jer 30:8 2114
days in the land where ye be *s* ... Jer 35:7 1481
for *s* are come into the ... Jer 51:51 2114
Our inheritance is turned to *s* ... Lam 5:2 2114
the hands of the *s* for a prey ... Eze 7:21 2114
deliver you into the hands of *s* ... Eze 11:9 2114
which taketh *s* instead of her ... Eze 16:32 2114
I will bring *s* upon thee, the ... Eze 28:7 2114
uncircumcised by the hand of *s* ... Eze 28:10 2114
that is therein, by the hand of *s* ... Eze 30:12 2114
And *s*, the terrible of the nations ... Eze 31:12 2114
have brought into my sanctuary *s* ... Eze 44:7 1121,5236
to the *s* that sojourn among you, ... Eze 47:22 1616
S have devoured his strength, and ... Hos 7:9 2114
the *s* shall swallow it up ... Hos 8:7 2114
there shall no *s* pass through her ... Joel 3:17 2114
in the day that the *s* carried ... Obad 11 2114
of their own children, or of *s* ... Mt 17:25 *245*
Peter saith unto him, Of *s* ... Mt 17:26 *245*
the potter's field, to bury *s* in ... Mt 27:7 *3581*
for they know not the voice of *s* ... Jn 10:5 *245*
s of Rome, Jews and proselytes, ... Acts 2:10 *1927*
dwelt as *s* in the land of Egypt ... Acts 13:17 *1722,3940*
s which were there spent their ... Acts 17:21 *3581*
s from the covenants of promise, ... Eph 2:12 *3581*
Now therefore ye are no more *s* ... Eph 2:19 *3581*
up children, if she have lodged *s* ... 1Ti 5:10 *3580*
and confessed that they were *s* ... Heb 11:13 *3581*
Be not forgetful to entertain *s* ... Heb 13:2 *5381*
to the *s* scattered throughout ... 1Pet 1:1 *3927*
beloved, I beseech you as *s* ... 1Pet 2:11 *3941*
doest to the brethren, and to *s* ... 3Jn 5 *3581*

STRANGERS' {1}
thine own, and not *s* with thee ... Prov 5:17 2114

STRANGLED {4}
s for his lionesses, and filled ... Nah 2:12 2614
fornication, and from things *s* ... Acts 15:20 *4156*
and from blood, and from things *s* ... Acts 15:29 *4156*
idols, and from blood, and from *s* ... Acts 21:25 *4156*

STRANGLING {1}
So that my soul chooseth *s* ... Job 7:15 4267

STRAW {16}
moreover unto him, We have both *s* ... Gen 24:25 8401
he ungirded his camels, and gave *s* ... Gen 24:32 8401
give the people *s* to make brick ... Ex 5:7 8401
go and gather *s* for themselves ... Ex 5:7 8401
Pharaoh, I will not give you *s* ... Ex 5:10 8401
get you *s* where ye can find it ... Ex 5:11 8401
to gather stubble instead of *s* ... Ex 5:12 8401
daily tasks, as when there was *s* ... Ex 5:13 8401
There is no *s* given unto thy ... Ex 5:16 8401
for there shall no *s* be given you ... Ex 5:18 8401
Yet there is both *s* and provender ... Judg 19:19 8401
s for the horses and dromedaries ... 1Kin 4:28 8401
He esteemeth iron as *s*, and brass ... Job 41:27 8401
the lion shall eat *s* like the ox ... Is 11:7 8401
even as *s* is trodden down for the ... Is 25:10 4963
lion shall eat *s* like the bullock ... Is 65:25 8401

STRAWED {5}
s it upon the water, and made the ... Ex 32:20 2219
the trees, and *s* them in the way ... Mt 21:8 *4766*
gathering where thou hast not *s* ... Mt 25:24 *1287*
not, and gather where I have not *s* ... Mt 25:26 *1287*
the trees, and *s* them in the way ... Mk 11:8 *4766*

STREAM {12}
at the *s* of the brooks that goeth ... Num 21:15 793
as the *s* of brooks they pass away ... Job 6:15 650
the *s* had gone over our soul ... Ps 124:4 5158
of the river unto the *s* of Egypt ... Is 27:12 5158
his breath, as an overflowing *s* ... Is 30:28 5158
like a *s* of brimstone, doth ... Is 30:33 5158
stones of the *s* is thy portion ... Is 57:6 5158
of the Gentiles like a flowing *s* ... Is 66:12 5158
A fiery *s* issued and came forth ... Dan 7:10 5103
and righteousness as a mighty *s* ... Amos 5:24 5158
the *s* beat vehemently upon that ... Lk 6:48 *4215*
against which the *s* did beat ... Lk 6:49 *4215*

STREAMS {12}
the waters of Egypt, upon their *s* ... Ex 7:19 5104
hand with thy rod over the *s* ... Ex 8:5 5104
the *s* whereof shall make glad the ... Ps 46:4 6388
He brought *s* also out of the rock ... Ps 78:16 5140
gushed out, and the *s* overflowed ... Ps 78:20 5158
O LORD, as the *s* in the south ... Ps 126:4 650
living waters, and *s* from Lebanon ... Song 4:15 5140
and shall smite it in the seven *s* ... Is 11:15 5158
s of waters in the day of the ... Is 30:25 2988
us a place of broad rivers and *s* ... Is 33:21 2975
the *s* thereof shall be turned ... Is 34:9 5158
break out, and *s* in the desert ... Is 35:6 5158

STREET {37}
we will abide in the *s* all night ... Gen 19:2 7339
into the midst of the *s* thereof ... Deut 13:16 7339
the doors of thy house into the *s* ... Josh 2:19 2351
sat him down in a *s* of the city ... Judg 19:15 7339
man in the *s* of the city ... Judg 19:17 7339
only lodge not in the *s* ... Judg 19:20 7339
them from the *s* of Beth-shan ... 2Sa 21:12 7339
stamp them as the mire of the *s* ... 2Sa 22:43 2351
them together into the east *s* ... 2Chr 29:4 7339
in the *s* of the gate of the city ... 2Chr 32:6 7339
sat in the *s* of the house of God ... Ezr 10:9 7339
together as one man into the *s* ... Neh 8:1 7339
he read therein before the *s* that ... Neh 8:3 7339
in the *s* of the water gate, and in ... Neh 8:16 7339
in the *s* of the gate of Ephraim ... Neh 8:16 7339
Mordecai unto the *s* of the city ... Est 4:6 7339

S

through the *s* of the city	Est 6:9	7339
through the *s* of the city	Est 6:11	7339
and he shall have no name in the *s*	Job 18:17	2351,6440
when I prepared my seat in the *s*	Job 29:7	7339
stranger did not lodge in the *s*	Job 31:32	2351
through the *s* near her corner	Prov 7:8	7784
his voice to be heard in the *s*	Is 42:2	2351
body as the ground, and as the *s*	Is 51:23	2351
for truth is fallen in the *s*	Is 59:14	7339
of bread out of the bakers' *s*	Jer 37:21	2351
for hunger in the top of every *s*	Lam 2:19	2351
poured out in the top of every *s*	Lam 4:1	2351
thee an high place in every *s*	Eze 16:24	7339
thine high place in every *s*	Eze 16:31	7339
pestilence, and blood into her *s*	Eze 28:23	7339
the *s* shall be built again, and	Dan 9:25	7339
go into the *s* which is called	Acts 9:11	*4505*
out, and passed on through one *s*	Acts 12:10	*4505*
lie in the *s* of the great city	Rev 11:8	*4113*
the *s* of the city was pure gold,	Rev 21:21	*4113*
In the midst of the *s* of it	Rev 22:2	*4113*

STREETS {64}

it not in the *s* of Askelon	2Sa 1:20	2351
thou shalt make *s* for thee in	1Kin 20:34	2351
them out as the dirt in the *s*	Ps 18:42	2351
and guile depart not from her *s*	Ps 55:11	7339
and ten thousands in our *s*	Ps 144:13	2351
there be no complaining in our *s*	Ps 144:14	7339
she uttereth her voice in the *s*	Prov 1:20	7339
and rivers of waters in the *s*	Prov 5:16	7339
Now is she without, now in the *s*	Prov 7:12	7339
I shall be slain in the *s*	Prov 22:13	7339
a lion is in the *s*	Prov 26:13	7339
the doors shall be shut in the *s*	Eccl 12:4	7784
and the mourners go about the *s*	Eccl 12:5	7784
and go about the city in the *s*	Song 3:2	7784
were torn in the midst of the *s*	Is 5:25	2351
them down like the mire of the *s*	Is 10:6	2351
In their *s* they shall gird	Is 15:3	2351
of their houses, and in their *s*	Is 15:3	7339
is a crying for wine in the *s*	Is 24:11	2351
they lie at the head of all the *s*	Is 51:20	2351
and fro through the *s* of Jerusalem	Jer 5:1	2351
of Judah and in the *s* of Jerusalem	Jer 7:17	2351
from the *s* of Jerusalem, the	Jer 7:34	2351
and the young men from the *s*	Jer 9:21	7339
in the *s* of Jerusalem, saying,	Jer 11:6	2351
the *s* of Jerusalem have ye set up	Jer 11:13	2351
shall be cast out in the *s* of	Jer 14:16	2351
in the *s* of Jerusalem, that are	Jer 33:10	2351
of Judah and in the *s* of Jerusalem	Jer 44:6	2351
Judah, and in the *s* of Jerusalem	Jer 44:9	2351
Judah, and in the *s* of Jerusalem	Jer 44:17	2351
in the *s* of Jerusalem, ye, and	Jer 44:21	2351
of Moab, and in the *s* thereof	Jer 48:38	7339
her young men shall fall in her *s*	Jer 49:26	7339
shall her young men fall in the *s*	Jer 50:30	7339
that are thrust through in her *s*	Jer 51:4	2351
swoon in the *s* of the city	Lam 2:11	7339
the wounded in the *s* of the city	Lam 2:12	7339
old lie on the ground in the *s*	Lam 2:21	2351
delicately are desolate in the *s*	Lam 4:5	2351
they are not known in the *s*	Lam 4:8	2351
wandered as blind men in the *s*	Lam 4:14	2351
steps, that we cannot go in our *s*	Lam 4:18	7339
shall cast their silver in the *s*	Eze 7:19	2351
ye have filled the *s* thereof with	Eze 11:6	2351
shall he tread down all thy *s*	Eze 26:11	2351
Wailing shall be in all *s*	Amos 5:16	7339
trodden down as the mire of the *s*	Mic 7:10	2351
The chariots shall rage in the *s*	Nah 2:4	2351
in pieces at the top of all the *s*	Nah 3:10	2351
I made their *s* waste, that none	Zeph 3:6	2351
women dwell in the *s* of Jerusalem	Zec 8:4	7339
the *s* of the city shall be full	Zec 8:5	7339
and girls playing in the *s* thereof	Zec 8:5	7339
and fine gold as the mire of the *s*	Zec 9:3	2351
the mire of the *s* in the battle	Zec 10:5	2351
do in the synagogues and in the *s*	Mt 6:2	*4505*
and in the corners of the *s*	Mt 6:5	*4113*
any man hear his voice in the *s*	Mt 12:19	*4113*
they laid the sick in the *s*	Mk 6:56	*58*
ways out into the *s* of the same	Lk 10:10	*4113*
and thou hast taught in our *s*	Lk 13:26	*4113*
Go out quickly into the *s*	Lk 14:21	*4113*
brought forth the sick into the *s*	Acts 5:15	*4113*

STRENGTH {242}

henceforth yield unto thee her *s*	Gen 4:12	3581
might, and the beginning of my *s*	Gen 49:3	202
But his bow abode in *s*, and the	Gen 49:24	386
for by *s* of hand the LORD brought	Ex 13:3	2392
By *s* of hand the LORD brought us	Ex 13:14	2392
for by *s* of hand the LORD brought	Ex 13:16	2392
the sea returned to his *s* when	Ex 14:27	386
The LORD is my *s* and song, and he	Ex 15:2	5797
in thy *s* unto thy holy habitation	Ex 15:13	5797
your *s* shall be spent in vain	Lev 26:20	3581
as it were the *s* of a unicorn	Num 23:22	8443
as it were the *s* of a unicorn	Num 24:8	8443
for he is the beginning of his *s*	Deut 21:17	202
and as thy days, so shall thy *s* be	Deut 33:25	1679
that stood still in their *s*	Josh 11:13	8510
as my *s* was then, even so is my	Josh 14:11	3581
was then, even so is my *s* now	Josh 14:11	3581
my soul, thou hast trodden down *s*	Judg 5:21	5797
for as the man is, so is his *s*	Judg 8:21	1369
and see wherein his great *s* lieth	Judg 16:5	3581
thee, wherein thy great *s* lieth	Judg 16:6	3581
So his *s* was not known	Judg 16:9	3581
told me wherein thy great *s* lieth	Judg 16:15	3581
then my *s* will go from me, and I	Judg 16:17	3581
him, and his *s* went from him	Judg 16:19	3581
that stumbled are girded with *s*	1Sa 2:4	2428
for by *s* shall no man prevail	1Sa 2:9	3581
and he shall give *s* unto his king	1Sa 2:10	5797
also the *S* of Israel will not lie	1Sa 15:29	5331
and there was no *s* in him	1Sa 28:20	3581
and eat, that thou mayest have *s*	1Sa 28:22	3581
God is my *s* and power	2Sa 22:33	4581
hast girded me with *s* to battle	2Sa 22:40	2428
went in the *s* of that meat forty	1Kin 19:8	3581
Jehu drew a bow with his full *s*	2Kin 9:24	3027
I have counsel and *s* for the war	2Kin 18:20	1369
there is not *s* to bring forth	2Kin 19:3	3581
Seek the LORD and his *s*, seek his	1Chr 16:11	5797
s and gladness are in his place	1Chr 16:27	5797
give unto the LORD glory and *s*	1Chr 16:28	5797
able men for *s* for the service,	1Chr 26:8	3581
make great, and to give *s* unto all	1Chr 29:12	2388
place, thou, and the ark of thy *s*	2Chr 6:41	5797
s again in the days of Abijah	2Chr 13:20	3581
The *s* of the bearers of burdens	Neh 4:10	3581
for the joy of the LORD is your *s*	Neh 8:10	4581
What is my *s*, that I should hope	Job 6:11	3581
Is my *s* the *s* of stones	Job 6:12	3581
is wise in heart, and mighty in *s*	Job 9:4	3581
If I speak of *s*, lo, he is strong	Job 9:19	3581
With him is wisdom and *s*, he hath	Job 12:13	1369
With him is *s* and wisdom	Job 12:16	5797
and weakeneth the *s* of the mighty	Job 12:21	4206
The steps of his *s* shall be	Job 18:7	202
His *s* shall be hungerbitten, and	Job 18:12	202
It shall devour the *s* of his skin	Job 18:13	905
of death shall devour his *s*	Job 18:13	905
One dieth in his full *s*, being	Job 21:23	6106
but he would put *s* in me	Job 23:6	
thou the arm that hath no *s*	Job 26:2	5797
whereto might the *s* of their	Job 30:2	3581
he is mighty in *s* and wisdom	Job 36:5	3581
not gold, nor all the forces of *s*	Job 36:19	3581
and to the great rain of his *s*	Job 37:6	5797
trust him, because his *s* is great	Job 39:11	3581
Hath thou given the horse *s*	Job 39:19	1369
the valley, and rejoiceth in his *s*	Job 39:21	3581
his *s* is in his loins, and his	Job 40:16	3581
In his neck remaineth *s*, and	Job 41:22	5797
s because of thine enemies	Ps 8:2	5797
I will love thee, O LORD, my *s*	Ps 18:1	2391
my God, my *s*, in whom I will	Ps 18:2	6697
It is God that girdeth me with *s*	Ps 18:32	2428
girded me with *s* unto the battle	Ps 18:39	2428
in thy sight, O LORD, my *s*	Ps 19:14	6697
the saving *s* of his right hand	Ps 20:6	1369
The king shall joy in thy *s*	Ps 21:1	5797
exalted, LORD, in thine own *s*	Ps 21:13	5797
My *s* is dried up like a potsherd	Ps 22:15	3581
O my *s*, haste thee to help me	Ps 22:19	360
the LORD is the *s* of my life	Ps 27:1	4581
The LORD is my *s* and my shield	Ps 28:7	5797
The LORD is their *s*, and he is the	Ps 28:8	5797
is the saving *s* of his anointed	Ps 28:8	4581
give unto the LORD glory and *s*	Ps 29:1	5797
LORD will give *s* unto his people	Ps 29:11	5797
for thou art my *s*	Ps 31:4	4581
my *s* faileth because of mine	Ps 31:10	3581
man is not delivered by much *s*	Ps 33:16	3581
he deliver any by his great *s*	Ps 33:17	2428
he is their *s* in the time of	Ps 37:39	4581
My heart panteth, my *s* faileth me	Ps 38:10	3581
O spare me, that I may recover *s*	Ps 39:13	1082
For thou art the God of my *s*	Ps 43:2	4581
God is our refuge and *s*, a very	Ps 46:1	5797
the man that made not God his *s*	Ps 52:7	4581
by thy name, and judge me by thy *s*	Ps 54:1	1369
Because of his *s* will I wait upon	Ps 59:9	5797
Unto thee, O my *s*, will I sing	Ps 59:17	5797
also is the *s* of mine head	Ps 60:7	4581
the rock of my *s*, and my refuge,	Ps 62:7	5797
Which by his *s* setteth fast the	Ps 65:6	3581
Thy God hath commanded thy *s*	Ps 68:28	5797
Ascribe ye *s* unto God	Ps 68:34	5797
Israel, and his *s* is in the clouds	Ps 68:34	5797
God of Israel is he that giveth *s*	Ps 68:35	5797
forsake me not when my *s* faileth	Ps 71:9	3581
will go in the *s* of the Lord GOD	Ps 71:16	1369
shewed thy *s* unto this generation	Ps 71:18	2220
but their *s* is firm	Ps 73:4	193
but God is the *s* of my heart	Ps 73:26	6697
didst divide the sea by thy *s*	Ps 74:13	5797
declared thy *s* among the people	Ps 77:14	5797
the praises of the LORD, and his *s*	Ps 78:4	5807
the chief of their *s* in the	Ps 78:51	202
delivered his *s* into captivity,	Ps 78:61	5797
and Manasseh stir up thy *s*	Ps 80:2	1369
Sing aloud unto God our *s*	Ps 81:1	5797
is the man whose *s* is in thee	Ps 84:5	5797
They go from *s* to *s*	Ps 84:7	2428
give thy *s* unto thy servant, and	Ps 86:16	5797
I am as a man that hath no *s*	Ps 88:4	353
For thou art the glory of their *s*	Ps 89:17	5797
if by reason of *s* they be	Ps 90:10	1369
years, yet is their *s* labour	Ps 90:10	7296
the LORD is clothed with *s*	Ps 93:1	5797
the *s* of the hills is his also	Ps 95:4	8443
s and beauty are in his sanctuary	Ps 96:6	5797
give unto the LORD glory and *s*	Ps 96:7	5797
The king's *s* also loveth judgment	Ps 99:4	5797
He weakened my *s* in the way	Ps 102:23	3581
ye his angels, that excel in *s*	Ps 103:20	3581
Seek the LORD, and his *s*	Ps 105:4	5797
land, the chief of all their *s*	Ps 105:36	202
also is the *s* of mine head	Ps 108:8	4581
send the rod of thy *s* out of Zion	Ps 110:2	5797
The LORD is my *s* and song, and is	Ps 118:14	5797
thou, and the ark of thy *s*	Ps 132:8	5797
me with *s* in my soul	Ps 138:3	5797
the *s* of my salvation, thou hast	Ps 140:7	5797
Blessed be the LORD my *s*, which	Ps 144:1	6697
not in the *s* of the horse	Ps 147:10	1369
I have *s*	Prov 8:14	1369
of the LORD is *s* to the upright	Prov 10:29	4581
increase is by the *s* of the ox	Prov 14:4	3581
The glory of young men is their *s*	Prov 20:29	3581
casteth down the *s* of the	Prov 21:22	5797
a man of knowledge increaseth *s*	Prov 24:5	3581
day of adversity, thy *s* is small	Prov 24:10	3581
Give not thy *s* unto women	Prov 31:3	2428
She girdeth her loins with *s*	Prov 31:17	5797
S and honour are her clothing	Prov 31:25	5797
said I, Wisdom is better than *s*	Eccl 9:16	1369
edge, then must he put to more *s*	Eccl 10:10	2428
princes eat in due season, for *s*	Eccl 10:17	1369
men of *s* to mingle strong drink	Is 5:22	2428
By the *s* of my hand I have done	Is 10:13	3581
for the LORD JEHOVAH is my *s*	Is 12:2	5797
been mindful of the rock of thy *s*	Is 17:10	4581
even the *s* of the sea, saying, I	Is 23:4	4581
there is no more *s*	Is 23:10	4206
for your *s* is laid waste	Is 23:14	4581
thou hast been a *s* to the poor	Is 25:4	4581
a *s* to the needy in his distress,	Is 25:4	4581
the LORD JEHOVAH is everlasting *s*	Is 26:4	6697
Or let him take hold of my *s*	Is 27:5	4581
for *s* to them that turn the	Is 28:6	1369
themselves in the *s* of Pharaoh	Is 30:2	4581
Therefore shall the *s* of Pharaoh	Is 30:3	4581
this, Their *s* is to sit still	Is 30:7	7293
and in confidence shall be your *s*	Is 30:15	1369
of thy times, and *s* of salvation	Is 33:6	2633
I have counsel and *s* for war	Is 36:5	1369
there is not *s* to bring forth	Is 37:3	3581
tidings, lift up thy voice with *s*	Is 40:9	3581
have no might he increaseth *s*	Is 40:29	6109
upon the LORD shall renew their *s*	Is 40:31	3581
and let the people renew their *s*	Is 41:1	3581
of his anger, and the *s* of battle	Is 42:25	5807
worketh it with the *s* of his arms	Is 44:12	3581
he is hungry, and his *s* faileth	Is 44:12	3581
LORD have I righteousness and *s*	Is 45:24	5797
I have spent my *s* for nought	Is 49:4	3581
the LORD, and my God shall be my *s*	Is 49:5	5797
Awake, awake, put on *s*, O arm of	Is 51:9	5797
put on thy *s*, O Zion	Is 52:1	5797
hand, and by the arm of his *s*	Is 62:8	5797
in the greatness of his *s*	Is 63:1	3581
bring down their *s* to the earth	Is 63:6	5332
where is thy zeal and thy *s*	Is 63:15	1369
O LORD, my *s*, and my fortress, and	Jer 16:19	5797
deliver all the *s* of this city	Jer 20:5	2633
fortify the height of her *s*	Jer 51:53	5797
gone without *s* before the pursuer	Lam 1:6	3581
he hath made my *s* to fall	Lam 1:14	3581
And I said, My *s* and my hope is	Lam 3:18	5331
the excellency of your *s*	Eze 24:21	5797
day when I take from them their *s*	Eze 24:25	4581
my fury upon Sin, the *s* of Egypt	Eze 30:15	4581
the pomp of her *s* shall cease in	Eze 30:18	5797
and the pomp of her *s* shall cease	Eze 33:28	5797
given thee a kingdom, power, and *s*	Dan 2:37	8632
be in it of the *s* of the iron	Dan 2:41	5326
and there remained no *s* in me	Dan 10:8	3581
corruption, and I retained no *s*	Dan 10:8	3581
upon me, and I have retained no *s*	Dan 10:16	3581
there remained no *s* in me	Dan 10:17	3581
by his *s* through his riches he	Dan 11:2	2394
shall there be any *s* to withstand	Dan 11:15	3581
with the *s* of his whole kingdom	Dan 11:17	8633
shall pollute the sanctuary of *s*	Dan 11:31	4581
Strangers have devoured his *s*	Hos 7:9	3581
by his *s* he had power with God	Hos 12:3	202
tree and the vine do yield their *s*	Joel 2:22	2428
the *s* of the children of Israel	Joel 3:16	4581
shall bring down thy *s* from thee	Amos 3:11	5797
taken to us horns by our own *s*	Amos 6:13	2392
and feed in the *s* of the LORD	Mic 5:4	5797
Ethiopia and Egypt were her *s*	Nah 3:9	6109
shalt seek *s* because of the enemy	Nah 3:11	4581
The LORD God is my *s*, and he will	Hab 3:19	2428
I will destroy the *s* of the	Hag 2:22	2392
of Jerusalem shall be my *s* in the	Zec 12:5	556
all thy mind, and with all thy *s*	Mk 12:30	*2479*
all the soul, and with all the *s*	Mk 12:33	*2479*
He hath shewed *s* with his arm	Lk 1:51	*2904*
all thy soul, and with all thy *s*	Lk 10:27	*2479*
feet and ancle bones received *s*	Acts 3:7	*4732*
But Saul increased the more in *s*	Acts 9:22	*1743*
For when we were yet without *s*	Rom 5:6	*772*
and the *s* of sin is the law	1Cor 15:56	*1411*
pressed out of measure, above *s*	2Cor 1:8	*1411*
for my *s* is made perfect in	2Cor 12:9	*1411*
otherwise it is of no *s* at all	Heb 9:17	*2480*
received *s* to conceive seed	Heb 11:11	*1411*
was as the sun shineth in his *s*	Rev 1:16	*1411*

for thou hast a little s, and hast ... Rev 3:8 1411
power, and riches, and wisdom, and s ... Rev 5:12 2479
Now is come salvation, and s ... Rev 12:10 1411
their power and s unto the beast ... Rev 17:13 1849

STRENGTHEN {32}
and encourage him, and s him ... Deut 3:28 553
s me, I pray thee, only this once ... Judg 16:28 2388
s thyself, and mark, and see what ... 1Kin 20:22 2388
to s their hands in the work of ... Ezr 6:22 2388
Now therefore, O God, s my hands ... Neh 6:9 2388
But I would s you with my mouth, ... Job 16:5 553
sanctuary, and s thee out of Zion ... Ps 20:2 5582
and he shall s thine heart ... Ps 27:14 553
he shall s your heart, all ye ... Ps 31:24 553
The LORD will s him upon the bed ... Ps 41:3 5582
s, O God, that which thou hast ... Ps 68:28 5810
mine arm also shall s him ... Ps 89:21 553
s thou me according unto thy word ... Ps 119:28 6965
s him with thy girdle, and I will ... Is 22:21 2388
to s themselves in the strength ... Is 30:2 5810
they could not well s their mast ... Is 33:23 2388
S ye the weak hands, and confirm ... Is 35:3 2388
I will s thee ... Is 41:10 553
thy cords, and s thy stakes ... Is 54:2 2388
they s also the hands of ... Jer 23:14 2388
neither shall any s himself in ... Eze 7:13 2388
neither did she s the hand of the ... Eze 16:49 2388
I will s the arms of the king of ... Eze 30:24 2388
But I will s the arms of the king ... Eze 30:25 2388
will s that which was sick ... Eze 34:16 2388
I, stood to confirm and to s him ... Dan 11:1 4581
the strong shall not s his force ... Amos 2:14 553
I will s the house of Judah, and I ... Zec 10:6 1396
I will s them in the LORD ... Zec 10:12 1396
art converted, s thy brethren ... Lk 22:32 4741
make you perfect, stablish, s ... 1Pet 5:10 4599
s the things which remain, that ... Rev 3:2 4741

STRENGTHENED {39}
Israel s himself, and sat upon the ... Gen 48:2 2388
the LORD s Eglon the king of Moab ... Judg 3:12 2388
be s to go down unto the host ... Judg 7:11 2388
the wood, and s his hand in God ... 1Sa 23:16 2388
Therefore now let your hands be s ... 2Sa 2:7 2388
who s themselves with him in his ... 1Chr 11:10 2388
son of David was s in his kingdom ... 2Chr 1:1 2388
So they s the kingdom of Judah, ... 2Chr 11:17 2388
had s himself, he forsook the law ... 2Chr 12:1 2394
So king Rehoboam s himself in ... 2Chr 12:13 2388
have s themselves against ... 2Chr 13:7 553
and s himself against Israel ... 2Chr 17:1 2388
he s himself, and slew all his ... 2Chr 21:4 2388
seventh year Jehoiada s himself ... 2Chr 23:1 2388
of God in his state, and s it ... 2Chr 24:13 553
And Amaziah s himself, and led ... 2Chr 25:11 2388
for he s himself exceedingly ... 2Chr 26:8 2388
and distressed him, but s him not ... 2Chr 28:20 2388
Also he s himself, and built up ... 2Chr 32:5 2388
s their hands with vessels of ... Ezr 1:6 2388
I was s as the hand of the LORD ... Ezr 7:28 2388
So they s their hands for this ... Neh 2:18 2388
thou hast s the weak hands ... Job 4:3 2388
thou hast s the feeble knees ... Job 4:4 553
s himself in his wickedness ... Ps 52:7 5810
For he hath s the bars of thy ... Ps 147:13 2388
when he s the fountains of the ... Prov 8:28 5810
s the hands of the wicked, that ... Eze 13:22 2388
The diseased have ye not s ... Eze 34:4 2388
appearance of a man, and he s me ... Dan 10:18 2388
he had spoken unto me, I was s ... Dan 10:19 2388
for thou hast s me ... Dan 10:19 2388
he that s her in these times ... Dan 11:6 2388
but he shall not be s by it ... Dan 11:12 5810
s their arms, yet do they imagine ... Hos 7:15 2388
he had received meat, he was s ... Acts 9:19 1765
to be s with might by his Spirit ... Eph 3:16 2901
S with all might, according to ... Col 1:11 1412
the Lord stood with me, and s me ... 2Ti 4:17 1743

STRENGTHENEDST {1}
s me with strength in my soul ... Ps 138:3 7292

STRENGTHENETH {7}
s himself against the Almighty ... Job 15:25 1396
and bread which s man's heart ... Ps 104:15 5582
with strength, and s her arms ... Prov 31:17 553
Wisdom s the wise more than ten ... Eccl 7:19 5810
which he s for himself among the ... Is 44:14 553
That s the spoiled against the ... Amos 5:9 1082
things through Christ which s me ... Phil 4:13 1743

STRENGTHENING {2}
angel unto him from heaven, s him ... Lk 22:43 1765
in order, s all the disciples ... Acts 18:23 1991

STRETCH {50}
I will s out my hand, and smite ... Ex 3:20 7971
when I s forth mine hand upon ... Ex 7:5 5186
s out thine hand upon the waters ... Ex 7:19 5186
S forth thine hand with thy rod ... Ex 8:5 5186
S out thy rod, and smite the dust ... Ex 8:16 5186
For now I will s out my hand ... Ex 9:15 7971
S forth thine hand toward heaven, ... Ex 9:22 5186
S out thine hand over the land of ... Ex 10:12 5186
S out thine hand toward heaven, ... Ex 10:21 5186
s out thine hand over the sea, and ... Ex 14:16 5186
S out thine hand over the sea, ... Ex 14:26 5186
the cherubim shall s forth their ... Ex 25:20 6566
S out the spear that is in thy ... Josh 8:18 5186
to s forth mine hand against him, ... 1Sa 24:6 7971
for who can s forth his hand ... 1Sa 26:9 7971
s forth mine hand against the ... 1Sa 26:11 7971
but I would not s forth mine hand ... 1Sa 26:23 7971
How wast thou not afraid to s ... 2Sa 1:14 7971
I will s over Jerusalem the line ... 2Kin 21:13 5186
s out thine hands toward him ... Job 11:13 6566
Howbeit he will not s out his ... Job 30:24 7971
s her wings toward the south ... Job 39:26 6566
Ethiopia shall soon s out her ... Ps 68:31 7323
thou shalt s forth thine hand ... Ps 138:7 7971
I s forth my hands unto thee ... Ps 143:6 6566
that a man can s himself on it ... Is 28:20 8311
the LORD shall s out his hand ... Is 31:3 5186
he shall s out upon it the line ... Is 34:11 5186
let them s forth the curtains of ... Is 54:2 5186
for I will s out my hand upon the ... Jer 6:12 5186
there is none to s forth my tent ... Jer 10:20 5186
therefore will I s out my hand ... Jer 15:6 5186
I will s out mine hand upon thee, ... Jer 51:25 5186
So will I s out my hand upon them ... Eze 6:14 5186
I will s out my hand upon him, and ... Eze 14:9 5186
then will I s out mine hand upon ... Eze 14:13 5186
therefore I will s out mine hand ... Eze 25:7 5186
I will also s out mine hand upon ... Eze 25:13 5186
I will s out mine hand upon the ... Eze 25:16 5186
he shall s it out upon the land ... Eze 30:25 5186
I will s out mine hand against ... Eze 35:3 5186
He shall s forth his hand also ... Dan 11:42 7971
s themselves upon their couches, ... Amos 6:4 5628
I will also s out mine hand upon ... Zeph 1:4 5186
he will s out his hand against ... Zeph 2:13 5186
he to the man, S forth thine hand ... Mt 12:13 1614
unto the man, S forth thine hand ... Mk 3:5 1614
unto the man, S forth thy hand ... Lk 6:10 1614
thou shalt s forth thy hands, and ... Jn 21:18 1614
For we s not ourselves beyond our ... 2Cor 10:14 5239

STRETCHED {71}
Abraham s forth his hand, and took ... Gen 22:10 7971
Israel s out his right hand, and ... Gen 48:14 7971
will redeem you with a s out arm ... Ex 6:6 5186
Aaron s out his hand over the ... Ex 8:6 5186
for Aaron s out his hand with his ... Ex 8:17 5186
Moses s forth his rod toward ... Ex 9:23 5186
Moses s forth his rod over the ... Ex 10:13 5186
Moses s forth his hand toward ... Ex 10:22 5186
Moses s out his hand over the sea ... Ex 14:21 5186
Moses s forth his hand over the ... Ex 14:27 5186
by a s out arm, and by great ... Deut 4:34 5186
a mighty hand and by a s out arm ... Deut 5:15 5186
the s out arm, whereby the LORD ... Deut 7:19 5186
mighty power and by thy s out arm ... Deut 9:29 5186
mighty hand, and his s out arm, ... Deut 11:2 5186
Joshua s out the spear that he ... Josh 8:18 5186
as soon as he had s out his hand ... Josh 8:19 5186
wherewith he s out the spear, ... Josh 8:26 5186
when the angel s out his hand ... 2Sa 24:16 7971
they s forth the wings of the ... 1Kin 6:27 6566
strong hand, and of thy s out arm ... 1Kin 8:42 5186
he s himself upon the child three ... 1Kin 17:21 4058
he s himself upon the child ... 2Kin 4:34 1457
and went up, and s himself upon him ... 2Kin 4:35 1457
a s out arm, him shall ye fear, ... 2Kin 17:36 5186
in his hand s out over Jerusalem ... 1Chr 21:16 5186
thy mighty hand, and thy s out arm ... 2Chr 6:32 5186
or who hath s the line upon it ... Job 38:5 5186
or s out our hands to a strange ... Ps 44:20 6566
I have s out my hands unto thee ... Ps 88:9 7849
To him that s out the earth above ... Ps 136:6 7554
strong hand, and with a s out arm ... Ps 136:12 5186
I have s out my hand, and no man ... Prov 1:24 5186
walk with s forth necks and wanton ... Is 3:16 5186
he hath s forth his hand against ... Is 5:25 5186
away, but his hand is s out still ... Is 5:25 5186
away, but his hand is s out still ... Is 9:12 5186
away, but his hand is s out still ... Is 9:17 5186
away, but his hand is s out still ... Is 9:21 5186
away, but his hand is s out still ... Is 10:4 5186
is s out upon all the nations ... Is 14:26 5186
and his hand is s out, and who ... Is 14:27 5186
her branches are s out, they are ... Is 16:8 5203
He s out his hand over the sea, ... Is 23:11 5186
the heavens, and s them out ... Is 42:5 5186
have s out the heavens, and all ... Is 45:12 5186
that hath s forth the heavens, and ... Is 51:13 5186
shadows of the evening are s out ... Jer 6:4 5186
hath s out the heavens by his ... Jer 10:12 5186
s out arm, and there is nothing ... Jer 32:17 5186
with a s out arm, and with great ... Jer 32:21 5186
hath s out the heaven by his ... Jer 51:15 5186
he hath s out a line, he hath not ... Lam 2:8 5186
and their wings were s upward ... Eze 1:11 6504
s forth over their heads above ... Eze 1:22 5186
one cherub s forth his hand from ... Eze 10:7 7971
therefore I have s out my hand ... Eze 16:27 5186
with a s out arm, and with fury ... Eze 20:33 5186
with a s out arm, and with fury ... Eze 20:34 5186
he s out his hand with scorners ... Hos 7:5 4900
the banquet of them that s ... Amos 6:7 5628
a line shall be s forth upon ... Zec 1:16 5186
And he s it forth ... Mt 12:13 1614
he s forth his hand toward his ... Mt 12:49 1614
Jesus s forth his hand, and caught ... Mt 14:31 1614
were with Jesus s out his hand ... Mt 26:51 1614
And he s it out ... Mk 3:5 1614
ye s forth no hands against me ... Lk 22:53 1614
s forth his hands to vex certain ... Acts 12:1 1911
Then Paul s forth the hand, and ... Acts 26:1 1614
All day long I have s forth my ... Rom 10:21 1600

STRETCHEDST {1}
Thou s out thy right hand, the ... Ex 15:12 5186

STRETCHEST {1}
who s out the heavens like a ... Ps 104:2 5186

STRETCHETH {7}
For he s out his hand against God ... Job 15:25 5186
He s out the north over the empty ... Job 26:7 5186
She s out her hand to the poor ... Prov 31:20 6566
that s out the heavens as a ... Is 40:22 5186
The carpenter s out his rule ... Is 44:13 5186
that s forth the heavens alone ... Is 44:24 5186
which s forth the heavens, and ... Zec 12:1 5186

STRETCHING {2}
the s out of his wings shall fill ... Is 8:8 4298
By s forth thine hand to heal ... Acts 4:30 1614

STRICKEN {18}
Sarah were old and well s in age ... Gen 18:11 935
Abraham was old, and well s in age ... Gen 24:1 935
Now Joshua was old and s in years ... Josh 13:1 935
s in years, and there remaineth ... Josh 13:1 935
that Joshua waxed old and s in age ... Josh 23:1 935
unto them, I am old and s in age ... Josh 23:2 935
pierced and s through his temples ... Judg 5:26 2498
king David was old and s in years ... 1Kin 1:1 935
if thou hast s thy hand with a ... Prov 6:1 8628
They have s me, shalt thou say, ... Prov 23:35 5221
Why should ye be s any more ... Is 1:5 5221
surely they are s ... Is 16:7 5218
yet we did esteem him s, smitten ... Is 53:4 5060
of my people was he s ... Is 53:8 5061
thou hast s them, but they have ... Jer 5:3 5221
s through for want of the fruits ... Lam 4:9 1856
both were now well s in years ... Lk 1:7 4260
man, and my wife well s in years ... Lk 1:18 4260

STRIFE {39}
there was a s between the herdmen ... Gen 13:7 7379
said unto Lot, Let there be no s ... Gen 13:8 4808
in the s of the congregation, to ... Num 27:14 4808
and your burden, and your s ... Deut 1:12 7379
my people were at great s with ... Judg 12:2 7379
And all the people were at s ... 2Sa 19:9 1777
a pavilion from the s of tongues ... Ps 31:20 7379
seen violence and s in the city ... Ps 55:9 7379
Thou makest us a s unto our ... Ps 80:6 4066
him also at the waters of s ... Ps 106:32 4808
A wrathful man stirreth up s ... Prov 15:18 4066
that is slow to anger appeaseth s ... Prov 15:18 7379
A froward man soweth s ... Prov 16:28 4066
house full of sacrifices with s ... Prov 17:1 7379
The beginning of s is as when one ... Prov 17:14 4066
transgression that loveth s ... Prov 17:19 4683
honour for a man to cease from s ... Prov 20:3 7379
yea, s and reproach shall cease ... Prov 22:10 1779
meddleth with s belonging not to ... Prov 26:17 7379
is no talebearer, the s ceaseth ... Prov 26:20 4066
is a contentious man to kindle s ... Prov 26:21 7379
is of a proud heart stirreth up s ... Prov 28:25 4066
An angry man stirreth up s ... Prov 29:22 4066
forcing of wrath bringeth forth s ... Prov 30:33 7379
Behold, ye fast for s and debate, ... Is 58:4 7379
thou hast borne me a man of s ... Jer 15:10 7379
even to the waters of s in Kadesh ... Eze 47:19 4808
unto the waters of s in Kadesh ... Eze 48:28 4808
and there are that raise up s ... Hab 1:3 7379
And there was also a s among them ... Lk 22:24 5379
and wantonness, not in s and ... Rom 13:13 2054
there is among you envying, and s ... 1Cor 3:3 2054
variance, emulations, wrath, s ... Gal 5:20 2052
preach Christ even of envy and s ... Phil 1:15 2054
be done through s or vainglory ... Phil 2:3 2052
of words, whereof cometh envy, s ... 1Ti 6:4 2054
is to them an end of all s ... Heb 6:16 485
s in your hearts, glory not, and ... Jas 3:14 2052
s is, there is confusion and every ... Jas 3:16 2052

STRIFES {4}
Hatred stirreth up s ... Prov 10:12 4090
be debates, envyings, wraths, s ... 2Cor 12:20 2052
s of words, whereof cometh envy, ... 1Ti 6:4 3055
knowing that they do gender s ... 2Ti 2:23 3163

STRIKE {12}
s it on the two side posts and on ... Ex 12:7 5414
s the lintel and the two side ... Ex 12:22 5060
shall s off the heifer's neck ... Deut 21:4
s his hand over the place, and ... 2Kin 5:11 5130
is he that will s hands with me ... Job 17:3 8628
bow of steel shall s him through ... Job 20:24 2498
LORD at thy right hand shall s ... Ps 110:5 4272
Till a dart s through his liver ... Prov 7:23 6398
nor to s princes for equity ... Prov 17:26 5221
not thou one of them that s hands ... Prov 22:26 8628
Thou didst s through with his ... Hab 3:14 5344
the servants did s him with the ... Mk 14:65 906

STRIKER {2}
Not given to wine, no s, not ... 1Ti 3:3 4131
angry, not given to wine, no s ... Titus 1:7 4131

STRIKETH {3}
He s them as wicked men in the ... Job 34:26 5606
man void of understanding s hands ... Prov 17:18 8628
of a scorpion, when he s a man ... Rev 9:5 3817

STRING {2}
make ready their arrow upon the s ... Ps 11:2 3499
the s of his tongue was loosed, ... Mk 7:35 1199

S

STRINGED {3}
praise him with *s* instruments... Ps 150:4 4482
we will sing my songs to the *s*... Is 38:20 5058
chief singer on my *s* instruments... Hab 3:19 5058

STRINGS {4}
thy *s* against the face of them... Ps 21:12 4340
and an instrument of ten *s*... Ps 33:2
Upon an instrument of ten *s*... Ps 92:3
an instrument of ten *s* will I... Ps 144:9

STRIP {7}
s Aaron of his garments, and put... Num 20:26 6584
Philistines came to *s* the slain... 1Sa 31:8 6584
Philistines came to *s* the slain... 1Chr 10:8 6584
s you, and make you bare, and gird... Is 32:11 6584
they shall *s* thee also of thy... Eze 16:39 6584
They shall also *s* thee out of thy... Eze 23:26 6584
Lest I *s* her naked, and set her as... Hos 2:3 6584

STRIPE {2}
wound for wound, *s* for *s*... Ex 21:25 2250

STRIPES {17}
Forty *s* he may give him, and not... Deut 25:3 5221
beat him above these with many *s*... Deut 25:3 4347
with the *s* of the children of men... 2Sa 7:14 5061
the rod, and their iniquity with *s*... Ps 89:32 5061
man than an hundred *s* into a fool... Prov 17:10 5221
and *s* for the back of fools... Prov 19:29 4112
so do *s* the inward parts of the... Prov 20:30 4347
and with his *s* we are healed... Is 53:5 2250
will, shall be beaten with many *s*... Lk 12:47
and did commit things worthy of *s*... Lk 12:48 *4127*
shall be beaten with few *s*... Lk 12:48 *4127*
they had laid many *s* upon them... Acts 16:23 *4127*
of the night, and washed their *s*... Acts 16:33 *4127*
In *s*, in imprisonments, in... 2Cor 6:5 *4127*
in *s* above measure, in prisons... 2Cor 11:23 *4127*
times received I forty *s* save one... 2Cor 11:24 *4127*
by whose *s* ye were healed... 1Pet 2:24 *3468*

STRIPLING {1}
Enquire thou whose son the *s* is... 1Sa 17:56 5958

STRIPPED {11}
And the children of Israel *s*... Ex 33:6 5337
Moses *s* Aaron of his garments, and... Num 20:28 6584
Jonathan *s* himself of the robe... 1Sa 18:4 6584
s off his armour, and sent into... 1Sa 31:9 6584
And when they had *s* him, they took... 1Chr 10:9 6584
which they *s* off for themselves,... 2Chr 20:25 5337
He hath *s* me of my glory, and... Job 19:9 6584
s the naked of their clothing... Job 22:6 6584
I will wail and howl, I will go *s*... Mic 1:8 7758
And they *s* him, and put on him a... Mt 27:28 *1562*
which *s* him of his raiment, and... Lk 10:30 *1562*

STRIPT {2}
that they *s* Joseph out of his... Gen 37:23 6584
he *s* off his clothes also, and... 1Sa 19:24

STRIVE {22}
shall not always *s* with man... Gen 6:3 1777
Gerar did *s* with Isaac's herdmen... Gen 26:20 7378
if men *s* together, and one smite... Ex 21:18 7378
If men *s*, and hurt a woman with... Ex 21:22 5327
When men *s* together one with... Deut 25:11 5327
with whom thou didst *s* at the... Deut 33:8 7378
did he ever *s* against Israel, or... Judg 11:25 7378
Why dost thou *s* against him... Job 33:13 7378
O LORD, with them that *s* with me... Ps 35:1 3401
S not with a man without cause,... Prov 3:30 7378
Go not forth hastily to *s*... Prov 25:8 7378
they that *s* with thee shall... Is 41:11 7379
Let the potsherd *s* with the... Is 45:9
Yet let no man *s*, nor reprove... Hos 4:4 7378
as they that *s* with the priest... Hos 4:4 7378
He shall not *s*, nor cry... Mt 12:19 *2051*
S to enter in at the strait gate... Lk 13:24 *75*
that ye *s* together with me in... Rom 15:30 *4865*
And if a man also *s* for masteries... 2Ti 2:5 *118*
not crowned, except he *s* lawfully... 2Ti 2:5 *118*
s not about words to no profit... 2Ti 2:14 *3054*
servant of the Lord must not *s*... 2Ti 2:24 *3164*

STRIVED {1}
so have I *s* to preach the gospel,... Rom 15:20 *5389*

STRIVEN {1}
thou hast *s* against the LORD... Jer 50:24 1624

STRIVETH {2}
unto him that *s* with his Maker... Is 45:9 7378
every man that *s* for the mastery... 1Cor 9:25 *75*

STRIVING {3}
with one mind *s* together for the... Phil 1:27 *4866*
s according to his working, which... Col 1:29 *75*
unto blood, *s* against sin... Heb 12:4 *464*

STRIVINGS {3}
me from the *s* of my people... 2Sa 22:44 7379
me from the *s* of the people... Ps 18:43 7379
contentions, and *s* about the law... Titus 3:9 *3163*

STROKE {11}
and plea, and between *s* and *s*... Deut 17:8 5061
his hand fetcheth a *s* with the... Deut 19:5
controversy and every *s* be tried... Deut 21:5 5061
enemies with the *s* of the sword... Est 9:5 4347
my *s* is heavier than my groaning... Job 23:2 3027
lest he take thee away with his *s*... Job 36:18 5607
Remove thy *s* away from me... Ps 39:10 5061
in wrath with a continual *s*... Is 14:6 4347
healeth the *s* of their wound... Is 30:26 4273
the desire of thine eyes with a *s*... Eze 24:16 4046

STROKES {1}
and his mouth calleth for *s*... Prov 18:6 4112

STRONG {255}
Issachar is a *s* ass couching down... Gen 49:14 1634
s by the hands of the mighty God... Gen 49:24 6339
for with a *s* hand shall he let... Ex 6:1 2389
with a *s* hand shall he drive them... Ex 6:1 2389
LORD turned a mighty *s* west wind... Ex 10:19 2389
for with a *s* hand hath the LORD... Ex 13:9 2389
by a *s* east wind all that night... Ex 14:21 5794
Do not drink wine nor *s* drink... Lev 10:9
s drink, and shall drink no... Num 6:3
of wine, or vinegar of *s* drink... Num 6:3
whether they be *s* or weak... Num 13:18 2389
whether in tents, or in *s* holds... Num 13:19 4013
be *s* that dwell in the land... Num 13:28 5794
much people, and with a *s* hand... Num 20:20 2389
of the children of Ammon was *s*... Num 21:24 5794
S is thy dwellingplace, and thou... Num 24:21 386
s wine to be poured unto the LORD... Num 28:7
was not one city too *s* for us... Deut 2:36 7682
you this day, that ye may be *s*... Deut 11:8 2388
or for wine, or for *s* drink... Deut 14:26
have ye drunk wine or *s* drink... Deut 29:6
Be *s* and of a good courage, fear... Deut 31:6 2388
in the sight of all Israel, Be *s*... Deut 31:7 2388
of Nun a charge, and said, Be *s*... Deut 31:23 2388
Be *s* and of a good courage... Josh 1:6 2388
Only be thou *s* and very courageous... Josh 1:7 2388
Be *s* and of a good courage... Josh 1:9 2388
only be *s* and of a good courage... Josh 1:18 2388
Fear not, nor be dismayed, be *s*... Josh 10:25 2388
As yet I am as *s* this day as I... Josh 14:11 2389
children of Israel were waxen *s*... Josh 17:13 2388
chariots, and though they be *s*... Josh 17:18 2389
to Ramah, and to the *s* city Tyre... Josh 19:29 4013
before you great nations and *s*... Josh 23:9 6099
came to pass, when Israel was *s*... Judg 1:28 2388
mountains, and caves, and *s* holds... Judg 6:2 4679
But there was a *s* tower within... Judg 9:51 5797
and drink not wine nor *s* drink... Judg 13:4
and now drink no wine nor *s* drink... Judg 13:7
let her drink wine or *s* drink... Judg 13:14
out of the *s* came forth sweetness... Judg 14:14 5794
saw that they were too *s* for him... Judg 18:26 2389
drunken neither wine nor *s* drink... 1Sa 1:15
Be *s*, and quit yourselves like men... 1Sa 4:9 2388
and when Saul saw any *s* man... 1Sa 14:52 1368
in the wilderness in *s* holds... 1Sa 23:14 4679
with us in *s* holds in the wood... 1Sa 23:19 4679
dwelt in *s* holds at En-gedi... 1Sa 23:29 4679
himself *s* for the house of Saul... 2Sa 3:6 2388
David took the *s* hold of Zion... 2Sa 5:7 4686
If the Syrians be too *s* for me... 2Sa 10:11 2388
of Ammon be too *s* for thee... 2Sa 10:11 2388
battle more *s* against the city... 2Sa 11:25 2388
And the conspiracy was *s*... 2Sa 15:12 533
of all that are with thee be *s*... 2Sa 16:21 2388
He delivered me from my *s* enemy... 2Sa 22:18 5794
for they were too *s* for me... 2Sa 22:18 553
came to the *s* hold of Tyre, and to... 2Sa 24:7 4013
be thou *s* therefore, and shew... 1Kin 2:2 2388
thy great name, and of thy *s* hand... 1Kin 8:42 2389
s wind rent the mountains, and... 1Kin 19:11 2389
be with thy servants fifty *s* men... 2Kin 2:16 2428
their *s* holds wilt thou set on... 2Kin 8:12 4013
a thousand, all that were *s*... 2Kin 24:16 1368
If the Syrians be too *s* for me... 1Chr 19:12 2388
of Ammon be too *s* for thee... 1Chr 19:12 2388
be *s*, and of good courage... 1Chr 22:13 2388
whose brethren were *s* men... 1Chr 26:7 2428
sons and brethren, *s* men, eighteen... 1Chr 26:9 2428
be *s*, and do it... 1Chr 28:10 2388
said to Solomon his son, Be *s*... 1Chr 28:20 2388
And he fortified the *s* holds... 2Chr 11:11 4694
spears, and made them exceeding *s*... 2Chr 11:12 2388
Rehoboam the son of Solomon *s*... 2Chr 11:17 559
Be ye *s* therefore, and let not... 2Chr 15:7 2388
to shew himself *s* in the behalf... 2Chr 16:9 2388
go, do it, be *s* for the battle... 2Chr 25:8 2388
helped, till he was *s*... 2Chr 26:15 2388
But when he was *s*, his heart was... 2Chr 26:16 2394
Be *s* and courageous, be not afraid... 2Chr 32:7 2388
that ye may be *s*, and eat the good... Ezr 9:12 2388
thy great power, and by thy *s* hand... Neh 1:10 2389
And they took *s* cities, and a fat... Neh 9:25 1219
of thy mouth be like a *s* wind... Job 8:2 3524
I speak of strength, lo, he is *s*... Job 9:19 533
with thy *s* hand thou opposest... Job 30:21 6108
of his bones with *s* pain... Job 33:19 386
spread out the sky, which is *s*... Job 37:18 2389
crag of the rock, and the *s* place... Job 39:28 4686
bones are as *s* pieces of brass... Job 40:18 650
the poor may fall by his *s* ones... Ps 10:10 6099
He delivered me from my *s* enemy... Ps 18:17 5794
for they were too *s* for me... Ps 18:17 553
rejoiceth as a *s* man to run a... Ps 19:5 1368
s bulls of Bashan have beset me... Ps 22:12 47
The LORD *s* and mighty, the LORD... Ps 24:8 5808
hast made my mountain to stand *s*... Ps 30:7 5797
be thou my *s* rock, for an house... Ps 31:2 4581
marvellous kindness in a *s* city... Ps 31:21 4692
from him that is too *s* for him... Ps 35:10 2389
enemies are lively, and they are *s*... Ps 38:19 6105
Who will bring me into the *s* city... Ps 60:9 4692
me, and a *s* tower from the enemy... Ps 61:3 5797
Be thou my *s* habitation,... Ps 71:3 6697
but thou art my *s* refuge... Ps 71:7 5797
that thou madest *s* for thyself... Ps 80:15 553
whom thou madest *s* for thyself... Ps 80:17 553
who is a *s* LORD like unto thee... Ps 89:8 2626
thine enemies with thy *s* arm... Ps 89:10 5797
s is thy hand, and high is thy... Ps 89:13 5810
hast brought his *s* holds to ruin... Ps 89:40 4013
Who will bring me into the *s* city... Ps 108:10 4013
With a *s* hand, and with a... Ps 136:12 2389
That our oxen may be *s* to labour... Ps 144:14
many *s* men have been slain by her... Prov 7:26 6099
rich man's wealth is his *s* city... Prov 10:15 5797
and *s* men retain riches... Prov 11:16 6184
fear of the LORD is *s* confidence... Prov 14:26 5797
The name of the LORD is a *s* tower... Prov 18:10 5797
rich man's wealth is his *s* city... Prov 18:11 5797
is harder to be won than a *s* city... Prov 18:19 5797
is a mocker, *s* drink is raging... Prov 20:1
and a reward in the bosom *s* wrath... Prov 21:14 5794
A wise man is *s*... Prov 24:5 5797
The ants are a people not *s*... Prov 30:25 5794
nor for princes *s* drink... Prov 31:4
Give *s* drink unto him that is... Prov 31:6
swift, nor the battle to the *s*... Eccl 9:11 1368
the *s* men shall bow themselves,... Eccl 12:3 2428
for love is *s* as death... Song 8:6 5794
the *s* shall be as tow, and the... Is 1:31 2634
that they may follow *s* drink... Is 5:11
men of strength to mingle *s* drink... Is 5:22
them the waters of the river, *s*... Is 8:7 6099
spake thus to me with a *s* hand... Is 8:11 2393
In that day shall his *s* cities be... Is 17:9 4581
to destroy the *s* holds thereof... Is 23:11 4581
s drink shall be bitter to them... Is 24:9
shall the *s* people glorify thee... Is 25:3 5794
We have a *s* city... Is 26:1 5797
s sword shall punish leviathan... Is 27:1 2389
s one, which as a tempest of hail... Is 28:2 533
through *s* drink are out of the... Is 28:7
have erred through *s* drink... Is 28:7
out of the way through *s* drink... Is 28:7
lest your bands be made *s*... Is 28:22 2388
stagger, but not with *s* drink... Is 29:9
horsemen, because they are very *s*... Is 31:1 6105
pass over to his *s* hold for fear... Is 31:9 5553
that are of a fearful heart, Be *s*... Is 35:4 2388
Lord GOD will come with *s* hand... Is 40:10 2389
might, for that he is *s* in power... Is 40:26 533
bring forth your *s* reasons... Is 41:21 6110
shall divide the spoil with the *s*... Is 53:12 6099
will fill ourselves with *s* drink... Is 56:12
and a small one a *s* nation... Is 60:22 6099
of the neighing of his *s* ones... Jer 8:16 47
outstretched hand and with a *s* arm... Jer 21:5 2389
and with wonders, and with a *s* hand... Jer 32:21 2389
of the hoofs of his *s* horses... Jer 47:3 47
are mighty and *s* men for the war... Jer 48:14 2428
How is the *s* staff broken, and the... Jer 48:17 5797
and he shall destroy thy *s* holds... Jer 48:18 4013
the *s* holds are surprised, and the... Jer 48:41 4679
against the habitation of the *s*... Jer 49:19 386
Their Redeemer is *s*... Jer 50:34 2389
unto the habitation of the *s*... Jer 50:44 386
of Babylon, make the watch *s*... Jer 51:12 2388
thrown down in his wrath the *s*... Lam 2:2 4013
he hath destroyed his *s* holds... Lam 2:5 4013
thy face *s* against their faces... Eze 3:8 2389
thy forehead *s* against their... Eze 3:8 2389
hand of the LORD was *s* upon me... Eze 3:14 2388
make the pomp of the *s* to cease... Eze 7:24 5794
she had *s* rods for the sceptres... Eze 19:11 5797
her *s* rods were broken and... Eze 19:12 5797
so that she hath no *s* rod to be a... Eze 19:14 5797
endure, or can thine hands be *s*... Eze 22:14 2388
thy *s* garrisons shall go down to... Eze 26:11 5797
city, which wast *s* in the sea... Eze 26:17 2389
to make it *s* to hold the sword... Eze 30:21 2388
and will break his arms, the *s*... Eze 30:22 2389
The *s* among the mighty shall... Eze 32:21 410
I will destroy the fat and the *s*... Eze 34:16 2389
fourth kingdom shall be *s* as iron... Dan 2:40 8624
so the kingdom shall be partly *s*... Dan 2:42 8624
The tree grew, and was *s*, and the... Dan 4:11 8631
thou sawest, which grew, and was *s*... Dan 4:20 8631
king, that art grown and become *s*... Dan 4:22 8631
and terrible, and *s* exceedingly... Dan 7:7 8624
and when he was *s*, the great horn... Dan 8:8 6105
unto thee, be *s*, yea, be *s*... Dan 10:19 2388
the king of the south shall be *s*... Dan 11:5 2388
and he shall be *s* above him... Dan 11:5 2388
shall become *s* with a small... Dan 11:23 6105
his devices against the *s* holds... Dan 11:24 4013
that do know their God shall be *s*... Dan 11:32 2388
most *s* holds with a strange god... Dan 11:39 4581
nation is come up upon my land, *s*... Joel 1:6 6099
a great people and a *s*... Joel 2:2 6099
as a *s* people set in battle array... Joel 2:5 6099
for he is *s* that executeth his... Joel 2:11 6099
let the weak say, I am *s*... Joel 3:10 1368
cedars, and he was *s* as the oaks... Amos 2:9 2364
the *s* shall not strengthen his... Amos 2:14 2389
the spoiled against the *s*... Amos 5:9 5794
unto thee of wine and of *s* drink... Mic 2:11 7941
rebuke *s* nations afar off... Mic 4:3 6099
that was cast far off a *s* nation... Mic 4:7 6099
the *s* hold of the daughter of... Mic 4:8 6076
and throw down all thy *s* holds... Mic 5:11 4013
ye *s* foundations of the earth... Mic 6:2 386

a *s* hold in the day of trouble ... Nah 1:7 4581
watch the way, make thy loins *s* ... Nah 2:1 2388
All thy *s* holds shall be like fig ... Nah 3:12 4013
the siege, fortify thy *s* holds ... Nah 3:14 4013
the morter, make *s* the brickkiln ... Nah 3:14 2388
they shall deride every *s* hold ... Hab 1:10 4013
Yet now be *s*, O Zerubbabel, saith ... Hag 2:4 2388
and be *s*, O Joshua, son of ... Hag 2:4 2388
and be *s*, all ye people of the ... Hag 2:4 2388
Let your hands be *s*, ye that hear ... Zec 8:9 2388
fear not, but let your hands be *s* ... Zec 8:13 2388
s nations shall come to seek the ... Zec 8:22 6099
Tyrus did build herself a *s* hold ... Zec 9:3 4692
Turn you to the *s* hold, ye ... Zec 9:12 1225
one enter into a *s* man's house ... Mt 12:29 *2478*
except he first bind the *s* man ... Mt 12:29 *2478*
can enter into a *s* man's house ... Mk 3:27 *2478*
he will first bind the *s* man ... Mk 3:27 *2478*
drink neither wine nor *s* drink ... Lk 1:15 *4608*
waxed *s* in spirit, and was in the ... Lk 1:80 *2901*
waxed *s* in spirit, filled with ... Lk 2:40 *2901*
When a *s* man armed keepeth his ... Lk 11:21 *2478*
in his name hath made this man *s* ... Acts 3:16 *4732*
but was *s* in faith, giving glory ... Rom 4:20 *1743*
We then that are *s* ought to bear ... Rom 15:1 *1415*
we are weak, but ye are *s* ... 1Cor 4:10 *2478*
faith, quit you like men, be *s* ... 1Cor 16:13 *2901*
to the pulling down of *s* holds ... 2Cor 10:4 *3794*
for when I am weak, then am I *s* ... 2Cor 12:10 *1415*
when we are weak, and ye are *s* ... 2Cor 13:9 *1415*
be *s* in the Lord, and in the power ... Eph 6:10 *1743*
God shall send them *s* delusion ... 2Th 2:11 *1753*
be *s* in the grace that is in ... 2Ti 2:1 *1743*
and supplications with *s* crying ... Heb 5:7 *2478*
need of milk, and not of *s* meat ... Heb 5:12 *4731*
But *s* meat belongeth to them that ... Heb 5:14 *4731*
we might have a *s* consolation ... Heb 6:18 *2478*
out of weakness were made *s* ... Heb 11:34 *1743*
you, young men, because ye are *s* ... 1Jn 2:14 *2478*
I saw a *s* angel proclaiming with ... Rev 5:2 *2478*
he cried mightily with a *s* voice ... Rev 18:2 *3173*
for *s* is the Lord God who judgeth ... Rev 18:8 *2478*

STRONGER {21}
shall be *s* than the other people ... Gen 25:23 553
whensoever the *s* cattle did ... Gen 30:41 7194
were Laban's, and the *s* Jacob's ... Gen 30:42 7194
for they are *s* than we ... Num 13:31 2389
And what is *s* than a lion ... Judg 14:18 5794
eagles, they were *s* than lions ... 2Sa 1:23 1396
but David waxed *s* and *s*, and ... 2Sa 3:1 2390
being *s* than she, forced her, and ... 2Sa 13:14 2388
therefore they were *s* than we ... 1Kin 20:23 2388
and surely we shall be *s* than they ... 1Kin 20:23 2388
and surely we shall be *s* than they ... 1Kin 20:25 2388
hands shall be *s* and *s* ... Job 17:9 555
made them *s* than their enemies ... Ps 105:24 6105
for they are *s* than I ... Ps 142:6 553
thou art *s* than I, and hast ... Jer 20:7 2388
hand of him that was *s* than he ... Jer 31:11 2388
But when a *s* than he shall come ... Lk 11:22 *2478*
the weakness of God is *s* than men ... 1Cor 1:25 *2478*
are we *s* than he ... 1Cor 10:22 *2478*

STRONGEST {1}
A lion which is *s* among beasts ... Prov 30:30 1368

STRONGLY {1}
the foundations thereof be *s* laid ... Ezr 6:3

STROVE {14}
because they *s* with him ... Gen 26:20 6229
another well, and *s* for that also ... Gen 26:21 7378
and for that they *s* not ... Gen 26:22 7378
two men of the Hebrews *s* together ... Ex 2:13 5327
a man of Israel *s* together in the ... Lev 24:10 5327
of Israel *s* with the LORD ... Num 20:13 7378
who *s* against Moses and against ... Num 26:9 5327
when they *s* against the LORD ... Num 26:9 5327
they two *s* together in the field ... 2Sa 14:6 5327
when he *s* with Aram-naharaim and ... Ps 60:*t* 5327
the heaven *s* upon the great sea ... Dan 7:2 1519
Jews therefore *s* among themselves ... Jn 6:52 *3164*
himself unto them as they *s* ... Acts 7:26 *3164*
the Pharisees' part arose, and *s* ... Acts 23:9 *1264*

STROWED {1}
s it upon the graves of them that ... 2Chr 34:4 2236

STRUCK {7}
he *s* it into the pan, or kettle ... 1Sa 2:14 5221
the LORD *s* the child that Uriah's ... 2Sa 12:15 5062
to the ground, and *s* him not again ... 2Sa 20:10 8138
and the LORD *s* him, and he died ... 2Chr 13:20 5062
s a servant of the high priest's ... Mt 26:51 *3960*
they *s* him on the face, and asked ... Lk 22:64 *5180*
of the officers which stood by *s* ... Jn 18:22 *1325,4475*

STRUGGLED {1}
the children *s* together within ... Gen 25:22 7533

STUBBLE {18}
to gather *s* instead of straw ... Ex 5:12 7179
wrath, which consumed them as *s* ... Ex 15:7 7179
and wilt thou pursue the dry *s* ... Job 13:25 7179
They are as *s* before the wind, and ... Job 21:18 8401
are turned with him into *s* ... Job 41:28 7179
Darts are counted as *s* ... Job 41:29 7179
as the *s* before the wind ... Ps 83:13 7179
as the fire devoureth the *s* ... Is 5:24 7179
chaff, ye shall bring forth *s* ... Is 33:11 7179
shall take them away as *s* ... Is 40:24 7179
sword, and as driven *s* to his bow ... Is 41:2 7179
Behold, they shall be as *s* ... Is 47:14 7179
will I scatter them as the *s* that ... Jer 13:24 7179
of fire that devoureth the *s* ... Joel 2:5 7179
flame, and the house of Esau for *s* ... Obad 18 7179
shall be devoured as *s* fully dry ... Nah 1:10 7179
all that do wickedly, shall be *s* ... Mal 4:1 7179
precious stones, wood, hay, *s* ... 1Cor 3:12 *2562*

STUBBORN {5}
If a man have a *s* and rebellious ... Deut 21:18 5637
of his city, This our son is *s* ... Deut 21:20 5637
own doings, nor from their *s* way ... Judg 2:19 7186
not be as their fathers, a *s* ... Ps 78:8 5637
(She is loud and *s* ... Prov 7:11 5637

STUBBORNNESS {2}
not unto the *s* of this people ... Deut 9:27 7190
s is as iniquity and idolatry ... 1Sa 15:23 6484

STUCK {3}
his spear *s* in the ground at his ... 1Sa 26:7 4600
I have *s* unto thy testimonies ... Ps 119:31 1692
and the forepart *s* fast, and ... Acts 27:41 *2043*

STUDIETH {2}
of the righteous *s* to answer ... Prov 15:28 1897
For their heart *s* destruction ... Prov 24:2 1897

STUDS {1}
borders of gold with *s* of silver ... Song 1:11 5351

STUDY {3}
much *s* is a weariness of the ... Eccl 12:12 3854
that ye *s* to be quiet, and to do ... 1Th 4:11 *5389*
S to shew thyself approved unto ... 2Ti 2:15 *4704*

STUFF {16}
thou hast searched all my *s* ... Gen 31:37 3627
thou found of all thy household *s* ... Gen 31:37 3627
Also regard not your *s* ... Gen 45:20 3627
his neighbour money or *s* to keep ... Ex 22:7 3627
For the *s* they had was sufficient ... Ex 36:7 4399
put it even among their own *s* ... Josh 7:11 3627
he hath hid himself among the *s* ... 1Sa 10:22 3627
and two hundred abode by the *s* ... 1Sa 25:13 3627
part be that tarrieth by the *s* ... 1Sa 30:24 3627
s of Tobiah out of the chamber ... Neh 13:8 3627
man, prepare thee *s* for removing ... Eze 12:3 3627
forth thy *s* by day in their sight ... Eze 12:4 3627
in their sight, as *s* for removing ... Eze 12:4 3627
I brought forth my *s* by day ... Eze 12:7 3627
as *s* for captivity, and in the ... Eze 12:7 3627
his *s* in the house, let him not ... Lk 17:31 *4632*

STUMBLE {19}
safely, and thy foot shall not *s* ... Prov 3:23 5062
thou runnest, thou shalt not *s* ... Prov 4:12 3782
they know not at what they *s* ... Prov 4:19 3782
shall be weary nor *s* among them ... Is 5:27 3782
And many among them shall *s* ... Is 8:15 3782
err in vision, they *s* in judgment ... Is 28:7 6328
we *s* at noonday as in the night ... Is 59:10 3782
that they should not *s* ... Is 63:13 3782
before your feet *s* upon the dark ... Jer 13:16 5062
they have caused them to *s* in ... Jer 18:15 3782
therefore my persecutors shall *s* ... Jer 20:11 3782
way, wherein they shall not *s* ... Jer 31:9 3782
they shall *s*, and fall toward the ... Jer 46:6 3782
And the most proud shall *s* ... Jer 50:32 3782
but he shall *s* and fall, and not be ... Dan 11:19 3782
they shall *s* in their walk ... Nah 2:5 3782
they *s* upon their corpses ... Nah 3:3 3782
have caused many to *s* at the law ... Mal 2:8 3782
even to them which *s* at the word ... 1Pet 2:8 *4350*

STUMBLED {6}
they that *s* are girded with ... 1Sa 2:4 3782
for the oxen *s* ... 1Chr 13:9 8058
me to eat up my flesh, they *s* ... Ps 27:2 3782
man hath *s* against the mighty ... Jer 46:12 3782
For they *s* at that stumblingstone ... Rom 9:32 *4350*
Have they *s* that they should fall ... Rom 11:11 *4417*

STUMBLETH {4}
not thine heart be glad when he *s* ... Prov 24:17 3782
he *s* not, because he seeth the ... Jn 11:9 *4350*
if a man walk in the night, he *s* ... Jn 11:10 *4350*
any thing whereby thy brother *s* ... Rom 14:21 *4350*

STUMBLING {3}
but for a stone of *s* and for a ... Is 8:14 5063
And a stone of *s*, and a rock of ... 1Pet 2:8
is none occasion of *s* in him ... 1Jn 2:10 *4625*

STUMBLINGBLOCK {12}
nor put a *s* before the blind, but ... Lev 19:14 4383
take up the *s* out of the way of ... Is 57:14 4383
I lay a *s* before him, he shall ... Eze 3:20 4383
it is the *s* of their iniquity ... Eze 7:19 4383
put the *s* of their iniquity ... Eze 14:3 4383
putteth the *s* of his iniquity ... Eze 14:4 4383
putteth the *s* of his iniquity ... Eze 14:7 4383
made a snare, and a trap, and a *s* ... Rom 11:9 *4625*
that no man put a *s* or an ... Rom 14:13 *4348*
crucified, unto the Jews a *s* ... 1Cor 1:23 *4625*
become a *s* to them that are weak ... 1Cor 8:9 *4348*
who taught Balac to cast a *s* ... Rev 2:14 *4625*

STUMBLINGBLOCKS {2}
I will lay *s* before this people ... Jer 6:21 4383
the sea, and the *s* with the wicked ... Zeph 1:3 4384

STUMBLINGSTONE {2}
For they stumbled at that *s* ... Rom 9:32 *3037,4348*
Behold, I lay in Sion a *s* ... Rom 9:33 *3037,4348*

STUMP {4}
only the *s* of Dagon was left to ... 1Sa 5:4
Nevertheless leave the *s* of his ... Dan 4:15 6136
yet leave the *s* of the roots ... Dan 4:23 6136
to leave the *s* of the tree roots ... Dan 4:26 6136

SUAH *(su'-ah)* {1} *Son of Zophah.*
S, and Harnepher, and Shual, and ... 1Chr 7:36 5477

SUBDUE {8}
and replenish the earth, and *s* it ... Gen 1:28 3533
Moreover I will *s* all thine ... 1Chr 17:10 3665
He shall *s* the people under us ... Ps 47:3 1696
holden, to *s* nations before him ... Is 45:1 7286
first, and he shall *s* three kings ... Dan 7:24 8214
he will *s* our iniquities ... Mic 7:19 3533
devour, and *s* with sling stones ... Zec 9:15 3533
even to *s* all things unto himself ... Phil 3:21 *5293*

SUBDUED {19}
the land be *s* before the LORD ... Num 32:22 3533
and the land shall be *s* before you ... Num 32:29 3533
war with thee, until it be *s* ... Deut 20:20 3381
And the land was *s* before them ... Josh 18:1 3533
So Moab was *s* that day under the ... Judg 3:30 3665
So God *s* on that day Jabin the ... Judg 4:23 3665
Thus was Midian *s* before the ... Judg 8:28 3665
s before the children of Israel ... Judg 11:33 3665
So the Philistines were *s* ... 1Sa 7:13 3665
smote the Philistines, and *s* them ... 2Sa 8:1 3665
of all nations which he *s* ... 2Sa 8:11 3533
against me hast thou *s* under me ... 2Sa 22:40 3766
s them, and took Gath and her towns ... 1Chr 18:1 3665
and they were *s* ... 1Chr 20:4 3665
the land is *s* before the LORD, and ... 1Chr 22:18 3533
thou hast *s* under me those that ... Ps 18:39 3766
should soon have *s* their enemies ... Ps 81:14 3665
all things shall be *s* unto him ... 1Cor 15:28 *5293*
Who through faith *s* kingdoms ... Heb 11:33 *2610*

SUBDUEDST {1}
land, and thou *s* before them the ... Neh 9:24 3665

SUBDUETH {3}
me, and *s* the people under me ... Ps 18:47 1696
who *s* my people under me ... Ps 144:2 7286
in pieces and *s* all things ... Dan 2:40 2827

SUBJECT {17}
to Nazareth, and was *s* unto them ... Lk 2:51 *5293*
even the devils are *s* unto us ... Lk 10:17 *5293*
that the spirits are *s* unto you ... Lk 10:20 *5293*
for it is not *s* to the law of God ... Rom 8:7 *5293*
the creature was made *s* to vanity ... Rom 8:20 *5293*
Let every soul be *s* unto the ... Rom 13:1 *5293*
Wherefore ye must needs be *s* ... Rom 13:5 *5293*
prophets are *s* to the prophets ... 1Cor 14:32 *5293*
be *s* unto him that put all things ... 1Cor 15:28 *5293*
as the church is *s* unto Christ ... Eph 5:24 *5293*
world, are ye *s* to ordinances ... Col 2:20 *1379*
in mind to be *s* to principalities ... Titus 3:1 *5293*
all their lifetime *s* to bondage ... Heb 2:15 *1777*
Elias was a man *s* to like ... Jas 5:17 *3663*
be *s* to your masters with all ... 1Pet 2:18 *5293*
and powers being made *s* unto him ... 1Pet 3:22 *5293*
all of you be *s* one to another ... 1Pet 5:5 *5293*

SUBJECTED {1}
him who hath *s* the same in hope ... Rom 8:20 *5293*

SUBJECTION {14}
brought into *s* under their hand ... Ps 106:42 3665
brought them into *s* for servants ... Jer 34:11 3533
to return, and brought them into *s* ... Jer 34:16 3533
under my body, and bring it into *s* ... 1Cor 9:27 *1396*
s into the gospel of Christ ... 2Cor 9:13 *5292*
To whom we gave place by *s* ... Gal 2:5 *5292*
woman learn in silence with all *s* ... 1Ti 2:11 *5292*
children in *s* with all gravity ... 1Ti 3:4 *5292*
he not put in *s* the world to come ... Heb 2:5 *5293*
all things in *s* under his feet ... Heb 2:8 *5293*
in that he put all in *s* under him ... Heb 2:8 *5293*
in *s* unto the Father of spirits ... Heb 12:9 *5293*
be in *s* to your own husbands ... 1Pet 3:1 *5293*
being in *s* unto their own ... 1Pet 3:5 *5293*

SUBMIT {12}
s thyself under her hands ... Gen 16:9 6031
Strangers shall *s* themselves unto ... 2Sa 22:45 3584
shall *s* themselves unto me ... Ps 18:44 3584
enemies *s* themselves unto thee ... Ps 66:3 3584
till every one *s* himself with ... Ps 68:30 7511
That ye *s* yourselves unto such ... 1Cor 16:16 *5293*
s yourselves unto your own ... Eph 5:22 *5293*
s yourselves unto your own ... Col 3:18 *5293*
rule over you, and *s* yourselves ... Heb 13:17 *5226*
S yourselves therefore to God ... Jas 4:7 *5293*
S yourselves to every ordinance ... 1Pet 2:13 *5293*
s yourselves unto the elder ... 1Pet 5:5 *5293*

SUBMITTED {3}
s themselves unto Solomon the ... 1Chr 29:24 5414,3027
should have *s* themselves unto him ... Ps 81:15 3584
have not *s* themselves unto the ... Rom 10:3 *5293*

SUBMITTING {1}
S yourselves one to another in ... Eph 5:21 *5293*

SUBORNED {1}
Then they *s* men, which said, We ... Acts 6:11 *5260*

SUBSCRIBE {2}
another shall *s* with his hand ... Is 44:5 3789
s evidences, and seal them, and ... Jer 32:44 3789

SUBSCRIBED {2}
I *s* the evidence, and sealed it, Jer 32:10 3789
that *s* the book of the purchase Jer 32:12 3789

SUBSTANCE {50}
every living *s* that I have made Gen 7:4 3351
every living *s* was destroyed Gen 7:23 3351
all their *s* that they had Gen 12:5 7399
for their *s* was great, so that Gen 13:6 7399
shall they come out with great *s* Gen 15:14 7399
Shall not their cattle and their *s* Gen 34:23 7075
and all his beasts, and all his *s* Gen 36:6 7075
all the *s* that was in their Deut 11:6 3351
Bless, LORD, his *s*, and accept the Deut 33:11 3428
for their cattle and for their *s* Josh 14:4 7075
of the *s* which was king David's 1Chr 27:31 7399
and the stewards over all the *s* 1Chr 28:1 7399
carried away all the *s* that was 2Chr 21:17 7399
of his *s* for the burnt offerings 2Chr 31:3 7399
for God had given him *s* very much 2Chr 32:29 7399
these were of the king's *s* 2Chr 35:7 7399
our little ones, and for all our *s* Ezr 8:21 7399
all his *s* should be forfeited, and Ezr 10:8 7399
His *s* also was seven thousand Job 1:3 4735
his *s* is increased in the land Job 1:10 4735
the robber swalloweth up their *s* Job 5:5 2428
Give a reward for me of your *s* Job 6:22 3581
neither shall his *s* continue Job 15:29 2428
according to his *s* shall the Job 20:18 2428
Whereas our *s* is not cut down, Job 22:20 7009
ride upon it, and dissolvest my *s* Job 30:22 7738
rest of their *s* to their babes Ps 17:14
his house, and ruler of all his *s* Ps 105:21 7075
My *s* was not hid from thee, when Ps 139:15 6108
Thine eyes did see my *s*, yet Ps 139:16 1564
We shall find all precious *s* Prov 1:13 1952
Honour the LORD with thy *s* Prov 3:9 1952
shall give all the *s* of his house Prov 6:31 1952
those that love me to inherit *s* Prov 8:21 3426
casteth away the *s* of the wicked Prov 10:3 1942
but the *s* of a diligent man is Prov 12:27 1952
and unjust gain increaseth his *s* Prov 28:8 1952
with harlots spendeth his *s* Prov 29:3 1952
all the *s* of his house for love Song 8:7 1952
whose *s* is in them, when they Is 6:13 4678
holy seed shall be the *s* thereof Is 6:13 4678
Thy *s* and thy treasures will I Jer 15:13 2428
in the field, I will give thy *s* Jer 17:3 2428
rich, I have found me out *s* Hos 12:8 202
s in the day of their calamity Obad 13 2428
their *s* unto the Lord of the Mic 4:13 2428
ministered unto him of their *s* Lk 8:3 *5224*
there wasted his *s* with riotous Lk 15:13 *3776*
heaven a better and an enduring *s* Heb 10:34 *5223*
Now faith is the *s* of things Heb 11:1 *5287*

SUBTIL {3}
Now the serpent was more *s* than Gen 3:1 6175
and Jonadab was a very *s* man 2Sa 13:3 2450
of an harlot, and *s* of heart Prov 7:10 5341

SUBTILLY {3}
is told me that he dealeth very *s* 1Sa 23:22 6191
to deal *s* with his servants Ps 105:25 5230
The same dealt *s* with our kindred Acts 7:19 *2686*

SUBTILTY {6}
he said, Thy brother came with *s* Gen 27:35 4820
But Jehu did it in *s*, to the 2Kin 10:19 6122
To give *s* to the simple, to the Prov 1:4 6195
that they might take Jesus by *s* Mt 26:4 *1388*
And said, O full of all *s* and all Acts 13:10 *1388*
beguiled Eve through his *s* 2Cor 11:3 *3834*

SUBURBS {116}
But the field of the *s* of their Lev 25:34 4054
give also unto the Levites *s* for Num 35:2 4054
the *s* of them shall be for their Num 35:3 4054
the *s* of the cities, which ye Num 35:4 4054
be to them the *s* of the cities Num 35:5 4054
them shall ye give with their *s* Num 35:7 4054
with their *s* for their cattle and Josh 14:4 4054
with the *s* thereof for our cattle Josh 21:2 4054
the LORD, these cities and their *s* Josh 21:3 4054
Levites these cities with their *s* Josh 21:8 4054
with the *s* thereof round about it Josh 21:11 4054
the priest Hebron with her *s* Josh 21:13 4054
and Libnah with her *s*, Josh 21:13 4054
And Jattir with her *s*, and Eshtemoa Josh 21:14 4054
and Eshtemoa with her *s* Josh 21:14 4054
And Holon with her *s*, and Debir Josh 21:15 4054
and Debir with her *s* Josh 21:15 4054
And Ain with her *s*, and Juttah with Josh 21:16 4054
and Juttah with her *s* Josh 21:16 4054
and Beth-shemesh with her *s* Josh 21:16 4054
of Benjamin, Gibeon with her *s* Josh 21:17 4054
Geba with her *s* Josh 21:17 4054
Anathoth with her *s*, and Almon Josh 21:18 4054
and Almon with her *s* Josh 21:18 4054
were thirteen cities with their *s* Josh 21:19 4054
with her *s* in mount Ephraim Josh 21:21 4054
and Gezer with her *s*, Josh 21:21 4054
And Kibzaim with her *s*, and Josh 21:22 4054
and Beth-horon with her *s* Josh 21:22 4054
tribe of Dan, Eltekeh with her *s* Josh 21:23 4054
Gibbethon with her *s* Josh 21:23 4054
Aijalon with her *s*, Gath-rimmon Josh 21:24 4054
Gath-rimmon with her *s* Josh 21:24 4054
of Manasseh, Tanach with her *s* Josh 21:25 4054
and Gath-rimmon with her *s* Josh 21:25 4054
their *s* for the families of the Josh 21:26 4054
gave Golan in Bashan with her *s* Josh 21:27 4054
and Beesh-terah with her *s* Josh 21:27 4054
of Issachar, Kishon with her *s* Josh 21:28 4054
Dabareh with her *s* Josh 21:28 4054
Jarmuth with her *s*, En-gannim Josh 21:29 4054
En-gannim with her *s* Josh 21:29 4054
tribe of Asher, Mishal with her *s* Josh 21:30 4054
Abdon with her *s* Josh 21:30 4054
Helkath with her *s*, and Rehob with Josh 21:31 4054
Rehob with her *s* Josh 21:31 4054
Kedesh in Galilee with her *s* Josh 21:32 4054
and Hammoth-dor with her *s* Josh 21:32 4054
and Kartan with her *s* Josh 21:32 4054
were thirteen cities with their *s* Josh 21:33 4054
of Zebulun, Jokneam with her *s* Josh 21:34 4054
and Kartah with her *s* Josh 21:34 4054
Dimnah with her *s*, Nahalal with Josh 21:35 4054
her *s*, Nahalal with her *s* Josh 21:35 4054
tribe of Reuben, Bezer with her *s* Josh 21:36
and Jahazah with her *s* Josh 21:36
Kedemoth with her *s*, and Mephaath Josh 21:37
and Mephaath with her *s* Josh 21:37
Gad, Ramoth in Gilead with her *s* Josh 21:38 4054
and Mahanaim with her *s*, Josh 21:38 4054
Heshbon with her *s*, Jazer with Josh 21:39 4054
Jazer with her *s* Josh 21:39 4054
and eight cities with their *s* Josh 21:41 4054
one with their *s* round about them Josh 21:42 4054
chamberlain, which was in the *s* 2Kin 23:11 6503
towns, and in all the *s* of Sharon 1Chr 5:16 4054
the *s* thereof round about it 1Chr 6:55 4054
of refuge, and Libnah with her *s* 1Chr 6:57 4054
Jattir, and Eshtemoa, with their *s* 1Chr 6:57 4054
And Hilen with her *s*, Debir with 1Chr 6:58 4054
Debir with her *s* 1Chr 6:58 4054
And Ashan with her *s*, and 1Chr 6:59 4054
and Beth-shemesh with her *s* 1Chr 6:59 4054
Geba with her *s* 1Chr 6:60 4054
and Alemeth with her *s* 1Chr 6:60 4054
and Anathoth with her *s* 1Chr 6:60 4054
Levites these cities with their *s* 1Chr 6:64 4054
in mount Ephraim with her *s* 1Chr 6:67 4054
they gave also Gezer with her *s* 1Chr 6:67 4054
And Jokmeam with her *s*, and 1Chr 6:68 4054
and Beth-horon with her *s* 1Chr 6:68 4054
And Aijalon with her *s*, and 1Chr 6:69 4054
and Gath-rimmon with her *s* 1Chr 6:69 4054
Aner with her *s*, and Bileam with 1Chr 6:70 4054
and Bileam with her *s* 1Chr 6:70 4054
Golan in Bashan with her *s* 1Chr 6:71 4054
and Ashtaroth with her *s* 1Chr 6:71 4054
Kedesh with her *s* 1Chr 6:72 4054
Daberath with her *s* 1Chr 6:72 4054
And Ramoth with her *s* 1Chr 6:73 4054
and Anem with her *s* 1Chr 6:73 4054
Mashal with her *s* 1Chr 6:74 4054
and Abdon with her *s* 1Chr 6:74 4054
And Hukok with her *s* 1Chr 6:75 4054
and Rehob with her *s* 1Chr 6:75 4054
Kedesh in Galilee with her *s* 1Chr 6:76 4054
and Hammon with her *s* 1Chr 6:76 4054
and Kirjathaim with her *s* 1Chr 6:76 4054
of Zebulun, Rimmon with her *s* 1Chr 6:77 4054
Tabor with her *s* 1Chr 6:77 4054
in the wilderness with her *s* 1Chr 6:78 4054
and Jahzah with her *s* 1Chr 6:78 4054
Kedemoth also with her *s*, and 1Chr 6:79 4054
and Mephaath with her *s* 1Chr 6:79 4054
Ramoth in Gilead with her *s* 1Chr 6:80 4054
and Mahanaim with her *s* 1Chr 6:80 4054
And Heshbon with her *s*, and Jazer 1Chr 6:81 4054
and Jazer with her *s* 1Chr 6:81 4054
which are in their cities and *s* 1Chr 13:2 4054
For the Levites left their *s* 2Chr 11:14 4054
fields of the *s* of their cities 2Chr 31:19 4054
The *s* shall shake at the sound of Eze 27:28 4054
round about for the *s* thereof Eze 45:2 4054
the city, for dwelling, and for *s* Eze 48:15 4054
the *s* of the city shall be toward Eze 48:17 4054

SUBVERT {2}
To *s* a man in his cause, the Lord Lam 3:36 5791
who *s* whole houses, teaching Titus 1:11 *396*

SUBVERTED {1}
Knowing that he that is such is *s* Titus 3:11 *1612*

SUBVERTING {2}
s your souls, saying, Ye must be Acts 15:24 *384*
but to the *s* of the hearers 2Ti 2:14 *2692*

SUCATHITES See SUCHATHITES.

SUCCEED {1}
which she beareth shall *s* in the Deut 25:6 6965

SUCCEEDED {3}
but the children of Esau *s* them Deut 2:12 3423
and they *s* them, and dwelt in their Deut 2:21 3423
and they *s* them, and dwelt in their Deut 2:22 3423

SUCCEEDEST {2}
to possess them, and thou *s* them Deut 12:29 3423
God giveth thee, and thou *s* them Deut 19:1 3423

SUCCESS {1}
and then thou shalt have good *s* Josh 1:8 7919

SUCCOTH *(suc'-coth)* {18}
1. A place east of the Jordan.
And Jacob journeyed to *S*, and built Gen 33:17 5523
the name of the place is called *S* Gen 33:17 5523
2. An Israelite encampment in the wilderness.
journeyed from Rameses to *S* Ex 12:37 5523
And they took their journey from *S* Ex 13:20 5523
from Rameses, and pitched in *S* Num 33:5 5523
And they departed from *S*, and Num 33:6 5523
3. A place in Gad.
Beth-aram, and Beth-nimrah, and *S* Josh 13:27 5523
And he said unto the men of *S* Judg 8:5 5523
And the princes of *S* said, Are the Judg 8:6 5523
as the men of *S* had answered him Judg 8:8 5523
a young man of the men of *S* Judg 8:14 5523
unto him the princes of *S* Judg 8:14 5523
And he came unto the men of *S* Judg 8:15 5523
with them he taught the men of *S* Judg 8:16 5523
4. A city in Ephraim.
in the clay ground between *S* 1Kin 7:46 5523
in the clay ground between *S* 2Chr 4:17 5523
and mete out the valley of *S* Ps 60:6 5523
and mete out the valley of *S* Ps 108:7 5523

SUCCOTH-BENOTH *(suc'-coth-be'-noth)* {1} *A Babylonian god.*
And the men of Babylon made *S* 2Kin 17:30 5524

SUCCOUR {3}
came to *s* Hadadezer king of Zobah 2Sa 8:5 5826
that thou *s* us out of the city 2Sa 18:3 5826
he is able to *s* them that are Heb 2:18 *997*

SUCCOURED {2}
Abishai the son of Zeruiah *s* him 2Sa 21:17 5826
day of salvation have I *s* thee 2Cor 6:2 *997*

SUCCOURER {1}
for she hath been a *s* of many Rom 16:2 *4368*

SUCH See APPENDIX.

SUCHATHITES *(soo'-kath-ites)* {1} *A family of scribes.*
the Shimeathites, and *S* 1Chr 2:55 7756

SUCK {19}
should have given children *s* Gen 21:7 3243
he made him to *s* honey out of the Deut 32:13 3243
for they shall *s* of the abundance Deut 33:19 3243
gave her son *s* until she weaned 1Sa 1:23 3243
in the morning to give my child *s* 1Kin 3:21 3243
why the breasts that I should *s* Job 3:12 3243
He shall *s* the poison of asps Job 20:16 3243
Her young ones also *s* up blood Job 39:30 5966
Thou shalt also *s* the milk of the Is 60:16 3243
shalt *s* the breast of kings Is 60:16 3243
That ye may *s*, and be satisfied Is 66:11 3243
then shall ye *s*, ye shall be Is 66:12 3243
they give *s* to their young ones Lam 4:3 3243
s it out, and thou shalt break the Eze 23:34 4680
and those that *s* the breasts Joel 2:16 3243
to them that give *s* in those days Mt 24:19 *2337*
to them that give *s* in those days Mk 13:17 *2337*
child, and to them that give *s* Lk 21:23 *2337*
and the paps which never gave *s* Lk 23:29 *2337*

SUCKED {2}
that *s* the breasts of my mother Song 8:1 3243
and the paps which thou hast *s* Lk 11:27 *2337*

SUCKING {5}
father beareth the *s* child Num 11:12 3243
And Samuel took a *s* lamb, and 1Sa 7:9 2461
the *s* child shall play on the Is 11:8 3243
Can a woman forget her *s* child Is 49:15 5764
The tongue of the *s* child Lam 4:4 3243

SUCKLING {3}
the *s* also with the man of gray Deut 32:25 3243
both man and woman, infant and *s* 1Sa 15:3 3243
man and woman, child and *s* Jer 44:7 3243

SUCKLINGS {4}
both men and women, children and *s* 1Sa 22:19 3243
s hast thou ordained strength Ps 8:2 3243
the *s* swoon in the streets of the Lam 2:11 3243
s thou hast perfected praise Mt 21:16 *2337*

SUDDEN {3}
thee, and *s* fear troubleth thee Job 22:10 6597
Be not afraid of *s* fear, neither Prov 3:25 6597
then *s* destruction cometh upon 1Th 5:3 *160*

SUDDENLY {41}
And if any man die very *s* by him Num 6:9 6597
And the LORD spake *s* unto Moses Num 12:4 6597
if he thrust him *s* without enmity Num 35:22 6621
against you, and destroy thee *s* Deut 7:4 4118
Joshua therefore came unto them *s* Josh 10:9 6597
them by the waters of Merom *s* Josh 11:7 6597
to depart, lest he overtake us *s* 2Sa 15:14 4116
for the thing was done *s* 2Chr 29:36 6597
but *s* I cursed his habitation Job 5:3 6597
If the scourge slay *s*, he will Job 9:23 6597
let them return and be ashamed *s* Ps 6:10 7281
s do they shoot at him, and fear Ps 64:4 6597
s shall they be wounded Ps 64:7 6597
shall his calamity come *s* Prov 6:15 6597
s shall he be broken without Prov 6:15 6621
For their calamity shall rise *s* Prov 24:22 6597
shall *s* be destroyed, and that Prov 29:1 6621
time, when it falleth *s* upon them Eccl 9:12 6597
yea, it shall be at an instant *s* Is 29:5 6597
breaking cometh *s* at an instant Is 30:13 6597
desolation shall come upon thee *s* Is 47:11 6597
I did them *s*, and they came to Is 48:3 6597
s are my tents spoiled, and my Jer 4:20 6597
the spoiler shall *s* come upon us Jer 6:26 6597
have caused him to fall upon it *s* Jer 15:8 6597
shalt bring a troop *s* upon them Jer 18:22 6597
but I will *s* make him run away Jer 49:19 7280

make them *s* run away from her ... Jer 50:44 7280
Babylon is *s* fallen and destroyed ... Jer 51:8 6597
rise up *s* that shall bite thee ... Hab 2:7 6621
shall *s* come to his temple, even ... Mal 3:1 6597
And *s*, when they had looked round ... Mk 9:8 *1819*
Lest coming *s* he find you ... Mk 13:36 *1810*
s there was with the angel a ... Lk 2:13 *1810*
taketh him, and he *s* crieth out ... Lk 9:39 *1810*
s there came a sound from heaven ... Acts 2:2 *869*
s there shined round about him a ... Acts 9:3 *1810*
s there was a great earthquake, ... Acts 16:26 *869*
s there shone from heaven a great ... Acts 22:6 *1810*
swollen, or fallen down dead *s* ... Acts 28:6 *869*
Lay hands *s* on no man, neither be ... 1Ti 5:22 *5030*

SUE {1}
if any man will *s* thee at the law ... Mt 5:40 *2919*

SUFFER {97}
will not *s* the destroyer to come ... Ex 12:23 5414
Thou shalt not *s* a witch to live ... Ex 22:18
neither shalt thou *s* the salt of ... Lev 2:13
neighbour, and not *s* sin upon him ... Lev 19:17 5375
Or *s* them to bear the iniquity of ... Lev 22:16 5375
Sihon would not *s* Israel to pass ... Num 21:23 5414
s them not to enter into their ... Josh 10:19 5414
for they would not *s* them to come ... Judg 1:34 5414
father would not *s* him to go in ... Judg 15:1 5414
S me that I may feel the pillars ... Judg 16:26 3240
that thou wouldest not *s* the ... 2Sa 14:11
that he might not *s* any to go out ... 1Kin 15:17 5414
for the king's profit to *s* them ... Est 3:8 3240
He will not *s* me to take my ... Job 9:18 5414
S me that I may speak ... Job 21:3 5375
their winepresses, and *s* thirst ... Job 24:11
S me a little, and I will shew ... Job 36:2 3803
which I *s* of them that hate me ... Ps 9:13
neither wilt thou *s* thine Holy ... Ps 16:10 5414
young lions do lack, and *s* hunger ... Ps 34:10
he shall never *s* the righteous to ... Ps 55:22 5414
while I *s* thy terrors I am ... Ps 88:15 5375
nor *s* my faithfulness to fail ... Ps 89:33
and a proud heart will not I *s* ... Ps 101:5 3201
He will not *s* thy foot to be ... Ps 121:3 5414
The LORD will not *s* the soul of ... Prov 10:3
and an idle soul shall *s* hunger ... Prov 19:15
of great wrath shall *s* punishment ... Prov 19:19 5375
S not thy mouth to cause thy ... Eccl 5:6 5414
the rich will not *s* him to sleep ... Eccl 5:12 3240
nor *s* their locks to grow long ... Eze 44:20
said unto him, *S* it to be so now ... Mt 3:15 *863*
s me first to go and bury my ... Mt 8:21 *2010*
s us to go away into the herd of ... Mt 8:31 *2010*
s many things of the elders and ... Mt 16:21 *3958*
also the Son of man *s* of them ... Mt 17:12 *3958*
how long shall I *s* you ... Mt 17:17 *430*
S little children, and forbid them ... Mt 19:14 *863*
neither *s* ye them that are ... Mt 23:13 *863*
ye *s* him no more to do ought for ... Mk 7:12 *863*
the Son of man must *s* many things ... Mk 8:31 *3958*
man, that he must *s* many things ... Mk 9:12 *3958*
how long shall I *s* you ... Mk 9:19 *430*
S the little children to come ... Mk 10:14 *863*
would not *s* that any man should ... Mk 11:16 *863*
would *s* them to enter into them ... Lk 8:32 *2010*
The Son of man must *s* many things ... Lk 9:22 *3958*
shall I be with you, and *s* you ... Lk 9:41 *430*
s me first to go and bury my ... Lk 9:59 *2010*
But first must he *s* many things ... Lk 17:25 *3958*
S little children to come unto me ... Lk 18:16 *863*
this passover with you before I *s* ... Lk 22:15 *3958*
answered and said, *S* ye thus far ... Lk 22:51 *1439*
and thus it behoved Christ to *s* ... Lk 24:46 *3958*
neither wilt thou *s* thine Holy ... Acts 2:27 *1325*
prophets, that Christ should *s* ... Acts 3:18 *3958*
worthy to *s* shame for his name ... Acts 5:41 *818*
And seeing one of them *s* wrong ... Acts 7:24
he must *s* for my name's sake ... Acts 9:16 *3958*
Thou shalt not *s* thine Holy One ... Acts 13:35 *1325*
s me to speak unto the people ... Acts 21:39 *2010*
That Christ should *s*, and that he ... Acts 26:23 *3805*
if so be that we *s* with him ... Rom 8:17 *4841*
shall be burned, he shall *s* loss ... 1Cor 3:15 *2210*
being persecuted, we *s* it ... 1Cor 4:12 *430*
why do ye not rather *s* yourselves ... 1Cor 6:7
but *s* all things, lest we should ... 1Cor 9:12 *4722*
who will not *s* you to be tempted ... 1Cor 10:13 *1439*
And whether one member *s*, all the ... 1Cor 12:26 *3958*
s, all the members *s* with it ... 1Cor 12:26 *4841*
same sufferings which we also *s* ... 2Cor 1:6 *3958*
For ye *s* fools gladly, seeing ye ... 2Cor 11:19 *430*
For ye *s*, if a man bring you into ... 2Cor 11:20 *430*
why do I yet *s* persecution ... Gal 5:11 *1377*
only lest they should *s* ... Gal 6:12 *1377*
but also to *s* for his sake ... Phil 1:29 *3958*
both to abound and to *s* need ... Phil 4:12 *5302*
that we should *s* tribulation ... 1Th 3:4
of God, for which ye also *s* ... 2Th 1:5
But I *s* not a woman to teach, nor ... 1Ti 2:12 *2010*
s reproach, because we trust in ... 1Ti 4:10
which cause I also *s* these things ... 2Ti 1:12 *3958*
Wherein I *s* trouble, as an evil ... 2Ti 2:9 *2553*
If we *s*, we shall also reign with ... 2Ti 2:12 *5278*
Christ Jesus shall *s* persecution ... 2Ti 3:12 *1377*
Choosing rather to *s* affliction ... Heb 11:25 *4778*
and them which *s* adversity ... Heb 13:3 *2558*
s the word of exhortation ... Heb 13:22 *430*
s for it, ye take it patiently, ... 1Pet 2:20 *3958*
if ye *s* for righteousness' sake, ... 1Pet 3:14 *3958*
that ye *s* for well doing, than ... 1Pet 3:17 *3958*
let none of you *s* as a murderer ... 1Pet 4:15 *3958*
Yet if any man *s* as a Christian ... 1Pet 4:16
Wherefore let them that *s* ... 1Pet 4:19 *3958*
those things which thou shalt *s* ... Rev 2:10 *3958*
shall not *s* their dead bodies to ... Rev 11:9 *863*

SUFFERED {50}
therefore *s* I thee not to touch ... Gen 20:6 5414
but God *s* him not to hurt me ... Gen 31:7 5414
hast not *s* me to kiss my sons and ... Gen 31:28 5203
s thee to hunger, and fed thee ... Deut 8:3
thy God hath not *s* thee so to do ... Deut 18:14 5414
Moab, and *s* not a man to pass over ... Judg 3:28 5414
s them not to rise against Saul ... 1Sa 24:7 5414
s neither the birds of the air to ... 2Sa 21:10 5414
He *s* no man to do them wrong ... 1Chr 16:21 3240
(Neither have I *s* my mouth to sin ... Job 31:30 5414
He *s* no man to do them wrong ... Ps 105:14 3240
that for thy sake I have *s* rebuke ... Jer 15:15 5375
Then he *s* him ... Mt 3:15 *863*
s you to put away your wives ... Mt 19:8 *2010*
would not have *s* his house to be ... Mt 24:43 *1439*
for I have *s* many things this day ... Mt 27:19 *3958*
s not the devils to speak, ... Mk 1:34 *863*
Howbeit Jesus *s* him not, but ... Mk 5:19 *863*
had *s* many things of many ... Mk 5:26 *3958*
he *s* no man to follow him, save ... Mk 5:37 *863*
Moses *s* to write a bill of ... Mk 10:4 *2010*
he rebuking them *s* them not to ... Lk 4:41 *1439*
And he *s* them ... Lk 8:32 *2010*
he *s* no man to go in, save Peter, ... Lk 8:51 *863*
not have *s* his house to be broken ... Lk 12:39 *863*
because they *s* such things ... Lk 13:2 *3958*
not Christ to have *s* these things ... Lk 24:26 *3958*
years *s* he their manners in the ... Acts 13:18 *5159*
Who in times past *s* all nations ... Acts 14:16 *1439*
but the Spirit *s* them not ... Acts 16:7 *1439*
that Christ must needs have *s* ... Acts 17:3 *3958*
people, the disciples *s* him not ... Acts 19:30 *1439*
but Paul was *s* to dwell by ... Acts 28:16 *2010*
nor for his cause that *s* wrong ... 2Cor 7:12
thrice I *s* shipwreck, a night and ... 2Cor 11:25
Have ye *s* so many things in vain ... Gal 3:4 *3958*
for whom I have *s* the loss of all ... Phil 3:8 *2210*
even after that we had *s* before ... 1Th 2:2 *4310*
for ye also have *s* like things of ... 1Th 2:14 *3958*
he himself hath *s* being tempted ... Heb 2:18 *3958*
by the things which he *s* ... Heb 5:8 *3958*
because they were not *s* to ... Heb 7:23 *2967*
s since the foundation of the ... Heb 9:26 *3958*
his own blood, *s* without the gate ... Heb 13:12 *3958*
because Christ also *s* for us ... 1Pet 2:21 *3958*
when he *s*, he threatened not ... 1Pet 2:23 *3958*
Christ also hath once *s* for sins ... 1Pet 3:18 *3958*
Christ hath *s* for us in the flesh ... 1Pet 4:1 *3958*
for he that hath *s* in the flesh ... 1Pet 4:1 *3958*
after that ye have *s* a while ... 1Pet 5:10 *3958*

SUFFEREST {1}
because thou *s* that woman Jezebel ... Rev 2:20 *1439*

SUFFERETH {5}
s not our feet to be moved ... Ps 66:9 5414
s not their cattle to decrease ... Ps 107:38
the kingdom of heaven *s* violence ... Mt 11:12 *971*
sea, yet vengeance *s* not to live ... Acts 28:4 *1439*
Charity *s* long, and is kind ... 1Cor 13:4 *3114*

SUFFERING {5}
against Cnidus, the wind not *s* us ... Acts 27:7 *4330*
the angels for the *s* of death ... Heb 2:9 *3804*
for an example of *s* affliction ... Jas 5:10 *2552*
God endure grief, *s* wrongfully ... 1Pet 2:19 *3958*
s the vengeance of eternal fire ... Jude 7 *5254*

SUFFERINGS {10}
For I reckon that the *s* of this ... Rom 8:18 *3804*
For as the *s* of Christ abound in ... 2Cor 1:5 *3804*
the same *s* which we also suffer ... 2Cor 1:6 *3804*
that as ye are partakers of the *s* ... 2Cor 1:7 *3804*
and the fellowship of his *s* ... Phil 3:10 *3804*
Who now rejoice in my *s* for you ... Col 1:24 *3804*
their salvation perfect through *s* ... Heb 2:10 *3804*
beforehand the *s* of Christ ... 1Pet 1:11 *3804*
as ye are partakers of Christ's *s* ... 1Pet 4:13 *3804*
and a witness of the *s* of Christ ... 1Pet 5:1 *3804*

SUFFICE {7}
be slain for them, to *s* them ... Num 11:22 4672
together for them, to *s* them ... Num 11:22 4672
LORD said unto me, Let it *s* thee ... Deut 3:26 7227
if the dust of Samaria shall *s* ... 1Kin 20:10 5606
Israel, let it *s* you of all your ... Eze 44:6 7227
Let it *s* you, O princes of Israel ... Eze 45:9 7227
the time past of our life may *s* ... 1Pet 4:3 *713*

SUFFICED {3}
and yet so they *s* them not ... Judg 21:14 4672
corn, and she did eat, and was *s* ... Ruth 2:14 7646
she had reserved after she was *s* ... Ruth 2:18 7648

SUFFICETH {1}
shew us the Father, and it *s* us ... Jn 14:8 *714*

SUFFICIENCY {3}
In the fulness of his *s* he shall ... Job 20:22 5607
but our *s* is of God ... 2Cor 3:5 *2426*
always having all *s* in all things ... 2Cor 9:8 *841*

SUFFICIENT {13}
For the stuff they had was *s* for ... Ex 36:7 1767
surely lend him *s* for his need ... Deut 15:8 1767
let his hands be *s* for him ... Deut 33:7 7227
eat so much as is *s* for thee ... Prov 25:16 1767
And Lebanon is not *s* to burn ... Is 40:16 1767
thereof *s* for a burnt offering ... Is 40:16 1767
S unto the day is the evil ... Mt 6:34 *713*
whether he have *s* to finish it ... Lk 14:28
of bread is not *s* for them ... Jn 6:7 *714*
S to such a man is this ... 2Cor 2:6 *2425*
who is *s* for these things ... 2Cor 2:16 *2425*
Not that we are *s* of ourselves to ... 2Cor 3:5 *2425*
unto me, My grace is *s* for thee ... 2Cor 12:9 *714*

SUFFICIENTLY {2}
had not sanctified themselves *s* ... 2Chr 30:3 4078
dwell before the LORD, to eat *s* ... Is 23:18 7654

SUIT {3}
a *s* of apparel, and thy victuals ... Judg 17:10 6187
any *s* or cause might come unto me ... 2Sa 15:4 7379
yea, many shall make *s* unto thee ... Job 11:19 2470

SUITS {1}
The changeable *s* of apparel ... Is 3:22

SUKKIIMS *(suk'-ke-ims)* {1} *An Egyptian tribe.*
the Lubim, the *S*, and the ... 2Chr 12:3 5525

SUM {21}
there be laid on him a *s* of money ... Ex 21:30 3724
When thou takest the *s* of the ... Ex 30:12 7218
This is the *s* of the tabernacle, ... Ex 38:21 6485
Take ye the *s* of all the ... Num 1:2 7218
neither take the *s* of them among ... Num 1:49 7218
Take the *s* of the sons of Kohath ... Num 4:2 7218
Take also the *s* of the sons of ... Num 4:22 7218
Take the *s* of all the ... Num 26:2 7218
Take the *s* of the people, from ... Num 26:4
Take the *s* of the prey that was ... Num 31:26 7218
the *s* of the men of war which are ... Num 31:49 7218
Joab gave up the *s* of the number ... 2Sa 24:9 4557
that he may *s* the silver which is ... 2Kin 22:4 8552
Joab gave the *s* of the number of ... 1Chr 21:5 4557
of the *s* of the money that Haman ... Est 4:7 6575
How great is the *s* of them ... Ps 139:17 7218
Thou sealest up the *s*, full of ... Eze 28:12 8508
told the *s* of the matters ... Dan 7:1 7217
that Abraham bought for a *s* of ... Acts 7:16 *5092*
With a great *s* obtained I this ... Acts 22:28 *2774*
we have spoken this is the *s* ... Heb 8:1 *2774*

SUMMER {27}
and harvest, and cold and heat, and *s* ... Gen 8:22 7019
and he was sitting in a *s* parlour ... Judg 3:20 4747
his feet in his *s* chamber ... Judg 3:24 4747
and an hundred of *s* fruits ... 2Sa 16:1 7019
s fruit for the young men to eat ... 2Sa 16:2 7019
is turned into the drought of *s* ... Ps 32:4 7019
thou hast made *s* and winter ... Ps 74:17 7019
Provideth her meat in the *s* ... Prov 6:8 7019
that gathereth in *s* is a wise son ... Prov 10:5 7019
As snow in *s*, and as rain in ... Prov 26:1 7019
they prepare their meat in the *s* ... Prov 30:25 7019
for the shouting for thy *s* fruits ... Is 16:9 7019
and the fowls shall *s* upon them ... Is 18:6 6972
as the hasty fruit before the *s* ... Is 28:4 7019
the *s* is ended, and we are not ... Jer 8:20 7019
s fruits, and oil, and put them in ... Jer 40:10 7019
wine and *s* fruits very much ... Jer 40:12 7019
is fallen upon thy *s* fruits ... Jer 48:32 7019
chaff of the *s* threshingfloors ... Dan 2:35 7007
the winter house with the *s* house ... Amos 3:15 7019
and behold a basket of *s* fruit ... Amos 8:1 7019
And I said, A basket of *s* fruit ... Amos 8:2 7019
they have gathered the *s* fruits ... Mic 7:1 7019
in *s* and in winter shall it be ... Zec 14:8 7019
leaves, ye know that *s* is nigh ... Mt 24:32 *2330*
leaves, ye know that *s* is near ... Mk 13:28 *2330*
selves that *s* is now nigh at hand ... Lk 21:30 *2330*

SUMPTUOUSLY {1}
fine linen, and fared *s* every day ... Lk 16:19 *2983*

SUN {160}
when the *s* was going down, a deep ... Gen 15:12 8121
when the *s* went down, and it was ... Gen 15:17 8121
The *s* was risen upon the earth ... Gen 19:23 8121
all night, because the *s* was set ... Gen 28:11 8121
over Penuel the *s* rose upon him ... Gen 32:31 8121
and, behold, the *s* and the moon and ... Gen 37:9 8121
when the *s* waxed hot, it melted ... Ex 16:21 8121
until the going down of the *s* ... Ex 17:12 8121
If the *s* be risen upon him, there ... Ex 22:3 8121
unto him by that the *s* goeth down ... Ex 22:26 8121
And when the *s* is down, he shall ... Lev 22:7 8121
s shall they of the standard of ... Num 2:3
up before the LORD against the *s* ... Num 25:4 8121
heaven, and when thou seest the *s* ... Deut 4:19 8121
by the way where the *s* goeth down ... Deut 11:30 8121
even, at the going down of the *s* ... Deut 16:6 8121
and worshipped them, either the *s* ... Deut 17:3 8121
and when the *s* is down, he shall ... Deut 23:11 8121
again when the *s* goeth down ... Deut 24:13 8121
shall the *s* go down upon it ... Deut 24:15 8121
fruits brought forth by the *s* ... Deut 33:14 8121
toward the going down of the *s* ... Josh 1:4 8121
and as soon as the *s* was down ... Josh 8:29 8121
he said in the sight of Israel, *S* ... Josh 10:12 8121
the *s* stood still, and the moon ... Josh 10:13 8121
So the *s* stood still in the midst ... Josh 10:13 8121
time of the going down of the *s* ... Josh 10:27 8121
Jordan toward the rising of the *s* ... Josh 12:1 8121
the *s* when he goeth forth in his ... Judg 5:31 8121
from battle before the *s* was up ... Judg 8:13 2775
morning, as soon as the *s* is up ... Judg 9:33 8121

S

day before the *s* went down .... Judg 14:18 2775
the *s* went down upon them when .... Judg 19:14 8121
morrow, by that time the *s* be hot 1Sa 11:9 8121
the *s* went down when they were 2Sa 2:24 8121
or ought else, till the *s* be down 2Sa 3:35 8121
thy wives in the sight of this *s* 2Sa 12:11 8121
all Israel, and before the *s* 2Sa 12:12 8121
of the morning, when the *s* riseth 2Sa 23:4 8121
about the going down of the *s* 1Kin 22:36 8121
the *s* shone upon the water, and 2Kin 3:22 8121
incense unto Baal, to the *s* 2Kin 23:5 8121
kings of Judah had given to the *s* 2Kin 23:11 8121
the chariots of the *s* with fire 2Kin 23:11 8121
time of the *s* going down he died 2Chr 18:34 8121
be opened until the *s* be hot .... Neh 7:3 8121
He is green before the *s*, and his .... Job 8:16 8121
Which commandeth the *s*, and it .... Job 9:7 2775
I went mourning without the *s* .... Job 30:28 2535
If I beheld the *s* when it shined .... Job 31:26 216
he set a tabernacle for the *s* .... Ps 19:4 8121
the *s* unto the going down thereof .... Ps 50:1 8121
that they may not see the *s* .... Ps 58:8 8121
shall fear thee as long as the *s* .... Ps 72:5 8121
be continued as long as the *s* .... Ps 72:17 8121
hast prepared the light and the *s* .... Ps 74:16 8121
For the LORD God is a *s* and shield .... Ps 84:11 8121
and his throne as the *s* before me .... Ps 89:36 8121
the *s* knoweth his going down .... Ps 104:19 8121
The *s* ariseth, they gather .... Ps 104:22 8121
From the rising of the *s* unto the .... Ps 113:3 8121
The *s* shall not smite thee by day .... Ps 121:6 8121
The *s* to rule by day .... Ps 136:8 8121
Praise ye him, *s* and moon .... Ps 148:3 8121
which he taketh under the *s* .... Eccl 1:3 8121
The *s* also ariseth .... Eccl 1:5 8121
the *s* goeth down, and hasteth to .... Eccl 1:5 8121
there is no new thing under the *s* .... Eccl 1:9 8121
works that are done under the *s* .... Eccl 1:14 8121
there was no profit under the *s* .... Eccl 2:11 8121
under the *s* is grievous unto me .... Eccl 2:17 8121
which I had taken under the *s* .... Eccl 2:18 8121
shewed myself wise under the *s* .... Eccl 2:19 8121
labour which I took under the *s* .... Eccl 2:20 8121
he hath laboured under the *s* .... Eccl 2:22 8121
under the *s* the place of judgment .... Eccl 3:16 8121
that are done under the *s* .... Eccl 4:1 8121
work that is done under the *s* .... Eccl 4:3 8121
and I saw vanity under the *s* .... Eccl 4:7 8121
the living which walk under the *s* .... Eccl 4:15 8121
which I have seen under the *s* .... Eccl 5:13 8121
the *s* all the days of his life .... Eccl 5:18 8121
which I have seen under the *s* .... Eccl 6:1 8121
Moreover he hath not seen the *s* .... Eccl 6:5 8121
shall be after him under the *s* .... Eccl 6:12 8121
is profit to them that see the *s* .... Eccl 7:11 8121
work that is done under the *s* .... Eccl 8:9 8121
hath no better thing under the *s* .... Eccl 8:15 8121
which God giveth him under the *s* .... Eccl 8:15 8121
the work that is done under the *s* .... Eccl 8:17 8121
things that are done under the *s* .... Eccl 9:3 8121
thing that is done under the *s* .... Eccl 9:6 8121
he hath given thee under the *s* .... Eccl 9:9 8121
which thou takest under the *s* .... Eccl 9:9 8121
I returned, and saw under the *s* .... Eccl 9:11 8121
have I seen also under the *s* .... Eccl 9:13 8121
which I have seen under the *s* .... Eccl 10:5 8121
is for the eyes to behold the *s* .... Eccl 11:7 8121
While the *s*, or the light, or the .... Eccl 12:2 8121
because the *s* hath looked upon me .... Song 1:6 8121
fair as the moon, clear as the *s* .... Song 6:10 2535
the *s* shall be darkened in his .... Is 13:10 8121
the *s* ashamed, when the LORD of .... Is 24:23 2535
shall be as the light of the *s* .... Is 30:26 2535
the light of the *s* shall be .... Is 30:26 8121
gone down in the *s* dial of Ahaz .... Is 38:8 8121
So the *s* returned ten degrees, by .... Is 38:8 8121
from the rising of the *s* shall he .... Is 41:25 8121
may know from the rising of the *s* .... Is 45:6 8121
shall the heat nor *s* smite them .... Is 49:10 8121
glory from the rising of the *s* .... Is 59:19 8121
The *s* shall be no more thy light .... Is 60:19 8121
Thy *s* shall no more go down .... Is 60:20 8121
shall spread them before the *s* .... Jer 8:2 8121
her *s* is gone down while it was .... Jer 15:9 8121
which giveth the *s* for a light by .... Jer 31:35 8121
worshipped the *s* toward the east .... Eze 8:16 8121
I will cover the *s* with a cloud .... Eze 32:7 8121
down of the *s* to deliver him .... Dan 6:14 8122
the *s* and the moon shall be dark, ... Joel 2:10 8121
The *s* shall be turned into .... Joel 2:31 8121
The *s* and the moon shall be .... Joel 3:15 8121
cause the *s* to go down at noon .... Amos 8:9 8121
when the *s* did arise, that God .... Jonah 4:8 8121
the *s* beat upon the head of Jonah .... Jonah 4:8 8121
the *s* shall go down over the .... Mic 3:6 8121
but when the *s* ariseth they flee .... Nah 3:17 8121
The *s* and moon stood still in .... Hab 3:11 8121
For from the rising of the *s* even .... Mal 1:11 8121
the *S* of righteousness arise with .... Mal 4:2 8121
for he maketh his *s* to rise on .... Mt 5:45 *2246*
And when the *s* was up, they were .... Mt 13:6 *2246*
righteous shine forth as the *s* in .... Mt 13:43 *2246*
and his face did shine as the *s* .... Mt 17:2 *2246*
days shall the *s* be darkened .... Mt 24:29 *2246*
And at even, when the *s* did set .... Mk 1:32 *2246*
But when the *s* was up, it was .... Mk 4:6 *2246*
the *s* shall be darkened, and the .... Mk 13:24 *2246*
sepulchre at the rising of the *s* .... Mk 16:2 *2246*
Now when the *s* was setting .... Lk 4:40 *2246*
And there shall be signs in the *s* .... Lk 21:25 *2246*
the *s* was darkened, and the veil .... Lk 23:45 *2246*
The *s* shall be turned into .... Acts 2:20 *2246*
not seeing the *s* for a season .... Acts 13:11 *2246*
above the brightness of the *s* .... Acts 26:13 *2246*
when neither *s* nor stars in many .... Acts 27:20 *2246*
There is one glory of the *s* 1Cor 15:41 *2246*
let not the *s* go down upon your .... Eph 4:26 *2246*
For the *s* is no sooner risen with .... Jas 1:11 *2246*
as the *s* shineth in his strength .... Rev 1:16 *2246*
the *s* became black as sackcloth .... Rev 6:12 *2246*
neither shall the *s* light on them .... Rev 7:16 *2246*
third part of the *s* was smitten .... Rev 8:12 *2246*
and the *s* and the air were darkened .... Rev 9:2 *2246*
and his face was as it were the *s* .... Rev 10:1 *2246*
a woman clothed with the *s* .... Rev 12:1 *2246*
poured out his vial upon the *s* .... Rev 16:8 *2246*
I saw an angel standing in the *s* .... Rev 19:17 *2246*
And the city had no need of the *s* .... Rev 21:23 *2246*
no candle, neither light of the *s* .... Rev 22:5 *2246*

SUNDER {7}
bow, and cutteth the spear in *s* .... Ps 46:9
death, and brake their bands in *s* .... Ps 107:14
and cut the bars of iron in *s* .... Ps 107:16
chalkstones that are beaten in *s* .... Is 27:9
cut in *s* the bars of iron .... Is 45:2
and will burst thy bonds in *s* .... Nah 1:13
not aware, and will cut him in *s* .... Lk 12:46

SUNDERED {1}
together, that they cannot be *s* .... Job 41:17 6504

SUNDRY {1}
God, who at *s* times and in divers .... Heb 1:1 *4181*

SUNG {5}
song be *s* in the land of Judah .... Is 26:1 7891
And when they had *s* an hymn .... Mt 26:30 *5214*
And when they had *s* an hymn .... Mk 14:26 *5214*
they *s* a new song, saying, Thou .... Rev 5:9 *103*
they *s* as it were a new song .... Rev 14:3 *103*

SUNK {7}
that the stone *s* into his 1Sa 17:49 2883
and he *s* down in his chariot 2Kin 9:24 3766
The heathen are *s* down in the pit .... Ps 9:15 2883
so Jeremiah *s* in the mire .... Jer 38:6 2883
thy feet are *s* in the mire .... Jer 38:22 2883
Her gates are *s* into the ground .... Lam 2:9 2883
he *s* down with sleep, and fell .... Acts 20:9 *2702*

SUNRISING {10}
is before Moab, toward the *s* .... Num 21:11 4217,8121
Jericho eastward, toward the *s* .... Num 34:15 4217
on this side Jordan toward the *s* .... Deut 4:41 4217,8121
on this side Jordan toward the *s* .... Deut 4:47 4217,8121
on this side Jordan toward the *s* .... Josh 1:15 4217,8121
and all Lebanon, toward the *s* .... Josh 13:5 4217,8121
toward the *s* unto the border of .... Josh 19:12 4217,8121
toward the *s* to Beth-dagon .... Josh 19:27 4217,8121
to Judah upon Jordan toward the *s* .... Josh 19:34 4217,8121
over against Gibeah toward the *s* .... Judg 20:43 4217,8121

SUP {3}
their faces shall *s* up as the .... Hab 1:9 4041
him, Make ready wherewith I may *s* .... Lk 17:8 *1172*
will *s* with him, and he with me .... Rev 3:20 *1172*

SUPERFLUITY {1}
s of naughtiness, and receive with .... Jas 1:21 *4050*

SUPERFLUOUS {3}
hath a flat nose, or any thing *s* .... Lev 21:18 8311
thing *s* or lacking in his parts .... Lev 22:23 8311
it is *s* for me to write to you 2Cor 9:1 *4053*

SUPERSCRIPTION {5}
them, Whose is this image and *s* .... Mt 22:20 *1923*
them, Whose is this image and *s* .... Mk 12:16 *1923*
the *s* of his accusation was .... Mk 15:26 *1923*
Whose image and *s* hath it .... Lk 20:24 *1923*
a *s* also was written over him in .... Lk 23:38 *1923*

SUPERSTITION {1}
against him of their own *s* .... Acts 25:19 *1175*

SUPERSTITIOUS {1}
that in all things ye are too *s* .... Acts 17:22 *1174*

SUPPED {1}
he took the cup, when he had *s* 1Cor 11:25 *1172*

SUPPER {14}
birthday made a *s* to his lords .... Mk 6:21 *1173*
When thou makest a dinner or a *s* .... Lk 14:12 *1173*
him, A certain man made a great *s* .... Lk 14:16 *1173*
sent his servant at *s* time to say .... Lk 14:17 *1173*
were bidden shall taste of my *s* .... Lk 14:24 *1173*
Likewise also the cup after *s* .... Lk 22:20 *1172*
There they made him a *s* .... Jn 12:2 *1173*
s being ended, the devil having .... Jn 13:2 *1173*
He riseth from *s*, and laid aside .... Jn 13:4 *1173*
also leaned on his breast at *s* .... Jn 21:20 *1173*
this is not to eat the Lord's *s* 1Cor 11:20 *1173*
one taketh before other his own *s* 1Cor 11:21 *1173*
unto the marriage *s* of the Lamb .... Rev 19:9 *1173*
unto the *s* of the great God .... Rev 19:17 *1173*

SUPPLANT {1}
for every brother will utterly *s* .... Jer 9:4 6117

SUPPLANTED {1}
for he hath *s* me these two times .... Gen 27:36 6117

SUPPLE {1}
thou washed in water to *s* thee .... Eze 16:4 4935

SUPPLIANTS {1}
the rivers of Ethiopia my *s* .... Zeph 3:10 6282

SUPPLICATION {39}
I have not made *s* unto the LORD 1Sa 13:12 2420
of thy servant, and to his *s* 1Kin 8:28 8467
thou to the *s* of thy servant 1Kin 8:30 8467
make *s* unto thee in this house 1Kin 8:33 2603
s soever be made by any man, or 1Kin 8:38 8467
in heaven their prayer and their *s* 1Kin 8:45 8467
make *s* unto thee in the land of 1Kin 8:47 2603
their *s* in heaven thy dwelling 1Kin 8:49 8467
be open unto the *s* of thy servant 1Kin 8:52 8467
unto the *s* of thy people Israel, ... 1Kin 8:52 8467
s unto the LORD, he arose from 1Kin 8:54 8467
I have made *s* before the LORD 1Kin 8:59 2603
I have heard thy prayer and thy *s* 1Kin 9:3 8467
of thy servant, and to his *s* 2Chr 6:19 8467
make *s* before thee in this house 2Chr 6:24 2603
Then what prayer or what *s* soever 2Chr 6:29 8467
heavens their prayer and their *s* 2Chr 6:35 8467
intreated of him, and heard his *s* 2Chr 33:13 8467
to make *s* unto him, and to make .... Est 4:8 2603
make thy *s* to the Almighty .... Job 8:5 2603
but I would make *s* to my judge .... Job 9:15 2603
The LORD hath heard my *s* .... Ps 6:9 8467
and unto the LORD I made *s* .... Ps 30:8 2603
and hide not thyself from my *s* .... Ps 55:1 8467
Let my *s* come before thee .... Ps 119:170 8467
unto the LORD did I make my *s* .... Ps 142:1 2603
thee, they shall make *s* unto thee .... Is 45:14 6419
present their *s* before the LORD .... Jer 36:7 8467
let my *s*, I pray thee, be .... Jer 37:20 8467
I presented my *s* before the king, ... Jer 38:26 8467
our *s* be accepted before thee, and .... Jer 42:2 8467
me to present your *s* before him .... Jer 42:9 8467
and making *s* before his God .... Dan 6:11 2604
presenting my *s* before the LORD .... Dan 9:20 8467
he wept, and made *s* unto him .... Hos 12:4 2603
with one accord in prayer and *s* .... Acts 1:14 *1162*
s in the Spirit, and watching .... Eph 6:18 *1162*
perseverance and *s* for all saints .... Eph 6:18 *1162*
s with thanksgiving let your .... Phil 4:6 *1162*

SUPPLICATIONS {21}
unto the *s* of thy servant 2Chr 6:21 8469
place, their prayer and their *s* 2Chr 6:39 8467
Will he make many *s* unto thee .... Job 41:3 8469
Hear the voice of my *s*, when I .... Ps 28:2 8469
he hath heard the voice of my *s* .... Ps 28:6 8469
of my *s* when I cried unto thee .... Ps 31:22 8469
and attend to the voice of my *s* .... Ps 86:6 8469
he hath heard my voice and my *s* .... Ps 116:1 8469
be attentive to the voice of my *s* .... Ps 130:2 8469
hear the voice of my *s*, O LORD .... Ps 140:6 8469
prayer, O LORD, give ear to my *s* .... Ps 143:1 8469
s of the children of Israel .... Jer 3:21 8469
and with *s* will I lead them .... Jer 31:9 8469
Lord God, to seek by prayer and *s* .... Dan 9:3 8469
prayer of thy servant, and his *s* .... Dan 9:17 8469
present our *s* before thee for our .... Dan 9:18 8469
At the beginning of thy *s* the .... Dan 9:23 8469
the spirit of grace and of *s* .... Zec 12:10 8469
therefore, that, first of all, *s* 1Ti 2:1 *1162*
in God, and continueth in *s* 1Ti 5:5 *1162*
s with strong crying and tears .... Heb 5:7 *2428*

SUPPLIED {2}
lacking on your part they have *s* 1Cor 16:17 *378*
which came from Macedonia *s* 2Cor 11:9 *4322*

SUPPLIETH {2}
not only *s* the want of the saints 2Cor 9:12 *4322*
by that which every joint *s* .... Eph 4:16 *2024*

SUPPLY {5}
may be a *s* for their want 2Cor 8:14
also may be a *s* for your want 2Cor 8:14
the *s* of the Spirit of Jesus .... Phil 1:19 *2024*
to *s* your lack of service toward .... Phil 2:30 *378*
But my God shall *s* all your need .... Phil 4:19 *4137*

SUPPORT {2}
labouring ye ought to *s* the weak .... Acts 20:35 *482*
s the weak, be patient toward all 1Th 5:14 *472*

SUPPOSE {10}
Let not my lord *s* that they have 2Sa 13:32 559
I *s* that he, to whom he forgave .... Lk 7:43 *5274*
S ye that I am come to give peace .... Lk 12:51 *1380*
S ye that these Galilaeans were .... Lk 13:2 *1380*
I *s* that even the world itself .... Jn 21:25 *3633*
these are not drunken, as ye *s* .... Acts 2:15 *5274*
I *s* therefore that this is good 1Cor 7:26 *3543*
For I *s* I was not a whit behind 2Cor 11:5 *3049*
s ye, shall he be thought worthy, ... Heb 10:29 *1380*
faithful brother unto you, as I *s* 1Pet 5:12 *3049*

SUPPOSED {8}
they *s* that they should have .... Mt 20:10 *3543*
they *s* it had been a spirit, and .... Mk 6:49 *1380*
being (as was *s*) the son of .... Lk 3:23 *3543*
s that they had seen a spirit .... Lk 24:37 *1380*
For he *s* his brethren would have .... Acts 7:25 *3543*
whom they *s* that Paul had brought .... Acts 21:29 *3543*
accusation of such things as I *s* .... Acts 25:18 *5282*
Yet I *s* it necessary to send to .... Phil 2:25 *2233*

SUPPOSING {7}
s him to have been in the company .... Lk 2:44 *3543*
s him to be the gardener, saith .... Jn 20:15 *1380*
of the city, *s* he had been dead .... Acts 14:19 *3543*
s that the prisoners had been .... Acts 16:27 *3543*
s that they had obtained their .... Acts 27:13 *1380*

s to add affliction to my bonds ... Phil 1:16 *3633*
truth, *s* that gain is godliness ... 1Ti 6:5 *3543*

SUPREME {1}
whether it be to the king, as *s* ... 1Pet 2:13 *5242*

SUR *(sur)* {1} *A gate of the Temple.*
part shall be at the gate of *S* ... 2Kin 11:6 5495

SURE {41}
borders round about, were made *s* ... Gen 23:17 6965
were made *s* unto Abraham for a ... Gen 23:20 6965
I am *s* that the king of Egypt ... Ex 3:19 3045
be *s* your sin will find you out ... Num 32:23 3045
Only be *s* that thou eat not the ... Deut 12:23 2388
and I will build him a *s* house ... 1Sa 2:35 539
then be *s* that evil is determined ... 1Sa 20:7 3045
certainly make my lord a *s* house ... 1Sa 25:28 539
because I was *s* that he could not ... 2Sa 1:10 3045
ordered in all things, and *s* ... 2Sa 23:5 8104
thee, and build thee a *s* house ... 1Kin 11:38 539
of all this we make a *s* covenant ... Neh 9:38 548
riseth up, and no man is *s* of life ... Job 24:22 539
the testimony of the LORD is *s* ... Ps 19:7 539
Thy testimonies are very *s* ... Ps 93:5 539
all his commandments are *s* ... Ps 111:7 539
thyself, and make *s* thy friend ... Prov 6:3 7292
and he that hateth suretiship is *s* ... Prov 11:15 982
righteousness shall be a *s* reward ... Prov 11:18 571
fasten him as a nail in a *s* place ... Is 22:23 539
in the *s* place be removed ... Is 22:25 539
corner stone, a *s* foundation ... Is 28:16 3245
in *s* dwellings, and in quiet ... Is 32:18 4009
his waters shall be *s* ... Is 33:16 539
even the *s* mercies of David ... Is 55:3 539
and the interpretation thereof *s* ... Dan 2:45 546
thy kingdom shall be *s* unto thee ... Dan 4:26 7011
be made *s* until the third day ... Mt 27:64 *805*
your way, make it as *s* as ye can ... Mt 27:65 *805*
went, and made the sepulchre *s* ... Mt 27:66 *805*
notwithstanding be ye *s* of this ... Lk 10:11 *1097*
are *s* that thou art that Christ, ... Jn 6:69 *1097*
Now are we *s* that thou knowest ... Jn 16:30 *1492*
give you the *s* mercies of David ... Acts 13:34 *4103*
But we are *s* that the judgment of ... Rom 2:2 *1492*
might be *s* to all the seed ... Rom 4:16 *949*
And I am *s* that, when I come unto ... Rom 15:29 *1492*
the foundation of God standeth *s* ... 2Ti 2:19 *4731*
as an anchor of the soul, both *s* ... Heb 6:19 *804*
make your calling and election *s* ... 2Pet 1:10 *949*
also a more *s* word of prophecy ... 2Pet 1:19 *949*

SURELY See APPENDIX.

SURETIES {1}
or of them that are *s* for debts ... Prov 22:26 6148

SURETISHIP {1}
and he that hateth *s* is sure ... Prov 11:15 8628

SURETY {14}
Know of a *s* that thy seed shall ... Gen 15:13 3045
Shall I of a *s* bear a child ... Gen 18:13 552
Behold, of a *s* she is thy wife ... Gen 26:9 389
I will be *s* for him ... Gen 43:9 6148
For thy servant became *s* for the ... Gen 44:32 6148
down now, put me in a *s* with thee ... Job 17:3 6148
Be *s* for thy servant for good ... Ps 119:122 6148
if thou be *s* for thy friend, if ... Prov 6:1 6148
He that is *s* for a stranger shall ... Prov 11:15 6148
becometh *s* in the presence of his ... Prov 17:18 6161
garment that is *s* for a stranger ... Prov 20:16 6148
garment that is *s* for a stranger ... Prov 27:13 6148
he said, Now I know of a *s* ... Acts 12:11 *230*
made a *s* of a better testament ... Heb 7:22 *1450*

SURFEITING {1}
your hearts be overcharged with *s* ... Lk 21:34 *2897*

SURMISINGS {1}
envy, strife, railings, evil *s* ... 1Ti 6:4 *5283*

SURNAME {8}
s himself by the name of Israel ... Is 44:5 3655
Lebbaeus, whose *s* was Thaddaeus ... Mt 10:3 *1941*
for one Simon, whose *s* is Peter ... Acts 10:5 *1941*
hither Simon, whose *s* is Peter ... Acts 10:32 *1941*
call for Simon, whose *s* is Peter ... Acts 11:13 *1941*
mother of John, whose *s* was Mark ... Acts 12:12 *1941*
with them John, whose *s* was Mark ... Acts 12:25 *1941*
with them John, whose *s* was Mark ... Acts 15:37 *2564*

SURNAMED {8}
I have *s* thee, though thou hast ... Is 45:4 3655
And Simon he *s* Peter ... Mk 3:16 *2007,3686*
he *s* them Boanerges, which is, ... Mk 3:17 *2007,3686*
Satan into Judas *s* Iscariot ... Lk 22:3 *1941*
called Barsabas, who was *s* Justus ... Acts 1:23 *1941*
by the apostles was *s* Barnabas ... Acts 4:36 *1941*
whether Simon, which was *s* Peter ... Acts 10:18 *1941*
Judas *s* Barsabas, and Silas, chief ... Acts 15:22 *1941*

SURPRISED {3}
fearfulness hath *s* the hypocrites ... Is 33:14 270
taken, and the strong holds are *s* ... Jer 48:41 8610
the praise of the whole earth *s* ... Jer 51:41 8610

SUSA See SHUSHAN, SUSANCHITES.

SUSANCHITES *(su'-san-kites)* {1} *Resettled foreigners in Israel.*
the Babylonians, the *S*, the ... Ezr 4:9 7801

SUSANNA *(su'-zan'-nah)* {1} *A woman follower of Jesus.*
of Chuza Herod's steward, and *S* ... Lk 8:3 *4677*

SUSI *(su'-si)* {1} *Father of Gaddi.*
of Manasseh, Gaddi the son of *S* ... Num 13:11 5485

SUSTAIN {4}
a widow woman there to *s* thee ... 1Kin 17:9 3557
thou *s* them in the wilderness ... Neh 9:21 3557
upon the LORD, and he shall *s* thee ... Ps 55:22 3557
of a man will *s* his infirmity ... Prov 18:14 3557

SUSTAINED {3}
and with corn and wine have I *s* him ... Gen 27:37 5564
for the LORD *s* me ... Ps 3:5 5564
and his righteousness, it *s* him ... Is 59:16 5564

SUSTENANCE {3}
left no *s* for Israel, neither ... Judg 6:4 4241
of *s* while he lay at Mahanaim ... 2Sa 19:32 3557
and our fathers found no *s* ... Acts 7:11 *5527*

SWADDLED {2}
those that I have *s* and brought up ... Lam 2:22 2946
not salted at all, nor *s* at all ... Eze 16:4 2853

SWADDLING {2}
son, and wrapped him in *s* clothes ... Lk 2:7 *4683*
the babe wrapped in *s* clothes ... Lk 2:12 *4683*

SWADDLINGBAND {1}
and thick darkness a *s* for it ... Job 38:9 2854

SWALLOW {23}
and *s* them up, with all that ... Num 16:30 1104
said, Lest the earth *s* us up also ... Num 16:34 1104
why wilt thou *s* up the ... 2Sa 20:19 1104
me, that I should *s* up or destroy ... 2Sa 20:20 1104
me alone till I *s* down my spittle ... Job 7:19 1104
restore, and shall not *s* it down ... Job 20:18 1104
the LORD shall *s* them up in his ... Ps 21:9 1104
for man would *s* me up ... Ps 56:1 7602
Mine enemies would daily *s* me up ... Ps 56:2 7602
of him that would *s* me up ... Ps 57:3 7602
me, neither let the deep *s* me up ... Ps 69:15 1104
the *s* a nest for herself, where ... Ps 84:3 1866
Let us *s* them up alive as the ... Prov 1:12 1104
as the *s* by flying, so the curse ... Prov 26:2 1866
lips of a fool will *s* up himself ... Eccl 10:12 1104
He will *s* up death in victory ... Is 25:8 1104
Like a crane or a *s*, so did I ... Is 38:14 5693
the *s* observe the time of their ... Jer 8:7 5693
the strangers shall *s* it up ... Hos 8:7 1104
O ye that *s* up the needy, even to ... Amos 8:4 7602
shall drink, and they shall *s* down ... Obad 16 3886
a great fish to *s* up Jonah ... Jonah 1:17 1104
strain at a gnat, and *s* a camel ... Mt 23:24 *2666*

SWALLOWED {26}
but Aaron's rod *s* up their rods ... Ex 7:12 1104
thy right hand, the earth *s* them ... Ex 15:12 1104
s them up, and their houses, and ... Num 16:32 1104
s them up together with Korah, ... Num 26:10 1104
s them up, and their households, ... Deut 11:6 1104
lest the king be *s* up, and all the ... 2Sa 17:16 1104
therefore my words are *s* up ... Job 6:3 3886
He hath *s* down riches, and he ... Job 20:15 1104
speak, surely he shall be *s* up ... Job 37:20 1104
them not say, We have *s* him up ... Ps 35:25 1104
s up Dathan, and covered the ... Ps 106:17 1104
Then they had *s* us up quick ... Ps 124:3 1104
they are *s* up of wine, they are ... Is 28:7 1104
they that *s* thee up shall be far ... Is 49:19 1104
he hath *s* me up like a dragon, he ... Jer 51:34 1104
his mouth that which he hath *s* up ... Jer 51:44 1105
The Lord hath *s* up all the ... Lam 2:2 1104
he hath *s* up Israel, he hath ... Lam 2:5 1104
he hath *s* up all her palaces ... Lam 2:5 1104
they say, We have *s* her up ... Lam 2:16 1104
s you up on every side, that ye ... Eze 36:3 7602
Israel is *s* up ... Hos 8:8 1104
written, Death is *s* up in victory ... 1Cor 15:54 *2666*
be *s* up with overmuch sorrow ... 2Cor 2:7 *2666*
mortality might be *s* up of life ... 2Cor 5:4 *2666*
s up the flood which the dragon ... Rev 12:16 *2666*

SWALLOWETH {2}
the robber *s* up their substance ... Job 5:5 7602
He *s* the ground with fierceness ... Job 39:24 1572

SWAN {2}
And the *s*, and the pelican, and the ... Lev 11:18 8580
owl, and the great owl, and the *s* ... Deut 14:16 8580

SWARE {78}
because there they *s* both of them ... Gen 21:31 7650
that *s* unto me, saying, Unto thy ... Gen 24:7 7650
s to him concerning that matter ... Gen 24:9 7650
and he *s* unto him ... Gen 25:33 7650
which I *s* unto Abraham thy father ... Gen 26:3 7650
the morning, and *s* one to another ... Gen 26:31 7650
Jacob *s* by the fear of his father ... Gen 31:53 7650
And he *s* unto him ... Gen 47:31 7650
the land which he *s* to Abraham ... Gen 50:24 7650
which he *s* unto thy fathers to ... Ex 13:5 7650
as he *s* unto thee and to thy ... Ex 13:11 7650
the land which I *s* unto Abraham ... Ex 33:1 7650
the land which he *s* unto them ... Num 14:16 7650
land which I *s* unto their fathers ... Num 14:23 7650
concerning which I *s* to make you ... Num 14:30 5375
kindled the same time, and he *s* ... Num 32:10 7650
the land which I *s* unto Abraham ... Num 32:11 7650
the LORD *s* unto your fathers ... Deut 1:8 7650
of your words, and was wroth, and *s* ... Deut 1:34 7650
which I *s* to give unto your ... Deut 1:35 7650
the host, as the LORD *s* unto them ... Deut 2:14 7650
s that I should not go over ... Deut 4:21 7650
thy fathers which he *s* unto them ... Deut 4:31 7650
land which he *s* unto thy fathers ... Deut 6:10 7650
which the LORD *s* unto thy fathers ... Deut 6:18 7650
land which he *s* unto our fathers ... Deut 6:23 7650
mercy which he *s* unto thy fathers ... Deut 7:12 7650
in the land which he *s* unto thy ... Deut 7:13 7650
the LORD *s* unto your fathers ... Deut 8:1 7650
which he *s* unto thy fathers ... Deut 8:18 7650
which the LORD *s* unto thy fathers ... Deut 9:5 7650
which I *s* unto their fathers to ... Deut 10:11 7650
which the LORD *s* unto your ... Deut 11:9 7650
in the land which the LORD *s* unto ... Deut 11:21 7650
s unto our fathers for to give us ... Deut 26:3 7650
in the land which the LORD *s* unto ... Deut 28:11 7650
which the LORD *s* unto thy fathers ... Deut 30:20 7650
land which I *s* unto their fathers ... Deut 31:20 7650
them into the land which I *s* ... Deut 31:21 7650
into the land which I *s* unto them ... Deut 31:23 7650
the land which I *s* unto Abraham ... Deut 34:4 7650
which I *s* unto their fathers to ... Josh 1:6 7650
unto whom the LORD *s* that he ... Josh 5:6 7650
which the LORD *s* unto their ... Josh 5:6 7650
that she hath, as ye *s* unto her ... Josh 6:22 7650
of the congregation *s* unto them ... Josh 9:15 7650
of the oath which we *s* unto them ... Josh 9:20 7650
Moses *s* on that day, saying, ... Josh 14:9 7650
he *s* to give unto their fathers ... Josh 21:43 7650
all that he *s* unto their fathers ... Josh 21:44 7650
land which I *s* unto your fathers ... Judg 2:1 7650
and Saul *s*, As the LORD liveth, he ... 1Sa 19:6 7650
David *s* moreover, and said, Thy ... 1Sa 20:3 7650
And David *s* unto Saul ... 1Sa 24:22 7650
Saul *s* to her by the LORD, saying ... 1Sa 28:10 7650
while it was yet day, David *s* ... 2Sa 3:35 7650
And the king *s* unto him ... 2Sa 19:23 7650
Then the men of David *s* unto him ... 2Sa 21:17 7650
And the king *s*, and said, As the ... 1Kin 1:29 7650
Even as I *s* unto thee by the LORD ... 1Kin 1:30 7650
I *s* to him by the LORD, saying, I ... 1Kin 2:8 7650
Then king Solomon *s* by the LORD ... 1Kin 2:23 7650
And Gedaliah *s* to them, and to ... 2Kin 25:24 7650
they *s* unto the LORD with a loud ... 2Chr 15:14 7650
And they *s* ... Ezr 10:5 7650
Unto whom I *s* in my wrath that ... Ps 95:11 7650
How he *s* unto the LORD, and vowed ... Ps 132:2 7650
So Zedekiah the king *s* secretly ... Jer 38:16 7650
the son of Shaphan *s* unto them ... Jer 40:9 7650
I *s* unto thee, and entered into a ... Eze 16:8 7650
s by him that liveth for ever ... Dan 12:7 7650
he *s* unto her, Whatsoever thou ... Mk 6:23 *3660*
The oath which he *s* to our father ... Lk 1:73 *3660*
So I *s* in my wrath, They shall ... Heb 3:11 *3660*
to whom *s* he that they should not ... Heb 3:18 *3660*
by no greater, he *s* by himself, ... Heb 6:13 *3660*
that said unto him, The Lord *s* ... Heb 7:21 *3660*
s by him that liveth for ever and ... Rev 10:6 *3660*

SWAREST {5}
to whom thou *s* by thine own self, ... Ex 32:13 7650
which thou *s* unto their fathers ... Num 11:12 7650
as thou *s* unto our fathers, a ... Deut 26:15 7650
thou *s* by the LORD thy God unto ... 1Kin 1:17 7650
which thou *s* unto David in thy ... Ps 89:49 7650

SWARM {3}
there came a grievous *s* of flies ... Ex 8:24 6157
by reason of the *s* of flies ... Ex 8:24 6157
and, behold, there was a *s* of bees ... Judg 14:8 5712

SWARMS {5}
I will send *s* of flies upon thee, ... Ex 8:21 6157
shall be full of *s* of flies ... Ex 8:21 6157
that no *s* of flies shall be there ... Ex 8:22 6157
the *s* of flies may depart from ... Ex 8:29 6157
he removed the *s* of flies from ... Ex 8:31 6157

SWEAR {60}
Now therefore *s* unto me here by ... Gen 21:23 7650
And Abraham said, I will *s* ... Gen 21:24 7650
And I will make thee *s* by the LORD ... Gen 24:3 7650
And my master made me *s*, saying, ... Gen 24:37 7650
And Jacob said, *S* to me this day ... Gen 25:33 7650
And he said, *S* unto me ... Gen 47:31 7650
My father made me *s*, saying, Lo, ... Gen 50:5 7650
according as he made thee *s* ... Gen 50:6 7650
I did *s* to give it to Abraham ... Ex 6:8 5375
Or if a soul *s*, pronouncing with ... Lev 5:4 7650
ye shall not *s* by my name falsely ... Lev 19:12 7650
or *s* an oath to bind his soul ... Num 30:2 7650
serve him, and shalt *s* by his name ... Deut 6:13 7650
thou cleave, and *s* by his name ... Deut 10:20 7650
s unto me by the LORD, since I ... Josh 2:12 7650
oath which thou hast made us *s* ... Josh 2:17 7650
oath which thou hast made us to *s* ... Josh 2:20 7650
gods, nor cause to *s* by them ... Josh 23:7 7650
S unto me, that ye will not fall ... Judg 15:12 7650
Jonathan caused David to *s* again ... 1Sa 20:17 7650
S now therefore unto me by the ... 1Sa 24:21 7650
S unto me by God, that thou wilt ... 1Sa 30:15 7650
for I *s* by the LORD, if thou go ... 2Sa 19:7 7650
s unto thine handmaid, saying, ... 1Kin 1:13 7650
Let king Solomon *s* unto me to day ... 1Kin 1:51 7650
I not make thee to *s* by the LORD ... 1Kin 2:42 7650
laid upon him to cause him to *s* ... 1Kin 8:31 422
be laid upon him to make him *s* ... 2Chr 6:22 422
who had made him *s* by God ... 2Chr 36:13 7650
Israel, to *s* that they should do ... Ezr 10:5 7650
their hair, and made them *s* by God ... Neh 13:25 7650
In that day shall he *s*, saying, I ... Is 3:7 5375
Canaan, and *s* to the LORD of hosts ... Is 19:18 7650
shall bow, every tongue shall *s* ... Is 45:23 7650
which *s* by the name of the LORD, ... Is 48:1 7650
earth shall *s* by the God of truth ... Is 65:16 7650

And thou shalt *s*, The LORD liveth,	Jer 4:2	7650
surely they *s* falsely	Jer 5:2	7650
s falsely, and burn incense unto	Jer 7:9	7650
to *s* by my name, The LORD liveth	Jer 12:16	7650
taught my people to *s* by Baal	Jer 12:16	7650
I *s* by myself, saith the LORD,	Jer 22:5	7650
which thou didst *s* to their	Jer 32:22	7650
go ye up to Beth-aven, nor *s*	Hos 4:15	7650
They that *s* by the sin of Samaria	Amos 8:14	7650
that *s* by the LORD	Zeph 1:5	7650
and that *s* by Malcham	Zeph 1:5	7650
But I say unto you, *S* not at all	Mt 5:34	*3660*
Neither shalt thou *s* by thy head	Mt 5:36	*3660*
Whosoever shall *s* by the temple	Mt 23:16	*3660*
but whosoever shall *s* by the gold	Mt 23:16	*3660*
Whosoever shall *s* by the altar	Mt 23:18	*3660*
therefore shall *s* by the altar	Mt 23:20	*3660*
whoso shall *s* by the temple,	Mt 23:21	*3660*
And he that shall *s* by heaven	Mt 23:22	*3660*
Then began he to curse and to *s*	Mt 26:74	*3660*
But he began to curse and to *s*	Mk 14:71	*3660*
because he could *s* by no greater	Heb 6:13	*3660*
For men verily *s* by the greater	Heb 6:16	*3660*
s not, neither by heaven, neither	Jas 5:12	*3660*

SWEARERS {1}

adulterers, and against false *s*	Mal 3:5	7650

SWEARETH {11}

lieth concerning it, and *s* falsely	Lev 6:3	7650
He that *s* to his own hurt, and	Ps 15:4	7650
every one that *s* by him shall	Ps 63:11	7650
and he that *s*, as he that feareth	Eccl 9:2	7650
he that *s* in the earth shall	Is 65:16	7650
every one that *s* shall be cut off	Zec 5:3	7650
of him that *s* falsely by my name	Zec 5:4	7650
but whosoever *s* by the gift that	Mt 23:18	*3660*
s by it, and by all things thereon	Mt 23:20	*3660*
s by it, and by him that dwelleth	Mt 23:21	*3660*
s by the throne of God, and by him	Mt 23:22	*3660*

SWEARING {4}

soul sin, and hear the voice of *s*	Lev 5:1	423
for because of *s* the land	Jer 23:10	423
By *s*, and lying, and killing, and	Hos 4:2	422
s falsely in making a covenant	Hos 10:4	422

SWEAT {3}

In the *s* of thy face shalt thou	Gen 3:19	2188
with any thing that causeth *s*	Eze 44:18	3154
his *s* was as it were great drops	Lk 22:44	*2402*

SWEEP {3}

I will *s* it with the besom of	Is 14:23	2894
the hail shall *s* away the refuge	Is 28:17	3261
s the house, and seek diligently	Lk 15:8	*4563*

SWEEPING {1}

a *s* rain which leaveth no food	Prov 28:3	5502

SWEET {108}

And the LORD smelled a *s* savour	Gen 8:21	5207
waters, the waters were made *s*	Ex 15:25	4985
anointing oil, and for *s* incense,	Ex 25:6	5561
it is a *s* savour, an offering	Ex 29:18	5207
for a *s* savour before the LORD	Ex 29:25	5207
for a *s* savour, an offering made	Ex 29:41	5207
thereon *s* incense every morning	Ex 30:7	5561
of *s* cinnamon half so much, even	Ex 30:23	1314
of *s* calamus two hundred and fifty	Ex 30:23	1314
Moses, Take unto thee *s* spices	Ex 30:34	5561
these *s* spices with pure	Ex 30:34	5561
s incense for the holy place	Ex 31:11	5561
oil, and for the *s* incense	Ex 35:8	5561
the *s* incense, and the hanging for	Ex 35:15	5561
oil, and for the *s* incense	Ex 35:28	5561
and the pure incense of *s* spices	Ex 37:29	5561
the *s* incense, and the hanging for	Ex 39:38	5561
he burnt *s* incense thereon	Ex 40:27	5561
of a *s* savour unto the LORD	Lev 1:9	5207
of a *s* savour unto the LORD	Lev 1:13	5207
of a *s* savour unto the LORD	Lev 1:17	5207
of a *s* savour unto the LORD	Lev 2:2	5207
of a *s* savour unto the LORD	Lev 2:9	5207
burnt on the altar for a *s* savour	Lev 2:12	5207
of a *s* savour unto the LORD	Lev 3:5	5207
made by fire for a *s* savour	Lev 3:16	5207
of *s* incense before the LORD	Lev 4:7	5561
for a *s* savour unto the LORD	Lev 4:31	5207
it upon the altar for a *s* savour	Lev 6:15	5207
for a *s* savour unto the LORD	Lev 6:21	5207
a burnt sacrifice for a *s* savour	Lev 8:21	5207
were consecrations for a *s* savour	Lev 8:28	5207
his hands full of *s* incense	Lev 16:12	5561
burn the fat for a *s* savour unto	Lev 17:6	5207
fire unto the LORD for a *s* savour	Lev 23:13	5207
of *s* savour unto the LORD	Lev 23:18	5207
smell the savour of your *s* odours	Lev 26:31	5207
the *s* incense, and the daily meat	Num 4:16	5561
to make a *s* savour unto the LORD,	Num 15:3	5207
for a *s* savour unto the LORD	Num 15:7	5207
of a *s* savour unto the LORD	Num 15:10	5207
of a *s* savour unto the LORD	Num 15:13	5207
of a *s* savour unto the LORD	Num 15:14	5207
for a *s* savour unto the LORD,	Num 15:24	5207
for a *s* savour unto the LORD	Num 18:17	5207
for a *s* savour unto me, shall ye	Num 28:2	5207
in mount Sinai for a *s* savour	Num 28:6	5207
of a *s* savour unto the LORD	Num 28:8	5207
a burnt offering of a *s* savour	Num 28:13	5207
of a *s* savour unto the LORD	Num 28:24	5207
for a *s* savour unto the LORD	Num 28:27	5207
for a *s* savour unto the LORD	Num 29:2	5207
for a *s* savour, a sacrifice made	Num 29:6	5207
unto the LORD for a *s* savour	Num 29:8	5207
of a *s* savour unto the LORD	Num 29:13	5207
of a *s* savour unto the LORD	Num 29:36	5207
the *s* psalmist of Israel, said,	2Sa 23:1	5273
and to burn before him *s* incense	2Chr 2:4	5561
burnt sacrifices and *s* incense	2Chr 13:11	5561
which was filled with *s* odours	2Chr 16:14	1314
they may offer sacrifices of *s*	Ezr 6:10	5208
way, eat the fat, and drink the *s*	Neh 8:10	4477
and six months with *s* odours	Est 2:12	1314
wickedness be *s* in his mouth	Job 20:12	4985
of the valley shall be *s* unto him	Job 21:33	4985
Canst thou bind the *s* influences	Job 38:31	4575
We took *s* counsel together, and	Ps 55:14	4985
My meditation of him shall be *s*	Ps 104:34	6148
How *s* are thy words unto my taste	Ps 119:103	4452
for they are *s*	Ps 141:6	5276
lie down, and thy sleep shall be *s*	Prov 3:24	6148
Stolen waters are *s*, and bread	Prov 9:17	4985
accomplished is *s* to the soul	Prov 13:19	6148
s to the soul, and health to the	Prov 16:24	4966
Bread of deceit is *s* to a man	Prov 20:17	6149
vomit up, and lose thy *s* words	Prov 23:8	5273
which is *s* to thy taste	Prov 24:13	4966
soul every bitter thing is *s*	Prov 27:7	4966
The sleep of a labouring man is *s*	Eccl 5:12	4966
Truly the light is *s*, and a	Eccl 11:7	4966
and his fruit was *s* to my taste	Song 2:3	4966
for *s* is thy voice, and thy	Song 2:14	6149
my fingers with *s* smelling myrrh	Song 5:5	5674
as a bed of spices, as *s* flowers	Song 5:13	4840
dropping *s* smelling myrrh	Song 5:13	5674
His mouth is most *s*	Song 5:16	4477
that instead of *s* smell there	Is 3:24	1314
bitter for *s*, and *s* for bitter	Is 5:20	4966
make *s* melody, sing many songs,	Is 23:16	3190
bought me no *s* cane with money	Is 43:24	
their own blood, as with *s* wine	Is 49:26	6071
the *s* cane from a far country	Jer 6:20	2896
nor your sacrifices *s* unto me	Jer 6:20	6148
and my sleep was *s* unto me	Jer 31:26	6148
offer *s* savour to all their idols	Eze 6:13	5207
set it before them for a *s* savour	Eze 16:19	5207
also they made their *s* savour	Eze 20:28	5207
accept you with your *s* savour	Eze 20:41	5207
an oblation and *s* odours unto him	Dan 2:46	5208
the mountains shall drop *s* wine	Amos 9:13	6071
s wine, but shalt not drink wine	Mic 6:15	8492
and Salome, had bought *s* spices	Mk 16:1	
are unto God a *s* savour of Christ	2Cor 2:15	*2175*
from you, an odour of a *s* smell	Phil 4:18	*2175*
forth at the same place *s* water	Jas 3:11	*1099*
shall be in thy mouth *s* as honey	Rev 10:9	*1099*
and it was in my mouth *s* as honey	Rev 10:10	*1099*

SWEETER {3}

went down, What is *s* than honey	Judg 14:18	4966
s also than honey and the	Ps 19:10	4966
yea, *s* than honey to my mouth	Ps 119:103	

SWEETLY {2}

the worm shall feed *s* on him	Job 24:20	4988
for my beloved, that goeth down *s*	Song 7:9	4339

SWEETNESS {5}

unto them, Should I forsake my *s*	Judg 9:11	4987
and out of the strong came forth *s*	Judg 14:14	4966
the *s* of the lips increaseth	Prov 16:21	4986
so doth the *s* of a man's friend	Prov 27:9	4986
it was in my mouth as honey for *s*	Eze 3:3	4966

SWEETSMELLING {1}

a sacrifice to God for a *s* savour	Eph 5:2	*2175*

SWELL {4}

thigh to rot, and thy belly to *s*	Num 5:21	6639
bowels, to make thy belly to *s*	Num 5:22	6638
bitter, and her belly shall *s*	Num 5:27	6638
upon thee, neither did thy foot *s*	Deut 8:4	1216

SWELLED {1}

not old, and their feet *s* not	Neh 9:21	1216

SWELLING {7}

shake with the *s* thereof	Ps 46:3	1346
s out in a high wall, whose	Is 30:13	1158
wilt thou do in the *s* of Jordan	Jer 12:5	1347
from the *s* of Jordan against the	Jer 49:19	1347
come up like a lion from the *s* of	Jer 50:44	1347
speak great *s* words of vanity	2Pet 2:18	*5246*
mouth speaketh great *s* words	Jude 16	*5246*

SWELLINGS {1}

backbitings, whisperings, *s*	2Cor 12:20	*5450*

SWEPT {4}

The river of Kishon *s* them away	Judg 5:21	1640
Why are thy valiant men *s* away	Jer 46:15	5502
is come, he findeth it empty, *s*	Mt 12:44	*4563*
when he cometh, he findeth it *s*	Lk 11:25	*4563*

SWERVED {1}

From which some having *s* have	1Ti 1:6	*795*

SWIFT {20}

earth, as *s* as the eagle flieth	Deut 28:49	
were as *s* as the roes upon the	1Chr 12:8	4116
are passed away as the *s* ships	Job 9:26	16
He is *s* as the waters	Job 24:18	7031
feet that be *s* in running to	Prov 6:18	4116
that the race is not to the *s*	Eccl 9:11	7031
ye *s* messengers, to a nation	Is 18:2	7031
the LORD rideth upon a *s* cloud	Is 19:1	7031
and, We will ride upon the *s*	Is 30:16	7031
shall they that pursue you be *s*	Is 30:16	7043
upon *s* beasts, to my holy	Is 66:20	3753
thou art a *s* dromedary traversing	Jer 2:23	7031
Let not the *s* flee away, nor the	Jer 46:6	7031
flight shall perish from the *s*	Amos 2:14	7031
he that is *s* of foot shall not	Amos 2:15	7031
bind the chariot to the *s* beast	Mic 1:13	7409
I will be a *s* witness against the	Mal 3:5	4116
Their feet are *s* to shed blood	Rom 3:15	*3691*
let every man be *s* to hear	Jas 1:19	*5036*
upon themselves *s* destruction	2Pet 2:1	*5031*

SWIFTER {6}

they were *s* than eagles, they	2Sa 1:23	7043
My days are *s* than a weaver's	Job 7:6	7043
Now my days are *s* than a post	Job 9:25	7043
his horses are *s* than eagles	Jer 4:13	7043
Our persecutors are *s* than the	Lam 4:19	7031
also are *s* than the leopards	Hab 1:8	7043

SWIFTLY {4}

his word runneth very *s*	Ps 147:15	4120
they shall come with speed *s*	Is 5:26	7031
beginning, being caused to fly *s*	Dan 9:21	3288
and if ye recompense me, *s*	Joel 3:4	7031

SWIM {6}

and the iron did *s*	2Kin 6:6	6687
all the night make I my bed to *s*	Ps 6:6	7811
spreadeth forth his hands to *s*	Is 25:11	7811
waters were risen, waters to *s* in	Eze 47:5	7813
lest any of them should *s* out	Acts 27:42	*1579*
s should cast themselves first	Acts 27:43	*2860*

SWIMMEST {1}

thy blood the land wherein thou *s*	Eze 32:6	6824

SWIMMETH {1}

as he that spreadeth forth his	Is 25:11	7811

SWINE {16}

And the *s*, though he divide the	Lev 11:7	2386
And the *s*, because it divideth the	Deut 14:8	2386
cast ye your pearls before *s*	Mt 7:6	*5519*
them an herd of many *s* feeding	Mt 8:30	*5519*
us to go away into the herd of *s*	Mt 8:31	*5519*
out, they went into the herd of *s*	Mt 8:32	*5519*
the whole herd of *s* ran violently	Mt 8:32	*5519*
a great herd of *s* feeding	Mk 5:11	*5519*
him, saying, Send us into the *s*	Mk 5:12	*5519*
went out, and entered into the *s*	Mk 5:13	*5519*
And they that fed the *s* fled	Mk 5:14	*5519*
devil, and also concerning the *s*	Mk 5:16	*5519*
of many feeding on the mountain	Lk 8:32	*5519*
of the man, and entered into the *s*	Lk 8:33	*5519*
him into his fields to feed *s*	Lk 15:15	*5519*
with the husks that the *s* did eat	Lk 15:16	*5519*

SWINE'S {4}

As a jewel of gold in a *s* snout	Prov 11:22	2386
the monuments, which eat *s* flesh	Is 65:4	2386
as if he offered *s* blood	Is 66:3	2386
tree in the midst, eating *s* flesh	Is 66:17	2386

SWOLLEN {1}

they looked when he should have *s*	Acts 28:6	*4092*

SWOON {1}

the sucklings *s* in the streets of	Lam 2:11	5848

SWOONED {1}

when they *s* as the wounded in the	Lam 2:12	5848

SWORD {424}

a flaming *s* which turned every	Gen 3:24	2719
by thy *s* shalt thou live, and	Gen 27:40	2719
as captives taken with the *s*	Gen 31:26	2719
brethren, took each man his *s*	Gen 34:25	2719
his son with the edge of the *s*	Gen 34:26	2719
the hand of the Amorite with my *s*	Gen 48:22	2719
us with pestilence, or with the *s*	Ex 5:3	2719
to put a *s* in their hand to slay	Ex 5:21	2719
I will draw my *s*, my hand shall	Ex 15:9	2719
his people with the edge of the *s*	Ex 17:13	2719
me from the *s* of Pharaoh	Ex 18:4	2719
and I will kill you with the *s*	Ex 22:24	2719
Put every man his *s* by his side	Ex 32:27	2719
neither shall the *s* go through	Lev 26:6	2719
shall fall before you by the *s*	Lev 26:7	2719
shall fall before you by the *s*	Lev 26:8	2719
And I will bring a *s* upon you	Lev 26:25	2719
and will draw out a *s* after you	Lev 26:33	2719
shall flee, as fleeing from a *s*	Lev 26:36	2719
another, as it were before a *s*	Lev 26:37	2719
unto this land, to fall by the *s*	Num 14:3	2719
you, and ye shall fall by the *s*	Num 14:43	2719
slain with a *s* in the open fields	Num 19:16	2719
come out against thee with the *s*	Num 20:18	2719
smote him with the edge of the *s*	Num 21:24	2719
way, and his *s* drawn in his hand	Num 22:23	2719
would there were a *s* in mine hand	Num 22:29	2719
way, and his *s* drawn in his hand	Num 22:31	2719
son of Beor they slew with the *s*	Num 31:8	2719
that city with the edge of the *s*	Deut 13:15	2719
thereof, with the edge of the *s*	Deut 13:15	2719
thereof with the edge of the *s*	Deut 20:13	2719
an extreme burning, and with the *s*	Deut 28:22	2719
The *s* without, and terror within,	Deut 32:25	2719
If I whet my glittering *s*	Deut 32:41	2719
blood, and my *s* shall devour flesh	Deut 32:42	2719
who is the *s* of thy excellency	Deut 33:29	2719
him with his *s* drawn in his hand	Josh 5:13	2719
and ass, with the edge of the *s*	Josh 6:21	2719
all fallen on the edge of the *s*	Josh 8:24	2719

smote it with the edge of the *s* ... Josh 8:24 2719
of Israel slew with the *s* ... Josh 10:11 2719
smote it with the edge of the *s* ... Josh 10:28 2719
smote it with the edge of the *s* ... Josh 10:30 2719
smote it with the edge of the *s* ... Josh 10:32 2719
smote it with the edge of the *s* ... Josh 10:35 2719
smote it with the edge of the *s* ... Josh 10:37 2719
smote them with the edge of the *s* ... Josh 10:39 2719
smote the king thereof with the *s* ... Josh 11:10 2719
therein with the edge of the *s* ... Josh 11:11 2719
smote them with the edge of the *s* ... Josh 11:12 2719
they smote with the edge of the *s* ... Josh 11:14 2719
of Israel slay with the *s* among ... Josh 13:22 2719
smote it with the edge of the *s* ... Josh 19:47 2719
but not with thy *s*, nor with thy ... Josh 24:12 2719
smitten it with the edge of the *s* ... Judg 1:8 2719
the city with the edge of the *s* ... Judg 1:25 2719
the edge of the *s* before Barak ... Judg 4:15 2719
fell upon the edge of the *s* ... Judg 4:16 2719
the *s* of Gideon the son of Joash ... Judg 7:14 2719
The *s* of the LORD, and of Gideon ... Judg 7:18
The *s* of the LORD, and of Gideon ... Judg 7:20 2719
every man's *s* against his fellow ... Judg 7:22 2719
twenty thousand men that drew *s* ... Judg 8:10 2719
But the youth drew not his *s* ... Judg 8:20 2719
and said unto him, Draw thy *s* ... Judg 9:54 2719
smote them with the edge of the *s* ... Judg 18:27 2719
thousand footmen that drew *s* ... Judg 20:2 2719
and six thousand men that drew *s* ... Judg 20:15 2719
hundred thousand men that drew *s* ... Judg 20:17 2719
all these drew the *s* ... Judg 20:25 2719
all these drew the *s* ... Judg 20:35 2719
the city with the edge of the *s* ... Judg 20:37 2719
five thousand men that drew the *s* ... Judg 20:46 2719
smote them with the edge of the *s* ... Judg 20:48 2719
with the edge of the *s*, with the ... Judg 21:10 2719
that there was neither *s* nor ... 1Sa 13:22 2719
every man's *s* was against his ... 1Sa 14:20 2719
the people with the edge of the *s* ... 1Sa 15:8 2719
said, As thy *s* hath made women ... 1Sa 15:33 2719
girded his *s* upon his armour ... 1Sa 17:39 2719
Thou comest to me with a *s* ... 1Sa 17:45 2719
that the LORD saveth not with *s* ... 1Sa 17:47 2719
but there was no *s* in the hand of ... 1Sa 17:50 2719
the Philistine, and took his *s* ... 1Sa 17:51 2719
and his garments, even to his *s* ... 1Sa 18:4 2719
here under thine hand spear or *s* ... 1Sa 21:8 2719
my *s* nor my weapons with me ... 1Sa 21:8 2719
The *s* of Goliath the Philistine, ... 1Sa 21:9 2719
gave him the *s* of Goliath the ... 1Sa 22:10 2719
thou hast given him bread, and a *s* ... 1Sa 22:13 2719
smote he with the edge of the *s* ... 1Sa 22:19 2719
and sheep, with the edge of the *s* ... 1Sa 22:19 2719
men, Gird ye on every man his *s* ... 1Sa 25:13 2719
And they girded on every man his *s* ... 1Sa 25:13 2719
and David also girded on his *s* ... 1Sa 25:13 2719
unto his armourbearer, Draw thy *s* ... 1Sa 31:4 2719
Therefore Saul took a *s*, and fell ... 1Sa 31:4 2719
dead, he fell likewise upon his *s* ... 1Sa 31:5 2719
because they were fallen by the *s* ... 2Sa 1:12 2719
the *s* of Saul returned not empty ... 2Sa 1:22 2719
thrust his *s* in his fellow's side ... 2Sa 2:16 2719
Shall the *s* devour for ever ... 2Sa 2:26 2719
a staff, or that falleth on the *s* ... 2Sa 3:29 2719
for the *s* devoureth one as well ... 2Sa 11:25 2719
Uriah the Hittite with the *s* ... 2Sa 12:9 2719
hast slain him with the *s* of the ... 2Sa 12:9 2719
Now therefore the *s* shall never ... 2Sa 12:10 2719
the city with the edge of the *s* ... 2Sa 15:14 2719
that day than the *s* devoured ... 2Sa 18:8 2719
upon it a girdle with a *s* ... 2Sa 20:8 2719
to the *s* that was in Joab's hand ... 2Sa 20:10 2719
he being girded with a new *s* ... 2Sa 21:16
and his hand clave unto the *s* ... 2Sa 23:10 2719
valiant men that drew the *s* ... 2Sa 24:9 2719
not slay his servant with the *s* ... 1Kin 1:51 2719
not put thee to death with the *s* ... 1Kin 2:8 2719
than he, and slew them with the *s* ... 1Kin 2:32 2719
And the king said, Bring me a *s* ... 1Kin 3:24 2719
they brought a *s* before the king ... 1Kin 3:24 2719
slain all the prophets with the *s* ... 1Kin 19:1 2719
and slain thy prophets with the *s* ... 1Kin 19:10 2719
and slain thy prophets with the *s* ... 1Kin 19:14 2719
the *s* of Hazael shall Jehu slay ... 1Kin 19:17 2719
the *s* of Jehu shall Elisha slay ... 1Kin 19:17 2719
hast taken captive with thy *s* ... 2Kin 6:22 2719
men wilt thou slay with the *s* ... 2Kin 8:12 2719
smote them with the edge of the *s* ... 2Kin 10:25 2719
followeth her kill with the *s* ... 2Kin 11:15 2719
the *s* beside the king's house ... 2Kin 11:20 2719
to fall by the *s* in his own land ... 2Kin 19:7 2719
his sons smote him with the *s* ... 2Kin 19:37 2719
men able to bear buckler and *s* ... 1Chr 5:18 2719
to his armourbearer, Draw thy *s* ... 1Chr 10:4 2719
So Saul took a *s*, and fell upon it ... 1Chr 10:4 2719
dead, he fell likewise on the *s* ... 1Chr 10:5 2719
hundred thousand men that drew *s* ... 1Chr 21:5 2719
and ten thousand men that drew *s* ... 1Chr 21:5 2719
while that the *s* of thine enemies ... 1Chr 21:12 2719
else three days the *s* of the LORD ... 1Chr 21:12 2719
having a drawn *s* in his hand ... 1Chr 21:16 2719
he put up his *s* again into the ... 1Chr 21:27 2719
of the *s* of the angel of the LORD ... 1Chr 21:30 2719
evil cometh upon us, as the *s* ... 2Chr 20:9 2719
slew all his brethren with the *s* ... 2Chr 21:4 2719
her, let him be slain with the *s* ... 2Chr 23:14 2719
had slain Athaliah with the *s* ... 2Chr 23:21 2719
our fathers have fallen by the *s* ... 2Chr 29:9 2719

bowels slew him there with the *s* ... 2Chr 32:21 2719
slew their young men with the *s* ... 2Chr 36:17 2719
the *s* carried he away to Babylon ... 2Chr 36:20 2719
the kings of the lands, to the *s* ... Ezr 9:7 2719
every one had his *s* girded by his ... Neh 4:18 2719
enemies with the stroke of the *s* ... Est 9:5 2719
servants with the edge of the *s* ... Job 1:15 2719
servants with the edge of the *s* ... Job 1:17 2719
But he saveth the poor from the *s* ... Job 5:15 2719
and in war from the power of the *s* ... Job 5:20 2719
and he is waited for of the *s* ... Job 15:22 2719
Be ye afraid of the *s* ... Job 19:29 2719
bringeth the punishments of the *s* ... Job 19:29 2719
the glittering *s* cometh out of ... Job 20:25 1300
be multiplied, it is for the *s* ... Job 27:14 2719
his life from perishing by the *s* ... Job 33:18 7973
not, they shall perish by the *s* ... Job 36:12 7973
turneth he back from the *s* ... Job 39:22 2719
make his *s* to approach unto him ... Job 40:19 2719
The *s* of him that layeth at him ... Job 41:26 2719
he turn not, he will whet his *s* ... Ps 7:12 2719
from the wicked, which is thy *s* ... Ps 17:13 2719
Deliver my soul from the *s* ... Ps 22:20 2719
The wicked have drawn out the *s* ... Ps 37:14 2719
Their *s* shall enter into their ... Ps 37:15 2719
As with a *s* in my bones, mine ... Ps 42:10 7524
land in possession by their own *s* ... Ps 44:3 2719
bow, neither shall my *s* save me ... Ps 44:6 2719
Gird thy *s* upon thy thigh, O most ... Ps 45:3 2719
arrows, and their tongue a sharp *s* ... Ps 57:4 2719
They shall fall by the *s* ... Ps 63:10 2719
Who whet their tongue like a *s* ... Ps 64:3 2719
of the bow, the shield, and the *s* ... Ps 76:3 2719
his people over also unto the *s* ... Ps 78:62 2719
Their priests fell by the *s* ... Ps 78:64 2719
also turned the edge of his *s* ... Ps 89:43 2719
his servant from the hurtful *s* ... Ps 144:10 2719
a twoedged *s* in their hand ... Ps 149:6 2719
wormwood, sharp as a twoedged *s* ... Prov 5:4 2719
like the piercings of a *s* ... Prov 12:18 2719
his neighbour is a maul, and a *s* ... Prov 25:18 2719
every man hath his *s* upon his ... Song 3:8 2719
ye shall be devoured with the *s* ... Is 1:20 2719
not lift up *s* against nation ... Is 2:4 2719
Thy men shall fall by the *s* ... Is 3:25 2719
unto them shall fall by the *s* ... Is 13:15 2719
slain, thrust through with a *s* ... Is 14:19 2719
from the swords, from the drawn *s* ... Is 21:15 2719
men are not slain with the *s* ... Is 22:2 2719
strong *s* shall punish leviathan ... Is 27:1 2719
the Assyrian fall with the *s* ... Is 31:8 2719
and the *s*, not of a mean man, ... Is 31:8 2719
but he shall flee from the *s* ... Is 31:8 2719
For my *s* shall be bathed in ... Is 34:5 2719
The *s* of the LORD is filled with ... Is 34:6 2719
to fall by the *s* in his own land ... Is 37:7 2719
his sons smote him with the *s* ... Is 37:38 2719
he gave them as the dust to his *s* ... Is 41:2 2719
hath made my mouth like a sharp *s* ... Is 49:2 2719
and the famine, and the *s* ... Is 51:19 2719
will I number you to the *s* ... Is 65:12 2719
by his *s* will the LORD plead with ... Is 66:16 2719
your own *s* hath devoured your ... Jer 2:30 2719
whereas the *s* reacheth unto the ... Jer 4:10 2719
neither shall we see *s* nor famine ... Jer 5:12 2719
thou trustedst, with the *s* ... Jer 5:17 2719
for the *s* of the enemy and fear is ... Jer 6:25 2719
and I will send a *s* after them ... Jer 9:16 2719
the young men shall die by the *s* ... Jer 11:22 2719
for the *s* of the LORD shall ... Jer 12:12 2719
but I will consume them by the *s* ... Jer 14:12 2719
unto them, Ye shall not see the *s* ... Jer 14:13 2719
I sent them not, yet they say, *S* ... Jer 14:15 2719
By *s* and famine shall those ... Jer 14:15 2719
because of the famine and the *s* ... Jer 14:16 2719
then behold the slain with the *s* ... Jer 14:18 2719
as are for the *s*, to the *s* ... Jer 15:2 2719
the *s* to slay, and the dogs to ... Jer 15:3 2719
to the *s* before their enemies ... Jer 15:9 2719
they shall be consumed by the *s* ... Jer 16:4 2719
their blood by the force of the *s* ... Jer 18:21 2719
men be slain by the *s* in battle ... Jer 18:21 2719
by the *s* before their enemies ... Jer 19:7 2719
fall by the *s* of their enemies ... Jer 20:4 2719
and shall slay them with the *s* ... Jer 20:4 2719
from the pestilence, from the *s* ... Jer 21:7 2719
smite them with the edge of the *s* ... Jer 21:7 2719
in this city shall die by the *s* ... Jer 21:9 2719
And I will send the *s*, the famine, ... Jer 24:10 2719
because of the *s* that I will send ... Jer 25:16 2719
because of the *s* which I will ... Jer 25:27 2719
for I will call for a *s* upon all ... Jer 25:29 2719
them that are wicked to the *s* ... Jer 25:31 2719
who slew him with the *s*, and cast ... Jer 26:23 2719
saith the LORD, with the *s* ... Jer 27:8 2719
die, thou and thy people, by the *s* ... Jer 27:13 2719
I will send upon them the *s* ... Jer 29:17 2719
I will persecute them with the *s* ... Jer 29:18 2719
s found grace in the wilderness ... Jer 31:2 2719
against it, because of the *s* ... Jer 32:24 2719
of the king of Babylon by the *s* ... Jer 32:36 2719
down by the mounts, and by the *s* ... Jer 33:4 2719
thee, Thou shalt not die by the *s* ... Jer 34:4 2719
for you, saith the LORD, to the *s* ... Jer 34:17 2719
in this city shall die by the *s* ... Jer 38:2 2719
and thou shalt not fall by the *s* ... Jer 39:18 2719
the son of Shaphan with the *s* ... Jer 41:2 2719
it shall come to pass, that the *s* ... Jer 42:16 2719

they shall die by the *s*, by the ... Jer 42:17 2719
that ye shall die by the *s* ... Jer 42:22 2719
as are for the *s* to the *s* ... Jer 43:11 2719
shall even be consumed by the *s* ... Jer 44:12 2719
even unto the greatest, by the *s* ... Jer 44:12 2719
have punished Jerusalem, by the *s* ... Jer 44:13 2719
and have been consumed by the *s* ... Jer 44:18 2719
Egypt shall be consumed by the *s* ... Jer 44:27 2719
a small number that escape the *s* ... Jer 44:28 2719
the *s* shall devour, and it shall ... Jer 46:10 2719
for the *s* shall devour round ... Jer 46:14 2719
nativity, from the oppressing *s* ... Jer 46:16 2719
O thou *s* of the LORD, how long ... Jer 47:6 2719
the *s* shall pursue thee ... Jer 48:2 2719
keepeth back his *s* from blood ... Jer 48:10 2719
and I will send the *s* after them ... Jer 49:37 2719
for fear of the oppressing *s* they ... Jer 50:16 2719
A *s* is upon the Chaldeans, saith ... Jer 50:35 2719
A *s* is upon the liars ... Jer 50:36 2719
a *s* is upon her mighty men ... Jer 50:36 2719
A *s* is upon their horses, and upon ... Jer 50:37 2719
a *s* is upon her treasures ... Jer 50:37 2719
Ye that have escaped the *s* ... Jer 51:50 2719
abroad the *s* bereaveth, at home ... Lam 1:20 2719
my young men are fallen by the *s* ... Lam 2:21 2719
They that be slain with the *s* are ... Lam 4:9 2719
of the *s* of the wilderness ... Lam 5:9 2719
and I will draw out a *s* after them ... Eze 5:2 2719
fall by the *s* round about thee ... Eze 5:12 2719
and I will draw out a *s* after them ... Eze 5:12 2719
and I will bring the *s* upon thee ... Eze 5:17 2719
even I, will bring a *s* upon you ... Eze 6:3 2719
escape the *s* among the nations ... Eze 6:8 2719
for they shall fall by the *s* ... Eze 6:11 2719
that is near shall fall by the *s* ... Eze 6:12 2719
The *s* is without, and the ... Eze 7:15 2719
in the field shall die with the *s* ... Eze 7:15 2719
Ye have feared the *s* ... Eze 11:8 2719
and I will bring a *s* upon you ... Eze 11:8 2719
Ye shall fall by the *s* ... Eze 11:10 2719
I will draw out the *s* after them ... Eze 12:14 2719
a few men of them from the *s* ... Eze 12:16 2719
a *s* upon that land, and say, *S* ... Eze 14:17 2719
judgments upon Jerusalem, the *s* ... Eze 14:21 2719
all his bands shall fall by the *s* ... Eze 17:21 2719
draw forth my *s* out of his sheath ... Eze 21:3 2719
therefore shall my *s* go forth out ... Eze 21:4 2719
forth my *s* out of his sheath ... Eze 21:5 2719
Say, A *s*, a *s* is sharpened, ... Eze 21:9 2719
this *s* is sharpened, and it is ... Eze 21:11 2719
of the *s* shall be upon my people ... Eze 21:12 2719
what if the *s* contemn even the ... Eze 21:13
let the *s* be doubled the third ... Eze 21:14 2719
third time, the *s* of the slain ... Eze 21:14 2719
it is the *s* of the great men that ... Eze 21:14 2719
of the *s* against all their gates ... Eze 21:15 2719
that the *s* of the king of Babylon ... Eze 21:19 2719
that the *s* may come to Rabbath of ... Eze 21:20 2719
thou, The *s*, the *s* is drawn ... Eze 21:28 2719
daughters, and slew her with the *s* ... Eze 23:10 2719
thy remnant shall fall by the *s* ... Eze 23:25 2719
ye have left shall fall by the *s* ... Eze 24:21 2719
they of Dedan shall fall by the *s* ... Eze 25:13 2719
the field shall be slain by the *s* ... Eze 26:6 2719
He shall slay with the *s* thy ... Eze 26:8 2719
he shall slay thy people by the *s* ... Eze 26:11 2719
by the *s* upon her on every side ... Eze 28:23 2719
I will bring a *s* upon thee ... Eze 29:8 2719
the *s* shall come upon Egypt, and ... Eze 30:4 2719
shall fall with them by the *s* ... Eze 30:5 2719
shall they fall in it by the *s* ... Eze 30:6 2719
of Pi-beseth shall fall by the *s* ... Eze 30:17 2719
to make it strong to hold the *s* ... Eze 30:21 2719
I will cause the *s* to fall out of ... Eze 30:22 2719
Babylon, and put my *s* in his hand ... Eze 30:24 2719
when I shall put my *s* into the ... Eze 30:25 2719
them that be slain with the *s* ... Eze 31:17 2719
with them that be slain by the *s* ... Eze 31:18 2719
I shall brandish my *s* before them ... Eze 32:10 2719
The *s* of the king of Babylon ... Eze 32:11 2719
of them that are slain by the *s* ... Eze 32:20 2719
she is delivered to the *s* ... Eze 32:20 2719
lie uncircumcised, slain by the *s* ... Eze 32:21 2719
of them slain, fallen by the *s* ... Eze 32:22 2719
of them slain, fallen by the *s* ... Eze 32:23 2719
of them slain, fallen by the *s* ... Eze 32:24 2719
uncircumcised, slain by the *s* ... Eze 32:25 2719
uncircumcised, slain by the *s* ... Eze 32:26 2719
them that are slain with the *s* ... Eze 32:28 2719
by them that were slain by the *s* ... Eze 32:29 2719
with them that be slain by the *s* ... Eze 32:30 2719
and all his army slain by the *s* ... Eze 32:31 2719
them that are slain with the *s* ... Eze 32:32 2719
When I bring the *s* upon a land ... Eze 33:2 2719
he seeth the *s* come upon the land ... Eze 33:3 2719
if the *s* come, and take him away, ... Eze 33:4 2719
if the watchman see the *s* come ... Eze 33:6 2719
if the *s* come, and take any person ... Eze 33:6 2719
Ye stand upon your *s*, ye work ... Eze 33:26 2719
in the wastes shall fall by the *s* ... Eze 33:27 2719
s in the time of their calamity ... Eze 35:5 2719
fall that are slain with the *s* ... Eze 35:8 2719
that is brought back from the *s* ... Eze 38:8 2719
I will call for a *s* against him ... Eze 38:21 2719
every man's *s* shall be against ... Eze 38:21 2719
so fell they all by the *s* ... Eze 39:23 2719
yet they shall fall by the *s* ... Dan 11:33 2719
not save them by bow, nor by *s* ... Hos 1:7 2719

and I will break the bow and the *s* .... Hos 2:18 2719
s for the rage of their tongue .... Hos 7:16 2719
the *s* shall abide on his cities, ... Hos 11:6 2719
they shall fall by the *s* .... Hos 13:16 2719
and when they fall upon the *s* .... Joel 2:8 7973
did pursue his brother with the *s* .... Amos 1:11 2719
young men have I slain with the *s* .... Amos 4:10 2719
the house of Jeroboam with the *s* .... Amos 7:9 2719
Jeroboam shall die by the *s* .... Amos 7:11 2719
thy daughters shall fall by the *s* .... Amos 7:17 2719
slay the last of them with the *s* .... Amos 9:1 2719
thence will I command the *s* .... Amos 9:4 2719
of my people shall die by the *s* .... Amos 9:10 2719
not lift up a *s* against nation .... Mic 4:3 2719
the land of Assyria with the *s* .... Mic 5:6 2719
will I give up to the *s* .... Mic 6:14 2719
the *s* shall devour thy young .... Nah 2:13 2719
lifteth up both the bright *s* .... Nah 3:3 2719
the *s* shall cut thee off, it .... Nah 3:15 2719
also, ye shall be slain by my *s* .... Zeph 2:12 2719
every one by the *s* of his brother .... Hag 2:22 2719
thee as the *s* of a mighty man .... Zec 9:13 2719
the *s* shall be upon his arm, and .... Zec 11:17 2719
Awake, O *s*, against my shepherd, ... Zec 13:7 2719
I came not to send peace, but a *s* .... Mt 10:34 *3162*
out his hand, and drew his *s* .... Mt 26:51 *3162*
Put up again thy *s* into his place .... Mt 26:52 *3162*
the *s* shall perish with the *s* .... Mt 26:52 *3162*
of them that stood by drew a *s* .... Mk 14:47 *3162*
a *s* shall pierce through thy own .... Lk 2:35 *4501*
shall fall by the edge of the *s* .... Lk 21:24 *3162*
and he that hath no *s*, let him .... Lk 22:36 *3162*
Lord, shall we smite with the *s* .... Lk 22:49 *3162*
Simon Peter having a *s* drew it .... Jn 18:10 *3162*
Put up thy *s* into the sheath .... Jn 18:11 *3162*
the brother of John with the *s* .... Acts 12:2 *3162*
doors open, he drew out his *s* .... Acts 16:27 *3162*
or nakedness, or peril, or *s* .... Rom 8:35 *3162*
for he beareth not the *s* in vain .... Rom 13:4 *3162*
the *s* of the Spirit, which is the .... Eph 6:17 *3162*
and sharper than any twoedged *s* .... Heb 4:12 *3162*
fire, escaped the edge of the *s* .... Heb 11:34 *3162*
tempted, were slain with the *s* .... Heb 11:37 *3162*
his mouth went a sharp twoedged *s* .... Rev 1:16 *4501*
hath the sharp *s* with two edges .... Rev 2:12 *4501*
them with the *s* of my mouth .... Rev 2:16 *4501*
was given unto him a great *s* .... Rev 6:4 *3162*
part of the earth, to kill with *s* .... Rev 6:8 *4501*
he that killeth with the *s* must .... Rev 13:10 *3162*
must be killed with the *s* .... Rev 13:10 *3162*
beast, which had the wound by a *s* .... Rev 13:14 *3162*
out of his mouth goeth a sharp *s* .... Rev 19:15 *4501*
s of him that sat upon the horse .... Rev 19:21 *4501*
which *s* proceeded out of his .... Rev 19:21

SWORDS {24}
the Hebrews make them *s* or spears 1Sa 13:19 2719
him seven hundred men that drew *s* 2Kin 3:26 2719
after their families with their *s* .... Neh 4:13 2719
than oil, yet were they drawn *s* .... Ps 55:21 6609
s are in their lips .... Ps 59:7 2719
generation, whose teeth are as *s* .... Prov 30:14 2719
They all hold *s*, being expert in .... Song 3:8 2719
beat their *s* into plowshares .... Is 2:4 2719
For they fled from the *s*, from .... Is 21:15 2719
thrust thee through with their *s* .... Eze 16:40 2719
and dispatch them with their *s* .... Eze 23:47 2719
they shall draw their *s* against .... Eze 28:7 2719
shall draw their *s* against Egypt .... Eze 30:11 2719
By the *s* of the mighty will I .... Eze 32:12 2719
laid their *s* under their heads .... Eze 32:27 2719
shields, all of them handling *s* .... Eze 38:4 2719
Beat your plowshares into *s* .... Joel 3:10 2719
beat their *s* into plowshares .... Mic 4:3 2719
with him a great multitude with *s* .... Mt 26:47 *3162*
out as against a thief with *s* .... Mt 26:55 *3162*
with him a great multitude with *s* .... Mk 14:43 *3162*
out, as against a thief, with *s* .... Mk 14:48 *3162*
Lord, behold, here are two *s* .... Lk 22:38 *3162*
out, as against a thief, with *s* .... Lk 22:52 *3162*

SWORN {48}
And said, By myself have I *s* .... Gen 22:16 7650
for he had straitly *s* the .... Ex 13:19 7650
Because the LORD hath *s* .... Ex 17:16 3027,5920,3676
about which he hath *s* falsely .... Lev 6:5 7650
which he had *s* unto your fathers .... Deut 7:8 7650
as he hath *s* unto thy fathers .... Deut 13:17 7650
as he hath *s* unto thy fathers, and .... Deut 19:8 7650
himself, as he hath *s* unto thee .... Deut 28:9 7650
as he hath *s* unto thy fathers, to .... Deut 29:13 7650
the land which the LORD hath *s* .... Deut 31:7 7650
s unto them by the LORD God of .... Josh 9:18 7650
We have *s* unto them by the LORD .... Josh 9:19 7650
and as the LORD had *s* unto them .... Judg 2:15 7650
the men of Israel had *s* in Mizpeh .... Judg 21:1 7650
seeing we have *s* by the LORD that .... Judg 21:7 7650
for the children of Israel have *s* .... Judg 21:18 7650
therefore I have *s* unto the house 1Sa 3:14 7650
forasmuch as we have *s* both of us 1Sa 20:42 7650
as the LORD hath *s* to David 2Sa 3:9 7650
of Israel had *s* unto them 2Sa 21:2 7650
for they had *s* with all their 2Chr 15:15 7650
were many in Judah *s* unto him ...... Neh 6:18 1167,7621
which thou hadst *s* to give them .... Neh 9:15 5375
unto vanity, nor *s* deceitfully .... Ps 24:4 7650
I have *s* unto David my servant, ... Ps 89:3 7650
Once have I *s* by my holiness that .... Ps 89:35 7650
mad against me are *s* against me .... Ps 102:8 7650
The LORD hath *s*, and will not .... Ps 110:4 7650
I have *s*, and I will perform it, ... Ps 119:106 7650
The LORD hath *s* in truth unto .... Ps 132:11 7650
The LORD of hosts hath *s*, saying, ... Is 14:24 7650
I have *s* by myself, the word is .... Is 45:23 7650
for as I have *s* that the waters .... Is 54:9 7650
so have I *s* that I would not be .... Is 54:9 7650
The LORD hath *s* by his right hand .... Is 62:8 7650
s by them that are no gods .... Jer 5:7 7650
which I have *s* unto your fathers .... Jer 11:5 7650
I have *s* by my great name, saith .... Jer 44:26 7650
For I have *s* by myself, saith the .... Jer 49:13 7650
LORD of hosts hath *s* by himself .... Jer 51:14 7650
sight, to them that have *s* oaths .... Eze 21:23 7650
Lord GOD hath *s* by his holiness .... Amos 4:2 7650
The Lord GOD hath *s* by himself .... Amos 6:8 7650
The LORD hath *s* by the excellency .... Amos 8:7 7650
which thou hast *s* unto our .... Mic 7:20 7650
God had *s* with an oath to him .... Acts 2:30 *3660*
nigh, which God had *s* to Abraham .... Acts 7:17 *3660*
As I have *s* in my wrath, if they .... Heb 4:3 *3660*

SYCAMINE {1}
ye might say unto this *s* tree .... Lk 17:6 *4807*

SYCHAR *(si'-kar)* {1} See SHECHEM. *A city in Samaria.*
of Samaria, which is called *S* .... Jn 4:5 *4965*

SYCHEM *(si'-kem)* {2} See SHECHEM. *Same as Shechem.*
And were carried over into *S* .... Acts 7:16 *4966*
the sons of Emmor the father of *S* .... Acts 7:16 *4966*

SYCOMORE {7}
the *s* trees that are in the vale 1Kin 10:27 8256
the *s* trees that were in the low 1Chr 27:28 8256
cedar trees made he as the *s* 2Chr 1:15 8256
the *s* trees that are in the low 2Chr 9:27 8256
hail, and their *s* trees with frost .... Ps 78:47 8256
herdman, and a gatherer of *s* fruit .... Amos 7:14 8256
up into a *s* tree to see him .... Lk 19:4 *4809*

SYCOMORES {1}
the *s* are cut down, but we will .... Is 9:10 8256

SYENE *(si-e'-ne)* {2} *An Egyptian city.*
from the tower of *S* even unto the .... Eze 29:10 5482
from the tower of *S* shall they .... Eze 30:6 5482

SYNAGOGUE {43}
thence, he went into their *s* .... Mt 12:9 *4864*
he taught them in their *s* .... Mt 13:54 *4864*
sabbath day he entered into the *s* .... Mk 1:21 *4864*
there was in their *s* a man with .... Mk 1:23 *4864*
when they were come out of the *s* .... Mk 1:29 *4864*
And he entered again into the *s* .... Mk 3:1 *4864*
cometh one of the rulers of the *s* .... Mk 5:22 *752*
he saith unto the ruler of the *s* .... Mk 5:36 *752*
the house of the ruler of the *s* .... Mk 5:38 *752*
come, he began to teach in the *s* .... Mk 6:2 *4864*
he went into the *s* on the sabbath .... Lk 4:16 *4864*
in the *s* were fastened on him .... Lk 4:20 *4864*
And all they in the *s*, when they .... Lk 4:28 *4864*
in the *s* there was a man, which .... Lk 4:33 *4864*
And he arose out of the *s*, and .... Lk 4:38 *4864*
that he entered into the *s* .... Lk 6:6 *4864*
nation, and he hath built us a *s* .... Lk 7:5 *4864*
and he was a ruler of the *s* .... Lk 8:41 *4864*
the ruler of the *s* answered with .... Lk 13:14 *752*
These things said he in the *s* .... Jn 6:59 *4864*
he should be put out of the *s* .... Jn 9:22 *656*
they should be put out of the *s* .... Jn 12:42 *656*
I ever taught in the *s*, and in the .... Jn 18:20 *4864*
Then there arose certain of the *s* .... Acts 6:9 *4864*
is called the *s* of the Libertines .... Acts 6:9 *4864*
went into the *s* on the sabbath .... Acts 13:14 *4864*
rulers of the *s* sent unto them .... Acts 13:15 *752*
the Jews were gone out of the *s* .... Acts 13:42 *4864*
together into the *s* of the Jews .... Acts 14:1 *4864*
where was a *s* of the Jews .... Acts 17:1 *4864*
went into the *s* of the Jews .... Acts 17:10 *4864*
he in the *s* with the Jews .... Acts 17:17 *4864*
reasoned in the *s* every sabbath .... Acts 18:4 *4864*
whose house joined hard to the *s* .... Acts 18:7 *4864*
Crispus, the chief ruler of the *s* .... Acts 18:8 *752*
the chief ruler of the *s* .... Acts 18:17 *752*
but he himself entered into the *s* .... Acts 18:19 *4864*
he began to speak boldly in the *s* .... Acts 18:26 *4864*
And he went into the *s*, and spake .... Acts 19:8 *4864*
beat in every *s* them that .... Acts 22:19 *4864*
And I punished them oft in every *s* .... Acts 26:11 *4864*
are not, but are the *s* of Satan .... Rev 2:9 *4864*
will make them of the *s* of Satan .... Rev 3:9 *4864*

SYNAGOGUE'S {2}
of the *s* house certain which said .... Mk 5:35 *752*
one from the ruler of the *s* house .... Lk 8:49 *752*

SYNAGOGUES {24}
up all the *s* of God in the land .... Ps 74:8 4150
all Galilee, teaching in their *s* .... Mt 4:23 *4864*
as the hypocrites do in the *s* .... Mt 6:2 *4864*
love to pray standing in the *s* .... Mt 6:5 *4864*
and villages, teaching in their *s* .... Mt 9:35 *4864*
they will scourge you in their *s* .... Mt 10:17 *4864*
and the chief seats in the *s* .... Mt 23:6 *4864*
them shall ye scourge in your *s* .... Mt 23:34 *4864*
he preached in their *s* throughout .... Mk 1:39 *4864*
And the chief seats in the *s* .... Mk 12:39 *4864*
in the *s* ye shall be beaten .... Mk 13:9 *4864*
And he taught in their *s*, being .... Lk 4:15 *4864*
he preached in the *s* of Galilee .... Lk 4:44 *4864*
love the uppermost seats in the *s* .... Lk 11:43 *4864*
And when they bring you unto the *s* .... Lk 12:11 *4864*
in one of the *s* on the sabbath .... Lk 13:10 *4864*
and the highest seats in the *s* .... Lk 20:46 *4864*
you, delivering you up to the *s* .... Lk 21:12 *4864*
They shall put you out of the *s* .... Jn 16:2 *656*
him letters to Damascus to the *s* .... Acts 9:2 *4864*
he preached Christ in the *s* .... Acts 9:20 *4864*
word of God in the *s* of the Jews .... Acts 13:5 *4864*
read in the *s* every sabbath day .... Acts 15:21 *4864*
up the people, neither in the *s* .... Acts 24:12 *4864*

SYNTYCHE *(sin'-ti-ke)* {1} *A Christian at Philippi.*
I beseech Euodias, and beseech *S* .... Phil 4:2 *4941*

SYRACUSE *(sir'-a-cuse)* {1} *A city on Sicily.*
And landing at *S*, we tarried there .... Acts 28:12 *4946*

SYRIA *(sir'-e-ah)* {75} See ARAM, SYRIA-DAMASCUS, SYRIA-MAACHAH, SYRIAN. *Nation north of Israel.*
and Ashtaroth, and the gods of *S* .... Judg 10:6 758
put garrisons in *S* of Damascus 2Sa 8:6 758
Of *S*, and of Moab, and of the 2Sa 8:12 758
vow while I abode at Geshur in *S* 2Sa 15:8 758
Hittites, and for the kings of *S* 1Kin 10:29 758
Israel, and reigned over *S* 1Kin 11:25 758
the son of Hezion, king of *S* 1Kin 15:18 758
anoint Hazael to be king over *S* 1Kin 19:15 758
Ben-hadad the king of *S* gathered 1Kin 20:1 758
Ben-hadad the king of *S* escaped 1Kin 20:20 758
of *S* will come up against thee 1Kin 20:22 758
of the king of *S* said unto him 1Kin 20:23 758
three years without war between *S* 1Kin 22:1 758
out of the hand of the king of *S* 1Kin 22:3 758
But the king of *S* commanded his 1Kin 22:31 758
of the host of the king of *S* 2Kin 5:1 758
LORD had given deliverance unto *S* 2Kin 5:1 758
And the king of *S* said, Go to, go, ... 2Kin 5:5 758
Then the king of *S* warred against 2Kin 6:8 758
the heart of the king of *S* was 2Kin 6:11 758
So the bands of *S* came no more 2Kin 6:23 758
king of *S* gathered all his host 2Kin 6:24 758
uttermost part of the camp of *S* 2Kin 7:5 758
Ben-hadad the king of *S* was sick 2Kin 8:7 758
king of *S* hath sent me to thee 2Kin 8:9 758
me that thou shalt be king over *S* 2Kin 8:13 758
Hazael king of *S* in Ramoth-gilead 2Kin 8:28 758
fought against Hazael king of *S* 2Kin 8:29 758
because of Hazael king of *S* 2Kin 9:14 758
he fought with Hazael king of *S* 2Kin 9:15 758
Then Hazael king of *S* went up 2Kin 12:17 758
and sent it to Hazael king of *S* 2Kin 12:18 758
into the hand of Hazael king of *S* 2Kin 13:3 758
the king of *S* oppressed them 2Kin 13:4 758
for the king of *S* had destroyed 2Kin 13:7 758
the arrow of deliverance from *S* 2Kin 13:17 758
then hadst thou smitten *S* till 2Kin 13:19 758
now thou shalt smite *S* but thrice 2Kin 13:19 758
But Hazael king of *S* oppressed 2Kin 13:22 758
So Hazael king of *S* died 2Kin 13:24 758
against Judah Rezin the king of *S* 2Kin 15:37 758
Then Rezin king of *S* and Pekah son 2Kin 16:5 758
of *S* recovered Elath to *S* 2Kin 16:6 758
out of the hand of the king of *S* 2Kin 16:7 758
Hittites, and for the kings of *S* 2Chr 1:17 758
and sent to Ben-hadad king of *S* 2Chr 16:2 758
thou hast relied on the king of *S* 2Chr 16:7 758
of *S* escaped out of thine hand 2Chr 16:7 758
push *S* until they be consumed 2Chr 18:10 758
Now the king of *S* had commanded 2Chr 18:30 758
beyond the sea on this side *S* 2Chr 20:2 758
Hazael king of *S* at Ramoth-gilead 2Chr 22:5 758
he fought with Hazael king of *S* 2Chr 22:6 758
that the host of *S* came up 2Chr 24:23 758
into the hand of the king of *S* 2Chr 28:5 758
gods of the kings of *S* help them 2Chr 28:23 758
Judah, that Rezin the king of *S* .... Is 7:1 758
S is confederate with Ephraim .... Is 7:2 758
the fierce anger of Rezin with *S* .... Is 7:4 758
Because *S*, Ephraim, and the son of .... Is 7:5 758
For the head of *S* is Damascus .... Is 7:8 758
Damascus, and the remnant of *S* .... Is 17:3 758
reproach of the daughters of *S* .... Eze 16:57 758
S was thy merchant by reason of .... Eze 27:16 758
Jacob fled into the country of *S* .... Hos 12:12 758
the people of *S* shall go into .... Amos 1:5 758
And his fame went throughout all *S* .... Mt 4:24 *4947*
when Cyrenius was governor of *S* .... Lk 2:2 *4947*
of the Gentiles in Antioch and *S* .... Acts 15:23 *4947*
And he went through *S* and Cilicia, ... Acts 15:41 *4947*
brethren, and sailed thence into *S* .... Acts 18:18 *4947*
as he was about to sail into *S* .... Acts 20:3 *4947*
the left hand, and sailed into *S* .... Acts 21:3 *4947*
I came into the regions of *S* .... Gal 1:21 *4947*

SYRIACK *(sir'-e-ak)* {1} See SYRIAN. *Language of the Syrians.*
the Chaldeans to the king in *S* .... Dan 2:4 762

SYRIA-DAMASCUS *(sir'-e-ah-da-mas'-cus)* {1} See SYRIA, DAMASCUS. *Same as Damascus.*
Then David put garrisons in *S* 1Chr 18:6 758,1834

SYRIA-MAACHAH *(sir'-e-ah-ma-a-kah)* {1} *A Syrian city-state.*
out of Mesopotamia, and out of *S* 1Chr 19:6 758

SYRIAN *(sir'-e-un)* {12} See ARAMITES, SYRIANS, SYROPHENICIAN.
1. An inhabitant of Syria.
of Bethuel the *S* of Padan-aram .... Gen 25:20 761
the sister to Laban the *S* .... Gen 25:20 761
unto Laban, son of Bethuel the *S* .... Gen 28:5 761
away unawares to Laban the *S* .... Gen 31:20 761

Laban the *S* in a dream by night ... Gen 31:24 761
A *S* ready to perish was my father ... Deut 26:5 761
master hath spared Naaman this *S* ... 2Kin 5:20 761
was cleansed, saving Naaman the *S* ... Lk 4:27 *4948*
2. The language of Syria.
to thy servants in the *S* language ... 2Kin 18:26 762
was written in the *S* tongue ... Ezr 4:7 762
and interpreted in the *S* tongue ... Ezr 4:7 762
thy servants in the *S* language ... Is 36:11 762

SYRIANS {61}
when the *S* of Damascus came to ... 2Sa 8:5 758
of Zobah, David slew of the *S* two ... 2Sa 8:5 758
the *S* became servants to David, ... 2Sa 8:6 758
of the *S* in the valley of salt ... 2Sa 8:13 758
hired the *S* of Beth-rehob, and the ... 2Sa 10:6 758
the *S* of Zoba, twenty thousand ... 2Sa 10:6 758
the *S* of Zoba, and of Rehob, and ... 2Sa 10:8 758
put them in array against the *S* ... 2Sa 10:9 758
If the *S* be too strong for me, ... 2Sa 10:11 758
unto the battle against the *S* ... 2Sa 10:13 758
of Ammon saw that the *S* were fled ... 2Sa 10:14 758
when the *S* saw that they were ... 2Sa 10:15 758
brought out the *S* that were ... 2Sa 10:16 758
the *S* set themselves in array ... 2Sa 10:17 758
And the *S* fled before Israel ... 2Sa 10:18 758
seven hundred chariots of the *S* ... 2Sa 10:18 758
So the *S* feared to help the ... 2Sa 10:19 758
and the *S* fled ... 1Kin 20:20 758
slew the *S* with a great slaughter ... 1Kin 20:21 758
that Ben-hadad numbered the *S* ... 1Kin 20:26 758
but the *S* filled the country ... 1Kin 20:27 758
the LORD, Because the *S* have said ... 1Kin 20:28 758
S an hundred thousand footmen in ... 1Kin 20:29 758
With these shalt thou push the *S* ... 1Kin 22:11 758
up in his chariot against the *S* ... 1Kin 22:35 758
the *S* had gone out by companies, ... 2Kin 5:2 758
for thither the *S* are come down ... 2Kin 6:9 758
us fall unto the host of the *S* ... 2Kin 7:4 758
to go unto the camp of the *S* ... 2Kin 7:5 758
the *S* to hear a noise of chariots ... 2Kin 7:6 758
We came to the camp of the *S* ... 2Kin 7:10 758
you what the *S* have done to us ... 2Kin 7:12 758
king sent after the host of the *S* ... 2Kin 7:14 758
which the *S* had cast away in ... 2Kin 7:15 758
and spoiled the tents of the *S* ... 2Kin 7:16 758
and the *S* wounded Joram ... 2Kin 8:28 761
the *S* had given him at Ramah ... 2Kin 8:29 761
wounds which the *S* had given him ... 2Kin 9:15 761
out from under the hand of the *S* ... 2Kin 13:5 758
thou shalt smite the *S* in Aphek ... 2Kin 13:17 758
the *S* came to Elath, and dwelt ... 2Kin 16:6 758
the Chaldees, and bands of the *S* ... 2Kin 24:2 758
when the *S* of Damascus came to ... 1Chr 18:5 758
of Zobah, David slew of the *S* two ... 1Chr 18:5 758
the *S* became David's servants, and ... 1Chr 18:6 758
put them in array against the *S* ... 1Chr 19:10 758
If the *S* be too strong for me, ... 1Chr 19:12 758
nigh before the *S* unto the battle ... 1Chr 19:14 758
of Ammon saw that the *S* were fled ... 1Chr 19:15 758
when the *S* saw that they were put ... 1Chr 19:16 758
drew forth the *S* that were beyond ... 1Chr 19:16 758
the battle in array against the *S* ... 1Chr 19:17 758
But the *S* fled before Israel ... 1Chr 19:18 758
David slew of the *S* seven ... 1Chr 19:18 758
neither would the *S* help the ... 1Chr 19:19 758
against the *S* until the even ... 2Chr 18:34 758
and the *S* smote Joram ... 2Chr 22:5 761
For the army of the *S* came with a ... 2Chr 24:24 758
The *S* before, and the Philistines ... Is 9:12 758
and for fear of the army of the *S* ... Jer 35:11 758
from Caphtor, and the *S* from Kir ... Amos 9:7 758

SYROPHENICIAN *(sy'-ro-fe-ne'-she-un)* {1} *A citizen of Phenicia in Syria.*
woman was a Greek, a *S* by nation ... Mk 7:26 *4949*

SYRTIS See QUICKSANDS.

T

TAANACH *(ta'-a-nak)* {6} See TANACH. *A Levitical city in Manasseh.*
The king of *T*, one ... Josh 12:21 8590
towns, and the inhabitants of *T* ... Josh 17:11 8590
of Beth-shean and her towns, nor *T* ... Judg 1:27 8590
in *T* by the waters of Megiddo ... Judg 5:19 8590
to him pertained *T* and Megiddo, and ... 1Kin 4:12 8590
Beth-shean and her towns, *T* ... 1Chr 7:29 8590

TAANATH-SHILOH *(ta'-a-nath-shi'-lo)* {1} *A city on the border of Benjamin.*
border went about eastward unto *T* ... Josh 16:6 8387

TABALIAH See TEBALIAH.

TABBAOTH *(tab'-ba-oth)* {2} *A family of exiles.*
of Hasupha, the children of *T* ... Ezr 2:43 2884
of Hashupha, the children of *T* ... Neh 7:46 2884

TABBATH *(tab'-bath)* {1} *A city in Issachar.*
border of Abel-meholah, unto *T* ... Judg 7:22 2888

TABEAL *(tab'-e-al)* {1} See TABEEL. *Father of a would-be king of Israel.*
midst of it, even the son of *T* ... Is 7:6 2870

TABEEL *(tab'-e-el)* {1} See TABEAL. *A Persian official in Samaria.*
wrote Bishlam, Mithredath, *T* ... Ezr 4:7 2870

TABERAH *(tab'-e-rah)* {2} *A place in the wilderness of Paran.*
he called the name of the place *T* ... Num 11:3 8404
And at *T*, and at Massah, and at ... Deut 9:22 8404

TABERING {1}
of doves, *t* upon their breasts ... Nah 2:7 8608

TABERNACLE {328}
thee, after the pattern of the *t* ... Ex 25:9 4908
the *t* with ten curtains of fine ... Ex 26:1 4908
and it shall be one *t* ... Ex 26:6 4908
hair to be a covering upon the *t* ... Ex 26:7 4908
curtain in the forefront of the *t* ... Ex 26:9 168
hang over the backside of the *t* ... Ex 26:12 4908
the sides of the *t* on this side ... Ex 26:13 4908
the *t* of shittim wood standing up ... Ex 26:15 4908
make for all the boards of the *t* ... Ex 26:17 4908
shalt make the boards for the *t* ... Ex 26:18 4908
for the second side of the *t* on ... Ex 26:20 4908
for the sides of the *t* westward ... Ex 26:22 4908
corners of the *t* in the two sides ... Ex 26:23 4908
boards of the one side of the *t* ... Ex 26:26 4908
boards of the other side of the *t* ... Ex 26:27 4908
the boards of the side of the *t* ... Ex 26:27 4908
And thou shalt rear up the *t* ... Ex 26:30 4908
side of the *t* toward the south ... Ex 26:35 4908
shalt make the court of the *t* ... Ex 27:9 4908
All the vessels of the *t* in all ... Ex 27:19 4908
In the *t* of the congregation ... Ex 27:21 168
in unto the *t* of the congregation ... Ex 28:43 168
door of the *t* of the congregation ... Ex 29:4 168
before the *t* of the congregation ... Ex 29:10 168
by the door of the *t* of the ... Ex 29:11 168
when he cometh into the *t* of the ... Ex 29:30 168
by the door of the *t* of the ... Ex 29:32 168
t of the congregation before the ... Ex 29:42 168
the *t* shall be sanctified by my ... Ex 29:43
the *t* of the congregation ... Ex 29:44 168
of the *t* of the congregation ... Ex 30:16 168
between the *t* of the congregation ... Ex 30:18 168
go into the *t* of the congregation ... Ex 30:20 168
thou shalt anoint the *t* of the ... Ex 30:26 168
in the *t* of the congregation ... Ex 30:36 168
The *t* of the congregation, and the ... Ex 31:7 168
and all the furniture of the *t* ... Ex 31:7 168
And Moses took the *t*, and pitched ... Ex 33:7 168
camp, and called it the *T* of the ... Ex 33:7 168
unto the *t* of the congregation ... Ex 33:7 168
when Moses went out unto the *t* ... Ex 33:8 168
until he was gone into the *t* ... Ex 33:8 168
pass, as Moses entered into the *t* ... Ex 33:9 168
and stood at the door of the *t* ... Ex 33:9 168
cloudy pillar stand at the *t* door ... Ex 33:10 168
man, departed not out of the *t* ... Ex 33:11 168
The *t*, his tent, and his covering, ... Ex 35:11 4908
door at the entering in of the *t* ... Ex 35:15 4908
The pins of the *t*, and the pins of ... Ex 35:18 4908
work of the *t* of the congregation ... Ex 35:21 168
the *t* made ten curtains of fine ... Ex 36:8 4908
so it became one *t* ... Ex 36:13 4908
hair for the tent over the *t* ... Ex 36:14 4908
boards for the *t* of shittim wood ... Ex 36:20 4908
make for all the boards of the *t* ... Ex 36:22 4908
And he made boards for the *t* ... Ex 36:23 4908
And for the other side of the *t* ... Ex 36:25 4908
for the sides of the *t* westward ... Ex 36:27 4908
corners of the *t* in the two sides ... Ex 36:28 4908
boards of the one side of the *t* ... Ex 36:31 4908
boards of the other side of the *t* ... Ex 36:32 4908
of the *t* for the sides westward ... Ex 36:32 4908
an hanging for the *t* door of blue ... Ex 36:37 168
door of the *t* of the congregation ... Ex 38:8 168
And all the pins of the *t*, and of ... Ex 38:20 4908
This is the sum of the *t*, even of ... Ex 38:21 4908
even of the *t* of testimony, as it ... Ex 38:21 4908
door of the *t* of the congregation ... Ex 38:30 168
gate, and all the pins of the *t* ... Ex 38:31 4908
Thus was all the work of the *t* of ... Ex 39:32 4908
And they brought the *t* unto Moses ... Ex 39:33 4908
and the hanging for the *t* door ... Ex 39:38 168
vessels of the service of the *t* ... Ex 39:40 4908
month shalt thou set up the *t* of ... Ex 40:2 4908
the hanging of the door to the *t* ... Ex 40:5 4908
t of the tent of the congregation ... Ex 40:6 4908
anointing oil, and anoint the *t* ... Ex 40:9 4908
door of the *t* of the congregation ... Ex 40:12 168
month, that the *t* was reared up ... Ex 40:17 4908
And Moses reared up the *t*, and ... Ex 40:18 4908
spread abroad the tent over the *t* ... Ex 40:19 4908
And he brought the ark into the *t* ... Ex 40:21 4908
upon the side of the *t* northward ... Ex 40:22 4908
on the side of the *t* southward ... Ex 40:24 4908
the hanging at the door of the *t* ... Ex 40:28 4908
offering by the door of the *t* of ... Ex 40:29 4908
up the court round about the *t* ... Ex 40:33 4908
glory of the LORD filled the *t* ... Ex 40:34 4908
glory of the LORD filled the *t* ... Ex 40:35 4908
was taken up from over the *t* ... Ex 40:36 4908
of the LORD was upon the *t* by day ... Ex 40:38 4908
out of the *t* of the congregation ... Lev 1:1 168
will at the door of the *t* of the ... Lev 1:3 168
door of the *t* of the congregation ... Lev 1:5 168
door of the *t* of the congregation ... Lev 3:2 168
kill it before the *t* of the ... Lev 3:8 168
kill it before the *t* of the ... Lev 3:13 168
bullock unto the door of the *t* of ... Lev 4:4 168
and bring it to the *t* of the ... Lev 4:5 168
LORD, which is in the *t* of the ... Lev 4:7 168
door of the *t* of the congregation ... Lev 4:7 168
before the *t* of the congregation ... Lev 4:14 168
to the *t* of the congregation ... Lev 4:16 168
the LORD, that is in the *t* of the ... Lev 4:18 168
door of the *t* of the congregation ... Lev 4:18 168
in the court of the *t* of the ... Lev 6:16 168
of the *t* of the congregation ... Lev 6:26 168
into the *t* of the congregation to ... Lev 6:30 168
door of the *t* of the congregation ... Lev 8:3 168
door of the *t* of the congregation ... Lev 8:4 168
anointing oil, and anointed the *t* ... Lev 8:10 4908
door of the *t* of the congregation ... Lev 8:31 168
t of the congregation in seven ... Lev 8:33 168
of the *t* of the congregation day ... Lev 8:35 168
before the *t* of the congregation ... Lev 9:5 168
into the *t* of the congregation ... Lev 9:23 168
door of the *t* of the congregation ... Lev 10:7 168
go into the *t* of the congregation ... Lev 10:9 168
door of the *t* of the congregation ... Lev 12:6 168
at the door of the *t* of the ... Lev 14:11 168
door of the *t* of the congregation ... Lev 14:23 168
door of the *t* of the congregation ... Lev 15:14 168
to the door of the *t* of the ... Lev 15:29 168
defile my *t* that is among them ... Lev 15:31 4908
door of the *t* of the congregation ... Lev 16:7 168
do for the *t* of the congregation ... Lev 16:16 168
the *t* of the congregation when he ... Lev 16:17 168
the *t* of the congregation, and the ... Lev 16:20 168
into the *t* of the congregation ... Lev 16:23 168
for the *t* of the congregation ... Lev 16:33 168
door of the *t* of the congregation ... Lev 17:4 168
the LORD before the *t* of the LORD ... Lev 17:4 4908
door of the *t* of the congregation ... Lev 17:5 168
door of the *t* of the congregation ... Lev 17:6 168
door of the *t* of the congregation ... Lev 17:9 168
door of the *t* of the congregation ... Lev 19:21 168
in the *t* of the congregation, ... Lev 24:3 168
And I will set my *t* among you ... Lev 26:11 4908
in the *t* of the congregation, on ... Num 1:1 168
Levites over the *t* of testimony ... Num 1:50 4908
they shall bear the *t*, and all the ... Num 1:50 4908
and shall encamp round about the *t* ... Num 1:50 4908
when the *t* setteth forward, the ... Num 1:51 4908
when the *t* is to be pitched, the ... Num 1:51 4908
round about the *t* of testimony ... Num 1:53 4908
the charge of the *t* of testimony ... Num 1:53 4908
far off about the *t* of the ... Num 2:2 168
Then the *t* of the congregation ... Num 2:17 168
before the *t* of the congregation ... Num 3:7 168
to do the service of the *t* ... Num 3:7 4908
of the *t* of the congregation ... Num 3:8 168
to do the service of the *t* ... Num 3:8 4908
shall pitch behind the *t* westward ... Num 3:23 4908
t of the congregation shall be ... Num 3:25 168
the congregation shall be the *t* ... Num 3:25 4908
door of the *t* of the congregation ... Num 3:25 168
of the court, which is by the *t* ... Num 3:26 4908
on the side of the *t* southward ... Num 3:29 4908
on the side of the *t* northward ... Num 3:35 4908
shall be the boards of the *t* ... Num 3:36 4908
before the *t* toward the east ... Num 3:38 4908
even before the *t* of the ... Num 3:38 168
work in the *t* of the congregation ... Num 4:3 168
in the *t* of the congregation ... Num 4:4 168
in the *t* of the congregation ... Num 4:15 168
and the oversight of all the *t* ... Num 4:16 4908
work in the *t* of the congregation ... Num 4:23 168
shall bear the curtains of the *t* ... Num 4:25 4908
the *t* of the congregation, his ... Num 4:25 168
door of the *t* of the congregation ... Num 4:25 168
of the court, which is by the *t* ... Num 4:26 4908
in the *t* of the congregation ... Num 4:28 168
work of the *t* of the congregation ... Num 4:30 168
in the *t* of the congregation ... Num 4:31 168
the boards of the *t*, and the bars ... Num 4:31 4908
in the *t* of the congregation, ... Num 4:33 168
work in the *t* of the congregation ... Num 4:35 168
in the *t* of the congregation ... Num 4:37 168
work in the *t* of the congregation ... Num 4:39 168
in the *t* of the congregation ... Num 4:41 168
work in the *t* of the congregation ... Num 4:43 168
in the *t* of the congregation ... Num 4:47 168
of the *t* the priest shall take ... Num 5:17 4908
to the door of the *t* of the ... Num 6:10 168
door of the *t* of the congregation ... Num 6:13 168
door of the *t* of the congregation ... Num 6:18 168
that Moses had fully set up the *t* ... Num 7:1 4908
and they brought them before the *t* ... Num 7:3 4908
of the *t* of the congregation ... Num 7:5 168
t of the congregation to speak ... Num 7:89 168

before the *t* of the congregation Num 8:9 168
of the *t* of the congregation Num 8:15 168
in the *t* of the congregation Num 8:19 168
the *t* of the congregation before Num 8:22 168
of the *t* of the congregation Num 8:24 168
in the *t* of the congregation Num 8:26 168
on the day that the *t* was reared Num 9:15 4908
reared up the cloud covered the *t* Num 9:15 4908
at even there was upon the *t* as Num 9:15 4908
the cloud was taken up from the *t* Num 9:17 168
the *t* they rested in their tents Num 9:18 4908
tarried long upon the *t* many days Num 9:19 4908
cloud was a few days upon the *t* Num 9:20 4908
that the cloud tarried upon the *t* Num 9:22 4908
door of the *t* of the congregation Num 10:3 168
from off the *t* of the testimony Num 10:11 4908
And the *t* was taken down Num 10:17 4908
Merari set forward, bearing the *t* Num 10:17 4908
set up the *t* against they came Num 10:21 4908
unto the *t* of the congregation Num 11:16 168
and set them round about the *t* Num 11:24 168
but went not out unto the *t* Num 11:26 168
unto the *t* of the congregation Num 12:4 168
and stood in the door of the *t* Num 12:5 168
the cloud departed from off the *t* Num 12:10 168
of the LORD appeared in the *t* of Num 14:10 168
the service of the *t* of the LORD Num 16:9 4908
stood in the door of the *t* of the Num 16:18 168
door of the *t* of the congregation Num 16:19 168
you up from about the *t* of Korah Num 16:24 4908
they gat up from the *t* of Korah Num 16:27 4908
toward the *t* of the congregation Num 16:42 168
before the *t* of the congregation Num 16:43 168
door of the *t* of the congregation Num 16:50 168
thou shalt lay them up in the *t* Num 17:4 168
the LORD in the *t* of witness Num 17:7 168
Moses went into the *t* of witness Num 17:8 168
unto the *t* of the LORD shall die Num 17:13 4908
minister before the *t* of witness Num 18:2 168
and the charge of all the *t* Num 18:3 168
of the *t* of the congregation Num 18:4 168
for all the service of the *t* Num 18:4 168
of the *t* of the congregation Num 18:6 168
of the *t* of the congregation Num 18:21 168
nigh the *t* of the congregation Num 18:22 168
of the *t* of the congregation Num 18:23 168
in the *t* of the congregation Num 18:31 168
her blood directly before the *t* Num 19:4 168
defileth the *t* of the LORD Num 19:13 4908
door of the *t* of the congregation Num 20:6 168
door of the *t* of the congregation Num 25:6 168
by the door of the *t* of the Num 27:2 168
the charge of the *t* of the LORD Num 31:30 4908
the charge of the *t* of the LORD Num 31:47 4908
it into the *t* of the congregation Num 31:54 168
in the *t* of the congregation Deut 31:14 168
in the *t* of the congregation Deut 31:14 168
in the *t* in a pillar of a cloud Deut 31:15 168
stood over the door of the *t* Deut 31:15 168
set up the *t* of the congregation Josh 18:1 168
at the door of the *t* of the Josh 19:51 168
wherein the LORD's *t* dwelleth Josh 22:19 4908
LORD our God that is before his *t* Josh 22:29 4908
door of the *t* of the congregation 1Sa 2:22 168
in the midst of the *t* that David 2Sa 6:17 168
have walked in a tent and in a *t* 2Sa 7:6 4908
took an horn of oil out of the *t* 1Kin 1:39 168
Joab fled unto the *t* of the LORD 1Kin 2:28 168
was fled unto the *t* of the LORD 1Kin 2:29 168
Benaiah came to the *t* of the LORD 1Kin 2:30 168
the *t* of the congregation, and all 1Kin 8:4 168
holy vessels that were in the *t* 1Kin 8:4 168
of the *t* of the congregation with 1Chr 6:32 168
of the *t* of the house of God 1Chr 6:48 4908
keepers of the gates of the *t* 1Chr 9:19 168
door of the *t* of the congregation 1Chr 9:21 168
LORD, namely, the house of the *t* 1Chr 9:23 168
before the *t* of the LORD in the 1Chr 16:39 4908
to tent, and from one *t* to another 1Chr 17:5 4908
For the *t* of the LORD, which 1Chr 21:29 4908
they shall no more carry the *t* 1Chr 23:26 4908
of the *t* of the congregation 1Chr 23:32 168
for there was the *t* of the 2Chr 1:3 168
he put before the *t* of the LORD 2Chr 1:5 4908
which was at the *t* of the 2Chr 1:6 168
from before the *t* of the 2Chr 1:13 168
the *t* of the congregation, and all 2Chr 5:5 168
holy vessels that were in the *t* 2Chr 5:5 168
of Israel, for the *t* of witness 2Chr 24:6 168
know that thy *t* shall be in peace Job 5:24 168
The light shall be dark in his *t* Job 18:6 168
shall be rooted out of his *t* Job 18:14 168
It shall dwell in his *t*, because Job 18:15 168
me, and encamp round about my *t* Job 19:12 168
with him that is left in his *t* Job 20:26 168
the secret of God was upon my *t* Job 29:4 168
If the men of my *t* said not Job 31:31 168
the clouds, or the noise of his *t* Job 36:29 5521
Lord, who shall abide in thy *t* Ps 15:1 168
them hath he set a *t* for the sun Ps 19:4 168
secret of his *t* shall he hide me Ps 27:5 168
offer in his *t* sacrifices of joy Ps 27:6 168
I will abide in thy *t* for ever Ps 61:4 168
In Salem also is his *t*, and his Ps 76:2 5520
that he forsook the *t* of Shiloh Ps 78:60 4908
he refused the *t* of Joseph Ps 78:67 168
not come into the *t* of my house Ps 132:3 168
but the *t* of the upright shall Prov 14:11 168
there shall be a *t* for a shadow Is 4:6 5521
it in truth in the *t* of David Is 16:5 168
a *t* that shall not be taken down Is 33:20 168
My *t* is spoiled, and all my cords Jer 10:20 168
in the *t* of the daughter of Zion Lam 2:4 168
hath violently taken away his *t* Lam 2:6 7900
My *t* also shall be with them Eze 37:27 4908
which was the breadth of the *t* Eze 41:1 168
have borne the *t* of your Moloch Amos 5:26 5522
up the *t* of David that is fallen Amos 9:11 5521
Yea, ye took up the *t* of Moloch Acts 7:43 *4633*
Our fathers had the *t* of witness Acts 7:44 *4633*
desired to find a *t* for the God Acts 7:46 *4638*
will build again the *t* of David Acts 15:16 *4633*
house of this *t* were dissolved 2Cor 5:1 *4636*
we that are in this *t* do groan 2Cor 5:4 *4636*
the sanctuary, and of the true *t* Heb 8:2 *4633*
when he was about to make the *t* Heb 8:5 *4633*
For there was a *t* made Heb 9:2 *4633*
the *t* which is called the Holiest Heb 9:3 *4633*
went always into the first *t* Heb 9:6 *4633*
as the first *t* was yet standing Heb 9:8 *4633*
by a greater and more perfect *t* Heb 9:11 *4633*
sprinkled with blood both the *t* Heb 9:21 *4633*
no right to eat which serve the *t* Heb 13:10 *4633*
meet, as long as I am in this *t* 2Pet 1:13 *4638*
shortly I must put off this my *t* 2Pet 1:14 *4638*
to blaspheme his name, and his *t* Rev 13:6 *4633*
the temple of the *t* of the Rev 15:5 *4633*
the *t* of God is with men, and he Rev 21:3 *4633*

TABERNACLES {30}
month shall be the feast of *t* for Lev 23:34 5521
are thy tents, O Jacob, and thy *t* Num 24:5 4908
observe the feast of *t* seven days Deut 16:13 5521
of weeks, and in the feast of *t* Deut 16:16 5521
of release, in the feast of *t* Deut 31:10 5521
of weeks, and in the feast of *t* 2Chr 8:13 5521
They kept also the feast of *t* Ezr 3:4 5521
let not wickedness dwell in thy *t* Job 11:14 168
The *t* of robbers prosper, and they Job 12:6 168
shall consume the *t* of bribery Job 15:34 168
put away iniquity far from thy *t* Job 22:23 168
unto thy holy hill, and to thy *t* Ps 43:3 4908
place of the *t* of the most High Ps 46:4 4908
of their strength in the *t* of Ham Ps 78:51 168
The *t* of Edom, and the Ishmaelites Ps 83:6 168
How amiable are thy *t*, O LORD of Ps 84:1 4908
is in the *t* of the righteous Ps 118:15 168
We will go into his *t* Ps 132:7 4908
he shall plant the *t* of his Dan 11:45 168
thorns shall be in their *t* Hos 9:6 168
will yet make thee to dwell in *t* Hos 12:9 168
hosts, and to keep the feast of *t* Zec 14:16 5521
not up to keep the feast of *t* Zec 14:18 5521
not up to keep the feast of *t* Zec 14:19 5521
scholar, out of the *t* of Jacob Mal 2:12 168
wilt, let us make here three *t* Mt 17:4 *4633*
and let us make three *t* Mk 9:5 *4633*
and let us make three *t* Lk 9:33 *4633*
the Jews' feast of *t* was at hand Jn 7:2 *4634*
country, dwelling in *t* with Isaac Heb 11:9 *4633*

TABITHA *(tab'-ith-ah)* {2} *Woman raised from the dead by Peter.*
Joppa a certain disciple named *T* Acts 9:36 *5000*
turning him to the body said, *T* Acts 9:40 *5000*

TABLE {73}
also make a *t* of shittim wood Ex 25:23 7979
of the staves to bear the *t* Ex 25:27 7979
that the *t* may be borne with them Ex 25:28 7979
thou shalt set upon the *t* Ex 25:30 7979
shalt set the *t* without the vail Ex 26:35 7979
candlestick over against the *t* on Ex 26:35 7979
shalt put the *t* on the north side Ex 26:35 7979
And the *t* and all his vessels, and Ex 30:27 7979
And the *t* and his furniture, and the Ex 31:8 7979
The *t*, and his staves, and all his Ex 35:13 7979
he made the *t* of shittim wood Ex 37:10 7979
for the staves to bear the *t* Ex 37:14 7979
them with gold, to bear the *t* Ex 37:15 7979
the vessels which were upon the *t* Ex 37:16 7979
The *t*, and all the vessels thereof Ex 39:36 7979
And thou shalt bring in the *t* Ex 40:4 7979
he put the *t* in the tent of the Ex 40:22 7979
congregation, over against the *t* Ex 40:24 7979
upon the pure *t* before the LORD Lev 24:6 7979
charge shall be the ark, and the *t* Num 3:31 7979
upon the *t* of shewbread they Num 4:7 7979
gathered their meat under my *t* Judg 1:7 7979
he cometh not unto the king's *t* 1Sa 20:29 7979
arose from the *t* in fierce anger 1Sa 20:34 7979
eat bread at my *t* continually 2Sa 9:7 7979
son shall eat bread alway at my *t* 2Sa 9:10 7979
the king, he shall eat at my *t* 2Sa 9:11 7979
eat continually at the king's *t* 2Sa 9:13 7979
them that did eat at thine own *t* 2Sa 19:28 7979
be of those that eat at thy *t* 1Kin 2:7 7979
that came unto king Solomon's *t* 1Kin 4:27 7979
the *t* of gold, whereupon the 1Kin 7:48 7979
And the meat of his *t*, and the 1Kin 10:5 7979
to pass, as they sat at the *t* 1Kin 13:20 7979
hundred, which eat at Jezebel's *t* 1Kin 18:19 7979
set for him there a bed, and a *t* 2Kin 4:10 7979
tables of shewbread, for every *t* 1Chr 28:16 7979
And the meat of his *t*, and the 2Chr 9:4 7979
set they in order upon the pure *t* 2Chr 13:11 7979
thereof, and the shewbread *t* 2Chr 29:18 7979
there were at my *t* an hundred Neh 5:17 7979
thy *t* should be full of fatness Job 36:16 7979
Thou preparest a *t* before me in Ps 23:5 7979
Let their *t* become a snare before Ps 69:22 7979
God furnish a *t* in the wilderness Ps 78:19 7979
olive plants round about thy *t* Ps 128:3 7979
them upon the *t* of thine heart Prov 3:3 3871
them upon the *t* of thine heart Prov 7:3 3871
she hath also furnished her *t* Prov 9:2 7979
While the king sitteth at his *t* Song 1:12 4524
Prepare the *t*, watch in the Is 21:5 7979
go, write it before them in a *t* Is 30:8 3871
that prepare a *t* for that troop Is 65:11 7979
graven upon the *t* of their heart Jer 17:1 3871
a *t* prepared before it, whereupon Eze 23:41 7979
be filled at my *t* with horses Eze 39:20 7979
This is the *t* that is before the Eze 41:22 7979
and they shall come near to my *t* Eze 44:16 7979
and they shall speak lies at one *t* Dan 11:27 7979
The *t* of the LORD is contemptible Mal 1:7 7979
The *t* of the LORD is polluted Mal 1:12 7979
which fall from their masters' *t* Mt 15:27 *5132*
yet the dogs under the *t* eat of Mk 7:28 *5132*
And he asked for a writing *t* Lk 1:63 *4093*
which fell from the rich man's *t* Lk 16:21 *5132*
betrayeth me is with me on the *t* Lk 22:21 *5132*
drink at my *t* in my kingdom, and Lk 22:30 *5132*
them that sat at the *t* with him Jn 12:2
Now no man at the *t* knew for what Jn 13:28 *345*
Let their *t* be made a snare, and a Rom 11:9 *5132*
be partakers of the Lord's *t* 1Cor 10:21 *5132*
and of the *t* of devils 1Cor 10:21 *5132*
was the candlestick, and the *t* Heb 9:2 *5132*

TABLES {57}
and I will give thee *t* of stone Ex 24:12 3871
two *t* of testimony, *t* of Ex 31:18 3871
t of stone, written with the Ex 31:18 3871
the two *t* of the testimony were Ex 32:15 3871
the *t* were written on both their Ex 32:15 3871
the *t* were the work of God, and Ex 32:16 3871
writing of God, graven upon the *t* Ex 32:16 3871
he cast the *t* out of his hands Ex 32:19 3871
Hew thee two *t* of stone like unto Ex 34:1 3871
I will write upon these *t* the Ex 34:1 3871
words that were in the first *t* Ex 34:1 3871
he hewed two *t* of stone like unto Ex 34:4 3871
in his hand the two *t* of stone Ex 34:4 3871
he wrote upon the *t* the words of Ex 34:28 3871
two *t* of testimony in Moses' hand Ex 34:29 3871
he wrote them upon two *t* of stone Deut 4:13 3871
he wrote them in two *t* of stone Deut 5:22 3871
mount to receive the *t* of stone Deut 9:9 3871
even the *t* of the covenant which Deut 9:9 3871
two *t* of stone written with the Deut 9:10 3871
LORD gave me the two *t* of stone Deut 9:11 3871
even the *t* of the covenant Deut 9:11 3871
the two *t* of the covenant were in Deut 9:15 3871
And I took the two *t*, and cast them Deut 9:17 3871
Hew thee two *t* of stone like unto Deut 10:1 3871
I will write on the *t* the words Deut 10:2 3871
in the first *t* which thou brakest Deut 10:2 3871
hewed two *t* of stone like unto Deut 10:3 3871
having the two *t* in mine hand Deut 10:3 3871
And he wrote on the *t*, according Deut 10:4 3871
put the *t* in the ark which I had Deut 10:5 3871
the ark save the two *t* of stone 1Kin 8:9 3871
gave gold for the *t* of shewbread 1Chr 28:16 7979
silver for the *t* of silver 1Chr 28:16 7979
He made also ten *t*, and placed 2Chr 4:8 7979
the *t* whereon the shewbread was 2Chr 4:19 7979
two *t* which Moses put therein at 2Chr 5:10 3871
For all *t* are full of vomit and Is 28:8 7979
the gate were two *t* on this side Eze 40:39 7979
two *t* on that side, to slay Eze 40:39 7979
of the north gate, were two *t* Eze 40:40 7979
the porch of the gate, were two *t* Eze 40:40 7979
Four *t* were on this side, and four Eze 40:41 7979
four *t* on that side, by the side Eze 40:41 7979
eight *t*, whereupon they slew Eze 40:41 7979
the four *t* were of hewn stone for Eze 40:42 7979
upon the *t* was the flesh of the Eze 40:43 7979
vision, and make it plain upon *t* Hab 2:2 3871
temple, and overthrew the *t* of the Mt 21:12 *5132*
and pots, brasen vessels, and of *t* Mk 7:4 *2825*
temple, and overthrew the *t* of the Mk 11:15 *5132*
money, and overthrew the *t* Jn 2:15 *5132*
leave the word of God, and serve *t* Acts 6:2 *5132*
not in *t* of stone, but in fleshly 2Cor 3:3 *4109*
but in fleshly *t* of the heart 2Cor 3:3 *4109*
budded, and the *t* of the covenant Heb 9:4 *4109*

TABLETS {3}
and earrings, and rings, and *t* Ex 35:22 3558
bracelets, rings, earrings, and *t* Num 31:50 3558
legs, and the headbands, and the *t* Is 3:20 1004,5315

TABOR *(ta'-bor)* {10}
1. A mountain in Issachar and Zebulun.
And the coast reacheth to *T* Josh 19:22 8396
saying, Go and draw toward mount *T* Judg 4:6 8396
of Abinoam was gone up to mount *T* Judg 4:12 8396
So Barak went down from mount *T* Judg 4:14 8396
men were they whom ye slew at *T* Judg 8:18 8396
T and Hermon shall rejoice in thy Ps 89:12 8396
hosts, Surely as *T* is among the Jer 46:18 8396
on Mizpah, and a net spread upon *T* Hos 5:1 8396
2. A plain in Benjamin.
thou shalt come to the plain of *T* 1Sa 10:3 8396
3. A Levitical city in Zebulun.
her suburbs, *T* with her suburbs 1Chr 6:77 8396

TABRET {4}
with mirth, and with songs, with *t* ... Gen 31:27 8596
place with a psaltery, and a *t* ... 1Sa 10:5 8596
and aforetime I was as a *t* ... Job 17:6 8611
And the harp, and the viol, the *t* ... Is 5:12 8596

TABRETS {5}
to meet king Saul, with *t* ... 1Sa 18:6 8596
The mirth of *t* ceaseth, the noise ... Is 24:8 8596
lay upon him, it shall be with *t* ... Is 30:32 8596
shalt again be adorned with thy *t* ... Jer 31:4 8596
the workmanship of thy *t* and of ... Eze 28:13 8596

TABRIMMON See TABRIMON.

TABRIMON *(tab'-rim-on)* {1} *Father of Ben-hadad, king of Syria.*
them to Ben-hadad, the son of *T* ... 1Kin 15:18 2886

TACHES {10}
thou shalt make fifty *t* of gold ... Ex 26:6 7165
the curtains together with the *t* ... Ex 26:6 7165
thou shalt make fifty *t* of brass ... Ex 26:11 7165
put the *t* into the loops, and ... Ex 26:11 7165
hang up the vail under the *t* ... Ex 26:33 7165
his tent, and his covering, his *t* ... Ex 35:11 7165
And he made fifty *t* of gold ... Ex 36:13 7165
one unto another with the *t* ... Ex 36:13 7165
he made fifty *t* of brass to ... Ex 36:18 7165
tent, and all his furniture, his *t* ... Ex 39:33 7165

TACHMONITE *(tak'-mun-ite)* {1} See HACHMONITE. *Family name of a "mighty man" of David.*
The *T* that sat in the seat, chief ... 2Sa 23:8 8461

TACKLING {1}
our own hands the *t* of the ship ... Acts 27:19 *4631*

TACKLINGS {1}
Thy *t* are loosed ... Is 33:23 2256

TADMOR *(tad'-mor)* {2} *A city rebuilt by Solomon.*
T in the wilderness, in the land ... 1Kin 9:18 8412
he built *T* in the wilderness, and ... 2Chr 8:4 8412

TAHAN *(ta'-han)* {2} See TAHANITES.
1. A son of Ephraim.
of *T*, the family of the Tahanites ... Num 26:35 8465
2. A descendant of Ephraim.
and Telah his son, and *T* his son ... 1Chr 7:25 8465

TAHANITES *(ta'-han-ites)* {1} *Descendants of Tahan 1.*
of Tahan, the family of the *T* ... Num 26:35 8470

TAHAPANES *(ta-hap'-a-neze)* {1} See TAHAPANHES. *A city in Egypt.*
T have broken the crown of thy ... Jer 2:16 8471

TAHASH See THAHASH.

TAHATH *(ta'-hath)* {6}
1. An Israelite encampment in the wilderness.
from Makheloth, and encamped at *T* ... Num 33:26 8480
And they departed from *T*, and ... Num 33:27 8480
2. Father of Uriel.
T his son, Uriel his son, Uzziah ... 1Chr 6:24 8480
The son of *T*, the son of Assir ... 1Chr 6:37 8480
3. Father of Eladah.
T his son, and Eladah his son, and ... 1Chr 7:20 8480
4. Son of Eladah.
and Eladah his son, and *T* his son ... 1Chr 7:20 8480

TAHCHEMONITE See TACHMONITE.

TAHKEMONITE See TACHMONITE.

TAHPANHES *(tah'-pan-heze)* {5} See TAHAPANES, TAHPENES, TEHAPHNEHES. *Same as Tahapanes.*
thus came they even to *T* ... Jer 43:7 8471
of the LORD unto Jeremiah in *T* ... Jer 43:8 8471
the entry of Pharaoh's house in *T* ... Jer 43:9 8471
which dwell at Migdol, and at *T* ... Jer 44:1 8471
and publish in Noph and in *T* ... Jer 46:14 8471

TAHPENES *(tah'-pe-neze)* {3} See TAHPANHES. *Queen of a pharaoh.*
wife, the sister of *T* the queen ... 1Kin 11:19 8472
the sister of *T* bare him Genubath ... 1Kin 11:20 8472
whom *T* weaned in Pharaoh's house ... 1Kin 11:20 8472

TAHREA *(tah'-re-ah)* {1} See TAREA. *Son of Micah.*
were, Pithon, and Melech, and *T* ... 1Chr 9:41 8475

TAHTIM-HODSHI *(tah'-tim-hod'-shi)* {1} *A district north of Gilead in Bashan.*
to Gilead, and to the land of *T* ... 2Sa 24:6 8483

TAIL {10}
thine hand, and take it by the *t* ... Ex 4:4 2180
make thee the head, and not the *t* ... Deut 28:13 2180
the head, and thou shalt be the *t* ... Deut 28:44 2180
firebrands, and turned *t* to *t* ... Judg 15:4 2180
He moveth his *t* like a cedar ... Job 40:17 2180
cut off from Israel head and *t* ... Is 9:14 2180
that teacheth lies, he is the *t* ... Is 9:15 2180
for Egypt, which the head or *t* ... Is 19:15 2180
his *t* drew the third part of the ... Rev 12:4 *3769*

TAILS {6}
in the midst between two *t* ... Judg 15:4 2180
two *t* of these smoking firebrands ... Is 7:4 2180
they had *t* like unto scorpions ... Rev 9:10 *3769*
and there were stings in their *t* ... Rev 9:10 *3769*
is in their mouth, and in their *t* ... Rev 9:19 *3769*
for their *t* were like unto ... Rev 9:19 *3769*

TAKE {874}
t also of the tree of life, and ... Gen 3:22 3947
t thou unto thee of all food that ... Gen 6:21 3947
thou shalt *t* to thee by sevens ... Gen 7:2 3947
thy wife, *t* her, and go thy way ... Gen 12:19 3947
if thou wilt *t* the left hand ... Gen 13:9 3947
and *t* the goods to thyself ... Gen 14:21 3947
That I will not *t* from a thread ... Gen 14:23 3947
that I will not *t* any thing that ... Gen 14:23 3947
let them *t* their portion ... Gen 14:24 3947
T me an heifer of three years old ... Gen 15:9 3947
t thy wife, and thy two daughters ... Gen 19:15 3947
the mountain, lest some evil *t* me ... Gen 19:19 1692
ewe lambs shalt thou *t* of my hand ... Gen 21:30 3947
T now thy son, thine only son ... Gen 22:2 3947
t it of me, and I will bury my ... Gen 23:13 3947
that thou shalt not *t* a wife unto ... Gen 24:3 3947
t a wife unto my son Isaac ... Gen 24:4 3947
thou shalt *t* a wife unto my son ... Gen 24:7 3947
Thou shalt not *t* a wife to my son ... Gen 24:37 3947
kindred, and *t* a wife unto my son ... Gen 24:38 3947
thou shalt *t* a wife for my son of ... Gen 24:40 3947
t my master's brother's daughter ... Gen 24:48 3947
t her, and go, and let her be thy ... Gen 24:51 3947
Now therefore *t*, I pray thee, thy ... Gen 27:3 5375
the field, and *t* me some venison ... Gen 27:3 6679
if Jacob *t* a wife of the ... Gen 27:46 3947
Thou shalt not *t* a wife of the ... Gen 28:1 3947
t thee a wife from thence of the ... Gen 28:2 3947
to *t* him a wife from thence ... Gen 28:6 3947
Thou shalt not *t* a wife of the ... Gen 28:6 3947
wouldest thou *t* away my son's ... Gen 30:15 3947
T heed that thou speak not to ... Gen 31:24
T thou heed that thou speak not ... Gen 31:29
Peradventure thou wouldest *t* by ... Gen 31:31 1497
is thine with me, and *t* it to thee ... Gen 31:32 3947
or if thou shalt *t* other wives ... Gen 31:50 3947
T, I pray thee, my blessing that ... Gen 33:11 3947
Let us *t* our journey, and let us ... Gen 33:12
us, and *t* our daughters unto you ... Gen 34:9 3947
we will *t* your daughters to us ... Gen 34:16 3947
then will we *t* our daughter ... Gen 34:17 3947
let us *t* their daughters to us ... Gen 34:21 3947
Let her *t* it to her, lest we be ... Gen 38:23 3947
t up the fifth part of the land ... Gen 41:34
t food for the famine of your ... Gen 42:33 3947
not, and ye will *t* Benjamin away ... Gen 42:36 3947
t of the best fruits in the land ... Gen 43:11 3947
t double money in your hand ... Gen 43:12 3947
T also your brother, and arise, go ... Gen 43:13 3947
t us for bondmen, and our asses ... Gen 43:18 3947
if ye *t* this also from me, and ... Gen 44:29 3947
t your father and your households ... Gen 45:18 3947
t you wagons out of the land of ... Gen 45:19 3947
T this child away, and nurse it ... Ex 2:9 3212
thine hand, and *t* it by the tail ... Ex 4:4 270
that thou shalt *t* of the water of ... Ex 4:9 3947
thou shalt *t* this rod in thine ... Ex 4:17 3947
I will *t* you to me for a people ... Ex 6:7 3947
T thy rod, and cast it before ... Ex 7:9 3947
shalt thou *t* in thine hand ... Ex 7:15 3947
T thy rod, and stretch out thine ... Ex 7:19 3947
that he may *t* away the frogs from ... Ex 8:8 5493
T to you handfuls of ashes of the ... Ex 9:8 3947
that he may *t* away from me this ... Ex 10:17 5493
for thereof must we *t* to serve ... Ex 10:26 3947
t heed to thyself, see my face no ... Ex 10:28
shall *t* to them every man a lamb ... Ex 12:3 3947
t it according to the number of ... Ex 12:4 3947
ye shall *t* it out from the sheep ... Ex 12:5 3947
they shall *t* of the blood, and ... Ex 12:7 3947
t you a lamb according to your ... Ex 12:21 3947
ye shall *t* a bunch of hyssop, and ... Ex 12:22 3947
Also *t* your flocks and your herds ... Ex 12:32 3947
sorrow shall *t* hold on the ... Ex 15:14 270
trembling shall *t* hold upon them ... Ex 15:15 270
t ye every man for them which are ... Ex 16:16 3947
T a pot, and put an omer full of ... Ex 16:33 3947
t with thee of the elders of ... Ex 17:5 3947
the river, *t* in thine hand, and go ... Ex 17:5 3947
T heed to yourselves, that ye go ... Ex 19:12
Thou shalt not *t* the name of the ... Ex 20:7 5375
If he *t* him another wife ... Ex 21:10 3947
thou shalt *t* him from mine altar ... Ex 21:14 3947
If thou at all *t* thy neighbour's ... Ex 22:26 2254
And thou shalt *t* no gift ... Ex 23:8 3947
I will *t* sickness away from the ... Ex 23:25 5493
his heart ye shall *t* my offering ... Ex 25:2 3947
offering which ye shall *t* of them ... Ex 25:3 3947
that the loops may *t* hold one of ... Ex 26:5 6901
t thou unto thee Aaron thy ... Ex 28:1 7126
And they shall *t* gold, and blue, and ... Ex 28:5 3947
thou shalt *t* two onyx stones, and ... Ex 28:9 3947
T one young bullock, and two rams ... Ex 29:1 3947
thou shalt *t* the garments, and put ... Ex 29:5 3947
Then shalt thou *t* the anointing ... Ex 29:7 3947
thou shalt *t* of the blood of the ... Ex 29:12 3947
thou shalt *t* all the fat that ... Ex 29:13 3947
Thou shalt also *t* one ram ... Ex 29:15 3947
ram, and thou shalt *t* his blood ... Ex 29:16 3947
thou shalt *t* the other ram ... Ex 29:19 3947
t of his blood, and put it upon ... Ex 29:20 3947
thou shalt *t* of the blood that is ... Ex 29:21 3947
Also thou shalt *t* of the ram the ... Ex 29:22 3947
thou shalt *t* the breast of the ... Ex 29:26 3947
thou shalt *t* the ram of the ... Ex 29:31 3947
thou shalt *t* the atonement money ... Ex 30:16 3947
T thou also unto thee principal ... Ex 30:23 3947
T unto thee sweet spices, stacte ... Ex 30:34 3947
I will *t* away mine hand, and thou ... Ex 33:23 5493
t us for thine inheritance ... Ex 34:9
T heed to thyself, lest thou make ... Ex 34:12
thou *t* of their daughters unto ... Ex 34:16 3947
T ye from among you an offering ... Ex 35:5 3947
thou shalt *t* the anointing oil ... Ex 40:9 3947
he shall *t* thereout his handful ... Lev 2:2 7061
the priest shall *t* from the meat ... Lev 2:9 7311
the kidneys, it shall he *t* away ... Lev 3:4 5493
it shall he *t* off hard by the ... Lev 3:9 5493
the kidneys, it shall he *t* away ... Lev 3:10 5493
the kidneys, it shall he *t* away ... Lev 3:15 5493
shall *t* of the bullock's blood ... Lev 4:5 3947
he shall *t* off from it all the ... Lev 4:8 3318
the kidneys, it shall he *t* away ... Lev 4:9 5493
he shall *t* all his fat from him ... Lev 4:19 7311
the priest shall *t* of the blood ... Lev 4:25 3947
the priest shall *t* of the blood ... Lev 4:30 3947
he shall *t* away all the fat ... Lev 4:31 5493
the priest shall *t* of the blood ... Lev 4:34 3947
he shall *t* away all the fat ... Lev 4:35 5493
the priest shall *t* his handful of ... Lev 5:12 7061
t up the ashes which the fire ... Lev 6:10 7311
he shall *t* of it his handful, of ... Lev 6:15 7311
the kidneys, it shall he *t* away ... Lev 7:4 5493
T Aaron and his sons with him, and ... Lev 8:2 3947
T thee a young calf for a sin ... Lev 9:2 3947
T ye a kid of the goats for a sin ... Lev 9:3 3947
left, *T* the meat offering that ... Lev 10:12 3947
shall the priest command to *t* for ... Lev 14:4 3947
the living bird, he shall *t* it ... Lev 14:6 3947
on the eighth day he shall *t* two ... Lev 14:10 3947
And the priest shall *t* one he lamb ... Lev 14:12 3947
the priest shall *t* some of the ... Lev 14:14 3947
the priest shall *t* some of the ... Lev 14:15 3947
then he shall *t* one lamb for a ... Lev 14:21 3947
the priest shall *t* the lamb of ... Lev 14:24 3947
the priest shall *t* some of the ... Lev 14:25 3947
t away the stones in which the ... Lev 14:40 2502
they shall *t* other stones, and put ... Lev 14:42 3947
he shall *t* other morter, and shall ... Lev 14:42 3947
he shall *t* to cleanse the house ... Lev 14:49 3947
he shall *t* the cedar wood, and the ... Lev 14:51 3947
he shall *t* to him two turtledoves ... Lev 15:14 3947
she shall *t* unto her two turtles ... Lev 15:29 3947
he shall *t* of the congregation of ... Lev 16:5 3947
he shall *t* the two goats, and ... Lev 16:7 3947
he shall *t* a censer full of ... Lev 16:12 3947
he shall *t* of the blood of the ... Lev 16:14 3947
shall *t* of the blood of the ... Lev 16:18 3947
shalt thou *t* her son's daughter ... Lev 18:17 3947
Neither shalt thou *t* a wife to ... Lev 18:18 3947
And if a man *t* a wife and her ... Lev 20:14 3947
And if a man shall *t* his sister ... Lev 20:17 3947
if a man shall *t* his brother's ... Lev 20:21 3947
They shall not *t* a wife that is a ... Lev 21:7 3947
neither shall they *t* a woman put ... Lev 21:7 3947
And he shall *t* a wife in her ... Lev 21:13 3947
an harlot, these shall he not *t* ... Lev 21:14 3947
but he shall *t* a virgin of his ... Lev 21:14 3947
man of whom he may *t* uncleanness ... Lev 22:5
ye shall *t* you on the first day ... Lev 23:40 3947
And thou shalt *t* fine flour ... Lev 24:5 3947
T thou no usury of him, or ... Lev 25:36 3947
ye shall *t* them as an inheritance ... Lev 25:46
T ye the sum of all the ... Num 1:2 5375
neither *t* the sum of them among ... Num 1:49 5375
the Levites shall *t* it down ... Num 1:51 3381
t the number of their names ... Num 3:40 5375
thou shalt *t* the Levites for me ... Num 3:41 3947
T the Levites instead of all the ... Num 3:45 3947
Thou shalt even *t* five shekels ... Num 3:47 3947
the sanctuary shalt thou *t* them ... Num 3:47 3947
T the sum of the sons of Kohath ... Num 4:2 5375
they shall *t* down the covering ... Num 4:5 3381
they shall *t* a cloth of blue, and ... Num 4:9 3947
they shall *t* all the instruments ... Num 4:12 3947
they shall *t* away the ashes from ... Num 4:13 1878
T also the sum of the sons of ... Num 4:22 5375
the priest shall *t* holy water in ... Num 5:17 3947
the tabernacle the priest shall *t* ... Num 5:17 3947
Then the priest shall *t* the ... Num 5:25 3947
the priest shall *t* an handful of ... Num 5:26 7061
shall *t* the hair of the head of ... Num 6:18 3947
the priest shall *t* the sodden ... Num 6:19 3947
T it of them, that they may be to ... Num 7:5 3947
T the Levites from among the ... Num 8:6 3947
Then let them *t* a young bullock ... Num 8:8 3947
shalt thou *t* for a sin offering ... Num 8:8 3947
south side shall *t* their journey ... Num 10:6
I will *t* of the spirit which is ... Num 11:17 680
Ye *t* too much upon you, seeing ... Num 16:3
T you censers, Korah, and all his ... Num 16:6 3947
ye *t* too much upon you, ye sons ... Num 16:7
t every man his censer, and put ... Num 16:17 3947
that he *t* up the censers out of ... Num 16:37 7311
T a censer, and put fire therein ... Num 16:46 3947
t of every one of them a rod ... Num 17:2 3947
thou shalt quite *t* away their ... Num 17:10 3615
When ye *t* of the children of ... Num 18:26 3947
Eleazar the priest shall *t* of her ... Num 19:4 3947
And the priest shall *t* cedar wood ... Num 19:6 3947
shall *t* of the ashes of the burnt ... Num 19:17 3947
And a clean person shall *t* hyssop ... Num 19:18 3947
T the rod, and gather thou the ... Num 20:8 3947
T Aaron and Eleazar his son, and ... Num 20:25 3947
that he *t* away the serpents from ... Num 21:7 5493
Must I not *t* heed to speak that ... Num 23:12
T all the heads of the people, and ... Num 25:4 3947
T the sum of all the congregation ... Num 26:2 5375
T the sum of the people, from ... Num 26:4
T thee Joshua the son of Nun, a ... Num 27:18 3947
T the sum of the prey that was ... Num 31:26 5375
T it of their half, and give it ... Num 31:29 3947

T

thou shalt *t* one portion of fifty	Num 31:30	3947
ye shall *t* one prince of every	Num 34:18	3947
Moreover ye shall *t* no	Num 35:31	3947
ye shall *t* no satisfaction for	Num 35:32	3947
t your journey, and go to the	Deut 1:7	
T you wise men, and understanding,	Deut 1:13	3051
you, and *t* your journey into the	Deut 1:40	
t ye good heed unto yourselves	Deut 2:4	
t your journey, and pass over the	Deut 2:24	
Only *t* heed to thyself, and keep	Deut 4:9	
T ye therefore good heed unto	Deut 4:15	
T heed unto yourselves, lest ye	Deut 4:23	
t him a nation from the midst of	Deut 4:34	3947
Thou shalt not *t* the name of the	Deut 5:11	5375
shalt thou *t* unto thy son	Deut 7:3	3947
the LORD will *t* away from thee	Deut 7:15	5493
nor *t* it unto thee, lest thou be	Deut 7:25	3947
t thy journey before the people,	Deut 10:11	
T heed to yourselves, that your	Deut 11:16	
T heed to thyself that thou offer	Deut 12:13	
T heed to thyself that thou	Deut 12:19	
hast, and thy vows, thou shalt *t*	Deut 12:26	5375
T heed to thyself that thou be	Deut 12:30	
Then thou shalt *t* an aul, and	Deut 15:17	3947
respect persons, neither *t* a gift	Deut 16:19	3947
the battle, and another man *t* her	Deut 20:7	3947
shalt thou *t* unto thyself	Deut 20:14	962
in making war against it to *t* it	Deut 20:19	8610
of that city shall *t* an heifer	Deut 21:3	3947
thou shalt not *t* the dam with the	Deut 22:6	3947
dam go, and *t* the young to thee	Deut 22:7	3947
If any man *t* a wife, and go in	Deut 22:13	3947
of the damsel, and her mother, *t*	Deut 22:15	3947
of that city shall *t* that man	Deut 22:18	3947
A man shall not *t* his father's	Deut 22:30	3947
may not *t* her again to be his	Deut 24:4	3947
No man shall *t* the nether or the	Deut 24:6	2254
T heed in the plague of leprosy,	Deut 24:8	
nor *t* a widow's raiment to pledge	Deut 24:17	2254
t her to him to wife, and perform	Deut 25:5	3947
like not to *t* his brother's wife	Deut 25:7	3947
it, and say, I like not to *t* her	Deut 25:8	3947
That thou shalt *t* of the first of	Deut 26:2	3947
the priest shall *t* the basket out	Deut 26:4	3947
T heed, and hearken, O Israel	Deut 27:9	5535
T this book of the law, and put it	Deut 31:26	3947
mine hand *t* hold on judgment	Deut 32:41	270
T up the ark of the covenant, and	Josh 3:6	5375
Now therefore *t* you twelve men	Josh 3:12	3947
T you twelve men out of the	Josh 4:2	3947
T you hence out of the midst of	Josh 4:3	5375
t you up every man of you a stone	Josh 4:5	7311
T up the ark of the covenant, and	Josh 6:6	5375
when ye *t* of the accursed thing,	Josh 6:18	3947
until ye *t* away the accursed	Josh 7:13	5493
shall *t* shall come by households	Josh 7:14	3920
shall *t* shall come man by man	Josh 7:14	3920
t all the people of war with thee	Josh 8:1	3947
shall ye *t* for a prey unto	Josh 8:2	962
commanded that they should *t* his	Josh 8:29	3381
T victuals with you for the	Josh 9:11	3947
land did Joshua *t* at one time	Josh 10:42	3920
the kings of them, did Joshua *t*	Josh 11:12	3920
they shall *t* him into the city	Josh 20:4	622
But *t* diligent heed to do the	Josh 22:5	
and *t* possession among us	Josh 22:19	270
T good heed therefore unto	Josh 23:11	
t with thee ten thousand men of	Judg 4:6	3947
necks of them that *t* the spoil	Judg 5:30	
T the flesh and the unleavened	Judg 6:20	3947
T thy father's young bullock,	Judg 6:25	3947
t the second bullock, and offer a	Judg 6:26	3947
t before them the waters unto	Judg 7:24	3920
that thou goest to *t* a wife of	Judg 14:3	3947
after a time he returned to *t* her	Judg 14:8	3947
ye called us to *t* that we have	Judg 14:15	3423
t her, I pray thee, instead of	Judg 15:2	1961
t advice, and speak your minds	Judg 19:30	
we will *t* ten men of an hundred	Judg 20:10	3947
thou shouldest *t* knowledge of me	Ruth 2:10	
he that did *t* knowledge of thee	Ruth 2:19	
then *t* as much as thy soul	1Sa 2:16	3947
and if not, I will *t* it by force	1Sa 2:16	3947
t two milch kine, on which there	1Sa 6:7	3947
t the ark of the LORD, and lay it	1Sa 6:8	3947
He will *t* your sons, and appoint	1Sa 8:11	3947
he will *t* your daughters to be	1Sa 8:13	3947
he will *t* your fields, and your	1Sa 8:14	3947
he will *t* the tenth of your seed,	1Sa 8:15	
he will *t* your menservants, and	1Sa 8:16	3947
He will *t* the tenth of your sheep	1Sa 8:17	
T now one of the servants with	1Sa 9:3	3947
the asses, and *t* thought for us	1Sa 9:5	
T an heifer with thee, and say, I	1Sa 16:2	3947
T now for thy brethren an ephah	1Sa 17:17	3947
brethren fare, and *t* their pledge	1Sa 17:18	3947
thee, and *t* thine head from thee	1Sa 17:46	5493
t heed to thyself until the	1Sa 19:2	
Saul sent messengers to *t* David	1Sa 19:14	3947
Saul sent messengers to *t* David	1Sa 19:20	3947
are on this side of thee, *t* them	1Sa 20:21	3947
if thou wilt *t* that, *t* it	1Sa 21:9	3947
t knowledge of all the lurking	1Sa 23:23	
and his men round about to *t* them	1Sa 23:26	8610
yet thou huntest my soul to *t* it	1Sa 24:11	3947
Shall I then *t* my bread, and my	1Sa 25:11	3947
Abigail, to *t* her to him to wife	1Sa 25:39	3947
thee, to *t* thee to him to wife	1Sa 25:40	3947
t thou now the spear that is at	1Sa 26:11	3947
young men, and *t* thee his armour	2Sa 2:21	3947
t you away from the earth	2Sa 4:11	1197
Except thou *t* away the blind and	2Sa 5:6	5493
he spared to *t* of his own flock	2Sa 12:4	3947
I will *t* thy wives before thine	2Sa 12:11	3947
encamp against the city, and *t* it	2Sa 12:28	3920
lest I *t* the city, and it be	2Sa 12:28	3920
the king *t* the thing to his heart	2Sa 13:33	7760
thou, and *t* back thy brethren	2Sa 15:20	7725
I pray thee, and *t* off his head	2Sa 16:9	5493
the king should *t* it to his heart	2Sa 19:19	7760
unto the king, Yea, let him *t* all	2Sa 19:30	3947
t thou thy lord's servants, and	2Sa 20:6	3947
t away the iniquity of thy	2Sa 24:10	5674
David, Let my lord the king *t*	2Sa 24:22	3947
T with you the servants of your	1Kin 1:33	3947
If thy children *t* heed to their	1Kin 2:4	
that thou mayest *t* away the	1Kin 2:31	5493
thy children *t* heed to their way	1Kin 8:25	
to Jeroboam, *T* thee ten pieces	1Kin 11:31	3947
Howbeit I will not *t* the whole	1Kin 11:34	3947
But I will *t* the kingdom out of	1Kin 11:35	3947
And I will *t* thee, and thou shalt	1Kin 11:37	3947
t with thee ten loaves, and	1Kin 14:3	3947
will *t* away the remnant of the	1Kin 14:10	1197
I will *t* away the posterity of	1Kin 16:3	1197
unto them, *T* the prophets of Baal	1Kin 18:40	8610
now, O LORD, *t* away my life	1Kin 19:4	3947
they seek my life, to *t* it away	1Kin 19:10	3947
they seek my life, to *t* it away	1Kin 19:14	3947
it in their hand, and *t* it away	1Kin 20:6	3947
come out for peace, *t* them alive	1Kin 20:18	8610
be come out for war, *t* them alive	1Kin 20:18	8610
T the kings away, every man out	1Kin 20:24	5493
t possession of the vineyard of	1Kin 21:15	3423
Jezreelite, to *t* possession of it	1Kin 21:16	3423
will *t* away thy posterity, and	1Kin 21:21	1197
t it not out of the hand of the	1Kin 22:3	3947
T Micaiah, and carry him back unto	1Kin 22:26	3947
when the LORD would *t* up Elijah	2Kin 2:1	5927
t away thy master from thy head	2Kin 2:3	3947
t away thy master from thy head	2Kin 2:5	3947
the creditor is come to *t* unto	2Kin 4:1	3947
t my staff in thine hand, and go	2Kin 4:29	3947
unto him, he said, *T* up thy son	2Kin 4:36	5375
t a blessing of thy servant	2Kin 5:15	3947
And he urged him to *t* it	2Kin 5:16	3947
after him, and *t* somewhat of him	2Kin 5:20	3947
said, Be content, *t* two talents	2Kin 5:23	3947
t thence every man a beam, and let	2Kin 6:2	3947
said he, *T* it up to thee	2Kin 6:7	7311
hath sent to *t* away mine head	2Kin 6:32	5493
answered and said, Let some *t*	2Kin 7:13	3947
T a present in thine hand, and go,	2Kin 8:8	3947
t this box of oil in thine hand,	2Kin 9:1	3947
Then *t* the box of oil, and pour it	2Kin 9:3	3947
T an horseman, and send to meet	2Kin 9:17	3947
T up, and cast him in the portion	2Kin 9:25	5375
Now therefore *t* and cast him into	2Kin 9:26	5375
t ye the heads of the men your	2Kin 10:6	3947
And he said, *T* them alive	2Kin 10:14	8610
Let the priests *t* it to them	2Kin 12:5	3947
said unto him, *T* bow and arrows	2Kin 13:15	3947
And he said, *T* the arrows	2Kin 13:18	3947
t you away to a land like your	2Kin 18:32	3947
shall yet again *t* root downward	2Kin 19:30	3947
And Isaiah said, *T* a lump of figs	2Kin 20:7	3947
shalt beget, shall they *t* away	2Kin 20:18	3947
came down to *t* away their cattle	1Chr 7:21	3947
I will not *t* my mercy away from	1Chr 17:13	5493
T it to thee, and let my lord the	1Chr 21:23	3947
for I will not *t* that which is	1Chr 21:24	5375
T heed now	1Chr 28:10	7200
yet so that thy children *t* heed	2Chr 6:16	
T ye Micaiah, and carry him back	2Chr 18:25	3947
to the judges, *T* heed what ye do	2Chr 19:6	7200
t heed and do it	2Chr 19:7	
his people came to *t* away the	2Chr 20:25	962
that they might *t* the city	2Chr 32:18	3920
so that they will *t* heed to do	2Chr 33:8	
T heed now that ye fail not to do	Ezr 4:22	2095
those did Cyrus the king *t* out of	Ezr 5:14	5312
T these vessels, go, carry them	Ezr 5:15	5376
neither *t* their daughters unto	Ezr 9:12	5375
therefore we *t* up corn for them,	Neh 5:2	3947
let us *t* counsel together	Neh 6:7	
nor *t* their daughters for our	Neh 10:30	3947
when the Levites *t* tithes	Neh 10:38	
nor *t* their daughters unto your	Neh 13:25	5375
to *t* the spoil of them for a prey	Est 3:13	3947
to *t* away his sackcloth from him	Est 4:4	5493
t the apparel and the horse, as	Est 6:10	3947
to *t* the spoil of them for a prey	Est 8:11	
and *t* away mine iniquity	Job 7:21	5674
will not suffer me to *t* my breath	Job 9:18	7725
Let him *t* his rod away from me,	Job 9:34	5493
that I may *t* comfort a little,	Job 10:20	
thou shalt *t* thy rest in safety	Job 11:18	7901
Wherefore do I *t* my flesh in my	Job 13:14	5375
The gin shall *t* him by the heel,	Job 18:9	270
They *t* the timbrel and harp, and	Job 21:12	5375
But he knoweth the way that I *t*	Job 23:10	5978
they violently *t* away flocks	Job 24:2	1497
they *t* the widow's ox for a	Job 24:3	2254
breast, and *t* a pledge of the poor	Job 24:9	2254
they *t* away the sheaf from the	Job 24:10	5375
Terrors *t* hold on him as waters,	Job 27:20	5381
and my sinews *t* no rest	Job 30:17	7901
Surely I would *t* it upon my	Job 31:36	5375
my maker would soon *t* me away	Job 32:22	5375
and justice *t* hold on thee	Job 36:17	8551
beware lest he *t* thee away with	Job 36:18	5496
T heed, regard not iniquity	Job 36:21	
That it might *t* hold of the ends	Job 38:13	270
That thou shouldest *t* it to the	Job 38:20	3947
wilt thou *t* him for a servant for	Job 41:4	3947
Therefore *t* unto you now seven	Job 42:8	3947
the rulers *t* counsel together,	Ps 2:2	
enemy persecute my soul, and *t* it	Ps 7:5	5381
How long shall I *t* counsel in my	Ps 13:2	7896
nor *t* up their names into my lips	Ps 16:4	5375
me, then the LORD will *t* me up	Ps 27:10	622
they devised to *t* away my life	Ps 31:13	3947
T hold of shield and buckler, and	Ps 35:2	2388
I will *t* heed to my ways, that I	Ps 39:1	
I will *t* no bullock out of thy	Ps 50:9	3947
or that thou shouldest *t* my	Ps 50:16	5375
t not thy holy spirit from me	Ps 51:11	3947
he shall *t* thee away, and pluck	Ps 52:5	2846
he shall *t* them away as with a	Ps 58:9	8175
and I looked for some to *t* pity	Ps 69:20	
thy wrathful anger *t* hold of them	Ps 69:24	5381
for my soul *t* counsel together	Ps 71:10	
persecute and *t* him	Ps 71:11	8610
and didst cause it to *t* deep root	Ps 80:9	
T a psalm, and bring hither the	Ps 81:2	5375
Let us *t* to ourselves the houses	Ps 83:12	3423
will I not utterly *t* from him	Ps 89:33	6331
For thy servants *t* pleasure in	Ps 102:14	
t me not away in the midst of my	Ps 102:24	5927
and let another *t* his office	Ps 109:8	3947
I will *t* the cup of salvation, and	Ps 116:13	5375
t not the word of truth utterly	Ps 119:43	5337
If I *t* the wings of the morning,	Ps 139:9	5375
thine enemies *t* thy name in vain	Ps 139:20	5375
neither *t* they hold of the paths	Prov 2:19	5381
T fast hold of instruction	Prov 4:13	2388
her steps *t* hold on hell	Prov 5:5	8551
shall *t* the wicked himself	Prov 5:22	3920
neither let her *t* thee with her	Prov 6:25	3947
Can a man *t* fire in his bosom, and	Prov 6:27	2846
let us *t* our fill of love until	Prov 7:18	
T his garment that is surety for	Prov 20:16	3947
t a pledge of him for a strange	Prov 20:16	2254
why should he *t* away thy bed from	Prov 22:27	3947
T away the dross from the silver,	Prov 25:4	1898
T away the wicked from before the	Prov 25:5	1898
T his garment that is surety for	Prov 27:13	3947
t a pledge of him for a strange	Prov 27:13	2254
t the name of my God in vain	Prov 30:9	8610
shall *t* nothing of his labour,	Eccl 5:15	5375
to *t* his portion, and to rejoice	Eccl 5:19	5375
thou shouldest *t* hold of this	Eccl 7:18	270
Also *t* no heed unto all words	Eccl 7:21	5414
T us the foxes, the little foxes,	Song 2:15	270
I will *t* hold of the boughs	Song 7:8	270
thy dross, and *t* away all thy tin	Is 1:25	5493
doth *t* away from Jerusalem and	Is 3:1	5493
When a man shall *t* hold of his	Is 3:6	8610
will *t* away the bravery of their	Is 3:18	5493
women shall *t* hold of one man	Is 4:1	2388
thy name, to *t* away our reproach	Is 4:1	622
I will *t* away the hedge thereof,	Is 5:5	5493
t away the righteousness of the	Is 5:23	5493
say unto him, *T* heed, and be quiet	Is 7:4	
T thee a great roll, and write in	Is 8:1	3947
T counsel together, and it shall	Is 8:10	
to *t* away the right from the poor	Is 10:2	1497
to *t* the spoil, and to	Is 10:6	7997
to *t* the prey, and to tread them	Is 10:6	962
and sorrows shall *t* hold of them	Is 13:8	270
And the people shall *t* them	Is 14:2	3947
they shall *t* them captives, whose	Is 14:2	
That thou shalt *t* up this proverb	Is 14:4	5375
T counsel, execute judgment	Is 16:3	935
I will *t* my rest, and I will	Is 18:4	
t away and cut down the branches	Is 18:5	5493
T an harp, go about the city,	Is 23:16	3947
he *t* away from off all the earth	Is 25:8	5493
Or let him *t* hold of my strength,	Is 27:5	2388
them that come of Jacob to *t* root	Is 27:6	2388
all the fruit to *t* away his sin	Is 27:9	5493
it goeth forth it shall *t* you	Is 28:19	3947
that *t* counsel, but not of me	Is 30:1	6213
a sherd to *t* fire from the hearth	Is 30:14	2846
or to *t* water withal out of the	Is 30:14	2834
the lame *t* the prey	Is 33:23	962
t you away to a land like your	Is 36:17	3947
Judah shall again *t* root downward	Is 37:31	
Let them *t* a lump of figs, and lay	Is 38:21	5375
shall beget, shall they *t* away	Is 39:7	3947
shall not *t* root in the earth	Is 40:24	3947
the whirlwind shall *t* them away	Is 40:24	5375
for he will *t* thereof, and warm	Is 44:15	3947
let them *t* counsel together	Is 45:21	
T the millstones, and grind meal	Is 47:2	3947
I will *t* vengeance, and I will not	Is 47:3	3947
me, and *t* hold of my covenant	Is 56:4	2388
vanity shall *t* them	Is 57:13	3947
t up the stumblingblock out of	Is 57:14	7311
they *t* delight in approaching to	Is 58:2	
If thou *t* away from the midst of	Is 58:9	5493
up himself to *t* hold of thee	Is 64:7	2388
I will also *t* of them for priests	Is 66:21	3947
t thee much sope, yet thine	Jer 2:22	

I will *t* you one of a city, and	Jer 3:14	3947
t away the foreskins of your	Jer 4:4	5493
t away her battlements	Jer 5:10	5493
t up a lamentation on high places	Jer 7:29	5375
T ye heed every one of his	Jer 9:4	
mountains will I *t* up a weeping	Jer 9:10	5375
t up a wailing for us, that our	Jer 9:18	5375
T the girdle that thou hast got,	Jer 13:4	3947
t the girdle from thence, which I	Jer 13:6	3947
shall not sorrows *t* thee, as a	Jer 13:21	270
t me not away in thy	Jer 15:15	3947
if thou *t* forth the precious from	Jer 15:19	3318
Thou shalt not *t* thee a wife	Jer 16:2	3947
T heed to yourselves, and bear no	Jer 17:21	
they have digged a pit to *t* me	Jer 18:22	3920
t of the ancients of the people,	Jer 19:1	
t them, and carry them to Babylon	Jer 20:5	3947
we shall *t* our revenge on him	Jer 20:10	3947
t all the families of the north,	Jer 25:9	3947
Moreover I will *t* from them the	Jer 25:10	6
T the wine cup of this fury at my	Jer 25:15	3947
if they refuse to *t* the cup at	Jer 25:28	3947
T ye wives, and beget sons and	Jer 29:6	3947
t wives for your sons, and give	Jer 29:6	3947
king of Babylon, and he shall *t* it	Jer 32:3	3920
T these evidences, this evidence	Jer 32:14	3947
are come unto the city to *t* it	Jer 32:24	3920
field for money, and *t* witnesses	Jer 32:25	5749
king of Babylon, and he shall *t* it	Jer 32:28	3920
t witnesses in the land of	Jer 32:44	5749
so that I will not *t* any of his	Jer 33:26	3947
t it, and burn it with fire	Jer 34:22	3920
T thee a roll of a book, and write	Jer 36:2	3947
T in thine hand the roll wherein	Jer 36:14	3947
to *t* Baruch the scribe and	Jer 36:26	3947
T thee again another roll, and	Jer 36:28	3947
t it, and burn it with fire	Jer 37:8	3920
Babylon's army, which shall *t* it	Jer 38:3	3920
T from hence thirty men with thee	Jer 38:10	3947
t up Jeremiah the prophet out of	Jer 38:10	3947
T him, and look well to him, and do	Jer 39:12	3947
T great stones in thine hand, and	Jer 43:9	3947
t Nebuchadrezzar the king of	Jer 43:10	3947
I will *t* the remnant of Judah,	Jer 44:12	3947
t balm, O virgin, the daughter of	Jer 46:11	3947
and their flocks shall they *t* away	Jer 49:29	3947
they shall *t* to themselves their	Jer 49:29	5375
t vengeance upon her	Jer 50:15	
t balm for her pain, if so be she	Jer 51:8	3947
they shall not *t* of thee a stone	Jer 51:26	3947
cause, and *t* vengeance for thee	Jer 51:36	
What thing shall I *t* to witness	Lam 2:13	
t thee a tile, and lay it before	Eze 4:1	3947
Moreover *t* thou unto thee an iron	Eze 4:3	3947
T thou also unto thee wheat, and	Eze 4:9	3947
t thee a sharp knife	Eze 5:1	3947
t thee a barber's razor, and cause	Eze 5:1	3947
then *t* thee balances to weigh, and	Eze 5:1	3947
thou shalt *t* a third part, and	Eze 5:2	3947
Thou shalt also *t* thereof a few	Eze 5:3	3947
Then *t* of them again, and cast	Eze 5:4	3947
T fire from between the wheels,	Eze 10:6	3947
they shall *t* away all the	Eze 11:18	5493
I will *t* the stony heart out of	Eze 11:19	5493
That I may *t* the house of Israel	Eze 14:5	8610
or will men *t* a pin of it to hang	Eze 15:3	3947
And of thy garments thou didst *t*	Eze 16:16	3947
shall *t* thy fair jewels, and leave	Eze 16:39	3947
I will also *t* of the highest	Eze 17:22	3947
Moreover *t* thou up a lamentation	Eze 19:1	5375
the diadem, and *t* off the crown	Eze 21:26	7311
thou shalt *t* thine inheritance in	Eze 22:16	
they shall *t* away thy nose and	Eze 23:25	5493
they shall *t* thy sons and thy	Eze 23:25	3947
and *t* away thy fair jewels	Eze 23:26	3947
shall *t* away all thy labour, and	Eze 23:29	3947
T the choice of the flock, and	Eze 24:5	3947
fury to come up to *t* vengeance	Eze 24:8	
I *t* away from thee the desire of	Eze 24:16	3947
when I *t* from them their strength	Eze 24:25	3947
they shall *t* up a lamentation for	Eze 26:17	5375
t up a lamentation for Tyrus	Eze 27:2	5375
shall *t* up a lamentation for thee	Eze 27:32	5375
t up a lamentation upon the king	Eze 28:12	5375
he shall *t* her multitude	Eze 29:19	5375
multitude, and *t* her spoil	Eze 29:19	7997
her spoil, and *t* her prey	Eze 29:19	962
they shall *t* away her multitude,	Eze 30:4	3947
t up a lamentation for Pharaoh	Eze 32:2	5375
the land *t* a man of their coasts	Eze 33:2	3947
t him away, his blood shall be	Eze 33:4	3947
t any person from among them, he	Eze 33:6	3947
For I will *t* you from among the	Eze 36:24	3947
I will *t* away the stony heart out	Eze 36:26	5493
t thee one stick, and write upon	Eze 37:16	3947
then *t* another stick, and write	Eze 37:16	3947
I will *t* the stick of Joseph,	Eze 37:19	3947
I will *t* the children of Israel	Eze 37:21	3947
To *t* a spoil, and to	Eze 38:12	7997
a spoil, and to *t* a prey	Eze 38:12	962
thee, Art thou come to *t* a spoil	Eze 38:13	7997
gathered thy company to *t* a prey	Eze 38:13	962
to *t* away cattle and goods, to	Eze 38:13	3947
and goods, to *t* a great spoil	Eze 38:13	3947
So that they shall *t* no wood out	Eze 39:10	5375
thou shalt *t* of the blood thereof	Eze 43:20	3947
Thou shalt *t* the bullock also of	Eze 43:21	3947
Neither shall they *t* for their	Eze 44:22	3947
but they shall *t* maidens of the	Eze 44:22	3947
t away your exactions from my	Eze 45:9	7311
thou shalt *t* a young bullock	Eze 45:18	3947
the priest shall *t* of the blood	Eze 45:19	3947
Moreover the prince shall not *t*	Eze 46:18	3947
should *t* Daniel up out of the den	Dan 6:23	5267
the most High shall *t* the kingdom	Dan 7:18	6902
they shall *t* away his dominion,	Dan 7:26	5709
and *t* the most fenced cities	Dan 11:15	3920
unto the isles, and shall *t* many	Dan 11:18	3920
shall *t* away the daily sacrifice,	Dan 11:31	5493
t unto thee a wife of whoredoms	Hos 1:2	3947
but I will utterly *t* them away	Hos 1:6	5375
t away my corn in the time	Hos 2:9	3947
For I will *t* away the names of	Hos 2:17	5493
left off to *t* heed to the LORD	Hos 4:10	
new wine *t* away the heart	Hos 4:11	3947
I will *t* away, and none shall	Hos 5:14	5375
that *t* off the yoke on their jaws	Hos 11:4	7311
T with you words, and turn to the	Hos 14:2	3947
T away all iniquity, and receive	Hos 14:2	5375
shall one *t* up a snare from the	Amos 3:5	5927
that he will *t* you away with	Amos 4:2	5375
word which I *t* up against you	Amos 5:1	5375
ye *t* from him burdens of wheat	Amos 5:11	3947
they *t* a bribe, and they turn	Amos 5:12	3947
T thou away from me the noise of	Amos 5:23	5493
And a man's uncle shall *t* him up	Amos 6:10	5375
thence shall mine hand *t* them	Amos 9:2	3947
will search and *t* them out thence	Amos 9:3	3947
T me up, and cast me forth into	Jonah 1:12	5375
Therefore now, O LORD, *t*, I	Jonah 4:3	3947
fields, and *t* them by violence	Mic 2:2	5375
and houses, and *t* them away	Mic 2:2	5375
In that day shall one *t* up a	Mic 2:4	5375
them, that they shall not *t* shame	Mic 2:6	5253
and thou shalt *t* hold, but shalt	Mic 6:14	5253
the LORD will *t* vengeance on his	Nah 1:2	
T ye the spoil of silver	Nah 2:9	962
t the spoil of gold	Nah 2:9	962
for they shall heap dust, and *t* it	Hab 1:10	3920
They *t* up all of them with the	Hab 1:15	5927
Shall not all these *t* up a	Hab 2:6	5375
for then I will *t* away out of the	Zeph 3:11	5493
I will *t* pleasure in it, and I	Hag 1:8	
the LORD of hosts, will I *t* thee	Hag 2:23	3947
did they not *t* hold of your	Zec 1:6	5381
T away the filthy garments from	Zec 3:4	5493
T of them of the captivity, even	Zec 6:10	3947
Then *t* silver and gold, and make	Zec 6:11	3947
that ten men shall *t* hold out of	Zec 8:23	2388
even shall *t* hold of the skirt of	Zec 8:23	2388
I will *t* away his blood out of	Zec 9:7	5493
T unto thee yet the instruments	Zec 11:15	3947
t of them, and seethe therein	Zec 14:21	3947
one shall *t* you away with it	Mal 2:3	5375
Therefore *t* heed to your spirit,	Mal 2:15	
therefore *t* heed to your spirit,	Mal 2:16	
fear not to *t* unto thee Mary thy	Mt 1:20	*3880*
t the young child and his mother,	Mt 2:13	*3880*
t the young child and his mother,	Mt 2:20	*3880*
t away thy coat, let him have thy	Mt 5:40	*2983*
T heed that ye do not your alms	Mt 6:1	
T no thought for your life, what	Mt 6:25	
why *t* ye thought for raiment	Mt 6:28	
Therefore *t* no thought, saying,	Mt 6:31	
T therefore no thought for the	Mt 6:34	
for the morrow shall *t* thought	Mt 6:34	
t up thy bed, and go unto thine	Mt 9:6	*142*
t no thought how or what ye shall	Mt 10:19	
and the violent *t* it by force	Mt 11:12	*726*
T my yoke upon you, and learn of	Mt 11:29	*142*
and said, It is not meet to *t* the	Mt 15:26	*2983*
they had forgotten to *t* bread	Mt 16:5	*2983*
T heed and beware of the leaven of	Mt 16:6	
t up his cross, and follow me	Mt 16:24	*142*
of the earth *t* custom or tribute	Mt 17:25	*2983*
t up the fish that first cometh	Mt 17:27	*142*
that *t*, and give unto them for me	Mt 17:27	*2983*
T heed that ye despise not one of	Mt 18:10	
then *t* with thee one or two more,	Mt 18:16	*3880*
which would *t* account of his	Mt 18:23	*4868*
T that thine is, and go thy way	Mt 20:14	*142*
t him away, and cast him into	Mt 22:13	*142*
T heed that no man deceive you	Mt 24:4	
to *t* any thing out of his house	Mt 24:17	*142*
return back to *t* his clothes	Mt 24:18	*142*
T therefore the talent from him,	Mt 25:28	*142*
they might *t* Jesus by subtilty	Mt 26:4	*2902*
it to the disciples, and said, *T*	Mt 26:26	*2983*
Sleep on now, and *t* your rest	Mt 26:45	
for all they that *t* the sword	Mt 26:52	*2983*
with swords and staves for to *t* me	Mt 26:55	*4815*
Arise, and *t* up thy bed, and walk	Mk 2:9	*142*
t up thy bed, and go thy way into	Mk 2:11	*142*
unto them, *T* heed what ye hear	Mk 4:24	
t nothing for their journey	Mk 6:8	*142*
meet to *t* the children's bread	Mk 7:27	*2983*
had forgotten to *t* bread, neither	Mk 8:14	*2983*
T heed, beware of the leaven of	Mk 8:15	
t up his cross, and follow me	Mk 8:34	*142*
t up the cross, and follow me	Mk 10:21	*142*
his brother should *t* his wife	Mk 12:19	*2983*
T heed lest any man deceive you	Mk 13:5	
But *t* heed to yourselves	Mk 13:9	
t no thought beforehand what ye	Mk 13:11	
to *t* any thing out of his house	Mk 13:15	*142*
again for to *t* up his garment	Mk 13:16	*142*
But *t* ye heed	Mk 13:23	
T ye heed, watch and pray	Mk 13:33	
how they might *t* him by craft	Mk 14:1	*2902*
it and gave to them, and said, *T*	Mk 14:22	*2983*
t away this cup from me	Mk 14:36	*3911*
Sleep on now, and *t* your rest	Mk 14:41	
t him, and lead him away safely	Mk 14:44	*2902*
swords and with staves to *t* me	Mk 14:48	*4815*
them, what every man should *t*	Mk 15:24	*142*
Elias will come to *t* him down	Mk 15:36	*2507*
They shall *t* up serpents	Mk 16:18	*142*
to *t* away my reproach among men	Lk 1:25	*851*
t up thy couch, and go into thine	Lk 5:24	*142*
into the house of God, and did *t*	Lk 6:4	*2983*
forbid not to *t* thy coat also	Lk 6:29	
T heed therefore how ye hear	Lk 8:18	
T nothing for your journey,	Lk 9:3	*142*
t up his cross daily, and follow	Lk 9:23	*142*
and said unto him, *T* care of him	Lk 10:35	
T heed therefore that the light	Lk 11:35	*4648*
t ye no thought how or what thing	Lk 12:11	
T heed, and beware of covetousness	Lk 12:15	
t thine ease, eat, drink, and be	Lk 12:19	
T no thought for your life, what	Lk 12:22	
why *t* ye thought for the rest	Lk 12:26	
with shame to *t* the lowest room	Lk 14:9	*2722*
T thy bill, and sit down quickly,	Lk 16:6	*1209*
T thy bill, and write fourscore	Lk 16:7	*1209*
T heed to yourselves	Lk 17:3	
him not come down to *t* it away	Lk 17:31	*142*
T from him the pound, and give it	Lk 19:24	*142*
that they might *t* hold of his	Lk 20:20	*1949*
they could not *t* hold of his	Lk 20:26	*1949*
his brother should *t* his wife	Lk 20:28	*2983*
T heed that ye be not deceived	Lk 21:8	
t heed to yourselves, lest at any	Lk 21:34	
T this, and divide it among	Lk 22:17	*2983*
that hath a purse, let him *t* it	Lk 22:36	*142*
sold doves, *T* these things hence	Jn 2:16	*142*
him, Rise, *t* up thy bed, and walk	Jn 5:8	*142*
unto me, *T* up thy bed, and walk	Jn 5:11	*142*
unto thee, *T* up thy bed, and walk	Jn 5:12	*142*
every one of them may *t* a little	Jn 6:7	*2983*
t him by force, to make him a	Jn 6:15	*726*
Then they sought to *t* him	Jn 7:30	*4084*
priests sent officers to *t* him	Jn 7:32	*4084*
my life, that I might *t* it again	Jn 10:17	*2983*
and I have power to *t* it again	Jn 10:18	*2983*
they sought again to *t* him	Jn 10:39	*4084*
Jesus said, *T* ye away the stone	Jn 11:39	*142*
t away both our place and nation	Jn 11:48	*142*
shew it, that they might *t* him	Jn 11:57	*4084*
said I, that he shall *t* of mine	Jn 16:15	*2983*
shouldest *t* them out of the world	Jn 17:15	*142*
T ye him, and judge him according	Jn 18:31	*2983*
them, *T* ye him, and crucify him	Jn 19:6	*2983*
he might *t* away the body of Jesus	Jn 19:38	*142*
laid him, and I will *t* him away	Jn 20:15	*142*
and his bishoprick let another *t*	Acts 1:20	*2983*
That he may *t* part of this	Acts 1:25	*2983*
t heed to yourselves what ye	Acts 5:35	
proceeded further to *t* Peter also	Acts 12:3	*4815*
to *t* out of them a people for his	Acts 15:14	*2983*
determined to *t* with them John	Acts 15:37	*4838*
not good to *t* him with them	Acts 15:38	*4838*
there intending to *t* in Paul	Acts 20:13	*353*
Wherefore I *t* you to record this	Acts 20:26	
T heed therefore unto yourselves,	Acts 20:28	
Them *t*, and purify thyself with	Acts 21:24	*3880*
saying, *T* heed what thou doest	Acts 22:26	
to *t* him by force from among them	Acts 23:10	*726*
of whom thyself mayest *t*	Acts 24:8	
Paul besought them all to *t* meat	Acts 27:33	*3335*
I pray you to *t* some meat	Acts 27:34	*4355*
t heed lest he also spare not	Rom 11:21	
when I shall *t* away their sins	Rom 11:27	*851*
Whensoever I *t* my journey into	Rom 15:24	
But let every man *t* heed how he	1Cor 3:10	
Why do ye not rather *t* wrong	1Cor 6:7	
shall I then *t* the members of	1Cor 6:15	*142*
But *t* heed lest by any means this	1Cor 8:9	
Doth God *t* care for oxen	1Cor 9:9	
he standeth *t* heed lest he fall	1Cor 10:12	
thanks, he brake it, and said, *T*	1Cor 11:24	*2983*
t upon us the fellowship of the	2Cor 8:4	
man devour you, if a man *t* of you	2Cor 11:20	*2983*
Therefore I *t* pleasure in	2Cor 12:10	
t heed that ye be not consumed	Gal 5:15	
Wherefore *t* unto you the whole	Eph 6:13	*353*
t the helmet of salvation, and the	Eph 6:17	*1209*
T heed to the ministry which thou	Col 4:17	
how shall he *t* care of the church	1Ti 3:5	
T heed unto thyself, and unto the	1Ti 4:16	
T Mark, and bring him with thee	2Ti 4:11	*353*
T heed, brethren, lest there be	Heb 3:12	
have a commandment to *t* tithes of	Heb 7:5	
and of goats should *t* away sins	Heb 10:4	*851*
which can never *t* away sins	Heb 10:11	*4014*
T, my brethren, the prophets, who	Jas 5:10	*2983*
faults, ye shall *t* it patiently	1Pet 2:20	
ye *t* it patiently, this is	1Pet 2:20	
ye do well that ye *t* heed	2Pet 1:19	
was manifested to *t* away our sins	1Jn 3:5	*142*
hast, that no man *t* thy crown	Rev 3:11	*2983*
Thou art worthy to *t* the book	Rev 5:9	*2983*
thereon to *t* peace from the earth	Rev 6:4	*2983*
t the little book which is open	Rev 10:8	*2983*
said unto me, *T* it, and eat it up	Rev 10:9	*2983*

let him *t* the water of life Rev 22:17 *2902*
if any man shall *t* away from the Rev 22:19 *851*
God shall *t* away his part out of Rev 22:19 *851*

TAKEN {338}

which the LORD God had *t* from man Gen 2:22 3947
because she was *t* out of Man Gen 2:23 3947
for out of it wast thou *t* Gen 3:19 3947
the ground from whence he was *t* Gen 3:23 3947
shall be *t* on him sevenfold Gen 4:15
the woman was *t* into Pharaoh's Gen 12:15 3947
so I might have *t* her to me to Gen 12:19 3947
that his brother was *t* captive Gen 14:14
I have *t* upon me to speak unto Gen 18:27 2974
I have *t* upon me to speak unto Gen 18:31 2974
for the woman which thou hast *t* Gen 20:3 3947
servants had violently *t* away Gen 21:25 1497
where is he that hath *t* venison Gen 27:33 6679
and hath *t* away thy blessing Gen 27:35 3947
now he hath *t* away my blessing Gen 27:36 3947
that thou hast *t* my husband Gen 30:15 3947
God hath *t* away my reproach Gen 30:23 622
Jacob hath *t* away all that was Gen 31:1 3947
Thus God hath *t* away the cattle Gen 31:9 5337
which God hath *t* from our father Gen 31:16 5337
as captives *t* with the sword Gen 31:26
Now Rachel had *t* the images Gen 31:34 3947
hast thou *t* us away to die in the Ex 14:11 3947
they shall not be *t* from it Ex 25:15 5493
when the cloud was *t* up from over Ex 40:36 5927
But if the cloud were not *t* up Ex 40:37 5927
not till the day that it was *t* up Ex 40:37 5927
As it was *t* off from the bullock Lev 4:10 7311
as the fat is *t* away from off the Lev 4:31 7311
as the fat of the lamb is *t* away Lev 4:35 7311
or in a thing *t* away by violence, Lev 6:2 1497
the heave shoulder have I *t* of Lev 7:34 3947
that he hath *t* away the stones Lev 14:43 2502
being *t* from the children of among Lev 24:8
I have *t* the Levites from among Num 3:12 3947
neither she be *t* with the manner Num 5:13 8610
of Israel, have I *t* them unto me Num 8:16 3947
I have *t* the Levites for all the Num 8:18 3947
when the cloud was *t* up from the Num 9:17 5927
the cloud was *t* up in the morning Num 9:21 5927
by night that the cloud was *t* up Num 9:21 5927
but when it was *t* up, they Num 9:22 5927
that the cloud was *t* up from off Num 10:11 5927
And the tabernacle was *t* down Num 10:17 3381
I have not *t* one ass from them, Num 16:15 5375
I have *t* your brethren the Num 18:6 3947
t all his land out of his hand, Num 21:26 3947
the sum of the prey that was *t* Num 31:26 7628
Thy servants have *t* the sum of Num 31:49 5375
(For the men of war had *t* spoil Num 31:53
be *t* from the inheritance of our Num 36:3 1639
so shall it be *t* from the lot of Num 36:3 1639
be *t* away from the inheritance of Num 36:4 1639
But the LORD hath *t* you, and Deut 4:20 3947
a wife, and hath not *t* her Deut 20:7 3947
thou hast *t* them captive, Deut 21:10 7617
When a man hath *t* a wife, and Deut 24:1 3947
When a man hath *t* a new wife Deut 24:5 3947
cheer up his wife which he hath *t* Deut 24:5 3947
neither have I *t* away ought Deut 26:14 1197
t away from before thy face Deut 28:31 1497
for they have even *t* of the Josh 7:11 3947
that he that is *t* with the Josh 7:15 3920
and the tribe of Judah was *t* Josh 7:16 3920
and Zabdi was *t* Josh 7:17 3920
of the tribe of Judah, was *t* Josh 7:18 3920
shall be, when ye have *t* the city Josh 8:8 8610
that the ambush had *t* the city Josh 8:21 3920
had heard how Joshua had *t* Ai Josh 10:1 3920
against Jerusalem, and had *t* it Judg 1:8 3920
forasmuch as the LORD hath *t* Judg 11:36 6213
he told not them that he had *t* Judg 14:9 7287
because he had *t* his wife Judg 15:6 3947
of silver that were *t* from thee Judg 17:2 3947
Ye have *t* away my gods which I Judg 18:24 3947
And the ark of God was *t* 1Sa 4:11 3947
are dead, and the ark of God is *t* 1Sa 4:17 3947
tidings that the ark of God was *t* 1Sa 4:19 3947
because the ark of God was *t* 1Sa 4:21 3947
for the ark of God is *t* 1Sa 4:22 3947
which the Philistines had *t* from 1Sa 7:14 3947
near, the tribe of Benjamin was *t* 1Sa 10:20 3920
the family of Matri was *t* 1Sa 10:21 3920
and Saul the son of Kish was *t* 1Sa 10:21 3920
whose ox have I *t* 1Sa 12:3 3947
or whose ass have I *t* 1Sa 12:3 3947
neither hast thou *t* ought of any 1Sa 12:4 3947
And Saul and Jonathan were *t* 1Sa 14:41 3920
And Jonathan was *t* 1Sa 14:42 3920
that was *t* from before the LORD, 1Sa 21:6 5493
in the day when it was *t* away 1Sa 21:6 3947
had *t* the women captives, that 1Sa 30:2
their daughters, were *t* captives 1Sa 30:3
David's two wives were *t* captives 1Sa 30:5
they had *t* out of the land of the 1Sa 30:16 3947
any thing that they had *t* to them 1Sa 30:19 3947
hast *t* his wife to be thy wife, 2Sa 12:9 3947
hast *t* the wife of Uriah the 2Sa 12:10 3947
have *t* the city of waters 2Sa 12:27 3920
thou art *t* in thy mischief, 2Sa 16:8
he was *t* up between the heaven and 2Sa 18:9 5414
Now Absalom in his lifetime had *t* 2Sa 18:18 3947
they cannot be *t* with hands 2Sa 23:6 3947

daughter, whom he had *t* to wife 1Kin 7:8 3947
have *t* hold upon other gods, and 1Kin 9:9 2388
t Gezer, and burnt it with fire, 1Kin 9:16 3920
Zimri saw that the city was *t* 1Kin 16:18 3920
thou killed, and also *t* possession 1Kin 21:19
the high places were not *t* away 1Kin 22:43 5493
before I be *t* away from thee 2Kin 2:9 3947
thou see me when I am *t* from thee 2Kin 2:10 3947
Spirit of the LORD hath *t* him up 2Kin 2:16 5375
And when he had *t* him, and brought 2Kin 4:20 5375
hast *t* captive with thy sword 2Kin 6:22
the high places were not *t* away 2Kin 12:3 5493
which he had *t* out of the hand of 2Kin 13:25 3947
the high places were not *t* away 2Kin 14:4 5493
king of Israel, Samaria was *t* 2Kin 18:10 3920
whose altars Hezekiah hath *t* away 2Kin 18:22 5493
for the king of Babylon had *t* 2Kin 24:7 3947
household being *t* for Eleazar 1Chr 24:6 270
for Eleazar, and one *t* for Ithamar 1Chr 24:6 270
which he had *t* from mount Ephraim 2Chr 15:8 3920
were not *t* away out of Israel 2Chr 15:17 5493
which Asa his father had *t* 2Chr 17:2 3920
in that thou hast *t* away the 2Chr 19:3 1197
the high places were not *t* away 2Chr 20:33 5493
which ye have *t* captive of your 2Chr 28:11
had *t* Beth-shemesh, and Ajalon, and 2Chr 28:18 3920
For the king had *t* counsel 2Chr 30:2
Hezekiah *t* away his high places 2Chr 32:12 5493
For they have *t* of their Ezr 9:2 5375
have *t* strange wives of the Ezr 10:2 3427
have *t* strange wives, to increase Ezr 10:10 3427
let all them which have *t* strange Ezr 10:14 3427
end with all the men that had *t* Ezr 10:17 3427
found that had *t* strange wives Ezr 10:18 3427
All these had *t* strange wives Ezr 10:44 5375
had *t* of them bread and wine, Neh 5:15 3947
his son Johanan had *t* the Neh 6:18 3947
who had *t* her for his daughter, Est 2:15 3947
So Esther was *t* unto king Est 2:16 3947
ring, which he had *t* from Haman Est 8:2 5674
gave, and the LORD hath *t* away Job 1:21 3947
he hath also *t* me by my neck, and Job 16:12 247
and *t* the crown from my head Job 19:9 5493
because he hath violently *t* away Job 20:19 1497
For thou hast *t* a pledge from thy Job 22:6 2254
they are *t* out of the way as all Job 24:24 7092
who hath *t* away my judgment Job 27:2 5493
Iron is *t* out of the earth, and Job 28:2 3947
of affliction have *t* hold upon me Job 30:16 270
God hath *t* away my judgment Job 34:5 5493
shall be *t* away without hand Job 34:20 5493
they hid is their own foot *t* Ps 9:15 3920
let them be *t* in the devices that Ps 10:2 8610
iniquities have *t* hold upon me Ps 40:12 5381
let them even be *t* in their pride Ps 59:12 3920
They have *t* crafty counsel Ps 83:3
Thou hast *t* away all thy wrath Ps 85:3 5375
Horror hath *t* hold upon me Ps 119:53 270
Thy testimonies have I *t* as an Ps 119:111
and anguish have *t* hold on me Ps 119:143 4672
shall keep thy foot from being *t* Prov 3:26 3921
and their sleep is *t* away, unless Prov 4:16 1497
thou art *t* with the words of thy Prov 6:2 3920
He hath *t* a bag of money with him Prov 7:20 3947
be *t* in their own naughtiness Prov 11:6 3920
which I had *t* under the sun Eccl 2:18 6001
to it, nor any thing *t* from it Eccl 3:14 1639
but the sinner shall be *t* by her Eccl 7:26 3920
fishes that are *t* in an evil net Eccl 9:12 270
which he had *t* with the tongs Is 6:6 3947
and thine iniquity is *t* away Is 6:7 5493
have *t* evil counsel against thee, Is 7:5
the spoil of Samaria shall be *t* Is 8:4 5375
be broken, and be snared, and be *t* Is 8:15 3920
that his burden shall be *t* away Is 10:27 5493
they have *t* up their lodging at Is 10:29 3885
And gladness is *t* away, and joy out Is 16:10 622
Damascus is *t* away from being a Is 17:1 5493
pangs have *t* hold upon me, as the Is 21:3 270
Who hath *t* this counsel against Is 23:8
the pit shall be *t* in the snare Is 24:18 3920
and be broken, and snared, and *t* Is 28:13 3920
that shall not be *t* down Is 33:20 6813
whose altars Hezekiah hath *t* away Is 36:7 5493
Thou whom I have *t* from the ends Is 41:9 2388
the prey be *t* from the mighty Is 49:24 3947
of the mighty shall be *t* away Is 49:25 3947
I have *t* out of thine hand the Is 51:22 3947
my people is *t* away for nought Is 52:5 3947
He was *t* from prison and from Is 53:8 3947
and merciful men are *t* away Is 57:1 622
that the righteous is *t* away from Is 57:1 622
like the wind, have *t* us away Is 64:6 5375
husband with the wife shall be *t* Jer 6:11 3920
anguish hath *t* hold of us Jer 6:24 2388
ashamed, they are dismayed and *t* Jer 8:9
astonishment hath *t* hold on me Jer 8:21 2388
them, yea, they have *t* root Jer 12:2
for I have *t* away my peace from Jer 16:5 622
of them shall be *t* up a curse by Jer 29:22 3947
his hand, but shalt surely be *t* Jer 34:3 8610
but shalt be *t* by the hand of the Jer 38:23 8610
the day that Jerusalem was *t* Jer 38:28 3920
he was there when Jerusalem was *t* Jer 38:28 3920
and when they had *t* him, they Jer 39:5 3947
when he had *t* him being bound in Jer 40:1 3947
in your cities that ye have *t* Jer 40:10 8610
Kiriathaim is confounded and *t* Jer 48:1 3920

treasures, thou shalt also be *t* Jer 48:7 3920
gladness is *t* from the plentiful Jer 48:33 622
Kerioth is *t*, and the strong holds Jer 48:41 3920
the pit shall be *t* in the snare Jer 48:44 3920
for thy sons are *t* captives Jer 48:46 3947
LORD, that he hath *t* against Edom Jer 49:20 3289
anguish and sorrows have *t* her Jer 49:24 270
hath *t* counsel against you Jer 49:30
say, Babylon is *t*, Bel is Jer 50:2 3920
from thence she shall be *t* Jer 50:9 3920
for thee, and thou art also *t* Jer 50:24 3920
that he hath *t* against Babylon Jer 50:45 3289
that his city is *t* at one end Jer 51:31 3920
How is Sheshach *t* Jer 51:41 3920
Babylon, and her mighty men are *t* Jer 51:56 3920
he hath violently *t* away his Lam 2:6
was *t* in their pits, of whom we Lam 4:20 3920
him, and he shall be *t* in my snare Eze 12:13 8610
Shall wood be *t* thereof to do any Eze 15:3 3947
Thou hast also *t* thy fair jewels Eze 16:17 3947
Moreover thou hast *t* thy sons Eze 16:20 3947
with whom thou hast *t* pleasure Eze 16:37
hath *t* the king thereof, and the Eze 17:12 3947
hath *t* of the king's seed, and Eze 17:13 3947
him, and hath *t* an oath of him Eze 17:13 935
he hath also *t* the mighty of the Eze 17:13 3947
him, and he shall be *t* in my snare Eze 17:20 8610
neither hath *t* any increase Eze 18:8 3947
upon usury, and hath *t* increase Eze 18:13 3947
That hath *t* off his hand from the Eze 18:17 7725
he was *t* in their pit, and they Eze 19:4 8610
he was *t* in their pit Eze 19:8 8610
the iniquity, that they may be *t* Eze 21:23 8610
ye shall be *t* with the hand Eze 21:24 8610
In thee have they *t* gifts to shed Eze 22:12 3947
thou hast *t* usury and increase, and Eze 22:12 3947
they have *t* the treasure and Eze 22:25 3947
and have *t* vengeance with a Eze 25:15
they have *t* cedars from Lebanon Eze 27:5 3947
he is *t* away in his iniquity Eze 33:6 3947
ye are *t* up in the lips of Eze 36:3 5927
his father Nebuchadnezzar had *t* Dan 5:2 5312
the golden vessels that were *t* Dan 5:3 5312
So Daniel was *t* up out of the den Dan 6:23 5267
they had their dominion *t* away Dan 7:12 5709
the daily sacrifice was *t* away Dan 8:11 7311
when he hath *t* away the multitude Dan 11:12 5375
daily sacrifice shall be *t* away Dan 12:11 5493
of the sea also shall be *t* away Hos 4:3 622
Because ye have *t* my silver Joel 3:5 3947
of his den, if he have *t* nothing Amos 3:4 3920
earth, and have *t* nothing at all Amos 3:5 3947
be *t* out that dwell in Samaria in Amos 3:12 5337
sword, and have *t* away your horses Amos 4:10 7628
Have we not *t* to us horns by our Amos 6:13 3947
have ye *t* away my glory for ever Mic 2:9 3947
for pangs have *t* thee as a woman Mic 4:9 2388
The LORD hath *t* away thy Zeph 3:15 5493
and the city shall be *t*, and the Zec 14:2 3947
that were *t* with divers diseases Mt 4:24 *4912*
bridegroom shall be *t* from them Mt 9:15 *522*
from him shall be *t* away even Mt 13:12 *142*
It is because we have *t* no bread Mt 16:7 *2983*
of God shall be *t* from you Mt 21:43 *142*
the one shall be *t*, and the other Mt 24:40 *3880*
the one shall be *t*, and the other Mt 24:41 *3880*
be *t* away even that which he hath Mt 25:29 *142*
And when Joseph had *t* the body Mt 27:59 *2983*
had *t* counsel, they gave large Mt 28:12 *2983*
shall be *t* away from them Mk 2:20 *522*
from him shall be *t* even that Mk 4:25 *142*
when he had *t* the five loaves and Mk 6:41 *2983*
when he had *t* him in his arms, he Mk 9:36 *1723*
Forasmuch as many have *t* in hand Lk 1:1 *2021*
mother was *t* with a great fever Lk 4:38 *4912*
all the night, and have *t* nothing Lk 5:5 *2983*
of the fishes which they had *t* Lk 5:9 *4815*
a man which was *t* with a palsy Lk 5:18
shall be *t* away from them Lk 5:35 *522*
the piece that was *t* out of the Lk 5:36
from him shall be *t* even that Lk 8:18 *142*
for they were *t* with great fear Lk 8:37 *4912*
there was *t* up of fragments that Lk 9:17 *142*
shall not be *t* away from her Lk 10:42 *851*
for ye have *t* away the key of Lk 11:52 *142*
the one shall be *t*, and the other Lk 17:34 *3880*
the one shall be *t*, and the other Lk 17:35 *3880*
the one shall be *t*, and the other Lk 17:36 *3880*
if I have *t* any thing from any Lk 19:8
he hath shall be *t* away from him Lk 19:26 *142*
And some of them would have *t* him Jn 7:44 *4084*
unto him a woman *t* in adultery Jn 8:3 *2638*
this woman was *t* in adultery Jn 8:4 *2638*
had *t* his garments, and was set Jn 13:12 *2983*
and that they might be *t* away Jn 19:31 *142*
seeth the stone *t* away from the Jn 20:1 *142*
They have *t* away the Lord out of Jn 20:2 *142*
Because they have *t* away my Lord Jn 20:13 *142*
the day in which he was *t* up Acts 1:2 *353*
while they beheld, he was *t* up Acts 1:9 *1869*
which is *t* up from you into Acts 1:11 *353*
same day that he was *t* up from us Acts 1:22 *353*
foreknowledge of God, ye have *t* Acts 2:23 *2983*
many *t* with palsies, and that were Acts 8:7
his judgment was *t* away Acts 8:33 *142*
for his life is *t* from the earth Acts 8:33 *142*

when they had *t* security of Jason ... Acts 17:9 *2983*
the third loft, and was *t* up dead ... Acts 20:9 *142*
when we had *t* our leave one of ... Acts 21:6 *782*
This man was *t* of the Jews ... Acts 23:27 *4815*
Which when they had *t* up, they ... Acts 27:17 *142*
should be saved was then *t* away ... Acts 27:20 *4014*
fasting, having *t* nothing ... Acts 27:33 *4355*
when they had *t* up the anchors, ... Acts 27:40 *4014*
word of God hath *t* none effect ... Rom 9:6
might be *t* away from among you ... 1Cor 5:2 *1808*
There hath no temptation *t* you ... 1Cor 10:13 *2983*
Lord, the vail shall be *t* away ... 2Cor 3:16 *4014*
being *t* from you for a short time ... 1Th 2:17 *642*
until he be *t* out of the way ... 2Th 2:7 *1096*
Let not a widow be *t* into the ... 1Ti 5:9 *2639*
who are *t* captive by him at his ... 2Ti 2:26 *2221*
For every high priest *t* from ... Heb 5:1 *2983*
brute beasts, made to be *t* ... 2Pet 2:12 *259*
And when he had *t* the book ... Rev 5:8 *2983*
because thou hast *t* to thee thy ... Rev 11:17 *2983*
And the beast was *t*, and with him ... Rev 19:20 *4084*

TAKER {1}
as with the *t* of usury, so with ... Is 24:2

TAKEST {9}
the water which thou *t* out of the ... Ex 4:9 3947
When thou *t* the sum of the ... Ex 30:12 5375
the journey that thou *t* shall not ... Judg 4:9 1980
if thou *t* heed to fulfil the ... 1Chr 22:13 8104
thou *t* away their breath, they ... Ps 104:29 622
that thou *t* knowledge of him ... Ps 144:3 3947
labour which thou *t* under the sun ... Eccl 9:9 6001
our soul, and thou *t* no knowledge ... Is 58:3
thou *t* up that thou layedst not ... Lk 19:21 *142*

TAKETH {74}
guiltless that *t* his name in vain ... Ex 20:7 5375
guiltless that *t* his name in vain ... Deut 5:11 5375
not persons, nor *t* reward ... Deut 10:17 3947
for he *t* a man's life to pledge ... Deut 24:6 2254
her hand, and *t* him by the secrets ... Deut 25:11 2388
Cursed be he that *t* reward to ... Deut 27:25 3947
t them, beareth them on her wings ... Deut 32:11 3947
t shall come according to the ... Josh 7:14 3920
t it, to him will I give Achsah ... Josh 15:16 3920
t it, to him will I give Achsah ... Judg 1:12 3920
t away the reproach from Israel ... 1Sa 17:26 5493
as a man *t* away dung, till it be ... 1Kin 14:10 1197
t it even out of the thorns, and ... Job 5:5 3947
He *t* the wise in their own ... Job 5:13 3920
he *t* away, who can hinder him ... Job 9:12 2862
t away the understanding of the ... Job 12:20 3947
He *t* away the heart of the chief ... Job 12:24 5493
trembling *t* hold on my flesh ... Job 21:6 270
gained, when God *t* away his soul ... Job 27:8 7953
He *t* it with his eyes ... Job 40:24 3947
nor *t* up a reproach against his ... Ps 15:3 5375
nor *t* reward against the innocent ... Ps 15:5 3947
The LORD *t* my part with them that ... Ps 118:7
Happy shall he be, that *t* ... Ps 137:9 270
he *t* not pleasure in the legs of ... Ps 147:10
The LORD *t* pleasure in them that ... Ps 147:11
For the LORD *t* pleasure in his ... Ps 149:4
which *t* away the life of the ... Prov 1:19 3947
his spirit than he that *t* a city ... Prov 16:32 3920
A wicked man *t* a gift out of the ... Prov 17:23 3947
As he that *t* away a garment in ... Prov 25:20 5710
is like one that *t* a dog by the ... Prov 26:17 2388
The spider *t* hold with her hands, ... Prov 30:28 8610
labour which he *t* under the sun ... Eccl 1:3 5998
his heart *t* not rest in the night ... Eccl 2:23
t under the sun all the days of ... Eccl 5:18 5998
and as a sheep that no man *t* up ... Is 13:14 6908
he *t* up the isles as a very ... Is 40:15 5190
t the cypress and the oak, which ... Is 44:14 3947
neither is there any that *t* her ... Is 51:18 2388
it, and *t* hold of my covenant ... Is 56:6 2388
which *t* strangers instead of her ... Eze 16:32 3947
of the trumpet, and *t* not warning ... Eze 33:4
But he that *t* warning shall ... Eze 33:5
As the shepherd *t* out of the ... Amos 3:12 5337
Then the devil *t* him up into the ... Mt 4:5 *3880*
the devil *t* him up into an ... Mt 4:8 *3880*
to fill it up *t* from the garment ... Mt 9:16 *142*
he that *t* not his cross, and ... Mt 10:38 *2983*
t with himself seven other ... Mt 12:45 *3880*
And after six days Jesus *t* Peter ... Mt 17:1 *3880*
filled it up *t* away from the old ... Mk 2:21 *142*
t away the word that was sown in ... Mk 4:15 *142*
he *t* the father and the mother of ... Mk 5:40 *3880*
six days Jesus *t* with him Peter ... Mk 9:2 *3880*
And wheresoever he *t* him, he ... Mk 9:18 *2638*
he *t* with him Peter and James and ... Mk 14:33 *3880*
him that *t* away thy cloke forbid ... Lk 6:29 *142*
of him that *t* away thy goods ask ... Lk 6:30 *142*
t away the word out of their ... Lk 8:12 *142*
And, lo, a spirit *t* him, and he ... Lk 9:39 *2983*
he *t* from him all his armour ... Lk 11:22 *142*
t to him seven other spirits more ... Lk 11:26 *3880*
for my lord *t* away from me the ... Lk 16:3 *851*
which *t* away the sin of the world ... Jn 1:29 *142*
No man *t* it from me, but I lay it ... Jn 10:18 *142*
that beareth not fruit he *t* away ... Jn 15:2 *142*
and your joy no man *t* from you ... Jn 16:22 *142*
t bread, and giveth them, and fish ... Jn 21:13 *2983*
God unrighteous who *t* vengeance ... Rom 3:5 *2018*
He *t* the wise in their own ... 1Cor 3:19 *1405*
For in eating every one *t* before ... 1Cor 11:21 *4301*
no man *t* this honour unto himself ... Heb 5:4 *2983*
He *t* away the first, that he may ... Heb 10:9 *337*

TAKING {20}
of persons, nor *t* of gifts ... 2Chr 19:7 4727
I have seen the foolish *t* root ... Job 5:3
by *t* heed thereto according to ... Ps 119:9
At the noise of the *t* of Babylon ... Jer 50:46 8610
the house of Judah by *t* vengeance ... Eze 25:12
also to go, *t* them by their arms ... Hos 11:3 3947
Which of you by *t* thought can add ... Mt 6:27
man is as a man *t* a far journey ... Mk 13:34
t him up into an high mountain, ... Lk 4:5 *321*
which of you with *t* thought can ... Lk 12:25
t up that I laid not down, and ... Lk 19:22 *142*
had spoken of *t* of rest in sleep ... Jn 11:13
t occasion by the commandment, ... Rom 7:8 *2983*
t occasion by the commandment, ... Rom 7:11 *2983*
but *t* my leave of them, I went ... 2Cor 2:13
t wages of them, to do you ... 2Cor 11:8 *2983*
t the shield of faith, wherewith ... Eph 6:16 *353*
In flaming fire *t* vengeance on ... 2Th 1:8 *1325*
t the oversight thereof, not by ... 1Pet 5:2
t nothing of the Gentiles ... 3Jn 7 *2983*

TALE {5}
the *t* of the bricks, which they ... Ex 5:8 4971
shall ye deliver the *t* of bricks ... Ex 5:18 8506
gave them in full *t* to the king ... 1Sa 18:27
should bring them in and out by *t* ... 1Chr 9:28 4557
our years as a *t* that is told ... Ps 90:9 1899

TALEBEARER {6}
down as a *t* among thy people ... Lev 19:16 7400
A *t* revealeth secrets ... Prov 11:13 1980,7400
The words of a *t* are as wounds ... Prov 18:8 5372
about as a *t* revealeth secrets ... Prov 20:19 7400
so where there is no *t*, the ... Prov 26:20 5372
The words of a *t* are as wounds ... Prov 26:22 5372

TALENT {14}
Of a *t* of pure gold shall he make ... Ex 25:39 3603
Of a *t* of pure gold made he it, ... Ex 37:24 3603
hundred talents, a *t* for a socket ... Ex 38:27 3603
the weight whereof was a *t* of ... 2Sa 12:30 3603
else thou shalt pay a *t* of silver ... 1Kin 20:39 3603
a *t* of silver, and two changes of ... 2Kin 5:22 3603
talents of silver, and a *t* of gold ... 2Kin 23:33 3603
and found it to weigh a *t* of gold ... 1Chr 20:2 3603
talents of silver and a *t* of gold ... 2Chr 36:3 3603
there was lifted up a *t* of lead ... Zec 5:7 3603
which had received the one *t* came ... Mt 25:24 *5007*
and went and hid thy *t* in the earth ... Mt 25:25 *5007*
Take therefore the *t* from him ... Mt 25:28 *5007*
stone about the weight of a *t* ... Rev 16:21 *5006*

TALENTS {51}
offering, was twenty and nine *t* ... Ex 38:24 3603
the congregation was an hundred *t* ... Ex 38:25 3603
of the hundred *t* of silver were ... Ex 38:27 3603
hundred sockets of the hundred *t* ... Ex 38:27 3603
of the offering was seventy *t* ... Ex 38:29 3603
to the king sixscore *t* of gold ... 1Kin 9:14 3603
gold, four hundred and twenty *t* ... 1Kin 9:28 3603
twenty *t* of gold, and of spices ... 1Kin 10:10 3603
threescore and six *t* of gold, ... 1Kin 10:14 3603
of Shemer for two *t* of silver ... 1Kin 16:24 3603
and took with him ten *t* of silver ... 2Kin 5:5 3603
said, Be content, take two *t* ... 2Kin 5:23 3603
bound two *t* of silver in two bags ... 2Kin 5:23 3603
gave Pul a thousand *t* of silver ... 2Kin 15:19 3603
Judah three hundred *t* of silver ... 2Kin 18:14 3603
of silver and thirty *t* of gold ... 2Kin 18:14 3603
tribute of an hundred *t* of silver ... 2Kin 23:33 3603
of Ammon sent a thousand *t* of ... 1Chr 19:6 3603
an hundred thousand *t* of gold ... 1Chr 22:14 3603
a thousand thousand *t* of silver ... 1Chr 22:14 3603
Even three thousand *t* of gold ... 1Chr 29:4 3603
seven thousand *t* of refined ... 1Chr 29:4 3603
of God of gold five thousand *t* ... 1Chr 29:7 3603
and of silver ten thousand *t* ... 1Chr 29:7 3603
and of brass eighteen thousand *t* ... 1Chr 29:7 3603
and one hundred thousand *t* of iron ... 1Chr 29:7 3603
gold, amounting to six hundred *t* ... 2Chr 3:8 3603
fifty *t* of gold, and brought them ... 2Chr 8:18 3603
twenty *t* of gold, and of spices ... 2Chr 9:9 3603
and threescore and six *t* of gold ... 2Chr 9:13 3603
Israel for an hundred *t* of silver ... 2Chr 25:6 3603
shall we do for the hundred *t* ... 2Chr 25:9 3603
same year an hundred *t* of silver ... 2Chr 27:5 3603
land in an hundred *t* of silver ... 2Chr 36:3 3603
Unto an hundred *t* of silver ... Ezr 7:22 3604
fifty *t* of silver, and silver ... Ezr 8:26 3603
and silver vessels an hundred *t* ... Ezr 8:26 3603
and of gold an hundred *t* ... Ezr 8:26 3603
I will pay ten thousand *t* of ... Est 3:9 3603
which owed him ten thousand *t* ... Mt 18:24 *5007*
And unto one he gave five *t* ... Mt 25:15 *5007*
that had received the five *t* went ... Mt 25:16 *5007*
same, and made them other five *t* ... Mt 25:16 *5007*
he that had received five *t* came ... Mt 25:20 *5007*
came and brought other five *t* ... Mt 25:20 *5007*
thou deliveredst unto me five *t* ... Mt 25:20 *5007*
gained beside them five *t* more ... Mt 25:20 *5007*
also that had received two *t* came ... Mt 25:22 *5007*
thou deliveredst unto me two *t* ... Mt 25:22 *5007*
gained two other *t* beside them ... Mt 25:22 *5007*
give it unto him which hath ten *t* ... Mt 25:28 *5007*

TALES {2}
men that carry *t* to shed blood ... Eze 22:9 7400
words seemed to them as idle *t* ... Lk 24:11 *3026*

TALITHA *(tal'-ith-ah)* {1} *Aramaic for damsel.*
hand, and said unto her, *T* cumi ... Mk 5:41 *5008*

TALK {24}
come down and *t* with thee there ... Num 11:17 1696
this day that God doth *t* with man ... Deut 5:24 1696
shalt *t* of them when thou sittest ... Deut 6:7 1696
T no more so exceeding proudly ... 1Sa 2:3 1696
t not with us in the Jews' ... 2Kin 18:26 1696
t ye of all his wondrous works ... 1Chr 16:9 7878
a man full of *t* be justified ... Job 11:2 8193
and *t* deceitfully for him ... Job 13:7 1696
he reason with unprofitable *t* ... Job 15:3 1697
they *t* to the grief of those whom ... Ps 69:26 5608
My tongue also shall *t* of thy ... Ps 71:24 1897
all thy work, and *t* of thy doings ... Ps 77:12 7878
t ye of all his wondrous works ... Ps 105:2 7878
so shall I *t* of thy wondrous ... Ps 119:27 7878
of thy kingdom, and *t* of thy power ... Ps 145:11 1696
awakest, it shall *t* with thee ... Prov 6:22 7878
but the *t* of the lips tendeth ... Prov 14:23 1697
and their lips *t* of mischief ... Prov 24:2 1696
the end of his *t* is mischievous ... Eccl 10:13 6310
yet let me *t* with thee of thy ... Jer 12:1 1696
and I will there *t* with thee ... Eze 3:22 1696
this my lord *t* with this my lord ... Dan 10:17 1696
they might entangle him in his *t* ... Mt 22:15 *3056*
I will not *t* much with you ... Jn 14:30 *2980*

TALKED {42}
Cain *t* with Abel his brother ... Gen 4:8 559
and God *t* with him, saying, ... Gen 17:3 1696
in the place where he *t* with him ... Gen 35:13 1696
in the place where he *t* with him ... Gen 35:14 1696
that his brethren *t* with him ... Gen 45:15 1696
I have *t* with you from heaven ... Ex 20:22 1696
and the LORD *t* with Moses ... Ex 33:9 1696
face shone while he *t* with him ... Ex 34:29 1696
and Moses *t* with them ... Ex 34:31 1696
The LORD *t* with you face to face ... Deut 5:4 1696
he went down, and *t* with the woman ... Judg 14:7 1696
while Saul *t* unto the priest, ... 1Sa 14:19 1696
as he *t* with them, behold, there ... 1Sa 17:23 1696
lo, while she yet *t* with the king ... 1Kin 1:22 1696
pass, as they still went on, and *t* ... 2Kin 2:11 1696
And while he yet *t* with them ... 2Kin 6:33 1696
the king *t* with Gehazi the ... 2Kin 8:4 1696
as he *t* with him, that the king ... 2Chr 25:16 1696
hear that I have *t* with thee ... Jer 38:25 1696
t with me, and said, O Daniel, I ... Dan 9:22 1696
the angel that *t* with me said ... Zec 1:9 1696
that *t* with me with good words ... Zec 1:13 1696
unto the angel that *t* with me ... Zec 1:19 1696
the angel that *t* with me went ... Zec 2:3 1696
the angel that *t* with me came ... Zec 4:1 1696
spake to the angel that *t* with me ... Zec 4:4 1696
the angel that *t* with me answered ... Zec 4:5 1696
angel that *t* with me went forth ... Zec 5:5 1696
I to the angel that *t* with me ... Zec 5:10 1696
unto the angel that *t* with me ... Zec 6:4 1696
While he yet *t* to the people, ... Mt 12:46 *2980*
And immediately he *t* with them ... Mk 6:50 *2980*
there *t* with him two men, which ... Lk 9:30 *4814*
they *t* together of all these ... Lk 24:14 *3656*
while he *t* with us by the way, and ... Lk 24:32 *2980*
that he *t* with the woman ... Jn 4:27 *2980*
as he *t* with him, he went in, and ... Acts 10:27 *4926*
t a long while, even till break ... Acts 20:11 *3656*
they *t* between themselves, saying ... Acts 26:31 *2980*
t with me, saying unto me, Come ... Rev 17:1 *2980*
t with me, saying, Come hither, I ... Rev 21:9 *2980*
he that *t* with me had a golden ... Rev 21:15 *2980*

TALKERS {2}
ye are taken up in the lips of *t* ... Eze 36:3 3956
there are many unruly and vain *t* ... Titus 1:10 *3151*

TALKEST {3}
me a sign that thou *t* with me ... Judg 6:17 1696
while thou yet *t* there with the ... 1Kin 1:14 1696
or, Why *t* thou with her ... Jn 4:27 *2980*

TALKETH {2}
and his tongue *t* of judgment ... Ps 37:30 1696
him, and it is he that *t* with thee ... Jn 9:37 *2980*

TALKING {9}
And he left off *t* with him ... Gen 17:22 1696
either he is *t*, or he is pursuing ... 1Kin 18:27 7879
And while they were yet *t* with him ... Est 6:14 1696
The princes refrained *t*, and laid ... Job 29:9 4405
of thy people still are *t* against ... Eze 33:30 1696
them Moses and Elias *t* with him ... Mt 17:3 *4814*
and they were *t* with Jesus ... Mk 9:4 *4814*
Neither filthiness, nor foolish *t* ... Eph 5:4 *3473*
as it were of a trumpet *t* with me ... Rev 4:1 *2980*

TALL {5}
a people great, and many, and *t* ... Deut 2:10 7311
A people great, and many, and *t* ... Deut 2:21 7311
A people great and *t*, the children ... Deut 9:2 7311
will cut down the *t* cedar trees ... 2Kin 19:23 6967
cut down the *t* cedars thereof ... Is 37:24 6967

TALLER {1}
people is greater and *t* than we ... Deut 1:28 7311

TALMAI *(tal'-mahee)* {6}
1. A son of Anak.
where Ahiman, Sheshai, and *T* ... Num 13:22 8526
of Anak, Sheshai, and Ahiman, and *T* ... Josh 15:14 8526
slew Sheshai, and Ahiman, and *T* ... Judg 1:10 8526

2. A king of Geshur.
the daughter of *T* king of Geshur ... 2Sa 3:3 8526
But Absalom fled, and went to *T* ... 2Sa 13:37 8526
the daughter of *T* king of Geshur ... 1Chr 3:2 8526

TALMON *(tal'-mon)* {5} *A Levite in Jerusalem.*
were, Shallum, and Akkub, and *T* ... 1Chr 9:17 2929
of Ater, the children of *T* ... Ezr 2:42 2929
of Ater, the children of *T* ... Neh 7:45 2929
Moreover the porters, Akkub, *T* ... Neh 11:19 2929
Bakbukiah, Obadiah, Meshullam, *T* ... Neh 12:25 2929

TAMAH *(ta'-mah)* {1} See THAMAH. *A family of exiles.*
of Sisera, the children of *T* ... Neh 7:55 8547

TAMAR *(ta'-mar)* {24} See THAMAR.
1. Wife of Er.
his firstborn, whose name was *T* ... Gen 38:6 8559
Then said Judah to *T* his daughter ... Gen 38:11 8559
T went and dwelt in her father's ... Gen 38:11 8559
And it was told *T*, saying, Behold ... Gen 38:13 8559
T thy daughter in law hath played ... Gen 38:24 8559
whom *T* bare unto Judah, of the ... Ruth 4:12 8559
T his daughter in law bare him ... 1Chr 2:4 8559
2. A daughter of David.
a fair sister, whose name was *T* ... 2Sa 13:1 8559
he fell sick for his sister *T* ... 2Sa 13:2 8559
And Amnon said unto him, I love *T* ... 2Sa 13:4 8559
I pray thee, let my sister *T* come ... 2Sa 13:5 8559
let *T* my sister come, and make me ... 2Sa 13:6 8559
Then David sent home to *T* ... 2Sa 13:7 8559
So *T* went to her brother Amnon's ... 2Sa 13:8 8559
And Amnon said unto *T*, Bring the ... 2Sa 13:10 8559
T took the cakes which she had ... 2Sa 13:10 8559
T put ashes on her head, and rent ... 2Sa 13:19 8559
So *T* remained desolate in her ... 2Sa 13:20 8559
he had forced his sister *T* ... 2Sa 13:22 8559
day that he forced his sister *T* ... 2Sa 13:32 8559
the concubines, and *T* their sister ... 1Chr 3:9 8559
3. A daughter of Absalom.
and one daughter, whose name was *T* ... 2Sa 14:27 8559
4. A city in Judah.
from *T* even to the waters of ... Eze 47:19 8559
T unto the waters of strife in ... Eze 48:28 8559

TAME {2}
neither could any man *t* him ... Mk 5:4 *1150*
But the tongue can no man *t* ... Jas 3:8 *1150*

TAMED {2}
and of things in the sea, is *t* ... Jas 3:7 *1150*
and hath been *t* of mankind ... Jas 3:7 *1150*

TAMMUZ *(tam'-muz)* {1} *A Syrian god.*
there sat women weeping for *T* ... Eze 8:14 8542

TANACH *(ta'-nak)* {1} See TAANACH. *Same as Taanach.*
Manasseh, *T* with her suburbs, and ... Josh 21:25 8590

TANHUMETH *(tan'-hu-meth)* {2} *Father of Seraiah.*
the son of *T* the Netophathite ... 2Kin 25:23 8576
Kareah, and Seraiah the son of *T* ... Jer 40:8 8576

TANNER {3}
days in Joppa with one Simon a *t* ... Acts 9:43 *1038*
He lodgeth with one Simon a *t* ... Acts 10:6 *1038*
of one Simon a *t* by the sea side ... Acts 10:32 *1038*

TAPESTRY {2}
decked my bed with coverings of *t* ... Prov 7:16
She maketh herself coverings of *t* ... Prov 31:22

TAPHATH *(ta'-fath)* {1} *A daughter of Solomon.*
which had *T* the daughter of ... 1Kin 4:11 2955

TAPPUAH *(tap'-pu-ah)* {6}
1. A city in Judah.
The king of *T*, one ... Josh 12:17 8599
And Zanoah, and En-gannim, *T* ... Josh 15:34 8599
2. A city in Ephraim.
The border went out from *T* ... Josh 16:8 8599
Now Manasseh had the land of *T* ... Josh 17:8 8599
but *T* on the border of Manasseh ... Josh 17:8 8599
3. A son of Hebron.
Korah, and *T*, and Rekem, and Shema ... 1Chr 2:43 8599

TARAH *(ta'-rah)* {2} *An Israelite encampment in the wilderness.*
from Tahath, and pitched at *T* ... Num 33:27 8646
And they removed from *T*, and ... Num 33:28 8646

TARALAH *(tar'-a-lah)* {1} *A city in Benjamin.*
And Rekem, and Irpeel, and *T* ... Josh 18:27 8634

TARE {4}
t his garments, and lay on the ... 2Sa 13:31 7167
t forty and two children of them ... 2Kin 2:24 1234
him, straightway the spirit *t* him ... Mk 9:20 *4682*
devil threw him down, and *t* him ... Lk 9:42 *4952*

TAREA *(ta'-re-ah)* {1} See TAHREA. *A son of Micah.*
were, Pithon, and Melech, and *T* ... 1Chr 8:35 8390

TARES {8}
sowed *t* among the wheat, and went ... Mt 13:25 *2215*
fruit, then appeared the *t* also ... Mt 13:26 *2215*
from whence then hath it *t* ... Mt 13:27 *2215*
lest while ye gather up the *t* ... Mt 13:29 *2215*
Gather ye together first the *t* ... Mt 13:30 *2215*
the parable of the *t* of the field ... Mt 13:36 *2215*
but the *t* are the children of the ... Mt 13:38 *2215*
As therefore the *t* are gathered ... Mt 13:40 *2215*

TARGET {3}
legs, and a *t* of brass between his ... 1Sa 17:6 3591
shekels of gold went to one *t* ... 1Kin 10:16 6793
of beaten gold went to one *t* ... 2Chr 9:15 6793

TARGETS {3}
made two hundred *t* of beaten gold ... 1Kin 10:16 6793
made two hundred *t* of beaten gold ... 2Chr 9:15 6793
had an army of men that bare *t* ... 2Chr 14:8 6793

TARPELITES *(tar'-pel-ites)* {1} *Foreigners resettled in Israel.*
the Apharsathchites, the *T* ... Ezr 4:9 2967

TARRIED {32}
were with him, and *t* all night ... Gen 24:54 3885
t there all night, because the ... Gen 28:11 3885
and *t* all night in the mount ... Gen 31:54 3885
when the cloud *t* long upon the ... Num 9:19 748
that the cloud *t* upon the ... Num 9:22 748
they *t* till they were ashamed ... Judg 3:25 2342
And Ehud escaped while they *t* ... Judg 3:26 4102
they *t* until afternoon, and they ... Judg 19:8 4102
that she *t* a little in the house ... Ruth 2:7 3427
he *t* seven days, according to the ... 1Sa 13:8 3176
Saul *t* in the uttermost part of ... 1Sa 14:2 3427
But David *t* still at Jerusalem ... 2Sa 11:1 3427
t in a place that was far off ... 2Sa 15:17 5975
and they *t* there ... 2Sa 15:29 3427
but he *t* longer than the set time ... 2Sa 20:5 3186
(for he *t* at Jericho,) he said ... 2Kin 2:18 3427
But David *t* at Jerusalem ... 1Chr 20:1 3427
she that *t* at home divided the ... Ps 68:12 5116
While the bridegroom *t*, they all ... Mt 25:5 *5549*
marvelled that he *t* so long in ... Lk 1:21 *5549*
the child Jesus *t* behind in ... Lk 2:43 *5278*
there he *t* with them, and baptized ... Jn 3:22 *1304*
that he *t* many days in Joppa with ... Acts 9:43 *3306*
And after they had *t* there a space ... Acts 15:33 *4160*
Paul after this *t* there yet a ... Acts 18:18 *4357*
going before *t* for us at Troas ... Acts 20:5 *3306*
at Samos, and *t* at Trogyllium ... Acts 20:15 *3306*
disciples, we *t* there seven days ... Acts 21:4 *1961*
as we *t* there many days, there ... Acts 21:10 *1961*
when he had *t* among them more ... Acts 25:6 *1304*
the fourteenth day that ye have *t* ... Acts 27:33 *4328*
Syracuse, we *t* there three days ... Acts 28:12 *1961*

TARRIEST {1}
And now why *t* thou ... Acts 22:16 *3195*

TARRIETH {2}
his part be that *t* by the stuff ... 1Sa 30:24 3427
that *t* not for man, nor waiteth ... Mic 5:7 6960

TARRY {51}
t all night, and wash your feet, ... Gen 19:2 3885
t with him a few days, until thy ... Gen 27:44 3427
found favour in thine eyes, *t* ... Gen 30:27
come down unto me, *t* not ... Gen 45:9 5975
out of Egypt, and could not *t* ... Ex 12:39 4102
T ye here for us, until we come ... Ex 24:14 3427
shall *t* abroad out of his tent ... Lev 14:8 3427
t ye also here this night, that I ... Num 22:19 3427
Why *t* the wheels of his chariots ... Judg 5:28 309
I will *t* until thou come again ... Judg 6:18 3427
t all night, and let thine heart ... Judg 19:6 3885
evening, I pray you *t* all night ... Judg 19:9 3885
the man would not *t* that night ... Judg 19:10 3885
Would ye *t* for them till they ... Ruth 1:13 7663
T this night, and it shall be in ... Ruth 3:13 3885
t until thou have weaned him ... 1Sa 1:23 3427
seven days shalt thou *t*, till I ... 1Sa 10:8 3176
unto us, *T* until we come to you ... 1Sa 14:9 1826
T at Jericho until your beards be ... 2Sa 10:5 3427
T here to day also, and to morrow ... 2Sa 11:12 3427
I will *t* in the plain of the ... 2Sa 15:28 4102
I may not *t* thus with thee ... 2Sa 18:14 3176
there will not *t* one with thee ... 2Sa 19:7 3885
unto Elisha, *T* here, I pray thee ... 2Kin 2:2 3427
him, Elisha, *t* here, I pray thee ... 2Kin 2:4 3427
And Elijah said unto him, *T* ... 2Kin 2:6 3427
if we *t* till the morning light ... 2Kin 7:9 2442
open the door, and flee, and *t* not ... 2Kin 9:3 2442
glory of this, and *t* at home ... 2Kin 14:10 3427
T at Jericho until your beards be ... 1Chr 19:5 3427
lies shall not *t* in my sight ... Ps 101:7 3559
They that *t* long at the wine ... Prov 23:30 309
off, and my salvation shall not *t* ... Is 46:13 309
turneth aside to *t* for a night ... Jer 14:8 3885
though it *t*, wait for it ... Hab 2:3 4102
will surely come, it will not *t* ... Hab 2:3 309
t ye here, and watch with me ... Mt 26:38 *3306*
t ye here, and watch ... Mk 14:34 *3306*
And he went in to *t* with them ... Lk 24:29 *3306*
but *t* ye in the city of Jerusalem ... Lk 24:49 *2523*
him that he would *t* with them ... Jn 4:40 *3306*
If I will that he *t* till I come ... Jn 21:22 *3306*
If I will that he *t* till I come ... Jn 21:23 *3306*
prayed they him to *t* certain days ... Acts 10:48 *1961*
him to *t* longer time with them ... Acts 18:20 *3306*
were desired to *t* with them seven ... Acts 28:14 *1961*
to eat, *t* one for another ... 1Cor 11:33 *1551*
but I trust to *t* a while with you ... 1Cor 16:7 *1961*
But I will *t* at Ephesus until ... 1Cor 16:8 *1961*
But if I *t* long, that thou mayest ... 1Ti 3:15 *1019*
come will come, and will not *t* ... Heb 10:37 *5549*

TARRYING {2}
make no *t*, O my God ... Ps 40:17 309
O LORD, make no *t* ... Ps 70:5 309

TARSHISH *(tar'-shish)* {24} See THARSHISH.
1. A son of Javan.
Elishah, and *T*, Kittim, and Dodanim ... Gen 10:4 8659
Elishah, and *T*, Kittim, and Dodanim ... 1Chr 1:7 8659
2. Spain.
to *T* with the servants of Huram ... 2Chr 9:21 8659
came the ships of *T* bringing gold ... 2Chr 9:21 8659
with him to make ships to go to *T* ... 2Chr 20:36 8659
they were not able to go to *T* ... 2Chr 20:37 8659
the ships of *T* with an east wind ... Ps 48:7 8659
The kings of *T* and of the isles ... Ps 72:10 8659
And upon all the ships of *T* ... Is 2:16 8659
Howl, ye ships of *T* ... Is 23:1 8659
Pass ye over to *T* ... Is 23:6 8659
land as a river, O daughter of *T* ... Is 23:10 8659
Howl, ye ships of *T* ... Is 23:14 8659
for me, and the ships of *T* first ... Is 60:9 8659
of them unto the nations, to *T* ... Is 66:19 8659
into plates is brought from *T* ... Jer 10:9 8659
T was thy merchant by reason of ... Eze 27:12 8659
The ships of *T* did sing of thee ... Eze 27:25 8659
and Dedan, and the merchants of *T* ... Eze 38:13 8659
T from the presence of the LORD ... Jonah 1:3 8659
and he found a ship going to *T* ... Jonah 1:3 8659
to go with them unto *T* from the ... Jonah 1:3 8659
Therefore I fled before unto *T* ... Jonah 4:2 8659
3. A prince of Persia.
was Carshena, Shethar, Admatha, *T* ... Est 1:14 8659

TARSHISHAH See TARSHISH.

TARSUS *(tar'-sus)* {5} *Capital of Roman province of Cilicia.*
Judas for one called Saul, of *T* ... Acts 9:11 *5018*
Caesarea, and sent him forth to *T* ... Acts 9:30 *5019*
Then departed Barnabas to *T* ... Acts 11:25 *5019*
I am a man which am a Jew of *T* ... Acts 21:39 *5018*
a man which am a Jew, born in *T* ... Acts 22:3 *5019*

TARTAK *(tar'-tak)* {1} *A god of the Avites.*
And the Avites made Nibhaz and *T* ... 2Kin 17:31 8662

TARTAN *(tar'-tan)* {2} *The commander of the Assyrian army.*
And the king of Assyria sent *T* ... 2Kin 18:17 8661
the year that *T* came unto Ashdod ... Is 20:1 8661

TASK {2}
have ye not fulfilled your *t* in ... Ex 5:14 2706
from your bricks of your daily *t* ... Ex 5:19 1697

TASKMASTERS {6}
they did set over them *t* to ... Ex 1:11
their cry by reason of their *t* ... Ex 3:7 5065
the same day the *t* of the people ... Ex 5:6 5065
the *t* of the people went out, and ... Ex 5:10 5065
the *t* hasted them, saying, Fulfil ... Ex 5:13 5065
which Pharaoh's *t* had set over ... Ex 5:14 5065

TASKS {1}
Fulfil your works, your daily *t* ... Ex 5:13 1697

TASTE {22}
the *t* of it was like wafers made ... Ex 16:31 2940
the *t* of it was as the ... Num 11:8 2940
of it was as the *t* of fresh oil ... Num 11:8 2940
I did but *t* a little honey with ... 1Sa 14:43 2938
if I *t* bread, or ought else, till ... 2Sa 3:35 2938
can thy servant *t* what I eat or ... 2Sa 19:35 2938
or is there any *t* in the white of ... Job 6:6 2940
cannot my *t* discern perverse ... Job 6:30 2441
and the mouth *t* his meat ... Job 12:11 2938
O *t* and see that the LORD is good ... Ps 34:8 2938
How sweet are thy words unto my *t* ... Ps 119:103 2441
which is sweet to thy *t* ... Prov 24:13 2441
and his fruit was sweet to my *t* ... Song 2:3 2441
therefore his *t* remained in him, ... Jer 48:11 2940
herd nor flock, *t* any thing ... Jonah 3:7 2938
here, which shall not *t* of death ... Mt 16:28 *1089*
here, which shall not *t* of death ... Mk 9:1 *1089*
here, which shall not *t* of death ... Lk 9:27 *1089*
were bidden shall *t* of my supper ... Lk 14:24 *1089*
saying, he shall never *t* of death ... Jn 8:52 *1089*
t not ... Col 2:21 *1089*
God should *t* death for every man ... Heb 2:9 *1089*

TASTED {8}
So none of the people *t* any food ... 1Sa 14:24 2938
because I *t* a little of this ... 1Sa 14:29 2938
Belshazzar, whiles he *t* the wine ... Dan 5:2 2942
and when he had *t* thereof, he ... Mt 27:34 *1089*
t the water that was made wine ... Jn 2:9 *1089*
have *t* of the heavenly gift, and ... Heb 6:4 *1089*
have *t* the good word of God, and ... Heb 6:5 *1089*
If so be ye have *t* that the Lord ... 1Pet 2:3 *1089*

TASTETH {1}
trieth words, as the mouth *t* meat ... Job 34:3 2938

TATNAI *(tat'-nahee)* {4} *Persian governor of Samaria.*
At the same time came to them *T* ... Ezr 5:3 8674
The copy of the letter that *T* ... Ezr 5:6 8674
Now therefore, *T*, governor beyond ... Ezr 6:6 8674
Then *T*, governor on this side the ... Ezr 6:13 8674

TATTENAI See TATNAI.

TATTLERS {1}
but *t* also and busybodies, ... 1Ti 5:13 *5397*

TAUGHT {81}
Behold, I have *t* you statutes and ... Deut 4:5 3925
t it the children of Israel ... Deut 31:22 3925
with them he *t* the men of Succoth ... Judg 8:16 3045
t them how they should fear the ... 2Kin 17:28 3384
when thou hast *t* them the good ... 2Chr 6:27 3384
they *t* in Judah, and had the book ... 2Chr 17:9 3925
cities of Judah, and *t* the people ... 2Chr 17:9 3925
and such as to *t* to sing praise ... 2Chr 23:13 3045
unto all the Levites that *t* the ... 2Chr 30:22 7919

the Levites that *t* all Israel ... 2Chr 35:3 4000
and the Levites that *t* the people ... Neh 8:9 995
thou hast *t* me from my youth ... Ps 71:17 3925
for thou hast *t* me ... Ps 119:102 3384
when thou hast *t* me thy statutes ... Ps 119:171 3925
He *t* me also, and said unto me, ... Prov 4:4 3384
I have *t* thee in the way of ... Prov 4:11 3384
prophecy that his mother *t* him ... Prov 31:1 3256
he still *t* the people knowledge ... Eccl 12:9 3925
me is *t* by the precept of men ... Is 29:13 3925
being his counsellor hath *t* him ... Is 40:13 3045
t him in the path of judgment, and ... Is 40:14 3925
t him knowledge, and shewed to him ... Is 40:14 3925
children shall be *t* of the LORD ... Is 54:13 3928
also *t* the wicked ones thy ways ... Jer 2:33 3925
they have *t* their tongue to speak ... Jer 9:5 3925
which their fathers *t* them ... Jer 9:14 3925
as they *t* my people to swear by ... Jer 12:16 3925
for thou hast *t* them to be ... Jer 13:21 3925
because thou hast *t* rebellion ... Jer 28:16 1696
because he hath *t* rebellion ... Jer 29:32 1696
though I *t* them, rising up early ... Jer 32:33 3925
that all women may be *t* not to do ... Eze 23:48 3256
Ephraim is as an heifer that is *t* ... Hos 10:11 3925
I *t* Ephraim also to go, taking ... Hos 11:3 8637
for man *t* me to keep cattle from ... Zec 13:5
his mouth, and *t* them, saying, ... Mt 5:2 1321
For he *t* them as one having ... Mt 7:29 2258,1321
he *t* them in their synagogue, ... Mt 13:54 1321
the money, and did as they were *t* ... Mt 28:15 1321
entered into the synagogue, and *t* ... Mk 1:21 1321
for he *t* them as one that had ... Mk 1:22 2258,1321
resorted unto him, and he *t* them ... Mk 2:13 1321
he *t* them many things by parables ... Mk 4:2 1321
they had done, and what they had *t* ... Mk 6:30 1321
For he *t* his disciples, and said ... Mk 9:31 1321
as he was wont, he *t* them again ... Mk 10:1 1321
And he *t*, saying unto them, Is it ... Mk 11:17 1321
while he *t* in the temple, How say ... Mk 12:35 1321
he *t* in their synagogues, being ... Lk 4:15 1321
t them on the sabbath days ... Lk 4:31 2258,1321
t the people out of the ship ... Lk 5:3 1321
entered into the synagogue and *t* ... Lk 6:6 1321
as John also *t* his disciples ... Lk 11:1 1321
thou hast *t* in our streets ... Lk 13:26 1321
And he *t* daily in the temple ... Lk 19:47 2258,1321
as he *t* the people in the temple, ... Lk 20:1 1321
And they shall be all *t* of God ... Jn 6:45 1318
synagogue, as he *t* in Capernaum ... Jn 6:59 1321
went up into the temple, and *t* ... Jn 7:14 1321
cried Jesus in the temple as he *t* ... Jn 7:28 1321
and he sat down, and *t* them ... Jn 8:2 1321
treasury, as he *t* in the temple ... Jn 8:20 1321
but as my Father hath *t* me ... Jn 8:28 1321
I ever *t* in the synagogue, and in ... Jn 18:20 1321
grieved that they *t* the people ... Acts 4:2 1321
temple early in the morning, and *t* ... Acts 5:21 1321
with the church, and *t* much people ... Acts 11:26 1321
had *t* many, they returned again ... Acts 14:21 3100
down from Judaea *t* the brethren ... Acts 15:1 1321
t diligently the things of the ... Acts 18:25 1321
have *t* you publickly, and from ... Acts 20:20 1321
t according to the perfect manner ... Acts 22:3 3811
it of man, neither was I *t* it ... Gal 1:12 1321
Let him that is *t* in the word ... Gal 6:6 2727
heard him, and have been *t* by him ... Eph 4:21 1321
in the faith, as ye have been *t* ... Col 2:7 1321
for ye yourselves are *t* of God to ... 1Th 4:9 2312
traditions which ye have been *t* ... 2Th 2:15 1321
faithful word as he hath been *t* ... Titus 1:9 1322
no lie, and even as it hath *t* you ... 1Jn 2:27 1321
of Balaam, who *t* Balac to cast a ... Rev 2:14 1321

TAUNT {2}
be a reproach and a proverb, a *t* ... Jer 24:9 8148
So it shall be a reproach and a *t* ... Eze 5:15 1422

TAUNTING {1}
a *t* proverb against him, and say, ... Hab 2:6 4426

TAVERNS {1}
as Appii forum, and The three *t* ... Acts 28:15 4999

TAXATION {1}
of every one according to his *t* ... 2Kin 23:35 6187

TAXED {4}
but he *t* the land to give the ... 2Kin 23:35 6186
that all the world should be *t* ... Lk 2:1 582
And all went to be *t*, every one ... Lk 2:3 582
To be *t* with Mary his espoused ... Lk 2:5 582

TAXES {1}
of *t* in the glory of the kingdom ... Dan 11:20 5065

TAXING {2}
this *t* was first made when ... Lk 2:2 583
of Galilee in the days of the *t* ... Acts 5:37 583

TEACH {109}
t thee what thou shalt say ... Ex 4:12 3384
will *t* you what ye shall do ... Ex 4:15 3384
thou shalt *t* them ordinances and ... Ex 18:20 2094
that thou mayest *t* them ... Ex 24:12 3384
put in his heart that he may *t* ... Ex 35:34 3384
that ye may *t* the children of ... Lev 10:11 3384
To *t* when it is unclean, and when ... Lev 14:57 3384
unto the judgments, which I *t* you ... Deut 4:1 3925
but *t* them thy sons, and thy sons' ... Deut 4:9 3045
that they may *t* their children ... Deut 4:10 3925
me at that time to *t* you statutes ... Deut 4:14 3925
which thou shalt *t* them, that ... Deut 5:31 3925
LORD your God commanded to *t* you ... Deut 6:1 3925
thou shalt *t* them diligently unto ... Deut 6:7 8150
ye shall *t* them your children, ... Deut 11:19 3925
the law which they shall *t* thee ... Deut 17:11 3384
That they *t* you not to do after ... Deut 20:18 3925
priests the Levites shall *t* you ... Deut 24:8 3384
t it the children of Israel ... Deut 31:19 3925
They shall *t* Jacob thy judgments, ... Deut 33:10 3384
to *t* them war, at the least such ... Judg 3:2 3925
t us what we shall do unto the ... Judg 13:8 3384
but I will *t* you the good and the ... 1Sa 12:23 3384
(Also he bade them *t* the children ... 2Sa 1:18 3925
that thou *t* them the good way ... 1Kin 8:36 3384
let him *t* them the manner of the ... 2Kin 17:27 3384
to *t* in the cities of Judah ... 2Chr 17:7 3925
to *t* in Israel statutes and ... Ezr 7:10 3925
t ye them that know them not ... Ezr 7:25 3046
T me, and I will hold my tongue ... Job 6:24 3384
Shall not they *t* thee, and tell ... Job 8:10 3384
the beasts, and they shall *t* thee ... Job 12:7 3384
to the earth, and it shall *t* thee ... Job 12:8 3384
Shall any *t* God knowledge ... Job 21:22 3925
I will *t* you by the hand of God ... Job 27:11 3384
of years should *t* wisdom ... Job 32:7 3045
peace, and I shall *t* thee wisdom ... Job 33:33 502
That which I see not *t* thou me ... Job 34:32 3384
T us what we shall say unto him ... Job 37:19 3045
t me thy paths ... Ps 25:4 3925
Lead me in thy truth, and *t* me ... Ps 25:5 3925
therefore will he *t* sinners in ... Ps 25:8 3384
and the meek will he *t* his way ... Ps 25:9 3925
him shall he *t* in the way that he ... Ps 25:12 3384
T me thy way, O LORD, and lead me ... Ps 27:11 3384
t thee in the way which thou ... Ps 32:8 3384
I will *t* you the fear of the LORD ... Ps 34:11 3925
hand shall *t* thee terrible things ... Ps 45:4 3384
Then will I *t* transgressors thy ... Ps 51:13 3925
Michtam of David, to *t* ... Ps 60:*t* 3925
T me thy way, O LORD ... Ps 86:11 3384
So *t* us to number our days, that ... Ps 90:12 3045
and *t* his senators wisdom ... Ps 105:22
t me thy statutes ... Ps 119:12 3925
t me thy statutes ... Ps 119:26 3925
T me, O LORD, the way of thy ... Ps 119:33 3384
t me thy statutes ... Ps 119:64 3925
T me good judgment and knowledge ... Ps 119:66 3925
t me thy statutes ... Ps 119:68 3925
O LORD, and *t* me thy judgments ... Ps 119:108 3925
thy mercy, and *t* me thy statutes ... Ps 119:124 3925
and *t* me thy statutes ... Ps 119:135 3925
my testimony that I shall *t* them ... Ps 132:12 3925
T me to do thy will ... Ps 143:10 3925
t a just man, and he will increase ... Prov 9:9 3045
he will *t* us of his ways, and we ... Is 2:3 3384
Whom shall he *t* knowledge ... Is 28:9 3384
him to discretion, and doth *t* him ... Is 28:26 3384
t your daughters wailing, and ... Jer 9:20 3925
they shall *t* no more every man ... Jer 31:34 3925
they shall *t* my people the ... Eze 44:23 3384
and whom they might *t* the learning ... Dan 1:4 3925
and the priests thereof *t* for hire ... Mic 3:11 3384
he will *t* us of his ways, and we ... Mic 4:2 3384
the dumb stone, Arise, it shall *t* ... Hab 2:19 3384
shall *t* men so, he shall be ... Mt 5:19 1321
t them, the same shall be called ... Mt 5:19 1321
he departed thence to *t* and to ... Mt 11:1 1321
t all nations, baptizing them in ... Mt 28:19 3100
began again to *t* by the sea side ... Mk 4:1 1321
he began to *t* in the synagogue ... Mk 6:2 1321
he began to *t* them many things ... Mk 6:34 1321
And he began to *t* them, that the ... Mk 8:31 1321
t us to pray, as John also taught ... Lk 11:1 1321
For the Holy Ghost shall *t* you in ... Lk 12:12 1321
the Gentiles, and *t* the Gentiles ... Jn 7:35 1321
born in sins, and dost thou *t* us ... Jn 9:34 1321
he shall *t* you all things, and ... Jn 14:26 1321
that Jesus began both to do and *t* ... Acts 1:1 1321
at all nor *t* in the name of Jesus ... Acts 4:18 1321
that ye should not *t* in this name ... Acts 5:28 1321
every house, they ceased not to *t* ... Acts 5:42 1321
t customs, which are not lawful ... Acts 16:21 2605
as I *t* every where in every ... 1Cor 4:17 1321
Doth not even nature itself *t* you ... 1Cor 11:14 1321
by my voice I might *t* others also ... 1Cor 14:19 2727
that they *t* no other doctrine ... 1Ti 1:3 2085
But I suffer not a woman to *t* ... 1Ti 2:12 1321
given to hospitality, apt to *t* ... 1Ti 3:2 1317
These things command and *t* ... 1Ti 4:11 1321
These things *t* and exhort ... 1Ti 6:2 1321
If any man *t* otherwise, and ... 1Ti 6:3 2085
shall be able to *t* others also ... 2Ti 2:2 1321
be gentle unto all men, apt to *t* ... 2Ti 2:24 1317
That they may *t* the young women ... Titus 2:4 4994
ye have need that one *t* you again ... Heb 5:12 1321
they shall not *t* every man his ... Heb 8:11 1321
and ye need not that any man *t* you ... 1Jn 2:27 1321
herself a prophetess, to *t* ... Rev 2:20 1321

TEACHER {6}
the great, the *t* as the scholar ... 1Chr 25:8 995
a *t* of lies, that the maker of ... Hab 2:18 3384
that thou art a *t* come from God ... Jn 3:2 1320
a *t* of babes, which hast the form ... Rom 2:20 1320
a *t* of the Gentiles in faith and ... 1Ti 2:7 1320
apostle, and a *t* of the Gentiles ... 2Ti 1:11 1320

TEACHERS {14}
more understanding than all my *t* ... Ps 119:99 3925
have not obeyed the voice of my *t* ... Prov 5:13 3384
yet shall not thy *t* be removed ... Is 30:20 3384
but thine eyes shall see thy *t* ... Is 30:20 3384
thy *t* have transgressed against ... Is 43:27 3887
at Antioch certain prophets and *t* ... Acts 13:1 1320
secondarily prophets, thirdly *t* ... 1Cor 12:28 1320
are all *t*? ... 1Cor 12:29 1320
and some, pastors and *t* ... Eph 4:11 1320
Desiring to be *t* of the law ... 1Ti 1:7 3547
shall they heap to themselves *t* ... 2Ti 4:3 1320
to much wine, *t* of good things ... Titus 2:3 2567
for the time ye ought to be *t* ... Heb 5:12 1320
there shall be false *t* among you ... 2Pet 2:1 5572

TEACHEST {8}
O LORD, and *t* him out of thy law ... Ps 94:12 3925
t the way of God in truth, ... Mt 22:16 1321
but *t* the way of God in truth ... Mk 12:14 1321
t rightly, neither acceptest thou ... Lk 20:21 1321
but *t* the way of God truly ... Lk 20:21 1321
that thou *t* all the Jews which ... Acts 21:21 1321
Thou therefore which *t* another ... Rom 2:21 1321
t thou not thyself? ... Rom 2:21 1321

TEACHETH {16}
He *t* my hands to war ... 2Sa 22:35 3925
Who *t* us more than the beasts of ... Job 35:11 502
who *t* like him ... Job 36:22 3384
He *t* my hands to war, so that a ... Ps 18:34 3925
he that *t* man knowledge, shall ... Ps 94:10 3925
which *t* my hands to war, and my ... Ps 144:1 3925
his feet, he *t* with his fingers ... Prov 6:13 3384
The heart of the wise *t* his mouth ... Prov 16:23 7919
and the prophet that *t* lies ... Is 9:15 3384
thy God which *t* thee to profit ... Is 48:17 3925
that *t* all men every where ... Acts 21:28 1321
or he that *t*, on teaching ... Rom 12:7 1321
in the words which man's wisdom *t* ... 1Cor 2:13 1318
but which the Holy Ghost *t* ... 1Cor 2:13 1318
him that *t* in all good things ... Gal 6:6 2727
anointing *t* you of all things ... 1Jn 2:27 1321

TEACHING {25}
true God, and without a *t* priest ... 2Chr 15:3 3384
t them, yet they have not ... Jer 32:33 3925
t in their synagogues, and ... Mt 4:23 1321
t in their synagogues, and ... Mt 9:35 1321
t for doctrines the commandments ... Mt 15:9 1321
people came unto him as he was *t* ... Mt 21:23 1321
daily with you *t* in the temple ... Mt 26:55 1321
T them to observe all things ... Mt 28:20 1321
went round about the villages, *t* ... Mk 6:6 1321
t for doctrines the commandments ... Mk 7:7 1321
daily with you in the temple *t* ... Mk 14:49 1321
on a certain day, as he was *t* ... Lk 5:17 1321
he was *t* in one of the synagogues ... Lk 13:10 1321
through the cities and villages, *t* ... Lk 13:22 1321
day time he was *t* in the temple ... Lk 21:37 1321
t throughout all Jewry, beginning ... Lk 23:5 1321
in the temple, and *t* the people ... Acts 5:25 1321
Barnabas continued in Antioch, *t* ... Acts 15:35 1321
t the word of God among them ... Acts 18:11 1321
t those things which concern the ... Acts 28:31 1321
or he that teacheth, on *t* ... Rom 12:7 1319
t every man in all wisdom ... Col 1:28 1321
t and admonishing one another in ... Col 3:16 1321
t things which they ought not, ... Titus 1:11 1321
T us that, denying ungodliness and ... Titus 2:12 3811

TEAR {13}
then I will *t* your flesh with the ... Judg 8:7 1758
Lest he *t* my soul like a lion, ... Ps 7:2 2963
they did *t* me, and ceased not ... Ps 35:15 7167
lest I *t* you in pieces, and there ... Ps 50:22 2963
sword to slay, and the dogs to *t* ... Jer 15:3 5498
Neither shall men *t* themselves ... Jer 16:7 6536
I will *t* them from your arms, and ... Eze 13:20 7167
Your kerchiefs also will I *t* ... Eze 13:21 7167
I, even I, will *t* and go away ... Hos 5:14 2963
the wild beast shall *t* them ... Hos 13:8 1234
and his anger did *t* perpetually ... Amos 1:11 2963
The lion did *t* in pieces enough ... Nah 2:12 2963
fat, and *t* their claws in pieces ... Zec 11:16 6561

TEARETH {6}
t the arm with the crown of the ... Deut 33:20 2963
He *t* me in his wrath, who hateth ... Job 16:9 2963
He *t* himself in his anger ... Job 18:4 2963
t in pieces, and none can deliver ... Mic 5:8 2963
he taketh him, he *t* him ... Mk 9:18 4486
it *t* him that he foameth again, ... Lk 9:39 4682

TEARS {36}
thy prayer, I have seen thy *t* ... 2Kin 20:5 1832
besought him with *t* to put away ... Est 8:3 1058
mine eye poureth out *t* unto God ... Job 16:20
I water my couch with my *t* ... Ps 6:6 1832
hold not thy peace at my *t* ... Ps 39:12 1832
My *t* have been my meat day and ... Ps 42:3 1832
put thou my *t* into thy bottle ... Ps 56:8 1832
feedest them with the bread of *t* ... Ps 80:5 1832
givest them *t* to drink in great ... Ps 80:5 1832
soul from death, mine eyes from *t* ... Ps 116:8 1832
They that sow in *t* shall reap in ... Ps 126:5 1832
behold the *t* of such as were ... Eccl 4:1 1832
I will water thee with my *t* ... Is 16:9 1832
wipe away *t* from off all faces ... Is 25:8 1832
thy prayer, I have seen thy *t* ... Is 38:5 1832
and mine eyes a fountain of *t* ... Jer 9:1 1832
that our eyes may run down with *t* ... Jer 9:18 1832
weep sore, and run down with *t* ... Jer 13:17 1832
mine eyes run down with *t* night ... Jer 14:17 1832

T

weeping, and thine eyes from *t* .... Jer 31:16 1832
night, and her *t* are on her cheeks.......... Lam 1:2 1832
Mine eyes do fail with *t*, my.......... Lam 2:11 1832
let *t* run down like a river day.......... Lam 2:18 1832
neither shall thy *t* run down.......... Eze 24:16 1832
the altar of the LORD with *t*.......... Mal 2:13 1832
child cried out, and said with *t*.......... Mk 9:24 *1144*
and began to wash his feet with *t*.......... Lk 7:38 *1144*
she hath washed my feet with *t*.......... Lk 7:44 *1144*
humility of mind, and with many *t*.......... Acts 20:19 *1144*
every one night and day with *t*.......... Acts 20:31 *1144*
I wrote unto you with many *t*.......... 2Cor 2:4 *1144*
see thee, being mindful of thy *t*.......... 2Ti 1:4 *1144*
t unto him that was able to save.......... Heb 5:7 *1144*
he sought it carefully with *t*.......... Heb 12:17 *1144*
wipe away all *t* from their eyes.......... Rev 7:17 *1144*
wipe away all *t* from their eyes.......... Rev 21:4 *1144*

TEATS {3}
They shall lament for the *t*.......... Is 32:12 7699
bruised the *t* of their virginity.......... Eze 23:3 1717
youth, in bruising thy *t* by the.......... Eze 23:21 1717

TEBAH *(te'-bah)* {1} *A son of Nahor.*
name was Reumah, she bare also *T*.......... Gen 22:24 2875

TEBALIAH *(teb-a-li'-ah)* {1} *A sanctuary servant.*
T the third, Zechariah the fourth.......... 1Chr 26:11 2882

TEBETH *(te'-beth)* {1} *Tenth month of the Hebrew year.*
tenth month, which is the month *T*.......... Est 2:16 2887

TEDIOUS {1}
that I be not further *t* unto thee.......... Acts 24:4 *1465*

TEETH {50}
wine, and his *t* white with milk.......... Gen 49:12 8127
the flesh was yet between their *t*.......... Num 11:33 8127
send the *t* of beasts upon them.......... Deut 32:24 8127
fleshhook of three *t* in his hand.......... 1Sa 2:13 8127
the *t* of the young lions, are.......... Job 4:10 8127
do I take my flesh in my *t*.......... Job 13:14 8127
he gnasheth upon me with his *t*.......... Job 16:9 8127
am escaped with the skin of my *t*.......... Job 19:20 8127
and plucked the spoil out of his *t*.......... Job 29:17 8127
his *t* are terrible round about.......... Job 41:14 8127
hast broken the *t* of the ungodly.......... Ps 3:7 8127
they gnashed upon me with their *t*.......... Ps 35:16 8127
and gnasheth upon him with his *t*.......... Ps 37:12 8127
whose *t* are spears and arrows, and.......... Ps 57:4 8127
Break their *t*, O God, in their.......... Ps 58:6 8127
the great *t* of the young lions.......... Ps 58:6 4973
he shall gnash with his *t*.......... Ps 112:10 8127
not given us as a prey to their *t*.......... Ps 124:6 8127
As vinegar to the *t*, and as smoke.......... Prov 10:26 8127
whose *t* are as swords, and their.......... Prov 30:14 8127
swords, and their jaw *t* as knives.......... Prov 30:14 4973
Thy *t* are like a flock of sheep.......... Song 4:2 8127
Thy *t* are as a flock of sheep.......... Song 6:6 8127
threshing instrument having *t*.......... Is 41:15 6374
the children's *t* are set on edge.......... Jer 31:29 8127
his *t* shall be set on edge.......... Jer 31:30 8127
they hiss and gnash the *t*.......... Lam 2:16 8127
broken my *t* with gravel stones.......... Lam 3:16 8127
the children's *t* are set on edge.......... Eze 18:2 8127
mouth of it between the *t* of it.......... Dan 7:5 8128
and it had great iron *t*.......... Dan 7:7 8128
whose *t* were of iron, and his.......... Dan 7:19 8128
whose *t* are the.......... Joel 1:6 8127
are the *t* of a lion.......... Joel 1:6 8127
hath the cheek *t* of a great lion.......... Joel 1:6 4973
cleanness of *t* in all your cities.......... Amos 4:6 8127
err, that bite with their *t*.......... Mic 3:5 8127
abominations from between his *t*.......... Zec 9:7 8127
shall be weeping and gnashing of *t*.......... Mt 8:12 *3599*
shall be wailing and gnashing of *t*.......... Mt 13:42 *3599*
shall be wailing and gnashing of *t*.......... Mt 13:50 *3599*
shall be weeping and gnashing of *t*.......... Mt 22:13 *3599*
shall be weeping and gnashing of *t*.......... Mt 24:51 *3599*
shall be weeping and gnashing of *t*.......... Mt 25:30 *3599*
with him, cast the same in his *t*.......... Mt 27:44 *3679*
foameth, and gnasheth with his *t*.......... Mk 9:18 *3599*
shall be weeping and gnashing of *t*.......... Lk 13:28 *3599*
they gnashed on him with their *t*.......... Acts 7:54 *3599*
their *t* were as the.......... Rev 9:8 *3599*
were as the *t* of lions.......... Rev 9:8

TEHAPHNEHES *(te-haf'-ne-heze)* {1} *Same as Tahpanhes.*
At *T* also the day shall be.......... Eze 30:18 8471

TEHINNAH *(te-hin'-nah)* {1} *A descendant of Judah.*
T the father of Ir-nahash.......... 1Chr 4:12 8468

TEIL {1}
as a *t* tree, and as an oak, whose.......... Is 6:13 424

TEKEL *(te'-kel)* {2} *Part of the "handwriting of the wall."*
that was written, MENE, MENE, *T*.......... Dan 5:25 8625
T; Thou art weighed.......... Dan 5:27 8625

TEKOA *(te'-ko-ah)* {6} See TEKOAH, TEKOITE.
1. Son of Ashur.
bare him Ashur the father of *T*.......... 1Chr 2:24 8620
the father of *T* had two wives.......... 1Chr 4:5 8620
2. A city in Judah.
even Beth-lehem, and Etam, and *T*.......... 2Chr 11:6 8620
forth into the wilderness of *T*.......... 2Chr 20:20 8620
and blow the trumpet in *T*.......... Jer 6:1 8620
who was among the herdmen of *T*.......... Amos 1:1 8620

TEKOAH *(te'-ko-ah)* {3} See TEKOA. *Same as Tekoa 2.*
And Joab sent to *T*, and fetched.......... 2Sa 14:2 8620
the woman of *T* spake to the king.......... 2Sa 14:4 8621
the woman of *T* said unto the king.......... 2Sa 14:9 8621

TEKOITE *(te'-ko-ite)* {3} See TEKOITES. *An inhabitant of Tekoa.*
Ira the son of Ikkesh the *T*.......... 2Sa 23:26 8621
Ira the son of Ikkesh the *T*.......... 1Chr 11:28 8621
was Ira the son of Ikkesh the *T*.......... 1Chr 27:9 8621

TEKOITES *(te'-ko-ites)* {2}
And next unto them the *T* repaired.......... Neh 3:5 8621
After them the *T* repaired another.......... Neh 3:27 8621

TEL-ABIB *(tel-a'-bib)* {1} *Town on the River Chebar.*
to them of the captivity at *T*.......... Eze 3:15 8512

TELAH *(te'-lah)* {1} *Father of Tahan.*
T his son, and Tahan his son,.......... 1Chr 7:25 8520

TELAIM *(tel'-a-im)* {1} See TELEM. *A place in Judah.*
together, and numbered them in *T*.......... 1Sa 15:4 2923

TELASSAR *(te-las'-sar)* {1} See THELASAR. *A city in Mesopotamia.*
children of Eden which were in *T*.......... Is 37:12 8515

TEL AVIV See TEL-ABIB.

TELEM *(te'-lem)* {2} See TELAIM.
1. A city in Judah.
Ziph, and *T*, and Bealoth,.......... Josh 15:24 2928
2. Married a foreigner in exile.
Shallum, and *T*, and Uri.......... Ezr 10:24 2928

TEL-HARESHA *(tel-ha-re'-sha)* {1} See TEL-HARSA. *A Babylonian settlement of exiles.*
went up also from Tel-melah, *T*.......... Neh 7:61 8521

TEL-HARSA *(tel'-har-sah)* {1} See TEL-HARESHA. *Same as Tel-haresha.*
which went up from Tel-melah, *T*.......... Ezr 2:59 8521

TELL {217}
why didst thou not *t* me that she.......... Gen 12:18 5046
t the stars, if thou be able to.......... Gen 15:5 5608
neither didst thou *t* me, neither.......... Gen 21:26 5046
mountains which I will *t* thee of.......... Gen 22:2 559
t me, I pray thee.......... Gen 24:23 5046
and truly with my master, *t* me.......... Gen 24:49 5046
and if not, *t* me.......... Gen 24:49 5046
the land which I shall *t* thee of.......... Gen 26:2 559
t me, what shall thy wages be.......... Gen 29:15 5046
and didst not *t* me, that I might.......... Gen 31:27 5046
and I have sent to *t* my lord.......... Gen 32:5 5046
T me, I pray thee, thy name.......... Gen 32:29 5046
t me, I pray thee, where they.......... Gen 37:16 5046
t me them, I pray you.......... Gen 40:8 5608
as to *t* the man whether ye had.......... Gen 43:6 5046
we cannot *t* who put our money in.......... Gen 43:22 3045
ye shall *t* my father of all my.......... Gen 45:13 5046
that I may *t* you that which shall.......... Gen 49:1 5046
t him, Thus saith the LORD God of.......... Ex 9:1 1696
that thou mayest *t* in the ears of.......... Ex 10:2 5608
word that we did *t* thee in Egypt.......... Ex 14:12 1696
and *t* the children of Israel.......... Ex 19:3 5046
t the priest, saying, It seemeth.......... Lev 14:35 5046
they will *t* it to the inhabitants.......... Num 14:14 559
heard *t* that Israel came by the.......... Num 21:1
he sheweth me I will *t* thee.......... Num 23:3 5046
judgment which they shall *t* thee.......... Deut 17:11 559
thy elders, and they will *t* thee.......... Deut 32:7 559
t me now what thou hast done.......... Josh 7:19 5046
my mother, and shall I *t* it thee.......... Judg 14:16 5046
T me, I pray thee, wherein thy.......... Judg 16:6 5046
now *t* me, I pray thee, wherewith.......... Judg 16:10 5046
t me wherewith thou mightest be.......... Judg 16:13 5046
T us, how was this wickedness.......... Judg 20:3 1696
he will *t* thee what thou shalt do.......... Ruth 3:4 5046
wilt not redeem it, then *t* me.......... Ruth 4:4 5046
t us wherewith we shall send it.......... 1Sa 6:2 3045
the man of God, to *t* us our way.......... 1Sa 9:8 5046
T me, I pray thee, where the.......... 1Sa 9:18 5046
will *t* thee all that is in thine.......... 1Sa 9:19 5046
T me, I pray thee, what Samuel.......... 1Sa 10:15 5046
T me what thou hast done.......... 1Sa 14:43 5046
I will *t* thee what the LORD hath.......... 1Sa 15:16 5046
soul liveth, O king, I cannot *t*.......... 1Sa 17:55 3045
and what I see, that I will *t* thee.......... 1Sa 19:3 5046
thee, then would not I *t* it thee.......... 1Sa 20:9 5046
David to Jonathan, Who shall *t* me.......... 1Sa 20:10 5046
that he would surely *t* Saul.......... 1Sa 22:22 5046
I beseech thee, *t* thy servant.......... 1Sa 23:11 5046
saying, Lest they should *t* on us.......... 1Sa 27:11 5046
I pray thee, *t* me.......... 2Sa 1:4 5046
T it not in Gath, publish it not.......... 2Sa 1:20 5046
t my servant David, Thus saith.......... 2Sa 7:5 559
to *t* him that the child was dead.......... 2Sa 12:18 5046
if we *t* him that the child is.......... 2Sa 12:18 559
Who can *t* whether GOD will be.......... 2Sa 12:22 3045
wilt thou not *t* me.......... 2Sa 13:4 5046
thou shalt *t* it to Zadok and.......... 2Sa 15:35 5046
t David, saying, Lodge not this.......... 2Sa 17:16 5046
Go *t* the king what thou hast seen.......... 2Sa 18:21 5046
that thou shouldest *t* them who.......... 1Kin 1:20 5046
he shall *t* thee what shall become.......... 1Kin 14:3 5046
t Jeroboam, Thus saith the LORD.......... 1Kin 14:7 559
t thy lord, Behold, Elijah is.......... 1Kin 18:8 559
t thy lord, Behold, Elijah is.......... 1Kin 18:11 559
t Ahab, and he cannot find thee,.......... 1Kin 18:12 5046
t thy lord, Behold, Elijah is.......... 1Kin 18:14 559
T my lord the king, All that thou.......... 1Kin 20:9 559
T him, Let not him that girdeth.......... 1Kin 20:11 1696
t me nothing but that which is.......... 1Kin 22:16 1696
Did I not *t* thee that he would.......... 1Kin 22:18 559
t me, what hast thou in the house.......... 2Kin 4:2 5046
may go and *t* the king's household.......... 2Kin 7:9 5046
T me, I pray thee, all the great.......... 2Kin 8:4 5608
t us now.......... 2Kin 9:12 5046
the city to go to *t* it in Jezreel.......... 2Kin 9:15 5046
t Hezekiah the captain of my.......... 2Kin 20:5 559
T the man that sent you to me,.......... 2Kin 22:15 559
t David my servant, Thus saith.......... 1Chr 17:4 559
Furthermore I *t* thee that the.......... 1Chr 17:10 5046
t David, saying, Thus saith the.......... 1Chr 21:10 1696
Did I not *t* thee that he would.......... 2Chr 18:17 559
T ye the man that sent you to me,.......... 2Chr 34:23 559
I only am escaped alone to *t* thee.......... Job 1:15 5046
I only am escaped alone to *t* thee.......... Job 1:16 5046
I only am escaped alone to *t* thee.......... Job 1:17 5046
I only am escaped alone to *t* thee.......... Job 1:19 5046
t thee, and utter words out of.......... Job 8:10 559
of the air, and they shall *t* thee.......... Job 12:7 5046
Let men of understanding *t* me.......... Job 34:34 559
I may *t* all my bones.......... Ps 22:17 5608
t of all thy wondrous works.......... Ps 26:7 5608
t the towers thereof.......... Ps 48:12 5608
that ye may *t* it to the.......... Ps 48:13 5608
I were hungry, I would not *t* thee.......... Ps 50:12 559
his son's name, if thou canst *t*.......... Prov 30:4 3045
for who can *t* a man what shall be.......... Eccl 6:12 5046
for who can *t* him when it shall.......... Eccl 8:7 5046
a man cannot *t* what shall be.......... Eccl 10:14 5046
shall be after him, who can *t* him.......... Eccl 10:14 5046
hath wings shall *t* the matter.......... Eccl 10:20 5046
T me, O thou whom my soul loveth,.......... Song 1:7 5046
ye find my beloved, that ye *t* him.......... Song 5:8 5046
I will *t* you what I will do to my.......... Is 5:5 3045
t this people, Hear ye indeed,.......... Is 6:9 559
and let them *t* thee now, and let.......... Is 19:12 5046
they spring forth I *t* you of them.......... Is 42:9 8085
T ye, and bring them near.......... Is 45:21 5046
t this, utter it even to the end.......... Is 48:20 8085
then thou shalt *t* them, Thus.......... Jer 15:2 559
the words that I shall *t* thee.......... Jer 19:2 1696
they *t* every man to his neighbour.......... Jer 23:27 5608
hath a dream, let him *t* a dream.......... Jer 23:28 5608
do *t* them, and cause my people to.......... Jer 23:32 5608
t Hananiah, saying, Thus saith.......... Jer 28:13 559
t him, Thus saith the LORD.......... Jer 34:2 559
t the men of Judah and the.......... Jer 35:13 559
We will surely *t* the king of all.......... Jer 36:16 5046
T us now, How didst thou write.......... Jer 36:17 5046
t ye it in Arnon, that Moab is.......... Jer 48:20 5046
t them, Thus saith the Lord GOD.......... Eze 3:11 559
T them therefore, Thus saith the.......... Eze 12:23 559
t them, Behold, the king of.......... Eze 17:12 559
Wilt thou not *t* us what these.......... Eze 24:19 5046
t thy servants the dream, and we.......... Dan 2:4 560
Let the king *t* his servants the.......... Dan 2:7 560
therefore *t* me the dream, and I.......... Dan 2:9 560
we will *t* the interpretation.......... Dan 2:36 560
t me the visions of my dream that.......... Dan 4:9 560
T ye your children of it, and let.......... Joel 1:3 5608
your children *t* their children.......... Joel 1:3
T us, we pray thee, for whose.......... Jonah 1:8 5046
Who can *t* if God will turn and.......... Jonah 3:9 3045
saith unto him, See thou *t* no man.......... Mt 8:4 *2036*
What I *t* you in darkness, that.......... Mt 10:27 *3004*
t no man that he was Jesus the.......... Mt 16:20 *2036*
T the vision to no man, until the.......... Mt 17:9 *2036*
t him his fault between thee and.......... Mt 18:15 *1650*
hear them, *t* it unto the church.......... Mt 18:17 *2036*
T ye the daughter of Sion, Behold.......... Mt 21:5 *2036*
you one thing, which if ye *t* me.......... Mt 21:24 *2036*
I in like wise will *t* you by what.......... Mt 21:24 *2046*
Jesus, and said, We cannot *t*.......... Mt 21:27 *1492*
Neither *t* I you by what authority.......... Mt 21:27 *3004*
T them which are bidden, Behold,.......... Mt 22:4 *2036*
T us therefore, What thinkest.......... Mt 22:17 *2036*
T us, when shall these things be.......... Mt 24:3 *2036*
that thou *t* us whether thou be.......... Mt 26:63 *2036*
t his disciples that he is risen.......... Mt 28:7 *2036*
as they went to *t* his disciples.......... Mt 28:9 *518*
go *t* my brethren that they go.......... Mt 28:10 *518*
fever, and anon they *t* him of her.......... Mk 1:30 *3004*
t them how great things the Lord.......... Mk 5:19 *312*
them that they should *t* no man.......... Mk 7:36 *2036*
nor *t* it to any in the town.......... Mk 8:26 *2036*
that they should *t* no man of him.......... Mk 8:30 *3004*
t no man what things they had.......... Mk 9:9 *1334*
began to *t* them what things.......... Mk 10:32 *3004*
I will *t* you by what authority I.......... Mk 11:29 *2046*
and said unto Jesus, We cannot *t*.......... Mk 11:33 *1492*
Neither do I *t* you by what.......... Mk 11:33 *3004*
T us, when shall these things be.......... Mk 13:4 *2036*
t his disciples and Peter that he.......... Mk 16:7 *2036*
But I *t* you of a truth, many.......... Lk 4:25 *3004*
And he charged him to *t* no man.......... Lk 5:14 *2036*
t John what things ye have seen.......... Lk 7:22 *518*
T me therefore, which of them.......... Lk 7:42 *2036*
should *t* no man what was done.......... Lk 8:56 *2036*
them to *t* no man that thing.......... Lk 9:21 *2036*
But I *t* you of a truth, there be.......... Lk 9:27 *3004*
For I *t* you, that many prophets.......... Lk 10:24 *3004*
I *t* you, Nay.......... Lk 12:51 *3004*
I *t* thee, thou shalt not depart.......... Lk 12:59 *3004*
I *t* you, Nay.......... Lk 13:3 *3004*
I *t* you, Nay.......... Lk 13:5 *3004*
I *t* you, I know you not whence ye.......... Lk 13:27 *3004*
t that fox, Behold, I cast out.......... Lk 13:32 *2036*
I *t* you, in that night there.......... Lk 17:34 *3004*
I *t* you that he will avenge them.......... Lk 18:8 *3004*
I *t* you, this man went down to.......... Lk 18:14 *3004*

I *t* you that, if these should ... Lk 19:40 *3004*
T us, by what authority doest ... Lk 20:2 *2036*
they could not *t* whence it was ... Lk 20:7 *1492*
Neither *t* I you by what authority ... Lk 20:8 *3004*
I *t* thee, Peter, the cock shall ... Lk 22:34 *3004*
Art thou the Christ? *t* us ... Lk 22:67 *2036*
And he said unto them, If I *t* you ... Lk 22:67 *2036*
but canst not *t* whence it cometh, ... Jn 3:8 *1492*
if I *t* you of heavenly things ... Jn 3:12 *2036*
is come, he will *t* us all things ... Jn 4:25 *312*
but ye cannot *t* whence I come ... Jn 8:14 *1492*
because I *t* you the truth, ye ... Jn 8:45 *3004*
thou be the Christ, *t* us plainly ... Jn 10:24 *2036*
and again Andrew and Philip *t* Jesus ... Jn 12:22 *3004*
Now I *t* you before it come, that, ... Jn 13:19 *3004*
Nevertheless I *t* you the truth ... Jn 16:7 *3004*
we cannot *t* what he saith ... Jn 16:18 *1492*
or did others *t* it thee of me ... Jn 18:34 *2036*
t me where thou hast laid him, and ... Jn 20:15 *2036*
T me whether ye sold the land for ... Acts 5:8 *2036*
he shall *t* thee what thou ... Acts 10:6 *2980*
Who shall *t* thee words, whereby ... Acts 11:14 *2980*
who shall also *t* you the same ... Acts 15:27 *518*
in nothing else, but either to *t* ... Acts 17:21 *3004*
unto him, *T* me, art thou a Roman ... Acts 22:27 *3004*
he hath a certain thing to *t* him ... Acts 23:17 *518*
What is that thou hast to *t* me ... Acts 23:19 *518*
See thou *t* no man that thou hast ... Acts 23:22 *1583*
(whether in the body, I cannot *t* ... 2Cor 12:2 *1492*
out of the body, I cannot *t* ... 2Cor 12:2 *1492*
or out of the body, I cannot *t* ... 2Cor 12:3 *1492*
because I *t* you the truth ... Gal 4:16 *226*
T me, ye that desire to be under ... Gal 4:21 *3004*
of the which I *t* you before ... Gal 5:21 *4302*
now *t* you even weeping, that they ... Phil 3:18 *3004*
time would fail me to *t* of Gedeon ... Heb 11:32 *1334*
I will *t* thee the mystery of the ... Rev 17:7 *2046*

TELLEST {1}
Thou *t* my wanderings ... Ps 56:8 5608

TELLETH {7}
Also the LORD *t* thee that he will ... 2Sa 7:11 5046
t the king of Israel the words ... 2Kin 6:12 5046
when he goeth abroad, he *t* it ... Ps 41:6 1696
he that *t* lies shall not tarry in ... Ps 101:7 1696
He *t* the number of the stars ... Ps 147:4 4487
the hands of him that *t* them ... Jer 33:13 4487
Philip cometh and *t* Andrew ... Jn 12:22 *3004*

TELLING {3}
Gideon heard the *t* of the dream ... Judg 7:15 4557
When thou hast made an end of *t* ... 2Sa 11:19 1696
as he was *t* the king how he had ... 2Kin 8:5 5608

TEL-MELAH *(tel-me'-lah)* {2} *A place where the exiles lived.*
were they which went up from *T* ... Ezr 2:59 8528
they which went up also from *T* ... Neh 7:61 8528

TEMA *(te'-mah)* {5}
1. A son of Ishmael.
Hadar, and *T*, Jetur, Naphish, and ... Gen 25:15 8485
and Dumah, Massa, Hadad, and *T* ... 1Chr 1:30 8485
T brought water to him that was ... Is 21:14 8485
Dedan, and *T*, and Buz, and all that ... Jer 25:23 8485
2. A city in northern Arabia.
The troops of *T* looked, the ... Job 6:19 8485

TEMAH See THAMAH.

TEMAN *(te'-man)* {11} See TEMANITE.
1. A son of Eliphaz.
And the sons of Eliphaz were *T* ... Gen 36:11 8487
duke *T*, duke Omar, duke Zepho, ... Gen 36:15 8487
Duke Kenaz, duke *T*, duke Mibzar, ... Gen 36:42 8487
T, and Omar, Zephi, and Gatam, ... 1Chr 1:36 8487
Duke Kenaz, duke *T*, duke Mibzar, ... 1Chr 1:53 8487
2. A race and district of Edom.
Is wisdom no more in *T* ... Jer 49:7 8487
against the inhabitants of *T* ... Jer 49:20 8487
and I will make it desolate from *T* ... Eze 25:13 8487
But I will send a fire upon *T* ... Amos 1:12 8487
And thy mighty men, O *T*, shall be ... Obad 9 8487
God came from *T*, and the Holy One ... Hab 3:3 8487

TEMANI *(te'-ma-ni)* {1} See TEMANITE. *A son of Ashur.*
land of *T* reigned in his stead ... Gen 36:34 8489

TEMANITE *(te'-man-ite)* {6} See TEMANI, TEMANITES. *An inhabitant of Teman 2.*
Eliphaz the *T*, and Bildad the ... Job 2:11 8489
Then Eliphaz the *T* answered ... Job 4:1 8489
Then answered Eliphaz the *T* ... Job 15:1 8489
Then Eliphaz the *T* answered ... Job 22:1 8489
the LORD said to Eliphaz the *T* ... Job 42:7 8489
So Eliphaz the *T* and Bildad the ... Job 42:9 8489

TEMANITES *(te'-man-ites)* {1}
of the *T* reigned in his stead ... 1Chr 1:45 8489

TEMENI *(tem'-e-ni)* {1} *A descendant of Caleb.*
bare him Ahuzam, and Hepher, and *T* ... 1Chr 4:6 8488

TEMPER {1}
of oil, to *t* with the fine flour ... Eze 46:14 7450

TEMPERANCE {4}
he reasoned of righteousness, *t* ... Acts 24:25 *1466*
Meekness, *t* ... Gal 5:23 *1466*
And to knowledge *t* ... 2Pet 1:6 *1466*
and to *t* patience ... 2Pet 1:6 *1466*

TEMPERATE {3}
the mastery is *t* in all things ... 1Cor 9:25 *1467*
of good men, sober, just, holy, *t* ... Titus 1:8 *1468*
the aged men be sober, grave, *t* ... Titus 2:2 *4998*

TEMPERED {3}
and cakes unleavened *t* with oil ... Ex 29:2 1101
t together, pure and holy ... Ex 30:35 4414
but God hath *t* the body together, ... 1Cor 12:24 *4786*

TEMPEST {18}
For he breaketh me with a *t* ... Job 9:17 8183
a *t* stealeth him away in the ... Job 27:20 5492
and brimstone, and an horrible *t* ... Ps 11:6 7307
escape from the windy storm and *t* ... Ps 55:8 5591
So persecute them with thy *t* ... Ps 83:15 5591
strong one, which as a *t* of hail ... Is 28:2 2230
and great noise, with storm and *t* ... Is 29:6 5591
fire, with scattering, and *t* ... Is 30:30 2230
the wind, and a covert from the *t* ... Is 32:2 2230
O thou afflicted, tossed with *t* ... Is 54:11 5590
with a *t* in the day of the ... Amos 1:14 5591
there was a mighty *t* in the sea ... Jonah 1:4 5591
my sake this great *t* is upon you ... Jonah 1:12 5591
there arose a great *t* in the sea ... Mt 8:24 *4578*
being exceedingly tossed with a *t* ... Acts 27:18 *5492*
no small *t* lay on us, all hope ... Acts 27:20 *5494*
unto blackness, and darkness, and *t* ... Heb 12:18 *2366*
clouds that are carried with a *t* ... 2Pet 2:17 *2978*

TEMPESTUOUS {4}
shall be very *t* round about him ... Ps 50:3 8175
for the sea wrought, and was *t* ... Jonah 1:11 5490
wrought, and was *t* against them ... Jonah 1:13 5490
there arose against it a *t* wind ... Acts 27:14 *5189*

TEMPLE {204}
by a post of the *t* of the LORD ... 1Sa 1:9 1964
God went out in the *t* of the LORD ... 1Sa 3:3 1964
he did hear my voice out of his *t* ... 2Sa 22:7 1964
porch before the *t* of the house ... 1Kin 6:3 1964
house round about, both of the *t* ... 1Kin 6:5 1964
the *t* before it, was forty cubits ... 1Kin 6:17 1964
door of the *t* posts of olive tree ... 1Kin 6:33 1964
the pillars in the porch of the *t* ... 1Kin 7:21 1964
of the house, to wit, of the *t* ... 1Kin 7:50 1964
that were in the *t* of the LORD ... 2Kin 11:10 1004
the *t* to the left corner of the ... 2Kin 11:11 1004
to the left corner of the *t* ... 2Kin 11:11 1004
along by the altar and the *t* ... 2Kin 11:11 1004
the people into the *t* of the LORD ... 2Kin 11:13 1004
the doors of the *t* of the LORD ... 2Kin 18:16 1964
to bring forth out of the *t* of ... 2Kin 23:4 1964
had made in the *t* of the LORD ... 2Kin 24:13 1964
the priest's office in the *t* that ... 1Chr 6:10 1004
his head in the *t* of Dagon ... 1Chr 10:10 1004
up the pillars before the *t* ... 2Chr 3:17 1964
their form, and set them in the *t* ... 2Chr 4:7 1964
tables, and placed them in the *t* ... 2Chr 4:8 1964
the doors of the house of the *t* ... 2Chr 4:22 1964
from the right side of the *t* to ... 2Chr 23:10 1004
to the left side of the *t* ... 2Chr 23:10 1004
along by the altar and the *t* ... 2Chr 23:10 1004
went into the *t* of the LORD to ... 2Chr 26:16 1964
not into the *t* of the LORD ... 2Chr 27:2 1964
that they found in the *t* of the ... 2Chr 29:16 1964
when Josiah had prepared the *t* ... 2Chr 35:20 1004
and put them in his *t* at Babylon ... 2Chr 36:7 1964
But the foundation of the *t* of ... Ezr 3:6 1964
foundation of the *t* of the LORD ... Ezr 3:10 1964
the *t* unto the LORD God of Israel ... Ezr 4:1 1964
of the *t* that was in Jerusalem ... Ezr 5:14 1965
them into the *t* of Babylon ... Ezr 5:14 1965
king take out of the *t* of Babylon ... Ezr 5:14 1965
carry them into the *t* that is in ... Ezr 5:15 1965
of the *t* which is at Jerusalem ... Ezr 6:5 1965
unto the *t* which is at Jerusalem ... Ezr 6:5 1965
in the house of God, within the *t* ... Neh 6:10 1964
and let us shut the doors of the *t* ... Neh 6:10 1964
go into the *t* to save his life ... Neh 6:11 1964
will I worship toward thy holy *t* ... Ps 5:7 1964
The LORD is in his holy *t* ... Ps 11:4 1964
he heard my voice out of his *t* ... Ps 18:6 1964
the LORD, and to enquire in his *t* ... Ps 27:4 1964
in his *t* doth every one speak of ... Ps 29:9 1964
O God, in the midst of thy *t* ... Ps 48:9 1964
of thy house, even of thy holy *t* ... Ps 65:4 1964
Because of thy *t* at Jerusalem ... Ps 68:29 1964
thy holy *t* have they defiled ... Ps 79:1 1964
I will worship toward thy holy *t* ... Ps 138:2 1964
up, and his train filled the *t* ... Is 6:1 1964
and to the *t*, Thy foundation shall ... Is 44:28 1964
from the city, a voice from the *t* ... Is 66:6 1964
The *t* of the LORD ... Jer 7:4 1964
The *t* of the LORD ... Jer 7:4 1964
The *t* of the LORD, are these ... Jer 7:4 1964
were set before the *t* of the LORD ... Jer 24:1 1964
our God, the vengeance of his *t* ... Jer 50:28 1964
the LORD, the vengeance of his *t* ... Jer 51:11 1964
at the door of the *t* of the LORD ... Eze 8:16 1964
backs toward the *t* of the LORD ... Eze 8:16 1964
Afterward he brought me to the *t* ... Eze 41:1 1964
twenty cubits, before the *t* ... Eze 41:4 1964
hundred cubits, with the inner *t* ... Eze 41:15 1964
made, and on the wall of the *t* ... Eze 41:20 1964
The posts of the *t* were squared ... Eze 41:21 1964
And the *t* and the sanctuary had two ... Eze 41:23 1964
on them, on the doors of the *t* ... Eze 41:25 1964
before the *t* were an hundred ... Eze 42:8 1964
had taken out of the *t* which was ... Dan 5:2 1965
that were taken out of the *t* of ... Dan 5:3 1965
the songs of the *t* shall be ... Amos 8:3 1964
will look again toward thy holy *t* ... Jonah 2:4 1964
in unto thee, into thine holy *t* ... Jonah 2:7 1964
you, the Lord from his holy *t* ... Mic 1:2 1964
But the LORD is in his holy *t* ... Hab 2:20 1964
upon a stone in the *t* of the LORD ... Hag 2:15 1964
of the LORD's *t* was laid, ... Hag 2:18 1964
he shall build the *t* of the LORD ... Zec 6:12 1964
he shall build the *t* of the LORD ... Zec 6:13 1964
a memorial in the *t* of the LORD ... Zec 6:14 1964
and build in the *t* of the LORD ... Zec 6:15 1964
that the *t* might be built ... Zec 8:9 1964
shall suddenly come to his *t* ... Mal 3:1 1964
him on a pinnacle of the *t* ... Mt 4:5 *2411*
in the *t* profane the sabbath ... Mt 12:5 *2411*
place is one greater than the *t* ... Mt 12:6 *2411*
And Jesus went into the *t* of God ... Mt 21:12 *2411*
them that sold and bought in the *t* ... Mt 21:12 *2411*
and the lame came to him in the *t* ... Mt 21:14 *2411*
and the children crying in the *t* ... Mt 21:15 *2411*
And when he was come into the *t* ... Mt 21:23 *2411*
Whosoever shall swear by the *t* ... Mt 23:16 *3485*
shall swear by the gold of the *t* ... Mt 23:16 *3485*
or the *t* that sanctifieth the ... Mt 23:17 *3485*
And whoso shall swear by the *t* ... Mt 23:21 *3485*
whom ye slew between the *t* ... Mt 23:35 *3485*
went out, and departed from the *t* ... Mt 24:1 *2411*
shew him the buildings of the *t* ... Mt 24:1 *2411*
daily with you teaching in the *t* ... Mt 26:55 *2411*
I am able to destroy the *t* of God ... Mt 26:61 *3485*
the pieces of silver in the *t* ... Mt 27:5 *3485*
Thou that destroyest the *t* ... Mt 27:40 *3485*
the veil of the *t* was rent in ... Mt 27:51 *3485*
into Jerusalem, and into the *t* ... Mk 11:11 *2411*
and Jesus went into the *t*, and ... Mk 11:15 *2411*
them that sold and bought in the *t* ... Mk 11:15 *2411*
carry any vessel through the *t* ... Mk 11:16 *2411*
and as he was walking in the *t* ... Mk 11:27 *2411*
and said, while he taught in the *t* ... Mk 12:35 *2411*
And as he went out of the *t* ... Mk 13:1 *2411*
of Olives over against the *t* ... Mk 13:3 *2411*
daily with you in the *t* teaching ... Mk 14:49 *2411*
I will destroy this *t* that is ... Mk 14:58 *3485*
Ah, thou that destroyest the *t* ... Mk 15:29 *3485*
the veil of the *t* was rent in ... Mk 15:38 *3485*
he went into the *t* of the Lord ... Lk 1:9 *3485*
that he tarried so long in the *t* ... Lk 1:21 *3485*
he had seen a vision in the *t* ... Lk 1:22 *3485*
he came by the Spirit into the *t* ... Lk 2:27 *2411*
which departed not from the *t* ... Lk 2:37 *2411*
days they found him in the *t* ... Lk 2:46 *2411*
and set him on a pinnacle of the *t* ... Lk 4:9 *2411*
between the altar and the *t* ... Lk 11:51 *3624*
men went up into the *t* to pray ... Lk 18:10 *2411*
And he went into the *t*, and began ... Lk 19:45 *2411*
And he taught daily in the *t* ... Lk 19:47 *2411*
as he taught the people in the *t* ... Lk 20:1 *2411*
And as some spake of the *t* ... Lk 21:5 *2411*
day time he was teaching in the *t* ... Lk 21:37 *2411*
in the morning to him in the *t* ... Lk 21:38 *2411*
priests, and captains of the *t* ... Lk 22:52 *2411*
I was daily with you in the *t* ... Lk 22:53 *2411*
the veil of the *t* was rent in the ... Lk 23:45 *3485*
And were continually in the *t* ... Lk 24:53 *2411*
found in the *t* those that sold ... Jn 2:14 *2411*
he drove them all out of the *t* ... Jn 2:15 *2411*
and said unto them, Destroy this *t* ... Jn 2:19 *3485*
six years was this *t* in building ... Jn 2:20 *3485*
But he spake of the *t* of his body ... Jn 2:21 *3485*
Jesus findeth him in the *t* ... Jn 5:14 *2411*
feast Jesus went up into the *t* ... Jn 7:14 *2411*
cried Jesus in the *t* as he taught ... Jn 7:28 *2411*
morning he came again into the *t* ... Jn 8:2 *2411*
treasury, as he taught in the *t* ... Jn 8:20 *2411*
hid himself, and went out of the *t* ... Jn 8:59 *2411*
in the *t* in Solomon's porch ... Jn 10:23 *2411*
as they stood in the *t*, What ... Jn 11:56 *2411*
in the synagogue, and in the *t* ... Jn 18:20 *2411*
daily with one accord in the *t* ... Acts 2:46 *2411*
into the *t* at the hour of prayer ... Acts 3:1 *2411*
the *t* which is called Beautiful ... Acts 3:2 *2411*
of them that entered into the *t* ... Acts 3:2 *2411*
to go into the *t* asked an alms ... Acts 3:3 *2411*
and entered with them into the *t* ... Acts 3:8 *2411*
at the Beautiful gate of the *t* ... Acts 3:10 *2411*
priests, and the captain of the *t* ... Acts 4:1 *2411*
speak in the *t* to the people all ... Acts 5:20 *2411*
into the *t* early in the morning ... Acts 5:21 *2411*
priest and the captain of the *t* ... Acts 5:24 *2411*
in prison are standing in the *t* ... Acts 5:25 *2411*
And daily in the *t*, and in every ... Acts 5:42 *2411*
but also that the *t* of the great ... Acts 19:27 *2411*
with them entered into the *t* ... Acts 21:26 *2411*
Asia, when they saw him in the *t* ... Acts 21:27 *2411*
brought Greeks also into the *t* ... Acts 21:28 *2411*
that Paul had brought into the *t* ... Acts 21:29 *2411*
Paul, and drew him out of the *t* ... Acts 21:30 *2411*
even while I prayed in the *t* ... Acts 22:17 *2411*
hath gone about to profane the *t* ... Acts 24:6 *2411*
in the *t* disputing with any man ... Acts 24:12 *2411*
Asia found me purified in the *t* ... Acts 24:18 *2411*
the Jews, neither against the *t* ... Acts 25:8 *2411*
the Jews caught me in the *t* ... Acts 26:21 *2411*
ye not that ye are the *t* of God ... 1Cor 3:16 *3485*
If any man defile the *t* of God ... 1Cor 3:17 *3485*
for the *t* of God is holy, which ... 1Cor 3:17 *3485*
of God is holy, which *t* ye are ... 1Cor 3:17
ye not that your body is the *t* of ... 1Cor 6:19 *3485*

- sit at meat in the idol's *t* 1Cor 8:10
- live of the things of the *t* 1Cor 9:13 *2411*
- hath the *t* of God with idols 2Cor 6:16 *3485*
- for ye are the *t* of the living 2Cor 6:16 *3485*
- unto an holy *t* in the Lord Eph 2:21 *3485*
- he as God sitteth in the *t* of God 2Th 2:4 *3485*
- make a pillar in the *t* of my God Rev 3:12 *3485*
- serve him day and night in his *t* Rev 7:15 *3485*
- Rise, and measure the *t* of God Rev 11:1 *3485*
- which is without the *t* leave out Rev 11:2 *3485*
- the *t* of God was opened in heaven Rev 11:19 *3485*
- there was seen in his *t* the ark Rev 11:19 *3485*
- another angel came out of the *t* Rev 14:15 *3485*
- out of the *t* which is in heaven Rev 14:17 *3485*
- the *t* of the tabernacle of the Rev 15:5 *3485*
- seven angels came out of the *t* Rev 15:6 *3485*
- the *t* was filled with smoke from Rev 15:8 *3485*
- man was able to enter into the *t* Rev 15:8 *3485*
- the *t* saying to the seven angels Rev 16:1 *3485*
- voice out of the *t* of heaven Rev 16:17 *3485*
- And I saw no *t* therein Rev 21:22 *3485*
- and the Lamb are the *t* of it Rev 21:22 *3485*

TEMPLES {9}

- him, and smote the nail into his *t* Judg 4:21 7541
- dead, and the nail was in his *t* Judg 4:22 7541
- pierced and stricken through his *t* Judg 5:26 7541
- thy *t* are like a piece of a Song 4:3 7541
- are thy *t* within thy locks Song 6:7 7541
- his Maker, and buildeth *t* Hos 8:14 1964
- have carried into your *t* my Joel 3:5 1964
- dwelleth not in *t* made with hands Acts 7:48 *3485*
- dwelleth not in *t* made with hands Acts 17:24 *3485*

TEMPORAL {1}

- the things which are seen are *t* 2Cor 4:18 *4340*

TEMPT {14}

- things, that God did *t* Abraham Gen 22:1 5254
- wherefore do ye *t* the LORD Ex 17:2 5254
- Ye shall not *t* the LORD your God, Deut 6:16 5254
- ask, neither will I *t* the LORD Is 7:12 5254
- yea, they that *t* God are even Mal 3:15 974
- Thou shalt not *t* the Lord thy God Mt 4:7 *1598*
- Why *t* ye me, ye hypocrites Mt 22:18 *3985*
- said unto them, Why *t* ye me Mk 12:15 *3985*
- Thou shalt not *t* the Lord thy God Lk 4:12 *1598*
- and said unto them, Why *t* ye me Lk 20:23 *3985*
- to *t* the Spirit of the Lord Acts 5:9 *3985*
- Now therefore why *t* ye God Acts 15:10 *3985*
- that Satan *t* you not for your 1Cor 7:5 *3985*
- Neither let us *t* Christ, as some 1Cor 10:9 *1598*

TEMPTATION {16}

- as in the day of *t* in the Ps 95:8 4531
- And lead us not into *t*, but Mt 6:13 *3986*
- and pray, that ye enter not into *t* Mt 26:41 *3986*
- ye and pray, lest ye enter into *t* Mk 14:38 *3986*
- the devil had ended all the *t* Lk 4:13 *3986*
- and in time of *t* fall away Lk 8:13 *3986*
- And lead us not into *t* Lk 11:4 *3986*
- Pray that ye enter not into *t* Lk 22:40 *3986*
- and pray, lest ye enter into *t* Lk 22:46 *3986*
- There hath no *t* taken you but 1Cor 10:13 *3986*
- but will with the *t* also make a 1Cor 10:13 *3986*
- my *t* which was in my flesh ye Gal 4:14 *3986*
- that will be rich fall into *t* 1Ti 6:9 *3986*
- in the day of *t* in the wilderness Heb 3:8 *3986*
- is the man that endureth *t* Jas 1:12 *3986*
- will keep thee from the hour of *t* Rev 3:10 *3986*

TEMPTATIONS {8}

- the midst of another nation, by *t* Deut 4:34 4531
- The great *t* which thine eyes saw, Deut 7:19 4531
- The great *t* which thine eyes have Deut 29:3 4531
- have continued with me in my *t* Lk 22:28 *3986*
- of mind, and with many tears, and *t* Acts 20:19 *3986*
- joy when ye fall into divers *t* Jas 1:2 *3986*
- in heaviness through manifold *t* 1Pet 1:6 *3986*
- how to deliver the godly out of *t* 2Pet 2:9 *3986*

TEMPTED {25}

- and because they *t* the LORD Ex 17:7 5254
- have *t* me now these ten times, and Num 14:22 5254
- your God, as ye *t* him in Massah Deut 6:16 5254
- they *t* God in their heart by Ps 78:18 5254
- *t* God, and limited the Holy One of Ps 78:41 5254
- Yet they *t* and provoked the most Ps 78:56 5254
- When your fathers *t* me, proved me Ps 95:9 5254
- and *t* God in the desert Ps 106:14 5254
- wilderness to be *t* of the devil Mt 4:1 *3985*
- wilderness forty days, *t* of Satan Mk 1:13 *3985*
- Being forty days *t* of the devil Lk 4:2 *3985*
- *t* him, saying, Master, what shall Lk 10:25 *1598*
- Christ, as some of them also *t* 1Cor 10:9 *3985*
- to be *t* above that ye are able 1Cor 10:13 *3985*
- thyself, lest thou also be *t* Gal 6:1 *3985*
- some means the tempter have *t* you 1Th 3:5 *3985*
- he himself hath suffered being *t* Heb 2:18 *3985*
- able to succour them that are *t* Heb 2:18 *3985*
- When your fathers *t* me, proved me Heb 3:9 *3985*
- in all points *t* like as we are Heb 4:15 *3985*
- they were sawn asunder, were *t* Heb 11:37 *3985*
- when he is *t*, I am *t* of God Jas 1:13 *3985*
- for God cannot be *t* with evil Jas 1:13 *551*
- But every man is *t*, when he is Jas 1:14 *3985*

TEMPTER {2}

- when the *t* came to him, he said, Mt 4:3 *3985*
- some means the *t* have tempted you 1Th 3:5 *3985*

TEMPTETH {1}

- with evil, neither *t* he any man Jas 1:13 *3985*

TEMPTING {7}

- *t* desired him that he would shew Mt 16:1 *3985*
- *t* him, and saying unto him, Is it Mt 19:3 *3985*
- him a question, *t* him, and saying, Mt 22:35 *3985*
- of him a sign from heaven, *t* him Mk 8:11 *3985*
- put away his wife? *t* him Mk 10:2 *3985*
- *t* him, sought of him a sign from Lk 11:16 *3985*
- *t* him, that they might have to Jn 8:6 *3985*

TEN {247}

- were nine hundred and *t* years Gen 5:14 6235
- after Abram had dwelt *t* years in Gen 16:3 6235
- Peradventure *t* shall be found Gen 18:32 6235
- the servant took *t* camels of the Gen 24:10 6235
- hands of *t* shekels weight of gold Gen 24:22 6235
- us a few days, at the least *t* Gen 24:55 6218
- me, and changed my wages *t* times Gen 31:7 6235
- hast changed my wages *t* times Gen 31:41 6235
- *t* bulls, twenty she asses Gen 32:15 6235
- twenty she asses, and *t* foals Gen 32:15 6235
- Joseph's *t* brethren went down to Gen 42:3 6235
- *t* asses laden with the good Gen 45:23 6235
- *t* she asses laden with corn and Gen 45:23 6235
- into Egypt, were threescore and *t* Gen 46:27
- for him threescore and *t* days Gen 50:3
- lived an hundred and *t* years Gen 50:22 6235
- being an hundred and *t* years old Gen 50:26 6235
- and threescore and *t* palm trees Ex 15:27
- *t* curtains of fine twined linen Ex 26:1 6235
- *T* cubits shall be the length of a Ex 26:16 6235
- pillars *t*, and their sockets *t* Ex 27:12 6235
- the covenant, the *t* commandments Ex 34:28 6235
- *t* curtains of fine twined linen Ex 36:8 6235
- length of a board was *t* cubits Ex 36:21 6235
- pillars *t*, and their sockets *t* Ex 38:12 6235
- shall put *t* thousand to flight Lev 26:8 7233
- *t* women shall bake your bread in Lev 26:26 6235
- and for the female *t* shekels Lev 27:5 6235
- and for the female *t* shekels Lev 27:7 6235
- One spoon of *t* shekels of gold, Num 7:14 6235
- One spoon of gold of *t* shekels Num 7:20 6235
- One golden spoon of *t* shekels Num 7:26 6235
- One golden spoon of *t* shekels Num 7:32 6235
- One golden spoon of *t* shekels Num 7:38 6235
- One golden spoon of *t* shekels Num 7:44 6235
- One golden spoon of *t* shekels Num 7:50 6235
- One golden spoon of *t* shekels Num 7:56 6235
- One golden spoon of *t* shekels Num 7:62 6235
- One golden spoon of *t* shekels Num 7:68 6235
- One golden spoon of *t* shekels Num 7:74 6235
- One golden spoon of *t* shekels Num 7:80 6235
- weighing *t* shekels apiece, after Num 7:86 6235
- nor five days, neither *t* days Num 11:19 6235
- gathered least gathered *t* homers Num 11:32 6235
- have tempted me now these *t* times Num 14:22 6235
- And on the fourth day *t* bullocks Num 29:23 6235
- and threescore and *t* palm trees Num 33:9
- to perform, even *t* commandments Deut 4:13 6235
- the *t* commandments, which the Deut 10:4 6235
- with threescore and *t* persons Deut 10:22
- two put *t* thousand to flight, Deut 32:30 7233
- he came with *t* thousands of Deut 33:2 7233
- they are the *t* thousands of Deut 33:17 7233
- *t* cities with their villages Josh 15:57 6235
- there fell *t* portions to Manasseh Josh 17:5 6235
- half tribe of Manasseh, *t* cities Josh 21:5 6235
- All the cities were *t* with their Josh 21:26 6235
- And with him *t* princes, of each Josh 22:14 6235
- being an hundred and *t* years old Josh 24:29 6235
- of them in Bezek *t* thousand men Judg 1:4 6235
- *t* kings, having their thumbs and Judg 1:7
- being an hundred and *t* years old Judg 2:8 6235
- at that time about *t* thousand men Judg 3:29 6235
- take with thee *t* thousand men of Judg 4:6 6235
- he went up with *t* thousand men at Judg 4:10 6235
- and *t* thousand men after him Judg 4:14 6235
- Then Gideon took *t* men of his Judg 6:27 6235
- and there remained *t* thousand Judg 7:3 6235
- *t* sons of his body begotten Judg 8:30
- *t* persons, reign over you, or Judg 9:2
- *t* pieces of silver out of the Judg 9:4
- *t* persons, upon one stone Judg 9:5
- *t* persons, upon one stone, and Judg 9:18
- *t* sons of Jerubbaal might come, Judg 9:24
- and he judged Israel *t* years Judg 12:11 6235
- rode on threescore and *t* ass colts Judg 12:14
- I will give thee *t* shekels of Judg 17:10 6235
- we will take *t* men of an hundred Judg 20:10 6235
- and a thousand out of *t* thousand Judg 20:10 7233
- there came against Gibeah *t* Judg 20:34 6235
- they dwelled there about *t* years Ruth 1:4 6235
- he took *t* men of the elders of Ruth 4:2 6235
- not I better to thee than *t* sons 1Sa 1:8 6235
- thousand and threescore and *t* men 1Sa 6:19
- and *t* thousand men of Judah 1Sa 15:4 6235
- these *t* loaves, and run to the 1Sa 17:17 6235
- carry these *t* cheeses unto the 1Sa 17:18 6235
- and David his *t* thousands 1Sa 18:7 7233
- ascribed unto David *t* thousands 1Sa 18:8 7233
- and David his *t* thousands 1Sa 21:11 7233
- And David sent out *t* young men 1Sa 25:5 6235
- came to pass about *t* days after 1Sa 25:38 6235
- and David his *t* thousands 1Sa 29:5 7233
- And the king left *t* women, which 2Sa 15:16 6235
- thou art worth *t* thousand of us 2Sa 18:3 6235
- given thee *t* shekels of silver 2Sa 18:11 6235
- *t* young men that bare Joab's 2Sa 18:15 6235
- We have *t* parts in the king, and 2Sa 19:43 6235
- the king took the *t* women his 2Sa 20:3 6235
- *T* fat oxen, and twenty oxen out of 1Kin 4:23 6235
- *t* thousand a month by courses 1Kin 5:14 6235
- *t* thousand that bare burdens, and 1Kin 5:15
- *t* cubits was the breadth thereof 1Kin 6:3 6235
- of olive tree, each *t* cubits high 1Kin 6:23 6235
- part of the other were *t* cubits 1Kin 6:24 6235
- And the other cherub was *t* cubits 1Kin 6:25 6235
- of the one cherub was *t* cubits 1Kin 6:26 6235
- great stones, stones of *t* cubits 1Kin 7:10 6235
- *t* cubits from the one brim to the 1Kin 7:23 6235
- *t* in a cubit, compassing the sea 1Kin 7:24 6235
- And he made *t* bases of brass 1Kin 7:27 6235
- this manner he made the *t* bases 1Kin 7:37 6235
- Then made he *t* lavers of brass 1Kin 7:38 6235
- one of the *t* bases one laver 1Kin 7:38 6235
- bases, and *t* lavers on the bases 1Kin 7:43 6235
- to Jeroboam, Take thee *t* pieces 1Kin 11:31 6235
- will give *t* tribes to thee 1Kin 11:31 6235
- give it unto thee, even *t* tribes 1Kin 11:35 6235
- And take with thee *t* loaves 1Kin 14:3 6235
- took with him *t* talents of silver 2Kin 5:5 6235
- of gold, and *t* changes of raiment 2Kin 5:5 6235
- *t* chariots, and *t* thousand 2Kin 13:7 6235
- in the valley of salt *t* thousand 2Kin 14:7 6235
- reigned *t* years in Samaria 2Kin 15:17 6235
- *t* degrees, or go back *t* degrees 2Kin 20:9 6235
- the shadow to go down *t* degrees 2Kin 20:10 6235
- shadow return backward *t* degrees 2Kin 20:10 6235
- the shadow *t* degrees backward 2Kin 20:11 6235
- even *t* thousand captives, and all 2Kin 24:14 6235
- *t* men with him, and smote Gedaliah 2Kin 25:25 6235
- of Manasseh, by lot, *t* cities 1Chr 6:61 6235
- *t* thousand men that drew sword 1Chr 21:5
- *t* thousand drams, and of silver 1Chr 29:7 7239
- of silver *t* thousand talents, and 1Chr 29:7 6235
- *t* thousand men to bear burdens, 2Chr 2:2
- *t* thousand of them to be bearers 2Chr 2:18
- *t* cubits the height thereof 2Chr 4:1 6235
- sea of *t* cubits from brim to brim 2Chr 4:2 6235
- *t* in a cubit, compassing the sea 2Chr 4:3 6235
- He made also *t* lavers, and put 2Chr 4:6 6235
- he made *t* candlesticks of gold 2Chr 4:7 6235
- He made also *t* tables, and placed 2Chr 4:8 6235
- days the land was quiet *t* years 2Chr 14:1 6235
- the children of Seir *t* thousand 2Chr 25:11 6235
- other *t* thousand left alive did 2Chr 25:12 6235
- *t* thousand measures of wheat 2Chr 27:5 6235
- and *t* thousand of barley 2Chr 27:5 6235
- *t* bullocks, an hundred rams, and 2Chr 29:32
- bullocks and *t* thousand sheep 2Chr 30:24 6235
- months and *t* days in Jerusalem 2Chr 36:9 6235
- to fulfil threescore and *t* years 2Chr 36:21
- a second sort four hundred and *t* Ezr 1:10 6235
- and with him an hundred and *t* males Ezr 8:12 6235
- *t* of their brethren with them, Ezr 8:24 6235
- came, they said unto us *t* times Neh 4:12 6235
- once in *t* days store of all sorts Neh 5:18 6235
- to bring one of *t* to dwell in Neh 11:1 6235
- I will pay *t* thousand talents of Est 3:9 6235
- The *t* sons of Haman the son of Est 9:10 6235
- palace, and the *t* sons of Haman Est 9:12 6235
- let Haman's *t* sons be hanged upon Est 9:13 6235
- and they hanged Haman's *t* sons Est 9:14 6235
- These *t* times have ye reproached Job 19:3 6235
- afraid of *t* thousands of people Ps 3:6 7233
- and an instrument of *t* strings Ps 33:2 6218
- years are threescore years and *t* Ps 90:10
- *t* thousand at thy right hand Ps 91:7 7233
- Upon an instrument of *t* strings Ps 92:3 6218
- an instrument of *t* strings will I Ps 144:9 6218
- *t* thousands in our streets Ps 144:13 7231
- the wise more than *t* mighty men Eccl 7:19 6235
- the chiefest among *t* thousand Song 5:10 7233
- *t* acres of vineyard shall yield Is 5:10 6235
- dial of Ahaz, *t* degrees backward Is 38:8 6235
- So the sun returned *t* degrees Is 38:8 6235
- even *t* men with him, came unto Jer 41:1 6235
- the *t* men that were with him, and Jer 41:2 6235
- But *t* men were found among them Jer 41:8 6235
- And it came to pass after *t* days Jer 42:7 6235
- the entry of the gate, *t* cubits Eze 40:11 6235
- breadth of the door was *t* cubits Eze 41:2 6235
- a walk of *t* cubits breadth inward Eze 42:4 6235
- the breadth shall be *t* thousand Eze 45:1 6235
- and the breadth of *t* thousand Eze 45:3 6235
- the *t* thousand of breadth, shall Eze 45:5 6235
- cor, which is an homer of *t* baths Eze 45:14 6235
- for *t* baths are an homer Eze 45:14 6235
- and of *t* thousand in breadth Eze 48:9 6235
- toward the west *t* thousand in Eze 48:10 6235
- toward the east *t* thousand in Eze 48:10 6235
- length, and *t* thousand in breadth Eze 48:13 6235
- and the breadth *t* thousand Eze 48:13 6235
- shall be *t* thousand eastward Eze 48:18 6235
- and *t* thousand westward Eze 48:18 6235
- servants, I beseech thee, *t* days Dan 1:12 6235
- matter, and proved them *t* days Dan 1:14 6235
- at the end of *t* days their Dan 1:15 6235
- he found them *t* times better than Dan 1:20 6235
- and it had *t* horns Dan 7:7 6236
- unto him, and *t* thousand times Dan 7:10 7240
- *t* thousand stood before him Dan 7:10 7240
- of the *t* horns that were in his Dan 7:20 6236
- the *t* horns out of this kingdom Dan 7:24 6236
- are *t* kings that shall arise Dan 7:24 6236

shall cast down many *t* thousands .... Dan 11:12 7239
forth by an hundred shall leave *t* .... Amos 5:3 6235
if there remain *t* men in one .... Amos 6:9 6235
or with *t* thousands of rivers of .... Mic 6:7 7233
twenty measures, there were but *t* .... Hag 2:16 6235
these threescore and *t* years .... Zec 1:12
and the breadth thereof *t* cubits .... Zec 5:2 6235
that *t* men shall take hold out of .... Zec 8:23 6235
which owed him *t* thousand talents .... Mt 18:24 *3463*
And when the *t* heard it, they were .... Mt 20:24 *1176*
heaven be likened unto *t* virgins .... Mt 25:1 *1176*
it unto him which hath *t* talents .... Mt 25:28 *1176*
And when the *t* heard it, they .... Mk 10:41 *1176*
whether he be able with *t* .... Lk 14:31 *1176*
woman having *t* pieces of silver .... Lk 15:8 *1176*
there met him *t* men that were .... Lk 17:12 *1176*
said, Were there not *t* cleansed .... Lk 17:17 *1176*
And he called his *t* servants .... Lk 19:13 *1176*
and delivered them *t* pounds .... Lk 19:13 *1176*
thy pound hath gained *t* pounds .... Lk 19:16 *1176*
have thou authority over *t* cities .... Lk 19:17 *1176*
give it to him that hath *t* pounds .... Lk 19:24 *1176*
unto him, Lord, he hath *t* pounds .... Lk 19:25 *1176*
and horsemen threescore and *t* .... Acts 23:23
among them more than *t* days .... Acts 25:6 *1176*
For though ye have *t* thousand 1Cor 4:15 *3463*
than *t* thousand words in an 1Cor 14:19 *3463*
the Lord cometh with *t* thousands .... Jude 14 *3461*
ye shall have tribulation *t* days .... Rev 2:10 *1176*
the number of them was *t* thousand .... Rev 5:11 *3461*
thousand times *t* thousand .... Rev 5:11 *3461*
t horns, and seven crowns upon his .... Rev 12:3 *1176*
t horns, and upon his horns .... Rev 13:1 *1176*
and upon his horns *t* crowns .... Rev 13:1 *1176*
having seven heads and *t* horns .... Rev 17:3 *1176*
hath the seven heads and *t* horns .... Rev 17:7 *1176*
the *t* horns which thou sawest are .... Rev 17:12 *1176*
which thou sawest are *t* kings .... Rev 17:12 *1176*
the *t* horns which thou sawest .... Rev 17:16 *1176*

TEND {1}
diligent *t* only to plenteousness .... Prov 21:5

TENDER {39}
unto the herd, and fetcht a calf *t* .... Gen 18:7 7390
Leah was *t* eyed .... Gen 29:17 7390
knoweth that the children are *t* .... Gen 33:13 7390
that the man that is *t* among you .... Deut 28:54 7390
The *t* and delicate woman among you .... Deut 28:56 7390
as the small rain upon the *t* herb .... Deut 32:2
as the *t* grass springing out of 2Sa 23:4
Because thine heart was *t* 2Kin 22:19 7401
Solomon my son is young and *t* 1Chr 22:5 7390
hath chosen, is yet young and *t* 1Chr 29:1 7390
Because thine heart was *t* 2Chr 34:27 7401
that the *t* branch thereof will .... Job 14:7 3127
bud of the *t* herb to spring forth .... Job 38:27
O LORD, thy *t* mercies and thy .... Ps 25:6
not thou thy *t* mercies from me .... Ps 40:11
of thy *t* mercies blot out my .... Ps 51:1
to the multitude of thy *t* mercies .... Ps 69:16
he in anger shut up his *t* mercies .... Ps 77:9
let thy *t* mercies speedily .... Ps 79:8
with lovingkindness and *t* mercies .... Ps 103:4
Let thy *t* mercies come unto me, ... Ps 119:77
Great are thy *t* mercies, O LORD .... Ps 119:156
his *t* mercies are over all his .... Ps 145:9
For I was my father's son, *t* .... Prov 4:3 7390
but the *t* mercies of the wicked .... Prov 12:10
the *t* grass sheweth itself, and .... Prov 27:25
the vines with the *t* grape give a .... Song 2:13
for our vines have *t* grapes .... Song 2:15
whether the *t* grape appear, and .... Song 7:12
thou shalt no more be called *t* .... Is 47:1 7390
grow up before him as a *t* plant .... Is 53:2 3126
top of his young twigs a *t* one .... Eze 17:22 7390
t love with the prince of the .... Dan 1:9
in the *t* grass of the field .... Dan 4:15
in the *t* grass of the field .... Dan 4:23
When his branch is yet *t*, and .... Mt 24:32 *527*
When her branch is yet *t*, and .... Mk 13:28 *527*
Through the *t* mercy of our God .... Lk 1:78 *4698*
is very pitiful, and of *t* mercy .... Jas 5:11 *3629*

TENDERHEARTED {2}
when Rehoboam was young and *t* ... 2Chr 13:7 7390,3824
And be ye kind one to another, *t* .... Eph 4:32 *2155*

TENDERNESS {1}
the ground for delicateness and *t* .... Deut 28:56 7391

TENDETH {5}
labour of the righteous *t* to life .... Prov 10:16
As righteousness *t* to life .... Prov 11:19
than is meet, but it *t* to poverty .... Prov 11:24
talk of the lips *t* only to penury .... Prov 14:23
The fear of the LORD *t* to life .... Prov 19:23

TENONS {6}
Two *t* shall there be in one board .... Ex 26:17 3027
under one board for his two *t* .... Ex 26:19 3027
under another board for his two *t* .... Ex 26:19 3027
One board had two *t*, equally .... Ex 36:22 3027
under one board for his two *t* .... Ex 36:24 3027
under another board for his two *t* .... Ex 36:24 3027

TENOR {2}
according to the *t* of these words .... Gen 43:7 6310
for after the *t* of these words I .... Ex 34:27 6310

TEN'S {1}
I will not destroy it for *t* sake .... Gen 18:32 6235

TENS {3}
rulers of fifties, and rulers of *t* .... Ex 18:21 6235
rulers of fifties, and rulers of *t* .... Ex 18:25 6235
over fifties, and captains over *t* .... Deut 1:15 6235

TENT {98}
and he was uncovered within his *t* .... Gen 9:21 168
east of Beth-el, and pitched his *t* .... Gen 12:8 168
unto the place where his *t* had .... Gen 13:3 168
pitched his *t* toward Sodom .... Gen 13:12 167
Then Abram removed his *t*, and came .... Gen 13:18 167
he sat in the *t* door in the heat .... Gen 18:1 168
ran to meet them from the *t* door .... Gen 18:2 168
hastened into the *t* unto Sarah .... Gen 18:6 168
And he said, Behold, in the *t* .... Gen 18:9 168
And Sarah heard it in the *t* door .... Gen 18:10 168
her into his mother Sarah's *t* .... Gen 24:67 168
pitched his *t* in the valley of .... Gen 26:17
the LORD, and pitched his *t* there .... Gen 26:25 168
had pitched his *t* in the mount .... Gen 31:25 168
Jacob's *t*, and into Leah's *t* .... Gen 31:33 168
Then went he out of Leah's *t* .... Gen 31:33 168
and entered into Rachel's *t* .... Gen 31:33 168
And Laban searched all the *t* .... Gen 31:34 168
pitched his *t* before the city .... Gen 33:18
field, where he had spread his *t* .... Gen 33:19 168
spread his *t* beyond the tower of .... Gen 35:21 168
and they came into the *t* .... Ex 18:7 168
loops, and couple the *t* together .... Ex 26:11 168
of the curtains of the *t*, the .... Ex 26:12 168
length of the curtains of the *t* .... Ex 26:13 168
for the *t* of rams' skins dyed red .... Ex 26:14 168
an hanging for the door of the *t* .... Ex 26:36 168
and stood every man at his *t* door .... Ex 33:8 168
every man in his *t* door .... Ex 33:10 168
The tabernacle, his *t*, and his .... Ex 35:11 168
for the *t* over the tabernacle .... Ex 36:14 168
of brass to couple the *t* together .... Ex 36:18 168
for the *t* of rams' skins dyed red .... Ex 36:19 168
t of the congregation finished .... Ex 39:32 168
the tabernacle unto Moses, the *t* .... Ex 39:33 168
for the *t* of the congregation, ... Ex 39:40 168
of the *t* of the congregation .... Ex 40:2 168
of the *t* of the congregation .... Ex 40:6 168
between the *t* of the congregation .... Ex 40:7 168
abroad the *t* over the tabernacle .... Ex 40:19 168
covering of the *t* above upon it .... Ex 40:19 168
in the *t* of the congregation .... Ex 40:22 168
in the *t* of the congregation .... Ex 40:24 168
t of the congregation before the .... Ex 40:26 168
of the *t* of the congregation .... Ex 40:29 168
between the *t* of the congregation .... Ex 40:30 168
into the *t* of the congregation .... Ex 40:32 168
covered the *t* of the congregation .... Ex 40:34 168
into the *t* of the congregation .... Ex 40:35 168
abroad out of his *t* seven days .... Lev 14:8 168
shall be the tabernacle, and the *t* .... Num 3:25 168
namely, the *t* of the testimony .... Num 9:15 168
every man in the door of his *t* .... Num 11:10 168
the law, when a man dieth in a *t* .... Num 19:14 168
all that come into the *t*, and all .... Num 19:14 168
and all that is in the *t* .... Num 19:14 168
water, and sprinkle it upon the *t* .... Num 19:18 168
the man of Israel into the *t* .... Num 25:8 6898
in the earth in the midst of my *t* .... Josh 7:21 168
and they ran unto the *t* .... Josh 7:22 168
and, behold, it was hid in his *t* .... Josh 7:22 168
them out of the midst of the *t* .... Josh 7:23 168
his asses, and his sheep, and his *t* .... Josh 7:24 168
pitched his *t* unto the plain of .... Judg 4:11 168
fled away on his feet to the *t* of .... Judg 4:17 168
had turned in unto her into the *t* .... Judg 4:18 168
her, Stand in the door of the *t* .... Judg 4:20 168
Heber's wife took a nail of the *t* .... Judg 4:21 168
And when he came into her *t* .... Judg 4:22
shall she be above women in the *t* .... Judg 5:24 168
of Israel every man unto his *t* .... Judg 7:8 168
host of Midian, and came unto a *t* .... Judg 7:13 168
it, that the *t* lay along .... Judg 7:13 168
We will not any of us go to his *t* .... Judg 20:8 168
and they fled every man into his *t* 1Sa 4:10 168
people he sent every man to his *t* 1Sa 13:2 168
but he put his armour in his *t* 1Sa 17:54 168
this day, but have walked in a *t* 2Sa 7:6 168
So they spread Absalom a *t* upon 2Sa 16:22 168
Israel fled every one to his *t* 2Sa 18:17 168
had fled every man to his *t* 2Sa 19:8 168
from the city, every man to his *t* 2Sa 20:22 168
of the camp, they went into one *t* 2Kin 7:8 168
again, and entered into another *t* 2Kin 7:8 168
ark of God, and pitched for it a *t* 1Chr 15:1 168
set it in the midst of the *t* that 1Chr 16:1 168
but have gone from *t* to *t* 1Chr 17:5 168
pitched a *t* for it at Jerusalem 2Chr 1:4 168
and they fled every man to his *t* 2Chr 25:22 168
the *t* which he placed among men .... Ps 78:60 168
shall the Arabian pitch *t* there .... Is 13:20 167
removed from me as a shepherd's *t* .... Is 38:12 168
them out as a *t* to dwell in .... Is 40:22 168
Enlarge the place of thy *t* .... Is 54:2 168
to stretch forth my *t* any more .... Jer 10:20 168
they rise up every man in his *t* .... Jer 37:10 168

TENTH {81}
continually until the *t* month .... Gen 8:5 6224
in the *t* month, on the first day .... Gen 8:5 6224
will surely give the *t* unto thee .... Gen 28:22 6237
In the *t* day of this month they .... Ex 12:3 6218
an omer is the *t* part of an ephah .... Ex 16:36 6224
with the one lamb a *t* deal of .... Ex 29:40 6241
bring for his offering the *t* part .... Lev 5:11 6224
the *t* part of an ephah of fine .... Lev 6:20 6224
three *t* deals of fine flour for a .... Lev 14:10 6241
one *t* deal of fine flour mingled .... Lev 14:21 6241
on the *t* day of the month, ye .... Lev 16:29 6218
two *t* deals of fine flour mingled .... Lev 23:13 6241
two wave loaves of two *t* deals .... Lev 23:17 6241
Also on the *t* day of this seventh .... Lev 23:27 6218
two *t* deals shall be in one cake .... Lev 24:5 6241
on the *t* day of the seventh month .... Lev 25:9 6218
the *t* shall be holy unto the LORD .... Lev 27:32 6224
the *t* part of an ephah of barley .... Num 5:15 6224
On the *t* day Ahiezer the son of .... Num 7:66 6224
t deal of flour mingled with the .... Num 15:4 6241
t deals of flour mingled with the .... Num 15:6 6241
a meat offering of three *t* deals .... Num 15:9 6241
t in Israel for an inheritance .... Num 18:21 4643
even a *t* part of the tithe .... Num 18:26 4643
a *t* part of an ephah of flour for .... Num 28:5 6224
two *t* deals of flour for a meat .... Num 28:9 6241
three *t* deals of flour for a meat .... Num 28:12 6241
two *t* deals of flour for a meat .... Num 28:12 6241
a several *t* deal of flour mingled .... Num 28:13 6241
three *t* deals shall ye offer for .... Num 28:20 6241
bullock, and two *t* deals for a ram .... Num 28:20 6241
A several *t* deal shalt thou offer .... Num 28:21 6241
three *t* deals unto one bullock, ... Num 28:28 6241
two *t* deals unto one ram, ... Num 28:28 6241
A several *t* deal unto one lamb, ... Num 28:29 6241
three *t* deals for a bullock .... Num 29:3 6241
and two *t* deals for a ram, ... Num 29:3 6241
And one *t* deal for one lamb, ... Num 29:4 6241
ye shall have on the *t* day of .... Num 29:7 6218
three *t* deals to a bullock .... Num 29:9 6241
and two *t* deals to one ram, ... Num 29:9 6241
A several *t* deal for one lamb, ... Num 29:10 6241
three *t* deals unto every bullock .... Num 29:14 6241
two *t* deals to each ram of the .... Num 29:14 6241
a several *t* deal to each lamb of .... Num 29:15 6241
even to his *t* generation shall he .... Deut 23:2 6224
even to their *t* generation shall .... Deut 23:3 6224
on the *t* day of the first month .... Josh 4:19 6218
he will take the *t* of your seed 1Sa 8:15 6237
He will take the *t* of your sheep 1Sa 8:17 6237
year of his reign, in the *t* month 2Kin 25:1 6218
in the *t* day of the month, that 2Kin 25:1 6218
Jeremiah the *t*, Machbanai the 1Chr 12:13 6224
to Jeshua, the *t* to Shecaniah, ... 1Chr 24:11 6224
The *t* to Shimei, he, his sons, and 1Chr 25:17 6224
The *t* captain for the *t* month 1Chr 27:13 6224
the *t* month to examine the matter .... Ezr 10:16 6224
his house royal in the *t* month .... Est 2:16 6224
But yet in it shall be a *t* .... Is 6:13 6224
Jeremiah from the LORD in the *t* .... Jer 32:1 6224
king of Judah, in the *t* month .... Jer 39:1 6224
year of his reign, in the *t* month .... Jer 52:4 6224
in the *t* day of the month, that .... Jer 52:4 6218
in the *t* day of the month, which .... Jer 52:12 6218
the *t* day of the month, that .... Eze 20:1 6218
in the ninth year, in the *t* month .... Eze 24:1 6224
in the *t* day of the month, the .... Eze 24:1 6218
In the *t* year, in the *t* month .... Eze 29:1 6224
of our captivity, in the *t* month .... Eze 33:21 6224
in the *t* day of the month, in the .... Eze 40:1 6218
contain the *t* part of an homer .... Eze 45:11 4643
the ephah the *t* part of an homer .... Eze 45:11 4643
ye shall offer the *t* part of a .... Eze 45:14 4643
the seventh, and the fast of the *t* .... Zec 8:19 6224
for it was about the *t* hour .... Jn 1:39 *1182*
also Abraham gave a *t* part of all .... Heb 7:2 *1181*
Abraham gave the *t* of the spoils .... Heb 7:4 *1181*
the *t* part of the city fell, and .... Rev 11:13 *1182*
the *t*, a chrysoprasus .... Rev 21:20 *1182*

TENTMAKERS {1}
by their occupation they were *t* .... Acts 18:3 *4635*

TENTS {66}
the father of such as dwell in *t* .... Gen 4:20 168
he shall dwell in the *t* of Shem .... Gen 9:27 168
Abram, had flocks, and herds, and *t* .... Gen 13:5 168
was a plain man, dwelling in *t* .... Gen 25:27 168
and into the two maidservants' *t* .... Gen 31:33 168
man for them which are in his *t* .... Ex 16:16 168
of Israel shall pitch their *t* .... Num 1:52
of Israel pitched their *t* .... Num 9:17
tabernacle they rested in their *t* .... Num 9:18
of the LORD they abode in their *t* .... Num 9:20
of Israel abode in their *t* .... Num 9:22
of the LORD they rested in the *t* .... Num 9:23
that they dwell in, whether in *t* .... Num 13:19 4264
from the *t* of these wicked men, ... Num 16:26 168
and stood in the door of their *t* .... Num 16:27 168
his *t* according to their tribes .... Num 24:2
How goodly are thy *t*, O Jacob, and .... Num 24:5 168
And ye murmured in your *t*, and said .... Deut 1:27 168
out a place to pitch your *t* in .... Deut 1:33
them, Get you into your *t* again .... Deut 5:30 168
and their households, and their *t* .... Deut 11:6 168
in the morning, and go unto thy *t* .... Deut 16:7 168
and, Issachar, in thy *t* .... Deut 33:18 168
the people removed from their *t* .... Josh 3:14 168
return ye, and get you unto your *t* .... Josh 22:4 168
and they went unto their *t* .... Josh 22:6 168
sent them away also unto their *t* .... Josh 22:7 168
with much riches unto your *t* .... Josh 22:8 168
up with their cattle and their *t* .... Judg 6:5 168
dwelt in *t* on the east of Nobah .... Judg 8:11 168

T

and they spoiled their *t* 1Sa 17:53 4264
and Israel, and Judah, abide in *t* 2Sa 11:11 5521
every man to his *t*, O Israel 2Sa 20:1 168
king, and went unto their *t* joyful 1Kin 8:66 168
to your *t*, O Israel 1Kin 12:16 168
So Israel departed unto their *t* 1Kin 12:16 168
in the twilight, and left their *t* 2Kin 7:7 168
asses tied, and the *t* as they were 2Kin 7:10 168
spoiled the *t* of the Syrians 2Kin 7:16 4264
and the people fled into their *t* 2Kin 8:21 168
of Israel dwelt in their *t* 2Kin 13:5 168
and they fled every man to their *t* 2Kin 14:12 168
king of Judah, and smote their *t* 1Chr 4:41 168
they dwelt in their *t* throughout 1Chr 5:10 168
sent the people away into their *t* 2Chr 7:10 168
every man to your *t*, O Israel, and 2Chr 10:16 168
So all Israel went to their *t* 2Chr 10:16 168
They smote also the *t* of cattle 2Chr 14:15 168
in the gates of the *t* of the LORD 2Chr 31:2 4264
and there abode we in *t* three days Ezr 8:15 2583
and let none dwell in their *t* Ps 69:25 168
of Israel to dwell in their *t* Ps 78:55 168
to dwell in the *t* of wickedness Ps 84:10 168
But murmured in their *t*, and Ps 106:25 168
that I dwell in the *t* of Kedar Ps 120:5 168
as the *t* of Kedar, as the Song 1:5 168
thy kids beside the shepherds' *t* Song 1:8 4908
suddenly are my *t* spoiled Jer 4:20 168
they shall pitch their *t* against Jer 6:3 168
again the captivity of Jacob's *t* Jer 30:18 168
all your days ye shall dwell in *t* Jer 35:7 168
But we have dwelt in *t*, and have Jer 35:10 168
Their *t* and their flocks shall Jer 49:29 168
I saw the *t* of Cushan in Hab 3:7 168
shall save the *t* of Judah first Zec 12:7 168
beasts that shall be in these *t* Zec 14:15 4264

TERAH *(te'-rah)* {11} See THARA. *Father of Abraham.*
nine and twenty years, and begat *T* Gen 11:24 8646
lived after he begat *T* an hundred Gen 11:25 8646
T lived seventy years, and begat Gen 11:26 8646
these are the generations of *T* Gen 11:27 8646
T begat Abram, Nahor, and Haran Gen 11:27 8646
T in the land of his nativity Gen 11:28 8646
T took Abram his son, and Lot the Gen 11:31 8646
the days of *T* were two hundred and Gen 11:32 8646
and *T* died in Haran Gen 11:32 8646
of the flood in old time, even *T* Josh 24:2 8646
Serug, Nahor, *T*, 1Chr 1:26 8646

TERAPHIM {6}
of gods, and made an ephod, and *t* Judg 17:5 8655
is in these houses an ephod, and *t* Judg 18:14 8655
image, and the ephod, and the *t* Judg 18:17 8655
carved image, the ephod, and the *t* Judg 18:18 8655
and he took the ephod, and the *t* Judg 18:20 8655
and without an ephod, and without *t* Hos 3:4 8655

TERESH *(te'-resh)* {2} *A servant of King Ahasuerus.*
king's chamberlains, Bigthan and *T* Est 2:21 8657
had told of Bigthana and *T* Est 6:2 8657

TERMED {2}
Thou shalt no more be *t* Forsaken Is 62:4 559
thy land any more be *t* Desolate Is 62:4 559

TERRACES {1}
trees *t* to the house of the LORD 2Chr 9:11 4546

TERRESTRIAL {2}
celestial bodies, and bodies *t* 1Cor 15:40 *1919*
and the glory of the *t* is another 1Cor 15:40 *1919*

TERRIBLE {52}
for it is a *t* thing that I will Ex 34:10 3372
t wilderness, which ye saw by the Deut 1:19 3372
is among you, a mighty God and *t* Deut 7:21 3372
t wilderness, wherein were fiery Deut 8:15 3372
a great God, a mighty, and a *t* Deut 10:17 3372
t things, which thine eyes have Deut 10:21 3372
of an angel of God, very *t* Judg 13:6 3372
to do for you great things and *t* 2Sa 7:23 3372
t God, that keepeth covenant and Neh 1:5 3372
the LORD, which is great and *t* Neh 4:14 3372
great, the mighty, and the *t* God Neh 9:32 3372
with God is *t* majesty Job 37:22 3372
the glory of his nostrils is *t* Job 39:20 367
his teeth are *t* round about Job 41:14 367
hand shall teach thee *t* things Ps 45:4 3372
For the LORD most high is *t* Ps 47:2 3372
By *t* things in righteousness wilt Ps 65:5 3372
How *t* art thou in thy works Ps 66:3 3372
he is *t* in his doing toward the Ps 66:5 3372
thou art *t* out of thy holy places Ps 68:35 3372
he is *t* to the kings of the earth Ps 76:12 3372
them praise thy great and *t* name Ps 99:3 3372
Ham, and *t* things by the Red sea Ps 106:22 3372
speak of the might of thy *t* acts Ps 145:6 3372
t as an army with banners Song 6:4 366
t as an army with banners Song 6:10 366
lay low the haughtiness of the *t* Is 13:11 6184
peeled, to a people *t* from their Is 18:2 3372
from a people *t* from their Is 18:7 3372
from the desert, from a *t* land Is 21:1 3372
the city of the *t* nations shall Is 25:3 6184
when the blast of the *t* ones is Is 25:4 6184
the branch of the *t* ones shall be Is 25:5 6184
the multitude of the *t* ones shall Is 29:5 6184
For the *t* one is brought to Is 29:20 6184
the prey of the *t* shall be Is 49:25 6184
When thou didst *t* things which we Is 64:3 3372
thee out of the hand of the *t* Jer 15:21 6184
LORD is with me as a mighty *t* one Jer 20:11 6184
an oven because of the *t* famine Lam 5:10 2152
as the colour of the *t* crystal Eze 1:22 3372
upon thee, the *t* of the nations Eze 28:7 6184
the *t* of the nations, shall be Eze 30:11 6184
the *t* of the nations, have cut Eze 31:12 6184
the *t* of the nations, all of them Eze 32:12 6184
and the form thereof was *t* Dan 2:31 1763
a fourth beast, dreadful and *t* Dan 7:7 574
of the LORD is great and very *t* Joel 2:11 3372
the *t* day of the LORD come Joel 2:31 3372
They are *t* and dreadful Hab 1:7 366
The LORD will be *t* unto them Zeph 2:11 3372
so *t* was the sight, that Moses Heb 12:21 *5398*

TERRIBLENESS {3}
outstretched arm, and with great *t* Deut 26:8 4172
thee a name of greatness and *t* 1Chr 17:21 3372
Thy *t* hath deceived thee, and the Jer 49:16 8606

TERRIBLY {3}
he ariseth to shake *t* the earth Is 2:19 6206
he ariseth to shake *t* the earth Is 2:21 6206
the fir trees shall be *t* shaken Nah 2:3

TERRIFIED {4}
neither be ye *t* because of them Deut 20:3 6206
of wars and commotions, be not *t* Lk 21:9 *4422*
But they were *t* and affrighted, and Lk 24:37 *4422*
in nothing *t* by your adversaries Phil 1:28 *4426*

TERRIFIEST {1}
dreams, and *t* me through visions Job 7:14 1204

TERRIFY {4}
let the blackness of the day *t* it Job 3:5 1204
from me, and let not his fear *t* me Job 9:34 1204
did the contempt of families *t* me Job 31:34 2865
as if I would *t* you by letters 2Cor 10:9 *1629*

TERROR {29}
the *t* of God was upon the cities Gen 35:5 2847
I will even appoint over you *t* Lev 26:16 928
t within, shall destroy both the Deut 32:25 367
in all the great *t* which Moses Deut 34:12 4172
that your *t* is fallen upon us, and Josh 2:9 367
from God was a *t* to me, and by Job 31:23 6343
my *t* shall not make thee afraid Job 33:7 367
not be afraid for the *t* by night Ps 91:5 6343
hosts, shall lop the bough with *t* Is 10:33 4637
of Judah shall be a *t* unto Egypt Is 19:17 2283
Thine heart shall meditate *t* Is 33:18 367
and from *t* Is 54:14 4288
Be not a *t* unto me Jer 17:17 4288
I will make thee a *t* to thyself Jer 20:4 4032
out arm, and with great *t* Jer 32:21 4172
which cause their *t* to be on all Eze 26:17 2851
I will make thee a *t*, and thou Eze 26:21 1091
thou shalt be a *t*, and never shalt Eze 27:36 1091
thou shalt be a *t*, and never shalt Eze 28:19 1091
which caused *t* in the land of the Eze 32:23 2851
which caused their *t* in the land Eze 32:24 2851
though their *t* was caused in the Eze 32:25 2851
though they caused their *t* in the Eze 32:26 2851
though they were the *t* of the Eze 32:27 2851
with their *t* they are ashamed of Eze 32:30 2851
For I have caused my *t* in the Eze 32:32 2851
rulers are not a *t* to good works Rom 13:3 *5401*
therefore the *t* of the Lord 2Cor 5:11 *5401*
and be not afraid of their *t* 1Pet 3:14 *5401*

TERRORS {15}
stretched out arm, and by great *t* Deut 4:34 4172
the *t* of God do set themselves in Job 6:4 1161
T shall make him afraid on every Job 18:11 1091
shall bring him to the king of *t* Job 18:14 1091
t are upon him Job 20:25 367
they are in the *t* of the shadow Job 24:17 1091
T take hold on him as waters, a Job 27:20 1091
T are turned upon me Job 30:15 1091
the *t* of death are fallen upon me Ps 55:4 367
they are utterly consumed with *t* Ps 73:19 1091
I suffer thy *t* I am distracted Ps 88:15 367
thy *t* have cut me off Ps 88:16 1161
it suddenly, and *t* upon the city Jer 15:8 928
in a solemn day my *t* round about Lam 2:22 4032
t by reason of the sword shall be Eze 21:12 4048

TERTIUS *(tur'-she-us)* {1} *An assistant of Paul.*
I *T*, who wrote this epistle, Rom 16:22 *5060*

TERTULLUS *(tur-tul'-lus)* {2} *An orator who opposed Paul.*
and with a certain orator named *T* Acts 24:1 *5061*
T began to accuse him, saying, Acts 24:2 *5061*

TESTAMENT {14}
For this is my blood of the new *t* Mt 26:28 *1242*
This is my blood of the new *t* Mk 14:24 *1242*
This cup is the new *t* in my blood Lk 22:20 *1242*
This cup is the new *t* in my blood 1Cor 11:25 *1242*
us able ministers of the new *t* 2Cor 3:6 *1242*
away in the reading of the old *t* 2Cor 3:14 *1242*
Jesus made a surety of a better *t* Heb 7:22 *1242*
he is the mediator of the new *t* Heb 9:15 *1242*
that were under the first *t* Heb 9:15 *1242*
For where a *t* is, there must also Heb 9:16 *1242*
For a *t* is of force after men are Heb 9:17 *1242*
t was dedicated without blood Heb 9:18
This is the blood of the *t* which Heb 9:20 *1248*
in his temple the ark of his *t* Rev 11:19 *1248*

TESTATOR {2}
necessity be the death of the *t* Heb 9:16 *1303*
at all while the *t* liveth Heb 9:17 *1303*

TESTIFIED {24}
and it hath been *t* to his owner Ex 21:29 5749
hath *t* falsely against his Deut 19:18 6030
seeing the LORD hath *t* against me Ruth 1:21 6030
for thy mouth hath *t* against thee 2Sa 1:16 6030
Yet the LORD *t* against Israel, and 2Kin 17:13 5749
which he *t* against them 2Kin 17:15 5749
and they *t* against them 2Chr 24:19 5749
slew thy prophets which *t* against Neh 9:26 5749
I *t* against them in the day Neh 13:15 5749
Then I *t* against them, and said Neh 13:21 5749
the saying of the woman, which *t* Jn 4:39 *3140*
For Jesus himself *t*, that a Jn 4:44 *3140*
he was troubled in spirit, and *t* Jn 13:21 *3140*
And they, when they had *t* and Acts 8:25 *1263*
t to the Jews that Jesus was Acts 18:5 *1263*
for as thou hast *t* of me in Acts 23:11 *1263*
t the kingdom of God, persuading Acts 28:23 *1263*
because we have *t* of God that he 1Cor 15:15 *3140*
we also have forewarned you and *t* 1Th 4:6 *1263*
for all, to be *t* in due time 1Ti 2:6 *3142*
But one in a certain place *t* Heb 2:6 *1263*
signify, when it *t* beforehand the 1Pet 1:11 *4303*
of God which he hath *t* of his Son 1Jn 5:9 *3140*
t of the truth that is in thee, 3Jn 3 *3140*

TESTIFIEDST {2}
t against them, that thou Neh 9:29 5749
t against them by thy spirit in Neh 9:30 5749

TESTIFIETH {5}
the pride of Israel *t* to his face Hos 7:10 6030
he hath seen and heard, that he *t* Jn 3:32 *3140*
disciple which *t* of these things Jn 21:24 *3140*
For he *t*, Thou art a priest for Heb 7:17 *3140*
He which *t* these things saith, Rev 22:20 *3140*

TESTIFY {29}
but one witness shall not *t* Num 35:30 6030
I *t* against you this day that ye Deut 8:19 5749
rise up against any man to *t* Deut 19:16 6030
that this song shall *t* against Deut 31:21 6030
which I *t* among you this day Deut 32:46 5749
thou didst *t* against them Neh 9:34 5749
thine own lips *t* against thee Job 15:6 6030
Israel, and I will *t* against thee Ps 50:7 5749
my people, and I will *t* unto thee Ps 81:8 5749
thee, and our sins *t* against us Is 59:12 6030
our iniquities *t* against us Jer 14:7 6030
of Israel doth *t* to his face Hos 5:5 6030
t in the house of Jacob, saith Amos 3:13 5749
t against me Mic 6:3 6030
that he may *t* unto them, lest Lk 16:28 *1263*
not that any should *t* of man Jn 2:25 *3140*
do know, and *t* that we have seen Jn 3:11 *3140*
and they are they which *t* of me Jn 5:39 *3140*
me it hateth, because I *t* of it Jn 7:7 *3140*
from the Father, he shall *t* of me Jn 15:26 *3140*
And with many other words did he *t* Acts 2:40 *1263*
to *t* that it is he which was Acts 10:42 *1263*
to *t* the gospel of the grace of Acts 20:24 *1263*
the beginning, if they would *t* Acts 26:5 *3140*
For I *t* again to every man that Gal 5:3 *3143*
t in the Lord, that ye henceforth Eph 4:17 *3143*
do *t* that the Father sent the Son 1Jn 4:14 *3140*
to *t* unto you these things in the Rev 22:16 *3140*
For I *t* unto every man that Rev 22:18 *4828*

TESTIFYING {3}
T both to the Jews, and also to Acts 20:21 *1263*
was righteous, God *t* of his gifts Heb 11:4 *3140*
t that this is the true grace of 1Pet 5:12 *1957*

TESTIMONIES {36}
These are the *t*, and the statutes, Deut 4:45 5713
of the LORD your God, and his *t* Deut 6:17 5713
to come, saying, What mean the *t* Deut 6:20 5713
and his judgments, and his *t* 1Kin 2:3 5715
his *t* which he testified against 2Kin 17:15 5715
to keep his commandments and his *t* 2Kin 23:3 5715
to keep thy commandments, thy *t* 1Chr 29:19 5715
keep his commandments, and his *t* 2Chr 34:31 5715
unto thy commandments and thy *t* Neh 9:34 5715
as keep his covenant and his *t* Ps 25:10 5713
most high God, and kept not his *t* Ps 78:56 5713
Thy *t* are very sure Ps 93:5 5713
they kept his *t*, and the ordinance Ps 99:7 5713
Blessed are they that keep his *t* Ps 119:2 5713
have rejoiced in the way of thy *t* Ps 119:14 5715
for I have kept thy *t* Ps 119:22 5713
Thy *t* also are my delight, and my Ps 119:24 5713
I have stuck unto thy *t* Ps 119:31 5715
Incline my heart unto thy *t* Ps 119:36 5715
speak of thy *t* also before kings Ps 119:46 5713
and turned my feet unto thy *t* Ps 119:59 5713
and those that have known thy *t* Ps 119:79 5713
but I will consider thy *t* Ps 119:95 5713
for thy *t* are my meditation Ps 119:99 5715
Thy *t* have I taken as an heritage Ps 119:111 5715
therefore I love thy *t* Ps 119:119 5713
that I may know thy *t* Ps 119:125 5713
Thy *t* are wonderful Ps 119:129 5715
Thy *t* that thou hast commanded Ps 119:138 5713
of thy *t* is everlasting Ps 119:144 5715
save me, and I shall keep thy *t* Ps 119:146 5713
Concerning thy *t*, I have known of Ps 119:152 5713
yet do I not decline from thy *t* Ps 119:157 5715
My soul hath kept thy *t* Ps 119:167 5713
I have kept thy precepts and thy *t* Ps 119:168 5713
nor in his statutes, nor in his *t* Jer 44:23 5715

TESTIMONY {76}
so Aaron laid it up before the *T* ... Ex 16:34 5715
ark the *t* which I shall give thee ... Ex 25:16 5715
put the *t* that I shall give thee ... Ex 25:21 5715
which are upon the ark of the *t* ... Ex 25:22 5715
within the vail the ark of the *t* ... Ex 26:33 5715
of the *t* in the most holy place ... Ex 26:34 5715
the vail, which is before the *t* ... Ex 27:21 5715
vail that is by the ark of the *t* ... Ex 30:6 5715
the mercy seat that is over the *t* ... Ex 30:6 5715
therewith, and the ark of the *t* ... Ex 30:26 5715
put of it before the *t* in the ... Ex 30:36 5715
congregation, and the ark of the *t* ... Ex 31:7 5715
upon mount Sinai, two tables of *t* ... Ex 31:18 5715
tables of the *t* were in his hand ... Ex 32:15 5715
two tables of *t* in Moses' hand ... Ex 34:29 5715
even of the tabernacle of *t* ... Ex 38:21 5715
The ark of the *t*, and the staves ... Ex 39:35 5715
put therein the ark of the *t* ... Ex 40:3 5715
incense before the ark of the *t* ... Ex 40:5 5715
put the *t* into the ark, and set ... Ex 40:20 5715
and covered the ark of the *t* ... Ex 40:21 5715
the mercy seat that is upon the *t* ... Lev 16:13 5715
Without the vail of the *t* ... Lev 24:3 5715
Levites over the tabernacle of *t* ... Num 1:50 5715
round about the tabernacle of *t* ... Num 1:53 5715
the charge of the tabernacle of *t* ... Num 1:53 5715
and cover the ark of *t* with it ... Num 4:5 5715
seat that was upon the ark of *t* ... Num 7:89 5715
namely, the tent of the *t* ... Num 9:15 5715
from off the tabernacle of the *t* ... Num 10:11 5715
of the congregation before the *t* ... Num 17:4 5715
Aaron's rod again before the *t* ... Num 17:10 5715
that bear the ark of the *t* ... Josh 4:16 5715
and this was a *t* in Israel ... Ruth 4:7 8584
crown upon him, and gave him the *t* ... 2Kin 11:12 5715
him the crown, and gave him the *t* ... 2Chr 23:11 5715
the *t* of the LORD is sure, making ... Ps 19:7 5715
For he established a *t* in Jacob ... Ps 78:5 5715
he ordained in Joseph for a *t* ... Ps 81:5 5715
shall I keep the *t* of thy mouth ... Ps 119:88 5715
unto the *t* of Israel, to give ... Ps 122:4 5715
my *t* that I shall teach them ... Ps 132:12 5713
Bind up the *t*, seal the law among ... Is 8:16 8584
To the law and to the *t* ... Is 8:20 8584
commanded, for a *t* unto them ... Mt 8:4 *3142*
for a *t* against them and the ... Mt 10:18 *3142*
commanded, for a *t* unto them ... Mk 1:44 *3142*
your feet for a *t* against them ... Mk 6:11 *3142*
for my sake, for a *t* against them ... Mk 13:9 *3142*
commanded, for a *t* unto them ... Lk 5:14 *3142*
your feet for a *t* against them ... Lk 9:5 *3142*
And it shall turn to you for a *t* ... Lk 21:13 *3142*
and no man receiveth his *t* ... Jn 3:32 *3141*
He that hath received his *t* hath ... Jn 3:33 *3141*
But I receive not *t* from man ... Jn 5:34 *3141*
that the *t* of two men is true ... Jn 8:17 *3141*
and we know that his *t* is true ... Jn 21:24 *3141*
to whom also he gave *t*, and said, ... Acts 13:22 *3140*
which gave *t* unto the word of his ... Acts 14:3 *3140*
not receive thy *t* concerning me ... Acts 22:18 *3141*
Even as the *t* of Christ was ... 1Cor 1:6 *3142*
declaring unto you the *t* of God ... 1Cor 2:1 *3142*
the *t* of our conscience, that in ... 2Cor 1:12 *3142*
them that believe (because our *t* ... 2Th 1:10 *3142*
ashamed of the *t* of our Lord ... 2Ti 1:8 *3142*
for a *t* of those things which ... Heb 3:5 *3142*
his translation he had this *t* ... Heb 11:5 *3140*
of the *t* of Jesus Christ, and of ... Rev 1:2 *3141*
for the *t* of Jesus Christ ... Rev 1:9 *3141*
for the *t* which they held ... Rev 6:9 *3141*
they shall have finished their *t* ... Rev 11:7 *3141*
Lamb, and by the word of their *t* ... Rev 12:11 *3141*
have the *t* of Jesus Christ ... Rev 12:17 *3141*
of the *t* in heaven was opened ... Rev 15:5 *3142*
brethren that have the *t* of Jesus ... Rev 19:10 *3141*
for the *t* of Jesus is the spirit ... Rev 19:10 *3141*

TETRARCH {7}
At that time Herod the *t* heard of ... Mt 14:1 *5076*
and Herod being *t* of Galilee ... Lk 3:1 *5075*
his brother Philip *t* of Ituraea ... Lk 3:1 *5075*
and Lysanias the *t* of Abilene ... Lk 3:1 *5075*
But Herod the *t*, being reproved ... Lk 3:19 *5076*
Now Herod the *t* heard of all that ... Lk 9:7 *5076*
been brought up with Herod the *t* ... Acts 13:1 *5076*

THADDAEUS *(thad-de'-us)* {2} See JUDE, LEBBAEUS. *A disciple of Jesus.*
and Lebbaeus, whose surname was *T* ... Mt 10:3 *2280*
James the son of Alphaeus, and *T* ... Mk 3:18 *2280*

THAHASH *(tha'-hash)* {1} *A son of Reumah.*
bare also Tebah, and Gaham, and *T* ... Gen 22:24 8477

THAMAH *(tha'-mah)* {1} See TAMAH. *A family of exiles.*
of Sisera, the children of *T* ... Ezr 2:53 8547

THAMAR *(tha'-mar)* {1} See TAMAR. *Mother of Phares and Zara; ancestor of Jesus.*
Judas begat Phares and Zara of *T* ... Mt 1:3 *2283*

THAN See APPENDIX.

THANK {27}
the LORD, and to record, and to *t* ... 1Chr 16:4 3034
delivered first this psalm to *t* ... 1Chr 16:7 3034
And to stand every morning to *t* ... 1Chr 23:30 3034
we *t* thee, and praise thy glorious ... 1Chr 29:13 3034
t offerings into the house of the ... 2Chr 29:31 8426
in sacrifices and *t* offerings ... 2Chr 29:31 8426
t offerings, and commanded Judah ... 2Chr 33:16 8426
I *t* thee, and praise thee, O thou ... Dan 2:23 3029
I *t* thee, O Father, Lord of ... Mt 11:25 *1843*
which love you, what *t* have ye ... Lk 6:32 *5485*
do good to you, what *t* have ye ... Lk 6:33 *5485*
hope to receive, what *t* have ye ... Lk 6:34 *5485*
I *t* thee, O Father, Lord of ... Lk 10:21 *1843*
Doth he *t* that servant because he ... Lk 17:9 *2192,5485*
I *t* thee, that I am not as other ... Lk 18:11 *2168*
I *t* thee that thou hast heard me ... Jn 11:41 *2168*
I *t* my God through Jesus Christ ... Rom 1:8 *2168*
I *t* God through Jesus Christ our ... Rom 7:25 *2168*
I *t* my God always on your behalf, ... 1Cor 1:4 *2168*
I *t* God that I baptized none of ... 1Cor 1:14 *2168*
I *t* my God, I speak with tongues ... 1Cor 14:18 *2168*
I *t* my God upon every remembrance ... Phil 1:3 *2168*
For this cause also *t* we God ... 1Th 2:13 *2168*
We are bound to *t* God always for ... 2Th 1:3 *2168*
I *t* Christ Jesus our Lord, who ... 1Ti 1:12 *2192,5485*
I *t* God, whom I serve from my ... 2Ti 1:3 *2192,5485*
I *t* my God, making mention of ... Philem 4 *2168*

THANKED {3}
and bowed himself, and *t* the king ... 2Sa 14:22 1288
he *t* God, and took courage ... Acts 28:15 *2168*
But God be *t*, that ye were the ... Rom 6:17 *5485*

THANKFUL {3}
be *t* unto him, and bless his name ... Ps 100:4 3034
him not as God, neither were *t* ... Rom 1:21 *2168*
and be ye *t* ... Col 3:15 *2170*

THANKFULNESS {1}
most noble Felix, with all *t* ... Acts 24:3 *2169*

THANKING {1}
heard in praising and *t* the LORD ... 2Chr 5:13 3034

THANKS {73}
Therefore I will give *t* unto thee ... 2Sa 22:50 3034
Give *t* unto the LORD, call upon ... 1Chr 16:8 3034
O give *t* unto the LORD ... 1Chr 16:34 3034
we may give *t* to thy holy name ... 1Chr 16:35 3034
to give *t* to the LORD, because ... 1Chr 16:41 3034
prophesied with a harp, to give *t* ... 1Chr 25:3 3034
to minister, and to give *t* ... 2Chr 31:2 3034
and giving *t* unto the LORD ... Ezr 3:11 3034
them, to praise and to give *t* ... Neh 12:24 3034
companies of them that gave *t* ... Neh 12:31 8426
gave *t* went over against them ... Neh 12:38 8426
that gave *t* in the house of God ... Neh 12:40 8426
the grave who shall give thee *t* ... Ps 6:5 3034
Therefore will I give *t* unto thee ... Ps 18:49 3034
give *t* at the remembrance of his ... Ps 30:4 3034
I will give *t* unto thee for ever ... Ps 30:12 3034
I will give thee *t* in the great ... Ps 35:18 3034
Unto thee, O God, do we give *t* ... Ps 75:1 3034
unto thee do we give *t* ... Ps 75:1 3034
pasture will give thee *t* for ever ... Ps 79:13 3034
thing to give *t* unto the LORD ... Ps 92:1 3034
give *t* at the remembrance of his ... Ps 97:12 3034
O give *t* unto the LORD ... Ps 105:1 3034
O give *t* unto the LORD ... Ps 106:1 3034
to give *t* unto thy holy name, and ... Ps 106:47 3034
O give *t* unto the LORD, for he is ... Ps 107:1 3034
O give *t* unto the LORD ... Ps 118:1 3034
O give *t* unto the LORD ... Ps 118:29 3034
give *t* unto thee because of thy ... Ps 119:62 3034
to give *t* unto the name of the ... Ps 122:4 3034
O Give *t* unto the LORD ... Ps 136:1 3034
O give *t* unto the God of gods ... Ps 136:2 3034
O give *t* to the Lord of lords ... Ps 136:3 3034
O give *t* unto the God of heaven ... Ps 136:26 3034
shall give *t* unto thy name ... Ps 140:13 3034
gave *t* before his God, as he did ... Dan 6:10 3029
loaves and the fishes, and gave *t* ... Mt 15:36 *2168*
And he took the cup, and gave *t* ... Mt 26:27 *2168*
took the seven loaves, and gave *t* ... Mk 8:6 *2168*
the cup, and when he had given *t* ... Mk 14:23 *2168*
gave *t* likewise unto the Lord ... Lk 2:38 *437*
face at his feet, giving him *t* ... Lk 17:16 *2168*
And he took the cup, and gave *t* ... Lk 22:17 *2168*
And he took bread, and gave *t* ... Lk 22:19 *2168*
and when he had given *t*, he ... Jn 6:11 *2168*
after that the Lord had given *t* ... Jn 6:23 *2168*
gave *t* to God in presence of them ... Acts 27:35 *2168*
to the Lord, for he giveth God *t* ... Rom 14:6 *2168*
he eateth not, and giveth God *t* ... Rom 14:6 *2168*
unto whom not only I give *t* ... Rom 16:4 *2168*
of for that for which I give *t* ... 1Cor 10:30 *2168*
And when he had given *t*, he brake ... 1Cor 11:24 *2168*
say Amen at thy giving of *t* ... 1Cor 14:16 *2169*
For thou verily givest *t* well ... 1Cor 14:17 *2168*
But *t* be to God, which giveth us ... 1Cor 15:57 *5485*
t may be given by many on our ... 2Cor 1:11 *2168*
Now *t* be unto God, which always ... 2Cor 2:14 *5485*
But *t* be to God, which put the ... 2Cor 8:16 *5485*
T be unto God for his unspeakable ... 2Cor 9:15 *5485*
Cease not to give *t* for you ... Eph 1:16 *2168*
but rather giving of *t* ... Eph 5:4 *2169*
Giving *t* always for all things ... Eph 5:20 *2168*
We give *t* to God and the Father of ... Col 1:3 *2168*
Giving *t* unto the Father, which ... Col 1:12 *2168*
the Lord Jesus, giving *t* to God ... Col 3:17 *2168*
We give *t* to God always for you ... 1Th 1:2 *2168*
For what *t* can we render to God ... 1Th 3:9 *2169*
In every thing give *t* ... 1Th 5:18 *2168*
to give *t* alway to God for you ... 2Th 2:13 *2168*
intercessions, and giving of *t* ... 1Ti 2:1 *2169*
of our lips giving *t* to his name ... Heb 13:15 *3670*
t to him that sat on the throne, ... Rev 4:9 *2169*
Saying, We give thee *t*, O Lord ... Rev 11:17 *2168*

THANKSGIVING {27}
If he offer it for a *t*, then he ... Lev 7:12 8426
offer with the sacrifice of *t* ... Lev 7:12 8426
of *t* of his peace offerings ... Lev 7:13 8426
of his peace offerings for *t* ... Lev 7:15 8426
a sacrifice of *t* unto the LORD ... Lev 22:29 8426
to begin the *t* in prayer ... Neh 11:17 3034
Mattaniah, which was over the *t* ... Neh 12:8 1960
and songs of praise and *t* unto God ... Neh 12:46
I may publish with the voice of *t* ... Ps 26:7 3034
Offer unto God *t* ... Ps 50:14 8426
song, and will magnify him with *t* ... Ps 69:30 8426
come before his presence with *t* ... Ps 95:2 8426
Enter into his gates with *t* ... Ps 100:4 8426
sacrifice the sacrifices of *t* ... Ps 107:22 8426
offer to thee the sacrifice of *t* ... Ps 116:17 8426
Sing unto the LORD with *t* ... Ps 147:7 8426
shall be found therein, *t* ... Is 51:3 8426
And out of them shall proceed *t* ... Jer 30:19 8426
a sacrifice of *t* with leaven ... Amos 4:5 8426
unto thee with the voice of *t* ... Jonah 2:9 8426
grace might through the *t* of many ... 2Cor 4:15 *2169*
which causeth through us *t* to God ... 2Cor 9:11 *2169*
supplication with *t* let your ... Phil 4:6 *2169*
taught, abounding therein with *t* ... Col 2:7 *2169*
and watch in the same with *t* ... Col 4:2 *2169*
with *t* of them which believe ... 1Ti 4:3 *2169*
refused, if it be received with *t* ... 1Ti 4:4 *2169*
and glory, and wisdom, and *t* ... Rev 7:12 *2169*

THANKSGIVINGS {2}
with gladness, both with *t* ... Neh 12:27 8426
abundant also by many *t* unto God ... 2Cor 9:12 *2169*

THANKWORTHY {1}
For this is *t*, if a man for ... 1Pet 2:19 *5485*

THARA *(tha'-rah)* {1} See TERAH. *Greek form of Terah.*
Abraham, which was the son of *T* ... Lk 3:34 *2291*

THARSHISH *(thar'-shish)* {4} See TARSHISH.
1. Ships fitted for long voyages.
navy of *T* with the navy of Hiram ... 1Kin 10:22 8659
in three years came the navy of *T* ... 1Kin 10:22 8659
of *T* to go to Ophir for gold ... 1Kin 22:48 8659
2. Son of Bilhan.
and Chenaanah, and Zethan, and *T* ... 1Chr 7:10 8659

THAT See APPENDIX.

THE See APPENDIX.

THEATRE {2}
rushed with one accord into the *t* ... Acts 19:29 *2302*
not adventure himself into the *t* ... Acts 19:31 *2302*

THEBES See THEBEZ.

THEBEZ *(the'-bez)* {4} *A city in Ephraim.*
Then went Abimelech to *T*, and ... Judg 9:50 8405
to *T*, and encamped against *T* ... Judg 9:50 8405
from the wall, that he died in *T* ... 2Sa 11:21 8405

THEE See APPENDIX.

THEE-WARD {1}
works have been to *t* very good ... 1Sa 19:4

THEFT {2}
then he shall be sold for his *t* ... Ex 22:3 1591
If the *t* be certainly found in ... Ex 22:4 1591

THEFTS {3}
adulteries, fornications, *t* ... Mt 15:19 *2829*
T, covetousness, wickedness, ... Mk 7:22 *2829*
their fornication, nor of their *t* ... Rev 9:21 *2804*

THEIR See APPENDIX.

THEIR'S {1}
thing in Israel shall be *t* ... Eze 44:29 1992

THEIRS See APPENDIX.

THELASAR *(the-la'-sar)* {1} See TELASSAR. *Same as Telassar.*
children of Eden which were in *T* ... 2Kin 19:12 8515

THEM See APPENDIX.

THEMSELVES See APPENDIX.

THEN See APPENDIX.

THENCE {145}
from *t* it was parted, and became ... Gen 2:10 8033
t upon the face of all the earth ... Gen 11:8 8033
from *t* did the LORD scatter them ... Gen 11:9 8033
he removed from *t* unto a mountain ... Gen 12:8 8033
And the men rose up from *t* ... Gen 18:16 8033
the men turned their faces from *t* ... Gen 18:22 8033
Abraham journeyed from *t* toward ... Gen 20:1 8033
take a wife unto my son from *t* ... Gen 24:7 8033
And Isaac departed *t*, and pitched ... Gen 26:17 8033
And he removed from *t*, and digged ... Gen 26:22 8033
he went up from *t* to Beer-sheba ... Gen 26:23 8033
fetch me from *t* two good kids of ... Gen 27:9 8033
I will send, and fetch thee from *t* ... Gen 27:45 8033
take thee a wife from *t* of the ... Gen 28:2 8033
to take him a wife from *t* ... Gen 28:6 8033
removing from *t* all the speckled ... Gen 30:32 8033
thither, and buy for us from *t* ... Gen 42:2 8033
with the corn, and departed *t* ... Gen 42:26 8033
(from *t* is the shepherd, the ... Gen 49:24 8033
cut down from *t* a branch with one ... Num 13:23 8033
of Israel cut down from *t* ... Num 13:24 8033
From *t* they removed, and pitched ... Num 21:12 8033
From *t* they removed, and pitched ... Num 21:13 8033
And from *t* they went to Beer ... Num 21:16 8033
that *t* he might see the utmost ... Num 22:41 8033
and curse me them from *t* ... Num 23:13 8033
thou mayest curse me them from *t* ... Num 23:27 8033

T

But if from t thou shalt seek the............Deut 4:29 8033
thee out t through a mighty hand...........Deut 5:15 8033
And he brought us out from t ....Deut 6:23 8033
From t they journeyed unto......................Deut 10:7 8033
city shall send and fetch him t.................Deut 19:12 8033
house, if any man fall from t....................Deut 22:8
the LORD thy God redeemed thee t ....Deut 24:18 8033
from t will the LORD thy God...................Deut 30:4 8033
from t will he fetch thee........................Deut 30:4 8033
house, and bring out t the woman ....Josh 6:22 8033
From t it passed toward Azmon, and ......Josh 15:4
Caleb drove t the three sons of.................Josh 15:14 8033
he went up t to the inhabitants.................Josh 15:15 8033
went over from t toward Luz ....Josh 18:13 8033
And the border was drawn t ....Josh 18:14
from t passeth on along on the..................Josh 19:13 8033
and goeth out from t to Hukkok ....Josh 19:34 8033
from t he went against the ....Judg 1:11 8033
he expelled t the three sons of ....Judg 1:20 8033
And he went up t to Penuel.......................Judg 8:8 8033
there went from t of the family.................Judg 18:11 8033
they passed t unto mount Ephraim,...........Judg 18:13 8033
from t am I ....Judg 19:18 8033
of Israel departed t at that time...............Judg 21:24 8033
they went out from t every man to............Judg 21:24 8033
that they might bring from t the...............1Sa 4:4 8033
shalt thou go on forward from t...............1Sa 10:3 8033
And they ran and fetched him t................1Sa 10:23 8033
took t a stone, and slang it, and...............1Sa 17:49 8033
David therefore departed t.........................1Sa 22:1 8033
David went t to Mizpeh of Moab 1Sa 22:3 8033
And David went up from t, and dwelt 1Sa 23:29 8033
to bring up from t the ark of God............2Sa 6:2 8033
fetched t a wise woman, and said 2Sa 14:2 8033
t came out a man of the family of.............2Sa 16:5 8033
up from t the bones of Saul........................2Sa 21:13 8033
they are come up from t rejoicing............1Kin 1:45 8033
and go not forth t any whither..................1Kin 2:36 8033
to Ophir, and fetched from t gold.............1Kin 9:28 8033
and went out from t, and built..................1Kin 12:25 8033
So he departed t, and found Elisha...........1Kin 19:19 8033
there shall not be from t any.....................2Kin 2:21 8033
And he went up from t unto Beth-el.........2Kin 2:23 8033
he went from t to mount Carmel,...............2Kin 2:25 8033
from t he returned to Samaria 2Kin 2:25 8033
take t every man a beam, and let 2Kin 6:2 8033
eat and drink, and carried t silver 2Kin 7:8 8033
another tent, and carried t also.................2Kin 7:8 8033
And when he was departed t.......................2Kin 10:15 8033
priests whom ye brought from t................2Kin 17:27 8033
whom they carried away from t 2Kin 17:33 8033
down, and brake them down from t...........2Kin 23:12 8033
And he carried out t all the.......................2Kin 24:13 8033
to bring up t the ark of God the 1Chr 13:6 8033
took t four hundred and fifty.....................2Chr 8:18 8033
and they thrust him out from t 2Chr 26:20 8033
the river, be ye far from t ....Ezr 6:6 8536
yet will I gather them from t.....................Neh 1:9 8033
From t she seeketh the prey, and...............Job 39:29 8033
ye, depart ye, go ye out from t...................Is 52:11 8033
be no more t an infant of days ....Is 65:20 8033
out t shall be torn in pieces.......................Jer 5:6 2007
and take the girdle from t ....Jer 13:6 8033
hand, yet would I pluck thee t ....Jer 22:24 8033
shall cause to cease from t man ....Jer 36:29
to separate himself t in the ....Jer 37:12 8033
took t old cast clouts and old....................Jer 38:11 8033
he shall go forth from t in peace ....Jer 43:12 8033
I will bring thee down from t....................Jer 49:16 8033
and will destroy from t the king ....Jer 49:38 8033
from t she shall be taken............................Jer 50:9 8033
the abominations thereof from t ....Eze 11:18
give her her vineyards from t ....Hos 2:15 8033
from t go ye to Hamath the great...............Amos 6:2 8033
t shall mine hand take them.......................Amos 9:2 8033
heaven, t will I bring them down ....Amos 9:2 8033
I will search and take them out t ....Amos 9:3 8033
t will I command the serpent, and ....Amos 9:3 8033
t will I command the sword, and it............Amos 9:4 8033
t will I bring thee down, saith....................Obad 4 8033
And going on from t, he saw other.............Mt 4:21 1564
Thou shalt by no means come out t ....Mt 5:26 1564
And as Jesus passed forth from t ....Mt 9:9 1564
And when Jesus departed t, two ....Mt 9:27 1564
and there abide till ye go t ....Mt 10:11
disciples, he departed t to teach................Mt 11:1 1564
And when he was departed t.......................Mt 12:9 1564
it, he withdrew himself from t ....Mt 12:15 1564
these parables, he departed t ....Mt 13:53 1564
he departed t by ship into a ....Mt 14:13 1564
Then Jesus went t, and departed.................Mt 15:21 1564
And Jesus departed from t, and came.........Mt 15:29 1564
his hands on them, and departed t..............Mt 19:15 1564
he had gone a little farther t ....Mk 1:19 1564
And he went out from t, and came..............Mk 6:1 1564
nor hear you, when ye depart t ....Mk 6:11 1564
from t he arose, and went into the ....Mk 7:24 1564
And they departed t, and passed.................Mk 9:30 1564
And he arose from t, and cometh ....Mk 10:1 1564
into, there abide, and t depart ....Lk 9:4 1564
thee, thou shalt not depart t.......................Lk 12:59 1564
to us, that would come from t.....................Lk 16:26 1564
Now after two days he departed t................Jn 4:43 1564
but went t unto a country near to ....Jn 11:54 1564
and from t, when his father was ....Acts 7:4 1564
from t they sailed to Cyprus.......................Acts 13:4 1564
t sailed to Antioch, from whence ....Acts 14:26 1564
from t to Philippi, which is the..................Acts 16:12 1564
And he departed t, and entered into ....Acts 18:7 1564
sailed t into Syria, and with him...............Acts 18:18
And we sailed t, and came the next ....Acts 20:15 1564
Rhodes, and from t unto Patara ....Acts 21:1 1564
And when we had launched from t ....Acts 27:4 1564
part advised to depart t also ....Acts 27:12 1564
obtained their purpose, loosing t ....Acts 27:13 1564
from t we fetched a compass, and...............Acts 28:13 3606
And from t, when the brethren ....Acts 28:15 1564
I went from t into Macedonia.....................2Cor 2:13

THENCEFORTH {4}
t it shall be accepted for an..........................Lev 22:27 1973
the sight of all nations from t 2Chr 32:23 310,3651
it is t good for nothing, but to..................Mt 5:13 2089
from t Pilate sought to release ....Jn 19:12 1537,5127

THEOPHILUS *(the-of'-il-us)* {2} *To whom the gospel of Luke and the Acts of the Apostles are addressed.*
thee in order, most excellent T....................Lk 1:3 2321
former treatise have I made, O T...............Acts 1:1 2321

THERE See APPENDIX.

THEREABOUT {1}
as they were much perplexed t.........Lk 24:4 4012,5127

THEREAT {3}
wash their hands and their feet t..............Ex 30:19
their hands and their feet t ....Ex 40:31
and many there be which go in t.....Mt 7:13 1223,846

THEREBY See APPENDIX.

THEREFORE See APPENDIX.

THEREFROM {3}
that ye turn not aside t to the ....Josh 23:6
he departed not t 2Kin 3:3
he departed not t 2Kin 13:2

THEREIN See APPENDIX.

THEREINTO {1}
that are in the countries enter t......Lk 21:21 1519,846

THEREOF See APPENDIX.

THEREON See APPENDIX.

THEREOUT {2}
he shall take t his handful of ....Lev 2:2 8033
in the jaw, and there came water t............Judg 15:19

THERETO See APPENDIX.

THEREUNTO {9}
it, and have sacrificed t, and said ....Ex 32:8
he made t four pillars of shittim...............Ex 36:36
made t a crown of gold round ....Ex 37:11
Also he made t a border of an...................Ex 37:12
and unto all the places nigh t ....Deut 1:7
t with all perseverance ....Eph 6:18 1519,846,5124
know that we are appointed t 1Th 3:3 1519,5124
make the comers t perfect.........................Heb 10:1 4334
knowing that ye are t called...........1Pet 3:9 1519,5124

THEREUPON See APPENDIX.

THEREWITH {36}
corn, or the field, be consumed t...............Ex 22:6
tabernacle of the congregation t ....Ex 30:26
t he made the sockets to the door ....Ex 38:30
maketh atonement t shall have it...............Lev 7:7
the ephod, and bound it unto him t............Lev 8:7
goeth from him, and is defiled t................Lev 15:32
any beast to defile thyself t ....Lev 18:23
shall not eat to defile himself t ....Lev 22:8
shalt thou eat unleavened bread t..............Deut 16:3 5921
thyself abroad, thou shalt dig t ....Deut 23:13
took it, and slew a thousand men t............Judg 15:15
took new ropes, and bound him t...............Judg 16:12
any bribe to blind mine eyes t...................1Sa 12:3
slew him, and cut off his head t.................1Sa 17:51
thy sword, and thrust me through t 1Sa 31:4
so he smote him t in the fifth......................2Sa 20:10
I have t sent Naaman my servant...............2Kin 5:6
repaired t the house of the LORD...............2Kin 12:14
thy sword, and thrust me through t 1Chr 10:4
I made, said David, to praise t...................1Chr 23:5
and he built t Geba and Mizpah 2Chr 16:6
than great treasure and trouble t................Prov 15:16
is, than a stalled ox and hatred t ....Prov 15:17
is a dry morsel, and quietness t..................Prov 17:1
for thee, lest thou be filled t.......................Prov 25:16
the sons of man to be exercised t...............Eccl 1:13
to water t the wood that bringeth..............Eccl 2:6
removeth stones shall be hurt t..................Eccl 10:9
itself against him that heweth t ....Is 10:15
and thou shalt prepare thy bread t ....Eze 4:15 5921
oil, and ye shall be satisfied t.....................Joel 2:19 854
state I am, t to be content ....Phil 4:11
and raiment let us be t content....................1Ti 6:8 5125
T bless we God, even the Father.......Jas 3:9 1722,846
t curse we men, which are made .....Jas 3:9 1722,846
and not content t, neither doth he ..3Jn 10 1909,5125

THESE See APPENDIX.

THESSALONIANS *(thes-sa-lo'-ne-uns)* {5} *The inhabitants of Thessalonica.*
and of the T, Aristarchus and...................Acts 20:4 2331
unto the church of the T which is 1Th 1:1 2331
the T was written from Athens ....1Th s 2331
church of the T in God our Father 2Th 1:1 2331
to the T was written from Athens..............2Th s 2331

THESSALONICA *(thes-sa-lo-ni'-cah)* {6} *A city in Macedonia.*
and Apollonia, they came to T..................Acts 17:1 2332
were more noble than those in T...............Acts 17:11 2332
But when the Jews of T had.......................Acts 17:13 2332
Aristarchus, a Macedonian of T ....Acts 27:2 2331
For even in T ye sent once and.................Phil 4:16 2332
world, and is departed unto T....................2Ti 4:10 2332

THEUDAS *(thew'-das)* {1} *A false Jewish Messiah.*
For before these days rose up T...............Acts 5:36 2333

THEY See APPENDIX.

THICK {39}
there was a t darkness in all the ....Ex 10:22 653
Lo, I come unto thee in a t cloud.............Ex 19:9 5645
a t cloud upon the mount, and the.............Ex 19:16 3515
unto the t darkness where God was...........Ex 20:21
trees, and the boughs of t trees ....Lev 23:40 5687
darkness, clouds, and t darkness ....Deut 4:11
of the t darkness, with a great ....Deut 5:22
art waxen fat, thou art grown t...................Deut 32:15 5666
under the t boughs of a great oak............2Sa 18:9
waters, and t clouds of the skies 2Sa 22:12
the t beam were before them......................1Kin 7:6
And it was an hand breadth t 1Kin 7:26 5672
he would dwell in the t darkness 1Kin 8:12
morrow, that he took a t cloth....................2Kin 8:15
he would dwell in the t darkness 2Chr 6:1
branches, and branches of t trees................Neh 8:15 5687
upon the t bosses of his bucklers ....Job 15:26 5672
T clouds are a covering to him,...................Job 22:14
up the waters in his t clouds......................Job 26:8
watering he wearieth the t cloud ....Job 37:11
t darkness a swaddlingband for it ....Job 38:9
waters and t clouds of the skies..................Ps 18:11
before him his t clouds passed ....Ps 18:12
lifted up axes upon the t trees ....Ps 74:5 5441
as a t cloud, thy transgressions,..................Is 44:22
green tree, and under every t oak...............Eze 6:13 5687
a t cloud of incense went up ....Eze 8:11 6282
was exalted among the t branches..............Eze 19:11 5688
high hill, and all the t trees........................Eze 20:28 5687
and his top was among the t boughs...........Eze 31:3 5688
up his top among the t boughs....................Eze 31:10 5688
up their top among the t boughs.................Eze 31:14 5688
was five cubits t round about......................Eze 41:12 7341
there were t planks upon the face...............Eze 41:25 5645
of the house, and t planks ....Eze 41:26
of t darkness, as the morning......................Joel 2:2
that ladeth himself with t clay....................Hab 2:6
a day of clouds and t darkness,...................Zeph 1:15
people were gathered t together..................Lk 11:29

THICKER {2}
shall be t than my father's loins.................1Kin 12:10 5666
shall be t than my father's loins.................2Chr 10:10 5666

THICKET {2}
a ram caught in a t by his horns ....Gen 22:13 5442
The lion is come up from his t ....Jer 4:7 5441

THICKETS {4}
hide themselves in caves, and in t..............1Sa 13:6 2337
kindle in the t of the forest ....Is 9:18 5442
he shall cut down the t of the ....Is 10:34 5442
they shall go into t, and climb up ....Jer 4:29 5645

THICKNESS {4}
the t of it was an handbreadth,...................2Chr 4:5 5672
the t thereof was four fingers.....................Jer 52:21 5672
The t of the wall, which was for ....Eze 41:9 7341
The chambers were in the t of the.............Eze 42:10 7341

THIEF {28}
If a t be found breaking up, and ....Ex 22:2 1590
if the t be found, let him pay ....Ex 22:7 1590
If the t be not found, then the....................Ex 22:8 1590
then that t shall die ....Deut 24:7 1590
needy, and in the night is as a t..................Job 24:14 1590
cried after them as after a t ....Job 30:5 1590
When thou sawest a t, then thou................Ps 50:18 1590
Men do not despise a t, if he ....Prov 6:30 1590
with a t hateth his own soul.......................Prov 29:24 1590
As the t is ashamed when he is ....Jer 2:26 1590
the t cometh in, and the troop of ....Hos 7:1 1590
enter in at the windows like a t ....Joel 2:9 1590
enter into the house of the t........................Zec 5:4 1590
in what watch the t would come.................Mt 24:43 2812
out as against a t with swords.....................Mt 26:55 3027
Are ye come out, as against a t ....Mk 14:48 3027
where no t approacheth, neither ....Lk 12:33 2812
known what hour the t would come ....Lk 12:39 2812
Be ye come out, as against a t.....................Lk 22:52 3027
some other way, the same is a t...................Jn 10:1 2812
The t cometh not, but for to........................Jn 10:10 2812
but because he was a t, and had ....Jn 12:6 2812
so cometh as a t in the night.......................1Th 5:2 2812
day should overtake you as a t 1Th 5:4 2812
suffer as a murderer, or as a t 1Pet 4:15 2812
will come as a t in the night........................2Pet 3:10 2812
watch, I will come on thee as a t.................Rev 3:3 2812
Behold, I come as a t...................................Rev 16:15 2812

THIEVES {16}
rebellious, and companions of t ....Is 1:23 1590
was he found among t ....Jer 48:27 1590
if t by night, they will destroy....................Jer 49:9 1590
If t came to thee, if robbers by..................Obad 5 1590
where t break through and steal.................Mt 6:19 2812
where t do not break through nor ....Mt 6:20 2812
but ye have made it a den of t....................Mt 21:13 3027
there two t crucified with him ....Mt 27:38 3027
The t also, which were crucified ....Mt 27:44 3027
but ye have made it a den of t....................Mk 11:17 3027
And with him they crucify two t.................Mk 15:27 3027
to Jericho, and fell among t.......................Lk 10:30 3027

unto him that fell among the *t* ... Lk 10:36 *3027*
but ye have made it a den of *t* ... Lk 19:46 *3027*
that ever came before me are *t* ... Jn 10:8 *2812*
Nor *t*, nor covetous, nor ... 1Cor 6:10 *2812*

THIGH {21}
I pray thee, thy hand under my *t* ... Gen 24:2 3409
under the *t* of Abraham his master ... Gen 24:9 3409
he touched the hollow of his *t* ... Gen 32:25 3409
of Jacob's *t* was out of joint ... Gen 32:25 3409
upon him, and he halted upon his *t* ... Gen 32:31 3409
which is upon the hollow of the *t* ... Gen 32:32 3409
t in the sinew that shrank ... Gen 32:32 3409
I pray thee, thy hand under my *t* ... Gen 47:29 3409
the LORD doth make thy *t* to rot ... Num 5:21 3409
belly to swell, and thy *t* to rot ... Num 5:22 3409
shall swell, and her *t* shall rot ... Num 5:27 3409
his raiment upon his right *t* ... Judg 3:16 3409
took the dagger from his right *t* ... Judg 3:21 3409
hip and *t* with a great slaughter ... Judg 15:8 3409
Gird thy sword upon thy *t* ... Ps 45:3 3409
man hath his sword upon his *t* ... Song 3:8 3409
make bare the leg, uncover the *t* ... Is 47:2 7785
was instructed, I smote upon my *t* ... Jer 31:19 3409
smite therefore upon thy *t* ... Eze 21:12 3409
it, even every good piece, the *t* ... Eze 24:4 3409
on his *t* a name written, KING OF ... Rev 19:16 *3382*

THIGHS {3}
even unto the *t* they shall reach ... Ex 28:42 3409
joints of thy *t* are like jewels ... Song 7:1 3409
his belly and his *t* of brass, ... Dan 2:32 3410

THIMNATHAH *(thim'-nath-ah)* {1} See TIMNAH. *A city in Dan.*
And Elon, and *T*, and Ekron, ... Josh 19:43 8553

THIN {9}
And, behold, seven *t* ears and ... Gen 41:6 1851
the seven *t* ears devoured the ... Gen 41:7 1851
behold, seven ears, withered, *t* ... Gen 41:23 1851
the *t* ears devoured the seven ... Gen 41:24 1851
And the seven *t* and ill favoured ... Gen 41:27 7534
did beat the gold into *t* plates ... Ex 39:3
and there be in it a yellow *t* hair ... Lev 13:30 1851
certain additions made of *t* work ... 1Kin 7:29 4174
glory of Jacob shall be made *t* ... Is 17:4 1809

THINE See APPENDIX.

THING See APPENDIX.

THINGS See APPENDIX.

THINGS' {1}
For which *t* sake the wrath of God ... Col 3:6

THINK {65}
But *t* on me when it shall be well ... Gen 40:14 2142
them marry to whom they *t* best ... Num 36:6 5869
to *t* that all the king's sons are ... 2Sa 13:33 559
now ye *t* to withstand the kingdom ... 2Chr 13:8 559
T upon me, my God, for good, ... Neh 5:19 2142
that thou and the Jews *t* to rebel ... Neh 6:6 2803
t thou upon Tobiah and Sanballat ... Neh 6:14 2142
T not with thyself that thou ... Est 4:13 1819
why then should I *t* upon a maid ... Job 31:1 995
one would *t* the deep to be hoary ... Job 41:32 2803
though a wise man *t* to know it ... Eccl 8:17 559
so, neither doth his heart *t* so ... Is 10:7 2803
Which *t* to cause my people to ... Jer 23:27 2803
the thoughts that I *t* toward you ... Jer 29:11 2803
thou shalt *t* an evil thought ... Eze 38:10 2803
t to change times and laws ... Dan 7:25 5452
if so be that God will *t* upon us ... Jonah 1:6 6245
And I said unto them, If ye *t* good ... Zec 11:12 5869
t not to say within yourselves, ... Mt 3:9 *1380*
T not that I am come to destroy ... Mt 5:17 *3543*
for they *t* that they shall be ... Mt 6:7 *1380*
Wherefore *t* ye evil in your ... Mt 9:4 *1760*
T not that I am come to send ... Mt 10:34 *3543*
How *t* ye? ... Mt 18:12 *1380*
But what *t* ye ... Mt 21:28 *1380*
Saying, What *t* ye of Christ ... Mt 22:42 *1380*
as ye *t* not the Son of man cometh ... Mt 24:44 *1380*
What *t* ye? ... Mt 26:66 *1380*
what *t* ye? ... Mk 14:64 *5316*
cometh at an hour when ye *t* not ... Lk 12:40 *1380*
t ye that they were sinners above ... Lk 13:4 *1380*
for in them ye *t* ye have eternal ... Jn 5:39 *1380*
Do not *t* that I will accuse you ... Jn 5:45 *1380*
stood in the temple, What *t* ye ... Jn 11:56 *1380*
will *t* that he doeth God service ... Jn 16:2 *1380*
he said, Whom *t* ye that I am ... Acts 13:25 *5282*
we ought not to *t* that the ... Acts 17:29 *3543*
I *t* myself happy, king Agrippa, ... Acts 26:2 *2233*
not to *t* of himself more highly ... Rom 12:3 *5252*
more highly than he ought to *t* ... Rom 12:3 *5426*
but to *t* soberly, according as ... Rom 12:3 *5426*
to *t* of men above that which is ... 1Cor 4:6 *5426*
For I *t* that God hath set forth ... 1Cor 4:9 *1380*
But if any man *t* that he behaveth ... 1Cor 7:36 *3543*
I *t* also that I have the Spirit ... 1Cor 7:40 *1380*
if any man *t* that he knoweth any ... 1Cor 8:2 *1380*
which we *t* to be less honourable, ... 1Cor 12:23 *1380*
If any man *t* himself to be a ... 1Cor 14:37 *1380*
to *t* any thing as of ourselves ... 2Cor 3:5 *3049*
wherewith I *t* to be bold against ... 2Cor 10:2 *3049*
which *t* of us as if we walked ... 2Cor 10:2 *3049*
let him of himself *t* this again ... 2Cor 10:7 *3049*
Let such an one *t* this, that, ... 2Cor 10:11 *3049*
say again, Let no man *t* me a fool ... 2Cor 11:16 *1380*
lest any man should *t* of me above ... 2Cor 12:6 *3049*
t ye that we excuse ourselves ... 2Cor 12:19 *1380*
For if a man *t* himself to be ... Gal 6:3 *1380*
above all that we ask or *t* ... Eph 3:20 *3539*
meet for me to *t* this of you all ... Phil 1:7 *5426*
be any praise, *t* on these things ... Phil 4:8 *3049*
For let not that man *t* that he ... Jas 1:7 *3633*
Do ye *t* that the scripture saith ... Jas 4:5 *1380*
Wherein they *t* it strange that ye ... 1Pet 4:4
t it not strange concerning the ... 1Pet 4:12
I *t* it meet, as long as I am in ... 2Pet 1:13 *2233*

THINKEST {9}
T thou that David doth honour thy ... 2Sa 10:3 5869
T thou that David doth honour thy ... 1Chr 19:3 5869
T thou this to be right, that ... Job 35:2 2803
him, saying, What *t* thou, Simon ... Mt 17:25 *1380*
Tell us therefore, What *t* thou ... Mt 22:17 *1380*
T thou that I cannot now pray to ... Mt 26:53 *1380*
t thou, was neighbour unto him ... Lk 10:36 *1380*
to hear of thee what thou *t* ... Acts 28:22 *5426*
t thou this, O man, that judgest ... Rom 2:3 *3049*

THINKETH {6}
Me *t* the running of the foremost ... 2Sa 18:27 7200
yet the Lord *t* upon me ... Ps 40:17 2803
For as he *t* in his heart, so is ... Prov 23:7 8176
Wherefore let him that *t* he ... 1Cor 10:12 *1380*
is not easily provoked, *t* no evil ... 1Cor 13:5 *3049*
If any other man *t* that he hath ... Phil 3:4 *1380*

THINKING {2}
t to have brought good tidings, I ... 2Sa 4:10 1931,1961
t, David cannot come in ... 2Sa 5:6 559

THIRD {182}
and the morning were the *t* day ... Gen 1:13 7992
the name of the *t* river is ... Gen 2:14 7992
t stories shalt thou make it ... Gen 6:16 7992
Then on the *t* day Abraham lifted ... Gen 22:4 7992
on the *t* day that Jacob was fled ... Gen 31:22 7992
commanded he the second, and the *t* ... Gen 32:19 7992
And it came to pass on the *t* day ... Gen 34:25 7992
And it came to pass the *t* day ... Gen 40:20 7992
Joseph said unto them the *t* day ... Gen 42:18 7992
children of the *t* generation ... Gen 50:23 8029
In the *t* month, when the children ... Ex 19:1 7992
And be ready against the *t* day ... Ex 19:11 7992
for the *t* day the LORD will come ... Ex 19:11 7992
Be ready against the *t* day ... Ex 19:15 7969
pass on the *t* day in the morning ... Ex 19:16 7992
upon the children unto the *t* ... Ex 20:5 8029
the *t* row a ligure, an agate, and ... Ex 28:19 7992
children's children, unto the *t* ... Ex 34:7 8029
And the *t* row, a ligure, an agate, ... Ex 39:12 7992
t day shall be burnt with fire ... Lev 7:17 7992
be eaten at all on the *t* day ... Lev 7:18 7992
if ought remain until the *t* day ... Lev 19:6 7992
it be eaten at all on the *t* day ... Lev 19:7 7992
shall go forward in the *t* rank ... Num 2:24 7992
On the *t* day Eliab the son of ... Num 7:24 7992
upon the children unto the *t* ... Num 14:18 8029
with the *t* part of an hin of oil ... Num 15:6 7992
the *t* part of an hin of wine ... Num 15:7 7992
himself with it on the *t* day ... Num 19:12 7992
he purify not himself the *t* day ... Num 19:12 7992
upon the unclean on the *t* day ... Num 19:19 7992
the *t* part of an hin unto a ram, ... Num 28:14 7992
on the *t* day eleven bullocks, two ... Num 29:20 7992
and your captives on the *t* day ... Num 31:19 7992
upon the children unto the *t* ... Deut 5:9 8029
of the LORD in their *t* generation ... Deut 23:8 7992
of thine increase the *t* year ... Deut 26:12 7992
unto their cities on the *t* day ... Josh 9:17 7992
the *t* lot came up for the ... Josh 19:10 7992
children of Benjamin on the *t* day ... Judg 20:30 7992
called Samuel again the *t* time ... 1Sa 3:8 7992
him Abinadab, and the *t* Shammah ... 1Sa 17:13 7992
sent messengers again the *t* time ... 1Sa 19:21 7992
the field unto the *t* day at even ... 1Sa 20:5 7992
to morrow any time, or the *t* day ... 1Sa 20:12 7992
were come to Ziklag on the *t* day ... 1Sa 30:1 7992
It came even to pass on the *t* day ... 2Sa 1:2 7992
and the *t*, Absalom the son of ... 2Sa 3:3 7992
David sent forth a *t* part of the ... 2Sa 18:2 7992
a *t* part under the hand of ... 2Sa 18:2 7992
a *t* part under the hand of Ittai ... 2Sa 18:2 7992
it came to pass the *t* day after ... 1Kin 3:18 7992
the *t* was seven cubits broad ... 1Kin 6:6 7992
and out of the middle into the *t* ... 1Kin 6:8 7992
people came to Rehoboam the *t* day ... 1Kin 12:12 7992
Come to me again the *t* day ... 1Kin 12:12 7992
Even in the *t* year of Asa king of ... 1Kin 15:28 7969
In the *t* year of Asa king of ... 1Kin 15:33 7969
LORD came to Elijah in the *t* year ... 1Kin 18:1 7992
And he said, Do it the *t* time ... 1Kin 18:34 8027
And they did it the *t* time ... 1Kin 18:34 8027
And it came to pass in the *t* year ... 1Kin 22:2 7992
of the *t* fifty with his fifty ... 2Kin 1:13 7992
the *t* captain of fifty went up, ... 2Kin 1:13 7992
A *t* part of you that enter in on ... 2Kin 11:5 7992
a *t* part shall be at the gate of ... 2Kin 11:6 7992
a *t* part at the gate behind the ... 2Kin 11:6 7992
Now it came to pass in the *t* year ... 2Kin 18:1 7969
in the *t* year sow ye, and reap, and ... 2Kin 19:29 7992
on the *t* day thou shalt go up ... 2Kin 20:5 7992
the house of the LORD the *t* day ... 2Kin 20:8 7992
the second, and Shimma the *t* ... 1Chr 2:13 7992
The *t*, Absalom the son of Maachah ... 1Chr 3:2 7992
the *t* Zedekiah, the fourth ... 1Chr 3:15 7992
the second, and Aharah the *t* ... 1Chr 8:1 7992
the second, and Eliphelet the *t* ... 1Chr 8:39 7992
Obadiah the second, Eliab the *t* ... 1Chr 12:9 7992
the second, Jahaziel the *t* ... 1Chr 23:19 7992
The *t* to Harim, the fourth to ... 1Chr 24:8 7992
the second, Jahaziel the *t* ... 1Chr 24:23 7992
The *t* to Zaccur, he, his sons, and ... 1Chr 25:10 7992
the second, Zebadiah the *t* ... 1Chr 26:2 7992
Jehozabad the second, Joah the *t* ... 1Chr 26:4 7992
the second, Tebaliah the *t* ... 1Chr 26:11 7992
The *t* captain of the host for the ... 1Chr 27:5 7992
captain of the host for the *t* ... 1Chr 27:5 7992
came to Rehoboam on the *t* day ... 2Chr 10:12 7992
Come again to me on the *t* day ... 2Chr 10:12 7992
at Jerusalem in the *t* month ... 2Chr 15:10 7992
Also in the *t* year of his reign ... 2Chr 17:7 7969
A *t* part of you entering on the ... 2Chr 23:4 7992
a *t* part shall be at the king's ... 2Chr 23:5 7992
a *t* part at the gate of the ... 2Chr 23:5 7992
both the second year, and the *t* ... 2Chr 27:5 7992
In the *t* month they began to lay ... 2Chr 31:7 7992
on the *t* day of the month Adar ... Ezr 6:15 8531
the *t* part of a shekel for the ... Neh 10:32 7992
In the *t* year of his reign, he ... Est 1:3 7969
Now it came to pass on the *t* day ... Est 5:1 7992
at that time in the *t* month ... Est 8:9 7992
and the name of the *t*, ... Job 42:14 7992
shall Israel be the *t* with Egypt ... Is 19:24 7992
in the *t* year sow ye, and reap, and ... Is 37:30 7992
t entry that is in the house of ... Jer 38:14 7992
Thou shalt burn with fire a *t* ... Eze 5:2 7992
and thou shalt take a *t* part ... Eze 5:2 7992
a *t* part thou shalt scatter in ... Eze 5:2 7992
A *t* part of thee shall die with ... Eze 5:12 7992
a *t* part shall fall by the sword ... Eze 5:12 7992
I will scatter a *t* part into all ... Eze 5:12 7992
the *t* the face of a lion, and the ... Eze 10:14 7992
the sword be doubled the *t* time ... Eze 21:14 7992
the eleventh year, in the *t* month ... Eze 31:1 7992
the *t* part of an hin of oil, to ... Eze 46:14 7992
In the *t* year of the reign of ... Dan 1:1 7969
another *t* kingdom of brass, which ... Dan 2:39 8523
shall be the *t* ruler in the ... Dan 5:7 8523
shalt be the *t* ruler in the ... Dan 5:16 8531
be the *t* ruler in the kingdom ... Dan 5:29 8531
In the *t* year of the reign of ... Dan 8:1 7969
In the *t* year of Cyrus king of ... Dan 10:1 7969
in the *t* day he will raise us up, ... Hos 6:2 7992
in the *t* chariot white horses ... Zec 6:3 7992
but the *t* shall be left therein ... Zec 13:8 7992
I will bring the *t* part through ... Zec 13:9 7992
and be raised again the *t* day ... Mt 16:21 *5154*
the *t* day he shall be raised ... Mt 17:23 *5154*
And he went out about the *t* hour ... Mt 20:3 *5154*
the *t* day he shall rise again ... Mt 20:19 *5154*
the second also, and the *t* ... Mt 22:26 *5154*
away again, and prayed the *t* time ... Mt 26:44 *5154*
be made sure until the *t* day ... Mt 27:64 *5154*
killed, he shall rise the *t* day ... Mk 9:31 *5154*
the *t* day he shall rise again ... Mk 10:34 *5154*
and the *t* likewise ... Mk 12:21 *5154*
And he cometh the *t* time, and saith ... Mk 14:41 *5154*
And it was the *t* hour, and they ... Mk 15:25 *5154*
be slain, and be raised the *t* day ... Lk 9:22 *5154*
watch, or come in the *t* watch ... Lk 12:38 *5154*
the *t* day I shall be perfected ... Lk 13:32 *5154*
the *t* day he shall rise again ... Lk 18:33 *5154*
And again he sent a *t* ... Lk 20:12 *5154*
And the *t* took her ... Lk 20:31 *5154*
And he said unto them the *t* time ... Lk 23:22 *5154*
and the *t* day rise again ... Lk 24:7 *5154*
to day is the *t* day since these ... Lk 24:21 *5154*
to rise from the dead the *t* day ... Lk 24:46 *5154*
the *t* day there was a marriage in ... Jn 2:1 *5154*
This is now the *t* time that Jesus ... Jn 21:14 *5154*
He saith unto him the *t* time ... Jn 21:17 *5154*
he said unto him the *t* time ... Jn 21:17 *5154*
it is but the *t* hour of the day ... Acts 2:15 *5154*
Him God raised up the *t* day ... Acts 10:40 *5154*
and fell down from the *t* loft ... Acts 20:9 *5152*
at the *t* hour of the night ... Acts 23:23 *5154*
the *t* day we cast out with our ... Acts 27:19 *5154*
that he rose again the *t* day ... 1Cor 15:4 *5154*
an one caught up to the *t* heaven ... 2Cor 12:2 *5154*
the *t* time I am ready to come to ... 2Cor 12:14 *5154*
This is the *t* time I am coming to ... 2Cor 13:1 *5154*
the *t* beast had a face as a man, ... Rev 4:7 *5154*
And when he had opened the *t* seal ... Rev 6:5 *5154*
I heard the *t* beast say ... Rev 6:5 *5154*
the *t* part of trees was burnt up, ... Rev 8:7 *5154*
the *t* part of the sea became ... Rev 8:8 *5154*
the *t* part of the creatures which ... Rev 8:9 *5154*
the *t* part of the ships were ... Rev 8:9 *5154*
the *t* angel sounded, and there ... Rev 8:10 *5154*
it fell upon the *t* part of the ... Rev 8:10 *5154*
the *t* part of the waters became ... Rev 8:11 *5154*
the *t* part of the sun was smitten ... Rev 8:12 *5154*
the *t* part of the moon, and the ... Rev 8:12 *5154*
moon, and the *t* part of the stars ... Rev 8:12 *5154*
so as the *t* part of them was ... Rev 8:12 *5154*
day shone not for a *t* part of it ... Rev 8:12 *5154*
for to slay the *t* part of men ... Rev 9:15 *5154*
was the *t* part of men killed ... Rev 9:18 *5154*
behold, the *t* woe cometh quickly ... Rev 11:14 *5154*
his tail drew the *t* part of the ... Rev 12:4 *5154*
the *t* angel followed them, saying ... Rev 14:9 *5154*
the *t* angel poured out his vial ... Rev 16:4 *5154*
the *t*, a chalcedony ... Rev 21:19 *5154*

THIRDLY {1}
t teachers, after that miracles, 1Cor 12:28 *5154*

THIRST {31}
our children and our cattle with *t* Ex 17:3 6772
against thee, in hunger, and in *t* Deut 28:48 6772
heart, to add drunkenness to *t* Deut 29:19 6771
and now shall I die for *t*, and fall Judg 15:18 6772
to die by famine and by *t*, saying, 2Chr 32:11 6772
them out of the rock for their *t* Neh 9:15 6772
and gavest them water for their *t* Neh 9:20 6772
their winepresses, and suffer *t* Job 24:11 6770
in my *t* they gave me vinegar to Ps 69:21 6772
the wild asses quench their *t* Ps 104:11 6772
their multitude dried up with *t* Is 5:13 6772
and their tongue faileth for *t* Is 41:17 6772
They shall not hunger nor *t* Is 49:10 6770
there is no water, and dieth for *t* Is 50:2 6772
unshod, and thy throat from *t* Jer 2:25 6773
down from thy glory, and sit in *t* Jer 48:18 6772
to the roof of his mouth for *t* Lam 4:4 6772
a dry land, and slay her with *t* Hos 2:3 6772
nor a *t* for water, but of hearing Amos 8:11 6772
virgins and young men faint for *t* Amos 8:13 6772
hunger and *t* after righteousness Mt 5:6 *1372*
of this water shall *t* again Jn 4:13 *1372*
I shall give him shall never *t* Jn 4:14 *1372*
give me this water, that I *t* not Jn 4:15 *1372*
believeth on me shall never *t* Jn 6:35 *1372*
and cried, saying, If any man *t* Jn 7:37 *1372*
might be fulfilled, saith, I *t* Jn 19:28 *1372*
if he *t*, give him drink Rom 12:20 *1372*
present hour we both hunger, and *t* 1Cor 4:11 *1372*
watchings often, in hunger and *t* 2Cor 11:27 *1373*
no more, neither *t* any more Rev 7:16 *1372*

THIRSTED {2}
the people *t* there for water Ex 17:3 6770
they *t* not when he led them Is 48:21 6770

THIRSTETH {4}
My soul *t* for God, for the living Ps 42:2 6770
my soul *t* for thee, my flesh Ps 63:1 6770
my soul *t* after thee, as a Ps 143:6
Ho, every one that *t*, come ye to Is 55:1 6771

THIRSTY {17}
for I am *t* Judg 4:19 6770
people is hungry, and weary, and *t* 2Sa 17:29 6771
t land, where no water is Ps 63:1
Hungry and *t*, their soul fainted Ps 107:5 6771
thirsteth after thee, as a *t* land Ps 143:6
and if he be *t*, give him water to Prov 25:21 6771
As cold waters to a *t* soul Prov 25:25
brought water to him that was *t* Is 21:14 6771
or as when a *t* man dreameth Is 29:8 6771
cause the drink of the *t* to fail Is 32:6 6771
the *t* land springs of water Is 35:7 6774
pour water upon him that is *t* Is 44:3 6771
shall drink, but ye shall be *t* Is 65:13 6770
wilderness, in a dry and *t* ground Eze 19:13 6772
I was *t*, and ye gave me drink Mt 25:35 *1372*
or *t*, and gave thee drink Mt 25:37 *1372*
I was *t*, and ye gave me no drink Mt 25:42 *1372*

THIRTEEN {15}
Ishmael his son was *t* years old Gen 17:25 7969,6240
two hundred and threescore and *t* Num 3:43 7969
t of the firstborn of the Num 3:46 7969
t young bullocks, two rams, and Num 29:13 7969,6240
every bullock of the *t* bullocks Num 29:14 7969,6240
t cities and their villages Josh 19:6 7969,6240
the tribe of Benjamin, *t* cities Josh 21:4 7969,6240
of Manasseh in Bashan, *t* cities Josh 21:6 7969,6240
were *t* cities with their suburbs Josh 21:19 7969,6240
to their families were *t* cities Josh 21:33 7969,6240
building his own house *t* years 1Kin 7:1 7969,6240
their families were *t* cities 1Chr 6:60 7969,6240
of Manasseh in Bashan, *t* cities 1Chr 6:62 7969,6240
sons and brethren of Hosah were *t* 1Chr 26:11 7969,6240
the length of the gate, *t* cubits Eze 40:11 7969,6240

THIRTEENTH {11}
in the *t* year they rebelled Gen 14:4 7969,6240
The *t* to Huppah, the fourteenth 1Chr 24:13 7969,6240
The *t* to Shubael, he, his sons, 1Chr 25:20 7969,6240
on the *t* day of the first month Est 3:12 7969,6240
even upon the *t* day of the Est 3:13 7969,6240
upon the *t* day of the twelfth Est 8:12 7969,6240
on the *t* day of the same, when Est 9:1 7969,6240
On the *t* day of the month Adar Est 9:17 7969,6240
together on the *t* day thereof Est 9:18 7969,6240
in the *t* year of his reign Jer 1:2 7969,6240
From the *t* year of Josiah the son Jer 25:3 7969,6240

THIRTIETH {9}
t year of Uzziah king of Judah 2Kin 15:13 7970
t year of Azariah king of Judah 2Kin 15:17 7970
t year of the captivity of 2Kin 25:27 7970
t year of the reign of Asa 2Chr 15:19 7970
t year of the reign of Asa Baasha 2Chr 16:1 7970
t year of Artaxerxes the king, Neh 5:14 7970
t year of Artaxerxes king of Neh 13:6 7970
t year of the captivity of Jer 52:31 7970
Now it came to pass in the *t* year Eze 1:1 7970

THIRTY {174}
t years, and begat a son in his Gen 5:3 7970
were nine hundred and *t* years Gen 5:5 7970
t years, and begat sons and Gen 5:16 7970
and the height of it *t* cubits Gen 6:15 7970
five and *t* years, and begat Salah Gen 11:12 7970
And Salah lived *t* years, and begat Gen 11:14 7970
four and *t* years, and begat Peleg Gen 11:16 7970
t years, and begat sons and Gen 11:17 7970
And Peleg lived *t* years, and begat Gen 11:18 7970
two and *t* years, and begat Serug Gen 11:20 7970
And Serug lived *t* years, and begat Gen 11:22 7970
there shall *t* be found there Gen 18:30 7970
will not do it, if I find *t* there Gen 18:30 7970
life of Ishmael, an hundred and *t* Gen 25:17 7970
T milch camels with their colts, Gen 32:15 7970
Joseph was *t* years old when he Gen 41:46 7970
his sons and his daughters were *t* Gen 46:15 7970
are an hundred and *t* years Gen 47:9 7970
life of Levi were an hundred *t* Ex 6:16 7970
life of Kohath were an hundred *t* Ex 6:18 7970
of Amram were an hundred and *t* Ex 6:20 7970
was four hundred and *t* years Ex 12:40 7970
t years, even the selfsame day it Ex 12:41 7970
their master *t* shekels of silver Ex 21:32 7970
of one curtain shall be *t* cubits Ex 26:8 7970
of one curtain was *t* cubits Ex 36:15 7970
t shekels, after the shekel of Ex 38:24 7970
of her purifying three and *t* days Lev 12:4 7970
thy estimation shall be *t* shekels Lev 27:4 7970
of the tribe of Manasseh, were *t* Num 1:35 7970
of the tribe of Benjamin, were *t* Num 1:37 7970
were numbered of them, were *t* Num 2:21 7970
were numbered of them, were *t* Num 2:23 7970
From *t* years old and upward even Num 4:3 7970
From *t* years old and upward until Num 4:23 7970
From *t* years old and upward even Num 4:30 7970
From *t* years old and upward even Num 4:35 7970
From *t* years old and upward even Num 4:39 7970
two thousand and six hundred and *t* Num 4:40 7970
From *t* years old and upward even Num 4:43 7970
From *t* years old and upward even Num 4:47 7970
t shekels, one silver bowl of Num 7:13 7970
t shekels, one silver bowl of Num 7:19 7970
t shekels, one silver bowl of Num 7:25 7970
t shekels, one silver bowl of Num 7:31 7970
t shekels, one silver bowl of Num 7:37 7970
t shekels, a silver bowl of Num 7:43 7970
t shekels, one silver bowl of Num 7:49 7970
t shekels, one silver bowl of Num 7:55 7970
t shekels, one silver bowl of Num 7:61 7970
t shekels, one silver bowl of Num 7:67 7970
t shekels, one silver bowl of Num 7:73 7970
t shekels, one silver bowl of Num 7:79 7970
t shekels, each bowl seventy Num 7:85 7970
they mourned for Aaron *t* days Num 20:29 7970
thousand and seven hundred and *t* Num 26:7 7970
that were numbered of them, *t* Num 26:37 7970
and a thousand seven hundred and *t* Num 26:51 7970
And *t* and two thousand persons in Num 31:35 7970
t thousand and five hundred sheep Num 31:36 7970
And the beeves were *t* and six Num 31:38 7970
And the asses were *t* thousand Num 31:39 7970
of which the LORD's tribute was *t* Num 31:40 7970
t thousand and seven thousand and Num 31:43 7970
And *t* and six thousand beeves, Num 31:44 7970
t thousand asses and five hundred, Num 31:45 7970
come over the brook Zered, was *t* Deut 2:14 7970
in the plains of Moab *t* days Deut 34:8 7970
men of Ai smote of them about *t* Josh 7:5 7970
Joshua chose out *t* thousand Josh 8:3 7970
all the kings *t* and one Josh 12:24 7970
he had *t* sons that rode Judg 10:4 7970
sons that rode on *t* ass colts Judg 10:4 7970
ass colts, and they had *t* cities Judg 10:4 7970
And he had *t* sons Judg 12:9 7970
t daughters, whom he sent abroad, Judg 12:9 7970
took in *t* daughters from abroad Judg 12:9 7970
sons and *t* nephews, that rode on Judg 12:14 7970
that they brought *t* companions to Judg 14:11 7970
then I will give you *t* sheets Judg 14:12 7970
sheets and *t* change of garments Judg 14:12 7970
then shall ye give me *t* sheets Judg 14:13 7970
sheets and *t* change of garments Judg 14:13 7970
slew *t* men of them, and took their Judg 14:19 7970
the field, about *t* men of Israel Judg 20:31 7970
the men of Israel about *t* persons Judg 20:39 7970
fell of Israel *t* thousand footmen 1Sa 4:10 7970
which were about *t* persons 1Sa 9:22 7970
and the men of Judah *t* thousand 1Sa 11:8 7970
t thousand chariots, and six 1Sa 13:5 7970
David was *t* years old when he 2Sa 5:4 7970
and in Jerusalem he reigned *t* 2Sa 5:5 7970
chosen men of Israel, *t* thousand 2Sa 6:1 7970
three of the *t* chief went down, 2Sa 23:13 7970
He was more honourable than the *t* 2Sa 23:23 7970
brother of Joab was one of the *t* 2Sa 23:24 7970
t and seven in all 2Sa 23:39 7970
years reigned he in Hebron, and *t* 1Kin 2:11 7970
day was *t* measures of fine flour 1Kin 4:22 7970
and the levy was *t* thousand men 1Kin 5:13 7970
and the height thereof *t* cubits 1Kin 6:2 7970
and the height thereof *t* cubits 1Kin 7:2 7970
and the breadth thereof *t* cubits 1Kin 7:6 7970
a line of *t* cubits did compass it 1Kin 7:23 7970
In the *t* and first year of Asa 1Kin 16:23 7970
And in the *t* and eighth year of Asa 1Kin 16:29 7970
and there were *t* and two kings with 1Kin 20:1 7970
and they were two hundred and *t* two 1Kin 20:15 7970
pavilions, he and the kings, the *t* 1Kin 20:16 7970
the king of Syria commanded his *t* 1Kin 22:31 7970
Jehoshaphat was *t* and five years 1Kin 22:42 7970
T and two years old was he when he 2Kin 8:17 7970
In the *t* and seventh year of Joash 2Kin 13:10 7970
In the *t* and eighth year of 2Kin 15:8 7970
of silver and *t* talents of gold 2Kin 18:14 7970
began to reign, and he reigned *t* 2Kin 22:1 7970
and in Jerusalem he reigned *t* 1Chr 3:4 7970
for war, six and *t* thousand men 1Chr 7:4 7970
twenty and two thousand and *t* 1Chr 7:7 7970
Now three of the *t* captains went 1Chr 11:15 7970
he was honourable among the *t* 1Chr 11:25 7970
of the Reubenites, and *t* with him, 1Chr 11:42 7970
among the *t*, and over the *t* 1Chr 12:4 7970
with them with shield and spear *t* 1Chr 12:34 7970
and his brethren an hundred and *t* 1Chr 15:7 7970
So they hired *t* and two thousand 1Chr 19:7 7970
numbered from the age of *t* years 1Chr 23:3 7970
by their polls, man by man, was *t* 1Chr 23:3 7970
among the *t*, and above the *t* 1Chr 27:6 7970
years reigned he in Hebron, and *t* 1Chr 29:27 7970
before the house two pillars of *t* 2Chr 3:15 7970
a line of *t* cubits did compass it 2Chr 4:2 7970
And Asa in the *t* and ninth year of 2Chr 16:12 7970
he was *t* and five years old when 2Chr 20:31 7970
Jehoram was *t* and two years old 2Chr 21:5 7970
T and two years old was he when he 2Chr 21:20 7970
t years old was he when he died 2Chr 24:15 7970
in Jerusalem one and *t* years 2Chr 34:1 7970
to the number of *t* thousand 2Chr 35:7 7970
t chargers of gold, a thousand Ezr 1:9 7970
T basons of gold, silver basons Ezr 1:10 7970
thousand and six hundred and *t* Ezr 2:35 7970
of Shobai, in all an hundred *t* Ezr 2:42 7970
seven thousand three hundred *t* Ezr 2:65 7970
Their horses were seven hundred *t* Ezr 2:66 7970
Their camels, four hundred *t* Ezr 2:67 7970
three thousand nine hundred and *t* Neh 7:38 7970
children of Shobai, an hundred *t* Neh 7:45 7970
seven thousand three hundred *t* Neh 7:67 7970
Their horses, seven hundred *t* Neh 7:68 7970
Their camels, four hundred *t* Neh 7:69 7970
hundred and *t* priests' garments Neh 7:70 7970
in unto the king these *t* days Est 4:11 7970
Take from hence *t* men with thee Jer 38:10 7970
from Jerusalem eight hundred *t* Jer 52:29 7970
t chambers were upon the pavement Eze 40:17 7970
one over another, and *t* in order Eze 41:6 7970
of forty cubits long and *t* broad Eze 46:22 7970
of any God or man for *t* days Dan 6:7 8533
of any God or man within *t* days Dan 6:12 8533
three hundred and five and *t* days Dan 12:12 7970
for my price *t* pieces of silver Zec 11:12 7970
I took the *t* pieces of silver, and Zec 11:13 7970
hundredfold, some sixty, some *t* Mt 13:23 *5144*
with him for *t* pieces of silver Mt 26:15 *5144*
brought again the *t* pieces of Mt 27:3 *5144*
they took the *t* pieces of silver, Mt 27:9 *5144*
and brought forth, some *t*, and some Mk 4:8 *5144*
began to be about *t* years of age Lk 3:23 *5144*
there, which had an infirmity *t* Jn 5:5 *5144*
five and twenty or *t* furlongs Jn 6:19 *5144*
t years after, cannot disannul, Gal 3:17 *5144*

THIRTYFOLD {2}
some sixtyfold, some *t* Mt 13:8 *5144*
it, and bring forth fruit, some *t* Mk 4:20 *5144*

THIS See APPENDIX.

THISTLE {5}
The *t* that was in Lebanon sent to 2Kin 14:9 2336
in Lebanon, and trode down the *t* 2Kin 14:9 2336
The *t* that was in Lebanon sent to 2Chr 25:18 2336
in Lebanon, and trode down the *t* 2Chr 25:18 2336
the *t* shall come up on their Hos 10:8 1863

THISTLES {3}
t shall it bring forth to thee Gen 3:18 1863
Let *t* grow instead of wheat, and Job 31:40 2336
grapes of thorns, or figs of *t* Mt 7:16 *5146*

THITHER {95}
Oh, let me escape *t*, (is it not a Gen 19:20
Haste thee, escape *t* Gen 19:22
do any thing till thou be come *t* Gen 19:22
thou bring not my son *t* again Gen 24:6
only bring not my son *t* again Gen 24:8 8033
t were all the flocks gathered Gen 29:3 8033
which had brought him down *t* Gen 39:1 8033
get you down *t*, and buy for us Gen 42:2 8033
serve the LORD, until we come *t* Ex 10:26 8033
that thou mayest bring in *t* Ex 26:33 8033
the manslayer, that he may flee *t* Num 35:6 8033
that the slayer may flee *t* Num 35:11 8033
any person unawares may flee *t* Num 35:15 8033
Thou also shalt not go in *t* Deut 1:37 8033
before thee, he shall go in *t* Deut 1:38 8033
good and evil, they shall go in *t* Deut 1:39 8033
That the slayer might flee *t* Deut 4:42 8033
ye seek, and *t* thou shalt come Deut 12:5 8033
t ye shall bring your burnt Deut 12:6 8033
t shall ye bring all that I Deut 12:11 8033
that every slayer may flee *t* Deut 19:3 8033
of the slayer, which shall flee *t* Deut 19:4 8033
but thou shalt not go *t* unto the Deut 32:52 8033
but thou shalt not go over *t* Deut 34:4 8033
not all the people to labour *t* Josh 7:3 8033
So there went up *t* of the people Josh 7:4 8033
and unwittingly may flee *t* Josh 20:3 8033
person at unawares might flee *t* Josh 20:9 8033
all Israel went *t* a whoring after Judg 8:27 8033
t fled all the men and women, and Judg 9:51 8033
and they turned in *t*, and said unto Judg 18:3 8033
the land went up, and came in *t* Judg 18:17 8033
And they turned aside *t*, to go in Judg 19:15 8033

the congregation sent t twelve .... Judg 21:10 8033
all the Israelites that came t.................. 1Sa 2:14 8033
ark of the God of Israel about t 1Sa 5:8 8033
now let us go t 1Sa 9:6 8033
when thou art come t to the city 1Sa 10:5 8033
And when they came t to the hill 1Sa 10:10 8033
if the man should yet come t 1Sa 10:22 1988
he went t to Naioth in Ramah 1Sa 19:23 8033
heard it, they went down t to him 1Sa 22:1 8033
Abiathar brought t the ephod to 1Sa 30:7
So David went up t, and his two 2Sa 2:2 8033
they came t into the midst of the 2Sa 4:6
ready before it was brought t 1Kin 6:7
he came t unto a cave, and lodged 1Kin 19:9 8033
and they were divided hither and t 2Kin 2:8 2008
waters, they parted hither and t 2Kin 2:14 2008
by, he turned in t to eat bread 2Kin 4:8 8033
to us, that he shall turn in t 2Kin 4:10 8033
it fell on a day, that he came t 2Kin 4:11 8033
cut down a stick, and cast it in t 2Kin 6:6 8033
for t the Syrians are come down 2Kin 6:9 8033
Therefore sent he t horses 2Kin 6:14 8033
And when thou comest t, look out 2Kin 9:2 8033
Carry t one of the priests whom 2Kin 17:27 8033
Solomon went up t to the brasen 2Chr 1:6 8033
and when he came t, he did eat no .... Ezr 10:6 8033
the trumpet, resort ye t unto us .... Neh 4:20 8033
were gathered t unto the work .... Neh 5:16 8033
t brought I again the vessels of .... Neh 13:9 8033
womb, and naked shall I return t .... Job 1:21 8033
they came t, and were ashamed .... Job 6:20 5704
rivers come, t they return again .... Eccl 1:7 8033
and with bows shall men come t .... Is 7:24 8033
not come t the fear of briers .... Is 7:25 8033
that send forth t the feet of the .... Is 32:20
from heaven, and returneth not t .... Is 55:10 8033
even t wentest thou up to offer .... Is 57:7 8033
He shall not return t any more .... Jer 22:11 8033
return, t shall they not return .... Jer 22:27 8033
a great company shall return t .... Jer 31:8 2008
convenient for thee to go, t go .... Jer 40:4 8033
went, t was their spirit to go .... Eze 1:20 8033
And they shall come t, and they .... Eze 11:18 8033
was upon me, and brought me, t .... Eze 40:1 8033
And he brought me t, and, behold, ... Eze 40:3 8033
because these waters shall come t .... Eze 47:9
t cause thy mighty ones to come .... Joel 3:11
Herod, he was afraid to go t .... Mt 2:22 1563
ran afoot t out of all cities, and .... Mk 6:33 1563
t will the eagles be gathered .... Lk 17:37 1563
poor widow casting in t two mites .... Lk 21:2 1563
and where I am, t ye cannot come .... Jn 7:34
and where I am, t ye cannot come .... Jn 7:36
and goest thou t again .... Jn 11:8 1563
resorted t with his disciples .... Jn 18:2 1563
cometh t with lanterns and torches .... Jn 18:3 1563
And Philip ran t to him, and heard .... Acts 8:30 4370
there came t certain Jews from .... Acts 14:19 1904
unto the women which resorted t .... Acts 16:13
who coming t went into the .... Acts 17:10 3854
Paul at Berea, they came t also .... Acts 17:13 1563
he himself would depart shortly t .... Acts 25:4

THITHERWARD {3}
And they turned t, and came to the .... Judg 18:15 8033
way to Zion with their faces t .... Jer 50:5 2008
to be brought on my way t by you .... Rom 15:24 1563

THOMAS *(tom'-us)* {12} See DIDYMUS. *One of the twelve apostles.*
T, and Matthew the publican .... Mt 10:3 2381
and Bartholomew, and Matthew, and T .... Mk 3:18 2381
Matthew and T, James the son of .... Lk 6:15 2381
Then said T, which is called .... Jn 11:16 2381
T saith unto him, Lord, we know .... Jn 14:5 2381
But T, one of the twelve, called .... Jn 20:24 2381
were within, and T with them .... Jn 20:26 2381
Then saith he to T, Reach hither .... Jn 20:27 2381
T answered and said unto him, My .... Jn 20:28 2381
Jesus saith unto him, T, because .... Jn 20:29 2381
T called Didymus, and Nathanael of .... Jn 21:2 2381
and John, and Andrew, Philip, and T .... Acts 1:13 2381

THONGS {1}
And as they bound him with t .... Acts 22:25 2438

THORN {7}
or bore his jaw through with a t .... Job 41:2 2336
As a t goeth up into the hand of .... Prov 26:9 2336
Instead of the t shall come .... Is 55:13 5285
nor any grieving t of all that .... Eze 28:24 6975
the t and the thistle shall come .... Hos 10:8 6975
upright is sharper than a t hedge .... Mic 7:4 4534
was given to me a t in the flesh 2Cor 12:7 4647

THORNS {50}
T also and thistles shall it bring .... Gen 3:18 6975
If fire break out, and catch in t .... Ex 22:6 6975
t in your sides, and shall vex you .... Num 33:55 6975
t in your eyes, until ye perish .... Josh 23:13 6975
they shall be as t in your sides .... Judg 2:3
with the t of the wilderness .... Judg 8:7 6975
t of the wilderness and briers, and .... Judg 8:16 6975
be all of them as t thrust away 2Sa 23:6 6975
which took Manasseh among the t 2Chr 33:11 2336
and taketh it even out of the t .... Job 5:5 6791
Before your pots can feel the t .... Ps 58:9 329
are quenched as the fire of t .... Ps 118:12 6975
slothful man is as an hedge of t .... Prov 15:19 2312
T and snares are in the way of the .... Prov 22:5 6791
lo, it was all grown over with t .... Prov 24:31 7063
as the crackling of t under a pot .... Eccl 7:6 5518
As the lily among t, so is my .... Song 2:2 2336
there shall come up briers and t .... Is 5:6 7898
holes of the rocks, and upon all t .... Is 7:19 5285
it shall even be for briers and t .... Is 7:23 7898
the land shall become briers and t .... Is 7:24 7898
thither the fear of briers and t .... Is 7:25 7898
it shall devour the briers and t .... Is 9:18 7898
and it shall burn and devour his t .... Is 10:17 7898
briers and t against me in battle .... Is 27:4 7898
land of my people shall come up t .... Is 32:13 6975
as t cut up shall they be burned .... Is 33:12 6975
t shall come up in her palaces, ... Is 34:13 5518
fallow ground, and sow not among t .... Jer 4:3 6975
have sown wheat, but shall reap t .... Jer 12:13 6975
t be with thee, and thou dost .... Eze 2:6 5544
I will hedge up thy way with t .... Hos 2:6 5518
t shall be in their tabernacles .... Hos 9:6 2336
they be folden together as t .... Nah 1:10 5518
Do men gather grapes of t .... Mt 7:16 173
And some fell among t .... Mt 13:7 173
the t sprung up, and choked them .... Mt 13:7 173
the t is he that heareth the word .... Mt 13:22 173
they had platted a crown of t .... Mt 27:29 173
And some fell among t, and the .... Mk 4:7 173
the t grew up, and choked it, and .... Mk 4:7 173
are they which are sown among t .... Mk 4:18 173
purple, and platted a crown of t .... Mk 15:17 174
For of t men do not gather figs, ... Lk 6:44 173
And some fell among t .... Lk 8:7 173
the t sprang up with it, and .... Lk 8:7 173
that which fell among t are they .... Lk 8:14 173
the soldiers platted a crown of t .... Jn 19:2 173
forth, wearing the crown of t .... Jn 19:5 174
But that which beareth t and .... Heb 6:8 173

THOROUGHLY {2}
and shall cause him to be t healed .... Ex 21:19 7495
his images brake they in pieces t 2Kin 11:18 3190

THOSE See APPENDIX.

THOU See APPENDIX.

THOUGH See APPENDIX.

THOUGHT {81}
And Abraham said, Because I t .... Gen 20:11 559
saw her, he t her to be an harlot .... Gen 38:15 2803
I had not t to see thy face .... Gen 48:11 6419
as for you, ye t evil against me .... Gen 50:20 2803
which he t to do unto his people .... Ex 32:14 1696
I t to promote thee unto great .... Num 24:11 559
unto you, as I t to do unto them .... Num 33:56 1819
be not a t in thy wicked heart .... Deut 15:9 1697
as he had t to have done unto his .... Deut 19:19 2161
I verily t that thou hadst .... Judg 15:2 559
by night, and t to have slain me .... Judg 20:5 1819
I t to advertise thee, saying, ... Ruth 4:4 559
therefore Eli t she had been 1Sa 1:13 2803
for the asses, and take t for us 1Sa 9:5 1672
But Saul t to make David fall by 1Sa 18:25 2803
for he t, Something hath befallen 1Sa 20:26 559
who t that I would have given him 2Sa 4:10
Amnon t it hard for him to do any 2Sa 13:2 5869
Wherefore then hast thou t such a 2Sa 14:13 2803
and to do what he t good 2Sa 19:18 5869
new sword, t to have slain David 2Sa 21:16 559
went away, and said, Behold, I t 2Kin 5:11 559
for he t to make him king 2Chr 11:22
t to win them for himself 2Chr 32:1 559
But they t to do me mischief .... Neh 6:2 2803
he t scorn to lay hands on .... Est 3:6 5869
Now Haman t in his heart, To whom .... Est 6:6 559
in the t of him that is at ease .... Job 12:5 6248
that no t can be withholden from .... Job 42:2 4209
We have t of thy lovingkindness, ... Ps 48:9 1819
Their inward t is, that their .... Ps 49:11
both the inward t of every one of .... Ps 64:6
When I t to know this, it was too .... Ps 73:16 2803
I t on my ways, and turned my feet .... Ps 119:59 2803
thou understandest my t afar off .... Ps 139:2 7454
The t of foolishness is sin .... Prov 24:9 2154
thyself, or if thou hast t evil .... Prov 30:32 2161
not the king, no not in thy t .... Eccl 10:20 4093
sworn, saying, Surely as I have t .... Is 14:24 1819
the evil that I t to do unto them .... Jer 18:8 2803
and thou shalt think an evil t .... Eze 38:10 4284
I t it good to shew the signs and .... Dan 4:2 8232,6925
the king t to set him over the .... Dan 6:3 6246
declareth unto man what is his t .... Amos 4:13 7807
the LORD of hosts t to do unto us .... Zec 1:6 2161
As I t to punish you, when your .... Zec 8:14 2161
So again have I t in these days .... Zec 8:15 2161
the LORD, and that t upon his name .... Mal 3:16 2803
But while he t on these things, ... Mt 1:20 1760
Take no t for your life, what ye .... Mt 6:25 3309
Which of you by taking t can add .... Mt 6:27 3309
And why take ye t for raiment .... Mt 6:28 3309
Therefore take no t, saying, What .... Mt 6:31 3309
therefore no t for the morrow .... Mt 6:34 3309
take t for the things of itself .... Mt 6:34 3309
take no t how or what ye shall .... Mt 10:19 3309
take no t beforehand what ye .... Mk 13:11 4305
And when he t thereon, he wept .... Mk 14:72 1911
Wherefore neither t I myself .... Lk 7:7
perceiving the t of their heart .... Lk 9:47 1261
take ye no t how or what thing ye .... Lk 12:11 3309
he t within himself, saying, What .... Lk 12:17 1260
Take no t for your life, what ye .... Lk 12:22 3309
which of you with taking t can .... Lk 12:25 3309
why take ye t for the rest .... Lk 12:26 3309
because they t that the kingdom .... Lk 19:11 1380
but they t that he had spoken of .... Jn 11:13 1380
For some of them t, because Judas .... Jn 13:29 1380
because thou hast t that the gift .... Acts 8:20 3543
if perhaps the t of thine heart .... Acts 8:22 1963
While Peter t on the vision, the .... Acts 10:19 1760
but t he saw a vision .... Acts 12:9 1380
But Paul t not good to take him .... Acts 15:38
Why should it be t a thing .... Acts 26:8 2919
I verily t with myself, that I .... Acts 26:9 1380
as a child, I t as a child 1Cor 13:11 3049
Therefore I t it necessary to 2Cor 9:5 2233
t to the obedience of Christ 2Cor 10:5 3540
t it not robbery to be equal with .... Phil 2:6 2233
we t it good to be left at Athens 1Th 3:1 2106
suppose ye, shall he be t worthy .... Heb 10:29

THOUGHTEST {1}
thou t that I was altogether such .... Ps 50:21 1819

THOUGHTS {57}
the t of his heart was only evil .... Gen 6:5 4284
there were great t of heart .... Judg 5:15 2711
all the imaginations of the t 1Chr 28:9 4284
the t of the heart of thy people 1Chr 29:18 4284
In t from the visions of the .... Job 4:13 5587
off, even the t of my heart .... Job 17:11 4180
Therefore do my t cause me to .... Job 20:2 5587
Behold, I know your t, and the .... Job 21:27 4284
God is not in all his t .... Ps 10:4 4209
the t of his heart to all .... Ps 33:11 4284
thy t which are to us-ward .... Ps 40:5 4284
all their t are against me for .... Ps 56:5 4284
and thy t are very deep .... Ps 92:5 4284
The LORD knoweth the t of man .... Ps 94:11 4284
In the multitude of my t within .... Ps 94:19 8312
I hate vain t .... Ps 119:113 5588
precious also are thy t unto me .... Ps 139:17 7454
try me, and know my t .... Ps 139:23 8312
in that very day his t perish .... Ps 146:4 6250
The t of the righteous are right .... Prov 12:5 4284
The t of the wicked are an .... Prov 15:26 4284
thy t shall be established .... Prov 16:3 4284
The t of the diligent tend only .... Prov 21:5 4284
way, and the unrighteous man his t .... Is 55:7 4284
For my t are not your t, ... Is 55:8 4284
ways, and my t than your t .... Is 55:9 4284
their t are t of iniquity .... Is 59:7 4284
was not good, after their own t .... Is 65:2 4284
For I know their works and their t .... Is 66:18 4284
thy vain t lodge within thee .... Jer 4:14 4284
people, even the fruit of their t .... Jer 6:19 4284
have performed the t of his heart .... Jer 23:20 4209
For I know the t that I think .... Jer 29:11 4284
t of peace, and not of evil, to .... Jer 29:11 4284
thy t came into thy mind upon thy .... Dan 2:29 7476
mightest know the t of thy heart .... Dan 2:30 7476
the t upon my bed and the visions .... Dan 4:5 2031
one hour, and his t troubled him .... Dan 4:19 7476
his t troubled him, so that the .... Dan 5:6 7476
let not thy t trouble thee, nor .... Dan 5:10 7476
they know not the t of the LORD .... Mic 4:12 4284
And Jesus knowing their t said .... Mt 9:4 1761
And Jesus knew their t, and said .... Mt 12:25 1761
out of the heart proceed evil t .... Mt 15:19 1261
the heart of men, proceed evil t .... Mk 7:21 1261
that the t of many hearts may be .... Lk 2:35 1261
But when Jesus perceived their t .... Lk 5:22 1261
But he knew their t, and said to .... Lk 6:8 1261
But he, knowing their t, said .... Lk 11:17 1270
why do t arise in your hearts .... Lk 24:38 1261
their t the mean while accusing .... Rom 2:15 3053
Lord knoweth the t of the wise 1Cor 3:20 1261
and is a discerner of the t .... Heb 4:12 1761
and are become judges of evil t .... Jas 2:4 1261

THOUSAND {525}
thy brother a t pieces of silver .... Gen 20:16 505
about six hundred t on foot that .... Ex 12:37 505
people that day about three t men .... Ex 32:28 505
a t seven hundred and threescore .... Ex 38:25 505
six hundred t and three t .... Ex 38:26 505
of the t seven hundred seventy and .... Ex 38:28 505
was seventy talents, and two t .... Ex 38:29 505
of you shall put ten t to flight .... Lev 26:8 7233
of Reuben, were forty and six t .... Num 1:21 505
of Simeon, were fifty and nine t .... Num 1:23 505
five t six hundred and fifty .... Num 1:25 505
were threescore and fourteen t .... Num 1:27 505
of Issachar, were fifty and four t .... Num 1:29 505
of Zebulun, were fifty and seven t .... Num 1:31 505
tribe of Ephraim, were forty t .... Num 1:33 505
of Manasseh, were thirty and two t .... Num 1:35 505
Benjamin, were thirty and five t .... Num 1:37 505
of Dan, were threescore and two t .... Num 1:39 505
of Asher, were forty and one t .... Num 1:41 505
Naphtali, were fifty and three t .... Num 1:43 505
were numbered were six hundred t .... Num 1:46 505
six hundred t and three t .... Num 1:46 505
were threescore and fourteen t .... Num 2:4 505
thereof, were fifty and four t .... Num 2:6 505
thereof, were fifty and seven t .... Num 2:8 505
camp of Judah were an hundred t .... Num 2:9 505
and fourscore t and six t .... Num 2:9 505
thereof, were forty and six t .... Num 2:11 505
of them, were fifty and nine t .... Num 2:13 505
of them, were forty and five t .... Num 2:15 505
camp of Reuben were an hundred t .... Num 2:16 505
t and fifty and one t .... Num 2:16 505

numbered of them, were forty *t* Num 2:19 505
of them, were thirty and two *t* Num 2:21 505
of them, were thirty and five *t* Num 2:23 505
an hundred *t* and eight *t* Num 2:24 505
of them, were threescore and two *t* Num 2:26 505
of them, were forty and one *t* Num 2:28 505
of them, were fifty and three *t* Num 2:30 505
the camp of Dan were an hundred *t* Num 2:31 505
and fifty and seven *t* Num 2:31 505
six hundred *t* and three *t* Num 2:32 505
numbered of them were seven *t* Num 3:22 505
month old and upward, were eight *t* Num 3:28 505
a month old and upward, were six *t* Num 3:34 505
and upward, were twenty and two *t* Num 3:39 505
two *t* two hundred and threescore Num 3:43 505
a *t* three hundred and threescore Num 3:50 505
families were two *t* seven hundred Num 4:36 505
of their fathers, were two *t* Num 4:40 505
their families, were three *t* Num 4:44 505
numbered of them, were eight *t* Num 4:48 505
the silver vessels weighed two *t* Num 7:85 505
I am, are six hundred *t* footmen Num 11:21 505
in the plague were fourteen *t* Num 16:49 505
the plague were twenty and four *t* Num 25:9 505
of them were forty and three *t* Num 26:7 505
the Simeonites, twenty and two *t* Num 26:14 505
were numbered of them, forty *t* Num 26:18 505
of them, threescore and sixteen *t* Num 26:22 505
of them, threescore and four *t* Num 26:25 505
numbered of them, threescore *t* Num 26:27 505
numbered of them, fifty and two *t* Num 26:34 505
numbered of them, thirty and two *t* Num 26:37 505
of them were forty and five *t* Num 26:41 505
them, were threescore and four *t* Num 26:43 505
who were fifty and three *t* Num 26:47 505
of them were forty and five *t* Num 26:50 505
children of Israel, six hundred *t* Num 26:51 505
a *t* seven hundred and thirty Num 26:51 505
of them were twenty and three *t* Num 26:62 505
Of every tribe a *t*, throughout Num 31:4 505
a *t* of every tribe, twelve Num 31:5 505
tribe, twelve *t* armed for war Num 31:5 505
a *t* of every tribe, them and Num 31:6 505
war had caught, was six hundred *t* Num 31:32 505
seventy *t* and five *t* sheep, Num 31:32 505
And threescore and twelve *t* beeves Num 31:33 505
And threescore and one *t* asses, Num 31:34 505
two *t* persons in all, of women Num 31:35 505
was in number three hundred *t* Num 31:36 505
and seven and thirty *t* Num 31:36 505
the beeves were thirty and six *t* Num 31:38 505
And the asses were thirty *t* Num 31:39 505
And the persons were sixteen *t* Num 31:40 505
congregation was three hundred *t* Num 31:43 505
and thirty *t* and seven *t* Num 31:43 505
And thirty and six *t* beeves, Num 31:44 505
And thirty *t* asses and five hundred Num 31:45 505
And sixteen *t* persons Num 31:46 505
was sixteen *t* seven hundred and Num 31:52 505
outward a *t* cubits round about Num 35:4 505
on the east side two *t* cubits Num 35:5 505
and on the south side two *t* cubits Num 35:5 505
and on the west side two *t* cubits Num 35:5 505
and on the north side two *t* cubits Num 35:5 505
a *t* times so many more as ye are Deut 1:11 505
commandments to a *t* generations Deut 7:9 505
How should one chase a *t*, and two Deut 32:30 505
and two put ten *t* to flight Deut 32:30 505
about two *t* cubits by measure Josh 3:4 505
About forty *t* prepared for war Josh 4:13 505
about two or three *t* men go up Josh 7:3 505
of the people about three *t* men Josh 7:4 505
out thirty *t* mighty men of valour Josh 8:3 505
And he took about five *t* men Josh 8:12 505
of men and women, were twelve *t* Josh 8:25 505
One man of you shall chase a *t* Josh 23:10 505
slew of them in Bezek ten *t* men Judg 1:4 505
Moab at that time about ten *t* men Judg 3:29 505
take with thee ten *t* men of the Judg 4:6 505
up with ten *t* men at his feet Judg 4:10 505
Tabor, and ten *t* men after him Judg 4:14 505
seen among forty *t* in Israel Judg 5:8 505
of the people twenty and two *t* Judg 7:3 505
and there remained ten *t* Judg 7:3 505
with them, about fifteen *t* men Judg 8:10 505
twenty *t* men that drew sword Judg 8:10 505
that he requested was a *t* Judg 8:26 505
Shechem died also, about a *t* men Judg 9:49 505
of the Ephraimites forty and two *t* Judg 12:6 505
Then three *t* men of Judah went to Judg 15:11 505
it, and slew a *t* men therewith Judg 15:15 505
of an ass have I slain a *t* men Judg 15:16 505
upon the roof about three *t* men Judg 16:27 505
four hundred *t* footmen that drew Judg 20:2 505
of Israel, and an hundred of a *t* Judg 20:10 505
and a *t* out of ten *t* Judg 20:10 7233
six *t* men that drew sword, beside Judg 20:15 505
hundred *t* men that drew sword Judg 20:17 505
that day twenty and two *t* men Judg 20:21 505
of Israel again eighteen *t* men Judg 20:25 505
t chosen men out of all Israel Judg 20:34 505
that day twenty and five *t* Judg 20:35 505
fell of Benjamin eighteen *t* men Judg 20:44 505
them in the highways five *t* men Judg 20:45 505
Gidom, and slew two *t* men of them Judg 20:45 505
five *t* men that drew the sword Judg 20:46 505
sent thither twelve *t* men of the Judg 21:10 505
in the field about four *t* men 1Sa 4:2 505

fell of Israel thirty *t* footmen 1Sa 4:10 505
he smote of the people fifty *t* 1Sa 6:19 505
of Israel were three hundred *t* 1Sa 11:8 505
and the men of Judah thirty *t* 1Sa 11:8 505
chose him three *t* men of Israel 1Sa 13:2 505
whereof two *t* were with Saul in 1Sa 13:2 505
a *t* were with Jonathan in Gibeah 1Sa 13:2 505
thirty *t* chariots, and six 1Sa 13:5 505
six *t* horsemen, and people as the 1Sa 13:5 505
in Telaim, two hundred *t* footmen 1Sa 15:4 505
footmen, and ten *t* men of Judah 1Sa 15:4 505
coat was five *t* shekels of brass 1Sa 17:5 505
unto the captain of their *t* 1Sa 17:18 505
and made him his captain over a *t* 1Sa 18:13 505
Then Saul took three *t* chosen men 1Sa 24:2 505
great, and he had three *t* sheep 1Sa 25:2 505
sheep, and a *t* goats 1Sa 25:2 505
having three *t* chosen men of 1Sa 26:2 505
chosen men of Israel, thirty *t* 2Sa 6:1 505
David took from him a *t* chariots 2Sa 8:4 505
horsemen, and twenty *t* footmen 2Sa 8:4 505
the Syrians two and twenty *t* men 2Sa 8:5 505
of salt, being eighteen *t* men 2Sa 8:13 505
twenty *t* footmen, and of king 2Sa 10:6 505
and of king Maacah a *t* men 2Sa 10:6 505
and of Ish-tob twelve *t* men 2Sa 10:6 505
forty *t* horsemen, and smote 2Sa 10:18 505
me now choose out twelve *t* men 2Sa 17:1 505
now thou art worth ten *t* of us 2Sa 18:3 505
that day of twenty *t* men 2Sa 18:7 505
Though I should receive a *t* 2Sa 18:12 505
there were a *t* men of Benjamin 2Sa 19:17 505
were in Israel eight hundred *t* 2Sa 24:9 505
of Judah were five hundred *t* men 2Sa 24:9 505
even to Beer-sheba seventy *t* men 2Sa 24:15 505
a *t* burnt offerings did Solomon 1Kin 3:4 505
Solomon had forty *t* stalls of 1Kin 4:26 505
chariots, and twelve *t* horsemen 1Kin 4:26 505
And he spake three *t* proverbs 1Kin 4:32 505
and his songs were a *t* and five 1Kin 4:32 505
Solomon gave Hiram twenty *t* 1Kin 5:11 505
and the levy was thirty *t* men 1Kin 5:13 505
Lebanon, ten *t* a month by courses 1Kin 5:14 505
ten *t* that bare burdens, and 1Kin 5:15 505
fourscore *t* hewers in the 1Kin 5:15 505
which were over the work, three *t* 1Kin 5:16 505
it contained two *t* baths 1Kin 7:26 505
the LORD, two and twenty *t* oxen 1Kin 8:63 505
and an hundred and twenty *t* sheep 1Kin 8:63 505
and he had a *t* and four hundred 1Kin 10:26 505
twelve *t* horsemen, whom he 1Kin 10:26 505
fourscore *t* chosen men, which 1Kin 12:21 505
I have left me seven *t* in Israel 1Kin 19:18 505
children of Israel, being seven *t* 1Kin 20:15 505
an hundred *t* footmen in one day 1Kin 20:29 505
seven *t* of the men that were left 1Kin 20:30 505
king of Israel an hundred *t* lambs 2Kin 3:4 505
lambs, and an hundred *t* rams 2Kin 3:4 505
six *t* pieces of gold, and ten 2Kin 5:5 505
and ten chariots, and ten *t* footmen 2Kin 13:7 505
Edom in the valley of salt ten *t* 2Kin 14:7 505
gave Pul a *t* talents of silver 2Kin 15:19 505
I will deliver thee two *t* horses 2Kin 18:23 505
an hundred fourscore and five *t* 2Kin 19:35 505
of valour, even ten *t* captives 2Kin 24:14 505
the men of might, even seven *t* 2Kin 24:16 505
and craftsmen and smiths a *t* 2Kin 24:16 505
four and forty *t* seven hundred and 1Chr 5:18 505
of their camels fifty *t*, and of 1Chr 5:21 505
fifty *t*, and of asses two *t* 1Chr 5:21 505
and of men an hundred *t* 1Chr 5:21 505
the days of David two and twenty *t* 1Chr 7:2 505
for war, six and thirty *t* men 1Chr 7:4 505
genealogies fourscore and seven *t* 1Chr 7:5 505
their genealogies twenty and two *t* 1Chr 7:7 505
men of valour, was twenty *t* 1Chr 7:9 505
men of valour, were seventeen *t* 1Chr 7:11 505
to battle was twenty and six *t* men 1Chr 7:40 505
the house of their fathers, a *t* 1Chr 9:13 505
hundred, and the greatest over a *t* 1Chr 12:14 505
bare shield and spear were six *t* 1Chr 12:24 505
of valour for the war, seven *t* 1Chr 12:25 505
Of the children of Levi four *t* 1Chr 12:26 505
and with him were three *t* 1Chr 12:27 505
the kindred of Saul, three *t* 1Chr 12:29 505
the children of Ephraim twenty *t* 1Chr 12:30 505
half tribe of Manasseh eighteen *t* 1Chr 12:31 505
all instruments of war, fifty *t* 1Chr 12:33 505
And of Naphtali a *t* captains 1Chr 12:34 505
shield and spear thirty and seven *t* 1Chr 12:34 505
expert in war twenty and eight *t* 1Chr 12:35 505
to battle, expert in war, forty *t* 1Chr 12:36 505
battle, an hundred and twenty *t* 1Chr 12:37 505
he commanded to a *t* generations 1Chr 16:15 505
David took from him a *t* chariots 1Chr 18:4 505
seven *t* horsemen, and twenty 1Chr 18:4 505
horsemen, and twenty *t* footmen 1Chr 18:4 505
the Syrians two and twenty *t* men 1Chr 18:5 505
in the valley of salt eighteen *t* 1Chr 18:12 505
the children of Ammon sent a *t* 1Chr 19:6 505
two *t* chariots, and the king of 1Chr 19:7 505
t men which fought in chariots 1Chr 19:18 505
forty *t* footmen, and killed 1Chr 19:18 505
they of Israel were a *t* *t* 1Chr 21:5 505
an hundred *t* men that drew sword 1Chr 21:5 505
ten *t* men that drew sword 1Chr 21:5 505
fell of Israel seventy *t* men 1Chr 21:14 505
LORD an hundred *t* talents of gold 1Chr 22:14 505

a *t* *t* talents of silver 1Chr 22:14 505
man by man, was thirty and eight *t* 1Chr 23:3 505
four *t* were to set forward the 1Chr 23:4 505
six *t* were officers and judges 1Chr 23:4 505
Moreover four *t* were porters 1Chr 23:5 505
four *t* praised the LORD with the 1Chr 23:5 505
his brethren, men of valour, a *t* 1Chr 26:30 505
men of valour, were two *t* 1Chr 26:32 505
course were twenty and four *t* 1Chr 27:1 505
his course were twenty and four *t* 1Chr 27:2 505
likewise were twenty and four *t* 1Chr 27:4 505
his course were twenty and four *t* 1Chr 27:5 505
his course were twenty and four *t* 1Chr 27:7 505
his course were twenty and four *t* 1Chr 27:8 505
his course were twenty and four *t* 1Chr 27:9 505
his course were twenty and four *t* 1Chr 27:10 505
his course were twenty and four *t* 1Chr 27:11 505
his course were twenty and four *t* 1Chr 27:12 505
his course were twenty and four *t* 1Chr 27:13 505
his course were twenty and four *t* 1Chr 27:14 505
his course were twenty and four *t* 1Chr 27:15 505
Even three *t* talents of gold, of 1Chr 29:4 505
seven *t* talents of refined silver 1Chr 29:4 505
of God of gold five *t* talents 1Chr 29:7 505
ten *t* drams, and of silver ten 1Chr 29:7 7239
drams, and of silver ten *t* talents 1Chr 29:7 505
and of brass eighteen *t* talents 1Chr 29:7 7239,505
one hundred *t* talents of iron 1Chr 29:7 505
even a *t* bullocks, a *t* 1Chr 29:21 505
a *t* rams, and a *t* lambs, 1Chr 29:21 505
offered a *t* burnt offerings upon 2Chr 1:6 505
and he had a *t* and four hundred 2Chr 1:14 505
twelve *t* horsemen, which he 2Chr 1:14 505
ten *t* men to bear burdens, and 2Chr 2:2 505
fourscore *t* to hew in the 2Chr 2:2 505
hew in the mountain, and three *t* 2Chr 2:2 505
twenty *t* measures of beaten wheat 2Chr 2:10 505
twenty *t* measures of barley, and 2Chr 2:10 505
twenty *t* baths of wine, and twenty 2Chr 2:10 505
of wine, and twenty *t* baths of oil 2Chr 2:10 505
and fifty *t* and three *t* 2Chr 2:17 505
ten *t* of them to be bearers of 2Chr 2:18 505
fourscore *t* to be hewers in the 2Chr 2:18 505
in the mountain, and three *t* 2Chr 2:18 505
it received and held three *t* baths 2Chr 4:5 505
two *t* oxen, and an hundred and 2Chr 7:5 505
and an hundred and twenty *t* sheep 2Chr 7:5 505
Solomon had four *t* stalls for 2Chr 9:25 505
and chariots, and twelve *t* horsemen 2Chr 9:25 505
fourscore *t* chosen men, which 2Chr 11:1 505
and threescore *t* horsemen 2Chr 12:3 505
even four hundred *t* chosen men 2Chr 13:3 505
with eight hundred *t* chosen men 2Chr 13:3 505
Israel five hundred *t* chosen men 2Chr 13:17 505
out of Judah three hundred *t* 2Chr 14:8 505
bows, two hundred and fourscore *t* 2Chr 14:8 505
with an host of a *t* *t* 2Chr 14:9 505
hundred oxen and seven *t* sheep 2Chr 15:11 505
brought him flocks, seven *t* 2Chr 17:11 505
and seven hundred rams, and seven *t* 2Chr 17:11 505
men of valour three hundred *t* 2Chr 17:14 505
him two hundred and fourscore *t* 2Chr 17:15 505
hundred *t* mighty men of valour 2Chr 17:16 505
with bow and shield two hundred *t* 2Chr 17:17 505
fourscore *t* ready prepared for 2Chr 17:18 505
them three hundred *t* choice men 2Chr 25:5 505
He hired also an hundred *t* mighty 2Chr 25:6 505
of the children of Seir ten *t* 2Chr 25:11 505
other ten *t* left alive did the 2Chr 25:12 505
and smote three *t* of them 2Chr 25:13 505
mighty men of valour were two *t* 2Chr 26:12 505
three hundred *t* and seven *t* 2Chr 26:13 505
ten *t* measures of wheat, and ten 2Chr 27:5 505
of wheat, and ten *t* of barley 2Chr 27:5 505
twenty *t* in one day, which were 2Chr 28:6 505
of their brethren two hundred *t* 2Chr 28:8 505
six hundred oxen and three *t* sheep 2Chr 29:33 505
to the congregation a *t* bullocks 2Chr 30:24 505
bullocks and seven *t* sheep 2Chr 30:24 505
to the congregation a *t* bullocks 2Chr 30:24 505
t bullocks and ten *t* sheep 2Chr 30:24 505
to the number of thirty *t* 2Chr 35:7 505
and three *t* bullocks 2Chr 35:7 505
for the passover offerings two *t* 2Chr 35:8 505
offerings five *t* small cattle 2Chr 35:9 505
a *t* chargers of silver, nine and Ezr 1:9 505
and ten, and other vessels a *t* Ezr 1:10 505
of gold and of silver were five *t* Ezr 1:11 505
two *t* an hundred seventy and two Ezr 2:3 505
two *t* eight hundred and twelve Ezr 2:6 505
a *t* two hundred fifty and four Ezr 2:7 505
a *t* two hundred twenty and two Ezr 2:12 505
of Bigvai, two *t* fifty and six Ezr 2:14 505
a *t* two hundred fifty and four Ezr 2:31 505
The children of Senaah, three *t* Ezr 2:35 505
of Immer, a *t* fifty and two Ezr 2:37 505
a *t* two hundred forty and seven Ezr 2:38 505
The children of Harim, a *t* Ezr 2:39 505
two *t* three hundred and threescore Ezr 2:64 505
were seven *t* three hundred thirty Ezr 2:65 505
six *t* seven hundred and twenty Ezr 2:67 505
one *t* drams of gold, and five Ezr 2:69 505
five *t* pound of silver, and one Ezr 2:69 505
basons of gold, of a *t* drams Ezr 8:27 505
a *t* cubits on the wall unto the Neh 3:13 505
two *t* an hundred seventy and two Neh 7:8 505
children of Jeshua and Joab, two *t* Neh 7:11 505
a *t* two hundred fifty and four Neh 7:12 505

two *t* three hundred twenty and two ...... Neh 7:17 505
two *t* threescore and seven ...... Neh 7:19 505
a *t* two hundred fifty and four ...... Neh 7:34 505
three *t* nine hundred and thirty ...... Neh 7:38 505
of Immer, a *t* fifty and two ...... Neh 7:40 505
a *t* two hundred forty and seven ...... Neh 7:41 505
The children of Harim, a *t* ...... Neh 7:42 505
two *t* three hundred and threescore ...... Neh 7:66 505
were seven *t* three hundred thirty ...... Neh 7:67 505
six *t* seven hundred and twenty ...... Neh 7:69 505
to the treasure a *t* drams of gold ...... Neh 7:70 505
the work twenty *t* drams of gold ...... Neh 7:71 7239
of gold, and two *t* ...... Neh 7:71 505
gave was twenty *t* drams of gold ...... Neh 7:72 505
two *t* pounds of silver, and ...... Neh 7:72 7239
I will pay ten *t* talents of ...... Est 3:9 505
of their foes seventy and five *t* ...... Est 9:16 505
substance also was seven *t* sheep ...... Job 1:3 505
three *t* camels, and five hundred ...... Job 1:3 505
he cannot answer him one of a *t* ...... Job 9:3 505
an interpreter, one among a *t* ...... Job 33:23 505
for he had fourteen *t* sheep ...... Job 42:12 505
six *t* camels, and a *t* yoke ...... Job 42:12 505
yoke of oxen, and a *t* she asses ...... Job 42:12 505
and the cattle upon a *t* hills ...... Ps 50:10 505
in the valley of salt twelve *t* ...... Ps 60:*t* 505
The chariots of God are twenty *t* ...... Ps 68:17 7239
in thy courts is better than a *t* ...... Ps 84:10 505
For a *t* years in thy sight are ...... Ps 90:4 505
A *t* shall fall at thy side, and ...... Ps 91:7 505
side, and ten *t* at thy right hand ...... Ps 91:7 7233
he commanded to a *t* generations ...... Ps 105:8 505
he live a *t* years twice told ...... Eccl 6:6 505
one man among a *t* have I found ...... Eccl 7:28 505
whereon there hang a *t* bucklers ...... Song 4:4 505
ruddy, the chiefest among ten *t* ...... Song 5:10 7233
was to bring a *t* pieces of silver ...... Song 8:11 505
thou, O Solomon, must have a *t* ...... Song 8:12 505
t vines at a *t* silverlings ...... Is 7:23 505
One *t* shall flee at the rebuke of ...... Is 30:17 505
and I will give thee two *t* horses ...... Is 36:8 505
an hundred and fourscore and five *t* ...... Is 37:36 505
A little one shall become a *t* ...... Is 60:22 505
in the seventh year three *t* Jews ...... Jer 52:28 505
all the persons were four *t* ...... Jer 52:30 505
length of five and twenty *t* reeds ...... Eze 45:1 505
and the breadth shall be ten *t* ...... Eze 45:1 505
the length of five and twenty *t* ...... Eze 45:3 505
and the breadth of ten *t* ...... Eze 45:3 505
twenty *t* of length, and the ten ...... Eze 45:5 505
the ten *t* of breadth, shall also ...... Eze 45:5 505
of the city five *t* broad, and five ...... Eze 45:6 505
broad, and five and twenty *t* long ...... Eze 45:6 505
eastward, he measured a *t* cubits ...... Eze 47:3 505
Again he measured a *t*, and brought ...... Eze 47:4 505
Again he measured a *t*, and brought ...... Eze 47:4 505
Afterward he measured a *t* ...... Eze 47:5 505
twenty *t* reeds in breadth, and in ...... Eze 48:8 505
twenty *t* in length, and of ten ...... Eze 48:9 505
in length, and of ten *t* in breadth ...... Eze 48:9 505
twenty *t* in length, and toward the ...... Eze 48:10 505
toward the west ten *t* in breadth ...... Eze 48:10 505
toward the east ten *t* in breadth ...... Eze 48:10 505
south five and twenty *t* in length ...... Eze 48:10 505
twenty *t* in length, and ten ...... Eze 48:13 505
in length, and ten *t* in breadth ...... Eze 48:13 505
length shall be five and twenty *t* ...... Eze 48:13 505
and the breadth ten *t* ...... Eze 48:13 505
And the five *t*, that are left in ...... Eze 48:15 505
over against the five and twenty *t* ...... Eze 48:15 505
the north side four *t* and five ...... Eze 48:16 505
hundred, and the south side four *t* ...... Eze 48:16 505
and on the east side four *t* ...... Eze 48:16 505
hundred, and the west side four *t* ...... Eze 48:16 505
portion shall be ten *t* eastward ...... Eze 48:18 505
eastward, and ten *t* westward ...... Eze 48:18 505
twenty *t* by five and twenty ...... Eze 48:20 505
by five and twenty *t* ...... Eze 48:20 505
twenty *t* of the oblation toward ...... Eze 48:21 505
twenty *t* toward the west border, ... Eze 48:21 505
city on the north side, four *t* ...... Eze 48:30 505
And at the east side four *t* ...... Eze 48:32 505
And at the south side four *t* ...... Eze 48:33 505
At the west side four *t* and five ...... Eze 48:34 505
round about eighteen *t* measures ...... Eze 48:35 505
a great feast to a *t* of his lords ...... Dan 5:1 506
lords, and drank wine before the *t* ...... Dan 5:1 506
t thousands ministered unto him, ... Dan 7:10 506
ten *t* times ten *t* stood ...... Dan 7:10 7240
And he said unto me, Unto two *t* ...... Dan 8:14 505
there shall be a *t* two hundred ...... Dan 12:11 505
and cometh to the *t* three hundred ...... Dan 12:12 505
out by a *t* shall leave an hundred ...... Amos 5:3 505
t persons that cannot discern ...... Jonah 4:11 7239
had eaten were about five *t* men ...... Mt 14:21 *4000*
they that did eat were four *t* men ...... Mt 15:38 *5070*
the five loaves of the five *t* ...... Mt 16:9 *4000*
the seven loaves of the four *t* ...... Mt 16:10 *5070*
him, which owed him ten *t* talents ...... Mt 18:24 *3463*
the sea, (they were about two *t* ...... Mk 5:13 *1367*
the loaves were about five *t* men ...... Mk 6:44 *4000*
that had eaten were about four *t* ...... Mk 8:9 *5070*
the five loaves among five *t* ...... Mk 8:19 *4000*
And when the seven among four *t* ...... Mk 8:20 *5070*
For they were about five *t* men ...... Lk 9:14 *4000*
whether he be able with ten *t* to ...... Lk 14:31 *5505*
cometh against him with twenty *t* ...... Lk 14:31 *5505*
sat down, in number about five *t* ...... Jn 6:10 *4000*
unto them about three *t* souls ...... Acts 2:41 *5153*
of the men was about five *t* ...... Acts 4:4 *5505*
found it fifty *t* pieces of silver ...... Acts 19:19 *3461*
four *t* men that were murderers ...... Acts 21:38 *5070*
reserved to myself seven *t* men ...... Rom 11:4 *2035*
have ten *t* instructers in Christ 1Cor 4:15 *3463*
fell in one day three and twenty *t* 1Cor 10:8 *5505*
than ten *t* words in an unknown 1Cor 14:19 *3463*
day is with the Lord as a *t* years 2Pet 3:8 *5507*
years, and a *t* years as one day 2Pet 3:8 *5507*
them was ten *t* times ten *t* ...... Rev 5:11 *3461*
four *t* of all the tribes of the ...... Rev 7:4 *5505*
of Juda were sealed twelve *t* ...... Rev 7:5 *5505*
of Reuben were sealed twelve *t* ...... Rev 7:5 *5505*
tribe of Gad were sealed twelve *t* ...... Rev 7:5 *5505*
of Aser were sealed twelve *t* ...... Rev 7:6 *5505*
of Nepthalim were sealed twelve *t* ...... Rev 7:6 *5505*
of Manasses were sealed twelve *t* ...... Rev 7:6 *5505*
of Simeon were sealed twelve *t* ...... Rev 7:7 *5505*
of Levi were sealed twelve *t* ...... Rev 7:7 *5505*
of Issachar were sealed twelve *t* ...... Rev 7:7 *5505*
of Zabulon were sealed twelve *t* ...... Rev 7:8 *5505*
of Joseph were sealed twelve *t* ...... Rev 7:8 *5505*
of Benjamin were sealed twelve *t* ...... Rev 7:8 *5505*
were two hundred *t t* ...... Rev 9:16 *3461*
shall prophesy a *t* two hundred ...... Rev 11:3 *5507*
were slain of men seven *t* ...... Rev 11:13 *5505*
feed her there a *t* two hundred ...... Rev 12:6 *5507*
him an hundred forty and four *t* ...... Rev 14:1 *5505*
the hundred and forty and four *t* ...... Rev 14:3 *5505*
bridles, by the space of a *t* ...... Rev 14:20 *5507*
and Satan, and bound him a *t* years ...... Rev 20:2 *5507*
till the *t* years should be ...... Rev 20:3 *5507*
and reigned with Christ a *t* years ...... Rev 20:4 *5507*
until the *t* years were finished ...... Rev 20:5 *5507*
and shall reign with him a *t* years ...... Rev 20:6 *5507*
when the *t* years are expired, ... Rev 20:7 *5507*
with the reed, twelve *t* furlongs ...... Rev 21:16 *5505*

THOUSANDS {62}
thou the mother of *t* of millions ...... Gen 24:60 505
such over them, to be rulers of *t* ...... Ex 18:21 505
over the people, rulers of *t* ...... Ex 18:25 505
shewing mercy unto *t* of them that ...... Ex 20:6 505
Keeping mercy for *t*, forgiving ...... Ex 34:7 505
fathers, heads of *t* in Israel ...... Num 1:16 505
are heads of the *t* of Israel ...... Num 10:4 505
O LORD, unto the many *t* of Israel ...... Num 10:36 505
delivered out of the *t* of Israel ...... Num 31:5 505
host, with the captains over *t* ...... Num 31:14 505
which were over *t* of the host ...... Num 31:48 505
of the host, the captains of *t* ...... Num 31:48 505
to the LORD, of the captains of *t* ...... Num 31:52 505
the gold of the captains of *t* ...... Num 31:54 505
heads over you, captains over *t* ...... Deut 1:15 505
shewing mercy unto *t* of them that ...... Deut 5:10 505
and he came with ten *t* of saints ...... Deut 33:2 7233
and they are the ten *t* of Ephraim ...... Deut 33:17 7233
and they are the *t* of Manasseh ...... Deut 33:17 505
fathers among the *t* of Israel ...... Josh 22:14 505
unto the heads of the *t* of Israel ...... Josh 22:21 505
heads of the *t* of Israel which ...... Josh 22:30 505
will appoint him captains over *t* 1Sa 8:12 505
LORD by your tribes, and by your *t* 1Sa 10:19 505
his *t*, and David his ten *t* 1Sa 18:7 505
have ascribed unto David ten *t* 1Sa 18:8 7233
and to me they have ascribed but *t* 1Sa 18:8 505
saying, Saul hath slain his *t* 1Sa 21:11 505
and David his ten *t* 1Sa 21:11 7233
and make you all captains of *t* 1Sa 22:7 505
out throughout all the *t* of Judah 1Sa 23:23 505
passed on by hundreds, and by *t* 1Sa 29:2 505
dances, saying, Saul slew his *t* 1Sa 29:5 7233
and David his ten *t* 1Sa 29:5 505
with him, and set captains of *t* 2Sa 18:1 505
came out by hundreds and by *t* 2Sa 18:4 505
captains of the *t* that were of 1Chr 12:20 505
consulted with the captains of *t* 1Chr 13:1 505
of Israel, and the captains over *t* 1Chr 15:25 505
fathers, the captains over *t* 1Chr 26:26 505
chief fathers and captains of *t* 1Chr 27:1 505
and the captains over the *t* 1Chr 28:1 505
of Israel, and the captains of *t* 1Chr 29:6 505
all Israel, to the captains of *t* 2Chr 1:2 505
Of Judah, the captains of *t* 2Chr 17:14 505
and made them captains over *t* 2Chr 25:5 505
not be afraid of ten *t* of people ...... Ps 3:6 7233
twenty thousand, even *t* of angels ...... Ps 68:17 505
is better unto me than *t* of gold ...... Ps 119:72 505
that our sheep may bring forth *t* ...... Ps 144:13 503
and ten *t* in our streets ...... Ps 144:13 7232
shewest lovingkindness unto *t* ...... Jer 32:18 505
thousand *t* ministered unto him, ... Dan 7:10 506
and he shall cast down many ten *t* ...... Dan 11:12 7239
be little among the *t* of Judah ...... Mic 5:2 505
LORD be pleased with *t* of rams ...... Mic 6:7 505
or with ten *t* of rivers of oil ...... Mic 6:7 7233
how many *t* of Jews there are ...... Acts 21:20 *3461*
cometh with ten *t* of his saints ...... Jude 14 *3461*
ten thousand, and *t* of *t* ...... Rev 5:11 *5505*

THREAD {7}
from a *t* even to a shoelatchet ...... Gen 14:23 2339
bound upon his hand a scarlet *t* ...... Gen 38:28 2339
had the scarlet *t* upon his hand ...... Gen 38:30 2339
t in the window which thou didst ...... Josh 2:18 2339
as a *t* of tow is broken when it ...... Judg 16:9 6616
them from off his arms like a *t* ...... Judg 16:12 2339
Thy lips are like a *t* of scarlet ...... Song 4:3 2339

THREATEN {1}
people, let us straitly *t* them ...... Acts 4:17 *546*

THREATENED {2}
So when they had further *t* them ...... Acts 4:21 *4324*
when he suffered, he *t* not 1Pet 2:23 *546*

THREATENING {1}
things unto them, forbearing *t* ...... Eph 6:9 *547*

THREATENINGS {2}
And now, Lord, behold their *t* ...... Acts 4:29 *547*
And Saul, yet breathing out *t* ...... Acts 9:1 *547*

THREE {485}
begat Methuselah *t* hundred years ...... Gen 5:22 7969
of Enoch were *t* hundred sixty ...... Gen 5:23 7969
And Noah begat *t* sons, Shem, Ham, ... Gen 6:10 7969
the ark shall be *t* hundred cubits ...... Gen 6:15 7969
the *t* wives of his sons with them ...... Gen 7:13 7969
These are the *t* sons of Noah ...... Gen 9:19 7969
lived after the flood *t* hundred ...... Gen 9:28 7969
t years, and begat sons and ...... Gen 11:13 7969
t years, and begat sons and ...... Gen 11:15 7969
t hundred and eighteen, and pursued ...... Gen 14:14 7969
Take me an heifer of *t* years old ...... Gen 15:9 8027
old, and a she goat of *t* years old ...... Gen 15:9 8027
a ram of *t* years old, and a ...... Gen 15:9 8027
and, lo, *t* men stood by him ...... Gen 18:2 7969
Make ready quickly *t* measures of ...... Gen 18:6 7969
there were *t* flocks of sheep ...... Gen 29:2 7969
because I have born him *t* sons ...... Gen 29:34 7969
he set *t* days' journey betwixt ...... Gen 30:36 7969
came to pass about *t* months after ...... Gen 38:24 7969
And in the vine were *t* branches ...... Gen 40:10 7969
The *t* branches are *t* days ...... Gen 40:12 7969
Yet within *t* days shall Pharaoh ...... Gen 40:13 7969
I had *t* white baskets on my head ...... Gen 40:16 7969
The *t* baskets are *t* days ...... Gen 40:18 7969
Yet within *t* days shall Pharaoh ...... Gen 40:19 7969
all together into ward *t* days ...... Gen 42:17 7969
but to Benjamin he gave *t* hundred ...... Gen 45:22 7969
and his daughters were thirty and *t* ...... Gen 46:15 7969
child, she hid him *t* months ...... Ex 2:2 7969
thee, *t* days' journey into the ...... Ex 3:18 7969
t days' journey into the desert, ... Ex 5:3 7969
were an hundred thirty and *t* years ...... Ex 6:18 7969
t years old, when they spake unto ...... Ex 7:7 7969
We will go *t* days' journey into ...... Ex 8:27 7969
in all the land of Egypt *t* days ...... Ex 10:22 7969
any from his place for *t* days ...... Ex 10:23 7969
and they went *t* days in the ...... Ex 15:22 7969
And if he do not these *t* unto her ...... Ex 21:11 7969
T times thou shalt keep a feast ...... Ex 23:14 7969
T times in the year all thy males ...... Ex 23:17 7969
t branches of the candlestick out ...... Ex 25:32 7969
t branches of the candlestick out ...... Ex 25:32 7969
T bowls made like unto almonds, ... Ex 25:33 7969
t bowls made like almonds in the ...... Ex 25:33 7969
height thereof shall be *t* cubits ...... Ex 27:1 7969
pillars *t*, and their sockets *t* ...... Ex 27:14 7969
pillars *t*, and their sockets *t* ...... Ex 27:15 7969
that day about *t* thousand men ...... Ex 32:28 7969
t branches of the candlestick out ...... Ex 37:18 7969
t branches of the candlestick out ...... Ex 37:18 7969
T bowls made after the fashion of ...... Ex 37:19 7969
t bowls made like almonds in ...... Ex 37:19 7969
t cubits the height thereof ...... Ex 38:1 7969
pillars *t*, and their sockets *t* ...... Ex 38:14 7969
pillars *t*, and their sockets *t* ...... Ex 38:15 7969
t thousand and five hundred and ...... Ex 38:26 7969
in the blood of her purifying *t* ...... Lev 12:4 7969
t tenth deals of fine flour for a ...... Lev 14:10 7969
t years shall it be as ...... Lev 19:23 7969
bring forth fruit for *t* years ...... Lev 25:21 7969
shall be *t* shekels of silver ...... Lev 27:6 7969
and nine thousand and *t* hundred ...... Num 1:23 7969
t thousand and four hundred ...... Num 1:43 7969
t thousand and five hundred and ...... Num 1:46 7969
and nine thousand and *t* hundred ...... Num 2:13 7969
t thousand and four hundred ...... Num 2:30 7969
t thousand and five hundred and ...... Num 2:32 7969
a thousand *t* hundred and ...... Num 3:50 7969
were *t* thousand and two hundred ...... Num 4:44 7969
mount of the LORD *t* days' journey ...... Num 10:33 7969
them in the *t* days' journey ...... Num 10:33 7969
Come out ye *t* unto the tabernacle ...... Num 12:4 7969
And they *t* came out ...... Num 12:4 7969
of *t* tenth deals of flour mingled ...... Num 15:9 7969
hast smitten me these *t* times ...... Num 22:28 7969
smitten thine ass these *t* times ...... Num 22:32 7969
and turned from me these *t* times ...... Num 22:33 7969
blessed them these *t* times ...... Num 24:10 7969
t thousand and seven hundred and ...... Num 26:7 7969
and four thousand and *t* hundred ...... Num 26:25 7969
t thousand and four hundred ...... Num 26:47 7969
t thousand, all males from a ...... Num 26:62 7969
t tenth deals of flour for a meat ...... Num 28:12 7969
t tenth deals shall ye offer for ...... Num 28:20 7969
t tenth deals unto one bullock, ... Num 28:28 7969
t tenth deals for a bullock, and ...... Num 29:3 7969
t tenth deals to a bullock, and ...... Num 29:9 7969
t tenth deals unto every bullock ...... Num 29:14 7969
was in number *t* hundred thousand ...... Num 31:36 7969
was *t* hundred thousand and thirty ...... Num 31:43 7969
went *t* days' journey in the ...... Num 33:8 7969
t years old when he died in mount ...... Num 33:39 7969
Ye shall give *t* cities on this ...... Num 35:14 7969
t cities shall ye give in the ...... Num 35:14 7969
Then Moses severed *t* cities on ...... Deut 4:41 7969

At the end of *t* years thou shalt	Deut 14:28	7969
T times in a year shall all thy	Deut 16:16	7969
or *t* witnesses, shall he that is	Deut 17:6	7969
Thou shalt separate *t* cities for	Deut 19:2	7969
into *t* parts, that every slayer	Deut 19:3	8027
shalt separate *t* cities for thee	Deut 19:7	7969
then shalt thou add *t* cities more	Deut 19:9	7969
more for thee, beside these *t*	Deut 19:9	7969
or at the mouth of *t* witnesses	Deut 19:15	7969
for within *t* days ye shall pass	Josh 1:11	7969
and hide yourselves there *t* days	Josh 2:16	7969
mountain, and abode there *t* days	Josh 2:22	7969
And it came to pass after *t* days	Josh 3:2	7969
about two or *t* thousand men go up	Josh 7:3	7969
the people about *t* thousand men	Josh 7:4	7969
of *t* days after they had made a	Josh 9:16	7969
drove thence the *t* sons of Anak	Josh 15:14	7969
and her towns, even *t* countries	Josh 17:11	7969
among you *t* men for each tribe	Josh 18:4	7969
with her suburbs; *t* cities	Josh 21:32	7969
thence the *t* sons of Anak	Judg 1:20	7969
their mouth, were *t* hundred men	Judg 7:6	7969
By the *t* hundred men that lapped	Judg 7:7	7969
and retained those *t* hundred men	Judg 7:8	7969
he divided the *t* hundred men into	Judg 7:16	7969
hundred men into *t* companies	Judg 7:16	7969
the *t* companies blew the trumpets	Judg 7:20	7969
the *t* hundred blew the trumpets,	Judg 7:22	7969
the *t* hundred men that were with	Judg 8:4	7969
had reigned *t* years over Israel	Judg 9:22	7969
and divided them into *t* companies	Judg 9:43	7969
t years, and died, and was buried	Judg 10:2	7969
coasts of Arnon, *t* hundred years	Judg 11:26	7969
they could not in *t* days expound	Judg 14:14	7969
caught *t* hundred foxes, and took	Judg 15:4	7969
Then *t* thousand men of Judah went	Judg 15:11	7969
thou hast mocked me these *t* times	Judg 16:15	7969
the roof about *t* thousand men	Judg 16:27	7969
and he abode with him *t* days	Judg 19:4	7969
with *t* bullocks, and one ephah of	1Sa 1:24	7969
fleshhook of *t* teeth in his hand	1Sa 2:13	7969
she conceived, and bare *t* sons	1Sa 2:21	7969
asses that were lost *t* days ago	1Sa 9:20	7969
there shall meet thee *t* men going	1Sa 10:3	7969
to Beth-el, one carrying *t* kids	1Sa 10:3	7969
carrying *t* loaves of bread	1Sa 10:3	7969
of Israel were *t* hundred thousand	1Sa 11:8	7969
put the people in *t* companies	1Sa 11:11	7969
Saul chose him *t* thousand men of	1Sa 13:2	7969
of the Philistines in *t* companies	1Sa 13:17	7969
the *t* eldest sons of Jesse went	1Sa 17:13	7969
the names of his *t* sons that went	1Sa 17:13	7969
the *t* eldest followed Saul	1Sa 17:14	7969
And when thou hast stayed *t* days	1Sa 20:19	8027
I will shoot *t* arrows on the side	1Sa 20:20	7969
ground, and bowed himself *t* times	1Sa 20:41	7969
kept from us about these *t* days	1Sa 21:5	8032
Then Saul took *t* thousand chosen	1Sa 24:2	7969
he had *t* thousand sheep, and a	1Sa 25:2	7969
having *t* thousand chosen men of	1Sa 26:2	7969
any water, *t* days and *t* nights	1Sa 30:12	7969
because *t* days agone I fell sick	1Sa 30:13	7969
his *t* sons, and his armourbearer,	1Sa 31:6	7969
his *t* sons fallen in mount Gilboa	1Sa 31:8	7969
there were *t* sons of Zeruiah	2Sa 2:18	7969
of Abner's men, so that *t* hundred	2Sa 2:31	7969
t years over all Israel and Judah	2Sa 5:5	7969
of Obed-edom the Gittite *t* months	2Sa 6:11	7969
to Geshur, and was there *t* years	2Sa 13:38	7969
Absalom there were born *t* sons	2Sa 14:27	7969
he took *t* darts in his hand, and	2Sa 18:14	7969
me the men of Judah within *t* days	2Sa 20:4	7969
in the days of David *t* years	2Sa 21:1	7969
t hundred shekels of brass in	2Sa 21:16	7969
one of the *t* mighty men with	2Sa 23:9	7969
t of the thirty chief went down,	2Sa 23:13	7991
the *t* mighty men brake through	2Sa 23:16	7969
things did these *t* mighty men	2Sa 23:17	7969
son of Zeruiah, was chief among *t*	2Sa 23:18	7992
up his spear against *t* hundred	2Sa 23:18	7969
them, and had the name among *t*	2Sa 23:18	7969
Was he not most honourable of *t*	2Sa 23:19	7969
he attained not unto the first *t*	2Sa 23:19	7969
had the name among *t* mighty men	2Sa 23:22	7969
he attained not to the first *t*	2Sa 23:23	7969
the LORD, I offer thee *t* things	2Sa 24:12	7969
or wilt thou flee *t* months before	2Sa 24:13	7969
or that there be *t* days'	2Sa 24:13	7969
t years reigned he in Jerusalem	1Kin 2:11	7969
to pass at the end of *t* years	1Kin 2:39	7969
he spake *t* thousand proverbs	1Kin 4:32	7969
t thousand and *t* hundred,	1Kin 5:16	7969
court with *t* rows of hewed stone	1Kin 6:36	7969
And there were windows in *t* rows	1Kin 7:4	7969
was against light in *t* ranks	1Kin 7:4	7969
was against light in *t* ranks	1Kin 7:5	7969
was with *t* rows of hewed stones	1Kin 7:12	7969
t looking toward the north, and	1Kin 7:25	7969
t looking toward the west, and	1Kin 7:25	7969
t looking toward the south, and	1Kin 7:25	7969
t looking toward the east	1Kin 7:25	7969
t cubits the height of it	1Kin 7:27	7969
t times in a year did Solomon	1Kin 9:25	7969
he made *t* hundred shields of	1Kin 10:17	7969
t pound of gold went to one	1Kin 10:17	7969
once in *t* years came the navy of	1Kin 10:22	7969
and *t* hundred concubines	1Kin 11:3	7969
unto them, Depart yet for *t* days	1Kin 12:5	7969
T years reigned he in Jerusalem	1Kin 15:2	7969
himself upon the child *t* times	1Kin 17:21	7969
they continued *t* years without	1Kin 22:1	7969
and they sought *t* days, but found	2Kin 2:17	7969
called these *t* kings together	2Kin 3:10	7969
called these *t* kings together	2Kin 3:13	7969
out to him two or *t* eunuchs	2Kin 9:32	7969
But it was so, that in the *t*	2Kin 12:6	7969
In the *t* and twentieth year of	2Kin 13:1	7969
T times did Joash beat him, and	2Kin 13:25	7969
Samaria, and besieged it *t* years	2Kin 17:5	7969
at the end of *t* years they took	2Kin 18:10	7969
Judah *t* hundred talents of silver	2Kin 18:14	7969
t years old when he began to	2Kin 23:31	7969
he reigned *t* months in Jerusalem	2Kin 23:31	7969
became his servant *t* years	2Kin 24:1	7969
he reigned in Jerusalem *t* months	2Kin 24:8	7969
height of the chapiter *t* cubits	2Kin 25:17	7969
the *t* keepers of the door	2Kin 25:18	7969
which *t* were born unto him of the	1Chr 2:3	7969
Abishai, and Joab, and Asahel, *t*	1Chr 2:16	7969
And Segub begat Jair, who had *t*	1Chr 2:22	7969
he reigned thirty and *t* years	1Chr 3:4	7969
and Hezekiah, and Azrikam, *t*	1Chr 3:23	7969
Bela, and Becher, and Jediael, *t*	1Chr 7:6	7969
his *t* sons, and all his house died	1Chr 10:6	7969
t hundred slain by him at one	1Chr 11:11	7969
who was one of the *t* mighties	1Chr 11:12	7969
Now *t* of the thirty captains went	1Chr 11:15	7969
the *t* brake through the host of	1Chr 11:18	7969
things did these *t* mightiest	1Chr 11:19	7969
of Joab, he was chief of the *t*	1Chr 11:20	7969
up his spear against *t* hundred	1Chr 11:20	7969
them, and had a name among the *t*	1Chr 11:20	7969
Of the *t*, he was more honourable	1Chr 11:21	7969
he attained not to the first *t*	1Chr 11:21	7969
had the name among the *t* mighties	1Chr 11:24	7969
but attained not to the first *t*	1Chr 11:25	7969
and with him were *t* thousand	1Chr 12:27	7969
the kindred of Saul, *t* thousand	1Chr 12:29	7969
there they were with David *t* days	1Chr 12:39	7969
Obed-edom in his house *t* months	1Chr 13:14	7969
the LORD, I offer thee *t* things	1Chr 21:10	7969
Either *t* years' famine	1Chr 21:12	7969
or *t* months to be destroyed	1Chr 21:12	7969
or else *t* days the sword of the	1Chr 21:12	7969
was Jehiel, and Zetham, and Joel, *t*	1Chr 23:8	7969
Shelomith, and Haziel, and Haran, *t*	1Chr 23:9	7969
Mahli, and Eder, and Jeremoth, *t*	1Chr 23:23	7969
The *t* and twentieth to Delaiah,	1Chr 24:18	7969
fourteen sons and *t* daughters	1Chr 25:5	7969
The *t* and twentieth to Mahazioth,	1Chr 25:30	7969
Even *t* thousand talents of gold,	1Chr 29:4	7969
t years reigned he in Jerusalem	1Chr 29:27	7969
t thousand and six hundred to	2Chr 2:2	7969
t thousand and six hundred	2Chr 2:17	7969
t thousand and six hundred	2Chr 2:18	7969
t looking toward the north, and	2Chr 4:4	7969
t looking toward the west, and	2Chr 4:4	7969
t looking toward the south, and	2Chr 4:4	7969
t looking toward the east	2Chr 4:4	7969
received and held *t* thousand baths	2Chr 4:5	7969
t cubits high, and had set it in	2Chr 6:13	7969
And on the *t* and twentieth day of	2Chr 7:10	7969
t times in the year, even in the	2Chr 8:13	7969
t hundred shields made he of	2Chr 9:16	7969
t hundred shekels of gold went to	2Chr 9:16	7969
every *t* years once came the ships	2Chr 9:21	7969
Come again unto me after *t* days	2Chr 10:5	7969
son of Solomon strong, *t* years	2Chr 11:17	7969
for *t* years they walked in the	2Chr 11:17	7969
He reigned *t* years in Jerusalem	2Chr 13:2	7969
out of Judah *t* hundred thousand	2Chr 14:8	7969
thousand, and *t* hundred chariots	2Chr 14:9	7969
men of valour *t* hundred thousand	2Chr 17:14	7969
they were *t* days in gathering of	2Chr 20:25	7969
found them *t* hundred thousand	2Chr 25:5	7969
smote *t* thousand of them, and took	2Chr 25:13	7969
t hundred thousand and seven	2Chr 26:13	7969
hundred oxen and *t* thousand sheep	2Chr 29:33	7969
from *t* years old and upward, even	2Chr 31:16	7969
thousand, and *t* thousand bullocks	2Chr 35:7	7969
small cattle, and *t* hundred oxen	2Chr 35:8	7969
t years old when he began to	2Chr 36:2	7969
he reigned *t* months in Jerusalem	2Chr 36:2	7969
to reign, and he reigned *t* months	2Chr 36:9	7969
t hundred seventy and two	Ezr 2:4	7969
of Bebai, six hundred twenty and *t*	Ezr 2:11	7969
Bezai, *t* hundred twenty and *t*	Ezr 2:17	7969
Hashum, two hundred twenty and *t*	Ezr 2:19	7969
an hundred twenty and *t*	Ezr 2:21	7969
seven hundred and forty and *t*	Ezr 2:25	7969
and Ai, two hundred twenty and *t*	Ezr 2:28	7969
of Harim, *t* hundred and twenty	Ezr 2:32	7969
Jericho, *t* hundred forty and five	Ezr 2:34	7969
t thousand and six hundred and	Ezr 2:35	7969
Jeshua, nine hundred seventy and *t*	Ezr 2:36	7969
were *t* hundred ninety and two	Ezr 2:58	7969
forty and two thousand *t* hundred	Ezr 2:64	7969
seven thousand *t* hundred thirty	Ezr 2:65	7969
With *t* rows of great stones, and a	Ezr 6:4	8532
and with him *t* hundred males	Ezr 8:5	7969
and there abode we in tents *t* days	Ezr 8:15	7969
Jerusalem, and abode there *t* days	Ezr 8:32	7969
would not come within *t* days	Ezr 10:8	7969
unto Jerusalem within *t* days	Ezr 10:9	7969
to Jerusalem, and was there *t* days	Neh 2:11	7969
t hundred seventy and two	Neh 7:9	7969
two thousand *t* hundred twenty and	Neh 7:17	7969
t hundred twenty and eight	Neh 7:22	7969
Bezai, *t* hundred twenty and four	Neh 7:23	7969
Beeroth, seven hundred forty and *t*	Neh 7:29	7969
and Ai, an hundred twenty and *t*	Neh 7:32	7969
of Harim, *t* hundred and twenty	Neh 7:35	7969
Jericho, *t* hundred forty and five	Neh 7:36	7969
t thousand nine hundred and thirty	Neh 7:38	7969
Jeshua, nine hundred seventy and *t*	Neh 7:39	7969
were *t* hundred ninety and two	Neh 7:60	7969
forty and two thousand *t* hundred	Neh 7:66	7969
seven thousand *t* hundred thirty	Neh 7:67	7969
and neither eat nor drink *t* days	Est 4:16	7969
is, the month Sivan, on the *t*	Est 8:9	7969
slew *t* hundred men at Shushan	Est 9:15	7969
him seven sons and *t* daughters	Job 1:2	7969
t thousand camels, and five	Job 1:3	7969
called for their *t* sisters to eat	Job 1:4	7969
The Chaldeans made out *t* bands	Job 1:17	7969
Now when Job's *t* friends heard of	Job 2:11	7969
So these *t* men ceased to answer	Job 32:1	7969
Also against his *t* friends was	Job 32:3	7969
in the mouth of these *t* men	Job 32:5	7969
also seven sons and *t* daughters	Job 42:13	7969
There are *t* things that are never	Prov 30:15	7969
There be *t* things which are too	Prov 30:18	7969
For *t* things the earth is	Prov 30:21	7969
There be *t* things which go well,	Prov 30:29	7969
Zoar, an heifer of *t* years old	Is 15:5	7992
spoken, saying, Within *t* years	Is 16:14	7969
two or *t* berries in the top of	Is 17:6	7969
barefoot *t* years for a sign and	Is 20:3	7969
even unto this day, that is the *t*	Jer 25:3	7969
Jehudi had read *t* or four leaves	Jer 36:23	7969
as an heifer of *t* years old	Jer 48:34	7992
the *t* keepers of the door	Jer 52:24	7969
year *t* thousand Jews and *t*	Jer 52:28	7969
In the *t* and twentieth year of	Jer 52:30	7969
days, *t* hundred and ninety days	Eze 4:5	7969
t hundred and ninety days shalt	Eze 4:9	7969
Though these *t* men, Noah, Daniel,	Eze 14:14	7969
Though these *t* men were in it, as	Eze 14:16	7969
Though these *t* men were in it, as	Eze 14:18	7969
gate eastward were *t* on this side	Eze 40:10	7969
on this side, and *t* on that side	Eze 40:10	7969
they *t* were of one measure	Eze 40:10	7969
thereof were *t* on this side	Eze 40:21	7969
on this side and *t* on that side	Eze 40:21	7969
gate was *t* cubits on this side	Eze 40:48	7969
side, and *t* cubits on that side	Eze 40:48	7969
And the side chambers were *t*	Eze 41:6	7969
round about on their *t* stories	Eze 41:16	7969
altar of wood was *t* cubits high	Eze 41:22	7969
against gallery in *t* stories	Eze 42:3	7992
For they were in *t* stories	Eze 42:6	8027
t gates northward	Eze 48:31	7969
five hundred: and *t* gates	Eze 48:32	7969
hundred measures: and *t* gates	Eze 48:33	7969
five hundred, with their *t* gates	Eze 48:34	7969
so nourishing them *t* years	Dan 1:5	7969
And these *t* men, Shadrach, Meshach	Dan 3:23	8532
Did not we cast *t* men bound into	Dan 3:24	8532
And over these *t* presidents	Dan 6:2	8532
upon his knees *t* times a day	Dan 6:10	8532
maketh his petition *t* times a day	Dan 6:13	8532
it had *t* ribs in the mouth of it	Dan 7:5	8532
before whom there were *t* of the	Dan 7:8	8532
came up, and before whom *t* fell	Dan 7:20	8532
first, and he shall subdue *t* kings	Dan 7:24	8532
two thousand and *t* hundred days	Dan 8:14	7969
Daniel was mourning *t* full weeks	Dan 10:2	7969
till *t* whole weeks were fulfilled	Dan 10:3	7969
stand up yet *t* kings in Persia	Dan 11:2	7969
cometh to the thousand *t* hundred	Dan 12:12	7969
For *t* transgressions of Damascus,	Amos 1:3	7969
For *t* transgressions of Gaza, and	Amos 1:6	7969
For *t* transgressions of Tyrus, and	Amos 1:9	7969
For *t* transgressions of Edom, and	Amos 1:11	7969
For *t* transgressions of the	Amos 1:13	7969
For *t* transgressions of Moab, and	Amos 2:1	7969
For *t* transgressions of Judah, and	Amos 2:4	7969
For *t* transgressions of Israel,	Amos 2:6	7969
and your tithes after *t* years	Amos 4:4	7969
when there were yet *t* months to	Amos 4:7	7969
So two or *t* cities wandered unto	Amos 4:8	7969
the fish *t* days and *t* nights	Jonah 1:17	7969
great city of *t* days' journey	Jonah 3:3	7969
T shepherds also I cut off in one	Zec 11:8	7969
For as Jonas was *t* days	Mt 12:40	*5140*
t nights in the whale's belly	Mt 12:40	*5140*
so shall the Son of man be *t* days	Mt 12:40	*5140*
t nights in the heart of the	Mt 12:40	*5140*
hid in *t* measures of meal, till	Mt 13:33	*5140*
they continue with me now *t* days	Mt 15:32	*5140*
let us make here *t* tabernacles	Mt 17:4	*5140*
or *t* witnesses every word may be	Mt 18:16	*5140*
For where two or *t* are gathered	Mt 18:20	*5140*
of God, and to build it in *t* days	Mt 26:61	*5140*
temple, and buildest it in *t* days	Mt 27:40	*5140*
After *t* days I will rise again	Mt 27:63	*5140*
they have now been with me *t* days	Mk 8:2	*5140*
and after *t* days rise again	Mk 8:31	*5140*
and let us make *t* tabernacles	Mk 9:5	*5140*
for more than *t* hundred pence	Mk 14:5	*5145*
within *t* days I will build	Mk 14:58	*5140*
temple, and buildest it in *t* days	Mk 15:29	*5140*
abode with her about *t* months	Lk 1:56	*5140*
that after *t* days they found him	Lk 2:46	*5140*

the heaven was shut up *t* years ... Lk 4:25 *5140*
and let us make *t* tabernacles ... Lk 9:33 *5140*
Which now of these *t*, thinkest ... Lk 10:36 *5140*
him, Friend, lend me *t* loaves ... Lk 11:5 *5140*
t against two, and two against ... Lk 12:52 *5140*
against two, and two against *t* ... Lk 12:52 *5140*
these *t* years I come seeking ... Lk 13:7 *5140*
hid in *t* measures of meal, till ... Lk 13:21 *5140*
two or *t* firkins apiece ... Jn 2:6 *5140*
in *t* days I will raise it up ... Jn 2:19 *5140*
and wilt thou rear it up in *t* days ... Jn 2:20 *5140*
ointment sold for *t* hundred pence ... Jn 12:5 *5145*
fishes, an hundred and fifty and *t* ... Jn 21:11 *5140*
unto them about *t* thousand souls ... Acts 2:41 *5153*
about the space of *t* hours after ... Acts 5:7 *5140*
up in his father's house *t* months ... Acts 7:20 *5140*
he was *t* days without sight, and ... Acts 9:9 *5140*
unto him, Behold, *t* men seek thee ... Acts 10:19 *5140*
And this was done *t* times ... Acts 11:10 *5151*
immediately there were *t* men ... Acts 11:11 *5140*
t sabbath days reasoned with them ... Acts 17:2 *5140*
boldly for the space of *t* months ... Acts 19:8 *5140*
And there abode *t* months ... Acts 20:3 *5140*
that by the space of *t* years I ... Acts 20:31 *5148*
after *t* days he ascended from ... Acts 25:1 *5140*
lodged us *t* days courteously ... Acts 28:7 *5140*
after *t* months we departed in a ... Acts 28:11 *5140*
Syracuse, we tarried there *t* days ... Acts 28:12 *5140*
as Appii forum, and The *t* taverns ... Acts 28:15 *5140*
that after *t* days Paul called the ... Acts 28:17 *5140*
committed, and fell in one day *t* ... 1Cor 10:8 *5140*
faith, hope, charity, these *t* ... 1Cor 13:13 *5140*
it be by two, or at the most by *t* ... 1Cor 14:27 *5140*
Let the prophets speak two or *t* ... 1Cor 14:29 *5140*
In the mouth of two or *t* ... 2Cor 13:1 *5140*
Then after *t* years I went up to ... Gal 1:18 *5140*
but before two or *t* witnesses ... 1Ti 5:19 *5140*
mercy under two or *t* witnesses ... Heb 10:28 *5140*
was hid *t* months of his parents, ... Heb 11:23 *5150*
the earth by the space of *t* years ... Jas 5:17 *5140*
For there are *t* that bear record ... 1Jn 5:7 *5140*
and these *t* are one ... 1Jn 5:7 *5140*
there are *t* that bear witness in ... 1Jn 5:8 *5140*
and these *t* agree in one ... 1Jn 5:8 *5140*
t measures of barley for a penny ... Rev 6:6 *5140*
of the trumpet of the *t* angels ... Rev 8:13 *5140*
By these *t* was the third part of ... Rev 9:18 *5140*
see their dead bodies *t* days ... Rev 11:9 *5140*
And after *t* days and an half the ... Rev 11:11 *5140*
I saw *t* unclean spirits like ... Rev 16:13 *5140*
city was divided into *t* parts ... Rev 16:19 *5140*
On the east *t* gates ... Rev 21:13 *5140*
on the north *t* gates ... Rev 21:13 *5140*
on the south *t* gates ... Rev 21:13 *5140*
and on the west *t* gates ... Rev 21:13 *5140*

THREEFOLD {1}
a *t* cord is not quickly broken ... Eccl 4:12 8027

THREESCORE {93}
life which he lived, an hundred *t* ... Gen 25:7 7657
Isaac was *t* years old when she ... Gen 25:26 8346
sons' wives, all the souls were *t* ... Gen 46:26 8346
which came into Egypt, were *t* ... Gen 46:27 7657
the Egyptians mourned for him *t* ... Gen 50:3 7657
were twelve wells of water, and *t* ... Ex 15:27 7657
and a thousand seven hundred and *t* ... Ex 38:25 7657
in the blood of her purifying *t* ... Lev 12:5 8346
of the tribe of Judah, were *t* ... Num 1:27 7657
even of the tribe of Dan, were *t* ... Num 1:39 8346
were numbered of them, were *t* ... Num 2:4 7657
were numbered of them, were *t* ... Num 2:26 8346
and two thousand two hundred and *t* ... Num 3:43 7657
redeemed of the two hundred and *t* ... Num 3:46 7657
a thousand three hundred and *t* ... Num 3:50 8346
that were numbered of them, *t* ... Num 26:22 7657
that were numbered of them, *t* ... Num 26:25 8346
t thousand and five hundred ... Num 26:27 8346
were numbered of them, were *t* ... Num 26:43 8346
And *t* and twelve thousand beeves, ... Num 31:33 7657
And *t* and one thousand asses, ... Num 31:34 8346
of the sheep was six hundred and *t* ... Num 31:37 7657
of which the LORD's tribute was *t* ... Num 31:38 7657
of which the LORD's tribute was *t* ... Num 31:39 8346
twelve fountains of water, and *t* ... Num 33:9 7657
t cities, all the region of Argob ... Deut 3:4 8346
went down into Egypt with *t* ... Deut 10:22 7657
which are in Bashan, *t* cities ... Josh 13:30 8346
And Adoni-bezek said, *T* and ten ... Judg 1:7 7657
and the elders thereof, even *t* ... Judg 8:14 7657
And Gideon had *t* and ten sons of ... Judg 8:30 7657
sons of Jerubbaal, which are *t* ... Judg 9:2 7657
And they gave him *t* and ten pieces ... Judg 9:4 7657
the sons of Jerubbaal, being *t* ... Judg 9:5 7657
day, and have slain his sons, *t* ... Judg 9:18 7657
That the cruelty done to the *t* ... Judg 9:24 7657
and thirty nephews, that rode on *t* ... Judg 12:14 7657
of the people fifty thousand and *t* ... 1Sa 6:19 7657
that three hundred and *t* men died ... 2Sa 2:31 8346
t great cities with walls and ... 1Kin 4:13 8346
flour, and *t* measures of meal, ... 1Kin 4:22 8346
And Solomon had *t* and ten thousand ... 1Kin 5:15 7657
the length thereof was *t* cubits ... 1Kin 6:2 8346
in one year was six hundred *t* ... 1Kin 10:14 8346
t men of the people of the land ... 2Kin 25:19 8346
married when he was *t* years old ... 1Chr 2:21 8346
the towns thereof, even *t* cities ... 1Chr 2:23 8346
forty thousand seven hundred and *t* ... 1Chr 5:18 8346
a thousand and seven hundred and *t* ... 1Chr 9:13 8346
Obed-edom with their brethren, *t* ... 1Chr 16:38 8346
and Judah was four hundred *t* ... 1Chr 21:5 7657
strength for the service, were *t* ... 1Chr 26:8 8346
And Solomon told out *t* and ten ... 2Chr 2:2 7657
And he set *t* and ten thousand of ... 2Chr 2:18 7657
the first measure was *t* cubits ... 2Chr 3:3 8346
in one year was six hundred and *t* ... 2Chr 9:13 8346
eighteen wives, and *t* concubines ... 2Chr 11:21 8346
and eight sons, and *t* daughters ... 2Chr 11:21 8346
chariots, and *t* thousand horsemen ... 2Chr 12:3 8346
the congregation brought, was *t* ... 2Chr 29:32 7657
she kept sabbath, to fulfil *t* ... 2Chr 36:21 7657
of Zaccai, seven hundred and *t* ... Ezr 2:9 8346
two thousand three hundred and *t* ... Ezr 2:64 8346
unto the treasure of the work *t* ... Ezr 2:69 7239
the height thereof *t* cubits ... Ezr 6:3 8361
and the breadth thereof *t* cubits ... Ezr 6:3 8361
and with him an hundred and *t* males ... Ezr 8:10 8346
and Shemaiah, and with them *t* males ... Ezr 8:13 8346
of Zaccai, seven hundred and *t* ... Neh 7:14 8346
of Adonikam, six hundred *t* ... Neh 7:18 8346
of Bigvai, two thousand *t* ... Neh 7:19 8346
two thousand three hundred and *t* ... Neh 7:66 8346
thousand pounds of silver, and *t* ... Neh 7:72 8346
at Jerusalem were four hundred *t* ... Neh 11:6 8346
The days of our years are *t* years ... Ps 90:10 7657
t valiant men are about it, of ... Song 3:7 7657
There are *t* queens, and fourscore ... Song 6:8 7657
and within *t* and five years shall ... Is 7:8 7657
t men of the people of the land, ... Jer 52:25 7657
He made also posts of *t* cubits ... Eze 40:14 7657
gold, whose height was *t* cubits ... Dan 3:1 8361
took the kingdom, being about *t* ... Dan 5:31 8361
Prince shall be seven weeks, and *t* ... Dan 9:25 8346
And after *t* and two weeks shall ... Dan 9:26 8346
thou hast had indignation these *t* ... Zec 1:12 7657
from Jerusalem about *t* furlongs ... Lk 24:13 *1835*
to him, and all his kindred, *t* ... Acts 7:14 *1440*
to go to Caesarea, and horsemen *t* ... Acts 23:23 *1440*
in all in the ship two hundred *t* ... Acts 27:37 *1440*
into the number under *t* years old ... 1Ti 5:9 *1835*
t days, clothed in sackcloth ... Rev 11:3 *1835*
a thousand two hundred and *t* days ... Rev 12:6 *1835*
and his number is six hundred *t* ... Rev 13:18 *5516*

THRESH {4}
thou shalt *t* the mountains, and ... Is 41:15 1758
it is time to *t* her ... Jer 51:33 1869
Arise and *t*, O daughter of Zion ... Mic 4:13 1758
thou didst *t* the heathen in anger ... Hab 3:12 1758

THRESHED {3}
his son Gideon *t* wheat by the ... Judg 6:11 2251
For the fitches are not *t* with a ... Is 28:27 1758
because they have *t* Gilead with ... Amos 1:3 1758

THRESHETH {1}
that he that *t* in hope should be ... 1Cor 9:10 *248*

THRESHING {10}
your *t* shall reach unto the ... Lev 26:5 1786
and *t* instruments and other ... 2Sa 24:22 4173
had made them like the dust by *t* ... 2Kin 13:7 1758
Now Ornan was *t* wheat ... 1Chr 21:20 1758
the *t* instruments for wood, and ... 1Chr 21:23 4173
O my *t*, and the corn of my floor ... Is 21:10 4098
not threshed with a *t* instrument ... Is 28:27 2742
because he will not ever be *t* it ... Is 28:28 1758
sharp *t* instrument having teeth ... Is 41:15 4173
Gilead with *t* instruments of iron ... Amos 1:3 2742

THRESHINGFLOOR {17}
And they came to the *t* of Atad ... Gen 50:10 1637
ye do the heave offering of the *t* ... Num 15:20 1637
though it were the corn of the *t* ... Num 18:27 1637
Levites as the increase of the *t* ... Num 18:30 1637
barley to night in the *t* ... Ruth 3:2 1637
And when they came to Nachon's *t* ... 2Sa 6:6 1637
in the *t* of Araunah the Jebusite ... 2Sa 24:18 1637
David said, To buy the *t* of thee ... 2Sa 24:21 1637
So David bought the *t* and the oxen ... 2Sa 24:24 1637
they came unto the *t* of Chidon ... 1Chr 13:9 1637
by the *t* of Ornan the Jebusite ... 1Chr 21:15 1637
in the *t* of Ornan the Jebusite ... 1Chr 21:18 1637
saw David, and went out of the *t* ... 1Chr 21:21 1637
Grant me the place of this *t* ... 1Chr 21:22 1637
in the *t* of Ornan the Jebusite ... 1Chr 21:28 1637
in the *t* of Ornan the Jebusite ... 2Chr 3:1 1637
daughter of Babylon is like a *t* ... Jer 51:33 1637

THRESHINGFLOORS {2}
against Keilah, and they rob the *t* ... 1Sa 23:1 1637
like the chaff of the summer *t* ... Dan 2:35 147

THRESHINGPLACE {1}
by the *t* of Araunah the Jebusite ... 2Sa 24:16 1637

THRESHOLD {14}
and her hands were upon the *t* ... Judg 19:27 5592
his hands were cut off upon the *t* ... 1Sa 5:4 4670
tread on the *t* of Dagon in Ashdod ... 1Sa 5:5 4670
she came to the *t* of the door ... 1Kin 14:17 5592
he was, to the *t* of the house ... Eze 9:3 4670
and stood over the *t* of the house ... Eze 10:4 4670
from off the *t* of the house ... Eze 10:18 4670
and measured the *t* of the gate ... Eze 40:6 5592
the other *t* of the gate, which ... Eze 40:6 5592
the *t* of the gate by the porch of ... Eze 40:7 5592
of their *t* by my thresholds ... Eze 43:8 5592
worship at the *t* of the gate ... Eze 46:2 4670
under the *t* of the house eastward ... Eze 47:1 4670
all those that leap on the *t* ... Zeph 1:9 4670

THRESHOLDS {3}
the ward at the *t* of the gates ... Neh 12:25 624
of their threshold by my *t* ... Eze 43:8 5592
desolation shall be in the *t* ... Zeph 2:14 5592

THREW {6}
t stones at him, and cast dust ... 2Sa 16:13 5619
So they *t* her down ... 2Kin 9:33 8058
t down the high places and the ... 2Chr 31:1 5422
she *t* in two mites, which make a ... Mk 12:42 *906*
a coming, the devil *t* him down ... Lk 9:42 *4952*
clothes, and *t* dust into the air, ... Acts 22:23 *906*

THREWEST {1}
persecutors thou *t* into the deeps ... Neh 9:11 7993

THRICE {15}
T in the year shall all your men ... Ex 34:23 7060,6471
the LORD thy God *t* in the year ... Ex 34:24 7969,6471
And he smote *t*, and stayed ... 2Kin 13:18 7969,6471
now thou shalt smite Syria but *t* ... 2Kin 13:19 7969,6471
cock crow, thou shalt deny me *t* ... Mt 26:34 *5151*
cock crow, thou shalt deny me *t* ... Mt 26:75 *5151*
crow twice, thou shalt deny me *t* ... Mk 14:30 *5151*
crow twice, thou shalt deny me *t* ... Mk 14:72 *5151*
before that thou shalt *t* deny ... Lk 22:34 *5151*
cock crow, thou shalt deny me *t* ... Lk 22:61 *5151*
crow, till thou hast denied me *t* ... Jn 13:38 *5151*
This was done *t* ... Acts 10:16 *5151*
T was I beaten with rods, once ... 2Cor 11:25 *5151*
t I suffered shipwreck, a night ... 2Cor 11:25 *5151*
this thing I besought the Lord *t* ... 2Cor 12:8 *5151*

THROAT {7}
their *t* is an open sepulchre ... Ps 5:9 1627
my *t* is dried ... Ps 69:3 1627
speak they through their *t* ... Ps 115:7 1627
And put a knife to thy *t*, if thou ... Prov 23:2 3930
unshod, and thy *t* from thirst ... Jer 2:25 1627
on him, and took him by the *t* ... Mt 18:28 *4155*
Their *t* is an open sepulchre ... Rom 3:13 *2995*

THRONE {176}
only in the *t* will I be greater ... Gen 41:40 3678
Pharaoh that sitteth upon his *t* ... Ex 11:5 3678
his *t* unto the firstborn of the ... Ex 12:29 3678
sitteth upon the *t* of his kingdom ... Deut 17:18 3678
make them inherit the *t* of glory ... 1Sa 2:8 3678
to set up the *t* of David over ... 2Sa 3:10 3678
I will stablish the *t* of his ... 2Sa 7:13 3678
thy *t* shall be established for ... 2Sa 7:16 3678
and the king and his *t* be guiltless ... 2Sa 14:9 3678
me, and he shall sit upon my *t* ... 1Kin 1:13 3678
me, and he shall sit upon my *t* ... 1Kin 1:17 3678
t of my lord the king after him ... 1Kin 1:20 3678
me, and he shall sit upon my *t* ... 1Kin 1:24 3678
who should sit on the *t* of my ... 1Kin 1:27 3678
shall sit upon my *t* in my stead ... 1Kin 1:30 3678
that he may come and sit upon my *t* ... 1Kin 1:35 3678
make his *t* greater than the ... 1Kin 1:37 3678
than the *t* of my lord king David ... 1Kin 1:37 3678
sitteth on the *t* of the kingdom ... 1Kin 1:46 3678
his *t* greater than thy *t* ... 1Kin 1:47 3678
given one to sit on my *t* this day ... 1Kin 1:48 3678
said he) a man on the *t* of Israel ... 1Kin 2:4 3678
upon the *t* of David his father ... 1Kin 2:12 3678
unto her, and sat down on his *t* ... 1Kin 2:19 3678
set me on the *t* of David my ... 1Kin 2:24 3678
and upon his house, and upon his *t* ... 1Kin 2:33 3678
and the *t* of David shall be ... 1Kin 2:45 3678
given him a son to sit on his *t* ... 1Kin 3:6 3678
I will set upon thy *t* in thy room ... 1Kin 5:5 3678
for the *t* where he might judge ... 1Kin 7:7 3678
father, and sit on the *t* of Israel ... 1Kin 8:20 3678
sight to sit on the *t* of Israel ... 1Kin 8:25 3678
Then I will establish the *t* of ... 1Kin 9:5 3678
thee a man upon the *t* of Israel ... 1Kin 9:5 3678
to set thee on the *t* of Israel ... 1Kin 10:9 3678
the king made a great *t* of ivory ... 1Kin 10:18 3678
The *t* had six steps, and the top ... 1Kin 10:19 3678
the top of the *t* was round behind ... 1Kin 10:19 3678
reign, as soon as he sat on his *t* ... 1Kin 16:11 3678
king of Judah sat each on his *t* ... 1Kin 22:10 3678
I saw the LORD sitting on his *t* ... 1Kin 22:19 3678
and set him on his father's *t* ... 2Kin 10:3 3678
shall sit on the *t* of Israel ... 2Kin 10:30 3678
And he sat on the *t* of the kings ... 2Kin 11:19 3678
and Jeroboam sat upon his *t* ... 2Kin 13:13 3678
the *t* of Israel unto the fourth ... 2Kin 15:12 3678
set his *t* above the *t* of the ... 2Kin 25:28 3678
and I will stablish his *t* for ever ... 1Chr 17:12 3678
his *t* shall be established for ... 1Chr 17:14 3678
I will establish the *t* of his ... 1Chr 22:10 3678
Solomon my son to sit upon the *t* ... 1Chr 28:5 3678
Then Solomon sat on the *t* of the ... 1Chr 29:23 3678
and am set on the *t* of Israel ... 2Chr 6:10 3678
sight to sit upon the *t* of Israel ... 2Chr 6:16 3678
I stablish the *t* of thy kingdom ... 2Chr 7:18 3678
in thee to set thee on his *t* ... 2Chr 9:8 3678
the king made a great *t* of ivory ... 2Chr 9:17 3678
And there were six steps to the *t* ... 2Chr 9:18 3678
which were fastened to the *t* ... 2Chr 9:18 3678
Judah sat either of them on his *t* ... 2Chr 18:9 3678
I saw the LORD sitting upon his *t* ... 2Chr 18:18 3678
king upon the *t* of the kingdom ... 2Chr 23:20 3678
unto the *t* of the governor on ... Neh 3:7 3678
sat on the *t* of his kingdom ... Est 1:2 3678
his royal *t* in the royal house ... Est 5:1 3678
He holdeth back the face of his *t* ... Job 26:9 3678
but with kings are they on the *t* ... Job 36:7 3678
satest in the *t* judging right ... Ps 9:4 3678

T

hath prepared his *t* for judgment .... Ps 9:7 3678
the LORD's *t* is in heaven .... Ps 11:4 3678
Thy *t*, O God, is for ever and ever .... Ps 45:6 3678
upon the *t* of his holiness .... Ps 47:8 3678
build up thy *t* to all generations .... Ps 89:4 3678
are the habitation of thy *t* .... Ps 89:14 3678
his *t* as the days of heaven .... Ps 89:29 3678
his *t* as the sun before me .... Ps 89:36 3678
cast his *t* down to the ground .... Ps 89:44 3678
Thy *t* is established of old .... Ps 93:2 3678
Shall the *t* of iniquity have .... Ps 94:20 3678
are the habitation of his *t* .... Ps 97:2 3678
prepared his *t* in the heavens .... Ps 103:19 3678
of thy body will I set upon thy *t* .... Ps 132:11 3678
also sit upon thy *t* for evermore .... Ps 132:12 3678
for the *t* is established by .... Prov 16:12 3678
A king that sitteth in the *t* of .... Prov 20:8 3678
his *t* is upholden by mercy .... Prov 20:28 3678
his *t* shall be established in .... Prov 25:5 3678
his *t* shall be established for .... Prov 29:14 3678
also the Lord sitting upon a *t* .... Is 6:1 3678
be no end, upon the *t* of David .... Is 9:7 3678
I will exalt my *t* above the stars .... Is 14:13 3678
mercy shall the *t* be established .... Is 16:5 3678
glorious *t* to his father's house .... Is 22:23 3678
there is no *t*, O daughter of the .... Is 47:1 3678
the LORD, The heaven is my *t* .... Is 66:1 3678
they shall set every one his *t* at .... Jer 1:15 3678
call Jerusalem the *t* of the LORD .... Jer 3:17 3678
the kings that sit upon David's *t* .... Jer 13:13 3678
not disgrace the *t* of thy glory .... Jer 14:21 3678
A glorious high *t* from the .... Jer 17:12 3678
sitting upon the *t* of David .... Jer 17:25 3678
that sittest upon the *t* of David .... Jer 22:2 3678
kings sitting upon the *t* of David .... Jer 22:4 3678
sitting upon the *t* of David .... Jer 22:30 3678
that sitteth upon the *t* of David .... Jer 29:16 3678
upon the *t* of the house of Israel .... Jer 33:17 3678
have a son to reign upon his *t* .... Jer 33:21 3678
none to sit upon the *t* of David .... Jer 36:30 3678
will set his *t* upon these stones .... Jer 43:10 3678
And I will set my *t* in Elam .... Jer 49:38 3678
set his *t* above the *t* of the .... Jer 52:32 3678
thy *t* from generation to .... Lam 5:19 3678
heads was the likeness of a *t* .... Eze 1:26 3678
of the *t* was the likeness as the .... Eze 1:26 3678
appearance of the likeness of a *t* .... Eze 10:1 3678
me, Son of man, the place of my *t* .... Eze 43:7 3678
he was deposed from his kingly *t* .... Dan 5:20 3764
his *t* was like the fiery flame, ... Dan 7:9 3764
Nineveh, and he arose from his *t* .... Jonah 3:6 3678
will overthrow the *t* of kingdoms .... Hag 2:22 3678
and shall sit and rule upon his *t* .... Zec 6:13 3678
he shall be a priest upon his *t* .... Zec 6:13 3678
for it is God's *t* .... Mt 5:34 *2362*
shall sit in the *t* of his glory .... Mt 19:28 *2362*
heaven, sweareth by the *t* of God .... Mt 23:22 *2362*
he sit upon the *t* of his glory .... Mt 25:31 *2362*
him the *t* of his father David .... Lk 1:32 *2362*
raise up Christ to sit on his *t* .... Acts 2:30 *2362*
Heaven is my *t*, and earth is my .... Acts 7:49 *2362*
in royal apparel, sat upon his *t* .... Acts 12:21 *968*
But unto the Son he saith, Thy *t* .... Heb 1:8 *2362*
come boldly unto the *t* of grace .... Heb 4:16 *2362*
t of the Majesty in the heavens .... Heb 8:1 *2362*
at the right hand of the *t* of God .... Heb 12:2 *2362*
Spirits which are before his *t* .... Rev 1:4 *2362*
I grant to sit with me in my *t* .... Rev 3:21 *2362*
set down with my Father in his *t* .... Rev 3:21 *2362*
a *t* was set in heaven, and one sat .... Rev 4:2 *2362*
in heaven, and one sat on the *t* .... Rev 4:2 *2362*
was a rainbow round about the *t* .... Rev 4:3 *2362*
And round about the *t* were four .... Rev 4:4 *2362*
out of the *t* proceeded lightnings .... Rev 4:5 *2362*
of fire burning before the *t* .... Rev 4:5 *2362*
before the *t* there was a sea of .... Rev 4:6 *2362*
and in the midst of the *t*, and .... Rev 4:6 *2362*
and round about the *t* .... Rev 4:6 *2362*
thanks to him that sat on the *t* .... Rev 4:9 *2362*
down before him that sat on the *t* .... Rev 4:10 *2362*
and cast their crowns before the *t* .... Rev 4:10 *2362*
on the *t* a book written within .... Rev 5:1 *2362*
and, lo, in the midst of the *t* .... Rev 5:6 *2362*
hand of him that sat upon the *t* .... Rev 5:7 *2362*
of many angels round about the *t* .... Rev 5:11 *2362*
unto him that sitteth upon the *t* .... Rev 5:13 *2362*
face of him that sitteth on the *t* .... Rev 6:16 *2362*
and tongues, stood before the *t* .... Rev 7:9 *2362*
our God which sitteth upon the *t* .... Rev 7:10 *2362*
angels stood round about the *t* .... Rev 7:11 *2362*
fell before the *t* on their faces .... Rev 7:11 *2362*
are they before the *t* of God .... Rev 7:15 *2362*
on the *t* shall dwell among them .... Rev 7:15 *2362*
midst of the *t* shall feed them .... Rev 7:17 *2362*
altar which was before the *t* .... Rev 8:3 *2362*
caught up unto God, and to his *t* .... Rev 12:5 *2362*
it were a new song before the *t* .... Rev 14:3 *2362*
without fault before the *t* of God .... Rev 14:5 *2362*
the temple of heaven, from the *t* .... Rev 16:17 *2362*
worshipped God that sat on the *t* .... Rev 19:4 *2362*
And a voice came out of the *t* .... Rev 19:5 *2362*
And I saw a great white *t*, and him .... Rev 20:11 *2362*
And he that sat upon the *t* said .... Rev 21:5 *2362*
proceeding out of the *t* of God .... Rev 22:1 *2362*
but the *t* of God and of the Lamb .... Rev 22:3 *2362*

THRONES {9}
For there are set *t* of judgment .... Ps 122:5 3678
the *t* of the house of David .... Ps 122:5 3678
t all the kings of the nations .... Is 14:9 3678
sea shall come down from their *t* .... Eze 26:16 3678
beheld till the *t* were cast down .... Dan 7:9 3764
ye also shall sit upon twelve *t* .... Mt 19:28 *2362*
sit on *t* judging the twelve .... Lk 22:30 *2362*
and invisible, whether they be *t* .... Col 1:16 *2362*
And I saw *t*, and they sat upon them .... Rev 20:4 *2362*

THRONG {2}
multitude, lest they should *t* him .... Mk 3:9 *2346*
Master, the multitude *t* thee .... Lk 8:45 *4912*

THRONGED {2}
people followed him, and *t* him .... Mk 5:24 *4918*
But as he went the people *t* him .... Lk 8:42 *4846*

THRONGING {1}
Thou seest the multitude *t* thee .... Mk 5:31 *4918*

THROUGH See APPENDIX.

THROUGHLY {12}
let us make brick, and burn them *t* .... Gen 11:3
O that my grief were *t* weighed .... Job 6:2
Wash me *t* from mine iniquity, and .... Ps 51:2 7235
They shall *t* glean the remnant of .... Jer 6:9
For if ye *t* amend your ways and .... Jer 7:5
if ye *t* execute judgment between .... Jer 7:5
he shall *t* plead their cause, ... Jer 50:34
I *t* washed away thy blood from .... Eze 16:9
he will *t* purge his floor, and .... Mt 3:12 *1245*
he will *t* purge his floor, and .... Lk 3:17 *1245*
but we have been *t* made manifest .. 2Cor 11:6 *1722,3956*
t furnished unto all good works 2Ti 3:17 *1822*

THROUGHOUT See APPENDIX.

THROW {9}
ye shall *t* down their altars .... Judg 2:2 5422
t down the altar of Baal that thy .... Judg 6:25 2040
battered the wall, to *t* it down 2Sa 20:15 5307
And he said, *T* her down 2Kin 9:33 8058
to *t* down, to build, and to plant .... Jer 1:10 2040
to *t* down, and to destroy, and to .... Jer 31:28 2040
they shall *t* down thine eminent .... Eze 16:39 2040
t down all thy strong holds .... Mic 5:11 2040
shall build, but I will *t* down .... Mal 1:4 2040

THROWING {1}
And if he smite him with *t* a stone .... Num 35:17 3027

THROWN {19}
his rider hath he *t* into the sea .... Ex 15:1 7411
his rider hath he *t* into the sea .... Ex 15:21
because he hath *t* down his altar .... Judg 6:32 5422
his head shall be *t* to thee over 2Sa 20:21 7993
t down thine altars, and slain thy 1Kin 19:10 2040
t down thine altars, and slain thy 1Kin 19:14 2040
nor *t* down any more for ever .... Jer 31:40 2040
which are *t* down by the mounts, ... Jer 33:4 5422
are fallen, her walls are *t* down .... Jer 50:15 2040
he hath *t* down in his wrath the .... Lam 2:2 2040
he hath *t* down, and hath not .... Lam 2:17 2040
I will leave thee *t* into the .... Eze 29:5
and the mountains shall be *t* down .... Eze 38:20 2040
and the rocks are *t* down by him .... Nah 1:6 5422
another, that shall not be *t* down .... Mt 24:2 *2647*
another, that shall not be *t* down .... Mk 13:2 *2647*
the devil had *t* him in the midst .... Lk 4:35 *4496*
another, that shall not be *t* down .... Lk 21:6 *2647*
that great city Babylon be *t* down .... Rev 18:21 *906*

THRUST {50}
he shall surely *t* you out hence .... Ex 11:1 1644
because they were *t* out of Egypt .... Ex 12:39 1644
she *t* herself unto the wall, and .... Num 22:25 3905
t both of them through, the man .... Num 25:8 1856
But if he *t* him of hatred, or .... Num 35:20 1920
But if he *t* him suddenly without .... Num 35:22 1920
to *t* thee out of the way which .... Deut 13:5 5080
because he hath sought to *t* thee .... Deut 13:10 5080
t it through his ear unto the .... Deut 15:17 5414
he shall *t* out the enemy from .... Deut 33:27 1644
thigh, and *t* it into his belly .... Judg 3:21 8628
t the fleece together, and wringed .... Judg 6:38 2115
Zebul *t* out Gaal and his brethren, ... Judg 9:41 1644
And his young man *t* him through .... Judg 9:54 1856
they *t* out Jephthah, and said unto .... Judg 11:2 1644
that I may *t* out all your right 1Sa 11:2 5365
sword, and *t* me through therewith 1Sa 31:4 1856
t me through, and abuse me 1Sa 31:4 1856
t his sword in his fellow's side 2Sa 2:16
t them through the heart of 2Sa 18:14 8628
be all of them as thorns *t* away 2Sa 23:6 5074
So Solomon *t* out Abiathar from 1Kin 2:27 1644
Gehazi came near to *t* her away 2Kin 4:27 1920
sword, and *t* me through therewith 1Chr 10:4 1856
they *t* him out from thence 2Chr 26:20 926
Thou hast *t* sore at me that I .... Ps 118:13 1760
that is found shall be *t* through .... Is 13:15 1856
t through with a sword, that go .... Is 14:19 2944
they that are *t* through in her .... Jer 51:4 1856
t thee through with their swords .... Eze 16:40 1333
Because ye have *t* with side .... Eze 34:21 1920
to *t* them out of their possession .... Eze 46:18 3238
Neither shall one *t* another .... Joel 2:8 1766
t him through when he prophesieth .... Zec 13:3 1856
t him out of the city, and led him .... Lk 4:29 *1544*
prayed him that he would *t* out a .... Lk 5:3 *1877*
heaven, shalt be *t* down to hell .... Lk 10:15 *2601*
of God, and you yourselves *t* out .... Lk 13:28 *1544*
t my hand into his side, I will .... Jn 20:25 *906*
thy hand, and *t* it into my side .... Jn 20:27 *906*
his neighbour wrong *t* him away .... Acts 7:27 *683*
but *t* him from them, and in their .... Acts 7:39 *683*
t them into the inner prison, and .... Acts 16:24 *906*
now do they *t* us out privily .... Acts 16:37 *1544*
were possible, to *t* in the ship .... Acts 27:39 *1856*
stoned, or *t* through with a dart .... Heb 12:20 *2700*
cloud, *T* in thy sickle, and reap .... Rev 14:15 *3992*
he that sat on the cloud *t* in his .... Rev 14:16 *906*
T in thy sharp sickle, and gather .... Rev 14:18 *3992*
the angel *t* in his sickle into .... Rev 14:19 *906*

THRUSTETH {1}
God *t* him down, not man .... Job 32:13 5086

THUMB {6}
upon the *t* of their right hand, ... Ex 29:20 931
upon the *t* of his right hand, and .... Lev 8:23 931
upon the *t* of his right hand, and .... Lev 14:14 931
upon the *t* of his right hand, and .... Lev 14:17 931
upon the *t* of his right hand, and .... Lev 14:25 931
upon the *t* of his right hand, and .... Lev 14:28 931

THUMBS {3}
upon the *t* of their right hands, ... Lev 8:24 931
and caught him, and cut off his *t* .... Judg 1:6 931,3027
and ten kings, having their *t* .... Judg 1:7 931,3027

THUMMIM *(thum'-mim)* {5} *A symbolic object in the High Priest's breastplate.*
of judgment the Urim and the *T* .... Ex 28:30 8550
the breastplate the Urim and the *T* .... Lev 8:8 8550
And of Levi he said, Let thy *T* .... Deut 33:8 8550
up a priest with Urim and with *T* .... Ezr 2:63 8550
stood up a priest with Urim and *T* .... Neh 7:65 8550

THUNDER {19}
and the LORD sent *t* and hail, and .... Ex 9:23 6963
the *t* shall cease, neither shall .... Ex 9:29 6963
of heaven shall he *t* upon them 1Sa 2:10 7481
a great *t* on that day upon the 1Sa 7:10 6963
unto the LORD, and he shall send *t* 1Sa 12:17 6963
and the LORD sent *t* and rain that 1Sa 12:18 6963
but the *t* of his power who can .... Job 26:14 7482
a way for the lightning of the *t* .... Job 28:26 6963
or a way for the lightning of *t* .... Job 38:25 6963
hast thou clothed his neck with *t* .... Job 39:19 7483
the *t* of the captains, and the .... Job 39:25 7482
or canst thou *t* with a voice like .... Job 40:9 7481
The voice of thy *t* was in the .... Ps 77:18 7482
thee in the secret place of *t* .... Ps 81:7 7482
voice of thy *t* they hasted away .... Ps 104:7 7482
of the LORD of hosts with *t* .... Is 29:6 7482
which is, The sons of *t* .... Mk 3:17 *1027*
heard, as it were the noise of *t* .... Rev 6:1 *1027*
and as the voice of a great *t* .... Rev 14:2 *1027*

THUNDERBOLTS {1}
hail, and their flocks to hot *t* .... Ps 78:48 7565

THUNDERED {4}
but the LORD *t* with a great 1Sa 7:10 7481
The LORD *t* from heaven, and the 2Sa 22:14 7481
The LORD also *t* in the heavens, ... Ps 18:13 7481
by, and heard it, said that it *t* .... Jn 12:29 *1027,1096*

THUNDERETH {3}
he *t* with the voice of his .... Job 37:4 7481
God *t* marvellously with his voice .... Job 37:5 7481
the God of glory *t* .... Ps 29:3 7481

THUNDERINGS {6}
that there be no more mighty *t* .... Ex 9:28 6963
And all the people saw the *t* .... Ex 20:18 6963
throne proceeded lightnings and *t* .... Rev 4:5 *1027*
and there were voices, and *t* .... Rev 8:5 *1027*
were lightnings, and voices, and *t* .... Rev 11:19 *1027*
and as the voice of mighty *t* .... Rev 19:6 *1027*

THUNDERS {7}
and the *t* and hail ceased, and the .... Ex 9:33 6963
the *t* were ceased, he sinned yet .... Ex 9:34 6963
in the morning, that there were *t* .... Ex 19:16 6963
seven *t* uttered their voices .... Rev 10:3 *1027*
when the seven *t* had uttered .... Rev 10:4 *1027*
things which the seven *t* uttered .... Rev 10:4 *1027*
And there were voices, and *t* .... Rev 16:18 *1027*

THUS See APPENDIX.

THY See APPENDIX.

THYATIRA *(thi-a-ti'-rah)* {4} *A city in Lydia in Asia Minor.*
of purple, of the city of *T* .... Acts 16:14 *2363*
and unto Pergamos, and unto *T* .... Rev 1:11 *2363*
angel of the church in *T* write .... Rev 2:18 *2363*
you I say, and unto the rest in *T* .... Rev 2:24 *2363*

THYINE {1}
all *t* wood, and all manner vessels .... Rev 18:12 *2367*

THYSELF {216}
separate *t*, I pray thee, from me .... Gen 13:9
persons, and take the goods to *t* .... Gen 14:21
and submit *t* under her hands .... Gen 16:9
keep that thou hast unto *t* .... Gen 33:9
exaltest thou *t* against my people .... Ex 9:17
thou refuse to humble *t* before me .... Ex 10:3
Get thee from me, take heed to *t* .... Ex 10:28
why sittest thou *t* alone, and all .... Ex 18:14 859
not able to perform it *t* alone .... Ex 18:18
so shall it be easier for *t* .... Ex 18:22
Thou shalt not bow down *t* to them .... Ex 20:5
present *t* there to me in the top .... Ex 34:2
Take heed to *t*, lest thou make a .... Ex 34:12
and make an atonement for *t* .... Lev 9:7

wife, to defile *t* with her ... Lev 18:20
any beast to defile *t* therewith ... Lev 18:23
shalt love thy neighbour as *t* ... Lev 19:18
you, and thou shalt love him as *t* ... Lev 19:34
that thou bear it not *t* alone ... Num 11:17
except thou make *t* altogether a ... Num 16:13
Only take heed to *t*, and keep thy ... Deut 4:9
shalt not bow down *t* unto them ... Deut 5:9
greater and mightier than *t* ... Deut 9:1
Take heed to *t* that thou offer ... Deut 12:13
Take heed to *t* that thou forsake ... Deut 12:19
Take heed to *t* that thou be not ... Deut 12:30
thereof, shalt thou take unto *t* ... Deut 20:14
go astray, and hide *t* from them ... Deut 22:1
thou mayest not hide *t* ... Deut 22:3
by the way, and hide *t* from them ... Deut 22:4
wherewith thou coverest *t* ... Deut 22:12
be, when thou wilt ease *t* abroad ... Deut 23:13
shalt not anoint *t* with the oil ... Deut 28:40
cut down for *t* there in the land ... Josh 17:15
Wash *t* therefore, and anoint thee, ... Ruth 3:3
but make not *t* known unto the man ... Ruth 3:3
redeem thou my right to *t* ... Ruth 4:6
take heed to *t* until the morning, ... 1Sa 19:2
in a secret place, and hide *t* ... 1Sa 19:2
be in me iniquity, slay me *t* ... 1Sa 20:8 859
t when the business was in hand ... 1Sa 20:19
from avenging *t* with thine own ... 1Sa 25:26
that then thou shalt bestir *t* ... 2Sa 5:24
to *t* thy people Israel to be a ... 2Sa 7:24
down on thy bed, and make *t* sick ... 2Sa 13:5
feign *t* to be a mourner, and put ... 2Sa 14:2
apparel, and anoint not *t* with oil ... 2Sa 14:2
thou *t* wouldest have set *t* ... 2Sa 18:13 859
wouldest have set *t* against me ... 2Sa 18:13
thou wilt shew *t* merciful ... 2Sa 22:26
man thou wilt shew *t* upright ... 2Sa 22:26
the pure thou wilt shew *t* pure ... 2Sa 22:27
thou wilt shew *t* unsavoury ... 2Sa 22:27
strong therefore, and shew *t* a man ... 1Kin 2:2
and whithersoever thou turnest *t* ... 1Kin 2:3
and hast not asked for *t* long life ... 1Kin 3:11
neither hast asked riches for *t* ... 1Kin 3:11
but hast asked for *t* ... 1Kin 3:11
Come home with me, and refresh *t* ... 1Kin 13:7
Arise, I pray thee, and disguise *t* ... 1Kin 14:2
why feignest thou *t* to be another ... 1Kin 14:6
hide *t* by the brook Cherith, that ... 1Kin 17:3
saying, Go, shew *t* unto Ahab ... 1Kin 18:1
said unto him, Go, strengthen *t* ... 1Kin 20:22
t hast decided it ... 1Kin 20:40
because thou hast sold *t* to work ... 1Kin 21:20
into an inner chamber to hide *t* ... 1Kin 22:25
hast humbled *t* before the LORD ... 2Kin 22:19
Now therefore advise *t* what word ... 1Chr 21:12
asked wisdom and knowledge for *t* ... 2Chr 1:11
into an inner chamber to hide *t* ... 2Chr 18:24
thou hast joined *t* with Ahaziah ... 2Chr 20:37
house, which were better than *t* ... 2Chr 21:13
and thou didst humble *t* before God ... 2Chr 34:27
thereof, and humbledst *t* before me ... 2Chr 34:27
Think not with *t* that thou shalt ... Est 4:13 5315
prepare *t* to the search of their ... Job 8:8
thou shewest *t* marvellous upon me ... Job 10:16
and dost thou restrain wisdom to *t* ... Job 15:8 413
Acquaint now *t* with him, and be at ... Job 22:21
hand thou opposest *t* against me ... Job 30:21
Deck *t* now with majesty and ... Job 40:10
array *t* with glory and beauty ... Job 40:10
lift up *t* because of the rage of ... Ps 7:6
why hidest thou *t* in times of ... Ps 10:1
thou wilt shew *t* merciful ... Ps 18:25
man thou wilt shew *t* upright ... Ps 18:25
the pure thou wilt shew *t* pure ... Ps 18:26
froward thou wilt shew *t* froward ... Ps 18:26
Stir up *t*, and awake to my ... Ps 35:23
Fret not *t* because of evildoers, ... Ps 37:1
Delight *t* also in the LORD ... Ps 37:4
fret not *t* because of him who ... Ps 37:7
fret not *t* in any wise to do evil ... Ps 37:8
thee, when thou doest well to *t* ... Ps 49:18
I was altogether such an one as *t* ... Ps 50:21
Why boastest thou *t* in mischief ... Ps 52:1
hide not *t* from my supplication ... Ps 55:1
O turn *t* to us again ... Ps 60:1
that thou madest strong for *t* ... Ps 80:15
man whom thou madest strong for *t* ... Ps 80:17
thou hast turned *t* from the ... Ps 85:3
wilt thou hide *t* for ever ... Ps 89:46
whom vengeance belongeth, shew *t* ... Ps 94:1
Lift up *t*, thou judge of the ... Ps 94:2
Who coverest *t* with light as with ... Ps 104:2
Do this now, my son, and deliver *t* ... Prov 6:3
go, humble *t*, and make sure thy ... Prov 6:3
Deliver *t* as a roe from the hand ... Prov 6:5
be wise, thou shalt be wise for *t* ... Prov 9:12
Fret not *t* because of evil men, ... Prov 24:19
and make it fit for *t* in the field ... Prov 24:27
Put not forth *t* in the presence ... Prov 25:6
Boast not *t* of to morrow ... Prov 27:1
done foolishly in lifting up *t* ... Prov 30:32
neither make *t* over wise ... Eccl 7:16
why shouldest thou destroy *t* ... Eccl 7:16
t likewise hast cursed others ... Eccl 7:22 859
hide *t* as it were for a little ... Is 26:20
at the lifting up of *t* the ... Is 33:3
thou art a God that hidest *t* ... Is 45:15
Shake *t* from the dust ... Is 52:2

loose *t* from the bands of thy ... Is 52:2
discovered *t* to another than me ... Is 57:8
didst debase *t* even unto hell ... Is 57:9
that thou hide not *t* from thine ... Is 58:7
shalt thou delight *t* in the LORD ... Is 58:14
to make *t* a glorious name ... Is 63:14
thou refrain *t* for these things ... Is 64:12
Which say, Stand by *t*, come not ... Is 65:5
thou not procured this unto *t* ... Jer 2:17
thou clothest *t* with crimson ... Jer 4:30
in vain shalt thou make *t* fair ... Jer 4:30
sackcloth, and wallow *t* in ashes ... Jer 6:26
And thou, even *t*, shalt ... Jer 17:4
I will make thee a terror to *t* ... Jer 20:4
because thou closest *t* in cedar ... Jer 22:15
buy it for *t* ... Jer 32:8
seekest thou great things for *t* ... Jer 45:5
furnish *t* to go into captivity ... Jer 46:19
how long wilt thou cut *t* ... Jer 47:5
put up *t* into thy scabbard, rest, ... Jer 47:6
give *t* no rest ... Lam 2:18
Thou hast covered *t* with a cloud ... Lam 3:44
be drunken, and shalt make *t* naked ... Lam 4:21
shut *t* within thine house ... Eze 3:24
madest to *t* images of men, and ... Eze 16:17
hast defiled *t* in thine idols ... Eze 22:4
in *t* in the sight of the heathen ... Eze 22:16
for whom thou didst wash *t* ... Eze 23:40
deckedst *t* with ornaments, ... Eze 23:40
thou hast lifted up *t* in height ... Eze 31:10
thou prepared, and prepare for *t* ... Eze 38:7
the king, Let thy gifts be to *t* ... Dan 5:17
But hast lifted up *t* against the ... Dan 5:23
to chasten *t* before thy God, thy ... Dan 10:12
O Israel, thou hast destroyed *t* ... Hos 13:9
Though thou exalt *t* as the eagle ... Obad 4
of Aphrah roll *t* in the dust ... Mic 1:10
Now gather *t* in troops, O ... Mic 5:1
make *t* many as the cankerworm, ... Nah 3:15
make *t* many as the locusts ... Nah 3:15
Deliver *t*, O Zion, that dwellest ... Zec 2:7
be the Son of God, cast *t* down ... Mt 4:6 *4572*
time, Thou shalt not forswear *t* ... Mt 5:33
shew *t* to the priest, and offer ... Mt 8:4 *4572*
shalt love thy neighbour as *t* ... Mt 19:19 *4572*
shalt love thy neighbour as *t* ... Mt 22:39 *4572*
buildest it in three days, save *t* ... Mt 27:40 *4572*
shew *t* to the priest, and offer ... Mk 1:44 *4572*
shalt love thy neighbour as *t* ... Mk 12:31 *4572*
Save *t*, and come down from the ... Mk 15:30 *4572*
of God, cast *t* down from hence ... Lk 4:9 *4572*
this proverb, Physician, heal *t* ... Lk 4:23 *4572*
shew *t* to the priest, and offer ... Lk 5:14 *4572*
when thou *t* beholdest not the ... Lk 6:42 *846*
unto him, Lord, trouble not *t* ... Lk 7:6
and thy neighbour as *t* ... Lk 10:27 *4572*
wherewith I may sup, and gird *t* ... Lk 17:8
be the king of the Jews, save *t* ... Lk 23:37 *4572*
saying, If thou be Christ, save *t* ... Lk 23:39 *4572*
What sayest thou of *t* ... Jn 1:22 *4572*
these things, shew *t* to the world ... Jn 7:4 *4572*
him, Thou bearest record of *t* ... Jn 8:13 *4572*
whom makest thou *t* ... Jn 8:53 *4572*
thou, being a man, makest *t* God ... Jn 10:33 *4572*
that thou wilt manifest *t* unto us ... Jn 14:22 *4572*
him, Sayest thou this thing of *t* ... Jn 18:34 *1438*
thou wast young, thou girdedst *t* ... Jn 21:18 *4572*
near, and join *t* to this chariot ... Acts 8:29
the angel said unto him, Gird *t* ... Acts 12:8
loud voice, saying, Do *t* no harm ... Acts 16:28 *4572*
purify *t* with them, and be at ... Acts 21:24
but that thou *t* also walkest ... Acts 21:24 *846*
by examining of whom *t* mayest ... Acts 24:8 *846*
Thou art permitted to speak for *t* ... Acts 26:1 *4572*
voice, Paul, thou art beside *t* ... Acts 26:24
another, thou condemnest *t* ... Rom 2:1 *4572*
heart treasurest up unto *t* wrath ... Rom 2:5 *4572*
art confident that thou *t* art a ... Rom 2:19 *4572*
another, teachest thou not *t* ... Rom 2:21 *4572*
shalt love thy neighbour as *t* ... Rom 13:9 *1438*
have it to *t* before God ... Rom 14:22 *4572*
shalt love thy neighbour as *t* ... Gal 5:14 *1438*
considering *t*, lest thou also be ... Gal 6:1 *4572*
to behave *t* in the house of God ... 1Ti 3:15
exercise *t* rather unto godliness ... 1Ti 4:7 *4572*
give *t* wholly to them ... 1Ti 4:15
Take heed unto *t*, and unto the ... 1Ti 4:16 *4572*
doing this thou shalt both save *t* ... 1Ti 4:16 *4572*
keep *t* pure ... 1Ti 5:22 *4572*
from such withdraw *t* ... 1Ti 6:5
Study to shew *t* approved unto God ... 2Ti 2:15 *4572*
In all things shewing *t* a pattern ... Titus 2:7 *4572*
shalt love thy neighbour as *t* ... Jas 2:8 *4572*

TIARAS See HOODS.

TIBERIAS *(ti-be'-re-as)* {3} *A city on the Sea of Galilee.*
of Galilee, which is the sea of *T* ... Jn 6:1 *5085*
there came other boats from *T* ... Jn 6:23 *5085*
to the disciples at the sea of *T* ... Jn 21:1 *5085*

TIBERIUS *(ti-be'-re-us)* {1} See CAESAR. *A Roman emperor.*
year of the reign of *T* Caesar ... Lk 3:1 *5086*

TIBHATH *(tib'-hath)* {1} *A city in Aram Zobah.*
Likewise from *T*, and from Chun, ... 1Chr 18:8 2880

TIBNI *(tib'-ni)* {3} *Son of Ginath.*
followed *T* the son of Ginath ... 1Kin 16:21 8402
that followed *T* the son of Ginath ... 1Kin 16:22 8402
so *T* died, and Omri reigned ... 1Kin 16:22 8402

TIDAL *(ti'-dal)* {2} *A king of Goyim.*
of Elam, and *T* king of nations ... Gen 14:1 8413
with *T* king of nations, and ... Gen 14:9 8413

TIDINGS {46}
when Laban heard the *t* of Jacob ... Gen 29:13 8088
the people heard these evil *t* ... Ex 33:4 1697
when she heard the *t* that the ark ... 1Sa 4:19 8052
told the *t* in the ears of the ... 1Sa 11:4 1697
they told him the *t* of the men of ... 1Sa 11:5 1697
upon Saul when he heard those *t* ... 1Sa 11:6 1697
woman alive, to bring *t* to Gath ... 1Sa 27:11
years old when the *t* came of Saul ... 2Sa 4:4 8052
thinking to have brought good *t* ... 2Sa 4:10 1319
have given him a reward for his *t* ... 2Sa 4:10 1309
that *t* came to David, saying, ... 2Sa 13:30 8052
me now run, and bear the king *t* ... 2Sa 18:19 1319
Thou shalt not bear *t* this day ... 2Sa 18:20 1309
but thou shalt bear *t* another day ... 2Sa 18:20 1319
but this day thou shalt bear no *t* ... 2Sa 18:20 1319
seeing that thou hast no *t* ready ... 2Sa 18:22 1309
be alone, there is *t* in his mouth ... 2Sa 18:25 1309
the king said, He also bringeth *t* ... 2Sa 18:26 1319
a good man, and cometh with good *t* ... 2Sa 18:27 1309
and Cushi said, *T*, my lord the ... 2Sa 18:31 1319
a valiant man, and bringest good *t* ... 1Kin 1:42 1319
Then *t* came to Joab ... 1Kin 2:28 8052
I am sent to thee with heavy *t* ... 1Kin 14:6
this day is a day of good *t* ... 2Kin 7:9 1309
to carry *t* unto their idols, and ... 1Chr 10:9 1319
He shall not be afraid of evil *t* ... Ps 112:7 8052
O Zion, that bringest good *t* ... Is 40:9 1319
O Jerusalem, that bringest good *t* ... Is 40:9 1319
one that bringeth good *t* ... Is 41:27 1319
feet of him that bringeth good *t* ... Is 52:7 1319
that bringeth good *t* of good ... Is 52:7 1319
me to preach good *t* unto the meek ... Is 61:1 1319
man who brought *t* to my father ... Jer 20:15 1319
Jerusalem heard *t* of them ... Jer 37:5 8088
for they have heard evil *t* ... Jer 49:23 8052
that thou shalt answer, For the *t* ... Eze 21:7 8052
But *t* out of the east and out of ... Dan 11:44 8052
feet of him that bringeth good *t* ... Nah 1:15 1319
and to shew thee these glad *t* ... Lk 1:19 *2097*
I bring you good *t* of great joy ... Lk 2:10 *2097*
shewing the glad *t* of the kingdom ... Lk 8:1 *2097*
Then *t* of these things came unto ... Acts 11:22 *3056*
And we declare unto you glad *t* ... Acts 13:32 *2097*
t came unto the chief captain of ... Acts 21:31 *5334*
bring glad *t* of good things ... Rom 10:15 *2097*
brought us good *t* of your faith ... 1Th 3:6 *2097*

TIE {2}
t the kine to the cart, and bring ... 1Sa 6:7 631
heart, and *t* them about thy neck ... Prov 6:21 6029

TIED {9}
they *t* unto it a lace of blue, to ... Ex 39:31 5414
t them to the cart, and shut up ... 1Sa 6:10 631
voice of man, but horses *t* ... 2Kin 7:10 631
man, but horses *t*, and asses *t* ... 2Kin 7:10 631
ye shall find an ass *t*, and a colt ... Mt 21:2 *1210*
into it, ye shall find a colt *t* ... Mk 11:2 *1210*
found the colt *t* by the door ... Mk 11:4 *1210*
entering ye shall find a colt *t* ... Lk 19:30 *1210*

TIGLATH-PILESER *(tig'-lath-pi-le'-zur)* {3} See TILGATH-PILNESER. *An Assyrian king.*
of Israel came *T* king of Assyria ... 2Kin 15:29 8407
messengers to *T* king of Assyria ... 2Kin 16:7 8407
to meet *T* king of Assyria ... 2Kin 16:10 8407

TIGRIS See HIDDEKEL.

TIKVAH *(tik'-vah)* {2} See TIKVATH.
1. Father-in-law of Huldah.
the wife of Shallum the son of *T* ... 2Kin 22:14 8616
2. Father of Jahaziah.
Jahaziah the son of *T* were ... Ezr 10:15 8616

TIKVATH *(tik'-vath)* {1} See TIKVAH. *Same as Tikvah 1.*
the wife of Shallum the son of *T* ... 2Chr 34:22 8616

TIL {1}
t the Assyrian founded it for ... Is 23:13

TILE {1}
also, son of man, take thee a *t* ... Eze 4:1 3843

TILGATH-PILNESER *(til'-gath-pil-ne'-zur)* {3} See TIGLATH-PILESER. *Same as Tiglath-pileser.*
whom *T* king of Assyria carried ... 1Chr 5:6 8407
the spirit of *T* king of Assyria, ... 1Chr 5:26 8407
T king of Assyria came unto him, ... 2Chr 28:20 8407

TILING {1}
let him down through the *t* with ... Lk 5:19 *2766*

TILL See APPENDIX.

TILLAGE {3}
did the work of the field for *t* ... 1Chr 27:26 5656
tithes in all the cities of our *t* ... Neh 10:37 5656
Much food is in the *t* of the poor ... Prov 13:23 5215

TILLED {2}
turn unto you, and ye shall be *t* ... Eze 36:9 5647
And the desolate land shall be *t* ... Eze 36:34 5647

TILLER {1}
but Cain was a *t* of the ground ... Gen 4:2 5647

TILLEST {1}
When thou *t* the ground, it shall ... Gen 4:12 5647

TILLETH {2}
He that *t* his land shall be ... Prov 12:11 5647
He that *t* his land shall have ... Prov 28:19 5647

TILON *(ti'-lon)* {1} *A descendant of Judah.*
and Rinnah, Ben-hanan, and *T* ... 1Chr 4:20 8436

TIMAEUS *(ti-me'-us)* {1} See BARTIMAEUS. *Father of Bartimaeus.*
blind Bartimaeus, the son of *T* ... Mk 10:46 *5090*

TIMBER {26}
to set them, and in carving of *t* ... Ex 31:5 6086
the *t* thereof, and all the morter ... Lev 14:45 6086
to hew *t* like unto the Sidonians ... 1Kin 5:6 6086
thy desire concerning *t* of cedar ... 1Kin 5:8 6086
of cedar, and concerning *t* of fir ... 1Kin 5:8 6086
so they prepared *t* and stones to ... 1Kin 5:18 6086
on the house with *t* of cedar ... 1Kin 6:10 6086
the *t* thereof, wherewith Baasha ... 1Kin 15:22 6086
and hewers of stone, and to buy *t* ... 2Kin 12:12 6086
builders, and masons, and to buy *t* ... 2Kin 22:6 6086
t of cedars, with masons and ... 1Chr 14:1 6086
t also and stone have I prepared ... 1Chr 22:14 6086
hewers and workers of stone and *t* ... 1Chr 22:15 6086
can skill to cut *t* in Lebanon ... 2Chr 2:8 6086
Even to prepare me *t* in abundance ... 2Chr 2:9 6086
servants, the hewers that cut *t* ... 2Chr 2:10 6086
brass, in iron, in stone, and in *t* ... 2Chr 2:14 6086
the *t* thereof, wherewith Baasha ... 2Chr 16:6 6086
t for couplings, and to floor the ... 2Chr 34:11 6086
t is laid in the walls, and this ... Ezr 5:8 636
great stones, and a row of new *t* ... Ezr 6:4 636
let *t* be pulled down from his ... Ezr 6:11 636
that he may give me *t* to make ... Neh 2:8 6086
shall lay thy stones and thy *t* ... Eze 26:12 6086
beam out of the *t* shall answer it ... Hab 2:11 6086
consume it with the *t* thereof ... Zec 5:4 6086

TIMBREL {5}
of Aaron, took a *t* in her hand ... Ex 15:20 8596
They take the *t* and harp, and ... Job 21:12 8596
a psalm, and bring hither the *t* ... Ps 81:2 8596
sing praises unto him with the *t* ... Ps 149:3 8596
Praise him with the *t* and dance ... Ps 150:4 8596

TIMBRELS {5}
women went out after her with *t* ... Ex 15:20 8596
came out to meet him with *t* ... Judg 11:34 8596
harps, and on psalteries, and on *t* ... 2Sa 6:5 8596
and with psalteries, and with *t* ... 1Chr 13:8 8596
were the damsels playing with *t* ... Ps 68:25 8608

TIME {617}
in process of *t* it came to pass, ... Gen 4:3 3117
at this set *t* in the next year ... Gen 17:21 4150
thee according to the *t* of life ... Gen 18:10 6256
At the *t* appointed I will return ... Gen 18:14 4150
thee, according to the *t* of life ... Gen 18:14 6256
at the set *t* of which God had ... Gen 21:2 4150
And it came to pass at that *t* ... Gen 21:22 6256
out of heaven the second *t* ... Gen 22:15
of water at the *t* of the evening ... Gen 24:11 6256
even the *t* that women go out to ... Gen 24:11 6256
when he had been there a long *t* ... Gen 26:8 3117
neither is it *t* that the cattle ... Gen 29:7 6256
Now this *t* will my husband be ... Gen 29:34 6471
answer for me in *t* to come ... Gen 30:33 3117
it came to pass at the *t* that the ... Gen 31:10 6256
And it came to pass at that *t* ... Gen 38:1 6256
in process of *t* the daughter of ... Gen 38:12 3117
to pass in the *t* of her travail ... Gen 38:27 6256
it came to pass from the *t* that ... Gen 39:5
And it came to pass about this *t* ... Gen 39:11 3117
he slept and dreamed the second *t* ... Gen 41:5
now we had returned this second *t* ... Gen 43:10 6471
at the first *t* are we brought in ... Gen 43:18 8462
down at the first *t* to buy food ... Gen 43:20 8462
the *t* drew nigh that Israel must ... Gen 47:29 3117
it came to pass in process of *t* ... Ex 2:23 3117
hardened his heart at this *t* also ... Ex 8:32 6471
And the LORD appointed a set *t* ... Ex 9:5 4150
For I will at this *t* send all my ... Ex 9:14 6471
to morrow about this *t* I will ... Ex 9:18 6256
unto them, I have sinned this *t* ... Ex 9:27 6471
thy son asketh thee in *t* to come ... Ex 13:14 4279
shall pay for the loss of his *t* ... Ex 21:19 7674
to push with his horn in *t* past ... Ex 21:29 8543
ox hath used to push in *t* past ... Ex 21:36 8543
in the *t* appointed of the month ... Ex 23:15 4150
in the *t* of the month Abib ... Ex 34:18 4150
in earing *t* and in harvest thou ... Ex 34:21
it shall be washed the second *t* ... Lev 13:58
out of the *t* of her separation ... Lev 15:25 6256
beyond the *t* of her separation ... Lev 15:25 6256
beside the other in her life *t* ... Lev 18:18
may the Levites redeem at any *t* ... Lev 25:32
according to the *t* of an hired ... Lev 25:50 3117
shall reach unto the sowing *t* ... Lev 26:5
ye blow an alarm the second *t* ... Num 10:6
Now the *t* was the *t* of the ... Num 13:20 3117
we have dwelt in Egypt a long *t* ... Num 20:15 3117
king of the Moabites at that *t* ... Num 22:4 6256
according to this *t* it shall be ... Num 23:23 6256
what *t* the fire devoured two ... Num 26:10
anger was kindled the same *t* ... Num 32:10 3117
t come without the border of the ... Num 35:26
And I spake unto you at that *t* ... Deut 1:9 6256
I charged your judges at that *t* ... Deut 1:16 6256
I commanded you at that *t* all the ... Deut 1:18 6256
giants dwelt therein in old *t* ... Deut 2:20 6440
we took all his cities at that *t* ... Deut 2:34 6256
we took all his cities at that *t* ... Deut 3:4 6256
we took at that *t* out of the hand ... Deut 3:8 6256
which we possessed at that *t* ... Deut 3:12 6256
And I commanded you at that *t* ... Deut 3:18 6256
And I commanded Joshua at that *t* ... Deut 3:21 6256
And I besought the LORD at that *t* ... Deut 3:23 6256
at that *t* to teach you statutes ... Deut 4:14 6256
between the LORD and you at that *t* ... Deut 5:5 6256
thy son asketh thee in *t* to come ... Deut 6:20 4279
hearkened unto me at that *t* also ... Deut 9:19 6471
prayed for Aaron also the same *t* ... Deut 9:20 6256
At that *t* the LORD said unto me, ... Deut 10:1 6256
At that *t* the LORD separated the ... Deut 10:8 6256
mount, according to the first *t* ... Deut 10:10 3117
hearkened unto me at that *t* also ... Deut 10:10 6471
the seven weeks from such *t* as ... Deut 16:9
whom he hated not in *t* past ... Deut 19:4 8543
as he hated him not in *t* past ... Deut 19:6 8543
which they of old *t* have set in ... Deut 19:14 7223
shalt besiege a city a long *t* ... Deut 20:19 3117
their foot shall slide in due *t* ... Deut 32:35 6256
the *t* of shutting of the gate ... Josh 2:5
his banks all the *t* of harvest ... Josh 3:15 3117
ask their fathers in *t* to come ... Josh 4:6 4279
ask their fathers in *t* to come ... Josh 4:21 4279
At that *t* the LORD said unto ... Josh 5:2 6256
children of Israel the second *t* ... Josh 5:2
it came to pass at the seventh *t* ... Josh 6:16 6471
And Joshua adjured them at that *t* ... Josh 6:26 6256
at a *t* appointed, before the ... Josh 8:14 4150
it came to pass at the *t* of the ... Josh 10:27 6256
land did Joshua take at one *t* ... Josh 10:42 6471
for to morrow about this *t* will I ... Josh 11:6 6256
And Joshua at that *t* turned back ... Josh 11:10 6256
war a long *t* with all those kings ... Josh 11:18 3117
at that *t* came Joshua, and cut off ... Josh 11:21 6256
In *t* to come your children might ... Josh 22:24 4279
say to our children in *t* to come ... Josh 22:27 4279
to our generations in *t* to come ... Josh 22:28 4279
it came to pass a long *t* after ... Josh 23:1 3117
other side of the flood in old *t* ... Josh 24:2 5769
at that *t* about ten thousand men ... Judg 3:29 6256
she judged Israel at that *t* ... Judg 4:4 6256
The trees went forth on a *t* to ... Judg 9:8
you in the *t* of your tribulation ... Judg 10:14 6256
it came to pass in process of *t* ... Judg 11:4 3117
ye not recover them within that *t* ... Judg 11:26 6256
there fell at that *t* of the ... Judg 12:6 6256
nor would as at this *t* have told ... Judg 13:23 6256
for at that *t* the Philistines had ... Judg 14:4 6256
after a *t* he returned to take her ... Judg 14:8 3117
in the *t* of wheat harvest, that ... Judg 15:1 3117
all the *t* that the house of God ... Judg 18:31 3117
that *t* out of the cities twenty ... Judg 20:15 3117
And Benjamin came again at that *t* ... Judg 21:14 6256
did not give unto them at this *t* ... Judg 21:22 6256
Israel departed thence at that *t* ... Judg 21:24 6256
this was the manner in former *t* ... Ruth 4:7 6440
when the *t* was that Elkanah ... 1Sa 1:4 3117
when the *t* was come about after ... 1Sa 1:20 3117
And it came to pass at that *t* ... 1Sa 3:2 3117
called Samuel again the third *t* ... 1Sa 3:8
about the *t* of her death the ... 1Sa 4:20 6256
that the *t* was long ... 1Sa 7:2 3117
for about this *t* ye shall find ... 1Sa 9:13 3117
To morrow about this *t* I will ... 1Sa 9:16 6256
for unto this *t* hath it been kept ... 1Sa 9:24 4150
by that *t* the sun be hot, ye ... 1Sa 11:9
according to the set *t* that ... 1Sa 13:8 4150
t with the children of Israel ... 1Sa 14:18 3117
the Philistines before that *t* ... 1Sa 14:21 8032
the *t* when Merab Saul's daughter ... 1Sa 18:19 6256
sent messengers again the third *t* ... 1Sa 19:21
my father about to morrow any *t* ... 1Sa 20:12 6256
at the *t* appointed with David ... 1Sa 20:35 4150
I will not smite him the second *t* ... 1Sa 26:8
the *t* that David dwelt in the ... 1Sa 27:7 3117
the *t* that David was king in ... 2Sa 2:11 3117
Also in *t* past, when Saul was ... 2Sa 5:2 865,8032
dwelt in any house since the *t* ... 2Sa 7:6 3117
as since the *t* that I commanded ... 2Sa 7:11 3117
at the *t* when kings go forth to ... 2Sa 11:1 6256
had a long *t* mourned for the dead ... 2Sa 14:2 3117
when he sent again the second *t* ... 2Sa 14:29
hath given is not good at this *t* ... 2Sa 17:7 6471
set *t* which he had appointed him ... 2Sa 20:5 4150
They were wont to speak in old *t* ... 2Sa 20:18 7223
hundred, whom he slew at one *t* ... 2Sa 23:8 6471
t unto the cave of Adullam ... 2Sa 23:13
the midst of a pit in *t* of snow ... 2Sa 23:20 3117
morning even to the *t* appointed ... 2Sa 24:15 6256
displeased him at any *t* in saying ... 1Kin 1:6 3117
not at this *t* put thee to death ... 1Kin 2:26 3117
at that *t* Solomon held a feast, ... 1Kin 8:65 6256
appeared to Solomon the second *t* ... 1Kin 9:2
it came to pass at that *t* when ... 1Kin 11:29 6256
the *t* that Solomon reigned in ... 1Kin 11:42 3117
At that *t* Abijah the son of ... 1Kin 14:1 6256
Nevertheless in the *t* of his old ... 1Kin 15:23 6256
they prophesied until the *t* of ... 1Kin 18:29
And he said, Do it the second *t* ... 1Kin 18:34
And they did it the second *t* ... 1Kin 18:34
And he said, Do it the third *t* ... 1Kin 18:34
And they did it the third *t* ... 1Kin 18:34
it came to pass at the *t* of the ... 1Kin 18:36
it came to pass at the seventh *t* ... 1Kin 18:44
of them by to morrow about this *t* ... 1Kin 19:2 6256
the LORD came again the second *t* ... 1Kin 19:7
unto thee to morrow about this *t* ... 1Kin 20:6 6256
went out of Samaria the same *t* ... 2Kin 3:6 3117
according to the *t* of life ... 2Kin 4:16 6256
her, according to the *t* of life ... 2Kin 4:17 6256
Is it a *t* to receive money, and to ... 2Kin 5:26 6256
To morrow about this *t* shall a ... 2Kin 7:1 6256
this *t* in the gate of Samaria ... 2Kin 7:18 6256
Libnah revolted at the same *t* ... 2Kin 8:22 6256
a letter the second *t* to them ... 2Kin 10:6
me to Jezreel by to morrow this *t* ... 2Kin 10:6 6256
the *t* that Jehu reigned over ... 2Kin 10:36 3117
At that *t* Rezin king of Syria ... 2Kin 16:6 6256
At that *t* did Hezekiah cut off ... 2Kin 18:16 6256
At that *t* Berodach-baladan, the ... 2Kin 20:12 6256
At that *t* the servants of ... 2Kin 24:10 6256
was the ruler over them in *t* past ... 1Chr 9:20 6440
days from *t* to *t* with them ... 1Chr 9:25 6256
And moreover in *t* past, even when ... 1Chr 11:2 8543
hundred slain by him at one *t* ... 1Chr 11:11 6471
For at that *t* day by day there ... 1Chr 12:22 6256
since the *t* that I commanded ... 1Chr 17:10 3117
at the *t* that kings go out to ... 1Chr 20:1 6256
at which *t* Sibbechai the ... 1Chr 20:4 227
At that *t* when David saw that the ... 1Chr 21:28 6256
son of David king the second *t* ... 1Chr 29:22
the *t* that he reigned over Israel ... 1Chr 29:27 3117
Also at the same *t* Solomon kept ... 2Chr 7:8 6256
were brought under at that *t* ... 2Chr 13:18 6256
offered unto the LORD the same *t* ... 2Chr 15:11 3117
at that *t* Hanani the seer came to ... 2Chr 16:7 6256
some of the people the same *t* ... 2Chr 16:10 6256
about the *t* of the sun going down ... 2Chr 18:34 6256
The same *t* also did Libnah revolt ... 2Chr 21:10 6256
to pass, that in process of *t* ... 2Chr 21:19 3117
that at what *t* the chest was ... 2Chr 24:11 6256
Now after the *t* that Amaziah did ... 2Chr 25:27 6256
At that *t* did king Ahaz send unto ... 2Chr 28:16 6256
in the *t* of his distress did he ... 2Chr 28:22 6256
they could not keep it at that *t* ... 2Chr 30:3 6256
t in such sort as it was written ... 2Chr 30:5
for since the *t* of Solomon the ... 2Chr 30:26 3117
kept the passover at that *t* ... 2Chr 35:17 6256
side the river, and at such a *t* ... Ezr 4:10 3706
side the river, and at such a *t* ... Ezr 4:11 3706
sedition within the same of old *t* ... Ezr 4:15 3118
the river, Peace, and at such a *t* ... Ezr 4:17 3706
t hath made insurrection against ... Ezr 4:19 3118
At the same *t* came to them Tatnai ... Ezr 5:3 2166
since that *t* even until now hath ... Ezr 5:16 116
perfect peace, and at such a *t* ... Ezr 7:12 3706
the weight was written at that *t* ... Ezr 8:34 6256
it is a *t* of much rain, and we are ... Ezr 10:13 6256
and I set him a *t* ... Neh 2:6 2165
it came to pass from that *t* forth ... Neh 4:16 3117
Likewise at the same *t* said I ... Neh 4:22 6256
Moreover from the *t* that I was ... Neh 5:14 3117
(though at that *t* I had not set ... Neh 6:1 6256
me in like manner the fifth *t* ... Neh 6:5 6471
in the *t* of their trouble, when ... Neh 9:27 6256
since the *t* of the kings of ... Neh 9:32 3117
at that *t* were some appointed ... Neh 12:44 3117
But in all this *t* was not I at ... Neh 13:6
From that *t* forth came they no ... Neh 13:21 6256
gathered together the second *t* ... Est 2:19
holdest thy peace at this *t* ... Est 4:14 6256
the kingdom for such a *t* as this ... Est 4:14 6256
at that *t* in the third month ... Est 8:9 6256
to their appointed *t* every year ... Est 9:27 2165
What *t* they wax warm, they vanish ... Job 6:17 6256
an appointed *t* to man upon earth ... Job 7:1 6635
who shall set me a *t* to plead ... Job 9:19
thou wouldest appoint me a set *t* ... Job 14:13
of my appointed *t* will I wait ... Job 14:14 6635
be accomplished before his *t* ... Job 15:32 3117
Which were cut down out of *t* ... Job 22:16 6256
wilderness in former *t* desolate ... Job 30:3 570
reserved against the *t* of trouble ... Job 38:23 6256
Knowest thou the *t* when the wild ... Job 39:1 6256
or knowest thou the *t* when they ... Job 39:2 6256
What *t* she lifteth up herself on ... Job 39:18 6256
than in the *t* that their corn ... Ps 4:7 6256
oven in the *t* of thine anger ... Ps 21:9 6256
For in the *t* of trouble he shall ... Ps 27:5 3117
in a *t* when thou mayest be found ... Ps 32:6 6256
not be ashamed in the evil *t* ... Ps 37:19 6256
strength in the *t* of trouble ... Ps 37:39 6256
will deliver him in *t* of trouble ... Ps 41:1 3117
What *t* I am afraid, I will trust ... Ps 56:3 3117
thee, O LORD, in an acceptable *t* ... Ps 69:13 6256
me not off in the *t* of old age ... Ps 71:9 6256
many a *t* turned he his anger away ... Ps 78:38
in the *t* appointed, on our solemn ... Ps 81:3
but their *t* should have endured ... Ps 81:15 6256
Remember how short my *t* is ... Ps 89:47 2465
for the *t* to favour her, yea, the ... Ps 102:13 6256
to favour her, yea, the set *t* ... Ps 102:13 4150
Until the *t* that his word came ... Ps 105:19 6256
of the LORD from this *t* forth ... Ps 113:2 6258
bless the LORD from this *t* forth ... Ps 115:18 6258
It is *t* for thee, LORD, to work ... Ps 119:126 6256
thy coming in from this *t* forth ... Ps 121:8 6258
Many a *t* have they afflicted me ... Ps 129:1 7227
Many a *t* have they afflicted me ... Ps 129:2 7227
cold of snow in the *t* of harvest ... Prov 25:13 3117
in an unfaithful man in *t* of ... Prov 25:19 3117
and she shall rejoice in *t* to come ... Prov 31:25 3117
it hath been already of old *t* ... Eccl 1:10 5769
a *t* to every purpose under the ... Eccl 3:1 6256

A *t* to be born, and a *t* to die ... Eccl 3:2 6256
a *t* to plant, and a *t* to pluck ... Eccl 3:2 6256
A *t* to kill, and a *t* to heal ... Eccl 3:3 6256
a *t* to break down ... Eccl 3:3 6256
and a *t* to build up ... Eccl 3:3 6256
A *t* to weep, and a *t* to laugh ... Eccl 3:4 6256
a *t* to mourn, and a *t* to dance ... Eccl 3:4 6256
A *t* to cast away stones, and a ... Eccl 3:5 6256
a *t* to gather stones together ... Eccl 3:5 6256
a *t* to embrace ... Eccl 3:5 6256
a *t* to refrain from embracing ... Eccl 3:5 6256
A *t* to get, and a *t* to lose ... Eccl 3:6 6256
t to keep, and a *t* to cast away ... Eccl 3:6 6256
A *t* to rend, and a *t* to sew ... Eccl 3:7 6256
a *t* to keep silence ... Eccl 3:7 6256
and a *t* to speak ... Eccl 3:7 6256
A *t* to love, and a *t* to hate ... Eccl 3:8 6256
a *t* of war, and a *t* of peace ... Eccl 3:8 6256
every thing beautiful in his *t* ... Eccl 3:11 6256
for there is a *t* there for every ... Eccl 3:17 6256
shouldest thou die before thy *t* ... Eccl 7:17 6256
man's heart discerneth both *t* ... Eccl 8:5 6256
to every purpose there is *t* ... Eccl 8:6 6256
there is a *t* wherein one man ... Eccl 8:9 6256
but *t* and chance happeneth to them ... Eccl 9:11 6256
For man also knoweth not his *t* ... Eccl 9:12 6256
sons of men snared in an evil *t* ... Eccl 9:12 6256
the *t* of the singing of birds is ... Song 2:12 6256
t to recover the remnant of his ... Is 11:11
her *t* is near to come, and her ... Is 13:22 6256
concerning Moab since that *t* ... Is 16:13 227
In that *t* shall the present be ... Is 18:7 6256
At the same *t* spake the LORD by ... Is 20:2 6256
near the *t* of her delivery ... Is 26:17
From the *t* that it goeth forth it ... Is 28:19 1767
may be for the *t* to come for ever ... Is 30:8 3117
also in the *t* of trouble ... Is 33:2 6256
At that *t* Merodach-baladan, the ... Is 39:1 6256
I have long *t* holden my peace ... Is 42:14 5769
hearken and hear for the *t* to come ... Is 42:23 268
have not I told thee from that *t* ... Is 44:8 227
hath declared this from ancient *t* ... Is 45:21 6924
who hath told it from that *t* ... Is 45:21 227
thee new things from this *t* ... Is 48:6 6258
from that *t* that thine ear was ... Is 48:8 227
from the *t* that it was, there am ... Is 48:16 6256
In an acceptable *t* have I heard ... Is 49:8 6256
the LORD will hasten it in his *t* ... Is 60:22 6256
LORD came unto me the second *t* ... Jer 1:13
For of old *t* I have broken thy ... Jer 2:20 5769
but in the *t* of their trouble ... Jer 2:27 6256
save thee in the *t* of thy trouble ... Jer 2:28 6256
thou not from this *t* cry unto me ... Jer 3:4 6258
At that *t* they shall call ... Jer 3:17 6256
At that *t* shall it be said to ... Jer 4:11 6256
at the *t* that I visit them they ... Jer 6:15 6256
At that *t*, saith the LORD, they ... Jer 8:1 6256
observe the *t* of their coming ... Jer 8:7 6256
in the *t* of their visitation they ... Jer 8:12 6256
for a *t* of health, and behold ... Jer 8:15 6256
in the *t* of their visitation they ... Jer 10:15 6256
at all in the *t* of their trouble ... Jer 11:12 6256
t that they cry unto me for their ... Jer 11:14 6256
LORD came unto me the second *t* ... Jer 13:3
saviour thereof in *t* of trouble ... Jer 14:8 6256
for the *t* of healing, and behold ... Jer 14:19 6256
thee well in the *t* of evil ... Jer 15:11 6256
of evil and in the *t* of affliction ... Jer 15:11 6256
with them in the *t* of thine anger ... Jer 18:23 6256
until the very *t* of his land come ... Jer 27:7 6256
it is even the *t* of Jacob's ... Jer 30:7 6256
At the same *t*, saith the LORD, ... Jer 31:1 6256
came unto Jeremiah the second *t* ... Jer 33:1
In those days, and at that *t* ... Jer 33:15 6256
vineyards and fields at the same *t* ... Jer 39:10 3117
he hath passed the *t* appointed ... Jer 46:17 4150
the *t* of their visitation ... Jer 46:21 6256
the *t* that I will visit him ... Jer 49:8 6256
and who will appoint me the *t* ... Jer 49:19
In those days, and in that *t* ... Jer 50:4 6256
the sickle in the *t* of harvest ... Jer 50:16 6256
In those days, and in that *t* ... Jer 50:20 6256
the *t* of their visitation ... Jer 50:27 6256
the *t* that I will visit thee ... Jer 50:31 6256
and who will appoint me the *t* ... Jer 50:44
for this is the *t* of the LORD's ... Jer 51:6 6256
in the *t* of their visitation they ... Jer 51:18 6256
it is *t* to thresh her ... Jer 51:33 6256
the *t* of her harvest shall come ... Jer 51:33 6256
for ever, and forsake us so long *t* ... Lam 5:20 3117
from *t* to *t* shalt thou eat it ... Eze 4:10 6256
from *t* to *t* shalt thou drink ... Eze 4:11 6256
the *t* is come, the day of trouble ... Eze 7:7 6256
The *t* is come, the day draweth ... Eze 7:12 6256
thy *t* was the *t* of love ... Eze 16:8 6256
as at the *t* of thy reproach of ... Eze 16:57 6256
the sword be doubled the third *t* ... Eze 21:14
midst of it, that her *t* may come ... Eze 22:3 6256
the pit, with the people of old *t* ... Eze 26:20 5769
In the *t* when thou shalt be ... Eze 27:34 6256
it shall be the *t* of the heathen ... Eze 30:3 6256
sword in the *t* of their calamity ... Eze 35:5 6256
in the *t* that their iniquity had ... Eze 35:5 6256
that at the same *t* shall things ... Eze 38:10 3117
t by my servants the prophets of ... Eze 38:17 3117
shall come to pass at the same *t* ... Eze 38:18 3117
that ye would gain the *t*, because ... Dan 2:8 5732
before me, till the *t* be changed ... Dan 2:9 5732
the king that he would give him *t* ... Dan 2:16 2166
That at what *t* ye hear the sound ... Dan 3:5 5732
Therefore at that *t*, when all the ... Dan 3:7 2166
Wherefore at that *t* certain ... Dan 3:8 2166
t ye hear the sound of the cornet ... Dan 3:15 5732
At the same *t* my reason returned ... Dan 4:36 2166
were prolonged for a season and *t* ... Dan 7:12 5732
the *t* came that the saints ... Dan 7:22 2166
be given into his hand until a *t* ... Dan 7:25 5732
and times and the dividing of *t* ... Dan 7:25 5732
for at the *t* of the end shall be ... Dan 8:17 6256
for at the *t* appointed the end ... Dan 8:19 4150
in the latter *t* of their kingdom, ... Dan 8:23 319
touched me about the *t* of the ... Dan 9:21 6256
but the *t* appointed was long ... Dan 10:1
the strong holds, even for a *t* ... Dan 11:24 6256
end shall be at the *t* appointed ... Dan 11:27 4150
At the *t* appointed he shall ... Dan 11:29 4150
white, even to the *t* of the end ... Dan 11:35 6256
it is yet for a *t* appointed ... Dan 11:35 4150
at the *t* of the end shall the ... Dan 11:40 6256
at that *t* shall Michael stand up, ... Dan 12:1 6256
and there shall be a *t* of trouble ... Dan 12:1 6256
was a nation even to that same *t* ... Dan 12:1 6256
at that *t* thy people shall be ... Dan 12:1 6256
book, even to the *t* of the end ... Dan 12:4 6256
for ever that it shall be for a *t* ... Dan 12:7 4150
and sealed till the *t* of the end ... Dan 12:9 6256
from the *t* that the daily ... Dan 12:11 6256
away my corn in the *t* thereof ... Hos 2:9 6256
in the fig tree at her first *t* ... Hos 9:10 7225
for it is *t* to seek the LORD, ... Hos 10:12 6256
in those days, and in that *t* ... Joel 3:1 6256
shall keep silence in that *t* ... Amos 5:13 6256
for it is an evil *t* ... Amos 5:13 6256
LORD came unto Jonah the second *t* ... Jonah 3:1
for this *t* is evil ... Mic 2:3 6256
hide his face from them at that *t* ... Mic 3:4 6256
until the *t* that she which ... Mic 5:3 6256
shall not rise up the second *t* ... Nah 1:9 6471
vision is yet for an appointed *t* ... Hab 2:3 4150
it shall come to pass at that *t* ... Zeph 1:12 6256
at that *t* I will undo all that ... Zeph 3:19 6256
At that *t* will I bring you again, ... Zeph 3:20 6256
even in the *t* that I gather you ... Zeph 3:20 6256
The *t* is not come ... Hag 1:2 6256
the *t* that the LORD's house ... Hag 1:2 6256
Is it *t* for you, O ye, to dwell ... Hag 1:4 6256
rain in the *t* of the latter rain ... Zec 10:1 6256
that at evening *t* it shall be ... Zec 14:7 6256
fruit before the *t* in the field ... Mal 3:11
about the *t* they were carried ... Mt 1:11 *1909*
what *t* the star appeared ... Mt 2:7 *5550*
according to the *t* which he had ... Mt 2:16 *5550*
lest at any *t* thou dash thy foot ... Mt 4:6 *3379*
From that *t* Jesus began to preach ... Mt 4:17 *5119*
that it was said by them of old *t* ... Mt 5:21 *744*
lest at any *t* the adversary ... Mt 5:25 *3379*
that it was said by them of old *t* ... Mt 5:27 *744*
hath been said by them of old *t* ... Mt 5:33 *744*
hither to torment us before the *t* ... Mt 8:29 *2540*
At that *t* Jesus answered and said, ... Mt 11:25 *2540*
At that *t* Jesus went on the ... Mt 12:1 *2540*
lest at any *t* they should see ... Mt 13:15 *3379*
in the *t* of harvest I will say to ... Mt 13:30 *2540*
At that *t* Herod the tetrarch ... Mt 14:1 *2540*
place, and the *t* is now past ... Mt 14:15 *5610*
From that *t* forth began Jesus to ... Mt 16:21 *5119*
At the same *t* came the disciples ... Mt 18:1 *5610*
when the *t* of the fruit drew near ... Mt 21:34 *2540*
beginning of the world to this *t* ... Mt 24:21 *2540*
After a long *t* the lord of those ... Mt 25:19 *5550*
from that *t* he sought opportunity ... Mt 26:16 *5119*
The Master saith, My *t* is at hand ... Mt 26:18 *2540*
He went away again the second *t* ... Mt 26:42
away again, and prayed the third *t* ... Mt 26:44
The *t* is fulfilled, and the ... Mk 1:15 *2540*
lest at any *t* they should be ... Mk 4:12 *3379*
and so endure but for a *t* ... Mk 4:17 *4340*
place, and now the *t* is far passed ... Mk 6:35 *5610*
an hundredfold now in this *t* ... Mk 10:30 *2540*
for the *t* of figs was not yet ... Mk 11:13 *2540*
which God created unto this *t* ... Mk 13:19 *3568*
for ye know not when the *t* is ... Mk 13:33 *2540*
And he cometh the third *t*, and ... Mk 14:41
the second *t* the cock crew ... Mk 14:72
without at the *t* of incense ... Lk 1:10 *5610*
Now Elisabeth's full *t* came that ... Lk 1:57 *5550*
of the world in a moment of *t* ... Lk 4:5 *5550*
lest at any *t* thou dash thy foot ... Lk 4:11 *3379*
in the *t* of Eliseus the prophet ... Lk 4:27 *1909*
but this woman since the *t* I came ... Lk 7:45
in *t* of temptation fall away ... Lk 8:13 *2540*
man, which had devils long *t* ... Lk 8:27 *5550*
when the *t* was come that he ... Lk 9:51 *2250*
In the mean *t*, when there were ... Lk 12:1
it that ye do not discern this *t* ... Lk 12:56 *2540*
until the *t* come when ye shall ... Lk 13:35
sent his servant at supper *t* to ... Lk 14:17 *5610*
I at any *t* thy commandment ... Lk 15:29
since that *t* the kingdom of God ... Lk 16:16 *5119*
manifold more in this present *t* ... Lk 18:30 *2540*
not the *t* of thy visitation ... Lk 19:44 *2540*
into a far country for a long *t* ... Lk 20:9 *5550*
and the *t* draweth near ... Lk 21:8 *2540*
lest at any *t* your hearts be ... Lk 21:34 *3379*
in the day *t* he was teaching in ... Lk 21:37 *2250*
also was at Jerusalem at that *t* ... Lk 23:7 *2250*
And he said unto them the third *t* ... Lk 23:22
No man hath seen God at any *t* ... Jn 1:18 *4455*
second *t* into his mother's womb ... Jn 3:4 *1208*
been now a long *t* in that case ... Jn 5:6 *5550*
neither heard his voice at any *t* ... Jn 5:37 *4455*
From that *t* many of his disciples ... Jn 6:66
unto them, My *t* is not yet come ... Jn 7:6 *2540*
but your *t* is alway ready ... Jn 7:6 *2540*
for my *t* is not yet full come ... Jn 7:8 *2540*
him, Lord, by this *t* he stinketh ... Jn 11:39 *2235*
Have I been so long *t* with you ... Jn 14:9 *5550*
the *t* cometh, that whosoever ... Jn 16:2 *5610*
you, that when the *t* shall come ... Jn 16:4 *5610*
but the *t* cometh, when I shall no ... Jn 16:25 *5610*
This is now the third *t* that ... Jn 21:14
saith to him again the second *t* ... Jn 21:16
He saith unto him the third *t* ... Jn 21:17
he said unto him the third *t* ... Jn 21:17
wilt thou at this *t* restore again ... Acts 1:6 *5550*
the *t* that the Lord Jesus went in ... Acts 1:21 *5550*
at the second *t* Joseph was made ... Acts 7:13
But when the *t* of the promise ... Acts 7:17 *5550*
In which *t* Moses was born, and was ... Acts 7:20 *2540*
at that *t* there was a great ... Acts 8:1 *2250*
because that of long *t* he had ... Acts 8:11 *5550*
spake unto him again the second *t* ... Acts 10:15
at any *t* entered into my mouth ... Acts 11:8
Now about that *t* Herod the king ... Acts 12:1 *2540*
about the *t* of forty years ... Acts 13:18 *5550*
Long *t* therefore abode they ... Acts 14:3 *5550*
abode long *t* with the disciples ... Acts 14:28 *5550*
For Moses of old *t* hath in every ... Acts 15:21 *1074*
spent their *t* in nothing else ... Acts 17:21 *2119*
him to tarry longer *t* with them ... Acts 18:20 *5550*
after he had spent some *t* there ... Acts 18:23 *5550*
the same *t* there arose no small ... Acts 19:23 *2540*
he would not spend the *t* in Asia ... Acts 20:16 *5551*
answered, Go thy way for this *t* ... Acts 24:25 *3568*
Now when much *t* was spent ... Acts 27:9 *5550*
at this *t* his righteousness ... Rom 3:26 *2540*
in due *t* Christ died for the ... Rom 5:6 *2540*
t are not worthy to be compared ... Rom 8:18 *2540*
At this *t* will I come, and Sarah ... Rom 9:9 *2540*
present *t* also there is a remnant ... Rom 11:5 *2540*
And that, knowing the *t*, that now ... Rom 13:11 *2540*
that now it is high *t* to awake ... Rom 13:11 *5610*
judge nothing before the *t* ... 1Cor 4:5 *2540*
except it be with consent for a *t* ... 1Cor 7:5 *2540*
I say, brethren, the *t* is short ... 1Cor 7:29 *2540*
warfare any *t* at his own charges ... 1Cor 9:7 *4218*
also, as of one born out of due *t* ... 1Cor 15:8
was not at all to come at this *t* ... 1Cor 16:12 *3598*
when he shall have convenient *t* ... 1Cor 16:12 *2119*
I have heard thee in a *t* accepted ... 2Cor 6:2 *2540*
behold, now is the accepted *t* ... 2Cor 6:2 *2540*
that now at this *t* your abundance ... 2Cor 8:14 *2540*
the third *t* I am ready to come to ... 2Cor 12:14
This is the third *t* I am coming ... 2Cor 13:1
if I were present, the second *t* ... 2Cor 13:2
in *t* past in the Jews' religion ... Gal 1:13 *4218*
governors until the *t* appointed ... Gal 4:2 *4287*
the fulness of the *t* was come ... Gal 4:4 *5550*
as I have also told you in *t* past ... Gal 5:21
Wherein in *t* past ye walked ... Eph 2:2 *4218*
that ye being in *t* past Gentiles ... Eph 2:11 *4218*
That at that *t* ye were without ... Eph 2:12 *2540*
Redeeming the *t*, because the days ... Eph 5:16 *2540*
the which ye also walked some *t* ... Col 3:7 *4218*
that are without, redeeming the *t* ... Col 4:5 *2540*
For neither at any *t* used we ... 1Th 2:5 *4218*
you for a short *t* in presence ... 1Th 2:17 *2540*
he might be revealed in his *t* ... 2Th 2:6 *2540*
for all, to be testified in due *t* ... 1Ti 2:6 *2540*
foundation against the *t* to come ... 1Ti 6:19 *3195*
For the *t* will come when they ... 2Ti 4:3 *2540*
the *t* of my departure is at hand ... 2Ti 4:6 *2540*
brought before Nero the second *t* ... 2Ti *s*
Which in *t* past was to thee ... Philem 11 *4218*
in divers manners spake in *t* past ... Heb 1:1 *3819*
of the angels said he at any *t* ... Heb 1:5 *4218*
lest at any *t* we should let them ... Heb 2:1 *4218*
David, To day, after so long a *t* ... Heb 4:7 *5550*
find grace to help in *t* of need ... Heb 4:16 *2121*
For when for the *t* ye ought to be ... Heb 5:12 *5550*
a figure for the *t* then present ... Heb 9:9 *2540*
them until the *t* of reformation ... Heb 9:10 *2540*
t without sin unto salvation ... Heb 9:28
for the *t* would fail me to tell ... Heb 11:32 *5550*
that appeareth for a little *t* ... Jas 4:14
to be revealed in the last *t* ... 1Pet 1:5 *2540*
or what manner of *t* the Spirit of ... 1Pet 1:11 *2540*
pass the *t* of your sojourning ... 1Pet 1:17 *5550*
Which in *t* past were not a people ... 1Pet 2:10 *4218*
in the old *t* the holy women also ... 1Pet 3:5 *4218*
should live the rest of his *t* in ... 1Pet 4:2 *5550*
For the *t* past of our life may ... 1Pet 4:3 *5550*
For the *t* is come that judgment ... 1Pet 4:17 *2540*
that he may exalt you in due *t* ... 1Pet 5:6 *2540*
not in old *t* by the will of man ... 2Pet 1:21 *4218*
now of a long *t* lingereth not ... 2Pet 2:3 *1597*
Little children, it is the last *t* ... 1Jn 2:18 *5610*
we know that it is the last *t* ... 1Jn 2:18 *5610*
No man hath seen God at any *t* ... 1Jn 4:12 *4455*
should be mockers in the last *t* ... Jude 18 *5550*
for the *t* is at hand ... Rev 1:3 *2540*
that there should be *t* no longer ... Rev 10:6 *5550*
the *t* of the dead, that they ... Rev 11:18 *2540*
that he hath but a short *t* ... Rev 12:12 *2540*

for a *t*, and times, and half a *t* ... Rev 12:14 *2540*
for the *t* is come for thee to ... Rev 14:15 *5610*
for the *t* is at hand ... Rev 22:10 *2540*

TIMES {147}
he hath supplanted me these two *t* ... Gen 27:36 6471
me, and changed my wages ten *t* ... Gen 31:7 4489
thou hast changed my wages ten *t* ... Gen 31:41 4489
himself to the ground seven *t* ... Gen 33:3 6471
five *t* so much as any of theirs ... Gen 43:34 3027
Three *t* thou shalt keep a feast ... Ex 23:14 7272
Three *t* in the year all thy males ... Ex 23:17 6471
the blood seven *t* before the LORD ... Lev 4:6 6471
it seven *t* before the LORD ... Lev 4:17 6471
thereof upon the altar seven *t* ... Lev 8:11 6471
cleansed from the leprosy seven *t* ... Lev 14:7 6471
finger seven *t* before the LORD ... Lev 14:16 6471
left hand seven *t* before the LORD ... Lev 14:27 6471
and sprinkle the house seven *t* ... Lev 14:51 6471
that he come not at all *t* into ... Lev 16:2 6256
the blood with his finger seven *t* ... Lev 16:14 6471
upon it with his finger seven *t* ... Lev 16:19 6471
ye use enchantment, nor observe *t* ... Lev 19:26
unto thee, seven *t* seven years ... Lev 25:8 6471
you seven *t* more for your sins ... Lev 26:18
I will bring seven *t* more plagues ... Lev 26:21
you yet seven *t* for your sins ... Lev 26:24
you seven *t* for your sins ... Lev 26:28
have tempted me now these ten *t* ... Num 14:22
of the congregation seven *t* ... Num 19:4
hast smitten me these three *t* ... Num 22:28
smitten thine ass these three *t* ... Num 22:32
and turned from me these three *t* ... Num 22:33
he went not, as at other *t* ... Num 24:1 6471
blessed them these three *t* ... Num 24:10
thousand *t* so many more as ye are ... Deut 1:11 6471
The Emims dwelt therein in *t* past ... Deut 2:10 6440
and hated him not in *t* past ... Deut 4:42 8543
Three *t* in a year shall all thy ... Deut 16:16 6471
divination, or an observer of *t* ... Deut 18:10
hearkened unto observers of *t* ... Deut 18:14
ye shall compass the city seven *t* ... Josh 6:4 6471
after the same manner seven *t* ... Josh 6:15 6471
they compassed the city seven *t* ... Josh 6:15 6471
at *t* in the camp of Dan between ... Judg 13:25
thou hast mocked me these three *t* ... Judg 16:15 6471
will go out as at other *t* before ... Judg 16:20 6471
against Gibeah, as at other *t* ... Judg 20:30 6471
people, and kill, as at other *t* ... Judg 20:31 6471
and stood, and called as at other *t* ... 1Sa 3:10 6471
with his hand, as at other *t* ... 1Sa 18:10 3117
was in his presence, as in *t* past ... 1Sa 19:7 865,8632
sat upon his seat, as at other *t* ... 1Sa 20:25 6471
ground, and bowed himself three *t* ... 1Sa 20:41 6471
Ye sought for David in *t* past to ... 2Sa 3:17 8543
of his people Israel at all *t* ... 1Kin 8:59 3117
three *t* in a year did Solomon ... 1Kin 9:25 6471
himself upon the child three *t* ... 1Kin 17:21 6471
And he said, Go again seven *t* ... 1Kin 18:43 6471
How many *t* shall I adjure thee ... 1Kin 22:16 6471
and the child sneezed seven *t* ... 2Kin 4:35 6471
Go and wash in Jordan seven *t* ... 2Kin 5:10 6471
dipped himself seven *t* in Jordan ... 2Kin 5:14 6471
have smitten five or six *t* ... 2Kin 13:19 6471
Three *t* did Joash beat him, and ... 2Kin 13:25 6471
of ancient *t* that I have formed ... 2Kin 19:25 3117
through the fire, and observed *t* ... 2Kin 21:6
that had understanding of the *t* ... 1Chr 12:32 6256
hundred *t* so many more as they be ... 1Chr 21:3 6471
the *t* that went over him, and over ... 1Chr 29:30 6256
three *t* in the year, even in the ... 2Chr 8:13 6471
in those *t* there was no peace to ... 2Chr 15:5 6256
How many *t* shall I adjure thee ... 2Chr 18:15 6471
also he observed *t*, and used ... 2Chr 33:6
in our cities come at appointed *t* ... Ezr 10:14 6256
came, they said unto us ten *t* ... Neh 4:12 6471
unto me four *t* after this sort ... Neh 6:4 6471
many *t* didst thou deliver them ... Neh 9:28 6256
at *t* appointed year by year, to ... Neh 10:34 6256
at *t* appointed, and for the ... Neh 13:31 6256
to the wise men, which knew the *t* ... Est 1:13 6256
of Purim in their *t* appointed ... Est 9:31 2165
These ten *t* have ye reproached me ... Job 19:3 6471
seeing *t* are not hidden from the ... Job 24:1 6256
a refuge in *t* of trouble ... Ps 9:9 6256
thou thyself in *t* of trouble ... Ps 10:1 6256
of earth, purified seven *t* ... Ps 12:6
My *t* are in thy hand ... Ps 31:15 6256
I will bless the LORD at all *t* ... Ps 34:1 6256
in their days, in the *t* of old ... Ps 44:1 3117
Trust in him at all *t* ... Ps 62:8 6256
of old, the years of ancient *t* ... Ps 77:5 5769
that doeth righteousness at all *t* ... Ps 106:3 6256
Many *t* did he deliver them ... Ps 106:43 6471
hath unto thy judgments at all *t* ... Ps 119:20 6256
Seven *t* a day do I praise thee ... Ps 119:164
her breasts satisfy thee at all *t* ... Prov 5:19 6256
A friend loveth at all *t*, and a ... Prov 17:17 6256
For a just man falleth seven *t* ... Prov 24:16
a sinner do evil an hundred *t* ... Eccl 8:12
shall be alone in his appointed *t* ... Is 14:31 4151
shall be the stability of thy *t* ... Is 33:6 6256
and of ancient *t*, that I have ... Is 37:26 3117
from ancient *t* the things that ... Is 46:10 6924
heaven knoweth her appointed *t* ... Jer 8:7 6256
of the *t* that are far off ... Eze 12:27 6256
he found them ten *t* better than ... Dan 1:20
And he changeth the *t* and the ... Dan 2:21 5732
heat the furnace one seven *t* more ... Dan 3:19
let seven *t* pass over him ... Dan 4:16 5732
till seven *t* pass over him ... Dan 4:23 5732
seven *t* shall pass over thee, ... Dan 4:25 5732
seven *t* shall pass over thee, ... Dan 4:32 5732
upon his knees three *t* a day ... Dan 6:10 2166
maketh his petition three *t* a day ... Dan 6:13 2166
ten thousand *t* ten thousand stood ... Dan 7:10
most High, and think to change *t* ... Dan 7:25 2166
into his hand until a time and *t* ... Dan 7:25 5732
and the wall, even in troublous *t* ... Dan 9:25 6256
that strengthened her in these *t* ... Dan 11:6 6256
in those *t* there shall many stand ... Dan 11:14 6256
that it shall be for a time, *t* ... Dan 12:7 4150
ye not discern the signs of the *t* ... Mt 16:3 *2540*
till seven *t* ... Mt 18:21 *2034*
say not unto thee, Until seven *t* ... Mt 18:22 *2034*
but, Until seventy *t* seven ... Mt 18:22 *1441*
against thee seven *t* in a day ... Lk 17:4 *2034*
seven *t* in a day turn again to ... Lk 17:4 *2034*
until the *t* of the Gentiles be ... Lk 21:24 *2540*
you to know the *t* or the seasons ... Acts 1:7 *5550*
when the *t* of refreshing shall ... Acts 3:19 *2540*
t of restitution of all things ... Acts 3:21 *5550*
And this was done three *t* ... Acts 11:10 *5151*
Who in *t* past suffered all ... Acts 14:16 *1074*
determined the *t* before appointed ... Acts 17:26 *2540*
the *t* of this ignorance God ... Acts 17:30 *5550*
For as ye in *t* past have not ... Rom 11:30 *4218*
Of the Jews five *t* received I ... 2Cor 11:24 *3999*
in *t* past preacheth the faith ... Gal 1:23 *4218*
Ye observe days, and months, and *t* ... Gal 4:10 *2540*
dispensation of the fulness of *t* ... Eph 1:10 *2540*
t past in the lusts of our flesh ... Eph 2:3 *4218*
But of the *t* and the seasons, ... 1Th 5:1 *2540*
that in the latter *t* some shall ... 1Ti 4:1 *5550*
Which in his *t* he shall shew, who ... 1Ti 6:15 *5550*
last days perilous *t* shall come ... 2Ti 3:1 *5550*
But hath in due *t* manifested his ... Titus 1:3 *5550*
God, who at sundry *t* and in divers ... Heb 1:1
of the angels said he at any *t* ... Heb 1:13
manifest in these last *t* for you ... 1Pet 1:20 *5550*
was ten thousand *t* ten thousand ... Rev 5:11
she is nourished for a time, and *t* ... Rev 12:14 *2540*

TIMNA *(tim'-nah)* {4} See TIMNATH.
1. Concubine of Eliphaz.
T was concubine to Eliphaz Esau's ... Gen 36:12 8555
2. Daughter of Seir.
and Lotan's sister was *T* ... Gen 36:22 8555
and *T* was Lotan's sister ... 1Chr 1:39 8555
3. A son of Eliphaz.
Zephi, and Gatam, Kenaz, and *T* ... 1Chr 1:36 8555

TIMNAH *(tim'-nah)* {5} See TIMNA, TIMNATH.
1. A chief of Edom.
duke *T*, duke Alvah, duke Jetheth, ... Gen 36:40 8555
duke *T*, duke Aliah, duke Jetheth, ... 1Chr 1:51 8555
2. A city in Judah.
Cain, Gibeah, and *T* ... Josh 15:57 8553
3. A city in Dan.
Beth-shemesh, and passed on to *T* ... Josh 15:10 8553
T with the villages thereof, ... 2Chr 28:18 8553

TIMNATH *(tim'-nath)* {8} See THIMNATHAH, TIMNAH.
1. Same as Timnah 2.
up unto his sheepshearers to *T* ... Gen 38:12 8553
goeth up to *T* to shear his sheep ... Gen 38:13 8553
place, which is by the way to *T* ... Gen 38:14 8553
2. Same as Timnah 3.
And Samson went down to *T*, and saw ... Judg 14:1 8553
saw a woman in *T* of the daughters ... Judg 14:1 8553
I have seen a woman in *T* of the ... Judg 14:2 8553
and his father and his mother, to *T* ... Judg 14:5 8553
and came to the vineyards of *T* ... Judg 14:5 8553

TIMNATH-HERES *(tim'-nath-he'-rez)* {1} See TIMNATH-SERAH. *Land near Mount Ephraim.*
border of his inheritance in *T* ... Judg 2:9 8556

TIMNATH-SERAH *(tim'-nath-se'-rah)* {2} See TIMNATH-HERES. *Same as Timnath-heres.*
he asked, even *T* in mount Ephraim ... Josh 19:50 8556
border of his inheritance in *T* ... Josh 24:30 8556

TIMNITE *(tim'-nite)* {1} *An inhabitant of Timnath.*
Samson, the son in law of the *T* ... Judg 15:6 8554

TIMON *(ti'-mon)* {1} *A leader in the Jerusalem church.*
and Prochorus, and Nicanor, and *T* ... Acts 6:5 *5096*

TIMOTHEOUS {1}
and Fortunatus, and Achaicus, and *T* ... 1Cor *s* *5095*

TIMOTHEUS *(tim-o'-the-us)* {18} See TIMOTHY. *Same as Timothy.*
disciple was there, named *T* ... Acts 16:1 *5095*
but Silas and *T* abode there still ... Acts 17:14 *5095*
T for to come to him with all ... Acts 17:15 *5095*
T were come from Macedonia, Paul ... Acts 18:5 *5095*
them that ministered unto him, *T* ... Acts 19:22 *5095*
and Gaius of Derbe, and *T* ... Acts 20:4 *5095*
T my workfellow, and Lucius, and ... Rom 16:21 *5095*
this cause have I sent unto you *T* ... 1Cor 4:17 *5095*
Now if *T* come, see that he may be ... 1Cor 16:10 *5095*
us, even by me and Silvanus and *T* ... 2Cor 1:19 *5095*
Paul and *T*, the servants of Jesus ... Phil 1:1 *5095*
Jesus to send *T* shortly unto you ... Phil 2:19 *5095*
will of God, and *T* our brother, ... Col 1:1 *5095*
Paul, and Silvanus, and *T*, unto the ... 1Th 1:1 *5095*
And sent *T*, our brother, and ... 1Th 3:2 *5095*
But now when *T* came from you unto ... 1Th 3:6 *5095*
Paul, and Silvanus, and *T*, unto the ... 2Th 1:1 *5095*
The second epistle unto *T* ... 2Ti *s* *5095*

TIMOTHY *(tim'-o-thy)* {9} See TIMOTHEUS. *A co-worker with Paul.*
T our brother, unto the church of ... 2Cor 1:1 *5095*
Unto *T*, my own son in the faith ... 1Ti 1:2 *5095*
charge I commit unto thee, son *T* ... 1Ti 1:18 *5095*
O *T*, keep that which is committed ... 1Ti 6:20 *5095*
The first to *T* was written from ... 1Ti *s* *5095*
To *T*, my dearly beloved son ... 2Ti 1:2 *5095*
T our brother, unto Philemon our ... Philem 1 *5095*
our brother *T* is set at liberty ... Heb 13:23 *5095*
to the Hebrews from Italy by *T* ... Heb *s* *5095*

TIN {5}
the brass, the iron, the *t* ... Num 31:22 913
thy dross, and take away all thy *t* ... Is 1:25 913
all they are brass, and *t*, and iron ... Eze 22:18 913
and brass, and iron, and lead, and *t* ... Eze 22:20 913
with silver, iron, *t*, and lead, ... Eze 27:12 913

TINGLE {3}
every one that heareth it shall *t* ... 1Sa 3:11 6750
of it, both his ears shall *t* ... 2Kin 21:12 6750
heareth, his ears shall *t* ... Jer 19:3 6750

TINKLING {3}
making a *t* with their feet ... Is 3:16 5913
t ornaments about their feet ... Is 3:18
as sounding brass, or a *t* cymbal ... 1Cor 13:1 *214*

TIP {9}
put it upon the *t* of the right ... Ex 29:20 8571
upon the *t* of the right ear of ... Ex 29:20 8571
put it upon the *t* of Aaron's ... Lev 8:23 8571
upon the *t* of their right ear ... Lev 8:24 8571
priest shall put it upon the *t* of ... Lev 14:14 8571
shall the priest put upon the *t* ... Lev 14:17 8571
put it upon the *t* of the right ... Lev 14:25 8571
that is in his hand upon the *t* of ... Lev 14:28 8571
that he may dip the *t* of his ... Lk 16:24 *206*

TIPHSAH *(tif'-sah)* {2}
1. A city on the Euphrates River.
from *T* even to Azzah, over all ... 1Kin 4:24 8607
2. A city in Judah.
Then Menahem smote *T*, and all that ... 2Kin 15:16 8607

TIRAS *(Ti'-ras)* {2} *A son of Japheth.*
Javan, and Tubal, and Meshech, and *T* ... Gen 10:2 8493
Javan, and Tubal, and Meshech, and *T* ... 1Chr 1:5 8493

TIRATHITES *(ti'-rath-ites)* {1} *A family of scribes.*
the *T*, the Shimeathites, and ... 1Chr 2:55 8654

TIRE {1}
bind the *t* of thine head upon ... Eze 24:17 6287

TIRED {1}
t her head, and looked out at a ... 2Kin 9:30 3190

TIRES {2}
their round *t* like the moon, ... Is 3:18 7720
your *t* shall be upon your heads, ... Eze 24:23 6287

TIRHAKAH *(tur-ha'-kah)* {2} *A king of Ethiopia.*
heard say of *T* king of Ethiopia ... 2Kin 19:9 8640
say concerning *T* king of Ethiopia ... Is 37:9 8640

TIRHANAH *(tur-ha'-nah)* {1} *A son of Caleb.*
concubine, bare Sheber, and *T* ... 1Chr 2:48 8647

TIRIA *(tir'-e-ah)* {1} *A descendant of Judah.*
Ziph, and Ziphah, *T*, and Asareel ... 1Chr 4:16 8493

TIRSHATHA *(tur'-sha-thah)* {5} *Persian governors of Judah.*
the *T* said unto them, that they ... Ezr 2:63 8660
the *T* said unto them, that they ... Neh 7:65 8660
The *T* gave to the treasure a ... Neh 7:70 8660
And Nehemiah, which is the *T* ... Neh 8:9 8660
that sealed were, Nehemiah, the *T* ... Neh 10:1 8660

TIRZAH *(tur'-zah)* {18}
1. A daughter of Zelophehad.
and Noah, Hoglah, Milcah, and *T* ... Num 26:33 8656
Noah, and Hoglah, and Milcah, and *T* ... Num 27:1 8656
For Mahlah, *T*, and Hoglah, and ... Num 36:11 8656
and Noah, Hoglah, Milcah, and *T* ... Josh 17:3 8656
2. A city in Ephraim.
The king of *T*, one ... Josh 12:24 8656
arose, and departed, and came to *T* ... 1Kin 14:17 8656
building of Ramah, and dwelt in *T* ... 1Kin 15:21 8656
to reign over all Israel in *T* ... 1Kin 15:33 8656
his fathers, and was buried in *T* ... 1Kin 16:6 8656
Baasha to reign over Israel in *T* ... 1Kin 16:8 8656
against him, as he was in *T* ... 1Kin 16:9 8656
of Arza steward of his house in *T* ... 1Kin 16:9 8656
did Zimri reign seven days in *T* ... 1Kin 16:15 8656
with him, and they besieged *T* ... 1Kin 16:17 8656
six years reigned he in *T* ... 1Kin 16:23 8656
the son of Gadi went up from *T* ... 2Kin 15:14 8656
and the coasts thereof from *T* ... 2Kin 15:16 8656
art beautiful, O my love, as *T* ... Song 6:4 8656

TISHBE See TISHBITE.

TISHBITE *(tish'-bite)* {6} *An inhabitant of Tishbeh.*
And Elijah the *T*, who was of the ... 1Kin 17:1 8664
of the LORD came to Elijah the *T* ... 1Kin 21:17 8664
of the LORD came to Elijah the *T* ... 1Kin 21:28 8664
of the LORD said to Elijah the *T* ... 2Kin 1:3 8664
And he said, It is Elijah the *T* ... 2Kin 1:8 8664
spake by his servant Elijah the *T* ... 2Kin 9:36 8664

TITHE {14}
all the *t* of the land, whether of ... Lev 27:30 4643
And concerning the *t* of the herd ... Lev 27:32 4643
LORD, even a tenth part of the *t* ... Num 18:26 4643
thy gates the *t* of thy corn ... Deut 12:17 4643
Thou shalt truly *t* all the ... Deut 14:22 6237
the *t* of thy corn, of thy wine, ... Deut 14:23 4643

thou shalt bring forth all the *t* ... Deut 14:28 4643
the *t* of all things brought they ... 2Chr 31:5 4643
also brought in the *t* of oxen ... 2Chr 31:6 4643
the *t* of holy things which were ... 2Chr 31:6 4643
the Levites shall bring up the *t* ... Neh 10:38 4643
all Judah the *t* of the corn ... Neh 13:12 4643
for ye pay *t* of mint and anise and ... Mt 23:23 *586*
for ye *t* mint and rue and all ... Lk 11:42 *586*

TITHES {24}
And he gave him *t* of all ... Gen 14:20 4643
will at all redeem ought of his *t* ... Lev 27:31 4643
But the *t* of the children of ... Num 18:24 4643
the *t* which I have given you from ... Num 18:26 4643
unto the LORD of all your *t* ... Num 18:28 4643
and your sacrifices, and your *t* ... Deut 12:6 4643
and your sacrifices, your *t* ... Deut 12:11 4643
the *t* of thine increase the third ... Deut 26:12 4643
brought in the offerings and the *t* ... 2Chr 31:12 4643
the *t* of our ground unto the ... Neh 10:37 4643
the *t* in all the cities of our ... Neh 10:37 6237
Levites, when the Levites take *t* ... Neh 10:38 6237
the *t* unto the house of our God ... Neh 10:38 4643
for the firstfruits, and for the *t* ... Neh 12:44 4643
the *t* of the corn, the new wine, ... Neh 13:5 4643
and your *t* after three years ... Amos 4:4 4643
In *t* and offerings ... Mal 3:8 4643
Bring ye all the *t* into the ... Mal 3:10 4643
I give *t* of all that I possess ... Lk 18:12 *586*
have a commandment to take *t* of ... Heb 7:5 *586*
from them received *t* of Abraham ... Heb 7:6 *1183*
And here men that die receive *t* ... Heb 7:8 *1181*
say, Levi also, who receiveth *t* ... Heb 7:9 *1183*
payed *t* in Abraham ... Heb 7:9 *1183*

TITHING {2}
end of *t* all the tithes of thine ... Deut 26:12 6237
year, which is the year of *t* ... Deut 26:12 4643

TITIUS See JUSTUS.

TITIUS JUSTUS See JUSTUS.

TITLE {3}
What *t* is that that I see ... 2Kin 23:17 6725
And Pilate wrote a *t*, and put it on ... Jn 19:19 *5102*
This *t* then read many of the Jews ... Jn 19:20 *5102*

TITLES {2}
let me give flattering *t* unto man ... Job 32:21
I know not to give flattering *t* ... Job 32:22

TITTLE {2}
one jot or one *t* shall in no wise ... Mt 5:18 *2762*
than one *t* of the law to fail ... Lk 16:17 *2762*

TITUS *(ti'-tus)* {15} *A co-worker with Paul.*
because I found not *T* my brother ... 2Cor 2:13 *5103*
comforted us by the coming of *T* ... 2Cor 7:6 *5103*
more joyed we for the joy of *T* ... 2Cor 7:13 *5103*
boasting, which I made before *T* ... 2Cor 7:14 *5103*
Insomuch that we desired *T* ... 2Cor 8:6 *5103*
care into the heart of *T* for you ... 2Cor 8:16 *5103*
Whether any do enquire of *T* ... 2Cor 8:23 *5103*
I desired *T*, and with him I sent a ... 2Cor 12:18 *5103*
Did *T* make a gain of you ... 2Cor 12:18 *5103*
a city of Macedonia, by *T* ... 2Cor *s* *5103*
Barnabas, and took *T* with me also ... Gal 2:1 *5103*
But neither *T*, who was with me, ... Gal 2:3 *5103*
to Galatia, *T* unto Dalmatia ... 2Ti 4:10 *5103*
To *T*, mine own son after the ... Titus 1:4 *5103*
It was written to *T*, ordained the ... Titus *s* *5103*

TIZITE *(ti'-zite)* {1} *Family name of Joha.*
and Joha his brother, the *T* ... 1Chr 11:45 8491

TO See APPENDIX.

TOAH *(to'-ah)* {1} See NAHATH, TOHU. *An ancestor of Samuel.*
the son of Eliel, the son of *T* ... 1Chr 6:34 8430

TOB *(tob)* {2} *A district in Syria.*
and dwelt in the land of *T* ... Judg 11:3 2897
Jephthah out of the land of *T* ... Judg 11:5 2897

TOB-ADONIJAH *(tob'-ad-o-ni-jah)* {1} *A Levite messenger of King Jehoshaphat.*
and Adonijah, and Tobijah, and *T* ... 2Chr 17:8 2899

TOBIAH *(to-bi'-ah)* {15} See TOBIJAH.
1. A family of exiles.
of Delaiah, the children of *T* ... Ezr 2:60 2900
of Delaiah, the children of *T* ... Neh 7:62 2900
2. An Ammonite who opposed Nehemiah.
T the servant, the Ammonite, ... Neh 2:10 2900
T the servant, the Ammonite, and ... Neh 2:19 2900
Now *T* the Ammonite was by him, and ... Neh 4:3 2900
pass, that when Sanballat, and *T* ... Neh 4:7 2900
to pass, when Sanballat, and *T* ... Neh 6:1 2900
for *T* and Sanballat had hired him ... Neh 6:12 2900
My God, think thou upon *T* ... Neh 6:14 2900
of Judah sent many letters unto *T* ... Neh 6:17 2900
the letters of *T* came unto them ... Neh 6:17 2900
T sent letters to put me in fear ... Neh 6:19 2900
of our God, was allied unto *T* ... Neh 13:4 2900
the evil that Eliashib did for *T* ... Neh 13:7 2900
stuff of *T* out of the chamber ... Neh 13:8 2900

TOBIJAH *(to-bi'-jah)* {3} See TOBIAH.
1. A Levite messenger of King Jehoshaphat.
and Jehonathan, and Adonijah, and *T* ... 2Chr 17:8 2900
2. A clan leader of exiles.
captivity, even of Heldai, of *T* ... Zec 6:10 2900
crowns shall be to Helem, and to *T* ... Zec 6:14 2900

TOCHEN *(to'-ken)* {1} *A city in Simeon.*
were, Etam, and Ain, Rimmon, and *T* ... 1Chr 4:32 8507

TODAY {3}
glorious was the king of Israel *t* ... 2Sa 6:20
T thy servant knoweth that I have ... 2Sa 14:22
T shall the house of Israel ... 2Sa 16:3

TOE {6}
upon the great *t* of their right ... Ex 29:20 931
upon the great *t* of his right ... Lev 8:23 931
upon the great *t* of his right ... Lev 14:14 931
upon the great *t* of his right ... Lev 14:17 931
upon the great *t* of his right ... Lev 14:25 931
upon the great *t* of his right ... Lev 14:28 931

TOES {7}
upon the great *t* of their right ... Lev 8:24 931
cut off his thumbs and his great *t* ... Judg 1:6 931,7272
thumbs and their great *t* cut off ... Judg 1:7 931,7272
fingers, and on every foot six *t* ... 2Sa 21:20 676
t were four and twenty, six on ... 1Chr 20:6 676
whereas thou sawest the feet and *t* ... Dan 2:41 677
as the *t* of the feet were part of ... Dan 2:42 677

TOGARMAH *(to-gar'-mah)* {4} *A son of Gomer.*
Ashkenaz, and Riphath, and *T* ... Gen 10:3 8425
Ashchenaz, and Riphath, and *T* ... 1Chr 1:6 8425
They of the house of *T* traded in ... Eze 27:14 8425
the house of *T* of the north ... Eze 38:6 8425

TOGETHER See APPENDIX.

TOHU *(to'-hu)* {1} See NAHATH, TOAH. *An ancestor of Samuel.*
the son of Elihu, the son of *T* ... 1Sa 1:1 8459

TOI *(to'-i)* {3} See TOU. *King of Hamath.*
When *T* king of Hamath heard that ... 2Sa 8:9 8583
Then *T* sent Joram his son unto ... 2Sa 8:10 8583
for Hadadezer had wars with *T* ... 2Sa 8:10 8583

TOIL {4}
t of our hands, because of the ... Gen 5:29 6093
he, hath made me forget all my *t* ... Gen 41:51 5999
they *t* not, neither do they spin ... Mt 6:28 *2872*
they *t* not, they spin not ... Lk 12:27 *2872*

TOILED {1}
we have *t* all the night, and have ... Lk 5:5 *2872*

TOILING {1}
And he saw them *t* in rowing ... Mk 6:48 *928*

TOKEN {14}
This is the *t* of the covenant ... Gen 9:12 226
it shall be for a *t* of a covenant ... Gen 9:13 226
This is the *t* of the covenant, ... Gen 9:17 226
it shall be a *t* of the covenant ... Gen 17:11 226
and this shall be a *t* unto thee ... Ex 3:12 226
a *t* upon the houses where ye are ... Ex 12:13 226
shall be for a *t* upon thine hand ... Ex 13:16 226
to be kept for a *t* against the ... Num 17:10 226
house, and give me a true *t* ... Josh 2:12 226
Shew me a *t* for good ... Ps 86:17 226
betrayed him had given them a *t* ... Mk 14:44 *4953*
to them an evident *t* of perdition ... Phil 1:28 *1732*
Which is a manifest *t* of the ... 2Th 1:5 *1730*
which is the *t* in every epistle ... 2Th 3:17 *4592*

TOKENS {7}
bring forth the *t* of the damsel's ... Deut 22:15
yet these are the *t* of my ... Deut 22:17
the *t* of virginity be not found ... Deut 22:20
and do ye not know their *t* ... Job 21:29 226
parts are afraid at thy *t* ... Ps 65:8 226
Who sent *t* and wonders into the ... Ps 135:9 226
frustrateth the *t* of the liars ... Is 44:25 226

TOKHATH See TIKVATH.

TOLA *(to'-lah)* {6} See TOLAITES.
1. A son of Issachar.
T, and Phuvah, and Job, and Shimron ... Gen 46:13 8439
of *T*, the family of the Tolaites ... Num 26:23 8439
Now the sons of Issachar were, *T* ... 1Chr 7:1 8439
And the sons of *T* ... 1Chr 7:2 8439
father's house, to wit, of *T* ... 1Chr 7:2 8439
2. A judge of Israel.
defend Israel *T* the son of Puah ... Judg 10:1 8439

TOLAD *(to'-lad)* {1} See EL-TOLAD. *A city in Simeon.*
And at Bilhah, and at Ezem, and at *T* ... 1Chr 4:29 8434

TOLAITES *(to'-lah-ites)* {1} *Descendants of Tola.*
of Tola, the family of the *T* ... Num 26:23 8440

TOLD See APPENDIX.

TOLERABLE {6}
It shall be more *t* for the land ... Mt 10:15 *414*
you, It shall be more *t* for Tyre ... Mt 11:22 *414*
That it shall be more *t* for the ... Mt 11:24 *414*
you, It shall be more *t* for Sodom ... Mk 6:11 *414*
be more *t* in that day for Sodom ... Lk 10:12 *414*
But it shall be more *t* for Tyre ... Lk 10:14 *414*

TOLL {3}
again, then will they not pay *t* ... Ezr 4:13 4061
and *t*, tribute, and custom, was ... Ezr 4:20 4061
shall not be lawful to impose *t* ... Ezr 7:24 4061

TOMB {3}
grave, and shall remain in the *t* ... Job 21:32 1430
And laid it in his own new *t* ... Mt 27:60 *3419*
up his corpse, and laid it in a *t* ... Mk 6:29 *3419*

TOMBS {6}
with devils, coming out of the *t* ... Mt 8:28 *3419*
ye build the *t* of the prophets ... Mt 23:29 *5028*
there met him out of the *t* a man ... Mk 5:2 *3419*
Who had his dwelling among the *t* ... Mk 5:3 *3419*
was in the mountains, and in the *t* ... Mk 5:5 *3418*
abode in any house, but in the *t* ... Lk 8:27 *3418*

TONGS {6}
the *t* thereof, and the snuffdishes ... Ex 25:38 4457
the light, and his lamps, and his *t* ... Num 4:9 4457
and the lamps, and the *t* of gold, ... 1Kin 7:49 4457
flowers, and the lamps, and the *t* ... 2Chr 4:21 4457
with the *t* from off the altar ... Is 6:6 4457
The smith with the *t* both worketh ... Is 44:12 4621

TONGUE {129}
every one after his *t*, after ... Gen 10:5 3956
am slow of speech, and of a slow *t* ... Ex 4:10 3956
Israel shall not a dog move his *t* ... Ex 11:7 3956
a nation whose *t* thou shalt not ... Deut 28:49 3956
none moved his *t* against any of ... Josh 10:21 3956
lappeth of the water with his *t* ... Judg 7:5 3956
by me, and his word was in my *t* ... 2Sa 23:2 3956
was written in the Syrian *t* ... Ezr 4:7 762
and interpreted in the Syrian *t* ... Ezr 4:7 762
and bondwomen, I had held my *t* ... Est 7:4 2790
be hid from the scourge of the *t* ... Job 5:21 3956
Teach me, and I will hold my *t* ... Job 6:24 2790
Is there iniquity in my *t* ... Job 6:30 3956
for now, if I hold my *t*, I shall ... Job 13:19 2790
thou choosest the *t* of the crafty ... Job 15:5 3956
though he hide it under his *t* ... Job 20:12 3956
the viper's *t* shall slay him ... Job 20:16 3956
wickedness, nor my *t* utter deceit ... Job 27:4 3956
their *t* cleaved to the roof of ... Job 29:10 3956
my *t* hath spoken in my mouth ... Job 33:2 3956
or his *t* with a cord which thou ... Job 41:1 3956
they flatter with their *t* ... Ps 5:9 3956
under his *t* is mischief and vanity ... Ps 10:7 3956
the *t* that speaketh proud things ... Ps 12:3 3956
With our *t* will we prevail ... Ps 12:4 3956
He that backbiteth not with his *t* ... Ps 15:3 3956
and my *t* cleaveth to my jaws ... Ps 22:15 3956
Keep thy *t* from evil, and thy lips ... Ps 34:13 3956
And my *t* shall speak of thy ... Ps 35:28 3956
his *t* talketh of judgment ... Ps 37:30 3956
my ways, that I sin not with my *t* ... Ps 39:1 3956
then spake I with my *t* ... Ps 39:3 3956
my *t* is the pen of a ready writer ... Ps 45:1 3956
to evil, and thy *t* frameth deceit ... Ps 50:19 3956
my *t* shall sing aloud of thy ... Ps 51:14 3956
Thy *t* deviseth mischiefs ... Ps 52:2 3956
words, O thou deceitful *t* ... Ps 52:4 3956
arrows, and their *t* a sharp sword ... Ps 57:4 3956
Who whet their *t* like a sword ... Ps 64:3 3956
own *t* to fall upon themselves ... Ps 64:8 3956
and he was extolled with my *t* ... Ps 66:17 3956
the *t* of thy dogs in the same ... Ps 68:23 3956
My *t* also shall talk of thy ... Ps 71:24 3956
their *t* walketh through the earth ... Ps 73:9 3956
spoken against me with a lying *t* ... Ps 109:2 3956
My *t* shall speak of thy word ... Ps 119:172 3956
lying lips, and from a deceitful *t* ... Ps 120:2 3956
be done unto thee, thou false *t* ... Ps 120:3 3956
laughter, and our *t* with singing ... Ps 126:2 3956
let my *t* cleave to the roof of my ... Ps 137:6 3956
For there is not a word in my *t* ... Ps 139:4 3956
A proud look, a lying *t*, and hands ... Prov 6:17 3956
of the *t* of a strange woman ... Prov 6:24 3956
The *t* of the just is as choice ... Prov 10:20 3956
but the froward *t* shall be cut ... Prov 10:31 3956
but the *t* of the wise is health ... Prov 12:18 3956
but a lying *t* is but for a moment ... Prov 12:19 3956
The *t* of the wise useth knowledge ... Prov 15:2 3956
A wholesome *t* is a tree of life ... Prov 15:4 3956
in man, and the answer of the *t* ... Prov 16:1 3956
a liar giveth ear to a naughty *t* ... Prov 17:4 3956
perverse *t* falleth into mischief ... Prov 17:20 3956
and life are in the power of the *t* ... Prov 18:21 3956
a lying *t* is a vanity tossed to ... Prov 21:6 3956
his *t* keepeth his soul from ... Prov 21:23 3956
a soft *t* breaketh the bone ... Prov 25:15 3956
angry countenance a backbiting *t* ... Prov 25:23 3956
A lying *t* hateth those that are ... Prov 26:28 3956
he that flattereth with the *t* ... Prov 28:23 3956
in her *t* is the law of kindness ... Prov 31:26 3956
honey and milk are under thy *t* ... Song 4:11 3956
because their *t* and their doings ... Is 3:8 3956
destroy the *t* of the Egyptian sea ... Is 11:15 3956
another *t* will he speak to this ... Is 28:11 3956
his *t* as a devouring fire ... Is 30:27 3956
the *t* of the stammerers shall be ... Is 32:4 3956
of a stammering *t*, that thou ... Is 33:19 3956
hart, and the *t* of the dumb sing ... Is 35:6 3956
their *t* faileth for thirst, I the ... Is 41:17 3956
shall bow, every *t* shall swear ... Is 45:23 3956
given me the *t* of the learned ... Is 50:4 3956
every *t* that shall rise against ... Is 54:17 3956
a wide mouth, and draw out the *t* ... Is 57:4 3956
your *t* hath muttered perverseness ... Is 59:3 3956
have taught their *t* to speak lies ... Jer 9:5 3956
Their *t* is as an arrow shot out ... Jer 9:8 3956
and let us smite him with the *t* ... Jer 18:18 3956
The *t* of the sucking child ... Lam 4:4 3956
I will make thy *t* cleave to the ... Eze 3:26 3956
and the *t* of the Chaldeans ... Dan 1:4 3956
the sword for the rage of their *t* ... Hos 7:16 3956
Then shall he say, Hold thy *t* ... Amos 6:10 2013
their *t* is deceitful in their ... Mic 6:12 3956
holdest thy *t* when the wicked ... Hab 1:13 2790
t be found in their mouth ... Zeph 3:13 3956
their *t* shall consume away in ... Zec 14:12 3956
and he spit, and touched his *t* ... Mk 7:33 *1100*
and the string of his *t* was loosed ... Mk 7:35 *1100*
his *t* loosed, and he spake, and ... Lk 1:64 *1100*

T

his finger in water, and cool my *t* Lk 16:24 *1100*
called in the Hebrew *t* Bethesda Jn 5:2 *1447*
field is called in their proper *t* Acts 1:19 *1258*
hear we every man in our own *t* Acts 2:8 *1258*
heart rejoice, and my *t* was glad Acts 2:26 *1100*
spake unto them in the Hebrew *t* Acts 21:40 *1258*
he spake in the Hebrew *t* to them Acts 22:2 *1258*
me, and saying in the Hebrew *t* Acts 26:14 *1258*
every *t* shall confess to God Rom 14:11 *1100*
unknown *t* speaketh not unto men 1Cor 14:2 *1100*
in an unknown *t* edifieth himself 1Cor 14:4 *1100*
except ye utter by the *t* words 1Cor 14:9 *1100*
t pray that he may interpret 1Cor 14:13 *1100*
For if I pray in an unknown *t* 1Cor 14:14 *1100*
thousand words in an unknown *t* 1Cor 14:19 *1100*
psalm, hath a doctrine, hath a *t* 1Cor 14:26 *1100*
If any man speak in an unknown *t* 1Cor 14:27 *1100*
that every *t* should confess that Phil 2:11 *1100*
religious, and bridleth not his *t* Jas 1:26 *1100*
Even so the *t* is a little member, Jas 3:5 *1100*
the *t* is a fire, a world of Jas 3:6 *1100*
so is the *t* among our members, Jas 3:6 *1100*
But the *t* can no man tame Jas 3:8 *1100*
let him refrain his *t* from evil 1Pet 3:10 *1100*
us not love in word, neither in *t* 1Jn 3:18 *1100*
blood out of every kindred, and *t* Rev 5:9 *1100*
name in the Hebrew *t* is Abaddon Rev 9:11 *1447*
but in the Greek *t* hath his name Rev 9:11
to every nation, and kindred, and *t* Rev 14:6 *1100*
called in the Hebrew *t* Armageddon Rev 16:16 *1447*

TONGUES {36}
their families, after their *t* Gen 10:20 3956
their families, after their *t* Gen 10:31 3956
a pavilion from the strife of *t* Ps 31:20 3956
O Lord, and divide their *t* Ps 55:9 3956
they lied unto him with their *t* Ps 78:36 3956
sharpened their *t* like a serpent Ps 140:3 3956
I will gather all nations and *t* Is 66:18 3956
they bend their *t* like their bow Jer 9:3 3956
saith the LORD, that use their *t* Jer 23:31 3956
they shall speak with new *t* Mk 16:17 *1100*
them cloven *t* like as of fire Acts 2:3 *1100*
and began to speak with other *t* Acts 2:4 *1100*
our *t* the wonderful works of God Acts 2:11 *1100*
For they heard them speak with *t* Acts 10:46 *1100*
and they spake with *t*, and Acts 19:6 *1100*
with their *t* they have used Rom 3:13 *1100*
to another divers kinds of *t* 1Cor 12:10 *1100*
another the interpretation of *t* 1Cor 12:10 *1100*
governments, diversities of *t* 1Cor 12:28 *1100*
do all speak with *t* 1Cor 12:30 *1100*
Though I speak with the *t* of men 1Cor 13:1 *1100*
whether there be *t*, they shall 1Cor 13:8 *1100*
I would that ye all spake with *t* 1Cor 14:5 *1100*
than he that speaketh with *t* 1Cor 14:5 *1100*
I come unto you speaking with *t* 1Cor 14:6 *1100*
I speak with *t* more than ye all 1Cor 14:18 *1100*
is written, With men of other *t* 1Cor 14:21 *2084*
Wherefore *t* are for a sign, not 1Cor 14:22 *1100*
one place, and all speak with *t* 1Cor 14:23 *1100*
and forbid not to speak with *t* 1Cor 14:39 *1100*
and kindreds, and people, and *t* Rev 7:9 *1100*
many peoples, and nations, and *t* Rev 10:11 *1100*
of the people and kindreds and *t* Rev 11:9 *1100*
given him over all kindreds, and *t* Rev 13:7 *1100*
and they gnawed their *t* for pain Rev 16:10 *1100*
and multitudes, and nations, and *t* Rev 17:15 *1100*

TOO See APPENDIX.

TOOK {752}
And the LORD God *t* the man Gen 2:15 3947
he *t* one of his ribs, and closed Gen 2:21 3947
she *t* of the fruit thereof, and Gen 3:6 3947
Lamech *t* unto him two wives Gen 4:19 3947
for God *t* him Gen 5:24 3947
they *t* them wives of all which Gen 6:2 3947
t her, and pulled her in unto him Gen 8:9 3947
t of every clean beast, and of Gen 8:20 3947
Japheth *t* a garment, and laid it Gen 9:23 3947
And Abram and Nahor *t* them wives Gen 11:29 3947
Terah *t* Abram his son, and Lot the Gen 11:31 3947
Abram *t* Sarai his wife, and Lot Gen 12:5 3947
they *t* all the goods of Sodom and Gen 14:11 3947
And they *t* Lot, Abram's brother's Gen 14:12 3947
he *t* unto him all these, and Gen 15:10 3947
Sarai Abram's wife *t* Hagar her Gen 16:3 3947
Abraham *t* Ishmael his son, and all Gen 17:23 3947
he *t* butter, and milk, and the calf Gen 18:8 3947
king of Gerar sent, and *t* Sarah Gen 20:2 3947
And Abimelech *t* sheep, and oxen, and Gen 20:14 3947
t bread, and a bottle of water, and Gen 21:14 3947
his mother *t* him a wife out of Gen 21:21 3947
And Abraham *t* sheep and oxen, and Gen 21:27 3947
t two of his young men with him, Gen 22:3 3947
Abraham *t* the wood of the burnt Gen 22:6 3947
he *t* the fire in his hand, and a Gen 22:6 3947
t the knife to slay his son Gen 22:10 3947
t the ram, and offered him up for Gen 22:13 3947
which *t* me from my father's house Gen 24:7 3947
the servant *t* ten camels of the Gen 24:10 3947
that the man *t* a golden earring Gen 24:22 3947
and the servant *t* Rebekah, and went Gen 24:61 3947
therefore she *t* a vail, and Gen 24:65 3947
t Rebekah, and she became his wife Gen 24:67 3947
Then again Abraham *t* a wife Gen 25:1 3947
old when he *t* Rebekah to wife Gen 25:20 3947
his hand *t* hold on Esau's heel Gen 25:26
was forty years old when he *t* to Gen 26:34 3947
Rebekah *t* goodly raiment of her Gen 27:15 3947
he *t* away my birthright Gen 27:36 3947
t unto the wives which he had Gen 28:9 3947
he *t* of the stones of that place, Gen 28:11 3947
t the stone that he had put for Gen 28:18 3947
that he *t* Leah his daughter, and Gen 29:23 3947
she *t* Zilpah her maid, and gave Gen 30:9 3947
Jacob *t* him rods of green poplar, Gen 30:37 3947
he *t* his brethren with him, and Gen 31:23 3947
Jacob *t* a stone, and set it up for Gen 31:45 3947
they *t* stones, and made an heap Gen 31:46 3947
t of that which came to his hand Gen 32:13 3947
t his two wives, and his two Gen 32:22 3947
he *t* them, and sent them over the Gen 32:23 3947
And he urged him, and he *t* it Gen 33:11 3947
he *t* her, and lay with her, and Gen 34:2 3947
t each man his sword, and came Gen 34:25 3947
t Dinah out of Shechem's house, Gen 34:26 3947
They *t* their sheep, and their oxen Gen 34:28 3947
their wives *t* they captive, and Gen 34:29
Esau *t* his wives of the daughters Gen 36:2 3947
Esau *t* his wives, and his sons, and Gen 36:6 3947
And they *t* him, and cast him into a Gen 37:24 3947
they *t* Joseph's coat, and killed a Gen 37:31 3947
he *t* her, and went in unto her Gen 38:2 3947
Judah *t* a wife for Er his Gen 38:6 3947
and the midwife *t* and bound upon Gen 38:28 3947
And Joseph's master *t* him, and put Gen 39:20 3947
I *t* the grapes, and pressed them Gen 40:11 3947
Pharaoh *t* off his ring from his Gen 41:42 5493
t from them Simeon, and bound him Gen 42:24 3947
t us for spies of the country Gen 42:30 5414
the men *t* that present, and they Gen 43:15 3947
they *t* double money in their hand Gen 43:15 3947
And he *t* and sent messes unto them Gen 43:34 5375
Then they speedily *t* down every Gen 44:11 3381
Israel *t* his journey with all Gen 46:1
they *t* their cattle, and their Gen 46:6 3947
he *t* some of his brethren, even Gen 47:2 3947
he *t* with him his two sons, Gen 48:1 3947
Joseph *t* them both, Ephraim in Gen 48:13 3947
which I *t* out of the hand of the Gen 48:22 3947
Joseph *t* an oath of the children Gen 50:25
t to wife a daughter of Levi Ex 2:1 3947
she *t* for him an ark of bulrushes Ex 2:3 3947
And the woman *t* the child, and Ex 2:9 3947
and when he *t* it out, behold, his Ex 4:6 3318
Moses *t* his wife and his sons, and Ex 4:20 3947
Moses *t* the rod of God in his Ex 4:20 3947
Then Zipporah *t* a sharp stone Ex 4:25 3947
Amram *t* him Jochebed his father's Ex 6:20 3947
Aaron *t* him Elisheba, daughter of Ex 6:23 3947
Eleazar Aaron's son *t* him one of Ex 6:25 3947
they *t* ashes of the furnace, and Ex 9:10 3947
which *t* away the locusts, and cast Ex 10:19 5375
the people *t* their dough before Ex 12:34 5375
Moses *t* the bones of Joseph with Ex 13:19 3947
they *t* their journey from Succoth Ex 13:20
He *t* not away the pillar of the Ex 13:22 4185
chariot, and *t* his people with him Ex 14:6 3947
he *t* six hundred chosen chariots, Ex 14:7 3947
t off their chariot wheels, that Ex 14:25 5493
of Aaron, *t* a timbrel in her hand Ex 15:20 3947
they *t* their journey from Elim, Ex 16:1
they *t* a stone, and put it under Ex 17:12 3947
t Zipporah, Moses' wife, after he Ex 18:2 3947
t a burnt offering and sacrifices Ex 18:12 3947
Moses *t* half of the blood, and put Ex 24:6 3947
he *t* the book of the covenant, and Ex 24:7 3947
Moses *t* the blood, and sprinkled Ex 24:8 3947
he *t* the calf which they had made Ex 32:20 3947
Moses *t* the tabernacle, and Ex 33:7 3947
t in his hand the two tables of Ex 34:4 3947
he *t* the vail off, until he came Ex 34:34 5493
And he *t* and put the testimony into Ex 40:20 3947
that which he *t* violently away Lev 6:4 1497
Moses *t* the anointing oil, and Lev 8:10 3947
Moses *t* the blood, and put it upon Lev 8:15 3947
he *t* all the fat that was upon Lev 8:16 3947
Moses *t* of the blood of it, and Lev 8:23 3947
he *t* the fat, and the rump, and all Lev 8:25 3947
he *t* one unleavened cake, and a Lev 8:26 3947
Moses *t* them from off their hands Lev 8:28 3947
Moses *t* the breast, and waved it Lev 8:29 3947
Moses *t* of the anointing oil, and Lev 8:30 3947
t the goat, which was the sin Lev 9:15 3947
t an handful thereof, and burnt it Lev 9:17
t either of them his censer, and Lev 10:1 3947
Aaron *t* these men which are Num 1:17 3947
Moses *t* the redemption money of Num 3:49 3947
children of Israel *t* he the money Num 3:50 3947
Moses *t* the wagons and the oxen, Num 7:6 3947
the children of Israel *t* their Num 10:12 3947
they first *t* their journey Num 10:13
t of the spirit that was upon him Num 11:25 680
of Peleth, sons of Reuben, *t* men Num 16:1 3947
they *t* every man his censer, and Num 16:18 3947
the priest *t* the brasen censers Num 16:39 3947
Aaron *t* as Moses commanded, and Num 16:47 3947
looked, and *t* every man his rod Num 17:9 3947
Moses *t* the rod from before the Num 20:9 3947
and *t* some of them prisoners Num 21:1 7617
Israel *t* all these cities Num 21:25 3947
they *t* the villages thereof, and Num 21:32 3920
the morrow, that Balak *t* Balaam Num 22:41 3947
he *t* up his parable, and said, Num 23:7 5375
I *t* thee to curse mine enemies, Num 23:11 3947
he *t* up his parable, and said, Num 23:18 5375
he *t* up his parable, and said, Num 24:3 5375
he *t* up his parable, and said, Num 24:15 5375
he *t* up his parable, and said, Num 24:20 5375
t up his parable, and said, Strong Num 24:21 5375
he *t* up his parable, and said, Num 24:23 5375
and *t* a javelin in his hand Num 25:7 3947
he *t* Joshua, and set him before Num 27:22 3947
the children of Israel *t* all the Num 31:9
t the spoil of all their cattle, Num 31:9
they *t* all the spoil, and all the Num 31:11 3947
them that *t* the war upon them Num 31:27 8610
Moses *t* one portion of fifty, Num 31:47 3947
the priest *t* the gold of them Num 31:51 3947
Eleazar the priest *t* the gold of Num 31:54 3947
t it, and dispossessed the Amorite Num 32:39 3920
t the small towns thereof, and Num 32:41 3920
t Kenath, and the villages thereof Num 32:42 3920
they *t* their journey out of the Num 33:12 5265
So I *t* the chief of your tribes, Deut 1:15 3947
I *t* twelve men of you, one of a Deut 1:23 3947
they *t* of the fruit of the land Deut 1:25 3947
t our journey into the wilderness Deut 2:1 5265
we *t* all his cities at that time, Deut 2:34 3920
Only the cattle we *t* for a prey Deut 2:35
spoil of the cities which we *t* Deut 2:35 3920
we *t* all his cities at that time, Deut 3:4 3920
a city which we *t* not from them Deut 3:4 3947
we *t* for a prey to ourselves Deut 3:7
we *t* at that time out of the hand Deut 3:8 3947
Jair the son of Manasseh *t* all Deut 3:14 3947
I *t* the two tables, and cast them Deut 9:17 8610
I *t* your sin, the calf which ye Deut 9:21 3947
the children of Israel *t* their Deut 10:6
I *t* this woman, and when I came to Deut 22:14 3947
which *t* her to be his wife Deut 24:3 3947
we *t* their land, and gave it for Deut 29:8 3947
the woman *t* the two men, and hid Josh 2:4 3947
they *t* up the ark of the covenant Josh 3:6 5375
t up twelve stones out of the Josh 4:8 5375
which they *t* out of Jordan, did Josh 4:20 3947
the priests *t* up the ark of the Josh 6:12 5375
before him, and they *t* the city Josh 6:20 3920
of Judah, *t* of the accursed thing Josh 7:1 3947
he *t* the family of the Zarhites Josh 7:17 3920
then I coveted them, and *t* them Josh 7:21 3947
they *t* them out of the midst of Josh 7:23 3947
t Achan the son of Zerah, and the Josh 7:24 3947
he *t* about five thousand men, and Josh 8:12 3947
t it, and hasted and set the city Josh 8:19 3920
And the king of Ai they *t* alive Josh 8:23 8610
t for a prey unto themselves Josh 8:27
t old sacks upon their asses, and Josh 9:4 3947
This our bread we *t* hot for our Josh 9:12
the men *t* of their victuals, and Josh 9:14 3947
they *t* them down off the trees, Josh 10:27 3381
And that day Joshua *t* Makkedah Josh 10:28 3920
which *t* it on the second day, and Josh 10:32 3920
they *t* it on that day, and smote Josh 10:35 3920
And they *t* it, and smote it with Josh 10:37 3920
And he *t* it, and the king thereof, Josh 10:39 3920
t Hazor, and smote the king Josh 11:10 3920
the children of Israel *t* for a Josh 11:14
So Joshua *t* all that land, the Josh 11:16 3947
and all their kings he *t*, and smote Josh 11:17 3920
all other they *t* in battle Josh 11:19 3947
So Joshua *t* the whole land, Josh 11:23 3947
Kenaz, the brother of Caleb, *t* it Josh 15:17 3920
and Ephraim, *t* their inheritance Josh 16:4
t it, and smote it with the edge Josh 19:47 3920
I *t* your father Abraham from the Josh 24:3 3947
t a great stone, and set it up Josh 24:26 3947
Caleb's younger brother, *t* it Judg 1:13 3920
Also Judah *t* Gaza with the coast Judg 1:18 3920
they *t* their daughters to be Judg 3:6 3947
t the dagger from his right thigh Judg 3:21 3947
therefore they *t* a key, and opened Judg 3:25 3947
t the fords of Jordan toward Moab Judg 3:28 3920
Heber's wife *t* a nail of the tent Judg 4:21 3947
t an hammer in her hand, and went Judg 4:21 7760
they *t* no gain of money Judg 5:19 3947
Then Gideon *t* ten men of his Judg 6:27 3947
So the people *t* victuals in their Judg 7:8 3947
t the waters unto Beth-barah and Judg 7:24 3920
they *t* two princes of the Judg 7:25 3920
t the two kings of Midian, Zebah Judg 8:12 3920
he *t* the elders of the city, and Judg 8:16 3947
t away the ornaments that were on Judg 8:21 3947
he *t* the people, and divided them Judg 9:43 3947
he *t* the city, and slew the people Judg 9:45 3920
Abimelech *t* an axe in his hand, Judg 9:48 3947
t it, and laid it on his shoulder, Judg 9:48 5375
encamped against Thebez, and *t* it Judg 9:50 3920
Because Israel *t* away my land Judg 11:13 3947
Israel *t* not away the land of Judg 11:15 3947
the Gileadites *t* the passages of Judg 12:5 3920
Then they *t* him, and slew him at Judg 12:6 270
t in thirty daughters from abroad Judg 12:9 935
So Manoah *t* a kid with a meat Judg 13:19 3947
he *t* thereof in his hands, and Judg 14:9 7287
t their spoil, and gave change of Judg 14:19 3947
t firebrands, and turned tail to Judg 15:4 3947
t it, and slew a thousand men Judg 15:15 3947
t the doors of the gate of the Judg 16:3 270
Delilah therefore *t* new ropes Judg 16:12 3947
But the Philistines *t* him Judg 16:21 270
Samson *t* hold of the two middle Judg 16:29
t him, and brought him up, and Judg 16:31 5375
I *t* it Judg 17:2 3947

his mother *t* two hundred shekels	Judg 17:4	3947
t the graven image, and the ephod,	Judg 18:17	3947
he *t* the ephod, and the teraphim,	Judg 18:20	3947
they *t* the things which Micah had	Judg 18:27	3947
who *t* to him a concubine out of	Judg 19:1	3947
for there was no man that *t* them	Judg 19:15	622
so the man *t* his concubine, and	Judg 19:25	2388
Then the man *t* her up upon an ass	Judg 19:28	3947
he *t* a knife, and laid hold on his	Judg 19:29	3947
I *t* my concubine, and cut her in	Judg 20:6	270
t them wives, according to their	Judg 21:23	5375
they *t* them wives of the women of	Ruth 1:4	5375
she *t* it up, and went into the	Ruth 2:18	5375
he *t* ten men of the elders of the	Ruth 4:2	3947
So Boaz *t* Ruth, and she was his	Ruth 4:13	3947
Naomi *t* the child, and laid it in	Ruth 4:16	3947
she *t* him up with her, with three	1Sa 1:24	5927
up the priest *t* for himself	1Sa 2:14	3947
the Philistines *t* the ark of God	1Sa 5:1	3947
the Philistines *t* the ark of God	1Sa 5:2	3947
they *t* Dagon, and set him in his	1Sa 5:3	3947
t two milch kine, and tied them to	1Sa 6:10	3947
the kine *t* the straight way to	1Sa 6:12	
the Levites *t* down the ark of the	1Sa 6:15	3381
Samuel *t* a sucking lamb, and	1Sa 7:9	3947
Then Samuel *t* a stone, and set it	1Sa 7:12	3947
t bribes, and perverted judgment	1Sa 8:3	3947
And Samuel *t* Saul and his servant,	1Sa 9:22	3947
the cook *t* up the shoulder, and	1Sa 9:24	7311
Then Samuel *t* a vial of oil, and	1Sa 10:1	3947
he *t* a yoke of oxen, and hewed	1Sa 11:7	3947
t sheep, and oxen, and calves, and	1Sa 14:32	3947
So Saul *t* the kingdom over Israel	1Sa 14:47	3920
valiant man, he *t* him unto him	1Sa 14:52	622
he *t* Agag the king of the	1Sa 15:8	8610
But the people *t* of the spoil	1Sa 15:21	3947
Then Samuel *t* the horn of oil, and	1Sa 16:13	3947
Jesse *t* an ass laden with bread,	1Sa 16:20	3947
upon Saul, that David *t* an harp	1Sa 16:23	3947
the sheep with a keeper, and *t*	1Sa 17:20	5375
t a lamb out of the flock	1Sa 17:34	5375
he *t* his staff in his hand, and	1Sa 17:40	3947
t thence a stone, and slang it, and	1Sa 17:49	3947
t his sword, and drew it out of	1Sa 17:51	3947
And David *t* the head of the	1Sa 17:54	3947
of the Philistine, Abner *t* him	1Sa 17:57	3947
Saul *t* him that day, and would let	1Sa 18:2	3947
Michal *t* an image, and laid it in	1Sa 19:13	3947
Then Saul *t* three thousand chosen	1Sa 24:2	3947
t two hundred loaves, and two	1Sa 25:18	3947
David also *t* Ahinoam of Jezreel	1Sa 25:43	3947
So David *t* the spear and the cruse	1Sa 26:12	3947
t away the sheep, and the oxen, and	1Sa 27:9	3947
t flour, and kneaded it, and did	1Sa 28:24	3947
David *t* all the flocks and the	1Sa 30:20	3947
Therefore Saul *t* a sword, and fell	1Sa 31:4	3947
t the body of Saul and the bodies	1Sa 31:12	3947
they *t* their bones, and buried	1Sa 31:13	3947
I *t* the crown that was upon his	2Sa 1:10	3947
Then David *t* hold on his clothes,	2Sa 1:11	
t Ish-bosheth the son of Saul, and	2Sa 2:8	3947
they *t* up Asahel, and buried him	2Sa 2:32	5375
t her from her husband, even from	2Sa 3:15	3947
Joab *t* him aside in the gate to	2Sa 3:27	
And all the people *t* notice of it	2Sa 3:36	5384
of Jezreel, and his nurse *t* him up	2Sa 4:4	5375
t his head, and gat them away	2Sa 4:7	3947
I *t* hold of him, and slew him in	2Sa 4:10	
But they *t* the head of	2Sa 4:12	3947
Nevertheless David *t* the strong	2Sa 5:7	3920
David *t* him more concubines and	2Sa 5:13	3947
the ark of God, and *t* hold of it	2Sa 6:6	
I *t* thee from the sheepcote, from	2Sa 7:8	3947
as I *t* it from Saul, whom I put	2Sa 7:15	5493
David *t* Metheg-ammah out of the	2Sa 8:1	3947
David *t* from him a thousand	2Sa 8:4	3920
David *t* the shields of gold that	2Sa 8:7	3947
king David *t* exceeding much brass	2Sa 8:8	3947
Wherefore Hanun *t* David's	2Sa 10:4	3947
David sent messengers, and *t* her	2Sa 11:4	3947
but *t* the poor man's lamb, and	2Sa 12:4	3947
of Ammon, and *t* the royal city	2Sa 12:26	3920
and fought against it, and *t* it	2Sa 12:29	3920
he *t* their king's crown from off	2Sa 12:30	3947
she *t* flour, and kneaded it, and	2Sa 13:8	3947
she *t* a pan, and poured them out	2Sa 13:9	3947
Tamar *t* the cakes which she had	2Sa 13:10	3947
he *t* hold of her, and said unto	2Sa 13:11	
his hand, and *t* him, and kissed him	2Sa 15:5	2388
And the woman *t* and spread a	2Sa 17:19	3947
he *t* three darts in his hand, and	2Sa 18:14	3947
they *t* Absalom, and cast him into	2Sa 18:17	3947
the king *t* the ten women his	2Sa 20:3	3947
Joab *t* Amasa, by the beard with	2Sa 20:9	270
But Amasa *t* no heed to the sword	2Sa 20:10	
But the king *t* the two sons of	2Sa 21:8	3947
the daughter of Aiah *t* sackcloth	2Sa 21:10	3947
t the bones of Saul and the bones	2Sa 21:12	3947
He sent from above, he *t* me	2Sa 22:17	3947
t it, and brought it to David	2Sa 23:16	5375
Zadok the priest *t* an horn of oil	1Kin 1:39	3947
t Pharaoh's daughter, and brought	1Kin 3:1	3947
t my son from beside me, while	1Kin 3:20	3947
he also *t* Basmath the daughter of	1Kin 4:15	3947
came, and the priests *t* up the ark	1Kin 8:3	5375
they *t* men with them out of Paran	1Kin 11:18	3947
Whereupon the king *t* counsel	1Kin 12:28	
the prophet *t* up the carcase of	1Kin 13:29	5375
he *t* away the treasures of the	1Kin 14:26	3947
he even *t* away all	1Kin 14:26	3947
he *t* away all the shields of gold	1Kin 14:26	3947
he *t* away the sodomites out of	1Kin 15:12	5674
Then Asa *t* all the silver and the	1Kin 15:18	3947
they *t* away the stones of Ramah,	1Kin 15:22	5375
that he *t* to wife Jezebel the	1Kin 16:31	3947
he *t* him out of her bosom, and	1Kin 17:19	3947
Elijah *t* the child, and brought	1Kin 17:23	3947
that Obadiah *t* an hundred	1Kin 18:4	3947
he *t* an oath of the kingdom and	1Kin 18:10	
they *t* the bullock which was	1Kin 18:26	3947
Elijah *t* twelve stones, according	1Kin 18:31	3947
And they *t* them	1Kin 18:40	8610
t a yoke of oxen, and slew them,	1Kin 19:21	3947
which my father *t* from thy father	1Kin 20:34	3947
t the ashes away from his face	1Kin 20:41	5493
father Asa, he *t* out of the land	1Kin 22:46	1197
Elijah *t* his mantle, and wrapped	2Kin 2:8	3947
he *t* hold of his own clothes, and	2Kin 2:12	
He *t* up also the mantle of Elijah	2Kin 2:13	7311
he *t* the mantle of Elijah that	2Kin 2:14	3947
he *t* with him seven hundred men	2Kin 3:26	3947
Then he *t* his eldest son that	2Kin 3:27	3947
t up her son, and went out	2Kin 4:37	5375
t with him ten talents of silver,	2Kin 5:5	3947
he *t* them from their hand, and	2Kin 5:24	3947
And he put out his hand, and *t* it	2Kin 6:7	3947
t counsel with his servants,	2Kin 6:8	
They *t* therefore two chariot	2Kin 7:14	3947
t a present with him, even of	2Kin 8:9	3947
that he *t* a thick cloth, and	2Kin 8:15	3947
t every man his garment, and put	2Kin 9:13	3947
that they *t* the king's sons, and	2Kin 10:7	3947
they *t* them alive, and slew them	2Kin 10:14	8610
he *t* him up to him into the	2Kin 10:15	5927
But Jehu *t* no heed to walk in the	2Kin 10:31	
t Joash the son of Ahaziah, and	2Kin 11:2	3947
t an oath of them in the house of	2Kin 11:4	
they *t* every man his men that	2Kin 11:9	3947
he *t* the rulers over hundreds, and	2Kin 11:19	3947
But Jehoiada the priest *t* a chest	2Kin 12:9	3947
and fought against Gath, and *t* it	2Kin 12:17	3920
Jehoash king of Judah *t* all the	2Kin 12:18	3947
he *t* unto him bow and arrows	2Kin 13:15	3947
And he *t* them	2Kin 13:18	3947
t again out of the hand of	2Kin 13:25	3947
t Selah by war, and called the	2Kin 14:7	8610
of Israel *t* Amaziah king of Judah	2Kin 14:13	8610
he *t* all the gold and silver, and	2Kin 14:14	3947
all the people of Judah *t* Azariah	2Kin 14:21	3947
t Ijon, and Abel-beth-maachah, and	2Kin 15:29	3947
Ahaz *t* the silver and gold that	2Kin 16:8	3947
t it, and carried the people of it	2Kin 16:9	8610
t down the sea from off the	2Kin 16:17	3381
the king of Assyria *t* Samaria	2Kin 17:6	3920
the end of three years they *t* it	2Kin 18:10	3920
fenced cities of Judah, and *t* them	2Kin 18:13	8610
And they *t* and laid it on the boil,	2Kin 20:7	3947
he *t* away the horses that the	2Kin 23:11	7673
t the bones out of the sepulchres	2Kin 23:16	3947
the LORD to anger, Josiah *t* away	2Kin 23:19	5493
the people of the land *t* Jehoahaz	2Kin 23:30	3947
to Jehoiakim, and *t* Jehoahaz away	2Kin 23:34	3947
the king of Babylon *t* him in the	2Kin 24:12	3947
So they *t* the king, and brought	2Kin 25:6	8610
they ministered, *t* they away	2Kin 25:14	3947
the captain of the guard *t* away	2Kin 25:15	3947
guard *t* Seraiah the chief priest	2Kin 25:18	3947
out of the city he *t* an officer	2Kin 25:19	3947
captain of the guard *t* these	2Kin 25:20	3947
Caleb *t* unto him Ephrath, which	1Chr 2:19	3947
he *t* Geshur, and Aram, with the	1Chr 2:23	3947
of Pharaoh, which Mered *t*	1Chr 4:18	3947
And they *t* away their cattle	1Chr 5:21	7617
Machir *t* to wife the sister of	1Chr 7:15	3947
So Saul *t* a sword, and fell upon	1Chr 10:4	3947
they *t* his head, and his armour,	1Chr 10:9	5375
t away the body of Saul, and the	1Chr 10:12	5375
David *t* the castle of Zion	1Chr 11:5	3920
t it, and brought it to David	1Chr 11:18	5375
David *t* more wives at Jerusalem	1Chr 14:3	3947
I *t* thee from the sheepcote, even	1Chr 17:7	3947
as I *t* it from him that was	1Chr 17:13	5493
t Gath and her towns out of the	1Chr 18:1	3947
David *t* from him a thousand	1Chr 18:4	3920
David *t* the shields of gold that	1Chr 18:7	3947
Wherefore Hanun *t* David's	1Chr 19:4	3947
David *t* the crown of their king	1Chr 20:2	3947
brethren the sons of Kish *t* them	1Chr 23:22	5375
But David *t* not the number of	1Chr 27:23	5375
and the Levites *t* up the ark	2Chr 5:4	5375
t thence four hundred and fifty	2Chr 8:18	3947
king Rehoboam *t* counsel with the	2Chr 10:6	
t counsel with the young men that	2Chr 10:8	
Rehoboam *t* him Mahalath the	2Chr 11:18	3947
after her he *t* Maachah the	2Chr 11:20	3947
(for he *t* eighteen wives, and	2Chr 11:21	5375
he *t* the fenced cities which	2Chr 12:4	3920
t away the treasures of the house	2Chr 12:9	3947
he *t* all	2Chr 12:9	3947
t cities from him, Beth-el with	2Chr 13:19	3920
For he *t* away the altars of the	2Chr 14:3	5493
Also he *t* away out of all the	2Chr 14:5	5493
he *t* courage, and put away the	2Chr 15:8	
Then Asa the king *t* all Judah	2Chr 16:6	3947
moreover he *t* away the high	2Chr 17:6	5493
t Joash the son of Ahaziah, and	2Chr 22:11	3947
t the captains of hundreds,	2Chr 23:1	3947
t every man his men that were to	2Chr 23:8	3947
he *t* the captains of hundreds, and	2Chr 23:20	3947
Jehoiada *t* for him two wives	2Chr 24:3	5375
t it, and carried it to his place	2Chr 24:11	5375
thousand of them, and *t* much spoil	2Chr 25:13	
Amaziah king of Judah *t* advice	2Chr 25:17	
of Israel *t* Amaziah king of Judah	2Chr 25:23	8610
he *t* all the gold and the sliver,	2Chr 25:24	
all the people of Judah *t* Uzziah	2Chr 26:1	3947
t also away much spoil from them,	2Chr 28:8	962
t the captives, and with the spoil	2Chr 28:15	2388
For Ahaz *t* away a portion out of	2Chr 28:21	2505
And the Levites *t* it, to carry it	2Chr 29:16	6901
t away the altars that were in	2Chr 30:14	5493
altars for incense *t* they away	2Chr 30:14	5493
the whole assembly *t* counsel to	2Chr 30:23	
He *t* counsel with his princes and	2Chr 32:3	
which *t* Manasseh among the thorns	2Chr 33:11	3920
he *t* away the strange gods, and	2Chr 33:15	5493
And Josiah *t* away all the	2Chr 34:33	5493
His servants therefore *t* him out	2Chr 35:24	5674
land *t* Jehoahaz the son of Josiah	2Chr 36:1	3947
Necho *t* Jehoahaz his brother, and	2Chr 36:4	3947
which *t* a wife of the daughters	Ezr 2:61	3947
which Nebuchadnezzar *t* out of the	Ezr 5:14	5312
which Nebuchadnezzar *t* forth out	Ezr 6:5	5312
So *t* the priests and the Levites	Ezr 8:30	6901
I *t* up the wine, and gave it unto	Neh 2:1	5375
t great indignation, and mocked	Neh 4:1	
t an oath of them, that they	Neh 5:12	
which *t* one of the daughters of	Neh 7:63	3947
they *t* strong cities, and a fat	Neh 9:25	3920
were dead, *t* for his own daughter	Est 2:7	3947
the king *t* his ring from his hand	Est 3:10	5493
Then *t* Haman the apparel and the	Est 6:11	3947
the king *t* off his ring, which he	Est 8:2	5493
t upon them, and upon their seed,	Est 9:27	6901
fell upon them, and *t* them away	Job 1:15	3947
he *t* him a potsherd to scrape	Job 2:8	3947
He sent from above, he *t* me	Ps 18:16	3947
art he that *t* me out of the womb	Ps 22:9	1518
while they *t* counsel together	Ps 31:13	
Fear *t* hold upon them there, and	Ps 48:6	
We *t* sweet counsel together, and	Ps 55:14	
the Philistines *t* him in Gath	Ps 56:*t*	270
restored that which I *t* not away	Ps 69:4	1497
thou art he that *t* me out of my	Ps 71:6	1491
t him from the sheepfolds	Ps 78:70	3947
not that which he *t* in hunting	Prov 12:27	
labour which I *t* under the sun	Eccl 2:20	5998
the walls *t* away my veil from me	Song 5:7	5375
I *t* unto me faithful witnesses to	Is 8:2	
and fought against Ashdod, and *t* it	Is 20:1	3920
cities of Judah, and *t* them	Is 36:1	8610
With whom *t* he counsel, and who	Is 40:14	
t the girdle from the place where	Jer 13:7	3947
Then *t* I the cup at the LORD's	Jer 25:17	3947
prophets and all the people *t* him	Jer 26:8	8610
king of Babylon *t* not, when he	Jer 27:20	3947
of Babylon *t* away from this place	Jer 28:3	3947
Then Hananiah the prophet *t* the	Jer 28:10	3947
t them by the hand to bring them	Jer 31:32	2388
t witnesses, and weighed him the	Jer 32:10	
So I *t* the evidence of the	Jer 32:11	3947
Then I *t* Jaazaniah the son of	Jer 35:3	3947
of Neriah *t* the roll in his hand	Jer 36:14	3947
he *t* it out of Elishama the	Jer 36:21	3947
Then *t* Jeremiah another roll, and	Jer 36:32	3947
he *t* Jeremiah the prophet, saying	Jer 37:13	8610
so Irijah *t* Jeremiah, and brought	Jer 37:14	8610
the king sent, and *t* him out	Jer 37:17	3947
Then *t* they Jeremiah, and cast him	Jer 38:6	3947
So Ebed-melech *t* the men with him	Jer 38:11	3947
t thence old cast clouts and old	Jer 38:11	3947
t him up out of the dungeon	Jer 38:13	5927
t Jeremiah the prophet unto him	Jer 38:14	3947
t Jeremiah out of the court of	Jer 39:14	3947
captain of the guard *t* Jeremiah	Jer 40:2	3947
Then they *t* all the men, and went	Jer 41:12	3947
Then *t* Johanan the son of Kareah,	Jer 41:16	3947
t all the remnant of Judah, that	Jer 43:5	3947
all that *t* them captives held	Jer 50:33	
anguish *t* hold of him, and pangs	Jer 50:43	
Then they *t* the king, and carried	Jer 52:9	8610
they ministered, *t* they away	Jer 52:18	3947
t the captain of the guard away	Jer 52:19	3947
guard *t* Seraiah the chief priest	Jer 52:24	3947
He *t* also out of the city an	Jer 52:25	3947
the captain of the guard *t* them	Jer 52:26	3947
They *t* the young men to grind, and	Lam 5:13	5375
Then the spirit *t* me up, and I	Eze 3:12	5375
me up, and *t* me away, and I went in	Eze 3:14	3947
t me by a lock of mine head	Eze 8:3	3947
t thereof, and put it into the	Eze 10:7	5375
who *t* it, and went out	Eze 10:7	3947
Afterwards the spirit *t* me up	Eze 11:24	5375
therefore I *t* them away as I saw	Eze 16:50	5493
t the highest branch of the cedar	Eze 17:3	3947
He *t* also of the seed of the land	Eze 17:5	3947
then she *t* another of her whelps,	Eze 19:5	3947
they *t* her sons and her daughters,	Eze 23:10	3947
that they *t* both one way,	Eze 23:13	
When they *t* hold of thee by thy	Eze 29:7	8610
of the trumpet, and *t* not warning	Eze 33:5	
So the spirit *t* me up, and brought	Eze 43:5	5375
Thus Melzar *t* away the portion of	Dan 1:16	5375
slew those men that *t* up Shadrach	Dan 3:22	5267

they t his glory from him ... Dan 5:20 5709
Darius the Median t the kingdom ... Dan 5:31 6902
t Gomer the daughter of Diblaim ... Hos 1:3 3947
He t his brother by the heel in ... Hos 12:3 6117
anger, and t him away in my wrath ... Hos 13:11 3947
the LORD t me as I followed the ... Amos 7:15 3947
So they t up Jonah, and cast him ... Jonah 1:15 5375
And I t unto me two staves ... Zec 11:7 3947
I t my staff, even Beauty, and cut ... Zec 11:10 3947
I t the thirty pieces of silver, ... Zec 11:13 3947
him, and t unto him his wife ... Mt 1:24 3880
he t the young child and his ... Mt 2:14 3880
t the young child and his mother, ... Mt 2:21 3880
Himself t our infirmities, and ... Mt 8:17 2983
t her by the hand, and the maid ... Mt 9:25 2902
of mustard seed, which a man t ... Mt 13:31 2983
like unto leaven, which a woman t ... Mt 13:33 2983
t up the body, and buried it, and ... Mt 14:12 142
t the five loaves, and the two ... Mt 14:19 2983
they t up of the fragments that ... Mt 14:20 142
he t the seven loaves and the ... Mt 15:36 2983
they t up of the broken meat that ... Mt 15:37 142
t ship, and came into the coasts ... Mt 15:39 1684
and how many baskets ye t up ... Mt 16:9 2983
and how many baskets ye t up ... Mt 16:10 2983
Then Peter t him, and began to ... Mt 16:22 4355
t him by the throat, saying, Pay ... Mt 18:28 2902
Jesus going up to Jerusalem t the ... Mt 20:17 3880
And the husbandmen t his servants ... Mt 21:35 2983
because they t him for a prophet ... Mt 21:46 2192
the remnant t his servants, and ... Mt 22:6 2902
t counsel how they might entangle ... Mt 22:15 2983
flood came, and t them all away ... Mt 24:39 142
which t their lamps, and went ... Mt 25:1 2983
that were foolish t their lamps ... Mt 25:3 2983
lamps, and t no oil with them ... Mt 25:3 2983
But the wise t oil in their ... Mt 25:4 2983
and straightway t his journey ... Mt 25:15 589
I was a stranger, and ye t me in ... Mt 25:35 4863
we thee a stranger, and t thee in ... Mt 25:38 4863
was a stranger, and ye t me not in ... Mt 25:43 4863
they were eating, Jesus t bread ... Mt 26:26 2983
he t the cup, and gave thanks, and ... Mt 26:27 2983
he t with him Peter and the two ... Mt 26:37 3880
and laid hands on Jesus, and t him ... Mt 26:50 2902
elders of the people t counsel ... Mt 27:1 2983
chief priests t the silver pieces ... Mt 27:6 2983
they t counsel, and bought with ... Mt 27:7 2983
they t the thirty pieces of ... Mt 27:9 2983
he t water, and washed his hands ... Mt 27:24 2983
t Jesus into the common hall ... Mt 27:27 3880
t the reed, and smote him on the ... Mt 27:30 2983
they t the robe off from him, and ... Mt 27:31 1562
t a spunge, and filled it with ... Mt 27:48 2983
So they t the money, and did as ... Mt 28:15 2983
t her by the hand, and lifted her ... Mk 1:31 2902
t up the bed, and went forth ... Mk 2:12 142
straightway t counsel with the ... Mk 3:6 4160
they t him even as he was in the ... Mk 4:36 3880
he t the damsel by the hand, and ... Mk 5:41 2902
t up his corpse, and laid it in a ... Mk 6:29 142
they t up twelve baskets full of ... Mk 6:43 142
he t him aside from the multitude ... Mk 7:33 618
he t the seven loaves, and gave ... Mk 8:6 2983
they t up of the broken meat that ... Mk 8:8 142
baskets full of fragments t ye up ... Mk 8:19 142
baskets full of fragments t ye up ... Mk 8:20 142
he t the blind man by the hand, ... Mk 8:23 1949
And Peter t him, and began to ... Mk 8:32 4355
But Jesus t him by the hand, and ... Mk 9:27 2902
he t a child, and set him in the ... Mk 9:36 2983
he t them up in his arms, put his ... Mk 10:16 1723
he t again the twelve, and began ... Mk 10:32 3880
And they t him, and killed him, and ... Mk 12:8 2983
and the first t a wife, and dying ... Mk 12:20 2983
And the second t her, and died, ... Mk 12:21 2983
And as they did eat, Jesus t bread ... Mk 14:22 2983
he t the cup, and when he had ... Mk 14:23 2983
laid their hands on him, and t him ... Mk 14:46 2902
temple teaching, and ye t me not ... Mk 14:49 2902
they t off the purple from him, ... Mk 15:20 1562
t him down, and wrapped him in the ... Mk 15:46 2507
Then t he him up in his arms, and ... Lk 2:28 1209
t up that whereon he lay, and ... Lk 5:25 142
t her by the hand, and called, ... Lk 8:54 2902
And he t them, and went aside ... Lk 9:10 3880
Then he t the five loaves and the ... Lk 9:16 2983
he t Peter and John and James, and ... Lk 9:28 3880
t a child, and set him by him, ... Lk 9:47 1949
him to an inn, and t care of him ... Lk 10:34 1959
he t out two pence, and gave them ... Lk 10:35 1544
of mustard seed, which a man t ... Lk 13:19 2983
is like leaven, which a woman t ... Lk 13:21 2983
he t him, and healed him, and let ... Lk 14:4 1949
t his journey into a far country, ... Lk 15:13 589
Then he t unto him the twelve, and ... Lk 18:31 3830
and the first t a wife, and died ... Lk 20:29 2983
the second t her to wife, and he ... Lk 20:30 2983
And the third t her ... Lk 20:31 2983
he t the cup, and gave thanks, and ... Lk 22:17 1209
he t bread, and gave thanks, and ... Lk 22:19 2983
Then t they him, and led him, and ... Lk 22:54 4815
he t it down, and wrapped it in ... Lk 23:53 2507
he t bread, and blessed it, and ... Lk 24:30 2983
And he t it, and did eat before ... Lk 24:43 2983
whole, and t up his bed, and walked ... Jn 5:9 142
And Jesus t the loaves ... Jn 6:11 2983
disciples, they also t shipping ... Jn 6:24 1684
Then t they up stones to cast at ... Jn 8:59 142
Then the Jews t up stones again ... Jn 10:31 941
Then they t away the stone from ... Jn 11:41 142
Then from that day forth they t ... Jn 11:53 4823
Then t Mary a pound of ointment ... Jn 12:3 2983
T branches of palm trees, and went ... Jn 12:13 2983
t a towel, and girded himself ... Jn 13:4 2983
and officers of the Jews t Jesus ... Jn 18:12 4815
Then Pilate therefore t Jesus ... Jn 19:1 2983
they t Jesus, and led him away ... Jn 19:16 3880
t his garments, and made four ... Jn 19:23 2983
disciple t her unto his own home ... Jn 19:27 2983
therefore, and t the body of Jesus ... Jn 19:38 142
Then t they the body of Jesus, and ... Jn 19:40 2983
was guide to them that t Jesus ... Acts 1:16 4815
he t him by the right hand, and ... Acts 3:7 4084
they t knowledge of them, that ... Acts 4:13 1921
heart, and t counsel to slay them ... Acts 5:33 1011
out, Pharaoh's daughter t him up ... Acts 7:21 337
ye t up the tabernacle of Moloch, ... Acts 7:43 353
the Jews t counsel to kill him ... Acts 9:23 4823
Then the disciples t him by night ... Acts 9:25 2983
But Barnabas t him, and brought ... Acts 9:27 1949
But Peter t him up, saying, Stand ... Acts 10:26 1453
t with them John, whose surname ... Acts 12:25 4838
they t him down from the tree, and ... Acts 13:29 2507
and so Barnabas t Mark, and sailed ... Acts 15:39 3880
and t and circumcised him because ... Acts 16:3 2983
he t them the same hour of the ... Acts 16:33 3880
t unto them certain lewd fellows ... Acts 17:5 4355
And they t him, and brought him ... Acts 17:19 1949
Then all the Greeks t Sosthenes ... Acts 18:17 1949
then t his leave of the brethren, ... Acts 18:18 657
heard, they t him unto them, and ... Acts 18:26 4355
t upon them to call over them ... Acts 19:13 2021
we t him in, and came to Mitylene ... Acts 20:14 353
leave one of another, we t ship ... Acts 21:6 1519
he t Paul's girdle, and bound his ... Acts 21:11 142
those days we t up our carriages ... Acts 21:15 643
Then Paul t the men, and the next ... Acts 21:26 3880
and they t Paul, and drew him out ... Acts 21:30 1949
Who immediately t soldiers ... Acts 21:32 3880
t him, and commanded him to be ... Acts 21:33 1949
So he t him, and brought him to ... Acts 23:18 3880
chief captain t him by the hand ... Acts 23:19 1949
t Paul, and brought him by night ... Acts 23:31 353
whom we t, and would have judged ... Acts 24:6 2902
with great violence t him away ... Acts 24:7 520
he t bread, and gave thanks to God ... Acts 27:35 2983
cheer, and they also t some meat ... Acts 27:36 4355
saw, he thanked God, and t courage ... Acts 28:15 2983
in which he was betrayed t bread ... 1Cor 11:23 2983
the same manner also he t the cup ... 1Cor 11:25
Barnabas, and t Titus with me also ... Gal 2:1 4838
t upon him the form of a servant, ... Phil 2:7 2983
t it out of the way, nailing it ... Col 2:14 142
likewise t part of the same ... Heb 2:14 3348
For verily he t not on him the ... Heb 2:16 1949
but he t on him the seed of ... Heb 2:16 1949
in the day when I t them by the ... Heb 8:9 1949
he t the blood of calves and of ... Heb 9:19 2983
t joyfully the spoiling of your ... Heb 10:34 4327
t the book out of the right hand ... Rev 5:7 2983
the angel t the censer, and filled ... Rev 8:5 2983
I t the little book out of the ... Rev 10:10 2983
a mighty angel t up a stone like ... Rev 18:21 142

TOOKEST {2}
though thou t vengeance of their ... Ps 99:8
t thy broidered garments, and ... Eze 16:18 3947

TOOL {4}
for if thou lift up thy t upon it ... Ex 20:25 2719
and fashioned it with a graving t ... Ex 32:4
not lift up any iron t upon them ... Deut 27:5
any t of iron heard in the house ... 1Kin 6:7 3627

TOOTH {11}
Eye for eye, t for t, hand ... Ex 21:24 8127
he smite out his manservant's t ... Ex 21:27 8127
or his maidservant's t ... Ex 21:27 8127
breach, eye for eye, t for t ... Lev 24:20 8127
life, eye for eye, t for t ... Deut 19:21 8127
of trouble is like a broken t ... Prov 25:19 8127
for an eye, and a t for a t ... Mt 5:38 3599

TOOTH'S {1}
let him go free for his t sake ... Ex 21:27 8127

TOP {91}
whose t may reach unto heaven ... Gen 11:4 7218
the t of it reached to heaven ... Gen 28:12 7218
and poured oil upon the t of it ... Gen 28:18 7218
to morrow I will stand on the t ... Ex 17:9 7218
Hur went up to the t of the hill ... Ex 17:10 7218
Sinai, on the t of the mount ... Ex 19:20 7218
Moses up to the t of the mount ... Ex 19:20 7218
was like devouring fire on the t ... Ex 24:17 7218
shall be an hole in the t of it ... Ex 28:32 7218
the t thereof, and the sides ... Ex 30:3 1406
there to me in the t of the mount ... Ex 34:2 7218
with pure gold, both the t of it ... Ex 37:26 1406
up into the t of the mountain ... Num 14:40 7218
presumed to go up unto the hill t ... Num 14:44 7218
died there in the t of the mount ... Num 20:28 7218
to the t of Pisgah, which looketh ... Num 21:20 7218
For from the t of the rocks I see ... Num 23:9 7218
to the t of Pisgah, and built ... Num 23:14 7218
brought Balaam unto the t of Peor ... Num 23:28 7218
Get thee up into the t of Pisgah ... Deut 3:27 7218
thy foot unto the t of thy head ... Deut 28:35 6936
upon the t of the head of him ... Deut 33:16 6936
to the t of Pisgah, that is over ... Deut 34:1 7218
the border went up to the t of ... Josh 15:8 7218
t of the hill unto the fountain ... Josh 15:9 7218
thy God upon the t of this rock ... Judg 6:26 7218
stood in the t of mount Gerizim, ... Judg 9:7 7218
for him in the t of the mountains ... Judg 9:25 7218
down from the t of the mountains ... Judg 9:36 7218
gat them up to the t of the tower ... Judg 9:51 1406
dwelt in the t of the rock Etam ... Judg 15:8 5585
went to the t of the rock Etam ... Judg 15:11 5585
carried them up to the t of an ... Judg 16:3 7218
with Saul upon the t of the house ... 1Sa 9:25 1406
called Saul to the t of the house ... 1Sa 9:26 1406
stood on the t of an hill afar ... 1Sa 26:13 7218
and stood on the t of an hill ... 2Sa 2:25 7218
was come to the t of the mount ... 2Sa 15:32 7218
a little past the t of the hill ... 2Sa 16:1 7218
a tent upon the t of the house ... 2Sa 16:22 1406
were upon the t of the pillars ... 1Kin 7:17 7218
chapiters that were upon the t ... 1Kin 7:18 7218
the t of the pillars were of lily ... 1Kin 7:19 7218
upon the t of the pillars was ... 1Kin 7:22 7218
in the t of the base was there a ... 1Kin 7:35 7218
on the t of the base the ledges ... 1Kin 7:35 7218
were on the t of the two pillars ... 1Kin 7:41 7218
were upon the t of the pillars ... 1Kin 7:41 7218
the t of the throne was round ... 1Kin 10:19 7218
Elijah went up to the t of Carmel ... 1Kin 18:42 7218
he sat on the t of an hill ... 2Kin 1:9 7218
under him on the t of the stairs ... 2Kin 9:13 1634
the altars that were on the t of ... 2Kin 23:12 1406
the chapiter that was on the t of ... 2Chr 3:15 7218
were on the t of the two pillars ... 2Chr 4:12 7218
were on the t of the pillars ... 2Chr 4:12 7218
them unto the t of the rock ... 2Chr 25:12 7218
them down from the t of the rock ... 2Chr 25:12 7218
touched the t of the sceptre ... Est 5:2 7218
earth upon the t of the mountains ... Ps 72:16 7218
a sparrow alone upon the house t ... Ps 102:7 1406
standeth in the t of high places ... Prov 8:2 7218
that lieth upon the t of a mast ... Prov 23:34 7218
look from the t of Amana, from ... Song 4:8 7218
from the t of Shenir and Hermon, ... Song 4:8 7218
in the t of the mountains ... Is 2:2 7218
in the t of the uppermost bough ... Is 17:6 7218
a beacon upon the t of a mountain ... Is 30:17 7218
shout from the t of the mountains ... Is 42:11 7218
hunger in the t of every street ... Lam 2:19 7218
out in the t of every street ... Lam 4:1 7218
off the t of his young twigs ... Eze 17:4 7218
I will crop off from the t of his ... Eze 17:22 7218
she set it upon the t of a rock ... Eze 24:7 6706
her blood upon the t of a rock ... Eze 24:8 6706
and make her like the t of a rock ... Eze 26:4 6706
make thee like the t of a rock ... Eze 26:14 6706
his t was among the thick boughs ... Eze 31:3 6788
he hath shot up his t among the ... Eze 31:10 6788
up their t among the thick boughs ... Eze 31:14 6788
Upon the t of the mountain the ... Eze 43:12 7218
the t of Carmel shall wither ... Amos 1:2 7218
themselves in the t of Carmel ... Amos 9:3 7218
in the t of the mountains ... Mic 4:1 7218
at the t of all the streets ... Nah 3:10 7218
with a bowl upon the t of it ... Zec 4:2 7218
which are upon the t thereof ... Zec 4:2 7218
in twain from the t to the bottom ... Mt 27:51 509
in twain from the t to the bottom ... Mk 15:38 509
seam, woven from the t throughout ... Jn 19:23 509
leaning upon the t of his staff ... Heb 11:21 206

TOPAZ {5}
first row shall be a sardius, a t ... Ex 28:17 6357
the first row was a sardius, a t ... Ex 39:10 6357
The t of Ethiopia shall not equal ... Job 28:19 6357
was thy covering, the sardius, t ... Eze 28:13 6357
the ninth, a t ... Rev 21:20 5116

TOPHEL *(to'-fel)* {1} *A place in the Sinai wilderness.*
the Red sea, between Paran, and T ... Deut 1:1 8603

TOPHET *(to'-fet)* {9} See TOPHETH. *A place in the valley of Hinnom.*
For T is ordained of old ... Is 30:33 8613
have built the high places of T ... Jer 7:31 8612
that it shall no more be called T ... Jer 7:32 8612
for they shall bury in T, till ... Jer 7:32 8612
place shall no more be called T ... Jer 19:6 8612
and they shall bury them in T ... Jer 19:11 8612
and even make this city as T ... Jer 19:12 8612
be defiled as the place of T ... Jer 19:13 8612
Then came Jeremiah from T ... Jer 19:14 8612

TOPHETH *(to'-feth)* {1} See TOPHET. *Same as Tophet.*
And he defiled T, which is in the ... 2Kin 23:10 8612

TOPS {11}
were the t of the mountains seen ... Gen 8:5 7218
in the t of the mulberry trees ... 2Sa 5:24 7218
to set upon the t of the pillars ... 1Kin 7:16 7218
herb, as the grass on the house t ... 2Kin 19:26 1406
in the t of the mulberry trees ... 1Chr 14:15 7218
cut off as the t of the ears of ... Job 24:24 7218
into the t of the ragged rocks, ... Is 2:21 5585
on the t of their houses, and in ... Is 15:3 1406
in all the t of the mountains, and ... Eze 6:13 7218
upon the t of the mountains ... Hos 4:13 7218
t of mountains shall they leap ... Joel 2:5 7218

TORCH {1}
like a t of fire in a sheaf ... Zec 12:6 3940

TORCHES {3}
t in the day of his preparation ... Nah 2:3 6393
they shall seem like *t*, they ... Nah 2:4 3940
cometh thither with lanterns and *t* ... Jn 18:3 *2985*

TORMENT {12}
hither to *t* us before the time ... Mt 8:29 *928*
thee by God, that thou *t* me not ... Mk 5:7 *928*
I beseech thee, *t* me not ... Lk 8:28 *928*
also come into this place of *t* ... Lk 16:28 *931*
because fear hath *t* ... 1Jn 4:18 *2851*
their *t* was as the *t* of a ... Rev 9:5 *929*
was as the *t* of a scorpion ... Rev 9:5 *929*
the smoke of their *t* ascendeth up ... Rev 14:11 *929*
and lived deliciously, so much *t* ... Rev 18:7 *929*
afar off for the fear of her *t* ... Rev 18:10 *929*
afar off for the fear of her *t* ... Rev 18:15 *929*

TORMENTED {8}
sick of the palsy, grievously *t* ... Mt 8:6 *928*
for I am *t* in this flame ... Lk 16:24 *3600*
he is comforted, and thou art *t* ... Lk 16:25 *3600*
being destitute, afflicted, *t* ... Heb 11:37 *2558*
that they should be *t* five months ... Rev 9:5 *928*
because these two prophets *t* them ... Rev 11:10 *928*
and he shall be *t* with fire ... Rev 14:10 *928*
prophet are, and shall be *t* day ... Rev 20:10 *928*

TORMENTORS {1}
wroth, and delivered him to the *t* ... Mt 18:34 *930*

TORMENTS {2}
taken with divers diseases and *t* ... Mt 4:24 *931*
he lift up his eyes, being in *t* ... Lk 16:23 *931*

TORN {17}
That which was *t* of beasts I ... Gen 31:39 2966
I said, Surely he is *t* in pieces ... Gen 44:28 2963
If it be *t* in pieces, then let ... Ex 22:13 2963
not make good that which was *t* ... Ex 22:13 2966
that is *t* of beasts in the field ... Ex 22:31 2966
of that which is *t* with beasts ... Lev 7:24 2966
or that which was *t* with beasts ... Lev 17:15 2966
or is *t* with beasts, he shall not ... Lev 22:8 2966
unto the lion, which hath *t* him ... 1Kin 13:26 7665
eaten the carcase, nor *t* the ass ... 1Kin 13:28 7665
their carcases were *t* in the ... Is 5:25 5478
out thence shall be *t* in pieces ... Jer 5:6 2963
of itself, or is *t* in pieces ... Eze 4:14 2966
that is dead of itself, or *t* ... Eze 44:31 2966
for he hath *t*, and he will heal us ... Hos 6:1 2963
and ye brought that which was *t* ... Mal 1:13 1497
when the unclean spirit had *t* him ... Mk 1:26 *4682*

TORTOISE {1}
mouse, and the *t* after his kind, ... Lev 11:29 6632

TORTURED {1}
and others were *t*, not accepting ... Heb 11:35 *5178*

TOSS {2}
t thee like a ball into a large ... Is 22:18 6802
the waves thereof *t* themselves ... Jer 5:22 1607

TOSSED {7}
I am *t* up and down as the locust ... Ps 109:23 5287
a lying tongue is a vanity *t* to ... Prov 21:6 5086
t with tempest, and not comforted, ... Is 54:11
midst of the sea, *t* with waves ... Mt 14:24 *928*
exceedingly *t* with a tempest ... Acts 27:18 *5492*
t to and fro, and carried about ... Eph 4:14 *2831*
the sea driven with the wind and *t* ... Jas 1:6 *4494*

TOSSINGS {1}
and I am full of *t* to and fro unto ... Job 7:4 5076

TOTTERING {1}
wall shall ye be, and as a *t* fence ... Ps 62:3 1760

TOU *(to'-u)* {2} See TOI. *Same as Toi.*
Now when *T* king of Hamath heard ... 1Chr 18:9 8583
(for Hadarezer had war with *T* ... 1Chr 18:10 8583

TOUCH {48}
eat of it, neither shall ye *t* it ... Gen 3:3 5060
suffered I thee not to *t* her ... Gen 20:6 5060
the mount, or *t* the border of it ... Ex 19:12 5060
There shall not an hand *t* it ... Ex 19:13 5060
Or if a soul *t* any unclean thing, ... Lev 5:2 5060
Or if he *t* the uncleanness of man ... Lev 5:3 5060
Whatsoever shall *t* the flesh ... Lev 6:27 5060
that shall *t* any unclean thing ... Lev 7:21 5060
and their carcase shall ye not *t* ... Lev 11:8 5060
whosoever doth *t* them, when they ... Lev 11:31 5060
she shall *t* no hallowed thing, ... Lev 12:4 5060
they shall not *t* any holy thing ... Num 4:15 5060
t nothing of theirs, lest ye be ... Num 16:26 5060
flesh, nor *t* their dead carcase ... Deut 14:8 5060
now therefore we may not *t* them ... Josh 9:19 5060
men that they shall not *t* thee ... Ruth 2:9 5060
he shall not *t* thee any more ... 2Sa 14:10 5060
Beware that none *t* the young man ... 2Sa 18:12
But the man that shall *t* them ... 2Sa 23:7 5060
T not mine anointed, and do my ... 1Chr 16:22 5060
t all that he hath, and he will ... Job 1:11 5060
t his bone and his flesh, and he ... Job 2:5 5060
seven there shall no evil *t* thee ... Job 5:19 5060
to *t* are as my sorrowful meat ... Job 6:7 5060
T not mine anointed, and do my ... Ps 105:15 5060
t the mountains, and they shall ... Ps 144:5 5060
from thence, *t* no unclean thing ... Is 52:11 5060
that *t* the inheritance which I ... Jer 12:14 5060
men could not *t* their garments ... Lam 4:14 5060
depart, depart, *t* not ... Lam 4:15 5060
and with his skirt do *t* bread ... Hag 2:12 5060
by a dead body *t* any of these ... Hag 2:13 5060
If I may but *t* his garment ... Mt 9:21 *680*
only *t* the hem of his garment ... Mt 14:36 *680*
pressed upon him for to *t* him ... Mk 3:10 *680*
If I may *t* but his clothes, I ... Mk 5:28 *680*
t if it were but the border of ... Mk 6:56 *680*
him, and besought him to *t* him ... Mk 8:22 *680*
to him, that he should *t* them ... Mk 10:13 *680*
whole multitude sought to *t* him ... Lk 6:19 *680*
ye yourselves *t* not the burdens ... Lk 11:46 *4379*
infants, that he would *t* them ... Lk 18:15 *680*
Jesus saith unto her, *T* me not ... Jn 20:17 *680*
good for a man not to *t* a woman ... 1Cor 7:1 *680*
Lord, and *t* not the unclean thing ... 2Cor 6:17 *680*
T not; taste not ... Col 2:21 *680*
the firstborn should *t* them ... Heb 11:28 *2345*
so much as a beast *t* the mountain ... Heb 12:20 *2345*

TOUCHED {49}
us no hurt, as we have not *t* thee ... Gen 26:29 5060
he *t* the hollow of his thigh ... Gen 32:25 5060
because he *t* the hollow of ... Gen 32:32 5060
The soul which hath *t* any such ... Lev 22:6 5060
there, and upon him that *t* a bone ... Num 19:18 5060
and whosoever hath *t* any slain ... Num 31:19 5060
t the flesh and the unleavened ... Judg 6:21 5060
of men, whose hearts God had *t* ... 1Sa 10:26 5060
wing of the one *t* the one wall ... 1Kin 6:27 5060
the other cherub *t* the other wall ... 1Kin 6:27 5060
their wings *t* one another in the ... 1Kin 6:27 5060
tree, behold, then an angel *t* him ... 1Kin 19:5 5060
t him, and said, Arise and eat ... 1Kin 19:7 5060
t the bones of Elisha, he revived ... 2Kin 13:21 5060
near, and *t* the top of the sceptre ... Est 5:2 5060
for the hand of God hath *t* me ... Job 19:21 5060
and said, Lo, this hath *t* thy lips ... Is 6:7 5060
put forth his hand, and *t* my mouth ... Jer 1:9 5060
creatures that *t* one another ... Eze 3:13 5401
whole earth, and *t* not the ground ... Dan 8:5 5060
but he *t* me, and set me upright ... Dan 8:18 5060
t me about the time of the ... Dan 9:21 5060
And, behold, an hand *t* me, which ... Dan 10:10 5060
of the sons of men *t* my lips ... Dan 10:16 5060
t me one like the appearance of a ... Dan 10:18 5060
hand, and *t* him, saying, I will ... Mt 8:3 *680*
he *t* her hand, and the fever left ... Mt 8:15 *680*
him, and *t* the hem of his garment ... Mt 9:20 *680*
Then *t* he their eyes, saying, ... Mt 9:29 *680*
as many as *t* were made perfectly ... Mt 14:36 *680*
t them, and said, Arise, and be not ... Mt 17:7 *680*
on them, and *t* their eyes ... Mt 20:34 *680*
t him, and saith unto him, I will ... Mk 1:41 *680*
press behind, and *t* his garment ... Mk 5:27 *680*
press, and said, Who *t* my clothes ... Mk 5:30 *680*
thee, and sayest thou, Who *t* me ... Mk 5:31 *680*
as many as *t* him were made whole ... Mk 6:56 *680*
ears, and he spit, and *t* his tongue ... Mk 7:33 *680*
hand, and *t* him, saying, I will ... Lk 5:13 *680*
And he came and *t* the bier ... Lk 7:14 *680*
t the border of his garment ... Lk 8:44 *680*
And Jesus said, Who *t* me ... Lk 8:45 *680*
thee, and sayest thou, Who *t* me ... Lk 8:45 *680*
And Jesus said, Somebody hath *t* me ... Lk 8:46 *680*
for what cause she had *t* him ... Lk 8:47 *680*
he *t* his ear, and healed him ... Lk 22:51 *680*
And the next day we *t* at Sidon ... Acts 27:3 *2609*
be *t* with the feeling of our ... Heb 4:15 *4834*
unto the mount that might be *t* ... Heb 12:18 *5584*

TOUCHETH {40}
He that *t* this man or his wife ... Gen 26:11 5060
whosoever *t* the mount shall be ... Ex 19:12 5060
whatsoever *t* the altar shall be ... Ex 29:37 5060
whatsoever *t* them shall be holy ... Ex 30:29 5060
every one that *t* them shall be ... Lev 6:18 5060
the flesh that *t* any unclean ... Lev 7:19 5060
whosoever *t* the carcase of them ... Lev 11:24 5060
every one that *t* them shall be ... Lev 11:26 5060
whoso *t* their carcase shall be ... Lev 11:27 5060
but that which *t* their carcase ... Lev 11:36 5060
he that *t* the carcase thereof ... Lev 11:39 5060
whosoever *t* his bed shall wash ... Lev 15:5 5060
he that *t* the flesh of him that ... Lev 15:7 5060
whosoever *t* any thing that was ... Lev 15:10 5060
whomsoever he *t* that hath the ... Lev 15:11 5060
that he *t* which hath the issue, ... Lev 15:12 5060
whosoever *t* her shall be unclean ... Lev 15:19 5060
whosoever *t* her bed shall wash ... Lev 15:21 5060
whosoever *t* any thing that she ... Lev 15:22 5060
whereon she sitteth, when he *t* it ... Lev 15:23 5060
whosoever *t* those things shall be ... Lev 15:27 5060
whoso *t* any thing that is unclean ... Lev 22:4 5060
Or whosoever *t* any creeping thing ... Lev 22:5 5060
He that *t* the dead body of any ... Num 19:11 5060
Whosoever *t* the dead body of any ... Num 19:13 5060
whosoever *t* one that is slain ... Num 19:16 5060
he that *t* the water of separation ... Num 19:21 5060
unclean person *t* shall be unclean ... Num 19:22 5060
the soul that *t* it shall be ... Num 19:22 5060
tow is broken when it *t* the fire ... Judg 16:9 7306
it *t* thee, and thou art troubled ... Job 4:5 5060
he *t* the hills, and they smoke ... Ps 104:32 5060
whosoever *t* her shall not be ... Prov 6:29 5060
wither, when the east wind *t* it ... Eze 17:10 5060
they break out, and blood *t* blood ... Hos 4:2 5060
of hosts is he that *t* the land ... Amos 9:5 5060
for he that *t* you ... Zec 2:8 5060
you *t* the apple of his eye ... Zec 2:8 5060
of woman this is that *t* him ... Lk 7:39 *680*
and that wicked one *t* him not ... 1Jn 5:18 *680*

TOUCHING {30}
as *t* thee, doth comfort himself, ... Gen 27:42
make an atonement for him as *t* ... Lev 5:13 413
unto the Levites *t* their charge ... Num 8:26
as *t* the matter which thou and I ... 1Sa 20:23
As *t* the words which thou hast ... 2Kin 22:18
that *t* any of the priests and ... Ezr 7:24
T the Almighty, we cannot find ... Job 37:23
which I have made *t* the king ... Ps 45:1
song of my beloved *t* his vineyard ... Is 5:1
them *t* all their wickedness ... Jer 1:16 5921
t the house of the king of Judah, ... Jer 21:11
For thus saith the LORD *t* Shallum ... Jer 22:11 413
for the vision is *t* the whole ... Eze 7:13 413
t any thing that they shall ask ... Mt 18:19 *4012*
But as *t* the resurrection of the ... Mt 22:31 *4012*
as *t* the dead, that they rise ... Mk 12:26 *4012*
t those things whereof ye accuse ... Lk 23:14
ye intend to do as *t* these men ... Acts 5:35 *1909*
As *t* the Gentiles which believe, ... Acts 21:25 *4012*
T the resurrection of the dead I ... Acts 24:21 *4012*
t all the things whereof I am ... Acts 26:2 *4012*
but as *t* the election, they are ... Rom 11:28 *2596*
Now as *t* things offered unto ... 1Cor 8:1 *4012*
As *t* our brother Apollos, I ... 1Cor 16:12 *4012*
For as *t* the ministering to the ... 2Cor 9:1 *4012*
as *t* the law, a Pharisee ... Phil 3:5 *2596*
t the righteousness which is in ... Phil 3:6 *2596*
(*t* whom ye received commandments ... Col 4:10 *4012*
But as *t* brotherly love ye need ... 1Th 4:9 *4012*
have confidence in the Lord *t* you ... 2Th 3:4 *1909*

TOW {3}
as a thread of *t* is broken when ... Judg 16:9 5296
And the strong shall be as *t* ... Is 1:31 5296
extinct, they are quenched as *t* ... Is 43:17 6594

TOWARD See APPENDIX.

TOWEL {2}
and took a *t*, and girded himself ... Jn 13:4 *3012*
to wipe them with the *t* wherewith ... Jn 13:5 *3012*

TOWER {48}
to, let us build us a city and a *t* ... Gen 11:4 4026
down to see the city and the *t* ... Gen 11:5 4026
his tent beyond the *t* of Edar ... Gen 35:21 4026
peace, I will break down this *t* ... Judg 8:9 4026
And he beat down the *t* of Penuel ... Judg 8:17 4026
of the *t* of Shechem heard that ... Judg 9:46 4026
that all the men of the *t* of ... Judg 9:47 4026
men of the *t* of Shechem died also ... Judg 9:49 4026
was a strong *t* within the city ... Judg 9:51 4026
gat them up to the top of the *t* ... Judg 9:51 4026
And Abimelech came unto the *t* ... Judg 9:52 4026
of the *t* to burn it with fire ... Judg 9:52 4026
horn of my salvation, my high *t* ... 2Sa 22:3 4869
He is the *t* of salvation for his ... 2Sa 22:51 1431
And when he came to the *t*, he took ... 2Kin 5:24 6076
a watchman on the *t* in Jezreel ... 2Kin 9:17 4026
from the *t* of the watchmen to the ... 2Kin 17:9 4026
from the *t* of the watchmen to the ... 2Kin 18:8 4026
the watch *t* in the wilderness ... 2Chr 20:24
even unto the *t* of Meah they ... Neh 3:1 4026
it, unto the *t* of Hananeel ... Neh 3:1 4026
piece, and the *t* of the furnaces ... Neh 3:11 4026
the *t* which lieth out from the ... Neh 3:25 4026
the east, and the *t* that lieth out ... Neh 3:26 4026
the great *t* that lieth out ... Neh 3:27 4026
from beyond the *t* of the furnaces ... Neh 12:38 4026
the *t* of Hananeel ... Neh 12:39 4026
the *t* of Meah, even unto the ... Neh 12:39 4026
of my salvation, and my high *t* ... Ps 18:2 4869
a strong *t* from the enemy ... Ps 61:3 4026
my high *t*, and my deliverer ... Ps 144:2 4869
name of the LORD is a strong *t* ... Prov 18:10 4026
Thy neck is like the *t* of David ... Song 4:4 4026
Thy neck is as a *t* of ivory ... Song 7:4 4026
thy nose is as the *t* of Lebanon ... Song 7:4 4026
And upon every high *t*, and upon ... Is 2:15 4026
built a *t* in the midst of it, and ... Is 5:2 4026
I have set thee for a *t* and a ... Jer 6:27 969
t of Hananeel unto the gate of ... Jer 31:38 4026
from the *t* of Syene even unto the ... Eze 29:10 4024
from the *t* of Syene shall they ... Eze 30:6 4024
O *t* of the flock, the strong hold ... Mic 4:8 4026
my watch, and set me upon the *t* ... Hab 2:1 4692
from the *t* of Hananeel unto the ... Zec 14:10 4026
a winepress in it, and built a *t* ... Mt 21:33 *4444*
for the winefat, and built a *t* ... Mk 12:1 *4444*
upon whom the *t* in Siloam fell, ... Lk 13:4 *4444*
of you, intending to build a *t* ... Lk 14:28 *4444*

TOWERS {17}
and make about them walls, and *t* ... 2Chr 14:7 4026
Moreover Uzziah built *t* in ... 2Chr 26:9 4026
Also he built *t* in the desert ... 2Chr 26:10 4026
by cunning men, to be on the *t* ... 2Chr 26:15 4026
the forests he built castles and *t* ... 2Chr 27:4 4026
broken, and raised it up to the *t* ... 2Chr 32:5 4026
tell the *t* thereof ... Ps 48:12 4026
I am a wall, and my breasts like *t* ... Song 8:10 4026
they set up the *t* thereof ... Is 23:13 971
great slaughter, when the *t* fall ... Is 30:25 4026
t shall be for dens for ever, a ... Is 32:14 975
where is he that counted the *t* ... Is 33:18 4026
of Tyrus, and break down her *t* ... Eze 26:4 4026
axes he shall break down thy *t* ... Eze 26:9 4026
and the Gammadims were in thy *t* ... Eze 27:11 4026
cities, and against the high *t* ... Zeph 1:16 6438
their *t* are desolate ... Zeph 3:6 6438

TOWN {13}
for her house was upon the *t* wall — Josh 2:15 — 7023
the elders of the *t* trembled at — 1Sa 16:4 — 7023
entering into a *t* that hath gates — 1Sa 23:7 — 5892
a place in some *t* in the country — 1Sa 27:5 — 5892
him that buildeth a *t* with blood — Hab 2:12 — 5892
city or *t* ye shall enter, enquire — Mt 10:11 — *2968*
the hand, and led him out of the *t* — Mk 8:23 — *2968*
saying, Neither go into the *t* — Mk 8:26 — *2968*
nor tell it to any in the *t* — Mk 8:26 — *2968*
come out of every *t* of Galilee — Lk 5:17 — *2968*
out of the *t* of Bethlehem, where — Jn 7:42 — *2968*
the *t* of Mary and her sister — Jn 11:1 — *2968*
Jesus was not yet come into the *t* — Jn 11:30 — *2968*

TOWNCLERK {1}
when the *t* had appeased the — Acts 19:35 — *1122*

TOWNS {44}
these are their names, by their *t* — Gen 25:16 — 2691
went and took the small *t* thereof — Num 32:41 — 2333
beside unwalled *t* a great many — Deut 3:5 — 5892
of Bashan, and all the *t* of Jair — Josh 13:30 — 2333
Ekron, with her *t* and her villages — Josh 15:45 — 1323
Ashdod with her *t* and her villages — Josh 15:47 — 1323
and her villages, Gaza with her *t* — Josh 15:47 — 1323
and in Asher Beth-shean and her *t* — Josh 17:11 — 1323
and Ibleam and her *t* — Josh 17:11 — 1323
the inhabitants of Dor and her *t* — Josh 17:11 — 1323
inhabitants of En-dor and her *t* — Josh 17:11 — 1323
inhabitants of Taanach and her *t* — Josh 17:11 — 1323
inhabitants of Megiddo and her *t* — Josh 17:11 — 1323
who are of Beth-shean and her *t* — Josh 17:16 — 1323
of Beth-shean and her *t*, nor — Judg 1:27 — 1323
nor Taanach and her *t* — Judg 1:27 — 1323
the inhabitants of Dor and her *t* — Judg 1:27 — 1323
inhabitants of Ibleam and her *t* — Judg 1:27 — 1323
inhabitants of Megiddo and her *t* — Judg 1:27 — 1323
Israel dwelt in Heshbon and her *t* — Judg 11:26 — 1323
and in Aroer and her *t* — Judg 11:26 — 1323
to him pertained the *t* of Jair — 1Kin 4:13 — 2333
and Aram, with the *t* of Jair — 1Chr 2:23 — 2333
the *t* thereof, even threescore — 1Chr 2:23 — 1323
in Gilead in Bashan, and in her *t* — 1Chr 5:16 — 1323
the *t* thereof, and eastward Naaran — 1Chr 7:28 — 1323
Gezer, with the *t* thereof — 1Chr 7:28 — 1323
unto Gaza and the *t* thereof — 1Chr 7:28 — 1323
of Manasseh, Beth-shean and her *t* — 1Chr 7:29
Taanach and her *t* — 1Chr 7:29
Megiddo and her *t* — 1Chr 7:29
Dor and her *t* — 1Chr 7:29
Ono, and Lod, with the *t* thereof — 1Chr 8:12 — 1323
her *t* out of the hand of the — 1Chr 18:1 — 1323
him, Beth-el with the *t* thereof — 2Chr 13:19 — 1323
and Jeshanah with the *t* thereof — 2Chr 13:19 — 1323
and Ephrain with the *t* thereof — 2Chr 13:19 — 1323
that dwelt in the unwalled *t* — Est 9:19 — 5892
upon all her *t* all the evil that — Jer 19:15 — 5892
t without walls for the multitude — Zec 2:4 — 6519
them, Let us go into the next *t* — Mk 1:38 — *2969*
into the *t* of Caesarea Philippi — Mk 8:27 — *2968*
departed, and went through the *t* — Lk 9:6 — *2968*
away, that they may go into the *t* — Lk 9:12 — *2968*

TRACHONITIS *(trak-o-ni'-tis)* {1} *A rocky district east of the Jordan.*
of Ituraea and of the region of *T* — Lk 3:1 — *5139*

TRADE {5}
dwell and *t* ye therein, and get you — Gen 34:10 — 5503
dwell in the land, and *t* therein — Gen 34:21 — 5503
for their *t* hath been to feed — Gen 46:32 — 582
Thy servants' *t* hath been about — Gen 46:34 — 582
sailors, and as many as *t* by sea — Rev 18:17 — *2038*

TRADED {5}
tin, and lead, they *t* in thy fairs — Eze 27:12 — 5414
they *t* the persons of men and — Eze 27:13 — 5414
t in thy fairs with horses — Eze 27:14 — 5414
they *t* in thy market wheat of — Eze 27:17 — 5414
t with the same, and made them — Mt 25:16 — *2038*

TRADING {1}
much every man had gained by *t* — Lk 19:15 — *1281*

TRADITION {11}
transgress the *t* of the elders — Mt 15:2 — *3862*
the commandment of God by your *t* — Mt 15:3 — *3862*
of God of none effect by your *t* — Mt 15:6 — *3862*
holding the *t* of the elders — Mk 7:3 — *3862*
according to the *t* of the elders — Mk 7:5 — *3862*
of God, ye hold the *t* of men — Mk 7:8 — *3862*
God, that ye may keep your own *t* — Mk 7:9 — *3862*
God of none effect through your *t* — Mk 7:13 — *3862*
vain deceit, after the *t* of men — Col 2:8 — *3862*
not after the *t* which he received — 2Th 3:6 — *3862*
received by *t* from your fathers — 1Pet 1:18 — *3862*

TRADITIONS {2}
zealous of the *t* of my fathers — Gal 1:14 — *3862*
hold the *t* which ye have been — 2Th 2:15 — *3862*

TRAFFICK {5}
and ye shall *t* in the land — Gen 42:34 — 5503
of the *t* of the spice merchants — 1Kin 10:15 — 4536
and carried it into a land of *t* — Eze 17:4 — 3667
by thy *t* hast thou increased thy — Eze 28:5 — 7404
by the iniquity of thy *t* — Eze 28:18 — 7404

TRAFFICKERS {1}
whose *t* are the honourable of the — Is 23:8 — 3669

TRAIN {3}
to Jerusalem with a very great *t* — 1Kin 10:2 — 2428
T up a child in the way he should — Prov 22:6 — 2596
up, and his *t* filled the temple — Is 6:1 — 7757

TRAINED {1}
captive, he armed his *t* servants — Gen 14:14 — 2593

TRAITOR {1}
Iscariot, which also was the *t* — Lk 6:16 — *4273*

TRAITORS {1}
T, heady, highminded, lovers of — 2Ti 3:4 — *4273*

TRAMPLE {3}
dragon shalt thou *t* under feet — Ps 91:13 — 7429
mine anger, and *t* them in my fury — Is 63:3 — 7429
lest they *t* them under their feet — Mt 7:6 — *2662*

TRANCE {5}
of the Almighty, falling into a *t* — Num 24:4
of the Almighty, falling into a *t* — Num 24:16
they made ready, he fell into a *t* — Acts 10:10 — *1611*
in a *t* I saw a vision, A certain — Acts 11:5 — *1611*
in the temple, I was in a *t* — Acts 22:17 — *1611*

TRANQUILITY {1}
it may be a lengthening of thy *t* — Dan 4:27 — 7963

TRANSFERRED {1}
I have in a figure *t* to myself — 1Cor 4:6 — *3345*

TRANSFIGURED {2}
And was *t* before them — Mt 17:2 — *3339*
and he was *t* before them — Mk 9:2 — *3339*

TRANSFORMED {3}
but be ye *t* by the renewing of — Rom 12:2 — *3339*
for Satan himself is *t* into an — 2Cor 11:14 — *3345*
also be *t* as the ministers of — 2Cor 11:15 — *3345*

TRANSFORMING {1}
t themselves into the apostles of — 2Cor 11:13 — *3345*

TRANSGRESS {14}
Wherefore now do ye *t* the — Num 14:41 — 5674
ye make the LORD's people to *t* — 1Sa 2:24 — 5674
Why *t* ye the commandments of the — 2Chr 24:20 — 5674
servant Moses, saying, If ye *t* — Neh 1:8 — 4603
to *t* against our God in marrying — Neh 13:27 — 4603
that my mouth shall not *t* — Ps 17:3 — 5674
be ashamed which *t* without cause — Ps 25:3 — 898
a piece of bread that man will *t* — Prov 28:21 — 6586
and thou saidst, I will not *t* — Jer 2:20 — 5647
rebels, and them that *t* against me — Eze 20:38 — 6586
Come to Beth-el, and *t* — Amos 4:4 — 6586
Why do thy disciples *t* the — Mt 15:2 — *3845*
Why do ye also *t* the commandment — Mt 15:3 — *3845*
and circumcision dost *t* the law — Rom 2:27 — *3848*

TRANSGRESSED {34}
I have not *t* thy commandments, — Deut 26:13 — 5674
they have also *t* my covenant — Josh 7:11 — 5674
because he hath *t* the covenant of — Josh 7:15 — 5674
When ye have *t* the covenant of — Josh 23:16 — 5674
t my covenant which I commanded — Judg 2:20 — 5674
And he said, Ye have *t* — 1Sa 14:33 — 898
for I have *t* the commandment of — 1Sa 15:24 — 5674
wherein they have *t* against thee — 1Kin 8:50 — 6586
but *t* his covenant, and all that — 2Kin 18:12 — 5674
who *t* in the thing accursed — 1Chr 2:7 — 4603
they *t* against the God of their — 1Chr 5:25 — 4603
they had *t* against the LORD — 2Chr 12:2 — 4603
for he *t* against the LORD his God — 2Chr 26:16 — 4603
naked, and *t* sore against the LORD — 2Chr 28:19 — 4603
t very much after all the — 2Chr 36:14 — 4603
up, and said unto them, Ye have *t* — Ezr 10:10 — 4603
many that have *t* in this thing — Ezr 10:13 — 6586
because they have *t* the laws — Is 24:5 — 5674
and thy teachers have *t* against me — Is 43:27 — 6586
of the men that have *t* against me — Is 66:24 — 6586
the pastors also *t* against me — Jer 2:8 — 6586
ye all have *t* against me, saith — Jer 2:29 — 6586
that thou hast *t* against the LORD — Jer 3:13 — 6586
and whereby they have *t* against me — Jer 33:8 — 6586
the men that have *t* my covenant — Jer 34:18 — 5674
We have *t* and have rebelled — Lam 3:42 — 6586
their fathers have *t* against me — Eze 2:3 — 6586
transgressions, whereby ye have *t* — Eze 18:31 — 6586
Yea, all Israel have *t* thy law — Dan 9:11 — 5674
they like men have *t* the covenant — Hos 6:7 — 5674
because they have *t* against me — Hos 7:13 — 6586
because they have *t* my covenant — Hos 8:1 — 5674
wherein thou hast *t* against me — Zeph 3:11 — 6586
neither *t* I at any time thy — Lk 15:29 — *3928*

TRANSGRESSEST {1}
Why *t* thou the king's commandment — Est 3:3 — 5674

TRANSGRESSETH {4}
his mouth *t* not in judgment — Prov 16:10 — 4603
Yea also, because he *t* by wine — Hab 2:5 — 898
committeth sin *t* also the law — 1Jn 3:4 — *458,4160*
Whosoever *t*, and abideth not in — 2Jn 9 — *3845*

TRANSGRESSING {2}
LORD thy God, in *t* his covenant, — Deut 17:2 — 5674
In *t* and lying against the LORD, — Is 59:13 — 6586

TRANSGRESSION {51}
forgiving iniquity and *t* and sin, — Ex 34:7 — 6588
mercy, forgiving iniquity and *t* — Num 14:18 — 6588
or if in *t* against the LORD, — Josh 22:22 — 4604
neither evil nor *t* in mine hand — 1Sa 24:11 — 6588
away to Babylon for their *t* — 1Chr 9:1 — 4604
So Saul died for his *t* which he — 1Chr 10:13 — 4604
his reign did cast away in his *t* — 2Chr 29:19 — 4604
because of the *t* of those that — Ezr 9:4 — 4604
t of them that had been carried — Ezr 10:6 — 4604
And why dost thou not pardon my *t* — Job 7:21 — 6588
have cast them away for their *t* — Job 8:4 — 6588
make me to know my *t* and my sin — Job 13:23 — 6588
My *t* is sealed up in a bag, and — Job 14:17 — 6588
I am clean without *t*, I am — Job 33:9 — 6588
my wound is incurable without *t* — Job 34:6 — 6588
be innocent from the great *t* — Ps 19:13 — 6588
Blessed is he whose *t* is forgiven — Ps 32:1 — 6588
The *t* of the wicked saith within — Ps 36:1 — 6588
not for my *t*, nor for my sin, O — Ps 59:3 — 6588
will I visit their *t* with the rod — Ps 89:32 — 6588
Fools, because of their *t* — Ps 107:17 — 6588
is snared by the *t* of his lips — Prov 12:13 — 6588
He that covereth a *t* seeketh love — Prov 17:9 — 6588
He loveth *t* that loveth strife — Prov 17:19 — 6588
it is his glory to pass over a *t* — Prov 19:11 — 6588
For the *t* of a land many are the — Prov 28:2 — 6588
his mother, and saith, It is no *t* — Prov 28:24 — 6588
In the *t* of an evil man there is — Prov 29:6 — 6588
are multiplied, *t* increaseth — Prov 29:16 — 6588
and a furious man aboundeth in *t* — Prov 29:22 — 6588
the *t* thereof shall be heavy upon — Is 24:20 — 6588
for the *t* of my people was he — Is 53:8 — 6588
are ye not children of *t*, a seed — Is 57:4 — 6588
and shew my people their *t* — Is 58:1 — 6588
them that turn from *t* in Jacob — Is 59:20 — 6588
deliver him in the day of his *t* — Eze 33:12 — 6588
daily sacrifice by reason of *t* — Dan 8:12 — 6588
the *t* of desolation, to give both — Dan 8:13 — 6588
thy holy city, to finish the *t* — Dan 9:24 — 6588
at Gilgal multiply *t* — Amos 4:4 — 6586
For the *t* of Jacob is all this, — Mic 1:5 — 6588
What is the *t* of Jacob — Mic 1:5 — 6588
to declare unto Jacob his *t* — Mic 3:8 — 6588
I give my firstborn for my *t* — Mic 6:7 — 6588
passeth by the *t* of the remnant — Mic 7:18 — 6588
from which Judas by *t* fell — Acts 1:25 — *3845*
where no law is, there is no *t* — Rom 4:15 — *3847*
after the similitude of Adam's *t* — Rom 5:14 — *3847*
woman being deceived was in the *t* — 1Ti 2:14 — *3847*
angels was stedfast, and every *t* — Heb 2:2 — *3847*
for sin is the *t* of the law — 1Jn 3:4 — *458*

TRANSGRESSIONS {48}
for he will not pardon your *t* — Ex 23:21 — 6588
because of their *t* in all their — Lev 16:16 — 6588
all their *t* in all their sins, — Lev 16:21 — 6588
not forgive your *t* nor your sins — Josh 24:19 — 6588
all their *t* wherein they have — 1Kin 8:50 — 6588
If I covered my *t* as Adam — Job 31:33 — 6588
or if thy *t* be multiplied, what — Job 35:6 — 6588
their *t* that they have exceeded — Job 36:9 — 6588
out in the multitude of their *t* — Ps 5:10 — 6588
the sins of my youth, nor my *t* — Ps 25:7 — 6588
I will confess my *t* unto the LORD — Ps 32:5 — 6588
Deliver me from all my *t* — Ps 39:8 — 6588
thy tender mercies blot out my *t* — Ps 51:1 — 6588
For I acknowledge my *t* — Ps 51:3 — 6588
as for our *t*, thou shalt purge — Ps 65:3 — 6588
far hath he removed our *t* from us — Ps 103:12 — 6588
out thy *t* for mine own sake — Is 43:25 — 6588
out, as a thick cloud, thy *t* — Is 44:22 — 6588
for your *t* is your mother put — Is 50:1 — 6588
But he was wounded for our *t* — Is 53:5 — 6588
For our *t* are multiplied before — Is 59:12 — 6588
for our *t* are with us — Is 59:12 — 6588
because their *t* are many, and — Jer 5:6 — 6588
her for the multitude of her *t* — Lam 1:5 — 6588
The yoke of my *t* is bound by his — Lam 1:14 — 6588
hast done unto me for all my *t* — Lam 1:22 — 6588
any more with all their *t* — Eze 14:11 — 6588
All his *t* that he hath committed, — Eze 18:22 — 6588
all his *t* that he hath committed — Eze 18:28 — 6588
turn yourselves from all your *t* — Eze 18:30 — 6588
Cast away from you all your *t* — Eze 18:31 — 6588
in that your *t* are discovered, so — Eze 21:24 — 6588
Thus ye speak, saying, If our *t* — Eze 33:10 — 6588
things, nor with any of their *t* — Eze 37:23 — 6588
according to their *t* have I done — Eze 39:24 — 6588
For three *t* of Damascus, and for — Amos 1:3 — 6588
For three *t* of Gaza, and for four, — Amos 1:6 — 6588
For three *t* of Tyrus, and for four — Amos 1:9 — 6588
For three *t* of Edom, and for four, — Amos 1:11 — 6588
For three *t* of the children of — Amos 1:13 — 6588
For three *t* of Moab, and for four, — Amos 2:1 — 6588
For three *t* of Judah, and for four — Amos 2:4 — 6588
For three *t* of Israel, and for — Amos 2:6 — 6588
t of Israel upon him I will also — Amos 3:14 — 6588
For I know your manifold *t* — Amos 5:12 — 6588
for the *t* of Israel were found in — Mic 1:13 — 6588
It was added because of *t* — Gal 3:19 — *3847*
the *t* that were under the first — Heb 9:15 — *3847*

TRANSGRESSOR {5}
and the *t* for the upright — Prov 21:18 — 898
overthroweth the words of the *t* — Prov 22:12 — 898
and wast called a *t* from the womb — Is 48:8 — 6586
I destroyed, I make myself a *t* — Gal 2:18 — *3848*
thou art become a *t* of the law — Jas 2:11 — *3848*

TRANSGRESSORS {20}
But the *t* shall be destroyed — Ps 37:38 — 6586
Then will I teach *t* thy ways — Ps 51:13 — 6586
be not merciful to any wicked *t* — Ps 59:5 — 898
I beheld the *t*, and was grieved — Ps 119:158 — 898
the *t* shall be rooted out of it — Prov 2:22 — 898
of *t* shall destroy them — Prov 11:3 — 898
but *t* shall be taken in their own — Prov 11:6 — 898
soul of the *t* shall eat violence — Prov 13:2 — 898
but the way of *t* is hard — Prov 13:15 — 898

and increaseth the *t* among men — Prov 23:28 — 898
the fool, and rewardeth *t* — Prov 26:10 — 5674
And the destruction of the *t* — Is 1:28 — 6586
bring it again to mind, O ye *t* — Is 46:8 — 6586
and he was numbered with the *t* — Is 53:12 — 6586
and made intercession for the *t* — Is 53:12 — 6586
when the *t* are come to the full, — Dan 8:23 — 6586
but the *t* shall fall therein — Hos 14:9 — 6586
And he was numbered with the *t* — Mk 15:28 — *459*
And he was reckoned among the *t* — Lk 22:37 — *459*
and are convinced of the law as *t* — Jas 2:9 — *3848*

TRANSLATE {1}
To *t* the kingdom from the house — 2Sa 3:10 — 5674

TRANSLATED {3}
hath *t* us into the kingdom of his — Col 1:13 — *3179*
By faith Enoch was *t* that he — Heb 11:5 — *3346*
not found, because God had *t* him — Heb 11:5 — *3346*

TRANSLATION {1}
for before his *t* he had this — Heb 11:5 — *3331*

TRANSPARENT {1}
was pure gold, as it were *t* glass — Rev 21:21 — *1307*

TRAP {4}
ground, and a *t* for him in the way — Job 18:10 — 4434
their welfare, let it become a *t* — Ps 69:22 — 4170
they set a *t*, they catch men — Jer 5:26 — 4889
table be made a snare, and a *t* — Rom 11:9 — *2339*

TRAPS {1}
t unto you, and scourges in your — Josh 23:13 — 4170

TRAVAIL {29}
came to pass in the time of her *t* — Gen 38:27 — 3205
all the *t* that had come upon them — Ex 18:8 — 8513
and pain, as of a woman in *t* — Ps 48:6 — 3205
this sore *t* hath God given to the — Eccl 1:13 — 6045
days are sorrows, and his *t* grief — Eccl 2:23 — 6045
but to the sinner he giveth *t* — Eccl 2:26 — 6045
I have seen the *t*, which God hath — Eccl 3:10 — 6045
Again, I considered all *t* — Eccl 4:4 — 5999
than both the hands full with *t* — Eccl 4:6 — 5999
also vanity, yea, it is a sore *t* — Eccl 4:8 — 6045
But those riches perish by evil *t* — Eccl 5:14 — 6045
I *t* not, nor bring forth children — Is 23:4 — 2342
He shall see of the *t* of his soul — Is 53:11 — 5999
thou that didst not *t* with child — Is 54:1 — 2342
heard a voice as of a woman in *t* — Jer 4:31 — 2470
us, and pain, as of a woman in *t* — Jer 6:24 — 3205
take thee, as a woman in *t* — Jer 13:21 — 3205
thee, the pain as of a woman in *t* — Jer 22:23 — 3205
whether a man doth *t* with child — Jer 30:6 — 3205
on his loins, as a woman in *t* — Jer 30:6 — 3205
have taken her, as a woman in *t* — Jer 49:24 — 3205
him, and pangs as of a woman in *t* — Jer 50:43 — 3205
have taken thee as a woman in *t* — Mic 4:9 — 3205
of Zion, like a woman in *t* — Mic 4:10 — 3205
when she is in *t* hath sorrow — Jn 16:21 — *5088*
of whom I *t* in birth again until — Gal 4:19 — *5605*
brethren, our labour and *t* — 1Th 2:9 — *3449*
as *t* upon a woman with child — 1Th 5:3 — *5604*
t night and day, that we might not — 2Th 3:8 — *3449*

TRAVAILED {5}
and Rachel *t*, and she had hard — Gen 35:16 — 3205
And it came to pass, when she *t* — Gen 38:28 — 3205
were dead, she bowed herself and *t* — 1Sa 4:19 — 3205
Before she *t*, she brought forth — Is 66:7 — 2342
for as soon as Zion *t*, she — Is 66:8 — 2342

TRAVAILEST {1}
forth and cry, thou that *t* not — Gal 4:27 — *5605*

TRAVAILETH {7}
The wicked man *t* with pain all — Job 15:20 — 2342
he *t* with iniquity, and hath — Ps 7:14 — 2254
be in pain as a woman that *t* — Is 13:8 — 3205
as the pangs of a woman that *t* — Is 21:3 — 3205
her that *t* with child together — Jer 31:8 — 3205
she which *t* hath brought forth — Mic 5:3 — 3205
t in pain together until now — Rom 8:22 — *4944*

TRAVAILING {3}
now will I cry like a *t* woman — Is 42:14 — 3205
The sorrows of a *t* woman shall — Hos 13:13 — 3205
t in birth, and pained to be — Rev 12:2 — *5605*

TRAVEL {4}
Thou knowest all the *t* that hath — Num 20:14 — 8513
and compassed me with gall and *t* — Lam 3:5 — 8513
Macedonia, Paul's companions in *t* — Acts 19:29 — *4898*
to *t* with us with this grace — 2Cor 8:19 — *4898*

TRAVELERS {1}
the *t* walked through byways — Judg 5:6

TRAVELLED {1}
about Stephen *t* as far as Phenice — Acts 11:19 — *1330*

TRAVELLER {2}
there came a *t* unto the rich man, — 2Sa 12:4 — 1982
but I opened my doors to the *t* — Job 31:32 — 734

TRAVELLETH {2}
thy poverty come as one that *t* — Prov 6:11 — 1980
thy poverty come as one that *t* — Prov 24:34 — 1980

TRAVELLING {3}
O ye *t* companies of Dedanim — Is 21:13 — 736
t in the greatness of his — Is 63:1 — 6808
is as a man *t* into a far country — Mt 25:14 — *589*

TRAVERSING {1}
art a swift dromedary *t* her ways — Jer 2:23 — 8308

TREACHEROUS {9}
the *t* dealer dealeth — Is 21:2 — 898
the *t* dealers have dealt — Is 24:16 — 898
the *t* dealers have dealt very — Is 24:16 — 898
her *t* sister Judah saw it — Jer 3:7 — 901
yet her *t* sister Judah feared not — Jer 3:8 — 898
yet for all this her *t* sister — Jer 3:10 — 901
herself more than *t* Judah — Jer 3:11 — 898
adulterers, an assembly of *t* men — Jer 9:2 — 898
prophets are light and *t* persons — Zeph 3:4 — 900

TREACHEROUSLY {23}
of Shechem dealt *t* with Abimelech — Judg 9:23 — 898
the treacherous dealer dealeth *t* — Is 21:2 — 898
treacherous dealers have dealt *t* — Is 24:16 — 898
dealers have dealt very *t* — Is 24:16 — 898
and dealest *t*, and they dealt not — Is 33:1 — 898
and they dealt not *t* with thee — Is 33:1 — 898
thou shalt make an end to deal *t* — Is 33:1 — 898
they shall deal *t* with thee — Is 33:1 — 898
that thou wouldest deal very *t* — Is 48:8 — 898
Surely as a wife *t* departeth from — Jer 3:20 — 898
so have ye dealt *t* with me — Jer 3:20 — 898
have dealt very *t* against me — Jer 5:11 — 898
all they happy that deal very *t* — Jer 12:1 — 898
even they have dealt *t* with thee — Jer 12:6 — 898
her friends have dealt *t* with her — Lam 1:2 — 898
They have dealt *t* against the — Hos 5:7 — 898
have they dealt *t* against me — Hos 6:7 — 898
thou upon them that deal *t* — Hab 1:13 — 898
why do we deal *t* every man — Mal 2:10 — 898
Judah hath dealt *t*, and an — Mal 2:11 — 898
against whom thou hast dealt *t* — Mal 2:14 — 898
let none deal *t* against the wife — Mal 2:15 — 898
your spirit, that ye deal not *t* — Mal 2:16 — 898

TREACHERY {1}
and said to Ahaziah, There is *t* — 2Kin 9:23 — 4820

TREAD {33}
your feet shall *t* shall be yours — Deut 11:24 — 1869
all the land that ye shall *t* upon — Deut 11:25 — 1869
thou shalt *t* upon their high — Deut 33:29 — 1869
sole of your foot shall *t* upon — Josh 1:3 — 1869
t on the threshold of Dagon in — 1Sa 5:5 — 1869
t their winepresses, and suffer — Job 24:11 — 1869
t down the wicked in their place — Job 40:12 — 1915
let him *t* down my life upon the — Ps 7:5 — 7429
through thy name will we *t* them — Ps 44:5 — 947
is that shall *t* down our enemies — Ps 60:12 — 947
Thou shalt *t* upon the lion and — Ps 91:13 — 1869
is that shall *t* down our enemies — Ps 108:13 — 947
this at your hand, to *t* my courts — Is 1:12 — 7429
to *t* them down like the mire of — Is 10:6 — 7760,4823
my mountains *t* him under foot — Is 14:25 — 947
the treaders shall *t* out no wine — Is 16:10 — 1869
The foot shall *t* it down, even — Is 26:6 — 7429
for I will *t* them in mine anger, — Is 63:3 — 1869
I will *t* down the people in mine — Is 63:6 — 947
shout, as they that *t* the grapes — Jer 25:30 — 1869
none shall *t* with shouting — Jer 48:33 — 1869
shall he *t* down all thy streets — Eze 26:11 — 7429
but ye must *t* down with your feet — Eze 34:18 — 7429
shall *t* it down, and break it in — Dan 7:23 — 1759
and loveth to *t* out the corn — Hos 10:11 — 1758
t upon the high places of the — Mic 1:3 — 1869
when he shall *t* in our palaces, — Mic 5:5 — 1869
thou shalt *t* the olives, but thou — Mic 6:15 — 1869
t the morter, make strong the — Nah 3:14 — 7429
which *t* down their enemies in the — Zec 10:5 — 947
ye shall *t* down the wicked — Mal 4:3 — 6072
unto you power to *t* on serpents — Lk 10:19 — *3961*
shall they *t* under foot forty — Rev 11:2 — *3961*

TREADER {1}
the *t* of grapes him that soweth — Amos 9:13 — 1869

TREADERS {1}
the *t* shall tread out no wine in — Is 16:10 — 1869

TREADETH {10}
the ox when he *t* out the corn — Deut 25:4 — 1758
t upon the waves of the sea — Job 9:8 — 1869
morter, and as the potter *t* clay — Is 41:25 — 7429
like him that *t* in the winefat — Is 63:2 — 1869
t upon the high places of the — Amos 4:13 — 1869
when he *t* within our borders — Mic 5:6 — 1869
if he go through, both *t* down — Mic 5:8 — 7429
of the ox that *t* out the corn — 1Cor 9:9 — *248*
muzzle the ox that *t* out the corn — 1Ti 5:18 — *248*
he *t* the winepress of the — Rev 19:15 — *3961*

TREADING {4}
some *t* winepresses on the sabbath — Neh 13:15 — 1869
for the *t* of lesser cattle — Is 7:25 — 4823
of *t* down, and of perplexity by — Is 22:5 — 4001
as your *t* is upon the poor — Amos 5:11 — 1318

TREASON {7}
his *t* that he wrought, are they — 1Kin 16:20 — 7195
rent her clothes, and cried, *T* — 2Kin 11:14 — 7195
her clothes, and cried, *T, T* — 2Kin 11:14 — 7195
rent her clothes, and said, *T* — 2Chr 23:13 — 7195
her clothes, and said, *T, T* — 2Chr 23:13 — 7195

TREASURE {37}
hath given you *t* in your sacks — Gen 43:23 — 4301
they built for Pharaoh *t* cities — Ex 1:11 — 4543
t unto me above all people — Ex 19:5
shall open unto thee his good *t* — Deut 28:12 — 214
to the *t* of the house of the LORD — 1Chr 29:8 — 214
unto the *t* of the work threescore — Ezr 2:69 — 214
search made in the king's *t* house — Ezr 5:17 — 1596
it out of the king's *t* house — Ezr 7:20 — 1596
to the *t* a thousand drams of gold — Neh 7:70 — 214
of the fathers gave to the *t* of — Neh 7:71 — 214
to the chambers, into the *t* house — Neh 10:38 — 214
belly thou fillest with thy hid *t* — Ps 17:14
and Israel for his peculiar *t* — Ps 135:4
house of the righteous is much *t* — Prov 15:6 — 2633
the fear of the LORD than great *t* — Prov 15:16 — 214
There is *t* to be desired and oil — Prov 21:20 — 214
gold, and the peculiar *t* of kings — Eccl 2:8
the fear of the LORD is his *t* — Is 33:6 — 214
they have taken the *t* and precious — Eze 22:25 — 2633
into the *t* house of his god — Dan 1:2 — 214
he shall spoil the *t* of all — Hos 13:15 — 214
For where your *t* is, there will — Mt 6:21 — *2344*
A good man out of the good *t* of — Mt 12:35 — *2344*
evil *t* bringeth forth evil things — Mt 12:35 — *2344*
is like unto *t* hid in a field — Mt 13:44 — *2344*
forth out of his *t* things new — Mt 13:52 — *2344*
and thou shalt have *t* in heaven — Mt 19:21 — *2344*
and thou shalt have *t* in heaven — Mk 10:21 — *2344*
A good man out of the good *t* of — Lk 6:45 — *2344*
t of his heart bringeth forth — Lk 6:45 — *2344*
he that layeth up *t* for himself — Lk 12:21 — *2343*
a *t* in the heavens that faileth — Lk 12:33 — *2344*
For where your *t* is, there will — Lk 12:34 — *2344*
and thou shalt have *t* in heaven — Lk 18:22 — *2344*
who had the charge of all her *t* — Acts 8:27 — *1047*
But we have this *t* in earthen — 2Cor 4:7 — *2344*
Ye have heaped *t* together for the — Jas 5:3 — *2343*

TREASURED {1}
it shall not be *t* nor laid up — Is 23:18 — 686

TREASURER {2}
by the hand of Mithredath the *t* — Ezr 1:8 — 1489
hosts, Go, get thee unto this *t* — Is 22:15 — 5532

TREASURERS {4}
the *t* which are beyond the river — Ezr 7:21 — 1490
I made *t* over the treasuries, — Neh 13:13 — 686
the captains, the judges, the *t* — Dan 3:2 — 1411
and captains, the judges, the *t* — Dan 3:3 — 1411

TREASURES {62}
with me, and sealed up among my *t* — Deut 32:34 — 214
the seas, and of *t* hid in the sand — Deut 33:19 — 8226
did he put among the *t* of the — 1Kin 7:51 — 214
he took away the *t* of the house — 1Kin 14:26 — 214
the *t* of the king's house — 1Kin 14:26 — 214
in the *t* of the house of the LORD — 1Kin 15:18 — 214
the *t* of the king's house, and — 1Kin 15:18 — 214
in the *t* of the house of the LORD — 2Kin 12:18 — 214
in the *t* of the king's house, and — 2Kin 14:14 — 214
in the *t* of the king's house, and — 2Kin 16:8 — 214
in the *t* of the king's house — 2Kin 18:15 — 214
and all that was found in his *t* — 2Kin 20:13 — 214
there is nothing among my *t* that — 2Kin 20:15 — 214
the *t* of the house of the LORD — 2Kin 24:13 — 214
the *t* of the king's house, and cut — 2Kin 24:13 — 214
over the *t* of the house of God — 1Chr 26:20 — 214
over the *t* of the dedicated — 1Chr 26:20 — 214
which were over the *t* of the — 1Chr 26:22 — 214
son of Moses, was ruler of the *t* — 1Chr 26:24 — 214
all the *t* of the dedicated things — 1Chr 26:26 — 214
over the king's *t* was Azmaveth — 1Chr 27:25 — 214
put he among the *t* of the house — 2Chr 5:1 — 214
any matter, or concerning the *t* — 2Chr 8:15 — 214
took away the *t* of the house of — 2Chr 12:9 — 214
the *t* of the king's house — 2Chr 12:9 — 214
gold out of the *t* of the house of — 2Chr 16:2 — 214
the *t* of the king's house, the — 2Chr 25:24 — 214
the *t* of the house of the LORD, — 2Chr 36:18 — 214
the *t* of the king, and of his — 2Chr 36:18 — 214
where the *t* were laid up in — Ezr 6:1 — 1596
over the chambers for the *t* — Neh 12:44 — 214
and dig for it more than for hid *t* — Job 3:21 — 4301
entered into the *t* of the snow — Job 38:22 — 214
hast thou seen the *t* of the hail — Job 38:22 — 214
and searchest for her as for hid *t* — Prov 2:4 — 4301
and I will fill their *t* — Prov 8:21 — 214
T of wickedness profit nothing — Prov 10:2 — 214
The getting of *t* by a lying — Prov 21:6 — 214
is there any end of their *t* — Is 2:7 — 214
people, and have robbed their *t* — Is 10:13 — 6259
their *t* upon the bunches of — Is 30:6 — 214
and all that was found in his *t* — Is 39:2 — 214
there is nothing among my *t* that — Is 39:4 — 214
will give thee the *t* of darkness — Is 45:3 — 214
forth the wind out of his *t* — Jer 10:13 — 214
thy *t* will I give to the spoil — Jer 15:13 — 214
all thy *t* to the spoil, and thy — Jer 17:3 — 214
all the *t* of the kings of Judah — Jer 20:5 — 214
for we have *t* in the field, of — Jer 41:8 — 4301
trusted in thy works and in thy *t* — Jer 48:7 — 214
that trusted in her *t*, saying, — Jer 49:4 — 214
a sword is upon her *t* — Jer 50:37 — 214
upon many waters, abundant in *t* — Jer 51:13 — 214
forth the wind out of his *t* — Jer 51:16 — 214
gotten gold and silver into thy *t* — Eze 28:4 — 214
have power over the *t* of gold — Dan 11:43 — 4362
Are there yet the *t* of wickedness — Mic 6:10 — 214
and when they had opened their *t* — Mt 2:11 — *2344*
up for yourselves *t* upon earth — Mt 6:19 — *2344*
lay up for yourselves *t* in heaven — Mt 6:20 — *2344*
whom are hid all the *t* of wisdom — Col 2:3 — *2344*
riches than the *t* in Egypt — Heb 11:26 — *2344*

TREASUREST {1}
impenitent heart *t* up unto — Rom 2:5 — *2343*

TREASURIES {10}
chambers and *t* of the house of God — 1Chr 9:26 — 214
of the *t* thereof, and of the upper — 1Chr 28:11 — 1597
of the *t* of the house of God, and — 1Chr 28:12 — 214
of the *t* of the dedicated things — 1Chr 28:12 — 214

T

and he made himself *t* for silver ... 2Chr 32:27 214
new wine and the oil unto the *t* ... Neh 13:12 214
And I made treasurers over the *t* ... Neh 13:13 214
to bring it into the king's *t* ... Est 3:9 1595
pay to the king's *t* for the Jews ... Est 4:7 1595
he bringeth the wind out of his *t* ... Ps 135:7 214

TREASURY {9}
shall come into the *t* of the LORD ... Josh 6:19 214
they put into the *t* of the house ... Josh 6:24 214
the house of the king under the *t* ... Jer 38:11 214
lawful for to put them into the *t* ... Mt 27:6 *2878*
And Jesus sat over against the *t* ... Mk 12:41 *1049*
the people cast money into the *t* ... Mk 12:41 *1049*
they which have cast into the *t* ... Mk 12:43 *1049*
casting their gifts into the *t* ... Lk 21:1 *1049*
These words spake Jesus in the *t* ... Jn 8:20 *1049*

TREATISE {1}
The former *t* have I made, O ... Acts 1:1 *3056*

TREE {204}
the fruit *t* yielding fruit after ... Gen 1:11 6086
the *t* yielding fruit, whose seed ... Gen 1:12 6086
face of all the earth, and every *t* ... Gen 1:29 6086
is the fruit of a *t* yielding seed ... Gen 1:29 6086
t that is pleasant to the sight ... Gen 2:9 6086
the *t* of life also in the midst ... Gen 2:9 6086
the *t* of knowledge of good and ... Gen 2:9 6086
Of every *t* of the garden thou ... Gen 2:16 6086
But of the *t* of the knowledge of ... Gen 2:17 6086
not eat of every *t* of the garden ... Gen 3:1 6086
But of the fruit of the *t* which ... Gen 3:3 6086
saw that the *t* was good for food ... Gen 3:6 6086
a *t* to be desired to make one ... Gen 3:6 6086
Hast thou eaten of the *t*, whereof ... Gen 3:11 6086
be with me, she gave me of the *t* ... Gen 3:12 6086
thy wife, and hast eaten of the *t* ... Gen 3:17 6086
and take also of the *t* of life ... Gen 3:22 6086
to keep the way of the *t* of life ... Gen 3:24 6086
and rest yourselves under the *t* ... Gen 18:4 6086
and he stood by them under the *t* ... Gen 18:8 6086
and of the hazel and chesnut *t* ... Gen 30:37
thee, and shall hang thee on a *t* ... Gen 40:19 6086
brake every *t* of the field ... Ex 9:25 6086
shall eat every *t* which groweth ... Ex 10:5 6086
and the LORD shewed him a *t* ... Ex 15:25 6086
land, or of the fruit of the *t* ... Lev 27:30 6086
that is made of the vine *t* ... Num 6:4
the hills, and under every green *t* ... Deut 12:2 6086
with the axe to cut down the *t* ... Deut 19:5 6086
not cut them down (for the *t* of ... Deut 20:19 6086
to death, and thou hang him on a *t* ... Deut 21:22 6086
not remain all night upon the *t* ... Deut 21:23 6086
before thee in the way in any *t* ... Deut 22:6 6086
When thou beatest thine olive *t* ... Deut 24:20
he hanged on a *t* until eventide ... Josh 8:29 6086
take his carcase down from the *t* ... Josh 8:29 6086
palm *t* of Deborah between Ramah ... Judg 4:5
and they said unto the olive *t* ... Judg 9:8
But the olive *t* said unto them, ... Judg 9:9
And the trees said to the fig *t* ... Judg 9:10 6086
But the fig *t* said unto them, ... Judg 9:11 6086
pomegranate *t* which is in Migron ... 1Sa 14:2
in Gibeah under a *t* in Ramah ... 1Sa 22:6 815
buried them under a *t* at Jabesh ... 1Sa 31:13 815
under his vine and under his fig *t* ... 1Kin 4:25
from the cedar *t* that is in ... 1Kin 4:33 6086
he made two cherubims of olive *t* ... 1Kin 6:23 6086
oracle he made doors of olive *t* ... 1Kin 6:31 6086
two doors also were of olive *t* ... 1Kin 6:32 6086
of the temple posts of olive *t* ... 1Kin 6:33 6086
And the two doors were of fir *t* ... 1Kin 6:34 6086
high hill, and under every green *t* ... 1Kin 14:23 6086
and sat down under a juniper *t* ... 1Kin 19:4
he lay and slept under a juniper *t* ... 1Kin 19:5
city, and shall fell every good *t* ... 2Kin 3:19 6086
the hills, and under every green *t* ... 2Kin 16:4 6086
high hill, and under every green *t* ... 2Kin 17:10 6086
vine, and every one of his fig *t* ... 2Kin 18:31
house he cieled with fir *t* ... 2Chr 3:5 6086
the hills, and under every green *t* ... 2Chr 28:4 6086
they were both hanged on a *t* ... Est 2:23 6086
For there is hope of a *t*, if it ... Job 14:7 6086
hope hath he removed like a *t* ... Job 19:10 6086
wickedness shall be broken as a *t* ... Job 24:20 6086
he shall be like a *t* planted by ... Ps 1:3 6086
himself like a green bay *t* ... Ps 37:35
green olive *t* in the house of God ... Ps 52:8
shall flourish like the palm *t* ... Ps 92:12
She is a *t* of life to them that ... Prov 3:18 6086
of the righteous is a *t* of life ... Prov 11:30 6086
desire cometh, it is a *t* of life ... Prov 13:12 6086
A wholesome tongue is a *t* of life ... Prov 15:4 6086
Whoso keepeth the fig *t* shall eat ... Prov 27:18
if the *t* fall toward the south, ... Eccl 11:3 6086
in the place where the *t* falleth ... Eccl 11:3 6086
the almond *t* shall flourish, and ... Eccl 12:5
As the apple *t* among the trees of ... Song 2:3 6086
The fig *t* putteth forth her green ... Song 2:13
thy stature is like to a palm *t* ... Song 7:7
said, I will go up to the palm *t* ... Song 7:8
raised thee up under the apple *t* ... Song 8:5
as a teil *t*, and as an oak, whose ... Is 6:13
it, as the shaking of an olive *t* ... Is 17:6
be as the shaking of an olive *t* ... Is 24:13
as a falling fig from the fig *t* ... Is 34:4
vine, and every one of his fig *t* ... Is 36:16
chooseth a *t* that will not rot ... Is 40:20 6086
the cedar, the shittah *t*, and the ... Is 41:19 6086
t, and the myrtle, and the oil *t* ... Is 41:19 6086
will set in the desert the fir *t* ... Is 41:19
the pine, and the box *t* together ... Is 41:19
I fall down to the stock of a *t* ... Is 44:19 6086
O forest, and every *t* therein ... Is 44:23 6086
the thorn shall come up the fir *t* ... Is 55:13
brier shall come up the myrtle *t* ... Is 55:13
eunuch say, Behold, I am a dry *t* ... Is 56:3 6086
with idols under every green *t* ... Is 57:5 6086
shall come unto thee, the fir *t* ... Is 60:13
thee, the fir *t*, the pine *t* ... Is 60:13
for as the days of a *t* are the ... Is 65:22 6086
gardens behind one *t* in the midst ... Is 66:17
said, I see a rod of an almond *t* ... Jer 1:11
every green *t* thou wanderest ... Jer 2:20 6086
mountain and under every green *t* ... Jer 3:6 6086
the strangers under every green *t* ... Jer 3:13 6086
the vine, nor figs on the fig *t* ... Jer 8:13
one cutteth a *t* out of the forest ... Jer 10:3 6086
They are upright as the palm *t* ... Jer 10:5
called thy name, A green olive *t* ... Jer 11:16
Let us destroy the *t* with the ... Jer 11:19 6086
For he shall be as a *t* planted by ... Jer 17:8 6086
mountains, and under every green *t* ... Eze 6:13 6086
is the vine *t* more than any *t* ... Eze 15:2 6086
As the vine *t* among the trees of ... Eze 15:6 6086
waters, and set it as a willow *t* ... Eze 17:5
LORD have brought down the high *t* ... Eze 17:24 6086
have exalted the low *t* ... Eze 17:24 6086
t, have dried up the green *t* ... Eze 17:24 6086
have made the dry *t* to flourish ... Eze 17:24 6086
devour every green *t* in thee ... Eze 20:47 6086
and every dry *t* ... Eze 20:47 6086
the rod of my son, as every *t* ... Eze 21:10 6086
nor any *t* in the garden of God ... Eze 31:8 6086
the *t* of the field shall yield ... Eze 34:27 6086
will multiply the fruit of the *t* ... Eze 36:30 6086
so that a palm *t* was between a ... Eze 41:18
toward the palm *t* on the one side ... Eze 41:19
the palm *t* on the other side ... Eze 41:19
behold a *t* in the midst of the ... Dan 4:10 363
The *t* grew, and was strong, and the ... Dan 4:11 363
and said thus, Hew down the *t* ... Dan 4:14 363
The *t* that thou sawest, which ... Dan 4:20 363
heaven, and saying, Hew the *t* down ... Dan 4:23 363
to leave the stump of the *t* roots ... Dan 4:26 363
in the fig *t* at her first time ... Hos 9:10
beauty shall be as the olive *t* ... Hos 14:6
I am like a green fir *t* ... Hos 14:8
my vine waste, and barked my fig *t* ... Joel 1:7
up, and the fig *t* languisheth ... Joel 1:12
pomegranate *t*, the palm *t* also ... Joel 1:12
also, and the apple *t* ... Joel 1:12
for the *t* beareth her fruit, the ... Joel 2:22 6086
beareth her fruit, the fig *t* ... Joel 2:22
under his vine and under his fig *t* ... Mic 4:4
Although the fig *t* shall not ... Hab 3:17
as yet the vine, and the fig *t* ... Hag 2:19
the pomegranate, and the olive *t* ... Hag 2:19 6086
under the vine and under the fig *t* ... Zec 3:10
Howl, fir *t* ... Zec 11:2
therefore every *t* which bringeth ... Mt 3:10 *1186*
Even so every good *t* bringeth ... Mt 7:17 *1186*
but a corrupt *t* bringeth forth ... Mt 7:17 *1186*
A good *t* cannot bring forth evil ... Mt 7:18 *1186*
neither can a corrupt *t* bring ... Mt 7:18 *1186*
Every *t* that bringeth not forth ... Mt 7:19 *1186*
Either make the *t* good, and his ... Mt 12:33 *1186*
or else make the *t* corrupt ... Mt 12:33 *1186*
for the *t* is known by his fruit ... Mt 12:33 *1186*
among herbs, and becometh a *t* ... Mt 13:32 *1186*
And when he saw a fig *t* in the way ... Mt 21:19 *4808*
presently the fig *t* withered away ... Mt 21:19 *4808*
soon is the fig *t* withered away ... Mt 21:20 *4808*
this which is done to the fig *t* ... Mt 21:21 *4808*
Now learn a parable of the fig *t* ... Mt 24:32 *4808*
seeing a fig *t* afar off having ... Mk 11:13 *4808*
they saw the fig *t* dried up from ... Mk 11:20 *4808*
the fig *t* which thou cursedst is ... Mk 11:21 *4808*
Now learn a parable of the fig *t* ... Mk 13:28 *4808*
every *t* therefore which bringeth ... Lk 3:9 *1186*
For a good *t* bringeth not forth ... Lk 6:43 *1186*
corrupt *t* bring forth good fruit ... Lk 6:43 *1186*
For every *t* is known by his own ... Lk 6:44 *1186*
a fig *t* planted in his vineyard ... Lk 13:6 *4808*
come seeking fruit on this fig *t* ... Lk 13:7 *4808*
and it grew, and waxed a great *t* ... Lk 13:19 *1186*
ye might say unto this sycamine *t* ... Lk 17:6
up into a sycomore *t* to see him ... Lk 19:4 *4809*
Behold the fig *t*, and all the ... Lk 21:29 *4808*
they do these things in a green *t* ... Lk 23:31 *3586*
when thou wast under the fig *t* ... Jn 1:48 *4808*
thee, I saw thee under the fig *t* ... Jn 1:50 *4808*
whom ye slew and hanged on a *t* ... Acts 5:30 *3586*
whom they slew and hanged on a *t* ... Acts 10:39 *3586*
they took him down from the *t* ... Acts 13:29 *3586*
and thou, being a wild olive *t* ... Rom 11:17 *65*
root and fatness of the olive *t* ... Rom 11:17
olive *t* which is wild by nature ... Rom 11:24 *65*
to nature into a good olive *t* ... Rom 11:24 *2565*
be graffed into their own olive *t* ... Rom 11:24
is every one that hangeth on a *t* ... Gal 3:13 *3586*
Can the fig *t*, my brethren, bear ... Jas 3:12 *4808*
our sins in his own body on the *t* ... 1Pet 2:24 *3586*
I give to eat of the *t* of life ... Rev 2:7 *3586*
even as a fig *t* casteth her ... Rev 6:13 *4808*
nor on the sea, nor on any *t* ... Rev 7:1 *1186*
any green thing, neither any *t* ... Rev 9:4 *1186*
river, was there the *t* of life ... Rev 22:2 *3586*
the leaves of the *t* were for the ... Rev 22:2 *3586*
may have right to the *t* of life ... Rev 22:14 *3586*

TREES {157}
the fruit of the *t* of the garden ... Gen 3:2 6086
God amongst the *t* of the garden ... Gen 3:8 6086
all the *t* that were in the field, ... Gen 23:17 6086
all the fruit of the *t* which the ... Ex 10:15 6086
not any green thing in the *t* ... Ex 10:15 6086
and threescore and ten palm *t* ... Ex 15:27
planted all manner of *t* for food ... Lev 19:23 6086
first day the boughs of goodly *t* ... Lev 23:40 6086
branches of palm *t* ... Lev 23:40
and the boughs of thick *t* ... Lev 23:40 6086
the *t* of the field shall yield ... Lev 26:4 6086
neither shall the *t* of the land ... Lev 26:20 6086
as the *t* of lign aloes which the ... Num 24:6
as cedar *t* beside the waters ... Num 24:6
and threescore and ten palm *t* ... Num 33:9
not, vineyards and olive *t* ... Deut 6:11
and barley, and vines, and fig *t* ... Deut 8:8
not plant thee a grove of any *t* ... Deut 16:21 6086
the *t* thereof by forcing an ax ... Deut 20:19 6086
Only the *t* which thou knowest ... Deut 20:20 6086
that they be not *t* for meat ... Deut 20:20 6086
Thou shalt have olive *t* ... Deut 28:40
All thy *t* and fruit of thy land ... Deut 28:42 6086
of Jericho, the city of palm *t* ... Deut 34:3
them, and hanged them on five *t* ... Josh 10:26 6086
upon the *t* until the evening ... Josh 10:26 6086
and they took them down off the *t* ... Josh 10:27 6086
t with the children of Judah into ... Judg 1:16
and possessed the city of palm *t* ... Judg 3:13
The *t* went forth on a time to ... Judg 9:8 6086
and go to be promoted over the *t* ... Judg 9:9 6086
the *t* said to the fig tree, Come ... Judg 9:10 6086
and go to be promoted over the *t* ... Judg 9:11 6086
Then said the *t* unto the vine ... Judg 9:12 6086
and go to be promoted over the *t* ... Judg 9:13 6086
said all the *t* unto the bramble ... Judg 9:14 6086
And the bramble said unto the *t* ... Judg 9:15 6086
and cut down a bough from the *t* ... Judg 9:48 6086
messengers to David, and cedar *t* ... 2Sa 5:11 6086
them over against the mulberry *t* ... 2Sa 5:23
in the tops of the mulberry *t* ... 2Sa 5:24
And he spake of *t*, from the cedar ... 1Kin 4:33 6086
hew me cedar *t* out of Lebanon ... 1Kin 5:6
So Hiram gave Solomon cedar *t* ... 1Kin 5:10 6086
fir *t* according to all his desire ... 1Kin 5:10 6086
figures of cherubims and palm *t* ... 1Kin 6:29
carvings of cherubims and palm *t* ... 1Kin 6:32
the cherubims, and upon the palm *t* ... 1Kin 6:32
thereon cherubims and palm *t* ... 1Kin 6:35
cherubims, lions, and palm *t* ... 1Kin 7:36
Solomon with cedar *t* and fir *t* ... 1Kin 9:11 6086
Ophir great plenty of almug *t* ... 1Kin 10:11 6086
the king made of the almug *t* ... 1Kin 10:12 6086
there came no such almug *t* ... 1Kin 10:12 6086
sycomore *t* that are in the vale ... 1Kin 10:27
water, and felled all the good *t* ... 2Kin 3:25 6086
cut down the tall cedar *t* thereof ... 2Kin 19:23
and the choice fir *t* thereof ... 2Kin 19:23
them over against the mulberry *t* ... 1Chr 14:14
in the tops of the mulberry *t* ... 1Chr 14:15
Then shall the *t* of the wood sing ... 1Chr 16:33 6086
Also cedar *t* in abundance ... 1Chr 22:4 6086
And over the olive *t* and the ... 1Chr 27:28
the sycomore *t* that were in the ... 1Chr 27:28
cedar *t* made he as the sycomore ... 2Chr 1:15
t that are in the vale for ... 2Chr 1:15
Send me also cedar *t* ... 2Chr 2:8 6086
fir *t*, and algum *t* ... 2Chr 2:8
fine gold, and set thereon palm *t* ... 2Chr 3:5
gold from Ophir, brought algum *t* ... 2Chr 9:10 6086
the king made of the algum *t* ... 2Chr 9:11 6086
cedar *t* made he as the sycomore ... 2Chr 9:27
t that are in the low plains in ... 2Chr 9:27
to Jericho, the city of palm *t* ... 2Chr 28:15
to bring cedar *t* from Lebanon to ... Ezr 3:7 6086
branches, and branches of thick *t* ... Neh 8:15 6086
and fruit *t* in abundance ... Neh 9:25 6086
firstfruits of all fruit of all *t* ... Neh 10:35 6086
and the fruit of all manner of *t* ... Neh 10:37 6086
He lieth under the shady *t* ... Job 40:21
The shady *t* cover him with their ... Job 40:22
lifted up axes upon the thick *t* ... Ps 74:5 6086
and their sycomore *t* with frost ... Ps 78:47
then shall all the *t* of the wood ... Ps 96:12 6086
The *t* of the LORD are full of sap ... Ps 104:16 6086
stork, the fir *t* are her house ... Ps 104:17
their vines also and their fig *t* ... Ps 105:33
brake the *t* of their coasts ... Ps 105:33 6086
fruitful *t*, and all cedars ... Ps 148:9 6086
I planted *t* in them of all kind ... Eccl 2:5 6086
the wood that bringeth forth *t* ... Eccl 2:6 6086
tree among the *t* of the wood ... Song 2:3 6086
with all *t* of frankincense ... Song 4:14 6086
as the *t* of the wood are moved ... Is 7:2 6086
the rest of the *t* of his forest ... Is 10:19 6086
the fir *t* rejoice at thee, and the ... Is 14:8
and the choice fir *t* thereof ... Is 37:24
himself among the *t* of the forest ... Is 44:14 6086
all the *t* of the field shall clap ... Is 55:12 6086
be called *t* of righteousness ... Is 61:3 352
eat up thy vines and thy fig *t* ... Jer 5:17
LORD of hosts said, Hew ye down *t* ... Jer 6:6 6097
upon the *t* of the field, and upon ... Jer 7:20 6086

the green *t* upon the high hills ... Jer 17:2 6086
is among the *t* of the forest ... Eze 15:2 6086
tree among the *t* of the forest ... Eze 15:6 6086
all the *t* of the field shall know ... Eze 17:24 6086
high hill, and all the thick *t* ... Eze 20:28 6086
thy ship boards of fir *t* of Senir ... Eze 27:5
unto all the *t* of the field ... Eze 31:4 6086
above all the *t* of the field ... Eze 31:5 6086
the fir *t* were not like his ... Eze 31:8
the chesnut *t* were not like his ... Eze 31:8
so that all the *t* of Eden ... Eze 31:9 6086
t by the waters exalt themselves ... Eze 31:14 6086
neither their *t* stand up in their ... Eze 31:14 352
all the *t* of the field fainted ... Eze 31:15 6086
and all the *t* of Eden, the choice ... Eze 31:16 6086
in greatness among the *t* of Eden ... Eze 31:18 6086
t of Eden unto the nether parts ... Eze 31:18 6086
and upon each post were palm *t* ... Eze 40:16
and their arches, and their palm *t* ... Eze 40:22
and it had palm *t*, one on this ... Eze 40:26
palm *t* were upon the posts ... Eze 40:31
palm *t* were upon the posts ... Eze 40:34
palm *t* were upon the posts ... Eze 40:37
was made with cherubims and palm *t* ... Eze 41:18
were cherubims and palm *t* made ... Eze 41:20
the temple, cherubims and palm *t* ... Eze 41:25
palm *t* on the one side and on the ... Eze 41:26
were very many *t* on the one side ... Eze 47:7 6086
side, shall grow all *t* for meat ... Eze 47:12 6086
destroy her vines and her fig *t* ... Hos 2:12
tree, even all the *t* of the field ... Joel 1:12 6086
burned all the *t* of the field ... Joel 1:19 6086
and your vineyards and your fig *t* ... Amos 4:9
and your olive *t* increased ... Amos 4:9
the fir *t* shall be terribly ... Nah 2:3
fig *t* with the firstripe figs ... Nah 3:12
myrtle *t* that were in the bottom ... Zec 1:8
stood among the myrtle *t* answered ... Zec 1:10
that stood among the myrtle *t* ... Zec 1:11
And two olive *t* by it, one upon ... Zec 4:3
What are these two olive *t* upon ... Zec 4:11
ax is laid unto the root of the *t* ... Mt 3:10 *1186*
cut down branches from the *t* ... Mt 21:8 *1186*
up, and said, I see men as *t* ... Mk 8:24 *1186*
cut down branches off the *t* ... Mk 11:8 *1186*
is laid unto the root of the *t* ... Lk 3:9 *1186*
Behold the fig tree, and all the *t* ... Lk 21:29 *1186*
Took branches of palm *t*, and went ... Jn 12:13
t whose fruit withereth, without ... Jude 12 *1186*
earth, neither the sea, nor the *t* ... Rev 7:3 *1186*
the third part of *t* was burnt up ... Rev 8:7 *1186*
These are the two olive *t* ... Rev 11:4

TREMBLE {29}

hear report of thee, and shall *t* ... Deut 2:25 7264
faint, fear not, and do not *t* ... Deut 20:3 2648
lord, and of those that *t* at the ... Ezr 10:3 2730
place, and the pillars thereof *t* ... Job 9:6 6426
The pillars of heaven *t*, and are ... Job 26:11 7322
Thou hast made the earth to *t* ... Ps 60:2 7493
let the people *t* ... Ps 99:1 7264
T, thou earth, at the presence of ... Ps 114:7 2342
the keepers of the house shall *t* ... Eccl 12:3 2111
and the hills did *t*, and their ... Is 5:25 7264
the man that made the earth to *t* ... Is 14:16 7264
T, ye women that are at ease ... Is 32:11 2729
the nations may *t* at thy presence ... Is 64:2 7264
the LORD, ye that *t* at his word ... Is 66:5 2730
will ye not *t* at my presence, ... Jer 5:22 2342
at his wrath the earth shall *t* ... Jer 10:10 7493
t for all the goodness and for all ... Jer 33:9 7264
And the land shall *t* and sorrow ... Jer 51:29 7493
shall *t* at every moment, and be ... Eze 26:16 2729
Now shall the isles *t* in the day ... Eze 26:18 2729
they shall *t* at every moment, ... Eze 32:10 2729
dominion of my kingdom men *t* ... Dan 6:26 2112
children shall *t* from the west ... Hos 11:10 2729
They shall *t* as a bird out of ... Hos 11:11 2729
all the inhabitants of the land *t* ... Joel 2:1 7264
the heavens shall *t* ... Joel 2:10 7493
Shall not the land *t* for this ... Amos 8:8 7264
of the land of Midian did *t* ... Hab 3:7 7264
the devils also believe, and *t* ... Jas 2:19 *5425*

TREMBLED {21}

Isaac *t* very exceedingly, and said ... Gen 27:33 2729
the people that was in the camp *t* ... Ex 19:16 2729
of the field of Edom, the earth *t* ... Judg 5:4 7493
for his heart *t* for the ark of ... 1Sa 4:13 2730
and the spoilers, they also *t* ... 1Sa 14:15 2729
of the town *t* at his coming ... 1Sa 16:4 2729
afraid, and his heart greatly *t* ... 1Sa 28:5 2729
Then the earth shook and *t* ... 2Sa 22:8 7493
unto me every one that *t* at the ... Ezr 9:4 2730
Then the earth shook and *t* ... Ps 18:7 7493
the earth *t* and shook ... Ps 77:18 7264
the earth saw, and *t* ... Ps 97:4 2342
the mountains, and, lo, they *t* ... Jer 4:24 7493
the whole land *t* at the sound of ... Jer 8:16 7493
people, nations, and languages, *t* ... Dan 5:19 2112
The mountains saw thee, and they *t* ... Hab 3:10 2342
When I heard, my belly *t* ... Hab 3:16 7364
I *t* in myself, that I might rest ... Hab 3:16 7264
for they *t* and were amazed ... Mk 16:8 *2192,5156*
Then Moses *t*, and durst not ... Acts 7:32 *1790,1096*
and judgment to come, Felix *t* ... Acts 24:25 *1719,1096*

TREMBLETH {4}

At this also my heart *t*, and is ... Job 37:1 2729
He looketh on the earth, and it *t* ... Ps 104:32 7460
My flesh *t* for fear of thee ... Ps 119:120 5568
contrite spirit, and *t* at my word ... Is 66:2 2730

TREMBLING {26}

t shall take hold upon them ... Ex 15:15 7460
shall give thee there a *t* heart ... Deut 28:65 7268
and all the people followed him *t* ... 1Sa 13:7 2729
there was *t* in the host, in the ... 1Sa 14:15 2731
so it was a very great *t* ... 1Sa 14:15 2731
t because of this matter, and for ... Ezr 10:9 7460
Fear came upon me, and *t*, which ... Job 4:14 7460
t taketh hold on my flesh ... Job 21:6 6427
LORD with fear, and rejoice with *t* ... Ps 2:11 7460
t are come upon me, and horror ... Ps 55:5 7460
drunken the dregs of the cup of *t* ... Is 51:17 8653
out of thine hand the cup of *t* ... Is 51:22 8653
We have heard a voice of *t* ... Jer 30:5 2731
and drink thy water with *t* ... Eze 12:18 7269
shall clothe themselves with *t* ... Eze 26:16 2731
this word unto me, I stood *t* ... Dan 10:11 7460
When Ephraim spake *t*, he exalted ... Hos 13:1 7578
I will make Jerusalem a cup of *t* ... Zec 12:2 7478
But the woman fearing and *t* ... Mk 5:33 *5141*
that she was not hid, she came *t* ... Lk 8:47 *5141*
And he *t* and astonished said, Lord, ... Acts 9:6 *5141*
a light, and sprang in, and came *t* ... Acts 16:29 *1096,1790*
and in fear, and in much *t* ... 1Cor 2:3 *5156*
with fear and *t* ye received him ... 2Cor 7:15 *5156*
to the flesh, with fear and *t* ... Eph 6:5 *5156*
your own salvation with fear and *t* ... Phil 2:12 *5156*

TRENCH {8}

and he came to the *t*, as the host ... 1Sa 17:20 4570
and Saul lay in the *t*, and the ... 1Sa 26:5 4570
Saul lay sleeping within the *t* ... 1Sa 26:7 4570
the city, and it stood in the *t* ... 2Sa 20:15 2426
he made a *t* about the altar, as ... 1Kin 18:32 8585
he filled the *t* also with water ... 1Kin 18:35 8565
up the water that was in the *t* ... 1Kin 18:38 8565
enemies shall cast a *t* about thee ... Lk 19:43 *5482*

TRESPASS {82}

and said to Laban, What is my *t* ... Gen 31:36 6588
the *t* of thy brethren, and their ... Gen 50:17 6588
forgive the *t* of the servants of ... Gen 50:17 6588
For all manner of *t*, whether it ... Ex 22:9 6588
he shall bring his *t* offering ... Lev 5:6 817
then he shall bring for his *t* ... Lev 5:7 817
If a soul commit a *t* and sin ... Lev 5:15 4604
his *t* unto the LORD a ram without ... Lev 5:15 817
the sanctuary, for a *t* offering ... Lev 5:15 817
with the ram of the *t* offering ... Lev 5:16 817
for a *t* offering, unto the priest ... Lev 5:18 817
It is a *t* offering ... Lev 5:19 817
commit a *t* against the LORD, and ... Lev 6:2 4604
in the day of his *t* offering ... Lev 6:5 819
he shall bring his *t* offering ... Lev 6:6 817
for a *t* offering, unto the priest ... Lev 6:6 817
offering, and as the *t* offering ... Lev 6:17 817
this is the law of the *t* offering ... Lev 7:1 817
shall they kill the *t* offering ... Lev 7:2 817
it is a *t* offering ... Lev 7:5 817
offering is, so is the *t* offering ... Lev 7:7 817
of the *t* offering, and of the ... Lev 7:37 817
and offer him for a *t* offering ... Lev 14:12 817
priest's, so is the *t* offering ... Lev 14:13 817
of the blood of the *t* offering ... Lev 14:14 817
upon the blood of the *t* offering ... Lev 14:17 817
lamb for a *t* offering to be waved ... Lev 14:21 817
take the lamb of the *t* offering ... Lev 14:24 817
kill the lamb of the *t* offering ... Lev 14:25 817
of the blood of the *t* offering ... Lev 14:25 817
of the blood of the *t* offering ... Lev 14:28 817
he shall bring his *t* offering ... Lev 19:21 817
even a ram for a *t* offering ... Lev 19:21 817
for him with the ram of the *t* ... Lev 19:22 817
them to bear the iniquity of *t* ... Lev 22:16 819
fathers, with their *t* which they ... Lev 26:40 4604
to do a *t* against the LORD, and ... Num 5:6 4604
he shall recompense his *t* with ... Num 5:7 817
kinsman to recompense the *t* unto ... Num 5:8 817
let the *t* be recompensed unto the ... Num 5:8 817
aside, and commit a *t* against him, ... Num 5:12 4604
have done *t* against her husband, ... Num 5:27 4604
the first year for a *t* offering ... Num 6:12 817
every *t* offering of theirs, which ... Num 18:9 817
to commit *t* against the LORD in ... Num 31:16 4604
a *t* in the accursed thing ... Josh 7:1 4604
What *t* is this that ye have ... Josh 22:16 4604
commit a *t* in the accursed thing ... Josh 22:20 4604
committed this *t* against the LORD ... Josh 22:31 4604
any wise return him a *t* offering ... 1Sa 6:3 817
What shall be the *t* offering ... 1Sa 6:4 817
ye return him for a *t* offering ... 1Sa 6:8 817
for a *t* offering unto the LORD ... 1Sa 6:17 817
forgive the *t* of thine handmaid ... 1Sa 25:28 6588
If any man *t* against his ... 1Kin 8:31 2398
The *t* money and sin money was not ... 2Kin 12:16 817
will he be a cause of *t* to Israel ... 1Chr 21:3 819
that they *t* not against the LORD ... 2Chr 19:10 816
this do, and ye shall not *t* ... 2Chr 19:10 816
and Jerusalem for this their *t* ... 2Chr 24:18 819
add more to our sins and to our *t* ... 2Chr 28:13 819
for our *t* is great, and there is ... 2Chr 28:13 819
he *t* yet more against the LORD ... 2Chr 28:22 4603
of him, and all his sin, and his *t* ... 2Chr 33:19 4604
rulers hath been chief in this *t* ... Ezr 9:2 4604
our *t* is grown up unto the ... Ezr 9:6 819
been in a great *t* unto this day ... Ezr 9:7 819
evil deeds, and for our great *t* ... Ezr 9:13 819
to increase the *t* of Israel ... Ezr 10:10 819
a ram of the flock for their *t* ... Ezr 10:19 819
because they have committed a *t* ... Eze 15:8 4604
plead with him there for his *t* ... Eze 17:20 4604
in his *t* that he hath trespassed, ... Eze 18:24 4604
have committed a *t* against me ... Eze 20:27 4604
sin offering and the *t* offering ... Eze 40:39 817
sin offering, and the *t* offering ... Eze 42:13 817
sin offering, and the *t* offering ... Eze 44:29 817
priests shall boil the *t* offering ... Eze 46:20 817
because of their *t* that they have ... Dan 9:7 4604
thy brother shall *t* against thee ... Mt 18:15 *264*
If thy brother *t* against thee ... Lk 17:3 *264*
if he *t* against thee seven times ... Lk 17:4 *264*

TRESPASSED {15}

hath certainly *t* against the LORD ... Lev 5:19 816
trespass which they *t* against me ... Lev 26:40 4604
unto him against whom he hath *t* ... Num 5:7 816
Because ye *t* against me among the ... Deut 32:51 4603
for thou hast *t* ... 2Chr 26:18 4603
For our fathers have *t*, and done ... 2Chr 29:6 4603
which *t* against the LORD God of ... 2Chr 30:7 4603
but Amon *t* more and more ... 2Chr 33:23 819
We have *t* against our God, and ... Ezr 10:2 4603
that he hath *t* against me ... Eze 17:20 4604
in his trespass that he hath *t* ... Eze 18:24 4604
because they *t* against me ... Eze 39:23 4603
whereby they have *t* against me ... Eze 39:26 4603
that they have *t* against thee ... Dan 9:7 4603
my covenant, and *t* against my law ... Hos 8:1

TRESPASSES {12}

we are before thee in our *t* ... Ezr 9:15 819
an one as goeth on still in his *t* ... Ps 68:21 817
all their *t* whereby they have ... Eze 39:26 4604
For if ye forgive men their *t* ... Mt 6:14 *3900*
But if ye forgive not men their *t* ... Mt 6:15 *3900*
will your Father forgive your *t* ... Mt 6:15 *3900*
not every one his brother their *t* ... Mt 18:35 *3900*
in heaven may forgive you your *t* ... Mk 11:25 *3900*
which is in heaven forgive your *t* ... Mk 11:26 *3900*
not imputing their *t* unto them ... 2Cor 5:19 *3900*
he quickened, who were dead in *t* ... Eph 2:1 *3900*
him, having forgiven you all *t* ... Col 2:13 *3900*

TRESPASSING {2}

that he hath done in *t* therein ... Lev 6:7 819
against me by *t* grievously ... Eze 14:13 4603

TRIAL {6}

laugh at the *t* of the innocent ... Job 9:23 4531
Because it is a *t*, and what if the ... Eze 21:13 974
How that in a great *t* of ... 2Cor 8:2 *1382*
others had *t* of cruel mockings and ... Heb 11:36 *3984*
That the *t* of your faith, being ... 1Pet 1:7 *1383*
the fiery *t* which is to try you ... 1Pet 4:12

TRIBE {242}

the son of Hur, of the *t* of Judah ... Ex 31:2 4294
son of Ahisamach, of the *t* of Dan ... Ex 31:6 4294
the son of Hur, of the *t* of Judah ... Ex 35:30 4294
son of Ahisamach, of the *t* of Dan ... Ex 35:34 4294
of the *t* of Judah, made all that ... Ex 38:22 4294
son of Ahisamach, of the *t* of Dan ... Ex 38:23 4294
of Dibri, of the *t* of Dan ... Lev 24:11 4294
there shall be a man of every *t* ... Num 1:4 4294
of the *t* of Reuben ... Num 1:5
of them, even of the *t* of Reuben ... Num 1:21 4294
of them, even of the *t* of Simeon ... Num 1:23 4294
of them, even of the *t* of Gad ... Num 1:25 4294
of them, even of the *t* of Judah ... Num 1:27 4294
them, even of the *t* of Issachar ... Num 1:29 4294
of them, even of the *t* of Zebulun ... Num 1:31 4294
of them, even of the *t* of Ephraim ... Num 1:33 4294
them, even of the *t* of Manasseh ... Num 1:35 4294
them, even of the *t* of Benjamin ... Num 1:37 4294
of them, even of the *t* of Dan ... Num 1:39 4294
of them, even of the *t* of Asher ... Num 1:41 4294
them, even of the *t* of Naphtali ... Num 1:43 4294
the *t* of their fathers were not ... Num 1:47 4294
shalt not number the *t* of Levi ... Num 1:49 4294
him shall be the *t* of Issachar ... Num 2:5 4294
Then the *t* of Zebulun ... Num 2:7 4294
by him shall be the *t* of Simeon ... Num 2:12 4294
Then the *t* of Gad ... Num 2:14 4294
by him shall be the *t* of Manasseh ... Num 2:20 4294
Then the *t* of Benjamin ... Num 2:22 4294
by him shall be the *t* of Asher ... Num 2:27 4294
Then the *t* of Naphtali ... Num 2:29 4294
Bring the *t* of Levi near, and ... Num 3:6 4294
Cut ye not off the *t* of the ... Num 4:18 7626
of Amminadab, of the *t* of Judah ... Num 7:12 4294
over the host of the *t* of the ... Num 10:15 4294
over the host of the *t* of the ... Num 10:16 4294
over the host of the *t* of the ... Num 10:19 4294
over the host of the *t* of the ... Num 10:20 4294
over the host of the *t* of the ... Num 10:23 4294
over the host of the *t* of the ... Num 10:24 4294
over the host of the *t* of the ... Num 10:26 4294
over the host of the *t* of the ... Num 10:27 4294
of every *t* of their fathers shall ... Num 13:2 4294
of the *t* of Reuben, Shammua the ... Num 13:4 4294
Of the *t* of Simeon, Shaphat the ... Num 13:5 4294
Of the *t* of Judah, Caleb the son ... Num 13:6 4294
Of the *t* of Issachar, Igal the ... Num 13:7 4294
Of the *t* of Ephraim, Oshea the ... Num 13:8 4294
Of the *t* of Benjamin, Palti the ... Num 13:9 4294
Of the *t* of Zebulun, Gaddiel the ... Num 13:10 4294
Of the *t* of Joseph, namely, of ... Num 13:11 4294
of the *t* of Manasseh, Gaddi the ... Num 13:11 4294

T

Of the *t* of Dan, Ammiel the son .... Num 13:12 4294
Of the *t* of Asher, Sethur the son .... Num 13:13 4294
Of the *t* of Naphtali, Nahbi the........ Num 13:14 4294
Of the *t* of Gad, Geuel the son of........ Num 13:15 4294
brethren also of the *t* of Levi .... Num 18:2 4294
the *t* of thy father, bring thou .... Num 18:2 7626
Of every *t* a thousand, throughout .... Num 31:4 4294
of Israel, a thousand of every *t*........ Num 31:5 4294
to the war, a thousand of every *t*........ Num 31:6 4294
unto half the *t* of Manasseh the .... Num 32:33 7626
the nine tribes, and to the half *t* .... Num 34:13 4294
For the *t* of the children of........ Num 34:14 4294
the *t* of the children of Gad........ Num 34:14 4294
half the *t* of Manasseh have .... Num 34:14 4294
the half *t* have received their........ Num 34:15 4294
shall take one prince of every *t*........ Num 34:18 4294
Of the *t* of Judah, Caleb the son........ Num 34:19 4294
of the *t* of the children of .... Num 34:20 4294
Of the *t* of Benjamin, Elidad the........ Num 34:21 4294
the prince of the *t* of the .... Num 34:22 4294
for the *t* of the children of........ Num 34:23 4294
the prince of the *t* of the .... Num 34:24 4294
the prince of the *t* of the .... Num 34:25 4294
the prince of the *t* of the .... Num 34:26 4294
the prince of the *t* of the .... Num 34:27 4294
the prince of the *t* of the .... Num 34:28 4294
the *t* whereunto they are received........ Num 36:3 4294
the *t* whereunto they are received........ Num 36:4 4294
of the *t* of our fathers........ Num 36:4 4294
The *t* of the sons of Joseph hath........ Num 36:5 4294
only to the family of the *t* of .... Num 36:6 4294
of Israel remove from *t* to *t* .... Num 36:7 4294
of the *t* of his fathers........ Num 36:7 4294
an inheritance in any *t* of the........ Num 36:8 4294
the family of the *t* of her father .... Num 36:8 4294
from one *t* to another *t*........ Num 36:9 4294
inheritance remained in the *t* of........ Num 36:12 4294
twelve men of you, one of a *t* .... Deut 1:23 7626
I unto the half *t* of Manasseh .... Deut 3:13 7626
the LORD separated the *t* of Levi .... Deut 10:8 7626
the Levites, and all the *t* of Levi........ Deut 18:1 7626
and to the half *t* of Manasseh .... Deut 29:8 7626
man, or woman, or family, or *t*........ Deut 29:18 7626
and to half the *t* of Manasseh .... Josh 1:12 7626
of Israel, out of every *t* a man .... Josh 3:12 7626
the people, out of every *t* a man........ Josh 4:2 7626
of Israel, out of every *t* a man .... Josh 4:4 7626
half the *t* of Manasseh, passed .... Josh 4:12 7626
of the *t* of Judah, took of the........ Josh 7:1 4294
that the *t* which the LORD taketh........ Josh 7:14 7626
and the *t* of Judah was taken .... Josh 7:16 7626
of the *t* of Judah, was taken........ Josh 7:18 4294
and the half *t* of Manasseh........ Josh 12:6 7626
and the half *t* of Manasseh,........ Josh 13:7 7626
Only unto the *t* of Levi he gave........ Josh 13:14 7626
Moses gave unto the *t* of the........ Josh 13:15 4294
inheritance unto the *t* of Gad........ Josh 13:24 4294
unto the half *t* of Manasseh .... Josh 13:29 7626
t of the children of Manasseh by........ Josh 13:29 4294
But unto the *t* of Levi Moses gave........ Josh 13:33 7626
nine tribes, and for the half *t*........ Josh 14:2 4294
an half *t* on the other side .... Josh 14:3 4294
the *t* of the children of Judah by........ Josh 15:1 4294
of the *t* of the children of Judah .... Josh 15:20 4294
the uttermost cities of the *t* of........ Josh 15:21 4294
t of the children of Ephraim by........ Josh 16:8 4294
also a lot for the *t* of Manasseh........ Josh 17:1 4294
among you three men for each *t*........ Josh 18:4 7626
half the *t* of Manasseh, have .... Josh 18:7 7626
the lot of the *t* of the children .... Josh 18:11 4294
Now the cities of the *t* of the........ Josh 18:21 4294
even for the *t* of the children of .... Josh 19:1 4294
the *t* of the children of Simeon .... Josh 19:8 4294
the *t* of the children of Issachar .... Josh 19:23 4294
the *t* of the children of Asher........ Josh 19:24 4294
of the *t* of the children of Asher........ Josh 19:31 4294
the *t* of the children of Naphtali .... Josh 19:39 4294
for the *t* of the children of Dan........ Josh 19:40 4294
of the *t* of the children of Dan .... Josh 19:48 4294
the plain out of the *t* of Reuben........ Josh 20:8 4294
in Gilead out of the *t* of Gad........ Josh 20:8 4294
Bashan out of the *t* of Manasseh........ Josh 20:8 4294
had by lot out of the *t* of Judah .... Josh 21:4 4294
Judah, and out of the *t* of Simeon........ Josh 21:4 4294
out of the *t* of Benjamin,........ Josh 21:4 4294
the families of the *t* of Ephraim........ Josh 21:5 4294
Ephraim, and out of the *t* of Dan........ Josh 21:5 4294
and out of the half *t* of Manasseh .... Josh 21:5 4294
the families of the *t* of Issachar........ Josh 21:6 4294
and out of the *t* of Asher........ Josh 21:6 4294
out of the *t* of Naphtali, and out........ Josh 21:6 4294
out of the half *t* of Manasseh in........ Josh 21:6 4294
had out of the *t* of Reuben .... Josh 21:7 4294
of Reuben, and out of the *t* of Gad .... Josh 21:7 4294
Gad, and out of the *t* of Zebulun .... Josh 21:7 4294
they gave out of the *t* of the........ Josh 21:9 4294
out of the *t* of the children of........ Josh 21:9 4294
out of the *t* of Benjamin, Gibeon .... Josh 21:17 4294
their lot out of the *t* of Ephraim .... Josh 21:20 4294
And out of the *t* of Dan, Eltekeh........ Josh 21:23 4294
And out of the half *t* of Manasseh .... Josh 21:25 4294
out of the other half *t* of........ Josh 21:27 4294
out of the *t* of Issachar, Kishon .... Josh 21:28 4294
And out of the *t* of Asher, Mishal........ Josh 21:30 4294
out of the *t* of Naphtali, Kedesh .... Josh 21:32 4294
Levites, out of the *t* of Zebulun .... Josh 21:34 4294
And out of the *t* of Reuben........ Josh 21:36
And out of the *t* of Gad, Ramoth in........ Josh 21:38 4294

and the half *t* of Manasseh,........ Josh 22:1 4294
Now to the one half of the *t* of........ Josh 22:7 7626
the half *t* of Manasseh returned,........ Josh 22:9 7626
the half *t* of Manasseh built........ Josh 22:10 7626
the half *t* of Manasseh have built........ Josh 22:11 7626
Gad, and to the half *t* of Manasseh........ Josh 22:13 7626
Gad, and to the half *t* of Manasseh........ Josh 22:15 7626
the half *t* of Manasseh answered,........ Josh 22:21 7626
in those days the *t* of the .... Judg 18:1 7626
or that thou be a priest unto a *t*........ Judg 18:19 7626
the *t* of Dan until the day of the .... Judg 18:30 7626
men through all the *t* of Benjamin........ Judg 20:12 7626
be to day one *t* lacking in Israel........ Judg 21:3 7626
There is one *t* cut off from........ Judg 21:6 7626
that a *t* be not destroyed out of........ Judg 21:17 7626
at that time, every man to his *t*........ Judg 21:24 7626
the families of the *t* of Benjamin 1Sa 9:21 7626
the *t* of Benjamin was taken 1Sa 10:20 7626
When he had caused the *t* of........ 1Sa 10:21 7626
widow's son of the *t* of Naphtali 1Kin 7:14 4294
but will give one *t* to thy son........ 1Kin 11:13 7626
(But he shall have one *t* for my 1Kin 11:32 7626
And unto his son will I give one *t* 1Kin 11:36 7626
of David, but the *t* of Judah only........ 1Kin 12:20 7626
with the *t* of Benjamin, an 1Kin 12:21 7626
none left but the *t* of Judah only........ 2Kin 17:18 7626
half the *t* of Manasseh, of........ 1Chr 5:18 7626
the children of the half *t* of 1Chr 5:23 7626
the half *t* of Manasseh, and........ 1Chr 5:26 7626
And out of the *t* of Benjamin 1Chr 6:60 4294
were left of the family of that *t*........ 1Chr 6:61 4294
cities given out of the half *t* 1Chr 6:61 4294
out of the half *t* of Manasseh 1Chr 6:61
families out of the *t* of Issachar 1Chr 6:62 4294
and out of the *t* of Asher........ 1Chr 6:62 4294
out of the *t* of Naphtali, and out........ 1Chr 6:62 4294
out of the *t* of Manasseh in 1Chr 6:62 4294
families, out of the *t* of Reuben........ 1Chr 6:63 4294
of Reuben, and out of the *t* of Gad 1Chr 6:63 4294
Gad, and out of the *t* of Zebulun 1Chr 6:63 4294
of the *t* of the children of Judah 1Chr 6:65 4294
out of the *t* of the children of........ 1Chr 6:65 4294
out of the *t* of the children of........ 1Chr 6:65 4294
coasts out of the *t* of Ephraim........ 1Chr 6:66 4294
And out of the half *t* of Manasseh 1Chr 6:70 4294
family of the half *t* of Manasseh 1Chr 6:71 4294
And out of the *t* of Issachar 1Chr 6:72 4294
And out of the *t* of Asher 1Chr 6:74 4294
And out of the *t* of Naphtali 1Chr 6:76 4294
given out of the *t* of Zebulun 1Chr 6:77 4294
given them out of the *t* of Reuben........ 1Chr 6:78 4294
And out of the *t* of Gad........ 1Chr 6:80 4294
of the half *t* of Manasseh........ 1Chr 12:31 4294
and of the half *t* of Manasseh 1Chr 12:37 7626
sons were named of the *t* of Levi 1Chr 23:14 7626
the half *t* of Manasseh, for every........ 1Chr 26:32 7626
of the half *t* of Manasseh........ 1Chr 27:20 7626
Of the half *t* of Manasseh in........ 1Chr 27:21
and chose not the *t* of Ephraim........ Ps 78:67 7626
But chose the *t* of Judah, the........ Ps 78:68 7626
that in what *t* the stranger........ Eze 47:23 7626
of Phanuel, of the *t* of Aser .... Lk 2:36 *5443*
Cis, a man of the *t* of Benjamin .... Acts 13:21 *5443*
of Abraham, of the *t* of Benjamin .... Rom 11:1 *5443*
of the *t* of Benjamin, an Hebrew........ Phil 3:5 *5443*
spoken pertaineth to another *t*........ Heb 7:13 *5443*
of which *t* Moses spake nothing .... Heb 7:14 *5443*
behold, the Lion of the *t* of Juda........ Rev 5:5 *5443*
Of the *t* of Juda were sealed .... Rev 7:5 *5443*
Of the *t* of Reuben were sealed .... Rev 7:5 *5443*
Of the *t* of Gad were sealed........ Rev 7:5 *5443*
Of the *t* of Aser were sealed........ Rev 7:6 *5443*
Of the *t* of Nepthalim were sealed .... Rev 7:6 *5443*
Of the *t* of Manasses were sealed .... Rev 7:6 *5443*
Of the *t* of Simeon were sealed .... Rev 7:7 *5443*
Of the *t* of Levi were sealed .... Rev 7:7 *5443*
Of the *t* of Issachar were sealed........ Rev 7:7 *5443*
Of the *t* of Zabulon were sealed........ Rev 7:8 *5443*
Of the *t* of Joseph were sealed........ Rev 7:8 *5443*
Of the *t* of Benjamin were sealed .... Rev 7:8 *5443*

TRIBES {113}

people, as one of the *t* of Israel .... Gen 49:16 7626
these are the twelve *t* of Israel .... Gen 49:28 7626
to the twelve *t* of Israel .... Ex 24:4 7626
they be according to the twelve *t*........ Ex 28:21 7626
name, according to the twelve *t* .... Ex 39:14 7626
princes of the *t* of their fathers .... Num 1:16 4294
who were the princes of the *t*........ Num 7:2 4294
in his tents according to their *t*........ Num 24:2 7626
the *t* of their fathers they shall .... Num 26:55 4294
the *t* concerning the children of........ Num 30:1 4294
throughout all the *t* of Israel........ Num 31:4 4294
the chief fathers of the *t* of the .... Num 32:28 4294
according to the *t* of your........ Num 33:54 4294
commanded to give unto the nine *t*........ Num 34:13 4294
The two *t* and the half tribe have........ Num 34:15 4294
other *t* of the children of Israel........ Num 36:3 7626
but every one of the *t* of the........ Num 36:9 4294
and known among your *t*, and I will........ Deut 1:13 7626
So I took the chief of your *t* .... Deut 1:15 7626
tens, and officers among your *t*........ Deut 1:15 7626
me, even all the heads of your *t* .... Deut 5:23 7626
all your *t* to put his name there .... Deut 12:5 7626
LORD shall choose in one of thy *t*........ Deut 12:14 7626
God giveth thee, throughout thy *t*........ Deut 16:18 7626
hath chosen him out of all thy *t*........ Deut 18:5 7626
your captains of your *t*, your........ Deut 29:10 7626

evil out of all the *t* of Israel .... Deut 29:21 7626
unto me all the elders of your *t*........ Deut 31:28 7626
the *t* of Israel were gathered .... Deut 33:5 7626
twelve men out of the *t* of Israel .... Josh 3:12 7626
unto the number of the *t* of the........ Josh 4:5 7626
the *t* of the children of Israel .... Josh 4:8 7626
be brought according to your *t*........ Josh 7:14 7626
and brought Israel by their *t*........ Josh 7:16 7626
to their divisions by their *t*........ Josh 11:23 7626
the *t* of Israel for a possession........ Josh 12:7 7626
an inheritance unto the nine *t*........ Josh 13:7 7626
the *t* of the children of Israel .... Josh 14:1 4294
the hand of Moses, for the nine *t* .... Josh 14:2 4294
given the inheritance of two *t* .... Josh 14:3 4294
the children of Joseph were two *t* .... Josh 14:4 4294
the children of Israel seven *t*........ Josh 18:2 7626
the *t* of the children of Israel .... Josh 19:51 4294
the *t* of the children of Israel .... Josh 21:1 4294
nine cities out of those two *t*........ Josh 21:16 7626
throughout all the *t* of Israel........ Josh 22:14 4294
to be an inheritance for your *t*........ Josh 23:4 7626
all the *t* of Israel to Shechem .... Josh 24:1 7626
unto them among the *t* of Israel........ Judg 18:1 7626
even of all the *t* of Israel .... Judg 20:2 7626
throughout all the *t* of Israel........ Judg 20:10 7626
the *t* of Israel sent men through........ Judg 20:12 7626
Who is there among all the *t* of........ Judg 21:5 7626
What one is there of the *t* of .... Judg 21:8 7626
made a breach in the *t* of Israel .... Judg 21:15 7626
the *t* of Israel to be my priest........ 1Sa 2:28 7626
the smallest of the *t* of Israel 1Sa 9:21 7626
before the LORD by your *t* 1Sa 10:19 7626
all the *t* of Israel to come near........ 1Sa 10:20 7626
made the head of the *t* of Israel 1Sa 15:17 7626
Then came all the *t* of Israel to 2Sa 5:1 7626
word with any of the *t* of Israel 2Sa 7:7 7626
is of one of the *t* of Israel 2Sa 15:2 7626
throughout all the *t* of Israel........ 2Sa 15:10 7626
throughout all the *t* of Israel........ 2Sa 19:9 7626
all the *t* of Israel unto Abel........ 2Sa 20:14 7626
now through all the *t* of Israel 2Sa 24:2 7626
Israel, and all the heads of the *t* 1Kin 8:1 4294
the *t* of Israel to build an house........ 1Kin 8:16 7626
and will give ten *t* to thee 1Kin 11:31 7626
chosen out of all the *t* of Israel 1Kin 11:32 7626
give it unto thee, even ten *t*........ 1Kin 11:35 7626
choose out of all the *t* of Israel........ 1Kin 14:21 7626
of the *t* of the sons of Jacob 1Kin 18:31 7626
chosen out of all *t* of Israel 2Kin 21:7 7626
Furthermore over the *t* of Israel........ 1Chr 27:16 7626
the princes of the *t* of Israel........ 1Chr 27:22 7626
of Israel, the princes of the *t*........ 1Chr 28:1 7626
and princes of the *t* of Israel........ 1Chr 29:6 7626
Israel, and all the heads of the *t* 2Chr 5:2 4294
I chose no city among all the *t*........ 2Chr 6:5 7626
after them out of all the *t* of 2Chr 11:16 7626
chosen out of all the *t* of Israel 2Chr 12:13 7626
chosen before all the *t* of Israel........ 2Chr 33:7 7626
to the number of the *t* of Israel........ Ezr 6:17 7625
made the *t* of Israel to dwell in........ Ps 78:55 7626
one feeble person among their *t*........ Ps 105:37 7626
Whither the *t* go up, the *t*........ Ps 122:4 7626
the *t* of the LORD, unto the........ Ps 122:4 7626
are the stay of the *t* thereof........ Is 19:13 7626
to raise up the *t* of Jacob........ Is 49:6 7626
the *t* of thine inheritance........ Is 63:17 7626
the *t* of Israel his fellows, and........ Eze 37:19 7626
of Israel according to their *t* .... Eze 45:8 7626
to the twelve *t* of Israel .... Eze 47:13 7626
you according to the *t* of Israel .... Eze 47:21 7626
with you among the *t* of Israel .... Eze 47:22 7626
Now these are the names of the *t*........ Eze 48:1 7626
it out of all the *t* of Israel........ Eze 48:19 7626
As for the rest of the *t*, from .... Eze 48:23 7626
the *t* of Israel for inheritance .... Eze 48:29 7626
the names of the *t* of Israel .... Eze 48:31 7626
among the *t* of Israel have I made........ Hos 5:9 7626
according to the oaths of the *t* .... Hab 3:9 4294
of man, as of all the *t* of Israel........ Zec 9:1 7626
judging the twelve *t* of Israel........ Mt 19:28 *5443*
all the *t* of the earth mourn........ Mt 24:30 *5443*
judging the twelve *t* of Israel........ Lk 22:30 *5443*
Unto which promise our twelve *t*........ Acts 26:7 *1429*
to the twelve *t* which are........ Jas 1:1 *5443*
four thousand of all the *t* of the........ Rev 7:4 *5443*
t of the children of Israel .... Rev 21:12 *5443*

TRIBULATION {22}

When thou art in *t*, and all these .... Deut 4:30 6862
deliver you in the time of your *t*........ Judg 10:14 6869
let him deliver me out of all *t*........ 1Sa 26:24 6869
for when *t* or persecution ariseth........ Mt 13:21 *2347*
For then shall be great *t*........ Mt 24:21 *2347*
Immediately after the *t* of those........ Mt 24:29 *2347*
But in those days, after that *t*........ Mk 13:24 *2347*
In the world ye shall have *t*........ Jn 16:33 *2347*
that we must through much *t* enter .... Acts 14:22 *2347*
T and anguish, upon every soul of .... Rom 2:9 *2347*
knowing that *t* worketh patience .... Rom 5:3 *2347*
shall *t*, or distress, or........ Rom 8:35 *2347*
patient in *t*........ Rom 12:12 *2347*
Who comforteth us in all our *t*........ 2Cor 1:4 *2347*
am exceeding joyful in all our *t* 2Cor 7:4 *2347*
before that we should suffer *t* 1Th 3:4 *2346*
t to them that trouble you........ 2Th 1:6 *2347*
your brother, and companion in *t* .... Rev 1:9 *2347*
I know thy works, and *t*, and........ Rev 2:9 *2347*
and ye shall have *t* ten days........ Rev 2:10 *2347*

adultery with her into great *t* Rev 2:22 2347
they which came out of great *t* Rev 7:14 2347

TRIBULATIONS {4}
of all your adversities and your *t* 1Sa 10:19 6869
only so, but we glory in *t* also Rom 5:3 2347
that ye faint not at my *t* for you Eph 3:13 2347
persecutions and *t* that ye endure 2Th 1:4 2347

TRIBUTARIES {4}
therein shall be *t* unto thee Deut 20:11 4522
dwelt among them, and became *t* Judg 1:30 4522
of Beth-anath became *t* unto them Judg 1:33 4522
prevailed, so that they became *t* Judg 1:35 4522

TRIBUTARY {1}
provinces, how is she become *t* Lam 1:1 4522

TRIBUTE {37}
bear, and became a servant unto *t* Gen 49:15 4522
levy a *t* unto the LORD of the men Num 31:28 4371
the LORD's *t* of the sheep was six Num 31:37 4371
which the LORD's *t* was threescore Num 31:38 4371
which the LORD's *t* was threescore Num 31:39 4371
of which the LORD's *t* was thirty Num 31:40 4371
And Moses gave the *t*, which was Num 31:41 4371
unto the LORD thy God with a *t* of Deut 16:10 4530
unto this day, and serve under *t* Josh 16:10 4522
that they put the Canaanites to *t* Josh 17:13 4522
that they put the Canaanites to *t* Judg 1:28 4522
And Adoram was over the *t* 2Sa 20:24 4522
the son of Abda was over the *t* 1Kin 4:6 4522
a *t* of bondservice unto this day 1Kin 9:21 4522
sent Adoram, who was over the *t* 1Kin 12:18 4522
put the land to a *t* of an hundred 2Kin 23:33 6066
make to pay *t* until this day 2Chr 8:8 4522
sent Hadoram that was over the *t* 2Chr 10:18 4522
Jehoshaphat presents, and *t* silver 2Chr 17:11 4853
then will they not pay toll, *t* Ezr 4:13 1093
and toll, *t*, and custom, was paid Ezr 4:20 1093
even of the *t* beyond the river, Ezr 6:8 4061
not be lawful to impose toll, *t* Ezr 7:24 1093
borrowed money for the king's *t* Neh 5:4 4060
Ahasuerus laid a *t* upon the land Est 10:1 4522
but the slothful shall be under *t* Prov 12:24 4522
they that received *t* money came Mt 17:24 1323
said, Doth not your master pay *t* Mt 17:24 1323
of the earth take custom or *t* Mt 17:25 2778
it lawful to give *t* unto Caesar Mt 22:17 2778
Shew me the *t* money Mt 22:19 2778
Is it lawful to give *t* to Caesar Mk 12:14 2778
for us to give *t* unto Caesar Lk 20:22 5411
and forbidding to give *t* to Caesar Lk 23:2 5411
For for this cause pay ye *t* also Rom 13:6 5411
t to whom *t* is due Rom 13:7 5411

TRICKLETH {1}
Mine eye *t* down, and ceaseth not, Lam 3:49 5064

TRIED {20}
controversy and every stroke be *t* Deut 21:5
the word of the LORD is *t* 2Sa 22:31 6884
when he hath *t* me, I shall come Job 23:10 974
is that Job may be *t* unto the end Job 34:36 974
as silver *t* in a furnace of earth Ps 12:6 6884
thou hast *t* me, and shalt find Ps 17:3 6884
the word of the LORD is *t* Ps 18:30 6884
hast *t* us, as silver is *t* Ps 66:10 6884
the word of the LORD *t* him Ps 105:19 6884
a *t* stone, a precious corner Is 28:16 976
me, and *t* mine heart toward thee Jer 12:3 974
be purified, and made white, and *t* Dan 12:10 6884
and will try them as gold is *t* Zec 13:9 974
By faith Abraham, when he was *t* Heb 11:17 3985
for when he is *t*, he shall Jas 1:12 1384
though it be *t* with fire 1Pet 1:7 1381
thou hast *t* them which say they Rev 2:2 3985
you into prison, that ye may be *t* Rev 2:10 3985
to buy of me gold *t* in the fire Rev 3:18 4448

TRIEST {3}
my God, that thou *t* the heart 1Chr 29:17 974
that *t* the reins and the heart, Jer 11:20 974
that *t* the righteous, and seest Jer 20:12 974

TRIETH {5}
For the ear *t* words, as the mouth Job 34:3 974
the righteous God *t* the hearts Ps 7:9 974
The LORD *t* the righteous Ps 11:5 974
but the LORD *t* the hearts Prov 17:3 974
men, but God, which *t* our hearts 1Th 2:4 1381

TRIMMED {2}
nor *t* his beard, nor washed his 2Sa 19:24 6213
virgins arose, and *t* their lamps Mt 25:7 2885

TRIMMEST {1}
Why *t* thou thy way to seek love Jer 2:33 3190

TRIUMPH {10}
daughters of the uncircumcised *t* 2Sa 1:20 5937
let not mine enemies *t* over me Ps 25:2 5970
mine enemy doth not *t* over me Ps 41:11 7321
unto God with the voice of *t* Ps 47:1 7440
Philistia, *t* thou because of me Ps 60:8 7321
I will *t* in the works of thy Ps 92:4 7442
how long shall the wicked *t* Ps 94:3 5937
holy name, and to *t* in thy praise Ps 106:47 7623
over Philistia will I *t* Ps 108:9 7321
always causeth us to *t* in Christ 2Cor 2:14 2358

TRIUMPHED {2}
LORD, for he hath *t* gloriously Ex 15:1 1342
LORD, for he hath *t* gloriously Ex 15:21 1342

TRIUMPHING {2}
That the *t* of the wicked is short Job 20:5 7445
of them openly, *t* over them in it Col 2:15 2358

TROAS *(tro'-as)* {6} *A seaport of Phrygia in Asia Minor.*
passing by Mysia came down to *T* Acts 16:8 5174
Therefore loosing from *T*, we came Acts 16:11 5174
going before tarried for us at *T* Acts 20:5 5174
came unto them to *T* in five days Acts 20:6 5174
when I came to *T* to preach 2Cor 2:12 5174
that I left at *T* with Carpus 2Ti 4:13 5174

TRODDEN {27}
give the land that he hath *t* upon Deut 1:36 1869
have *t* shall be thine inheritance Josh 14:9 1869
thou hast *t* down strength Judg 5:21 1869
old way which wicked men have *t* Job 22:15 1869
The lion's whelps have not *t* it Job 28:8 1869
Thou hast *t* down all them that Ps 119:118 5541
thereof, and it shall be *t* down Is 5:5 4823
as a carcase *t* under feet Is 14:19 947
t down, whose land the rivers Is 18:2 4001
t under foot, whose land the Is 18:7 4001
Moab shall be *t* down under him, Is 25:10 1758
even as straw is *t* down for the Is 25:10 1758
of Ephraim, shall be *t* under feet Is 28:3 7429
then ye shall be *t* down by it Is 28:18 4823
I have *t* the winepress alone Is 63:3 1869
have *t* down thy sanctuary Is 63:18 947
they have *t* my portion under foot Jer 12:10 947
The Lord hath *t* under foot all my Lam 1:15 5541
the Lord hath *t* the virgin Lam 1:15 1869
which ye have *t* with your feet Eze 34:19 7429
and the host to be *t* under foot Dan 8:13 4823
now shall she be *t* down as the Mic 7:10 4823
to be *t* under foot of men Mt 5:13 2662
and it was *t* down, and the fowls of Lk 8:5 2662
Jerusalem shall be *t* down of the Lk 21:24 3961
who hath *t* under foot the Son of Heb 10:29 2662
winepress was *t* without the city Rev 14:20 3961

TRODE {8}
t the grapes, and made merry, and Judg 9:27 1869
t them down with ease over Judg 20:43 1869
the people *t* upon him in the gate 2Kin 7:17 7429
for the people *t* upon him in the 2Kin 7:20 7429
and he *t* her under foot 2Kin 9:33 7429
in Lebanon, and *t* down the thistle 2Kin 14:9 7429
in Lebanon, and *t* down the thistle 2Chr 25:18 7429
that they *t* one upon another Lk 12:1 2662

TROGYLLIUM *(tro-jil'-le-um)* {1} *A coastal town in Ionia in Asia Minor.*
arrived at Samos, and tarried at *T* Acts 20:15 5175

TROOP {13}
And Leah said, A *t* cometh Gen 30:11 1409
Gad, a *t* shall overcome him Gen 49:19 1416
Shall I pursue after this *t* 1Sa 30:8 1416
after Abner, and became one *t* 2Sa 2:25 92
and Joab came from pursuing a *t* 2Sa 3:22 1416
by thee I have run through a *t* 2Sa 22:30 1416
were gathered together into a *t* 2Sa 23:11 2416
the *t* of the Philistines pitched 2Sa 23:13 2416
by thee I have run through a *t* Ps 18:29 1416
that prepare a table for that *t* Is 65:11 1409
bring a *t* suddenly upon them Jer 18:22 1416
the *t* of robbers spoileth without Hos 7:1 1416
hath founded his *t* in the earth Amos 9:6 92

TROOPS {7}
The *t* of Tema looked, the Job 6:19 734
His *t* come together, and raise up Job 19:12 1416
by *t* in the harlots' houses Jer 5:7
as *t* of robbers wait for a man, Hos 6:9 1416
in *t*, O daughter of *t* Mic 5:1 1416
he will invade them with his *t* Hab 3:16

TROPHIMUS *(trof'-im-us)* {3} *A companion of Paul.*
and of Asia, Tychicus and *T* Acts 20:4 5161
him in the city *T* an Ephesian Acts 21:29 5161
but *T* have I left at Miletum sick 2Ti 4:20 5161

TROUBLE {110}
camp of Israel a curse, and *t* it Josh 6:18 5916
the LORD shall *t* thee this day Josh 7:25 5916
and thou art one of them that *t* me Judg 11:35 5916
Hezekiah, This day is a day of *t* 2Kin 19:3 6869
in my *t* I have prepared for the 1Chr 22:14 6040
But when they in their *t* did turn 2Chr 15:4 6862
and he hath delivered them to *t* 2Chr 29:8 2189
to affright them, and to *t* them 2Chr 32:18 926
and in the time of their *t* Neh 9:27 6869
let not all the *t* seem little Neh 9:32 8513
yet *t* came Job 3:26 7267
neither doth *t* spring out of the Job 5:6 5999
Yet man is born unto *t*, as the Job 5:7 5999
is of few days, and full of *t* Job 14:1 7267
T and anguish shall make him Job 15:24 6862
his cry when *t* cometh upon him Job 27:9 6869
not I weep for him that was in *t* Job 30:25 7186,3117
quietness, who then can make *t* Job 34:29 7561
reserved against the time of *t* Job 38:23 6862
how are they increased that *t* me Ps 3:1 6862
oppressed, a refuge in times of *t* Ps 9:9 6869
consider my *t* which I suffer of Ps 9:13 6040
hidest thou thyself in times of *t* Ps 10:1 6869
those that *t* me rejoice when I am Ps 13:4 6862
LORD hear thee in the day of *t* Ps 20:1 6869
for *t* is near Ps 22:11 6869
For in the time of *t* he shall Ps 27:5 7451
for thou hast considered my *t* Ps 31:7 6040
upon me, O LORD, for I am in *t* Ps 31:9 6887
thou shalt preserve me from *t* Ps 32:7 6862
their strength in the time of *t* Ps 37:39 6869
will deliver him in time of *t* Ps 41:1 7451
a very present help in *t* Ps 46:1 6869
And call upon me in the day of *t* Ps 50:15 6869
he hath delivered me out of all *t* Ps 54:7 6869
and refuge in the day of my *t* Ps 59:16 6862
Give us help from *t* Ps 60:11 6862
hath spoken, when I was in *t* Ps 66:14 6862
for I am in *t* Ps 69:17 6887
They are not in *t* as other men Ps 73:5 5999
In the day of my *t* I sought the Ps 77:2 6869
in vanity, and their years in *t* Ps 78:33 928
wrath, and indignation, and *t* Ps 78:49 6869
Thou calledst in *t*, and I Ps 81:7 6869
In the day of my *t* I will call Ps 86:7 6869
I will be with him in *t* Ps 91:15 6869
from me in the day when I am in *t* Ps 102:2 6862
cried unto the LORD in their *t* Ps 107:6 6862
cried unto the LORD in their *t* Ps 107:13 6862
they cry unto the LORD in their *t* Ps 107:19 6862
their soul is melted because of *t* Ps 107:26 7451
they cry unto the LORD in their *t* Ps 107:28 6862
Give us help from *t* Ps 108:12 6862
I found *t* and sorrow Ps 116:3 6869
T and anguish have taken hold on Ps 119:143 6862
Though I walk in the midst of *t* Ps 138:7 6869
I shewed before him my *t* Ps 142:2 6869
sake bring my soul out of *t* Ps 143:11 6869
righteous is delivered out of *t* Prov 11:8 6869
but the just shall come out of *t* Prov 12:13 6869
the revenues of the wicked is *t* Prov 15:6 5916
great treasure and *t* therewith Prov 15:16 4103
time of *t* is like a broken tooth Prov 25:19 6869
they are a *t* unto me Is 1:14 2960
and behold *t* and darkness, dimness Is 8:22 6869
And behold at eveningtide *t* Is 17:14 1091
For it is a day of *t*, and of Is 22:5 4103
in *t* have they visited thee Is 26:16 6862
into the land of *t* and anguish, Is 30:6 6869
salvation also in the time of *t* Is 33:2 6869
Hezekiah, This day is a day of *t* Is 37:3 6869
answer, nor save him out of his *t* Is 46:7 6869
in vain, nor bring forth for *t* Is 65:23 928
the time of their *t* they will say Jer 2:27 7451
save thee in the time of thy *t* Jer 2:28 7451
for a time of health, and behold *t* Jer 8:15 1205
at all in the time of their *t* Jer 11:12 7451
that they cry unto me for their *t* Jer 11:14 7451
the saviour thereof in time of *t* Jer 14:8 6869
the time of healing, and behold *t* Jer 14:19 1205
it is even the time of Jacob's *t* Jer 30:7 6869
for in the day of *t* they shall be Jer 51:2 7451
mine enemies have heard of my *t* Lam 1:21 7451
is come, the day of *t* is near Eze 7:7 4103
the foot of man *t* them any more Eze 32:13 4103
nor the hoofs of beasts *t* them Eze 32:13 1804
interpretation thereof, *t* thee Dan 4:19 927
let not thy thoughts *t* thee Dan 5:10 927
and out of the north shall *t* him Dan 11:44 926
and there shall be a time of *t* Dan 12:1 6869
a strong hold in the day of *t* Nah 1:7 6869
that I might rest in the day of *t* Hab 3:16 6869
day is a day of wrath, a day of *t* Zeph 1:15 6869
unto them, Why *t* ye the woman Mt 26:10 2873,3930
why *t* ye her Mk 14:6 3930
unto him, Lord, *t* not thyself Lk 7:6 4660
t not the Master Lk 8:49 4660
shall answer and say, *T* me not Lk 11:7 2873
that we *t* not them, which from Acts 15:19 3926
Jews, do exceedingly *t* our city Acts 16:20 1613
him said, *T* not yourselves Acts 20:10 2350
such shall have *t* in the flesh 1Cor 7:28 2347
comfort them which are in any *t* 2Cor 1:4 2347
of our *t* which came to us in Asia 2Cor 1:8 2347
but there be some that *t* you Gal 1:7 5015
were even cut off which *t* you Gal 5:12 387
From henceforth let no man *t* me Gal 6:17 2873,3930
tribulation to them that *t* you 2Th 1:6 2346
Wherein I suffer *t*, as an evil 2Ti 2:9 2553
of bitterness springing up *t* you Heb 12:15 1776

TROUBLED {68}
Ye have *t* me to make me to stink Gen 34:30 5916
the morning that his spirit was *t* Gen 41:8 6470
for they were *t* at his presence Gen 45:3 926
t the host of the Egyptians, Ex 14:24 2000
Joshua said, Why hast thou *t* us Josh 7:25 5916
My father hath *t* the land 1Sa 14:29 5916
evil spirit from the LORD *t* him 1Sa 16:14 1204
Saul, and saw that he was sore *t* 1Sa 28:21 926
and all the Israelites were *t* 2Sa 4:1 926
he answered, I have not *t* Israel 1Kin 18:18 5916
Syria was sore *t* for this thing 2Kin 6:11 5590
of Judah, and *t* them in building, Ezr 4:4 1089
it toucheth thee, and thou art *t* Job 4:5 926
so, why should not my spirit be *t* Job 21:4 7114
Therefore am I *t* at his presence Job 23:15 926
the people shall be *t* at midnight Job 34:20 1607
didst hide thy face, and I was *t* Ps 30:7 926
I am *t* Ps 38:6 5753
the waters thereof roar and be *t* Ps 46:3 2560
they were *t*, and hasted away Ps 48:5 926
I remembered God, and was *t* Ps 77:3 1993
I am so *t* that I cannot speak Ps 77:4 6470
the depths also were *t* Ps 77:16 7264
them be confounded and *t* for ever Ps 83:17 926
anger, and by thy wrath are we *t* Ps 90:7 926

Thou hidest thy face, they are *t* ... Ps 104:29 926
the wicked is as a *t* fountain ... Prov 25:26 7515
Many days and years shall ye be *t* ... Is 32:10 7264
be *t*, ye careless ones ... Is 32:11 7264
But the wicked are like the *t* sea ... Is 57:20 1644
therefore my bowels are *t* for him ... Jer 31:20 1993
my bowels are *t* ... Lam 1:20 2560
fail with tears, my bowels are *t* ... Lam 2:11 2560
the people of the land shall be *t* ... Eze 7:27 926
sea shall be *t* at thy departure ... Eze 26:18 926
afraid, they shall be *t* in their ... Eze 27:35 7481
wherewith his spirit was *t* ... Dan 2:1 6470
my spirit was *t* to know the dream ... Dan 2:3 6470
and the visions of my head *t* me ... Dan 4:5 927
one hour, and his thoughts *t* him ... Dan 4:19 927
changed, and his thoughts *t* him ... Dan 5:6 927
was king Belshazzar greatly *t* ... Dan 5:9 927
and the visions of my head *t* me ... Dan 7:15 927
Daniel, my cogitations much *t* me ... Dan 7:28 927
their way as a flock, they were *t* ... Zec 10:2 6031
had heard these things, he was *t* ... Mt 2:3 *5015*
walking on the sea, they were *t* ... Mt 14:26 *5015*
see that ye be not *t* ... Mt 24:6 *2360*
For they all saw him, and were *t* ... Mk 6:50 *5015*
and rumours of wars, be ye not *t* ... Mk 13:7 *2360*
when Zacharias saw him, he was *t* ... Lk 1:12 *5015*
she was *t* at his saying, and cast ... Lk 1:29 *1298*
careful and *t* about many things ... Lk 10:41 *5182*
he said unto them, Why are ye *t* ... Lk 24:38 *5015*
into the pool, and *t* the water ... Jn 5:4 *5015*
have no man, when the water is *t* ... Jn 5:7 *5015*
groaned in the spirit, and was *t* ... Jn 11:33 *5015,1438*
Now is my soul *t* ... Jn 12:27 *5015*
he was *t* in spirit, and testified, ... Jn 13:21 *5015*
Let not your heart be *t* ... Jn 14:1 *5015*
Let not your heart be *t*, neither ... Jn 14:27 *5015*
out from us have *t* you with words ... Acts 15:24 *5015*
they *t* the people and the rulers ... Acts 17:8 *5015*
We are *t* on every side, yet not ... 2Cor 4:8 *2346*
but we were *t* on every side ... 2Cor 7:5 *2346*
And to you who are *t* rest with us ... 2Th 1:7 *2346*
not soon shaken in mind, or be *t* ... 2Th 2:2 *2360*
of their terror, neither be *t* ... 1Pet 3:14 *5015*

TROUBLEDST {1}
t the waters with thy feet, and ... Eze 32:2 1804

TROUBLER {1}
the *t* of Israel, who transgressed ... 1Chr 2:7 5916

TROUBLES {12}
many evils and *t* shall befall them ... Deut 31:17 6869
t are befallen them, that this ... Deut 31:21 6869
He shall deliver thee in six *t* ... Job 5:19 6869
The *t* of my heart are enlarged ... Ps 25:17 6869
Israel, O God, out of all his *t* ... Ps 25:22 6869
and saved him out of all his *t* ... Ps 34:6 6869
them out of all their *t* ... Ps 34:17 6869
hast shewed me great and sore *t* ... Ps 71:20 6869
For my soul is full of *t* ... Ps 88:3 7451
tongue keepeth his soul from *t* ... Prov 21:23 6869
the former *t* are forgotten ... Is 65:16 6869
and there shall be famines and *t* ... Mk 13:8 *5016*

TROUBLEST {1}
why *t* thou the Master any further ... Mk 5:35 *4660*

TROUBLETH {10}
an evil spirit from God *t* thee ... 1Sa 16:15 1204
him, Art thou he that *t* Israel ... 1Kin 18:17 5916
about thee, and sudden fear *t* thee ... Job 22:10 926
heart soft, and the Almighty *t* me ... Job 23:16 926
he that is cruel *t* his own flesh ... Prov 11:17 5916
He that *t* his own house shall ... Prov 11:29 5916
is greedy of gain *t* his own house ... Prov 15:27 5916
is in thee, and no secret *t* thee ... Dan 4:9 598
Yet because this widow *t* me ... Lk 18:5 *3930,2873*
but he that *t* you shall bear his ... Gal 5:10 *5015*

TROUBLING {2}
There the wicked cease from *t* ... Job 3:17 7267
the *t* of the water stepped in was ... Jn 5:4 *5015*

TROUBLOUS {1}
and the wall, even in *t* times ... Dan 9:25 5916

TROUGH {1}
and emptied her pitcher into the *t* ... Gen 24:20 8268

TROUGHS {2}
t when the flocks came to drink ... Gen 30:38 8268
filled the *t* to water their ... Ex 2:16 7298

TROW {1}
I *t* not ... Lk 17:9 *1380*

TRUCEBREAKERS {1}
Without natural affection, *t* ... 2Ti 3:3 *786*

TRUE {81}
we are *t* men, thy servants are no ... Gen 42:11 3651
If ye be *t* men, let one of your ... Gen 42:19 3651
And we said unto him, We are *t* men ... Gen 42:31 3651
shall I know that ye are *t* men ... Gen 42:33 3651
no spies, but that ye are *t* men ... Gen 42:34 3651
diligently, and, behold, it be *t* ... Deut 17:4 571
But if this thing be *t*, and the ... Deut 22:20 571
house, and give me a *t* token ... Josh 2:12 571
now it is *t* that I am thy near ... Ruth 3:12 551
art that God, and thy words be *t* ... 2Sa 7:28 571
It was a *t* report that I heard in ... 1Kin 10:6 571
is *t* in the name of the LORD ... 1Kin 22:16 571
It was a *t* report which I heard ... 2Chr 9:5 571
hath been without the *t* God ... 2Chr 15:3 571
and *t* laws, good statutes and ... Neh 9:13 571
the judgments of the LORD are *t* ... Ps 19:9 571
Thy word is *t* from the beginning ... Ps 119:160 571
A *t* witness delivereth souls ... Prov 14:25 571
But the LORD is the *t* God ... Jer 10:10 571
said to Jeremiah, The LORD be a *t* ... Jer 42:5 571
hath executed *t* judgment between ... Eze 18:8 571
spake and said unto them, Is it *t* ... Dan 3:14 6656
answered and said unto the king, *T* ... Dan 3:24 3330
answered and said, The thing is *t* ... Dan 6:12 3330
the morning which was told is *t* ... Dan 8:26 571
and the thing was *t*, but the time ... Dan 10:1 571
Execute *t* judgment, and shew mercy ... Zec 7:9 571
Master, we know that thou art *t* ... Mt 22:16 *227*
Master, we know that thou art *t* ... Mk 12:14 *227*
commit to your trust the *t* riches ... Lk 16:11 *228*
That was the *t* Light, which ... Jn 1:9 *228*
set to his seal that God is *t* ... Jn 3:33 *227*
when the *t* worshippers shall ... Jn 4:23 *228*
And herein is that saying *t* ... Jn 4:37 *228*
of myself, my witness is not *t* ... Jn 5:31 *227*
which he witnesseth of me is *t* ... Jn 5:32 *227*
you the *t* bread from heaven ... Jn 6:32 *228*
that sent him, the same is *t* ... Jn 7:18 *227*
myself, but he that sent me is *t* ... Jn 7:28 *228*
thy record is not *t* ... Jn 8:13 *227*
of myself, yet my record is *t* ... Jn 8:14 *227*
yet if I judge, my judgment is *t* ... Jn 8:16 *227*
the testimony of two men is *t* ... Jn 8:17 *227*
but he that sent me is *t* ... Jn 8:26 *227*
John spake of this man were *t* ... Jn 10:41 *227*
I am the *t* vine, and my Father is ... Jn 15:1 *228*
might know thee the only *t* God ... Jn 17:3 *228*
bare record, and his record is *t* ... Jn 19:35 *228*
and he knoweth that he saith *t* ... Jn 19:35 *2227*
we know that his testimony is *t* ... Jn 21:24 *227*
wist not that it was *t* which was ... Acts 12:9 *227*
yea, let God be *t*, but every man ... Rom 3:4 *227*
But as God is *t*, our word toward ... 2Cor 1:18 *4103*
as deceivers, and yet *t* ... 2Cor 6:8 *227*
in righteousness and *t* holiness ... Eph 4:24 *3588,225*
t yokefellow, help those women ... Phil 4:3 *1103*
brethren, whatsoever things are *t* ... Phil 4:8 *227*
to serve the living and *t* God ... 1Th 1:9 *228*
This is a *t* saying, If a man ... 1Ti 3:1 *4103*
This witness is *t* ... Titus 1:13 *227*
of the *t* tabernacle, which the ... Heb 8:2 *228*
which are the figures of the *t* ... Heb 9:24 *228*
Let us draw near with a *t* heart ... Heb 10:22 *228*
testifying that this is the *t* ... 1Pet 5:12 *227*
them according to the *t* proverb ... 2Pet 2:22 *227*
unto you, which thing is *t* in him ... 1Jn 2:8 *227*
past, and the *t* light now shineth ... 1Jn 2:8 *228*
that we may know him that is *t* ... 1Jn 5:20 *228*
and we are in him that is *t* ... 1Jn 5:20 *228*
This is the *t* God, and eternal ... 1Jn 5:20 *228*
and ye know that our record is *t* ... 3Jn 12 *227*
he that is holy, he that is *t* ... Rev 3:7 *228*
t witness, the beginning of the ... Rev 3:14 *228*
How long, O Lord, holy and *t* ... Rev 6:10 *228*
t are thy ways, thou King of ... Rev 15:3 *228*
Even so, Lord God Almighty, *t* ... Rev 16:7 *228*
For *t* and righteous are his ... Rev 19:2 *228*
These are the *t* sayings of God ... Rev 19:9 *228*
upon him was called Faithful and *T* ... Rev 19:11 *228*
for these words are *t* and faithful ... Rev 21:5 *228*
These sayings are faithful and *t* ... Rev 22:6 *228*

TRULY {42}
t Lamech seventy and sevenfold ... Gen 4:24 571
t with my master, tell me ... Gen 24:49 571
and deal kindly and *t* with me ... Gen 47:29 571
but *t* his younger brother shall ... Gen 48:19 199
But as *t* as I live, all the earth ... Num 14:21 199
As *t* as I live, saith the LORD, ... Num 14:28
Thou shalt *t* tithe all the ... Deut 14:22
will deal kindly and *t* with thee ... Josh 2:14 571
T the LORD hath delivered into ... Josh 2:24 3588
Now therefore, if ye have done *t* ... Judg 9:16 571
If ye then have dealt *t* and ... Judg 9:19 571
but *t* as the LORD liveth, and as ... 1Sa 20:3 199
For *t* my words shall not be false ... Job 36:4 551
T my soul waiteth upon God ... Ps 62:1 389
T God is good to Israel, even to ... Ps 73:1 389
O LORD, *t* I am thy servant ... Ps 116:16 577
they that deal *t* are his delight ... Prov 12:22 530
T the light is sweet, and a ... Eccl 11:7
T in vain is salvation hoped for ... Jer 3:23 403
t in the LORD our God is the ... Jer 3:23 403
T this is a grief, and I must bear ... Jer 10:19 389
that the LORD hath *t* sent him ... Jer 28:9 571
hath kept my judgments, to deal *t* ... Eze 18:9 571
But *t* I am full of power by the ... Mic 3:8 199
The harvest *t* is plenteous, but ... Mt 9:37 *3303*
Elias *t* shall first come, and ... Mt 17:11 *3303*
T this was the Son of God ... Mt 27:54 *230*
The spirit *t* is ready, but the ... Mk 14:38 *3303*
T this man was the Son of God ... Mk 15:39 *230*
unto them, The harvest *t* is great ... Lk 10:2 *3303*
T ye bear witness that ye allow ... Lk 11:48 *686*
but teachest the way of God *t* ... Lk 20:21 *1909,225*
t the Son of man goeth, as it was ... Lk 22:22 *3303*
in that saidst thou *t* ... Jn 4:18 *227*
many other signs *t* did Jesus in ... Jn 20:30 *3303*
For John *t* baptized with water ... Acts 1:5 *3303*
For Moses *t* said unto the fathers ... Acts 3:22 *3303*
The prison *t* found we shut with ... Acts 5:23 *3303*
T the signs of an apostle were ... 2Cor 12:12 *3303*
they *t* were many priests, because ... Heb 7:23 *3303*
And *t*, if they had been mindful of ... Heb 11:15 *3303*
t our fellowship is with the ... 1Jn 1:3 *1161*

TRUMP {4}
O my soul, the sound of the *t* ... Jer 4:19 7782
in Gibeah, and the *t* in Ramah ... Hos 5:8 2689
of an eye, at the last *t* ... 1Cor 15:52 *4536*
archangel, and with the *t* of God ... 1Th 4:16 *4536*

TRUMPET {59}
when the *t* soundeth long, they ... Ex 19:13 3104
the voice of the *t* exceeding loud ... Ex 19:16 7782
the voice of the *t* sounded long ... Ex 19:19 7782
lightnings, and the noise of the *t* ... Ex 20:18 7782
Then shalt thou cause the *t* of ... Lev 25:9 7782
t sound throughout all your land ... Lev 25:9 7782
And if they blow but with one *t* ... Num 10:4
when ye hear the sound of the *t* ... Josh 6:5 7782
people heard the sound of the *t* ... Josh 6:20 7782
that he blew a *t* in the mountain ... Judg 3:27 7782
came upon Gideon, and he blew a *t* ... Judg 6:34 7782
he put a *t* in every man's hand ... Judg 7:16 7782
When I blow with a *t*, I and all ... Judg 7:18 7782
Saul blew the *t* throughout all ... 1Sa 13:3 7782
So Joab blew a *t*, and all the ... 2Sa 2:28 7782
and with the sound of the *t* ... 2Sa 6:15 7782
as ye hear the sound of the *t* ... 2Sa 15:10 7782
And Joab blew the *t*, and the people ... 2Sa 18:16 7782
and he blew a *t*, and said, We have ... 2Sa 20:1 7782
And he blew a *t*, and they retired ... 2Sa 20:22 7782
and blow ye with the *t*, and say, ... 1Kin 1:34 7782
And they blew the *t* ... 1Kin 1:39 7782
Joab heard the sound of the *t* ... 1Kin 1:41 7782
he that sounded the *t* was by me ... Neh 4:18 7782
ye hear the sound of the *t* ... Neh 4:20 7782
he that it is the sound of the *t* ... Job 39:24 7782
the LORD with the sound of a *t* ... Ps 47:5 7782
Blow up the *t* in the new moon, in ... Ps 81:3 7782
him with the sound of the *t* ... Ps 150:3 7782
and when he bloweth a *t*, hear ye ... Is 18:3 7782
that the great *t* shall be blown ... Is 27:13 7782
not, lift up thy voice like a *t* ... Is 58:1 7782
and say, Blow ye the *t* in the land ... Jer 4:5 7782
and hear the sound of the *t* ... Jer 4:21 7782
Jerusalem, and blow the *t* in Tekoa ... Jer 6:1 7782
Hearken to the sound of the *t* ... Jer 6:17 7782
war, nor hear the sound of the *t* ... Jer 42:14 7782
blow the *t* among the nations ... Jer 51:27 7782
They have blown the *t*, even to ... Eze 7:14 8628
come upon the land, he blow the *t* ... Eze 33:3 7782
heareth the sound of the *t* ... Eze 33:4 7782
He heard the sound of the *t* ... Eze 33:5 7782
the sword come, and blow not the *t* ... Eze 33:6 7782
Set the *t* to thy mouth ... Hos 8:1 7782
Blow ye the *t* in Zion, and sound ... Joel 2:1 7782
Blow the *t* in Zion, sanctify a ... Joel 2:15 7782
and with the sound of the *t* ... Amos 2:2 7782
Shall a *t* be blown in the city, ... Amos 3:6 7782
A day of the *t* and alarm against ... Zeph 1:16 7782
and the Lord GOD shall blow the *t* ... Zec 9:14 7782
do not sound a *t* before thee ... Mt 6:2 *4537*
angels with a great sound of a *t* ... Mt 24:31 *4536*
For if the *t* give an uncertain ... 1Cor 14:8 *4536*
for the *t* shall sound, and the ... 1Cor 15:52
And the sound of a *t*, and the voice ... Heb 12:19 *4536*
me a great voice, as of a *t* ... Rev 1:10 *4536*
as it were of a *t* talking with me ... Rev 4:1 *4536*
of the *t* of the three angels ... Rev 8:13 *4536*
the sixth angel which had the *t* ... Rev 9:14 *4536*

TRUMPETERS {4}
the *t* by the king, and all the ... 2Kin 11:14 2689
It came even to pass, as the *t* ... 2Chr 5:13 2689
singers sang, and the *t* sounded ... 2Chr 29:28 2690
and musicians, and of pipers, and *t* ... Rev 18:22 *4538*

TRUMPETS {51}
a memorial of blowing of *t* ... Lev 23:24
Make thee two *t* of silver ... Num 10:2 2689
priests, shall blow with the *t* ... Num 10:8 2689
ye shall blow an alarm with the *t* ... Num 10:9 2689
ye shall blow with the *t* over ... Num 10:10 2689
a day of blowing the *t* unto you ... Num 29:1
the *t* to blow in his hand ... Num 31:6 2689
the ark seven *t* of rams' horns ... Josh 6:4 7782
the priests shall blow with the *t* ... Josh 6:4 7782
let seven priests bear seven *t* of ... Josh 6:6 7782
t of rams' horns passed on before ... Josh 6:8 7782
the LORD, and blew with the *t* ... Josh 6:8 7782
the priests that blew with the *t* ... Josh 6:9 7782
going on, and blowing with the *t* ... Josh 6:9 7782
seven priests bearing seven *t* of ... Josh 6:13 7782
continually, and blew with the *t* ... Josh 6:13 7782
going on, and blowing with the *t* ... Josh 6:13 7782
when the priests blew with the *t* ... Josh 6:16 7782
when the priests blew with the *t* ... Josh 6:20 7782
in their hand, and their *t* ... Judg 7:8 7782
then blow ye the *t* also on every ... Judg 7:18 7782
and they blew the *t*, and brake the ... Judg 7:19 7782
And the three companies blew the *t* ... Judg 7:20 7782
the *t* in their right hands to ... Judg 7:20 7782
And the three hundred blew the *t* ... Judg 7:22 7782
top of the stairs, and blew with *t* ... 2Kin 9:13 7782
the land rejoiced, and blew with *t* ... 2Kin 11:14
of silver, snuffers, basons, *t* ... 2Kin 12:13 2689
and with cymbals, and with *t* ... 1Chr 13:8 2689
did blow with the *t* before the ... 1Chr 15:24 2689
sound of the cornet, and with *t* ... 1Chr 15:28 2689
Jahaziel the priests with *t* ... 1Chr 16:6 2689
them Heman and Jeduthun with *t* ... 1Chr 16:42 2689

and twenty priests sounding with *t* 2Chr 5:12 2689
lifted up their voice with the *t* 2Chr 5:13
the priests sounded *t* before them 2Chr 7:6
t to cry alarm against you 2Chr 13:12 2689
and the priests sounded with the *t* 2Chr 13:14 2689
and with shouting, and with *t* 2Chr 15:14 2689
t unto the house of the LORD 2Chr 20:28 2689
the princes and the *t* by the king 2Chr 23:13 2689
land rejoiced, and sounded with *t* 2Chr 23:13 2689
David, and the priests with the *t* 2Chr 29:26 2689
of the LORD began also with the *t* 2Chr 29:27 2689
priests in their apparel with *t* .... Ezr 3:10 2689
of the priests' sons with *t* .... Neh 12:35 2689
Zechariah, and Hananiah, with *t* .... Neh 12:41 2689
He saith among the *t*, Ha, ha .... Job 39:25 7782
With *t* and sound of cornet make a .... Ps 98:6 2689
and to them were given seven *t* .... Rev 8:2 *4536*
angels which had the seven *t* .... Rev 8:6 *4536*

TRUST {134}

come and put your *t* in my shadow .... Judg 9:15 2620
whose wings thou art come to *t* .... Ruth 2:12 2620
in him will I *t* 2Sa 22:3 2620
buckler to all them that *t* in him 2Sa 22:31 2620
Now on whom dost thou *t*, that 2Kin 18:20 982
of Egypt unto all that *t* on him 2Kin 18:21 982
unto me, We *t* in the LORD our God 2Kin 18:22 982
put thy *t* on Egypt for chariots 2Kin 18:24 982
Hezekiah make you *t* in the LORD 2Kin 18:30 982
because they put their *t* in him 1Chr 5:20 982
king of Assyria, Whereon do ye *t* 2Chr 32:10 982
he put no *t* in his servants .... Job 4:18 539
whose *t* shall be a spider's web .... Job 8:14 4009
he slay me, yet will I *t* in him .... Job 13:15 3176
he putteth no *t* in his saints .... Job 15:15 539
him that is deceived *t* in vanity .... Job 15:31 539
therefore *t* thou in him .... Job 35:14 2342
Wilt thou *t* him, because his .... Job 39:11 982
all they that put their *t* in him .... Ps 2:12 2620
and put your *t* in the LORD .... Ps 4:5 982
that put their *t* in thee rejoice .... Ps 5:11 2620
my God, in thee do I put my *t* .... Ps 7:1 2620
thy name will put their *t* in thee .... Ps 9:10 982
In the LORD put I my *t* .... Ps 11:1 2620
for in thee do I put my *t* .... Ps 16:1 2620
t in thee from those that rise up .... Ps 17:7 2620
my strength, in whom I will *t* .... Ps 18:2 2620
to all those that *t* in him .... Ps 18:30 2620
Some *t* in chariots, and some in .... Ps 20:7
O my God, I *t* in thee .... Ps 25:2 982
for I put my *t* in thee .... Ps 25:20 2620
In thee, O LORD, do I put my *t* .... Ps 31:1 2620
but I *t* in the LORD .... Ps 31:6 982
t in thee before the sons of men .... Ps 31:19 2620
none of them that *t* in him shall .... Ps 34:22 2620
t under the shadow of thy wings .... Ps 36:7 2620
T in the LORD, and do good .... Ps 37:3 982
t also in him .... Ps 37:5 982
save them, because they *t* in him .... Ps 37:40 2620
and fear, and shall *t* in the LORD .... Ps 40:3 982
man that maketh the LORD his *t* .... Ps 40:4 4009
For I will not *t* in my bow .... Ps 44:6 982
They that *t* in their wealth, and .... Ps 49:6 982
I *t* in the mercy of God for ever .... Ps 52:8 982
but I will *t* in thee .... Ps 55:23 982
I am afraid, I will *t* in thee .... Ps 56:3 982
his word, in God I have put my *t* .... Ps 56:4 982
In God have I put my *t* .... Ps 56:11 982
I will *t* in the covert of thy .... Ps 61:4 2620
T in him at all times .... Ps 62:8 982
T not in oppression, and become .... Ps 62:10 982
in the LORD, and shall *t* in him .... Ps 64:10 2620
In thee, O LORD, do I put my *t* .... Ps 71:1 2620
thou art my *t* from my youth .... Ps 71:5 4004
I have put my *t* in the Lord GOD, ... Ps 73:28 4268
in him will I *t* .... Ps 91:2 982
and under his wings shalt thou *t* .... Ps 91:4 2620
O Israel, *t* thou in the LORD .... Ps 115:9 982
O house of Aaron, *t* in the LORD .... Ps 115:10 982
that fear the LORD, *t* in the LORD .... Ps 115:11 982
It is better to *t* in the LORD .... Ps 118:8 2620
It is better to *t* in the LORD .... Ps 118:9 2620
for I *t* in thy word .... Ps 119:42 982
They that *t* in the LORD shall be .... Ps 125:1 982
in thee is my *t* .... Ps 141:8 2620
for in thee do I *t* .... Ps 143:8 982
my shield, and he in whom I *t* .... Ps 144:2 2620
Put not your *t* in princes .... Ps 146:3 982
T in the LORD with all thine .... Prov 3:5 982
That thy *t* may be in the LORD, I .... Prov 22:19 4009
but he that putteth his *t* in the .... Prov 28:25 982
but whoso putteth his *t* in the .... Prov 29:25 982
unto them that put their *t* in him .... Prov 30:5 2620
her husband doth safely *t* in her .... Prov 31:11 982
I will *t*, and not be afraid .... Is 12:2 982
poor of his people shall *t* in it .... Is 14:32 2620
T ye in the LORD for ever .... Is 26:4 982
to *t* in the shadow of Egypt .... Is 30:2 2620
the *t* in the shadow of Egypt your .... Is 30:3 2622
t in oppression and perverseness, ... Is 30:12 982
t in chariots, because they are .... Is 31:1 982
now on whom dost thou *t*, that .... Is 36:5 982
of Egypt to all that *t* in him .... Is 36:6 982
to me, We *t* in the LORD our God .... Is 36:7 982
put thy *t* on Egypt for chariots .... Is 36:9 982
Hezekiah make you *t* in the LORD .... Is 36:15 982
that *t* in graven images, that say .... Is 42:17 982
let him *t* in the name of the LORD .... Is 50:10 982
me, and on mine arm shall they *t* .... Is 51:5 3176
but he that putteth his *t* in me .... Is 57:13 2620
they *t* in vanity, and speak lies .... Is 59:4 982
T ye not in lying words, saying, ... Jer 7:4 982
ye *t* in lying words, that cannot .... Jer 7:8 982
called by my name, wherein ye *t* .... Jer 7:14 982
and *t* ye not in any brother .... Jer 9:4 982
makest this people to *t* in a lie .... Jer 28:15 982
and he caused you to *t* in a lie .... Jer 29:31 982
because thou hast put thy *t* in me .... Jer 39:18 982
and all them that *t* in him .... Jer 46:25 982
and let thy widows *t* in me .... Jer 49:11 982
But thou didst *t* in thine own .... Eze 16:15 982
if he *t* to his own righteousness, ... Eze 33:13 982
because thou didst *t* in thy way .... Hos 10:13 982
t in the mountain of Samaria, ... Amos 6:1 982
T ye not in a friend, put ye not .... Mic 7:5 539
and he knoweth them that *t* in him .... Nah 1:7 2620
they shall *t* in the name of the .... Zeph 3:12 2620
in his name shall the Gentiles *t* .... Mt 12:21 *1679*
t in riches to enter into the .... Mk 10:24 *3982*
commit to your *t* the true riches .... Lk 16:11 *4100*
you, even Moses, in whom ye *t* .... Jn 5:45 *1679*
in him shall the Gentiles *t* .... Rom 15:12 *1679*
for I *t* to see you in my journey, ... Rom 15:24 *1679*
but I *t* to tarry a while with you 1Cor 16:7 *1679*
that we should not *t* in ourselves 2Cor 1:9 *3982*
in whom we *t* that he will yet 2Cor 1:10 *1679*
I *t* ye shall acknowledge even to 2Cor 1:13 *1679*
such *t* have we through Christ to 2Cor 3:4 *4006*
I *t* also are made manifest in 2Cor 5:11 *1679*
If any man *t* to himself that he 2Cor 10:7 *3982*
But I *t* that ye shall know that 2Cor 13:6 *1679*
But I *t* in the Lord Jesus to send .... Phil 2:19 *1679*
But I *t* in the Lord that I also .... Phil 2:24 *3982*
whereof he might *t* in the flesh .... Phil 3:4 *3982*
to be put in *t* with the gospel 1Th 2:4 *4100*
God, which was committed to my *t* 1Ti 1:11 *4100*
because we *t* in the living God, ... 1Ti 4:10 *1679*
nor *t* in uncertain riches, but in 1Ti 6:17 *1679*
that which is committed to thy *t* 1Ti 6:20
for I *t* that through your prayers .... Philem 22 *1679*
And again, I will put my *t* in him .... Heb 2:13 *3982*
for we *t* we have a good .... Heb 13:18 *3982*
but I *t* to come unto you, and 2Jn 12 *1679*
But I *t* I shall shortly see thee, ... 3Jn 14 *1679*

TRUSTED {29}

gods, their rock in whom they *t* .... Deut 32:37 2620
But Sihon *t* not Israel to pass .... Judg 11:20 539
because they *t* unto the liers in .... Judg 20:36 982
He *t* in the LORD God of Israel 2Kin 18:5 982
But I have *t* in thy mercy .... Ps 13:5 982
Our fathers *t* in thee .... Ps 22:4 982
they *t*, and thou didst deliver .... Ps 22:4 982
they *t* in thee, and were not .... Ps 22:5 982
He *t* on the LORD that he would .... Ps 22:8 1556
I have *t* also in the LORD .... Ps 26:1 982
my heart *t* in him, and I am helped .... Ps 28:7 982
But I *t* in thee, O LORD .... Ps 31:14 982
because we have *t* in his holy .... Ps 33:21 982
own familiar friend, in whom I *t* .... Ps 41:9 982
but *t* in the abundance of his .... Ps 52:7 982
in God, and *t* not in his salvation .... Ps 78:22 982
For thou hast *t* in thy wickedness .... Is 47:10 982
forgotten me, and *t* in falsehood .... Jer 13:25 982
because thou hast *t* in thy works .... Jer 48:7 982
that *t* in her treasures, saying, ... Jer 49:4 982
his servants that *t* in him .... Dan 3:28 7365
she *t* not in the LORD .... Zeph 3:2 982
He *t* in God .... Mt 27:43 *3982*
him all his armour wherein he *t* .... Lk 11:22 *3982*
t in themselves that they were .... Lk 18:9 *3982*
But we *t* that it had been he .... Lk 24:21 *1679*
his glory, who first *t* in Christ .... Eph 1:12 *4276*
In whom ye also *t*, after that ye .... Eph 1:13
who *t* in God, adorned themselves, ... 1Pet 3:5 *1679*

TRUSTEDST {3}

walls come down, wherein thou *t* .... Deut 28:52 982
thy fenced cities, wherein thou *t* .... Jer 5:17 982
the land of peace, wherein thou *t* .... Jer 12:5 982

TRUSTEST {6}

confidence is this wherein thou *t* 2Kin 18:19 982
thou *t* upon the staff of this 2Kin 18:21 982
God in whom thou *t* deceive thee 2Kin 19:10 982
confidence is this wherein thou *t* .... Is 36:4 982
thou *t* in the staff of this .... Is 36:6 982
Let not thy God, in whom thou *t* .... Is 37:10 982

TRUSTETH {17}

he *t* that he can draw up Jordan .... Job 40:23 982
For the king *t* in the LORD .... Ps 21:7 982
but he that *t* in the LORD .... Ps 32:10 982
blessed is the man that *t* in him .... Ps 34:8 2620
for my soul *t* in thee .... Ps 57:1 2620
blessed is the man that *t* in thee .... Ps 84:12 982
save thy servant that *t* in thee .... Ps 86:2 982
so is every one that *t* in them .... Ps 115:8 982
so is every one that *t* in them .... Ps 135:18 982
He that *t* in his riches shall .... Prov 11:28 982
whoso *t* in the LORD, happy is he .... Prov 16:20 982
He that *t* in his own heart is a .... Prov 28:26 982
because he *t* in thee .... Is 26:3 982
Cursed be the man that *t* in man .... Jer 17:5 982
is the man that *t* in the LORD .... Jer 17:7 982
the maker of his work *t* therein .... Hab 2:18 982
t in God, and continueth in 1Ti 5:5 *1679*

TRUSTING {1}

his heart is fixed, *t* in the LORD .... Ps 112:7 982

TRUSTY {1}

removeth away the speech of the *t* .... Job 12:20 539

TRUTH {235}

my master of his mercy and his *t* .... Gen 24:27 571
all the mercies, and of all the *t* .... Gen 32:10 571
whether there be any *t* in you .... Gen 42:16 571
men, such as fear God, men of *t* .... Ex 18:21 571
and abundant in goodness and *t* .... Ex 34:6 571
and, behold, if it be *t*, and the .... Deut 13:14 571
a God of *t* and without iniquity, ... Deut 32:4 530
and serve him in sincerity and in *t* .... Josh 24:14 571
If in *t* ye anoint me king over .... Judg 9:15 571
serve him in *t* with all your 1Sa 12:24 571
Of a *t* women have been kept from . 1Sa 21:5 3588,518
LORD shew kindness and *t* unto you 2Sa 2:6 571
mercy and *t* be with thee 2Sa 15:20 571
me in *t* with all their heart 1Kin 2:4 571
as he walked before thee in *t* 1Kin 3:6 571
of the LORD in thy mouth is *t* 1Kin 17:24 571
Of a *t*, LORD, the kings of 2Kin 19:17 551
I have walked before thee in *t* 2Kin 20:3 571
good, if peace and *t* be in my days 2Kin 20:19 571
t to me in the name of the LORD 2Chr 18:15 571
t before the LORD his God 2Chr 31:20 571
with words of peace and *t* .... Est 9:30 571
I know it is so of a *t* .... Job 9:2 551
and speaketh the *t* in his heart .... Ps 15:2 571
Lead me in thy *t*, and teach me .... Ps 25:5 571
t unto such as keep his covenant .... Ps 25:10 571
and I have walked in thy *t* .... Ps 26:3 571
shall it declare thy *t* .... Ps 30:9 571
hast redeemed me, O LORD God of *t* .... Ps 31:5 571
and all his works are done in *t* .... Ps 33:4 530
thy *t* from the great congregation .... Ps 40:10 571
thy *t* continually preserve me .... Ps 40:11 571
O send out thy light and thy *t* .... Ps 43:3 571
ride prosperously because of *t* .... Ps 45:4 571
thou desirest *t* in the inward .... Ps 51:6 571
cut them off in thy *t* .... Ps 54:5 571
send forth his mercy and his *t* .... Ps 57:3 571
heavens, and thy *t* unto the clouds .... Ps 57:10 571
may be displayed because of the *t* .... Ps 60:4 7189
O prepare mercy and *t*, which may .... Ps 61:7 571
in the *t* of thy salvation .... Ps 69:13 571
with the psaltery, even thy *t* .... Ps 71:22 571
Mercy and *t* are met together .... Ps 85:10 571
T shall spring out of the earth .... Ps 85:11 571
I will walk in thy *t* .... Ps 86:11 571
and plenteous in mercy and *t* .... Ps 86:15 571
t shall go before thy face .... Ps 89:14 571
thou swarest unto David in thy *t* .... Ps 89:49 530
his *t* shall be thy shield and .... Ps 91:4 571
and the people with his *t* .... Ps 96:13 530
his *t* toward the house of Israel .... Ps 98:3 530
his *t* endureth to all generations .... Ps 100:5 530
thy *t* reacheth unto the clouds .... Ps 108:4 571
ever and ever, and are done in *t* .... Ps 111:8 571
the *t* of the LORD endureth for .... Ps 117:2 571
I have chosen the way of *t* .... Ps 119:30 530
take not the word of *t* utterly .... Ps 119:43 571
and thy law is the *t* .... Ps 119:142 571
and all thy commandments are *t* .... Ps 119:151 571
LORD hath sworn in *t* unto David .... Ps 132:11 571
thy lovingkindness and for thy *t* .... Ps 138:2 571
to all that call upon him in *t* .... Ps 145:18 571
which keepeth *t* for ever .... Ps 146:6 571
Let not mercy and *t* forsake thee .... Prov 3:3 571
For my mouth shall speak *t* .... Prov 8:7 571
He that speaketh *t* sheweth forth .... Prov 12:17 530
The lip of *t* shall be established .... Prov 12:19 571
t shall be to them that devise .... Prov 14:22 571
By mercy and *t* iniquity is purged .... Prov 16:6 571
Mercy and *t* preserve the king .... Prov 20:28 571
the certainty of the words of *t* .... Prov 22:21 571
of *t* to them that send unto thee .... Prov 22:21 571
Buy the *t*, and sell it not .... Prov 23:23 571
was upright, even words of *t* .... Eccl 12:10 571
Of a *t* many houses shall be .... Is 5:9 518,3808
the Holy One of Israel, in *t* .... Is 10:20 571
he shall sit upon it in *t* in the .... Is 16:5 571
of old are faithfulness and *t* .... Is 25:1 544
which keepeth the *t* may enter in .... Is 26:2 529
Of a *t*, LORD, the kings of .... Is 37:18 551
I have walked before thee in *t* .... Is 38:3 571
the pit cannot hope for thy *t* .... Is 38:18 571
children shall make known thy *t* .... Is 38:19 571
shall be peace and *t* in my days .... Is 39:8 571
shall bring forth judgment unto *t* .... Is 42:3 571
or let them hear, and say, It is *t* .... Is 43:9 571
the God of Israel, but not in *t* .... Is 48:1 571
justice, nor any pleadeth for *t* .... Is 59:4 530
for *t* is fallen in the street, and .... Is 59:14 571
Yea, *t* faileth .... Is 59:15 571
and I will direct their work in *t* .... Is 61:8 571
bless himself in the God of *t* .... Is 65:16 548
earth shall swear by the God of *t* .... Is 65:16 548
swear, The LORD liveth, in *t* .... Jer 4:2 571
judgment, that seeketh the *t* .... Jer 5:1 530
are not thine eyes upon the *t* .... Jer 5:3 530
t is perished, and is cut off from .... Jer 7:28 530
valiant for the *t* upon the earth .... Jer 9:3 530
and will not speak the *t* .... Jer 9:5 571
for of a *t* the LORD hath sent me .... Jer 26:15 571
them the abundance of peace and *t* .... Jer 33:6 571
Of a *t* it is, that your God is a .... Dan 2:47 7187

T

of heaven, all whose works are *t* Dan 4:37 7187
and asked him the *t* of all this Dan 7:16 3330
know the *t* of the fourth beast Dan 7:19 3321
it cast down the *t* to the ground Dan 8:12 571
iniquities, and understand thy *t* Dan 9:13 571
is noted in the scripture of *t* Dan 10:21 571
And now will I shew thee the *t* Dan 11:2 571
the land, because there is no *t* Hos 4:1 571
Thou wilt perform the *t* to Jacob Mic 7:20 571
shall be called a city of *t* Zec 8:3 571
and I will be their God, in *t* Zec 8:8 571
every man the *t* to his neighbour Zec 8:16 571
execute the judgment of *t* Zec 8:16 571
therefore love the *t* and peace Zec 8:19 571
The law of *t* was in his mouth, and Mal 2:6 571
Of a *t* thou art the Son of God Mt 14:33 230
And she said, *T*, Lord Mt 15:27 3483
and teachest the way of God in *t* Mt 22:16 225
before him, and told him all the *t* Mk 5:33 225
but teachest the way of God in *t* Mk 12:14 225
Master, thou hast said the *t* Mk 12:32 225
But I tell you of a *t*, many Lk 4:25 225
But I tell you of a *t*, there be Lk 9:27 230
Of a *t* I say unto you, that he Lk 12:44 230
Of a *t* I say unto you, that this Lk 21:3 230
Of a *t* this fellow also was with Lk 22:59 225
the Father,) full of grace and *t* Jn 1:14 225
grace and *t* came by Jesus Christ Jn 1:17 225
But he that doeth *t* cometh to the Jn 3:21 225
the Father in spirit and in *t* Jn 4:23 225
worship him in spirit and in *t* Jn 4:24 225
and he bare witness unto the *t* Jn 5:33 225
This is of a *t* that prophet that Jn 6:14 230
Of a *t* this is the Prophet Jn 7:40 230
And ye shall know the *t*, and the Jn 8:32 225
the *t* shall make you free Jn 8:32 225
a man that hath told you the *t* Jn 8:40 225
beginning, and abode not in the *t* Jn 8:44 225
because there is no *t* in him Jn 8:44 225
And because I tell you the *t* Jn 8:45 225
And if I say the *t*, why do ye not Jn 8:46 225
unto him, I am the way, the *t* Jn 14:6 225
Even the Spirit of *t* Jn 14:17 225
the Father, even the Spirit of *t* Jn 15:26 225
Nevertheless I tell you the *t* Jn 16:7 225
Howbeit when he, the Spirit of *t* Jn 16:13 225
he will guide you into all *t* Jn 16:13 225
Sanctify them through thy *t* Jn 17:17 225
thy word is *t* Jn 17:17 225
might be sanctified through the *t* Jn 17:19 225
I should bear witness unto the *t* Jn 18:37 225
that is of the *t* heareth my voice Jn 18:37 225
Pilate saith unto him, What is *t* Jn 18:38 225
For of a *t* against thy holy child Acts 4:27 225
Of a *t* I perceive that God is no Acts 10:34 225
but speak forth the words of *t* Acts 26:25 225
who hold the *t* in unrighteousness Rom 1:18 225
Who changed the *t* of God into a Rom 1:25 225
t against them which commit such Rom 2:2 225
contentious, and do not obey the *t* Rom 2:8 225
knowledge and of the *t* in the law Rom 2:20 225
For if the *t* of God hath more Rom 3:7 225
I say the *t* in Christ, I lie not, Rom 9:1 225
the circumcision for the *t* of God Rom 15:8 225
bread of sincerity and *t* 1Cor 5:8 225
iniquity, but rejoiceth in the *t* 1Cor 13:6 225
report that God is in you of a *t* 1Cor 14:25 3689
but by manifestation of the *t* 2Cor 4:2 225
By the word of *t*, by the power of 2Cor 6:7 225
we spake all things to you in *t* 2Cor 7:14 225
I made before Titus, is found a *t* 2Cor 7:14 225
As the *t* of Christ is in me, no 2Cor 11:10 225
for I will say the *t* 2Cor 12:6 225
against the *t*, but for the *t* 2Cor 13:8 225
that the *t* of the gospel might Gal 2:5 225
according to the *t* of the gospel Gal 2:14 225
that ye should not obey the *t* Gal 3:1 225
enemy, because I tell you the *t* Gal 4:16 226
you that ye should not obey the *t* Gal 5:7 225
after that ye heard the word of *t* Eph 1:13 225
But speaking the *t* in love Eph 4:15 226
by him, as the *t* is in Jesus Eph 4:21 225
speak every man *t* with his Eph 4:25 226
goodness and righteousness and *t* Eph 5:9 226
your loins girt about with *t* Eph 6:14 226
way, whether in pretence, or in *t* Phil 1:18 226
the word of the *t* of the gospel Col 1:5 226
it, and knew the grace of God in *t* Col 1:6 226
word of men, but as it is in *t* 1Th 2:13 230
received not the love of the *t* 2Th 2:10 225
be damned who believed not the *t* 2Th 2:12 225
of the Spirit and belief of the *t* 2Th 2:13 225
come unto the knowledge of the *t* 1Ti 2:4 225
apostle, (I speak the *t* in Christ 1Ti 2:7 225
the pillar and ground of the *t* 1Ti 3:15 225
them which believe and know the *t* 1Ti 4:3 225
minds, and destitute of the *t* 1Ti 6:5 225
rightly dividing the word of *t* 2Ti 2:15 225
Who concerning the *t* have erred 2Ti 2:18 225
to the acknowledging of the *t* 2Ti 2:25 225
to come to the knowledge of the *t* 2Ti 3:7 225
so do these also resist the *t* 2Ti 3:8 225
turn away their ears from the *t* 2Ti 4:4 225
of the *t* which is after godliness Titus 1:1 225
of men, that turn from the *t* Titus 1:14 225
received the knowledge of the *t* Heb 10:26 225
begat he us with the word of *t* Jas 1:18 225
not, and lie not against the *t* Jas 3:14 225
if any of you do err from the *t* Jas 5:19 225
the *t* through the Spirit unto 1Pet 1:22 225
be established in the present *t* 2Pet 1:12 225
way of *t* shall be evil spoken of 2Pet 2:2 225
darkness, we lie, and do not the *t* 1Jn 1:6 225
ourselves, and the *t* is not in us 1Jn 1:8 225
is a liar, and the *t* is not in him 1Jn 2:4 225
you because ye know not the *t* 1Jn 2:21 225
it, and that no lie is of the *t* 1Jn 2:21 225
you of all things, and is *t* 1Jn 2:27 227
but in deed and in *t* 1Jn 3:18 225
we know that we are of the *t* 1Jn 3:19 225
Hereby know we the spirit of *t* 1Jn 4:6 225
witness, because the Spirit is *t* 1Jn 5:6 225
children, whom I love in the *t* 2Jn 1 225
all they that have known the *t* 2Jn 1 225
the Son of the Father, in *t* 2Jn 3 225
of thy children walking in *t* 2Jn 4 225
Gaius, whom I love in the *t* 3Jn 1 225
of the *t* that is in thee, even as 3Jn 3 225
even as thou walkest in the *t* 3Jn 3 225
hear that my children walk in *t* 3Jn 4 225
might be fellowhelpers to the *t* 3Jn 8 225
of all men, and of the *t* itself 3Jn 12 225

TRUTH'S {2}
for thy mercy, and for thy *t* sake Ps 115:1 571
For the *t* sake, which dwelleth in 2Jn 2 225

TRY {17}
I will *t* them for thee there Judg 7:4 6884
to *t* him, that he might know all 2Chr 32:31 5254
morning, and *t* him every moment Job 7:18 974
Doth not the ear *t* words Job 12:11 974
his eyes behold, his eyelids *t* Ps 11:4 974
t my reins and my heart Ps 26:2 6884
t me, and know my thoughts Ps 139:23 974
thou mayest know and *t* their way Jer 6:27 974
I will melt them, and *t* them Jer 9:7 974
I *t* the reins, even to give every Jer 17:10 974
t our ways, and turn again to the Lam 3:40 2713
to *t* them, and to purge, and to Dan 11:35 6884
will *t* them as gold is tried Zec 13:9 974
the fire shall *t* every man's work 1Cor 3:13 1381
the fiery trial which is to *t* you 1Pet 4:12 4314,3986
but *t* the spirits whether they 1Jn 4:1 1381
to *t* them that dwell upon the Rev 3:10 3985

TRYING {1}
that the *t* of your faith worketh Jas 1:3 1383

TRYPHAENA See TRYPHENA.

TRYPHENA *(tri-fe'-nah)* {1} *A Christian in Rome.*
Salute *T* and Tryphosa, who labour Rom 16:12 5170

TRYPHOSA *(tri-fo'-sah)* {1} *A Christian in Rome.*
Salute Tryphena and *T*, who labour Rom 16:12 5173

TUBAL *(tu'-bal)* {8}
1. A son of Japeth.
Magog, and Madai, and Javan, and *T* Gen 10:2 8422
Magog, and Madai, and Javan, and *T* 1Chr 1:5 8422
2. Migrants to Sicily and Spain.
and Lud, that draw the bow, to *T* Is 66:19 8422
Javan, *T*, and Meshech, they were Eze 27:13 8422
There is Meshech, *T*, and all her Eze 32:26 8422
the chief prince of Meshech and *T* Eze 38:2 8422
the chief prince of Meshech and *T* Eze 38:3 8422
the chief prince of Meshech and *T* Eze 39:1 8422

TUBAL-CAIN *(tu'-bal-cain)* {2} *Son of Lamech.*
And Zillah, she also bare *T* Gen 4:22 8423
and the sister of *T* was Naamah Gen 4:22 8423

TUMBLED {1}
a cake of barley bread *t* into the Judg 7:13 2015

TUMULT {16}
What meaneth the noise of this *t* 1Sa 4:14 1995
me thy servant, I saw a great *t* 2Sa 18:29 1995
thy *t* is come up into mine ears, 2Kin 19:28 7600
waves, and the *t* of the people Ps 65:7 1995
the *t* of those that rise up Ps 74:23 7588
For, lo, thine enemies make a *t* Ps 83:2 1993
noise of the *t* the people fled Is 33:3 1995
thy rage against me, and thy *t* Is 37:29 7600
with the noise of a great *t* he Jer 11:16 1999
Therefore shall a *t* arise among Hos 10:14 7588
and Moab shall die with *t*, with Amos 2:2 7588
that a great *t* from the LORD Zec 14:13 4103
but that rather a *t* was made Mt 27:24 2351
of the synagogue, and seeth the *t* Mk 5:38 2351
not know the certainty for the *t* Acts 21:34 2351
with multitude, nor with *t* Acts 24:18 2351

TUMULTS {3}
behold the great *t* in the midst Amos 3:9 4103
stripes, in imprisonments, in *t* 2Cor 6:5 181
whisperings, swellings, *t* 2Cor 12:20 181

TUMULTUOUS {3}
a *t* noise of the kingdoms of Is 13:4 7588
of stirs, a *t* city, a joyous city Is 22:2 1993
crown of the head of the *t* ones Jer 48:45 1121,7588

TURN {283}
t in, I pray you, into your Gen 19:2 5493
that I may *t* to the right hand, Gen 24:49 6437
until thy brother's fury *t* away Gen 27:44 7725
brother's anger *t* away from thee Gen 27:45 7725
And Moses said, I will now *t* aside Ex 3:3 5493
children of Israel, that they *t* Ex 14:2 7725
enemies *t* their backs unto thee Ex 23:27
T from thy fierce wrath, and Ex 32:12 7725
Or if the raw flesh *t* again Lev 13:16 7725
T ye not unto idols, nor make to Lev 19:4 6437
To morrow *t* you, and get you into Num 14:25 6437
we will not *t* to the right hand Num 20:17 5186
we will not *t* into the fields, or Num 21:22 5186
the ass, to *t* her into the way Num 22:23 5186
where was no way to *t* either to Num 22:26 5186
For if ye *t* away from after him, Num 32:15 7725
your border shall *t* from the Num 34:4 5437
T you, and take your journey, and Deut 1:7 6437
t you, and take your journey into Deut 1:40 6437
t you northward Deut 2:3 6437
I will neither *t* unto the right Deut 2:27 5493
if thou *t* to the LORD thy God, and Deut 4:30 7725
ye shall not *t* aside to the right Deut 5:32 5493
For they will *t* away thy son from Deut 7:4 5493
ye *t* aside, and serve other gods, Deut 11:16 5493
but *t* aside out of the way which Deut 11:28 5493
because he hath spoken to *t* you Deut 13:5 5627
that the LORD may *t* from the Deut 13:17 7725
Then shalt thou *t* it into money Deut 14:25 5414
thou shalt *t* in the morning, and Deut 16:7 6437
that his heart *t* not away Deut 17:17 5493
that he *t* not aside from the Deut 17:20 5493
dig therewith, and shalt *t* back Deut 23:13 7725
in thee, and *t* away from thee Deut 23:14 7725
LORD thy God will *t* thy captivity Deut 30:3 7725
if thou *t* unto the LORD thy God Deut 30:10 7725
But if thine heart *t* away Deut 30:17 6437
then will they *t* unto other gods, Deut 31:20 6437
t aside from the way which I have Deut 31:29 5493
t not from it to the right hand Josh 1:7 5493
to *t* away this day from following Josh 22:16 7725
But that ye must *t* away this day Josh 22:18 7725
to *t* from following the LORD Josh 22:23 7725
t this day from following the Josh 22:29 7725
that ye *t* not aside therefrom to Josh 23:6 5493
strange gods, then he will *t* Josh 24:20 7725
T in, my lord, *t* in to me Judg 4:18 5493
Therefore we *t* again to thee now, Judg 11:8 7725
let us *t* in into this city of the Judg 19:11 5493
We will not *t* aside hither into Judg 19:12 5493
we any of us *t* into his house Judg 20:8 5493
Naomi said, *T* again, my daughters Ruth 1:11 7725
T again, my daughters, go your Ruth 1:12 7725
t aside, sit down here Ruth 4:1 5493
yet *t* not aside from following 1Sa 12:20 5493
And *t* ye not aside 1Sa 12:21 5493
t thee; behold, I am 1Sa 14:7 5186
t again with me, that I may 1Sa 15:25 7725
t again with me, that I may 1Sa 15:30 7725
footmen that stood about him, *T* 1Sa 22:17 5437
T thou, and fall upon the priests 1Sa 22:18 5437
T thee aside to thy right hand or 2Sa 2:21 5186
But Asahel would not *t* aside from 2Sa 2:21 5493
T thee aside from following me 2Sa 2:22 5493
Howbeit he refused to *t* aside 2Sa 2:23 5493
none can *t* to the right hand or 2Sa 14:19
Let him *t* to his own house, and 2Sa 14:24 5437
t the counsel of Ahithophel into 2Sa 15:31
unto him, *T* aside, and stand here 2Sa 18:30 5437
t back again, that I may die in 2Sa 19:37 7725
shall *t* again to thee, and confess 1Kin 8:33 7725
t from their sin, when thou 1Kin 8:35 7725
shall at all *t* from following me 1Kin 9:6 7725
for surely they will *t* away your 1Kin 11:2 5186
people *t* again unto their lord 1Kin 12:27 7725
nor *t* again by the same way that 1Kin 13:9 7725
nor *t* again to go by the way that 1Kin 13:17 7725
t thee eastward, and hide thyself 1Kin 17:3 6437
T thine hand, and carry me out of 1Kin 22:34 2015
t again unto the king that sent 2Kin 1:6 7725
to us, that he shall *t* in thither 2Kin 4:10 5493
t thee behind me 2Kin 9:18 5437
t thee behind me 2Kin 9:19 5437
T ye from your evil ways, and keep 2Kin 17:13 7725
How then wilt thou *t* away the 2Kin 18:24 7725
I will *t* thee back by the way by 2Kin 19:28 7725
T again, and tell Hezekiah the 2Kin 20:5 7725
to *t* the kingdom of Saul to him, 1Chr 12:23 5437
t away from them, and come upon 1Chr 14:14 5437
t from their sin, when thou dost 2Chr 6:26 7725
they are carried captive, and *t* 2Chr 6:37 7725
t not away the face of thine 2Chr 6:42 7725
face, and *t* from their wicked ways 2Chr 7:14 7725
But if ye *t* away, and forsake my 2Chr 7:19 7725
did *t* unto the LORD God of Israel 2Chr 15:4 7725
T thine hand, that thou mayest 2Chr 18:33 2015
t away from following the LORD 2Chr 25:27 5493
fierce wrath may *t* away from us 2Chr 29:10 7725
t again unto the LORD God of 2Chr 30:6 7725
of his wrath may *t* away from you 2Chr 30:8 7725
For if ye *t* again unto the LORD, 2Chr 30:9 7725
will not *t* away his face from you 2Chr 30:9 5493
would not *t* his face from him 2Chr 35:22 5437
But if ye *t* unto me, and keep my Neh 1:9 7725
t their reproach upon their own Neh 4:4 7725
against them to *t* them to thee Neh 9:26 7725
Now when every maid's *t* was come Est 2:12 8447
Now when the *t* of Esther, the Est 2:15 8447
which of the saints wilt thou *t* Job 5:1 6437
T from him, that he may rest, Job 14:6 8159
is in one mind, and who can *t* him Job 23:13 7725
They *t* the needy out of the way Job 24:4 5186
man shall *t* again unto dust Job 34:15 7725
how long will ye *t* my glory into Ps 4:2
If he *t* not, he will whet his Ps 7:12 7725
neither did I *t* again till they Ps 18:37 7725
shalt thou make them *t* their back Ps 21:12
shall remember and *t* unto the LORD Ps 22:27 7725

T thee unto me, and have mercy	Ps 25:16	6437
nor such as *t* aside to lies	Ps 40:4	7750
Thou makest us to *t* back from the	Ps 44:10	7725
then shall mine enemies *t* back	Ps 56:9	7725
O *t* thyself to us again	Ps 60:1	7725
t unto me according to the	Ps 69:16	6437
T us again, O God, and cause thy	Ps 80:3	7725
T us again, O God of hosts, and	Ps 80:7	7725
T us again, O LORD God of hosts,	Ps 80:19	7725
T us, O God of our salvation, and	Ps 85:4	7725
but let them not *t* again to folly	Ps 85:8	7725
O *t* unto me, and have mercy upon	Ps 86:16	6437
the work of them that *t* aside	Ps 101:3	7750
that they *t* not again to cover	Ps 104:9	7725
to *t* away his wrath, lest he	Ps 106:23	7725
T away mine eyes from beholding	Ps 119:37	5674
T away my reproach which I fear	Ps 119:39	5674
those that fear thee *t* unto me	Ps 119:79	7725
As for such as *t* aside unto their	Ps 125:5	5186
T again our captivity, O LORD, as	Ps 126:4	7725
sake *t* not away the face of thine	Ps 132:10	7725
he will not *t* from it	Ps 132:11	7725
T you at my reproof	Prov 1:23	7725
by it, *t* from it, and pass away	Prov 4:15	7847
T not to the right hand nor to	Prov 4:27	5186
is simple, let him *t* in hither	Prov 9:4	5493
is simple, let him *t* in hither	Prov 9:16	5493
he *t* away his wrath from him	Prov 24:18	7725
shame, and thine infamy *t* not away	Prov 25:10	7725
but wise men *t* away wrath	Prov 29:8	7725
the dust, and all *t* to dust again	Eccl 3:20	7725
and the shadows flee away, *t*	Song 2:17	5437
T away thine eyes from me, for	Song 6:5	5437
I will *t* my hand upon thee, and	Is 1:25	7725
To *t* aside the needy from	Is 10:2	5186
every man *t* to his own people	Is 13:14	6437
out, and who shall *t* it back	Is 14:27	7725
they shall *t* the rivers far away	Is 19:6	2186
He will surely violently *t*	Is 22:18	6801
she shall *t* to her hire, and shall	Is 23:17	7725
that *t* the battle to the gate	Is 28:6	7725
t aside the just for a thing of	Is 29:21	5186
t aside out of the path, cause	Is 30:11	5186
when ye *t* to the right hand, and	Is 30:21	
hand, and when ye *t* to the left	Is 30:21	
T ye unto him from whom the	Is 31:6	7725
How then wilt thou *t* away the	Is 36:9	7725
I will *t* thee back by the way by	Is 37:29	7725
If thou *t* away thy foot from the	Is 58:13	7725
to Zion, and unto them that *t* from	Is 59:20	7725
her occasion who can *t* her away	Jer 2:24	7725
surely his anger shall *t* from me	Jer 2:35	7725
all these things, *T* thou unto me	Jer 3:7	7725
T, O backsliding children, saith	Jer 3:14	7725
and shalt not *t* away from me	Jer 3:19	7725
neither will I *t* back from it	Jer 4:28	7725
t back thine hand as a	Jer 6:9	7725
shall he *t* away, and not return	Jer 8:4	7725
he *t* it into the shadow of death,	Jer 13:16	7760
t from their evil, I will repent	Jer 18:8	7725
to *t* away thy wrath from them	Jer 18:20	7725
I will *t* back the weapons of war	Jer 21:4	5437
T ye again now every one from his	Jer 25:5	7725
t every man from his evil way,	Jer 26:3	7725
I will *t* away your captivity, and	Jer 29:14	7725
for I will *t* their mourning into	Jer 31:13	2015
t thou me, and I shall be turned	Jer 31:18	7725
t again, O virgin of Israel	Jer 31:21	7725
t again to these thy cities	Jer 31:21	7725
that I will not *t* away from them	Jer 32:40	7725
ear to *t* from their wickedness	Jer 44:5	7725
t back, dwell deep, O inhabitants	Jer 49:8	6437
shall *t* every one to his people	Jer 50:16	6437
iniquity, to *t* away thy captivity	Lam 2:14	7725
To *t* aside the right of a man	Lam 3:35	5186
our ways, and *t* again to the LORD	Lam 3:40	7725
T thou us unto thee, O LORD, and	Lam 5:21	7725
he *t* not from his wickedness, nor	Eze 3:19	7725
man doth *t* from his righteousness	Eze 3:20	7725
thou shalt not *t* thee from one	Eze 4:8	2015
My face will I *t* also from them	Eze 7:22	5437
but *t* thee yet again, and thou	Eze 8:6	7725
T thee yet again, and thou shalt	Eze 8:13	7725
t thee yet again, and thou shalt	Eze 8:15	7725
t yourselves from your idols	Eze 14:6	7725
t away your faces from all your	Eze 14:6	7725
But if the wicked will *t* from all	Eze 18:21	7725
t yourselves from all your	Eze 18:30	7725
wherefore *t* yourselves, and live	Eze 18:32	7725
wicked of his way to *t* from it	Eze 33:9	7725
if he do not *t* from his way	Eze 33:9	7725
that the wicked *t* from his way	Eze 33:11	7725
t ye, *t* ye from your evil ways	Eze 33:11	7725
if he *t* from his sin, and do that	Eze 33:14	7725
But if the wicked *t* from his	Eze 33:19	7725
I will *t* unto you, and ye shall be	Eze 36:9	6437
I will *t* thee back, and put hooks	Eze 38:4	7725
to *t* thine hand upon the desolate	Eze 38:12	7725
I will *t* thee back, and leave but	Eze 39:2	7725
our God, that we might *t* from our	Dan 9:13	7725
After this shall he *t* his face	Dan 11:18	7725
he shall cause it to *t* upon him	Dan 11:18	7725
Then he shall *t* his face toward	Dan 11:19	7725
they that *t* many to righteousness	Dan 12:3	
their doings to *t* unto their God	Hos 5:4	7725
Therefore *t* thou to thy God	Hos 12:6	7725
with you words, and *t* to the LORD	Hos 14:2	7725
t ye even to me with all your	Joel 2:12	7725
and *t* unto the LORD your God	Joel 2:13	7725
I will not *t* away the punishment	Amos 1:3	7725
I will not *t* away the punishment	Amos 1:6	7725
I will *t* mine hand against Ekron	Amos 1:8	7725
I will not *t* away the punishment	Amos 1:9	7725
I will not *t* away the punishment	Amos 1:11	7725
I will not *t* away the punishment	Amos 1:13	7725
I will not *t* away the punishment	Amos 2:1	7725
I will not *t* away the punishment	Amos 2:4	7725
I will not *t* away the punishment	Amos 2:6	7725
t aside the way of the meek	Amos 2:7	5186
Ye who *t* judgment to wormwood, and	Amos 5:7	2015
they *t* aside the poor in the gate	Amos 5:12	5186
I will *t* your feasts into	Amos 8:10	2015
let them *t* every one from his	Jonah 3:8	7725
Who can tell if God will *t*	Jonah 3:9	7725
t away from his fierce anger,	Jonah 3:9	7725
He will *t* again, he will have	Mic 7:19	7725
them, and *t* away their captivity	Zeph 2:7	7725
For then will I *t* to the people a	Zeph 3:9	2015
when I *t* back your captivity	Zeph 3:20	7725
T ye unto me, saith the LORD of	Zec 1:3	7725
I will *t* unto you, saith the LORD	Zec 1:3	7725
T ye now from your evil ways, and	Zec 1:4	7725
T you to the strong hold, ye	Zec 9:12	7725
with their children, and *t* again	Zec 10:9	7725
I will *t* mine hand upon the	Zec 13:7	7725
did *t* many away from iniquity	Mal 2:6	7725
that *t* aside the stranger from	Mal 3:5	5186
he shall *t* the heart of the	Mal 4:6	7725
cheek, *t* to him the other also	Mt 5:39	4762
borrow of thee *t* not thou away	Mt 5:42	654
feet, and *t* again and rend you	Mt 7:6	4762
him that is in the field not *t*	Mk 13:16	1994
shall he *t* to the Lord their God	Lk 1:16	1994
to *t* the hearts of the fathers to	Lk 1:17	1994
if not, it shall *t* to you again	Lk 10:6	344
times in a day *t* again to thee	Lk 17:4	1994
it shall *t* to you for a testimony	Lk 21:13	576
seeking to *t* away the deputy from	Acts 13:8	1294
life, lo, we *t* to the Gentiles	Acts 13:46	4762
t from these vanities unto the	Acts 14:15	1994
to *t* them from darkness to light,	Acts 26:18	1994
t to God, and do works meet for	Acts 26:20	1994
shall *t* away ungodliness from	Rom 11:26	654
when it shall *t* to the Lord	2Cor 3:16	1994
how *t* ye again to the weak and	Gal 4:9	1994
For I know that this shall *t* to	Phil 1:19	576
from such *t* away	2Ti 3:5	665
they shall *t* away their ears from	2Ti 4:4	654
of men, that *t* from the truth	Titus 1:14	654
if we *t* away from him that	Heb 12:25	654
we *t* about their whole body	Jas 3:3	3329
to *t* from the holy commandment	2Pet 2:21	1994
over waters to *t* them to blood	Rev 11:6	4762

TURNED {287}

a flaming sword which *t* every way	Gen 3:24	2015
the men *t* their faces from thence	Gen 18:22	6437
they *t* in unto him, and entered	Gen 19:3	5493
t in to a certain Adullamite,	Gen 38:1	5186
he *t* unto her by the way, and said	Gen 38:16	5186
he *t* himself about from them, and	Gen 42:24	5437
LORD saw that he *t* aside to see	Ex 3:4	5493
it was *t* again as his other flesh	Ex 4:7	7725
the rod which was *t* to a serpent	Ex 7:15	2015
and they shall be *t* to blood	Ex 7:17	2015
were in the river were *t* to blood	Ex 7:20	2015
And Pharaoh *t* and went into his	Ex 7:23	6437
he *t* himself, and went out from	Ex 10:6	6437
the LORD *t* a mighty strong west	Ex 10:19	2015
servants was *t* against the people	Ex 14:5	2015
They have *t* aside quickly out of	Ex 32:8	5493
And Moses *t*, and went down from the	Ex 32:15	6437
And he *t* again into the camp	Ex 33:11	7725
the hair in the plague is *t* white	Lev 13:3	2015
the hair thereof be not *t* white	Lev 13:4	2015
it have *t* the hair white, and	Lev 13:10	2015
it is all *t* white	Lev 13:13	2015
if the plague be *t* into white	Lev 13:17	2015
and the hair thereof be *t* white	Lev 13:20	2015
in the bright spot be *t* white	Lev 13:25	2015
because ye are *t* away from the	Num 14:43	7725
wherefore Israel *t* away from him	Num 20:21	5186
And they *t* and went up by the way	Num 21:33	6437
the ass *t* aside out of the way,	Num 22:23	5186
t from me these three times	Num 22:33	5186
unless she had *t* from me, surely	Num 22:33	5186
LORD may be *t* away from Israel	Num 25:4	7725
hath *t* my wrath away from the	Num 25:11	7725
t again unto Pi-hahiroth, which	Num 33:7	7725
And they *t* and went up into the	Deut 1:24	6437
Then we *t*, and took our journey	Deut 2:1	6437
Elath, and from Ezion-gaber, we *t*	Deut 2:8	6437
Then we *t*, and went up the way to	Deut 3:1	6437
they are quickly *t* aside out of	Deut 9:12	5493
So I *t* and came down from the	Deut 9:15	6437
ye had *t* aside quickly out of the	Deut 9:16	5493
I *t* myself and came down from the	Deut 10:5	6437
but the LORD thy God *t* the curse	Deut 23:5	2015
that they are *t* unto other gods	Deut 31:18	6437
but *t* their backs before their	Josh 7:12	6437
So the LORD *t* from the fierceness	Josh 7:26	7725
t back upon the pursuers	Josh 8:20	2015
city ascended, then they *t* again	Josh 8:21	7725
And Joshua at that time *t* back	Josh 11:10	7725
t from Sarid eastward toward the	Josh 19:12	7725
they *t* quickly out of the way	Judg 2:17	5493
But he himself *t* again from the	Judg 3:19	7725
when he had *t* in unto her into	Judg 4:18	5493
the children of Israel *t* again	Judg 8:33	7725
he *t* aside to see the carcase of	Judg 14:8	5493
and *t* tail to tail, and put a	Judg 15:4	6437
they *t* in thither, and said unto	Judg 18:3	5493
they *t* thitherward, and came to	Judg 18:15	5493
So they *t* and departed, and put the	Judg 18:21	6437
they *t* their faces, and said unto	Judg 18:23	5437
were too strong for him, he *t*	Judg 18:26	6437
they *t* aside thither, to go in and	Judg 19:15	5493
And when the men of Israel *t* again	Judg 20:41	2015
Therefore they *t* their backs	Judg 20:42	6437
And they *t* and fled toward the	Judg 20:45	6437
But six hundred men *t* and fled to	Judg 20:47	6437
the men of Israel *t* again upon	Judg 20:48	7725
the man was afraid, and *t* himself	Ruth 3:8	3943
And he *t* aside, and sat down	Ruth 4:1	5493
t not aside to the right hand or	1Sa 6:12	5493
but *t* aside after lucre, and took	1Sa 8:3	5186
shalt be *t* into another man	1Sa 10:6	2015
that when he had *t* his back to go	1Sa 10:9	6437
one company *t* unto the way that	1Sa 13:17	6437
another company *t* the way to	1Sa 13:18	6437
another company *t* to the way of	1Sa 13:18	6437
even they also *t* to be with the	1Sa 14:21	
and whithersoever he *t* himself	1Sa 14:47	6437
for he is *t* back from following	1Sa 15:11	7725
as Samuel *t* about to go away, he	1Sa 15:27	5437
So Samuel *t* again after Saul	1Sa 15:31	7725
he *t* from him toward another, and	1Sa 17:30	5437
And Doeg the Edomite *t*, and he fell	1Sa 22:18	5437
So David's young men *t* their way	1Sa 25:12	2015
the bow of Jonathan *t* not back	2Sa 1:22	7734
in going he *t* not to the right	2Sa 2:19	5186
he *t* aside, and stood still	2Sa 18:30	5437
the victory that day was *t* into	2Sa 19:2	
t not again until I had consumed	2Sa 22:38	7725
howbeit the kingdom is *t* about	1Kin 2:15	5437
for Joab had *t* after Adonijah,	1Kin 2:28	5186
though he *t* not after Absalom	1Kin 2:28	5186
the king *t* his face about, and	1Kin 8:14	5437
So she *t* and went to her own	1Kin 10:13	6437
his wives *t* away his heart	1Kin 11:3	5186
that his wives *t* away his heart	1Kin 11:4	5186
because his heart was *t* from the	1Kin 11:9	5186
t not aside from any thing that	1Kin 15:5	5493
that thou hast *t* their heart back	1Kin 18:37	5437
and, behold, a man *t* aside	1Kin 20:39	5493
t away his face, and would eat no	1Kin 21:4	5437
they *t* aside to fight against him	1Kin 22:32	5493
that they *t* back from pursuing	1Kin 22:33	7725
he *t* not aside from it, doing	1Kin 22:43	5493
the messengers *t* back unto him	2Kin 1:5	7725
unto them, Why are ye now *t* back	2Kin 1:5	7725
he *t* back, and looked on them, and	2Kin 2:24	6437
he *t* in thither to eat bread	2Kin 4:8	5493
he *t* into the chamber, and lay	2Kin 4:11	5493
So he *t* and went away in a rage	2Kin 5:12	6437
when the man *t* again from his	2Kin 5:26	2015
Joram *t* his hands, and fled, and	2Kin 9:23	2015
So the king of Assyria *t* back	2Kin 15:20	7725
t he from the house of the LORD	2Kin 16:18	5437
Then he *t* his face to the wall,	2Kin 20:2	5437
t not aside to the right hand or	2Kin 22:2	5493
And as Josiah *t* himself, he spied	2Kin 23:16	6437
that *t* to the LORD with all his	2Kin 23:25	7725
Notwithstanding the LORD *t* not	2Kin 23:26	7725
t his name to Jehoiakim, and took	2Kin 23:34	5437
then he *t* and rebelled against him	2Kin 24:1	7725
t the kingdom unto David the son	1Chr 10:14	5437
And Ornan *t* back, and saw the angel	1Chr 21:20	7725
And the king *t* his face, and	2Chr 6:3	5437
So she *t*, and went away to her own	2Chr 9:12	2015
the wrath of the LORD *t* from him	2Chr 12:12	7725
they *t* back again from pursuing	2Chr 18:32	7725
Egypt, but they *t* from them, and	2Chr 20:10	5493
have *t* away their faces from the	2Chr 29:6	5437
of the LORD, and *t* their backs	2Chr 29:6	5414
and *t* his name to Jehoiakim	2Chr 36:4	5437
t the heart of the king of	Ezr 6:22	5437
God for this matter be *t* from us	Ezr 10:14	7725
t back, and entered by the gate of	Neh 2:15	7725
neither *t* they from their wicked	Neh 9:35	7725
howbeit our God *t* the curse into	Neh 13:2	2015
(though it was *t* to the contrary,	Est 9:1	2015
the month which was *t* unto them	Est 9:22	2015
paths of his way are *t* aside	Job 6:18	3943
t me over into the hands of the	Job 16:11	3399
whom I loved are *t* against me	Job 19:19	2015
Yet his meat in his bowels is *t*	Job 20:14	2015
under it is *t* up as it were fire	Job 28:5	2015
Terrors are *t* upon me	Job 30:15	2015
My harp also is *t* to mourning	Job 30:31	
If my step hath *t* out of the way	Job 31:7	5186
Because they *t* back from him, and	Job 34:27	5493
it is *t* round about by his	Job 37:12	2015
It is *t* as clay to the seal	Job 38:14	2015
sorrow is *t* into joy before him	Job 41:22	1750
slingstones are *t* with him into	Job 41:28	2015
the LORD *t* the captivity of Job,	Job 42:10	7725
When mine enemies are *t* back	Ps 9:3	7725
The wicked shall be *t* into hell	Ps 9:17	7725
Thou hast *t* for me my mourning	Ps 30:11	2015
my moisture is *t* into the drought	Ps 32:4	2015
let them be *t* back and brought to	Ps 35:4	5472
Our heart is not *t* back, neither	Ps 44:18	5472
He *t* the sea into dry land	Ps 66:6	2015

T

which hath not *t* away my prayer ... Ps 66:20 5493
let them be *t* backward, and put to ... Ps 70:2 5472
Let them be *t* back for a reward ... Ps 70:3 7725
t back in the day of battle ... Ps 78:9 2015
many a time *t* he his anger away, ... Ps 78:38 7725
Yea, they *t* back and tempted God, ... Ps 78:41 7725
had *t* their rivers into blood ... Ps 78:44 2015
But *t* back, and dealt unfaithfully ... Ps 78:57 5472
they were *t* aside like a ... Ps 78:57 2015
and *t* my hand against their ... Ps 81:14 7725
thou hast *t* thyself from the ... Ps 85:3 7725
Thou hast also *t* the edge of his ... Ps 89:43 7725
He *t* their heart to hate his ... Ps 105:25 2015
He *t* their waters into blood, and ... Ps 105:29 2015
Which *t* the rock into a standing ... Ps 114:8 2015
t my feet unto thy testimonies ... Ps 119:59 7725
When the LORD *t* again the ... Ps 126:1 7725
and *t* back that hate Zion ... Ps 129:5 5472
I *t* myself to behold wisdom, and ... Eccl 2:12 6437
whither is thy beloved *t* aside ... Song 6:1 6437
all this his anger is not *t* away ... Is 5:25 7725
all this his anger is not *t* away ... Is 9:12 7725
all this his anger is not *t* away ... Is 9:17 7725
all this his anger is not *t* away ... Is 9:21 7725
all this his anger is not *t* away ... Is 10:4 7725
with me, thine anger is *t* away ... Is 12:1 7725
hath he *t* into fear unto me ... Is 21:4 7760
wheel *t* about upon the cummin ... Is 28:27 5437
Lebanon shall be *t* into a ... Is 29:17 7725
thereof shall be *t* into pitch ... Is 34:9 2015
Then Hezekiah *t* his face toward ... Is 38:2 5437
They shall be *t* back, they shall ... Is 42:17 5472
a deceived heart hath *t* him aside ... Is 44:20 5186
rebellious, neither *t* away back ... Is 50:5 5472
we have *t* every one to his own ... Is 53:6 6437
judgment is *t* away backward, and ... Is 59:14 5253
therefore he was *t* to be their ... Is 63:10 2015
how then art thou *t* into the ... Jer 2:21 2015
for they have *t* their back unto ... Jer 2:27 6437
sister Judah hath not *t* unto me ... Jer 3:10 7725
of the LORD is not *t* back from us ... Jer 4:8 7725
have *t* away these things, and your ... Jer 5:25 5186
houses shall be *t* unto others ... Jer 6:12 5437
every one *t* to his course, as the ... Jer 8:6 7725
They are *t* back to the iniquities ... Jer 11:10 7725
then they should have *t* them from ... Jer 23:22 7725
and all faces are *t* into paleness ... Jer 30:6 2015
turn thou me, and I shall be *t* ... Jer 31:18 7725
Surely after that I was *t* ... Jer 31:19 7725
they have *t* unto me the back, and ... Jer 32:33 6437
But afterward they *t*, and caused ... Jer 34:11 7725
And ye were now *t*, and had done ... Jer 34:15 7725
But ye *t* and polluted my name, and ... Jer 34:16 7725
the mire, and they are *t* away back ... Jer 38:22 5472
seen them dismayed and *t* away back ... Jer 46:5 5472
for they also are *t* back, and are ... Jer 46:21 6437
how hath Moab *t* the back with ... Jer 48:39 6437
they have *t* them away on the ... Jer 50:6 7725
for my feet, he hath *t* me back ... Lam 1:13 7725
mine heart is *t* within me ... Lam 1:20 2015
Surely against me is he *t* ... Lam 3:3 7725
He hath *t* aside my ways, and ... Lam 3:11 5493
Our inheritance is *t* to strangers ... Lam 5:2 2015
our dance is *t* into mourning ... Lam 5:15 2015
thee, O LORD, and we shall be *t* ... Lam 5:21 7725
they *t* not when they went ... Eze 1:9 5437
they *t* not when they went ... Eze 1:12 5437
they *t* not when they went ... Eze 1:17 5437
they *t* not as they went, but to ... Eze 10:11 5437
they *t* not as they went ... Eze 10:11 5437
also *t* not from beside them ... Eze 10:16 5437
whose branches *t* toward him ... Eze 17:6 6437
she is *t* unto me ... Eze 26:2 5437
He *t* about to the west side, and ... Eze 42:19 5437
thy fury be *t* away from thy city ... Dan 9:16 7725
was *t* in me into corruption ... Dan 10:8 2015
vision my sorrows are *t* upon me ... Dan 10:16 2015
Ephraim is a cake not *t* ... Hos 7:8 2015
mine heart is *t* within me ... Hos 11:8 2015
for mine anger is *t* away from him ... Hos 14:4 7725
The sun shall be *t* into darkness ... Joel 2:31 2015
for ye have *t* judgment into gall, ... Amos 6:12 2015
that they *t* from their evil way ... Jonah 3:10 7725
For the LORD hath *t* away the ... Nah 2:2 7725
right hand shall be *t* unto thee ... Hab 2:16 5437
them that are *t* back from the ... Zeph 1:6 5472
yet ye *t* not to me, saith the ... Hag 2:17
Then I *t*, and lifted up mine eyes, ... Zec 5:1 7725
And I *t*, and lifted up mine eyes, ... Zec 6:1 7725
All the land shall be *t* as a ... Zec 14:10 5437
he *t* aside into the parts of ... Mt 2:22 *402*
But Jesus *t* him about, and when he ... Mt 9:22 *1994*
But he *t*, and said unto Peter, Get ... Mt 16:23 *4672*
t him about in the press, and said ... Mk 5:30 *1994*
But when he had *t* about and looked ... Mk 8:33 *1994*
they *t* back again to Jerusalem, ... Lk 2:45 *5290*
t him about, and said unto the ... Lk 7:9 *4762*
he *t* to the woman, and said unto ... Lk 7:44 *4762*
But he *t*, and rebuked them, and ... Lk 9:55 *4762*
he *t* him unto his disciples, and ... Lk 10:23 *4762*
and he *t*, and said unto them, ... Lk 14:25 *4762*
t back, and with a loud voice ... Lk 17:15 *5290*
And the Lord *t*, and looked upon ... Lk 22:61 *4762*
Then Jesus *t*, and saw them ... Jn 1:38 *4762*
your sorrow shall be *t* into joy ... Jn 16:20 *1096*
she *t* herself back, and saw Jesus ... Jn 20:14 *4762*
She *t* herself, and saith unto him, ... Jn 20:16 *4762*
The sun shall be *t* into darkness ... Acts 2:20 *4762*
in their hearts *t* back again into ... Acts 7:39 *4762*
Then God *t*, and gave them up to ... Acts 7:42 *4762*
Saron saw him, and *t* to the Lord ... Acts 9:35 *1994*
believed, and *t* unto the Lord ... Acts 11:21 *1994*
among the Gentiles are *t* to God ... Acts 15:19 *1994*
But Paul, being grieved, *t* ... Acts 16:18 *1994*
These that have *t* the world ... Acts 17:6 *387*
t away much people, saying that ... Acts 19:26 *3179*
how ye *t* to God from idols to ... 1Th 1:9 *1994*
have *t* aside unto vain jangling ... 1Ti 1:6 *1824*
are already *t* aside after Satan ... 1Ti 5:15 *1824*
are in Asia be *t* away from me ... 2Ti 1:15 *654*
truth, and shall be *t* unto fables ... 2Ti 4:4 *654*
t to flight the armies of the ... Heb 11:34 *2827*
which is lame be *t* out of the way ... Heb 12:13 *1624*
yet are they *t* about with a very ... Jas 3:4 *3329*
your laughter be *t* to mourning ... Jas 4:9 *3344*
The dog is *t* to his own vomit ... 2Pet 2:22 *1994*
I *t* to see the voice that spake ... Rev 1:12 *1994*
And being *t*, I saw seven golden ... Rev 1:12 *1994*

TURNEST {3}

and whithersoever thou *t* thyself ... 1Kin 2:3 6437
That thou *t* thy spirit against ... Job 15:13 7725
Thou *t* man to destruction ... Ps 90:3 7725

TURNETH {33}

the soul that *t* after such as ... Lev 20:6 6437
whose heart *t* away this day from ... Deut 29:18 6437
when Israel *t* their backs before ... Josh 7:8 2015
t toward the sunrising to ... Josh 19:27 7725
And then the coast *t* to Ramah ... Josh 19:29 7725
and the coast *t* to Hosah ... Josh 19:29 7725
then the coast *t* westward to ... Josh 19:34 7725
neither *t* he back from the sword ... Job 39:22 7725
He *t* rivers into a wilderness, and ... Ps 107:33 7760
He *t* the wilderness into a ... Ps 107:35 7760
of the wicked he *t* upside down ... Ps 146:9 5791
A soft answer *t* away wrath ... Prov 15:1 7725
whithersoever it *t*, it prospereth ... Prov 17:8 6437
he *t* it whithersoever he will ... Prov 21:1 5186
As the door *t* upon his hinges, so ... Prov 26:14 5437
He that *t* away his ear from ... Prov 28:9 5493
beasts, and *t* not away for any ... Prov 30:30 7725
south, and *t* about unto the north ... Eccl 1:6 5437
that *t* aside by the flocks of thy ... Song 1:7 5844
For the people *t* not unto him ... Is 9:13 7725
t it upside down, and scattereth ... Is 24:1 5753
that *t* wise men backward, and ... Is 44:25 7725
as a wayfaring man that *t* aside ... Jer 14:8 5186
t herself to flee, and fear hath ... Jer 49:24 6437
yea, she sigheth, and *t* backward ... Lam 1:8 7725
he *t* his hand against me all the ... Lam 3:3 7725
But when the righteous *t* away ... Eze 18:24 7725
When a righteous man *t* away from ... Eze 18:26 7725
when the wicked man *t* away from ... Eze 18:27 7725
and *t* away from all his ... Eze 18:28 7725
day that he *t* from his wickedness ... Eze 33:12 7725
When the righteous *t* from his ... Eze 33:18 7725
t the shadow of death into the ... Amos 5:8 2015

TURNING {18}

wiping it, and *t* it upside down ... 2Kin 21:13 2015
gate, and at the *t* of the wall, and ... 2Chr 26:9 4740
hardened his heart from *t* unto ... 2Chr 36:13 7257
the armoury at the *t* of the wall ... Neh 3:19 4740
from the *t* of the wall unto the ... Neh 3:20 4740
of Azariah unto the *t* of the wall ... Neh 3:24 4740
over against the *t* of the wall ... Neh 3:25 4740
For the *t* away of the simple ... Prov 1:32 4878
Surely your *t* of things upside ... Is 29:16 2017
two leaves apiece, two *t* leaves ... Eze 41:24 4142
t away he hath divided our fields ... Mic 2:4 7725
But Jesus *t* unto them said, ... Lk 23:28 *4762*
t about, seeth the disciple whom ... Jn 21:20 *1994*
in *t* away every one of you from ... Acts 3:26 *654*
t him to the body said, Tabitha, ... Acts 9:40 *1994*
variableness, neither shadow of *t* ... Jas 1:17 *5157*
t the cities of Sodom and Gomorrah ... 2Pet 2:6 *5077*
t the grace of our God into ... Jude 4 *3346*

TURTLE {2}

the voice of the *t* is heard in ... Song 2:12 8449
and the *t* and the crane and the ... Jer 8:7 8449

TURTLEDOVE {3}

a ram of three years old, and a *t* ... Gen 15:9 8449
and a young pigeon, or a *t* ... Lev 12:6 8449
thy *t* unto the multitude of the ... Ps 74:19 8449

TURTLEDOVES {7}

he shall bring his offering of *t* ... Lev 1:14 8449
which he hath committed, two *t* ... Lev 5:7 8449
if he be not able to bring two *t* ... Lev 5:11 8449
And two *t*, or two young pigeons, ... Lev 14:22 8449
he shall offer the one of the *t* ... Lev 14:30 8449
day he shall take to him two *t* ... Lev 15:14 8449
the law of the Lord, A pair of *t* ... Lk 2:24 *5167*

TURTLES {3}

lamb, then she shall bring two *t* ... Lev 12:8 8449
day she shall take unto her two *t* ... Lev 15:29 8449
eighth day he shall bring two *t* ... Num 6:10 8449

TUTORS {1}

But is under *t* and governors until ... Gal 4:2 *2012*

TWAIN {17}

my son in law in the one of the *t* ... 1Sa 18:21 8147
and shut the door upon them *t* ... 2Kin 4:33 8147
with *t* he covered his face, and ... Is 6:2 8147
with *t* he covered his feet, and ... Is 6:2 8147
his feet, and with *t* he did fly ... Is 6:2 8147
me, when they cut the calf in *t* ... Jer 34:18 8147
both *t* shall come forth out of ... Eze 21:19 8147
thee to go a mile, go with him *t* ... Mt 5:41 *1417*
they *t* shall be one flesh ... Mt 19:5 *1417*
Wherefore they are no more *t* ... Mt 19:6 *1417*
Whether of them *t* did the will of ... Mt 21:31 *1417*
Whether of the *t* will ye that I ... Mt 27:21 *1417*
in *t* from the top to the bottom ... Mt 27:51 *1417*
they *t* shall be one flesh ... Mk 10:8 *1417*
so then they are no more *t* ... Mk 10:8 *1417*
in *t* from the top to the bottom ... Mk 15:38 *1417*
make in himself of *t* one new man ... Eph 2:15 *1417*

TWELFTH {23}

On the *t* day Ahira the son of ... Num 7:78 8147,6240
oxen before him, and he with the *t* . 1Kin 19:19 8147,6240
In the *t* year of Joram the son of ... 2Kin 8:25 8147,6240
In the *t* year of Ahaz king of ... 2Kin 17:1 8147,6240
king of Judah, in the *t* month ... 2Kin 25:27 8147,6240
to Eliashib, the *t* to Jakim, ... 1Chr 24:12 8147,6240
The *t* to Hashabiah, he, his sons, ... 1Chr 25:19 8147,6240
The *t* captain for the *t* ... 1Chr 27:15 8147,6240
in the *t* year he began to purge ... 2Chr 34:3 8147,6240
on the *t* day of the first month ... Ezr 8:31 8147,6240
in the *t* year of king Ahasuerus, ... Est 3:7 8147,6240
month to month, to the *t* month ... Est 3:7 8147,6240
the thirteenth day of the *t* month ... Est 3:13 8147,6240
the thirteenth day of the *t* month ... Est 8:12 8147,6240
Now in the *t* month, that is, the ... Est 9:1 8147,6240
king of Judah, in the *t* month ... Jer 52:31 8147,6240
in the *t* day of the month, the ... Eze 29:1 8147,6240
the *t* year, in the *t* month ... Eze 32:1 8147,6240
came to pass also in the *t* year ... Eze 32:17 8147,6240
in the *t* year of our captivity ... Eze 33:21 8147,6240
the *t*, an amethyst ... Rev 21:20 *1428*

TWELVE {189}

Seth were nine hundred and *t* ... Gen 5:8 8147,6240
T years they served Chedorlaomer, .. Gen 14:4 8147,6240
t princes shall he beget, and I ... Gen 17:20 8147,6240
t princes according to their ... Gen 25:16 8147,6240
Now the sons of Jacob were *t* ... Gen 35:22 8147,6240
said, Thy servants are *t* brethren ... Gen 42:13 8147,6240
We be *t* brethren, sons of our ... Gen 42:32 8147,6240
these are the *t* tribes of Israel ... Gen 49:28 8147,6240
where were *t* wells of water, and ... Ex 15:27 8147,6240
t pillars, according to the ... Ex 24:4 8147,6240
to the *t* tribes of Israel ... Ex 24:4 8147,6240
of the children of Israel, *t* ... Ex 28:21 8147,6240
they be according to the *t* tribes ... Ex 28:21 8147,6240
of the children of Israel, *t* ... Ex 39:14 8147,6240
name, according to the *t* tribes ... Ex 39:14 8147,6240
flour, and bake *t* cakes thereof ... Lev 24:5 8147,6240
princes of Israel, being *t* men ... Num 1:44 8147,6240
six covered wagons, and *t* oxen ... Num 7:3 8147,6240
t chargers of silver ... Num 7:84 8147,6240
t silver bowls, *t* spoons of ... Num 7:84 8147,6240
The golden spoons were *t*, full of ... Num 7:86 8147,6240
were *t* bullocks, the rams *t* ... Num 7:87 8147,6240
the lambs of the first year *t* ... Num 7:87 8147,6240
of the goats for sin offering *t* ... Num 7:87 8147,6240
the house of their fathers *t* rods ... Num 17:2 8147,6240
fathers' houses, even *t* rods ... Num 17:6 8147,6240
ye shall offer *t* young bullocks ... Num 29:17 8147,6240
tribe, *t* thousand armed for war ... Num 31:5 8147,6240
threescore and *t* thousand beeves, ... Num 31:33 8147
tribute was threescore and *t* ... Num 31:38 8147
in Elim were *t* fountains of water ... Num 33:9 8147,6240
I took *t* men of you, one of a ... Deut 1:23 8147,6240
Now therefore take you *t* men out ... Josh 3:12 8147,6240
Take you *t* men out of the people, ... Josh 4:2 8147,6240
t stones, and ye shall carry them ... Josh 4:3 8147,6240
Then Joshua called the *t* men ... Josh 4:4 8147,6240
took up *t* stones out of the midst ... Josh 4:8 8147,6240
Joshua set up *t* stones in the ... Josh 4:9 8147,6240
those *t* stones, which they took ... Josh 4:20 8147,6240
were *t* thousand, even all the men ... Josh 8:25 8147,6240
t cities with their villages ... Josh 18:24 8147,6240
t cities with their villages ... Josh 19:15 8147,6240
of the tribe of Zebulun, *t* cities ... Josh 21:7 8147,6240
were by their lot *t* cities ... Josh 21:40 8147,6240
into *t* pieces, and sent her into ... Judg 19:29 8147,6240
the congregation sent thither *t* ... Judg 21:10 8147,6240
over by number *t* of Benjamin ... 2Sa 2:15 8147,6240
t of the servants of David ... 2Sa 2:15 8147,6240
of Ish-tob *t* thousand men ... 2Sa 10:6 8147,6240
me now choose out *t* thousand ... 2Sa 17:1 8147,6240
Solomon had *t* officers over all ... 1Kin 4:7 8147,6240
chariots, and *t* thousand horsemen . 1Kin 4:26 8147,6240
a line of *t* cubits did compass ... 1Kin 7:15 8147,6240
It stood upon *t* oxen, three ... 1Kin 7:25 8147,6240
one sea, and *t* oxen under the sea ... 1Kin 7:44 8147,6240
t lions stood there on the one ... 1Kin 10:20 8147,6240
t thousand horsemen, whom he ... 1Kin 10:26 8147,6240
on him, and rent it in *t* pieces ... 1Kin 11:30 8147,6240
to reign over Israel, *t* years ... 1Kin 16:23 8147,6240
And Elijah took *t* stones, ... 1Kin 18:31 8147,6240
who was plowing with *t* yoke of ... 1Kin 19:19 8147,6240
king of Judah, and reigned *t* years .. 2Kin 3:1 8147,6240
Manasseh was *t* years old when ... 2Kin 21:1 8147,6240
of the tribe of Zebulun, *t* cities ... 1Chr 6:63 8147,6240
the gates were two hundred and *t* ... 1Chr 9:22 8147,6240
and his brethren an hundred and *t* . 1Chr 15:10 8147,6240
with his brethren and sons were *t* ... 1Chr 25:9 8147,6240
his sons, and his brethren, were *t* ... 1Chr 25:10 8147,6240
his sons, and his brethren, were *t* ... 1Chr 25:11 8147,6240
his sons, and his brethren, were *t* ... 1Chr 25:12 8147,6240
his sons, and his brethren, were *t* ... 1Chr 25:13 8147,6240
his sons, and his brethren, were *t* ... 1Chr 25:14 8147,6240
his sons, and his brethren, were *t* ... 1Chr 25:15 8147,6240

his sons, and his brethren, were *t*	1Chr 25:16	8147,6240
his sons, and his brethren, were *t*	1Chr 25:17	8147,6240
his sons, and his brethren, were *t*	1Chr 25:18	8147,6240
his sons, and his brethren, were *t*	1Chr 25:19	8147,6240
his sons, and his brethren, were *t*	1Chr 25:20	8147,6240
his sons, and his brethren, were *t*	1Chr 25:21	8147,6240
his sons, and his brethren, were *t*	1Chr 25:22	8147,6240
his sons, and his brethren, were *t*	1Chr 25:23	8147,6240
his sons, and his brethren, were *t*	1Chr 25:24	8147,6240
his sons, and his brethren, were *t*	1Chr 25:25	8147,6240
his sons, and his brethren, were *t*	1Chr 25:26	8147,6240
his sons, and his brethren, were *t*	1Chr 25:27	8147,6240
his sons, and his brethren, were *t*	1Chr 25:28	8147,6240
his sons, and his brethren, were *t*	1Chr 25:29	8147,6240
his sons, and his brethren, were *t*	1Chr 25:30	8147,6240
his sons, and his brethren, were *t*	1Chr 25:31	8147,6240
t thousand horsemen, which he	2Chr 1:14	8147,6240
It stood upon *t* oxen, three	2Chr 4:4	8147,6240
One sea, and *t* oxen under it	2Chr 4:15	8147,6240
t lions stood there on the one	2Chr 9:19	8147,6240
chariots, and *t* thousand horsemen	2Chr 9:25	8147,6240
With *t* hundred chariots, and	2Chr 12:3	505
Manasseh was *t* years old when	2Chr 33:1	8147,6240
two thousand eight hundred and *t*	Ezr 2:6	8147,6240
of Jorah, an hundred and *t*	Ezr 2:18	8147,6240
t he goats, according to the	Ezr 6:17	8648,6236
Then I separated *t* of the chief	Ezr 8:24	8147,6240
t bullocks for all Israel, ninety	Ezr 8:35	8147,6240
t he goats for a sin offering	Ezr 8:35	8147,6240
t years, I and my brethren have	Neh 5:14	8147,6240
of Hariph, an hundred and *t*	Neh 7:24	8147,6240
after that she had been *t* months	Est 2:12	8147,6240
in the valley of salt *t* thousand	Ps 60:*t*	8147,6240
t brasen bulls that were under	Jer 52:20	8147,6240
a fillet of *t* cubits did compass	Jer 52:21	8147,6240
the altar shall be *t* cubits long	Eze 43:16	8147,6240
t broad, square in the four	Eze 43:16	8147,6240
to the *t* tribes of Israel	Eze 47:13	8147,6240
At the end of *t* months he walked	Dan 4:29	8648,6236
with an issue of blood *t* years	Mt 9:20	*1427*
called unto him his *t* disciples	Mt 10:1	*1427*
names of the *t* apostles are these	Mt 10:2	*1427*
These *t* Jesus sent forth, and	Mt 10:5	*1427*
end of commanding his *t* disciples	Mt 11:1	*1427*
that remained *t* baskets full	Mt 14:20	*1427*
ye also shall sit upon *t* thrones	Mt 19:28	*1427*
judging the *t* tribes of Israel	Mt 19:28	*1427*
the *t* disciples apart in the way	Mt 20:17	*1427*
Then one of the *t*, called Judas	Mt 26:14	*1427*
was come, he sat down with the *t*	Mt 26:20	*1427*
spake, lo, Judas, one of the *t*	Mt 26:47	*1427*
me more than *t* legions of angels	Mt 26:53	*1427*
And he ordained *t*, that they	Mk 3:14	*1427*
the *t* asked of him the parable	Mk 4:10	*1427*
had an issue of blood *t* years	Mk 5:25	*1427*
for she was of the age of *t* years	Mk 5:42	*1427*
And he called unto him the *t*	Mk 6:7	*1427*
they took up *t* baskets full of	Mk 6:43	*1427*
They say unto him, *T*	Mk 8:19	*1427*
And he sat down, and called the *t*	Mk 9:35	*1427*
And he took again the *t*, and began	Mk 10:32	*1427*
went out unto Bethany with the *t*	Mk 11:11	*1427*
And Judas Iscariot, one of the *t*	Mk 14:10	*1427*
the evening he cometh with the *t*	Mk 14:17	*1427*
unto them, It is one of the *t*	Mk 14:20	*1427*
spake, cometh Judas, one of the *t*	Mk 14:43	*1427*
And when he was *t* years old	Lk 2:42	*1427*
and of them he chose *t*, whom also	Lk 6:13	*1427*
and the *t* were with him,	Lk 8:1	*1427*
about *t* years of age, and she lay	Lk 8:42	*1427*
having an issue of blood *t* years	Lk 8:43	*1427*
called his *t* disciples together	Lk 9:1	*1427*
to wear away, then came the *t*	Lk 9:12	*1427*
that remained to them *t* baskets	Lk 9:17	*1427*
Then he took unto him the *t*	Lk 18:31	*1427*
being of the number of the *t*	Lk 22:3	*1427*
down, and the *t* apostles with him	Lk 22:14	*1427*
judging the *t* tribes of Israel	Lk 22:30	*1427*
was called Judas, one of the *t*	Lk 22:47	*1427*
filled *t* baskets with the	Jn 6:13	*1427*
Then said Jesus unto the *t*	Jn 6:67	*1427*
them, Have not I chosen you *t*	Jn 6:70	*1427*
betray him, being one of the *t*	Jn 6:71	*1427*
Are there not *t* hours in the day	Jn 11:9	*1427*
But Thomas, one of the *t*, called	Jn 20:24	*1427*
Then the *t* called the multitude	Acts 6:2	*1427*
and Jacob begat the *t* patriarchs	Acts 7:8	*1427*
And all the men were about *t*	Acts 19:7	*1177*
that there are yet but *t* days	Acts 24:11	*1177*
Unto which promise our *t* tribes	Acts 26:7	*1429*
was seen of Cephas, then of the *t*	1Cor 15:5	*1427*
to the *t* tribes which are	Jas 1:1	*1427*
of Juda were sealed *t* thousand	Rev 7:5	*1427*
of Reuben were sealed *t* thousand	Rev 7:5	*1427*
of Gad were sealed *t* thousand	Rev 7:5	*1427*
of Aser were sealed *t* thousand	Rev 7:6	*1427*
Nepthalim were sealed *t* thousand	Rev 7:6	*1427*
Manasses were sealed *t* thousand	Rev 7:6	*1427*
of Simeon were sealed *t* thousand	Rev 7:7	*1427*
of Levi were sealed *t* thousand	Rev 7:7	*1427*
Issachar were sealed *t* thousand	Rev 7:7	*1427*
of Zabulon were sealed *t* thousand	Rev 7:8	*1427*
of Joseph were sealed *t* thousand	Rev 7:8	*1427*
Benjamin were sealed *t* thousand	Rev 7:8	*1427*
upon her head a crown of *t* stars	Rev 12:1	*1427*
had *t* gates, and at the gates	Rev 21:12	*1427*
gates, and at the gates *t* angels	Rev 21:12	*1427*
the *t* tribes of the children of	Rev 21:12	*1427*
of the city had *t* foundations	Rev 21:14	*1427*
of the *t* apostles of the Lamb	Rev 21:14	*1427*
the reed, *t* thousand furlongs	Rev 21:16	*1427*
the *t* gates were *t* pearls	Rev 21:21	*1427*
which bare *t* manner of fruits, and	Rev 22:2	*1427*

TWENTIETH {36}

t day of the month, was the earth	Gen 8:14	6242
t day of the month at even	Ex 12:18	6242
it came to pass on the *t* day of	Num 10:11	6242
in the *t* year of Jeroboam king of	1Kin 15:9	6242
t year of king Jehoash the	2Kin 12:6	6242
t year of Joash the son of	2Kin 13:1	6242
in the *t* year of Jotham the son	2Kin 15:30	6242
seven and *t* day of the month, that	2Kin 25:27	6242
to Pethahiah, the *t* to Jehezekel,	1Chr 24:16	6242
t to Jachin, the two and	1Chr 24:17	6242
to Jachin, the two and *t* to Gamul,	1Chr 24:17	6242
t to Delaiah, the four and	1Chr 24:18	6242
Delaiah, the four and *t* to Maaziah	1Chr 24:18	6242
The *t* to Eliathah, he, his sons,	1Chr 25:27	6242
t to Hothir, he, his sons, and his	1Chr 25:28	6242
t to Giddalti, he, his sons, and	1Chr 25:29	6242
t to Mahazioth, he, his sons, and	1Chr 25:30	6242
t to Romamti-ezer, he, his sons,	1Chr 25:31	6242
t day of the seventh month he	2Chr 7:10	6242
on the *t* day of the month	Ezr 10:9	6242
the month Chisleu, in the *t* year	Neh 1:1	6242
in the *t* year of Artaxerxes the	Neh 2:1	6242
from the *t* year even unto the two	Neh 5:14	6242
on the three and *t* day thereof	Est 8:9	6242
t year, the word of the LORD hath	Jer 25:3	6242
three and *t* year of Nebuchadrezzar	Jer 52:30	6242
five and *t* day of the month, that	Jer 52:31	6242
t year, in the first month, in	Eze 29:17	6242
t year of our captivity, in the	Eze 40:1	6242
t day of the first month, as I	Dan 10:4	6242
t day of the sixth month, in the	Hag 1:15	6242
t day of the month, came the word	Hag 2:1	6242
t day of the ninth month, in the	Hag 2:10	6242
t day of the ninth month, even	Hag 2:18	6242
t day of the month, saying,	Hag 2:20	6242
t day of the eleventh month,	Zec 1:7	6242

TWENTY {}

shall be an hundred and *t* years	Gen 6:3	6242
nine and *t* years, and begat Terah	Gen 11:24	6242
there shall be *t* found there	Gen 18:31	6242
hundred and seven and *t* years old	Gen 23:1	6242
This *t* years have I been with	Gen 31:38	6242
Thus have I been *t* years in thy	Gen 31:41	6242
t he goats, two hundred ewes, and	Gen 32:14	6242
two hundred ewes, and *t* rams,	Gen 32:14	6242
t she asses, and ten foals	Gen 32:15	6242
for *t* pieces of silver	Gen 37:28	6242
t cubits, and the breadth of one	Ex 26:2	6242
t boards on the south side	Ex 26:18	6242
of silver under the *t* boards	Ex 26:19	6242
side there shall be *t* boards	Ex 26:20	6242
the *t* pillars thereof and their	Ex 27:10	6242
their *t* sockets shall be of brass	Ex 27:10	6242
his *t* pillars and their *t*	Ex 27:11	6242
shall be an hanging of *t* cubits	Ex 27:16	6242
(a shekel is *t* gerahs	Ex 30:13	6242
from *t* years old and above, shall	Ex 30:14	6242
The length of one curtain was *t*	Ex 36:9	6242
t boards for the south side	Ex 36:23	6242
silver he made under the *t* boards	Ex 36:24	6242
north corner, he made *t* boards	Ex 36:25	6242
Their pillars were *t*, and their	Ex 38:10	6242
and their brasen sockets *t*	Ex 38:10	6242
cubits, their pillars were *t*	Ex 38:11	6242
and their sockets of brass *t*	Ex 38:11	6242
t cubits was the length, and the	Ex 38:18	6242
the gold of the offering, was *t*	Ex 38:24	6242
from *t* years old and upward, for	Ex 38:26	6242
shall be of the male from *t* years	Lev 27:3	6242
years old even unto *t* years old	Lev 27:5	6242
shall be of the male *t* shekels	Lev 27:5	6242
t gerahs shall be the shekel	Lev 27:25	6242
From *t* years old and upward, all	Num 1:3	6242
from *t* years old and upward, by	Num 1:18	6242
every male from *t* years old	Num 1:20	6242
every male from *t* years old	Num 1:22	6242
from *t* years old and upward, all	Num 1:24	6242
from *t* years old and upward, all	Num 1:26	6242
from *t* years old and upward, all	Num 1:28	6242
from *t* years old and upward, all	Num 1:30	6242
from *t* years old and upward, all	Num 1:32	6242
from *t* years old and upward, all	Num 1:34	6242
from *t* years old and upward, all	Num 1:36	6242
from *t* years old and upward, all	Num 1:38	6242
from *t* years old and upward, all	Num 1:40	6242
from *t* years old and upward, all	Num 1:42	6242
from *t* years old and upward, all	Num 1:45	6242
a month old and upward, were *t*	Num 3:39	6242
were numbered of them, were *t*	Num 3:43	6242
(the shekel is *t* gerahs	Num 3:47	6242
was an hundred and *t* shekels	Num 7:86	6242
of the peace offerings were *t*	Num 7:88	6242
from *t* and five years old and	Num 8:24	6242
neither ten days, nor *t* days	Num 11:19	6242
from *t* years old and upward, which	Num 14:29	6242
the sanctuary, which is *t* gerahs	Num 18:16	6242
that died in the plague were *t*	Num 25:9	6242
from *t* years old and upward,	Num 26:2	6242
from *t* years old and upward	Num 26:4	6242
the families of the Simeonites, *t*	Num 26:14	6242
that were numbered of them were *t*	Num 26:62	6242
from *t* years old and upward, shall	Num 32:11	6242
And Aaron was an hundred and *t*	Num 33:39	6242
hundred and *t* years old this day	Deut 31:2	6242
and *t* years old when he died	Deut 34:7	6242
all the cities are *t* and nine,	Josh 15:32	6242
t and two cities with their	Josh 19:30	6242
t years he mightily oppressed the	Judg 4:3	6242
And there returned of the people *t*	Judg 7:3	6242
t thousand men that drew sword	Judg 8:10	6242
And he judged Israel *t* and three	Judg 10:2	6242
a Gileadite, and judged Israel *t*	Judg 10:3	6242
even *t* cities, and unto the plain	Judg 11:33	6242
days of the Philistines *t* years	Judg 15:20	6242
And he judged Israel *t* years	Judg 16:31	6242
at that time out of the cities *t*	Judg 20:15	6242
of the Israelites that day *t*	Judg 20:21	6242
of the Benjamites that day *t*	Judg 20:35	6242
fell that day of Benjamin were *t*	Judg 20:46	6242
for it was *t* years	1Sa 7:2	6242
made, was about *t* men, within as	1Sa 14:14	6242
to Hebron, and *t* men with him	2Sa 3:20	6242
horsemen, and *t* thousand footmen	2Sa 8:4	6242
the Syrians two and *t* thousand men	2Sa 8:5	6242
had fifteen sons and *t* servants	2Sa 9:10	6242
t thousand footmen, and of king	2Sa 10:6	6242
that day of *t* thousand men	2Sa 18:7	6242
sons and his *t* servants with him	2Sa 19:17	6242
six toes, four and *t* in number	2Sa 21:20	6242
the end of nine months and *t* days	2Sa 24:8	6242
t oxen out of the pastures, and an	1Kin 4:23	6242
Solomon gave Hiram *t* thousand	1Kin 5:11	6242
and *t* measures of pure oil	1Kin 5:11	6242
and the breadth thereof *t* cubits	1Kin 6:2	6242
t cubits was the length thereof,	1Kin 6:3	6242
he built *t* cubits on the sides of	1Kin 6:16	6242
forepart was *t* cubits in length	1Kin 6:20	6242
t cubits in breadth	1Kin 6:20	6242
t cubits in the height thereof	1Kin 6:20	6242
t thousand oxen, and an hundred and	1Kin 8:63	6242
and an hundred and *t* thousand sheep	1Kin 8:63	6242
to pass at the end of *t* years	1Kin 9:10	6242
then king Solomon gave Hiram *t*	1Kin 9:11	6242
t talents, and brought it to king	1Kin 9:28	6242
t talents of gold, and of spices	1Kin 10:10	6242
reigned were two and *t* years	1Kin 14:20	6242
over all Israel in Tirzah, *t*	1Kin 15:33	6242
In the *t* and sixth year of Asa	1Kin 16:8	6242
him, and killed him, in the *t*	1Kin 16:10	6242
In the *t* and seventh year of Asa	1Kin 16:15	6242
reigned over Israel in Samaria *t*	1Kin 16:29	6242
and there a wall fell upon *t*	1Kin 20:30	6242
and he reigned *t* and five years in	1Kin 22:42	6242
t loaves of barley, and full ears	2Kin 4:42	6242
t years old was Ahaziah when he	2Kin 8:26	6242
over Israel in Samaria was *t*	2Kin 10:36	6242
He was *t* and five years old when	2Kin 14:2	6242
he began to reign, and reigned *t*	2Kin 14:2	6242
In the *t* and seventh year of	2Kin 15:1	6242
in Samaria, and reigned *t* years	2Kin 15:27	6242
t years old was he when he began	2Kin 15:33	6242
T years old was Ahaz when he	2Kin 16:2	6242
T and five years old was he when	2Kin 18:2	6242
and he reigned *t* and nine years in	2Kin 18:2	6242
Amon was *t* and two years old when	2Kin 21:19	6242
Jehoahaz was *t* and three years old	2Kin 23:31	6242
Jehoiakim was *t* and five years old	2Kin 23:36	6242
Zedekiah was *t* and one years old	2Kin 24:18	6242
t cities in the land of Gilead	1Chr 2:22	6242
t thousand and six hundred	1Chr 7:2	6242
reckoned by their genealogies *t*	1Chr 7:7	6242
was *t* thousand and two hundred	1Chr 7:9	6242
apt to the war and to battle was *t*	1Chr 7:40	6242
and of his father's house *t*	1Chr 12:28	6242
children of Ephraim *t* thousand	1Chr 12:30	6242
And of the Danites expert in war *t*	1Chr 12:35	6242
battle, an hundred and *t* thousand	1Chr 12:37	6242
and his brethren an hundred and *t*	1Chr 15:5	6242
and his brethren two hundred and *t*	1Chr 15:6	6242
horsemen, and *t* thousand footmen	1Chr 18:4	6242
the Syrians two and *t* thousand men	1Chr 18:5	6242
fingers and toes were four and *t*	1Chr 20:6	6242
Of which, *t* and four thousand were	1Chr 23:4	6242
the LORD, from the age of *t* years	1Chr 23:24	6242
were numbered from *t* years old	1Chr 23:27	6242
the year, of every course were *t*	1Chr 27:1	6242
and in his course were *t* and four	1Chr 27:2	6242
in his course likewise were *t*	1Chr 27:4	6242
and in his course were *t* and four	1Chr 27:5	6242
and in his course were *t* and four	1Chr 27:7	6242
and in his course were *t* and four	1Chr 27:8	6242
and in his course were *t* and four	1Chr 27:9	6242
and in his course were *t* and four	1Chr 27:10	6242
and in his course were *t* and four	1Chr 27:11	6242
and in his course were *t* and four	1Chr 27:12	6242
and in his course were *t* and four	1Chr 27:13	6242
and in his course were *t* and four	1Chr 27:14	6242
and in his course were *t* and four	1Chr 27:15	6242
number of them from *t* years old	1Chr 27:23	6242
t thousand measures of beaten	2Chr 2:10	6242
t thousand measures of barley, and	2Chr 2:10	6242
t thousand baths of wine, and	2Chr 2:10	6242
wine, and *t* thousand baths of oil	2Chr 2:10	6242
cubits, and the breadth *t* cubits	2Chr 3:3	6242
t cubits, and the height was an	2Chr 3:4	6242
and the height was an hundred and *t*	2Chr 3:4	6242
t cubits, and the breadth thereof	2Chr 3:8	6242
and the breadth thereof *t* cubits	2Chr 3:8	6242
the cherubims were *t* cubits long	2Chr 3:11	6242

spread themselves forth *t* cubits 2Chr 3:13 6242
t cubits the length thereof, and 2Chr 4:1 6242
t cubits the breadth thereof, and 2Chr 4:1 6242
t priests sounding with trumpets 2Chr 5:12 6242
Solomon offered a sacrifice of *t* 2Chr 7:5 6242
and an hundred and *t* thousand sheep 2Chr 7:5 6242
to pass at the end of *t* years 2Chr 8:1 6242
t talents of gold, and of spices 2Chr 9:9 6242
and begat *t* and eight sons, and 2Chr 11:21 6242
fourteen wives, and begat *t* 2Chr 13:21 6242
began to reign, and he reigned *t* 2Chr 20:31 6242
Amaziah was *t* and five years old 2Chr 25:1 6242
began to reign, and he reigned *t* 2Chr 25:1 6242
he numbered them from *t* years old 2Chr 25:5 6242
Jotham was *t* and five years old 2Chr 27:1 6242
t years old when he began to 2Chr 27:8 6242
Ahaz was *t* years old when he 2Chr 28:1 6242
t thousand in one day, which were 2Chr 28:6 6242
t years old, and he reigned nine 2Chr 29:1 6242
nine and *t* years in Jerusalem 2Chr 29:1 6242
and the Levites from *t* years old 2Chr 31:17 6242
t years old when he began to 2Chr 33:21 6242
Jehoahaz was *t* and three years old 2Chr 36:2 6242
Jehoiakim was *t* and five years old 2Chr 36:5 6242
t years old when he began to 2Chr 36:11 6242
of silver, nine and *t* knives, ... Ezr 1:9 6242
children of Bebai, six hundred *t* .... Ezr 2:11 6242
Azgad, a thousand two hundred *t* .... Ezr 2:12 6242
of Bezai, three hundred *t* .... Ezr 2:17 6242
children of Hashum, two hundred *t* .... Ezr 2:19 6242
of Beth-lehem, an hundred *t* .... Ezr 2:21 6242
The men of Anathoth, an hundred *t* .... Ezr 2:23 6242
of Ramah and Gaba, six hundred *t* .... Ezr 2:26 6242
The men of Michmas, an hundred *t* .... Ezr 2:27 6242
of Beth-el and Ai, two hundred *t* .... Ezr 2:28 6242
of Harim, three hundred and *t* .... Ezr 2:32 6242
Hadid, and Ono, seven hundred *t* .... Ezr 2:33 6242
children of Asaph, an hundred *t* .... Ezr 2:41 6242
six thousand seven hundred and *t* .... Ezr 2:67 6242
from *t* years old and upward, to .... Ezr 3:8 6242
the son of Bebai, and with him *t* .... Ezr 8:11 6242
his brethren and their sons, *t* .... Ezr 8:19 6242
two hundred and *t* Nethinims .... Ezr 8:20 6242
Also *t* basons of gold, of a .... Ezr 8:27 6242
So the wall was finished in the *t* .... Neh 6:15 6242
children of Bebai, six hundred *t* .... Neh 7:16 6242
two thousand three hundred *t* .... Neh 7:17 6242
of Hashum, three hundred *t* .... Neh 7:22 6242
of Bezai, three hundred *t* .... Neh 7:23 6242
The men of Anathoth, an hundred *t* .... Neh 7:27 6242
of Ramah and Gaba, six hundred *t* .... Neh 7:30 6242
men of Michmas, an hundred and *t* .... Neh 7:31 6242
of Beth-el and Ai, an hundred *t* .... Neh 7:32 6242
of Harim, three hundred and *t* .... Neh 7:35 6242
Hadid, and Ono, seven hundred *t* .... Neh 7:37 6242
thousand seven hundred and *t* asses .... Neh 7:69 6242
the work *t* thousand drams of gold .... Neh 7:71 7239
gave was *t* thousand drams of gold .... Neh 7:72 7239
Now in the *t* and fourth day of .... Neh 9:1 6242
Gabbai, Sallai, nine hundred *t* .... Neh 11:8 6242
of the house were eight hundred *t* .... Neh 11:12 6242
men of valour, an hundred *t* .... Neh 11:14 6242
hundred and seven and *t* provinces .... Est 1:1 6242
India unto Ethiopia, an hundred *t* .... Est 8:9 6242
all the Jews, to the hundred *t* .... Est 9:30 6242
chariots of God are *t* thousand .... Ps 68:17 7239
t years old when he began to .... Jer 52:1 6242
three thousand Jews and three and *t* .... Jer 52:28 6242
be by weight, *t* shekels a day .... Eze 4:10 6242
t men, with their backs toward .... Eze 8:16 6242
door of the gate five and *t* men .... Eze 11:1 6242
t cubits, door against door .... Eze 40:13 6242
and the breadth five and *t* cubits .... Eze 40:21 6242
and the breadth five and *t* cubits .... Eze 40:25 6242
long, and five and *t* cubits broad .... Eze 40:29 6242
t cubits long, and five cubits .... Eze 40:30 6242
long, and five and *t* cubits broad .... Eze 40:33 6242
and the breadth five and *t* cubits .... Eze 40:36 6242
length of the porch was *t* cubits .... Eze 40:49 6242
and the breadth, *t* cubits .... Eze 41:2 6242
the length thereof, *t* cubits .... Eze 41:4 6242
t cubits, before the temple .... Eze 41:4 6242
chambers was the wideness of *t* .... Eze 41:10 6242
Over against the *t* cubits which .... Eze 42:3 6242
t thousand reeds, and the breadth .... Eze 45:1 6242
t thousand, and the breadth of ten .... Eze 45:3 6242
t thousand of length, and the ten .... Eze 45:5 6242
for a possession for *t* chambers .... Eze 45:5 6242
t thousand long, over against the .... Eze 45:6 6242
And the shekel shall be *t* gerahs .... Eze 45:12 6242
t shekels, five and *t* shekels .... Eze 45:12 6242
t thousand reeds in breadth, and .... Eze 48:8 6242
t thousand in length, and of ten .... Eze 48:9 6242
t thousand in length, and toward .... Eze 48:10 6242
five and *t* thousand in length .... Eze 48:10 6242
t thousand in length, and ten .... Eze 48:13 6242
t thousand, and the breadth ten .... Eze 48:13 6242
t thousand, shall be a profane .... Eze 48:15 6242
t thousand by five and .... Eze 48:20 6242
thousand by five and *t* thousand .... Eze 48:20 6242
t thousand of the oblation toward .... Eze 48:21 6242
t thousand toward the west border .... Eze 48:21 6242
t princes, which should be over .... Dan 6:1 6243
Persia withstood me one and *t* days .... Dan 10:13 6242
one came to an heap of *t* measures .... Hag 2:16 6242
of the press, there were but *t* .... Hag 2:16 6242
the length thereof is *t* cubits .... Zec 5:2 6242
against him with *t* thousand .... Lk 14:31 *1501*
t or thirty furlongs, they see .... Jn 6:19 *1501*
were about an hundred and *t* .... Acts 1:15 *1501*
And sounded, and found it *t* fathoms .... Acts 27:28 *1501*
in one day three and *t* thousand 1Cor 10:8 *1501*
the throne were four and *t* seats .... Rev 4:4 *1501*
t elders sitting, clothed in .... Rev 4:4 *1501*
t elders fall down before him .... Rev 4:10 *1501*
t elders fell down before the .... Rev 5:8 *1501*
t elders fell down and worshipped .... Rev 5:14 *1501*
t elders, which sat before God on .... Rev 11:16 *1501*
t elders and the four beasts fell .... Rev 19:4 *1501*

TWENTY'S {1}
I will not destroy it for *t* sake .... Gen 18:31 6242

TWICE {17}
dream was doubled unto Pharaoh *t* .... Gen 41:32 6471
it shall be *t* as much as they .... Ex 16:5 4932
day they gathered *t* as much bread .... Ex 16:22 4932
with his rod he smote the rock *t* .... Num 20:11 6471
avoided out of his presence *t* 1Sa 18:11 6471
which had appeared unto him *t* 1Kin 11:9 6471
himself there, not once nor *t* 2Kin 6:10 8147
without Jerusalem once or *t* .... Neh 13:20 8147
For God speaketh once, yea *t* .... Job 33:14 8147
will not answer: yea, *t* .... Job 40:5 8147
also the LORD gave Job *t* as much .... Job 42:10 4932
t have I heard this .... Ps 62:11 8147
he live a thousand years *t* told .... Eccl 6:6 6471
night, before the cock crow *t* .... Mk 14:30 *1364*
unto him, Before the cock crow *t* .... Mk 14:72 *1364*
I fast *t* in the week, I give .... Lk 18:12 *1364*
t dead, plucked up by the roots .... Jude 12 *1364*

TWIGS {2}
off the top of his young *t* .... Eze 17:4 3242
top of his young *t* a tender one .... Eze 17:22 3127

TWILIGHT {9}
David smote them from the *t* even 1Sa 30:17 5399
And they rose up in the *t*, to go 2Kin 7:5 5399
they arose and fled in the *t* 2Kin 7:7 5399
stars of the *t* thereof be dark .... Job 3:9 5399
the adulterer waiteth for the *t* .... Job 24:15 5399
In the *t*, in the evening, in the .... Prov 7:9 5399
and carry it forth in the *t* .... Eze 12:6 5939
I brought it forth in the *t* .... Eze 12:7 5939
bear upon his shoulder in the *t* .... Eze 12:12 5939

TWINED {21}
with ten curtains of fine *t* linen .... Ex 26:1 7806
fine *t* linen of cunning work .... Ex 26:31 7806
fine *t* linen, wrought with .... Ex 26:36 7806
hangings for the court of fine *t* .... Ex 27:9 7806
fine *t* linen, wrought with .... Ex 27:16 7806
five cubits of fine *t* linen .... Ex 27:18 7806
fine *t* linen, with cunning work .... Ex 28:6 7806
and scarlet, and fine *t* linen .... Ex 28:8 7806
and of scarlet, and of fine *t* linen .... Ex 28:15 7806
made ten curtains of fine *t* linen .... Ex 36:8 7806
and scarlet, and fine *t* linen .... Ex 36:35 7806
fine *t* linen, of needlework .... Ex 36:37 7806
of the court were of fine *t* linen .... Ex 38:9 7806
round about were of fine *t* linen .... Ex 38:16 7806
and scarlet, and fine *t* linen .... Ex 38:18 7806
and scarlet, and fine *t* linen .... Ex 39:2 7806
and scarlet, and fine *t* linen .... Ex 39:5 7806
and scarlet, and fine *t* linen .... Ex 39:8 7806
and purple, and scarlet, and *t* linen .... Ex 39:24 7806
and linen breeches of fine *t* linen .... Ex 39:28 7806
And a girdle of fine *t* linen .... Ex 39:29 7806

TWINKLING {1}
in the *t* of an eye, at the last 1Cor 15:52 *4493*

TWINS {6}
behold, there were *t* in her womb .... Gen 25:24 8380
that, behold, *t* were in her womb .... Gen 38:27 8380
whereof every one bear *t*, and none .... Song 4:2 8382
like two young roes that are *t* .... Song 4:5 8380
whereof every one beareth *t* .... Song 6:6 8382
like two young roes that are *t* .... Song 7:3 8380

TWO See APPENDIX.

TWOEDGED {4}
mouth, and a *t* sword in their hand .... Ps 149:6 6374
as wormwood, sharp as a *t* sword .... Prov 5:4 6310
and sharper than any *t* sword .... Heb 4:12 *1366*
of his mouth went a sharp *t* sword .... Rev 1:16 *1366*

TWOFOLD {1}
ye make him *t* more the child of .... Mt 23:15 *1366*

TYCHICUS *(tik'-ik-us)* {7} *A co-worker with Paul.*
and of Asia, *T* and Trophimus .... Acts 20:4 *5190*
know my affairs, and how I do, *T* .... Eph 6:21 *5190*
from Rome unto the Ephesians by *T* .... Eph *s* *5190*
my state shall *T* declare unto you .... Col 4:7 *5190*
from Rome to the Colossians by *T* .... Col *s* *5190*
And *T* have I sent to Ephesus 2Ti 4:12 *5190*
send Artemas unto thee, or *T* .... Titus 3:12 *5190*

TYRANNUS *(ti-ran'-nus)* {1} *An Ephesian schoolmaster.*
daily in the school of one *T* .... Acts 19:9 *5181*

TYRE *(tire)* {37} See TYRUS. *A coastal city of Phoenicia.*
to Ramah, and to the strong city *T* .... Josh 19:29 6865
Hiram king of *T* sent messengers 2Sa 5:11 6865
And came to the strong hold of *T* 2Sa 24:7 6865
Hiram king of *T* sent his servants 1Kin 5:1 6865
sent and fetched Hiram out of *T* 1Kin 7:13 6865
and his father was a man of *T* 1Kin 7:14 6876
(Now Hiram the king of *T* had 1Kin 9:11 6865
Hiram came out from *T* to see the 1Kin 9:12 6865
Now Hiram king of *T* sent 1Chr 14:1 6865
they of *T* brought much cedar wood 1Chr 22:4 6876
sent to Huram the king of *T* 2Chr 2:3 6865
the king of *T* answered in writing 2Chr 2:11 6865
Dan, and his father was a man of *T* 2Chr 2:14 6876
them of Zidon, and to them of *T* .... Ezr 3:7 6876
There dwelt men of *T* also therein .... Neh 13:16 6876
the daughter of *T* shall be there .... Ps 45:12 6865
with the inhabitants of *T* .... Ps 83:7 6865
behold Philistia, and *T*, with .... Ps 87:4 6865
The burden of *T* .... Is 23:1 6865
sorely pained at the report of *T* .... Is 23:5 6865
hath taken this counsel against *T* .... Is 23:8 6865
that *T* shall be forgotten seventy .... Is 23:15 6865
years shall *T* sing as an harlot .... Is 23:15 6865
years, that the LORD will visit *T* .... Is 23:17 6865
what have ye to do with me, O *T* .... Joel 3:4 6865
done in you, had been done in *T* .... Mt 11:21 *5184*
It shall be more tolerable for *T* .... Mt 11:22 *5184*
and departed into the coasts of *T* .... Mt 15:21 *5184*
and they about *T* and Sidon, a great .... Mk 3:8 *5184*
and went into the borders of *T* .... Mk 7:24 *5184*
departing from the coasts of *T* .... Mk 7:31 *5184*
and from the sea coast of *T* .... Lk 6:17 *5184*
mighty works had been done in *T* .... Lk 10:13 *5184*
it shall be more tolerable for *T* .... Lk 10:14 *5184*
highly displeased with them of *T* .... Acts 12:20 *5185*
sailed into Syria, and landed at *T* .... Acts 21:3 *5184*
we had finished our course from *T* .... Acts 21:7 *5184*

TYRIAN See TYRE.

TYRUS *(ti'-rus)* {22} See TYRE. *Same as Tyre.*
And all the kings of *T*, and all the .... Jer 25:22 6865
Ammonites, and to the king of *T* .... Jer 27:3 6865
Philistines, and to cut off from *T* .... Jer 47:4 6865
because that *T* hath said against .... Eze 26:2 6865
Behold, I am against thee, O *T* .... Eze 26:3 6865
they shall destroy the walls of *T* .... Eze 26:4 6865
Behold, I will bring upon *T* .... Eze 26:7 6865
Thus saith the Lord GOD to *T* .... Eze 26:15 6865
man, take up a lamentation for *T* .... Eze 27:2 6865
And say unto *T*, O thou that art .... Eze 27:3 6865
O *T*, thou hast said, I am of .... Eze 27:3 6865
thy wise men, O *T*, that were in .... Eze 27:8 6865
thee, saying, What city is like *T* .... Eze 27:32 6865
of man, say unto the prince of *T* .... Eze 28:2 6865
a lamentation upon the king of *T* .... Eze 28:12 6865
serve a great service against *T* .... Eze 29:18 6865
he no wages, nor his army, for *T* .... Eze 29:18 6865
Ephraim, as I saw *T*, is planted .... Hos 9:13 6865
For three transgressions of *T* .... Amos 1:9 6865
will send a fire on the wall of *T* .... Amos 1:10 6865
T, and Zidon, though it be very .... Zec 9:2 6865
T did build herself a strong hold .... Zec 9:3 6865

U

UCAL *(u'-cal)* {1} *An obscure name.*
Ithiel, even unto Ithiel and *U* .... Prov 30:1 401

UEL *(u'-el)* {1} *Married a foreigner in exile.*
Maadai, Amram, and *U*, ... Ezr 10:34 177

ULAI *(u'-lahee)* {2} *A river near Susa.*
and I was by the river of *U* .... Dan 8:2 195
voice between the banks of *U* .... Dan 8:16 195

ULAM *(u'-lam)* {1}
1. A son of Sheresh.
and his sons were *U* and Rakem 1Chr 7:16 198
And the sons of *U* 1Chr 7:17 198
2. A son of Eshek.
U his firstborn, Jehush the 1Chr 8:39 198
the sons of *U* were mighty men of 1Chr 8:40 198

ULLA *(ul'-la)* {1} *An Asherite chief.*
And the sons of *U* 1Chr 7:39 5925

UMMAH *(um'-mah)* {1} *A city in Asher.*
U also, and Aphek, and Rehob .... Josh 19:30 5981

UNACCUSTOMED {1}
as a bullock *u* to the yoke .... Jer 31:18 3808,3925

UNADVISEDLY {1}
so that he spake *u* with his lips .... Ps 106:33 981

UNAWARES {12}
Jacob stole away *u* to Laban the .... Gen 31:20 3820,3824
thou hast stolen away *u* to me .... Gen 31:26 3820,3824
which killeth any person at *u* .... Num 35:11 7684
any person *u* may flee thither .... Num 35:15 7684
which should kill his neighbour *u* .... Deut 4:42 1097,1847
slayer that killeth any person *u* .... Josh 20:3 7684
person at *u* might flee thither .... Josh 20:9 7684
destruction come upon him at *u* .... Ps 35:8 3045
and so that day come upon you *u* .... Lk 21:34 *160*
of false brethren *u* brought in .... Gal 2:4 *3920*
some have entertained angels *u* .... Heb 13:2 *2990*
there are certain men crept in *u* .... Jude 4 *3921*

UNBELIEF {16}

works there because of their *u*	Mt 13:58	*570*
said unto them, Because of your *u*	Mt 17:20	*570*
he marvelled because of their *u*	Mk 6:6	*570*
help thou mine *u*	Mk 9:24	*570*
and upbraided them with their *u*	Mk 16:14	*570*
shall their *u* make the faith of	Rom 3:3	*570*
at the promise of God through *u*	Rom 4:20	*570*
because of *u* they were broken off	Rom 11:20	*570*
if they abide not still in *u*	Rom 11:23	*570*
obtained mercy through their *u*	Rom 11:30	*543*
God hath concluded them all in *u*	Rom 11:32	*543*
because I did it ignorantly in *u*	1Ti 1:13	*570*
in any of you an evil heart of *u*	Heb 3:12	*570*
could not enter in because of *u*	Heb 3:19	*570*
entered not in because of *u*	Heb 4:6	*543*
fall after the same example of *u*	Heb 4:11	*543*

UNBELIEVERS {4}

him his portion with the *u*	Lk 12:46	*571*
brother, and that before the *u*	1Cor 6:6	*571*
in those that are unlearned, or *u*	1Cor 14:23	*571*
unequally yoked together with *u*	2Cor 6:14	*571*

UNBELIEVING {6}

But the *u* Jews stirred up the	Acts 14:2	*544*
For the *u* husband is sanctified	1Cor 7:14	*571*
the *u* wife is sanctified by the	1Cor 7:14	*571*
But if the *u* depart, let him	1Cor 7:15	*571*
are defiled and *u* is nothing pure	Titus 1:15	*571*
But the fearful, and *u*, and the	Rev 21:8	*571*

UNBLAMEABLE {2}

death, to present you holy and *u*	Col 1:22	*299*
hearts *u* in holiness before God	1Th 3:13	*299*

UNBLAMEABLY {1}

u we behaved ourselves among you	1Th 2:10	*274*

UNCERTAIN {2}

if the trumpet give an *u* sound	1Cor 14:8	*82*
highminded, nor trust in *u* riches	1Ti 6:17	*83*

UNCERTAINLY {1}

I therefore so run, not as *u*	1Cor 9:26	*82*

UNCHANGEABLE {1}

ever, hath an *u* priesthood	Heb 7:24	*531*

UNCIRCUMCISED {43}

the *u* man child whose flesh of	Gen 17:14	6189
give our sister to one that is *u*	Gen 34:14	6189
Pharaoh hear me, who am of *u* lips	Ex 6:12	6189
the LORD, Behold, I am of *u* lips	Ex 6:30	6189
for no *u* person shall eat thereof	Ex 12:48	6189
count the fruit thereof as *u*	Lev 19:23	6189
years shall it be as *u* unto you	Lev 19:23	6189
if then their *u* hearts be humbled	Lev 26:41	6189
for they were *u*, because they had	Josh 5:7	6189
take a wife of the *u* Philistines	Judg 14:3	6189
and fall into the hand of the *u*	Judg 15:18	6189
over unto the garrison of these *u*	1Sa 14:6	6189
for who is this *u* Philistine	1Sa 17:26	6189
this *u* Philistine shall be as one	1Sa 17:36	6189
lest these *u* come and thrust me	1Sa 31:4	6189
the daughters of the *u* triumph	2Sa 1:20	6189
lest these *u* come and abuse me	1Chr 10:4	6189
no more come into thee the *u*	Is 52:1	6189
behold, their ear is *u*, and they	Jer 6:10	6189
which are circumcised with the *u*	Jer 9:25	6190
for all these nations are *u*	Jer 9:26	6189
of Israel are *u* in the heart	Jer 9:26	6189
of the *u* by the hand of strangers	Eze 28:10	6189
shalt lie in the midst of the *u*	Eze 31:18	6189
down, and be thou laid with the *u*	Eze 32:19	6189
they are gone down, they lie *u*	Eze 32:21	6189
which are gone down *u* into the	Eze 32:24	6189
all of them *u*, slain by the sword	Eze 32:25	6189
all of them *u*, slain by the sword	Eze 32:26	6189
mighty that are fallen of the *u*	Eze 32:27	6189
be broken in the midst of the *u*	Eze 32:28	6189
they shall lie with the *u*	Eze 32:29	6189
they lie *u* with them that be	Eze 32:30	6189
be laid in the midst of the *u*	Eze 32:32	6189
u in heart, and *u* in flesh	Eze 44:7	6189
u in heart, nor *u* in flesh	Eze 44:9	6189
u in heart and ears, ye do always	Acts 7:51	*564*
Saying, Thou wentest in to men *u*	Acts 11:3	*203,2192*
faith which he had yet being *u*	Rom 4:11	*1722,3588,203*
which he had being yet *u*	Rom 4:12	*1722,3588,203*
let him not become *u*	1Cor 7:18	*1986*

UNCIRCUMCISION {16}

law, thy circumcision is made *u*	Rom 2:25	*203*
Therefore if the *u* keep the	Rom 2:26	*203*
shall not his *u* be counted for	Rom 2:26	*203*
shall not *u* which is by nature,	Rom 2:27	*203*
by faith, and *u* through faith	Rom 3:30	*203*
only, or upon the *u* also	Rom 4:9	*203*
he was in circumcision, or in *u*	Rom 4:10	*203*
Not in circumcision, but in *u*	Rom 4:10	*203*
Is any called in *u*	1Cor 7:18	*203*
u is nothing, but the keeping of	1Cor 7:19	*203*
of the *u* was committed unto me	Gal 2:7	*203*
availeth any thing, nor *u*	Gal 5:6	*203*
availeth any thing, nor *u*	Gal 6:15	*203*
who are called *U* by that which is	Eph 2:11	*203*
the *u* of your flesh, hath he	Col 2:13	*203*
Greek nor Jew, circumcision nor *u*	Col 3:11	*203*

UNCLE {10}

the sons of Uzziel the *u* of Aaron	Lev 10:4	1730
Either his *u*, or his uncle's son,	Lev 25:49	1730
Saul's *u* said unto him and to his	1Sa 10:14	1730
And Saul's *u* said, Tell me, I pray	1Sa 10:15	1730
And Saul said unto his *u*, He told	1Sa 10:16	1730
Abner, the son of Ner, Saul's *u*	1Sa 14:50	1730
David's *u* was a counsellor	1Chr 27:32	1730
of Abihail the *u* of Mordecai	Est 2:15	1730
thine *u* shall come unto thee	Jer 32:7	1730
a man's *u* shall take him up, and	Amos 6:10	1730

UNCLEAN {194}

Or if a soul touch any *u* thing	Lev 5:2	2931
it be a carcase of an *u* beast	Lev 5:2	2931
or a carcase of *u* cattle	Lev 5:2	2931
the carcase of *u* creeping things	Lev 5:2	2931
he also shall be *u*, and guilty	Lev 5:2	2931
any *u* thing shall not be eaten	Lev 7:19	2931
soul that shall touch any *u* thing	Lev 7:21	2932
of man, or any *u* beast, or any	Lev 7:21	2931
or any abominable *u* thing	Lev 7:21	2931
holy and unholy, and between *u*	Lev 10:10	2931
he is *u* unto you	Lev 11:4	2931
he is *u* unto you	Lev 11:5	2931
he is *u* unto you	Lev 11:6	2931
he is *u* to you	Lev 11:7	2931
they are *u* to you	Lev 11:8	2931
And for these ye shall be *u*	Lev 11:24	2930
of them shall be *u* until the even	Lev 11:24	2930
clothes, and be *u* until the even	Lev 11:25	2930
cheweth the cud, are *u* unto you	Lev 11:26	2931
one that toucheth them shall be *u*	Lev 11:26	2930
on all four, those are *u* unto you	Lev 11:27	2931
carcase shall be *u* until the even	Lev 11:27	2930
clothes, and be *u* until the even	Lev 11:28	2930
they are *u* unto you	Lev 11:28	2931
These also shall be *u* unto you	Lev 11:29	2931
These are *u* to you among all that	Lev 11:31	2931
shall be *u* until the even	Lev 11:31	2930
dead, doth fall, it shall be *u*	Lev 11:32	2930
it shall be *u* until the even	Lev 11:32	2930
whatsoever is in it shall be *u*	Lev 11:33	2930
such water cometh shall be *u*	Lev 11:34	2930
in every such vessel shall be *u*	Lev 11:34	2930
their carcase falleth shall be *u*	Lev 11:35	2930
for they are *u*, and shall be	Lev 11:35	2931
and shall be *u* unto you	Lev 11:35	2931
toucheth their carcase shall be *u*	Lev 11:36	2930
thereon, it shall be *u* unto you	Lev 11:38	2931
thereof shall be *u* until the even	Lev 11:39	2930
clothes, and be *u* until the even	Lev 11:40	2930
clothes, and be *u* until the even	Lev 11:40	2930
ye make yourselves *u* with them	Lev 11:43	2930
make a difference between the *u*	Lev 11:47	2931
then she shall be *u* seven days	Lev 12:2	2930
for her infirmity shall she be *u*	Lev 12:2	2930
then she shall be *u* two weeks	Lev 12:5	2930
look on him, and pronounce him *u*	Lev 13:3	2930
the priest shall pronounce him *u*	Lev 13:8	2930
the priest shall pronounce him *u*	Lev 13:11	2930
for he is *u*	Lev 13:11	2931
appeareth in him, he shall be *u*	Lev 13:14	2930
flesh, and pronounce him to be *u*	Lev 13:15	2930
for the raw flesh is *u*	Lev 13:15	2931
the priest shall pronounce him *u*	Lev 13:20	2930
the priest shall pronounce him *u*	Lev 13:22	2930
the priest shall pronounce him *u*	Lev 13:25	2930
the priest shall pronounce him *u*	Lev 13:27	2930
the priest shall pronounce him *u*	Lev 13:30	2930
he is *u*	Lev 13:36	2931
He is a leprous man, he is *u*	Lev 13:44	2931
shall pronounce him utterly *u*	Lev 13:44	2930
lip, and shall cry, *U*, *u*	Lev 13:45	2931
he is *u*	Lev 13:46	2931
it is *u*	Lev 13:51	2931
it is *u*	Lev 13:55	2931
it clean, or to pronounce it *u*	Lev 13:59	2930
is in the house be not made *u*	Lev 14:36	2930
into an *u* place without the city	Lev 14:40	2931
without the city into an *u* place	Lev 14:41	2931
it is *u*	Lev 14:44	2931
out of the city into an *u* place	Lev 14:45	2931
shut up shall be *u* until the even	Lev 14:46	2930
To teach when it is *u*, and when it	Lev 14:57	2931
because of his issue he is *u*	Lev 15:2	2931
lieth that hath the issue, is *u*	Lev 15:4	2930
whereon he sitteth, shall be *u*	Lev 15:4	2930
in water, and be *u* until the even	Lev 15:5	2930
in water, and be *u* until the even	Lev 15:6	2930
in water, and be *u* until the even	Lev 15:7	2930
in water, and be *u* until the even	Lev 15:8	2930
that hath the issue shall be *u*	Lev 15:9	2930
him shall be *u* until the even	Lev 15:10	2930
in water, and be *u* until the even	Lev 15:10	2930
in water, and be *u* until the even	Lev 15:11	2930
in water, and be *u* until the even	Lev 15:16	2930
water, and be *u* until the even	Lev 15:17	2930
in water, and be *u* until the even	Lev 15:18	2930
her shall be *u* until the even	Lev 15:19	2930
upon in her separation shall be *u*	Lev 15:20	2930
that she sitteth upon shall be *u*	Lev 15:20	2930
in water, and be *u* until the even	Lev 15:21	2930
in water, and be *u* until the even	Lev 15:22	2930
he shall be *u* until the even	Lev 15:23	2930
him, he shall be *u* seven days	Lev 15:24	2930
bed whereon he lieth shall be *u*	Lev 15:24	2930
she shall be *u*	Lev 15:25	2931
she sitteth upon shall be *u*	Lev 15:26	2931
toucheth those things shall be *u*	Lev 15:27	2930
in water, and be *u* until the even	Lev 15:27	2930
him that lieth with her that is *u*	Lev 15:33	2931
in water, and be *u* until the even	Lev 17:15	2930
brother's wife, it is an *u* thing	Lev 20:21	5079
between clean beasts and *u*	Lev 20:25	2931
and between *u* fowls	Lev 20:25	2931
I have separated from you as *u*	Lev 20:25	2930
any thing that is *u* by the dead	Lev 22:4	2931
thing, whereby he may be made *u*	Lev 22:5	2930
any such shall be *u* until even	Lev 22:6	2930
And if it be any *u* beast, of which	Lev 27:11	2931
And if it be of an *u* beast	Lev 27:27	2931
not make himself *u* for his father	Num 6:7	2930
be *u* by reason of a dead body	Num 9:10	2931
the firstling of *u* beasts shalt	Num 18:15	2931
priest shall be *u* until the even	Num 19:7	2930
shall be *u* until the even	Num 19:8	2930
clothes, and be *u* until the even	Num 19:10	2930
of any man shall be *u* seven days	Num 19:11	2930
sprinkled upon him, he shall be *u*	Num 19:13	2931
the tent, shall be *u* seven days	Num 19:14	2930
no covering bound upon it, is *u*	Num 19:15	2931
or a grave, shall be *u* seven days	Num 19:16	2930
for an *u* person they shall take	Num 19:17	2931
upon the *u* on the third day	Num 19:19	2931
But the man that shall be *u*	Num 19:20	2930
he is *u*	Num 19:20	2931
separation shall be *u* until even	Num 19:21	2930
whatsoever the *u* person toucheth	Num 19:22	2931
person toucheth shall be *u*	Num 19:22	2930
toucheth it shall be *u* until even	Num 19:22	2930
the *u* and the clean may eat	Deut 12:15	2931
the *u* and the clean shall eat of	Deut 12:22	2931
therefore they are *u* unto you	Deut 14:7	2931
not the cud, it is *u* unto you	Deut 14:8	2931
it is *u* unto you	Deut 14:10	2931
thing that flieth is *u* unto you	Deut 14:19	2931
the *u* and the clean person shall	Deut 15:22	2931
that he see no *u* thing in thee	Deut 23:14	6172
away ought thereof for any *u* use	Deut 26:14	2931
the land of your possession be *u*	Josh 22:19	2931
drink, and eat not any *u* thing	Judg 13:4	2931
drink, neither eat any *u* thing	Judg 13:7	2932
strong drink, nor eat any *u* thing	Judg 13:14	2932
that none which was *u* in any	2Chr 23:19	2931
is an *u* land with the filthiness	Ezr 9:11	5079
bring a clean thing out of an *u*	Job 14:4	2931
and their life is among the *u*	Job 36:14	6945
good and to the clean, and to the *u*	Eccl 9:2	2931
because I am a man of *u* lips	Is 6:5	2931
the midst of a people of *u* lips	Is 6:5	2931
the *u* shall not pass over it	Is 35:8	2931
thee the uncircumcised and the *u*	Is 52:1	2931
out from thence, touch no *u* thing	Is 52:11	2931
But we are all as an *u* thing	Is 64:6	2931
it is *u*	Lam 4:15	2931
shewed difference between the *u*	Eze 22:26	2931
them to discern between the *u*	Eze 44:23	2931
they shall eat *u* things in	Hos 9:3	2931
If one that is *u* by a dead body	Hag 2:13	2931
touch any of these, shall it be *u*	Hag 2:13	2930
answered and said, It shall be *u*	Hag 2:13	2930
that which they offer there is *u*	Hag 2:14	2931
the *u* spirit to pass out of the	Zec 13:2	2932
gave them power against *u* spirits	Mt 10:1	*169*
When the *u* spirit is gone out of	Mt 12:43	*169*
synagogue a man with an *u* spirit	Mk 1:23	*169*
when the *u* spirit had torn him,	Mk 1:26	*169*
commandeth he even the *u* spirits	Mk 1:27	*169*
u spirits, when they saw him,	Mk 3:11	*169*
they said, He hath an *u* spirit	Mk 3:30	*169*
the tombs a man with an *u* spirit	Mk 5:2	*169*
out of the man, thou *u* spirit	Mk 5:8	*169*
the *u* spirits went out, and	Mk 5:13	*169*
and gave them power over *u* spirits	Mk 6:7	*169*
young daughter had an *u* spirit	Mk 7:25	*169*
which had a spirit of an *u* devil	Lk 4:33	*169*
power he commandeth the *u* spirits	Lk 4:36	*169*
that were vexed with *u* spirits	Lk 6:18	*169*
(For he had commanded the *u*	Lk 8:29	*169*
And Jesus rebuked the *u* spirit	Lk 9:42	*169*
When the *u* spirit is gone out of	Lk 11:24	*169*
which were vexed with *u* spirits	Acts 5:16	*169*
For *u* spirits, crying with loud	Acts 8:7	*169*
any thing that is common or *u*	Acts 10:14	*169*
not call any man common or *u*	Acts 10:28	*169*
for nothing common or *u* hath at	Acts 11:8	*169*
that there is nothing *u* of itself	Rom 14:14	*2839*
that esteemeth any thing to be *u*	Rom 14:14	*2839*
to him it is *u*	Rom 14:14	*2839*
else were your children *u*	1Cor 7:14	*169*
Lord, and touch not the *u* thing	2Cor 6:17	*169*
nor *u* person, nor covetous man,	Eph 5:5	*169*
of an heifer sprinkling the *u*	Heb 9:13	*2840*
I saw three *u* spirits like frogs	Rev 16:13	*169*
foul spirit, and a cage of every *u*	Rev 18:2	*169*

UNCLEANNESS {40}

Or if he touch the *u* of man	Lev 5:3	2932
whatsoever *u* it be that a man	Lev 5:3	2932
the LORD, having his *u* upon him	Lev 7:20	2932
unclean thing, as the *u* of man	Lev 7:21	2932
that is to be cleansed from his *u*	Lev 14:19	2932
this shall be his *u* in his issue	Lev 15:3	2932
from his issue, it is his *u*	Lev 15:3	2932
her *u* shall be as the days of her	Lev 15:25	2932
as the *u* of her separation	Lev 15:26	2932
the LORD for the issue of her *u*	Lev 15:30	2932
children of Israel from their *u*	Lev 15:31	2932
that they die not in their *u*	Lev 15:31	2932

U

because of the *u* of the children Lev 16:16 2932
them in the midst of their *u* Lev 16:16 2932
hallow it from the *u* of the Lev 16:19 2932
as she is put apart for her *u* Lev 18:19 2932
the LORD, having his *u* upon him Lev 22:3 2932
or a man of whom he may take *u* Lev 22:5 2930
whatsoever *u* he hath Lev 22:5 2932
to *u* with another instead of thy Num 5:19 2932
his *u* is yet upon him Num 19:13 2932
of *u* that chanceth him by night Deut 23:10 7137
he hath found some *u* in her Deut 24:1 6172
for she was purified from her *u* 2Sa 11:4 2932
brought out all the *u* that they 2Chr 29:16 2932
one end to another with their *u* Ezr 9:11 2932
me as the *u* of a removed woman Eze 36:17 2932
According to their *u* and according Eze 39:24 2932
of Jerusalem for sin and for *u* Zec 13:1 5079
of dead men's bones, and of all *u* Mt 23:27 *167*
God also gave them up to *u* Rom 1:24 *167*
your members servants to *u* Rom 6:19 *167*
and have not repented of the *u* 2Cor 12:21 *167*
Adultery, fornication, *u*, Gal 5:19 *167*
to work all *u* with greediness Eph 4:19 *167*
But fornication, and all *u* Eph 5:3 *167*
fornication, *u*, inordinate Col 3:5 *167*
was not of deceit, nor of *u* 1Th 2:3 *167*
For God hath not called us unto *u* 1Th 4:7 *167*
after the flesh in the lust of *u* 2Pet 2:10 *3394*

UNCLEANNESSES {1}
also save you from all your *u* Eze 36:29 2932

UNCLE'S {7}
a man shall lie with his *u* wife Lev 20:20 1733
he hath uncovered his *u* nakedness Lev 20:20 1730
Either his uncle, or his *u* son Lev 25:49 1733
that is, Esther, his *u* daughter Est 2:7 1733
So Hanameel mine *u* son came to me Jer 32:8 1733
the field of Hanameel my *u* son Jer 32:9 1733
the sight of Hanameel mine *u* son Jer 32:12 1733

UNCLOTHED {1}
not for that we would be *u* 2Cor 5:4 *1562*

UNCOMELY {2}
himself *u* toward his virgin 1Cor 7:36 *807*
our *u* parts have more abundant 1Cor 12:23 *809*

UNCONDEMNED {2}
They have beaten us openly *u* Acts 16:37 *178*
a man that is a Roman, and *u* Acts 22:25 *178*

UNCORRUPTIBLE {1}
changed the glory of the *u* God Rom 1:23 *862*

UNCORRUPTNESS {1}
in doctrine shewing *u*, gravity, Titus 2:7 *90*

UNCOVER {26}
U not your heads, neither rend Lev 10:6 6544
kin to him, to *u* their nakedness Lev 18:6 1540
of thy mother, shalt thou not *u* Lev 18:7 1540
thou shalt not *u* her nakedness Lev 18:7 1540
father's wife shalt thou not *u* Lev 18:8 1540
their nakedness thou shalt not *u* Lev 18:9 1540
their nakedness thou shalt not *u* Lev 18:10 1540
thou shalt not *u* her nakedness Lev 18:11 1540
Thou shalt not *u* the nakedness of Lev 18:12 1540
Thou shalt not *u* the nakedness of Lev 18:13 1540
Thou shalt not *u* the nakedness of Lev 18:14 1540
Thou shalt not *u* the nakedness of Lev 18:15 1540
thou shalt not *u* her nakedness Lev 18:15 1540
Thou shalt not *u* the nakedness of Lev 18:16 1540
Thou shalt not *u* the nakedness of Lev 18:17 1540
daughter, to *u* her nakedness Lev 18:17 1540
to *u* her nakedness, beside the Lev 18:18 1540
unto a woman to *u* her nakedness Lev 18:19 1540
and shall *u* her nakedness Lev 20:18 1540
thou shalt not *u* the nakedness of Lev 20:19 1540
garments, shall not *u* his head Lev 21:10 6544
u the woman's head, and put the Num 5:18 6544
u his feet, and lay thee down Ruth 3:4 1540
u thy locks, make bare the leg, Is 47:2 1540
u the thigh, pass over the rivers Is 47:2 1540
for he shall *u* the cedar work Zeph 2:14 6168

UNCOVERED {17}
and he was *u* within his tent Gen 9:21 1540
hath *u* his father's nakedness Lev 20:11 1540
he hath *u* his sister's nakedness Lev 20:17 1540
she hath *u* the fountain of her Lev 20:18 1540
he hath *u* his uncle's nakedness Lev 20:20 1540
he hath *u* his brother's nakedness Lev 20:21 1540
u his feet, and laid her down Ruth 3:7 1540
of Israel today, who *u* himself 2Sa 6:20 1540
even with their buttocks *u* Is 20:4 2834
and horsemen, and Kir *u* the shield Is 22:6 6168
Thy nakedness shall be *u*, yea, Is 47:3 1540
I have *u* his secret places, and he Jer 49:10 1540
and thine arm shall be *u*, and thou Eze 4:7 2834
also, and let thy foreskin be *u* Hab 2:16
they *u* the roof where he was Mk 2:4 *648*
her head *u* dishonoureth her head 1Cor 11:5 *177*
that a woman pray unto God *u* 1Cor 11:13 *177*

UNCOVERETH {3}
for he *u* his near kin Lev 20:19 6168
because he *u* his father's skirt Deut 27:20 1540
fellows shamelessly *u* himself 2Sa 6:20 1540

UNCTION {1}
But ye have an *u* from the Holy 1Jn 2:20 *5545*

UNDEFILED {7}
Blessed are the *u* in the way Ps 119:1 8549
my sister, my love, my dove, my *u* Song 5:2 8535
My dove, my *u* is but one Song 6:9 8535
us, who is holy, harmless, *u* Heb 7:26 *283*
honourable in all, and the bed *u* Heb 13:4 *283*
u before God and the Father is Jas 1:27 *283*
inheritance incorruptible, and *u* 1Pet 1:4 *283*

UNDER See APPENDIX.

UNDERGIRDING {1}
up, they used helps, *u* the ship Acts 27:17 *5269*

UNDERNEATH See APPENDIX.

UNDERSETTERS {4}
and the four corners thereof had *u* 1Kin 7:30 3802
under the laver were *u* molten 1Kin 7:30 3802
there were four *u* to the four 1Kin 7:34 3802
the *u* were of the very base 1Kin 7:34 3802

UNDERSTAND {91}
that they may not *u* one another's Gen 11:7 8085
that thou canst *u* a dream to Gen 41:15 8085
then ye shall *u* that these men Num 16:30 3045
U therefore this day, that the Deut 9:3 3045
U therefore, that the LORD thy Deut 9:6 3045
whose tongue thou shalt not *u* Deut 28:49 8085
for we *u* it 2Kin 18:26 8085
the LORD made me *u* in writing by 1Chr 28:19 7919
the women, and those that could *u* Neh 8:3 995
caused the people to *u* the law Neh 8:7 995
and caused them to *u* the reading Neh 8:8 995
even to *u* the words of the law Neh 8:13 7919
cause me to *u* wherein I have Job 6:24 995
u what he would say unto me Job 23:5 995
thunder of his power who can *u* Job 26:14 995
neither do the aged *u* judgment Job 32:9 995
Also can any *u* the spreadings of Job 36:29 995
see if there were any that did *u* Ps 14:2 7919
Who can *u* his errors Ps 19:12 995
see if there were any that did *u* Ps 53:2 7919
know not, neither will they *u* Ps 82:5 995
neither doth a fool *u* this Ps 92:6 995
U, ye brutish among the people Ps 94:8 995
things, even they shall *u* the Ps 107:43 995
Make me to *u* the way of thy Ps 119:27 995
I *u* more than the ancients, Ps 119:100 995
To *u* a proverb, and the Prov 1:6 995
Then shalt thou *u* the fear of the Prov 2:5 995
Then shalt thou *u* righteousness Prov 2:9 995
O ye simple, *u* wisdom Prov 8:5 995
of the prudent is to *u* his way Prov 14:8 995
and he will *u* knowledge Prov 19:25 995
how can a man then *u* his own way Prov 20:24 995
Evil men *u* not judgment Prov 28:5 995
that seek the LORD *u* all things Prov 28:5 995
for though he *u* he will not Prov 29:19 995
people, Hear ye indeed, but *u* not Is 6:9 995
u with their heart, and convert, Is 6:10 995
whom shall he make to *u* doctrine Is 28:9 995
a vexation only to *u* the report Is 28:19 995
of the rash shall *u* knowledge Is 32:4 995
tongue, that thou canst not *u* Is 33:19 998
for we *u* it Is 36:11 8085
u together, that the hand of the Is 41:20 7919
and believe me, and *u* that I am he Is 43:10 995
their hearts, that they cannot *u* Is 44:18 7919
they are shepherds that cannot *u* Is 56:11 995
is the wise man, that may *u* this Jer 9:12 995
whose words thou canst not *u* Eze 3:6 8085
make this man to *u* the vision Dan 8:16 995
but he said unto me, *U*, O son of Dan 8:17 995
our iniquities, and *u* thy truth Dan 9:13 7919
therefore *u* the matter, and Dan 9:23 995
Know therefore and *u*, that from Dan 9:25 7919
u the words that I speak unto Dan 10:11 995
thou didst set thine heart to *u* Dan 10:12 995
Now I am come to make thee *u* what Dan 10:14 995
they that *u* among the people Dan 11:33 7919
and none of the wicked shall *u* Dan 12:10 995
but the wise shall *u* Dan 12:10 995
people that doth not *u* shall fall Hos 4:14 995
wise, and he shall *u* these things Hos 14:9 995
neither *u* they his counsel Mic 4:12 995
they hear not, neither do they *u* Mt 13:13 *4920*
ye shall hear, and shall not *u* Mt 13:14 *4920*
should *u* with their heart, and Mt 13:15 *4920*
and said unto them, Hear, and *u* Mt 15:10 *4920*
Do not ye yet *u*, that whatsoever Mt 15:17 *3539*
Do ye not yet *u*, neither remember Mt 16:9 *3539*
How is it that ye do not *u* that I Mt 16:11 *3539*
place, (whoso readeth, let him *u* Mt 24:15 *3539*
hearing they may hear, and not *u* Mk 4:12 *4920*
unto me every one of you, and *u* Mk 7:14 *4920*
perceive ye not yet, neither *u* Mk 8:17 *4920*
them, How is it that ye do not *u* Mk 8:21 *4920*
not, (let him that readeth *u* Mk 13:14 *3539*
neither *u* I what thou sayest Mk 14:68 *1987*
see, and hearing they might not *u* Lk 8:10 *4920*
that they might *u* the scriptures Lk 24:45 *4920*
Why do ye not *u* my speech Jn 8:43 *1097*
nor *u* with their heart, and be Jn 12:40 *3539*
Because that thou mayest *u* Acts 24:11 *1097*
ye shall hear, and shall not *u* Acts 28:26 *4920*
u with their heart, and should be Acts 28:27 *4920*
they that have not heard shall *u* Rom 15:21 *4920*
Wherefore I give you to *u* 1Cor 12:3 *1107*
u all mysteries, and all knowledge 1Cor 13:2 *1492*
ye may *u* my knowledge in the Eph 3:4 *3539*
But I would ye should *u*, brethren Phil 1:12 *1097*
Through faith we *u* that the Heb 11:3 *3539*
of the things that they *u* not 2Pet 2:12 *50*

UNDERSTANDEST {4}
what *u* thou, which is not in us Job 15:9 995
thou *u* my thought afar off Ps 139:2 995
not, neither *u* what they say Jer 5:15 8085
and said, *U* thou what thou readest Acts 8:30 *1097*

UNDERSTANDETH {11}
u all the imaginations of the 1Chr 28:9 995
God *u* the way thereof, and he Job 28:23 995
u not, is like the beasts that Ps 49:20 995
They are all plain to him that *u* Prov 8:9 995
knowledge is easy unto him that *u* Prov 14:6 995
glorieth glory in this, that he *u* Jer 9:24 7919
u it not, then cometh the wicked Mt 13:19 *4920*
he that heareth the word, and *u* it Mt 13:23 *4920*
There is none that *u*, there is Rom 3:11 *4920*
for no man *u* him 1Cor 14:2 *191*
seeing he *u* not what thou sayest 1Cor 14:16 *1492*

UNDERSTANDING {160}
spirit of God, in wisdom, and in *u* Ex 31:3 8394
spirit of God, in wisdom, in *u* Ex 35:31 8394
u to know how to work all manner Ex 36:1 8394
Take you wise men, and *u*, and known Deut 1:13 995
your *u* in the sight of the Deut 4:6 998
nation is a wise and *u* people Deut 4:6 995
neither is there any *u* in them Deut 32:28 8394
and she was a woman of good *u* 1Sa 25:3 7922
an *u* heart to judge thy people 1Kin 3:9 8085
for thyself *u* to discern judgment 1Kin 3:11 995
given thee a wise and an *u* heart 1Kin 3:12 995
u exceeding much, and largeness of 1Kin 4:29 8394
he was filled with wisdom, and *u* 1Kin 7:14 8394
were men that had *u* of the times 1Chr 12:32 998
the LORD give thee wisdom and *u* 1Chr 22:12 998
son, endued with prudence and *u* 2Chr 2:12 998
sent a cunning man, endued with *u* 2Chr 2:13 998
who had *u* in the visions of God 2Chr 26:5 995
and for Elnathan, men of *u* Ezr 8:16 995
us they brought us a man of *u* Ezr 8:18 7922
and all that could hear with *u* Neh 8:2 995
one having knowledge, and having *u* Neh 10:28 995
But I have *u* as well as you Job 12:3 3824
and in length of days *u* Job 12:12 8394
and strength, he hath counsel and *u* Job 12:13 8394
and taketh away the *u* of the aged Job 12:20 2940
thou hast hid their heart from *u* Job 17:4 7922
the spirit of my *u* causeth me to Job 20:3 998
by his *u* he smiteth through the Job 26:12 8394
and where is the place of *u* Job 28:12 998
and where is the place of *u* Job 28:20 998
and to depart from evil is *u* Job 28:28 998
of the Almighty giveth them *u* Job 32:8 995
hearken unto me, ye men of *u* Job 34:10 3824
If now thou hast *u*, hear this Job 34:16 998
Let men of *u* tell me, and let a Job 34:34 3824
declare, if thou hast *u* Job 38:4 998
or who hath given *u* to the heart Job 38:36 998
neither hath he imparted to her *u* Job 39:17 998
or as the mule, which have no *u* Ps 32:9 995
sing ye praises with *u* Ps 47:7 7919
of my heart shall be of *u* Ps 49:3 8394
a good *u* have all they that do Ps 111:10 7922
Give me *u*, and I shall keep thy Ps 119:34 995
give me *u*, that I may learn thy Ps 119:73 995
I have more *u* than all my Ps 119:99 7919
Through thy precepts I get *u* Ps 119:104 995
give me *u*, that I may know thy Ps 119:125 995
it giveth *u* unto the simple Ps 119:130 995
give me *u*, and I shall live Ps 119:144 995
give me *u* according to thy word Ps 119:169 995
his *u* is infinite Ps 147:5 8394
to perceive the words of *u* Prov 1:2 998
a man of *u* shall attain unto wise Prov 1:5 995
wisdom, and apply thine heart to *u* Prov 2:2 8394
and liftest up thy voice for *u* Prov 2:3 8394
his mouth cometh knowledge and *u* Prov 2:6 8394
preserve thee, *u* shall keep thee Prov 2:11 8394
good *u* in the sight of God and man Prov 3:4 7922
and lean not unto thine own *u* Prov 3:5 998
wisdom, and the man that getteth *u* Prov 3:13 8394
by *u* hath he established the Prov 3:19 8394
of a father, and attend to know *u* Prov 4:1 998
Get wisdom, get *u* Prov 4:5 998
and with all thy getting get *u* Prov 4:7 998
wisdom, and bow thine ear to my *u* Prov 5:1 8394
adultery with a woman lacketh *u* Prov 6:32 3820
and call *u* thy kinswoman Prov 7:4 998
the youths, a young man void of *u* Prov 7:7 3820
and *u* put forth her voice Prov 8:1 8394
and, ye fools, be ye of an *u* heart Prov 8:5 995
I am *u* Prov 8:14 998
as for him that wanteth *u* Prov 9:4 3820
and go in the way of *u* Prov 9:6 998
and the knowledge of the holy is *u* Prov 9:10 998
and as for him that wanteth *u* Prov 9:16 3820
him that hath *u* wisdom is found Prov 10:13 995
the back of him that is void of *u* Prov 10:13 3820
but a man of *u* hath wisdom Prov 10:23 8394
but a man of *u* holdeth his peace Prov 11:12 8394
vain persons is void of *u* Prov 12:11 3820
Good *u* giveth favour Prov 13:15 7922
is slow to wrath is of great *u* Prov 14:29 8394
in the heart of him that hath *u* Prov 14:33 995
him that hath *u* seeketh knowledge Prov 15:14 995
but a man of *u* walketh uprightly Prov 15:21 8394
he that heareth reproof getteth *u* Prov 15:32 3820
to get *u* rather to be chosen than Prov 16:16 998
U is a wellspring of life unto Prov 16:22 7922

A man void of *u* striketh hands, Prov 17:18 3820
Wisdom is before him that hath *u* Prov 17:24 995
a man of *u* is of an excellent Prov 17:27 8394
his lips is esteemed a man of *u* Prov 17:28 995
A fool hath no delight in *u* Prov 18:2 8394
he that keepeth *u* shall find good Prov 19:8 8394
and reprove one that hath *u* Prov 19:25 995
but a man of *u* will draw it out Prov 20:5 8394
the way of *u* shall remain in the Prov 21:16 7919
There is no wisdom nor *u* nor Prov 21:30 8394
also wisdom, and instruction, and *u* Prov 23:23 998
and by *u* it is established Prov 24:3 8394
the vineyard of the man void of *u* Prov 24:30 3820
but by a man of *u* and knowledge Prov 28:2 995
that hath *u* searcheth him out Prov 28:11 995
The prince that wanteth *u* is also Prov 28:16 8394
man, and have not the *u* of a man Prov 30:2 998
wise, nor yet riches to men of *u* Eccl 9:11 995
him, the spirit of wisdom and *u* Is 11:2 998
quick *u* in the fear of the LORD Is 11:3 7306
for it is a people of no *u* Is 27:11 998
the *u* of their prudent men shall Is 29:14 998
him that framed it, He had no *u* Is 29:16 995
erred in spirit shall come to *u* Is 29:24 998
and shewed to him the way of *u* Is 40:14 8394
there is no searching of his *u* Is 40:28 8394
is there knowledge nor *u* to say Is 44:19 8394
feed you with knowledge and *u* Jer 3:15 7919
children, and they have none *u* Jer 4:22 995
O foolish people, and without *u* Jer 5:21 3820
stretched out the heaven by his *u* Jer 51:15 8394
with thine *u* thou hast gotten Eze 28:4 8394
u science, and such as had ability Dan 1:4 995
Daniel had *u* in all visions and Dan 1:17 995
And in all matters of wisdom and *u* Dan 1:20 998
and knowledge to them that know *u* Dan 2:21 999
mine *u* returned unto me, and I Dan 4:34 4486
the days of thy father light and *u* Dan 5:11 7924
spirit, and knowledge, and *u* Dan 5:12 7924
is in thee, and that light and *u* Dan 5:14 7924
u dark sentences, shall stand up Dan 8:23 995
forth to give thee skill and *u* Dan 9:22 998
the thing, and had *u* of the vision Dan 10:1 998
And some of them of *u* shall fall Dan 11:35 7919
and idols according to their own *u* Hos 13:2 8394
there is none *u* in him Obad 7 8394
u out of the mount of Esau Obad 8 8394
said, Are ye also yet without *u* Mt 15:16 *801*
them, Are ye so without *u* also Mk 7:18 *801*
all the heart, and with all the *u* Mk 12:33 *4907*
having had perfect *u* of all Lk 1:3 *3877*
him were astonished at his *u* Lk 2:47 *4907*
Then opened he their *u*, that they Lk 24:45 *3563*
Without *u*, covenantbreakers, Rom 1:31 *801*
to nothing the *u* of the prudent 1Cor 1:19 *4907*
prayeth, but my *u* is unfruitful 1Cor 14:14 *3563*
and I will pray with the *u* also 1Cor 14:15 *3563*
and I will sing with the *u* also 1Cor 14:15 *3563*
rather speak five words with my *u* 1Cor 14:19 *3563*
Brethren, be not children in *u* 1Cor 14:20 *5424*
be ye children, but in *u* be men 1Cor 14:20 *5424*
The eyes of your *u* being Eph 1:18 *1271*
Having the *u* darkened, being Eph 4:18 *1271*
but *u* what the will of the Lord Eph 5:17 *4920*
peace of God, which passeth all *u* Phil 4:7 *3563*
will in all wisdom and spiritual *u* Col 1:9 *4907*
riches of the full assurance of *u* Col 2:2 *4907*
u neither what they say, nor 1Ti 1:7 *4920*
Lord give thee *u* in all things 2Ti 2:7 *4907*
is come, and hath given us an *u* 1Jn 5:20 *1271*
Let him that hath *u* count the Rev 13:18 *3563*

UNDERSTOOD {37}
they knew not that Joseph *u* them Gen 42:23 8085
they were wise, that they *u* this Deut 32:29 7919
they *u* that the ark of the LORD 1Sa 4:6 3045
u that Saul was come in very deed 1Sa 26:4 3045
all Israel *u* that day that it was 2Sa 3:37 3045
because they had *u* the words that Neh 8:12 995
u of the evil that Eliashib did Neh 13:7 995
this, mine ear hath heard and *u* it Job 13:1 995
have I uttered that I *u* not Job 42:3 995
then *u* I their end Ps 73:17 995
I heard a language that I *u* not Ps 81:5 3045
Our fathers *u* not thy wonders in Ps 106:7 7919
have ye not *u* from the Is 40:21 995
They have not known nor *u* Is 44:18 995
at the vision, but none *u* it Dan 8:27 995
u by books the number of the Dan 9:2 995
and he *u* the thing, and had Dan 10:1 995
And I heard, but I *u* not Dan 12:8 995
Have ye *u* all these things Mt 13:51 *4920*
Then *u* they how that he bade them Mt 16:12 *4920*
Then the disciples *u* that he Mt 17:13 *4920*
When Jesus *u* it, he said unto Mt 26:10 *1097*
But they *u* not that saying, and Mk 9:32 *50*
they *u* not the saying which he Lk 2:50 *4920*
But they *u* not this saying, and it Lk 9:45 *50*
they *u* none of these things Lk 18:34 *4920*
They *u* not that he spake to them Jn 8:27 *1097*
but they *u* not what things they Jn 10:6 *1097*
These things *u* not his disciples Jn 12:16 *1097*
his brethren would have *u* how Acts 7:25 *4920*
but they *u* not Acts 7:25 *4920*
having *u* that he was a Roman Acts 23:27 *3129*
when he *u* that he was of Cilicia Acts 23:34 *4441*
being *u* by the things that are Rom 1:20 *3539*
I *u* as a child, I thought as a 1Cor 13:11 *5426*
by the tongue words easy to be *u* 1Cor 14:9 *2154*
are some things hard to be *u* 2Pet 3:16 *1425*

UNDERTAKE {1}
oppressed; *u* for me Is 38:14 6148

UNDERTOOK {1}
the Jews *u* to do as they had Est 9:23 6901

UNDO {2}
to *u* the heavy burdens, and to let Is 58:6 5425
at that time I will *u* all that Zeph 3:19 6213

UNDONE {5}
thou art *u*, O people of Chemosh Num 21:29 6
he left nothing *u* of all that the Josh 11:15 5493
for I am *u* Is 6:5 1820
done, and not to leave the other *u* Mt 23:23
done, and not to leave the other *u* Lk 11:42

UNDRESSED {2}
gather the grapes of thy vine *u* Lev 25:5 5139
the grapes in it of thy vine *u* Lev 25:11 5139

UNEQUAL {2}
are not your ways *u* Eze 18:25 3808,8505
are not your ways *u* Eze 18:29 3808,8505

UNEQUALLY {1}
Be ye not *u* yoked together with 2Cor 6:14 *2086*

UNFAITHFUL {1}
Confidence in an *u* man in time of Prov 25:19 898

UNFAITHFULLY {1}
dealt *u* like their fathers Ps 78:57 898

UNFEIGNED {4}
by the Holy Ghost, by love *u* 2Cor 6:6 *505*
a good conscience, and of faith *u* 1Ti 1:5 *505*
the *u* faith that is in thee 2Ti 1:5 *505*
unto *u* love of the brethren 1Pet 1:22 *505*

UNFRUITFUL {6}
choke the word, and he becometh *u* Mt 13:22 *175*
choke the word, and it becometh *u* Mk 4:19 *175*
but my understanding is *u* 1Cor 14:14 *175*
with the *u* works of darkness Eph 5:11 *175*
uses, that they be not *u* Titus 3:14 *175*
u in the knowledge of our Lord 2Pet 1:8 *175*

UNGIRDED {1}
he *u* his camels, and gave straw and Gen 24:32 6605

UNGODLINESS {4}
from heaven against all *u* Rom 1:18 *763*
and shall turn away *u* from Jacob Rom 11:26 *763*
they will increase unto more *u* 2Ti 2:16 *763*
Teaching us that, denying *u* Titus 2:12 *763*

UNGODLY {27}
the floods of *u* men made me 2Sa 22:5 1100
Shouldest thou help the *u* 2Chr 19:2 7563
God hath delivered me to the *u* Job 16:11 5760
and to princes, Ye are *u* Job 34:18 7563
not in the counsel of the *u* Ps 1:1 7563
The *u* are not so Ps 1:4 7563
Therefore the *u* shall not stand Ps 1:5 7563
but the way of the *u* shall perish Ps 1:6 7563
hast broken the teeth of the *u* Ps 3:7 7563
the floods of *u* men made me Ps 18:4 1100
my cause against an *u* nation Ps 43:1 3808,2623
Behold, these are the *u*, who Ps 73:12 7563
An *u* man diggeth up evil Prov 16:27 1100
An *u* witness scorneth judgment Prov 19:28 1100
on him that justifieth the *u* Rom 4:5 *765*
in due time Christ died for the *u* Rom 5:6 *765*
lawless and disobedient, for the *u* 1Ti 1:9 *765*
be saved, where shall the *u* 1Pet 4:18 *765*
the flood upon the world of the *u* 2Pet 2:5 *765*
those that after should live *u* 2Pet 2:6 *764*
of judgment and perdition of *u* men 2Pet 3:7 *765*
u men, turning the grace of our Jude 4 *765*
to convince all that are *u* among Jude 15 *763*
u deeds which they have Jude 15 *763*
deeds which they have *u* committed Jude 15 *764*
all their hard speeches which *u* Jude 15 *765*
walk after their own *u* lusts Jude 18 *763*

UNHOLY {4}
put difference between holy and *u* Lev 10:10 2455
the ungodly and for sinners, for *u* 1Ti 1:9 *462*
to parents, unthankful, *u* 2Ti 3:2 *462*
an *u* thing, and hath done despite Heb 10:29 *2839*

UNICORN {6}
as it were the strength of a *u* Num 23:22 7214
as it were the strength of a *u* Num 24:8 7214
Will the *u* be willing to serve Job 39:9 7214
Canst thou bind the *u* with his Job 39:10 7214
Lebanon and Sirion like a young *u* Ps 29:6 7214
thou exalt like the horn of an *u* Ps 92:10 7214

UNICORNS {3}
his horns are like the horns of *u* Deut 33:17 7214
heard me from the horns of the *u* Ps 22:21 7214
the *u* shall come down with them, Is 34:7 7214

UNITE {1}
u my heart to fear thy name Ps 86:11 3161

UNITED {1}
mine honour, be not thou *u* Gen 49:6 3161

UNITY {3}
brethren to dwell together in *u* Ps 133:1 3162
Endeavouring to keep the *u* of the Eph 4:3 *1775*
we all come in the *u* of the faith Eph 4:13 *1775*

UNJUST {17}
me from the deceitful and *u* man Ps 43:1 5766
the hope of *u* men perisheth Prov 11:7 205
u gain increaseth his substance, Prov 28:8 8636
An *u* man is an abomination to the Prov 29:27 5766
but the *u* knoweth no shame Zeph 3:5 5767
rain on the just and on the *u* Mt 5:45 *94*
the lord commended the *u* steward Lk 16:8 *93*
he that is *u* in the least is Lk 16:10 *94*
in the least is *u* also in much Lk 16:10 *94*
said, Hear what the *u* judge saith Lk 18:6 *93*
as other men are, extortioners, *u* Lk 18:11 *94*
the dead, both of the just and *u* Acts 24:15 *94*
another, go to law before the *u* 1Cor 6:1 *94*
for sins, the just for the *u* 1Pet 3:18 *94*
to reserve the *u* unto the day of 2Pet 2:9 *94*
He that is *u*, let him be *u* Rev 22:11 *91*

UNJUSTLY {2}
How long will ye judge *u*, and Ps 82:2 5766
of uprightness will he deal *u* Is 26:10 5765

UNKNOWN {9}
this inscription, TO THE *U* GOD Acts 17:23 *57*
For he that speaketh in an *u* 1Cor 14:2
He that speaketh in an *u* tongue 1Cor 14:4
in an *u* tongue pray that he may 1Cor 14:13
For if I pray in an *u* tongue 1Cor 14:14
ten thousand words in an *u* tongue 1Cor 14:19
If any man speak in an *u* tongue 1Cor 14:27
As *u*, and yet well known 2Cor 6:9 *50*
was *u* by face unto the churches Gal 1:22 *50*

UNLADE {1}
the ship was to *u* her burden Acts 21:3 *670*

UNLAWFUL {2}
Ye know how that it is an *u* thing Acts 10:28 *111*
day to day with their *u* deeds 2Pet 2:8 *459*

UNLEARNED {6}
and perceived that they were *u* Acts 4:13 *62*
the *u* say Amen at thy giving of 1Cor 14:16 *2399*
and there come in those that are *u* 1Cor 14:23 *2399*
one that believeth not, or one *u* 1Cor 14:24 *2399*
u questions avoid, knowing that 2Ti 2:23 *521*
understood, which they that are *u* 2Pet 3:16 *261*

UNLEAVENED {61}
them a feast, and did bake *u* bread Gen 19:3 4682
roast with fire, and *u* bread Ex 12:8 4682
Seven days shall ye eat *u* bread Ex 12:15 4682
observe the feast of *u* bread Ex 12:17 4682
at even, ye shall eat *u* bread Ex 12:18 4682
habitations shall ye eat *u* bread Ex 12:20 4682
they baked *u* cakes of the dough Ex 12:39 4682
Seven days thou shalt eat *u* bread Ex 13:6 4682
U bread shall be eaten seven days Ex 13:7 4682
shalt keep the feast of *u* bread Ex 23:15 4682
(thou shalt eat *u* bread seven Ex 23:15 4682
u bread, and cakes *u* Ex 29:2 4682
wafers *u* anointed with oil Ex 29:2 4682
u bread that is before the LORD Ex 29:23 4682
The feast of *u* bread shalt thou Ex 34:18 4682
Seven days thou shalt eat *u* bread Ex 34:18 4682
it shall be *u* cakes of fine flour Lev 2:4 4682
or *u* wafers anointed with oil Lev 2:4 4682
pan, it shall be of fine flour *u* Lev 2:5 4682
with *u* bread shall it be eaten in Lev 6:16 4682
u cakes mingled with oil, and Lev 7:12 4682
u wafers anointed with oil, and Lev 7:12 4682
two rams, and a basket of *u* bread Lev 8:2 4682
And out of the basket of *u* bread Lev 8:26 4682
the LORD, he took one *u* cake Lev 8:26 4682
feast of *u* bread unto the LORD Lev 23:6 4682
seven days ye must eat *u* bread Lev 23:6 4682
And a basket of *u* bread, cakes of Num 6:15 4682
wafers of *u* bread anointed with Num 6:15 4682
LORD, with the basket of *u* bread Num 6:17 4682
one *u* cake out of the basket, and Num 6:19 4682
one *u* wafer, and shall put them Num 6:19 4682
keep it, and eat it with *u* bread Num 9:11 4682
seven days shall *u* bread be eaten Num 28:17 4682
shalt thou eat *u* bread therewith Deut 16:3 4682
Six days thou shalt eat *u* bread Deut 16:8 4682
in the feast of *u* bread, and in Deut 16:16 4682
u cakes, and parched corn in the Josh 5:11 4682
u cakes of an ephah of flour Judg 6:19 4682
the *u* cakes, and lay them upon Judg 6:20 4682
touched the flesh and the *u* cakes Judg 6:21 4682
consumed the flesh and the *u* cakes Judg 6:21 4682
it, and did bake *u* bread thereof 1Sa 28:24 4682
but they did eat of the *u* bread 2Kin 23:9 4682
meat offering, and for the *u* cakes 1Chr 23:29 4682
even in the feast of *u* bread 2Chr 8:13 4682
of *u* bread in the second month 2Chr 30:13 4682
of *u* bread seven days with great 2Chr 30:21 4682
the feast of *u* bread seven days 2Chr 35:17 4682
kept the feast of *u* bread seven Ezr 6:22 4682
u bread shall be eaten Eze 45:21 4682
of *u* bread the disciples came to Mt 26:17 *106*
of the passover, and of *u* bread Mk 14:1 *106*
And the first day of *u* bread Mk 14:12 *106*
the feast of *u* bread drew nigh Lk 22:1 *106*
Then came the day of *u* bread Lk 22:7 *106*
(Then were the days of *u* bread Acts 12:3 *106*
after the days of *u* bread Acts 20:6 *106*
ye may be a new lump, as ye are *u* 1Cor 5:7 *106*
but with the *u* bread of sincerity 1Cor 5:8 *106*

UNLESS See APPENDIX.

UNLOOSE {3}
am not worthy to stoop down and *u* Mk 1:7 *3089*
whose shoes I am not worthy to *u* Lk 3:16 *3089*
latchet I am not worthy to *u* Jn 1:27 *3089*

UNMARRIED {4}
I say therefore to the *u* and 1Cor 7:8 *22*
if she depart, let her remain *u* 1Cor 7:11 *22*
He that is *u* careth for the 1Cor 7:32 *22*
The *u* woman careth for the things 1Cor 7:34 *22*

UNMERCIFUL {1}
natural affection, implacable, *u* ...... Rom 1:31 *415*

UNMINDFUL {1}
Rock that begat thee thou art *u* ...... Deut 32:18 7876

UNMOVABLE {1}
brethren, be ye stedfast, *u* 1Cor 15:58 *277*

UNMOVEABLE {1}
stuck fast, and remained *u* ...... Acts 27:41 *761*

UNNI *(un'-nee)* {3} *A Levite.*
and Shemiramoth, and Jehiel, and *U* 1Chr 15:18 6042
and Shemiramoth, and Jehiel, and *U* 1Chr 15:20 6042
Also Bakbukiah and *U*, their ...... Neh 12:9 6042

UNOCCUPIED {1}
days of Jael, the highways were *u* ...... Judg 5:6 2308

UNPERFECT {1}
did see my substance, yet being *u* ...... Ps 139:16

UNPREPARED {1}
come with me, and find you *u* 2Cor 9:4 *532*

UNPROFITABLE {7}
Should he reason with *u* talk ...... Job 15:3 5532
cast ye the *u* servant into outer ...... Mt 25:30 *888*
you, say, We are *u* servants ...... Lk 17:10 *888*
way, they are together become *u* ...... Rom 3:12 *889*
for they are *u* and vain ...... Titus 3:9 *512*
Which in time past was to thee *u* ...... Philem 11 *890*
for that is *u* for you ...... Heb 13:17 *255*

UNPROFITABLENESS {1}
for the weakness and *u* thereof ...... Heb 7:18 *512*

UNPUNISHED {11}
hand, the wicked shall not be *u* ...... Prov 11:21 5352
join in hand, he shall not be *u* ...... Prov 16:5 5352
glad at calamities shall not be *u* ...... Prov 17:5 5352
A false witness shall not be *u* ...... Prov 19:5 5352
A false witness shall not be *u* ...... Prov 19:9 5352
name, and should ye be utterly *u* ...... Jer 25:29 5352
Ye shall not be *u* ...... Jer 25:29 5352
will not leave thee altogether *u* ...... Jer 30:11 5352
will I not leave thee wholly *u* ...... Jer 46:28 5352
he that shall altogether go *u* ...... Jer 49:12 5352
thou shalt not go *u*, but thou ...... Jer 49:12 5352

UNQUENCHABLE {2}
burn up the chaff with *u* fire ...... Mt 3:12 *762*
chaff he will burn with fire *u* ...... Lk 3:17 *762*

UNREASONABLE {2}
to me *u* to send a prisoner ...... Acts 25:27 *249*
that we may be delivered from *u* 2Th 3:2 *824*

UNREBUKEABLE {1}
this commandment without spot, *u* 1Ti 6:14 *423*

UNREPROVEABLE {1}
and unblameable and *u* in his sight ...... Col 1:22 *410*

UNRIGHTEOUS {9}
the wicked to be an *u* witness ...... Ex 23:1 2555
riseth up against me as the *u* ...... Job 27:7 5767
wicked, out of the hand of the *u* ...... Ps 71:4 5765
unto them that decree *u* decrees ...... Is 10:1 205
way, and the *u* man his thoughts ...... Is 55:7 205
not been faithful in the *u* mammon ...... Lk 16:11 *94*
Is God *u* who taketh vengeance ...... Rom 3:5 *94*
Know ye not that the *u* shall not 1Cor 6:9 *94*
For God is not *u* to forget your ...... Heb 6:10 *94*

UNRIGHTEOUSLY {1}
do such things, and all that do *u* ...... Deut 25:16 5766

UNRIGHTEOUSNESS {21}
Ye shall do no *u* in judgment ...... Lev 19:15 5766
Ye shall do no *u* in judgment ...... Lev 19:35 5766
my rock, and there is no *u* in him ...... Ps 92:15 5766
him that buildeth his house by *u* .... Jer 22:13 3808,6664
friends of the mammon of *u* ...... Lk 16:9 *93*
same is true, and no *u* is in him ...... Jn 7:18 *93*
u of men, who hold the truth in ...... Rom 1:18 *93*
of men, who hold the truth in *u* ...... Rom 1:18 *93*
Being filled with all *u*, ... Rom 1:29 *93*
do not obey the truth, but obey *u* ...... Rom 2:8 *93*
But if our *u* commend the ...... Rom 3:5 *93*
as instruments of *u* unto sin ...... Rom 6:13 *93*
Is there *u* with God ...... Rom 9:14 *93*
hath righteousness with *u* 2Cor 6:14 *458*
of *u* in them that perish 2Th 2:10 *93*
the truth, but had pleasure in *u* 2Th 2:12 *93*
For I will be merciful to their *u* ...... Heb 8:12 *93*
And shall receive the reward of *u* 2Pet 2:13 *93*
Bosor, who loved the wages of *u* 2Pet 2:15 *93*
sins, and to cleanse us from all *u* 1Jn 1:9 *93*
All *u* is sin 1Jn 5:17 *93*

UNRIPE {1}
shake off his *u* grape as the vine ...... Job 15:33 1154

UNRULY {4}
brethren, warn them that are *u* 1Th 5:14 *813*
children not accused of riot or *u* ...... Titus 1:6 *506*
For there are many *u* and vain ...... Titus 1:10 *506*
it is an *u* evil, full of deadly ...... Jas 3:8 *183*

UNSATIABLE {1}
Assyrians, because thou wast *u* ...... Eze 16:28 1115,7654

UNSAVOURY {2}
froward thou wilt shew thyself *u* 2Sa 22:27 6617
Can that which is *u* be eaten ...... Job 6:6 8602

UNSEARCHABLE {5}
Which doeth great things and *u* ...... Job 5:9 369,2714
and his greatness is *u* ...... Ps 145:3 369,2714
depth, and the heart of kings is *u* ... Prov 25:3 369,2714
how *u* are his judgments, and his ...... Rom 11:33 *419*
Gentiles the *u* riches of Christ ...... Eph 3:8 *421*

UNSEEMLY {2}
with men working that which is *u* ...... Rom 1:27 *808*
Doth not behave itself *u*, seeketh 1Cor 13:5

UNSHOD {1}
Withhold thy foot from being *u* ...... Jer 2:25 *3182*

UNSKILFUL {1}
is *u* in the word of righteousness ...... Heb 5:13 *552*

UNSPEAKABLE {3}
Thanks be unto God for his *u* gift 2Cor 9:15 *411*
into paradise, and heard *u* words 2Cor 12:4 *731*
believing, ye rejoice with joy *u* 1Pet 1:8 *412*

UNSPOTTED {1}
to keep himself *u* from the world ...... Jas 1:27 *784*

UNSTABLE {4}
U as water, thou shalt not excel ...... Gen 49:4 6349
minded man is *u* in all his ways ...... Jas 1:8 *182*
beguiling *u* souls 2Pet 2:14 *793*
u wrest, as they do also the 2Pet 3:16 *793*

UNSTOPPED {1}
the ears of the deaf shall be *u* ...... Is 35:5 6605

UNTAKEN {1}
day remaineth the same vail *u* 2Cor 3:14 *3361,348*

UNTEMPERED {5}
others daubed it with *u* morter ...... Eze 13:10 8602
them which daub it with *u* morter ...... Eze 13:11 8602
that ye have daubed with *u* morter ...... Eze 13:14 8602
that have daubed it with *u* morter ...... Eze 13:15 8602
have daubed them with *u* morter ...... Eze 22:28 8602

UNTHANKFUL {2}
for he is kind unto the *u* ...... Lk 6:35 *884*
disobedient to parents, *u* 2Ti 3:2 *884*

UNTIL See APPENDIX.

UNTIMELY {4}
Or as an hidden *u* birth I had not ...... Job 3:16 5309
like the *u* birth of a woman, that ...... Ps 58:8 5309
that an *u* birth is better than he ...... Eccl 6:3 5309
as a fig tree casteth her *u* figs ...... Rev 6:13 *3653*

UNTO See APPENDIX.

UNTOWARD {1}
yourselves from this *u* generation ...... Acts 2:40 *4646*

UNWALLED {3}
beside *u* towns a great many ...... Deut 3:5 6521
that dwelt in the *u* towns ...... Est 9:19 6519
go up to the land of *u* villages ...... Eze 38:11

UNWASHEN {3}
but to eat with *u* hands defileth ...... Mt 15:20 *449*
defiled, that is to say, with *u* ...... Mk 7:2 *449*
but eat bread with *u* hands ...... Mk 7:5 *449*

UNWEIGHED {1}
And Solomon left all the vessels *u* 1Kin 7:47

UNWISE {4}
the LORD, O foolish people and *u* ... Deut 32:6 3808,2450
he is an *u* son ...... Hos 13:13 3808,2450
both to the wise, and to the *u* ...... Rom 1:14 *453*
Wherefore be ye not *u*, but ...... Eph 5:17 *878*

UNWITTINGLY {3}
if a man eat of the holy thing *u* ...... Lev 22:14 7684
unawares and *u* may flee thither ..... Josh 20:3 1097,1847
because he smote his neighbour *u* ... Josh 20:5 1097,1847

UNWORTHILY {2}
and drink this cup of the Lord, *u* 1Cor 11:27 *371*
For he that eateth and drinketh *u* 1Cor 11:29 *371*

UNWORTHY {2}
judge yourselves *u* of everlasting .... Acts 13:46 *3756,514*
are ye *u* to judge the smallest 1Cor 6:2 *370*

UP See APPENDIX.

UPBRAID {2}
Zalmunna, with whom ye did *u* me ...... Judg 8:15 2778
Then began he to *u* the cities ...... Mt 11:20 *3679*

UPBRAIDED {1}
u them with their unbelief and ...... Mk 16:14 *3679*

UPBRAIDETH {1}
to all men liberally, and *u* not ...... Jas 1:5 *3679*

UPHARSIN *(u-far'-sin)* {1} See PERES. *Part of the "handwriting on the wall."*
written, MENE, MENE, TEKEL, *U* ...... Dan 5:25 6537

UPHAZ *(u'-faz)* {2} *A place in southern Arabia.*
from Tarshish, and gold from *U* ...... Jer 10:9 210
were girded with fine gold of *U* ...... Dan 10:5 210

UPHELD {1}
and my fury, it *u* me ...... Is 63:5 5564

UPHOLD {8}
u me with thy free spirit ...... Ps 51:12 5564
Lord is with them that *u* my soul ...... Ps 54:4 5564
U me according unto thy word, ... Ps 119:116 5564
but honour shall *u* the humble in ...... Prov 29:23 8551
I will *u* thee with the right hand ...... Is 41:10 8551
Behold my servant, whom I *u* ...... Is 42:1 8551
wondered that there was none to *u* ...... Is 63:5 5564
They also that *u* Egypt shall fall ...... Eze 30:6 5564

UPHOLDEN {2}
Thy words have *u* him that was ...... Job 4:4 6965
and his throne is *u* by mercy ...... Prov 20:28 5582

UPHOLDEST {1}
thou *u* me in mine integrity, and ...... Ps 41:12 8551

UPHOLDETH {4}
but the LORD *u* the righteous ...... Ps 37:17 5564
for the LORD *u* him with his hand ...... Ps 37:24 5564
thy right hand *u* me ...... Ps 63:8 8551
The LORD *u* all that fall, and ...... Ps 145:14 5564

UPHOLDING {1}
u all things by the word of his ...... Heb 1:3 *5342*

UPON See APPENDIX.

UPPER {25}
on the *u* door post of the houses, ... Ex 12:7 4947
put a covering upon his *u* lip ...... Lev 13:45 8222
or the *u* millstone to pledge ...... Deut 24:6 7393
And he gave her the *u* springs ...... Josh 15:19 5942
unto Beth-horon the *u* ...... Josh 16:5 5945
And Caleb gave her the *u* springs ...... Judg 1:15 5942
his *u* chamber that was in Samaria 2Kin 1:2 5944
by the conduit of the *u* pool 2Kin 18:17 5945
the top of the *u* chamber of Ahaz 2Kin 23:12 5944
Beth-horon the nether, and the *u* 1Chr 7:24 5945
of the *u* chambers thereof, and of 1Chr 28:11 5944
he overlaid the *u* chambers with 2Chr 3:9 5944
Also he built Beth-horon the *u* 2Chr 8:5 5945
the *u* watercourse of Gihon 2Chr 32:30 5945
the *u* pool in the highway of the ...... Is 7:3 5945
the *u* pool in the highway of the ...... Is 36:2 5945
Now the *u* chambers were shorter ...... Eze 42:5 5945
lodge in the *u* lintels of it ...... Zeph 2:14 3730
shew you a large *u* room furnished ...... Mk 14:15 *508*
shew you a large *u* room furnished ...... Lk 22:12 *508*
in, they went up into an *u* room ...... Acts 1:13 *5253*
they laid her in an *u* chamber ...... Acts 9:37 *5253*
brought him into the *u* chamber ...... Acts 9:39 *5253*
the *u* coasts came to Ephesus ...... Acts 19:1 *510*
were many lights in the *u* chamber ...... Acts 20:8 *5250*

UPPERMOST {6}
in the *u* basket there was of all ...... Gen 40:17 5945
berries in the top of the *u* bough ...... Is 17:6
an *u* branch, which they left ...... Is 17:9
love the *u* rooms at feasts, and ...... Mt 23:6 *4411*
and the *u* rooms at feasts ...... Mk 12:39 *4411*
for ye love the *u* seats in the ...... Lk 11:43 *4410*

UPRIGHT {68}
my sheaf arose, and also stood *u* ...... Gen 37:7
the floods stood *u* as an heap ...... Ex 15:8
of your yoke, and made you go *u* ...... Lev 26:13 6968
the LORD liveth, thou hast been *u* 1Sa 29:6 3477
I was also *u* before him, and have 2Sa 22:24 8549
with the *u* man thou wilt shew 2Sa 22:26 8549
man thou wilt shew thyself *u* 2Sa 22:26 8552
for the Levites were more *u* in 2Chr 29:34 3477
and that man was perfect and *u* ...... Job 1:1 3477
an *u* man, one that feareth God, ... Job 1:8 3477
an *u* man, one that feareth God, ... Job 2:3 3477
If thou wert pure and *u* ...... Job 8:6 3477
the just *u* man is laughed to ...... Job 12:4 8549
U men shall be astonied at this, ... Job 17:8 3477
God, which saveth the *u* in heart ...... Ps 7:10 3477
privily shoot at the *u* in heart ...... Ps 11:2 3477
his countenance doth behold the *u* ...... Ps 11:7 3477
I was also *u* before him, and I ...... Ps 18:23 8549
with an *u* man thou wilt shew ...... Ps 18:25 8549
man thou wilt shew thyself *u* ...... Ps 18:25 8549,8552
then shall I be *u*, and I shall be ...... Ps 19:13 8552
but we are risen, and stand *u* ...... Ps 20:8
Good and *u* is the LORD ...... Ps 25:8 3477
joy, all ye that are *u* in heart ...... Ps 32:11 3477
for praise is comely for the *u* ...... Ps 33:1 3477
righteousness to the *u* in heart ...... Ps 36:10 3477
slay such as be of *u* conversation ...... Ps 37:14 3477
LORD knoweth the days of the *u* ...... Ps 37:18 8549
the perfect man, and behold the *u* ...... Ps 37:37 3477
the *u* shall have dominion over ...... Ps 49:14 3477
all the *u* in heart shall glory ...... Ps 64:10 3477
To shew that the LORD is *u* ...... Ps 92:15 3477
all the *u* in heart shall follow ...... Ps 94:15 3477
and gladness for the *u* in heart ...... Ps 97:11 3477
heart, in the assembly of the *u* ...... Ps 111:1 3477
of the *u* shall be blessed ...... Ps 112:2 3477
Unto the *u* there ariseth light in ...... Ps 112:4 3477
O LORD, and *u* are thy judgments ...... Ps 119:137 3477
them that are *u* in their hearts ...... Ps 125:4 3477
the *u* shall dwell in thy presence ...... Ps 140:13 3477
For the *u* shall dwell in the land ...... Prov 2:21 3477
of the LORD is strength to the *u* ...... Prov 10:29 8537
of the *u* shall guide them ...... Prov 11:3 3477
of the *u* shall deliver them ...... Prov 11:6 3477
of the *u* the city is exalted ...... Prov 11:11 3477
but such as are *u* in their way ...... Prov 11:20 8549
mouth of the *u* shall deliver them ...... Prov 12:6 3477
keepeth him that is *u* in the way ...... Prov 13:6 8537
of the *u* shall flourish ...... Prov 14:11 3477
prayer of the *u* is his delight ...... Prov 15:8 3477
The highway of the *u* is to depart ...... Prov 16:17 3477
and the transgressor for the *u* ...... Prov 21:18 3477
but as for the *u*, he directeth ...... Prov 21:29 3477
but the *u* shall have good things ...... Prov 28:10 8549
The bloodthirsty hate the *u* ...... Prov 29:10 8535
he that is *u* in the way is ...... Prov 29:27 3477
I found, that God hath made man *u* ...... Eccl 7:29 3477
and that which was written was *u* ...... Eccl 12:10 3476

the *u* love thee ... Song 1:4 4339
thou, most *u*, dost weigh the path ... Is 26:7 3477
They are *u* as the palm tree, but ... Jer 10:5 4749
but he touched me, and set me *u* ... Dan 8:18 5977
I speak unto thee, and stand *u* ... Dan 10:11 5977
whole kingdom, and *u* ones with him ... Dan 11:17 3477
and there is none *u* among men ... Mic 7:2 3477
the most *u* is sharper than a ... Mic 7:4 3477
is lifted up is not *u* in him ... Hab 2:4 3474
a loud voice, Stand *u* on thy feet ... Acts 14:10 *3717*

UPRIGHTLY {12}
He that walketh *u*, and worketh ... Ps 15:2 8549
do ye judge *u*, O ye sons of men ... Ps 58:1 4339
the congregation I will judge *u* ... Ps 75:2 4339
he withhold from them that walk *u* ... Ps 84:11 8549
is a buckler to them that walk *u* ... Prov 2:7 8537
He that walketh *u* walketh surely ... Prov 10:9 8537
a man of understanding walketh *u* ... Prov 15:21 3474
Whoso walketh *u* shall be saved ... Prov 28:18 8549
righteously, and speaketh *u* ... Is 33:15 4339
and they abhor him that speaketh *u* ... Amos 5:10 8549
do good to him that walketh *u* ... Mic 2:7 3477
u according to the truth of the ... Gal 2:14 *3716*

UPRIGHTNESS {19}
or for the *u* of thine heart, dost ... Deut 9:5 3476
and in *u* of heart with thee ... 1Kin 3:6 3483
in integrity of heart, and in *u* ... 1Kin 9:4 3476
the heart, and hast pleasure in *u* ... 1Chr 29:17 3476
in the *u* of mine heart I have ... 1Chr 29:17 4339
thy hope, and the *u* of thy ways ... Job 4:6 8537
shall be of the *u* of my heart ... Job 33:3 3476
thousand, to shew unto man his *u* ... Job 33:23 3476
judgment to the people in *u* ... Ps 9:8 4339
Let integrity and *u* preserve me ... Ps 25:21 3476
ever, and are done in truth and *u* ... Ps 111:8 3477
will praise thee with *u* of heart ... Ps 119:7 3476
lead me into the land of *u* ... Ps 143:10 4334
Who leave the paths of *u*, to walk ... Prov 2:13 3476
walketh in his *u* feareth the LORD ... Prov 14:2 3476
is the poor that walketh in his *u* ... Prov 28:6 8537
The way of the just is *u* ... Is 26:7 4339
in the land of *u* will he deal ... Is 26:10 5229
beds, each one walking in his *u* ... Is 57:2 5228

UPRISING {1}
knowest my downsitting and mine *u* ... Ps 139:2 6965

UPROAR {8}
noise of the city being in an *u* ... 1Kin 1:41 1993
there be an *u* among the people ... Mt 26:5 *2351*
lest there be an *u* of the people ... Mk 14:2 *2351*
and set all the city on an *u* ... Acts 17:5 *2350*
in question for this day's *u* ... Acts 19:40 *4714*
after the *u* was ceased, Paul ... Acts 20:1 *2351*
that all Jerusalem was in an *u* ... Acts 21:31 *4797*
before these days madest an *u* ... Acts 21:38 *387*

UPSIDE {5}
wiping it, and turning it *u* down ... 2Kin 21:13 5921,6440
of the wicked he turneth *u* down ... Ps 146:9
it waste, and turneth it *u* down ... Is 24:1 5921,6440
u down shall be esteemed as the ... Is 29:16
world *u* down are come hither also ... Acts 17:6 *389*

UPWARD {61}
Fifteen cubits *u* did the waters ... Gen 7:20 4605
from twenty years old and *u* ... Ex 38:26 4605
From twenty years old and *u* ... Num 1:3 4605
names, from twenty years old and *u* ... Num 1:18 4605
male from twenty years old and *u* ... Num 1:20 4605
male from twenty years old and *u* ... Num 1:22 4605
names, from twenty years old and *u* ... Num 1:24 4605
names, from twenty years old and *u* ... Num 1:26 4605
names, from twenty years old and *u* ... Num 1:28 4605
names, from twenty years old and *u* ... Num 1:30 4605
names, from twenty years old and *u* ... Num 1:32 4605
names, from twenty years old and *u* ... Num 1:34 4605
names, from twenty years old and *u* ... Num 1:36 4605
names, from twenty years old and *u* ... Num 1:38 4605
names, from twenty years old and *u* ... Num 1:40 4605
names, from twenty years old and *u* ... Num 1:42 4605
from twenty years old and *u* ... Num 1:45 4605
old and *u* shalt thou number them ... Num 3:15 4605
the males, from a month old and *u* ... Num 3:22 4605
the males, from a month old and *u* ... Num 3:28 4605
the males, from a month old and *u* ... Num 3:34 4605
the males from a month old and *u* ... Num 3:39 4605
of Israel from a month old and *u* ... Num 3:40 4605
of names, from a month old and *u* ... Num 3:43 4605
u even until fifty years old, all ... Num 4:3 4605
u until fifty years old shalt ... Num 4:23 4605
u even unto fifty years old shalt ... Num 4:30 4605
u even unto fifty years old, ... Num 4:35 4605
u even unto fifty years old, ... Num 4:39 4605
u even unto fifty years old, ... Num 4:43 4605
u even unto fifty years old, ... Num 4:47 4605
u they shall go in to wait upon ... Num 8:24 4605
from twenty years old and *u* ... Num 14:29 4605
from twenty years old and *u* ... Num 26:2 4605
from twenty years old and *u* ... Num 26:4 4605
all males from a month old and *u* ... Num 26:62 4605
Egypt, from twenty years old and *u* ... Num 32:11 4605
to Akrabbim, from the rock, and *u* ... Judg 1:36 4605
u he was higher than any of the ... 1Sa 9:2 4605
people from his shoulders and *u* ... 1Sa 10:23 4605
were able to put on armour, and *u* ... 2Kin 3:21 4605
root downward, and bear fruit *u* ... 2Kin 19:30 4605
from the age of thirty years and *u* ... 1Chr 23:3 4605
from the age of twenty years and *u* ... 1Chr 23:24 4605
males, from three years old and *u* ... 2Chr 31:16 4605
from twenty years old and *u* ... 2Chr 31:17 4605
from twenty years old and *u* ... Ezr 3:8 4605
unto trouble, as the sparks fly *u* ... Job 5:7 1361
the spirit of man that goeth *u* ... Eccl 3:21 4605
king and their God, and look *u* ... Is 8:21 4605
root downward, and bear fruit *u* ... Is 37:31 4605
mine eyes fail with looking *u* ... Is 38:14 4791
and their wings were stretched *u* ... Eze 1:11 4605
appearance of his loins even *u* ... Eze 1:27 4605
and from his loins even *u*, as the ... Eze 8:2 4605
still *u* to the side chambers ... Eze 41:7 4605
still *u* round about the house ... Eze 41:7 4605
breadth of the house was still *u* ... Eze 41:7 4605
altar and *u* shall be four horns ... Eze 43:15 4605
you, consider from this day and *u* ... Hag 2:15 4605
Consider now from this day and *u* ... Hag 2:18 4605

UR *(ur)* {5}
1. A district in Mesopotamia.
nativity, in *U* of the Chaldees ... Gen 11:28 218
with them from *U* of the Chaldees ... Gen 11:31 218
thee out of *U* of the Chaldees ... Gen 15:7 218
forth out of *U* of the Chaldees ... Neh 9:7 218
2. Father of Eliphal.
Hararite, Eliphal the son of *U* ... 1Chr 11:35 218

URBANE *(ur'-bane)* {1} *A Christian in Rome.*
Salute *U*, our helper in Christ, ... Rom 16:9 *3779*

URBANUS See URBANE.

URGE {1}
began to *u* him vehemently ... Lk 11:53 *1758*

URGED {6}
And he *u* him, and he took it ... Gen 33:11 6484
u him, so that his soul was vexed ... Judg 16:16 509
depart, his father in law *u* him ... Judg 19:7 6484
when they *u* him till he was ... 2Kin 2:17 6484
And he *u* him to take it ... 2Kin 5:16 6484
he *u* him, and bound two talents of ... 2Kin 5:23 6555

URGENT {2}
Egyptians were *u* upon the people ... Ex 12:33 2388
the king's commandment was *u* ... Dan 3:22 2685

URI *(u'-ri)* {8}
1. Father of Bezaleel.
by name Bezaleel the son of *U* ... Ex 31:2 221
by name Bezaleel the son of *U* ... Ex 35:30 221
And Bezaleel the son of *U*, the son ... Ex 38:22 221
And Hur begat *U* ... 1Chr 2:20 221
and *U* begat Bezaleel ... 1Chr 2:20 221
altar, that Bezaleel the son of *U* ... 2Chr 1:5 221
2. Father of Geber.
Geber the son of *U* was in the ... 1Kin 4:19 221
Shallum, and Telem, and *U* ... Ezr 10:24 221

URIAH *(u-ri'-ah)* {27} See URIAH'S, URIAS, URIJAH.
1. Husband of Bathsheba.
Eliam, the wife of *U* the Hittite ... 2Sa 11:3 223
saying, Send me *U* the Hittite ... 2Sa 11:6 223
And Joab sent *U* to David ... 2Sa 11:6 223
when *U* was come unto him, David ... 2Sa 11:7 223
And David said to *U*, Go down to ... 2Sa 11:8 223
U departed out of the king's ... 2Sa 11:8 223
But *U* slept at the door of the ... 2Sa 11:9 223
U went not down unto his house, ... 2Sa 11:10 223
unto his house, David said unto *U* ... 2Sa 11:10 223
U said unto David, The ark, and ... 2Sa 11:11 223
And David said to *U*, Tarry here to ... 2Sa 11:12 223
So *U* abode in Jerusalem that day, ... 2Sa 11:12 223
Joab, and sent it by the hand of *U* ... 2Sa 11:14 223
Set ye *U* in the forefront of the ... 2Sa 11:15 223
that he assigned *U* unto a place ... 2Sa 11:16 223
and *U* the Hittite died also ... 2Sa 11:17 223
Thy servant *U* the Hittite is dead ... 2Sa 11:21 223
thy servant *U* the Hittite is dead ... 2Sa 11:24 223
when the wife of *U* heard that ... 2Sa 11:26 223
heard that *U* her husband was dead ... 2Sa 11:26 223
thou hast killed *U* the Hittite ... 2Sa 12:9 223
hast taken the wife of *U* the ... 2Sa 12:10 223
U the Hittite ... 2Sa 23:39 223
in the matter of *U* the Hittite ... 1Kin 15:5 223
U the Hittite, Zabad the son of ... 1Chr 11:41 223
2. A rebuilder of Jerusalem's wall.
Meremoth the son of *U* the priest ... Ezr 8:33 223
3. A priest who aided Isaiah.
U the priest, and Zechariah the ... Is 8:2 223

URIAH'S *(u-ri'-ahz)* {1} *Refers to Uriah 1.*
child that *U* wife bare unto David ... 2Sa 12:15 223

URIAS *(u-ri'-as)* {1} *Greek form of Uriah 1.*
her that had been the wife of *U* ... Mt 1:6 *3774*

URIEL *(u'-re-el)* {4}
1. Son of Tahath.
U his son, Uzziah his son, and ... 1Chr 6:24 222
U the chief, and his brethren an ... 1Chr 15:5 222
and for the Levites, for *U* ... 1Chr 15:11 222
2. Father of Micaiah.
the daughter of *U* of Gibeah ... 2Chr 13:2 222

URIJAH *(u-ri'-jah)* {11} See URIAH.
1. A priest in Jerusalem.
king Ahaz sent to *U* the priest ... 2Kin 16:10 223
U the priest built an altar ... 2Kin 16:11 223
so *U* the priest made it against ... 2Kin 16:11 223
king Ahaz commanded *U* the priest ... 2Kin 16:15 223
Thus did *U* the priest, according ... 2Kin 16:16 223
2. A priest who rebuilt the wall.
repaired Meremoth the son of *U* ... Neh 3:4 223
of *U* the son of Koz another piece ... Neh 3:21 223
3. A priest who aided Ezra.
and Shema, and Anaiah, and *U* ... Neh 8:4 223
4. A prophet killed by Jehoiakim.
LORD, *U* the son of Shemaiah of ... Jer 26:20 223
but when *U* heard it, he was ... Jer 26:21 223
they fetched forth *U* out of Egypt ... Jer 26:23 223

URIM *(u'-rim)* {7} *A symbolic object in the High Priest's breastplate.*
the breastplate of judgment the *U* ... Ex 28:30 224
he put in the breastplate the *U* ... Lev 8:8 224
the judgment of *U* before the LORD ... Num 27:21 224
thy *U* be with thy holy one, whom ... Deut 33:8 224
not, neither by dreams, nor by *U* ... 1Sa 28:6 224
there stood up a priest with *U* ... Ezr 2:63 224
there stood up a priest with *U* ... Neh 7:65 224

US See APPENDIX.

USE See APPENDIX.

USED See APPENDIX.

USES See APPENDIX.

USEST {1}
as thou *u* to do unto those that ... Ps 119:132 4941

USETH {7}
or that *u* divination, or an ... Deut 18:10
brought which the king *u* to wear ... Est 6:8
of the wise *u* knowledge aright ... Prov 15:2
The poor *u* intreaties ... Prov 18:23 1696
that *u* his neighbour's service ... Jer 22:13
every one that *u* proverbs shall ... Eze 16:44
For every one that *u* milk is ... Heb 5:13 *3348*

USING See APPENDIX.

USURER {1}
thou shalt not be to him as a *u* ... Ex 22:25 5383

USURP {1}
nor to *u* authority over the man, ... 1Ti 2:12 *831*

USURY {24}
neither shalt thou lay upon him *u* ... Ex 22:25 5392
Take thou no *u* of him, or ... Lev 25:36 5392
not give him thy money upon *u* ... Lev 25:37 5392
not lend upon *u* to thy brother ... Deut 23:19 5391
u of money, *u* of victuals, ... Deut 23:19 5392
u of any thing that is lent upon ... Deut 23:19 5392
of any thing that is lent upon *u* ... Deut 23:19 5391
stranger thou mayest lend upon *u* ... Deut 23:20 5391
thou shalt not lend upon *u* ... Deut 23:20 5391
and said unto them, Ye exact *u* ... Neh 5:7 5383
pray you, let us leave off this *u* ... Neh 5:10 5383
putteth not out his money to *u* ... Ps 15:5 5392
He that by *u* and unjust gain ... Prov 28:8 5392
as with the taker of *u* ... Is 24:2 5383
so with the giver of *u* to him ... Is 24:2 5378
I have neither lent on *u* ... Jer 15:10 5383
nor men have lent to me on *u* ... Jer 15:10 5383
that hath not given forth upon *u* ... Eze 18:8 5392
Hath given forth upon *u*, and hath ... Eze 18:13 5392
hath not received *u* nor increase ... Eze 18:17 5392
thou hast taken *u* and increase, and ... Eze 22:12 5392
have received mine own with *u* ... Mt 25:27 *5110*
have required mine own with *u* ... Lk 19:23 *5110*

US-WARD {3}
and thy thoughts which are to *u* ... Ps 40:5 413
of his power to *u* who believe ... Eph 1:19 *1519,2248*
but is longsuffering to *u* ... 2Pet 3:9 *1519,2248*

UTHAI *(u'-thahee)* {2}
1. Son of Ammihud.
U the son of Ammihud, the son of ... 1Chr 9:4 5793
2. A clan leader with Ezra.
U, and Zabbud, and with them ... Ezr 8:14 5793

UTMOST {11}
of my progenitors unto the *u* ... Gen 49:26
of Arnon, which is in the *u* coast ... Num 22:36 7097
see the *u* part of the people ... Num 22:41 7097
shalt see but the *u* part of them ... Num 23:13 7097
the land of Judah, unto the *u* sea ... Deut 34:2 314
and all that are in the *u* corners ... Jer 9:26 7112
and all that are in the *u* corners ... Jer 25:23 7112
them that are in the *u* corners ... Jer 49:32 7112
against her from the *u* border ... Jer 50:26 7093
his hinder part toward the *u* sea ... Joel 2:20 314
for she came from the *u* parts of ... Lk 11:31 *4009*

UTTER {45}
if he do not *u* it, then he shall ... Lev 5:1 5046
if ye *u* not this our business ... Josh 2:14 5046
if thou *u* this our business, then ... Josh 2:20 5046
awake, awake, *u* a song ... Judg 5:12 1696
whom I appointed to *u* destruction ... 1Kin 20:42
u words out of their heart ... Job 8:10 3318
a wise man *u* vain knowledge ... Job 15:2 6030
nor my tongue *u* deceit ... Job 27:4 1897
my lips shall *u* knowledge clearly ... Job 33:3 4448
I will *u* dark sayings of old ... Ps 78:2 5042
How long shall they *u* and speak ... Ps 94:4 5042
Who can *u* the mighty acts of the ... Ps 106:2 4448
My lips shall *u* praise, when thou ... Ps 119:171 5042
They shall abundantly *u* the ... Ps 145:7 5042
but a false witness will *u* lies ... Prov 14:5 6315
heart shall *u* perverse things ... Prov 23:33 1696
man cannot *u* it ... Eccl 1:8 1696
hasty to *u* any thing before God ... Eccl 5:2 3318
to *u* error against the LORD, to ... Is 32:6 1696
u it even to the end of the earth ... Is 48:20 3318
I will *u* my judgments against ... Jer 1:16 1696
u his voice from his holy ... Jer 25:30 5414
u a parable unto the rebellious ... Eze 24:3 4911
thereof were toward the *u* court ... Eze 40:31 2435
thereof were toward the *u* court ... Eze 40:37 2435

brought me forth into the *u* court .... Eze 42:1 2435
which was for the *u* court .... Eze 42:3 2435
toward the *u* court on the .... Eze 42:7 2435
in the *u* court was fifty cubits .... Eze 42:8 2435
goeth into them from the *u* court .... Eze 42:9 2435
the holy place into the *u* court .... Eze 42:14 2435
they go forth into the *u* court .... Eze 44:19 2435
even into the *u* court to the .... Eze 44:19 2435
them not out into the *u* court .... Eze 46:20 2435
brought me forth into the *u* court .... Eze 46:21 2435
u gate by the way that looketh .... Eze 47:2 2531
the LORD shall *u* his voice before .... Joel 2:11 5414
u his voice from Jerusalem .... Joel 3:16 5414
u his voice from Jerusalem .... Amos 1:2 5414
flood he will make an *u* end of .... Nah 1:8 3617
he will make an *u* end .... Nah 1:9 3617
shall be no more *u* destruction .... Zec 14:11
I will *u* things which have been .... Mt 13:35 *2044*
except ye *u* by the tongue words 1Cor 14:9 *1325*
it is not lawful for a man to *u* 2Cor 12:4 *2980*

UTTERANCE {5}
as the Spirit gave them *u* .... Acts 2:4 *669*
ye are enriched by him, in all *u* 1Cor 1:5 *3056*
in every thing, in faith, and *u* 2Cor 8:7 *3056*
that *u* may be given unto me, that .... Eph 6:19 *3056*
would open unto us a door of *u* .... Col 4:3 *3056*

UTTERED {17}
or *u* ought out of her lips, ... Num 30:6 4008
and that which she *u* with her lips .... Num 30:8 4008
Jephthah *u* all his words before .... Judg 11:11 1696
and the most High *u* his voice 2Sa 22:14 5414
before me, and *u* my words to him .... Neh 6:19 3318
To whom hast thou *u* words .... Job 26:4 5046
therefore have I *u* that I .... Job 42:3 5046
he *u* his voice, the earth melted .... Ps 46:6 5414
Which my lips have *u*, and my mouth .... Ps 66:14 6475
have they *u* their voice, from .... Jer 48:34 5414
a noise of their voice is *u* .... Jer 51:55 5414
the deep *u* his voice, and lifted .... Hab 3:10 5414
with groanings which cannot be *u* .... Rom 8:26 *215*
things to say, and hard to be *u* .... Heb 5:11 *3004*
seven thunders *u* their voices .... Rev 10:3 *2980*
seven thunders had *u* their voices .... Rev 10:4 *2980*
things which the seven thunders *u* .... Rev 10:4 *2980*

UTTERETH {19}
For thy mouth *u* thine iniquity, ... Job 15:5 502
Day unto day *u* speech, and night .... Ps 19:2 5042
she *u* her voice in the streets .... Prov 1:20 5414
in the city she *u* her words .... Prov 1:21 559
he that *u* a slander, is a fool .... Prov 10:18 3318
A fool *u* all his mind .... Prov 29:11 3318
When he *u* his voice, there is a .... Jer 10:13 5414
When he *u* his voice, there is a .... Jer 51:16 5414
he *u* his mischievous desire .... Mic 7:3 1696

UTTERING {1}
u from the heart words of .... Is 59:13 1897

UTTERLY {1}
for I will *u* put out the .... Ex 17:14
If her father *u* refuse to give .... Ex 22:17
only, he shall be *u* destroyed .... Ex 22:20
but thou shalt *u* overthrow them .... Ex 23:24
shall pronounce him *u* unclean .... Lev 13:44
I abhor them, to destroy them *u* .... Lev 26:44 3615
that soul shall *u* be cut off .... Num 15:31
then I will *u* destroy their .... Num 21:2
they *u* destroyed them and their .... Num 21:3
But if her husband hath *u* made .... Num 30:12
u destroyed the men, and the women .... Deut 2:34
we *u* destroyed them, as we did .... Deut 3:6
u destroying the men, women, and .... Deut 3:6
that ye shall soon *u* perish from .... Deut 4:26
upon it, but shall *u* be destroyed .... Deut 4:26
smite them, and *u* destroy them .... Deut 7:2
but thou shalt *u* detest it .... Deut 7:26
and thou shalt *u* abhor it .... Deut 7:26
Ye shall *u* destroy all the places .... Deut 12:2
of the sword, destroying it *u* .... Deut 13:15
But thou shalt *u* destroy them .... Deut 20:17
ye will *u* corrupt yourselves .... Deut 31:29
Sihon and Og, whom ye *u* destroyed .... Josh 2:10
they *u* destroyed all that was in .... Josh 6:21
until he had *u* destroyed all the .... Josh 8:26
taken Ai, and had *u* destroyed it .... Josh 10:1
the king thereof he *u* destroyed .... Josh 10:28
therein he *u* destroyed that day .... Josh 10:35
but destroyed it *u*, and all the .... Josh 10:37
u destroyed all the souls that .... Josh 10:39
but *u* destroyed all that breathed .... Josh 10:40
of the sword, *u* destroying them .... Josh 11:11
he *u* destroyed them, as Moses the .... Josh 11:12
that he might destroy them *u* .... Josh 11:20
them *u* with their cities .... Josh 11:21
but did not *u* drive them out .... Josh 17:13
Zephath, and *u* destroyed it .... Judg 1:17
and did not *u* drive them out .... Judg 1:28
that thou hadst *u* hated her .... Judg 15:2
Ye shall *u* destroy every male, and .... Judg 21:11
u destroy all that they have, and 1Sa 15:3
u destroyed all the people with 1Sa 15:8
good, and would not *u* destroy them 1Sa 15:9
and refuse, that they destroyed *u* 1Sa 15:9
and the rest we have *u* destroyed 1Sa 15:15
u destroy the sinners the 1Sa 15:18
have *u* destroyed the Amalekites 1Sa 15:20
should have been *u* destroyed 1Sa 15:21
his people Israel *u* to abhor him 1Sa 27:12
the heart of a lion, shall *u* melt 2Sa 17:10
they shall be *u* burned with fire 2Sa 23:7
also were not able *u* to destroy 1Kin 9:21
all lands, by destroying them *u* 2Kin 19:11
and destroyed them *u* unto this day 1Chr 4:41
u to slay and destroy them 2Chr 20:23
until they had *u* destroyed them 2Chr 31:1
that my fathers *u* destroyed 2Chr 32:14
thou didst not *u* consume them .... Neh 9:31
fall, he shall not be *u* cast down .... Ps 37:24
they are *u* consumed with terrors .... Ps 73:19
will I not *u* take from him .... Ps 89:33
O forsake me not *u* .... Ps 119:8 3966
word of truth *u* out of my mouth .... Ps 119:43 3966
for love, it would *u* be contemned .... Song 8:7
And the idols he shall *u* abolish .... Is 2:18 3632
man, and the land be *u* desolate .... Is 6:11
the LORD shall *u* destroy the .... Is 11:15
be *u* emptied, and *u* spoiled .... Is 24:3
The earth is *u* broken down .... Is 24:19
he hath *u* destroyed them, he hath .... Is 34:2
to all lands by destroying them *u* .... Is 37:11
and the young men shall *u* fall .... Is 40:30
The LORD hath *u* separated me from .... Is 56:3
those nations shall be *u* wasted .... Is 60:12
for every brother will *u* supplant .... Jer 9:4
I will *u* pluck up and destroy that .... Jer 12:17
Hast thou *u* rejected Judah .... Jer 14:19
will *u* forget you, and I will .... Jer 23:39
will *u* destroy them, and make them .... Jer 25:9
and should ye be *u* unpunished .... Jer 25:29
u destroy after them, saith the .... Jer 50:21
her up as heaps, and destroy her *u* .... Jer 50:26
destroy ye *u* all her host .... Jer 51:3
of Babylon shall be *u* broken .... Jer 51:58
But thou hast *u* rejected us .... Lam 5:22
Slay *u* old and young, both maids, ... Eze 9:6
shall it not *u* wither, when the .... Eze 17:10
make themselves *u* bald for thee .... Eze 27:31
make the land of Egypt *u* waste .... Eze 29:10
destroy, and *u* to make away many .... Dan 11:44
but I will *u* take them away .... Hos 1:6
the king of Israel *u* be cut off .... Hos 10:15
saving that I will not *u* destroy .... Amos 9:8
and say, We be *u* spoiled .... Mic 2:4 7703
he is *u* cut off .... Nah 1:15 3605
I will *u* consume all things from .... Zeph 1:2
his right eye shall be *u* darkened .... Zec 11:17
there is *u* a fault among you 1Cor 6:7 *3654*
shall *u* perish in their own 2Pet 2:12 *2704*
she shall be *u* burned with fire .... Rev 18:8 *2618*

UTTERMOST {28}
in the *u* edge of another curtain .... Ex 26:4 7020
in the *u* side of another curtain .... Ex 36:11 7020
the *u* edge of the curtain in the .... Ex 36:17 7020
were in the *u* parts of the camp .... Num 11:1 7097
a city in the *u* of thy border .... Num 20:16 7097
even unto the *u* sea shall your .... Deut 11:24 314
was the *u* part of the south coast .... Josh 15:1 7097
the sea at the *u* part of Jordan .... Josh 15:5 7097
the *u* cities of the tribe of the .... Josh 15:21 7097
Saul tarried in the *u* part of 1Sa 14:2 7097
from the *u* part of the one wing 1Kin 6:24 7098
the *u* part of the other were ten 1Kin 6:24 7098
the *u* part of the camp of Syria 2Kin 7:5 7097
came to the *u* part of the camp 2Kin 7:8 7097
out unto the *u* part of the heaven .... Neh 1:9 7097
the *u* parts of the earth for thy .... Ps 2:8 657
They also that dwell in the *u* .... Ps 65:8 7098
dwell in the *u* parts of the sea .... Ps 139:9 319
the *u* part of the rivers of Egypt .... Is 7:18 7097
From the *u* part of the earth have .... Is 24:16 3671
thou hast paid the *u* farthing .... Mt 5:26 *2078*
for she came from the *u* parts of .... Mt 12:42 *4009*
from the *u* part of the earth to .... Mk 13:27 *206*
the earth to the *u* part of heaven .... Mk 13:27 *206*
unto the *u* part of the earth .... Acts 1:8 *2078*
I will know the *u* of your matter .... Acts 24:22 *1231*
wrath is come upon them to the *u* 1Th 2:16 *5056*
the *u* that come unto God by him .... Heb 7:25 *3838*

UZ *(uz)* {7} *A son of Aram.*
U, and Hul, and Gether, and Mash .... Gen 10:23 5780
are these; *U*, and Aran .... Gen 36:28 5780
Arphaxad, and Lud, and Aram, and *U* 1Chr 1:17 5780
of Dishan; *U*, and Aran 1Chr 1:42 5780
There was a man in the land of *U* .... Job 1:1 5780
and all the kings of the land of *U* .... Jer 25:20 5780
that dwellest in the land of *U* .... Lam 4:21 5780

UZAI *(u'-zahee)* {1} *Father of Palal.*
Palal the son of *U*, over against .... Neh 3:25 186

UZAL *(u'-zal)* {2} *A son of Joktan.*
And Hadoram, and *U*, and Diklah, ... Gen 10:27 187
Hadoram also, and *U*, and Diklah, ... 1Chr 1:21 187

UZZA *(uz'-zah)* {10} See UZZAH.
1. Name of the burial ground of Manasseh and Amon.
his own house, in the garden of *U* 2Kin 21:18 5798
his sepulchre in the garden of *U* 2Kin 21:26 5798
2. Son of Shimei.
son, Shimei his son, *U* his son, ... 1Chr 6:29 5798
3. A brother of Ahihud.
Gera, he removed them, and begat *U* 1Chr 8:7 5798
4. Touched the Ark and died.
and *U* and Ahio drave the cart 1Chr 13:7 5798
U put forth his hand to hold the 1Chr 13:9 5798
of the LORD was kindled against *U* 1Chr 13:10 5798
the LORD had made a breach upon *U* 1Chr 13:11 5798
5. A family of Nethinims.
The children of *U*, the children .... Ezr 2:49 5798
of Gazzam, the children of *U* .... Neh 7:51 5798

UZZAH *(uz'-zah)* {4} See UZZA. *Same as Uzza 4.*
and *U* and Ahio, the sons of 2Sa 6:3 5798
U put forth his hand to the ark 2Sa 6:6 5798
of the LORD was kindled against *U* 2Sa 6:7 5798
the LORD had made a breach upon *U* 2Sa 6:8 5798

UZZEN-SHEERAH See UZZEN-SHERAH.

UZZEN-SHERAH *(uz'-zen-she'-rah)* {1} *A city in Ephraim.*
the nether, and the upper, and *U* 1Chr 7:24 242

UZZI *(uz'-zi)* {11}
1. A son of Bukki.
begat Bukki, and Bukki begat *U* 1Chr 6:5 5813
U begat Zerahiah, and Zerahiah 1Chr 6:6 5813
U his son, Zerahiah his son, ... 1Chr 6:51 5813
The son of Zerahiah, the son of *U* .... Ezr 7:4 5813
2. Father of Izrahiah.
U, and Rephaiah, and Jeriel, and 1Chr 7:2 5813
And the sons of *U* 1Chr 7:3 5813
3. Son of Bela.
Ezbon, and *U*, and Uzziel, and 1Chr 7:7 5813
4. A family of exiles.
of Jeroham, and Elah the son of *U* 1Chr 9:8 5813
5. An overseer of Levites.
Jerusalem was *U* the son of Bani .... Neh 11:22 5813
6. A priest descended from Jedaiah.
of Jedaiah, *U* .... Neh 12:19 5813
and Shemaiah, and Eleazar, and *U* .... Neh 12:42 5813

UZZIA *(uz-zi'-ah)* {1} *A "mighty man" of David.*
U the Ashterathite, Shama and 1Chr 11:44 5814

UZZIAH *(uz-zi'-ah)* {27}
1. A king of Judah.
thirtieth year of *U* king of Judah 2Kin 15:13 5818
year of Jotham the son of *U* 2Kin 15:30 5818
son of *U* king of Judah to reign 2Kin 15:32 5818
to all that his father *U* had done 2Kin 15:34 5818
all the people of Judah took *U* 2Chr 26:1 5818
Sixteen years old was *U* when he 2Chr 26:3 5818
And the Ammonites gave gifts to *U* 2Chr 26:8 5818
Moreover *U* built towers in 2Chr 26:9 5818
Moreover *U* had an host of 2Chr 26:11 5818
U prepared for them throughout 2Chr 26:14 5818
And they withstood *U* the king 2Chr 26:18 5818
It appertaineth not unto thee, *U* 2Chr 26:18 5818
Then *U* was wroth, and had a censer 2Chr 26:19 5818
U the king was a leper unto the 2Chr 26:21 5818
Now the rest of the acts of *U* 2Chr 26:22 5818
So *U* slept with his fathers, and 2Chr 26:23 5818
to all that his father *U* did 2Chr 27:2 5818
and Jerusalem in the days of *U* .... Is 1:1 5818
In the year that king *U* died I .... Is 6:1 5818
the son of Jotham, the son of *U* .... Is 7:1 5818
son of Beeri, in the days of *U* .... Hos 1:1 5818
in the days of *U* king of Judah .... Amos 1:1 5818
in the days of *U* king of Judah .... Zec 14:5 5818
2. Son of Uriel.
U his son, and Shaul his son 1Chr 6:24 5818
3. Father of Jehonathan.
was Jehonathan the son of *U* 1Chr 27:25 5818
4. Married a foreigner in exile.
and Shemaiah, and Jehiel, and *U* .... Ezr 10:21 5818
5. A family of exiles.
Athaiah the son of *U*, the son of .... Neh 11:4 5818

UZZIEL *(uz-zi'-el)* {16}
1. A son of Kohath.
Amram, and Izhar, and Hebron, and *U* .... Ex 6:18 5816
And the sons of *U* .... Ex 6:22 5816
the sons of *U* the uncle of Aaron, ... Lev 10:4 5816
Amram, and Izehar, Hebron, and *U* .... Num 3:19 5816
shall be Elizaphan the son of *U* .... Num 3:30 5816
Amram, Izhar, and Hebron, and *U* 1Chr 6:2 5816
Amram, and Izhar, and Hebron, and *U* 1Chr 6:18 5816
Of the sons of *U* 1Chr 15:10 5816
Amram, Izhar, Hebron, and *U* 1Chr 23:12 5816
Of the sons of *U* 1Chr 23:20 5816
Of the sons of *U* 1Chr 24:24 5816
2. A son of Ishi.
and Neariah, and Rephaiah, and *U* 1Chr 4:42 5816
3. A son of Bela.
Ezbon, and Uzzi, and *U*, and Jerimoth 1Chr 7:7 5816
4. A sanctuary servant.
Bukkiah, Mattaniah, *U*, Shebuel, ... 1Chr 25:4 5816
5. A Levite who cleansed the Temple.
Shemaiah, and *U* 2Chr 29:14 5816
6. A repairer of Jerusalem's wall.
repaired *U* the son of Harhaiah .... Neh 3:8 5816

UZZIELITES *(uz-zi'-el-ites)* {2} *Descendants of Uzziel 1.*
and the family of the *U* .... Num 3:27 5817
the Hebronites, and the *U* 1Chr 26:23 5817

V

VAGABOND {3}
a v shalt thou be in the earth ... Gen 4:12 5110
be a fugitive and a v in the earth ... Gen 4:14 5110
Then certain of the v Jews ... Acts 19:13 *4022*

VAGABONDS {1}
Let his children be continually v ... Ps 109:10 5128

VAIL {38}
therefore she took a v, and ... Gen 24:65 6809
from her, and covered her with a v ... Gen 38:14 6809
away, and laid by her v from her ... Gen 38:19 6809
And thou shalt make a v of blue ... Ex 26:31 6532
hang up the v under the taches ... Ex 26:33 6532
the v the ark of the testimony ... Ex 26:33 6532
the v shall divide unto you ... Ex 26:33 6532
shalt set the table without the v ... Ex 26:35 6532
of the congregation without the v ... Ex 27:21 6532
the v that is by the ark of the ... Ex 30:6 6532
with them, he put a v on his face ... Ex 34:33 4533
speak with him, he took the v off ... Ex 34:34 4533
Moses put the v upon his face ... Ex 34:35 4533
seat, and the v of the covering, ... Ex 35:12 6532
And he made a v of blue, and purple ... Ex 36:35 6532
and the sockets of the v ... Ex 38:27 6532
skins, and the v of the covering, ... Ex 39:34 6532
and cover the ark with the v ... Ex 40:3 6532
set up the v of the covering, and ... Ex 40:21 6532
northward, without the v ... Ex 40:22 6532
of the congregation before the v ... Ex 40:26 6532
before the v of the sanctuary ... Lev 4:6 6532
the LORD, even before the v ... Lev 4:17 6532
the v before the mercy seat ... Lev 16:2 6532
small, and bring it within the v ... Lev 16:12 6532
and bring his blood within the v ... Lev 16:15 6532
he shall not go in unto the v ... Lev 21:23 6532
Without the v of the testimony, ... Lev 24:3 6532
shall take down the covering v ... Num 4:5 6532
of the altar, and within the v ... Num 18:7 6532
Bring the v that thou hast upon ... Ruth 3:15 4304
And he made the v of blue, and ... 2Chr 3:14 6532
the v that is spread over all ... Is 25:7 4541
which put a v over his face, that ... 2Cor 3:13 *2571*
this day remaineth the same v ... 2Cor 3:14 *2571*
which v is done away in Christ ... 2Cor 3:14
the v is upon their heart ... 2Cor 3:15 *2571*
the v shall be taken away ... 2Cor 3:16 *2571*

VAILS {1}
linen, and the hoods, and the v ... Is 3:23 7289

VAIN {112}
and let them not regard v words ... Ex 5:9 8267
the name of the LORD thy God in v ... Ex 20:7 7723
that taketh his name in v ... Ex 20:7 7723
and ye shall sow your seed in v ... Lev 26:16 7385
your strength shall be spent in v ... Lev 26:20 7385
the name of the LORD thy God in v ... Deut 5:11 7723
that taketh his name in v ... Deut 5:11 7723
For it is not a v thing for you ... Deut 32:47 7386
wherewith Abimelech hired v ... Judg 9:4 7386
were gathered v men to Jephthah ... Judg 11:3 7386
then should ye go after v things ... 1Sa 12:21 8414
for they are v ... 1Sa 12:21 8414
Surely in v have I kept all that ... 1Sa 25:21 8267
servants, as one of the v fellows ... 2Sa 6:20 7386
they followed vanity, and became v ... 2Kin 17:15 1891
sayest, (but they are but v words ... 2Kin 18:20 8193
there are gathered unto him v men ... 2Chr 13:7 7386
be wicked, why then labour I in v ... Job 9:29 1892
For he knoweth v men ... Job 11:11 7723
For v man would be wise, though ... Job 11:12 5014
a wise man utter v knowledge ... Job 15:2 7307
Shall v words have an end ... Job 16:3 7307
How then comfort ye me in v ... Job 21:34 1892
why then are ye thus altogether v ... Job 27:12 1891
doth Job open his mouth in v ... Job 35:16 1892
her labour is in v without fear ... Job 39:16 7385
Behold, the hope of him is in v ... Job 41:9 3576
and the people imagine a v thing ... Ps 2:1 7385
I have not sat with v persons ... Ps 26:4 7723
An horse is a v thing for safety ... Ps 33:17 8267
every man walketh in a v shew ... Ps 39:6
surely they are disquieted in v ... Ps 39:6 1892
for v is the help of man ... Ps 60:11 7723
and become not v in robbery ... Ps 62:10 1891
I have cleansed my heart in v ... Ps 73:13 7385
hast thou made all men in v ... Ps 89:47 7723
for v is the help of man ... Ps 108:12 7723
I hate v thoughts ... Ps 119:113
they labour in v that build it ... Ps 127:1 7723
the watchman waketh but in v ... Ps 127:1 7723
It is v for you to rise up early, ... Ps 127:2 7723
thine enemies take thy name in v ... Ps 139:20 7723
Surely in v the net is spread in ... Prov 1:17 2600
followeth v persons is void of ... Prov 12:11 7386
v persons shall have poverty ... Prov 28:19 7386
and take the name of my God in v ... Prov 30:9
is deceitful, and beauty is v ... Prov 31:30 1892
all the days of his v life which ... Eccl 6:12 1892
Bring no more v oblations ... Is 1:13 7723
For the Egyptians shall help in v ... Is 30:7 1892
(but they are but v words) I have ... Is 36:5 8193
it, he created it not in v ... Is 45:18 8414
seed of Jacob, Seek ye me in v ... Is 45:19 8414
Then I said, I have laboured in v ... Is 49:4 7385
my strength for nought, and in v ... Is 49:4 1892
They shall not labour in v ... Is 65:23 7385
after vanity, and are become v ... Jer 2:5 1891
In v have I smitten your children ... Jer 2:30 7723
Truly in v is salvation hoped for ... Jer 3:23 8267
How long shall thy v thoughts ... Jer 4:14 205
in v shalt thou make thyself fair ... Jer 4:30 7723
the founder melteth in v ... Jer 6:29 7723
Lo, certainly in v made he it ... Jer 8:8 8267
the pen of the scribes is in v ... Jer 8:8 8267
the customs of the people are v ... Jer 10:3 1892
they make you v ... Jer 23:16 1891
in v shalt thou use many ... Jer 46:11 7723
none shall return in v ... Jer 50:9 7387
and the people shall labour in v ... Jer 51:58 7385
Thy prophets have seen v and ... Lam 2:14 7723
eyes as yet failed for our v help ... Lam 4:17 1892
that I have not said in v that I ... Eze 6:10 2600
more any v vision nor flattering ... Eze 12:24 7723
Have ye not seen a v vision ... Eze 13:7 7723
they comfort in v ... Zec 10:2 1892
have said, It is v to serve God ... Mal 3:14 7723
use not v repetitions, as the ... Mt 6:7
But in v they do worship me, ... Mt 15:9 *3155*
Howbeit in v do they worship me, ... Mk 7:7 *3155*
and the people imagine v things ... Acts 4:25 *2756*
but became v in their ... Rom 1:21 *3154*
for he beareth not the sword in v ... Rom 13:4 *1500*
of the wise, that they are v ... 1Cor 3:20 *3152*
you, unless ye have believed in v ... 1Cor 15:2 *1500*
was bestowed upon me was not in v ... 1Cor 15:10 *2756*
risen, then is our preaching v ... 1Cor 15:14 *2756*
and your faith is also v ... 1Cor 15:14 *2756*
be not raised, your faith is v ... 1Cor 15:17 *3152*
labour is not in v in the Lord ... 1Cor 15:58 *2756*
receive not the grace of God in v ... 2Cor 6:1 *2756*
you should be in v in this behalf ... 2Cor 9:3 *2761*
I should run, or had run, in v ... Gal 2:2 *2756*
the law, then Christ is dead in v ... Gal 2:21 *1432*
ye suffered so many things in v ... Gal 3:4 *1500*
if it be yet in v ... Gal 3:4 *1500*
bestowed upon you labour in v ... Gal 4:11 *1500*
Let us not be desirous of v glory ... Gal 5:26 *2755*
no man deceive you with v words ... Eph 5:6 *2756*
Christ, that I have not run in v ... Phil 2:16 *2756*
neither laboured in v ... Phil 2:16 *2756*
v deceit, after the tradition of ... Col 2:8 *2756*
in unto you, that it was not in v ... 1Th 2:1 *2756*
you, and our labour be in v ... 1Th 3:5 *2756*
have turned aside unto v jangling ... 1Ti 1:6 *3150*
v babblings, and oppositions of ... 1Ti 6:20 *2757*
But shun profane and v babblings ... 2Ti 2:16 *2757*
v talkers and deceivers, specially ... Titus 1:10 *3151*
for they are unprofitable and v ... Titus 3:9 *3152*
heart, this man's religion is v ... Jas 1:26 *3152*
O v man, that faith without works ... Jas 2:20 *2756*
that the scripture saith in v ... Jas 4:5 *2761*
from your v conversation received ... 1Pet 1:18 *3152*

VAINGLORY {1}
be done through strife or v ... Phil 2:3 *2754*

VAINLY {1}
v puffed up by his fleshly mind, ... Col 2:18 *1500*

VAIZATHA See VAJEZATHA.

VAJEZATHA *(va-jez'-a-thah)* {1} *A son of Haman.*
and Arisai, and Aridai, and V ... Est 9:9 2055

VALE {9}
together in the v of Siddim ... Gen 14:3 6010
with them in the v of Siddim ... Gen 14:8 6010
the v of Siddim was full of ... Gen 14:10 6010
sent him out of the v of Hebron ... Gen 37:14 6010
plain, in the hills, and in the v ... Deut 1:7 8219
and of the south, and of the v ... Josh 10:40 8219
sycomore trees that are in the v ... 1Kin 10:27 8219
that are in the v for abundance ... 2Chr 1:15 8219
mountains, in the cities of the v ... Jer 33:13 8219

VALIANT {32}
saw any strong man, or any v man ... 1Sa 14:52 2428
in playing, and a mighty v man ... 1Sa 16:18 2428
only be thou v for me, and fight ... 1Sa 18:17 1121,2428
to Abner, Art not thou a v man ... 1Sa 26:15
All the v men arose, and went all ... 1Sa 31:12 2428
be strengthened, and be ye v ... 2Sa 2:7 1121,2428
where he knew that v men were ... 2Sa 11:16 2428
be courageous, and be v ... 2Sa 13:28 1121,2428
And he also that is v, whose heart ... 2Sa 17:10 1121,2428
they which be with him are v men ... 2Sa 17:10 2428
of Jehoiada, the son of a v man ... 2Sa 23:20 2428
v men that drew the sword ... 2Sa 24:9 2428
for thou art a v man, and bringest ... 1Kin 1:42 2428
of v men, men able to bear ... 1Chr 5:18 2428
they were v men of might in their ... 1Chr 7:2 1368
of Issachar were v men of might ... 1Chr 7:5 1368
They arose, all the v men ... 1Chr 10:12 2428
the son of a v man of Kabzeel, ... 1Chr 11:22 2428
Also the v men of the armies were ... 1Chr 11:26 1368
mighty men, and with all the v men ... 1Chr 28:1 2428
with an army of v men of war ... 2Chr 13:3 1368
of the LORD, that were v men ... 2Chr 26:17 2428
in one day, which were all v men ... 2Chr 28:6 2428
hundred threescore and eight v men ... Neh 11:6 2428
threescore v men are about it, of ... Song 3:7 1368
are about it, of the v of Israel ... Song 3:7 1368
down the inhabitants like a v man ... Is 10:13 3524
their v ones shall cry without ... Is 33:7 691
but they are not v for the truth ... Jer 9:3 1396
Why are thy v men swept away ... Jer 46:15 47
red, the v men are in scarlet ... Nah 2:3 2428
waxed v in fight, turned to ... Heb 11:34 *2478*

VALIANTEST {1}
twelve thousand men of the v ... Judg 21:10 1121,2428

VALIANTLY {6}
and Israel shall do v ... Num 24:18 2428
behave ourselves v for our people ... 1Chr 19:13 2388
Through God we shall do v ... Ps 60:12 2428
Through God we shall do v ... Ps 108:13 2428
right hand of the LORD doeth v ... Ps 118:15 2428
right hand of the LORD doeth v ... Ps 118:16 2428

VALLEY {140}
at the v of Shaveh, which is the ... Gen 14:17 6010
his tent in the v of Gerar ... Gen 26:17 5158
Isaac's servants digged in the v ... Gen 26:19 5158
and the Canaanites dwelt in the v ... Num 14:25 6010
and pitched in the v of Zared ... Num 21:12 5158
And from Bamoth in the v, that is ... Num 21:20 1516
they went up unto the v of Eshcol ... Num 32:9 5158
and came unto the v of Eshcol ... Deut 1:24 5158
unto the river Arnon half the v ... Deut 3:16 5158
So we abode in the v over against ... Deut 3:29 1516
in the v over against Beth-peor, ... Deut 4:46 1516
down the heifer unto a rough v ... Deut 21:4 5158
the heifer's neck there in the v ... Deut 21:4 5158
heifer that is beheaded in the v ... Deut 21:6 5158
and the plain of the v of Jericho ... Deut 34:3 1237
he buried him in a v in the land ... Deut 34:6 1516
brought them unto the v of Achor ... Josh 7:24 6010
The v of Achor, unto this day ... Josh 7:26 6010
now there was a v between them ... Josh 8:11 1516
night into the midst of the v ... Josh 8:13 6010
and thou, Moon, in the v of Ajalon ... Josh 10:12 6010
south of Chinneroth, and in the v ... Josh 11:2 8219
unto the v of Mizpeh eastward ... Josh 11:8 1237
all the land of Goshen, and the v ... Josh 11:16 8219
of Israel, and the v of the same ... Josh 11:16 8219
even unto Baal-gad in the v of ... Josh 11:17 1237
from Baal-gad in the v of Lebanon ... Josh 12:7 1237
in the mount of the v, ... Josh 13:19 6010
And in the v, Beth-aram, and ... Josh 13:27 6010
toward Debir from the v of Achor ... Josh 15:7 6010
the border went up by the v of ... Josh 15:8 1516
before the v of Hinnom westward ... Josh 15:8 1516
of the v of the giants northward ... Josh 15:8 6010
And in the v, Eshtaol, and Zoreah, ... Josh 15:33 8219
of the v have chariots of iron ... Josh 17:16 6010
they who are of the v of Jezreel ... Josh 17:16 6010
before the v of the son of Hinnom ... Josh 18:16 1516
which is in the v of the giants ... Josh 18:16 6010
and descended to the v of Hinnom ... Josh 18:16 1516
Beth-hoglah, and the v of Keziz, ... Josh 18:21 6010
are in the v of Jiphthah-el ... Josh 19:14 1516
to the v of Jiphthah-el toward ... Josh 19:27 1516
and in the south, and in the v ... Judg 1:9 8219
out the inhabitants of the v ... Judg 1:19 6010
suffer them to come down to the v ... Judg 1:34 6010
he was sent on foot into the v ... Judg 5:15 6010
and pitched in the v of Jezreel ... Judg 6:33 6010
by the hill of Moreh, in the v ... Judg 7:1 6010
Midian was beneath him in the v ... Judg 7:8 6010
of the east lay along in the v ... Judg 7:12 6010
loved a woman in the v of Sorek ... Judg 16:4 5158
it was in the v that lieth by ... Judg 18:28 6010
their wheat harvest in the v ... 1Sa 6:13 6010
the border that looketh to the v ... 1Sa 13:18 1516
of Amalek, and laid wait in the v ... 1Sa 15:5 5158
and pitched by the v of Elah ... 1Sa 17:2 6010
there was a v between them ... 1Sa 17:3 1516
of Israel, were in the v of Elah ... 1Sa 17:19 6010
until thou come to the v ... 1Sa 17:52 1516
thou slewest in the v of Elah ... 1Sa 21:9 6010
were on the other side of the v ... 1Sa 31:7 6010
themselves in the v of Rephaim ... 2Sa 5:18 6010
themselves in the v of Rephaim ... 2Sa 5:22 6010
of the Syrians in the v of salt ... 2Sa 8:13 1516
pitched in the v of Rephaim ... 2Sa 23:13 6010
some mountain, or into some v ... 2Kin 2:16 1516
Make this v full of ditches ... 2Kin 3:16 5158
yet that v shall be filled with ... 2Kin 3:17 5158
in the v of salt ten thousand ... 2Kin 14:7 1516
which is in the v of the children ... 2Kin 23:10 1516
the father of the v of Charashim ... 1Chr 4:14 1516
even unto the east side of the v ... 1Chr 4:39 1516
were in the v saw that they fled ... 1Chr 10:7 6010
encamped in the v of Rephaim ... 1Chr 11:15 6010
themselves in the v of Rephaim ... 1Chr 14:9 6010
spread themselves abroad in the v ... 1Chr 14:13 6010
the v of salt eighteen thousand ... 1Chr 18:12 1516
in the v of Zephathah at Mareshah ... 2Chr 14:10 1516
themselves in the v of Berachah ... 2Chr 20:26 6010
The v of Berachah, unto this day ... 2Chr 20:26 6010
people, and went to the v of salt ... 2Chr 25:11 1516
the corner gate, and at the v gate ... 2Chr 26:9 1516
in the v of the son of Hinnom ... 2Chr 28:3 1516
in the v of the son of Hinnom ... 2Chr 33:6 1516
the west side of Gihon, in the v ... 2Chr 33:14 5158
came to fight in the v of Megiddo ... 2Chr 35:22 1237
out by night by the gate of the v ... Neh 2:13 1516
and entered by the gate of the v ... Neh 2:15 1516
The v gate repaired Hanun, and the ... Neh 3:13 1516
Beer-sheba unto the v of Hinnom ... Neh 11:30 1516
Lod, and Ono, the v of craftsmen ... Neh 11:35 1516
The clods of the v shall be sweet ... Job 21:33 5158
He paweth in the v, and rejoiceth ... Job 39:21 6010

the *v* of the shadow of death ... Ps 23:4 1516
smote of Edom in the *v* of salt ... Ps 60:*t* 1516
and mete out the *v* of Succoth ... Ps 60:6 6010
the *v* of Baca make it a well ... Ps 84:6 6010
and mete out the *v* of Succoth ... Ps 108:7 6010
ravens of the *v* shall pick it out ... Prov 30:17 5158
nuts to see the fruits of the *v* ... Song 6:11 5158
ears in the *v* of Rephaim ... Is 17:5 6010
The burden of the *v* of vision ... Is 22:1 1516
God of hosts in the *v* of vision ... Is 22:5 1516
which is on the head of the fat *v* ... Is 28:4 1516
be wroth as in the *v* of Gibeon ... Is 28:21 6010
Every *v* shall be exalted, and ... Is 40:4 1516
As a beast goeth down into the *v* ... Is 63:14 1237
the *v* of Achor a place for the ... Is 65:10 6010
see thy way in the *v*, know what ... Jer 2:23 1516
which is in the *v* of the son of ... Jer 7:31 1516
nor the *v* of the son of Hinnom, ... Jer 7:32 1516
of Hinnom, but the *v* of slaughter ... Jer 7:32 1516
go forth unto the *v* of the son of ... Jer 19:2 1516
nor The *v* of the son of Hinnom, ... Jer 19:6 1516
of Hinnom, but The *v* of slaughter ... Jer 19:6 1516
thee, O inhabitant of the *v* ... Jer 21:13 6010
the whole *v* of the dead bodies, ... Jer 31:40 6010
which are in the *v* of the son of ... Jer 32:35 1516
and in the cities of the *v* ... Jer 32:44 8219
off with the remnant of their *v* ... Jer 47:5 6010
the *v* also shall perish, and the ... Jer 48:8 6010
in the valleys, thy flowing *v* ... Jer 49:4 6010
of the *v* which was full of bones ... Eze 37:1 1237
were very many in the open *v* ... Eze 37:2 1237
the *v* of the passengers on the ... Eze 39:11 1516
shall call it The *v* of Hamon-gog ... Eze 39:11 1516
buried it in the *v* of Hamon-gog ... Eze 39:15 1516
bow of Israel in the *v* of Jezreel ... Hos 1:5 6010
the *v* of Achor for a door of hope ... Hos 2:15 6010
down into the *v* of Jehoshaphat ... Joel 3:2 6010
come up to the *v* of Jehoshaphat ... Joel 3:12 6010
multitudes in the *v* of decision ... Joel 3:14 6010
Lord is near in the *v* of decision ... Joel 3:14 6010
and shall water the *v* of Shittim ... Joel 3:18 5158
the stones thereof into the *v* ... Mic 1:6 1516
Hadadrimmon in the *v* of Megiddon ... Zec 12:11 1237
and there shall be a very great *v* ... Zec 14:4 1516
flee to the *v* of the mountains ... Zec 14:5 1516
for the *v* of the mountains shall ... Zec 14:5 1516
Every *v* shall be filled, and every ... Lk 3:5 *5327*

VALLEYS {28}
As the *v* are they spread forth, ... Num 24:6 5158
and depths that spring out of *v* ... Deut 8:7 1237
it, is a land of hills and *v* ... Deut 11:11 1237
Jordan, in the hills, and in the *v* ... Josh 9:1 8219
In the mountains, and in the *v* ... Josh 12:8 8219
hills, but he is not God of the *v* ... 1Kin 20:28 6010
put to flight all them of the *v* ... 1Chr 12:15 6010
v was Shaphat the son of Adlai ... 1Chr 27:29 6010
To dwell in the cliffs of the *v* ... Job 30:6 5158
will he harrow the *v* after thee ... Job 39:10 6010
the *v* also are covered over with ... Ps 65:13 6010
they go down by the *v* unto the ... Ps 104:8 1237
He sendeth the springs into the *v* ... Ps 104:10 5158
of Sharon, and the lily of the *v* ... Song 2:1 6010
all of them in the desolate *v* ... Is 7:19 5158
that thy choicest *v* shall be full ... Is 22:7 6010
are on the head of the fat *v* of ... Is 28:1 1516
fountains in the midst of the *v* ... Is 41:18 1237
slaying the children in the *v* ... Is 57:5 5158
Wherefore gloriest thou in the *v* ... Jer 49:4 6010
hills, to the rivers, and to the *v* ... Eze 6:3 1516
the mountains like doves of the *v* ... Eze 7:16 1516
in all the *v* his branches are ... Eze 31:12 1516
fill the *v* with thy height ... Eze 32:5 1516
in thy hills, and in thy *v* ... Eze 35:8 1516
hills, to the rivers, and to the *v* ... Eze 36:4 1516
hills, to the rivers, and to the *v* ... Eze 36:6 1516
the *v* shall be cleft, as wax ... Mic 1:4 6010

VALOUR {37}
armed, all the mighty men of *v* ... Josh 1:14 2428
thereof, and the mighty men of *v* ... Josh 6:2 2428
thirty thousand mighty men of *v* ... Josh 8:3 2428
him, and all the mighty men of *v* ... Josh 10:7 2428
men, all lusty, and all men of *v* ... Judg 3:29 2428
with thee, thou mighty man of *v* ... Judg 6:12 2428
Gileadite was a mighty man of *v* ... Judg 11:1 2428
men from their coasts, men of *v* ... Judg 18:2 2428
all these were men of *v* ... Judg 20:44 2428
all these were men of *v* ... Judg 20:46 2428
Jeroboam was a mighty man of *v* ... 1Kin 11:28 2428
he was also a mighty man in *v* ... 2Kin 5:1 2428
and all the mighty men of *v* ... 2Kin 24:14 2428
and Jahdiel, mighty men of *v* ... 1Chr 5:24 2428
of their fathers, mighty men of *v* ... 1Chr 7:7 2428
of their fathers, mighty men of *v* ... 1Chr 7:9 2428
of their fathers, mighty men of *v* ... 1Chr 7:11 2428
house, choice and mighty men of *v* ... 1Chr 7:40 2428
sons of Ulam were mighty men of *v* ... 1Chr 8:40 2428
for they were all mighty men of *v* ... 1Chr 12:21 2428
mighty men of *v* for the war ... 1Chr 12:25 2428
And Zadok, a young man mighty of *v* ... 1Chr 12:28 2428
and eight hundred, mighty men of *v* ... 1Chr 12:30 2428
for they were mighty men of *v* ... 1Chr 26:6 2428
and his brethren, men of *v* ... 1Chr 26:30 2428
men of *v* at Jazer of Gilead ... 1Chr 26:31 2428
And his brethren, men of *v* ... 1Chr 26:32 2428
chosen men, being mighty men of *v* ... 2Chr 13:3 2428
all these were mighty men of *v* ... 2Chr 14:8 2428
the men of war, mighty men of *v* ... 2Chr 17:13 2428
men of *v* three hundred thousand ... 2Chr 17:14 2428
hundred thousand mighty men of *v* ... 2Chr 17:16 2428
Eliada a mighty man of *v*, and with ... 2Chr 17:17 2428
of *v* out of Israel for an hundred ... 2Chr 25:6 2428
mighty men of *v* were two thousand ... 2Chr 26:12 2428
cut off all the mighty men of *v* ... 2Chr 32:21 2428
their brethren, mighty men of *v* ... Neh 11:14 2428

VALUE {7}
priest, and the priest shall *v* him ... Lev 27:8 6186
that vowed shall the priest *v* him ... Lev 27:8 6186
And the priest shall *v* it, whether ... Lev 27:12 6186
ye are all physicians of no *v* ... Job 13:4 457
ye are of more *v* than many ... Mt 10:31 *1308*
of the children of Israel did *v* ... Mt 27:9 *5091*
ye are of more *v* than many ... Lk 12:7 *1308*

VALUED {4}
be *v* at fifty shekels of silver ... Lev 27:16
It cannot be *v* with the gold of ... Job 28:16 5541
shall it be *v* with pure gold ... Job 28:19 5541
the price of him that was *v* ... Mt 27:9 *5091*

VALUEST {1}
as thou *v* it, who art the priest, ... Lev 27:12 6187

VANIAH *(va-ni'-ah)* {1} *Married a foreigner in exile.*
V, Meremoth, Eliashib, ... Ezr 10:36 2057

VANISH {4}
What time they wax warm, they *v* ... Job 6:17 6789
heavens shall *v* away like smoke ... Is 51:6 4414
be knowledge, it shall *v* away ... 1Cor 13:8 *2673*
and waxeth old is ready to *v* away ... Heb 8:13 *854*

VANISHED {2}
is their wisdom *v* ... Jer 49:7 5628
and he *v* out of their sight ... Lk 24:31 *1096,855*

VANISHETH {2}
the cloud is consumed and *v* away ... Job 7:9 3212
for a little time, and then *v* away ... Jas 4:14 *853*

VANITIES {13}
provoked me to anger with their *v* ... Deut 32:21 1892
of Israel to anger with their *v* ... 1Kin 16:13 1892
of Israel to anger with their *v* ... 1Kin 16:26 1892
hated them that regard lying *v* ... Ps 31:6 1892
Vanity of *v*, saith the Preacher, ... Eccl 1:2 1892
saith the Preacher, vanity of *v* ... Eccl 1:2 1892
words there are also divers *v* ... Eccl 5:7 1892
Vanity of *v*, saith the preacher ... Eccl 12:8 1892
graven images, and with strange *v* ... Jer 8:19 1892
the stock is a doctrine of *v* ... Jer 10:8 1892
Are there any among the *v* of the ... Jer 14:22 1892
lying *v* forsake their own mercy ... Jonah 2:8 1892
from these *v* unto the living God ... Acts 14:15 *3152*

VANITY {86}
and they followed *v*, and became ... 2Kin 17:15 1892
am I made to possess months of *v* ... Job 7:3 7723
for my days are *v* ... Job 7:16 1892
him that is deceived trust in *v* ... Job 15:31 7723
for *v* shall be his recompence ... Job 15:31 7723
mischief, and bring forth *v* ... Job 15:35 205
If I have walked with *v*, or if my ... Job 31:5 7723
Surely God will not hear *v* ... Job 35:13 7723
how long will ye love *v*, and seek ... Ps 4:2 7385
under his tongue is mischief and *v* ... Ps 10:7 205
They speak *v* every one with his ... Ps 12:2 7723
not lifted up his soul unto *v* ... Ps 24:4 7723
at his best state is altogether *v* ... Ps 39:5 1892
surely every man is *v* ... Ps 39:11 1892
he come to see me, he speaketh *v* ... Ps 41:6 7723
Surely men of low degree are *v* ... Ps 62:9 1892
are altogether lighter than *v* ... Ps 62:9 1892
their days did he consume in *v* ... Ps 78:33 1892
thoughts of man, that they are *v* ... Ps 94:11 1892
away mine eyes from beholding *v* ... Ps 119:37 7723
Man is like to *v* ... Ps 144:4 1892
Whose mouth speaketh *v*, and their ... Ps 144:8 7723
children, whose mouth speaketh *v* ... Ps 144:11 7723
Wealth gotten by *v* shall be ... Prov 13:11 1892
a lying tongue is a *v* tossed to ... Prov 21:6 1892
that soweth iniquity shall reap *v* ... Prov 22:8 205
Remove far from me *v* and lies ... Prov 30:8 7723
V of vanities, saith the Preacher ... Eccl 1:2 1892
saith the Preacher, *v* of vanities ... Eccl 1:2 1892
all is *v* ... Eccl 1:2 1892
and, behold, all is *v* and vexation ... Eccl 1:14 1892
and, behold, this also is *v* ... Eccl 2:1 1892
and, behold, all was *v* and vexation ... Eccl 2:11 1892
in my heart, that this also is *v* ... Eccl 2:15 1892
for all is *v* and vexation of ... Eccl 2:17 1892
This also is *v* ... Eccl 2:19 1892
This also is *v* and a great evil ... Eccl 2:21 1892
This also is *v* ... Eccl 2:23 1892
This also is *v* and vexation of ... Eccl 2:26 1892
for all is *v* ... Eccl 3:19 1892
This also is *v* and vexation of ... Eccl 4:4 1892
and I saw *v* under the sun ... Eccl 4:7 1892
This is also *v*, yea, it is a sore ... Eccl 4:8 1892
Surely this also is *v* and vexation ... Eccl 4:16 1892
this is also *v* ... Eccl 5:10 1892
this is *v*, and it is an evil ... Eccl 6:2 1892
For he cometh in with *v*, and ... Eccl 6:4 1892
this is also *v* and vexation of ... Eccl 6:9 1892
be many things that increase *v* ... Eccl 6:11 1892
this also is *v* ... Eccl 7:6 1892
have I seen in the days of my *v* ... Eccl 7:15 1892
this is also *v* ... Eccl 8:10 1892
There is a *v* which is done upon ... Eccl 8:14 1892
I said that this also is *v* ... Eccl 8:14 1892
all the days of the life of thy *v* ... Eccl 9:9 1892
the sun, all the days of thy *v* ... Eccl 9:9 1892
All that cometh is *v* ... Eccl 11:8 1892
for childhood and youth are *v* ... Eccl 11:10 1892
V of vanities, saith the preacher ... Eccl 12:8 1892
all is *v* ... Eccl 12:8 1892
draw iniquity with cords of *v* ... Is 5:18 7723
the nations with the sieve of *v* ... Is 30:28 7723
to him less than nothing, and *v* ... Is 40:17 8414
the judges of the earth as *v* ... Is 40:23 8414
Behold, they are all *v* ... Is 41:29 205
a graven image are all of them *v* ... Is 44:9 8414
v shall take them ... Is 57:13 1892
of the finger, and speaking *v* ... Is 58:9 205
they trust in *v*, and speak lies ... Is 59:4 8414
from me, and have walked after *v* ... Jer 2:5 1892
They are *v*, and the work of errors ... Jer 10:15 1892
fathers have inherited lies, *v* ... Jer 16:19 1892
me, they have burned incense to *v* ... Jer 18:15 7723
They are *v*, the work of errors ... Jer 51:18 1892
They have seen *v* and lying ... Eze 13:6 7723
Because ye have spoken *v*, and seen ... Eze 13:8 7723
be upon the prophets that see *v* ... Eze 13:9 7723
Therefore ye shall see no more *v* ... Eze 13:23 7723
Whiles they see *v* unto thee ... Eze 21:29 7723
with untempered morter, seeing *v* ... Eze 22:28 7723
surely they are *v* ... Hos 12:11 7723
shall weary themselves for very *v* ... Hab 2:13 7385
For the idols have spoken *v* ... Zec 10:2 205
creature was made subject to *v* ... Rom 8:20 *3153*
walk, in the *v* of their mind, ... Eph 4:17 *3153*
speak great swelling words of *v* ... 2Pet 2:18 *3153*

VAPORS {2}
he causeth the *v* to ascend from ... Jer 10:13 5387
he causeth the *v* to ascend from ... Jer 51:16 5387

VAPOUR {4}
rain according to the *v* thereof ... Job 36:27 108
the cattle also concerning the *v* ... Job 36:33 5927
blood, and fire, and *v* of smoke ... Acts 2:19 *822*
It is even a *v*, that appeareth ... Jas 4:14 *822*

VAPOURS {2}
He causeth the *v* to ascend from ... Ps 135:7 5387
and hail; snow, and *v* ... Ps 148:8 7008

VARIABLENESS {1}
of lights, with whom is no *v* ... Jas 1:17 *3883*

VARIANCE {2}
set a man at *v* against his father ... Mt 10:35 *1369*
Idolatry, witchcraft, hatred, *v* ... Gal 5:20 *2054*

VASHNI *(vash'-ni)* {1} *A son of Samuel.*
the firstborn *V*, and Abiah ... 1Chr 6:28 2059

VASHTI *(vash'-ti)* {10} *A Persian queen, succeeded by Esther.*
Also *V* the queen made a feast for ... Est 1:9 2060
To bring *V* the queen before the ... Est 1:11 2060
But the queen *V* refused to come ... Est 1:12 2060
unto the queen *V* according to law ... Est 1:15 2060
V the queen hath not done wrong ... Est 1:16 2060
V the queen to be brought in ... Est 1:17 2060
That *V* come no more before king ... Est 1:19 2060
was appeased, he remembered *V* ... Est 2:1 2060
the king be queen instead of *V* ... Est 2:4 2060
and made her queen instead of *V* ... Est 2:17 2060

VAUNT {1}
lest Israel *v* themselves against ... Judg 7:2 6286

VAUNTETH {1}
charity *v* not itself, is not ... 1Cor 13:4 *4068*

VEDAN See Dan.

VEHEMENT {3}
fire, which hath a most *v* flame ... Song 8:6 3050
that God prepared a *v* east wind ... Jonah 4:8 2759
what *v* desire, yea, what zeal, ... 2Cor 7:11 *1972*

VEHEMENTLY {5}
But he spake the more *v*, If I ... Mk 14:31 *1722*,4053
the stream beat *v* upon that house ... Lk 6:48 *4366*
which the stream did beat *v* ... Lk 6:49 *4366*
the Pharisees began to urge him *v* ... Lk 11:53 *1171*
and scribes stood and *v* accused him ... Lk 23:10 *2159*

VEIL {7}
the walls took away my *v* from me ... Song 5:7 7289
the *v* of the temple was rent in ... Mt 27:51 *2665*
the *v* of the temple was rent in ... Mk 15:38 *2665*
the *v* of the temple was rent in ... Lk 23:45 *2665*
entereth into that within the *v* ... Heb 6:19 *2665*
And after the second *v*, the ... Heb 9:3 *2665*
consecrated for us, through the *v* ... Heb 10:20 *2665*

VEIN {1}
there is a *v* for the silver ... Job 28:1 4161

VENGEANCE {45}
v shall be taken on him sevenfold ... Gen 4:15 5358
To me belongeth *v*, and recompence ... Deut 32:35 5359
I will render *v* to mine enemies, ... Deut 32:41 5359
will render *v* to his adversaries, ... Deut 32:43 5359
as the Lord hath taken *v* for thee ... Judg 11:36 5360
shall rejoice when he seeth the *v* ... Ps 58:10 5359
O LORD God, to whom *v* belongeth ... Ps 94:1 5360
to whom *v* belongeth, shew thyself ... Ps 94:1 5360
tookest *v* of their inventions ... Ps 99:8 5358
To execute *v* upon the heathen, and ... Ps 149:7 5360
he will not spare in the day of *v* ... Prov 6:34 5359
For it is the day of the Lord's *v* ... Is 34:8 5359
behold, your God will come with *v* ... Is 35:4 5359
I will take *v*, and I will not meet ... Is 47:3 5359
on the garments of *v* for clothing ... Is 59:17 5359
Lord, and the day of *v* of our God ... Is 61:2 5359

For the day of v is in mine heart ... Is 63:4 5359
heart, let me see thy v on them ... Jer 11:20 5360
heart, let me see thy v on them ... Jer 20:12 5360
the Lord GOD of hosts, a day of v ... Jer 46:10 5360
for it is the v of the LORD ... Jer 50:15 5360
take v upon her ... Jer 50:15 5358
in Zion the v of the LORD our God ... Jer 50:28 5360
LORD our God, the v of his temple ... Jer 50:28 5360
this is the time of the LORD's v ... Jer 51:6 5360
because it is the v of the LORD ... Jer 51:11 5360
of the LORD, the v of his temple ... Jer 51:11 5360
thy cause, and take v for thee ... Jer 51:36 5360
Thou hast seen all their v ... Lam 3:60 5360
cause fury to come up to take v ... Eze 24:8 5359
the house of Judah by taking v ... Eze 25:12 5359
I will lay my v upon Edom by the ... Eze 25:14 5360
and they shall know my v, saith ... Eze 25:14 5360
have taken v with a despiteful ... Eze 25:15 5359
I will execute great v upon them ... Eze 25:17 5360
when I shall lay my v upon them ... Eze 25:17 5360
And I will execute v in anger ... Mic 5:15 5359
will take v on his adversaries ... Nah 1:2 5358
For these be the days of v ... Lk 21:22 1557
yet v suffereth not to live ... Acts 28:4 1349
Is God unrighteous who taketh v ... Rom 3:5 3709
for it is written, V is mine ... Rom 12:19 1557
In flaming fire taking v on them ... 2Th 1:8 1557
V belongeth unto me, I will ... Heb 10:30 1557
suffering the v of eternal fire ... Jude 7 1349

VENISON {8}
Esau, because he did eat of his v ... Gen 25:28 6718
to the field, and take me some v ... Gen 27:3 6720
went to the field to hunt for v ... Gen 27:5 6718
Bring me v, and make me savoury ... Gen 27:7 6718
I pray thee, sit and eat of my v ... Gen 27:19 6718
me, and I will eat of my son's v ... Gen 27:25 6718
arise, and eat of his son's v ... Gen 27:31 6718
where is he that hath taken v ... Gen 27:33 6718

VENOM {1}
dragons, and the cruel v of asps ... Deut 32:33 7219

VENOMOUS {1}
saw the v beast hang on his hand ... Acts 28:4

VENT {1}
belly is as wine which hath no v ... Job 32:19 6605

VENTURE {2}
a certain man drew a bow at a v ... 1Kin 22:34 8537
a certain man drew a bow at a v ... 2Chr 18:33 8537

VERIFIED {3}
so shall your words be v, and ye ... Gen 42:20 539
let thy word, I pray thee, be v ... 1Kin 8:26 539
God of Israel, let thy word be v ... 2Chr 6:17 539

VERILY {140}
We are v guilty concerning our ... Gen 42:21 61
V my sabbaths ye shall keep ... Ex 31:13 389
I v thought that thou hadst ... Judg 15:2 559
V our lord king David hath made ... 1Kin 1:43 61
V she hath no child, and her ... 2Kin 4:14 61
but I will v buy it for the full ... 1Chr 21:24 7069
are v estranged from me ... Job 19:13 389
the land, and v thou shalt be fed ... Ps 37:3 530
v every man at his best state is ... Ps 39:5 389
V there is a reward for the ... Ps 58:11 389
v he is a God that judgeth in the ... Ps 58:11 389
But v God hath heard me ... Ps 66:19 403
V I have cleansed my heart in ... Ps 73:13 389
V thou art a God that hidest ... Is 45:15 403
V it shall be well with thy ... Jer 15:11 518,3808
v I will cause the enemy to ... Jer 15:11 518
For v I say unto you, Till heaven ... Mt 5:18 281
V I say unto thee, Thou shalt by ... Mt 5:26 281
V I say unto you, They have their ... Mt 6:2 281
V I say unto you, They have their ... Mt 6:5 281
V I say unto you, They have their ... Mt 6:16 281
V I say unto you, I have not ... Mt 8:10 281
V I say unto you, It shall be ... Mt 10:15 281
for v I say unto you, Ye shall ... Mt 10:23 281
v I say unto you, he shall in no ... Mt 10:42 281
V I say unto you, Among them that ... Mt 11:11 281
For v I say unto you, That many ... Mt 13:17 281
V I say unto you, There be some ... Mt 16:28 281
for v I say unto you, If ye have ... Mt 17:20 281
V I say unto you, Except ye be ... Mt 18:3 281
v I say unto you, he rejoiceth ... Mt 18:13 281
V I say unto you, Whatsoever ye ... Mt 18:18 281
V I say unto you, That a rich man ... Mt 19:23 281
V I say unto you, That ye which ... Mt 19:28 281
V I say unto you, If ye have ... Mt 21:21 281
V I say unto you, That the ... Mt 21:31 281
V I say unto you, All these ... Mt 23:36 281
v I say unto you, There shall not ... Mt 24:2 281
V I say unto you, This generation ... Mt 24:34 281
V I say unto you, That he shall ... Mt 24:47 281
V I say unto you, I know you not ... Mt 25:12 281
V I say unto you, Inasmuch as ye ... Mt 25:40 281
V I say unto you, Inasmuch as ye ... Mt 25:45 281
V I say unto you, Wheresoever ... Mt 26:13 281
V I say unto you, that one of you ... Mt 26:21 281
V I say unto thee, That this ... Mt 26:34 281
V I say unto you, All sins shall ... Mk 3:28 281
V I say unto you, It shall be ... Mk 6:11 281
v I say unto you, There shall no ... Mk 8:12 281
V I say unto you, That there be ... Mk 9:1 281
them, Elias v cometh first, and ... Mk 9:12 3303
v I say unto you, he shall not ... Mk 9:41 281
V I say unto you, Whosoever shall ... Mk 10:15 281
V I say unto you, There is no man ... Mk 10:29 281
For v I say unto you, That ... Mk 11:23 281
V I say unto you, That this poor ... Mk 12:43 281
V I say unto you, that this ... Mk 13:30 281
V I say unto you, Wheresoever ... Mk 14:9 281
V I say unto you, One of you ... Mk 14:18 281
V I say unto you, I will drink no ... Mk 14:25 281
V I say unto thee, That this day ... Mk 14:30 281
V I say unto you, No prophet is ... Lk 4:24 281
v I say unto you, It shall be ... Lk 11:51 3483
v I say unto you, that he shall ... Lk 12:37 281
v I say unto you, Ye shall not ... Lk 13:35 281
V I say unto you, Whosoever shall ... Lk 18:17 281
V I say unto you, There is no man ... Lk 18:29 281
V I say unto you, This generation ... Lk 21:32 281
V I say unto thee, To day shalt ... Lk 23:43 281
And he saith unto him, V, v ... Jn 1:51 281
and said unto him, V, v ... Jn 3:3 281
Jesus answered, V, v ... Jn 3:5 281
V, v, I say unto thee, We ... Jn 3:11 281
and said unto them, V, v ... Jn 5:19 281
V, v, I say unto you, He ... Jn 5:24 281
V, v, I say unto you, The ... Jn 5:25 281
answered them and said, V, v ... Jn 6:26 281
Jesus said unto them, V, v ... Jn 6:32 281
V, v, I say unto you, He ... Jn 6:47 281
Jesus said unto them, V, v ... Jn 6:53 281
Jesus answered them, V, v ... Jn 8:34 281
V, v, I say unto you, If a ... Jn 8:51 281
Jesus said unto them, V, v ... Jn 8:58 281
V, v, I say unto you, He ... Jn 10:1 281
Jesus unto them again, V, v ... Jn 10:7 281
V, v, I say unto you, Except ... Jn 12:24 281
V, v, I say unto you, The ... Jn 13:16 281
V, v, I say unto you, He ... Jn 13:20 281
and testified, and said, V, v ... Jn 13:21 281
V, v, I say unto thee, The ... Jn 13:38 281
V, v, I say unto you, He ... Jn 14:12 281
V, v, I say unto you, That ... Jn 16:20 281
V, v, I say unto you ... Jn 16:23 281
V, v, I say unto thee, When ... Jn 21:18 281
nay v; but let them ... Acts 16:37 1063
John v baptized with the baptism ... Acts 19:4 3303
I am v a man which am a Jew, born ... Acts 22:3 3303
I v thought with myself, that I ... Acts 26:9 3303,3767
For circumcision v profiteth ... Rom 2:25 3303
Yes v, their sound went into all ... Rom 10:18 3304
It hath pleased them v ... Rom 15:27 1063
For I v, as absent in body, but ... 1Cor 5:3 3303
V that, when I preach the gospel, ... 1Cor 9:18
For thou v givest thanks well, ... 1Cor 14:17 3303
v righteousness should have been ... Gal 3:21 3689
For v, when we were with you, we ... 1Th 3:4 2532
For v he took not on him the ... Heb 2:16 1222
Moses v was faithful in all his ... Heb 3:5 3303
For men v swear by the greater ... Heb 6:16 3303
v they that are of the sons of ... Heb 7:5 3303
For there is v a disannulling of ... Heb 7:18 3303
Then v the first covenant had ... Heb 9:1 3303
For they v for a few days ... Heb 12:10 3303
Who v was foreordained before the ... 1Pet 1:20 3303
in him v is the love of God ... 1Jn 2:5 230

VERITY {2}
The works of his hands are v ... Ps 111:7 571
of the Gentiles in faith and v ... 1Ti 2:7 225

VERMILION {2}
with cedar, and painted with v ... Jer 22:14 8350
the Chaldeans pourtrayed with v ... Eze 23:14 8350

VERY See APPENDIX.

VESSEL {46}
But the earthen v wherein it is ... Lev 6:28 3627
whether it be any v of wood ... Lev 11:32 3627
skin, or sack, whatsoever v it be ... Lev 11:32 3627
And every earthen v, whereinto any ... Lev 11:33 3627
in every such v shall be unclean ... Lev 11:34 3627
an earthen v over running water ... Lev 14:5 3627
an earthen v over running water ... Lev 14:50 3627
the v of earth, that he toucheth ... Lev 15:12 3627
every v of wood shall be rinsed ... Lev 15:12 3627
take holy water in an earthen v ... Num 5:17 3627
And every open v, which hath no ... Num 19:15 3627
water shall be put thereto in a v ... Num 19:17 3627
thou shalt not put any in thy v ... Deut 23:24 3627
were sanctified this day in the v ... 1Sa 21:5 3627
pray thee, a little water in a v ... 1Kin 17:10 3627
unto her son, Bring me yet a v ... 2Kin 4:6 3627
unto her, There is not a v more ... 2Kin 4:6 3627
them in pieces like a potter's v ... Ps 2:9 3627
I am like a broken v ... Ps 31:12 3627
come forth a v for the finer ... Prov 25:4 3627
v that is broken in pieces ... Is 30:14 5035
v into the house of the LORD ... Is 66:20 3627
the v that he made of clay was ... Jer 18:4 3627
so he made it again another v ... Jer 18:4 3627
as one breaketh a potter's v ... Jer 19:11 3627
is he a v wherein is no pleasure ... Jer 22:28 3627
ye shall fall like a pleasant v ... Jer 25:34 3627
and put them in an earthen v ... Jer 32:14 3627
not been emptied from v to v ... Jer 48:11 3627
like a v wherein is no pleasure ... Jer 48:38 3627
me, he hath made me an empty v ... Jer 51:34 3627
and fitches, and put them in one v ... Eze 4:9 3627
a pin of it to hang any v thereon ... Eze 15:3 3627
as a v wherein is no pleasure ... Hos 8:8 3627
carry any v through the temple ... Mk 11:16 4632
a candle, covereth it with a v ... Lk 8:16 4632
there was set a v full of vinegar ... Jn 19:29 4632
for he is a chosen v unto me ... Acts 9:15 4632
a certain v descending unto him, ... Acts 10:11 4632
the v was received up again into ... Acts 10:16 4632
saw a vision, A certain v descend ... Acts 11:5 4632
lump to make one v unto honour ... Rom 9:21 4632
possess his v in sanctification ... 1Th 4:4 4632
he shall be a v unto honour ... 2Ti 2:21 4632
the wife, as unto the weaker v ... 1Pet 3:7 4632

VESSELS {154}
best fruits in the land in your v ... Gen 43:11 3627
v of wood, and in v of stone ... Ex 7:19
he make it, with all these v ... Ex 25:39 3627
all the v thereof thou shalt make ... Ex 27:3 3627
All the v of the tabernacle in ... Ex 27:19 3627
And the table and all his v ... Ex 30:27 3627
and the candlestick and his v ... Ex 30:27 3627
of burnt offering with all his v ... Ex 30:28 3627
and his staves, and all his v ... Ex 35:13 3627
grate, his staves, and all his v ... Ex 35:16 3627
he made the v which were upon the ... Ex 37:16 3627
made he it, and all the v thereof ... Ex 37:24 3627
And he made all the v of the altar ... Ex 38:3 3627
all the v thereof made he of ... Ex 38:3 3627
it, and all the v of the altar, ... Ex 38:30 3627
The table, and all the v thereof ... Ex 39:36 3627
in order, and all the v thereof ... Ex 39:37 3627
brass, his staves, and all his v ... Ex 39:39 3627
all the v of the service of the ... Ex 39:40 3627
hallow it, and all the v thereof ... Ex 40:9 3627
the burnt offering, and all his v ... Ex 40:10 3627
anointed the altar and all his v ... Lev 8:11 3627
and over all the v thereof ... Num 1:50 3627
tabernacle, and all the v thereof ... Num 1:50 3627
the v of the sanctuary wherewith ... Num 3:31 3627
thereof, and all the v thereof ... Num 3:36 3627
and all the oil v thereof ... Num 4:9 3627
all the v thereof within a ... Num 4:10 3627
put upon it all the v thereof ... Num 4:14 3627
basons, all the v of the altar ... Num 4:14 3627
all the v of the sanctuary, as ... Num 4:15 3627
sanctuary, and in the v thereof ... Num 4:16 3627
the altar and all the v thereof ... Num 7:1 3627
all the silver v weighed two ... Num 7:85 3627
come nigh the v of the sanctuary ... Num 18:3 3627
upon the tent, and upon all the v ... Num 19:18 3627
gold, and v of brass and iron, are ... Josh 6:19 3627
the v of brass and of iron, they ... Josh 6:24 3627
thou art athirst, go unto the v ... Ruth 2:9 3627
for the bread is spent in our v ... 1Sa 9:7 3627
the v of the young men are holy, ... 1Sa 21:5 3627
brought with him v of silver ... 2Sa 8:10 3627
and v of gold, and v of brass ... 2Sa 8:10 3627
beds, and basons, and earthen v ... 2Sa 17:28 3627
and all these v, which Hiram made ... 1Kin 7:45 3627
Solomon left all the v unweighed ... 1Kin 7:47 3627
Solomon made all the v that ... 1Kin 7:48 3627
the silver, and the gold, and the v ... 1Kin 7:51 3627
all the holy v that were in the ... 1Kin 8:4 3627
Solomon's drinking v were of gold ... 1Kin 10:21 3627
all the v of the house of the ... 1Kin 10:21 3627
v of silver, and v of gold, ... 1Kin 10:25 3627
the LORD, silver, and gold, and v ... 1Kin 15:15 3627
borrow thee v abroad of all thy ... 2Kin 4:3 3627
all thy neighbours, even empty v ... 2Kin 4:3 3627
shalt pour out into all those v ... 2Kin 4:4 3627
sons, who brought the v to her ... 2Kin 4:5
when the v were full, that she ... 2Kin 4:6 3627
the way was full of garments and v ... 2Kin 7:15 3627
any v of gold ... 2Kin 12:13 3627
or v of silver, of the money that ... 2Kin 12:13 3627
all the v that were found in the ... 2Kin 14:14 3627
all the v that were made for Baal ... 2Kin 23:4 3627
cut in pieces all the v of gold ... 2Kin 24:13 3627
all the v of brass wherewith they ... 2Kin 25:14 3627
of all these v was without weight ... 2Kin 25:16 3627
the charge of the ministering v ... 1Chr 9:28 3627
were appointed to oversee the v ... 1Chr 9:29 3627
and the pillars, and the v of brass ... 1Chr 18:8 3627
with him all manner of v of gold ... 1Chr 18:10 3627
of the LORD, and the holy v of God ... 1Chr 22:19 3627
nor any v of it for the service ... 1Chr 23:26 3627
for all the v of service in the ... 1Chr 28:13 3627
all these v in great abundance ... 2Chr 4:18 3627
Solomon made all the v that were ... 2Chr 4:19 3627
all the holy v that were in the ... 2Chr 5:5 3627
all the drinking v of king ... 2Chr 9:20 3627
all the v of the house of the ... 2Chr 9:20 3627
v of silver, and v of gold, ... 2Chr 9:24 3627
dedicated, silver, and gold, and v ... 2Chr 15:18 3627
whereof were made v for the house ... 2Chr 24:14 3627
even v to minister, and to offer ... 2Chr 24:14 3627
and spoons, and v of gold and silver ... 2Chr 24:14 3627
all the v that were found in the ... 2Chr 25:24 3627
the v of the house of God ... 2Chr 28:24 3627
cut in pieces the v of the house ... 2Chr 28:24 3627
offering, with all the v thereof ... 2Chr 29:18 3627
table, with all the v thereof ... 2Chr 29:18 3627
Moreover all the v, which king ... 2Chr 29:19 3627
also carried of the v of the ... 2Chr 36:7 3627
with the goodly v of the house of ... 2Chr 36:10 3627
all the v of the house of God, ... 2Chr 36:18 3627
all the goodly v thereof ... 2Chr 36:19 3627
their hands with v of silver ... Ezr 1:6 3627
the v of the house of the LORD ... Ezr 1:7 3627
and ten, and other v a thousand ... Ezr 1:10 3627
All the v of gold and of silver ... Ezr 1:11 3627

the *v* also of gold and silver of Ezr 5:14 3984
And said unto him, Take these *v* Ezr 5:15 3984
silver *v* of the house of God, Ezr 6:5 3984
The *v* also that are given thee Ezr 7:19 3984
the silver, and the gold, and the *v* Ezr 8:25 3627
silver *v* an hundred talents, and Ezr 8:26 3627
two *v* of fine copper, precious as Ezr 8:27 3627
the *v* are holy also Ezr 8:28 3627
the silver, and the gold, and the *v* Ezr 8:30 3627
the *v* weighed in the house of our Ezr 8:33 3627
where are the *v* of the sanctuary, Neh 10:39 3627
the frankincense, and the *v* Neh 13:5 3627
I again the *v* of the house of God Neh 13:9 3627
they gave them drink in *v* of gold Est 1:7 3627
(the *v* being diverse one from Est 1:7 3627
even in *v* of bulrushes upon the Is 18:2 3627
all *v* of small quantity, from the Is 22:24 3627
quantity, from the *v* of cups Is 22:24 3627
even to all the *v* of flagons Is 22:24 3627
that bear the *v* of the LORD Is 52:11 3627
abominable things is in their *v* Is 65:4 3627
they returned with their *v* empty Jer 14:3 3627
the *v* of the LORD's house shall Jer 27:16 3627
that the *v* which are left in the Jer 27:18 3627
of the *v* that remain in this city Jer 27:19 3627
concerning the *v* that remain in Jer 27:21 3627
all the *v* of the LORD's house Jer 28:3 3627
to bring again the *v* of the Jer 28:6 3627
and oil, and put them in your *v* Jer 40:10 3627
to wander, and shall empty his *v* Jer 48:12 3627
their curtains, and all their *v* Jer 49:29 3627
all the *v* of brass wherewith they Jer 52:18 3627
of all these *v* was without weight Jer 52:20 3627
men and *v* of brass in thy market Eze 27:13 3627
with part of the *v* of the house Dan 1:2 3627
he brought the *v* into the Dan 1:2 3627
silver *v* which his father Dan 5:2 3984
v that were taken out of the Dan 5:3 3984
they have brought the *v* of his Dan 5:23 3984
with their precious *v* of silver Dan 11:8 3627
the treasure of all pleasant *v* Hos 13:15 3627
draw out fifty *v* out of the press Hag 2:16
down, and gathered the good into *v* Mt 13:48 *30*
oil in their *v* with their lamps Mt 25:4 *30*
of cups, and pots, brasen *v* Mk 7:4
with much longsuffering the *v* of Rom 9:22 *4632*
of his glory on the *v* of mercy Rom 9:23 *4632*
have this treasure in earthen *v* 2Cor 4:7 *4632*
there are not only *v* of gold 2Ti 2:20 *4632*
all the *v* of the ministry Heb 9:21 *4632*
as the *v* of a potter shall they Rev 2:27 *4632*
wood, and all manner *v* of ivory Rev 18:12 *4632*
all manner *v* of most precious Rev 18:12 *4632*

VESTMENTS {2}
Bring forth *v* for all the 2Kin 10:22 3830
And he brought them forth *v* 2Kin 10:22 4403

VESTRY {1}
said unto him that was over the *v* 2Kin 10:22 4458

VESTURE {8}
upon the four quarters of thy *v* Deut 22:12 3682
them, and cast lots upon my *v* Ps 22:18 3830
as a *v* shalt thou change them, and Ps 102:26 3830
upon my *v* did they cast lots Mt 27:35 *2441*
for my *v* they did cast lots Jn 19:24 *2441*
as a *v* shalt thou fold them up, Heb 1:12 *4018*
clothed with a *v* dipped in blood Rev 19:13 *2440*
And he hath on his *v* and on his Rev 19:16 *2440*

VESTURES {1}
and arrayed him in *v* of fine linen Gen 41:42 899

VEX {15}
Thou shalt neither *v* a stranger Ex 22:21 3238
sister, to *v* her, to uncover her Lev 18:18 6887
in your land, ye shall not *v* him Lev 19:33 3238
V the Midianites, and smite them Num 25:17 6887
For they *v* you with their wiles Num 25:18 6887
shall *v* you in the land wherein Num 33:55 6887
how will he then *v* himself 2Sa 12:18 6213,7451
for God did *v* them with all 2Chr 15:6 2000
How long will ye *v* my soul Job 19:2 3013
v them in his sore displeasure Ps 2:5 926
v it, and let us make a breach Is 7:6 6973
and Judah shall not *v* Ephraim Is 11:13 6887
I will also *v* the hearts of many Eze 32:9 3707
thee, and awake that shall *v* thee Hab 2:7 2111
hands to *v* certain of the church Acts 12:1 *2559*

VEXATION {14}
shall send upon thee cursing, *v* Deut 28:20 4103
all is vanity and *v* of spirit Eccl 1:14 7469
that this also is *v* of spirit Eccl 1:17 7475
v of spirit, and there was no Eccl 2:11 7469
for all is vanity and *v* of spirit Eccl 2:17 7469
of the *v* of his heart, wherein he Eccl 2:22 7475
also is vanity and *v* of spirit Eccl 2:26 7469
is also vanity and *v* of spirit Eccl 4:4 7469
full with travail and *v* of spirit Eccl 4:6 7469
also is vanity and *v* of spirit Eccl 4:16 7475
is also vanity and *v* of spirit Eccl 6:9 7469
shall not be such as was in her *v* Is 9:1 4164
and it shall be a *v* only to Is 28:19 2113
and shall howl for *v* of spirit Is 65:14 7667

VEXATIONS {1}
but great *v* were upon all the 2Chr 15:5 4103

VEXED {22}
and the Egyptians *v* us, and our Num 20:15 7489
that oppressed them and *v* them Judg 2:18 1766
And that year they *v* and oppressed Judg 10:8 7492
so that his soul was *v* unto death Judg 16:16 7114
he turned himself, he *v* them 1Sa 14:47 7561
And Amnon was so *v*, that he fell 2Sa 13:2 3334
for her soul is *v* within her 2Kin 4:27 4843
hand of their enemies, who *v* them Neh 9:27 6887
the Almighty, who hath *v* my soul Job 27:2 4843
for my bones are *v* Ps 6:2 926
My soul is also sore *v* Ps 6:3 926
mine enemies be ashamed and sore *v* Ps 6:10 926
rebelled, and *v* his holy Spirit Is 63:10 6087
which art infamous and much *v* Eze 22:5 4103
thee have they *v* the fatherless Eze 22:7 3238
and have *v* the poor and needy Eze 22:29 3238
is grievously *v* with a devil Mt 15:22 *1139*
for he is lunatick, and sore *v* Mt 17:15 *3958*
they that were *v* with unclean Lk 6:18 *3791*
them which were *v* with unclean Acts 5:16 *3791*
v with the filthy conversation of 2Pet 2:7 *2669*
v his righteous soul from day to 2Pet 2:8 *928*

VIAL {8}
Then Samuel took a *v* of oil 1Sa 10:1 6378
poured out his *v* upon the earth Rev 16:2 *5357*
poured out his *v* upon the sea Rev 16:3 *5357*
poured out his *v* upon the rivers Rev 16:4 *5357*
poured out his *v* upon the sun Rev 16:8 *5357*
his *v* upon the seat of the beast Rev 16:10 *5357*
v upon the great river Euphrates Rev 16:12 *5357*
poured out his *v* into the air Rev 16:17 *5357*

VIALS {5}
golden *v* full of odours, which Rev 5:8 *5357*
golden *v* full of the wrath of God Rev 15:7 *5357*
pour out the *v* of the wrath of Rev 16:1 *5357*
angels which had the seven *v* Rev 17:1 *5357*
angels which had the seven *v* full Rev 21:9 *5357*

VICTORY {12}
the *v* that day was turned into 2Sa 19:2 8668
LORD wrought a great *v* that day 2Sa 23:10 8668
and the LORD wrought a great *v* 2Sa 23:12 8668
the power, and the glory, and the *v* 1Chr 29:11 5331
holy arm, hath gotten him the *v* Ps 98:1 3467
He will swallow up death in *v* Is 25:8 5331
he send forth judgment unto *v* Mt 12:20 *3534*
Death is swallowed up in *v* 1Cor 15:54 *3534*
O grave, where is thy *v* 1Cor 15:55 *3534*
which giveth us the *v* through our 1Cor 15:57 *3534*
this is the *v* that overcometh the 1Jn 5:4 *3529*
had gotten the *v* over the beast Rev 15:2 *3528*

VICTUAL {5}
prepared for themselves any *v* Ex 12:39 6720
to fetch *v* for the people, that Judg 20:10 6720
provided *v* for king Solomon 1Kin 4:27 3557
captains in them, and store of *v* 2Chr 11:11 3978
and he gave them *v* in abundance 2Chr 11:23 4202

VICTUALS {17}
Sodom and Gomorrah, and all their *v* Gen 14:11 400
nor lend him thy *v* for increase Lev 25:37 400
usury of money, usury of *v* Deut 23:19 400
the people, saying, Prepare you *v* Josh 1:11 6720
Take *v* with you for the journey, Josh 9:11 6720
And the men took of their *v* Josh 9:14 6718
the people took *v* in their hand Judg 7:8 6720
and a suit of apparel, and thy *v* Judg 17:10 4241
the LORD for him, and gave him *v* 1Sa 22:10 6720
which provided *v* for the king 1Kin 4:7 3557
him an house, and appointed him *v* 1Kin 11:18 3899
any *v* on the sabbath day to sell Neh 10:31 7668
in the day wherein they sold *v* Neh 13:15 6718
captain of the guard gave him *v* Jer 40:5 737
for then had we plenty of *v* Jer 44:17 3899
the villages, and buy themselves *v* Mt 14:15 *1033*
round about, and lodge, and get *v* Lk 9:12 *1979*

VIEW {4}
Go *v* the land, even Jericho Josh 2:1 7200
saying, Go up and *v* the country Josh 7:2 7270
went, and stood to *v* afar off 2Kin 2:7 5048
were to *v* at Jericho saw him 2Kin 2:15 5048

VIEWED {4}
And the men went up and *v* Ai Josh 7:2 7370
I *v* the people, and the priests, Ezr 8:15 995
v the walls of Jerusalem, which Neh 2:13 7663
v the wall, and turned back, and Neh 2:15 7663

VIGILANT {2}
the husband of one wife, *v* 1Ti 3:2 *3524*
Be sober, be *v* 1Pet 5:8 *1127*

VILE {19}
brother should seem *v* unto thee Deut 25:3 7034
unto this man do not so *v* a thing Judg 19:24 5039
his sons made themselves *v* 1Sa 3:13 7043
but every thing that was *v* 1Sa 15:9 5240
And I will yet be more *v* than thus 2Sa 6:22 7043
and reputed *v* in your sight Job 18:3 2933
Behold, I am *v* Job 40:4 7043
In whose eyes a *v* person is Ps 15:4 959
The *v* person shall be no more Is 32:5 5036
For the *v* person will speak Is 32:6 5036
forth the precious from the *v* Jer 15:19 2151
and will make them like *v* figs Jer 29:17 8182
for I am become *v* Lam 1:11 2151
estate shall stand up a *v* person Dan 11:21 959
for thou art *v* Nah 1:14 7043
filth upon thee, and make thee *v* Nah 3:6 5034
gave them up unto *v* affections Rom 1:26 *819*
Who shall change our *v* body Phil 3:21 *5014*
in also a poor man in *v* raiment Jas 2:2 *4508*

VILELY {1}
of the mighty is *v* cast away 2Sa 1:21 1602

VILER {1}
they were *v* than the earth Job 30:8 5217

VILEST {1}
when the *v* men are exalted Ps 12:8 2149

VILLAGE {10}
Go into the *v* over against you, Mt 21:2 *2968*
way into the *v* over against you Mk 11:2 *2968*
went throughout every city and *v* Lk 8:1 *2968*
went, and entered into a *v* of the Lk 9:52 *2968*
And they went to another *v* Lk 9:56 *2968*
that he entered into a certain *v* Lk 10:38 *2968*
And as he entered into a certain *v* Lk 17:12 *2968*
Go ye into the *v* over against you Lk 19:30 *2968*
same day to a *v* called Emmaus Lk 24:13 *2968*
And they drew nigh unto the *v* Lk 24:28 *2968*

VILLAGES {75}
out of the houses, out of the *v* Ex 8:13 2691
But the houses of the *v* which Lev 25:31 2691
Heshbon, and in all the *v* thereof Num 21:25 1323
and they took the *v* thereof Num 21:32 1323
the *v* thereof, and called it Nobah Num 32:42 1323
the cities and the *v* thereof Josh 13:23 2691
families, the cities, and their *v* Josh 13:28 2691
are twenty and nine, with their *v* Josh 15:32 2691
fourteen cities with their *v* Josh 15:36 2691
sixteen cities with their *v* Josh 15:41 2691
nine cities with their *v* Josh 15:44 2691
Ekron, with her towns and her *v* Josh 15:45 2691
lay near Ashdod, with their *v* Josh 15:46 2691
Ashdod with her towns and her *v* Josh 15:47 2691
Gaza with her towns and her *v* Josh 15:47 2691
eleven cities with their *v* Josh 15:51 2691
nine cities with their *v* Josh 15:54 2691
ten cities with their *v* Josh 15:57 2691
six cities with their *v* Josh 15:59 2691
two cities with their *v* Josh 15:60 2691
six cities with their *v* Josh 15:62 2691
all the cities with their *v* Josh 16:9 2691
twelve cities with their *v* Josh 18:24 2691
fourteen cities with their *v* Josh 18:28 2691
thirteen cities and their *v* Josh 19:6 2691
four cities and their *v* Josh 19:7 2691
all the *v* that were round about Josh 19:8 2691
twelve cities with their *v* Josh 19:15 2691
these cities with their *v* Josh 19:16 2691
sixteen cities with their *v* Josh 19:22 2691
families, the cities and their *v* Josh 19:23 2691
twenty and two cities with their *v* Josh 19:30 2691
these cities with their *v* Josh 19:31 2691
nineteen cities with their *v* Josh 19:38 2691
families, the cities and their *v* Josh 19:39 2691
these cities with their *v* Josh 19:48 2691
the *v* thereof, gave they to Caleb Josh 21:12 2691
The inhabitants of the *v* ceased Judg 5:7 6520
inhabitants of his *v* in Israel Judg 5:11 6520
of fenced cities, and of country *v* 1Sa 6:18 3724
And their *v* were, Etam, and Ain, 1Chr 4:32 2691
all their *v* that were round about 1Chr 4:33 2691
the *v* thereof, they gave to Caleb 1Chr 6:56 2691
that dwelt in the *v* of the 1Chr 9:16 2691
by their genealogy in their *v* 1Chr 9:22 2691
brethren, which were in their *v* 1Chr 9:25 2691
in the cities, and in the *v* 1Chr 27:25 3723
and Shocho with the *v* thereof 2Chr 28:18 1323
and Timnah with the *v* thereof 2Chr 28:18 1323
Gimzo also and the *v* thereof 2Chr 28:18 1323
one of the *v* in the plain of Ono Neh 6:2 3715
And for the *v*, with their fields, Neh 11:25 2691
in the *v* thereof, and at Dibon, and Neh 11:25 2691
in the *v* thereof, and at Jekabzeel Neh 11:25 1323
Jekabzeel, and in the *v* thereof, Neh 11:25 1323
Beer-sheba, and in the *v* thereof, Neh 11:27 1323
at Mekonah, and in the *v* thereof, Neh 11:28 1323
Zanoah, Adullam, and in their *v* Neh 11:30 2691
at Azekah, and in the *v* thereof Neh 11:30 1323
Aija, and Beth-el, and in their *v* Neh 11:31 1323
and from the *v* of Netophathi Neh 12:28 2691
them *v* round about Jerusalem Neh 12:29 2691
Therefore the Jews of the *v* Est 9:19 6521
in the lurking places of the *v* Ps 10:8 2691
let us lodge in the *v* Song 7:11 3723
the *v* that Kedar doth inhabit Is 42:11 2691
go up to the land of unwalled *v* Eze 38:11 6519
with his staves the head of his *v* Hab 3:14 6518
went about all the cities and *v* Mt 9:35 *2968*
away, that they may go into the *v* Mt 14:15 *2968*
And he went round about the *v* Mk 6:6 *2968*
round about, and into the *v* Mk 6:36 *2968*
whithersoever he entered, into *v* Mk 6:56 *2968*
he went through the cities and *v* Lk 13:22 *2968*
in many *v* of the Samaritans Acts 8:25 *2968*

VILLANY {2}
For the vile person will speak *v* Is 32:6 5039
they have committed *v* in Israel Jer 29:23 5039

VINE {62}
dream, behold, a *v* was before me Gen 40:9 1612
in the *v* were three branches Gen 40:10 1612
Binding his foal unto the *v* Gen 49:11 1612
his ass's colt unto the choice *v* Gen 49:11 8321
the grapes of thy *v* undressed Lev 25:5 5139
grapes in it of thy *v* undressed Lev 25:11 5139
that is made of the *v* tree Num 6:4 3196
their *v* is of the *v* of Sodom Deut 32:32 1612
Then said the trees unto the *v* Judg 9:12 1612

the *v* said unto them, Should I ... Judg 9:13 1612
of any thing that cometh of the *v* ... Judg 13:14 1612
safely, every man under his *v* ... 1Kin 4:25 1612
gather herbs, and found a wild *v* ... 2Kin 4:39 1612
eat ye every man of his own *v* ... 2Kin 18:31 1612
v dressers in the mountains, and ... 2Chr 26:10 3755
off his unripe grape as the *v* ... Job 15:33 1612
hast brought a *v* out of Egypt ... Ps 80:8 1612
and behold, and visit this *v* ... Ps 80:14 1612
v by the sides of thine house ... Ps 128:3 1612
to see whether the *v* flourished ... Song 6:11 1612
shall be as clusters of the *v* ... Song 7:8 1612
let us see if the *v* flourish ... Song 7:12 1612
and planted it with the choicest *v* ... Is 5:2 8321
languish, and the *v* of Sibmah ... Is 16:8 1612
weeping of Jazer the *v* of Sibmah ... Is 16:9 1612
the *v* languisheth, all the ... Is 24:7 1612
fields, for the fruitful *v* ... Is 32:12 1612
the leaf falleth off from the *v* ... Is 34:4 1612
and eat ye every one of his *v* ... Is 36:16 1612
Yet I had planted thee a noble *v* ... Jer 2:21 8321
plant of a strange *v* unto me ... Jer 2:21 1612
the remnant of Israel as a *v* ... Jer 6:9 1612
there shall be no grapes on the *v* ... Jer 8:13 1612
O *v* of Sibmah, I will weep for ... Jer 48:32 1612
What is the *v* tree more than any ... Eze 15:2 1612
As the *v* tree among the trees of ... Eze 15:6 1612
a spreading *v* of low stature ... Eze 17:6 1612
so it became a *v*, and brought ... Eze 17:6 1612
this *v* did bend her roots toward ... Eze 17:7 1612
that it might be a goodly *v* ... Eze 17:8 1612
mother is like a *v* in thy blood ... Eze 19:10 1612
Israel is an empty *v*, he bringeth ... Hos 10:1 1612
as the corn, and grow as the *v* ... Hos 14:7 1612
He hath laid my *v* waste, and ... Joel 1:7 1612
The *v* is dried up, and the fig ... Joel 1:12 1612
the *v* do yield their strength ... Joel 2:22 1612
shall sit every man under his *v* ... Mic 4:4 1612
out, and marred their *v* branches ... Nah 2:2 2156
yea, as yet the *v*, and the fig ... Hag 2:19 1612
man his neighbour under the *v* ... Zec 3:10 1612
the *v* shall give her fruit, and ... Zec 8:12 1612
neither shall your *v* cast her ... Mal 3:11 1612
henceforth of this fruit of the *v* ... Mt 26:29 *288*
no more of the fruit of the *v* ... Mk 14:25 *288*
not drink of the fruit of the *v* ... Lk 22:18 *288*
I am the true *v*, and my Father is ... Jn 15:1 *288*
itself, except it abide in the *v* ... Jn 15:4 *288*
I am the *v*, ye are the branches ... Jn 15:5 *288*
either a *v*, figs? ... Jas 3:12 *288*
clusters of the *v* of the earth ... Rev 14:18 *288*
and gathered the *v* of the earth ... Rev 14:19 *288*

VINEDRESSERS {4}
of the poor of the land to be *v* ... 2Kin 25:12 3755
shall be your plowmen and your *v* ... Is 61:5 3755
of the poor of the land for *v* ... Jer 52:16 3755
howl, O ye *v*, for the wheat and ... Joel 1:11 3755

VINEGAR {13}
and shall drink no *v* of wine ... Num 6:3 2558
or *v* of strong drink, neither ... Num 6:3 2558
bread, and dip thy morsel in the *v* ... Ruth 2:14 2558
my thirst they gave me *v* to drink ... Ps 69:21 2558
As *v* to the teeth, and as smoke to ... Prov 10:26 2558
as *v* upon nitre, so is he that ... Prov 25:20 2558
They gave him *v* to drink mingled ... Mt 27:34 *3690*
a spunge, and filled it with *v* ... Mt 27:48 *3690*
ran and filled a spunge full of *v* ... Mk 15:36 *3690*
coming to him, and offering him *v* ... Lk 23:36 *3690*
there was set a vessel full of *v* ... Jn 19:29 *3690*
and they filled a spunge with *v* ... Jn 19:29 *3690*
therefore had received the *v* ... Jn 19:30 *3690*

VINES {12}
of seed, or of figs, or of *v* ... Num 20:5 1612
A land of wheat, and barley, and *v* ... Deut 8:8 1612
He destroyed their *v* with hail ... Ps 78:47 1612
He smote their *v* also and their ... Ps 105:33 1612
the *v* with the tender grape give ... Song 2:13 1612
little foxes, that spoil the *v* ... Song 2:15 3754
for our *v* have tender grapes ... Song 2:15 3754
v at a thousand silverlings ... Is 7:23 1612
they shall eat up thy *v* and thy ... Jer 5:17 1612
Thou shalt yet plant *v* upon the ... Jer 31:5 3754
And I will destroy her *v* and her ... Hos 2:12 1612
neither shall fruit be in the *v* ... Hab 3:17 1612

VINEYARD {69}
an husbandman, and he planted a *v* ... Gen 9:20 3754
cause a field or *v* to be eaten ... Ex 22:5 3754
and of the best of his own *v* ... Ex 22:5 3754
manner thou shalt deal with thy *v* ... Ex 23:11 3754
And thou shalt not glean thy *v* ... Lev 19:10 3754
thou gather every grape of thy *v* ... Lev 19:10 3754
six years thou shalt prune thy *v* ... Lev 25:3 3754
sow thy field, nor prune thy *v* ... Lev 25:4 3754
man is he that hath planted a *v* ... Deut 20:6 3754
not sow thy *v* with divers seeds ... Deut 22:9 3754
hast sown, and the fruit of thy *v* ... Deut 22:9 3754
comest into thy neighbour's *v* ... Deut 23:24 3754
gatherest the grapes of thy *v* ... Deut 24:21 3754
thou shalt plant a *v*, and shalt ... Deut 28:30 3754
Naboth the Jezreelite had a *v* ... 1Kin 21:1 3754
Naboth, saying, Give me thy *v* ... 1Kin 21:2 3754
thee for it a better *v* than it ... 1Kin 21:2 3754
unto him, Give me thy *v* for money ... 1Kin 21:6 3754
I will give thee another *v* for it ... 1Kin 21:6 3754
I will not give thee my *v* ... 1Kin 21:6 3754
I will give thee the *v* of Naboth ... 1Kin 21:7 3754
take possession of the *v* of ... 1Kin 21:15 3754
to the *v* of Naboth the Jezreelite ... 1Kin 21:16 3754
behold, he is in the *v* of Naboth ... 1Kin 21:18 3754
the *v* which thy right hand hath ... Ps 80:15 3657
by the *v* of the man void of ... Prov 24:30 3754
of her hands she planteth a *v* ... Prov 31:16 3754
but mine own *v* have I not kept ... Song 1:6 3754
Solomon had a *v* at Baal-hamon ... Song 8:11 3754
he let out the *v* unto keepers ... Song 8:11 3754
My *v*, which is mine, is before me ... Song 8:12 3754
Zion is left as a cottage in a *v* ... Is 1:8 3754
for ye have eaten up the *v* ... Is 3:14 3754
song of my beloved touching his *v* ... Is 5:1 3754
My wellbeloved hath a *v* in a very ... Is 5:1 3754
I pray you, betwixt me and my *v* ... Is 5:3 3754
could have been done more to my *v* ... Is 5:4 3754
tell you what I will do to my *v* ... Is 5:5 3754
For the *v* of the LORD of hosts is ... Is 5:7 3754
ten acres of *v* shall yield one ... Is 5:10 3754
sing ye unto her, A *v* of red wine ... Is 27:2 3754
Many pastors have destroyed my *v* ... Jer 12:10 3754
house, nor sow seed, nor plant *v* ... Jer 35:7 3754
neither have we *v*, nor field, nor ... Jer 35:9 3754
the field, and as plantings of a *v* ... Mic 1:6 3754
to hire labourers into his *v* ... Mt 20:1 *290*
a day, he sent them into his *v* ... Mt 20:2 *290*
Go ye also into the *v*, and ... Mt 20:4 *290*
unto them, Go ye also into the *v* ... Mt 20:7 *290*
the lord of the *v* saith unto his ... Mt 20:8 *290*
said, Son, go work to day in my *v* ... Mt 21:28 *290*
householder, which planted a *v* ... Mt 21:33 *290*
him, and cast him out of the *v* ... Mt 21:39 *290*
lord therefore of the *v* cometh ... Mt 21:40 *290*
will let out his *v* unto other ... Mt 21:41 *290*
A certain man planted a *v* ... Mk 12:1 *290*
husbandmen of the fruit of the *v* ... Mk 12:2 *290*
him, and cast him out of the *v* ... Mk 12:8 *290*
therefore the lord of the *v* do ... Mk 12:9 *290*
and will give the *v* unto others ... Mk 12:9 *290*
had a fig tree planted in his *v* ... Lk 13:6 *290*
said he unto the dresser of his *v* ... Lk 13:7 *289*
A certain man planted a *v* ... Lk 20:9 *290*
give him of the fruit of the *v* ... Lk 20:10 *290*
Then said the lord of the *v* ... Lk 20:13 *290*
So they cast him out of the *v* ... Lk 20:15 *290*
the lord of the *v* do unto them ... Lk 20:15 *290*
and shall give the *v* to others ... Lk 20:16 *290*
who planteth a *v*, and eateth not ... 1Cor 9:7 *290*

VINEYARDS {45}
us inheritance of fields and *v* ... Num 16:14 3754
the fields, or through the *v* ... Num 20:17 3754
into the fields, or into the *v* ... Num 21:22 3754
the LORD stood in a path of the *v* ... Num 22:24 3754
which thou diggedst not, *v* ... Deut 6:11 3754
Thou shalt plant *v*, and dress them ... Deut 28:39 3754
of the *v* and oliveyards which ye ... Josh 24:13 3754
the fields, and gathered their *v* ... Judg 9:27 3754
and unto the plain of the *v* ... Judg 11:33 3754
and came to the *v* of Timnath ... Judg 14:5 3754
the standing corn, with the *v* ... Judg 15:5 3754
Go and lie in wait in the *v* ... Judg 21:20 3754
dances, then come ye out of the *v* ... Judg 21:21 3754
will take your fields, and your *v* ... 1Sa 8:14 3754
tenth of your seed, and of your *v* ... 1Sa 8:15 3754
give every one of you fields and *v* ... 1Sa 22:7 3754
garments, and oliveyards, and *v* ... 2Kin 5:26 3754
and wine, a land of bread and *v* ... 2Kin 18:32 3754
year sow ye, and reap, and plant *v* ... 2Kin 19:29 3754
over the *v* was Shimei the ... 1Chr 27:27 3754
over the increase of the *v* for ... 1Chr 27:27 3754
We have mortgaged our lands, *v* ... Neh 5:3 3754
and that upon our lands and *v* ... Neh 5:4 3754
for other men have our lands and *v* ... Neh 5:5 3754
this day, their lands, their *v* ... Neh 5:11 3754
of all goods, wells digged, *v* ... Neh 9:25 3754
he beholdeth not the way of the *v* ... Job 24:18 3754
And sow the fields, and plant *v* ... Ps 107:37 3754
I planted me *v* ... Eccl 2:4 3754
they made me the keeper of the *v* ... Song 1:6 3754
of camphire in the *v* of En-gedi ... Song 1:14 3754
Let us get up early to the *v* ... Song 7:12 3754
in the *v* there shall be no ... Is 16:10 3754
and wine, a land of bread and *v* ... Is 36:17 3754
year sow ye, and reap, and plant *v* ... Is 37:30 3754
and they shall plant *v*, and eat the ... Is 65:21 3754
v shall be possessed again in ... Jer 32:15 3754
the land of Judah, and gave them *v* ... Jer 39:10 3754
and shall build houses, and plant *v* ... Eze 28:26 3754
I will give her her *v* from thence ... Hos 2:15 3754
when your gardens and your *v* ... Amos 4:9 3754
ye have planted pleasant *v* ... Amos 5:11 3754
in all *v* shall be wailing ... Amos 5:17 3754
and they shall plant *v*, and drink ... Amos 9:14 3754
and they shall plant *v*, but not ... Zeph 1:13 3754

VINTAGE {10}
threshing shall reach unto the *v* ... Lev 26:5 1210
the *v* shall reach unto the sowing ... Lev 26:5 1210
better than the *v* of Abi-ezer ... Judg 8:2 1210
they gather the *v* of the wicked ... Job 24:6 3754
made their *v* shouting to cease ... Is 16:10
grapes when the *v* is done ... Is 24:13 1210
for the *v* shall fail, the ... Is 32:10 1210
thy summer fruits and upon thy *v* ... Jer 48:32 1210
as the grapegleanings of the *v* ... Mic 7:1 1210
the forest of the *v* is come down ... Zec 11:2 1208

VIOL {2}
And the harp, and the *v*, the tabret ... Is 5:12 5035
That chant to the sound of the *v* ... Amos 6:5 5035

VIOLATED {1}
Her priests have *v* my law ... Eze 22:26 2554

VIOLENCE {57}
and the earth was filled with *v* ... Gen 6:11 2555
is filled with *v* through them ... Gen 6:13 2555
or in a thing taken away by *v* ... Lev 6:2 1498
thou savest me from *v* ... 2Sa 22:3 2555
him that loveth *v* his soul hateth ... Ps 11:5 2555
for I have seen *v* and strife in ... Ps 55:9 2555
ye weigh the *v* of your hands in ... Ps 58:2 2555
their soul from deceit and *v* ... Ps 72:14 2555
v covereth them as a garment ... Ps 73:6 2555
and drink the wine of *v* ... Prov 4:17 2555
but *v* covereth the mouth of the ... Prov 10:6 2555
but *v* covereth the mouth of the ... Prov 10:11 2555
of the transgressors shall eat *v* ... Prov 13:2 2555
A man that doeth *v* to the blood ... Prov 28:17 6231
because he had done no *v*, neither ... Is 53:9 2555
the act of *v* is in their hands ... Is 59:6 2555
V shall no more be heard in thy ... Is 60:18 2555
v and spoil is heard in her ... Jer 6:7 2555
I spake, I cried out, I cried *v* ... Jer 20:8 2555
do no *v* to the stranger, the ... Jer 22:3 2554
and for oppression, and for *v* ... Jer 22:17 4835
The *v* done to me and to my flesh ... Jer 51:35 2555
v in the land, ruler against ... Jer 51:46 2555
V is risen up into a rod of ... Eze 7:11 2555
crimes, and the city is full of *v* ... Eze 7:23 2555
they have filled the land with *v* ... Eze 8:17 2555
because of the *v* of all them that ... Eze 12:19 2555
pledge, hath spoiled none by *v* ... Eze 18:7 1500
poor and needy, hath spoiled by *v* ... Eze 18:12 1500
pledge, neither hath spoiled by *v* ... Eze 18:16 1500
spoiled his brother by *v* ... Eze 18:18 1499
filled the midst of thee with *v* ... Eze 28:16 2555
remove *v* and spoil, and execute ... Eze 45:9 2555
for the *v* against the children of ... Joel 3:19 2555
saith the LORD, who store up *v* ... Amos 3:10 2555
cause the seat of *v* to come near ... Amos 6:3 2555
For thy *v* against thy brother ... Obad 10 2555
from the *v* that is in their hands ... Jonah 3:8 2555
covet fields, and take them by *v* ... Mic 2:2 1497
rich men thereof are full of *v* ... Mic 6:12 2555
even cry out unto thee of *v* ... Hab 1:2 2555
for spoiling and *v* are before me ... Hab 1:3 2555
They shall come all for *v* ... Hab 1:9 2555
for the *v* of the land, of the ... Hab 2:8 2555
For the *v* of Lebanon shall cover ... Hab 2:17 2555
for the *v* of the land, of the ... Hab 2:17 2555
fill their masters' houses with *v* ... Zeph 1:9 2555
they have done *v* to the law ... Zeph 3:4 2554
one covereth *v* with his garment ... Mal 2:16 2555
the kingdom of heaven suffereth *v* ... Mt 11:12 *971*
Do *v* to no man, neither accuse ... Lk 3:14 *1286*
and brought them without *v* ... Acts 5:26 *970*
soldiers for the *v* of the people ... Acts 21:35 *970*
with great *v* took him away out of ... Acts 24:7 *970*
broken with the *v* of the waves ... Acts 27:41 *970*
Quenched the *v* of fire, escaped ... Heb 11:34 *1411*
Thus with *v* shall that great city ... Rev 18:21 *3731*

VIOLENT {10}
hast delivered me from the *v* man ... 2Sa 22:49 2555
his *v* dealing shall come down ... Ps 7:16 2555
hast delivered me from the *v* man ... Ps 18:48 2555
the assemblies of *v* men have ... Ps 86:14 6184
preserve me from the *v* man ... Ps 140:1 2555
preserve me from the *v* man ... Ps 140:4 2555
evil shall hunt the *v* man to ... Ps 140:11 2555
A *v* man enticeth his neighbour, ... Prov 16:29 2555
v perverting of judgment and ... Eccl 5:8 1499
and the *v* take it by force ... Mt 11:12 *973*

VIOLENTLY {10}
servants had *v* taken away ... Gen 21:25 1497
restore that which he took *v* away ... Lev 6:4 1500
thine ass shall be *v* taken away ... Deut 28:31 1497
because he hath *v* taken away an ... Job 20:19 1497
they *v* take away flocks, and feed ... Job 24:2 1497
He will surely *v* turn and toss ... Is 22:18
And he hath *v* taken away his ... Lam 2:6 2554
the whole herd of swine ran *v* ... Mt 8:32
the herd ran *v* down a steep place ... Mk 5:13
the herd ran *v* down a steep place ... Lk 8:33

VIOLS {2}
the grave, and the noise of thy *v* ... Is 14:11 5035
will not hear the melody of thy *v* ... Amos 5:23 5035

VIPER {3}
come the young and old lion, the *v* ... Is 30:6 660
is crushed breaketh out into a *v* ... Is 59:5 660
there came a *v* out of the heat, ... Acts 28:3 *2191*

VIPER'S {1}
the *v* tongue shall slay him ... Job 20:16 660

VIPERS {4}
said unto them, O generation of *v* ... Mt 3:7 *2191*
O generation of *v*, how can ye, ... Mt 12:34 *2191*
Ye serpents, ye generation of *v* ... Mt 23:33 *2191*
of him, O generation of *v* ... Lk 3:7 *2191*

VIRGIN {33}
was very fair to look upon, a *v* ... Gen 24:16 1330
that when the *v* cometh forth to ... Gen 24:43 5959
And for his sister a *v*, that is ... Lev 21:3 1330
but he shall take a *v* of his own ... Lev 21:14 1330
an evil name upon a *v* of Israel ... Deut 22:19 1330

If a damsel that is a *v* be .... Deut 22:23 1330
a man find a damsel that is a *v* .... Deut 22:28 1330
both the young man and the *v* .... Deut 32:25 1330
for she was a *v* 2Sa 13:2 1330
for my lord the king a young *v* 1Kin 1:2 1330
The *v* the daughter of Zion hath 2Kin 19:21 1330
a *v* shall conceive, and bear a son .... Is 7:14 5959
more rejoice, O thou oppressed *v* .... Is 23:12 1330
The *v*, the daughter of Zion, hath .... Is 37:22 1330
O *v* daughter of Babylon, sit on .... Is 47:1 1330
For as a young man marrieth a *v* .... Is 62:5 1330
for the *v* daughter of my people .... Jer 14:17 1330
the *v* of Israel hath done a very .... Jer 18:13 1330
shalt be built, O *v* of Israel .... Jer 31:4 1330
Then shall the *v* rejoice in the .... Jer 31:13 1330
O *v* of Israel, turn again to .... Jer 31:21 1330
up into Gilead, and take balm, O *v* .... Jer 46:11 1330
the Lord hath trodden the *v* .... Lam 1:15 1330
thee, O *v* daughter of Zion .... Lam 2:13 1330
Lament like a *v* girded with .... Joel 1:8 1330
The *v* of Israel is fallen .... Amos 5:2 1330
a *v* shall be with child, and shall .... Mt 1:23 *3933*
To a *v* espoused to a man whose .... Lk 1:27 *3933*
if a *v* marry, she hath not sinned 1Cor 7:28 *3933*
also between a wife and a *v* 1Cor 7:34 *3933*
himself uncomely toward his *v* 1Cor 7:36 *3933*
his heart that he will keep his *v* 1Cor 7:37 *3933*
you as a chaste *v* to Christ 2Cor 11:2 *3933*

VIRGINITY {9}
And he shall take a wife in her *v* .... Lev 21:13 1331
the tokens of the damsel's *v* unto .... Deut 22:15 1331
are the tokens of my daughter's *v* .... Deut 22:17 1331
the tokens of *v* be not found for .... Deut 22:20 1331
the mountains, and bewail my *v* .... Judg 11:37 1331
bewailed her *v* upon the mountains .... Judg 11:38 1331
they bruised the teats of their *v* .... Eze 23:3 1331
they bruised the breasts of her *v* .... Eze 23:8 1331
an husband seven years from her *v* .... Lk 2:36 *3932*

VIRGIN'S {1}
and the *v* name was Mary .... Lk 1:27 *3933*

VIRGINS {22}
money according to the dowry of *v* .... Ex 22:17 1330
four hundred young *v*, that had .... Judg 21:12 1330
daughters that were *v* apparelled 2Sa 13:18 1330
fair young *v* sought for the king .... Est 2:2 1330
young *v* unto Shushan the palace .... Est 2:3 1330
in his sight more than all the *v* .... Est 2:17 1330
when the *v* were gathered together .... Est 2:19 1330
the *v* her companions that follow .... Ps 45:14 1330
therefore do the *v* love thee .... Song 1:3 5959
concubines, and *v* without number .... Song 6:8 5959
up young men, nor bring up *v* .... Is 23:4 1330
her *v* are afflicted, and she is in .... Lam 1:4 1330
my *v* and my young men are gone .... Lam 1:18 1330
the *v* of Jerusalem hang down .... Lam 2:10 1330
my *v* and my young men are fallen .... Lam 2:21 1330
In that day shall the fair *v* .... Amos 8:13 1330
of heaven be likened unto ten *v* .... Mt 25:1 *3933*
Then all those *v* arose, and .... Mt 25:7 *3933*
Afterward came also the other *v* .... Mt 25:11 *3933*
same man had four daughters, *v* .... Acts 21:9 *3933*
Now concerning *v* I have no 1Cor 7:25 *3933*
for they are *v* .... Rev 14:4 *3933*

VIRTUE {7}
that *v* had gone out of him .... Mk 5:30 *1411*
for there went *v* out of him .... Lk 6:19 *1411*
perceive that *v* is gone out of me .... Lk 8:46 *1411*
if there be any *v*, and if there be .... Phil 4:8 *703*
that hath called us to glory and *v* 2Pet 1:3 *703*
diligence, add to your faith *v* 2Pet 1:5 *703*
and to *v* knowledge 2Pet 1:5 *703*

VIRTUOUS {3}
doth know that thou art a *v* woman .... Ruth 3:11 2428
A *v* woman is a crown to her .... Prov 12:4 2428
Who can find a *v* woman .... Prov 31:10 2428

VIRTUOUSLY {1}
Many daughters have done *v* .... Prov 31:29 2428

VISAGE {3}
his *v* was so marred more than any .... Is 52:14 4758
Their *v* is blacker than a coal .... Lam 4:8 8389
the form of his *v* was changed .... Dan 3:19 600

VISIBLE {1}
heaven, and that are in earth, *v* .... Col 1:16 *3707*

VISION {79}
the LORD came unto Abram in a *v* .... Gen 15:1 4236
make myself known unto him in a *v* .... Num 12:6 4758
which saw the *v* of the Almighty, ... Num 24:4 4236
which saw the *v* of the Almighty, ... Num 24:16 4236
there was no open *v* 1Sa 3:1 2377
Samuel feared to shew Eli the *v* 1Sa 3:15 4758
words, and according to all this *v* 2Sa 7:17 2384
words, and according to all this *v* 1Chr 17:15 2377
in the *v* of Isaiah the prophet 2Chr 32:32 2377
chased away as a *v* of the night .... Job 20:8 2384
in a *v* of the night, when deep .... Job 33:15 2384
thou spakest in *v* to thy holy one .... Ps 89:19 2377
Where there is no *v*, the people .... Prov 29:18 2377
The *v* of Isaiah the son of Amoz, ... Is 1:1 2377
A grievous *v* is declared unto me .... Is 21:2 2380
The burden of the valley of *v* .... Is 22:1 2384
GOD of hosts in the valley of *v* .... Is 22:5 2384
they err in *v*, they stumble in .... Is 28:7 7203
shall be as a dream of a night *v* .... Is 29:7 2377
the *v* of all is become unto you .... Is 29:11 2380
they prophesy unto you a false *v* .... Jer 14:14 2377
they speak a *v* of their own heart .... Jer 23:16 2377
also find no *v* from the LORD .... Lam 2:9 2377
for the *v* is touching the whole .... Eze 7:13 2377
they seek a *v* of the prophet .... Eze 7:26 2377
according to the *v* that I saw in .... Eze 8:4 4758
brought me in a *v* by the Spirit .... Eze 11:24 4758
So the *v* that I had seen went up .... Eze 11:24 4758
are prolonged, and every *v* faileth .... Eze 12:22 2377
at hand, and the effect of every *v* .... Eze 12:23 2377
vain *v* nor flattering divination .... Eze 12:24 2377
The *v* that he seeth is for many .... Eze 12:27 2377
Have ye not seen a vain *v* .... Eze 13:7 4236
appearance of the *v* which I saw .... Eze 43:3 4758
even according to the *v* that I .... Eze 43:3 4758
the visions were like the *v* that .... Eze 43:3 4758
revealed unto Daniel in a night *v* .... Dan 2:19 2376
and said, I saw in my *v* by night .... Dan 7:2 2376
Belshazzar a *v* appeared unto me .... Dan 8:1 2377
And I saw in a *v* .... Dan 8:2 2377
and I saw in a *v*, and I was by the .... Dan 8:2 2377
spake, How long shall be the *v* .... Dan 8:13 2377
I, even I Daniel, had seen the *v* .... Dan 8:15 2377
make this man to understand the *v* .... Dan 8:16 4758
time of the end shall be the *v* .... Dan 8:17 4758
the *v* of the evening and the .... Dan 8:26 4758
wherefore shut thou up the *v* .... Dan 8:26 2377
and I was astonished at the *v* .... Dan 8:27 4758
seen in the *v* at the beginning .... Dan 9:21 2377
the matter, and consider the *v* .... Dan 9:23 2377
and to seal up the *v* and prophecy, ... Dan 9:24 2377
and had understanding of the *v* .... Dan 10:1 4758
And I Daniel alone saw the *v* .... Dan 10:7 4759
that were with me saw not the *v* .... Dan 10:7 4759
left alone, and saw this great *v* .... Dan 10:8 4759
for yet the *v* is for many days .... Dan 10:14 2377
by the *v* my sorrows are turned .... Dan 10:16 4758
themselves to establish the *v* .... Dan 11:14 2377
The *v* of Obadiah .... Obad 1 2377
you, that ye shall not have a *v* .... Mic 3:6 2377
The book of the *v* of Nahum the .... Nah 1:1 2377
answered me, and said, Write the *v* .... Hab 2:2 2377
For the *v* is yet for an appointed .... Hab 2:3 2377
be ashamed every one of his *v* .... Zec 13:4 2384
Tell the *v* to no man, until the .... Mt 17:9 *3705*
he had seen a *v* in the temple .... Lk 1:22 *3701*
they had also seen a *v* of angels .... Lk 24:23 *3701*
and to him said the Lord in a *v* .... Acts 9:10 *3705*
hath seen in a *v* a man named .... Acts 9:12 *3705*
He saw in a *v* evidently about the .... Acts 10:3 *3705*
doubted in himself what this *v* .... Acts 10:17 *3705*
While Peter thought on the *v* .... Acts 10:19 *3705*
and in a trance I saw a *v*, A .... Acts 11:5 *3705*
but thought he saw a *v* .... Acts 12:9 *3705*
a *v* appeared to Paul in the night .... Acts 16:9 *3705*
And after he had seen the *v* .... Acts 16:10 *3705*
Lord to Paul in the night by a *v* .... Acts 18:9 *3705*
disobedient unto the heavenly *v* .... Acts 26:19 *3705*
And thus I saw the horses in the *v* .... Rev 9:17 *3706*

VISIONS {24}
unto Israel in the *v* of the night .... Gen 46:2 4759
in the *v* of Iddo the seer against 2Chr 9:29 2378
had understanding in the *v* of God 2Chr 26:5 7200
thoughts from the *v* of the night .... Job 4:13 2384
and terrifiest me through *v* .... Job 7:14 2384
were opened, and I saw *v* of God .... Eze 1:1 4759
brought me in the *v* of God to .... Eze 8:3 4759
which see *v* of peace for her, and .... Eze 13:16 2377
In the *v* of God brought he me .... Eze 40:2 4759
the *v* were like the vision that I .... Eze 43:3 4759
Daniel had understanding in all *v* .... Dan 1:17 2377
the *v* of thy head upon thy bed, ... Dan 2:28 2376
the *v* of my head troubled me .... Dan 4:5 2376
tell me the *v* of my dream that I .... Dan 4:9 2376
Thus were the *v* of mine head in .... Dan 4:10 2376
I saw in the *v* of my head upon my .... Dan 4:13 2376
v of his head upon his bed .... Dan 7:1 2376
After this I saw in the night *v* .... Dan 7:7 2376
I saw in the night *v*, and, behold, ... Dan 7:13 2376
the *v* of my head troubled me .... Dan 7:15 2376
prophets, and I have multiplied *v* .... Hos 12:10 2377
your young men shall see *v* .... Joel 2:28 2384
and your young men shall see *v* .... Acts 2:17 *3706*
I will come to *v* and revelations 2Cor 12:1 *3701*

VISIT {38}
and God will surely *v* you, and .... Gen 50:24 6485
saying, God will surely *v* you .... Gen 50:25 6485
saying, God will surely *v* you .... Ex 13:19 6485
I *v* I will *v* their sin upon .... Ex 32:34 6485
therefore I do *v* the iniquity .... Lev 18:25 6485
thou shalt *v* thy habitation, and .... Job 5:24 6485
shouldest *v* him every morning .... Job 7:18 6485
awake to *v* all the heathen .... Ps 59:5 6485
heaven, and behold, and *v* this vine .... Ps 80:14 6485
Then will I *v* their transgression .... Ps 89:32 6485
O *v* me with thy salvation .... Ps 106:4 6485
years, that the LORD will *v* Tyre .... Is 23:17 6485
neither shall they *v* it .... Jer 3:16 6485
Shall I not *v* for these things .... Jer 5:9 6485
Shall I not *v* for these things .... Jer 5:29 6485
at the time that I *v* them they .... Jer 6:15 6485
Shall I not *v* them for these .... Jer 9:9 6485
their iniquity, and *v* their sins .... Jer 14:10 6485
v me, and revenge me of my .... Jer 15:15 6485
I will *v* upon you the evil of .... Jer 23:2 6485
be until the day that I *v* them .... Jer 27:22 6485
at Babylon I will *v* you, and .... Jer 29:10 6485
there shall he be until I *v* him .... Jer 32:5 6485
him, the time that I will *v* him .... Jer 49:8 6485
come, the time that I will *v* thee .... Jer 50:31 6485
he will *v* thine iniquity, O .... Lam 4:22 6485
I will *v* upon her the days of .... Hos 2:13 6485
their iniquity, and *v* their sins .... Hos 8:13 6485
iniquity, he will *v* their sins .... Hos 9:9 6485
v the transgressions of Israel .... Amos 3:14 6485
will also *v* the altars of Beth-el .... Amos 3:14 6485
the LORD their God shall *v* them .... Zeph 2:7 6485
which shall not *v* those that be .... Zec 11:16 6485
it came into his heart to *v* his .... Acts 7:23 *1980*
at the first did *v* the Gentiles .... Acts 15:14 *1980*
v our brethren in every city .... Acts 15:36 *1980*
To *v* the fatherless and widows in .... Jas 1:27 *1980*

VISITATION {15}
be visited after the *v* of all men .... Num 16:29 6486
thy *v* hath preserved my spirit .... Job 10:12 6486
what will ye do in the day of *v* .... Is 10:3 6486
in the time of their *v* they shall .... Jer 8:12 6486
time of their *v* they shall perish .... Jer 10:15 6486
even the year of their *v* .... Jer 11:23 6486
them, even the year of their *v* .... Jer 23:12 6486
upon them, and the time of their *v* .... Jer 46:21 6486
upon Moab, the year of their *v* .... Jer 48:44 6486
day is come, the time of their *v* .... Jer 50:27 6486
time of their *v* they shall perish .... Jer 51:18 6486
The days of *v* are come, the days .... Hos 9:7 6486
of thy watchmen and thy *v* cometh .... Mic 7:4 6486
knewest not the time of thy *v* .... Lk 19:44 *1984*
glorify God in the day of *v* 1Pet 2:12 *1984*

VISITED {23}
the LORD *v* Sarah as he had said, ... Gen 21:1 6485
me, saying, I have surely *v* you .... Ex 3:16 6485
LORD had *v* the children of Israel .... Ex 4:31 6485
or if they be *v* after the .... Num 16:29 6485
that Samson *v* his wife with a kid .... Judg 15:1 6485
of Moab how that the LORD had *v* .... Ruth 1:6 6485
And the LORD *v* Hannah, so that she 1Sa 2:21 6485
is not so, he hath *v* in his anger .... Job 35:15 6485
thou hast *v* me in the night .... Ps 17:3 6485
he shall not be *v* with evil .... Prov 19:23 6485
after many days shall they be *v* .... Is 24:22 6485
therefore hast thou *v* and .... Is 26:14 6485
LORD, in trouble have they *v* thee .... Is 26:16 6485
Thou shalt be *v* of the LORD of .... Is 29:6 6485
this is the city to be *v* .... Jer 6:6 6485
them away, and have not *v* them .... Jer 23:2 6485
After many days thou shalt be *v* .... Eze 38:8 6485
for the LORD of hosts hath *v* his .... Zec 10:3 6485
I was sick, and ye *v* me .... Mt 25:36 *1980*
and in prison, and ye *v* me not .... Mt 25:43 *1980*
for he hath *v* and redeemed his .... Lk 1:68 *1980*
dayspring from on high hath *v* us .... Lk 1:78 *1980*
and, That God hath *v* his people .... Lk 7:16 *1980*

VISITEST {3}
the son of man, that thou *v* him .... Ps 8:4 6485
Thou *v* the earth, and waterest it .... Ps 65:9 6485
the son of man, that thou *v* him .... Heb 2:6 *1980*

VISITETH {1}
and when he *v*, what shall I answer .... Job 31:14 6485

VISITING {4}
v the iniquity of the fathers .... Ex 20:5 6485
v the iniquity of the fathers .... Ex 34:7 6485
v the iniquity of the fathers .... Num 14:18 6485
v the iniquity of the fathers .... Deut 5:9 6485

VOCATION {1}
of the *v* wherewith ye are called .... Eph 4:1 *2821*

VOICE {505}
they heard the *v* of the LORD God .... Gen 3:8 6963
I heard thy *v* in the garden, and I .... Gen 3:10 6963
hearkened unto the *v* of thy wife .... Gen 3:17 6963
the *v* of thy brother's blood .... Gen 4:10 6963
wives, Adah and Zillah, Hear my *v* .... Gen 4:23 6963
Abram hearkened to the *v* of Sarai .... Gen 16:2 6963
unto thee, hearken unto her *v* .... Gen 21:12 6963
against him, and lift up her *v* .... Gen 21:16 6963
And God heard the *v* of the lad .... Gen 21:17 6963
the *v* of the lad where he is .... Gen 21:17 6963
because thou hast obeyed my *v* .... Gen 22:18 6963
Because that Abraham obeyed my *v* .... Gen 26:5 6963
obey my *v* according to that which .... Gen 27:8 6963
only obey my *v*, and go fetch me .... Gen 27:13 6963
and said, The *v* is Jacob's *v* .... Gen 27:22 6963
And Esau lifted up his *v*, and wept .... Gen 27:38 6963
Now therefore, my son, obey my *v* .... Gen 27:43 6963
kissed Rachel, and lifted up his *v* .... Gen 29:11 6963
me, and hath also heard my *v* .... Gen 30:6 6963
with me, and I cried with a loud *v* .... Gen 39:14 6963
he heard that I lifted up my *v* .... Gen 39:15 6963
came to pass, as I lifted up my *v* .... Gen 39:18 6963
And they shall hearken to thy *v* .... Ex 3:18 6963
believe me, nor hearken unto my *v* .... Ex 4:1 6963
to the *v* of the first sign .... Ex 4:8 6963
believe the *v* of the latter sign .... Ex 4:8 6963
signs, neither hearken unto thy *v* .... Ex 4:9 6963
obey his *v* to let Israel go .... Ex 5:2 6963
to the *v* of the LORD thy God .... Ex 15:26 6963
Hearken now unto my *v*, I will .... Ex 18:19 6963
to the *v* of his father in law .... Ex 18:24 6963
if ye will obey my *v* indeed .... Ex 19:5 6963
the *v* of the trumpet exceeding .... Ex 19:16 6963
when the *v* of the trumpet sounded .... Ex 19:19 6963
spake, and God answered him by a *v* .... Ex 19:19 6963
Beware of him, and obey his *v* .... Ex 23:21 6963
if thou shalt indeed obey his *v* .... Ex 23:22 6963
the people answered with one *v* .... Ex 24:3 6963

It is not the *v* of them that	Ex 32:18	6963
neither is it the *v* of them that	Ex 32:18	6963
hear the *v* of swearing, and is a	Lev 5:1	6963
then he heard the *v* of one	Num 7:89	6963
congregation lifted up their *v*	Num 14:1	6963
and have not hearkened to my *v*	Num 14:22	6963
unto the LORD, he heard our *v*	Num 20:16	6963
LORD hearkened to the *v* of Israel	Num 21:3	6963
LORD heard the *v* of your words	Deut 1:34	6963
LORD would not hearken to your *v*	Deut 1:45	6963
ye heard the *v* of the words	Deut 4:12	6963
only ye heard a *v*	Deut 4:12	6963
and shalt be obedient unto his *v*	Deut 4:30	6963
Did ever people hear the *v* of God	Deut 4:33	6963
heaven he made thee to hear his *v*	Deut 4:36	6963
thick darkness, with a great *v*	Deut 5:22	6963
when ye heard the *v* out of the	Deut 5:23	6963
we have heard his *v* out of the	Deut 5:24	6963
if we hear the *v* of the LORD our	Deut 5:25	6963
that hath heard the *v* of the	Deut 5:26	6963
LORD heard the *v* of your words	Deut 5:28	6963
I have heard the *v* of the words	Deut 5:28	6963
unto the *v* of the LORD your God	Deut 8:20	6963
him not, nor hearkened to his *v*	Deut 9:23	6963
his commandments, and obey his *v*	Deut 13:4	6963
to the *v* of the LORD thy God	Deut 13:18	6963
unto the *v* of the LORD thy God	Deut 15:5	6963
again the *v* of the LORD my God	Deut 18:16	6963
will not obey the *v* of his father	Deut 21:18	6963
or the *v* of his mother, and that,	Deut 21:18	6963
he will not obey our *v*	Deut 21:20	6963
our fathers, the LORD heard our *v*	Deut 26:7	6963
to the *v* of the LORD my God	Deut 26:14	6963
and to hearken unto his *v*	Deut 26:17	6963
obey the *v* of the LORD thy God	Deut 27:10	6963
the men of Israel with a loud *v*	Deut 27:14	6963
unto the *v* of the LORD thy God	Deut 28:1	6963
unto the *v* of the LORD thy God	Deut 28:2	6963
unto the *v* of the LORD thy God	Deut 28:15	6963
unto the *v* of the LORD thy God	Deut 28:45	6963
obey the *v* of the LORD thy God	Deut 28:62	6963
shalt obey his *v* according to all	Deut 30:2	6963
obey the *v* of the LORD, and do all	Deut 30:8	6963
unto the *v* of the LORD thy God	Deut 30:10	6963
and that thou mayest obey his *v*	Deut 30:20	6963
the *v* of Judah, and bring him unto	Deut 33:7	6963
they obeyed not the *v* of the LORD	Josh 5:6	6963
nor make any noise with your *v*	Josh 6:10	6963
hearkened unto the *v* of a man	Josh 10:14	6963
have obeyed my *v* in all that I	Josh 22:2	6963
we serve, and his *v* will we obey	Josh 24:24	6963
but ye have not obeyed my *v*	Judg 2:2	6963
that the people lifted up their *v*	Judg 2:4	6963
and have not hearkened unto my *v*	Judg 2:20	6963
but ye have not obeyed my *v*	Judg 6:10	6963
mount Gerizim, and lifted up his *v*	Judg 9:7	6963
God hearkened to the *v* of Manoah	Judg 13:9	6963
they knew the *v* of the young man	Judg 18:3	6963
Let not thy *v* be heard among us,	Judg 18:25	6963
would not hearken to the *v* of	Judg 20:13	6963
and they lifted up their *v*	Ruth 1:9	6963
And they lifted up their *v*	Ruth 1:14	6963
moved, but her *v* was not heard	1Sa 1:13	6963
not unto the *v* of their father	1Sa 2:25	6963
Hearken unto the *v* of the people	1Sa 8:7	6963
therefore hearken unto their *v*	1Sa 8:9	6963
refused to obey the *v* of Samuel	1Sa 8:19	6963
to Samuel, Hearken unto their *v*	1Sa 8:22	6963
I have hearkened unto your *v* in	1Sa 12:1	6963
LORD, and serve him, and obey his *v*	1Sa 12:14	6963
will not obey the *v* of the LORD	1Sa 12:15	6963
the *v* of the words of the LORD	1Sa 15:1	6963
thou not obey the *v* of the LORD	1Sa 15:19	6963
I have obeyed the *v* of the LORD	1Sa 15:20	6963
as in obeying the *v* of the LORD	1Sa 15:22	6963
the people, and obeyed their *v*	1Sa 15:24	6963
hearkened unto the *v* of Jonathan	1Sa 19:6	6963
that Saul said, Is this thy *v*	1Sa 24:16	6963
And Saul lifted up his *v*, and wept	1Sa 24:16	6963
see, I have hearkened to thy *v*	1Sa 25:35	6963
And Saul knew David's *v*	1Sa 26:17	6963
and said, Is this thy *v*	1Sa 26:17	6963
And David said, It is my *v*	1Sa 26:17	6963
Samuel, she cried with a loud *v*	1Sa 28:12	6963
obeyedst not the *v* of the LORD	1Sa 28:18	6963
thine handmaid hath obeyed thy *v*	1Sa 28:21	6963
also unto the *v* of thine handmaid	1Sa 28:22	6963
and he hearkened unto their *v*	1Sa 28:23	6963
were with him lifted up their *v*	1Sa 30:4	6963
and the king lifted up his *v*	2Sa 3:32	6963
he would not hearken unto our *v*	2Sa 12:18	6963
he would not hearken unto her *v*	2Sa 13:14	6963
sons came, and lifted up their *v*	2Sa 13:36	6963
the country wept with a loud *v*	2Sa 15:23	6963
and the king cried with a loud *v*	2Sa 19:4	6963
any more the *v* of singing men	2Sa 19:35	6963
he did hear my *v* out of his	2Sa 22:7	6963
and the most High uttered his *v*	2Sa 22:14	6963
of Israel with a loud *v*, saying,	1Kin 8:55	6963
And the LORD heard the *v* of Elijah	1Kin 17:22	6963
But there was no *v*, nor any that	1Kin 18:26	6963
that there was neither *v*	1Kin 18:29	6963
and after the fire a still small *v*	1Kin 19:12	6963
behold, there came a *v* unto him	1Kin 19:13	6963
And he hearkened unto their *v*	1Kin 20:25	6963
hast not obeyed the *v* of the LORD	1Kin 20:36	6963
but there was neither *v*, nor	2Kin 4:31	6963
no man there, neither *v* of man	2Kin 7:10	6963
and if ye will hearken unto my *v*	2Kin 10:6	6963
not the *v* of the LORD their God	2Kin 18:12	6963
cried with a loud *v* in the Jews'	2Kin 18:28	6963
whom hast thou exalted thy *v*	2Kin 19:22	6963
by lifting up the *v* with joy	1Chr 15:16	6963
up their *v* with the trumpets	2Chr 5:13	6963
sware unto the LORD with a loud *v*	2Chr 15:14	6963
of Israel with a loud *v* on high	2Chr 20:19	6963
their *v* was heard, and their	2Chr 30:27	6963
Then they cried with a loud *v* in	2Chr 32:18	6963
their eyes, wept with a loud *v*	Ezr 3:12	6963
answered and said with a loud *v*	Ezr 10:12	6963
cried with a loud *v* unto the LORD	Neh 9:4	6963
him not, they lifted up their *v*	Job 2:12	6963
let no joyful *v* come therein	Job 3:7	6963
hear not the *v* of the oppressor	Job 3:18	6963
the *v* of the fierce lion, and the	Job 4:10	6963
there was silence, and I heard a *v*	Job 4:16	6963
that he had hearkened unto my *v*	Job 9:16	6963
into the *v* of them that weep	Job 30:31	6963
I have heard the *v* of thy words	Job 33:8	6963
hearken to the *v* of my words	Job 34:16	6963
attentively the noise of his *v*	Job 37:2	6963
After it a *v* roareth	Job 37:4	6963
with the *v* of his excellency	Job 37:4	6963
not stay them when his *v* is heard	Job 37:4	6963
marvellously with his *v*	Job 37:5	6963
thou lift up thy *v* to the clouds	Job 38:34	6963
thou thunder with a *v* like him	Job 40:9	6963
I cried unto the LORD with my *v*	Ps 3:4	6963
Hearken unto the *v* of my cry	Ps 5:2	6963
My *v* shalt thou hear in the	Ps 5:3	6963
hath heard the *v* of my weeping	Ps 6:8	6963
he heard my *v* out of his temple,	Ps 18:6	6963
and the Highest gave his *v*	Ps 18:13	6963
where their *v* is not heard	Ps 19:3	6963
with the *v* of thanksgiving	Ps 26:7	6963
O LORD, when I cry with my *v*	Ps 27:7	6963
Hear the *v* of my supplications,	Ps 28:2	6963
heard the *v* of my supplications	Ps 28:6	6963
The *v* of the LORD is upon the	Ps 29:3	6963
The *v* of the LORD is powerful	Ps 29:4	6963
the *v* of the LORD is full of	Ps 29:4	6963
The *v* of the LORD breaketh the	Ps 29:5	6963
The *v* of the LORD divideth the	Ps 29:7	6963
The *v* of the LORD shaketh the	Ps 29:8	6963
The *v* of the LORD maketh the	Ps 29:9	6963
the *v* of my supplications when I	Ps 31:22	6963
house of God, with the *v* of joy	Ps 42:4	6963
For the *v* of him that reproacheth	Ps 44:16	6963
he uttered his *v*, the earth	Ps 46:6	6963
unto God with the *v* of triumph	Ps 47:1	6963
Because of the *v* of the enemy	Ps 55:3	6963
and he shall hear my *v*	Ps 55:17	6963
not hearken to the *v* of charmers	Ps 58:5	6963
Hear my *v*, O God, in my prayer	Ps 64:1	6963
make the *v* of his praise to be	Ps 66:8	6963
attended to the *v* of my prayer	Ps 66:19	6963
out his *v*, and that a mighty *v*	Ps 68:33	6963
Forget not the *v* of thine enemies	Ps 74:23	6963
I cried unto God with my *v*	Ps 77:1	6963
even unto God with my *v*	Ps 77:1	6963
The *v* of thy thunder was in the	Ps 77:18	6963
people would not hearken to my *v*	Ps 81:11	6963
and attend to the *v* of my	Ps 86:6	6963
the floods have lifted up their *v*	Ps 93:3	6963
To day if ye will hear his *v*	Ps 95:7	6963
the harp, and the *v* of a psalm	Ps 98:5	6963
By reason of the *v* of my groaning	Ps 102:5	6963
hearkening unto the *v* of his word	Ps 103:20	6963
at the *v* of thy thunder they	Ps 104:7	6963
not unto the *v* of the LORD	Ps 106:25	6963
LORD, because he hath heard my *v*	Ps 116:1	6963
The *v* of rejoicing and salvation	Ps 118:15	6963
Hear my *v* according unto thy	Ps 119:149	6963
Lord, hear my *v*	Ps 130:2	6963
to the *v* of my supplications	Ps 130:2	6963
hear the *v* of my supplications, O	Ps 140:6	6963
give ear unto my *v*, when I cry	Ps 141:1	6963
I cried unto the LORD with my *v*	Ps 142:1	6963
with my *v* unto the LORD did I	Ps 142:1	6963
she uttereth her *v* in the streets	Prov 1:20	6963
and liftest up thy *v* for	Prov 2:3	6963
not obeyed the *v* of my teachers	Prov 5:13	6963
and understanding put forth her *v*	Prov 8:1	6963
my *v* is to the sons of man	Prov 8:4	6963
blesseth his friend with a loud *v*	Prov 27:14	6963
a fool's *v* is known by multitude	Eccl 5:3	6963
should God be angry at thy *v*	Eccl 5:6	6963
bird of the air shall carry the *v*	Eccl 10:20	6963
rise up at the *v* of the bird	Eccl 12:4	6963
The *v* of my beloved	Song 2:8	6963
the *v* of the turtle is heard in	Song 2:12	6963
countenance, let me hear thy *v*	Song 2:14	6963
for sweet is thy *v*, and thy	Song 2:14	6963
it is the *v* of my beloved that	Song 5:2	6963
the companions hearken to thy *v*	Song 8:13	6963
moved at the *v* of him that cried	Is 6:4	6963
Also I heard the *v* of the Lord	Is 6:8	6963
Lift up thy *v*, O daughter of	Is 10:30	6963
mountain, exalt the *v* unto them	Is 13:2	6963
their *v* shall be heard even unto	Is 15:4	6963
They shall lift up their *v*	Is 24:14	6963
Give ye ear, and hear my *v*	Is 28:23	6963
thy *v* shall be, as of one that	Is 29:4	6963
unto thee at the *v* of thy cry	Is 30:19	6963
cause his glorious *v* to be heard	Is 30:30	6963
For through the *v* of the LORD	Is 30:31	6963
he will not be afraid of their *v*	Is 31:4	6963
hear my *v*, ye careless daughters	Is 32:9	6963
cried with a loud *v* in the Jews'	Is 36:13	6963
whom hast thou exalted thy *v*	Is 37:23	6963
The *v* of him that crieth in the	Is 40:3	6963
The *v* said, Cry	Is 40:6	6963
lift up thy *v* with strength	Is 40:9	6963
nor cause his *v* to be heard in	Is 42:2	6963
cities thereof lift up their *v*	Is 42:11	
with a *v* of singing declare ye,	Is 48:20	6963
that obeyeth the *v* of his servant	Is 50:10	6963
thanksgiving, and the *v* of melody	Is 51:3	6963
Thy watchmen shall lift up the *v*	Is 52:8	6963
with the *v* together shall they	Is 52:8	6963
lift up thy *v* like a trumpet, and	Is 58:1	6963
to make your *v* to be heard on	Is 58:4	6963
the *v* of weeping shall be no more	Is 65:19	6963
heard in her, nor the *v* of crying	Is 65:19	6963
A *v* of noise from the city	Is 66:6	6963
a *v* from the temple	Is 66:6	6963
a *v* of the LORD that rendereth	Is 66:6	6963
tree, and ye have not obeyed my *v*	Jer 3:13	6963
A *v* was heard upon the high	Jer 3:21	6963
obeyed the *v* of the LORD our God	Jer 3:25	6963
For a *v* declareth from Dan, and	Jer 4:15	6963
give out their *v* against the	Jer 4:16	6963
For I have heard a *v* as of a	Jer 4:31	6963
the *v* of the daughter of Zion,	Jer 4:31	6963
their *v* roareth like the sea	Jer 6:23	6963
I them, saying, Obey my *v*	Jer 7:23	6963
not the *v* of the LORD their God	Jer 7:28	6963
the *v* of mirth	Jer 7:34	6963
the *v* of gladness	Jer 7:34	6963
the *v* of the bridegroom	Jer 7:34	6963
and the *v* of the bride	Jer 7:34	6963
Behold the *v* of the cry of the	Jer 8:19	6963
can men hear the *v* of the cattle	Jer 9:10	6963
them, and have not obeyed my *v*	Jer 9:13	6963
For a *v* of wailing is heard out	Jer 9:19	6963
When he uttereth his *v*, there is	Jer 10:13	6963
iron furnace, saying, Obey my *v*	Jer 11:4	6963
and protesting, saying, Obey my *v*	Jer 11:7	6963
the *v* of mirth	Jer 16:9	6963
the *v* of gladness	Jer 16:9	6963
the *v* of the bridegroom	Jer 16:9	6963
and the *v* of the bride	Jer 16:9	6963
my sight, that it obey not my *v*	Jer 18:10	6963
hearken to the *v* of them that	Jer 18:19	6963
and lift up thy *v* in Bashan	Jer 22:20	6963
that thou obeyedst not my *v*	Jer 22:21	6963
take from them the *v* of mirth	Jer 25:10	6963
the *v* of gladness	Jer 25:10	6963
the *v* of the bridegroom	Jer 25:10	6963
the *v* of the bride	Jer 25:10	6963
utter his *v* from his holy	Jer 25:30	6963
A *v* of the cry of the shepherds,	Jer 25:36	6963
obey the *v* of the LORD your God	Jer 26:13	6963
We have heard a *v* of trembling	Jer 30:5	6963
the *v* of them that make merry	Jer 30:19	6963
A *v* was heard in Ramah,	Jer 31:15	6963
Refrain thy *v* from weeping, and	Jer 31:16	6963
but they obeyed not thy *v*	Jer 32:23	6963
The *v* of joy	Jer 33:11	6963
the *v* of gladness	Jer 33:11	6963
the *v* of the bridegroom	Jer 33:11	6963
the *v* of the bride	Jer 33:11	6963
the *v* of them that shall say,	Jer 33:11	6963
Thus have we obeyed the *v* of	Jer 35:8	6963
the *v* of the LORD, which I speak	Jer 38:20	6963
LORD, and have not obeyed his *v*	Jer 40:3	6963
we will obey the *v* of the LORD	Jer 42:6	6963
when we obey the *v* of the LORD	Jer 42:6	6963
neither obey the *v* of the LORD	Jer 42:13	6963
obeyed the *v* of the LORD your God	Jer 42:21	6963
obeyed not the *v* of the LORD	Jer 43:4	6963
they obeyed not the *v* of the LORD	Jer 43:7	6963
have not obeyed the *v* of the LORD	Jer 44:23	6963
The *v* thereof shall go like a	Jer 46:22	6963
A *v* of crying shall be from	Jer 48:3	6963
Jahaz, have they uttered their *v*	Jer 48:34	6963
The *v* of them that flee and escape	Jer 50:28	6963
their *v* shall roar like the sea,	Jer 50:42	6963
When he uttereth his *v*, there is	Jer 51:16	6963
destroyed out of her the great *v*	Jer 51:55	6963
a noise of their *v* is uttered	Jer 51:55	6963
Thou hast heard my *v*	Lam 3:56	6963
as the *v* of the Almighty, the	Eze 1:24	6963
the *v* of speech, as the noise of	Eze 1:24	6963
there was a *v* from the firmament	Eze 1:25	6963
I heard a *v* of one that spake	Eze 1:28	6963
behind me a *v* of a great rushing	Eze 3:12	6963
cry in mine ears with a loud *v*	Eze 8:18	6963
also in mine ears with a loud *v*	Eze 9:1	6963
as the *v* of the Almighty God when	Eze 10:5	6963
my face, and cried with a loud *v*	Eze 11:13	6963
that his *v* should no more be	Eze 19:9	6963
to lift up the *v* with shouting	Eze 21:22	6963
a *v* of a multitude being at ease	Eze 23:42	6963
shall cause their *v* to be heard	Eze 27:30	6963
of one that hath a pleasant *v*	Eze 33:32	6963
his *v* was like a noise of many	Eze 43:2	6963
mouth, there fell a *v* from heaven	Dan 4:31	7032
with a lamentable *v* unto Daniel	Dan 6:20	7032
v of the great words which the	Dan 7:11	7032
I heard a man's *v* between the	Dan 8:16	6963
obeyed the *v* of the LORD our God	Dan 9:10	6963
that they might not obey thy *v*	Dan 9:11	6963
for we obeyed not his *v*	Dan 9:14	6963

the *v* of his words like the ... Dan 10:6 6963
words like the *v* of a multitude ... Dan 10:6 6963
Yet heard I the *v* of his words ... Dan 10:9 6963
when I heard the *v* of his words ... Dan 10:9 6963
shall utter his *v* before his army ... Joel 2:11 6963
utter his *v* from Jerusalem ... Joel 3:16 6963
utter his *v* from Jerusalem ... Amos 1:2 6963
cried I, and thou heardest my *v* ... Jonah 2:2 6963
thee with the *v* of thanksgiving ... Jonah 2:9 6963
and let the hills hear thy *v* ... Mic 6:1 6963
The LORD's *v* crieth unto the city ... Mic 6:9 6963
lead her as with the *v* of doves ... Nah 2:7 6963
the *v* of thy messengers shall no ... Nah 2:13 6963
the deep uttered his *v*, and lifted ... Hab 3:10 6963
my lips quivered at the *v* ... Hab 3:16 6963
even the *v* of the day of the LORD ... Zeph 1:14 6963
their *v* shall sing in the windows ... Zeph 2:14 6963
She obeyed not the *v* ... Zeph 3:2 6963
obeyed the *v* of the LORD their ... Hag 1:12 6963
obey the *v* of the LORD your God ... Zec 6:15 6963
There is a *v* of the howling of ... Zec 11:3 6963
a *v* of the roaring of young lions ... Zec 11:3 6963
In Rama was there a *v* heard ... Mt 2:18 *5456*
The *v* of one crying in the ... Mt 3:3 *5456*
lo a *v* from heaven, saying, This ... Mt 3:17 *5456*
any man hear his *v* in the streets ... Mt 12:19 *5456*
behold a *v* out of the cloud, ... Mt 17:5 *5456*
hour Jesus cried with a loud *v* ... Mt 27:46 *5456*
he had cried again with a loud *v* ... Mt 27:50 *5456*
The *v* of one crying in the ... Mk 1:3 *5456*
And there came a *v* from heaven ... Mk 1:11 *5456*
torn him, and cried with a loud *v* ... Mk 1:26 *5456*
And cried with a loud *v*, and said, ... Mk 5:7 *5456*
a *v* came out of the cloud, saying ... Mk 9:7 *5456*
hour Jesus cried with a loud *v* ... Mk 15:34 *5456*
And Jesus cried with a loud *v* ... Mk 15:37 *5456*
And she spake out with a loud *v* ... Lk 1:42 *5456*
For, lo, as soon as the *v* of thy ... Lk 1:44 *5456*
The *v* of one crying in the ... Lk 3:4 *5456*
a *v* came from heaven, which said, ... Lk 3:22 *5456*
devil, and cried out with a loud *v* ... Lk 4:33 *5456*
before him, and with a loud *v* said ... Lk 8:28 *5456*
there came a *v* out of the cloud, ... Lk 9:35 *5456*
And when the *v* was past, Jesus was ... Lk 9:36 *5456*
of the company lifted up her *v* ... Lk 11:27 *5456*
with a loud *v* glorified God, ... Lk 17:15 *5456*
praise God with a loud *v* for all ... Lk 19:37 *5456*
Jesus had cried with a loud *v* ... Lk 23:46 *5456*
I am the *v* of one crying in the ... Jn 1:23 *5456*
because of the bridegroom's *v* ... Jn 3:29 *5456*
hear the *v* of the Son of God ... Jn 5:25 *5456*
in the graves shall hear his *v* ... Jn 5:28 *5456*
neither heard his *v* at any time ... Jn 5:37 *5456*
and the sheep hear his *v* ... Jn 10:3 *5456*
for they know his *v* ... Jn 10:4 *5456*
they know not the *v* of strangers ... Jn 10:5 *5456*
bring, and they shall hear my *v* ... Jn 10:16 *5456*
My sheep hear my *v*, and I know ... Jn 10:27 *5456*
spoken, he cried with a loud *v* ... Jn 11:43 *5456*
Then came there a *v* from heaven ... Jn 12:28 *5456*
This *v* came not because of me, ... Jn 12:30 *5456*
that is of the truth heareth my *v* ... Jn 18:37 *5456*
with the eleven, lifted up his *v* ... Acts 2:14 *5456*
they lifted up their *v* to God ... Acts 4:24 *5456*
the *v* of the Lord came unto him, ... Acts 7:31 *5456*
Then they cried out with a loud *v* ... Acts 7:57 *5456*
down, and cried with a loud *v* ... Acts 7:60 *5456*
spirits, crying with loud *v* ... Acts 8:7 *5456*
heard a *v* saying unto him, Saul, ... Acts 9:4 *5456*
him stood speechless, hearing a *v* ... Acts 9:7 *5456*
And there came a *v* to him, Rise, ... Acts 10:13 *5456*
the *v* spake unto him again the ... Acts 10:15 *5456*
I heard a *v* saying unto me, Arise ... Acts 11:7 *5456*
But the *v* answered me again from ... Acts 11:9 *5456*
And when she knew Peter's *v* ... Acts 12:14 *5456*
saying, It is the *v* of a god ... Acts 12:22 *5456*
Said with a loud *v*, Stand upright ... Acts 14:10 *5456*
But Paul cried with a loud *v* ... Acts 16:28 *5456*
all with one *v* about the space of ... Acts 19:34 *5456*
heard a *v* saying unto me, Saul, ... Acts 22:7 *5456*
but they heard not the *v* of him ... Acts 22:9 *5456*
shouldest hear the *v* of his mouth ... Acts 22:14 *5456*
Except it be for this one *v* ... Acts 24:21 *5456*
death, I gave my *v* against them ... Acts 26:10 *5586*
I heard a *v* speaking unto me, and ... Acts 26:14 *5456*
Festus said with a loud *v* ... Acts 26:24 *5456*
I know not the meaning of the *v* ... 1Cor 14:11 *5456*
that by my *v* I might teach others ... 1Cor 14:19
with you now, and to change my *v* ... Gal 4:20 *5456*
with the *v* of the archangel, and ... 1Th 4:16 *5456*
To day if ye will hear his *v* ... Heb 3:7 *5456*
To day if ye will hear his *v* ... Heb 3:15 *5456*
To day if ye will hear his *v* ... Heb 4:7 *5456*
of a trumpet, and the *v* of words ... Heb 12:19 *5456*
which *v* they that heard intreated ... Heb 12:19
Whose *v* then shook the earth ... Heb 12:26 *5456*
when there came such a *v* to him ... 2Pet 1:17 *5456*
this *v* which came from heaven we ... 2Pet 1:18 *5456*
man's *v* forbad the madness of the ... 2Pet 2:16 *5456*
day, and heard behind me a great *v* ... Rev 1:10 *5456*
to see the *v* that spake with me ... Rev 1:12 *5456*
his *v* as the sound of many waters ... Rev 1:15 *5456*
if any man hear my *v*, and open the ... Rev 3:20 *5456*
the first *v* which I heard was as ... Rev 4:1 *5456*
angel proclaiming with a loud *v* ... Rev 5:2 *5456*
I heard the *v* of many angels ... Rev 5:11 *5456*
Saying with a loud *v*, Worthy is ... Rev 5:12 *5456*
I heard a *v* in the midst of the ... Rev 6:6 *5456*
I heard the *v* of the fourth beast ... Rev 6:7 *5456*
And they cried with a loud *v* ... Rev 6:10 *5456*
with a loud *v* to the four angels ... Rev 7:2 *5456*
And cried with a loud *v*, saying, ... Rev 7:10 *5456*
of heaven, saying with a loud *v* ... Rev 8:13 *5456*
I heard a *v* from the four horns ... Rev 9:13 *5456*
And cried with a loud *v*, as when a ... Rev 10:3 *5456*
I heard a *v* from heaven saying ... Rev 10:4 *5456*
of the *v* of the seventh angel ... Rev 10:7 *5456*
the *v* which I heard from heaven ... Rev 10:8 *5456*
they heard a great *v* from heaven ... Rev 11:12 *5456*
I heard a loud *v* saying in heaven ... Rev 12:10 *5456*
I heard a *v* from heaven ... Rev 14:2 *5456*
as the *v* of many waters ... Rev 14:2 *5456*
as the *v* of a great thunder ... Rev 14:2 *5456*
I heard the *v* of harpers harping ... Rev 14:2 *5456*
Saying with a loud *v*, Fear God, ... Rev 14:7 *5456*
them, saying with a loud *v* ... Rev 14:9 *5456*
I heard a *v* from heaven saying ... Rev 14:13 *5456*
crying with a loud *v* to him that ... Rev 14:15 *5456*
I heard a great *v* out of the ... Rev 16:1 *5456*
there came a great *v* out of the ... Rev 16:17 *5456*
he cried mightily with a strong *v* ... Rev 18:2 *5456*
And I heard another *v* from heaven ... Rev 18:4 *5456*
the *v* of harpers, and musicians, ... Rev 18:22 *5456*
the *v* of the bridegroom and of the ... Rev 18:23 *5456*
great *v* of much people in heaven ... Rev 19:1 *5456*
a *v* came out of the throne, ... Rev 19:5 *5456*
were the *v* of a great multitude ... Rev 19:6 *5456*
as the *v* of many waters ... Rev 19:6 *5456*
as the *v* of mighty thunderings, ... Rev 19:6 *5456*
and he cried with a loud *v* ... Rev 19:17 *5456*
I heard a great *v* out of heaven ... Rev 21:3 *5456*

VOICES {17}
before God, and lifted up their *v* ... Judg 21:2 6963
all the people lifted up their *v* ... 1Sa 11:4 6963
And they lifted up their *v* ... Lk 17:13 *5456*
And they were instant with loud *v* ... Lk 23:23 *5456*
the *v* of them and of the chief ... Lk 23:23 *5456*
nor yet the *v* of the prophets ... Acts 13:27 *5456*
had done, they lifted up their *v* ... Acts 14:11 *5456*
word, and then lifted up their *v* ... Acts 22:22 *5456*
so many kinds of *v* in the world ... 1Cor 14:10 *5456*
lightnings and thunderings and *v* ... Rev 4:5 *5456*
and there were *v*, and thunderings, ... Rev 8:5 *5456*
v of the trumpet of the three ... Rev 8:13 *5456*
seven thunders uttered their *v* ... Rev 10:3 *5456*
thunders had uttered their *v* ... Rev 10:4 *5456*
and there were great *v* in heaven ... Rev 11:15 *5456*
and there were lightnings, and *v* ... Rev 11:19 *5456*
And there were *v*, and thunders, and ... Rev 16:18 *5456*

VOID {24}
the earth was without form, and *v* ... Gen 1:2 922
them *v* on the day he heard them ... Num 30:12 6565
her husband hath made them *v* ... Num 30:12 6565
it, or her husband may make it *v* ... Num 30:13 6565
v after that he hath heard them ... Num 30:15 6565
they are a nation *v* of counsel ... Deut 32:28 6
in a *v* place in the entrance of ... 1Kin 22:10 1637
they sat in a *v* place at the ... 2Chr 18:9 1637
Thou hast made *v* the covenant of ... Ps 89:39 5010
for they have made *v* thy law ... Ps 119:126 6565
a young man *v* of understanding, ... Prov 7:7 2638
of him that is *v* of understanding ... Prov 10:13 2638
He that is *v* of wisdom despiseth ... Prov 11:12 2638
persons is *v* of understanding ... Prov 12:11 2638
A man *v* of understanding striketh ... Prov 17:18 2638
of the man *v* of understanding ... Prov 24:30 2638
it shall not return unto me *v* ... Is 55:11 7387
and, lo, it was without form, and *v* ... Jer 4:23 922
I will make *v* the counsel of ... Jer 19:7 1238
She is empty, and *v*, and waste ... Nah 2:10 4003
v of offence toward God, and ... Acts 24:16 *677*
Do we then make *v* the law through ... Rom 3:31 *2673*
the law be heirs, faith is made *v* ... Rom 4:14 *2758*
any man should make my glorying *v* ... 1Cor 9:15 *2758*

VOLUME {2}
in the *v* of the book it is ... Ps 40:7 4039
I come (in the *v* of the book it ... Heb 10:7 *2777*

VOLUNTARILY {1}
peace offerings *v* unto the LORD ... Eze 46:12 5071

VOLUNTARY {4}
his own *v* will at the door of the ... Lev 1:3 7522
or a *v* offering, it shall be ... Lev 7:16 5071
a *v* burnt offering or peace ... Eze 46:12 5071
of your reward in a *v* humility ... Col 2:18 *2309*

VOMIT {8}
and he shall *v* them up again ... Job 20:15 6958
thou hast eaten shalt thou *v* up ... Prov 23:8 6958
thou be filled therewith, and *v* it ... Prov 25:16 6958
As a dog returneth to his *v* ... Prov 26:11 6892
a drunken man staggereth in his *v* ... Is 19:14 6892
For all tables are full of *v* ... Is 28:8 6892
Moab also shall wallow in his *v* ... Jer 48:26 6892
dog is turned to his own *v* again ... 2Pet 2:22 *1829*

VOMITED {1}
it *v* out Jonah upon the dry land ... Jonah 2:10 6958

VOMITETH {1}
the land itself *v* out her ... Lev 18:25 6958

VOPHSI *(vof'-si)* {1} *A spy sent to the Promised Land.*
of Naphtali, Nahbi the son of *V* ... Num 13:14 2058

VOW {41}
And Jacob vowed a *v*, saying, If ... Gen 28:20 5088
and where thou vowedst a *v* unto me ... Gen 31:13 5088
sacrifice of his offering be a *v* ... Lev 7:16 5088
unto the LORD to accomplish his *v* ... Lev 22:21 5088
but for a *v* it shall not be ... Lev 22:23 5088
a man shall make a singular *v* ... Lev 27:2 5088
separate themselves to *v* ... Num 6:2 5087
a *v* of a Nazarite, to ... Num 6:2 5088
All the days of the *v* of his ... Num 6:5 5088
according to the *v* which he vowed ... Num 6:21 5088
or a sacrifice in performing a *v* ... Num 15:3 5088
for a sacrifice in performing a *v* ... Num 15:8 5088
And Israel vowed a *v* unto the LORD ... Num 21:2 5088
If a man *v* a ... Num 30:2 5087
a *v* unto the LORD ... Num 30:2 5088
If a woman also *v* a ... Num 30:3 5087
a *v* unto the LORD ... Num 30:3 5088
And her father hear her *v*, and her ... Num 30:4 5088
shall make her *v* which she vowed ... Num 30:8 5088
But every *v* of a widow, and of her ... Num 30:9 5088
Every *v*, and every binding oath to ... Num 30:13 5088
vows which ye *v* unto the LORD ... Deut 12:11 5087
of the LORD thy God for any *v* ... Deut 23:18 5088
When thou shalt *v* a ... Deut 23:21 5087
a *v* unto the LORD thy God ... Deut 23:21 5088
But if thou shalt forbear to *v* ... Deut 23:22 5087
Jephthah vowed a *v* unto the LORD ... Judg 11:30 5088
to his *v* which he had vowed ... Judg 11:39 5088
And she vowed a *v*, and said, O LORD ... 1Sa 1:11 5088
the yearly sacrifice, and his *v* ... 1Sa 1:21 5088
pray thee, let me go and pay my *v* ... 2Sa 15:7 5088
For thy servant vowed a *v* while I ... 2Sa 15:8 5088
thee shall the *v* be performed ... Ps 65:1 5088
V, and pay unto the LORD your God ... Ps 76:11 5087
When thou vowest a *v* unto God ... Eccl 5:4 5088
is it that thou shouldest not *v* ... Eccl 5:5 5087
than that thou shouldest *v* ... Eccl 5:5 5087
oblation; yea, they shall *v* ... Is 19:21 5087
a *v* unto the LORD ... Is 19:21 5088
for he had a *v* ... Acts 18:18 *2171*
four men which have a *v* on them ... Acts 21:23 *2171*

VOWED {18}
And Jacob *v* a vow, saying, If God ... Gen 28:20 5087
that *v* shall the priest value him ... Lev 27:8 5087
law of the Nazarite who hath *v* ... Num 6:21 5087
according to the vow which he *v* ... Num 6:21 5087
Israel *v* a vow unto the LORD, and ... Num 21:2 5087
had at all an husband, when she *v* ... Num 30:6 5088
he shall make her vow which she *v* ... Num 30:8 5088
if she *v* in her husband's house, ... Num 30:10 5087
thou hast *v* unto the LORD thy God ... Deut 23:23 5087
Jephthah *v* a vow unto the LORD, ... Judg 11:30 5087
to his vow which he had *v* ... Judg 11:39 5087
she *v* a vow, and said, O LORD of ... 1Sa 1:11 5087
which I have *v* unto the LORD, in ... 2Sa 15:7 5087
For thy servant *v* a vow while I ... 2Sa 15:8 5087
v unto the mighty God of Jacob ... Ps 132:2 5087
pay that which thou hast *v* ... Eccl 5:4 5087
perform our vows that we have *v* ... Jer 44:25 5087
I will pay that that I have *v* ... Jonah 2:9 5087

VOWEDST {1}
where thou *v* a vow unto me ... Gen 31:13 5087

VOWEST {2}
nor any of thy vows which thou *v* ... Deut 12:17 5087
When thou *v* a vow unto God, defer ... Eccl 5:4 5087

VOWETH {1}
hath in his flock a male, and *v* ... Mal 1:14 5087

VOWS {30}
offer his oblation for all his *v* ... Lev 22:18 5088
your gifts, and beside all your *v* ... Lev 23:38 5088
in your set feasts, beside your *v* ... Num 29:39 5088
then all her *v* shall stand ... Num 30:4 5088
not any of her *v*, or of her bonds ... Num 30:5 5088
then her *v* shall stand, and her ... Num 30:7 5088
then all her *v* shall stand ... Num 30:11 5088
out of her lips concerning her *v* ... Num 30:12 5088
then he establisheth all her *v* ... Num 30:14 5088
offerings of your hand, and your *v* ... Deut 12:6 5088
all your choice *v* which ye vow ... Deut 12:11 5088
nor any of thy *v* which thou ... Deut 12:17 5088
things which thou hast, and thy *v* ... Deut 12:26 5088
thee, and thou shalt pay thy *v* ... Job 22:27 5088
I will pay my *v* before them that ... Ps 22:25 5088
pay thy *v* unto the most High ... Ps 50:14 5088
Thy *v* are upon me, O God ... Ps 56:12 5088
For thou, O God, hast heard my *v* ... Ps 61:5 5088
that I may daily perform my *v* ... Ps 61:8 5088
I will pay thee my *v*, ... Ps 66:13 5088
I will pay my *v* unto the LORD now ... Ps 116:14 5088
I will pay my *v* unto the LORD now ... Ps 116:18 5088
this day have I payed my *v* ... Prov 7:14 5088
holy, and after *v* to make enquiry ... Prov 20:25 5088
and what, the son of my *v* ... Prov 31:2 5088
perform our *v* that we have vowed ... Jer 44:25 5088
ye will surely accomplish your *v* ... Jer 44:25 5088
and surely perform your *v* ... Jer 44:25 5088
unto the LORD, and made *v* ... Jonah 1:16 5088
thy solemn feasts, perform thy *v* ... Nah 1:15 5088

VOYAGE {1}
that this *v* will be with hurt ... Acts 27:10 *4144*

VULTURE {2}
And the *v*, and the kite after his ... Lev 11:14 1676
kite, and the *v* after his kind, ... Deut 14:13 1772

VULTURE'S {1}
which the *v* eye hath not seen ... Job 28:7 344

VULTURES {1}
there shall the *v* also be ... Is 34:15 1772

W

WADI ZERED See ZARED.

WAFER {3}
- one *w* out of the basket of the Ex 29:23 7550
- a cake of oiled bread, and one *w* Lev 8:26 7550
- the basket, and one unleavened *w* Num 6:19 7550

WAFERS {5}
- of it was like *w* made with honey Ex 16:31 6838
- *w* unleavened anointed with oil Ex 29:2 7550
- or unleavened *w* anointed with oil Lev 2:4 7550
- unleavened *w* anointed with oil, Lev 7:12 7550
- *w* of unleavened bread anointed Num 6:15 7550

WAG {3}
- be astonished, and *w* his head Jer 18:16 5110
- *w* their head at the daughter of Lam 2:15 5128
- by her shall hiss, and *w* his hand Zeph 2:15 5128

WAGES {18}
- tell me, what shall thy *w* be Gen 29:15 4909
- And he said, Appoint me thy *w* Gen 30:28 7939
- me, and changed my *w* ten times Gen 31:7 4909
- thus, The speckled shall be thy *w* Gen 31:8 7939
- thou hast changed my *w* ten times Gen 31:41 4909
- for me, and I will give thee thy *w* Ex 2:9 7939
- the *w* of him that is hired shall Lev 19:13 6468
- his neighbour's service without *w* Jer 22:13 2600
- yet had he no *w*, nor his army, Eze 29:18 7939
- and it shall be the *w* for his army Eze 29:19 7939
- he that earneth *w* earneth *w* Hag 1:6 7936
- oppress the hireling in his *w* Mal 3:5 7939
- and be content with your *w* Lk 3:14 *3800*
- And he that reapeth receiveth *w* Jn 4:36 *3408*
- For the *w* of sin is death Rom 6:23 *3800*
- taking *w* of them, to do you 2Cor 11:8 *3800*
- son of Bosor, who loved the *w* of 2Pet 2:15 *3408*

WAGGING {2}
- by reviled him, *w* their heads, Mt 27:39 *2795*
- *w* their heads, and saying, Ah, Mk 15:29 *2795*

WAGON {1}
- a *w* for two of the princes, and Num 7:3 5699

WAGONS {9}
- take you *w* out of the land of Gen 45:19 5699
- and Joseph gave them *w*, according Gen 45:21 5699
- when he saw the *w* which Joseph Gen 45:27 5699
- in the *w* which Pharaoh had sent Gen 46:5 5699
- before the LORD, six covered *w* Num 7:3 5699
- And Moses took the *w* and the oxen, Num 7:6 5699
- Two *w* and four oxen he gave unto Num 7:7 5699
- And four *w* and eight oxen he gave Num 7:8 5699
- against thee with chariots, *w* Eze 23:24 7393

WAHEB See DID.

WAIL {3}
- *w* for the multitude of Egypt, and Eze 32:18 5091
- Therefore I will *w* and howl, I Mic 1:8 5594
- the earth shall *w* because of him Rev 1:7 *2875*

WAILED {1}
- and them that wept and *w* greatly Mk 5:38 *214*

WAILING {16}
- and fasting, and weeping, and *w* Est 4:3 4553
- will I take up a weeping and *w* Jer 9:10 5092
- make haste, and take up a *w* for us Jer 9:18 5092
- For a voice of *w* is heard out of Jer 9:19 5092
- mouth, and teach your daughters *w* Jer 9:20 5092
- neither shall there be *w* for them Eze 7:11 5089
- bitterness of heart and bitter *w* Eze 27:31 4553
- in their *w* they shall take up a Eze 27:32 5204
- *W* shall be in all streets Amos 5:16 4553
- are skilful of lamentation to *w* Amos 5:16 4553
- And in all vineyards shall be *w* Amos 5:17 4553
- I will make a *w* like the dragons, Mic 1:8 4553
- there shall be *w* and gnashing of Mt 13:42 *2805*
- there shall be *w* and gnashing of Mt 13:50 *2805*
- fear of her torment, weeping and *w* Rev 18:15 *3996*
- heads, and cried, weeping and *w* Rev 18:19 *3996*

WAIT {106}
- And if a man lie not in *w*, but God Ex 21:13 6658
- they shall *w* on their priest's Num 3:10 8104
- in to *w* upon the service of the Num 8:24 6633
- or hurl at him by laying of *w* Num 35:20 6660
- him any thing without laying of *w* Num 35:22 6660
- lie in *w* for him, and rise up Deut 19:11 693
- ye shall lie in *w* against the Josh 8:4 693
- their liers in *w* on the west of Josh 8:13 6119
- in *w* for him in the top of the Judg 9:25 693
- thee, and lie in *w* in the field Judg 9:32 693
- they laid *w* against Shechem in Judg 9:34 693
- were with him, from lying in *w* Judg 9:35 3993
- laid *w* in the field, and looked, Judg 9:43 693
- laid *w* for him all night in the Judg 16:2 693
- Now there were men lying in *w* Judg 16:9 693
- there were liers in *w* abiding in Judg 16:12 693
- set liers in *w* round about Gibeah Judg 20:29 693
- the liers in *w* of Israel came Judg 20:33 693
- in *w* which they had set beside Judg 20:36 693
- And the liers in *w* hasted, and Judg 20:37 693
- the liers in *w* drew themselves Judg 20:37 693
- men of Israel and the liers in *w* Judg 20:38 693
- lie in *w* in the vineyards Judg 21:20 693
- how he laid *w* for him in the way, 1Sa 15:2
- Amalek, and laid *w* in the valley 1Sa 15:5 693
- servant against me, to lie in *w* 1Sa 22:8 693
- rise against me, to lie in *w* 1Sa 22:13 693
- what should I *w* for the LORD any 2Kin 6:33 3176
- Because their office was to *w* on 1Chr 23:28 3027
- and did not then *w* by course 2Chr 5:11 8104
- the Levites *w* upon their business 2Chr 13:10
- and of such as lay in *w* by the way Ezr 8:31 693
- of my appointed time will I *w* Job 14:14 3176
- If I *w*, the grave is mine house Job 17:13 6960
- or if I have laid *w* at my Job 31:9 693
- abide in the covert to lie in *w* Job 38:40 695
- He lieth in *w* secretly as a lion Ps 10:9 693
- he lieth in *w* to catch the poor Ps 10:9 693
- let none that *w* on thee be Ps 25:3 6960
- on thee do I *w* all the day Ps 25:5 6960
- for I *w* on thee Ps 25:21 6960
- *W* on the LORD Ps 27:14 6960
- *w*, I say, on the LORD Ps 27:14 6960
- the LORD, and *w* patiently for him Ps 37:7 2342
- but those that *w* upon the LORD Ps 37:9 6960
- *W* on the LORD, and keep his way, Ps 37:34 6960
- And now, Lord, what *w* I for Ps 39:7 6960
- and I will *w* on thy name Ps 52:9 6960
- my steps, when they *w* for my soul Ps 56:6 6960
- lo, they lie in *w* for my soul Ps 59:3 693
- his strength will I *w* upon thee Ps 59:9 8104
- My soul, *w* thou only upon God Ps 62:5 1826
- eyes fail while I *w* for my God Ps 69:3 3176
- Let not them that *w* on thee Ps 69:6 6960
- they that lay *w* for my soul take Ps 71:10 8104
- These *w* all upon thee Ps 104:27 7663
- so our eyes *w* upon the LORD our Ps 123:2
- *w* for the LORD, my soul doth *w* Ps 130:5 6960
- The eyes of all *w* upon thee Ps 145:15 7663
- with us, let us lay *w* for blood Prov 1:11 693
- they lay *w* for their own blood Prov 1:18 693
- lieth in *w* at every corner Prov 7:12 693
- wicked are to lie in *w* for blood Prov 12:6 693
- but *w* on the LORD, and he shall Prov 20:22 6960
- She also lieth in *w* as for a prey Prov 23:28 693
- Lay not *w*, O wicked man, against Prov 24:15 693
- I will *w* upon the LORD, that Is 8:17 2442
- And therefore will the LORD *w* Is 30:18 2442
- are all they that *w* for him Is 30:18 2442
- But they that *w* upon the LORD Is 40:31 6960
- and the isles shall *w* for his law Is 42:4 3176
- not be ashamed that *w* for me Is 49:23 6960
- the isles shall *w* upon me Is 51:5 6960
- we *w* for light, but behold Is 59:9 6960
- Surely the isles shall *w* for me Is 60:9 6960
- they lay *w*, as he that setteth Jer 5:26 7789
- but in heart he layeth his *w* Jer 9:8 696
- therefore we will *w* upon thee Jer 14:22 6960
- was unto me as a bear lying in *w* Lam 3:10 693
- is good unto them that *w* for him Lam 3:25 6960
- quietly *w* for the salvation of Lam 3:26 1748
- they laid *w* for us in the Lam 4:19 693
- as troops of robbers *w* for a man Hos 6:9 2442
- an oven, whiles they lie in *w* Hos 7:6 693
- and *w* on thy God continually Hos 12:6 6960
- they all lie in *w* for blood Mic 7:2 693
- I will *w* for the God of my Mic 7:7 3176
- though it tarry, *w* for it Hab 2:3 2442
- Therefore *w* ye upon me, saith the Zeph 3:8 2442
- that a small ship should *w* on him Mk 3:9 *4342*
- Laying *w* for him, and seeking to Lk 11:54 *1748*
- unto men that *w* for their lord Lk 12:36 *4327*
- but *w* for the promise of the Acts 1:4 *4037*
- And when the Jews laid *w* for him Acts 20:3 *1096,1917*
- me by the lying in *w* of the Jews Acts 20:19 *1917*
- son heard of their lying in *w* Acts 23:16 *1747*
- for there lie in *w* for him of Acts 23:21 *1748*
- that the Jews laid *w* for the man Acts 23:30 *1917*
- laying *w* in the way to kill him Acts 25:3 *4160,1747*
- then do we with patience *w* for it Rom 8:25 *553*
- let us *w* on our ministering Rom 12:7
- they which *w* at the altar are 1Cor 9:13 *4332*
- For we through the Spirit *w* for Gal 5:5 *553*
- whereby they lie in *w* to deceive Eph 4:14 *3180*
- to *w* for his Son from heaven, 1Th 1:10 *362*

WAITED {35}
- I have *w* for thy salvation, O Gen 49:18 6960
- *w* for the king by the way, and 1Kin 20:38 5975
- and she *w* on Naaman's wife 2Kin 5:2 1961,6440
- then they *w* on their office 1Chr 6:32 5975
- they that *w* with their children 1Chr 6:33 5975
- Who hitherto *w* in the king's gate 1Chr 9:18
- the priests *w* on their offices 2Chr 7:6 5975
- These *w* on the king, beside those 2Chr 17:19 8334
- the porters *w* at every gate 2Chr 35:15
- priests and for the Levites that *w* Neh 12:44 5975
- the companies of Sheba *w* for them Job 6:19 6960
- and he is *w* for of the sword Job 15:22 6822
- Unto me men gave ear, and *w* Job 29:21 3176
- they *w* for me as for the rain Job 29:23 3176
- when I *w* for light, there came Job 30:26 3176
- Now Elihu had *w* till Job had Job 32:4 2442
- Behold, I *w* for your words Job 32:11 3176
- When I had *w*, (for they spake not Job 32:16 3176
- I *w* patiently for the LORD Ps 40:1 6960
- they *w* not for his counsel Ps 106:13 2442
- The wicked have *w* for me to Ps 119:95 6960
- we have *w* for him, and he will Is 25:9 6960
- we have *w* for him, we will be Is 25:9 6960
- O LORD, have we *w* for thee Is 26:8 6960
- we have *w* for thee Is 33:2 6960
- Now when she saw that she had *w* Eze 19:5 3176
- of Maroth *w* carefully for good Mic 1:12 2342
- *w* upon me knew that it was the Zec 11:11 8104
- which also *w* for the kingdom of Mk 15:43 *4327*
- the people *w* for Zacharias, and Lk 1:21 *4328*
- who also himself *w* for the Lk 23:51 *4327*
- of them that *w* on him continually Acts 10:7 *4342*
- And Cornelius *w* for them, and had Acts 10:24 *4328*
- Now while Paul *w* for them at Acts 17:16 *1551*
- of God *w* in the days of Noah 1Pet 3:20 *1551*

WAITETH {11}
- the adulterer *w* for the twilight Job 24:15 8104
- Our soul *w* for the LORD Ps 33:20 2442
- Truly my soul *w* upon God Ps 62:1 1747
- Praise *w* for thee, O God in Sion Ps 65:1 1747
- My soul *w* for the Lord more than Ps 130:6
- so he that *w* on his master shall Prov 27:18 8104
- prepared for him that *w* for him Is 64:4 2442
- Blessed is he that *w*, and cometh Dan 12:12 2442
- nor *w* for the sons of men Mic 5:7 3176
- expectation of the creature *w* for Rom 8:19 *553*
- the husbandman *w* for the precious Jas 5:7 *1551*

WAITING {8}
- cease *w* upon the service thereof Num 8:25 6635
- *w* at the posts of my doors Prov 8:34 8104
- *w* for the consolation of Israel Lk 2:25 *4327*
- for they were all *w* for him Lk 8:40 *4328*
- *w* for the moving of the water Jn 5:3 *1551*
- *w* for the adoption, to wit, the Rom 8:23 *553*
- *w* for the coming of our Lord 1Cor 1:7 *553*
- and into the patient *w* for Christ 2Th 3:5

WAKE {4}
- sleep a perpetual sleep, and not *w* Jer 51:39 6974
- sleep a perpetual sleep, and not *w* Jer 51:57 6974
- *w* up the mighty men, let all the Joel 3:9 5782
- us, that, whether we *w* or sleep 1Th 5:10 *1127*

WAKED {1}
- *w* me, as a man that is wakened Zec 4:1 5782

WAKENED {2}
- Let the heathen be *w*, and come up Joel 3:12 5782
- a man that is *w* out of his sleep Zec 4:1 5782

WAKENETH {2}
- he *w* morning by morning Is 50:4 5782
- he *w* mine ear to hear as the Is 50:4 5782

WAKETH {2}
- city, the watchman *w* but in vain Ps 127:1 8245
- I sleep, but my heart *w* Song 5:2 5782

WAKING {1}
- Thou holdest mine eyes *w* Ps 77:4 8109

WALK {212}
- *w* through the land in the length Gen 13:17 1980
- *w* before me, and be thou perfect Gen 17:1 1980
- me, The LORD, before whom I *w* Gen 24:40 1980
- my fathers Abraham and Isaac did *w* Gen 48:15 1980
- whether they will *w* in my law Ex 16:4 3212
- them the way wherein they must *w* Ex 18:20 3212
- *w* abroad upon his staff, then Ex 21:19 1980
- neither shall ye *w* in their Lev 18:3 3212
- mine ordinances, to *w* therein Lev 18:4 3212
- ye shall not *w* in the manners of Lev 20:23 3212
- If ye *w* in my statutes, and keep Lev 26:3 3212
- I will *w* among you, and will be Lev 26:12 1980
- if ye *w* contrary unto me, and will Lev 26:21 3212
- but will *w* contrary unto me Lev 26:23 1980
- Then will I also *w* contrary unto Lev 26:24 1980
- unto me, but *w* contrary unto me Lev 26:27 1980
- Then I will *w* contrary unto you Lev 26:28 1980
- Ye shall *w* in all the ways which Deut 5:33 3212
- to *w* in his ways, and to fear him Deut 8:6 3212
- *w* after other gods, and serve them Deut 8:19 1980
- to *w* in all his ways, and to love Deut 10:12 3212
- to *w* in all his ways, and to Deut 11:22 3212
- Ye shall *w* after the LORD your Deut 13:4 3212
- thy God commanded thee to *w* in Deut 13:5 3212
- thy God, and to *w* ever in his ways Deut 19:9 3212
- to *w* in his ways, and to keep his Deut 26:17 3212
- LORD thy God, and *w* in his ways Deut 28:9 1980
- though I *w* in the imagination of Deut 29:19 3212
- to *w* in his ways, and to keep his Deut 30:16 3212
- *w* through the land, and describe Josh 18:8 1980
- to *w* in all his ways, and to keep Josh 22:5 3212
- the way of the LORD to *w* therein Judg 2:22 3212
- sit in judgment, and *w* by the way Judg 5:10 1980
- should *w* before me for ever 1Sa 2:30 1980
- he shall *w* before mine anointed 1Sa 2:35 1980
- thy sons *w* not in thy ways 1Sa 8:5 1980
- to *w* in his ways, to keep his 1Kin 2:3 3212
- to *w* before me in truth with all 1Kin 2:4 3212
- And if thou wilt *w* in my ways 1Kin 3:14 3212
- as thy father David did *w* 1Kin 3:14 1980
- if thou wilt *w* in my statutes, and 1Kin 6:12 3212
- all my commandments to *w* in them 1Kin 6:12 3212
- that *w* before thee with all their 1Kin 8:23 1980
- that they *w* before me as thou 1Kin 8:25 3212
- good way wherein they should *w* 1Kin 8:36 3212
- to *w* in all his ways, and to keep 1Kin 8:58 3212
- to *w* in his statutes, and to keep 1Kin 8:61 3212
- And if thou wilt *w* before me 1Kin 9:4 3212
- wilt *w* in my ways, and do that is 1Kin 11:38 1980
- been a light thing for him to *w* 1Kin 16:31 3212
- But Jehu took no heed to *w* in the 2Kin 10:31 3212
- to *w* after the LORD, and to keep 2Kin 23:3 3212
- that *w* before thee with all their 2Chr 6:14 1980
- heed to their way to *w* in my law 2Chr 6:16 3212
- good way, wherein they should *w* 2Chr 6:27 3212
- to *w* in thy ways, so long as they 2Chr 6:31 3212

W

thee, if thou wilt *w* before me 2Chr 7:17 3212
to *w* after the LORD, and to keep 2Chr 34:31 3212
ought ye not to *w* in the fear of Neh 5:9 3212
to *w* in God's law, which was Neh 10:29 3212
The wicked *w* on every side, when Ps 12:8 1980
though I *w* through the valley of Ps 23:4 3212
I will *w* in mine integrity Ps 26:11 3212
W about Zion, and go round about Ps 48:12 5437
that I may *w* before God in the Ps 56:13 1980
God, and refused to *w* in his law Ps 78:10 3212
they *w* on in darkness Ps 82:5 1980
from them that *w* uprightly Ps 84:11 1980
I will *w* in thy truth Ps 86:11 1980
they shall *w*, O LORD, in the Ps 89:15 1980
my law, and *w* not in my judgments Ps 89:30 3212
I will *w* within my house with a Ps 101:2 1980
feet have they, but they *w* not Ps 115:7 1980
I will *w* before the LORD in the Ps 116:9 1980
who *w* in the law of the LORD Ps 119:1 1980
they *w* in his ways Ps 119:3 1980
And I will *w* at liberty Ps 119:45 1980
Though I *w* in the midst of Ps 138:7 3212
know the way wherein I should *w* Ps 143:8 3212
w not thou in the way with them Prov 1:15 3212
buckler to them that *w* uprightly Prov 2:7 1980
to *w* in the ways of darkness Prov 2:13 3212
That thou mayest *w* in the way of Prov 2:20 3212
Then shalt thou *w* in thy way Prov 3:23 3212
the living which *w* under the sun Eccl 4:15 1980
that knoweth to *w* before the Eccl 6:8 1980
w in the ways of thine heart, and Eccl 11:9 1980
ways, and we will *w* in his paths Is 2:3 3212
let us *w* in the light of the LORD Is 2:5 3212
w with stretched forth necks and Is 3:16 3212
not *w* in the way of this people Is 8:11 3212
That *w* to go down into Egypt, and Is 30:2 1980
w ye in it, when ye turn to the Is 30:21 3212
but the redeemed shall *w* there Is 35:9 1980
and they shall *w*, and not faint Is 40:31 3212
and spirit to them that *w* therein Is 42:5 1980
for they would not *w* in his ways Is 42:24 1980
w in the light of your fire, and Is 50:11 3212
brightness, but we *w* in darkness Is 59:9 1980
neither shall they *w* any more Jer 3:17 3212
shall *w* with the house of Israel Jer 3:18 3212
w therein, and ye shall find rest Jer 6:16 3212
they said, We will not *w* therein Jer 6:16 3212
into the field, nor *w* by the way Jer 6:25 3212
neither *w* after other gods to Jer 7:6 3212
w after other gods whom ye know Jer 7:9 1980
w ye in all the ways that I have Jer 7:23 1980
neighbour will *w* with slanders Jer 9:4 1980
which *w* in the imagination of Jer 13:10 1980
w after other gods, to serve them Jer 13:10 1980
behold, ye *w* every one after the Jer 16:12 1980
but we will *w* after our own Jer 18:12 1980
to *w* in paths, in a way not cast Jer 18:15 1980
commit adultery, and *w* in lies Jer 23:14 1980
to *w* in my law, which I have set Jer 26:4 1980
I will cause them to *w* by the Jer 31:9 1980
shew us the way wherein we may *w* Jer 42:3 1980
is desolate, the foxes *w* upon it Lam 5:18 1980
That they may *w* in my statutes, Eze 11:20 3212
W ye not in the statutes of your Eze 20:18 3212
w in my statutes, and keep my Eze 20:19 3212
w in the statutes of life, Eze 33:15 1980
I will cause men to *w* upon you Eze 36:12 3212
cause you to *w* in my statutes, and Eze 36:27 3212
they shall also *w* in my judgments Eze 37:24 3212
before the chambers was a *w* of Eze 42:4 4109
those that *w* in pride he is able Dan 4:37 1981
to *w* in his laws, which he set Dan 9:10 3212
They shall *w* after the LORD Hos 11:10 3212
and the just shall *w* in them Hos 14:9 3212
they shall *w* every one in his Joel 2:8 3212
Can two *w* together, except they Amos 3:3 3212
ways, and we will *w* in his paths Mic 4:2 3212
For all people will *w* every one Mic 4:5 3212
we will *w* in the name of the LORD Mic 4:5 3212
and to *w* humbly with thy God Mic 6:8 3212
Ahab, and ye *w* in their counsels Mic 6:16 3212
they shall stumble in their *w* Nah 2:5 1979
Thou didst *w* through the sea with Hab 3:15 1869
he will make me to *w* upon mine Hab 3:19 1869
that they shall *w* like blind men Zeph 1:17 1980
whom the LORD hath sent to *w* to Zec 1:10 1980
If thou wilt *w* in my ways Zec 3:7 3212
to *w* among these that stand by Zec 3:7 4108
sought to go that they might *w* to Zec 6:7 1980
w to and fro through the earth Zec 6:7 1980
and they shall *w* up and down in his Zec 10:12 1980
or to say, Arise, and *w* Mt 9:5 4043
their sight, and the lame *w* Mt 11:5 4043
maimed to be whole, the lame to *w* Mt 15:31 4043
Arise, and take up thy bed, and *w* Mk 2:9 4043
Why *w* not thy disciples according Mk 7:5 4043
or to say, Rise up and *w* Lk 5:23 4043
that the blind see, the lame *w* Lk 7:22 4043
the men that *w* over them are not Lk 11:44 4043
Nevertheless I must *w* to day Lk 13:33 4198
which desire to *w* in long robes Lk 20:46 4043
ye have one to another, as ye *w* Lk 24:17 4043
him, Rise, take up thy bed, and *w* Jn 5:8 4043
unto me, Take up thy bed, and *w* Jn 5:11 4043
unto thee, Take up thy bed, and *w* Jn 5:12 4043
for he would not *w* in Jewry Jn 7:1 4043
me shall not *w* in darkness Jn 8:12 4043
If any man *w* in the day, he Jn 11:9 4043
But if a man *w* in the night Jn 11:10 4043
W while ye have the light, lest Jn 12:35 4043
Christ of Nazareth rise up and *w* Acts 3:6 4043
we had made this man to *w* Acts 3:12 4043
nations to *w* in their own ways Acts 14:16 4198
neither to *w* after the customs Acts 21:21 4043
but who also *w* in the steps of Rom 4:12 4748
also should *w* in newness of life Rom 6:4 4043
who *w* not after the flesh, but Rom 8:1 4043
who *w* not after the flesh, but Rom 8:4 4043
Let us *w* honestly, as in the day Rom 13:13 4043
are ye not carnal, and *w* as men 1Cor 3:3 4043
called every one, so let him *w* 1Cor 7:17 4043
(For we *w* by faith, not by sight 2Cor 5:7 4043
will dwell in them, and *w* in them 2Cor 6:16 1704
For though we *w* in the flesh 2Cor 10:3 4043
W in the Spirit, and ye shall not Gal 5:16 4043
let us also *w* in the Spirit Gal 5:25 4748
as many as *w* according to this Gal 6:16 4748
ordained that we should *w* in them Eph 2:10 4043
beseech you that ye *w* worthy of Eph 4:1 4043
w not as other Gentiles *w* Eph 4:17 4043
w in love, as Christ also hath Eph 5:2 4043
w as children of light Eph 5:8 4043
See then that ye *w* circumspectly Eph 5:15 4043
let us *w* by the same rule, let us Phil 3:16 4748
mark them which *w* so as ye have Phil 3:17 4043
(For many *w*, of whom I have told Phil 3:18 4043
That ye might *w* worthy of the Col 1:10 4043
Jesus the Lord, so *w* ye in him Col 2:6 4043
W in wisdom toward them that are Col 4:5 4043
That ye would *w* worthy of God 1Th 2:12 4043
received of us how ye ought to *w* 1Th 4:1 4043
That ye may *w* honestly toward 1Th 4:12 4043
some which *w* among you disorderly 2Th 3:11 4043
But chiefly them that *w* after the 2Pet 2:10 4198
w in darkness, we lie, and do not 1Jn 1:6 4043
But if we *w* in the light, as he 1Jn 1:7 4043
in him ought himself also so to *w* 1Jn 2:6 4043
that we *w* after his commandments 2Jn 6 4043
the beginning, ye should *w* in it 2Jn 6 4043
hear that my children *w* in truth 3Jn 4 4043
who should *w* after their own Jude 18 4198
they shall *w* with me in white Rev 3:4 4043
neither can see, nor hear, nor *w* Rev 9:20 4043
his garments, lest he *w* naked Rev 16:15 4043
saved shall *w* in the light of it Rev 21:24 4043

WALKED {122}

Enoch *w* with God after he begat Gen 5:22 1980
And Enoch *w* with God Gen 5:24 1980
generations, and Noah *w* with God Gen 6:9 1980
her maidens *w* along by the Ex 2:5 1980
But the children of Israel *w* upon Ex 14:29 1980
also they have *w* contrary unto me Lev 26:40 1980
that I also have *w* contrary unto Lev 26:41 3212
For the children of Israel *w* Josh 5:6 1980
the way which their fathers *w* in Judg 2:17 1980
the travellers *w* through byways Judg 5:6 3212
w through the wilderness unto the Judg 11:16 3212
his sons *w* not in his ways, but 1Sa 8:3 1980
I have *w* before you from my 1Sa 12:2 1980
his men *w* all that night through 2Sa 2:29 1980
but have *w* in a tent and in a 2Sa 7:6 1980
all the places wherein I have *w* 2Sa 7:7 1980
w upon the roof of the king's 2Sa 11:2 1980
according as he *w* before thee in 1Kin 3:6 1980
me as thou hast *w* before me 1Kin 8:25 1980
before me, as David thy father *w* 1Kin 9:4 1980
have not *w* in my ways, to do that 1Kin 11:33 1980
he *w* in all the sins of his 1Kin 15:3 3212
w in the way of his father, and in 1Kin 15:26 3212
w in the way of Jeroboam, and in 1Kin 15:34 3212
thou hast *w* in the way of 1Kin 16:2 3212
For he *w* in all the way of 1Kin 16:26 3212
he *w* in all the ways of Asa his 1Kin 22:43 3212
w in the way of his father, and in 1Kin 22:52 3212
and *w* in the house to and fro 2Kin 4:35 3212
he *w* in the way of the kings of 2Kin 8:18 3212
he *w* in the way of the house of 2Kin 8:27 3212
made Israel sin, but *w* therein 2Kin 13:6 1980
but he *w* therein 2Kin 13:11 1980
But he *w* in the way of the kings 2Kin 16:3 3212
w in the statutes of the heathen, 2Kin 17:8 3212
but *w* in the statutes of Israel 2Kin 17:19 3212
For the children of Israel *w* in 2Kin 17:22 3212
how I have *w* before thee in truth 2Kin 20:3 1980
he *w* in all the way that his 2Kin 21:21 3212
all the way that his father *w* in 2Kin 21:21 1980
w not in the way of the LORD 2Kin 21:22 1980
w in all the way of David his 2Kin 22:2 3212
I have *w* with all Israel, spake I 1Chr 17:6 1980
thee whithersoever thou hast *w* 1Chr 17:8
my law, as thou hast *w* before me 2Chr 6:16 3212
before me, as David thy father *w* 2Chr 7:17 1980
years they *w* in the way of David 2Chr 11:17 1980
because he *w* in the first ways of 2Chr 17:3 1980
w in his commandments, and not 2Chr 17:4 1980
he *w* in the way of Asa his father 2Chr 20:32 3212
he *w* in the way of the kings of 2Chr 21:6 3212
Because thou hast not *w* in the 2Chr 21:12 1980
But hast *w* in the way of the 2Chr 21:13 3212
He also *w* in the ways of the 2Chr 22:3 1980
He *w* also after their counsel, and 2Chr 22:5 1980
For he *w* in the ways of the kings 2Chr 28:2 3212
w in the ways of David his father 2Chr 34:2 3212
Mordecai *w* every day before the Est 2:11 1980
by his light I *w* through darkness Job 29:3 3212
If I have *w* with vanity, or if my Job 31:5 1980
mine heart *w* after mine eyes, and Job 31:7 1980
or hast thou *w* in the search of Job 38:16 1980
for I have *w* in mine integrity Ps 26:1 1980
and I have *w* in thy truth Ps 26:3 1980
w unto the house of God in Ps 55:14 1980
they *w* in their own counsels Ps 81:12 3212
me, and Israel had *w* in my ways Ps 81:13 1980
In the way wherein I *w* have they Ps 142:3 1980
The people that *w* in darkness Is 9:2 1980
as my servant Isaiah hath *w* naked Is 20:3 1980
how I have *w* before thee in truth Is 38:3 1980
have *w* after vanity, and are Jer 2:5 3212
w after things that do not profit Jer 2:8 1980
but *w* in the counsels and in the Jer 7:24 3212
served, and after whom they have *w* Jer 8:2 1980
my voice, neither *w* therein Jer 9:13 1980
But have *w* after the imagination Jer 9:14 3212
their ear, but *w* every one in the Jer 11:8 3212
have *w* after other gods, and have Jer 16:11 3212
thy voice, neither *w* in thy law Jer 32:23 1980
nor *w* in my law, nor in my Jer 44:10 1980
nor *w* in his law, nor in his Jer 44:23 1980
statutes, they have not *w* in them Eze 5:6 1980
have not *w* in my statutes, Eze 5:7 1980
for ye have not *w* in my statutes Eze 11:12 1980
hast thou not *w* after their ways Eze 16:47 1980
Hath *w* in my statutes, and hath Eze 18:9 1980
judgments, hath *w* in my statutes Eze 18:17 1980
they *w* not in my statutes, and Eze 20:13 1980
w not in my statutes, but Eze 20:16 1980
they *w* not in my statutes, Eze 20:21 1980
Thou hast *w* in the way of thy Eze 23:31 1980
thou hast *w* up and down in the Eze 28:14 1980
At the end of twelve months he *w* Dan 4:29 1981
because he willingly *w* after the Hos 5:11 1980
the which their fathers have *w* Amos 2:4 1980
the lion, even the old lion, *w* Nah 2:11 1980
trees, and said, We have *w* to Zec 1:11 1980
So they *w* to and fro through the Zec 6:7 1980
he *w* with me in peace and equity, Mal 2:6 1980
that we have *w* mournfully before Mal 3:14 1980
he *w* on the water, to go to Jesus Mt 14:29 4043
Now as he *w* by the sea of Galilee Mk 1:16 4043
the damsel arose, and *w* Mk 5:42 4043
form unto two of them, as they *w* Mk 16:12 4043
And looking upon Jesus as he *w* Jn 1:36 4043
whole, and took up his bed, and *w* Jn 5:9 4043
went back, and *w* no more with him Jn 6:66 4043
these things Jesus *w* in Galilee Jn 7:1 4043
And Jesus *w* in the temple in Jn 10:23 4043
Jesus therefore *w* no more openly Jn 11:54 4043
And he leaping up stood, and *w* Acts 3:8 4043
mother's womb, who never had *w* Acts 14:8 4043
And he leaped and *w* Acts 14:10 4043
as if we *w* according to the flesh 2Cor 10:2 4043
w we not in the same spirit 2Cor 12:18 4043
w we not in the same steps 2Cor 12:18 4043
But when I saw that they *w* not Gal 2:14 3716
Wherein in time past ye *w* Eph 2:2 4043
In the which ye also *w* some time Col 3:7 4043
when we *w* in lasciviousness, 1Pet 4:3 4198
also so to walk, even as he *w* 1Jn 2:6 4043

WALKEDST {1}

and *w* whither thou wouldest Jn 21:18 4043

WALKEST {7}

when thou *w* by the way, and when Deut 6:7 3212
when thou *w* by the way, when thou Deut 11:19 3212
w abroad any whither, that thou 1Kin 2:42 1980
when thou *w* through the fire, Is 43:2 3212
that thou thyself also *w* orderly Acts 21:24 4748
now *w* thou not charitably Rom 14:15 4043
thee, even as thou *w* in the truth 3Jn 3 4043

WALKETH {41}

What man is this that *w* in the Gen 24:65 1980
For the LORD thy God *w* in the Deut 23:14 1980
behold, the king *w* before you 1Sa 12:2 1980
own feet, and he *w* upon a snare Job 18:8 1980
he *w* in the circuit of heaven Job 22:14 1980
of iniquity, and *w* with wicked men Job 34:8 3212
Blessed is the man that *w* not in Ps 1:1 1980
He that *w* uprightly, and worketh Ps 15:2 1980
Surely every man *w* in a vain shew Ps 39:6 1980
their tongue *w* through the earth Ps 73:9 1980
the pestilence that *w* in darkness Ps 91:6 1980
he that *w* in a perfect way, he Ps 101:6 1980
who *w* upon the wings of the wind Ps 104:3 1980
that *w* in his ways Ps 128:1 1980
man, *w* with a froward mouth Prov 6:12 1980
that *w* uprightly *w* surely Prov 10:9 3212
He that *w* with wise men shall be Prov 13:20 1980
He that *w* in his uprightness Prov 14:2 1980
man of understanding *w* uprightly Prov 15:21 1980
the poor that *w* in his integrity Prov 19:1 1980
The just man *w* in his integrity Prov 20:7 1980
poor that *w* in his uprightness Prov 28:6 1980
Whoso *w* uprightly shall be saved Prov 28:18 1980
but whoso *w* wisely, he shall be Prov 28:26 1980
but the fool *w* in darkness Eccl 2:14 1980
he that is a fool *w* by the way Eccl 10:3 1980
He that *w* righteously, and Is 33:15 1980
that *w* in darkness, and hath no Is 50:10 1980
which *w* in a way that was not Is 65:2 1980
in man that *w* to direct his steps Jer 10:23 1980
w after the imagination of his Jer 23:17 1980
heart *w* after the heart of their Eze 11:21 1980
do good to him that *w* uprightly Mic 2:7 1980

he *w* through dry places, seeking .... Mt 12:43 *1330*
he *w* through dry places, seeking .... Lk 11:24 *1330*
for he that *w* in darkness knoweth .... Jn 12:35 *4043*
every brother that *w* disorderly 2Th 3:6 *4043*
w about, seeking whom he may 1Pet 5:8 *4043*
w in darkness, and knoweth not 1Jn 2:11 *4043*
who *w* in the midst of the seven .... Rev 2:1 *4043*

WALKING {30}
w in the garden in the cool of .... Gen 3:8 1980
he knoweth thy *w* through this .... Deut 2:7 3212
w in the statutes of David his 1Kin 3:3 3212
in *w* in the way of Jeroboam, and 1Kin 16:19 3212
and fro in the earth, and from *w* up .... Job 1:7 1980
and fro in the earth, and from *w* up .... Job 2:2 1980
or the moon *w* in brightness .... Job 31:26 1980
princes *w* as servants upon the .... Eccl 10:7 1980
forth necks and wanton eyes, *w* .... Is 3:16 1980
And he did so, *w* naked and barefoot .... Is 20:2 1980
each one *w* in his uprightness .... Is 57:2 1980
revolters, *w* with slanders .... Jer 6:28 1980
w in the midst of the fire, and .... Dan 3:25 1981
If a man *w* in the spirit and .... Mic 2:11 1980
w by the sea of Galilee, saw two .... Mt 4:18 *4043*
went unto them, *w* on the sea .... Mt 14:25 *4043*
disciples saw him *w* on the sea .... Mt 14:26 *4043*
w upon the sea, and would have .... Mk 6:48 *4043*
when they saw him *w* upon the sea .... Mk 6:49 *4043*
and said, I see men as trees, *w* .... Mk 8:24 *4043*
as he was *w* in the temple, there .... Mk 11:27 *4043*
w in all the commandments and .... Lk 1:6 *4198*
they see Jesus *w* on the sea .... Jn 6:19 *4043*
with them into the temple, *w* .... Acts 3:8 *4043*
And all the people saw him *w* .... Acts 3:9 *4043*
w in the fear of the Lord, and in .... Acts 9:31 *4198*
not *w* in craftiness, nor handling 2Cor 4:2 *4043*
w after their own lusts, ... 2Pet 3:3 *4198*
found of thy children *w* in truth 2Jn 4 *4043*
w after their own lusts .... Jude 16 *4198*

WALL {179}
selfwill they digged down a *w* .... Gen 49:6 7794
whose branches run over the *w* .... Gen 49:22 7791
the waters were a *w* unto them on .... Ex 14:22 2346
the waters were a *w* unto them on .... Ex 14:29 2346
in sight are lower than the *w* .... Lev 14:37 7023
no *w* round about them shall be .... Lev 25:31 2346
a *w* being on this side, and a *w* .... Num 22:24 1447
she thrust herself unto the *w* .... Num 22:25 7023
Balaam's foot against the *w* .... Num 22:25 7023
reach from the *w* of the city .... Num 35:4 7023
for her house was upon the town *w* .... Josh 2:15 2346
and she dwelt upon the *w* .... Josh 2:15 2346
the *w* of the city shall fall down .... Josh 6:5 2346
that the *w* fell down flat, so .... Josh 6:20 2346
smite David even to the *w* with it 1Sa 18:11 7023
even to the *w* with the javelin 1Sa 19:10 7023
he smote the javelin into the *w* 1Sa 19:10 7023
times, even upon a seat by the *w* 1Sa 20:25 7023
They were a *w* unto us both by 1Sa 25:16 2346
any that pisseth against the *w* 1Sa 25:22 7023
any that pisseth against the *w* 1Sa 25:34 2346
his body to the *w* of Beth-shan 1Sa 31:10 7023
his sons from the *w* of Beth-shan 1Sa 31:12 2346
that they would shoot from the *w* 2Sa 11:20 2346
a millstone upon him from the *w* 2Sa 11:21 2346
why went ye nigh the *w* 2Sa 11:21 2346
from off the *w* upon thy servants 2Sa 11:24 2346
the roof over the gate unto the *w* 2Sa 18:24 2346
were with Joab battered the *w* 2Sa 20:15 2346
be thrown to thee over the *w* 2Sa 20:21 2346
by my God have I leaped over a *w* 2Sa 22:30 7791
the *w* of Jerusalem round about 1Kin 3:1 2346
that springeth out of the *w* 1Kin 4:33 7023
against the *w* of the house he 1Kin 6:5 7023
for without in the *w* of the house 1Kin 6:6
wing of the one touched the one *w* 1Kin 6:27 7023
other cherub touched the other *w* 1Kin 6:27 7023
posts were a fifth part of the *w* 1Kin 6:31
tree, a fourth part of the *w* 1Kin 6:33
the *w* of Jerusalem, and Hazor, and 1Kin 9:15 2346
him that pisseth against the *w* 1Kin 14:10 7023
not one that pisseth against a *w* 1Kin 16:11 7023
there a *w* fell upon twenty and 1Kin 20:30 2346
him that pisseth against the *w* 1Kin 21:21 7023
eat Jezebel by the *w* of Jezreel 1Kin 21:23 2426
for a burnt offering upon the *w* 2Kin 3:27 2346
chamber, I pray thee, on the *w* 2Kin 4:10 7023
Israel was passing by upon the *w* 2Kin 6:26 2346
and he passed by upon the *w* 2Kin 6:30 2346
him that pisseth against the *w* 2Kin 9:8 7023
her blood was sprinkled on the *w* 2Kin 9:33 7023
brake down the *w* of Jerusalem 2Kin 14:13 2346
of the people that are on the *w* 2Kin 18:26 2346
me to the men which sit on the *w* 2Kin 18:27 2346
Then he turned his face to the *w* 2Kin 20:2 7023
reaching to the *w* of the house 2Chr 3:11 7023
reaching to the *w* of the house 2Chr 3:12 7023
brake down the *w* of Jerusalem 2Chr 25:23 2346
and brake down the *w* of Gath 2Chr 26:6 2346
the *w* of Jabneh, and the 2Chr 26:6 2346
the *w* of Ashdod, and built cities 2Chr 26:6 2346
gate, and at the turning of the *w* 2Chr 26:9
on the *w* of Ophel he built much 2Chr 27:3 2346
up all the *w* that was broken 2Chr 32:5 2346
the towers, and another *w* without 2Chr 32:5 2346
of Jerusalem that were on the *w* 2Chr 32:18 2346
a *w* without the city of David 2Chr 33:14 2346
and brake down the *w* of Jerusalem 2Chr 36:19 2346
this house, and to make up this *w* .... Ezr 5:3 846
and to give us a *w* in Judah .... Ezr 9:9 1447
the *w* of Jerusalem also is broken .... Neh 1:3 2346
for the *w* of the city, and for the .... Neh 2:8 2346
by the brook, and viewed the *w* .... Neh 2:15 2346
us build up the *w* of Jerusalem .... Neh 2:17 2346
Jerusalem unto the broad *w* .... Neh 3:8 2346
on the *w* unto the dung gate .... Neh 3:13 2346
the *w* of the pool of Siloah by .... Neh 3:15 2346
armoury at the turning of the *w* .... Neh 3:19
from the turning of the *w* unto .... Neh 3:20
Azariah unto the turning of the *w* .... Neh 3:24
over against the turning of the *w* .... Neh 3:25
out, even unto the *w* of Ophel .... Neh 3:27 2346
heard that we builded the *w* .... Neh 4:1 2346
even break down their stone *w* .... Neh 4:3 2346
So built we the *w* .... Neh 4:6 2346
all the *w* was joined together .... Neh 4:6 2346
we are not able to build the *w* .... Neh 4:10 2346
in the lower places behind the *w* .... Neh 4:13 2346
we returned all of us to the *w* .... Neh 4:15 2346
They which builded on the *w* .... Neh 4:17 2346
and we are separated upon the *w* .... Neh 4:19 2346
I continued in the work of this *w* .... Neh 5:16 2346
heard that I had builded the *w* .... Neh 6:1 2346
which cause thou buildest the *w* .... Neh 6:6 2346
So the *w* was finished in the .... Neh 6:15 2346
when the *w* was built, and I had .... Neh 7:1 2346
at the dedication of the *w* of .... Neh 12:27 2346
people, and the gates, and the *w* .... Neh 12:30 2346
the princes of Judah upon the *w* .... Neh 12:31 2346
upon the *w* toward the dung gate .... Neh 12:31 2346
David, at the going up of the *w* .... Neh 12:37 2346
the half of the people upon the *w* .... Neh 12:38 2346
furnaces even unto the broad *w* .... Neh 12:38 2346
them, Why lodge ye about the *w* .... Neh 13:21 2346
by my God have I leaped over a *w* .... Ps 18:29 7791
as a bowing *w* shall ye be .... Ps 62:3 7023
as an high *w* in his own conceit .... Prov 18:11 2346
the stone *w* thereof was broken .... Prov 24:31 1444
behold, he standeth behind our *w* .... Song 2:9 3796
If she be a *w*, we will build upon .... Song 8:9 2346
I am a *w*, and my breasts like .... Song 8:10 2346
tower, and upon every fenced *w* .... Is 2:15 2346
and break down the *w* thereof .... Is 5:5 1447
ye broken down to fortify the *w* .... Is 22:10 2346
ones is as a storm against the *w* .... Is 25:4 7023
to fall, swelling out in a high *w* .... Is 30:13 2346
of the people that are on the *w* .... Is 36:11 2346
me to the men that sit upon the *w* .... Is 36:12 2346
turned his face toward the *w* .... Is 38:2 7023
We grope for the *w* like the blind .... Is 59:10 7023
this people a fenced brasen *w* .... Jer 15:20 2346
a fire in the *w* of Damascus .... Jer 49:27 2346
the *w* of Babylon shall fall .... Jer 51:44 2346
the *w* of the daughter of Zion .... Lam 2:8 2346
the rampart and the *w* to lament .... Lam 2:8 2346
O *w* of the daughter of Zion, let .... Lam 2:18 2346
set it for a *w* of iron between .... Eze 4:3 7023
I looked, behold a hole in the *w* .... Eze 8:7 7023
me, Son of man, dig now in the *w* .... Eze 8:8 7023
and when I had digged in the *w* .... Eze 8:8 7023
pourtrayed upon the *w* round about .... Eze 8:10 7023
thou through the *w* in their sight .... Eze 12:5 7023
through the *w* with mine hand .... Eze 12:7 7023
the *w* to carry out thereby .... Eze 12:12 7023
and one built up a *w*, and, lo, ... Eze 13:10 2434
when the *w* is fallen, shall it .... Eze 13:12 7023
the *w* that ye have daubed with .... Eze 13:14 7023
I accomplish my wrath upon the *w* .... Eze 13:15 7023
The *w* is no more, neither they .... Eze 13:15 7023
she saw men pourtrayed upon the *w* .... Eze 23:14 7023
every *w* shall fall to the ground .... Eze 38:20 2346
behold a *w* on the outside of the .... Eze 40:5 2346
he measured the *w* of the house .... Eze 41:5 7023
they entered into the *w* which was .... Eze 41:6 7023
not hold in the *w* of the house .... Eze 41:6 7023
The thickness of the *w*, which was .... Eze 41:9 7023
the *w* of the building was five .... Eze 41:12 7023
by all the *w* round about within .... Eze 41:17 7023
made, and on the *w* of the temple .... Eze 41:20 7023
the *w* that was without over .... Eze 42:7 1447
w of the court toward the east .... Eze 42:10 1444
before the *w* toward the east .... Eze 42:12 1448
it had a *w* round about, five .... Eze 42:20 2346
the *w* between me and them, they .... Eze 43:8 7023
of the *w* of the king's palace .... Dan 5:5 3797
shall be built again, and the *w* .... Dan 9:25 2742
thy way with thorns, and make a *w* .... Hos 2:6 1447
shall climb the *w* like men of war .... Joel 2:7 2346
they shall run upon the *w* .... Joel 2:9 2346
will send a fire on the *w* of Gaza .... Amos 1:7 2346
send a fire on the *w* of Tyrus .... Amos 1:10 2346
kindle a fire in the *w* of Rabbah .... Amos 1:14 2346
and leaned his hand on the *w* .... Amos 5:19 7023
upon a *w* made by a plumbline .... Amos 7:7 2346
shall make haste to the *w* thereof .... Nah 2:5 2346
sea, and her *w* was from the sea .... Nah 3:8 2346
the stone shall cry out of the *w* .... Hab 2:11 7023
will be unto her a *w* of fire .... Zec 2:5 2346
let him down by the *w* in a basket .... Acts 9:25 *5038*
shall smite thee, thou whited *w* .... Acts 23:3 *5109*
a basket was I let down by the *w* 2Cor 11:33 *5038*
middle *w* of partition between us .... Eph 2:14
And had a *w* great and high, and had .... Rev 21:12 *5038*
the *w* of the city had twelve .... Rev 21:14 *5038*
gates thereof, and the *w* thereof .... Rev 21:15 *5038*
And he measured the *w* thereof .... Rev 21:17 *5038*
of the *w* of it was of jasper .... Rev 21:18 *5038*
the foundations of the *w* of the .... Rev 21:19 *5038*

WALLED {4}
sell a dwelling house in a *w* city .... Lev 25:29 2346
w city shall be established for .... Lev 25:30 2346
in the land, and the cities are *w* .... Num 13:28 1219
are great and *w* up to heaven .... Deut 1:28 1219

WALLOW {4}
sackcloth, and *w* thyself in ashes .... Jer 6:26 6428
w yourselves in the ashes, ye .... Jer 25:34 6428
Moab also shall *w* in his vomit .... Jer 48:26 5606
they shall *w* themselves in the .... Eze 27:30 6428

WALLOWED {2}
Amasa *w* in blood in the midst of 2Sa 20:12 1556
fell on the ground, and *w* foaming .... Mk 9:20 *2947*

WALLOWING {1}
was washed to her *w* in the mire 2Pet 2:22 *2946*

WALLS {66}
if the plague be in the *w* of the .... Lev 14:37 7023
be spread in the *w* of the house .... Lev 14:39 7023
cities were fenced with high *w* .... Deut 3:5 2346
fenced *w* come down, wherein thou .... Deut 28:52 2346
threescore great cities with *w* 1Kin 4:13 2346
against the *w* of the house round 1Kin 6:5 7023
be fastened in the *w* of the house 1Kin 6:6 7023
he built the *w* of the house 1Kin 6:15 7023
house, and the *w* of the cieling 1Kin 6:15 7023
the *w* with boards of cedar 1Kin 6:16 7023
he carved all the *w* of the house 1Kin 6:29 7023
the way of the gate between two *w* 2Kin 25:4 2346
brake down the *w* of Jerusalem 2Kin 25:10 2346
to overlay the *w* of the houses 1Chr 29:4 7023
the *w* thereof, and the doors 2Chr 3:7 7023
and graved cherubims on the *w* 2Chr 3:7 7023
the nether, fenced cities, with *w* 2Chr 8:5 2346
cities, and make about them *w* 2Chr 14:7 2346
and have set up the *w* thereof .... Ezr 4:12 7791
the *w* set up again, then will .... Ezr 4:13 7791
the *w* thereof set up, by this .... Ezr 4:16 7791
and timber is laid in the *w* .... Ezr 5:8 3797
this house, and to make up these *w* .... Ezr 5:9 846
viewed the *w* of Jerusalem, which .... Neh 2:13 2346
heard that the *w* of Jerusalem .... Neh 4:7 2346
Which make oil within their *w* .... Job 24:11 7791
build thou the *w* of Jerusalem .... Ps 51:18 2346
go about it upon the *w* thereof .... Ps 55:10 2346
Peace be within thy *w*, and .... Ps 122:7 2426
that is broken down, and without *w* .... Prov 25:28 2346
the keepers of the *w* took away my .... Song 5:7 2346
of vision, breaking down the *w* .... Is 22:5 7023
also a ditch between the two *w* .... Is 22:11 2346
fort of thy *w* shall he bring down .... Is 25:12 2346
salvation will God appoint for *w* .... Is 26:1 2346
thy *w* are continually before me .... Is 49:16 2346
mine house and within my *w* a place .... Is 56:5 2346
of strangers shall build up thy *w* .... Is 60:10 2346
thou shalt call thy *w* Salvation .... Is 60:18 2346
I have set watchmen upon thy *w* .... Is 62:6 2346
against all the *w* thereof round .... Jer 1:15 2346
brasen *w* against the whole land, ... Jer 1:18 2346
Go ye up upon her *w*, and destroy .... Jer 5:10 8284
which besiege you without the *w* .... Jer 21:4 2346
by the gate betwixt the two *w* .... Jer 39:4 2346
and brake down the *w* of Jerusalem .... Jer 39:8 2346
are fallen, her *w* are thrown down .... Jer 50:15 2346
standard upon the *w* of Babylon .... Jer 51:12 2346
The broad *w* of Babylon shall be .... Jer 51:58 2346
way of the gate between the two *w* .... Jer 52:7 2346
brake down all the *w* of Jerusalem .... Jer 52:14 2346
of the enemy the *w* of her palaces .... Lam 2:7 2346
they shall destroy the *w* of Tyrus .... Eze 26:4 2346
set engines of war against thy *w* .... Eze 26:9 2346
thy *w* shall shake at the noise of .... Eze 26:10 2346
and they shall break down thy *w* .... Eze 26:12 2346
army were upon thy *w* round about .... Eze 27:11 2346
shields upon thy *w* round about .... Eze 27:11 2346
are talking against thee by the *w* .... Eze 33:30 7023
all of them dwelling without *w* .... Eze 38:11 2346
the building, with the *w* thereof .... Eze 41:13 7023
the *w* thereof, were of wood .... Eze 41:22 7023
like as were made upon the *w* .... Eze 41:25 7023
day that thy *w* are to be built .... Mic 7:11 1447
w for the multitude of men .... Zec 2:4
By faith the *w* of Jericho fell .... Heb 11:30 *5038*

WANDER {14}
when God caused me to *w* from my .... Gen 20:13 8582
your children shall *w* in the .... Num 14:33 7462
he made them *w* in the wilderness .... Num 32:13 5128
the blind to *w* out of the way .... Deut 27:18 7686
causeth them to *w* in a wilderness .... Job 12:24 8582
unto God, they *w* for lack of meat .... Job 38:41 8582
Lo, then would I *w* far off .... Ps 55:7 5074
Let them *w* up and down for meat, ... Ps 59:15 5128
and causeth them to *w* in the .... Ps 107:40 8582
O let me not *w* from thy .... Ps 119:10 7686
they shall *w* every one to his .... Is 47:15 8582
people, Thus have they loved to *w* .... Jer 14:10 5128
that shall cause him to *w* .... Jer 48:12 6808
they shall *w* from sea to sea, and .... Amos 8:12 5128

WANDERED {10}
w in the wilderness of Beer-sheba .... Gen 21:14 8582
of Israel *w* in the wilderness .... Josh 14:10 1980
They *w* in the wilderness in a .... Ps 107:4 8582
they *w* through the wilderness .... Is 16:8 8582
They have *w* as blind men in the .... Lam 4:14 5128

when they fled away and *w*, they ... Lam 4:15 5128
My sheep *w* through all the ... Eze 34:6 7686
or three cities *w* unto one city ... Amos 4:8 5128
they *w* about in sheepskins and ... Heb 11:37 *4022*
they *w* in deserts, and in ... Heb 11:38 *4105*

WANDERERS {2}
LORD, that I will send unto him *w* ... Jer 48:12 6808
they shall be *w* among the nations ... Hos 9:17 5074

WANDEREST {1}
and under every green tree thou *w* ... Jer 2:20 6808

WANDERETH {6}
He *w* abroad for bread, saying, ... Job 15:23 5074
The man that *w* out of the way of ... Prov 21:16 8582
As a bird that *w* from her nest ... Prov 27:8 5074
so is a man that *w* from his place ... Prov 27:8 5074
bewray not him that *w* ... Is 16:3 5074
none shall gather up him that *w* ... Jer 49:5 5074

WANDERING {6}
and, behold, he was *w* in the field ... Gen 37:15 8582
As the bird by *w*, as the swallow ... Prov 26:2 5110
the eyes than the *w* of the desire ... Eccl 6:9 1981
as a *w* bird cast out of the nest, ... Is 16:2 5074
w about from house to house ... 1Ti 5:13 *4022*
w stars, to whom is reserved the ... Jude 13 *4107*

WANDERINGS {1}
Thou tellest my *w* ... Ps 56:8 5112

WANT {31}
nakedness, and in *w* of all things ... Deut 28:48 2640
for she shall eat them for *w* of ... Deut 28:57 2640
a place where there is no *w* of ... Judg 18:10 4270
there is no *w* of any thing ... Judg 19:19 4270
the rock for *w* of a shelter ... Job 24:8 1097
For *w* and famine they were ... Job 30:3 2639
seen any perish for *w* of clothing ... Job 31:19 1097
I shall not *w* ... Ps 23:1 2637
for there is no *w* to them that ... Ps 34:9 4270
LORD shall not *w* any good thing ... Ps 34:10 2637
and thy *w* as an armed man ... Prov 6:11 4270
but fools die for *w* of wisdom ... Prov 10:21 2638
is destroyed for *w* of judgment ... Prov 13:23 3808
the belly of the wicked shall *w* ... Prov 13:25 2637
but in the *w* of people is the ... Prov 14:28 657
every one that is hasty only to *w* ... Prov 21:5 4270
the rich, shall surely come to *w* ... Prov 22:16 4270
and thy *w* as an armed man ... Prov 24:34 4270
shall fail, none shall *w* her mate ... Is 34:16 6485
David shall never *w* a man to sit ... Jer 33:17 3772
shall the priests the Levites *w* a ... Jer 33:18 3772
the son of Rechab shall not *w* a ... Jer 35:19 3772
stricken through for *w* of the ... Lam 4:9
That they may *w* bread and water, ... Eze 4:17 2637
w of bread in all your places ... Amos 4:6 2640
but she of her *w* did cast in all ... Mk 12:44 *5304*
and he began to be in *w* ... Lk 15:14 *5302*
may be a supply for their *w* ... 2Cor 8:14 *5303*
also may be a supply for your *w* ... 2Cor 8:14 *5303*
supplieth the *w* of the saints ... 2Cor 9:12 *5303*
Not that I speak in respect of *w* ... Phil 4:11 *5304*

WANTED {3}
we have *w* all things, and have ... Jer 44:18 2637
And when they *w* wine, the mother ... Jn 2:3 *5302*
when I was present with you, and *w* ... 2Cor 11:9 *5302*

WANTETH {7}
for his need, in that which he *w* ... Deut 15:8 2637
as for him that *w* understanding ... Prov 9:4 2638
as for him that *w* understanding ... Prov 9:16 2638
of words there *w* not sin ... Prov 10:19 2308
The prince that *w* understanding ... Prov 28:16 2638
so that he *w* nothing for his soul ... Eccl 6:2 2638
round goblet, which *w* not liquor ... Song 7:2 2637

WANTING {8}
let none be *w* ... 2Kin 10:19 6485
whosoever shall be *w*, he shall ... 2Kin 10:19 6485
with words, yet they are *w* to him ... Prov 19:7 3808
that which is *w* cannot be ... Eccl 1:15 2642
in the balances, and art found *w* ... Dan 5:27 2627
in order the things that are *w* ... Titus 1:5 *3007*
that nothing be *w* unto them ... Titus 3:13 *3007*
be perfect and entire, *w* nothing ... Jas 1:4 *3007*

WANTON {3}
w eyes, walking and mincing as ... Is 3:16 8265
begun to wax *w* against Christ ... 1Ti 5:11 *2691*
pleasure on the earth, and been *w* ... Jas 5:5 *4684*

WANTONNESS {2}
not in chambering and *w*, not in ... Rom 13:13 *766*
of the flesh, through much *w* ... 2Pet 2:18 *766*

WANTS {2}
let all thy *w* lie upon me ... Judg 19:20 4270
and he that ministered to my *w* ... Phil 2:25 *5532*

WAR {225}
That these made *w* with Bera king ... Gen 14:2 4421
when there falleth out any *w* ... Ex 1:10 4421
the people repent when they see *w* ... Ex 13:17 4421
The LORD is a man of *w* ... Ex 15:3 4421
sworn that the LORD will have *w* ... Ex 17:16 4421
There is a noise of *w* in the camp ... Ex 32:17 4421
able to go forth to *w* in Israel ... Num 1:3 6635
that were able to go forth to *w* ... Num 1:20 6635
that were able to go forth to *w* ... Num 1:22 6635
that were able to go forth to *w* ... Num 1:24 6635
that were able to go forth to *w* ... Num 1:26 6635
that were able to go forth to *w* ... Num 1:28 6635
that were able to go forth to *w* ... Num 1:30 6635
that were able to go forth to *w* ... Num 1:32 6635
that were able to go forth to *w* ... Num 1:34 6635
that were able to go forth to *w* ... Num 1:36 6635
that were able to go forth to *w* ... Num 1:38 6635
that were able to go forth to *w* ... Num 1:40 6635
that were able to go forth to *w* ... Num 1:42 6635
able to go forth to *w* in Israel ... Num 1:45 6635
if ye go to *w* in your land ... Num 10:9 4421
are able to go to *w* in Israel ... Num 26:2 6635
Arm some of yourselves unto the *w* ... Num 31:3 6635
of Israel, shall ye send to the *w* ... Num 31:4 6635
twelve thousand armed for *w* ... Num 31:5 6635
And Moses sent them to the *w* ... Num 31:6 6635
of Eleazar the priest, to the *w* ... Num 31:6 6635
men of *w* which went to the battle ... Num 31:21 6635
them that took the *w* upon them ... Num 31:27 4421
men of *w* which went out to battle ... Num 31:28 4421
which the men of *w* had caught ... Num 31:32 6635
of them that went out to *w* ... Num 31:36 6635
of *w* which are under our charge ... Num 31:49 4421
(For the men of *w* had taken spoil ... Num 31:53 6635
Shall your brethren go to *w* ... Num 32:6 4421
go armed before the LORD to *w* ... Num 32:20 4421
pass over, every man armed for *w* ... Num 32:27 6635
on every man his weapons of *w* ... Deut 1:41 4421
the generation of the men of *w* ... Deut 2:14 4421
all the men of *w* were consumed ... Deut 2:16 4421
all that are meet for the *w* ... Deut 3:18 2438
by signs, and by wonders, and by *w* ... Deut 4:34 4421
but will make *w* against thee ... Deut 20:12 4421
in making *w* against it to take it ... Deut 20:19 3898
the city that maketh *w* with thee ... Deut 20:20 4421
forth to *w* against thine enemies ... Deut 21:10 4421
wife, he shall not go out to *w* ... Deut 24:5 6635
for *w* passed over before the LORD ... Josh 4:13 6635
were males, even all the men of *w* ... Josh 5:4 4421
all the people that were men of *w* ... Josh 5:6 4421
compass the city, all ye men of *w* ... Josh 6:3 4421
all the people of *w* with thee ... Josh 8:1 4421
arose, and all the people of *w* ... Josh 8:3 4421
people of *w* that were with him ... Josh 8:11 4421
Gibeon, and made *w* against it ... Josh 10:5 3898
and all the people of *w* with him ... Josh 10:7 4421
the men of *w* which went with him ... Josh 10:24 4421
and all the people of *w* with him ... Josh 11:7 4421
Joshua made *w* a long time with ... Josh 11:18 4421
And the land rested from *w* ... Josh 11:23 4421
even so is my strength now, for *w* ... Josh 14:11 4421
And the land had rest from *w* ... Josh 14:15 4421
because he was a man of *w* ... Josh 17:1 4421
to go up to *w* against them ... Josh 22:12 6635
might know, to teach them *w* ... Judg 3:2 4421
judged Israel, and went out to *w* ... Judg 3:10 4421
then was *w* in the gates ... Judg 5:8 3901
of Ammon made *w* against Israel ... Judg 11:4 3898
of Ammon made *w* against Israel ... Judg 11:5 3898
doest me wrong to *w* against me ... Judg 11:27 3898
men appointed with weapons of *w* ... Judg 18:11 4421
appointed with their weapons of *w* ... Judg 18:16 4421
were appointed with weapons of *w* ... Judg 18:17 4421
all these were men of *w* ... Judg 20:17 4421
not to each man his wife in the *w* ... Judg 21:22 4421
and to make his instruments of *w* ... 1Sa 8:12 4421
there was sore *w* against the ... 1Sa 14:52 4421
mighty valiant man, and a man of *w* ... 1Sa 16:18 4421
he a man of *w* from his youth ... 1Sa 17:33 4421
and Saul set him over the men of *w* ... 1Sa 18:5 4421
And there was *w* again ... 1Sa 19:8 4421
all the people together to *w* ... 1Sa 23:8 4421
the Philistines make *w* against me ... 1Sa 28:15 3898
and the weapons of *w* perished ... 2Sa 1:27 4421
Now there was long *w* between the ... 2Sa 3:1 4421
while there was *w* between the ... 2Sa 3:6 4421
did, and how the *w* prospered ... 2Sa 11:7 4421
all the things concerning the *w* ... 2Sa 11:18 4421
matters of the *w* unto the king ... 2Sa 11:19 4421
and thy father is a man of *w* ... 2Sa 17:8 4421
had yet *w* again with Israel ... 2Sa 21:15 4421
He teacheth my hands to *w* ... 2Sa 22:35 4421
and shed the blood of *w* in peace ... 1Kin 2:5 4421
put the blood of *w* upon his ... 1Kin 2:5 4421
but they were men of *w*, and his ... 1Kin 9:22 4421
there was *w* between Rehoboam and ... 1Kin 14:30 4421
there was *w* between Rehoboam and ... 1Kin 15:6 4421
there was *w* between Abijam and ... 1Kin 15:7 4421
there was *w* between Asa and Baasha ... 1Kin 15:16 4421
there was *w* between Asa and Baasha ... 1Kin 15:32 4421
or whether they be come out for *w* ... 1Kin 20:18 4421
years without *w* between Syria ... 1Kin 22:1 4421
Joram the son of Ahab to the *w* ... 2Kin 8:28 4421
hand of Jehoahaz his father by *w* ... 2Kin 13:25 4421
ten thousand, and took Selah by *w* ... 2Kin 14:7 4421
Israel came up to Jerusalem to *w* ... 2Kin 16:5 4421
counsel and strength for the *w* ... 2Kin 18:20 4421
all that were strong and apt for *w* ... 2Kin 24:16 4421
all the men of *w* fled by night by ... 2Kin 25:4 4421
that was set over the men of *w* ... 2Kin 25:19 4421
they made *w* with the Hagarites ... 1Chr 5:10 4421
shoot with bow, and skilful in *w* ... 1Chr 5:18 4421
that went out to the *w* ... 1Chr 5:18 6635
they made *w* with the Hagarites, ... 1Chr 5:19 4421
slain, because the *w* was of God ... 1Chr 5:22 4421
were bands of soldiers for *w* ... 1Chr 7:4 4421
soldiers, fit to go out for *w* ... 1Chr 7:11 6635
of them that were apt to the *w* ... 1Chr 7:40 6635
the mighty men, helpers of the *w* ... 1Chr 12:1 4421
men of *w* fit for the battle, that ... 1Chr 12:8 6635
that were ready armed to the *w* ... 1Chr 12:23 6635
hundred, ready armed to the *w* ... 1Chr 12:24 6635
mighty men of valour for the *w* ... 1Chr 12:25 6635
went forth to battle, expert in *w* ... 1Chr 12:33 4421
with all instruments of *w* ... 1Chr 12:33 4421
of the Danites expert in *w* twenty ... 1Chr 12:35 4421
went forth to battle, expert in *w* ... 1Chr 12:36 4421
instruments of *w* for the battle ... 1Chr 12:37 6635
All these men of *w*, that could ... 1Chr 12:38 4421
(for Hadarezer had *w* with Tou ... 1Chr 18:10 4421
that there arose *w* at Gezer with ... 1Chr 20:4 4421
there was *w* again with the ... 1Chr 20:5 4421
And yet again there was *w* at Gath ... 1Chr 20:6 4421
because thou hast been a man of *w* ... 1Chr 28:3 4421
If thy people go out to *w* against ... 2Chr 6:34 4421
but they were men of *w*, and chief ... 2Chr 8:9 4421
there was *w* between Abijah and ... 2Chr 13:2 4421
with an army of valiant men of *w* ... 2Chr 13:3 4421
he had no *w* in those years ... 2Chr 14:6 4421
there was no more *w* unto the five ... 2Chr 15:19 4421
made no *w* against Jehoshaphat ... 2Chr 17:10 3898
and the men of *w*, mighty men of ... 2Chr 17:13 4421
thousand ready prepared for the *w* ... 2Chr 17:18 6635
and we will be with thee in the *w* ... 2Chr 18:3 4421
son of Ahab king of Israel to *w* ... 2Chr 22:5 4421
choice men, able to go forth to *w* ... 2Chr 25:5 6635
men, that went out to *w* by bands ... 2Chr 26:11 6635
that made *w* with mighty power, to ... 2Chr 26:13 4421
against them that came from the *w* ... 2Chr 28:12 6635
set captains of *w* over the people ... 2Chr 32:6 4421
put captains of *w* in all the ... 2Chr 33:14 2428
the house wherewith I have *w* ... 2Chr 35:21 4421
in *w* from the power of the sword ... Job 5:20 4421
changes and *w* are against me ... Job 10:17 6635
against the day of battle and *w* ... Job 38:23 4421
He teacheth my hands to *w* ... Ps 18:34 4421
though *w* should rise against me, ... Ps 27:3 4421
butter, but *w* was in his heart ... Ps 55:21 7128
thou the people that delight in *w* ... Ps 68:30 7128
but when I speak, they are for *w* ... Ps 120:7 4421
are they gathered together for *w* ... Ps 140:2 4421
which teacheth my hands to *w* ... Ps 144:1 4421,7128
and with good advice make *w* ... Prov 20:18 4421
counsel thou shalt make thy *w* ... Prov 24:6 4421
a time of *w*, and a time of peace ... Eccl 3:8 4421
there is no discharge in that *w* ... Eccl 8:8 4421
is better than weapons of *w* ... Eccl 9:18 7128
hold swords, being expert in *w* ... Song 3:8 4421
shall they learn *w* any more ... Is 2:4 4421
The mighty man, and the man of *w* ... Is 3:2 4421
the sword, and thy mighty in the *w* ... Is 3:25 4421
toward Jerusalem to *w* against it ... Is 7:1 4421
and from the grievousness of *w* ... Is 21:15 4421
I have counsel and strength for *w* ... Is 36:5 4421
is come forth to make *w* with thee ... Is 37:9 3898
they that *w* against thee shall be ... Is 41:12 4421
stir up jealousy like a man of *w* ... Is 42:13 4421
of the trumpet, the alarm of *w* ... Jer 4:19 4421
Prepare ye *w* against her ... Jer 6:4 4421
array as men for *w* against thee ... Jer 6:23 4421
of Babylon maketh *w* against us ... Jer 21:2 3898
of *w* that are in your hands ... Jer 21:4 4421
and against great kingdoms, of *w* ... Jer 28:8 4421
the hands of the men of *w* that ... Jer 38:4 4421
saw them, and all the men of *w* ... Jer 39:4 4421
were found there, and the men of *w* ... Jer 41:3 4421
of Ahikam, even mighty men of *w* ... Jer 41:16 4421
of Egypt, where we shall see no *w* ... Jer 42:14 4421
mighty and strong men for the *w* ... Jer 48:14 4421
of *w* to be heard in Rabbah of the ... Jer 49:2 4421
all the men of *w* shall be cut off ... Jer 49:26 4421
all her men of *w* shall be cut off ... Jer 50:30 4421
art my battle ax and weapons of *w* ... Jer 51:20 4421
the men of *w* are affrighted ... Jer 51:32 4421
up, and all the men of *w* fled ... Jer 52:7 4421
had the charge of the men of *w* ... Jer 52:25 4421
company make for him in the *w* ... Eze 17:17 4421
engines of *w* against thy walls ... Eze 26:9 6904
were in thine army, thy men of *w* ... Eze 27:10 4421
merchandise, and all thy men of *w* ... Eze 27:27 4421
to hell with their weapons of *w* ... Eze 32:27 4421
mighty men, and with all men of *w* ... Eze 39:20 4421
same horn made *w* with the saints ... Dan 7:21 7129
unto the end of the *w* desolations ... Dan 9:26 4421
climb the wall like men of *w* ... Joel 2:7 4421
Prepare *w*, wake up the mighty men ... Joel 3:9 4421
let all the men of *w* draw near ... Joel 3:9 4421
by securely as men averse from *w* ... Mic 2:8 4421
they even prepare *w* against him ... Mic 3:5 4421
shall they learn *w* any more ... Mic 4:3 4421
going to make *w* against another ... Lk 14:31 *4171*
his men of *w* set him at nought ... Lk 23:11 *4753*
we do not *w* after the flesh ... 2Cor 10:3 *4754*
by them mightest *w* a good warfare ... 1Ti 1:18 *4754*
your lusts that *w* in your members ... Jas 4:1 *4754*
ye fight and *w*, yet ye have not, ... Jas 4:2 *4170*
lusts, which *w* against the soul ... 1Pet 2:11 *4754*
pit shall make *w* against them ... Rev 11:7 *4171*
And there was *w* in heaven ... Rev 12:7 *4171*
went to make *w* with the remnant ... Rev 12:17 *4171*
who is able to make *w* with him ... Rev 13:4 *4170*
him to make *w* with the saints ... Rev 13:7 *4171*
These shall make *w* with the Lamb ... Rev 17:14 *4170*
he doth judge and make *w* ... Rev 19:11 *4170*
gathered together to make *w* ... Rev 19:19 *4171*

WARD {22}
he put them in *w* in the house of ... Gen 40:3 4929
and they continued a season in *w* ... Gen 40:4 4929
him in the *w* of his lord's house ... Gen 40:7 4929

put me in *w* in the captain of the... Gen 41:10 4929
all together into *w* three days... Gen 42:17 4929
And they put him in *w*, that the... Lev 24:12 4929
And they put him in *w*, because it... Num 15:34 4929
keep the house, and put them in *w*... 2Sa 20:3 4931
kept the *w* of the house of Saul... 1Chr 12:29 4931
And they cast lots, *w* against... 1Chr 25:8 4931
against *w*, as well... 1Chr 25:8 4929
of the going up, *w* against *w*... 1Chr 26:16 4929
man of God, *w* over against *w*... Neh 12:24 4929
were porters keeping the *w* at the... Neh 12:25 4929
porters kept the *w* of their God... Neh 12:45 4931
the *w* of the purification,... Neh 12:45 4931
and I am set in my *w* whole nights... Is 21:8 4931
a captain of the *w* was there... Jer 37:13 6488
And they put him in *w* in chains... Eze 19:9 5474
past the first and the second *w*... Acts 12:10 *5438*

WARDROBE {2}
son of Harhas, keeper of the *w*... 2Kin 22:14 899
son of Hasrah, keeper of the *w*... 2Chr 34:22 899

WARDS {3}
the house of the tabernacle, by *w*... 1Chr 9:23 4931
having *w* one against another, to... 1Chr 26:12 4931
appointed the *w* of the priests and... Neh 13:30 4931

WARE {6}
w or any victuals on the sabbath... Neh 10:31 4728
brought fish, and all manner of *w*... Neh 13:16 4377
sellers of all kind of *w* lodged... Neh 13:20 4465
w no clothes, neither abode in... Lk 8:27 *1737*
They were *w* of it, and fled unto... Acts 14:6 *4894*
Of whom be thou *w* also... 2Ti 4:15 *5442*

WARES {5}
Gather up thy *w* out of the land,... Jer 10:17 3666
multitude of the *w* of thy making... Eze 27:16 4639
multitude of the *w* of thy making... Eze 27:18 4639
When thy *w* went forth out of the... Eze 27:33 5801
cast forth the *w* that were in the... Jonah 1:5 3627

WARFARE {5}
their armies together for *w*... 1Sa 28:1 6635
that her *w* is accomplished, that... Is 40:2 6635
Who goeth a *w* any time at his own... 1Cor 9:7 *4754*
weapons of our *w* are not carnal... 2Cor 10:4 *4752*
by them mightest war a good *w*... 1Ti 1:18 *4752*

WARM {8}
and the flesh of the child waxed *w*... 2Kin 4:34 2552
What time they wax *w*, they vanish... Job 6:17 2215
How thy garments are *w*, when he... Job 37:17 2525
but how can one be *w* alone... Eccl 4:11 3179
will take thereof, and *w* himself... Is 44:15 2552
himself, and saith, Aha, I am *w*... Is 44:16 2552
there shall not be a coal to *w* at... Is 47:14 2552
clothe you, but there is none *w*... Hag 1:6 2527

WARMED {6}
if he were not *w* with the fleece... Job 31:20 2552
and *w* himself at the fire... Mk 14:54 *2328*
and they *w* themselves... Jn 18:18 *2328*
stood with them, and *w* himself... Jn 18:18 *2328*
And Simon Peter stood and *w* himself... Jn 18:25 *2328*
them, Depart in peace, be ye *w*... Jas 2:16 *2328*

WARMETH {2}
the earth, and *w* them in the dust,... Job 39:14 2552
he *w* himself, and saith, Aha, I am... Is 44:16 2552

WARMING {1}
And when she saw Peter *w* himself... Mk 14:67 *2328*

WARN {11}
ye shall even *w* them that they... 2Chr 19:10 2094
nor speakest to *w* the wicked from... Eze 3:18 2094
Yet if thou *w* the wicked, and he... Eze 3:19 2094
if thou *w* the righteous man... Eze 3:21 2094
blow the trumpet, and *w* the people... Eze 33:3 2094
at my mouth, and *w* them from me... Eze 33:7 2094
to *w* the wicked from his way... Eze 33:8 2094
if thou *w* the wicked of his way... Eze 33:9 2094
I ceased not to *w* every one night... Acts 20:31 *3560*
but as my beloved sons I *w* you... 1Cor 4:14 *3560*
w them that are unruly, comfort... 1Th 5:14 *3560*

WARNED {10}
w him of, and saved himself there,... 2Kin 6:10 2094
Moreover by them is thy servant *w*... Ps 19:11 2094
surely live, because he is *w*... Eze 3:21 2094
trumpet, and the people be not *w*... Eze 33:6 2094
being *w* of God in a dream that... Mt 2:12 *5537*
being *w* of God in a dream, he... Mt 2:22 *5537*
who hath *w* you to flee from the... Mt 3:7 *5263*
who hath *w* you to flee from the... Lk 3:7 *5263*
was *w* from God by an holy angel... Acts 10:22 *5537*
being *w* of God of things not seen... Heb 11:7 *5537*

WARNING {8}
To whom shall I speak, and give *w*... Jer 6:10 5749
my mouth, and give them *w* from me... Eze 3:17 2094
and thou givest him not *w*, nor... Eze 3:18 2094
because thou hast not given him *w*... Eze 3:20 2094
of the trumpet, and taketh not *w*... Eze 33:4 2094
of the trumpet, and took not *w*... Eze 33:5 2094
But he that taketh *w* shall... Eze 33:5 2094
w every man, and teaching every... Col 1:28 *3560*

WARP {9}
Whether it be in the *w*, or woof... Lev 13:48 8359
or in the skin, either in the *w*... Lev 13:49 8359
in the garment, either in the *w*... Lev 13:51 8359
that garment, whether *w* or woof... Lev 13:52 8359
in the garment, either in the *w*... Lev 13:53 8359
out of the skin, or out of the *w*... Lev 13:56 8359
in the garment, either in the *w*... Lev 13:57 8359
And the garment, either *w*, or woof... Lev 13:58 8359
woollen or linen, either in the *w*... Lev 13:59 8359

WARRED {9}
they *w* against the Midianites, as... Num 31:7 6633
Moses divided from the men that *w*... Num 31:42 6633
w against Israel, and sent and... Josh 24:9 3898
of the acts of Jeroboam, how he *w*... 1Kin 14:19 3898
besieged Samaria, and *w* against it... 1Kin 20:1 3898
might that he shewed, and how he *w*... 1Kin 22:45 3898
king of Syria *w* against Israel... 2Kin 6:8 3898
he did, and his might, how he *w*... 2Kin 14:28 3898
w against the Philistines, and... 2Chr 26:6 3898

WARRETH {1}
No man that *w* entangleth himself... 2Ti 2:4 *4754*

WARRING {3}
king of Assyria *w* against Libnah... 2Kin 19:8 3898
king of Assyria *w* against Libnah... Is 37:8 3898
w against the law of my mind, and... Rom 7:23 *497*

WARRIOR {1}
of the *w* is with confused noise... Is 9:5 5431

WARRIORS {2}
chosen men, which were *w*... 1Kin 12:21 6213,4421
chosen men, which were *w*... 2Chr 11:1 6213,4421

WARS {15}
in the book of the *w* of the LORD... Num 21:14 4421
had not known all the *w* of Canaan... Judg 3:1 4421
for Hadadezer had *w* with Toi... 2Sa 8:10 4421
of the LORD his God for the *w*... 1Kin 5:3 4421
abundantly, and hast made great *w*... 1Chr 22:8 4421
there were *w* between Rehoboam and... 2Chr 12:15 4421
from henceforth thou shalt have *w*... 2Chr 16:9 4421
the acts of Jotham, and all his *w*... 2Chr 27:7 4421
He maketh *w* to cease unto the end... Ps 46:9 4421
hear of *w* and rumours of *w*... Mt 24:6 *4171*
hear of *w* and rumours of *w*... Mk 13:7 *4171*
But when ye shall hear of *w*... Lk 21:9 *4171*
From whence come *w* and fightings... Jas 4:1 *4171*

WAS See APPENDIX.

WASH {45}
w your feet, and rest yourselves... Gen 18:4 7364
w your feet, and ye shall rise up... Gen 19:2 7364
camels, and water to *w* his feet... Gen 24:32 7364
down to *w* herself at the river... Ex 2:5 7364
let them *w* their clothes,... Ex 19:10 3526
and shalt *w* them with water... Ex 29:4 7364
w the inwards of him, and his legs... Ex 29:17 7364
foot also of brass, to *w* withal... Ex 30:18 7364
and his sons shall *w* their hands... Ex 30:19 7364
they shall *w* with water, that... Ex 30:20 7364
So they shall *w* their hands... Ex 30:21 7364
and *w* them with water... Ex 40:12 7364
and put water there, to *w* withal... Ex 40:30 7364
and his legs shall he *w* in water... Lev 1:9 7364
But he shall *w* the inwards... Lev 1:13 7364
thou shalt *w* that whereon it was... Lev 6:27 3526
he did *w* the inwards and the legs,... Lev 9:14 7364
of them shall *w* his clothes... Lev 11:25 3526
of them shall *w* his clothes... Lev 11:28 3526
carcase of it shall *w* his clothes... Lev 11:40 3526
carcase of it shall *w* his clothes... Lev 11:40 3526
he shall *w* his clothes, and be... Lev 13:6 3526
he shall *w* his clothes, and be... Lev 13:34 3526
priest shall command that they *w*... Lev 13:54 3526
of skin it be, which thou shalt *w*... Lev 13:58 3526
be cleansed shall *w* his clothes... Lev 14:8 3526
w himself in water, that he may... Lev 14:8 7364
he shall *w* his clothes, also he... Lev 14:9 3526
also he shall *w* his flesh in... Lev 14:9 7364
in the house shall *w* his clothes... Lev 14:47 3526
in the house shall *w* his clothes... Lev 14:47 3526
his bed shall *w* his clothes... Lev 15:5 3526
the issue shall *w* his clothes... Lev 15:6 3526
the issue shall *w* his clothes... Lev 15:7 3526
then he shall *w* his clothes... Lev 15:8 3526
those things shall *w* his clothes... Lev 15:10 3526
he shall *w* his clothes, and bathe... Lev 15:11 3526
w his clothes, and bathe his flesh... Lev 15:13 3526
then he shall *w* all his flesh in... Lev 15:16 7364
her bed shall *w* his clothes... Lev 15:21 3526
she sat upon shall *w* his clothes... Lev 15:22 3526
shall *w* his clothes, and bathe... Lev 15:27 3526
shall he *w* his flesh in water... Lev 16:4 7364
he shall *w* his flesh with water... Lev 16:24 7364
the scapegoat shall *w* his clothes... Lev 16:26 3526
burneth them shall *w* his clothes... Lev 16:28 3526
he shall both *w* his clothes... Lev 17:15 3526
But if he *w* them not, nor bathe... Lev 17:16 3526
unless he *w* his flesh with water... Lev 22:6 7364
let them *w* their clothes, and so... Num 8:7 3526
the priest shall *w* his clothes... Num 19:7 3526
her shall *w* his clothes in water... Num 19:8 3526
of the heifer shall *w* his clothes... Num 19:10 3526
w his clothes, and bathe himself... Num 19:19 3526
of separation shall *w* his clothes... Num 19:21 3526
ye shall *w* your clothes on the... Num 31:24 3526
shall *w* their hands over the... Deut 21:6 7364
he shall *w* himself with water... Deut 23:11 7364
W thyself therefore, and anoint... Ruth 3:3 7364
w the feet of the servants of my... 1Sa 25:41 7364
down to thy house, and *w* thy feet... 2Sa 11:8 7364
w in Jordan seven times, and thy... 2Kin 5:10 7364
may I not *w* in them, and be clean... 2Kin 5:12 7364
then, when he saith to thee, *W*... 2Kin 5:13 7364
and five on the left, to *w* in them... 2Chr 4:6 7364
sea was for the priests to *w* in... 2Chr 4:6 7364
If I *w* myself with snow water, and... Job 9:30 7364
I will *w* mine hands in innocency... Ps 26:6 7364
W me throughly from mine iniquity... Ps 51:2 3526
w me, and I shall be whiter than... Ps 51:7 3526
he shall *w* his feet in the blood... Ps 58:10 7364
W you, make you clean... Is 1:16 7364
For though thou *w* thee with nitre... Jer 2:22 3526
w thine heart from wickedness,... Jer 4:14 3526
for whom thou didst *w* thyself... Eze 23:40 7364
anoint thine head, and *w* thy face... Mt 6:17 *3538*
for they *w* not their hands when... Mt 15:2 *3538*
except they *w* their hands oft,... Mk 7:3 *3538*
from the market, except they *w*... Mk 7:4 *907*
began to *w* his feet with tears,... Lk 7:38 *1026*
w in the pool of Siloam, (which... Jn 9:7 *3538*
Go to the pool of Siloam, and *w*... Jn 9:11 *3538*
began to *w* the disciples' feet,... Jn 13:5 *3538*
him, Lord, dost thou *w* my feet... Jn 13:6 *3538*
him, Thou shalt never *w* my feet... Jn 13:8 *3538*
If I *w* thee not, thou hast no... Jn 13:8 *3538*
needeth not save to *w* his feet... Jn 13:10 *3538*
ye also ought to *w* one another's... Jn 13:14 *3538*
w away thy sins, calling on the... Acts 22:16 *628*

WASHED {1}
them water, and they *w* their feet... Gen 43:24 7364
he *w* his face, and went out, and... Gen 43:31 7364
he *w* his garments in wine, and his... Gen 49:11 3526
and they *w* their clothes... Ex 19:14 3526
his sons *w* their hands and their... Ex 40:31 7364
came near unto the altar, they *w*... Ex 40:32 7364
and his sons, and *w* them with water... Lev 8:6 7364
he *w* the inwards and the legs in... Lev 8:21 7364
on the plague, after that it is *w*... Lev 13:55 3526
it shall be *w* the second time... Lev 13:58 3526
shall be *w* with water, and be... Lev 15:17 3526
purified, and they *w* their clothes... Num 8:21 3526
they *w* their feet, and did eat and... Judg 19:21 7364
David arose from the earth, and *w*... 2Sa 12:20 7364
nor *w* his clothes, from the day... 2Sa 19:24 3526
one *w* the chariot in the pool of... 1Kin 22:38 7857
and they *w* his armour... 1Kin 22:38 7364
the burnt offering they *w* in them... 2Chr 4:6 1740
When I *w* my steps with butter, and... Job 29:6 7364
vain, and *w* my hands in innocency... Ps 73:13 7364
eyes, and yet is not *w* from their... Prov 30:12 7364
I have *w* my feet... Song 5:3 7364
w with milk, and fitly set... Song 5:12 7364
When the Lord shall have *w* away... Is 4:4 7364
neither wast thou *w* in water to... Eze 16:4 7364
Then *w* I thee with water... Eze 16:9 7364
I throughly *w* away thy blood from... Eze 16:9 7857
where they *w* the burnt offering... Eze 40:38 1740
w his hands before the multitude,... Mt 27:24 *633*
but she hath *w* my feet with tears... Lk 7:44 *1026*
he had not first *w* before dinner... Lk 11:38 *907*
He went his way therefore, and *w*... Jn 9:7 *3538*
and I went and *w*, and I received... Jn 9:11 *3538*
put clay upon mine eyes, and I *w*... Jn 9:15 *3538*
He that is *w* needeth not save to... Jn 13:10 *3068*
So after he had *w* their feet... Jn 13:12 *3538*
Lord and Master, have *w* your feet... Jn 13:14 *3538*
whom when they had *w*, they laid... Acts 9:37 *3068*
of the night, and *w* their stripes... Acts 16:33 *3068*
but ye are *w*, but ye are... 1Cor 6:11 *628*
if she have *w* the saints' feet,... 1Ti 5:10 *3538*
our bodies *w* with pure water... Heb 10:22 *3068*
the sow that was *w* to her... 2Pet 2:22 *3068*
w us from our sins in his own... Rev 1:5 *3068*
have *w* their robes, and made them... Rev 7:14 *4150*

WASHEST {1}
thou *w* away the things which grow... Job 14:19 7857

WASHING {10}
somewhat dark after the *w* of it... Lev 13:56 3526
the roof he saw a woman *w* herself... 2Sa 11:2 7364
that every one put them off for *w*... Neh 4:23 4325
shorn, which came up from the *w*... Song 4:2 7367
of sheep which go up from the *w*... Song 6:6 7367
as the *w* of cups, and pots, brasen... Mk 7:4 *909*
of men, as the *w* of pots and cups... Mk 7:8 *909*
out of them, and were *w* their nets... Lk 5:2 *637*
cleanse it with the *w* of water by... Eph 5:26 *3067*
by the *w* of regeneration, and... Titus 3:5 *3067*

WASHINGS {1}
in meats and drinks, and divers *w*... Heb 9:10 *909*

WASHPOT {2}
Moab is my *w*... Ps 60:8 5518,7366
Moab is my *w*... Ps 108:9 5518,7366

WAST {66}
Who told thee that thou *w* naked... Gen 3:11
for out of it *w* thou taken... Gen 3:19
of God, and thou *w* pleased with me... Gen 33:10
manner when thou *w* his butler... Gen 40:13 1961
remember that thou *w* a servant in... Deut 5:15 1961
thou shalt remember that thou *w* a... Deut 15:15 1961
that thou *w* a bondman in Egypt... Deut 16:12 1961
because thou *w* a stranger in his... Deut 23:7 1961
that thou *w* a bondman in Egypt... Deut 24:18 1961
thou shalt remember that thou *w* a... Deut 24:22 1961
behind thee, when thou *w* faint... Deut 25:18
of Egypt, which thou *w* afraid of... Deut 28:60
with whose maidens thou *w*... Ruth 3:2
When thou *w* little in thine own... 1Sa 15:17
w thou not made the head of the... 1Sa 15:17
How *w* thou not afraid to stretch... 2Sa 1:14
thou *w* slain in thine high places... 2Sa 1:25
thou *w* he that leddest out and... 2Sa 5:2 1961

thou *w* he that leddest out and ... 1Chr 11:2
or *w* thou made before the hills ... Job 15:7
Where *w* thou when I laid the ... Job 38:4 1961
thou it, because thou *w* then born ... Job 38:21
thou *w* a God that forgavest them, ... Ps 99:8 1961
Jordan, that thou *w* driven back ... Ps 114:5
though thou *w* angry with me, ... Is 12:1
wherein thou *w* made to serve ... Is 14:3
spoilest, and thou *w* not spoiled ... Is 33:1
Since thou *w* precious in my sight ... Is 43:4
w called a transgressor from the ... Is 48:8
of youth, when thou *w* refused ... Is 54:6
therefore thou *w* not grieved ... Is 57:10
as thou *w* ashamed of Assyria ... Jer 2:36
O Babylon, and thou *w* not aware ... Jer 50:24
in the day thou *w* born thy navel ... Eze 16:4
neither *w* thou washed in water to ... Eze 16:4
thou *w* not salted at all, nor ... Eze 16:4
but thou *w* cast out in the open ... Eze 16:5
in the day that thou *w* born ... Eze 16:5
thee when thou *w* in thy blood ... Eze 16:6
thee when thou *w* in thy blood ... Eze 16:6
is grown, whereas thou *w* naked ... Eze 16:7
Thus *w* thou decked with gold and ... Eze 16:13
thou *w* exceeding beautiful, and ... Eze 16:13
of thy youth, when thou *w* naked ... Eze 16:22 1961
bare, and *w* polluted in thy blood ... Eze 16:22 1961
because thou *w* unsatiable ... Eze 16:28
yet thou *w* not satisfied herewith ... Eze 16:29
thou *w* corrupted more than they ... Eze 16:47
in the place where thou *w* created ... Eze 21:30
thou *w* not purged, thou shalt not ... Eze 24:13
that *w* inhabited of seafaring men ... Eze 26:17
which *w* strong in the sea, she and ... Eze 26:17
thou *w* replenished, and made very ... Eze 27:25
in the day that thou *w* created ... Eze 28:13
thou *w* upon the holy mountain of ... Eze 28:14 1961
Thou *w* perfect in thy ways from ... Eze 28:15
from the day that thou *w* created ... Eze 28:15
even thou *w* as one of them ... Obad 11
Thou also *w* with Jesus of Galilee ... Mt 26:69 *2258*
thou also *w* with Jesus of ... Mk 14:67 *2258*
when thou *w* under the fig tree, I ... Jn 1:48 *5607*
Thou *w* altogether born in sins, ... Jn 9:34
say unto thee, When thou *w* young ... Jn 21:18 *2258*
for thou *w* slain, and hast ... Rev 5:9
God Almighty, which art, and *w* ... Rev 11:17 *2258*
O Lord, which art, and *w*, and ... Rev 16:5 *2258*

WASTE {64}
And I will make your cities *w* ... Lev 26:31 2723
be desolate, and your cities *w* ... Lev 26:33 2723
have laid them *w* even unto Nophah ... Num 21:30 8074
in the *w* howling wilderness ... Deut 32:10 8414
The barrel of meal shall not *w* ... 1Kin 17:14 3615
lay *w* fenced cities into ruinous ... 2Kin 19:25 7582
of wickedness *w* them any more ... 1Chr 17:9 1086
my fathers' sepulchres, lieth *w* ... Neh 2:3 2720
we are in, how Jerusalem lieth *w* ... Neh 2:17 2720
in former time desolate and *w* ... Job 30:3 4875
satisfy the desolate and *w* ground ... Job 38:27 4875
laid *w* his dwelling place ... Ps 79:7 8074
boar out of the wood doth *w* it ... Ps 80:13 3765
And I will lay it *w* ... Is 5:6 1326
the *w* places of the fat ones ... Is 5:17 2723
in the night Ar of Moab is laid *w* ... Is 15:1 7703
the night Kir of Moab is laid *w* ... Is 15:1 7703
for it is laid *w*, so that there ... Is 23:1 7703
for your strength is laid *w* ... Is 23:14 7703
the earth empty, and maketh it *w* ... Is 24:1 1110
The highways lie *w*, the wayfaring ... Is 33:8 8074
to generation it shall lie *w* ... Is 34:10 2717
have laid *w* all the nations ... Is 37:18 2717
w defenced cities into ruinous ... Is 37:26 7582
I will make *w* mountains and hills, ... Is 42:15 2717
they that made thee *w* shall go ... Is 49:17 2717
For thy *w* and thy desolate places, ... Is 49:19 2723
he will comfort all her *w* places ... Is 51:3 2723
ye *w* places of Jerusalem ... Is 52:9 2723
thee shall build the old *w* places ... Is 58:12 2723
and they shall repair the *w* cities ... Is 61:4 2721
our pleasant things are laid *w* ... Is 64:11 2723
yelled, and they made his land *w* ... Jer 2:15 8047
and thy cities shall be laid *w* ... Jer 4:7 5327
should this city be laid *w* ... Jer 27:17 2723
for Noph shall be *w* and desolate ... Jer 46:19 8047
a desolation, a reproach, a *w* ... Jer 49:13 2721
w and utterly destroy after them, ... Jer 50:21 2717
Moreover I will make thee *w* ... Eze 5:14 2723
the cities shall be laid *w* ... Eze 6:6 2717
that your altars may be laid *w* ... Eze 6:6 2717
are inhabited shall be laid *w* ... Eze 12:20 2717
and he laid *w* their cities ... Eze 19:7 2717
be replenished, now she is laid *w* ... Eze 26:2 2717
of Egypt shall be desolate and *w* ... Eze 29:9 2723
make the land of Egypt utterly *w* ... Eze 29:10 2723
w shall be desolate forty years ... Eze 29:12 2717
and I will make the land *w* ... Eze 30:12 8074
I will lay thy cities *w*, and thou ... Eze 35:4 2723
and the *w* and desolate and ruined ... Eze 36:35 2720
so shall the *w* cities be filled ... Eze 36:38 2720
Israel, which have been always *w* ... Eze 38:8 2723
He hath laid my vine *w*, and barked ... Joel 1:7 8047
of Israel shall be laid *w* ... Amos 7:9 2717
and they shall build the *w* cities ... Amos 9:14 8074
they shall *w* the land of Assyria ... Mic 5:6 7489
She is empty, and void, and *w* ... Nah 2:10 1110
thee, and say, Nineveh is laid *w* ... Nah 3:7 7703

I made their streets *w*, that none ... Zeph 3:6 2717
houses, and this house lie *w* ... Hag 1:4 2720
Because of mine house that is *w* ... Hag 1:9 2720
his heritage *w* for the dragons of ... Mal 1:3 8077
saying, To what purpose is this *w* ... Mt 26:8 *684*
Why was this *w* of the ointment ... Mk 14:4 *684*

WASTED {16}
carcases be *w* in the wilderness ... Num 14:33 8552
the Kenite shall be *w*, until ... Num 24:22 1197
of the men of war were *w* out from ... Deut 2:14 8552
And the barrel of meal *w* not ... 1Kin 17:16 3615
w the country of the children of ... 1Chr 20:1 7843
they that *w* us required of us ... Ps 137:3 8437
cities be *w* without inhabitant ... Is 6:11 7582
the sea, and the river shall be *w* ... Is 19:5 2717
those nations shall be utterly *w* ... Is 60:12 2717
and they are *w* and desolate, as at ... Jer 44:6 2723
midst of the cities that are *w* ... Eze 30:7 2717
The field is *w*, the land mourneth ... Joel 1:10 7703
for the corn is *w* ... Joel 1:10 7703
there *w* his substance with ... Lk 15:13 *1287*
unto him that he had *w* his goods ... Lk 16:1 *1287*
the church of God, and *w* it ... Gal 1:13 *4199*

WASTENESS {1}
trouble and distress, a day of *w* ... Zeph 1:15 7722

WASTER {2}
brother to him that is a great *w* ... Prov 18:9 7843
I have created the *w* to destroy ... Is 54:16 7843

WASTES {7}
And they shall build the old *w* ... Is 61:4 2723
thereof shall be perpetual *w* ... Jer 49:13 2723
they that inhabit those *w* of the ... Eze 33:24 2723
in the *w* shall fall by the sword ... Eze 33:27 2723
to the valleys, to the desolate *w* ... Eze 36:4 2723
and the *w* shall be builded ... Eze 36:10 2723
cities, and the *w* shall be builded ... Eze 36:33 2723

WASTETH {3}
But man dieth, and *w* away ... Job 14:10 2522
the destruction that *w* at noonday ... Ps 91:6 7736
He that *w* his father, and chaseth ... Prov 19:26 7703

WASTING {2}
w and destruction are in their ... Is 59:7 7701
w nor destruction within thy ... Is 60:18 7701

WATCH {61}
The LORD *w* between me and thee, ... Gen 31:49 6822
that in the morning *w* the LORD ... Ex 14:24 821
in the beginning of the middle *w* ... Judg 7:19 821
and they had but newly set the *w* ... Judg 7:19 8104
of the host in the morning *w* ... 1Sa 11:11 821
to *w* him, and to slay him in the ... 1Sa 19:11 8104
kept the *w* lifted up his eyes ... 2Sa 13:34 6822
of the *w* of the king's house ... 2Kin 11:5 4931
shall ye keep the *w* of the house ... 2Kin 11:6 4931
even they shall keep the *w* of the ... 2Kin 11:7 4931
the *w* tower in the wilderness ... 2Chr 20:24 4707
shall keep the *w* of the LORD ... 2Chr 23:6 4931
W ye, and keep them, until ye ... Ezr 8:29 8245
set a *w* against them day and night ... Neh 4:9 4929
of Jerusalem, every one in his *w* ... Neh 7:3 4929
that thou settest a *w* over me ... Job 7:12 4929
dost thou not *w* over my sin ... Job 14:16 8104
is past, and as a *w* in the night ... Ps 90:4 821
I *w*, and am as a sparrow alone ... Ps 102:7 8245
than they that *w* for the morning ... Ps 130:6 8104
than they that *w* for the morning ... Ps 130:6 8104
Set a *w*, O LORD, before my mouth ... Ps 141:3 8108
w in the watchtower, eat, drink ... Is 21:5 6822
all that *w* for iniquity are cut ... Is 29:20 8245
a leopard shall *w* over their ... Jer 5:6 8245
so will I *w* over them, to build, ... Jer 31:28 8245
I will *w* over them for evil, and ... Jer 44:27 8245
of Babylon, make the *w* strong ... Jer 51:12 4929
w the way, make thy loins strong, ... Nah 2:1 6822
I will stand upon my *w*, and set me ... Hab 2:1 4931
will *w* to see what he will say ... Hab 2:1 6822
in the fourth *w* of the night ... Mt 14:25 *5438*
W therefore ... Mt 24:42 *1127*
in what *w* the thief would come ... Mt 24:43 *5438*
W therefore, for ye know neither ... Mt 25:13 *1127*
tarry ye here, and *w* with me ... Mt 26:38 *1127*
could ye not *w* with me one hour ... Mt 26:40 *1127*
W and pray, that ye enter not into ... Mt 26:41 *1127*
said unto them, Ye have a *w* ... Mt 27:65 *2892*
sealing the stone, and setting a *w* ... Mt 27:66 *2892*
some of the *w* came into the city, ... Mt 28:11 *2892*
about the fourth *w* of the night ... Mk 6:48 *5438*
Take ye heed, *w* and pray ... Mk 13:33 *69*
and commanded the porter to *w* ... Mk 13:34 *1127*
W ye therefore ... Mk 13:35 *1127*
I say unto you I say unto all, *W* ... Mk 13:37 *1127*
tarry ye here, and *w* ... Mk 14:34 *1127*
couldest not thou *w* one hour ... Mk 14:37 *1127*
W ye and pray, lest ye enter into ... Mk 14:38 *1127*
keeping *w* over their flock by ... Lk 2:8 *5438*
if he shall come in the second *w* ... Lk 12:38 *5438*
or come in the third *w* ... Lk 12:38 *5438*
W ye therefore, and pray always, ... Lk 21:36 *69*
Therefore *w*, and remember, that by ... Acts 20:31 *1127*
W ye, stand fast in the faith, ... 1Cor 16:13 *1127*
w in the same with thanksgiving ... Col 4:2 *1127*
but let us *w* and be sober ... 1Th 5:6 *1127*
But *w* thou in all things, endure ... 2Ti 4:5 *3525*
for they *w* for your souls, as ... Heb 13:17 *69*
therefore sober, and *w* unto prayer ... 1Pet 4:7 *3525*
If therefore thou shalt not *w* ... Rev 3:3 *1127*

WATCHED {13}
they *w* the house to kill him ... Ps 59:*t* 8104
All my familiars *w* for my halting ... Jer 20:10 8104
that like as I have *w* over them ... Jer 31:28 8245
in our watching we have *w* for a ... Lam 4:17 6822
hath the LORD *w* upon the evil ... Dan 9:14 8245
thief would come, he would have *w* ... Mt 24:43 *1127*
And sitting down they *w* him there ... Mt 27:36 *5083*
And they *w* him, whether he would ... Mk 3:2 *3906*
And the scribes and Pharisees *w* him ... Lk 6:7 *3906*
thief would come, he would have *w* ... Lk 12:39 *1127*
the sabbath day, that they *w* him ... Lk 14:1 *3906*
And they *w* him, and sent forth ... Lk 20:20 *3906*
they *w* the gates day and night to ... Acts 9:24 *3906*

WATCHER {2}
head upon my bed, and, behold, a *w* ... Dan 4:13 5894
And whereas the king saw a *w* ... Dan 4:23 5894

WATCHERS {2}
that *w* come from a far country, ... Jer 4:16 5341
matter is by the decree of the *w* ... Dan 4:17 5894

WATCHES {5}
appoint *w* of the inhabitants of ... Neh 7:3 4931
were over against them in the *w* ... Neh 12:9 4931
meditate on thee in the night *w* ... Ps 63:6 821
Mine eyes prevent the night *w* ... Ps 119:148 821
in the beginning of the *w* pour ... Lam 2:19 821

WATCHETH {3}
The wicked *w* the righteous, and ... Ps 37:32 6822
it *w* for thee ... Eze 7:6 6974
Blessed is he that *w*, and keepeth ... Rev 16:15 *1127*

WATCHFUL {1}
Be *w*, and strengthen the things ... Rev 3:2 *1127*

WATCHING {6}
sat upon a seat by the wayside *w* ... 1Sa 4:13 6822
w daily at my gates, waiting at ... Prov 8:34 8245
in our *w* we have watched for a ... Lam 4:17 6822
w Jesus, saw the earthquake, and ... Mt 27:54 *5083*
lord when he cometh shall find *w* ... Lk 12:37 *1127*
w thereunto with all perseverance ... Eph 6:18 *69*

WATCHINGS {2}
in tumults, in labours, in *w* ... 2Cor 6:5 *70*
in *w* often, in hunger and thirst, ... 2Cor 11:27 *70*

WATCHMAN {18}
the *w* went up to the roof over ... 2Sa 18:24 6822
the *w* cried, and told the king ... 2Sa 18:25 6822
the *w* saw another man running ... 2Sa 18:26 6822
the *w* called unto the porter, and ... 2Sa 18:26 6822
the *w* said, Me thinketh the ... 2Sa 18:27 6822
there stood a *w* on the tower in ... 2Kin 9:17 6822
the *w* told, saying, The messenger ... 2Kin 9:18 6822
the *w* told, saying, He came even ... 2Kin 9:20 6822
city, the *w* waketh but in vain ... Ps 127:1 8104
Lord said unto me, Go, set a *w* ... Is 21:6 6822
He calleth to me out of Seir, *W* ... Is 21:11 8104
W, what of the night ... Is 21:11 8104
The *w* said, The morning cometh, ... Is 21:12 8104
I have made thee a *w* unto the ... Eze 3:17 6822
coasts, and set him for their *w* ... Eze 33:2 6822
But if the *w* see the sword come, ... Eze 33:6 6822
I have set thee a *w* unto the ... Eze 33:7 6822
The *w* of Ephraim was with my God ... Hos 9:8 6822

WATCHMAN'S {1}
will I require at the *w* hand ... Eze 33:6 6822

WATCHMEN {12}
the *w* of Saul in Gibeah of ... 1Sa 14:16 6822
tower of the *w* to the fenced city ... 2Kin 17:9 5341
tower of the *w* to the fenced city ... 2Kin 18:8 5341
The *w* that go about the city ... Song 3:3 8104
The *w* that went about the city ... Song 5:7 8104
Thy *w* shall lift up the voice ... Is 52:8 6822
His *w* are blind ... Is 56:10 6822
I have set *w* upon thy walls, O ... Is 62:6 8104
Also I set *w* over you, saying, ... Jer 6:17 6822
that the *w* upon the mount Ephraim ... Jer 31:6 5341
the watch strong, set up the *w* ... Jer 51:12 8104
the day of thy *w* and thy ... Mic 7:4 6822

WATCHTOWER {2}
Prepare the table, watch in the *w* ... Is 21:5 6844
upon the *w* in the daytime ... Is 21:8 4707

WATER {396}
went out of Eden to *w* the garden ... Gen 2:10 8248
a fountain of *w* in the wilderness ... Gen 16:7 4325
Let a little *w*, I pray you, be ... Gen 18:4 4325
and took bread, and a bottle of *w* ... Gen 21:14 4325
the *w* was spent in the bottle, and ... Gen 21:15 4325
her eyes, and she saw a well of *w* ... Gen 21:19 4325
went, and filled the bottle with *w* ... Gen 21:19 4325
Abimelech because of a well of *w* ... Gen 21:25 4325
of *w* at the time of the evening ... Gen 24:11 4325
time that women go out to draw *w* ... Gen 24:11
I stand here by the well of *w* ... Gen 24:13 4325
of the city come out to draw *w* ... Gen 24:13 4325
drink a little *w* of thy pitcher ... Gen 24:17 4325
I will draw *w* for thy camels also ... Gen 24:19 4325
ran again unto the well to draw *w* ... Gen 24:20 4325
w to wash his feet, and the men's ... Gen 24:32 4325
Behold, I stand by the well of *w* ... Gen 24:43 4325
the virgin cometh forth to draw *w* ... Gen 24:43
a little *w* of thy pitcher to ... Gen 24:43 4325
down unto the well, and drew *w* ... Gen 24:45 4325
Isaac digged again the wells of *w* ... Gen 26:18 4325
found there a well of springing *w* ... Gen 26:19 4325
herdmen, saying, The *w* is ours ... Gen 26:20 4325
and said unto him, We have found *w* ... Gen 26:32 4325

w ye the sheep, and go and feed	Gen 29:7	8248
then we *w* the sheep	Gen 29:8	8248
was empty, there was no *w* in it	Gen 37:24	4325
Joseph's house, and gave them *w*	Gen 43:24	4325
Unstable as *w*, thou shalt not	Gen 49:4	4325
Because I drew him out of the *w*	Ex 2:10	4325
and they came and drew *w*, and filled	Ex 2:16	
troughs to *w* their father's flock	Ex 2:16	8248
also drew *w* enough for us, and	Ex 2:19	
shalt take of the *w* of the river	Ex 4:9	4325
the *w* which thou takest out of	Ex 4:9	4325
lo, he goeth out unto the *w*	Ex 7:15	4325
to drink of the *w* of the river	Ex 7:18	4325
and upon all their pools of *w*	Ex 7:19	4325
not drink of the *w* of the river	Ex 7:21	4325
about the river for *w* to drink	Ex 7:24	4325
not drink of the *w* of the river	Ex 7:24	4325
lo, he cometh forth to the *w*	Ex 8:20	4325
it raw, nor sodden at all with *w*	Ex 12:9	4325
in the wilderness, and found no *w*	Ex 15:22	4325
where were twelve wells of *w*	Ex 15:27	4325
there was no *w* for the people to	Ex 17:1	4325
Give us *w* that we may drink	Ex 17:2	4325
the people thirsted there for *w*	Ex 17:3	4325
and there shall come *w* out of it	Ex 17:6	4325
that is in the *w* under the earth	Ex 20:4	4325
shall bless thy bread, and thy *w*	Ex 23:25	4325
and shalt wash them with *w*	Ex 29:4	4325
and thou shalt put *w* therein	Ex 30:18	4325
they shall wash with *w*, that	Ex 30:20	4325
powder, and strawed it upon the *w*	Ex 32:20	4325
neither eat bread, nor drink *w*	Ex 34:28	4325
the altar, and shalt put *w* therein	Ex 40:7	4325
congregation, and wash them with *w*	Ex 40:12	4325
put *w* there, to wash withal	Ex 40:30	4325
and his legs shall he wash in *w*	Lev 1:9	4325
the inwards and the legs with *w*	Lev 1:13	4325
be both scoured, and rinsed in *w*	Lev 6:28	4325
his sons, and washed them with *w*	Lev 8:6	4325
the inwards and the legs in *w*	Lev 8:21	4325
is done, it must be put into *w*	Lev 11:32	4325
that on which such *w* cometh shall	Lev 11:34	4325
pit, wherein there is plenty of *w*	Lev 11:36	4325
But if any *w* be put upon the seed	Lev 11:38	4325
an earthen vessel over running *w*	Lev 14:5	4325
was killed over the running *w*	Lev 14:6	4325
his hair, and wash himself in *w*	Lev 14:8	4325
also he shall wash his flesh in *w*	Lev 14:9	4325
an earthen vessel over running *w*	Lev 14:50	4325
slain bird, and in the running *w*	Lev 14:51	4325
the bird, and with the running *w*	Lev 14:52	4325
clothes, and bathe himself in *w*	Lev 15:5	4325
clothes, and bathe himself in *w*	Lev 15:6	4325
clothes, and bathe himself in *w*	Lev 15:7	4325
clothes, and bathe himself in *w*	Lev 15:8	4325
clothes, and bathe himself in *w*	Lev 15:10	4325
and hath not rinsed his hands in *w*	Lev 15:11	4325
clothes, and bathe himself in *w*	Lev 15:11	4325
of wood shall be rinsed in *w*	Lev 15:12	4325
and bathe his flesh in running *w*	Lev 15:13	4325
he shall wash all his flesh in *w*	Lev 15:16	4325
shall be washed with *w*, and be	Lev 15:17	4325
shall both bathe themselves in *w*	Lev 15:18	4325
clothes, and bathe himself in *w*	Lev 15:21	4325
clothes, and bathe himself in *w*	Lev 15:22	4325
clothes, and bathe himself in *w*	Lev 15:27	4325
shall he wash his flesh in *w*	Lev 16:4	4325
flesh with *w* in the holy place	Lev 16:24	4325
clothes, and bathe his flesh in *w*	Lev 16:26	4325
clothes, and bathe his flesh in *w*	Lev 16:28	4325
clothes, and bathe himself in *w*	Lev 17:15	4325
unless he wash his flesh with *w*	Lev 22:6	4325
take holy *w* in an earthen vessel	Num 5:17	4325
shall take, and put it into the *w*	Num 5:17	4325
bitter *w* that causeth the curse	Num 5:18	4325
bitter *w* that causeth the curse	Num 5:19	4325
this *w* that causeth the curse	Num 5:22	4325
blot them out with the bitter *w*	Num 5:23	4325
bitter *w* that causeth the curse	Num 5:24	4325
the *w* that causeth the curse	Num 5:24	4325
cause the woman to drink the *w*	Num 5:26	4325
he hath made her to drink the *w*	Num 5:27	4325
that the *w* that causeth the curse	Num 5:27	4325
Sprinkle *w* of purifying upon them	Num 8:7	4325
and he shall bathe his flesh in *w*	Num 19:7	4325
her shall wash his clothes in *w*	Num 19:8	4325
and bathe his flesh in *w*	Num 19:8	4325
of Israel for a *w* of separation	Num 19:9	4325
because the *w* of separation was	Num 19:13	4325
running *w* shall be put thereto in	Num 19:17	4325
take hyssop, and dip it in the *w*	Num 19:18	4325
clothes, and bathe himself in *w*	Num 19:19	4325
the *w* of separation hath not been	Num 19:20	4325
that he that sprinkleth the *w* of	Num 19:21	4325
he that toucheth the *w* of	Num 19:21	4325
And there was no *w* for the	Num 20:2	4325
neither is there any *w* to drink	Num 20:5	4325
and it shall give forth his *w*	Num 20:8	4325
forth to them *w* out of the rock	Num 20:8	4325
we fetch you *w* out of this rock	Num 20:10	4325
the *w* came out abundantly, and the	Num 20:11	4325
This is the *w* of Meribah	Num 20:13	4325
we drink of the *w* of the wells	Num 20:17	4325
if I and my cattle drink of thy *w*	Num 20:19	4325
my word at the *w* of Meribah	Num 20:24	4325
no bread, neither is there any *w*	Num 21:5	4325
together, and I will give them *w*	Num 21:16	4325
He shall pour the *w* out of his	Num 24:7	4325
me at the *w* before their eyes	Num 27:14	4325
that is the *w* of Meribah in	Num 27:14	4325
purified with the *w* of separation	Num 31:23	4325
ye shall make go through the *w*	Num 31:23	4325
Elim were twelve fountains of *w*	Num 33:9	4325
where was no *w* for the people to	Num 33:14	4325
also buy *w* of them for money	Deut 2:6	4325
give me *w* for money, that I may	Deut 2:28	4325
good land, a land of brooks of *w*	Deut 8:7	4325
and drought, where there was no *w*	Deut 8:15	4325
who brought thee forth *w* out of	Deut 8:15	4325
neither did eat bread nor drink *w*	Deut 9:9	4325
neither eat bread, nor drink *w*	Deut 9:18	4325
how he made the *w* of the Red sea	Deut 11:4	4325
drinketh *w* of the rain of heaven	Deut 11:11	4325
shall pour it upon the earth as *w*	Deut 12:16	4325
shalt pour it upon the earth as *w*	Deut 12:24	4325
pour it upon the ground as *w*	Deut 15:23	4325
with *w* in the way, when ye came	Deut 23:4	4325
on, he shall wash himself with *w*	Deut 23:11	4325
thy wood unto the drawer of thy *w*	Deut 29:11	4325
up the *w* of the Red sea for you	Josh 2:10	4325
to the brink of the *w* of Jordan	Josh 3:8	4325
were dipped in the brim of the *w*	Josh 3:15	4325
the people melted, and became as *w*	Josh 7:5	4325
drawers of *w* unto all the	Josh 9:21	4325
drawers of *w* for the house of my	Josh 9:23	4325
drawers of *w* for the congregation	Josh 9:27	4325
the fountain of the *w* of Nephtoah	Josh 15:9	4325
give me also springs of *w*	Josh 15:19	4325
unto the *w* of Jericho on the east	Josh 16:1	4325
give me also springs of *w*	Judg 1:15	4325
I pray thee, a little *w* to drink	Judg 4:19	4325
the clouds also dropped *w*	Judg 5:4	4325
in the places of drawing *w*	Judg 5:11	4325
He asked *w*, and she gave him milk	Judg 5:25	4325
of the fleece, a bowl full of *w*	Judg 6:38	4325
bring them down unto the *w*	Judg 7:4	4325
down the people unto the *w*	Judg 7:5	4325
lappeth of the *w* with his tongue	Judg 7:5	4325
down upon their knees to drink *w*	Judg 7:6	4325
the jaw, and there came *w* thereout	Judg 15:19	4325
together to Mizpeh, and drew *w*	1Sa 7:6	4325
young maidens going out to draw *w*	1Sa 9:11	4325
I then take my bread, and my *w*	1Sa 25:11	4325
at his bolster, and the cruse of *w*	1Sa 26:11	4325
the cruse of *w* from Saul's	1Sa 26:12	4325
the cruse of *w* that was at his	1Sa 26:16	4325
and they made him drink *w*	1Sa 30:11	4325
eaten no bread, nor drunk any *w*	1Sa 30:12	4325
are as *w* spilt on the ground,	2Sa 14:14	4325
They be gone over the brook of *w*	2Sa 17:20	4325
Arise, and pass quickly over the *w*	2Sa 17:21	4325
the beginning of harvest until *w*	2Sa 21:10	4325
the *w* of the well of Beth-lehem	2Sa 23:15	4325
drew *w* out of the well of	2Sa 23:16	4325
bread nor drink *w* in this place	1Kin 13:8	4325
saying, Eat no bread, nor drink *w*	1Kin 13:9	4325
drink *w* with thee in this place	1Kin 13:16	4325
eat no bread nor drink *w* there	1Kin 13:17	4325
that he may eat bread and drink *w*	1Kin 13:18	4325
bread in his house, and drank *w*	1Kin 13:19	4325
drunk *w* in the place, of the	1Kin 13:22	4325
thee, Eat no bread, and drink no *w*	1Kin 13:22	4325
as a reed is shaken in the *w*	1Kin 14:15	4325
a little *w* in a vessel, that I	1Kin 17:10	4325
cave, and fed them with bread and *w*	1Kin 18:4	4325
the land, unto all fountains of *w*	1Kin 18:5	4325
cave, and fed them with bread and *w*	1Kin 18:13	4325
and said, Fill four barrels with *w*	1Kin 18:33	4325
the *w* ran round about the altar	1Kin 18:35	4325
he filled the trench also with *w*	1Kin 18:35	4325
licked up the *w* that was in the	1Kin 18:38	4325
and a cruse of *w* at his head	1Kin 19:6	4325
with *w* of affliction, until I	1Kin 22:27	4325
but the *w* is naught, and the	2Kin 2:19	4325
and there was no *w* for the host	2Kin 3:9	4325
which poured *w* on the hands of	2Kin 3:11	4325
valley shall be filled with *w*	2Kin 3:17	4325
good tree, and stop all wells of *w*	2Kin 3:19	4325
there came *w* by the way of Edom,	2Kin 3:20	4325
and the country was filled with *w*	2Kin 3:20	4325
and the sun shone upon the *w*	2Kin 3:22	4325
the Moabites saw the *w* on the	2Kin 3:22	4325
they stopped all the wells of *w*	2Kin 3:25	4325
beam, the ax head fell into the *w*	2Kin 6:5	4325
w before them, that they may eat	2Kin 6:22	4325
a thick cloth, and dipped it in *w*	2Kin 8:15	4325
brought *w* into the city, are they	2Kin 20:20	4325
the *w* of the well of Beth-lehem	1Chr 11:17	4325
drew *w* out of the well of	1Chr 11:18	4325
with *w* of affliction, until I	2Chr 18:26	4325
of Assyria come, and find much *w*	2Chr 32:4	4325
he did eat no bread, nor drink *w*	Ezr 10:6	4325
the *w* gate toward the east	Neh 3:26	4325
street that was before the *w* gate	Neh 8:1	4325
the *w* gate from the morning until	Neh 8:3	4325
and in the street of the *w* gate	Neh 8:16	4325
broughtest forth *w* for them out	Neh 9:15	4325
gavest them *w* for their thirst	Neh 9:20	4325
even unto the *w* gate eastward	Neh 12:37	4325
of Israel with bread and with *w*	Neh 13:2	4325
can the flag grow without *w*	Job 8:11	4325
If I wash myself with snow *w*	Job 9:30	1119
the scent of *w* it will bud	Job 14:9	4325
which drinketh iniquity like *w*	Job 15:16	4325
Thou hast not given *w* to the	Job 22:7	4325
who drinketh up scorning like *w*	Job 34:7	4325
he maketh small the drops of *w*	Job 36:27	4325
a tree planted by the rivers of *w*	Ps 1:3	4325
I *w* my couch with my tears	Ps 6:6	4529
I am poured out like *w*, and all my	Ps 22:14	4325
hart panteth after the *w* brooks	Ps 42:1	4325
and thirsty land, where no *w* is	Ps 63:1	4325
river of God, which is full of *w*	Ps 65:9	4325
we went through fire and through *w*	Ps 66:12	4325
as showers that *w* the earth	Ps 72:6	2222
The clouds poured out *w*	Ps 77:17	4325
shed like *w* round about Jerusalem	Ps 79:3	4325
came round about me daily like *w*	Ps 88:17	4325
the wilderness into a standing *w*	Ps 107:35	4325
it come into his bowels like *w*	Ps 109:18	4325
turned the rock into a standing *w*	Ps 114:8	4325
no fountains abounding with *w*	Prov 8:24	4325
is as when one letteth out *w*	Prov 17:14	4325
the heart of man is like deep *w*	Prov 20:5	4325
of the LORD, as the rivers of *w*	Prov 21:1	4325
be thirsty, give him *w* to drink	Prov 25:21	4325
As in *w* face answereth to face,	Prov 27:19	4325
earth that is not filled with *w*	Prov 30:16	4325
I made me pools of *w*	Eccl 2:6	4325
to *w* therewith the wood that	Eccl 2:6	8248
dross, thy wine mixed with *w*	Is 1:22	4325
and as a garden that hath no *w*	Is 1:30	4325
of bread, and the whole stay of *w*	Is 3:1	4325
with joy shall ye draw *w* out of	Is 12:3	4325
for the bittern, and pools of *w*	Is 14:23	4325
I will *w* thee with my tears, O	Is 16:9	7301
brought *w* to him that was thirsty	Is 21:14	4325
walls for the *w* of the old pool	Is 22:11	4325
I will *w* it every moment	Is 27:3	8248
or to take *w* withal out of the	Is 30:14	4325
the *w* of affliction, yet shall	Is 30:20	4325
as rivers of *w* in a dry place, as	Is 32:2	4325
and the thirsty land springs of *w*	Is 35:7	4325
I have digged, and drunk *w*	Is 37:25	4325
When the poor and needy seek *w*	Is 41:17	4325
make the wilderness a pool of *w*	Is 41:18	4325
and the dry land springs of *w*	Is 41:18	4325
For I will pour *w* upon him that	Is 44:3	4325
as willows by the *w* courses	Is 44:4	4325
he drinketh no *w*, and is faint	Is 44:12	4325
springs of *w* shall he guide them	Is 49:10	4325
stinketh, because there is no *w*	Is 50:2	4325
garden, and like a spring of *w*	Is 58:11	4325
arm, dividing the *w* before them	Is 63:12	4325
cisterns, that can hold no *w*	Jer 2:13	4325
given us *w* of gall to drink,	Jer 8:14	4325
give them *w* of gall to drink	Jer 9:15	4325
thy loins, and put it not in *w*	Jer 13:1	4325
came to the pits, and found no *w*	Jer 14:3	4325
and make them drink the *w* of gall	Jer 23:15	4325
And in the dungeon there was no *w*	Jer 38:6	4325
eye, mine eye runneth down with *w*	Lam 1:16	4325
pour out thine heart like *w*	Lam 2:19	4325
of *w* for the destruction of the	Lam 3:48	4325
We have drunken our *w* for money	Lam 5:4	4325
shalt drink also *w* by measure	Eze 4:11	4325
and they shall drink *w* by measure	Eze 4:16	4325
That they may want bread and *w*	Eze 4:17	4325
and all knees shall be weak as *w*	Eze 7:17	4325
drink thy *w* with trembling and	Eze 12:18	4325
drink their *w* with astonishment,	Eze 12:19	4325
thou washed in *w* to supple thee	Eze 16:4	4325
Then washed I thee with *w*	Eze 16:9	4325
that he might *w* it by the furrows	Eze 17:7	8248
and all knees shall be weak as *w*	Eze 21:7	4325
set it on, and also pour *w* into it	Eze 24:3	4325
and thy dust in the midst of the *w*	Eze 26:12	4325
in their height, all that drink *w*	Eze 31:14	4325
best of Lebanon, all that drink *w*	Eze 31:16	4325
I will also *w* with thy blood the	Eze 32:6	8248
will I sprinkle clean *w* upon you	Eze 36:25	4325
us pulse to eat, and *w* to drink	Dan 1:12	4325
that give me my bread and my *w*	Hos 2:5	4325
out my wrath upon them like *w*	Hos 5:10	4325
is cut off as the foam upon the *w*	Hos 10:7	4325
shall *w* the valley of Shittim	Joel 3:18	8248
unto one city, to drink *w*	Amos 4:8	4325
of bread, nor a thirst for *w*	Amos 8:11	4325
let them not feed, nor drink *w*	Jonah 3:7	4325
is of old like a pool of *w*	Nah 2:8	4325
overflowing of the *w* passed by	Hab 3:10	4325
out of the pit wherein is no *w*	Zec 9:11	4325
you with *w* unto repentance	Mt 3:11	*5204*
went up straightway out of the *w*	Mt 3:16	*5204*
w only in the name of a disciple	Mt 10:42	
bid me come unto thee on the *w*	Mt 14:28	*5204*
of the ship, he walked on the *w*	Mt 14:29	*5204*
into the fire, and oft into the *w*	Mt 17:15	*5204*
a tumult was made, he took *w*	Mt 27:24	*5204*
I indeed have baptized you with *w*	Mk 1:8	*5204*
coming up out of the *w*, he saw	Mk 1:10	*5204*
a cup of *w* to drink in my name	Mk 9:41	*5204*
you a man bearing a pitcher of *w*	Mk 14:13	*5204*
all, I indeed baptize you with *w*	Lk 3:16	*5204*
thou gavest me no *w* for my feet	Lk 7:44	*5204*
and they were filled with *w*	Lk 8:23	
the wind and the raging of the *w*	Lk 8:24	*5204*
he commandeth even the winds and *w*	Lk 8:25	*5204*
dip the tip of his finger in *w*	Lk 16:24	*5204*
meet you, bearing a pitcher of *w*	Lk 22:10	*5204*
them, saying, I baptize with *w*	Jn 1:26	*5204*
am I come baptizing with *w*	Jn 1:31	*5204*
he that sent me to baptize with *w*	Jn 1:33	*5204*
them, Fill the waterpots with *w*	Jn 2:7	*5204*

tasted the *w* that was made wine ... Jn 2:9 *5204*
servants which drew the *w* knew ... Jn 2:9 *5204*
thee, Except a man be born of *w* ... Jn 3:5 *5204*
because there was much *w* there ... Jn 3:23 *5204*
a woman of Samaria to draw *w* ... Jn 4:7 *5204*
he would have given thee living *w* ... Jn 4:10 *5204*
then hast thou that living *w* ... Jn 4:11 *5204*
of this *w* shall thirst again ... Jn 4:13 *5204*
the *w* that I shall give him shall ... Jn 4:14 *5204*
but the *w* that I shall give him ... Jn 4:14 *5204*
w springing up into everlasting ... Jn 4:14 *5204*
unto him, Sir, give me this *w* ... Jn 4:15 *5204*
Galilee, where he made the *w* wine ... Jn 4:46 *5204*
waiting for the moving of the *w* ... Jn 5:3 *5204*
into the pool, and troubled the *w* ... Jn 5:4 *5204*
after the troubling of the *w* ... Jn 5:4 *5204*
when the *w* is troubled, to put me ... Jn 5:7 *5204*
shall flow rivers of living *w* ... Jn 7:38 *5204*
that he poureth *w* into a bason ... Jn 13:5 *5204*
came there out blood and *w* ... Jn 19:34 *5204*
For John truly baptized with *w* ... Acts 1:5 *5204*
way, they came unto a certain *w* ... Acts 8:36 *5204*
the eunuch said, See, here is *w* ... Acts 8:36 *5204*
and they went down both into the *w* ... Acts 8:38 *5204*
they were come up out of the *w* ... Acts 8:39 *5204*
Can any man forbid *w*, that these ... Acts 10:47 *5204*
said, John indeed baptized with *w* ... Acts 11:16 *5204*
with the washing of *w* by the word ... Eph 5:26 *5204*
Drink no longer *w*, but use a ... 1Ti 5:23 *5202*
of calves and of goats, with *w* ... Heb 9:19 *5204*
and our bodies washed with pure *w* ... Heb 10:22 *5204*
forth at the same place sweet *w* ... Jas 3:11
can no fountain both yield salt *w* ... Jas 3:12 *5204*
is, eight souls were saved by *w* ... 1Pet 3:20 *5204*
These are wells without *w* ... 2Pet 2:17 *504*
out of the *w* and in the *w* ... 2Pet 3:5 *5204*
then was, being overflowed with *w* ... 2Pet 3:6 *5204*
This is he that came by *w* ... 1Jn 5:6 *5204*
not by *w* only, but by *w* ... 1Jn 5:6 *5204*
in earth, the spirit, and the *w* ... 1Jn 5:8 *5204*
clouds they are without *w* ... Jude 12 *504*
w as a flood after the woman ... Rev 12:15 *5204*
the *w* thereof was dried up, that ... Rev 16:12 *5204*
fountain of the *w* of life freely ... Rev 21:6 *5204*
me a pure river of *w* of life ... Rev 22:1 *5204*
let him take the *w* of life freely ... Rev 22:17 *5204*

WATERCOURSE {2}
also stopped the upper *w* of Gihon . 2Chr 32:30 4161,4325
Who hath divided a *w* for the ... Job 38:25 8585

WATERED {11}
w the whole face of the ground ... Gen 2:6 8248
that it was well *w* every where ... Gen 13:10 4945
of that well they *w* the flocks ... Gen 29:2 8248
w the sheep, and put the stone ... Gen 29:3 8248
w the flock of Laban his mother's ... Gen 29:10 8248
and helped them, and *w* their flock ... Ex 2:17 8248
enough for us, and *w* the flock ... Ex 2:19 8248
watereth shall be *w* also himself ... Prov 11:25 3384
and thou shalt be like a *w* garden ... Is 58:11 7302
their soul shall be as a *w* garden ... Jer 31:12 7302
I have planted, Apollos *w* ... 1Cor 3:6 *4222*

WATEREDST {1}
w it with thy foot, as a garden ... Deut 11:10 8248

WATEREST {2}
Thou visitest the earth, and *w* it ... Ps 65:9 7783
Thou *w* the ridges thereof ... Ps 65:10 7301

WATERETH {5}
He *w* the hills from his chambers ... Ps 104:13 8248
he that *w* shall be watered also ... Prov 11:25 7301
but *w* the earth, and maketh it ... Is 55:10 7301
any thing, neither he that *w* ... 1Cor 3:7 *4222*
planteth and he that *w* are one ... 1Cor 3:8 *4222*

WATERFLOOD {1}
Let not the *w* overflow me ... Ps 69:15 7641,4325

WATERING {3}
flocks in the gutters in the *w* ... Gen 30:38 4325
Also by *w* he wearieth the thick ... Job 37:11 7377
the stall, and lead him away to *w* ... Lk 13:15 *4222*

WATERPOT {1}
The woman then left her *w* ... Jn 4:28 *5201*

WATERPOTS {2}
were set there six *w* of stone ... Jn 2:6 *5201*
unto them, Fill the *w* with water ... Jn 2:7 *5201*

WATERS {287}
God moved upon the face of the *w* ... Gen 1:2 4325
a firmament in the midst of the *w* ... Gen 1:6 4325
it divide the *w* from the *w* ... Gen 1:6 4325
divided the *w* which were under ... Gen 1:7 4325
under the firmament from the *w* ... Gen 1:7 4325
Let the *w* under the heaven be ... Gen 1:9 4325
together of the *w* called he Seas ... Gen 1:10 4325
Let the *w* bring forth abundantly ... Gen 1:20 4325
which the *w* brought forth ... Gen 1:21 4325
fill the *w* in the seas, and let ... Gen 1:22 4325
bring a flood of *w* upon the earth ... Gen 6:17 4325
the flood of *w* was upon the earth ... Gen 7:6 4325
because of the *w* of the flood ... Gen 7:7 4325
that the *w* of the flood were upon ... Gen 7:10 4325
the *w* increased, and bare up the ... Gen 7:17 4325
And the *w* prevailed, and were ... Gen 7:18 4325
ark went upon the face of the *w* ... Gen 7:18 4325
the *w* prevailed exceedingly upon ... Gen 7:19 4325
cubits upward did the *w* prevail ... Gen 7:20 4325
the *w* prevailed upon the earth an ... Gen 7:24 4325
over the earth, and the *w* asswaged ... Gen 8:1 4325
the *w* returned from off the earth ... Gen 8:3 4325
and fifty days the *w* were abated ... Gen 8:3 4325
the *w* decreased continually until ... Gen 8:5 4325
until the *w* were dried up from ... Gen 8:7 4325
to see if the *w* were abated from ... Gen 8:8 4325
for the *w* were on the face of the ... Gen 8:9 4325
so Noah knew that the *w* were ... Gen 8:11 4325
the *w* were dried up from off the ... Gen 8:13 4325
off any more by the *w* of a flood ... Gen 9:11 4325
the *w* shall no more become a ... Gen 9:15 4325
upon the *w* which are in the river ... Ex 7:17 4325
thine hand upon the *w* of Egypt ... Ex 7:19 4325
smote the *w* that were in the ... Ex 7:20 4325
all the *w* that were in the river ... Ex 7:20 4325
out his hand over the *w* of Egypt ... Ex 8:6 4325
dry land, and the *w* were divided ... Ex 14:21 4325
the *w* were a wall unto them on ... Ex 14:22 4325
that the *w* may come again upon ... Ex 14:26 4325
the *w* returned, and covered the ... Ex 14:28 4325
the *w* were a wall unto them on ... Ex 14:29 4325
the *w* were gathered together ... Ex 15:8 4325
they sank as lead in the mighty *w* ... Ex 15:10 4325
again the *w* of the sea upon them ... Ex 15:19 4325
could not drink of the *w* of Marah ... Ex 15:23 4325
which when he had cast into the *w* ... Ex 15:25 4325
the *w* were made sweet ... Ex 15:25 4325
and they encamped there by the *w* ... Ex 15:27 4325
ye eat of all that are in the *w* ... Lev 11:9 4325
hath fins and scales in the *w* ... Lev 11:9 4325
rivers, of all that move in the *w* ... Lev 11:10 4325
living thing which is in the *w* ... Lev 11:10 4325
hath no fins nor scales in the *w* ... Lev 11:12 4325
creature that moveth in the *w* ... Lev 11:46 4325
not drink of the *w* of the well ... Num 21:22 4325
and as cedar trees beside the *w* ... Num 24:6 4325
and his seed shall be in many *w* ... Num 24:7 4325
is in the *w* beneath the earth ... Deut 4:18 4325
is in the *w* beneath the earth ... Deut 5:8 4325
to Jotbath, a land of rivers of *w* ... Deut 10:7 4325
eat of all that are in the *w* ... Deut 14:9 4325
Israel at the *w* of Meribah-kadesh ... Deut 32:51 4325
didst strive at the *w* of Meribah ... Deut 33:8 4325
shall rest in the *w* of Jordan ... Josh 3:13 4325
that the *w* of Jordan shall be cut ... Josh 3:13 4325
the *w* that come down from above ... Josh 3:13 4325
That the *w* which came down from ... Josh 3:16 4325
That the *w* of Jordan were cut off ... Josh 4:7 4325
the *w* of Jordan were cut off ... Josh 4:7 4325
that the *w* of Jordan returned ... Josh 4:18 4325
the *w* of Jordan from before you ... Josh 4:23 4325
the *w* of Jordan from before the ... Josh 5:1 4325
together at the *w* of Merom ... Josh 11:5 4325
them by the *w* of Merom suddenly ... Josh 11:7 4325
passed toward the *w* of En-shemesh ... Josh 15:7 4325
out to the well of *w* of Nephtoah ... Josh 18:15 4325
in Taanach by the *w* of Megiddo ... Judg 5:19 4325
before them the *w* unto Beth-barah ... Judg 7:24 4325
took the *w* unto Beth-barah and ... Judg 7:24 4325
before me, as the breach of *w* ... 2Sa 5:20 4325
and have taken the city of *w* ... 2Sa 12:27 4325
pavilions round about him, dark *w* ... 2Sa 22:12 4325
he drew me out of many *w* ... 2Sa 22:17 4325
it together, and smote the *w* ... 2Kin 2:8 4325
fell from him, and smote the *w* ... 2Kin 2:14 4325
and when he also had smitten the *w* ... 2Kin 2:14 4325
forth unto the spring of the *w* ... 2Kin 2:21 4325
the LORD, I have healed these *w* ... 2Kin 2:21 4325
So the *w* were healed unto this ... 2Kin 2:22 4325
better than all the *w* of Israel ... 2Kin 5:12 4325
ye every one the *w* of his cistern ... 2Kin 18:31 4325
I have digged and drunk strange *w* ... 2Kin 19:24 4325
hand like the breaking forth of *w* ... 1Chr 14:11 4325
his mighty men to stop the *w* of ... 2Chr 32:3 4325
as a stone into the mighty *w* ... Neh 9:11 4325
are poured out like the *w* ... Job 3:24 4325
sendeth *w* upon the fields ... Job 5:10 4325
remember it as *w* that pass away ... Job 11:16 4325
Behold, he withholdeth the *w* ... Job 12:15 4325
As the *w* fail from the sea, and ... Job 14:11 4325
The *w* wear the stones ... Job 14:19 4325
and abundance of *w* cover thee ... Job 22:11 4325
He is swift as the *w* ... Job 24:18 4325
and heat consume the snow *w* ... Job 24:19 4325
are formed from under the *w* ... Job 26:5 4325
He bindeth up the *w* in his thick ... Job 26:8 4325
hath compassed the *w* with bounds ... Job 26:10 4325
Terrors take hold on him as *w* ... Job 27:20 4325
even the *w* forgotten of the foot ... Job 28:4 4325
and he weigheth the *w* by measure ... Job 28:25 4325
My root was spread out by the *w* ... Job 29:19 4325
me as a wide breaking in of *w* ... Job 30:14 4325
breadth of the *w* is straitened ... Job 37:10 4325
for the overflowing of *w*, or a ... Job 38:25 4325
The *w* are hid as with a stone, and ... Job 38:30 4325
abundance of *w* may cover thee ... Job 38:34 4325
round about him were dark *w* ... Ps 18:11 4325
Then the channels of *w* were seen ... Ps 18:15 4325
took me, he drew me out of many *w* ... Ps 18:16 4325
he leadeth me beside the still *w* ... Ps 23:2 4325
voice of the LORD is upon the *w* ... Ps 29:3 4325
the LORD is upon many *w* ... Ps 29:3 4325
w they shall not come nigh unto ... Ps 32:6 4325
He gathereth the *w* of the sea ... Ps 33:7 4325
Though the *w* thereof roar and be ... Ps 46:3 4325
away as *w* which run continually ... Ps 58:7 4325
for the *w* are come in unto my ... Ps 69:1 4325
I am come into deep *w*, where the ... Ps 69:2 4325
hate me, and out of the deep *w* ... Ps 69:14 4325
w of a full cup are wrung out to ... Ps 73:10 4325
the heads of the dragons in the *w* ... Ps 74:13 4325
The *w* saw thee, O God, the *w* ... Ps 77:16 4325
sea, and thy path in the great *w* ... Ps 77:19 4325
he made the *w* to stand as an heap ... Ps 78:13 4325
caused *w* to run down like rivers ... Ps 78:16 4325
that the *w* gushed out, and the ... Ps 78:20 4325
I proved thee at the *w* of Meribah ... Ps 81:7 4325
mightier than the noise of many *w* ... Ps 93:4 4325
beams of his chambers in the *w* ... Ps 104:3 4325
the *w* stood above the mountains ... Ps 104:6 4325
He turned their *w* into blood ... Ps 105:29 4325
the rock, and the *w* gushed out ... Ps 105:41 4325
the *w* covered their enemies ... Ps 106:11 4325
him also at the *w* of strife ... Ps 106:32 4325
that do business in great *w* ... Ps 107:23 4325
the flint into a fountain of *w* ... Ps 114:8 4325
Rivers of *w* run down mine eyes, ... Ps 119:136 4325
Then the *w* had overwhelmed us, ... Ps 124:4 4325
Then the proud *w* had gone over ... Ps 124:5 4325
out the earth above the *w* ... Ps 136:6 4325
me, and deliver me out of great *w* ... Ps 144:7 4325
his wind to blow, and the *w* flow ... Ps 147:18 4325
ye *w* that be above the heavens ... Ps 148:4 4325
Drink *w* out of thine own cistern, ... Prov 5:15 4325
running *w* out of thine own well ... Prov 5:15
rivers of *w* in the streets ... Prov 5:16 4325
that the *w* should not pass his ... Prov 8:29 4325
Stolen *w* are sweet, and bread ... Prov 9:17 4325
of a man's mouth are as deep *w* ... Prov 18:4 4325
As cold *w* to a thirsty soul, so ... Prov 25:25 4325
who hath bound the *w* in a garment ... Prov 30:4 4325
Cast thy bread upon the *w* ... Eccl 11:1 4325
of gardens, a well of living *w* ... Song 4:15 4325
eyes of doves by the rivers of *w* ... Song 5:12 4325
Many *w* cannot quench love, ... Song 8:7 4325
the *w* of Shiloah that go softly ... Is 8:6 4325
up upon them the *w* of the river ... Is 8:7 4325
the LORD, as the *w* cover the sea ... Is 11:9 4325
For the *w* of Nimrim shall be ... Is 15:6 4325
For the *w* of Dimon shall be full ... Is 15:9 4325
like the rushing of mighty *w* ... Is 17:12 4325
rush like the rushing of many *w* ... Is 17:13 4325
vessels of bulrushes upon the *w* ... Is 18:2 4325
the *w* shall fail from the sea, and ... Is 19:5 4325
nets upon the *w* shall languish ... Is 19:8 4325
together the *w* of the lower pool ... Is 22:9 4325
by great *w* the seed of Sihor, the ... Is 23:3 4325
a flood of mighty *w* overflowing ... Is 28:2 4325
the *w* shall overflow the hiding ... Is 28:17 4325
streams of *w* in the day of the ... Is 30:25 4325
are ye that sow beside all *w* ... Is 32:20 4325
his *w* shall be sure ... Is 33:16 4325
the wilderness shall *w* break out ... Is 35:6 4325
one the *w* of his own cistern ... Is 36:16 4325
Who hath measured the *w* in the ... Is 40:12 4325
When thou passest through the *w* ... Is 43:2 4325
sea, and a path in the mighty *w* ... Is 43:16 4325
because I give *w* in the ... Is 43:20 4325
come forth out of the *w* of Judah ... Is 48:1 4325
he caused the *w* to flow out of ... Is 48:21 4325
rock also, and the *w* gushed out ... Is 48:21 4325
the sea, the *w* of the great deep ... Is 51:10 4325
this is as the *w* of Noah unto me ... Is 54:9 4325
for as I have sworn that the *w* of ... Is 54:9 4325
that thirsteth, come ye to the *w* ... Is 55:1 4325
whose *w* cast up mire and dirt ... Is 57:20 4325
spring of water, whose *w* fail not ... Is 58:11 4325
the fire causeth the *w* to boil ... Is 64:2 4325
me the fountain of living *w* ... Jer 2:13 4325
of Egypt, to drink the *w* of Sihor ... Jer 2:18 4325
to drink the *w* of the river ... Jer 2:18 4325
As a fountain casteth out her *w* ... Jer 6:7 4325
Oh that my head were *w*, and mine ... Jer 9:1 4325
and our eyelids gush out with *w* ... Jer 9:18 4325
a multitude of *w* in the heavens ... Jer 10:13 4325
sent their little ones to the *w* ... Jer 14:3 4325
me as a liar, and as *w* that fail ... Jer 15:18 4325
be as a tree planted by the *w* ... Jer 17:8 4325
LORD, the fountain of living *w* ... Jer 17:13 4325
or shall the cold flowing *w* that ... Jer 18:14 4325
the rivers of *w* in a straight way ... Jer 31:9 4325
by the great *w* that are in Gibeon ... Jer 41:12 4325
whose *w* are moved as the rivers ... Jer 46:7 4325
his *w* are moved like the rivers ... Jer 46:8 4325
w rise up out of the north, and ... Jer 47:2 4325
for the *w* also of Nimrim shall be ... Jer 48:34 4325
A drought is upon her *w* ... Jer 50:38 4325
O thou that dwellest upon many *w* ... Jer 51:13 4325
a multitude of *w* in the heavens ... Jer 51:16 4325
her waves do roar like great *w* ... Jer 51:55 4325
W flowed over mine head ... Lam 3:54 4325
wings, like the noise of great *w* ... Eze 1:24 4325
he placed it by great *w*, and set ... Eze 17:5 4325
planted in a good soil by great *w* ... Eze 17:8 4325
in thy blood, planted by the *w* ... Eze 19:10 4325
of branches by reason of many *w* ... Eze 19:10 4325
thee, and great *w* shall cover thee ... Eze 26:19 4325
have brought thee into great *w* ... Eze 27:26 4325
depths of the *w* thy merchandise ... Eze 27:34 4325
The *w* made him great, the deep ... Eze 31:4 4325
because of the multitude of *w* ... Eze 31:5 4325
for his root was by great *w* ... Eze 31:7 4325
the *w* exalt themselves for their ... Eze 31:14 4325
and the great *w* were stayed ... Eze 31:15 4325
and troubledst the *w* with thy feet ... Eze 32:2 4325
thereof from beside the great *w* ... Eze 32:13 4325

Then will I make their *w* deep Eze 32:14 4325
and to have drunk of the deep *w* Eze 34:18 4325
voice was like a noise of many *w* Eze 43:2 4325
w issued out from under the Eze 47:1 4325
the *w* came down from under from Eze 47:1 4325
there ran out *w* on the right side Eze 47:2 4325
and he brought me through the *w* Eze 47:3 4325
the *w* were to the ancles Eze 47:3 4325
and brought me through the *w* Eze 47:4 4325
the *w* were to the knees Eze 47:4 4325
the *w* were to the loins Eze 47:4 4325
for the *w* were risen Eze 47:5 4325
w to swim in, a river that could Eze 47:5 4325
These *w* issue out toward the east Eze 47:8 4325
the sea, the *w* shall be healed Eze 47:8 4325
because these *w* shall come Eze 47:9 4325
because their *w* they issued Eze 47:12 4325
even to the *w* of strife in Kadesh Eze 47:19 4325
unto the *w* of strife in Kadesh Eze 48:28 4325
which was upon the *w* of the river Dan 12:6 4325
which was upon the *w* of the river Dan 12:7 4325
for the rivers of *w* are dried up Joel 1:20 4325
rivers of Judah shall flow with *w* Joel 3:18 4325
that calleth for the *w* of the sea Amos 5:8 4325
But let judgment run down as *w* Amos 5:24 4325
that calleth for the *w* of the sea Amos 9:6 4325
The *w* compassed me about, even to Jonah 2:5 4325
as the *w* that are poured down a Mic 1:4 4325
that had the *w* round about it, Nah 3:8 4325
Draw thee *w* for the siege, Nah 3:14 4325
the LORD, as the *w* cover the sea Hab 2:14 4325
through the heap of great *w* Hab 3:15 4325
that living *w* shall go out from Zec 14:8 4325
the sea, and perished in the *w* Mt 8:32 *5204*
him into the fire, and into the *w* Mk 9:22 *5204*
journeyings often, in perils of *w* 2Cor 11:26 *4215*
his voice as the sound of many *w* Rev 1:15 *5204*
them unto living fountains of *w* Rev 7:17 *5204*
and upon the fountains of *w* Rev 8:10 *5204*
part of the *w* became wormwood Rev 8:11 *5204*
and many men died of the *w* Rev 8:11 *5204*
have power over *w* to turn them to Rev 11:6 *5204*
heaven, as the voice of many *w* Rev 14:2 *5204*
and the sea, and the fountains of *w* Rev 14:7 *5204*
upon the rivers and fountains of *w* Rev 16:4 *5204*
And I heard the angel of the *w* say Rev 16:5 *5204*
whore that sitteth upon many *w* Rev 17:1 *5204*
The *w* which thou sawest, where Rev 17:15 *5204*
and as the voice of many *w* Rev 19:6 *5204*

WATERSPOUTS {1}
unto deep at the noise of thy *w* Ps 42:7 6794

WATERSPRINGS {2}
and the *w* into dry ground Ps 107:33 4161,4325
water, and dry ground into *w* Ps 107:35 4161,4325

WAVE {32}
shalt *w* them for a Ex 29:24 5130
them for a *w* offering Ex 29:24 8573
and *w* it for a Ex 29:26 5130
it for a *w* offering before Ex 29:26 8573
the breast of the *w* offering Ex 29:27 8573
for a *w* offering before the LORD Lev 7:30 8573
For the *w* breast and the heave Lev 7:34 8573
waved them for a *w* offering Lev 8:27 8573
waved it for a *w* offering before Lev 8:29 8573
for a *w* offering before the LORD Lev 9:21 8573
the *w* breast and heave shoulder Lev 10:14 8573
the *w* breast shall they bring Lev 10:15 8573
to *w* it for a *w* offering Lev 10:15 5130
w them for a Lev 14:12 5130
them for a *w* offering before Lev 14:12 8573
the priest shall *w* them for a Lev 14:24 5130
for a *w* offering before the LORD Lev 14:24 8573
he shall *w* the sheaf before the Lev 23:11 5130
the sabbath the priest shall *w* it Lev 23:11 5130
ye *w* the sheaf an he lamb without Lev 23:12 5130
the sheaf of the *w* offering Lev 23:15 8573
two *w* loaves of two tenth deals Lev 23:17 8573
the priest shall *w* them with the Lev 23:20 5130
for a *w* offering before the LORD Lev 23:20 8573
shall *w* the offering before the Num 5:25 5130
the priest shall *w* them for a Num 6:20 5130
for a *w* offering before the LORD Num 6:20 8573
for the priest, with the *w* breast Num 6:20 8573
with all the *w* offerings of the Num 18:11 8573
shall be thine, as the *w* breast Num 18:18 8573
For he that wavereth is like a *w* Jas 1:6 *2830*

WAVED {6}
of the heave offering, which is *w* Ex 29:27 5130
that the breast may be *w* for a Lev 7:30 5130
w them for a wave offering before Lev 8:27 5130
w it for a wave offering before Lev 8:29 5130
the right shoulder Aaron *w* for a Lev 9:21 5130
for a trespass offering to be *w* Lev 14:21 8573

WAVERETH {1}
For he that *w* is like a wave of Jas 1:6 *1252*

WAVERING {2}
profession of our faith without *w* Heb 10:23 *186*
let him ask in faith, nothing *w* Jas 1:6 *1252*

WAVES {26}
When the *w* of death compassed me, 2Sa 22:5 4867
and treadeth upon the *w* of the sea Job 9:8 1116
here shall thy proud *w* be stayed Job 38:11 1530
all thy *w* and thy billows are gone Ps 42:7 4867
of the seas, the noise of their *w* Ps 65:7 1530
hast afflicted me with all thy *w* Ps 88:7 4867
when the *w* thereof arise, thou Ps 89:9 1530
the floods lift up their *w* Ps 93:3 1796
yea, than the mighty *w* of the sea Ps 93:4 4867
which lifteth up the *w* thereof Ps 107:25 1530
so that the *w* thereof are still Ps 107:29 1530
righteousness as the *w* of the sea Is 48:18 1530
divided the sea, whose *w* roared Is 51:15 1530
though the *w* thereof toss Jer 5:22 1530
the sea when the *w* thereof roar Jer 31:35 1530
the multitude of the *w* thereof Jer 51:42 1530
when her *w* do roar like great Jer 51:55 1530
the sea causeth his *w* to come up Eze 26:3 1530
billows and thy *w* passed over me Jonah 2:3 1530
and shall smite the *w* in the sea Zec 10:11 1530
the ship was covered with the *w* Mt 8:24 *2949*
midst of the sea, tossed with *w* Mt 14:24 *2949*
the *w* beat into the ship, so that Mk 4:37 *2949*
the sea and the *w* roaring Lk 21:25 *4535*
broken with the violence of the *w* Acts 27:41 *2949*
Raging *w* of the sea, foaming out Jude 13 *2949*

WAX {24}
And my wrath shall *w* hot, and I Ex 22:24
my wrath may *w* hot against them Ex 32:10
why doth thy wrath *w* hot against Ex 32:11
not the anger of my lord *w* hot Ex 32:22
or stranger *w* rich by thee Lev 25:47
that dwelleth by him *w* poor Lev 25:47
place, and his eyes began to *w* dim 1Sa 3:2
What time they *w* warm, they Job 6:17
root thereof *w* old in the earth Job 14:8
my heart is like *w* Ps 22:14 1749
as *w* melteth before the fire, so Ps 68:2 1749
The hills melted like *w* at the Ps 97:5 1749
all of them shall *w* old like a Ps 102:26
fatness of his flesh shall *w* lean Is 17:4
neither shall his face now *w* pale Is 29:22
they all shall *w* old as a garment Is 50:9
the earth shall *w* old like a Is 51:6
our hands *w* feeble Jer 6:24
as *w* before the fire, and as the Mic 1:4 1749
the love of many shall *w* cold Mt 24:12 *5594*
yourselves bags which *w* not old Lk 12:33 *3822*
begun to *w* wanton against Christ 1Ti 5:11 *2691*
men and seducers shall *w* worse 2Ti 3:13 *4298*
they all shall *w* old as doth a Heb 1:11 *3822*

WAXED {37}
After I am *w* old shall I have Gen 18:12
And the man *w* great, and went Gen 26:13
the famine *w* sore in the land of Gen 41:56
multiplied, and *w* exceeding mighty Ex 1:7
multiplied, and *w* very mighty Ex 1:20
and when the sun *w* hot, it melted Ex 16:21
w louder and louder, Moses spake, Ex 19:19
and Moses' anger *w* hot, and he cast Ex 32:19
Moses, Is the LORD's hand *w* short Num 11:23
Thy raiment *w* not old upon thee, Deut 8:4
But Jeshurun *w* fat, and kicked Deut 32:15
round about, that Joshua *w* old Josh 23:1
hath many children is *w* feeble 1Sa 2:5
but David *w* stronger and stronger, 2Sa 3:1 1980
and the house of Saul *w* weaker 2Sa 3:1 1980
and David *w* faint 2Sa 21:15
and the flesh of the child *w* warm 2Kin 4:34
So David *w* greater and greater 1Chr 11:9 1980
But Abijah *w* mighty, and married 2Chr 13:21
Jehoshaphat *w* great exceedingly 2Chr 17:12 1980
But Jehoiada *w* old, and was full 2Chr 24:15
their clothes *w* not old, and their Neh 9:21
for this man Mordecai *w* greater Est 9:4 1980
my bones *w* old through my roaring Ps 32:3
Damascus is *w* feeble, and turneth Jer 49:24
of them, and his hands *w* feeble Jer 50:43
the he goat *w* very great Dan 8:8
which *w* exceeding great, toward Dan 8:9
it *w* great, even to the host of Dan 8:10
this people's heart is *w* gross Mt 13:15 *3975*
w strong in spirit, and was in the Lk 1:80 *2901*
w strong in spirit, filled with Lk 2:40 *2901*
and it grew, and *w* a great tree Lk 13:19 *1096*
Then Paul and Barnabas *w* bold Acts 13:46 *3955*
heart of this people is *w* gross Acts 28:27 *3975*
w valiant in fight, turned to Heb 11:34 *1096*
w rich through the abundance of Rev 18:3 *4147*

WAXEN {12}
because the cry of them is *w* Gen 19:13
If thy brother be *w* poor, and hath Lev 25:25
And if thy brother be *w* poor Lev 25:35
that dwelleth by thee be *w* poor Lev 25:39
clothes are not *w* old upon you Deut 29:5
thy shoe is not *w* old upon thy Deut 29:5
and filled themselves, and *w* fat Deut 31:20
thou art *w* fat, thou art grown Deut 32:15
children of Israel were *w* strong Josh 17:13
they are become great, and *w* rich Jer 5:27
They are *w* fat, they shine Jer 5:28
w great, and thou art come to Eze 16:7

WAXETH {2}
it *w* old because of all mine Ps 6:7
w old is ready to vanish away Heb 8:13 *1095*

WAXING {1}
w confident by my bonds, are much Phil 1:14 *3982*

WAY {664}
sword which turned every *w* Gen 3:24
to keep the *w* of the tree of life Gen 3:24 1870
corrupted his *w* upon the earth Gen 6:12 1870
thy wife, take her, and go thy *w* Gen 12:19
their victuals, and went their *w* Gen 14:11 3212
by the fountain in the *w* to Shur Gen 16:7 1870
with them to bring them on the *w* Gen 18:16 7971
they shall keep the *w* of the LORD Gen 18:19 1870
And the LORD went his *w*, as soon Gen 18:33 3212
over against him a good *w* off Gen 21:16 7368
I being in the *w*, the LORD led me Gen 24:27 1870
angel with thee, and prosper thy *w* Gen 24:40 1870
thou do prosper my *w* which I go Gen 24:42 1870
w to take my master's brother's Gen 24:48 1870
the LORD hath prospered my *w* Gen 24:56 1870
took Rebekah, and went his *w* Gen 24:61 3212
Isaac came from the *w* of the well Gen 24:62 935
drink, and rose up, and went his *w* Gen 25:34 3212
will keep me in this *w* that I go Gen 28:20 1870
And Jacob went on his *w*, and the Gen 32:1 1870
that day on his *w* unto Seir Gen 33:16 1870
was with me in the *w* which I went Gen 35:3 1870
but a little *w* to come to Ephrath Gen 35:16 776
and was buried in the *w* to Ephrath Gen 35:19 1870
which is by the *w* to Timnath Gen 38:14 1870
And he turned unto her by the *w* Gen 38:16 1870
that was openly by the *w* side Gen 38:21 1870
to give them provision for the *w* Gen 42:25 1870
him by the *w* in the which ye go Gen 42:38 1870
and gave them provision for the *w* Gen 45:21 1870
and meat for his father by the *w* Gen 45:23 1870
See that ye fall not out by the *w* Gen 45:24 1870
me in the land of Canaan in the *w* Gen 48:7 1870
a little *w* to come unto Ephrath Gen 48:7 776
her there in the *w* of Ephrath Gen 48:7 1870
Dan shall be a serpent by the *w* Gen 49:17 1870
And he looked this *w* and that *w*, Ex 2:12 3541
came to pass by the *w* in the inn Ex 4:24 1870
and Aaron, who stood in the *w* Ex 5:20 7125
God led them not through the *w* of Ex 13:17 1870
through the *w* of the wilderness Ex 13:18 1870
of a cloud, to lead them the *w* Ex 13:21 1870
of that had come upon them by the *w* Ex 18:8 1870
shalt shew them the *w* wherein Ex 18:20 1870
he went his *w* into his own land Ex 18:27
thee, to keep thee in the *w* Ex 23:20 1870
of the *w* which I commanded them Ex 32:8 1870
lest I consume thee in the *w* Ex 33:3 1870
in thy sight, shew me now thy *w* Ex 33:13 1870
them, Get you up this *w* southward Num 13:17
by the *w* of the Red sea Num 14:25 1870
we will go by the king's high *w* Num 20:17 1870
him, We will go by the high *w* Num 20:19 4546
Israel came by the *w* of the spies Num 21:1 1870
mount Hor by the *w* of the Red sea Num 21:4 1870
much discouraged because of the *w* Num 21:4 1870
go along by the king's high *w* Num 21:22 1870
and went up by the *w* of Bashan Num 21:33 1870
w for an adversary against him Num 22:22 1870
of the LORD standing in the *w* Num 22:23 1870
the ass turned aside out of the *w* Num 22:23 1870
the ass, to turn her into the *w* Num 22:23 1870
where was no *w* to turn either to Num 22:26 1870
of the LORD standing in the *w* Num 22:31 1870
because thy *w* is perverse before Num 22:32 1870
thou stoodest in the *w* against me Num 22:34 1870
and Balak also went his *w* Num 24:25 1870
Horeb by the *w* of mount Seir unto Deut 1:2 1870
which ye saw by the *w* of the Deut 1:19 1870
again by what *w* we must go up Deut 1:22 1870
in all the *w* that ye went, until Deut 1:31 1870
Who went in the *w* before you Deut 1:33 1870
shew you by what *w* ye should go Deut 1:33 1870
by the *w* of the Red sea Deut 1:40 1870
by the *w* of the Red sea, as the Deut 2:1 1870
through the *w* of the plain from Deut 2:8 1870
passed by the *w* of the wilderness Deut 2:8 1870
I will go along by the high *w* Deut 2:27 1870
and went up the *w* to Bashan Deut 3:1 1870
and when thou walkest by the *w* Deut 6:7 1870
thou shalt remember all the *w* Deut 8:2 1870
of the *w* which I commanded them Deut 9:12 1870
w which the LORD had commanded Deut 9:16 1870
and when thou walkest by the *w* Deut 11:19 1870
but turn aside out of the *w* which Deut 11:28 1870
by the *w* where the sun goeth down Deut 11:30 1870
of the *w* which the LORD thy God Deut 13:5 1870
if the *w* be too long for thee, so Deut 14:24 1870
henceforth return no more that *w* Deut 17:16 1870
Thou shalt prepare thee a *w* Deut 19:3 1870
him, because the *w* is long Deut 19:6 1870
ass or his ox fall down by the *w* Deut 22:4 1870
before thee in the *w* in any tree Deut 22:6 1870
with bread and with water in the *w* Deut 23:4 1870
thy God did unto Miriam by the *w* Deut 24:9 1870
Amalek did unto thee by the *w* Deut 25:17 1870
How he met thee by the *w*, and Deut 25:18 1870
the blind to wander out of the *w* Deut 27:18 1870
shall come out against thee one *w* Deut 28:7 1870
shalt go out one *w* against them Deut 28:25 1870
by the *w* whereof I spake unto Deut 28:68 1870
turn aside from the *w* which I Deut 31:29 1870
thou shalt make thy *w* prosperous Josh 1:8 1870
the *w* to Jordan unto the fords Josh 2:7 1870
and afterward may ye go your *w* Josh 2:16 1870
sought them throughout all the *w* Josh 2:22 1870
know the *w* by which ye must go Josh 3:4 1870
have not passed this *w* heretofore Josh 3:4 1870
died in the wilderness by the *w* Josh 5:4 1870
born in the wilderness by the *w* Josh 5:5 1870
had not circumcised them by the *w* Josh 5:7 1870
fled by the *w* of the wilderness Josh 8:15 1870

power to flee this *w* or that *w*	Josh 8:20	2008
chased them along the *w* that	Josh 10:10	1870
the east, the *w* to Beth-jeshimoth	Josh 12:3	1870
I am going the *w* of all the earth	Josh 23:14	1870
us in all the *w* wherein we went	Josh 24:17	1870
w which their fathers walked in	Judg 2:17	1870
doings, nor from their stubborn *w*	Judg 2:19	1870
whether they will keep the *w* of	Judg 2:22	1870
sit in judgment, and walk by the *w*	Judg 5:10	1870
Gideon went up by the *w* of them	Judg 8:11	1870
that came along that *w* by them	Judg 9:25	1870
that we may know whether our *w*	Judg 18:5	1870
the LORD is your *w* wherein ye go	Judg 18:6	1870
when they were a good *w* from the	Judg 18:22	7368
the children of Dan went their *w*	Judg 18:26	1870
of bread, and afterward go your *w*	Judg 19:5	
to morrow get you early on your *w*	Judg 19:9	1870
And they passed on and went their *w*	Judg 19:14	3212
house, and went out to go his *w*	Judg 19:27	1870
unto the *w* of the wilderness	Judg 20:42	1870
they went on the *w* to return unto	Ruth 1:7	1870
again, my daughters, go your *w*	Ruth 1:12	1870
So the woman went her *w*, and did	1Sa 1:18	1870
up by the *w* of his own coast to	1Sa 6:9	1870
w to the *w* of Beth-shemesh	1Sa 6:12	1870
shew us our *w* that we should go	1Sa 9:6	1870
the man of God, to tell us our *w*	1Sa 9:8	1870
teach you the good and the right *w*	1Sa 12:23	1870
unto the *w* that leadeth to Ophrah	1Sa 13:17	1870
turned the *w* to Beth-horon	1Sa 13:18	1870
w of the border that looketh to	1Sa 13:18	1870
how he laid wait for him in the *w*	1Sa 15:2	1870
have gone the *w* which the LORD	1Sa 15:20	1870
fell down by the *w* to Shaaraim	1Sa 17:52	1870
go thy *w*	1Sa 20:22	3212
came to the sheepcotes by the *w*	1Sa 24:3	1870
out of the cave, and went on his *w*	1Sa 24:7	1870
David's young men turned their *w*	1Sa 25:12	1870
is before Jeshimon, by the *w*	1Sa 26:3	1870
So David went on his *w*, and Saul	1Sa 26:25	1870
when thou goest on thy *w*	1Sa 28:22	1870
them away, and went on their *w*	1Sa 30:2	1870
the *w* of the wilderness of Gibeon	2Sa 2:24	1870
to pass, while they were in the *w*	2Sa 13:30	1870
the *w* of the hill side behind him	2Sa 13:34	1870
and stood beside the *w* of the gate	2Sa 15:2	1870
toward the *w* of the wilderness	2Sa 15:23	1870
as David and his men went by the *w*	2Sa 16:13	1870
Ahimaaz ran by the *w* of the plain	2Sa 18:23	1870
w over Jordan with the king	2Sa 19:36	
As for God, his *w* is perfect	2Sa 22:31	1870
and he maketh my *w* perfect	2Sa 22:33	1870
rose up, and went every man his *w*	1Kin 1:49	1870
I go the *w* of all the earth	1Kin 2:2	1870
thy children take heed to their *w*	1Kin 2:4	1870
thy children take heed to their *w*	1Kin 8:25	1870
to bring his *w* upon his head	1Kin 8:32	1870
good *w* wherein they should walk	1Kin 8:36	1870
the Shilonite found him in the *w*	1Kin 11:29	1870
by the same *w* that thou camest	1Kin 13:9	1870
So he went another *w*, and returned	1Kin 13:10	1870
returned not by the *w* that he	1Kin 13:10	1870
said unto them, What *w* went he	1Kin 13:12	1870
seen what *w* the man of God went	1Kin 13:12	1870
to go by the *w* that thou camest	1Kin 13:17	1870
was gone, a lion met him by the *w*	1Kin 13:24	1870
and his carcase was cast in the *w*	1Kin 13:24	1870
and saw the carcase cast in the *w*	1Kin 13:25	1870
him back from the *w* heard thereof	1Kin 13:26	1870
found his carcase cast in the *w*	1Kin 13:28	1870
returned not from his evil *w*	1Kin 13:33	1870
and walked in the *w* of his father	1Kin 15:26	1870
and walked in the *w* of Jeroboam	1Kin 15:34	1870
hast walked in the *w* of Jeroboam	1Kin 16:2	1870
in walking in the *w* of Jeroboam	1Kin 16:19	1870
For he walked in all the *w* of	1Kin 16:26	1870
Ahab went one *w* by himself	1Kin 18:6	1870
Obadiah went another *w* by himself	1Kin 18:6	1870
And as Obadiah was in the *w*	1Kin 18:7	1870
return on thy *w* to the wilderness	1Kin 19:15	1870
and waited for the king by the *w*	1Kin 20:38	1870
Which *w* went the Spirit of the	1Kin 22:24	2088
and walked in the *w* of his father	1Kin 22:52	1870
in the *w* of his mother, and in the	1Kin 22:52	1870
in the *w* of Jeroboam the son of	1Kin 22:52	1870
and as he was going up by the *w*	2Kin 2:23	1870
he said, Which *w* shall we go up	2Kin 3:8	1870
The *w* through the wilderness of	2Kin 3:8	1870
there came water by the *w* of Edom	2Kin 3:20	1870
staff in thine hand, and go thy *w*	2Kin 4:29	1870
he departed from him a little *w*	2Kin 5:19	776
said unto them, This is not the *w*	2Kin 6:19	1870
all the *w* was full of garments and	2Kin 7:15	1870
he walked in the *w* of the kings	2Kin 8:18	1870
he walked in the *w* of the house	2Kin 8:27	1870
he fled by the *w* of the garden	2Kin 9:27	1870
at the shearing house in the *w*	2Kin 10:12	1870
she went by the *w* by the which	2Kin 11:16	1870
came by the *w* of the gate of the	2Kin 11:19	1870
But he walked in the *w* of the	2Kin 16:3	1870
by the *w* by which thou camest	2Kin 19:28	1870
By the *w* that he came, by the	2Kin 19:33	1870
he walked in all the *w* that his	2Kin 21:21	1870
walked not in the *w* of the LORD	2Kin 21:22	1870
walked in all the *w* of David his	2Kin 22:2	1870
w of the gate between two walls	2Kin 25:4	1870
king went the *w* toward the plain	2Kin 25:4	1870
heed to their *w* to walk in my law	2Chr 6:16	1870
his *w* upon his own head	2Chr 6:23	1870
thou hast taught them the good *w*	2Chr 6:27	1870
the *w* that thou shalt send them	2Chr 6:34	1870
they walked in the *w* of David	2Chr 11:17	1870
Which *w* went the Spirit of the	2Chr 18:23	1870
he walked in the *w* of Asa his	2Chr 20:32	1870
he walked in the *w* of the kings	2Chr 21:6	1870
in the *w* of the kings of Israel	2Chr 21:13	1870
to seek of him a right *w* for us	Ezr 8:21	1870
us against the enemy in the *w*	Ezr 8:22	1870
of such as lay in wait by the *w*	Ezr 8:31	1870
Then he said unto them, Go your *w*	Neh 8:10	1870
the people went their *w* to eat	Neh 8:12	1870
in the *w* wherein they should go	Neh 9:12	1870
by day, to lead them in the *w*	Neh 9:19	1870
the *w* wherein they should go	Neh 9:19	1870
So Mordecai went his *w*, and did	Est 4:17	
given to a man whose *w* is hid	Job 3:23	1870
paths of their *w* are turned aside	Job 6:18	1870
Behold, this is the joy of his *w*	Job 8:19	1870
a wilderness where there is no *w*	Job 12:24	1870
then I shall go the *w* whence I	Job 16:22	734
also shall hold on his *w*, and he	Job 17:9	1870
and a trap for him in the *w*	Job 18:10	5410
fenced up my *w* that I cannot pass	Job 19:8	734
and raise up their *w* against me	Job 19:12	1870
not asked them that go by the *w*	Job 21:29	1870
shall declare his *w* to his face	Job 21:31	1870
Hast thou marked the old *w* which	Job 22:15	734
But he knoweth the *w* that I take	Job 23:10	1870
his *w* have I kept, and not	Job 23:11	1870
They turn the needy out of the *w*	Job 24:4	1870
not the *w* of the vineyards	Job 24:18	1870
taken out of the *w* as all other	Job 24:24	1870
God understandeth the *w* thereof	Job 28:23	1870
a *w* for the lightning of the	Job 28:26	1870
I chose out their *w*, and sat chief	Job 29:25	1870
my step hath turned out of the *w*	Job 31:7	1870
Who hath enjoined him his *w*	Job 36:23	1870
Where is the *w* where light	Job 38:19	1870
By what *w* is the light parted,	Job 38:24	1870
or a *w* for the lightning of	Job 38:25	1870
nor standeth in the *w* of sinners	Ps 1:1	1870
knoweth the *w* of the righteous	Ps 1:6	1870
but the *w* of the ungodly shall	Ps 1:6	1870
be angry, and ye perish from the *w*	Ps 2:12	
make thy *w* straight before my	Ps 5:8	1870
As for God, his *w* is perfect	Ps 18:30	1870
strength, and maketh my *w* perfect	Ps 18:32	1870
will he teach sinners in the *w*	Ps 25:8	1870
and the meek will he teach his *w*	Ps 25:9	1870
in the *w* that he shall choose	Ps 25:12	1870
Teach me thy *w*, O LORD, and lead	Ps 27:11	1870
teach thee in the *w* which thou	Ps 32:8	1870
stop the *w* against them that	Ps 35:3	
Let their *w* be dark and slippery	Ps 35:6	1870
himself in a *w* that is not good	Ps 36:4	1870
Commit thy *w* unto the LORD	Ps 37:5	1870
of him who prospereth in his *w*	Ps 37:7	1870
and he delighteth in his *w*	Ps 37:23	1870
Wait on the LORD, and keep his *w*	Ps 37:34	1870
our steps declined from thy *w*	Ps 44:18	734
This their *w* is their folly	Ps 49:13	1870
That thy *w* may be known upon	Ps 67:2	1870
Thy *w*, O God, is in the sanctuary	Ps 77:13	1870
Thy *w* is in the sea, and thy path	Ps 77:19	1870
He made a *w* to his anger	Ps 78:50	5410
which pass by the *w* do pluck her	Ps 80:12	1870
set us in the *w* of his steps	Ps 85:13	1870
Teach me thy *w*, O LORD	Ps 86:11	1870
All that pass by the *w* spoil him	Ps 89:41	1870
myself wisely in a perfect *w*	Ps 101:2	1870
he that walketh in a perfect *w*	Ps 101:6	1870
He weakened my strength in the *w*	Ps 102:23	1870
in the wilderness in a solitary *w*	Ps 107:4	1870
he led them forth by the right *w*	Ps 107:7	1870
wilderness, where there is no *w*	Ps 107:40	1870
shall drink of the brook in the *w*	Ps 110:7	1870
are the undefiled in the *w*	Ps 119:1	1870
shall a young man cleanse his *w*	Ps 119:9	734
in the *w* of thy testimonies	Ps 119:14	1870
understand the *w* of thy precepts	Ps 119:27	1870
Remove from me the *w* of lying	Ps 119:29	1870
I have chosen the *w* of truth	Ps 119:30	1870
I will run the *w* of thy	Ps 119:32	1870
me, O LORD, the *w* of thy statutes	Ps 119:33	1870
and quicken thou me in thy *w*	Ps 119:37	1870
my feet from every evil *w*	Ps 119:101	734
therefore I hate every false *w*	Ps 119:104	734
and I hate every false *w*	Ps 119:128	734
if there be any wicked *w* in me	Ps 139:24	1870
and lead me in the *w* everlasting	Ps 139:24	1870
In the *w* wherein I walked have	Ps 142:3	734
cause me to know the *w* wherein I	Ps 143:8	1870
but the *w* of the wicked he	Ps 146:9	1870
walk not thou in the *w* with them	Prov 1:15	1870
eat of the fruit of their own *w*	Prov 1:31	1870
and preserveth the *w* of his saints	Prov 2:8	1870
thee from the *w* of the evil man	Prov 2:12	1870
mayest walk in the *w* of good men	Prov 2:20	1870
shalt thou walk in thy *w* safely	Prov 3:23	1870
taught thee in the *w* of wisdom	Prov 4:11	1870
and go not in the *w* of evil men	Prov 4:14	1870
The *w* of the wicked is as	Prov 4:19	1870
Remove thy *w* far from her, and	Prov 5:8	1870
of instruction are the *w* of life	Prov 6:23	1870
he went the *w* to her house,	Prov 7:8	1870
Her house is the *w* to hell	Prov 7:27	1870
by the *w* in the places of the	Prov 8:2	1870
and arrogancy, and the evil *w*	Prov 8:13	1870
I lead in the *w* of righteousness,	Prov 8:20	734
me in the beginning of his *w*	Prov 8:22	1870
go in the *w* of understanding	Prov 9:6	1870
He is in the *w* of life that	Prov 10:17	734
The *w* of the LORD is strength to	Prov 10:29	1870
of the perfect shall direct his *w*	Prov 11:5	1870
in their *w* are his delight	Prov 11:20	1870
The *w* of a fool is right in his	Prov 12:15	1870
but the *w* of the wicked seduceth	Prov 12:26	1870
In the *w* of righteousness is life	Prov 12:28	734
him that is upright in the *w*	Prov 13:6	1870
but the *w* of transgressors is	Prov 13:15	1870
prudent is to understand his *w*	Prov 14:8	1870
There is a *w* which seemeth right	Prov 14:12	1870
The *w* of the wicked is an	Prov 15:9	1870
unto him that forsaketh the *w*	Prov 15:10	734
The *w* of the slothful man is as	Prov 15:19	1870
but the *w* of the righteous is	Prov 15:19	734
The *w* of life is above to the	Prov 15:24	734
A man's heart deviseth his *w*	Prov 16:9	1870
keepeth his *w* preserveth his soul	Prov 16:17	1870
There is a *w* that seemeth right	Prov 16:25	1870
him into the *w* that is not good	Prov 16:29	1870
found in the *w* of righteousness	Prov 16:31	1870
of man perverteth his *w*	Prov 19:3	1870
but when he is gone his *w*	Prov 20:14	
a man then understand his own *w*	Prov 20:24	1870
Every *w* of a man is right in his	Prov 21:2	1870
The *w* of man is froward and	Prov 21:8	1870
w of understanding shall remain	Prov 21:16	1870
the upright, he directeth his *w*	Prov 21:29	1870
are in the *w* of the froward	Prov 22:5	1870
up a child in the *w* he should go	Prov 22:6	1870
and guide thine heart in the *w*	Prov 23:19	1870
saith, There is a lion in the *w*	Prov 26:13	1870
to go astray in an evil *w*	Prov 28:10	1870
he that is upright in the *w* is	Prov 29:27	1870
The *w* of an eagle in the air	Prov 30:19	1870
the *w* of a serpent upon a rock	Prov 30:19	1870
the *w* of a ship in the midst of	Prov 30:19	1870
the *w* of a man with a maid	Prov 30:19	1870
Such is the *w* of an adulterous	Prov 30:20	1870
Go thy *w*, eat thy bread with joy,	Eccl 9:7	
that is a fool walketh by the *w*	Eccl 10:3	1870
not what is the *w* of the spirit	Eccl 11:5	1870
high, and fears shall be in the *w*	Eccl 12:5	1870
go thy *w* forth by the footsteps	Song 1:8	1870
destroy the *w* of thy paths	Is 3:12	1870
not walk in the *w* of this people	Is 8:11	1870
afflict her by the *w* of the sea	Is 9:1	1870
for in the *w* of Horonaim they	Is 15:5	1870
The *w* of the just is uprightness	Is 26:7	734
in the *w* of thy judgments, O LORD	Is 26:8	734
strong drink are out of the *w*	Is 28:7	8582
they are out of the *w* through	Is 28:7	8582
Get you out of the *w*, turn aside	Is 30:11	1870
thee, saying, This is the *w*	Is 30:21	1870
an highway shall be there, and a *w*	Is 35:8	1870
shall be called The *w* of holiness	Is 35:8	1870
by the *w* by which thou camest	Is 37:29	1870
By the *w* that he came, by the	Is 37:34	1870
Prepare ye the *w* of the LORD	Is 40:3	1870
to him the *w* of understanding	Is 40:14	1870
My *w* is hid from the LORD, and my	Is 40:27	1870
even by the *w* that he had not	Is 41:3	734
blind by a *w* that they knew not	Is 42:16	1870
LORD, which maketh a *w* in the sea	Is 43:16	1870
even make a *w* in the wilderness	Is 43:19	1870
and he shall make his *w* prosperous	Is 48:15	1870
by the *w* that thou shouldest go	Is 48:17	1870
I will make all my mountains a *w*	Is 49:11	1870
made the depths of the sea a *w*	Is 51:10	1870
turned every one to his own *w*	Is 53:6	1870
Let the wicked forsake his *w*	Is 55:7	1870
they all look to their own *w*	Is 56:11	1870
wearied in the greatness of thy *w*	Is 57:10	1870
ye up, cast ye up, prepare the *w*	Is 57:14	1870
out of the *w* of my people	Is 57:14	1870
frowardly in the *w* of his heart	Is 57:17	1870
The *w* of peace they know not	Is 59:8	1870
prepare ye the *w* of the people	Is 62:10	1870
walketh in a *w* that was not good	Is 65:2	1870
God, when he led thee by the *w*	Jer 2:17	1870
hast thou to do in the *w* of Egypt	Jer 2:18	1870
thou to do in the *w* of Assyria	Jer 2:18	1870
see thy *w* in the valley, know	Jer 2:23	1870
trimmest thou thy *w* to seek love	Jer 2:33	1870
about so much to change thy *w*	Jer 2:36	1870
for they have perverted their *w*	Jer 3:21	1870
of the Gentiles is on his *w*	Jer 4:7	5265
Thy *w* and thy doings have procured	Jer 4:18	1870
they know not the *w* of the LORD	Jer 5:4	1870
they have known the *w* of the LORD	Jer 5:5	1870
old paths, where is the good *w*	Jer 6:16	1870
into the field, nor walk by the *w*	Jer 6:25	1870
thou mayest know and try their *w*	Jer 6:27	1870
Learn not the *w* of the heathen,	Jer 10:2	1870
I know that the *w* of man is not	Jer 10:23	1870
Wherefore doth the *w* of the	Jer 12:1	1870
ye now every one from his evil *w*	Jer 18:11	1870
walk in paths, in a *w* not cast up	Jer 18:15	1870
w of life, and the *w* of death	Jer 21:8	1870
Wherefore their *w* shall be unto	Jer 23:12	1870
turned them from their evil *w*	Jer 23:22	1870
now every one from his evil *w*	Jer 25:5	1870
shepherds shall have no *w* to flee	Jer 25:35	4498

and turn every man from his evil *w* .... Jer 26:3 1870
the prophet Jeremiah went his *w* .... Jer 28:11 1870
rivers of waters in a straight *w* .... Jer 31:9 1870
even the *w* which thou wentest .... Jer 31:21 1870
give them one heart, and one *w* .... Jer 32:39 1870
ye now every man from his evil *w* .... Jer 35:15 1870
return every man from his evil *w* .... Jer 36:3 1870
return every one from his evil *w* .... Jer 36:7 1870
by the *w* of the king's garden, by .... Jer 39:4 1870
and he went out the *w* of the plain .... Jer 39:4 1870
shew us the *w* wherein we may walk .... Jer 42:3 1870
of Aroer, stand by the *w*, and espy .... Jer 48:19 1870
They shall ask the *w* to Zion with .... Jer 50:5 1870
the *w* of the gate between the two .... Jer 52:7 1870
they went by the *w* of the plain .... Jer 52:7 1870
warn the wicked from his wicked *w* .... Eze 3:18 1870
wickedness, nor from his wicked *w* .... Eze 3:19 1870
I will do unto them after their *w* .... Eze 7:27 1870
eyes now the *w* toward the north .... Eze 8:5 1870
mine eyes the *w* toward the north .... Eze 8:5 1870
from the *w* of the higher gate .... Eze 9:2 1870
their *w* upon their head .... Eze 9:10 1870
their *w* upon their own heads .... Eze 11:21 1870
not return from his wicked *w* .... Eze 13:22 1870
unto you, and ye shall see their *w* .... Eze 14:22 1870
high place at every head of the *w* .... Eze 16:25 1870
which are ashamed of thy lewd *w* .... Eze 16:27 1870
place in the head of every *w* .... Eze 16:31 1870
recompense thy *w* upon thine head .... Eze 16:43 1870
The *w* of the Lord is not equal .... Eze 18:25 1870
Is not my *w* equal .... Eze 18:25 1870
The *w* of the Lord is not equal .... Eze 18:29 1870
Go thee one *w* or other, either on .... Eze 21:16
at the head of the *w* to the city .... Eze 21:19 1870
Appoint a *w*, that the sword may .... Eze 21:20 1870
stood at the parting of the *w* .... Eze 21:21 1870
their own *w* have I recompensed .... Eze 22:31 1870
that they took both one *w* .... Eze 23:13 1870
walked in the *w* of thy sister .... Eze 23:31 1870
to warn the wicked from his *w* .... Eze 33:8 1870
wicked of his *w* to turn from it .... Eze 33:9 1870
if he do not turn from his *w* .... Eze 33:9 1870
that the wicked turn from his *w* .... Eze 33:11 1870
The *w* of the Lord is not equal .... Eze 33:17 1870
as for them, their *w* is not equal .... Eze 33:17 1870
The *w* of the Lord is not equal .... Eze 33:20 1870
they defiled it by their own *w* .... Eze 36:17 1870
their *w* was before me as the .... Eze 36:17 1870
according to their *w* and according .... Eze 36:19 1870
court, the *w* toward the north .... Eze 42:1 1870
breadth inward, a *w* of one cubit .... Eze 42:4 1870
the *w* before them was like the .... Eze 42:11 1870
was a door in the head of the *w* .... Eze 42:12 1870
even the *w* directly before the .... Eze 42:12 1870
came from the *w* of the east .... Eze 43:2 1870
w of the gate whose prospect is .... Eze 43:4 1870
the *w* of the gate of the outward .... Eze 44:1 1870
he shall enter by the *w* of the .... Eze 44:3 1870
shall go out by the *w* of the same .... Eze 44:3 1870
Then brought he me the *w* of the .... Eze 44:4 1870
the *w* of the porch of that gate .... Eze 46:2 1870
he shall go in by the *w* of the .... Eze 46:8 1870
shall go forth by the *w* thereof .... Eze 46:8 1870
he that entereth in by the *w* of .... Eze 46:9 1870
go out by the *w* of the south gate .... Eze 46:9 1870
he that entereth by the *w* of the .... Eze 46:9 1870
forth by the *w* of the north gate .... Eze 46:9 1870
he shall not return by the *w* of .... Eze 46:9 1870
of the *w* of the gate northward .... Eze 47:2 1870
led me about the *w* without unto .... Eze 47:2 1870
by the *w* that looketh eastward .... Eze 47:2 1870
the *w* of Hethlon, as men go to .... Eze 47:15 1870
to the coast of the *w* of Hethlon .... Eze 48:1 1870
And he said, Go thy *w*, Daniel .... Dan 12:9
But go thou thy *w* till the end be .... Dan 12:13 1870
I will hedge up thy *w* with thorns .... Hos 2:6 1870
murder in the *w* by consent .... Hos 6:9 1870
because thou didst trust in thy *w* .... Hos 10:13 1870
by the *w* will I observe them .... Hos 13:7 1870
and turn aside the *w* of the meek .... Amos 2:7 1870
turn every one from his evil *w* .... Jonah 3:8 1870
they turned from their evil *w* .... Jonah 3:10 1870
LORD hath his *w* in the whirlwind .... Nah 1:3 1870
keep the munition, watch the *w* .... Nah 2:1 1870
they went their *w* as a flock .... Zec 10:2
But ye are departed out of the *w* .... Mal 2:8 1870
he shall prepare the *w* before me .... Mal 3:1 1870
into their own country another *w* .... Mt 2:12 *3598*
Prepare ye the *w* of the Lord .... Mt 3:3 *3598*
by the *w* of the sea, beyond .... Mt 4:15 *3598*
before the altar, and go thy *w* .... Mt 5:24
whiles thou art in the *w* with him .... Mt 5:25 *3598*
is the gate, and broad is the *w* .... Mt 7:13 *3598*
is the gate, and narrow is the *w* .... Mt 7:14 *3598*
but go thy *w*, shew thyself to the .... Mt 8:4
said unto the centurion, Go thy *w* .... Mt 8:13
that no man might pass by that *w* .... Mt 8:28 *3598*
there was a good *w* off from them .... Mt 8:30 *3112*
Go not into the *w* of the Gentiles .... Mt 10:5 *3598*
shall prepare thy *w* before thee .... Mt 11:10 *3598*
some seeds fell by the *w* side .... Mt 13:4 *3598*
which received seed by the *w* side .... Mt 13:19 *3598*
among the wheat, and went his *w* .... Mt 13:25
fasting, lest they faint in the *w* .... Mt 15:32 *3598*
And they went their *w* .... Mt 20:4
Take that thine is, and go thy *w* .... Mt 20:14 *3598*
twelve disciples apart in the *w* .... Mt 20:17 *3598*
blind men sitting by the *w* side .... Mt 20:30 *3598*

spread their garments in the *w* .... Mt 21:8 *3598*
trees, and strawed them in the *w* .... Mt 21:8 *3598*
when he saw a fig tree in the *w* .... Mt 21:19 *3598*
you in the *w* of righteousness .... Mt 21:32 *3598*
teachest the *w* of God in truth .... Mt 22:16 *3598*
and left him, and went their *w* .... Mt 22:22
go your *w*, make it as sure as ye .... Mt 27:65
shall prepare thy *w* before thee .... Mk 1:2 *3598*
Prepare ye the *w* of the Lord .... Mk 1:3 *3598*
but go thy *w*, shew thyself to the .... Mk 1:44
go thy *w* into thine house .... Mk 2:11
he sowed, some fell by the *w* side .... Mk 4:4 *3598*
And these are they by the *w* side .... Mk 4:15 *3598*
her, For this saying go thy *w* .... Mk 7:29
houses, they will faint by the *w* .... Mk 8:3 *3598*
by the *w* he asked his disciples .... Mk 8:27 *3598*
among yourselves by the *w* .... Mk 9:33 *3598*
for by the *w* they had disputed .... Mk 9:34 *3598*
when he was gone forth into the *w* .... Mk 10:17 *3598*
go thy *w*, sell whatsoever thou .... Mk 10:21
they were in the *w* going up to .... Mk 10:32 *3598*
And Jesus said unto him, Go thy *w* .... Mk 10:52
sight, and followed Jesus in the *w* .... Mk 10:52 *3598*
Go your *w* into the village over .... Mk 11:2
And they went their *w*, and found .... Mk 11:4
spread their garments in the *w* .... Mk 11:8 *3598*
trees, and strawed them in the *w* .... Mk 11:8 *3598*
and they left him, and went their *w* .... Mk 12:12
teachest the *w* of God in truth .... Mk 12:14 *3598*
But go your *w*, tell his disciples .... Mk 16:7
our feet into the *w* of peace .... Lk 1:79 *3598*
Prepare ye the *w* of the Lord .... Lk 3:4 *3598*
the midst of them went his *w* .... Lk 4:30
they could not find by what *w* .... Lk 5:19
said unto them, Go your *w* .... Lk 7:22
shall prepare thy *w* before thee .... Lk 7:27 *3598*
he sowed, some fell by the *w* side .... Lk 8:5 *3598*
Those by the *w* side are they that .... Lk 8:12 *3598*
And he went his *w*, and published .... Lk 8:39
pass, that, as they went in the *w* .... Lk 9:57 *3598*
and salute no man by the *w* .... Lk 10:4 *3598*
came down a certain priest that *w* .... Lk 10:31 *3598*
magistrate, as thou art in the *w* .... Lk 12:58 *3598*
the other is yet a great *w* off .... Lk 14:32 *4206*
But when he was yet a great *w* off .... Lk 15:20 *3112*
he said unto him, Arise, go thy *w* .... Lk 17:19
man sat by the *w* side begging .... Lk 18:35 *3598*
for he was to pass that *w* .... Lk 19:4
they that were sent went their *w* .... Lk 19:32
spread their clothes in the *w* .... Lk 19:36 *3598*
but teachest the *w* of God truly .... Lk 20:21 *3598*
And he went his *w*, and communed .... Lk 22:4
while he talked with us by the *w* .... Lk 24:32 *3598*
what things were done in the *w* .... Lk 24:35 *3598*
Make straight the *w* of the Lord .... Jn 1:23 *3598*
went her *w* into the city, and .... Jn 4:28
Jesus saith unto him, Go thy *w* .... Jn 4:50
spoken unto him, and he went his *w* .... Jn 4:50
Jesus again unto them, I go my *w* .... Jn 8:21
He went his *w* therefore, and .... Jn 9:7
but climbeth up some other *w* .... Jn 10:1 *237*
she had so said, she went her *w* .... Jn 11:28
I go ye know, and the *w* ye know .... Jn 14:4 *3598*
and how can we know the *w* .... Jn 14:5 *3598*
Jesus saith unto him, I am the *w* .... Jn 14:6 *3598*
But now I go my *w* to him that .... Jn 16:5
ye seek me, let these go their *w* .... Jn 18:8
go toward the south unto the *w* .... Acts 8:26 *3598*
And as they went on their *w* .... Acts 8:36 *3598*
and he went on his *w* rejoicing .... Acts 8:39 *3598*
that if he found any of this *w* .... Acts 9:2 *3598*
the Lord said unto him, Go thy *w* .... Acts 9:15
And Ananias went his *w*, and entered .... Acts 9:17
unto thee in the *w* as thou camest .... Acts 9:17 *3598*
how he had seen the Lord in the *w* .... Acts 9:27 *3598*
brought on their *w* by the church .... Acts 15:3 *4311*
shew unto us the *w* of salvation .... Acts 16:17 *3598*
instructed in the *w* of the Lord .... Acts 18:25 *3598*
him the *w* of God more perfectly .... Acts 18:26 *3598*
of that *w* before the multitude .... Acts 19:9 *3598*
arose no small stir about that *w* .... Acts 19:23 *3598*
days, we departed and went our *w* .... Acts 21:5 *4311*
and they all brought us on our *w* .... Acts 21:5 *4311*
persecuted this *w* unto the death .... Acts 22:4 *3598*
that after the *w* which they call .... Acts 24:14 *3598*
more perfect knowledge of that *w* .... Acts 24:22 *3598*
answered, Go thy *w* for this time .... Acts 24:25
laying wait in the *w* to kill him .... Acts 25:3 *3598*
I saw in the *w* a light from .... Acts 26:13 *3598*
Much every *w*: chiefly .... Rom 3:2 *5158*
They are all gone out of the *w* .... Rom 3:12
the *w* of peace have they not .... Rom 3:17 *3598*
to fall in his brother's *w* .... Rom 14:13
on my *w* thitherward by you .... Rom 15:24 *4311*
also make a *w* to escape, that ye 1Cor 10:13 *1545*
I unto you a more excellent *w* 1Cor 12:31 *3598*
I will not see you now by the *w* 1Cor 16:7 *3938*
be brought on my *w* toward Judaea 2Cor 1:16 *4311*
notwithstanding, every *w*, whether .... Phil 1:18 *5158*
to us, and took it out of the *w* .... Col 2:14 *3319*
Christ, direct our *w* unto you 1Th 3:11 *3598*
until he be taken out of the *w* 2Th 2:7 *3319*
and on them that are out of the *w* .... Heb 5:2 *4105*
that the *w* into the holiest of .... Heb 9:8 *3598*
By a new and living *w*, which he .... Heb 10:20 *3598*
is lame be turned out of the *w* .... Heb 12:13 *1624*
beholdeth himself, and goeth his *w* .... Jas 1:24
and had sent them out another *w* .... Jas 2:25 *3598*

w shall save a soul from death .... Jas 5:20 *3598*
by reason of whom the *w* of truth 2Pet 2:2 *3598*
Which have forsaken the right *w* 2Pet 2:15 *3598*
following the *w* of Balaam the son 2Pet 2:15 *3598*
have known the *w* of righteousness 2Pet 2:21 *3598*
pure minds by *w* of remembrance 2Pet 3:1 *1722*
they have gone in the *w* of Cain .... Jude 11 *3598*
that the *w* of the kings of the .... Rev 16:12 *3598*

WAYFARING {6}
he saw a *w* man in the street of .... Judg 19:17 732
to dress for the *w* man that was 2Sa 12:4 732
lie waste, the *w* man ceaseth .... Is 33:8 5674,734
the *w* men, though fools, shall .... Is 35:8 1980,1870
a lodging place of *w* men .... Jer 9:2 732
as a *w* man that turneth aside to .... Jer 14:8 732

WAYMARKS {1}
Set thee up *w*, make thee high .... Jer 31:21 6725

WAYS {205}
rise up early, and go on your *w* .... Gen 19:2 1870
w hide their eyes from the man .... Lev 20:4
your high *w* shall be desolate .... Lev 26:22 1870
But if he shall any *w* make them .... Num 30:15
Ye shall walk in all the *w* which .... Deut 5:33 1870
LORD thy God, to walk in his *w* .... Deut 8:6 1870
thy God, to walk in all his *w* .... Deut 10:12 1870
your God, to walk in all his *w* .... Deut 11:22 1870
thy God, and to walk ever in his *w* .... Deut 19:9 1870
be thy God, and to walk in his *w* .... Deut 26:17 1870
way, and flee before thee seven *w* .... Deut 28:7 1870
LORD thy God, and walk in his *w* .... Deut 28:9 1870
them, and flee seven *w* before them .... Deut 28:25 1870
thou shalt not prosper in thy *w* .... Deut 28:29 1870
LORD thy God, to walk in his *w* .... Deut 30:16 1870
for all his *w* are judgment .... Deut 32:4 1870
your God, and to walk in all his *w* .... Josh 22:5 1870
And his sons walked not in his *w* 1Sa 8:3 1870
and thy sons walk not in thy *w* 1Sa 8:5 1870
himself wisely in all his *w* 1Sa 18:14 1870
For I have kept the *w* of the LORD 2Sa 22:22 1870
LORD thy God, to walk in his *w* 1Kin 2:3 1870
And if thou wilt walk in my *w* 1Kin 3:14 1870
to every man according to his *w* 1Kin 8:39 1870
unto him, to walk in all his *w* 1Kin 8:58 1870
Ammon, and have not walked in my *w* 1Kin 11:33 1870
thee, and wilt walk in my *w* 1Kin 11:38 1870
in all the *w* of Asa his father 1Kin 22:43 1870
saying, Turn ye from your evil *w* 2Kin 17:13 1870
man according unto all his *w* 2Chr 6:30 1870
may fear thee, to walk in thy *w* 2Chr 6:31 1870
face, and turn from their wicked *w* 2Chr 7:14 1870
of the acts of Abijah, and his *w* 2Chr 13:22 1870
the first *w* of his father David 2Chr 17:3 1870
lifted up in the *w* of the LORD 2Chr 17:6 1870
the *w* of Jehoshaphat thy father 2Chr 21:12 1870
nor in the *w* of Asa king of Judah 2Chr 21:12 1870
in the *w* of the house of Ahab 2Chr 22:3 1870
his *w* before the LORD his God 2Chr 27:6 1870
Jotham, and all his wars, and his *w* 2Chr 27:7 1870
For he walked in the *w* of the 2Chr 28:2 1870
rest of his acts and of all his *w* 2Chr 28:26 1870
the nations of those lands any *w* 2Chr 32:13 1870
walked in the *w* of David his 2Chr 34:2 1870
hope, and the uprightness of thy *w* .... Job 4:6 1870
maintain mine own *w* before him .... Job 13:15 1870
desire not the knowledge of thy *w* .... Job 21:14 1870
that thou makest thy *w* perfect .... Job 22:3 1870
the light shall shine upon thy *w* .... Job 22:28 1870
they know not the *w* thereof .... Job 24:13 1870
yet his eyes are upon their *w* .... Job 24:23 1870
Lo, these are parts of his *w* .... Job 26:14 1870
me the *w* of their destruction .... Job 30:12 734
Doth not he see my *w*, and count .... Job 31:4 1870
man to find according to his *w* .... Job 34:11 734
his eyes are upon the *w* of man .... Job 34:21 1870
would not consider any of his *w* .... Job 34:27 1870
He is the chief of the *w* of God .... Job 40:19 1870
His *w* are always grievous .... Ps 10:5 1870
For I have kept the *w* of the LORD .... Ps 18:21 1870
Shew me thy *w*, O LORD .... Ps 25:4 1870
I said, I will take heed to my *w* .... Ps 39:1 1870
will I teach transgressors thy *w* .... Ps 51:13 1870
me, and Israel had walked in my *w* .... Ps 81:13 1870
in whose heart are the *w* of them .... Ps 84:5 4546
thee, to keep thee in all thy *w* .... Ps 91:11 1870
and they have not known my *w* .... Ps 95:10 1870
He made known his *w* unto Moses .... Ps 103:7 1870
they walk in his *w* .... Ps 119:3 1870
O that my *w* were directed to keep .... Ps 119:5 1870
and have respect unto thy *w* .... Ps 119:15 734
I have declared my *w*, and thou .... Ps 119:26 1870
I thought on my *w*, and turned my .... Ps 119:59 1870
for all my *w* are before thee .... Ps 119:168 1870
turn aside unto their crooked *w* .... Ps 125:5
that walketh in his *w* .... Ps 128:1 1870
shall sing in the *w* of the LORD .... Ps 138:5 1870
and art acquainted with all my *w* .... Ps 139:3 1870
LORD is righteous in all his *w* .... Ps 145:17 1870
So are the *w* of every one that is .... Prov 1:19 734
to walk in the *w* of darkness .... Prov 2:13 1870
Whose *w* are crooked, and they .... Prov 2:15 734
In all thy *w* acknowledge him, and .... Prov 3:6 1870
Her *w* are *w* of pleasantness, ... Prov 3:17 1870
and choose none of his *w* .... Prov 3:31 1870
let all thy *w* be established .... Prov 4:26 1870
her *w* are moveable, that thou .... Prov 5:6 4570
For the *w* of man are before the .... Prov 5:21 1870
consider her *w*, and be wise .... Prov 6:6 1870

W

not thine heart decline to her *w* ... Prov 7:25 1870
blessed are they that keep my *w* ... Prov 8:32 1870
who go right on their *w* ... Prov 9:15 734
perverteth his *w* shall be known ... Prov 10:9 1870
perverse in his *w* despiseth him ... Prov 14:2 1870
end thereof are the *w* of death ... Prov 14:12 1870
shall be filled with his own *w* ... Prov 14:14 1870
All the *w* of a man are clean in ... Prov 16:2 1870
When a man's *w* please the LORD, ... Prov 16:7 1870
end thereof are the *w* of death ... Prov 16:25 1870
to pervert the *w* of judgment ... Prov 17:23 734
he that despiseth his *w* shall die ... Prov 19:16 1870
Lest thou learn his *w*, and get a ... Prov 22:25 734
and let thine eyes observe my *w* ... Prov 23:26 1870
than he that is perverse in his *w* ... Prov 28:6 1870
in his *w* shall fall at once ... Prov 28:18 1870
women, nor thy *w* to that which ... Prov 31:3 1870
well to the *w* of her household ... Prov 31:27 1979
walk in the *w* of thine heart, and ... Eccl 11:9 1870
in the broad *w* I will seek him ... Song 3:2 7339
and he will teach us of his *w* ... Is 2:3 1870
for they would not walk in his *w* ... Is 42:24 1870
and I will direct all his *w* ... Is 45:13 1870
They shall feed in the *w*, and ... Is 49:9 1870
neither are your *w* my *w* ... Is 55:8 1870
so are my *w* higher than your *w* ... Is 55:9 1870
I have seen his *w*, and will heal ... Is 57:18 1870
me daily, and delight to know my *w* ... Is 58:2 1870
honour him, not doing thine own *w* ... Is 58:13 1870
thou made us to err from thy *w* ... Is 63:17 1870
those that remember thee in thy *w* ... Is 64:5 1870
Yea, they have chosen their own *w* ... Is 66:3 1870
swift dromedary traversing her *w* ... Jer 2:23 1870
also taught the wicked ones thy *w* ... Jer 2:33 1870
In the *w* hast thou sat for them, ... Jer 3:2 1870
hast scattered thy *w* to the ... Jer 3:13 1870
saith the LORD, Stand ye in the *w* ... Jer 6:16 1870
the God of Israel, Amend your *w* ... Jer 7:3 1870
For if ye throughly amend your *w* ... Jer 7:5 1870
walk ye in all the *w* that I have ... Jer 7:23 1870
learn the *w* of my people, to ... Jer 12:16 1870
they return not from their *w* ... Jer 15:7 1870
mine eyes are upon all their *w* ... Jer 16:17 1870
give every man according to his *w* ... Jer 17:10 1870
from his evil way, and make your *w* ... Jer 18:11 1870
in their *w* from the ancient paths ... Jer 18:15 1870
as slippery *w* in the darkness ... Jer 23:12
Therefore now amend your *w* ... Jer 26:13 1870
upon all the *w* of the sons of men ... Jer 32:19 1870
give every one according to his *w* ... Jer 32:19 1870
The *w* of Zion do mourn, because ... Lam 1:4 1870
inclosed my *w* with hewn stone ... Lam 3:9 1870
He hath turned aside my *w* ... Lam 3:11 1870
Let us search and try our *w* ... Lam 3:40 1870
judge thee according to thy *w* ... Eze 7:3 1870
I will recompense thy *w* upon thee ... Eze 7:4 1870
judge thee according to thy *w* ... Eze 7:8 1870
thee according to thy *w* and thine ... Eze 7:9 1870
comfort you, when ye see their *w* ... Eze 14:23 1870
thou not walked after their *w* ... Eze 16:47 1870
more than they in all thy *w* ... Eze 16:47 1870
Then thou shalt remember thy *w* ... Eze 16:61 1870
that he should return from his *w* ... Eze 18:23 1870
are not your *w* unequal ... Eze 18:25 1870
of Israel, are not my *w* equal ... Eze 18:29 1870
are not your *w* unequal ... Eze 18:29 1870
every one according to his *w* ... Eze 18:30 1870
And there shall ye remember your *w* ... Eze 20:43 1870
not according to your wicked *w* ... Eze 20:44 1870
son of man, appoint thee two *w* ... Eze 21:19 1870
the way, at the head of the two *w* ... Eze 21:21 1870
according to thy *w*, and according ... Eze 24:14 1870
Thou wast perfect in thy *w* from ... Eze 28:15 1870
turn ye, turn ye from your evil *w* ... Eze 33:11 1870
judge you every one after his *w* ... Eze 33:20 1870
shall ye remember your own evil *w* ... Eze 36:31 1870
and confounded for your own *w* ... Eze 36:32 1870
are truth, and his *w* judgment ... Dan 4:37 735
breath is, and whose are all thy *w* ... Dan 5:23 735
and I will punish them for their *w* ... Hos 4:9 1870
a snare of a fowler in all his *w* ... Hos 9:8 1870
punish Jacob according to his *w* ... Hos 12:2 1870
for the *w* of the LORD are right, ... Hos 14:9 1870
shall march every one on his *w* ... Joel 2:7 1870
and he will teach us of his *w* ... Mic 4:2 1870
against another in the broad *w* ... Nah 2:4
his *w* are everlasting ... Hab 3:6 1979
Consider your *w* ... Hag 1:5 1870
Consider your *w* ... Hag 1:7 1870
Turn ye now from your evil *w* ... Zec 1:4 1870
to do unto us, according to our *w* ... Zec 1:6 1870
If thou wilt walk in my *w* ... Zec 3:7 1870
as ye have not kept my *w*, but ... Mal 2:9 1870
went their *w* into the city, and ... Mt 8:33
made light of it, and went their *w* ... Mt 22:5
in a place where two *w* met ... Mk 11:4 *296*
face of the Lord to prepare his *w* ... Lk 1:76 *3598*
the rough *w* shall be made smooth ... Lk 3:5 *3598*
Go your *w* ... Lk 10:3
go your *w* out into the streets of ... Lk 10:10
went their *w* to the Pharisees ... Jn 11:46
made known to me the *w* of life ... Acts 2:28 *3598*
pervert the right *w* of the Lord ... Acts 13:10 *3598*
nations to walk in their own *w* ... Acts 14:16 *3598*
and misery are in their *w* ... Rom 3:16 *3598*
and his *w* past finding out ... Rom 11:33 *3598*
of my *w* which be in Christ ... 1Cor 4:17 *3598*
and they have not known my *w* ... Heb 3:10 *3598*
man is unstable in all his *w* ... Jas 1:8 *3598*
the rich man fade away in his *w* ... Jas 1:11 *4197*
shall follow their pernicious *w* ... 2Pet 2:2 *684*
just and true are thy *w*, thou King ... Rev 15:3 *3598*
to the seven angels, Go your *w* ... Rev 16:1

WAYSIDE {2}
sat upon a seat by the *w* watching ... 1Sa 4:13 3197,1870
they have spread a net by the *w* ... Ps 140:5 3027,4570

WE See APPENDIX.

WEAK {47}
whether they be strong or *w* ... Num 13:18 7504
never dried, then shall I be *w* ... Judg 16:7 2470
were occupied, then shall I be *w* ... Judg 16:11 2470
go from me, and I shall become *w* ... Judg 16:17 2470
And I am this day *w*, though ... 2Sa 3:39 7390
w handed, and will make him afraid ... 2Sa 17:2 7504
and let not your hands be *w* ... 2Chr 15:7 7503
hast strengthened the *w* hands ... Job 4:3 7504
for I am *w* ... Ps 6:2 536
My knees are *w* through fasting ... Ps 109:24 3782
Art thou also become *w* as we ... Is 14:10 2470
Strengthen ye the *w* hands ... Is 35:3 7504
and all knees shall be *w* as water ... Eze 7:17 3212
How *w* is thine heart, saith the ... Eze 16:30 535
and all knees shall be *w* as water ... Eze 21:7 3212
let the *w* say, I am strong ... Joel 3:10 2523
is willing, but the flesh is *w* ... Mt 26:41 *772*
is ready, but the flesh is *w* ... Mk 14:38 *772*
ye ought to support the *w* ... Acts 20:35 *770*
And being not *w* in faith, he ... Rom 4:19 *770*
in that it was *w* through the ... Rom 8:3 *770*
Him that is *w* in the faith ... Rom 14:1 *770*
another, who is *w*, eateth herbs ... Rom 14:2 *770*
or is offended, or is made *w* ... Rom 14:21 *770*
to bear the infirmities of the *w* ... Rom 15:1 *102*
God hath chosen the *w* things of ... 1Cor 1:27 *772*
we are *w*, but ye are strong ... 1Cor 4:10 *772*
conscience being *w* is defiled ... 1Cor 8:7 *772*
stumblingblock to them that are *w* ... 1Cor 8:9 *770*
is *w* be emboldened to eat those ... 1Cor 8:10 *772*
shall the *w* brother perish ... 1Cor 8:11 *770*
and wound their *w* conscience ... 1Cor 8:12 *770*
To the *w* became I as *w* ... 1Cor 9:22 *770*
as *w*, that I might gain the *w* ... 1Cor 9:22 *770*
For this cause many are *w* ... 1Cor 11:30 *770*
but his bodily presence is *w* ... 2Cor 10:10 *770*
reproach, as though we had been *w* ... 2Cor 11:21 *770*
Who is *w*, and I am not *w* ... 2Cor 11:29 *770*
for when I am *w*, then am I strong ... 2Cor 12:10 *770*
in me, which to you-ward is not *w* ... 2Cor 13:3 *770*
For we also are *w* in him, but we ... 2Cor 13:4 *770*
For we are glad, when we are *w* ... 2Cor 13:9 *770*
God, how turn ye again to the *w* ... Gal 4:9 *772*
the feebleminded, support the *w* ... 1Th 5:14 *772*

WEAKEN {1}
ground, which didst *w* the nations ... Is 14:12 2522

WEAKENED {3}
land *w* the hands of the people of ... Ezr 4:4 7503
hands shall be *w* from the work ... Neh 6:9 7503
He *w* my strength in the way ... Ps 102:23 6031

WEAKENETH {2}
w the strength of the mighty ... Job 12:21 7503
for thus he *w* the hands of the ... Jer 38:4 7503

WEAKER {3}
house of Saul waxed *w* and *w* ... 2Sa 3:1 1800
the wife, as unto the *w* vessel ... 1Pet 3:7 *772*

WEAKNESS {7}
the *w* of God is stronger than men ... 1Cor 1:25 *772*
And I was with you in *w*, and in ... 1Cor 2:3 *769*
it is sown in *w* ... 1Cor 15:43 *769*
my strength is made perfect in *w* ... 2Cor 12:9 *769*
though he was crucified through *w* ... 2Cor 13:4 *769*
going before for the *w* and ... Heb 7:18 *772*
out of *w* were made strong, waxed ... Heb 11:34 *769*

WEALTH {27}
And all their *w*, and all their ... Gen 34:29 2428
mine hand hath gotten me this *w* ... Deut 8:17 2428
that giveth thee power to get *w* ... Deut 8:18 2428
her husband's, a mighty man of *w* ... Ruth 2:1 2428
in all the *w* which God shall give ... 1Sa 2:32
even of all the mighty men of *w* ... 2Kin 15:20 2428
and thou hast not asked riches, *w* ... 2Chr 1:11 5233
and I will give thee riches, and *w* ... 2Chr 1:12 5233
their peace or their *w* for ever ... Ezr 9:12 2896
seeking the *w* of his people, and ... Est 10:3 2896
They spend their days in *w* ... Job 21:13 2896
I rejoiced because my *w* was great ... Job 31:25 2428
not increase thy *w* by their price ... Ps 44:12
They that trust in their *w* ... Ps 49:6 2428
and leave their *w* to others ... Ps 49:10 2428
W and riches shall be in his house ... Ps 112:3 1952
strangers be filled with thy *w* ... Prov 5:10 3581
The rich man's *w* is his strong ... Prov 10:15 1952
W gotten by vanity shall be ... Prov 13:11 1952
the *w* of the sinner is laid up ... Prov 13:22 2428
The rich man's *w* is his strong ... Prov 18:11 1952
W maketh many friends ... Prov 19:4 1952
whom God hath given riches and *w* ... Eccl 5:19 5233
to whom God hath given riches, *w* ... Eccl 6:2 5233
the *w* of all the heathen round ... Zec 14:14 2428
that by this craft we have our *w* ... Acts 19:25 *2142*
own, but every man another's *w* ... 1Cor 10:24

WEALTHY {2}
broughtest us out into a *w* place ... Ps 66:12 7310
get you up unto the *w* nation ... Jer 49:31 7961

WEANED {12}
And the child grew, and was *w* ... Gen 21:8 1580
the same day that Isaac was *w* ... Gen 21:8 1580
not go up until the child be *w* ... 1Sa 1:22 1580
tarry until thou have *w* him ... 1Sa 1:23 1580
gave her son suck until she *w* him ... 1Sa 1:23 1580
And when she had *w* him, she took ... 1Sa 1:24 1580
whom Tahpenes *w* in Pharaoh's ... 1Kin 11:20 1580
a child that is *w* of his mother ... Ps 131:2 1580
my soul is even as a *w* child ... Ps 131:2 1580
the *w* child shall put his hand on ... Is 11:8 1580
them that are *w* from the milk ... Is 28:9 1580
Now when she had *w* Lo-ruhamah ... Hos 1:8 1580

WEAPON {8}
smite him with an hand *w* of wood ... Num 35:18 3627
shalt have a paddle upon thy *w* ... Deut 23:13 240
man having his *w* in his hand ... 2Chr 23:10 7973
and with the other hand held a *w* ... Neh 4:17 7973
He shall flee from the iron *w* ... Job 20:24 5402
No *w* that is formed against thee ... Is 54:17 3627
with his destroying *w* in his hand ... Eze 9:1 3627
man a slaughter *w* in his hand ... Eze 9:2 3627

WEAPONS {21}
take, I pray thee, thy *w*, thy ... Gen 27:3 3627
girded on every man his *w* of war ... Deut 1:41 3627
men appointed with *w* of war ... Judg 18:11 3627
men appointed with their *w* of war ... Judg 18:16 3627
that were appointed with *w* of war ... Judg 18:17 3627
brought my sword nor my *w* with me ... 1Sa 21:8 3627
fallen, and the *w* of war perished ... 2Sa 1:27 3627
every man with his *w* in his hand ... 2Kin 11:8 3627
every man with his *w* in his hand ... 2Kin 11:11 3627
every man with his *w* in his hand ... 2Chr 23:7 3627
Wisdom is better than *w* of war ... Eccl 9:18 3627
the *w* of his indignation, to ... Is 13:5 3627
I will turn back the *w* of war ... Jer 21:4 3627
thee, every one with his *w* ... Jer 22:7 3627
forth the *w* of his indignation ... Jer 50:25 3627
Thou art my battle ax and *w* of war ... Jer 51:20 3627
down to hell with their *w* of war ... Eze 32:27 3627
shall set on fire and burn the *w* ... Eze 39:9 5402
they shall burn the *w* with fire ... Eze 39:10 5402
with lanterns and torches and *w* ... Jn 18:3 *3696*
(For the *w* of our warfare are not ... 2Cor 10:4 *3696*

WEAR {12}
Thou wilt surely *w* away, both ... Ex 18:18 5034
The woman shall not *w* that which ... Deut 22:5 1961
Thou shalt not *w* a garment of ... Deut 22:11 3847
incense, to *w* an ephod before me ... 1Sa 2:28 5375
persons that did *w* a linen ephod ... 1Sa 22:18 5375
brought which the king useth to *w* ... Est 6:8 3847
The waters *w* the stones ... Job 14:19 7833
own bread, and *w* our own apparel ... Is 4:1 3847
shall *w* out the saints of the ... Dan 7:25 1080
neither shall they *w* a rough ... Zec 13:4 3847
they that *w* soft clothing are in ... Mt 11:8 *5409*
And when the day began to *w* away ... Lk 9:12 *2827*

WEARETH {1}
to him that *w* the gay clothing ... Jas 2:3 *5409*

WEARIED {14}
so that they *w* themselves to find ... Gen 19:11 3811
offering, nor *w* thee with incense ... Is 43:23 3021
thou hast *w* me with thine ... Is 43:24 3021
Thou art *w* in the multitude of ... Is 47:13 3811
Thou art *w* in the greatness of ... Is 57:10 3021
for my soul is *w* because of ... Jer 4:31 5888
the footmen, and they have *w* thee ... Jer 12:5 3811
thou trustedst, they *w* thee ... Jer 12:5
She hath *w* herself with lies, and ... Eze 24:12 3811
and wherein have I *w* thee ... Mic 6:3 3811
Ye have *w* the LORD with your ... Mal 2:17 3021
Yet ye say, Wherein have we *w* him ... Mal 2:17 3021
being *w* with his journey, sat ... Jn 4:6 *2872*
against himself, lest ye be *w* ... Heb 12:3 *2577*

WEARIETH {2}
by watering he *w* the thick cloud ... Job 37:11 2959
the foolish *w* every one of them ... Eccl 10:15 3021

WEARINESS {3}
and much study is a *w* of the flesh ... Eccl 12:12 3024
said also, Behold, what a *w* is it ... Mal 1:13 4972
In *w* and painfulness, in watchings ... 2Cor 11:27 *2873*

WEARING {3}
priest in Shiloh, *w* an ephod ... 1Sa 14:3 5375
w the crown of thorns, and the ... Jn 19:5 *5409*
of *w* of gold, or of putting on of ... 1Pet 3:3 *4025*

WEARISOME {1}
w nights are appointed to me ... Job 7:3 5999

WEARY {42}
I am *w* of my life because of the ... Gen 27:46 6973
thee, when thou wast faint and *w* ... Deut 25:18 3023
for he was fast asleep and *w* ... Judg 4:21 5774
bread unto thy men that are *w* ... Judg 8:15 3286
people that were with him, came *w* ... 2Sa 16:14 5889
will come upon him while he is *w* ... 2Sa 17:2 3023
said, The people is hungry, and *w* ... 2Sa 17:29 5889
Philistines until his hand was *w* ... 2Sa 23:10 3021
and there the *w* be at rest ... Job 3:17 3019
My soul is *w* of my life ... Job 10:1 5354
But now he hath made me *w* ... Job 16:7 3811
not given water to the *w* to drink ... Job 22:7 5889
I am *w* with my groaning ... Ps 6:6 3021

thine inheritance, when it was *w* ... Ps 68:9 3811
I am *w* of my crying ... Ps 69:3 3021
neither be *w* of his correction ... Prov 3:11 6973
lest he be *w* of thee, and so hate ... Prov 25:17 7646
I am *w* to bear them ... Is 1:14 3811
None shall be *w* nor stumble among ... Is 5:27 5889
it a small thing for you to *w* men ... Is 7:13 3811
but will ye *w* my God also ... Is 7:13 3811
that Moab is *w* on the high place ... Is 16:12 3811
ye may cause the *w* to rest ... Is 28:12 5889
of a great rock in a *w* land ... Is 32:2 5889
earth, fainteth not, neither is *w* ... Is 40:28 3021
the youths shall faint and be *w* ... Is 40:30 3021
they shall run, and not be *w* ... Is 40:31 3021
but thou hast been *w* of me ... Is 43:22 3021
they are a burden to the *w* beast ... Is 46:1 5889
a word in season to him that is *w* ... Is 50:4 3287
seek her will not *w* themselves ... Jer 2:24 3286
I am *w* with holding in ... Jer 6:11 3811
w themselves to commit iniquity ... Jer 9:5 3811
I am *w* with repenting ... Jer 15:6 3811
I was *w* with forbearing, and I ... Jer 20:9 3811
For I have satiated the *w* soul ... Jer 31:25 5889
in the fire, and they shall be *w* ... Jer 51:58 3286
and they shall be *w* ... Jer 51:64 3286
the people shall *w* themselves for ... Hab 2:13 3286
by her continual coming she *w* me ... Lk 18:5 *5299*
And let us not be *w* in well doing ... Gal 6:9 *1573*
brethren, be not *w* in well doing ... 2Th 3:13 *1573*

WEASEL {1}
the *w*, and the mouse, and the ... Lev 11:29 2467

WEATHER {4}
Fair *w* cometh out of the north ... Job 37:22 2091
taketh away a garment in cold *w* ... Prov 25:20 3117
ye say, It will be fair *w* ... Mt 16:2 *2105*
morning, It will be foul *w* to day ... Mt 16:3 *5494*

WEAVE {2}
flax, and they that *w* networks ... Is 19:9 707
eggs, and *w* the spider's web ... Is 59:5 707

WEAVER {2}
and in fine linen, and of the *w* ... Ex 35:35 707
I have cut off like a *w* my life ... Is 38:12 707

WEAVER'S {5}
of his spear was like a *w* beam ... 1Sa 17:7 707
of whose spear was like a *w* beam ... 2Sa 21:19 707
hand was a spear like a *w* beam ... 1Chr 11:23 707
spear staff was like a *w* beam ... 1Chr 20:5 707
days are swifter than a *w* shuttle ... Job 7:6

WEAVEST {1}
If thou *w* the seven locks of my ... Judg 16:13 707

WEB {4}
seven locks of my head with the *w* ... Judg 16:13 4545
pin of the beam, and with the *w* ... Judg 16:14 4545
whose trust shall be a spider's *w* ... Job 8:14 1004
eggs, and weave the spider's *w* ... Is 59:5 6980

WEBS {1}
Their *w* shall not become garments ... Is 59:6 6980

WEDDING {7}
them that were bidden to the *w* ... Mt 22:3 *1062*
The *w* is ready, but they which ... Mt 22:8 *1062*
the *w* was furnished with guests ... Mt 22:10 *1062*
man which had not on a *w* garment ... Mt 22:11 *1062*
in hither not having a *w* garment ... Mt 22:12 *1062*
when he will return from the *w* ... Lk 12:36 *1062*
thou art bidden of any man to a *w* ... Lk 14:8 *1062*

WEDGE {3}
a *w* of gold of fifty shekels ... Josh 7:21 3956
the *w* of gold, and his sons, and ... Josh 7:24 3956
a man than the golden *w* of Ophir ... Is 13:12

WEDLOCK {1}
judge thee, as women that break *w* ... Eze 16:38 5003

WEEDS {1}
the *w* were wrapped about my head ... Jonah 2:5 5488

WEEK {13}
Fulfil her *w*, and we will give ... Gen 29:27 7620
Jacob did so, and fulfilled her *w* ... Gen 29:28 7620
the covenant with many for one *w* ... Dan 9:27 7620
in the midst of the *w* he shall ... Dan 9:27 7620
toward the first day of the *w* ... Mt 28:1 *4521*
morning the first day of the *w* ... Mk 16:2 *4521*
early the first day of the *w* ... Mk 16:9 *4521*
I fast twice in the *w*, I give ... Lk 18:12 *4521*
Now upon the first day of the *w* ... Lk 24:1 *4521*
The first day of the *w* cometh ... Jn 20:1 *4521*
being the first day of the *w* ... Jn 20:19 *4521*
And upon the first day of the *w* ... Acts 20:7 *4521*
Upon the first day of the *w* let ... 1Cor 16:2 *4521*

WEEKS {15}
thou shalt observe the feast of *w* ... Ex 34:22 7620
then she shall be unclean two *w* ... Lev 12:5 7620
the LORD, after your *w* be out ... Num 28:26 7620
Seven *w* shalt thou number unto ... Deut 16:9 7620
seven *w* from such time as thou ... Deut 16:9 7620
of *w* unto the LORD thy God with a ... Deut 16:10 7620
bread, and in the feast of *w* ... Deut 16:16 7620
bread, and in the feast of *w* ... 2Chr 8:13 7620
us the appointed *w* of the harvest ... Jer 5:24 7620
Seventy *w* are determined upon thy ... Dan 9:24 7620
the Prince shall be seven *w* ... Dan 9:25 7620
and threescore and two *w* ... Dan 9:25 7620
two *w* shall Messiah be cut off, ... Dan 9:26 7620
Daniel was mourning three full *w* ... Dan 10:2 7620
till three whole *w* were fulfilled ... Dan 10:3 7620

WEEP {49}
mourn for Sarah, and to *w* for her ... Gen 23:2 1058
and he sought where to *w* ... Gen 43:30 1058
w throughout their families ... Num 11:10 1058
for they *w* unto me, saying, Give ... Num 11:13 1058
aileth the people that they *w* ... 1Sa 11:5 1058
until they had no more power to *w* ... 1Sa 30:4 1058
w over Saul, who clothed you in ... 2Sa 1:24 1058
w for the child, while it was ... 2Sa 12:21 1058
rend thy clothes, and *w* before me ... 2Chr 34:27 1058
mourn not, nor *w* ... Neh 8:9 1058
and his widows shall not *w* ... Job 27:15 1058
Did not I *w* for him that was in ... Job 30:25 1058
into the voice of them that *w* ... Job 30:31 1058
A time to *w*, and a time to laugh ... Eccl 3:4 1058
to Dibon, the high places, to *w* ... Is 15:2 1065
I will *w* bitterly, labour not to ... Is 22:4 1065
thou shalt *w* no more ... Is 30:19 1058
of peace shall *w* bitterly ... Is 33:7 1058
of tears, that I might *w* day ... Jer 9:1 1058
my soul shall *w* in secret places ... Jer 13:17 1058
and mine eye shall *w* sore, and run ... Jer 13:17 1830
W ye not for the dead, neither ... Jer 22:10 1058
but *w* sore for him that goeth ... Jer 22:10 1058
I will *w* for thee with the ... Jer 48:32 1058
For these things I *w* ... Lam 1:16 1058
neither shalt thou mourn nor *w* ... Eze 24:16 1058
ye shall not mourn nor *w* ... Eze 24:23 1058
they shall *w* for thee with ... Eze 27:31 1058
Awake, ye drunkards, and *w* ... Joel 1:5 1058
w between the porch and the altar ... Joel 2:17 1058
it not at Gath, *w* ye not at all ... Mic 1:10 1058
Should I *w* in the fifth month, ... Zec 7:3 1058
them, Why make ye this ado, and *w* ... Mk 5:39 *2799*
Blessed are ye that *w* now ... Lk 6:21 *2799*
for ye shall mourn and *w* ... Lk 6:25 *2799*
on her, and said unto her, *W* not ... Lk 7:13 *2799*
but he said, *W* not ... Lk 8:52 *2799*
w not for me, but *w* for ... Lk 23:28 *2799*
goeth unto the grave to *w* there ... Jn 11:31 *2799*
I say unto you, That ye shall *w* ... Jn 16:20 *2799*
Paul answered, What mean ye to *w* ... Acts 21:13 *2799*
rejoice, and *w* with them that *w* ... Rom 12:15 *2799*
And they that *w*, as though they ... 1Cor 7:30 *2799*
Be afflicted, and mourn, and *w* ... Jas 4:9 *2799*
Go to now, ye rich men, *w* ... Jas 5:1 *2799*
the elders saith unto me, *W* not ... Rev 5:5 *2799*
merchants of the earth shall *w* ... Rev 18:11 *2799*

WEEPEST {3}
to her, Hannah, why *w* thou ... 1Sa 1:8 1058
say unto her, Woman, why *w* thou ... Jn 20:13 *2799*
saith unto her, Woman, why *w* thou ... Jn 20:15 *2799*

WEEPETH {4}
was told Joab, Behold, the king *w* ... 2Sa 19:1 1058
And Hazael said, Why *w* my lord ... 2Kin 8:12 1058
He that goeth forth and *w*, bearing ... Ps 126:6 1058
She *w* sore in the night, and her ... Lam 1:2 1058

WEEPING {44}
who were *w* before the door of the ... Num 25:6 1058
so the days of *w* and mourning for ... Deut 34:8 1065
her along *w* behind her to Bahurim ... 2Sa 3:16 1058
they went up, *w* as they went up ... 2Sa 15:30 1058
the noise of the *w* of the people ... Ezr 3:13 1065
and when he had confessed, *w* ... Ezr 10:1 1058
among the Jews, and fasting, and *w* ... Est 4:3 1065
My face is foul with *w*, and on my ... Job 16:16 1065
LORD hath heard the voice of my *w* ... Ps 6:8 1065
w may endure for a night, but joy ... Ps 30:5 1065
bread, and mingled my drink with *w* ... Ps 102:9 1065
one shall howl, *w* abundantly ... Is 15:3 1065
Luhith with *w* shall they go it up ... Is 15:5 1065
I will bewail with the *w* of Jazer ... Is 16:9 1065
the Lord GOD of hosts call to *w* ... Is 22:12 1065
the voice of *w* shall be no more ... Is 65:19 1065
was heard upon the high places, *w* ... Jer 3:21 1065
the mountains will I take up a *w* ... Jer 9:10 1065
They shall come with *w*, and with ... Jer 31:9 1065
Ramah, lamentation, and bitter *w* ... Jer 31:15 1065
Rahel *w* for her children refused ... Jer 31:15 1058
Refrain thy voice from *w*, and ... Jer 31:16 1065
meet them, *w* all along as he went ... Jer 41:6 1058
of Luhith continual *w* shall go up ... Jer 48:5 1065
weep for thee with the *w* of Jazer ... Jer 48:32 1065
of Judah together, going and *w* ... Jer 50:4 1058
there sat women *w* for Tammuz ... Eze 8:14 1058
heart, and with fasting, and with *w* ... Joel 2:12 1065
of the LORD with tears, with *w* ... Mal 2:13 1065
a voice heard, lamentation, and *w* ... Mt 2:18 *2805*
Rachel *w* for her children, and ... Mt 2:18 *2799*
there shall be *w* and gnashing of ... Mt 8:12 *2805*
there shall be *w* and gnashing of ... Mt 22:13 *2805*
there shall be *w* and gnashing of ... Mt 24:51 *2805*
there shall be *w* and gnashing of ... Mt 25:30 *2805*
And stood at his feet behind him *w* ... Lk 7:38 *2799*
There shall be *w* and gnashing of ... Lk 13:28 *2805*
When Jesus therefore saw her *w* ... Jn 11:33 *2799*
the Jews also *w* which came with ... Jn 11:33 *2799*
stood without at the sepulchre *w* ... Jn 20:11 *2799*
and all the widows stood by him *w* ... Acts 9:39 *2799*
you often, and now tell you even *w* ... Phil 3:18 *2799*
for the fear of her torment, *w* ... Rev 18:15 *2799*
dust on their heads, and cried, *w* ... Rev 18:19 *2799*

WEIGH {6}
found it to *w* a talent of gold, ... 1Chr 20:2 4948
until ye *w* them before the chief ... Ezr 8:29 8254
ye *w* the violence of your hands ... Ps 58:2 6424
dost *w* the path of the just ... Is 26:7 6424
w silver in the balance, and hire ... Is 46:6 8254
then take thee balances to *w* ... Eze 5:1 4948

WEIGHED {17}
Abraham *w* to Ephron the silver, ... Gen 23:16 8254
the silver vessels *w* two thousand ... Num 7:85
and by him actions are *w* ... 1Sa 2:3 8505
his spear's head *w* six hundred ... 1Sa 17:7
he *w* the hair of his head at two ... 2Sa 14:26 8254
the weight of whose spear *w* three ... 2Sa 21:16
w unto them the silver, and the ... Ezr 8:25 8254
I even *w* unto their hand six ... Ezr 8:26 8254
the vessels *w* in the house of our ... Ezr 8:33 8254
O that my grief were throughly *w* ... Job 6:2 8254
silver be *w* for the price thereof ... Job 28:15 8254
Let me be *w* in an even balance, ... Job 31:6 8254
w the mountains in scales, and the ... Is 40:12 8254
w him the money, even seventeen ... Jer 32:9 8254
w him the money in the balances ... Jer 32:10 8254
Thou art *w* in the balances, and ... Dan 5:27 8625
So they *w* for my price thirty ... Zec 11:12 8254

WEIGHETH {2}
he *w* the waters by measure ... Job 28:25 8505
but the LORD *w* the spirits ... Prov 16:2 8505

WEIGHING {2}
charger of silver *w* an hundred ... Num 7:85
w ten shekels apiece, after the ... Num 7:86

WEIGHT {58}
golden earring of half a shekel *w* ... Gen 24:22 4948
hands of ten shekels *w* of gold ... Gen 24:22 4948
of his sack, our money in full *w* ... Gen 43:21 4948
of each shall there be a like *w* ... Ex 30:34
in judgment, in meteyard, in *w* ... Lev 19:35 4948
deliver you your bread again by *w* ... Lev 26:26 4948
the *w* thereof was an hundred and ... Num 7:13
the *w* whereof was an hundred and ... Num 7:19
the *w* whereof was an hundred and ... Num 7:25
charger of the *w* of an hundred ... Num 7:31 4948
the *w* whereof was an hundred and ... Num 7:37 4948
charger of the *w* of an hundred ... Num 7:43 4948
the *w* whereof was an hundred and ... Num 7:49 4948
charger of the *w* of an hundred ... Num 7:55 4948
the *w* whereof was an hundred and ... Num 7:61 4948
the *w* whereof was an hundred and ... Num 7:67 4948
the *w* whereof was an hundred and ... Num 7:73 4948
the *w* whereof was an hundred and ... Num 7:79 4948
shalt have a perfect and just *w* ... Deut 25:15 68
wedge of gold of fifty shekels *w* ... Josh 7:21 4948
the *w* of the golden earrings that ... Judg 8:26 4948
the *w* of the coat was five ... 1Sa 17:5 4948
the *w* whereof was a talent of ... 2Sa 12:30 4948
shekels after the king's *w* ... 2Sa 14:26 68
the *w* of whose spear weighed ... 2Sa 21:16 4948
hundred shekels of brass in *w* ... 2Sa 21:16 4948
neither was the *w* of the brass ... 1Kin 7:47 4948
Now the *w* of gold that came to ... 1Kin 10:14 4948
all these vessels was without *w* ... 2Kin 25:16 4948
six hundred shekels of gold by *w* ... 1Chr 21:25 4948
and brass in abundance without *w* ... 1Chr 22:3 4948
and of brass and iron without *w* ... 1Chr 22:14 4948
of gold by *w* for things of gold ... 1Chr 28:14 4948
all instruments of silver by *w* ... 1Chr 28:14 4948
Even the *w* for the candlesticks ... 1Chr 28:15 4948
by *w* for every candlestick, and ... 1Chr 28:15 4948
the candlesticks of silver by *w* ... 1Chr 28:15 4948
by *w* he gave gold for the tables ... 1Chr 28:16 4948
he gave gold by *w* for every bason ... 1Chr 28:17 4948
likewise silver by *w* for every ... 1Chr 28:17 4948
of incense refined gold by *w* ... 1Chr 28:18 4948
the *w* of the nails was fifty ... 2Chr 3:9 4948
for the *w* of the brass could not ... 2Chr 4:18 4948
Now the *w* of gold that came to ... 2Chr 9:13 4948
the Levites the *w* of the silver ... Ezr 8:30 4948
By number and by *w* of every one ... Ezr 8:34 4948
all the *w* was written at that ... Ezr 8:34 4948
To make the *w* for the winds ... Job 28:25 4948
but a just *w* is his delight ... Prov 11:1 68
A just *w* and balance are the ... Prov 16:11 6425
all these vessels was without *w* ... Jer 52:20 4948
thou shalt eat shall be by *w* ... Eze 4:10 4946
and they shall eat bread by *w* ... Eze 4:16 4948
he cast the *w* of lead upon the ... Zec 5:8 68
aloes, about an hundred pound *w* ... Jn 19:39
exceeding and eternal *w* of glory ... 2Cor 4:17 *922*
let us lay aside every *w* ... Heb 12:1 *3591*
stone about the *w* of a talent ... Rev 16:21 *5006*

WEIGHTIER {1}
have omitted the *w* matters of the ... Mt 23:23 *926*

WEIGHTS {6}
Just balances, just *w*, a just ... Lev 19:36 68
not have in thy bag divers *w* ... Deut 25:13 68
all the *w* of the bag are his work ... Prov 16:11 68
Divers *w*, and divers measures, ... Prov 20:10 68
Divers *w* are an abomination unto ... Prov 20:23 68
and with the bag of deceitful *w* ... Mic 6:11 68

WEIGHTY {2}
A stone is heavy, and the sand *w* ... Prov 27:3 5192
For his letters, say they, are *w* ... 2Cor 10:10 *926*

WELFARE {7}
And he asked them of their *w* ... Gen 43:27 7965
they asked each other of their *w* ... Ex 18:7 7965
king David, to enquire of his *w* ... 1Chr 18:10 7965
the *w* of the children of Israel ... Neh 2:10 2896
my *w* passeth away as a cloud ... Job 30:15 3444

should have been for their *w* Ps 69:22 7965
seeketh not the *w* of this people Jer 38:4 7965

WELL {256}
If thou doest *w*, shalt thou not Gen 4:7 3190
and if thou doest not *w*, sin lieth Gen 4:7 3190
that it may be *w* with me for thy Gen 12:13 3190
he entreated Abram *w* for her sake Gen 12:16 3190
that it was *w* watered every where Gen 13:10
Wherefore the *w* was called Gen 16:14 875
were old and *w* stricken in age Gen 18:11
her eyes, and she saw a *w* of water Gen 21:19 875
Abimelech because of a *w* of water Gen 21:25 875
me, that I have digged this *w* Gen 21:30 875
was old, and *w* stricken in age Gen 24:1
down without the city by a *w* of Gen 24:11 875
I stand here by the *w* of water Gen 24:13 5869
and she went down to the *w* Gen 24:16 5869
again unto the *w* to draw water Gen 24:20 875
ran out unto the man, unto the *w* Gen 24:29 5869
he stood by the camels at the *w* Gen 24:30 5869
And I came this day unto the *w* Gen 24:42 5869
Behold, I stand by the *w* of water Gen 24:43 5869
and she went down unto the *w* Gen 24:45 5869
from the way of the *w* Lahai-roi Gen 24:62
and Isaac dwelt by the *w* Lahai-roi Gen 25:11 883
found there a *w* of springing Gen 26:19 875
he called the name of the *w* Esek Gen 26:20 875
And they digged another *w*, and Gen 26:21 875
from thence, and digged another *w* Gen 26:22 875
there Isaac's servants digged a *w* Gen 26:25 875
the *w* which they had digged Gen 26:32 875
behold a *w* in the field, and, lo, Gen 29:2 875
for out of that *w* they watered Gen 29:2 875
And he said unto them, Is he *w* Gen 29:6 7965
And they said, He is *w* Gen 29:6 7965
was beautiful and *w* favoured Gen 29:17 3303
and I will deal *w* with thee Gen 32:9 3190
whether it be *w* with thy brethren Gen 37:14 7965
and *w* with the flocks Gen 37:14 7965
a goodly person, and *w* favoured Gen 39:6 3303
me when it shall be *w* with thee Gen 40:14 3190
the river seven *w* favoured kine Gen 41:2 3303
did eat up the seven *w* favoured Gen 41:4 3303
kine, fatfleshed and *w* favoured Gen 41:18 3303
and said, Is your father *w* Gen 43:27 7965
and it pleased Pharaoh *w*, and his Gen 45:16
even a fruitful bough by a *w* Gen 49:22 5869
God dealt *w* with the midwives Ex 1:20 3190
and he sat down by a *w* Ex 2:15 875
I know that he can speak *w* Ex 4:14
And Moses said, Thou hast spoken *w* Ex 10:29 3651
as *w* the stranger, as he that is Lev 24:16
as *w* for the stranger, as for one Lev 24:22
for it was *w* with us in Egypt Num 11:18 2895
for we are *w* able to overcome it Num 13:30
that is the *w* whereof the LORD Num 21:16 875
sang this song, Spring up, O *w* Num 21:17 875
The princes digged the *w*, the Num 21:18 875
not drink of the waters of the *w* Num 21:22 875
of the sons of Joseph hath said *w* Num 36:5 3651
hear the small as *w* as the great Deut 1:17
And the saying pleased me *w* Deut 1:23
as *w* as unto you, and until they Deut 3:20
day, that it may go *w* with thee Deut 4:40 3190
maidservant may rest as *w* as thou Deut 5:14
and that it may go *w* with thee Deut 5:16 3190
they have *w* said all that they Deut 5:28 3190
that it might be *w* with them Deut 5:29 3190
and that it may be *w* with you Deut 5:33 2895
that it may be *w* with thee Deut 6:3 3190
that it may be *w* with thee Deut 6:18 3190
but shalt *w* remember what the Deut 7:18
that it may go *w* with thee Deut 12:25 3190
thee, that it may go *w* with thee Deut 12:28 3190
house, because he is *w* with thee Deut 15:16 2895
They have *w* spoken that which Deut 18:17 3190
that it may go *w* with thee Deut 19:13 2895
heart faint as *w* as his heart Deut 20:8
that it may be *w* with thee Deut 22:7 3190
as *w* the stranger, as he that was Josh 8:33
went out to the *w* of waters of Josh 18:15 4599
and pitched beside the *w* of Harod Judg 7:1 5878
if ye have dealt *w* with Jerubbaal Judg 9:16 2895
for she pleaseth me *w* Judg 14:3
and she pleased Samson *w* Judg 14:7
as *w* the men of every city, as Judg 20:48 3190
thee, that it may be *w* with thee Ruth 3:1 3190
thee the part of a kinsman, *w* Ruth 3:13 2896
said Saul to his servant, *W* said 1Sa 9:10 2896
with his hand, and thou shalt be *w* 1Sa 16:16 2895
me now a man that can play *w* 1Sa 16:17 3190
so Saul was refreshed, and was *w* 1Sa 16:23 2895
it pleased David *w* to be the 1Sa 18:26
came to a great *w* that is in 1Sa 19:22 953
If he say thus, It is *w* 1Sa 20:7 2896
that thou hast dealt *w* with me 1Sa 24:18 2896
enemy, will he let him go *w* away 1Sa 24:19 2896
I know *w* that thou shalt surely 1Sa 24:20
shall have dealt *w* with my lord 1Sa 25:31 3190
And he said, *W* 2Sa 3:13 2896
him again from the *w* of Sirah 2Sa 3:26 953
as *w* to the women as men, to 2Sa 6:19
devoureth one as *w* as another 2Sa 11:25 2090
And the saying pleased Absalom *w* 2Sa 17:4
which had a *w* in his court 2Sa 17:18 375
that they came up out of the *w* 2Sa 17:21 375
and said unto the king, All is *w* 2Sa 18:28 7965
day, then it had pleased thee *w* 2Sa 19:6
the water of the *w* of Beth-lehem 2Sa 23:15 953
water out of the *w* of Beth-lehem 2Sa 23:16 953
And Bath-sheba said, *W* 1Kin 2:18 2896
thou didst *w* that it was in thine 1Kin 8:18 3190
answered and said, It is *w* spoken 1Kin 18:24 2896
And she said, It shall be *w* 2Kin 4:23 7965
say unto her, Is it *w* with thee 2Kin 4:26 7965
is it *w* with thy husband 2Kin 4:26 7965
is it *w* with the child 2Kin 4:26 7965
And she answered, It is *w* 2Kin 4:26 7965
to meet him, and said, Is all *w* 2Kin 5:21 7965
And he said, All is *w* 2Kin 5:22 7965
said one to another, We do not *w* 2Kin 7:9 3651
and one said unto him, Is all *w* 2Kin 9:11 7965
Because thou hast done *w* in 2Kin 10:30 2895
and it shall be *w* with you 2Kin 25:24 3190
the water of the *w* of Beth-lehem 1Chr 11:17 953
water out of the *w* of Beth-lehem 1Chr 11:18 953
as *w* the small as the great, the 1Chr 25:8
as *w* the small as the great, 1Chr 26:13
thou didst *w* in that it was in 2Chr 6:8 2895
and also in Judah things went *w* 2Chr 12:12 2896
as *w* to the great as to the small 2Chr 31:15
valley, even before the dragon *w* Neh 2:13 5869
I have understanding as *w* as you Job 12:3 71
Mark *w*, O Job, hearken unto me Job 33:31 7181
Mark ye *w* her bulwarks, consider Ps 48:13
when thou doest *w* to thyself Ps 49:18 3190
my steps had *w* nigh slipped Ps 73:2 369
So they did eat, and were *w* filled Ps 78:29 3966
the valley of Baca make it a *w* Ps 84:6 4599
As *w* the singers as the players Ps 87:7
Thou hast dealt *w* with thy Ps 119:65 2896
be, and it shall be *w* with thee Ps 128:2 2896
and that my soul knoweth right *w* Ps 139:14
running waters out of thine own *w* Prov 5:15 875
of a righteous man is a *w* of life Prov 10:11 4726
When it goeth *w* with the Prov 11:10 2898
but with the *w* advised is wisdom Prov 13:10
man looketh *w* to his going Prov 14:15 995
Then I saw, and considered it *w* Prov 24:32 3190
flocks, and look *w* to thy herds Prov 27:23
There be three things which go *w* Prov 30:29 3190
She looketh *w* to the ways of her Prov 31:27 6822
be *w* with them that fear God Eccl 8:12 2896
it shall not be *w* with the wicked Eccl 8:13 2896
a *w* of living waters, and streams Song 4:15 875
Learn to do *w* Is 1:17 3190
that it shall be *w* with him Is 3:10 2896
instead of *w* set hair baldness Is 3:24 4639
of wines on the lees *w* refined Is 25:6
they could not *w* strengthen their Is 33:23 3651
The LORD is *w* pleased for his Is 42:21 2654
LORD unto me, Thou hast *w* seen Jer 1:12 3190
you, that it may be *w* unto you Jer 7:23 3190
it shall be *w* with thy remnant Jer 15:11 2896
thee *w* in the time of evil Jer 15:11
and then it was *w* with him Jer 22:15 2896
then it was *w* with him Jer 22:16 2896
so it shall be *w* unto thee Jer 38:20 3190
look *w* to him, and do him no harm Jer 39:12
and I will look *w* unto thee Jer 40:4
and it shall be *w* with you Jer 40:9 3190
that it may be *w* with us, when we Jer 42:6 2896
we plenty of victuals, and were *w* Jer 44:17 2896
bones under it, and make it boil *w* Eze 24:5 7571
consume the flesh, and spice it *w* Eze 24:10
can play *w* on an instrument Eze 33:32
said unto me, Son of man, mark *w* Eze 44:5
mark *w* the entering in of the Eze 44:5
inherit it, one as *w* as another Eze 47:14
but *w* favoured, and skilful in all Dan 1:4 2896
which I have made; *w* Dan 3:15
LORD, Doest thou *w* to be angry Jonah 4:4 3190
Doest thou *w* to be angry for the Jonah 4:9 3190
I do *w* to be angry, even unto Jonah 4:9 3190
these days to do *w* unto Jerusalem Zec 8:15 3190
Son, in whom I am *w* pleased Mt 3:17 *2106*
to do *w* on the sabbath days Mt 12:12 *2573*
in whom my soul is *w* pleased Mt 12:18 *2106*
w did Esaias prophesy of you, Mt 15:7 *2573*
Son, in whom I am *w* pleased Mt 17:5 *2106*
W done, thou good and faithful Mt 25:21 *2095*
W done, good and faithful servant Mt 25:23 *2095*
Son, in whom I am *w* pleased Mk 1:11 *2106*
W hath Esaias prophesied of you Mk 7:6 *2573*
Full *w* ye reject the commandment Mk 7:9 *2573*
saying, He hath done all things *w* Mk 7:37 *2573*
that he had answered them *w* Mk 12:28 *2573*
And the scribe said unto him, *W* Mk 12:32 *2573*
both were now *w* stricken in years Lk 1:7 *4260*
my wife *w* stricken in years Lk 1:18 *4260*
in thee I am *w* pleased Lk 3:22 *2106*
when all men shall speak *w* of you Lk 6:26 *2573*
And if it bear fruit, *w* Lk 13:9 *2573*
And he said unto him, *W*, thou good Lk 19:17 *2095*
said, Master, thou hast *w* said Lk 20:39 *2573*
and when men have *w* drunk, then Jn 2:10 *3184*
Now Jacob's *w* was there Jn 4:6 *4077*
his journey, sat thus on the *w* Jn 4:6 *4077*
to draw with, and the *w* is deep Jn 4:11 *5421*
father Jacob, which gave us the *w* Jn 4:12 *5421*
a *w* of water springing up into Jn 4:14 *4077*
said unto her, Thou hast *w* said Jn 4:17 *2573*
Say we not *w* that thou art a Jn 8:48 *2573*
Lord, if he sleep, he shall do *w* Jn 11:12 *4982*
and ye say *w* Jn 13:13 *2573*
but if *w*, why smitest thou me Jn 18:23 *2573*
thou hast *w* done that thou art Acts 10:33 *2573*
the Holy Ghost as *w* as we Acts 10:47 *2532*
ye keep yourselves, ye shall do *w* Acts 15:29 *2095*
Fare ye *w* Acts 15:29 *2095*
Which was *w* reported of by the Acts 16:2 *3140*
no wrong, as thou very *w* knowest Acts 25:10 *2573*
W spake the Holy Ghost by Esaias Acts 28:25 *2573*
in *w* doing seek for glory Rom 2:7 *18*
W; because of unbelief Rom 11:20 *2573*
he will keep his virgin, doeth *w* 1Cor 7:37 *2573*
giveth her in marriage doeth *w* 1Cor 7:38 *2573*
as *w* as other apostles, and as the 1Cor 9:5 *2532*
of them God was not *w* pleased 1Cor 10:5 *2106*
For thou verily givest thanks *w* 1Cor 14:17 *2573*
As unknown, and yet *w* known 2Cor 6:9 *1921*
ye might *w* bear with him 2Cor 11:4 *2573*
zealously affect you, but not *w* Gal 4:17 *2573*
Ye did run *w* Gal 5:7 *2573*
And let us not be weary in *w* doing Gal 6:9 *2570*
That it may be *w* with thee Eph 6:3 *2095*
Notwithstanding ye have *w* done Phil 4:14 *2573*
for this is *w* pleasing unto the Col 3:20 *2101*
brethren, be not weary in *w* doing 2Th 3:13 *2569*
One that ruleth *w* his own house 1Ti 3:4 *2573*
children and their own houses *w* 1Ti 3:12 *2573*
used the office of a deacon *w* 1Ti 3:13 *2573*
W reported of for good works 1Ti 5:10 *3140*
Let the elders that rule *w* be 1Ti 5:17 *2573*
at Ephesus, thou knowest very *w* 2Ti 1:18 *957*
and to please them *w* in all things Titus 2:9 *1510,2101*
preached, as *w* as unto them Heb 4:2 *2509*
such sacrifices God is *w* pleased Heb 13:16 *2100*
thy neighbour as thyself, ye do *w* Jas 2:8 *2573*
thou doest *w* Jas 2:19 *2573*
for the praise of them that do *w* 1Pet 2:14 *17*
that with *w* doing ye may put to 1Pet 2:15 *15*
but if, when ye do *w*, and suffer 1Pet 2:20 *15*
ye are, as long as ye do *w* 1Pet 3:6 *15*
be so, that ye suffer for *w* doing 1Pet 3:17 *15*
of their souls to him in *w* doing 1Pet 4:19 *16*
Son, in whom I am *w* pleased 2Pet 1:17 *2106*
whereunto ye do *w* that ye take 2Pet 1:19 *2573*
a godly sort, thou shalt do *w* 3Jn 6 *2573*

WELLBELOVED {6}
A bundle of myrrh is my *w* unto me Song 1:13 1730
Now will I sing to my *w* a song of Is 5:1 3039
My *w* hath a vineyard in a very Is 5:1 3039
yet therefore one son, his *w* Mk 12:6 *27*
Salute my *w* Epaenetus, who is the Rom 16:5 *27*
The elder unto the *w* Gaius 3Jn 1 *27*

WELLFAVOURED {1}
of the whoredoms of the *w* harlot Nah 3:4

WELLPLEASING {2}
a sacrifice acceptable, *w* to God Phil 4:18 *2101*
you that which is *w* in his sight Heb 13:21 *2101*

WELL'S {6}
great stone was upon the *w* mouth Gen 29:2 875
rolled the stone from the *w* mouth Gen 29:3 875
upon the *w* mouth in his place Gen 29:3 875
roll the stone from the *w* mouth Gen 29:8 875
rolled the stone from the *w* mouth Gen 29:10 875
a covering over the *w* mouth 2Sa 17:19 875

WELLS {11}
For all the *w* which his father's Gen 26:15 875
Isaac digged again the *w* of water Gen 26:18 875
where were twelve *w* of water Ex 15:27 5869
we drink of the water of the *w* Num 20:17 875
w digged, which thou diggedst not Deut 6:11 953
good tree, and stop all *w* of water 2Kin 3:19 4599
they stopped all the *w* of water 2Kin 3:25 4599
in the desert, and digged many *w* 2Chr 26:10 953
goods, *w* digged, vineyards, and Neh 9:25 953
water out of the *w* of salvation Is 12:3 4599
These are *w* without water, clouds 2Pet 2:17 *4077*

WELLSPRING {2}
Understanding is a *w* of life unto Prov 16:22 4726
the *w* of wisdom as a flowing Prov 18:4 4726

WEN {1}
broken, or maimed, or having a *w* Lev 22:22 2990

WENCH {1}
and a *w* went and told them 2Sa 17:17 8198

WENT See APPENDIX.

WENTEST {14}
because thou *w* up to thy father's Gen 49:4 5927
when thou *w* out of Seir, when Judg 5:4 3318
when thou *w* to fight with the Judg 8:1 1980
which thou *w* to seek are found 1Sa 10:2 1980
with thee whithersoever thou *w* 2Sa 7:9 1980
why *w* thou not with thy friend 2Sa 16:17 1980
Wherefore *w* not thou with me, 2Sa 19:25 1980
when thou *w* forth before thy Ps 68:7 3318
even thither *w* thou up to offer Is 57:7 5927
thou *w* to the king with ointment, Is 57:9 7788
when thou *w* after me in the Jer 2:2 3212
even the way which thou *w* Jer 31:21 1980
Thou *w* forth for the salvation of Hab 3:13 3318
Thou *w* in to men uncircumcised, Acts 11:3 *1525*

WEPT {71}
him, and lift up her voice, and *w* Gen 21:16 1058
And Esau lifted up his voice, and *w* Gen 27:38 1058
and lifted up his voice, and *w* Gen 29:11 1058
and they *w* Gen 33:4 1058
Thus his father *w* for him Gen 37:35 1058

himself about from them, and *w* Gen 42:24 1058
into his chamber, and *w* there Gen 43:30 1058
And he *w* aloud Gen 45:2
his brother Benjamin's neck, and *w* Gen 45:14 1058
and Benjamin *w* upon his neck Gen 45:14 1058
all his brethren, and *w* upon them Gen 45:15 1058
w on his neck a good while Gen 46:29 1058
w upon him, and kissed him Gen 50:1 1058
Joseph *w* when they spake unto him Gen 50:17 1058
and, behold, the babe *w* Ex 2:6 1058
children of Israel also *w* again Num 11:4 1058
for ye have *w* in the ears of the Num 11:18 1058
have *w* before him, saying, Why Num 11:20 1058
and the people *w* that night Num 14:1 1058
ye returned and *w* before the LORD Deut 1:45 1058
the children of Israel *w* for Deut 34:8 1058
lifted up their voice, and *w* Judg 2:4 1058
And Samson's wife *w* before him Judg 14:16 1058
she *w* before him the seven days, Judg 14:17 1058
w before the LORD until even, and Judg 20:23 1058
came unto the house of God, and *w* Judg 20:26 1058
lifted up their voices, and *w* sore Judg 21:2 1058
they lifted up their voice, and *w* Ruth 1:9 1058
lifted up their voice, and *w* again Ruth 1:14 1058
therefore she *w*, and did not eat 1Sa 1:7 1058
prayed unto the LORD, and *w* sore 1Sa 1:10 1058
lifted up their voices, and *w* 1Sa 11:4 1058
w one with another, until David 1Sa 20:41 1058
And Saul lifted up his voice, and *w* 1Sa 24:16 1058
him lifted up their voice and *w* 1Sa 30:4 1058
And they mourned, and *w*, and fasted 2Sa 1:12 1058
voice, and *w* at the grave of Abner 2Sa 3:32 1058
and all the people *w* 2Sa 3:32 1058
all the people *w* again over him 2Sa 3:34 1058
was yet alive, I fasted and *w* 2Sa 12:22 1058
and lifted up their voice and *w* 2Sa 13:36 1058
and all his servants *w* very sore 2Sa 13:36 1058
all the country *w* with a loud 2Sa 15:23 1058
w as he went up, and had his head 2Sa 15:30 1058
the chamber over the gate, and *w* 2Sa 18:33 1058
and the man of God *w* 2Kin 8:11 1058
w over his face, and said, O my 2Kin 13:14 1058
And Hezekiah *w* sore 2Kin 20:3 1058
rent thy clothes, and *w* before me 2Kin 22:19 1058
their eyes, *w* with a loud voice Ezr 3:12 1058
for the people *w* very sore Ezr 10:1 1058
these words, that I sat down and *w* Neh 1:4 1058
For all the people *w*, when they Neh 8:9 1058
they lifted up their voice, and *w* Job 2:12 1058
When I *w*, and chastened my soul Ps 69:10 1058
there we sat down, yea, we *w* Ps 137:1 1058
And Hezekiah *w* sore Is 38:3 1058
he *w*, and made supplication unto Hos 12:4 1058
And he went out, and *w* bitterly Mt 26:75 *2799*
seeth the tumult, and them that *w* Mk 5:38 *2799*
And when he thought thereon, he *w* Mk 14:72 *2799*
with him, as they mourned and *w* Mk 16:10 *2799*
mourned to you, and ye have not *w* Lk 7:32 *2799*
And all *w*, and bewailed her Lk 8:52 *2799*
he beheld the city, and *w* over it, Lk 19:41 *2799*
And Peter went out, and *w* bitterly Lk 22:62 *2799*
Jesus *w* Jn 11:35 *1145*
and as she *w*, she stooped down, and Jn 20:11 *2799*
And they all *w* sore, and fell on Acts 20:37
that weep, as though they *w* not 1Cor 7:30 *2799*
I *w* much, because no man was Rev 5:4 *2799*

WERE See APPENDIX.

WERT {6}
If thou *w* pure and upright Job 8:6
O that thou *w* as my brother, that Song 8:1
w graffed in among them, and with Rom 11:17
For if thou *w* cut out of the Rom 11:24
w graffed contrary to nature into Rom 11:24
I would thou *w* cold or hot Rev 3:15 *1498*

WEST {69}
his tent, having Beth-el on the *w* Gen 12:8 3220
thou shalt spread abroad to the *w* Gen 28:14 3220
turned a mighty strong *w* wind Ex 10:19 3220
w side shall be hangings of fifty Ex 27:12 3220
for the *w* side were hangings of Ex 38:12 3220
On the *w* side shall be the Num 2:18 3220
this shall be your *w* border Num 34:6 3220
on the *w* side two thousand cubits Num 35:5 3220
of the LORD, possess thou the *w* Deut 33:23 3220
and Ai, on the *w* side of Ai Josh 8:9 3220
on the *w* side of the city Josh 8:12 3220
in wait on the *w* of the city Josh 8:13 3220
and in the borders of Dor on the *w* Josh 11:2 3220
Canaanite on the east and on the *w* Josh 11:3 3220
on this side Jordan on the *w* Josh 12:7 3220
the *w* border was to the great sea Josh 15:12 3220
this was the *w* quarter Josh 18:14 3220
and the border went out on the *w* Josh 18:15 3220
reacheth to Asher on the *w* side Josh 19:34 3220
and three looking toward the *w* 1Kin 7:25 3220
the porters, toward the east, *w* 1Chr 9:24 3220
toward the east, and toward the *w* 1Chr 12:15 4628
and three looking toward the *w* 2Chr 4:4 3220
the *w* side of the city of David 2Chr 32:30 4628
on the *w* side of Gihon, in the 2Chr 33:14 4628
from the east, nor from the *w* Ps 75:6 4628
As far as the east is from the *w* Ps 103:12 4628
from the east, and from the *w* Ps 107:3 4628
of the Philistines toward the *w* Is 11:14 3220
east, and gather thee from the *w* Is 43:5 4628
rising of the sun, and from the *w* Is 45:6 4628
from the north and from the *w* Is 49:12 3220
the name of the LORD from the *w* Is 59:19 4628
the *w* was seventy cubits broad Eze 41:12 3220
He turned about to the *w* side Eze 42:19 3220
from the *w* side westward, and from Eze 45:7 3220
from the *w* border unto the east Eze 45:7 3220
The *w* side also shall be the Eze 47:20 3220
This is the *w* side Eze 47:20 3220
for these are his sides east and *w* Eze 48:1 3220
the east side unto the *w* side Eze 48:2 3220
east side even unto the *w* side Eze 48:3 3220
the east side unto the *w* side Eze 48:4 3220
the east side unto the *w* side Eze 48:5 3220
east side even unto the *w* side Eze 48:6 3220
the east side unto the *w* side Eze 48:7 3220
the east side unto the *w* side Eze 48:8 3220
the east side unto the *w* side Eze 48:8 3220
toward the *w* ten thousand in Eze 48:10 3220
the *w* side four thousand and five Eze 48:16 3220
toward the *w* two hundred and fifty Eze 48:17 3220
thousand toward the *w* border Eze 48:21 3220
the east side unto the *w* side Eze 48:23 3220
the east side unto the *w* side Eze 48:24 3220
the east side unto the *w* side Eze 48:25 3220
the east side unto the *w* side Eze 48:26 3220
the east side unto the *w* side Eze 48:27 3220
At the *w* side four thousand and Eze 48:34 3220
an he goat came from the *w* on the Dan 8:5 4628
children shall tremble from the *w* Hos 11:10 3220
country, and from the *w* country Zec 8:7 3996,8121
toward the east and toward the *w* Zec 14:4 3220
shall come from the east and *w* Mt 8:11 *1424*
east, and shineth even unto the *w* Mt 24:27 *1424*
ye see a cloud rise out of the *w* Lk 12:54 *1424*
come from the east, and from the *w* Lk 13:29 *1424*
and lieth toward the south *w* Acts 27:12 *3047*
and north *w* Acts 27:12 *5566*
and on the *w* three gates Rev 21:13 *1424*

WESTERN {1}
And as for the *w* border, ye shall Num 34:6 3220

WESTWARD {26}
and southward, and eastward, and *w* Gen 13:14 3220
w thou shalt make six boards Ex 26:22 3220
tabernacle, for the two sides *w* Ex 26:27 3220
tabernacle *w* he made six boards Ex 36:27 3220
of the tabernacle for the sides *w* Ex 36:32 3220
pitch behind the tabernacle *w* Num 3:23 3220
Pisgah, and lift up thine eyes *w* Deut 3:27 3220
were on the side of Jordan *w* Josh 5:1 3220
before the valley of Hinnom *w* Josh 15:8 3220
from Baalah *w* unto mount Seir Josh 15:10 3220
goeth down *w* to the coast of Josh 16:3 3220
Tappuah *w* unto the river Kanah Josh 16:8 3220
went up through the mountains *w* Josh 18:12 3220
and reacheth to Carmel *w*, and to Josh 19:26 3220
coast turneth *w* to Aznoth-tabor Josh 19:34 3220
brethren on this side Jordan *w* Josh 22:7 3220
off, even unto the great sea *w* Josh 23:4 3996,8121
w Gezer, with the towns thereof 1Chr 7:28 4628
and Hosah the lot came forth *w* 1Chr 26:16 4628
At Parbar *w*, four at the causeway 1Chr 26:18 4628
of Israel on this side Jordan *w* 1Chr 26:30 4628
of the city, from the west side *w* Eze 45:7 3220
was a place on the two sides *w* Eze 46:19 3220
eastward, and ten thousand *w* Eze 48:18 3220
w over against the five and twenty Eze 48:21 3220
I saw the ram pushing *w*, and Dan 8:4 3220

WET {6}
They are *w* with the showers of Job 24:8 7372
let it be *w* with the dew of Dan 4:15 6647
let it be *w* with the dew of Dan 4:23 6647
they shall *w* thee with the dew of Dan 4:25 6647
his body was *w* with the dew of Dan 4:33 6647
his body was *w* with the dew of Dan 5:21 6647

WHALE {2}
Am I a sea, or a *w*, that thou Job 7:12 8577
and thou art as a *w* in the seas Eze 32:2 8565

WHALE'S {1}
and three nights in the *w* belly Mt 12:40 *2785*

WHALES {1}
And God created great *w*, and every Gen 1:21 8577

WHAT See APPENDIX.

WHATSOEVER See APPENDIX.

WHEAT {51}
went in the days of *w* harvest Gen 30:14 2406
But the *w* and the rie were not Ex 9:32 2406
of the firstfruits of *w* harvest Ex 34:22 2406
the best of the wine, and of the *w* Num 18:12 1715
A land of *w*, and barley, and vines, Deut 8:8 2406
with the fat of kidneys of *w* Deut 32:14 2406
threshed *w* by the winepress Judg 6:11 2406
after, in the time of *w* harvest Judg 15:1 2406
of barley harvest and of *w* harvest Ruth 2:23 2406
their *w* harvest in the valley 1Sa 6:13 2406
Is it not *w* harvest to day 1Sa 12:17 2406
though they would have fetched *w* 2Sa 4:6 2406
basons, and earthen vessels, and *w* 2Sa 17:28 2406
of *w* for food to his household 1Kin 5:11 2406
Now Ornan was threshing *w* 1Chr 21:20 2406
the *w* for the meat offering 1Chr 21:23 2406
thousand measures of beaten *w* 2Chr 2:10 2406
Now therefore the *w*, and the 2Chr 2:15 2406
and ten thousand measures of *w* 2Chr 27:5 2406
offerings of the God of heaven, *w* Ezr 6:9 2591
and to an hundred measures of *w* Ezr 7:22 2591
Let thistles grow instead of *w* Job 31:40 2406
also with the finest of the *w* Ps 81:16 2406
thee with the finest of the *w* Ps 147:14 2406
in a mortar among *w* with a pestle Prov 27:22 7383
heap of *w* set about with lilies Song 7:2 2406
and cast in the principal *w* Is 28:25 2406
They have sown *w*, but shall reap Jer 12:13 2406
What is the chaff to the *w* Jer 23:28 1250
the goodness of the LORD, for *w* Jer 31:12 1715
have treasures in the field, of *w* Jer 41:8 2406
Take thou also unto thee *w* Eze 4:9 2406
traded in thy market *w* of Minnith Eze 27:17 2406
part of an ephah of an homer of *w* Eze 45:13 2406
O ye vinedressers, for the *w* Joel 1:11 2406
And the floors shall be full of *w* Joel 2:24 1250
and ye take from him burdens of *w* Amos 5:11 1250
sabbath, that we may set forth *w* Amos 8:5 1250
yea, and sell the refuse of the *w* Amos 8:6 1250
gather his *w* into the garner Mt 3:12 *4621*
came and sowed tares among the *w* Mt 13:25 *4621*
ye root up also the *w* with them Mt 13:29 *4621*
but gather the *w* into my barn Mt 13:30 *4621*
will gather the *w* into his garner Lk 3:17 *4621*
he said, An hundred measures of *w* Lk 16:7 *4621*
you, that he may sift you as *w* Lk 22:31 *4621*
Except a corn of *w* fall into the Jn 12:24 *4621*
and cast out the *w* into the sea Acts 27:38 *4621*
bare grain, it may chance of *w* 1Cor 15:37 *4621*
say, A measure of *w* for a penny Rev 6:6 *4621*
wine, and oil, and fine flour, and *w* Rev 18:13 *4621*

WHEATEN {1}
of *w* flour shalt thou make them Ex 29:2 2406

WHEEL {15}
and the height of a *w* was a cubit 1Kin 7:32 212
was like the work of a chariot *w* 1Kin 7:33 212
O my God, make them like a *w* Ps 83:13 1534
and bringeth the *w* over them Prov 20:26 212
or the *w* broken at the cistern Eccl 12:6 1534
neither is a cart *w* turned about Is 28:27 212
break it with the *w* of his cart Is 28:28 1536
behold one *w* upon the earth by Eze 1:15 212
were a *w* in the middle of a *w* Eze 1:16 212
one *w* by one cherub, and another Eze 10:9 212
another *w* by another cherub Eze 10:9 212
as if a *w* had been in the midst Eze 10:10 212
had been in the midst of a *w* Eze 10:10 212
unto them in my hearing, O *w* Eze 10:13 1534

WHEELS {33}
And took off their chariot *w* Ex 14:25 212
Why tarry the *w* of his chariots Judg 5:28 6471
And every base had four brasen *w* 1Kin 7:30 212
And under the borders were four *w* 1Kin 7:32 212
the axletrees of the *w* were 1Kin 7:32 212
the work of the *w* was like the 1Kin 7:33 212
and their *w* like a whirlwind Is 5:28 1534
he wrought a work on the *w* Jer 18:3 70
and at the rumbling of his *w* Jer 47:3 1534
The appearance of the *w* and their Eze 1:16 212
went, the *w* went by them Eze 1:19 212
the earth, the *w* were lifted up Eze 1:19 212
the *w* were lifted up over against Eze 1:20 212
the living creature was in the *w* Eze 1:20 212
the *w* were lifted up over against Eze 1:21 212
the living creature was in the *w* Eze 1:21 212
the noise of the *w* over against Eze 3:13 212
and said, Go in between the *w* Eze 10:2 1534
Take fire from between the *w* Eze 10:6 1534
he went in, and stood beside the *w* Eze 10:6 212
looked, behold the four *w* by the Eze 10:9 212
the appearance of the *w* was as Eze 10:9 212
hands, and their wings, and the *w* Eze 10:12 212
even the *w* that they four had Eze 10:12 212
As for the *w*, it was cried unto Eze 10:13 212
went, the *w* went by them Eze 10:16 212
the same *w* also turned not from Eze 10:16 212
the *w* also were beside them, and Eze 10:19 212
their wings, and the *w* beside them Eze 11:22 212
thee with chariots, wagons, and *w* Eze 23:24 1534
of the horsemen, and of the *w* Eze 26:10 1534
flame, and his *w* as burning fire Dan 7:9 1535
noise of the rattling of the *w* Nah 3:2 212

WHELP {3}
Judah is a lion's *w* Gen 49:9 1482
of Dan he said, Dan is a lion's *w* Deut 33:22 1482
old lion, walked, and the lion's *w* Nah 2:11 1482

WHELPS {10}
bear robbed of her *w* in the field 2Sa 17:8
the stout lion's *w* are scattered Job 4:11 1121
The lion's *w* have not trodden it, Job 28:8 1121
a bear robbed of her *w* meet a man Prov 17:12
they shall yell as lions' *w* Jer 51:38 1484
nourished her *w* among young lions Eze 19:2 1482
And she brought up one of her *w* Eze 19:3 1482
then she took another of her *w* Eze 19:5 1482
a bear that is bereaved of her *w* Hos 13:8
tear in pieces enough for his *w* Nah 2:12 1484

WHEN See APPENDIX.

WHENCE See APPENDIX.

WHENSOEVER {3}
w the stronger cattle did Gen 30:41 3605
w ye will ye may do them good Mk 14:7 *3752*
W I take my journey into Spain, Rom 15:24 *5613,1437*

WHERE See APPENDIX.

WHEREABOUT {1}
of the business *w* I send thee 1Sa 21:2 834

W

WHEREAS See APPENDIX.
WHEREBY See APPENDIX.
WHEREFORE See APPENDIX.
WHEREIN See APPENDIX.
WHEREINSOEVER {1}
Howbeit *w* any is bold ... 2Cor 11:21 *1722,3739,302*
WHEREINTO {3}
w any of them falleth, ... Lev 11:33 834,413,8432
I bring into the land *w* he went ... Num 14:24 824,8432
save that one *w* his disciples ... Jn 6:22 *1519,3739*
WHEREOF See APPENDIX.
WHEREON {27}
the land *w* thou liest, to thee ... Gen 28:13 834,5921
for the place *w* thou standest is ... Ex 3:5 834,5921
and also the ground *w* they are ... Ex 8:21 834,5921
thou shalt wash that *w* it was ... Lev 6:27 834,5921
w he lieth that hath the issue, ... Lev 15:4
w he sitteth, shall be unclean ... Lev 15:4
w he sat that hath the issue ... Lev 15:6 834,5921
w is the seed of copulation, ... Lev 15:17 834,5921
or on any thing *w* she sitteth ... Lev 15:23 834,5921
all the bed *w* he lieth shall be ... Lev 15:24 834,5921
Every bed *w* she lieth all the ... Lev 15:26 834,5921
Every place *w* the soles of your ... Deut 11:24 834
for the place *w* thou standest is ... Josh 5:15 834,5921
Surely the land *w* thy feet have ... Josh 14:9 834
w they set down the ark of the ... 1Sa 6:18 834,5921
the tables *w* the shewbread was ... 2Chr 4:19 5921
W do ye trust, that ye abide in ... 2Chr 32:10 5921,4100
fallen upon the bed *w* Esther was ... Est 7:8
him to be in safety, *w* he resteth ... Job 24:23
w there hang a thousand bucklers, ... Song 4:4 5921
w if a man lean, it will go into ... Is 36:6 834,5921
the sticks *w* thou writest shall ... Eze 37:20 834,5921
find a colt tied, *w* never man sat ... Mk 11:2 *1909,3739*
the hill *w* their city was built ... Lk 4:29 *1909,3739*
them, and took up that *w* he lay ... Lk 5:25 *1909,3739*
a colt tied, *w* yet never man sat ... Lk 19:30 *1909,3739*
reap that *w* ye bestowed no labour ... Jn 4:38 *3739*
WHERESOEVER See APPENDIX.
WHERETO {3}
w might the strength of their ... Job 30:2 4100
prosper in the thing *w* I sent it ... Is 55:11 834
w we have already attained, let ... Phil 3:16 *1519,3739*
WHEREUNTO See APPENDIX.
WHEREUPON See APPENDIX.
WHEREWITH {110}
blessing *w* his father blessed him ... Gen 27:41 834
w the Egyptians oppress them ... Ex 3:9 834
thine hand, *w* thou shalt do signs ... Ex 4:17 834
the bread *w* I have fed you in the ... Ex 16:32 834
w thou smotest the river, take in ... Ex 17:5 834
things *w* the atonement was made ... Ex 29:33 834
of the sanctuary *w* they minister ... Num 3:31 834
w the odd number of them is to be ... Num 3:48
thereof, *w* they minister unto it ... Num 4:9 834
w they minister in the sanctuary, ... Num 4:12 834
w they minister about it, even ... Num 4:14 834
w they that were burnt had ... Num 16:39 834
w they have beguiled you in the ... Num 25:18 834
her bond *w* she hath bound her ... Num 30:4 834
every bond *w* she hath bound her ... Num 30:4 834
or of her bonds *w* she hath bound ... Num 30:5 834
of her lips, *w* she bound her soul ... Num 30:6 834
her bonds *w* she bound her soul ... Num 30:7 834
w she bound her soul, of none ... Num 30:8 834
w they have bound their souls, ... Num 30:9 834
every bond *w* she bound her soul ... Num 30:11 834
w he may die, and he die, he is a ... Num 35:17 834
w he may die, and he die, he is a ... Num 35:18 834
w a man may die, seeing him not, ... Num 35:23 834
w the LORD was wroth against you ... Deut 9:19 834
of that *w* the LORD thy God hath ... Deut 15:14 834
vesture, *w* thou coverest thyself ... Deut 22:12 834
w thine enemies shall distress ... Deut 28:53 834
w thine enemies shall distress ... Deut 28:55 834
w thine enemy shall distress thee ... Deut 28:57 834
of thine heart *w* thou shalt fear ... Deut 28:67 834
w Moses the man of God blessed ... Deut 33:1 834
w he stretched out the spear, ... Josh 8:26 834
Oh my Lord, *w* shall I save Israel ... Judg 6:15 4100
w Abimelech hired vain and light ... Judg 9:4
w by me they honour God and man, ... Judg 9:9 834
w thou saidst, Who is Abimelech, ... Judg 9:38 834
w thou mightest be bound to ... Judg 16:6 4100
thee, *w* thou mightest be bound ... Judg 16:10 4100
tell me *w* thou mightest be bound ... Judg 16:13 834
tell us *w* we shall send it to his ... 1Sa 6:2 4100
w they have forsaken me, and ... 1Sa 8:8
for *w* should he reconcile himself ... 1Sa 29:4 4100
so that the hatred *w* he hated her ... 2Sa 13:15 834
than the love *w* he had loved her ... 2Sa 13:15 834
w shall I make the atonement, ... 2Sa 21:3 4100
w I have made supplication before ... 1Kin 8:59 834
thereof, *w* Baasha had builded ... 1Kin 15:22 834
in his sin *w* he made Israel to ... 1Kin 15:26 834
by his provocation *w* he provoked ... 1Kin 15:30 834
in his sin *w* he made Israel to ... 1Kin 15:34 834
in his sin *w* he made Israel to ... 1Kin 16:26 834
for the provocation *w* thou hast ... 1Kin 21:22 834
And the LORD said unto him, *W* ... 1Kin 22:22 4100
his might *w* he fought against ... 2Kin 13:12 834
beside his sin *w* he made Judah to ... 2Kin 21:16 834
w his anger was kindled against ... 2Kin 23:26 834
of brass *w* they ministered ... 2Kin 25:14 834
w Solomon made the brasen sea, and ... 1Chr 18:8
after the numbering *w* David his ... 2Chr 2:17 834
thereof, *w* Baasha was building ... 2Chr 16:6 834
And the LORD said unto him, *W* ... 2Chr 18:20 4100
against the house *w* I have war ... 2Chr 35:21
w thou didst testify against them ... Neh 9:34 834
or with speeches *w* he can do no ... Job 15:3
w they have reproached thee, O ... Ps 79:12 834
W thine enemies have reproached, ... Ps 89:51 834
w they have reproached the ... Ps 89:51 834
w he hath girded himself ... Ps 93:1
for a girdle *w* he is girded ... Ps 109:19
So shall I have *w* to answer him ... Ps 119:42 1697
W the mower filleth not his hand ... Ps 129:7
king Solomon with the crown *w* his ... Song 3:11
This is the rest *w* ye may cause ... Is 28:12 834
w the servants of the king of ... Is 37:6 834
w I said I would benefit them ... Jer 18:10 834
w their enemies, and they that ... Jer 19:9 834
w ye fight against the king of ... Jer 21:4 834
this is the name *w* she shall be ... Jer 33:16 834
of brass *w* they ministered ... Jer 52:18 834
w the LORD hath afflicted me in ... Lam 1:12 834
the daubing *w* ye have daubed it ... Eze 13:12 834
w ye there hunt the souls to make ... Eze 13:20 834
w I fed thee, thou hast even set ... Eze 16:19
his labour *w* he served against it ... Eze 29:20 834
w they shall lament her ... Eze 32:16
for their idols *w* they had ... Eze 36:18
w they slew the burnt offering ... Eze 40:42 834
w his spirit was troubled, and his ... Dan 2:1
W shall I come before the LORD, ... Mic 6:6 4100
this shall be the plague *w* the ... Zec 14:12 834
w the LORD will smite the heathen ... Zec 14:18 834
him for the fear *w* he feared me ... Mal 2:5
his savour, *w* shall it be salted ... Mt 5:13 *1722,5101*
blasphemies *w* soever they shall ... Mk 3:28 *3745*
his saltness, *w* will ye season it ... Mk 9:50 *1722,5101*
savour, *w* shall it be seasoned ... Lk 14:34 *1722,5101*
unto him, Make ready *w* I may sup ... Lk 17:8 *5101*
with the towel *w* he was girded ... Jn 13:5 *3739*
that the love *w* thou hast loved ... Jn 17:26 *3739*
things *w* one may edify another ... Rom 14:19
by the comfort *w* we ourselves are ... 2Cor 1:4 *3739*
but by the consolation *w* he was ... 2Cor 7:7 *3739*
w I think to be bold against some ... 2Cor 10:2 *3739*
w Christ hath made us free ... Gal 5:1 *3739*
for his great love *w* he loved us ... Eph 2:4 *3739*
of the vocation *w* ye are called ... Eph 4:1 *3739*
w ye shall be able to quench all ... Eph 6:16 *1722,3739*
for all the joy *w* we joy for your ... 1Th 3:9 *3739*
w he was sanctified, an unholy ... Heb 10:29 *1722,3739*
WHEREWITHAL {2}
W shall a young man cleanse his ... Ps 119:9
or, *W* shall we be clothed ... Mt 6:31 *5101*
WHET {4}
If I *w* my glittering sword, and ... Deut 32:41 8150
he turn not, he will *w* his sword ... Ps 7:12 3913
Who *w* their tongue like a sword, ... Ps 64:3 8150
be blunt, and he do not *w* the edge ... Eccl 10:10 7043
WHETHER See APPENDIX.
WHICH See APPENDIX.
WHILE See APPENDIX.
WHILES {10}
W they see vanity unto thee, ... Eze 21:29
w they divine a lie unto thee, to ... Eze 21:29
w they minister in the gates of ... Eze 44:17
w he tasted the wine, commanded ... Dan 5:2
w I was speaking, and praying, and ... Dan 9:20 5750
w I was speaking in prayer, even ... Dan 9:21
like an oven, *w* they lie in wait ... Hos 7:6
w thou art in the way with him ... Mt 5:25 *2193,3755*
W it remained, was it not thine ... Acts 5:4
W by the experiment of this ... 2Cor 9:13
WHILST {10}
put to death *w* it is yet morning ... Judg 6:31 5704
w I leave it, and come down to you ... Neh 6:3 834
W it is yet in his greenness, and ... Job 8:12 5704
w ye searched out what to say ... Job 32:11 5704
own nets, *w* that I withal escape ... Ps 141:10 5704
W their children remember their ... Jer 17:2
w we are at home in the body, we ... 2Cor 5:6
w he remembereth the obedience of ... 2Cor 7:15
w ye were made a gazingstock both ... Heb 10:33
w ye became companions of them ... Heb 10:33
WHIP {2}
A *w* for the horse, a bridle for ... Prov 26:3 7752
The noise of a *w*, and the noise of ... Nah 3:2 7752
WHIPS {4}
father hath chastised you with *w* ... 1Kin 12:11 7752
father also chastised you with *w* ... 1Kin 12:14 7752
my father chastised you with *w* ... 2Chr 10:11 7752
my father chastised you with *w* ... 2Chr 10:14 7752
WHIRLETH {1}
it *w* about continually, and the ... Eccl 1:6 1980
WHIRLWIND {27}
take up Elijah into heaven by a *w* ... 2Kin 2:1 5591
Elijah went up by a *w* into heaven ... 2Kin 2:11 5591
Out of the south cometh the *w* ... Job 37:9 5492
LORD answered Job out of the *w* ... Job 38:1 5591
the LORD unto Job out of the *w* ... Job 40:6 5591
shall take them away as with a *w* ... Ps 58:9 8175
and your destruction cometh as a *w* ... Prov 1:27 5492
As the *w* passeth, so is the ... Prov 10:25 5492
flint, and their wheels like a *w* ... Is 5:28 5492
like a rolling thing before the *w* ... Is 17:13 5492
the *w* shall take them away as ... Is 40:24 5591
away, and the *w* shall scatter them ... Is 41:16 5591
and with his chariots like a *w* ... Is 66:15 5492
and his chariots shall be as a *w* ... Jer 4:13 5492
a *w* of the LORD is gone forth in ... Jer 23:19 5591
forth in fury, even a grievous *w* ... Jer 23:19 5591
a great *w* shall be raised up from ... Jer 25:32 5591
the *w* of the LORD goeth forth ... Jer 30:23 5591
forth with fury, a continuing *w* ... Jer 30:23 5591
a *w* came out of the north, a ... Eze 1:4 7307,5591
shall come against him like a *w* ... Dan 11:40 8175
wind, and they shall reap the *w* ... Hos 8:7 5492
with the *w* out of the floor ... Hos 13:3 5590
a tempest in the day of the *w* ... Amos 1:14 5492
the LORD hath his way in the *w* ... Nah 1:3 5492
came out as a *w* to scatter me ... Hab 3:14 5590
But I scattered them with a *w* ... Zec 7:14 5590
WHIRLWINDS {2}
As *w* in the south pass through ... Is 21:1 5492
and shall go with *w* of the south ... Zec 9:14 5591
WHISPER {2}
All that hate me *w* together ... Ps 41:7 3907
speech shall *w* out of the dust ... Is 29:4 6850
WHISPERED {1}
David saw that his servants *w* ... 2Sa 12:19 3907
WHISPERER {1}
a *w* separateth chief friends ... Prov 16:28 5372
WHISPERERS {1}
deceit, malignity; *w*, ... Rom 1:29 *5588*
WHISPERINGS {1}
wraths, strifes, backbitings, *w* ... 2Cor 12:20 *5587*
WHIT {5}
and all the spoil thereof every *w* ... Deut 13:16 3632
And Samuel told him every *w* ... 1Sa 3:18 1697
every *w* whole on the sabbath day ... Jn 7:23 *3650*
his feet, but is clean every *w* ... Jn 13:10 *3650*
not a *w* behind the very chiefest ... 2Cor 11:5 *3367*
WHITE {75}
every one that had some *w* in it ... Gen 30:35 3836
pilled *w* strakes in them ... Gen 30:37 3836
made the *w* appear which was in ... Gen 30:37 3836
I had three *w* baskets on my head ... Gen 40:16 2751
wine, and his teeth *w* with milk ... Gen 49:12 3836
and it was like coriander seed, *w* ... Ex 16:31 3836
hair in the plague is turned *w* ... Lev 13:3 3836
If the bright spot be *w* in the ... Lev 13:4 3836
the hair thereof be not turned *w* ... Lev 13:4 3836
if the rising be *w* in the skin ... Lev 13:10 3836
and it have turned the hair *w* ... Lev 13:10 3836
it is all turned *w* ... Lev 13:13 3836
turn again, and be changed unto *w* ... Lev 13:16 3836
if the plague be turned into *w* ... Lev 13:17 3836
of the boil there be a *w* rising ... Lev 13:19 3836
or a bright spot, *w* ... Lev 13:19 3836
and the hair thereof be turned *w* ... Lev 13:20 3836
there be no *w* hairs therein, and ... Lev 13:21 3836
that burneth have a *w* bright spot ... Lev 13:24 3836
somewhat reddish, or *w* ... Lev 13:24 3836
in the bright spot be turned *w* ... Lev 13:25 3836
there be no *w* hair in the bright ... Lev 13:26 3836
bright spots, even *w* bright spots ... Lev 13:38 3836
skin of their flesh be darkish *w* ... Lev 13:39 3836
bald forehead, a *w* reddish sore ... Lev 13:42 3836
be *w* reddish in his bald head ... Lev 13:43 3836
Miriam became leprous, *w* as snow ... Num 12:10
Speak, ye that ride on *w* asses ... Judg 5:10 6715
his presence a leper as *w* as snow ... 2Kin 5:27
being arrayed in *w* linen ... 2Chr 5:12
Where were *w*, green, and blue, ... Est 1:6 2353
a pavement of red, and blue, and *w* ... Est 1:6 1858
in royal apparel of blue and *w* ... Est 8:15 2353
any taste in the *w* of an egg ... Job 6:6 7388
it was *w* as snow in Salmon ... Ps 68:14
Let thy garments be always *w* ... Eccl 9:8 3836
My beloved is *w* and ruddy, the ... Song 5:10 6703
they shall be as *w* as snow ... Is 1:18 3835
in the wine of Helbon, and *w* wool ... Eze 27:18 6713
sit, whose garment was *w* as snow ... Dan 7:9
and to purge, and to make them *w* ... Dan 11:35 3835
Many shall be purified, and made *w* ... Dan 12:10 3835
the branches thereof are made *w* ... Joel 1:7 3835
there red horses, speckled, and *w* ... Zec 1:8 3836
And in the third chariot *w* horses ... Zec 6:3 3836
the *w* go forth after them ... Zec 6:6 3836
not make one hair *w* or black ... Mt 5:36 *3022*
and his raiment was *w* as the light ... Mt 17:2 *3022*
and his raiment *w* as snow ... Mt 28:3 *3022*
shining, exceeding *w* as snow ... Mk 9:3 *3022*
as no fuller on earth can *w* them ... Mk 9:3 *3021*
side, clothed in a long *w* garment ... Mk 16:5 *3022*
was altered, and his raiment was *w* ... Lk 9:29 *3022*
for they are *w* already to harvest ... Jn 4:35 *3022*
And seeth two angels in *w* sitting ... Jn 20:12 *3022*
men stood by them in *w* apparel ... Acts 1:10 *3022*
w like wool, as *w* as snow ... Rev 1:14 *3022*
manna, and will give him a *w* stone ... Rev 2:17 *3022*
and they shall walk with me in *w* ... Rev 3:4 *3022*
shall be clothed in *w* raiment ... Rev 3:5 *3022*
w raiment, that thou mayest be ... Rev 3:18 *3022*
sitting, clothed in *w* raiment ... Rev 4:4 *3022*
And I saw, and behold a *w* horse ... Rev 6:2 *3022*
w robes were given unto every one ... Rev 6:11 *3022*

the Lamb, clothed with *w* robes ... Rev 7:9 *3022*
which are arrayed in *w* robes ... Rev 7:13 *3022*
made them *w* in the blood of the ... Rev 7:14 *3021*
And I looked, and behold a *w* cloud ... Rev 14:14 *3022*
w linen, and having their breasts ... Rev 15:6 *2986*
arrayed in fine linen, clean and *w* ... Rev 19:8 *2986*
opened, and behold a *w* horse ... Rev 19:11 *3022*
heaven followed him upon *w* horses ... Rev 19:14 *3022*
clothed in fine linen, *w* ... Rev 19:14 *3022*
And I saw a great *w* throne ... Rev 20:11 *3022*

WHITED {2}
for ye are like unto *w* sepulchres ... Mt 23:27 *2867*
God shall smite thee, thou *w* wall ... Acts 23:3 *2867*

WHITER {2}
me, and I shall be *w* than snow ... Ps 51:7 3835
than snow, they were *w* than milk ... Lam 4:7 6705

WHITHER See APPENDIX.

WHITHERSOEVER {29}
thou mayest prosper *w* thou goest ... Josh 1:7 3605,834
thy God is with thee *w* thou goest .. Josh 1:9 3605,834
w thou sendest us, we will go ... Josh 1:16 3605,834
W they went out, the hand of the ... Judg 2:15 3605,834
w he turned himself, he vexed ... 1Sa 14:47 3605,834
David went out *w* Saul sent him ... 1Sa 18:5 3605,834
Keilah, and went *w* they could go ... 1Sa 23:13 834
I was with thee *w* thou wentest ... 2Sa 7:9 3605,834
LORD preserved David *w* he went .. 2Sa 8:6 3605,834
LORD preserved David *w* he went .. 2Sa 8:14 3605,834
and *w* thou turnest thyself ... 1Kin 2:3 3605,834,8033
w thou shalt send them, and shall .. 1Kin 8:44 1870,834
he prospered *w* he went forth ... 2Kin 18:7 3605,834
with thee *w* thou hast walked ... 1Chr 17:8 3605,834
LORD preserved David *w* he went ... 1Chr 18:6 3605,834
LORD preserved David *w* he went .. 1Chr 18:13 3605,834
w the king's commandment ... Est 4:3 4725,834
w the king's commandment and his ... Est 8:17 834
w it turneth, it prospereth ... Prov 17:8 413,3605,834
he turneth it *w* he will ... Prov 21:1 5921,3605,834
W the spirit was to go, they ... Eze 1:20 5921,834,8033
or on the left, *w* thy face is set ... Eze 21:16 575
w the rivers shall come, ... Eze 47:9 413,3605,834,8033
I will follow thee *w* thou goest ... Mt 8:19 *3699,1437*
w he entered, into villages, or ... Mk 6:56 *3699,302*
I will follow thee *w* thou goest ... Lk 9:57 *3699,302*
bring me on my journey *w* I go ... 1Cor 16:6 *3757,1437*
helm, *w* the governor listeth ... Jas 3:4 *3699,302*
which follow the Lamb *w* he goeth . Rev 14:4 *3699,302*

WHO See APPENDIX.

WHOLE {250}
watered the *w* face of the ground ... Gen 2:6 854,3605
compasseth the *w* land of Havilah .. Gen 2:11 854,3605
compasseth the *w* land of Ethiopia . Gen 2:13 854,3605
that were under the *w* heaven ... Gen 7:19 3605
were on the face of the *w* earth ... Gen 8:9 3605
and of them was the *w* earth ... Gen 9:19 3605
the *w* earth was of one language, ... Gen 11:1 3605
upon the face of the *w* earth ... Gen 11:4 3605
Is not the *w* land before thee ... Gen 13:9 3605
so the *w* age of Jacob was an ... Gen 47:28 3605
covered the face of the *w* earth ... Ex 10:15 3605
and the *w* assembly of the ... Ex 12:6 3605
the *w* congregation of the ... Ex 16:2 3605
to kill this *w* assembly with ... Ex 16:3 854,3605
as Aaron spake unto the *w* ... Ex 16:10 3605
the *w* mount quaked greatly ... Ex 19:18 3605
burn the *w* ram upon the altar ... Ex 29:18 854,3605
the *w* rump, it shall he take off ... Lev 3:9 8549
Even the *w* bullock shall he carry ... Lev 4:12 854,3605
if the *w* congregation of Israel ... Lev 4:13 3605
he shall offer one out of the *w* ... Lev 7:14 3605
Moses burnt the *w* ram upon the ... Lev 8:21 854,3605
the *w* house of Israel, bewail the ... Lev 10:6 3605
within a *w* year after it is sold ... Lev 25:29 8552
the charge of the *w* congregation ... Num 3:7 3605
thou shalt gather the *w* assembly ... Num 8:9 854,3605
of a *w* piece shalt thou make them ... Num 10:2 4749
But even a *w* month, until it come ... Num 11:20 3117
that they may eat a *w* month ... Num 11:21 3117
the *w* congregation said unto them ... Num 14:2 3605
you, according to your *w* number ... Num 14:29 3605
even the *w* congregation, into the ... Num 20:1 3605
Israel, even the *w* congregation, ... Num 20:22 3605
that are under the *w* heaven ... Deut 2:25 3605
all nations under the *w* heaven ... Deut 4:19 3605
of the LORD thy God of *w* stones ... Deut 27:6 8003
that the *w* land thereof is ... Deut 29:23 3605
w burnt sacrifice upon thine ... Deut 33:10 3632
in the camp, till they were *w* ... Josh 5:8 2421
of Moses, an altar of *w* stones ... Josh 8:31 8003
not to go down about a *w* day ... Josh 10:13 8549
So Joshua took the *w* land ... Josh 11:23 854,3605
the *w* congregation of the ... Josh 18:1 3605
the *w* congregation of the ... Josh 22:12 3605
Thus saith the *w* congregation of ... Josh 22:16 3605
with the *w* congregation of Israel ... Josh 22:18 3605
and was there four *w* months ... Judg 19:2 3117
the *w* congregation sent some to ... Judg 21:13 3605
because my life is yet *w* in me ... 2Sa 1:9 3605
good to the *w* house of Benjamin ... 2Sa 3:19 3605
even among the *w* multitude of ... 2Sa 6:19 3605
the *w* family is risen against ... 2Sa 14:7 3605
the *w* house he overlaid with gold ... 1Kin 6:22 3605
also the *w* altar that was by the ... 1Kin 6:22 3605
the *w* kingdom out of his hand ... 1Kin 11:34 854,3605
For the *w* house of Ahab shall ... 2Kin 9:8 3605
blessed the *w* congregation of ... 2Chr 6:3 854,3605
and sought him with their *w* desire ... 2Chr 15:15 3605
to and fro throughout the *w* earth ... 2Chr 16:9 3605
The *w* number of the chief of the ... 2Chr 26:12 3605
the *w* assembly took counsel to ... 2Chr 30:23 3605
them, according to the *w* law ... 2Chr 33:8 3605
The *w* congregation together was ... Ezr 2:64 3605
The *w* congregation together was ... Neh 7:66 3605
the *w* kingdom of Ahasuerus ... Est 3:6 3605
he woundeth, and his hands make *w* ... Job 5:18 7495
and seeth under the *w* heaven ... Job 28:24 3605
Or who hath disposed the *w* world ... Job 34:13 3605
directeth it under the *w* heaven ... Job 37:3 3605
is under the *w* heaven is mine ... Job 41:11 3605
thee, O LORD, with my *w* heart ... Ps 9:1 3605
situation, the joy of the *w* earth ... Ps 48:2 3605
offering and *w* burnt offering ... Ps 51:19 3632
let the *w* earth be filled with ... Ps 72:19 854,3605
of the LORD of the *w* earth ... Ps 97:5 3605
he brake the *w* staff of bread ... Ps 105:16 3605
praise the LORD with my *w* heart ... Ps 111:1 3605
and that seek him with the *w* heart ... Ps 119:2 3605
With my *w* heart have I sought ... Ps 119:10 3605
shall observe it with my *w* heart ... Ps 119:34 3605
thy favour with my *w* heart ... Ps 119:58 3605
keep thy precepts with my *w* heart ... Ps 119:69 3605
I cried with my *w* heart ... Ps 119:145
will praise thee with my *w* heart ... Ps 138:1 3605
and *w*, as those that go down into ... Prov 1:12 8549
but the *w* disposing thereof is of ... Prov 16:33 3605
shewed before the *w* congregation ... Prov 26:26
the conclusion of the *w* matter ... Eccl 12:13 3605
for this is the *w* duty of man ... Eccl 12:13 3605
the *w* head is sick ... Is 1:5 3605
and the *w* heart faint ... Is 1:5 3605
the *w* stay of bread ... Is 3:1 3605
and the *w* stay of water ... Is 3:1 3605
the *w* earth is full of his glory ... Is 6:3 3605
his *w* work upon mount Zion ... Is 10:12 854,3605
to destroy the *w* land ... Is 13:5 3605
The *w* earth is at rest, and is ... Is 14:7 3605
that is purposed upon the *w* earth ... Is 14:26 3605
w Palestina, because the rod of ... Is 14:29 3605
w Palestina, art dissolved ... Is 14:31 3605
and I am set in my ward *w* nights ... Is 21:8 3605
even determined upon the *w* earth ... Is 28:22 3605
The God of the *w* earth shall he ... Is 54:5 3605
brasen walls against the *w* land ... Jer 1:18 3605
turned unto me with her *w* heart ... Jer 3:10 3605
for the *w* land is spoiled ... Jer 4:20 3605
The *w* land shall be desolate ... Jer 4:27 3605
The *w* city shall flee for the ... Jer 4:29 3605
even the *w* seed of Ephraim ... Jer 7:15 3605
the *w* land trembled at the sound ... Jer 8:16 3605
the *w* land is made desolate, ... Jer 12:11 3605
unto me the *w* house of Israel ... Jer 13:11 3605
the *w* house of Judah, saith the ... Jer 13:11 3605
man of contention to the *w* earth ... Jer 15:10 3605
that cannot be made *w* again ... Jer 19:11 7495
return unto me with their *w* heart ... Jer 24:7 3605
this *w* land shall be a desolation ... Jer 25:11 3605
the *w* valley of the dead bodies, ... Jer 31:40 3605
my *w* heart and with my *w* soul ... Jer 32:41 3605
the *w* house of the Rechabites ... Jer 35:3 3605
the *w* army of the Chaldeans that ... Jer 37:10 3605
I will pluck up, even this *w* land ... Jer 45:4 3605
of the *w* earth cut in asunder ... Jer 50:23 3605
praise of the *w* earth surprised ... Jer 51:41 3605
her *w* land shall be confounded, ... Jer 51:47 3605
of beauty, The joy of the *w* earth ... Lam 2:15 3605
the *w* remnant of thee will I ... Eze 5:10 3605
touching the *w* multitude thereof ... Eze 7:13 3605
And their *w* body, and their backs, ... Eze 10:12 3605
Behold, when it was *w*, it was ... Eze 15:5 8549
beasts of the *w* earth with thee ... Eze 32:4 3605
When the *w* earth rejoiceth, I ... Eze 35:14 3605
bones are the *w* house of Israel ... Eze 37:11 3605
mercy upon the *w* house of Israel ... Eze 39:25 3605
they may keep the *w* form thereof ... Eze 43:11 3605
the top of the mountain the *w* ... Eze 43:12 3605
be for the *w* house of Israel ... Eze 45:6 3605
mountain, and filled the *w* earth ... Dan 2:35 3606
over the *w* province of Babylon ... Dan 2:48 3606
should be over the *w* kingdom ... Dan 6:1 3606
to set him over the *w* realm ... Dan 6:3 3606
and shall devour the *w* earth ... Dan 7:23 3606
of the kingdom under the *w* heaven ... Dan 7:27 3606
west on the face of the *w* earth ... Dan 8:5 3605
for under the *w* heaven hath not ... Dan 9:12 3605
till three *w* weeks were fulfilled ... Dan 10:3 3117
the strength of his *w* kingdom ... Dan 11:17 3605
away captive the *w* captivity ... Amos 1:6 8003
up the *w* captivity to Edom ... Amos 1:9 8003
against the *w* family which I ... Amos 3:1 3605
unto the Lord of the *w* earth ... Mic 4:13 3605
but the *w* land shall be devoured ... Zeph 1:18 3605
run to and fro through the *w* earth ... Zec 4:10 3605
stand by the Lord of the *w* earth ... Zec 4:14 3605
over the face of the *w* earth ... Zec 5:3 3605
robbed me, even this *w* nation ... Mal 3:9 3605
not that thy *w* body should be ... Mt 5:29 *3650*
not that thy *w* body should be ... Mt 5:30 *3650*
thy *w* body shall be full of light ... Mt 6:22 *3650*
thy *w* body shall be full of ... Mt 6:23 *3650*
the *w* herd of swine ran violently ... Mt 8:32 *3956*
the *w* city came out to meet Jesus ... Mt 8:34 *3956*
They that be *w* need not a ... Mt 9:12 *2480*
touch his garment, I shall be *w* ... Mt 9:21 *4982*
thy faith hath made thee *w* ... Mt 9:22 *4982*
woman was made *w* from that hour ... Mt 9:22 *4982*
and it was restored *w*, like as the ... Mt 12:13 *5199*
the *w* multitude stood on the ... Mt 13:2 *3956*
of meal, till the *w* was leavened ... Mt 13:33 *3650*
as touched were made perfectly *w* ... Mt 14:36 *1295*
was made *w* from that very hour ... Mt 15:28 *3390*
dumb to speak, the maimed to be *w* ... Mt 15:31 *5199*
if he shall gain the *w* world ... Mt 16:26 *3650*
shall be preached in the *w* world ... Mt 26:13 *3650*
unto him the *w* band of soldiers ... Mt 27:27 *3650*
They that are *w* have no need of ... Mk 2:17 *2480*
hand was restored *w* as the other ... Mk 3:5 *5199*
the *w* multitude was by the sea on ... Mk 4:1 *3956*
but his clothes, I shall be *w* ... Mk 5:28 *4982*
thy faith hath made thee *w* ... Mk 5:34 *4982*
in peace, and be *w* of thy plague ... Mk 5:34 *5199*
ran through that *w* region round ... Mk 6:55 *3650*
many as touched him were made *w* ... Mk 6:56 *4982*
man, if he shall gain the *w* world ... Mk 8:36 *3650*
thy faith hath made thee *w* ... Mk 10:52 *4982*
more than all *w* burnt offerings ... Mk 12:33 *3646*
preached throughout the *w* world ... Mk 14:9 *3650*
the *w* council, and bound Jesus, and ... Mk 15:1 *3650*
and they call together the *w* band ... Mk 15:16 *3650*
the *w* land until the ninth hour ... Mk 15:33 *3650*
the *w* multitude of the people ... Lk 1:10 *3956*
They that are *w* need not a ... Lk 5:31 *5198*
hand was restored *w* as the other ... Lk 6:10 *5199*
the *w* multitude sought to touch ... Lk 6:19 *3956*
found the servant *w* that had been ... Lk 7:10 *5198*
Then the *w* multitude of the ... Lk 8:37 *537*
published throughout the *w* city ... Lk 8:39 *3650*
thy faith hath made thee *w* ... Lk 8:48 *4982*
only, and she shall be made *w* ... Lk 8:50 *4982*
if he gain the *w* world, and lose ... Lk 9:25 *3650*
thy *w* body also is full of light ... Lk 11:34 *3650*
If thy *w* body therefore be full ... Lk 11:36 *3650*
the *w* shall be full of light, as ... Lk 11:36 *3650*
of meal, till the *w* was leavened ... Lk 13:21 *3650*
thy faith hath made thee *w* ... Lk 17:19 *4982*
the *w* multitude of the disciples ... Lk 19:37 *537*
dwell on the face of the *w* earth ... Lk 21:35 *3956*
the *w* multitude of them arose, and ... Lk 23:1 *537*
himself believed, and his *w* house ... Jn 4:53 *3650*
w of whatsoever disease he had ... Jn 5:4 *5199*
unto him, Wilt thou be made *w* ... Jn 5:6 *5199*
immediately the man was made *w* ... Jn 5:9 *5199*
answered them, He that made me *w* ... Jn 5:11 *5199*
unto him, Behold, thou art made *w* ... Jn 5:14 *5199*
was Jesus, which had made him *w* ... Jn 5:15 *5199*
every whit *w* on the sabbath day ... Jn 7:23 *5199*
that the *w* nation perish not ... Jn 11:50 *3650*
man, by what means he is made *w* ... Acts 4:9 *4982*
this man stand here before you *w* ... Acts 4:10 *5199*
saying pleased the *w* multitude ... Acts 6:5 *3956*
Jesus Christ maketh thee *w* ... Acts 9:34 *2390*
that a *w* year they assembled ... Acts 11:26 *3650*
sabbath day came almost the *w* ... Acts 13:44 *3956*
and elders, with the *w* church ... Acts 15:22 *3650*
the *w* city was filled with ... Acts 19:29 *3650*
Paul dwelt two *w* years in his own ... Acts 28:30 *3650*
spoken of throughout the *w* world ... Rom 1:8 *3650*
know that the *w* creation groaneth ... Rom 8:22 *3956*
mine host, and of the *w* church ... Rom 16:23 *3650*
leaven leaveneth the *w* lump ... 1Cor 5:6 *3650*
If the *w* body were an eye, where ... 1Cor 12:17 *3650*
If the *w* were hearing, where were ... 1Cor 12:17 *3650*
If therefore the *w* church be come ... 1Cor 14:23 *3650*
he is a debtor to do the *w* law ... Gal 5:3 *3650*
leaven leaveneth the *w* lump ... Gal 5:9 *3650*
Of whom the *w* family in heaven and ... Eph 3:15 *3958*
From whom the *w* body fitly joined ... Eph 4:16 *3958*
Put on the *w* armour of God, that ... Eph 6:11
take unto you the *w* armour of God ... Eph 6:13
and I pray God your *w* spirit ... 1Th 5:23 *3648*
be stopped, who subvert *w* houses ... Titus 1:11 *3650*
whosoever shall keep the *w* law ... Jas 2:10 *3650*
and able also to bridle the *w* body ... Jas 3:2 *3650*
and we turn about their *w* body ... Jas 3:3 *3650*
that it defileth the *w* body ... Jas 3:6 *3650*
also for the sins of the *w* world ... 1Jn 2:2 *3650*
the *w* world lieth in wickedness ... 1Jn 5:19 *3650*
which deceiveth the *w* world ... Rev 12:9 *3650*
of the earth and of the *w* world ... Rev 16:14 *3650*

WHOLESOME {2}
A *w* tongue is a tree of life ... Prov 15:4 4832
and consent not to *w* words ... 1Ti 6:3 *5198*

WHOLLY {29}
it shall be *w* burnt ... Lev 6:22 3632
for the priest shall be *w* burnt ... Lev 6:23 3632
thou shalt not *w* reap the corners ... Lev 19:9 3615
they are *w* given unto him out of ... Num 3:9
spread over it a cloth *w* of blue ... Num 4:6 3632
For they are *w* given unto me from ... Num 8:16
they have not *w* followed me ... Num 32:11 4390
for they have *w* followed the LORD ... Num 32:12 4390
because he hath *w* followed the ... Deut 1:36 4390
but I *w* followed the LORD my God ... Josh 14:8 4390
because thou hast *w* followed the ... Josh 14:9 4390
because that he *w* followed the ... Josh 14:14 4390
I had *w* dedicated the silver unto ... Judg 17:3 6942
a burnt offering *w* unto the LORD ... 1Sa 7:9 3632
will be *w* at thy commandment ... 1Chr 28:21 3605
being *w* at ease and quiet ... Job 21:23 3605
that thou art *w* gone up to the ... Is 22:1 3605
thee a noble vine, *w* a right seed ... Jer 2:21 3605
she is *w* oppression in the midst ... Jer 6:6 3605

W

it shall be *w* carried away Jer 13:19 7965
If ye *w* set your faces to enter Jer 42:15 7760
I not leave thee *w* unpunished Jer 46:28 5352
but it shall be *w* desolate Jer 50:13 3605
and all the house of Israel *w* Eze 11:15 3605
and it shall rise up *w* as a flood Amos 8:8 3605
it shall rise up *w* like a flood Amos 9:5 3605
saw the city *w* given to idolatry Acts 17:16
very God of peace sanctify you *w* 1Th 5:23 *3651*
give thyself *w* to them 1Ti 4:15 *1510,1722*

WHOM See APPENDIX.

WHOMSOEVER {20}
With *w* thou findest thy gods, let Gen 31:32 834
With *w* of thy servants it be Gen 44:9 834
w he toucheth that hath the issue Lev 15:11 3605,834
of *w* I say unto thee, This shall Judg 7:4 834
So *w* the LORD our God shall drive Judg 11:24 3605,834
of men, and giveth it to *w* he will Dan 4:17 4479
of men, and giveth it to *w* he will Dan 4:25 4479
of men, and giveth it to *w* he will Dan 4:32 4479
he appointeth over it *w* he will Dan 5:21 4479,1768
he to *w* the Son will reveal him Mt 11:27 *3739,1437*
but on *w* it shall fall, it will Mt 21:44 *3739,302*
W I shall kiss, that same is he Mt 26:48 *3739,302*
W I shall kiss, that same is he Mk 14:44 *3739,302*
them one prisoner, *w* they desired Mk 15:6 *3746*
and to *w* I will I give it Lk 4:6 *3739,1437*
For unto *w* much is given, of him Lk 12:48 *3956,3739*
but on *w* it shall fall, it will Lk 20:18 *3739,302*
He that receiveth *w* I send Jn 13:20 *1437,1500*
that on *w* I lay hands, he may Acts 8:19 *3739,302*
w ye shall approve by your 1Cor 16:3 *3739,1437*

WHORE {14}
daughter, to cause her to be a *w* Lev 19:29 2181
shall not take a wife that is a *w* Lev 21:7 2181
profane herself by playing the *w* Lev 21:9 2181
to play the *w* in her father's Deut 22:21 2181
There shall be no *w* of the Deut 23:17 6948
shalt not bring the hire of a *w* Deut 23:18 2181
played the *w* against him, and went Judg 19:2 2181
For a *w* is a deep ditch Prov 23:27 2181
seed of the adulterer and the *w* Is 57:3 2181
Thou hast played the *w* also with Eze 16:28 2181
w that sitteth upon many waters Rev 17:1 *4204*
thou sawest, where the *w* sitteth Rev 17:15 *4204*
the beast, these shall hate the *w* Rev 17:16 *4204*
for he hath judged the great *w* Rev 19:2 *4204*

WHOREDOM {22}
behold, she is with child by *w* Gen 38:24 2183
lest the land fall to *w*, and the Lev 19:29 2181
to commit *w* with Molech, from Lev 20:5 2181
w with the daughters of Moab Num 25:1 2181
through the lightness of her *w* Jer 3:9 2184
neighings, the lewdness of thy *w* Jer 13:27 2184
men, and didst commit *w* with them Eze 16:17 2181
unto thee on every side for thy *w* Eze 16:33 8457
and commit ye *w* after their Eze 20:30 2181
and poured their *w* upon her Eze 23:8 8457
and they defiled her with their *w* Eze 23:17 8457
thy *w* brought from the land of Eze 23:27 2184
they, nor their kings, by their *w* Eze 43:7 2184
Now let them put away their *w* Eze 43:9 2184
the land hath committed great *w* Hos 1:2 2181
they shall commit *w*, and shall not Hos 4:10 2181
W and wine and new wine take away Hos 4:11 2184
your daughters shall commit *w* Hos 4:13 2181
your daughters when they commit *w* Hos 4:14 2181
they have committed *w* continually Hos 4:18 2181
now, O Ephraim, thou committest *w* Hos 5:3 2181
there is the *w* of Ephraim Hos 6:10 2184

WHOREDOMS {32}
forty years, and bear your *w* Num 14:33 2184
so long as the *w* of thy mother 2Kin 9:22 2183
like to the *w* of the house of 2Chr 21:13 2181
hast polluted the land with thy *w* Jer 3:2 2184
Is this of thy *w* a small matter Eze 16:20 8457
thy *w* thou hast not remembered Eze 16:22 8457
passed by, and multiplied thy *w* Eze 16:25 8457
and hast increased thy *w*, to Eze 16:26 8457
in thee from other women in thy *w* Eze 16:34 8457
none followeth thee to commit *w* Eze 16:34 2181
through thy *w* with thy lovers Eze 16:36 8457
And they committed *w* in Egypt Eze 23:3
they committed *w* in their youth Eze 23:3
she committed her *w* with them Eze 23:7 8457
left she her *w* brought from Egypt Eze 23:8 8457
in her *w* more than her sister in Eze 23:11 8457
more than her sister in her *w* Eze 23:11 2183
And that she increased her *w* Eze 23:14 8457
So she discovered her *w*, and Eze 23:18 8457
Yet she multiplied her *w*, in Eze 23:19 8457
of thy *w* shall be discovered Eze 23:29 2183
both thy lewdness and thy *w* Eze 23:29 8457
thou also thy lewdness and thy *w* Eze 23:35 8457
Will they now commit *w* with her Eze 23:43 8457
Go, take unto thee a wife of *w* Hos 1:2 2183
and children of *w* Hos 1:2 2183
put away her *w* out of her sight Hos 2:2 2183
for they be the children of *w* Hos 2:4 2183
for the spirit of *w* hath caused Hos 4:12 2183
for the spirit of *w* is in the Hos 5:4 2183
the *w* of the wellfavoured harlot Nah 3:4 2183
selleth nations through her *w* Nah 3:4 2183

WHOREMONGER {1}
For this ye know, that no *w* Eph 5:5 *4205*

WHOREMONGERS {4}
For *w*, for them that defile 1Ti 1:10 *4205*
but *w* and adulterers God will Heb 13:4 *4205*
abominable, and murderers, and *w* Rev 21:8 *4205*
are dogs, and sorcerers, and *w* Rev 22:15 *4205*

WHORE'S {1}
and thou hadst a *w* forehead Jer 3:3 2181

WHORES {2}
They give gifts to all *w* Eze 16:33 2181
themselves are separated with *w* Hos 4:14 2181

WHORING {19}
they go a *w* after their gods, and Ex 34:15 2181
daughters go a *w* after their gods Ex 34:16 2181
thy sons go a *w* after their gods Ex 34:16 2181
after whom they have gone a *w* Lev 17:7 2181
off, and all that go a *w* after him Lev 20:5 2181
to go a *w* after them, I will even Lev 20:6 2181
after which ye use to go a *w* Num 15:39 2181
go a *w* after the gods of the Deut 31:16 2181
but they went a *w* after other Judg 2:17 2181
Israel went thither a *w* after it Judg 8:27 2181
went a *w* after Baalim, and made Judg 8:33 2181
went a *w* after the gods of the 1Chr 5:25 2181
of Jerusalem to go a *w*, like to 2Chr 21:13 2181
all them that go a *w* from thee Ps 73:27 2181
works, and went a *w* with their own Ps 106:39 2181
which go a *w* after their idols Eze 6:9 2181
hast gone a *w* after the heathen Eze 23:30 2181
they have gone a *w* from under Hos 4:12 2181
thou hast gone a *w* from thy God Hos 9:1 2181

WHORISH {3}
For by means of a *w* woman a man Prov 6:26 2181
I am broken with their *w* heart Eze 6:9 2181
the work of an imperious *w* woman Eze 16:30 2181

WHOSE See APPENDIX.

WHOSO See APPENDIX.

WHOSOEVER {183}
Therefore *w* slayeth Cain, Gen 4:15 3605
for *w* eateth leavened bread from Ex 12:15 3605
for *w* eateth that which is Ex 12:19 3605
w toucheth the mount shall be Ex 19:12 3605
W lieth with a beast shall surely Ex 22:19 3605
W compoundeth any like it Ex 30:33 376
or *w* putteth any of it upon a Ex 30:33 834
W shall make like unto that, to Ex 30:38 834
for *w* doeth any work therein, Ex 31:14 3605
w doeth any work in the sabbath Ex 31:15 3605
W hath any gold, let them break Ex 32:24 4310
W hath sinned against me, him Ex 32:33 834
w doeth work therein shall be put Ex 35:2 3605
w is of a willing heart, let him Ex 35:5 3605
For *w* eateth the fat of the beast Lev 7:25 3605
w toucheth the carcase of them Lev 11:24 3605
w beareth ought of the carcase of Lev 11:25 3605
w doth touch them, when they be Lev 11:31 3605
w toucheth his bed shall wash his Lev 15:5 376,834
w toucheth any thing that was Lev 15:10 3605
w toucheth her shall be unclean Lev 15:19 3605
w toucheth her bed shall wash his Lev 15:21 3605
w toucheth any thing that she sat Lev 15:22 3605
w toucheth those things shall be Lev 15:27 3605
w eateth it shall be cut off Lev 17:14 3605
For *w* shall commit any of these Lev 18:29 3605,834
w lieth carnally with a woman, Lev 19:20 376
W he be of the children of Israel Lev 20:2 376
W he be of thy seed in their Lev 21:17 376
W he be of all your seed among Lev 22:3 3605,376
Or *w* toucheth any creeping thing, Lev 22:5 376,834
w offereth a sacrifice of peace Lev 22:21 376
W curseth his God shall bear his Lev 24:15 376
and *w* is defiled by the dead Num 5:2 3605
or *w* be among you in your Num 15:14 834
W cometh any thing near unto the Num 17:13 3605
W toucheth the dead body of any Num 19:13 3605
w toucheth one that is slain with Num 19:16 3695,834
w hath killed any person, and Num 31:19 3605
w hath touched any slain, purify Num 31:19 3605
that *w* will not hearken unto my Deut 18:19 376,834
W he be that doth rebel against Josh 1:18 3605
that *w* shall go out of the doors Josh 2:19 3605,834
w shall be with thee in the house Josh 2:19 3605,834
that *w* killeth any person at Josh 20:9 3605
W is fearful and afraid, let him Judg 7:3 4310
W cometh not forth after Saul and 1Sa 11:7 834
W getteth up to the gutter, and 2Sa 5:8 3605
W saith ought unto thee, bring 2Sa 14:10
that *w* heareth it will say, There 2Sa 17:9
w would, he consecrated him, and 1Kin 13:33
w shall be wanting, he shall not 2Kin 10:19 3605,834
that *w* heareth of it, both his 2Kin 21:12 3605
W smiteth the Jebusites first 1Chr 11:6 3605
w had dedicated any thing, it was 1Chr 26:28 3605
so that *w* cometh to consecrate 2Chr 13:9 3605
That *w* would not seek the LORD 2Chr 15:13 3605
w else cometh into the house, he 2Chr 23:7
w remaineth in any place where he Ezr 1:4 3605
that *w* shall alter this word, let Ezr 6:11 3605
w will not do the law of thy God, Ezr 7:26 3605
that *w* would not come within Ezr 10:8 3605
king's provinces, do know, that *w* Est 4:11 834
w toucheth her shall not be Prov 6:29 3605
w is deceived thereby is not wise Prov 20:1 3605
W hideth her hideth the wind, and Prov 27:16
w shall gather together against Is 54:15 4310
w goeth therein shall not know Is 59:8 3605
this place, the which *w* heareth Jer 19:3 3605
Then *w* heareth the sound of the Eze 33:4
W shall read this writing, and Dan 5:7 3605
that *w* shall ask a petition of Dan 6:7 3605
that *w* shall call on the name of Joel 2:32 834
W therefore shall break one of Mt 5:19 *3739,1437*
but *w* shall do and teach them, the Mt 5:19 *3739,302*
w shall kill shall be in danger Mt 5:21 *3739,302*
That *w* is angry with his brother Mt 5:22 *3956,3588*
w shall say to his brother, Raca, Mt 5:22 *3739,302*
but *w* shall say, Thou fool, shall Mt 5:22 *3739,302*
That *w* looketh on a woman to lust Mt 5:28 *3956,3588*
W shall put away his wife, let Mt 5:31 *3739,302*
That *w* shall put away his wife, Mt 5:32 *3739,302*
w shall marry her that is Mt 5:32 *3739,1437*
but *w* shall smite thee on thy Mt 5:39 *3748*
w shall compel thee to go a mile, Mt 5:41 *3748*
Therefore *w* heareth these sayings Mt 7:24 *3956,3748*
w shall not receive you, nor hear Mt 10:14 *3739,1437*
W therefore shall confess me Mt 10:32 *3956,3748*
But *w* shall deny me before men Mt 10:33 *3748,302*
w shall give to drink unto one of Mt 10:42 *3739,302*
w shall not be offended in me Mt 11:6 *3739,1437*
w speaketh a word against the Son Mt 12:32 *3739,302*
but *w* speaketh against the Holy Mt 12:32 *3739,302*
For *w* shall do the will of my Mt 12:50 *3748,302*
For *w* hath, to him shall be given Mt 13:12 *3748*
but *w* hath not, from him shall be Mt 13:12 *3748*
W shall say to his father or his Mt 15:5 *3739,302*
For *w* will save his life shall Mt 16:25 *3739,302*
w will lose his life for my sake Mt 16:25 *3739,302*
W therefore shall humble himself Mt 18:4 *3748*
W shall put away his wife, except Mt 19:9 *3739,302*
but *w* will be great among you, Mt 20:26 *3739,1437*
w will be chief among you, let Mt 20:27 *3737,1437*
w shall fall on this stone shall Mt 21:44 *3588*
w shall exalt himself shall be Mt 23:12 *3748*
W shall swear by the temple, it Mt 23:16 *3739,302*
but *w* shall swear by the gold of Mt 23:16 *3739,302*
W shall swear by the altar, it is Mt 23:18 *3739,1437*
but *w* sweareth by the gift that Mt 23:18 *3739,302*
For *w* shall do the will of God, Mk 3:35 *3739,302*
w shall not receive you, nor hear Mk 6:11 *3745,302*
W will come after me, let him Mk 8:34 *3748*
For *w* will save his life shall Mk 8:35 *3739,302*
but *w* shall lose his life for my Mk 8:35 *3739,302*
W therefore shall be ashamed of Mk 8:38 *3739,302*
W shall receive one of such Mk 9:37 *3739,1437*
w shall receive me, receiveth not Mk 9:37 *3739,1437*
For *w* shall give you a cup of Mk 9:41 *3739,302*
w shall offend one of these Mk 9:42 *3739,302*
W shall put away his wife, and Mk 10:11 *3739,1437*
W shall not receive the kingdom Mk 10:15 *3739,1437*
but *w* will be great among you, Mk 10:43 *3739,1437*
w of you will be the chiefest, Mk 10:44 *3739,302*
That *w* shall say unto this Mk 11:23 *3739,302*
W cometh to me, and heareth my Lk 6:47 *3956,3588*
w shall not be offended in me Lk 7:23 *3739,1437*
for *w* hath, to him shall be given Lk 8:18 *3739,302*
w hath not, from him shall be Lk 8:18 *3739,302*
w will not receive you, when ye Lk 9:5 *3745,302*
For *w* will save his life shall Lk 9:24 *3739,302*
but *w* will lose his life for my Lk 9:24 *3739,302*
For *w* shall be ashamed of me and Lk 9:26 *3739,302*
W shall receive this child in my Lk 9:48 *3739,1437*
w shall receive me receiveth him Lk 9:48 *3739,1437*
W shall confess me before men, Lk 12:8 *3956,3739,302*
w shall speak a word against the Lk 12:10 *3956,3739*
For *w* exalteth himself shall be Lk 14:11 *3956,3588*
w doth not bear his cross, and Lk 14:27 *3748*
w he be of you that forsaketh not Lk 14:33 *3956*
W putteth away his wife, and Lk 16:18 *3956,3588*
w marrieth her that is put away Lk 16:18 *3956,3588*
W shall seek to save his life Lk 17:33 *3739,1437*
w shall lose his life shall Lk 17:33 *3739,1437*
W shall not receive the kingdom Lk 18:17 *3739,1437*
W shall fall upon that stone Lk 20:18 *3956,3588*
That *w* believeth in him should Jn 3:15 *3956,3588*
that *w* believeth in him should Jn 3:16 *3956,3588*
W drinketh of this water shall Jn 4:13 *3756,3588*
But *w* drinketh of the water that Jn 4:14 *3739,302*
w then first after the troubling Jn 5:4 *3588*
W committeth sin is the servant Jn 8:34 *3956,3588*
w liveth and believeth in me shall Jn 11:26 *3956,3588*
that *w* believeth on me should not Jn 12:46 *3956,3588*
that *w* killeth you will think Jn 16:2 *3956,3588*
w maketh himself a king speaketh Jn 19:12 *3956,3588*
that *w* shall call on the name Acts 2:21 *3956,3739,302*
that through his name *w* believeth Acts 10:43 *3956,3588*
w among you feareth God, to you Acts 13:26 *3588*
O man, *w* thou art that judgest Rom 2:1 *3956,3588*
w believeth on him shall not be Rom 9:33 *3956,3588*
W believeth on him shall not be Rom 10:11 *3956,3588*
For *w* shall call upon the name Rom 10:13 *3956,3739,302*
W therefore resisteth the power, Rom 13:2 *3588*
Wherefore *w* shall eat this bread, 1Cor 11:27 *3739,302*
w of you are justified by the law Gal 5:4 *3748*
shall bear his judgment, *w* he be Gal 5:10 *3748,302*
For *w* shall keep the whole law, Jas 2:10 *3748*
w therefore will be a friend of Jas 4:4 *3739,302*
W denieth the Son, the same hath 1Jn 2:23 *3956,3588*
W committeth sin transgresseth 1Jn 3:4 *3456,3588*
W abideth in him sinneth not 1Jn 3:6 *3956,3588*
w sinneth hath not seen him, 1Jn 3:6 *3956,3588*
W is born of God doth not commit 1Jn 3:9 *3956,3588*
w doeth not righteousness is not 1Jn 3:10 *3956,3588*
W hateth his brother is a 1Jn 3:15 *3956,3588*
W shall confess that Jesus is the 1Jn 4:15 *3739,302*

W believeth that Jesus is the ... 1Jn 5:1 *3956,3588*
We know that *w* is born of God ... 1Jn 5:18 *3956,3588*
W transgresseth, and abideth not ... 2Jn 9 *3956,3588*
w receiveth the mark of his name ... Rev 14:11 *1536*
w was not found written in the ... Rev 20:15 *1536*
and *w* loveth and maketh a lie ... Rev 22:15 *3956,3588*
w will, let him take the water of ... Rev 22:17 *3588*

WHY See APPENDIX.

WICKED {344}

But the men of Sodom were *w* ... Gen 13:13 7451
destroy the righteous with the *w* ... Gen 18:23 7563
to slay the righteous with the *w* ... Gen 18:25 7563
the righteous should be as the *w* ... Gen 18:25 7563
was *w* in the sight of the LORD ... Gen 38:7 7451
and I and my people are *w* ... Ex 9:27 7563
put not thine hand with the *w* to ... Ex 23:1 7563
for I will not justify the *w* ... Ex 23:7 7563
it is a *w* thing ... Lev 20:17 2617
from the tents of these *w* men ... Num 16:26 7563
be not a thought in thy *w* heart ... Deut 15:9 1100
which have committed that *w* thing ... Deut 17:5 7451
then keep thee from every *w* thing ... Deut 23:9 7451
the righteous, and condemn the *w* ... Deut 25:1 7563
if the *w* man be worthy to be ... Deut 25:2 7563
the *w* shall be silent in darkness ... 1Sa 2:9 7563
Wickedness proceedeth from the *w* ... 1Sa 24:13 7563
Then answered all the *w* men ... 1Sa 30:22 7451
as a man falleth before *w* men ... 2Sa 3:34 5766
when *w* men have slain a righteous ... 2Sa 4:11 7563
thy servants, condemning the *w* ... 1Kin 8:32 7563
wrought *w* things to provoke the ... 2Kin 17:11 7451
thy servants, by requiting the *w* ... 2Chr 6:23 7563
face, and turn from their *w* ways ... 2Chr 7:14 7451
that *w* woman, had broken up the ... 2Chr 24:7 4849
turned they from their *w* works ... Neh 9:35 7451
and enemy is this *w* Haman ... Est 7:6 7451
by letters that his *w* device ... Est 9:25 7451
There the *w* cease from troubling ... Job 3:17 7563
of the *w* shall come to nought ... Job 8:22 7563
destroyeth the perfect and the *w* ... Job 9:22 7563
is given into the hand of the *w* ... Job 9:24 7563
If I be *w*, why then labour I in ... Job 9:29 7561
shine upon the counsel of the *w* ... Job 10:3 7563
Thou knowest that I am not *w* ... Job 10:7 7561
If I be *w*, woe unto me ... Job 10:15 7561
But the eyes of the *w* shall fail ... Job 11:20 7563
The *w* man travaileth with pain ... Job 15:20 7563
me over into the hands of the *w* ... Job 16:11 7563
light of the *w* shall be put out ... Job 18:5 7563
such are the dwellings of the *w* ... Job 18:21 5767
the triumphing of the *w* is short ... Job 20:5 7563
every hand of the *w* shall come ... Job 20:22 6001
the portion of a *w* man from God ... Job 20:29 7563
Wherefore do the *w* live, become ... Job 21:7 7563
counsel of the *w* is far from me ... Job 21:16 7563
is the candle of the *w* put out ... Job 21:17 7563
are the dwelling places of the *w* ... Job 21:28 7563
That the *w* is reserved to the day ... Job 21:30 7451
old way which *w* men have trodden ... Job 22:15 205
counsel of the *w* is far from me ... Job 22:18 7563
they gather the vintage of the *w* ... Job 24:6 7563
Let mine enemy be as the *w* ... Job 27:7 7563
the portion of a *w* man with God ... Job 27:13 7563
And I brake the jaws of the *w* ... Job 29:17 5767
Is not destruction to the *w* ... Job 31:3 5767
iniquity, and walketh with *w* men ... Job 34:8 7562
fit to say to a king, Thou art *w* ... Job 34:18 1100
He striketh them as *w* men in the ... Job 34:26 7563
because of his answers for *w* men ... Job 34:36 205
preserveth not the life of the *w* ... Job 36:6 7563
fulfilled the judgment of the *w* ... Job 36:17 7563
that the *w* might be shaken out of ... Job 38:13 7563
from the *w* their light is ... Job 38:15 7563
tread down the *w* in their place ... Job 40:12 7563
of the *w* come to an end ... Ps 7:9 7563
God is angry with the *w* every day ... Ps 7:11
thou hast destroyed the *w* ... Ps 9:5 7563
the *w* is snared in the work of ... Ps 9:16 7563
The *w* shall be turned into hell ... Ps 9:17 7563
The *w* in his pride doth persecute ... Ps 10:2 7563
For the *w* boasteth of his heart's ... Ps 10:3 7563
The *w*, through the pride of his ... Ps 10:4 7563
Wherefore doth the *w* contemn God ... Ps 10:13 7563
Break thou the arm of the *w* ... Ps 10:15 7563
the *w* bend their bow, they make ... Ps 11:2 7563
but the *w* and him that loveth ... Ps 11:5 7563
Upon the *w* he shall rain snares, ... Ps 11:6 7563
The *w* walk on every side, when ... Ps 12:8 7563
From the *w* that oppress me, from ... Ps 17:9 7563
deliver my soul from the *w* ... Ps 17:13 7563
of the *w* have inclosed me ... Ps 22:16 7489
and will not sit with the *w* ... Ps 26:5 7563
When the *w*, even mine enemies and ... Ps 27:2 7489
Draw me not away with the *w* ... Ps 28:3 7563
let the *w* be ashamed, and let them ... Ps 31:17 7563
Many sorrows shall be to the *w* ... Ps 32:10 7563
Evil shall slay the *w* ... Ps 34:21 7563
of the *w* saith within my heart ... Ps 36:1 7563
not the hand of the *w* remove me ... Ps 36:11 7563
who bringeth *w* devices to pass ... Ps 37:7 4209
while, and the *w* shall not be ... Ps 37:10 7563
The *w* plotteth against the just, ... Ps 37:12 7563
The *w* have drawn out the sword, ... Ps 37:14 7563
better than the riches of many *w* ... Ps 37:16 7563
the arms of the *w* shall be broken ... Ps 37:17 7563
But the *w* shall perish, and the ... Ps 37:20 7563
The *w* borroweth, and payeth not ... Ps 37:21 7563
seed of the *w* shall be cut off ... Ps 37:28 7563
The *w* watcheth the righteous, and ... Ps 37:32 7563
when the *w* are cut off, thou ... Ps 37:34 7563
I have seen the *w* in great power ... Ps 37:35 7563
the end of the *w* shall be cut off ... Ps 37:38 7563
he shall deliver them from the *w* ... Ps 37:40 7563
bridle, while the *w* is before me ... Ps 39:1 7563
But unto the *w* God saith, What ... Ps 50:16 7563
of the oppression of the *w* ... Ps 55:3 7563
The *w* are estranged from the womb ... Ps 58:3 7563
his feet in the blood of the *w* ... Ps 58:10 7563
merciful to any *w* transgressors ... Ps 59:5 205
from the secret counsel of the *w* ... Ps 64:2 7489
so let the *w* perish at the ... Ps 68:2 7563
my God, out of the hand of the *w* ... Ps 71:4 7563
I saw the prosperity of the *w* ... Ps 73:3 7563
unto the multitude of the *w* ... Ps 74:19
and to the *w*, Lift not up the horn ... Ps 75:4 7563
all the *w* of the earth shall ... Ps 75:8 7563
of the *w* also will I cut off ... Ps 75:10 7563
and accept the persons of the *w* ... Ps 82:2 7563
rid them out of the hand of the *w* ... Ps 82:4 7563
behold and see the reward of the *w* ... Ps 91:8 7563
When the *w* spring as the grass, ... Ps 92:7 7563
of the *w* that rise up against me ... Ps 92:11 7489
LORD, how long shall the *w* ... Ps 94:3 7563
how long shall the *w* triumph ... Ps 94:3 7563
until the pit be digged for the *w* ... Ps 94:13 7563
them out of the hand of the *w* ... Ps 97:10 7563
I will set no *w* thing before mine ... Ps 101:3 1100
I will not know a *w* person ... Ps 101:4 7451
destroy all the *w* of the land ... Ps 101:8 7563
that I may cut off all *w* doers ... Ps 101:8 205
earth, and let the *w* be no more ... Ps 104:35 7563
the flame burned up the *w* ... Ps 106:18 7563
For the mouth of the *w* and the ... Ps 109:2 7563
Set thou a *w* man over him ... Ps 109:6 7563
The *w* shall see it, and be grieved ... Ps 112:10 7563
the desire of the *w* shall perish ... Ps 112:10 7563
of the *w* that forsake thy law ... Ps 119:53 7563
The bands of the *w* have robbed me ... Ps 119:61 7563
The *w* have waited for me to ... Ps 119:95 7563
The *w* have laid a snare for me ... Ps 119:110 7563
all the *w* of the earth like dross ... Ps 119:119 7563
Salvation is far from the *w* ... Ps 119:155 7563
For the rod of the *w* shall not ... Ps 125:3 7562
cut asunder the cords of the *w* ... Ps 129:4 7563
Surely thou wilt slay the *w* ... Ps 139:19 7563
see if there be any *w* way in me ... Ps 139:24 6090
O LORD, from the hands of the *w* ... Ps 140:4 7563
not, O LORD, the desires of the *w* ... Ps 140:8 7563
further not his *w* device ... Ps 140:8 2162
to practise *w* works with men that ... Ps 141:4 7562
Let the *w* fall into their own ... Ps 141:10 7563
but all the *w* will he destroy ... Ps 145:20 7563
but the way of the *w* he turneth ... Ps 146:9 7563
he casteth the *w* down to the ... Ps 147:6 7563
in the frowardness of the *w* ... Prov 2:14 7451
But the *w* shall be cut off from ... Prov 2:22 7563
of the desolation of the *w* ... Prov 3:25 7563
the LORD is in the house of the *w* ... Prov 3:33 7563
Enter not into the path of the *w* ... Prov 4:14 7563
The way of the *w* is as darkness ... Prov 4:19 7563
shall take the *w* himself, and he ... Prov 5:22 7563
a *w* man, walketh with a froward ... Prov 6:12 205
that deviseth *w* imaginations ... Prov 6:18 205
he that rebuketh a *w* man getteth ... Prov 9:7 7563
away the substance of the *w* ... Prov 10:3 7563
covereth the mouth of the *w* ... Prov 10:6 7563
but the name of the *w* shall rot ... Prov 10:7 7563
covereth the mouth of the *w* ... Prov 10:11 7563
the fruit of the *w* to sin ... Prov 10:16 7563
heart of the *w* is little worth ... Prov 10:20 7563
The fear of the *w*, it shall come ... Prov 10:24 7563
passeth, so is the *w* no more ... Prov 10:25 7563
years of the *w* shall be shortened ... Prov 10:27 7563
expectation of the *w* shall perish ... Prov 10:28 7563
but the *w* shall not inhabit the ... Prov 10:30 7563
of the *w* speaketh frowardness ... Prov 10:32 7563
but the *w* shall fall by his own ... Prov 11:5 7563
When a *w* man dieth, his ... Prov 11:7 7563
the *w* cometh in his stead ... Prov 11:8 7563
and when the *w* perish, there is ... Prov 11:10 7563
overthrown by the mouth of the *w* ... Prov 11:11 7563
The *w* worketh a deceitful work ... Prov 11:18 7563
the *w* shall not be unpunished ... Prov 11:21 7451
the expectation of the *w* is wrath ... Prov 11:23 7563
much more the *w* and the sinner ... Prov 11:31 7563
but a man of *w* devices will he ... Prov 12:2 4209
the counsels of the *w* are deceit ... Prov 12:5 7563
The words of the *w* are to lie in ... Prov 12:6 7563
The *w* are overthrown, and are not ... Prov 12:7 7563
tender mercies of the *w* are cruel ... Prov 12:10 7563
The *w* desireth the net of evil ... Prov 12:12 7563
The *w* is snared by the ... Prov 12:13 7451
but the *w* shall be filled with ... Prov 12:21 7563
the way of the *w* seduceth them ... Prov 12:26 7563
but a *w* man is loathsome, and ... Prov 13:5 7563
lamp of the *w* shall be put out ... Prov 13:9 7563
A *w* messenger falleth into ... Prov 13:17 7563
but the belly of the *w* shall want ... Prov 13:25 7563
The house of the *w* shall be ... Prov 14:11 7563
a man of *w* devices is hated ... Prov 14:17 4209
the *w* at the gates of the ... Prov 14:19 7563
The *w* is driven away in his ... Prov 14:32 7563
the revenues of the *w* is trouble ... Prov 15:6 7563
The sacrifice of the *w* is an ... Prov 15:8 7563
The way of the *w* is an ... Prov 15:9 7563
The thoughts of the *w* are an ... Prov 15:26 7451
but the mouth of the *w* poureth ... Prov 15:28 7563
The LORD is far from the *w* ... Prov 15:29 7563
even the *w* for the day of evil ... Prov 16:4 7563
A *w* doer giveth heed to false ... Prov 17:4 7489
He that justifieth the *w*, and he ... Prov 17:15 7563
A *w* man taketh a gift out of the ... Prov 17:23 7563
When the *w* cometh, then cometh ... Prov 18:3 7563
to accept the person of the *w* ... Prov 18:5 7563
the mouth of the *w* devoureth ... Prov 19:28 7563
A wise king scattereth the *w* ... Prov 20:26 7563
heart, and the plowing of the *w* ... Prov 21:4 7563
of the *w* shall destroy them ... Prov 21:7 7563
The soul of the *w* desireth evil ... Prov 21:10 7563
considereth the house of the *w* ... Prov 21:12 7563
the *w* for their wickedness ... Prov 21:12 7563
The *w* shall be a ransom for the ... Prov 21:18 7563
sacrifice of the *w* is abomination ... Prov 21:27 7563
when he bringeth it with a *w* mind ... Prov 21:27 2154
A *w* man hardeneth his face ... Prov 21:29 7563
O *w* man, against the dwelling of ... Prov 24:15 7563
but the *w* shall fall into ... Prov 24:16 7563
neither be thou envious at the *w* ... Prov 24:19 7563
candle of the *w* shall be put out ... Prov 24:20 7563
He that saith unto the *w*, Thou ... Prov 24:24 7563
Take away the *w* from before the ... Prov 25:5 7563
the *w* is as a troubled fountain ... Prov 25:26 7563
a *w* heart are like a potsherd ... Prov 26:23 7451
The *w* flee when no man pursueth ... Prov 28:1 7563
that forsake the law praise the *w* ... Prov 28:4 7563
but when the *w* rise, a man is ... Prov 28:12 7563
so is a *w* ruler over the poor ... Prov 28:15 7563
When the *w* rise, men hide ... Prov 28:28 7563
but when the *w* beareth rule ... Prov 29:2 7563
but the *w* regardeth not to know ... Prov 29:7 7563
to lies, all his servants are *w* ... Prov 29:12 7563
When the *w* are multiplied, ... Prov 29:16 7563
the way is abomination to the *w* ... Prov 29:27 7563
judge the righteous and the *w* ... Eccl 3:17 7563
there is a *w* man that prolongeth ... Eccl 7:15 7563
Be not over much *w*, neither be ... Eccl 7:17 7561
And so I saw the *w* buried, who had ... Eccl 8:10 7563
it shall not be well with the *w* ... Eccl 8:13 7563
according to the work of the *w* ... Eccl 8:14 7563
again, there be *w* men, to whom it ... Eccl 8:14 7563
to the righteous, and to the *w* ... Eccl 9:2 7563
Woe unto the *w* ... Is 3:11 7563
Which justify the *w* for reward ... Is 5:23 7563
of his lips shall he slay the *w* ... Is 11:4 7563
evil, and the *w* for their iniquity ... Is 13:11 7563
hath broken the staff of the *w* ... Is 14:5 7563
Let favour be shewed to the *w* ... Is 26:10 7563
he deviseth *w* devices to destroy ... Is 32:7 2154
peace, saith the LORD, unto the *w* ... Is 48:22 7563
And he made his grave with the *w* ... Is 53:9 7563
Let the *w* forsake his way, and the ... Is 55:7 7563
But the *w* are like the troubled ... Is 57:20 7563
no peace, saith my God, to the *w* ... Is 57:21 7563
also taught the *w* ones thy ways ... Jer 2:33 7451
among my people are found *w* men ... Jer 5:26 7563
they overpass the deeds of the *w* ... Jer 5:28 7451
for the *w* are not plucked away ... Jer 6:29 7451
doth the way of the *w* prosper ... Jer 12:1 7563
thee out of the hand of the *w* ... Jer 15:21 7451
all things, and desperately *w* ... Jer 17:9 605
grievously upon the head of the *w* ... Jer 23:19 7563
give them that are *w* to the sword ... Jer 25:31 7563
with pain upon the head of the *w* ... Jer 30:23 7563
When I say unto the *w*, Thou shalt ... Eze 3:18 7563
to warn the *w* from his *w* way ... Eze 3:18 7563
the same *w* man shall die in his ... Eze 3:18 7563
Yet if thou warn the *w*, and he ... Eze 3:19 7563
wickedness, nor from his *w* way ... Eze 3:19 7563
to the *w* of the earth for a spoil ... Eze 7:21 7563
behold the *w* abominations that ... Eze 8:9 7451
give *w* counsel in this city ... Eze 11:2 7451
strengthened the hands of the *w* ... Eze 13:22 7451
should not return from his *w* way ... Eze 13:22 7563
of the *w* shall be upon him ... Eze 18:20 7563
But if the *w* will turn from all ... Eze 18:21 7563
at all that the *w* should die ... Eze 18:23 7563
abominations that the *w* man doeth ... Eze 18:24 7563
when the *w* man turneth away from ... Eze 18:27 7563
not according to your *w* ways ... Eze 20:44 7451
from thee the righteous and the *w* ... Eze 21:3 7563
from thee the righteous and the *w* ... Eze 21:4 7563
profane *w* prince of Israel, whose ... Eze 21:25 7563
of them that are slain, of the *w* ... Eze 21:29 7563
the land into the hand of the *w* ... Eze 30:12 7451
When I say unto the *w* ... Eze 33:8 7563
O *w* man, thou shalt surely die ... Eze 33:8 7563
speak to warn the *w* from his way ... Eze 33:8 7563
that *w* man shall die in his ... Eze 33:8 7563
if thou warn the *w* of his way to ... Eze 33:9 7563
no pleasure in the death of the *w* ... Eze 33:11 7563
but that the *w* turn from his way ... Eze 33:11 7563
as for the wickedness of the *w* ... Eze 33:12 7563
Again, when I say unto the *w* ... Eze 33:14 7563
If the *w* restore the pledge, give ... Eze 33:15 7563
But if the *w* turn from his ... Eze 33:19 7563
but the *w* shall do wickedly ... Dan 12:10 7563
none of the *w* shall understand ... Dan 12:10 7563
wickedness in the house of the *w* ... Mic 6:10 7563
them pure with the *w* balances ... Mic 6:11 7562
and will not at all acquit the *w* ... Nah 1:3 7563
against the LORD, a *w* counsellor ... Nah 1:11 1100
for the *w* shall no more pass ... Nah 1:15 1100
for the *w* doth compass about the ... Hab 1:4 7563

W

holdest thy tongue when the *w* ... Hab 1:13 7563
head out of the house of the *w* ... Hab 3:13 7563
and the stumblingblocks with the *w* ... Zeph 1:3 7563
between the righteous and the *w* ... Mal 3:18 7563
And ye shall tread down the *w* ... Mal 4:3 7563
other spirits more *w* than himself ... Mt 12:45 *4191*
it be also unto this *w* generation ... Mt 12:45 *4190*
it not, then cometh the *w* one ... Mt 13:19 *4190*
are the children of the *w* one ... Mt 13:38 *4190*
sever the *w* from among the just, ... Mt 13:49 *4190*
A *w* and adulterous generation ... Mt 16:4 *4190*
O thou *w* servant, I forgave thee ... Mt 18:32 *4190*
miserably destroy those *w* men ... Mt 21:41 *2556*
answered and said unto him, Thou *w* ... Mt 25:26 *4190*
other spirits more *w* than himself ... Lk 11:26 *4191*
will I judge thee, thou *w* servant ... Lk 19:22 *4190*
by *w* hands have crucified and ... Acts 2:23 *459*
a matter of wrong or *w* lewdness ... Acts 18:14 *4190*
among yourselves that *w* person ... 1Cor 5:13 *4190*
all the fiery darts of the *w* ... Eph 6:16 *4190*
enemies in your mind by *w* works ... Col 1:21 *4190*
And then shall that *W* be revealed ... 2Th 2:8 *459*
from unreasonable and *w* men ... 2Th 3:2 *4190*
the filthy conversation of the *w* ... 2Pet 2:7 *113*
led away with the error of the *w* ... 2Pet 3:17 *113*
ye have overcome the *w* one ... 1Jn 2:13 *4190*
and ye have overcome the *w* one ... 1Jn 2:14 *4190*
as Cain, who was of that *w* one ... 1Jn 3:12 *4190*
that *w* one toucheth him not ... 1Jn 5:18 *4190*

WICKEDLY {23}

I pray you, brethren, do not so *w* ... Gen 19:7 7489
in doing *w* in the sight of the ... Deut 9:18 7561
nay, I pray you, do not so *w* ... Judg 19:23 7489
But if ye shall still do *w* ... 1Sa 12:25 7489
have not *w* departed from my God ... 2Sa 22:22 7561
I have sinned, and I have done *w* ... 2Sa 24:17 5753
hath done *w* above all that the ... 2Kin 21:11 7489
have done amiss, and have dealt *w* ... 2Chr 6:37 7561
king of Israel, who did very *w* ... 2Chr 20:35 7561
mother was his counsellor to do *w* ... 2Chr 22:3 7561
done right, but we have done *w* ... Neh 9:33 7561
Will ye speak *w* for God ... Job 13:7 5766
Yea, surely God will not do *w* ... Job 34:12 7561
have not *w* departed from my God ... Ps 18:21 7561
speak *w* concerning oppression ... Ps 73:8 7451
hath done *w* in the sanctuary ... Ps 74:3 7489
iniquity, we have done *w* ... Ps 106:6 7561
For they speak against thee *w* ... Ps 139:20 4209
iniquity, and have done *w*, and have ... Dan 9:5 7561
we have sinned, we have done *w* ... Dan 9:15 7561
such as do *w* against the covenant ... Dan 11:32 7561
but the wicked shall do *w* ... Dan 12:10 7561
the proud, yea, and all that do *w* ... Mal 4:1 7564

WICKEDNESS {127}

God saw that the *w* of man was ... Gen 6:5 7451
how then can I do this great *w* ... Gen 39:9 7451
it is *w* ... Lev 18:17 2154
and the land become full of *w* ... Lev 19:29 2154
a wife and her mother, it is *w* ... Lev 20:14 2154
that there be no *w* among you ... Lev 20:14 2154
but for the *w* of these nations ... Deut 9:4 7564
but for the *w* of these nations ... Deut 9:5 7564
of this people, nor to their *w* ... Deut 9:27 7562
any such *w* as this is among you ... Deut 13:11 7451
that hath wrought *w* in the sight ... Deut 17:2 7451
because of the *w* of thy doings ... Deut 28:20 7455
God rendered the *w* of Abimelech ... Judg 9:56 7451
Israel, Tell us, how was this *w* ... Judg 20:3 7451
What *w* is this that is done among ... Judg 20:12 7451
and see that your *w* is great ... 1Sa 12:17 7451
ye have done all this *w* ... 1Sa 12:20 7451
W proceedeth from the wicked ... 1Sa 24:13 7562
the *w* of Nabal upon his own head ... 1Sa 25:39 7451
doer of evil according to his *w* ... 2Sa 3:39 7451
of *w* afflict them any more ... 2Sa 7:10 5766
but if *w* shall be found in him, ... 1Kin 1:52 7451
Thou knowest all the *w* which ... 1Kin 2:44 7451
return thy *w* upon thine own head ... 1Kin 2:44 7451
perversely, we have committed *w* ... 1Kin 8:47 7561
work *w* in the sight of the LORD ... 1Kin 21:25 7451
he wrought much *w* in the sight of ... 2Kin 21:6 7451
children of *w* waste them any more ... 1Chr 17:9 5766
they that plow iniquity, and sow *w* ... Job 4:8 5999
he seeth *w* also ... Job 11:11 205
away, and let not *w* dwell in thy ... Job 11:14 5766
Though *w* be sweet in his mouth, ... Job 20:12 7451
Is not thy *w* great ... Job 22:5 7451
w shall be broken as a tree ... Job 24:20 5766
My lips shall not speak *w* ... Job 27:4 5766
it from God, that he should do *w* ... Job 34:10 7562
Thy *w* may hurt a man as thou art ... Job 35:8 7562
not a God that hath pleasure in *w* ... Ps 5:4 7562
their inward part is very *w* ... Ps 5:9 1942
Oh let the *w* of the wicked come ... Ps 7:9 7451
seek out his *w* till thou find ... Ps 10:15 7562
according to the *w* of their ... Ps 28:4 7455
lovest righteousness, and hatest *w* ... Ps 45:7 7562
and strengthened himself in his *w* ... Ps 52:7 1942
W is in the midst thereof ... Ps 55:11 1942
for *w* is in their dwellings, and ... Ps 55:15 7451
Yea, in heart ye work *w* ... Ps 58:2 5766
than to dwell in the tents of *w* ... Ps 84:10 7562
nor the son of *w* afflict him ... Ps 89:22 5766
shall cut them off in their own *w* ... Ps 94:23 7451
for the *w* of them that dwell ... Ps 107:34 7451
For they eat the bread of *w* ... Prov 4:17 7562
w is an abomination to my lips ... Prov 8:7 7562
Treasures of *w* profit nothing ... Prov 10:2 7562
wicked shall fall by his own *w* ... Prov 11:5 7564
man shall not be established by *w* ... Prov 12:3 7562
but *w* overthroweth the sinner ... Prov 13:6 7564
wicked is driven away in his *w* ... Prov 14:32 7451
abomination to kings to commit *w* ... Prov 16:12 7562
the wicked for their *w* ... Prov 21:12 7451
his *w* shall be shewed before the ... Prov 26:26 7451
mouth, and saith, I have done no *w* ... Prov 30:20 205
of judgment, that *w* was there ... Eccl 3:16 7562
that prolongeth his life in his *w* ... Eccl 7:15 7451
things, and to know the *w* of folly ... Eccl 7:25 7562
neither shall *w* deliver those ... Eccl 8:8 7562
For *w* burneth as the fire ... Is 9:18 7564
For thou hast trusted in thy *w* ... Is 47:10 7451
and to smite with the fist of *w* ... Is 58:4 7562
to loose the bands of *w*, to undo ... Is 58:6 7562
against them touching all their *w* ... Jer 1:16 7451
Thine own *w* shall correct thee, ... Jer 2:19 7451
with thy whoredoms and with thy *w* ... Jer 3:2 7451
wash thine heart from *w*, that ... Jer 4:14 7451
this is thy *w*, because it is ... Jer 4:18 7451
waters, so she casteth out her *w* ... Jer 6:7 7451
it for the *w* of my people Israel ... Jer 7:12 7451
no man repented him of his *w* ... Jer 8:6 7451
for the *w* of them that dwell ... Jer 12:4 7451
for I will pour their *w* upon them ... Jer 14:16 7451
We acknowledge, O LORD, our *w* ... Jer 14:20 7562
and confounded for all thy *w* ... Jer 22:22 7451
in my house have I found their *w* ... Jer 23:11 7451
that none doth return from his *w* ... Jer 23:14 7451
for all whose *w* I have hid my ... Jer 33:5 7451
Because of their *w* which they ... Jer 44:3 7451
their ear to turn from their *w* ... Jer 44:5 7451
forgotten the *w* of your fathers ... Jer 44:9 7451
the *w* of the kings of Judah, and ... Jer 44:9 7451
the *w* of their wives, and your own ... Jer 44:9 7451
of their wives, and your own *w* ... Jer 44:9 7451
the *w* of your wives, which they ... Jer 44:9 7451
Let all their *w* come before thee ... Lam 1:22 7451
wicked, and he turn not from his *w* ... Eze 3:19 7562
into *w* more than the nations ... Eze 5:6 7564
is risen up into a rod of *w* ... Eze 7:11 7562
it came to pass after all thy *w* ... Eze 16:23 7451
Before thy *w* was discovered, as ... Eze 16:57 7451
the *w* of the wicked shall be upon ... Eze 18:20 7564
from his *w* that he hath committed ... Eze 18:27 7564
I have driven him out for his *w* ... Eze 31:11 7562
as for the *w* of the wicked, he ... Eze 33:12 7564
day that he turneth from his *w* ... Eze 33:12 7562
But if the wicked turn from his *w* ... Eze 33:19 7564
discovered, and the *w* of Samaria ... Hos 7:1 7451
that I remember all their *w* ... Hos 7:2 7451
make the king glad with their *w* ... Hos 7:3 7451
All their *w* is in Gilgal ... Hos 9:15 7451
for the *w* of their doings I will ... Hos 9:15 7455
Ye have plowed *w*, ye have reaped ... Hos 10:13 7562
unto you because of your great *w* ... Hos 10:15 7451
for their *w* is great ... Joel 3:13 7451
for their *w* is come up before me ... Jonah 1:2 7451
of *w* in the house of the wicked ... Mic 6:10 7562
hath not thy *w* passed continually ... Nah 3:19 7451
And he said, This is *w* ... Zec 5:8 7564
shall call them, The border of *w* ... Mal 1:4 7564
yea, they that work *w* are set up ... Mal 3:15 7564
But Jesus perceived their *w* ... Mt 22:18 *4189*
Thefts, covetousness, *w*, deceit, ... Mk 7:22 *4189*
part is full of ravening and *w* ... Lk 11:39 *4189*
Repent therefore of this thy *w* ... Acts 8:22 *2549*
man, if there be any *w* in him ... Acts 25:5 *5129,824*
unrighteousness, fornication, *w* ... Rom 1:29 *4189*
with the leaven of malice and *w* ... 1Cor 5:8 *4189*
spiritual *w* in high places ... Eph 6:12 *4189*
and the whole world lieth in *w* ... 1Jn 5:19 *4190*

WIDE {15}

shalt open thine hand *w* unto him ... Deut 15:8 6605
thine hand *w* unto thy brother ... Deut 15:11 6605
and good, and the land was *w* ... 1Chr 4:40 7342,3027
mouth *w* as for the latter rain ... Job 29:23
me as a *w* breaking in of waters ... Job 30:14 7342
opened their mouth *w* against me ... Ps 35:21 7337
open thy mouth *w*, and I will fill ... Ps 81:10 7337
w sea, wherein are things ... Ps 104:25 7342,3027
but he that openeth *w* his lips ... Prov 13:3
a brawling woman and in a *w* house ... Prov 21:9 2267
a brawling woman and in a *w* house ... Prov 25:24 2267
against whom make ye a *w* mouth ... Is 57:4 7337
saith, I will build me a *w* house ... Jer 22:14 4060
be set *w* open unto thine enemies ... Nah 3:13 6605
for *w* is the gate, and broad is ... Mt 7:13 *4116*

WIDENESS {1}

w of twenty cubits round about ... Eze 41:10 7341

WIDOW {50}

Remain a *w* at thy father's house, ... Gen 38:11 490
Ye shall not afflict any *w* ... Ex 22:22 490
A *w*, or a divorced woman, or ... Lev 21:14 490
if the priest's daughter be a *w* ... Lev 22:13 490
But every vow of a *w*, and of her ... Num 30:9 490
judgment of the fatherless and *w* ... Deut 10:18 490
and the fatherless, and the *w* ... Deut 14:29 490
and the fatherless, and the *w* ... Deut 16:11 490
and the fatherless, and the *w* ... Deut 16:14 490
for the fatherless, and for the *w* ... Deut 24:19 490
for the fatherless, and for the *w* ... Deut 24:20 490
for the fatherless, and for the *w* ... Deut 24:21 490
the fatherless, and the *w* ... Deut 26:12 490
to the fatherless, and to the *w* ... Deut 26:13 490
of the stranger, fatherless, and *w* ... Deut 27:19 490
answered, I am indeed a *w* woman ... 2Sa 14:5 490
a *w* woman, even he lifted up his ... 1Kin 11:26 490
I have commanded a *w* woman there ... 1Kin 17:9 490
the *w* woman was there gathering ... 1Kin 17:10 490
upon the *w* with whom I sojourn ... 1Kin 17:20 490
and doeth not good to the *w* ... Job 24:21 490
caused the eyes of the *w* to fail ... Job 31:16 490
They slay the *w* and the stranger, ... Ps 94:6 490
be fatherless, and his wife a *w* ... Ps 109:9 490
he relieveth the fatherless and *w* ... Ps 146:9 490
establish the border of the *w* ... Prov 15:25 490
the fatherless, plead for the *w* ... Is 1:17 490
the cause of the *w* come unto them ... Is 1:23 490
I shall not sit as a *w*, neither ... Is 47:8 490
the fatherless, and the *w* ... Jer 7:6 490
the fatherless, nor the *w* ... Jer 22:3 490
how is she become as a *w* ... Lam 1:1 490
vexed the fatherless and the *w* ... Eze 22:7 490
they take for their wives a *w* ... Eze 44:22 490
or a *w* that had a priest before ... Eze 44:22 490
And oppress not the *w*, nor the ... Zec 7:10 490
the hireling in his wages, the *w* ... Mal 3:5 490
And there came a certain poor *w* ... Mk 12:42 *5503*
That this poor *w* hath cast more ... Mk 12:43 *5503*
she was a *w* of about fourscore and ... Lk 2:37 *5503*
Sidon, unto a woman that was a *w* ... Lk 4:26 *5503*
son of his mother, and she was a *w* ... Lk 7:12 *5503*
there was a *w* in that city ... Lk 18:3 *5503*
Yet because this *w* troubleth me ... Lk 18:5 *5503*
he saw also a certain poor *w* ... Lk 21:2 *5503*
that this poor *w* hath cast in ... Lk 21:3 *5503*
But if any *w* have children or ... 1Ti 5:4 *5503*
Now she that is a *w* indeed ... 1Ti 5:5 *5503*
Let not a *w* be taken into the ... 1Ti 5:9 *5503*
heart, I sit a queen, and am no *w* ... Rev 18:7 *5503*

WIDOWHOOD {4}

and put on the garments of her *w* ... Gen 38:19 491
day of their death, living in *w* ... 2Sa 20:3 491
day, the loss of children, and *w* ... Is 47:9 489
the reproach of thy *w* any more ... Is 54:4 491

WIDOW'S {5}

she put her *w* garments off from ... Gen 38:14 491
nor take a *w* raiment to pledge ... Deut 24:17 490
He was a *w* son of the tribe of ... 1Kin 7:14 490
they take the *w* ox for a pledge ... Job 24:3 490
I caused the *w* heart to sing for ... Job 29:13 490

WIDOWS {23}

and your wives shall be *w*, and your ... Ex 22:24 490
Thou hast sent *w* away empty ... Job 22:9 490
and his *w* shall not weep ... Job 27:15 490
fatherless, and a judge of the *w* ... Ps 68:5 490
their *w* made no lamentation ... Ps 78:64 490
mercy on their fatherless and *w* ... Is 9:17 490
that *w* may be their prey, and that ... Is 10:2 490
Their *w* are increased to me above ... Jer 15:8 490
of their children, and be *w* ... Jer 18:21 490
and let thy *w* trust in me ... Jer 49:11 490
fatherless, our mothers are as *w* ... Lam 5:3 490
her many *w* in the midst thereof ... Eze 22:25 490
many *w* were in Israel in the days ... Lk 4:25 *5503*
because their *w* were neglected in ... Acts 6:1 *5503*
all the *w* stood by him weeping, ... Acts 9:39 *5503*
he had called the saints and *w* ... Acts 9:41 *5503*
therefore to the unmarried and *w* ... 1Cor 7:8 *5503*
Honour *w* that are *w* indeed ... 1Ti 5:3 *5503*
But the younger *w* refuse ... 1Ti 5:11 *5503*
or woman that believeth have *w* ... 1Ti 5:16 *5503*
relieve them that are *w* indeed ... 1Ti 5:16 *5503*
w in their affliction, and to keep ... Jas 1:27 *5503*

WIDOWS' {3}

for ye devour *w* houses, and for a ... Mt 23:14 *5503*
Which devour *w* houses, and for a ... Mk 12:40 *5503*
Which devour *w* houses, and for a ... Lk 20:47 *5503*

WIFE {396}

and shall cleave unto his *w* ... Gen 2:24 802
were both naked, the man and his *w* ... Gen 2:25 802
his *w* hid themselves from the ... Gen 3:8 802
hearkened unto the voice of thy *w* ... Gen 3:17 802
to his *w* did the LORD God make ... Gen 3:21 802
And Adam knew Eve his *w* ... Gen 4:1 802
And Cain knew his *w* ... Gen 4:17 802
And Adam knew his *w* again ... Gen 4:25 802
ark, thou, and thy sons, and thy *w* ... Gen 6:18 802
went in, and his sons, and his *w* ... Gen 7:7 802
the sons of Noah, and Noah's *w* ... Gen 7:13 802
forth of the ark, thou, and thy *w* ... Gen 8:16 802
went forth, and his sons, and his *w* ... Gen 8:18 802
the name of Abram's *w* was Sarai ... Gen 11:29 802
and the name of Nahor's *w*, Milcah, ... Gen 11:29 802
in law, his son Abram's *w* ... Gen 11:31 802
And Abram took Sarai his *w* ... Gen 12:5 802
that he said unto Sarai his *w* ... Gen 12:11 802
they shall say, This is his *w* ... Gen 12:12 802
because of Sarai Abram's *w* ... Gen 12:17 802
not tell me that she was thy *w* ... Gen 12:18 802
I might have taken her to me to *w* ... Gen 12:19 802
now therefore behold thy *w* ... Gen 12:19 802
and they sent him away, and his *w* ... Gen 12:20 802
up out of Egypt, he, and his *w* ... Gen 13:1 802
Now Sarai Abram's *w* bare him no ... Gen 16:1 802
Sarai Abram's *w* took Hagar her ... Gen 16:3 802
to her husband Abram to be his *w* ... Gen 16:3 802
unto Abraham, As for Sarai thy *w* ... Gen 17:15 802
Sarah thy *w* shall bear thee a son ... Gen 17:19 802
unto him, Where is Sarah thy *w* ... Gen 18:9 802

Sarah thy *w* shall have a son	Gen 18:10	802
Lot, saying, Arise, take thy *w*	Gen 19:15	802
hand, and upon the hand of his *w*	Gen 19:16	802
But his *w* looked back from behind	Gen 19:26	802
And Abraham said of Sarah his *w*	Gen 20:2	802
for she is a man's *w*	Gen 20:3	1166
therefore restore the man his *w*	Gen 20:7	802
and she became my *w*	Gen 20:12	802
and restored him Sarah his *w*	Gen 20:14	802
and God healed Abimelech, and his *w*	Gen 20:17	802
because of Sarah Abraham's *w*	Gen 20:18	802
his mother took him a *w* out of	Gen 21:21	802
Abraham buried Sarah his *w* in the	Gen 23:19	802
that thou shalt not take a *w* unto	Gen 24:3	802
take a *w* unto my son Isaac	Gen 24:4	802
thou shalt take a *w* unto my son	Gen 24:7	802
the *w* of Nahor, Abraham's brother	Gen 24:15	802
Sarah my master's *w* bare a son to	Gen 24:36	802
Thou shalt not take a *w* to my son	Gen 24:37	802
kindred, and take a *w* unto my son	Gen 24:38	802
thou shalt take a *w* for my son of	Gen 24:40	802
let her be thy master's son's *w*	Gen 24:51	802
took Rebekah, and she became his *w*	Gen 24:67	802
Then again Abraham took a *w*	Gen 25:1	802
Abraham buried, and Sarah his *w*	Gen 25:10	802
old when he took Rebekah to *w*	Gen 25:20	802
intreated the LORD for his *w*	Gen 25:21	802
him, and Rebekah his *w* conceived	Gen 25:21	802
of the place asked him of his *w*	Gen 26:7	802
for he feared to say, She is my *w*	Gen 26:7	802
was sporting with Rebekah his *w*	Gen 26:8	802
Behold, of a surety she is thy *w*	Gen 26:9	802
lightly have lien with thy *w*	Gen 26:10	802
w shall surely be put to death	Gen 26:11	802
to *w* Judith the daughter of Beeri	Gen 26:34	802
if Jacob take a *w* of the	Gen 27:46	802
Thou shalt not take a *w* of the	Gen 28:1	802
take thee a *w* from thence of the	Gen 28:2	802
to take him a *w* from thence	Gen 28:6	802
Thou shalt not take a *w* of the	Gen 28:6	802
sister of Nebajoth, to be his *w*	Gen 28:9	802
said unto Laban, Give me my *w*	Gen 29:21	802
him Rachel his daughter to *w* also	Gen 29:28	802
gave him Bilhah her handmaid to *w*	Gen 30:4	802
her maid, and gave her Jacob to *w*	Gen 30:9	802
saying, Get me this damsel to *w*	Gen 34:4	802
I pray you give her him to *w*	Gen 34:8	802
but give me the damsel to *w*	Gen 34:12	802
the son of Adah the *w* of Esau	Gen 36:10	802
son of Bashemath the *w* of Esau	Gen 36:10	802
were the sons of Adah Esau's *w*	Gen 36:12	802
the sons of Bashemath Esau's *w*	Gen 36:13	802
the daughter of Zibeon, Esau's *w*	Gen 36:14	802
the sons of Bashemath Esau's *w*	Gen 36:17	802
the sons of Aholibamah Esau's *w*	Gen 36:18	802
the daughter of Anah, Esau's *w*	Gen 36:18	802
Judah took a *w* for Er his	Gen 38:6	802
Onan, Go in unto thy brother's *w*	Gen 38:8	802
he went in unto his brother's *w*	Gen 38:9	802
daughter of Shuah Judah's *w* died	Gen 38:12	802
she was not given unto him to *w*	Gen 38:14	802
that his master's *w* cast her eyes	Gen 39:7	802
and said unto his master's *w*	Gen 39:8	802
but thee, because thou art his *w*	Gen 39:9	802
master heard the words of his *w*	Gen 39:19	802
he gave him to *w* Asenath the	Gen 41:45	802
Ye know that my *w* bare me two	Gen 44:27	802
The sons of Rachel Jacob's *w*	Gen 46:19	802
buried Abraham and Sarah his *w*	Gen 49:31	802
buried Isaac and Rebekah his *w*	Gen 49:31	802
took to *w* a daughter of Levi	Ex 2:1	
And Moses took his *w* and his sons,	Ex 4:20	802
Jochebed his father's sister to *w*	Ex 6:20	802
sister of Naashon, to *w*	Ex 6:23	802
of the daughters of Putiel to *w*	Ex 6:25	802
in law, took Zipporah, Moses' *w*	Ex 18:2	802
his *w* unto Moses into the	Ex 18:5	802
am come unto thee, and thy *w*	Ex 18:6	802
shalt not covet thy neighbour's *w*	Ex 20:17	802
then his *w* shall go out with him	Ex 21:3	802
If his master have given him a *w*	Ex 21:4	802
the *w* and her children shall be	Ex 21:4	802
say, I love my master, my *w*	Ex 21:5	802
If he take him another *w*	Ex 21:10	
surely endow her to be his *w*	Ex 22:16	802
father's *w* shalt thou not uncover	Lev 18:8	802
thou shalt not approach to his *w*	Lev 18:14	802
she is thy son's *w*	Lev 18:15	802
the nakedness of thy brother's *w*	Lev 18:16	802
shalt thou take a *w* to her sister	Lev 18:18	802
carnally with thy neighbour's *w*	Lev 18:20	802
adultery with another man's *w*	Lev 20:10	802
adultery with his neighbour's *w*	Lev 20:10	802
w hath uncovered his father's	Lev 20:11	802
And if a man take a *w* and her	Lev 20:14	802
man shall lie with his uncle's *w*	Lev 20:20	1753
a man shall take his brother's *w*	Lev 20:21	802
not take a *w* that is a whore	Lev 21:7	802
And he shall take a *w* in her	Lev 21:13	802
a virgin of his own people to *w*	Lev 21:14	802
them, If any man's *w* go aside	Num 5:12	802
him, and he be jealous of his *w*	Num 5:14	802
him, and he be jealous of his *w*	Num 5:14	802
man bring his *w* unto the priest	Num 5:15	802
when a *w* goeth aside to another	Num 5:29	802
him, and he be jealous over his *w*	Num 5:30	802
name of Amram's *w* was Jochebed	Num 26:59	802
Moses, between a man and his *w*	Num 30:16	802
shall be *w* unto one of the family	Num 36:8	802
thou desire thy neighbour's *w*	Deut 5:21	802
or the *w* of thy bosom, or thy	Deut 13:6	802
is there that hath betrothed a *w*	Deut 20:7	802
thou wouldest have her to thy *w*	Deut 21:11	802
husband, and she shall be thy *w*	Deut 21:13	802
If any man take a *w*, and go in	Deut 22:13	802
my daughter unto this man to *w*	Deut 22:16	802
and she shall be his *w*	Deut 22:19	802
he hath humbled his neighbour's *w*	Deut 22:24	802
of silver, and she shall be his *w*	Deut 22:29	802
man shall not take his father's *w*	Deut 22:30	802
When a man hath taken a *w*	Deut 24:1	802
she may go and be another man's *w*	Deut 24:2	
die, which took her to be his *w*	Deut 24:3	802
not take her again to be his *w*	Deut 24:4	802
When a man hath taken a new *w*	Deut 24:5	802
shall cheer up his *w* which he	Deut 24:5	802
the *w* of the dead shall not marry	Deut 25:5	802
unto her, and take her to him to *w*	Deut 25:5	802
like not to take his brother's *w*	Deut 25:7	2994
then let his brother's *w* go up to	Deut 25:7	2994
Then shall his brother's *w* come	Deut 25:9	2994
the *w* of the one draweth near for	Deut 25:11	802
he that lieth with his father's *w*	Deut 27:20	802
Thou shalt betroth a *w*, and	Deut 28:30	802
toward the *w* of his bosom, and	Deut 28:54	802
I give Achsah my daughter to *w*	Josh 15:16	802
gave him Achsah his daughter to *w*	Josh 15:17	802
I give Achsah my daughter to *w*	Judg 1:12	802
gave him Achsah his daughter to *w*	Judg 1:13	802
the *w* of Lapidoth, she judged	Judg 4:4	802
of Jael the *w* of Heber the Kenite	Judg 4:17	802
Then Jael Heber's *w* took a nail	Judg 4:21	802
Jael the *w* of Heber the Kenite be	Judg 5:24	802
And Gilead's *w* bare him sons	Judg 11:2	802
his *w* was barren, and bare not	Judg 13:2	802
Manoah arose, and went after his *w*	Judg 13:11	802
and Manoah and his *w* looked on	Judg 13:19	802
his *w* looked on it, and fell on	Judg 13:20	802
more appear to Manoah and to his *w*	Judg 13:21	802
And Manoah said unto his *w*	Judg 13:22	802
But his *w* said unto him, If the	Judg 13:23	802
now therefore get her for me to *w*	Judg 14:2	802
to take a *w* of the uncircumcised	Judg 14:3	802
that they said unto Samson's *w*	Judg 14:15	802
Samson's *w* wept before him, and	Judg 14:16	802
But Samson's *w* was given to his	Judg 14:20	802
Samson visited his *w* with a kid	Judg 15:1	802
go in to my *w* into the chamber	Judg 15:1	802
because he had taken his *w*	Judg 15:6	802
his daughter unto Benjamin to *w*	Judg 21:1	802
be he that giveth a *w* to Benjamin	Judg 21:18	802
catch you every man his *w* of the	Judg 21:21	802
not to each man his *w* in the war	Judg 21:22	802
the country of Moab, he, and his *w*	Ruth 1:1	802
and the name of his *w* Naomi	Ruth 1:2	802
the *w* of the dead, to raise up	Ruth 4:5	802
the *w* of Mahlon, have I purchased	Ruth 4:10	802
have I purchased to be my *w*	Ruth 4:10	802
Boaz took Ruth, and she was his *w*	Ruth 4:13	802
he gave to Peninnah his *w*	1Sa 1:4	802
and Elkanah knew Hannah his *w*	1Sa 1:19	802
And Eli blessed Elkanah and his *w*	1Sa 2:20	802
his daughter in law, Phinehas' *w*	1Sa 4:19	802
the name of Saul's *w* was Ahinoam	1Sa 14:50	802
Merab, her will I give thee to *w*	1Sa 18:17	802
unto Adriel the Meholathite to *w*	1Sa 18:19	802
gave him Michal his daughter to *w*	1Sa 18:27	802
and Michal David's *w* told him	1Sa 19:11	802
and the name of his *w* Abigail	1Sa 25:3	802
young men told Abigail, Nabal's *w*	1Sa 25:14	802
his *w* had told him these things,	1Sa 25:37	802
Abigail, to take her to him to *w*	1Sa 25:39	802
thee, to take thee to him to *w*	1Sa 25:40	802
of David, and became his *w*	1Sa 25:42	802
Michal his daughter, David's *w*	1Sa 25:44	802
the Carmelitess, Nabal's *w*	1Sa 27:3	802
Abigail the *w* of Nabal the	1Sa 30:5	802
save to every man his *w* and his	1Sa 30:22	802
Abigail Nabal's *w* the Carmelite	2Sa 2:2	802
of Abigail the *w* of Nabal the	2Sa 3:3	802
Ithream, by Eglah David's *w*	2Sa 3:5	802
saying, Deliver me my *w* Michal	2Sa 3:14	802
the *w* of Uriah the Hittite	2Sa 11:3	802
and to drink, and to lie with my *w*	2Sa 11:11	802
when the *w* of Uriah heard that	2Sa 11:26	802
to his house, and she became his *w*	2Sa 11:27	802
hast taken his *w* to be thy *w*	2Sa 12:9	802
hast taken the *w* of Uriah the	2Sa 12:10	802
of Uriah the Hittite to be thy *w*	2Sa 12:10	802
that Uriah's *w* bare unto David	2Sa 12:15	802
David comforted Bath-sheba his *w*	2Sa 12:24	802
me Abishag the Shunammite to *w*	1Kin 2:17	802
to Adonijah thy brother to *w*	1Kin 2:21	802
the daughter of Solomon to *w*	1Kin 4:11	802
the daughter of Solomon to *w*	1Kin 4:15	802
daughter, whom he had taken to *w*	1Kin 7:8	
unto his daughter, Solomon's *w*	1Kin 9:16	802
so that he gave him to *w* the	1Kin 11:19	802
the sister of his own *w*	1Kin 11:19	802
And Jeroboam said to his *w*	1Kin 14:2	802
not known to be the *w* of Jeroboam	1Kin 14:2	802
And Jeroboam's *w* did so, and arose,	1Kin 14:4	802
the *w* of Jeroboam cometh to ask a	1Kin 14:5	802
said, Come in, thou *w* of Jeroboam	1Kin 14:6	802
And Jeroboam's *w* arose, and	1Kin 14:17	802
that he took to *w* Jezebel the	1Kin 16:31	802
But Jezebel his *w* came to him	1Kin 21:5	802
Jezebel his *w* said unto him, Dost	1Kin 21:7	802
whom Jezebel his *w* stirred up	1Kin 21:25	802
and she waited on Naaman's *w*	2Kin 5:2	802
the daughter of Ahab was his *w*	2Kin 8:18	802
Give thy daughter to my son to *w*	2Kin 14:9	802
the *w* of Shallum the son of	2Kin 22:14	802
begat children of Azubah his *w*	1Chr 2:18	802
then Abiah Hezron's *w* bare him	1Chr 2:24	802
Jerahmeel had also another *w*	1Chr 2:26	802
the name of the *w* of Abishur was	1Chr 2:29	802
to Jarha his servant to *w*	1Chr 2:35	802
the sixth, Ithream by Eglah his *w*	1Chr 3:3	802
his *w* Jehudijah bare Jered the	1Chr 4:18	802
the sons of his *w* Hodiah the	1Chr 4:19	802
Machir took to *w* the sister of	1Chr 7:15	802
Maachah the *w* of Machir bare a	1Chr 7:16	802
And when he went in to his *w*	1Chr 7:23	802
And he begat of Hodesh his *w*	1Chr 8:9	802
My *w* shall not dwell in the house	2Chr 8:11	802
of Jerimoth the son of David to *w*	2Chr 11:18	802
he had the daughter of Ahab to *w*	2Chr 21:6	802
the *w* of Jehoiada the priest,	2Chr 22:11	802
Give thy daughter to my son to *w*	2Chr 25:18	802
the *w* of Shallum the son of	2Chr 34:22	802
which took a *w* of the daughters	Ezr 2:61	802
of Barzillai the Gileadite to *w*	Neh 7:63	802
for his friends, and Zeresh his *w*	Est 5:10	802
Then said Zeresh his *w* and all his	Est 5:14	802
And Haman told Zeresh his *w*	Est 6:13	802
wise men and Zeresh his *w* unto him	Est 6:13	802
Then said his *w* unto him, Dost	Job 2:9	802
My breath is strange to my *w*	Job 19:17	802
Then let my *w* grind unto another,	Job 31:10	802
be fatherless, and his *w* a widow	Ps 109:9	802
Thy *w* shall be as a fruitful vine	Ps 128:3	802
rejoice with the *w* of thy youth	Prov 5:18	802
goeth in to his neighbour's *w*	Prov 6:29	802
Whoso findeth a *w* findeth a good	Prov 18:22	802
the contentions of a *w* are a	Prov 19:13	802
a prudent *w* is from the LORD	Prov 19:14	802
Live joyfully with the *w* whom	Eccl 9:9	802
the children of the married *w*	Is 54:1	
a *w* of youth, when thou wast	Is 54:6	802
They say, If a man put away his *w*	Jer 3:1	802
Surely as a *w* treacherously	Jer 3:20	802
neighed after his neighbour's *w*	Jer 5:8	802
husband with the *w* shall be taken	Jer 6:11	802
Thou shalt not take thee a *w*	Jer 16:2	802
But as a *w* that committeth	Eze 16:32	802
hath defiled his neighbour's *w*	Eze 18:6	802
and defiled his neighbour's *w*	Eze 18:11	802
not defiled his neighbour's *w*	Eze 18:15	802
with his neighbour's *w*	Eze 22:11	802
and at even my *w* died	Eze 24:18	802
every one his neighbour's *w*	Eze 33:26	802
take unto thee a *w* of whoredoms	Hos 1:2	802
for she is not my *w*, neither am I	Hos 2:2	802
Syria, and Israel served for a *w*	Hos 12:12	802
and for a *w* he kept sheep	Hos 12:12	802
Thy *w* shall be an harlot in the	Amos 7:17	802
the *w* of thy youth, against whom	Mal 2:14	802
and the *w* of thy covenant	Mal 2:14	802
against the *w* of his youth	Mal 2:15	802
her that had been the *w* of Urias	Mt 1:6	
not to take unto thee Mary thy *w*	Mt 1:20	*1135*
him, and took unto him his *w*	Mt 1:24	*1135*
Whosoever shall put away his *w*	Mt 5:31	*1135*
whosoever shall put away his *w*	Mt 5:32	*1135*
sake, his brother Philip's *w*	Mt 14:3	*1135*
him to be sold, and his *w*, and	Mt 18:25	*1135*
to put away his *w* for every cause	Mt 19:3	*1135*
mother, and shall cleave to his *w*	Mt 19:5	*1135*
Whosoever shall put away his *w*	Mt 19:9	*1135*
case of the man be so with his *w*	Mt 19:10	*1135*
or father, or mother, or *w*	Mt 19:29	*1135*
his brother shall marry his *w*	Mt 22:24	*1135*
first, when he had married a *w*	Mt 22:25	
left his *w* unto his brother	Mt 22:25	*1135*
whose *w* shall she be of the seven	Mt 22:28	*1135*
his *w* sent unto him, saying, Have	Mt 27:19	*1135*
sake, his brother Philip's *w*	Mk 6:17	*1135*
for thee to have thy brother's *w*	Mk 6:18	*1135*
for a man to put away his *w*	Mk 10:2	*1135*
and mother, and cleave to his *w*	Mk 10:7	*1135*
Whosoever shall put away his *w*	Mk 10:11	*1135*
or father, or mother, or *w*	Mk 10:29	*1135*
leave his *w* behind him, and leave	Mk 12:19	*1135*
his brother should take his *w*	Mk 12:19	*1135*
and the first took a *w*, and dying	Mk 12:20	*1135*
whose *w* shall she be of them	Mk 12:23	*1135*
for the seven had her to *w*	Mk 12:23	*1135*
his *w* was of the daughters of	Lk 1:5	*1135*
thy *w* Elisabeth shall bear thee a	Lk 1:13	*1135*
my *w* well stricken in years	Lk 1:18	*1135*
days his *w* Elisabeth conceived	Lk 1:24	*1135*
be taxed with Mary his espoused *w*	Lk 2:5	*1135*
Herodias his brother Philip's *w*	Lk 3:19	*1135*
Joanna the *w* of Chuza Herod's	Lk 8:3	*1135*
another said, I have married a *w*	Lk 14:20	*1135*
not his father, and mother, and *w*	Lk 14:26	*1135*
Whosoever putteth away his *w*	Lk 16:18	*1135*
Remember Lot's *w*	Lk 17:32	*1135*
or parents, or brethren, or *w*	Lk 18:29	*1135*
any man's brother die, having a *w*	Lk 20:28	*1135*
his brother should take his *w*	Lk 20:28	*1135*
and the first took a *w*, and died	Lk 20:29	*1135*
And the second took her to *w*	Lk 20:30	*1135*

whose *w* of them is she	Lk 20:33	*1135*
for seven had her to *w*	Lk 20:33	*1135*
Mary the *w* of Cleophas, and Mary	Jn 19:25	
Ananias, with Sapphira his *w*	Acts 5:1	*1135*
his *w* also being privy to it, and	Acts 5:2	*1135*
of three hours after, when his *w*	Acts 5:7	*1135*
from Italy, with his *w* Priscilla	Acts 18:2	*1135*
Felix came with his *w* Drusilla	Acts 24:24	*1135*
one should have his father's *w*	1Cor 5:1	*1135*
let every man have his own *w*	1Cor 7:2	*1135*
render unto the *w* due benevolence	1Cor 7:3	*1135*
also the *w* unto the husband	1Cor 7:3	*1135*
The *w* hath not power of her own	1Cor 7:4	*1135*
power of his own body, but the *w*	1Cor 7:4	*1135*
Let not the *w* depart from her	1Cor 7:10	*1135*
not the husband put away his *w*	1Cor 7:11	*1135*
hath a *w* that believeth not	1Cor 7:12	*1135*
husband is sanctified by the *w*	1Cor 7:14	*1135*
the unbelieving *w* is sanctified	1Cor 7:14	*1135*
For what knowest thou, O *w*	1Cor 7:16	*1135*
whether thou shalt save thy *w*	1Cor 7:16	*1135*
Art thou bound unto a *w*	1Cor 7:27	*1135*
Art thou loosed from a *w*	1Cor 7:27	*1135*
seek not a *w*	1Cor 7:27	*1135*
world, how he may please his *w*	1Cor 7:33	*1135*
is difference also between a *w*	1Cor 7:34	*1135*
The *w* is bound by the law as long	1Cor 7:39	*1135*
power to lead about a sister, a *w*	1Cor 9:5	*1135*
the husband is the head of the *w*	Eph 5:23	*1135*
that loveth his *w* loveth himself	Eph 5:28	*1135*
and shall be joined unto his *w*	Eph 5:31	*1135*
so love his *w* even as himself	Eph 5:33	*1135*
the *w* see that she reverence her	Eph 5:33	*1135*
blameless, the husband of one *w*	1Ti 3:2	*1135*
deacons be the husbands of one *w*	1Ti 3:12	*1135*
old, having been the *w* of one man	1Ti 5:9	*1135*
blameless, the husband of one *w*	Titus 1:6	*1135*
giving honour unto the *w*	1Pet 3:7	*1134*
his *w* hath made herself ready	Rev 19:7	*1135*
shew thee the bride, the Lamb's *w*	Rev 21:9	*1135*

WIFE'S {11}

And Adam called his *w* name Eve	Gen 3:20	802
they will slay me for my *w* sake	Gen 20:11	802
his *w* name was Mehetabel, the	Gen 36:39	802
of thy father's *w* daughter	Lev 18:11	802
his *w* sons grew up, and they	Judg 11:2	802
his *w* name was Mehetabel, the	1Chr 1:50	802
whose *w* name was Maachah	1Chr 8:29	802
Jehiel, whose *w* name was Maachah	1Chr 9:35	802
he saw his *w* mother laid, and sick	Mt 8:14	*3994*
But Simon's *w* mother lay sick of	Mk 1:30	*3994*
Simon's *w* mother was taken with a	Lk 4:38	*3994*

WILD {44}

And he will be a *w* man	Gen 16:12	6501
will also send *w* beasts among you	Lev 26:22	7704
the *w* goat, and the pygarg	Deut 14:5	689
the pygarg, and the *w* ox	Deut 14:5	8377
to the *w* beasts of the earth	1Sa 17:46	2416
men upon the rocks of the *w* goats	1Sa 24:2	3277
was as light of foot as a *w* roe	2Sa 2:18	7704
gather herbs, and found a *w* vine	2Kin 4:39	7704
gathered thereof *w* gourds his lap	2Kin 4:39	7704
there passed by a *w* beast that	2Kin 14:9	7704
there passed by a *w* beast that	2Chr 25:18	7704
Doth the *w* ass bray when he hath	Job 6:5	6501
man be born like a *w* ass's colt	Job 11:12	6501
as *w* asses in the desert, go they	Job 24:5	6501
w goats of the rock bring forth	Job 39:1	3277
Who hath sent out the *w* ass free	Job 39:5	6501
loosed the bands of the *w* ass	Job 39:5	6171
or that the *w* beast may break	Job 39:15	7704
the *w* beasts of the field are	Ps 50:11	2123
the *w* beast of the field doth	Ps 80:13	2123
the *w* asses quench their thirst	Ps 104:11	6501
are a refuge for the *w* goats	Ps 104:18	3277
and it brought forth *w* grapes	Is 5:2	891
grapes, brought it forth *w* grapes	Is 5:4	891
But *w* beasts of the desert shall	Is 13:21	6728
the *w* beasts of the islands shall	Is 13:22	338
dens for ever, a joy of *w* asses	Is 32:14	6501
The *w* beasts of the desert shall	Is 34:14	6728
with the *w* beasts of the island	Is 34:14	338
the streets, as a *w* bull in a net	Is 51:20	8377
A *w* ass used to the wilderness,	Jer 2:24	6501
the *w* asses did stand in the high	Jer 14:6	6501
Therefore the *w* beasts of the	Jer 50:39	6728
the *w* beasts of the islands shall	Jer 50:39	338
his dwelling was with the *w* asses	Dan 5:21	6167
Assyria, a *w* ass alone by himself	Hos 8:9	6501
the *w* beast shall tear them	Hos 13:8	7704
his meat was locusts and *w* honey	Mt 3:4	*66*
and he did eat locusts and *w* honey	Mk 1:6	*66*
and was with the *w* beasts	Mk 1:13	*2342*
w beasts, and creeping things, and	Acts 10:12	*2342*
w beasts, and creeping things, and	Acts 11:6	*2342*
being a *w* olive tree, wert	Rom 11:17	*65*
olive tree which is *w* by nature	Rom 11:24	*65*

WILDERNESS {305}

unto El-paran, which is by the *w*	Gen 14:6	4057
by a fountain of water in the *w*	Gen 16:7	4057
wandered in the *w* of Beer-sheba	Gen 21:14	4057
and he grew, and dwelt in the *w*	Gen 21:20	4057
And he dwelt in the *w* of Paran	Gen 21:21	4057
that found the mules in the *w*	Gen 36:24	4057
into this pit that is in the *w*	Gen 37:22	4057
three days' journey into the *w*	Ex 3:18	4057
Go into the *w* to meet Moses	Ex 4:27	4057
may hold a feast unto me in the *w*	Ex 5:1	4057
that they may serve me in the *w*	Ex 7:16	4057
go three days' journey into the *w*	Ex 8:27	4057
to the LORD your God in the *w*	Ex 8:28	4057
the way of the *w* of the Red sea	Ex 13:18	4057
in Etham, in the edge of the *w*	Ex 13:20	4057
the land, the *w* hath shut them in	Ex 14:3	4057
taken us away to die in the *w*	Ex 14:11	4057
than that we should die in the *w*	Ex 14:12	4057
they went out into the *w* of Shur	Ex 15:22	4057
and they went three days in the *w*	Ex 15:22	4057
of Israel came unto the *w* of Sin	Ex 16:1	4057
against Moses and Aaron in the *w*	Ex 16:2	4057
have brought us forth into this *w*	Ex 16:3	4057
that they looked toward the *w*	Ex 16:10	4057
upon the face of the *w* there lay	Ex 16:14	4057
wherewith I have fed you in the *w*	Ex 16:32	4057
journeyed from the *w* of Sin	Ex 17:1	4057
and his wife unto Moses into the *w*	Ex 18:5	4057
day came they into the *w* of Sinai	Ex 19:1	4057
of Sinai, and had pitched in the *w*	Ex 19:2	4057
unto the LORD, in the *w* of Sinai	Lev 7:38	4057
him go for a scapegoat into the *w*	Lev 16:10	4057
the hand of a fit man into the *w*	Lev 16:21	4057
he shall let go the goat in the *w*	Lev 16:22	4057
unto Moses in the *w* of Sinai	Num 1:1	4057
numbered them in the *w* of Sinai	Num 1:19	4057
in the *w* of Sinai, and they had no	Num 3:4	4057
unto Moses in the *w* of Sinai	Num 3:14	4057
unto Moses in the *w* of Sinai	Num 9:1	4057
month at even in the *w* of Sinai	Num 9:5	4057
journeys out of the *w* of Sinai	Num 10:12	4057
cloud rested in the *w* of Paran	Num 10:12	4057
how we are to encamp in the *w*	Num 10:31	4057
and pitched in the *w* of Paran	Num 12:16	4057
sent them from the *w* of Paran	Num 13:3	4057
land from the *w* of Zin unto Rehob	Num 13:21	4057
of Israel, unto the *w* of Paran	Num 13:26	4057
would God we had died in this *w*	Num 14:2	4057
he hath slain them in the *w*	Num 14:16	4057
which I did in Egypt and in the *w*	Num 14:22	4057
get you into the *w* by the way of	Num 14:25	4057
carcases shall fall in this *w*	Num 14:29	4057
they shall fall in this *w*	Num 14:32	4057
shall wander in the *w* forty years	Num 14:33	4057
your carcases be wasted in the *w*	Num 14:33	4057
in this *w* they shall be consumed,	Num 14:35	4057
children of Israel were in the *w*	Num 15:32	4057
and honey, to kill us in the *w*	Num 16:13	4057
of the LORD into this *w*, that we	Num 20:4	4057
up out of Egypt to die in the *w*	Num 21:5	4057
in the *w* which is before Moab,	Num 21:11	4057
which is in the *w* that cometh out	Num 21:13	4057
from the *w* they went to Mattanah	Num 21:18	4057
out against Israel into the *w*	Num 21:23	4057
but he set his face toward the *w*	Num 24:1	4057
of Israel in the *w* of Sinai	Num 26:64	4057
They shall surely die in the *w*	Num 26:65	4057
Our father died in the *w*, and he	Num 27:3	4057
Meribah in Kadesh in the *w* of Zin	Num 27:14	4057
them wander in the *w* forty years	Num 32:13	4057
yet again leave them in the *w*	Num 32:15	4057
which is in the edge of the *w*	Num 33:6	4057
the midst of the sea into the *w*	Num 33:8	4057
days' journey in the *w* of Etham	Num 33:8	4057
sea, and encamped in the *w* of Sin	Num 33:11	4057
their journey out of the *w* of Sin	Num 33:12	4057
and pitched in the *w* of Sinai	Num 33:15	4057
and pitched in the *w* of Zin	Num 33:36	4057
w of Zin along by the coast of	Num 34:3	4057
on this side Jordan in the *w*	Deut 1:1	4057
all that great and terrible *w*	Deut 1:19	4057
And in the *w*, where thou hast seen	Deut 1:31	4057
the *w* by the way of the Red sea	Deut 1:40	4057
the *w* by the way of the Red sea	Deut 2:1	4057
thy walking through this great *w*	Deut 2:7	4057
by the way of the *w* of Moab	Deut 2:8	4057
I sent messengers out of the *w* of	Deut 2:26	4057
Namely, Bezer in the *w*, in the	Deut 4:43	4057
thee these forty years in the *w*	Deut 8:2	4057
through that great and terrible *w*	Deut 8:15	4057
Who fed thee in the *w* with manna	Deut 8:16	4057
LORD thy God to wrath in the *w*	Deut 9:7	4057
them out to slay them in the *w*	Deut 9:28	4057
And what he did unto you in the *w*	Deut 11:5	4057
from the *w* and Lebanon, from the	Deut 11:24	4057
have led you forty years in the *w*	Deut 29:5	4057
land, and in the waste howling *w*	Deut 32:10	3452
Meribah-kadesh, in the *w* of Zin	Deut 32:51	4057
From the *w* and this Lebanon even	Josh 1:4	4057
of war, died in the *w* by the way	Josh 5:4	4057
people that were born in the *w* by	Josh 5:5	4057
walked forty years in the *w*	Josh 5:6	4057
them, and fled by the way of the *w*	Josh 8:15	4057
the people that fled to the *w*	Josh 8:20	4057
in the *w* wherein they chased them	Josh 8:24	4057
and in the springs, and in the *w*	Josh 12:8	4057
of Israel wandered in the *w*	Josh 14:10	4057
the *w* of Zin southward was the	Josh 15:1	4057
In the *w*, Beth-arabah, Middin, and	Josh 15:61	4057
to the *w* that goeth up from	Josh 16:1	4057
were at the *w* of Beth-aven	Josh 18:12	4057
they assigned Bezer in the *w* upon	Josh 20:8	4057
ye dwelt in the *w* a long season	Josh 24:7	4057
of Judah into the *w* of Judah	Judg 1:16	4057
flesh with the thorns of the *w*	Judg 8:7	4057
of the city, and thorns of the *w*	Judg 8:16	4057
through the *w* unto the Red sea	Judg 11:16	4057
they went along through the *w*	Judg 11:18	4057
from the *w* even unto Jordan	Judg 11:22	4057
of Israel unto the way of the *w*	Judg 20:42	4057
fled toward the *w* unto the rock	Judg 20:45	4057
fled to the *w* unto the rock	Judg 20:47	4057
with all the plagues in the *w*	1Sa 4:8	4057
the valley of Zeboim toward the *w*	1Sa 13:18	4057
left those few sheep in the *w*	1Sa 17:28	4057
abode in the *w* in strong holds	1Sa 23:14	4057
in a mountain in the *w* of Ziph	1Sa 23:14	4057
David was in the *w* of Ziph in a	1Sa 23:15	4057
and his men were in the *w* of Maon	1Sa 23:24	4057
a rock, and abode in the *w* of Maon	1Sa 23:25	4057
after David in the *w* of Maon	1Sa 23:25	4057
David is in the *w* of En-gedi	1Sa 24:1	4057
and went down to the *w* of Paran	1Sa 25:1	4057
David heard in the *w* that Nabal	1Sa 25:4	4057
out of the *w* to salute our master	1Sa 25:14	4057
that this fellow hath in the *w*	1Sa 25:21	4057
and went down to the *w* of Ziph	1Sa 26:2	4057
to seek David in the *w* of Ziph	1Sa 26:2	4057
But David abode in the *w*, and he	1Sa 26:3	4057
Saul came after him into the *w*	1Sa 26:3	4057
by the way of the *w* of Gibeon	2Sa 2:24	4057
over, toward the way of the *w*	2Sa 15:23	4057
will tarry in the plain of the *w*	2Sa 15:28	4057
as be faint in the *w* may drink	2Sa 16:2	4057
this night in the plains of the *w*	2Sa 17:16	4057
and weary, and thirsty, in the *w*	2Sa 17:29	4057
buried in his own house in the *w*	1Kin 2:34	4057
And Baalath, and Tadmor in the *w*	1Kin 9:18	4057
went a day's journey into the *w*	1Kin 19:4	4057
on thy way to the *w* of Damascus	1Kin 19:15	4057
The way through the *w* of Edom	2Kin 3:8	4057
of the *w* from the river Euphrates	1Chr 5:9	4057
Bezer in the *w* with her suburbs,	1Chr 6:78	4057
the hold to the *w* men of might	1Chr 12:8	4057
LORD, which Moses made in the *w*	1Chr 21:29	4057
of the LORD had made in the *w*	2Chr 1:3	4057
And he built Tadmor in the *w*	2Chr 8:4	4057
the brook, before the *w* of Jeruel	2Chr 20:16	4057
and went forth into the *w* of Tekoa	2Chr 20:20	4057
toward the watch tower in the *w*	2Chr 20:24	4057
of God laid upon Israel in the *w*	2Chr 24:9	4057
forsookest them not in the *w*	Neh 9:19	4057
didst thou sustain them in the *w*	Neh 9:21	4057
came a great wind from the *w*	Job 1:19	4057
in a *w* where there is no way	Job 12:24	8414
the *w* yieldeth food for them and	Job 24:5	6160
fleeing into the *w* in former time	Job 30:3	6723
on the *w*, wherein there is no man	Job 38:26	4057
Whose house I have made the *w*	Job 39:6	6160
voice of the LORD shaketh the *w*	Ps 29:8	4057
the LORD shaketh the *w* of Kadesh	Ps 29:8	4057
far off, and remain in the *w*	Ps 55:7	4057
when he was in the *w* of Judah	Ps 63:*t*	4057
drop upon the pastures of the *w*	Ps 65:12	4057
thou didst march through the *w*	Ps 68:7	3452
in the *w* shall bow before him	Ps 72:9	6728
to the people inhabiting the *w*	Ps 74:14	6728
He clave the rocks in the *w*	Ps 78:15	4057
provoking the most High in the *w*	Ps 78:17	6723
Can God furnish a table in the *w*	Ps 78:19	4057
oft did they provoke him in the *w*	Ps 78:40	4057
guided them in the *w* like a flock	Ps 78:52	4057
in the day of temptation in the *w*	Ps 95:8	4057
I am like a pelican of the *w*	Ps 102:6	4057
the depths, as through the *w*	Ps 106:9	4057
But lusted exceedingly in the *w*	Ps 106:14	4057
them, to overthrow them in the *w*	Ps 106:26	4057
in the *w* in a solitary way	Ps 107:4	4057
He turneth rivers into a *w*	Ps 107:33	4057
He turneth the *w* into a standing	Ps 107:35	4057
causeth them to wander in the *w*	Ps 107:40	8414
led his people through the *w*	Ps 136:16	4057
It is better to dwell in the *w*	Prov 21:19	4057
of the *w* like pillars of smoke	Song 3:6	4057
is this that cometh up from the *w*	Song 8:5	4057
That made the world as a *w*	Is 14:17	4057
of the land from Sela to the *w*	Is 16:1	4057
they wandered through the *w*	Is 16:8	4057
it for them that dwell in the *w*	Is 23:13	6728
forsaken, and left like a *w*	Is 27:10	4057
the *w* be a fruitful field, and the	Is 32:15	4057
judgment shall dwell in the *w*	Is 32:16	4057
Sharon is like a *w*	Is 33:9	6160
The *w* and the solitary place shall	Is 35:1	4057
for in the *w* shall waters break	Is 35:6	4057
voice of him that crieth in the *w*	Is 40:3	4057
I will make the *w* a pool of water	Is 41:18	4057
I will plant in the *w* the cedar	Is 41:19	4057
Let the *w* and the cities thereof	Is 42:11	4057
I will even make a way in the *w*	Is 43:19	4057
because I give waters in the *w*	Is 43:20	4057
up the sea, I make the rivers a *w*	Is 50:2	4057
and he will make her *w* like Eden	Is 51:3	4057
the deep, as an horse in the *w*	Is 63:13	4057
are a *w*, Zion is a *w*	Is 64:10	4057
thou wentest after me in the *w*	Jer 2:2	4057
Egypt, that led us through the *w*	Jer 2:6	4057
A wild ass used to the *w*, that	Jer 2:24	4057
Have I been a *w* unto Israel	Jer 2:31	4057
for them, as the Arabian in the *w*	Jer 3:2	4057
the *w* toward the daughter of my	Jer 4:11	4057
lo, the fruitful place was a *w*	Jer 4:26	4057
Oh that I had in the *w* a lodging	Jer 9:2	4057
of the *w* a lamentation, because	Jer 9:10	4057
and is burned up like a *w*, that	Jer 9:12	4057

corners, that dwell in the *w* ... Jer 9:26 4057
my pleasant portion a desolate *w* ... Jer 12:10 4057
all high places through the *w* ... Jer 12:12 4057
passeth away by the wind of the *w* ... Jer 13:24 4057
the parched places in the *w* ... Jer 17:6 4057
yet surely I will make thee a *w* ... Jer 22:6 4057
places of the *w* are dried up ... Jer 23:10 4057
of the sword found grace in the *w* ... Jer 31:2 4057
and be like the heath in the *w* ... Jer 48:6 4057
of the nations shall be a *w* ... Jer 50:12 4057
a desolation, a dry land, and a *w* ... Jer 51:43 6160
like the ostriches in the *w* ... Lam 4:3 4057
they laid wait for us in the *w* ... Lam 4:19 4057
because of the sword of the *w* ... Lam 5:9 4057
than the *w* toward Diblath ... Eze 6:14 4057
And now she is planted in the *w* ... Eze 19:13 4057
Egypt, and brought them into the *w* ... Eze 20:10 4057
rebelled against me in the *w* ... Eze 20:13 4057
out my fury upon them in the *w* ... Eze 20:13 4057
up my hand unto them in the *w* ... Eze 20:15 4057
I make an end of them in the *w* ... Eze 20:17 4057
said unto their children in the *w* ... Eze 20:18 4057
my anger against them in the *w* ... Eze 20:21 4057
mine hand unto them also in the *w* ... Eze 20:23 4057
you into the *w* of the people ... Eze 20:35 4057
in the *w* of the land of Egypt ... Eze 20:36 4057
were brought Sabeans from the *w* ... Eze 23:42 4057
will leave thee thrown into the *w* ... Eze 29:5 4057
they shall dwell safely in the *w* ... Eze 34:25 4057
she was born, and make her as a *w* ... Hos 2:3 4057
her, and bring her into the *w* ... Hos 2:14 4057
found Israel like grapes in the *w* ... Hos 9:10 4057
I did know thee in the *w*, in the ... Hos 13:5 4057
the LORD shall come up from the *w* ... Hos 13:15 4057
devoured the pastures of the *w* ... Joel 1:19 4057
devoured the pastures of the *w* ... Joel 1:20 4057
them, and behind them a desolate *w* ... Joel 2:3 4057
the pastures of the *w* do spring ... Joel 2:22 4057
and Edom shall be a desolate *w* ... Joel 3:19 4057
led you forty years through the *w* ... Amos 2:10 4057
and offerings in the *w* forty years ... Amos 5:25 4057
of Hemath unto the river of the *w* ... Amos 6:14 6166
a desolation, and dry like a *w* ... Zeph 2:13 4057
waste for the dragons of the *w* ... Mal 1:3 4057
preaching in the *w* of Judaea ... Mt 3:1 *2048*
The voice of one crying in the *w* ... Mt 3:3 *2048*
the *w* to be tempted of the devil ... Mt 4:1 *2048*
went ye out into the *w* to see ... Mt 11:7 *2048*
we have so much bread in the *w* ... Mt 15:33 *2047*
The voice of one crying in the *w* ... Mk 1:3 *2048*
John did baptize in the *w* ... Mk 1:4 *2048*
the spirit driveth him into the *w* ... Mk 1:12 *2048*
he was there in the *w* forty days ... Mk 1:13 *2048*
men with bread here in the *w* ... Mk 8:4 *2047*
the son of Zacharias in the *w* ... Lk 3:2 *2048*
The voice of one crying in the *w* ... Lk 3:4 *2048*
was led by the Spirit into the *w* ... Lk 4:1 *2048*
And he withdrew himself into the *w* ... Lk 5:16 *2048*
went ye out into the *w* for to see ... Lk 7:24 *2048*
driven of the devil into the *w* ... Lk 8:29 *2048*
leave the ninety and nine in the *w* ... Lk 15:4 *2048*
the voice of one crying in the *w* ... Jn 1:23 *2048*
lifted up the serpent in the *w* ... Jn 3:14 *2048*
fathers did eat manna in the *w* ... Jn 6:49 *2048*
unto a country near to the *w* ... Jn 11:54 *2048*
there appeared to him in the *w* of ... Acts 7:30 *2048*
Red sea, and in the *w* forty years ... Acts 7:36 *2048*
w with the angel which spake to ... Acts 7:38 *2048*
the space of forty years in the *w* ... Acts 7:42 *2048*
tabernacle of witness in the *w* ... Acts 7:44 *2048*
he their manners in the *w* ... Acts 13:18 *2048*
leddest out into the *w* four ... Acts 21:38 *2048*
for they were overthrown in the *w* ... 1Cor 10:5 *2048*
in the city, in perils in the *w* ... 2Cor 11:26 *2047*
in the day of temptation in the *w* ... Heb 3:8 *2048*
whose carcases fell in the *w* ... Heb 3:17 *2048*
And the woman fled into the *w* ... Rev 12:6 *2048*
that she might fly into the *w* ... Rev 12:14 *2048*
me away in the spirit into the *w* ... Rev 17:3 *2048*

WILES {2}

For they vex you with their *w* ... Num 25:18 5231
stand against the *w* of the devil ... Eph 6:11 *3180*

WILFULLY {1}

For if we sin *w* after that we ... Heb 10:26 *1596*

WILILY {1}

They did work *w*, and went and made ... Josh 9:4 6195

WILL {3840}

I *w* make him an help meet for him ... Gen 2:18
I *w* put enmity between thee and ... Gen 3:15
I *w* greatly multiply thy sorrow ... Gen 3:16
I *w* destroy man whom I have ... Gen 6:7
I *w* destroy them with the earth ... Gen 6:13
But with thee *w* I establish my ... Gen 6:18
I *w* cause it to rain upon the ... Gen 7:4
substance that I have made *w* I ... Gen 7:4
I *w* not again curse the ground ... Gen 8:21
neither *w* I again smite any more ... Gen 8:21
blood of your lives *w* I require ... Gen 9:5
of every beast *w* I require it ... Gen 9:5
w I require the life of man ... Gen 9:5
I *w* establish my covenant with ... Gen 9:11
I *w* remember my covenant, which ... Gen 9:15
I *w* look upon it, that I may ... Gen 9:16
now nothing *w* be restrained from ... Gen 11:6
unto a land that I *w* shew thee ... Gen 12:1
I *w* make of thee a great nation, ... Gen 12:2
I *w* bless thee, and make thy name ... Gen 12:2
I *w* bless them that bless thee, ... Gen 12:3
Unto thy seed *w* I give this land ... Gen 12:7
they *w* kill me, but they *w* ... Gen 12:12
hand, then I *w* go to the right ... Gen 13:9
hand, then I *w* go to the left ... Gen 13:9
to thee *w* I give it, and to thy ... Gen 13:15
I *w* make thy seed as the dust of ... Gen 13:16
for I *w* give it unto thee ... Gen 13:17
That I *w* not take from a thread ... Gen 14:23
that I *w* not take any thing that ... Gen 14:23
whom they shall serve, *w* I judge ... Gen 15:14
I *w* multiply thy seed exceedingly ... Gen 16:10
And he *w* be a wild man ... Gen 16:12
his hand *w* be against every man, ... Gen 16:12
I *w* make my covenant between me ... Gen 17:2
w multiply thee exceedingly ... Gen 17:2
I *w* make thee exceeding fruitful, ... Gen 17:6
I *w* make nations of thee, and ... Gen 17:6
I *w* establish my covenant between ... Gen 17:7
I *w* give unto thee, and to thy ... Gen 17:8
and I *w* be their God ... Gen 17:8
I *w* bless her, and give thee a son ... Gen 17:16
I *w* bless her, and she shall be a ... Gen 17:16
I *w* establish my covenant with ... Gen 17:19
w make him fruitful ... Gen 17:20
w multiply him exceedingly ... Gen 17:20
I *w* make him a great nation ... Gen 17:20
But my covenant *w* I establish ... Gen 17:21
I *w* fetch a morsel of bread, and ... Gen 18:5
I *w* certainly return unto thee ... Gen 18:10
appointed I *w* return unto thee ... Gen 18:14
that he *w* command his children and ... Gen 18:19
I *w* go down now, and see whether ... Gen 18:21
and if not, I *w* know ... Gen 18:21
then I *w* spare all the place for ... Gen 18:26
forty and five, I *w* not destroy it ... Gen 18:28
I *w* not do it for forty's sake ... Gen 18:29
the LORD be angry, and I *w* speak ... Gen 18:30
I *w* not do it, if I find thirty ... Gen 18:30
I *w* not destroy it for twenty's ... Gen 18:31
I *w* speak yet but this once ... Gen 18:32
I *w* not destroy it for ten's sake ... Gen 18:32
but we *w* abide in the street all ... Gen 19:2
sojourn, and he *w* needs be a judge ... Gen 19:9
now *w* we deal worse with thee, ... Gen 19:9
For we *w* destroy this place, ... Gen 19:13
for the LORD *w* destroy this city ... Gen 19:14
that I *w* not overthrow this city, ... Gen 19:21
we *w* lie with him, that we may ... Gen 19:32
they *w* slay me for my wife's sake ... Gen 20:11
all that hear *w* laugh with me ... Gen 21:6
the bondwoman *w* I make a nation ... Gen 21:13
for I *w* make him a great nation ... Gen 21:18
And Abraham said, I *w* swear ... Gen 21:24
mountains which I *w* tell thee of ... Gen 22:2
the lad *w* go yonder and worship, ... Gen 22:5
God *w* provide himself a lamb for ... Gen 22:8
That in blessing I *w* bless thee ... Gen 22:17
in multiplying I *w* multiply thy ... Gen 22:17
I *w* give thee money for the field ... Gen 23:13
of me, and I *w* bury my dead there ... Gen 23:13
I *w* make thee swear by the LORD, ... Gen 24:3
Peradventure the woman *w* not be ... Gen 24:5
Unto thy seed *w* I give this land ... Gen 24:7
if the woman *w* not be willing to ... Gen 24:8
I *w* give thy camels drink also ... Gen 24:14
I *w* draw water for thy camels ... Gen 24:19
I *w* not eat, until I have told ... Gen 24:33
the woman *w* not follow me ... Gen 24:39
w send his angel with thee, and ... Gen 24:40
I *w* also draw for thy camels ... Gen 24:44
I *w* give thy camels drink also ... Gen 24:46
now if ye *w* deal kindly and truly ... Gen 24:49
We *w* call the damsel, and enquire ... Gen 24:57
And she said, I *w* go ... Gen 24:58
I *w* be with thee ... Gen 26:3
and *w* bless thee ... Gen 26:3
I *w* give all these countries, and ... Gen 26:3
I *w* perform the oath which I ... Gen 26:3
I *w* make thy seed to multiply as ... Gen 26:4
w give unto thy seed all these ... Gen 26:4
w bless thee, and multiply thy ... Gen 26:24
I *w* make them savoury meat for ... Gen 27:9
My father peradventure *w* feel me ... Gen 27:12
I *w* eat of my son's venison, that ... Gen 27:25
then *w* I slay my brother Jacob ... Gen 27:41
then I *w* send, and fetch thee from ... Gen 27:45
to thee *w* I give it, and to thy ... Gen 28:13
w keep thee in all places whither ... Gen 28:15
w bring thee again into this land ... Gen 28:15
for I *w* not leave thee, until I ... Gen 28:15
If God *w* be with me ... Gen 28:20
w keep me in this way that I go, ... Gen 28:20
w give me bread to eat, and ... Gen 28:20
all that thou shalt give me I *w* ... Gen 28:22
I *w* serve thee seven years for ... Gen 29:18
we *w* give thee this also for the ... Gen 29:27
therefore my husband *w* love me ... Gen 29:32
Now this time *w* my husband be ... Gen 29:34
she said, Now *w* I praise the LORD ... Gen 29:35
the daughters *w* call me blessed ... Gen 30:13
now *w* my husband dwell with me, ... Gen 30:20
me thy wages, and I *w* give it ... Gen 30:28
I *w* again feed and keep thy flock ... Gen 30:31
I *w* pass through all thy flock to ... Gen 30:32
and I *w* be with thee ... Gen 31:3
that I *w* not pass over this heap ... Gen 31:52
and I *w* deal well with thee ... Gen 32:9
for I fear him, lest he *w* come ... Gen 32:11
I *w* surely do thee good, and make ... Gen 32:12
I *w* appease him with the present ... Gen 32:20
afterward I *w* see his face ... Gen 32:20
peradventure he *w* accept of me ... Gen 32:20
I *w* not let thee go, except thou ... Gen 32:26
let us go, and I *w* go before thee ... Gen 33:12
them one day, all the flock *w* die ... Gen 33:13
I *w* lead on softly, according as ... Gen 33:14
ye shall say unto me I *w* give ... Gen 34:11
I *w* give according as ye shall ... Gen 34:12
But in this *w* we consent unto you ... Gen 34:15
If ye *w* be as we be, that every ... Gen 34:15
Then *w* we give our daughters unto ... Gen 34:16
we *w* take your daughters to us, ... Gen 34:16
we *w* dwell with you ... Gen 34:16
and we *w* become one people ... Gen 34:16
But if ye *w* not hearken unto us, ... Gen 34:17
then *w* we take our daughter, and ... Gen 34:17
our daughter, and we *w* be gone ... Gen 34:17
Only herein *w* the men consent ... Gen 34:22
them, and they *w* dwell with us ... Gen 34:23
I *w* make there an altar unto God, ... Gen 35:3
and Isaac, to thee I *w* give it ... Gen 35:12
seed after thee *w* I give the land ... Gen 35:12
come, and I *w* send thee unto them ... Gen 37:13
we *w* say, Some evil beast hath ... Gen 37:20
we shall see what *w* become of his ... Gen 37:20
For I *w* go down into the grave ... Gen 37:35
I *w* send thee a kid from the ... Gen 38:17
God *w* shortly bring it to pass ... Gen 41:32
only in the throne *w* I be greater ... Gen 41:40
so *w* I deliver you your brother, ... Gen 42:34
not, and ye *w* take Benjamin away ... Gen 42:36
I *w* bring him to thee again ... Gen 42:37
we *w* go down and buy thee food ... Gen 43:4
not send him, we *w* not go down ... Gen 43:5
lad with me, and we *w* arise and go ... Gen 43:8
I *w* be surety for him ... Gen 43:9
we also *w* be my lord's bondmen ... Gen 44:9
be with us, then *w* we go down ... Gen 44:26
lad is not with us, that he *w* die ... Gen 44:31
And there *w* I nourish thee ... Gen 45:11
I *w* give you the good of the land ... Gen 45:18
I *w* go and see him before I die ... Gen 45:28
for I *w* there make of thee a ... Gen 46:3
I *w* go down with thee into Egypt ... Gen 46:4
I *w* also surely bring thee up ... Gen 46:4
I *w* go up, and shew Pharaoh, and ... Gen 46:31
I *w* give you for your cattle, if ... Gen 47:16
We *w* not hide it from my lord, ... Gen 47:18
our land *w* be servants unto ... Gen 47:19
we *w* be Pharaoh's servants ... Gen 47:25
But I *w* lie with my fathers, and ... Gen 47:30
he said, I *w* do as thou hast said ... Gen 47:30
I *w* make thee fruitful, and ... Gen 48:4
I *w* make of thee a multitude of ... Gen 48:4
w give this land to thy seed ... Gen 48:4
thee, unto me, and I *w* bless them ... Gen 48:9
I *w* divide them in Jacob, and ... Gen 49:7
bury my father, and I *w* come again ... Gen 50:5
Joseph *w* peradventure hate us, and ... Gen 50:15
w certainly requite us all the ... Gen 50:15
I *w* nourish you, and your little ... Gen 50:21
God *w* surely visit you, and bring ... Gen 50:24
God *w* surely visit you, and ye ... Gen 50:25
me, and I *w* give thee thy wages ... Ex 2:9
I *w* now turn aside, and see this ... Ex 3:3
I *w* send thee unto Pharaoh, that ... Ex 3:10
Certainly I *w* be with thee ... Ex 3:12
I *w* bring you up out of the ... Ex 3:17
king of Egypt *w* not let you go ... Ex 3:19
I *w* stretch out my hand, and smite ... Ex 3:20
which I *w* do in the midst thereof ... Ex 3:20
and after that he *w* let you go ... Ex 3:20
I *w* give this people favour in ... Ex 3:21
they *w* not believe me, nor ... Ex 4:1
for they *w* say, The LORD hath not ... Ex 4:1
if they *w* not believe thee, ... Ex 4:8
that they *w* believe the voice of ... Ex 4:8
if they *w* not believe also these ... Ex 4:9
I *w* be with thy mouth, and teach ... Ex 4:12
he *w* be glad in his heart ... Ex 4:14
I *w* be with thy mouth, and with ... Ex 4:15
w teach you what ye shall do ... Ex 4:15
but I *w* harden his heart, that he ... Ex 4:21
I *w* slay thy son, even thy ... Ex 4:23
neither *w* I let Israel go ... Ex 5:2
Pharaoh, I *w* not give you straw ... Ex 5:10
thou see what I *w* do to Pharaoh ... Ex 6:1
I *w* bring you out from under the ... Ex 6:6
I *w* rid you out of their bondage, ... Ex 6:6
I *w* redeem you with a stretched ... Ex 6:6
I *w* take you to me for a people, ... Ex 6:7
and I *w* be to you a God ... Ex 6:7
I *w* bring you in unto the land, ... Ex 6:8
I *w* give it you for an heritage ... Ex 6:8
I *w* harden Pharaoh's heart, and ... Ex 7:3
I *w* smite with the rod that is in ... Ex 7:17
I *w* smite all thy borders with ... Ex 8:2
I *w* let the people go, that they ... Ex 8:8
I *w* send swarms of flies upon ... Ex 8:21
I *w* sever in that day the land of ... Ex 8:22
I *w* put a division between my ... Ex 8:23
eyes, and *w* they not stone us ... Ex 8:26
We *w* go three days' journey into ... Ex 8:27
I *w* let you go, that ye may ... Ex 8:28

I *w* intreat the LORD that the ... Ex 8:29
For I *w* at this time send all my ... Ex 9:14
For now I *w* stretch out my hand, ... Ex 9:15
time I *w* cause it to rain a very ... Ex 9:18
I *w* let you go, and ye shall stay ... Ex 9:28
I *w* spread abroad my hands unto ... Ex 9:29
I know that ye *w* not yet fear the ... Ex 9:30
to morrow *w* I bring the locusts ... Ex 10:4
We *w* go with our young and with ... Ex 10:9
flocks and with our herds *w* we go ... Ex 10:9
as I *w* let you go, and your little ... Ex 10:10
I *w* see thy face again no more ... Ex 10:29
Yet *w* I bring one plague more ... Ex 11:1
afterwards he *w* let you go hence ... Ex 11:1
About midnight *w* I go out into ... Ex 11:4
and after that I *w* go out ... Ex 11:8
For I *w* pass through the land of ... Ex 12:12
w smite all the firstborn in the ... Ex 12:12
of Egypt I *w* execute judgment ... Ex 12:12
I *w* pass over you, and the plague ... Ex 12:13
For the LORD *w* pass through to ... Ex 12:23
the LORD *w* pass over the door, and ... Ex 12:23
w not suffer the destroyer to ... Ex 12:23
land which the LORD *w* give you ... Ex 12:25
w keep the passover to the LORD, ... Ex 12:48
saying, God *w* surely visit you ... Ex 13:19
For Pharaoh *w* say of the children ... Ex 14:3
I *w* harden Pharaoh's heart, that ... Ex 14:4
I *w* be honoured upon Pharaoh, and ... Ex 14:4
which he *w* shew to you to day ... Ex 14:13
I *w* harden the hearts of the ... Ex 14:17
I *w* get me honour upon Pharaoh, ... Ex 14:17
I *w* sing unto the LORD, for he ... Ex 15:1
I *w* prepare him an habitation ... Ex 15:2
my father's God, and I *w* exalt him ... Ex 15:2
I *w* pursue, I *w* overtake, I ... Ex 15:9
overtake, I *w* divide the spoil ... Ex 15:9
I *w* draw my sword, my hand shall ... Ex 15:9
I *w* put none of these diseases ... Ex 15:26
I *w* rain bread from heaven for ... Ex 16:4
whether they *w* walk in my law, or ... Ex 16:4
bake that which ye *w* bake to day ... Ex 16:23
and seethe that ye *w* seethe ... Ex 16:23
I *w* stand before thee there upon ... Ex 17:6
to morrow I *w* stand on the top of ... Ex 17:9
for I *w* utterly put out the ... Ex 17:14
LORD *w* have war with Amalek from ... Ex 17:16
I *w* give thee counsel, and God ... Ex 18:19
if ye *w* obey my voice indeed, and ... Ex 19:5
that the LORD hath spoken we *w* do ... Ex 19:8
for the third day the LORD *w* come ... Ex 19:11
for the LORD *w* not hold him ... Ex 20:7
Speak thou with us, and we *w* hear ... Ex 20:19
record my name I *w* come unto thee ... Ex 20:24
come unto thee, and I *w* bless thee ... Ex 20:24
I *w* not go out free ... Ex 21:5
then I *w* appoint thee a place ... Ex 21:13
woman's husband *w* lay upon him ... Ex 21:22
I *w* surely hear their cry ... Ex 22:23
I *w* kill you with the sword ... Ex 22:24
he crieth unto me, that I *w* hear ... Ex 22:27
for I *w* not justify the wicked ... Ex 23:7
for he *w* not pardon your ... Ex 23:21
then I *w* be an enemy unto thine ... Ex 23:22
and I *w* cut them off ... Ex 23:23
I *w* take sickness away from the ... Ex 23:25
the number of thy days I *w* fulfil ... Ex 23:26
I *w* send my fear before thee, and ... Ex 23:27
w destroy all the people to whom ... Ex 23:27
I *w* make all thine enemies turn ... Ex 23:27
I *w* send hornets before thee, ... Ex 23:28
I *w* not drive them out from ... Ex 23:29
little I *w* drive them out from ... Ex 23:30
I *w* set thy bounds from the Red ... Ex 23:31
for I *w* deliver the inhabitants ... Ex 23:31
it *w* surely be a snare unto thee ... Ex 23:33
which the LORD hath said *w* we do ... Ex 24:3
that the LORD hath said *w* we do ... Ex 24:7
I *w* give thee tables of stone, and ... Ex 24:12
there I *w* meet with thee, and I ... Ex 25:22
I *w* commune with thee from above ... Ex 25:22
of all things which I *w* give thee ... Ex 25:22
where I *w* meet you, to speak ... Ex 29:42
there I *w* meet with the children ... Ex 29:43
I *w* sanctify the tabernacle of ... Ex 29:44
I *w* sanctify also both Aaron and ... Ex 29:44
I *w* dwell among the children of ... Ex 29:45
of Israel, and *w* be their God ... Ex 29:45
where I *w* meet with thee ... Ex 30:6
where I *w* meet with thee ... Ex 30:36
I *w* make of thee a great nation ... Ex 32:10
I *w* multiply your seed as the ... Ex 32:13
spoken of *w* I give unto your seed ... Ex 32:13
now I *w* go up unto the LORD ... Ex 32:30
him *w* I blot out of my book ... Ex 32:33
I *w* visit their sin upon them ... Ex 32:34
saying, Unto thy seed *w* I give it ... Ex 33:1
I *w* send an angel before thee ... Ex 33:2
I *w* drive out the Canaanite, the ... Ex 33:2
for I *w* not go up in the midst of ... Ex 33:3
I *w* come up into the midst of ... Ex 33:5
with thee, and I *w* give thee rest ... Ex 33:14
I *w* do this thing also that thou ... Ex 33:17
I *w* make all my goodness pass ... Ex 33:19
I *w* proclaim the name of the LORD ... Ex 33:19
w be gracious to whom ... Ex 33:19
gracious to whom I *w* be gracious ... Ex 33:19
w shew mercy on whom ... Ex 33:19
on whom I *w* shew mercy ... Ex 33:19
that I *w* put thee in a clift of ... Ex 33:22
w cover thee with my hand while I ... Ex 33:22
I *w* take away mine hand, and thou ... Ex 33:23
I *w* write upon these tables the ... Ex 34:1
that *w* by no means clear the ... Ex 34:7
all thy people I *w* do marvels ... Ex 34:10
thing that I *w* do with thee ... Ex 34:10
For I *w* cast out the nations ... Ex 34:24
w at the door of the tabernacle ... Lev 1:3 7522
when any *w* offer a meat offering ... Lev 2:1
to day the LORD *w* appear unto you ... Lev 9:4
I *w* be sanctified in them that ... Lev 10:3
all the people I *w* be glorified ... Lev 10:3
for I *w* appear in the cloud upon ... Lev 16:2
I *w* even set my face against that ... Lev 17:10
w cut him off from among his ... Lev 17:10
ye shall offer it at your own *w* ... Lev 19:5 7522
I *w* set my face against that man, ... Lev 20:3
w cut him off from among his ... Lev 20:3
Then I *w* set my face against that ... Lev 20:5
w cut him off, and all that go a ... Lev 20:5
I *w* even set my face against that ... Lev 20:6
w cut him off from among his ... Lev 20:6
I *w* give it unto you to possess ... Lev 20:24
that *w* offer his oblation for all ... Lev 22:18
which they *w* offer unto the LORD ... Lev 22:18
your own *w* a male without blemish ... Lev 22:19 7522
when ye *w* offer a sacrifice of ... Lev 22:29
the LORD, offer it at your own *w* ... Lev 22:29 7522
but I *w* be hallowed among the ... Lev 22:32
the same soul *w* I destroy from ... Lev 23:30
Then I *w* command my blessing upon ... Lev 25:21
Then I *w* give you rain in due ... Lev 26:4
I *w* give peace in the land, and ye ... Lev 26:6
I *w* rid evil beasts out of the ... Lev 26:6
For I *w* have respect unto you, and ... Lev 26:9
I *w* set my tabernacle among you ... Lev 26:11
I *w* walk among you ... Lev 26:12
w be your God, and ye shall be my ... Lev 26:12
But if ye *w* not hearken unto me, ... Lev 26:14
w not do all these commandments ... Lev 26:14
so that ye *w* not do all my ... Lev 26:15
I also *w* do this unto you ... Lev 26:16
I *w* even appoint over you terror, ... Lev 26:16
I *w* set my face against you, and ... Lev 26:17
if ye *w* not yet for all this ... Lev 26:18
then I *w* punish you seven times ... Lev 26:18
I *w* break the pride of your power ... Lev 26:19
I *w* make your heaven as iron, and ... Lev 26:19
unto me, and *w* not hearken unto me ... Lev 26:21 14
I *w* bring seven times more ... Lev 26:21
I *w* also send wild beasts among ... Lev 26:22
if ye *w* not be reformed by me by ... Lev 26:23
but *w* walk contrary unto me ... Lev 26:23
Then *w* I also walk contrary unto ... Lev 26:24
w punish you yet seven times for ... Lev 26:24
I *w* bring a sword upon you, that ... Lev 26:25
I *w* send the pestilence among you ... Lev 26:25
if ye *w* not for all this hearken ... Lev 26:27
Then I *w* walk contrary unto you ... Lev 26:28
w chastise you seven times for ... Lev 26:28
I *w* destroy your high places, and ... Lev 26:30
I *w* make your cities waste, and ... Lev 26:31
I *w* not smell the savour of your ... Lev 26:31
And I *w* bring the land into ... Lev 26:32
I *w* scatter you among the heathen ... Lev 26:33
w draw out a sword after you ... Lev 26:33
I *w* send a faintness into their ... Lev 26:36
Then *w* I remember my covenant ... Lev 26:42
with Abraham *w* I remember ... Lev 26:42
and I *w* remember the land ... Lev 26:42
I *w* not cast them away ... Lev 26:44
neither *w* I abhor them, to ... Lev 26:44
But I *w* for their sakes remember ... Lev 26:45
But if he *w* at all redeem it, ... Lev 27:13
sanctified it *w* redeem his house ... Lev 27:15
the field *w* in any wise redeem it ... Lev 27:19
if he *w* not redeem the field, or ... Lev 27:20
if a man *w* at all redeem ought of ... Lev 27:31
and I *w* bless them ... Num 6:27
I *w* hear what the LORD ... Num 9:8
the LORD *w* command concerning you ... Num 9:8
w keep the passover unto the LORD ... Num 9:14
the LORD said, I *w* give it you ... Num 10:29
with us, and we *w* do thee good ... Num 10:29
And he said unto him, I *w* not go ... Num 10:30
but I *w* depart to mine own land, ... Num 10:30
the same *w* we do unto thee ... Num 10:32
I *w* come down and talk with thee ... Num 11:17
I *w* take of the spirit which is ... Num 11:17
upon thee, and *w* put it upon them ... Num 11:17
the LORD *w* give you flesh ... Num 11:18
I *w* give them flesh, that they ... Num 11:21
I the LORD *w* make myself known ... Num 12:6
w speak unto him in a dream ... Num 12:6
With him *w* I speak mouth to mouth ... Num 12:8
then he *w* bring us into this land ... Num 14:8
How long *w* this people provoke me ... Num 14:11
how long *w* it be ere they believe ... Num 14:11
I *w* smite them with the ... Num 14:12
w make of thee a greater nation ... Num 14:12
they *w* tell it to the inhabitants ... Num 14:14
heard the fame of thee *w* speak ... Num 14:15
him *w* I bring into the land ... Num 14:24
in mine ears, so *w* I do to you ... Num 14:28
them *w* I bring in, and they shall ... Num 14:31
I *w* surely do it unto all this ... Num 14:35
w go up unto the place which the ... Num 14:40
the LORD *w* not be with you ... Num 14:43
w make an offering by fire unto ... Num 15:3
w offer an offering made by fire, ... Num 15:14
the LORD *w* shew who are his ... Num 16:5
w cause him to come near unto him ... Num 16:5
even him whom he hath chosen *w* he ... Num 16:5
which said, We *w* not come up ... Num 16:12
we *w* not come up ... Num 16:14
where I *w* meet with you ... Num 17:4
I *w* make to cease from me the ... Num 17:5
we *w* not pass through the fields, ... Num 20:17
neither *w* we drink of the water ... Num 20:17
we *w* go by the king's high way, ... Num 20:17
we *w* not turn to the right hand ... Num 20:17
unto him, We *w* go by the high way ... Num 20:19
of thy water, then I *w* pay for it ... Num 20:19
I *w* only, without doing any thing ... Num 20:19
then I *w* utterly destroy their ... Num 21:2
together, and I *w* give them water ... Num 21:16
we *w* not turn into the fields, or ... Num 21:22
we *w* not drink of the waters of ... Num 21:22
but we *w* go along by the king's ... Num 21:22
I *w* bring you word again, as the ... Num 22:8
For I *w* promote thee unto very ... Num 22:17
I *w* do whatsoever thou sayest ... Num 22:17
what the LORD *w* say unto me more ... Num 22:19
thee, I *w* get me back again ... Num 22:34
by thy burnt offering, and I *w* go ... Num 23:3
the LORD *w* come to meet me ... Num 23:3
he sheweth me I *w* tell thee ... Num 23:3
I *w* bring thee unto another place ... Num 23:27
peradventure it *w* please God that ... Num 23:27
the LORD saith, that *w* I speak ... Num 24:13
I *w* advertise thee what this ... Num 24:14
he *w* yet again leave them in the ... Num 32:15
We *w* build sheepfolds here for ... Num 32:16
But we ourselves *w* go ready armed ... Num 32:17
We *w* not return unto our houses, ... Num 32:18
For we *w* not inherit with them on ... Num 32:19
If ye *w* do this thing ... Num 32:20
if ye *w* go armed before the LORD ... Num 32:20
w go all of you armed over Jordan ... Num 32:21
But if ye *w* not do so, behold, ye ... Num 32:23
be sure your sin *w* find you out ... Num 32:23
Thy servants *w* do as my lord ... Num 32:25
But thy servants *w* pass over ... Num 32:27
the children of Reuben *w* pass ... Num 32:29
But if they *w* not pass over with ... Num 32:30
unto thy servants, so *w* we do ... Num 32:31
We *w* pass over armed before the ... Num 32:32
But if ye *w* not drive out the ... Num 33:55
I *w* make them rulers over you ... Deut 1:13
bring it unto me, and I *w* hear it ... Deut 1:17
We *w* send men before us, and they ... Deut 1:22
to him *w* I give the land that he ... Deut 1:36
thither, and unto them *w* I give it ... Deut 1:39
we *w* go up and fight, according to ... Deut 1:41
for I *w* not give you of their ... Deut 2:5
for I *w* not give thee of their ... Deut 2:9
for I *w* not give thee of the land ... Deut 2:19
This day *w* I begin to put the ... Deut 2:25
I *w* go along by the high way ... Deut 2:27
I *w* neither turn unto the right ... Deut 2:27
only I *w* pass through on my feet ... Deut 2:28
for I *w* deliver him, and all his ... Deut 3:2
I *w* make them hear my words, that ... Deut 4:10
he *w* not forsake thee ... Deut 4:31
for the LORD *w* not hold him ... Deut 5:11
for this great fire *w* consume us ... Deut 5:25
and we *w* hear it, and do it ... Deut 5:27
I *w* speak unto thee all the ... Deut 5:31
For they *w* turn away thy son from ... Deut 7:4
so *w* the anger of the LORD be ... Deut 7:4
he *w* not be slack to him that ... Deut 7:10
he *w* repay him to his face ... Deut 7:10
he *w* love thee, and bless thee, and ... Deut 7:13
he *w* also bless the fruit of thy ... Deut 7:13
the LORD *w* take away from thee ... Deut 7:15
w put none of the evil diseases ... Deut 7:15
but *w* lay them upon all them that ... Deut 7:15
for that *w* be a snare unto thee ... Deut 7:16
Moreover the LORD thy God *w* send ... Deut 7:20
the LORD thy God *w* put out those ... Deut 7:22
I *w* make of thee a nation ... Deut 9:14
I *w* write on the tables the words ... Deut 10:2
That I *w* give you the rain of ... Deut 11:14
I *w* send grass in thy fields for ... Deut 11:15
Then *w* the LORD drive out all ... Deut 11:23
if ye *w* not obey the commandments ... Deut 11:28
I *w* eat flesh, because thy soul ... Deut 12:20
even so *w* I do likewise ... Deut 12:30
I *w* not go away from thee ... Deut 15:16
the man that *w* do presumptuously, ... Deut 17:12
w not hearken unto the priest ... Deut 17:12
I *w* set a king over me, like as ... Deut 17:14
The LORD thy God *w* raise up unto ... Deut 18:15
I *w* raise them up a Prophet from ... Deut 18:18
w put my words in his mouth ... Deut 18:18
that whosoever *w* not hearken unto ... Deut 18:19
in my name, I *w* require it of him ... Deut 18:19
if it *w* make no peace with thee, ... Deut 20:12
but *w* make war against thee, then ... Deut 20:12
shall let her go whither she *w* ... Deut 21:14 5315
which *w* not obey the voice of his ... Deut 21:18
him, *w* not hearken unto them ... Deut 21:18
he *w* not obey our voice ... Deut 21:20
for the LORD thy God *w* surely ... Deut 23:21

he *w* not perform the duty of my ... Deut 25:7 14
that *w* not build up his brother's ... Deut 25:9
that the LORD thy God *w* set thee ... Deut 28:1
The LORD *w* smite thee with the ... Deut 28:27
So that he *w* not give to any of ... Deut 28:55
Then the LORD *w* make thy plagues ... Deut 28:59
Moreover he *w* bring upon thee all ... Deut 28:60
them *w* the LORD bring upon thee, ... Deut 28:61
so the LORD *w* rejoice over you to ... Deut 28:63
The LORD *w* not spare him, but ... Deut 29:20 14
LORD thy God *w* turn thy captivity ... Deut 30:3
w return and gather thee from all ... Deut 30:3
from thence *w* the LORD thy God ... Deut 30:4
from thence *w* he fetch thee ... Deut 30:4
the LORD thy God *w* bring thee ... Deut 30:5
he *w* do thee good, and multiply ... Deut 30:5
the LORD thy God *w* circumcise ... Deut 30:6
the LORD thy God *w* put all these ... Deut 30:7
the LORD thy God *w* make thee ... Deut 30:9
for the LORD *w* again rejoice over ... Deut 30:9
he *w* go over before thee, and he ... Deut 31:3
he *w* destroy these nations from ... Deut 31:3
he *w* not fail thee, nor forsake ... Deut 31:6
he *w* be with thee ... Deut 31:8
he *w* not fail thee, neither ... Deut 31:8
and this people *w* rise up, and go a ... Deut 31:16
w forsake me, and break my ... Deut 31:16
I *w* forsake them ... Deut 31:17
I *w* hide my face from them, and ... Deut 31:17
so that they *w* say in that day, ... Deut 31:17
I *w* surely hide my face in that ... Deut 31:18
then *w* they turn unto other gods, ... Deut 31:20
and I *w* be with thee ... Deut 31:23
ye *w* utterly corrupt yourselves ... Deut 31:29
evil *w* befall you in the latter ... Deut 31:29
because ye *w* do evil in the sight ... Deut 31:29
ear, O ye heavens, and I *w* speak ... Deut 32:1
Because I *w* publish the name of ... Deut 32:3
ask thy father, and he *w* shew thee ... Deut 32:7
thy elders, and they *w* tell thee ... Deut 32:7
I *w* hide my face from them ... Deut 32:20
I *w* see what their end shall be ... Deut 32:20
I *w* move them to jealousy with ... Deut 32:21
I *w* provoke them to anger with a ... Deut 32:21
I *w* heap mischiefs upon them ... Deut 32:23
I *w* spend mine arrows upon them ... Deut 32:23
I *w* also send the teeth of beasts ... Deut 32:24
I *w* render vengeance to mine ... Deut 32:41
w reward them that hate me ... Deut 32:41
I *w* make mine arrows drunk with ... Deut 32:42
for he *w* avenge the blood of his ... Deut 32:43
w render vengeance to his ... Deut 32:43
w be merciful unto his land, and ... Deut 32:43
for the good *w* of him that dwelt ... Deut 33:16 7522
I *w* give it unto thy seed ... Deut 34:4
with Moses, so I *w* be with thee ... Josh 1:5
I *w* not fail thee, nor forsake ... Josh 1:5
that thou commandest us we *w* do ... Josh 1:16
thou sendest us, we *w* go ... Josh 1:16
so *w* we hearken unto thee ... Josh 1:17
w not hearken unto thy words in ... Josh 1:18
that ye *w* also shew kindness unto ... Josh 2:12
that ye *w* save alive my father, ... Josh 2:13
that we *w* deal kindly and truly ... Josh 2:14
We *w* be blameless of this thine ... Josh 2:17
his head, and we *w* be guiltless ... Josh 2:19
then we *w* be quit of thine oath ... Josh 2:20
the LORD *w* do wonders among you ... Josh 3:5
This day *w* I begin to magnify ... Josh 3:7
with Moses, so I *w* be with thee ... Josh 3:7
that he *w* without fail drive out ... Josh 3:10
neither *w* I be with you any more, ... Josh 7:12
with me, *w* approach unto the city ... Josh 8:5
that we *w* flee before them, ... Josh 8:5
(For they *w* come out after us) ... Josh 8:6
for they *w* say, They flee before ... Josh 8:6
therefore we *w* flee before them ... Josh 8:6
for the LORD your God *w* deliver ... Josh 8:7
for I *w* give it into thine hand ... Josh 8:18
This we *w* do to them ... Josh 9:20
we *w* even let them live, lest ... Josh 9:20
w I deliver them up all slain ... Josh 11:6
them *w* I drive out from before ... Josh 13:6
if so be the LORD *w* be with me ... Josh 14:12
to him *w* I give Achsah my ... Josh 15:16
I *w* send them, and they shall rise ... Josh 18:4
and it *w* be, seeing ye rebel to ... Josh 22:18
that to morrow he *w* be wroth with ... Josh 22:18
that the LORD your God *w* no more ... Josh 23:13
you this day whom ye *w* serve ... Josh 24:15
and my house, we *w* serve the LORD ... Josh 24:15
therefore *w* we also serve the ... Josh 24:18
he *w* not forgive your ... Josh 24:19
strange gods, then he *w* turn ... Josh 24:20
but we *w* serve the LORD ... Josh 24:21
The LORD our God *w* we serve ... Josh 24:24
we serve, and his voice *w* we obey ... Josh 24:24
I likewise *w* go with thee into ... Judg 1:3
to him *w* I give Achsah my ... Judg 1:12
the city, and we *w* shew thee mercy ... Judg 1:24
I *w* never break my covenant with ... Judg 2:1
I *w* not drive them out from ... Judg 2:3
I also *w* not henceforth drive out ... Judg 2:21
whether they *w* keep the way of ... Judg 2:22
I *w* draw unto thee to the river ... Judg 4:7
I *w* deliver him into thine hand ... Judg 4:7
thou wilt go with me, then I *w* go ... Judg 4:8
not go with me, then I *w* not go ... Judg 4:8

she said, I *w* surely go with thee ... Judg 4:9
I *w* shew thee the man whom thou ... Judg 4:22
I, even I, *w* sing unto the LORD ... Judg 5:3
I *w* sing praise to the LORD God ... Judg 5:3
Surely I *w* be with thee, and thou ... Judg 6:16
I *w* tarry until thou come again ... Judg 6:18
against him, *W* ye plead for Baal ... Judg 6:31
w ye save him ... Judg 6:31
he that *w* plead for him, let him ... Judg 6:31
I *w* put a fleece of wool in the ... Judg 6:37
me, and I *w* speak but this once ... Judg 6:39
I *w* try them for thee there ... Judg 7:4
men that lapped *w* I save you ... Judg 7:7
then I *w* tear your flesh with the ... Judg 8:7
I *w* break down this tower ... Judg 8:9
I *w* not rule over you, neither ... Judg 8:23
We *w* willingly give them ... Judg 8:25
wherefore I *w* deliver you no more ... Judg 10:13
What man is he that *w* begin to ... Judg 10:18
from before us, them *w* we possess ... Judg 11:24
I *w* offer it up for a burnt ... Judg 11:31
we *w* burn thine house upon thee ... Judg 12:1
me, I *w* not eat of thy bread ... Judg 13:16
I *w* now put forth a riddle unto ... Judg 14:12
then I *w* give you thirty sheets ... Judg 14:12
I *w* go in to my wife into the ... Judg 15:1
yet *w* I be avenged of you, and ... Judg 15:7
of you, and after that I *w* cease ... Judg 15:7
that ye *w* not fall upon me ... Judg 15:12
but we *w* bind thee fast, and ... Judg 15:13
but surely we *w* not kill thee ... Judg 15:13
we *w* give thee every one of us ... Judg 16:5
then my strength *w* go from me ... Judg 16:17
I *w* go out as at other times ... Judg 16:20
now therefore I *w* restore it unto ... Judg 17:3
I *w* give thee ten shekels of ... Judg 17:10
know I that the LORD *w* do me good ... Judg 17:13
We *w* not turn aside hither into ... Judg 19:12
we *w* pass over to Gibeah ... Judg 19:12
them I *w* bring out now, and humble ... Judg 19:24
We *w* not any of us go to his tent ... Judg 20:8
neither *w* we any of us turn into ... Judg 20:8
the thing which we *w* do to Gibeah ... Judg 20:9
we *w* go up by lot against it ... Judg 20:9
we *w* take ten men of an hundred ... Judg 20:10
for to morrow I *w* deliver them ... Judg 20:28
w not give them of our daughters ... Judg 21:7
that we *w* say unto them, Be ... Judg 21:22
Surely we *w* return with thee unto ... Ruth 1:10
why *w* ye go with me ... Ruth 1:11
for whither thou goest, I *w* go ... Ruth 1:16
and where thou lodgest, I *w* lodge ... Ruth 1:16
w I die, and there *w* I be ... Ruth 1:17
he *w* tell thee what thou shalt do ... Ruth 3:4
that thou sayest unto me I *w* do ... Ruth 3:5
I *w* do to thee all that thou ... Ruth 3:11
that if he *w* perform unto thee ... Ruth 3:13
but if he *w* not do the part of a ... Ruth 3:13 2654
then *w* I do the part of a kinsman ... Ruth 3:13
thou know how the matter *w* fall ... Ruth 3:18
for the man *w* not be in rest, ... Ruth 3:18
And he said, I *w* redeem it ... Ruth 4:4
then I *w* give him unto the LORD ... 1Sa 1:11
I *w* not go up until the child be ... 1Sa 1:22
then I *w* bring him, that he may ... 1Sa 1:22
He *w* keep the feet of his saints, ... 1Sa 2:9
for he *w* not have sodden flesh of ... 1Sa 2:15
and if not, I *w* take it by force ... 1Sa 2:16
them that honour me I *w* honour ... 1Sa 2:30
that I *w* cut off thine arm, and ... 1Sa 2:31
I *w* raise me up a faithful priest ... 1Sa 2:35
I *w* build him a sure house ... 1Sa 2:35
I *w* do a thing in Israel, at ... 1Sa 3:11
In that day I *w* perform against ... 1Sa 3:12
I begin, I *w* also make an end ... 1Sa 3:12
For I have told him that I *w* ... 1Sa 3:13
peradventure he *w* lighten his ... 1Sa 6:5
he *w* deliver you out of the hand ... 1Sa 7:3
I *w* pray for you unto the LORD ... 1Sa 7:5
that he *w* save us out of the hand ... 1Sa 7:8
This *w* be the manner of the king ... 1Sa 8:11
He *w* take your sons, and appoint ... 1Sa 8:11
he *w* appoint him captains over ... 1Sa 8:12
w set them to ear his ground, and ... 1Sa 8:12
he *w* take your daughters to be ... 1Sa 8:13
he *w* take your fields, and your ... 1Sa 8:14
he *w* take the tenth of your seed, ... 1Sa 8:15
he *w* take your menservants, and ... 1Sa 8:16
He *w* take the tenth of your sheep ... 1Sa 8:17
the LORD *w* not hear you in that ... 1Sa 8:18
but we *w* have a king over us ... 1Sa 8:19
that *w* I give to the man of God, ... 1Sa 9:8
for the people *w* not eat until he ... 1Sa 9:13
To morrow about this time I *w* ... 1Sa 9:16
day, and to morrow I *w* let thee go ... 1Sa 9:19
w tell thee all that is in thine ... 1Sa 9:19
they *w* say unto thee, The asses ... 1Sa 10:2
they *w* salute thee, and give thee ... 1Sa 10:4
of the LORD *w* come upon thee ... 1Sa 10:6
I *w* come down unto thee, to offer ... 1Sa 10:8
with us, and we *w* serve thee ... 1Sa 11:1
On this condition *w* I make a ... 1Sa 11:2
to save us, we *w* come out to thee ... 1Sa 11:3
To morrow we *w* come out unto you, ... 1Sa 11:10
and I *w* restore it you ... 1Sa 12:3
our enemies, and we *w* serve thee ... 1Sa 12:10
If ye *w* fear the LORD, and serve ... 1Sa 12:14
But if ye *w* not obey the voice of ... 1Sa 12:15

which the LORD *w* do before your ... 1Sa 12:16
I *w* call unto the LORD, and he ... 1Sa 12:17
For the LORD *w* not forsake his ... 1Sa 12:22
but I *w* teach you the good and the ... 1Sa 12:23
The Philistines *w* come down now ... 1Sa 13:12
be that the LORD *w* work for us ... 1Sa 14:6
we *w* pass over unto these men, and ... 1Sa 14:8
we *w* discover ourselves unto them ... 1Sa 14:8
then we *w* stand still in our ... 1Sa 14:9
place, and *w* not go up unto them ... 1Sa 14:9
then we *w* go up ... 1Sa 14:10
to us, and we *w* shew you a thing ... 1Sa 14:12
Jonathan my son *w* be on the other ... 1Sa 14:40
I *w* tell thee what the LORD hath ... 1Sa 15:16
Saul, I *w* not return with thee ... 1Sa 15:26
of Israel *w* not lie nor repent ... 1Sa 15:29
I *w* send thee to Jesse the ... 1Sa 16:1
if Saul hear it, he *w* kill me ... 1Sa 16:2
I *w* shew thee what thou shalt do ... 1Sa 16:3
for we *w* not sit down till he ... 1Sa 16:11
then *w* we be your servants ... 1Sa 17:9
the king *w* enrich him with great ... 1Sa 17:25
w give him his daughter, and make ... 1Sa 17:25
thy servant *w* go and fight with ... 1Sa 17:32
he *w* deliver me out of the hand ... 1Sa 17:37
I *w* give thy flesh unto the fowls ... 1Sa 17:44
This day *w* the LORD deliver thee ... 1Sa 17:46
I *w* smite thee, and take thine ... 1Sa 17:46
I *w* give the carcases of the host ... 1Sa 17:46
he *w* give you into our hands ... 1Sa 17:47
I *w* smite David even to the wall ... 1Sa 18:11
her *w* I give thee to wife ... 1Sa 18:17
I *w* give him her, that she may be ... 1Sa 18:21
I *w* go out and stand beside my ... 1Sa 19:3
I *w* commune with my father of ... 1Sa 19:3
and what I see, that I *w* tell thee ... 1Sa 19:3
my father *w* do nothing either ... 1Sa 20:2
small, but that he *w* shew it me ... 1Sa 20:2
desireth, I *w* even do it for thee ... 1Sa 20:4
then I *w* shew it thee, and send ... 1Sa 20:13
because thy seat *w* be empty ... 1Sa 20:18
I *w* shoot three arrows on the ... 1Sa 20:20
I *w* send a lad, saying, Go, find ... 1Sa 20:21
till I know what God *w* do for me ... 1Sa 22:3
w the son of Jesse give every one ... 1Sa 22:7
for I *w* deliver the Philistines ... 1Sa 23:4
W the men of Keilah deliver me up ... 1Sa 23:11
w Saul come down, as thy servant ... 1Sa 23:11
And the LORD said, He *w* come down ... 1Sa 23:11
W the men of Keilah deliver me and ... 1Sa 23:12
LORD said, They *w* deliver thee up ... 1Sa 23:12
the certainty, and I *w* go with you ... 1Sa 23:23
the land, that I *w* search him out ... 1Sa 23:23
I *w* deliver thine enemy into ... 1Sa 24:4
I *w* not put forth mine hand ... 1Sa 24:10
w he let him go well away ... 1Sa 24:19
young men, and they *w* shew thee ... 1Sa 25:8
for the LORD *w* certainly make my ... 1Sa 25:28
Who *w* go down with me to Saul to ... 1Sa 26:6
said, I *w* go down with thee ... 1Sa 26:6
I *w* not smite him the second time ... 1Sa 26:8
for I *w* no more do thee harm, ... 1Sa 26:21
so *w* be his manner all the while ... 1Sa 27:11
Therefore *w* I make thee keeper of ... 1Sa 28:2
Moreover the LORD *w* also deliver ... 1Sa 28:19
he refused, and said, I *w* not eat ... 1Sa 28:23
I *w* bring thee down to this ... 1Sa 30:15
we *w* not give them ought of the ... 1Sa 30:22
For who *w* hearken unto you in ... 1Sa 30:24
I also *w* requite you this ... 2Sa 2:6
knowest thou not that it *w* be ... 2Sa 2:26
I *w* make a league with thee ... 2Sa 3:13
I *w* save my people Israel out of ... 2Sa 3:18
I *w* arise and go ... 2Sa 3:21
w gather all Israel unto my lord ... 2Sa 3:21
for I *w* doubtless deliver the ... 2Sa 5:19
therefore *w* I play before the ... 2Sa 6:21
I *w* yet be more vile than thus, ... 2Sa 6:22
w be base in mine own sight ... 2Sa 6:22
Moreover I *w* appoint a place for ... 2Sa 7:10
w plant them, that they may dwell ... 2Sa 7:10
thee that he *w* make thee an house ... 2Sa 7:11
I *w* set up thy seed after thee, ... 2Sa 7:12
I *w* establish his kingdom ... 2Sa 7:12
I *w* stablish the throne of his ... 2Sa 7:13
I *w* be his father, and he shall be ... 2Sa 7:14
I *w* chasten him with the rod of ... 2Sa 7:14
saying, I *w* build thee an house ... 2Sa 7:27
for I *w* surely shew thee kindness ... 2Sa 9:7
w restore thee all the land of ... 2Sa 9:7
I *w* shew kindness unto Hanun the ... 2Sa 10:2
strong for thee, then I *w* come ... 2Sa 10:11
liveth, I *w* not do this thing ... 2Sa 11:11
to morrow I *w* let thee depart ... 2Sa 11:12
I *w* raise up evil against thee ... 2Sa 12:11
I *w* take thy wives before thine ... 2Sa 12:11
but I *w* do this thing before all ... 2Sa 12:12
how *w* he then vex himself, if we ... 2Sa 12:18
whether GOD *w* be gracious to me ... 2Sa 12:22
for he *w* not withhold me from ... 2Sa 13:13
we *w* destroy the heir also ... 2Sa 14:7
I *w* give charge concerning thee ... 2Sa 14:8
I *w* now speak unto the king ... 2Sa 14:15
it may be that the king *w* perform ... 2Sa 14:15
For the king *w* hear, to deliver ... 2Sa 14:16
the LORD thy God *w* be with thee ... 2Sa 14:17
then I *w* serve the LORD ... 2Sa 15:8
even there also *w* thy servant be ... 2Sa 15:21

he *w* bring me again, and shew me ... 2Sa 15:25
I *w* tarry in the plain of the ... 2Sa 15:28
I *w* be thy servant, O king ... 2Sa 15:34
so *w* I now also be thy servant ... 2Sa 15:34
LORD *w* look on mine affliction ... 2Sa 16:12
that the LORD *w* requite me good ... 2Sa 16:12
his *w* I be ... 2Sa 16:18
and with him *w* I abide ... 2Sa 16:18
so *w* I be in thy presence ... 2Sa 16:19
I *w* arise and pursue after David ... 2Sa 17:1
I *w* come upon him while he is ... 2Sa 17:2
weak handed, and *w* make him afraid ... 2Sa 17:2
and I *w* smite the king only ... 2Sa 17:2
I *w* bring back all the people ... 2Sa 17:3
w not lodge with the people ... 2Sa 17:8
it *w* come to pass, when some of ... 2Sa 17:9
that whosoever heareth it *w* say ... 2Sa 17:9
we *w* light upon him as the dew ... 2Sa 17:12
we *w* draw it into the river, ... 2Sa 17:13
I *w* surely go forth with you ... 2Sa 18:2
flee away, they *w* not care for us ... 2Sa 18:3
of us die, *w* they care for us ... 2Sa 18:3
What seemeth you best I *w* do ... 2Sa 18:4
there *w* not tarry one with thee ... 2Sa 19:7
that *w* be worse unto thee than ... 2Sa 19:7
I *w* saddle me an ass, that I may ... 2Sa 19:26
me, and I *w* feed thee with me in ... 2Sa 19:33
Thy servant *w* go a little way ... 2Sa 19:36
I *w* do to him that which shall ... 2Sa 19:38
of me, that *w* I do for thee ... 2Sa 19:38
only, and I *w* depart from the city ... 2Sa 20:21
We *w* have no silver nor gold of ... 2Sa 21:4
ye shall say, that *w* I do for you ... 2Sa 21:4
we *w* hang them up unto the LORD ... 2Sa 21:6
And the king said, I *w* give them ... 2Sa 21:6
in him *w* I trust ... 2Sa 22:3
I *w* call on the LORD, who is ... 2Sa 22:4
the LORD *w* lighten my darkness ... 2Sa 22:29
Therefore I *w* give thanks unto ... 2Sa 22:50
but I *w* surely buy it of thee at ... 2Sa 24:24
neither *w* I offer burnt offerings ... 2Sa 24:24
himself, saying, I *w* be king ... 1Kin 1:5
I also *w* come in after thee, and ... 1Kin 1:14
even so *w* I certainly do this day ... 1Kin 1:30
swear unto me to day that he *w* ... 1Kin 1:51
If he *w* shew himself a worthy man ... 1Kin 1:52
I *w* not put thee to death with ... 1Kin 2:8
(for he *w* not say thee nay,) that ... 1Kin 2:17
I *w* speak for thee unto the king ... 1Kin 2:18
for I *w* not say thee nay ... 1Kin 2:20
but I *w* not at this time put thee ... 1Kin 2:26
but I *w* die here ... 1Kin 2:30
hath said, so *w* thy servant do ... 1Kin 2:38
then I *w* lengthen thy days ... 1Kin 3:14
whom I *w* set upon thy throne in ... 1Kin 5:5
unto thee *w* I give hire for thy ... 1Kin 5:6
I *w* do all thy desire concerning ... 1Kin 5:8
I *w* convey them by sea in floats ... 1Kin 5:9
w cause them to be discharged ... 1Kin 5:9
then *w* I perform my word with ... 1Kin 6:12
I *w* dwell among the children of ... 1Kin 6:13
w not forsake my people Israel ... 1Kin 6:13
But *w* God indeed dwell on the ... 1Kin 8:27
Then I *w* establish the throne of ... 1Kin 9:5
w not keep my commandments and my .. 1Kin 9:6
Then *w* I cut off Israel out of ... 1Kin 9:7
my name, *w* I cast out of my sight ... 1Kin 9:7
for surely they *w* turn away your ... 1Kin 11:2
I *w* surely rend the kingdom from ... 1Kin 11:11
thee, and *w* give it to thy servant ... 1Kin 11:11
days I *w* not do it for David thy ... 1Kin 11:12
but I *w* rend it out of the hand ... 1Kin 11:12
Howbeit I *w* not rend away all the ... 1Kin 11:13
but *w* give one tribe to thy son ... 1Kin 11:13
I *w* rend the kingdom out of the ... 1Kin 11:31
w give ten tribes to thee ... 1Kin 11:31
Howbeit I *w* not take the whole ... 1Kin 11:34
but I *w* make him prince all the ... 1Kin 11:34
But I *w* take the kingdom out of ... 1Kin 11:35
w give it unto thee, even ten ... 1Kin 11:35
unto his son *w* I give one tribe, ... 1Kin 11:36
I *w* take thee, and thou shalt ... 1Kin 11:37
that I *w* be with thee, and build ... 1Kin 11:38
David, and *w* give Israel unto thee ... 1Kin 11:38
I *w* for this afflict the seed of ... 1Kin 11:39
us, lighter, and we *w* serve thee ... 1Kin 12:4
then they *w* be thy servants for ... 1Kin 12:7
heavy yoke, I *w* add to your yoke ... 1Kin 12:11
but I *w* chastise you with ... 1Kin 12:11
heavy, and I *w* add to your yoke ... 1Kin 12:14
but I *w* chastise you with ... 1Kin 12:14
and I *w* give thee a reward ... 1Kin 13:7
I *w* not go in with thee ... 1Kin 13:8
neither *w* I eat bread nor drink ... 1Kin 13:8
neither *w* I eat bread nor drink ... 1Kin 13:16
I *w* bring evil upon the house of ... 1Kin 14:10
w cut off from Jeroboam him that ... 1Kin 14:10
w take away the remnant of the ... 1Kin 14:10
I *w* take away the posterity of ... 1Kin 16:3
w make thy house like the house ... 1Kin 16:3
I *w* send rain upon the earth ... 1Kin 18:1
I *w* surely shew myself unto him ... 1Kin 18:15
I *w* dress the other bullock, and ... 1Kin 18:23
I *w* call on the name of the LORD ... 1Kin 18:24
mother, and then I *w* follow thee ... 1Kin 19:20
Yet I *w* send my servants unto ... 1Kin 20:6
thy servant at the first I *w* do ... 1Kin 20:9
I *w* deliver it into thine hand ... 1Kin 20:13

of Syria *w* come up against thee ... 1Kin 20:22
we *w* fight against them in the ... 1Kin 20:25
therefore *w* I deliver all this ... 1Kin 20:28
peradventure he *w* save thy life ... 1Kin 20:31
took from thy father, I *w* restore ... 1Kin 20:34
I *w* send thee away with this ... 1Kin 20:34
I *w* give thee for it a better ... 1Kin 21:2
I *w* give thee the worth of it in ... 1Kin 21:2
I *w* not give thee the inheritance ... 1Kin 21:4
I *w* give thee another vineyard ... 1Kin 21:6
I *w* not give thee my vineyard ... 1Kin 21:6
I *w* give thee the vineyard of ... 1Kin 21:7
I *w* bring evil upon thee ... 1Kin 21:21
w take away thy posterity, and ... 1Kin 21:21
w cut off from Ahab him that ... 1Kin 21:21
w make thine house like the house ... 1Kin 21:22
I *w* not bring the evil in his ... 1Kin 21:29
but in his son's days *w* I bring ... 1Kin 21:29
saith unto me, that *w* I speak ... 1Kin 22:14
LORD, and said, I *w* persuade him ... 1Kin 22:21
I *w* go forth ... 1Kin 22:22
I *w* be a lying spirit in the ... 1Kin 22:22
I *w* disguise myself, and enter ... 1Kin 22:30
soul liveth, I *w* not leave thee ... 2Kin 2:2
Knowest thou that the LORD *w* take ... 2Kin 2:3
soul liveth, I *w* not leave thee ... 2Kin 2:4
Knowest thou that the LORD *w* take ... 2Kin 2:5
soul liveth, I *w* not leave thee ... 2Kin 2:6
And he said, I *w* go up ... 2Kin 3:7
he *w* deliver the Moabites also ... 2Kin 3:18
soul liveth, I *w* not leave thee ... 2Kin 4:30
I *w* send a letter unto the king ... 2Kin 5:5
He *w* surely come out to me, and ... 2Kin 5:11
whom I stand, I *w* receive none ... 2Kin 5:16
for thy servant *w* henceforth ... 2Kin 5:17
I *w* run after him, and take ... 2Kin 5:20
And he answered, I *w* go ... 2Kin 6:3
W ye not shew me which of us is ... 2Kin 6:11
I *w* bring you to the man whom ye ... 2Kin 6:19
we *w* eat my son to morrow ... 2Kin 6:28
We *w* enter into the city, then ... 2Kin 7:4
some mischief *w* come upon us ... 2Kin 7:9
I *w* now shew you what the Syrians ... 2Kin 7:12
I *w* cut off from Ahab him that ... 2Kin 9:8
I *w* make the house of Ahab like ... 2Kin 9:9
I *w* requite thee in this plat, ... 2Kin 9:26
w do all that thou shalt bid us ... 2Kin 10:5
we *w* not make any king ... 2Kin 10:5
if ye *w* hearken unto my voice, ... 2Kin 10:6
which thou puttest on me *w* I bear ... 2Kin 18:14
it *w* go into his hand, and pierce ... 2Kin 18:21
I *w* deliver thee two thousand ... 2Kin 18:23
The LORD *w* surely deliver us, and ... 2Kin 18:30
saying, The LORD *w* deliver us ... 2Kin 18:32
thy God *w* hear all the words of ... 2Kin 19:4
w reprove the words which the ... 2Kin 19:4
I *w* send a blast upon him, and he ... 2Kin 19:7
I *w* cause him to fall by the ... 2Kin 19:7
w cut down the tall cedar trees ... 2Kin 19:23
I *w* enter into the lodgings of ... 2Kin 19:23
therefore I *w* put my hook in thy ... 2Kin 19:28
I *w* turn thee back by the way by ... 2Kin 19:28
For I *w* defend this city, to save ... 2Kin 19:34
behold, I *w* heal thee ... 2Kin 20:5
I *w* add unto thy days fifteen ... 2Kin 20:6
I *w* deliver thee and this city out ... 2Kin 20:6
I *w* defend this city for mine own ... 2Kin 20:6
the sign that the LORD *w* heal me ... 2Kin 20:8
that the LORD *w* do the thing that ... 2Kin 20:9
In Jerusalem *w* I put my name ... 2Kin 21:4
Israel, *w* I put my name for ever ... 2Kin 21:7
Neither *w* I make the feet of ... 2Kin 21:8
only if they *w* observe to do ... 2Kin 21:8
I *w* stretch over Jerusalem the ... 2Kin 21:13
I *w* wipe Jerusalem as a man ... 2Kin 21:13
I *w* forsake the remnant of mine ... 2Kin 21:14
I *w* bring evil upon this place, ... 2Kin 22:16
I *w* gather thee unto thy fathers, ... 2Kin 22:20
which I *w* bring upon this place ... 2Kin 22:20
I *w* remove Judah also out of my ... 2Kin 23:27
w cast off this city Jerusalem ... 2Kin 23:27
He *w* fall to his master Saul to ... 1Chr 12:19
for I *w* deliver them into thine ... 1Chr 14:10
Unto thee *w* I give the land of ... 1Chr 16:18
Also I *w* ordain a place for my ... 1Chr 17:9
w plant them, and they shall dwell ... 1Chr 17:9
Moreover I *w* subdue all thine ... 1Chr 17:10
the LORD *w* build thee an house ... 1Chr 17:10
that I *w* raise up thy seed after ... 1Chr 17:11
I *w* establish his kingdom ... 1Chr 17:11
I *w* stablish his throne for ever ... 1Chr 17:12
I *w* be his father, and he shall be ... 1Chr 17:13
I *w* not take my mercy away from ... 1Chr 17:13
But I *w* settle him in mine house ... 1Chr 17:14
I *w* shew kindness unto Hanun the ... 1Chr 19:2
for thee, then I *w* help thee ... 1Chr 19:12
why *w* he be a cause of trespass ... 1Chr 21:3
but I *w* verily buy it for the ... 1Chr 21:24
for I *w* not take that which is ... 1Chr 21:24
I *w* therefore now make ... 1Chr 22:5
I *w* give him rest from all his ... 1Chr 22:9
I *w* give peace and quietness unto ... 1Chr 22:9
be my son, and I *w* be his father ... 1Chr 22:10
I *w* establish the throne of his ... 1Chr 22:10
be my son, and I *w* be his father ... 1Chr 28:6
Moreover I *w* establish his ... 1Chr 28:7
seek him, he *w* be found of thee ... 1Chr 28:9
he *w* cast thee off for ever ... 1Chr 28:9

God, even my God, *w* be with thee ... 1Chr 28:20
he *w* not fail thee, nor forsake ... 1Chr 28:20
all the people *w* be wholly at thy ... 1Chr 28:21
I *w* give thee riches, and wealth, ... 2Chr 1:12
I *w* give to thy servants, the ... 2Chr 2:10
we *w* cut wood out of Lebanon, as ... 2Chr 2:16
we *w* bring it to thee in flotes ... 2Chr 2:16
But *w* God in very deed dwell with ... 2Chr 6:18
then *w* I hear from heaven, and ... 2Chr 7:14
w forgive their sin ... 2Chr 7:14
and *w* heal their land ... 2Chr 7:14
Then *w* I stablish the throne of ... 2Chr 7:18
Then *w* I pluck them up by the ... 2Chr 7:20
w I cast out of my sight ... 2Chr 7:20
w make it to be a proverb and a ... 2Chr 7:20
put upon us, and we *w* serve thee ... 2Chr 10:4
they *w* be thy servants for ever ... 2Chr 10:7
I *w* put more to your yoke ... 2Chr 10:11
but I *w* chastise you with ... 2Chr 10:11
yoke heavy, but I *w* add thereto ... 2Chr 10:14
but I *w* chastise you with ... 2Chr 10:14
therefore I *w* not destroy them, ... 2Chr 12:7
but I *w* grant them some ... 2Chr 12:7
ye seek him, he *w* be found of you ... 2Chr 15:2
ye forsake him, he *w* forsake you ... 2Chr 15:2
we *w* be with thee in the war ... 2Chr 18:3
for God *w* deliver it into the ... 2Chr 18:5
what my God saith, that *w* I speak ... 2Chr 18:13
the LORD, and said, I *w* entice him ... 2Chr 18:20
I *w* go out, and be a lying spirit ... 2Chr 18:21
I *w* disguise myself ... 2Chr 18:29
and *w* go to the battle ... 2Chr 18:29
for the LORD *w* be with you ... 2Chr 20:17
with a great plague *w* the LORD ... 2Chr 21:14
therefore *w* I sacrifice to them, ... 2Chr 28:23
he *w* return to the remnant of you ... 2Chr 30:6
w not turn away his face from you ... 2Chr 30:9
Israel, *w* I put my name for ever ... 2Chr 33:7
Neither *w* I any more remove the ... 2Chr 33:8
so that they *w* take heed to do ... 2Chr 33:8
I *w* bring evil upon this place, ... 2Chr 34:24
I *w* gather thee to thy fathers, ... 2Chr 34:28
that I *w* bring upon this place ... 2Chr 34:28
but we ourselves together *w* build ... Ezr 4:3
then *w* they not pay toll, tribute ... Ezr 4:13
that do after the *w* of your God ... Ezr 7:18 7470
whosoever *w* not do the law of thy ... Ezr 7:26
we also *w* be with thee ... Ezr 10:4
I *w* scatter you abroad among the ... Neh 1:8
yet *w* I gather them from thence, ... Neh 1:9
w bring them unto the place that ... Neh 1:9
w ye rebel against the king ... Neh 2:19
God of heaven, he *w* prosper us ... Neh 2:20
therefore we his servants *w* arise ... Neh 2:20
w they fortify themselves ... Neh 4:2
w they sacrifice ... Neh 4:2
w they make an end in a day ... Neh 4:2
w they revive the stones out of ... Neh 4:2
return unto us they *w* be upon you ... Neh 4:12
w ye even sell your brethren ... Neh 5:8
We *w* restore them ... Neh 5:12
w require nothing of them ... Neh 5:12
so *w* we do as thou sayest ... Neh 5:12
for they *w* come to slay thee ... Neh 6:10
in the night *w* they come to slay ... Neh 6:10
I *w* not go in ... Neh 6:11
we *w* not forsake the house of our ... Neh 10:39
do so again, I *w* lay hands on you ... Neh 13:21
I *w* pay ten thousand talents of ... Est 3:9
my maidens *w* fast likewise ... Est 4:16
so *w* I go in unto the king, which ... Est 4:16
I *w* do to morrow as the king hath ... Est 5:8
W he force the queen also before ... Est 7:8
he *w* curse thee to thy face ... Job 1:11
all that a man hath *w* he give for ... Job 2:4
he *w* curse thee to thy face ... Job 2:5
there be any that *w* answer thee ... Job 5:1
Teach me, and I *w* hold my tongue ... Job 6:24
Therefore I *w* not refrain my ... Job 7:11
I *w* speak in the anguish of my ... Job 7:11
I *w* complain in the bitterness of ... Job 7:11
God *w* not cast away a perfect man ... Job 8:20
neither *w* he help the evil doers ... Job 8:20
If he *w* contend with him, he ... Job 9:3 2654
who *w* say unto him, What doest ... Job 9:12
If God *w* not withdraw his anger, ... Job 9:13
He *w* not suffer me to take my ... Job 9:18
he *w* laugh at the trial of the ... Job 9:23
I *w* forget my complaint ... Job 9:27
I *w* leave off my heaviness, and ... Job 9:27
I *w* leave my complaint upon ... Job 10:1
I *w* speak in the bitterness of my ... Job 10:1
I *w* say unto God, Do not condemn ... Job 10:2
yet *w* I not lift up my head ... Job 10:15
w he not then consider it ... Job 11:11
W ye speak wickedly for God ... Job 13:7
W ye accept his person ... Job 13:8
w ye contend for God ... Job 13:8
He *w* surely reprove you, if ye do ... Job 13:10
speak, and let come on me what *w* ... Job 13:13
he slay me, yet *w* I trust in him ... Job 13:15
but I *w* maintain mine own ways ... Job 13:15
Who is he that *w* plead with me ... Job 13:19
then I *w* not hide myself from ... Job 13:20
Then call thou, and I *w* answer ... Job 13:22
that it *w* sprout again, and that ... Job 14:7
tender branch thereof *w* not cease ... Job 14:7
the scent of water it *w* bud ... Job 14:9

of my appointed time *w* I wait ... Job 14:14
shalt call, and I *w* answer thee ... Job 14:15
I *w* shew thee, hear me ... Job 15:17
which I have seen I *w* declare ... Job 15:17
who is he that *w* strike hands ... Job 17:3
How long *w* it be ere ye make an ... Job 18:2
mark, and afterwards we *w* speak ... Job 18:2
How long *w* ye vex my soul, and ... Job 19:2
If indeed ye *w* magnify yourselves ... Job 19:5
W he reprove thee for fear of ... Job 22:4
w he enter with thee into ... Job 22:4
W he plead against me with his ... Job 23:6
who *w* make me a liar, and make my ... Job 24:25
till I die I *w* not remove mine ... Job 27:5
I hold fast, and *w* not let it go ... Job 27:6
W God hear his cry when trouble ... Job 27:9
W he delight himself in the ... Job 27:10
w he always call upon God ... Job 27:10
I *w* teach you by the hand of God ... Job 27:11
with the Almighty *w* I not conceal ... Job 27:11
Howbeit he *w* not stretch out his ... Job 30:24
I also *w* shew mine opinion ... Job 32:10
neither *w* I answer him with your ... Job 32:14
I *w* answer also my part ... Job 32:17
I also *w* shew mine opinion ... Job 32:17
I *w* speak, that I may be ... Job 32:20
I *w* open my lips and answer ... Job 32:20
I *w* answer thee, that God is ... Job 33:12
he *w* be favourable unto him ... Job 33:26
for he *w* render unto man his ... Job 33:26
He *w* deliver his soul from going ... Job 33:28
hold thy peace, and I *w* speak ... Job 33:31
surely God *w* not do wickedly, ... Job 34:12
neither *w* the Almighty pervert ... Job 34:12
For he *w* not lay upon man more ... Job 34:23
I *w* not offend any more ... Job 34:31
done iniquity, I *w* do no more ... Job 34:32
he *w* recompense it, whether thou ... Job 34:33
What advantage *w* it be unto thee ... Job 35:3
I *w* answer thee, and thy ... Job 35:4
Surely God *w* not hear vanity, ... Job 35:13
neither *w* the Almighty regard it ... Job 35:13
I *w* shew thee that I have yet to ... Job 36:2
I *w* fetch my knowledge from afar, ... Job 36:3
w ascribe righteousness to my ... Job 36:3
W he esteem thy riches ... Job 36:19
he *w* not stay them when his voice ... Job 37:4
he *w* not afflict ... Job 37:23
for I *w* demand of thee, and answer ... Job 38:3
W the unicorn be willing to serve ... Job 39:9
or *w* he harrow the valleys after ... Job 39:10
that he *w* bring home thy seed, and ... Job 39:12
I *w* lay mine hand upon my mouth ... Job 40:4
but I *w* not answer ... Job 40:5
but I *w* proceed no further ... Job 40:5
I *w* demand of thee, and declare ... Job 40:7
Then *w* I also confess unto thee ... Job 40:14
W he make many supplications unto ... Job 41:3
w he speak soft words unto thee ... Job 41:3
W he make a covenant with thee ... Job 41:4
I *w* not conceal his parts, nor ... Job 41:12
I beseech thee, and I *w* speak ... Job 42:4
I *w* demand of thee, and declare ... Job 42:4
for him *w* I accept ... Job 42:8
I *w* declare the decree ... Ps 2:7
I *w* not be afraid of ten ... Ps 3:6
how long *w* ye turn my glory into ... Ps 4:2
how long *w* ye love vanity, and ... Ps 4:2
the LORD *w* hear when I call unto ... Ps 4:3
that say, Who *w* shew us any good ... Ps 4:6
I *w* both lay me down in peace, and ... Ps 4:8
for unto thee *w* I pray ... Ps 5:2
in the morning *w* I direct my ... Ps 5:3
my prayer unto thee, and *w* look up ... Ps 5:3
the LORD *w* abhor the bloody and ... Ps 5:6
I *w* come into thy house in the ... Ps 5:7
in thy fear *w* I worship toward ... Ps 5:7
the LORD *w* receive my prayer ... Ps 6:9
he turn not, he *w* whet his sword ... Ps 7:12
I *w* praise the LORD according to ... Ps 7:17
w sing praise to the name of the ... Ps 7:17
I *w* praise thee, O LORD, with my ... Ps 9:1
I *w* shew forth all thy marvellous ... Ps 9:1
I *w* be glad and rejoice in thee ... Ps 9:2
I *w* sing praise to thy name, O ... Ps 9:2
The LORD also *w* be a refuge for ... Ps 9:9
name *w* put their trust in thee ... Ps 9:10
I *w* rejoice in thy salvation ... Ps 9:14
countenance, *w* not seek after God ... Ps 10:4
he *w* never see it ... Ps 10:11
With our tongue *w* we prevail ... Ps 12:4
now *w* I arise, saith the LORD ... Ps 12:5
I *w* set him in safety from him ... Ps 12:5
I *w* sing unto the LORD, because ... Ps 13:6
offerings of blood *w* I not offer ... Ps 16:4
I *w* bless the LORD, who hath ... Ps 16:7
As for me, I *w* behold thy face in ... Ps 17:15
I *w* love thee, O LORD, my ... Ps 18:1
my strength, in whom I *w* trust ... Ps 18:2
I *w* call upon the LORD, who is ... Ps 18:3
the LORD my God *w* enlighten my ... Ps 18:28
Therefore *w* I give thanks unto ... Ps 18:49
We *w* rejoice in thy salvation, and ... Ps 20:5
our God we *w* set up our banners ... Ps 20:5
he *w* hear him from his holy ... Ps 20:6
but we *w* remember the name of the ... Ps 20:7
so *w* we sing and praise thy power ... Ps 21:13
I *w* declare thy name unto my ... Ps 22:22
the congregation *w* I praise thee ... Ps 22:22
I *w* pay my vows before them that ... Ps 22:25
shadow of death, I *w* fear no evil ... Ps 23:4
I *w* dwell in the house of the ... Ps 23:6
therefore *w* he teach sinners in ... Ps 25:8
The meek *w* he guide in judgment ... Ps 25:9
the meek *w* he teach his way ... Ps 25:9
he *w* shew them his covenant ... Ps 25:14
persons, neither *w* I go in with ... Ps 26:4
w not sit with the wicked ... Ps 26:5
I *w* wash mine hands in innocency ... Ps 26:6
so *w* I compass thine altar, O ... Ps 26:6
I *w* walk in mine integrity ... Ps 26:11
congregations *w* I bless the LORD ... Ps 26:12
me, in this *w* I be confident ... Ps 27:3
of the LORD, that *w* I seek after ... Ps 27:4
therefore *w* I offer in his ... Ps 27:6
I *w* sing, yea, I *w* sing ... Ps 27:6
thee, Thy face, LORD, *w* I seek ... Ps 27:8
me, then the LORD *w* take me up ... Ps 27:10
over unto the *w* of mine enemies ... Ps 27:12 5315
Unto thee *w* I cry, O LORD my rock ... Ps 28:1
and with my song *w* I praise him ... Ps 28:7
The LORD *w* give strength unto his ... Ps 29:11
the LORD *w* bless his people with ... Ps 29:11
I *w* extol thee, O LORD ... Ps 30:1
I *w* give thanks unto thee for ... Ps 30:12
I *w* be glad and rejoice in thy ... Ps 31:7
I *w* confess my transgressions ... Ps 32:5
I *w* instruct thee and teach thee ... Ps 32:8
I *w* guide thee with mine eye ... Ps 32:8
I *w* bless the LORD at all times ... Ps 34:1
I *w* teach you the fear of the ... Ps 34:11
I *w* give thee thanks in the great ... Ps 35:18
I *w* praise thee among much people ... Ps 35:18
The LORD *w* not leave him in his ... Ps 37:33
For I *w* declare mine iniquity ... Ps 38:18
I *w* be sorry for my sin ... Ps 38:18
I *w* take heed to my ways, that I ... Ps 39:1
I *w* keep my mouth with a bridle, ... Ps 39:1
I delight to do thy *w*, O my God ... Ps 40:8 7522
the LORD *w* deliver him in time of ... Ps 41:1
The LORD *w* preserve him, and keep ... Ps 41:2
him unto the *w* of his enemies ... Ps 41:2 5315
The LORD *w* strengthen him upon ... Ps 41:3
therefore *w* I remember thee from ... Ps 42:6
Yet the LORD *w* command his ... Ps 42:8
I *w* say unto God my rock, Why ... Ps 42:9
Then *w* I go unto the altar of God ... Ps 43:4
upon the harp *w* I praise thee ... Ps 43:4
Through thee *w* we push down our ... Ps 44:5
through thy name *w* we tread them ... Ps 44:5
For I *w* not trust in my bow, ... Ps 44:6
I *w* make thy name to be ... Ps 45:17
Therefore *w* not we fear, though ... Ps 46:2
I *w* be exalted among the heathen, ... Ps 46:10
I *w* be exalted in the earth ... Ps 46:10
God *w* establish it for ever ... Ps 48:8
he *w* be our guide even unto death ... Ps 48:14
I *w* incline mine ear to a parable ... Ps 49:4
I *w* open my dark saying upon the ... Ps 49:4
But God *w* redeem my soul from the ... Ps 49:15
men *w* praise thee, when thou ... Ps 49:18
Hear, O my people, and I *w* speak ... Ps 50:7
and I *w* testify against thee ... Ps 50:7
I *w* not reprove thee for thy ... Ps 50:8
I *w* take no bullock out of thy ... Ps 50:9
W I eat the flesh of bulls, or ... Ps 50:13
I *w* deliver thee, and thou shalt ... Ps 50:15
but I *w* reprove thee, and set them ... Ps 50:21
his conversation aright *w* I shew ... Ps 50:23
Then *w* I teach transgressors thy ... Ps 51:13
I *w* praise thee for ever, because ... Ps 52:9
and I *w* wait on thy name ... Ps 52:9
I *w* freely sacrifice unto thee ... Ps 54:6
I *w* praise thy name, O LORD ... Ps 54:6
As for me, I *w* call upon God ... Ps 55:16
at noon, *w* I pray, and cry aloud ... Ps 55:17
but I *w* trust in thee ... Ps 55:23
I am afraid, I *w* trust in thee ... Ps 56:3
In God I *w* praise his word, in ... Ps 56:4
I *w* not fear what flesh can do ... Ps 56:4
In God *w* I praise his word ... Ps 56:10
in the LORD *w* I praise his word ... Ps 56:10
I *w* not be afraid what man can do ... Ps 56:11
I *w* render praises unto thee ... Ps 56:12
of thy wings *w* I make my refuge ... Ps 57:1
I *w* cry unto God most high ... Ps 57:2
I *w* sing and give praise ... Ps 57:7
I myself *w* awake early ... Ps 57:8
I *w* praise thee, O Lord, among ... Ps 57:9
I *w* sing unto thee among the ... Ps 57:9
Which *w* not hearken to the voice ... Ps 58:5
his strength *w* I wait upon thee ... Ps 59:9
But I *w* sing of thy power ... Ps 59:16
I *w* sing aloud of thy mercy in ... Ps 59:16
thee, O my strength, *w* I sing ... Ps 59:17
I *w* rejoice, I *w* divide ... Ps 60:6
over Edom *w* I cast out my shoe ... Ps 60:8
Who *w* bring me into the strong ... Ps 60:9
who *w* lead me into Edom ... Ps 60:9
of the earth *w* I cry unto thee ... Ps 61:2
I *w* abide in thy tabernacle for ... Ps 61:4
I *w* trust in the covert of thy ... Ps 61:4
So *w* I sing praise unto thy name ... Ps 61:8
How long *w* ye imagine mischief ... Ps 62:3
early *w* I seek thee ... Ps 63:1
Thus *w* I bless thee while I live ... Ps 63:4
I *w* lift up my hands in thy name ... Ps 63:4
shadow of thy wings *w* I rejoice ... Ps 63:7
I *w* go into thy house with burnt ... Ps 66:13
I *w* pay thee my vows, ... Ps 66:13
I *w* offer unto thee burnt ... Ps 66:15
I *w* offer bullocks with goats ... Ps 66:15
I *w* declare what he hath done for ... Ps 66:16
my heart, the Lord *w* not hear me ... Ps 66:18
the LORD *w* dwell in it for ever ... Ps 68:16
I *w* bring again from Bashan ... Ps 68:22
I *w* bring my people again from ... Ps 68:22
I *w* praise the name of God with a ... Ps 69:30
w magnify him with thanksgiving ... Ps 69:30
For God *w* save Zion ... Ps 69:35
w build the cities of Judah ... Ps 69:35
But I *w* hope continually ... Ps 71:14
w yet praise thee more and more ... Ps 71:14
I *w* go in the strength of the ... Ps 71:16
I *w* make mention of thy ... Ps 71:16
I *w* also praise thee with the ... Ps 71:22
unto thee *w* I sing with the harp, ... Ps 71:22
If I say, I *w* speak thus ... Ps 73:15
congregation I *w* judge uprightly ... Ps 75:2
But I *w* declare for ever ... Ps 75:9
I *w* sing praises to the God of ... Ps 75:9
of the wicked also *w* I cut off ... Ps 75:10
W the Lord cast off for ever ... Ps 77:7
w he be favourable no more ... Ps 77:7
but I *w* remember the years of the ... Ps 77:10
I *w* remember the works of the ... Ps 77:11
surely I *w* remember thy wonders ... Ps 77:11
I *w* meditate also of all thy work ... Ps 77:12
I *w* open my mouth in a parable ... Ps 78:2
I *w* utter dark sayings of old ... Ps 78:2
We *w* not hide them from their ... Ps 78:4
sheep of thy pasture *w* give thee ... Ps 79:13
we *w* shew forth thy praise to all ... Ps 79:13
So *w* not we go back from thee ... Ps 80:18
us, and we *w* call upon thy name ... Ps 80:18
people, and I *w* testify unto thee ... Ps 81:8
thy mouth wide, and I *w* fill it ... Ps 81:10
How long *w* ye judge unjustly, and ... Ps 82:2
neither *w* they understand ... Ps 82:5
they *w* be still praising thee ... Ps 84:4
the LORD *w* give grace and glory ... Ps 84:11
no good thing *w* he withhold from ... Ps 84:11
I *w* hear what God the ... Ps 85:8
God the LORD *w* speak ... Ps 85:8
for he *w* speak peace unto his ... Ps 85:8
of my trouble I *w* call upon thee ... Ps 86:7
I *w* walk in thy truth ... Ps 86:11
I *w* praise thee, O Lord my God, ... Ps 86:12
I *w* glorify thy name for evermore ... Ps 86:12
I *w* make mention of Rahab and ... Ps 87:4
I *w* sing of the mercies of the ... Ps 89:1
with my mouth *w* I make known thy ... Ps 89:1
Thy seed *w* I establish for ever, ... Ps 89:4
I *w* beat down his foes before his ... Ps 89:23
I *w* set his hand also in the sea, ... Ps 89:25
Also I *w* make him my firstborn, ... Ps 89:27
My mercy *w* I keep for him for ... Ps 89:28
His seed also *w* I make to endure ... Ps 89:29
Then *w* I visit their ... Ps 89:32
w I not utterly take from him ... Ps 89:33
My covenant *w* I not break ... Ps 89:34
that I *w* not lie unto David ... Ps 89:35
I *w* say of the LORD, He is my ... Ps 91:2
in him *w* I trust ... Ps 91:2
therefore *w* I deliver him ... Ps 91:14
I *w* set him on high, because he ... Ps 91:14
call upon me, and I *w* answer him ... Ps 91:15
I *w* be with him in trouble ... Ps 91:15
I *w* deliver him, and honour him ... Ps 91:15
With long life *w* I satisfy him ... Ps 91:16
I *w* triumph in the works of thy ... Ps 92:4
and ye fools, when *w* ye be wise ... Ps 94:8
For the LORD *w* not cast off his ... Ps 94:14
people, neither *w* he forsake his ... Ps 94:14
Who *w* rise up for me against the ... Ps 94:16
or who *w* stand up for me against ... Ps 94:16
To day if ye *w* hear his voice, ... Ps 95:7
I *w* sing of mercy and judgment ... Ps 101:1
unto thee, O LORD, *w* I sing ... Ps 101:1
I *w* behave myself wisely in a ... Ps 101:2
I *w* walk within my house with a ... Ps 101:2
I *w* set no wicked thing before ... Ps 101:3
I *w* not know a wicked person ... Ps 101:4
his neighbour, him *w* I cut off ... Ps 101:5
and a proud heart *w* not I suffer ... Ps 101:5
I *w* early destroy all the wicked ... Ps 101:8
He *w* regard the prayer of the ... Ps 102:17
He *w* not always chide ... Ps 103:9
neither *w* he keep his anger for ... Ps 103:9
I *w* sing unto the LORD as long as ... Ps 104:33
I *w* sing praise to my God while I ... Ps 104:33
I *w* be glad in the LORD ... Ps 104:34
Unto thee *w* I give the land of ... Ps 105:11
w observe these things, even they ... Ps 107:43
I *w* sing and give praise, even ... Ps 108:1
I myself *w* awake early ... Ps 108:2
I *w* praise thee, O LORD, among ... Ps 108:3
I *w* sing praises unto thee among ... Ps 108:3
I *w* rejoice, I *w* divide ... Ps 108:7
over Edom *w* I cast out my shoe ... Ps 108:9
over Philistia *w* I triumph ... Ps 108:9
Who *w* bring me into the strong ... Ps 108:10
who *w* lead me into Edom ... Ps 108:10
I *w* greatly praise the LORD with ... Ps 109:30

yea, I *w* praise him among the ... Ps 109:30
w not repent, Thou art a priest ... Ps 110:4
I *w* praise the LORD with my whole ... Ps 111:1
he *w* ever be mindful of his ... Ps 111:5
he *w* guide his affairs with ... Ps 112:5
he *w* bless us ... Ps 115:12
he *w* bless the house of Israel ... Ps 115:12
he *w* bless the house of Aaron ... Ps 115:12
He *w* bless them that fear the ... Ps 115:13
But we *w* bless the LORD from this ... Ps 115:18
therefore *w* I call upon him as ... Ps 116:2
I *w* walk before the LORD in the ... Ps 116:9
I *w* take the cup of salvation, and ... Ps 116:13
I *w* pay my vows unto the LORD now ... Ps 116:14
I *w* offer to thee the sacrifice ... Ps 116:17
w call upon the name of the LORD ... Ps 116:17
I *w* pay my vows unto the LORD now ... Ps 116:18
I *w* not fear ... Ps 118:6
name of the LORD *w* I destroy them ... Ps 118:10
name of the LORD I *w* destroy them ... Ps 118:11
name of the LORD I *w* destroy them ... Ps 118:12
I *w* go into them ... Ps 118:19
I *w* praise the LORD ... Ps 118:19
I *w* praise thee ... Ps 118:21
we *w* rejoice and be glad in it ... Ps 118:24
art my God, and I *w* praise thee ... Ps 118:28
thou art my God, I *w* exalt thee ... Ps 118:28
I *w* praise thee with uprightness ... Ps 119:7
I *w* keep thy statutes ... Ps 119:8
I *w* meditate in thy precepts, and ... Ps 119:15
I *w* delight myself in thy ... Ps 119:16
I *w* not forget thy word ... Ps 119:16
I *w* run the way of thy ... Ps 119:32
And I *w* walk at liberty ... Ps 119:45
I *w* speak of thy testimonies also ... Ps 119:46
before kings, and *w* not be ashamed ... Ps 119:46
I *w* delight myself in thy ... Ps 119:47
My hands also *w* I lift up unto ... Ps 119:48
I *w* meditate in thy statutes ... Ps 119:48
At midnight I *w* rise to give ... Ps 119:62
but I *w* keep thy precepts with my ... Ps 119:69
They that fear thee *w* be glad ... Ps 119:74
but I *w* meditate in thy precepts ... Ps 119:78
I *w* never forget thy precepts ... Ps 119:93
but I *w* consider thy testimonies ... Ps 119:95
I *w* perform it ... Ps 119:106
that I *w* keep thy righteous ... Ps 119:106
for I *w* keep the commandments of ... Ps 119:115
I *w* have respect unto thy ... Ps 119:117
so *w* I keep thy precepts ... Ps 119:134
I *w* keep thy statutes ... Ps 119:145
I *w* lift up mine eyes unto the ... Ps 121:1
He *w* not suffer thy foot to be ... Ps 121:3
that keepeth thee *w* not slumber ... Ps 121:3
I *w* now say, Peace be within thee ... Ps 122:8
LORD our God I *w* seek thy good ... Ps 122:9
Surely I *w* not come into the ... Ps 132:3
I *w* not give sleep to mine eyes, ... Ps 132:4
We *w* go into his tabernacles ... Ps 132:7
we *w* worship at his footstool ... Ps 132:7
he *w* not turn from it ... Ps 132:11
thy body *w* I set upon thy throne ... Ps 132:11
If thy children *w* keep my ... Ps 132:12
here *w* I dwell ... Ps 132:14
I *w* abundantly bless her ... Ps 132:15
I *w* satisfy her poor with bread ... Ps 132:15
I *w* also clothe her priests with ... Ps 132:16
There *w* I make the horn of David ... Ps 132:17
His enemies *w* I clothe with shame ... Ps 132:18
For the LORD *w* judge his people, ... Ps 135:14
he *w* repent himself concerning ... Ps 135:14
I *w* praise thee with my whole ... Ps 138:1
before the gods *w* I sing praise ... Ps 138:1
I *w* worship toward thy holy ... Ps 138:2
The LORD *w* perfect that which ... Ps 138:8
I *w* praise thee ... Ps 139:14
I know that the LORD *w* maintain ... Ps 140:12
Teach me to do thy *w* ... Ps 143:10 7522
I *w* sing a new song unto thee, O ... Ps 144:9
w I sing praises unto thee ... Ps 144:9
I *w* extol thee, my God, O king ... Ps 145:1
I *w* bless thy name for ever and ... Ps 145:1
Every day *w* I bless thee ... Ps 145:2
I *w* praise thy name for ever and ... Ps 145:2
I *w* speak of the glorious honour ... Ps 145:5
I *w* declare thy greatness ... Ps 145:6
He *w* fulfil the desire of them ... Ps 145:19
he also *w* hear their cry ... Ps 145:19
and *w* save them ... Ps 145:19
but all the wicked *w* he destroy ... Ps 145:20
While I live *w* I praise the LORD ... Ps 146:2
I *w* sing praises unto my God ... Ps 146:2
he *w* beautify the meek with ... Ps 149:4
A wise man *w* hear ... Prov 1:5
and *w* increase learning ... Prov 1:5
simple ones, *w* ye love simplicity ... Prov 1:22
I *w* pour out my spirit unto you, ... Prov 1:23
I *w* make known my words unto you ... Prov 1:23
I also *w* laugh at your calamity ... Prov 1:26
I *w* mock when your fear cometh ... Prov 1:26
call upon me, but I *w* not answer ... Prov 1:28
come again, and to morrow I *w* give ... Prov 3:28
the adulteress *w* hunt for the ... Prov 6:26
therefore he *w* not spare in the ... Prov 6:34
He *w* not regard any ransom ... Prov 6:35
neither *w* he rest content, though ... Prov 6:35
w come home at the day appointed ... Prov 7:20
for I *w* speak of excellent things ... Prov 8:6

and I *w* fill their treasures ... Prov 8:21
a wise man, and he *w* love thee ... Prov 9:8
a wise man, and he *w* be yet wiser ... Prov 9:9
he *w* increase in learning ... Prov 9:9
The LORD *w* not suffer the soul of ... Prov 10:3
The wise in heart *w* receive ... Prov 10:8
of wicked devices *w* he condemn ... Prov 12:2
A faithful witness *w* not lie ... Prov 14:5
but a false witness *w* utter lies ... Prov 14:5
neither *w* he go unto the wise ... Prov 15:12
The LORD *w* destroy the house of ... Prov 15:25
but he *w* establish the border of ... Prov 15:25
but a wise man *w* pacify it ... Prov 16:14
The spirit of a man *w* sustain his ... Prov 18:14
Many *w* intreat the favour of the ... Prov 19:6
he hath given *w* he pay him again ... Prov 19:17
w not so much as bring it to his ... Prov 19:24
a scorner, and the simple *w* beware ... Prov 19:25
he *w* understand knowledge ... Prov 19:25
but every fool *w* be meddling ... Prov 20:3
The sluggard *w* not plow by reason ... Prov 20:4
of understanding *w* draw it out ... Prov 20:5
Most men *w* proclaim every one his ... Prov 20:6
Say not thou, I *w* recompense evil ... Prov 20:22
he turneth it whithersoever he *w* ... Prov 21:1 2654
is old, he *w* not depart from it ... Prov 22:6
For the LORD *w* plead their cause, ... Prov 22:23
for he *w* despise the wisdom of ... Prov 23:9
I *w* seek it yet again ... Prov 23:35
I *w* do so to him as he hath done ... Prov 24:29
I *w* render to the man according ... Prov 24:29
a stone, it *w* return upon him ... Prov 26:27
yet *w* not his foolishness depart ... Prov 27:22
it for him that *w* pity the poor ... Prov 28:8
of bread that man *w* transgress ... Prov 28:21
A servant *w* not be corrected by ... Prov 29:19
he understand he *w* not answer ... Prov 29:19
She *w* do him good and not evil all ... Prov 31:12
I *w* prove thee with mirth, ... Eccl 2:1
the one *w* lift up his fellow ... Eccl 4:10
who *w* no more be admonished ... Eccl 4:13 3045
rich *w* not suffer him to sleep ... Eccl 5:12
the living *w* lay it to his heart ... Eccl 7:2
I said, I *w* be wise ... Eccl 7:23
Surely the serpent *w* bite without ... Eccl 10:11
of a fool *w* swallow up himself ... Eccl 10:12
God *w* bring thee into judgment ... Eccl 11:9
Draw me, we *w* run after thee ... Song 1:4
we *w* be glad and rejoice in thee, ... Song 1:4
we *w* remember thy love more than ... Song 1:4
We *w* make thee borders of gold ... Song 1:11
I *w* rise now, and go about the ... Song 3:2
in the broad ways I *w* seek him ... Song 3:2
I *w* get me to the mountain of ... Song 4:6
What *w* ye see in the Shulamite ... Song 6:13
I *w* go up to the palm tree ... Song 7:8
I *w* take hold of the boughs ... Song 7:8
there *w* I give thee my loves ... Song 7:12
we *w* build upon her a palace of ... Song 8:9
we *w* inclose her with boards of ... Song 8:9
ye *w* revolt more and more ... Is 1:5
I *w* hide mine eyes from you ... Is 1:15
make many prayers, I *w* not hear ... Is 1:15
I *w* ease me of mine adversaries, ... Is 1:24
I *w* turn my hand upon thee, and ... Is 1:25
I *w* restore thy judges as at the ... Is 1:26
he *w* teach us of his ways ... Is 2:3
and we *w* walk in his paths ... Is 2:3
I *w* give children to be their ... Is 3:4
saying, I *w* not be an healer ... Is 3:7
The LORD *w* enter into judgment ... Is 3:14
Therefore the Lord *w* smite with a ... Is 3:17
the LORD *w* discover their secret ... Is 3:17
In that day the Lord *w* take away ... Is 3:18
We *w* eat our own bread, and wear ... Is 4:1
the LORD *w* create upon every ... Is 4:5
Now *w* I sing to my wellbeloved a ... Is 5:1
I *w* tell you what I *w* do to my ... Is 5:5
I *w* take away the hedge thereof, ... Is 5:5
And I *w* lay it waste ... Is 5:6
I *w* also command the clouds that ... Is 5:6
he *w* lift up an ensign to the ... Is 5:26
w hiss unto them from the end of ... Is 5:26
shall I send, and who *w* go for us ... Is 6:8
If ye *w* not believe, surely ye ... Is 7:9
I *w* not ask, neither *w* I tempt ... Is 7:12
but *w* ye weary my God also ... Is 7:13
I *w* wait upon the LORD, that ... Is 8:17
of Jacob, and I *w* look for him ... Is 8:17
the LORD of hosts *w* perform this ... Is 9:7
but we *w* build with hewn stones ... Is 9:10
but we *w* change them into cedars ... Is 9:10
Therefore the LORD *w* cut off from ... Is 9:14
what *w* ye do in the day of ... Is 10:3
to whom *w* ye flee for help ... Is 10:3
where *w* ye leave your glory ... Is 10:3
I *w* send him against an ... Is 10:6
of my wrath *w* I give him a charge ... Is 10:6
I *w* punish the fruit of the stout ... Is 10:12
say, O LORD, I *w* praise thee ... Is 12:1
I *w* trust, and not be afraid ... Is 12:2
I *w* punish the world for their ... Is 13:11
I *w* cause the arrogancy of the ... Is 13:11
w lay low the haughtiness of the ... Is 13:11
I *w* make a man more precious than ... Is 13:12
Therefore I *w* shake the heavens, ... Is 13:13
I *w* stir up the Medes against ... Is 13:17
For the LORD *w* have mercy on ... Is 14:1

w yet choose Israel, and set them ... Is 14:1
I *w* ascend into heaven ... Is 14:13
I *w* exalt my throne above the ... Is 14:13
I *w* sit also upon the mount of ... Is 14:13
I *w* ascend above the heights of ... Is 14:14
I *w* be like the most High ... Is 14:14
For I *w* rise up against them, ... Is 14:22
I *w* also make it a possession for ... Is 14:23
I *w* sweep it with the besom of ... Is 14:23
That I *w* break the Assyrian in my ... Is 14:25
I *w* kill thy root with famine, and ... Is 14:30
for I *w* bring more upon Dimon, ... Is 15:9
Therefore I *w* bewail with the ... Is 16:9
I *w* water thee with my tears, O ... Is 16:9
I *w* take my rest ... Is 18:4
I *w* consider in my dwelling place ... Is 18:4
I *w* set the Egyptians against the ... Is 19:2
I *w* destroy the counsel thereof ... Is 19:3
the Egyptians *w* I give over into ... Is 19:4
if ye *w* enquire, enquire ye ... Is 21:12
I *w* weep bitterly, labour not to ... Is 22:4
the LORD *w* carry thee away with a ... Is 22:17
captivity, and *w* surely cover thee ... Is 22:17
He *w* surely violently turn and ... Is 22:18
I *w* drive thee from thy station, ... Is 22:19
that I *w* call my servant Eliakim ... Is 22:20
I *w* clothe him with thy robe, and ... Is 22:21
I *w* commit thy government into ... Is 22:21
David *w* I lay upon his shoulder ... Is 22:22
I *w* fasten him as a nail in a ... Is 22:23
years, that the LORD *w* visit Tyre ... Is 23:17
I *w* exalt thee, I *w* praise thy ... Is 25:1
he *w* destroy in this mountain the ... Is 25:7
He *w* swallow up death in victory ... Is 25:8
the Lord GOD *w* wipe away tears ... Is 25:8
waited for him, and he *w* save us ... Is 25:9
we *w* be glad and rejoice in his ... Is 25:9
salvation *w* God appoint for walls ... Is 26:1
within me *w* I seek thee early ... Is 26:9
the world *w* learn righteousness ... Is 26:9
yet *w* he not learn righteousness ... Is 26:10
of uprightness *w* he deal unjustly ... Is 26:10
w not behold the majesty of the ... Is 26:10
hand is lifted up, they *w* not see ... Is 26:11
but by thee only *w* we make ... Is 26:13
I *w* water it every moment ... Is 27:3
hurt it, I *w* keep it night and day ... Is 27:3
them *w* not have mercy on them ... Is 27:11
formed them *w* shew them no favour ... Is 27:11
another tongue *w* he speak to this ... Is 28:11
Judgment also *w* I lay to the line ... Is 28:17
because he *w* not ever be ... Is 28:28
Yet I *w* distress Ariel, and there ... Is 29:2
I *w* camp against thee round about ... Is 29:3
w lay siege against thee with a ... Is 29:3
I *w* raise forts against thee ... Is 29:3
I *w* proceed to do a marvellous ... Is 29:14
they *w* carry their riches upon ... Is 30:6
children that *w* not hear the law ... Is 30:9 14
for we *w* flee upon horses ... Is 30:16
and, We *w* ride upon the swift ... Is 30:16
therefore *w* the LORD wait, that ... Is 30:18
therefore *w* he be exalted, that ... Is 30:18
he *w* be very gracious unto thee ... Is 30:19
shall hear it, he *w* answer thee ... Is 30:19
of shaking *w* he fight with it ... Is 30:32
w bring evil, and *w* not call ... Is 31:2
but *w* arise against the house of ... Is 31:2
he *w* not be afraid of their voice ... Is 31:4
so *w* the LORD of hosts defend ... Is 31:5
defending also he *w* deliver it ... Is 31:5
and passing over he *w* preserve it ... Is 31:5
the vile person *w* speak villany ... Is 32:6
his heart *w* work iniquity, to ... Is 32:6
he *w* cause the drink of the ... Is 32:6
Now *w* I rise, saith the LORD ... Is 33:10
now *w* I be exalted ... Is 33:10
now *w* I lift up myself ... Is 33:10
w be unto us a place of broad ... Is 33:21
he *w* save us ... Is 33:22
your God *w* come with vengeance, ... Is 35:4
he *w* come and save you ... Is 35:4
it *w* go into his hand, and pierce ... Is 36:6
I *w* give thee two thousand horses ... Is 36:8
The LORD *w* surely deliver us ... Is 36:15
saying, The LORD *w* deliver us ... Is 36:18
It may be the LORD thy God *w* hear ... Is 37:4
w reprove the words which the ... Is 37:4
I *w* send a blast upon him, and he ... Is 37:7
I *w* cause him to fall by the ... Is 37:7
I *w* cut down the tall cedars ... Is 37:24
I *w* enter into the height of his ... Is 37:24
therefore *w* I put my hook in thy ... Is 37:29
I *w* turn thee back by the way by ... Is 37:29
For I *w* defend this city to save ... Is 37:35
I *w* add unto thy days fifteen ... Is 38:5
I *w* deliver thee and this city out ... Is 38:6
and I *w* defend this city ... Is 38:6
that the LORD *w* do this thing ... Is 38:7
I *w* bring again the shadow of the ... Is 38:8
he *w* cut me off with pining ... Is 38:12
so *w* he break all my bones ... Is 38:13
therefore we *w* sing my songs to ... Is 38:20
the Lord GOD *w* come with strong ... Is 40:10
To whom then *w* ye liken God ... Is 40:18
or what likeness *w* ye compare ... Is 40:18
chooseth a tree that *w* not rot ... Is 40:20
To whom then *w* ye liken me ... Is 40:25

I *w* strengthen thee ... Is 41:10
yea, I *w* help thee ... Is 41:10
I *w* uphold thee with the right ... Is 41:10
thy God *w* hold thy right hand ... Is 41:13
I *w* help thee ... Is 41:13
I *w* help thee, saith the LORD, and ... Is 41:14
I *w* make thee a new sharp ... Is 41:15
thirst, I the LORD *w* hear them ... Is 41:17
God of Israel *w* not forsake them ... Is 41:17
I *w* open rivers in high places, ... Is 41:18
I *w* make the wilderness a pool of ... Is 41:18
I *w* plant in the wilderness the ... Is 41:19
I *w* set in the desert the fir ... Is 41:19
I *w* give to Jerusalem one that ... Is 41:27
w hold thine hand ... Is 42:6
w keep thee, and give thee for a ... Is 42:6
my glory *w* I not give to another, ... Is 42:8
now *w* I cry like a travailing ... Is 42:14
I *w* destroy and devour at once ... Is 42:14
I *w* make waste mountains and hills ... Is 42:15
I *w* make the rivers islands ... Is 42:15
and I *w* dry up the pools ... Is 42:15
I *w* bring the blind by a way that ... Is 42:16
I *w* lead them in paths that they ... Is 42:16
I *w* make darkness light before ... Is 42:16
These things *w* I do unto them, and ... Is 42:16
he *w* magnify the law, and make it ... Is 42:21
Who among you *w* give ear to this ... Is 42:23
who *w* hearken and hear for the ... Is 42:23
the waters, I *w* be with thee ... Is 43:2
therefore *w* I give men for thee, ... Is 43:4
I *w* bring thy seed from the east, ... Is 43:5
I *w* say to the north, Give up ... Is 43:6
I *w* work, and who shall let it ... Is 43:13
Behold, I *w* do a new thing ... Is 43:19
I *w* even make a way in the ... Is 43:19
sake, and *w* not remember thy sins ... Is 43:25
from the womb, which *w* help thee ... Is 44:2
For I *w* pour water upon him that ... Is 44:3
I *w* pour my spirit upon thy seed, ... Is 44:3
for he *w* take thereof, and warm ... Is 44:15
I *w* raise up the decayed places ... Is 44:26
Be dry, and I *w* dry up thy rivers ... Is 44:27
I *w* loose the loins of kings, to ... Is 45:1
I *w* go before thee, and make the ... Is 45:2
I *w* break in pieces the gates of ... Is 45:2
I *w* give thee the treasures of ... Is 45:3
and I *w* direct all his ways ... Is 45:13
even to hoar hairs *w* I carry you ... Is 46:4
I have made, and I *w* bear ... Is 46:4
I *w* carry, and *w* deliver you ... Is 46:4
To whom *w* ye liken me, and make me ... Is 46:5
stand, and I *w* do all my pleasure ... Is 46:10
I *w* also bring it to pass ... Is 46:11
have purposed it, I *w* also do it ... Is 46:11
I *w* place salvation in Zion for ... Is 46:13
I *w* take vengeance ... Is 47:3
I *w* not meet thee as a man ... Is 47:3
and *w* not ye declare it ... Is 48:6
name's sake *w* I defer mine anger ... Is 48:9
for my praise *w* I refrain for ... Is 48:9
even for mine own sake, *w* I do it ... Is 48:11
I *w* not give my glory unto ... Is 48:11
he *w* do his pleasure on Babylon, ... Is 48:14
Israel, in whom I *w* be glorified ... Is 49:3
I *w* also give thee for a light to ... Is 49:6
I *w* preserve thee, and give thee ... Is 49:8
I *w* make all my mountains a way, ... Is 49:11
w have mercy upon his afflicted ... Is 49:13
forget, yet *w* I not forget thee ... Is 49:15
I *w* lift up mine hand to the ... Is 49:22
for I *w* contend with him that ... Is 49:25
thee, and I *w* save thy children ... Is 49:25
I *w* feed them that oppress thee ... Is 49:26
For the Lord GOD *w* help me ... Is 50:7
who *w* contend with me ... Is 50:8
Behold, the Lord GOD *w* help me ... Is 50:9
he *w* comfort all her waste places ... Is 51:3
he *w* make her wilderness like ... Is 51:3
I *w* make my judgment to rest for ... Is 51:4
But I *w* put it into the hand of ... Is 51:23
for the LORD *w* go before you ... Is 52:12
God of Israel *w* be your rereward ... Is 52:12
Therefore *w* I divide him a ... Is 53:12
great mercies *w* I gather thee ... Is 54:7
kindness *w* I have mercy on thee ... Is 54:8
I *w* lay thy stones with fair ... Is 54:11
I *w* make thy windows of agates, ... Is 54:12
I *w* make an everlasting covenant ... Is 55:3
LORD, and he *w* have mercy upon him ... Is 55:7
for he *w* abundantly pardon ... Is 55:7
Even unto them *w* I give in mine ... Is 56:5
I *w* give them an everlasting name ... Is 56:5
Even them *w* I bring to my holy ... Is 56:7
Yet *w* I gather others to him, ... Is 56:8
I *w* fetch wine ... Is 56:12
we *w* fill ourselves with strong ... Is 56:12
I *w* declare thy righteousness, and ... Is 57:12
For I *w* not contend for ever, ... Is 57:16
neither *w* I be always wroth ... Is 57:16
have seen his ways, and *w* heal him ... Is 57:18
I *w* lead him also, and restore ... Is 57:18
and I *w* heal him ... Is 57:19
I *w* cause thee to ride upon the ... Is 58:14
face from you, that he *w* not hear ... Is 59:2
deeds, accordingly he *w* repay ... Is 59:18
the islands he *w* repay recompence ... Is 59:18
I *w* glorify the house of my glory ... Is 60:7
kingdom that *w* not serve thee ... Is 60:12
I *w* make the place of my feet ... Is 60:13
thee, I *w* make thee an eternal ... Is 60:15
For brass I *w* bring gold, and for ... Is 60:17
for iron I *w* bring silver, and for ... Is 60:17
I *w* also make thy officers peace, ... Is 60:17
I the LORD *w* hasten it in his ... Is 60:22
I *w* direct their work in truth, ... Is 61:8
I *w* make an everlasting covenant ... Is 61:8
I *w* greatly rejoice in the LORD, ... Is 61:10
so the Lord GOD *w* cause ... Is 61:11
For Zion's sake *w* I not hold my ... Is 62:1
for Jerusalem's sake I *w* not rest ... Is 62:1
Surely I *w* no more give thy corn ... Is 62:8
for I *w* tread them in mine anger, ... Is 63:3
and I *w* stain all my raiment ... Is 63:3
I *w* tread down the people in mine ... Is 63:6
I *w* bring down their strength to ... Is 63:6
I *w* mention the lovingkindnesses ... Is 63:7
people, children that *w* not lie ... Is 63:8
I *w* not keep silence ... Is 65:6
but *w* recompense, even recompense ... Is 65:6
therefore *w* I measure their ... Is 65:7
so *w* I do for my servants' sakes, ... Is 65:8
I *w* bring forth a seed out of ... Is 65:9
Therefore *w* I number you to the ... Is 65:12
I *w* rejoice in Jerusalem, and joy ... Is 65:19
that before they call, I *w* answer ... Is 65:24
they are yet speaking, I *w* hear ... Is 65:24
but to this man *w* I look, even to ... Is 66:2
I also *w* choose their delusions, ... Is 66:4
w bring their fears upon them ... Is 66:4
I *w* extend peace to her like a ... Is 66:12
comforteth, so *w* I comfort you ... Is 66:13
the LORD *w* come with fire, and ... Is 66:15
by his sword *w* the LORD plead ... Is 66:16
that I *w* gather all nations and ... Is 66:18
I *w* set a sign among them ... Is 66:19
I *w* send those that escape of ... Is 66:19
I *w* also take of them for priests ... Is 66:21
and the new earth, which I *w* make ... Is 66:22
for I *w* hasten my word to perform ... Jer 1:12
I *w* call all the families of the ... Jer 1:15
I *w* utter my judgments against ... Jer 1:16
Wherefore I *w* yet plead with you, ... Jer 2:9
children's children *w* I plead ... Jer 2:9
thou saidst, I *w* not transgress ... Jer 2:20
seek her *w* not weary themselves ... Jer 2:24
strangers, and after them *w* I go ... Jer 2:25
time of their trouble they *w* say ... Jer 2:27
Wherefore *w* ye plead with me ... Jer 2:29
we *w* come no more unto thee ... Jer 2:31
I *w* plead with thee, because thou ... Jer 2:35
W he reserve his anger for ever ... Jer 3:5
w he keep it to the end ... Jer 3:5
I *w* not cause mine anger to fall ... Jer 3:12
I *w* not keep anger for ever ... Jer 3:12
I *w* take you one of a city, and ... Jer 3:14
family, and I *w* bring you to Zion ... Jer 3:14
I *w* give you pastors according to ... Jer 3:15
I *w* heal your backslidings ... Jer 3:22
for I *w* bring evil from the north ... Jer 4:6
now also *w* I give sentence ... Jer 4:12
yet *w* I not make a full end ... Jer 4:27
w not repent ... Jer 4:28
neither *w* I turn back from it ... Jer 4:28
thy lovers *w* despise thee, they ... Jer 4:30
thee, they *w* seek thy life ... Jer 4:30
and I *w* pardon it ... Jer 5:1
I *w* get me unto the great ... Jer 5:5
and *w* speak unto them ... Jer 5:5
I *w* make my words in thy mouth ... Jer 5:14
I *w* bring a nation upon you from ... Jer 5:15
I *w* not make a full end with you ... Jer 5:18
w ye not tremble at my presence, ... Jer 5:22
what *w* ye do in the end thereof ... Jer 5:31
I *w* pour it out upon the children ... Jer 6:11
for I *w* stretch out my hand upon ... Jer 6:12
they said, We *w* not walk therein ... Jer 6:16
But they said, We *w* not hearken ... Jer 6:17
I *w* bring evil upon this people, ... Jer 6:19
I *w* lay stumblingblocks before ... Jer 6:21
I *w* cause you to dwell in this ... Jer 7:3
Then *w* I cause you to dwell in ... Jer 7:7
W ye steal, murder, and commit ... Jer 7:9
Therefore *w* I do unto this house, ... Jer 7:14
I *w* cast you out of my sight, as ... Jer 7:15
for I *w* not hear thee ... Jer 7:16
I *w* be your God, and ye shall be ... Jer 7:23
but they *w* not hearken to thee ... Jer 7:27
but they *w* not answer thee ... Jer 7:27
Then *w* I cause to cease from the ... Jer 7:34
Therefore *w* I give their wives ... Jer 8:10
I *w* surely consume them, saith ... Jer 8:13
I *w* send serpents, cockatrices, ... Jer 8:17
which *w* not be charmed, and they ... Jer 8:17
every brother *w* utterly supplant ... Jer 9:4
every neighbour *w* walk with ... Jer 9:4
they *w* deceive every one his ... Jer 9:5
and *w* not speak the truth ... Jer 9:5
I *w* melt them, and try them ... Jer 9:7
For the mountains *w* I take up a ... Jer 9:10
I *w* make Jerusalem heaps, and a ... Jer 9:11
I *w* make the cities of Judah ... Jer 9:11
I *w* feed them, even this people, ... Jer 9:15
I *w* scatter them also among the ... Jer 9:16
I *w* send a sword after them, till ... Jer 9:16
that I *w* punish all them which ... Jer 9:25
I *w* sling out the inhabitants of ... Jer 10:18
w distress them, that they may ... Jer 10:18
be my people, and I *w* be your God ... Jer 11:4
therefore I *w* bring upon them all ... Jer 11:8
I *w* bring evil upon them, which ... Jer 11:11
I *w* not hearken unto them ... Jer 11:11
for I *w* not hear them in the time ... Jer 11:14
of hosts, Behold, I *w* punish them ... Jer 11:22
for I *w* bring evil upon the men ... Jer 11:23
I *w* pluck them out of their land, ... Jer 12:14
have plucked them out I *w* return ... Jer 12:15
w bring them again, every man to ... Jer 12:15
if they *w* diligently learn the ... Jer 12:16
But if they *w* not obey ... Jer 12:17
I *w* utterly pluck up and destroy ... Jer 12:17
After this manner *w* I mar the ... Jer 13:9
I *w* fill all the inhabitants of ... Jer 13:13
I *w* dash them one against another ... Jer 13:14
I *w* not pity, nor spare, nor have ... Jer 13:14
But if ye *w* not hear it, my soul ... Jer 13:17
Therefore *w* I scatter them as the ... Jer 13:24
Therefore *w* I discover thy skirts ... Jer 13:26
he *w* now remember their iniquity, ... Jer 14:10
they fast, I *w* not hear their cry ... Jer 14:12
an oblation, I *w* not accept them ... Jer 14:12
but I *w* consume them by the sword ... Jer 14:12
but I *w* give you assured peace in ... Jer 14:13
for I *w* pour their wickedness ... Jer 14:16
therefore we *w* wait upon thee ... Jer 14:22
I *w* appoint over them four kinds, ... Jer 15:3
I *w* cause them to be removed into ... Jer 15:4
therefore *w* I stretch out my hand ... Jer 15:6
I *w* fan them with a fan in the ... Jer 15:7
I *w* bereave them of children ... Jer 15:7
I *w* destroy my people, since they ... Jer 15:7
the residue of them *w* I deliver ... Jer 15:9
verily I *w* cause the enemy to ... Jer 15:11
thy treasures *w* I give to the ... Jer 15:13
I *w* make thee to pass with thine ... Jer 15:14
then *w* I bring thee again, and ... Jer 15:19
I *w* make thee unto this people a ... Jer 15:20
I *w* deliver thee out of the hand ... Jer 15:21
I *w* redeem thee out of the hand ... Jer 15:21
I *w* cause to cease out of this ... Jer 16:9
Therefore *w* I cast you out of ... Jer 16:13
where I *w* not shew you favour ... Jer 16:13
I *w* bring them again into their ... Jer 16:15
I *w* send for many fishers, saith ... Jer 16:16
after *w* I send for many hunters, ... Jer 16:16
first I *w* recompense their ... Jer 16:18
I *w* this once cause them to know, ... Jer 16:21
I *w* cause them to know mine hand ... Jer 16:21
I *w* give thy substance and all thy ... Jer 17:3
I *w* cause thee to serve thine ... Jer 17:4
But if ye *w* not hearken unto me ... Jer 17:27
then *w* I kindle a fire in the ... Jer 17:27
there I *w* cause thee to hear my ... Jer 18:2
I *w* repent of the evil that I ... Jer 18:8
then I *w* repent of the good, ... Jer 18:10
but we *w* walk after our own ... Jer 18:12
we *w* every one do the imagination ... Jer 18:12
W a man leave the snow of Lebanon ... Jer 18:14
I *w* scatter them as with an east ... Jer 18:17
I *w* shew them the back, and not ... Jer 18:17
I *w* bring evil upon this place, ... Jer 19:3
I *w* make void the counsel of ... Jer 19:7
I *w* cause them to fall by the ... Jer 19:7
their carcases *w* I give to be ... Jer 19:7
I *w* make this city desolate, and ... Jer 19:8
I *w* cause them to eat the flesh ... Jer 19:9
Even so *w* I break this people and ... Jer 19:11
Thus *w* I do unto this place, ... Jer 19:12
I *w* bring upon this city and upon ... Jer 19:15
I *w* make thee a terror to thyself ... Jer 20:4
I *w* give all Judah into the hand ... Jer 20:4
Moreover I *w* deliver all the ... Jer 20:5
w I give into the hand of their ... Jer 20:5
I *w* not make mention of him, nor ... Jer 20:9
say they, and we *w* report it ... Jer 20:10
Peradventure he *w* be enticed ... Jer 20:10
if so be that the LORD *w* deal ... Jer 21:2
I *w* turn back the weapons of war ... Jer 21:4
I *w* assemble them into the midst ... Jer 21:4
I myself *w* fight against you with ... Jer 21:5
I *w* smite the inhabitants of this ... Jer 21:6
I *w* deliver Zedekiah king of ... Jer 21:7
But I *w* punish you according to ... Jer 21:14
I *w* kindle a fire in the forest ... Jer 21:14
But if ye *w* not hear these words, ... Jer 22:5
yet surely I *w* make thee a ... Jer 22:6
I *w* prepare destroyers against ... Jer 22:7
I *w* build me a wide house and ... Jer 22:14
but thou saidst, I *w* not hear ... Jer 22:21
I *w* give thee into the hand of ... Jer 22:25
I *w* cast thee out, and thy mother ... Jer 22:26
I *w* visit upon you the evil of ... Jer 23:2
I *w* gather the remnant of my ... Jer 23:3
w bring them again to their folds ... Jer 23:3
I *w* set up shepherds over them ... Jer 23:4
that I *w* raise unto David a ... Jer 23:5
for I *w* bring evil upon them, ... Jer 23:12
I *w* feed them with wormwood, and ... Jer 23:15
I *w* even forsake you, saith the ... Jer 23:33
I *w* even punish that man and his ... Jer 23:34
w utterly forget you ... Jer 23:39
I *w* forsake you, and the city that ... Jer 23:39
I *w* bring an everlasting reproach ... Jer 23:40
so *w* I acknowledge them that are ... Jer 24:5

For I *w* set mine eyes upon them ... Jer 24:6
I *w* bring them again to this land ... Jer 24:6
I *w* build them, and not pull them ... Jer 24:6
I *w* plant them, and not pluck them ... Jer 24:6
I *w* give them an heart to know me ... Jer 24:7
be my people, and I *w* be their God ... Jer 24:7
So *w* I give Zedekiah the king of ... Jer 24:8
I *w* deliver them to be removed ... Jer 24:9
I *w* send the sword, the famine, ... Jer 24:10
and I *w* do you no hurt ... Jer 25:6
I *w* send and take all the families ... Jer 25:9
w bring them against this land, ... Jer 25:9
w utterly destroy them, and make ... Jer 25:9
Moreover I *w* take from them the ... Jer 25:10
that I *w* punish the king of ... Jer 25:12
w make it perpetual desolations ... Jer 25:12
I *w* bring upon that land all my ... Jer 25:13
I *w* recompense them according to ... Jer 25:14
sword that I *w* send among them ... Jer 25:16
sword which I *w* send among you ... Jer 25:27
for I *w* call for a sword upon all ... Jer 25:29
he *w* plead with all flesh ... Jer 25:31
he *w* give them that are wicked to ... Jer 25:31
If so be they *w* hearken, and turn ... Jer 26:3
If ye *w* not hearken to me, to ... Jer 26:4
Then *w* I make this house like ... Jer 26:6
w make this city a curse to all ... Jer 26:6
the LORD *w* repent him of the evil ... Jer 26:13
kingdom which *w* not serve the ... Jer 27:8
that *w* not put their neck under ... Jer 27:8
Babylon, that nation *w* I punish ... Jer 27:8
those *w* I let remain still in ... Jer 27:11
Why *w* ye die, thou and thy people, ... Jer 27:13
w not serve the king of Babylon ... Jer 27:13
then *w* I bring them up, and ... Jer 27:22
Within two full years *w* I bring ... Jer 28:3
I *w* bring again to this place ... Jer 28:4
for I *w* break the yoke of the ... Jer 28:4
Even so *w* I break the yoke of ... Jer 28:11
I *w* cast thee from off the face ... Jer 28:16
at Babylon I *w* visit you, and ... Jer 29:10
unto me, and I *w* hearken unto you ... Jer 29:12
I *w* be found of you, saith the ... Jer 29:14
I *w* turn away your captivity, and ... Jer 29:14
I *w* gather you from all the ... Jer 29:14
I *w* bring you again into the ... Jer 29:14
I *w* send upon them the sword, the ... Jer 29:17
w make them like vile figs, that ... Jer 29:17
I *w* persecute them with the sword ... Jer 29:18
w deliver them to be removed to ... Jer 29:18
I *w* deliver them into the hand of ... Jer 29:21
Behold, I *w* punish Shemaiah the ... Jer 29:32
good that I *w* do for my people ... Jer 29:32
LORD, that I *w* bring again the ... Jer 30:3
I *w* cause them to return to the ... Jer 30:3
that I *w* break his yoke from off ... Jer 30:8
w burst thy bonds, and strangers ... Jer 30:8
whom I *w* raise up unto them ... Jer 30:9
I *w* save thee from afar, and thy ... Jer 30:10
yet *w* I not make a full end of ... Jer 30:11
but I *w* correct thee in measure, ... Jer 30:11
w not leave thee altogether ... Jer 30:11
upon thee *w* I give for a prey ... Jer 30:16
For I *w* restore health unto thee, ... Jer 30:17
I *w* heal thee of thy wounds, ... Jer 30:17
I *w* bring again the captivity of ... Jer 30:18
I *w* multiply them, and they shall ... Jer 30:19
I *w* also glorify them, and they ... Jer 30:19
I *w* punish all that oppress them ... Jer 30:20
I *w* cause him to draw near, and he ... Jer 30:21
be my people, and I *w* be your God ... Jer 30:22
w I be the God of all the ... Jer 31:1
Again I *w* build thee, and thou ... Jer 31:4
I *w* bring them from the north ... Jer 31:8
with supplications *w* I lead them ... Jer 31:9
I *w* cause them to walk by the ... Jer 31:9
scattered Israel *w* gather him ... Jer 31:10
for I *w* turn their mourning into ... Jer 31:13
w comfort them, and make them ... Jer 31:13
I *w* satiate the soul of the ... Jer 31:14
I *w* surely have mercy upon him, ... Jer 31:20
that I *w* sow the house of Israel ... Jer 31:27
so *w* I watch over them, to build, ... Jer 31:28
that I *w* make a new covenant with ... Jer 31:31
shall be the covenant that I *w* ... Jer 31:33
I *w* put my law in their inward ... Jer 31:33
w be their God, and they shall be ... Jer 31:33
for I *w* forgive their iniquity, ... Jer 31:34
I *w* remember their sin no more ... Jer 31:34
I *w* also cast off all the seed of ... Jer 31:37
I *w* give this city into the hand ... Jer 32:3
I *w* give this city into the hand ... Jer 32:28
I *w* gather them out of all ... Jer 32:37
I *w* bring them again unto this ... Jer 32:37
I *w* cause them to dwell safely ... Jer 32:37
be my people, and I *w* be their God ... Jer 32:38
I *w* give them one heart, and one ... Jer 32:39
I *w* make an everlasting covenant ... Jer 32:40
that I *w* not turn away from them, ... Jer 32:40
but I *w* put my fear in their ... Jer 32:40
I *w* rejoice over them to do them ... Jer 32:41
I *w* plant them in this land ... Jer 32:41
so *w* I bring upon them all the ... Jer 32:42
for I *w* cause their captivity to ... Jer 32:44 7522
I *w* answer thee, and shew thee ... Jer 33:3
I *w* bring it health and cure ... Jer 33:6
I *w* cure them, and *w* reveal ... Jer 33:6
I *w* cause the captivity of Judah ... Jer 33:7
w build them, as at the first ... Jer 33:7
I *w* cleanse them from all their ... Jer 33:8
I *w* pardon all their iniquities, ... Jer 33:8
For I *w* cause to return the ... Jer 33:11
that I *w* perform that good thing ... Jer 33:14
time, *w* I cause the Branch of ... Jer 33:15
so *w* I multiply the seed of David ... Jer 33:22
Then *w* I cast away the seed of ... Jer 33:26
so that I *w* not take any of his ... Jer 33:26
for I *w* cause their captivity to ... Jer 33:26
I *w* give this city into the hand ... Jer 34:2
they *w* lament thee, saying, Ah ... Jer 34:5
I *w* make you to be removed into ... Jer 34:17
I *w* give the men that have ... Jer 34:18
I *w* even give them into the hand ... Jer 34:20
his princes *w* I give into the ... Jer 34:21
I *w* command, saith the LORD, and ... Jer 34:22
I *w* make the cities of Judah a ... Jer 34:22
But they said, We *w* drink no wine ... Jer 35:6
W ye not receive instruction to ... Jer 35:13
I *w* bring upon Judah and upon all ... Jer 35:17
Judah *w* hear all the evil which I ... Jer 36:3
It may be they *w* present their ... Jer 36:7
w return every one from his evil ... Jer 36:7
We *w* surely tell the king of all ... Jer 36:16
I *w* punish him and his seed and his ... Jer 36:31
I *w* bring upon them, and upon the ... Jer 36:31
Jeremiah, I *w* ask thee a thing ... Jer 38:14
I *w* not put thee to death, ... Jer 38:16
neither *w* I give thee into the ... Jer 38:16
we *w* not put thee to death ... Jer 38:25
I *w* bring my words upon this city ... Jer 39:16
But I *w* deliver thee in that day, ... Jer 39:17
For I *w* surely deliver thee, and ... Jer 39:18
and I *w* look well unto thee ... Jer 40:4
I *w* dwell at Mizpah to serve the ... Jer 40:10
Chaldeans, which *w* come unto us ... Jer 40:10
I *w* slay Ishmael the son of ... Jer 40:15
I *w* pray unto the LORD your God ... Jer 42:4
you, I *w* declare it unto you ... Jer 42:4
I *w* keep nothing back from you ... Jer 42:4
we *w* obey the voice of the LORD ... Jer 42:6
If ye *w* still abide in this land, ... Jer 42:10
then *w* I build you, and not pull ... Jer 42:10
I *w* plant you, and not pluck you ... Jer 42:10
I *w* shew mercies unto you, that ... Jer 42:12
We *w* not dwell in this land, ... Jer 42:13
but we *w* go into the land of ... Jer 42:14
and there *w* we dwell ... Jer 42:14
the evil that I *w* bring upon them ... Jer 42:17
so declare unto us, and we *w* do it ... Jer 42:20
I *w* send and take Nebuchadrezzar ... Jer 43:10
w set his throne upon these ... Jer 43:10
I *w* kindle a fire in the houses ... Jer 43:12
I *w* set my face against you for ... Jer 44:11
I *w* take the remnant of Judah, ... Jer 44:12
For I *w* punish them that dwell in ... Jer 44:13
we *w* not hearken unto thee ... Jer 44:16
But we *w* certainly do whatsoever ... Jer 44:17
We *w* surely perform our vows that ... Jer 44:25
ye *w* surely accomplish your vows, ... Jer 44:25
I *w* watch over them for evil, and ... Jer 44:27
that I *w* punish you in this place ... Jer 44:29
I *w* give Pharaoh-hophra king of ... Jer 44:30
which I have built *w* I break down ... Jer 45:4
which I have planted I *w* pluck up ... Jer 45:4
I *w* bring evil upon all flesh, ... Jer 45:5
but thy life *w* I give unto thee ... Jer 45:5
I *w* go up, and *w* cover the ... Jer 46:8
I *w* destroy the city and the ... Jer 46:8
I *w* punish the multitude of No, ... Jer 46:25
I *w* deliver them into the hand of ... Jer 46:26
I *w* save thee from afar off, and ... Jer 46:27
for I *w* make a full end of all ... Jer 46:28
but I *w* not make a full end of ... Jer 46:28
yet *w* I not leave thee wholly ... Jer 46:28
for the LORD *w* spoil the ... Jer 47:4
how long *w* it be ere thou be ... Jer 47:6
that I *w* send unto him wanderers, ... Jer 48:12
Therefore *w* I howl for Moab ... Jer 48:31
I *w* cry out for all Moab ... Jer 48:31
I *w* weep for thee with the ... Jer 48:32
Moreover I *w* cause to cease in ... Jer 48:35
for I *w* bring upon it, even upon ... Jer 48:44
Yet *w* I bring again the captivity ... Jer 48:47
that I *w* cause an alarm of war to ... Jer 49:2
I *w* bring a fear upon thee, saith ... Jer 49:5
afterward I *w* bring again the ... Jer 49:6
for I *w* bring the calamity of ... Jer 49:8
him, the time that I *w* visit him ... Jer 49:8
they *w* destroy till they have ... Jer 49:9
children, I *w* preserve them alive ... Jer 49:11
I *w* make thee small among the ... Jer 49:15
I *w* bring thee down from thence, ... Jer 49:16
but I *w* suddenly make him run ... Jer 49:19
who *w* appoint me the time ... Jer 49:19
shepherd that *w* stand before me ... Jer 49:19
I *w* kindle a fire in the wall of ... Jer 49:27
I *w* scatter into all winds them ... Jer 49:32
I *w* bring their calamity from all ... Jer 49:32
I *w* break the bow of Elam, the ... Jer 49:35
upon Elam *w* I bring the four ... Jer 49:36
w scatter them toward all those ... Jer 49:36
For I *w* cause Elam to be dismayed ... Jer 49:37
I *w* bring evil upon them, even my ... Jer 49:37
I *w* send the sword after them, ... Jer 49:37
I *w* set my throne in Elam, and ... Jer 49:38
w destroy from thence the king and ... Jer 49:38
days, that I *w* bring again the ... Jer 49:39
I *w* raise and cause to come up ... Jer 50:9
I *w* punish the king of Babylon and ... Jer 50:18
I *w* bring Israel again to his ... Jer 50:19
for I *w* pardon them whom I ... Jer 50:20
the time that I *w* visit thee ... Jer 50:31
I *w* kindle a fire in his cities, ... Jer 50:32
are cruel, and *w* not shew mercy ... Jer 50:42
but I *w* make them suddenly run ... Jer 50:44
who *w* appoint me the time ... Jer 50:44
shepherd that *w* stand before me ... Jer 50:44
I *w* raise up against Babylon, and ... Jer 51:1
w send unto Babylon fanners, that ... Jer 51:2
he *w* render unto her a recompence ... Jer 51:6
Surely I *w* fill thee with men, as ... Jer 51:14
for with thee *w* I break in pieces ... Jer 51:20
with thee *w* I destroy kingdoms ... Jer 51:20
with thee *w* I break in pieces the ... Jer 51:21
with thee *w* I break in pieces the ... Jer 51:21
With thee also *w* I break in ... Jer 51:22
with thee *w* I break in pieces old ... Jer 51:22
with thee *w* I break in pieces the ... Jer 51:22
I *w* also break in pieces with ... Jer 51:23
with thee *w* I break in pieces the ... Jer 51:23
with thee *w* I break in pieces ... Jer 51:23
I *w* render unto Babylon and to all ... Jer 51:24
I *w* stretch out mine hand upon ... Jer 51:25
w make thee a burnt mountain ... Jer 51:25
I *w* plead thy cause, and take ... Jer 51:36
I *w* dry up her sea, and make her ... Jer 51:36
In their heat I *w* make their ... Jer 51:39
I *w* make them drunken, that they ... Jer 51:39
I *w* bring them down like lambs to ... Jer 51:40
I *w* punish Bel in Babylon ... Jer 51:44
I *w* bring forth out of his mouth ... Jer 51:44
that I *w* do judgment upon the ... Jer 51:47
that I *w* do judgment upon her ... Jer 51:52
I *w* make drunk her princes, and ... Jer 51:57
the evil that I *w* bring upon her ... Jer 51:64
therefore *w* I hope in him ... Lam 3:24
For the Lord *w* not cast off for ... Lam 3:31
grief, yet *w* he have compassion ... Lam 3:32
he *w* no more regard them ... Lam 4:16
he *w* no more carry thee away into ... Lam 4:22
he *w* visit thine iniquity, O ... Lam 4:22
he *w* discover thy sins ... Lam 4:22
thy feet, and I *w* speak unto thee ... Eze 2:1
And they, whether they *w* hear ... Eze 2:5
or whether they *w* forbear ... Eze 2:5
unto them, whether they *w* hear ... Eze 2:7
or whether they *w* forbear ... Eze 2:7
of Israel *w* not hearken unto thee ... Eze 3:7 14
for they *w* not hearken unto me ... Eze 3:7 14
whether they *w* hear ... Eze 3:11
or whether they *w* forbear ... Eze 3:11
but his blood *w* I require at ... Eze 3:18
but his blood *w* I require at ... Eze 3:20
and I *w* there talk with thee ... Eze 3:22
I *w* make thy tongue cleave to the ... Eze 3:26
I *w* open thy mouth, and thou shalt ... Eze 3:27
I *w* lay bands upon thee, and thou ... Eze 4:8
Gentiles, whither I *w* drive them ... Eze 4:13
I *w* break the staff of bread in ... Eze 4:16
I *w* draw out a sword after them ... Eze 5:2
w execute judgments in the midst ... Eze 5:8
I *w* do in thee that which I have ... Eze 5:9
whereunto I *w* not do any more the ... Eze 5:9
I *w* execute judgments in thee, and ... Eze 5:10
the whole remnant of thee *w* I ... Eze 5:10
therefore *w* I also diminish thee ... Eze 5:11
neither *w* I have any pity ... Eze 5:11
I *w* scatter a third part into all ... Eze 5:12
I *w* draw out a sword after them ... Eze 5:12
I *w* cause my fury to rest upon ... Eze 5:13
upon them, and I *w* be comforted ... Eze 5:13
Moreover I *w* make thee waste, and ... Eze 5:14
which I *w* send to destroy you ... Eze 5:16
I *w* increase the famine upon you, ... Eze 5:16
w break your staff of bread ... Eze 5:16
So *w* I send upon you famine and ... Eze 5:17
I *w* bring the sword upon thee ... Eze 5:17
w bring a sword upon you ... Eze 6:3
I *w* destroy your high places ... Eze 6:3
I *w* cast down your slain men ... Eze 6:4
I *w* lay the dead carcases of the ... Eze 6:5
I *w* scatter your bones round ... Eze 6:5
Yet *w* I leave a remnant, that ye ... Eze 6:8
thus *w* I accomplish my fury upon ... Eze 6:12
So *w* I stretch out my hand upon ... Eze 6:14
I *w* send mine anger upon thee, and ... Eze 7:3
w judge thee according to thy ... Eze 7:3
w recompense upon thee all thine ... Eze 7:3
spare thee, neither *w* I have pity ... Eze 7:4
but I *w* recompense thy ways upon ... Eze 7:4
Now *w* I shortly pour out my fury ... Eze 7:8
I *w* judge thee according to thy ... Eze 7:8
w recompense thee for all thine ... Eze 7:8
not spare, neither *w* I have pity ... Eze 7:9
I *w* recompense thee according to ... Eze 7:9
I *w* give it into the hands of the ... Eze 7:21
My face *w* I turn also from them, ... Eze 7:22
Wherefore I *w* bring the worst of ... Eze 7:24
I *w* also make the pomp of the ... Eze 7:24
I *w* do unto them after their way, ... Eze 7:27
to their deserts *w* I judge them ... Eze 7:27
Therefore *w* I also deal in fury ... Eze 8:18
not spare, neither *w* I have pity ... Eze 8:18
loud voice, yet *w* I not hear them ... Eze 8:18

neither *w* I have pity Eze 9:10
but I *w* recompense their way upon Eze 9:10
but I *w* bring you forth out of Eze 11:7
I *w* bring a sword upon you, saith Eze 11:8
I *w* bring you out of the midst Eze 11:9
w execute judgments among you Eze 11:9
I *w* judge you in the border of Eze 11:10
but I *w* judge you in the border Eze 11:11
yet *w* I be to them as a little Eze 11:16
I *w* even gather you from the Eze 11:17
I *w* give you the land of Israel Eze 11:17
I *w* give them one heart Eze 11:19
I *w* put a new spirit within you Eze 11:19
I *w* take the stony heart out of Eze 11:19
w give them an heart of flesh Eze 11:19
be my people, and I *w* be their God Eze 11:20
I *w* recompense their way upon Eze 11:21
it may be they *w* consider Eze 12:3
My net also *w* I spread upon him, Eze 12:13
I *w* bring him to Babylon to the Eze 12:13
I *w* scatter toward every wind all Eze 12:14
I *w* draw out the sword after them Eze 12:14
But I *w* leave a few men of them Eze 12:16
I *w* make this proverb to cease, Eze 12:23
I *w* speak, and the word that I Eze 12:25
w I say the word Eze 12:25
w perform it, saith the Lord GOD Eze 12:25
I *w* even rend it with a stormy Eze 13:13
So *w* I break down the wall that Eze 13:14
Thus *w* I accomplish my wrath upon Eze 13:15
w say unto you, The wall is no Eze 13:15
W ye hunt the souls of my people, Eze 13:18
w ye save the souls alive that Eze 13:18
w ye pollute me among my people Eze 13:19
I *w* tear them from your arms, and Eze 13:20
w let the souls go, even the Eze 13:20
Your kerchiefs also *w* I tear Eze 13:21
for I *w* deliver my people out of Eze 13:23
I the LORD *w* answer him that Eze 14:4
I the LORD *w* answer him by myself Eze 14:7
I *w* set my face against that man, Eze 14:8
w make him a sign and a proverb, Eze 14:8
I *w* cut him off from the midst of Eze 14:8
I *w* stretch out my hand upon him, Eze 14:9
w destroy him from the midst of Eze 14:9
then *w* I stretch out mine hand Eze 14:13
w break the staff of the bread Eze 14:13
w send famine upon it Eze 14:13
w cut off man and beast from it Eze 14:13
or *w* men take a pin of it to hang Eze 15:3
so *w* I give the inhabitants of Eze 15:6
I *w* set my face against them Eze 15:7
I *w* make the land desolate, Eze 15:8
unto the *w* of them that hate thee Eze 16:27 5315
therefore I *w* gather all thy Eze 16:37
I *w* even gather them round about Eze 16:37
w discover thy nakedness unto Eze 16:37
I *w* judge thee, as women that Eze 16:38
I *w* give thee blood in fury and Eze 16:38
I *w* also give thee into their Eze 16:39
I *w* cause thee to cease from Eze 16:41
So *w* I make my fury toward thee Eze 16:42
I *w* be quiet Eze 16:42
and *w* be no more angry Eze 16:42
therefore I also *w* recompense thy Eze 16:43
then *w* I bring again the Eze 16:53
I *w* even deal with thee as thou Eze 16:59
Nevertheless I *w* remember my Eze 16:60
I *w* establish unto thee an Eze 16:60
I *w* give them unto thee for Eze 16:61
I *w* establish my covenant with Eze 16:62
even it *w* I recompense upon his Eze 17:19
I *w* spread my net upon him, and he Eze 17:20
I *w* bring him to Babylon Eze 17:20
w plead with him there for his Eze 17:20
I *w* also take of the highest Eze 17:22
of the high cedar, and *w* set it Eze 17:22
I *w* crop off from the top of his Eze 17:22
w plant it upon an high mountain Eze 17:22
the height of Israel *w* I plant it Eze 17:23
But if the wicked *w* turn from all Eze 18:21
Therefore I *w* judge you, O house Eze 18:30
for why *w* ye die, O house of Eze 18:31
I *w* not be enquired of by you Eze 20:3
I *w* pour out my fury upon them, Eze 20:8
I *w* not be enquired of by you Eze 20:31
We *w* be as the heathen, as the Eze 20:32
poured out, *w* I rule over you Eze 20:33
I *w* bring you out from the people Eze 20:34
w gather you out of the countries Eze 20:34
I *w* bring you into the wilderness Eze 20:35
there *w* I plead with you face to Eze 20:35
so *w* I plead with you, saith the Eze 20:36
I *w* cause you to pass under the Eze 20:37
I *w* bring you into the bond of Eze 20:37
I *w* purge out from among you the Eze 20:38
I *w* bring them forth out of the Eze 20:38
if ye *w* not hearken unto me Eze 20:39
there *w* I accept them Eze 20:40
there *w* I require your offerings, Eze 20:40
I *w* accept you with your sweet Eze 20:41
I *w* be sanctified in you before Eze 20:41
I *w* kindle a fire in thee, and it Eze 20:47
w draw forth my sword out of his Eze 21:3
w cut off from thee the righteous Eze 21:3
Seeing then that I *w* cut off from Eze 21:4
I *w* also smite mine hands Eze 21:17
I *w* cause my fury to rest Eze 21:17
but he *w* call to remembrance the Eze 21:23
I *w* overturn, overturn, overturn, Eze 21:27
and I *w* give it him Eze 21:27
I *w* judge thee in the place where Eze 21:30
I *w* pour out mine indignation Eze 21:31
I *w* blow against thee in the fire Eze 21:31
LORD have spoken it, and *w* do it Eze 22:14
I *w* scatter thee among the Eze 22:15
w consume thy filthiness out of Eze 22:15
therefore I *w* gather you into the Eze 22:19
so *w* I gather you in mine anger Eze 22:20
I *w* leave you there, and melt you Eze 22:20
I *w* gather you, and blow upon you Eze 22:21
I *w* raise up thy lovers against Eze 23:22
I *w* bring them against thee on Eze 23:22
I *w* set judgment before them, and Eze 23:24
I *w* set my jealousy against thee, Eze 23:25
Thus *w* I make thy lewdness to Eze 23:27
I *w* deliver thee into the hand of Eze 23:28
I *w* do these things unto thee, Eze 23:30
therefore *w* I give her cup into Eze 23:31
W they now commit whoredoms with Eze 23:43
I *w* bring up a company upon them, Eze 23:46
w give them to be removed and Eze 23:46
Thus *w* I cause lewdness to cease Eze 23:48
I *w* even make the pile for fire Eze 24:9
shall come to pass, and I *w* do it Eze 24:14
I *w* not go back Eze 24:14
not go back, neither *w* I spare Eze 24:14
w I spare, neither *w* I repent Eze 24:14
I *w* profane my sanctuary, the Eze 24:21
therefore I *w* deliver thee to the Eze 25:4
I *w* make Rabbah a stable for Eze 25:5
therefore I *w* stretch out mine Eze 25:7
w deliver thee for a spoil to the Eze 25:7
I *w* cut thee off from the people, Eze 25:7
I *w* cause thee to perish out of Eze 25:7
I *w* destroy thee Eze 25:7
I *w* open the side of Moab from Eze 25:9
w give them in possession, that Eze 25:10
I *w* execute judgments upon Moab Eze 25:11
I *w* also stretch out mine hand Eze 25:13
w cut off man and beast from it Eze 25:13
I *w* make it desolate from Teman Eze 25:13
I *w* lay my vengeance upon Edom by Eze 25:14
I *w* stretch out mine hand upon Eze 25:16
I *w* cut off the Cherethims, and Eze 25:16
I *w* execute great vengeance upon Eze 25:17
w cause many nations to come up Eze 26:3
I *w* also scrape her dust from her Eze 26:4
Behold, I *w* bring upon Tyrus Eze 26:7
I *w* cause the noise of thy songs Eze 26:13
I *w* make thee like the top of a Eze 26:14
I *w* make thee a terror, and thou Eze 26:21
therefore I *w* bring strangers Eze 28:7
therefore I *w* cast thee as Eze 28:16
I *w* destroy thee, O covering Eze 28:16
I *w* cast thee to the ground Eze 28:17
I *w* lay thee before kings, that Eze 28:17
therefore *w* I bring forth a fire Eze 28:18
I *w* bring thee to ashes upon the Eze 28:18
I *w* be glorified in the midst of Eze 28:22
For I *w* send into her pestilence, Eze 28:23
But I *w* put hooks in thy jaws, and Eze 29:4
I *w* cause the fish of thy rivers Eze 29:4
I *w* bring thee up out of the Eze 29:4
I *w* leave thee thrown into the Eze 29:5
I *w* bring a sword upon thee, and Eze 29:8
I *w* make the land of Egypt Eze 29:10
I *w* make the land of Egypt Eze 29:12
I *w* scatter the Egyptians among Eze 29:12
w disperse them through the Eze 29:12
At the end of forty years *w* I Eze 29:13
I *w* bring again the captivity of Eze 29:14
w cause them to return into the Eze 29:14
for I *w* diminish them, that they Eze 29:15
I *w* give the land of Egypt unto Eze 29:19
In that day *w* I cause the horn of Eze 29:21
I *w* give thee the opening of the Eze 29:21
I *w* also make the multitude of Eze 30:10
I *w* make the rivers dry, and sell Eze 30:12
I *w* make the land waste, and all Eze 30:12
I *w* also destroy the idols Eze 30:13
I *w* cause their images to cease Eze 30:13
I *w* put a fear in the land of Eze 30:13
I *w* make Pathros desolate, and Eze 30:14
w set fire in Zoan Eze 30:14
w execute judgments in No Eze 30:14
I *w* pour my fury upon Sin, the Eze 30:15
I *w* cut off the multitude of No Eze 30:15
And I *w* set fire in Egypt Eze 30:16
Thus *w* I execute judgments in Eze 30:19
w break his arms, the strong, and Eze 30:22
I *w* cause the sword to fall out Eze 30:22
I *w* scatter the Egyptians among Eze 30:23
w disperse them through the Eze 30:23
I *w* strengthen the arms of the Eze 30:24
but I *w* break Pharaoh's arms, and Eze 30:24
But I *w* strengthen the arms of Eze 30:25
I *w* scatter the Egyptians among Eze 30:26
I *w* therefore spread out my net Eze 32:3
Then *w* I leave thee upon the land Eze 32:4
I *w* cast thee forth upon the open Eze 32:4
w cause all the fowls of the Eze 32:4
I *w* fill the beasts of the whole Eze 32:4
I *w* lay thy flesh upon the Eze 32:5
I *w* also water with thy blood the Eze 32:6
I *w* cover the heaven, and make the Eze 32:7
I *w* cover the sun with a cloud, Eze 32:7
of heaven *w* I make dark over thee Eze 32:8
I *w* also vex the hearts of many Eze 32:9
I *w* make many people amazed at Eze 32:10
By the swords of the mighty *w* I Eze 32:12
I *w* destroy also all the beasts Eze 32:13
Then *w* I make their waters deep, Eze 32:14
but his blood *w* I require at the Eze 33:6
but his blood *w* I require at Eze 33:8
for why *w* ye die, O house of Eze 33:11
I *w* judge you every one after his Eze 33:20
w I give to the beasts to be Eze 33:27
For I *w* lay the land most Eze 33:28
thy words, but they *w* not do them Eze 33:31
it *w* come,) then shall they know Eze 33:33
I *w* require my flock at their Eze 34:10
for I *w* deliver my flock from Eze 34:10
w both search my sheep, and seek Eze 34:11
so *w* I seek out my sheep Eze 34:12
w deliver them out of all places Eze 34:12
I *w* bring them out from the Eze 34:13
w bring them to their own land, Eze 34:13
I *w* feed them in a good pasture, Eze 34:14
I *w* feed my flock Eze 34:15
I *w* cause them to lie down, saith Eze 34:15
I *w* seek that which was lost, and Eze 34:16
w bind up that which was broken, Eze 34:16
w strengthen that which was sick Eze 34:16
but I *w* destroy the fat and the Eze 34:16
I *w* feed them with judgment Eze 34:16
w judge between the fat cattle and Eze 34:20
Therefore *w* I save my flock, and Eze 34:22
I *w* judge between cattle and Eze 34:22
I *w* set up one shepherd over them Eze 34:23
I the LORD *w* be their God, and my Eze 34:24
I *w* make with them a covenant of Eze 34:25
w cause the evil beasts to cease Eze 34:25
I *w* make them and the places round Eze 34:26
I *w* cause the shower to come down Eze 34:26
I *w* raise up for them a plant of Eze 34:29
I *w* stretch out mine hand against Eze 35:3
I *w* make thee most desolate Eze 35:3
I *w* lay thy cities waste, and thou Eze 35:4
I *w* prepare thee unto blood, and Eze 35:6
Thus *w* I make mount Seir most Eze 35:7
I *w* fill his mountains with his Eze 35:8
I *w* make thee perpetual Eze 35:9
shall be mine, and we *w* possess it Eze 35:10
I *w* even do according to thine Eze 35:11
I *w* make myself known among them, Eze 35:11
rejoiceth, I *w* make thee desolate Eze 35:14
was desolate, so *w* I do unto thee Eze 35:15
I *w* turn unto you, and ye shall be Eze 36:9
I *w* multiply men upon you, all Eze 36:10
I *w* multiply upon you man and Eze 36:11
I *w* settle you after your old Eze 36:11
w do better unto you than at your Eze 36:11
I *w* cause men to walk upon you, Eze 36:12
Neither *w* I cause men to hear in Eze 36:15
I *w* sanctify my great name, which Eze 36:23
For I *w* take you from among the Eze 36:24
w bring you into your own land Eze 36:24
Then *w* I sprinkle clean water Eze 36:25
all your idols, *w* I cleanse you Eze 36:25
A new heart also *w* I give you Eze 36:26
a new spirit *w* I put within you Eze 36:26
I *w* take away the stony heart out Eze 36:26
I *w* give you an heart of flesh Eze 36:26
I *w* put my spirit within you, and Eze 36:27
be my people, and I *w* be your God Eze 36:28
I *w* also save you from all your Eze 36:29
I *w* call for the corn Eze 36:29
w increase it, and lay no famine Eze 36:29
I *w* multiply the fruit of the Eze 36:30
w also cause you to dwell in the Eze 36:33
LORD have spoken it, and I *w* do it Eze 36:36
I *w* yet for this be enquired of Eze 36:37
I *w* increase them with men like a Eze 36:37
I *w* cause breath to enter into Eze 37:5
I *w* lay sinews upon you Eze 37:6
w bring up flesh upon you, and Eze 37:6
I *w* open your graves, and cause Eze 37:12
I *w* take the stick of Joseph, Eze 37:19
w put them with him, even with Eze 37:19
I *w* take the children of Israel Eze 37:21
w gather them on every side, and Eze 37:21
I *w* make them one nation in the Eze 37:22
but I *w* save them out of all Eze 37:23
have sinned, and *w* cleanse them Eze 37:23
be my people, and I *w* be their God Eze 37:23
Moreover I *w* make a covenant of Eze 37:26
I *w* place them, and multiply them, Eze 37:26
w set my sanctuary in the midst Eze 37:26
I *w* be their God, and they shall Eze 37:27
I *w* turn thee back, and put hooks Eze 38:4
I *w* bring thee forth, and all Eze 38:4
I *w* go up to the land of unwalled Eze 38:11
I *w* go to them that are at rest, Eze 38:11
I *w* bring thee against my land, Eze 38:16
I *w* call for a sword against him Eze 38:21
I *w* plead against him with Eze 38:22
I *w* rain upon him, and upon his Eze 38:22
Thus *w* I magnify myself, and Eze 38:23
I *w* be known in the eyes of many Eze 38:23
I *w* turn thee back, and leave but Eze 39:2
w cause thee to come up from the Eze 39:2
w bring thee upon the mountains Eze 39:2
I *w* smite thy bow out of thy left Eze 39:3

w cause thine arrows to fall out Eze 39:3
I *w* give thee unto the ravenous Eze 39:4
I *w* send a fire on Magog, and Eze 39:6
So *w* I make my holy name known in Eze 39:7
I *w* not let them pollute my holy Eze 39:7
that I *w* give unto Gog a place Eze 39:11
I *w* set my glory among the Eze 39:21
Now *w* I bring again the captivity Eze 39:25
w be jealous for my holy name Eze 39:25
Neither *w* I hide my face any more Eze 39:29
where I *w* dwell in the midst of Eze 43:7
I *w* dwell in the midst of them Eze 43:9
I *w* accept you, saith the Lord Eze 43:27
But I *w* make them keepers of the Eze 44:14
we *w* shew the interpretation Dan 2:4
if ye *w* not make known unto me Dan 2:5
we *w* shew the interpretation of Dan 2:7
But if ye *w* not make known unto Dan 2:9
I *w* shew unto the king the Dan 2:24
that *w* make known unto the king Dan 2:25
we *w* tell the interpretation Dan 2:36
he *w* deliver us out of thine hand Dan 3:17
that we *w* not serve thy gods, nor Dan 3:18
and giveth it to whomsoever he *w* Dan 4:17 6634
and giveth it to whomsoever he *w* Dan 4:25 6634
and giveth it to whomsoever he *w* Dan 4:32 6634
to his *w* in the army of heaven Dan 4:35 6634
he *w* shew the interpretation Dan 5:12
yet I *w* read the writing unto the Dan 5:17
over it whomsoever he *w* Dan 5:21 6634
continually, he *w* deliver thee Dan 6:16
but he did according to his *w* Dan 8:4 7522
I *w* make thee know what shall be Dan 8:19
now *w* I return to fight with the Dan 10:20
But I *w* shew thee that which is Dan 10:21
now *w* I shew thee the truth Dan 11:2
and do according to his *w* Dan 11:3 7522
shall do according to his own *w* Dan 11:16 7522
king shall do according to his *w* Dan 11:36 7522
I *w* avenge the blood of Jezreel Hos 1:4
w cause to cease the kingdom of Hos 1:4
that I *w* break the bow of Israel Hos 1:5
for I *w* no more have mercy upon Hos 1:6
but I *w* utterly take them away Hos 1:6
But I *w* have mercy upon the house Hos 1:7
w save them by the LORD their God Hos 1:7
w not save them by bow, nor by Hos 1:7
my people, and I *w* not be your God Hos 1:9
I *w* not have mercy upon her Hos 2:4
I *w* go after my lovers, that give Hos 2:5
I *w* hedge up thy way with thorns, Hos 2:6
I *w* go and return to my first Hos 2:7
Therefore *w* I return, and take Hos 2:9
w recover my wool and my flax Hos 2:9
now *w* I discover her lewdness in Hos 2:10
I *w* also cause all her mirth to Hos 2:11
I *w* destroy her vines and her fig Hos 2:12
I *w* make them a forest, and the Hos 2:12
I *w* visit upon her the days of Hos 2:13
I *w* allure her, and bring her into Hos 2:14
I *w* give her her vineyards from Hos 2:15
For I *w* take away the names of Hos 2:17
in that day *w* I make a covenant Hos 2:18
I *w* break the bow and the sword and Hos 2:18
w make them to lie down safely Hos 2:18
I *w* betroth thee unto me for ever Hos 2:19
I *w* betroth thee unto me in Hos 2:19
I *w* even betroth thee unto me in Hos 2:20
I *w* hear, saith the LORD Hos 2:21
I *w* hear the heavens, and they Hos 2:21
I *w* sow her unto me in the earth Hos 2:23
I *w* have mercy upon her that had Hos 2:23
I *w* say to them which were not my Hos 2:23
so *w* I also be for thee Hos 3:3
night, and I *w* destroy thy mother Hos 4:5
I *w* also reject thee, that thou Hos 4:6
I *w* also forget thy children Hos 4:6
therefore *w* I change their glory Hos 4:7
I *w* punish them for their ways, Hos 4:9
I *w* not punish your daughters Hos 4:14
now the LORD *w* feed them as a Hos 4:16
They *w* not frame their doings to Hos 5:4
therefore I *w* pour out my wrath Hos 5:10
Therefore *w* I be unto Ephraim as Hos 5:12
For I *w* be unto Ephraim as a lion Hos 5:14
I, even I, *w* tear and go away Hos 5:14
I *w* take away, and none shall Hos 5:14
I *w* go and return to my place, Hos 5:15
affliction they *w* seek me early Hos 5:15
for he hath torn, and he *w* heal us Hos 6:1
hath smitten, and he *w* bind us up Hos 6:1
After two days *w* he revive us Hos 6:2
in the third day he *w* raise us up Hos 6:2
I *w* spread my net upon them Hos 7:12
I *w* bring them down as the fowls Hos 7:12
I *w* chastise them, as their Hos 7:12
how long *w* it be ere they attain Hos 8:5
now *w* I gather them, and they Hos 8:10
now *w* he remember their iniquity, Hos 8:13
but I *w* send a fire upon his Hos 8:14
What *w* ye do in the solemn day, Hos 9:5
therefore he *w* remember their Hos 9:9
iniquity, he *w* visit their sins Hos 9:9
yet *w* I bereave them, that there Hos 9:12
I *w* drive them out of mine house Hos 9:15
I *w* love them no more Hos 9:15
yet *w* I slay even the beloved Hos 9:16
My God *w* cast them away, because Hos 9:17
I *w* make Ephraim to ride Hos 10:11
I *w* not execute the fierceness of Hos 11:9
I *w* not return to destroy Ephraim Hos 11:9
I *w* not enter into the city Hos 11:9
I *w* place them in their houses, Hos 11:11
w punish Jacob according to his Hos 12:2
to his doings *w* he recompense him Hos 12:2
Egypt *w* yet make thee to dwell in Hos 12:9
Therefore I *w* be unto them as a Hos 13:7
by the way *w* I observe them Hos 13:7
I *w* meet them as a bear that is Hos 13:8
w rend the caul of their heart, Hos 13:8
there *w* I devour them like a lion Hos 13:8
I *w* be thy king Hos 13:10 165
I *w* ransom them from the power of Hos 13:14
I *w* redeem them from death Hos 13:14
O death, I *w* be thy plagues Hos 13:14 165
O grave, I *w* be thy destruction Hos 13:14 165
so *w* we render the calves of our Hos 14:2
we *w* not ride upon horses Hos 14:3
neither *w* we say any more to the Hos 14:3
I *w* heal their backsliding Hos 14:4
I *w* love them freely Hos 14:4
I *w* be as the dew unto Israel Hos 14:5
O LORD, to thee *w* I cry Joel 1:19
Who knoweth if he *w* return Joel 2:14
Then *w* the LORD be jealous for Joel 2:18
Yea, the LORD *w* answer and say Joel 2:19
I *w* send you corn, and wine, and Joel 2:19
I *w* no more make you a reproach Joel 2:19
But I *w* remove far off from you Joel 2:20
w drive him into a land barren and Joel 2:20
for the LORD *w* do great things Joel 2:21
he *w* cause to come down for you Joel 2:23
I *w* restore to you the years that Joel 2:25
that I *w* pour out my spirit upon Joel 2:28
those days *w* I pour out my spirit Joel 2:29
I *w* shew wonders in the heavens Joel 2:30
I *w* also gather all nations, and Joel 3:2
w bring them down into the valley Joel 3:2
w plead with them there for my Joel 3:2
w ye render me a recompence Joel 3:4
and speedily *w* I return your Joel 3:4
I *w* raise them out of the place Joel 3:7
w return your recompence upon Joel 3:7
I *w* sell your sons and your Joel 3:8
for there *w* I sit to judge all Joel 3:12
but the LORD *w* be the hope of his Joel 3:16
For I *w* cleanse their blood that Joel 3:21
The LORD *w* roar from Zion, and Amos 1:2
I *w* not turn away the punishment Amos 1:3
But I *w* send a fire into the Amos 1:4
I *w* break also the bar of Amos 1:5
I *w* not turn away the punishment Amos 1:6
But I *w* send a fire on the wall Amos 1:7
I *w* cut off the inhabitant from Amos 1:8
I *w* turn mine hand against Ekron Amos 1:8
I *w* not turn away the punishment Amos 1:9
But I *w* send a fire on the wall Amos 1:10
I *w* not turn away the punishment Amos 1:11
But I *w* send a fire upon Teman, Amos 1:12
I *w* not turn away the punishment Amos 1:13
But I *w* kindle a fire in the wall Amos 1:14
I *w* not turn away the punishment Amos 2:1
But I *w* send a fire upon Moab, and Amos 2:2
I *w* cut off the judge from the Amos 2:3
w slay all the princes thereof Amos 2:3
I *w* not turn away the punishment Amos 2:4
But I *w* send a fire upon Judah, Amos 2:5
I *w* not turn away the punishment Amos 2:6
his father *w* go in unto the same Amos 2:7
therefore I *w* punish you for all Amos 3:2
W a lion roar in the forest, when Amos 3:4
w a young lion cry out of his den Amos 3:4
Surely the Lord GOD *w* do nothing Amos 3:7
lion hath roared, who *w* not fear Amos 3:8
of Israel upon him I *w* also visit Amos 3:14
I *w* smite the winter house with Amos 3:15
that he *w* take you away with Amos 4:2
Therefore thus *w* I do unto thee Amos 4:12
because I *w* do this unto thee, Amos 4:12
be that the LORD God of hosts *w* Amos 5:15
for I *w* pass through thee, saith Amos 5:17
I *w* not smell in your solemn Amos 5:21
offerings, I *w* not accept them Amos 5:22
neither *w* I regard the peace Amos 5:22
for I *w* not hear the melody of Amos 5:23
Therefore *w* I cause you to go Amos 5:27
therefore *w* I deliver up the city Amos 6:8
he *w* smite the great house with Amos 6:11
w one plow there with oxen Amos 6:12
I *w* raise up against you a nation Amos 6:14
I *w* set a plumbline in the midst Amos 7:8
I *w* not again pass by them any Amos 7:8
I *w* rise against the house of Amos 7:9
I *w* not again pass by them any Amos 8:2
When *w* the new moon be gone, that Amos 8:5
Surely I *w* never forget any of Amos 8:7
that I *w* cause the sun to go down Amos 8:9
I *w* darken the earth in the clear Amos 8:9
I *w* turn your feasts into Amos 8:10
I *w* bring up sackcloth upon all Amos 8:10
I *w* make it as the mourning of an Amos 8:10
that I *w* send a famine in the Amos 8:11
I *w* slay the last of them with Amos 9:1
thence *w* I bring them down Amos 9:2
I *w* search and take them out Amos 9:3
thence *w* I command the serpent, Amos 9:3
thence *w* I command the sword, and Amos 9:4
I *w* set mine eyes upon them for Amos 9:4
I *w* destroy it from off the face Amos 9:8
saving that I *w* not utterly Amos 9:8
I *w* command Amos 9:9
I *w* sift the house of Israel Amos 9:9
In that day *w* I raise up the Amos 9:11
I *w* raise up his ruins, and I *w* Amos 9:11
I *w* build it as in the days of Amos 9:11
I *w* bring again the captivity of Amos 9:14
I *w* plant them upon their land, Amos 9:15
thence *w* I bring thee down, saith Obad 4
if so be that God *w* think upon us Jonah 1:6
yet I *w* look again toward thy Jonah 2:4
But I *w* sacrifice unto thee with Jonah 2:9
I *w* pay that that I have vowed Jonah 2:9
Who can tell if God *w* turn Jonah 3:9
w come down, and tread upon the Mic 1:3
Therefore I *w* make Samaria as an Mic 1:6
I *w* pour down the stones thereof Mic 1:6
I *w* discover the foundations Mic 1:6
idols thereof *w* I lay desolate Mic 1:7
I *w* wail and howl Mic 1:8
I *w* go stripped and naked Mic 1:8
I *w* make a wailing like the Mic 1:8
Yet *w* I bring an heir unto thee, Mic 1:15
I *w* prophesy unto thee of wine and Mic 2:11
I *w* surely assemble, O Jacob, all Mic 2:12
I *w* surely gather the remnant of Mic 2:12
I *w* put them together as the Mic 2:12
the LORD, but he *w* not hear them Mic 3:4
he *w* even hide his face from them Mic 3:4
yet *w* they lean upon the LORD, and Mic 3:11
he *w* teach us of his ways Mic 4:2
and we *w* walk in his paths Mic 4:2
For all people *w* walk every one Mic 4:5
we *w* walk in the name of the LORD Mic 4:5
w I assemble her that halteth, and Mic 4:6
I *w* gather her that is driven out Mic 4:6
I *w* make her that halted a Mic 4:7
I *w* make thine horn iron Mic 4:13
and I *w* make thy hoofs brass Mic 4:13
I *w* consecrate their gain unto Mic 4:13
Therefore *w* he give them up, Mic 5:3
that I *w* cut off thy horses out Mic 5:10
thee, and I *w* destroy thy chariots Mic 5:10
I *w* cut off the cities of thy Mic 5:11
I *w* cut off witchcrafts out of Mic 5:12
graven images also *w* I cut off Mic 5:13
I *w* pluck up thy groves out of Mic 5:14
so *w* I destroy thy cities Mic 5:14
I *w* execute vengeance in anger and Mic 5:15
people, and he *w* plead with Israel Mic 6:2
W the LORD be pleased with Mic 6:7
Therefore also *w* I make thee sick Mic 6:13
w I give up to the sword Mic 6:14
Therefore I *w* look unto the LORD Mic 7:7
I *w* wait for the God of my Mic 7:7
my God *w* hear me Mic 7:7
I *w* bear the indignation of the Mic 7:9
he *w* bring me forth to the light, Mic 7:9
w I shew unto him marvellous Mic 7:15
He *w* turn again Mic 7:19
he *w* have compassion upon us Mic 7:19
he *w* subdue our iniquities Mic 7:19
the LORD *w* take vengeance on his Nah 1:2
w not at all acquit the wicked Nah 1:3
with an overrunning flood he *w* Nah 1:8
he *w* make an utter end Nah 1:9
thee, I *w* afflict thee no more Nah 1:12
For now *w* I break his yoke from Nah 1:13
w burst thy bonds in sunder Nah 1:13
gods *w* I cut off the graven image Nah 1:14
I *w* make thy grave Nah 1:14
I *w* burn her chariots in the Nah 2:13
I *w* cut off thy prey from the Nah 2:13
I *w* discover thy skirts upon thy Nah 3:5
face, and I *w* shew the nations thy Nah 3:5
I *w* cast abominable filth upon Nah 3:6
w set thee as a gazingstock Nah 3:6
who *w* bemoan her Nah 3:7
for I *w* work a work in your days, Hab 1:5
which ye *w* not believe, though it Hab 1:5
I *w* stand upon my watch, and set Hab 2:1
w watch to see what Hab 2:1
to see what he *w* say unto me Hab 2:1
because it *w* surely come Hab 2:3
it *w* not tarry Hab 2:3
he *w* invade them with his troops Hab 3:16
Yet I *w* rejoice in the LORD Hab 3:18
I *w* joy in the God Hab 3:18
he *w* make my feet like hinds' Hab 3:19
he *w* make me to walk upon mine Hab 3:19
I *w* utterly consume all things Zeph 1:2
I *w* consume man and beast Zeph 1:3
I *w* consume the fowls of the Zeph 1:3
I *w* cut off man from off the land Zeph 1:3
I *w* also stretch out mine hand Zeph 1:4
I *w* cut off the remnant of Baal Zeph 1:4
that I *w* punish the princes, and Zeph 1:8
In the same day also *w* I punish Zeph 1:9
that I *w* search Jerusalem with Zeph 1:12
LORD *w* not do good Zeph 1:12
neither *w* he do evil Zeph 1:12
I *w* bring distress upon men, that Zeph 1:17
I *w* even destroy thee, that there Zeph 2:5
The LORD *w* be terrible unto them Zeph 2:11
for he *w* famish all the gods of Zeph 2:11

he *w* stretch out his hand against	Zeph 2:13	
w make Nineveh a desolation, and	Zeph 2:13	
he *w* not do iniquity	Zeph 3:5	
For then *w* I turn to the people a	Zeph 3:9	
for then I *w* take away out of the	Zeph 3:11	
I *w* also leave in the midst of	Zeph 3:12	
he *w* save, he *w* rejoice over	Zeph 3:17	
he *w* rejoice over thee with joy	Zeph 3:17	
he *w* rest in his love	Zeph 3:17	
he *w* joy over thee with singing	Zeph 3:17	
I *w* gather them that are	Zeph 3:18	
at that time I *w* undo all that	Zeph 3:19	
I *w* save her that halteth, and	Zeph 3:19	
I *w* get them praise and fame in	Zeph 3:19	
At that time *w* I bring you again,	Zeph 3:20	
for I *w* make you a name and a	Zeph 3:20	
I *w* take pleasure in it	Hag 1:8	
I *w* be glorified, saith the LORD	Hag 1:8	
I *w* shake the heavens, and the	Hag 2:6	
I *w* shake all nations, and the	Hag 2:7	
I *w* fill this house with glory,	Hag 2:7	
and in this place *w* I give peace	Hag 2:9	
from this day *w* I bless you	Hag 2:19	
I *w* shake the heavens and the	Hag 2:21	
I *w* overthrow the throne of	Hag 2:22	
I *w* destroy the strength of the	Hag 2:22	
I *w* overthrow the chariots, and	Hag 2:22	
w I take thee, O Zerubbabel, my	Hag 2:23	
LORD, and *w* make thee as a signet	Hag 2:23	
I *w* turn unto you, saith the LORD	Zec 1:3	
I *w* shew thee what these be	Zec 1:9	
w be unto her a wall of fire	Zec 2:5	
w be the glory in the midst of	Zec 2:5	
I *w* shake mine hand upon them, and	Zec 2:9	
I *w* dwell in the midst of thee,	Zec 2:10	
I *w* dwell in the midst of thee,	Zec 2:11	
I *w* clothe thee with change of	Zec 3:4	
I *w* give thee places to walk	Zec 3:7	
I *w* bring forth my servant the	Zec 3:8	
I *w* engrave the graving thereof,	Zec 3:9	
I *w* remove the iniquity of that	Zec 3:9	
I *w* bring it forth, saith the	Zec 5:4	
if ye *w* diligently obey the voice	Zec 6:15	
w dwell in the midst of Jerusalem	Zec 8:3	
I *w* save my people from the east	Zec 8:7	
I *w* bring them, and they shall	Zec 8:8	
I *w* be their God, in truth and in	Zec 8:8	
But now I *w* not be unto the	Zec 8:11	
I *w* cause the remnant of this	Zec 8:12	
so *w* I save you, and ye shall be a	Zec 8:13	
I *w* go also	Zec 8:21	
a Jew, saying, We *w* go with you	Zec 8:23	
the Lord *w* cast her out	Zec 9:4	
he *w* smite her power in the sea	Zec 9:4	
I *w* cut off the pride of the	Zec 9:6	
I *w* take away his blood out of	Zec 9:7	
I *w* encamp about mine house	Zec 9:8	
I *w* cut off the chariot from	Zec 9:10	
that I *w* render double unto thee	Zec 9:12	
I *w* strengthen the house of Judah	Zec 10:6	
I *w* save the house of Joseph, and	Zec 10:6	
I *w* bring them again to place	Zec 10:6	
LORD their God, and *w* hear them	Zec 10:6	
I *w* hiss for them, and gather them	Zec 10:8	
I *w* sow them among the people	Zec 10:9	
I *w* bring them again also out of	Zec 10:10	
I *w* bring them into the land of	Zec 10:10	
I *w* strengthen them in the LORD	Zec 10:12	
For I *w* no more pity the	Zec 11:6	
I *w* deliver the men every one	Zec 11:6	
their hand I *w* not deliver them	Zec 11:6	
I *w* feed the flock of slaughter,	Zec 11:7	
Then said I, I *w* not feed you	Zec 11:9	
I *w* raise up a shepherd in the	Zec 11:16	
I *w* make Jerusalem a cup of	Zec 12:2	
in that day *w* I make Jerusalem a	Zec 12:3	
I *w* smite every horse with	Zec 12:4	
I *w* open mine eyes upon the house	Zec 12:4	
w smite every horse of the people	Zec 12:4	
In that day *w* I make the	Zec 12:6	
that I *w* seek to destroy all the	Zec 12:9	
I *w* pour upon the house of David,	Zec 12:10	
that I *w* cut off the names of the	Zec 13:2	
also I *w* cause the prophets and	Zec 13:2	
I *w* turn mine hand upon the	Zec 13:7	
I *w* bring the third part through	Zec 13:9	
w refine them as silver is	Zec 13:9	
w try them as gold is tried	Zec 13:9	
call on my name, and I *w* hear them	Zec 13:9	
I *w* say, It is my people	Zec 13:9	
For I *w* gather all nations	Zec 14:2	
the plague wherewith the LORD *w*	Zec 14:12	
that whoso *w* not come up of all	Zec 14:17	
wherewith the LORD *w* smite the	Zec 14:18	
are impoverished, but we *w* return	Mal 1:4	
shall build, but I *w* throw down	Mal 1:4	
The LORD *w* be magnified from the	Mal 1:5	
w he be pleased with thee, or	Mal 1:8	
God that he *w* be gracious unto us	Mal 1:9	
w he regard your persons	Mal 1:9	
neither *w* I accept an offering at	Mal 1:10	
If ye *w* not hear	Mal 2:2	
if ye *w* not lay it to heart, to	Mal 2:2	
I *w* even send a curse upon you,	Mal 2:2	
and I *w* curse your blessings	Mal 2:2	
I *w* corrupt your seed, and spread	Mal 2:3	
The LORD *w* cut off the man that	Mal 2:12	
it with good *w* at your hand	Mal 2:13	7522
I *w* send my messenger, and he	Mal 3:1	
I *w* come near to you to judgment	Mal 3:5	
I *w* be a swift witness against	Mal 3:5	
I *w* return unto you, saith the	Mal 3:7	
W a man rob God	Mal 3:8	
if I *w* not open you the windows	Mal 3:10	
I *w* rebuke the devourer for your	Mal 3:11	
I *w* spare them, as a man spareth	Mal 3:17	
I *w* send you Elijah the prophet	Mal 4:5	
for Herod *w* seek the young child	Mt 2:13	3195
he *w* throughly purge his floor,	Mt 3:12	
but he *w* burn up the chaff with	Mt 3:12	
All these things *w* I give thee	Mt 4:9	
I *w* make you fishers of men	Mt 4:19	
if any man *w* sue thee at the law,	Mt 5:40	2309
Thy *w* be done in earth, as it is	Mt 6:10	2307
Father *w* also forgive you	Mt 6:14	
neither *w* your Father forgive	Mt 6:15	
there *w* your heart be also	Mt 6:21	
for either he *w* hate the one	Mt 6:24	
or else he *w* hold to the one, and	Mt 6:24	
ask bread, *w* he give him a stone	Mt 7:9	
a fish, *w* he give him a serpent	Mt 7:10	
but he that doeth the *w* of my	Mt 7:21	2307
Many *w* say to me in that day,	Mt 7:22	
then *w* I profess unto them, I	Mt 7:23	
I *w* liken him unto a wise man,	Mt 7:24	
hand, and touched him, saying, I *w*	Mt 8:3	2309
unto him, I *w* come and heal him	Mt 8:7	
I *w* follow thee whithersoever	Mt 8:19	
I *w* have mercy, and not sacrifice	Mt 9:13	2309
but the days *w* come, when the	Mt 9:15	
that he *w* send forth labourers	Mt 9:38	
for they *w* deliver you up to the	Mt 10:17	
they *w* scourge you in their	Mt 10:17	
him *w* I confess also before my	Mt 10:32	
him *w* I also deny before my	Mt 10:33	
if ye *w* receive it, this is Elias	Mt 11:14	2309
whomsoever the Son *w* reveal him	Mt 11:27	1014
heavy laden, and I *w* give you rest	Mt 11:28	
I *w* have mercy, and not sacrifice,	Mt 12:7	2309
w he not lay hold on it, and lift	Mt 12:11	
I *w* put my Spirit upon him, and he	Mt 12:18	
then he *w* spoil his house	Mt 12:29	
I *w* return into my house from	Mt 12:44	
For whosoever shall do the *w* of	Mt 12:50	2307
of harvest I *w* say to the reapers	Mt 13:30	
I *w* open my mouth in parables	Mt 13:35	
I *w* utter things which have been	Mt 13:35	
I *w* not send them away fasting,	Mt 15:32	2309
ye say, It *w* be fair weather	Mt 16:2	
It *w* be foul weather to day	Mt 16:3	
this rock I *w* build my church	Mt 16:18	
I *w* give unto thee the keys of	Mt 16:19	
If any man *w* come after me, let	Mt 16:24	2309
For whosoever *w* save his life	Mt 16:25	2309
whosoever *w* lose his life for my	Mt 16:25	
Even so it is not the *w* of your	Mt 18:14	2307
But if he *w* not hear thee, then	Mt 18:16	
with me, and I *w* pay thee all	Mt 18:26	
with me, and I *w* pay thee all	Mt 18:29	
whatsoever is right I *w* give you	Mt 20:4	
I *w* give unto this last, even as	Mt 20:14	2309
me to do what I *w* with mine own	Mt 20:15	2309
but whosoever *w* be great among	Mt 20:26	2309
whosoever *w* be chief among you,	Mt 20:27	2309
What *w* ye that I shall do unto	Mt 20:32	2309
and straightway he *w* send them	Mt 21:3	
I also *w* ask you one thing, which	Mt 21:24	
I in like wise *w* tell you by what	Mt 21:24	
he *w* say unto us, Why did ye not	Mt 21:25	
He answered and said, I *w* not	Mt 21:29	2309
twain did the *w* of his father	Mt 21:31	2307
saying, They *w* reverence my son	Mt 21:37	
cometh, what *w* he do unto those	Mt 21:40	
He *w* miserably destroy those	Mt 21:41	
w let out his vineyard unto other	Mt 21:41	
fall, it *w* grind him to powder	Mt 21:44	
but they themselves *w* not move	Mt 23:4	2309
there *w* the eagles be gathered	Mt 24:28	
I *w* make thee ruler over many	Mt 25:21	
I *w* make thee ruler over many	Mt 25:23	
What *w* ye give me	Mt 26:15	2309
and I *w* deliver him unto you	Mt 26:15	
I *w* keep the passover at thy	Mt 26:18	
I *w* not drink henceforth of this	Mt 26:29	
I *w* smite the shepherd, and the	Mt 26:31	
I *w* go before you into Galilee	Mt 26:32	
yet *w* I never be offended	Mt 26:33	
with thee, yet *w* I not deny thee	Mt 26:35	
nevertheless not as I *w*, but as	Mt 26:39	2309
except I drink it, thy *w* be done	Mt 26:42	2307
Whom *w* ye that I release unto you	Mt 27:17	2309
Whether of the twain *w* ye that I	Mt 27:21	2309
the cross, and we *w* believe him	Mt 27:42	
deliver him now, if he *w* have him	Mt 27:43	2309
whether Elias *w* come to save him	Mt 27:49	
After three days I *w* rise again	Mt 27:63	
we *w* persuade him, and secure you	Mt 28:14	
I *w* make you to become fishers of	Mk 1:17	
him, and saith unto him, I *w*	Mk 1:41	2309
But the days *w* come, when the	Mk 2:20	
and the bottles *w* be marred	Mk 2:22	
except he *w* first bind the strong	Mk 3:27	
then he *w* spoil his house	Mk 3:27	
whosoever shall do the *w* of God	Mk 3:35	2307
how then *w* ye know all parables	Mk 4:13	
thou wilt, and I *w* give it thee	Mk 6:22	
I *w* give it thee, unto the half	Mk 6:23	
I *w* that thou give me by and by in	Mk 6:25	2309
houses, they *w* faint by the way	Mk 8:3	
Whosoever *w* come after me, let	Mk 8:34	2309
For whosoever *w* save his life	Mk 8:35	2309
wherewith *w* ye season it	Mk 9:50	
but whosoever *w* be great among	Mk 10:43	2309
of you *w* be the chiefest, shall	Mk 10:44	2309
straightway he *w* send him hither	Mk 11:3	
neither *w* your Father which is in	Mk 11:26	
I *w* also ask of you one question,	Mk 11:29	
I *w* tell you by what authority I	Mk 11:29	
he *w* say, Why then did ye not	Mk 11:31	
saying, They *w* reverence my son	Mk 12:6	
he *w* come and destroy the	Mk 12:9	
w give the vineyard unto others	Mk 12:9	
whensoever ye *w* ye may do them	Mk 14:7	2309
he *w* shew you a large upper room	Mk 14:15	
I *w* drink no more of the fruit of	Mk 14:25	
I *w* smite the shepherd, and the	Mk 14:27	
I *w* go before you into Galilee	Mk 14:28	
shall be offended, yet *w* not I	Mk 14:29	
I *w* not deny thee in any wise	Mk 14:31	
nevertheless not what I *w*,	Mk 14:36	2309
I *w* destroy this temple that is	Mk 14:58	
within three days I *w* build	Mk 14:58	
W ye that I release unto you the	Mk 15:9	2309
What *w* ye then that I shall do	Mk 15:12	2309
Elias *w* come to take him down	Mk 15:36	
on earth peace, good *w* toward men	Lk 2:14	2107
he *w* throughly purge his floor,	Lk 3:17	
w gather the wheat into his	Lk 3:17	
but the chaff he *w* burn with fire	Lk 3:17	
him, All this power *w* I give thee	Lk 4:6	
and to whomsoever I *w* I give it	Lk 4:6	2309
Ye *w* surely say unto me this	Lk 4:23	
at thy word I *w* let down the net	Lk 5:5	
hand, and touched him, saying, I *w*	Lk 5:13	2309
But the days *w* come, when the	Lk 5:35	
the new wine *w* burst the bottles	Lk 5:37	
unto them, I *w* ask you one thing	Lk 6:9	
I *w* shew you to whom he is like	Lk 6:47	
which of them *w* love him most	Lk 7:42	
whosoever *w* not receive you, when	Lk 9:5	
If any man *w* come after me, let	Lk 9:23	2309
For whosoever *w* save his life	Lk 9:24	2309
but whosoever *w* lose his life for	Lk 9:24	
I *w* follow thee whithersoever	Lk 9:57	
also said, Lord, I *w* follow thee	Lk 9:61	
he to whom the Son *w* reveal him	Lk 10:22	1014
when I come again, I *w* repay thee	Lk 10:35	
Thy *w* be done, as in heaven, so	Lk 11:2	2307
unto you, Though he *w* not rise	Lk 11:8	
of his importunity he *w* rise	Lk 11:8	
a father, *w* he give him a stone	Lk 11:11	
w he for a fish give him a	Lk 11:11	
w he offer him a scorpion	Lk 11:12	
I *w* return unto my house whence I	Lk 11:24	
I *w* send them prophets and	Lk 11:49	
But I *w* forewarn you whom ye	Lk 12:5	
And he said, This *w* I do	Lk 12:18	
I *w* pull down my barns, and build	Lk 12:18	
there *w* I bestow all my fruits and	Lk 12:18	
I *w* say to my soul, Soul, thou	Lk 12:19	
how much more *w* he clothe you	Lk 12:28	
there *w* your heart be also	Lk 12:34	
when he *w* return from the wedding	Lk 12:36	
w come forth and serve them	Lk 12:37	
that he *w* make him ruler over all	Lk 12:44	
The lord of that servant *w* come	Lk 12:46	
w cut him in sunder	Lk 12:46	
w appoint him his portion with	Lk 12:46	
servant, which knew his lord's *w*	Lk 12:47	2307
neither did according to his *w*	Lk 12:47	2307
of him they *w* ask the more	Lk 12:48	
and what *w* I, if it be already	Lk 12:49	2309
blow, ye say, There *w* be heat	Lk 12:55	
w seek to enter in, and shall not	Lk 13:24	
for Herod *w* kill thee	Lk 13:31	2309
w not straightway pull him out on	Lk 14:5	
I *w* arise and go to my father, and	Lk 15:18	
w say unto him, Father, I have	Lk 15:18	
who *w* commit to your trust the	Lk 16:11	
for either he *w* hate the one	Lk 16:13	
or else he *w* hold to the one, and	Lk 16:13	
them from the dead, they *w* repent	Lk 16:30	
neither *w* they be persuaded,	Lk 16:31	
but that offences *w* come	Lk 17:1	
w say unto him by and by, when he	Lk 17:7	
w not rather say unto him, Make	Lk 17:8	
the disciples, The days *w* come	Lk 17:22	
thither *w* the eagles be gathered	Lk 17:37	
I *w* avenge her, lest by her	Lk 18:5	
I tell you that he *w* avenge them	Lk 18:8	
We *w* not have this man to reign	Lk 19:14	2309
of thine own mouth *w* I judge thee	Lk 19:22	
I *w* also ask you one thing	Lk 20:3	
he *w* say, Why then believed ye	Lk 20:5	
all the people *w* stone us	Lk 20:6	
I *w* send my beloved son	Lk 20:13	
it may be they *w* reverence him	Lk 20:13	
fall, it *w* grind him to powder	Lk 20:18	
which ye behold, the days *w* come	Lk 21:6	
what sign *w* there be when these	Lk 21:7	
For I *w* give you a mouth and	Lk 21:15	
I *w* not any more eat thereof,	Lk 22:16	
I *w* not drink of the fruit of the	Lk 22:18	
nevertheless not my *w*, but thine,	Lk 22:42	2307

If I tell you, ye *w* not believe	Lk 22:67	
ye *w* not answer me, nor let me go	Lk 22:68	
I *w* therefore chastise him, and	Lk 23:16	
I *w* therefore chastise him, and	Lk 23:22	
but he delivered Jesus to their *w*	Lk 23:25	*2307*
nor of the *w* of the flesh	Jn 1:13	*2307*
nor of the *w* of man	Jn 1:13	*2307*
and in three days I *w* raise it up	Jn 2:19	
is come, he *w* tell us all things	Jn 4:25	
to do the *w* of him that sent me	Jn 4:34	*2307*
and wonders, ye *w* not believe	Jn 4:48	
he *w* shew him greater works than	Jn 5:20	
so the Son quickeneth whom he *w*	Jn 5:21	*2309*
because I seek not mine own *w*	Jn 5:30	*2307*
but the *w* of the Father which	Jn 5:30	*2307*
ye *w* not come to me, that ye	Jn 5:40	*2309*
in his own name, him ye *w* receive	Jn 5:43	
Do not think that I *w* accuse you	Jn 5:45	
to me I *w* in no wise cast out	Jn 6:37	
from heaven, not to do mine own *w*	Jn 6:38	*2307*
but the *w* of him that sent me	Jn 6:38	*2307*
the Father's *w* which hath sent me	Jn 6:39	*2307*
this is the *w* of him that sent me	Jn 6:40	*2307*
I *w* raise him up at the last day	Jn 6:40	
I *w* raise him up at the last day	Jn 6:44	
bread that I *w* give is my flesh	Jn 6:51	
which I *w* give for the life of	Jn 6:51	
I *w* raise him up at the last day	Jn 6:54	
the twelve, *W* ye also go away	Jn 6:67	*2309*
If any man *w* do his	Jn 7:17	*2309*
do his *w*, he shall	Jn 7:17	*2307*
w he do more miracles than these	Jn 7:31	
among themselves, Whither *w* he go	Jn 7:35	*3195*
w he go unto the dispersed among	Jn 7:35	*3195*
said the Jews, *W* he kill himself	Jn 8:22	
the lusts of your father ye *w* do	Jn 8:44	*2309*
w ye also be his disciples	Jn 9:27	*2309*
worshipper of God, and doeth his *w*	Jn 9:31	*2307*
a stranger *w* they not follow	Jn 10:5	
but *w* flee from him	Jn 10:5	
ask of God, God *w* give it thee	Jn 11:22	
alone, all men *w* believe on him	Jn 11:48	
that he *w* not come to the feast	Jn 11:56	
serve me, him *w* my Father honour	Jn 12:26	
it, and *w* glorify it again	Jn 12:28	
the earth, *w* draw all men unto me	Jn 12:32	
I *w* lay down my life for thy sake	Jn 13:37	
I *w* come again, and receive you	Jn 14:3	
shall ask in my name, that *w* I do	Jn 14:13	
any thing in my name, I *w* do it	Jn 14:14	
I *w* pray the Father, and he shall	Jn 14:16	
I *w* not leave you comfortless	Jn 14:18	
I *w* come to you	Jn 14:18	
I *w* love him	Jn 14:21	
and *w* manifest myself to him	Jn 14:21	
a man love me, he *w* keep my words	Jn 14:23	
and my Father *w* love him	Jn 14:23	
we *w* come unto him, and make our	Jn 14:23	
whom the Father *w* send in my name	Jn 14:26	
Hereafter I *w* not talk much with	Jn 14:30	
in you, ye shall ask what ye *w*	Jn 15:7	*2309*
they *w* also persecute you	Jn 15:20	
my saying, they *w* keep yours also	Jn 15:20	
But all these things *w* they do	Jn 15:21	
whom I *w* send unto you from the	Jn 15:26	
that whosoever killeth you *w*	Jn 16:2	
these things *w* they do unto you,	Jn 16:3	
the Comforter *w* not come unto you	Jn 16:7	
I depart, I *w* send him unto you	Jn 16:7	
he *w* reprove the world of sin, and	Jn 16:8	
he *w* guide you into all truth	Jn 16:13	
he *w* shew you things to come	Jn 16:13	
but I *w* see you again, and your	Jn 16:22	
in my name, he *w* give it you	Jn 16:23	
that I *w* pray the Father for you	Jn 16:26	
I *w* that they also, whom thou	Jn 17:24	*2309*
them thy name, and *w* declare it	Jn 17:26	
w ye therefore that I release	Jn 18:39	*1014*
laid him, and I *w* take him away	Jn 20:15	
into his side, I *w* not believe	Jn 20:25	
If I *w* that he tarry till I come,	Jn 21:22	*2309*
If I *w* that he tarry till I come,	Jn 21:23	*2309*
I *w* pour out of my Spirit upon	Acts 2:17	
on my handmaidens I *w* pour out in	Acts 2:18	
I *w* shew wonders in heaven above,	Acts 2:19	
which *w* not hear that prophet,	Acts 3:23	
be of men, it *w* come to nought	Acts 5:38	
But we *w* give ourselves	Acts 6:4	
shall be in bondage *w* I judge	Acts 7:7	
come, I *w* send thee into Egypt	Acts 7:34	
I *w* carry you away beyond Babylon	Acts 7:43	
what house *w* ye build me	Acts 7:49	
For I *w* shew him how great things	Acts 9:16	
which shall fulfil all my *w*	Acts 13:22	*2307*
I *w* give you the sure mercies of	Acts 13:34	
own generation by the *w* of God	Acts 13:36	*1012*
After this I *w* return	Acts 15:16	
w build again the tabernacle of	Acts 15:16	
I *w* build again the ruins thereof	Acts 15:16	
ruins thereof, and I *w* set it up	Acts 15:16	
said, What *w* this babbler say	Acts 17:18	*2309*
in the which he *w* judge the world	Acts 17:31	*3195*
We *w* hear thee again of this	Acts 17:32	
from henceforth I *w* go unto the	Acts 18:6	
for I *w* be no judge of such	Acts 18:15	*1014*
I *w* return again unto you	Acts 18:21	
return again unto you, if God *w*	Acts 18:21	*2309*
The *w* of the Lord be done	Acts 21:14	*2307*
for they *w* hear that thou art	Acts 21:22	
that thou shouldest know his *w*	Acts 22:14	*2307*
for they *w* not receive thy	Acts 22:18	
for I *w* send thee far hence unto	Acts 22:21	
that we *w* eat nothing until we	Acts 23:14	
that they *w* neither eat nor drink	Acts 23:21	
I *w* hear thee, said he, when	Acts 23:35	
I *w* know the uttermost of your	Acts 24:22	
season, I *w* call for thee	Acts 24:25	
in the which I *w* appear unto thee	Acts 26:16	
that this voyage *w* be with hurt	Acts 27:10	*3195*
Gentiles, and that they *w* hear it	Acts 28:28	
by the *w* of God to come unto you	Rom 1:10	*2307*
Who *w* render to every man	Rom 2:6	
And knowest his *w*, and approvest	Rom 2:18	*2307*
to whom the Lord *w* not impute sin	Rom 4:8	
for a righteous man *w* one die	Rom 5:7	
for to *w* is present with me	Rom 7:18	*2309*
saints according to the *w* of God	Rom 8:27	
of promise, At this time *w* I come	Rom 9:9	
I *w* have mercy on whom	Rom 9:15	
on whom I *w* have mercy	Rom 9:15	
I *w* have compassion on whom I	Rom 9:15	
on whom I *w* have compassion	Rom 9:15	
he mercy on whom he *w* have mercy	Rom 9:18	*2309*
and whom he *w* he hardeneth	Rom 9:18	*2309*
For who hath resisted his *w*	Rom 9:19	*1013*
I *w* call them my people, which	Rom 9:25	
For he *w* finish the work, and cut	Rom 9:28	
because a short work *w* the Lord	Rom 9:28	
I *w* provoke you to jealousy by	Rom 10:19	
by a foolish nation I *w* anger you	Rom 10:19	
acceptable, and perfect, *w* of God	Rom 12:2	*2307*
I *w* repay, saith the Lord	Rom 12:19	
For this cause I *w* confess to	Rom 15:9	
For I *w* not dare to speak of any	Rom 15:18	
into Spain, I *w* come to you	Rom 15:24	
I *w* come by you into Spain	Rom 15:28	
unto you with joy by the *w* of God	Rom 15:32	*2307*
Jesus Christ through the *w* of God	1Cor 1:1	*2307*
I *w* destroy the wisdom of the	1Cor 1:19	
wise, and *w* bring to nothing the	1Cor 1:19	
who both *w* bring to light the	1Cor 4:5	
w make manifest the counsels of	1Cor 4:5	
I *w* come to you shortly	1Cor 4:19	
to you shortly, if the Lord *w*	1Cor 4:19	*2309*
w know, not the speech of them	1Cor 4:19	
What *w* ye	1Cor 4:21	*2309*
but I *w* not be brought under the	1Cor 6:12	
w also raise up us by his own	1Cor 6:14	
so require, let him do what he *w*	1Cor 7:36	*2309*
but hath power over his own *w*	1Cor 7:37	*2307*
heart that he *w* keep his virgin	1Cor 7:37	
to be married to whom she *w*	1Cor 7:39	*2309*
I *w* eat no flesh while the world	1Cor 8:13	
but if against my *w*, a	1Cor 9:17	*210*
who *w* not suffer you to be	1Cor 10:13	
but *w* with the temptation also	1Cor 10:13	
the rest *w* I set in order when I	1Cor 11:34	
to every man severally as he *w*	1Cor 12:11	*1014*
I *w* pray with the spirit	1Cor 14:15	
I *w* pray with the understanding	1Cor 14:15	
I *w* sing with the spirit	1Cor 14:15	
I *w* sing with the understanding	1Cor 14:15	
other lips *w* I speak unto this	1Cor 14:21	
for all that *w* they not hear me	1Cor 14:21	
w they not say that ye are mad	1Cor 14:23	
down on his face he *w* worship God	1Cor 14:25	
if they *w* learn any thing, let	1Cor 14:35	*2309*
But some man *w* say, How are the	1Cor 15:35	
them *w* I send to bring your	1Cor 16:3	
Now I *w* come unto you, when I	1Cor 16:5	
And it may be that I *w* abide	1Cor 16:6	
For I *w* not see you now by the	1Cor 16:7	*2309*
But I *w* tarry at Ephesus until	1Cor 16:8	
but his *w* was not at all to come	1Cor 16:12	*2307*
but he *w* come when he shall have	1Cor 16:12	
of Jesus Christ by the *w* of God	2Cor 1:1	*2307*
we trust that he *w* yet deliver us	2Cor 1:10	
I *w* dwell in them, and walk in	2Cor 6:16	
I *w* be their God, and they shall	2Cor 6:16	
and I *w* receive you,	2Cor 6:17	
w be a Father unto you, and ye	2Cor 6:18	
Lord, and unto us by the *w* of God	2Cor 8:5	*2307*
as there was a readiness to *w*	2Cor 8:11	*2309*
such *w* we be also in deed when we	2Cor 10:11	
But we *w* not boast of things	2Cor 10:13	
unto you, and so *w* I keep myself	2Cor 11:9	
But what I do, that I *w* do	2Cor 11:12	
after the flesh, I *w* glory also	2Cor 11:18	
I *w* glory of the things which	2Cor 11:30	
I *w* come to visions and	2Cor 12:1	
Of such an one *w* I glory	2Cor 12:5	
yet of myself I *w* not glory	2Cor 12:5	
for I *w* say the truth	2Cor 12:6	
therefore *w* I rather glory in my	2Cor 12:9	
I *w* not be burdensome to you	2Cor 12:14	
I *w* very gladly spend and be spent	2Cor 12:15	
my God *w* humble me among you, and	2Cor 12:21	
if I come again, I *w* not spare	2Cor 13:2	
world, according to the *w* of God	Gal 1:4	*2307*
that ye *w* be none otherwise	Gal 5:10	
of Jesus Christ by the *w* of God	Eph 1:1	*2307*
to the good pleasure of his *w*	Eph 1:5	*2307*
unto us the mystery of his *w*	Eph 1:9	*2307*
after the counsel of his own *w*	Eph 1:11	*2307*
what the *w* of the Lord is	Eph 5:17	*2307*
doing the *w* of God from the heart	Eph 6:6	*2307*
With good *w* doing service, as to	Eph 6:7	*2133*
you *w* perform it until the day of	Phil 1:6	
and some also of good *w*	Phil 1:15	*2107*
do rejoice, yea, and *w* rejoice	Phil 1:18	
which worketh in you both to *w*	Phil 2:13	*2309*
who *w* naturally care for your	Phil 2:20	
I shall see how it *w* go with me	Phil 2:23	
of Jesus Christ by the *w* of God	Col 1:1	*2307*
knowledge of his *w* in all wisdom	Col 1:9	*2307*
a shew of wisdom in *w* worship	Col 2:23	*1479*
and complete in all the *w* of God	Col 4:12	*2307*
For this is the *w* of God, even	1Th 4:3	*2307*
in Jesus *w* God bring with him	1Th 4:14	
for this is the *w* of God in	1Th 5:18	*2307*
calleth you, who also *w* do it	1Th 5:24	
only he who now letteth *w* let	2Th 2:7	
w do the things which we command	2Th 3:4	
Who *w* have all men to be saved,	1Ti 2:4	*2309*
I *w* therefore that men pray every	1Ti 2:8	*1014*
against Christ, they *w* marry	1Ti 5:11	*2309*
I *w* therefore that the younger	1Ti 5:14	*1014*
But they that *w* be rich fall into	1Ti 6:9	*1014*
of Jesus Christ by the *w* of God	2Ti 1:1	*2307*
if we deny him, he also *w* deny us	2Ti 2:12	
for they *w* increase unto more	2Ti 2:16	
their word *w* eat as doth a canker	2Ti 2:17	
if God peradventure *w* give them	2Ti 2:25	
are taken captive by him at his *w*	2Ti 2:26	*2307*
all that *w* live godly in Christ	2Ti 3:12	*2309*
For the time *w* come when they	2Ti 4:3	
they *w* not endure sound doctrine	2Ti 4:3	
w preserve me unto his heavenly	2Ti 4:18	
these things I *w* that thou affirm	Titus 3:8	*1014*
with mine own hand, I *w* repay it	Philem 19	
I *w* be to him a Father, and he	Heb 1:5	
Ghost, according to his own *w*	Heb 2:4	*2308*
I *w* declare thy name unto my	Heb 2:12	
church *w* I sing praise unto thee	Heb 2:12	
And again, I *w* put my trust in him	Heb 2:13	
To day if ye *w* hear his voice,	Heb 3:7	
To day if ye *w* hear his voice,	Heb 3:15	
To day if ye *w* hear his voice,	Heb 4:7	
this *w* we do, if God permit	Heb 6:3	
Surely blessing I *w* bless thee	Heb 6:14	
and multiplying I *w* multiply thee	Heb 6:14	
w not repent, Thou art a priest	Heb 7:21	
when I *w* make a new covenant with	Heb 8:8	
I *w* make with the house of Israel	Heb 8:10	
I *w* put my laws into their mind,	Heb 8:10	
I *w* be to them a God, and they	Heb 8:10	
For I *w* be merciful to their	Heb 8:12	
their iniquities *w* I remember no	Heb 8:12	
it is written of me,) to do thy *w*	Heb 10:7	*2307*
said he, Lo, I come to do thy *w*	Heb 10:9	*2307*
By the which *w* we are sanctified	Heb 10:10	*2307*
This is the covenant that I *w*	Heb 10:16	
I *w* put my laws into their hearts	Heb 10:16	
and in their minds *w* I write them	Heb 10:16	
iniquities *w* I remember no more	Heb 10:17	
I *w* recompense, saith the Lord	Heb 10:30	
after ye have done the *w* of God	Heb 10:36	*2307*
and he that shall come *w* come	Heb 10:37	
w come, and *w* not tarry	Heb 10:37	
and adulterers God *w* judge	Heb 13:4	
I *w* never leave thee, nor forsake	Heb 13:5	
I *w* not fear what man shall do	Heb 13:6	
in every good work to do his *w*	Heb 13:21	*2307*
if he come shortly, I *w* see you	Heb 13:23	
Of his own *w* begat he us with the	Jas 1:18	*1014*
I *w* shew thee my faith by my	Jas 2:18	
whosoever therefore *w* be a friend	Jas 4:4	*1014*
the devil, and he *w* flee from you	Jas 4:7	
to God, and he *w* draw nigh to you	Jas 4:8	
morrow we *w* go into such a city	Jas 4:13	
ye ought to say, If the Lord *w*	Jas 4:15	*2309*
For so is the *w* of God, that with	1Pet 2:15	*2307*
For he that *w* love life, and see	1Pet 3:10	*2309*
And who is he that *w* harm you	1Pet 3:13	
if the *w* of God be so, that ye	1Pet 3:17	*2307*
lusts of men, but to the *w* of God	1Pet 4:2	*2307*
wrought the *w* of the Gentiles	1Pet 4:3	*2307*
w of God commit the keeping of	1Pet 4:19	*2307*
Wherefore I *w* not be negligent to	2Pet 1:12	
Moreover I *w* endeavour that ye	2Pet 1:15	
not in old time by the *w* of man	2Pet 1:21	*2307*
But the day of the Lord *w* come as	2Pet 3:10	
but he that doeth the *w* of God	1Jn 2:17	*2307*
ask any thing according to his *w*	1Jn 5:14	*2307*
I *w* remember his deeds which he	3Jn 10	
but I *w* not with ink and pen write	3Jn 13	*2309*
I *w* therefore put you in	Jude 5	*1014*
or else I *w* come unto thee	Rev 2:5	
w remove thy candlestick out of	Rev 2:5	
To him that overcometh *w* I give	Rev 2:7	
I *w* give thee a crown of life	Rev 2:10	
or else I *w* come unto thee	Rev 2:16	
w fight against them with the	Rev 2:16	
To him that overcometh *w* I give	Rev 2:17	
w give him a white stone, and in	Rev 2:17	
I *w* cast her into a bed, and them	Rev 2:22	
I *w* kill her children with death	Rev 2:23	
I *w* give unto every one of you	Rev 2:23	
I *w* put upon you none other	Rev 2:24	
to him *w* I give power over the	Rev 2:26	
I *w* give him the morning star	Rev 2:28	
I *w* come on thee as a thief, and	Rev 3:3	
know what hour I *w* come upon thee	Rev 3:3	
I *w* not blot out his name out of	Rev 3:5	

but I *w* confess his name before ..... Rev 3:5
I *w* make them of the synagogue of ..... Rev 3:9
I *w* make them to come and worship ..... Rev 3:9
I also *w* keep thee from the hour ..... Rev 3:10
Him that overcometh *w* I make a ..... Rev 3:12
I *w* write upon him the name of my ..... Rev 3:12
I *w* write upon him my new name ..... Rev 3:12
I *w* spue thee out of my mouth ..... Rev 3:16 *3195*
I *w* come in to him ..... Rev 3:20
w sup with him, and he with me ..... Rev 3:20
To him that overcometh *w* I grant ..... Rev 3:21
I *w* shew thee things which must ..... Rev 4:1
I *w* give power unto my two ..... Rev 11:3
And if any man *w* hurt them ..... Rev 11:5 *2309*
and if any man *w* hurt them ..... Rev 11:5 *2309*
all plagues, as often as they *w* ..... Rev 11:6 *2309*
I *w* shew unto thee the judgment ..... Rev 17:1
I *w* tell thee the mystery of the ..... Rev 17:7
in their hearts to fulfil his *w* ..... Rev 17:17 *1106*
he *w* dwell with them, and they ..... Rev 21:3
I *w* give unto him that is athirst ..... Rev 21:6
I *w* be his God, and he shall be my ..... Rev 21:7
I *w* shew thee the bride, the ..... Rev 21:9
And whosoever *w*, let him take the ..... Rev 22:17 *2309*

WILLETH {1}
So then it is not of him that *w* ..... Rom 9:16 *2309*

WILLING See APPENDIX.

WILLINGLY See APPENDIX.

WILLOW {1}
waters, and set it as a *w* tree ..... Eze 17:5 6851

WILLOWS {5}
of thick trees, and *w* of the brook ..... Lev 23:40 6155
the *w* of the brook compass him ..... Job 40:22 6155
upon the *w* in the midst thereof ..... Ps 137:2 6155
carry away to the brook of the *w* ..... Is 15:7 6155
as *w* by the water courses ..... Is 44:4 6155

WILT {245}
if thou *w* take the left hand, ... Gen 13:9
what *w* thou give me, seeing I go ..... Gen 15:2
and whither *w* thou go ..... Gen 16:8
W thou also destroy the righteous ..... Gen 18:23
w thou also destroy and not spare ..... Gen 18:24
w thou destroy all the city for ..... Gen 18:28
w thou slay also a righteous ..... Gen 20:4
thou *w* not deal falsely with me ..... Gen 21:23
saying, But if thou *w* give it ..... Gen 23:13
unto her, *W* thou go with this man ..... Gen 24:58
That thou *w* do us no hurt, as we ..... Gen 26:29
if thou *w* do this thing for me, I ..... Gen 30:31
What *w* thou give me, that thou ..... Gen 38:16
W thou give me a pledge, till ..... Gen 38:17
If thou *w* send our brother with ..... Gen 43:4
But if thou *w* not send him, we ..... Gen 43:5
the hand of him whom thou *w* send ..... Ex 4:13
if thou *w* not let my people go, ... Ex 8:21
them go, and *w* hold them still, ... Ex 9:2
that thou *w* not let them go ..... Ex 9:17
How long *w* thou refuse to humble ..... Ex 10:3
if thou *w* not redeem it, then ..... Ex 13:13
If thou *w* diligently hearken to ..... Ex 15:26
w do that which is right in his ..... Ex 15:26
w give ear to his commandments, ... Ex 15:26
Thou *w* surely wear away, both ..... Ex 18:18
if thou *w* make me an altar of ..... Ex 20:25
if thou *w* forgive their sin ..... Ex 32:32
me know whom thou *w* send with me ..... Ex 33:12
w thou put out the eyes of these ..... Num 16:14
w thou be wroth with all the ..... Num 16:22
If thou *w* indeed deliver this ..... Num 21:2
when thou *w* ease thyself abroad, ... Deut 23:13
if thou *w* not hearken unto the ..... Deut 28:15
If thou *w* not observe to do all ..... Deut 28:58
away, so that thou *w* not hear ..... Deut 30:17
what *w* thou do unto thy great ..... Josh 7:9
Caleb said unto her, What *w* thou ..... Judg 1:14
If thou *w* go with me, then I will ..... Judg 4:8
but if thou *w* not go with me, ... Judg 4:8
If thou *w* save Israel by mine ..... Judg 6:36
thou *w* save Israel by mine hand ..... Judg 6:37
W not thou possess that which ..... Judg 11:24
if thou *w* offer a burnt offering, ... Judg 13:16
If thou *w* redeem it, redeem it ..... Ruth 4:4
but if thou *w* not redeem it, then ..... Ruth 4:4
if thou *w* indeed look on the 1Sa 1:11
but *w* give unto thine handmaid a 1Sa 1:11
How long *w* thou be drunken 1Sa 1:14
w thou deliver them into the hand 1Sa 14:37
How long *w* thou mourn for Saul, ... 1Sa 16:1
wherefore then *w* thou sin against 1Sa 19:5
if thou *w* take that, take it 1Sa 21:9
that thou *w* not cut off my seed 1Sa 24:21
that thou *w* not destroy my name 1Sa 24:21
know and consider what thou *w* do 1Sa 25:17
that thou *w* neither kill me, nor 1Sa 30:15
w thou deliver them into mine 2Sa 5:19
w thou not tell me 2Sa 13:4
Joab said, Wherefore *w* thou run 2Sa 18:22
why *w* thou swallow up the 2Sa 20:19
thou *w* shew thyself merciful 2Sa 22:26
man thou *w* shew thyself upright 2Sa 22:26
the pure thou *w* shew thyself pure 2Sa 22:27
with the froward thou *w* shew 2Sa 22:27
the afflicted people thou *w* save 2Sa 22:28
or *w* thou flee three months 2Sa 24:13
if thou *w* walk in my ways, to 1Kin 3:14
if thou *w* walk in my statutes, and 1Kin 6:12
if thou *w* walk before me, as 1Kin 9:4
thee, and *w* keep my statutes and my 1Kin 9:4
if thou *w* hearken unto all that I 1Kin 11:38
w walk in my ways, and do that is 1Kin 11:38
If thou *w* be a servant unto this 1Kin 12:7
w serve them, and answer them, and 1Kin 12:7
If thou *w* give me half thine 1Kin 13:8
W thou go with me to battle to 1Kin 22:4
w thou go with me against Moab to 2Kin 3:7
Wherefore *w* thou go to him to day 2Kin 4:23
I know the evil that thou *w* do 2Kin 8:12
strong holds *w* thou set on fire 2Kin 8:12
their young men *w* thou slay with 2Kin 8:12
w dash their children, and rip up 2Kin 8:12
How then *w* thou turn away the 2Kin 18:24
w thou deliver them into mine 1Chr 14:10
that thou *w* build him an house 1Chr 17:25
if thou *w* walk before me, as 2Chr 7:17
of Judah, *W* thou go with me to 2Chr 18:3
our affliction, then thou *w* hear 2Chr 20:9
O our God, *w* thou not judge them 2Chr 20:12
But if thou *w* go, do it, be 2Chr 25:8
and when *w* thou return ..... Neh 2:6
the king unto her, What *w* thou ..... Est 5:3
with thee, *w* thou be grieved ..... Job 4:2
which of the saints *w* thou turn ..... Job 5:1
How long *w* thou not depart from ..... Job 7:19
How long *w* thou speak these ..... Job 8:2
I know that thou *w* not hold me ..... Job 9:28
w thou bring me into dust again ..... Job 10:9
thou *w* not acquit me from mine ..... Job 10:14
W thou break a leaf driven to and ..... Job 13:25
w thou pursue the dry stubble ..... Job 13:25
thou *w* have a desire to the work ..... Job 14:15
that thou *w* bring me to death ..... Job 30:23
w thou condemn him that is most ..... Job 34:17
W thou hunt the prey for the lion ..... Job 38:39
W thou trust him, because his ..... Job 39:11
or *w* thou leave thy labour to him ..... Job 39:11
W thou believe him, that he will ..... Job 39:12
W thou also disannul my judgment ..... Job 40:8
w thou condemn me, that thou ..... Job 40:8
w thou take him for a servant for ..... Job 41:4
W thou play with him as with a ..... Job 41:5
or *w* thou bind him for thy ..... Job 41:5
thou, LORD, *w* bless the righteous ..... Ps 5:12
with favour *w* thou compass him as ..... Ps 5:12
his heart, Thou *w* not require it ..... Ps 10:13
thou *w* prepare their heart ..... Ps 10:17
thou *w* cause thine ear to hear ..... Ps 10:17
How long *w* thou forget me, O LORD ..... Ps 13:1
how long *w* thou hide thy face ..... Ps 13:1
For thou *w* not leave my soul in ..... Ps 16:10
neither *w* thou suffer thine Holy ..... Ps 16:10
Thou *w* shew me the path of life ..... Ps 16:11
upon thee, for thou *w* hear me ..... Ps 17:6
thou *w* shew thyself merciful ..... Ps 18:25
man thou *w* shew thyself upright ..... Ps 18:25
the pure thou *w* shew thyself pure ..... Ps 18:26
thou *w* shew thyself froward ..... Ps 18:26
For thou *w* save the afflicted ..... Ps 18:27
but *w* bring down high looks ..... Ps 18:27
For thou *w* light my candle ..... Ps 18:28
LORD, how long *w* thou look on ..... Ps 35:17
thou *w* hear, O Lord my God ..... Ps 38:15
thou *w* not deliver him unto the ..... Ps 41:2
thou *w* make all his bed in his ..... Ps 41:3
heart, O God, thou *w* not despise ..... Ps 51:17
w not thou deliver my feet from ..... Ps 56:13
W not thou, O God, which hadst ..... Ps 60:10
Thou *w* prolong the king's life ..... Ps 61:6
in righteousness *w* thou answer us ..... Ps 65:5
w thou be angry for ever ..... Ps 79:5
how long *w* thou be angry against ..... Ps 80:4
if thou *w* hearken unto me ..... Ps 81:8
W thou be angry with us for ever ..... Ps 85:5
w thou draw out thine anger to ..... Ps 85:5
W thou not revive us again ..... Ps 85:6
for thou *w* answer me ..... Ps 86:7
W thou shew wonders to the dead ..... Ps 88:10
w thou hide thyself for ever ..... Ps 89:46
O when *w* thou come unto me ..... Ps 101:2
W not thou, O God, who hast cast ..... Ps 108:11
w not thou, O God, go forth with ..... Ps 108:11
saying, When *w* thou comfort me ..... Ps 119:82
when *w* thou execute judgment on ..... Ps 119:84
of trouble, thou *w* revive me ..... Ps 138:7
Surely thou *w* slay the wicked, O ..... Ps 139:19
if thou *w* receive my words, and ..... Prov 2:1
why *w* thou, my son, be ravished ..... Prov 5:20
How long *w* thou sleep, O sluggard ..... Prov 6:9
when *w* thou arise out of thy ..... Prov 6:9
W thou set thine eyes upon that ..... Prov 23:5
Thou *w* keep him in perfect peace, ... Is 26:3
thou *w* ordain peace for us ..... Is 26:12
forth, thou *w* debate with it ..... Is 27:8
How then *w* thou turn away the ..... Is 36:9
to night *w* thou make an end of me ..... Is 38:12
to night *w* thou make an end of me ..... Is 38:13
so *w* thou recover me, and make me ..... Is 38:16
w thou call this a fast, and an ..... Is 58:5
W thou refrain thyself for these ..... Is 64:12
w thou hold thy peace, and afflict ..... Is 64:12
W thou not from this time cry ..... Jer 3:4
If thou *w* return, O Israel, saith ..... Jer 4:1
and if thou *w* put away thine ..... Jer 4:1
thou art spoiled, what *w* thou do ..... Jer 4:30
then how *w* thou do in the ..... Jer 12:5
What *w* thou say when he shall ..... Jer 13:21
w thou not be made clean ..... Jer 13:27
w thou be altogether unto me as a ..... Jer 15:18
How long *w* thou go about, O thou ..... Jer 31:22
w thou not surely put me to death ..... Jer 38:15
w thou not hearken unto me ..... Jer 38:15
If thou *w* assuredly go forth unto ..... Jer 38:17
But if thou *w* not go forth to the ..... Jer 38:18
how long *w* thou cut thyself ..... Jer 47:5
thou *w* bring the day that thou ..... Lam 1:21
w thou destroy all the residue of ..... Eze 9:8
w thou make a full end of the ..... Eze 11:13
W thou judge them, son of man, ... Eze 20:4
son of man, *w* thou judge them ..... Eze 20:4
w thou judge, *w* thou judge the ..... Eze 22:2
w thou judge Aholah and Aholibah ..... Eze 23:36
W thou not tell us what these ..... Eze 24:19
W thou yet say before him that ..... Eze 28:9
W thou not shew us what thou ..... Eze 37:18
what *w* thou give ..... Hos 9:14
thou *w* cast all their sins into ..... Mic 7:19
Thou *w* perform the truth to Jacob ..... Mic 7:20
shall I cry, and thou *w* not hear ..... Hab 1:2
of violence, and thou *w* not save ..... Hab 1:2
I said, Surely thou *w* fear me ..... Zeph 3:7
thou *w* receive instruction ..... Zeph 3:7
how long *w* thou not have mercy on ..... Zec 1:12
If thou *w* walk in my ways ..... Zec 3:7
if thou *w* keep my charge, then ..... Zec 3:7
if thou *w* fall down and worship me ..... Mt 4:9
Or how *w* thou say to thy brother, ... Mt 7:4
him, saying, Lord, if thou *w* ..... Mt 8:2 *2309*
W thou then that we go and gather ..... Mt 13:28 *2309*
be it unto thee even as thou *w* ..... Mt 15:28 *2309*
if thou *w*, let us make here three ..... Mt 17:4 *2309*
but if thou *w* enter into life, ... Mt 19:17 *2309*
If thou *w* be perfect, go and sell ..... Mt 19:21 *2309*
And he said unto her, What *w* thou ..... Mt 20:21 *2309*
Where *w* thou that we prepare for ..... Mt 26:17 *2309*
not as I will, but as thou *w* ..... Mt 26:39
and saying unto him, If thou *w* ..... Mk 1:40 *2309*
Ask of me whatsoever thou *w* ..... Mk 6:22 *2309*
What *w* thou that I should do unto ..... Mk 10:51 *2309*
Where *w* thou that we go and ..... Mk 14:12 *2309*
not what I will, but what thou *w* ..... Mk 14:36 *2309*
If thou therefore *w* worship me ..... Lk 4:7
him, saying, Lord, if thou *w* ..... Lk 5:12 *2309*
w thou that we command fire to ..... Lk 9:54 *2309*
What *w* thou that I shall do unto ..... Lk 18:41
Where *w* thou that we prepare ..... Lk 22:9 *2309*
w thou rear it up in three days ..... Jn 2:20
unto him, *W* thou be made whole ..... Jn 5:6 *2309*
now, whatsoever thou *w* ask of God ..... Jn 11:22
W thou lay down thy life for my ..... Jn 13:38
how is it that thou *w* manifest ..... Jn 14:22
w thou at this time restore again ..... Acts 1:6
Because thou *w* not leave my soul ..... Acts 2:27
neither *w* thou suffer thine Holy ..... Acts 2:27
W thou kill me, as thou diddest ..... Acts 7:28 *2309*
what *w* thou have me to do ..... Acts 9:6 *2309*
w thou not cease to pervert the ..... Acts 13:10
W thou go up to Jerusalem, and ..... Acts 25:9
Thou *w* say then unto me, Why doth ..... Rom 9:19
Thou *w* say then, The branches ..... Rom 11:19
W thou then not be afraid of the ..... Rom 13:3 *2309*
knowing that thou *w* also do more ..... Philem 21
But *w* thou know, O vain man, that ..... Jas 2:20 *2309*

WIMPLES {1}
apparel, and the mantles, and the *w* ..... Is 3:22 4304

WIN {2}
thought to *w* them for himself 2Chr 32:1 1234
but dung, that I may *w* Christ ..... Phil 3:8 *2770*

WIND {123}
God made a *w* to pass over the ..... Gen 8:1 7307
the east *w* sprung up after them ..... Gen 41:6
thin, and blasted with the east *w* ..... Gen 41:23
ears blasted with the east *w* ..... Gen 41:27
the LORD brought an east *w* upon ..... Ex 10:13 7307
the east *w* brought the locusts ..... Ex 10:13 7307
turned a mighty strong west *w* ..... Ex 10:19 7307
by a strong east *w* all that night ..... Ex 14:21 7307
Thou didst blow with thy *w* ..... Ex 15:10 7307
went forth a *w* from the LORD ..... Num 11:31 7307
was seen upon the wings of the *w* 2Sa 22:11 7307
heaven was black with clouds and *w* 1Kin 18:45 7307
strong *w* rent the mountains, and 1Kin 19:11 7307
but the LORD was not in the *w* 1Kin 19:11 7307
after the *w* an earthquake 1Kin 19:11 7307
the LORD, Ye shall not see *w* 2Kin 3:17 7307
there came a great *w* from the ..... Job 1:19 7307
that is desperate, which are as *w* ..... Job 6:26 7307
O remember that my life is *w* ..... Job 7:7 7307
of thy mouth be like a strong *w* ..... Job 8:2 7307
and fill his belly with the east *w* ..... Job 15:2 7307
They are as stubble before the *w* ..... Job 21:18 7307
The east *w* carrieth him away, and ..... Job 27:21
they pursue my soul as the *w* ..... Job 30:15 7307
Thou liftest me up to the *w* ..... Job 30:22 7307
quieteth the earth by the south *w* ..... Job 37:17
but the *w* passeth, and cleanseth ..... Job 37:21 7307
the east *w* upon the earth ..... Job 38:24
chaff which the *w* driveth away ..... Ps 1:4 7307
did fly upon the wings of the *w* ..... Ps 18:10 7307
small as the dust before the *w* ..... Ps 18:42 7307
Let them be as chaff before the *w* ..... Ps 35:5 7307
ships of Tarshish with an east *w* ..... Ps 48:7 7307
He caused an east *w* to blow in ..... Ps 78:26

power he brought in the south *w* ... Ps 78:26
a *w* that passeth away, and cometh ... Ps 78:39 7307
as the stubble before the *w* ... Ps 83:13 7307
For the *w* passeth over it, and it ... Ps 103:16 7307
walketh upon the wings of the *w* ... Ps 104:3 7307
and raiseth the stormy *w*, which ... Ps 107:25 7307
he bringeth the *w* out of his ... Ps 135:7 7307
he causeth his *w* to blow, and the ... Ps 147:18 7307
stormy *w* fulfilling his word ... Ps 148:8 7307
his own house shall inherit the *w* ... Prov 11:29 7307
is like clouds and *w* without rain ... Prov 25:14 7307
The north *w* driveth away rain ... Prov 25:23 7307
Whosoever hideth her hideth the *w* ... Prov 27:16 7307
hath gathered the *w* in his fists ... Prov 30:4 7307
The *w* goeth toward the south, and ... Eccl 1:6 7307
the *w* returneth again according ... Eccl 1:6 7307
he that hath laboured for the *w* ... Eccl 5:16 7307
observeth the *w* shall not sow ... Eccl 11:4 7307
Awake, O north *w* ... Song 4:16
of the wood are moved with the *w* ... Is 7:2 7307
with his mighty *w* shall he shake ... Is 11:15 7307
of the mountains before the *w* ... Is 17:13 7307
have as it were brought forth *w* ... Is 26:18 7307
he stayeth his rough *w* in the day ... Is 27:8 7307
the day of the east *w* ... Is 27:8
be as an hiding place from the *w* ... Is 32:2 7307
the *w* shall carry them away, and ... Is 41:16 7307
their molten images are *w* ... Is 41:29 7307
but the *w* shall carry them all ... Is 57:13 7307
and our iniquities, like the *w* ... Is 64:6 7307
snuffeth up the *w* at her pleasure ... Jer 2:24 7307
A dry *w* of the high places in the ... Jer 4:11 7307
Even a full *w* from those places ... Jer 4:12 7307
And the prophets shall become *w* ... Jer 5:13 7307
bringeth forth the *w* out of his ... Jer 10:13 7307
away by the *w* of the wilderness ... Jer 13:24 7307
snuffed up the *w* like dragons ... Jer 14:6 7307
with an east *w* before the enemy ... Jer 18:17 7307
The *w* shall eat up all thy ... Jer 22:22 7307
up against me, a destroying *w* ... Jer 51:1 7307
bringeth forth the *w* out of his ... Jer 51:16 7307
part thou shalt scatter in the *w* ... Eze 5:2 7307
I will scatter toward every *w* all ... Eze 12:14 7307
and a stormy *w* shall rend it ... Eze 13:11 7307
it with a stormy *w* in my fury ... Eze 13:13 7307
when the east *w* toucheth it ... Eze 17:10 7307
the east *w* dried up her fruit ... Eze 19:12 7307
the east *w* hath broken thee in ... Eze 27:26 7307
he unto me, Prophesy unto the *w* ... Eze 37:9 7307
son of man, and say to the *w* ... Eze 37:9 7307
the *w* carried them away, that no ... Dan 2:35 7308
The *w* hath bound her up in her ... Hos 4:19 7307
For they have sown the *w*, and they ... Hos 8:7 7307
Ephraim feedeth on *w* ... Hos 12:1 7307
and followeth after the east *w* ... Hos 12:1
an east *w* shall come ... Hos 13:15
the *w* of the LORD shall come up ... Hos 13:15 7307
the mountains, and createth the *w* ... Amos 4:13 7307
sent out a great *w* into the sea ... Jonah 1:4 7307
God prepared a vehement east *w* ... Jonah 4:8 7307
faces shall sup up as the east *w* ... Hab 1:9
and the *w* was in their wings ... Zec 5:9 7307
A reed shaken with the *w* ... Mt 11:7 *417*
for the *w* was contrary ... Mt 14:24 *417*
But when he saw the *w* boisterous ... Mt 14:30 *417*
come into the ship, the *w* ceased ... Mt 14:32 *417*
And there arose a great storm of *w* ... Mk 4:37 *417*
And he arose, and rebuked the *w* ... Mk 4:39 *417*
the *w* ceased, and there was a ... Mk 4:39 *417*
of man is this, that even the *w* ... Mk 4:41 *417*
for the *w* was contrary unto them ... Mk 6:48 *417*
and the *w* ceased ... Mk 6:51 *417*
A reed shaken with the *w* ... Lk 7:24 *417*
down a storm of *w* on the lake ... Lk 8:23 *417*
Then he arose, and rebuked the *w* ... Lk 8:24 *417*
And when ye see the south *w* blow ... Lk 12:55
The *w* bloweth where it listeth ... Jn 3:8 *4151*
by reason of a great *w* that blew ... Jn 6:18 *417*
heaven as of a rushing mighty *w* ... Acts 2:2 *4157*
the *w* not suffering us, we sailed ... Acts 27:7 *417*
And when the south *w* blew softly ... Acts 27:13
arose against it a tempestuous *w* ... Acts 27:14 *417*
and could not bear up into the *w* ... Acts 27:15 *417*
hoised up the mainsail to the *w* ... Acts 27:40 *4154*
and after one day the south *w* blew ... Acts 28:13
about with every *w* of doctrine ... Eph 4:14 *417*
wave of the sea driven with the *w* ... Jas 1:6 *416*
when she is shaken of a mighty *w* ... Rev 6:13 *417*
that the *w* should not blow on the ... Rev 7:1 *417*

WINDING {3}

they went up with *w* stairs into ... 1Kin 6:8 3583
a *w* about still upward to the ... Eze 41:7 5437
for the *w* about of the house went ... Eze 41:7 4141

WINDOW {16}

A *w* shalt thou make to the ark, ... Gen 6:16 6672
that Noah opened the *w* of the ark ... Gen 8:6 2474
the Philistines looked out at a *w* ... Gen 26:8 2474
them down by a cord through the *w* ... Josh 2:15 2474
line of scarlet thread in the *w* ... Josh 2:18 2474
bound the scarlet line in the *w* ... Josh 2:21 2474
of Sisera looked out at a *w* ... Judg 5:28 2474
Michal let David down through a *w* ... 1Sa 19:12 2474
daughter looked through a *w* ... 2Sa 6:16 2474
her head, and looked out at a *w* ... 2Kin 9:30 2474
And he lifted up his face to the *w* ... 2Kin 9:32 2474
And he said, Open the *w* eastward ... 2Kin 13:17 2474
out at a *w* saw king David dancing ... 1Chr 15:29 2474
For at the *w* of my house I looked ... Prov 7:6 2474
there sat in a *w* a certain young ... Acts 20:9 *2376*
through a *w* in a basket was I let ... 2Cor 11:33 *2376*

WINDOWS {30}

the *w* of heaven were opened ... Gen 7:11 699
the *w* of heaven were stopped, and ... Gen 8:2 699
house he made *w* of narrow lights ... 1Kin 6:4 2474
there were *w* in three rows, and ... 1Kin 7:4 8261
and posts were square, with the *w* ... 1Kin 7:5 8260
the LORD would make *w* in heaven ... 2Kin 7:2 699
the LORD should make *w* in heaven ... 2Kin 7:19 699
look out of the *w* be darkened ... Eccl 12:3 699
wall, he looketh forth at the *w* ... Song 2:9 2474
for the *w* from on high are open, ... Is 24:18 699
And I will make thy *w* of agates ... Is 54:12 8121
cloud, and as the doves to their *w* ... Is 60:8 699
For death is come up into our *w* ... Jer 9:21 2474
chambers, and cutteth him out *w* ... Jer 22:14 2474
there were narrow *w* to the little ... Eze 40:16 2474
w were round about inward ... Eze 40:16 2474
And their *w*, and their arches, and ... Eze 40:22 2474
And there were *w* in it and in the ... Eze 40:25 2474
thereof round about, like those *w* ... Eze 40:25 2474
and there were *w* in it and in the ... Eze 40:29 2474
and there were *w* therein and in the ... Eze 40:33 2474
and the *w* to it round about ... Eze 40:36 2474
The door posts, and the narrow *w* ... Eze 41:16 2474
and from the ground up to the *w* ... Eze 41:16 2474
and the *w* were covered ... Eze 41:16 2474
And there were narrow *w* and palm ... Eze 41:26 2474
his *w* being open in his chamber ... Dan 6:10 3551
enter in at the *w* like a thief ... Joel 2:9 2474
their voice shall sing in the *w* ... Zeph 2:14 2474
will not open you the *w* of heaven ... Mal 3:10 699

WINDS {23}

To make the weight for the *w* ... Job 28:25 7307
I will scatter into all *w* them ... Jer 49:32 7307
four *w* from the four quarters of ... Jer 49:36 7307
scatter them toward all those *w* ... Jer 49:36 7307
will I scatter into all the *w* ... Eze 5:10 7307
a third part into all the *w* ... Eze 5:12 7307
shall be scattered toward all *w* ... Eze 17:21 7307
Come from the four *w*, O breath, ... Eze 37:9 7307
the four *w* of the heaven strove ... Dan 7:2 7308
ones toward the four *w* of heaven ... Dan 8:8 7307
toward the four *w* of heaven ... Dan 11:4 7307
as the four *w* of the heaven ... Zec 2:6 7307
the *w* blew, and beat upon that ... Mt 7:25 *417*
the *w* blew, and beat upon that ... Mt 7:27 *417*
Then he arose, and rebuked the *w* ... Mt 8:26 *417*
of man is this, that even the *w* ... Mt 8:27 *417*
his elect from the four *w* ... Mt 24:31 *417*
his elect from the four *w* ... Mk 13:27 *417*
for he commandeth even the *w* ... Lk 8:25 *417*
because the *w* were contrary ... Acts 27:4 *417*
great, and are driven of fierce *w* ... Jas 3:4 *417*
without water, carried about of *w* ... Jude 12 *417*
holding the four *w* of the earth ... Rev 7:1 *417*

WINDY {1}

hasten my escape from the *w* storm ... Ps 55:8 7307

WINE {230}

And he drank of the *w*, and was ... Gen 9:21 3196
Noah awoke from his *w*, and knew ... Gen 9:24 3196
of Salem brought forth bread and *w* ... Gen 14:18 3196
let us make our father drink *w* ... Gen 19:32 3196
their father drink *w* that night ... Gen 19:33 3196
make him drink *w* this night also ... Gen 19:34 3196
father drink *w* that night also ... Gen 19:35 3196
and he brought him *w*, and he drank ... Gen 27:25 3196
the earth, and plenty of corn and *w* ... Gen 27:28 8492
corn and *w* have I sustained him ... Gen 27:37 8492
he washed his garments in *w* ... Gen 49:11 3196
His eyes shall be red with *w* ... Gen 49:12 3196
an hin of *w* for a drink offering ... Ex 29:40 3196
Do not drink *w* nor strong drink, ... Lev 10:9 3196
offering thereof shall be of *w* ... Lev 23:13 3196
He shall separate himself from *w* ... Num 6:3 3196
and shall drink no vinegar of *w* ... Num 6:3 3196
that the Nazarite may drink *w* ... Num 6:20 3196
the fourth part of an hin of *w* ... Num 15:5 3196
the third part of an hin of *w* ... Num 15:7 3196
a drink offering half an hin of *w* ... Num 15:10 3196
the oil, and all the best of the *w* ... Num 18:12 8492
shalt thou cause the strong *w* to ... Num 28:7 7491
half an hin of *w* unto a bullock ... Num 28:14 3196
of thy land, thy corn, and thy *w* ... Deut 7:13 8492
gather in thy corn, and thy *w* ... Deut 11:14 8492
tithe of thy corn, or of thy *w* ... Deut 12:17 8492
the tithe of thy corn, of thy *w* ... Deut 14:23 8492
for oxen, or for sheep, or for *w* ... Deut 14:26 3196
gathered in thy corn and thy *w* ... Deut 16:13 3342
also of thy corn, of thy *w* ... Deut 18:4 8492
but shalt neither drink of the *w* ... Deut 28:39 3196
not leave thee either corn, *w* ... Deut 28:51 8492
have ye drunk *w* or strong drink ... Deut 29:6 3196
Their *w* is the poison of dragons, ... Deut 32:33 3196
drank the *w* of their drink ... Deut 32:38 3196
shall be upon a land of corn and *w* ... Deut 33:28 8492
w bottles, old, and rent, and bound ... Josh 9:4 3196
And these bottles of *w*, which we ... Josh 9:13 3196
unto them, Should I leave my *w* ... Judg 9:13 8492
drink not *w* nor strong drink, and ... Judg 13:4 3196
now drink no *w* nor strong drink, ... Judg 13:7 3196
let her drink *w* or strong drink ... Judg 13:14 3196
w also for me, and for thy ... Judg 19:19 3196
put away thy *w* from thee ... 1Sa 1:14 3196
neither *w* nor strong drink ... 1Sa 1:15 3196
ephah of flour, and a bottle of *w* ... 1Sa 1:24 3196
and another carrying a bottle of *w* ... 1Sa 10:3 3196
with bread, and a bottle of *w* ... 1Sa 16:20 3196
loaves, and two bottles of *w* ... 1Sa 25:18 3196
when the *w* was gone out of Nabal, ... 1Sa 25:37 3196
piece of flesh, and a flagon of *w* ... 2Sa 6:19
Amnon's heart is merry with *w* ... 2Sa 13:28 3196
summer fruits, and a bottle of *w* ... 2Sa 16:1 3196
and the *w*, that such as be faint ... 2Sa 16:2 3196
own land, a land of corn and *w* ... 2Kin 18:32 8492
and the fine flour, and the *w* ... 1Chr 9:29 3196
figs, and bunches of raisins, and *w* ... 1Chr 12:40 3196
piece of flesh, and a flagon of *w* ... 1Chr 16:3
of the vineyards for the *w* ... 1Chr 27:27 3196
and twenty thousand baths of *w* ... 2Chr 2:10 3196
and the barley, the oil, and the *w* ... 2Chr 2:15 3196
store of victual, and of oil and *w* ... 2Chr 11:11 3196
the firstfruits of corn, *w* ... 2Chr 31:5 8492
for the increase of corn, and *w* ... 2Chr 32:28 8492
the God of heaven, wheat, salt, *w* ... Ezr 6:9 2562
and to an hundred baths of *w* ... Ezr 7:22 2562
the king, that *w* was before him ... Neh 2:1 3196
and I took up the *w*, and gave it ... Neh 2:1 3196
the money, and of the corn, the *w* ... Neh 5:11 8492
and had taken of them bread and *w* ... Neh 5:15 3196
ten days store of all sorts of *w* ... Neh 5:18 3196
of all manner of trees, of *w* ... Neh 10:37 8492
of the corn, of the new *w* ... Neh 10:39 8492
the tithes of the corn, the new *w* ... Neh 13:5 8492
tithe of the corn and the new *w* ... Neh 13:12 8492
as also *w*, grapes, and figs, and ... Neh 13:15 3196
royal *w* in abundance, according ... Est 1:7 3196
of the king was merry with *w* ... Est 1:10 3196
unto Esther at the banquet of *w* ... Est 5:6 3196
second day at the banquet of *w* ... Est 7:2 3196
of *w* in his wrath went into the ... Est 7:7 3196
the place of the banquet of *w* ... Est 7:8 3196
drinking *w* in their eldest ... Job 1:13 3196
drinking *w* in their eldest ... Job 1:18 3196
my belly is as *w* which hath no ... Job 32:19 3196
their corn and their *w* increased ... Ps 4:7 8492
us to drink the *w* of astonishment ... Ps 60:3 3196
there is a cup, and the *w* is red ... Ps 75:8 3196
man that shouteth by reason of *w* ... Ps 78:65 3196
w that maketh glad the heart of ... Ps 104:15 3196
shall burst out with new *w* ... Prov 3:10 8492
and drink the *w* of violence ... Prov 4:17 3196
she hath mingled her *w* ... Prov 9:2 3196
drink of the *w* which I have ... Prov 9:5 3196
W is a mocker, strong drink is ... Prov 20:1 3196
he that loveth *w* and oil shall not ... Prov 21:17 3196
They that tarry long at the *w* ... Prov 23:30 3196
they that go to seek mixed *w* ... Prov 23:30 4469
thou upon the *w* when it is red ... Prov 23:31 3196
it is not for kings to drink *w* ... Prov 31:4 3196
w unto those that be of heavy ... Prov 31:6 3196
mine heart to give myself unto *w* ... Eccl 2:3 3196
drink thy *w* with a merry heart ... Eccl 9:7 3196
for laughter, and *w* maketh merry ... Eccl 10:19 3196
for thy love is better than *w* ... Song 1:2 3196
remember thy love more than *w* ... Song 1:4 3196
much better is thy love than *w* ... Song 4:10 3196
I have drunk my *w* with my milk ... Song 5:1 3196
like the best *w* for my beloved ... Song 7:9 3196
cause thee to drink of spiced *w* ... Song 8:2 3196
dross, thy *w* mixed with water ... Is 1:22 5435
until night, till *w* inflame them ... Is 5:11 3196
viol, the tabret, and pipe, and *w* ... Is 5:12 3196
them that are mighty to drink *w* ... Is 5:22 3196
tread out no *w* in their presses ... Is 16:10 3196
eating flesh, and drinking *w* ... Is 22:13 3196
The new *w* mourneth, the vine ... Is 24:7 8492
shall not drink *w* with a song ... Is 24:9 3196
is a crying for *w* in the streets ... Is 24:11 3196
ye unto her, A vineyard of red *w* ... Is 27:2 2561
of them that are overcome with *w* ... Is 28:1 3196
they also have erred through *w* ... Is 28:7 3196
drink, they are swallowed up of *w* ... Is 28:7 3196
they are drunken, but not with *w* ... Is 29:9 3196
own land, a land of corn and *w* ... Is 36:17 8492
their own blood, as with sweet *w* ... Is 49:26 6071
and drunken, but not with *w* ... Is 51:21 3196
yea, come, buy *w* and milk without ... Is 55:1 3196
Come ye, say they, I will fetch *w* ... Is 56:12 3196
stranger shall not drink thy *w* ... Is 62:8 8492
As the new *w* is found in the ... Is 65:8 8492
bottle shall be filled with *w* ... Jer 13:12 3196
bottle shall be filled with *w* ... Jer 13:12 3196
like a man whom *w* hath overcome ... Jer 23:9 3196
Take the *w* cup of this fury at my ... Jer 25:15 3196
of the LORD, for wheat, and for *w* ... Jer 31:12 8492
chambers, and give them *w* to drink ... Jer 35:2 3196
of the Rechabites pots full of *w* ... Jer 35:5 3196
and I said unto them, Drink ye *w* ... Jer 35:5 3196
But they said, We will drink no *w* ... Jer 35:6 3196
us, saying, Ye shall drink no *w* ... Jer 35:6 3196
to drink no *w* all our days, we, ... Jer 35:8 3196
commanded his sons not to drink *w* ... Jer 35:14 3196
but ye, gather ye *w*, and summer ... Jer 40:10 3196
unto Mizpah, and gathered *w* ... Jer 40:12 3196
I have caused *w* to fail from the ... Jer 48:33 3196
the nations have drunken of her *w* ... Jer 51:7 3196
their mothers, Where is corn and *w* ... Lam 2:12 3196
in the *w* of Helbon, and white wool ... Eze 27:18 3196
Neither shall any priest drink *w* ... Eze 44:21 3196
meat, and of the *w* which he drank ... Dan 1:5 3196
nor with the *w* which he drank ... Dan 1:8 3196

the *w* that they should drink ... Dan 1:16 3196
drank *w* before the thousand ... Dan 5:1 2562
whiles he tasted the *w*, ... Dan 5:2 2562
They drank *w*, and praised the gods ... Dan 5:4 2562
concubines, have drunk *w* in them ... Dan 5:23 2562
came flesh nor *w* in my mouth ... Dan 10:3 3196
know that I gave her corn, and *w* ... Hos 2:8 8492
my *w* in the season thereof, and ... Hos 2:9 8492
shall hear the corn, and the *w*, ... Hos 2:22 8492
other gods, and love flagons of *w* ... Hos 3:1 6025
Whoredom and *w* and new ... Hos 4:11 3196
new *w* take away the heart ... Hos 4:11 8492
made him sick with bottles of *w* ... Hos 7:5 3196
assemble themselves for corn and *w* ... Hos 7:14 8492
the new *w* shall fail in her ... Hos 9:2 8492
They shall not offer *w* offerings ... Hos 9:4 8492
shall be as the *w* of Lebanon ... Hos 14:7 8492
and howl, all ye drinkers of *w* ... Joel 1:5 3196
because of the new *w* ... Joel 1:5 6071
the new *w* is dried up, the oil ... Joel 1:10 8492
I will send you corn, and *w* ... Joel 2:19 8492
and the fats shall overflow with *w* ... Joel 2:24 8492
an harlot, and sold a girl for *w* ... Joel 3:3 3196
mountains shall drop down new *w* ... Joel 3:18 6071
they drink the *w* of the condemned ... Amos 2:8 3196
ye gave the Nazarites *w* to drink ... Amos 2:12 3196
but ye shall not drink *w* of them ... Amos 5:11 3196
That drink *w* in bowls, and anoint ... Amos 6:6 3196
the mountains shall drop sweet *w* ... Amos 9:13 6071
vineyards, and drink the *w* thereof ... Amos 9:14 3196
I will prophesy unto thee of *w* ... Mic 2:11 3196
with oil; and sweet *w* ... Mic 6:15 8492
but shalt not drink *w* ... Mic 6:15 3196
because he transgresseth by *w* ... Hab 2:5 3196
but not drink the *w* thereof ... Zeph 1:13 3196
upon the corn, and upon the new *w* ... Hag 1:11 8492
do touch bread, or pottage, or *w* ... Hag 2:12 3196
and make a noise as through *w* ... Zec 9:15 3196
men cheerful, and new *w* the maids ... Zec 9:17 8492
heart shall rejoice as through *w* ... Zec 10:7 3196
do men put new *w* into old bottles ... Mt 9:17 *3631*
the *w* runneth out, and the bottles ... Mt 9:17 *3631*
they put new *w* into new bottles ... Mt 9:17 *3631*
putteth new *w* into old bottles ... Mk 2:22 *3631*
else the new *w* doth burst the ... Mk 2:22 *3631*
the *w* is spilled, and the bottles ... Mk 2:22 *3631*
but new *w* must be put into new ... Mk 2:22 *3631*
him to drink *w* mingled with myrrh ... Mk 15:23 *3631*
drink neither *w* nor strong drink ... Lk 1:15 *3631*
putteth new *w* into old bottles ... Lk 5:37 *3631*
else the new *w* will burst the ... Lk 5:37 *3631*
But new *w* must be put into new ... Lk 5:38 *3631*
old *w* straightway desireth new ... Lk 5:39
eating bread nor drinking *w* ... Lk 7:33 *3631*
his wounds, pouring in oil and *w* ... Lk 10:34 *3631*
And when they wanted *w*, the mother ... Jn 2:3 *3631*
saith unto him, They have no *w* ... Jn 2:3 *3631*
tasted the water that was made *w* ... Jn 2:9 *3631*
beginning doth set forth good *w* ... Jn 2:10 *3631*
hast kept the good *w* until now ... Jn 2:10 *3631*
where he made the water *w* ... Jn 4:46 *3631*
said, These men are full of new *w* ... Acts 2:13 *1098*
to eat flesh, nor to drink *w* ... Rom 14:21 *3631*
And be not drunk with *w*, wherein ... Eph 5:18 *3631*
Not given to *w*, no striker, not ... 1Ti 3:3 *3943*
not given to much *w*, not greedy ... 1Ti 3:8 *3631*
but use a little *w* for thy ... 1Ti 5:23 *3631*
not soon angry, not given to *w* ... Titus 1:7 *3943*
accusers, not given to much *w* ... Titus 2:3 *3631*
lusts, excess of *w*, revellings, ... 1Pet 4:3 *3632*
thou hurt not the oil and the *w* ... Rev 6:6 *3631*
made all nations drink of the *w* ... Rev 14:8 *3631*
of the *w* of the wrath of God ... Rev 14:10 *3631*
w of the fierceness of his wrath ... Rev 16:19 *3631*
with the *w* of her fornication ... Rev 17:2 *3631*
all nations have drunk of the *w* ... Rev 18:3 *3631*
ointments, and frankincense, and *w* ... Rev 18:13 *3631*

WINEBIBBER {2}
Behold a man gluttonous, and a *w* ... Mt 11:19 *3630*
Behold a gluttonous man, and a *w* ... Lk 7:34

WINEBIBBERS {1}
Be not among *w* ... Prov 23:20 5433,3196

WINEFAT {2}
like him that treadeth in the *w* ... Is 63:2 1660
it, and digged a place for the *w* ... Mk 12:1 *5276*

WINEPRESS {15}
and as the fulness of the *w* ... Num 18:27 3342
and as the increase of the *w* ... Num 18:30 3342
out of thy floor, and out of thy *w* ... Deut 15:14 3342
Gideon threshed wheat by the *w* ... Judg 6:11 1660
Zeeb they slew at the *w* of Zeeb ... Judg 7:25 3342
of the barnfloor, or out of the *w* ... 2Kin 6:27 3342
of it, and also made a *w* therein ... Is 5:2 3342
I have trodden the *w* alone ... Is 63:3 6333
the daughter of Judah, as in a *w* ... Lam 1:15 1660
the *w* shall not feed them, and the ... Hos 9:2 3342
round about, and digged a *w* in it ... Mt 21:33 *3025*
the great *w* of the wrath of God ... Rev 14:19 *3025*
the *w* was trodden without the ... Rev 14:20 *3025*
city, and blood came out of the *w* ... Rev 14:20 *3025*
and he treadeth the *w* of the ... Rev 19:15 *3025,3631*

WINEPRESSES {4}
some treading *w* on the sabbath ... Neh 13:15 1660
their walls, and tread their *w* ... Job 24:11 3342
caused wine to fail from the *w* ... Jer 48:33 3342
of Hananeel unto the king's *w* ... Zec 14:10 3342

WINES {2}
a feast of *w* on the lees, of fat ... Is 25:6 8105
of *w* on the lees well refined ... Is 25:6 8105

WING {13}
was the one *w* of the cherub ... 1Kin 6:24 3671
cubits the other *w* of the cherub ... 1Kin 6:24 3671
the uttermost part of the one *w* ... 1Kin 6:24 3671
so that the *w* of the one touched ... 1Kin 6:27 3671
the *w* of the other cherub touched ... 1Kin 6:27 3671
one *w* of the one cherub was five ... 2Chr 3:11 3671
the other *w* was likewise five ... 2Chr 3:11 3671
reaching to the *w* of the other ... 2Chr 3:11 3671
one *w* of the other cherub was ... 2Chr 3:12 3671
the other *w* was five cubits also, ... 2Chr 3:12 3671
joining to the *w* of the other ... 2Chr 3:12 3671
there was none that moved the *w* ... Is 10:14 3671
shall dwell all fowl of every *w* ... Eze 17:23 3671

WINGED {2}
every *w* fowl after his kind ... Gen 1:21 3671
the likeness of any *w* fowl that ... Deut 4:17 3671

WINGS {76}
and how I bare you on eagles' *w* ... Ex 19:4 3671
stretch forth their *w* on high ... Ex 25:20 3671
the mercy seat with their *w* ... Ex 25:20 3671
spread out their *w* on high ... Ex 37:9 3671
covered with their *w* over the ... Ex 37:9 3671
cleave it with the *w* thereof ... Lev 1:17 3671
her young, spreadeth abroad her *w* ... Deut 32:11 3671
them, beareth them on her *w* ... Deut 32:11 84
under whose *w* thou art come to ... Ruth 2:12 3671
was seen upon the *w* of the wind ... 2Sa 22:11 3671
forth the *w* of the cherubims ... 1Kin 6:27 3671
their *w* touched one another in ... 1Kin 6:27 3671
even under the *w* of the cherubims ... 1Kin 8:6 3671
spread forth their two *w* over the ... 1Kin 8:7 3671
that spread out their *w*, and ... 1Chr 28:18
the *w* of the cherubims were ... 2Chr 3:11 3671
The *w* of these cherubims spread ... 2Chr 3:13 3671
even under the *w* of the cherubims ... 2Chr 5:7 3671
their *w* over the place of the ark ... 2Chr 5:8 3671
the goodly *w* unto the peacocks ... Job 39:13 3671
or *w* and feathers unto the ostrich ... Job 39:13 34
stretch her *w* toward the south ... Job 39:26 3671
hide me under the shadow of thy *w* ... Ps 17:8 3671
he did fly upon the *w* of the wind ... Ps 18:10 3671
trust under the shadow of thy *w* ... Ps 36:7 3671
said, Oh that I had *w* like a dove ... Ps 55:6 83
in the shadow of thy *w* will I ... Ps 57:1 3671
will trust in the covert of thy *w* ... Ps 61:4 3671
shadow of thy *w* will I rejoice ... Ps 63:7 3671
yet shall ye be as the *w* of a ... Ps 68:13 3671
under his *w* shalt thou trust ... Ps 91:4 3671
walketh upon the *w* of the wind ... Ps 104:3 3671
If I take the *w* of the morning, ... Ps 139:9 3671
certainly make themselves *w* ... Prov 23:5 3671
that which hath *w* shall tell the ... Eccl 10:20 3671
each one had six *w* ... Is 6:2 3671
the stretching out of his *w* shall ... Is 8:8 3671
Woe to the land shadowing with *w* ... Is 18:1 3671
shall mount up with *w* as eagles ... Is 40:31 83
Give *w* unto Moab, that it may ... Jer 48:9 6731
and shall spread his *w* over Moab ... Jer 48:40 3671
and spread his *w* over Bozrah ... Jer 49:22 3671
faces, and every one had four *w* ... Eze 1:6 3671
under their *w* on their four sides ... Eze 1:8 3671
four had their faces and their *w* ... Eze 1:8 3671
Their *w* were joined one to ... Eze 1:9 3671
their *w* were stretched upward ... Eze 1:11 3671
two *w* of every one were joined ... Eze 1:11
firmament were their *w* straight ... Eze 1:23 3671
I heard the noise of their *w* ... Eze 1:24 3671
they stood, they let down their *w* ... Eze 1:24 3671
stood, and had let down their *w* ... Eze 1:25 3671
w of the living creatures that ... Eze 3:13 3671
w was heard even to the outer ... Eze 10:5 3671
of a man's hand under their *w* ... Eze 10:8 3671
backs, and their hands, and their *w* ... Eze 10:12 3671
w to mount up from the earth ... Eze 10:16 3671
the cherubims lifted up their *w* ... Eze 10:19 3671
faces apiece, and every one four *w* ... Eze 10:21 3671
hands of a man was under their *w* ... Eze 10:21 3671
did the cherubims lift up their *w* ... Eze 11:22 3671
A great eagle with great *w* ... Eze 17:3 3671
another great eagle with great *w* ... Eze 17:7 3671
was like a lion, and had eagle's *w* ... Dan 7:4 1611
I beheld till the *w* thereof were ... Dan 7:4 1611
the back of it four *w* of a fowl ... Dan 7:6 1611
wind hath bound her up in her *w* ... Hos 4:19 3671
women, and the wind was in their *w* ... Zec 5:9 3671
had *w* like the *w* of a stork ... Zec 5:9 3671
arise with healing in his *w* ... Mal 4:2 3671
her chickens under her *w*, and ye ... Mt 23:37 *4420*
doth gather her brood under her *w* ... Lk 13:34 *4420*
had each of them six *w* about him ... Rev 4:8 *4420*
the sound of their *w* was as the ... Rev 9:9 *4420*
were given two *w* of a great eagle ... Rev 12:14 *4420*

WINK {2}
and what do thy eyes *w* at, ... Job 15:12 7335
neither let them *w* with the eye ... Ps 35:19 7169

WINKED {1}
times of this ignorance God *w* at ... Acts 17:30 *5237*

WINKETH {2}
He *w* with his eyes, he speaketh ... Prov 6:13 7169
He that *w* with the eye causeth ... Prov 10:10 7169

WINNETH {1}
and he that *w* souls is wise ... Prov 11:30 3947

WINNOWED {1}
which hath been *w* with the shovel ... Is 30:24 2219

WINNOWETH {1}
he *w* barley to night in the ... Ruth 3:2 2219

WINTER {14}
and cold and heat, and summer and *w* ... Gen 8:22 2779
thou hast made summer and *w* ... Ps 74:17 2779
the *w* is past, the rain is over ... Song 2:11 5638
of the earth shall *w* upon them ... Is 18:6 2778
I will smite the *w* house with the ... Amos 3:15 2779
in summer and in *w* shall it be ... Zec 14:8 2778
that your flight be not in the *w* ... Mt 24:20 *5494*
that your flight be not in the *w* ... Mk 13:18 *5494*
of the dedication, and it was *w* ... Jn 10:22 *5494*
haven was not commodious to *w* in ... Acts 27:12 *3915*
attain to Phenice, and there to *w* ... Acts 27:12 *3914*
w with you, that ye may bring me ... 1Cor 16:6 *3914*
Do thy diligence to come before *w* ... 2Ti 4:21 *5494*
for I have determined there to *w* ... Titus 3:12 *3914*

WINTERED {1}
which had *w* in the isle, whose ... Acts 28:11 *3916*

WINTERHOUSE {1}
sat in the *w* in the ninth month ... Jer 36:22 2779

WIPE {8}
I will *w* Jerusalem as a man ... 2Kin 21:13 4229
w not out my good deeds that I ... Neh 13:14 4229
the Lord GOD will *w* away tears ... Is 25:8 4229
did *w* them with the hairs of her ... Lk 7:38 *1591*
on us, we do *w* off against you ... Lk 10:11 *631*
feet, and to *w* them with the towel ... Jn 13:5 *1591*
God shall *w* away all tears from ... Rev 7:17 *1813*
God shall *w* away all tears from ... Rev 21:4 *1813*

WIPED {4}
his reproach shall not be *w* away ... Prov 6:33 4229
w them with the hairs of her head ... Lk 7:44 *1591*
w his feet with her hair, whose ... Jn 11:2 *1591*
and *w* his feet with her hair ... Jn 12:3 *1591*

WIPETH {2}
wipe Jerusalem as a man *w* a dish ... 2Kin 21:13 4229
w her mouth, and saith, I have ... Prov 30:20 4229

WIPING {1}
w it, and turning it upside down ... 2Kin 21:13 4229

WIRES {1}
thin plates, and cut it into *w* ... Ex 39:3 6616

WISDOM {234}
have filled with the spirit of *w* ... Ex 28:3 2451
him with the spirit of God, in *w* ... Ex 31:3 2451
are wise hearted I have put *w* ... Ex 31:6 2451
them up in *w* spun goats' hair ... Ex 35:26 2451
him with the spirit of God, in *w* ... Ex 35:31 2451
hath he filled with *w* of heart ... Ex 35:35 2451
man, in whom the LORD put *w* ... Ex 36:1 2451
in whose heart the LORD had put *w* ... Ex 36:2 2451
for this is your *w* and your ... Deut 4:6 2451
Nun was full of the spirit of *w* ... Deut 34:9 2451
according to the *w* of an angel of ... 2Sa 14:20 2451
went unto all the people in her *w* ... 2Sa 20:22 2451
Do therefore according to thy *w* ... 1Kin 2:6 2451
saw that the *w* of God was in him ... 1Kin 3:28 2451
And God gave Solomon *w* and ... 1Kin 4:29 2451
Solomon's *w* excelled the *w* ... 1Kin 4:30 2451
country, and all the *w* of Egypt ... 1Kin 4:30 2451
people to hear the *w* of Solomon ... 1Kin 4:34 2451
earth, which had heard of his *w* ... 1Kin 4:34 2451
And the LORD gave Solomon *w* ... 1Kin 5:12 2451
and he was filled with *w*, and ... 1Kin 7:14 2451
of Sheba had seen all Solomon's *w* ... 1Kin 10:4 2451
own land of thy acts and of thy *w* ... 1Kin 10:6 2451
thy *w* and prosperity exceedeth the ... 1Kin 10:7 2451
before thee, and that hear thy *w* ... 1Kin 10:8 2451
of the earth for riches and for *w* ... 1Kin 10:23 2451
sought to Solomon, to hear his *w* ... 1Kin 10:24 2451
and all that he did, and his *w* ... 1Kin 11:41 2451
Only the LORD give thee *w* ... 1Chr 22:12 7922
Give me now *w* and knowledge, that ... 2Chr 1:10 2451
but hast asked *w* and knowledge for ... 2Chr 1:11 2451
W and knowledge is granted unto ... 2Chr 1:12 2451
Sheba had seen the *w* of Solomon ... 2Chr 9:3 2451
land of thine acts, and of thy *w* ... 2Chr 9:5 2451
of thy *w* was not told me ... 2Chr 9:6 2451
before thee, and hear thy *w* ... 2Chr 9:7 2451
kings of the earth in riches and *w* ... 2Chr 9:22 2451
of Solomon, to hear his *w* ... 2Chr 9:23 2451
after the *w* of thy God, that is ... Ezr 7:25 2452
they die, even without *w* ... Job 4:21 2451
is *w* driven quite from me ... Job 6:13 8454
would shew thee the secrets of *w* ... Job 11:6 2451
people, and *w* shall die with you ... Job 12:2 2451
With the ancient is *w* ... Job 12:12 2451
With him is *w* and strength, he ... Job 12:13 2451
With him is strength and *w* ... Job 12:16 8454
and it should be your *w* ... Job 13:5 2451
dost thou restrain *w* to thyself ... Job 15:8 2451
thou counseled him that hath no *w* ... Job 26:3 2451
But where shall *w* be found ... Job 28:12 2451
the price of *w* is above rubies ... Job 28:18 2451
Whence then cometh *w* ... Job 28:20 2451
the fear of the LORD, that is *w* ... Job 28:28 2451
multitude of years should teach *w* ... Job 32:7 2451
should say, We have found out *w* ... Job 32:13 2451
peace, and I shall teach thee *w* ... Job 33:33 2451
and his words were without *w* ... Job 34:35 7919

W

he is mighty in strength and *w* Job 36:5 3820
Who hath put *w* in the inward Job 38:36 2451
Who can number the clouds in *w* Job 38:37 2451
God hath deprived her of *w* Job 39:17 2451
Doth the hawk fly by thy *w* Job 39:26 998
mouth of the righteous speaketh *w* Ps 37:30 2451
My mouth shall speak of *w* Ps 49:3 2454
part thou shalt make me to know *w* Ps 51:6 2451
we may apply our hearts unto *w* Ps 90:12 2451
In *w* hast thou made them all Ps 104:24 2451
and teach his senators *w* Ps 105:22 2449
of the LORD is the beginning of *w* Ps 111:10 2451
To him that by *w* made the heavens Ps 136:5 8394
To know *w* and instruction Prov 1:2 2451
To receive the instruction of *w* Prov 1:3 7919
but fools despise *w* and Prov 1:7 2451
W crieth without Prov 1:20 2454
thou incline thine ear unto *w* Prov 2:2 2451
For the LORD giveth *w* Prov 2:6 2451
up sound *w* for the righteous Prov 2:7 8454
When *w* entereth into thine heart, Prov 2:10 2451
Happy is the man that findeth *w* Prov 3:13 2451
The LORD by *w* hath founded the Prov 3:19 2451
keep sound *w* and discretion Prov 3:21 8454
Get *w*, get understanding Prov 4:5 2451
W is the principal thing Prov 4:7 2451
therefore get *w* Prov 4:7 2451
have taught thee in the way of *w* Prov 4:11 2451
My son, attend unto my *w*, and bow Prov 5:1 2451
Say unto *w*, Thou art my sister Prov 7:4 2451
Doth not *w* cry Prov 8:1 2451
O ye simple, understand *w* Prov 8:5 6195
For *w* is better than rubies Prov 8:11 2451
I *w* dwell with prudence, and find Prov 8:12 2451
Counsel is mine, and sound *w* Prov 8:14 8454
W hath builded her house, she Prov 9:1 2454
of the LORD is the beginning of *w* Prov 9:10 2451
hath understanding *w* is found Prov 10:13 2451
but fools die for want of *w* Prov 10:21 3820
but a man of understanding hath *w* Prov 10:23 2451
of the just bringeth forth *w* Prov 10:31 2451
but with the lowly is *w* Prov 11:2 2451
He that is void of *w* despiseth Prov 11:12 3820
be commended according to his *w* Prov 12:8 7922
but with the well advised is *w* Prov 13:10 2451
A scorner seeketh *w*, and findeth Prov 14:6 2451
The *w* of the prudent is to Prov 14:8 2451
W resteth in the heart of him Prov 14:33 2451
joy to him that is destitute of *w* Prov 15:21 3820
the LORD is the instruction of *w* Prov 15:33 2451
better is it to get *w* than gold Prov 16:16 2451
in the hand of a fool to get *w* Prov 17:16 2451
W is before him that hath Prov 17:24 2451
and intermeddleth with all *w* Prov 18:1 8454
the wellspring of *w* as a flowing Prov 18:4 2451
He that getteth *w* loveth his own Prov 19:8 3820
There is no *w* nor understanding Prov 21:30 2451
cease from thine own *w* Prov 23:4 998
will despise the *w* of thy words Prov 23:9 7922
also *w*, and instruction, and Prov 23:23 2451
Through *w* is an house builded Prov 24:3 2451
W is too high for a fool Prov 24:7 2454
knowledge of *w* be unto thy soul Prov 24:14 2451
Whoso loveth *w* rejoiceth his Prov 29:3 2451
The rod and reproof give *w* Prov 29:15 2451
I neither learned *w*, nor have the Prov 30:3 2451
She openeth her mouth with *w* Prov 31:26 2451
search out by *w* concerning all Eccl 1:13 2451
have gotten more *w* than all they Eccl 1:16 2451
heart had great experience of *w* Eccl 1:16 2451
And I gave my heart to know *w* Eccl 1:17 2451
For in much *w* is much grief Eccl 1:18 2451
yet acquainting mine heart with *w* Eccl 2:3 2451
also my *w* remained with me Eccl 2:9 2451
And I turned myself to behold *w* Eccl 2:12 2451
Then I saw that *w* excelleth folly Eccl 2:13 2451
is a man whose labour is in *w* Eccl 2:21 2451
a man that is good in his sight *w* Eccl 2:26 2451
W is good with an inheritance Eccl 7:11 2451
For *w* is a defence, and money is a Eccl 7:12 2451
that *w* giveth life to them that Eccl 7:12 2451
W strengtheneth the wise more Eccl 7:19 2451
All this have I proved by *w* Eccl 7:23 2451
and to search, and to seek out *w* Eccl 7:25 2451
a man's *w* maketh his face to Eccl 8:1 2451
I applied mine heart to know *w* Eccl 8:16 2451
nor device, nor knowledge, nor *w* Eccl 9:10 2451
This *w* have I seen also under the Eccl 9:13 2451
he by his *w* delivered the city Eccl 9:15 2451
W is better than strength Eccl 9:16 2451
the poor man's *w* is despised Eccl 9:16 2451
W is better than weapons of war Eccl 9:18 2451
him that is in reputation for *w* Eccl 10:1 2451
his *w* faileth him, and he saith to Eccl 10:3 3820
but *w* is profitable to direct Eccl 10:10 2451
hand I have done it, and by my *w* Is 10:13 2451
rest upon him, the spirit of *w* Is 11:2 2451
for the *w* of their wise men shall Is 29:14 2451
And *w* and knowledge shall be the Is 33:6 2451
Thy *w* and thy knowledge, it hath Is 47:10 2451
and what *w* is in them Jer 8:9 2451
not the wise man glory in his *w* Jer 9:23 2451
established the world by his *w* Jer 10:12 2451
Is *w* no more in Teman Jer 49:7 2451
is their *w* vanished Jer 49:7 2451
established the world by his *w* Jer 51:15 2451
With thy *w* and with thine Eze 28:4 2451
By thy great *w* and by thy traffick Eze 28:5 2451
against the beauty of thy *w* Eze 28:7 2451
sealest up the sum, full of *w* Eze 28:12 2451
thou hast corrupted thy *w* by Eze 28:17 2451
favoured, and skilful in all *w* Dan 1:4 2451
and skill in all learning and *w* Dan 1:17 2451
And in all matters of *w* and Dan 1:20 2451
w to Arioch the captain of the Dan 2:14 2942
for *w* and might are his Dan 2:20 2452
he giveth *w* unto the wise, and Dan 2:21 2452
my fathers, who hast given me *w* Dan 2:23 2452
any *w* that I have more than any Dan 2:30 2452
light and understanding and *w* Dan 5:11 2452
like the *w* of the gods, was found Dan 5:11 2452
excellent *w* is found in thee Dan 5:14 2452
the man of *w* shall see thy name Mic 6:9 8454
But *w* is justified of her Mt 11:19 *4678*
earth to hear the *w* of Solomon Mt 12:42 *4678*
said, Whence hath this man this *w* Mt 13:54 *4678*
what *w* is this which is given Mk 6:2 *4678*
disobedient to the *w* of the just Lk 1:17 *5428*
strong in spirit, filled with *w* Lk 2:40 *4678*
And Jesus increased in *w* and Lk 2:52 *4678*
But *w* is justified of all her Lk 7:35 *4678*
earth to hear the *w* of Solomon Lk 11:31 *4678*
Therefore also said the *w* of God Lk 11:49 *4678*
For I will give you a mouth and *w* Lk 21:15 *4678*
full of the Holy Ghost and *w* Acts 6:3 *4678*
were not able to resist the *w* Acts 6:10 *4678*
w in the sight of Pharaoh king of Acts 7:10 *4678*
in all the *w* of the Egyptians Acts 7:22 *4678*
depth of the riches both of the *w* Rom 11:33 *4678*
not with *w* of words, lest the 1Cor 1:17 *4678*
I will destroy the *w* of the wise 1Cor 1:19 *4678*
made foolish the *w* of this world 1Cor 1:20 *4678*
For after that in the *w* of God 1Cor 1:21 *4678*
God the world by *w* knew not God 1Cor 1:21 *4678*
sign, and the Greeks seek after *w* 1Cor 1:22 *4678*
the power of God, and the *w* of God 1Cor 1:24 *4678*
who of God is made unto us *w* 1Cor 1:30 *4678*
with excellency of speech or of *w* 1Cor 2:1 *4678*
with enticing words of man's *w* 1Cor 2:4 *4678*
should not stand in the *w* of men 1Cor 2:5 *4678*
Howbeit we speak *w* among them 1Cor 2:6 *4678*
yet not the *w* of this world, nor 1Cor 2:6 *4678*
But we speak the *w* of God in a 1Cor 2:7 *4678*
in a mystery, even the hidden *w* 1Cor 2:7
the words which man's *w* teacheth 1Cor 2:13 *4678*
For the *w* of this world is 1Cor 3:19 *4678*
given by the Spirit the word of *w* 1Cor 12:8 *4678*
sincerity, not with fleshly *w* 2Cor 1:12 *4678*
hath abounded toward us in all *w* Eph 1:8 *4678*
may give unto you the spirit of *w* Eph 1:17 *4678*
the church the manifold *w* of God Eph 3:10 *4678*
knowledge of his will in all *w* Col 1:9 *4678*
and teaching every man in all *w* Col 1:28 *4678*
are hid all the treasures of *w* Col 2:3 *4678*
a shew of *w* in will worship Col 2:23 *4678*
dwell in you richly in all *w* Col 3:16 *4678*
Walk in *w* toward them that are Col 4:5 *4678*
If any of you lack *w*, let him ask Jas 1:5 *4678*
his works with meekness of *w* Jas 3:13 *4678*
This *w* descendeth not from above, Jas 3:15 *4678*
But the *w* that is from above is Jas 3:17 *4678*
Paul also according to the *w* 2Pet 3:15 *4678*
to receive power, and riches, and *w* Rev 5:12 *4678*
Blessing, and glory, and *w*, and Rev 7:12 *4678*
Here is *w* Rev 13:18 *4678*
And here is the mind which hath *w* Rev 17:9 *4678*

WISE {247}

tree to be desired to make one *w* Gen 3:6 7919
Egypt, and all the *w* men thereof Gen 41:8 2450
look out a man discreet and *w* Gen 41:33 2450
none so discreet and *w* as thou art Gen 41:39 2450
Pharaoh also called the *w* men Ex 7:11 2450
If thou afflict them in any *w* Ex 22:23 6031
for the gift blindeth the *w* Ex 23:8 6493
speak unto all that are *w* hearted Ex 28:3 2450
are *w* hearted I have put wisdom Ex 31:6 2450
every *w* hearted among you shall Ex 35:10 2450
all the women that were *w* hearted Ex 35:25 2450
every *w* hearted man, in whom the Ex 36:1 2450
every *w* hearted man, in whose Ex 36:2 2450
And all the *w* men, that wrought Ex 36:4 2450
every *w* hearted man among them Ex 36:8 2450
but ye shall in no *w* eat of it Lev 7:24
thou shalt in any *w* rebuke thy Lev 19:17 3198
the field will in any *w* redeem it Lev 27:19
On this *w* ye shall bless the Num 6:23
Take you *w* men, and understanding, Deut 1:13 2450
w men, and known, and made them Deut 1:15 2450
Surely this great nation is a *w* Deut 4:6 2450
gift doth blind the eyes of the *w* Deut 16:19 2450
Thou shalt in any *w* set him king Deut 17:15
shalt in any *w* bury him that day Deut 21:23
shalt in any *w* let the dam go Deut 22:7
O that they were *w*, that they Deut 32:29 2449
in any *w* keep yourselves from the Josh 6:18
Else if ye do in any *w* go back Josh 23:12
Her *w* ladies answered her, yea, Judg 5:29 2450
but in any *w* return him a 1Sa 6:3
and fetched thence a *w* woman 2Sa 14:2 2450
and my lord is *w*, according to the 2Sa 14:20 2450
Then cried a *w* woman out of the 2Sa 20:16 2450
for thou art a *w* man, and knowest 1Kin 2:9 2450
lo, I have given thee a *w* 1Kin 3:12 2450
living child, and in no *w* slay it 1Kin 3:26
living child, and in no *w* slay it 1Kin 3:27
a *w* son over this great people 1Kin 5:7 2450
howbeit let me go in any *w* 1Kin 11:22
a *w* counsellor, they cast lots 1Chr 26:14 7922
counsellor, a *w* man, and a scribe 1Chr 27:32 995
given to David the king a *w* son 2Chr 2:12 2450
Then the king said to the *w* men Est 1:13 2450
Then said his *w* men and Zeresh his Est 6:13 2450
He taketh the *w* in their own Job 5:13 2450
He is *w* in heart, and mighty in Job 9:4 2450
For vain man would be *w*, though Job 11:12 3823
Should a *w* man utter vain Job 15:2 2450
Which *w* men have told from their Job 15:18 2450
I cannot find one *w* man among you Job 17:10 2450
as he that is *w* may be profitable Job 22:2 7919
Great men are not always *w* Job 32:9 2449
Hear my words, O ye *w* men Job 34:2 2450
let a *w* man hearken unto me Job 34:34 2450
not any that are *w* of heart Job 37:24 2450
Be *w* now therefore, O ye kings Ps 2:10 7919
LORD is sure, making *w* the simple Ps 19:7 2449
he hath left off to be *w*, and to Ps 36:3 7919
not thyself in any *w* to do evil Ps 37:8
For he seeth that *w* men die Ps 49:10 2450
and ye fools, when will ye be *w* Ps 94:8 7919
Whoso is *w*, and will observe these Ps 107:43 2450
A *w* man will hear, and will Prov 1:5 2450
shall attain unto *w* counsels Prov 1:5
the words of the *w*, and their dark Prov 1:6 2450
Be not *w* in thine own eyes Prov 3:7 2450
The *w* shall inherit glory Prov 3:35 2450
consider her ways, and be *w* Prov 6:6 2449
Hear instruction, and be *w* Prov 8:33 2449
rebuke a *w* man, and he will love Prov 9:8 2450
Give instruction to a *w* man Prov 9:9 2450
If thou be *w*, thou shalt Prov 9:12 2449
thou shalt be *w* for thyself Prov 9:12 2449
A *w* son maketh a glad father Prov 10:1 2450
gathereth in summer is a *w* son Prov 10:5 7919
The *w* in heart will receive Prov 10:8 2450
W men lay up knowledge Prov 10:14 2450
he that refraineth his lips is *w* Prov 10:19 7919
be servant to the *w* of heart Prov 11:29 2450
and he that winneth souls is *w* Prov 11:30 2450
that hearkeneth unto counsel is *w* Prov 12:15 2450
but the tongue of the *w* is health Prov 12:18 2450
A *w* son heareth his father's Prov 13:1 2450
The law of the *w* is a fountain of Prov 13:14 2450
walketh with *w* men shall Prov 13:20 2450
men shall be *w* Prov 13:20 2449
Every *w* woman buildeth her house Prov 14:1 2454
lips of the *w* shall preserve them Prov 14:3 2450
A *w* man feareth, and departeth Prov 14:16 2450
crown of the *w* is their riches Prov 14:24 2450
favour is toward a *w* servant Prov 14:35 7919
The tongue of the *w* useth Prov 15:2 2450
The lips of the *w* disperse Prov 15:7 2450
neither will he go unto the *w* Prov 15:12 2450
A *w* son maketh a glad father Prov 15:20 2450
The way of life is above to the *w* Prov 15:24 7919
of life abideth among the *w* Prov 15:31 2450
but a *w* man will pacify it Prov 16:14 2450
The *w* in heart shall be called Prov 16:21 2450
The heart of the *w* teacheth his Prov 16:23 2450
A *w* servant shall have rule over Prov 17:2 7919
a *w* man than an hundred stripes Prov 17:10 995
holdeth his peace, is counted *w* Prov 17:28 2450
and the ear of the *w* seeketh Prov 18:15 2450
mayest be *w* in thy latter end Prov 19:20 2449
is deceived thereby is not *w* Prov 20:1 2449
A *w* king scattereth the wicked, Prov 20:26 2450
is punished, the simple is made *w* Prov 21:11 2449
when the *w* is instructed, he Prov 21:11 2449
and oil in the dwelling of the *w* Prov 21:20 2450
A *w* man scaleth the city of the Prov 21:22 2450
ear, and hear the words of the *w* Prov 22:17 2450
My son, if thine heart be *w* Prov 23:15 2449
Hear thou, my son, and be *w* Prov 23:19 2449
he that begetteth a *w* child shall Prov 23:24 2450
A *w* man is strong Prov 24:5 2450
For by *w* counsel thou shalt make Prov 24:6
These things also belong to the *w* Prov 24:23 2450
so is a *w* reprover upon an Prov 25:12 2450
lest he be *w* in his own conceit Prov 26:5 2450
Seest thou a man *w* in his own Prov 26:12 2450
My son, be *w*, and make my heart Prov 27:11 2449
Whoso keepeth the law is a *w* son Prov 28:7 995
The rich man is *w* in his own Prov 28:11 2450
but *w* men turn away wrath Prov 29:8 2450
If a *w* man contendeth with a Prov 29:9 2450
but a *w* man keepeth it in till Prov 29:11 2450
earth, but they are exceeding *w* Prov 30:24 2450
The *w* man's eyes are in his head Eccl 2:14 2450
and why was I then more *w* Eccl 2:15 2449
w more than of the fool for ever Eccl 2:16 2450
And how dieth the *w* man Eccl 2:16 2450
he shall be a *w* man or a fool Eccl 2:19 2450
shewed myself *w* under the sun Eccl 2:19 2449
a *w* child than an old and foolish Eccl 4:13 2450
For what hath the *w* more than the Eccl 6:8 2450
The heart of the *w* is in the Eccl 7:4 2450
to hear the rebuke of the *w* Eccl 7:5 2450
oppression maketh a *w* man mad Eccl 7:7 2450
neither make thyself over *w* Eccl 7:16 2449
Wisdom strengtheneth the *w* more Eccl 7:19 2450
I said, I will be *w* Eccl 7:23 2449
Who is as the *w* man Eccl 8:1 2450
a *w* man's heart discerneth both Eccl 8:5 2450
though a *w* man think to know it, Eccl 8:17 2450

that the righteous, and the *w* ... Eccl 9:1 2450
neither yet bread to the *w* ... Eccl 9:11 2450
was found in it a poor *w* man ... Eccl 9:15 2450
The words of *w* men are heard in ... Eccl 9:17 2450
A *w* man's heart is at his right ... Eccl 10:2 2450
The words of a *w* man's mouth are ... Eccl 10:12 2450
because the preacher was *w* ... Eccl 12:9 2450
The words of the *w* are as goads ... Eccl 12:11 2450
them that are *w* in their own eyes ... Is 5:21 2450
the counsel of the *w* counsellors ... Is 19:11 2450
Pharaoh, I am the son of the *w* ... Is 19:11 2450
where are thy *w* men ... Is 19:12 2450
of their *w* men shall perish ... Is 29:14 2450
Yet he also is *w*, and will bring ... Is 31:2 2450
that turneth *w* men backward ... Is 44:25 2450
they are *w* to do evil, but to do ... Jer 4:22 2450
How do ye say, We are *w*, and the ... Jer 8:8 2450
The *w* men are ashamed, they are ... Jer 8:9 2450
Who is the *w* man, that may ... Jer 9:12 2450
Let not the *w* man glory in his ... Jer 9:23 2450
all the *w* men of the nations ... Jer 10:7 2450
priest, nor counsel from the *w* ... Jer 18:18 2450
her princes, and upon her *w* men ... Jer 50:35 2450
drunk her princes, and her *w* men ... Jer 51:57 2450
thy *w* men, O Tyrus, that were in ... Eze 27:8 2450
the *w* men thereof were in thee ... Eze 27:9 2450
destroy all the *w* men of Babylon ... Dan 2:12 2445
that the *w* men should be slain ... Dan 2:13 2445
to slay the *w* men of Babylon ... Dan 2:14 2445
the rest of the *w* men of Babylon ... Dan 2:18 2445
he giveth wisdom unto the *w* ... Dan 2:21 2445
to destroy the *w* men of Babylon ... Dan 2:24 2445
Destroy not the *w* men of Babylon ... Dan 2:24 2445
hath demanded cannot the *w* men ... Dan 2:27 2445
over all the *w* men of Babylon ... Dan 2:48 2445
the *w* men of Babylon before me ... Dan 4:6 2445
forasmuch as all the *w* men of my ... Dan 4:18 2445
said to the *w* men of Babylon, ... Dan 5:7 2445
Then came in all the king's *w* men ... Dan 5:8 2445
And now the *w* men, the astrologers ... Dan 5:15 2445
they that be *w* shall shine as the ... Dan 12:3 7919
but the *w* shall understand ... Dan 12:10 7919
Who is *w*, and he shall understand ... Hos 14:9 2450
destroy the *w* men out of Edom ... Obad 8 2450
and Zidon, though it be very *w* ... Zec 9:2 2449
of Jesus Christ was on this *w* ... Mt 1:18 *3779*
there came *w* men from the east to ... Mt 2:1 *3097*
he had privily called the *w* men ... Mt 2:7 *3097*
that he was mocked of the *w* men ... Mt 2:16 *3097*
diligently enquired of the *w* men ... Mt 2:16 *3097*
shall in no *w* pass from the law ... Mt 5:18 *3364*
I will liken him unto a *w* man ... Mt 7:24 *5429*
be ye therefore *w* as serpents ... Mt 10:16 *5429*
he shall in no *w* lose his reward ... Mt 10:42 *3364*
hast hid these things from the *w* ... Mt 11:25 *4680*
I in like *w* will tell you by what ... Mt 21:24
prophets, and *w* men, and scribes ... Mt 23:34 *4680*
w servant, whom his lord hath ... Mt 24:45 *5429*
And five of them were *w*, and five ... Mt 25:2 *5429*
But the *w* took oil in their ... Mt 25:4 *5429*
And the foolish said unto the *w* ... Mt 25:8 *5429*
But the *w* answered, saying, Not ... Mt 25:9 *5429*
I will not deny thee in any *w* ... Mk 14:31
hast hid these things from the *w* ... Lk 10:21 *4680*
w steward, whom his lord shall ... Lk 12:42 *5429*
could in no *w* lift up herself ... Lk 13:11 *3588,3838*
child shall in no *w* enter therein ... Lk 18:17
to me I will in no *w* cast out ... Jn 6:37
on this *w* shewed he himself ... Jn 21:1 *3779*
And God spake on this *w*, That his ... Acts 7:6 *3779*
to corruption, he said on this *w* ... Acts 13:34 *3779*
which ye shall in no *w* believe ... Acts 13:41
both to the *w*, and to the unwise ... Rom 1:14 *4680*
Professing themselves to be *w* ... Rom 1:22 *4680*
No, in no *w*: ... Rom 3:9 *3843*
is of faith speaketh on this *w* ... Rom 10:6 *3779*
lest ye should be *w* in your own ... Rom 11:25 *5429*
Be not *w* in your own conceits ... Rom 12:16 *5429*
you *w* unto that which is good ... Rom 16:19 *4680*
To God only *w*, be glory through ... Rom 16:27 *4680*
will destroy the wisdom of the *w* ... 1Cor 1:19 *4680*
Where is the *w* ... 1Cor 1:20 *4680*
how that not many *w* men after the ... 1Cor 1:26 *4680*
of the world to confound the *w* ... 1Cor 1:27 *4680*
as a *w* masterbuilder, I have laid ... 1Cor 3:10 *4680*
you seemeth to be *w* in this world ... 1Cor 3:18 *4680*
become a fool, that he may be *w* ... 1Cor 3:18 *4680*
He taketh the *w* in their own ... 1Cor 3:19 *4680*
knoweth the thoughts of the *w* ... 1Cor 3:20 *4680*
sake, but ye are *w* in Christ ... 1Cor 4:10 *5429*
there is not a *w* man among you ... 1Cor 6:5 *4680*
I speak as to *w* men ... 1Cor 10:15 *5429*
among themselves, are not *w* ... 2Cor 10:12 *4920*
seeing ye yourselves are *w* ... 2Cor 11:19 *5429*
not as fools, but as *w*, ... Eph 5:15 *4680*
invisible, the only *w* God ... 1Ti 1:17 *4680*
which are able to make thee *w* ... 2Ti 3:15 *4679*
of the seventh day on this *w* ... Heb 4:4 *3779*
Who is a *w* man and endued with ... Jas 3:13 *4680*
To the only *w* God our Saviour, be ... Jude 25 *4680*
there shall in no *w* enter into it ... Rev 21:27

WISELY {14}
Come on, let us deal *w* with them ... Ex 1:10 2449
sent him, and behaved himself *w* ... 1Sa 18:5 7919
behaved himself *w* in all his ways ... 1Sa 18:14 7919
that he behaved himself very *w* ... 1Sa 18:15 7919
w than all the servants of Saul ... 1Sa 18:30 7919
And he dealt *w*, and dispersed of ... 2Chr 11:23 995
of charmers, charming never so *w* ... Ps 58:5 2449
for they shall *w* consider of his ... Ps 64:9 7919
behave myself *w* in a perfect way ... Ps 101:2 7919
a matter *w* shall find good ... Prov 16:20 7919
The righteous man *w* considereth ... Prov 21:12 7919
but whoso walketh *w*, he shall be ... Prov 28:26 2451
not enquire *w* concerning this ... Eccl 7:10 2451
steward, because he had done *w* ... Lk 16:8 *5430*

WISER {8}
For he was *w* than all men ... 1Kin 4:31 2449
maketh us *w* than the fowls of ... Job 35:11 2449
hast made me *w* than mine enemies ... Ps 119:98 2449
a wise man, and he will be yet *w* ... Prov 9:9 2449
The sluggard is *w* in his own ... Prov 26:16 2450
Behold, thou art *w* than Daniel ... Eze 28:3 2450
w than the children of light ... Lk 16:8 *5429*
foolishness of God is *w* than men ... 1Cor 1:25 *4680*

WISH {6}
according to thy *w* in God's stead ... Job 33:6 6310
and put to shame that *w* me evil ... Ps 40:14 2655
they have more than heart could *w* ... Ps 73:7 4906
For I could *w* that myself were ... Rom 9:3 *2172*
and this also we *w*, even your ... 2Cor 13:9 *2172*
I *w* above all things that thou ... 3Jn 2 *2172*

WISHED {2}
w in himself to die, and said, It ... Jonah 4:8 7592
of the stern, and *w* for the day ... Acts 27:29 *2172*

WISHING {1}
to sin by *w* a curse to his soul ... Job 31:30 7592

WIST {13}
for they *w* not what it was ... Ex 16:15 3045
that Moses *w* not that the skin of ... Ex 34:29 3045
though he *w* it not, yet is he ... Lev 5:17 3045
w it not, and it shall be forgiven ... Lev 5:18 3045
but I *w* not whence they were ... Josh 2:4 3045
but he *w* not that there were ... Josh 8:14 3045
he *w* not that the LORD was ... Judg 16:20 3045
For he *w* not what to say ... Mk 9:6 *1492*
neither *w* they what to answer ... Mk 14:40 *1492*
w ye not that I must be about my ... Lk 2:49 *1492*
that was healed *w* not who it was ... Jn 5:13 *1492*
w not that it was true which was ... Acts 12:9 *1492*
I *w* not, brethren, that he was ... Acts 23:5 *1492*

WIT {21}
to *w* whether the LORD had made ... Gen 24:21 3045
to *w* what would be done to him ... Ex 2:4 3045
to *w*, for Machir the firstborn of ... Josh 17:1
David not knowing thereof, to *w* ... 1Kin 2:32
for the doors of the house, to *w* ... 1Kin 7:50
he saddled for him the ass, to *w* ... 1Kin 13:23
not from after them, to *w* ... 2Kin 10:29
of their father's house, to *w* ... 1Chr 7:2
Israel after their number, to *w* ... 1Chr 27:1
To *w*, the two pillars, and the ... 2Chr 4:12
the LORD is not with Israel, to *w* ... 2Chr 25:7
Then Amaziah separated them, to *w* ... 2Chr 25:10
for the burnt offerings, to *w* ... 2Chr 31:3
possession in their cities, to *w* ... Neh 11:3
purifications accomplished, to *w* ... Est 2:12
To *w*, Jerusalem, and the cities of ... Jer 25:18
serve himself of them, to *w* ... Jer 34:9
To *w*, the prophets of Israel ... Eze 13:16
waiting for the adoption, to *w* ... Rom 8:23
To *w*, that God was in Christ, ... 2Cor 5:19 *5613*
we do you to *w* of the grace of ... 2Cor 8:1 *1107*

WITCH {2}
Thou shalt not suffer a *w* to live ... Ex 22:18 3784
of times, or an enchanter, or a *w* ... Deut 18:10 3784

WITCHCRAFT {3}
For rebellion is as the sin of *w* ... 1Sa 15:23 7081
and used enchantments, and used *w* ... 2Chr 33:6 3784
Idolatry, *w*, hatred, variance, ... Gal 5:20 *5331*

WITCHCRAFTS {4}
Jezebel and her *w* are so many ... 2Kin 9:22 3785
I will cut off *w* out of thine ... Mic 5:12 3785
harlot, the mistress of *w* ... Nah 3:4 3785
and families through her *w* ... Nah 3:4 3785

WITH See APPENDIX.

WITHAL {33}
and bowls thereof, to cover *w* ... Ex 25:29 2004
for the staves to bear it *w* ... Ex 30:4 1992
his foot also of brass, to wash *w* ... Ex 30:18
of the sanctuary, to make it *w* ... Ex 36:3
bowls, and his covers to cover *w* ... Ex 37:16 2004
for the staves to bear it *w* ... Ex 37:27
sides of the altar, to bear it *w* ... Ex 38:7
and put water there, to wash *w* ... Ex 40:30
be that a man shall be defiled *w* ... Lev 5:3
to reconcile *w* in the holy place ... Lev 6:30
feet, to leap *w* upon the earth ... Lev 11:21 2004
be holy to praise the LORD *w* ... Lev 19:24
the bowls, and covers to cover *w* ... Num 4:7
in their right hands to blow *w* ... Judg 7:20
w of a beautiful countenance, and ... 1Sa 16:12 5973
w how he had slain all the ... 1Kin 19:1 834,3605
that Manasseh had provoked him *w* ... 2Kin 23:26
overlay the walls of the houses *w* ... 1Chr 29:4
to minister, and to offer *w* ... 2Chr 24:14
to shoot arrows and great stones *w* ... 2Chr 26:15
man *w* whom the king delighteth to ... Est 6:9
a potsherd to scrape himself *w* ... Job 2:8
own nets, whilst that I *w* escape ... Ps 141:10 3162
they shall *w* be fitted in thy ... Prov 22:18 3162
or to take water *w* out of the pit ... Is 30:14
that thou shalt sow the ground *w* ... Is 30:23
baptized *w* shall ye be baptized ... Mk 10:39
w it shall be measured to you ... Lk 6:38
not *w* to signify the crimes laid ... Acts 25:27
is given to every man to profit *w* ... 1Cor 12:7
W praying also for us, that God ... Col 4:3 *260*
And *w* they learn to be idle, ... 1Ti 5:13 *260*
But *w* prepare me also a lodging ... Philem 22 *260*

WITHDRAW {11}
unto the priest, *W* thine hand ... 1Sa 14:19 622
If God will not *w* his anger ... Job 9:13 7725
W thine hand far from me ... Job 13:21 7368
That he may *w* man from his ... Job 33:17 5493
W thy foot from thy neighbour's ... Prov 25:17 3365
also from this *w* not thine hand ... Eccl 7:18 3240
neither shall thy moon *w* itself ... Is 60:20 622
the stars shall *w* their shining ... Joel 2:10 622
the stars shall *w* their shining ... Joel 3:15 622
that ye *w* yourselves from every ... 2Th 3:6 *4724*
from such *w* thyself ... 1Ti 6:5 *868*

WITHDRAWEST {1}
Why *w* thou thy hand, even thy ... Ps 74:11 7725

WITHDRAWETH {1}
He *w* not his eyes from the ... Job 36:7 1639

WITHDRAWN {6}
have *w* the inhabitants of their ... Deut 13:13 5080
but my beloved had *w* himself ... Song 5:6 2559
he hath not *w* his hand from ... Lam 2:8 7725
that hath *w* his hand from ... Eze 18:8 7725
he hath *w* himself from them ... Hos 5:6 2502
he was *w* from them about a ... Lk 22:41 *645*

WITHDREW {6}
w the shoulder, and hardened their. Neh 9:29 5414,5437
Nevertheless I *w* mine hand ... Eze 20:22 7725
knew it, he *w* himself from thence ... Mt 12:15 *402*
But Jesus *w* himself with his ... Mk 3:7 *402*
he *w* himself into the wilderness, ... Lk 5:16 *5298*
but when they were come, he *w* ... Gal 2:12 *5288*

WITHER {11}
his leaf also shall not *w* ... Ps 1:3 5034
the grass, and *w* as the green herb ... Ps 37:2 5034
the reeds and flags shall *w* ... Is 19:6 7060
thing sown by the brooks, shall *w* ... Is 19:7 3001
blow upon them, and they shall *w* ... Is 40:24 3001
and the herbs of every field *w* ... Jer 12:4 3001
off the fruit thereof, that it *w* ... Eze 17:9 3001
it shall *w* in all the leaves of ... Eze 17:9 3001
shall it not utterly *w*, when the ... Eze 17:10 3001
it shall *w* in the furrows where ... Eze 17:10 3001
and the top of Carmel shall *w* ... Amos 1:2 3001

WITHERED {25}
And, behold, seven ears, *w* ... Gen 41:23 6798
heart is smitten, and *w* like grass ... Ps 102:4 3001
and I am *w* like grass ... Ps 102:11 3001
for the hay is *w* away, the grass ... Is 15:6 3001
When the boughs thereof are *w* ... Is 27:11 3001
it is *w*, it is become like a ... Lam 4:8 3001
her strong rods were broken and *w* ... Eze 19:12 3001
all the trees of the field, are *w* ... Joel 1:12 3001
because joy is *w* away from the ... Joel 1:12 3001
for the corn is *w* ... Joel 1:17 3001
piece whereupon it rained not *w* ... Amos 4:7 3001
and it smote the gourd that it *w* ... Jonah 4:7 3001
was a man which had his hand *w* ... Mt 12:10 *3584*
they had no root, they *w* away ... Mt 13:6 *3583*
And presently the fig tree *w* away ... Mt 21:19 *3583*
How soon is the fig tree *w* away ... Mt 21:20 *3583*
a man there which had a *w* hand ... Mk 3:1 *3583*
unto the man which had the *w* hand ... Mk 3:3 *3583*
because it had no root, it *w* away ... Mk 4:6 *3583*
which thou cursedst is *w* away ... Mk 11:21 *3583*
was a man whose right hand was *w* ... Lk 6:6 *3584*
to the man which had the *w* hand ... Lk 6:8 *3584*
it *w* away, because it lacked ... Lk 8:6 *3583*
impotent folk, of blind, halt, *w* ... Jn 5:3 *3584*
cast forth as a branch, and is *w* ... Jn 15:6 *3583*

WITHERETH {8}
it *w* before any other herb ... Job 8:12 3001
the evening it is cut down, and *w* ... Ps 90:6 3001
which *w* afore it groweth up ... Ps 129:6 3001
The grass *w*, the flower fadeth ... Is 40:7 3001
The grass *w*, the flower fadeth ... Is 40:8 3001
but it *w* the grass, and the flower ... Jas 1:11 *3583*
The grass *w*, and the flower ... 1Pet 1:24 *3583*
trees whose fruit *w*, without ... Jude 12 *5352*

WITHHELD {6}
for I also *w* thee from sinning ... Gen 20:6 2820
seeing thou hast not *w* thy son ... Gen 22:12 2820
this thing, and hast not *w* thy son ... Gen 22:16 2820
who hath *w* from thee the fruit of ... Gen 30:2 4513
If I have *w* the poor from their ... Job 31:16 4513
I *w* not my heart from any joy ... Eccl 2:10 4513

WITHHELDEST {1}
w not thy manna from their mouth, ... Neh 9:20 4513

WITHHOLD {9}
none of us shall *w* from thee his ... Gen 23:6 3607
for he will not *w* me from thee ... 2Sa 13:13 4513
but who can *w* himself from ... Job 4:2 6113
W not thou thy tender mercies ... Ps 40:11 3607
no good thing will he *w* from them ... Ps 84:11 4513
W not good from them to whom it ... Prov 3:27 4513
W not correction from the child ... Prov 23:13 4513

in the evening *w* not thine hand ... Eccl 11:6 3240
W thy foot from being unshod, and ... Jer 2:25 4513

WITHHOLDEN {10}
seeing the LORD hath *w* thee from ... 1Sa 25:26 4513
thou hast *w* bread from the hungry ... Job 22:7 4513
from the wicked their light is *w* ... Job 38:15 4513
no thought can be *w* from thee ... Job 42:2 1219
hast not *w* the request of his ... Ps 21:2 4513
Therefore the showers have been *w* ... Jer 3:3 4513
your sins have *w* good things from ... Jer 5:25 4513
hath not *w* the pledge, neither ... Eze 18:16 2254
the drink offering is *w* from the ... Joel 1:13 4513
also I have *w* the rain from you, ... Amos 4:7 4513

WITHHOLDETH {4}
he *w* the waters, and they dry up ... Job 12:15 6113
there is that *w* more than is meet ... Prov 11:24 2820
He that *w* corn, the people shall ... Prov 11:26 4513
now ye know what *w* that he might ... 2Th 2:6 2722

WITHIN See APPENDIX.

WITHOUT See APPENDIX.

WITHS {3}
green *w* that were never dried ... Judg 16:7 3499
green *w* which had not been dried ... Judg 16:8 3499
And he brake the *w*, as a thread of ... Judg 16:9 3499

WITHSTAND {10}
behold, I went out to *w* thee ... Num 22:32 7854
and could not *w* them ... 2Chr 13:7 2388
now ye think to *w* the kingdom of ... 2Chr 13:8 2388
so that none is able to *w* thee ... 2Chr 20:6 3320
and no man could *w* them ... Est 9:2 5975
against him, two shall *w* him ... Eccl 4:12 5975
the arms of the south shall not *w* ... Dan 11:15 5975
shall there be any strength to *w* ... Dan 11:15 5975
what was I, that I could *w* God ... Acts 11:17 2967
may be able to *w* in the evil day ... Eph 6:13 436

WITHSTOOD {6}
they *w* Uzziah the king, and said ... 2Chr 26:18 5975
of the kingdom of Persia *w* me one ... Dan 10:13 5975
name by interpretation) *w* them ... Acts 13:8 436
I *w* him to the face, because he ... Gal 2:11 436
Now as Jannes and Jambres *w* Moses ... 2Ti 3:8 436
for he hath greatly *w* our words ... 2Ti 4:15 436

WITNESS {135}
that they may be a *w* unto me ... Gen 21:30 5713
and let it be for a *w* between me ... Gen 31:44 5707
said, This heap is a *w* between me ... Gen 31:48 5707
God is *w* betwixt me and thee ... Gen 31:50 5707
This heap be *w* ... Gen 31:52 5707
and this pillar be *w* ... Gen 31:52 5711
false *w* against thy neighbour ... Ex 20:16 5707
then let him bring it for *w* ... Ex 22:13 5707
the wicked to be an unrighteous *w* ... Ex 23:1 5707
the voice of swearing, and is a *w* ... Lev 5:1 5707
and there be no *w* against her ... Num 5:13 5707
the LORD in the tabernacle of *w* ... Num 17:7 5715
went into the tabernacle of *w* ... Num 17:8 5715
before the tabernacle of *w* ... Num 18:2 5715
but one *w* shall not testify ... Num 35:30 5707
earth to *w* against you this day, ... Deut 4:26 5749
false *w* against thy neighbour ... Deut 5:20 5707
but at the mouth of one *w* he ... Deut 17:6 5707
One *w* shall not rise up against a ... Deut 19:15 5707
If a false *w* rise up against any ... Deut 19:16 5707
if the *w* be a false *w* ... Deut 19:18 5707
that this song may be a *w* for me ... Deut 31:19 5707
shall testify against them as a *w* ... Deut 31:21 5707
may be there for a *w* against thee ... Deut 31:26 5707
But that it may be a *w* between us ... Josh 22:27 5707
but it is a *w* between us and you ... Josh 22:28 5707
for it shall be a *w* between us ... Josh 22:34 5707
this stone shall be a *w* unto us ... Josh 24:27 5713
shall be therefore a *w* unto you ... Josh 24:27 5713
The LORD be *w* between us ... Judg 11:10 8085
w against me before the LORD, and ... 1Sa 12:3 6030
them, The LORD is *w* against you ... 1Sa 12:5 5707
and his anointed is *w* this day ... 1Sa 12:5 5707
And they answered, He is *w* ... 1Sa 12:5 5707
to bear *w* against him, saying, ... 1Kin 21:10 5749
Israel, for the tabernacle of *w* ... 2Chr 24:6 5715
wrinkles, which is a *w* against me ... Job 16:8 5707
up in me beareth *w* to my face ... Job 16:8 6030
my *w* is in heaven, and my record ... Job 16:19 5707
the eye saw me, it gave *w* to me ... Job 29:11 5749
and as a faithful *w* in heaven ... Ps 89:37 5707
A false *w* that speaketh lies, and ... Prov 6:19 5707
but a false *w* deceit ... Prov 12:17 5707
A faithful *w* will not lie ... Prov 14:5 5707
but a false *w* will utter lies ... Prov 14:5 5707
A true *w* delivereth souls ... Prov 14:25 5707
but a deceitful *w* speaketh lies ... Prov 14:25
A false *w* shall not be unpunished ... Prov 19:5 5707
A false *w* shall not be unpunished ... Prov 19:9 5707
An ungodly *w* scorneth judgment ... Prov 19:28 5707
A false *w* shall perish ... Prov 21:28 5707
Be not a *w* against thy neighbour ... Prov 24:28 5707
A man that beareth false *w* ... Prov 25:18 5707
countenance doth *w* against them ... Is 3:9 5707
for a *w* unto the LORD of hosts in ... Is 19:20 5707
given him for a *w* to the people ... Is 55:4 5707
even I know, and am a *w*, saith the ... Jer 29:23 5707
faithful *w* between us, if we do ... Jer 42:5 5707
thing shall I take to *w* for thee ... Lam 2:13 5749
let the Lord GOD be *w* against you ... Mic 1:2 5707
the LORD hath been *w* between thee ... Mal 2:14 5749
I will be a swift *w* against the ... Mal 3:5 5707
fornications, thefts, false *w* ... Mt 15:19 5577
Thou shalt not bear false *w* ... Mt 19:18 5576
world for a *w* unto all nations ... Mt 24:14 3142
sought false *w* against Jesus, to ... Mt 26:59 5577
is it which these *w* against thee ... Mt 26:62 2649
many things they *w* against thee ... Mt 27:13 2649
Do not steal, Do not bear false *w* ... Mk 10:19 5576
all the council sought for *w* ... Mk 14:55 3141
For many bare false *w* against him ... Mk 14:56 5576
but their *w* agreed not together ... Mk 14:56 3141
bare false *w* against him, saying, ... Mk 14:57 5576
so did their *w* agree together ... Mk 14:59 3141
is it which these *w* against thee ... Mk 14:60 2649
many things they *w* against thee ... Mk 15:4 2649
And all bare him *w*, and wondered at ... Lk 4:22 3140
Truly ye bear *w* that ye allow the ... Lk 11:48 3140
Do not steal, Do not bear false *w* ... Lk 18:20 5576
said, What need we any further *w* ... Lk 22:71 3141
The same came for a *w* ... Jn 1:7 3141
to bear *w* of the Light, that all ... Jn 1:7 3140
was sent to bear *w* of that Light ... Jn 1:8 3140
John bare *w* of him, and cried, ... Jn 1:15 3140
and ye receive not our *w* ... Jn 3:11 3141
Jordan, to whom thou barest *w* ... Jn 3:26 3140
Ye yourselves bear me *w*, that I ... Jn 3:28 3140
If I bear *w* of myself ... Jn 5:31 3140
of myself, my *w* is not true ... Jn 5:31 3141
is another that beareth *w* of me ... Jn 5:32 3140
I know that the *w* which he ... Jn 5:32 3141
John, and he bare *w* unto the truth ... Jn 5:33 3140
have greater *w* than that of John ... Jn 5:36 3141
bear *w* of me, that the Father ... Jn 5:36 3140
hath sent me, hath borne *w* of me ... Jn 5:37 3140
I am one that bear *w* of myself ... Jn 8:18 3140
that sent me beareth *w* of me ... Jn 8:18 3140
Father's name, they bear *w* of me ... Jn 10:25 3140
And ye also shall bear *w*, because ... Jn 15:27 3140
spoken evil, bear *w* of the evil ... Jn 18:23 3140
I should bear *w* unto the truth ... Jn 18:37 3140
a *w* with us of his resurrection ... Acts 1:22 3144
great power gave the apostles *w* ... Acts 4:33 3142
tabernacle of *w* in the wilderness ... Acts 7:44 3142
To him give all the prophets *w* ... Acts 10:43 3140
he left not himself without *w* ... Acts 14:17 267
knoweth the hearts, bare them *w* ... Acts 15:8 3140
the high priest doth bear me *w* ... Acts 22:5 3140
For thou shalt be his *w* unto all ... Acts 22:15 3144
so must thou bear *w* also at Rome ... Acts 23:11 3140
a *w* both of these things which ... Acts 26:16 3144
For God is my *w*, whom I serve ... Rom 1:9 3144
their conscience also bearing *w* ... Rom 2:15 4828
itself beareth *w* with our spirit ... Rom 8:16 4828
bearing me *w* in the Holy Ghost ... Rom 9:1 4828
Thou shalt not bear false *w* ... Rom 13:9 5576
God is *w* ... 1Th 2:5 3144
This *w* is true ... Titus 1:13 3141
God also bearing them *w*, both ... Heb 2:4 4901
the Holy Ghost also is a *w* to us ... Heb 10:15 3140
by which he obtained *w* that he ... Heb 11:4 3140
of them shall be a *w* against you ... Jas 5:3 3142
a *w* of the sufferings of Christ, ... 1Pet 5:1 3144
and we have seen it, and bear *w* ... 1Jn 1:2 3140
it is the Spirit that beareth *w* ... 1Jn 5:6 3140
are three that bear *w* in earth ... 1Jn 5:8 3140
If we receive the *w* of men ... 1Jn 5:9 3141
the *w* of God is greater ... 1Jn 5:9 3141
for this is the *w* of God which he ... 1Jn 5:9 3141
Son of God hath the *w* in himself ... 1Jn 5:10 3141
Which have borne *w* of thy charity ... 3Jn 6 3140
Christ, who is the faithful *w* ... Rev 1:5 3144
the Amen, the faithful and true *w* ... Rev 3:14 3144
were beheaded for the *w* of Jesus ... Rev 20:4 3141

WITNESSED {4}
the men of Belial *w* against him ... 1Kin 21:13 5749
being *w* by the law and the ... Rom 3:21 3140
Pilate *w* a good confession ... 1Ti 6:13 3140
of whom it is *w* that he liveth ... Heb 7:8 3140

WITNESSES {49}
be put to death by the mouth of *w* ... Num 35:30 5707
of two *w*, or three *w* ... Deut 17:6 5707
The hands of the *w* shall be first ... Deut 17:7 5707
at the mouth of two *w* ... Deut 19:15 5707
or at the mouth of three *w* ... Deut 19:15 5707
Ye are *w* against yourselves that ... Josh 24:22 5707
And they said, We are *w* ... Josh 24:22 5707
Ye are *w* this day, that I have ... Ruth 4:9 5707
ye are *w* this day ... Ruth 4:10 5707
and the elders, said, We are *w* ... Ruth 4:11 5707
Thou renewest thy *w* against me ... Job 10:17 5707
for false *w* are risen up against ... Ps 27:12 5707
False *w* did rise up ... Ps 35:11 5707
took unto me faithful *w* to record ... Is 8:2 5707
let them bring forth their *w* ... Is 43:9 5707
Ye are my *w*, saith the LORD, and ... Is 43:10 5707
therefore ye are my *w*, saith the ... Is 43:12 5707
ye are even my *w* ... Is 44:8 5707
and they are their own *w* ... Is 44:9 5707
evidence, and sealed it, and took *w* ... Jer 32:10 5707
in the presence of the *w* that ... Jer 32:12 5707
the field for money, and take *w* ... Jer 32:25 5707
take *w* in the land of Benjamin, ... Jer 32:44 5707
in the mouth of two or three *w* ... Mt 18:16 3144
Wherefore ye be *w* unto yourselves ... Mt 23:31 3140
yea, though many false *w* came ... Mt 26:60 5575
At the last came two false *w* ... Mt 26:60 5575
what further need have we of *w* ... Mt 26:65 3144
saith, What need we any further *w* ... Mk 14:63 3144
And ye are *w* of these things ... Lk 24:48 3144
ye shall be *w* unto me both in ... Acts 1:8 3144
raised up, whereof we all are *w* ... Acts 2:32 3144
whereof we are *w* ... Acts 3:15 3144
we are his *w* of these things ... Acts 5:32 3144
And set up false *w*, which said, ... Acts 6:13 3144
the *w* laid down their clothes at ... Acts 7:58 3144
we are *w* of all things which he ... Acts 10:39 3144
but unto *w* chosen before of God, ... Acts 10:41 3144
who are his *w* unto the people ... Acts 13:31 3144
and we are found false *w* of God ... 1Cor 15:15 5575
In the mouth of two or three *w* ... 2Cor 13:1 3144
Ye are *w*, and God also, how holily ... 1Th 2:10 3144
but before two or three *w* ... 1Ti 5:19 3144
a good profession before many *w* ... 1Ti 6:12 3144
hast heard of me among many *w* ... 2Ti 2:2 3144
mercy under two or three *w* ... Heb 10:28 3144
about with so great a cloud of *w* ... Heb 12:1 3144
I will give power unto my two *w* ... Rev 11:3 3144

WITNESSETH {2}
witness which he *w* of me is true ... Jn 5:32 3140
the Holy Ghost *w* in every city ... Acts 20:23 1263

WITNESSING {1}
w both to small and great, saying ... Acts 26:22 3140

WIT'S {1}
man, and are at their *w* end ... Ps 107:27 2451

WITTINGLY {1}
head, guiding his hands *w* ... Gen 48:14 7919

WITTY {1}
out knowledge of *w* inventions ... Prov 8:12

WIVES {132}
And Lamech took unto him two *w* ... Gen 4:19 802
And Lamech said unto his *w* ... Gen 4:23 802
ye *w* of Lamech, hearken unto my ... Gen 4:23 802
they took them *w* of all which ... Gen 6:2 802
wife, and thy sons' *w* with thee ... Gen 6:18 802
his wife, and his sons' *w* with him ... Gen 7:7 802
the three *w* of his sons with them ... Gen 7:13 802
sons, and thy sons' *w* with thee ... Gen 8:16 802
his wife, and his sons' *w* with him ... Gen 8:18 802
And Abram and Nahor took them *w* ... Gen 11:29 802
took unto the *w* which he had ... Gen 28:9 802
Give me my *w* and my children, for ... Gen 30:26 802
set his sons and his *w* upon camels ... Gen 31:17 802
take other *w* beside my daughters ... Gen 31:50 802
up that night, and took his two *w* ... Gen 32:22 802
take their daughters to us for *w* ... Gen 34:21 802
their *w* took they captive, and ... Gen 34:29 802
Esau took his *w* of the daughters ... Gen 36:2 802
And Esau took his *w*, and his sons, ... Gen 36:6 802
sons of Zilpah, his father's *w* ... Gen 37:2 802
your little ones, and for your *w* ... Gen 45:19 802
and their little ones, and their *w* ... Gen 46:5 802
loins, besides Jacob's sons' *w* ... Gen 46:26 802
come not at your *w* ... Ex 19:15 802
your *w* shall be widows, and your ... Ex 22:24 802
which are in the ears of your *w* ... Ex 32:2 802
to fall by the sword, that our *w* ... Num 14:3 802
door of their tents, and their *w* ... Num 16:27 802
Our little ones, our *w*, our ... Num 32:26 802
But your *w*, and your little ones, ... Deut 3:19 802
shall he multiply *w* to himself ... Deut 17:17 802
If a man have two *w*, one beloved, ... Deut 21:15 802
Your little ones, your *w*, and thy ... Deut 29:11 802
Your *w*, your little ones, and your ... Josh 1:14 802
their daughters to be their *w* ... Judg 3:6 802
for he had many *w* ... Judg 8:30 802
How shall we do for *w* for them ... Judg 21:7 802
give them of our daughters to *w* ... Judg 21:7 802
they gave them *w* which they had ... Judg 21:14 802
How shall we do for *w* for them ... Judg 21:16 802
not give them *w* of our daughters ... Judg 21:18 802
Benjamin did so, and took them *w* ... Judg 21:23 802
they took them *w* of the women of ... Ruth 1:4 802
And he had two *w* ... 1Sa 1:2 802
they were also both of them his *w* ... 1Sa 25:43 802
even David with his two *w* ... 1Sa 27:3 802
and their *w*, and their sons, and ... 1Sa 30:3 802
David's two *w* were taken captives ... 1Sa 30:5 802
and David rescued his two *w* ... 1Sa 30:18 802
up thither, and his two *w* also ... 2Sa 2:2 802
w out of Jerusalem, after he was ... 2Sa 5:13 802
thy master's *w* into thy bosom, and ... 2Sa 12:8 802
I will take thy *w* before thine ... 2Sa 12:11 802
he shall lie with thy *w* in the ... 2Sa 12:11 802
daughters, and the lives of thy *w* ... 2Sa 19:5 802
And he had seven hundred *w* ... 1Kin 11:3 802
his *w* turned away his heart ... 1Kin 11:3 802
that his *w* turned away his heart ... 1Kin 11:4 802
did he for all his strange *w* ... 1Kin 11:8 802
thy *w* also and thy children, even ... 1Kin 20:3 802
thy silver, and thy gold, and thy *w* ... 1Kin 20:5 802
for he sent unto me for my *w* ... 1Kin 20:7 802
the *w* of the sons of the prophets ... 2Kin 4:1 802
king's mother, and the king's *w* ... 2Kin 24:15 802
the father of Tekoa had two *w* ... 1Chr 4:5 802
for they had many *w* and sons ... 1Chr 7:4 802
Hushim and Baara were his *w* ... 1Chr 8:8 802
And David took more *w* at Jerusalem ... 1Chr 14:3 802
of Absalom above all his *w* ... 2Chr 11:21 802
(for he took eighteen *w*, and ... 2Chr 11:21 802
And he desired many *w* ... 2Chr 11:23 802
mighty, and married fourteen *w* ... 2Chr 13:21 802
with their little ones, their *w* ... 2Chr 20:13 802
people, and thy children, and thy *w* ... 2Chr 21:14 802
house, and his sons also, and his *w* ... 2Chr 21:17 802

And Jehoiada took for him two *w* 2Chr 24:3 802
our *w* are in captivity for this 2Chr 29:9 802
of all their little ones, their *w* 2Chr 31:18 802
have taken strange *w* of the Ezr 10:2 802
our God to put away all the *w* Ezr 10:3 802
and have taken strange *w*, to Ezr 10:10 802
the land, and from the strange *w* Ezr 10:11 802
them which have taken strange *w* Ezr 10:14 802
w by the first day of the first Ezr 10:17 802
found that had taken strange *w* Ezr 10:18 802
that they would put away their *w* Ezr 10:19 802
All these had taken strange *w* Ezr 10:44 802
some of them had *w* by whom they Ezr 10:44 802
sons, and your daughters, your *w* Neh 4:14 802
of their *w* against their brethren Neh 5:1 802
unto the law of God, their *w* Neh 10:28 802
the *w* also and the children Neh 12:43 802
Jews that had married *w* of Ashdod Neh 13:23 802
our God in marrying strange *w* Neh 13:27 802
all the *w* shall give to their Est 1:20 802
be spoiled, and their *w* ravished Is 13:16 802
with their fields and *w* together Jer 6:12 802
will I give their *w* unto others Jer 8:10 802
none to bury them, them, their *w* Jer 14:16 802
let their *w* be bereaved of their Jer 18:21 802
Take ye *w*, and beget sons and Jer 29:6 802
take *w* for your sons, and give Jer 29:6 802
adultery with their neighbours' *w* Jer 29:23 802
no wine all our days, we, our *w* Jer 35:8 802
So they shall bring out all thy *w* Jer 38:23 802
and the wickedness of their *w* Jer 44:9 802
and the wickedness of your *w* Jer 44:9 802
w had burned incense unto other Jer 44:15 802
your *w* have both spoken with your Jer 44:25 802
they take for their *w* a widow Eze 44:22 802
the king, and his princes, his *w* Dan 5:2 7695
the king, and his princes, his *w* Dan 5:3 7695
and thou, and thy lords, thy *w* Dan 5:23 7695
them, their children, and their *w* Dan 6:24 5389
of David apart, and their *w* apart Zec 12:12 802
of Nathan apart, and their *w* apart Zec 12:12 802
of Levi apart, and their *w* apart Zec 12:13 802
of Shimei apart, and their *w* apart Zec 12:13 802
family apart, and their *w* apart Zec 12:14 802
suffered you to put away your *w* Mt 19:8 *1135*
eat, they drank, they married *w* Lk 17:27 *1135*
all brought us on our way, with *w* Acts 21:5 *1135*
that both they that have *w* be as 1Cor 7:29 *1135*
W, submit yourselves unto your Eph 5:22 *1135*
so let the *w* be to their own Eph 5:24 *1135*
Husbands, love your *w*, even as Eph 5:25 *1135*
love their *w* as their own bodies Eph 5:28 *1135*
W, submit yourselves unto your Col 3:18 *1135*
Husbands, love your *w*, and be not Col 3:19 *1135*
Even so must their *w* be grave 1Ti 3:11 *1135*
Likewise, ye *w*, be in subjection 1Pet 3:1 *1135*
won by the conversation of the *w* 1Pet 3:1 *1135*

WIVES' {1}
old *w* fables, and exercise thyself 1Ti 4:7 *1126*

WIZARD {2}
a familiar spirit, or that is a *w* Lev 20:27 3049
with familiar spirits, or a *w* Deut 18:11 3049

WIZARDS {9}
spirits, neither seek after *w* Lev 19:31 3049
have familiar spirits, and after *w* Lev 20:6 3049
had familiar spirits, and the *w* 1Sa 28:3 3049
have familiar spirits, and the *w* 1Sa 28:9 3049
dealt with familiar spirits and *w* 2Kin 21:6 3049
with familiar spirits, and the *w* 2Kin 23:24 3049
with a familiar spirit, and with *w* 2Chr 33:6 3049
unto *w* that peep, and that mutter Is 8:19 3049
familiar spirits, and to the *w* Is 19:3 3049

WOE {108}
W to thee, Moab Num 21:29 188
And they said, *W* unto us 1Sa 4:7 188
W unto us 1Sa 4:8 188
If I be wicked, *w* unto me Job 10:15 480
W is me, that I sojourn in Mesech Ps 120:5 190
Who hath *w* Prov 23:29 188
but *w* to him that is alone when Eccl 4:10 337
W to thee, O land, when thy king Eccl 10:16 337
W unto their soul Is 3:9 188
W unto the wicked Is 3:11 188
W unto them that join house to Is 5:8 1945
W unto them that rise up early in Is 5:11 1945
W unto them that draw iniquity Is 5:18 1945
W unto them that call evil good, Is 5:20 1945
W unto them that are wise in Is 5:21 1945
W unto them that are mighty to Is 5:22 1945
Then said I, *W* is me Is 6:5 188
W unto them that decree Is 10:1 1945
W to the multitude of many people Is 17:12 1945
W to the land shadowing with Is 18:1 1945
leanness, my leanness, *w* unto me Is 24:16 188
W to the crown of pride, to the Is 28:1 1945
W to Ariel, to Ariel, the city Is 29:1 1945
W unto them that seek deep to Is 29:15 1945
W to the rebellious children, Is 30:1 1945
W to them that go down to Egypt Is 31:1 1945
W to thee that spoilest, and thou Is 33:1 1945
W unto him that striveth with his Is 45:9 1945
W unto him that saith unto his Is 45:10 1945
W unto us Jer 4:13 188
her hands, saying, *W* is me now Jer 4:31 188
W unto us Jer 6:4 188
W is me for my hurt Jer 10:19 188
W unto thee, O Jerusalem Jer 13:27 188
W is me, my mother, that thou Jer 15:10 188
W unto him that buildeth his Jer 22:13 1945
W be unto the pastors that Jer 23:1 1945
Thou didst say, *W* is me now Jer 45:3 188
W unto Nebo Jer 48:1 1945
W be unto thee, O Moab Jer 48:46 188
w unto them Jer 50:27 1945
w unto us, that we have sinned Lam 5:16 188
lamentations, and mourning, and *w* Eze 2:10 1958
W unto the foolish prophets, that Eze 13:3 1945
W to the women that sew pillows Eze 13:18 1945
w, *w* unto thee Eze 16:23 188
W to the bloody city, to the pot Eze 24:6 188
W to the bloody city Eze 24:9 188
Howl ye, *W* worth the day Eze 30:2 1929
W be to the shepherds of Israel Eze 34:2 1945
W unto them Hos 7:13 188
w also to them when I depart from Hos 9:12 188
W unto you that desire the day of Amos 5:18 1945
W to them that are at ease in Amos 6:1 1945
W to them that devise iniquity, Mic 2:1 1945
W is me Mic 7:1 480
W to the bloody city Nah 3:1 1945
W to him that increaseth that Hab 2:6 1945
W to him that coveteth an evil Hab 2:9 1945
W to him that buildeth a town Hab 2:12 1945
W unto him that giveth his Hab 2:15 1945
W unto him that saith to the wood Hab 2:19 1945
W unto the inhabitants of the sea Zeph 2:5 1945
W to her that is filthy and Zeph 3:1 1945
W to the idol shepherd that Zec 11:17 1945
W unto thee, Chorazin Mt 11:21 *3759*
w unto thee, Bethsaida Mt 11:21 *3759*
W unto the world because of Mt 18:7 *3759*
but *w* to that man by whom the Mt 18:7 *3759*
But *w* unto you, scribes and Mt 23:13 *3759*
W unto you, scribes and Pharisees, Mt 23:14 *3759*
W unto you, scribes and Pharisees, Mt 23:15 *3759*
W unto you, ye blind guides, Mt 23:16 *3759*
W unto you, scribes and Pharisees, Mt 23:23 *3759*
W unto you, scribes and Pharisees, Mt 23:25 *3759*
W unto you, scribes and Pharisees, Mt 23:27 *3759*
W unto you, scribes and Pharisees, Mt 23:29 *3759*
w unto them that are with child, Mt 24:19 *3759*
but *w* unto that man by whom the Mt 26:24 *3759*
But *w* to them that are with child Mk 13:17 *3759*
but *w* to that man by whom the Son Mk 14:21 *3759*
But *w* unto you that are rich Lk 6:24 *3759*
W unto you that are full Lk 6:25 *3759*
W unto you that laugh now Lk 6:25 *3759*
W unto you, when all men shall Lk 6:26 *3759*
W unto thee, Chorazin Lk 10:13 *3759*
w unto thee, Bethsaida Lk 10:13 *3759*
But *w* unto you, Pharisees Lk 11:42 *3759*
W unto you, Pharisees Lk 11:43 *3759*
W unto you, scribes and Pharisees, Lk 11:44 *3759*
W unto you also, ye lawyers Lk 11:46 *3759*
W unto you! for ye build the Lk 11:47 *3759*
W unto you, lawyers Lk 11:52 *3759*
but *w* unto him, through whom they Lk 17:1 *3759*
But *w* unto them that are with Lk 21:23 *3759*
but *w* unto that man by whom he is Lk 22:22 *3759*
w is unto me, if I preach not the 1Cor 9:16 *3759*
W unto them Jude 11 *3759*
saying with a loud voice, *W*, *w* Rev 8:13 *3759*
with a loud voice, *W*, *w*, *w* Rev 8:13 *3759*
One *w* is past Rev 9:12 *3759*
The second *w* is past Rev 11:14 *3759*
the third *w* cometh quickly Rev 11:14 *3759*
W to the inhabiters of the earth Rev 12:12 *3759*

WOEFUL {1}
neither have I desired the *w* day Jer 17:16 605

WOES {1}
there come two *w* more hereafter Rev 9:12 *3759*

WOLF {6}
Benjamin shall ravin as a *w* Gen 49:27 2061
The *w* also shall dwell with the Is 11:6 2061
The *w* and the lamb shall feed Is 65:25 2061
a *w* of the evenings shall spoil Jer 5:6 2061
sheep are not, seeth the *w* coming Jn 10:12 *3074*
and the *w* catcheth them, and Jn 10:12 *3074*

WOLVES {7}
are like *w* ravening the prey Eze 22:27 2061
more fierce than the evening *w* Hab 1:8 2061
her judges are evening *w* Zeph 3:3 2061
but inwardly they are ravening *w* Mt 7:15 *3074*
forth as sheep in the midst of *w* Mt 10:16 *3074*
I send you forth as lambs among *w* Lk 10:3 *3074*
grievous *w* enter in among you Acts 20:29 *3074*

WOMAN {361}
had taken from man, made he a *w* Gen 2:22 802
she shall be called *W*, because Gen 2:23 802
And he said unto the *w*, Yea, hath Gen 3:1 802
the *w* said unto the serpent, We Gen 3:2 802
And the serpent said unto the *w* Gen 3:4 802
when the *w* saw that the tree was Gen 3:6 802
The *w* whom thou gavest to be with Gen 3:12 802
And the LORD God said unto the *w* Gen 3:13 802
the *w* said, The serpent beguiled Gen 3:13 802
put enmity between thee and the *w* Gen 3:15 802
Unto the *w* he said, I will Gen 3:16 802
thou art a fair *w* to look upon Gen 12:11 802
the *w* that she was very fair Gen 12:14 802
the *w* was taken into Pharaoh's Gen 12:15 802
for the *w* which thou hast taken Gen 20:3 802
Peradventure the *w* will not be Gen 24:5 802
if the *w* will not be willing to Gen 24:8 802
Peradventure the *w* will not Gen 24:39 802
let the same be the *w* whom the Gen 24:44 802
Shaul the son of a Canaanitish *w* Gen 46:10
the *w* conceived, and bare a son Ex 2:2 802
the *w* took the child, and nursed Ex 2:9 802
But every *w* shall borrow of her Ex 3:22 802
Shaul the son of a Canaanitish *w* Ex 6:15
every *w* of her neighbour, jewels Ex 11:2 802
hurt a *w* with child, so that her Ex 21:22 802
If an ox gore a man or a *w* Ex 21:28 802
that he hath killed a man or a *w* Ex 21:29 802
unto the LORD, every man and *w* Ex 35:29 802
Let neither man nor *w* make any Ex 36:6 802
If a *w* have conceived seed, and Lev 12:2 802
If a man or *w* have a plague upon Lev 13:29 802
If a man also or a *w* have in the Lev 13:38 802
The *w* also with whom man shall Lev 15:18 802
if a *w* have an issue, and her Lev 15:19 802
if a *w* have an issue of her blood Lev 15:25 802
an issue, of the man, and of the *w* Lev 15:33 5347
not uncover the nakedness of a *w* Lev 18:17 802
unto a *w* to uncover her nakedness Lev 18:19 802
neither shall any *w* stand before Lev 18:23 802
whosoever lieth carnally with a *w* Lev 19:20 802
mankind, as he lieth with a *w* Lev 20:13 802
if a *w* approach unto any beast, Lev 20:16 802
thereto, thou shalt kill the *w* Lev 20:16 802
lie with a *w* having her sickness Lev 20:18 802
A man also or *w* that hath a Lev 20:27 802
a *w* put away from her husband Lev 21:7 802
A widow, or a divorced *w*, or Lev 21:14
And the son of an Israelitish *w* Lev 24:10 802
and this son of the Israelitish *w* Lev 24:10
When a man or *w* shall commit any Num 5:6 802
shall set the *w* before the LORD Num 5:18 802
her by an oath, and say unto the *w* Num 5:19 802
the *w* with an oath of cursing Num 5:21 802
the priest shall say unto the *w* Num 5:21 802
the *w* shall say, Amen, amen Num 5:22 802
he shall cause the *w* to drink the Num 5:24 802
cause the *w* to drink the water Num 5:26 802
the *w* shall be a curse among her Num 5:27 802
if the *w* be not defiled, but be Num 5:28 802
shall set the *w* before the LORD, Num 5:30 802
this *w* shall bear her iniquity Num 5:31 802
When either man or *w* shall Num 6:2 802
Ethiopian *w* whom he had married Num 12:1 802
for he had married an Ethiopian *w* Num 12:1 802
w in the sight of Moses, and in Num 25:6
and the *w* through her belly Num 25:8 802
was slain with the Midianitish *w* Num 25:14
w that was slain was Cozbi Num 25:15 802
If a *w* also vow a vow unto the Num 30:3 802
kill every *w* that hath known man Num 31:17 802
an Hebrew man, or an Hebrew *w* Deut 15:12
thy God giveth thee, man or *w* Deut 17:2 802
bring forth that man or that *w* Deut 17:5 802
gates, even that man or that *w* Deut 17:5 802
among the captives a beautiful *w* Deut 21:11 802
The *w* shall not wear that which Deut 22:5 802
upon her, and say, I took this *w* Deut 22:14 802
with a *w* married to an husband Deut 22:22 802
that lay with the *w*, and the *w* Deut 22:22 802
delicate *w* among you, which would Deut 28:56
should be among you man, or *w* Deut 29:18 802
the *w* took the two men, and hid Josh 2:4 802
was in the city, both man and *w* Josh 6:21 802
house, and bring out thence the *w* Josh 6:22 802
sell Sisera into the hand of a *w* Judg 4:9 802
a certain *w* cast a piece of a Judg 9:53 802
men say not of me, A *w* slew him Judg 9:54 802
thou art the son of a strange *w* Judg 11:2 802
of the LORD appeared unto the *w* Judg 13:3 802
Then the *w* came and told her Judg 13:6 802
the *w* as she sat in the field Judg 13:9 802
the *w* made haste, and ran, and Judg 13:10 802
the man that spakest unto the *w* Judg 13:11 802
I said unto the *w* let her beware Judg 13:13 802
the *w* bare a son, and called his Judg 13:24 802
saw a *w* in Timnath of the Judg 14:1 802
I have seen a *w* in Timnath of the Judg 14:2 802
Is there never a *w* among the Judg 14:3 802
went down, and talked with the *w* Judg 14:7 802
his father went down unto the *w* Judg 14:10 802
that he loved a *w* in the valley Judg 16:4 802
Then came the *w* in the dawning of Judg 19:26 802
the *w* his concubine was fallen Judg 19:27 802
husband of the *w* that was slain Judg 20:4 802
every *w* that hath lain by man Judg 21:11 802
the *w* was left of her two sons and Ruth 1:5 802
and, behold, a *w* lay at his feet Ruth 3:8 802
know that thou art a virtuous *w* Ruth 3:11 802
that a *w* came into the floor Ruth 3:14 802
The LORD make the *w* that is come Ruth 4:11 802
shall give thee of this young *w* Ruth 4:12 5291
I am a *w* of a sorrowful spirit 1Sa 1:15 802
So the *w* went her way, and did eat 1Sa 1:18 802
So the *w* abode, and gave her son 1Sa 1:23 802
I am the *w* that stood by thee 1Sa 1:26 802
w for the loan which is lent to 1Sa 2:20 802
but slay both man and *w*, infant and 1Sa 15:3 802
son of the perverse rebellious *w* 1Sa 20:30
she was a *w* of good understanding 1Sa 25:3 802
and left neither man nor *w* alive 1Sa 27:9 802
saved neither man nor *w* alive 1Sa 27:11 802
Seek me a *w* that hath a familiar 1Sa 28:7 802

there is a *w* that hath a familiar ... 1Sa 28:7 802
and they came to the *w* by night ... 1Sa 28:8 802
the *w* said unto him, Behold, thou ... 1Sa 28:9 802
Then said the *w*, Whom shall I ... 1Sa 28:11 802
when the *w* saw Samuel, she cried ... 1Sa 28:12 802
the *w* spake to Saul, saying, Why ... 1Sa 28:12 802
the *w* said unto Saul, I saw gods ... 1Sa 28:13 802
the *w* came unto Saul, and saw that ... 1Sa 28:21 802
his servants, together with the *w* ... 1Sa 28:23 802
the *w* had a fat calf in the house ... 1Sa 28:24 802
with a fault concerning this *w* ... 2Sa 3:8 802
roof he saw a *w* washing herself ... 2Sa 11:2 802
the *w* was very beautiful to look ... 2Sa 11:2 802
sent and enquired after the *w* ... 2Sa 11:3 802
the *w* conceived, and sent and told ... 2Sa 11:5 802
did not a *w* cast a piece of a ... 2Sa 11:21 802
said, Put now this *w* out from me ... 2Sa 13:17
and fetched thence a wise *w* ... 2Sa 14:2 802
but be as a *w* that had a long ... 2Sa 14:2 802
when the *w* of Tekoah spake to the ... 2Sa 14:4 802
answered, I am indeed a widow *w* ... 2Sa 14:5 802
And the king said unto the *w* ... 2Sa 14:8 802
the *w* of Tekoah said unto the ... 2Sa 14:9 802
Then the *w* said, Let thine ... 2Sa 14:12 802
the *w* said, Wherefore then hast ... 2Sa 14:13 802
king answered and said unto the *w* ... 2Sa 14:18 802
the *w* said, Let my lord the king ... 2Sa 14:18 802
the *w* answered and said, As thy ... 2Sa 14:19 802
she was a *w* of a fair countenance ... 2Sa 14:27 802
the *w* took and spread a covering ... 2Sa 17:19 802
came to the *w* to the house ... 2Sa 17:20 802
the *w* said unto them, They be ... 2Sa 17:20 802
cried a wise *w* out of the city ... 2Sa 20:16 802
the *w* said, Art thou Joab ... 2Sa 20:17 802
the *w* said unto Joab, Behold, his ... 2Sa 20:21 802
Then the *w* went unto all the ... 2Sa 20:22 802
And the one *w* said, O my lord, I ... 1Kin 3:17 802
this *w* dwell in one house ... 1Kin 3:17 802
that this *w* was delivered also ... 1Kin 3:18 802
And the other *w* said, Nay ... 1Kin 3:22 802
Then spake the *w* whose the living ... 1Kin 3:26 802
name was Zeruah, a widow *w* ... 1Kin 11:26 802
feign herself to be another *w* ... 1Kin 14:5
a widow *w* there to sustain thee ... 1Kin 17:9 802
the widow *w* was there gathering ... 1Kin 17:10 802
things, that the son of the *w* ... 1Kin 17:17 802
the *w* said to Elijah, Now by this ... 1Kin 17:24 802
Now there cried a certain *w* of ... 2Kin 4:1 802
to Shunem, where was a great *w* ... 2Kin 4:8 802
the *w* conceived, and bare a son at ... 2Kin 4:17 802
wall, there cried a *w* unto him ... 2Kin 6:26 802
This *w* said unto me, Give thy son ... 2Kin 6:28 802
the king heard the words of the *w* ... 2Kin 6:30 802
Then spake Elisha unto the *w* ... 2Kin 8:1 802
the *w* arose, and did after the ... 2Kin 8:2 802
that the *w* returned out of the ... 2Kin 8:3 802
body to life, that, behold, the *w* ... 2Kin 8:5 802
My lord, O king, this is the *w* ... 2Kin 8:5 802
And when the king asked the *w* ... 2Kin 8:6 802
said, Go, see now this cursed *w* ... 2Kin 9:34
one of Israel, both man and *w* ... 1Chr 16:3 802
The son of a *w* of the daughters ... 2Chr 2:14 802
small or great, whether man or *w* ... 2Chr 15:13 802
sons of Athaliah, that wicked *w* ... 2Chr 24:7
that whosoever, whether man or *w* ... Est 4:11 802
is born of a *w* is of few days ... Job 14:1 802
and he which is born of a *w* ... Job 15:14 802
he be clean that is born of a *w* ... Job 25:4 802
heart have been deceived by a *w* ... Job 31:9 802
and pain, as of a *w* in travail ... Ps 48:6
like the untimely birth of a *w* ... Ps 58:8 802
maketh the barren *w* to keep house ... Ps 113:9
deliver thee from the strange *w* ... Prov 2:16 802
a strange *w* drop as an honeycomb ... Prov 5:3
son, be ravished with a strange *w* ... Prov 5:20
To keep thee from the evil *w* ... Prov 6:24 802
of the tongue of a strange *w* ... Prov 6:24
For by means of a whorish *w* a man ... Prov 6:26 802
with a *w* lacketh understanding ... Prov 6:32 802
may keep thee from the strange *w* ... Prov 7:5 802
there met him a *w* with the attire ... Prov 7:10 802
A foolish *w* is clamorous ... Prov 9:13 802
A gracious *w* retaineth honour ... Prov 11:16 802
so is a fair *w* which is without ... Prov 11:22 802
A virtuous *w* is a crown to her ... Prov 12:4 802
Every wise *w* buildeth her house ... Prov 14:1 802
a pledge of him for a strange *w* ... Prov 20:16
housetop, than with a brawling *w* ... Prov 21:9 802
with a contentious and an angry *w* ... Prov 21:19 802
a strange *w* is a narrow pit ... Prov 23:27
housetop, than with a brawling *w* ... Prov 25:24 802
a pledge of him for a strange *w* ... Prov 27:13
day and a contentious *w* are alike ... Prov 27:15 802
is the way of an adulterous *w* ... Prov 30:20 802
For an odious *w* when she is ... Prov 30:23
Who can find a virtuous *w* ... Prov 31:10 802
but a *w* that feareth the LORD, ... Prov 31:30 802
find more bitter than death the *w* ... Eccl 7:26 802
but a *w* among all those have I ... Eccl 7:28 802
be in pain as a *w* that travaileth ... Is 13:8
the pangs of a *w* that travaileth ... Is 21:3
Like as a *w* with child, that ... Is 26:17
will I cry like a travailing *w* ... Is 42:14
or to the *w*, What hast thou ... Is 45:10 802
Can a *w* forget her sucking child, ... Is 49:15 802
hath called thee as a *w* forsaken ... Is 54:6 802
a voice as of a *w* in travail ... Jer 4:31
of Zion to a comely and delicate *w* ... Jer 6:2
us, and pain, as of a *w* in travail ... Jer 6:24
take thee, as a *w* in travail ... Jer 13:21 802
the pain as of a *w* in travail ... Jer 22:23
as a *w* in travail, and all faces ... Jer 30:6
the *w* with child and her that ... Jer 31:8
earth, A *w* shall compass a man ... Jer 31:22 5347
to cut off from you man and *w* ... Jer 44:7 802
as the heart of a *w* in her pangs ... Jer 48:41 802
as the heart of a *w* in her pangs ... Jer 49:22 802
have taken her, as a *w* in travail ... Jer 49:24
and pangs as of a *w* in travail ... Jer 50:43
will I break in pieces man and *w* ... Jer 51:22 802
is as a menstruous *w* among them ... Lam 1:17
work of an imperious whorish *w* ... Eze 16:30 802
hath come near to a menstruous *w* ... Eze 18:6 802
as they go in unto a *w* that ... Eze 23:44 802
as the uncleanness of a removed *w* ... Eze 36:17
love a *w* beloved of her friend, ... Hos 3:1 802
travailing *w* shall come upon him ... Hos 13:13
have taken thee as a *w* in travail ... Mic 4:9
of Zion, like a *w* in travail ... Mic 4:10
this is a *w* that sitteth in the ... Zec 5:7 802
on a *w* to lust after her hath ... Mt 5:28 *1135*
And, behold, a *w*, which was ... Mt 9:20 *1135*
the *w* was made whole from that ... Mt 9:22 *1135*
like unto leaven, which a *w* took ... Mt 13:33 *1135*
a *w* of Canaan came out of the ... Mt 15:22 *1135*
answered and said unto her, O *w* ... Mt 15:28 *1135*
And last of all the *w* died also ... Mt 22:27 *1135*
There came unto him a *w* having an ... Mt 26:7 *1135*
unto them, Why trouble ye the *w* ... Mt 26:10 *1135*
also this, that this *w* hath done ... Mt 26:13
And a certain *w*, which had an ... Mk 5:25 *1135*
But the *w* fearing and trembling, ... Mk 5:33 *1135*
For a certain *w*, whose young ... Mk 7:25 *1135*
The *w* was a Greek, a ... Mk 7:26 *1135*
if a *w* shall put away her husband ... Mk 10:12 *1135*
last of all the *w* died also ... Mk 12:22 *1135*
at meat, there came a *w* having an ... Mk 14:3 *1135*
unto a *w* that was a widow ... Lk 4:26 *1135*
a *w* in the city, which was a ... Lk 7:37 *1135*
what manner of *w* this is that ... Lk 7:39 *1135*
And he turned to the *w*, and said ... Lk 7:44 *1135*
unto Simon, Seest thou this *w* ... Lk 7:44
but this *w* since the time I came ... Lk 7:45
but this *w* hath anointed my feet ... Lk 7:46
And he said to the *w*, Thy faith ... Lk 7:50 *1135*
a *w* having an issue of blood ... Lk 8:43 *1135*
when the *w* saw that she was not ... Lk 8:47 *1135*
a certain *w* named Martha received ... Lk 10:38 *1135*
a certain *w* of the company lifted ... Lk 11:27 *1135*
there was a *w* which had a spirit ... Lk 13:11 *1135*
her to him, and said unto her, *W*, ... Lk 13:12 *1135*
And ought not this *w*, being a ... Lk 13:16
It is like leaven, which a *w* took ... Lk 13:21 *1135*
Either what *w* having ten pieces ... Lk 15:8 *1135*
Last of all the *w* died also ... Lk 20:32 *1135*
And he denied him, saying, *W*, ... Lk 22:57 *1135*
Jesus saith unto her, *W*, what ... Jn 2:4 *1135*
There cometh a *w* of Samaria to ... Jn 4:7 *1135*
Then saith the *w* of Samaria unto ... Jn 4:9 *1135*
of me, which am a *w* of Samaria ... Jn 4:9 *1135*
The *w* saith unto him, Sir, thou ... Jn 4:11 *1135*
The *w* saith unto him, Sir, give ... Jn 4:15 *1135*
The *w* answered and said, I have no ... Jn 4:17 *1135*
The *w* saith unto him, Sir, I ... Jn 4:19 *1135*
Jesus saith unto her, *W*, believe ... Jn 4:21 *1135*
The *w* saith unto him, I know that ... Jn 4:25 *1135*
that he talked with the *w* ... Jn 4:27 *1135*
The *w* then left her waterpot, and ... Jn 4:28 *1135*
on him for the saying of the *w* ... Jn 4:39 *1135*
And said unto the *w*, Now we ... Jn 4:42 *1135*
unto him a *w* taken in adultery ... Jn 8:3 *1135*
this *w* was taken in adultery, in ... Jn 8:4 *1135*
the *w* standing in the midst ... Jn 8:9 *1135*
up himself, and saw none but the *w* ... Jn 8:10 *1135*
he said unto her, *W*, ... Jn 8:10 *1135*
A *w* when she is in travail hath ... Jn 16:21 *1135*
he saith unto his mother, *W*, ... Jn 19:26 *1135*
And they say unto her, *W*, why ... Jn 20:13 *1135*
Jesus saith unto her, *W*, why ... Jn 20:15 *1135*
this *w* was full of good works and ... Acts 9:36
Timotheus, the son of a certain *w* ... Acts 16:1 *1135*
a certain *w* named Lydia, a seller ... Acts 16:14 *1135*
a *w* named Damaris, and others with ... Acts 17:34 *1135*
leaving the natural use of the *w* ... Rom 1:27 *2338*
For the *w* which hath an husband ... Rom 7:2 *1135*
good for a man not to touch a *w* ... 1Cor 7:1 *1135*
let every *w* have her own husband ... 1Cor 7:2
the *w* which hath an husband that ... 1Cor 7:13 *1135*
The unmarried *w* careth for the ... 1Cor 7:34 *1135*
and the head of the *w* is the man ... 1Cor 11:3 *1135*
But every *w* that prayeth or ... 1Cor 11:5 *1135*
For if the *w* be not covered, let ... 1Cor 11:6 *1135*
for a *w* to be shorn or shaven ... 1Cor 11:6 *1135*
but the *w* is the glory of the man ... 1Cor 11:7 *1135*
For the man is not of the *w* ... 1Cor 11:8 *1135*
but the *w* of the man ... 1Cor 11:8 *1135*
was the man created for the *w* ... 1Cor 11:9 *1135*
but the *w* for the man ... 1Cor 11:9 *1135*
For this cause ought the *w* to ... 1Cor 11:10 *1135*
neither is the man without the *w* ... 1Cor 11:11 *1135*
neither the *w* without the man, in ... 1Cor 11:11 *1135*
For as the *w* is of the man ... 1Cor 11:12 *1135*
even so is the man also by the *w* ... 1Cor 11:12 *1135*
is it comely that a *w* pray unto ... 1Cor 11:13 *1135*
But if a *w* have long hair, it is ... 1Cor 11:15 *1135*
sent forth his Son, made of a *w* ... Gal 4:4 *1135*
heir with the son of the free *w* ... Gal 4:30 *1658*
as travail upon a *w* with child ... 1Th 5:3
Let the *w* learn in silence with ... 1Ti 2:11 *1135*
But I suffer not a *w* to teach ... 1Ti 2:12 *1135*
but the *w* being deceived was in ... 1Ti 2:14 *1135*
If any man or *w* that believeth ... 1Ti 5:16
thou sufferest that *w* Jezebel ... Rev 2:20 *1135*
a *w* clothed with the sun, and the ... Rev 12:1 *1135*
the dragon stood before the *w* ... Rev 12:4 *1135*
the *w* fled into the wilderness, ... Rev 12:6 *1135*
he persecuted the *w* which brought ... Rev 12:13 *1135*
to the *w* were given two wings of ... Rev 12:14 *1135*
water as a flood after the *w* ... Rev 12:15 *1135*
And the earth helped the *w* ... Rev 12:16 *1135*
the dragon was wroth with the *w* ... Rev 12:17 *1135*
I saw a *w* sit upon a scarlet ... Rev 17:3 *1135*
the *w* was arrayed in purple and ... Rev 17:4 *1135*
I saw the *w* drunken with the ... Rev 17:6 *1135*
tell thee the mystery of the *w* ... Rev 17:7 *1135*
mountains, on which the *w* sitteth ... Rev 17:9 *1135*
the *w* which thou sawest is that ... Rev 17:18 *1135*

WOMANKIND {1}

not lie with mankind, as with *w* ... Lev 18:22 802

WOMAN'S {7}

his pledge from the *w* hand ... Gen 38:20 802
according as the *w* husband will ... Ex 21:22 802
the Israelitish *w* son blasphemed ... Lev 24:11 802
the LORD, and uncover the *w* head ... Num 5:18 802
offering out of the *w* hand ... Num 5:25 802
shall a man put on a *w* garment ... Deut 22:5 802
this *w* child died in the night ... 1Kin 3:19 802

WOMB {71}

her, Two nations are in thy *w* ... Gen 25:23 990
behold, there were twins in her *w* ... Gen 25:24 990
Leah was hated, he opened her *w* ... Gen 29:31 7358
from thee the fruit of the *w* ... Gen 30:2 990
hearkened to her, and opened her *w* ... Gen 30:22 7358
that, behold, twins were in her *w* ... Gen 38:27 990
of the breasts, and of the *w* ... Gen 49:25 7356
whatsoever openeth the *w* among ... Ex 13:2 7358
instead of such as open every *w* ... Num 8:16 7358
he cometh out of his mother's *w* ... Num 12:12 7358
also bless the fruit of thy *w* ... Deut 7:13 990
be a Nazarite unto God from the *w* ... Judg 13:5 990
the *w* to the day of his death ... Judg 13:7 990
unto God from my mother's *w* ... Judg 16:17 990
there yet any more sons in my *w* ... Ruth 1:11 4578
but the LORD had shut up her *w* ... 1Sa 1:5 7358
the LORD had shut up her *w* ... 1Sa 1:6 7358
Naked came I out of my mother's *w* ... Job 1:21 990
not up the doors of my mother's *w* ... Job 3:10 990
Why died I not from the *w* ... Job 3:11 7358
brought me forth out of the *w* ... Job 10:18 7358
carried from the *w* to the grave ... Job 10:19 990
The *w* shall forget him ... Job 24:20 7358
he that made me in the *w* make him ... Job 31:15 990
did not one fashion us in the *w* ... Job 31:15 7358
guided her from my mother's *w* ... Job 31:18 990
as if it had issued out of the *w* ... Job 38:8 7358
Out of whose *w* came the ice ... Job 38:29 990
art he that took me out of the *w* ... Ps 22:9 990
I was cast upon thee from the *w* ... Ps 22:10 7358
wicked are estranged from the *w* ... Ps 58:3 7358
have I been holden up from the *w* ... Ps 71:6 990
from the *w* of the morning ... Ps 110:3 7358
the fruit of the *w* is his reward ... Ps 127:3 990
hast covered me in my mother's *w* ... Ps 139:13 990
and the barren *w* ... Prov 30:16 7356
and what, the son of my *w* ... Prov 31:2 990
he came forth of his mother's *w* ... Eccl 5:15 990
the *w* of her that is with child ... Eccl 11:5 990
no pity on the fruit of the *w* ... Is 13:18 990
thee, and formed thee from the *w* ... Is 44:2 990
and he that formed thee from the *w* ... Is 44:24 990
which are carried from the *w* ... Is 46:3 7356
called a transgressor from the *w* ... Is 48:8 990
LORD hath called me from the *w* ... Is 49:1 990
me from the *w* to be his servant ... Is 49:5 990
compassion on the son of her *w* ... Is 49:15 990
to bring forth, and shut the *w* ... Is 66:9
out of the *w* I sanctified thee ... Jer 1:5 7358
Because he slew me not from the *w* ... Jer 20:17 7358
her *w* to be always great with me ... Jer 20:17 7358
forth out of the *w* to see labour ... Jer 20:18 7358
the fire all that openeth the *w* ... Eze 20:26 7356
from the birth, and from the *w* ... Hos 9:11 990
give them a miscarrying *w* ... Hos 9:14 7358
even the beloved fruit of their *w* ... Hos 9:16 990
his brother by the heel in the *w* ... Hos 12:3 990
so born from their mother's *w* ... Mt 19:12 *2836*
Ghost, even from his mother's *w* ... Lk 1:15 *2836*
thou shalt conceive in thy *w* ... Lk 1:31 *1064*
of Mary, the babe leaped in her *w* ... Lk 1:41 *2836*
and blessed is the fruit of thy *w* ... Lk 1:42 *2836*
the babe leaped in my *w* for joy ... Lk 1:44 *2836*
before he was conceived in the *w* ... Lk 2:21 *2836*
the *w* shall be called holy to the ... Lk 2:23 *3388*
Blessed is the *w* that bare thee ... Lk 11:27 *2836*
second time into his mother's *w* ... Jn 3:4 *2836*
from his mother's *w* was carried ... Acts 3:2 *2836*
a cripple from his mother's *w* ... Acts 14:8 *2836*
yet the deadness of Sarah's *w* ... Rom 4:19 *3388*
separated me from my mother's *w* ... Gal 1:15 *2836*

WOMBS {2}

the *w* of the house of Abimelech ... Gen 20:18 7358
the *w* that never bare, and the ... Lk 23:29 *2836*

WOMEN {178}
the *w* also, and the people ... Gen 14:16 802
with Sarah after the manner of *w* ... Gen 18:11 802
even the time that *w* go out to ... Gen 24:11
for the custom of *w* is upon me ... Gen 31:35 802
lifted up his eyes, and saw the *w* ... Gen 33:5 802
of a midwife to the Hebrew *w* ... Ex 1:16
Because the Hebrew *w* are not as ... Ex 1:19 802
not as the Egyptian *w* ... Ex 1:19 802
to thee a nurse of the Hebrew *w* ... Ex 2:7
all the *w* went out after her with ... Ex 15:20 802
And they came, both men and *w* ... Ex 35:22 802
all the *w* that were wise hearted ... Ex 35:25 802
all the *w* whose heart stirred ... Ex 35:26 802
of the *w* assembling, which ... Ex 38:8
ten *w* shall bake your bread in ... Lev 26:26 802
took all the *w* of Midian captives ... Num 31:9 802
Have ye saved all the *w* alive ... Num 31:15 5347
But all the *w* children, that have ... Num 31:18 802
of *w* that had not known man by ... Num 31:35 802
destroyed the men, and the *w* ... Deut 2:34 802
utterly destroying the men, *w* ... Deut 3:6 802
But the *w*, and the little ones, and ... Deut 20:14 802
the people together, men, and *w* ... Deut 31:12 802
fell that day, both of men and *w* ... Josh 8:25 802
of Israel, with the *w*, and the ... Josh 8:35 802
Blessed above *w* shall Jael the ... Judg 5:24 802
shall she be above *w* in the tent ... Judg 5:24 802
also, about a thousand men and *w* ... Judg 9:49 802
and thither fled all the men and *w* ... Judg 9:51 802
the house was full of men and *w* ... Judg 16:27 802
about three thousand men and *w* ... Judg 16:27 802
the edge of the sword, with the *w* ... Judg 21:10 802
alive of the *w* of Jabesh-gilead ... Judg 21:14 802
seeing the *w* are destroyed out of ... Judg 21:16 802
took them wives of the *w* of Moab ... Ruth 1:4 802
the *w* said unto Naomi, Blessed be ... Ruth 4:14 802
the *w* her neighbours gave it a ... Ruth 4:17
how they lay with the *w* that ... 1Sa 2:22 802
w that stood by her said unto her ... 1Sa 4:20
thy sword hath made *w* childless ... 1Sa 15:33 802
thy mother be childless among *w* ... 1Sa 15:33 802
that the *w* came out of all cities ... 1Sa 18:6 802
the *w* answered one another as ... 1Sa 18:7 802
kept themselves at least from *w* ... 1Sa 21:4 802
Of a truth *w* have been kept from ... 1Sa 21:5 802
edge of the sword, both men and *w* ... 1Sa 22:19 802
And had taken the *w* captives ... 1Sa 30:2 802
wonderful, passing the love of *w* ... 2Sa 1:26 802
Israel, as well to the *w* as men ... 2Sa 6:19 802
And the king left ten *w*, which ... 2Sa 15:16 802
voice of singing men and singing *w* ... 2Sa 19:35
took the ten *w* his concubines ... 2Sa 20:3 802
Then came there two *w*, that were ... 1Kin 3:16 802
king Solomon loved many strange *w* ... 1Kin 11:1 802
w of the Moabites, Ammonites, ... 1Kin 11:1
and rip up their *w* with child ... 2Kin 8:12
all the *w* therein that were with ... 2Kin 15:16
where the *w* wove hangings for the ... 2Kin 23:7 802
brethren two hundred thousand, *w* ... 2Chr 28:8 802
the singing *w* spake of Josiah in ... 2Chr 35:25
hundred singing men and singing *w* ... Ezr 2:65
great congregation of men and *w* ... Ezr 10:1 802
and five singing men and singing *w* ... Neh 7:67
the congregation both of men and *w* ... Neh 8:2 802
midday, before the men and the *w* ... Neh 8:3 802
him did outlandish *w* cause to sin ... Neh 13:26 802
the *w* in the royal house which ... Est 1:9 802
shall come abroad unto all *w* ... Est 1:17 802
the palace, to the house of the *w* ... Est 2:3 802
chamberlain, keeper of the *w* ... Est 2:3 802
custody of Hegai, keeper of the *w* ... Est 2:8 802
best place of the house of the *w* ... Est 2:9 802
according to the manner of the *w* ... Est 2:12 802
things for the purifying of the *w* ... Est 2:12 802
of the *w* unto the king's house ... Est 2:13 802
into the second house of the *w* ... Est 2:14 802
chamberlain, the keeper of the *w* ... Est 2:15 802
king loved Esther above all the *w* ... Est 2:17 802
and old, little children and *w* ... Est 3:13 802
them, both little ones and *w* ... Est 8:11 802
as one of the foolish *w* speaketh ... Job 2:10
in all the land were no *w* found ... Job 42:15 802
were among thy honourable *w* ... Ps 45:9
mouth of strange *w* is a deep pit ... Prov 22:14
Thine eyes shall behold strange *w* ... Prov 23:33
Give not thy strength unto *w* ... Prov 31:3 802
w singers, and the delights of the ... Eccl 2:8
know not, O thou fairest among *w* ... Song 1:8 802
beloved, O thou fairest among *w* ... Song 5:9 802
gone, O thou fairest among *w* ... Song 6:1 802
oppressors, and *w* rule over them ... Is 3:12 802
in that day seven *w* shall take ... Is 4:1 802
day shall Egypt be like unto *w* ... Is 19:16 802
the *w* come, and set them on fire ... Is 27:11 802
Rise up, ye *w* that are at ease ... Is 32:9 802
ye be troubled, ye careless *w* ... Is 32:10
Tremble, ye *w* that are at ease ... Is 32:11
the *w* knead their dough, to make ... Jer 7:18 802
ye, and call for the mourning *w* ... Jer 9:17
and send for cunning *w*, that they ... Jer 9:17
hear the word of the LORD, O ye *w* ... Jer 9:20 802
all the *w* that are left in the ... Jer 38:22 802
those *w* shall say, Thy friends ... Jer 38:22
had committed unto him men, and *w* ... Jer 40:7 802
even mighty men of war, and the *w* ... Jer 41:16 802
Even men, and *w*, and children, and ... Jer 43:6 802
all the *w* that stood by, a great ... Jer 44:15 802
people, to the men, and to the *w* ... Jer 44:20 802
all the people, and to all the *w* ... Jer 44:24 802
and they shall become as *w* ... Jer 50:37 802
they became as *w* ... Jer 51:30 802
Shall the *w* eat their fruit, and ... Lam 2:20 802
The hands of the pitiful *w* have ... Lam 4:10 802
They ravished the *w* in Zion ... Lam 5:11 802
there sat *w* weeping for Tammuz ... Eze 8:14 802
maids, and little children, and *w* ... Eze 9:6 802
Woe to the *w* that sew pillows to ... Eze 13:18
from other *w* in thy whoredoms ... Eze 16:34 802
as *w* that break wedlock and shed ... Eze 16:38
upon thee in the sight of many *w* ... Eze 16:41 802
Son of man, there were two *w* ... Eze 23:2 802
and she became famous among *w* ... Eze 23:10 802
and unto Aholibah, the lewd *w* ... Eze 23:44 802
the manner of *w* that shed blood ... Eze 23:45
that all *w* may be taught not to ... Eze 23:48 802
shall give him the daughter of *w* ... Dan 11:17 802
his fathers, nor the desire of *w* ... Dan 11:37 802
their *w* with child shall be ... Hos 13:16
up the *w* with child of Gilead ... Amos 1:13
The *w* of my people have ye cast ... Mic 2:9 802
people in the midst of thee are *w* ... Nah 3:13 802
and, behold, there came out two *w* ... Zec 5:9 802
old *w* dwell in the streets of ... Zec 8:4
houses rifled, and the *w* ravished ... Zec 14:2 802
Among them that are born of *w* ... Mt 11:11 *1135*
about five thousand men, beside *w* ... Mt 14:21 *1135*
were four thousand men, beside *w* ... Mt 15:38 *1135*
Two *w* shall be grinding at the ... Mt 24:41
many *w* were there beholding afar ... Mt 27:55 *1135*
angel answered and said unto the *w* ... Mt 28:5 *1135*
There were also *w* looking on afar ... Mk 15:40 *1135*
many other *w* which came up with ... Mk 15:41
blessed art thou among *w* ... Lk 1:28 *1135*
and said, Blessed art thou among *w* ... Lk 1:42 *1135*
Among those that are born of *w* ... Lk 7:28 *1135*
And certain *w*, which had been ... Lk 8:2 *1135*
Two *w* shall be grinding together ... Lk 17:35
great company of people, and of *w* ... Lk 23:27 *1135*
the *w* that followed him from ... Lk 23:49 *1135*
the *w* also, which came with him ... Lk 23:55 *1135*
other *w* that were with them, ... Lk 24:10
certain *w* also of our company ... Lk 24:22 *1135*
it even so as the *w* had said ... Lk 24:24 *1135*
and supplication, with the *w* ... Acts 1:14 *1135*
Lord, multitudes both of men and *w* ... Acts 5:14 *1135*
w committed them to prison ... Acts 8:3 *1135*
they were baptized, both men and *w* ... Acts 8:12 *1135*
way, whether they were men or *w* ... Acts 9:2 *1135*
up the devout and honourable *w* ... Acts 13:50 *1135*
spake unto the *w* which resorted ... Acts 16:13 *1135*
and of the chief *w* not a few ... Acts 17:4 *1135*
of honourable *w* which were Greeks ... Acts 17:12 *1135*
into prisons both men and *w* ... Acts 22:4 *1135*
for even their *w* did change the ... Rom 1:26 *2338*
Let your *w* keep silence in the ... 1Cor 14:34 *1135*
for it is a shame for *w* to speak ... 1Cor 14:35 *1135*
help those *w* which laboured with ... Phil 4:3
that *w* adorn themselves in modest ... 1Ti 2:9 *1135*
that (which becometh *w* professing ... 1Ti 2:10 *1135*
The elder *w* as mothers ... 1Ti 5:2
that the younger *w* marry, bear ... 1Ti 5:14
captive silly *w* laden with sins ... 2Ti 3:6 *1133*
The aged *w* likewise, that they be ... Titus 2:3 *4247*
may teach the young *w* to be sober ... Titus 2:4
W received their dead raised to ... Heb 11:35 *1135*
in the old time the holy *w* also ... 1Pet 3:5 *1135*
And they had hair as the hair of *w* ... Rev 9:8 *1135*
which were not defiled with *w* ... Rev 14:4 *1135*

WOMEN'S {1}
before the court of the *w* house ... Est 2:11 802

WOMENSERVANTS {3}
and oxen, and menservants, and *w* ... Gen 20:14 8198
flocks, and menservants, and *w* ... Gen 32:5 8198
took his two wives, and his two *w* ... Gen 32:22 8198

WON {3}
Out of the spoils *w* in battles ... 1Chr 26:27
harder to be *w* than a strong city ... Prov 18:19
be *w* by the conversation of the ... 1Pet 3:1 *2770*

WONDER {15}
and giveth thee a sign or a *w* ... Deut 13:1 4159
And the sign or the *w* come to pass ... Deut 13:2 4159
upon thee for a sign and for a *w* ... Deut 28:46 4159
the *w* that was done in the land ... 2Chr 32:31 4159
I am as a *w* unto many ... Ps 71:7 4159
w upon Egypt and upon Ethiopia ... Is 20:3 4159
Stay yourselves, and *w* ... Is 29:9 8539
even a marvellous work and a *w* ... Is 29:14 6382
and the prophets shall *w* ... Jer 4:9 8539
and regard, and *w* marvellously ... Hab 1:5 8539
and they were filled with *w* ... Acts 3:10 *2285*
Behold, ye despisers, and *w* ... Acts 13:41 *2296*
appeared a great *w* in heaven ... Rev 12:1 *4592*
appeared another *w* in heaven ... Rev 12:3 *4592*
that dwell on the earth shall *w* ... Rev 17:8 *2296*

WONDERED {15}
w that there was no intercessor ... Is 59:16 8074
I *w* that there was none to uphold ... Is 63:5 8074
for they are men *w* at ... Zec 3:8 4159
Insomuch that the multitude *w* ... Mt 15:31 *2296*
themselves beyond measure, and *w* ... Mk 6:51 *2296*
all they that heard it *w* at those ... Lk 2:18 *2296*
w at the gracious words which ... Lk 4:22 *2296*
And they being afraid *w*, saying ... Lk 8:25 *2296*
But while they *w* every one at all ... Lk 9:43 *2296*
and the people *w* ... Lk 11:14 *2296*
yet believed not for joy, and *w* ... Lk 24:41 *2296*
Moses saw it, he *w* at the sight ... Acts 7:31 *2296*
he continued with Philip, and *w* ... Acts 8:13 *1839*
all the world *w* after the beast ... Rev 13:3 *2296*
I *w* with great admiration ... Rev 17:6 *2296*

WONDERFUL {21}
the LORD will make thy plagues *w* ... Deut 28:59 6381
thy love to me was *w*, passing the ... 2Sa 1:26 6381
about to build shall be *w* great ... 2Chr 2:9 6381
things too *w* for me, which I knew ... Job 42:3 6381
are thy *w* works which thou hast ... Ps 40:5 6381
his *w* works that he hath done ... Ps 78:4 6381
for his *w* works to the children ... Ps 107:8 6381
for his *w* works to the children ... Ps 107:15 6381
for his *w* works to the children ... Ps 107:21 6381
for his *w* works to the children ... Ps 107:31 6381
He hath made his *w* works to be ... Ps 111:4 6381
Thy testimonies are *w* ... Ps 119:129 6382
Such knowledge is too *w* for me ... Ps 139:6 6383
things which are too *w* for me ... Prov 30:18 6381
and his name shall be called *W* ... Is 9:6 6382
for thou hast done *w* things ... Is 25:1 6382
which is *w* in counsel, and ... Is 28:29 6381
A *w* and horrible thing is ... Jer 5:30 8047
and in thy name done many *w* works ... Mt 7:22 *1411*
scribes saw the *w* things that he ... Mt 21:15 *2297*
in our tongues the *w* works of God ... Acts 2:11 *3167*

WONDERFULLY {4}
when he had wrought *w* among them ... 1Sa 6:6 5953
for I am fearfully and *w* made ... Ps 139:14 6395
therefore she came down *w* ... Lam 1:9 6382
and he shall destroy *w*, and shall ... Dan 8:24 6381

WONDERING {3}
the man *w* at her held his peace, ... Gen 24:21 7583
w in himself at that which was ... Lk 24:12 *2296*
is called Solomon's, greatly *w* ... Acts 3:11 *1569*

WONDEROUSLY {1}
and the angel did *w* ... Judg 13:19 6381

WONDERS {55}
smite Egypt with all my *w* which I ... Ex 3:20 6381
do all those *w* before Pharaoh ... Ex 4:21 4159
my *w* in the land of Egypt ... Ex 7:3 4159
that my *w* may be multiplied in ... Ex 11:9 4159
did all these *w* before Pharaoh ... Ex 11:10 4159
fearful in praises, doing *w* ... Ex 15:11 6382
by temptations, by signs, and by *w* ... Deut 4:34 4159
And the LORD shewed signs and *w* ... Deut 6:22 4159
eyes saw, and the signs, and the *w* ... Deut 7:19 4159
and with signs, and with *w* ... Deut 26:8 4159
In all the signs and the *w* ... Deut 34:11 4159
the LORD will do *w* among you ... Josh 3:5 6381
works that he hath done, his *w* ... 1Chr 16:12 4159
w upon Pharaoh, and on all his ... Neh 9:10 4159
thy *w* that thou didst among them ... Neh 9:17 6381
yea, and *w* without number ... Job 9:10 6381
I will remember thy *w* of old ... Ps 77:11 6382
Thou art the God that doest *w* ... Ps 77:14 6382
his *w* that he had shewed them ... Ps 78:11 6381
his *w* in the field of Zoan ... Ps 78:43 4159
Wilt thou shew *w* to the dead ... Ps 88:10 6382
Shall thy *w* be known in the dark ... Ps 88:12 6382
And the heavens shall praise thy *w* ... Ps 89:5 6382
heathen, his *w* among all people ... Ps 96:3 6381
his *w*, and the judgments of his ... Ps 105:5 4159
them, and *w* in the land of Ham ... Ps 105:27 4159
understood not thy *w* in Egypt ... Ps 106:7 6381
of the LORD, and his *w* in the deep ... Ps 107:24 6381
w into the midst of thee, O Egypt ... Ps 135:9 4159
To him who alone doeth great *w* ... Ps 136:4 6381
for *w* in Israel from the LORD of ... Is 8:18 4159
w in the land of Egypt, even unto ... Jer 32:20 4159
of Egypt with signs, and with *w* ... Jer 32:21 4159
w that the high God hath wrought ... Dan 4:2 8540
and how mighty are his *w* ... Dan 4:3 8540
w in heaven and in earth, who hath ... Dan 6:27 8540
shall it be to the end of these *w* ... Dan 12:6 6382
I will shew *w* in the heavens and ... Joel 2:30 4159
and shall shew great signs and *w* ... Mt 24:24 *5059*
rise, and shall shew signs and *w* ... Mk 13:22 *5059*
him, Except ye see signs and *w* ... Jn 4:48 *5059*
I will shew *w* in heaven above, and ... Acts 2:19 *5059*
of God among you by miracles and *w* ... Acts 2:22 *5059*
and many *w* and signs were done by ... Acts 2:43 *5059*
w may be done by the name of thy ... Acts 4:30 *5059*
w wrought among the people ... Acts 5:12 *5059*
of faith and power, did great *w* ... Acts 6:8 *5059*
out, after that he had shewed *w* ... Acts 7:36 *5059*
w to be done by their hands ... Acts 14:3 *5059*
w God had wrought among the ... Acts 15:12 *5059*
Through mighty signs and *w* ... Rom 15:19 *5059*
in all patience, in signs, and *w* ... 2Cor 12:12 *5059*
all power and signs and lying *w* ... 2Th 2:9 *5059*
witness, both with signs and *w* ... Heb 2:4 *5059*
And he doeth great *w*, so that he ... Rev 13:13 *4592*

WONDROUS {15}
him, talk ye of all his *w* works ... 1Chr 16:9 6381
and consider the *w* works of God ... Job 37:14 6381
the *w* works of him which is ... Job 37:16 4652
and tell of all thy *w* works ... Ps 26:7 6381
have I declared thy *w* works ... Ps 71:17 6381
Israel, who only doeth *w* things ... Ps 72:18 6381
name is near thy *w* works declare ... Ps 75:1 6381
and believed not for his *w* works ... Ps 78:32 6381
thou art great, and doest *w* things ... Ps 86:10 6381

talk ye of all his *w* works ... Ps 105:2 6381
W works in the land of Ham, and ... Ps 106:22 6381
that I may behold *w* things out of ... Ps 119:18 6381
so shall I talk of thy *w* works ... Ps 119:27 6381
of thy majesty, and of thy *w* works ... Ps 145:5 6381
us according to all his *w* works ... Jer 21:2 6381

WONDROUSLY {1}
God, that hath dealt *w* with you ... Joel 2:26 6381

WONT {9}
But if the ox were *w* to push with ... Ex 21:29 5056
was I ever *w* to do so unto thee ... Num 22:30 5532
and his men were *w* to haunt ... 1Sa 30:31 1980
They were *w* to speak in old time, ... 2Sa 20:18 1696
more than it was *w* to be heated ... Dan 3:19 2370
w to release unto the people a ... Mt 27:15 *1486*
and, as he was *w*, he taught them ... Mk 10:1 *1486*
came out, and went, as he was *w* ... Lk 22:39 *2596,1485*
where prayer was *w* to be made ... Acts 16:13 *3543*

WOOD {140}
Make thee an ark of gopher *w* ... Gen 6:14 6086
clave the *w* for the burnt ... Gen 22:3 6086
Abraham took the *w* of the burnt ... Gen 22:6 6086
he said, Behold the fire and the *w* ... Gen 22:7 6086
there, and laid the *w* in order ... Gen 22:9 6086
laid him on the altar upon the *w* ... Gen 22:9 6086
of Egypt, both in vessels of *w* ... Ex 7:19 6086
and badgers' skins, and shittim *w* ... Ex 25:5 6086
shall make an ark of shittim *w* ... Ex 25:10 6086
shalt make staves of shittim *w* ... Ex 25:13 6086
also make a table of shittim *w* ... Ex 25:23 6086
make the staves of shittim *w* ... Ex 25:28 6086
of shittim *w* standing up ... Ex 26:15 6086
thou shalt make bars of shittim *w* ... Ex 26:26 6086
of shittim *w* overlaid with gold ... Ex 26:32
hanging five pillars of shittim *w* ... Ex 26:37
shalt make an altar of shittim *w* ... Ex 27:1 6086
the altar, staves of shittim *w* ... Ex 27:6 6086
of shittim *w* shalt thou make it ... Ex 30:1 6086
make the staves of shittim *w* ... Ex 30:5 6086
and badgers' skins, and shittim *w* ... Ex 35:7 6086
w for any work of the service ... Ex 35:24 6086
to set them, and in carving of *w* ... Ex 35:33 6086
for the tabernacle of shittim *w* ... Ex 36:20 6086
And he made bars of shittim *w* ... Ex 36:31 6086
four pillars of shittim *w* ... Ex 36:36
made the ark of shittim *w* ... Ex 37:1 6086
And he made staves of shittim *w* ... Ex 37:4 6086
And he made the table of shittim *w* ... Ex 37:10 6086
he made the staves of shittim *w* ... Ex 37:15 6086
the incense altar of shittim *w* ... Ex 37:25 6086
he made the staves of shittim *w* ... Ex 37:28 6086
of burnt offering of shittim *w* ... Ex 38:1 6086
he made the staves of shittim *w* ... Ex 38:6 6086
lay the *w* in order upon the fire ... Lev 1:7 6086
in order upon the *w* that is on ... Lev 1:8 6086
w that is on the fire which is ... Lev 1:12 6086
upon the *w* that is upon the fire ... Lev 1:17 6086
which is upon the *w* that is on ... Lev 3:5 6086
and burn him on the *w* with fire ... Lev 4:12 6086
shall burn *w* on it every morning ... Lev 6:12 6086
whether it be any vessel of *w* ... Lev 11:32 6086
birds alive and clean, and cedar *w* ... Lev 14:4 6086
he shall take it, and the cedar *w* ... Lev 14:6 6086
the house two birds, and cedar *w* ... Lev 14:49 6086
And he shall take the cedar *w* ... Lev 14:51 6086
living bird, and with the cedar *w* ... Lev 14:52 6086
every vessel of *w* shall be rinsed ... Lev 15:12 6086
lean, whether there be *w* therein ... Num 13:20 6086
And the priest shall take cedar *w* ... Num 19:6 6086
hair, and all things made of *w* ... Num 31:20 6086
him with an hand weapon of *w* ... Num 35:18 6086
gods, the work of men's hands, *w* ... Deut 4:28 6086
mount, and make thee an ark of *w* ... Deut 10:1 6086
And I made an ark of shittim *w* ... Deut 10:3 6086
As when a man goeth into the *w* ... Deut 19:5 3293
his neighbour to hew *w* ... Deut 19:5 6086
shalt thou serve other gods, *w* ... Deut 28:36 6086
thy fathers have known, even *w* ... Deut 28:64 6086
from the hewer of thy *w* unto the ... Deut 29:11 6086
abominations, and their idols, *w* ... Deut 29:17 6086
but let them be hewers of *w* ... Josh 9:21 6086
being bondmen, and hewers of *w* ... Josh 9:23 6086
made them that day hewers of *w* ... Josh 9:27 6086
then get thee up to the *w* country ... Josh 17:15 3293
for it is a *w*, and thou shalt cut ... Josh 17:18 3293
a burnt sacrifice with the *w* of ... Judg 6:26 6086
and they clave the *w* of the cart ... 1Sa 6:14 6086
all they of the land came to a *w* ... 1Sa 14:25 3293
the people were come into the *w* ... 1Sa 14:26 3293
in the wilderness of Ziph in a *w* ... 1Sa 23:15 2793
and went to David into the *w* ... 1Sa 23:16 2793
and David abode in the *w*, and ... 1Sa 23:18 2793
with us in strong holds in the *w* ... 1Sa 23:19 2793
of instruments made of fir *w* ... 2Sa 6:5 6086
battle was in the *w* of Ephraim ... 2Sa 18:6 3293
the *w* devoured more people that ... 2Sa 18:8 3293
him into a great pit in the *w* ... 2Sa 18:17 3293
instruments of the oxen for *w* ... 2Sa 24:22 6086
covered them on the inside with *w* ... 1Kin 6:15 6086
cut it in pieces, and lay it on *w* ... 1Kin 18:23 6086
the other bullock, and lay it on *w* ... 1Kin 18:23 6086
And he put the *w* in order, and cut ... 1Kin 18:33 6086
in pieces, and laid him on the *w* ... 1Kin 18:33 6086
the burnt sacrifice, and on the *w* ... 1Kin 18:33 6086
the burnt sacrifice, and the *w* ... 1Kin 18:38 6086
forth two she bears out of the *w* ... 2Kin 2:24 3293
came to Jordan, they cut down *w* ... 2Kin 6:4 6086
but the work of men's hands, *w* ... 2Kin 19:18 6086
Then shall the trees of the *w* ... 1Chr 16:33 3293
the threshing instruments for *w* ... 1Chr 21:23 6086
brought much cedar *w* to David ... 1Chr 22:4 6086
of iron, and *w* for things of *w* ... 1Chr 29:2 6086
we will cut *w* out of Lebanon, as ... 2Chr 2:16 6086
scribe stood upon a pulpit of *w* ... Neh 8:4 6086
for the *w* offering, to bring it ... Neh 10:34 6086
for the *w* offering, at times ... Neh 13:31 6086
as straw, and brass as rotten *w* ... Job 41:27 6086
boar out of the *w* doth waste it ... Ps 80:13 3293
As the fire burneth a *w*, and as ... Ps 83:14 3293
all the trees of the *w* rejoice ... Ps 96:12 3293
found it in the fields of the *w* ... Ps 132:6 3293
cleaveth *w* upon the earth ... Ps 141:7
Where no *w* is, there the fire ... Prov 26:20 6086
to burning coals, and *w* to fire ... Prov 26:21 6086
to water therewith the *w* that ... Eccl 2:6 3293
he that cleaveth *w* shall be ... Eccl 10:9 6086
tree among the trees of the *w* ... Song 2:3 3293
a chariot of the *w* of Lebanon ... Song 3:9 6086
as the trees of the *w* are moved ... Is 7:2 3293
up itself, as if it were no *w* ... Is 10:15 6086
pile thereof is fire and much *w* ... Is 30:33 6086
but the work of men's hands, *w* ... Is 37:19 6086
up the *w* of their graven image ... Is 45:20 6086
for *w* brass, and for stones iron ... Is 60:17 6086
thy mouth fire, and this people *w* ... Jer 5:14 6086
The children gather *w*, and the ... Jer 7:18 6086
Thou hast broken the yokes of *w* ... Jer 28:13 6086
her with axes, as hewers of *w* ... Jer 46:22 6086
our *w* is sold unto us ... Lam 5:4 6086
and the children fell under the *w* ... Lam 5:13 6086
Shall *w* be taken thereof to do ... Eze 15:3 6086
of the countries, to serve *w* ... Eze 20:32 6086
Heap on *w*, kindle the fire, ... Eze 24:10 6086
shall take no *w* out of the field ... Eze 39:10 6086
door, cieled with *w* round about ... Eze 41:16 6086
The altar of *w* was three cubits ... Eze 41:22 6086
and the walls thereof, were of *w* ... Eze 41:22 6086
silver, of brass, of iron, of *w* ... Dan 5:4 636
and gold, of brass, iron, *w* ... Dan 5:23 636
which dwell solitarily in the *w* ... Mic 7:14 3293
Woe unto him that saith to the *w* ... Hab 2:19 6086
Go up to the mountain, and bring *w* ... Hag 1:8 6086
an hearth of fire among the *w* ... Zec 12:6 6086
gold, silver, precious stones, *w* ... 1Cor 3:12 *3586*
gold and of silver, but also of *w* ... 2Ti 2:20 *3585*
and brass, and stone, and of *w* ... Rev 9:20 *3585*
silk, and scarlet, and all thyine *w* ... Rev 18:12 *3586*
manner vessels of most precious *w* ... Rev 18:12 *3586*

WOODS {1}
the wilderness, and sleep in the *w* ... Eze 34:25 3264

WOOF {9}
Whether it be in the warp, or *w* ... Lev 13:48 6154
either in the warp, or in the *w* ... Lev 13:49 6154
either in the warp, or in the *w* ... Lev 13:51 6154
that garment, whether warp or *w* ... Lev 13:52 6154
either in the warp, or in the *w* ... Lev 13:53 6154
out of the warp, or out of the *w* ... Lev 13:56 6154
either in the warp, or in the *w* ... Lev 13:57 6154
And the garment, either warp, or *w* ... Lev 13:58 6154
linen, either in the warp, or *w* ... Lev 13:59 6154

WOOL {14}
put a fleece of *w* in the floor ... Judg 6:37 6785
hundred thousand rams, with the *w* ... 2Kin 3:4 6785
He giveth snow like *w* ... Ps 147:16 6785
She seeketh *w*, and flax, and ... Prov 31:13 6785
like crimson, they shall be as *w* ... Is 1:18 6785
and the worm shall eat them like *w* ... Is 51:8 6785
in the wine of Helbon, and white *w* ... Eze 27:18 6785
fat, and ye clothe you with the *w* ... Eze 34:3 6785
no *w* shall come upon them, whiles ... Eze 44:17 6785
hair of his head like the pure *w* ... Dan 7:9 6015
me my bread and my water, my *w* ... Hos 2:5 6785
thereof, and will recover my *w* ... Hos 2:9 6785
goats, with water, and scarlet *w* ... Heb 9:19 *2053*
and his hairs were white like *w* ... Rev 1:14 *2053*

WOOLLEN {6}
is in, whether it be a *w* garment ... Lev 13:47 6785
of linen, or of *w* ... Lev 13:48 6785
in *w* or in linen, or any thing of ... Lev 13:52 6785
in a garment of *w* or linen ... Lev 13:59 6785
of linen and *w* come upon thee ... Lev 19:19 8162
garment of divers sorts, as of *w* ... Deut 22:11 6785

WORD {97}
After these things the *w* of the ... Gen 15:1 1697
the *w* of the LORD came unto him, ... Gen 15:4 1697
it might be according to thy *w* ... Gen 30:34 1697
and bring me *w* again ... Gen 37:14 1697
according unto thy *w* shall all my ... Gen 41:40 6310
to the *w* that Joseph had spoken ... Gen 44:2 1697
speak a *w* in my lord's ears, and ... Gen 44:18 1697
he said, Be it according to thy *w* ... Ex 8:10 1697
did according to the *w* of Moses ... Ex 8:13 1697
did according to the *w* of Moses ... Ex 8:31 1697
He that feared the *w* of the LORD ... Ex 9:20 1697
he that regarded not the *w* of the ... Ex 9:21 1697
did according to the *w* of Moses ... Ex 12:35 1697
Is not this the *w* that we did ... Ex 14:12 1697
did according to the *w* of Moses ... Ex 32:28 1697
did according to the *w* of Moses ... Lev 10:7 1697
according to the *w* of the LORD ... Num 3:16 6310
according to the *w* of the LORD ... Num 3:51 6310
the *w* of the LORD by the hand of ... Num 4:45 6310
thou shalt see now whether my *w* ... Num 11:23 1697
and brought back *w* unto them ... Num 13:26 1697
have pardoned according to thy *w* ... Num 14:20 1697
hath despised the *w* of the LORD ... Num 15:31 1697
my *w* at the water of Meribah ... Num 20:24 6310
and I will bring you *w* again ... Num 22:8 1697
beyond the *w* of the LORD my God ... Num 22:18 6310
but yet the *w* which I shall say ... Num 22:20 1697
but only the *w* that I shalt speak ... Num 22:35 1697
the *w* that God putteth in my ... Num 22:38 1697
the LORD put a *w* in Balaam's ... Num 23:5 1697
put a *w* in his mouth, and said, Go ... Num 23:16 1697
at his *w* shall they go out ... Num 27:21 6310
at his *w* they shall come in, both ... Num 27:21 6310
he shall not break his *w*, he ... Num 30:2 1697
according to the *w* of the LORD ... Num 36:5 6310
bring us *w* again by what way we ... Deut 1:22 1697
unto us, and brought us *w* again ... Deut 1:25 1697
unto the *w* which I command you ... Deut 4:2 1697
to shew you the *w* of the LORD ... Deut 5:5 1697
but by every *w* that proceedeth ... Deut 8:3
that he may perform the *w* which ... Deut 9:5 1697
presume to speak a *w* in my name ... Deut 18:20 1697
How shall we know the *w* which the ... Deut 18:21 1697
and by their *w* shall every ... Deut 21:5 6310
But the *w* is very nigh unto thee, ... Deut 30:14 1697
for they have observed thy *w* ... Deut 33:9 565
according to the *w* of the LORD ... Deut 34:5 6310
Remember the *w* which Moses the ... Josh 1:13 1697
neither shall any *w* proceed out ... Josh 6:10 1697
according unto the *w* of the LORD ... Josh 8:27 1697
There was not a *w* of all that ... Josh 8:35 1697
I brought him *w* again as it was ... Josh 14:7 1697
the LORD spake this *w* unto Moses ... Josh 14:10 1697
According to the *w* of the LORD ... Josh 19:50 6310
according to the *w* of the LORD by ... Josh 22:9 6310
Israel, and brought them *w* again ... Josh 22:32 1697
only the LORD establish his *w* ... 1Sa 1:23 1697
the *w* of the LORD was precious in ... 1Sa 3:1 1697
neither was the *w* of the LORD yet ... 1Sa 3:7 1697
in Shiloh by the *w* of the LORD ... 1Sa 3:21 1697
the *w* of Samuel came to all ... 1Sa 4:1 1697
that I may shew thee the *w* of God ... 1Sa 9:27 1697
Then came the *w* of the LORD unto ... 1Sa 15:10 1697
hast rejected the *w* of the LORD ... 1Sa 15:23 1697
hast rejected the *w* of the LORD ... 1Sa 15:26 1697
could not answer Abner a *w* again ... 2Sa 3:11 1697
that the *w* of the LORD came unto ... 2Sa 7:4 1697
I a *w* with any of the tribes of ... 2Sa 7:7 1697
the *w* that thou hast spoken ... 2Sa 7:25 1697
speak one *w* unto my lord the king ... 2Sa 14:12 1697
The *w* of my lord the king shall ... 2Sa 14:17 1697
until there come *w* from you to ... 2Sa 15:28 1697
not a *w* of bringing the king back ... 2Sa 19:10
they sent this *w* unto the king ... 2Sa 19:14
the *w* of the LORD is tried ... 2Sa 22:31 565
by me, and his *w* was in my tongue ... 2Sa 23:2 4405
king's *w* prevailed against Joab ... 2Sa 24:4 1697
the *w* of the LORD came unto the ... 2Sa 24:11 1697
w which he spake concerning me ... 1Kin 2:4 1697
this *w* against his own life ... 1Kin 2:23 1697
he might fulfil the *w* of the LORD ... 1Kin 2:27 1697
Benaiah brought the king *w* again ... 1Kin 2:30 1697
The *w* that I have heard is good ... 1Kin 2:42 1697
the *w* of the LORD came to Solomon ... 1Kin 6:11 1697
will I perform my *w* with thee ... 1Kin 6:12 1697
performed his *w* that he spake ... 1Kin 8:20 1697
now, O God of Israel, let thy *w* ... 1Kin 8:26 1697
one *w* of all his good promise ... 1Kin 8:56 1697
But the *w* of God came unto ... 1Kin 12:22 1697
therefore to the *w* of the LORD ... 1Kin 12:24 1697
according to the *w* of the LORD ... 1Kin 12:24 1697
by the *w* of the LORD unto Beth-el ... 1Kin 13:1 1697
the altar in the *w* of the LORD ... 1Kin 13:2 1697
had given by the *w* of the LORD ... 1Kin 13:5 1697
charged me by the *w* of the LORD ... 1Kin 13:9 1697
said to me by the *w* of the LORD ... 1Kin 13:17 1697
unto me by the *w* of the LORD ... 1Kin 13:18 1697
that the *w* of the LORD came unto ... 1Kin 13:20 1697
unto the *w* of the LORD ... 1Kin 13:26 6310
according to the *w* of the LORD ... 1Kin 13:26 1697
saying which he cried by the *w* of ... 1Kin 13:32 1697
according to the *w* of the LORD ... 1Kin 14:18 1697
Then the *w* of the LORD came to ... 1Kin 16:1 1697
the *w* of the LORD against Baasha ... 1Kin 16:7 1697
according to the *w* of the LORD ... 1Kin 16:12 1697
according to the *w* of the LORD ... 1Kin 16:34 1697
years, but according to my *w* ... 1Kin 17:1 1697
the *w* of the LORD came unto him, ... 1Kin 17:2 1697
according unto the *w* of the LORD ... 1Kin 17:5 1697
the *w* of the LORD came unto him, ... 1Kin 17:8 1697
according to the *w* of the LORD ... 1Kin 17:16 1697
that the *w* of the LORD in thy ... 1Kin 17:24 1697
that the *w* of the LORD came to ... 1Kin 18:1 1697
the people answered him not a *w* ... 1Kin 18:21 1697
unto whom the *w* of the LORD came, ... 1Kin 18:31 1697
done all these things at thy *w* ... 1Kin 18:36 1697
the *w* of the LORD came to him, and ... 1Kin 19:9 1697
departed, and brought him *w* again ... 1Kin 20:9 1697
neighbour in the *w* of the LORD ... 1Kin 20:35 1697
displeased because of the *w* which ... 1Kin 21:4 1697
the *w* of the LORD came to Elijah ... 1Kin 21:17 1697
the *w* of the LORD came to Elijah ... 1Kin 21:28 1697
at the *w* of the LORD to day ... 1Kin 22:5 1697
let thy *w*, I pray thee ... 1Kin 22:13 1697
be like the *w* of one of them, and ... 1Kin 22:13 1697
thou therefore the *w* of the LORD ... 1Kin 22:19 1697
according unto the *w* of the LORD ... 1Kin 22:38 1697
God in Israel to enquire of his *w* ... 2Kin 1:16 1697

So he died according to the *w* of	2Kin 1:17	1697
The *w* of the LORD is with him	2Kin 3:12	1697
according to the *w* of the LORD	2Kin 4:44	1697
according to the *w* of Elisha	2Kin 6:18	1697
said, Hear ye the *w* of the LORD	2Kin 7:1	1697
according to the *w* of the LORD	2Kin 7:16	1697
according to the *w* of the LORD	2Kin 9:26	1697
said, This is the *w* of the LORD	2Kin 9:36	1697
nothing of the *w* of the LORD	2Kin 10:10	1697
according to the *w* of the LORD	2Kin 14:25	1697
This was the *w* of the LORD which	2Kin 15:12	1697
Hear the *w* of the great king, the	2Kin 18:28	1697
peace, and answered him not a *w*	2Kin 18:36	1697
This is the *w* that the LORD hath	2Kin 19:21	1697
that the *w* of the LORD came to	2Kin 20:4	1697
Hezekiah, Hear the *w* of the LORD	2Kin 20:16	1697
Good is the *w* of the LORD which	2Kin 20:19	1697
king, and brought the king *w* again	2Kin 22:9	1697
And they brought the king *w* again	2Kin 22:20	1697
according to the *w* of the LORD	2Kin 23:16	1697
according to the *w* of the LORD	2Kin 24:2	1697
even against the *w* of the LORD	1Chr 10:13	1697
according to the *w* of the LORD by	1Chr 11:3	1697
according to the *w* of the LORD	1Chr 11:10	1697
according to the *w* of the LORD	1Chr 12:23	6310
according to the *w* of the LORD	1Chr 15:15	1697
the *w* which he commanded to a	1Chr 16:15	1697
that the *w* of God came to Nathan,	1Chr 17:3	1697
spake I a *w* to any of the judges	1Chr 17:6	1697
king's *w* prevailed against Joab	1Chr 21:4	1697
for the king's *w* was abominable	1Chr 21:6	1697
therefore advise thyself what *w* I	1Chr 21:12	1697
But the *w* of the LORD came to me,	1Chr 22:8	1697
his *w* that he hath spoken	2Chr 6:10	1697
let thy *w* be verified, which thou	2Chr 6:17	1697
that the LORD might perform his *w*	2Chr 10:15	1697
But the *w* of the LORD came to	2Chr 11:2	1697
the *w* of the LORD came to	2Chr 12:7	1697
at the *w* of the LORD to day	2Chr 18:4	1697
let thy *w* therefore, I pray thee,	2Chr 18:12	1697
Therefore hear the *w* of the LORD	2Chr 18:18	1697
the princes, by the *w* of the LORD	2Chr 30:12	1697
and brought the king *w* back again	2Chr 34:16	1697
have not kept the *w* of the LORD	2Chr 34:21	1697
So they brought the king *w* again	2Chr 34:28	1697
the *w* of the LORD by the hand of	2Chr 35:6	1697
To fulfil the *w* of the LORD by	2Chr 36:21	1697
that the *w* of the LORD spoken by	2Chr 36:22	1697
that the *w* of the LORD by the	Ezr 1:1	1697
that whosoever shall alter this *w*	Ezr 6:11	6600
should do according to this *w*	Ezr 10:5	1697
the *w* that thou commandedst thy	Neh 1:8	1697
did according to the *w* of Memucan	Est 1:21	1697
As the *w* went out of the king's	Est 7:8	1697
and none spake a *w* unto him	Job 2:13	1697
by the *w* of thy lips I have kept	Ps 17:4	1697
the *w* of the LORD is tried	Ps 18:30	565
For the *w* of the LORD is right	Ps 33:4	1697
By the *w* of the LORD were the	Ps 33:6	1697
In God I will praise his *w*	Ps 56:4	1697
In God will I praise his *w*	Ps 56:10	1697
in the LORD will I praise his *w*	Ps 56:10	1697
The Lord gave the *w*	Ps 68:11	562
unto the voice of his *w*	Ps 103:20	1697
the *w* which he commanded to a	Ps 105:8	1697
Until the time that his *w* came	Ps 105:19	1697
the *w* of the LORD tried him	Ps 105:19	565
they rebelled not against his *w*	Ps 105:28	1697
land, they believed not his *w*	Ps 106:24	1697
He sent his *w*, and healed them, and	Ps 107:20	1697
heed thereto according to thy *w*	Ps 119:9	1697
Thy *w* have I hid in mine heart,	Ps 119:11	565
I will not forget thy *w*	Ps 119:16	1697
that I may live, and keep thy *w*	Ps 119:17	1697
thou me according to thy *w*	Ps 119:25	1697
thou me according unto thy *w*	Ps 119:28	1697
Stablish thy *w* unto thy servant,	Ps 119:38	565
thy salvation, according to thy *w*	Ps 119:41	565
for I trust in thy *w*	Ps 119:42	1697
take not the *w* of truth utterly	Ps 119:43	1697
Remember the *w* unto thy servant,	Ps 119:49	1697
for thy *w* hath quickened me	Ps 119:50	565
unto me according to thy *w*	Ps 119:58	565
O LORD, according unto thy *w*	Ps 119:65	1697
but now have I kept thy *w*	Ps 119:67	565
because I have hoped in thy *w*	Ps 119:74	1697
to thy *w* unto thy servant	Ps 119:76	565
but I hope in thy *w*	Ps 119:81	1697
Mine eyes fail for thy *w*, saying,	Ps 119:82	565
thy *w* is settled in heaven	Ps 119:89	1697
evil way, that I might keep thy *w*	Ps 119:101	1697
Thy *w* is a lamp unto my feet, and	Ps 119:105	1697
me, O LORD, according unto thy *w*	Ps 119:107	1697
I hope in thy *w*	Ps 119:114	1697
Uphold me according unto thy *w*	Ps 119:116	565
for the *w* of thy righteousness	Ps 119:123	565
Order my steps in thy *w*	Ps 119:133	565
Thy *w* is very pure	Ps 119:140	565
I hoped in thy *w*	Ps 119:147	1697
that I might meditate in thy *w*	Ps 119:148	565
quicken me according to thy *w*	Ps 119:154	565
because they kept not thy *w*	Ps 119:158	565
Thy *w* is true from the beginning	Ps 119:160	1697
my heart standeth in awe of thy *w*	Ps 119:161	1697
I rejoice at thy *w*, as one that	Ps 119:162	565
understanding according to thy *w*	Ps 119:169	1697
deliver me according to thy *w*	Ps 119:170	565
My tongue shall speak of thy *w*	Ps 119:172	565
doth wait, and in his *w* do I hope	Ps 130:5	1697
thy *w* above all thy name	Ps 138:2	565
For there is not a *w* in my tongue	Ps 139:4	4405
his *w* runneth very swiftly	Ps 147:15	1697
He sendeth out his *w*, and melteth	Ps 147:18	1697
He sheweth his *w* unto Jacob	Ps 147:19	1697
stormy wind fulfilling his *w*	Ps 148:8	1697
but a good *w* maketh it glad	Prov 12:25	1697
the *w* shall be destroyed	Prov 13:13	1697
The simple believeth every *w*	Prov 14:15	1697
a *w* spoken in due season, how	Prov 15:23	1697
A *w* fitly spoken is like apples	Prov 25:11	1697
Every *w* of God is pure	Prov 30:5	565
Where the *w* of a king is, there	Eccl 8:4	1697
Hear the *w* of the LORD, ye rulers	Is 1:10	1697
The *w* that Isaiah the son of Amoz	Is 2:1	1697
the *w* of the LORD from Jerusalem	Is 2:3	1697
despised the *w* of the Holy One of	Is 5:24	565
speak the *w*, and it shall not	Is 8:10	1697
speak not according to this *w*	Is 8:20	1697
The Lord sent a *w* into Jacob	Is 9:8	1697
This is the *w* that the LORD hath	Is 16:13	1697
for the LORD hath spoken this *w*	Is 24:3	1697
But the *w* of the LORD was unto	Is 28:13	1697
Wherefore hear the *w* of the LORD	Is 28:14	1697
make a man an offender for a *w*	Is 29:21	1697
Israel, Because ye despise this *w*	Is 30:12	1697
ears shall hear a *w* behind thee	Is 30:21	1697
peace, and answered him not a *w*	Is 36:21	1697
This is the *w* which the LORD hath	Is 37:22	1697
Then came the *w* of the LORD to	Is 38:4	1697
Hear the *w* of the LORD of hosts	Is 39:5	1697
Good is the *w* of the LORD which	Is 39:8	1697
but the *w* of our God shall stand	Is 40:8	1697
I asked of them, could answer a *w*	Is 41:28	1697
confirmeth the *w* of his servant	Is 44:26	1697
the *w* is gone out of my mouth in	Is 45:23	1697
I should know how to speak a *w* in	Is 50:4	1697
So shall my *w* be that goeth forth	Is 55:11	1697
spirit, and trembleth at my *w*	Is 66:2	1697
Hear the *w* of the LORD	Is 66:5	1697
ye that tremble at his *w*	Is 66:5	1697
To whom the *w* of the LORD came in	Jer 1:2	1697
Then the *w* of the LORD came unto	Jer 1:4	1697
Moreover the *w* of the LORD came	Jer 1:11	1697
I will hasten my *w* to perform it	Jer 1:12	1697
the *w* of the LORD came unto me	Jer 1:13	1697
Moreover the *w* of the LORD came	Jer 2:1	1697
Hear ye the *w* of the LORD	Jer 2:4	1697
see ye the *w* of the LORD	Jer 2:31	1697
wind, and the *w* is not in them	Jer 5:13	1699
of hosts, Because ye speak this *w*	Jer 5:14	1697
the *w* of the LORD is unto them a	Jer 6:10	1697
The *w* that came to Jeremiah from	Jer 7:1	1697
house, and proclaim there this *w*	Jer 7:2	1697
Hear the *w* of the LORD, all ye of	Jer 7:2	1697
have rejected the *w* of the LORD	Jer 8:9	1697
Yet hear the *w* of the LORD	Jer 9:20	1697
ear receive the *w* of his mouth	Jer 9:20	1697
Hear ye the *w* which the LORD	Jer 10:1	1697
The *w* that came to Jeremiah from	Jer 11:1	1697
according to the *w* of the LORD	Jer 13:2	1697
the *w* of the LORD came unto me	Jer 13:3	1697
Then the *w* of the LORD came unto	Jer 13:8	1697
thou shalt speak unto them this *w*	Jer 13:12	1697
The *w* of the LORD that came to	Jer 14:1	1697
thou shalt say this *w* unto them	Jer 14:17	1697
thy *w* was unto me the joy and	Jer 15:16	1697
The *w* of the LORD came also unto	Jer 16:1	1697
me, Where is the *w* of the LORD	Jer 17:15	1697
them, Hear ye the *w* of the LORD	Jer 17:20	1697
The *w* which came to Jeremiah from	Jer 18:1	1697
Then the *w* of the LORD came to me	Jer 18:5	1697
nor the *w* from the prophet	Jer 18:18	1697
And say, Hear ye the *w* of the LORD	Jer 19:3	1697
because the *w* of the LORD was	Jer 20:8	1697
But his *w* was in mine heart as a	Jer 20:9	
The *w* which came unto Jeremiah	Jer 21:1	1697
say, Hear ye the *w* of the LORD	Jer 21:11	1697
of Judah, and speak there this *w*	Jer 22:1	1697
Hear the *w* of the LORD, O king of	Jer 22:2	1697
earth, hear the *w* of the LORD	Jer 22:29	1697
and hath perceived and heard his *w*	Jer 23:18	1697
who hath marked his *w*, and heard	Jer 23:18	1697
and he that hath my *w*	Jer 23:28	1697
let him speak my *w* faithfully	Jer 23:28	1697
Is not my *w* like as a fire	Jer 23:29	1697
for every man's *w* shall be his	Jer 23:36	1697
Because ye say this *w*, The burden	Jer 23:38	1697
Again the *w* of the LORD came unto	Jer 24:4	1697
The *w* that came to Jeremiah	Jer 25:1	1697
the *w* of the LORD hath come unto	Jer 25:3	1697
Judah came this *w* from the LORD	Jer 26:1	1697
diminish not a *w*	Jer 26:2	1697
w unto Jeremiah from the LORD	Jer 27:1	1697
if the *w* of the LORD be with them	Jer 27:18	1697
this *w* that I speak in thine ears	Jer 28:7	1697
when the *w* of the prophet shall	Jer 28:9	1697
Then the *w* of the LORD came unto	Jer 28:12	1697
and perform my good *w* toward you	Jer 29:10	1697
ye therefore the *w* of the LORD	Jer 29:20	1697
Then came the *w* of the LORD unto	Jer 29:30	1697
The *w* that came to Jeremiah from	Jer 30:1	1697
Hear the *w* of the LORD, O ye	Jer 31:10	1697
The *w* that came to Jeremiah from	Jer 32:1	1697
The *w* of the LORD came unto me,	Jer 32:6	1697
according to the *w* of the LORD	Jer 32:8	1697
that this was the *w* of the LORD	Jer 32:8	1697
Then came the *w* of the LORD unto	Jer 32:26	1697
Moreover the *w* of the LORD came	Jer 33:1	1697
the *w* of the LORD came unto	Jer 33:19	1697
Moreover the *w* of the LORD came	Jer 33:23	1697
The *w* which came unto Jeremiah	Jer 34:1	1697
Yet hear the *w* of the LORD	Jer 34:4	1697
for I have pronounced the *w*	Jer 34:5	1697
This is the *w* that came unto	Jer 34:8	1697
Therefore the *w* of the LORD came	Jer 34:12	1697
The *w* which came unto Jeremiah	Jer 35:1	1697
Then came the *w* of the LORD unto	Jer 35:12	1697
that this *w* came unto Jeremiah	Jer 36:1	1697
Then the *w* of the LORD came to	Jer 36:27	1697
Then came the *w* of the LORD unto	Jer 37:6	1697
Is there any *w* from the LORD	Jer 37:17	1697
this is the *w* that the LORD hath	Jer 38:21	1697
Now the *w* of the LORD came unto	Jer 39:15	1697
The *w* that came to Jeremiah from	Jer 40:1	1697
that the *w* of the LORD came unto	Jer 42:7	1697
therefore hear the *w* of the LORD	Jer 42:15	1697
Then came the *w* of the LORD unto	Jer 43:8	1697
The *w* that came to Jeremiah	Jer 44:1	1697
As for the *w* that thou hast	Jer 44:16	1697
Hear the *w* of the LORD, all Judah	Jer 44:24	1697
hear ye the *w* of the LORD	Jer 44:26	1697
The *w* that Jeremiah the prophet	Jer 45:1	1697
The *w* of the LORD which came to	Jer 46:1	1697
The *w* that the LORD spake to	Jer 46:13	1697
The *w* of the LORD that came to	Jer 47:1	1697
The *w* of the LORD that came to	Jer 49:34	1697
The *w* that the LORD spake against	Jer 50:1	1697
The *w* which Jeremiah the prophet	Jer 51:59	1697
he hath fulfilled his *w* that he	Lam 2:17	565
The *w* of the LORD came expressly	Eze 1:3	1697
that the *w* of the LORD came unto	Eze 3:16	1697
therefore hear the *w* at my mouth	Eze 3:17	1697
the *w* of the LORD came unto me,	Eze 6:1	1697
hear the *w* of the Lord GOD	Eze 6:3	1697
Moreover the *w* of the LORD came	Eze 7:1	1697
Again the *w* of the LORD came unto	Eze 11:14	1697
The *w* of the LORD also came unto	Eze 12:1	1697
came the *w* of the LORD unto me	Eze 12:8	1697
Moreover the *w* of the LORD came	Eze 12:17	1697
the *w* of the LORD came unto me,	Eze 12:21	1697
the *w* that I shall speak shall	Eze 12:25	1697
house, will I say the *w*, and will	Eze 12:25	1697
Again the *w* of the LORD came to	Eze 12:26	1697
but the *w* which I have spoken	Eze 12:28	1697
the *w* of the LORD came unto me,	Eze 13:1	1697
hearts, Hear ye the *w* of the LORD	Eze 13:2	1697
that they would confirm the *w*	Eze 13:6	1697
the *w* of the LORD came unto me,	Eze 14:2	1697
The *w* of the LORD came again to	Eze 14:12	1697
the *w* of the LORD came unto me,	Eze 15:1	1697
Again the *w* of the LORD came unto	Eze 16:1	1697
O harlot, hear the *w* of the LORD	Eze 16:35	1697
the *w* of the LORD came unto me,	Eze 17:1	1697
Moreover the *w* of the LORD came	Eze 17:11	1697
The *w* of the LORD came unto me	Eze 18:1	1697
Then came the *w* of the LORD unto	Eze 20:2	1697
Moreover the *w* of the LORD came	Eze 20:45	1697
drop thy *w* toward the south, and	Eze 20:46	
the south, Hear the *w* of the LORD	Eze 20:47	1697
the *w* of the LORD came unto me,	Eze 21:1	1697
drop thy *w* toward the holy places	Eze 21:2	
Again the *w* of the LORD came unto	Eze 21:8	1697
The *w* of the LORD came unto me	Eze 21:18	1697
Moreover the *w* of the LORD came	Eze 22:1	1697
the *w* of the LORD came unto me,	Eze 22:17	1697
the *w* of the LORD came unto me,	Eze 22:23	1697
The *w* of the LORD came again unto	Eze 23:1	1697
the *w* of the LORD came unto me,	Eze 24:1	1697
Also the *w* of the LORD came unto	Eze 24:15	1697
The *w* of the LORD came unto me,	Eze 24:20	1697
The *w* of the LORD came again unto	Eze 25:1	1697
Hear the *w* of the Lord GOD	Eze 25:3	1697
that the *w* of the LORD came unto	Eze 26:1	1697
The *w* of the LORD came again unto	Eze 27:1	1697
The *w* of the LORD came again unto	Eze 28:1	1697
Moreover the *w* of the LORD came	Eze 28:11	1697
Again the *w* of the LORD came unto	Eze 28:20	1697
the *w* of the LORD came unto me,	Eze 29:1	1697
the *w* of the LORD came unto me,	Eze 29:17	1697
The *w* of the LORD came again unto	Eze 30:1	1697
that the *w* of the LORD came unto	Eze 30:20	1697
that the *w* of the LORD came unto	Eze 31:1	1697
that the *w* of the LORD came unto	Eze 32:1	1697
that the *w* of the LORD came unto	Eze 32:17	1697
Again the *w* of the LORD came unto	Eze 33:1	1697
thou shalt hear the *w* at my mouth	Eze 33:7	1697
Then the *w* of the LORD came unto	Eze 33:23	1697
hear what is the *w* that cometh	Eze 33:30	1697
the *w* of the Lord came unto me,	Eze 34:1	1697
shepherds, hear the *w* of the LORD	Eze 34:7	1697
shepherds, hear the *w* of the LORD	Eze 34:9	1697
Moreover the *w* of the LORD came	Eze 35:1	1697
of Israel, hear the *w* of the LORD	Eze 36:1	1697
hear the *w* of the Lord GOD	Eze 36:4	1697
Moreover the *w* of the LORD came	Eze 36:16	1697
dry bones, hear the *w* of the LORD	Eze 37:4	1697
The *w* of the LORD came again unto	Eze 37:15	1697
the *w* of the LORD came unto me,	Eze 38:1	1697
him, and have changed the king's *w*	Dan 3:28	4406
demand by the *w* of the holy ones	Dan 4:17	3983
While the *w* was in the king's	Dan 4:31	4406
whereof the *w* of the LORD came to	Dan 9:2	1697
when he had spoken this *w* unto me	Dan 10:11	1697
The *w* of the LORD that came unto	Hos 1:1	1697

of the *w* of the LORD by Hosea ... Hos 1:2 1699
Hear the *w* of the LORD, ye ... Hos 4:1 1697
The *w* of the LORD that came to ... Joel 1:1 1697
he is strong that executeth his *w* ... Joel 2:11 1697
Hear this *w* that the LORD hath ... Amos 3:1 1697
Hear this *w*, ye kine of Bashan, ... Amos 4:1 1697
Hear ye this *w* which I take up ... Amos 5:1 1697
hear thou the *w* of the LORD ... Amos 7:16 1697
drop not thy *w* against the house ... Amos 7:16
and fro to seek the *w* of the LORD ... Amos 8:12 1697
Now the *w* of the LORD came unto ... Jonah 1:1 1697
the *w* of the LORD came unto Jonah ... Jonah 3:1 1697
according to the *w* of the LORD ... Jonah 3:3 1697
For *w* came unto the king of ... Jonah 3:6 1697
The *w* of the LORD that came to ... Mic 1:1 1697
the *w* of the LORD from Jerusalem ... Mic 4:2 1697
oaths of the tribes, even thy *w* ... Hab 3:9 562
The *w* of the LORD which came unto ... Zeph 1:1 1697
the *w* of the LORD is against you ... Zeph 2:5 1697
came the *w* of the LORD by Haggai ... Hag 1:1 1697
Then came the *w* of the LORD by ... Hag 1:3 1697
came the *w* of the LORD by the ... Hag 2:1 1697
According to the *w* that I ... Hag 2:5 1697
came the *w* of the LORD by Haggai ... Hag 2:10 1697
again the *w* of the LORD came unto ... Hag 2:20 1697
came the *w* of the LORD unto ... Zec 1:1 1697
came the *w* of the LORD unto ... Zec 1:7 1697
This is the *w* of the LORD unto ... Zec 4:6 1697
Moreover the *w* of the LORD came ... Zec 4:8 1697
the *w* of the LORD came unto me, ... Zec 6:9 1697
that the *w* of the LORD came unto ... Zec 7:1 1697
Then came the *w* of the LORD of ... Zec 7:4 1697
the *w* of the LORD came unto ... Zec 7:8 1697
Again the *w* of the LORD of hosts ... Zec 8:1 1697
the *w* of the LORD of hosts came ... Zec 8:18 1697
The burden of the *w* of the LORD ... Zec 9:1 1697
that it was the *w* of the LORD ... Zec 11:11 1697
The burden of the *w* of the LORD ... Zec 12:1 1697
The burden of the *w* of the LORD ... Mal 1:1 1697
have found him, bring me *w* again ... Mt 2:8 *518*
thou there until I bring thee *w* ... Mt 2:13 *2036*
but by every *w* that proceedeth ... Mt 4:4 *4487*
but speak the *w* only, and my ... Mt 8:8 *3056*
cast out the spirits with his *w* ... Mt 8:16 *3056*
whosoever speaketh a *w* against ... Mt 12:32 *3056*
That every idle *w* that men shall ... Mt 12:36 *4487*
one heareth the *w* of the kingdom ... Mt 13:19 *3056*
the same is he that heareth the *w* ... Mt 13:20 *3056*
ariseth because of the *w*, by and ... Mt 13:21 *3056*
thorns is he that heareth the *w* ... Mt 13:22 *3056*
of riches, choke the *w*, and he ... Mt 13:22 *3056*
ground is he that heareth the *w* ... Mt 13:23 *3056*
But he answered her not a *w* ... Mt 15:23 *3056*
every *w* may be established ... Mt 18:16 *4487*
no man was able to answer him a *w* ... Mt 22:46 *3056*
Peter remembered the *w* of Jesus ... Mt 26:75 *4487*
And he answered him to never a *w* ... Mt 27:14 *4487*
did run to bring his disciples *w* ... Mt 28:8 *518*
and he preached the *w* unto them ... Mk 2:2 *3056*
The sower soweth the *w* ... Mk 4:14 *3056*
the way side, where the *w* is sown ... Mk 4:15 *3056*
taketh away the *w* that was sown ... Mk 4:15 *3056*
who, when they have heard the *w* ... Mk 4:16 *3056*
such as hear the *w*, ... Mk 4:18 *3056*
things entering in, choke the *w* ... Mk 4:19 *3056*
such as hear the *w*, and receive it ... Mk 4:20 *3056*
parables spake he the *w* unto them ... Mk 4:33 *3056*
Jesus heard the *w* that was spoken ... Mk 5:36 *3056*
Making the *w* of God of none ... Mk 7:13 *3056*
the *w* that Jesus said unto him ... Mk 14:72 *4487*
confirming the *w* with signs ... Mk 16:20 *3056*
and ministers of the *w* ... Lk 1:2 *3056*
be it unto me according to thy *w* ... Lk 1:38 *4487*
in peace, according to thy *w* ... Lk 2:29 *4487*
the *w* of God came unto John the ... Lk 3:2 *4487*
alone, but by every *w* of God ... Lk 4:4 *4487*
for his *w* was with power ... Lk 4:32 *3056*
saying, What a *w* is this ... Lk 4:36 *3056*
upon him to hear the *w* of God ... Lk 5:1 *3056*
nevertheless at thy *w* I will let ... Lk 5:5 *4487*
but say in a *w*, and my servant ... Lk 7:7 *3056*
The seed is the *w* of God ... Lk 8:11 *3056*
taketh away the *w* out of their ... Lk 8:12 *3056*
they hear, receive the *w* with joy ... Lk 8:13 *3056*
and good heart, having heard the *w* ... Lk 8:15 *3056*
are these which hear the *w* of God ... Lk 8:21 *3056*
at Jesus' feet, and heard his *w* ... Lk 10:39 *3056*
are they that hear the *w* of God ... Lk 11:28 *3056*
speak a *w* against the Son of man ... Lk 12:10 *3056*
remembered the *w* of the Lord ... Lk 22:61 *3056*
w before God and all the people ... Lk 24:19 *3056*
In the beginning was the *W* ... Jn 1:1 *3056*
the *W* was with God ... Jn 1:1 *3056*
and the *W* was God ... Jn 1:1 *3056*
the *W* was made flesh, and dwelt ... Jn 1:14 *3056*
the *w* which Jesus had said ... Jn 2:22 *3056*
believed because of his own *w* ... Jn 4:41 *3056*
the man believed the *w* that Jesus ... Jn 4:50 *3056*
unto you, He that heareth my *w* ... Jn 5:24 *3056*
ye have not his *w* abiding in you ... Jn 5:38 *3056*
on him, If ye continue in my *w* ... Jn 8:31 *3056*
because my *w* hath no place in you ... Jn 8:37 *3056*
even because ye cannot hear my *w* ... Jn 8:43 *3056*
gods, unto whom the *w* of God came ... Jn 10:35 *3056*
the *w* that I have spoken, the ... Jn 12:48 *3056*
the *w* which ye hear is not mine, ... Jn 14:24 *3056*
w which I have spoken unto you ... Jn 15:3 *3056*
Remember the *w* that I said unto ... Jn 15:20 *3056*
that the *w* might be fulfilled ... Jn 15:25 *3056*
and they have kept thy *w* ... Jn 17:6 *3056*
I have given them thy *w* ... Jn 17:14 *3056*
thy *w* is truth ... Jn 17:17 *3056*
believe on me through their *w* ... Jn 17:20 *3056*
received his *w* were baptized ... Acts 2:41 *3056*
them which heard the *w* believed ... Acts 4:4 *3056*
all boldness they may speak thy *w* ... Acts 4:29 *3056*
they spake the *w* of God with ... Acts 4:31 *3056*
that we should leave the *w* of God ... Acts 6:2 *3056*
and to the ministry of the *w* ... Acts 6:4 *3056*
And the *w* of God increased ... Acts 6:7 *3056*
went every where preaching the *w* ... Acts 8:4 *3056*
Samaria had received the *w* of God ... Acts 8:14 *3056*
and preached the *w* of the Lord ... Acts 8:25 *3056*
The *w* which God sent unto the ... Acts 10:36 *3056*
That *w*, I say, ye know, which was ... Acts 10:37 *4487*
on all them which heard the *w* ... Acts 10:44 *3056*
had also received the *w* of God ... Acts 11:1 *3056*
remembered I the *w* of the Lord ... Acts 11:16 *4487*
preaching the *w* to none but unto ... Acts 11:19 *3056*
But the *w* of God grew and ... Acts 12:24 *3056*
they preached the *w* of God in the ... Acts 13:5 *3056*
and desired to hear the *w* of God ... Acts 13:7 *3056*
if ye have any *w* of exhortation ... Acts 13:15 *3056*
to you is the *w* of this salvation ... Acts 13:26 *3056*
together to hear the *w* of God ... Acts 13:44 *3056*
It was necessary that the *w* of ... Acts 13:46 *3056*
and glorified the *w* of the Lord ... Acts 13:48 *3056*
the *w* of the Lord was published ... Acts 13:49 *3056*
testimony unto the *w* of his grace ... Acts 14:3 *3056*
they had preached the *w* in Perga ... Acts 14:25 *3056*
should hear the *w* of the gospel ... Acts 15:7 *3056*
and preaching the *w* of the Lord ... Acts 15:35 *3056*
have preached the *w* of the Lord ... Acts 15:36 *3056*
Ghost to preach the *w* in Asia ... Acts 16:6 *3056*
spake unto him the *w* of the Lord ... Acts 16:32 *3056*
in that they received the *w* with ... Acts 17:11 *3056*
had knowledge that the *w* of God ... Acts 17:13 *3056*
teaching the *w* of God among them ... Acts 18:11 *3056*
heard the *w* of the Lord Jesus ... Acts 19:10 *3056*
So mightily grew the *w* of God ... Acts 19:20 *3056*
to the *w* of his grace, which is ... Acts 20:32 *3056*
gave him audience unto this *w* ... Acts 22:22 *3056*
after that Paul had spoken one *w* ... Acts 28:25 *4487*
Not as though the *w* of God hath ... Rom 9:6 *3056*
For this is the *w* of promise ... Rom 9:9 *3056*
The *w* is nigh thee, even in thy ... Rom 10:8 *4487*
the *w* of faith, which we preach ... Rom 10:8 *4487*
and hearing by the *w* of God ... Rom 10:17 *4487*
make the Gentiles obedient, by *w* ... Rom 15:18 *3056*
the kingdom of God is not in *w* ... 1Cor 4:20 *3056*
by the Spirit the *w* of wisdom ... 1Cor 12:8 *3056*
to another the *w* of knowledge by ... 1Cor 12:8 *3056*
came the *w* of God out from you ... 1Cor 14:36 *3056*
our *w* toward you was not yea and ... 2Cor 1:18 *3056*
many, which corrupt the *w* of God ... 2Cor 2:17 *3056*
nor handling the *w* of God ... 2Cor 4:2 *3056*
unto us the *w* of reconciliation ... 2Cor 5:19 *3056*
By the *w* of truth, by the power ... 2Cor 6:7 *3056*
such as we are in *w* by letters ... 2Cor 10:11 *3056*
shall every *w* be established ... 2Cor 13:1 *4487*
all the law is fulfilled in one *w* ... Gal 5:14 *3056*
the *w* communicate unto him that ... Gal 6:6 *3056*
that ye heard the *w* of truth ... Eph 1:13 *3056*
the washing of water by the *w* ... Eph 5:26 *4487*
the Spirit, which is the *w* of God ... Eph 6:17 *4487*
bold to speak the *w* without fear ... Phil 1:14 *3056*
Holding forth the *w* of life ... Phil 2:16 *3056*
the *w* of the truth of the gospel ... Col 1:5 *3056*
for you, to fulfil the *w* of God ... Col 1:25 *3056*
Let the *w* of Christ dwell in you ... Col 3:16 *3056*
And whatsoever ye do in *w* or deed ... Col 3:17 *3056*
came not unto you in *w* only ... 1Th 1:5 *3056*
received the *w* in much affliction ... 1Th 1:6 *3056*
out the *w* of the Lord not only in ... 1Th 1:8 *3056*
when ye received the *w* of God ... 1Th 2:13 *3056*
received it not as the *w* of men ... 1Th 2:13 *3056*
the *w* of God, which effectually ... 1Th 2:13 *3056*
say unto you by the *w* of the Lord ... 1Th 4:15 *3056*
neither by spirit, nor by *w* ... 2Th 2:2 *3056*
ye have been taught, whether by *w* ... 2Th 2:15 *3056*
and stablish you in every good *w* ... 2Th 2:17 *3056*
that the *w* of the Lord may have ... 2Th 3:1 *3056*
obey not our *w* by this epistle ... 2Th 3:14 *3056*
it is sanctified by the *w* of God ... 1Ti 4:5 *3056*
an example of the believers, in *w* ... 1Ti 4:12 *3056*
they who labour in the *w* and ... 1Ti 5:17 *3056*
but the *w* of God is not bound ... 2Ti 2:9 *3056*
rightly dividing the *w* of truth ... 2Ti 2:15 *3056*
their *w* will eat as doth a canker ... 2Ti 2:17 *3056*
Preach the *w* ... 2Ti 4:2 *3056*
his *w* through preaching, which is ... Titus 1:3 *3056*
faithful *w* as he hath been taught ... Titus 1:9 *3056*
that the *w* of God be not ... Titus 2:5 *3056*
all things by the *w* of his power ... Heb 1:3 *4487*
For if the *w* spoken by angels was ... Heb 2:2 *3056*
but the *w* preached did not profit ... Heb 4:2 *3056*
For the *w* of God is quick, and ... Heb 4:12 *3056*
in the *w* of righteousness ... Heb 5:13 *3056*
And have tasted the good *w* of God ... Heb 6:5 *4487*
but the *w* of the oath, which was ... Heb 7:28 *3056*
were framed by the *w* of God ... Heb 11:3 *4487*
w should not be spoken to them ... Heb 12:19 *3056*
And this *w*, Yet once more, ... Heb 12:27
have spoken unto you the *w* of God ... Heb 13:7 *3056*
suffer the *w* of exhortation ... Heb 13:22 *3056*
begat he us with the *w* of truth ... Jas 1:18 *3056*
with meekness the engrafted *w* ... Jas 1:21 *3056*
But be ye doers of the *w*, and not ... Jas 1:22 *3056*
For if any be a hearer of the *w* ... Jas 1:23 *3056*
If any man offend not in *w* ... Jas 3:2 *3056*
of incorruptible, by the *w* of God ... 1Pet 1:23 *3056*
But the *w* of the Lord endureth ... 1Pet 1:25 *4487*
this is the *w* which by the gospel ... 1Pet 1:25 *4487*
desire the sincere milk of the *w* ... 1Pet 2:2 *3050*
to them which stumble at the *w* ... 1Pet 2:8 *3056*
that, if any obey not the *w* ... 1Pet 3:1 *3056*
they also may without the *w* be ... 1Pet 3:1 *3056*
also a more sure *w* of prophecy ... 2Pet 1:19 *3056*
that by the *w* of God the heavens ... 2Pet 3:5 *3056*
by the same *w* are kept in store, ... 2Pet 3:7 *3056*
have handled, of the *W* of life ... 1Jn 1:1 *3056*
him a liar, and his *w* is not in us ... 1Jn 1:10 *3056*
But whoso keepeth his *w*, in him ... 1Jn 2:5 *3056*
The old commandment is the *w* ... 1Jn 2:7 *3056*
the *w* of God abideth in you, and ... 1Jn 2:14 *3056*
children, let us not love in *w* ... 1Jn 3:18 *3056*
in heaven, the Father, the *W* ... 1Jn 5:7 *3056*
Who bare record of the *w* of God ... Rev 1:2 *3056*
called Patmos, for the *w* of God ... Rev 1:9 *3056*
strength, and hast kept my *w* ... Rev 3:8 *3056*
hast kept the *w* of my patience ... Rev 3:10 *3056*
that were slain for the *w* of God ... Rev 6:9 *3056*
by the *w* of their testimony ... Rev 12:11 *3056*
his name is called The *W* of God ... Rev 19:13 *3056*
of Jesus, and for the *w* of God ... Rev 20:4 *3056*

WORD'S {2}

For thy *w* sake, and according to ... 2Sa 7:21 1697
ariseth for the *w* sake, ... Mk 4:17 *3056*

WORDS {549}

when he heard the *w* of Rebekah ... Gen 24:30 1697
Abraham's servant heard their *w* ... Gen 24:52 1697
Esau heard the *w* of his father ... Gen 27:34 1697
these *w* of Esau her elder son ... Gen 27:42 1697
he heard the *w* of Laban's sons, ... Gen 31:1 1697
their *w* pleased Hamor, and Shechem ... Gen 34:18 1697
more for his dreams, and for his *w* ... Gen 37:8 1697
unto him according to these *w* ... Gen 39:17 1697
master heard the *w* of his wife ... Gen 39:19 1697
that your *w* may be proved, ... Gen 42:16 1697
so shall your *w* be verified ... Gen 42:20 1697
according to the tenor of these *w* ... Gen 43:7 1697
he spake unto them these same *w* ... Gen 44:6 1697
Wherefore saith my lord these *w* ... Gen 44:7 1697
let it be according unto your *w* ... Gen 44:10 1697
we told him the *w* of my lord ... Gen 44:24 1697
they told him all the *w* of Joseph ... Gen 45:27 1697
he giveth goodly *w* ... Gen 49:21 561
unto him, and put *w* in his mouth ... Ex 4:15 1697
Moses told Aaron all the *w* of the ... Ex 4:28 1697
Aaron spake all the *w* which the ... Ex 4:30 1697
and let them not regard vain *w* ... Ex 5:9 1697
These are the *w* which thou shalt ... Ex 19:6 1697
w which the LORD commanded him ... Ex 19:7 1697
Moses returned the *w* of the ... Ex 19:8 1697
Moses told the *w* of the people ... Ex 19:9 1697
And God spake all these *w*, saying, ... Ex 20:1 1697
perverteth the *w* of the righteous ... Ex 23:8 1697
the people all the *w* of the LORD ... Ex 24:3 1697
All the *w* which the LORD hath ... Ex 24:3 1697
Moses wrote all the *w* of the LORD ... Ex 24:4 1697
with you concerning all these *w* ... Ex 24:8 1697
write upon these tables the *w* ... Ex 34:1 1697
unto Moses, Write thou these *w* ... Ex 34:27 1697
w I have made a covenant with ... Ex 34:27 1697
the tables the *w* of the covenant ... Ex 34:28 1697
These are the *w* which the LORD ... Ex 35:1 1697
told the people the *w* of the LORD ... Num 11:24 1697
And he said, Hear now my *w* ... Num 12:6 1697
an end of speaking all these *w* ... Num 16:31 1697
and spake unto him the *w* of Balak ... Num 22:7 1697
said, which heard the *w* of God ... Num 24:4 561
said, which heard the *w* of God ... Num 24:16 561
These be the *w* which Moses spake ... Deut 1:1 1697
LORD heard the voice of your *w* ... Deut 1:34 1697
king of Heshbon with *w* of peace ... Deut 2:26 1697
and I will make them hear my *w* ... Deut 4:10 1697
ye heard the voice of the *w* ... Deut 4:12 1697
thou heardest his *w* out of the ... Deut 4:36 1697
These *w* the LORD spake unto all ... Deut 5:22 1697
LORD heard the voice of your *w* ... Deut 5:28 1697
the voice of the *w* of this people ... Deut 5:28 1697
And these *w*, which I command thee ... Deut 6:6 1697
written according to all the *w* ... Deut 9:10 1697
w that were in the first tables ... Deut 10:2 1697
lay up these my *w* in your heart ... Deut 11:18 1697
hear all these *w* which I command ... Deut 12:28 1697
unto the *w* of that prophet ... Deut 13:3 1697
pervert the *w* of the righteous ... Deut 16:19 1697
to keep all the *w* of this law ... Deut 17:19 1697
will put my *w* in his mouth ... Deut 18:18 1697
will not hearken unto my *w* which ... Deut 18:19 1697
upon them all the *w* of this law ... Deut 27:3 1697
the *w* of this law very plainly ... Deut 27:8 1697
all the *w* of this law to do them ... Deut 27:26 1697
not go aside from any of the *w* ... Deut 28:14 1697
wilt not observe to do all the *w* ... Deut 28:58 1697
These are the *w* of the covenant, ... Deut 29:1 1697
therefore the *w* of this covenant ... Deut 29:9 1697
he heareth the *w* of this curse ... Deut 29:19 1697
we may do all the *w* of this law ... Deut 29:29 1697
spake these *w* unto all Israel ... Deut 31:1 1697
to do all the *w* of this law ... Deut 31:12 1697
the *w* of this law in a book ... Deut 31:24 1697

I may speak these *w* in their ears Deut 31:28 1697
of Israel the *w* of this song Deut 31:30 1697
hear, O earth, the *w* of my mouth Deut 32:1 561
spake all the *w* of this song in Deut 32:44 1697
all these *w* to all Israel Deut 32:45 1697
Set your hearts unto all the *w* Deut 32:46 1697
to do, all the *w* of this law Deut 32:46 1697
every one shall receive of thy *w* Deut 33:3 1703
will not hearken unto thy *w* in Josh 1:18 1697
she said, According unto your *w* Josh 2:21 1697
hear the *w* of the LORD your God Josh 3:9 1697
he read all the *w* of the law Josh 8:34 1697
heard the *w* that the children of Josh 22:30 1697
Joshua wrote these *w* in the book Josh 24:26 1697
for it hath heard all the *w* of Josh 24:27 561
angel of the LORD spake these *w* Judg 2:4 1697
the men of Shechem all these *w* Judg 9:3 1697
the *w* of Gaal the son of Ebed Judg 9:30 1697
we do not so according to thy *w* Judg 11:10 1697
Jephthah uttered all his *w* before Judg 11:11 1697
w of Jephthah which he sent him Judg 11:28 1697
Now let thy *w* come to pass Judg 13:12 1697
she pressed him daily with her *w* Judg 16:16 1697
none of his *w* fall to the ground 1Sa 3:19 1697
Samuel told all the *w* of the LORD 1Sa 8:10 1697
heard all the *w* of the people 1Sa 8:21 1697
the voice of the *w* of the LORD 1Sa 15:1 1697
commandment of the LORD, and thy *w* 1Sa 15:24 1697
heard those *w* of the Philistine 1Sa 17:11 1697
and spake according to the same *w* 1Sa 17:23 1697
when the *w* were heard which David 1Sa 17:31 1697
those *w* in the ears of David 1Sa 18:23 1697
his servants told David these *w* 1Sa 18:26 1697
laid up these *w* in his heart 1Sa 21:12 1697
stayed his servants with these *w* 1Sa 24:7 1697
Wherefore hearest thou men's *w* 1Sa 24:9 1697
end of speaking these *w* unto Saul 1Sa 24:16 1697
all those *w* in the name of David 1Sa 25:9 1697
hear the *w* of thine handmaid 1Sa 25:24 1697
king hear the *w* of his servant 1Sa 26:19 1697
because of the *w* of Samuel 1Sa 28:20 1697
have hearkened unto thy *w* which 1Sa 28:21 1697
wroth for the *w* of Ish-bosheth 2Sa 3:8 1697
According to all these *w*, and 2Sa 7:17 1697
thy *w* be true, and thou hast 2Sa 7:28 1697
So Joab put the *w* in her mouth 2Sa 14:3 1697
he put all these *w* in the mouth 2Sa 14:19 1697
the *w* of the men of Judah were 2Sa 19:43 1697
than the *w* of the men of Israel 2Sa 19:43 1697
Hear the *w* of thine handmaid 2Sa 20:17 1697
unto the LORD the *w* of this song 2Sa 22:1 1697
Now these be the last *w* of David 2Sa 23:1 1697
in after thee, and confirm thy *w* 1Kin 1:14 1697
I have done according to thy *w* 1Kin 3:12 1697
when Hiram heard the *w* of Solomon 1Kin 5:7 1697
And let these my *w*, wherewith I 1Kin 8:59 1697
Howbeit I believed not the *w* 1Kin 10:7 1697
them, and speak good *w* to them 1Kin 12:7 1697
the *w* which he had spoken unto 1Kin 13:11 1697
to pass, when Ahab heard those *w* 1Kin 21:27 1697
the *w* of the prophets declare 1Kin 22:13 1697
to meet you, and told you these *w* 2Kin 1:7 1697
the *w* that thou speakest in thy 2Kin 6:12 1697
the king heard the *w* of the woman 2Kin 6:30 1697
sayest, (but they are but vain *w* 2Kin 18:20 1697
and to thee, to speak these *w* 2Kin 18:27 1697
told him the *w* of Rab-shakeh 2Kin 18:37 1697
will hear all the *w* of Rab-shakeh 2Kin 19:4 1697
will reprove the *w* which the LORD 2Kin 19:4 1697
Be not afraid of the *w* which thou 2Kin 19:6 1697
hear the *w* of Sennacherib, which 2Kin 19:16 1697
the *w* of the book of the law 2Kin 22:11 1697
concerning the *w* of this book 2Kin 22:13 1697
hearkened unto the *w* of this book 2Kin 22:13 1697
even all the *w* of the book which 2Kin 22:16 1697
As touching the *w* which thou hast 2Kin 22:18 1697
the *w* of the book of the covenant 2Kin 23:2 1697
to perform the *w* of this covenant 2Kin 23:3 1697
who proclaimed these *w* 2Kin 23:16 1697
that he might perform the *w* of 2Kin 23:24 1697
According to all these *w*, and 1Chr 17:15 1697
For by the last *w* of David the 1Chr 23:27 1697
the king's seer in the *w* of God 1Chr 25:5 1697
Howbeit I believed not their *w* 2Chr 9:6 1697
them, and speak good *w* to them 2Chr 10:7 1697
And they obeyed the *w* of the LORD 2Chr 11:4 1697
And when Asa heard these *w* 2Chr 15:8 1697
the *w* of the prophets declare 2Chr 18:12 1697
by the *w* of the LORD, to cleanse 2Chr 29:15 1697
unto the LORD with the *w* of David 2Chr 29:30 1697
the *w* of Hezekiah king of Judah 2Chr 32:8 1697
the *w* of the seers that spake to 2Chr 33:18 1697
king had heard the *w* of the law 2Chr 34:19 1697
concerning the *w* of the book that 2Chr 34:21 1697
the *w* which thou hast heard 2Chr 34:26 1697
heardest his *w* against this place 2Chr 34:27 1697
the *w* of the book of the covenant 2Chr 34:30 1697
to perform the *w* of the covenant 2Chr 34:31 1697
hearkened not unto the *w* of Necho 2Chr 35:22 1697
of God, and despised his *w* 2Chr 36:16 1697
even a scribe of the *w* of the Ezr 7:11 1697
at the *w* of the God of Israel Ezr 9:4 1697
The *w* of Nehemiah the son of Neh 1:1 1697
to pass, when I heard these *w* Neh 1:4 1697
as also the king's *w* that he had Neh 2:18 1697
when I heard their cry and these *w* Neh 5:6 1697
their king, according to these *w* Neh 6:6 1697
to the king according to these *w* Neh 6:7 1697
before me, and uttered my *w* to him Neh 6:19 1697
when they heard the *w* of the law Neh 8:9 1697
w that were declared unto them Neh 8:12 1697
to understand the *w* of the law Neh 8:13 1697
his seed, and hast performed thy *w* Neh 9:8 1697
and told Esther the *w* of Mordecai Est 4:9 1697
they told to Mordecai Esther's *w* Est 4:12 1697
for all the *w* of this letter Est 9:26 1697
with *w* of peace and truth, Est 9:30 1697
Thy *w* have upholden him that was Job 4:4 4405
therefore my *w* are swallowed up Job 6:3 1697
concealed the *w* of the Holy One Job 6:10 561
How forcible are right *w* Job 6:25 561
Do ye imagine to reprove *w* Job 6:26 4405
how long shall the *w* of thy mouth Job 8:2 561
utter *w* out of their heart Job 8:10 4405
choose out my *w* to reason with Job 9:14 1697
the multitude of *w* be answered Job 11:2 1697
Doth not the ear try *w* Job 12:11 4405
lettest such *w* go out of thy Job 15:13 4405
Shall vain *w* have an end Job 16:3 1697
I could heap up *w* against you Job 16:4 4405
it be ere ye make an end of *w* Job 18:2 4405
and break me in pieces with *w* Job 19:2 4405
Oh that my *w* were now written Job 19:23 4405
lay up his *w* in thine heart Job 22:22 561
I would know the *w* which he would Job 23:5 4405
I have esteemed the *w* of his Job 23:12 561
To whom hast thou uttered *w* Job 26:4 4405
After my *w* they spake not again Job 29:22 1697
The *w* of Job are ended Job 31:40 1697
Behold, I waited for your *w* Job 32:11 1697
Job, or that answered his *w* Job 32:12 561
not directed his *w* against me Job 32:14 4405
speeches, and hearken to all my *w* Job 33:1 1697
My *w* shall be of the uprightness Job 33:3 561
set thy *w* in order before me, Job 33:5
I have heard the voice of thy *w* Job 33:8 4405
Hear my *w*, O ye wise men Job 34:2 4405
For the ear trieth *w*, as the Job 34:3 4405
hearken to the voice of my *w* Job 34:16 4405
his *w* were without wisdom Job 34:35 1697
and multiplieth his *w* against God Job 34:37 561
he multiplieth *w* without Job 35:16 4405
For truly my *w* shall not be false Job 36:4 4405
counsel by *w* without knowledge Job 38:2 4405
will he speak soft *w* unto thee Job 41:3
LORD had spoken these *w* unto Job Job 42:7 1697
Give ear to my *w*, O LORD Ps 5:1 561
concerning the *w* of Cush the Ps 7:*t* 1697
The *w* of the LORD Ps 12:6 565
the LORD are pure *w* Ps 12:6 565
Concerning the *w* of men, by the Ps 17:4
who spake unto the LORD the *w* of Ps 18:*t* 1697
their *w* to the end of the world Ps 19:4 4405
Let the *w* of my mouth, and the Ps 19:14 561
me, and from the *w* of my roaring Ps 22:1 1697
The *w* of his mouth are iniquity Ps 36:3 1697
and castest my *w* behind thee Ps 50:17 1697
Thou lovest all devouring *w* Ps 52:4 1697
give ear to the *w* of my mouth Ps 54:2 561
The *w* of his mouth were smoother Ps 55:21
his *w* were softer than oil, yet Ps 55:21 1697
Every day they wrest my *w* Ps 56:5 1697
the *w* of their lips let them even Ps 59:12 1697
shoot their arrows, even bitter *w* Ps 64:3 1697
your ears to the *w* of my mouth Ps 78:1 561
Then believed they his *w* Ps 106:12 1697
rebelled against the *w* of God Ps 107:11 561
me about also with *w* of hatred Ps 109:3 1697
have said that I would keep thy *w* Ps 119:57 1697
How sweet are thy *w* unto my taste Ps 119:103 565
entrance of thy *w* giveth light Ps 119:130 1697
mine enemies have forgotten thy *w* Ps 119:139 1697
when they hear the *w* of thy mouth Ps 138:4 561
places, they shall hear my *w* Ps 141:6 561
to perceive the *w* of Prov 1:2 561
the *w* of the wise, and their dark Prov 1:6 1697
in the city she uttereth her *w* Prov 1:21 561
I will make known my *w* unto you Prov 1:23 1697
My son, if thou wilt receive my *w* Prov 2:1 561
which flattereth with her *w* Prov 2:16 561
me, Let thine heart retain my *w* Prov 4:4 1697
decline from the *w* of my mouth Prov 4:5 561
My son, attend to my *w* Prov 4:20 1697
depart not from the *w* of my mouth Prov 5:7 561
snared with the *w* of thy mouth Prov 6:2 561
art taken with the *w* of thy mouth Prov 6:2 561
My son, keep my *w*, and lay up my Prov 7:1 561
which flattereth with her *w* Prov 7:5 561
and attend to the *w* of my mouth Prov 7:24 561
All the *w* of my mouth are in Prov 8:8 561
In the multitude of *w* there Prov 10:19 1697
The *w* of the wicked are to lie in Prov 12:6 1697
but grievous *w* stir up anger Prov 15:1 1697
but the *w* of the pure are Prov 15:26
the pure are pleasant *w* Prov 15:26
Pleasant *w* are as an honeycomb, Prov 16:24 561
that hath knowledge spareth his *w* Prov 17:27 561
The *w* of a man's mouth are as Prov 18:4 1697
The *w* of a talebearer are as Prov 18:8 1697
he pursueth them with *w*, yet they Prov 19:7 561
to err from the *w* of knowledge Prov 19:27 561
the *w* of the transgressor Prov 22:12 1697
hear the *w* of the wise, and apply Prov 22:17 1697
the certainty of the *w* of truth Prov 22:21 561
that thou mightest answer the *w* Prov 22:21 561
vomit up, and lose thy sweet *w* Prov 23:8 1697
will despise the wisdom of thy *w* Prov 23:9 4405
thine ears to the *w* of knowledge Prov 23:12 561
The *w* of a talebearer are as Prov 26:22 1697
will not be corrected by *w* Prov 29:19 1697
thou a man that is hasty in his *w* Prov 29:20 1697
The *w* of Agur the son of Jakeh, Prov 30:1 1697
Add thou not unto his *w*, lest he Prov 30:6 1697
The *w* of king Lemuel, the Prov 31:1 1697
The *w* of the Preacher, the son of Eccl 1:1 1697
therefore let thy *w* be few Eccl 5:2 1697
voice is known by multitude of *w* Eccl 5:3 1697
many *w* there are also divers Eccl 5:7 1697
heed unto all *w* that are spoken Eccl 7:21 1697
despised, and his *w* are not heard Eccl 9:16 1697
The *w* of wise men are heard in Eccl 9:17 1697
The *w* of a wise man's mouth are Eccl 10:12 1697
The beginning of the *w* of his Eccl 10:13 1697
A fool also is full of *w* Eccl 10:14 1697
sought to find out acceptable *w* Eccl 12:10 1697
was upright, even *w* of truth Eccl 12:10 1697
The *w* of the wise are as goads, Eccl 12:11 1697
as the *w* of a book that is sealed Is 29:11 1697
the deaf hear the *w* of the book Is 29:18 1697
evil, and will not call back his *w* Is 31:2 1697
to destroy the poor with lying *w* Is 32:7 561
are but vain *w*) I have counsel Is 36:5 1697
and to thee to speak these *w* Is 36:12 1697
Hear ye the *w* of the great king, Is 36:13 1697
and told him the *w* of Rabshakeh Is 36:22 1697
God will hear the *w* of Rabshakeh Is 37:4 1697
will reprove the *w* which the LORD Is 37:4 1697
of the *w* that thou hast heard Is 37:6 1697
hear all the *w* of Sennacherib, Is 37:17 1697
there is none that heareth your *w* Is 41:26 561
And I have put my *w* in thy mouth Is 51:16 1697
nor speaking thine own *w* Is 58:13 1697
from the heart *w* of falsehood Is 59:13 1697
my *w* which I have put in thy Is 59:21 1697
The *w* of Jeremiah the son of Jer 1:1 1697
I have put my *w* in thy mouth Jer 1:9 1697
proclaim these *w* toward the north Jer 3:12 1697
I will make my *w* in thy mouth Jer 5:14 1697
they have not hearkened unto my *w* Jer 6:19 1697
Trust ye not in lying *w*, saying, Jer 7:4 1697
Behold, ye trust in lying *w* Jer 7:8 1697
shalt speak all these *w* unto them Jer 7:27 1697
Hear ye the *w* of this covenant, Jer 11:2 1697
not the *w* of this covenant Jer 11:3 1697
Proclaim all these *w* in the Jer 11:6 1697
Hear ye the *w* of this covenant, Jer 11:6 1697
them all the *w* of this covenant Jer 11:8 1697
which refused to hear my *w* Jer 11:10 1697
they speak fair *w* unto thee Jer 12:6
people, which refuse to hear my *w* Jer 13:10 1697
Thy *w* were found, and I did eat Jer 15:16 1697
shew this people all these *w* Jer 16:10 1697
I will cause thee to hear my *w* Jer 18:2 1697
us not give heed to any of his *w* Jer 18:18 1697
proclaim there the *w* that I shall Jer 19:2 1697
that they might not hear my *w* Jer 19:15 1697
But if ye will not hear these *w* Jer 22:5 1697
because of the *w* of his holiness Jer 23:9 1697
Hearken not unto the *w* of the Jer 23:16 1697
had caused my people to hear my *w* Jer 23:22 1697
that steal my *w* every one from Jer 23:30 1697
perverted the *w* of the living God Jer 23:36 1697
Because ye have not heard my *w* Jer 25:8 1697
bring upon that land all my *w* Jer 25:13 1697
thou against them all these *w* Jer 25:30 1697
all the *w* that I command thee to Jer 26:2 1697
To hearken to the *w* of my Jer 26:5 1697
these *w* in the house of the LORD Jer 26:7 1697
city all the *w* that ye have heard Jer 26:12 1697
to speak all these *w* in your ears Jer 26:15 1697
to all the *w* of Jeremiah Jer 26:20 1697
and all the princes, heard his *w* Jer 26:21 1697
of Judah according to all these *w* Jer 27:12 1697
Therefore hearken not unto the *w* Jer 27:14 1697
Hearken not to the *w* of your Jer 27:16 1697
the LORD perform thy *w* which thou Jer 28:6 1697
Now these are the *w* of the letter Jer 29:1 1697
they have not hearkened to my *w* Jer 29:19 1697
and have spoken lying *w* in my name Jer 29:23 1697
Write thee all the *w* that I have Jer 30:2 1697
these are the *w* that the LORD Jer 30:4 1697
the prophet spake all these *w* Jer 34:6 1697
which have not performed the *w* of Jer 34:18 1697
instruction to hearken to my *w* Jer 35:13 1697
The *w* of Jonadab the son of Jer 35:14 1697
write therein all the *w* that I Jer 36:2 1697
of Jeremiah all the *w* of the LORD Jer 36:4 1697
the *w* of the LORD in the ears of Jer 36:6 1697
reading in the book the *w* of the Jer 36:8 1697
read Baruch in the book the *w* of Jer 36:10 1697
of the book all the *w* of the LORD Jer 36:11 1697
them all the *w* that he had heard Jer 36:13 1697
when they had heard all the *w* Jer 36:16 1697
tell the king of all these *w* Jer 36:16 1697
write all these *w* at his mouth Jer 36:17 1697
these *w* unto me with his mouth Jer 36:18 1697
told all the *w* in the ears of the Jer 36:20 1697
servants that heard all these *w* Jer 36:24 1697
the *w* which Baruch wrote at the Jer 36:27 1697
write in it all the former *w* that Jer 36:28 1697
the *w* of the book which Jehoiakim Jer 36:32 1697
besides unto them many like *w* Jer 36:32 1697
hearken unto the *w* of the LORD Jer 37:2 1697
heard the *w* that Jeremiah had Jer 38:1 1697

in speaking such *w* unto them	Jer 38:4	1697
Let no man know of these *w*	Jer 38:24	1697
w that the king had commanded	Jer 38:27	1697
I will bring my *w* upon this city	Jer 39:16	1697
LORD your God according to your *w*	Jer 42:4	1697
all the *w* of the LORD their God	Jer 43:1	1697
him to them, even all these *w*	Jer 43:1	1697
shall know whose *w* shall stand	Jer 44:28	1697
that ye may know that my *w* shall	Jer 44:29	1697
these *w* in a book at the mouth of	Jer 45:1	1697
even all these *w* that are written	Jer 51:60	1697
see, and shalt read all these *w*	Jer 51:61	1697
Thus far are the *w* of Jeremiah	Jer 51:64	1697
neither be afraid of their *w*	Eze 2:6	1697
be not afraid of their *w*, nor be	Eze 2:6	1697
thou shalt speak my *w* unto them	Eze 2:7	1697
and speak with my *w* unto them	Eze 3:4	1697
whose *w* thou canst not understand	Eze 3:6	1697
all my *w* that I shall speak unto	Eze 3:10	1697
of my *w* be prolonged any more	Eze 12:28	1697
as my people, and they hear thy *w*	Eze 33:31	1697
for they hear thy *w*, but they do	Eze 33:32	1697
have multiplied your *w* against me	Eze 35:13	1697
corrupt *w* to speak before me,	Dan 2:9	4406
by reason of the *w* of the king	Dan 5:10	4406
the king, when he heard these *w*	Dan 6:14	4406
the great *w* which the horn spake	Dan 7:11	4406
he shall speak great *w* against	Dan 7:25	4406
And he hath confirmed his *w*	Dan 9:12	1697
the voice of his *w* like the voice	Dan 10:6	1697
Yet heard I the voice of his *w*	Dan 10:9	1697
when I heard the voice of his *w*	Dan 10:9	1697
understand the *w* that I speak	Dan 10:11	1697
thy *w* were heard	Dan 10:12	1697
and I am come for thy *w*	Dan 10:12	1697
when he had spoken such *w* unto me	Dan 10:15	1697
But thou, O Daniel, shut up the *w*	Dan 12:4	1697
for the *w* are closed up and sealed	Dan 12:9	1697
slain them by the *w* of my mouth	Hos 6:5	561
They have spoken *w*, swearing	Hos 10:4	1697
Take with you *w*, and turn to the	Hos 14:2	1697
The *w* of Amos, who was among the	Amos 1:1	1697
is not able to bear all his *w*	Amos 7:10	1697
but of hearing the *w* of the LORD	Amos 8:11	1697
do not my *w* do good to him that	Mic 2:7	1697
the *w* of Haggai the prophet, as	Hag 1:12	1697
But my *w* and my statutes, which I	Zec 1:6	1697
that talked with me with good *w*	Zec 1:13	1697
and comfortable *w*	Zec 1:13	1697
Should ye not hear the *w* which	Zec 7:7	1697
the *w* which the LORD of hosts	Zec 7:12	1697
w by the mouth of the prophets	Zec 8:9	1697
have wearied the LORD with your *w*	Mal 2:17	1697
Your *w* have been stout against me	Mal 3:13	1697
not receive you, nor hear your *w*	Mt 10:14	*3056*
For by thy *w* thou shalt be	Mt 12:37	*3056*
by thy *w* thou shalt be condemned	Mt 12:37	*3056*
When they had heard these *w*	Mt 22:22	
but my *w* shall not pass away	Mt 24:35	*3056*
the third time, saying the same *w*	Mt 26:44	*3056*
of my *w* in this adulterous and	Mk 8:38	*3056*
were astonished at his *w*	Mk 10:24	*3056*
Herodians, to catch him in his *w*	Mk 12:13	*3056*
but my *w* shall not pass away	Mk 13:31	*3056*
and prayed, and spake the same *w*	Mk 14:39	*3056*
because thou believest not my *w*	Lk 1:20	*3056*
of the *w* of Esaias the prophet	Lk 3:4	*3056*
wondered at the gracious *w* which	Lk 4:22	*3056*
shall be ashamed of me and of my *w*	Lk 9:26	*3056*
they might take hold of his *w*	Lk 20:20	*3056*
hold of his *w* before the people	Lk 20:26	*4487*
but my *w* shall not pass away	Lk 21:33	*3056*
he questioned with him in many *w*	Lk 23:9	*3056*
And they remembered his *w*,	Lk 24:8	*4487*
their *w* seemed to them as idle	Lk 24:11	*4487*
These are the *w* which I spake	Lk 24:44	*3056*
hath sent speaketh the *w* of God	Jn 3:34	*4487*
how shall ye believe my *w*	Jn 5:47	*4487*
the *w* that I speak unto you, they	Jn 6:63	*4487*
thou hast the *w* of eternal life	Jn 6:68	*4487*
he had said these *w* unto them	Jn 7:9	
These *w* spake Jesus in the	Jn 8:20	*4487*
As he spake these *w*, many	Jn 8:30	
He that is of God heareth God's *w*	Jn 8:47	*4487*
These *w* spake his parents,	Jn 9:22	
which were with him heard these *w*	Jn 9:40	
These are not the *w* of him that	Jn 10:21	*4487*
And if any man hear my *w*, and	Jn 12:47	*4487*
me, and receiveth not my *w*	Jn 12:48	*4487*
the *w* that I speak unto you I	Jn 14:10	*4487*
a man love me, he will keep my *w*	Jn 14:23	*3056*
my *w* abide in you, ye shall ask	Jn 15:7	*4487*
These *w* spake Jesus, and lifted up	Jn 17:1	
them the *w* which thou gavest me	Jn 17:8	*4487*
When Jesus had spoken these *w*	Jn 18:1	
unto you, and hearken to my *w*	Acts 2:14	*4487*
Ye men of Israel, hear these *w*	Acts 2:22	*3056*
with many other *w* did he testify	Acts 2:40	*3056*
Ananias hearing these *w* fell down	Acts 5:5	*3056*
the people all the *w* of this life	Acts 5:20	*4487*
speak blasphemous *w* against Moses	Acts 6:11	*4487*
w against this holy place	Acts 6:13	*4487*
the Egyptians, and was mighty in *w*	Acts 7:22	*3056*
his house, and to hear *w* of thee	Acts 10:22	*4487*
While Peter yet spake these *w*	Acts 10:44	*4487*
Who shall tell thee *w*, whereby	Acts 11:14	*4487*
Gentiles besought that these *w*	Acts 13:42	*4487*
this agree the *w* of the prophets	Acts 15:15	*3056*
from us have troubled you with *w*	Acts 15:24	*3056*
exhorted the brethren with many *w*	Acts 15:32	*3056*
told these *w* unto the magistrates	Acts 16:38	*4487*
But if it be a question of *w*	Acts 18:15	*3056*
to remember the *w* of the Lord	Acts 20:35	*3056*
of all for the *w* which he spake	Acts 20:38	*3056*
hear us of thy clemency a few *w*	Acts 24:4	
but speak forth the *w* of truth	Acts 26:25	*4487*
And when he had said these *w*	Acts 28:29	
their *w* unto the ends of the	Rom 10:18	*4487*
and by good *w* and fair speeches	Rom 16:18	*5542*
not with wisdom of *w*, lest the	1Cor 1:17	*3056*
with enticing *w* of man's wisdom	1Cor 2:4	*3056*
not in the *w* which man's wisdom	1Cor 2:13	*3056*
tongue *w* easy to be understood	1Cor 14:9	*3056*
five *w* with my understanding	1Cor 14:19	*3056*
than ten thousand *w* in an unknown	1Cor 14:19	*3056*
paradise, and heard unspeakable *w*	2Cor 12:4	*4487*
(as I wrote afore in few *w*	Eph 3:3	
no man deceive you with vain *w*	Eph 5:6	*3056*
beguile you with enticing *w*	Col 2:4	*4086*
at any time used we flattering *w*	1Th 2:5	*3056*
comfort one another with these *w*	1Th 4:18	*3056*
nourished up in the *w* of faith	1Ti 4:6	*3056*
and consent not to wholesome *w*	1Ti 6:3	*3056*
even the *w* of our Lord Jesus	1Ti 6:3	
about questions and strifes of *w*	1Ti 6:4	*3055*
Hold fast the form of sound *w*	2Ti 1:13	*3056*
strive not about *w* to no profit	2Ti 2:14	*3054*
he hath greatly withstood our *w*	2Ti 4:15	*3056*
of a trumpet, and the voice of *w*	Heb 12:19	*4487*
a letter unto you in few *w*	Heb 13:22	
feigned *w* make merchandise of you	2Pet 2:3	*3056*
speak great swelling *w* of vanity	2Pet 2:18	
That ye may be mindful of the *w*	2Pet 3:2	*4487*
against us with malicious *w*	3Jn 10	*3056*
mouth speaketh great swelling *w*	Jude 16	
remember ye the *w* which were	Jude 17	*4487*
that hear the *w* of this prophecy	Rev 1:3	*3056*
until the *w* of God shall be	Rev 17:17	*4487*
for these *w* are true and faithful	Rev 21:5	*3056*
w of the prophecy of this book	Rev 22:18	*3056*
w of the book of this prophecy	Rev 22:19	*3056*

WORK {419}

God ended his *w* which he had made	Gen 2:2	4399
from all his *w* which he had made	Gen 2:2	4399
from all his *w* which God created	Gen 2:3	4399
shall comfort us concerning our *w*	Gen 5:29	4639
Let there more *w* be laid upon the	Ex 5:9	5656
of your *w* shall be diminished	Ex 5:11	5656
Go therefore now, and *w*	Ex 5:18	5647
no manner of *w* shall be done in	Ex 12:16	4399
Israel saw that great *w* which the	Ex 14:31	3027
walk, and the *w* that they must do	Ex 18:20	4640
thou labour, and do all thy *w*	Ex 20:9	4399
in it thou shalt not do any *w*	Ex 20:10	4399
Six days thou shalt do thy *w*	Ex 23:12	4639
a paved *w* of a sapphire stone	Ex 24:10	4639
of beaten *w* shalt thou make them,	Ex 25:18	4749
of beaten *w* shall the candlestick	Ex 25:31	4749
be one beaten *w* of pure gold	Ex 25:36	4749
of cunning *w* shalt thou make them	Ex 26:1	4639
and fine twined linen of cunning *w*	Ex 26:31	4639
fine twined linen, with cunning *w*	Ex 28:6	4639
same, according to the *w* thereof	Ex 28:8	4639
With the *w* of an engraver in	Ex 28:11	4639
of wreathen *w* shalt thou make	Ex 28:14	4639
of judgment with cunning *w*	Ex 28:15	4639
after the *w* of the ephod thou	Ex 28:15	4639
ends of wreathen *w* of pure gold	Ex 28:22	4639
w round about the hole of it	Ex 28:32	4639
to *w* in gold, and in silver, and in	Ex 31:4	6213
to *w* in all manner of workmanship	Ex 31:5	6213
for whosoever doeth any *w* therein	Ex 31:14	4399
Six days may *w* be done	Ex 31:15	4399
doeth any *w* in the sabbath day	Ex 31:15	4399
And the tables were the *w* of God	Ex 32:16	4639
art shall see the *w* of the LORD	Ex 34:10	4639
Six days thou shalt *w*, but on the	Ex 34:21	5627
Six days shall *w* be done, but on	Ex 35:2	4399
whosoever doeth *w* therein shall	Ex 35:2	4399
to the *w* of the tabernacle of the	Ex 35:21	4399
wood for any *w* of the service	Ex 35:24	4399
to bring for all manner of *w*	Ex 35:29	4399
to *w* in gold, and in silver, and in	Ex 35:32	6213
to make any manner of cunning *w*	Ex 35:33	4399
to *w* all manner of	Ex 35:35	6213
all manner of *w*	Ex 35:35	4399
even of them that do any *w*	Ex 35:35	4399
and of those that devise cunning *w*	Ex 35:35	
to *w* all manner of	Ex 36:1	6213
of *w* for the service of the	Ex 36:1	4399
up to come unto the *w* to do it	Ex 36:2	4399
of Israel had brought for the *w*	Ex 36:3	4399
all the *w* of the sanctuary	Ex 36:4	4399
man from his *w* which they made	Ex 36:4	4399
enough for the service of the *w*	Ex 36:5	4399
more *w* for the offering of the	Ex 36:6	4399
for all the *w* to make it, and too	Ex 36:7	4399
the *w* of the tabernacle made ten	Ex 36:8	4399
of cunning *w* made he them	Ex 36:8	4639
cherubims made he it of cunning *w*	Ex 36:35	4639
of beaten *w* made he the	Ex 37:17	4749
it was one beaten *w* of pure gold	Ex 37:22	4749
according to the *w* of the	Ex 37:29	4639
the *w* in all the *w* of the holy	Ex 38:24	4399
to *w* it in the blue, and in the	Ex 39:3	6213
in the fine linen, with cunning *w*	Ex 39:3	4639
same, according to the *w* thereof	Ex 39:5	4639
made the breastplate of cunning *w*	Ex 39:8	4639
like the *w* of the ephod	Ex 39:8	4639
of wreathen *w* of pure gold	Ex 39:15	4639
the robe of the ephod of woven *w*	Ex 39:22	4639
fine linen of woven *w* for Aaron	Ex 39:27	4639
Thus was all the *w* of the	Ex 39:32	5656
children of Israel made all the *w*	Ex 39:42	5656
And Moses did look upon all the *w*	Ex 39:43	4399
So Moses finished the *w*	Ex 40:33	4399
it be, wherein any *w* is done	Lev 11:32	4399
or in any *w* that is made of skin	Lev 13:51	4399
do no *w* at all, whether it be one	Lev 16:29	4399
Six days shall *w* be done	Lev 23:3	4399
ye shall do no *w* therein	Lev 23:3	4399
ye shall do no servile *w* therein	Lev 23:7	4399
ye shall do no servile *w* therein	Lev 23:8	4399
ye shall do no servile *w* therein	Lev 23:21	4399
Ye shall do no servile *w* therein	Lev 23:25	4399
ye shall do no *w* in that same day	Lev 23:28	4399
that doeth any *w* in that same day	Lev 23:30	4399
Ye shall do no manner of *w*	Lev 23:31	4399
ye shall do no servile *w* therein	Lev 23:35	4399
ye shall do no servile *w* therein	Lev 23:36	4399
to do the *w* in the tabernacle of	Num 4:3	4399
to do the *w* in the tabernacle of	Num 4:23	5656
to do the *w* of the tabernacle of	Num 4:30	5656
for the *w* in the tabernacle of	Num 4:35	5656
for the *w* in the tabernacle of	Num 4:39	5656
for the *w* in the tabernacle of	Num 4:43	5656
this *w* of the candlestick was of	Num 8:4	4639
the flowers thereof, was beaten *w*	Num 8:4	
do no manner of servile *w* therein	Num 28:18	4399
ye shall do no servile *w*	Num 28:25	4399
ye shall do no servile *w*	Num 28:26	4399
ye shall do no servile *w*	Num 29:1	4399
ye shall not do any *w* therein	Num 29:7	4399
ye shall do no servile *w*, and ye	Num 29:12	4399
ye shall do no servile *w* therein	Num 29:35	4399
all *w* of goats' hair, and all	Num 31:20	4639
the *w* of men's hands, wood and	Deut 4:28	4639
shalt labour, and do all thy *w*	Deut 5:13	4399
in it thou shalt not do any *w*	Deut 5:14	4399
God may bless thee in all the *w*	Deut 14:29	4639
thou shalt do no *w* with the	Deut 15:19	5647
thou shalt do no *w* therein	Deut 16:8	4399
thee in all the *w* of thine hands	Deut 24:19	4639
the *w* of the hands of the	Deut 27:15	4639
to bless all the *w* of thine hand	Deut 28:12	4639
in every *w* of thine hand, in the	Deut 30:9	4639
anger through the *w* of your hands	Deut 31:29	4639
He is the Rock, his *w* is perfect	Deut 32:4	6467
accept the *w* of his hands	Deut 33:11	6467
They did *w* wilily, and went and	Josh 9:4	6213
his *w* out of the field at even	Judg 19:16	4639
The LORD recompense thy *w*	Ruth 2:12	6467
your asses, and put them to his *w*	1Sa 8:16	4399
be that the LORD will *w* for us	1Sa 14:6	6213
officers which were over the *w*	1Kin 5:16	4399
the people that wrought in the *w*	1Kin 5:16	4399
gold fitted upon the carved *w*	1Kin 6:35	
porch, which was of the like *w*	1Kin 7:8	4649
cunning to *w* all works in brass	1Kin 7:14	6213
Solomon, and wrought all his *w*	1Kin 7:14	4399
And nets of checker *w*	1Kin 7:17	4639
and wreaths of chain *w*	1Kin 7:17	4639
were of lily *w* in the porch	1Kin 7:19	4639
the top of the pillars was lily *w*	1Kin 7:22	4639
so was the *w* of the pillars	1Kin 7:22	4399
the *w* of the bases was on this	1Kin 7:28	4639
certain additions made of thin *w*	1Kin 7:29	4639
was round after the *w* of the base	1Kin 7:31	4639
the *w* of the wheels was like the	1Kin 7:33	4639
was like the *w* of a chariot wheel	1Kin 7:33	4639
made an end of doing all the *w*	1Kin 7:40	4399
So was ended all the *w* that king	1Kin 7:51	4399
that were over Solomon's *w*	1Kin 9:23	4399
the people that wrought in the *w*	1Kin 9:23	4399
to anger with the *w* of his hands	1Kin 16:7	4639
thou hast sold thyself to *w* evil	1Kin 21:20	6213
which did sell himself to *w*	1Kin 21:25	6213
the hands of them that did the *w*	2Kin 12:11	4399
but the *w* of men's hands, wood and	2Kin 19:18	4639
the hand of the doers of the *w*	2Kin 22:5	4399
give it to the doers of the *w*	2Kin 22:5	4399
the hand of them that do the *w*	2Kin 22:9	4399
and the wreathen *w*, and	2Kin 25:17	7639
the second pillar with wreathen *w*	2Kin 25:17	7639
dwelt with the king for his *w*	1Chr 4:23	4399
all the *w* of the place most holy	1Chr 6:49	4399
very able men for the *w* of the	1Chr 9:13	4399
were over the *w* of the service,	1Chr 9:19	4399
they were employed in that *w* day	1Chr 9:33	4399
as every day's *w* required	1Chr 16:37	1697
cunning men for every manner of *w*	1Chr 22:15	4399
were to set forward the *w* of the	1Chr 23:4	4399
that did the *w* for the service of	1Chr 23:24	4399
the *w* of the service of the house	1Chr 23:28	4639
over them that did the *w* of the	1Chr 27:26	4399
for all the *w* of the service of	1Chr 28:13	4399
thou hast finished all the *w* for	1Chr 28:20	4399
and tender, and the *w* is great	1Chr 29:1	4399
for all manner of *w* to be made by	1Chr 29:5	4399
with the rulers of the king's *w*	1Chr 29:6	4399
a man cunning to *w* in gold	2Chr 2:7	6213
man of Tyre, skilful to *w* in gold	2Chr 2:14	6213
overseers to set the people a *w*	2Chr 2:18	5647

he made two cherubims of image *w* 2Chr 3:10 4639
like the *w* of the brim of a cup 2Chr 4:5 4639
Huram finished the *w* that he was 2Chr 4:11 4399
Thus all the *w* that Solomon made 2Chr 5:1 4399
make no servants for his *w* 2Chr 8:9 4399
Now all the *w* of Solomon was 2Chr 8:16 4399
for your *w* shall be rewarded 2Chr 15:7 6468
of Ramah, and let his *w* cease 2Chr 16:5 4399
gave it to such as did the *w* of 2Chr 24:12 4399
the *w* was perfected by them, and 2Chr 24:13 4399
till the *w* was ended, and until 2Chr 29:34 4399
in every *w* that he began in the 2Chr 31:21 4639
which were the *w* of the hands of 2Chr 32:19 4639
And the men did the *w* faithfully 2Chr 34:12 4399
of all that wrought the *w* in any 2Chr 34:13 4399
the treasure of the *w* threescore Ezr 2:69 4399
to set forward the *w* of the house Ezr 3:8 4399
Then ceased the *w* of the house of Ezr 4:24 5673
and this *w* goeth fast on, and Ezr 5:8 5673
Let the *w* of this house of God Ezr 6:7 5673
in the *w* of the house of God Ezr 6:22 4399
is this a *w* of one day or two Ezr 10:13 4399
nor to the rest that did the *w* Neh 2:16 4399
their hands for this good *w* Neh 2:18
necks to the *w* of their Lord Neh 3:5 5656
for the people had a mind to *w* Neh 4:6 6213
them, and cause the *w* to cease Neh 4:11 4399
to the wall, every one unto his *w* Neh 4:15 4399
of my servants wrought in the *w* Neh 4:16 4399
one of his hands wrought in the *w* Neh 4:17 4399
The *w* is great and large, and we Neh 4:19 4399
So we laboured in the *w* Neh 4:21 4399
I continued in the *w* of this wall Neh 5:16 4399
were gathered thither unto the *w* Neh 5:16 4399
saying, I am doing a great *w* Neh 6:3 4399
why should the *w* cease, whilst I Neh 6:3 4399
shall be weakened from the *w* Neh 6:9 4399
this *w* was wrought of our God Neh 6:16 4399
of the fathers gave unto the *w* Neh 7:70 4399
gave to the treasure of the *w* Neh 7:71 4399
for all the *w* of the house of our Neh 10:33 4399
their brethren that did the *w* of Neh 11:12 4399
and the singers, that did the *w* Neh 13:10 4399
hast blessed the *w* of his hands Job 1:10 4639
looketh for the reward of his *w* Job 7:2 6467
despise the *w* of thine hands Job 10:3 3018
a desire to the *w* of thine hands Job 14:15 4639
On the left hand, where he doth *w* Job 23:9 6213
desert, go they forth to their *w* Job 24:5 6467
For the *w* of a man shall he Job 34:11 6467
they all are the *w* of his hands Job 34:19 4639
Then he sheweth them their *w* Job 36:9 6467
Remember that thou magnify his *w* Job 36:24 6467
that all men may know his *w* Job 37:7 4639
the *w* of thy fingers, the moon and Ps 8:3 4639
snared in the *w* of his own hands Ps 9:16 6467
them after the *w* of their hands Ps 28:4 4639
what *w* thou didst in their days, Ps 44:1 6467
Yea, in heart ye *w* wickedness Ps 58:2 6466
to every man according to his *w* Ps 62:12 4639
and shall declare the *w* of God Ps 64:9 6467
w thereof at once with axes Ps 74:6 6603
I will meditate also of all thy *w* Ps 77:12 6467
Let thy *w* appear unto thy Ps 90:16 6467
establish thou the *w* of our hands Ps 90:17 4639
the *w* of our hands establish thou Ps 90:17 4639
hast made me glad through thy *w* Ps 92:4 6467
me, proved me, and saw my *w* Ps 95:9 6467
I hate the *w* of them that turn Ps 101:3 6213
heavens are the *w* of thy hands Ps 102:25 4639
Man goeth forth unto his *w* Ps 104:23 6467
His *w* is honourable and glorious Ps 111:3 6467
and gold, the *w* of men's hands Ps 115:4 4639
It is time for thee, LORD, to *w* Ps 119:126 6213
and gold, the *w* of men's hands Ps 135:15 4639
works with men that *w* iniquity Ps 141:4 5950
I muse on the *w* of thy hands Ps 143:5 4639
The wicked worketh a deceitful *w* Prov 11:18 6468
the weights of the bag are his *w* Prov 16:11 4639
his *w* is brother to him that is a Prov 18:9 4399
his doings, whether his *w* be pure Prov 20:11 6467
as for the pure, his *w* is right Prov 21:8 6467
Prepare thy *w* without, and make it Prov 24:27 4399
to the man according to his *w* Prov 24:29 6467
because the *w* that is wrought Eccl 2:17 4639
the *w* that God maketh from the Eccl 3:11 4639
for every purpose and for every *w* Eccl 3:17 4639
evil *w* that is done under the sun Eccl 4:3 4639
all travail, and every right *w* Eccl 4:4 4639
destroy the *w* of thine hands Eccl 5:6 4639
Consider the *w* of God Eccl 7:13 4639
w that is done under the sun Eccl 8:9 4639
evil *w* is not executed speedily Eccl 8:11 4639
according to the *w* of the wicked Eccl 8:14 4639
to the *w* of the righteous Eccl 8:14 4639
Then I beheld all the *w* of God Eccl 8:17 4639
the *w* that is done under the sun Eccl 8:17 4639
for there is no *w*, nor device, Eccl 9:10 4639
shall bring every *w* into judgment Eccl 12:14 4639
the *w* of the hands of a cunning Song 7:1 4639
they worship the *w* of their own Is 2:8 4639
they regard not the *w* of the LORD Is 5:12 6467
him make speed, and hasten his *w* Is 5:19 4639
his whole *w* upon mount Zion Is 10:12 4639
the *w* of his hands, neither shall Is 17:8 4639
Moreover they that *w* in fine flax Is 19:9 5647
Egypt to err in every *w* thereof Is 19:14 4639
shall there be any *w* for Egypt Is 19:15 4639
and Assyria the *w* of my hands Is 19:25 4639
he may do his *w*, his strange *w* Is 28:21 4639
a marvellous *w* among this people Is 29:14 6381
this people, even a marvellous *w* Is 29:14 6381
for shall the *w* say of him that Is 29:16 4639
the *w* of mine hands, in the midst Is 29:23 4639
the help of them that *w* iniquity Is 31:2 6213
and his heart will *w* iniquity Is 32:6 6213
the *w* of righteousness shall be Is 32:17 4639
but the *w* of men's hands, wood and Is 37:19 4639
is with him, and his *w* before him Is 40:10 6468
of nothing, and your *w* of nought Is 41:24 6467
I will *w*, and who shall let it Is 43:13 6466
or thy *w*, He hath no hands Is 45:9 6467
concerning the *w* of my hands Is 45:11 6467
the LORD, and my *w* with my God Is 49:4 6468
forth an instrument for his *w* Is 54:16 4639
the *w* of my hands, that I may be Is 60:21 4639
and I will direct their *w* in truth Is 61:8 6468
is with him, and his *w* before him Is 62:11 6468
and we all are the *w* of thy hand Is 64:8 4639
their former *w* into their bosom Is 65:7 6468
long enjoy the *w* of their hands Is 65:22 4639
the *w* of the hands of the workman Jer 10:3 4639
the *w* of the workman, and of the Jer 10:9 4639
they are all the *w* of cunning men Jer 10:9 4639
are vanity, and the *w* of errors Jer 10:15 4639
sabbath day, neither do ye any *w* Jer 17:22 4399
sabbath day, to do no *w* therein Jer 17:24 4399
he wrought a *w* on the wheels Jer 18:3 4399
and giveth him not for his *w* Jer 22:13 6467
for thy *w* shall be rewarded, Jer 31:16 6468
Great in counsel, and mighty in *w* Jer 32:19 5950
anger with the *w* of their hands Jer 32:30 4639
the *w* of the LORD deceitfully Jer 48:10 4399
for this is the *w* of the Lord GOD Jer 50:25 4399
recompense her according to her *w* Jer 50:29 6467
in Zion the *w* of the LORD our God Jer 51:10 4639
They are vanity, the *w* of errors Jer 51:18 4639
according to the *w* of their hands Lam 3:64 4639
the *w* of the hands of the potter Lam 4:2 4639
their *w* was like unto the colour Eze 1:16 4639
their *w* was as it were a wheel in Eze 1:16 4639
wood be taken thereof to do any *w* Eze 15:3 4399
is it meet for any *w* Eze 15:4 4399
was whole, it was meet for no *w* Eze 15:5 4399
shall it be meet yet for any *w* Eze 15:5 4399
thee also with broidered *w* Eze 16:10 7553
linen, and silk, and broidered *w* Eze 16:13 7553
the *w* of an imperious whorish Eze 16:30 4639
Fine linen with broidered *w* from Eze 27:7 7553
emeralds, purple, and broidered *w* Eze 27:16 7553
in blue clothes, and broidered *w* Eze 27:24 7553
ye *w* abomination, and ye defile Eze 33:26 6213
with him he shall *w* deceitfully Dan 11:23 6213
is a city of them that *w* iniquity Hos 6:8 6466
all of it the *w* of the craftsmen Hos 13:2 4639
any more to the *w* of our hands Hos 14:3 4639
and *w* evil upon their beds Mic 2:1 6466
more worship the *w* of thine hands Mic 5:13 4639
for I will *w* a Hab 1:5 6466
a *w* in your days Hab 1:5 6467
maker of his *w* trusteth therein Hab 2:18 3336
revive thy *w* in the midst of the Hab 3:2 6467
for he shall uncover the cedar *w* Zeph 2:14 731
did *w* in the house of the LORD of Hag 1:14 4399
of the land, saith the LORD, and *w* Hag 2:4 6213
so is every *w* of their hands Hag 2:14 4639
they that *w* wickedness are set up Mal 3:15 6213
from me, ye that *w* iniquity Mt 7:23 *2038*
go *w* to day in my vineyard Mt 21:28 *2038*
she hath wrought a good *w* upon me Mt 26:10 *2041*
And he could there do no mighty *w* Mk 6:5 *1411*
servants, and to every man his *w* Mk 13:34 *2041*
she hath wrought a good *w* on me Mk 14:6 *2041*
six days in which men ought to *w* Lk 13:14 *2038*
that sent me, and to finish his *w* Jn 4:34 *2041*
Father worketh hitherto, and I *w* Jn 5:17 *2038*
that we might *w* the works of God Jn 6:28 *2038*
unto them, This is the *w* of God Jn 6:29 *2041*
what dost thou *w* Jn 6:30 *2038*
said unto them, I have done one *w* Jn 7:21 *2041*
I must *w* the works of him that Jn 9:4 *2038*
night cometh, when no man can *w* Jn 9:4 *2038*
For a good *w* we stone thee not Jn 10:33 *2041*
I have finished the *w* which thou Jn 17:4 *2041*
this counsel or this *w* be of men Acts 5:38 *2041*
Saul for the *w* whereunto I have Acts 13:2 *2041*
for I *w* a Acts 13:41 *2038*
a *w* in your days Acts 13:41 *2040*
a *w* which ye shall in no wise Acts 13:41 *2041*
for the *w* which they fulfilled Acts 14:26 *2041*
and went not with them to the *w* Acts 15:38 *2041*
had much *w* to come by the boat Acts 27:16 *3433,2480*
Which shew the *w* of the law Rom 2:15 *2041*
did *w* in our members to bring Rom 7:5 *1754*
we know that all things *w* Rom 8:28 *4903*
For he will finish the *w*, and cut Rom 9:28 *3056*
because a short *w* will the Lord Rom 9:28 *3056*
otherwise *w* is no more *w* Rom 11:6 *2041*
For meat destroy not the *w* of God Rom 14:20 *2041*
Every man's *w* shall be made 1Cor 3:13 *2041*
every man's *w* of what sort it is 1Cor 3:13 *2041*
If any man's *w* abide which he 1Cor 3:14 *2041*
If any man's *w* shall be burned, 1Cor 3:15 *2041*
are not ye my *w* in the Lord 1Cor 9:1 *2041*
abounding in the *w* of the Lord 1Cor 15:58 *2041*
for he worketh the *w* of the Lord 1Cor 16:10 *2041*
may abound to every good *w* 2Cor 9:8 *2041*
But let every man prove his own *w* Gal 6:4 *2041*
for the *w* of the ministry, for Eph 4:12 *2041*
to *w* all uncleanness with Eph 4:19 *2039*
w in you will perform it until Phil 1:6 *2041*
w out your own salvation with Phil 2:12 *2716*
Because for the *w* of Christ he Phil 2:30 *2041*
being fruitful in every good *w* Col 1:10 *2041*
without ceasing your *w* of faith 1Th 1:3 *2041*
to *w* with your own hands, as we 1Th 4:11 *2038*
the *w* of faith with power 2Th 1:11 *2041*
of iniquity doth already *w* 2Th 2:7 *1754*
you in every good word and *w* 2Th 2:17 *2041*
you, that if any would not *w* 2Th 3:10 *2038*
that with quietness they *w* 2Th 3:12 *2038*
of a bishop, he desireth a good *w* 1Ti 3:1 *2041*
diligently followed every good *w* 1Ti 5:10 *2041*
and prepared unto every good *w* 2Ti 2:21 *2041*
do the *w* of an evangelist, make 2Ti 4:5 *2041*
deliver me from every evil *w* 2Ti 4:18 *2041*
and unto every good *w* reprobate Titus 1:16 *2041*
to be ready to every good *w* Titus 3:1 *2041*
not unrighteous to forget your *w* Heb 6:10 *2041*
in every good *w* to do his will Heb 13:21 *2041*
let patience have her perfect *w* Jas 1:4 *2041*
hearer, but a doer of the *w* Jas 1:25 *2041*
is confusion and every evil *w* Jas 3:16 *4229*
according to every man's *w* 1Pet 1:17 *2041*
man according as his *w* shall be Rev 22:12 *2041*

WORKER {1}

was a man of Tyre, a *w* in brass 1Kin 7:14 2790

WORKERS {28}

Moreover the *w* with familiar 2Kin 23:24
w of stone and timber, and all 1Chr 22:15 2796
punishment to the *w* of iniquity Job 31:3 6466
in company with the *w* of iniquity Job 34:8 6466
where the *w* of iniquity may hide Job 34:22 6466
thou hatest all *w* of iniquity Ps 5:5 6466
from me, all ye *w* of iniquity Ps 6:8 6466
Have all the *w* of iniquity no Ps 14:4 6466
with the *w* of iniquity, which Ps 28:3 6466
There are the *w* of iniquity Ps 36:12 6466
envious against the *w* of iniquity Ps 37:1 6213
Have the *w* of iniquity no Ps 53:4 6466
Deliver me from the *w* of iniquity Ps 59:2 6466
insurrection of the *w* of iniquity Ps 64:2 6466
when all the *w* of iniquity do Ps 92:7 6466
all the *w* of iniquity shall be Ps 92:9 6466
all the *w* of iniquity boast Ps 94:4 6466
for me against the *w* of iniquity Ps 94:16 6466
them forth with the *w* of iniquity Ps 125:5 6466
and the gins of the *w* of iniquity Ps 141:9 6466
shall be to the *w* of iniquity Prov 10:29 6466
shall be to the *w* of iniquity Prov 21:15 6466
from me, all ye *w* of iniquity Lk 13:27 *2040*
are all *w* of miracles 1Cor 12:29 *1411*
as *w* together with him, beseech 2Cor 6:1 *4903*
are false apostles, deceitful *w* 2Cor 11:13 *2040*
Beware of dogs, beware of evil *w* Phil 3:2 *2040*
fellow *w* unto the kingdom of God Col 4:11

WORKETH {37}

all these things *w* God oftentimes Job 33:29 6466
w righteousness, and speaketh the Ps 15:2 6466
He that *w* deceit shall not dwell Ps 101:7 6213
The wicked *w* a deceitful work Prov 11:18 6213
and a flattering mouth *w* ruin Prov 26:28 6213
w willingly with her hands Prov 31:13 6213
What profit hath he that *w* in Eccl 3:9 6213
the tongs both *w* in the coals Is 44:12 6466
w it with the strength of his Is 44:12 6466
w righteousness, those that Is 64:5 6213
he *w* signs and wonders in heaven Dan 6:27 5648
them, My Father *w* hitherto Jn 5:17 *2038*
w righteousness, is accepted with Acts 10:35 *2038*
peace, to every man that *w* good Rom 2:10 *2038*
Now to him that *w* is the reward Rom 4:4 *2038*
But to him that *w* not, but Rom 4:5 *2038*
Because the law *w* wrath Rom 4:15 *2716*
that tribulation *w* patience Rom 5:3 *2716*
Love *w* no ill to his neighbour Rom 13:10 *2038*
the same God which *w* all in all 1Cor 12:6 *1754*
But all these *w* that one and the 1Cor 12:11 *1754*
for he *w* the work of the Lord, as 1Cor 16:10 *2038*
So then death *w* in us, but life 2Cor 4:12 *1754*
w for us a far more exceeding and 2Cor 4:17 *2716*
For godly sorrow *w* repentance to 2Cor 7:10 *2716*
the sorrow of the world *w* death 2Cor 7:10 *2716*
w miracles among you, doeth he it Gal 3:5 *1754*
but faith which *w* by love Gal 5:6 *1754*
to the purpose of him who *w* all Eph 1:11 *1754*
the spirit that now *w* in the Eph 2:2 *1754*
to the power that *w* in us Eph 3:20 *1754*
God which *w* in you both to will Phil 2:13 *1754*
working, which *w* in me mightily Col 1:29 *1754*
which effectually *w* also in you 1Th 2:13 *1754*
trying of your faith *w* patience Jas 1:3 *2716*
For the wrath of man *w* not the Jas 1:20 *2716*
neither whatsoever *w* abomination Rev 21:27 *4160*

WORKFELLOW {1}

Timotheus my *w*, and Lucius, and Rom 16:21 *4904*

WORKING {20}

like a sharp rasor, *w* deceitfully Ps 52:2 6213
w salvation in the midst of the Ps 74:12 6466
in counsel, and excellent in *w* Is 28:29 8454
east shall be shut the six *w* days Eze 46:1 4639
where, the Lord *w* with them, and Mk 16:20 *4903*

W

men with men *w* that which is	Rom 1:27	*2716*
w death in me by that which is	Rom 7:13	*2716*
And labour, *w* with our own hands	1Cor 4:12	*2038*
have not we power to forbear *w*	1Cor 9:6	*2038*
To another the *w* of miracles	1Cor 12:10	*1755*
according to the *w* of his mighty	Eph 1:19	*1753*
by the effectual *w* of his power	Eph 3:7	*1753*
according to the effectual *w* in	Eph 4:16	*1753*
w with his hands the thing which	Eph 4:28	*2038*
according to the *w* whereby he is	Phil 3:21	*1753*
striving according to his *w*	Col 1:29	*1753*
the *w* of Satan with all power	2Th 2:9	*1753*
w not at all, but are busybodies	2Th 3:11	*2038*
his will, *w* in you that which is	Heb 13:21	*4160*
w miracles, which go forth unto	Rev 16:14	*4160*

WORKMAN {10}

the engraver, and of the cunning *w*	Ex 35:35	2803
Dan, an engraver, and a cunning *w*	Ex 38:23	2803
work of the hands of a cunning *w*	Song 7:1	542
The *w* melteth a graven image, and	Is 40:19	2796
w to prepare a graven image	Is 40:20	2796
the work of the hands of the *w*	Jer 10:3	2796
from Uphaz, the work of the *w*	Jer 10:9	2796
the *w* made it	Hos 8:6	2796
for the *w* is worthy of his meat	Mt 10:10	*2040*
a *w* that needeth not to be	2Ti 2:15	*2040*

WORKMANSHIP {7}

knowledge, and in all manner of *w*	Ex 31:3	4399
to work in all manner of *w*	Ex 31:5	4399
knowledge, and in all manner of *w*	Ex 35:31	4399
according to all the *w* thereof	2Kin 16:10	4639
of *w* every willing skilful man	1Chr 28:21	4399
the *w* of thy tabrets and of thy	Eze 28:13	4399
For we are his *w*, created in	Eph 2:10	*4161*

WORKMEN {11}

But they gave that to the *w*	2Kin 12:14	6213,4399
the money to be bestowed on *w*	2Kin 12:15	6213,4399
Moreover there are *w* with thee in	1Chr 22:15	6213,4399
the number of the *w* according to	1Chr 25:1	582,4399
So the *w* wrought, and the work	2Chr 24:13	6213,4399
w that had the oversight of the	2Chr 34:10	6213,4399
they gave it to the *w* that	2Chr 34:10	6213,4399
and to the hand of the *w*	2Chr 34:17	6213,4399
to set forward the *w* in the house	Ezr 3:9	
and the *w*, they are of men	Is 44:11	2796
with the *w* of like occupation	Acts 19:25	*2040*

WORKMEN'S {1}

and her right hand to the *w* hammer	Judg 5:26	6001

WORK'S {1}

highly in love for their *w* sake	1Th 5:13	*2041*

WORKS {235}

let the people from their *w*	Ex 5:4	4639
them, saying, Fulfil your *w*	Ex 5:13	4639
serve them, nor do after their *w*	Ex 23:24	4639
To devise cunning *w*, to work in	Ex 31:4	
And to devise curious *w*, to work	Ex 35:32	
hath sent me to do all these *w*	Num 16:28	4639
thee in all the *w* of thy hand	Deut 2:7	4639
that can do according to thy *w*	Deut 3:24	4639
God shall bless thee in all thy *w*	Deut 15:10	4639
in all the *w* of thine hands,	Deut 16:15	4639
had known all the *w* of the LORD	Josh 24:31	4639
seen all the great *w* of the LORD	Judg 2:7	4639
nor yet the *w* which he had done	Judg 2:10	4639
According to all the *w* which they	1Sa 8:8	4639
because his *w* have been to	1Sa 19:4	4639
and cunning to work all *w* in brass	1Kin 7:14	4399
told him all the *w* that the man	1Kin 13:11	4639
with all the *w* of their hands	2Kin 22:17	4639
talk ye of all his wondrous *w*	1Chr 16:9	
marvellous *w* that he hath done	1Chr 16:12	
his marvellous *w* among all	1Chr 16:24	
even all the *w* of this pattern	1Chr 28:19	4399
the LORD hath broken thy *w*	2Chr 20:37	4639
Hezekiah prospered in all his *w*	2Chr 32:30	4639
with all the *w* of their hands	2Chr 34:25	4639
according to these their *w*	Neh 6:14	4639
turned they from their wicked *w*	Neh 9:35	4611
Therefore he knoweth their *w*	Job 34:25	4566
and consider the wondrous *w* of God	Job 37:14	
the wondrous *w* of him which is	Job 37:16	
dominion over the *w* of thy hands	Ps 8:6	4639
shew forth all thy marvellous *w*	Ps 9:1	
they have done abominable *w*	Ps 14:1	5949
and tell of all thy wondrous *w*	Ps 26:7	
they regard not the *w* of the LORD	Ps 28:5	6468
all his *w* are done in truth	Ps 33:4	4640
he considereth all their *w*	Ps 33:15	4640
are thy wonderful *w* which thou	Ps 40:5	
behold the *w* of the LORD, what	Ps 46:8	4659
How terrible art thou in thy *w*	Ps 66:3	4639
Come and see the *w* of God	Ps 66:5	4659
have I declared thy wondrous *w*	Ps 71:17	
GOD, that I may declare all thy *w*	Ps 73:28	4399
is near thy wondrous *w* declare	Ps 75:1	
I will remember the *w* of the LORD	Ps 77:11	4611
his wonderful *w* that he hath done	Ps 78:4	
God, and not forget the *w* of God	Ps 78:7	4611
And forgat his *w*, and his wonders	Ps 78:11	5949
believed not for his wondrous *w*	Ps 78:32	
there any *w* like unto thy *w*	Ps 86:8	4639
triumph in the *w* of thy hands	Ps 92:4	4639
O LORD, how great are thy *w*	Ps 92:5	4639
all his *w* in all places of his	Ps 103:22	4639
satisfied with the fruit of thy *w*	Ps 104:13	4639
O LORD, how manifold are thy *w*	Ps 104:24	4639
the LORD shall rejoice in his *w*	Ps 104:31	4639
talk ye of all his wondrous *w*	Ps 105:2	
marvellous *w* that he hath done	Ps 105:5	
They soon forgat his *w*	Ps 106:13	4639
Wondrous *w* in the land of Ham, and	Ps 106:22	
the heathen, and learned their *w*	Ps 106:35	4639
they defiled with their own *w*	Ps 106:39	4639
for his wonderful *w* to the	Ps 107:8	
for his wonderful *w* to the	Ps 107:15	
for his wonderful *w* to the	Ps 107:21	
declare his *w* with rejoicing	Ps 107:22	4639
These see the *w* of the LORD	Ps 107:24	4639
for his wonderful *w* to the	Ps 107:31	
The *w* of the LORD are great,	Ps 111:2	4639
his wonderful *w* to be remembered	Ps 111:4	
his people the power of his *w*	Ps 111:6	4639
The *w* of his hands are verity and	Ps 111:7	4639
and declare the *w* of the LORD	Ps 118:17	4639
so shall I talk of thy wondrous *w*	Ps 119:27	
forsake not the *w* of thine own	Ps 138:8	4639
marvellous are thy *w*	Ps 139:14	4639
to practise wicked *w* with men	Ps 141:4	5949
I meditate on all thy *w*	Ps 143:5	6467
shall praise thy *w* to another	Ps 145:4	4639
thy majesty, and of thy wondrous *w*	Ps 145:5	1697
tender mercies are over all his *w*	Ps 145:9	4639
All thy *w* shall praise thee, O	Ps 145:10	4639
his ways, and holy in all his *w*	Ps 145:17	4639
of tapestry, with carved *w*	Prov 7:16	
of his way, before his *w* of old	Prov 8:22	4659
Commit thy *w* unto the LORD, and	Prov 16:3	4639
to every man according to his *w*	Prov 24:12	6467
let her own *w* praise her in the	Prov 31:31	4639
I have seen all the *w* that are	Eccl 1:14	4639
I made me great *w*	Eccl 2:4	4639
Then I looked on all the *w* that	Eccl 2:11	4639
a man should rejoice in his own *w*	Eccl 3:22	4639
and the wise, and their *w*, are in	Eccl 9:1	5652
for God now accepteth thy *w*	Eccl 9:7	4639
not the *w* of God who maketh all	Eccl 11:5	4639
also hast wrought all our *w* in us	Is 26:12	4639
their *w* are in the dark, and they	Is 29:15	4639
their *w* are nothing	Is 41:29	4639
thy righteousness, and thy *w*	Is 57:12	4639
cover themselves with their *w*	Is 59:6	4639
their *w* are *w* of iniquity	Is 59:6	4639
For I know their *w* and their	Is 66:18	4639
worshipped the *w* of their own	Jer 1:16	4639
because ye have done all these *w*	Jer 7:13	4639
according to all his wondrous *w*	Jer 21:2	
to anger with the *w* of your hands	Jer 25:6	4639
provoke me to anger with the *w* of	Jer 25:7	4639
according to the *w* of their own	Jer 25:14	4639
wrath with the *w* of your hands	Jer 44:8	4639
thou hast trusted in thy *w*	Jer 48:7	4639
down, and your *w* may be abolished	Eze 6:6	4639
of heaven, all whose *w* are truth	Dan 4:37	4567
in all his *w* which he doeth	Dan 9:14	4639
will never forget any of their *w*	Amos 8:7	4639
And God saw their *w*, that they	Jonah 3:10	4639
all the *w* of the house of Ahab,	Mic 6:16	4639
that they may see your good *w*	Mt 5:16	*2041*
in thy name done many wonderful *w*	Mt 7:22	
in the prison the *w* of Christ	Mt 11:2	*2041*
most of his mighty *w* were done	Mt 11:20	
for if the mighty *w*, which were	Mt 11:21	
for if the mighty *w*, which have	Mt 11:23	
this wisdom, and these mighty *w*	Mt 13:54	
he did not many mighty *w* there	Mt 13:58	
therefore mighty *w* do shew forth	Mt 14:2	
every man according to his *w*	Mt 16:27	*4234*
but do not ye after their *w*	Mt 23:3	*2041*
But all their *w* they do for to be	Mt 23:5	*2041*
that even such mighty *w* are	Mk 6:2	
therefore mighty *w* do shew forth	Mk 6:14	
for if the mighty *w* had been done	Lk 10:13	
the mighty *w* that they had seen	Lk 19:37	
shew him greater *w* than these	Jn 5:20	*2041*
for the *w* which the Father hath	Jn 5:36	*2041*
the same *w* that I do, bear	Jn 5:36	*2041*
that we might work the *w* of God	Jn 6:28	*2041*
may see the *w* that thou doest	Jn 7:3	*2041*
that the *w* thereof are evil	Jn 7:7	*2041*
ye would do the *w* of Abraham	Jn 8:39	*2041*
but that the *w* of God should be	Jn 9:3	*2041*
I must work the *w* of him that	Jn 9:4	*2041*
the *w* that I do in my Father's	Jn 10:25	*2041*
Many good *w* have I shewed you	Jn 10:32	*2041*
which of those *w* do ye stone me	Jn 10:32	*2041*
If I do not the *w* of my Father	Jn 10:37	*2041*
ye believe not me, believe the *w*	Jn 10:38	*2041*
dwelleth in me, he doeth the *w*	Jn 14:10	*2041*
the *w* that I do shall he do also	Jn 14:12	*2041*
greater *w* than these shall he do	Jn 14:12	*2041*
the *w* which none other man did	Jn 15:24	*2041*
tongues the wonderful *w* of God	Acts 2:11	
rejoiced in the *w* of their own	Acts 7:41	*2041*
this woman was full of good *w*	Acts 9:36	*2041*
Known unto God are all his *w* from	Acts 15:18	*2041*
God, and do *w* meet for repentance	Acts 26:20	*2041*
what law? of *w*?	Rom 3:27	*2041*
if Abraham were justified by *w*	Rom 4:2	*2041*
imputeth righteousness without *w*	Rom 4:6	*2041*
to election might stand, not of *w*	Rom 9:11	*2041*
as it were by the *w* of the law	Rom 9:32	*2041*
by grace, then is it no more of *w*	Rom 11:6	*2041*
But if it be of *w*, then is it no	Rom 11:6	*2041*
rulers are not a terror to good *w*	Rom 13:3	*2041*
cast off the *w* of darkness	Rom 13:12	*2041*
end shall be according to their *w*	2Cor 11:15	*2041*
not justified by the *w* of the law	Gal 2:16	*2041*
and not by the *w* of the law	Gal 2:16	*2041*
for by the *w* of the law shall no	Gal 2:16	*2041*
ye the Spirit by the *w* of the law	Gal 3:2	*2041*
doeth he it by the *w* of the law	Gal 3:5	*2041*
For as many as are of the *w* of	Gal 3:10	*2041*
Now the *w* of the flesh are	Gal 5:19	*2041*
Not of *w*, lest any man should	Eph 2:9	*2041*
in Christ Jesus unto good *w*	Eph 2:10	*2041*
with the unfruitful *w* of darkness	Eph 5:11	*2041*
enemies in your mind by wicked *w*	Col 1:21	*2041*
professing godliness) with good *w*	1Ti 2:10	*2041*
Well reported of for good *w*	1Ti 5:10	*2041*
Likewise also the good *w* of some	1Ti 5:25	*2041*
good, that they be rich in good *w*	1Ti 6:18	*2041*
calling, not according to our *w*	2Ti 1:9	*2041*
furnished unto all good *w*	2Ti 3:17	*2041*
reward him according to his *w*	2Ti 4:14	*2041*
but in *w* they deny him, being	Titus 1:16	*2041*
thyself a pattern of good *w*	Titus 2:7	*2041*
people, zealous of good *w*	Titus 2:14	*2041*
Not by *w* of righteousness which	Titus 3:5	*2041*
be careful to maintain good *w*	Titus 3:8	*2041*
good *w* for necessary uses	Titus 3:14	*2041*
heavens are the *w* of thine hands	Heb 1:10	*2041*
set him over the *w* of thy hands	Heb 2:7	*2041*
me, and saw my *w* forty years	Heb 3:9	*2041*
although the *w* were finished from	Heb 4:3	*2041*
the seventh day from all his *w*	Heb 4:4	*2041*
also hath ceased from his own *w*	Heb 4:10	*2041*
of repentance from dead *w*	Heb 6:1	*2041*
dead *w* to serve the living God	Heb 9:14	*2041*
to provoke unto love and to good *w*	Heb 10:24	*2041*
say he hath faith, and have not *w*	Jas 2:14	*2041*
Even so faith, if it hath not *w*	Jas 2:17	*2041*
say, Thou hast faith, and I have *w*	Jas 2:18	*2041*
shew me thy faith without thy *w*	Jas 2:18	*2041*
I will shew thee my faith by my *w*	Jas 2:18	*2041*
man, that faith without *w* is dead	Jas 2:20	*2041*
Abraham our father justified by *w*	Jas 2:21	*2041*
thou how faith wrought with his *w*	Jas 2:22	*2041*
by *w* was faith made perfect	Jas 2:22	*2041*
how that by *w* a man is justified	Jas 2:24	*2041*
Rahab the harlot justified by *w*	Jas 2:25	*2041*
so faith without *w* is dead also	Jas 2:26	*2041*
his *w* with meekness of wisdom	Jas 3:13	*2041*
they may by your good *w*, which	1Pet 2:12	*2041*
the *w* that are therein shall be	2Pet 3:10	*2041*
might destroy the *w* of the devil	1Jn 3:8	*2041*
Because his own *w* were evil	1Jn 3:12	*2041*
I know thy *w*, and thy labour, and	Rev 2:2	*2041*
and repent, and do the first *w*	Rev 2:5	*2041*
I know thy *w*, and tribulation, and	Rev 2:9	*2041*
I know thy *w*, and where thou	Rev 2:13	*2041*
I know thy *w*, and charity, and	Rev 2:19	*2041*
faith, and thy patience, and thy *w*	Rev 2:19	*2041*
one of you according to your *w*	Rev 2:23	*2041*
keepeth my *w* unto the end, to him	Rev 2:26	*2041*
I know thy *w*, that thou hast a	Rev 3:1	*2041*
found thy *w* perfect before God	Rev 3:2	*2041*
I know thy *w*	Rev 3:8	*2041*
I know thy *w*, that thou art	Rev 3:15	*2041*
not of the *w* of their hands	Rev 9:20	*2041*
and their *w* do follow them	Rev 14:13	*2041*
Great and marvellous are thy *w*	Rev 15:3	*2041*
her double according to her *w*	Rev 18:6	*2041*
the books, according to their *w*	Rev 20:12	*2041*
every man according to their *w*	Rev 20:13	*2041*

WORKS' {1}

believe me for the very *w* sake	Jn 14:11	*2041*

WORLD {287}

and he hath set the *w* upon them	1Sa 2:8	8398
of the *w* were discovered, at the	2Sa 22:16	8398
the *w* also shall be stable, that	1Chr 16:30	8398
darkness, and chased out of the *w*	Job 18:18	8398
Or who hath disposed the whole *w*	Job 34:13	8398
the face of the *w* in the earth	Job 37:12	8398
judge the *w* in righteousness	Ps 9:8	8398
hand, O LORD, from men of the *w*	Ps 17:14	2465
the foundations of the *w* were	Ps 18:15	8398
their words to the end of the *w*	Ps 19:4	8398
the ends of the *w* shall remember	Ps 22:27	776
the *w*, and they that dwell therein	Ps 24:1	8398
of the *w* stand in awe of him	Ps 33:8	8398
ear, all ye inhabitants of the *w*	Ps 49:1	2465
for the *w* is mine, and the fulness	Ps 50:12	8398
the ungodly, who prosper in the *w*	Ps 73:12	5769
the lightnings lightened the *w*	Ps 77:18	8398
as for the *w* and the fulness	Ps 89:11	8398
hadst formed the earth and the *w*	Ps 90:2	8398
the *w* also is stablished, that it	Ps 93:1	8398
the *w* also shall be established	Ps 96:10	8398
judge the *w* with righteousness	Ps 96:13	8398
His lightnings enlightened the *w*	Ps 97:4	8398
the *w*, and they that dwell therein	Ps 98:7	8398
shall he judge the *w*, and the	Ps 98:9	8398
highest part of the dust of the *w*	Prov 8:26	8398
he hath set the *w* in their heart	Eccl 3:11	5769
will punish the *w* for their evil	Is 13:11	8398
That made the *w* as a wilderness,	Is 14:17	8398
the face of the *w* with cities	Is 14:21	8398
All ye inhabitants of the *w*	Is 18:3	8398
the *w* upon the face of the earth	Is 23:17	776
the *w* languisheth and fadeth away,	Is 24:4	8398
the inhabitants of the *w* will	Is 26:9	8398

the inhabitants of the *w* fallen ... Is 26:18 8398
fill the face of the *w* with fruit ... Is 27:6 8398
the *w*, and all things that come ... Is 34:1 8398
with the inhabitants of the *w* ... Is 38:11 2309
nor confounded *w* without end ... Is 45:17 5769
proclaimed unto the end of the *w* ... Is 62:11 776
of the *w* men have not heard ... Is 64:4 5769
established the *w* by his wisdom ... Jer 10:12 8398
and all the kingdoms of the *w* ... Jer 25:26 776
established the *w* by his wisdom ... Jer 51:15 8398
and all the inhabitants of the *w* ... Lam 4:12 8398
at his presence, yea, the *w* ... Nah 1:5 8398
him all the kingdoms of the *w* ... Mt 4:8 2889
Ye are the light of the *w* ... Mt 5:14 2889
forgiven him, neither in this *w* ... Mt 12:32 165
neither in the *w* to come ... Mt 12:32
and the care of this *w*, and the ... Mt 13:22 165
from the foundation of the *w* ... Mt 13:35 2889
The field is the *w* ... Mt 13:38 2889
the harvest is the end of the *w* ... Mt 13:39 165
shall it be in the end of this *w* ... Mt 13:40 165
shall it be at the end of the *w* ... Mt 13:49 165
if he shall gain the whole *w* ... Mt 16:26 2889
Woe unto the *w* because of ... Mt 18:7 2889
coming, and of the end of the *w* ... Mt 24:3 165
shall be preached in all the *w* ... Mt 24:14 3625
beginning of the *w* to this time ... Mt 24:21 2889
you from the foundation of the *w* ... Mt 25:34 2889
shall be preached in the whole *w* ... Mt 26:13 2889
alway, even unto the end of the *w* ... Mt 28:20 165
And the cares of this *w*, and the ... Mk 4:19 165
man, if he shall gain the whole *w* ... Mk 8:36 2889
in the *w* to come eternal life ... Mk 10:30 165
preached throughout the whole *w* ... Mk 14:9 2889
unto them, Go ye into all the *w* ... Mk 16:15 2889
which have been since the *w* began ... Lk 1:70 165
that all the *w* should be taxed ... Lk 2:1 3625
of the *w* in a moment of time ... Lk 4:5 3625
if he gain the whole *w*, and lose ... Lk 9:25 2889
shed from the foundation of the *w* ... Lk 11:50 2889
the nations of the *w* seek after ... Lk 12:30 2889
for the children of this *w* are in ... Lk 16:8 165
in the *w* to come life everlasting ... Lk 18:30 165
The children of this *w* marry ... Lk 20:34 165
accounted worthy to obtain that *w* ... Lk 20:35 165
every man that cometh into the *w* ... Jn 1:9 2889
He was in the *w* ... Jn 1:10 2889
the *w* was made by him, and the ... Jn 1:10 2889
by him, and the *w* knew him not ... Jn 1:10 2889
taketh away the sin of the *w* ... Jn 1:29 2889
For God so loved the *w*, that he ... Jn 3:16 2889
into the *w* to condemn the *w* ... Jn 3:17 2889
but that the *w* through him might ... Jn 3:17 2889
that light is come into the *w* ... Jn 3:19 2889
the Christ, the Saviour of the *w* ... Jn 4:42 2889
that should come into the *w* ... Jn 6:14 2889
heaven, and giveth life unto the *w* ... Jn 6:33 2889
I will give for the life of the *w* ... Jn 6:51 2889
things, shew thyself to the *w* ... Jn 7:4 2889
The *w* cannot hate you ... Jn 7:7 2889
saying, I am the light of the *w* ... Jn 8:12 2889
ye are of this *w* ... Jn 8:23 2889
I am not of this *w* ... Jn 8:23 2889
I speak to the *w* those things ... Jn 8:26 2889
As long as I am in the *w* ... Jn 9:5 2889
I am the light of the *w* ... Jn 9:5 2889
Since the *w* began was it not ... Jn 9:32 165
judgment I am come into this *w* ... Jn 9:39 2889
sanctified, and sent into the *w* ... Jn 10:36 2889
he seeth the light of this *w* ... Jn 11:9 2889
God, which should come into the *w* ... Jn 11:27 2889
behold, the *w* is gone after him ... Jn 12:19 2889
w shall keep it unto life eternal ... Jn 12:25 2889
Now is the judgment of this *w* ... Jn 12:31 2889
the prince of this *w* be cast out ... Jn 12:31 2889
I am come a light into the *w* ... Jn 12:46 2889
for I came not to judge the *w* ... Jn 12:47 2889
but to save the *w* ... Jn 12:47 2889
out of this *w* unto the Father ... Jn 13:1 2889
loved his own which were in the *w* ... Jn 13:1 2889
whom the *w* cannot receive ... Jn 14:17 2889
while, and the *w* seeth me no more ... Jn 14:19
unto us, and not unto the *w* ... Jn 14:22 2889
not as the *w* giveth, give I unto ... Jn 14:27 2889
for the prince of this *w* cometh ... Jn 14:30 2889
But that the *w* may know that I ... Jn 14:31 2889
If the *w* hate you, ye know that ... Jn 15:18 2889
If ye were of the *w* ... Jn 15:19 2889
the *w* would love his own ... Jn 15:19 2889
but because ye are not of the *w* ... Jn 15:19 2889
I have chosen you out of the *w* ... Jn 15:19 2889
therefore the *w* hateth you ... Jn 15:19 2889
he will reprove the *w* of sin ... Jn 16:8 2889
the prince of this *w* is judged ... Jn 16:11 2889
lament, but the *w* shall rejoice ... Jn 16:20 2889
joy that a man is born into the *w* ... Jn 16:21 2889
the Father, and am come into the *w* ... Jn 16:28 2889
again, I leave the *w*, and go to ... Jn 16:28 2889
In the *w* ye shall have ... Jn 16:33 2889
I have overcome the *w* ... Jn 16:33 2889
I had with thee before the *w* was ... Jn 17:5 2889
which thou gavest me out of the *w* ... Jn 17:6 2889
I pray not for the *w*, but for ... Jn 17:9 2889
And now I am no more in the *w* ... Jn 17:11 2889
but these are in the *w* ... Jn 17:11 2889
While I was with them in the *w* ... Jn 17:12 2889
and these things I speak in the *w* ... Jn 17:13 2889
the *w* hath hated them ... Jn 17:14 2889
because they are not of the *w* ... Jn 17:14 2889
even as I am not of the *w* ... Jn 17:14 2889
shouldest take them out of the *w* ... Jn 17:15 2889
They are not of the *w* ... Jn 17:16 2889
even as I am not of the *w* ... Jn 17:16 2889
As thou hast sent me into the *w* ... Jn 17:18 2889
have I also sent them into the *w* ... Jn 17:18 2889
that the *w* may believe that thou ... Jn 17:21 2889
that the *w* may know that thou ... Jn 17:23 2889
me before the foundation of the *w* ... Jn 17:24 2889
the *w* hath not known thee ... Jn 17:25 2889
him, I spake openly to the *w* ... Jn 18:20 2889
My kingdom is not of this *w* ... Jn 18:36 2889
if my kingdom were of this *w* ... Jn 18:36 2889
for this cause came I into the *w* ... Jn 18:37 2889
I suppose that even the *w* itself ... Jn 21:25 2889
holy prophets since the *w* began ... Acts 3:21 165
great dearth throughout all the *w* ... Acts 11:28 3625
works from the beginning of the *w* ... Acts 15:18 165
These that have turned the *w* ... Acts 17:6 3625
God that made the *w* and all things ... Acts 17:24 2889
w in righteousness by that man ... Acts 17:31 3625
all Asia and the *w* worshippeth ... Acts 19:27 3625
all the Jews throughout the *w* ... Acts 24:5 3625
spoken of throughout the whole *w* ... Rom 1:8 2889
of the *w* are clearly seen ... Rom 1:20 2889
then how shall God judge the *w* ... Rom 3:6 2889
all the *w* may become guilty ... Rom 3:19 2889
he should be the heir of the *w* ... Rom 4:13 2889
by one man sin entered into the *w* ... Rom 5:12 2889
until the law sin was in the *w* ... Rom 5:13 2889
words unto the ends of the *w* ... Rom 10:18 3625
of them be the riches of the *w* ... Rom 11:12 2889
them be the reconciling of the *w* ... Rom 11:15 2889
And be not conformed to this *w* ... Rom 12:2 165
was kept secret since the *w* began ... Rom 16:25 166
where is the disputer of this *w* ... 1Cor 1:20 165
made foolish the wisdom of this *w* ... 1Cor 1:20 2889
God the *w* by wisdom knew not God ... 1Cor 1:21 2889
of the *w* to confound the wise ... 1Cor 1:27 2889
w to confound the things which ... 1Cor 1:27 2889
And base things of the *w*, and ... 1Cor 1:28 2889
yet not the wisdom of this *w* ... 1Cor 2:6 165
nor of the princes of this *w* ... 1Cor 2:6 165
before the *w* unto our glory ... 1Cor 2:7 165
of the princes of this *w* knew ... 1Cor 2:8 165
received, not the spirit of the *w* ... 1Cor 2:12 2889
you seemeth to be wise in this *w* ... 1Cor 3:18 165
For the wisdom of this *w* is ... 1Cor 3:19 2889
or Apollos, or Cephas, or the *w* ... 1Cor 3:22 2889
are made a spectacle unto the *w* ... 1Cor 4:9 2889
we are made as the filth of the *w* ... 1Cor 4:13 2889
with the fornicators of this *w* ... 1Cor 5:10 2889
must ye needs go out of the *w* ... 1Cor 5:10 2889
that the saints shall judge the *w* ... 1Cor 6:2 2889
if the *w* shall be judged by you ... 1Cor 6:2 2889
And they that use this *w*, as not ... 1Cor 7:31 2889
fashion of this *w* passeth away ... 1Cor 7:31 2889
for the things that are of the *w* ... 1Cor 7:33 2889
careth for the things of the *w* ... 1Cor 7:34 2889
that an idol is nothing in the *w* ... 1Cor 8:4 2889
eat no flesh while the *w* standeth ... 1Cor 8:13 165
whom the ends of the *w* are come ... 1Cor 10:11 165
not be condemned with the *w* ... 1Cor 11:32 2889
so many kinds of voices in the *w* ... 1Cor 14:10 2889
had our conversation in the *w* ... 2Cor 1:12 2889
In whom the god of this *w* hath ... 2Cor 4:4 165
reconciling the *w* unto himself ... 2Cor 5:19 2889
the sorrow of the *w* worketh death ... 2Cor 7:10 2889
us from this present evil *w* ... Gal 1:4 165
under the elements of the *w* ... Gal 4:3 2889
by whom the *w* is crucified unto ... Gal 6:14 2889
unto me, and I unto the *w* ... Gal 6:14 2889
before the foundation of the *w* ... Eph 1:4 2889
that is named, not only in this *w* ... Eph 1:21 165
according to the course of this *w* ... Eph 2:2 2889
no hope, and without God in the *w* ... Eph 2:12 2889
of the *w* hath been hid in God ... Eph 3:9 165
all ages, *w* without end ... Eph 3:21 165
rulers of the darkness of this *w* ... Eph 6:12 165
whom ye shine as lights in the *w* ... Phil 2:15 2889
unto you, as it is in all the *w* ... Col 1:6 2889
men, after the rudiments of the *w* ... Col 2:8 2889
from the rudiments of the *w* ... Col 2:20 2889
why, as though living in the *w* ... Col 2:20 2889
came into the *w* to save sinners ... 1Ti 1:15 2889
Gentiles, believed on in the *w* ... 1Ti 3:16 2889
we brought nothing into this *w* ... 1Ti 6:7 2889
them that are rich in this *w* ... 1Ti 6:17 165
Christ Jesus before the *w* began ... 2Ti 1:9 166
me, having loved this present *w* ... 2Ti 4:10 165
lie, promised before the *w* began ... Titus 1:2 166
and godly, in this present *w* ... Titus 2:12 165
in the firstbegotten into the *w* ... Heb 1:6 3625
put in subjection the *w* to come ... Heb 2:5 3625
from the foundation of the *w* ... Heb 4:3 2889
and the powers of the *w* to come ... Heb 6:5 165
since the foundation of the *w* ... Heb 9:26 2889
w hath he appeared to put away ... Heb 9:26 165
when he cometh into the *w* ... Heb 10:5 2889
by the which he condemned the *w* ... Heb 11:7 2889
(Of whom the *w* was not worthy ... Heb 11:38 2889
keep himself unspotted from the *w* ... Jas 1:27 2889
the poor of this *w* rich in faith ... Jas 2:5 2889
tongue is a fire, a *w* of iniquity ... Jas 3:6 2889
of the *w* is enmity with God ... Jas 4:4 2889
of the *w* is the enemy of God ... Jas 4:4 2889
before the foundation of the *w* ... 1Pet 1:20 2889
your brethren that are in the *w* ... 1Pet 5:9 2889
that is in the *w* through lust ... 2Pet 1:4 2889
And spared not the old *w*, but ... 2Pet 2:5 2889
flood upon the *w* of the ungodly ... 2Pet 2:5 2889
w through the knowledge of the ... 2Pet 2:20 2889
Whereby the *w* that then was ... 2Pet 3:6 2889
also for the sins of the whole *w* ... 1Jn 2:2 2889
Love not the *w*, neither the ... 1Jn 2:15 2889
the things that are in the *w* ... 1Jn 2:15 2889
If any man love the *w*, the love ... 1Jn 2:15 2889
For all that is in the *w*, the ... 1Jn 2:16 2889
of the Father, but is of the *w* ... 1Jn 2:16 2889
the *w* passeth away, and the lust ... 1Jn 2:17 2889
therefore the *w* knoweth us not ... 1Jn 3:1 2889
my brethren, if the *w* hate you ... 1Jn 3:13 2889
prophets are gone out into the *w* ... 1Jn 4:1 2889
even now already is it in the *w* ... 1Jn 4:3 2889
in you, than he that is in the *w* ... 1Jn 4:4 2889
They are of the *w* ... 1Jn 4:5 2889
therefore speak they of the *w* ... 1Jn 4:5 2889
and the *w* heareth them ... 1Jn 4:5 2889
his only begotten Son into the *w* ... 1Jn 4:9 2889
Son to be the Saviour of the *w* ... 1Jn 4:14 2889
as he is, so are we in this *w* ... 1Jn 4:17 2889
is born of God overcometh the *w* ... 1Jn 5:4 2889
the victory that overcometh the *w* ... 1Jn 5:4 2889
Who is he that overcometh the *w* ... 1Jn 5:5 2889
the whole *w* lieth in wickedness ... 1Jn 5:19 2889
deceivers are entered into the *w* ... 2Jn 7 2889
which shall come upon all the *w* ... Rev 3:10 3625
The kingdoms of this *w* are become ... Rev 11:15 2889
which deceiveth the whole *w* ... Rev 12:9 3625
all the *w* wondered after the ... Rev 13:3 1093
from the foundation of the *w* ... Rev 13:8 2889
of the earth and of the whole *w* ... Rev 16:14 3625
life from the foundation of the *w* ... Rev 17:8 2889

WORLDLY {2}
w lusts, we should live soberly ... Titus 2:12 2886
divine service, and a *w* sanctuary ... Heb 9:1 2886

WORLD'S {1}
But whoso hath this *w* good ... 1Jn 3:17 2889

WORLDS {2}
by whom also he made the *w* ... Heb 1:2 165
faith we understand that the *w* ... Heb 11:3 165

WORM {14}
neither was there any *w* therein ... Ex 16:24 7415
to the *w*, Thou art my mother, and ... Job 17:14 7415
the *w* shall feed sweetly on him ... Job 24:20 7415
How much less man, that is a *w* ... Job 25:6 7415
and the son of man, which is a *w* ... Job 25:6 8438
But I am a *w*, and no man ... Ps 22:6 8438
the *w* is spread under thee, and ... Is 14:11 7415
thou *w* Jacob, and ye men of Israel ... Is 41:14 8438
the *w* shall eat them like wool ... Is 51:8 5580
for their *w* shall not die ... Is 66:24 8438
But God prepared a *w* when the ... Jonah 4:7 8438
Where their *w* dieth not, and the ... Mk 9:44 4663
Where their *w* dieth not, and the ... Mk 9:46 4663
Where their *w* dieth not, and the ... Mk 9:48 4663

WORMS {8}
until the morning, and it bred *w* ... Ex 16:20 8438
for the *w* shall eat them ... Deut 28:39 8438
My flesh is clothed with *w* ... Job 7:5 7415
after my skin *w* destroy this body ... Job 19:26
dust, and the *w* shall cover them ... Job 21:26 7415
under thee, and the *w* cover thee ... Is 14:11 8438
their holes like *w* of the earth ... Mic 7:17 2119
and he was eaten of *w*, and gave up ... Acts 12:23 4662

WORMWOOD {9}
you a root that beareth gall and *w* ... Deut 29:18 3939
But her end is bitter as *w* ... Prov 5:4 3939
them, even this people, with *w* ... Jer 9:15 3939
Behold, I will feed them with *w* ... Jer 23:15 3939
he hath made me drunken with *w* ... Lam 3:15 3939
affliction and my misery, the *w* ... Lam 3:19 3939
Ye who turn judgment to *w* ... Amos 5:7 3939
the name of the star is called W ... Rev 8:11 894
third part of the waters became *w* ... Rev 8:11 894

WORSE See APPENDIX.

WORSHIP {108}
I and the lad will go yonder and *w* ... Gen 22:5 7812
and *w* ye afar off ... Ex 24:1 7812
For thou shalt *w* no other god ... Ex 34:14 7812
shouldest be driven to *w* them ... Deut 4:19 7812
w them, I testify against you ... Deut 8:19 7812
and serve other gods, and *w* them ... Deut 11:16 7812
w before the LORD thy God ... Deut 26:10 7812
w other gods, and serve them ... Deut 30:17 7812
his face to the earth, and did *w* ... Josh 5:14 7812
up out of his city yearly to *w* ... 1Sa 1:3 7812
with me, that I may *w* the LORD ... 1Sa 15:25 7812
that I may *w* the LORD thy God ... 1Sa 15:30 7812
go and serve other gods, and *w* them ... 1Kin 9:6 7812
people went to *w* before the one ... 1Kin 12:30
the house of Rimmon to *w* there ... 2Kin 5:18 7812
shall ye fear, and him shall ye *w* ... 2Kin 17:36 7812
Ye shall *w* before this altar in ... 2Kin 18:22 7812
w the LORD in the beauty of ... 1Chr 16:29 7812
go and serve other gods, and *w* them ... 2Chr 7:19 7812
Ye shall *w* before one altar, and ... 2Chr 32:12 7812
in thy fear will I *w* toward thy ... Ps 5:7 7812
the nations shall *w* before thee ... Ps 22:27 7812
be fat upon earth shall eat and *w* ... Ps 22:29 7812
w the LORD in the beauty of ... Ps 29:2 7812
and *w* thou him ... Ps 45:11 7812

W

All the earth shall *w* thee ... Ps 66:4 7812
shalt thou *w* any strange god ... Ps 81:9 7812
come and *w* before thee, O Lord ... Ps 86:9 7812
O come, let us *w* and bow down ... Ps 95:6 7812
O *w* the LORD in the beauty of ... Ps 96:9 7812
w him, all ye gods ... Ps 97:7 7812
our God, and *w* at his footstool ... Ps 99:5 7812
our God, and *w* at his holy hill ... Ps 99:9 7812
we will *w* at his footstool ... Ps 132:7 7812
I will *w* toward thy holy temple, ... Ps 138:2 7812
they *w* the work of their own ... Is 2:8 7812
made each one for himself to *w* ... Is 2:20 7812
shall *w* the LORD in the holy ... Is 27:13 7812
Ye shall *w* before this altar ... Is 36:7 7812
they fall down, yea, they *w* ... Is 46:6 7812
and arise, princes also shall *w* ... Is 49:7 7812
all flesh come to *w* before me ... Is 66:23 7812
in at these gates to *w* the LORD ... Jer 7:2 7812
to *w* them, shall even be as this ... Jer 13:10 7812
to *w* them, and provoke me not to ... Jer 25:6 7812
which come to *w* in the LORD's ... Jer 26:2 7812
did we make her cakes to *w* her ... Jer 44:19 6087
he shall *w* at the threshold of ... Eze 46:2 7812
the people of the land shall *w* at ... Eze 46:3 7812
w shall go out by the way of the ... Eze 46:9 7812
down and *w* the golden image that ... Dan 3:5 5457
fall down and *w* the golden image ... Dan 3:10 5457
nor *w* the golden image which thou ... Dan 3:12 5457
nor *w* the golden image which I ... Dan 3:14 5457
w the image which I have made ... Dan 3:15 5457
but if ye *w* not, ye shall be cast ... Dan 3:15 5457
nor *w* the golden image which thou ... Dan 3:18 5457
might not serve nor *w* any god ... Dan 3:28 5457
thou shalt no more *w* the work of ... Mic 5:13 7812
them that *w* the host of heaven ... Zeph 1:5 7812
and them that *w* and that swear by ... Zeph 1:5 7812
and men shall *w* him, every one ... Zeph 2:11 7812
from year to year to *w* the King ... Zec 14:16 7812
unto Jerusalem to *w* the King ... Zec 14:17 7812
in the east, and are come to *w* him ... Mt 2:2 *4352*
that I may come and *w* him also ... Mt 2:8 *4352*
if thou wilt fall down and *w* me ... Mt 4:9 *4352*
Thou shalt *w* the Lord thy God, and ... Mt 4:10 *4352*
But in vain they do *w* me, ... Mt 15:9 *4576*
Howbeit in vain do they *w* me ... Mk 7:7 *4576*
If thou therefore wilt *w* me ... Lk 4:7 *4352,1799*
Thou shalt *w* the Lord thy God, and ... Lk 4:8 *4352*
then shalt thou have *w* in the ... Lk 14:10 *1391*
is the place where men ought to *w* ... Jn 4:20 *4352*
yet at Jerusalem, *w* the Father ... Jn 4:21 *4352*
Ye *w* ye know not what ... Jn 4:22 *4352*
we know what we *w* ... Jn 4:22 *4352*
shall *w* the Father in spirit ... Jn 4:23 *4352*
the Father seeketh such to *w* him ... Jn 4:23 *4352*
they that *w* him must ... Jn 4:24 *4352*
must *w* him in spirit ... Jn 4:24 *4352*
that came up to *w* at the feast ... Jn 12:20 *4352*
gave them up to *w* the host of ... Acts 7:42 *3000*
figures which ye made to *w* them ... Acts 7:43 *4352*
and had come to Jerusalem for to *w* ... Acts 8:27 *4352*
Whom therefore ye ignorantly *w* ... Acts 17:23 *2151*
men to *w* God contrary to the law ... Acts 18:13 *4576*
I went up to Jerusalem for to *w* ... Acts 24:11 *4352*
so *w* I the God of my fathers, ... Acts 24:14 *3000*
down on his face he will *w* God ... 1Cor 14:25 *4352*
which *w* God in the spirit, and ... Phil 3:3 *3000*
indeed a shew of wisdom in will *w* ... Col 2:23 *1479*
let all the angels of God *w* him ... Heb 1:6 *4352*
w before thy feet, and to know ... Rev 3:9 *4352*
w him that liveth for ever and ... Rev 4:10 *4352*
that they should not *w* devils ... Rev 9:20 *4352*
the altar, and them that *w* therein ... Rev 11:1 *4352*
dwell upon the earth shall *w* him ... Rev 13:8 *4352*
therein to *w* the first beast ... Rev 13:12 *4352*
w the image of the beast should ... Rev 13:15 *4352*
w him that made heaven, and earth, ... Rev 14:7 *4352*
voice, If any man *w* the beast ... Rev 14:9 *4352*
who *w* the beast and his image, and ... Rev 14:11 *4352*
shall come and *w* before thee ... Rev 15:4 *4352*
And I fell at his feet to *w* him ... Rev 19:10 *4352*
w God ... Rev 19:10 *4352*
I fell down to *w* before the feet ... Rev 22:8 *4352*
w God ... Rev 22:9 *4352*

WORSHIPPED {70}
down his head, and *w* the LORD ... Gen 24:26 7812
w the LORD, and blessed the LORD ... Gen 24:48 7812
he *w* the LORD, bowing himself to ... Gen 24:52 7812
then they bowed their heads and *w* ... Ex 4:31 7812
And the people bowed the head and *w* ... Ex 12:27 7812
them a molten calf, and have *w* it ... Ex 32:8 7812
and all the people rose up and *w* ... Ex 33:10 7812
his head toward the earth, and *w* ... Ex 34:8 7812
w them, either the sun, or moon, ... Deut 17:3 7812
w them, gods whom they knew not, ... Deut 29:26 7812
interpretation thereof, that he *w* ... Judg 7:15 7812
w before the LORD, and returned, ... 1Sa 1:19 7812
And he *w* the LORD there ... 1Sa 1:28 7812
and Saul *w* the LORD ... 1Sa 15:31 7812
into the house of the LORD, and *w* ... 2Sa 12:20 7812
top of the mount, where he *w* God ... 2Sa 15:32 7812
upon other gods, and have *w* them ... 1Kin 9:9 7812
have *w* Ashtoreth the goddess of ... 1Kin 11:33 7812
and went and served Baal, and *w* him ... 1Kin 16:31 7812
w him, and provoked to anger the ... 1Kin 22:53 7812
w all the host of heaven, and ... 2Kin 17:16 7812
w all the host of heaven, and ... 2Kin 21:3 7812
that his father served, and *w* them ... 2Kin 21:21 7812
heads, and *w* the LORD, and the king ... 1Chr 29:20 7812
ground upon the pavement, and *w* ... 2Chr 7:3 7812
gods, and *w* them, and served them ... 2Chr 7:22 7812
And all the congregation *w* ... 2Chr 29:28 7812
with him bowed themselves, and *w* ... 2Chr 29:29 7812
and they bowed their heads and *w* ... 2Chr 29:30 7812
w all the host of heaven, and ... 2Chr 33:3 7812
w the LORD with their faces to ... Neh 8:6 7812
and *w* the LORD their God ... Neh 9:3 7812
fell down upon the ground, and *w* ... Job 1:20 7812
in Horeb, and *w* the molten image ... Ps 106:19 7812
w the works of their own hands ... Jer 1:16 7812
have sought, and whom they have *w* ... Jer 8:2 7812
have served them, and have *w* them ... Jer 16:11 7812
w other gods, and served them ... Jer 22:9 7812
they *w* the sun toward the east ... Eze 8:16 7812
w Daniel, and commanded that they ... Dan 2:46 5457
down and *w* the golden image that ... Dan 3:7 5457
mother, and fell down, and *w* him ... Mt 2:11 *4352*
w him, saying, Lord, if thou wilt ... Mt 8:2 *4352*
w him, saying, My daughter is ... Mt 9:18 *4352*
w him, saying, Of a truth thou ... Mt 14:33 *4352*
w him, saying, Lord, help me ... Mt 15:25 *4352*
w him, saying, Lord, have ... Mt 18:26 *4352*
and held him by the feet, and *w* him ... Mt 28:9 *4352*
And when they saw him, they *w* him ... Mt 28:17 *4352*
Jesus afar off, he ran and *w* him, ... Mk 5:6 *4352*
him, and bowing their knees *w* him ... Mk 15:19 *4352*
And they *w* him, and returned to ... Lk 24:52 *4352*
Our fathers *w* in this mountain ... Jn 4:20 *4352*
And he *w* him ... Jn 9:38 *4352*
fell down at his feet, and *w* him ... Acts 10:25 *4352*
the city of Thyatira, which *w* God ... Acts 16:14 *4576*
Neither is *w* with men's hands, as ... Acts 17:25 *2323*
named Justus, one that *w* God ... Acts 18:7 *4576*
the truth of God into a lie, and *w* ... Rom 1:25 *4573*
that is called God, or that is *w* ... 2Th 2:4 *4574*
and *w*, leaning upon the top of his ... Heb 11:21 *4352*
w him that liveth for ever and ... Rev 5:14 *4352*
throne on their faces, and *w* God, ... Rev 7:11 *4352*
fell upon their faces, and *w* God, ... Rev 11:16 *4352*
they *w* the dragon which gave ... Rev 13:4 *4352*
they *w* the beast, saying, Who is ... Rev 13:4 *4352*
and upon them which *w* his image ... Rev 16:2 *4352*
w God that sat on the throne, ... Rev 19:4 *4352*
beast, and them that had *w* his image ... Rev 19:20 *4352*
God, and which had not *w* the beast ... Rev 20:4 *4352*

WORSHIPPER {2}
but if any man be a *w* of God ... Jn 9:31 *2318*
is a *w* of the great goddess Diana ... Acts 19:35 *3511*

WORSHIPPERS {7}
he might destroy the *w* of Baal ... 2Kin 10:19 5647
all the *w* of Baal came, so that ... 2Kin 10:21 5647
vestments for all the *w* of Baal ... 2Kin 10:22 5647
Baal, and said unto the *w* of Baal ... 2Kin 10:23 5647
the LORD, but the *w* of Baal only ... 2Kin 10:23 5647
when the true *w* shall worship the ... Jn 4:23 *4353*
because that the *w* once purged ... Heb 10:2 *3000*

WORSHIPPETH {6}
and the host of heaven *w* thee ... Neh 9:6 7812
yea, he maketh a god, and *w* it ... Is 44:15 7812
w it, and prayeth unto it, and ... Is 44:17 7812
w shall the same hour be cast ... Dan 3:6 5457
And whoso falleth not down and *w* ... Dan 3:11 5457
whom all Asia and the world *w* ... Acts 19:27 *4576*

WORSHIPPING {5}
as he was *w* in the house of ... 2Kin 19:37 7812
fell before the LORD, *w* the LORD ... 2Chr 20:18 7812
as he was *w* in the house of ... Is 37:38 7812
w him, and desiring a certain ... Mt 20:20 *4352*
w of angels, intruding into those ... Col 2:18 *2356*

WORST See APPENDIX.

WORTH {9}
it is *w* he shall give it me for a ... Gen 23:9 4392
the land is *w* four hundred ... Gen 23:15
unto him the *w* of thy estimation ... Lev 27:23 4373
for he hath been *w* a double hired ... Deut 15:18 7939
but now thou art *w* ten thousand ... 2Sa 18:3 3644
give thee the *w* of it in money ... 1Kin 21:2 4242
liar, and make my speech nothing *w* ... Job 24:25
heart of the wicked is little *w* ... Prov 10:20
Howl ye, Woe *w* the day ... Eze 30:2

WORTHIES {1}
He shall recount his *w* ... Nah 2:5 117

WORTHILY {1}
do thou *w* in Ephratah, and be ... Ruth 4:11 2428

WORTHY {68}
I am not *w* of the least of all ... Gen 32:10 6994
shall he that is *w* of death be ... Deut 17:6
whereas he was not *w* of death ... Deut 19:6
have committed a sin *w* of death ... Deut 21:22
in the damsel no sin *w* of death ... Deut 22:26
the wicked man be *w* to be beaten ... Deut 25:2 1121
unto Hannah he gave a *w* portion ... 1Sa 1:5 639
the LORD liveth, ye are *w* to die ... 1Sa 26:16 1121
the LORD, who is *w* to be praised ... 2Sa 22:4
If he will shew himself a *w* man ... 1Kin 1:52 2428
for thou art *w* of death ... 1Kin 2:26 376
the LORD, who is *w* to be praised ... Ps 18:3
saying, This man is *w* to die ... Jer 26:11
This man is not *w* to die ... Jer 26:16
I, whose shoes I am not *w* to bear ... Mt 3:11 *2425*
I am not *w* that thou shouldest ... Mt 8:8 *2425*
for the workman is *w* of his meat ... Mt 10:10 *514*
enter, enquire who in it is *w* ... Mt 10:11 *514*
And if the house be *w*, let your ... Mt 10:13 *514*
but if it be not *w*, let your ... Mt 10:13 *514*
more than me is not *w* of me ... Mt 10:37 *514*
more than me is not *w* of me ... Mt 10:37 *514*
after me, is not *w* of me ... Mt 10:38 *514*
they which were bidden were not *w* ... Mt 22:8 *514*
shoes I am not *w* to stoop down ... Mk 1:7 *2425*
therefore fruits *w* of repentance ... Lk 3:8 *514*
whose shoes I am not *w* to unloose ... Lk 3:16 *2425*
That he was *w* for whom he should ... Lk 7:4 *514*
for I am not *w* that thou ... Lk 7:6 *2425*
I myself *w* to come unto thee ... Lk 7:7 *515*
for the labourer is *w* of his hire ... Lk 10:7 *514*
and did commit things *w* of stripes ... Lk 12:48 *514*
am no more *w* to be called thy son ... Lk 15:19 *514*
am no more *w* to be called thy son ... Lk 15:21 *514*
accounted *w* to obtain that world ... Lk 20:35 *2661*
that ye may be accounted *w* to ... Lk 21:36 *2661*
nothing *w* of death is done unto ... Lk 23:15 *514*
latchet I am not *w* to unloose ... Jn 1:27 *514*
that they were counted *w* to ... Acts 5:41 *2661*
of his feet I am not *w* to loose ... Acts 13:25 *514*
his charge *w* of death or of bonds ... Acts 23:29 *514*
that very *w* deeds are done unto ... Acts 24:2 *2735*
committed any thing *w* of death ... Acts 25:11 *514*
had committed nothing *w* of death ... Acts 25:25 *514*
nothing *w* of death or of bonds ... Acts 26:31 *514*
commit such things are *w* of death ... Rom 1:32 *514*
of this present time are not *w* to ... Rom 8:18 *514*
beseech you that ye walk *w* of the ... Eph 4:1 *516*
That ye might walk *w* of the Lord ... Col 1:10 *516*
That ye would walk *w* of God ... 1Th 2:12 *516*
counted *w* of the kingdom of God ... 2Th 1:5 *2661*
would count you *w* of this calling ... 2Th 1:11 *515*
w of all acceptation, that Christ ... 1Ti 1:15 *514*
saying and *w* of all acceptation ... 1Ti 4:9 *514*
be counted *w* of double honour ... 1Ti 5:17 *515*
The labourer is *w* of his reward ... 1Ti 5:18 *514*
their own masters *w* of all honour ... 1Ti 6:1 *514*
w of more glory than Moses ... Heb 3:3 *515*
suppose ye, shall he be thought *w* ... Heb 10:29 *515*
(Of whom the world was not *w* ... Heb 11:38 *514*
Do not they blaspheme that *w* name ... Jas 2:7 *2570*
for they are *w* ... Rev 3:4 *514*
Thou art *w*, O Lord, to receive ... Rev 4:11 *514*
Who is *w* to open the book, and to ... Rev 5:2 *514*
no man was found *w* to open ... Rev 5:4 *514*
Thou art *w* to take the book, and ... Rev 5:9 *514*
W is the Lamb that was slain to ... Rev 5:12 *514*
for they are *w* ... Rev 16:6 *514*

WOT {10}
I *w* not who hath done this thing ... Gen 21:26 3045
w ye not that such a man as I can ... Gen 44:15 3045
we *w* not what is become of him ... Ex 32:1 3045
we *w* not what is become of him ... Ex 32:23 3045
for I *w* that he whom thou ... Num 22:6 3045
whither the men went I *w* not ... Josh 2:5 3045
I *w* that through ignorance ye did ... Acts 3:17 *1492*
we *w* not what is become of him ... Acts 7:40 *1492*
W ye not what the scripture saith ... Rom 11:2 *1492*
yet what I shall choose I *w* not ... Phil 1:22 *1107*

WOTTETH {1}
my master *w* not what is with me ... Gen 39:8 3045

WOULD See APPENDIX.

WOULDEST See APPENDIX.

WOUND {25}
w for *w*, stripe for stripe ... Ex 21:25 6482
I *w*, and I heal ... Deut 32:39 4272
the blood ran out of the *w* into ... 1Kin 22:35 4347
my *w* is incurable without ... Job 34:6 2671
But God shall *w* the head of his ... Ps 68:21 4272
he shall *w* the heads over many ... Ps 110:6 4272
A *w* and dishonour shall he get ... Prov 6:33 5061
The blueness of a *w* cleanseth ... Prov 20:30 6482
and healeth the stroke of their *w* ... Is 30:26 4347
my *w* is grievous ... Jer 10:19 4347
my *w* incurable, which refuseth to ... Jer 15:18 4347
incurable, and thy *w* is grievous ... Jer 30:12 4347
thee with the *w* of an enemy ... Jer 30:14 4347
his sickness, and Judah saw his *w* ... Hos 5:13 4205
heal you, nor cure you of your *w* ... Hos 5:13 4205
bread have laid a *w* under thee ... Obad 7 4204
For her *w* is incurable ... Mic 1:9 4347
thy *w* is grievous ... Nah 3:19 4347
w it in linen clothes with the ... Jn 19:40 *1210*
w him up, and carried him out, and ... Acts 5:6 *4958*
w their weak conscience, ye sin ... 1Cor 8:12 *5180*
and his deadly *w* was healed ... Rev 13:3 *4127*
beast, whose deadly *w* was healed ... Rev 13:12 *4127*
beast, which had the *w* by a sword ... Rev 13:14 *4127*

WOUNDED {35}
He that is *w* in the stones, or ... Deut 23:1 1795
many were overthrown and *w* ... Judg 9:40 2491
the *w* of the Philistines fell ... 1Sa 17:52 2491
he was sore *w* of the archers ... 1Sa 31:3 2342
w them, that they could not arise ... 2Sa 22:39 4272
him, so that in smiting he *w* him ... 1Kin 20:37 6481
for I am *w* ... 1Kin 22:34 2470
and the Syrians *w* Joram ... 2Kin 8:28 5221
him, and he was *w* of the archers ... 1Chr 10:3 2342
for I am *w* ... 2Chr 18:33 2470
for I am sore *w* ... 2Chr 35:23 2470
and the soul of the *w* crieth out ... Job 24:12 2491
I have *w* them that they were not ... Ps 18:38 4272
suddenly shall they be *w* ... Ps 64:7 4347
grief of those whom thou hast *w* ... Ps 69:26 2491

needy, and my heart is *w* within me ... Ps 109:22 2490
For she hath cast down many *w* ... Prov 7:26 2491
but a *w* spirit who can bear ... Prov 18:14 5218
me, they smote me, they *w* me ... Song 5:7 6481
hath cut Rahab, and *w* the dragon ... Is 51:9 2490
But he was *w* for our ... Is 53:5 2490
for I have *w* thee with the wound ... Jer 30:14 5221
remained but *w* men among them ... Jer 37:10 1856
all her land the *w* shall groan ... Jer 51:52 2491
when they swooned as the *w* in the ... Lam 2:12 2491
sound of thy fall, when the *w* cry ... Eze 26:15 2491
the *w* shall be judged in the ... Eze 28:23 2491
the groanings of a deadly *w* man ... Eze 30:24 2491
the sword, they shall not be *w* ... Joel 2:8 1214
Those with which I was *w* in the ... Zec 13:6 5221
w him in the head, and sent him ... Mk 12:4
w him, and departed, leaving him ... Lk 10:30 *4127,2007*
they *w* him also, and cast him out ... Lk 20:12 *5135*
fled out of that house naked and *w* ... Acts 19:16 *5135*
his heads as it were *w* to death ... Rev 13:3 *4969*

WOUNDEDST {1}
thou *w* the head out of the house ... Hab 3:13 4272

WOUNDETH {1}
he *w*, and his hands make whole ... Job 5:18 4272

WOUNDING {1}
for I have slain a man to my *w* ... Gen 4:23 6482

WOUNDS {15}
to be healed in Jezreel of the *w* ... 2Kin 8:29 4347
to be healed in Jezreel of the *w* ... 2Kin 9:15 4347
in Jezreel because of the *w* which ... 2Chr 22:6 4347
and multiplieth my *w* without cause ... Job 9:17 6482
My *w* stink and are corrupt because ... Ps 38:5 2250
in heart, and bindeth up their *w* ... Ps 147:3 6094
words of a talebearer are as *w* ... Prov 18:8 3859
who hath *w* without cause ... Prov 23:29 6482
words of a talebearer are as *w* ... Prov 26:22 3859
Faithful are the *w* of a friend ... Prov 27:6 6482
but *w*, and bruises, and putrifying ... Is 1:6 6482
me continually is grief and *w* ... Jer 6:7 4347
and I will heal thee of thy *w* ... Jer 30:17 4347
What are these *w* in thine hands ... Zec 13:6 4347
And went to him, and bound up his *w* ... Lk 10:34 *5134*

WOVE {1}
where the women *w* hangings for ... 2Kin 23:7 707

WOVEN {4}
it shall have a binding of *w* work ... Ex 28:32 707
the robe of the ephod of *w* work ... Ex 39:22 707
of fine linen of *w* work for Aaron ... Ex 39:27 707
w from the top throughout ... Jn 19:23 *5307*

WRAP {2}
than that he can *w* himself in it ... Is 28:20 3664
so they *w* it up ... Mic 7:3 5686

WRAPPED {14}
w herself, and sat in an open ... Gen 38:14 5968
it is here *w* in a cloth behind ... 1Sa 21:9 3874
that he *w* his face in his mantle, ... 1Kin 19:13 3874
w it together, and smote the ... 2Kin 2:8 1563
His roots are *w* about the heap, ... Job 8:17 5440
of his stones are *w* together ... Job 40:17 8276
it is *w* up for the slaughter ... Eze 21:15 4593
the weeds were *w* about my head ... Jonah 2:5 2280
he *w* it in a clean linen cloth, ... Mt 27:59 *1794*
w him in the linen, and laid him ... Mk 15:46 *1750*
w him in swaddling clothes, and ... Lk 2:7 *4683*
the babe *w* in swaddling clothes ... Lk 2:12 *4683*
w it in linen, and laid it in a ... Lk 23:53 *1794*
but *w* together in a place by ... Jn 20:7 *1794*

WRATH {200}
that his *w* was kindled ... Gen 39:19 639
and their *w*, for it was cruel ... Gen 49:7 5678
thou sentest forth thy *w*, which ... Ex 15:7 2740
my *w* shall wax hot, and I will ... Ex 22:24 639
that my *w* may wax hot against ... Ex 32:10 639
why doth thy *w* wax hot against ... Ex 32:11 639
Turn from thy fierce *w*, and repent ... Ex 32:12 639
lest *w* come upon all the people ... Lev 10:6 7107
that there be no *w* upon the ... Num 1:53 7110
the *w* of the LORD was kindled ... Num 11:33 639
for there is *w* gone out from the ... Num 16:46 7110
that there be no *w* any more upon ... Num 18:5 7110
hath turned my *w* away from the ... Num 25:11 2534
thy God to *w* in the wilderness ... Deut 9:7 7107
Horeb ye provoked the LORD to *w* ... Deut 9:8 7107
ye provoked the LORD to *w* ... Deut 9:22 7107
then the LORD's *w* be kindled ... Deut 11:17 639
in his anger, and in his *w* ... Deut 29:23 2534
of their land in anger, and in *w* ... Deut 29:28 2534
that I feared the *w* of the enemy ... Deut 32:27 3708
lest *w* be upon us, because of the ... Josh 9:20 7110
w fell on all the congregation of ... Josh 22:20 7110
his fierce *w* upon Amalek, ... 1Sa 28:18 639
if so be that the king's *w* arise ... 2Sa 11:20 2534
for great is the *w* of the LORD ... 2Kin 22:13 2534
therefore my *w* shall be kindled ... 2Kin 22:17 2534
the fierceness of his great *w* ... 2Kin 23:26 639
because there fell *w* for it ... 1Chr 27:24 7110
my *w* shall not be poured out upon ... 2Chr 12:7 2534
the *w* of the LORD turned from him ... 2Chr 12:12 639
therefore is *w* upon thee from ... 2Chr 19:2 7110
so *w* come upon you, and upon your ... 2Chr 19:10 7110
w came upon Judah and Jerusalem ... 2Chr 24:18 7110
for the fierce *w* of the LORD is ... 2Chr 28:11 639
there is fierce *w* against Israel ... 2Chr 28:13 639
Wherefore the *w* of the LORD was ... 2Chr 29:8 7110
that his fierce *w* may turn away ... 2Chr 29:10 639
of his *w* may turn away from you ... 2Chr 30:8 639
therefore there was *w* upon him ... 2Chr 32:25 7110
so that the *w* of the LORD came ... 2Chr 32:26 7110
for great is the *w* of the LORD ... 2Chr 34:21 2534
therefore my *w* shall be poured ... 2Chr 34:25 2534
until the *w* of the LORD arose ... 2Chr 36:16 2534
provoked the God of heaven unto *w* ... Ezr 5:12 7265
for why should there be *w* against ... Ezr 7:23 7109
his *w* is against all them that ... Ezr 8:22 639
until the fierce *w* of our God for ... Ezr 10:14 639
yet ye bring more *w* upon Israel ... Neh 13:18 2740
arise too much contempt and *w* ... Est 1:18 7110
when the *w* of king Ahasuerus was ... Est 2:1 2534
then was Haman full of *w* ... Est 3:5 2534
his *w* went into the palace garden ... Est 7:7 2534
Then was the king's *w* pacified ... Est 7:10 2534
For *w* killeth the foolish man, and ... Job 5:2 3708
me secret, until thy *w* be past ... Job 14:13 639
He teareth me in his *w*, who ... Job 16:9 639
also kindled his *w* against me ... Job 19:11 639
for *w* bringeth the punishments of ... Job 19:29 2534
cast the fury of his *w* upon him ... Job 20:23 639
flow away in the day of his *w* ... Job 20:28 639
drink of the *w* of the Almighty ... Job 21:20 2534
be brought forth to the day of *w* ... Job 21:30 5678
Then was kindled the *w* of Elihu ... Job 32:2 639
against Job was his *w* kindled ... Job 32:2 639
three friends was his *w* kindled ... Job 32:3 639
three men, then his *w* was kindled ... Job 32:5 639
the hypocrites in heart heap up *w* ... Job 36:13 639
Because there is *w*, beware lest ... Job 36:18 2534
Cast abroad the rage of thy *w* ... Job 40:11 639
My *w* is kindled against thee, and ... Job 42:7 639
shall he speak unto them in his *w* ... Ps 2:5 639
when his *w* is kindled but a ... Ps 2:12 639
shall swallow them up in his *w* ... Ps 21:9 639
Cease from anger, and forsake *w* ... Ps 37:8 2534
O LORD, rebuke me not in thy *w* ... Ps 38:1 7110
upon me, and in *w* they hate me ... Ps 55:3 639
both living, and in his *w* ... Ps 58:9 2740
Consume them in *w*, consume them, ... Ps 59:13 2534
Surely the *w* of man shall praise ... Ps 76:10 2534
the remainder of *w* shalt thou ... Ps 76:10 2534
The *w* of God came upon them, and ... Ps 78:31 639
and did not stir up all his *w* ... Ps 78:38 2534
the fierceness of his anger, *w* ... Ps 78:49 5678
Pour out thy *w* upon the heathen ... Ps 79:6 2534
Thou hast taken away all thy *w* ... Ps 85:3 5678
Thy *w* lieth hard upon me, and thou ... Ps 88:7 2534
Thy fierce *w* goeth over me ... Ps 88:16 2740
shall thy *w* burn like fire ... Ps 89:46 2534
and by thy *w* are we troubled ... Ps 90:7 2534
our days are passed away in thy *w* ... Ps 90:9 5678
to thy fear, so is thy *w* ... Ps 90:11 5678
Unto whom I sware in my *w* that ... Ps 95:11 639
of thine indignation and thy *w* ... Ps 102:10 7110
in the breach, to turn away his *w* ... Ps 106:23 2534
Therefore was the *w* of the LORD ... Ps 106:40 639
through kings in the day of his *w* ... Ps 110:5 639
when their *w* was kindled against ... Ps 124:3 639
against the *w* of mine enemies ... Ps 138:7 639
Riches profit not in the day of *w* ... Prov 11:4 5678
expectation of the wicked is *w* ... Prov 11:23 5678
A fool's *w* is presently known ... Prov 12:16 3708
He that is slow to *w* is of great ... Prov 14:29 639
but his *w* is against him that ... Prov 14:35 5678
A soft answer turneth away *w* ... Prov 15:1 2534
The *w* of a king is as messengers ... Prov 16:14 2534
The king's *w* is as the roaring of ... Prov 19:12 2197
A man of great *w* shall suffer ... Prov 19:19 2534
and a reward in the bosom strong *w* ... Prov 21:14 2534
his name, who dealeth in proud *w* ... Prov 21:24 5678
and he turn away his *w* from him ... Prov 24:18 639
but a fool's *w* is heavier than ... Prov 27:3 3708
W is cruel, and anger is ... Prov 27:4 2534
but wise men turn away *w* ... Prov 29:8 639
so the forcing of *w* bringeth ... Prov 30:33 639
sorrow and *w* with his sickness ... Eccl 5:17 7110
Through the *w* of the LORD of ... Is 9:19 5678
of my *w* will I give him a charge ... Is 10:6 5678
LORD cometh, cruel both with *w* ... Is 13:9 5678
in the *w* of the LORD of hosts, and ... Is 13:13 5678
in *w* with a continual stroke ... Is 14:6 5678
and his pride, and his *w* ... Is 16:6 5678
In a little *w* I hid my face from ... Is 54:8 7110
for in my *w* I smote thee, but in ... Is 60:10 7110
forsaken the generation of his *w* ... Jer 7:29 5678
at his *w* the earth shall tremble, ... Jer 10:10 7110
and to turn away thy *w* from them ... Jer 18:20 2534
anger, and in fury, and in great *w* ... Jer 21:5 7110
and in my fury, and in great *w* ... Jer 32:37 7110
In that ye provoke me unto *w* with ... Jer 44:8 3707
I know his *w*, saith the LORD ... Jer 48:30 5678
Because of the *w* of the LORD it ... Jer 50:13 7110
in his *w* the strong holds of the ... Lam 2:2 5678
affliction by the rod of his *w* ... Lam 3:1 5678
for *w* is upon all the multitude ... Eze 7:12 2740
for my *w* is upon all the ... Eze 7:14 2740
in the day of the *w* of the LORD ... Eze 7:19 5678
I accomplish my *w* upon the wall ... Eze 13:15 2534
against thee in the fire of my *w* ... Eze 21:31 5678
blow upon you in the fire of my *w* ... Eze 22:21 5678
them with the fire of my *w* ... Eze 22:31 5678
in the fire of my *w* have I spoken ... Eze 38:19 5678
out my *w* upon them like water ... Hos 5:10 5678
anger, and took him away in my *w* ... Hos 13:11 5678
and he kept his *w* for ever ... Amos 1:11 5678
he reserveth *w* for his enemies ... Nah 1:2 2534
in *w* remember mercy ... Hab 3:2 7267
was thy *w* against the sea, that ... Hab 3:8 5678
That day is a day of *w*, a day of ... Zeph 1:15 5678
them in the day of the LORD's *w* ... Zeph 1:18 5678
a great *w* from the LORD of hosts ... Zec 7:12 7110
your fathers provoked me to *w* ... Zec 8:14 7107
you to flee from the *w* to come ... Mt 3:7 *3709*
you to flee from the *w* to come ... Lk 3:7 *3709*
these things, were filled with *w* ... Lk 4:28 *2372*
the land, and *w* upon this people ... Lk 21:23 *3709*
but the *w* of God abideth on him ... Jn 3:36 *3709*
sayings, they were full of *w* ... Acts 19:28 *2372*
For the *w* of God is revealed from ... Rom 1:18 *3709*
w against the day of *w* ... Rom 2:5 *3709*
w against the day of *w* ... Rom 2:5 *3709*
unrighteousness, indignation and *w* ... Rom 2:8 *3709*
Because the law worketh *w* ... Rom 4:15 *3709*
shall be saved from *w* through him ... Rom 5:9 *3709*
if God, willing to shew his *w* ... Rom 9:22 *3709*
of *w* fitted to destruction ... Rom 9:22 *3709*
but rather give place unto *w* ... Rom 12:19 *3709*
a revenger to execute *w* upon him ... Rom 13:4 *3709*
needs be subject, not only for *w* ... Rom 13:5 *3709*
hatred, variance, emulations, *w* ... Gal 5:20 *2372*
were by nature the children of *w* ... Eph 2:3 *3709*
not the sun go down upon your *w* ... Eph 4:26 *3950*
Let all bitterness, and *w*, and ... Eph 4:31 *2372*
of these things cometh the *w* of ... Eph 5:6 *3709*
provoke not your children to *w* ... Eph 6:4 *3949*
For which things' sake the *w* of ... Col 3:6 *3709*
anger, *w*, malice, blasphemy, ... Col 3:8 *2372*
delivered us from the *w* to come ... 1Th 1:10 *3709*
for the *w* is come upon them to ... 1Th 2:16 *3709*
God hath not appointed us to *w* ... 1Th 5:9 *3709*
lifting up holy hands, without *w* ... 1Ti 2:8 *3709*
So I sware in my *w*, They shall ... Heb 3:11 *3709*
he said, As I have sworn in my *w* ... Heb 4:3 *3709*
not fearing the *w* of the king ... Heb 11:27 *2372*
to hear, slow to speak, slow to *w* ... Jas 1:19 *3709*
For the *w* of man worketh not the ... Jas 1:20 *3709*
throne, and from the *w* of the Lamb ... Rev 6:16 *3709*
the great day of his *w* is come ... Rev 6:17 *3709*
thy *w* is come, and the time of the ... Rev 11:18 *3709*
down unto you, having great *w* ... Rev 12:12 *2372*
wine of the *w* of her fornication ... Rev 14:8 *2372*
drink of the wine of the *w* of God ... Rev 14:10 *2372*
great winepress of the *w* of God ... Rev 14:19 *2372*
in them is filled up the *w* of God ... Rev 15:1 *2372*
golden vials full of the *w* of God ... Rev 15:7 *2372*
of the *w* of God upon the earth ... Rev 16:1 *2372*
wine of the fierceness of his *w* ... Rev 16:19 *3709*
wine of the *w* of her fornication ... Rev 18:3 *2372*
fierceness and *w* of Almighty God ... Rev 19:15 *3709*

WRATHFUL {2}
let thy *w* anger take hold of them ... Ps 69:24 2740
A *w* man stirreth up strife ... Prov 15:18 2534

WRATHS {1}
there be debates, envyings, *w* ... 2Cor 12:20 *2372*

WREATH {1}
rows of pomegranates on each *w* ... 2Chr 4:13 7639

WREATHED {1}
they are *w*, and come up upon my ... Lam 1:14 8276

WREATHEN {10}
of *w* work shalt thou make them, ... Ex 28:14 5688
fasten the *w* chains to the ouches ... Ex 28:14 5688
the ends of *w* work of pure gold ... Ex 28:22 5688
thou shalt put the two *w* chains ... Ex 28:24 5688
the other two ends of the two *w* ... Ex 28:25 5688
the ends, of *w* work of pure gold ... Ex 39:15 5688
they put the two *w* chains of gold ... Ex 39:17 5688
the two ends of the two *w* chains ... Ex 39:18 5688
the *w* work, and pomegranates upon ... 2Kin 25:17 7639
had the second pillar with *w* work ... 2Kin 25:17 7639

WREATHS {3}
work, and *w* of chain work, for the ... 1Kin 7:17 1434
the two *w* to cover the two ... 2Chr 4:12 7639
hundred pomegranates on the two *w* ... 2Chr 4:13 7639

WREST {5}
decline after many to *w* judgment ... Ex 23:2 5186
Thou shalt not *w* the judgment of ... Ex 23:6 5186
Thou shalt not *w* judgment ... Deut 16:19 5186
Every day they *w* my words ... Ps 56:5 6087
that are unlearned and unstable *w* ... 2Pet 3:16 *4761*

WRESTLE {1}
For we *w* not against flesh and ... Eph 6:12 *2076,3823*

WRESTLED {3}
have I *w* with my sister, and I ... Gen 30:8 6617
there *w* a man with him until the ... Gen 32:24 79
out of joint, as he *w* with him ... Gen 32:25 79

WRESTLINGS {1}
With great *w* have I wrestled with ... Gen 30:8 5319

WRETCHED {2}
O *w* man that I am ... Rom 7:24 *5005*
and knowest not that thou art *w* ... Rev 3:17 *5005*

WRETCHEDNESS {1}
and let me not see my *w* ... Num 11:15 7451

WRING {3}
w off his head, and burn it on the ... Lev 1:15 4454
w off his head from his neck, but ... Lev 5:8 4454
of the earth shall *w* them out ... Ps 75:8 4680

WRINGED {1}
w the dew out of the fleece, a ... Judg 6:38 4680

W

WRINGING {1}
the *w* of the nose bringeth forth ... Prov 30:33 4330

WRINKLE {1}
church, not having spot, or *w* ... Eph 5:27 *4512*

WRINKLES {1}
And thou hast filled me with *w* ... Job 16:8 7059

WRITE {91}
W this for a memorial in a book, ... Ex 17:14 3789
I will *w* upon these tables the ... Ex 34:1 3789
unto Moses, *W* thou these words ... Ex 34:27 3789
the priest shall *w* these curses ... Num 5:23 3789
w thou every man's name upon his ... Num 17:2 3789
thou shalt *w* Aaron's name upon ... Num 17:3 3789
thou shalt *w* them upon the posts ... Deut 6:9 3789
I will *w* on the tables the words ... Deut 10:2 3789
thou shalt *w* them upon the door ... Deut 11:20 3789
that he shall *w* him a copy of ... Deut 17:18 3789
then let him *w* her a bill of ... Deut 24:1 3789
w her a bill of divorcement, and ... Deut 24:3 3789
thou shalt *w* upon them all the ... Deut 27:3 3789
thou shalt *w* upon the stones all ... Deut 27:8 3789
Now therefore *w* ye this song for ... Deut 31:19 3789
the prophet, the son of Amoz, *w* ... 2Chr 26:22 3789
that we might *w* the names of the ... Ezr 5:10 3790
we make a sure covenant, and *w* it ... Neh 9:38 3789
W ye also for the Jews, as it ... Est 8:8 3789
w them upon the table of thine ... Prov 3:3 3789
w them upon the table of thine ... Prov 7:3 3789
roll, and *w* in it with a man's pen ... Is 8:1 3789
that *w* grievousness which they ... Is 10:1 3789
be few, that a child may *w* them ... Is 10:19 3789
w it before them in a table, and ... Is 30:8 3789
W ye this man childless, a man ... Jer 22:30 3789
W thee all the words that I have ... Jer 30:2 3789
parts, and *w* it in their hearts ... Jer 31:33 3789
w therein all the words that I ... Jer 36:2 3789
How didst thou *w* all these words ... Jer 36:17 3789
w in it all the former words that ... Jer 36:28 3789
w thee the name of the day, even ... Eze 24:2 3789
w upon it, For Judah, and for the ... Eze 37:16 3789
w upon it, For Joseph, the stick ... Eze 37:16 3789
w it in their sight, that they ... Eze 43:11 3789
W the vision, and make it plain ... Hab 2:2 3789
Moses suffered to *w* a bill of ... Mk 10:4 *1125*
to *w* unto thee in order, most ... Lk 1:3 *1125*
and sit down quickly, and *w* fifty ... Lk 16:6 *1125*
Take thy bill, and *w* fourscore ... Lk 16:7 *1125*
the law, and the prophets, did *w* ... Jn 1:45 *1125*
W not, The King of the Jews ... Jn 19:21 *1125*
But that we *w* unto them, that ... Acts 15:20 *1989*
certain thing to *w* unto my lord ... Acts 25:26 *1125*
had, I might have somewhat to *w* ... Acts 25:26 *1125*
I *w* not these things to shame you ... 1Cor 4:14 *1125*
that the things that I *w* unto you ... 1Cor 14:37 *1125*
For we *w* none other things unto ... 2Cor 1:13 *1125*
For to this end also did I *w* ... 2Cor 2:9 *1125*
is superfluous for me to *w* to you ... 2Cor 9:1 *1125*
being absent now I *w* to them ... 2Cor 13:2 *1125*
Therefore I *w* these things being ... 2Cor 13:10 *1125*
Now the things which I *w* unto you ... Gal 1:20 *1125*
To *w* the same things to you, to ... Phil 3:1 *1125*
ye need not that I *w* unto you ... 1Th 4:9 *1125*
ye have no need that I *w* unto you ... 1Th 5:1 *1125*
so I *w* ... 2Th 3:17 *1125*
These things *w* I unto thee ... 1Ti 3:14 *1125*
mind, and *w* them in their hearts ... Heb 8:10 *1924*
and in their minds will I *w* them ... Heb 10:16 *1924*
beloved, I now *w* unto you ... 2Pet 3:1 *1125*
And these things *w* we unto you ... 1Jn 1:4 *1125*
these things *w* I unto you ... 1Jn 2:1 *1125*
I *w* no new commandment unto you, ... 1Jn 2:7 *1125*
a new commandment I *w* unto you ... 1Jn 2:8 *1125*
I *w* unto you, little children, ... 1Jn 2:12 *1125*
I *w* unto you, fathers, because ye ... 1Jn 2:13 *1125*
I *w* unto you, young men, because ... 1Jn 2:13 *1125*
I *w* unto you, little children, ... 1Jn 2:13 *1125*
Having many things to *w* unto you ... 2Jn 12 *1125*
I would not *w* with paper ... 2Jn 12
I had many things to *w*, but I ... 3Jn 13 *1125*
not with ink and pen *w* unto thee ... 3Jn 13 *1125*
to *w* unto you of the common ... Jude 3 *1125*
was needful for me to *w* unto you ... Jude 3 *1125*
w in a book, and send it unto the ... Rev 1:11 *1125*
W the things which thou hast seen ... Rev 1:19 *1125*
angel of the church of Ephesus *w* ... Rev 2:1 *1125*
angel of the church in Smyrna *w* ... Rev 2:8 *1125*
angel of the church in Pergamos *w* ... Rev 2:12 *1125*
angel of the church in Thyatira *w* ... Rev 2:18 *1125*
angel of the church in Sardis *w* ... Rev 3:1 *1125*
of the church in Philadelphia *w* ... Rev 3:7 *1125*
I will *w* upon him the name of my ... Rev 3:12 *1125*
I will *w* upon him my new name ... Rev 3:12
of the church of the Laodiceans *w* ... Rev 3:14 *1125*
their voices, I was about to *w* ... Rev 10:4 *1125*
thunders uttered, and *w* them not ... Rev 10:4 *1125*
from heaven saying unto me, *W* ... Rev 14:13 *1125*
And he saith unto me, *W*, Blessed ... Rev 19:9 *1125*
And he said unto me, *W* ... Rev 21:5 *1125*

WRITER {2}
they that handle the pen of the *w* ... Judg 5:14 5608
my tongue is the pen of a ready *w* ... Ps 45:1 5608

WRITER'S {2}
with a *w* inkhorn by his side ... Eze 9:2 5608
which had the *w* inkhorn by his ... Eze 9:3 5608

WRITEST {2}
For thou *w* bitter things against ... Job 13:26 3789
the sticks whereon thou *w* shall ... Eze 37:20 3789

WRITETH {1}
when he *w* up the people, that ... Ps 87:6 3789

WRITING {38}
the *w* was the *w* of God, ... Ex 32:16 4385
pure gold, and wrote upon it a *w* ... Ex 39:30 4385
tables, according to the first *w* ... Deut 10:4 4385
when Moses had made an end of *w* ... Deut 31:24 3789
in *w* by his hand upon me, even ... 1Chr 28:19 3791
the king of Tyre answered in *w* ... 2Chr 2:11 3791
there came a *w* to him from Elijah ... 2Chr 21:12 4385
according to the *w* of David king ... 2Chr 35:4 3791
according to the *w* of Solomon his ... 2Chr 35:4 4385
his kingdom, and put it also in *w* ... 2Chr 36:22 4385
his kingdom, and put it also in *w* ... Ezr 1:1 4385
the *w* of the letter was written ... Ezr 4:7 3791
according to the *w* thereof ... Est 1:22 3791
according to the *w* thereof ... Est 3:12 3791
The copy of the *w* for a ... Est 3:14 3791
he gave him the copy of the *w* of ... Est 4:8 3791
for the *w* which is written in the ... Est 8:8 3791
according to the *w* thereof ... Est 8:9 3791
to the Jews according to their *w* ... Est 8:9 3791
The copy of the *w* for a ... Est 8:13 3791
two days according to their *w* ... Est 9:27 3791
The *w* of Hezekiah king of Judah, ... Is 38:9 4385
in the *w* of the house of Israel ... Eze 13:9 3791
Whosoever shall read this *w* ... Dan 5:7 3792
but they could not read the *w* ... Dan 5:8 3792
me, that they should read this *w* ... Dan 5:15 3792
now if thou canst read the *w* ... Dan 5:16 3792
I will read the *w* unto the king ... Dan 5:17 3792
and this *w* was written ... Dan 5:24 3792
this is the *w* that was written, ... Dan 5:25 3792
the decree, and sign the *w* ... Dan 6:8 3792
king Darius signed the *w* and the ... Dan 6:9 3792
Daniel knew that the *w* was signed ... Dan 6:10 3792
him give her a *w* of divorcement ... Mt 5:31
to give a *w* of divorcement ... Mt 19:7 *975*
And he asked for a *w* table ... Lk 1:63 *4093*
the *w* was, JESUS OF NAZARETH ... Jn 19:19 *1125*

WRITINGS {1}
But if ye believe not his *w* ... Jn 5:47 *1121*

WRITTEN {291}
and commandments which I have *w* ... Ex 24:12 3789
stone, *w* with the finger of God ... Ex 31:18 3789
the tables were *w* on both their ... Ex 32:15 3789
side and on the other were they *w* ... Ex 32:15 3789
out of thy book which thou hast *w* ... Ex 32:32 3789
and they were of them that were *w* ... Num 11:26 3789
of stone *w* with the finger of God ... Deut 9:10 3789
on them was *w* according to all ... Deut 9:10
this law that are *w* in this book ... Deut 28:58 3789
which is not *w* in the book of ... Deut 28:61 3789
all the curses that are *w* in this ... Deut 29:20 3789
are *w* in this book of the law ... Deut 29:21 3789
curses that are *w* in this book ... Deut 29:27 3789
his statutes which are *w* in this ... Deut 30:10 3789
to all that is *w* therein ... Josh 1:8 3789
as it is *w* in the book of the law ... Josh 8:31 3789
that is *w* in the book of the law ... Josh 8:34 3789
Is not this *w* in the book of ... Josh 10:13 3789
to do all that is *w* in the book ... Josh 23:6 3789
it is *w* in the book of Jasher ... 2Sa 1:18 3789
as it is *w* in the law of Moses, ... 1Kin 2:3 3789
are they not *w* in the book of the ... 1Kin 11:41 3789
they are *w* in the book of the ... 1Kin 14:19 3789
are they not *w* in the book of the ... 1Kin 14:29 3789
are they not *w* in the book of the ... 1Kin 15:7 3789
are they not *w* in the book of the ... 1Kin 15:23 3789
are they not *w* in the book of the ... 1Kin 15:31 3789
are they not *w* in the book of the ... 1Kin 16:5 3789
are they not *w* in the book of the ... 1Kin 16:14 3789
are they not *w* in the book of the ... 1Kin 16:20 3789
are they not *w* in the book of the ... 1Kin 16:27 3789
as it was *w* in the letters which ... 1Kin 21:11 3789
are they not *w* in the book of the ... 1Kin 22:39 3789
are they not *w* in the book of the ... 1Kin 22:45 3789
are they not *w* in the book of the ... 2Kin 1:18 3789
are they not *w* in the book of the ... 2Kin 8:23 3789
are they not *w* in the book of the ... 2Kin 10:34 3789
are they not *w* in the book of the ... 2Kin 12:19 3789
are they not *w* in the book of the ... 2Kin 13:8 3789
are they not *w* in the book of the ... 2Kin 13:12 3789
according unto that which is *w* in ... 2Kin 14:6 3789
are they not *w* in the book of the ... 2Kin 14:15 3789
are they not *w* in the book of the ... 2Kin 14:18 3789
are they not *w* in the book of the ... 2Kin 14:28 3789
are they not *w* in the book of the ... 2Kin 15:6 3789
they are *w* in the book of the ... 2Kin 15:11 3789
they are *w* in the book of the ... 2Kin 15:15 3789
are they not *w* in the book of the ... 2Kin 15:21 3789
they are *w* in the book of the ... 2Kin 15:26 3789
they are *w* in the book of the ... 2Kin 15:31 3789
are they not *w* in the book of the ... 2Kin 15:36 3789
are they not *w* in the book of the ... 2Kin 16:19 3789
are they not *w* in the book of the ... 2Kin 20:20 3789
are they not *w* in the book of the ... 2Kin 21:17 3789
are they are not *w* in the book of ... 2Kin 21:25 3789
all that which is *w* concerning us ... 2Kin 22:13 3789
covenant that were *w* in this book ... 2Kin 23:3 3789
as it is *w* in the book of this ... 2Kin 23:21 3789
w in the book that Hilkiah the ... 2Kin 23:24 3789
are they not *w* in the book of the ... 2Kin 23:28 3789
are they not *w* in the book of the ... 2Kin 24:5 3789
these *w* by name came in the days ... 1Chr 4:41 3789
they were *w* in the book of the ... 1Chr 9:1 3789
that is *w* in the law of the LORD ... 1Chr 16:40 3789
they are *w* in the book of Samuel ... 1Chr 29:29 3789
are they not *w* in the book of ... 2Chr 9:29 3789
are they not *w* in the book of ... 2Chr 12:15 3789
are *w* in the story of the prophet ... 2Chr 13:22 3789
they are *w* in the book of the ... 2Chr 16:11 3789
they are *w* in the book of Jehu ... 2Chr 20:34 3789
as it is *w* in the law of Moses, ... 2Chr 23:18 3789
they are *w* in the story of the ... 2Chr 24:27 3789
but did as it is *w* in the law in ... 2Chr 25:4 3789
are they not *w* in the book of the ... 2Chr 25:26 3789
they are *w* in the book of the ... 2Chr 27:7 3789
they are *w* in the book of the ... 2Chr 28:26 3789
time in such sort as it was *w* ... 2Chr 30:5 3789
passover otherwise than it was *w* ... 2Chr 30:18 3789
as it is *w* in the law of the LORD ... 2Chr 31:3 3789
they are *w* in the vision of ... 2Chr 32:32 3789
they are *w* in the book of the ... 2Chr 33:18
they are *w* among the sayings of ... 2Chr 33:19 3789
after all that is *w* in this book ... 2Chr 34:21 3789
are *w* in the book which they have ... 2Chr 34:24 3789
covenant which are *w* in this book ... 2Chr 34:31 3789
as it is *w* in the book of Moses ... 2Chr 35:12 3789
they are *w* in the lamentations ... 2Chr 35:25 3789
was *w* in the law of the LORD ... 2Chr 35:26 3789
they are *w* in the book of the ... 2Chr 35:27 3789
they are *w* in the book of the ... 2Chr 36:8 3789
as it is *w* in the law of Moses ... Ezr 3:2 3789
feast of tabernacles, as it is *w* ... Ezr 3:4 3789
letter was *w* in the Syrian tongue ... Ezr 4:7 3789
unto him, wherein was *w* thus ... Ezr 5:7 3790
and therein was a record thus *w* ... Ezr 6:2 3790
as it is *w* in the book of Moses ... Ezr 6:18 3792
all the weight was *w* at that time ... Ezr 8:34 3789
Wherein was *w*, It is reported ... Neh 6:6 3789
at the first, and found *w* therein, ... Neh 7:5 3789
they found *w* in the law which the ... Neh 8:14 3789
trees, to make booths, as it is *w* ... Neh 8:15 3789
our God, as it is *w* in the law ... Neh 10:34 3789
as it is *w* in the law, and the ... Neh 10:36 3789
were *w* in the book of the ... Neh 12:23 3789
and therein was found *w*, that the ... Neh 13:1 3789
let it be *w* among the laws of the ... Est 1:19 3789
it was *w* in the book of the ... Est 2:23 3789
let it be *w* that they may be ... Est 3:9 3789
there was *w* according to all that ... Est 3:12 3789
name of king Ahasuerus was it *w* ... Est 3:12 3789
And it was found *w*, that Mordecai ... Est 6:2 3789
let it be *w* to reverse the ... Est 8:5 3789
which is *w* in the king's name ... Est 8:8 3789
it was *w* according to all that ... Est 8:9 3789
and as Mordecai had *w* unto them ... Est 9:23 3789
and it was *w* in the book ... Est 9:32 3789
are they not *w* in the book of the ... Est 10:2 3789
Oh that my words were now *w* ... Job 19:23 3789
that mine adversary had *w* a book ... Job 31:35 3789
volume of the book it is *w* of me ... Ps 40:7 3789
not be *w* with the righteous ... Ps 69:28 3789
This shall be *w* for the ... Ps 102:18 3789
in thy book all my members were *w* ... Ps 139:16 3789
execute upon them the judgment *w* ... Ps 149:9 3789
Have not I *w* to thee excellent ... Prov 22:20 3789
and that which was *w* was upright ... Eccl 12:10 3789
even every one that is *w* among ... Is 4:3 3789
Behold, it is *w* before me ... Is 65:6 3789
of Judah is *w* with a pen of iron ... Jer 17:1 3789
from me shall be *w* in the earth ... Jer 17:13 3789
even all that is *w* in this book ... Jer 25:13 3789
which thou hast *w* from my mouth ... Jer 36:6 3789
saying, Why hast thou *w* therein ... Jer 36:29 3789
when he had *w* these words in a ... Jer 45:1 3789
words that are *w* against Babylon ... Jer 51:60 3789
and it was *w* within and without ... Eze 2:10 3789
there was *w* therein lamentations, ... Eze 2:10 3789
neither shall they be *w* in the ... Eze 13:9 3789
and this writing was *w* ... Dan 5:24 7560
And this is the writing that was *w* ... Dan 5:25 7560
the oath that is *w* in the law of ... Dan 9:11 3789
As it is *w* in the law of Moses, ... Dan 9:13 3789
that shall be found *w* in the book ... Dan 12:1 3789
I have *w* to him the great things ... Hos 8:12 3789
a book of remembrance was *w* ... Mal 3:16 3789
for thus it is *w* by the prophet ... Mt 2:5 *1125*
But he answered and said, It is *w* ... Mt 4:4 *1125*
for it is *w*, He shall give his ... Mt 4:6 *1125*
said unto him, It is *w* again ... Mt 4:7 *1125*
for it is *w*, Thou shalt worship ... Mt 4:10 *1125*
For this is he, of whom it is *w* ... Mt 11:10 *1125*
And said unto them, It is *w* ... Mt 21:13 *1125*
of man goeth as it is *w* of him ... Mt 26:24 *1125*
for it is *w*, I will smite the ... Mt 26:31 *1125*
up over his head his accusation *w* ... Mt 27:37 *1125*
As it is *w* in the prophets, ... Mk 1:2 *1125*
of you hypocrites, as it is *w* ... Mk 7:6 *1125*
how it is *w* of the Son of man, ... Mk 9:12 *1125*
they listed, as it is *w* of him ... Mk 9:13 *1125*
saying unto them, Is it not *w* ... Mk 11:17 *1125*
indeed goeth, as it is *w* of him ... Mk 14:21 *1125*
for it is *w*, I will smite the ... Mk 14:27 *1125*
of his accusation was *w* over ... Mk 15:26 *1924*
(As it is *w* in the law of the ... Lk 2:23 *1125*
As it is *w* in the book of the ... Lk 3:4 *1125*
answered him, saying, It is *w* ... Lk 4:4 *1125*
for it is *w*, Thou shalt worship ... Lk 4:8 *1125*
For it is *w*, He shall give his ... Lk 4:10 *1125*

he found the place where it was *w*	Lk 4:17	*1125*
This is he, of whom it is *w*	Lk 7:27	*1125*
your names are *w* in heaven	Lk 10:20	*1125*
unto him, What is *w* in the law	Lk 10:26	*1125*
all things that are *w* by the	Lk 18:31	*1125*
Saying unto them, It is *w*	Lk 19:46	*1125*
said, What is this then that is *w*	Lk 20:17	*1125*
which are *w* may be fulfilled	Lk 21:22	*1125*
that this that is *w* must yet be	Lk 22:37	*1125*
a superscription also was *w* over	Lk 23:38	*1125*
which were *w* in the law of Moses,	Lk 24:44	*1125*
And said unto them, Thus it is *w*	Lk 24:46	*1125*
remembered that it was *w*, The	Jn 2:17	*1125*
as it is *w*, He gave them bread	Jn 6:31	*1125*
It is *w* in the prophets, And they	Jn 6:45	*1125*
It is also *w* in your law, that	Jn 8:17	*1125*
Is it not *w* in your law, I said,	Jn 10:34	*1125*
as it is *w*,	Jn 12:14	*1125*
that these things were *w* of him	Jn 12:16	*1125*
fulfilled that is *w* in their law	Jn 15:25	*1125*
it was *w* in Hebrew, and Greek, and	Jn 19:20	*1125*
What I have *w* I have *w*	Jn 19:22	*1125*
which are not *w* in this book	Jn 20:30	*1125*
But these are *w*, that ye might	Jn 20:31	*1125*
if they should be *w* every one	Jn 21:25	*1125*
the books that should be *w*	Jn 21:25	*1125*
For it is *w* in the book of Psalms	Acts 1:20	*1125*
as it is *w* in the book of the	Acts 7:42	*1125*
fulfilled all that was *w* of him	Acts 13:29	*1125*
as it is also *w* in the second	Acts 13:33	*1125*
as it is *w*,	Acts 15:15	*1125*
Gentiles which believe, we have *w*	Acts 21:25	*1989*
for it is *w*, Thou shalt not speak	Acts 23:5	*1125*
all things which are *w* in the law	Acts 24:14	*1125*
as it is *w*, The just shall live	Rom 1:17	*1125*
work of the law *w* in their hearts	Rom 2:15	*1123*
Gentiles through you, as it is *w*	Rom 2:24	*1125*
as it is *w*, That thou mightest be	Rom 3:4	*1125*
As it is *w*, There is none	Rom 3:10	*1125*
(As it is *w*, I have made thee a	Rom 4:17	*1125*
Now it was not *w* for his sake	Rom 4:23	*1125*
As it is *w*, For thy sake we are	Rom 8:36	*1125*
As it is *w*, Jacob have I loved,	Rom 9:13	*1125*
As it is *w*, Behold, I lay in Sion	Rom 9:33	*1125*
as it is *w*, How beautiful are the	Rom 10:15	*1125*
(According as it is *w*, God hath	Rom 11:8	*1125*
as it is *w*, There shall come out	Rom 11:26	*1125*
for it is *w*, Vengeance is mine	Rom 12:19	*1125*
For it is *w*, As I live, saith the	Rom 14:11	*1125*
but, as it is *w*, The reproaches	Rom 15:3	*1125*
For whatsoever things were *w*	Rom 15:4	*4270*
aforetime were *w* for our learning	Rom 15:4	*4270*
as it is *w*, For this cause I will	Rom 15:9	*1125*
I have *w* the more boldly unto you	Rom 15:15	*1125*
But as it is *w*, To whom he was	Rom 15:21	*1125*
W to the Romans from Corinthus,	Rom *s*	*1125*
For it is *w*, I will destroy the	1Cor 1:19	*1125*
That, according as it is *w*	1Cor 1:31	*1125*
But as it is *w*, Eye hath not seen	1Cor 2:9	*1125*
For it is *w*, He taketh the wise	1Cor 3:19	*1125*
of men above that which is *w*	1Cor 4:6	*1125*
But now I have *w* unto you not to	1Cor 5:11	*1125*
For it is *w* in the law of Moses,	1Cor 9:9	*1125*
our sakes, no doubt, this is *w*	1Cor 9:10	*1125*
neither have I *w* these things	1Cor 9:15	*1125*
as it is *w*, The people sat down	1Cor 10:7	*1125*
they are *w* for our admonition,	1Cor 10:11	*1125*
In the law it is *w*, With men of	1Cor 14:21	*1125*
And so it is *w*, The first man Adam	1Cor 15:45	*1125*
to pass the saying that is *w*	1Cor 15:54	*1125*
was *w* from Philippi by Stephanus	1Cor *s*	*1125*
are our epistle *w* in our hearts	2Cor 3:2	*1449*
w not with ink, but with the	2Cor 3:3	*1449*
if the ministration of death, *w*	2Cor 3:7	*1722,1121*
of faith, according as it is *w*	2Cor 4:13	*1125*
As it is *w*, He that had gathered	2Cor 8:15	*1125*
(As it is *w*, He hath dispersed	2Cor 9:9	*1125*
Corinthians was *w* from Philippi	2Cor *s*	*1125*
for it is *w*, Cursed is every one	Gal 3:10	*1125*
not in all things which are *w* in	Gal 3:10	*1125*
for it is *w*, Cursed is every one	Gal 3:13	*1125*
For it is *w*, that Abraham had two	Gal 4:22	*1125*
For it is *w*, Rejoice, thou barren	Gal 4:27	*1125*
w unto you with mine own hand	Gal 6:11	*1125*
Unto the Galatians *w* from Rome	Gal *s*	*1125*
W from Rome unto the Ephesians by	Eph *s*	*1125*
It was *w* to the Philippians from	Phil *s*	*1125*
W from Rome to the Colossians by	Col *s*	*1125*
Thessalonians was *w* from Athens	1Th *s*	*1125*
Thessalonians was *w* from Athens	2Th *s*	*1125*
The first to Timothy was *w* from	1Ti *s*	*1125*
was *w* from Rome, when Paul was	2Ti *s*	*1125*
It was *w* to Titus, ordained the	Titus *s*	*1125*
I Paul have *w* it with mine own	Philem 19	*1125*
W from Rome to Philemon, by	Philem *s*	*1125*
volume of the book it is *w* of me	Heb 10:7	*1125*
firstborn, which are *w* in heaven	Heb 12:23	*583*
for I have *w* a letter unto you in	Heb 13:22	*1989*
W to the Hebrews from Italy by	Heb *s*	*1125*
Because it is *w*, Be ye holy	1Pet 1:16	*1125*
I have *w* briefly, exhorting, and	1Pet 5:12	*1125*
given unto him hath *w* unto you	2Pet 3:15	*1125*
I have *w* unto you, fathers,	1Jn 2:14	*1125*
I have *w* unto you, young men,	1Jn 2:14	*1125*
I have not *w* unto you because ye	1Jn 2:21	*1125*
These things have I *w* unto you	1Jn 2:26	*1125*
These things have I *w* unto you	1Jn 5:13	*1125*
those things which are *w* therein	Rev 1:3	*1125*
and in the stone a new name *w*	Rev 2:17	*1125*
sat on the throne a book *w* within	Rev 5:1	*1125*
whose names are not *w* in the book	Rev 13:8	*1125*
name *w* in their foreheads	Rev 14:1	*1125*
And upon her forehead was a name *w*	Rev 17:5	*1125*
whose names were not *w* in the	Rev 17:8	*1125*
and he had a name *w*, that no man	Rev 19:12	*1125*
vesture and on his thigh a name *w*	Rev 19:16	*1125*
things which were *w* in the books	Rev 20:12	*1125*
whosoever was not found *w* in the	Rev 20:15	*1125*
names *w* thereon, which are the	Rev 21:12	*1924*
but they which are *w* in the	Rev 21:27	*1125*
plagues that are *w* in this book	Rev 22:18	*1125*
things which are *w* in this book	Rev 22:19	*1125*

WRONG {26}

unto Abram, My *w* be upon thee	Gen 16:5	2555
and he said to him that did the *w*	Ex 2:13	7563
against him that which is *w*	Deut 19:16	5627
thou doest me *w* to war against me	Judg 11:27	7451
there is no *w* in mine hands	1Chr 12:17	2555
He suffered no man to do them *w*	1Chr 16:21	6231
hath not done *w* to the king only	Est 1:16	5753
Behold, I cry out of *w*, but I am	Job 19:7	2555
He suffered no man to do them *w*	Ps 105:14	6231
and do no *w*, do no violence to the	Jer 22:3	3238
and his chambers by *w*	Jer 22:13	3808,4941
O LORD, thou hast seen my *w*	Lam 3:59	5792
therefore *w* judgment proceedeth	Hab 1:4	6127
and said, Friend, I do thee no *w*	Mt 20:13	*91*
And seeing one of them suffer *w*	Acts 7:24	*91*
why do ye *w* one to another	Acts 7:26	*91*
his neighbour *w* thrust him away	Acts 7:27	*91*
a matter of *w* or wicked lewdness	Acts 18:14	*92*
to the Jews have I done no *w*	Acts 25:10	*91*
Why do ye not rather take *w*	1Cor 6:7	*91*
Nay, ye do *w*, and defraud, and that	1Cor 6:8	*91*
for his cause that had done the *w*	2Cor 7:12	*91*
nor for his cause that suffered *w*	2Cor 7:12	*91*
forgive me this *w*	2Cor 12:13	*93*
But he that doeth *w* shall receive	Col 3:25	*91*
for the *w* which he hath done	Col 3:25	*91*

WRONGED {2}

we have *w* no man, we have	2Cor 7:2	*91*
If he hath *w* thee, or oweth thee	Philem 18	*91*

WRONGETH {1}

sinneth against me *w* his own soul	Prov 8:36	2554

WRONGFULLY {7}

which ye *w* imagine against me	Job 21:27	2554
mine enemies *w* rejoice over me	Ps 35:19	8267
that hate me *w* are multiplied	Ps 38:19	8267
destroy me, being mine enemies *w*	Ps 69:4	8267
they persecute me *w*	Ps 119:86	8267
have oppressed the stranger *w*	Eze 22:29	3808,4941
God endure grief, suffering *w*	1Pet 2:19	*95*

WROTE {62}

Moses *w* all the words of the LORD	Ex 24:4	3789
he *w* upon the tables the words of	Ex 34:28	3789
w upon it a writing, like to the	Ex 39:30	3789
And Moses *w* their goings out	Num 33:2	3789
he *w* them upon two tables of	Deut 4:13	3789
he *w* them in two tables of stone,	Deut 5:22	3789
he *w* on the tables, according to	Deut 10:4	3789
Moses *w* this law, and delivered it	Deut 31:9	3789
Moses therefore *w* this song the	Deut 31:22	3789
he *w* there upon the stones a copy	Josh 8:32	3789
which he *w* in the presence of the	Josh 8:32	3789
Joshua *w* these words in the book	Josh 24:26	3789
w it in a book, and laid it up	1Sa 10:25	3789
that David *w* a letter to Joab, and	2Sa 11:14	3789
he *w* in the letter, saying, Set	2Sa 11:15	3789
So she *w* letters in Ahab's name,	1Kin 21:8	3789
she *w* in the letters, saying,	1Kin 21:9	3789
Jehu *w* letters, and sent to	2Kin 10:1	3789
Then he *w* a letter the second	2Kin 10:6	3789
commandment, which he *w* for you	2Kin 17:37	3789
w them before the king, and the	1Chr 24:6	3789
w letters also to Ephraim and	2Chr 30:1	3789
He *w* also letters to rail on the	2Chr 32:17	3789
w they unto him an accusation	Ezr 4:6	3789
the days of Artaxerxes *w* Bishlam	Ezr 4:7	3789
Shimshai the scribe *w* a letter	Ezr 4:8	3790
Then *w* Rehum the chancellor, and	Ezr 4:9	
which he *w* to destroy the Jews	Est 8:5	3789
he *w* in the king Ahasuerus' name,	Est 8:10	3789
Mordecai *w* these things, and sent	Est 9:20	3789
w with all authority, to confirm	Est 9:29	3789
Baruch *w* from the mouth of	Jer 36:4	3789
I *w* them with ink in the book	Jer 36:18	3789
the words which Baruch *w* at the	Jer 36:27	3789
who *w* therein from the mouth of	Jer 36:32	3789
So Jeremiah *w* in a book all the	Jer 51:60	3789
w over against the candlestick	Dan 5:5	3790
saw the part of the hand that *w*	Dan 5:5	3790
king Darius *w* unto all people	Dan 6:25	3790
then he *w* the dream, and told the	Dan 7:1	3790
your heart he *w* you this precept	Mk 10:5	*1125*
Moses *w* unto us, If a man's	Mk 12:19	*1125*
asked for a writing table, and *w*	Lk 1:63	*1125*
Moses *w* unto us, If any man's	Lk 20:28	*1125*
for he *w* of me	Jn 5:46	*1125*
with his finger *w* on the ground	Jn 8:6	*1125*
stooped down, and *w* on the ground	Jn 8:8	*1125*
Pilate *w* a title, and put it on	Jn 19:19	*1125*
these things, and *w* these things	Jn 21:24	*1125*
they *w* letters by them after this	Acts 15:23	*1125*
pass into Achaia, the brethren *w*	Acts 18:27	*1125*
he *w* a letter after this manner	Acts 23:25	*1125*
who *w* this epistle, salute you in	Rom 16:22	*1125*
I *w* unto you in an epistle not to	1Cor 5:9	*1125*
the things whereof ye *w* unto me	1Cor 7:1	*1125*
I *w* this same unto you, lest,	2Cor 2:3	*1125*
anguish of heart I *w* unto you	2Cor 2:4	*1125*
Wherefore, though I *w* unto you	2Cor 7:12	*1125*
(as I *w* afore in few words,	Eph 3:3	*4270*
in thy obedience I *w* unto thee	Philem 21	*1125*
lady, not as though I *w* a new	2Jn 5	*1125*
I *w* unto the church	3Jn 9	*1125*

WROTH {49}

And Cain was very *w*, and his	Gen 4:5	2734
said unto Cain, Why art thou *w*	Gen 4:6	2734
And Jacob was *w*, and chode with	Gen 31:36	2734
were grieved, and they were very *w*	Gen 34:7	2734
Pharaoh was *w* against two of his	Gen 40:2	7107
Pharaoh was *w* with his servants,	Gen 41:10	7107
and Moses was *w* with them	Ex 16:20	7107
And Moses was very *w*, and said unto	Num 16:15	2734
wilt thou be *w* with all the	Num 16:22	7107
Moses was *w* with the officers of	Num 31:14	7107
the voice of your words, and was *w*	Deut 1:34	7107
But the LORD was *w* with me for	Deut 3:26	5674
wherewith the LORD was *w* against	Deut 9:19	7107
that to morrow he will be *w* with	Josh 22:18	7107
And Saul was very *w*, and the saying	1Sa 18:8	2734
but if he be very *w*, then be sure	1Sa 20:7	2734
the Philistines were *w* with him	1Sa 29:4	7107
Then was Abner very *w* for the	2Sa 3:8	2734
all these things, he was very *w*	2Sa 13:21	2734
moved and shook, because he was *w*	2Sa 22:8	2734
But Naaman was *w*, and went away,	2Kin 5:11	7107
And the man of God was *w* with him	2Kin 13:19	7107
Then Asa was *w* with the seer, and	2Chr 16:10	3707
Then Uzziah was *w*, and had a	2Chr 26:19	2196
while he was *w* with the priests,	2Chr 26:19	2196
of your fathers was *w* with Judah	2Chr 28:9	2534
we builded the wall, he was *w*	Neh 4:1	2734
be stopped, then they were very *w*	Neh 4:7	2734
therefore was the king very *w*	Est 1:12	7107
those which kept the door, were *w*	Est 2:21	7107
and were shaken, because he was *w*	Ps 18:7	2734
the LORD heard this, and was *w*	Ps 78:21	5674
When God heard this, he was *w*	Ps 78:59	5674
was *w* with his inheritance	Ps 78:62	5674
thou hast been *w* with thine	Ps 89:38	5674
he shall be *w* as in the valley of	Is 28:21	7264
I was *w* with my people, I have	Is 47:6	7107
that I would not be *w* with thee	Is 54:9	7107
ever, neither will I be always *w*	Is 57:16	7107
of his covetousness was I *w*	Is 57:17	7107
I hid me, and was *w*, and he went on	Is 57:17	7107
behold, thou art *w*	Is 64:5	7107
Be not *w* very sore, O LORD,	Is 64:9	7107
the princes were *w* with Jeremiah	Jer 37:15	7107
thou art very *w* against us	Lam 5:22	7107
of the wise men, was exceeding *w*	Mt 2:16	*2373*
And his lord was *w*, and delivered	Mt 18:34	*3710*
the king heard thereof, he was *w*	Mt 22:7	*3710*
the dragon was *w* with the woman	Rev 12:17	*3710*

WROUGHT {100}

because he had *w* folly in Israel	Gen 34:7	6213
what things I have *w* in Egypt	Ex 10:2	5953
twined linen, *w* with needlework	Ex 26:36	4639
twined linen, *w* with needlework	Ex 27:16	
Then *w* Bezaleel and Aholiab, and	Ex 36:1	6213
that *w* all the work of the	Ex 36:4	6213
hearted man among them that *w* the	Ex 36:8	6213
they *w* onyx stones inclosed in	Ex 39:6	6213
they have *w* confusion	Lev 20:12	6213
and of Israel, What hath God *w*	Num 23:23	6466
gold of them, even all *w* jewels	Num 31:51	4639
such abomination is *w* among you	Deut 13:14	6213
that hath *w* wickedness in the	Deut 17:2	6213
such abomination is *w* in Israel	Deut 17:4	6213
which hath not been *w* with	Deut 21:3	5647
she hath *w* folly in Israel	Deut 22:21	6213
the evils which they shall have *w*	Deut 31:18	6213
because he hath *w* folly in Israel	Josh 7:15	6213
folly that they have *w* in Israel	Judg 20:10	6213
mother in law with whom she had *w*	Ruth 2:19	6213
name with whom I *w* to day is Boaz	Ruth 2:19	6213
when he had *w* wonderfully among	1Sa 6:6	5953
LORD hath *w* salvation in Israel	1Sa 11:13	6213
who hath *w* this great salvation	1Sa 14:45	6213
for he hath *w* with God this day	1Sa 14:45	6213
the LORD *w* a great salvation for	1Sa 19:5	6213
Otherwise I should have *w*	2Sa 18:13	6213
the LORD *w* a great victory that	2Sa 23:10	6213
the LORD *w* a great victory	2Sa 23:12	6213
the people that *w* in the work	1Kin 5:16	6213
king Solomon, and *w* all his work	1Kin 7:14	6213
the brim thereof was *w* like the	1Kin 7:26	4639
the people that *w* in the work	1Kin 9:23	6213
Zimri, and his treason that he *w*	1Kin 16:20	7194
But Omri *w* evil in the eyes of	1Kin 16:25	6213
he *w* evil in the sight of the	2Kin 3:2	6213
that *w* upon the house of the LORD	2Kin 12:11	6213
w wicked things to provoke the	2Kin 17:11	6213
he *w* much wickedness in the sight	2Kin 21:6	6213
house of them that *w* fine linen	1Chr 4:21	5656
he set masons to hew *w* stones to	1Chr 22:2	1496
linen, and *w* cherubims thereon	2Chr 3:14	5927
he *w* that which was evil in the	2Chr 21:6	6213
the LORD, and also such as *w* iron	2Chr 24:12	2790
So the workmen *w*, and the work was	2Chr 24:13	6213

W

w that which was good and right and 2Chr 31:20 6213
he *w* much evil in the sight of 2Chr 33:6 6213
that *w* in the house of the LORD 2Chr 34:10 6213
that *w* the work in any manner of 2Chr 34:13 6213
half of my servants *w* in the work .... Neh 4:16 6213
one of his hands *w* in the work .... Neh 4:17 6213
that this work was *w* of our God .... Neh 6:16 6213
and had *w* great provocations .... Neh 9:18 6213
they *w* great provocations .... Neh 9:26 6213
the hand of the LORD hath *w* this .... Job 12:9 6213
who can say, Thou hast *w* iniquity .... Job 36:23 6466
which thou hast *w* for them that .... Ps 31:19 6466
her clothing is of *w* gold .... Ps 45:13 4865
that which thou hast *w* for us .... Ps 68:28 6466
How he had *w* his signs in Egypt, ... Ps 78:43 7760
curiously *w* in the lowest parts .... Ps 139:15 7551
all the works that my hands had *w* .... Eccl 2:11 6213
because the work that is *w* under .... Eccl 2:17 6213
for thou also hast *w* all our .... Is 26:12 6466
we have not *w* any deliverance in .... Is 26:18 6213
Who hath *w* and done it, calling .... Is 41:4 6466
seeing she hath *w* lewdness with .... Jer 11:15 6213
he *w* a work on the wheels .... Jer 18:3 6213
But I *w* for my name's sake, that .... Eze 20:9 6213
But I *w* for my name's sake, that .... Eze 20:14 6213
w for my name's sake, that it .... Eze 20:22 6213
when I have *w* with you for my .... Eze 20:44 6213
against it, because they *w* for me .... Eze 29:20 6213
the high God hath *w* toward me .... Dan 4:2 5648
for the sea *w*, and was tempestuous .... Jonah 1:11 1980
for the sea *w*, and was tempestuous .... Jonah 1:13 1980
which have *w* his judgment .... Zeph 2:3 6466
These last have *w* but one hour .... Mt 20:12 *4160*
for she hath *w* a good work upon .... Mt 26:10 *2038*
mighty works are *w* by his hands .... Mk 6:2 *1096*
she hath *w* a good work on me .... Mk 14:6 *2038*
manifest, that they are *w* in God .... Jn 3:21 *2038*
wonders *w* among the people .... Acts 5:12 *1096*
wonders God had *w* among the .... Acts 15:12 *4160*
craft, he abode with them, and *w* .... Acts 18:3 *2038*
God *w* special miracles by the .... Acts 19:11 *4160*
what things God had *w* among the .... Acts 21:19 *4160*
w in me all manner of .... Rom 7:8 *2716*
which Christ hath not *w* by me .... Rom 15:18 *2716*
Now he that hath *w* us for the 2Cor 5:5 *2716*
what carefulness it *w* in you 2Cor 7:11 *2716*
were *w* among you in all patience 2Cor 12:12 *2716*
(For he that *w* effectually in .... Gal 2:8 *1754*
Which he *w* in Christ, when he .... Eph 1:20 *1754*
but *w* with labour and travail 2Th 3:8 *2038*
w righteousness, obtained .... Heb 11:33 *2038*
thou how faith *w* with his works .... Jas 2:22 *4903*
have *w* the will of the Gentiles 1Pet 4:3 *2716*
not those things which we have *w* 2Jn 8 *2038*
that *w* miracles before him .... Rev 19:20 *4160*

WROUGHTEST {1}
and where *w* thou .... Ruth 2:19 6213

WRUNG {4}
the blood thereof shall be *w* out .... Lev 1:15 4680
w out at the bottom of the altar .... Lev 5:9 4680
of a full cup are *w* out to them .... Ps 73:10 4680
cup of trembling, and *w* them out .... Is 51:17 4680

XERXES See AHASUERUS.

XERXES' See AHASUERUS'.

Y

YAH See JAH.

YARN {4}
brought out of Egypt, and linen *y* 1Kin 10:28 4723
received the linen *y* at a price 1Kin 10:28 4723
brought out of Egypt, and linen *y* 2Chr 1:16 4723
received the linen *y* at a price 2Chr 1:16 4723

YE See APPENDIX.

YEA See APPENDIX.

YEAR {377}
six hundredth *y* of Noah's life .... Gen 7:11 8141
in the six hundredth and first *y* .... Gen 8:13 8141
in the thirteenth *y* they rebelled .... Gen 14:4 8141
fourteenth *y* came Chedorlaomer .... Gen 14:5 8141
at this set time in the next *y* .... Gen 17:21 8141
in the same *y* an hundredfold .... Gen 26:12 8141
for all their cattle for that *y* .... Gen 47:17 8141
When that *y* was ended, they came .... Gen 47:18 8141
they came unto him the second *y* .... Gen 47:18 8141
the first month of the *y* to you .... Ex 12:2 8141
blemish, a male of the first *y* .... Ex 12:5 8141
in his season from *y* to *y* .... Ex 13:10 3117
in his season from *y* to *y* .... Ex 13:10 3117
But the seventh *y* thou shalt let .... Ex 23:11
keep a feast unto me in the *y* .... Ex 23:14 8141
which is in the end of the *y* .... Ex 23:16 8141
Three times in the *y* all thy .... Ex 23:17 8141
out from before thee in one *y* .... Ex 23:29 8141
first *y* day by day continually .... Ex 29:38 8141
in a *y* with the blood of the sin .... Ex 30:10 8141
once in the *y* shall he make .... Ex 30:10 8141
Thrice in the *y* shall all your .... Ex 34:23 8141
the LORD thy God thrice in the *y* .... Ex 34:24 8141
the first month in the second *y* .... Ex 40:17 8141
and a lamb, both of the first *y* .... Lev 9:3 8141
the first *y* for a burnt offering .... Lev 12:6 8141
of the first *y* without blemish .... Lev 14:10 8141
for all their sins once a *y* .... Lev 16:34 8141
But in the fourth *y* all the fruit .... Lev 19:24 8141
in the fifth *y* shall ye eat of .... Lev 19:25 8141
without blemish of the first *y* .... Lev 23:12 8141
without blemish of the first *y* .... Lev 23:18 8141
two lambs of the first *y* for a .... Lev 23:19 8141
unto the LORD seven days in the *y* .... Lev 23:41 8141
But in the seventh *y* shall be a .... Lev 25:4 8141
for it is a *y* of rest unto the .... Lev 25:5 8141
And ye shall hallow the fiftieth *y* .... Lev 25:10 8141
shall that fiftieth *y* be unto you .... Lev 25:11 8141
In the *y* of this jubile ye shall .... Lev 25:13 8141
What shall we eat the seventh *y* .... Lev 25:20 8141
blessing upon you in the sixth *y* .... Lev 25:21 8141
And ye shall sow the eighth *y* .... Lev 25:22 8141
of old fruit until the ninth *y* .... Lev 25:22 8141
bought it until the *y* of jubile .... Lev 25:28 8141
within a whole *y* after it is sold .... Lev 25:29 8141
within a full *y* may he redeem it .... Lev 25:29 3117
within the space of a full *y* .... Lev 25:30 8141
shall go out in the *y* of jubile .... Lev 25:33
serve thee unto the *y* of jubile .... Lev 25:40 8141
y that he was sold to him unto .... Lev 25:50 8141
sold to him unto the *y* of jubile .... Lev 25:50 8141
few years unto the *y* of jubile .... Lev 25:52 8141
shall go out in the *y* of jubile .... Lev 25:54 8141
his field from the *y* of jubile .... Lev 27:17 8141
even unto the *y* of the jubile .... Lev 27:18 8141
even unto the *y* of the jubile .... Lev 27:23 8141
In the *y* of the jubile the field .... Lev 27:24 8141
in the second *y* after they were .... Num 1:1 8141
first *y* for a trespass offering .... Num 6:12 8141
one he lamb of the first *y* .... Num 6:14 8141
first *y* without blemish for a sin .... Num 6:14 8141
one ram, one lamb of the first *y* .... Num 7:15 8141
goats, five lambs of the first *y* .... Num 7:17 8141
one ram, one lamb of the first *y* .... Num 7:21 8141
goats, five lambs of the first *y* .... Num 7:23 8141
one ram, one lamb of the first *y* .... Num 7:27 8141
goats, five lambs of the first *y* .... Num 7:29 8141
one ram, one lamb of the first *y* .... Num 7:33 8141
goats, five lambs of the first *y* .... Num 7:35 8141
one ram, one lamb of the first *y* .... Num 7:39 8141
goats, five lambs of the first *y* .... Num 7:41 8141
one ram, one lamb of the first *y* .... Num 7:45 8141
goats, five lambs of the first *y* .... Num 7:47 8141
one ram, one lamb of the first *y* .... Num 7:51 8141
goats, five lambs of the first *y* .... Num 7:53 8141
one ram, one lamb of the first *y* .... Num 7:57 8141
goats, five lambs of the first *y* .... Num 7:59 8141
one ram, one lamb of the first *y* .... Num 7:63 8141
goats, five lambs of the first *y* .... Num 7:65 8141
one ram, one lamb of the first *y* .... Num 7:69 8141
goats, five lambs of the first *y* .... Num 7:71 8141
one ram, one lamb of the first *y* .... Num 7:75 8141
goats, five lambs of the first *y* .... Num 7:77 8141
one ram, one lamb of the first *y* .... Num 7:81 8141
goats, five lambs of the first *y* .... Num 7:83 8141
the lambs of the first *y* twelve .... Num 7:87 8141
the lambs of the first *y* sixty .... Num 7:88 8141
the first month of the second *y* .... Num 9:1 8141
were two days, or a month, or a *y* .... Num 9:22 3117
the second month, in the second *y* .... Num 10:11 8141
even forty days, each day for a *y* .... Num 14:34 8141
of the first *y* for a sin offering .... Num 15:27 8141
two lambs of the first *y* without .... Num 28:3 8141
lambs of the first *y* without spot .... Num 28:9 8141
lambs of the first *y* without spot .... Num 28:11 8141
throughout the months of the *y* .... Num 28:14 8141
and seven lambs of the first *y* .... Num 28:19 8141
ram, seven lambs of the first *y* .... Num 28:27 8141
of the first *y* without blemish .... Num 29:2 8141
and seven lambs of the first *y* .... Num 29:8 8141
and fourteen lambs of the first *y* .... Num 29:13 8141
lambs of the first *y* without spot .... Num 29:17 8141
of the first *y* without blemish .... Num 29:20 8141
of the first *y* without blemish .... Num 29:23 8141
lambs of the first *y* without spot .... Num 29:26 8141
of the first *y* without blemish .... Num 29:29 8141
of the first *y* without blemish .... Num 29:32 8141
of the first *y* without blemish .... Num 29:36 8141
in the fortieth *y* after the .... Num 33:38 8141
it came to pass in the fortieth *y* .... Deut 1:3 8141
from the beginning of the *y* even .... Deut 11:12 8141
y even unto the end of the *y* .... Deut 11:12 8141
field bringeth forth *y* by *y* .... Deut 14:22 8141
field bringeth forth *y* by *y* .... Deut 14:22 8141
of thine increase the same *y* .... Deut 14:28 8141
heart, saying, The seventh *y* .... Deut 15:9 8141
the *y* of release, is at hand .... Deut 15:9 8141
then in the seventh *y* thou shalt .... Deut 15:12 8141
y by *y* in the place which the .... Deut 15:20 8141
by *y* in the place which the LORD .... Deut 15:20 8141
Three times in a *y* shall all thy .... Deut 16:16 8141
he shall be free at home one *y* .... Deut 24:5 8141
of thine increase the third *y* .... Deut 26:12 8141
which is the *y* of tithing .... Deut 26:12 8141
the solemnity of the *y* of release .... Deut 31:10 8141
of the land of Canaan that *y* .... Josh 5:12 8141
that *y* they vexed and oppressed .... Judg 10:8 8141
the Gileadite four days in a *y* .... Judg 11:40 8141
ten shekels of silver by the *y* .... Judg 17:10 3117
And as he did so *y* by *y* 1Sa 1:7 8141
brought it to him from *y* to *y* 1Sa 2:19 3117
he went from *y* to *y* in circuit 1Sa 7:16 8141
Saul reigned one *y* 1Sa 13:1 8141
of the Philistines was a full *y* 1Sa 27:7
after the *y* was expired, at the 2Sa 11:1 8141
David three years, *y* after *y* 2Sa 21:1 8141
his month in a *y* made provision 1Kin 4:7 8141
gave Solomon to Hiram *y* by *y* 1Kin 5:11 8141
eightieth *y* after the children of 1Kin 6:1 8141
in the fourth *y* of Solomon's 1Kin 6:1 8141
In the fourth *y* was the 1Kin 6:37 8141
And in the eleventh *y*, in the 1Kin 6:38 8141
three times in a *y* did Solomon 1Kin 9:25 8141
one *y* was six hundred threescore 1Kin 10:14 8141
and mules, a rate *y* by *y* 1Kin 10:25 8141
in the fifth *y* of king Rehoboam 1Kin 14:25 8141
Now in the eighteenth *y* of king 1Kin 15:1 8141
in the twentieth *y* of Jeroboam 1Kin 15:9 8141
the second *y* of Asa king of Judah 1Kin 15:25 8141
Even in the third *y* of Asa king 1Kin 15:28 8141
In the third *y* of Asa king of 1Kin 15:33 8141
sixth *y* of Asa king of Judah 1Kin 16:8 8141
seventh *y* of Asa king of Judah, ... 1Kin 16:10 8141
seventh *y* of Asa king of Judah 1Kin 16:15 8141
first *y* of Asa king of Judah 1Kin 16:23 8141
eighth *y* of Asa king of Judah 1Kin 16:29 8141
came to Elijah in the third *y* 1Kin 18:1 8141
for at the return of the *y* the 1Kin 20:22 8141
to pass at the return of the *y* 1Kin 20:26 8141
And it came to pass in the third *y* 1Kin 22:2 8141
fourth *y* of Ahab king of Israel 1Kin 22:41 8141
in Samaria the seventeenth *y* of 1Kin 22:51 8141
second *y* of Jehoram the son of 2Kin 1:17 8141
in Samaria the eighteenth *y* of 2Kin 3:1 8141
in the fifth *y* of Joram the son 2Kin 8:16 8141
In the twelfth *y* of Joram the son 2Kin 8:25 8141
and he reigned one *y* in Jerusalem 2Kin 8:26 8141
in the eleventh *y* of Joram the 2Kin 9:29 8141
the seventh *y* Jehoiada sent and 2Kin 11:4 8141
In the seventh *y* of Jehu Jehoash 2Kin 12:1 8141
twentieth *y* of king Jehoash the 2Kin 12:6 8141
twentieth *y* of Joash the son of 2Kin 13:1 8141
seventh *y* of Joash king of Judah 2Kin 13:10 8141
land at the coming in of the *y* 2Kin 13:20 8141
In the second *y* of Joash son of 2Kin 14:1 8141
In the fifteenth *y* of Amaziah the 2Kin 14:23 8141
seventh *y* of Jeroboam king of 2Kin 15:1 8141
eighth *y* of Azariah king of Judah 2Kin 15:8 8141
thirtieth *y* of Uzziah king of 2Kin 15:13 8141
thirtieth *y* of Azariah king of 2Kin 15:17 8141
In the fiftieth *y* of Azariah king 2Kin 15:23 8141
fiftieth *y* of Azariah king of 2Kin 15:27 8141
in the twentieth *y* of Jotham the 2Kin 15:30 8141
In the second *y* of Pekah the son 2Kin 15:32 8141
In the seventeenth *y* of Pekah the 2Kin 16:1 8141
In the twelfth *y* of Ahaz king of 2Kin 17:1 8141
Assyria, as he had done *y* by *y* 2Kin 17:4 8141
In the ninth *y* of Hoshea the king 2Kin 17:6 8141
it came to pass in the third *y* of 2Kin 18:1 8141
in the fourth *y* of king Hezekiah 2Kin 18:9 8141
which was the seventh *y* of Hoshea 2Kin 18:9 8141
even in the sixth *y* of Hezekiah 2Kin 18:10 8141
that is the ninth *y* of Hoshea 2Kin 18:10 8141
fourteenth *y* of king Hezekiah did 2Kin 18:13 8141
Ye shall eat this *y* such things 2Kin 19:29 8141
in the second *y* that which 2Kin 19:29 8141
and in the third *y* sow ye, and reap 2Kin 19:29 8141

the eighteenth *y* of king Josiah ... 2Kin 22:3 8141
the eighteenth *y* of king Josiah ... 2Kin 23:23 8141
him in the eighth *y* of his reign ... 2Kin 24:12 8141
pass in the ninth *y* of his reign ... 2Kin 25:1 8141
the eleventh *y* of king Zedekiah ... 2Kin 25:2 8141
which is the nineteenth *y* of king ... 2Kin 25:8 8141
thirtieth *y* of the captivity of ... 2Kin 25:27 8141
king of Babylon in the *y* that he ... 2Kin 25:27 8141
that after the *y* was expired ... 1Chr 20:1 8141
In the fortieth *y* of the reign of ... 1Chr 26:31 8141
all the months of the *y*, of every ... 1Chr 27:1 8141
in the fourth *y* of his reign ... 2Chr 3:2 8141
feasts, three times in the *y* ... 2Chr 8:13 8141
Solomon in one *y* was six hundred ... 2Chr 9:13 8141
and mules, a rate *y* by *y* ... 2Chr 9:24 8141
that in the fifth *y* of king ... 2Chr 12:2 8141
Now in the eighteenth *y* of king ... 2Chr 13:1 8141
in the fifteenth *y* of the reign ... 2Chr 15:10 8141
thirtieth *y* of the reign of Asa ... 2Chr 15:19 8141
thirtieth *y* of the reign of Asa ... 2Chr 16:1 8141
ninth *y* of his reign was diseased ... 2Chr 16:12 8141
one and fortieth *y* of his reign ... 2Chr 16:13 8141
Also in the third *y* of his reign ... 2Chr 17:7 8141
and he reigned one *y* in Jerusalem ... 2Chr 22:2 8141
in the seventh *y* Jehoiada ... 2Chr 23:1 8141
house of your God from *y* to *y* ... 2Chr 24:5 8141
came to pass at the end of the *y* ... 2Chr 24:23 8141
of Ammon gave him the same *y* an ... 2Chr 27:5 8141
pay unto him, both the second *y* ... 2Chr 27:5 8141
He in the first *y* of his reign ... 2Chr 29:3 8141
For in the eighth *y* of his reign ... 2Chr 34:3 8141
in the twelfth *y* he began to ... 2Chr 34:3 8141
in the eighteenth *y* of his reign ... 2Chr 34:8 8141
In the eighteenth *y* of the reign ... 2Chr 35:19 8141
when the *y* was expired, king ... 2Chr 36:10 8141
Now in the first *y* of Cyrus king ... 2Chr 36:22 8141
Now in the first *y* of Cyrus king ... Ezr 1:1 8141
Now in the second *y* of their ... Ezr 3:8 8141
So it ceased unto the second *y* of ... Ezr 4:24 8140
But in the first *y* of Cyrus the ... Ezr 5:13 8140
In the first *y* of Cyrus the king ... Ezr 6:3 8140
which was in the sixth *y* of the ... Ezr 6:15 8140
in the seventh *y* of Artaxerxes ... Ezr 7:7 8141
was in the seventh *y* of the king ... Ezr 7:8 8141
month Chisleu, in the twentieth *y* ... Neh 1:1 8141
in the twentieth *y* of Artaxerxes ... Neh 2:1 8141
the twentieth *y* even unto the two ... Neh 5:14 8141
thirtieth *y* of Artaxerxes the ... Neh 5:14 8141
that we would leave the seventh *y* ... Neh 10:31 8141
at times appointed *y* by *y* ... Neh 10:34 8141
at times appointed *y* by *y* ... Neh 10:34 8141
all fruit of all trees, *y* by *y* ... Neh 10:35 8141
thirtieth *y* of Artaxerxes king of ... Neh 13:6 8141
In the third *y* of his reign ... Est 1:3 8141
in the seventh *y* of his reign ... Est 2:16 8141
Nisan, in the twelfth *y* of king ... Est 3:7 8141
to their appointed time every *y* ... Est 9:27 8141
be joined unto the days of the *y* ... Job 3:6 8141
crownest the *y* with thy goodness ... Ps 65:11 8141
In the *y* that king Uzziah died I ... Is 6:1 8141
In the *y* that king Ahaz died was ... Is 14:28 8141
In the *y* that Tartan came unto ... Is 20:1 8141
the Lord said unto me, Within a *y* ... Is 21:16 8141
add ye *y* to *y* ... Is 29:1 8141
the *y* of recompences for the ... Is 34:8 8141
the fourteenth *y* of king Hezekiah ... Is 36:1 8141
Ye shall eat this *y* such as ... Is 37:30 8141
the second *y* that which springeth ... Is 37:30 8141
and in the third *y* sow ye, and reap ... Is 37:30 8141
the acceptable *y* of the LORD ... Is 61:2 8141
the *y* of my redeemed is come ... Is 63:4 8141
in the thirteenth *y* of his reign ... Jer 1:2 8141
unto the end of the eleventh *y* of ... Jer 1:3 8141
even the *y* of their visitation ... Jer 11:23 8141
be careful in the *y* of drought ... Jer 17:8 8141
even the *y* of their visitation, ... Jer 23:12 8141
people of Judah in the fourth *y* ... Jer 25:1 8141
of Judah, that was the first *y* of ... Jer 25:1 8141
From the thirteenth *y* of Josiah ... Jer 25:3 8141
that is the three and twentieth *y* ... Jer 25:3 8141
And it came to pass the same *y* ... Jer 28:1 8141
king of Judah, in the fourth *y* ... Jer 28:1 8141
this *y* thou shalt die, because ... Jer 28:16 8141
the same *y* in the seventh month ... Jer 28:17 8141
tenth *y* of Zedekiah king of Judah ... Jer 32:1 8141
eighteenth *y* of Nebuchadrezzar ... Jer 32:1 8141
it came to pass in the fourth *y* ... Jer 36:1 8141
it came to pass in the fifth *y* of ... Jer 36:9 8141
In the ninth *y* of Zedekiah king ... Jer 39:1 8141
And in the eleventh *y* of Zedekiah ... Jer 39:2 8141
in the fourth *y* of Jehoiakim the ... Jer 45:1 8141
y of Jehoiakim the son of Josiah ... Jer 46:2 8141
the *y* of their visitation, saith ... Jer 48:44 8141
a rumour shall both come one *y* ... Jer 51:46 8141
in another *y* shall come a rumour ... Jer 51:46 8141
in the fourth *y* of his reign ... Jer 51:59 8141
pass in the ninth *y* of his reign ... Jer 52:4 8141
the eleventh *y* of king Zedekiah ... Jer 52:5 8141
which was the nineteenth *y* of ... Jer 52:12 8141
in the seventh *y* three thousand ... Jer 52:28 8141
In the eighteenth *y* of ... Jer 52:29 8141
twentieth *y* of Nebuchadrezzar ... Jer 52:30 8141
thirtieth *y* of the captivity of ... Jer 52:31 8141
king of Babylon in the first *y* of ... Jer 52:31 8141
came to pass in the thirtieth *y* ... Eze 1:1 8141
which was the fifth *y* of king ... Eze 1:2 8141
appointed thee each day for a *y* ... Eze 4:6 8141
And it came to pass in the sixth *y* ... Eze 8:1 8141
it came to pass in the seventh *y* ... Eze 20:1 8141
Again in the ninth *y*, in the ... Eze 24:1 8141
it came to pass in the eleventh *y* ... Eze 26:1 8141
In the tenth *y*, in the tenth ... Eze 29:1 8141
pass in the seven and twentieth *y* ... Eze 29:17 8141
it came to pass in the eleventh *y* ... Eze 30:20 8141
it came to pass in the eleventh *y* ... Eze 31:1 8141
it came to pass in the twelfth *y* ... Eze 32:1 8141
to pass also in the twelfth *y* ... Eze 32:17 8141
in the twelfth *y* of our captivity ... Eze 33:21 8141
twentieth *y* of our captivity, in ... Eze 40:1 8141
in the beginning of the *y* ... Eze 40:1 8141
in the fourteenth *y* after that ... Eze 40:1 8141
of the first *y* without blemish ... Eze 46:13 8141
shall be his to the *y* of liberty ... Eze 46:17 8141
In the third *y* of the reign of ... Dan 1:1 8141
unto the first *y* of king Cyrus ... Dan 1:21 8141
in the second *y* of the reign of ... Dan 2:1 8141
In the first *y* of Belshazzar king ... Dan 7:1 8140
In the third *y* of the reign of ... Dan 8:1 8141
In the first *y* of Darius the son ... Dan 9:1 8141
In the first *y* of his reign I ... Dan 9:2 8141
In the third *y* of Cyrus king of ... Dan 10:1 8141
in the first *y* of Darius the Mede ... Dan 11:1 8141
offerings, with calves of a *y* old ... Mic 6:6 8141
In the second *y* of Darius the ... Hag 1:1 8141
in the second *y* of Darius the ... Hag 1:15 8141
month, in the second *y* of Darius ... Hag 2:10 8141
month, in the second *y* of Darius ... Zec 1:1 8141
Sebat, in the second *y* of Darius ... Zec 1:7 8141
in the fourth *y* of king Darius ... Zec 7:1 8141
y to *y* to worship the King ... Zec 14:16 8141
y at the feast of the passover ... Lk 2:41 *2094*
Now in the fifteenth *y* of the ... Lk 3:1 *2094*
the acceptable *y* of the Lord ... Lk 4:19 *1763*
Lord, let it alone this *y* also ... Lk 13:8 *2094*
being the high priest that same *y* ... Jn 11:49 *1763*
but being high priest that *y* ... Jn 11:51 *1763*
was the high priest that same *y* ... Jn 18:13 *1763*
that a whole *y* they assembled ... Acts 11:26 *1763*
And he continued there a *y* ... Acts 18:11 *1763*
but also to be forward a *y* ago ... 2Cor 8:10 *4070*
that Achaia was ready a *y* ago ... 2Cor 9:2 *4070*
high priest alone once every *y* ... Heb 9:7 *1763*
every *y* with blood of others ... Heb 9:25 *1763*
y by *y* continually make the ... Heb 10:1 *1763*
which they offered *y* by *y* ... Heb 10:1 *1763*
again made of sins every *y* ... Heb 10:3 *1763*
a city, and continue there a *y* ... Jas 4:13 *1763*
and a day, and a month, and a *y* ... Rev 9:15 *1763*

YEARLY {9}

as a *y* hired servant shall he be ... Lev 25:53 8141
went *y* to lament the daughter of ... Judg 11:40 3117
y in a place which is on the ... Judg 21:19 3117
up out of his city *y* to worship ... 1Sa 1:3 3117
unto the LORD the *y* sacrifice ... 1Sa 1:21 3117
husband to offer the *y* sacrifice ... 1Sa 2:19 3117
for there is a *y* sacrifice there ... 1Sa 20:6 3117
to charge ourselves *y* with the ... Neh 10:32 8141
the fifteenth day of the same, *y* ... Est 9:21 8141

YEARN {1}

his bowels did *y* upon his brother ... Gen 43:30 3648

YEARNED {1}

for her bowels *y* upon her son ... 1Kin 3:26 3648

YEAR'S {2}

feast of ingathering at the *y* end ... Ex 34:22 8141
(for it was at every *y* end that ... 2Sa 14:26 3117

YEARS {538}

and for seasons, and for days, and *y* ... Gen 1:14 8141
Adam lived an hundred and thirty *y* ... Gen 5:3 8141
Seth were eight hundred *y* ... Gen 5:4 8141
were nine hundred and thirty *y* ... Gen 5:5 8141
Seth lived an hundred and five *y* ... Gen 5:6 8141
Enos eight hundred and seven *y* ... Gen 5:7 8141
were nine hundred and twelve *y* ... Gen 5:8 8141
And Enos lived ninety *y*, and begat ... Gen 5:9 8141
Cainan eight hundred and fifteen *y* ... Gen 5:10 8141
Enos were nine hundred and five *y* ... Gen 5:11 8141
And Cainan lived seventy *y* ... Gen 5:12 8141
eight hundred and forty *y*, and ... Gen 5:13 8141
Cainan were nine hundred and ten *y* ... Gen 5:14 8141
Mahalaleel lived sixty and five *y* ... Gen 5:15 8141
Jared eight hundred and thirty *y* ... Gen 5:16 8141
eight hundred ninety and five *y* ... Gen 5:17 8141
lived an hundred sixty and two *y* ... Gen 5:18 8141
he begat Enoch eight hundred *y* ... Gen 5:19 8141
were nine hundred sixty and two *y* ... Gen 5:20 8141
And Enoch lived sixty and five *y* ... Gen 5:21 8141
begat Methuselah three hundred *y* ... Gen 5:22 8141
three hundred sixty and five *y* ... Gen 5:23 8141
an hundred eighty and seven *y* ... Gen 5:25 8141
seven hundred eighty and two *y* ... Gen 5:26 8141
were nine hundred sixty and nine *y* ... Gen 5:27 8141
lived an hundred eighty and two *y* ... Gen 5:28 8141
five hundred ninety and five *y* ... Gen 5:30 8141
seven hundred seventy and seven *y* ... Gen 5:31 8141
And Noah was five hundred *y* old ... Gen 5:32 8141
shall be an hundred and twenty *y* ... Gen 6:3 8141
Noah was six hundred *y* old when ... Gen 7:6 8141
flood three hundred and fifty *y* ... Gen 9:28 8141
Noah were nine hundred and fifty *y* ... Gen 9:29 8141
Shem was an hundred *y* old ... Gen 11:10 8141
Arphaxad two *y* after the flood ... Gen 11:10 8141
he begat Arphaxad five hundred *y* ... Gen 11:11 8141
Arphaxad lived five and thirty *y* ... Gen 11:12 8141
Salah four hundred and three *y* ... Gen 11:13 8141
And Salah lived thirty *y*, and begat ... Gen 11:14 8141
Eber four hundred and three *y* ... Gen 11:15 8141
And Eber lived four and thirty *y* ... Gen 11:16 8141
Peleg four hundred and thirty *y* ... Gen 11:17 8141
And Peleg lived thirty *y*, and begat ... Gen 11:18 8141
begat Reu two hundred and nine *y* ... Gen 11:19 8141
And Reu lived two and thirty *y* ... Gen 11:20 8141
Serug two hundred and seven *y* ... Gen 11:21 8141
And Serug lived thirty *y*, and begat ... Gen 11:22 8141
he begat Nahor two hundred *y* ... Gen 11:23 8141
And Nahor lived nine and twenty *y* ... Gen 11:24 8141
Terah an hundred and nineteen *y* ... Gen 11:25 8141
And Terah lived seventy *y*, and ... Gen 11:26 8141
Terah were two hundred and five *y* ... Gen 11:32 8141
five *y* old when he departed out ... Gen 12:4 8141
Twelve *y* they served Chedorlaomer ... Gen 14:4 8141
Take me an heifer of three *y* old ... Gen 15:9 8027
old, and a she goat of three *y* old ... Gen 15:9 8027
old, and a ram of three *y* old ... Gen 15:9 3027
shall afflict them four hundred *y* ... Gen 15:13 8141
dwelt ten *y* in the land of Canaan ... Gen 16:3 8141
Abram was fourscore and six *y* old ... Gen 16:16 8141
And when Abram was ninety *y* old ... Gen 17:1 8141
unto him that is an hundred *y* old ... Gen 17:17 8141
shall Sarah, that is ninety *y* old ... Gen 17:17 8141
And Abraham was ninety *y* old ... Gen 17:24 8141
his son was thirteen *y* old ... Gen 17:25 8141
And Abraham was an hundred *y* old ... Gen 21:5 8141
hundred and seven and twenty *y* old ... Gen 23:1 8141
these were the *y* of the life of ... Gen 23:1 8141
these are the days of the *y* of ... Gen 25:7 8141
hundred threescore and fifteen *y* ... Gen 25:7 8141
old age, an old man, and full of *y* ... Gen 25:8
these are the *y* of the life of ... Gen 25:17 8141
an hundred and thirty and seven *y* ... Gen 25:17 8141
Isaac was forty *y* old when he ... Gen 25:20 8141
Isaac was threescore *y* old when ... Gen 25:26 8141
Esau was forty *y* old when he took ... Gen 26:34 8141
I will serve thee seven *y* for ... Gen 29:18 8141
Jacob served seven *y* for Rachel ... Gen 29:20 8141
serve with me yet seven other *y* ... Gen 29:27 8141
served with him yet seven other *y* ... Gen 29:30 8141
This twenty *y* have I been with ... Gen 31:38 8141
have I been twenty *y* in thy house ... Gen 31:41 8141
fourteen *y* for thy two daughters ... Gen 31:41 8141
and six *y* for thy cattle ... Gen 31:41 8141
were an hundred and fourscore *y* ... Gen 35:28 8141
Joseph, being seventeen *y* old ... Gen 37:2 8141
to pass at the end of two full *y* ... Gen 41:1 8141
The seven good kine are seven *y* ... Gen 41:26 8141
the seven good ears are seven *y* ... Gen 41:26 8141
came up after them are seven *y* ... Gen 41:27 8141
wind shall be seven *y* of famine ... Gen 41:27 8141
there come seven *y* of great ... Gen 41:29 8141
after them seven *y* of famine ... Gen 41:30 8141
of Egypt in the seven plenteous *y* ... Gen 41:34 8141
food of those good *y* that come ... Gen 41:35 8141
against the seven *y* of famine ... Gen 41:36 8141
Joseph was thirty *y* old when he ... Gen 41:46 8141
in the seven plenteous *y* the ... Gen 41:47 8141
up all the food of the seven *y* ... Gen 41:48 8141
sons before the *y* of famine came ... Gen 41:50 8141
the seven *y* of plenteousness, ... Gen 41:53 8141
the seven *y* of dearth began to ... Gen 41:54 8141
For these two *y* hath the famine ... Gen 45:6 8141
and yet there are five *y*, in the ... Gen 45:6 8141
yet there are five *y* of famine ... Gen 45:11 8141
Pharaoh, The days of the *y* of my ... Gen 47:9 8141
are an hundred and thirty *y* ... Gen 47:9 8141
the days of the *y* of my life been ... Gen 47:9 8141
y of the life of my fathers in ... Gen 47:9 8141
in the land of Egypt seventeen *y* ... Gen 47:28 8141
was an hundred forty and seven *y* ... Gen 47:28 8141
Joseph lived an hundred and ten *y* ... Gen 50:22 8141
being an hundred and ten *y* old ... Gen 50:26 8141
the *y* of the life of Levi were an ... Ex 6:16 8141
were an hundred thirty and seven *y* ... Ex 6:16 8141
the *y* of the life of Kohath were ... Ex 6:18 8141
were an hundred thirty and three *y* ... Ex 6:18 8141
the *y* of the life of Amram were ... Ex 6:20 8141
an hundred and thirty and seven *y* ... Ex 6:20 8141
And Moses was fourscore *y* old ... Ex 7:7 8141
and Aaron fourscore and three *y* old ... Ex 7:7 8141
was four hundred and thirty *y* ... Ex 12:40 8141
of the four hundred and thirty *y* ... Ex 12:41 8141
of Israel did eat manna forty *y* ... Ex 16:35 8141
servant, six *y* he shall serve ... Ex 21:2 8141
six *y* thou shalt sow thy land, and ... Ex 23:10 8141
are numbered, from twenty *y* old ... Ex 30:14 8141
to be numbered, from twenty *y* old ... Ex 38:26 8141
three *y* shall it be as ... Lev 19:23 8141
Six *y* thou shalt sow thy field, ... Lev 25:3 8141
six *y* thou shalt prune thy ... Lev 25:3 8141
seven sabbaths of *y* unto thee ... Lev 25:8 8141
unto thee, seven times seven *y* ... Lev 25:8 8141
of *y* shall be unto thee forty ... Lev 25:8 8141
be unto thee forty and nine *y* ... Lev 25:8 8141
According to the number of *y* ... Lev 25:15 8141
of *y* of the fruits he shall sell ... Lev 25:15 8141
y thou shalt increase the price ... Lev 25:16 8141
according to the fewness of *y* ... Lev 25:16 8141
according to the number of the *y* ... Lev 25:16 8141
bring forth fruit for three *y* ... Lev 25:21 8141
count the *y* of the sale thereof ... Lev 25:27 8141
be according unto the number of *y* ... Lev 25:50 8141
If there be yet many *y* behind ... Lev 25:51 8141
but few *y* unto the year of jubile ... Lev 25:52 8141
according unto his *y* shall he ... Lev 25:52 8141

Y

if he be not redeemed in these *y* ... Lev 25:54 8141
be of the male from twenty *y* old ... Lev 27:3 8141
even unto sixty *y* old ... Lev 27:3 8141
if it be from five *y* old even ... Lev 27:5 8141
y old even unto twenty *y* old ... Lev 27:5 8141
a month old even unto five *y* old ... Lev 27:6 8141
And if it be from sixty *y* old ... Lev 27:7 8141
according to the *y* that remain ... Lev 27:18 8141
From twenty *y* old and upward, all ... Num 1:3 8141
of the names, from twenty *y* old ... Num 1:18 8141
every male from twenty *y* old ... Num 1:20 8141
every male from twenty *y* old ... Num 1:22 8141
of the names, from twenty *y* old ... Num 1:24 8141
of the names, from twenty *y* old ... Num 1:26 8141
of the names, from twenty *y* old ... Num 1:28 8141
of the names, from twenty *y* old ... Num 1:30 8141
of the names, from twenty *y* old ... Num 1:32 8141
of the names, from twenty *y* old ... Num 1:34 8141
of the names, from twenty *y* old ... Num 1:36 8141
of the names, from twenty *y* old ... Num 1:38 8141
of the names, from twenty *y* old ... Num 1:40 8141
of the names, from twenty *y* old ... Num 1:42 8141
their fathers, from twenty *y* old ... Num 1:45 8141
From thirty *y* old and upward even ... Num 4:3 8141
and upward even until fifty *y* old ... Num 4:3 8141
From thirty *y* old and upward until ... Num 4:23 8141
upward until fifty *y* old shalt ... Num 4:23 8141
From thirty *y* old and upward even ... Num 4:30 8141
upward even unto fifty *y* old ... Num 4:30 8141
From thirty *y* old and upward even ... Num 4:35 8141
and upward even unto fifty *y* old ... Num 4:35 8141
From thirty *y* old and upward even ... Num 4:39 8141
and upward even unto fifty *y* old ... Num 4:39 8141
From thirty *y* old and upward even ... Num 4:43 8141
and upward even unto fifty *y* old ... Num 4:43 8141
From thirty *y* old and upward even ... Num 4:47 8141
and upward even unto fifty *y* old ... Num 4:47 8141
from twenty and five *y* old ... Num 8:24 8141
from the age of fifty *y* they ... Num 8:25 8141
seven *y* before Zoan in Egypt ... Num 13:22 8141
whole number, from twenty *y* old ... Num 14:29 8141
wander in the wilderness forty *y* ... Num 14:33 8141
your iniquities, even forty *y* ... Num 14:34 8141
of Israel, from twenty *y* old ... Num 26:2 8141
of the people, from twenty *y* old ... Num 26:4 8141
out of Egypt, from twenty *y* old ... Num 32:11 8141
wander in the wilderness forty *y* ... Num 32:13 8141
three *y* old when he died in mount ... Num 33:39 8141
these forty *y* the LORD thy God ... Deut 2:7 8141
Zered, was thirty and eight *y* ... Deut 2:14 8141
these forty *y* in the wilderness ... Deut 8:2 8141
did thy foot swell, these forty *y* ... Deut 8:4 8141
At the end of three *y* thou shalt ... Deut 14:28 8141
seven *y* thou shalt make a release ... Deut 15:1 8141
unto thee, and serve thee six *y* ... Deut 15:12 8141
to thee, in serving thee six *y* ... Deut 15:18 8141
led you forty *y* in the wilderness ... Deut 29:5 8141
hundred and twenty *y* old this day ... Deut 31:2 8141
At the end of every seven *y* ... Deut 31:10 8141
of old, consider the *y* of many ... Deut 32:7 8141
twenty *y* old when he died ... Deut 34:7 8141
walked forty *y* in the wilderness ... Josh 5:6 8141
Joshua was old and stricken in *y* ... Josh 13:1 8141
Thou art old and stricken in *y* ... Josh 13:1 8141
Forty *y* old was I when Moses the ... Josh 14:7 8141
as he said, these forty and five *y* ... Josh 14:10 8141
this day fourscore and five *y* old ... Josh 14:10 8141
being an hundred and ten *y* old ... Josh 24:29 8141
being an hundred and ten *y* old ... Judg 2:8 8141
served Chushan-rishathaim eight *y* ... Judg 3:8 8141
And the land had rest forty *y* ... Judg 3:11 8141
Eglon the king of Moab eighteen *y* ... Judg 3:14 8141
And the land had rest fourscore *y* ... Judg 3:30 8141
twenty *y* he mightily oppressed ... Judg 4:3 8141
And the land had rest forty *y* ... Judg 5:31 8141
into the hand of Midian seven *y* ... Judg 6:1 8141
the second bullock of seven *y* old ... Judg 6:25 8141
forty *y* in the days of Gideon ... Judg 8:28 8141
had reigned three *y* over Israel ... Judg 9:22 8141
judged Israel twenty and three *y* ... Judg 10:2 8141
and judged Israel twenty and two *y* ... Judg 10:3 8141
eighteen *y*, all the children of ... Judg 10:8 8141
coasts of Arnon, three hundred *y* ... Judg 11:26 8141
And Jephthah judged Israel six *y* ... Judg 12:7 8141
And he judged Israel seven *y* ... Judg 12:9 8141
and he judged Israel ten *y* ... Judg 12:11 8141
and he judged Israel eight *y* ... Judg 12:14 8141
hand of the Philistines forty *y* ... Judg 13:1 8141
days of the Philistines twenty *y* ... Judg 15:20 8141
And he judged Israel twenty *y* ... Judg 16:31 8141
and they dwelled there about ten *y* ... Ruth 1:4 8141
Now Eli was ninety and eight *y* old ... 1Sa 4:15 8141
And he had judged Israel forty *y* ... 1Sa 4:18 8141
for it was twenty *y* ... 1Sa 7:2 8141
he had reigned two *y* over Israel ... 1Sa 13:1 8141
with me these days, or these *y* ... 1Sa 29:3 8141
Saul's son was forty *y* old when ... 2Sa 2:10 8141
over Israel, and reigned two *y* ... 2Sa 2:10 8141
the house of Judah was seven *y* ... 2Sa 2:11 8141
He was five *y* old when the ... 2Sa 4:4 8141
David was thirty *y* old when he ... 2Sa 5:4 8141
to reign, and he reigned forty *y* ... 2Sa 5:4 8141
he reigned over Judah seven *y* ... 2Sa 5:5 8141
three *y* over all Israel and Judah ... 2Sa 5:5 8141
it came to pass after two full *y* ... 2Sa 13:23 8141
to Geshur, and was there three *y* ... 2Sa 13:38 8141
dwelt two full *y* in Jerusalem ... 2Sa 14:28 8141
And it came to pass after forty *y* ... 2Sa 15:7 8141
aged man, even fourscore *y* old ... 2Sa 19:32 8141
I am this day fourscore *y* old ... 2Sa 19:35 8141
in the days of David three *y* ... 2Sa 21:1 8141
Shall seven *y* of famine come unto ... 2Sa 24:13 8141
David was old and stricken in *y* ... 1Kin 1:1 3117
reigned over Israel were forty *y* ... 1Kin 2:11 8141
seven *y* reigned he in Hebron, and ... 1Kin 2:11 8141
three *y* reigned he in Jerusalem ... 1Kin 2:11 8141
to pass at the end of three *y* ... 1Kin 2:39 8141
So was he seven *y* in building it ... 1Kin 6:38 8141
building his own house thirteen *y* ... 1Kin 7:1 8141
to pass at the end of twenty *y* ... 1Kin 9:10 8141
once in three *y* came the navy of ... 1Kin 10:22 8141
over all Israel was forty *y* ... 1Kin 11:42 8141
reigned were two and twenty *y* ... 1Kin 14:20 8141
one *y* old when he began to reign, ... 1Kin 14:21 8141
reigned seventeen *y* in Jerusalem ... 1Kin 14:21 8141
Three *y* reigned he in Jerusalem ... 1Kin 15:2 8141
one *y* reigned he in Jerusalem ... 1Kin 15:10 8141
and reigned over Israel two *y* ... 1Kin 15:25 8141
in Tirzah, twenty and four *y* ... 1Kin 15:33 8141
over Israel in Tirzah, two *y* ... 1Kin 16:8 8141
to reign over Israel, twelve *y* ... 1Kin 16:23 8141
six *y* reigned he in Tirzah ... 1Kin 16:23 8141
Israel in Samaria twenty and two *y* ... 1Kin 16:29 8141
shall not be dew nor rain these *y* ... 1Kin 17:1 8141
they continued three *y* without ... 1Kin 22:1 8141
five *y* old when he began to reign ... 1Kin 22:42 8141
twenty and five *y* in Jerusalem ... 1Kin 22:42 8141
and reigned two *y* over Israel ... 1Kin 22:51 8141
of Judah, and reigned twelve *y* ... 2Kin 3:1 8141
also come upon the land seven *y* ... 2Kin 8:1 8141
land of the Philistines seven *y* ... 2Kin 8:2 8141
two *y* old was he when he began to ... 2Kin 8:17 8141
he reigned eight *y* in Jerusalem ... 2Kin 8:17 8141
twenty *y* old was Ahaziah when he ... 2Kin 8:26 8141
in Samaria was twenty and eight *y* ... 2Kin 10:36 8141
in the house of the LORD six *y* ... 2Kin 11:3 8141
Seven *y* old was Jehoash when he ... 2Kin 11:21 8141
forty *y* reigned he in Jerusalem ... 2Kin 12:1 8141
Samaria, and reigned seventeen *y* ... 2Kin 13:1 8141
in Samaria, and reigned sixteen *y* ... 2Kin 13:10 8141
five *y* old when he began to reign ... 2Kin 14:2 8141
twenty and nine *y* in Jerusalem ... 2Kin 14:2 8141
Jehoahaz king of Israel fifteen *y* ... 2Kin 14:17 8141
Azariah, which was sixteen *y* old ... 2Kin 14:21 8141
and reigned forty and one *y* ... 2Kin 14:23 8141
Sixteen *y* old was he when he ... 2Kin 15:2 8141
two and fifty *y* in Jerusalem ... 2Kin 15:2 8141
and reigned ten *y* in Samaria ... 2Kin 15:17 8141
in Samaria, and reigned two *y* ... 2Kin 15:23 8141
in Samaria, and reigned twenty *y* ... 2Kin 15:27 8141
twenty *y* old was he when he began ... 2Kin 15:33 8141
he reigned sixteen *y* in Jerusalem ... 2Kin 15:33 8141
Twenty *y* old was Ahaz when he ... 2Kin 16:2 8141
and reigned sixteen *y* in Jerusalem ... 2Kin 16:2 8141
in Samaria over Israel nine *y* ... 2Kin 17:1 8141
Samaria, and besieged it three *y* ... 2Kin 17:5 8141
five *y* old was he when he began ... 2Kin 18:2 8141
twenty and nine *y* in Jerusalem ... 2Kin 18:2 8141
the end of three *y* they took it ... 2Kin 18:10 8141
will add unto thy days fifteen *y* ... 2Kin 20:6 8141
Manasseh was twelve *y* old when he ... 2Kin 21:1 8141
fifty and five *y* in Jerusalem ... 2Kin 21:1 8141
two *y* old when he began to reign, ... 2Kin 21:19 8141
and he reigned two *y* in Jerusalem ... 2Kin 21:19 8141
Josiah was eight *y* old when he ... 2Kin 22:1 8141
thirty and one *y* in Jerusalem ... 2Kin 22:1 8141
three *y* old when he began to ... 2Kin 23:31 8141
five *y* old when he began to reign ... 2Kin 23:36 8141
he reigned eleven *y* in Jerusalem ... 2Kin 23:36 8141
became his servant three *y* ... 2Kin 24:1 8141
Jehoiachin was eighteen *y* old ... 2Kin 24:8 8141
one *y* old when he began to reign, ... 2Kin 24:18 8141
he reigned eleven *y* in Jerusalem ... 2Kin 24:18 8141
when he was threescore *y* old ... 1Chr 2:21 8141
and there he reigned seven *y* ... 1Chr 3:4 8141
he reigned thirty and three *y* ... 1Chr 3:4 8141
numbered from the age of thirty *y* ... 1Chr 23:3 8141
LORD, from the age of twenty *y* ... 1Chr 23:24 8141
were numbered from twenty *y* old ... 1Chr 23:27 8141
number of them from twenty *y* old ... 1Chr 27:23 8141
reigned over Israel was forty *y* ... 1Chr 29:27 8141
seven *y* reigned he in Hebron, and ... 1Chr 29:27 8141
three *y* reigned he in Jerusalem ... 1Chr 29:27 8141
to pass at the end of twenty *y* ... 2Chr 8:1 8141
every three *y* once came the ships ... 2Chr 9:21 8141
Jerusalem over all Israel forty *y* ... 2Chr 9:30 8141
son of Solomon strong, three *y* ... 2Chr 11:17 8141
for three *y* they walked in the ... 2Chr 11:17 8141
forty *y* old when he began to ... 2Chr 12:13 8141
reigned seventeen *y* in Jerusalem ... 2Chr 12:13 8141
He reigned three *y* in Jerusalem ... 2Chr 13:2 8141
his days the land was quiet ten *y* ... 2Chr 14:1 8141
rest, and he had no war in those *y* ... 2Chr 14:6 8141
after certain *y* he went down to ... 2Chr 18:2 8141
five *y* old when he began to reign ... 2Chr 20:31 8141
twenty and five *y* in Jerusalem ... 2Chr 20:31 8141
two *y* old when he began to reign, ... 2Chr 21:5 8141
he reigned eight *y* in Jerusalem ... 2Chr 21:5 8141
of time, after the end of two *y* ... 2Chr 21:19 3117
two *y* old was he when he began to ... 2Chr 21:20
he reigned in Jerusalem eight *y* ... 2Chr 21:20 8141
two *y* old was Ahaziah when he ... 2Chr 22:2 8141
hid in the house of God six *y* ... 2Chr 22:12 8141
Joash was seven *y* old when he ... 2Chr 24:1 8141
he reigned forty *y* in Jerusalem ... 2Chr 24:1 8141
thirty *y* old was he when he died ... 2Chr 24:15 8141
five *y* old when he began to reign ... 2Chr 25:1 8141
twenty and nine *y* in Jerusalem ... 2Chr 25:1 8141
numbered them from twenty *y* old ... 2Chr 25:5 8141
Jehoahaz king of Israel fifteen *y* ... 2Chr 25:25 8141
Uzziah, who was sixteen *y* old ... 2Chr 26:1 8141
Sixteen *y* old was Uzziah when he ... 2Chr 26:3 8141
fifty and two *y* in Jerusalem ... 2Chr 26:3 8141
five *y* old when he began to reign ... 2Chr 27:1 8141
he reigned sixteen *y* in Jerusalem ... 2Chr 27:1 8141
twenty *y* old when he began to ... 2Chr 27:8 8141
and reigned sixteen *y* in Jerusalem ... 2Chr 27:8 8141
Ahaz was twenty *y* old when he ... 2Chr 28:1 8141
he reigned sixteen *y* in Jerusalem ... 2Chr 28:1 8141
when he was five and twenty *y* old ... 2Chr 29:1 8141
nine and twenty *y* in Jerusalem ... 2Chr 29:1 8141
of males, from three *y* old ... 2Chr 31:16 8141
and the Levites from twenty *y* old ... 2Chr 31:17 8141
Manasseh was twelve *y* old when he ... 2Chr 33:1 8141
fifty and five *y* in Jerusalem ... 2Chr 33:1 8141
twenty *y* old when he began to ... 2Chr 33:21 8141
reigned two *y* in Jerusalem ... 2Chr 33:21 8141
Josiah was eight *y* old when he ... 2Chr 34:1 8141
in Jerusalem one and thirty *y* ... 2Chr 34:1 8141
three *y* old when he began to ... 2Chr 36:2 8141
five *y* old when he began to reign ... 2Chr 36:5 8141
he reigned eleven *y* in Jerusalem ... 2Chr 36:5 8141
Jehoiachin was eight *y* old when ... 2Chr 36:9 8141
twenty *y* old when he began to ... 2Chr 36:11 8141
and reigned eleven *y* in Jerusalem ... 2Chr 36:11 8141
to fulfil threescore and ten *y* ... 2Chr 36:21 8141
the Levites, from twenty *y* old ... Ezr 3:8 8141
that was builded these many *y* ago ... Ezr 5:11 8140
the king, that is, twelve *y* ... Neh 5:14 8141
forty *y* didst thou sustain them ... Neh 9:21 8141
Yet many *y* didst thou forbear ... Neh 9:30 8141
are thy *y* as man's days, ... Job 10:5 8141
the number of *y* is hidden to the ... Job 15:20 8141
When a few *y* are come, then I ... Job 16:22 8141
multitude of *y* should teach ... Job 32:7 8141
and their *y* in pleasures ... Job 36:11 8141
number of his *y* be searched out ... Job 36:26 8141
lived Job an hundred and forty *y* ... Job 42:16 8141
with grief, and my *y* with sighing ... Ps 31:10 8141
his *y* as many generations ... Ps 61:6 8141
of old, the *y* of ancient times ... Ps 77:5 8141
but I will remember the *y* of the ... Ps 77:10 8141
in vanity, and their *y* in trouble ... Ps 78:33 8141
For a thousand *y* in thy sight are ... Ps 90:4 8141
we spend our *y* as a tale that is ... Ps 90:9 8141
of our *y* are threescore *y* ... Ps 90:10 8141
of strength they be fourscore *y* ... Ps 90:10 8141
the *y* wherein we have seen evil ... Ps 90:15 8141
Forty *y* long was I grieved with ... Ps 95:10 8141
thy *y* are throughout all ... Ps 102:24 8141
same, and thy *y* shall have no end ... Ps 102:27 8141
the *y* of thy life shall be many ... Prov 4:10 8141
others, and thy *y* unto the cruel ... Prov 5:9 8141
the *y* of thy life shall be ... Prov 9:11 8141
but the *y* of the wicked shall be ... Prov 10:27 8141
hundred children, and live many *y* ... Eccl 6:3 8141
so that the days of his *y* be many ... Eccl 6:3 8141
he live a thousand *y* twice told ... Eccl 6:6 8141
But if a man live many *y*, and ... Eccl 11:8 8141
nor the *y* draw nigh, when thou ... Eccl 12:1 8141
five *y* shall Ephraim be broken, ... Is 7:8 8141
Zoar, an heifer of three *y* old ... Is 15:5
spoken, saying, Within three *y* ... Is 16:14 8141
as the *y* of an hireling, and the ... Is 16:14 8141
and barefoot three *y* for a sign ... Is 20:3 8141
according to the *y* of an hireling ... Is 21:16 8141
Tyre shall be forgotten seventy *y* ... Is 23:15 8141
after the end of seventy *y* shall ... Is 23:15 8141
pass after the end of seventy *y* ... Is 23:17 8141
y shall ye be troubled, ye ... Is 32:10 8141
will add unto thy days fifteen *y* ... Is 38:5 8141
deprived of the residue of my *y* ... Is 38:10 8141
I shall go softly all my *y* in the ... Is 38:15 8141
child shall die an hundred *y* old ... Is 65:20 8141
hundred *y* old shall be accursed ... Is 65:20 8141
the king of Babylon seventy *y* ... Jer 25:11 8141
when seventy *y* are accomplished, ... Jer 25:12 8141
Within two full *y* will I bring ... Jer 28:3 8141
within the space of two full *y* ... Jer 28:11 8141
the LORD, That after seventy *y* be ... Jer 29:10 8141
At the end of seven *y* let ye go ... Jer 34:14 8141
and when he hath served thee six *y* ... Jer 34:14 8141
as an heifer of three *y* old ... Jer 48:34
twenty *y* old when he began to ... Jer 52:1 8141
he reigned eleven *y* in Jerusalem ... Jer 52:1 8141
upon thee the *y* of their iniquity ... Eze 4:5 8141
near, and art come even unto thy *y* ... Eze 22:4 8141
shall it be inhabited forty *y* ... Eze 29:11 8141
waste shall be desolate forty *y* ... Eze 29:12 8141
At the end of forty *y* will I ... Eze 29:13 8141
in the latter *y* thou shalt come ... Eze 38:8 8141
prophesied in those days many *y* ... Eze 38:17 8141
shall burn them with fire seven *y* ... Eze 39:9 8141
so nourishing them three *y* ... Dan 1:5 8141
about threescore and two *y* old ... Dan 5:31 8140
by books the number of the *y* ... Dan 9:2 8141
he would accomplish seventy *y* in ... Dan 9:2 8141
in the end of *y* they shall join ... Dan 11:6 8141
he shall continue more *y* than the ... Dan 11:8 8141
after certain *y* with a great army ... Dan 11:13 8141
even to the *y* of many generations ... Joel 2:2 8141
I will restore to you the *y* that ... Joel 2:25 8141
two *y* before the earthquake ... Amos 1:1 8141
led you forty *y* through the ... Amos 2:10 8141

and your tithes after three y ... Amos 4:4 3117
in the wilderness forty y ... Amos 5:25 8141
thy work in the midst of the y ... Hab 3:2 8141
in the midst of the y make known ... Hab 3:2 8141
these threescore and ten y ... Zec 1:12 8141
as I have done these so many y ... Zec 7:3 8141
month, even those seventy y ... Zec 7:5 8141
days of old, and as in former y ... Mal 3:4 8141
coasts thereof, from two y old ... Mt 2:16 *1332*
with an issue of blood twelve y ... Mt 9:20 *2094*
had an issue of blood twelve y ... Mk 5:25 *2094*
she was of the age of twelve y ... Mk 5:42 *2094*
both were now well stricken in y ... Lk 1:7 *2250*
and my wife well stricken in y ... Lk 1:18 *2250*
seven y from her virginity ... Lk 2:36 *2094*
of about fourscore and four y ... Lk 2:37 *2094*
And when he was twelve y old ... Lk 2:42 *2094*
began to be about thirty y of age ... Lk 3:23 *2094*
the heaven was shut up three y ... Lk 4:25 *2094*
daughter, about twelve y of age ... Lk 8:42 *2094*
having an issue of blood twelve y ... Lk 8:43 *2094*
much goods laid up for many y ... Lk 12:19 *2094*
these three y I come seeking ... Lk 13:7 *2094*
a spirit of infirmity eighteen y ... Lk 13:11 *2094*
hath bound, lo, these eighteen y ... Lk 13:16 *2094*
these many y do I serve thee, ... Lk 15:29 *2094*
six y was this temple in building ... Jn 2:20 *2094*
an infirmity thirty and eight y ... Jn 5:5 *2094*
him, Thou art not yet fifty y old ... Jn 8:57 *2094*
For the man was above forty y old ... Acts 4:22 *2094*
entreat them evil four hundred y ... Acts 7:6 *2094*
And when he was full forty y old ... Acts 7:23 *5063*
when forty y were expired, there ... Acts 7:30 *2094*
sea, and in the wilderness forty y ... Acts 7:36 *2094*
of forty y in the wilderness ... Acts 7:42 *2094*
which had kept his bed eight y ... Acts 9:33 *2094*
about the time of forty y ... Acts 13:18 *5063*
space of four hundred and fifty y ... Acts 13:20 *2094*
Benjamin, by the space of forty y ... Acts 13:21 *2094*
continued by the space of two y ... Acts 19:10 *2094*
that by the space of three y I ... Acts 20:31 *5148*
many y a judge unto this nation ... Acts 24:10 *2094*
Now after many y I came to bring ... Acts 24:17 *2094*
But after two y Porcius Festus ... Acts 24:27 *1333*
Paul dwelt two whole y in his own ... Acts 28:30 *1333*
he was about an hundred y old ... Rom 4:19 *1541*
these many y to come unto you ... Rom 15:23 *2094*
in Christ above fourteen y ago ... 2Cor 12:2 *2094*
Then after three y I went up to ... Gal 1:18 *2094*
Then fourteen y after I went up ... Gal 2:1 *2094*
four hundred and thirty y after ... Gal 3:17 *2094*
days, and months, and times, and y ... Gal 4:10 *1763*
the number under threescore y old ... 1Ti 5:9 *2094*
the same, and thy y shall not fail ... Heb 1:12 *2094*
me, and saw my works forty y ... Heb 3:9 *2094*
with whom was he grieved forty y ... Heb 3:17 *2094*
Moses, when he was come to y ... Heb 11:24 *1096,3173*
the earth by the space of three y ... Jas 5:17 *1763*
is with the Lord as a thousand y ... 2Pet 3:8 *2094*
and a thousand y as one day ... 2Pet 3:8 *2094*
Satan, and bound him a thousand y ... Rev 20:2 *2094*
till the thousand y should be ... Rev 20:3 *2094*
reigned with Christ a thousand y ... Rev 20:4 *2094*
the thousand y were finished ... Rev 20:5 *2094*
shall reign with him a thousand y ... Rev 20:6 *2094*
when the thousand y are expired ... Rev 20:7 *2094*

YEARS' {2}
came to pass at the seven y end ... 2Kin 8:3 8141
Either three y famine ... 1Chr 21:12 8141

YELL {1}
they shall y as lions' whelps ... Jer 51:38 5286

YELLED {1}
lions roared upon him, and y ... Jer 2:15 5414,6963

YELLOW {4}
and there be in it a y thin hair ... Lev 13:30 6669
not, and there be in it no y hair ... Lev 13:32 6669
priest shall not seek for y hair ... Lev 13:36 6669
and her feathers with y gold ... Ps 68:13 3422

YES See APPENDIX.

YESTERDAY {9}
your task in making brick both y ... Ex 5:14 8543
son of Jesse to meat, neither y ... 1Sa 20:27 8543
Whereas thou camest but y ... 2Sa 15:20 8543
Surely I have seen y the blood of ... 2Kin 9:26 570
(For we are but of y, and know ... Job 8:9 8543
are but as y when it is past ... Ps 90:4 865
Y at the seventh hour the fever ... Jn 4:52 *5504*
as thou diddest the Egyptian y ... Acts 7:28 *5504*
Jesus Christ the same y, and to ... Heb 13:8 *5504*

YESTERNIGHT {3}
Behold, I lay y with my father ... Gen 19:34 570
of your father spake unto me y ... Gen 31:29 570
of my hands, and rebuked thee y ... Gen 31:42 570

YET See APPENDIX.

YIELD {30}
y unto thee her strength ... Gen 4:12 5414
he shall y royal dainties ... Gen 49:20 5414
that it may y unto you the ... Lev 19:25 3254
And the land shall y her fruit ... Lev 25:19 5414
and the land shall y her increase ... Lev 26:4 5414
of the field shall y their fruit ... Lev 26:4 5414
land shall not y her increase ... Lev 26:20 5414
trees of the land y their fruits ... Lev 26:20 5414
and that the land y not her fruit ... Deut 11:17 5414
but y yourselves unto the LORD, ... 2Chr 30:8 5414,3027
shall the earth y her increase ... Ps 67:6 5414
and our land shall y her increase ... Ps 85:12 5414
which may y fruits of increase ... Ps 107:37 6213
fair speech she caused him to y ... Prov 7:21 5186
of vineyard shall y one bath ... Is 5:10 6213
seed of an homer shall y an ephah ... Is 5:10 6213
of the field shall y her fruit ... Eze 34:27 5414
and the earth shall y her increase ... Eze 34:27 5414
y your fruit to my people of ... Eze 36:8 5375
the bud shall y no meal ... Hos 8:7 6213
if so be it y, the strangers ... Hos 8:7 6213
the vine do y their strength ... Joel 2:22 5414
and the fields shall y no meat ... Hab 3:17 6213
did y fruit that sprang up and ... Mk 4:8 *1325*
But do not thou y unto them ... Acts 23:21 *3982*
Neither y ye your members as ... Rom 6:13 *3936*
but y yourselves unto God, as ... Rom 6:13 *3936*
that to whom ye y yourselves ... Rom 6:16 *3936*
even so now y your members ... Rom 6:19 *3936*
can no fountain both y salt water ... Jas 3:12 *4160*

YIELDED {8}
y up the ghost, and was gathered ... Gen 49:33 1478
and bloomed blossoms, and y almonds ... Num 17:8 1580
y their bodies, that they might ... Dan 3:28 3052
with a loud voice, y up the ghost ... Mt 27:50 *863*
and choked it, and it y no fruit ... Mk 4:7 *1325*
at his feet, and y up the ghost ... Acts 5:10 *1634*
for as ye have y your members ... Rom 6:19 *3936*
and y her fruit every month ... Rev 22:2 *591*

YIELDETH {4}
it y much increase unto the kings ... Neh 9:37 7235
the wilderness y food for them ... Job 24:5
the root of the righteous y fruit ... Prov 12:12 5414
it y the peaceable fruit of ... Heb 12:11 *591*

YIELDING {7}
forth grass, the herb y seed ... Gen 1:11 2232
the fruit tree y fruit after his ... Gen 1:11 6213
herb y seed after his kind, and ... Gen 1:12 2232
his kind, and the tree y fruit ... Gen 1:12 6213
is the fruit of a tree y seed ... Gen 1:29 2232
for y pacifieth great offences ... Eccl 10:4 4832
neither shall cease from y fruit ... Jer 17:8 6213

YIRON See IRON

YOKE {59}
break his y from off thy neck ... Gen 27:40 5923
I have broken the bands of your y ... Lev 26:13 5923
and upon which never came y ... Num 19:2 5923
and which hath not drawn in the y ... Deut 21:3 5923
he shall put a y of iron upon thy ... Deut 28:48 5923
on which there hath come no y ... 1Sa 6:7 5923
And he took a y of oxen, and hewed ... 1Sa 11:7 6776
which a y of oxen might plow ... 1Sa 14:14 6776
Thy father made our y grievous ... 1Kin 12:4 5923
his heavy y which he put upon us, ... 1Kin 12:4 5923
Make the y which thy father did ... 1Kin 12:9 5923
Thy father made our y heavy ... 1Kin 12:10 5923
heavy y, I will add to your y ... 1Kin 12:11 5923
My father made your y heavy ... 1Kin 12:14 5923
and I will add to your y ... 1Kin 12:14 5923
with twelve y of oxen before him ... 1Kin 19:19 6776
took a y of oxen, and slew them, ... 1Kin 19:21 6776
Thy father made our y grievous ... 2Chr 10:4 5923
his heavy y that he put upon us, ... 2Chr 10:4 5923
Ease somewhat the y that thy ... 2Chr 10:9 5923
Thy father made our y heavy ... 2Chr 10:10 5923
my father put a heavy y upon you ... 2Chr 10:11 5923
you, I will put more to your y ... 2Chr 10:11 5923
My father made your y heavy ... 2Chr 10:14 5923
camels, and five hundred y of oxen ... Job 1:3 6776
camels, and a thousand y of oxen ... Job 42:12 6776
hast broken the y of his burden ... Is 9:4 5923
his y from off thy neck, and the ... Is 10:27 5923
the y shall be destroyed because ... Is 10:27 5923
then shall his y depart from off ... Is 14:25 5923
hast thou very heavily laid thy y ... Is 47:6 5923
go free, and that ye break every y ... Is 58:6 4133
away from the midst of thee the y ... Is 58:9 4133
of old time I have broken thy y ... Jer 2:20 5923
have altogether broken the y ... Jer 5:5 5923
the y of the king of Babylon ... Jer 27:8 5923
the y of the king of Babylon ... Jer 27:11 5923
the y of the king of Babylon ... Jer 27:12 5923
I have broken the y of the king ... Jer 28:2 5923
for I will break the y of the ... Jer 28:4 5923
Hananiah the prophet took the y ... Jer 28:10 4133
Even so will I break the y of ... Jer 28:11 5923
the y from off the neck of the ... Jer 28:12 4133
I have put a y of iron upon the ... Jer 28:14 5923
break his y from off thy neck ... Jer 30:8 5923
a bullock unaccustomed to the y ... Jer 31:18
the husbandman and his y of oxen ... Jer 51:23 6776
The y of my transgressions is ... Lam 1:14 5923
that he bear the y in his youth ... Lam 3:27 5923
have broken the bands of their y ... Eze 34:27 5923
that take off the y on their jaws ... Hos 11:4 5923
will I break his y from off thee ... Nah 1:13 4132
Take my y upon you, and learn of ... Mt 11:29 *2218*
For my y is easy, and my burden is ... Mt 11:30 *2218*
I have bought five y of oxen ... Lk 14:19 *2201*
to put a y upon the neck of the ... Acts 15:10 *2218*
again with the y of bondage ... Gal 5:1 *2218*
y count their own masters worthy ... 1Ti 6:1 *2218*

YOKED {1}
Be ye not unequally y together ... 2Cor 6:14 *2086*

YOKEFELLOW {1}
And I intreat thee also, true y ... Phil 4:3 *4805*

YOKES {4}
Make thee bonds and y, and put them ... Jer 27:2 4133
Thou hast broken the y of wood ... Jer 28:13 4133
shalt make for them y of iron ... Jer 28:13 4133
shall break there the y of Egypt ... Eze 30:18 4133

YONDER {7}
and I and the lad will go y ... Gen 22:5 3541
and scatter thou the fire y ... Num 16:37 1973
offering, while I meet the LORD y ... Num 23:15 3541
with them on y side Jordan ... Num 32:19 5676
Behold, y is that Shunammite ... 2Kin 4:25 5704,3541
mountain, Remove hence to y place ... Mt 17:20 *1563*
Sit ye here, while I go and pray y ... Mt 26:36 *1563*

YOU See APPENDIX.

YOUNG {301}
wounding, and a y man to my hurt ... Gen 4:23 3206
that which the y men have eaten ... Gen 14:24 5288
and a turtledove, and a y pigeon ... Gen 15:9 1469
and good, and gave it unto a y man ... Gen 18:7 5288
the house round, both old and y ... Gen 19:4 5288
and took two of his y men with him ... Gen 22:3 5288
And Abraham said unto his y men ... Gen 22:5 5288
Abraham returned unto his y men ... Gen 22:19 5288
she goats have not cast their y ... Gen 31:38
and herds with y are with me ... Gen 33:13 5763
the y man deferred not to do the ... Gen 34:19 5288
there was there with us a y man ... Gen 41:12 5288
Moses said, We will go with our y ... Ex 10:9 5288
There shall nothing cast their y ... Ex 23:26
he sent y men of the children of ... Ex 24:5 5288
Take one y bullock, and two rams ... Ex 29:1 1121,1241
a y man, departed not out of the ... Ex 33:11 5288
of turtledoves, or of y pigeons ... Lev 1:14 1121
a y bullock without blemish unto ... Lev 4:3 1121,1241
offer a y bullock for the sin ... Lev 4:14 1121,1241
or two y pigeons, unto the LORD ... Lev 5:7 1121
or two y pigeons, then he that ... Lev 5:11 1121
Take thee a y calf for a sin ... Lev 9:2 1121,1241
a y pigeon, or a turtledove, for ... Lev 12:6 1121
two turtles, or two y pigeons ... Lev 12:8 1121
or two y pigeons, such as he is ... Lev 14:22 1121
turtledoves, or of the y pigeons ... Lev 14:30 1121
or two y pigeons, and come before ... Lev 15:14 1121
or two y pigeons, and bring them ... Lev 15:29 1121
with a y bullock for a sin ... Lev 16:3 1121,1241
kill it and her y both in one day ... Lev 22:28 1121
one y bullock, and two rams ... Lev 23:18 1121,1241
or two y pigeons, to the priest, ... Num 6:10 1121
One y bullock, one ram, one lamb ... Num 7:15 1121,1241
One y bullock, one ram, one lamb ... Num 7:21 1121,1241
One y bullock, one ram, one lamb ... Num 7:27 1121,1241
One y bullock, one ram, one lamb ... Num 7:33 1121,1241
One y bullock, one ram, one lamb ... Num 7:39 1121,1241
One y bullock, one ram, one lamb ... Num 7:45 1121,1241
One y bullock, one ram, one lamb ... Num 7:51 1121,1241
One y bullock, one ram, one lamb ... Num 7:57 1121,1241
One y bullock, one ram, one lamb ... Num 7:63 1121,1241
One y bullock, one ram, one lamb ... Num 7:69 1121,1241
One y bullock, one ram, one lamb ... Num 7:75 1121,1241
One y bullock, one ram, one lamb ... Num 7:81 1121,1241
Then let them take a y bullock ... Num 8:8 1121,1241
another y bullock shalt thou take ... Num 8:8 1121,1241
And there ran a y man, and told ... Num 11:27 5288
of Moses, one of his y men ... Num 11:28 979
y bullock for a burnt offering ... Num 15:24 1121,1241
and lift up himself as a y lion ... Num 23:24
y bullocks, and one ram, seven ... Num 28:11 1121,1241
two y bullocks, and one ram, and ... Num 28:19 1121,1241
two y bullocks, one ram, seven ... Num 28:27 1121,1241
one y bullock, one ram, and seven ... Num 29:2 1121,1241
one y bullock, one ram, and seven ... Num 29:8 1121,1241
thirteen y bullocks, two rams, and ... Num 29:13 1121,1241
ye shall offer twelve y bullocks ... Num 29:17 1121,1241
ground, whether they be y ones ... Deut 22:6 667
and the dam sitting upon the y ... Deut 22:6 667
shalt not take the dam with the y ... Deut 22:6 1121
the dam go, and take the y to thee ... Deut 22:7 1121
the old, nor shew favour to the y ... Deut 28:50 5288
toward her y one that cometh out ... Deut 28:57 7988
her nest, fluttereth over her y ... Deut 32:11 1469
shall destroy both the y man ... Deut 32:25 970
in the city, both man and woman, y ... Josh 6:21 5288
the y men that were spies went in ... Josh 6:23 5288
him, Take thy father's y bullock ... Judg 6:25 6499
caught a y man of the men of ... Judg 8:14 5288
unto the y man his armourbearer ... Judg 9:54 5288
his y man thrust him through, and ... Judg 9:54 5288
a y lion roared against him ... Judg 14:5 3715
for so used the y men to do ... Judg 14:10 970
And there was a y man out of ... Judg 17:7 5288
the y man was unto him as one of ... Judg 17:11 5288
the y man became his priest, and ... Judg 17:12 5288
the voice of the y man the Levite ... Judg 18:3 5288
the house of the y man the Levite ... Judg 18:15 5288
for the y man which is with thy ... Judg 19:19 5288
four hundred y virgins, that had ... Judg 21:12 5291
have I not charged the y men that ... Ruth 2:9 5288
that which the y men have drawn ... Ruth 2:9 5288
glean, Boaz commanded his y men ... Ruth 2:15 5288
Thou shalt keep fast by my y men ... Ruth 2:21 5288
as thou followedst not y men ... Ruth 3:10 970
shall give thee of this y woman ... Ruth 4:12 5291
and the child was y ... 1Sa 1:24 5288

Wherefore the sin of the *y* men 1Sa 2:17 5288
and your goodliest *y* men, and your 1Sa 8:16 970
name was Saul, a choice *y* man 1Sa 9:2 970
they found *y* maidens going out to 1Sa 9:11 5291
the *y* man that bare his armour 1Sa 14:1 5288
Jonathan said to the *y* man that 1Sa 14:6 5288
Whose son art thou, thou *y* man 1Sa 17:58 5288
But if I say thus unto the *y* man 1Sa 20:22 5958
if the *y* men have kept themselves 1Sa 21:4 5288
the vessels of the *y* men are holy 1Sa 21:5 5288
And David sent out ten *y* men 1Sa 25:5 5288
men, and David said unto the *y* men 1Sa 25:5 5288
Ask thy *y* men, and they will shew 1Sa 25:8 5288
Wherefore let the *y* men find 1Sa 25:8 5288
And when David's *y* men came 1Sa 25:9 5288
So David's *y* men turned their way 1Sa 25:12 5288
But one of the *y* men told Abigail 1Sa 25:14 5288
saw not the *y* men of my lord 1Sa 25:25 5288
the *y* men that follow my lord 1Sa 25:27 5288
and let one of the *y* men come over 1Sa 26:22 5288
I am a *y* man of Egypt, servant to 1Sa 30:13 5288
of them, save four hundred *y* men 1Sa 30:17 5288
said unto the *y* man that told him 2Sa 1:5 5288
the *y* man that told him said, As 2Sa 1:6 5288
said unto the *y* man that told him 2Sa 1:13 5288
And David called one of the *y* men 2Sa 1:15 5288
Let the *y* men now arise, and play 2Sa 2:14 5288
lay thee hold on one of the *y* men 2Sa 2:21 5288
And David commanded his *y* men 2Sa 4:12 5288
And Mephibosheth had a *y* son 2Sa 9:12 6996
all the *y* men the king's sons 2Sa 13:32 5288
the *y* man that kept the watch 2Sa 13:34 5288
bring the *y* man Absalom again 2Sa 14:21 5288
summer fruit for the *y* men to eat 2Sa 16:2 5288
gently for my sake with the *y* man 2Sa 18:5 5288
that none touch the *y* man Absalom 2Sa 18:12 5288
ten *y* men that bare Joab's armour 2Sa 18:15 5288
Is the *y* man Absalom safe 2Sa 18:29 5288
Is the *y* man Absalom safe 2Sa 18:32 5288
do thee hurt, be as that *y* man is 2Sa 18:32 5288
for my lord the king a *y* virgin 1Kin 1:2 5291
Solomon seeing the *y* man that he 1Kin 11:28 5288
consulted with the *y* men that 1Kin 12:8 3206
the *y* men that were grown up with 1Kin 12:10 3206
after the counsel of the *y* men 1Kin 12:14 3206
Even by the *y* men of the princes 1Kin 20:14 5288
Then he numbered the *y* men of the 1Kin 20:15 5288
the *y* men of the princes of the 1Kin 20:17 5288
So these *y* men of the princes of 1Kin 20:19 5288
me, I pray thee, one of the *y* men 2Kin 4:22 5288
to me from mount Ephraim two *y* 2Kin 5:22 5288
LORD opened the eyes of the *y* man 2Kin 6:17 5288
their *y* men wilt thou slay with 2Kin 8:12 970
So the *y* man, even the *y* man 2Kin 9:4 5288
even the *y* man the prophet, went 2Kin 9:4 5288
a *y* man mighty of valour, and of 1Chr 12:28 5288
David said, Solomon my son is *y* 1Chr 22:5 5288
alone God hath chosen, is yet *y* 1Chr 29:1 5288
took counsel with the *y* men that 2Chr 10:8 3206
the *y* men that were brought up 2Chr 10:10 3206
after the advice of the *y* men 2Chr 10:14 3206
of Solomon, when Rehoboam was *y* 2Chr 13:7 5288
himself with a *y* bullock and seven 2Chr 13:9 1121,1241
of his reign, while he was yet *y* 2Chr 34:3 5288
who slew their *y* men with the 2Chr 36:17 970
compassion upon *y* man or maiden 2Chr 36:17 970
both *y* bullocks, and rams, and Ezr 6:9 1123
Let there be fair *y* virgins Est 2:2 5291
gather together all the fair *y* Est 2:3 5291
cause to perish, all Jews, both *y* Est 3:13 5288
mules, camels, and *y* dromedaries Est 8:10 1121
house, and it fell upon the *y* men Job 1:19 5288
lion, and the teeth of the *y* lions Job 4:10 3715
Yea, *y* children despised me Job 19:18
The *y* men saw me, and hid Job 29:8 5288
Buzite answered and said, I am *y* Job 32:6 6810,3117
fill the appetite of the *y* lions Job 38:39 3715
when his *y* ones cry unto God, Job 38:41 3206
they bring forth their *y* ones Job 39:3 3206
Their *y* ones are in good liking, Job 39:4 1121
is hardened against her *y* ones Job 39:16 1121
Her *y* ones also suck up blood Job 39:30 667
as it were a *y* lion lurking in Ps 17:12 3715
and Sirion like a *y* unicorn Ps 29:6 1121
The *y* lions do lack, and suffer Ps 34:10 3715
I have been *y*, and now am old Ps 37:25 5288
the great teeth of the *y* lions Ps 58:6 3715
The fire consumed their *y* men Ps 78:63 970
y he brought him to feed Jacob Ps 78:71 5763
herself, where she may lay her *y* Ps 84:3 667
the *y* lion and the dragon shalt Ps 91:13 3715
The *y* lions roar after their prey Ps 104:21 3715
shall a *y* man cleanse his way Ps 119:9 5288
to the *y* ravens which cry Ps 147:9 1121
Both *y* men, and maidens Ps 148:12 970
to the *y* man knowledge and Prov 1:4 5288
a *y* man void of understanding, Prov 7:7 5288
The glory of *y* men is their Prov 20:29 970
the *y* eagles shall eat it Prov 30:17 1121
Rejoice, O *y* man, in thy youth Eccl 11:9 970
beloved is like a roe or a *y* hart Song 2:9 6082
be thou like a roe or a *y* hart Song 2:17 6082
like two *y* roes that are twins Song 4:5 6082
like two *y* roes that are twins Song 7:3 6082
to a *y* hart upon the mountains of Song 8:14 6082
they shall roar like *y* lions Is 5:29 3715
that a man shall nourish a *y* cow Is 7:21 1241
shall have no joy in their *y* men Is 9:17 970
the *y* lion and the fatling Is 11:6 3715
their *y* ones shall lie down Is 11:7 3206
shall dash the *y* men to pieces Is 13:18 5288
and the Ethiopians captives, *y* Is 20:4 5288
neither do I nourish up *y* men Is 23:4 970
anguish, from whence come the *y* Is 30:6 3833
upon the shoulders of *y* asses Is 30:6
the *y* asses that ear the ground Is 30:24
the *y* lion roaring on his prey, Is 31:4 3715
his *y* men shall be discomfited Is 31:8 970
gently lead those that are with *y* Is 40:11 5763
the *y* men shall utterly fall Is 40:30 5288,970
For as a *y* man marrieth a virgin, Is 62:5 970
The *y* lions roared upon him, and Jer 2:15 3715
the assembly of *y* men together Jer 6:11 970
the *y* men from the streets Jer 9:21 970
the *y* men shall die by the sword Jer 11:22 970
of the *y* men a spoiler at noonday Jer 15:8 970
let their *y* men be slain by the Jer 18:21 970
for the *y* of the flock and of the Jer 31:12 1121
rejoice in the dance, both *y* men Jer 31:13 970
his chosen *y* men are gone down to Jer 48:15 970
Therefore her *y* men shall fall in Jer 49:26 970
Therefore shall her *y* men fall in Jer 50:30 970
and spare ye not her *y* men Jer 51:3 970
will I break in pieces old and *y* Jer 51:22 5288
will I break in pieces the *y* man Jer 51:22 970
against me to crush my *y* men Lam 1:15 970
my *y* men are gone into captivity Lam 1:18 970
for the life of thy *y* children Lam 2:19
The *y* and the old lie on the Lam 2:21 5288
my *y* men are fallen by the sword Lam 2:21 970
they give suck to their *y* ones Lam 4:3 1482
the *y* children ask bread, and no Lam 4:4
They took the *y* men to grind Lam 5:13 970
the *y* men from their musick Lam 5:14 970
Slay utterly old and *y*, both maids Eze 9:6 970
off the top of his *y* twigs Eze 17:4 3242
top of his *y* twigs a tender one Eze 17:22 3127
her whelps among *y* lions Eze 19:2 3715
it became a *y* lion, and it learned Eze 19:3 3715
her whelps, and made him a *y* lion Eze 19:5 3715
the lions, he became a *y* lion Eze 19:6 3715
all of them desirable *y* men Eze 23:6 970
all of them desirable *y* men Eze 23:12 970
all of them desirable *y* men Eze 23:23 970
The *y* men of Aven and of Pi-beseth Eze 30:17 970
of the field bring forth their *y* Eze 31:6
Thou art like a *y* lion of the Eze 32:2 3715
with all the *y* lions thereof, Eze 38:13 3715
the face of a *y* lion toward the Eze 41:19 3715
a *y* bullock for a sin offering Eze 43:19 1121,1241
thou shalt offer a *y* bullock Eze 43:23 1121,1241
shall also prepare a *y* bullock Eze 43:25 1121,1241
thou shalt take a *y* bullock Eze 45:18 1121,1241
be a *y* bullock without blemish Eze 46:6 1121,1241
as a *y* lion to the house of Judah Hos 5:14 3715
your *y* men shall see visions Joel 2:28 970
of your *y* men for Nazarites Amos 2:11 970
will a *y* lion cry out of his den, Amos 3:4 3715
your *y* men have I slain with the Amos 4:10 970
virgins and *y* men faint for thirst Amos 8:13 970
as a *y* lion among the flocks of Mic 5:8 3715
the feeding place of the *y* lions Nah 2:11 3715
sword shall devour thy *y* lions Nah 2:13 3715
her *y* children also were dashed Nah 3:10
him, Run, speak to this *y* man Zec 2:4 5288
shall make the *y* men cheerful Zec 9:17 970
a voice of the roaring of *y* lions Zec 11:3 3715
off, neither shall seek the *y* one Zec 11:16 5288
search diligently for the *y* child Mt 2:8 *3813*
stood over where the *y* child was Mt 2:9 *3813*
they saw the *y* child with Mary Mt 2:11 *3813*
Arise, and take the *y* child Mt 2:13 *3813*
seek the *y* child to destroy him Mt 2:13 *3813*
he arose, he took the *y* child Mt 2:14 *3813*
Arise, and take the *y* child Mt 2:20 *3813*
which sought the *y* child's life Mt 2:20 *3813*
And he arose, and took the *y* child Mt 2:21 *3813*
The *y* man saith unto him, All Mt 19:20 *3495*
But when the *y* man heard that Mt 19:22 *3495*
whose *y* daughter had an unclean Mk 7:25 *2365*
they brought *y* children to him, Mk 10:13 *3813*
followed him a certain *y* man Mk 14:51 *3495*
the *y* men laid hold on him Mk 14:51 *3495*
they saw a *y* man sitting on the Mk 16:5 *3495*
of turtledoves, or two *y* pigeons Lk 2:24 *3502*
Y man, I say unto thee, Arise Lk 7:14 *3495*
Jesus, when he had found a *y* ass Jn 12:14 *3678*
I say unto thee, When thou wast *y* Jn 21:18 *3501*
your *y* men shall see visions, and Acts 2:17 *3495*
the *y* men arose, wound him up, and Acts 5:6 *3501*
the *y* men came in, and found her Acts 5:10 *3495*
they cast out their *y* children Acts 7:19 *1025*
their clothes at a *y* man's feet Acts 7:58 *3494*
a certain *y* man named Eutychus Acts 20:9 *3494*
And they brought the *y* man alive Acts 20:12 *3816*
Bring this *y* man unto the chief Acts 23:17 *3494*
me to bring this *y* man unto thee Acts 23:18 *3494*
captain then let the *y* man depart Acts 23:22 *3494*
may teach the *y* women to be sober Titus 2:4 *3501*
Y men likewise exhort to be sober Titus 2:6 *3501*
y men, because ye have overcome 1Jn 2:13 *3495*
y men, because ye are strong, and 1Jn 2:14 *3495*

YOUNGER {31}

knew what his *y* son had done unto Gen 9:24 6996
And the firstborn said unto the *y* Gen 19:31 6810
the firstborn said unto the *y* Gen 19:34 6810
the *y* arose, and lay with him Gen 19:35 6810
And the *y*, she also bare a son, and Gen 19:38 6810
and the elder shall serve the *y* Gen 25:23 6810
and put them upon Jacob her *y* son Gen 27:15 6996
sent and called Jacob her *y* son Gen 27:42 6996
and the name of the *y* was Rachel Gen 29:16 6996
years for Rachel thy *y* daughter Gen 29:18 6996
country, to give the *y* before the Gen 29:26 6810
and said, Is this your *y* brother Gen 43:29 6996
Ephraim's head, who was the *y* Gen 48:14 6810
but truly his *y* brother shall be Gen 48:19 6996
son of Kenaz, Caleb's *y* brother Judg 1:13 6996
son of Kenaz, Caleb's *y* brother Judg 3:9 6996
is not her *y* sister fairer than Judg 15:2 6996
and the name of the *y* Michal 1Sa 14:49 6996
over against their *y* brethren 1Chr 24:31 6996
But now they that are *y* than I Job 30:1 6810,3117
thy *y* sister, that dwelleth at Eze 16:46 6996
thy sisters, thine elder and thy *y* Eze 16:61 6996
the *y* of them said to his father, Lk 15:12 *3501*
not many days after the *y* son Lk 15:13 *3501*
among you, let him be as the *y* Lk 22:26 *3501*
her, The elder shall serve the *y* Rom 9:12 *1640*
and the *y* men as brethren 1Ti 5:1 *3501*
the *y* as sisters, with all purity 1Ti 5:2 *3501*
But the *y* widows refuse 1Ti 5:11 *3501*
therefore that the *y* women marry 1Ti 5:14 *3501*
Likewise, ye *y*, submit yourselves 1Pet 5:5 *3501*

YOUNGEST {18}

the *y* is this day with our father Gen 42:13 6996
except your *y* brother come hither Gen 42:15 6996
But bring your *y* brother unto me Gen 42:20 6996
the *y* is this day with our father Gen 42:32 6996
bring your *y* brother unto me Gen 42:34 6996
the *y* according to his youth Gen 43:33 6810
cup, in the sack's mouth of the *y* Gen 44:2 6996
at the eldest, and left at the *y* Gen 44:12 6996
Except your *y* brother come down Gen 44:23 6996
if our *y* brother be with us, then Gen 44:26 6996
except our *y* brother be with us Gen 44:26 6996
in his *y* son shall he set up the Josh 6:26 6810
the *y* son of Jerubbaal was left Judg 9:5 6996
said, There remaineth yet the *y* 1Sa 16:11 6996
And David was the *y* 1Sa 17:14 6996
gates thereof in his *y* son Segub 1Kin 16:34 6810
save Jehoahaz, the *y* of his sons 2Chr 21:17 6996
his *y* son king in his stead 2Chr 22:1 6996

YOUR See APPENDIX.

YOURS See APPENDIX.

YOURSELVES See APPENDIX.

YOUTH {70}

of man's heart is evil from his *y* Gen 8:21 5271
the youngest according to his *y* Gen 43:33 6812
cattle from our *y* even until now Gen 46:34 5271
her father's house, as in her *y* Lev 22:13 5271
in her father's house in her *y* Num 30:3 5271
being yet in her *y* in her Num 30:16 5271
But the *y* drew not his sword Judg 8:20 5288
he feared, because he was yet a *y* Judg 8:20 5288
for thou art but a *y*, and he a man 1Sa 17:33 5288
and he a man of war from his *y* 1Sa 17:33 5271
for he was but a *y*, and ruddy, and 1Sa 17:42 5288
host, Abner, whose son is this *y* 1Sa 17:55 5288
befell thee from thy *y* until now 2Sa 19:7 5271
servant fear the LORD from my *y* 1Kin 18:12 5271
to possess the iniquities of my *y* Job 13:26 5271
are full of the sin of his *y* Job 20:11 5934
As I was in the days of my *y* Job 29:4 2779
Upon my right hand rise the *y* Job 30:12 6526
(For from my *y* he was brought up Job 31:18 5271
shall return to the days of his *y* Job 33:25 5934
They die in *y*, and their life is Job 36:14 5290
Remember not the sins of my *y* Ps 25:7 5271
thou art my trust from my *y* Ps 71:5 5271
thou hast taught me from my *y* Ps 71:17 5271
and ready to die from my *y* up Ps 88:15 5290
The days of his *y* hast thou Ps 89:45 5934
so that thy *y* is renewed like the Ps 103:5 5271
thou hast the dew of thy *y* Ps 110:3 3208
so are children of the *y* Ps 127:4 5271
have they afflicted me from my *y* Ps 129:1 5271
have they afflicted me from my *y* Ps 129:2 5271
be as plants grown up in their *y* Ps 144:12 5271
forsaketh the guide of her *y* Prov 2:17 5271
and rejoice with the wife of thy *y* Prov 5:18 5271
Rejoice, O young man, in thy *y* Eccl 11:9 3208
cheer thee in the days of thy *y* Eccl 11:9 979
for childhood and *y* are vanity Eccl 11:10 7839
thy Creator in the days of thy *y* Eccl 12:1 979
thou hast laboured from thy *y* Is 47:12 5271
even thy merchants, from thy *y* Is 47:15 5271
shalt forget the shame of thy *y* Is 54:4 5934
grieved in spirit, and a wife of *y* Is 54:6 5271
thee, the kindness of thy *y* Jer 2:2 5271
thou art the guide of my *y* Jer 3:4 5271
labour of our fathers from our *y* Jer 3:24 5271
from our *y* even unto this day, and Jer 3:25 5271
hath been thy manner from thy *y* Jer 22:21 5271
I did bear the reproach of my *y* Jer 31:19 5271
done evil before me from their *y* Jer 32:30 5271
Moab hath been at ease from his *y* Jer 48:11 5271

that he bear the yoke in his *y* ... Lam 3:27 5271
for from my *y* up even till now ... Eze 4:14 5271
not remembered the days of thy *y* ... Eze 16:22 5271
not remembered the days of thy *y* ... Eze 16:43 5271
with thee in the days of thy *y* ... Eze 16:60 5271
committed whoredoms in their *y* ... Eze 23:3 5271
for in her *y* they lay with her, ... Eze 23:8 5271
to remembrance the days of her *y* ... Eze 23:19 5271
remembrance the lewdness of thy *y* ... Eze 23:21 5271
Egyptians for the paps of thy *y* ... Eze 23:21 5271
there, as in the days of her *y* ... Hos 2:15 5271
for the husband of her *y* ... Joel 1:8 5271
me to keep cattle from my *y* ... Zec 13:5 5271
between thee and the wife of thy *y* ... Mal 2:14 5271
against the wife of his *y* ... Mal 2:15 5271
things have I kept from my *y* up ... Mt 19:20 *3503*
these have I observed from my *y* ... Mk 10:20 *3503*
these have I kept from my *y* up ... Lk 18:21 *3503*
My manner of life from my *y* ... Acts 26:4 *3503*
Let no man despise thy *y* ... 1Ti 4:12 *3503*

YOUTHFUL {1}
Flee also *y* lusts ... 2Ti 2:22 *3512*

YOUTHS {2}
ones, I discerned among the *y* ... Prov 7:7 1121
Even the *y* shall faint and be ... Is 40:30 5288

YOU-WARD {3}
world, and more abundantly to *y* ... 2Cor 1:12 *4314,5209*
which to *y* is not weak, but is ... 2Cor 13:3 *1519,5209*
of God which is given me to *y* ... Eph 3:2 *1519,5209*

Z

ZAANAIM *(za-an-a'-im)* {1} See ZAANANNIM. *A plain in Naphtali.*
his tent unto the plain of Z ... Judg 4:11 6815

ZAANAN *(za'-an-an)* {1} See ZENAN. *A city of Judah.*
the inhabitant of Z came not ... Mic 1:11 6630

ZA-ANANNIM See ZAANAIM.

ZAANANNIM *(za-an-an'-nim)* {1} *Same as Zaanaim.*
was from Heleph, from Allon to Z ... Josh 19:33 6815

ZAAVAN *(za'-av-an)* {1} See ZAVAN. *A son of Ezer.*
Bilhan, and Z, and Akan ... Gen 36:27 2190

ZABAD *(za'-bad)* {8} See JOSABAD, JOZACHAR.
1. A son of Nathan.
begat Nathan, and Nathan begat Z ... 1Chr 2:36 2066
Z begat Ephlal, and Ephlal begat ... 1Chr 2:37 2066
2. Son of Tahath.
Z his son, and Shuthelah his son, ... 1Chr 7:21 2066
3. A "mighty man" of David.
the Hittite, Z the son of Ahlai, ... 1Chr 11:41 2066
4. A son of Shimeath.
Z the son of Shimeath an ... 2Chr 24:26 2066
5. A son of Zatta.
Mattaniah, and Jeremoth, and Z ... Ezr 10:27 2066
6. A son of Hasham.
Mattenai, Mattathah, Z, Eliphelet ... Ezr 10:33 2066
7. A son of Nebo.
Jeiel, Mattithiah, Z, Zebina, ... Ezr 10:43 2066

ZABBAI *(zab'-bahee)* {2} See ZACCAI.
1. Married a foreigner in exile.
Jehohanan, Hananiah, Z, and Athlai ... Ezr 10:28 2079
2. Father of Baruch.
After him Baruch the son of Z ... Neh 3:20 2079

ZABBUD *(zab'-bud)* {1} See ZACCUR. *An exile with Ezra.*
Uthai, and Z, and with them seventy ... Ezr 8:14 2072

ZABDI *(zab'-di)* {6} See ZACCHUR, ZICHRI.
1. Father of Carmi.
the son of Carmi, the son of Z ... Josh 7:1 2067
and Z was taken ... Josh 7:17 2067
the son of Carmi, the son of Z ... Josh 7:18 2067
2. Son of Shimhi.
And Jakim, and Zichri, and Z ... 1Chr 8:19 2067
3. A storekeeper in David's court.
wine cellars was Z the Shiphmite ... 1Chr 27:27 2067
4. A Levite.
the son of Micha, the son of Z ... Neh 11:17 2067

ZABDIEL *(zab'-de-el)* {2}
1. Father of Jashobeam.
month was Jashobeam the son of Z ... 1Chr 27:2 2068
2. An overseer of priests.
and their overseer was Z, the son ... Neh 11:14 2068

ZABUD *(za'-bud)* {1} *A family of exiles.*
Z the son of Nathan was principal ... 1Kin 4:5 2071

ZABULON *(zab'-u-lon)* {3} See ZEBULUN. *Greek form of Zebulon.*
sea coast, in the borders of Z ... Mt 4:13 *2194*
The land of Z, and the land of ... Mt 4:15 *2194*
Of the tribe of Z were sealed ... Rev 7:8 *2194*

ZACCAI *(zac'-cahee)* {2} See ZABBAI. *A family of exiles.*
The children of Z, seven hundred ... Ezr 2:9 2140
The children of Z, seven hundred ... Neh 7:14 2140

ZACCHAEUS *(zak-ke'-us)* {3} *A tax collector visited by Jesus.*
behold, there was a man named Z ... Lk 19:2 *2195*
and saw him, and said unto him, Z ... Lk 19:5 *2195*
Z stood, and said unto the Lord ... Lk 19:8 *2195*

ZACCHUR *(zac'-cur)* {1} See ZACCUR. *Father of Shimei.*
Z his son, Shimei his son ... 1Chr 4:26 2139

ZACCUR *(zac'-cur)* {8} See ZABBUD, ZABDI, ZACCHUR, ZICHRI.
1. Father of Shammua.
of Reuben, Shammua the son of Z ... Num 13:4 2139
2. A sanctuary servant.
Beno, and Shoham, and Z, and Ibri ... 1Chr 24:27 2139
3. A son of Asaph.
Z, and Joseph, and Nethaniah, and ... 1Chr 25:2 2139
The third to Z, he, his sons, and ... 1Chr 25:10 2139
the son of Michaiah, the son of Z ... Neh 12:35 2139
4. A rebuilder of Jerusalem's wall.
to them builded Z the son of Imri ... Neh 3:2 2139
5. A Levite who renewed the covenant.
Z, Sherebiah, Shebaniah, ... Neh 10:12 2139
6. Father of Hanan.
to them was Hanan the son of Z ... Neh 13:13 2139

ZACHARIAH *(zak-a-ri'-ah)* {4} See ZECHARIAH.
1. A king of Israel.
Z his son reigned in his stead ... 2Kin 14:29 2148
of Azariah king of Judah did Z ... 2Kin 15:8 2148
And the rest of the acts of Z ... 2Kin 15:11 2148
2. Father of Abi.
also was Abi, the daughter of Z ... 2Kin 18:2 2148

ZACHARIAS *(zak'-a-ri'-as)* {11} See ZECHARIAH.
1. Son of Barachias.
the blood of Z son of Barachias ... Mt 23:35 *2197*
blood of Abel unto the blood of Z ... Lk 11:51 *2197*
2. Father of John the Baptist.
Judaea, a certain priest named Z ... Lk 1:5 *2197*
when Z saw him, he was troubled, ... Lk 1:12 *2197*
angel said unto him, Fear not, Z ... Lk 1:13 *2197*
Z said unto the angel, Whereby ... Lk 1:18 *2197*
And the people waited for Z ... Lk 1:21 *2197*
And entered into the house of Z ... Lk 1:40 *2197*
and they called him Z, after the ... Lk 1:59 *2197*
his father Z was filled with the ... Lk 1:67 *2197*
the son of Z in the wilderness ... Lk 3:2 *2197*

ZACHER *(za'-kur)* {1} See ZECHARIAH. *Father of Gibeon.*
And Gedor, and Ahio, and Z ... 1Chr 8:31 2144

ZADOK *(za'-dok)* {52} See ZADOK'S.
1. A priest in David's time.
Z the son of Ahitub, and Ahimelech ... 2Sa 8:17 6659
lo Z also, and all the Levites ... 2Sa 15:24 6659
And the king said unto Z, Carry ... 2Sa 15:25 6659
king said also unto Z the priest ... 2Sa 15:27 6659
Z therefore and Abiathar carried ... 2Sa 15:29 6659
hast thou not there with thee Z ... 2Sa 15:35 6659
house, thou shalt tell it to Z ... 2Sa 15:35 6659
Then said Hushai unto Z and to ... 2Sa 17:15 6659
Then said Ahimaaz the son of Z ... 2Sa 18:19 6659
the son of Z yet again to Joab ... 2Sa 18:22 6659
running of Ahimaaz the son of Z ... 2Sa 18:27 6659
And king David sent to Z and to ... 2Sa 19:11 6659
and Z and Abiathar were the priests ... 2Sa 20:25 6659
But Z the priest, and Benaiah the ... 1Kin 1:8 6659
Z the priest, and Benaiah the son ... 1Kin 1:26 6659
Call me Z the priest, and Nathan ... 1Kin 1:32 6659
let Z the priest and Nathan the ... 1Kin 1:34 6659
So Z the priest, and Nathan the ... 1Kin 1:38 6659
Z the priest took an horn of oil ... 1Kin 1:39 6659
hath sent with him Z the priest ... 1Kin 1:44 6659
Z the priest and Nathan the ... 1Kin 1:45 6659
Z the priest did the king put in ... 1Kin 2:35 6659
Azariah the son of Z the priest ... 1Kin 4:2 6659
and Z and Abiathar were the priests ... 1Kin 4:4 6659
And Ahitub begat Z ... 1Chr 6:8 6659
and Z begat Ahimaaz ... 1Chr 6:8 6659
Z his son, Ahimaaz his son ... 1Chr 6:53 6659
And David called for Z and Abiathar ... 1Chr 15:11 6659
Z the priest, and his brethren the ... 1Chr 16:39 6659
Z the son of Ahitub, and Abimelech ... 1Chr 18:16 6659
both Z of the sons of Eleazar, and ... 1Chr 24:3 6659
Z the priest, and Ahimelech the ... 1Chr 24:6 6659
presence of David the king, and Z ... 1Chr 24:31 6659
of the Aaronites, Z ... 1Chr 27:17 6659
chief governor, and Z to be priest ... 1Chr 29:22 6659
of the house of Z answered him ... 2Chr 31:10 6659
The son of Shallum, the son of Z ... Ezr 7:2 6659
these are the sons of Z among the ... Eze 40:46 6659
Levites that be of the seed of Z ... Eze 43:19 6659
the Levites, the sons of Z ... Eze 44:15 6659
are sanctified of the sons of Z ... Eze 48:11 6659
2. Father of Jerusha.
was Jerusha, the daughter of Z ... 2Kin 15:33 6659
was Jerushah, the daughter of Z ... 2Chr 27:1 6659
3. Son of Ahitub.
And Ahitub begat Z, and Zadok begat ... 1Chr 6:12 6659
begat Zadok, and Z begat Shallum, ... 1Chr 6:12 6659
son of Meshullam, the son of Z ... 1Chr 9:11 6659
4. A warrior in David's army.
And Z, a young man mighty of ... 1Chr 12:28 6659
5. The son of Baana.
them repaired Z the son of Baana ... Neh 3:4 6659
6. A priest who rebuilt the wall.
After them repaired Z the son of ... Neh 3:29 6659
7. A renewer of the covenant.
Meshezabeel, Z, Jaddua, ... Neh 10:21 6659
8. A son of Meraioth.
son of Meshullam, the son of Z ... Neh 11:11 6659
9. A Temple servant.
Z the scribe, and of the Levites, ... Neh 13:13 6659

ZADOKITES See ZADOK'S.

ZADOK'S *(za'-doks)* {1} *Refers to Zadok 1.*
their two sons, Ahimaaz Z son ... 2Sa 15:36 6659

ZAHAM *(za'-ham)* {1} *A son of Rehoboam.*
Jeush, and Shamariah, and Z ... 2Chr 11:19 2093

ZAIR *(za'-ur)* {1} *A city in Edom.*
So Joram went over to Z, and all ... 2Kin 8:21 6811

ZALAPH *(za'-laf)* {1} *Father of Hanun.*
and Hanun the sixth son of Z ... Neh 3:30 6764

ZALMON *(zal'-mon)* {2} See ILAI, SALMON.
1. A hill in Ephraim.
Abimelech gat him up to mount Z ... Judg 9:48 6756
2. A "mighty man" of David.
Z the Ahohite, Maharai the ... 2Sa 23:28 6756

ZALMONAH *(zal'-mo-nah)* {2} *An Israelite encampment in the wilderness.*
from mount Hor, and pitched in Z ... Num 33:41 6758
And they departed from Z, and ... Num 33:42 6758

ZALMUNNA *(zal-mun'-nah)* {12} *A Midianite king.*
and I am pursuing after Zebah and Z ... Judg 8:5 6759
Z now in thine hand, that we ... Judg 8:6 6759
Z into mine hand, then I will ... Judg 8:7 6759
Z were in Karkor, and their hosts ... Judg 8:10 6759
Z fled, he pursued after them, and ... Judg 8:12 6759
two kings of Midian, Zebah and Z ... Judg 8:12 6759
and said, Behold Zebah and Z ... Judg 8:15 6759
Z now in thine hand, that we ... Judg 8:15 6759
Then said he unto Zebah and Z ... Judg 8:18 6759
Z said, Rise thou, and fall upon ... Judg 8:21 6759
Gideon arose, and slew Zebah and Z ... Judg 8:21 6759
their princes as Zebah, and as Z ... Ps 83:11 6759

ZAMZUMMIMS *(zam-zum'-mims)* {1} See ZUZIMS. *A tribe in Canaan.*
and the Ammonites call them Z ... Deut 2:20 2157

ZAMZUMMITES See ZAMZUMMIMS.

ZANOAH *(za-no'-ah)* {5}
1. A city on the plain of Judah.
And Z, and En-gannim, Tappuah, and ... Josh 15:34 2182
Hanun, and the inhabitants of Z ... Neh 3:13 2182
Z, Adullam, and in their villages, ... Neh 11:30 2182
2. A city in the hills of Judah.
And Jezreel, and Jokdeam, and Z ... Josh 15:56 2182
3. A descendant of Caleb.
and Jekuthiel the father of Z ... 1Chr 4:18 2182

ZAPHENATH-PANEAH See ZAPHNATH-PAANEAH.

ZAPHNATH-PAANEAH *(zaf'-nath-pa-a-ne'-ah)* {1} *Name given to Joseph by Pharaoh.*
And Pharaoh called Joseph's name Z ... Gen 41:45 6847

ZAPHON *(za'-fon)* {1} *A city in Gad.*
and Beth-nimrah, and Succoth, and Z ... Josh 13:27 6829

ZARA *(za'-rah)* {1} See ZARAH, ZERAH. *Greek form of Zarah; an ancestor of Jesus.*
Judas begat Phares and Z of Thamar ... Mt 1:3 *2196*

ZARAH *(za'-rah)* {2} See ZARA, ZERAH. *A son of Judah.*
and his name was called Z ... Gen 38:30 2226
Onan, and Shelah, and Pharez, and Z ... Gen 46:12 2226

ZAREAH *(za'-re-ah)* {1} See ZAREATHITES, ZORAH. *A city in Judah.*
And at En-rimmon, and at Z, and at ... Neh 11:29 6881

ZAREATHITES *(za'-re-ath-ites)* {1} See ZORATHITES. *Descendants of Shobal.*
of them came the Z, and the ... 1Chr 2:53 6882

ZARED *(za'-red)* {1} See ZERED. *A brook near the Dead Sea.*
and pitched in the valley of Z ... Num 21:12 2218

ZAREPHATH *(zar'-e-fath)* {3} See SAREPTA. *A city in Phoenicia.*
Arise, get thee to Z, which ... 1Kin 17:9 6886
So he arose and went to Z ... 1Kin 17:10 6886
of the Canaanites, even unto Z ... Obad 20 6886

ZARETAN *(zar'-e-tan)* {1} See ZARTANAH, ZEREDATHAH. *A city in Ephraim.*
the city Adam, that is beside Z ... Josh 3:16 6891

ZARETHAN See ZARTHAN.

ZARETH-SHAHAR *(za'-reth-sha'-har)* {1} *A city in Reuben.*
Z in the mount of the valley, ... Josh 13:19 6890

ZARHITES *(zar'-hites)* {6}
1. Descendants of Zerah, the Simeonite.
Of Zerah, the family of the Z ... Num 26:13 2227
and he took the family of the Z ... Josh 7:17 2227
the family of the Z man by man ... Josh 7:17 2227
Sibbecai the Hushathite, of the Z ... 1Chr 27:11 2227
the Netophathite, of the Z ... 1Chr 27:13 2227

2. Descendants of Zerah, son of Judah.
of Zerah, the family of the Z ... Num 26:20 2227

ZARTANAH *(zar'-ta-nah)* {} See ZARETAN, ZARTHAN. *Same as Zaretan.*
which is by Z beneath Jezreel, ... 1Kin 4:12 6891

ZARTHAN *(zar'-than)* {1} See ZARETAN, ZARTANAH. *Same as Zaretan.*
clay ground between Succoth and Z ... 1Kin 7:46 6891

ZATTHU *(zath'-u)* {1} See ZATTU. *A renewer of the covenant.*
Parosh, Pahath-moab, Elam, Z ... Neh 10:14 2240

ZATTU *(zat'-tu)* {3} See ZATTHU. *A family of exiles.*
The children of Z, nine hundred ... Ezr 2:8 2240
And of the sons of Z ... Ezr 10:27 2240
The children of Z, eight hundred ... Neh 7:13 2240

ZAVAN *(za'-van)* {1} See ZAAVAN. *Son of Ezer.*
Bilhan, and Z, and Jakan ... 1Chr 1:42 2190

ZAZA *(za'-zah)* {1} *A son of Jonathan.*
Peleth, and Z ... 1Chr 2:33 2117

ZEAL {16}
his *z* to the children of Israel ... 2Sa 21:2 7065
with me, and see my *z* for the LORD ... 2Kin 10:16 7068
the *z* of the LORD of hosts shall ... 2Kin 19:31 7068
For the *z* of thine house hath ... Ps 69:9 7068
My *z* hath consumed me, because ... Ps 119:139 7068
The *z* of the LORD of hosts will ... Is 9:7 7068
the *z* of the LORD of hosts shall ... Is 37:32 7068
and was clad with *z* as a cloke ... Is 59:17 7068
where is thy *z* and thy strength, ... Is 63:15 7068
I the LORD have spoken it in my *z* ... Eze 5:13 7068
The *z* of thine house hath eaten ... Jn 2:17 *2205*
record that they have a *z* of God ... Rom 10:2 *2205*
what vehement desire, yea, what *z* ... 2Cor 7:11 *2205*
your *z* hath provoked very many ... 2Cor 9:2 *2205*
Concerning *z*, persecuting the ... Phil 3:6 *2205*
that he hath a great *z* for you ... Col 4:13 *2205*

ZEALOT See ZELOTES.

ZEALOUS {8}
while he was *z* for my sake among ... Num 25:11 7065
because he was *z* for his God ... Num 25:13 7065
and they are all *z* of the law ... Acts 21:20 *2207*
was *z* toward God, as ye all are ... Acts 22:3 *2207*
as ye are *z* of spiritual gifts ... 1Cor 14:12 *2207*
being more exceedingly *z* of the ... Gal 1:14 *2207*
peculiar people, *z* of good works ... Titus 2:14 *2207*
be *z* therefore, and repent ... Rev 3:19 *2206*

ZEALOUSLY {2}
They *z* affect you, but not well ... Gal 4:17 *2206*
But it is good to be *z* affected ... Gal 4:18 *2206*

ZEBADIAH *(zeb-ad-i'-ah)* {9}
1. Grandson of Elpael.
And Z, and Arad, and Ader, ... 1Chr 8:15 2069
2. A son of Elpael.
And Z, and Meshullam, and Hezeki ... 1Chr 8:17 2069
3. A warrior in David's army.
And Joelah, and Z, the sons of ... 1Chr 12:7 2069
4. A Levite gatekeeper.
Z the third, Jathniel the fourth, ... 1Chr 26:2 2069
5. A son of Asahel.
of Joab, and Z his son after him ... 1Chr 27:7 2069
6. A messenger for King Jehoshaphat.
even Shemaiah, and Nethaniah, and Z ... 2Chr 17:8 2069
7. Son of Ishmael.
Z the son of Ishmael, the ruler ... 2Chr 19:11 2069
8. A family of exiles.
Z the son of Michael, and with him ... Ezr 8:8 2069
9. Married a foreigner in exile.
Hanani, and Z ... Ezr 10:20 2069

ZEBAH *(ze'-bah)* {12} *A king of Midian.*
faint, and I am pursuing after Z ... Judg 8:5 2078
Succoth said, Are the hands of Z ... Judg 8:6 2078
when the LORD hath delivered Z ... Judg 8:7 2078
Now Z and Zalmunna were in Karkor, ... Judg 8:10 2078
And when Z and Zalmunna fled, he ... Judg 8:12 2078
took the two kings of Midian, Z ... Judg 8:12 2078
men of Succoth, and said, Behold Z ... Judg 8:15 2078
me, saying, Are the hands of Z ... Judg 8:15 2078
Then said he unto Z and Zalmunna, ... Judg 8:18 2078
Then Z and Zalmunna said, Rise ... Judg 8:21 2078
And Gideon arose, and slew Z ... Judg 8:21 2078
yea, all their princes as Z ... Ps 83:11 2078

ZEBAIM *(ze-ba'-im)* {2} *Residence of some exiles in Babylonia.*
the children of Pochereth of Z ... Ezr 2:57 6380
the children of Pochereth of Z ... Neh 7:59 6380

ZEBEDEE *(zeb'-e-dee)* {10} See ZEBEDEE'S. *Father of James and John.*
two brethren, James the son of Z ... Mt 4:21 *2199*
in a ship with Z their father ... Mt 4:21 *2199*
James the son of Z, and John his ... Mt 10:2 *2199*
him Peter and the two sons of Z ... Mt 26:37 *2199*
thence, he saw James the son of Z ... Mk 1:19 *2199*
they left their father Z in the ... Mk 1:20 *2199*
And James the son of Z, and John ... Mk 3:17 *2199*
And James and John, the sons of Z ... Mk 10:35 *2199*
James, and John, the sons of Z ... Lk 5:10 *2199*
Cana in Galilee, and the sons of Z ... Jn 21:2 *2199*

ZEBEDEE'S *(zeb'-e-dees)* {2}
of Z children with her sons ... Mt 20:20 *2199*
and the mother of Z children ... Mt 27:56 *2199*

ZEBIDAH See ZEBUDAH.

ZEBINA *(ze-bi'-nah)* {1} *Married a foreigner in exile.*
Jeiel, Mattithiah, Zabad, Z ... Ezr 10:43 2081

ZEBOIIM *(ze-boy'-im)* {2} See ZEBOIM. *City destroyed with Sodom and Gomorrah.*
of Admah, and Shemeber king of Z ... Gen 14:2 6636
king of Admah, and the king of Z ... Gen 14:8 6636

ZEBOIM *(ze-bo'-im)* {5} See ZEBOIIM.
1. Same as Zeboiim.
and Gomorrah, and Admah, and Z ... Gen 10:19 6636
Sodom, and Gomorrah, Admah, and Z ... Deut 29:23 6636
how shall I set thee as Z ... Hos 11:8 6636
2. A city in Benjamin.
valley of Z toward the wilderness ... 1Sa 13:18 6650
Hadid, Z, Neballat, ... Neh 11:34 6650

ZEBUDAH *(ze-bu'-dah)* {1} *Mother of King Jehoshaphat.*
And his mother's name was Z ... 2Kin 23:36 2081

ZEBUL *(ze'-bul)* {6} *A ruler of Shechem.*
and Z his officer ... Judg 9:28 2083
when Z the ruler of the city ... Judg 9:30 2083
Gaal saw the people, he said to Z ... Judg 9:36 2083
Z said unto him, Thou seest the ... Judg 9:36 2083
Then said Z unto him, Where is ... Judg 9:38 2083
Z thrust out Gaal and his brethren ... Judg 9:41 2083

ZEBULONITE *(zeb'-u-lon-ite)* {2} See ZEBULONITES. *A descendant of Zebulun 1.*
And after him Elon, a Z, judged ... Judg 12:11 2075
And Elon the Z died, and was buried ... Judg 12:12 2075

ZEBULUN *(zeb'-u-lun)* {44} See ZABULON, ZEBULONITE, ZEBULONITES.
1. A son of Jacob.
and she called his name Z ... Gen 30:20 2074
Levi, and Judah, and Issachar, and Z ... Gen 35:23 2074
And the sons of Z ... Gen 46:14 2074
Z shall dwell at the haven of the ... Gen 49:13 2074
Issachar, Z, and Benjamin, ... Ex 1:3 2074
Levi, and Judah, Issachar, and Z ... 1Chr 2:1 2074
2. Descendants of Zebulun.
Of Z; Eliab the ... Num 1:9 2074
Of the children of Z, by their ... Num 1:30 2074
of them, even of the tribe of Z ... Num 1:31 2074
Then the tribe of Z ... Num 2:7 2074
be captain of the children of Z ... Num 2:7 2074
prince of the children of Z ... Num 7:24 2074
of Z was Eliab the son of Helon ... Num 10:16 2074
Of the tribe of Z, Gaddiel the ... Num 13:10 2074
Of the sons of Z after their ... Num 26:26 2074
of the tribe of the children of Z ... Num 34:25 2074
Reuben, Gad, and Asher, and Z ... Deut 27:13 2074
And of Zebulun he said, Rejoice, Z ... Deut 33:18 2074
of Z according to their families ... Josh 19:10 2074
of Z according to their families ... Josh 19:16 2074
to Beth-dagon, and reacheth to Z ... Josh 19:27 2074
reacheth to Z on the south side, ... Josh 19:34 2074
of Gad, and out of the tribe of Z ... Josh 21:7 2074
Levites, out of the tribe of Z ... Josh 21:34 2074
Neither did Z drive out the ... Judg 1:30 2074
Naphtali and of the children of Z ... Judg 4:6 2074
And Barak called Z and Naphtali to ... Judg 4:10 2074
out of Z they that handle the pen ... Judg 5:14 2074
Z and Naphtali were a people that ... Judg 5:18 2074
messengers unto Asher, and unto Z ... Judg 6:35 2074
in Aijalon in the country of Z ... Judg 12:12 2074
of Gad, and out of the tribe of Z ... 1Chr 6:63 2074
were given out of the tribe of Z ... 1Chr 6:77 2074
Of Z, such as went forth to ... 1Chr 12:33 2074
them, even unto Issachar and Z ... 1Chr 12:40 2074
Of Z, Ishmaiah the son of Obadiah ... 1Chr 27:19 2074
Ephraim and Manasseh even unto Z ... 2Chr 30:10 2074
of Z humbled themselves, and came ... 2Chr 30:11 2074
and Manasseh, Issachar, and Z ... 2Chr 30:18 2074
their council, the princes of Z ... Ps 68:27 2074
lightly afflicted the land of Z ... Is 9:1 2074
unto the west side, Z a portion ... Eze 48:26 2074
And by the border of Z, from the ... Eze 48:27 2074
gate of Issachar, one gate of Z ... Eze 48:33 2074

ZEBULUNITES *(zeb'-u-lun-ites)* {1} *Descendants of Zebulun.*
Z according to those that were ... Num 26:27 2075

ZECHARIAH *(zek-a-ri'-ah)* {39} See ZACCUR, ZACHARIAH, ZACHARIAS, ZACHER.
1. A chief Reubenite.
were the chief, Jeiel, and Z ... 1Chr 5:7 2148
2. A Levite gatekeeper.
Z the son of Meshelemiah was ... 1Chr 9:21 2148
Z the firstborn, Jediael the ... 1Chr 26:2 2148
Then for Z his son, a wise ... 1Chr 26:14 2148
was Abijah, the daughter of Z ... 2Chr 29:1 2148
3. A Benjamite.
And Gedor, and Ahio, and Z, and ... 1Chr 9:37 2148
4. A Levite musician.
brethren of the second degree, Z ... 1Chr 15:18 2148
And Z, and Aziel, and Shemiramoth, ... 1Chr 15:20 2148
Asaph the chief, and next to him Z ... 1Chr 16:5 2148
5. A Tabernacle priest.
and Nethaneel, and Amasai, and Z ... 1Chr 15:24 2148
6. A son of Isshiah.
sons of Isshiah; Z ... 1Chr 24:25 2148
7. Son of Hosah.
Tebaliah the third, Z the fourth ... 1Chr 26:11 2148
8. A chief of Manasseh.
in Gilead, Iddo the son of Z ... 1Chr 27:21 2148
9. A messenger of King Jehoshaphat.
Ben-hail, and to Obadiah, and to Z ... 2Chr 17:7 2148
10. Father of Jehaziel.
Then upon Jahaziel the son of Z ... 2Chr 20:14 2148
11. A son of Jehoshaphat.
Azariah, and Jehiel, and Z ... 2Chr 21:2 2148
12. Son of Jehoida.
the Spirit of God came upon Z the ... 2Chr 24:20 2148
13. A prophet in King Uzziah's time.
And he sought God in the days of Z ... 2Chr 26:5 2148
14. A Levite who cleansed the Temple.
Z, and Mattaniah ... 2Chr 29:13 2148
15. An overseer of the Temple repairs.
and Z and Meshullam, of the sons of ... 2Chr 34:12 2148
16. A prince of Judah.
Hilkiah and Z and Jehiel, rulers of ... 2Chr 35:8 2148
17. A prophet in Judah.
Z the son of Iddo, prophesied ... Ezr 5:1 2148
the prophet and Z the son of Iddo ... Ezr 6:14 2148
came the word of the LORD unto Z ... Zec 1:1 2148
came the word of the LORD unto Z ... Zec 1:7 2148
Z in the fourth day of the ninth ... Zec 7:1 2148
the word of the LORD came unto Z ... Zec 7:8 2148
18. A son of Pharosh.
sons of Pharosh; Z ... Ezr 8:3 2148
19. A son of Bebai.
Z the son of Bebai, and with him ... Ezr 8:11 2148
Elnathan, and for Nathan, and for Z ... Ezr 8:16 2148
20. Married a foreigner in exile.
Mattaniah, Z, and Jehiel, and Abdi, ... Ezr 10:26 2148
21. A prince who aided Ezra.
and Hashum, and Hashbadana, Z ... Neh 8:4 2148
22. A descendant of Pharez.
the son of Uzziah, the son of Z ... Neh 11:4 2148
23. A son of Shiloni.
the son of Joiarib, the son of Z ... Neh 11:5 2148
24. Father of a resettler in Jerusalem.
the son of Amzi, the son of Z ... Neh 11:12 2148
25. A priest in Joiakim's time.
Of Iddo, Z ... Neh 12:16 2148
26. A priest who dedicated the wall.
Z the son of Jonathan, the son of ... Neh 12:35 2148
Miniamin, Michaiah, Elioenai, Z ... Neh 12:41 2148
27. Son of Jeber.
and Z the son of Jeberechiah ... Is 8:2 2148

ZECHER See ZACHER.

ZEDAD *(ze'-dad)* {2} *A place near Hamath.*
forth of the border shall be to Z ... Num 34:8 6657
way of Hethlon, as men go to Z ... Eze 47:15 6657

ZEDEKIAH *(zed-e-ki'-ah)* {61} See MATTANIAH, ZEDEKIAH'S, ZIDKIJAH.
1. A false prophet.
Z the son of Chenaanah made him ... 1Kin 22:11 6667
But Z the son of Chenaanah went ... 1Kin 22:24 6667
Z the son of Chenaanah had made ... 2Chr 18:10 6667
Then Z the son of Chenaanah came ... 2Chr 18:23 6667
2. Name given to Mattaniah by Nebuchadnezzar.
stead, and changed his name to Z ... 2Kin 24:17 6667
Z was twenty and one years old ... 2Kin 24:18 6667
that Z rebelled against the king ... 2Kin 24:20 6667
unto the eleventh year of king Z ... 2Kin 25:2 6667
the sons of Z before his eyes ... 2Kin 25:7 6667
eyes, and put out the eyes of Z ... 2Kin 25:7 6667
the second Jehoiakim, the third Z ... 1Chr 3:15 6667
made Z his brother king over ... 2Chr 36:10 6667
Z was one and twenty years old ... 2Chr 36:11 6667
Z the son of Josiah king of Judah ... Jer 1:3 6667
when king Z sent unto him Pashur ... Jer 21:1 6667
unto them, Thus shall ye say to Z ... Jer 21:3 6667
I will deliver Z king of Judah ... Jer 21:7 6667
So will I give Z the king of ... Jer 24:8 6667
to Jerusalem unto Z king of Judah ... Jer 27:3 6667
I spake also to Z king of Judah ... Jer 27:12 6667
of the reign of Z king of Judah ... Jer 28:1 6667
(whom Z king of Judah sent unto ... Jer 29:3 6667
the tenth year of Z king of Judah ... Jer 32:1 6667
For Z king of Judah had shut him ... Jer 32:3 6667
Z king of Judah shall not escape ... Jer 32:4 6667
And he shall lead Z to Babylon ... Jer 32:5 6667
speak to Z king of Judah, and tell ... Jer 34:2 6667
of the LORD, O Z king of Judah ... Jer 34:4 6667
unto Z king of Judah in Jerusalem ... Jer 34:6 6667
after that the king Z had made a ... Jer 34:8 6667
Z king of Judah and his princes ... Jer 34:21 6667
king Z the son of Josiah reigned ... Jer 37:1 6667
Z the king sent Jehucal the son ... Jer 37:3 6667
Then Z the king sent, and took him ... Jer 37:17 6667
Jeremiah said unto king Z ... Jer 37:18 6667
Then Z the king commanded that ... Jer 37:21 6667
Then Z the king said, Behold, he ... Jer 38:5 6667
Then Z the king sent, and took ... Jer 38:14 6667
Then Jeremiah said unto Z ... Jer 38:15 6667
So Z the king sware secretly unto ... Jer 38:16 6667
Then said Jeremiah unto Z ... Jer 38:17 6667
Z the king said unto Jeremiah, I ... Jer 38:19 6667
Then said Z unto Jeremiah, Let no ... Jer 38:24 6667
the ninth year of Z king of Judah ... Jer 39:1 6667
And in the eleventh year of Z ... Jer 39:2 6667
that when Z the king of Judah saw ... Jer 39:4 6667
overtook Z in the plains of ... Jer 39:5 6667
of Z in Riblah before his eyes ... Jer 39:6 6667
as I gave Z king of Judah into ... Jer 44:30 6667
of the reign of Z king of Judah ... Jer 49:34 6667
when he went with Z the king of ... Jer 51:59 6667
Z was one and twenty years old ... Jer 52:1 6667
that Z rebelled against the king ... Jer 52:3 6667
unto the eleventh year of king Z ... Jer 52:5 6667
overtook Z in the plains of ... Jer 52:8 6667

the sons of Z before his eyes ... Jer 52:10 6667
Then he put out the eyes of Z ... Jer 52:11 6667
3. Grandson of Jehoiakim.
Jeconiah his son, Z his son ... 1Chr 3:16 6667
4. A false prophet denounced by Jeremiah.
of Z the son of Maaseiah, which ... Jer 29:21 6667
saying, The LORD make thee like Z ... Jer 29:22 6667
5. A prince of Judah.
Z the son of Hananiah, and all the ... Jer 36:12 6667

ZEDEKIAH'S *(zed-e-ki'-ahs)* {1} *Refers to Zedekiah 2.*
Moreover he put out Z eyes ... Jer 39:7 6667

ZEEB *(ze'-eb)* {6} *A Midianite prince.*
of the Midianites, Oreb and Z ... Judg 7:25 2062
Z they slew at the winepress of ... Judg 7:25 2062
they slew at the winepress of Z ... Judg 7:25 2062
Z to Gideon on the other side ... Judg 7:25 2062
the princes of Midian, Oreb and Z ... Judg 8:3 2062
their nobles like Oreb, and like Z ... Ps 83:11 2062

ZELA See ZELAH.

ZELAH *(ze'-lah)* {2} *A city in Benjamin.*
And Z, Eleph, and Jebusi, which is ... Josh 18:28 6762
in the country of Benjamin in Z ... 2Sa 21:14 6762

ZELEK *(ze'-lek)* {2} *A "mighty man" of David.*
Z the Ammonite, Nahari the ... 2Sa 23:37 6768
Z the Ammonite, Naharai the ... 1Chr 11:39 6768

ZELOPHEHAD *(ze-lo'-fe-had)* {11} *Son of Hepher.*
Z the son of Hepher had no sons, ... Num 26:33 6765
of the daughters of Z were Mahlah ... Num 26:33 6765
Then came the daughters of Z ... Num 27:1 6765
The daughters of Z speak right ... Num 27:7 6765
Z our brother unto his daughters ... Num 36:2 6765
concerning the daughters of Z ... Num 36:6 6765
Moses, so did the daughters of Z ... Num 36:10 6765
and Noah, the daughters of Z ... Num 36:11 6765
But Z, the son of Hepher, the son ... Josh 17:3 6765
and the name of the second was Z ... 1Chr 7:15 6765
and Z had daughters ... 1Chr 7:15 6765

ZELOTES *(ze-lo-teze)* {2} See CANAANITE, SIMON. *Surname of Simon, disciple of Jesus.*
of Alphaeus, and Simon called Z ... Lk 6:15 *2208*
the son of Alphaeus, and Simon Z ... Acts 1:13 *2208*

ZELZAH *(zel'-zah)* {1} *A city in Benjamin.*
in the border of Benjamin at Z ... 1Sa 10:2 6766

ZEMARAIM *(zem-a-ra'-im)* {2} See ZEMARITE.
1. A city in Benjamin.
And Beth-arabah, and Z, and Beth-el, ... Josh 18:22 6787
2. A mountain in Ephraim.
And Abijah stood up upon mount Z ... 2Chr 13:4 6787

ZEMARITE {2} *A descendant of Canaan.*
And the Arvadite, and the Z ... Gen 10:18 6786
And the Arvadite, and the Z ... 1Chr 1:16 6786

ZEMIRA *(ze-mi'-rah)* {1} *A son of Becher.*
Z, and Joash, and Eliezer, and ... 1Chr 7:8 2160

ZEMIRAH See ZEMIRA.

ZENAN *(ze'-nan)* {1} See ZAANAN. *A city in Judah.*
Z, and Hadashah, and Migdal-gad, ... Josh 15:37 6799

ZENAS *(ze'-nas)* {1} *A Christian lawyer.*
Bring Z the lawyer and Apollos on ... Titus 3:13 *2211*

ZEPHANIAH *(zef-a-ni'-ah)* {10}
1. A priest in exile.
Z the second priest, and the three ... 2Kin 25:18 6846
Z the son of Maaseiah the priest, ... Jer 21:1 6846
to Z the son of Maaseiah the ... Jer 29:25 6846
Z the priest read this letter in ... Jer 29:29 6846
Z the son of Maaseiah the priest ... Jer 37:3 6846
Z the second priest, and the three ... Jer 52:24 6846
2. An ancestor of Samuel.
the son of Azariah, the son of Z ... 1Chr 6:36 6846
3. A prophet.
came unto Z the son of Cushi ... Zeph 1:1 6846
4. Son of Josiah the priest.
the house of Josiah the son of Z ... Zec 6:10 6846
Jedaiah, and to Hen the son of Z ... Zec 6:14 6846

ZEPHATH *(ze'-fath)* {1} See HORMAH. *A city in Simeon.*
the Canaanites that inhabited Z ... Judg 1:17 6857

ZEPHATHAH *(zef'-a-thah)* {1} *A valley in Judah.*
in the valley of Z at Mareshah ... 2Chr 14:10 6859

ZEPHI *(ze'-fi)* {1} See ZEPHO. *Son of Eliphaz.*
Teman, and Omar, Z, and Gatam, ... 1Chr 1:36 6825

ZEPHO *(ze'-fo)* {2} See ZEPHI. *Same as Zephi.*
of Eliphaz were Teman, Omar, Z ... Gen 36:11 6825
duke Teman, duke Omar, duke Z ... Gen 36:15 6825

ZEPHON *(ze'-fon)* {1} See ZEPHONITES, ZIPHION. *A son of Gad.*
of Z, the family of the ... Num 26:15 6827

ZEPHONITES *(zef'-on-ites)* {1} *Descendants of Zephon.*
of Zephon, the family of the Z ... Num 26:15 6831

ZER *(zur)* {1} *A city in Naphtali.*
the fenced cities are Ziddim, Z ... Josh 19:35 6863

ZERAH *(ze'-rah)* {19} See EZRAHITE, ZARAH, ZARHITES, ZOHAR.
1. A son of Reuel.
and Z, Shammah, and Mizzah ... Gen 36:13 2226
duke Nahath, duke Z, duke Shammah ... Gen 36:17 2226
Nahath, Z, Shammah, and Mizzah ... 1Chr 1:37 2226
2. Father of Jobab.
Jobab the son of Z of Bozrah ... Gen 36:33 2226
Jobab the son of Z of Bozrah ... 1Chr 1:44 2226
3. Son of Judah.
of Z, the family of the Zarhites ... Num 26:20 2226
the son of Zabdi, the son of Z ... Josh 7:1 2226
the son of Zabdi, the son of Z ... Josh 7:18 2226
with him, took Achan the son of Z ... Josh 7:24 2226
son of Z commit a trespass in the ... Josh 22:20 2226
in law bare him Pharez and Z ... 1Chr 2:4 2226
And the sons of Z ... 1Chr 2:6 2226
And of the sons of Z ... 1Chr 9:6 2226
children of Z the son of Judah ... Neh 11:24 2226
4. A son of Simeon.
Of Z, the family of the Zarhites ... Num 26:13 2226
were, Nemuel, and Jamin, Jarib, Z ... 1Chr 4:24 2226
5. Son of Iddo.
Z his son, Jeaterai his son ... 1Chr 6:21 2226
6. Father of Ethni.
The son of Ethni, the son of Z ... 1Chr 6:41 2226
7. An Ethiopian king.
there came out against them Z the ... 2Chr 14:9 2226

ZERAHIAH *(zer-a-hi'-ah)* {7}
1. An ancestor of Ezra.
And Uzzi begat Z, and Z ... 1Chr 6:6 2228
Z, and Z begat Meraioth, ... 1Chr 6:6 2228
his son, Uzzi his son, Z his son, ... 1Chr 6:51 2228
The son of Z, the son of Uzzi, ... Ezr 7:4 2228
2. Father of Elihoenai.
Elihoenai the son of Z, and with ... Ezr 8:4 2228

ZERAHITE See ZARHITES.

ZERED *(ze'-red)* {3} See ZARED. *Same as Zared.*
I, and get you over the brook Z ... Deut 2:13 2218
And we went over the brook Z ... Deut 2:13 2218
we were come over the brook Z ... Deut 2:14 2218

ZEREDA *(zer'-e-dah)* {1} *A city north of Mt. Ephraim.*
son of Nebat, an Ephrathite of Z ... 1Kin 11:26 6868

ZEREDAH See ZEREDATHAH.

ZEREDATHAH *(ze-red'-a-thah)* {1} See ZARTHAN, ZERERATH. *A city in Manasseh.*
clay ground between Succoth and Z ... 2Chr 4:17 6868

ZERERAH See ZERERATH.

ZERERATH *(zer'-e-rath)* {1} See ZARTHAN, ZEREDATHAH. *A district in Manasseh.*
host fled to Beth-shittah in Z ... Judg 7:22 6888

ZERESH *(ze'-resh)* {4} *Wife of Haman.*
for his friends, and Z his wife ... Est 5:10 2238
Then said Z his wife and all his ... Est 5:14 2238
And Haman told Z his wife and all ... Est 6:13 2238
Z his wife unto him, If Mordecai ... Est 6:13 2238

ZERETH *(ze'-reth)* {1} *A descendant of Judah.*
And the sons of Helah were, Z ... 1Chr 4:7 6889

ZERETH-SHAHAR See ZERETH.

ZERI *(ze'-ri)* {1} See IZRI. *Son of Jeduthun.*
Gedaliah, and Z, and Jeshaiah, ... 1Chr 25:3 6874

ZEROR *(ze'-ror)* {1} *Ancestor of King Saul.*
the son of Abiel, the son of Z ... 1Sa 9:1 6872

ZERUAH *(ze-ru'-ah)* {1} *Mother of Jeroboam 1.*
whose mother's name was Z ... 1Kin 11:26 6871

ZERUBBABEL *(ze-rub'-ba-bel)* {22} See SHESHBAZZAR, ZOROBABEL. *A leader of a group of exiles.*
And the sons of Pedaiah were, Z ... 1Chr 3:19 2216
and the sons of Z ... 1Chr 3:19 2216
Which came with Z ... Ezr 2:2 2216
Z the son of Shealtiel, and his ... Ezr 3:2 2216
began Z the son of Shealtiel, and ... Ezr 3:8 2216
Then they came to Z, and to the ... Ezr 4:2 2216
But Z, and Jeshua, and the rest of ... Ezr 4:3 2216
Then rose up Z the son of ... Ezr 5:2 2217
Who came with Z, Jeshua, Nehemiah ... Neh 7:7 2216
up with Z the son of Shealtiel ... Neh 12:1 2216
And all Israel in the days of Z ... Neh 12:47 2216
unto Z the son of Shealtiel ... Hag 1:1 2216
Then Z the son of Shealtiel, and ... Hag 1:12 2216
spirit of Z the son of Shealtiel ... Hag 1:14 2216
Speak now to Z the son of ... Hag 2:2 2216
Yet now be strong, O Z, saith the ... Hag 2:4 2216
Speak to Z, governor of Judah, ... Hag 2:21 2216
of hosts, will I take thee, O Z ... Hag 2:23 2216
is the word of the LORD unto Z ... Zec 4:6 2216
before Z thou shalt become a ... Zec 4:7 2216
The hands of Z have laid the ... Zec 4:9 2216
in the hand of Z with those seven ... Zec 4:10 2216

ZERUIAH *(ze-ru-i'-ah)* {26} *Sister of David.*
and to Abishai the son of Z ... 1Sa 26:6 6870
And Joab the son of Z, and the ... 2Sa 2:13 6870
there were three sons of Z there ... 2Sa 2:18 6870
the sons of Z be too hard for me ... 2Sa 3:39 6870
Joab the son of Z was over the ... 2Sa 8:16 6870
Now Joab the son of Z perceived ... 2Sa 14:1 6870
the son of Z unto the king ... 2Sa 16:9 6870
I to do with you, ye sons of Z ... 2Sa 16:10 6870
sister to Z Joab's mother ... 2Sa 17:25 6870
the hand of Abishai the son of Z ... 2Sa 18:2 6870
But Abishai the son of Z answered ... 2Sa 19:21 6870
I to do with you, ye sons of Z ... 2Sa 19:22 6870
the son of Z succoured him ... 2Sa 21:17 6870
the brother of Joab, the son of Z ... 2Sa 23:18 6870
armourbearer to Joab the son of Z ... 2Sa 23:37 6870
conferred with Joab the son of Z ... 1Kin 1:7 6870
what Joab the son of Z did to me ... 1Kin 2:5 6870
priest, and for Joab the son of Z ... 1Kin 2:22 6870
Whose sisters were Z, and Abigail ... 1Chr 2:16 6870
And the sons of Z ... 1Chr 2:16 6870
Joab the son of Z went first up ... 1Chr 11:6 6870
armourbearer of Joab the son of Z ... 1Chr 11:39 6870
Abishai the son Z slew of the ... 1Chr 18:12 6870
Joab the son of Z was over the ... 1Chr 18:15 6870
son of Ner, and Joab the son of Z ... 1Chr 26:28 6870
Joab the son of Z began to number ... 1Chr 27:24 6870

ZETHAM *(ze'-tham)* {2} *A descendant of Laadan.*
the chief was Jehiel, and Z ... 1Chr 23:8 2241
Z, and Joel his brother, which ... 1Chr 26:22 2241

ZETHAN *(ze'-than)* {1} *A son of Bilhan.*
and Ehud, and Chenaanah, and Z ... 1Chr 7:10 2133

ZETHAR *(ze'-thar)* {1} *A servant of King Ahasuerus.*
Harbona, Bigtha, and Abagtha, Z ... Est 1:10 2242

ZEUS See MERCURIUS.

ZIA *(zi'-ah)* {1} *A Gadite in Bashan.*
Sheba, and Jorai, and Jachan, and Z ... 1Chr 5:13 2127

ZIBA *(zi'-bah)* {16} *A servant of King Saul.*
Saul a servant whose name was Z ... 2Sa 9:2 6717
king said unto him, Art thou Z ... 2Sa 9:2 6717
Z said unto the king, Jonathan ... 2Sa 9:3 6717
Z said unto the king, Behold, he ... 2Sa 9:4 6717
Then the king called to Z ... 2Sa 9:9 6717
Now Z had fifteen sons and twenty ... 2Sa 9:10 6717
Then said Z unto the king, ... 2Sa 9:11 6717
all that dwelt in the house of Z ... 2Sa 9:12 6717
Z the servant of Mephibosheth met ... 2Sa 16:1 6717
And the king said unto Z, What ... 2Sa 16:2 6717
Z said, The asses be for the ... 2Sa 16:2 6717
Z said unto the king, Behold, he ... 2Sa 16:3 6717
Then said the king to Z, Behold, ... 2Sa 16:4 6717
Z said, I humbly beseech thee ... 2Sa 16:4 6717
Z the servant of the house of ... 2Sa 19:17 6717
said, Thou and Z divide the land ... 2Sa 19:29 6717

ZIBEON *(zib'-e-un)* {8}
1. Grandfather of Adah.
Anah the daughter of Z the Hivite ... Gen 36:2 6649
of Anah the daughter of Z ... Gen 36:14 6649
2. A son of Seir.
Lotan, and Shobal, and Z, and Anah, ... Gen 36:20 6649
And these are the children of Z ... Gen 36:24 6649
he fed the asses of Z his father ... Gen 36:24 6649
duke Lotan, duke Shobal, duke Z ... Gen 36:29 6649
Lotan, and Shobal, and Z, and Anah, ... 1Chr 1:38 6649
And the sons of Z ... 1Chr 1:40 6649

ZIBIA *(zib'-e-ah)* {1} *Son of Hodesh.*
of Hodesh his wife, Jobab, and Z ... 1Chr 8:9 6644

ZIBIAH *(zib'-e-ah)* {2} *Mother of King Jehoash.*
mother's name was Z of Beer-sheba ... 2Kin 12:1 6645
name also was Z of Beer-sheba ... 2Chr 24:1 6645

ZICHRI *(zik'-ri)* {12} See ZITHRI.
1. A son of Izhar.
Korah, and Nepheg, and Z ... Ex 6:21 2147
2. A Benjamite.
And Jakim, and Z, and Zabdi, ... 1Chr 8:19 2147
3. Son of Shishak.
And Abdon, and Z, and Hanan, ... 1Chr 8:23 2147
4. Son of Jeroham.
And Jaresiah, and Eliah, and Z ... 1Chr 8:27 2147
5. Son of Asaph.
the son of Micah, the son of Z ... 1Chr 9:15 2147
6. Descendant of Eliezer.
Z his son, and Shelomith his son ... 1Chr 26:25 2147
7. Father of Eliezer.
was Eliezer the son of Z ... 1Chr 27:16 2147
8. Father of Amasiah.
next him was Amasiah the son of Z ... 2Chr 17:16 2147
9. Father of Elishaphat.
and Elishaphat the son of Z ... 2Chr 23:1 2147
10. A "mighty man" of Ephraim.
And Z, a mighty man of Ephraim, ... 2Chr 28:7 2147
11. Father of Joel.
Joel the son of Z was their ... Neh 11:9 2147
12. A priest with Zerubbabel.
Of Abijah, Z ... Neh 12:17 2147

ZICRI See ZICHRI.

ZIDDIM *(zid'-dim)* {1} *A city in Naphtali.*
And the fenced cities are Z ... Josh 19:35 6661

ZIDKIJAH *(zid-ki'-jah)* {1} See ZEDEKIAH. *A clan leader who renewed the covenant.*
the son of Hachaliah, and Z ... Neh 10:1 6667

ZIDON *(zi'-don)* {21}
1. A city in Asher.
and his border shall be unto Z ... Gen 49:13 6721
them, and chased them unto great Z ... Josh 11:8 6721
and Kanah, even unto great Z ... Josh 19:28 6721
Accho, nor the inhabitants of Z ... Judg 1:31 6721
gods of Syria, and the gods of Z ... Judg 10:6 6721
because it was far from Z ... Judg 18:28 6721
came to Dan-jaan, and about to Z ... 2Sa 24:6 6721
Zarephath, which belongeth to Z ... 1Kin 17:9 6721
and drink, and oil, unto them of Z ... Ezr 3:7 6722
thou whom the merchants of Z ... Is 23:2 6721
Be thou ashamed, O Z ... Is 23:4 6721
oppressed virgin, daughter of Z ... Is 23:12 6721
of Tyrus, and all the kings of Z ... Jer 25:22 6721
of Tyrus, and to the king of Z ... Jer 27:3 6721
Z every helper that remaineth ... Jer 47:4 6721
The inhabitants of Z and Arvad ... Eze 27:8 6721
of man, set thy face against Z ... Eze 28:21 6721
Behold, I am against thee, O Z ... Eze 28:22 6721
ye to do with me, O Tyre, and Z ... Joel 3:4 6721
Tyrus, and Z, though it be very ... Zec 9:2 6721
2. A son of Canaan.
Canaan begat Z his firstborn, and ... 1Chr 1:13 6721

ZIDONIANS *(zi-do'-ne-uns)* {10} See SIDONIANS. *Inhabitants of Zidon.*
The Z also, and the Amalekites, and... Judg 10:12 6722
after the manner of the Z... Judg 18:7 6722
and they were far from the Z... Judg 18:7 6722
Moabites, Ammonites, Edomites, Z... 1Kin 11:1 6722
Ashtoreth the goddess of the Z... 1Kin 11:5 6722
Ashtoreth the goddess of the Z... 1Kin 11:33 6722
daughter of Ethbaal king of the Z... 1Kin 16:31 6722
the abomination of the Z, and for... 2Kin 23:13 6722
for the Z and they of Tyre brought... 1Chr 22:4 6722
north, all of them, and all the Z... Eze 32:30 6722

ZIF *(zif)* {2} *Second month of the Hebrew year.*
reign over Israel, in the month Z... 1Kin 6:1 2099
of the LORD laid, in the month Z... 1Kin 6:37 2099

ZIHA *(zi'-hah)* {3}
1. A family of exiles.
the children of Z, the children... Ezr 2:43 6727
the children of Z, the children... Neh 7:46 6727
2. An overseer of Temple servants.
and Z and Gispa were over the... Neh 11:21 6727

ZIKLAG *(zik'-lag)* {15} *A city in Judah.*
And Z, and Madmannah, and... Josh 15:31 6860
And Z, and Beth-marcaboth, and... Josh 19:5 6860
Then Achish gave him Z that day... 1Sa 27:6 6860
wherefore Z pertaineth unto the... 1Sa 27:6 6860
were come to Z on the third day... 1Sa 30:1 6860
south, and Z, and smitten Z... 1Sa 30:1 6860
and we burned Z with fire... 1Sa 30:14 6860
And when David came to Z, he sent... 1Sa 30:26 6860
And David had abode two days in Z... 2Sa 1:1 6860
hold of him, and slew him in Z... 2Sa 4:10 6860
at Bethuel, and at Hormah, and at Z... 1Chr 4:30 6860
are they that came to David to Z... 1Chr 12:1 6860
As he went to Z, there fell to... 1Chr 12:20 6860
And at Z, and at Mekonah, and in the... Neh 11:28 6860

ZILLAH *(zil'-lah)* {3} *A wife of Lamech.*
Adah, and the name of the other Z... Gen 4:19 6741
And Z, she also bare Tubal-cain,... Gen 4:22 6741
said unto his wives, Adah and Z... Gen 4:23 6741

ZILLETHAI See ZILTHAI.

ZILPAH *(zil'-pah)* {7} *Handmaid of Leah.*
Leah Z his maid for an handmaid... Gen 29:24 2153
left bearing, she took Z her maid... Gen 30:9 2153
Z Leah's maid bare Jacob a son... Gen 30:10 2153
Z Leah's maid bare Jacob a second... Gen 30:12 2153
And the sons of Z, Leah's handmaid... Gen 35:26 2153
of Bilhah, and with the sons of Z... Gen 37:2 2153
These are the sons of Z, whom... Gen 46:18 2153

ZILTHAI *(zil'-thahee)* {2}
1. Son of Shimhi.
And Elienai, and Z, and Eliel,... 1Chr 8:20 6769
2. A warrior in David's army.
and Jozabad, and Elihu, and Z... 1Chr 12:20 6769

ZIMMAH *(zim'-mah)* {3}
1. A son of Jahath.
son, Jahath his son, Z his son,... 1Chr 6:20 2155
2. A Gershonite.
The son of Ethan, the son of Z... 1Chr 6:42 2155
3. Father of Joah.
Joah the son of Z, and Eden the... 2Chr 29:12 2155

ZIMRAN *(zim'-ran)* {2} *A son of Abraham.*
And she bare him Z, and Jokshan, and... Gen 25:2 2175
she bare Z, and Jokshan, and Medan,... 1Chr 1:32 2175

ZIMRI *(zim'-ri)* {15}
1. A Simeonite.
with the Midianitish woman, was Z... Num 25:14 2174
2. A king of Israel.
And his servant Z, captain of half... 1Kin 16:9 2174
Z went in and smote him, and killed... 1Kin 16:10 2174
Thus did Z destroy all the house... 1Kin 16:12 2174
did Z reign seven days in Tirzah... 1Kin 16:15 2174
Z hath conspired, and hath also... 1Kin 16:16 2174
when Z saw that the city was... 1Kin 16:18 2174
Now the rest of the acts of Z... 1Kin 16:20 2174
Had Z peace, who slew his master... 2Kin 9:31 2174
3. A son of Zerah.
Z, and Ethan, and Heman, and Calcol,... 1Chr 2:6 2174
4. Son of Jehoadah.
begat Alemeth, and Azmaveth, and Z... 1Chr 8:36 2174
and Z begat Moza,... 1Chr 8:36 2174
begat Alemeth, and Azmaveth, and Z... 1Chr 9:42 2174
and Z begat Moza... 1Chr 9:42 2174
5. An unspecified place.
And all the kings of Z, and all the... Jer 25:25 2174

ZIN *(zin)* {10} *A wilderness south of Judah.*
the wilderness of Z unto Rehob... Num 13:21 6790
desert of Z in the first month... Num 20:1 6790
my commandment in the desert of Z... Num 27:14 6790
in Kadesh in the wilderness of Z... Num 27:14 6790
and pitched in the wilderness of Z... Num 33:36 6790
of Z along by the coast of Edom... Num 34:3 6790
of Akrabbim, and pass on to Z... Num 34:4 6790
in the wilderness of Z... Deut 32:51 6790
of Edom the wilderness of Z... Josh 15:1 6790
and passed along to Z, and... Josh 15:3 6790

ZINA *(zi'-nah)* {1} *A son of Shimei.*
sons of Shimei were, Jahath, Z... 1Chr 23:10 2126

ZION *(zi'-un)* {152} See SION, ZION'S. *A term for Jerusalem.*
David took the strong hold of Z... 2Sa 5:7 6726
of the city of David, which is Z... 1Kin 8:1 6726
daughter of Z hath despised thee... 2Kin 19:21 6726
they that escape out of mount Z... 2Kin 19:31 6726
David took the castle of Z... 1Chr 11:5 6726
of the city of David, which is Z... 2Chr 5:2 6726
my king upon my holy hill of Z... Ps 2:6 6726
to the LORD, which dwelleth in Z... Ps 9:11 6726
in the gates of the daughter of Z... Ps 9:14 6726
of Israel were come out of Z... Ps 14:7 6726
and strengthen thee out of Z... Ps 20:2 6726
of the whole earth, is mount Z... Ps 48:2 6726
Let mount Z rejoice, let the... Ps 48:11 6726
Walk about Z, and go round about... Ps 48:12 6726
Out of Z, the perfection of... Ps 50:2 6726
good in thy good pleasure unto Z... Ps 51:18 6726
of Israel were come out of Z... Ps 53:6 6726
For God will save Z, and will... Ps 69:35 6726
this mount Z, wherein thou hast... Ps 74:2 6726
and his dwelling place in Z... Ps 76:2 6726
the mount Z which he loved... Ps 78:68 6726
of them in Z appeareth before God... Ps 84:7 6726
The LORD loveth the gates of Z... Ps 87:2 6726
of Z it shall be said, This and... Ps 87:5 6726
Z heard, and was glad... Ps 97:8 6726
The LORD is great in Z... Ps 99:2 6726
shalt arise, and have mercy upon Z... Ps 102:13 6726
When the LORD shall build up Z... Ps 102:16 6726
declare the name of the LORD in Z... Ps 102:21 6726
the rod of thy strength out of Z... Ps 110:2 6726
in the LORD shall be as mount Z... Ps 125:1 6726
turned again the captivity of Z... Ps 126:1 6726
LORD shall bless thee out of Z... Ps 128:5 6726
and turned back that hate Z... Ps 129:5 6726
For the LORD hath chosen Z... Ps 132:13 6726
descended upon the mountains of Z... Ps 133:3 6726
and earth bless thee out of Z... Ps 134:3 6726
Blessed be the LORD out of Z... Ps 135:21 6726
we wept, when we remembered Z... Ps 137:1 6726
Sing us one of the songs of Z... Ps 137:3 6726
reign for ever, even thy God, O Z... Ps 146:10 6726
praise thy God, O Z... Ps 147:12 6726
let the children of Z be joyful... Ps 149:2 6726
Go forth, O ye daughters of Z... Song 3:11 6726
the daughter of Z is left as a... Is 1:8 6726
Z shall be redeemed with judgment... Is 1:27 6726
for out of Z shall go forth the... Is 2:3 6726
the daughters of Z are haughty... Is 3:16 6726
of the head of the daughters of Z... Is 3:17 6726
pass, that he that is left in Z... Is 4:3 6726
the filth of the daughters of Z... Is 4:4 6726
every dwelling place of mount Z... Is 4:5 6726
hosts, which dwelleth in mount Z... Is 8:18 6726
his whole work upon mount Z... Is 10:12 6726
O my people that dwellest in Z... Is 10:24 6726
the mount of the daughter of Z... Is 10:32 6726
and shout, thou inhabitant of Z... Is 12:6 6726
That the LORD hath founded Z... Is 14:32 6726
the mount of the daughter of Z... Is 16:1 6726
of the LORD of hosts, the mount Z... Is 18:7 6726
of hosts shall reign in mount Z... Is 24:23 6726
I lay in Z for a foundation a... Is 28:16 6726
be, that fight against mount Z... Is 29:8 6726
shall dwell in Z at Jerusalem... Is 30:19 6726
come down to fight for mount Z... Is 31:4 6726
the LORD, whose fire is in Z... Is 31:9 6726
he hath filled Z with judgment... Is 33:5 6726
The sinners in Z are afraid... Is 33:14 6726
Look upon Z, the city of our... Is 33:20 6726
for the controversy of Z... Is 34:8 6726
and come to Z with songs and... Is 35:10 6726
The virgin, the daughter of Z... Is 37:22 6726
they that escape out of mount Z... Is 37:32 6726
O Z, that bringest good tidings,... Is 40:9 6726
The first shall say to Z, Behold,... Is 41:27 6726
in Z for Israel my glory... Is 46:13 6726
But Z said, The LORD hath... Is 49:14 6726
For the LORD shall comfort Z... Is 51:3 6726
and come with singing unto Z... Is 51:11 6726
of the earth, and say unto Z... Is 51:16 6726
put on thy strength, O Z... Is 52:1 6726
thy neck, O captive daughter of Z... Is 52:2 6726
that saith unto Z, Thy God... Is 52:7 6726
when the LORD shall bring again Z... Is 52:8 6726
And the Redeemer shall come to Z... Is 59:20 6726
The Z of the Holy One of Israel... Is 60:14 6726
appoint unto them that mourn in Z... Is 61:3 6726
Say ye to the daughter of Z... Is 62:11 6726
Z is a wilderness, Jerusalem a... Is 64:10 6726
for as soon as Z travailed... Is 66:8 6726
family, and I will bring you to Z... Jer 3:14 6726
Set up the standard toward Z... Jer 4:6 6726
the voice of the daughter of Z... Jer 4:31 6726
the daughter of Z to a comely... Jer 6:2 6726
war against thee, O daughter of Z... Jer 6:23 6726
Is not the LORD in Z... Jer 8:19 6726
of wailing is heard out of Z... Jer 9:19 6726
hath thy soul lothed Z... Jer 14:19 6726
Z shall be plowed like a field,... Jer 26:18 6726
an Outcast, saying, This is Z... Jer 30:17 6726
let us go up to Z unto the LORD... Jer 31:6 6726
come and sing in the height of Z... Jer 31:12 6726
They shall ask the way to Z with... Jer 50:5 6726
to declare in Z the vengeance of... Jer 50:28 6726
let us declare in Z the work of... Jer 51:10 6726
they have done in Z in your sight... Jer 51:24 6726
shall the inhabitant of Z say... Jer 51:35 6726
The ways of Z do mourn, because... Lam 1:4 6726
from the daughter of Z all her... Lam 1:6 6726
Z spreadeth forth her hands, and... Lam 1:17 6726
of Z with a cloud in his anger... Lam 2:1 6726
tabernacle of the daughter of Z... Lam 2:4 6726
and sabbaths to be forgotten in Z... Lam 2:6 6726
the wall of the daughter of Z... Lam 2:8 6726
daughter of Z sit upon the ground... Lam 2:10 6726
thee, O virgin daughter of Z... Lam 2:13 6726
Lord, O wall of the daughter of Z... Lam 2:18 6726
The precious sons of Z,... Lam 4:2 6726
and hath kindled a fire in Z... Lam 4:11 6726
is accomplished, O daughter of Z... Lam 4:22 6726
They ravished the women in Z... Lam 5:11 6726
Because of the mountain of Z... Lam 5:18 6726
Blow ye the trumpet in Z, and... Joel 2:1 6726
Blow the trumpet in Z, sanctify a... Joel 2:15 6726
Be glad then, ye children of Z... Joel 2:23 6726
for in mount Z and in Jerusalem... Joel 2:32 6726
The LORD also shall roar out of Z... Joel 3:16 6726
the LORD your God dwelling in Z... Joel 3:17 6726
for the LORD dwelleth in Z... Joel 3:21 6726
said, The LORD will roar from Z... Amos 1:2 6726
Woe to them that are at ease in Z... Amos 6:1 6726
But upon mount Z shall be... Obad 17 6726
Z to judge the mount of Esau... Obad 21 6726
of the sin to the daughter of Z... Mic 1:13 6726
They build up Z with blood... Mic 3:10 6726
Therefore shall Z for your sake... Mic 3:12 6726
for the law shall go forth of Z... Mic 4:2 6726
them in mount Z from henceforth... Mic 4:7 6726
strong hold of the daughter of Z... Mic 4:8 6726
to bring forth, O daughter of Z... Mic 4:10 6726
and let our eye look upon Z... Mic 4:11 6726
Arise and thresh, O daughter of Z... Mic 4:13 6726
Sing, O daughter of Z... Zeph 3:14 6726
and to Z, Let not thine hands be... Zeph 3:16 6726
for Z with a great jealousy... Zec 1:14 6726
and the LORD shall yet comfort Z... Zec 1:17 6726
Deliver thyself, O Z, that... Zec 2:7 6726
Sing and rejoice, O daughter of Z... Zec 2:10 6726
I was jealous for Z with great... Zec 8:2 6726
I am returned unto Z, and will... Zec 8:3 6726
Rejoice greatly, O daughter of Z... Zec 9:9 6726
and raised up thy sons, O Z... Zec 9:13 6726

ZION'S *(zi'-uns)* {1}
For Z sake will I not hold my... Is 62:1 6726

ZIOR *(zi'-or)* {1} *A city in Judah.*
which is Hebron, and Z... Josh 15:54 6730

ZIPH *(zif)* {10} See ZIPHITES.
1. A city in southeast Judah.
Z, and Telem, and Bealoth,... Josh 15:24 2128
a mountain in the wilderness of Z... 1Sa 23:14 2128
in the wilderness of Z in a wood... 1Sa 23:15 2128
arose, and went to Z before Saul... 1Sa 23:24 2128
went down to the wilderness of Z... 1Sa 26:2 2128
seek David in the wilderness of Z... 1Sa 26:2 2128
And Gath, and Mareshah, and Z... 2Chr 11:8 2128
2. A city in Judah near Carmel.
Maon, Carmel, and Z, and Juttah,... Josh 15:55 2128
3. A descendant of Caleb.
which was the father of Z... 1Chr 2:42 2128
4. A son of Jehalaleel.
Z, and Ziphah, Tiria, and Asareel... 1Chr 4:16 2128

ZIPHAH *(zi'-fah)* {1} *A son of Jehalaleel.*
Ziph, and Z, Tiria, and Asareel... 1Chr 4:16 2129

ZIPHIMS *(zif'-ims)* {1} See ZIPHITES. *Same as Ziphites.*
A Psalm of David, when the Z came... Ps 54:*t* 2130

ZIPHION *(zif'-e-on)* {1} See ZEPHON. *A son of Gad.*
Z, and Haggi, Shuni, and Ezbon, Eri... Gen 46:16 6837

ZIPHITES *(zif'-ites)* {2} See ZIPHIMS. *Inhabitants of Ziph.*
Then came up the Z to Saul to... 1Sa 23:19 2130
the Z came unto Saul to Gibeah,... 1Sa 26:1 2130

ZIPHRON *(zif'-ron)* {1} *A place in northern Palestine.*
And the border shall go on to Z... Num 34:9 2202

ZIPPOR *(zip'-por)* {7} *Father of Balak.*
Balak the son of Z saw all that... Num 22:2 6834
Balak the son of Z was king of... Num 22:4 6834
said unto God, Balak the son of Z... Num 22:10 6834
Thus saith Balak the son of Z... Num 22:16 6834
hearken unto me, thou son of Z... Num 23:18 6834
Then Balak the son of Z, king of... Josh 24:9 6834
better than Balak the son of Z... Judg 11:25 6834

ZIPPORAH *(zip-po'-rah)* {3} *Wife of Moses.*
and he gave Moses Z his daughter... Ex 2:21 6855
Then Z took a sharp stone, and cut... Ex 4:25 6855
Moses' father in law, took Z... Ex 18:2 6855

ZITHRI *(zith'-ri)* {1} See ZICHRI. *A son of Uzziel.*
Mishael, and Elzaphan, and Z... Ex 6:22 5644

ZIV See ZIF.

ZIZ *(ziz)* {1} *A place in Judah.*
they come up by the cliff of Z... 2Chr 20:16 6732

ZIZA *(zi'-zah)* {2} See ZIZAH.
1. Son of Ziphi.
Z the son of Shiphi, the son of... 1Chr 4:37 2124
2. A son of Rehoboam.
bare him Abijah, and Attai, and Z... 2Chr 11:20 2124

ZIZAH *(zi'-zah)* {1} See ZINA, ZIZA. *Son of Shimei.*
was the chief, and Z the second... 1Chr 23:11 2125

ZOAN *(zo'-an)* {7} *An Egyptian city.*
seven years before Z in Egypt... Num 13:22 6814
land of Egypt, in the field of Z... Ps 78:12 6814
and his wonders in the field of Z... Ps 78:43 6814
Surely the princes of Z are fools... Is 19:11 6814
The princes of Z are become fools... Is 19:13 6814
For his princes were at Z... Is 30:4 6814
desolate, and will set fire in Z... Eze 30:14 6814

ZOAR *(zo'-ar)* {10} *A Canaanite city.*
of Egypt, as thou comest unto Z............Gen 13:10 6820
and the king of Bela, which is Z............Gen 14:2 6820
the king of Bela (the same is Z............Gen 14:8 6820
the name of the city was called Z..........Gen 19:22 6820
the earth when Lot entered into Z..........Gen 19:23 6820
And Lot went up out of Z, and dwelt.....Gen 19:30 6820
for he feared to dwell in Z.....................Gen 19:30 6820
the city of palm trees, unto Z.................Deut 34:3 6820
his fugitives shall flee unto Z.................Is 15:5 6820
from Z even unto Horonaim, as an.........Jer 48:34 6820

ZOBA *(zo'-bah)* {2} See ZOBAH. *A district in northern Syria.*
Beth-rehob, and the Syrians of Z...........2Sa 10:6 6678
and the Syrians of Z, and of Rehob,........2Sa 10:8 6678

ZOBAH *(zo'-bah)* {11} See ZOBA. *Same as Zoba.*
Edom, and against the kings of Z..........1Sa 14:47 6678
the son of Rehob, king of Z.....................2Sa 8:3 6678
to succour Hadadezer king of Z.............2Sa 8:5 6678
son of Rehob, king of Z..........................2Sa 8:12 6678
Igal the son of Nathan of Z....................2Sa 23:36 6678
from his lord Hadadezer king of Z.........1Kin 11:23 6678
a band, when David slew them of Z.......1Kin 11:24 6678
Hadarezer king of Z unto Hamath..........1Chr 18:3 6678
came to help Hadarezer king of Z............1Chr 18:5 6678
the host of Hadarezer king of Z..............1Chr 18:9 6678
out of Syria-maachah, and out of Z........1Chr 19:6 6678

ZOBEBAH *(zo-be'-bah)* {1} *A daughter of Coz.*
And Coz begat Anub, and Z, and the......1Chr 4:8 6637

ZOHAR *(zo'-har)* {4} See ZERAH, ZEROR.
1. Father of Ephron.
for me to Ephron the son of Z.................Gen 23:8 6714
Ephron the son of Z the Hittite..............Gen 25:9 6714
2. Son of Simeon.
Jamin, and Ohad, and Jachin, and Z......Gen 46:10 6714
Jamin, and Ohad, and Jachin, and Z......Ex 6:15 6714

ZOHELETH *(zo'-he-leth)* {1} *A stone near En-rogel.*
and fat cattle by the stone of Z..............1Kin 1:9 2120

ZOHETH *(zo'heth)* {1} *Son of Ishi.*
And the sons of Ishi were, Z...................1Chr 4:20 2105

ZOPHAH *(zo'-fah)* {2} *Son of Helem.*
Z, and Imna, and Shelesh, and Amal......1Chr 7:35 6690
The sons of Z..1Chr 7:36 6690

ZOPHAI *(zo'-fahee)* {1} See ZUPH. *Brother of Samuel.*
Z his son, and Nahath his son,................1Chr 6:26 6689

ZOPHAR *(zo'-far)* {4}
the Shuhite, and Z the Naamathite........Job 2:11 6691
Then answered Z the Naamathite,..........Job 11:1 6691
Then answered Z the Naamathite,..........Job 20:1 6691
Z the Naamathite went, and did............Job 42:9 6691

ZOPHIM *(zo'-fim)* {1} *A peak on Mt. Pisgah.*
brought him into the field of Z..............Num 23:14 6839

ZORAH *(zo'-rah)* {8} See ZAREAH, ZORATHITES, ZOREAH, ZORITES. *A city in Judah.*
coast of their inheritance was Z.............Josh 19:41 6681
And there was a certain man of Z..........Judg 13:2 6681
in the camp of Dan between Z................Judg 13:25 6681
him up, and buried him between Z.........Judg 16:31 6681
coasts, men of valour, from Z.................Judg 18:2 6681
came unto their brethren to Z................Judg 18:8 6681
family of the Danites, out of Z...............Judg 18:11 6681
And Z, and Aijalon, and Hebron,............2Chr 11:10 6681

ZORATHITES *(zo'-rath-ites)* {1} *Descendants of Shobal.*
These are the families of the Z..............1Chr 4:2 6882

ZOREAH *(zo'-re-ah)* {1} *Same as Zorah.*
And in the valley, Eshtaol, and Z...........Josh 15:33 6881

ZORITES *(zo'-rites)* {1} See ZAREATHITES, ZORATHITES. *Descendants of Salma.*
half of the Manahethites, the Z..............1Chr 2:54 6882

ZOROBABEL *(zo-rob'-a-bel)* {3} See ZERUBBABEL. *Father of Abiud; ancestor of Jesus.*
and Salathiel begat Z.............................Mt 1:12 *2216*
And Z begat Abiud..................................Mt 1:13 *2216*
of Rhesa, which was the son of Z...........Lk 3:27 *2216*

ZUAR *(zu'-ar)* {5} *Father of Nethaneel.*
Nethaneel the son of Z...........................Num 1:8 6686
Nethaneel the son of Z shall be.............Num 2:5 6686
second day Nethaneel the son of Z.........Num 7:18 6686
of Nethaneel the son of Z.......................Num 7:23 6686
was Nethaneel the son of Z.....................Num 10:15 6686

ZUPH *(zuf)* {3}
1. An ancestor of Samuel.
the son of Tohu, the son of Z...................1Sa 1:1 6689
The son of Z, the son of Elkanah,...........1Chr 6:35 6689
2. A district in Jerusalem.
they were come to the land of Z.............1Sa 9:5 6689

ZUPHITE See ZUPH.

ZUR *(zur)* {5}
1. Father of Cozbi.
was Cozbi, the daughter of Z.................Num 25:15 6698
namely, Evi, and Rekem, and Z..............Num 31:8 6698
of Midian, Evi, and Rekem, and Z...........Josh 13:21 6698
2. Son of Jeiel.
And his firstborn son Abdon, and Z.......1Chr 8:30 6698
his firstborn son Abdon, then Z..............1Chr 9:36 6698

ZURIEL *(zu'-re-el)* {1} *Son of Abihail.*
Merari was Z the son of Abihail............Num 3:35 6700

ZURISHADDAI *(zu-re-shad'-da-i)* {5} *Father of Shelumiel.*
Shelumiel the son of Z...........................Num 1:6 6701
shall be Shelumiel the son of Z..............Num 2:12 6701
fifth day Shelumiel the son of Z............Num 7:36 6701
of Shelumiel the son of Z.......................Num 7:41 6701
Simeon was Shelumiel the son of Z........Num 10:19 6701

ZUZIMS *(zu'-zims)* {1} See ZAMZUMMIMS. *A tribe in the land of Ham.*
the Z in Ham, and the Emims in.............Gen 14:5 2104

APPENDIX OF ARTICLES, CONJUNCTIONS, PREPOSITIONS, ETC.

A

Gen 1:6; 29; 2:5; 6; 7; 8; 10; 21; 22; 24; 3:6; 24; 4:1; 2(2); 12(2); 14(2); 15; 17; 23(2); 25; 26; 5:3; 28; 6:9; 16(2); 17; 8:1; 7; 8; 21; 9:11(2); 13(2); 14; 15; 20; 23; 25; 10:8; 9; 12; 30; 11:2; 4(3); 12:1; 2(2); 8; 10; 11; 13:7; 16; 14:23(2); 15:1; 9(4); 12; 13(3); 15; 17(2); 18; 16:7; 11; 12; 15; 17:4; 5; 7; 8; 11; 16(2); 17; 19; 20; 18:4; 5; 7(2); 10; 13(2); 14; 18; 19:3; 9; 20(2); 26; 28; 30; 31; 37; 38; 20:3(3); 4; 6; 7; 9; 16(2); 21:2; 7; 8; 13; 14; 16(2); 18; 19; 21; 25; 27; 30; 32; 33; 22:2; 6; 7; 8(2); 13(3); 23:4(4); 6; 9(2); 18; 20(2); 24:3; 4; 7; 11; 16; 17; 22(2); 29; 36; 37; 38; 40; 43; 55; 65; 25:1; 8; 27(3); 26:1; 8(2); 9; 19; 25; 28; 30; 35; 27:11(2); 12(3); 27; 34; 36; 44; 46; 28:1; 2; 3; 4; 6(3); 11; 12; 18; 20; 22; 29:2(2); 14; 20; 22; 32; 33; 34; 35; 30:5; 6; 7; 10; 11; 12; 15; 20; 21; 23; 30; 31:10; 11; 13; 24; 44(2); 45(2); 48; 32:13; 16; 18; 24; 28; 33:18; 19(2); 34:14; 35:11(2); 14(3); 16; 20; 37:1; 3; 5; 9; 15; 24; 25; 31; 38:1; 2(2); 3; 4; 5; 6; 11; 14; 17(2); 28; 39:2; 6; 14; 20; 40:4; 5; 8; 9; 19; 20; 41:2; 7; 11; 12; 15(2); 18; 33; 38(2); 42; 43:2; 6; 11(3); 44:15; 18; 19(2); 20(3); 25; 33; 45:7(2); 8(2); 46:3; 10; 29; 47:11; 22; 26; 48:4; 7; 16; 19(2); 49:6(2); 9(2); 10; 14; 15; 17; 19; 21; 22(3); 27; 30(2); 50:9; 10(2); 11; 13(2); 16; 26; **Ex** 1:8; 16(3); 2:1(2); 2(2); 7; 14(2); 15; 22(3); 3:2(2); 8(3); 12; 17; 19; 4:2; 3; 4; 10; 16; 25(2); 26; 5:1; 21; 6:1(2); 6; 7(2); 13; 15; 7:1; 9(2); 10; 15; 8:23; 24; 9:3; 5; 9; 10; 18; 24; 10:7; 9; 19; 22; 11:6; 7(2); 8; 12:3(2); 5; 13; 14(3); 19; 21; 22; 30(2); 38; 42; 45; 46; 48; 13:5; 6; 9(3); 12; 13; 16; 21(3); 14:20; 21; 22; 29; 15:3; 5; 16; 20; 25(2); 16:4; 14; 25; 33; 35; 17:12; 14(2); 18:3; 12; 16; 19:5; 6; 9; 16; 18(2); 19; 20:5; 21:4; 7(2); 8; 12; 13(2); 14; 16; 18; 20(2); 21; 22; 26; 28(2); 29(2); 30; 31(2); 32(2); 33(4); 22:1(3); 2; 5(2); 7; 10(2); 14; 16(2); 18; 19; 21; 25; 23:1; 2(2); 3; 7; 9(2); 14; 19; 33; 24:10(2); 12; 15; 25:8; 10(5); 11; 17(4); 23(4); 24; 25(2); 31; 33(4); 35(3); 39; 26:7; 13(2); 14(2); 16(3); 31; 27:4; 21; 28:4(5); 11; 12; 16(2); 17(3); 18(2); 19; 20(2); 21; 28; 29; 32; 34(4); 36(2); 37; 43; 29:9; 10; 14; 18(2); 22; 24; 25(2); 26; 28; 33; 36(2); 40(2); 41; 42; 30:2(2); 3; 8; 10; 12; 13(2); 15; 16; 18; 21; 33; 34; 35(2); 31:13; 16; 17; 32:4(2); 5; 8; 9; 10; 11; 17; 21; 29; 30; 31; 33:3(2); 5(2); 11(2); 21(2); 22; 34:9; 10(2); 12(2); 14; 15(2); 16(2); 20; 26; 27; 33; 35:2; 5; 29; 36:19(2); 21(3); 35; 37:1(5); 2; 6(2); 10(3); 11; 12(2); 19(4); 21(3); 24; 25(2); 26; 38:4; 23; 25; 26(2); 27(2); 39:7; 9(2); 10(3); 11(2); 12; 13(2); 14; 21; 23; 26(4); 28; 29; 30(2); 31; 40:34; **Lev** 1:3(2); 9(2); 10(2); 13(2); 17(2); 2:1; 2; 3; 4; 5(2); 6; 7; 9(2); 10; 12; 14; 15; 3:1(2); 5; 6; 7; 12; 16; 17; 4:2; 3(2); 12; 14; 20; 21; 22; 23(2); 24; 28(2); 31; 32(3); 33; 5:1(2); 2(3); 3; 4(2); 6(4); 7(3); 9; 10; 11(2); 12(2); 13; 15(4); 17; 18(2); 19; 6:2(3); 3; 6(2); 11; 15; 18; 20; 21(2); 22; 28; 7:5; 12; 16(2); 30; 34; 36; 8:2(2); 21(2); 26; 27; 28; 29; 9:2(4); 3(5); 4(3); 18; 21; 24; 10:9; 14; 15(2); 11:36; 47; 12:2(2); 5; 6(7); 7(2); 8(2); 13:2(3); 3; 5; 6; 8; 9; 12; 15; 18; 19(2); 20; 22; 23; 24(2); 25; 28; 29(2); 30(3); 37; 38(2); 39; 42(2); 44; 45; 47(2); 48; 49; 51(2); 52; 57; 59; 14:10; 12(2); 21(3); 22(2); 24; 31(2); 34(2); 35; 44; 55(2); 56(3); 15:2; 15(2); 19; 25; 30(2); 16:3(4); 4; 5(2); 9; 10; 12; 21; 22; 29(2); 31(2); 34; 17:6; 7(2); 8; 15; 18:5; 17; 18; 19; 23; 19:5; 14; 16; 19(2); 20(2); 21(2); 29; 33; 36(2); 20:5; 6; 12; 13(2); 14(2); 15(2); 16; 17(2); 18(2); 20; 21; 24; 27(3); 21:3; 4; 7(3); 13; 14(3); 18(4); 19; 20(2); 21(2); 23; 22:4(3); 5; 10; 12; 13; 14; 18; 19; 20; 21(2); 22; 23(4); 25; 27(3); 29; 23:10; 12; 13(2); 14; 16; 18; 19(2); 20; 21; 24(2); 27; 28; 31; 32; 36; 37(3); 39(3); 41(2); 24:3; 6; 7; 9; 10; 18; 19(2); 20(2); 21(2); 25:2; 4(2); 5; 10; 11; 24; 29(5); 30; 33; 35(2); 39; 40; 46; 47; 53; 26:1; 25; 33; 36(3); 37; 27:2(2); 4; 6; 7; 9; 10(4); 11; 13; 14; 16(3); 21; 22(2); 23; 27; 28; 31; **Num** 1:4; 3:15; 22; 28; 34; 39; 40; 43; 50; 4:6; 7; 8(2); 9; 10(2); 11(2); 12(3); 13; 14; 5:6(2); 12; 13; 21; 23; 27; 29; 6:2(2); 11(2); 12(2); 14(2); 15; 17; 20; 7:3; 13; 15; 16; 17; 19; 21; 22; 23; 25; 27; 28; 29; 31; 33; 34; 35; 37; 39; 40; 41; 43(2); 45; 46; 47; 49; 51; 52; 53; 55; 57; 58; 59; 61; 63; 64; 65; 67; 69; 70; 71; 73; 75; 76; 77; 79; 81; 82; 83; 8:8(2); 12(2); 19; 9:6; 7; 10(2); 13; 14; 20; 22(2); 10:2; 10; 33; 11:4; 8; 12; 20; 21; 25; 27; 31(3); 33; 12:6(3); 13:2(2); 23(2); 32(2); 14:3; 4; 8; 12; 14(3); 31; 34; 36; 15:3(5); 4(2); 5; 6(2); 7(2); 8(4); 9(2); 10(2); 11(2); 13; 14(2); 20; 24(3); 25; 27(2); 30; 32; 38; 39(2); 16:9; 13(3); 14; 21; 30; 35; 38(2); 39; 40; 45; 46; 17:2; 6; 10; 18:4; 6; 7; 11; 16; 17(4); 19(2); 23; 26; 19:2; 9(4); 10; 14(2); 16(5); 17; 18(3); 21; 20:15; 16; 20; 21:2; 8(2); 9(3); 28(2); 22:5; 11; 24(3); 26; 27; 29; 36; 23:2(2); 4(2); 5; 14(2); 16; 19; 21; 22; 24(2); 30(2); 24:4; 8; 9(2); 16; 17(2); 18(2); 21; 25:6; 7; 14(2); 15(2); 18; 26:10; 31; 62; 64; 65; 27:4; 7; 8; 11; 16; 18; 19; 23; 28:2; 3; 5(2); 6(3); 7; 8(2); 9; 11; 12(2); 13(5); 14(4); 15; 19(2); 20(2); 21; 22; 23; 24; 26; 27; 29; 29:1; 2(2); 3(2); 5; 6(2); 8(2); 9; 10; 11; 12; 13(3); 15; 16; 19; 22; 25; 28; 31; 34; 35; 36(3); 38; 30:2(3); 3(3); 9; 10; 16; 31:4; 5; 6; 16; 18; 28; 54; 32:1(2); 4; 5; 29; 34:5; 6; 35:4; 15; 16; 17(2); 18; 21; 23; 29; 31; **Deut** 1:11; 23; 25; 31; 33(2); 39; 2:5(2); 9(2); 10; 19; 20; 21; 35; 3:4; 5; 7; 11(2); 4:6; 12; 16; 20; 23; 24(2); 25; 31; 34(3); 5:2; 9; 15(3); 22; 6:8; 15; 21; 7:6; 8; 9; 16; 21; 23; 26(2); 8:5; 7(2); 8(2); 9(2); 9:2; 3; 6; 12; 13; 14; 16; 26; 10:7; 15; 17(3); 11:9; 10; 11; 12; 18; 26(2); 27; 28; 12:11; 13:1(4); 14:2; 21; 15:1; 3; 7; 9; 15; 18; 16:8; 10(2); 12; 15; 16; 19(2); 21; 17:8; 14; 15; 18(2); 18:3; 6; 10; 11(4); 15; 18; 20; 22; 19:3; 5(2); 15; 16; 18; 20:1; 5; 6; 7; 10; 19(2); 21:4; 11(2); 13; 15; 17; 18(2); 20(2); 22(3); 22:5(3); 6; 8(2); 11; 13; 14; 17; 19; 22(2); 23(3); 25(2); 26; 28(3); 30; 23:2; 5; 7; 12; 13; 17; 18(2); 20; 21; 23; 25; 24:1(3); 3; 5(2); 6; 7; 17; 18; 19; 22; 25:1; 2; 5; 7; 13(2); 14(2); 15(2); 26:2; 5(3); 8; 9; 15; 27:3; 14; 15; 28:22(2); 30(2); 33; 35; 36; 37(2); 46(2); 48; 49(2); 50; 65; 29:13(2); 18; 22; 31:6; 7; 14; 15(2); 16; 19; 21; 23(2); 24; 26; 32:4; 5; 10; 20; 21(2); 22; 28; 30; 47; 49; 33:2; 4; 20; 21; 22; 28; 34:6; 10; **Josh** 1:6; 9; 18; 2:12; 15; 3:4; 12; 4:2; 4; 5; 6; 7; 5:6; 13; 6:5(2); 18; 20; 7:1; 21(2); 26; 8:2; 11; 14; 17; 27; 28; 29(2); 32; 35; 9:6(2); 7; 9; 11; 15; 16; 10:2; 8; 10; 13; 14; 16; 17; 20; 11:14; 18; 19; 12:6; 7; 14:15; 15:3; 13; 18; 19(2); 17:1(2); 2; 14; 15; 17; 18; 18:9; 14; 20:4; 21:13; 21; 27; 32; 38; 44; 22:10; 14; 17; 20; 25; 27; 28; 34; 23:1; 10; 13; 24:7; 13; 19; 25(2); 26; 27(2); 32; 33; **Judg** 1:14; 15(2); 24; 26; 2:3; 17; 3:9; 15(4); 16(2); 17; 19; 20(2); 25; 27; 28; 29; 4:4; 9; 16; 18; 19(2); 21; 5:7; 8; 12; 14; 18; 25; 28; 30(3); 6:8; 17; 19(3); 26; 31; 34; 37; 38; 7:5; 13(5); 14; 16; 18; 8:14; 18; 20; 24; 25; 26; 27(2); 31; 32; 33; 9:8(2); 48; 49; 51; 53(3); 54; 10:1; 3; 11:1; 2; 30; 31; 33; 39; 40; 12:11; 13; 13:2; 3; 5(2); 6; 7(2); 15; 16; 19(3); 23(2); 24; 14:1; 2; 3(2); 5; 6; 8(2); 10; 12; 16; 18; 15:1(2); 3; 4; 8; 15(2); 16; 16:4; 9; 12; 17(2); 19; 23; 17:1; 3(2); 4(2); 7(2); 8; 9(2); 10(3); 13; 18:10(3); 14(2); 19(6); 22; 23; 27; 28; 19:1(2); 3; 5; 12; 15; 17; 24(2); 29; 20:10(2); 38; 40; 21:5; 15; 17; 18; 19(2); **Ruth** 1:1(2); 2:1(2); 3; 7; 10; 11; 12; 3:8; 9; 11; 12; 13(3); 14; 4:1; 3; 7(2); 13; 14; 15(2); 17(2); **1Sa** 1:1; 5; 9(2); 11(2); 15(2); 16; 20; 24; 25; 2:3; 13; 18(2); 19; 25; 27; 34; 35(2); 36(3); 3:11; 20; 4:5; 7; 10; 12; 13; 17; 20; 5:9; 11; 6:3; 7; 8(2); 9; 14(3); 17; 19; 7:9(2); 10; 12; 8:5; 6; 10; 19; 22; 9:1(3); 2(4); 6; 7; 8; 9(3); 12; 15; 16; 21; 27; 10:1; 3; 5(5); 10; 12; 19; 25; 26; 11:1; 2(2); 7; 13; 12:1; 12; 13; 17; 19; 13:2; 4; 6; 9; 12; 14; 21; 14:1; 2; 4(2); 10; 12; 14; 15; 20; 25; 29; 30; 33; 36; 39; 41; 43; 15:5; 12; 18; 28; 29; 16:1; 12; 16(2); 17; 18(4); 20(2); 17:3(3); 4(2); 5; 6; 7(2); 8(2); 10; 20; 29; 33(2); 34(3); 38; 40(2); 42(2); 43; 45(3); 46; 49; 50(2); 18:3; 10; 13; 21; 23(3); 19:2; 5(2); 8; 12; 13(2); 16; 22; 20:3; 6; 8; 16; 20; 21; 25; 29; 33; 35; 41; 21:2(2); 5(2); 7; 9; 22:2; 6; 8; 13; 18; 23:5; 7; 14; 15; 18; 25; 27; 24:3; 14(2); 19; 25:2(2); 3(2); 8; 10; 16; 17(2); 28; 29(2); 36(2); 37; 41; 26:12; 13; 15; 20(2); 27:5; 7; 10; 28:7(4); 9; 12; 14; 22; 24; 29:1; 30:12(2); 13; 17; 25; 26; 31:4; 13; **2Sa** 1:2; 13; 2:17; 18; 28; 3:7; 8(2); 11; 13; 20; 21; 22(2); 29(2); 33; 34; 38(2); 4:2; 4; 5; 10; 11; 5:2; 3; 23; 24; 6:3; 8; 14; 16; 19(3); 7:6(2); 7; 9; 10(2); 19(2); 23(2); 24; 8:2; 4; 13; 9:2; 3; 8; 12; 10:6; 11:2; 8; 14; 16; 21(3); 27; 12:3; 4; 24; 30; 13:1; 2; 3(2); 6; 9; 18; 14:2(4); 5; 13; 27(2); 15:2; 8; 13; 17; 19; 23; 27; 33; 16:1(3); 5; 8; 22; 23; 17:8(2); 9; 10(2); 13; 17; 18(3); 19; 25; 18:2(3); 7; 9(2); 10; 11; 12; 17(2); 18; 24; 27; 29; 19:4; 10; 16; 17; 18; 32(2); 35; 36(2); 20:1(3); 8(2); 12; 15; 16; 19(2); 21; 22; 26; 21:1; 16; 18; 19(3); 20(2); 22:9; 11; 20; 30(2); 31; 32; 35; 44; 23:4; 7; 10; 11(2); 12; 20(3); 21(3); 29; 24:14; 15; 23; 24; **1Kin** 1:2; 3(2); 6; 42; 52; 2:2; 4; 8(2); 9; 19; 42; 3:4; 5; 6; 7; 8; 9; 12; 15(2); 17; 24(2); 4:7; 32; 5:1; 7; 12; 13; 14(2); 6:21; 31; 33; 36; 7:3; 6; 7; 12; 14(3); 15; 23(2); 24; 26; 29; 31(2); 32(3); 33; 35(2); 8:9; 13; 21; 25; 41(2); 55; 63; 65(2); 9:5; 7(2); 16; 21; 25; 26; 10:2; 6; 18; 22; 25; 26; 28; 29; 11:17; 24; 26; 28; 29; 36; 38; 12:7; 11; 30; 32; 33; 13:1; 2; 3; 7; 18; 24; 14:3; 5; 10; 14; 15; 15:4; 13; 19(2); 22; 16:11; 31; 33; 17:7; 9; 10(2); 11; 12(4); 13; 19; 24; 18:2; 4; 13; 21; 22; 27(2); 32; 41; 44(2); 45; 19:2; 4(2); 5; 6(2); 9; 11; 12(2); 13; 21; 20:13; 21; 28; 30; 34; 35; 36(2); 39(3); 42; 21:1; 2(2); 9; 12; 22:7; 10; 17; 21; 22; 23; 34(3); 36; 47; **2Kin** 1:2; 3; 6(2); 8; 9; 10; 12; 13; 2:1; 9; 10; 11(2); 20; 3:4; 9; 11; 15; 18; 27; 4:1; 2; 3; 6(2); 8(2); 10(5); 11; 16; 17; 18; 19; 28; 38; 39; 42; 5:1(3); 2; 5; 7(2); 8; 10; 12; 14; 15; 19; 22; 26; 27; 6:2(2); 5; 6; 8; 9; 14; 25(2); 26; 32(2); 7:1(3); 2; 6(3); 9; 16(3); 18(3); 19; 8:1; 5; 6; 8; 9; 13; 15; 19; 20; 9:16; 17(2); 19; 24; 28; 30; 34; 10:2; 6; 8; 18; 19; 20; 21; 27; 11:4; 5; 6(2); 14; 17; 12:9(2); 20; 13:5; 21(2); 14:9; 19; 15:5(2); 13; 19; 25; 30; 16:8; 17; 17:16; 21; 35; 36; 18:17; 21; 28; 31; 32(4); 36; 19:3; 7(2); 17; 29; 31; 32; 20:3; 7; 10; 12; 14; 20(2); 21:3; 7; 13(2); 14(2); 22:10; 12; 19(2); 23:3(2); 8; 22; 30; 33(2); 24:16; 25:8; 23; 30(2); **1Chr** 2:34; 5:25; 6:33; 7:16; 23; 9:13; 10:4; 13; 11:3; 11; 13; 14; 20; 22(4); 23(4); 42; 12:2; 4; 14; 22; 28; 34; 38; 13:7; 11; 14:12; 15; 15:1(2); 13; 27; 28; 29; 16:3(3); 5; 15; 17; 19; 42; 17:6; 8; 9; 17(3); 21; 24; 18:4; 19:6; 20:2; 5; 6; 21:3; 5; 13; 16; 22:9(2); 14; 25:3; 26:14; 17(2); 30; 27:5; 32(3); 28:3; 9(2); 29:15; 19; 21(3); 28; **2Chr** 1:4; 6; 9; 14; 16; 17; 2:7; 12; 13; 14(2); 18; 4:2(2); 3; 5; 5:10; 13; 6:2; 5; 13; 16; 22; 32; 36; 7:5; 8; 9; 18; 20(2); 8:13; 9:1; 5; 17; 18; 24; 10:11; 13:5; 8; 9(2); 15; 17; 14:9; 15:3(2); 12; 14; 16; 16:3; 8; 10(2); 14; 17:17; 18:6; 9; 20; 21; 22; 33(3); 19:9; 20:2; 3; 8; 14; 19; 21:7; 8; 12; 13; 14; 17; 22:11; 23:3; 4; 5(2); 16; 24:8; 9; 24(2); 26; 25:2; 7; 15; 18; 27; 26:19; 21(3); 23; 28:5(2); 7; 9(2); 21; 29:10; 21; 31; 32; 30:5(2); 13; 18; 24(3); 32:18; 24; 33:6; 7; 14(2); 34:14; 18; 20; 31; 35:1; 3; 18; 36:3; 22; **Ezr** 1:1; 9; 10(2); 2:7; 12; 31; 37; 38; 39; 61; 63; 3:5; 11; 12; 13; 4:8; 10; 11; 15; 17; 5:7; 11; 13; 17; 6:1; 2(2); 3; 4; 8; 11(2); 12; 17; 7:6; 11; 12(2); 13; 21; 27; 8:18; 21(2); 22; 27; 28; 35(2); 9:7(2); 8(4); 9(2); 10:1; 3; 12; 13(2); 19; **Neh** 2:6; 8; 10; 17; 3:13; 4:2; 3; 4; 6; 9; 17; 22; 5:1; 7; 6:3; 7; 11; 7:2; 5; 12; 34; 40; 41; 42; 65; 70; 8:4; 18; 9:4; 8; 10; 11; 12(2); 17(2); 18; 25; 29; 31; 38; 10:29; 32; 11:23; 13:2; 5; 7; **Est** 1:3; 5; 6; 9; 19; 2:5(2); 18(2); 23; 3:4; 8; 13; 14; 4:1(2); 5; 14; 5:9; 14; 8:11; 13; 15(2); 17(2); 9:17; 18; 19(2); 22; 10:1; **Job** 1:1; 3; 6; 8; 13; 14; 19; 2:1; 3; 4; 8; 13; 3:3; 5; 23; 4:12(2); 15; 16; 17; 5:26(2); 6:15; 22; 27; 7:1; 2(2); 6; 12(3); 20(2); 8:2; 9; 14; 20; 9:2; 3; 17; 19; 25; 32; 10:16; 20; 22; 11:2; 12; 12:5; 14; 18; 24; 25; 13:25; 27; 28(2); 14:1; 3(2); 4; 7; 8; 10; 11; 16; 17; 15:2; 14; 21; 24; 16:8; 14; 21(2); 22; 17:3; 6(2); 7; 18:8(2); 10; 19:10; 15; 23; 29; 20:5; 8(2); 26; 29; 21:11; 13; 22:2; 6; 14; 16; 28; 24:3; 5; 8; 9; 14; 20; 24; 25; 25:4; 6(2); 26:14; 27:13; 18(2); 20; 21; 28:1(2); 7; 26(2); 29:14(2); 16; 25; 30:5; 14; 15; 29(2); 31:1(2); 3; 9; 12; 18; 23; 30; 34; 35; 36; 37; 32:8; 33:15(2); 23(2); 24; 25; 34:9; 11; 13; 18; 20; 29(2); 34; 35:8; 36:2; 16; 18; 37:4; 18; 20; 38:3; 9; 14; 25(2); 28; 30; 39:20; 40:7; 9; 17; 23; 41:1; 2; 4(2); 5; 6; 15; 18; 20; 21; 24(2); 29; 31(2); 32; 34; 42:8; 11; 12(2); **Ps** 1:3; 2:1; 9(2); 12; 3:t, 3; 4:t; 5:t, 4; 12; 6:t; 7:2; 15; 8:t, 5; 9:t, 6; 9(2); 10:9; 11:t, 1; 12:t, 2; 6; 13:t; 14:t; 15:t, 3; 4; 16:6; 17:t, 12(2); 18:t, 8; 10; 19; 29(2); 30; 31; 34; 43; 19:t, 4; 5(3); 20:t; 21:t, 3; 9; 11; 22:t, 6(2); 13(2); 15; 30(2); 31; 23:t, 5; 24:t, 4; 25:t; 26:t; 27:t, 5; 11; 28:t; 29:t, 6(2); 30:t, 5(2); 31:t, 8; 11(2); 12(2); 20; 21; 32:(2); 6; 33:3(2); 16; 17; 34:t, 18(2); 35:t, 7; 19; 36:t, 4; 6; 37:t, 10; 16(2); 23; 35; 38:t, 7; 13(2); 14; 39:t, 1; 6; 11; 12(2); 40:t, 2; 3; 15; 41:t, 42:4; 10; 44:3; 13(3); 14(2); 20; 45:(2); 1(2); 6; 12; 46:t, 1; 4; 47:t, 2; 5(2); 48:t, 3; 6; 49:t, 4; 7; 50:t, 3; 5; 10; 18; 51:t, 10(2); 17(3); 52:t, 2; 8; 53:t; 54:t; 55:t, 2; 6; 13; 56:t; 57:4; 6(2); 58:4; 8(2); 9; 11(3); 59:6(2); 14(2); 60:4; 61:t, 3(2); 62:t, 3(3); 8; 9; 63:t, 1; 10; 64:t, 3; 6; 65:t; 66:t, 1; 12; 67:t; 68:t, 5(2); 6; 9; 13; 33; 69:t, 4; 8; 11; 22(2); 30; 70:t, 3; 71:7; 72:t; 73:t, 1; 6(2); 10; 19; 20; 22; 27; 74:5; 75:t, 5; 8; 76:t, 6; 77:t, 13; 17; 20; 78:2; 5(2); 8(2); 14(2); 19; 21; 38; 39; 50; 52; 57; 65; 66; 79:t, 4(2); 80:t, 1; 6; 8; 81:t, 1; 2; 4(2); 5(2); 82:t; 83:t, 2; 4; 13; 14; 84:t, 3; 6; 10(3); 11; 85:t; 86:t, 15; 17; 87:t; 88:t, 4; 89:3; 8; 13; 37; 41; 90:t, 4(2); 5(2); 9; 91:7; 12; 92:t, 1; 3; 6(2); 12; 94:2; 20; 95:1; 2; 3(2); 10; 96:1; 97:3; 98:t, 1; 4(2); 5; 6; 99:8; 100:t, 1; 101:t, 2(2); 4(2); 5; 6; 102:t, 6; 7; 11; 26(2); 103:t, 13; 15; 104:2(2); 4; 6; 9; 18; 105:8; 10; 12; 16; 17(2); 39(2); 41; 106:18; 19; 36; 39; 107:4; 7; 27; 29; 33; 34; 35; 36; 41; 108:t; 109:t, 2; 3; 6; 9; 19; 25; 29; 110:t, 4; 111:10; 112:5; 113:9; 114:1; 8(2); 118:5; 119:9; 19; 63; 69; 78; 83; 105(2); 110; 161; 164; 176; 120:t, 2; 121:t; 122:t, 3; 123:t, 2; 124:t, 6; 7; 125:t; 126:t; 127:t, 4; 128:t, 3; 129:t, 1; 2; 130:t; 131:t, 2(2); 132:t, 5; 17; 133:t; 134:t, 136:12(2); 137:3; 4; 138:t; 139:t, 4; 140:t, 3; 5(2); 141:t, 3; 5; 142:t, 3; 143:t, 6; 144:t, 4; 8; 9(2); 11; 12; 15; 147:10; 148:6; 14; 149:1; 6; **Prov** 1:5(2); 6; 27; 2:7; 3:12; 18; 30; 4:1; 9; 24; 5:3; 4; 10; 20(2); 6:1; 5(2); 10(3); 12(3); 17(2); 19; 23; 24; 26(3); 27; 30; 32; 33; 34; 7:7; 10; 19; 20; 22; 23(2); 8:27; 9:7(3); 8(2); 9(2); 13; 14; 10:1(3); 4; 5(2); 8; 10; 11(2); 13; 18(2); 23(2); 11:1(2); 7; 12; 13(2); 15; 16; 18(2); 20; 22(3); 28; 30; 12:2(2); 3; 4(2); 8(2); 9; 10; 14(2); 15; 16(2); 17; 18; 19(2); 23; 25; 27; 13:1(2); 2; 5(2); 8; 12; 14; 16; 17(2); 20; 22; 14:3; 5(2); 6; 7; 9; 10; 12(2); 14; 16; 17; 25(2); 26; 27; 30; 34(2); 35; 15:1; 4(3); 5; 12; 13(2); 15(2); 17(2); 18; 20(3); 21; 23(2); 30; 16:2; 7; 8; 9; 10; 11; 14(2); 15; 18; 20; 22; 25(2); 27; 20(2); 29; 31; 32; 17:1; 2(2); 4(3); 7(2); 8(2); 9(2); 10(3); 11; 12(3); 16(2); 17(2); 18; 20(2); 21(2); 22(3); 23(2); 24; 25(2); 27; 28(2); 18:1; 2; 4(2); 6; 7; 8; 9; 10; 13; 14(2); 16; 19(3); 20; 22(2); 24(3); 19:1; 5; 6; 9; 10(2); 11(2); 12; 13(3); 14; 15; 19; 21; 22(3); 24; 25; 26; 20:1; 2(2); 3; 5; 6; 8; 11; 15(2); 16(3); 17; 19; 23; 24; 25; 26; 30; 21:2; 4; 6(2); 9(3); 14(2); 17; 18; 19; 20; 22; 27; 28; 29; 22:1; 3; 6; 9; 13; 14; 15; 18; 24; 25; 29; 23:1; 2(2); 9; 21; 24; 27(4); 28; 32; 34; 24:5(2); 7; 8; 14; 16; 25; 26; 28; 33(3); 25:2(2); 4; 9; 11; 12; 13; 14; 15(2); 18(4); 19(2); 20; 23; 24(2); 25(2); 26(3); 28; 26:1; 3(3); 4; 5; 6(2); 7; 8(3); 9(3); 11(2); 12(2); 13(2); 16; 17; 18; 21; 22; 23(2); 27(2); 28(2); 27:1; 2; 3(2); 6; 8(2); 9; 10(2); 12; 13(3); 14(2); 15(3); 17; 21; 22(3); 28:1; 2(2); 3(2); 7(2); 12; 15(3); 16; 17; 20; 21; 23; 24; 25; 26; 27; 29:5(2); 6; 8(2); 9(2); 11(2); 12; 15; 19; 20(2); 21; 22; 23; 24; 25; 30:2; 4; 5; 6; 10; 11; 12; 13; 14; 19(5); 22(2); 25; 26; 30; 31(2); 31:10; 15; 16(2); 30; **Eccl** 1:3; 2:19(2); 21(3); 24; 26; 3:1(2); 2(4); 3(4); 4(4); 5(4); 6(4); 7(4); 8(4); 12; 17; 19(2); 22; 4:4; 8(2); 9; 12; 13(2); 5:3(2); 4; 8; 12; 13; 14; 16; 6:2(2); 3; 6; 12(2); 7:1; 5; 6; 7(2); 8; 12(2); 15(2); 20; 28(2); 8:1(2); 4; 5; 9; 12; 13; 14; 15; 17(3); 9:4(2); 5; 6; 7; 14(2); 15; 10:1(2); 2(2); 3(2); 8(2); 11; 12(2); 14(2); 16; 19; 20; 11:2; 7; 8; 12:5; 12; **Song** 1:9; 13; 14; 2:9(2); 13; 17(2); 3:4; 9; 4:1; 2; 3(3); 4; 12(3); 15(2); 5:11; 13; 6:5; 6; 7(2); 7:1; 2; 4; 7; 13; 8:6(3); 7; 8; 9(3); 10; 11(2); 12; 14(2); **Is** 1:4(2); 8(5); 9; 14; 30; 31; 2:20; 3:6; 7; 16; 17; 24(4); 4:5(3); 6(4); 5:1(3); 2(2); 7; 9; 18; 28; 29; 6:1; 5(2); 6; 12; 13(2); 7:6(2); 8; 11; 13; 14(3); 20; 21(2); 23(2); 8:1(2); 3; 11; 12(2); 14(5); 19; 9:2; 6(2); 8; 10:6; 7; 13; 14; 16(2); 17(2); 18; 19; 22; 23; 24; 25; 26; 34; 11:1(2); 6; 10; 13:2; 4(3); 5; 6; 8; 12(2); 14; 14:6; 17; 19(2); 23; 30(2); 31; 15:5; 16:2; 4; 17:1(2); 7; 9; 11; 12(2); 13; 18:2(3); 3; 4(2); 7(3); 19:1; 4(2); 14(2); 17; 19; 20(4); 21; 23; 24; 20:3; 21:1; 2; 3; 6; 7(4); 8; 9(2); 16; 22:2(2); 5; 11; 16(2); 17; 18(2); 21; 23(3); 23:3; 10; 11; 24:9; 11; 20(2); 25:2(4); 4(5); 5(2); 6(2); 26:1; 16; 17; 20; 27:2; 10; 11; 28:1; 2(4); 4; 5(2); 6; 10(2); 13(2); 15; 16(5); 19; 20; 22; 27(4); 29:3; 4; 7(2); 8; 11; 14(3); 17(3); 21(4); 30:1; 5(3); 6; 8(2); 9; 13(2); 14; 17(2); 18; 20; 21; 22; 27; 28; 29(3); 30; 31; 33; 31:4; 7; 8(2); 32:1; 2(5); 14(2); 15(2); 18; 19; 33:9; 19(4); 20(2); 21; 23; 34:4(2); 6(2); 13; 14; 35:4(2); 7; 8; 36:2; 6; 13; 16; 17(3); 21; 37:3; 7(2); 18; 30; 32; 33; 38:3; 7; 12(2); 13; 14(3); 21(2); 39:1; 3; 40:3; 11; 12(2); 15(3); 16; 19; 20(3); 22(2); 41:12; 15; 18; 28; 42:3; 6(2); 10; 13(2); 14; 16; 22(3); 24; 43:16(2); 19(2); 44:8; 9; 10(2); 13(3); 15(3); 17; 19; 20(2); 22(2); 45:15; 19; 20; 21(2); 46:1; 6(2); 11(2); 47:3; 7; 8; 9; 14; 48:8; 18; 20; 49:2(2); 6(2); 7; 8(2); 11; 15; 18; 21; 50:2; 4; 7; 9; 11; 51:4(2); 6; 8; 10; 12; 20(2); 53:2(3); 3; 7(2); 12; 54:6(2); 7; 8(2); 55:4(2); 5; 13; 56:3; 5(2); 57:4(2); 6(2); 7; 8; 15; 58:1; 2; 5(5); 11(2); 13; 59:5; 15; 17(2); 19(2); 60:8; 15; 22(4); 61:10(2); 62:1; 2; 3(2); 5(2); 7; 10; 12; 63:14(2); 18; 64:6; 10(3); 65:1; 2(2); 3; 5(2); 8; 9; 10(2); 11; 15; 17; 18(2); 22; 66:2; 3(3); 6(3); 7; 8(2); 12(2); 15; 19; 20; **Jer** 1:5; 6; 7; 11; 13; 18; 2:2; 6(3); 7; 10; 11; 14(2); 21(3); 23; 24; 27(2); 30; 31(2); 32(2); 3:1; 3; 8; 14(2); 19(2); 20; 21; 4:6; 11; 12; 13; 15; 16; 17; 19; 20; 26; 27; 29; 31(2); 5:1; 3; 6(3); 9; 10; 15(3); 18; 19; 22; 23(2); 26; 27; 29; 30; 6:1; 2; 6; 7; 8; 9(2); 10; 20; 22(2); 24; 27(2); 7:5; 11; 28; 29; 8:5; 15; 19; 9:1; 2; 9; 10(2); 11; 12; 16; 18; 19; 10:3; 8; 13; 19; 22(2); 11:5; 9; 14; 16(2); 19; 12:6; 8; 9; 10; 13:1; 2; 4; 11(5); 21; 14:8(3); 9(2); 14(2); 17(2); 18; 15:7; 8; 10(2); 14(2); 18; 20; 16:2; 13; 20; 17:1(2); 4; 6; 8; 11; 12; 16; 17; 22; 27(2); 18:3; 7(2); 9(2); 11; 13; 14; 15; 16; 20; 22(3); 19:1; 11; 20:4; 8(2); 9; 11; 15; 21:5; 6; 9; 14; 22:5; 6; 14; 23; 28(3); 30; 23:5(2); 9(2); 16; 19(2); 23(2); 28(2); 29(2); 33; 40; 24:9(4); 25:11; 18(2); 29; 30; 31(2); 32; 34; 36; 26:2; 6; 15; 18(2); 20; 27:10; 14; 15; 16; 28:14; 15; 29:18(2); 21; 22; 23; 26; 27; 31; 32; 30:2; 5; 6(2); 11(2); 14; 16(2); 23; 31:6; 8; 9(2); 10; 12; 15; 18; 20; 22(3); 29; 31; 35(2); 36; 32:20; 21(2); 22; 31; 33:9(2); 17; 18; 21; 24; 34:8; 9; 13; 15; 17; 22; 35:4; 19; 36:2(2); 4(2); 9; 22; 37:13; 21; 38:2; 14; 39:18; 40:5; 8; 11; 42:2; 5; 18(2); 43:12(2); 44:2; 8(2); 12(2); 14; 15; 22(2); 28; 29; 45:1; 5; 46:7; 8; 10(2); 17; 20; 22; 28(2); 47:7; 48:2; 3; 4; 5; 27; 38; 39(2); 41; 42; 45(2); 49:2; 5; 13(4); 14; 17; 18; 19(2); 22; 24; 27; 30; 32(2); 33(2); 50:2; 3; 5; 9; 10; 12(3); 17; 22; 23; 24; 32; 35; 36(2); 37(2); 38; 41(2); 42; 43; 44(2); 51:1; 6; 7; 14; 16; 25; 26(3); 27(2); 29; 33(2); 34; 37; 39; 43(4); 46(2); 54(2); 55; 57; 59; 60; 63; 52:21; 22; 23; 34(2); **Lam** 1:1; 13; 15; 17; 2:1; 3; 6; 7(2); 8; 18; 20; 22; 3:10(2); 12; 14; 26; 27; 35; 36; 39(2); 44; 47; 52; 53; 64; 4:6; 8(2); 11; 17; **Eze** 1:4(4); 5; 7; 8; 10(2); 14; 16(3); 25; 26(3); 28; 2:3; 5(2); 6; 9(2); 3:5(2); 6; 9; 12(2); 13(2); 17; 20(2); 26(2); 27; 4:1; 2(2); 3(2); 6; 10; 5:1(2); 2(5); 3; 4; 12(4); 14; 15(2); 6:3; 8; 9; 7:11; 21(2); 23; 26; 8:2; 3; 7; 8; 11; 17; 18; 9:1; 2(2); 4; 10:1(2); 8; 9; 10(2); 14(3); 21; 11:8; 13(2); 16; 19; 24; 12:2(2); 3; 6; 16; 23; 13:7(2); 10; 11; 13; 14:7; 8(2); 9; 17; 19; 22; 15:2; 3; 8; 16:8; 11; 12(2); 13; 19; 20; 32; 34; 40; 47; 54; 17:2(2); 3; 4(2); 5(2); 6(2); 8(2); 13; 22; 23; 18:5; 6; 7; 10(3); 14; 16; 26; 31(2); 19:1; 2; 3; 5; 6; 10; 13; 14(4); 20:6; 11; 12; 13; 20; 21; 27; 33(2); 34(2); 47; 21:9(2); 10; 13; 19; 20; 22(2); 23; 29; 22:4(2); 25(2); 30; 23:30; 40; 41(2); 42(2); 44; 46; 24:3(2); 7; 8; 16; 24; 27; 25:4; 5(2); 7; 15; 26:4; 5(2); 7; 8(2); 10(2); 12(2); 14(2); 17; 19; 21; 27:2; 3; 15; 32; 36; 28:2(2); 9; 12; 18; 19; 24; 29:6; 7; 8; 14; 18; 30:3; 8; 13(2); 18; 21; 24; 31:3(2); 15; 32:2(3); 3; 7; 25; 33:2(2); 7; 32(2); 33; 34:8; 12; 14(3); 18; 22; 24; 25; 26; 28; 29; 35:5; 36:3; 4; 5; 17; 26(2); 37; 37:7(2); 26; 38:4; 7; 9(2); 12(2); 13(3); 15(2); 16; 19; 21; 39:6; 11; 13; 15(2); 17; 40:2(2); 3(3); 5(2); 17; 24; 27; 42(2); 41:7; 8; 18(3); 19(2); 42:4(2); 12; 20(2);

43:2; 13(4); 17(2); 19(2); 22(2); 23(2); 24; 25(4); 44:13; 22(3); 45:4; 5; 7; 10(2); 14; 15(2); 18; 21; 22(2); 23(3); 24(3); 46:4; 5; 6(2); 7(3); 11(2); 12; 13(2); 14(3); 15; 16; 17; 19; 21; 23; 47:3; 4(2); 5(3); 9; 10; 20; 48:1; 2; 3; 4; 5; 6; 7; 12; 15; 23; 24; 25; 26; 27; **Dan** 1:5; 2:3; 5; 10; 11; 19; 25; 28; 31; 34; 35; 37(2); 44; 47(4); 48; 3:6; 10; 11; 15; 29(2); 4:5; 6; 10; 13; 15; 16; 23(2); 27; 31; 5:1(2); 5; 7; 11; 16; 18; 29(2); 6:7(3); 10; 12(2); 13; 17; 20; 26; 7:1; 4(3); 5(2); 6(2); 7; 8; 10; 12; 14; 20; 25; 8:1; 2(2); 3; 5; 9; 15; 16; 18; 23; 9:12; 15; 16; 26; 10:1; 5; 6; 7; 9; 11; 18; 11:3; 5; 7; 10; 11; 13(2); 15; 18; 20; 21; 22; 23; 24; 25(2); 34; 35; 38; 39; 40; 12:1(2); 7; 11; **Hos** 1:2; 3; 4; 6; 8; 2:3(2); 6; 12; 15; 18; 3:1; 4(3); 4:1; 12; 16(3); 5:1(2); 2; 7; 12; 14(2); 6:4; 8; 9; 7:6; 8; 11; 16; 8:8; 9; 10; 12; 14; 9:1(2); 7; 8(2); 11; 12; 13; 14; 10:3; 4; 6; 14; 15; 11:1; 4; 10; 11(2); 12:1; 2; 7; 12(2); 13(2); 13:7(2); 8(2); 10; 11; 13; 14:8; **Joel** 1:6(3); 8; 14(2); 15; 2:2(4); 3(3); 5(2); 9; 14(3); 15(2); 19; 20; 3:3(2); 4; 8; 18; 19(2); **Amos** 1:4; 7; 10; 12; 14(2); 2:2; 5; 6; 7; 13; 3:4(2); 5(3); 6(2); 12(3); 4:5; 11; 5:1; 3; 12; 19(4); 24; 6:10; 13; 14; 7:4; 7(3); 8(2); 14; 17; 8:1; 2; 6; 8; 10; 11(3); 9:5; 9; **Obad** 1; 7; 12; 18(2); **Jonah** 1:3; 4(2); 16; 17; 3:4; 5; 4:2; 5; 6(2); 7; 8; 10(2); **Mic** 1:4; 6; 8; 14; 2:2(2); 4(2); 5; 10; 11; 3:6; 12; 4:3; 7(2); 9; 10; 5:1; 7; 8(2); 6:2; 6; 16; 7:2; 3; 4(2); 5(2); 6; 8; 17; 18; **Nah** 1:7; 11; 14; 2:8; 3:2; 3(2); 6; **Hab** 1:5; 10; 2:5; 6(2); 12(2); 18; 3:1; 14; **Zeph** 1:7; 10(2); 13(2); 15(5); 16; 18; 2:4; 9; 13(2); 15(2); 3:9; 13; 18; 20(2); **Hag** 1:6; 11; 2:6; 13; 15(2); 23; **Zec** 1:8(2); 14; 15; 16; 2:1(2); 5; 9; 3:2; 5(2); 4:1; 2(2); 7; 5:1; 2; 7(2); 9; 6:13; 14; 7:12; 14; 8:3; 13(2); 23; 9:3; 6; 7(2); 9; 13; 15; 16; 10:2(2); 7; 11:3(2); 13; 15; 16; 12:2; 3; 6(2); 11; 13:1; 4; 14:4; 10; 13; **Mal** 1:6(4); 11; 13; 14(3); 2:2; 11; 15; 3:2; 3; 5; 8; 9; 10; 12; 16; 17; 4:6; **Mt** 1:19(2); 20; 21; 23(2); 2:6; 12; 13; 18; 19; 22; 23(2); 3:4; 16; 17; 4:5; 6; 18; 21; 5:1; 14; 15(3); 22; 28; 31; 38(2); 41; 6:2; 16; 7:4; 9; 10(2); 17; 18(2); 24(2); 25; 26; 8:2; 4; 5; 9; 14; 19; 23; 24; 26; 30; 32; 9:1; 2(2); 9; 12; 16; 18; 20; 23; 32(2); 10:18; 29; 34; 35; 36; 41(6); 42(2); 11:7; 8; 9(2); 11; 18; 19(3); 12:10; 11; 12(2); 14; 20; 22; 29; 32; 35; 38; 39; 41; 42; 43; 13:2; 3; 21; 24; 31(2); 32; 33; 34; 42; 44(2); 45; 47; 52; 57; 14:5; 8; 11; 13; 14; 15; 22; 23; 26; 33; 15:5; 11(2); 20(2); 22(2); 23; 29; 33; 34; 16:1; 4(2); 26(2); 17:5(2); 14; 20; 27; 18:2; 6; 12; 17; 23; 19:3; 5; 7; 23; 24(3); 20:1; 2(2); 9; 10; 13; 20; 28; 29; 21:2; 5; 8; 13; 19; 26; 28; 33(5); 43; 46; 22:2(2); 11(2); 12; 19; 24; 25; 35(2); 46; 23:14; 16; 24(2); 37; 24:14; 31(2); 32; 45; 50; 25:6; 14(2); 19; 21; 23; 32; 35; 38; 43; 44; 26:7; 10; 13; 18; 36; 39; 47; 48; 51; 55; 69; 73; 27:14; 15; 16; 19; 24; 28; 29(2); 32; 33(3); 46; 48(2); 50; 57; 59; 60; 65; 66; 28:2; 16; **Mk** 1:6(2); 10; 11; 16; 19; 23; 26; 30; 35(2); 40; 44; 2:21; 3:1(2); 7; 8; 9; 13; 24; 25; 27; 4:1(2); 3; 17; 21(4); 26; 31; 34; 37; 38; 39; 5:2; 7; 11; 13; 25; 42; 6:4; 5; 8; 10; 11; 15; 19; 20; 21(2); 25; 28; 29; 31(2); 32; 34; 35; 46; 49; 7:11(2); 15; 25; 26(2); 36; 8:4; 7; 10; 11; 12; 22; 36; 37; 9:7(2); 14; 17; 21; 36; 39; 41; 42; 10:2; 4; 7; 12; 15; 25(3); 45; 46; 48; 11:2; 4; 13; 17; 32; 12:1(5); 2; 15; 19; 20; 40; 42(2); 13:9; 28; 34(2); 14:3; 6; 9; 13(2); 15; 32; 35; 43; 44; 47(2); 48; 51(2); 69; 70(2); 15:1; 17; 19; 21; 22; 34; 36(2); 37; 46(3); 16:5(2); **Lk** 1:1; 5; 13; 17; 22; 26; 27(2); 31; 34; 36; 39; 42; 45; 57; 63; 2:1; 7; 11; 12(2); 13; 16; 24(2); 25; 32; 34; 35; 36(2); 37; 44; 3:22(3); 4:5; 9; 11; 13; 14; 25; 26(3); 31; 33(3); 36; 38; 42; 5:3; 4; 6; 8; 12(2); 14; 15; 17; 18(3); 27; 29(2); 31; 36(4); 6:6; 12; 17; 39; 43(2); 44; 45; 48(3); 49(2); 7:2; 5; 7; 8; 11; 12(2); 16(2); 24; 25; 26(2); 28; 33; 34(3); 37(2); 39(2); 41; 8:4; 5; 6; 13; 16(4); 22(2); 23; 24; 27; 28; 33; 41(2); 42; 43; 9:5; 10; 12; 14; 25; 27; 28; 34; 35; 38; 39; 42; 46; 47; 52; 57; 10:13; 25; 30; 31; 32; 33; 38(2); 39; 11:1; 5; 6; 11(6); 12; 14; 16; 17(2); 21; 22; 24; 27; 29; 30; 31; 32; 33(4); 36; 37; 12:10; 14(2); 15; 16(2); 33; 44; 46; 50; 54(2); 13:6(2); 11(2); 16; 19(3); 21; 33; 34; 14:2; 5; 7; 8(2); 12(3); 13; 16(2); 18; 20; 28; 32; 15:8; 11; 13; 14; 15; 20; 22; 29; 16:1(2); 19; 20; 26; 17:2; 4(2); 6; 7; 12; 15; 16; 18:1; 2(2); 3; 4; 10(2); 13; 17; 18; 25(3); 35; 19:2; 4; 7(2); 9; 11; 12(3); 14; 17; 20; 30; 37; 43; 46; 20:6; 9(4); 10; 12; 24; 28; 29; 38; 47; 21:2; 3; 13; 15; 27; 29; 35; 22:10(2); 12; 24; 29; 36; 41; 47; 48; 52; 55; 56; 58; 59(2); 23:2; 6; 8; 11; 19; 26; 27; 31; 38; 44; 46; 47; 50(4); 51; 53; 24:13; 18; 19; 23; 37; 39; 42(2); **Jn** 1:6; 7; 30; 32; 42; 2:1; 15; 3:1(2); 2; 3; 4; 5; 10; 25; 27; 4:5; 7; 9(2); 14; 19; 24; 29; 44; 46; 5:1; 2; 3; 4; 5; 6; 13; 14; 35(3); 6:2; 3; 4; 5; 7; 9; 14; 15(2); 17; 18; 50; 70; 7:12; 20; 22; 23(2); 33; 40; 43; 8:3; 7; 40; 44(3); 48(2); 49; 51; 52(2); 55; 9:1; 11; 16(3); 17; 24; 25; 30; 31; 10:1(2); 5; 19; 20; 21(2); 33(2); 11:1; 10; 38(2); 43; 44; 47; 54(2); 57; 12:2; 3; 6; 14; 24; 28; 35; 46; 49; 13:4; 5; 26; 33; 34; 14:2; 3; 19; 23; 15:6(2); 13; 25; 16:16(2); 17(2); 18; 19(2); 21(2); 18:1; 3; 10; 18; 30; 35; 37(2); 39; 40; 19:2(2); 7; 12; 13; 17(2); 19; 23; 29(2); 34; 36; 38; 39; 41(2); 20:7; 21:3(2); 8; 9; **Acts** 1:9; 12; 18; 22; 2:2(2); 22; 30; 3:2; 14; 22; 4:16; 27; 36; 5:1(2); 2; 16; 30; 31(2); 34(3); 36; 6:1; 5(2); 7; 7:5; 6; 11; 16; 27(2); 29; 30(2); 35(4); 37; 41; 46; 57; 58; 60; 8:1; 9; 27; 32(2); 36; 9:3; 4; 7; 10(2); 12(2); 15; 25; 26; 33; 36; 43; 10:1(2); 2; 3; 4; 6; 7; 10; 11(2); 13; 22; 26; 28(2); 30; 32; 34; 39; 11:5(4); 7; 21; 24; 26; 12:7; 9; 11; 13; 21; 22(3); 13:6(3); 7; 11(3); 21(2); 22; 23; 29; 41(3); 47; 14:1; 8(2); 10; 15:7; 10; 14; 33; 16:1(4); 3; 9(2); 11; 12; 13; 14(2); 16(2); 24; 26; 28; 29; 17:1; 4(2); 5; 12; 15; 18; 31; 34; 18:2; 7; 9; 11; 14; 15; 18(2); 24; 19:14; 22; 24(2); 34; 35; 38; 39; 20:9(3); 11; 12; 21:1; 2; 10; 23; 39(4); 40; 22:3(3); 6; 7; 12(2); 17; 22; 25(2); 26; 27; 28; 29; 23:6(2); 7; 9(2); 10; 12; 14; 17; 21; 25; 27; 24:1; 4; 5(3); 10; 15; 16; 23; 24; 25; 27; 25:9; 14; 27; 26:5; 8; 13; 14; 16(2); 24; 26; 28; 27:1; 2(2); 5; 6; 8; 14; 16; 18; 26; 28; 39(2); 41; 28:2; 3(2); 4; 6(2); 8(2); 11; 13; 16; 23; **Rom** 1:1; 10; 25; 28; 2:14; 17; 19(2); 20; 21; 22; 25; 28; 29; 3:4; 5; 7; 25; 28; 4:11; 17; 5:7(2); 7:1; 21; 8:24; 9:9; 27; 28; 29; 33; 10:2; 14; 19; 21; 11:5; 9(4); 17; 24; 12:1; 13:3; 4; 14:13; 15:8; 12; 23; 26; 16:1; 2; 23; **1Cor** 1:22; 23; 2:7; 11; 3:10; 14; 18; 4:1; 2; 3; 6; 9; 21; 5:5; 6; 7; 11(4); 6:1; 5; 7; 18; 20; 7:1(2); 5; 12; 15(2); 21; 22; 23; 26; 27(3); 28; 34(2); 35; 8:7; 9; 9:5(2); 7(3); 8; 11; 17(2); 20; 24; 25; 27; 10:13; 27; 30; 11:6(2); 7; 13; 14(2); 15(3); 28; 12:31; 13:1; 11(5); 12; 14:7; 11(2); 22; 25; 26(4); 35; 37; 15:38; 44(4); 45(2); 51; 52; 16:7; 9; **2Cor** 1:10; 15; 23; 2:6; 7; 12; 15; 3:13; 18; 4:17(2); 5:1; 17; 6:2; 13; 18; 7:8(2); 9; 11; 14; 8:2; 10; 11(2); 12(2); 14(2); 9:2; 5; 7; 10:6; 13; 11:1; 2; 5; 16(3); 20(5); 23; 25(2); 32; 33(2); 12:2; 3; 4; 6; 7; 11; 17; 18(2); 13:3; S:1; **Gal** 2:3; 14; 16; 18; 3:13(2); 15; 19; 20(2); 21; 25; 4:1(2); 4; 7(3); 18; 22(2); 27; 5:3; 9; 6:1(2); 3; 7; 11; 12; 15; **Eph** 3:7; 4:13; 5:2(2); 12; 27; 31; 32; 6:21; **Phil** 1:6; 23(2); 2:7; 8; 9; 15; 22; 3:5; 4:17; 18(2); **Col** 1:7; 23; 25; 2:15; 17; 18; 23; 3:13; 4:1; 3; 7(2); 9; 11; 12; 13; **1Th** 2:5; 7; 11; 17; 4:16; 5:2; 3; 4; **2Th** 1:5; 6; 2:3; 11; 3:15; **1Ti** 1:5(2); 8; 9; 13(2); 15; 16; 18; 19; 2:2; 6; 7(2); 12; 3:1(4); 2; 3; 5; 6; 7; 9; 10; 13(2); 4:2; 6; 9; 5:1; 5; 9; 23; 6:9; 12; 13; 19; **2Ti** 1:7; 11(2); 2:3; 4; 5; 11; 15; 17; 20; 21(2); 22; 3:5; 15; 4:7; 8; **Titus** 1:1; 7; 8(2); 12; 2:7; 14; 3:8; 10; **Philem** 1:1; 9; 15; 16(3); 17; 22; S:1; **Heb** 1:4; 5(2); 7; 8; 11; 12; 2:2; 6; 7; 9; 17; 3:5(2); 6; 4:1; 4; 7(2); 9; 12; 14; 5:6; 8; 13; 6:18; 7:2; 3; 5; 12; 16; 17; 18; 19; 21; 22(2); 8:2; 4; 6(2); 8; 10(2); 13; 9:1; 2; 9; 11; 16; 17; 10:1; 3; 5; 15; 20; 22; 27; 31; 32; 33; 34; 37; 11:2; 4; 6; 8; 9; 10; 11; 14; 16(2); 19; 21; 23; 25; 35; 39; 12:1; 10; 19; 20(2); 28; 29; 13:9; 18; 22; **Jas** 1:1; 6; 8; 11; 18; 23(4); 25(2); 2:2(3); 3; 11; 14; 15; 18; 24; 3:2; 4; 5(3); 6(2); 11; 12; 13(2); 4:4; 11(2); 13(2); 14(2); 5:3; 5; 16; 17; 20(2); **1Pet** 1:3; 6; 19; 22; 2:4; 5; 6; 8(2); 9(3); 10; 16; 19; 3:4; 9; 15; 16; 20; 21; 4:15(3); 16; 19; 5:1(2); 2; 4; 8; 10; 12; 14; **2Pet** 1:1; 17; 19(3); 2:3; 5; 17; 19; 3:8(2); 10(2); 13; **1Jn** 1:10; 2:4; 8; 22; 3:15; 4:20(2); 5:10; 16(2); 17; **2Jn** 4; 5; 7; 8; **3Jn** 6; **Jude** 9; 22; **Rev** 1:10(2); 11; 13(2); 14; 15; 16; 2:10; 14(2); 17(2); 18; 20(2); 22; 27(2); 3:1; 3; 4; 8; 12; 4:1(2); 2; 3(3); 6; 7(5); 5:1; 2(2); 6; 9; 12; 6:2(3); 4; 5(2); 6(4); 8; 10; 11; 12; 13(2); 14; 7:2; 9; 10; 8:3; 8; 10(2); 12; 13; 9:1; 2(2); 5(2); 11; 13; 15(3); 10:1(2); 2; 3(2); 4; 11:1(2); 3; 12(2); 13; 12:1(3); 3; 5(2); 6(2); 10; 12; 14(3); 15; 13:1; 2(3); 5; 11(2); 14; 16; 18; 14:1; 2(2); 3; 7; 9; 13; 14(3); 15; 17; 18; 20; 15:2; 16:1; 2; 3; 15; 16; 17; 18; 21(2); 17:3(2); 4; 5; 10; 18:2(2); 7; 21(3); 22; 23; 19:1; 5; 6; 11; 12(2); 13; 15(2); 16; 17; 20; 20:1; 2; 3(2); 4; 6; 11; 21:1(2); 2; 3; 10; 11(2); 12; 15; 17; 19; 20(3); 27; 22:1; 15

ABOUT

Gen 23:17; 35:5; 37:7; 38:24; 39:11; 41:25; 28; 42; 48; 42:24; 46:34; **Ex** 7:24; 9:18; 11:4; 12:37; 13:18; 16:13; 19:12; 23; 25:11; 24; 25(2); 27:17; 28:32; 33(2); 34; 29:16; 20; 30:3(2); 32:28; 37:2; 11; 12(2); 26(2); 38:16; 20; 31(2); 39:23; 25; 26; 40:8; 33; **Lev** 1:5; 11; 3:2; 8; 13; 6:5; 7:2; 8:15; 19; 24; 9:12; 18; 14:41; 16:18; 25:31; 44; **Num** 1:50; 53; 2:2; 3:26; 37; 4:4; 14; 26; 32; 11:8; 24; 31; 32; 16:24; 34; 49; 22:4; 32:33; 34:12; 35:2; 4; **Deut** 6:14; 12:10; 13:7; 17:14; 21:2; 25:19; 31:21; 32:10; **Josh** 2:5; 3:4; 4:13; 6:3; 11; 15; 7:3; 4; 5; 8:12; 10:13; 11:6; 15:12; 16:6; 18:20; 19:8; 21:11; 42; 44; 23:1; **Judg** 2:12; 14; 3:29; 7:21; 8:10; 26; 9:49; 16:27; 17:2; 19:22; 20:5; 29; 31; 39; 43; **Ruth** 1:4; 19; 2:17; **1Sa** 1:20; 4:2; 20; 5:8(2); 9; 10; 9:13; 16; 22; 26; 13:15; 14:2; 14; 21; 15:12; 27; 17:42; 20:12; 21:5; 22:2; 6; 7; 17; 23:13; 26; 25:13; 38; 26:5; 7; 31:9; **2Sa** 3:12; 4:5; 5:9; 7:1; 14:20; 18:15; 20:26; 22:6; 12; 24:6; **1Kin** 2:5; 15; 3:1; 4:24; 31; 5:3; 6:5(3); 6; 29; 7:12; 15; 18; 20; 23(2); 24(2); 36; 8:14; 18:32; 35; 19:2; 20:6; 22:6; 36; **2Kin** 1:8; 3:25; 4:16; 6:14; 17; 7:1; 18; 8:21; 11:7; 8; 11; 17:15; 23:5; 25:1; 4; 10; 17; **1Chr** 4:33; 6:55; 9:27; 10:9; 11:8(2); 15:22; 18:17; 22:9; 28:12; **2Chr** 2:9; 4:2; 3(2); 13:13; 14:7; 14; 15:15; 17:9; 10; 18:31; 34; 20:30; 23:2; 7; 10; 26:6; 33:14; 34:6; **Ezr** 1:6; 10:15; **Neh** 5:17; 6:16; 12:28; 29; 13:21; **Job** 1:5; 10(3); 8:17; 10:8; 11:18; 16:13; 19:12; 20:23; 22:10; 29:5; 30:18; 37:12; 40:22; 41:14; **Ps** 3:6; 7:7; 17:9; 18:5; 11; 27:6; 32:7; 10; 34:7; 40:12; 44:13; 48:12(2); 49:5; 50:3; 55:10; 59:6; 14; 73:6; 76:11; 78:28; 79:3; 4; 88:17(2); 89:7; 8; 97:2; 3; 109:3; 118:10; 11(2); 12; 125:2(2); 128:3; 139:11; 140:9; 142:7; **Prov** 1:9; 3:3; 6:21; 20:19; **Eccl** 1:6(2); 2:20; 12:5; **Song** 3:2; 3; 7; 5:7; 7:2; **Is** 3:18; 15:8; 23:16; 26:20; 28:27; 29:3; 42:25; 49:18; 50:11; 60:4; **Jer** 1:15; 2:36; 4:17; 6:3; 12:9; 14:18; 17:26; 21:14; 25:9; 31:22; 39; 32:44; 33:13; 41:14; 46:5; 14; 48:17; 39; 49:5; 50:14; 15; 29; 32; 51:2; 52:4; 7; 14; 22; 23; **Lam** 1:17; 2:3; 22; 3:7; **Eze** 1:4; 18; 27(2); 28; 4:2; 5:2; 5; 6; 7(2); 12; 14; 15; 6:5; 13; 8:10; 16; 10:12; 11:12; 12:14; 16:10; 37; 57(2); 23:24; 27:11(2); 28:24; 26; 31:4; 32:22; 23; 24; 25; 26; 34:26; 36:4; 7; 36; 37:2; 40:5; 14; 16(2); 17; 25; 29; 30; 33; 36; 43; 41:5; 6; 7(3); 8; 10; 11; 12; 16(2); 17; 19; 42:15; 16; 17; 19; 20; 43:12; 13; 17(2); 20; 45:1; 2(2); 46:23(3); 47:2; 48:35; **Dan** 5:7; 16; 29; 31; 9:16; 21; **Hos** 7:2; 11:12; **Joel** 3:11; 12; **Amos** 3:11; **Jonah** 2:3; 5(3); 6; **Nah** 3:8; **Hab** 1:4; **Zec** 2:5; 7:7; 9:8; 12:2; 6; 14:14; **Mt** 1:11; 3:4; 5; 4:23; 8:18; 9:22; 35; 14:21; 35; 18:6; 20:3; 5; 6; 9; 21:33; 27:46; **Mk** 1:6; 28; 2:2; 3:5; 8; 32; 34(2); 4:10; 5:13; 30; 32; 6:6; 36; 44; 48; 55(2); 8:9; 33; 9:8; 14; 42; 10:23; 11:11; 12:1; 14:51; 15:17; **Lk** 1:56; 65; 2:9; 37; 49; 3:3; 23; 4:14; 37; 6:10; 7:9; 17; 8:37; 42; 9:12; 14; 28; 10:40; 41; 12:35; 13:8; 17:2; 19:43; 22:41; 49; 59; 23:44; 24:13; **Jn** 1:39; 3:25; 4:6; 6:10; 19; 7:14; 19; 20; 10:24; 11:18; 44; 19:14; 39; 20:7; 21:20; **Acts** 1:15; 2:10; 41; 3:3; 4:4; 5:7; 16; 36; 9:3; 29; 10:3; 9; 38; 11:19; 12:1; 8; 13:11; 18; 20; 14:6; 20; 15:2; 18:14; 19:7; 23; 34; 20:3; 21:31; 22:6(2); 24:6; 25:7; 15; 24; 26:13; 21; 27:27; 30; **Rom** 4:19; 10:3; 15:19; **1Cor** 9:5; 13; **2Cor** 4:10; **Eph** 4:14; 6:14; **1Ti** 5:13; 6:4; **2Ti** 2:14; **Titus** 3:9; **Heb** 8:5; 9:4; 11:30; 37; 12:1; 13:9; **Jas** 3:3; 4; **1Pet** 5:8; **Jude** 7; 9; 12; **Rev** 1:13; 4:3; 4; 6; 8; 5:11; 7:11(2); 8:1; 10:4; 16:21; 20:9

ABOVE

Gen 1:7; 20; 3:14(2); 6:16; 7:17; 27:39; 28:13; 48:22; 49:25; 26; **Ex** 18:11; 19:5; 20:4; 25:21; 22; 26:14; 24; 28:27; 28; 29:13; 22; 30:14; 36:19; 39:20; 21; 40:19; 20; **Lev** 3:4; 10; 15; 4:9; 7:4; 8:16; 25; 9:10; 19; 11:21; 27:7; **Num** 3:49; 4:25; 12:3; 16:3; **Deut** 4:39; 5:8; 7:6; 14; 10:15; 14:2; 17:20; 25:3; 26:19; 28:1; 13; 43; 30:5; **Josh** 2:11; 3:13; 16; **Judg** 5:24(2); **1Sa** 2:29; **2Sa** 22:17; 49; **1Kin** 7:3; 11; 20; 25; 29; 31; 8:7; 23; 14:9; 22; 16:30; **2Kin** 21:11; 25:28; **1Chr** 5:2; 16:25; 23:27; 27:6; 29:3; 11; **2Chr** 2:5; 4:4; 5:8; 11:21; 24:20; 25:5; 34:4; **Neh** 3:28; 7:2; 8:5; 9:5; 12:37; 39(3); **Est** 2:17; 3:1; 5:11; **Job** 3:4; 18:16; 28:18; 31:2; 28; **Ps** 8:1; 10:5; 18:16; 48; 27:6; 45:7; 50:4; 57:5(2); 11(2); 78:23; 95:3; 96:4; 97:9(2); 99:2; 103:11; 104:6; 108:4; 5(2); 113:4(2); 119:127(2); 135:5; 136:6; 137:6; 138:2; 144:7; 148:4; 13; **Prov** 8:28; 15:24; 31:10; **Eccl** 2:7; 3:19; **Is** 2:2; 6:2; 7:11; 14:13; 14; 45:8; **Jer** 4:28; 15:8; 17:9; 31:37; 35:4; 52:32; **Lam** 1:13; **Eze** 1:22; 26(2); 10:1; 19; 11:22; 16:43; 29:15; 31:5; 37:8; 41:17; 20; **Dan** 6:3; 11:5; 36; 37; **Amos** 2:9; **Mic** 4:1; **Nah** 3:16; **Mt** 10:24(2); **Lk** 3:20; 6:40; 13:2; 4; **Jn** 3:31(3); 6:13; 8:23; 19:11; **Acts** 2:19; 4:22; 26:13; **Rom** 10:6; 14:5; **1Cor** 4:6; 10:13; 15:6; **2Cor** 1:8; 11:23; 12:2; 6; 7(2); **Gal** 1:14; 4:26; **Eph** 1:21; 3:20; 4:6; 10; 6:16; **Phil** 2:9; **Col** 3:1; 2; 14; **2Th** 2:4; **Philem** 1:16; **Heb** 1:9; 10:8; **Jas** 1:17; 3:15; 17; 5:12; **1Pet** 4:8; **3Jn** 2

ACCORDING

Gen 6:22; 7:5; 18:10; 14; 21; 21:23; 25:13; 16; 27:8; 19; 30:34; 33:14; 34:12; 36:40; 43; 39:17; 40:5; 41:11; 12; 40; 54; 43:7; 33(2); 44:2; 7; 10; 45:21; 47:12; 49:28; 50:6; 12; **Ex** 6:16; 17; 19; 25; 26; 8:10; 13; 31; 12:3; 4(2); 21; 25; 35; 16:16(2); 18; 21; 17:1; 21:22; 31; 22:17; 24:4; 25:9; 35; 26:30; 28:8; 10; 21(2); 29:35; 41(2); 30:37; 31:11; 32:28; 36:1; 37:21; 29; 38:21; 39:5; 14(3); 32; 42; 40:16; **Lev** 4:3; 35; 5:10; 12; 9:16; 10:7; 12:2; 25:15(2); 16(3); 50(2); 51; 52; 26:21; 27:8; 16; 17; 18; 25; 27(2); **Num** 1:18; 20; 22; 24; 26; 28; 30; 32; 34; 36; 38; 40; 42; 54; 2:10; 18; 34(2); 3:16; 20; 22; 34; 51; 4:31; 33; 37; 41; 45; 49(3); 6:21; 7:5; 7; 8; 8:4; 20; 9:3(2); 5; 12; 14(2); 20(2); 10:13; 14; 18; 22; 28; 14:17; 19; 20; 29; 15:12(2); 24; 17:2(2); 6; 18:16; 23:23; 24:2; 26:18; 22; 25; 27; 37; 43; 47; 50; 53; 54; 55; 56; 29:6; 18; 21; 24; 27; 30; 33; 37; 40; 30:2; 33:2(2); 54; 34:14(2); 35:8; 24; 36:5; **Deut** 1:3; 30; 41; 46; 3:24(2); 4:34; 9:10; 10:4; 9; 10; 12:15; 16:10; 17; 17:10(2); 11(2); 18:16; 23:23; 24:8; 25:2; 26:13; 14; 29:21; 30:2; 31:5; 32:8; 34:5; **Josh** 1:7; 8; 17; 2:21; 4:5; 8; 10; 7:14(2); 8:8; 27; 34; 10:32; 35; 37; 11:23(2); 12:7; 13:15; 24; 15:12; 13; 20; 16:5; 17:4; 18:4; 10; 11; 20; 21; 28; 19:1; 8; 10; 16; 17; 23; 24; 31; 32; 39; 40; 48; 50; 21:33; 44; 22:9; 24:5; **Judg** 8:35; 9:16; 11:10; 36; 39; 20:10; 21:23; **Ruth** 3:6; **1Sa** 2:35; 6:4; 18; 8:8; 13:8; 14:7; 17:23; 23:20; 25:9; 30; **2Sa** 3:39; 7:17(2); 21; 22; 9:11; 14:20; 22:21(2); 25(2); 24:19; **1Kin** 2:6; 3:6; 12; 4:28; 5:6; 10; 6:3; 38; 7:9; 36; 8:32; 39; 43; 56; 9:4; 11; 11:37; 12:24; 13:5; 26; 14:18; 24; 15:29; 16:12; 34; 17:1; 5; 15; 16; 18:31; 20:4; 21:26; 22:38; 53; **2Kin** 1:17; 2:22; 4:16; 17; 44; 5:14; 6:18; 7:16; 9:26; 10:17; 30; 11:9; 14:3; 6; 25; 15:3; 34; 16:3; 10; 11; 16; 17:13; 18:3; 21:8(2); 22:13; 23:16; 19; 25; 32; 35(2); 37; 24:2; 3; 9; 19; **1Chr** 6:19; 32; 49; 9:9; 11:3; 10; 12:23; 15:15; 16:40; 17:15(2); 17; 19; 20; 23:11; 31; 24:3; 4; 19; 25:1; 2; 6; 26:13; 31; 28:15; **2Chr** 3:4; 8; 4:7; 6:23; 30; 33; 7:17; 18; 8:13; 14; 17:14; 23:8; 24:6; 25:5; 26:4; 11; 27:2; 29:2; 15; 25; 30:6; 16; 19; 31:2; 16; 32:25; 33:8; 34:32; 35:4(2); 5; 6; 10; 12; 13; 15; 16; 26; **Ezr** 3:4; 7; 6:9; 13; 14(2); 17; 7:6; 9; 14; 9:1; 10:3(2); 5; 8; **Neh** 2:8; 5:12; 13; 19; 6:6; 7; 14; 8:18; 9:27; 28; 12:24; 45; 13:22; 24; **Est** 1:7; 8(2); 15; 21; 22(2); 2:12; 18; 3:12(2); 4:16; 17; 8:9(4); 9:13; 27(2); 31; **Job** 1:5; 20:18; 33:6; 34:11; 33; 36:27; 42:9; **Ps** 7:8(2); 17; 18:20(2); 24(2); 20:4; 25:7; 28:4(2); 33:22; 35:24; 48:10; 51:1(2); 62:12; 69:16; 74:5; 78:72; 79:11; 90:11; 15; 103:10; 106:45; 109:26; 119:9; 25; 28; 41; 58; 65; 76; 91; 107; 116; 124; 149(2); 154; 156; 159; 169; 170; 150:2; **Prov** 12:8; 24:12; 29; 26:4; 5; **Eccl** 1:6; 8:14(2); **Is** 8:20; 9:3; 10:26; 21:16; 23:15; 27:7; 44:13; 59:18; 63:7(3); **Jer** 2:28; 3:15; 11:4; 13(2); 13:2; 17:10(2); 21:2; 14; 25:14(2); 26:20; 27:12; 31:32; 32:8; 11; 19(2); 35:10; 18; 36:8; 38:27; 40:3; 42:4; 5; 20; 50:21; 29(2); 52:2; **Lam** 3:32; 64; **Eze** 4:4; 5; 9; 5:7; 7:3; 8; 9; 27; 8:4; 14:4; 18:24; 30; 20:44(2); 23:24; 24:14(2); 24; 25:14(2); 35:11(2); 36:19(2); 39:24(2); 40:24; 28; 29; 32; 33; 35; 42:11(2); 12; 43:3(2); 44:24; 45:8; 25(4); 46:7; 47:10; 12; 13; 21; **Dan** 4:8; 35; 6:8; 12; 8:4; 9:16; 11:3; 4; 16; 36; **Hos** 3:1; 9:10; 10:1(2); 12:2(2); 13:2; 6; **Jonah** 3:3; **Mic** 7:15; **Hab** 3:9; **Hag** 2:5; **Zec** 1:6(2); 5:3(2); **Mal** 2:9; **Mt** 2:16; 9:29; 16:27; 25:15; **Mk** 7:5; **Lk** 1:9; 38; 2:22; 24; 29; 39; 5:14; 12:47; 23:56; **Jn** 7:24; 18:31; **Acts** 2:30; 4:35; 7:44; 11:29; 13:23; 22:3; 12; 24:6; **Rom** 1:3; 4; 2:2; 6; 16; 4:18; 8:27; 28; 9:3; 11; 10:2; 11:5; 8; 12:3; 6(2); 15:5; 16:25(2); 26; **1Cor** 1:31; 3:8; 10; 15:3; 4; **2Cor** 1:17; 4:13; 5:10; 8:12(2); 9:7; 10:2; 13; 15; 11:15; 13:10; **Gal** 1:4; 2:14; 3:29; 6:16; **Eph** 1:4; 5; 7; 9; 11; 19; 2:2(2); 3:7; 11; 16; 20; 4:7; 16; 22; 6:5; **Phil** 1:20; 3:21; 4:19; **Col** 1:11; 25; 29; 3:22; **2Th** 1:12; **1Ti** 1:11; 18; 6:3; **2Ti** 1:1; 8; 9(2); 2:8; 4:14; **Titus** 1:1; 3; 3:5; 7; **Heb** 2:4; 7:5; 8:4; 5; 9; 9:19; **Jas** 2:8; **1Pet** 1:2; 3; 14; 17; 3:7; 4:6(2); 19; **2Pet** 1:3; 2:22; 3:13; 15; **1Jn** 5:14; **Rev** 2:23; 18:6; 20:12; 13; 21:17; 22:12

AFAR

Gen 22:4; 37:18; **Ex** 2:4; 20:18; 21; 24:1; 33:7; **Num** 9:10; **1Sa** 26:13; **2Kin** 2:7; 4:25; **Ezr** 3:13; **Neh** 12:43; **Job** 2:12; 36:3; 25; 39:25; 29; **Ps** 10:1; 38:11; 65:5; 138:6; 139:2; **Prov** 31:14; **Is** 23:7; 59:14; 66:19; **Jer** 23:23; 30:10; 31:10; 46:27; 51:50; **Mic** 4:3; **Mt** 26:58; 27:55; **Mk** 5:6; 11:13; 14:54; 15:40; **Lk** 16:23; 17:12; 18:13; 22:54; 23:49; **Acts** 2:39; **Eph** 2:17; **Heb** 11:13; **2Pet** 1:9; **Rev** 18:10; 15; 17

AFTER

Gen 1:11; 12(2); 21(2); 24(2); 25(3); 26; 4:17; 5:3; 4; 7; 10; 13; 16; 19; 22; 26; 30; 6:4; 20(3); 7:10; 14(4); 8:3; 19; 9:9; 28; 10:1; 5(2); 20(2); 31(3); 32(2); 11:10; 11; 13; 15; 17; 19; 21; 23; 25; 13:14; 14:17; 15:1; 16:3; 13; 17:7(2); 8; 9; 10; 19; 18:5; 11; 12; 19; 25; 19:6; 31; 22:1; 20; 23:19; 24:55; 67; 25:11; 26; 26:18(2); 31:23; 30; 36; 32:29; 33:2; 7; 35:5; 12; 36:40; 37:17; 38:24; 39:7; 19; 40:1; 13; 41:3; 6; 19; 23; 27; 30; 44:4; 45:15; 23; 48:1; 4; 6(2); 50:14; **Ex** 3:20; 5:19; 7:25; 10:14; 11:8; 14:4; 8; 9; 10; 23; 28; 15:20; 16:1; 17:1; 18:2; 21:9; 23:2; 24; 25:9; 40; 28:15; 43; 29:29; 30:12; 13; 24; 25; 32; 35; 32:4; 33:8; 34:15; 16(2); 27; 37:19; 38:24; 25; 26; **Lev** 5:15; 11:14; 15; 16; 19; 22(4); 29; 13:7; 35; 55; 56; 14:8; 43(3); 48; 15:28; 16:1; 17:7; 18:3(2); 19:31; 20:5; 6(3); 23:11; 15; 16; 25:15; 29; 46; 48; 26:33; 27:3; 18; **Num** 1:1; 2; 18; 20; 22; 24; 26; 28; 30; 32; 34; 36; 38; 40; 42; 47; 2:34; 3:15; 47; 50; 4:2; 15; 29; 34(2); 44; 46(2); 6:19; 20; 21; 7:13; 19; 25; 31; 37; 43; 49; 55; 61; 67; 73; 79; 85; 86; 88; 8:15; 22; 9:1; 17; 12:14; 13:25; 14:34; 15:13; 39(2); 16:29; 18:16; 25:8; 13; 26:1; 12; 15; 20; 23; 26; 28; 35; 37; 38; 41; 42(2); 44; 48; 57; 27:21; 28:24; 26; 29:18; 21; 24; 27; 30; 33; 37; 30:15; 32:15; 42; 33:3; 38; 35:28; **Deut** 1:4; 8; 3:11; 14;

4:37; 40; 45; 46; 6:14; 8:19; 9:4; 10:15; 11:4; 28; 12:8; 15; 20; 21; 25; 28; 30(2); 13:2; 4; 14:13; 14; 15; 18; 26; 16:13; 18:9; 20:18; 21:13; 22:2; 24:4; 9; 28:14; 29:22; 31:16; 27; 29; **Josh** 1:1; 2:5; 7(2); 3:2; 3; 5:4; 11; 12; 6:9; 13; 15; 7:25; 8:6; 16(2); 17(2); 9:16; 10:14; 19; 13:23; 28; 19:47; 20:5; 22:27; 23:1; 24:6; 20; 29; **Judg** 1:1; 6; 2:10; 17; 3:22; 28(2); 31; 4:14; 16(2); 5:14; 6:34; 35; 7:23; 8:5; 12; 27; 33; 10:1; 3; 12:8; 11; 13; 13:11; 18; 14:8; 15:1; 7; 16:22; 18:7; 29; 19:3; 20:45; **Ruth** 1:15; 16; 2:2; 3; 7; 9; 18; 4:4; **1Sa** 1:9(2); 20; 5:9; 6:12; 7:2; 8:3; 10:5; 11:5; 7(2); 12:21; 13:4; 14; 14:12; 13(2); 22; 36; 37; 15:31; 17:27; 30(2); 35; 53; 18:30; 20:37; 38; 22:20; 23:25; 28; 24:8; 14(4); 21; 25:13; 19; 38; 42(2); 26:3; 18; 30:8; **2Sa** 1:1; 6; 10; 2:1; 19; 24; 25; 28; 3:26; 5:13; 7:12; 8:1; 10:1; 11:1; 3; 12:28; 13:1; 17; 18; 23; 14:26; 15:1; 7; 13; 16; 17; 18; 17:1; 6(2); 21; 18:16; 18; 22; 20:2; 6; 7(2); 10; 11; 13(2); 14; 21:1; 14; 18; 23:4; 9; 10; 11; 24:10; **1Kin** 1:6; 13; 14; 17; 20; 24; 27; 30; 35; 40; 2:28(2); 3:12; 10; 6:1; 7:11; 31; 37; 9:21; 11:2; 4; 5(2); 6; 10; 15; 12:14; 13:14; 23(2); 31; 33; 15:4; 16:24; 17:7; 13; 17; 18:1; 28; 19:11; 12(2); 20; 21; 20:15; 21:1; **2Kin** 1:1; 5:20; 21(2); 6:24; 7:14; 15; 8:2; 9:25; 27; 10:29; 14:17; 19; 22; 17:15; 33; 34(4); 40; 18:5; 21:2; 23:3; 25; 25:5; **1Chr** 2:24; 5:1; 25; 6:31; 7:4; 9; 8:8; 9:25; 10:2(2); 11:12; 14:14; 15:13; 17:11; 18:1; 19:1; 20:1; 4; 23:24; 24:30; 27:1; 7; 34; 28:8; 29:14; 21; **2Chr** 1:12; 2:17; 3:3; 4:20; 8:8; 13; 10:5; 14; 11:16; 20; 13:9; 19; 17:4; 18:2; 19(2); 20:1; 35; 21:18; 19; 22:4; 5; 23:21; 24:4; 17; 25:14; 15; 20; 25; 27(2); 26:2; 17; 28:3; 30:16; 31:2; 32:1; 9; 33:14; 34:3; 21; 31; 35:4; 5; 20; 36:14; **Ezr** 2:61; 69; 3:10; 5:4; 12; 7:1; 18; 25; 9:10; 13; 10:16; **Neh** 3:16; 17; 18; 20; 21; 22; 23(2); 24; 25; 27; 29(2); 30(2); 31; 4:13; 5:8; 6:4(2); 7:63; 9:28; 10:34; 11:8; 12:32; 38; 13:6; 19; **Est** 1:22; 2:1; 12; 8:9; 9:26; **Job** 3:1; 10:6(2); 18:20; 19:26; 21:3; 21; 33; 29:22; 30:5(2); 31:7; 37:4; 39:8; 10; 41:32; 42:7; 8; 16; **Ps** 4:2; 10:4; 16:4; 27:4; 28:4; 35:4; 38:12; 40:14; 42:1(2); 49:11; 17; 51:1; 54:3; 63:8; 68:25; 70:2; 78:34; 86:14; 103:10; 104:21; 110:4; 119:40; 85; 88; 150; 143:6; 144:12; **Prov** 2:3; 6:25; 7:22; 15:9; 20:7; 25; 21:21; 28:19; **Eccl** 1:11; 2:12; 18; 3:22; 4:16; 6:12; 7:14; 9:3; 10:14; 11:1; 12:2; **Song** 1:4; **Is** 1:23; 5:17; 10:24; 26; 11:3(2); 23:15; 17; 24:22; 43:10; 44:13; 45:14; 49:20; 51:1; 65:2; **Jer** 2:2; 5; 8; 23; 25; 3:7; 17; 5:8; 7:6; 9; 8:2; 9:14(2); 16; 22; 11:10; 12:6; 15; 13:6; 9; 10; 16:11; 12; 16; 18:12; 23:17; 24:1; 25:6; 26; 28:12; 29:2; 10; 30:17; 18; 31:19(2); 33; 32:18; 39; 34:8; 35:15; 36:27; 39:5; 40:1; 41:4; 16; 42:7; 16; 49:37; 50:21; 51:46; 52:8; **Eze** 5:2; 12; 6:9; 7:27; 9:5; 11:12; 21; 12:14; 16:23; 47(2); 20:16; 24; 30(2); 23:15; 30; 45(2); 48; 29:16; 33:20; 31; 34:6; 36:11; 38:8; 39:14; 36; 40:1; 31; 33; 34; 41:5; 43:13; 44:10; 26; 45:11; 46:12; 17; 19; 48:31; **Dan** 2:39; 3:29; 4:26; 7:6; 7; 24; 8:1; 9:26; 11:13; 18; 23; **Hos** 2:5; 7; 13; 5:8; 11; 6:2; 7:4; 11:10; 12:1; **Joel** 2:2; **Amos** 2:4; 7; 4:4; 10; 7:1; **Zec** 2:8; 6:6; 7:14; **Mt** 1:12; 3:11; 5:6; 28; 6:9; 32; 10:38; 12:39; 15:12; 23; 16:4; 24; 17:1; 18:32; 23:3; 24:29; 25:19; 26:2; 32; 73; 27:31; 53; 63; **Mk** 1:7; 14; 17; 20; 36; 2:1; 4:28; 8:12; 25; 31; 34; 9:2; 31; 12:34; 13:24; 14:1; 28; 70; 16:12; 14; 19; **Lk** 1:24; 59; 2:27; 42; 46; 5:27; 6:1; 7:11; 9:23; 28; 10:1; 12:4; 5; 30; 13:9; 14:27; 29; 15:4; 13; 17:23; 19:14; 20:40; 21:8; 26; 22:20; 58; 59; 23:26; 55; **Jn** 1:15; 27; 30; 35; 2:6; 12; 3:22; 4:43; 5:1; 4; 6:1; 23; 7:1; 8:15; 11:7; 11; 12:19; 13:5; 12; 27; 19:28; 38; 20:26; 21:1; 14; **Acts** 1:2; 3; 8; 3:24; 5:4; 7; 37(2); 7:5; 7; 36; 45; 9:23; 10:24; 37; 41; 12:4; 13:15; 20; 22; 25; 36; 14:24; 15:1; 13; 16; 17; 23; 33; 36; 16:7; 10; 17:27; 18:1; 18; 23; 19:4; 21(2); 20:1; 6; 18; 29; 30; 21:1; 15; 21; 36; 22:29; 23:3; 25; 24:1; 10; 14; 17; 24; 27; 25:1; 13; 26; 26:5; 27:14; 21; 28:6; 11; 13; 17; 25; **Rom** 2:5; 3:11; 5:14; 6:19; 7:22; 8:1(2); 4(2); 5(2); 12; 13; 9:30; 31; 10:20; 14:19; **1Cor** 1:21; 22; 26; 7:7(2); 40; 10:6; 8; 11:25; 12:28; 14:1; 15:6; 7; 32; **2Cor** 5:16(2); 7:9; 11; 9:14; 10:3; 7; 11:17; 18; **Gal** 1:18; 2:1; 14; 3:15; 17; 25; 4:9; 23; 29(2); **Eph** 1:11; 13(2); 15; 4:24; **Phil** 1:8; 2:26; 3:12; **Col** 2:8(3); 22; 3:10; **1Th** 2:2; **2Th** 2:9; 3:6; **1Ti** 5:15; 24; 6:10; 11; **2Ti** 4:3; **Titus** 1:1; 4; 3:4; 10; **Heb** 3:5; 4:7; 11; 5:6; 10; 6:15; 20; 7:2; 11(2); 15; 16(2); 17; 21; 8:10; 9:3; 17; 27; 10:12; 15; 16; 26; 32; 36; 11:8; 30; 12:10; **Jas** 3:9; **1Pet** 3:5; 5:10; **2Pet** 1:15; 2:6; 10; 20; 21; 3:3; **2Jn** 6; **3Jn** 6; **Jude** 7; 11; 16; 18; **Rev** 4:1; 7:1; 9; 11:11; 12:15; 13:3; 15:5; 18:1; 14; 19:1; 20:3

AFTERWARD

Gen 10:18; 15:14; 32:20; 38:30; **Ex** 5:1; 34:32; **Lev** 14:19; 36; 16:26; 28; 22:7; **Num** 5:26; 12:16; 19:7; 31:2; 24; 32:22; **Deut** 17:7; 24:21; **Josh** 2:16; 8:34; 10:26; 24:5; **Judg** 1:9; 7:11; 16:4; 19:5; **1Sa** 24:5; 8; **2Sa** 3:28; **1Chr** 2:21; **2Chr** 35:14; **Ezr** 3:5; **Neh** 6:10; **Ps** 73:24; **Is** 1:26; 9:1; **Jer** 21:7; 34:11; 46:26; 49:6; **Eze** 41:1; 43:1; 47:1; 5; **Dan** 8:27; **Hos** 3:5; **Joel** 2:28; **Mt** 4:2; 21:29; 32; 25:11; **Mk** 4:17; 16:14; **Lk** 4:2; 8:1; 17:8; 18:4; **Jn** 5:14; **Acts** 13:21; **1Cor** 15:23; 46; **Heb** 4:8; 12:11; 17; **Jude** 5

AGAIN

Gen 4:2; 25; 8:10; 12; 21(2); 14:16; 15:16; 18:29; 19:9; 22:5; 24:5; 6; 8; 20; 25:1; 26:18; 28:15; 21; 29:3; 33; 34; 35; 30:7; 19; 31; 35:9; 37:14; 22; 38:4; 5; 26; 40:21; 42:24; 37; 43:2; 12(2); 13; 21; 44:8; 25; 46:4; 48:21; 50:5; **Ex** 4:7(3); 10:8; 29; 14:13; 26; 15:19; 21:19; 23:4; 24:14; 33:11; 34:35; **Lev** 13:6; 7; 16; 14:39; 43; 20:2; 24:20; 25:48; 51; 52; 26:26; **Num** 11:4; 12:14; 15; 17:10; 22:8; 15; 25; 34; 23:16; 32:15; 33:7; 35:32; **Deut** 1:22; 25; 5:30; 13:16; 15:3; 18:16; 22:1; 2; 4; 23:11; 24:4; 13; 19; 20; 28:68(2); 30:9; 33:11; **Josh** 5:2; 8:21; 14:7; 18:4; 8; 9; 22:28; 32; **Judg** 3:12; 19; 4:1; 20; 6:18; 8:9; 33; 9:37; 10:6; 11:8; 9; 13; 14; 13:1; 8; 9; 15:19; 16:22; 19:3; 7; 20:22; 23; 25; 28; 41; 48; 21:14; **Ruth** 1:11; 12; 14; 21; 4:3; **1Sa** 3:5; 6(2); 8; 21; 4:5; 5:3; 11; 6:21; 9:8; 15:25; 30; 31; 16:10; 17:30; 19:8; 15; 21; 20:17; 23:4; 23; 25:12; 27:4; 29:4; 30:12; **2Sa** 1:9; 2:22; 3:11; 26; 34; 5:22; 6:1; 12:23; 14:13; 14; 21; 29; 15:8; 25; 29; 16:19; 18:22; 19:24; 30; 37; 20:10; 21:15; 18; 19; 22:38; 24:1; **1Kin** 1:45; 2:30; 41; 8:33; 34; 12:5; 12; 20; 21; 27(2); 13:4; 6(2); 9; 17; 33; 17:21; 22; 18:37; 43; 19:6; 7; 20; 20:5; 9; **2Kin** 1:6; 11; 13; 2:18; 4:22; 29; 31; 38; 43; 5:10; 14; 26; 7:8; 9:18; 20; 36; 13:25; 19:9; 30; 20:5; 21:3; 22:9; 20; 24:7; **1Chr** 13:3; 14:13; 14; 20:5; 6; 21:12; 27; **2Chr** 6:25; 10:5; 12; 11:1; 12:11; 13:20; 18:18; 32; 19:4; 20:27; 24:11; 19; 25:10; 28:11; 17; 30:6; 9(2); 32:25; 33:3; 13; 34:16; 28; **Ezr** 2:1; 4:13; 16; 6:5; 21; 9:14; **Neh** 7:6; 8:17; 9:28; 29; 13:9; 21; **Est** 4:10; 6:12; 7:2; 8:3; **Job** 2:1; 6:29; 10:9; 16; 12:14; 23; 14:7; 14; 20:15; 29:22; 34:15; **Ps** 18:37; 37:21; 60:1; 68:22(2); 71:20(2); 78:39; 80:3; 7; 19; 85:6; 8; 104:9; 107:26; 39; 126:1; 4; 6; 140:10; **Prov** 2:19; 3:28; 19:17; 19; 24; 23:35; 24:16; 26:15; **Eccl** 1:6; 7; 3:20; 4:4; 11; 8:14; **Is** 7:10; 8:5; 10:20; 11:11; 24:20; 37:31; 38:8; 46:8; 49:5; 20; 51:22; 52:8; **Jer** 3:1(2); 12:15; 15:19; 16:15; 18:4; 19:11; 23:3; 24:4; 6; 25:5; 27:16; 28:3; 4; 6; 29:14; 30:3; 18; 31:4(2); 16; 17; 21(2); 23; 32:15; 37; 33:10; 12; 13; 36:28; 37:8; 41:16; 46:16; 48:47; 49:6; 39; 50:19; **Lam** 3:40; **Eze** 3:20; 4:6; 5:4; 7:7; 8:6; 13; 15; 11:14; 12:26; 14:12; 16:1; 53(2); 18:1; 27; 21:8; 18; 23:1; 24:1; 25:1; 26:21; 27:1; 28:1; 20; 29:14; 30:1; 33:1; 14; 15; 34:4; 16; 37:4; 15; 39:25; 27; 47:1; 4(2); **Dan** 2:7; 9:25; 10:10; **Hos** 1:6; **Joel** 3:1; **Amos** 7:8; 13; 8:2; 14; 9:14; **Jonah** 2:4; **Mic** 7:19; **Zeph** 3:20; **Hag** 2:20; **Zec** 2:1; 12; 4:1; 12; 8:1; 15; 10:6; 9; 10; 12:6; **Mal** 2:13; **Mt** 2:8; 4:7; 8; 5:33; 7:2; 6; 11:4; 13:44; 45; 47; 16:21; 17:9; 23; 18:19; 19:24; 20:5; 19; 21:36; 22:1; 4; 26:32; 42; 43; 44; 52; 72; 27:3; 50; 63; **Mk** 2:1; 13; 3:1; 20; 4:1; 5:21; 7:31; 8:13; 25; 31; 10:1(2); 10; 24; 32; 34; 11:27; 12:4; 5; 13:16; 14:39; 40; 61; 69; 70(2); 15:4; 12; 13; **Lk** 2:34; 45; 4:20; 6:30; 34; 35; 38; 8:37; 55; 9:8; 19; 39; 42; 10:6; 17; 35; 13:20; 14:6; 12; 15:24; 32; 17:4; 18:33; 20:11; 12; 23:11; 20; 24:7; **Jn** 1:35; 3:3; 7; 4:3; 13; 46; 54; 6:15; 39; 8:2; 8; 12; 21; 9:15; 17; 24; 26; 27; 10:7; 17; 18; 19; 31; 39; 40; 11:7; 8; 23; 24; 38; 12:22; 28; 39; 13:12; 14:3; 28; 16:16; 17; 19; 22; 28; 18:7; 27; 33; 38; 40; 19:4; 9; 37; 20:9; 10; 21; 26; 21:1; 16; **Acts** 1:6; 7:26; 39; 10:15; 16; 11:9; 10; 13:33; 37; 14:21; 15:16(2); 36; 17:32; 18:21; 20:11; 21:6; 22:17; 27:28; **Rom** 4:25; 8:15; 34; 10:7; 11:23; 35; 15:10; 11; 12; **1Cor** 3:20; 7:5; 12:21; 15:4; **2Cor** 1:16; 2:1; 3:1; 5:12; 15; 10:7; 11:16; 12:19; 21; 13:2; **Gal** 1:9; 17; 2:1; 18; 4:9(2); 19; 5:1; 3; **Phil** 1:26; 2:28; 4:4; 10; 16; **1Th** 2:18; 3:9; 4:14; **Titus** 2:9; **Philem** 1:12; **Heb** 1:5; 6; 2:13(2); 4:5; 7; 5:12; 6:1; 6; 10:3; 30; 11:35; 13:20; **Jas** 5:18; **1Pet** 1:3; 23; 2:23; **2Pet** 2:20; 22; **1Jn** 2:8; **Rev** 10:8; 11; 19:3; 20:5

AGAINST

Gen 4:8; 14:15; 15:10; 16:12(2); 20:6; 21:16(2); 30:2; 32:25; 34:30; 37:18; 39:9; 40:2(3); 41:36; 42:22; 36; 43:18; 25; 44:18; 50:20; **Ex** 1:10; 4:14; 7:15; 8:12; 9:17; 10:16(2); 11:7(2); 12:12; 14:2; 5; 25; 27; 15:7; 24; 16:2; 7(2); 8(3); 17:3; 19:11; 15; 20:16; 23:29; 33; 25:27; 37; 26:17; 35; 28:27; 32:10; 11; 12; 33; 37:14; 39:20; 40:24; **Lev** 4:2(2); 13; 14; 22; 27; 5:19; 6:2; 17:10; 19:16; 18; 20:3; 5(2); 6; 26:17; 40; **Num** 5:6; 7; 12; 13; 27; 8:2; 3; 10:9; 21; 11:18; 33; 12:1; 8; 9; 13:31; 14:2(2); 9; 27(2); 29; 35; 36; 16:3(2); 11(2); 19; 38; 41(2); 42(2); 17:5; 10; 20:2(2); 18; 20; 24; 21:1; 5(2); 7(2); 23(2); 26; 33; 22:5; 22; 25; 34; 23:23(2); 24:10; 25:3; 4; 26:9(3); 27:3; 14; 30:9; 31:3; 7; 16; 32:13; 23; 35:30; **Deut** 1:1; 26; 41; 43; 44; 2:15; 19; 32; 3:1; 29; 4:26; 46; 5:20; 6:15; 7:4; 8:19; 9:7; 16; 19; 23; 24; 11:17; 30; 15:9(2); 19:11; 15; 16(2); 18; 20:1; 3; 4; 10; 12; 18; 19(2); 20; 21:10; 22:14; 17; 26; 23:4; 9; 24:15; 28:7(2); 25; 48; 49; 29:7; 20; 27; 30:19; 31:17; 19; 21; 26; 27; 28; 32:49; 51; 33:11; 34:1; 6; **Josh** 1:18; 3:16; 5:13; 7:1; 13; 20; 8:3; 4; 5; 14(2); 22; 33(2); 9:1; 18; 10:5; 6; 21; 25; 29; 31(2); 34(2); 36; 38; 11:5; 7; 20; 18:17; 18; 19:47; 22:11; 12; 16(2); 18; 19(2); 22; 29; 31; 33; 23:16; 24:9; 11; 22; **Judg** 1:1(2); 3; 5; 8; 9; 10; 11; 2:14; 15; 20; 3:8; 10; 12; 4:24; 5:14; 20; 23; 6:2; 3; 4; 31; 32; 39; 7:2; 22; 24; 9:18; 31; 33; 34; 43; 45; 50; 52; 10:7; 9(3); 10; 18; 11:4; 5; 8; 9; 12; 20; 25(2); 27(2); 32; 12:1; 3(2); 14:4; 5; 15:10; 14; 16:5; 18:9; 19:2; 10; 20:5; 9; 11; 14; 18; 19; 20(2); 23(2); 24; 25; 28; 30(2); 31; 34; 43; **Ruth** 1:13; 21; **1Sa** 2:25(2); 3:12; 4:1; 2; 5:9; 7:6; 7; 10; 13; 9:14; 11:1; 12:3; 5; 9; 12; 14; 15(3); 23; 14:5(2); 20; 33; 34; 47(6); 52; 15:7; 18; 17:2; 9; 21; 28; 33; 35; 55; 18:21; 19:4(3); 5; 20:30; 22:8(2); 13(2); 23:1; 3; 9; 28; 24:6; 7; 10; 11; 25:17(2); 20; 22; 34; 26:9; 11; 19; 23; 27:10(3); 28:15; 29:8; 30:23; 31:1; 3; **2Sa** 1:16; 3:8; 5:23; 6:7; 8:10; 10:9(2); 10; 13; 17; 11:23; 25; 12:5; 11; 13; 26; 27; 28; 29; 14:7; 13; 16:13; 17:21; 18:6; 12; 13(2); 28; 31; 32; 20:15; 21(2); 21:5; 15; 22:40; 49; 23:8; 18; 24:1(2); 4(2); 17(2); **1Kin** 2:23; 6:5(2); 10; 7:4; 5; 20; 39; 8:31; 33; 35; 44; 46; 50(2); 11:26; 27; 12:19; 21; 24; 13:2; 4(2); 32(2); 14:10; 25; 15:17; 20; 27; 16:1; 7(2); 9; 11; 12; 15; 22; 20:1; 12; 22; 23; 25; 26; 27; 29; 21:10; 13(2); 21; 22:6; 15; 32; 35; **2Kin** 1:1; 3:5; 7(2); 21; 27; 5:7; 6:8; 7:6; 8:28; 29; 9:8; 14; 21; 10:9; 12:17; 13:3; 12; 14:19; 15:10; 19; 25; 30; 37; 16:7; 9; 11; 17:3; 7; 9; 13(2); 15; 18:7; 9; 13; 17; 20; 25(2); 19:8; 9; 20; 22(2); 27; 28; 32; 21:23; 24; 22:13; 17; 19(2); 23:17; 26; 29(2); 24:1; 2(2); 10; 11; 20; 25:1(3); 4; **1Chr** 5:11; 20; 25; 8:32; 9:38; 10:1; 3; 13(2); 11:11; 20; 12:10; 21; 13:10; 14:8; 10; 14; 18:10; 19:10(2); 11; 17(2); 21:1; 4; 24:31(2); 25:8; 26:12; 16; 27:24; **2Chr** 4:10; 6:22; 24; 26; 34; 36; 39; 8:3; 9:29; 10:19; 11:1; 4(2); 12:2(2); 9; 13:3; 6; 7; 12(2); 14:9; 10; 11(2); 16:1; 4; 17:1; 10; 18:22; 34; 19:10; 20:1; 2; 12(2); 16; 17; 22(2); 23; 29; 37; 21:16; 22:5; 7; 24:19; 21; 23; 24; 25; 26; 25:10; 15; 27; 26:6; 7(2); 13; 16; 27:5; 28:10; 12; 13(2); 19; 22; 30:7; 32:1; 2; 9; 16(2); 17; 19(2); 33:24; 25; 34:27(2); 35:20(2); 21(2); 36:6; 13; 16; **Ezr** 4:5; 6; 8; 19; 7:23; 8:22(2); 10:2; **Neh** 1:6; 7; 2:19; 3:10; 16; 19; 23; 25; 26; 27; 28; 29; 30; 31; 4:8; 9; 5:1; 7; 6:12; 7:3; 9:10; 26(2); 29(2); 30; 34; 12:9; 24(2); 37; 38; 13:2; 15; 21; 27; **Est** 2:1; 3:14; 5:1(2); 9; 6:13; 7:7; 8:3; 13; 9:24; 25; **Job** 2:3; 6:4; 7:20; 8:4; 9:4; 10:17(2); 11:5; 13:26; 14:20; 15:6; 13; 24; 25(2); 16:4; 8; 10; 17:8; 18:9; 19:5(2); 11; 12; 18; 19; 20:27; 21:27; 23:6; 24:13; 27:7; 30:12; 21; 31:21; 38; 32:2; 3; 14; 33:10; 13; 34:6; 29(2); 37; 35:6; 38:23(2); 39:16; 23; 42:7(2); **Ps** 2:2(2); 3:1; 6; 5:10; 7:13; 10:8; 13:4; 15:3; 5; 17:7; 18:39; 48; 21:11; 12; 27:3(2); 12; 31:13; 18; 34:16; 35:1(2); 3; 15; 20; 21; 26; 36:11; 37:1; 12; 38:16; 41:4; 7(2); 9; 43:1; 44:5; 50:7; 20; 51:4; 53:5; 54:3; 55:12; 18; 20; 56:2; 5; 59:1; 3; 62:3; 65:3; 69:12; 71:10; 73:9; 15; 74:1; 23; 78:17; 19; 21(2); 79:8; 80:4; 81:14; 83:3(2); 5; 86:14; 91:12; 92:11; 94:16(2); 21; 102:8(2); 105:28; 106:26; 40; 107:11; 109:2(2); 3; 20; 119:11; 23; 69; 124:2; 3; 129:2; 137:9; 138:7; 139:20; 21; **Prov** 3:29; 8:36; 14:35; 17:11; 19:3; 20:2; 21:30; 31; 24:1; 15; 28; 25:18; 30:31; **Eccl** 4:12; 7:14; 8:11; 9:14(2); 10:4; **Is** 1:2; 2:4; 3:5(2); 8; 9; 5:25(2); 30; 7:1(2); 5; 6; 9:11; 21; 10:6(2); 15(3); 24; 32; 13:17; 14:4; 8; 22; 19:2(5); 17; 20:1; 23:8; 11; 25:4; 27:4; 29:3(3); 7(2); 8; 31:2(2); 4; 32:6; 36:1; 5; 10(2); 37:8; 21; 23(2); 28; 29; 33; 41:11; 12; 42:13; 24; 43:27; 45:24; 54:15; 17(2); 57:4(2); 59:12; 13; 19; 63:10; 66:24; **Jer** 1:15(2); 16; 18(5); 19(2); 2:8; 29; 3:13; 25; 4:12; 16(2); 17(2); 5:11; 6:3; 4; 6; 23; 8:14; 18; 11:17(2); 19; 12:8; 9; 14; 13:14; 14:7(2); 20; 15:6; 8; 20(2); 16:10(2); 18:8; 11(2); 18; 23; 19:15; 20:10; 21:2; 4(2); 5; 10; 13(2); 22:7; 23:2; 30; 31; 32; 25:9(3); 13(2); 30(2); 26:9; 11; 12(2); 13; 19(2); 20(2); 27:13; 28:8(2); 16; 29:32; 31:20; 39; 32:24; 29; 33:8(2); 34:1(2); 7(4); 22; 35:17; 36:2(3); 7; 31; 37:8; 10; 18(3); 19(2); 38:5; 22; 39:1; 40:3; 43:3; 44:7; 11; 23; 29; 46:1; 2(2); 12; 22; 47:1; 7(2); 48:1; 2; 26; 42; 49:14; 19; 20(2); 30(2); 34; 50:1(2); 3; 7; 9(2); 14(2); 15; 21(3); 24; 26; 29(4); 31; 42; 45(2); 51:1(3); 2; 3(2); 5; 11; 12; 14; 25; 27(3); 28; 29; 40; 60; 62; 52:3; 4(3); **Lam** 1:13; 15; 18; 2:3; 16; 3:3(2); 5; 46; 60; 61; 62(2); 5:22; **Eze** 1:20; 21; 2:3(2); 3:8(2); 13; 4:2(5); 3(2); 7; 5:8; 6:2; 11:4; 13:2; 8; 17(2); 20; 14:8; 13; 15:7(2); 16:37; 40; 44; 17:15; 20; 19:8; 20:8(2); 13; 21(2); 27; 38; 46; 21:2; 3; 4; 15; 22; 31; 22:3; 23:22(2); 24(2); 25; 24:2; 25:2(2); 3(3); 6; 12; 26:2; 3(2); 8(3); 9; 27:30; 28:7; 21(2); 22; 29:2(3); 3; 10(2); 18(2); 20; 30:11; 22; 33:30; 34:2; 10; 35:2(2); 3(2); 11; 12; 13(2); 36:2; 5(2); 38:2(2); 3; 8; 16(2); 17; 18; 21(2); 22; 39:1(2); 23; 26; 40:13; 18; 23; 41:15; 16; 42:1; 3(3); 7; 10(2); 44:12; 45:6; 7; 46:9; 47:20; 48:13; 15; 18(2); 21(3); **Dan** 3:19; 29; 5:5; 6; 23; 6:4; 5(2); 7:21; 25; 8:7; 12; 25; 9:7; 8; 9; 11; 12(2); 11:2; 7; 14; 16; 24; 25(2); 28; 30(2); 32; 36; 40; **Hos** 4:7; 5:7; 6:7; 7:13(2); 14; 15; 8:1(2); 5; 10:9; 10; 13:16; **Joel** 3:19; **Amos** 1:8; 3:1(2); 5:1; 9(2); 6:14; 7:9; 10; 16(2); **Obad** 1; 7; 10; **Jonah** 1:2; 13; **Mic** 1:2; 2:3; 4; 3:5; 4:3; 11; 5:1; 5; 6:3; 7:6(2); 8; 9; **Nah** 1:9; 11; 2:4; 13; 3:5; **Hab** 2:6(2); 10; 3:8(3); **Zeph** 1:16(2); 17; 2:5; 8; 10; 13; 3:11; **Zec** 1:12; 7:10; 8:10; 17; 9:13; 10:3; 12:2(2); 3; 7; 9; 13:7(2); 14:2; 3; 12; 13; 16; **Mal** 1:4; 2:10; 14; 15; 3:5(4); 13(2); **Mt** 4:6; 5:11; 23; 10:1; 18; 21; 35(3); 12:14; 25(2); 26; 30; 31; 32(2); 16:18; 18:15; 21; 20:11; 24; 21:2; 23:13; 24:7(2); 26:55; 59; 62; 27:1; 13; 61; **Mk** 3:6; 24; 25; 26; 29; 6:11; 19; 9:40; 10:11; 11:2; 25; 12:12; 41; 13:3; 8(2); 9; 12; 14:5; 48; 55; 56; 57; 60; 15:4; 39; **Lk** 2:34; 4:11; 5:30; 6:7; 49; 7:30; 8:26; 9:5; 50; 10:11; 11:17(2); 18; 23; 12:10(2); 52(2); 53(6); 14:31(2); 15:18; 21; 17:3; 4; 19:30; 20:19; 21:10(2); 22:52; 53; 65; **Jn** 12:7; 13:18; 29; 18:29; 19:11; 12; **Acts** 4:14; 26(2); 27; 5:39; 6:1; 11(2); 13; 8:1; 9:1; 5; 29; 13:45; 50; 51; 14:2; 16:22; 18:12; 19:16; 36; 38; 20:15; 21:28; 22:24; 23:9; 30; 24:1; 19; 25:2; 3; 7; 8(3); 15; 16; 18; 19; 27; 26:10; 11; 14; 27:7(2); 14; 28:17; 19; 22; **Rom** 1:18; 26; 2:2; 5; 4:18; 7:23; 8:7; 31; 9:20; 11:2; 18; **1Cor** 4:6; 6:1; 18; 8:12(2); 9:17; **2Cor** 10:2; 5; 13:8; **Gal** 3:21; 5:17(2); 23; **Eph** 6:11; 12(5); **Col** 2:14; 3:13; 19; **1Ti** 5:11; 19; 6:19; **2Ti** 1:12; **Heb** 12:3; 4; **Jas** 2:13; 3:14; 5:3; 9; **1Pet** 2:11; 12; 3:12; **2Pet** 2:11; 3:7; **3Jn** 10; **Jude** 9; 15; **Rev** 2:4; 14; 16; 20; 11:7; 12:7; 13:6; 19:19(2)

AGO

1Sa 9:20; **2Kin** 19:25; **Ezr** 5:11; **Is** 22:11; 37:26; **Mt** 11:21; **Mk** 9:21; **Lk** 10:13; **Acts** 10:30; 15:7; **2Cor** 8:10; 9:2; 12:2

AH

Ps 35:25; **Is** 1:4; 24; **Jer** 1:6; 4:10; 14:13; 22:18(4); 32:17; 34:5; **Eze** 4:14; 9:8; 11:13; 20:49; 21:15; **Mk** 15:29

AHA

Ps 35:21(2); 40:15(2); 70:3(2); **Is** 44:16; **Eze** 25:3; 26:2; 36:2

ALAS

Num 12:11; 24:23; **Josh** 7:7; **Judg** 6:22; 11:35; **1Kin** 13:30; **2Kin** 3:10; 6:5; 15; **Jer** 30:7; **Eze** 6:11; **Joel** 1:15; **Amos** 5:16(2); **Rev** 18:10(2); 16(2); 19(2)

ALIKE

Deut 12:22; 15:22; **1Sa** 30:24; **Job** 21:26; **Ps** 33:15; 139:12; **Prov** 20:10; 27:15; **Eccl** 9:2; 11:6; **Rom** 14:5

ALL

Gen 1:26; 29; 2:1; 2; 3; 20; 3:14(2); 17; 20; 4:21; 5:5; 8; 11; 14; 17; 20; 23; 27; 31; 6:2; 12; 13; 17; 19; 21; 22; 7:1; 3; 5; 11; 14; 15; 16; 19; 21; 22(2); 8:1; 17; 9:2(2); 3; 10; 11; 15(2); 16; 17; 29; 10:21; 29; 11:6; 8; 9(2); 12:3; 5; 20; 13:1; 10; 11; 15; 14:3; 7; 11(2); 16; 20; 15:10; 16:12; 17:8; 23(2); 27; 18:18; 25; 26; 28; 19:2(2); 4; 17; 25(2); 28; 31; 20:7; 8(2); 16(2); 18; 21:6; 12; 22; 22:18; 23:10; 17(2); 18; 24:1; 2; 10; 20; 36; 54; 66; 25:4; 5; 18; 25; 26:3; 4(2); 11; 15; 27:33; 37; 28:11; 14; 15; 22; 29:3; 8; 13; 22; 30:32(3); 35(2); 40; 31:1(2); 6; 8(2); 12(2); 16; 18(2); 21; 34; 37(2); 43; 54; 32:10(2); 19; 33:8; 13; 34:19; 24(2); 25; 29(3); 35:2; 4(2); 6; 36:6(3); 37:3; 4; 35(2); 39:3; 4; 5(2); 6; 8; 22; 40:17; 20; 41:8(2); 19; 29; 30; 35; 37; 39; 40; 41; 43; 44; 45; 46; 48; 51(2); 54(2); 55(2); 56(2); 57(2); 42:6; 11; 17; 29; 36; 45:1; 8(2); 9; 10; 11; 13(2); 15; 20; 22; 26; 27; 46:1; 6; 7; 15; 22; 25; 26(2); 27; 32; 47:1; 12; 13(2); 14; 15; 17; 20; 48:15; 16; 49:28; 50:7(2); 8; 14; 15; **Ex** 1:5; 6(2); 14(2); 22; 3:15; 20; 4:19; 21; 28(2); 29; 30; 5:12; 23; 6:29; 7:2; 19(2); 20; 21; 24; 8:2; 4; 16; 17(2); 24; 9:4; 6; 9(2); 11; 14(2); 16; 19; 22; 24; 25(2); 10:6(2); 12; 13(2); 14(2); 15(2); 19; 22; 23; 11:5(2); 6; 8(2); 10; 12:3; 9; 12(2); 20; 21; 29(2); 30(2); 33; 41; 42; 47; 48; 50; 13:2; 7; 12; 13; 15(3); 14:4; 7; 9; 17; 20; 21; 23; 28; 15:15; 20; 26; 16:1; 6; 9; 22; 17:1; 18:1; 8(2); 9; 11; 12; 14(2); 21; 22; 23; 24;

25; 26; 19:5(2); 7; 8(2); 11; 16; 20:1; 9; 11; 18; 24; 22:9; 23; 26; 23:13; 17; 22; 27(2); 24:3(4); 4; 7; 8; 25:9(2); 22; 36; 39; 26:8; 17; 27:3; 17; 19(4); 28:3; 31; 38; 29:12; 13; 24; 35; 30:27; 28; 31:3; 5; 6(2); 7; 8; 9; 11; 32:3; 13; 26; 33:8; 10(2); 16; 19; 34:3; 10(3); 19; 20; 23; 30; 31; 32(2); 35:1; 4; 10; 13; 16; 20; 21; 22; 25; 26; 29; 31; 35; 36:1(2); 3; 4(2); 7; 9; 22; 37:22; 24; 38:3(2); 16; 17; 20; 22; 24(2); 30; 31(2); 39:22; 32(2); 33; 36; 37; 39; 40; 42(2); 43; 40:9(2); 10; 16; 36; 38(2); **Lev** 1:9; 13; 2:2; 13; 16; 3:3; 9; 14; 16; 17; 4:7; 8(2); 11; 18; 19; 26; 30; 31; 34; 35; 6:3; 5; 7; 9; 15; 18; 29; 7:3; 9(2); 10; 18; 19; 8:3; 10; 11; 16; 25; 27; 36; 9:5; 23; 24; 10:3; 6; 11; 11:2; 9; 10(2); 20(2); 21; 23; 27(2); 31; 34(2); 42(2); 13:12; 13(2); 46; 14:8; 9(2); 36; 45; 46; 54; 15:16; 24(2); 25; 26; 16:2; 16; 17; 21(3); 22; 29; 30; 33; 34; 17:2; 14(2); 18:24; 27; 19:2; 7; 13; 20; 23; 24; 37(2); 20:5; 22(2); 23; 21:24; 22:3; 18(3); 23:3; 14; 21; 31; 38(2); 42; 24:14(2); 16; 25:7; 9; 10(2); 24; 26:14; 15; 18; 27; 44; 27:9; 10; 13; 25; 28; 30; 31; 33; **Num** 1:2; 3; 18; 20; 22; 24; 26; 28; 30; 32; 34; 36; 38; 40; 42; 45(2); 46; 50(3); 54; 2:9; 16; 24; 31; 32; 34; 3:8; 12; 13(3); 22; 26; 28; 31; 34; 36(2); 39(2); 40; 41(2); 42; 43; 45; 4:3; 9; 10; 12; 14(2); 15; 16(2); 23; 26(2); 27(4); 31; 32(2); 33; 37; 41; 46; 5:9; 30; 6:4; 5; 6; 8; 7:1(2); 85; 86; 87; 88; 8:7; 16; 17; 18; 20(2); 9:3(2); 5; 12; 10:3; 25; 11:6; 11; 12; 13; 14; 22; 29; 32(4); 12:3; 7; 13:3; 26(2); 32; 14:1; 2; 5; 7; 10(2); 11; 15; 21; 22; 29; 35; 36; 39; 15:13; 22; 23; 24; 25; 26(2); 33; 35; 36; 39; 40; 16:3; 5; 6; 10; 11; 16; 19(2); 22(2); 26; 28; 29(2); 30; 31; 32(2); 33; 34; 41; 17:2; 9(2); 12; 18:3; 4; 8; 11; 12(2); 15; 19; 21; 28; 29(2); 19:14(2); 18; 20:14; 27; 29(2); 21:23; 25(3); 26; 33; 34; 35; 22:2; 4; 38; 23:6; 13; 25(2); 26; 24:17; 25:4; 6; 26:2(2); 43; 62; 27:2; 16; 19; 20; 21(2); 22; 29:40; 30:2; 4; 6; 11; 14(2); 31:4; 7; 9(4); 10(2); 11(2); 13; 15; 18; 20(4); 23; 27; 30; 35; 51; 52; 32:13; 15; 21; 26; 33:3; 4; 52(4); 35:3; 7; 29; **Deut** 1:1; 3; 7; 18; 19; 30; 31; 41; 2:7; 14; 16; 32; 33; 34; 36; 3:1; 2; 3; 4(2); 5; 7; 10(3); 13(3); 14; 18; 21(2); 4:3; 6; 7; 8; 9; 10; 19(2); 29(2); 30; 34; 49; 5:1; 3; 13; 22; 23; 26; 27(2); 28; 29; 31; 33; 6:2(2); 5(3); 11; 19; 22; 24; 25; 7:6; 7; 14; 15(2); 16; 18; 19; 8:1; 2; 13; 19; 9:10; 18; 10:12(3); 14; 15; 11:3; 6(2); 7; 8; 13(2); 22(2); 23; 25; 32; 12:1; 2; 5; 7; 8; 10; 11(2); 14; 15; 18; 28; 13:3(2); 9; 11; 15; 16(2); 18; 14:2; 9(2); 11; 20; 22; 28; 29; 15:5; 10(2); 18; 19; 16:3; 4(2); 15(2); 16; 18; 17:7; 10; 13; 14; 19(2); 18:1; 5; 6(2); 7; 12; 16; 18; 19:8; 9; 20:11; 14(2); 15; 18; 21:6; 14; 17; 21(2); 23; 22:3; 5; 19; 29; 23:6; 20; 24:8; 19; 25:16(2); 18; 19; 26:2; 12; 13; 14; 16(2); 18; 19; 27:1; 3; 8; 9; 14; 15; 16; 17; 18; 19; 20; 21; 22; 23; 24; 25; 26(2); 28:1(2); 2; 8; 10; 12; 15(2); 20; 25; 26; 32; 33; 37; 40; 42; 45; 47; 48; 52(4); 55; 57; 58; 60; 64; 29:2(4); 9; 10(2); 20; 21(2); 24; 27; 29; 30:1(2); 2(3); 3; 6(2); 7; 8; 10(2); 31:1; 5; 7; 9; 11(2); 12; 18; 28; 30; 32:4; 27; 44; 45(2); 46(2); 33:3; 12; 34:1; 2(2); 11(3); 12(3); **Josh** 1:2; 4; 5; 7; 8; 14; 16; 17; 18; 2:3; 9; 13; 18; 22; 23; 24(2); 3:1; 7; 11; 13; 15(2); 17(2); 4:1; 10; 11; 14(2); 18; 24; 5:1(2); 4(2); 5(2); 6; 8; 6:3; 5; 17(2); 19; 21; 22; 23(2); 24; 25; 27; 7:3(2); 7; 9; 15; 23; 24(2); 25; 8:1; 3; 4; 5; 11; 13; 14; 15; 16; 21; 24(3); 25(2); 26; 33; 34(2); 35(2); 9:1(2); 5; 9; 10; 11; 18; 19(2); 21; 24(2); 10:2; 5; 6; 7(2); 9; 15; 21; 24; 25; 28; 29; 30; 31; 32(2); 34; 35(2); 36; 37(4); 38; 39(2); 40(3); 41; 42; 43; 11:4; 5; 6; 7; 10; 11; 12(2); 14; 15; 16(3); 17; 18; 19; 21(2); 23; 12:1; 5; 24; 13:2(2); 4; 5; 6(2); 9; 10; 11(2); 12; 16; 17; 21(2); 25; 30(3); 15:32; 46; 16:9; 17:16; 19:8; 20:9; 21:19; 26; 33; 39; 40; 41; 42; 43; 44(3); 45; 22:2(2); 5(3); 14; 20; 23:1; 2; 3(2); 4; 6; 14(5); 15(2); 24:1; 2; 3; 17(2); 18; 27(2); 31(3); **Judg** 1:25; 2:4; 7(3); 10; 18; 3:1; 3; 19; 29(2); 4:13(2); 15(2); 16; 5:31; 6:9; 13(2); 31; 33; 35; 37; 39; 40; 7:1; 6; 7; 8; 12; 14; 18(2); 21; 22; 23; 24(2); 8:10(2); 12; 27; 34; 35; 9:1; 2(2); 3(2); 6(2); 14; 25; 34; 44; 45; 46; 47; 48; 49(2); 51(2); 53; 57; 10:8; 18; 11:8; 11; 20; 21(2); 22; 26; 12:4; 13:13; 14; 23; 14:3; 16:2(2); 3; 17; 18(2); 27; 30(2); 31; 18:1; 31; 19:6; 9; 13; 20; 25; 29; 30; 20:1; 2(2); 6; 7; 8; 10(2); 11; 12; 16; 17; 25; 26(2); 33; 34; 35; 37; 44; 46(2); 48(2); 21:5; **Ruth** 1:19; 2:11; 21; 3:5; 6; 11(2); 16; 4:7; 9(3); 11; **1Sa** 1:4; 11; 21; 2:14(2); 22(2); 23; 28(2); 29; 32; 33; 3:12; 17; 20; 4:1; 5; 8; 13; 5:8; 11(2); 6:4; 18; 7:2; 3(2); 5; 13; 15; 16; 8:4; 5; 7; 8; 10; 20; 21; 9:6; 19; 20(2); 21; 10:9; 11; 18; 19; 20; 24(3); 25; 11:1; 2(2); 3; 4; 7; 10; 15(2); 12:1(2); 7; 18; 19(2); 20(2); 24; 13:3; 4; 7; 19; 20; 14:7; 15; 20; 22; 25; 34; 38; 39; 40; 47; 52; 15:3; 6; 8; 9; 11; 16:11; 17:11; 19; 24; 46; 47; 18:5; 6; 14; 16; 22; 30; 19:1; 5; 7; 18; 24(2); 20:6(2); 22:1; 4; 6; 7; 8; 11(2); 14; 15(2); 16; 22; 23:8; 20; 23(2); 24:2; 25:1; 6; 7; 9; 12; 16; 17; 21(2); 22; 28; 30; 26:12; 24; 27:11; 28:3; 4; 20(3); 29:1; 30:6; 8; 16(2); 18; 19; 20; 22; 31; 31:6; 12(2); **2Sa** 1:11; 2:9; 28; 29(2); 30; 32; 3:12; 18; 19; 21(2); 23; 25; 29; 31; 32; 34; 35; 36(2); 37(2); 4:1; 7; 9; 5:1; 3; 5; 17; 6:1; 2; 5(2); 11; 12; 14; 15; 19(2); 21; 7:1; 3; 7(2); 9; 11; 17(2); 21; 22; 8:4; 9; 11; 14(2); 15(2); 9:7; 9(2); 11; 12; 10:7; 9; 17; 19; 11:1; 9; 18; 22; 12:12; 16; 29; 31(2); 13:9; 21; 23; 25; 27; 29; 30; 31; 32; 33; 36; 14:19(2); 20; 25; 15:6; 10; 14; 16; 17; 18(4); 22(2); 23(3); 24(2); 30; 16:4; 6(3); 8; 11; 14; 15; 18; 21(2); 22; 23; 17:2; 3(3); 4; 10; 11; 12; 13; 14; 16; 22; 24; 18:4; 5(2); 8; 17; 28; 31; 32; 19:2; 5; 6; 7; 8(2); 9(2); 11; 14(2); 20; 28; 30; 39; 40; 41(2); 42(2); 20:7; 12; 13; 14(2); 15; 22; 23; 21:9; 14; 22:1; 23; 31; 23:5(3); 6; 39; 24:2; 7; 8; 23; **1Kin** 1:3; 9(2); 19; 20; 25; 29; 39; 40; 41; 49; 2:2; 3; 4(2); 15; 26; 44; 3:13; 15; 28; 4:1; 7; 10; 11; 12; 21(2); 24(3); 25; 27; 30(2); 31(2); 34(2); 5:6; 8; 10; 13; 6:10; 12; 18; 22; 29; 38(2); 7:1; 5; 9; 14(2); 23; 25; 33; 37; 40; 45; 47; 48; 51; 8:1; 2; 3; 4; 5; 14(2); 16; 22; 23; 38; 39; 40; 43(2); 48(2); 50; 52; 53; 54; 55; 56(2); 58; 59; 60; 62; 63; 65; 66; 9:1; 4; 6; 7; 9; 11; 19(2); 20; 10:2; 3; 4; 13; 15; 21(2); 23; 24; 29; 11:8; 13; 16; 25; 28; 32; 34; 37; 38; 41; 42; 12:1; 3; 12; 16; 18; 20(2); 21; 23; 13:11; 32; 14:8; 9; 10; 13; 18; 21; 22; 24; 26(2); 29; 30; 15:3; 5; 6; 7; 12; 14; 16; 18; 20(2); 22; 23(3); 27; 29; 31; 32; 33; 16:7; 11; 12; 13; 14; 16; 17; 25; 26; 30; 33; 18:5(3); 19; 20; 21; 24; 30(2); 36; 39; 19:1(2); 18; 20:1; 4; 7; 8(2); 9; 10; 13; 15(2); 27; 28; 21:26; 22:10; 12; 17; 19; 22; 23; 28; 39(2); 43; 53; **2Kin** 3:6; 19; 21(2); 25(2); 4:3; 4; 13; 5:12; 15(2); 21; 22; 6:24; 7:13(2); 15; 8:4; 6(2); 21; 23; 9:5; 7; 11; 14; 10:5; 9(2); 11(2); 17; 18; 19(3); 21(2); 22; 30; 31; 32; 33; 34(2); 11:1; 7; 9; 14; 18; 19; 20; 12:2; 4(2); 9; 12; 18(2); 19; 13:3; 8; 11; 12; 22; 14:3; 14(2); 21; 24; 28; 15:3; 6; 16(2); 18; 20; 21; 26; 29; 31; 34; 36; 16:10; 11; 15(3); 16; 17:5; 9; 11; 13(3); 16(2); 20; 22; 23; 39; 18:3; 5; 12; 13; 15; 21; 33; 35; 19:4; 11; 15; 19; 24; 35; 20:13(4); 15; 17; 20; 21:3; 5; 7; 8(2); 11; 14; 17; 21; 24; 22:2; 13(2); 16; 17; 20; 23:1; 2(4); 3(3); 4(2); 5; 8; 19(2); 20; 21; 22; 24; 25(4); 26; 28; 32; 37; 24:3; 5; 7; 9; 13(2); 14(4); 16(2); 19; 25:1; 4; 5; 9; 10; 14; 16; 17; 23; 26; 29; 30; **1Chr** 1:23; 33; 2:4; 6; 23; 3:9; 4:27; 33; 5:10; 16; 17; 20; 6:48; 49(2); 60; 7:3; 5(2); 8; 11; 40; 8:38; 40; 9:1; 9; 22; 29; 10:6; 7; 11(2); 12; 11:1; 3; 4; 10; 12:15(2); 21; 32; 33; 37; 38(3); 13:2(2); 4(2); 5; 6; 8(2); 14; 14:8(2); 17(2); 15:3; 27; 28; 16:9; 14; 23; 24; 25; 26; 30; 32; 36; 40; 43; 17:2; 6; 8; 10; 15(2); 19(2); 20; 18:4; 9; 10; 11; 13; 14(2); 19:8; 10; 17; 20:3(2); 21:3; 4; 5; 12; 23; 22:5; 9; 15; 17; 23:2; 28; 29; 31; 25:5; 6; 7; 26:8; 11; 26; 28; 30; 27:1; 3; 31; 28:1(3); 4(2); 5; 8(2); 9(2); 12(2); 13(2); 14(4); 19(2); 20; 21(3); 29:1; 2(2); 3; 5; 10; 11(2); 12(2); 14; 15; 16(2); 17; 19; 20(2); 21; 23; 24(2); 25; 26; 30(2); **2Chr** 1:2(2); 3; 17; 2:5; 17; 4:4; 16; 18; 19; 5:1(3); 2; 3; 4; 5; 6; 11; 12; 6:3; 5; 12; 13; 14; 29; 30; 33(2); 38(2); 7:3; 4; 5; 6; 8; 11; 17; 20; 22; 8:4; 6(4); 7; 16; 9:1; 2; 12; 14; 20(2); 22; 23; 26; 28; 30; 10:1; 3; 12; 16(2); 11:3; 13(2); 16; 21; 23(2); 12:1; 9; 13; 13:4; 15; 14:5; 8; 14(2); 15:2; 5; 6; 8; 9; 12(2); 15(2); 17; 16:4; 6; 17:2; 5; 9; 10; 19; 18:9; 11; 16; 18; 21; 27; 19:5; 11(2); 20:3; 4; 6; 13; 15; 18; 29; 21:2; 4; 9; 14; 17; 18; 22:1; 9; 10; 23:2; 3; 5; 6; 8(2); 10; 13; 16; 17; 20; 21; 24:2; 5; 7; 10(2); 14; 23(2); 25:5; 7; 12; 24(2); 26:1; 4; 14; 20; 27:2; 7; 28:6; 14; 15(2); 23; 26; 29:2; 16; 18(3); 19; 24(2); 28(2); 29; 32; 34; 36; 30:1; 2; 4; 5; 6; 14; 22; 25(2); 31:1(5); 5(2); 18(2); 19(2); 20; 21; 32:4; 5; 7; 9(2); 13; 14; 21; 22; 23; 27; 28; 30; 31; 33; 33:3; 5; 7; 8; 14; 15; 19; 22; 25; 34:7(2); 9(2); 12; 13; 16; 21; 24; 25; 28; 29; 30(3); 31(2); 32; 33(4); 35:3; 7(2); 13; 16; 18(2); 20; 24; 25; 36:14(2); 17; 18(2); 19(2); 22; 23(2); **Ezr** 1:1; 2; 3; 5; 6(2); 11(2); 2:42; 58; 70; 3:5; 8; 11; 4:5; 20; 5:7; 6:12; 17; 20(2); 21; 7:6; 13; 16(2); 21; 25(2); 28; 8:20; 21; 22(2); 25; 34; 35(2); 9:13; 10:3; 5; 7; 8; 9(2); 12; 14(2); 16; 17; 44; **Neh** 4:6; 8; 12; 15; 16; 5:13; 16; 18(2); 19; 6:9; 16(2); 7:60; 73; 8:1; 2; 3; 5(3); 6; 9(2); 11; 12; 13; 15; 17; 9:2; 5; 6(4); 10(2); 25; 32(2); 33; 38; 10:28; 29; 33; 35(2); 37(2); 11:2; 6; 18; 20; 24; 12:27; 47; 13:3; 6; 8; 12; 15; 16; 18; 20; 26; 27; 30; **Est** 1:3; 5; 8; 13; 16(3); 17; 18; 20(2); 22; 2:3(2); 15; 17(2); 18; 3:1; 2; 6; 8(2); 12; 13(2); 14; 4:1; 7; 11; 13; 16; 17; 5:11; 13; 14; 6:10; 13; 8:5; 9; 11; 12; 13; 9:2(2); 3; 4; 5; 20(2); 24; 26; 27; 29; 30; 10:2; 3; **Job** 1:3; 5; 10; 11; 12; 22; 2:4; 10; 11; 4:14; 8:13; 9:28; 12:9; 10; 13:1; 4; 27; 14:14; 15:20; 16:2; 7; 17:7; 10; 19:19; 20:26; 24:24; 27:3; 12; 28:3; 21; 29:19; 30:23; 31:4; 12; 33:1; 11; 29; 34:15; 19; 21; 36:19; 37:7; 38:7; 18; 40:20; 41:34(2); 42:11(4); 15; **Ps** 2:12; 3:7; 5:5; 11; 6:6; 7; 8; 10; 7:1; 8:1; 6; 7; 9; 9:1; 14; 17; 10:4; 5; 12:3; 14:3(2); 4; 16:3; 18:t, 22; 30; 19:4; 20:3; 4; 5; 21:8; 22:7; 14; 17; 23(2); 27(2); 29(2); 23:6; 25:5; 10; 18; 22; 26:7; 27:4; 31:11; 23; 24; 32:3; 11; 33:4; 6; 8(2); 11; 13; 14; 15; 34:1; 4; 6; 17; 19; 20; 35:10; 28; 38:6; 9; 12; 39:8; 12; 40:16; 41:3; 7; 42:7; 44:8; 17; 22; 45:8; 13; 16; 17; 47:1; 2; 7; 49:1(2); 11; 50:11; 51:9; 52:4; 54:7; 56:5; 57:2; 5; 11; 59:5; 8; 62:3; 8; 64:8; 9; 10; 65:2; 5; 66:1; 4; 16; 67:2; 3; 5; 7; 69:19; 70:4; 71:8; 15; 24; 72:5; 11(2); 17; 73:14; 27; 28; 74:3; 8; 17; 75:3; 8; 10; 76:9; 11; 77:12; 78:14; 32; 38; 51; 79:13; 80:12; 82:5; 6; 8; 83:11; 18; 85:2; 3; 5; 86:5; 9; 12; 87:2; 7; 88:7; 89:1; 4; 7; 16; 40; 41; 42; 47; 50; 90:1; 9; 14; 91:11; 92:7; 9; 94:4; 15; 95:3; 96:1; 3; 4; 5; 9; 12(2); 97:6; 7(2); 9(2); 98:3; 4; 99:2; 100:1; 5; 101:8(2); 102:8; 12; 15; 24; 26; 103:1; 2; 3(2); 6; 19; 21; 22(2); 104:20; 24; 27; 105:2; 7; 21; 31; 35; 36(2); 106:2; 3; 31; 46; 48; 107:18; 42; 108:5; 109:11; 111:2; 7; 10; 113:4; 116:11; 12; 14; 18; 117:1(2); 118:10; 119:6; 13; 14; 20; 63; 86; 90; 91; 96; 97; 99; 118; 119; 128(2); 151; 168; 172; 121:7; 128:5; 129:5; 130:8; 132:1; 134:1; 135:5; 6; 9; 11; 13; 136:25; 138:2; 4; 139:3; 16; 143:5; 12; 144:13; 145:9(2); 10; 13; 14(2); 15; 17(2); 18(2); 20(2); 21; 146:6; 10; 147:4; 148:2(2); 3; 7; 9(2); 10; 11(2); 14; 149:9; **Prov** 1:13; 14; 25; 30; 3:5; 6; 9; 15; 17; 4:7; 22; 23; 26; 5:14; 19; 21; 6:31; 8:8; 9; 11; 16; 36; 10:12; 14:23; 15:15; 16:2; 4; 11; 17:17; 18:1; 19:7; 20:8; 27; 21:26; 22:2; 23:17; 24:4; 31; 26:10; 28:5; 29:11; 12; 30:4; 27; 31:8; 12; 21; 29; **Eccl** 1:2; 3; 7; 8; 13; 14(2); 16; 2:3; 5; 7; 8; 9; 10(2); 11(2); 14; 16; 17; 18; 19; 20; 22; 23; 3:13; 19(2); 20(3); 4:1; 4; 8; 15; 16(2); 5:9; 16; 17; 18(2); 6:2; 6; 7; 12; 7:2; 15; 18; 21; 23; 28; 8:9; 17; 9:1(3); 2(2); 3(2); 4; 9(2); 11; 10:19; 11:5; 8(2); 9; 12:4; 8; **Song** 1:13; 3:6; 8; 4:4; 7; 10; 14(2); 7:13; 8:7; **Is** 1:25; 2:2; 13(2); 14(2); 16(2); 4:5; 5:25; 28; 7:19(3); 24; 25; 8:7(3); 9; 12; 9:9; 12; 17; 21; 10:4; 14; 23; 11:9; 12:5; 13:7; 14:9(2); 10; 18(2); 26; 15:2; 16:14; 18:3; 6; 19:8; 10; 21:2; 9; 16; 22:3(2); 24(3); 23:9(2); 17; 24:7; 11; 25:6; 7(2); 8(2); 26:12; 14; 15; 27:9(2); 28:8; 24; 29:7(2); 8; 11; 20; 30:5; 18; 31:3; 32:13; 20; 34:1(2); 2(2); 4(2); 12; 36:1; 6; 20; 37:11; 16; 17; 18; 20; 25; 36; 38:13; 15; 16; 17; 20; 39:2(3); 4; 6; 40:2; 5; 6(2); 17; 26; 41:11; 29; 42:10; 15; 22; 43:9; 14; 44:9; 11(2); 24; 28; 45:7; 12; 13; 16; 22; 24; 25; 46:3; 10; 48:6; 14; 49:9; 11; 18(2); 26; 50:2; 9; 11; 51:3; 18(2); 20; 52:10(2); 53:6(2); 54:12; 13; 55:12; 56:7; 9(2); 10(2); 11; 57:13; 58:3; 59:11; 60:4; 6; 7; 14; 21; 61:2; 9; 11; 62:2; 63:3; 7; 9(2); 64:6(3); 8; 9; 11; 65:2; 5; 8; 12; 25; 66:2(2); 10(2); 16; 18; 20(2); 23; 24; **Jer** 1:7; 14; 15(3); 16; 17; 2:3; 4; 24; 29; 34; 3:7; 8; 10; 17; 4:24; 25; 26; 5:16; 19; 6:15; 28(2); 7:2; 10; 13; 15; 23; 25; 27; 8:2; 3(2); 12; 16; 9:2; 25; 26(3); 10:7(2); 9; 16; 20; 21; 11:4; 6; 8; 12; 12:1; 9; 12; 14; 13:13(2); 19; 14:22; 15:4; 13(2); 16:10(2); 15; 17; 17:3(2); 9; 13; 19; 20(2); 18:23; 19:8; 13(2); 14; 15(2); 20:4(2); 5(4); 6(2); 10; 21:2; 14; 22:20; 22(2); 23:3; 8; 9; 14; 15; 32; 24:9(2); 25:1; 2(2); 4; 9(2); 13(3); 15; 17; 19; 20(3); 22(2); 23; 24(2); 25(3); 26(2); 29; 30(2); 31; 26:2(2); 6; 7; 8(3); 9; 11; 12(3); 15; 16; 17; 18; 19(2); 20; 21(2); 27:6; 7; 12; 16; 20; 28:1; 3; 4; 5; 6; 7; 11(2); 14; 29:1; 4; 13; 14(2); 16; 18(2); 20; 22; 25(2); 31; 30:2; 6; 11; 14; 16(3); 20; 31:1; 12; 24; 34; 37(2); 40; 32:12; 19; 23(2); 27; 32; 37; 42(2); 33:5; 8(2); 9(4); 12; 34:1(4); 6; 7; 8; 10(2); 17; 19; 35:3; 7; 8(2); 10; 15; 17(2); 18(2); 36:2(2); 3; 4; 6; 8; 9(2); 10; 11; 12(2); 13; 14; 16(2); 17; 18; 20; 21; 23; 24; 28; 31; 32; 37:21; 38:1; 4; 9; 22; 23; 27(2); 39:1; 3(2); 4; 6; 13; 40:1; 4; 7; 11(2); 12(2); 13; 15; 41:3; 6; 9; 10(2); 11(2); 12; 13(2); 14; 16(2); 42:1(2); 2; 5; 8(2); 17; 20; 43:1(3); 2; 4(2); 5(3); 44:1; 2(2); 4; 8; 11; 12; 15(3); 18; 20(2); 24(3); 26(2); 27; 28; 45:5(2); 46:25; 28; 47:2(2); 4; 48:17(2); 24; 31; 37; 38; 39; 49:5; 13; 17; 26; 29; 32(2); 36; 50:7; 10; 13; 14; 21; 27; 29(2); 30; 32; 33; 37; 51:3; 7; 19; 24(2); 25; 28(2); 47; 48; 49; 52; 60(2); 61; 52:2; 4; 7; 8; 10; 13(2); 14(2); 17; 18; 20; 22; 23; 30; 33; 34; **Lam** 1:2(2); 3; 4; 6; 7; 8; 10; 11; 12; 13; 15; 18; 21; 22(2); 2:2; 3; 4; 5; 15; 16; 3:3; 14(2); 34; 46; 51; 60(2); 61; 62; 4:12; **Eze** 3:7; 10; 5:4; 9; 10; 11(2); 12; 14; 6:6; 9; 11; 13(2); 14; 7:3; 8; 12; 14(2); 16; 17(2); 18(2); 8:10; 9:4; 8; 11:15; 18(2); 25; 12:10; 14(2); 16; 19(2); 13:18; 14:3; 5; 6; 11; 22; 23; 16:4(2); 22; 23; 30; 33(2); 36; 37(4); 43(2); 47; 51; 54; 57; 63; 17:9; 18; 21(3); 23; 24; 18:4; 13; 14; 19; 21(2); 22; 23; 24(2); 28; 30; 31; 20:6; 15; 26; 28; 31; 32; 40(3); 43(2); 47; 48; 21:4; 5; 7(2); 12; 15; 24; 22:2; 4; 18; 19; 23:6; 7(3); 12; 15; 23(4); 29; 48; 24:24; 25:6; 8; 26:11; 16; 17; 27:5; 9; 12; 18; 21; 22(2); 24; 27(2); 29(2); 34; 35; 28:18; 19; 24; 26; 29:2; 4; 5; 6; 7(2); 30:5; 8; 12; 31:4; 5; 6(3); 9; 12(3); 13(2); 14(3); 15; 16(2); 18; 32:4; 8; 12(2); 13; 15; 16; 20; 22(2); 23; 24(2); 25(2); 26(2); 29; 30(2); 31(2); 32; 33:13; 29; 34:5; 6(2); 12; 13; 21; 35:8; 12; 15(2); 36:5(2); 10(2); 24; 25(2); 29; 33; 34; 37:16; 22(2); 23; 24; 38:4(4); 5; 6(2); 7; 8; 9; 11; 13; 15; 20(2); 21; 39:4; 11; 13; 18; 20; 21; 23; 26; 40:4(2); 41:17; 19; 42:11; 43:11(6); 44:5(3); 6; 7; 14(2); 24; 30(3); 45:1; 16; 17; 22; 47:12; 48:13; 19; 20; **Dan** 1:4; 15; 17(2); 19; 20(3); 2:12; 38; 39; 40(2); 44; 48; 3:2; 3; 5; 7(3); 10; 15; 4:1(2); 6; 11; 12(2); 18; 20; 21; 28; 35; 37; 5:8; 19; 22; 23; 6:7; 24; 25(2); 7:7; 14; 16; 19; 23; 27; 9:6; 7(2); 11; 13; 14; 16(2); 10:3; 11:2(2); 37; 43; 12:7; **Hos** 2:11(2); 5:2; 7:2; 4; 6; 7(2); 10; 9:4; 8; 15(2); 10:14; 11:7; 12:8; 13:2; 10; 15; 14:2; **Joel** 1:2; 5; 12; 13; 14; 19; 2:1; 6; 12; 28; 3:2; 4; 9; 11; 12; 18; **Amos** 1:11; 2:3; 3:2(2); 5; 4:6(2); 5:16(2); 17; 6:8; 7:10; 8:10(2); 9:1; 5; 9; 10; 12; 13; **Obad** 7; 15; 16; **Jonah** 2:3; **Mic** 1:2(2); 5; 7(3); 10; 2:12; 3:7; 9; 4:5; 5:9; 11; 6:16; 7:2; 16; 19; **Nah** 1:3; 4; 5; 2:9; 10(2); 3:1; 7; 10(2); 12; 19; **Hab** 1:9; 15; 2:5(2); 6; 8(2); 17; 19; 20; **Zeph** 1:2; 4; 8; 9; 11(2); 18; 2:3; 11(2); 14; 3:7; 8(2); 9; 11; 14; 19; 20; **Hag** 1:11; 12; 14; 2:4; 7(2); 17; **Zec** 1:11; 2:13; 4:2; 5:6; 6:5; 7:5(2); 14; 8:10; 12; 17; 23; 9:1; 10:11; 11:10; 12:2; 3(3); 6; 9; 14; 13:8; 14:2; 5; 9; 10; 12; 14; 15; 16; 17; 19; 21; **Mal** 2:9; 10; 3:10; 12; 4:1(2); 4; **Mt** 1:17; 22; 2:3; 4; 16(2); 3:5(2); 15; 4:8; 9; 23(3); 24(2); 5:11; 15; 18; 34; 6:29; 32(2); 33; 7:12; 8:16; 9:26; 31; 35; 10:1(2); 22; 30; 11:13; 27; 28; 12:15; 23; 31; 13:32; 34; 41; 44; 46; 51; 56(2); 14:20; 35(2); 15:37; 17:11; 18:25; 26; 29; 31; 32; 34; 19:11; 20; 26; 27; 20:6; 21:4; 10; 12; 22; 26; 37; 22:4; 10; 27; 28; 37(3); 40; 23:3; 5; 8; 20; 27; 35; 36; 24:2; 6; 8; 9; 14(2); 30; 33; 34; 39; 47; 25:5; 7; 31; 32; 26:1; 27; 31; 33; 35; 52; 56(2); 59; 70; 27:1; 22; 25; 45; 28:9; 11; 18; 19; 20; **Mk** 1:5(2); 27; 28; 32; 33; 37; 39; 2:12(2); 13; 3:28; 4:11; 13; 31; 32; 34; 5:12; 20; 26; 33; 40; 6:30; 33; 39; 41; 42; 50; 7:3; 14; 19; 23; 37; 9:12; 15; 23; 35(2); 10:20; 27; 28; 44; 11:11; 17; 18; 32; 12:22; 28; 29; 30(4); 33(5); 43; 44(3); 13:4; 10; 13; 23; 30; 37; 14:23; 27; 29; 31; 36; 50; 53; 55; 64; 16:15; **Lk** 1:3; 6; 48; 63; 65(3); 66; 71; 75; 2:1; 3; 10; 18; 19; 20; 31; 38; 39; 47; 51; 3:3; 6; 15; 16; 19; 20; 21; 4:5; 6; 7; 13; 14; 15; 20; 22; 25; 28; 36; 40; 5:5; 9; 11; 26; 28; 6:10; 12; 17; 19; 26; 7:1; 16; 17(2); 18; 29; 35; 8:40; 43; 45; 47; 52; 54; 9:1; 7; 10; 13; 15; 17; 23; 43(2); 48; 10:19; 22; 27(4); 11:22; 41; 42; 50; 12:1; 7; 18; 27; 30; 31; 41; 44; 13:2; 3; 4; 5; 17(3); 27; 28; 14:17; 18; 29; 33; 15:1; 13; 14; 31; 16:14; 26; 17:10; 27; 29; 18:12; 21; 22; 28; 31; 43; 19:7; 37; 48; 20:6; 32; 38; 40; 45; 21:3; 4(2); 12; 15; 17; 22; 24; 29; 32; 35; 36; 38; 22:70; 23:5; 18; 44; 48; 49; 24:9(2); 14; 19; 21; 25; 27(2); 44; 47; **Jn** 1:3; 7; 16; 2:15; 24; 3:26; 31(2); 35; 4:25; 29; 39; 45; 5:20; 22; 23; 28; 6:37; 39; 45; 7:21; 8:2; 10:8; 29; 41; 11:48; 49; 12:32; 13:3; 10; 11; 18; 35; 14:26(2); 15:15; 21; 16:13; 15; 30; 17:2; 7; 10; 21; 18:4; 38; 40; 19:11; 28; 21:11; 17; **Acts** 1:1; 8; 14; 18; 19; 21; 24; 2:1; 2; 4; 7(2); 12; 14; 17; 32; 36; 39; 44(2); 45; 47; 3:9; 11; 16; 18; 21(2); 22; 24; 25; 4:10(2); 16; 18; 21; 23; 24; 29; 31; 32; 33; 5:5; 11; 12; 17; 20; 21; 23; 34; 36; 37; 6:15; 7:10(2); 11; 14; 22; 50; 8:1; 10; 27; 37; 40; 9:14; 21; 26; 31; 32; 35; 39; 40; 42; 10:2; 8; 12; 22; 33(2); 36; 37; 38; 39; 41; 43; 44; 11:10; 14; 23; 28; 12:11; 13:10(3); 22; 24; 29; 39(2); 49; 14:15; 16; 27; 15:3; 4; 12; 17(2); 18; 16:3; 26; 28; 32; 33; 34; 17:5; 7; 11; 15; 21; 22; 24; 25(2); 26(2); 30; 31; 18:2; 8; 17; 21; 23(2); 19:7; 10; 17(2); 19; 26; 27; 34; 20:18; 19; 25; 26; 27; 28; 32; 35; 36; 37; 38; 21:5; 18; 20; 21; 24; 27; 28; 30; 31; 22:3; 5; 10; 12; 15; 30; 23:1; 24:3(2); 5; 8; 14; 25:8; 24(2); 26:2; 3; 4; 14; 20; 29; 27:20; 24; 33; 35; 36; 37; 44; 28:30; 31; **Rom** 1:5; 7; 8; 18; 29; 3:9; 12; 19; 22(2); 23; 4:11; 16(2); 5:12(2); 18(2); 7:8; 8:28; 32(2); 36; 37; 9:5; 6; 7; 17; 10:12(2); 16; 18; 21; 11:26; 32(2); 36; 12:4; 17; 18; 13:7; 14:2; 10; 20; 15:11(2); 13; 14; 33; 16:4; 15; 19; 24; 26; **1Cor** 1:2; 5(2); 10; 2:10; 15; 3:21; 22; 4:13; 6:12(3); 7:7; 17; 8:1; 6(2); 9:12; 19(2); 22(3); 24; 25; 10:1(2); 2; 3; 4; 11; 17; 23(4); 31; 33(2); 11:2; 5; 12; 18; 12:6(2); 11; 12; 13(2); 19; 26(2); 29(4); 30(3); 13:2(3); 3; 7(4); 14:5; 18; 21; 23; 24(3); 26; 31(3); 33; 40; 15:3; 7; 8; 10; 19; 22(2); 24(2); 25; 27(3); 28(4); 29; 39; 51(2); 16:12; 14; 20; 24; **2Cor** 1:1(2); 3; 4; 20; 2:3(2); 5; 9; 3:2; 18; 4:15; 5:10; 14(2); 15; 17; 18; 6:4; 10; 7:1; 4; 11; 13; 14; 15; 16; 8:7; 18; 9:8(3); 11; 13; 10:6; 11:6; 9; 28; 12:12; 19; 13:2; 13; 14; **Gal** 1:2; 2:14; 3:8; 10; 22; 26; 28; 4:1; 12; 26; 5:14; 6:6; 10; **Eph** 1:3; 8; 10; 11; 15; 21; 22(2); 23(2); 2:3; 21; 3:8; 9(2); 18; 19; 20; 21; 4:2; 6(4); 10(2); 13; 15; 19; 31(2); 5:3; 9; 13; 20; 6:13; 16(2); 18(3); 21; 24; **Phil** 1:1; 4; 7(2); 8; 9; 13(2); 20; 25; 2:14; 17; 21; 26; 29; 3:8(2); 21; 4:5; 7; 12; 13; 18; 19; 22; 23; **Col** 1:4; 6; 9; 10; 11(2); 16(2); 17(2); 18; 19; 20; 28; 2:2; 3; 9; 10; 13; 19; 22; 3:8; 11(2); 14; 16; 17; 20; 22; 4:7; 9; 12; **1Th** 1:2; 7; 2:15; 3:7; 9; 12; 13; 4:6; 10(2); 5:5; 14; 15; 21; 22; 26; 27; **2Th** 1:3; 4; 10; 11; 2:4; 9; 10; 12; 3:2; 11; 16(2); 18; **1Ti** 1:15; 16; 2:1(2); 2(2); 4; 6; 11; 3:4; 11; 4:8; 9; 10; 15; 5:2; 20; 6:1; 10; 13; 17; **2Ti** 1:15; 2:7; 10; 24; 3:9; 11; 12; 16; 17; 4:2; 5; 8; 16; 17; 21; **Titus** 1:15; 2:7; 9; 10(2); 11; 14; 15; 3:2(2); 15(2); **Philem** 1:5; **Heb** 1:2; 3; 6; 11; 14; 2:8(3); 10(2); 11; 15; 17; 3:2; 4; 5; 16; 4:4; 13; 15; 5:9; 6:16; 7:2; 7; 8:5; 11; 9:3; 8; 17; 19(2); 21; 22; 10:10; 11:13; 39; 12:8; 14; 23; 13:4; 18; 24(2); 25; **Jas** 1:2; 5; 8; 21; 2:10; 3:2; 4:16; 5:12; **1Pet** 1:15; 24(2); 2:1(3); 17; 18; 3:8; 4:7; 8; 11; 5:5; 7; 10; 14; **2Pet** 1:3; 5; 3:4; 9; 11(2); 16; **1Jn** 1:5; 7; 9; 2:16; 19; 20; 27; 3:20; 5:17; **2Jn** 1; **3Jn** 2; 12; **Jude** 3; 15(4); **Rev** 1:2; 7; 2:23; 3:10; 4:11; 5:6; 13; 7:4; 9; 11; 17; 8:3; 7; 11:6; 12:5; 13:3; 7; 8; 12; 16; 14:8; 15:4; 18:3; 12(3); 14(2); 17; 19; 21; 22(2); 23(3); 24; 19:5; 17; 18; 21; 21:4; 5; 7; 8; 19; 25; 22:21

ALMOST

Ex 17:4; **Ps** 73:2; 94:17; 119:87; **Prov** 5:14; **Acts** 13:44; 19:26; 21:27; 26:28; 29; **Heb** 9:22

ALONE

Gen 2:18; 32:24; 42:38; 44:20; **Ex** 14:12; 18:14; 18; 24:2; 32:10; **Lev** 13:46; **Num** 11:14; 17; 23:9; **Deut** 1:9; 12; 9:14; 32:12; 33:28; **Josh** 22:20; **Judg** 3:20; 11:37; **1Sa** 21:1; **2Sa** 16:11; 18:24; 25; 26; **1Kin** 11:29; **2Kin** 4:27; 19:15; 23:18(2); **1Chr** 29:1; **Ezr** 6:7; **Neh** 9:6; **Est** 3:6; **Job** 1:15; 16; 17; 19; 7:16; 19; 9:8; 10:20; 13:13; 15:19; 31:17; **Ps** 83:18; 86:10; 102:7; 136:4; 148:13; **Prov** 9:12; **Eccl** 4:8; 10; 11; **Is** 2:11; 17; 5:8; 14:31; 37:16; 44:24; 49:21; 51:2; 63:3; **Jer** 15:17; 49:31; **Lam** 3:28; **Dan** 10:7; 8; **Hos** 4:17; 8:9; **Mt** 4:4; 14:23; 15:14; 18:15; **Mk** 1:24; 4:10; 34; 6:47; 14:6; 15:36; **Lk** 4:4; 34; 5:21; 6:4; 9:18; 36; 10:40; 13:8; **Jn** 6:15; 22; 8:9; 16; 29; 11:48; 12:7; 24; 16:32(2); 17:20; **Acts** 5:38; 19:26; **Rom** 4:23; 11:3; **Gal** 6:4; **1Th** 3:1; **Heb** 9:7; **Jas** 2:17

ALONG

Ex 2:5; 9:23; **Num** 21:22; 34:3; **Deut** 2:27; **Josh** 10:10; 15:3(2); 6; 10; 11; 16:2; 17:7; 18:18; 19; 19:13; **Judg** 7:12; 13; 9:25; 37; 11:18; 26; 20:37; **1Sa** 6:12; 28:20; **2Sa** 3:16; 16:13; **2Kin** 11:11; **2Chr** 23:10; **Jer** 41:6

ALREADY

Ex 1:5; **2Chr** 28:13; **Neh** 5:5; **Eccl** 1:10; 2:12; 3:15; 4:2; 6:10; **Mal** 2:2; **Mt** 5:28; 17:12; **Mk** 15:44; **Lk** 12:49; **Jn** 3:18; 4:35; 9:22; 27; 11:17; 19:33; **Acts** 11:11; 27:9; **1Cor** 5:3; **2Cor** 12:21; **Phil** 3:12(2); 16; **2Th** 2:7; **1Ti** 5:15; **2Ti** 2:18; **1Jn** 4:3; **Rev** 2:25

ALSO

Gen 1:16; 2:9; 3:6; 18; 21; 22; 4:4; 22; 26; 6:3; 4; 11; 7:3; 8:2; 8; 10:21; 12:15; 13:5; 16; 14:7; 16(2); 15:14; 16:13; 17:16; 18:12; 23; 24; 19:21; 34; 35; 38; 20:4; 6; 21:13; 22:20; 24; 24:14; 19; 44; 46(2); 53; 26:21; 27:31; 34; 38; 45; 29:27; 28; 30(2); 33; 30:3; 6; 15; 30; 31:15; 32:6; 18; 33:7; 35:17; 37:7; 38:10; 11; 22; 24; 40:15; 16; 42:22; 43:8; 13; 44:9; 10; 16; 29; 45:20; 46:4; 34; 47:3; 18; 48:11; 19(2); 50:18; 23; **Ex** 1:10; 2:19; 3:9; 4:9; 14; 6:4; 5; 7:11(2); 23; 8:21; 32; 10:24; 25; 26; 12:32(2); 38; 15:4; 18:23; 19:22; 21:6; 29; 35; 23:9; 24:11; 25:23; 29:15; 22; 44; 30:18(2); 23; 31:13; 33:12; 17; 35:14; 37:12; 26; **Lev** 5:2; 7:16; 8:8; 9; 9:4; 18; 11:29; 40; 13:18; 38; 47; 14:9; 15:18; 20; 18:19; 28; 20:13; 27; 22:12; 23:27; 39; 26:16; 22; 24; 28; 39; 40; 41; 42(2); 43; **Num** 3:1; 4:22; 6:17; 9:2; 10:10; 11:4; 10; 12:2; 15:15; 16:10; 17; 34; 18:2; 3; 8; 28; 20:11; 22:19; 33; 24:12; 18; 24; 25; 27:13; 28:26; 30:3; 31:8; 33:4; 35:2; **Deut** 1:37(2); 2:6; 11; 12; 20; 3:3; 17; 20; 7:13; 8:5; 9:8; 19; 20; 10:10; 14; 15:17; 18:4; 20:6; 23:12; 26:13; 28:51; 61; 29:15; 31:2; 32:24; 25; 33:28; **Josh** 1:15; 2:12; 7:11(3); 10:30; 39; 13:3; 22; 15:19; 17:1; 2; 9; 19:30; 20:1; 22:7; 24:5; 18; **Judg** 1:15; 18; 22; 2:3; 10; 21; 3:22; 31; 5:4; 15; 6:35; 7:18; 8:9; 22; 31; 9:2; 19; 49; 10:9; 10; 12; 15:5; 17:2; 19:10; 16; 19; 20:48; **Ruth** 1:5; 12(2); 17; 2:16; 21; 3:15; 4:5; **1Sa** 1:6; 28; 2:15; 26; 3:12; 17; 4:17(2); 8:8; 20; 10:11; 12; 26; 12:14; 13:4; 14:15; 21; 22; 44; 15:1; 23; 29; 17:38; 18:5; 19:11; 20; 21; 22; 23; 24(2); 20:15; 22:17; 23:17; 25; 24:8; 25:13; 22; 43(2); 26:25; 28:19(2); 22; 30:21; **2Sa** 1:4(2); 18; 2:2; 6; 7; 24; 3:9; 12; 19(2); 35; 4:2; 5:2; 15; 18; 7:11; 19; 8:3; 11; 10:14; 11:12; 17; 21; 24; 12:13; 14; 13:36; 14:7; 15:19(2); 21; 23; 24; 27; 34; 17:5; 10; 18:2; 22; 26; 19:13; 40; 43; 20:14; 26; 21:20; 22:10; 20; 24; 36; 41; 44; 49; 23:20; **1Kin** 1:6; 14; 22; 33; 46; 48; 2:5; 22; 23; 3:13; 18; 4:13; 15; 28; 33; 6:22; 32; 33; 7:2; 8; 20; 31; 8:24; 9:21; 10:11; 12; 12:14; 13:5; 11; 18; 24; 14:23; 24; 15:13; 16:7; 16; 17:20; 18:35; 19:2; 20:3; 10; 21:19; 23; 22:22; **2Kin** 1:11; 2:13; 14; 3:18; 5:1; 6:31; 7:4; 8; 8:1; 9:27; 10:2; 5; 11:17; 13:6; 16:14; 17:19; 18:2; 21:11; 22:19; 23:5; 19; 27; 24:4; **1Chr** 1:14; 21; 51; 2:9; 26; 49; 3:6; 18; 6:3; 48; 67; 79; 7:10; 12; 25; 28; 8:13; 18; 32; 9:29; 38; 10:13; 11:10; 22; 26; 12:38; 13:2; 15:27; 16:6; 25; 30; 38; 17:9; 17; 18:4; 11; 20:2; 6; 21:23; 22:4; 14; 17; 23:26; 24:30; 26:6; 10; 27:4; 30; 32; 28:13; 14; 15; 17; 21; 29:9; 17; **2Chr** 2:8; 14; 3:7; 12; 15; 4:2; 6; 8; 14; 16; 19; 5:6; 12; 7:6; 8; 8:5; 14; 9:4; 10; 12:5; 9; 12; 13:2; 3; 11; 14:5; 15; 15:16; 17:7; 11; 18:21; 19:11; 20:1; 21:4; 10; 13; 17; 22:2; 3; 5; 23:13; 18; 24:1; 7; 12; 20; 25:6; 24; 26:3; 10(2); 20; 27:1; 5; 28:2; 4; 5; 8; 18(2); 29:7; 22; 27; 35; 30:1; 12; 31:1; 3; 6; 19; 32:5; 17; 28; 30; 33:4; 6; 19; 34:13; 27; 35:9; 36:7; 13; 22; **Ezr** 1:1; 7; 3:4; 7; 4:20; 5:10; 14; 6:5; 11; 7:19; 24; 8:6; 14; 16; 20; 27; 28; 35; 10:4; 23; 24; 28; **Neh** 1:3; 2:6; 18; 3:3; 8; 29; 5:3; 4; 9; 11; 13; 16; 18; 6:7; 19; 7:61; 8:7; 18; 9:13; 20; 23; 37; 10:32; 36; 11:1; 15; 22; 31; 12:9; 10; 22; 29; 43(2); 13:15; 16; 22; 23; **Est** 1:9; 16; 2:8; 3:11; 4:8; 16; 5:12; 7:8; 9; 8:8; 9:13; 15; **Job** 1:3; 6; 16; 17; 18; 2:1; 5:25; 7:1; 9:11; 20; 11:11; 19; 12:15; 13:2; 16; 27; 14:2; 16:4; 12; 17; 19; 17:6; 7; 9; 19:11; 20:9; 22:28; 24:15; 22; 30:11; 31; 31:28; 32:3; 10; 17(2); 33:6; 19; 36:1; 10; 29; 33; 37:1; 11; 39:30; 40:8; 14; 42:9; 10; 11; 13; **Ps** 1:3; 5:11; 6:3; 7:13; 9:9; 16:7; 9; 18:7; 9; 13; 19; 23; 35; 40; 19:10; 13; 26:1; 27:7; 28:9; 29:6; 35:3; 37:4; 5; 38:10; 12; 20; 40:2; 45:10; 52:6; 55:10; 60:7; 62:12; 65:8; 13(2); 68:1; 8; 18; 69:11; 21; 31; 36; 71:18; 19; 22; 24; 72:8; 12; 15; 74:16; 75:10; 76:2; 77:12; 16; 17; 78:14; 16; 20; 21; 27; 46; 48; 55; 62; 70; 81:16; 83:8; 84:6; 89:5; 11; 21; 25; 27; 29; 43; 92:11; 93:1; 95:4; 96:10; 99:4; 105:23; 33; 36; 37; 106:9; 16; 27; 28; 32; 42; 46; 107:32; 38; 108:8; 109:3; 10; 25; 119:3; 23; 24; 41; 46; 48; 132:12; 16; 139:17; 141:5; 145:19; 148:6; 14; **Prov** 1:26; 4:4; 9:2; 11:25; 17:26; 18:3; 9; 19:2; 21:13; 23:23; 28; 24:23; 25:1; 26:4; 28:16; 30:31; 31:15; 28; **Eccl** 1:5; 17; 2:1; 7; 8; 9; 14; 15; 19; 21; 23; 24; 26; 3:11; 13; 4:4; 8; 14; 16(2); 5:7; 10; 16; 17; 19; 6:3; 9; 7:6; 14; 18; 21; 22; 8:10; 14; 16; 9:3; 6; 12; 13; 10:3; 14; 11:2; 12:5; **Song** 1:16; 7:8; **Is** 2:7(2); 8; 5:2; 6; 6:1; 8; 7:13; 20; 8:5; 11:6; 13; 12:2; 13:3; 16; 18; 14:10; 13; 23; 17:3; 19:8; 13; 21:12; 22:9; 11; 23:12; 24:5; 26:12; 21; 28:7; 17; 29; 29:19; 24; 30:5; 22; 31:2; 5; 32:4; 7; 33:2; 34:3; 11; 14(2); 15; 38:22; 40:24; 44:19; 45:16; 46:11(2); 48:12; 13; 19; 21; 49:6; 7; 56:6; 57:8; 15; 18; 60:14; 16; 17; 21; 62:3; 66:4; 21; **Jer** 1:3; 2:8; 16; 33; 34; 36; 3:6; 8; 4:12; 6:14; 17; 7:27; 9:16; 10:5; 13:23; 14:5; 16:1; 8; 19:5; 20:1; 23:14(2); 25:14; 26:20; 27:6; 12; 16; 28:14; 29:24; 30:19; 20; 31:36; 37; 33:21; 35:15; 36:6; 38:25; 39:6; 40:5; 41:3; 43:13; 46:21(2); 48:2; 7; 8; 26(2); 34; 49:17; 50:24(2); 51:22; 23; 52:10; 17; 18; 22; 25; **Lam** 2:9; 3:8; 16; 4:21; **Eze** 1:5; 10; 3:13; 21; 4:1; 2; 4; 9; 11; 5:3; 11; 7:2; 18; 22; 24; 8:13; 18; 9:1; 10; 10:16; 17; 19; 12:1; 13; 13:21; 16:10; 11; 17; 19; 24; 26; 28; 39(2); 40; 41; 43; 52(2); 17:5; 7; 13; 22; 18:4; 19:4; 20:12; 15; 23; 25; 28; 39; 21:9; 17; 19; 23:26; 35; 37; 24:3; 5; 15; 25; 25:13; 26:4; 27:19; 30:6; 10; 13; 18; 31:17; 32:6; 9; 13; 17; 33:30; 36:1; 26; 29; 33; 37:24; 27; 38:10; 39:16; 40:8; 12; 14; 42; 41:8; 14; 43:21; 25; 44:30; 45:5; 47:20; **Dan** 6:22; 7:6; 8:25(2); 10:6; 11:1; 8; 14; 17; 22; 41; 42; **Hos** 2:11; 3:3; 4:3; 5; 6(2); 5:5; 6:11; 7:11; 8:6; 9:12; 10:6; 8; 11:3; 12:2; 10; **Joel** 1:12; 20; 2:12; 29; 3:2; 6; 16; **Amos** 1:5; 2:10; 3:14; 4:6; 7; 7:6; 12; 9:14; **Jonah** 4:11; **Mic** 3:3; 4:11; 5:13; 6:13; 7:12; **Nah** 3:10; 11(2); **Hab** 1:8; 2:5; 15; 16; **Zeph** 1:4; 9; 13; 2:12; 3:12; **Zec** 3:7(2); 4:9; 8:6; 21; 9:2; 5; 11; 10:10; 11:8(2); 12:7; 13:2; 14:14; **Mal** 1:13; 2:9; **Mt** 2:8; 3:10; 5:39; 40; 6:14; 21; 10:4; 32; 33; 12:45; 13:22; 23; 26; 29; 15:3; 16; 16:1; 18; 17:12; 18:33; 35; 19:3; 28; 20:4; 7; 21:21; 24; 22:26; 27; 23:26; 28; 24:27; 37; 39; 44; 25:11; 17; 22; 41; 44; 26:13; 35; 69; 71; 73; 27:41; 44; 57; **Mk** 1:19; 38; 2:15; 21; 26; 28; 3:19; 4:36; 5:16; 7:18; 8:7; 34; 38; 11:25; 29; 12:6; 22; 14:9; 31; 67; 15:31; 40; 41; 43; **Lk** 1:3; 35; 36; 2:4; 35; 3:9; 12; 21; 4:23; 41; 43; 5:10; 36; 39; 6:4; 5; 6; 13; 14; 16; 29(2); 31; 32; 33; 34; 36; 7:8; 49; 8:36; 9:61; 10:1; 39; 11:1; 4; 18; 30; 34(2); 40; 45; 46; 49; 12:8(2); 34; 40; 54; 13:6; 8; 14:12(2); 26; 16:1; 10(2); 14; 22; 28; 17:24; 26; 28; 18:15; 19:9; 19; 20:3; 11; 12; 31; 32; 21:2; 22:20; 24; 39; 56; 58; 59; 68; 23:7; 27; 32; 35; 36; 38; 51; 55; 24:22; 23; **Jn** 3:23; 4:45; 5:18; 19; 27; 6:24; 36; 67; 7:3; 10; 47; 52; 8:17; 19; 9:15; 27; 40; 10:16; 11:16; 33; 52; 12:9; 10; 18; 26; 42; 13:9; 14; 32; 34; 14:1; 3; 7; 12; 19; 15:20(2); 23; 27; 17:1; 18; 19; 20; 21; 24; 18:2; 5; 17; 25; 19:23; 39; 20:8; 21:3; 20; 25; **Acts** 1:3; 11; 2:22; 26; 3:17; 5:2; 16; 32; 37; 7:45; 8:13; 19; 9:32; 10:26; 45; 11:1; 18; 30; 12:3; 13:5; 9; 22; 33; 35; 14:1; 5; 15; 15:27; 32; 35(2); 17:6; 12; 13; 28(2); 19:17; 19; 21; 27; 20:21; 30; 21:13; 16; 24; 28; 22:5(2); 20; 29; 23:11; 30; 33; 35; 24:6; 9; 15; 26; 25:22; 24; 26:10; 26; 29; 27:10; 12; 36; 28:9; 10; **Rom** 1:6; 13; 15; 16; 24; 27; 2:9; 10; 12; 15; 3:7; 29(2); 4:6; 9; 11; 12; 16; 21; 24; 5:2; 3; 11; 15; 6:4; 5; 8; 11; 7:4; 8:11; 17; 21; 23; 26; 29; 30(3); 32; 34; 9:1; 10; 24; 25; 27; 11:1; 5; 16; 21; 22; 23; 31(2); 13:5; 6; 15:7; 14(3); 22; 27; 16:2; 4; 7; **1Cor** 1:8; 16; 2:13; 4:8; 5:12; 6:14; 7:3; 4; 22; 34; 40; 9:8; 10:6; 9; 10; 13; 11:1; 6; 12; 19; 23; 25; 12:12; 13:12; 14:15(2); 19; 34; 15:1; 2; 3; 8; 14; 18; 21; 28; 40; 42; 48(2); 49; 16:4; 10; **2Cor** 1:5; 6; 7; 11; 14(2); 22; 2:9; 10; 3:6; 4:10; 11; 13; 14; 5:5; 11; 6:1; 13; 8:6(2); 7; 10; 11; 14; 19; 21; 9:6(2); 12; 10:11; 14; 11:15; 18; 21; 13:4; 9; **Gal** 2:1; 10; 13; 17; 5:21; 25; 6:1; 7; **Eph** 1:11; 13(2); 15; 21; 2:3; 22; 4:9; 10; 5:2; 25; 6:9; 21; **Phil** 1:15; 20; 29; 2:4; 5; 9; 18; 19; 24; 27; 3:4; 12; 20; 4:3(2); 10; 15; **Col** 1:6; 7; 8; 9; 29; 2:11; 12; 3:4; 7; 8; 13; 15; 4:1; 3(2); 16; **1Th** 1:5; 8; 2:8; 10; 13(2); 14; 3:6; 4:6; 8; 14; 5:11; 24; **2Th** 1:5; 11; **1Ti** 2:9; 3:10; 5:13; 20; 25; 6:12; **2Ti** 1:5; 12; 2:2; 5; 10; 11; 12(2); 20; 22; 3:1; 8; 9; 4:8; 15; **Titus** 3:3; 14; **Philem** 1:9; 21; 22; **Heb** 1:2; 2:4; 14; 3:2; 4:10; 5:2; 3; 5; 6; 7:2(2); 9; 12; 25; 8:3; 6; 9:1; 16; 10:15; 11:11; 19; 32; 12:1; 26; 13:3; 12; **Jas** 1:11; 2:2; 11; 19; 25; 26; 3:2; 4; 5:8; **1Pet** 2:5; 6; 8; 18; 21; 3:1; 5; 18; 19; 21; 4:6; 13; 5:1(2); **2Pet** 1:19; 2:1; 3:10; 15; 16(2); 17; **1Jn** 1:3; 2:2; 6; 23; 24; 3:4; 4:11; 21; 5:1; **2Jn** 1; **3Jn** 12; **Jude** 8; 14; **Rev** 1:7; 9; 2:6; 15; 3:10; 21; 6:11; 11:8; 14:17

ALTHOUGH

Ex 13:17; **Josh** 22:17; **2Sa** 23:5(2); **1Kin** 20:5; **Est** 7:4; **Job** 2:3; 5:6; 35:14; **Jer** 31:32; **Eze** 7:13; 11:16(2); **Hab** 3:17; **Mk** 14:29; **Heb** 4:3

ALTOGETHER

Gen 18:21; **Ex** 11:1; 19:18; **Num** 16:13; 23:11; 24:10; 30:14; **Deut** 16:20; **2Chr** 12:12; **Est** 4:14; **Job** 13:5; 27:12; **Ps** 19:9; 39:5; 50:21; 53:3; 62:9; 139:4; **Song** 5:16; **Is** 10:8; **Jer** 5:5; 10:8; 15:18; 30:11; 49:12; **Jn** 9:34; **Acts** 26:29; **1Cor** 5:10; 9:10

AM

Gen 4:9; 15:1; 7; 17:1; 18:12; 13; 27; 22:1; 7; 11; 23:4; 24:24; 34; 25:22; 30; 32; 26:24(2); 27:1; 2; 11; 18; 19; 24; 32; 46; 28:13; 15; 30:2; 13; 31:11; 13; 32:10(2); 35:11; 37:13; 38:25; 41:44; 43:14; 45:3; 4; 46:2; 3; 49:29; 50:19; **Ex** 3:4; 6; 8; 11; 14(3); 19; 4:10(2); 6:2; 6; 7; 8; 12; 29; 30; 7:5; 17; 8:22; 9:29; 10:2; 12:12; 14:4; 18; 15:26; 16:12; 18:6; 20:2; 5; 22:27; 29:46(2); 31:13; **Lev** 8:35; 10:13; 11:44(2); 45(2); 18:2; 4; 5; 6; 21; 30; 19:2; 3; 4; 10; 12; 14; 16; 18; 25; 28; 30; 31; 32; 34; 36; 37; 20:7; 8; 24; 26; 21:8; 12; 22:2; 3; 8; 30; 31; 32; 33; 23:22; 43; 24:22; 25:17; 38; 55; 26:1; 2; 13; 44; 45; **Num** 3:13; 41; 45; 10:10; 11:14; 21; 15:41(2); 18:20; 22:30; 37; 38; **Deut** 1:9; 42; 5:6; 9; 26:3; 29:6; 31:2; 27; 32:39; **Josh** 5:14; 14:10; 11; 17:14; 23:2; 14; **Judg** 4:19; 6:10; 15; 8:5; 9:2; 13:11; 17:9; 18:4; 19:18(2); **Ruth** 1:12; 2:10; 3:9; 12; 4:4; **1Sa** 1:8; 15; 26; 3:4; 5; 6; 8; 16; 4:16; 9:19; 21; 12:2; 3; 14:7; 16:2; 5; 17:8; 43; 58; 18:18; 23; 22:12; 28:15; 30:13; **2Sa** 1:3; 7; 8; 13; 26; 2:20; 3:8; 39; 7:18; 9:8; 11:5; 14:5; 15; 32; 15:26; 19:20; 22; 35; 20:17; 19; 24:14; **1Kin** 3:7; 8:20; 13:14; 18; 31; 14:6; 17:12; 18:8; 12; 36; 19:4; 10; 14; 20:4; 13; 28; 22:4; 34; **2Kin** 2:10; 3:7; 5:7; 16:7; 18:25; 19:23; 21:12; **1Chr** 17:16; 21:13; 29:14; **2Chr** 2:6; 9; 6:10(2); 18:3; 33; 35:23; **Ezr** 9:6; **Neh** 6:3; 11; **Est** 5:12; **Job** 1:15; 16; 17; 19; 7:3; 4; 8; 12; 20; 9:20; 28; 32; 10:7; 15; 11:4; 12:3; 4; 13:2; 16:6; 19:7; 10; 15; 20; 21:6; 23:15(2); 30:9(2); 19; 29; 32:6; 18; 33:6(2); 9(2); 34:5; 40:4; **Ps** 6:2; 6; 13:4; 17:3; 22:2; 6; 14; 25:16; 28:7; 31:9; 12(2); 22; 35:3; 37:25; 38:6(2); 8; 17; 39:4; 10; 12; 40:12; 17; 46:10; 50:7; 52:8; 56:3; 69:2; 3; 8; 17; 20; 29; 70:5; 71:7; 18; 73:23; 77:4; 81:10; 86:1; 2; 88:4(2); 8; 15(2); 102:2; 6(2); 7; 11; 109:22; 23(2); 116:16(2); 119:19; 63; 83; 94; 107; 120; 125; 141; 120:7; 139:14; 18; 21; 142:6; 143:12; **Prov** 8:14; 20:9; 26:19; 30:2; **Eccl** 1:16; **Song** 1:5; 6; 2:1; 5; 16; 5:1; 8; 6:3; 7:10; 8:10; **Is** 1:11; 14; 6:5(2); 8; 10:13; 19:11; 21:8; 29:12; 33:24; 36:10; 37:24; 38:10; 14; 41:4; 10(2); 42:8; 43:3; 5; 10; 11; 12; 13; 15; 25; 44:5; 6(2); 16; 24; 45:3; 5; 6; 18; 22; 46:4; 9(2); 47:8; 10; 48:12(3); 16; 17; 49:21; 23; 26; 51:12; 15; 52:6; 56:3; 58:9; 60:16; 65:1(2); 5; **Jer** 1:6; 7; 8; 19; 2:23; 35; 3:12; 14; 4:19; 6:11(2); 8:21(2); 9:24; 15:6; 16; 20; 20:7; 21:13; 23:9; 23; 30; 31; 32; 24:7; 26:14; 29:23; 30:11; 31:9; 32:27; 36:5; 38:19; 42:11; 46:28; 50:31; 51:25; **Lam** 1:11; 14; 20; 3:1; 54; 63; **Eze** 5:8; 6:7; 9; 10; 13; 14; 7:4; 9; 27; 11:10; 12; 12:11; 15; 16; 20; 25; 13:8; 9; 14; 20; 21; 23; 14:8; 15:7; 16:62; 63; 20:5; 7; 12; 19; 20; 26; 38; 42; 44; 21:3; 22:16; 26; 23:49; 24:24; 27; 25:5; 7; 11; 17; 26:3; 6; 27:3; 28:2; 9; 22(2); 23; 24; 26; 29:3; 6; 9; 10; 16; 21; 30:8; 19; 22; 25; 26; 32:15; 33:29; 34:10; 27; 30; 31; 35:3; 4; 9; 12; 15; 36:9; 11; 23; 38; 37:6; 13; 38:3; 23; 39:1; 6; 7; 22; 27; 28; 44:28(2); **Dan** 9:22; 23; 10:11; 12; 14; 20; **Hos** 2:2; 11:9; 12:8; 9; 13:4; 14:8; **Joel** 2:27(2); 3:10; 17; **Amos** 2:13; **Jonah** 1:9; 2:4; **Mic** 3:8; 7:1; **Nah** 2:13; 3:5; **Hab** 2:1; **Zeph** 2:15; **Hag** 1:13; 2:4; **Zec** 1:14; 15; 16; 8:3; 10:6; 11:5; 13:5(2); **Mal** 1:14; 3:6; **Mt** 3:11; 17; 5:17(2); 8:8; 9; 9:13; 28; 10:34; 35; 11:29; 15:24; 16:13; 15; 17:5; 18:20; 20:15; 22; 23; 22:32; 24:5; 26:32; 61; 27:24; 43; 28:20; **Mk** 1:7; 11; 8:27; 29; 10:38; 39; 12:26; 13:6; 14:28; 62; **Lk** 1:18; 19(2); 3:16; 22; 4:43; 5:8; 7:6; 8; 9:18; 20; 12:49; 50; 51; 15:19; 21; 16:3; 4(2); 24; 18:11; 21:8; 22:27; 33; 58; 70; **Jn** 1:20; 21; 23; 27; 31; 3:28(2); 4:9; 26; 5:7; 43; 6:35; 41; 48; 51; 7:28(2); 29; 33; 34; 36; 8:12; 16; 18; 23(2); 24; 28; 58; 9:5(2); 9; 39; 10:7; 9; 10; 11; 14(2); 36; 11:15; 25; 12:26; 46; 13:13; 19; 33; 14:3; 6; 10; 11; 20; 15:1; 5; 16:28; 32; 17:10; 11; 14; 16; 24; 18:5; 6; 8; 17; 25; 35; 37; 19:21; 20:17; **Acts** 7:32; 34; 9:5; 10; 10:21; 26; 13:25(3); 18:6; 10; 20:26; 21:13; 39(2); 22:3(2); 8; 23:6(2); 24:21; 26:2; 6; 7; 15; 25; 26; 29; 27:23; 28:20; **Rom** 1:14; 15; 16; 3:7; 7:14; 24; 8:38; 11:1; 3; 13; 14:14; 15:14; 29; 16:19; **1Cor** 1:12; 3:4(2); 4:4; 9:1(2); 2; 22; 10:30; 11:1; 12:15(2); 16(2); 13:1; 2; 12; 15:9(2); 10(2); 16:17; **2Cor** 7:4(2); 14; 10:1(2); 2; 11:2; 21; 22(3); 23; 29; 12:10(2); 11(2); 14; 13:1; **Gal** 2:19; 20; 4:11; 12(2); 16; 18; **Eph** 3:8; 6:20; **Phil** 1:17; 23; 3:12; 4:11; 12; 18; **Col** 1:23; 25; 2:5; 4:3; **1Ti** 1:15; 2:7; **2Ti** 1:5; 11; 12(2); 4:6; **Jas** 1:13; **1Pet** 1:16; 5:1; **2Pet** 1:13; 17; **Rev** 1:8; 9; 11; 17; 18(2); 2:23; 3:17; 21; 18:7; 19:10; 21:6; 22:9; 13; 16

AMONG

Gen 17:10; 12; 23; 23:6; 10; 24:3; 30:32(2); 33(2); 35; 41; 34:22; 30(2); 35:2; 36:30; 40:20; 42:5; 47:6; **Ex** 2:5; 7:5; 9:20; 10:2; 12:31; 49; 13:2; 13; 15:11; 17:7; 25:8; 28:1; 29:45; 46; 30:12; 13; 14; 31:14; 32:25; 34:9; 10; 19; 35:5; 10; 36:8; **Lev** 6:18; 29; 7:6; 33; 34; 11:2; 3; 13; 27; 29; 31; 42; 15:31; 16:16; 29; 17:4; 8; 9; 10(2); 12; 13; 18:26; 29; 19:8; 16; 34; 20:3; 5; 6; 14; 18; 21:1; 4; 10; 15; 22:3; 32; 23:29; 30; 24:10; 25:33; 45; 26:11; 12; 22; 25; 33; 38; **Num** 1:47; 49; 2:33; 3:12(2); 41(2); 42; 45; 4:2; 18; 5:21; 27; 8:6; 14; 16; 19(2); 9:7; 13; 14; 11:1; 3; 4; 20; 21; 12:6; 13:2; 14:11; 13; 14; 42; 15:14; 23; 26; 29(2); 30; 16:3; 21; 33; 45; 47; 17:6; 18:6; 20(2); 23; 24; 19:10; 20; 21:6; 23:9; 21; 25:7; 11; 14; 26:62(2); 64; 27:4(2); 7; 31:16; 17; 32:30; 33:4; 54; 35:6; 15; 34; **Deut** 1:13; 15; 42; 2:14; 15; 16; 4:3; 27(2); 6:15; 7:14(2); 20; 21; 13:1; 11; 13; 14; 14:6; 15:4; 7; 16:11; 17:2; 7; 15; 18:2; 10; 18; 19:19; 20; 21:9; 11; 21; 22:21; 24; 23:10; 16; 24:7; 26:11; 28:37; 54; 56; 64; 65; 29:17; 18(2); 30:1; 31:16; 17; 32:26; 34; 46; 51; **Josh** 3:5; 10; 4:6; 7:11; 12; 13; 21; 8:9; 33; 35; 9:7; 16; 22; 10:1; 13:13; 22; 14:3; 15; 15:13; 16:9; 10; 17:4(2); 6; 9; 18:2; 4; 7; 19:49; 20:4; 9; 22:7; 14; 19; 31; 23:7(2); 12; 24:5; 17; 23; **Judg** 1:16; 29; 30; 32; 33; 3:5; 5:8; 9; 13; 14; 16; 10:16; 12:4(2); 14:3(2); 18:1; 25; 20:12; 16; 21:5; 12; **Ruth** 2:7; 15; 4:10; **1Sa** 2:8; 4:3; 17; 6:6; 7:3; 9:2; 22; 10:10; 11(2); 12; 22; 23; 24; 14:15; 30; 34; 39; 15:6(2); 33; 16:1; 17:12; 19:24; 22:14; 31:9; **2Sa** 6:19(2); 15:31; 16:20; 17:9; 19:28; 22:50; 23:8; 18(2); 22; **1Kin** 3:13; 5:6; 6:13; 7:51; 8:53; 9:7; 11:20; 14:7; 21:9; 12; **2Kin** 4:13; 9:2; 11:2; 17:25; 26; 18:5; 35; 20:15; 23:9; **1Chr** 4:23; 7:5; 11:20; 24; 25; 12:1; 4; 16:8; 24(2); 31; 18:14; 21:6; 23:6; 24:4(2); 26:12(2); 19(2); 30; 31(3); 27:6; 28:4; **2Chr** 5:1; 6:5; 7:13; 20; 11:22; 20:25; 22:11; 24:16; 23; 26:6; 28:15; 31:19(2); 32:14; 33:11; 19; 35:13; 36:23; **Ezr** 1:3; 2:62; 65; 10:18; **Neh** 1:8; 4:11; 5:17; 6:6; 7:64; 9:17; 10:34; 11:17; 13:26; **Est** 1:19; 3:8; 4:3; 9:21; 28; 10:3; **Job** 1:6; 2:1; 8; 15:19; 17:10; 18:19; 28:10; 30:5; 7; 33:23; 34:4; 37; 36:14; 39:25; 41:6; 42:15; **Ps** 9:11; 12:1; 18:49; 21:10; 22:18; 28; 31:11(2); 35:18; 44:11; 14(2); 45:9; 12; 46:10; 55:15; 57:4(2); 9(2); 67:2; 68:13; 17; 18; 25; 74:9; 77:14; 78:45; 49; 60; 79:10; 80:6; 82:1; 86:8; 88:5; 89:6; 94:8; 96:3(2); 10; 99:6(2); 104:10; 12; 105:1; 27; 37; 106:27; 35; 47; 108:3(2); 109:30; 110:6; 126:2; 136:11; **Prov** 1:14; 6:19; 7:7(2); 14:9; 15:31; 17:2; 23:20(2); 28; 27:22; 30:14; 30; 31:23; **Eccl** 6:1; 7:28(2); 9:3; 17; **Song** 1:8; 2:2(2); 3(2); 16; 4:2; 5; 5:9; 10; 6:1; 3; 6; **Is** 2:4; 4:3; 5:27; 8:15; 16; 10:16; 12:4; 24:13; 29:14; 19; 33:14(2); 36:20; 39:4; 41:28; 42:23; 43:9; 12; 44:4; 14; 48:14; 50:10; 51:18; 57:6; 61:9(2); 65:4; 66:19(2); **Jer** 3:19; 4:3; 5:26; 6:15; 18; 27; 8:12; 17; 9:16; 10:7; 11:9(2); 12:14; 14:22; 18:13; 24:10; 25:16; 27; 29:18; 32; 31:7; 32:20; 37:4; 10; 39:14; 40:1; 5; 6; 11; 41:8(2); 44:8; 46:18; 48:27; 49:15(2); 50:2; 23; 46; 51:27; 41; **Lam** 1:1(2); 2; 3; 17; 2:9; 4:15; 20; **Eze** 1:1; 13; 2:5; 6; 3:15; 25; 4:13; 5:14; 6:8; 9; 13; 9:2; 11:1; 9; 16(2); 12:10; 12; 15; 16; 13:19; 15:2; 6; 16:14; 18:18; 19:2(2); 6; 11; 20:9; 23; 38; 22:15; 26; 30; 23:10; 25:10; 27:24; 36; 28:19; 25; 29:12(2); 30:23; 26(2); 31:3; 10; 14; 18; 32:9; 21; 33:6; 33; 34:12; 24; 35:11; 36:19; 21; 22; 23; 24; 30; 37:21; 39:6; 21; 28; 40:46; 44:9; 47:22(4); **Dan** 1:6; 19; 4:35; 7:8; 11:24; 33; **Hos** 5:9; 7:7; 8; 8:8; 10; 9:17; 10:14; 13:15; **Joel** 2:17; 19; 25; 3:2; 9; **Amos** 1:1; 2:16; 4:10; 9:9; **Obad** 1; 2; 4; **Mic** 3:11; 4:3; 5:2; 8(3); 7:2; **Nah** 3:8; **Hab** 1:5; **Zeph** 3:20; **Hag** 2:3; 5; **Zec** 1:8; 10; 11; 3:7; 7:14; 8:13; 10:9; 12:6; 8; 14:13; **Mal** 1:10; 11(2); 14; **Mt** 2:6; 4:23; 9:35; 11:11; 12:11; 13:7; 22; 25; 32; 49; 16:7; 8; 20:26(2); 27; 21:38; 23:11; 26:5; 27:35; 56; 28:15; **Mk** 1:27; 4:7; 18; 5:3; 6:4; 41; 8:16; 19; 20; 9:33; 34; 10:26; 43(2); 12:7;

13:10; 15:31; 40; 16:3; **Lk** 1:1; 25; 28; 42; 2:44; 4:36; 7:16; 28; 8:7; 14; 9:46; 48; 10:3; 30; 36; 16:15; 19:2; 39; 20:14; 22:17; 23; 24; 26; 27; 37; 55; 24:5; 47; **Jn** 1:14; 26; 6:9; 43; 52; 7:12; 35(2); 43; 8:7; 9:16; 10:19; 11:54; 56; 12:19; 20; 42; 15:24; 16:17; 19; 19:24(2); 21:23; **Acts** 1:21; 2:22; 3:23; 4:12; 15; 17; 34; 5:12; 34; 6:3; 8; 10:22; 12:18; 13:26; 14:14; 15:7; 12; 19; 22; 17:33; 34; 18:11; 20:25; 29; 32; 21:19; 21; 34; 23:10; 24:5; 21; 25:5; 6; 26:3; 4; 18; 27:22; 28:4; 25; 29; **Rom** 1:5; 6; 13(2); 2:24; 8:29; 11:17; 12:3; 15:9; 16:7; **1Cor** 1:10; 11; 2:2; 6; 3:3; 18; 5:1(2); 2; 13; 6:5; 7; 11:18; 19(2); 30; 15:12; **2Cor** 1:19; 6:17; 10:1; 12; 11:6; 26; 12:12; 21; **Gal** 1:16; 2:2; 3:1; 5; **Eph** 2:3; 3:8; 5:3; **Phil** 2:15; **Col** 1:27; 4:16; **1Th** 1:5; 2:7; 10; 5:12; 13; 15; **2Th** 1:10; 3:7; 11; **2Ti** 2:2; **Heb** 5:1; **Jas** 1:26; 3:6; 13; 4:1; 5:13; 14; **1Pet** 2:12; 4:8; 5:1; 2; **2Pet** 2:1(2); 8; **3Jn** 9; **Jude** 15; **Rev** 2:13; 7:15; 14:4

AN

Gen 2:18; 20; 4:3; 22; 5:3; 6; 18; 25; 28; 6:3; 14; 7:24; 8:11; 20; 9:20; 11:10; 25; 12:7; 8; 13:18; 15:9; 12; 16:1(2); 17:7; 8; 13; 17; 19; 21:5; 20; 22:9; 23:1; 25:7; 8; 17; 25; 26:12; 25; 28; 27:30; 29:24; 31:46; 33:17; 19; 20; 34:31; 35:1; 3; 7; 8; 28; 37:33; 36; 38:14; 15; 39:1(2); 14; 41:12; 16; 42:23; 43:12; 32; 44:20; 46:34; 47:9; 28; 48:4; 49:9; 13; 17; 33; 50:22; 25; 26; **Ex** 2:3; 11(2); 19; 4:20; 6:8; 16; 18; 20; 10:13; 26; 12:3; 14; 16(2); 17; 24; 45; 13:13; 14:8; 15:2; 8; 25; 16:16; 18; 32; 33; 36(2); 17:15; 18:3; 19:6; 13; 20:24; 25; 21:2; 6; 28; 33(2); 22:1(2); 10(2); 11; 15; 23:1; 20; 22(2); 24:4; 25:2; 10; 25; 26:36; 27:1; 9; 11; 16; 18; 28:4; 11; 18; 19(2); 20; 32(2); 29:18; 25; 28(2); 36; 37(2); 40(2); 41; 30:1; 10; 13; 14; 15(2); 16; 24; 25(3); 31; 31:18; 32:5; 30; 33:2; 34:20; 35:2; 5(2); 22; 24; 36:37; 37:12; 38:9; 11; 23(2); 25; 27; 39:11; 12(2); 13; 23(2); 40:10; 15; **Lev** 1:2; 9; 13; 17; 2:2; 4; 9; 16; 3:3; 5; 9; 14; 4:20; 26; 31; 35; 5:2; 4; 6; 10; 11; 13; 16; 18; 6:7; 20; 7:5; 14; 18; 25; 32; 8:21; 28; 33; 34; 9:7(2); 17; 11:10; 11; 12; 13; 20; 23; 41; 42; 12:7; 8; 13:11; 28; 14:5; 18; 19; 20; 21; 29; 31; 40; 41; 45; 50; 53; 15:13; 15; 19; 25; 30; 32; 33; 16:6; 10; 11; 16; 17(2); 18; 20; 24; 30; 33(3); 34(2); 17:3; 4; 11(2); 19:20; 22; 20:13; 21; 21:14; 22:10; 12; 22; 27; 23:3; 7; 8(2); 12; 13; 14; 18; 21; 24; 25; 27(2); 28; 35; 36(3); 37; 24:7; 8; 10(2); 25:40; 46; 50; 26:8(2); 27:9; 27; **Num** 2:9; 16; 24(2); 31; 4:15; 5:2; 8; 15(3); 17; 19; 21(2); 26; 6:11; 7:3; 13; 19; 25; 31; 37; 43; 49; 55; 61; 67; 73; 79; 85; 86; 8:11; 12; 13; 15; 19; 21(2); 9:7; 10:5; 6(2); 7; 8; 9; 12:1; 13:32; 14:7; 15:3; 4; 5; 6; 7; 9; 10(2); 13; 14; 15; 19; 20; 21; 25; 28(2); 16:31; 46; 47; 18:8; 17; 21; 24; 26; 28; 19:17; 20:16; 22:22; 23:3; 25:13(2); 26:53; 27:7; 28:5(2); 7; 14(3); 18; 22; 25; 26; 30; 29:1; 5; 7; 12; 30:2; 6; 10; 31:29; 50(2); 32:14; 33:3; 39; 54; 34:2; 35:16; 18; 36:2; 8; **Deut** 4:21; 38; 5:29; 7:6; 25; 26; 10:1; 3; 13:16; 14:2; 21(2); 15:4; 12(2); 17; 17:1; 18:10(2); 12; 19:10; 20:9; 16; 19; 21:3; 23; 22:10(2); 14; 19(2); 22; 23; 23:3; 7(2); 24:4; 14; 25:5; 16; 19; 26:1; 8; 12; 19; 27:5(2); 15; 25; 28:9; 22(2); 30; 37; 29:4; 8; 31:2; 24; 32:11; 45; 33:7; 34:7; **Josh** 1:6; 2:1; 3:13; 16; 7:13; 8:2; 24; 28; 30; 31; 10:20; 11:23; 13:6; 7; 14:3; 13; 17:4(2); 6; 19:49(2); 51(2); 22:10; 11; 14; 16; 19; 23; 26; 29; 23:4; 24:19; 25; 26; 29; 32; **Judg** 2:1; 8; 3:18; 31; 4:21; 6:11(2); 19; 22(2); 24; 26; 8:10; 27; 9:23; 46; 48; 11:1; 12:5; 13:6; 16; 21; 14:4; 15:15; 16(2); 17; 19; 16:1; 3; 17:5(2); 18:1; 14; 19:9; 16; 28; 20:10(2); 16; 35; 38; 21:4; 17; **Ruth** 1:12(2); 2:17; **1Sa** 1:1; 2:28; 31; 32(2); 3:12; 4:18; 7:17; 9:6; 10:13; 13:10; 14:3; 14; 27; 28; 35; 48; 16:2; 14; 15; 16; 20; 23; 17:5; 12; 17; 38; 18:1; 25; 19:13; 16; 20:36; 21:7; 23:6; 24:16; 25:18; 42; 26:13; 19; 28:14; 29:4; 9; 30:11; 13; 14; 25; **2Sa** 1:8; 13; 2:25; 3:14; 29; 5:11; 6:18; 7:2; 5; 7; 11; 13; 27; 8:4; 11:2; 19; 13:36; 14:17; 20; 15:19; 16:1(2); 17:25; 18:10; 19:26; 27; 23:5; 14; 21; 38(2); 24:3; 18; 21; 25; **1Kin** 1:39; 41(2); 52; 2:24; 36; 3:1; 9; 12; 4:23; 5:3; 5(2); 7:2; 8; 26; 31; 40; 8:13; 16; 17; 18; 20; 31; 36; 54; 63; 10:10; 29(2); 11:7; 14; 18; 25; 26; 12:21; 31; 13:11; 14; 18; 14:21; 31; 15:13; 16:32; 17:12; 18:4; 10; 13; 32; 19:5; 11; 20:20; 25; 29; 30; 22:9; 25; **2Kin** 1:8; 9; 3:4(2); 4:9; 24; 43; 6:15; 25; 9:2; 5; 17; 10:25; 11:4; 16:10; 11; 18:31; 19:32; 35; 23:33; 25:19; **1Chr** 2:34; 5:21; 6:49; 8:40; 11:23; 12:14; 37; 14:1; 15:5; 7; 10; 27; 16:2; 17; 29; 17:1; 4; 5; 6; 10; 12; 25; 18:4; 21:3; 5; 15; 18; 22; 26; 22:6; 7; 8; 10; 14; 27:4; 28:2; 3; 8; 10; 29:16; **2Chr** 1:17(2); 2:1(2); 3; 4(2); 6(2); 12(2); 17; 3:4; 16; 4:1; 5; 8; 5:12; 6:2; 5; 7; 8; 22; 27; 7:1; 5; 12; 21; 9:9; 11:1; 12:13; 13:3; 13; 14:8; 9; 15:16; 17:18; 18:24; 20:23; 21:18; 24:10; 15; 26; 25:6(2); 26:11; 13; 27:5; 28:6; 29:17; 24; 29; 32; 32:8; 21; 35:25; 36:3; 23; **Ezr** 1:2; 2:3; 18; 21; 23; 27; 30; 41; 42; 4:3; 6; 17; 6:17; 7:22(4); 8:3; 10; 12; 26(2); 9:11; 12; 10:17; **Neh** 4:2; 5:12; 17; 6:5; 13; 7:8; 24; 26; 27; 31; 32; 44; 45; 10:29; 33; 11:14; 19; **Est** 1:1; 4; 8:9; **Job** 1:8; 10; 2:3; 11; 3:16; 4:16; 6:6; 7:1; 13:16; 14:3; 4; 6; 16:3; 18:2; 19:15; 24; 20:19; 26:10; 28:3; 31:6; 11(2); 28; 33:23; 40:9; 15; 41:1; 2; 42:11; 16; **Ps** 5:9; 7:9; 11:6; 18:25; 26:12; 27:3; 31:2; 33:2; 7; 16; 17; 38:4; 39:5; 40:2; 41:8; 43:1; 48:7; 50:21; 55:12; 64:5; 7; 68:15; 21; 69:8; 13; 31; 72:16; 78:13; 26; 55; 84:3; 88:8; 92:3; 10; 96:8; 101:5; 102:3; 6; 105:10; 106:20; 119:96; 111; 142; 127:3; 132:5; 135:12(2); 136:21; 22; 140:11; 141:5; 144:9; 145:13; **Prov** 1:9; 4:9; 5:3; 6:11; 16; 18; 7:10; 13; 22; 8:5; 7; 10:25; 11:9; 13:22; 15:8; 9; 19; 26; 16:5; 12; 18; 19; 24; 27; 17:1; 10; 11; 27; 18:11; 19:15; 28; 20:3; 21; 23; 21:4; 19; 22:24; 23:5; 6; 18; 32; 24:3; 9; 34; 25:12(3); 19; 20; 23; 27:6; 7; 28:10; 22; 29:6; 22; 27(2); 30:19; 20; 23(2); 31; **Eccl** 4:6; 13; 5:6; 6:1; 2; 3(2); 7:11; 8:3; 11; 12; 9:2; 3; 12(2); 10:5(2); 8; **Song** 4:4; 13; 6:4; 10; 7:2; **Is** 1:13; 21; 30; 3:7; 5:10(2); 26; 6:13; 9:17(2); 10:6; 11:10; 12; 16; 14:19; 15:5; 16:4; 11; 14; 17:6; 9; 18:3; 19:19; 21:16; 22:16(2); 23:15; 16; 24:13; 25:2; 29:5; 8; 21; 30:5; 13; 17(2); 28; 32:2; 33:1; 34:13; 35:6; 8; 36:16; 37:33; 36; 38:12; 13; 41:24; 43:23; 44:14; 19; 45:17; 48:4; 49:8; 18; 53:10; 54:16; 55:3; 13; 56:5; 7; 58:5; 59:17; 60:15; 19; 61:8; 63:12; 13; 64:6; 65:9; 20(4); 66:3(3); 14; 20(2); 24; **Jer** 1:11; 14; 18; 2:7; 19; 3:18; 4:7; 5:15; 16; 6:26; 9:2; 8; 11; 10:10; 11:19; 14:12; 18:17; 19:8; 21:5; 22:19; 23:14; 40; 24:7; 25:9(2); 11; 18(2); 36; 26:8; 9; 29:11; 18(2); 30:14; 17; 31:3; 32; 32:14; 40; 33:9; 12; 34:9(2); 14; 22; 42:18(2); 43:1; 44:12(2); 22(2); 27; 46:19; 22; 47:2; 48:34; 40; 49:2; 14; 50:9; 51:29; 34; 37(3); 41; 63; 52:23; 25; **Lam** 1:15; 2:4(2); 5; 5:10; **Eze** 1:10(2); 24; 2:9; 3:5; 6; 9; 4:3; 11; 5:15(2); 7:2; 5(2); 6; 8:3; 10:14; 11:19; 13:11; 13; 16:3(2); 24(2); 30; 31; 45(2); 60; 17:13; 22; 20:17; 21:25; 29; 23:24; 31:3; 33:32; 35:5; 36:3; 26; 37:10; 26; 38:10; 40:5; 19; 23; 27; 42(2); 43; 47(2); 41:7; 13(2); 14; 15; 42:2; 8; 15; 43:13; 23; 44:28; 45:1(2); 4; 11(2); 13(4); 14(2); 24(4); 46:5(3); 7(4); 11(4); 14(2); 47:22; **Dan** 2:46; 3:1; 4; 27; 4:3; 13; 23; 34; 5:12; 6:1; 3; 7:14; 27; 8:5; 12; 9:24; 10:10; 11:6; 7; 12:7; **Hos** 3:1; 2(2); 4(2); 6:10; 11; 7:4; 6; 7; 8:1; 10:1; 11; 13:13; 15; **Joel** 2:1; 3:3; **Amos** 3:11; 12; 15; 5:3(2); 13; 7:2; 14(2); 17; 8:10; **Obad** 1; **Jonah** 1:9; 3:3; **Mic** 1:6; 7(2); 15; 2:3; 8; 6:16; **Nah** 1:8(2); 9; **Hab** 2:3; 9; **Zeph** 1:10; 3:12; **Hag** 2:16; **Zec** 5:6; 11; 7:12; 9:9(2); 16; 12:6; 13:5; **Mal** 1:10; 13; 2:11; 12; 3:3; 4:1; **Mt** 2:19; 4:2; 8; 5:14; 38(2); 8:30; 9:16; 20; 10:12; 11:1; 12:1; 3; 35; 39; 13:8; 23; 28; 52; 14:7; 16:23; 17:1; 27; 18:12; 17; 28; 19:29; 20:1; 21:2; 5(2); 24:44; 50; 25:24; 35; 37; 42; 44; 26:5; 7; 30; 72; **Mk** 1:23; 2:21; 25; 3:19; 26; 30; 4:8; 20; 5:2; 25; 6:20; 27; 7:22; 24; 25; 32; 9:2; 10:30; 12:1; 14:2; 3; 26; 15:43; **Lk** 1:11; 18; 69; 2:36; 4:5; 33; 5:36; 6:3; 7; 45; 48; 49; 7:37; 8:8; 15; 32; 43; 9:28; 10:34; 11:12; 29; 12:1; 40; 46; 14:5(2); 32; 15:4; 16:2; 6; 7; 19:21; 22; 21:18; 22:37; 43; 44; 24:42; **Jn** 1:22; 47; 2:16; 5:4; 5; 6:60; 10:12; 13; 12:15; 29; 13:15; 19:31; 39; 21:11; **Acts** 1:13; 15; 2:30; 3:3; 6:15; 7:30; 47; 8:27; 9:37; 10:3; 22; 28; 11:13; 12:21; 13:17; 14:5; 17:5; 23; 18:24; 19:40; 20:32; 21:16; 26; 29; 31; 38; 23:9; 21; 27; 25:11; 27:12; 34; **Rom** 1:1; 23; 2:20; 3:13; 4:19; 7:2; 3; 11:1; 14:13; 16:16; **1Cor** 1:1; 5:9; 11(3); 6:15; 16; 7:13; 8:4; 7; 9:1; 2; 25; 12:17; 14:2; 4; 8; 13; 14; 19; 26; 27; 15:9; 52; 16:20; **2Cor** 1:1; 2:11; 5:1; 6:15; 8:14; 10:11; 11:7; 14; 12:2; 5; 12; 13:12; **Gal** 1:1; 8; 2:5; 4:7; 14; 24; 5:13; 6:1; **Eph** 1:1; 11; 2:21; 22; 5:2; 5; 6:20; **Phil** 1:28; 3:5; 17; 4:18; **Col** 1:1; 2:16; **1Th** 5:8; 26; **2Th** 3:9; 15; **1Ti** 1:1; 2:7; 4:12; 5:1; 8; 19(2); **2Ti** 1:1; 9; 11; 2:9; 4:5; **Titus** 1:1; 3:10; **Philem** 1:9; **Heb** 3:12; 4:15; 5:5; 10; 6:6; 16(2); 17; 19; 20; 7:16; 20; 21(2); 24; 26; 8:1; 9:11; 13; 10:21; 22; 29; 34; 11:7; 8; 16; 12:22; 13:10; **Jas** 3:8; 5:10; **1Pet** 1:1; 4; 2:5; 9; 21; 3:15; 4:15; 5:1; **2Pet** 1:1; 11; 2:6(2); 14; **1Jn** 2:1; 7; 20; 5:20; **2Jn** 7; **Jude** 7; **Rev** 2:7; 11; 17; 29; 3:6; 8; 13; 22; 4:3; 7:4; 8:1; 5; 13; 9:15; 11:9; 11; 19; 13:9; 14; 14:1; 16:18; 19:17; 20:1; 21:17; 19; 20

AND

Gen 1:1; 2(4); 3(2); 4(2); 5(4); 6(2); 7(3); 8(3); 9(3); 10(3); 11(3); 12(4); 13(2); 14(5); 15(2); 16(2); 17; 18(4); 19(2); 20(2); 21(4); 22(4); 23(2); 24(4); 25(4); 26(6); 27; 28(8); 29(2); 30(4); 31(4); 2:1(2); 2(2); 3(3); 4(2); 5(3); 6; 7(3); 8(2); 9(4); 10(3); 12(2); 13; 14(2); 15(3); 16; 17; 18; 19(4); 20(3); 21(4); 22(2); 23(2); 24(3); 25(3); 3:1; 2; 4; 5(2); 6(6); 7(4); 8(3); 9(2); 10(3); 11; 12(2); 13(3); 14(3); 15(5); 16(3); 17(2); 18(2); 19; 20; 21(2); 22(6); 24(2); 4:1(4); 2(2); 3; 4(4); 5(3); 6(2); 7(3); 8(3); 9(2); 10; 11; 12; 13; 14(4); 15(2); 16(2); 17(5); 18(4); 19(2); 20(2); 21(2); 22(3); 23(3); 24; 25(3); 26(2); 5:2(3); 3(4); 4(3); 5(3); 6(3); 7(4); 8(3); 9(2); 10(4); 11(3); 12(2); 13(4); 14(3); 15(3); 16(4); 17(3); 18(3); 19(3); 20(3); 21(3); 22(3); 23(2); 24(2); 25(3); 26(4); 27(3); 28(3); 29(2); 30(4); 31(3); 32(3); 6:1(2); 2; 3(2); 4(2); 5(2); 6(2); 7(4); 9(2); 10(2); 11; 12(2); 13(2); 14(2); 15(2); 16(3); 17(2); 18(4); 19(2); 20; 21(4); 7:1(2); 2(3); 3; 4(3); 5; 6; 7(4); 8(3); 9(2); 10; 11; 12(2); 13(5); 14(4); 15(2); 16(3); 17(4); 18(3); 19(2); 20; 21(5); 23(7); 24(2); 8:1(5); 2(2); 3(3); 4; 5; 6; 7(2); 9(3); 10(2); 11(2); 12(2); 13(5); 14(2); 15; 16(3); 17(4); 18(4); 19(2); 20(4); 21(2); 22(7); 9:1(5); 2(4); 5(2); 7(3); 8(2); 9(2); 10(2); 11; 12(3); 13(2); 14; 15(4); 16(3); 17(2); 18(4); 19; 20(2); 21(3); 22(2); 23(7); 24(2); 25; 26(2); 27(2); 28(2); 29(3); 10:1(2); 2(6); 3(3); 4(3); 6(4); 7(7); 8; 10(4); 11(3); 12(2); 13(4); 14(3); 15(2); 16(3); 17(3); 18(4); 19(4); 20; 22(4); 23(4); 24(2); 25(2); 26(4); 27(3); 28(3); 29(3); 30; 32; 11:1(2); 2(2); 3(4); 4(3); 5(2); 6(4); 7; 8; 9; 10; 11(3); 12(3); 13(4); 14(2); 15(4); 16(3); 17(4); 18(2); 19(4); 20(3); 21(4); 22(2); 23(3); 24(3); 25(4); 26(3); 27(2); 28; 29(4); 31(6); 32(3); 12:1(2); 2(4); 3(3); 4(3); 5(6); 6(2); 7(3); 8(5); 9; 10(2); 11; 12; 13; 14; 15(2); 16(8); 17(2); 18(2); 19; 20(4); 13:1(4); 2(2); 3(2); 4; 5(3); 6; 7(4); 8(4); 10(3); 11(2); 12(2); 13; 14(5); 15; 16; 17; 18(3); 14:1(2); 2(3); 4; 5(5); 6; 7(4); 8(6); 9(3); 10(5); 11(4); 12(3); 13(4); 14(3); 15(4); 16(5); 17(2); 18(3); 19(3); 20(2); 21(2); 22(2); 23; 24(2); 15:1; 2(2); 3(2); 4; 5(4); 6(2); 7; 8; 9(5); 10(3); 11; 12(2); 13(3); 14(2); 15; 17(3); 19(2); 20(3); 21(4); 16:1; 2(2); 3(2); 4(3); 5(3); 6; 7; 8(3); 9(2); 10; 11(3); 12(3); 13; 14; 15(2); 16(2); 17:1(4); 2(3); 3(2); 4; 6(3); 7(4); 8(3); 9(2); 10(2); 11(3); 12; 13(2); 14; 15; 16(3); 17(3); 18; 19(4); 20(4); 22(2); 23(4); 24(2); 25; 26; 27(2); 18:1(2); 2(5); 3; 4(2); 5(3); 6(3); 7(5); 8(6); 9(2); 10(3); 11(3); 13; 14; 15; 16(3); 17; 18(2); 19(3); 20(3); 21(2); 22(2); 23(2); 24; 25; 26; 27(3); 28(2); 29(3); 30(3); 31(2); 32(3); 33(2); 19:1(4); 2(6); 3(6); 4; 5(2); 6(2); 7; 8; 9(5); 10(2); 11(2); 12(4); 13; 14(3); 15(2); 16(5); 17; 18; 19(3); 20(2); 21; 24(2); 25(4); 26; 27; 28(5); 29(2); 30(5); 31(2); 32; 33(4); 34(3); 35(4); 37(2); 38(2); 20:1(4); 2(3); 3; 4; 5(2); 6; 7(4); 8(3); 9(3); 10; 11(2); 12(2); 13; 14(6); 15; 16(2); 17(4); 21:1(2); 2; 3; 4; 5; 6; 7; 8(3); 9; 10; 11; 12(2); 13; 14(8); 15(2); 16(5); 17(3); 18; 19(5); 20(4); 21(2); 22(2); 23; 24; 25; 26; 27(4); 28; 29; 30; 32(2); 33(2); 34; 22:1(3); 2(3); 3(7); 4; 5(5); 6(5); 7(5); 8; 9(5); 10(2); 11(3); 12; 13(6); 14; 15; 16(2); 17(3); 18; 19(3); 20; 21(2); 22(5); 23; 24(4); 23:1(3); 2(3); 3(2); 4; 5; 7(2); 8(2); 10(2); 11; 12; 13(2); 14; 15; 16(2); 17(3); 19; 20(2); 24:1(3); 2; 3(2); 4(2); 5; 6; 7(4); 8; 9(2); 10(4); 11; 12(2); 13; 14(4); 15; 16(4); 17(2); 18(4); 19; 20(4); 21; 22(2); 23; 24; 25(2); 26(2); 27(2); 28(2); 29(3); 30(4); 31(2); 32(6); 33(2); 34; 35(10); 36(2); 37; 38(2); 39; 40(4); 41; 42(2); 43(2); 44(2); 45(4); 46(5); 47(5); 48(3); 49(3); 50(2); 51(2); 52; 53(5); 54(6); 55(2); 56; 57(2); 58(3); 59(4); 60(3); 61(6); 62; 63(4); 64(2); 65(2); 66; 67(5); 25:1; 2(6); 3(5); 4(5); 5; 6; 7(2); 8(3); 9(2); 10; 11(2); 13(4); 14(3); 15(2); 16(2); 17(6); 18(2); 19; 20; 21(3); 22(3); 23(4); 24; 25(2); 26(4); 27(3); 28; 29(3); 30; 31; 32(2); 33(3); 34(5); 26:1(2); 2(2); 3(4); 4(3); 5(2); 6; 7(2); 8(3); 9(4); 10(2); 11; 12(2); 13(3); 14(3); 15; 16; 17(3); 18(2); 19(2); 20(2); 21(3); 22(6); 23; 24(4); 25(4); 26(2); 27(2); 28(4); 29(2); 30(3); 31(4); 32(3); 33; 34(2); 35; 27:1(4); 2; 3(3); 4(2); 5(3); 6; 7(2); 9(2); 10(2); 11(2); 12(3); 13(2); 14(4); 15(2); 16(2); 17(2); 18(3); 19(2); 20(2); 21; 22(3); 23; 24(2); 25(6); 26(2); 27(5); 28(3); 29(3); 30(2); 31(4); 32(2); 33(6); 34(3); 35(2); 36(3); 37(6); 38(3); 39(3); 40(3); 41(2); 42(4); 43; 44; 45(2); 46; 28:1(4); 2; 3(3); 4(2); 5(3); 6(2); 7(3); 8; 9; 10(2); 11(5); 12(5); 13(4); 14(7); 15(3); 16(3); 17(3); 18(4); 19; 20(4); 22(2); 29:1; 2(4); 3(4); 4(2); 5(2); 6(3); 7(3); 8(2); 9; 10(4); 11(3); 12(4); 13(5); 14(3); 15; 16(2); 17; 18(2); 19; 20(2); 21; 22(2); 23(3); 24; 25(2); 26; 27; 28(3); 29; 30(3); 31; 32(3); 33(4); 34(3); 35(4); 30:1(2); 2(2); 3(2); 4(2); 5(2); 6(3); 7(2); 8(3); 9; 10; 11(2); 12; 13(2); 14(3); 15(3); 16(4); 17(3); 18(2); 19(2); 20(2); 21(2); 22(3); 23(3); 24(2); 25(2); 26(2); 27; 28(2); 29(2); 30(3); 31(3); 32(5); 33(2); 34; 35(7); 36(3); 37(5); 38; 39(3); 40(5); 41; 42; 43(6); 31:1(2); 2(2); 3(3); 4(3); 5; 6; 7(2); 8; 9; 10(4); 11(2); 12(3); 13(2); 14(3); 15; 16; 17(2); 18(2); 19(2); 20; 21(3); 22; 23(3); 24(2); 25; 26(2); 27(4); 28(2); 30; 31(2); 32; 33(4); 34(3); 35(2); 36(4); 37; 38(2); 40(2); 41(2); 42(3); 43(6); 44(3); 45(2); 46(4); 47; 48(2); 49(2); 50; 51(3); 52(3); 53(2); 54(3); 55(6); 32:1(2); 2(2); 3; 4(2); 5(5); 6(3); 7(5); 8(2); 9(4); 10(2); 11(2); 12(2); 13(2); 14(2); 15(2); 16(4); 17(4); 18; 19(3); 20(2); 21; 22(5); 23(3); 24(2); 25(2); 26(2); 27(2); 28(3); 29(4); 30(2); 31(2); 33:1(7); 2(6); 3(2); 4(5); 5(5); 6(2); 7(5); 8(2); 9; 10(2); 11(3); 12(3); 13(4); 14(2); 15(2); 17(3); 18(2); 19; 20(2); 34:1; 2(3); 3(3); 4; 5(2); 6; 7(3); 8; 9(3); 10(4); 11(3); 12(2); 13(3); 14; 16(3); 17; 18(2); 19(2); 20(3); 21(2); 23(3); 24(3); 25(4); 26(4); 27; 28(4); 29(4); 30(7); 31; 35:1(3); 2(3); 3(4); 4(3); 5(3); 6; 7(2); 8(2); 9(2); 10(2); 11(4); 12(3); 13; 14(3); 15; 16(4); 17; 18; 19(2); 20; 21(2); 22(3); 23(5); 24; 25(2); 26(2); 27(2); 28(2); 29(6); 36:2; 3; 4(2); 5(3); 6(8); 7; 9; 11(3); 12(2); 13(3); 14(4); 16; 17; 18; 19; 20(3); 21(3); 22(3); 23(4); 24(2); 25(2); 26(4); 27(2); 28; 31; 32(2); 33(2); 34(2); 35(3); 36(2); 37(2); 38(2); 39(4); 40; 37:1; 2(3); 3; 4(2); 5(3); 6; 7(4); 8(3); 9(6); 10(6); 11; 12; 13(3); 14(4); 15(3); 16; 17(3); 18; 19; 20(4); 21(3); 22(2); 23; 24(3); 25(6); 26(2); 27(4); 28(4); 29(3); 30(3); 31(3); 32(3); 33(2); 34(3); 35(3); 36(2); 38:1(2); 2(3); 3(3); 4(3); 5(4); 6; 7(2); 8(3); 9(2); 10; 11(2); 12(4); 13; 14(5); 16(3); 17(2); 18(7); 19(4); 20; 21; 22(3); 23(2); 24(4); 25(3); 26(3); 27; 28(3); 29(2); 30(2); 39:1(2); 2(3); 3(2); 4(4); 5(4); 6(4); 7(2); 8(2); 9; 10; 11(2); 12(4); 13(2); 14(2); 15(4); 16; 17; 18(3); 19; 20(3); 21(2); 22(2); 23; 40:1(2); 2(2); 3; 4(3); 5(2); 6(3); 7; 8(3); 9(2); 10(4); 11(4); 12; 13(2); 14(3); 15; 16; 17(2); 18(2); 19(2); 20(3); 21(2); 41:1(2); 2(3); 3(3); 4(3); 5(4); 6(2); 7(4); 8(5); 10(2); 11(2); 12(3); 13(2); 14(5); 15(3); 16; 17; 18(3); 19(3); 20(2); 21; 22(3); 23(2); 24(2); 25; 26; 27(3); 30(3); 31; 32(2); 33(2); 34(2); 35(3); 36; 37(2); 38; 39(2); 40; 41; 42(4); 43(3); 44(2); 45(3); 46(3); 47; 48(2); 49; 50; 51(2); 52; 53; 54(2); 55(2); 56(4); 57; 42:2(3); 3; 5; 6(4); 7(5); 8; 9(2); 10; 12; 13(3); 14; 16(2); 17; 18(2); 20(2); 21(2); 22(2); 23; 24(6); 25(3); 26(2); 27; 28(4); 29(2); 30; 31; 32; 33(3); 34(2); 35(3); 36(3); 37(2); 38(2); 43:1; 2; 3; 4; 6; 7(3); 8(6); 9; 11(5); 12(2); 13; 14(2); 15(6); 16(3); 17(2); 18(5); 19(2); 20; 21(3); 22; 23(3); 24(4); 25; 26(2); 27(2); 28(3); 29(4); 30(4); 31(4); 32(3); 33(3); 34(4); 44:1(2); 2(3); 3; 4(3); 5; 6(2); 7; 9; 10(2); 11; 12(4); 13(2); 14(3); 15; 16(2); 17(2); 18(2); 20(5); 21; 22; 23; 24; 25(2); 26; 27; 28(3); 29(2); 30; 31; 33; 34; 45:1(2); 2(3); 3(2); 4(3); 6; 7(2); 8(3); 9(2); 10(7); 11(3); 12(2); 13(4); 14(3); 15(2); 16(3); 17(2); 18(5); 19(3); 21(3); 22; 23(4); 24(2); 25(2); 26(3); 27(2); 28(2); 46:1(3); 2(3); 3; 4(2); 5(4); 6(4); 7(3); 8(2); 9(4); 10(6); 11(2); 12(8); 13(4); 14(3); 15(2); 16(5); 17(7); 18; 19; 20(2); 21(7); 23; 24(4); 25; 26; 27(2); 28(2); 29(5); 30; 31(5); 32(4); 33(2); 34; 47:1(7); 2(2); 3(3); 5(2); 6(2); 7(3); 8; 9(4); 10(2); 11(3); 12(3); 13(2); 14(3); 15(3); 16(2); 17(6); 18(2); 19(6); 20; 21; 22; 23(2); 24(5); 25(2); 26; 27(4); 28(2); 29(5); 30(3); 31(3); 48:1(3); 2(4); 3(2); 4(4); 5(3); 6(2); 7(2); 8(2); 9(3); 10(3); 11(2); 12(2); 13(3); 14(3); 15(3); 16(4); 17(2); 18; 19(4); 20(3); 21(2); 22; 49:1(2); 2(2); 3(2); 5; 6; 7(2); 9; 10; 11(2); 12; 13(2); 15(4); 20; 23(2); 24; 25(2); 26; 27; 28(2); 29(2); 31(3); 32; 33(3); 50:1(3); 2(2); 3(3); 4; 5(2); 6(2); 7(3); 8(5); 9(3); 10(4); 11; 12; 13; 14(3); 15(2); 16; 17(3); 18(3); 19; 21(3); 22(4); 23; 24(4); 25(2); 26(3); **Ex** 1:1; 2; 3; 4(2); 5; 6(3); 7(5); 9(2); 10(3); 11(2); 12(2); 13; 14(3); 15(2); 16(2); 17; 18(3); 19(2); 20(2); 21; 22(2); 2:1(2); 2(3); 3(5); 4; 5(3); 6(4); 7; 8(3); 9(5); 10(5); 11(3); 12(4); 13(2); 14(4); 15(2); 16(3); 17(4); 18; 19(3); 20(2); 21(2); 22(2); 23(4); 24(3); 25(2); 3:1(2); 2(4); 3(2); 4(3); 5; 6(2); 7(2); 8(9); 9; 10; 11(2); 12(2); 13(3); 14(2); 15(3); 16(4); 17(7); 18(5); 19; 20(3); 21(2); 22(6); 4:1(2); 2(2); 3(4); 4(5); 5; 6(3); 7(4); 8; 9(3); 10(2); 11; 12(2); 13; 14(4); 15(5); 16(3); 17; 18(6); 19; 20(5); 21; 22; 23(2); 24(2); 25(3); 27(4); 28(2); 29(3); 30(2); 31(4); 5:1(3); 2; 3(2); 4(2); 5(2); 6(2); 7; 8(2); 9; 10(3); 13; 14(3); 15; 16(2); 17; 18; 19; 20(2); 21(3); 22(2); 6:1; 2(2); 3(2); 4; 5(2); 6(4); 7(3); 8(3); 9(2); 10; 12; 13(4); 14(2); 15(6); 16(5); 17; 18(6); 19(2); 20(6); 21(3); 22(3); 23(4); 24(3); 25(2); 26; 27; 28; 30(2); 7:1(2); 2; 3(3); 4(2); 5(2); 6(2); 7(3); 8(2); 9(2); 10(6); 11; 12; 13; 14; 15(2); 16(2); 17; 18(3); 19(6); 20(6); 21(4); 22(2); 23(2); 24; 25; 8:1(2); 2; 3(8); 4(3); 5(3); 6(3); 7(2); 8(4); 9(4); 10(2); 11(4); 12(3); 13(3); 14(2); 15; 16(2); 17(4); 18(2); 19(2); 20(3); 21(5); 22; 23(2); 24(4); 25(3); 26(2); 27; 28; 29(3); 30(2); 31(3); 32; 9:1; 2; 3; 4(3); 5; 6(2); 7(4); 8(3); 9(3); 10(5); 11(2); 12(2); 13(3); 14(2); 15(2); 16(2); 19(5); 20; 21(2); 22(3); 23(5); 24; 25(4); 27(6); 28(3); 29(2); 30; 31(3); 32; 33(5); 34(5); 35; 10:1(2); 2(3); 3(3); 5(3); 6(5); 7; 8(3); 9(4); 10(2); 11(2); 12(2); 13(4); 14(2); 15(3); 16(3); 17; 18(2); 19(2); 21; 22(2); 24(3); 25(2); 26; 27; 28; 29; 11:1(2); 2(3); 3(2); 4; 5(2); 6; 7; 8(5); 9; 10(3); 12:1(2); 4(2); 6(2); 7(3); 8(3); 9; 10(2); 11(3); 12(3); 13(3); 14(2); 16(2); 17; 18; 21(3); 22(5); 23(3); 24(2); 25; 26; 27(3); 28(3); 29(2); 30(4); 31(6); 32(3); 33; 34; 35(4); 36(2); 37; 38(3); 39(2); 40; 41(2); 43(2); 45; 48(5); 49; 50; 51; 13:1; 2; 3; 5(6); 6; 7; 8; 9(2); 11(3); 12; 13(3); 14; 15(2); 16(2); 17(2); 18; 19(2); 20(2); 21(3); 14:1; 2(2); 4(4); 5(4); 6(2); 7(3); 8(3); 9(4); 10(4); 11; 13(2); 14; 15; 16(3); 17(5); 18(2); 19(4); 20(4); 21(4); 22(3); 23(3); 24(3); 25; 26(2); 27(4); 28(4); 29(2); 30; 31(4); 15:1(3); 2(4); 4; 7; 8(2); 14; 16; 17; 18; 19(2); 20(3); 21(2); 22(3); 23; 24; 25(4); 26(4); 27(4); 16:1(3); 2(2); 3(2); 4(2); 5(2); 6(2); 7(2); 8(3); 9; 10(2); 11; 12(2); 13(3); 14; 15(2); 17(2); 18(2); 19; 20(3); 21(2); 22(3); 23(3); 24(2); 25; 27(2); 28(2); 31(3); 32; 33(3); 35; 17:1(3); 2(2); 3(5); 4; 5(4); 6(3); 7(3); 8; 9(2); 10(3); 11(2); 12(7); 13(2); 14(2); 15(2); 18:1(2); 3; 4(2); 5(2); 6(3); 7(5); 8(4); 9; 10(2); 12(4); 13(2); 14(2); 15; 16(4); 17; 18; 19; 20(4); 21(3); 22(3); 23(2); 24; 25(3); 26; 27(2); 19:2(3); 3(3); 4(2); 5; 6(2); 7(3); 8(3); 9(3); 10(4); 11; 12; 14(3); 15; 16(4); 17(2); 18(3); 19(4); 20(3); 21(2); 22; 23(2); 24(4); 25; 20:1; 5; 6(2); 9; 11(4); 12; 18(6); 19(2); 20(2); 21(2); 22; 24(4); 25; 21:2; 4(3); 5(2); 6(2); 7; 9; 10; 11; 13; 15; 16(2); 17; 18(3); 19(2); 20(2); 22(3);

23; 26; 27; 28; 29(3); 32; 33(3); 34(2); 35(3); 36(2); 22:1(2); 2;
5(3); 6; 7; 9; 10; 11(2); 12; 13; 14(2); 16(2); 23; 24(4); 27; 29;
30; 31; 23:5; 7(2); 8(2); 10(2); 11(3); 12(4); 13(2); 15; 16(2); 20;
21; 22(2); 23(6); 24; 25(4); 27(2); 28(2); 29; 30(2); 31(3); 24:1(5);
2; 3(5); 4(4); 5(2); 6(3); 7(4); 8(3); 9(3); 10(3); 11(3); 12(5); 13(3);
14(3); 15(2); 16(3); 17; 18(4); 25:1; 3(3); 4(5); 5(3); 6; 7(2); 8;
9; 10(6); 11(3); 12(4); 13(2); 14; 16; 17(4); 18; 19(2); 20(2);
21(2); 22(2); 23(3); 24(2); 25(2); 26(2); 28(2); 29(4); 30; 31(3);
32(2); 33(3); 34(2); 35(3); 36; 37(2); 38(2); 40; 26:1(3); 2(3); 3;
4(2); 5; 6(3); 7; 8(2); 9(3); 10(2); 11(3); 12; 13(3); 14(2); 15;
16(2); 18; 19(2); 20; 21(2); 22; 23; 24(2); 25(3); 26; 27(2); 28;
29(3); 30; 31(4); 32; 33(3); 34; 35(3); 36(4); 37(4); 27:1(3); 2(2);
3(5); 4(2); 5; 6(2); 7(2); 9; 10(3); 11(4); 12(2); 13; 14; 15(2);
16(6); 17; 18(3); 19(2); 20; 21; 28:1(4); 2(2); 3; 4(7); 5(5); 6(3);
7; 8(4); 9(2); 10; 12(2); 13; 14(2); 15(4); 16; 17(2); 18(2); 19(2);
20(3); 21; 22; 23(2); 24; 25(2); 26(2); 27(2); 28(2); 29; 30(4);
31; 32; 33(4); 34(2); 35(3); 36(3); 37; 38(2); 39(3); 40(4); 41(5);
42; 43(4); 29:1(2); 2(3); 3(3); 4(3); 5(6); 6(2); 7(2); 8(2); 9(6);
10(3); 11; 12(3); 13(5); 14(2); 15(2); 16(3); 17(5); 18; 19(3);
20(6); 21(10); 22(6); 23(3); 24(3); 25(2); 26(3); 27(4); 28(3);
29(2); 30; 31(2); 32(3); 33(2); 34; 35(2); 36(3); 37(2); 39; 40(2);
41(3); 43(2); 44(3); 45(2); 46; 30:1; 2(2); 3(4); 4(2); 5(2); 6; 7;
8; 10; 11; 14; 15; 16(2); 17; 18(4); 19(2); 21(3); 23(4); 24(2); 25;
26(2); 27(5); 28(3); 29; 30(3); 31; 32; 34(3); 35(2); 36(2); 37;
31:1; 3(4); 4(2); 5(2); 6(2); 7(3); 8(4); 9(3); 10(3); 11(2); 12; 13;
17(4); 18; 32:1(2); 2(3); 3(2); 4(3); 5(3); 6(6); 7; 8(3); 9(2); 10(2);
11(3); 12(3); 13(4); 14; 15(4); 16(2); 17; 18; 19(5); 20(5); 21;
22; 24(2); 25; 26(2); 27(6); 28(2); 29; 30(2); 31(3); 32; 33; 35;
33:1(4); 2(5); 3; 4(2); 5; 6; 7(4); 8(3); 9(3); 10(3); 11(2); 12(3);
13; 14(2); 15; 16(2); 17(2); 18; 19(4); 20(2); 21(2); 22(2); 23(2);
34:1(2); 2(3); 3; 4(4); 5(3); 6(5); 7(5); 8(3); 9(4); 10(2); 11(5);
13; 15(4); 16(3); 19; 20(2); 21; 22(2); 24; 27(2); 28(3); 29; 30(3);
31(4); 32(2); 33; 34(2); 35(2); 35:1(2); 4; 5(2); 6(5); 7(3); 8(3);
9(3); 10(2); 11(3); 12(2); 13(3); 14(2); 15(5); 16(2); 17(2); 18(2);
19; 20; 21(5); 22(7); 23(7); 24(2); 25(5); 26; 27(3); 28(4); 29;
30; 31(3); 32(3); 33(2); 34(2); 35(6); 36:1(3); 2(3); 3(2); 4; 5;
6(2); 7; 8(4); 9(2); 10(2); 11; 12; 13(2); 14; 15; 16(2); 17(2); 18;
19(2); 20; 21(2); 23; 24(2); 25; 26(2); 27; 28; 29(2); 30(2); 31;
32(2); 33; 34(3); 35(4); 36(3); 37(4); 38(3); 37:1(6); 2(3); 3(2);
4(2); 5; 6(4); 7; 8; 9(2); 10(4); 11(2); 12; 13(2); 15(2); 16(4);
17(3); 18(2); 19(3); 20(2); 21(3); 22; 23(3); 24; 25(3); 26(3); 27;
28(2); 29(2); 38:1(3); 2(2); 3(5); 4; 5; 6(2); 7; 8(2); 9; 10(2);
11(3); 12(3); 13; 14; 15(3); 17(4); 18(6); 19(4); 20(2); 22; 23(6);
24(3); 25(4); 26(4); 27(2); 28(4); 29(3); 30(4); 31(4); 39:1(4);
2(4); 3(3); 5(4); 6; 7; 8(4); 9; 10(2); 11(2); 12(2); 13(2); 14; 15;
16(3); 17; 18(2); 19(2); 20(2); 21(2); 22; 23; 24(4); 25(2); 26(2);
27(2); 28(3); 29(4); 30(2); 31; 32; 33(4); 34(3); 35(2); 36(2);
37(2); 38(4); 39(3); 40(4); 41(2); 43(3); 40:1; 3(2); 4(4); 5(2); 6;
7(3); 8(2); 9(6); 10(4); 11(3); 12(3); 13(3); 14(2); 15; 17; 18(5);
19(2); 20(4); 21(3); 22; 23; 24; 25; 26; 27; 28; 29(3); 30(3); 31(4);
32; 33(3); 34; 35(2); 36; 38; **Lev** 1:1(2); 2(2); 4(2); 5(3); 6(2);
7(2); 8(2); 9(2); 10; 11(2); 12(3); 13(3); 14; 15(4); 16(2); 17(2);
2:1(3); 2(4); 3(2); 4; 5; 6; 7; 8(2); 9(2); 10(2); 13; 14; 15(2);
16(2); 3:1; 2(3); 3(2); 4(3); 5; 6; 8(3); 9(4); 10(3); 11; 12; 13(3);
14(2); 15(3); 16; 4:1; 2; 4(3); 5(2); 6(2); 7(2); 8(2); 9(3); 10;
11(5); 12; 13(4); 14; 15(2); 16; 17(2); 18(2); 19(2); 20(3); 21(2);
22(2); 24(2); 25(3); 26(3); 27(2); 29(2); 30(3); 31(4); 32; 33(2);
34(3); 35(4); 5:1(3); 2(2); 3; 4; 5; 6(2); 7(2); 8(2); 9(2); 10(3);
12(2); 13(3); 14; 15; 16(5); 17(3); 18(4); 6:1; 2(2); 3(2); 4; 5(2);
6; 7(2); 8; 9(2); 10(4); 11(3); 12(4); 14; 15(4); 16(2); 17; 19;
20(2); 21(2); 22; 24; 25; 27; 28(2); 30; 7:2; 3(2); 4(3); 5; 8; 9(3);
10(2); 11; 12(2); 14(2); 15; 16; 18(2); 19(2); 21; 22; 24(2); 28;
31(2); 32; 33; 34(3); 35; 37(4); 8:1; 2(6); 3; 4(2); 5; 6(3); 7(6);
8(2); 9; 10(4); 11(4); 12(2); 13(4); 14(3); 15(6); 16(5); 17(2);
18(3); 19(2); 20(4); 21(4); 22(3); 23(5); 24(5); 25(7); 26(5); 27(3);
28(2); 29(2); 30(10); 31(4); 32(2); 33; 35(2); 36; 9:1(3); 2(3);
3(3); 4(2); 5(3); 6(2); 7(7); 8; 9(4); 10(2); 11(2); 12(2); 13(3);
14(3); 15(4); 16(2); 17(3); 18(2); 19(5); 20(2); 21(2); 22(5); 23(5);
24(4); 10:1(5); 2(3); 3(2); 4(4); 5; 6(4); 7(2); 8; 10(4); 11; 12(4);
13(2); 14(5); 15(3); 16(4); 17; 19(4); 20; 11:1(2); 3(2); 5; 6; 7(2);
8; 9(2); 10(4); 13(3); 14(2); 16(4); 17(3); 18(3); 19(3); 22(3); 24;
25(2); 26; 27; 28(2); 29(2); 30(5); 32(2); 33(2); 34; 35(2); 37;
38; 39; 40(3); 41; 42; 44; 46(3); 47(3); 12:1; 2; 3; 4(2); 5(2);
6(2); 7(2); 8(4); 13:1(2); 2; 3(5); 4(2); 5(3); 6(5); 8; 10(4); 11(2);
12(2); 13; 15(2); 16; 17(2); 18; 19(3); 20(2); 21(2); 22; 23(2);
24; 25(2); 26(2); 27(2); 28(3); 30(2); 31(3); 32(4); 33; 34(4); 36;
37(2); 39; 40; 41; 42; 43; 45(4); 49(2); 50(2); 51; 53(2); 54;
55(3); 56(2); 57; 58(2); 14:1; 3(3); 4(4); 5; 6(5); 7(3); 8(5); 9(4);
10(4); 11(2); 12(4); 13(2); 14(4); 15(2); 16(2); 17(3); 18(2); 19(3);
20(4); 21(4); 22(3); 23; 24(3); 25(5); 26; 27; 28(3); 29; 30; 31(2);
33(2); 34; 35(2); 36; 37(2); 38; 39(3); 40; 41(2); 42(4); 43(4);
44(2); 45(4); 47(2); 48(3); 49(4); 50; 51(7); 52(6); 53(2); 54;
55(2); 56(3); 57; 15:1(2); 2; 3; 4; 5(3); 6(3); 7(3); 8(3); 9; 10(4);
11(4); 12(2); 13(4); 14(3); 15(3); 16(2); 17(3); 18; 19(3); 20;
21(3); 22(3); 23; 24(3); 25; 26; 27(4); 28; 29(2); 30(3); 32(2);
33(4); 16:1(2); 2; 3; 4(4); 5(2); 6(3); 7(2); 8(2); 9(2); 10; 11(4);
12(3); 13; 14(3); 15(4); 16(3); 17(4); 18(5); 19(3); 20(3); 21(4);
22(2); 23(3); 24(7); 25; 26(3); 27(5); 28(3); 29(2); 31; 32(3);
33(5); 34(2); 17:1; 2(3); 4(2); 5; 6(2); 7; 8; 9; 10(2); 11; 13(3);
15(3); 18:1; 2; 3; 4; 5; 17; 21; 25(2); 26(2); 27; 30; 19:1; 2; 3(2);
5; 6(2); 7; 8; 9; 10(2); 12; 16; 17; 19; 20(2); 21; 22(2); 23(2); 25;
29; 30; 32(2); 33; 34; 36; 37(2); 20:1; 3(3); 4(2); 5(3); 6(3); 7;
8(2); 10(2); 11; 12; 14(3); 15(2); 16(3); 17(4); 18(4); 19; 20; 21;
22(2); 23(2); 24(2); 25(4); 26(2); 21:1(2); 2(4); 3; 6(2); 9; 10(2);
13; 16; 22; 24(3); 22:1; 2(2); 4; 6; 7(2); 9; 11; 13(2); 14(2); 15;
17; 18(4); 21; 25; 26; 27(2); 28(2); 29; 31; 23:1; 2; 6; 9; 10(2);
11; 12; 13(2); 14; 15; 16; 18(4); 19; 20; 21; 22(2); 23; 26; 27(2);
28; 30; 32; 33; 36(2); 37(2); 38(3); 39; 40(4); 41; 44; 24:1; 5(2);
6; 7; 9(3); 10(3); 11(4); 12; 13; 14(2); 15; 16(2); 17; 18; 19;
21(2); 23(3); 25:1; 2; 3(2); 6(5); 7(2); 8(3); 10(4); 14; 15; 16;
18(3); 19(3); 20; 21; 22(2); 23; 24; 25(2); 26(2); 27; 28(2); 29;
30; 31; 32; 33(2); 35(2); 38; 39(2); 40(2); 41(4); 44(2); 45(2);
46; 47(3); 50(2); 52(2); 53(2); 54(2); 26:2; 3(2); 4(2); 5(4); 6(4);
7(2); 8(3); 9(3); 10(2); 11(2); 12(3); 13(2); 14; 15; 16(3); 17(3);
18; 19(3); 20; 21(2); 22(3); 23; 24; 25(3); 26(4); 27; 28; 29(2);
30(4); 31(3); 32(2); 33(4); 34(2); 36(4); 37(2); 38(2); 39(2); 40(2);
41(3); 42(3); 43(3); 44(2); 46(3); 27:1; 2; 3; 4; 5(2); 6(2); 7(3);
8; 9; 10(2); 11; 12; 14; 15(2); 16; 18; 19(2); 20; 22; 23; 25; 27(2);
28(2); 30; 31; 32; 33(2); **Num** 1:1; 3(2); 4; 5; 17(2); 18(3); 20(2);
21(2); 22; 23(2); 24; 25(2); 26; 27(2); 28; 29(2); 30; 31(2); 32;
33; 34; 35(2); 36; 37(2); 38; 39(2); 40; 41(2); 42; 43(2); 44(2);
45; 46(3); 50(5); 51(3); 52(2); 53; 54; 2:1(2); 3(2); 4(4); 5(2);
6(4); 7; 8(4); 9(3); 10; 11(4); 12(2); 13(4); 14; 15(5); 16(5); 18;
19(3); 20(2); 21(4); 22; 23(4); 24(3); 25; 26(4); 27(2); 28(4); 29;
30(4); 31(3); 32(3); 34(2); 3:1; 2(3); 4(5); 5; 6; 7(2); 8(2); 9(2);
10(4); 11; 12; 13; 14; 15; 16; 17(3); 18(2); 19(3); 20(2); 21;
22(2); 24; 25(3); 26(4); 27(4); 28(2); 30; 31(7); 32(2); 33; 34(3);
35; 36(7); 37(4); 38(3); 39(3); 40(3); 41(2); 42; 43(5); 44; 45(2);
46(3); 48(2); 49(2); 50(2); 51(2); 4:1(2); 3; 5(4); 6(3); 7(6); 8(3);
9(6); 10(3); 11(3); 12(4); 13(2); 14(5); 15(3); 16(7); 17(2); 19(4);
21; 23; 24; 25(4); 26(6); 27(3); 28; 30; 31(4); 32(6); 34(4); 35;
36(2); 37; 38(2); 39; 40(2); 41; 42; 43; 44; 45; 46(3); 47(2);
48(2); 49; 5:1; 2(2); 3; 4(2); 5; 6; 7(3); 9; 10; 11; 12(2); 13(5);
14(5); 15; 16(2); 17(3); 18(4); 19(3); 20(2); 21(3); 22(3); 23(2);
24(3); 25(2); 26(3); 27(3); 28(2); 29; 30(3); 31; 6:1; 2; 3(2); 5;
9(2); 10; 11(4); 12(2); 13; 14(3); 15(4); 16(3); 17(2); 18(3); 19(4);
20(3); 21; 22; 23; 24; 25; 26; 27(2); 7:1(7); 2; 3(4); 4; 5; 6(3); 7;
8(2); 10; 11; 12; 13(2); 17; 19; 23; 25; 29; 31; 35; 37; 41; 43;
47; 49; 53; 55; 59; 61; 65; 67; 71; 73; 77; 79; 83; 85(2); 86; 87;
88(2); 89(2); 8:1; 2; 3; 4; 5; 6; 7(4); 8; 9(2); 10(2); 11; 12(3);
13(3); 14; 15(3); 17; 18; 19(3); 20(3); 21(4); 22(2); 23; 24(2);
25(2); 26; 9:1; 3; 4; 5; 6(3); 7; 8(2); 9; 11(2); 13(2); 14(4); 15(2);
16; 17(2); 18; 19(2); 20(2); 21(2); 22; 23; 10:1; 2; 3; 4; 8(2);
9(3); 10(3); 11; 12(2); 13; 14; 15; 16; 17(3); 18(2); 19; 20;
21(2); 22(2); 23; 24; 25(2); 26; 27; 29(2); 30(2); 31(2); 32; 33(2);
34; 35(3); 36; 11:1(5); 2(2); 3; 4(3); 5(4); 7(2); 8(6); 9; 10; 11(2);
15(2); 16(3); 17(5); 18(3); 20(2); 21(2); 22; 23; 24(4); 25(6);
26(4); 27(4); 28(2); 29(2); 30(2); 31(5); 32(5); 33(2); 34; 35(2);
12:1(2); 2(2); 4(4); 5(5); 6(2); 8(2); 9(2); 10(4); 11(2); 13; 14(2);
15(2); 16(2); 13:1; 3; 4; 16; 17(3); 18(2); 19(2); 20(3); 21; 22(3);
23(5); 25; 26(7); 27(5); 28(3); 29(5); 30(3); 32(2); 33(3);
14:1(3); 2(3); 3(2); 4(2); 5; 6(2); 7; 8(2); 9; 10; 11(2); 12(3);
13; 14(4); 17; 18(4); 19; 20; 22(4); 24(2); 25(2); 26(2); 29(2);
30; 31; 33(2); 34; 35; 36(2); 38; 39(2); 40(3); 41; 43(2); 44;
45(3); 15:1; 2; 3; 5; 7; 8; 10; 14(2); 15; 16(2); 17; 18; 22(2); 23;
24(2); 25(4); 26(2); 27; 28(2); 29; 30; 31; 32; 33(3); 34; 35;
36(3); 37; 38(2); 39(5); 40(2); 16:1(3); 2(2); 3(4); 4; 5(4); 6; 7(3);
8; 9; 10(3); 11(2); 12(2); 13; 14(2); 15(2); 16(4); 17(5); 18(5);
19(2); 20(2); 22(3); 23; 24; 25(4); 26(2); 27(7); 28; 30(3); 31;
32(5); 33(3); 34; 35(3); 36; 37; 38; 39(2); 40; 41; 42(4); 43(2);
44; 45; 46(5); 47(5); 48(3); 49; 50(2); 17:1; 2; 3; 4; 5(2); 6(3); 7;
8(5); 9(3); 10(2); 11; 12; 18:1(5); 2(3); 3(3); 4(3); 5(2); 6; 7(4);
8(2); 9(3); 11(3); 12(2); 13; 15; 16; 17; 18(2); 19(3); 20(2); 21;
22; 23; 25; 26; 27(2); 28; 30; 31(2); 32; 19:1(2); 2; 3(2); 4(2); 5(3);
6(4); 7(3); 8(3); 9(3); 10(4); 12; 13(2); 14; 15; 16; 17(2); 18(6);
19(6); 20; 21(2); 22(2); 20:1(3); 2(3); 3(2); 4(2); 5; 6(4); 7; 8(6);
9; 10(3); 11(5); 12(2); 13; 14; 15(3); 16(4); 18; 19(3); 20(3);
22(2); 23(2); 25(2); 26(4); 27(2); 28(5); 29; 21:1(2); 2(2); 3(5);
4(2); 5(3); 6(3); 7(3); 8(3); 9(3); 10(2); 11(2); 12; 13(2); 14; 15(2);
16(2); 18; 19(2); 20; 21; 23(4); 24(2); 25(3); 26; 27; 28; 29; 30;
32(3); 33(4); 34(4); 35(3); 22:1(2); 2; 3(2); 4(2); 5; 6(2); 7(4);
8(3); 9(2); 10; 11; 12; 13(2); 14(3); 15(2); 16(2); 17; 18(3); 20(3);
21(3); 22(3); 23(5); 24; 25(3); 26(2); 27(3); 28(2); 29; 30(2);
31(4); 32; 33(3); 34; 35; 36; 37; 38; 39(2); 40(4); 41(2); 23:1(3);
2(4); 3(4); 4(4); 5(3); 6(3); 7(3); 9(2); 10(2); 11(2); 12(2); 13(3);
14(4); 15; 16(4); 17(3); 18(3); 19(2); 20(2); 21; 23; 24(2); 25;
26; 27; 28; 29(3); 30(3); 24:1; 2(3); 3(3); 5; 6; 7(3); 8(2); 9(2);
10(4); 12; 13; 14(2); 15(3); 16; 17(3); 18(2); 19; 20(2); 21(4);
23(2); 24(4); 25(4); 25:1(2); 2(3); 3(2); 4(2); 5; 6(3); 7(2); 8(3);
9(2); 10; 13(3); 15(2); 16; 17; 18; 26:1(2); 2; 3(2); 4(2); 7(4); 8;
9(5); 10(4); 14(2); 18; 19(3); 20; 21; 22(2); 25(2); 27; 28; 29;
31(2); 32(2); 33(4); 34(3); 36; 37(2); 40(3); 41(3); 43(2); 46;
47(2); 50(3); 51(2); 52; 54; 56; 57; 58; 59(4); 60(3); 61(2); 62(3);
63; 64; 65(2); 27:1(4); 2(4); 3(2); 5; 6; 7; 8(2); 9; 10; 11(3); 12(2);
13; 15; 17(3); 18(2); 19(3); 20; 21(3); 22(4); 23(2); 28:1; 2(2); 3;
4; 5; 7; 8(2); 9(3); 10; 11(2); 12(2); 13; 14(3); 15(2); 16; 17;
19(2); 20(2); 22; 24; 25; 28; 30; 31(2); 29:1; 2(2); 3(2); 4; 5;
6(4); 7(2); 8; 9(2); 11(3); 12(2); 13(2); 14; 15; 16(2); 17; 18(3);
19(3); 20; 21(3); 22(3); 23(2); 24(2); 25(2); 26(2); 27(3); 28(3);
29(2); 30(3); 31(2); 32(2); 33(3); 34(2); 37(2); 38(3); 39(4); 40;
30:1; 3; 4(4); 5; 6; 7(3); 8(2); 9; 10; 11(4); 12; 13; 16(2); 31:1;
3(3); 6(3); 7(2); 8(5); 9(5); 10(2); 11(3); 12(5); 13(3); 14(2); 15;
16; 17; 19(4); 20(4); 21; 22(2); 23(2); 24(3); 25; 26(3); 27(2);
28(4); 29; 30(3); 31(2); 32(3); 33(2); 34(2); 35(2); 36(4); 37(3);
38(3); 39(3); 40(2); 41; 42; 43(3); 44(2); 45(2); 46; 47(2); 48(2);
49(2); 50(2); 51(2); 52(3); 54(4); 32:1(3); 2(4); 3(8); 4; 5; 6(3);
7; 9; 10(2); 11(2); 12; 13(2); 14; 15; 16(3); 17; 20; 21; 22(4); 23;
24(2); 25(2); 26; 28(2); 29(3); 31(2); 33(4); 34(3); 35(3); 36(3);
37(3); 38(4); 39(3); 40(2); 41(3); 42(4); 33:1; 2(2); 3; 5(2); 6(2);
7(3); 8(4); 9(6); 10(2); 11(2); 12(2); 13(2); 14(2); 15(2); 16(2);
17(2); 18(2); 19(2); 20(2); 21(2); 22(2); 23(2); 24(2); 25(2); 26(2);
27(2); 28(2); 29(2); 30(2); 31(2); 32(2); 33(2); 34(2); 35(2);
36(2); 37(2); 38(2); 39(3); 40; 41(2); 42(2); 43(2); 44(2); 45(2);
46(2); 47(2); 48(2); 49; 50; 51; 52(3); 53(2); 54(3); 55(2); 34:1;
2; 3; 4(5); 5(2); 6; 7; 8; 9(2); 10; 11(3); 12(2); 13(2); 14(2); 15;
16; 17; 18; 19; 20; 22; 24; 25; 26; 27; 28; 35:1; 2; 3(4); 4(2);
5(5); 6(3); 7; 8; 9; 10; 12; 13; 14; 15(2); 16; 17(2); 18; 23(2); 24;
25(3); 27(2); 32; 33; 36:1(3); 2(2); 3(2); 4; 5; 8; 11(3); 12(2); 13;
Deut 1:1(4); 3; 4; 7(7); 8(3); 9; 10; 11; 12(2); 13(3); 14(2); 15(6);
16(4); 17(2); 18; 19(3); 20; 21; 22(5); 23(2); 24(4); 25(4); 27(2);
28(3); 31; 33; 34(3); 36(2); 39(4); 40; 41(3); 42; 43(2); 44(3);
45(2); 2:1(2); 2; 4(2); 6; 8(3); 9; 10(2); 12; 13(2); 14(2); 16; 19;
20; 21(4); 22(2); 23(2); 24(3); 25(3); 26; 28; 29; 30; 31(2); 32;
33(4); 34(4); 35; 36; 3:1(3); 2(4); 3(2); 4; 5; 6(2); 7; 8; 9; 10(3);
11; 12(4); 13(2); 14(2); 15; 16(3); 17(2); 18; 19(2); 20(2); 21;
23; 24(2); 25(2); 26(2); 27(5); 28(3); 4:1(3); 5; 6(4); 8(2); 9(3);
10(2); 11(4); 12; 13(2); 14(2); 16; 19(5); 20; 21(2); 22; 23; 25(5);
26; 27(2); 28(2); 29; 30(2); 32; 33; 34(6); 36(2); 37(2); 38; 39(2);
40(3); 42(2); 43(2); 44; 45(2); 46; 47(2); 49; 5:1(5); 5(2); 9; 10(2);
13; 14; 15(3); 16(2); 22(4); 23(2); 24(4); 26; 27(4); 28(2); 29(2);
31(3); 33(2); 6:1; 2(4); 3(3); 5(3); 6; 7(5); 8(2); 9(2); 10(3); 11(4);
13(2); 15; 17(2); 18(4); 20(3); 21; 22(4); 23; 24; 25; 7:1(8); 2(2);
4; 5(3); 8(2); 9(2); 10; 11(2); 12(3); 13(7); 15(2); 16; 18; 19(4);
20; 21; 22(2); 23; 24(2); 26; 8:1(3); 2(2); 3(3); 6; 7(2); 8(5); 9;
10; 11(2); 12(3); 13(5); 14; 15(3); 16; 17(2); 19(4); 9:1(2); 2(2);
3(2); 5(2); 7; 9; 10(2); 11(2); 12; 13; 14(3); 15(3); 16(3); 17(3);
18(2); 19; 20(2); 21(5); 22(3); 23(2); 25; 26(2); 27; 28; 29(2);
10:1(2); 2(2); 3(3); 4(2); 5(4); 6(3); 7; 8; 10(4); 11(2); 12(4); 13;
14; 15; 16; 17(2); 18(3); 20(2); 21(2); 22(2); 11:1(4); 2(3); 3(3);
4(3); 5; 6(6); 8(2); 9(3); 10; 11(2); 13(3); 14(3); 15(2); 16(3);
17(4); 18(2); 19(3); 20(2); 21; 22; 23(2); 24; 25; 26; 28; 29(2);
31(2); 32(2); 12:1; 2(2); 3(5); 5; 6(8); 7(3); 9; 10(2); 11(3); 12(6);
14; 15(3); 18(6); 20; 21(2); 22(2); 23; 25; 26(2); 27(4); 28(3);
29(2); 30; 31; 13:1; 2(2); 3; 4(5); 5(2); 6; 9; 10; 11(3); 13(2);
14(4); 15(2); 16(4); 17(4); 14:2; 4; 5(6); 6(3); 7(2); 8; 9; 10(2);
12(2); 13(3); 14; 15(4); 16(2); 17(3); 18(4); 19; 23(4); 24; 25(2);
26(4); 27; 28; 29(6); 15:2; 6(2); 8; 9(4); 10(2); 11; 12(2); 13;
14(2); 15(2); 16(2); 17(3); 18; 19; 20; 21; 22(2); 16:1; 2; 4; 7(4);
8; 10; 11(9); 12(3); 13; 14(8); 15; 16(3); 18(2); 19; 20; 17:3(3);
4(5); 5; 7; 8(5); 9(4); 10(2); 11; 12(3); 13(3); 14(3); 17; 18; 19(3);
20(2); 18:1(2); 3(4); 4(2); 5; 6(2); 12; 14; 17; 18(2); 19; 21;
19:1(3); 3; 4; 5(4); 6(2); 8(2); 9; 10; 11(4); 12(2); 17; 18(3); 20(3);
21; 20:1(3); 2(2); 3(2); 5(4); 6(4); 7(4); 8(4); 9; 11(3); 12; 13;
14(4); 17(3); 19; 20(2); 21:1; 2(2); 3(2); 4(2); 5(4); 6; 7(2); 8(2);
10(2); 11(2); 12(2); 13(7); 14; 15(4); 18(2); 19(3); 20(3); 21(3);
22(3); 22:1; 2(3); 3(3); 4; 6; 7(2); 9; 10; 11; 13(2); 14(4); 15(2);
16(2); 17(3); 18(2); 19(3); 20; 21; 22; 23(2); 24(2); 25(2); 26;
27(2); 28(3); 29; 23:4(2); 11; 13(4); 14(2); 21; 23; 24:1(4); 2(2);
3(4); 4; 5; 7(2); 8; 11; 12; 13(2); 14; 15(2); 18; 19(2); 20; 21; 22;
25:1(2); 2(2); 3(2); 5(4); 6; 7(2); 8(3); 9(4); 10; 11(3); 13; 14;
15(2); 16; 18(3); 26:1(3); 2(2); 3(2); 4(2); 5(6); 6(3); 7(4); 8(5);
9(3); 10(3); 11(4); 12(3); 13(3); 14; 15(3); 16(3); 17(5); 18(2);
19(4); 27:1; 2(2); 3(2); 4; 5; 6; 7(3); 8; 9(3); 10(2); 11; 12(5);
13(4); 14(2); 15(3); 16; 17; 18; 19(2); 20; 21; 22; 23; 24; 25; 26;
28:1(2); 2(2); 3; 4(3); 5; 6; 7; 8(2); 9; 10(2); 11(3); 12(3); 13(5);
14; 15(2); 16; 17; 18(2); 19; 20(2); 22(7); 23(2); 24; 25(2); 26(3);
27(3); 28(2); 29(5); 30(3); 31(3); 32(4); 33(3); 35; 36(3); 37(2);
38; 39; 41; 42; 43; 44(2); 45(3); 46(3); 47; 48(4); 51(2); 52(3);
53(3); 54(3); 55; 56(4); 57(3); 58; 59(4); 60; 61; 62; 63(4); 64(3);
65(3); 66(4); 67(2); 68(4); 29:2(4); 3; 4(2); 5(2); 7(3); 8(4); 9; 10;
11; 12; 13(3); 14; 15; 16; 17(4); 18(2); 19; 20(3); 21; 22(2);
23(6); 26(3); 27; 28(4); 29; 30:1(3); 2(4); 3(3); 4; 5(4); 6(3); 7(2);
8(3); 9(3); 10(3); 12(2); 13(2); 14; 15(3); 16(5); 17(2); 18; 19(4);
20(4); 31:1(2); 2(3); 3(3); 4(3); 5; 6; 7(4); 8; 9(3); 10; 12(6);
13(2); 14(5); 15(2); 16(5); 17(5); 18; 19; 20(7); 21(2); 22; 23(4);
24; 26; 27(2); 28(3); 29(2); 30; 32:1(2); 2; 4(2); 5; 6(2); 7(2); 10;
12; 13(2); 14(4); 15(2); 18; 19(2); 20; 21; 22(3); 24(2); 25(2);
27(2); 30(2); 32; 33; 34; 35(2); 36(2); 37; 38(3); 39(3); 40; 41(2);
42(3); 43(3); 44(3); 45; 46; 47; 48; 49; 50(3); 33:1; 2(3); 3;
5(2); 6(2); 7(4); 8(3); 9(2); 10(2); 11(2); 12(3); 13(2); 14(2); 15(2);
16(4); 17(3); 18(2); 19; 20(2); 21(3); 22; 23(3); 24(2); 25(2); 26;
27(3); 28; 29(3); 34:1(2); 2(4); 3(2); 4(2); 6; 7(2); 8(2); 9(3); 10;
11(3); 12(2); **Josh** 1:2; 4(2); 6; 7; 8(2); 9; 11; 12(3); 13; 14(2);
15(2); 16(2); 18(2); 2:1(4); 2; 3; 4(3); 5; 6; 7(2); 8; 9(3); 10(2);
11(2); 12; 13(6); 14(3); 15; 16(3); 17; 18(4); 19(3); 20; 21(4);
22(4); 23(4); 24; 3:1(5); 2; 3(3); 4; 5; 6(4); 7; 8; 9(2); 10(8);
13(2); 14(2); 15(2); 16(4); 17(2); 4:1; 3(3); 5(2); 7; 8(4); 9(2);
10(2); 11(2); 12(3); 14; 15; 18(3); 19(2); 20; 21; 5:1(2); 2; 3(2);
4; 6; 7; 8; 9; 10(2); 11(2); 12; 13(5); 14(4); 15(2); 6:1; 2(3);
3(2); 4(3); 5(4); 6(3); 7(3); 8(3); 9(3); 10; 11(2); 12(2); 13(4);
14(2); 15(2); 16; 17(3); 18(3); 19(3); 20(3); 21(6); 22(2); 23(8);
24(5); 25(4); 26(3); 27; 7:1; 2(5); 3(4); 4; 5(4); 6(4); 7(2); 9(4);
10; 11(4); 13; 14(3); 15(3); 16(2); 17(4); 18(2); 19(3); 20(4);
21(5); 22(3); 23(4); 24(13); 25(3); 26; 8:1(5); 2(4); 3(3); 4; 5(3); 7;
8; 9(3); 10(4); 11(5); 12(3); 13(2); 14(4); 15(3); 16(3); 17(3);
18(2); 19(6); 20(4); 21(4); 22(3); 23(2); 24(3); 25(2); 27; 28(2);
29(4); 31(2); 32; 33(6); 34(2); 35(2); 9:1(5); 2; 3(2); 4(6); 5(5);
6(3); 7(2); 8(3); 9(2); 10(2); 11(3); 12; 13(4); 14(2); 15(3); 16(2);
17(5); 18(2); 21(2); 22(2); 23(3); 24(4); 25(2); 26(2); 27(3);
10:1(5); 2(2); 3(3); 4(2); 5(4); 6(3); 7(2); 8; 9; 10(5); 11(3); 12(2);
13(3); 14; 15(2); 16; 17; 18(2); 19(2); 20(2); 21; 22; 23(3); 24(4);
25(2); 26(4); 27(4); 28(5); 29(2); 30(4); 31(4); 32(3); 33(2); 34(4);
35(3); 36(3); 37(6); 38(3); 39(7); 40(4); 41(2); 42(2); 43(2);
11:1(3); 2(4); 3(7); 4(3); 5(2); 6(2); 7(2); 8(5); 9(2); 10(3);
11(2); 12(4); 14(2); 15; 16(6); 17(3); 20; 21(4); 22; 23(2); 12:1(2);
2(3); 3(3); 4(2); 5(5); 6(4); 7(2); 8(7); 24; 13:1(4); 2; 3(2); 4; 5(2);
6; 7; 8; 9(2); 10; 11(5); 12(2); 13; 15; 16(3); 17(3); 18(3); 19(3);
20(3); 21(6); 23(3); 24; 25(3); 26(3); 27(5); 28; 29(2); 30(2);
31(3); 14:1(3); 2; 3; 4(2); 5; 6(2); 7; 9(2); 10(4); 11; 12(2); 13(2);
15(2); 15:2; 3(6); 4(2); 5(2); 6(3); 7(4); 8(2); 9(3); 10(4); 11(5);
12(2); 13; 14(3); 15(2); 16(2); 17(2); 18(3); 19(2); 21(3); 22(3);
23(3); 24(2); 25(3); 26(2); 27(3); 28(3); 29(2); 30(3); 31(3); 32(5);
33(3); 34(3); 35(2); 36(4); 37(2); 38(3); 39(2); 40(3); 41(3); 42(2);
43(3); 44(3); 45; 47(4); 48(3); 49(2); 50(3); 51(3); 52(2); 53(3);
54(3); 55(2); 56(3); 57; 58; 59(3); 60; 61; 62(3); 16:1; 2(2); 3(3);
4; 5; 6(3); 7(4); 8; 9; 10(2); 17:1; 2(5); 3(3); 4(3); 5(2); 6; 7(2);
9(2); 10(4); 11(13); 14(2); 15(3); 16(4); 17(3); 18(3); 18:1(3); 2;
3; 4(5); 5(2); 6; 7(3); 8(6); 9(4); 10(2); 11(3); 12(4); 13(2); 14(3);
15(3); 16(4); 17(4); 18(2); 19(2); 20; 21(2); 22(3); 23(3); 24(3);
25(2); 26(3); 27(3); 28(3); 19:1(2); 2(2); 3(3); 4(3); 5(3); 6(3);
7(3); 8; 10(2); 11(4); 12(3); 13(2); 14(2); 15(5); 17; 18(3);
19(3); 20(3); 21(4); 22(4); 23; 24; 25(4); 26(5); 27(5); 28(4);
29(4); 30(3); 33(4); 34(5); 35(3); 36(3); 37(3); 38(4); 39; 40;
41(3); 42(3); 43(3); 44(3); 45(3); 46(2); 47(6); 50(2); 51(2);
20:3(2); 4(3); 5(2); 6(4); 7(3); 8(3); 9(2); 21:1(2); 2; 3(2); 4(4);
5(3); 6(4); 7(2); 8; 9(2); 11; 12; 13; 14(2); 15(2); 16(3); 17; 18;
20; 21; 22(2); 23; 25(2); 27(2); 28; 30; 31; 32(3); 34(2); 36(2);
37; 38(2); 41; 43(3); 44(2); 22:1(2); 2(2); 4(3); 5(6); 6(2); 7; 8(6);
9(4); 10(3); 11(3); 12; 13(3); 14(2); 15(4); 18; 19; 20(2); 21(3);
22; 24; 25(2); 27(4); 28; 29; 30(5); 31(3); 32(4); 33(4); 34(2);
23:1(2); 2(7); 3; 5(3); 6; 9; 12(4); 13(3); 14(4); 16(4); 24:1(6);
2(3); 3(4); 4(4); 5(3); 6(4); 7(6); 8(4); 9(3); 11(9); 12; 13(4); 14(5);
15(2); 16(2); 17(4); 18; 19; 20(3); 21; 22(2); 23; 24(2); 25(2);
26(3); 27; 29(2); 30; 31(3); 32(2); 33(2); **Judg** 1:2; 3(2); 4(4);
5(4); 6(4); 7(5); 8(3); 9(3); 10(4); 11(2); 12(2); 13(2); 14(3); 15(3);
16(3); 17(4); 18(2); 19(2); 20(2); 21; 22(2); 23; 24(3); 25(2);
26(3); 27(5); 28(2); 30; 33; 34; 35; 36(2); 2:1(4); 2; 3; 4(2); 5(2);
6; 7(2); 8(2); 9; 10(2); 11(2); 12(4); 13(3); 14(3); 15(2); 17(2);
18(3); 19(3); 20(3); 3:3(3); 4; 5(5); 6(3); 7(4); 8(2); 9; 10(5);
11(2); 12(2); 13(5); 15; 16; 17(2); 18; 19(2); 20(4); 21(3); 22(3);
23(2); 24; 25(4); 26(3); 27(3); 28(4); 29(3); 30; 31(2); 4:1; 2;
3(2); 4; 5(3); 6(6); 7(3); 8; 9(3); 10(4); 11; 12; 13(2); 14(2); 15(4);
16(3); 17; 18(3); 19(4); 20(3); 21(5); 22(5); 24(2); 5:1; 4; 6; 10;
12; 14; 15(2); 17(2); 18; 19; 25; 26(3); 28; 31; 6:1(2); 2(4); 3(3);

4(3); 5(4); 6(2); 7; 8; 9(4); 10; 11(3); 12(2); 13(3); 14(3); 15(2);
16(2); 17; 18(3); 19(6); 20(5); 21(5); 22; 23; 24; 25(3); 26(3);
27(3); 28(3); 29(3); 30; 31; 33(4); 34(2); 35(5); 36; 37(2); 38(3);
39(3); 40(2); 7:1(2); 2; 3(5); 4(4); 5; 6; 7(3); 8(4); 9; 11(2);
12(4); 13(6); 14(3); 15(4); 16(3); 17(3); 18(3); 19(4); 20(6); 21(4);
22(4); 23(4); 24(5); 25(7); 8:1(2); 2; 3(2); 4(3); 5(3); 6(2); 7(3);
8(3); 9; 10(3); 11(3); 12(5); 13; 14(5); 15(4); 16(4); 17(2); 18(2);
19; 20(2); 21(6); 22(2); 23; 24; 25(3); 26(5); 27(4); 28; 29(2);
30(2); 31; 32(2); 33(3); 34; 9:1(3); 2(2); 3(2); 4(3); 5(3); 6(4);
7(5); 8; 9(2); 10(2); 11(2); 12; 13(3); 14; 15(4); 16(4); 17(2);
18(4); 19(3); 20(5); 21(4); 23(2); 24(3); 25(3); 26(3); 27(8); 28(3);
29(3); 30; 31(3); 32(2); 33(4); 34(3); 35(4); 36(2); 37(3); 38;
39(2); 40(4); 41(3); 42(2); 43(7); 44(5); 45(5); 46; 47; 48(8);
49(5); 50(2); 51(5); 52(3); 53(2); 54(4); 55; 57(2); 10:1(2); 2(4);
3(3); 4(2); 5(2); 6(10); 7(3); 8(2); 9(2); 10(2); 11(3); 12(4); 13;
14; 15; 16(3); 17(3); 18(2); 11:1(2); 2(4); 3(3); 4; 5; 6(2); 7(3);
8(3); 9(2); 10; 11(3); 12; 13(2); 14; 15; 16(2); 17(2); 18(4); 19(2);
20(2); 21(3); 22(2); 23; 25; 26(4); 27; 29(4); 30(2); 31; 32; 33(2);
34(4); 35(4); 36; 37(4); 38(4); 39(3); 12:1(4); 2(3); 3(3); 4(3);
5(2); 6(4); 7(2); 8; 9(4); 10; 11(2); 12(2); 13; 14(4); 15(2); 13:1(2);
2(3); 3(4); 4(2); 5(3); 6(2); 7(2); 8(2); 9(2); 10(4); 11(5); 12(2);
13; 15; 16(2); 17; 18; 19(4); 20(3); 21; 22; 23; 24(4); 25(2);
14:1(2); 2(4); 3(2); 4; 5(4); 6(3); 7(3); 8(4); 9(6); 10; 11; 12(3);
13(2); 14(3); 15(2); 16(6); 17(3); 18(3); 19(7); 15:1; 2; 3; 4(5);
5(4); 6(5); 7(2); 8(4); 9(2); 10(2); 11(2); 12(2); 13(4); 14(4); 15(4);
16; 17(2); 18(5); 19(3); 20; 16:1(2); 2(4); 3(8); 4; 5(5); 6(2); 7(2);
8; 9(2); 10(2); 11(2); 12(4); 13(3); 14(5); 15(2); 16(2); 17(3);
18(3); 19(5); 20(5); 21(4); 23; 24(2); 25(4); 26; 27(4); 28(3);
29(3); 30(4); 31(6); 17:1; 2(3); 3(2); 4(4); 5(4); 7(2); 8(2); 9(3);
10(6); 11(2); 12(3); 18:1; 2(4); 3(4); 4(4); 5; 6; 7(6); 8(3); 9(4); 10;
11(2); 12(2); 13(2); 14(4); 15(3); 16; 17(7); 18(4); 19(5); 20(5);
21(4); 22(2); 23(3); 24(5); 25(2); 26(3); 27(6); 28(5); 29; 30(3);
31; 19:1; 2(3); 3(6); 4(4); 5(3); 6(5); 7; 8(4); 9(4); 10(3); 11(4);
12; 13(2); 14(3); 15(3); 16(2); 17(3); 18(3); 19(5); 20; 21(4);
22(2); 23(2); 24(3); 25(4); 26; 27(5); 28(4); 29(4); 30(2); 20:1;
2; 4(3); 5(4); 6(4); 7; 8; 10(3); 12; 13; 15(2); 16; 17; 18(5); 19(2);
20(2); 21(3); 22(2); 23(4); 24; 25(2); 26(7); 27; 28(2); 29; 30(2);
31(5); 32(2); 33(3); 34(2); 35(4); 37(4); 38; 39(2); 40; 41; 42;
43(2); 44; 45(5); 46; 47(2); 48(3); 21:2(4); 3; 4(4); 5; 6(2); 8(2);
9; 10(4); 11(2); 12(2); 13(2); 14(3); 15; 17; 19; 20; 21(4); 22;
23(6); 24(3); **Ruth** 1:1(3); 2(6); 3(3); 4(3); 5(4); 7(2); 8(2); 9(2);
10; 11; 12; 14(3); 15(2); 16(3); 17(3); 19(2); 20; 21(2); 22(2);
2:1(2); 2(3); 3(4); 4(3); 6(2); 7(3); 9(3); 10(2); 11(6); 12; 13;
14(8); 15(2); 16(3); 17(2); 18(5); 19(4); 20(3); 21; 22; 23(2); 3:2;
3(4); 4(5); 5; 6(2); 7(6); 8(3); 9(2); 10; 11; 12; 13; 14(3); 15(4);
16(2); 17; 4:1(4); 2(3); 3; 4(4); 6; 7(3); 9(4); 10; 11(5); 12; 13(3);
14; 15(2); 16(3); 17(2); 19(2); 20(2); 21(2); 22(2); **1Sa** 1:1; 2(3);
3(4); 4(3); 6; 7(2); 8(2); 9; 10(3); 11(5); 12; 14; 15(2); 16; 17(2);
18(3); 19(6); 20; 21(3); 22(2); 23(2); 24(5); 25(2); 26; 27; 28;
2:1(2); 3; 4; 5(2); 6(2); 7(2); 8(3); 9; 10(2); 11(2); 13; 14; 15;
16(3); 19; 20(4); 21(4); 22(2); 23; 26(3); 27(2); 28(2); 29(2);
30(2); 31; 32(2); 33(3); 34(2); 35(4); 36(4); 3:1(2); 2(2); 3(2); 4;
5(5); 6(5); 8(5); 9(2); 10(3); 11; 13; 14; 15(3); 16(2); 17(2); 18(3);
19(3); 20; 21; 4:1(3); 2(3); 3; 4(2); 5; 6(2); 7(2); 9(2); 10(4);
11(3); 12(3); 13(3); 14(3); 15(2); 16(3); 17(6); 18(5); 19(5); 20;
21(3); 22; 5:1(2); 2; 3(3); 4(3); 6(3); 7(2); 8(4); 9(4); 10(2); 11(4);
12(2); 6:1; 2(2); 3(2); 4(2); 5(4); 6(2); 7(3); 8(4); 9; 10(4); 11(3);
12(4); 13(4); 14(4); 15(5); 16; 17; 18(2); 19(4); 20(2); 21(2);
7:1(4); 2(2); 3(5); 4(2); 5(2); 6(6); 7(2); 8; 9(4); 10(3); 11(3);
12(3); 13(2); 14(4); 15; 16(4); 17(3); 8:1; 2; 3(3); 4; 5(2); 6; 7;
8; 9; 10; 11(4); 12(6); 13(3); 14(4); 15(4); 16(5); 17; 18(2); 19;
20(3); 21(2); 22(3); 9:2(4); 3(3); 4(4); 5(3); 6(2); 7; 8(2); 9; 11(2);
12(2); 13; 14(2); 16; 17; 18; 19(4); 20(3); 21(3); 22(4); 23; 24(5);
25; 26(5); 27(2); 10:1(3); 2(3); 3(4); 4(2); 5(5); 6(3); 7; 8(4); 9(2);
10(3); 11; 12(2); 13; 14(4); 15; 16; 17; 18(4); 19(4); 20; 21(2);
22; 23(4); 24(3); 25(3); 26(2); 27(2); 11:1(3); 2(2); 3(2); 4(3);
5(3); 6(2); 7(6); 8(2); 9(4); 10; 11(4); 12; 13; 14(2); 15(5); 12:1(2);
2(5); 3(2); 4; 5(3); 6(3); 7; 8(3); 9(4); 10(5); 11(6); 12; 13(2);
14(4); 16; 17(3); 18(4); 19; 20; 21; 23; 24; 25; 13:1; 2(3); 3(3);
4(3); 5(5); 6(4); 7(3); 8(2); 9(3); 10(2); 11(4); 12(2); 13; 14;
15(3); 16(3); 17; 18(2); 20(3); 21(4); 22(2); 23; 14:1; 2(2); 3(2);
4(4); 5; 6(2); 7; 8; 9; 10; 11(2); 12(5); 13(5); 14(2); 15(4); 16(3);
17(3); 18; 19(3); 20(5); 21; 23; 24; 25(2); 26; 27(3); 28(2); 31(2);
32(6); 33; 34(8); 35; 36(4); 37; 38(3); 40(3); 41(2); 42(3); 43(3);
44(2); 45; 46; 47(6); 48(3); 49(4); 50(2); 51(2); 52(2); 15:3(7);
4(3); 5(2); 6; 7; 8(2); 9(8); 11(3); 12(5); 13(2); 14(2); 15(3); 16(2);
17(2); 18(4); 19; 20(4); 21; 22(3); 23(2); 24(3); 25; 26(2); 27(2);
28(2); 29; 30(2); 31; 32(2); 33(2); 34; 35(2); 16:1(2); 2(3); 3(3);
4(4); 5(5); 6(2); 8(2); 9; 10; 11(5); 12(5); 13(3); 14; 15; 16(2);
17(2); 18(6); 19; 20(4); 21(4); 22; 23(4); 17:1(3); 2(4); 3(3); 4(2);
5(3); 6(2); 7(3); 8(5); 9(3); 10; 11(2); 12(2); 13(5); 14(2); 15;
16(3); 17(3); 18(3); 19(2); 20(6); 21; 22(4); 23(3); 24(2); 25(4);
26(2); 27; 28(5); 29; 30(3); 31(2); 32(2); 33(2); 34(4); 35(6);
36(2); 37(3); 38(2); 39(4); 40(5); 41(3); 42(4); 43(2); 44(3); 45(2);
46(4); 47(3); 48(4); 49(5); 50(3); 51(6); 52(7); 53(2); 54(2); 55(2);
56; 57(2); 58(2); 18:1(2); 2(2); 3; 4(5); 5(5); 6(3); 7(3); 8(5);
9(2); 10(4); 11(2); 12(2); 13(3); 14(2); 16(2); 17(2); 18(2); 20(3);
21(2); 22(3); 23(3); 24; 25; 26(2); 27(6); 28(3); 29(2); 30; 19:1(2);
2(3); 3(4); 4(3); 5(3); 6(2); 7(4); 8(5); 9(2); 10(4); 11(2); 12(3);
13(4); 14; 15; 16; 17(3); 18(6); 19; 20(4); 21(4); 22(5); 23(4);
24(4); 20:1(4); 2(2); 3(5); 5(2); 9; 11(3); 12(4); 13(3); 14; 17; 18;
19(3); 20; 21(2); 23(3); 24; 25(4); 27(2); 28; 29(4); 30(2); 31;
32(2); 33; 34; 35(2); 36(2); 37(2); 38(3); 39; 40(2); 41(5); 42(7);
21:1(3); 2(5); 4(2); 5(4); 7; 8(2); 9(2); 10(3); 11(2); 12(2); 13(4);
22:1(3); 2(5); 3(4); 4(2); 5(3); 6(2); 7(3); 8(2); 9; 10(3); 11(2);
12(2); 13(4); 14(4); 16(2); 17(4); 18(6); 19(6); 20(2); 21; 22;
23:1; 2(4); 3; 4(2); 5(4); 6; 7(3); 8(2); 9(2); 11; 12(2); 13(5);
14(3); 15(2); 16(3); 17(4); 18(3); 20; 21; 22(3); 23(4); 24(3);
25(4); 26(6); 27; 28; 29(2); 24:1; 2(2); 3(4); 4(2); 5; 6; 7(2); 8(4);
9; 10(2); 11(3); 12(2); 15(5); 16(3); 17; 18; 20(2); 21; 22(3);
25:1(6); 2(5); 3(5); 4; 5(4); 6(3); 7; 8(2); 9(2); 10(3); 11(3); 12(3);
13(5); 14; 15; 16; 17(2); 18(7); 19; 20(4); 21; 22; 23(4); 24(4);
25; 26(3); 27; 28; 29(2); 30(2); 32; 33(3); 34; 35(2); 36(3); 37(2);
38; 39(4); 40; 41(3); 42(5); 43; 26:1; 2; 3(2); 4; 5(6); 6(3); 7(4);
8; 9(2); 10; 11(2); 12(3); 13; 14(3); 15(2); 16(2); 17(3); 18; 21;
22(4); 23; 24(2); 25(2); 27:1(2); 2(2); 3(3); 4(2); 5; 7(2); 8(5);
9(9); 10(4); 11(2); 12; 28:1(3); 2(2); 3(4); 4(5); 5(2); 6; 7(2); 8(7);
9(2); 10; 11; 12(2); 13(2); 14(6); 15(4); 16; 17(2); 19(2); 20(2);
21(5); 22(2); 23(3); 24(6); 25(4); 29:1; 2(3); 3(2); 4(3); 5; 6(3);
7; 8(2); 9(2); 10(2); 11(2); 30:1(5); 2(2); 3(5); 4(2); 5(2); 6(2);
7(2); 8(3); 9(2); 10; 11(5); 12(4); 13(4); 14(3); 15(3); 16(4); 17(3);
18(2); 19; 20(3); 21(4); 22(4); 23; 25(2); 26; 27(2); 28(3); 29(3);
30(3); 31(3); 31:1(2); 2(5); 3(3); 4(4); 5(2); 6(3); 7(7); 8(2); 9(4);
10(2); 11; 12(5); 13(3); **2Sa** 1:1; 2(3); 3(2); 4(6); 5(2); 6(3); 7(3);
8(2); 9; 10(4); 11(2); 12(6); 13(2); 14; 15(4); 16; 17(2); 22; 23(3);
27; 2:1(4); 2(2); 3(2); 4(3); 5(3); 6(3); 7(2); 8; 9(6); 10; 11(2);
12(2); 13(5); 14(3); 15(2); 16(2); 17(3); 18(4); 19(2); 20(2); 21(3);
22; 23(4); 24(2); 25(3); 26; 27; 28(2); 29(5); 30(3); 31(2); 32(5);
3:1(4); 2(2); 3(2); 4(2); 5; 6(2); 7(2); 8(3); 9; 10(2); 11; 12(2);
13; 14; 15(2); 16(2); 17; 18; 19(3); 20(3); 21(6); 22(4); 23(3);
24(2); 25(3); 26; 27(2); 28(2); 29(2); 30; 31(5); 32(4); 33(2); 34;
35(2); 36(2); 37; 38(2); 39(2); 4:1(2); 2(2); 3(2); 4(7); 5(3); 6(4);
7(5); 8(4); 9(3); 10; 11; 12(6); 5:1(2); 2(3); 3(2); 4; 5(4); 6(3);
8(6); 9(3); 10(3); 11(5); 12(2); 13(4); 14(4); 15(3); 16(3); 17(2);
18; 19(2); 20(3); 21(3); 22(2); 23(2); 24; 25(2); 6:2(2); 3(4); 4(2);
5(6); 6(2); 7(3); 8(2); 9(2); 11(3); 12(3); 13(2); 14(2); 15(2); 16(4);
17(4); 18(2); 19(3); 20(2); 21(2); 22(3); 7:1(2); 3; 4; 5; 6; 9(3);
10(2); 11(2); 12(3); 13; 14(2); 16(2); 17; 18(3); 19(2); 20; 21;
23(5); 24; 25(3); 26(2); 28(3); 29; 8:1(3); 2(5); 4(4); 5(2); 6(3);
7(2); 8(2); 10(5); 11; 12(5); 13; 14(3); 15(3); 16(2); 17(3); 18(3);
9:1; 2(3); 3(2); 4(2); 5; 6(3); 7(3); 8(2); 9(2); 10(4); 12(2); 13;
10:1(2); 2(2); 3(3); 4(3); 5(2); 6(5); 7(2); 8(6); 9(2); 10; 11(2);
12(3); 13(3); 14(3); 15; 16(4); 17(5); 18(4); 19(2); 11:1(5); 2(4);
3(3); 4(5); 5(4); 6(2); 7(3); 8(4); 9; 10; 11(8); 12(3); 13(4); 14(2);
15(3); 16; 17(4); 18; 19; 20(2); 22(2); 23(3); 24(3); 25(2); 26;
27(4); 12:1(4); 2; 3(6); 4(4); 5(2); 6(2); 7(2); 8(6); 9(2); 10; 11(3);
12; 13(2); 15(3); 16(3); 17(2); 18(3); 19; 20(7); 21(2); 22(2);
24(6); 25(2); 26(2); 27(3); 28(3); 29(4); 30(3); 31(7); 13:1(2);
2(2); 3; 4(2); 5(6); 6(3); 7; 8(5); 9(4); 10(3); 11(2); 12; 13(2); 14;
15; 16; 17(2); 18(2); 19(4); 20; 22; 23(2); 24(3); 25(2); 26; 27;
28(2); 29(3); 30(2); 31(3); 32(2); 34(3); 35; 36(5); 37(2); 38(2);
39; 14:2(5); 3(2); 4(3); 5(3); 6(4); 7(5); 8(2); 9(4); 10(2); 11; 12;
13; 14; 15; 16; 17; 18(2); 19(4); 20; 21; 22(4); 23(2); 24(3); 26;
27(2); 28; 29; 30(3); 31(2); 32(2); 33(4); 15:1(3); 2(5); 3(2); 4;
5(3); 6; 7(2); 9(2); 11(3); 12(2); 13; 14(4); 15; 16(3); 17(3); 18(4);
19(2); 20(3); 21(3); 22(5); 23(3); 24(4); 25(3); 27(2); 29(2); 30(6);
31(2); 32(2); 34; 35(3); 36(2); 37; 16:1(5); 2(5); 3(3); 4; 5(2);
6(5); 7(2); 8(2); 9; 10; 11(3); 12; 13(5); 14(3); 15(3); 16; 17;
18(4); 19; 21(2); 22; 23(2); 17:1(2); 2(5); 3; 4(2); 5; 6; 7; 8(4);
9; 10(2); 11; 12(3); 13; 14(2); 15(5); 16(2); 17(5); 18(2); 19(4);
20(5); 21(5); 22(2); 23(7); 24(2); 25; 26; 27(3); 28(9); 29(7);
18:1(3); 2(4); 4(4); 5(4); 6; 7; 8; 9(7); 10(3); 11(5); 12(3); 13;
14(2); 15(3); 16(2); 17(4); 18(3); 19; 20; 21(2); 22; 23(2); 24(5);
25(5); 26(4); 27(3); 28(4); 29(3); 30(4); 31(2); 32(3); 33(4);
19:1(2); 2; 3; 4; 5(6); 6(2); 7(2); 8(3); 9(3); 10; 11(2); 12; 13(3);
14(2); 15(2); 16(2); 17(5); 18(3); 19; 21; 22; 23; 24(2); 25; 26(2);
27; 29(2); 30; 31(2); 32; 33(2); 34; 35(3); 36; 37(3); 38(3); 39(4);
40(3); 41(5); 42; 43(4); 20:1(3); 2; 3(4); 4; 6(3); 7(5); 8(3); 9(2);
10(4); 11(3); 12(3); 14(5); 15(5); 17(3); 18; 19(2); 20(2); 21(2);
22(5); 23(2); 24(2); 25(3); 26; 21:1(3); 2(5); 3; 4(2); 5(2); 6(2);
7; 8(2); 9(4); 10(3); 11; 12(3); 13(3); 14(4); 15(4); 16; 17(2); 18;
19; 20(4); 21; 22(2); 22:1(2); 2(3); 3(2); 7(3); 8(2); 9; 10(2);
11(3); 12(2); 14; 15(3); 16; 18; 22; 23; 24; 26; 27; 28; 29; 32;
33(2); 34; 36; 38(2); 39(2); 43; 46; 47(2); 48; 49; 50; 51(2);
23:1(2); 2; 4; 5(2); 7(2); 9(2); 10(4); 11(3); 12(3); 13(3); 14(2);
15(2); 16(4); 17; 18(4); 20(2); 21(4); 22; 23; 39; 24:1(3); 2; 3(2);
4(3); 5(3); 6(3); 7(4); 8; 9(3); 10(3); 12; 13(3); 14(2); 15; 16(3);
17(4); 18(2); 19; 20(5); 21(2); 22(4); 23; 24(2); 25(4); **1Kin**
1:1(2); 2(3); 3(2); 4(3); 5(3); 6(3); 7(3); 8(5); 9(5); 10(3); 11; 12;
13(3); 14; 15(3); 16(3); 17(2); 18(2); 19(6); 20; 21; 22; 23(2);
24(2); 25(9); 26(3); 27; 28(3); 29(2); 30; 31(2); 32(4); 33(2);
34(4); 35(3); 36(2); 37; 38(6); 39(4); 40(3); 41(3); 42(3); 43(2);
44(6); 45(3); 46; 47(3); 48; 49(3); 50(4); 51; 52; 53(4); 2:1; 2;
3(5); 4; 5(5); 6; 7; 8(2); 9; 10; 11(3); 12; 13(3); 14; 15(3); 16(2);
17; 18; 19(5); 20; 21; 22(5); 23; 24(2); 25(2); 26(2); 28(2); 29(2);
30(5); 31(4); 32(4); 33(4); 34(3); 35(2); 36(5); 37; 38(2); 39(2);
40(5); 41(2); 42(6); 43; 45(2); 46(2); 3:1(5); 3(2); 4; 5; 6(4);
7(2); 8; 9; 10; 11(2); 12; 13(2); 14(2); 15(7); 16; 17(3); 18(2);
19; 20(4); 21; 22(4); 23(3); 24(2); 25(3); 26(2); 27(2); 28(2); 4:2;
3; 4(3); 5(3); 6(2); 7(2); 8; 9(3); 10; 12(2); 13; 16; 19(2); 20(3);
21(3); 22(2); 23(5); 24; 25(3); 26(2); 27(2); 28(2); 29(3); 30(2);
31(4); 32(3); 33(4); 34; 5:1; 2; 5; 6(2); 7(2); 8(3); 9(4); 10; 11(2);
12(4); 13(2); 14(3); 15(3); 16; 17(3); 18(4); 6:1(2); 2(3); 3(2); 4;
5(3); 6(2); 7; 8(2); 9(3); 10(2); 11; 12(2); 13(2); 14; 15(4); 16(2);
17; 18(2); 19; 20(5); 21(2); 22; 23; 24(2); 25(2); 26; 27(4); 28;
29(4); 30(2); 31(2); 32(6); 34(2); 35(4); 36(2); 38(2); 7:1; 2(2);
3; 4(2); 5(3); 6(5); 7; 8; 9(2); 10(2); 11(2); 12(3); 13(2); 14(6);
15; 16(2); 17(3); 18(3); 19; 20(2); 21(5); 22; 23(3); 24; 25(5);
26(2); 27(3); 28(2); 29(5); 30(3); 31(4); 32(4); 33(4); 34(2); 35(3);
36(3); 37; 38(2); 39(3); 40(3); 41(2); 42; 43(2); 44(2); 45(4); 46;
47; 48(2); 49(4); 50(7); 51(3); 8:1; 2; 3(2); 4(4); 5(3); 6; 7(2);
8(3); 10; 14(3); 15(2); 17; 18; 20(4); 21; 22(2); 23(2); 24; 26; 27;
28(2); 29; 30(4); 31(2); 32(3); 33(4); 34(2); 35(3); 36(3); 38(2);
39(3); 42(3); 43(2); 44(2); 45(2); 46(2); 47(3); 48(4); 49(2); 50(3);
51; 52; 54(2); 55(2); 58(3); 59(3); 60; 61; 62(2); 63(5); 64(4);
65(3); 66(4); 9:1(3); 3(4); 4(4); 6(4); 7(3); 8(4); 9(4); 10(2); 11(2);
12(2); 13(2); 14; 15(7); 16(4); 17(2); 18(2); 19(6); 20(2); 22(5);
23; 25(3); 26; 27; 28(4); 10:1; 2(4); 3; 4(2); 5(6); 6(2); 7(3); 8;
9; 10(4); 11(2); 12(3); 13(3); 14; 15(3); 16; 17(2); 18; 19(3);
20(2); 21(2); 22(3); 23; 24; 25(6); 26(6); 27(2); 28(2); 29(6);
11:1; 3(3); 4; 5; 6(2); 7; 8(2); 9; 10; 11(3); 13; 14; 15; 17; 18(6);
19; 20(2); 21(2); 22; 23; 24(5); 25(3); 26; 27(2); 28(2); 29(3);
30(2); 31(2); 32; 33(5); 34; 35; 36; 37(3); 38(6); 39; 40(3);
41(3); 42; 43(3); 12:1; 2(2); 3(4); 4(2); 5(2); 6(2); 7(4); 8(2); 9;
10; 11; 12; 13(2); 14(2); 18; 20(3); 21(2); 23(3); 24; 25(3); 26;
27(2); 28(2); 29(2); 30; 31(2); 32(3); 33(3); 13:1(2); 2(4); 3(2);
4(2); 5; 6(6); 7(3); 8; 10; 11(2); 12; 13(2); 14(4); 15; 16; 18(2);
19(2); 20; 21(2); 22(3); 23(2); 24(4); 25(5); 26(2); 27(2); 28(4);
29(5); 30(2); 31; 32; 33; 34(2); 14:2(3); 3(4); 4(4); 5(2); 6; 7;
8(4); 9(3); 10(4); 11; 12; 13(2); 15(2); 16(2); 17(4); 18(2); 19(2);
20(4); 21(4); 22(2); 23(3); 24(2); 25; 26(3); 27(2); 28(2); 29;
30(2); 31(4); 15:2; 3(2); 4; 5; 6(2); 7(3); 8(3); 9; 10(3); 11; 12(2);
13(3); 15(4); 16(2); 17(2); 18(4); 19(5); 20(5); 21(2); 22(4); 23(3);
24(3); 25(2); 26(3); 27(3); 28; 29; 30; 31; 32(2); 33; 34(3);
16:2(3); 3(2); 4; 5(2); 6(2); 7(3); 8; 9; 10(5); 11; 13(2); 14; 15(2);
16(2); 17(3); 18(3); 19; 20; 21; 22; 23; 24(3); 25; 26; 27; 28(2);
29(4); 30; 31(4); 32; 33(2); 34; 17:1; 2; 3(2); 4(2); 5(2); 6(5); 7;
8; 9; 10(4); 11(2); 12(6); 13(5); 15(5); 16; 17(2); 18(2); 19(4);
20(2); 21(3); 22(3); 23(4); 24(2); 18:1(2); 2(2); 3; 4(3); 5(3); 6;
7(4); 8; 9; 10(2); 11; 12(4); 13(2); 14(2); 15; 16(2); 17; 18(3);
19(4); 20; 21(3); 22; 23(7); 24(5); 25(3); 26(4); 27(3); 28(3);
29(2); 30(3); 31; 32(2); 33(6); 34(4); 35(2); 36(5); 37; 38(5);
39(2); 40(4); 41(2); 42(4); 43(5); 44(3); 45(5); 46(3); 19:1(2); 2;
3(4); 4(4); 5(4); 6(6); 7(4); 8(5); 9(4); 10(4); 11(7); 12(2); 13(5);
14(4); 15(2); 16(2); 17(2); 18; 19(4); 20(6); 21(8); 20:1(8); 2(2);
3(2); 4(3); 5(5); 6(4); 7(6); 8(2); 9(2); 10(3); 11(2); 12(3); 13(2);
14(3); 15(3); 16(3); 17(3); 18; 19; 20(4); 21(4); 22(4); 23(2);
24(2); 25(6); 26(2); 27(4); 28(4); 29(3); 30(4); 31(3); 32(4); 33(3);
34(3); 35(2); 36(2); 37(2); 38(2); 39(5); 40(3); 41(3); 42(2);
43(3); 21:1; 2(2); 3; 4(5); 5; 6(3); 7(3); 8(3); 9(2); 10(4); 11(3);
12; 13(5); 14; 15(2); 16; 17; 19(3); 20(2); 21(4); 22(3); 23; 24;
26; 27(5); 28; 22:1(2); 2; 3(3); 4(2); 5; 6(2); 7; 8(2); 9; 10(3);
11(2); 12(2); 13(2); 14; 15(3); 16; 17(2); 18; 19(3); 20(4); 21(3);
22(6); 23; 24(2); 25; 26(3); 27(3); 28(2); 29; 30(4); 31; 32(3);
33; 34(3); 35(4); 36(2); 37(2); 38(3); 39(3); 40; 41; 42(4); 43(2);
44; 45(2); 46; 50(3); 51; 52(4); 53(2); **2Kin** 1:2(4); 3; 4; 5; 6(3);
7(2); 8(3); 9(3); 10(7); 11(2); 12(7); 13(7); 14; 15(3); 16; 17; 2:1;
2(3); 3(3); 4(3); 5(3); 6(4); 7(3); 8(5); 9(2); 10; 11(5); 12(6); 13(2);
14(6); 15(3); 16(4); 17(2); 18; 19(2); 20(3); 21(3); 23(4); 24(6);
25(2); 3:1; 2(2); 4(3); 6(2); 7(4); 8(2); 9(5); 10; 11(2); 12(3);
13(3); 14; 15; 16; 17(2); 18; 19(5); 20(2); 21(3); 22(3); 23(2);
24(2); 25(6); 26; 27(4); 4:1(2); 2(2); 4(4); 5(3); 6(3); 7(5); 8(3);
9; 10(5); 11(3); 12(2); 13(2); 14(3); 15(2); 16(2); 17(2); 18; 19(2);
20(3); 21(4); 22(4); 23(2); 24(2); 25(2); 26(2); 27(4); 29(4); 30(4);
31(3); 32(2); 33(2); 34(7); 35(6); 36(3); 37(4); 38(5); 39(5); 40(3);
41(3); 42(4); 43(2); 44(2); 5:1; 2(3); 3; 4(3); 5(6); 6; 7(4); 8(2);
9(2); 10(4); 11(6); 12(3); 13(4); 14(3); 15(5); 16; 17; 18(2); 19;
20; 21(2); 22(2); 23(5); 24(4); 25(3); 26(8); 27(2); 6:1; 2(3); 3(3);
4; 5(2); 6(5); 7(2); 8(2); 9; 10(3); 11(2); 12; 13(4); 14(4); 15(4);
16; 17(6); 18(3); 19(2); 20(4); 21; 22(5); 23(4); 24(3); 25(3); 26;
27; 28(3); 29(3); 30(4); 31; 32(3); 33(2); 7:1; 2(2); 3(2); 4(4);
5(2); 6(3); 7(5); 8(13); 9(2); 10(5); 11(2); 12(3); 13(4); 14(2);
15(5); 16(3); 17(3); 18(2); 19(3); 20(2); 8:1(4); 2(4); 3(3); 4; 5(4);
6(2); 7(3); 8(3); 9(4); 10; 11(2); 12(5); 13(2); 14(2); 15(4); 16;
17(2); 18(2); 19; 20; 21(5); 23(2); 24(3); 26(3); 27(2); 28(2);
29(2); 9:1(4); 2(4); 3(4); 5(4); 6(4); 7(2); 8(3); 9(2); 10(4); 11(3);
12(3); 13(3); 14; 15; 16(2); 17(6); 18(3); 19(2); 20(3); 21(6);
22(3); 23(3); 24(4); 25(2); 26(3); 27(5); 28(2); 29; 30(4); 31;
32(3); 33(4); 34(4); 35(3); 36(2); 37; 10:1(4); 2(3); 3(3); 4; 5(4);
6(2); 7(4); 8(3); 9(4); 11(3); 12(4); 13(4); 14(4); 15(6); 16(2); 17;
18(2); 19; 20(2); 21(4); 22(2); 23(4); 24(3); 25(7); 26(2); 27(3);
29; 30(2); 32; 33(3); 34(2); 35(3); 36(2); 11:1(2); 2(3); 3(2); 4(7);
5; 6(2); 7; 8(4); 9(3); 10(2); 11(2); 12(7); 13(2); 14(7); 15(2);
16(3); 17(4); 18(5); 19(7); 20(3); 12:1(2); 2; 3; 4(2); 5; 6; 7(2);
8; 9(3); 10(4); 11(3); 12(5); 14; 16; 17(3); 18(8); 19(2); 20(3);
21(4); 13:1(2); 2(2); 3(3); 4(2); 5(2); 6; 7(3); 8(2); 9(3); 10(2);
11; 12(3); 13(3); 14(4); 15(4); 16(3); 17(5); 18(5); 19(2); 20(3);
21(5); 23(5); 24; 25(2); 14:2(4); 3; 4; 5; 7(2); 9(3); 10(3); 11(2);
12(2); 13(3); 14(6); 15(2); 16(3); 17; 18; 19(2); 20(2); 21(2); 22;
23(2); 24; 27; 28(4); 29(2); 15:1; 2(3); 3; 4; 5(3); 6(2); 7(2); 8;
9; 10(4); 11; 12; 13(2); 14(4); 15(2); 16(3); 17(2); 18; 19(2);
20(2); 21(2); 22(2); 23; 24; 25(5); 26(2); 27(2); 28; 29(8); 30(4);
31(2); 33(3); 34; 35; 36; 37; 38(3); 16:2(2); 3; 4(4); 5(2); 6(3);
7(3); 8(4); 9(4); 10(4); 11; 12(3); 13(4); 14(3); 15(9); 17(4); 18(2);
20(3); 17:2; 3(2); 4(3); 5(2); 6(4); 7; 8(2); 9(2); 10(3); 11(2);
13(5); 15(6); 16(5); 17(5); 18; 20(3); 21(3); 24(8); 25; 26(2);
27(3); 28(2); 29; 30(3); 31(4); 32; 33; 34; 35; 36(3); 37(5); 38;
39; 41(2); 18:2(3); 3; 4(4); 6; 7(4); 8; 9(2); 10; 11(4); 12(2); 13;
14(3); 15(2); 16(2); 17(7); 18(3); 19; 20; 21; 22(3); 23; 24(2);
25; 26(3); 27(2); 28(2); 30; 31(4); 32(6); 34(2); 36; 37(3); 19:1(3);
2(3); 3(4); 4; 6; 7(3); 8; 9; 11; 12(3); 13(3); 14(4); 15(3); 16(3);
17; 18(2); 21; 22(3); 23(5); 24(2); 25; 26(3); 27(3); 28(3); 29(6);
30(2); 31; 33; 34; 35(4); 36(3); 37(4); 20:1(3); 2; 3(3); 4; 5; 6(5);
7(4); 8(2); 9; 10; 11(2); 12; 13(7); 14(3); 15(2); 16; 17; 18(2);
19(2); 20(5); 21(2); 21:1(3); 2; 3(4); 4; 5; 6(5); 7(3); 8; 9; 10;
11(2); 12; 13(4); 14(4); 15; 17(2); 18(3); 19(3); 20; 21(3); 22(2);
23(2); 24(2); 26(2); 22:1(3); 2(3); 3; 5(2); 6(4); 8(3); 9(4); 10(2);
11; 12(5); 13(2); 14(5); 15; 16; 17(2); 19(5); 20(3); 23:1(3); 2(8);
3(7); 4(7); 5(5); 6(4); 7; 8(3); 10; 11(2); 12(4); 13(3); 14(3); 15(5);
16(5); 17(2); 18; 19(2); 20(3); 21; 24(5); 25(3); 27(3); 28; 29(2);
30(6); 31(3); 32; 33(3); 34(5); 35(3); 36(3); 37; 24:1(2); 2(5); 4;
5; 6; 7; 8(2); 9; 10; 11(2); 12(6); 13(3); 14(5); 15(5); 16(4); 17(2);
18(3); 19; 20; 25:1(4); 2; 3(2); 4(3); 5(3); 6(2); 7(4); 8; 9(4); 10;
11; 12; 13(4); 14(5); 15(4); 16; 17(5); 18(3); 19(4); 20(2); 21(2);
22; 23(6); 24(5); 25(4); 26(4); 27(3); 28(2); 29(2); 30; **1Chr** 1:4;
5(6); 6(3); 7(3); 8(2); 9(7); 10; 11(4); 12(3); 13(2); 14(2); 15(3);
16(3); 17(8); 18(2); 19(2); 20(4); 21(2); 22(3); 23(3); 28; 29(2);
30(2); 31; 32(7); 33(5); 34(2); 35(3); 36(4); 37; 38(7); 39(3);
40(5); 41(4); 42(3); 43; 44; 45; 46(2); 47; 48; 49; 50(3); 51;
2:1(2); 2(2); 3(4); 4(2); 5; 6(5); 7; 8; 9(2); 10(2); 11(2); 12(2);
13(3); 16(4); 17(2); 18(4); 19; 20(2); 21(2); 22(2); 23(3); 24;
25(5); 27(3); 28(4); 29(3); 30(2); 31(3); 32(3); 33(2); 34; 35(2);
36(2); 37(2); 38(2); 39(2); 40(2); 41(2); 42; 43(4); 44(2); 45(2);
46(4); 47(6); 48; 49(2); 52(2); 53(5); 54(2); 55(2); 3:4(4); 5(4);
6(2); 7(3); 8(3); 9; 10; 15; 16; 17; 18(3); 19(5); 20(4); 21(2);
22(6); 23(3); 24(7); 4:1(3); 2(3); 3(4); 4(2); 5(2); 6(4); 7(3); 8(3);
9(2); 10(5); 11; 12(3); 13(3); 14(2); 15(3); 16(3); 17(7); 18(4);
19(2); 20(5); 21(2); 22(6); 23(2); 24(2); 26; 27(2); 28(3); 29(3);
30(3); 31(4); 32(4); 33(2); 34(3); 35(2); 36(7); 37; 38; 39; 40(5);
41(5); 42(4); 43(2); 5:1; 2; 3(2); 7(2); 8(2); 9; 10(2); 11; 12(3);
13(7); 16(3); 17; 18(7); 19(3); 20(4); 21(5); 22; 23(3); 24(8);
25(2); 26(9); 6:1; 2(3); 3(5); 5(2); 6(2); 7; 8(2); 9(2); 10; 11(2);
12(2); 13(2); 14(2); 15(2); 16; 17(2); 18(4); 19(2); 23(2); 24;
25(2); 26; 28(2); 31; 32(2); 33; 39; 44; 49(4); 50; 55(2); 56;
57(4); 58; 59(2); 60(3); 61; 62(4); 63(2); 64; 65(3); 66; 67; 68(2);
69(2); 70(2); 71; 72; 73(2); 74(2); 75(2); 76(3); 78(2); 79; 80(2);
81(2); 7:1(2); 2(8); 3(4); 4(3); 5(2); 6(2); 7(9); 8(9); 9(2); 10(7);
11(2); 12(2); 13(3); 15(4); 16(5); 17; 18(3); 19(4); 20(5); 21(4);
22(2); 23(3); 24(3); 25(3); 28(7); 29(5); 30(4); 31(2); 32(4); 33(3);
34(3); 35(4); 36(4); 37(5); 38(3); 39(3); 40(4); 8:1; 2; 3(3); 4(3);
5(3); 6(2); 7(5); 8(2); 9(4); 10(3); 11(2); 12(3); 13; 14(2); 15(3);
16(3); 17(4); 18(2); 19(3); 20(3); 21(3); 22(3); 23(3); 24(3); 25(2);
26(3); 27(3); 29; 30(5); 31(3); 32(2); 33(6); 34(2); 35(4); 36(5);
37; 38(5); 39(2); 40(4); 9:1(2); 2; 3(4); 5(2); 6(3); 7; 8(3); 9(3);

5; 6; 9; 10; 12; 14; 15; 16; 17; 18(2); 19; 20; 21; 22; 24; 26; 28; 26:1; 3; 6; 10; 17; 18; 19; 21; 22; 23; 24; 27; 28; 27:2(2); 3; 4; 9; 10; 11; 12(2); 13; 15; 16; 20; 21; 23; 24; 25(2); 26; 27(2); 28:2; 8; 13; 15; 22; 24; 29:1; 6; 13; 15; 17; 22; 24; 27; 30:1; 2; 4; 6; 8; 9(4); 10; 11; 12; 13; 14(2); 16(2); 17(2); 19; 20(2); 21; 22; 23; 28; 30; 31; 33; 31:2(2); 5(2); 6; 7(2); 9(2); 12; 13(2); 15(2); 16; 17; 19; 22; 24(2); 25(2); 26; 27; 28(2); 30; 31; **Eccl** 1:4; 5(2); 6(2); 9(2); 13(2); 14(2); 15; 16(2); 17(3); 18; 2:1; 2; 3; 5(2); 7(3); 8(6); 9; 10(2); 11(4); 12(3); 14; 15; 16; 17; 19(2); 21(3); 22; 23; 24(2); 26(4); 3:1; 2(2); 3(2); 4(2); 5(2); 6(2); 7(2); 8(2); 12; 13(3); 14; 15(2); 16(2); 17(2); 18; 20; 21; 4:1(4); 4(2); 5; 6; 7; 8(2); 12(2); 13(2); 16; 5:1; 2(2); 3; 5; 6; 7; 8(3); 11; 14(2); 15; 16(2); 17(2); 18(3); 19(4); 6:1; 2(2); 3(3); 4(2); 7; 9; 10; 7:1; 2; 7; 8; 11; 12; 15; 20; 24; 25(5); 26(3); 8:1(2); 2; 4; 5(2); 6; 8; 9; 10(3); 12; 15(2); 16; 9:1(2); 2(5); 3(2); 6(2); 7; 8; 9; 11(2); 12; 13; 14(4); 15; 16; 10:1; 3; 6; 7; 8; 9; 10; 11; 13; 14; 16; 17(2); 18; 19; 20(2); 11:2; 3; 4; 6; 7; 8; 9(3); 10(2); 12:3(3); 4(3); 5(5); 7; 9(3); 10; 11; 12(2); 13; **Song** 1:4; 8; 17; 2:1; 3; 4; 6; 7; 10(2); 11; 12; 13(2); 14; 16; 17(2); 3:2(2); 4(2); 5; 6; 11(2); 4:2; 3; 6(2); 8; 10; 11(2); 14(3); 15; 16(2); 5:2; 4; 5(2); 6; 10; 11; 12; 16; 6:2; 3; 6; 8(2); 9(3); 10; 11(2); 7:5; 6; 7; 8; 9; 10; 12; 13(2); 8:2; 3; 8; 9; 10; 12; 14; **Is** 1:1(2); 2(3); 3; 5(2); 6(2); 7; 8; 9; 11(2); 13; 14; 15; 18; 19; 20; 23(2); 24; 25(3); 26(2); 27; 28(3); 29; 30; 31(4); 2:1; 2(3); 3(6); 4(4); 5; 6(2); 7; 9(2); 10(2); 11(2); 12(3); 13(3); 14(2); 15(2); 16(2); 17(3); 18; 19(3); 20(2); 21(2); 3:1(3); 2(4); 3(4); 4(2); 5(3); 6; 8(2); 9; 12(2); 13; 14; 15; 16(4); 17; 18(2); 19(2); 20(4); 21; 22(3); 23(3); 24(5); 25; 26(3); 4:1(2); 2(3); 3(2); 4(2); 5(4); 6(4); 5:2(7); 3(3); 5(4); 6(2); 7(2); 9; 10; 12(4); 13(2); 14(5); 15(3); 16; 17; 18; 19(3); 20(3); 21; 22; 23; 24(3); 25(4); 26(3); 28(2); 29(3); 30(4); 6:1(2); 2(2); 3(2); 4(2); 5; 7(4); 8; 9(3); 10(6); 11(3); 12(2); 13(3); 7:1(2); 2(3); 3; 4(3); 5; 6(3); 8(3); 9(2); 13; 14(2); 15(2); 16; 17(2); 18(2); 19(5); 20(2); 21(2); 22(2); 23(2); 24(2); 25(3); 8:1; 2(2); 3(3); 4(2); 6(2); 7(4); 8(3); 9(4); 10(2); 11; 13(2); 14(3); 15(5); 17(2); 18(2); 19(3); 20; 21(6); 22(4); 9:1(2); 3(2); 4; 5(2); 6(2); 7(4); 8; 9(3); 11; 12(2); 14(2); 15(2); 16; 17(3); 18(3); 19; 20(4); 21(2); 10:1; 2(2); 3(3); 4; 5; 6(3); 7; 10(2); 11(2); 12(2); 13(4); 14(3); 16; 17(5); 18(4); 19; 20(2); 24; 25(2); 26(2); 27(3); 33(2); 34(2); 11:1(2); 2(4); 3(2); 4(3); 5(2); 6(5); 7(3); 8(2); 10(2); 11(8); 12(3); 13(2); 14(2); 15(4); 16; 12:1(2); 2(2); 4; 6; 13:5; 7; 8(2); 9(2); 10(2); 11(4); 13(2); 14(3); 15; 16; 17; 18; 19(2); 21(3); 22(4); 14:1(4); 2(6); 3(3); 4; 5; 6; 7; 8; 10; 11(2); 16; 17; 19; 20; 22(4); 23(2); 24; 25(2); 26; 27(3); 29; 30(4); 31; 32; 15:1(2); 2(3); 3; 4(2); 7; 8; 9; 16:5(4); 6(2); 8; 9(2); 10(3); 11; 12; 14(3); 17:1; 2; 3(2); 4(2); 5(3); 7; 8; 9(2); 10(2); 11(2); 12; 13(3); 14(3); 18:2(2); 3(2); 4(2); 5(3); 6(3); 7(3); 19:1(3); 2(4); 3(6); 4(2); 5(3); 6(4); 7(2); 8(2); 9; 10(2); 12(2); 14; 16(2); 17; 18; 19; 20(5); 21(5); 22(5); 23(3); 24; 25(2); 20:1(2); 2(4); 3(4); 4(3); 5(3); 6(2); 21:2; 5; 7(3); 8(2); 9(4); 10; 12; 15(2); 16; 17; 22:5(3); 6(3); 7(2); 8(2); 9; 10(2); 12(4); 13(5); 14; 15; 16(2); 17; 18(2); 19(2); 20; 21(5); 22(4); 23(2); 24(2); 25(3); 23:3(2); 9; 12; 13; 15; 17(3); 18(3); 24:1(3); 2; 3; 4(2); 6(2); 12; 13; 17(2); 18(3); 20(5); 21(2); 22(3); 23(3); 25:1; 6; 7(2); 8(2); 9(3); 10; 11(2); 12(2); 26:1; 6; 8; 10; 11; 14(2); 17; 19(2); 20; 21; 27:1(3); 3; 4; 5; 6(2); 9(2); 10(4); 11(2); 12(2); 13(4); 28:2(2); 4(2); 5; 6(2); 7(2); 8; 9(2); 10; 11; 12; 13(5); 15(2); 17(3); 18(2); 19(2); 20; 21; 23(2); 24; 25(4); 26; 27; 29; 29:2(3); 3(3); 4(5); 5; 6(4); 7(3); 8(5); 9(2); 10(2); 11(2); 12(2); 13(2); 14(2); 15(3); 17(2); 18(3); 19; 20(2); 21(2); 23(2); 24; 30:1; 2(2); 3; 4; 5; 6(4); 7; 8(2); 10; 12(3); 14; 15(3); 16; 17; 18(2); 20(2); 21(2); 22; 23(3); 24(2); 25(3); 26(2); 27(2); 28(2); 29; 30(5); 32(3); 33(2); 31:1(3); 2(3); 3(5); 4(2); 5; 7; 8(2); 9(3); 32:1; 2(2); 3(2); 4; 6(3); 8; 10; 11(2); 13; 14; 15(2); 16; 17(3); 18(3); 19; 20; 33:1(4); 4(2); 5; 6(3); 9(4); 12; 13; 15(2); 21; 24; 34:1(3); 2; 3(2); 4(4); 5; 6(3); 7(4); 8; 9(3); 10; 11(4); 12; 13(4); 14(2); 15(3); 16(2); 17(2); 35:1(3); 2(4); 3; 4; 5; 6(2); 7(3); 8(3); 10(6); 36:1; 2(2); 3(2); 4; 5; 6; 7(3); 8; 9(2); 10(2); 11(3); 12(2); 13(2); 16(4); 17(3); 19(2); 21; 22(3); 37:1(3); 2(3); 3(4); 4; 6; 7(3); 8; 9(2); 11; 12(3); 13(3); 14(4); 15; 16; 17(3); 18; 19(2); 22; 23(3); 24(5); 25(2); 26; 27(3); 28(3); 29(3); 30(6); 31(2); 32; 34; 35; 36(4); 37(3); 38(4); 38:1(3); 2; 3(4); 5; 6(3); 7; 9; 12; 15; 16(2); 21(2); 39:1(2); 2(7); 3(3); 4; 6; 7(2); 8; 40:2; 4(4); 5(2); 6(2); 10(2); 11(2); 12(4); 14(4); 15; 16; 17(2); 19(2); 22(2); 24(3); 26; 27(2); 29; 30(2); 31(3); 41:1; 2(2); 3; 4(2); 5(2); 6; 7(2); 9(3); 11(2); 12(2); 14(2); 15(2); 16(4); 17(3); 18(2); 19(4); 20(4); 22(2); 23; 24; 25(3); 26; 27; 28(2); 29; 42:3; 4; 5(3); 6(3); 7; 8; 9; 10(3); 11; 12; 14(2); 15(4); 16(3); 18; 19; 21; 22(4); 23; 24; 25(3); 43:1; 2; 3; 4(2); 5; 6(2); 8; 9(3); 10(3); 11; 12(2); 13(2); 14(2); 16; 17(2); 19; 20(2); 25; 27; 28(2); 44:1; 2(2); 3(2); 4; 5(3); 6(3); 7(5); 8; 9(2); 11(2); 12(4); 13(2); 14(3); 15(4); 16(2); 17(4); 18; 19(3); 21; 22; 23(2); 24; 25(2); 26(3); 27; 28(2); 45:1(2); 2(2); 3(2); 4; 5; 6(2); 7(2); 8(3); 11(2); 12(2); 13(2); 14(5); 16; 18(2); 20(2); 21(3); 22(2); 23; 24(2); 25; 46:1; 3; 4(4); 5(2); 6(3); 7(2); 8; 9(2); 10(2); 13(2); 47:1(2); 2; 3; 5; 6; 7; 8; 9(2); 10(3); 11(2); 12; 13; 48:1(2); 2; 3(3); 4(2); 5(2); 6(2); 7; 8; 9; 11; 12; 13; 14(2); 15; 16(2); 18; 19; 21(2); 49:1; 2(2); 3; 4(2); 5(2); 6(2); 7(4); 8(3); 9; 11(2); 12(3); 13(3); 14; 17; 18(3); 19(3); 21(4); 22(3); 23(4); 25(2); 26(4); 50:1; 2; 3; 5; 6(2); 7; 10(2); 11; 51:1; 2(3); 3(4); 4(2); 5(2); 6(4); 8(2); 9; 11(5); 12; 13(4); 14; 16(4); 17; 19(3); 21; 22; 23(2); 52:1; 2; 3; 4; 5; 10; 12; 13(2); 14; 15; 53:1; 2(2); 3(4); 4(2); 5; 6; 7(2); 8(2); 9(2); 10; 11; 12(4); 54:1(2); 2(2); 3(3); 4; 5; 6(2); 10; 11(2); 12(3); 13(2); 14; 16(2); 17(2); 55:1(4); 2(3); 3(3); 4; 5(2); 7(4); 9; 10(5); 11; 12(3); 13(3); 56:1(2); 2(2); 4(2); 5(3); 6(2); 7(2); 11; 12(3); 57:1(2); 3; 4; 7; 8(3); 9(4); 11(3); 12; 13; 14; 15(4); 16; 17(3); 18(3); 19(2); 20; 58:1(2); 2(3); 3(3); 4(2); 5(3); 6(2); 7(2); 8(2); 9(3); 10(3); 11(5); 12(2); 13(2); 14(2); 59:2(2); 3; 4(2); 5(2); 6; 7(2); 8; 10; 11; 12(2); 13(4); 14(3); 15(3); 16(3); 17(3); 19; 20(2); 21(2); 60:1; 2(2); 3(2); 4(2); 5(3); 6(3); 7; 8; 9(3); 10(2); 11; 12; 13(2); 14(2); 15; 16(3); 17(4); 18; 19; 20; 22; 61:1; 2; 4(2); 5(4); 6; 7; 8(2); 9(2); 10; 11(2); 62:1(2); 2(3); 3; 4(2); 5; 7(2); 8(2); 9(2); 11; 12(2); 63:2; 3(4); 4; 5(4); 6(3); 7(3); 9(4); 10(2); 11; 15(4); 16; 17; 64:5(2); 6(3); 7(2); 8(2); 11(2); 12; 65:3; 4(2); 7(2); 8; 9(4); 10(2); 11; 12(2); 14; 15(2); 16(2); 17(2); 18(2); 19(3); 21(4); 22(3); 23; 24(2); 25(3); 66:1(2); 2(3); 3; 4(2); 5; 9(2); 10; 11(2); 12(2); 13; 14(4); 15(2); 16(2); 17(3); 18(4); 19(5); 20(5); 21(2); 22(2); 23(2); 24(3); **Jer** 1:5(2); 7; 9(2); 10(5); 11; 13(3); 15(4); 16(3); 17(2); 18(3); 19; 2:2; 3; 4; 5(2); 6(3); 7(3); 8(3); 9; 10(4); 12; 13; 15(2); 16; 18; 19(4); 20(3); 22; 25(2); 26(2); 27(3); 37(2); 3:1(2); 2(3); 3(2); 5; 6(2); 7(2);

8(3); 9(3); 10; 11; 12(4); 13(2); 14(3); 15(2); 16(2); 17; 18; 19(3); 21(2); 22; 23; 24(2); 25(3); 4:1; 2(4); 3(2); 4(3); 5(4); 6; 7(2); 8; 9(4); 10; 11; 13; 15; 16; 18; 20; 21; 22; 23(4); 24(2); 25(2); 26(3); 28(2); 29(3); 30; 31; 5:1(5); 2; 5(3); 6(2); 7(2); 9; 10; 11; 12; 13(2); 14(2); 17(5); 19(2); 20; 21(3); 22; 23(2); 24; 25; 27; 28; 30; 31(3); 6:1(3); 2; 4; 5(2); 6; 7(2); 10(2); 11; 12(2); 13; 16(4); 18; 20; 21(3); 22; 23(3); 24; 25; 26; 27(2); 28; 7:2(2); 3(2); 5(2); 6(2); 7; 9(4); 10(3); 12; 13(4); 14(2); 15; 17; 18(3); 20(6); 21; 23(3); 24(3); 25; 28; 29(3); 31(2); 33(3); 34(3); 8:1(4); 2(7); 3; 4(2); 6; 7(3); 8; 9(2); 10; 13(2); 14(3); 15(2); 16(3); 17; 19; 20; 9:1(2); 2; 3(2); 4(2); 5(3); 7; 10(3); 11(3); 12(2); 13(2); 14; 15; 16; 17(2); 18(3); 20(3); 21(2); 22(2); 24(2); 26(6); 10:2; 4(2); 6; 7; 8; 9(3); 10(2); 11(2); 12; 13(2); 14; 15; 16; 18; 19; 20(3); 21(2); 22(2); 25(4); 11:2(2); 3; 4(2); 5(2); 6(2); 7; 9(2); 10(2); 11; 12(2); 13; 15; 16(2); 17; 18(2); 19(2); 20; 22; 23; 12:2; 3(2); 4(2); 5(2); 6; 11; 13; 14; 15(4); 16; 17; 13:1(3); 2; 3; 4(2); 5; 6(2); 7(3); 9; 10(2); 11(4); 12; 13(3); 14(2); 15; 16(3); 17(2); 18; 19; 20; 21; 22(2); 25; 27(2); 14:2(2); 3(4); 5; 6; 8; 9; 10; 12(4); 14(3); 15(3); 16(3); 17(2); 18(2); 19(4); 20; 15:1(2); 2(4); 3(5); 4; 6; 7; 8; 9(2); 10; 11; 12; 13(2); 14; 15(2); 16(3); 18(2); 19(2); 20(3); 21(2); 16:3(3); 4(4); 5; 6; 8; 9(3); 10(2); 11(5); 12; 13(2); 15(2); 16(5); 18(3); 19(4); 20; 21(2); 17:1(2); 2; 3(2); 4(2); 5(2); 6(2); 7; 8(3); 9; 10; 11(3); 13; 14(2); 18; 19(3); 20(3); 21; 24; 25(5); 26(10); 27(3); 18:2(2); 3; 4; 7(3); 9(3); 11(4); 12(2); 15; 16(2); 17; 18(3); 19; 20; 21(4); 22; 19:1(3); 2(2); 3(2); 4(3); 7(6); 8(3); 9(5); 11(3); 12(2); 13(3); 14(2); 15; 20:2; 3; 4(6); 5(5); 6(6); 7(2); 8(2); 9(2); 10(3); 11; 12(2); 16(4); 17; 18; 21:1; 4(2); 5(4); 6(2); 7(8); 8(2); 9(4); 10(2); 11; 12(2); 13; 14(2); 22:1; 2(3); 3(2); 4(3); 6(2); 7(3); 8(2); 9(2); 12; 13(2); 14(4); 15(4); 16; 17(4); 19; 20(3); 22(2); 25(3); 26(3); 28(2); 30; 23:1; 2(2); 3(4); 4(2); 5(4); 6(2); 8(3); 9(2); 10(2); 11; 12; 13(2); 14(2); 15; 16; 17; 18(3); 20; 22(2); 23; 24; 28; 29; 31; 32(3); 33; 34(4); 35(2); 36; 37; 38; 39(4); 40(2); 24:1(4); 2; 3(2); 6(5); 7(3); 8(4); 9(3); 10(3); 25:2; 3(3); 4(2); 5(4); 6(4); 9(9); 10(3); 11(3); 12(4); 13; 14(3); 15; 16(3); 17; 18(4); 19(3); 20(7); 21(2); 22(3); 23(3); 24(2); 25(3); 26(4); 27(4); 28; 29; 30(2); 32; 33; 34(4); 35; 36; 37; 38; 26:2; 3; 4; 5; 6; 7(2); 8(2); 9(2); 10; 11(2); 12(2); 13(3); 14; 15(2); 16(2); 17; 18(3); 19(3); 20(2); 21(4); 22(2); 23(3); 27:2(2); 3(5); 4; 5(3); 6(2); 7(5); 8(5); 10(2); 11(3); 12(3); 13(2); 15(2); 16; 17; 18(3); 19(3); 20(2); 21(2); 22(2); 28:1(3); 3; 4; 5; 6; 7; 8(4); 10; 11(2); 13; 14(2); 29:1(3); 2(5); 3; 5(3); 6(6); 7(2); 8; 10; 11; 12(3); 13(2); 14(5); 16(2); 17(2); 18(6); 19; 21(2); 22(2); 23(3); 25(2); 26(2); 28(3); 29; 31(2); 32; 30:3(3); 4(2); 5; 6(2); 8(2); 9; 10(5); 11; 12; 16(3); 17; 18(3); 19(5); 20(2); 21(4); 22(2); 24; 31:1; 4(2); 5; 6; 7(2); 8(4); 9(2); 10(3); 11; 12(8); 13(3); 14(2); 15; 16(2); 17; 18(2); 19; 23(2); 24(3); 25; 26(2); 27(2); 28(6); 29; 31; 33(3); 34(3); 35(2); 37; 39(2); 40(3); 32:2; 3(2); 4(3); 5(2); 6; 8(2); 9(2); 10(4); 11(2); 12(2); 13; 14(2); 15(2); 17(3); 18; 19(2); 20(4); 21(5); 22(2); 23(2); 24(5); 25(2); 28(2); 29(4); 30; 31; 32(4); 33(3); 35(2); 36(3); 37(4); 38(2); 39(3); 40; 41(2); 43; 44(8); 33:3(3); 4(2); 5(2); 6(4); 7(3); 8(3); 9(5); 10(4); 11(3); 12(2); 13(4); 14; 15(3); 16(2); 18(2); 19; 20(3); 21; 22; 25(3); 26(3); 34:1(4); 2(3); 3(5); 5(2); 7(2); 9; 10(3); 11(4); 14; 15(3); 16(5); 17(3); 18(2); 19(3); 20(3); 21(4); 22(6); 35:2(3); 3; 4; 5(3); 10(2); 11(2); 13(2); 14; 15(5); 17(2); 18(3); 36:1; 2(3); 3; 4; 5; 6(2); 7(2); 8; 9(2); 12(6); 14(2); 15(2); 16(2); 17; 18; 19(2); 20(2); 21(3); 22; 23(2); 25(2); 26(3); 27; 28; 29(4); 30(2); 31(6); 32(2); 37:1; 32(2); 3; 4; 5; 8(4); 10(2); 11; 13(2); 14; 15(2); 16(2); 17(4); 21; 38:1(3); 2(2); 4; 6(3); 8; 9; 10; 11(4); 12(3); 13(2); 14(2); 15; 17(3); 18(2); 19(2); 20; 22(4); 23(3); 24; 25(3); 27(2); 28; 39:1(2); 2; 3(2); 4(4); 5(2); 7; 8(3); 9; 10(2); 12(2); 13(3); 14(2); 16(3); 17; 18; 40:1; 2(2); 3(2); 4(3); 5(3); 6; 7(5); 8(6); 9(4); 10(4); 11(4); 12(3); 13; 14; 15(3); 41:1(2); 2(3); 3(2); 4(2); 5(4); 6(2); 7(3); 8(4); 9; 10(3); 11; 12(2); 13; 14(2); 15; 16(4); 17(2); 42:1(3); 2(2); 3; 4; 5; 7; 8(2); 9; 10(3); 11; 12(2); 14; 15(2); 16(2); 17(2); 18(6); 20(2); 21; 22(2); 43:1; 2(2); 4; 5(2); 6(6); 9; 10(4); 11(4); 12(5); 13; 44:1(3); 2(3); 3; 4; 6(5); 7(2); 8(2); 9(5); 10; 11; 12(9); 13; 15; 17(6); 18(3); 19(3); 20(2); 21(5); 22(3); 23(2); 24; 25(4); 27(3); 28; 29; 30(2); 45:3; 4; 5; 46:3(2); 4(3); 5(4); 6; 8(4); 9(5); 10(3); 11; 12(2); 13; 14(4); 16(3); 18; 19; 21(2); 22; 23; 25(4); 26(4); 27(6); 47:2(5); 3; 4(2); 6; 7; 48:1(2); 2; 3; 6; 7(3); 8(3); 9; 10; 11(3); 12(2); 13; 14; 15(2); 16; 17(2); 18(2); 19(3); 20; 21(3); 22(3); 23(3); 24(3); 25; 26; 28(2); 29(3); 31; 32; 33(4); 34; 35; 36; 37(2); 38; 39; 40; 41(2); 42; 43(2); 44; 45(3); 46; 49:1; 2(2); 3(4); 5(2); 6; 10(4); 11; 12; 13(2); 14(3); 15; 16; 17; 18(2); 19(3); 20; 22(3); 23; 24(3); 26; 27(2); 28(2); 29(4); 30; 32(4); 33(2); 36(3); 37(3); 38(3); 50:1; 2(3); 3(2); 4(4); 5; 7; 8(2); 9(2); 10; 11; 12; 13; 16(2); 17; 18; 19(5); 20(4); 21(3); 22; 23; 24(3); 25; 26; 28; 30; 32(5); 33(2); 34; 35(3); 36(2); 37(4); 38(2); 39(2); 40(2); 41(2); 42(3); 43(2); 44(3); 45; 46; 51:1; 2(2); 3(2); 4; 6; 8; 9(2); 10; 12; 13; 14; 15; 16(2); 17; 19; 20(2); 21(4); 22(5); 23(5); 24(2); 25(3); 26; 27; 28(2); 29(2); 31; 32(3); 33; 35(2); 36(3); 37(2); 39(3); 41; 43; 44(3); 45; 46(4); 47(2); 48(2); 50; 52; 53; 54; 55; 56; 57(6); 58(4); 59; 61(3); 63(2); 64(3); 52:1(3); 2; 3; 4(4); 6; 7(3); 8(2); 9; 10; 11(3); 13(4); 14; 15(3); 16; 17(3); 18(5); 19(8); 20; 21(3); 22(4); 23(3); 24(3); 25(3); 26; 27(2); 28(2); 29; 30(3); 31(4); 32(2); 33(2); 34; **Lam** 1:1; 2; 3; 4; 6(2); 7(3); 8; 11; 12; 13(2); 14; 17; 18(2); 19; 21; 22(2); 2:1(2); 2(2); 3; 4; 5(2); 6(4); 8; 9(2); 10; 11; 12; 14(3); 15; 16; 17(2); 18; 20(3); 21(3); 22; 3:2; 4; 5(2); 8; 10; 11; 12; 14; 17; 18(2); 19(2); 20; 26; 28; 37; 38; 40(2); 42; 43; 45; 47(2); 49; 50; 53; 60; 61; 62; 63; 66; 4:4; 6; 11(2); 12(2); 13; 15; 21(2); 5:1; 3; 5; 6; 7(2); 11; 13; 20; 21; **Eze** 1:1; 3; 4(5); 5; 6(2); 7(3); 8(3); 10(2); 11(2); 12(2); 13(4); 14(2); 16(4); 17; 18; 19(2); 20; 21(2); 22; 23(2); 24; 25(2); 26(2); 27(3); 28(2); 2:1(2); 2(2); 3(2); 4(2); 5; 6(3); 7; 8; 9(2); 10(6); 3:1; 2; 3(3); 4(2); 5; 6; 7; 8; 10; 11(3); 12; 13(2); 14(2); 15(2); 16; 17; 18; 19; 20(3); 21; 22(3); 23(3); 24(3); 25(2); 26(2); 27(2); 4:1(2); 2(4); 3(5); 4; 5; 6(2); 7(2); 8(2); 9(8); 10; 12(2); 13; 15; 16(4); 17(3); 5:1(4); 2(4); 3; 4(2); 5; 6(3); 7; 8; 9(2); 10(3); 11; 12(4); 13(3); 14; 15(4); 16(3); 17(5); 6:1; 2; 3(4); 4(3); 5(2); 6(6); 7(2); 9(3); 10(2); 11(3); 12(3); 13(2); 14(2); 7:3(3); 4(3); 7; 8(3); 9(3); 15(4); 16; 17; 18(3); 19(2); 20; 21(3); 22(2); 23; 24(2); 25(2); 26(2); 27(4); 8:1(2); 2(2); 3(5); 4; 5; 6; 7(2); 8; 9(2); 10(4); 11(3); 13; 14; 15; 16(6); 17(2); 18; 9:2(5); 3(2); 4(3); 5(2); 6(4); 7(4); 8(4); 9(4); 10; 11; 10:1; 2(5); 3; 4(3); 5; 6(2); 7(4); 8; 9(3); 10; 12(5); 14(4); 15; 16(2); 17; 18; 19(4); 20; 21(2); 22(2); 11:1(4); 2; 3; 5(2); 6; 7; 8; 9(3); 10; 12; 13(3); 15; 16; 17(2); 18(3); 19(4); 20(4); 21; 22(2);

23(2); 24; 12:2(2); 3(2); 4; 5; 6; 7(3); 8; 10; 11; 12(2); 13(2); 14(3); 15(2); 16(2); 18(2); 19(3); 20(3); 21; 22; 23(2); 25(2); 27; 13:1; 2; 3; 6(3); 7; 8; 9(3); 10(3); 11(2); 13(2); 14(4); 15(2); 16(2); 17; 18(3); 19(3); 20(2); 21(3); 22; 23; 14:1; 2; 3; 4(3); 6(2); 7(3); 8(5); 9(3); 10; 11; 13(4); 14; 15; 17(2); 19(2); 20; 21(4); 22(4); 23(3); 15:1; 4; 5; 7(3); 8; 16:3(3); 4; 6(2); 7(5); 8(5); 9; 10(3); 11(2); 12(3); 13(8); 14; 15(2); 16(3); 17(3); 18(4); 19(3); 20(2); 21; 22(4); 23; 24; 25(3); 26; 27(2); 28; 29; 31(2); 33; 34(3); 36(3); 37(2); 38(4); 39(6); 40(2); 41(4); 42(3); 43; 45(4); 46(4); 48; 49(3); 50(2); 51; 52; 53(3); 54; 55(4); 57; 58; 60; 61(3); 62(2); 63(2); 17:1; 2; 3(2); 4; 5(2); 6(5); 7(3); 8; 9; 12(3); 13(3); 15(2); 16; 17(2); 18; 19; 20(4); 21(3); 22(3); 23(4); 24(3); 18:2; 5(2); 6; 7(2); 8; 9; 10; 11(2); 12(2); 13; 14(2); 16; 18; 19(3); 20; 21(3); 23(2); 24(3); 26(2); 27(2); 28; 30; 31(2); 32; 19:2; 3(2); 4; 5(2); 6(4); 7(4); 8; 9(2); 10; 11(3); 12(2); 13(2); 14(2); 20:1(2); 3; 5(3); 6; 7; 8; 10; 11(2); 12; 13(2); 15; 16; 19(2); 20(3); 22; 23; 24(2); 25; 26; 27; 28(4); 29; 30; 31; 32(2); 33(2); 34(4); 35(2); 37(2); 38(4); 39(2); 40(2); 41(2); 42; 43(3); 44; 46(2); 47(4); 48; 21:1; 2(2); 3(4); 4; 6; 7(6); 9(2); 11(2); 12; 13; 14(2); 15; 17; 19; 20; 22; 23; 25; 26(2); 27(2); 28(3); 31(3); 22:3; 4(4); 5(2); 7(2); 8; 9; 11(3); 12(3); 13; 14; 15(3); 16(2); 17; 18(3); 20(7); 21(2); 22; 23; 25; 26(5); 27; 28(3); 29(3); 30(2); 23:3(2); 4(6); 5(2); 6; 7; 8(2); 10(3); 11(2); 12; 14; 16(2); 17(4); 18; 20; 22; 23(6); 24(7); 25(6); 26; 27; 29(6); 30; 32(2); 33(2); 34(3); 35(2); 36; 37(3); 38; 39; 40(3); 41(3); 42(3); 43; 44; 45(3); 46(2); 47(4); 49(3); 24:3(3); 4; 5(3); 6; 10(2); 11(2); 12; 13; 14(2); 17(3); 18(2); 19; 21(3); 22; 23(3); 24; 25(2); 27(4); 25:2; 3(3); 4(3); 5(3); 6(2); 7(4); 8; 9; 10; 11(2); 12(2); 13(4); 14(4); 15; 16(2); 17(2); 26:1; 3; 4(3); 5; 6(2); 7(4); 8(3); 9(2); 10(2); 11; 12(7); 13(2); 14; 16(4); 17(3); 19; 20(2); 21; 27:3; 7; 8; 9; 10(3); 11; 12; 13(2); 14(2); 15; 16(4); 17(5); 18; 19(3); 21(3); 22(3); 23(3); 24(3); 25(2); 27(5); 29(2); 30(3); 31(4); 32(2); 33; 34; 35; 36; 28:2(2); 4(3); 5(2); 7(2); 8; 9; 12(2); 13(5); 14(2); 16(2); 18; 19; 21; 22(4); 23(3); 24(2); 25; 26(4); 29:2(2); 3(2); 4(3); 5(3); 6; 7(3); 8(2); 9(4); 10(3); 12(4); 14(3); 16; 17(2); 18; 19(4); 21(2); 30:2; 4(4); 5(5); 6; 7(2); 8(2); 9; 11(3); 12(4); 13(3); 14(3); 15(2); 16(3); 17(2); 18(2); 19; 20; 21; 22(3); 23(2); 24(3); 25(3); 26(3); 31:1; 2; 3(3); 4; 5(2); 6(2); 8; 10(2); 12(6); 13; 15(4); 16(2); 17; 18(2); 32:1; 2(5); 3; 4(2); 5(2); 6; 7(3); 8; 10(2); 12(2); 14; 15; 16; 18(2); 19; 20; 22; 23; 24; 26; 27(2); 28; 29(2); 30(3); 31(2); 32(2); 33:2(2); 3; 4(2); 5; 6(3); 7; 10(2); 11; 13; 14(2); 16; 18; 19(2); 21; 22(3); 24; 25(3); 26(2); 27(3); 28(2); 30(3); 31(3); 32(2); 33; 34:1; 2; 3; 4; 5(2); 6(2); 8(2); 10(2); 11; 12(2); 13(5); 14(2); 15; 16(4); 17(3); 18; 19(2); 20; 21(2); 22(3); 23(3); 24(2); 25(4); 26(3); 27(5); 28(2); 29(2); 30; 31(2); 35:2; 3(3); 4(2); 5; 6; 7(2); 8(3); 9(2); 10(2); 11(2); 12(2); 13; 15(2); 36:1; 3(4); 4(4); 5; 6(4); 8; 9(3); 10(3); 11(7); 12(3); 13; 17; 18; 19(3); 20(2); 23(2); 24(2); 25(2); 26(3); 27(4); 28(3); 29(3); 30(2); 31(3); 32; 33; 34; 35(5); 36(2); 38; 37:1(2); 2(3); 3(2); 4; 5; 6(6); 7(3); 8(3); 9(2); 10(3); 11; 12(3); 13(2); 14(4); 16(4); 17(2); 18; 19(4); 20; 21(3); 22(3); 23(2); 24(4); 25(5); 26(3); 27; 28; 38:1; 2(2); 3; 3(2); 4(6); 5(2); 6(3); 7(3); 8(2); 9(3); 10; 11(2); 12(3); 13(4); 14; 15(3); 16(2); 18; 19; 20(7); 21; 22(8); 23(3); 39:1(2); 2(4); 3(2); 4(3); 6(3); 7(2); 8; 9(8); 10(2); 11(5); 12; 13; 14; 15; 16; 17(4); 18(2); 19(2); 20(2); 21(3); 22; 23(2); 24(2); 25(2); 26(2); 27(2); 28; 40:1(2); 2; 3(4); 4(3); 5(4); 6(3); 7(4); 9(2); 10(4); 11(2); 12(3); 13; 15; 16(5); 17(2); 18; 19; 20(2); 21(6); 22(5); 23(3); 24(3); 25(4); 26(4); 27(2); 28(2); 29(7); 30(3); 31(3); 32(2); 33(7); 34(4); 35(2); 36(4); 37(4); 38(2); 39(4); 40(2); 41; 42(6); 43(2); 44(2); 45; 46; 47(2); 48(5); 49(4); 41:1(2); 2(5); 3(3); 4(2); 5; 6(3); 7(3); 9; 10; 11(3); 12(2); 13(2); 14; 15(4); 16(4); 17(3); 18(4); 19; 20(2); 21; 22(5); 23(2); 24(2); 25(3); 26(5); 42:1(2); 2; 3; 4(2); 5; 6; 7; 8; 9; 10; 11(4); 12; 13(4); 14(2); 15; 19; 20(2); 43:2(3); 3(3); 4; 5(2); 6(2); 7(3); 8(3); 9(2); 10; 11(11); 13(5); 14(4); 15(2); 16; 17(5); 18(2); 19; 20(5); 21; 22(2); 23; 24(3); 25; 26(2); 27(4); 44:1(2); 3; 4(3); 5(5); 6; 7(3); 8; 10; 11(3); 12(2); 13(2); 14; 15(2); 16(2); 17(3); 18; 19(4); 23(4); 24(5); 25; 26; 27; 28(2); 29(3); 30(2); 45:1(2); 2; 3(5); 4(2); 5(3); 6(3); 7(6); 8(2); 9(3); 10(2); 11(2); 12(2); 13; 15(3); 17(8); 18; 19(4); 20(2); 22(2); 23(3); 24(3); 25(2); 46:1; 2(5); 3; 4(2); 5(3); 6(3); 7(4); 8(2); 9; 10(2); 11(5); 12(3); 14(2); 15(2); 19; 20; 21(2); 22; 23(2); 47:1(2); 2(2); 3(2); 4(2); 5; 6(2); 7; 8(2); 9(3); 10; 11; 12(4); 14(2); 15; 16; 17(4); 18(5); 19(2); 22(3); 23; 48:1; 2; 3; 4; 5; 6; 7; 8(4); 9(2); 10(7); 12; 13(5); 14; 15(4); 16(8); 17(8); 18(4); 19; 20(2); 21(8); 22(2); 24; 25; 26; 27; 28(2); 29; 30(2); 31; 32(4); 33(3); 34; 35; **Dan** 1:1; 2(2); 3(3); 4(6); 5(2); 6; 7(3); 9; 10(2); 11; 12(2); 13(2); 14; 15(2); 16(2); 17(4); 19(3); 20(3); 21; 2:1(2); 2(4); 3(2); 4; 5(2); 6(4); 7(2); 8; 9(2); 10; 11(2); 12(2); 13(3); 14; 15; 16(2); 17(2); 18; 20(3); 21(4); 22(2); 23(3); 24(2); 25; 26(2); 27; 28(2); 29; 30; 31(2); 32(2); 33; 34(2); 35(5); 36; 37(2); 38(3); 39(2); 40(4); 41(3); 42(3); 43; 44(4); 45(4); 46(3); 47(3); 48(3); 49(2); 3:1; 2(2); 3(3); 4; 5(2); 6(2); 7(3); 8; 9; 10(3); 11(2); 12; 13(2); 14(2); 15(4); 16(2); 17; 19(3); 20(3); 21(3); 22(2); 23(2); 24(4); 25(3); 26(5); 27(3); 28(5); 29(3); 30; 4:1; 2; 3(2); 4; 5(2); 7(2); 8(2); 9(2); 10(2); 11(3); 12(4); 13(2); 14(4); 15(3); 16(2); 17(3); 19(4); 20(2); 21(3); 22(3); 23(7); 24; 25(5); 26; 27(2); 30(2); 32(4); 33(4); 34(6); 35(4); 36(6); 37(4); 5:1; 2(3); 3(3); 4(3); 5(2); 6(2); 7(6); 9(2); 10(3); 11(4); 12(5); 13(2); 14(3); 15(2); 16(5); 17(3); 18(3); 19(6); 20(2); 21(5); 22; 23(9); 24; 25; 26; 27; 28(2); 29(3); 31(2); 6:1; 2(2); 3(2); 4; 6(2); 7(3); 8(2); 9; 10(3); 11(2); 12(3); 13; 14(2); 15(2); 16(3); 17(4); 18(2); 19; 20(3); 22(2); 23(2); 24(6); 25; 26(4); 27(4); 28; 7:1(2); 2(2); 3; 4(4); 5(4); 6(2); 7(8); 8(3); 9(3); 10(3); 11(2); 12; 13(3); 14(5); 15; 16(2); 18(2); 19(2); 20(4); 21(2); 22(2); 23(3); 24(4); 25(7); 26(2); 27(5); 28; 8:2(4); 3(4); 4(3); 5(3); 6(2); 7(7); 8(2); 9(3); 10(4); 11(2); 12(4); 13(3); 14(2); 15(2); 16(2); 17(2); 18; 19; 20; 21(2); 23(2); 24(6); 25(3); 26(2); 27(4); 9:3(4); 4(6); 5(4); 6(2); 7(3); 8; 9; 11; 12(2); 13; 14; 15(2); 16(3); 17(2); 18(3); 19(2); 20(5); 22(4); 23(2); 24(7); 25(5); 26(6); 27(5); 10:1(3); 4(2); 5(2); 6(5); 7; 8(3); 9(2); 10(2); 11(3); 12(2); 13(2); 15(2); 16(4); 18(2); 19(3); 20(2); 21; 11:1; 2(3); 3(2); 4(3); 5(4); 6(4); 7(3); 8(4); 9; 10(5); 11(4); 12(2); 13(3); 14; 15(3); 16(2); 17(2); 18; 19(2); 21(2); 22(2); 23(2); 24(4); 25(4); 26(2); 27(2); 28(3); 29; 30(3); 31(4); 32(2); 33(3); 35(3); 36(5); 38(4); 39(3); 40(7); 41(3); 42; 43(4); 44(2); 45(2); 12:1(3); 2(3); 3(3); 4(3); 5(2); 6; 7(5); 8; 9(2); 10(3); 11(3); 12(3); 13; **Hos** 1:1(2); 2(2); 3(2); 4(3); 5; 6(3); 7(2); 8; 9; 10; 11(3); 2:1; 2; 3(4); 4; 5(3); 6; 7(3); 8(4); 9(4); 10(2); 11(2); 12(4); 13(5); 14(2); 15(4); 16(2); 17; 18(7); 19(4); 20; 21(2); 22(4);

23(4); 3:1; 2(2); 3(2); 4(5); 5(4); 4:2(5); 3(2); 5(2); 8; 9(3); 10(2); 11(2); 12(2); 13(4); 14; 15; 19; 5:1(3); 2; 3(2); 4; 5(2); 6; 8; 11; 12; 13(2); 14(3); 15(2); 6:1(3); 2; 3(2); 4; 5; 6(2); 8; 9; 7:1(3); 2; 3; 7; 9(2); 10(2); 14(3); 15; 8:1; 4(2); 7; 10; 13(2); 14(3); 9:2(2); 3; 5; 7; 8; 10(2); 11(2); 14; 17; 10:5; 6; 8(3); 10; 11(3); 12; 14; 11:1; 2; 4(2); 6(3); 7; 9(2); 11(2); 12(2); 12:1(4); 2; 3; 4(3); 6(2); 8; 9; 10(2); 12(3); 13(2); 14; 13:2(4); 3(2); 4; 6; 8(2); 10(2); 11; 15(2); 16; 14:2(2); 5; 6(2); 7; 8; 9(3); **Joel** 1:2; 3(2); 4(2); 5(2); 6(2); 7(2); 9; 11; 12(2); 13(2); 14(2); 15; 16; 19; 20; 2:1; 2(3); 3(3); 4; 7(2); 8; 9; 10(2); 11(3); 12(3); 13(6); 14(3); 16(2); 17(3); 18; 19(5); 20(5); 21; 22; 23(3); 24(3); 25(3); 26(4); 27(4); 28(3); 29(2); 30(4); 31(2); 32(3); 3:1(2); 2(4); 3(3); 4(5); 5(2); 6; 7; 8(3); 10; 11(2); 12; 15(2); 16(4); 17; 18(5); 19; 20; **Amos** 1:1; 2(4); 3; 5(3); 6; 8(4); 9(2); 11(4); 13; 14; 15(2); 2:1; 2(3); 3(2); 4(3); 5; 6(2); 7(3); 8(2); 9(2); 10; 11(2); 12; 14; 15; 16; 3:5; 6(2); 9(4); 10; 11(2); 12; 13; 14(2); 15(3); 4:1; 2; 3(2); 4(3); 5(3); 6(2); 7(4); 9(4); 10(2); 11(2); 12; 13(3); 5:3; 4; 5(2); 6(3); 7; 8(4); 10; 11; 12(2); 14(2); 15(2); 16(3); 17; 18; 19(3); 20(2); 21; 22; 24; 25; 26; 6:1; 2(2); 3; 4(3); 5; 6; 7; 8; 9; 10(4); 11(2); 12; 14; 7:1(2); 2; 4(3); 7; 8(2); 9(3); 11; 12(2); 13; 14(2); 15(2); 16; 17(5); 8:1; 2(2); 3; 5(3); 6(2); 8(4); 9(2); 10(6); 12(4); 13; 14(3); 9:1(4); 3(4); 4(4); 5(5); 6(2); 7(2); 8; 9; 11(3); 12; 13(3); 14(6); 15(2); **Obad** 1(2); 4; 7; 8; 9; 10; 11(2); 16(2); 17(2); 18(6); 19(5); 20(2); 21(2); **Jonah** 1:2; 3(3); 4; 5(4); 6; 7(3); 8(2); 9(3); 10; 11; 12(2); 13; 14(2); 15(2); 16(2); 17(2); 2:2(3); 3(2); 7; 10(2); 3:1; 2; 3; 4(4); 5(2); 6(4); 7(3); 8(3); 9(2); 10(3); 4:1; 2(5); 5(3); 6(2); 7; 8(4); 9(2); 10; 11(3); **Mic** 1:1(2); 2(2); 3(2); 4(3); 5(2); 6(3); 7(4); 8(3); 16; 2:1; 2(6); 4(2); 10; 11(2); 13(4); 3:1(2); 2(2); 3(4); 5(2); 6(3); 7; 8(3); 9(2); 10; 11(3); 12(2); 4:1(2); 2(7); 3(4); 4(2); 5(2); 6(2); 7(3); 8; 10(3); 11; 13(5); 5:4(3); 5(3); 6(3); 7; 8(3); 9; 10(2); 11(2); 12(2); 13(2); 14; 15(2); 6:1; 2(2); 3; 4(3); 5; 6; 8(3); 9(2); 10; 11; 12(2); 14(3); 15; 16(3); 7:2; 3(2); 4; 9(2); 10; 12(4); 14; 16; 17; 18; 19; 20; **Nah** 1:2(3); 3(4); 4(4); 5(3); 6(2); 7; 8; 10; 12; 13; 14(2); 2:2; 3; 5; 6; 7(2); 9; 10(6); 11(3); 12(3); 13(4); 3:1; 2(3); 3(4); 4; 5(3); 6(3); 7(2); 8; 9(3); 10(2); 14; 16; 17(2); 18; **Hab** 1:2(2); 3(4); 4; 5(2); 6; 7(2); 8(3); 9; 10(3); 11(2); 12; 13(2); 14; 15(2); 16(2); 17; 2:1(3); 2(3); 3; 5(3); 6(3); 7(2); 8(2); 10; 11; 12; 13; 15; 16(2); 17(3); 18; 19(2); 3:2; 3(2); 4(2); 5; 6(3); 7; 8; 10(2); 11(2); 16; 17(2); 19(2); **Zeph** 1:3(4); 4(3); 5(4); 6(2); 8(3); 9; 10(3); 12(2); 13(2); 14; 15(4); 16(2); 17(3); 2:4(2); 6(3); 7(2); 8(2); 9(4); 10; 11; 13(4); 14(2); 15(2); 3:1; 4; 7; 11; 12(2); 13(2); 14; 16; 19(4); 20; **Hag** 1:1; 4; 6(2); 8(4); 9(3); 10; 11(9); 12(3); 14(5); 15; 2:1; 2(2); 3; 4(3); 6(4); 7(3); 8; 9; 10; 12(3); 13(2); 14(4); 15(2); 17(2); 18(2); 19(3); 20(2); 21; 22(6); 23; **Zec** 1:3; 4; 5; 6(4); 7; 8(4); 9; 10(3); 11(5); 12(3); 13(2); 14; 15(2); 16; 17(2); 18(2); 19(3); 20; 21; 2:1(2); 2(2); 3(2); 4(2); 5; 6; 9(2); 10(2); 11(4); 12(2); 3:1(2); 2; 3; 4(4); 5(3); 6; 7(3); 8; 9; 10; 4:1(2); 2(5); 3(2); 4; 5(2); 6; 7; 9; 10(2); 11(2); 12(2); 13(3); 5:1(3); 2(3); 3; 4(5); 5(2); 6(2); 7(2); 8(3); 9(5); 11(3); 6:1(5); 2; 3(3); 4; 5(2); 6(2); 7(6); 8; 9; 10(3); 11(3); 12(3); 13(5); 14(4); 15(4); 7:1; 2(2); 3(2); 5(3); 6(3); 7(3); 8; 9(2); 10(2); 11(2); 12; 13(2); 8:2; 3(3); 4(2); 5(2); 7; 8(5); 12(3); 13(3); 14; 15; 16; 17(2); 18; 19(6); 20; 21(2); 22(2); 9:1; 2(2); 3(3); 4(2); 5(5); 6(2); 7(4); 8(3); 9(3); 10(6); 13(2); 14(4); 15(6); 16; 17(2); 10:1; 2(2); 3(2); 5(3); 6(5); 7(3); 8(2); 9(4); 10(4); 11(5); 12(3); 11:5(3); 6(3); 7(4); 8(2); 9(2); 10(2); 11(2); 12(2); 13(3); 14; 15; 16; 17(2); 12:1(2); 2; 3; 4(3); 5; 6(4); 7; 8(2); 9; 10(6); 12(3); 13(2); 14; 13:1(2); 2(4); 3(4); 4; 6; 7(3); 8(2); 9(5); 14:1; 2(5); 3; 4(6); 5(3); 6; 8(3); 9(2); 10(3); 11(2); 12(3); 13(3); 14(4); 15(3); 16(2); 17; 18(2); 19; 20; 21(5); **Mal** 1:3(3); 4(3); 5(2); 6(3); 7; 8(3); 9; 11(2); 12; 13(4); 14(3); 2:1; 2(2); 3(2); 4; 5(3); 6(3); 7; 9; 11(3); 12(2); 13(2); 14(2); 15(3); 17; 3:1(2); 2(2); 3(5); 4(2); 5(8); 7(2); 8; 10(2); 11(2); 12; 14(2); 15; 16(4); 17(2); 18(3); 4:1(3); 2(2); 3; 4; 5; 6(3); **Mt** 1:2(3); 3(4); 4(3); 5(3); 6(2); 7(3); 8(3); 9(3); 10(3); 11(2); 12(2); 13(3); 14(3); 15(3); 16; 17(2); 19; 21(2); 23(2); 24; 25(2); 2:2; 3; 4(2); 5; 6; 8(5); 9(2); 11(6); 12; 13(5); 14(2); 15; 16(4); 18(3); 20(3); 21(4); 23(2); 3:2; 4(4); 5(2); 6; 7; 9; 10(2); 11; 12(2); 14; 15; 16(4); 17; 4:2(2); 3; 4; 5; 6(2); 8(2); 9(2); 10; 11(2); 13(3); 15; 16(2); 17; 18(2); 19(2); 20(2); 21(3); 22(3); 23(4); 24(7); 25(5); 5:1(2); 2(2); 6; 11(2); 12; 13; 15(2); 16; 18; 19(2); 20; 21; 22; 23; 24(3); 25(2); 29(3); 30(3); 32; 38; 40(2); 41; 42; 43; 44(2); 45(3); 47; 6:2; 4; 5(2); 6(2); 12; 13(3); 17; 18; 19(3); 20; 24(3); 25; 28; 29; 30; 33(2); 7:2; 3; 4; 5; 6(2); 7(3); 8(2); 12; 13(2); 14(2); 19; 22(2); 23; 24; 25(5); 26(2); 27(6); 28; 29; 8:2(2); 3(3); 4(2); 5; 6; 7(2); 8(2); 9(6); 10; 11(5); 12; 13(3); 14(2); 15(4); 16(2); 17; 19(2); 20(2); 21(2); 22; 23; 24; 25(2); 26(4); 27; 28; 29; 30; 32(4); 33(4); 34(2); 9:1(3); 2(2); 3; 4; 5; 6; 7(2); 8; 9(4); 10(4); 11(2); 13(2); 14; 15(2); 16; 17(3); 18(3); 19(3); 20(2); 22(2); 23(3); 24; 25(2); 26; 27(2); 28(2); 30(2); 33(2); 35(5); 36; 10:1(3); 2(2); 3(3); 4; 5(2); 7; 11(2); 12; 13; 14; 15; 16; 17; 18(3); 21(4); 22; 25; 26; 27; 28(2); 29; 35(2); 36; 37; 38(2); 39; 40; 41; 42; 11:1(2); 3; 4(3); 5(3); 6; 7; 9; 12(2); 13; 14; 16; 17(3); 18; 19(4); 21(2); 22; 23; 25(4); 27(2); 28(2); 29(3); 30; 12:1(3); 3; 4; 5; 7; 9; 10(2); 11(3); 13(2); 14; 15(2); 16; 18; 20; 21; 22(4); 23(2); 25(3); 26; 27; 29(2); 30; 31; 32; 33(2); 35; 37; 38; 39(3); 40(2); 41(2); 42(2); 43; 44(2); 45(4); 46; 47; 48(2); 49(3); 50(2); 13:1; 2(3); 3; 4(3); 5; 6(2); 7(3); 8; 10(2); 11; 12; 13; 14(4); 15(6); 16; 17(4); 19(2); 20; 21; 22(3); 23(2); 25(2); 26; 27; 28; 30(2); 31; 32(2); 33; 34; 36(2); 37; 39; 40; 41(2); 42(2); 44(3); 46(2); 47; 48(2); 49; 50(2); 52; 53; 54(3); 55(4); 56; 57(2); 58; 14:2(2); 3(2); 5; 6; 8; 9(2); 10(2); 11(3); 12(5); 13; 14(4); 15(3); 17(2); 19(7); 20(3); 21(2); 22(2); 23(2); 25; 26(2); 28(2); 29(2); 30; 31(3); 32; 33; 34; 35(2); 36(2); 15:1; 3; 4(2); 6; 8; 10(3); 12; 13; 14; 15; 16; 17; 18; 21(2); 22(2); 23(2); 24; 25; 26(2); 27; 28(2); 29(4); 30(4); 31(2); 32(3); 33; 34(3); 35; 36(6); 37(3); 38(2); 39(3); 16:1; 2; 3(2); 4(4); 5; 6(2); 7; 9; 10; 11; 12; 14(2); 16(2); 17(3); 18(3); 19(3); 21(5); 22; 23; 24(2); 25; 26; 27; 17:1(3); 2(3); 3(2); 4(3); 5; 6(2); 7(4); 8; 9; 10; 11(3); 12; 14(2); 15(2); 16(2); 17(2); 18(3); 19; 20(3); 21; 22; 23(3); 24(2); 25; 27(5); 18:2(2); 3(2); 5; 6; 8; 9(2); 12(4); 13(2); 15(2); 17(2); 18; 21(2); 24; 25(4); 26(2); 27(2); 28(3); 29(3); 30(2); 31(2); 34(2); 19:1(2); 2(2); 3; 4(3); 5(4); 7; 9(3); 12(2); 13(2); 14; 15(2); 16(2); 17; 19(2); 21(5); 24; 26; 27(2); 28; 29(2); 30; 20:2; 3(2); 4(3); 5(2); 6(3); 7; 8; 9; 10; 11; 12(2); 13; 14; 16; 17(2); 18(3); 19(4); 20; 21(2); 22(2); 23(3); 24; 25(2); 27; 28; 29; 30; 31; 32(3); 34(3); 21:1(2); 2(3); 3(2); 5(2); 6(2); 7(4); 8(2); 9(2); 10; 11; 12(5); 13; 14(3); 15(4); 16(3); 17(3); 19(4); 20; 21(3); 22; 23(4); 24(2); 25; 27(3); 28(2); 29(2); 30(5);

31; 32(3); 33(5); 34; 35(4); 36; 38; 39(3); 41; 42; 43; 44; 45(2); 22:1(3); 3(2); 4(2); 5; 6(3); 7(3); 9; 10(3); 11; 12(2); 13(4); 15; 16(2); 18; 19; 20(2); 21; 22(2); 23; 24; 25(2); 26; 27; 29; 32(2); 33; 35; 37(2); 38; 39; 40; 46; 23:1; 2; 3(2); 4(2); 5; 6(2); 7(2); 8; 9; 12(2); 13; 14(2); 15(3); 17; 18; 19; 20; 21(2); 22(2); 23(6); 24; 25(3); 26; 27(2); 28; 29(2); 30; 34(6); 35; 37(2); 24:1(3); 2; 3(3); 4(2); 5; 6(2); 7(4); 9(2); 10(3); 11(2); 12; 14(2); 19(2); 22; 24(3); 27; 29(3); 30(4); 31(2); 32; 35; 36; 38(2); 39(2); 40; 41; 43; 45; 48; 49(3); 50; 51(3); 25:1; 2(2); 3; 5; 6; 7; 8; 9(2); 10(3); 12; 14; 15(3); 16(2); 17; 18(2); 19; 20(2); 21; 22; 23; 24(2); 25(3); 26(3); 27; 28; 29; 30(2); 31; 32(2); 33; 35(3); 36(3); 37(2); 38(2); 39; 40(2); 41; 42(2); 43(4); 44; 46; 26:1; 2; 3(2); 4(2); 7; 9; 15(3); 16; 18(2); 19(2); 21; 22(2); 23(2); 25; 26(5); 27(3); 30; 31; 33; 36(2); 37(4); 38; 39(3); 40(3); 41; 42; 43(2); 44(3); 45(3); 47(4); 49(3); 50(3); 51(4); 53; 55(2); 56; 57(2); 58(2); 59(2); 61(2); 62(2); 63(2); 64; 66; 67(2); 69; 71(2); 72; 73(2); 74(2); 75(3); 27:1; 2(2); 3(2); 4; 5(4); 6(2); 7(2); 9; 10; 11(3); 12(2); 14; 16; 20(2); 21; 23; 24; 25(2); 26; 27; 28(2); 29(4); 30(3); 31(3); 32; 33; 34; 35(3); 36; 37; 38; 39; 40(2); 41; 42; 46; 48(5); 51(3); 52(2); 53(3); 54(2); 55; 56(3); 58; 59; 60(3); 61(2); 62; 64(2); 66(2); 28:1; 2(4); 3; 4(2); 5(2); 7(3); 8(3); 9(4); 10; 11; 12(2); 13; 14(2); 15(2); 17; 18(3); 19(3); 20; **Mk** 1:4; 5(3); 6(4); 7(2); 9(2); 10(2); 11; 12; 13(3); 15(3); 16; 17(2); 18(2); 19(2); 20(3); 21(3); 22(2); 23(2); 25(2); 26(2); 27(2); 28; 29(2); 30; 31(5); 32(2); 33; 34(3); 35(3); 36(2); 37; 38; 39(2); 40(3); 41(3); 42(2); 43(2); 44(2); 45(3); 2:1(2); 2(2); 3; 4(2); 6; 8; 9(2); 11(2); 12(3); 13(3); 14(4); 15(4); 16(5); 18(5); 19; 20; 21; 22(3); 23(2); 24; 25(3); 26(2); 27(2); 3:1(2); 2; 3; 4; 5(3); 6(2); 7(2); 8(5); 9; 11(2); 12; 13(3); 14(2); 15(2); 16; 17(3); 18(8); 19(2); 20; 21; 22(2); 23(2); 24; 25; 26(2); 27(2); 28; 31(2); 32(3); 33; 34(3); 35(2); 4:1(4); 2(2); 4(3); 5(2); 6; 7(4); 8(6); 9; 10; 11; 12(4); 13(2); 15(2); 16; 17(2); 18; 19(4); 20(4); 21(2); 24(2); 25; 26; 27(5); 30; 32(2); 33; 34; 35; 36(2); 37(2); 38(3); 39(5); 40; 41(3); 5:1; 2; 3; 4(3); 5(4); 6; 7(2); 9(2); 10; 12; 13(5); 14(4); 15(6); 16(2); 17; 18; 19(2); 20(3); 21(2); 22(2); 23(3); 24(3); 25; 26(3); 27; 29(2); 30(2); 31(2); 32; 33(3); 34(2); 37(3); 38(4); 39(2); 40(4); 41(2); 42(3); 43(2); 6:1(3); 2(3); 3(5); 4(2); 5(2); 6(2); 7(4); 8; 9; 10; 11(2); 12(2); 13(3); 14(3); 15; 17(2); 19; 20(4); 21(2); 22(5); 23; 24(3); 25(3); 26(2); 27(4); 28(3); 29(3); 30(3); 31(4); 32; 33(5); 34(3); 35(3); 36(2); 37(4); 38(3); 39; 40(2); 41(6); 42(2); 43(2); 44; 45(2); 46; 47(2); 48(3); 49; 50(3); 51(4); 53(2); 54; 55(2); 56(3); 7:1; 2; 3; 4(4); 5; 6; 8(2); 9; 10(2); 12; 13; 14(2); 17; 18; 19; 20; 23; 24(5); 25(2); 26; 27; 28(2); 29; 30(2); 31(2); 32(3); 33(4); 34(2); 35(3); 36; 37(2); 8:1(2); 2; 3; 4; 5(2); 6(6); 7(3); 8(2); 9(2); 10(2); 11(2); 12(2); 13(2); 15(2); 16; 17; 18(2); 20(2); 21; 22(3); 23(4); 24(2); 25(3); 26; 27(3); 28(2); 29(3); 30; 31(6); 32(3); 33; 34(3); 35; 36; 38(2); 9:1; 2(5); 3; 4(2); 5(5); 7(2); 8; 9; 10; 11; 12(5); 13; 14(2); 15(2); 16; 17(2); 18(6); 19; 20(4); 21(2); 22(3); 24(2); 25(2); 26(4); 27(2); 28; 29(2); 30(3); 31(3); 32; 33(2); 35(4); 36(3); 37; 38(3); 42(2); 43; 44; 45; 46; 47; 48; 49; 50; 10:1(4); 2(2); 3(2); 4(2); 5(2); 6; 7(2); 8; 10; 11(2); 12(2); 13(2); 14(2); 16(2); 17(3); 18; 19; 20(2); 21(5); 22(2); 23(2); 24(2); 26; 27; 28; 29(3); 30(6); 31; 32(6); 33(4); 34(5); 35(2); 36; 37; 38; 39(3); 40; 41(2); 42(2); 44; 45; 46(3); 47(2); 48; 49(3); 50(2); 51(2); 52(3); 11:1(2); 2(3); 3(2); 4(3); 5; 6(2); 7(3); 8(3); 9(2); 11(4); 12; 13(2); 14(3); 15(6); 16; 17; 18(3); 19; 20; 21; 22; 23(2); 24; 25; 27(4); 28(2); 29(4); 31; 33(3); 12:1(6); 2; 3(3); 4(4); 5(4); 7; 8(3); 9(2); 10; 11; 12(3); 13(2); 14(2); 16(4); 17(3); 18; 19(3); 20(2); 21(3); 22(2); 24; 26(3); 28(3); 29; 30(4); 31; 32(2); 33(6); 34(2); 35(2); 37(2); 38(2); 39(2); 40; 41(3); 42(2); 43(2); 13:1(2); 2; 3(4); 4; 5; 6; 7(2); 8(4); 9(3); 10; 11; 12(3); 13; 15; 16; 17; 18; 20; 21; 22(3); 24; 25(2); 26(2); 27(2); 28; 31; 32; 33; 34(3); 37; 14:1(4); 3(3); 4(2); 5(2); 6; 7; 10; 11(3); 12(2); 13(3); 14; 15(2); 16(4); 17; 18(2); 19(3); 20(2); 22(5); 23(3); 24; 26; 27(2); 30; 32(2); 33(5); 34(2); 35(3); 36; 37(3); 38; 39(3); 40; 41(3); 43(5); 44(2); 45(3); 46(2); 47(3); 48(3); 49; 50(2); 51(2); 52(2); 53(4); 54(3); 55(3); 57(2); 58; 60(2); 61(2); 62(3); 63; 64; 65(5); 66; 67(3); 68(2); 69(2); 70(3); 71; 72(3); 15:1(6); 2(2); 3; 4; 7; 8; 12(2); 13; 14; 15(2); 16(2); 17(3); 18; 19(3); 20(3); 21(2); 22; 23; 24; 25(2); 26; 27(2); 28(2); 29(3); 30; 32(2); 33; 34; 35; 36(4); 37(2); 38; 39(2); 40(3); 41(2); 42; 43(2); 44(2); 45; 46(5); 47(2); 16:1(4); 2; 3; 4; 5(2); 6; 7; 8(3); 10(3); 11(2); 12; 13(2); 14(2); 15(2); 16; 17; 18(2); 19; 20(3); **Lk** 1:2; 5(2); 6(2); 7(2); 8; 10; 11; 12(2); 13(2); 14(3); 15(2); 16; 17(3); 18(2); 19(3); 20(2); 21(2); 22(3); 23; 24(2); 26; 27; 28(2); 29(2); 30; 31(3); 32(2); 33(2); 35(3); 36(2); 38(2); 39(2); 40(2); 41(2); 42(3); 43; 45; 46; 47; 49; 50; 52; 53; 55; 56(2); 57; 58(3); 59(2); 60(2); 61; 62; 63(3); 64(4); 65(2); 66(2); 67(2); 68; 69; 71; 72; 75; 76; 79; 80(3); 2:1; 2; 3; 4(2); 6; 7(3); 8; 9(3); 10; 12; 13(2); 14; 15(2); 16(4); 17; 18; 19; 20(3); 21; 22; 24; 25(4); 26; 27(2); 28(2); 32; 33(2); 34(4); 36(2); 37(4); 38(2); 39; 40(3); 42; 43(3); 44(2); 45; 46(2); 47(2); 48(3); 49; 50; 51(3); 52(4); 3:1(4); 2; 3; 5(4); 6; 8; 9(2); 10; 11(2); 12; 13; 14(4); 15(2); 16; 17(2); 18; 19; 21; 22(2); 23; 4:1(2); 2(2); 3; 4; 5; 6(3); 8(3); 9(3); 11; 12; 13; 14(2); 15; 16(3); 17(2); 18; 20(4); 21; 22(3); 23; 24; 25; 27(2); 28; 29(3); 31(2); 32; 33(2); 35(4); 36(4); 37; 38(4); 39(5); 40(2); 41(3); 42(5); 43; 44; 5:1; 2(2); 3(4); 4; 5(2); 6(2); 7(4); 9; 10(3); 11(2); 12(2); 13(3); 14(3); 15(2); 16(2); 17(5); 18(3); 19(2); 20; 21(2); 23; 24(2); 25(3); 26(3); 27(3); 28(2); 29(3); 30(3); 31; 33(4); 34; 35; 36(2); 37(3); 38; 6:1(3); 2; 3(2); 4(3); 5; 6(3); 7(2); 8(4); 10(3); 11(2); 12(2); 13(2); 14(3); 15(2); 16(2); 17(8); 18(2); 19(2); 20(2); 22(3); 23; 25; 28; 29(2); 30; 31; 33; 34; 35(5); 37(3); 38(3); 39; 41; 42; 45; 46(2); 47(2); 48(4); 49(3); 7:2(2); 3(2); 4; 5; 6; 7; 8(6); 9(2); 10; 11(3); 12(2); 13(2); 14(4); 15(3); 16(3); 17(2); 18; 19; 21(4); 22(2); 23; 24; 25; 26; 29(2); 30; 31(2); 32(4); 33; 34(4); 36(3); 37; 38(5); 39; 40(2); 41; 42; 43(2); 44(3); 48; 49; 50; 8:1(4); 2(2); 3(3); 4(2); 5(3); 6(2); 7(3); 8(4); 9; 10(2); 12(2); 13(2); 14(5); 15(2); 17; 18; 19(2); 20(2); 21(4); 22(2); 23(3); 24(6); 25(4); 26; 27(2); 28(2); 29(4); 30(2); 31; 32(3); 33(3); 34(3); 35(4); 37(2); 39(3); 40; 41(4); 42; 43; 44(2); 45(4); 46; 47(3); 48; 50; 51(5); 52(2); 53; 54(3); 55(3); 56; 9:1(3); 2(2); 3; 4(2); 5; 6(3); 7; 8(2); 9(2); 10(3); 11(4); 12(5); 13(3); 14; 15(2); 16(4); 17(3); 18(2); 19; 21(2); 22(5); 23(3); 25; 26(3); 28(4); 29(3); 30(2); 31; 32(3); 33(4); 34(2); 35; 36(3); 37; 38; 39(4); 40(2); 41(3); 42(5); 43; 45(2); 47(2); 48(2); 49(3); 50; 51; 52(3); 53; 54(3); 55(2); 56; 57; 58(2); 59(2); 60; 61; 62(2); 10:1(3); 4; 5; 6; 7(2); 8(2); 9(2); 10(2); 13(2); 14; 15; 16(2); 17; 18; 19(3); 21(4); 22(3); 23(2); 24(4); 25(2); 27(5); 28(2); 29;

30(4); 31(2); 32(3); 33; 34(6); 35(4); 37(2); 38; 39(2); 40(2); 41(3); 42; 11:1; 2; 4(2); 5(3); 6; 7(4); 8(2); 9(4); 10(2); 14(4); 16; 17; 19; 22(2); 23; 24; 25(2); 26(4); 27(3); 28; 29(2); 31(2); 32(2); 37(3); 38; 39(3); 41; 42(5); 43; 44(2); 45; 46(2); 47; 48; 49(3); 51; 52; 53(3); 54; 12:3; 4(2); 6; 10; 11(3); 13; 14; 15(2); 16; 17; 18(4); 19(2); 21; 22; 23; 24; 25; 27; 28; 29; 30; 31; 33; 35; 36(2); 37(3); 38(2); 39(2); 42(2); 45(6); 46(3); 47(2); 48(2); 49; 50; 52; 53(3); 54(2); 55(2); 56; 57; 58(2); 13:2; 4; 6(3); 7; 8(2); 9(2); 10; 11(3); 12(2); 13(3); 14(4); 15(2); 16; 17(2); 18; 19(4); 20; 21; 22(3); 23; 24; 25(5); 26(2); 28(5); 29(5); 30(2); 31; 32(5); 33(2); 34(2); 35; 14:1; 2; 3(2); 4(4); 5(2); 6; 7; 9(4); 10; 11; 12; 14; 15; 16; 17; 18(3); 19(2); 20(2); 21(6); 22(2); 23(3); 25(3); 26(7); 27(2); 28; 29; 30; 31; 32; 15:1; 2(3); 3; 4(2); 5; 6(2); 7; 8(2); 9(2); 11; 12(2); 13(3); 14(2); 15(3); 16(2); 17(3); 18(3); 19; 20(6); 21(3); 22(3); 23(4); 24(3); 25(3); 26(2); 27(3); 28(3); 29(2); 31(2); 32(4); 16:1(2); 2(2); 5; 6(4); 7(4); 8; 9; 10; 12; 13(3); 14(2); 15; 16(2); 17(2); 18(2); 19(2); 20; 21(2); 22(3); 23(3); 24(4); 25(2); 26(2); 29; 30; 31(2); 17:2; 3; 4(2); 5; 6(3); 7(2); 8(6); 11(2); 12; 13(2); 14(2); 15(2); 16(2); 17; 19; 20(2); 22(2); 23; 25; 26; 27(2); 29(2); 31(2); 33; 34; 35; 36; 37(3); 18:1(2); 3(2); 4; 6; 7(2); 9(2); 10; 11; 13; 14; 15; 16(2); 18; 19; 20; 21; 22(3); 23; 24; 26; 27; 28; 29; 30; 31(2); 32(3); 33(3); 34(2); 35; 36; 37; 38; 39; 40(3); 41; 42; 43(3); 19:1(2); 2(2); 3(2); 4(2); 5(4); 6(3); 7; 8(3); 9; 10; 11(3); 12; 13(3); 14; 15; 17; 18; 19; 20; 21; 22(2); 24(2); 25; 26; 27; 28; 29(2); 30; 31; 32(2); 33; 34; 35(3); 36; 37(2); 38; 39; 40(2); 41(2); 43(2); 44(3); 45(3); 47(3); 48; 20:1(3); 2; 3(3); 5; 6; 7; 8; 9(2); 10(2); 11(4); 12(3); 15; 16(3); 17(2); 19(3); 20(3); 21(2); 23; 24(2); 25(2); 26(3); 27; 28(2); 29(2); 30(2); 31(4); 34(2); 35; 36; 37(2); 40; 41; 42; 46(3); 47; 21:1(2); 2; 3; 5(2); 7(2); 8(2); 9(2); 10; 11(5); 12(3); 13; 15; 16(5); 17; 20; 21(2); 23(2); 24(3); 25(5); 26; 27(2); 28(2); 29(2); 30; 33; 34(4); 36(2); 37(3); 38; 22:2(2); 4(3); 5(2); 6(2); 8(3); 9; 10; 11; 12; 13(3); 14(2); 15; 17(4); 19(4); 22; 23; 24; 25(2); 26; 29; 30(2); 31; 32; 33(2); 34; 35(4); 36(3); 37; 38(2); 39(3); 40; 41(3); 43; 44(2); 45(2); 46(2); 47(3); 50(2); 51(4); 52(3); 53; 54(3); 55(2); 56(2); 57; 58(3); 59; 60(2); 61(3); 62(2); 63(2); 64(2); 65; 66(4); 67; 68; 70; 71; 23:1(2); 2(2); 3(3); 4; 5; 7; 8(2); 10(3); 11(4); 12(2); 13(3); 14; 15; 16; 18(2); 19; 22(2); 23(3); 24; 25(2); 26(2); 27(3); 28; 29(2); 30; 32; 33(3); 34(2); 35(2); 36(2); 37; 38(3); 39(2); 41; 42; 43; 44(2); 45(2); 46(2); 48(2); 49(2); 50(3); 51; 52; 53(3); 54(2); 55(3); 56(4); 24:1; 2; 3(2); 4; 5(2); 7(2); 8; 9(3); 10(3); 11(2); 12(3); 13; 14; 15(3); 17(2); 18(2); 19(4); 20(3); 21; 22; 23; 24(2); 25; 26; 27(2); 28(2); 29(2); 30(4); 31(3); 32(2); 33(4); 34; 35(2); 36(2); 37(2); 38(2); 39(3); 40(2); 41(2); 42(2); 43(2); 44(3); 46(3); 47(2); 48; 49; 50(3); 51(2); 52(2); 53(2); **Jn** 1:1(2); 3; 4; 5(2); 10(2); 11; 14(4); 15; 16(2); 17; 19(2); 20(2); 21(3); 24; 25(2); 29; 31; 32(2); 33(2); 34(2); 35; 36; 37(2); 38(2); 39(3); 40; 41; 42(2); 43(2); 44; 45(2); 46(2); 47; 48; 49; 50; 51(3); 2:1(2); 2(2); 3; 6; 7; 8(3); 9; 10(2); 11(2); 12(4); 13(2); 14(4); 15(5); 16; 17; 18; 19(2); 20(2); 22(2); 25; 3:2; 3; 4; 5; 6; 8(2); 9; 10(2); 11(2); 12; 13; 14; 19(2); 22(3); 23(3); 25; 26(3); 27; 29; 31; 32(3); 35; 36; 4:1; 3; 4; 6; 10(3); 11; 12(3); 13; 16; 17; 18; 20; 23(2); 24(2); 27(2); 28(2); 30; 34; 35(2); 36(3); 37(2); 38; 39; 40; 41; 42(2); 43; 46; 47(2); 48; 50(2); 51(2); 52; 53(2); 5:1; 4; 5(2); 6; 8; 9(4); 11; 12; 13; 14; 15; 16(2); 17; 19; 20(2); 21; 24(2); 25(2); 27; 29(2); 30; 32; 33; 35(2); 37; 38; 39; 40; 43; 44; 6:2; 3(2); 4; 5; 6; 9; 10; 11(4); 13(2); 15; 16; 17(4); 18; 19(3); 21; 22; 24; 25; 26(2); 29; 30; 33; 35(2); 36; 37; 39; 40(3); 42(2); 43; 44; 45(2); 49; 50; 51; 53; 54(2); 55; 56(2); 57; 58; 62; 63; 64; 65; 66; 69(2); 70; 7:3; 4; 11; 12; 14; 15; 16; 18; 19; 20; 21(2); 22; 26; 28(2); 29; 31(2); 32(2); 33; 34(2); 35; 36(2); 37(2); 42; 44; 45(2); 51; 52(2); 53; 8:1(2); 2(4); 3(3); 6; 7; 8(2); 9(3); 10; 11(2); 14(3); 16(2); 18; 20; 21(2); 23; 25; 26(2); 28; 29; 32(2); 33; 35; 38; 39; 42; 44(3); 45; 46; 48(2); 49; 50(2); 52(2); 53; 55(2); 56(2); 57; 59(2); 9:1; 2; 6(2); 7(3); 8(2); 11(7); 14(2); 15(2); 16; 18; 19; 20(2); 24; 25; 27; 28; 30(2); 31; 34(3); 35; 36; 37(2); 38(2); 39(2); 40(2); 10:1; 3(3); 4(2); 5; 8; 9(3); 10(3); 12(5); 13; 14(2); 15; 16(4); 18; 20(2); 22(2); 23; 24; 25; 27(2); 28(2); 29; 30; 33; 35; 36; 38(2); 40(2); 41(2); 42; 11:1; 2; 5(2); 8; 11; 15; 19(2); 20; 25; 26(2); 28(3); 29; 31(2); 32; 33(2); 34(2); 37; 38; 41(2); 42; 43; 44(4); 45; 46; 47(2); 48(3); 49; 50; 51; 52; 54; 55(2); 56; 57; 12:2; 3(3); 5; 6(2); 9; 11; 13(2); 14; 16; 17; 20; 21; 22(3); 23; 24; 25; 26; 27; 28; 29; 30; 32; 34; 36(2); 38; 40(3); 41; 44; 45; 47(2); 48; 49; 50; 13:2; 3(2); 4(3); 5(2); 6; 7; 9; 10; 12(2); 13(2); 14; 20; 21(2); 26; 27; 30; 31; 32; 33; 14:3(3); 4(2); 5; 6; 7(2); 8; 9(2); 10; 11; 12; 13; 16(2); 17; 19; 20(2); 21(4); 22; 23(4); 24; 26; 28; 29; 30; 31; 15:1; 2; 4; 5; 6(4); 7(2); 10; 11; 16(3); 22; 24(2); 27; 16:3; 4; 5; 8(3); 10; 13; 14; 15; 16(3); 17(4); 19(4); 20(2); 22(3); 23; 24; 26; 27; 28(2); 29; 30; 32(2); 17:1(2); 3(2); 5; 6(2); 8(3); 10(3); 11(2); 12; 13(2); 14; 19; 21; 22; 23(3); 25; 26(3); 18:1; 2; 3(4); 4; 5; 6; 7; 10(2); 12(3); 13; 15(3); 16(2); 18(5); 19; 20(2); 22; 25(3); 27; 28(2); 29; 30; 31; 33(2); 35; 37; 38(2); 19:1; 2(3); 3(2); 4; 5(2); 6(2); 7; 9(2); 10; 12; 13; 14(3); 16(2); 17; 18(2); 19(3); 20(3); 23(2); 24; 25(2); 26; 27; 29(3); 30(2); 31; 32(2); 33; 34(2); 35(3); 37; 38(3); 39(3); 40; 41; 20:1; 2(4); 3(2); 4(2); 5(2); 6(2); 7; 8(2); 11(2); 12(2); 13(2); 14(3); 15; 16; 17(4); 18(2); 19(2); 20(2); 22(2); 23; 25(2); 26(4); 27(4); 28(3); 29; 30; 31; 21:1; 2(4); 3(2); 6(3); 7; 8; 9(2); 11(4); 12(2); 13(3); 17; 18(3); 19; 20; 21; 24(2); 25; **Acts** 1:1; 3; 4; 7; 8(4); 9(2); 10; 13(8); 14(3); 15(3); 16; 17; 18(2); 19; 20(2); 21; 23(2); 24(2); 25; 26(3); 2:1; 2(2); 3(2); 4(2); 5; 6; 7(2); 8; 9(6); 10(4); 11; 12(2); 14(3); 17(5); 18(3); 19(4); 20(2); 21; 22(2); 23(3); 26; 29(3); 30; 33(2); 36; 37(3); 38(2); 39(2); 40(2); 41; 42(4); 43(3); 44(2); 45(3); 46(3); 47(2); 3:1; 2; 3; 4; 5; 6(2); 7(4); 8(5); 9(2); 10(3); 11(2); 12; 13(3); 14(2); 15; 16(2); 17; 19; 20; 23; 24(2); 25(2); 4:1(3); 2; 3(2); 4; 5(3); 6(5); 7; 8; 10; 13(4); 14; 16; 18(2); 19(2); 20; 23(3); 24(5); 25; 26(2); 27(2); 28; 29(2); 30(2); 31(3); 32(2); 33(2); 34; 35(2); 36(2); 37(2); 5:2(3); 3; 4; 5(3); 6(3); 7; 8(2); 9; 10(4); 11(2); 12(3); 13; 14(2); 15(2); 16(2); 17(2); 18(2); 19(2); 20; 21(6); 22(2); 23; 24(2); 25(2); 26; 27(2); 28(2); 29(2); 30; 31(2); 32(2); 33; 34; 35; 36(2); 37(2); 38(2); 40(4); 41; 42(3); 6:1; 2(2); 3; 4; 5(9); 6; 7(3); 8(3); 9(4); 10(2); 11; 12(6); 13(2); 14; 15; 7:2(2); 3(3); 4(2); 5(2); 6(3); 7(3); 8(5); 9; 10(5); 11(3); 13(2); 14(3); 15(2); 16(2); 17; 19; 20(2); 21(2); 22(3); 23; 24(3); 26(2); 27; 29; 30; 31; 32(3); 34(3); 35(2); 36(3); 38; 39; 41(3); 42(2); 43(2); 46; 49; 51(2); 52(2); 53; 54; 55(2); 56(2); 57(2); 58(3); 59(2); 60(3); 8:1(4); 2(2); 3(2); 5; 6(2); 7(2); 8; 9; 11; 12(2); 13(3); 14; 17; 18; 22; 23; 24; 25(3); 26(2);

27(4); 28; 29; 30(3); 31(3); 32; 33; 34(2); 35(2); 36(2); 37(3); 38(4); 39(2); 40; 9:1(2); 2; 3(2); 4(2); 5(2); 6(5); 7; 8(3); 9(2); 10(3); 11(3); 12(2); 14; 15(2); 17(4); 18(4); 19; 20; 21(2); 22; 23; 24(2); 25; 26(2); 27(4); 28(2); 29(2); 30; 31(5); 32; 33(2); 34(3); 35(3); 36; 37(2); 38(2); 39(4); 40(5); 41(4); 42(2); 43; 10:2(2); 3; 4(4); 5(2); 7(2); 8; 9; 10(2); 11(3); 12(3); 13(2); 15; 16; 17; 18(2); 20(2); 21; 22(4); 23(3); 24(4); 25(3); 27(2); 28; 30(3); 31(2); 32; 33; 34; 35; 37; 38(2); 39(3); 40; 41; 42(3); 45; 46; 48; 11:1(2); 2; 3; 4; 5(2); 6(4); 7(2); 10(2); 11; 12(2); 13(3); 14; 15; 18; 19(2); 20(2); 21(3); 22; 23(2); 24(3); 26(4); 27; 28(2); 30(2); 12:2; 3; 4(2); 6(2); 7(5); 8(5); 9(3); 10(4); 11(3); 12; 13; 14(2); 15; 16(2); 17(4); 19(5); 20(3); 21(2); 22(2); 23(3); 24; 25(3); 13:1(5); 2(2); 3(3); 4; 5(2); 6; 7(2); 10(2); 11(5); 13(2); 14(2); 15(3); 16(2); 17(2); 18; 19; 20(2); 21(2); 22(2); 25; 26(2); 27; 28; 29(2); 31; 32; 34; 36(2); 38; 39; 41(2); 42; 43(2); 44; 45(2); 46(3); 48(3); 49; 50(5); 51; 52(2); 14:1(3); 2; 3(2); 4(2); 5(3); 6(3); 7; 8; 9; 10(2); 11; 12(2); 13(2); 14(2); 15(5); 17(3); 18; 19(3); 20(2); 21(4); 22(2); 23(2); 24; 25; 26; 27(3); 28; 15:1(2); 2(5); 3(3); 4(4); 5; 6(2); 7(4); 8; 9(2); 12(3); 13(2); 15; 16(3); 17; 20(3); 22(3); 23(5); 24; 25; 27; 28; 29(3); 30; 32(3); 33; 35(2); 36(3); 37; 38; 39(3); 40(2); 41(2); 16:1(3); 2; 3(2); 4(2); 5(2); 6(2); 8; 9(3); 10; 11; 12(3); 13(3); 14; 15(4); 16; 17(2); 18(3); 19(3); 20; 21; 22(3); 23; 24; 25(4); 26(3); 27(3); 29(4); 30(2); 31(3); 32(2); 33(4); 34(2); 35; 36(2); 37(3); 38(2); 39(4); 40(4); 17:1; 2(2); 3(3); 4(5); 5(4); 6(2); 7; 8(2); 9(2); 10(2); 11; 12; 13; 14(2); 15(3); 17(2); 18(3); 19(2); 21; 22; 23; 24(2); 25(2); 26(3); 27; 28(2); 29; 30; 32(2); 34(3); 18:1; 2(2); 3(2); 4(3); 5(3); 6(3); 7(2); 8(3); 9; 10; 11(2); 12(2); 14; 15(2); 16; 17(2); 18(5); 19(3); 21; 22(3); 23(3); 24(2); 25(2); 26(3); 27; 28; 19:1(2); 2; 3(2); 6(3); 7; 8(3); 9(2); 10(2); 11; 12(2); 14(2); 15(3); 16(4); 17(4); 18(3); 19(3); 20; 21; 22; 23; 25; 26(2); 27(2); 28(2); 29(3); 30; 31; 32(2); 33(3); 35(2); 36; 38(2); 41; 20:1(3); 2(2); 3(2); 4(7); 6(2); 7(2); 8; 9(4); 10(3); 11(3); 12(2); 13(2); 14(2); 15(5); 17(2); 18; 19(2); 20(3); 21(2); 22; 23; 24; 25; 28; 31(2); 32(3); 34; 35; 36(2); 37(3); 38; 21:1(4); 2(2); 3(2); 4; 5(6); 6(2); 7(3); 8(4); 9; 10; 11(5); 12(2); 13; 14; 15(2); 16; 17; 18(2); 19; 20(3); 21; 24(4); 25(4); 26; 27(2); 28(4); 30(5); 31; 32(4); 33(4); 34(2); 35; 37; 38; 39; 40(3); 22:1; 2(2); 3(2); 4(3); 5(2); 6(2); 7(2); 8(2); 9(2); 10(4); 11; 12; 13(3); 14(3); 15; 16(3); 17; 18(2); 19(2); 20(3); 21; 22(3); 23(3); 24; 25(2); 26; 27; 28(2); 29(2); 30(4); 23:1(2); 2; 3; 4; 6(3); 7(3); 9(3); 10(3); 11(2); 12(2); 13; 14(3); 15; 16(3); 17; 18(3); 19(2); 20; 21; 22; 23(4); 24(2); 25; 27(2); 28; 30(2); 31; 32; 33; 34(2); 35; 24:1(2); 2(2); 3; 5(2); 6; 7; 9; 12; 14; 15(2); 16(2); 17; 19; 22(2); 23(3); 24(2); 25(3); 26; 27; 25:2(2); 3; 4; 5; 6(2); 7(3); 9(2); 13(2); 14; 15; 16; 17; 19; 20(2); 23(4); 24(3); 25; 26; 27; 26:1; 3; 6(2); 7; 10(2); 11(3); 12; 13; 14(2); 15(2); 16(3); 17; 18(3); 20(5); 21; 22(2); 23(3); 24; 25; 29(2); 30(4); 31; 27:1(2); 2; 3(3); 4; 5(2); 6(2); 7(2); 8; 9; 10(3); 11; 12(4); 13; 15(2); 16; 17(2); 18; 19; 20(2); 21(4); 22; 23; 24; 27; 28(4); 29; 30; 31; 32; 33(2); 35(3); 36; 37(2); 38(2); 39; 40(4); 41(3); 42(2); 43(2); 44(3); 28:1; 2(3); 3(3); 4; 5(2); 6(2); 7; 8(5); 9; 10; 11(2); 12; 13(4); 14(2); 15(3); 16; 17(3); 20; 21; 23(3); 24(2); 25; 26(4); 27(6); 28; 29(2); 30(2); 31; **Rom** 1:4; 5; 7(2); 12; 14(2); 16; 18; 20; 21; 23(4); 25(2); 27(2); 28; 2:3(2); 4(2); 5(2); 7(2); 8(2); 9(2); 10(2); 12; 15; 17(2); 18(2); 19; 20; 27(2); 29(2); 3:4; 8(2); 9; 14; 16; 17; 19; 21; 22; 23; 26; 30; 4:3; 7; 11; 12; 14; 17; 19; 21; 22; 25; 5:2; 3; 4(2); 5; 11; 12(2); 15; 16; 17; 6:13; 19; 22(2); 7:6; 9; 10; 11; 12(3); 23; 8:2; 3; 6; 10; 17(2); 22; 23; 27; 28; 30(2); 9:2; 4(5); 5; 9; 10; 15; 17; 18; 21; 22; 23; 25; 26; 28; 29(2); 33(2); 10:1; 3; 8; 9; 10; 12; 14(2); 15(2); 17; 18; 19; 20; 21; 11:3(3); 6; 7; 8; 9(4); 10; 12; 14; 16; 17(4); 20; 22; 23; 24; 26(2); 29; 33(2); 35; 36(2); 12:2(3); 4; 5; 14; 15; 13:2; 3; 9; 11; 12; 13(3); 14; 14:3; 6(3); 7; 8; 9(3); 11; 14; 17(3); 18; 19; 23; 15:1; 4; 5; 6; 9(2); 10; 11(2); 12(2); 13; 14; 18; 19(2); 21; 23; 24; 26; 27; 28; 29; 30; 31; 32; 16:2(2); 3; 7(2); 9; 12; 13(2); 14; 15(4); 17(2); 18(2); 19; 20; 21(3); 23(2); 25; 26; S:1; **1Cor** 1:1; 2; 3(2); 5; 10(2); 12(3); 14; 16; 19; 22; 23; 24(2); 25; 27; 28(3); 30(3); 2:1; 2; 3(3); 4(3); 3:1; 2; 3(3); 4; 5; 8(2); 10; 13; 16; 20; 23(2); 4:1; 5(2); 6(2); 7; 8; 9(2); 11(4); 12; 13; 17; 19; 21; 5:1; 2(2); 4; 8(2); 6:1; 2; 6; 8(2); 11(2); 13(3); 14(2); 15; 19; 20; 7:2; 3; 4; 5(2); 6; 7; 8; 10; 11(2); 12; 13(2); 14; 17; 19; 28(2); 30(3); 31; 34(2); 35(2); 36; 37; 40; 8:2; 4; 5; 6(3); 7; 11; 12; 9:4; 5(2); 6; 7(2); 10; 13; 20; 23; 25; 27; 10:1; 2(2); 3; 4(2); 7(2); 8(2); 9; 10; 11; 17; 20(2); 21(2); 26; 27; 28(2); 11:2; 3(2); 7; 18; 21(2); 22(2); 24(2); 26; 27(2); 28(2); 29(2); 30(2); 34(2); 12:3; 5; 6; 11; 12(2); 13; 16; 19; 21; 23(2); 26; 27; 28; 31; 13:1(2); 2(5); 3(3); 4; 9; 13; 14:1; 3(2); 7; 10; 11; 15(2); 21(2); 23(2); 24; 25(3); 27(2); 28(2); 29; 31; 32; 35; 39; 40; 15:1; 4(2); 5; 8; 10; 11; 14(2); 15; 17; 20; 24(2); 28; 30; 32; 34; 35; 37; 38; 39; 40(2); 41(2); 44; 45; 46; 48; 49; 50; 52(2); 53; 54; 56; 16:3; 4; 6(2); 9(2); 15; 16(2); 17(2); 18; 19; S:1(3); **2Cor** 1:1; 2(2); 3; 6(3); 7; 10; 12(2); 13; 15; 16(3); 17; 18; 19(3); 20; 21; 22; 2:3; 4; 7; 12; 14; 15; 16(2); 3:2; 4; 7; 13; 17; 4:5; 7; 13(2); 14; 17; 5:8(2); 11; 12; 15(2); 18(2); 19; 6:2; 7; 8(3); 9(3); 10; 14; 15; 16(4); 17(3); 18(3); 7:1; 3; 7; 13; 15(2); 8:2; 3; 4; 5(2); 7(4); 8; 10; 12; 13; 15; 18; 19(2); 22; 23(2); 24(2); 9:2; 4; 5(2); 6; 8; 10(2); 13(2); 14; 10:1; 5(2); 6; 8; 10(2); 12; 16; 11:1; 9(4); 14; 25; 27(3); 29(2); 31; 33(2); 12:1; 3; 4; 7; 9; 12(2); 14; 15(2); 18; 20; 21(5); 13:2(3); 9(2); 10; 11(2); 14(2); S:1; **Gal** 1:1; 2; 3(2); 4; 5; 7; 13; 14; 15; 16; 17; 18; 21; 22; 24; 2:1; 2(2); 4; 9(4); 12; 13; 14; 15; 16; 20(2); 3:5; 6; 8; 12; 16(3); 17(2); 19; 29(2); 4:2; 6; 7; 9; 10(3); 14; 15; 18; 20; 25(2); 27; 30; 5:1; 11; 15; 16; 17(2); 21; 24(2); 6:2; 4(2); 9; 14; 16(3); **Eph** 1:1; 2(2); 3; 4; 8; 10; 15; 17; 18; 19; 20; 21(4); 22(2); 2:1(2); 3(2); 6(2); 8; 12(2); 14; 16; 17(3); 19(2); 20(2); 3:5; 6(2); 9; 10; 12; 15; 17; 18(3); 19; 4:2; 4; 6(3); 8; 11(5); 13; 14(3); 16; 17; 21; 23; 24(2); 26; 30; 31(4); 32; 5:2(3); 3; 5; 9(2); 11; 14(2); 18; 19(3); 20; 23; 25; 26; 27; 29; 30; 31(3); 32; 33; 6:2; 3; 4(2); 5; 7; 9; 10; 12; 13; 14; 15; 17(2); 18(3); 19; 21(2); 22; 23(2); **Phil** 1:1(2); 2(2); 7(2); 9(3); 10; 11; 13; 14; 15(2); 18(2); 19; 20; 21; 23; 25(3); 27; 28(2); 30; 2:1; 7(2); 8(2); 9; 10(2); 11; 12; 13; 14; 15(2); 17(3); 18; 25(3); 26; 27; 28; 29; 3:3(2); 8(2); 9; 10(2); 13; 15; 17; 18; 19; 4:1(2); 2; 3(2); 4; 6; 7(2); 8; 9(4); 12(4); 15; 16; 18; 20(2); **Col** 1:1; 2(3); 3; 4; 6(2); 9(2); 10; 11; 13; 16(3); 17(2); 18; 20; 21(2); 22(2); 23(3); 24; 26; 28; 2:1(2); 2(3); 3; 4; 5(2); 7(2); 8(2); 10(2); 13(2); 14; 15(2); 18; 19(3); 22; 23(2); 3:3; 5; 10; 11; 12; 13; 14; 15(2); 16(3); 17(2); 19; 23(2); 25; 4:1; 2; 7(2); 8; 9; 10; 11; 12; 13(2); 14; 15(2); 16(2); 17; S:1; **1Th** 1:1(5); 3(3); 5(2); 6(2); 7; 8; 9(2); 10; 2:2; 9(2); 10(3); 11(2); 12; 15(4); 18; 20; 3:2(4); 4; 5; 6(3); 7; 10(2); 11(2); 12(3); 4:1(3); 4; 6(2); 10(2); 11(3); 12; 14; 15; 16(2); 17(2); 5:1; 3(2); 5; 6; 7; 8(2); 11; 12(3); 13(2); 15; 23(4); **2Th** 1:1(3); 2(2); 3; 4(2); 7; 8; 9; 10; 11(2); 12(2); 2:1; 3; 4; 6; 8(2); 9(2); 10; 11; 13; 15; 16(3); 17(2); 3:1; 2(2); 3; 4(2); 5(2); 6; 8(2); 12(2); 14(2); **1Ti** 1:1; 2(2); 4; 5(2); 9(4); 10; 12; 13(2); 14(2); 15; 17(2); 19; 20; 2:1; 2(3); 3; 4; 5(2); 7(3); 8; 9; 14; 15(2); 3:7; 10; 12; 13; 15; 16; 4:1; 3(2); 4; 5; 6; 7(2); 8; 9; 10; 11; 16(2); 5:1; 4(2); 5(4); 7; 8(2); 13(3); 16; 17; 18; 21(2); 23; 24; 25; 6:1; 2(3); 3(2); 4; 5; 7; 8(2); 9(4); 10; 11; 12; 13; 15(2); 16; 20(2); **2Ti** 1:2(2); 3; 5(2); 7(2); 9(2); 10(2); 11(2); 12; 13; 15; 16; 17; 18; 2:2; 5; 7; 16; 17(2); 18; 19; 20(4); 21(2); 23; 24; 26; 3:6; 7; 8; 12; 13(3); 14; 15; 16; 4:1(3); 2; 4(2); 6; 8; 10; 11; 12; 13; 17(3); 18(3); 19(2); 21(4); **Titus** 1:1(2); 4(2); 5; 9; 10(2); 14; 15(2); 16(2); 2:9; 12(2); 13(2); 14; 15(2); 3:1; 3(3); 4; 5; 8(2); 9(4); 10; 11; 13; 14; **Philem** 1:1(2); 2(3); 3(2); 5(2); 7; 9; 11; 16; **Heb** 1:1; 3(2); 5(2); 6(2); 7(2); 8; 9; 10(2); 11; 12(3); 2:2(2); 3; 4(3); 7(2); 9; 10; 11; 13(3); 14; 15; 17; 3:1; 5; 6; 9; 10(2); 18; 4:4; 5; 6; 12(7); 13; 16; 5:1; 2; 3; 4; 7(3); 9; 11; 12(2); 14; 6:1; 2(3); 3; 4(2); 5(2); 6; 7; 8(2); 9; 10(2); 11; 12; 14; 15; 16; 19(2); 7:1; 2; 5; 6; 7; 8; 9; 11; 15; 18; 20; 21; 23; 26; 27; 8:2(2); 3; 5; 8; 9; 10(3); 11(2); 12(2); 13; 9:1; 2(2); 3; 4(3); 5; 7; 9; 10(3); 11; 12; 13(2); 15; 19(5); 21; 22(2); 27; 28; 10:1; 4; 5; 6; 8(3); 11(2); 16; 17(2); 20; 21; 22; 24(2); 25; 27; 29(2); 30; 33(2); 34(2); 37(2); 11:4; 5; 6; 7; 8; 9; 10; 11; 12(2); 13(4); 15; 17; 20; 21; 22; 23; 28; 32(6); 35; 36(3); 37; 38(3); 39; 12:1(2); 2(2); 3; 5; 6; 8; 9(2); 12; 13; 14; 15; 18(3); 19(2); 20; 21(2); 22(2); 23(3); 24(2); 27; 28; 13:3; 4(2); 5; 6; 8(2); 9; 16; 17(2); 21; 22; 24; **Jas** 1:1; 4; 5(2); 6; 11(2); 14; 15; 17(2); 21(2); 22; 23; 24(2); 25; 26; 27(4); 2:2; 3(3); 4; 5; 6; 9; 10; 12; 13; 14; 15; 16(2); 18(2); 19; 22; 23(3); 24; 25; 3:2; 3; 4; 5; 6(3); 7(4); 9; 10; 11; 12; 13; 14(2); 16(2); 17(3); 18; 4:1; 2(4); 3; 4; 7; 8(2); 9(3); 10; 11(2); 12; 13(4); 14; 15; 17; 5:1; 2; 3(3); 4; 5; 6(2); 7(2); 10; 11(2); 12; 14; 15(3); 16; 17(3); 18(3); 19; 20; **1Pet** 1:1; 2(2); 3; 4(2); 7(2); 8; 10; 11; 13; 17; 18; 19; 21(2); 23; 24(2); 25; 2:1(4); 4; 6; 8(2); 11; 14; 16; 18; 20; 25; 3:3; 4; 6; 7; 10(2); 11(2); 12; 13; 14(2); 15(2); 19; 22(3); 4:3; 5; 7; 8; 11(2); 14; 17; 18(2); 5:1(2); 4; 5(2); 11(2); 12; 13; **2Pet** 1:1(2); 2(2); 3(2); 4; 5(2); 6(3); 7(2); 8; 9(2); 10; 11; 12; 16; 17; 18; 19; 2:1; 2; 3(2); 4; 5; 6(2); 7; 8; 9; 10; 11; 12(2); 13(2); 14; 15; 20(2); 22; 3:2(2); 4; 5(2); 7(2); 8; 10(2); 11; 12(2); 13; 14; 15; 16; 18(3); **1Jn** 1:1; 2(4); 3(3); 4; 5(2); 6(2); 7; 8; 9(2); 10; 2:1; 2(2); 3; 4(2); 8(2); 9; 10; 11(2); 14(2); 16(2); 17(2); 18; 20; 21; 22; 24; 25; 27(4); 28(2); 3:2; 3; 5(2); 9; 10; 12(3); 15; 16; 17(2); 18; 19(2); 20; 22(2); 23(2); 24(3); 4:3(3); 4; 5; 6; 7(2); 10; 12; 13; 14(2); 15; 16(4); 20; 21; 5:1; 2; 3; 4; 6(3); 7(2); 8(4); 11(2); 12; 13; 14; 15; 16; 17; 18; 19(2); 20(4); **2Jn** 1(2); 2; 3(3); 5; 6; 7; 9(2); 10; 12(2); **3Jn** 2; 3; 5; 10(3); 12(3); 13; 14; **Jude** 1(3); 2(2); 3; 4(2); 6; 7(3); 8; 11(2); 14; 15(2); 16; 22; 23; 24; 25(3); **Rev** 1:1(2); 2(2); 3(2); 4(4); 5(4); 6(5); 7(3); 8(4); 9(4); 10; 11(10); 12(2); 13(2); 14(2); 15(2); 16(3); 17(3); 18(4); 19(2); 20(2); 2:2(6); 3(4); 5(3); 8(3); 9(4); 10(2); 12; 13(3); 14; 16; 17(2); 18(2); 19(6); 20(2); 21(2); 22; 23(4); 24(2); 26(2); 27; 28; 3:1(3); 2; 3(4); 4; 5(2); 7(4); 8(3); 9(3); 12(4); 14(2); 16; 17(7); 18(3); 19(2); 20(4); 21; 4:1(3); 2(3); 3(3); 4(5); 5(4); 6(4); 7(4); 8(6); 9(4); 10(4); 11(4); 5:1(2); 2(2); 3; 4(2); 5(2); 6(5); 7(2); 8(4); 9(6); 10(3); 11(6); 12(6); 13(10); 14(5); 6:1(3); 2(6); 3(2); 4(4); 5(5); 6(4); 7(2); 8(8); 9(2); 10(3); 11(3); 12(4); 13; 14(3); 15(8); 16(4); 17; 7:1; 2(3); 4(4); 9(6); 10(2); 11(5); 12(7); 13(2); 14(4); 15(3); 17(2); 8:1; 2(2); 3(3); 4; 5(7); 6; 7(5); 8(3); 9(3); 10(4); 11(3); 12(6); 13(2); 9:1(3); 2(4); 3(2); 4; 5(2); 6(4); 7(3); 8(2); 9(2); 10(3); 11; 12; 13(2); 15(4); 16(2); 17(8); 18(2); 19(3); 20(6); 10:1(4); 2(3); 3(2); 4(3); 5(2); 6(7); 8(4); 9(5); 10(4); 11(4); 11:1(5); 2(3); 3(3); 4; 5(3); 6(2); 7(3); 8(2); 9(6); 10(3); 11(4); 12(3); 13(5); 14; 15(5); 16(3); 17(3); 18(8); 19(7); 12:1(3); 2(2); 3(4); 4(3); 5(3); 6(2); 7(4); 8; 9(3); 10(5); 11(3); 12(2); 13; 14(3); 15; 16(3); 17(3); 13:1(5); 2(6); 3(3); 4(2); 5(4); 6(3); 7(5); 8; 10; 11(3); 12(3); 13; 14(2); 15(2); 16(4); 17; 18(2); 14:1(4); 2(3); 3(6); 4; 5; 6(5); 7(5); 8; 9(3); 10(3); 11(5); 12; 13(2); 14(4); 15(2); 16(2); 17; 18(3); 19(3); 20(3); 15:1(2); 2(5); 3(4); 4(2); 5(2); 6(3); 7(2); 8(3); 16:1(2); 2(5); 3(3); 4(3); 5(3); 6(2); 7(2); 8(2); 9(3); 10(3); 11(3); 12(2); 13(3); 14; 15(2); 16; 17(2); 18(5); 19(3); 20(2); 21(2); 17:1(2); 2; 3(2); 4(6); 5(2); 6(3); 7(3); 8(6); 9; 10(4); 11(4); 12; 13(2); 14(5); 15(4); 16(5); 17(2); 18; 18:1(2); 2(5); 3(2); 4(2); 5; 6; 7(4); 8(3); 9(3); 11(2); 12(13); 13(14); 14(4); 15; 16(6); 17(4); 18; 19(3); 20(2); 21(3); 22(6); 23(3); 24(3); 19:1(4); 2(2); 3(3); 4(4); 5(3); 6(3); 7(3); 8(2); 9(2); 10(3); 11(6); 12(2); 13(2); 14(2); 15(4); 16(3); 17(3); 18(7); 19(4); 20(3); 21(2); 20:1(2); 2(3); 3(4); 4(8); 6(3); 7; 8(2); 9(5); 10(6); 11(4); 12(5); 13(4); 14(2); 15; 21:1(4); 2; 3(5); 4(2); 5(3); 6(3); 7(2); 8(8); 9(2); 10(3); 11; 12(5); 13; 14(2); 15(3); 16(5); 17(3); 18(2); 19; 21(2); 22(2); 23(2); 24(3); 25; 26(2); 27; 22:1(2); 2(3); 3(3); 4(2); 5(4); 6(3); 8(4); 9(2); 10; 11(3); 12(2); 13(3); 14; 15(6); 16(3); 17(5); 19(3)

ANOTHER

Gen 4:25; 11:3; 15:10; 26:21; 22; 31; 29:19; 30:24; 31:49; 37:9; 19; 42:1; 21; 28; 43:7; 33; **Ex** 10:23; 16:15; 18:16; 21:10; 18; 22:5; 9; 25:20; 26:3(2); 4; 5; 17; 19; 21; 25; 36:10(2); 11; 12; 13; 22; 24; 26; 37:8; 9; 19; **Lev** 7:10; 19:11; 20:10; 25:14; 17; 46; 26:37; 27:20; **Num** 5:19; 20; 29; 8:8; 14:4; 24; 23:13; 27; 36:9; **Deut** 4:34; 20:5; 6; 7; 21:15; 24:2; 25:11; 28:30; 32; 29:28; **Judg** 2:10; 6:29; 9:37; 10:18; 16:7; 11; **Ruth** 2:8; 3:14; **1Sa** 2:25; 10:3(2); 6; 9; 11; 13:18(2); 14:16; 17:30; 18:7; 20:41(2); 21:11; 29:5; **2Sa** 11:25; 18:20; 26(2); **1Kin** 6:27; 7:8; 11:23; 13:10; 14:5; 6; 18:6; 20:37; 21:6; 22:20; **2Kin** 1:11; 3:23; 7:3; 6; 8; 9; 10:21; 14:8; 11; 21:16; **1Chr** 2:26; 16:20; 17:5; 24:5; 26:12; **2Chr** 18:19; 20:23; 25:17; 21; 32:5; **Ezr** 4:21; 9:11; **Neh** 3:19; 21; 24; 27; 30; 4:19; 9:3; **Est** 1:7; 19; 4:14; 9:19; 22; **Job** 1:16; 17; 18; 13:9; 19:27; 21:25; 31:8; 10; 41:16; 17; **Ps** 16:4; 75:7; 105:13(2); 109:8; 145:4; **Prov** 25:9; 27:2; **Eccl** 1:4; 4:10; 8:9; **Song** 5:9(2); **Is** 3:5; 6:3; 13:8; 28:11; 42:8; 44:5(2); 48:11; 57:8; 65:15; 22(2); 66:23(2); **Jer** 3:1; 13:14; 18:4; 14; 22:26; 25:26; 36:28; 32; 46:16; 51:31(2); 46; **Eze** 1:9; 11; 3:13; 4:8; 17; 10:9(2); 12:3; 15:7; 17:7; 19:5; 22:11(2); 24:23; 33:30; 37:16; 17; 40:13; 26; 49; 41:6; 11; 47:14; **Dan** 2:39(2); 43; 5:6; 17; 7:3; 5; 6; 8; 24; 8:13; **Hos** 3:3; 4:4; **Joel** 1:3; 2:8; **Amos** 4:7; **Nah** 2:4; **Zec** 2:3; 8:21; 11:9; **Mal** 3:16; **Mt** 2:12; 8:9; 21; 10:23; 11:3; 13:24; 31; 33; 19:9; 21:33; 35(2); 22:5; 24:2; 10(2); 25:15(2); 32; 26:71; 27:38; **Mk** 4:41; 9:10; 50; 10:11; 12; 12:4; 5; 13:2; 14:19; 58; 16:12; **Lk** 2:15; 6:6; 11; 7:8; 19; 20; 32; 8:25; 9:56; 59; 61; 12:1; 14:19; 20; 31; 16:7; 12; 18; 19:20; 44; 20:11; 21:6; 22:58; 59; 24:17; 32; **Jn** 4:33; 37; 5:7; 32; 43; 44; 13:22; 34(2); 35; 14:16; 15:12; 17; 18:15; 19:37; 21:18; **Acts** 1:20; 2:7; 12; 7:18; 26; 10:28; 12:17; 13:35; 17:7; 19:32; 38; 21:6; 34; **Rom** 1:27; 2:1; 15; 21; 7:3(2); 4; 23; 9:21; 12:5; 10(2); 16; 13:8(2); 14:2; 4; 5(2); 13; 19; 15:5; 7; 14; 20; 16:16; **1Cor** 3:4; 10; 4:6; 7; 6:1; 7; 7:7; 10:29; 11:21; 33; 12:8; 9(2); 10(5); 25; 14:30; 15:39(3); 40; 41(3); 16:20; **2Cor** 10:16; 11:4(3); 13:12; **Gal** 1:6; 7; 5:13; 15(2); 26(2); 6:4; **Eph** 4:2; 25; 32(2); 5:21; **Col** 3:9; 13(2); 16; **1Th** 3:12; 4:9; 18; 5:11; **1Ti** 5:21; **Titus** 3:3; **Heb** 3:13; 4:8; 5:6; 7:11; 13; 15; 10:24; 25; **Jas** 2:25; 4:11; 12; 5:9; 16(2); **1Pet** 1:22; 3:8; 4:9; 10; 5:5; 14; **1Jn** 1:7; 3:11; 23; 4:7; 11; 12; **2Jn** 5; **Rev** 6:4(2); 7:2; 8:3; 10:1; 11:10; 12:3; 13:11; 14:6; 8; 15; 17; 18; 15:1; 16:7; 18:1; 4; 20:12

ANOTHER'S

Gen 11:7; **Ex** 21:35; **Jn** 13:14; **1Cor** 10:24; **Gal** 6:2

ANSWER

Gen 30:33; 41:16; 45:3; **Deut** 20:11; 21:7; 25:9; 27:15; **Josh** 4:7; **Judg** 5:29; **1Sa** 2:16; 20:10; **2Sa** 3:11; 24:13; **1Kin** 9:9; 12:6; 7; 9; 18:29; **2Kin** 4:29; 18:36; **2Chr** 10:6; 9; 10; **Ezr** 4:17; 5:5; 11; **Neh** 5:8; **Est** 4:13; 15; **Job** 5:1; 9:3; 14; 15; 32; 13:22(2); 14:15; 19:16; 20:2; 3; 23:5; 31:14; 35; 32:1; 3; 5; 14; 17; 20; 33:5; 12; 32; 35:4; 12; 38:3; 40:2; 4; 5; **Ps** 27:7; 65:5; 86:7; 91:15; 102:2; 108:6; 119:42; 143:1; **Prov** 1:28; 15:1; 23; 28; 16:1; 22:21; 24:26; 26:4; 5; 27:11; 29:19; **Song** 5:6; **Is** 14:32; 30:19; 36:21; 41:28; 46:7; 50:2; 58:9; 65:12; 24; 66:4; **Jer** 5:19; 7:27; 22:9; 33:3; 42:4; 44:20; **Eze** 14:4; 7; 21:7; **Dan** 3:16; **Joel** 2:19; **Mic** 3:7; **Hab** 2:1; 11; **Zec** 13:6; **Mt** 22:46; 25:37; 40; 44; 45; **Mk** 11:29; 30; 14:40; **Lk** 11:7; 12:11; 13:25; 14:6; 20:3; 26; 21:14; 22:68; **Jn** 1:22; 19:9; **Acts** 24:10; 25:16; 26:2; **Rom** 11:4; **1Cor** 9:3; **2Cor** 5:12; **Col** 4:6; **2Ti** 4:16; **1Pet** 3:15; 21

ANSWERED

Gen 18:27; 23:5; 10; 14; 24:50; 27:37; 39; 31:14; 31; 36; 43; 34:13; 35:3; 40:18; 41:16; 42:22; 43:28; **Ex** 4:1; 15:21; 19:8; 19; 24:3; **Num** 11:28; 22:18; 23:12; 26; 32:31; **Deut** 1:14; 41; **Josh** 1:16; 2:14; 7:20; 9:24; 15:19; 17:15; 22:21; 24:16; **Judg** 5:29; 7:14; 8:8(2); 18; 25; 11:13; 15:6; 10; 18:14; 19:28; 20:4; **Ruth** 2:4; 6; 11; 3:9; **1Sa** 1:15; 17; 3:4; 6; 10; 16; 4:17; 20; 5:8; 6:4; 9:8; 12; 19; 21; 10:12; 22; 11:2; 12:5; 14:12; 28; 37; 39; 44; 16:18; 17:27; 30; 58; 18:7; 19:17; 20:28; 32; 21:4; 5; 22:9; 12; 14; 23:4; 25:10; 26:6; 14; 22; 28:6; 15; 29:9; 30:8; 22; **2Sa** 1:4; 7; 8; 13; 2:20; 4:9; 9:6; 13:12; 32; 14:5; 18; 19; 32; 15:21; 18:3; 29; 32; 19:21; 26; 38; 42; 43; 20:17(2); 20; 21:1; 5; 22:42; **1Kin** 1:28; 36; 43; 2:22; 30; 3:27; 11:22; 12:13; 16; 13:6; 18:8; 18; 21; 24; 26; 20:4; 11; 14; 21:6; 20; 22:15; **2Kin** 1:8; 10; 11; 12; 2:5; 3:8; 11; 4:13; 14; 26; 6:2; 3; 16; 22; 28; 7:2; 13; 19; 8:12; 13; 14; 9:19; 22; 10:13; 15; 18:36; 20:10; 15; **1Chr** 12:17; 21:3; 26; 28; **2Chr** 2:11; 7:22; 10:13; 14; 16; 18:3; 25:9; 29:31; 31:10; 34:15; 23; **Ezr** 10:2; 12; **Neh** 2:20; 6:4; 8:6; **Est** 1:16; 5:4; 7; 6:7; 7:3; 5; **Job** 1:7; 9; 2:2; 4; 4:1; 6:1; 8:1; 9:1; 16; 11:1; 2; 12:1; 15:1; 16:1; 18:1; 19:1; 20:1; 21:1; 22:1; 23:1; 25:1; 26:1; 32:6; 12; 15; 16; 34:1; 38:1; 40:1; 3; 6; 42:1; **Ps** 18:41; 81:7; 99:6; 118:5; **Is** 6:11; 21:9; 36:21; 39:4; **Jer** 7:13; 11:5; 23:35; 37; 35:17; 36:18; 44:15; **Eze** 24:20; 37:3; **Dan** 2:5; 7; 8; 10; 14; 15; 20; 26; 27; 47; 3:16; 24; 25; 4:19; 5:17; 6:12; 13; **Amos** 7:14; **Mic** 6:5; **Hab** 2:2; **Hag** 2:12; 13; 14; **Zec** 1:10; 11; 12; 13; 19; 3:4; 4:4; 5; 6; 11; 12; 13; 5:2; 6:4; 5; **Mt** 4:4; 8:8; 11:4; 25; 12:38; 39; 48; 13:11; 37; 14:28; 15:3; 13; 15; 23; 24; 26; 28; 16:2; 16; 17; 17:4; 11; 17; 19:4; 27; 20:13; 22; 21:21; 24; 27; 29; 30; 22:1; 29; 24:4; 25:9; 12; 26; 26:23; 25; 33; 63; 66; 27:12; 14; 21; 25; 28:5; **Mk** 3:33; 5:9; 6:37; 7:6; 28; 8:4; 28; 9:5; 12; 17; 38; 10:3; 5; 20; 29; 51; 11:14; 29; 33; 12:28; 29; 34; 35; 14:20; 48; 61; 15:3; 5; 9; 12; **Lk** 1:35; 60; 3:16; 4:4; 8; 7:43; 8:21; 50; 9:49; 10:28; 41; 11:45; 13:14; 15; 14:5; 17:20; 37; 19:40; 20:3; 7; 24; 22:51; 23:3; 9; **Jn** 1:21; 26; 48; 49; 50; 2:18; 19; 3:3; 5; 9; 10; 27; 4:10; 13; 17; 5:7; 11; 17; 19; 6:7; 26; 29; 43; 68; 70; 7:16; 20; 21; 46; 47; 52; 8:14; 19; 33; 34; 39; 48; 49; 54; 9:3; 11; 20; 25; 27; 30; 34; 36; 10:25; 32; 33; 34; 11:9; 12:23; 30; 34; 13:7; 8; 26; 36; 38; 14:23; 16:31; 18:5; 8; 20; 23; 30; 34; 35; 36; 37; 19:7; 11; 15; 22; 20:28; 21:5; **Acts** 3:12; 4:19; 5:8; 29; 8:24; 34; 37; 9:13; 10:46; 11:9; 15:13; 19:15; 21:13; 22:8; 28; 24:10; 25; 25:4; 8; 9; 12; 16; 26:1; **Rev** 7:13

ANSWERING

Mt 3:15; **Mk** 11:22; 33; 12:17; 24; 13:2; 5; 15:2; **Lk** 1:19; 4:12; 5:5; 22; 31; 6:3; 7:22; 40; 9:19; 20; 41; 10:27; 30; 13:2; 8; 14:3; 15:29; 17:17; 20:34; 39; 23:40; 24:18; **Titus** 2:9

ANSWERS

Job 21:34; 34:36; **Lk** 2:47

ANY

Gen 3:1; 4:15; 8:12; 21(2); 9:11(2); 14:23; 17:5; 12; 18:14; 19:12; 22:12; 24:16; 30:31; 31:14; 35:10; 36:31; 39:9; 23; 42:16; 43:34; 47:6; **Ex** 1:10; 8:29; 9:29; 10:15; 23; 11:6; 7; 12:39; 16:24; 20:4(3); 10; 17; 21:23; 22:9; 10; 20; 22; 23; 25; 31; 24:14(2); 30:32; 33(2); 31:14; 15; 32:24; 34:3; 10; 24; 35:24; 33; 35; 36:6; **Lev** 1:2; 2:1; 11(2); 4:2(2); 13; 22; 27(2); 5:2; 11; 17; 6:3; 7; 27; 30; 7:8; 15; 18; 19; 21(3); 24; 26; 27; 11:10; 32(3); 33; 35; 37(2); 38(2); 39; 43; 44; 13:24; 48; 49; 51; 52; 53; 57; 59; 15:2; 6; 10(2); 16; 22; 23; 24; 17:10; 12; 13; 18:6; 21; 23(2); 24; 26(3); 29; 30; 19:17; 18; 26; 28(2); 20:2; 4; 16; 25; 21:5; 9; 11; 17; 18; 22:4; 5; 6; 11; 23; 24; 25; 23:22; 30; 24:17; 25:25; 32; 49; 26:1; 27:9; 11; 19; 20; **Num** 4:15; 5:6; 10; 12; 6:3; 9; 9:10; 12; 14:23; 15:27; 17:13; 18:5; 20; 19:11; 13; 20:5; 19; 21:5; 9; 22:38(2); 23:23; 29:7; 30:5; 15; 31:19(2); 35:11; 15; 22; 23; 26; 30(2); 36:3; 8; **Deut** 2:19; 37; 4:16; 17(2); 18(2); 23; 25; 32; 5:8(3); 14(2); 21; 25; 7:7; 8:9; 12:17; 13:11; 14:1; 3; 21; 15:7; 21(2); 16:4; 5; 21; 22; 17:1(2); 2; 3; 15; 18:6; 10; 16; 19:11; 15(3); 16; 20; 21:23; 22:1; 6; 7; 8; 13; 23:10; 18; 19; 24; 24:5; 7; 10; 13; 26:14; 27:5; 15; 21; 28:14; 55; 29:23; 30:4; 31:13; 32:28; 39; **Josh** 1:5; 2:11(2); 19; 5:1; 12; 6:10(2); 18; 7:12; 8:31; 10:21; 11:11; 14; 13:33; 20:3; 9; 21:45; 23:12; 13; **Judg** 2:14; 21; 4:20(2); 11:25; 13:4; 7; 14(2); 16:17; 18:7(2); 10; 28; 19:19; 20:8(2); 21:1; 12; **Ruth** 1:11; 2:22; **1Sa** 2:2; 13; 16; 3:17; 5:5; 6:3; 9:2; 10:23; 12:3; 4; 13:22; 14:24(2); 28; 52(2); 18:25; 20:12; 26; 39; 21:2; 22:15; 25:15; 22; 34; 27:1(2); 30:2; 12; 19; **2Sa** 2:1; 28; 7:6; 7; 10; 22; 9:1; 3; 10:19; 13:2; 14:10; 11; 14; 32; 15:2; 4; 5; 11; 19:22; 28; 29; 35; 42; 21:4; 5; **1Kin** 1:6; 2:36; 42; 3:12; 13; 5:6; 6:7; 8:31; 38; 10:3; 20; 11:22; 15:5; 17; 29; 18:26; 29(2); 20:33; 39; **2Kin** 2:21; 4:2; 29(2); 6:33; 10:5; 14; 24; 12:4; 5; 13; 14:26(3); 18:5; 33; 21:8; 23:25; 24:7; **1Chr** 1:43; 17:6; 9; 20; 19:19; 23:26; 26:28; 27:1; 28:21; 29:25; **2Chr** 1:12; 2:14; 6:5; 29; 8:15; 9:9; 19; 20; 23:19; 32:13; 15; 33:8; 34:13; **Ezr** 1:4; 7:24; **Neh** 2:12(2); 5:16; 10:31; **Job** 4:20; 5:1; 4; 6:6; 7:10; 8:12; 9:33; 10:22; 15:11; 16:17; 18:19; 20:9; 21:22; 22:3; 25:3; 31:7; 19(2); 32:21; 33:13; 27; 32; 34:27; 31; 36:5; 29; 37:24; **Ps** 4:6; 14:2; 33:17; 34:10; 37:8; 38:3; 49:7; 53:2; 59:5; 74:9(2); 81:9; 86:8; 91:10; 109:12; 115:17; 119:133; 135:17; 139:24; 141:4; 146:2; 147:20; **Prov** 1:17; 6:35; 14:34; 28:17; 30:2; 30; 31:5; **Eccl** 1:10; 11; 2:10; 3:14; 5:2; 6:5; 9:5(2); 6(2); **Is** 1:5; 2:4; 7(2); 19:15; 26:18; 27:3; 30:20; 33:20; 35:9; 36:18; 44:8; 51:18; 52:14; 53:9; 54:4; 56:2; 59:4; 62:4; **Jer** 3:16; 17; 5:1; 9:4; 10:20; 14:22; 17:22; 18:18; 20:9; 22:11; 30; 23:24; 31:12; 40; 32:27; 33:26; 34:10; 35:7; 36:24; 37:17; 38:5; 42:21; 44:26; 48:9; 49:33; 50:40; 51:43; 44; **Lam** 1:12; 3:49; **Eze** 5:9; 11; 7:11; 13; 9:6; 12:24; 28; 14:11; 15:2; 3(2); 4; 5; 16:5; 41; 63; 18:3; 7; 8; 10; 11; 16; 23; 21:5; 23:27; 24:13; 27:36; 28:19; 24; 29:15; 31:8; 32:13; 33:6; 34:10; 29; 36:14; 15(3); 37:22; 23(2); 39:7; 10; 15; 28; 29; 44:9; 13; 18; 21; 31; 46:16; **Dan** 2:10; 30(2); 3:28; 29; 6:4; 5; 7; 12; 8:4; 11:15; 37; **Hos** 13:10; 14:3; 8; **Joel** 2:2; 3:17; **Amos** 6:10; 7:8; 13; 8:2; 7; **Obad** 18; **Jonah** 3:7; **Mic** 4:3; **Zeph** 3:15; **Hag** 2:12; 13; **Zec** 8:10(2); 9:8; 13:3; **Mal** 2:13; **Mt** 4:6; 5:25; 40; 10:5; 11:27; 12:19; 13:15; 19; 16:24; 18:19; 21:3; 22:16; 46(2); 24:17; 23; **Mk** 1:44; 4:12; 22; 23; 5:4; 35; 7:16; 8:26; 9:8; 22; 30; 35; 11:3; 13; 16(2); 25; 12:21; 34; 13:5; 15; 21; 14:31; 63; 15:44; 16:8(2); 18; **Lk** 3:14; 4:11; 40; 8:17; 27; 43; 9:23; 36; 10:19; 11:11; 14:8; 26; 15:29; 19:8(2); 31; 20:21; 27; 28; 36; 40; 21:34; 22:16; 35; 71; 24:41; **Jn** 1:3; 18; 46; 2:25; 4:33; 5:37; 6:46; 51; 7:4; 17; 37; 48; 51; 8:33; 9:22; 31; 32; 10:9; 28; 11:9; 57; 12:26(2); 47; 14:14; 16:30; 18:31; 21:5; **Acts** 4:12; 32; 34; 9:2; 10:14; 28; 47; 11:8; 13:15; 17:25; 19:2; 38; 39; 24:12; 20; 25:5; 8; 11; 16; 17; 24; 27:12; 22; 34; 42; 28:21(2); **Rom** 1:10; 6:2; 8:9; 33; 39; 9:11; 11:14; 13:8; 9; 14:13; 14; 21; 15:18; **1Cor** 1:15; 16; 2:2; 3:7; 12; 14; 15; 17; 18; 5:11; 6:1; 12; 7:12; 18(2); 36; 8:2(2); 3; 9; 10; 9:7; 15; 27; 10:19(2); 27; 28; 11:16; 34; 14:27; 30; 35; 37; 38; 16:22; **2Cor** 1:4; 2:5; 10(2); 3:5; 5:17; 6:3; 7:14; 8:23; 10:7; 11:3; 21; 12:6; 17; **Gal** 1:8; 9(2); 2:2; 5:6; 6:15; **Eph** 2:9; 5:5; 27; 6:8; **Phil** 2:1(4); 3:4; 11; 15; 4:8(2); **Col** 2:4; 8; 23; 3:13(2); **1Th** 1:8; 2:5; 9; 4:6; 5:15; **2Th** 2:3; 3:8(2); 10; 14; **1Ti** 1:10; 5:4; 8; 16; 6:3; **Titus** 1:6; **Heb** 1:5; 13; 2:1; 3:12; 13; 4:1; 11; 12; 13; 10:38; 12:15(2); 16; 19; **Jas** 1:5; 7; 13; 23; 26; 3:2; 5:12; 13(2); 14; 19; **1Pet** 3:1; 6; 4:11(2); 16; **2Pet** 1:20; 3:9; **1Jn** 2:1; 15; 27; 4:12; 5:14; 16; **2Jn** 10; **Rev** 3:20; 7:1; 16(2); 9:4(2); 11:5(2); 12:8; 13:9; 14:9; 18:11; 22; 21:4; 27; 22:18; 19

APART

Ex 13:12; **Lev** 15:19; 18:19; **Ps** 4:3; **Eze** 22:10; **Zec** 12:12(5); 13(4); 14(2); **Mt** 14:13; 23; 17:1; 19; 20:17; **Mk** 6:31; 9:2; **Jas** 1:21

ARE

Gen 2:4; 6:9; 7:2; 8; 9:2; 19; 10:1; 20; 31; 32; 11:10; 27; 18:5; 24; 19:5; 15; 20:7; 16; 25:7; 12; 13; 16(2); 17; 19; 23; 27:22; 41; 46; 29:4; 21; 31:12; 15; 43(3); 49; 32:17; 33:5; 8; 13(2); 15; 34:21; 22; 35:2; 26; 36:1; 5; 9; 10; 13; 16; 17(3); 18; 19(2); 20; 21; 24; 26; 27; 28; 29; 30; 31; 40; 37:2; 17; 38:25(2); 40:12; 18; 41:26(2); 27; 42:9(2); 10; 11(3); 12; 13; 14; 16; 21; 31(2); 33; 34(2); 36; 43:18; 44:16; 45:6; 11; 16; 46:8; 18; 22; 25; 31; 32; 47:1(2); 3; 4; 5; 9; 48:5; 8; 9; 49:5(2); 28; 50:3(2); **Ex** 1:1; 9; 19(3); 2:18; 3:7; 4:18; 19; 5:5; 16; 17(2); 6:15; 16; 19; 24; 25; 26; 27(2); 7:17; 8:21; 9:27; 10:8; 11; 12:13; 14:3; 15:4; 16:7; 8(2); 16; 19:6; 21:1; 24:14; 25:22; 26; 28:3; 4; 24; 29:33; 30:13; 14; 31:6; 32:2; 22; 33:5; 16; 35:1; 39:6; 40:4; **Lev** 4:12(2); 13; 5:17; 10:14; 11:2(2); 8; 9; 13(2); 26; 27; 28; 31; 32; 35; 42; 12:6; 14:37; 16:4; 18:17; 24; 23:2; 4; 17; 37; 42; 25:7; 23; 33; 42; 44; 45; 55(2); 26:25; 36; 39; 46; 27:34; **Num** 1:3; 5; 17; 44; 2:32; 3:1; 2; 3; 9; 13; 18; 20; 21; 27; 33; 46(2); 4:15; 20; 41; 6:13; 8:16; 17; 9:7(2); 10:4; 29; 31; 11:21; 13:16; 28; 30; 31; 32; 14:9; 35; 43(2); 15:13; 15; 16:3; 5; 11; 37; 38; 18:6; 16; 17; 18; 20:16; 22:4; 6; 9; 12; 24:3; 5; 6; 15; 26:2; 7; 14; 18; 22; 25; 27; 30; 34; 35; 36; 37(2); 41; 42(2); 47; 50; 57; 58; 63; 27:1; 30:14; 16; 31:12; 49; 32:14; 33:1; 2; 51; 34:17; 19; 29; 35:33; 36:3; 4; 13; **Deut** 1:2; 10; 11; 20; 28; 2:4; 25; 3:18; 4:4; 20; 30; 32; 45; 5:3; 6:1; 14; 7:6; 17; 20; 8:9; 9:12; 29; 11:12; 30; 12:1; 9; 13:7; 13; 14:1; 2; 4; 7; 9; 12; 29; 16:11; 14; 17:14; 18:12; 20:2; 15(2); 21:2; 6; 22:5; 17; 23:8; 18; 24:14; 25:16; 27:12; 28:58; 29:1; 5; 20; 21; 27; 29; 30:1; 10; 31:17; 18; 21; 32:4; 5; 20; 21; 28; 32(2); 37; 33:3; 17(3); 27; **Josh** 2:3(2); 3:8; 4:9; 6:17(2); 19; 7:3; 21; 8:5; 9:8(2); 9; 11; 13; 22; 23; 25; 10:6; 17; 12:1; 7; 13:14; 17; 30; 32; 14:1; 15:32; 16:3; 17:3; 9; 16(2); 18:3; 19:14; 29; 35; 51; 21:9; 22:10; 17; 23:14; 15; 24:22(2); 23; **Judg** 3:1; 5:11; 6:2; 7:2(2); 4; 18; 8:6; 15(2); 9:2; 18; 10:4(2); 11:7(2); 12:3; 4; 15:10(2); 11; 12; 18:9; 24; 19:18; 20:7; 13; 32; 39; 21:16; **Ruth** 1:11; 4:9; 10; 11; 18; **1Sa** 2:3; 4(2); 8; 4:8; 17; 6:17; 9:20; 10:2; 7; 12:2; 21; 16:11; 16; 17:8; 19:22; 20:21; 22; 21:5; 26:16; 29:10; **2Sa** 1:4(3); 19; 25; 27; 3:28; 5:1; 8; 7:9; 11:11; 13:33; 14:14; 20; 15:3; 13; 15; 16:4; 21; 17:2; 10; 12; 16; 19:11; 12(3); 20:19; 22:28; 39; 24:14; **1Kin** 1:20; 45; 4:8; 13; 8:8; 9:13; 10:8(2); 27; 11:41; 13:3; 32; 14:19; 29; 15:7; 23; 31; 16:5; 14; 20; 27; 18:22; 25; 20:3; 17; 23; 31; 22:39; 45; **2Kin** 1:5; 18; 3:23; 5:12; 6:9; 16; 7:12; 13(5); 8:23; 9:22; 10:2(2); 5; 13(2); 34; 12:19; 13:8; 12; 14:15; 18; 28; 15:6; 11; 15; 21; 26; 31; 36; 16:19; 18:20; 26; 34(2); 35; 19:3; 4; 20:14; 15; 20; 21:17; 25(2); 23:28; 24:5; **1Chr** 1:29; 31; 33; 43; 54; 2:1; 18; 55; 4:2; 4; 12; 18; 22; 5:14; 6:19; 31; 33; 50; 54; 65; 7:8; 33; 8:6(2); 38; 40; 9:33; 44; 11:1; 10; 12:1; 15; 18; 23; 13:2(2); 14:4; 15:12; 16:14; 26; 27(2); 17:8; 19:3; 21:3; 13; 22:15; 24:1; 26:19; 29:15(2); 17; 29; **2Chr** 1:15; 2:7; 3:3; 6:37; 7:14; 8:11; 9:7(2); 27; 29; 11:10; 12:15; 13:7; 8; 9; 10; 22; 16:11; 17:14; 19:3; 20:12; 34; 23:6; 24:26; 27; 25:26; 26:18; 27:7; 28:10; 26; 29:9; 19; 30:6; 32:32; 33:18; 19; 34:21; 24; 31; 35:25; 27; 36:8; **Ezr** 2:1; 4:10; 12; 5:4; 11; 6:6; 9; 7:13; 19; 21; 25; 8:1; 13; 28(3); 9:6; 15; 10:3; 13(3); **Neh** 1:3(3); 10; 2:3; 17(2); 4:2; 4; 10; 19; 5:2; 5; 17; 6:8; 7:6; 9:6; 36(2); 37; 10:39; 11:3; 7; 12:1; **Est** 1:16; 3:8; 4:16; 7:4; 8:5; 9; 9:13; 10:2; **Job** 1:19; 3:8; 19; 22; 24; 4:9; 10; 11; 19; 20; 5:4(2); 6:3; 4; 7; 16; 17; 18; 21(2); 25; 26; 7:1; 3; 6(2); 8; 16; 8:9(2); 13; 17; 9:25; 26; 10:5(2); 17; 20; 11:6; 12:2; 6; 16; 13:4(2); 12; 23; 14:5(2); 21; 15:10; 11; 15; 28; 16:2; 22; 17:1(2); 2; 7; 11(2); 18:3; 21; 19:3; 13; 19; 22; 20:11; 25; 21:7; 9; 18; 22; 24(2); 28; 33; 22:10; 12; 14; 19; 29; 23:14; 24:1; 8; 13; 17; 23; 24(3); 25:2; 5; 26:5; 11; 14; 27:12; 28:4(2); 6; 30:1; 15; 17; 30; 31:40; 32:6; 9; 34:18; 19; 21; 25; 35:5; 36:7(2); 20; 37:17; 24; 38:6; 30; 35; 39:4; 30; 40:17; 18(2); 41:14; 15; 17; 18; 23(2); 25; 28; 29; 30; **Ps** 1:4(2); 2:12; 3:1(2); 6:2; 9:3; 6; 15; 10:5(2); 8; 16; 12:4; 6; 8; 14:1; 3(2); 16:3; 6; 11; 17:2; 10; 14(2); 18:38; 19:8; 9; 10; 20:8(2); 21:11; 22:14; 25:10; 15; 17; 19; 27:12; 31:10; 15; 32:11; 33:4; 34:15(2); 18; 19; 35:19; 20; 36:3; 6; 12(2); 37:23; 28; 34; 38:4(2); 5; 7; 14; 19(3); 20; 39:6; 40:5(3); 12; 42:7; 44:13; 22(2); 45:5; 47:9; 49:14; 50:11; 51:17; 53:1; 3; 54:3; 55:4; 5; 10; 56:5; 8; 12; 57:4(2); 6; 58:3; 4; 59:3; 7; 62:9(3); 65:5; 8; 13(2); 68:6; 17; 69:1; 4(2); 5; 9; 19; 71:13; 24(2); 72:20; 73:1; 4; 5(2); 8; 10; 12; 19(2); 27; 74:20; 75:3; 76:5; 6; 77:19; 79:1; 4(2); 8; 11; 82:5; 6(2); 83:5; 84:1; 4; 5; 85:10; 86:8; 14; 87:3; 7; 88:5; 89:7; 11; 14; 49; 90:4; 5(2); 7(2); 9; 10; 92:5(2); 93:5; 94:11; 95:4; 7; 96:5; 6(2); 97:2(2); 100:3; 102:3(2); 8(2); 11; 20; 22; 24; 25; 103:6; 14; 15; 104:16; 17; 18; 24; 25; 28; 29; 30; 105:7; 106:3; 107:17; 27; 29; 30; 38; 39; 109:2; 4; 24; 111:2; 7(2); 8; 113:6; 115:4; 8; 15; 16; 116:11; 118:12; 119:1; 2; 21; 24; 39; 75; 84; 85; 86; 91; 98; 99; 103; 111; 129; 137; 138; 143; 150; 151; 156; 157; 168; 172; 120:7; 122:5; 123:3; 4; 124:7; 125:2; 4; 126:3; 127:3; 4(2); 135:15; 18; 139:12; 14; 17; 18; 140:2; 141:6(2); 7; 8; 142:6; 144:4; 145:9; 146:8; **Prov** 1:19; 2:15; 3:15; 17(2); 20; 4:22; 23; 5:6; 11; 21; 6:16; 23; 8:8; 9; 11; 18; 32; 9:17; 18(2); 10:6; 11:20(4); 12:5(2); 6; 7(2); 10; 22(2); 13:8; 14:4; 12; 18; 15:3; 11; 15; 22(2); 26(2); 16:2; 11(2); 13; 24; 25; 17:6(2); 15; 24; 18:4; 7; 8; 19; 21; 19:7; 13; 14; 21; 29; 20:7; 10; 15; 23; 24; 22:3; 4; 5; 26; 23:3; 24:11(2); 21; 25:1; 26:7; 21; 22; 23; 25; 28; 27:6(2); 12; 15; 20(2); 24; 25; 26(2); 28:1; 2; 29:2; 12; 16; 30:12; 13(2); 14; 15(2); 18; 24(2); 25; 26; 29; 31:8; 21; 25; **Eccl** 1:8; 11; 13; 14; 2:14; 23; 3:18; 20; 4:1; 2(2); 9; 5:7; 11; 7:19; 21; 8:8; 13; 9:1; 3; 12(3); 16; 17; 10:12; 11:10; 12:3; 11(2); **Song** 1:10; 17; 3:7; 4:2(2); 3(2); 5(2); 11; 12; 13; 5:11; 12; 13; 14; 15; 6:6; 7; 8; 7:1(2); 3(2); 9; 13; 8:6; **Is** 1:4(2); 7; 14; 15; 23; 2:6; 13; 14; 3:8; 12; 16; 4:2; 5:12; 13(2); 21; 22; 28; 7:2; 8:18; 9:10(2); 16(2); 10:8; 14; 20; 29; 14:19; 16:4; 7; 8(3); 17:2; 19:11; 12(2); 13(3); 21:3; 22:2; 3(4); 9; 23:8(2); 24:6(2); 17; 18; 21; 22; 25:1; 26:9; 14(2); 27:7; 9; 11; 28:1(2); 7(3); 8; 9; 15; 27(2); 29:9; 15; 20; 30:18; 27; 31:1(2); 3; 32:7; 9; 11; 20; 33:13(2); 14; 23; 35:4; 36:5; 11; 19(2); 20; 37:3; 39:3; 40:11; 15(2); 17(2); 22; 41:23(2); 24; 29(3); 42:9; 17; 22(3); 43:10; 12; 17(2); 44:7; 8; 9(2); 11; 45:16; 19; 20; 24; 46:1; 2; 3(2); 10; 12; 48:1(2); 7; 49:9; 16; 51:1(2); 19; 20; 52:7; 53:5; 54:1; 55:8(2); 9(2); 56:8; 10(3); 11(2); 57:1; 4; 6; 20; 58:7; 59:3; 6; 7(2); 10; 12(2); 60:8; 61:1; 9; 11; 63:8; 15; 19; 64:6(2); 8(2); 9; 10; 11; 65:5; 11; 16(2); 22; 23; 24; **Jer** 2:5(2); 11; 15; 28(2); 31; 4:13(2); 17; 20; 22(2); 5:3; 4(2); 6(2); 7; 10; 16; 23; 26; 27(2); 28; 6:4; 28; 29; 28(3); 29(2); 7:4; 10; 8:8; 9(2); 10; 20; 9:3; 10(3); 19(2); 25; 26(3); 10:2; 3; 5; 8; 9; 15; 20(3); 21; 11:10; 16; 12:1; 4; 9; 12; 13:22; 23; 14:2; 7; 9; 18; 22; 15:2(4); 8; 16:3; 17(2); 20; 18:6; 21:4; 7; 22:6; 17; 20; 28(2); 23:10; 11; 14; 26; 24:2; 3; 5; 8; 25:12; 22; 23; 26; 31; 34; 37; 27:5; 18; 29:1; 4; 16; 17; 22; 25; 30:4; 6; 31:20; 29; 32:19; 24; 35; 33:4; 10; 34:21; 35:14; 37:19; 38:19; 22(3); 40:15; 41:12; 42:2; 11; 43:11(3); 44:2; 6; 10; 14; 24; 27; 28; 46:5(2); 7; 8; 12; 15; 21(3); 23(2); 48:14; 15; 17; 32; 36; 41; 46; 49:23; 32; 50:2(2); 11; 15(2); 37; 38; 42; 51:4; 7; 18; 30; 32(2); 43; 51(2); 56; 60; 64; **Lam** 1:2(2); 4(2); 5(2); 6(2); 14; 16; 18; 20; 21; 22; 2:9(2); 11; 21; 3:22; 23; 4:1; 2; 5; 8; 9; 18; 19; 5:3(2); 5; 7; 12; 17; **Eze** 2:4; 5; 7; 3:7; 26; 27; 5:2; 5; 6; 7(2); 14; 15; 7:9; 11:2; 7; 12; 15; 12:2; 10; 14; 20; 22; 23; 27; 13:4; 14:5; 16:7; 27; 38; 52; 57; 18:2; 4; 25; 29(2); 20:3; 30; 34; 21:14; 24(2); 29; 22:9; 18(2); 19; 27; 23:45; 24:19; 25:9; 26:6; 18; 19; 27:4; 27; 28:8; 24; 25; 29:12(2); 30:7(2); 31:12(3); 14; 32:20; 21; 22; 23; 24; 25; 26; 27(2); 28; 29; 30(2); 32; 33:24; 27; 30; 34:3; 12; 30; 31; 35:8; 12(2); 36:2; 3(2); 4(2); 7; 8; 20(2); 35(2); 36; 37:11(3); 38:7; 11; 12(2); 20; 22; 40:46; 42:13; 14(2); 43:13; 18; 27; 44:10; 45:14; 46:24; 48:1(2); 11; 15; 29; 30; **Dan** 1:10; 2:20; 28; 3:12; 16; 4:3(2); 18; 35; 37; 5:23; 7:17(2); 24; 8:20; 23; 9:7(2); 16(2); 19; 24; 26; 10:16; 12:9; **Hos** 1:9; 10(2); 2:12; 4:4; 6; 14; 5:2; 6:5; 7:2; 4; 7(2); 9; 16; 8:9; 9:6; 7(2); 15; 11:7; 8; 12:7; 11(2); 14:3; 9; **Joel** 1:6; 7; 12; 17(2); 18(2); 20; **Amos** 4:1; 5:16; 6:1(2); 6; 9:7; 8; 12; **Obad** 6(2); **Jonah** 4:11; **Mic** 1:4; 5(2); 16; 2:7; 13; 4:11; 6:10; 12; 16; 7:6; 11; **Nah** 1:3; 6; 10; 2:3; 3:13; 17(2); **Hab** 1:3(2); 6; 7; 8(2); 15; 3:6; **Zeph** 1:6; 8; 11(2); 12; 3:3(2); 4; 6(2); 18(2); **Hag** 1:9; **Zec** 1:5; 9; 10; 15; 19; 21(2); 3:8; 4:2; 4; 10; 11; 14; 6:4; 5; 6; 10; 15; 8:16; 17; 11:2; 13:6; **Mal** 1:4; 2:8; 3:6; 7; 9; 15(2); **Mt** 1:17(3); 2:18; 20; 5:3; 4; 5; 6; 7; 8; 9; 10(2); 11; 13; 14; 15; 6:5; 26; 7:15; 8:26; 9:12; 17; 37; 10:2; 28; 29; 30; 31; 11:5(2); 8; 11; 27; 28; 12:5; 48; 13:15; 16; 38(2); 39; 40; 56; 15:16; 20; 17:26; 18:20; 19:6; 12(2); 26; 30; 20:22(2); 25; 22:4(3); 14(2); 21(2); 30(2); 23:8; 13; 25; 27(2); 28; 31; 37; 24:8; 19; 25:8; 26:55; **Mk** 2:17(2); 4:11(2); 15; 16(2); 17; 18(2); 20(2); 40; 5:9; 6:2; 3; 7:15; 18; 9:23; 10:8; 27; 31; 42; 12:17(2); 25(3); 13:1; 8; 17; 25; 32; 14:36; 48; **Lk** 1:1; 4:18; 5:20; 31(2); 38; 6:21(2); 22; 24; 25; 7:22(2); 25(2); 28; 31; 32; 47(2); 48; 8:12; 13; 14(2); 15; 21; 9:12; 55; 61; 10:2; 8; 9; 17; 20(2); 22; 23; 11:7; 21; 28; 41; 44(2); 12:6; 7(2); 24; 37; 38; 13:14; 23; 25; 27; 30(2); 34; 14:17; 16:8; 15; 17:10(2); 17; 18; 18:11; 27(2); 31; 19:42; 20:34; 35; 36(2); 37; 21:21(3); 22; 23; 26; 22:10; 25; 28; 38; 23:29(2); 24:17(2); 18; 38; 44; 48; **Jn** 3:21; 4:35(2); 38; 5:28; 39; 6:9; 49; 58; 63(2); 64; 69; 7:7; 23; 47; 49; 8:10; 23(2); 31; 37; 44; 47; 53; 9:28; 40; 10:8; 12; 16; 21; 26; 30; 34; 11:9; 13:10; 11; 17; 35; 14:2; 15:3; 5; 6; 14; 19; 16:15; 30; 17:7; 9; 10(2); 11(2); 14; 16; 22; 20:23(2); 29; 30; 31; 21:25; **Acts** 2:7; 13; 15; 32; 39; 3:15; 25; 5:9; 25; 32; 7:1; 26; 10:4; 21; 31; 33(2); 39; 13:27; 31; 39; 14:11; 15(2); 15:18; 19; 23; 16:17; 21; 28; 17:6; 22; 28; 29; 19:15; 26; 37; 38(2); 40; 20:32; 21:20(2); 21(2); 24; 22:3; 10; 23:15; 21; 35; 24:2; 11; 14; 25:5; 24; 26:3; 18; 26; 28:27; **Rom** 1:6; 15; 20(3); 28; 32; 2:2; 8; 13; 14; 18; 19; 3:9(2); 12(2); 15; 16; 19; 25; 4:7(3); 12; 14; 6:2; 4; 13; 14; 15; 16; 21; 7:4; 6; 8:1; 5(2); 8; 9; 12; 14(2); 16; 18; 24; 28; 36(2); 37; 9:4; 5; 6(2); 7(2); 8(3); 26; 10:15; 19; 11:14; 16; 28(2); 29; 33; 36; 12:5; 13:1; 3; 6; 14:8; 20; 15:1; 14; 26; 27; 16:7; 10; 11; 14; 15; 18; **1Cor** 1:2; 5; 11(2); 18; 24; 26; 27; 28(3); 30; 2:6; 12; 14(2); 3:2; 3(2); 4; 8; 9(3); 16; 17; 20; 21; 22; 23; 4:8(2); 9; 10(6); 11(2); 13(2); 18; 19; 5:2; 4; 7; 12(2); 13; 6:2; 4; 11(3); 12(3); 15; 19; 20(2); 7:14; 23; 33; 8:4; 5; 6(2); 8(2); 9; 10; 9:1; 2; 12; 13; 20(2); 21(2); 10:11(2); 13; 17(2); 18; 22; 23(3); 11:19; 30; 32(2); 12:4; 5; 6; 12; 13; 20; 22; 27; 29(4); 14:10; 12; 22; 23(2); 25; 32; 34; 37; 15:2; 6; 15; 17; 18(2); 19; 23; 27; 29(2); 35; 40; 48(4); 16:9; 18; **2Cor** 1:1; 4(2); 7; 14(2); 20; 24; 2:11; 15(2); 16; 17; 3:2; 3; 5; 18; 4:3; 8(2); 11; 15; 18(6); 5:4; 6(3); 8; 11(2); 17(2); 18; 20; 6:12(2); 16; 7:3; 6; 8:23; 10:4; 7; 10; 11(3); 12; 14; 11:13; 19; 22(3); 23; 28; 13:4; 6; 9(3); **Gal** 1:2; 6; 2:15; 17; 3:3(2); 7(2); 9; 10(3); 25; 26; 28; 29; 4:6; 8; 9; 12; 24(2); 28; 31; 5:4(2); 17; 18; 19(2); 24; 6:1; 10; 13; **Eph** 1:1; 10(2); 2:5; 8; 10; 11; 13; 19; 20; 22; 4:1; 4; 25; 30; 5:4; 8; 12; 13(2); 16; 30; 6:5; **Phil** 1:1; 7; 10; 11; 13; 14; 2:21; 3:3; 13(2); 18; 4:3; 8(6); 21; 22; **Col** 1:2; 16(2); 2:3; 10; 11; 12; 17; 20; 22; 3:1; 3; 5; 15; 4:5; 9; 11(2); 13; 15; **1Th** 2:10; 14; 15; 19; 20; 3:3; 4:9; 10; 12; 13; 15(2); 17; 5:4; 5(2); 7; 8; 12; 14; **2Th** 1:3; 7; 2:13; 3:11(2); 12; **1Ti** 2:2; 3:7; 5:3; 15; 16; 24; 25(2); 6:1; 2(2); 17; **2Ti** 1:15(2); 2:19; 20; 26; 3:3; 6; 15; **Titus** 1:5; 10; 12; 15(2); 3:8; 9; 15; **Philem** 1:7; **Heb** 1:10; 14; 2:10(2); 11(2); 14; 18; 3:6; 14; 4:13; 15; 5:2; 11; 12; 14; 6:9; 7:5; 13; 8:4; 9:15; 17; 22; 24; 10:8; 10; 14; 39; 11:3; 12:1; 8(2); 11; 18; 22; 23; 27(2); 13:3; 11; **Jas** 1:1; 2:4(2); 7; 9; 16; 3:4(2); 9; 5:2(2); 4; 17; **1Pet** 1:5; 6; 12; 2:5; 9; 10; 14; 25; 3:6(2); 9; 12(2); 14; 4:6; 13; 14; 5:1; 9(2); 14; **2Pet** 1:4; 2:10(2); 11; 13; 15; 17(2); 19; 20; 3:5; 7(2); 10; 16(2); **1Jn** 2:5; 12; 14; 15; 18; 3:2; 10; 19; 22; 4:1(2); 4; 5; 6; 17; 5:3; 7(2); 8; 19; 20; **2Jn** 7; **Jude** 1; 4; 7; 12(2); 15; 16; **Rev** 1:3; 4(2); 11; 19; 20(2); 2:2(3); 9(3); 18; 3:2; 4; 9(2); 4:5; 11; 5:6; 8; 13(2); 7:13(2); 14; 15; 8:13; 9:14; 10:6(3); 11:4; 15; 13:8; 14:4(3); 5; 12; 13; 18; 15:3(2); 4; 16:6; 7; 14; 17:9; 10(2); 12; 14(2); 15; 18:3; 14(2); 19:2; 9(3); 20:7; 8; 10; 21:4; 5; 12; 16; 22; 24; 27; 22:6; 14; 15; 18; 19

ART

Gen 3:9; 14; 19; 4:6; 11; 12:11; 13; 13:14; 16:11; 17:8; 20:3; 23:6; 24:23; 47; 60; 26:16; 29; 27:18; 24; 32; 28:4; 29:14; 15; 32:17; 39:9; 41:39; 44:18; 45:19; 46:30; 47:8; 49:3; 8; 9; **Ex** 4:25; 26; 18:18; 30:25; 35; 33:3; 34:10; **Lev** 27:12; **Num** 14:14(2); 21:29; **Deut** 2:18; 4:30; 38; 7:6; 19; 8:10; 12; 9:1; 6; 14:2; 21; 24; 17:14; 18:9; 26:1; 27:3; 9; 28:10; 32:15(3); 18; 33:29; **Josh** 5:13; 13:1; 17:17; **Judg** 8:18; 11:2; 12; 25; 35; 12:5; 13:3; 11; **Ruth** 2:9; 11; 12; 3:9(2); 11; 16; **1Sa** 8:5; 10:2; 5; 17:28; 33(2); 58; 19:3; 21:1; 24:17; 26:14; 15; 28:12; 29:9; 30:13; **2Sa** 1:8; 13; 2:20; 7:22; 24; 28; 9:2; 12:7; 13:4; 15:2; 19; 27; 16:8(2); 21; 18:3; 19:13; 20:9; 17; 22:29; **1Kin** 1:42; 2:9; 26; 6:12; 13:14; 18; 17:18; 24; 18:7; 17; 36; 37; 20:36; 22:4; **2Kin** 1:4; 6; 16; 3:7; 4:4; 19:15; 19; **1Chr** 17:26; 29:11; **2Chr** 14:11; 16:14; 18:3; 20:6; 7; 25:16; **Ezr** 7:14; 9:15; **Neh** 2:2; 9:6; 7; 8; 17; 31; 33; **Est** 4:14; **Job** 4:5; 15:7; 17:14(2); 22:3; 30:21; 31:24; 33:12; 34:18; 35:8; **Ps** 2:7; 3:3; 5:4; 8:4; 10:14; 16:2; 22:1; 3; 9; 10; 23:4; 25:5; 31:3; 4; 14; 32:7; 40:17; 42:5(2); 11(2); 43:2; 5(2); 44:4; 45:2; 63:1; 65:5; 66:3; 68:35; 70:5; 71:3; 5(2); 6; 7; 76:4; 7(2); 77:14; 83:18; 86:5; 10(2); 15; 89:17; 26; 90:2; 92:8; 93:2; 97:9(2); 102:27; 104:1(2); 110:4; 118:21; 28(2); 119:12; 57; 68; 114; 137; 151; 137:8; 139:3; 8(2); 140:6; 142:5; 143:10; **Prov** 6:2(2); 3; 7:4; 24:24; **Eccl** 10:17; **Song** 1:15(2); 16; 2:14; 4:1(2); 7; 6:4; 7:6; **Is** 14:8; 10(2); 12(2); 19; 31; 22:1; 2; 25:1; 26:15; 37:16; 20; 41:8; 9; 43:1; 44:17; 21(2); 45:15; 47:8; 13; 48:4; 49:3; 51:9; 10; 12; 16; 57:8; 10; 63:2; 16(2); 64:5; 8; **Jer** 2:21; 23; 27; 3:4; 22; 4:30; 10:6; 12:1; 2; 14:9; 22; 15:6; 17:14; 17; 20:7; 22:6; 31:18; 39:17; 49:12; 50:24(2); 51:20; **Lam** 5:22; **Eze** 3:5; 16:7; 34; 45(2); 54; 22:4(2); 5; 24; 23:30; 26:17; 27:3(2); 28:2; 3; 14; 31:2; 18; 32:2(2); 33:32; 38:13; 17; 40:4; **Dan** 2:26; 37; 38; 4:18; 22; 5:13(2); 27(2); 9:23; **Hos** 2:23(2); **Obad** 2; 5; **Jonah** 1:8; 4:2; **Mic** 2:7; **Nah** 1:14; 3:8; **Hab** 1:12; 13; 2:16; **Zec** 4:7; **Mt** 2:6; 5:25; 6:9; 8:29; 11:3; 23; 14:33; 16:14; 16; 17; 18; 23; 22:16; 25:24; 26:50; 73; 27:11; **Mk** 1:11; 24(2); 3:11; 8:29; 12:14; 34; 14:61; 70(2); 15:2; **Lk** 1:28(2); 42; 3:22; 4:34(2); 41; 7:19; 20; 10:15; 41; 11:2; 12:58; 13:12; 14:8; 10; 15:31; 16:25; 19:21; 22:32; 58; 67; 70; 23:3; 40; 24:18; **Jn** 1:19; 21(2); 22; 42;

49(2); 3:2; 10; 4:12; 19; 5:14; 6:69; 7:52; 8:25; 48; 53; 57; 9:28; 11:27; 17:21; 18:17; 25; 33; 37; 19:9; 12; 21:12; **Acts** 4:24; 8:23; 9:5; 10:33; 12:15; 13:33; 17:29; 21:22; 38; 22:8; 27; 26:1; 15; 24; **Rom** 2:1(2); 17; 19(2); 3:4; 9:20; 14:4; **1Cor** 7:21; 27(2); **Gal** 4:7; **1Ti** 6:12; **Heb** 1:5; 12; 2:6; 5:5; 6; 7:17; 21; 12:5; **Jas** 2:11; 4:11; 12; **Rev** 2:5; 9; 3:1; 15; 16; 17; 4:11; 5:9; 11:17(2); 15:4; 16:5(2)

AS

Gen 3:5; 22; 4:20(2); 21; 7:9; 16; 8:21; 9:3; 10:9; 19(2); 30; 11:2; 12:4; 13:10(2); 16; 16:6; 17:4; 15; 20; 23; 18:5; 25; 33(2); 19:8; 14; 28; 21:1(2); 4; 16; 22:14; 17(2); 23:9(2); 24:22; 51; 25:18; 26:4; 29(2); 27:4; 9; 12; 14; 19; 23; 27; 30(2); 42; 46; 28:6; 14; 31:2; 5; 26; 32:12; 25; 28; 31; 33:10; 14; 34:12; 15; 22; 31; 35:18; 36:24; 38:11; 29; 39:10; 18; 40:10; 22; 41:13; 19; 21; 38; 39(2); 49; 54; 42:27; 35; 43:6; 17; 34; 44:1(2); 3(2); 15; 17; 18; 47:11; 21; 30; 48:5; 7; 20(2); 49:4; 9(2); 16; 27; 50:6; 12; 20(2); **Ex** 1:17; 19; 2:14; 4:6; 7; 5:7; 13; 14; 20; 7:6; 10; 13; 20; 22; 8:15; 19; 27; 9:12; 17; 18; 24; 29(2); 30; 35; 10:10; 14; 11:6; 12:25; 28; 31; 32; 36; 48; 50; 13:11; 14:28; 15:5; 7; 8; 10; 16(2); 16:5(2); 10; 14(2); 22; 24; 34; 17:10; 18:21; 19:18; 21:7; 22(2); 22:25; 23:15; 24:10(2); 27:8; 28:32; 30:37; 32:1; 13; 17; 19(2); 23; 33:9; 11; 34:4; 10; 18; 35:22(2); 38:21; 39:1; 5; 6; 7; 21; 23; 26; 29; 31; 43; 40:15; 19; 21; 23; 25; 27; 29; 32; **Lev** 2:12; 4:10; 20; 21; 26(2); 31; 35; 5:13(2); 6:17(2); 7:7; 10(2); 19; 21; 8:4; 9; 13; 17; 21; 29; 31; 34; 9:7; 10; 15; 21; 10:5; 15; 18; 11:4; 12:5; 13:43; 14:6; 13; 22; 30; 31; 35; 15:25; 26(2); 16:15; 34; 18:19(2); 22; 28; 19:16; 18; 23(2); 34(2); 20:6; 13; 25; 22:13; 24:16(2); 19; 20; 22(2); 23; 25:31; 39; 40(2); 42; 46; 53; 26:19(2); 34(2); 35(2); 36; 37; 27:12; 14; 21; 23; **Num** 1:19; 2:17; 33; 3:16; 42; 51; 4:15; 29; 49; 5:4; 8:3; 16; 19; 21; 22; 9:15; 18(2); 10:31; 11:7(2); 8; 12; 31(3); 12:10; 12; 13:21; 33; 14:15; 17; 19; 21(2); 28(3); 32; 15:14; 15; 20; 36; 16:31; 40(3); 45; 47; 17:11; 18:6; 7; 18(2); 24; 27(2); 30(2); 20:9; 27; 21:34; 22:4; 8; 23:2; 22; 24(2); 30; 24:1; 6(4); 8; 9(2); 26:4; 27:11; 13; 17; 22; 23; 28:8(2); 31:7; 31; 41; 47; 32:25; 27; 31; 33:56; 34:6; 36:10; **Deut** 1:10; 11(2); 17(2); 19; 21; 31; 40; 44; 2:1; 5; 10; 11; 12; 14; 21; 22; 29; 30; 3:2; 6; 20(2); 4:5; 7; 8; 20; 32; 33; 38; 5:12; 14(2); 16; 26; 31; 32; 6:3; 8; 16; 19; 24; 25; 8:5; 18; 20; 9:3(2); 18; 21(2); 25; 10:5; 9; 15; 22; 11:4; 10(2); 18; 21; 25; 12:9; 12; 15(2); 16; 19(2); 20; 21; 22; 24; 13:6; 11; 17; 14:7; 15:6; 21; 22(2); 23; 16:9; 10; 17; 17:14; 16; 18:2; 7; 14; 19:5; 6; 8; 19; 20:8(2); 17; 22:11; 26; 23:23; 24:8; 26:15; 18; 19; 27:3; 28:9; 29; 49(2); 62; 63; 29:13(2); 28; 30:9; 31:3; 4; 13(2); 21; 32:2(4); 10; 11; 31; 50; 33:20; 25; 34:9; **Josh** 1:3; 5; 15; 17(2); 2:7(2); 11(2); 3:7; 13(2); 15; 4:8(2); 12; 14; 18; 23; 5:5; 14; 6:22; 7:5; 8:2; 5; 6; 15; 19(2); 29(2); 31(2); 33(3); 9:4; 21; 25; 10:1; 2; 11; 28; 30; 39(2); 40; 11:4; 9; 12; 13; 15; 20; 13:6; 8; 14; 33; 14:2; 5; 7; 10; 11(4); 12; 15:18; 63; 17:14; 21:8; 22:4; 23:5; 8; 9; 10; 15; 24:15; **Judg** 1:7; 20; 2:3; 15(2); 22; 3:1(2); 2; 4:22; 5:31; 6:5; 16; 27; 36; 37; 7:5; 12; 17; 8:8; 18; 19; 21; 33(2); 9:33(3); 36; 48; 11:36; 13:9; 23(2); 14:6; 20; 15:10; 11; 14; 16:7; 9; 11; 20; 17:8; 11; 19:22; 20:1; 8; 11; 30; 31; 32; 39; 48(2); **Ruth** 1:8; 3:10; 13; **1Sa** 1:7; 12; 26; 28(2); 2:2; 16(2); 3:10; 4:9; 5:10; 6:6; 12; 7:10; 9:11; 13(2); 20; 27; 10:7; 12:15; 23; 13:5; 7; 10(2); 14:14; 39; 45; 15:22(2); 23(2); 27; 33; 16:7; 17:20(2); 23; 36; 55; 57; 18:1; 3; 6; 7; 10; 19:6; 7; 9; 20; 20:3(2); 13; 17; 20; 21; 23; 25; 31(2); 36; 41(2); 42; 22:8; 13; 14; 23:11; 24:4; 13; 18; 25:15(2); 20; 25; 26(3); 29; 34; 37; 26:10; 16; 20; 24; 27:8; 28:10; 17; 29:6; 8; 9; 10(2); 30:24; **2Sa** 1:6; 21; 2:18(2); 23(2); 27; 3:9; 33; 34; 36; 4:4; 6; 9; 5:20; 25; 6:16; 18(2); 19(2); 20; 7:10; 11; 15; 25; 8:3; 9:8; 11(2); 10:2; 11:11(2); 25(2); 12:3; 5; 13:13(2); 29; 35; 36(2); 14:2; 11; 13; 14; 17; 19; 25; 15:10(2); 21(2); 26; 30(2); 34; 16:2; 5; 13(2); 19; 23; 17:3; 8; 10; 11; 12(2); 18:32; 33; 19:3; 14; 18; 27; 30; 20:8; 22:23; 31; 43(3); 45(2); 23:4(2); 6; 24:19; 23; **1Kin** 1:29; 30; 37; 41; 2:3; 24(2); 31; 38; 3:6(2); 14; 4:20; 29; 5:5; 12; 8:20; 24; 25; 43; 53; 57; 59; 61; 9:2; 4; 5; 10:10; 27(2); 11:4; 6; 11; 33; 38(2); 12:12; 17; 13:6; 18; 20; 21; 14:6; 7; 8; 10; 15; 15:3; 11; 16:2; 9; 11(2); 31; 17:1; 11; 12; 13; 18:7; 10; 12(2); 15; 32(2); 19:2; 5; 20:11; 12; 34; 36(4); 39; 40; 21:11(2); 26; 22:4(3); 14; 17; **2Kin** 1:16; 2:2(2); 4(2); 6(2); 11; 19; 23; 3:7(3); 14; 22(2); 4:8(2); 30(2); 40; 5:16; 20; 27(2); 6:5; 26; 7:7; 10; 13(2); 17; 18; 8:5; 18; 19; 27; 9:17; 22; 31; 37; 10:2(2); 12; 15; 25(2); 11:8(2); 14; 12:9; 13:5; 21; 23; 14:3; 4; 5(2); 15:9; 17:2; 4; 11; 23; 41; 19:12; 26(4); 29; 37; 21:3; 13; 20; 22:18; 23:16; 21; 27; 24:13; 25:15; 22; **1Chr** 5:1; 6:26; 12:8(2); 20; 33; 36; 14:16; 15:15; 29; 16:37; 17:1; 9; 13; 23; 18:3; 21:3; 15; 17; 21; 22:7; 11; 23:24; 24:19; 25:8(3); 26:13(2); 21; 28:2; 7; 29:11; 15(2); 17; 23; 25; **2Chr** 1:12; 15(3); 2:3; 16(2); 3:16; 4:6; 5:13(2); 6:8; 10; 15; 16; 31; 33; 7:17(2); 18; 8:7; 14; 9:9; 27(2); 10:12; 17; 11:16; 13:10; 15; 16:3; 18:3(2); 13; 16; 20:9; 20; 21; 33; 21:6; 7; 23:3; 13; 18(2); 24:12(2); 25:4; 16; 26:5(2); 29:8; 31(2); 30:5; 7; 8; 31:3; 5(2); 15(2); 32:17; 19; 33:22; 23; 34:26; 35:12; 18; 36:21(2); **Ezr** 2:62; 3:1; 2; 4(2); 4:2; 3; 6:18; 21; 7:14; 25; 27; 28; 8:27; 31; 9:7; 13; 15; 10:3; 12; **Neh** 1:1; 2:16; 18; 5:5(2); 12; 6:8; 11(2); 7:64; 8:1; 15; 9:10; 11; 23; 24; 10:34; 36; 13:15; **Est** 2:9; 20(2); 3:11; 4:14; 5:5; 8; 13; 6:10; 7:8; 8:8; 9:2; 22; 23(2); 27(2); 31(2); **Job** 2:10; 3:6; 16(2); 4:8; 5:7; 14; 25; 26; 6:7; 15(2); 26; 7:2(2); 9; 20; 9:26(2); 32; 10:4; 5(2); 9; 10; 16; 19; 22(2); 11:8(2); 16; 17; 20; 12:3(3); 4; 5; 13:9; 28(2); 14:2; 6; 11; 15:24; 33(2); 16:4; 21; 17:6; 7; 10; 15; 18:3; 20; 19:11; 22; 20:8(2); 21:4; 18(2); 33; 22:2; 8; 24(2); 23:10; 24:5; 14; 17; 18; 20; 24(2); 26:3; 27:2; 6; 7(2); 16(2); 18(2); 20; 21; 28:5(2); 29:2(2); 4; 14; 18; 23(2); 25(2); 30:5; 14; 15(2); 18; 31:18; 33; 36; 37; 32:19; 34:3; 26; 35:8; 37:18; 38:8; 14(2); 19; 30; 39:16; 20; 40:15; 18; 41:5; 15; 20; 24(4); 27(2); 29; 42:7; 9; 10(2); 15; **Ps** 5:7; 12; 10:5; 9; 11:1; 12:6; 14:4; 17:8; 12(2); 15; 18:30; 42(2); 44(2); 19:5(2); 21:9; 22:13; 25:10; 26:11; 27:12; 31:12; 32:9(2); 33:7; 22; 34:18; 35:5; 13; 14(2); 37:2; 6(2); 14; 20; 22; 38:4; 10; 13(2); 14; 39:5(2); 12; 40:4; 16; 41:12; 42:1; 10; 44:22; 48:6; 8; 50:21; 53:4; 55:16; 20; 58:3(2); 7(2); 8; 9; 61:6; 62:3(2); 63:2; 5; 65:3; 66:10; 68:2(2); 13; 14; 15(2); 17; 21; 69:13; 70:4; 71:7; 72:5(2); 6; 7; 17(2); 73:1; 2; 5; 6(2); 19; 20; 22; 74:5; 77:13; 78:8; 13; 15; 27(2); 65; 83:9(3); 10; 11(2); 13; 14(2); 87:7(2); 88:4; 89:10; 11; 29; 36; 37(2); 90:4(2); 5(2); 9; 92:7; 95:8(2); 102:3; 7; 26; 103:11; 12(2); 13; 15(3); 18; 104:2; 6; 17; 33(2); 106:9; 107:10; 109:17(2); 18(2); 19; 23; 29; 116:2(2); 118:12; 119:14(2); 70(2); 111; 132; 162; 122:3; 123:2(2); 124:6; 7; 125:1; 2; 5(2); 126:4; 127:4; 128:3; 129:6; 131:2(2); 133:3(2); 137:8; 139:12; 16; 140:9; 141:2(2); 7; 143:3; 6; 144:4; 12(2); 147:20; **Prov** 1:12(2); 27(2); 2:4(2); 3:12; 4:18; 19; 5:3; 4(2); 19; 6:5(2); 11(2); 7:2; 22(2); 23; 8:26; 30; 9:4; 16; 10:20; 23; 25; 26(2); 11:19; 20; 22; 28; 12:4; 15:19; 16:14; 15; 24; 27; 17:8; 14; 18:4(2); 8; 11; 19:12(2); 24; 20:2; 19; 21:1; 8; 29; 23:5; 7; 28; 34(2); 24:29; 34(2); 25:12; 13; 16; 20(2); 25; 26; 26:1(2); 2(2); 8; 9; 11; 14; 18; 21; 22; 27:8; 19; 21; 28:1; 4; 15; 30:14(2); 31:8; **Eccl** 2:8; 13(2); 15; 16; 3:19; 4:1; 5:15(2); 16; 6:12; 7:6; 26; 8:1; 13; 9:2(2); 12(2); 10:5; 7; 11:5; 12:7; 11(2); **Song** 1:3; 5(2); 7; 14; 2:2; 3; 4:1; 11; 5:11(2); 12; 13(2); 14(2); 15(3); 6:4(3); 5; 6; 7; 10(4); 13; 7:4(2); 8; 8:1; 6(4); 10; **Is** 1:7; 8(3); 9; 18(4); 26(2); 30(2); 31(2); 3:9; 12; 16; 5:18; 24(3); 6:13(2); 7:2; 8:6; 9:1; 3; 4; 18; 19; 10:9(3); 10; 11; 14(2); 15(3); 18; 20; 22; 26; 32; 11:9; 16; 13:4; 6; 8(2); 14(2); 17; 19; 14:10; 17; 19(2); 24(2); 16:2; 3; 14; 17:3; 5(2); 6; 9; 13; 19:14; 20:3; 21:1; 3; 22:16; 23; 23:5; 10; 15; 24:2(6); 13(2); 22; 25:4; 5; 10; 11; 26:17; 18; 19; 20; 27:7; 9; 28:2(2); 4; 21(2); 29:2; 4; 5; 7; 8(2); 11; 13; 16; 17; 30:13; 14; 17(2); 22; 26(2); 27; 28; 29(2); 31:4; 5; 32:2(3); 33:4; 11; 12(2); 34:4(3); 35:1; 6; 37:12; 27(4); 30; 38; 38:12; 13; 14; 19; 40:6; 15(3); 17; 22(3); 23; 24; 31; 41:2(2); 11; 12(2); 15; 25(2); 42:13; 19(3); 43:17; 44:4(2); 7; 22(2); 47:3; 4; 8; 14; 48:18(2); 19; 49:18(3); 26; 50:4; 9; 51:9; 12; 13; 20; 23(2); 52:14; 53:2(2); 3; 7(2); 54:6; 9(2); 55:9; 10; 56:12; 58:2; 4; 5; 8; 10; 59:10(3); 12; 17(2); 21; 60:8(2); 61:10(2); 11(2); 62:1(2); 5(2); 63:13; 14; 64:2; 6(3); 65:8; 22; 66:3(4); 8(2); 13; 20; 22; **Jer** 2:26; 36; 3:2; 5; 20; 4:13(2); 17; 31(2); 5:8; 9; 16; 19; 26; 27; 29; 6:7; 9(2); 23; 24; 26; 7:14; 15; 8:6; 9:8; 9; 22(2); 10:5; 6; 7; 11:5; 12:8; 9; 16; 13:5; 10; 11; 21(2); 24; 14:8(2); 9(2); 15:2(4); 18(2); 19; 16:4; 17:8; 11; 16; 22; 18:4; 6(2); 17; 19:11; 12; 13; 20:9; 11; 16; 21:7; 22:23; 24; 23:12; 14(2); 27; 29; 34; 24:8; 25:18; 30; 38; 26:11; 14(2); 18; 27:13; 30:6; 20; 31:5; 10; 12; 18; 23; 28; 32:20; 31; 42; 33:7; 11; 22; 38:16; 39:12; 40:3; 10; 41:6(2); 42:2; 18; 43:11(3); 12; 44:6; 13; 14; 16; 17; 22; 23; 30; 46:7(2); 18(3); 22; 26; 48:8; 13; 34; 40; 41; 49:16(2); 18; 22(2); 24; 50:8; 9; 11(2); 15; 18; 26; 37; 40; 43; 51:14; 27; 30; 38; 49; **Lam** 1:1; 15; 17; 20; 22; 2:4; 5; 6; 7; 12; 22; 3:6; 10(2); 12; 45; 4:2; 6; 14; 17(2); 5:3; 21; **Eze** 1:1; 4; 10; 13; 14; 15; 16; 18; 22; 24(2); 26(2); 27(3); 28; 3:3; 9; 23; 4:12; 5:11; 7:17; 20; 8:1; 2(3); 9:10; 11; 10:1(2); 5; 9; 10(2); 11(2); 13; 11:16; 21; 12:4(2); 7(2); 11; 23; 14:10; 16; 18; 20; 15:6; 16:4; 7; 31; 32; 38; 44; 47; 48(2); 50; 57; 59; 17:5; 16; 19; 18:3; 4; 18; 20:3; 31; 32(2); 33; 36; 39; 21:7; 10; 23; 22:20; 22; 23:16(2); 18; 20; 44; 24:18; 22; 26:3; 10; 28:2; 6; 16; 30:9; 18; 32:2; 33:11; 12; 17; 27; 31(2); 32; 34:8; 12; 17; 19; 35:6; 11; 15; 36:17; 38(2); 37:7(2); 10; 38:16; 40:2; 40; 41:21; 25; 42:6; 9; 11(4); 12; 43:22; 46:5; 7; 11; 12; 47:10; 14(2); 15; 22; 48:1; 8; 11; 23; **Dan** 1:4; 13; 17; 2:29; 30; 40(3); 41; 42; 43; 45; 4:18; 25; 32; 33; 35; 5:12; 6:4; 10; 22; 7:4; 9(2); 12; 28; 8:5; 15; 18; 9:7; 12; 13; 15; 10:4; 6(2); 17; 11:29(2); 32; 12:1; 3(2); **Hos** 1:10; 2:3(2); 15(2); 4:4; 7; 16(2); 5:12(2); 14(2); 6:3(3); 4(2); 5; 9; 7:4; 6; 7; 12(2); 8:1; 8; 12; 9:1; 4; 9; 10(2); 11; 13; 10:4; 7(2); 11; 14; 11:2; 4; 8(2); 11(2); 12:9; 11; 13:3(4); 7(2); 8; 14:5(3); 6(2); 7(3); **Joel** 1:15; 2:2; 3; 4(2); 5; 32; **Amos** 2:9; 13; 3:12; 4:11(2); 5:11; 14; 16; 19; 24(2); 7:15; 8:8(2); 10(2); 9:5; 7; 9; 11; **Obad** 4; 11; 15; 16(2); **Jonah** 1:14; **Mic** 1:4(2); 6(2); 8; 16; 2:8(2); 12(2); 3:3(2); 4; 12(2); 4:9; 12; 5:7(2); 8(2); 15; 7:1(2); 4; 10; 14; **Nah** 1:10(3); 2:2; 7; 3:6; 15(2); 17(2); **Hab** 1:8; 9(2); 14(2); 2:5(2); 14; 3:4; 14(2); **Zeph** 1:8; 17(2); 2:2; 9(3); **Hag** 1:12; 2:3; 19; 23; **Zec** 1:4; 6; 2:4; 6; 4:1; 5:3(2); 7:3; 12; 13; 8:11; 13; 14; 9:1; 3(2); 7(2); 11; 13; 14; 15(2); 16(3); 10:2; 3; 5; 6; 7; 8; 12:8(3); 10(2); 11; 13:9(2); 14:3; 5; 10; 15; **Mal** 2:9; 3:3(2); 4(2); 17; 4:1; 2; **Mt** 1:18; 24; 5:48; 6:2; 5; 7; 10; 12; 16; 7:29(2); 8:13; 9:9; 10; 15(2); 32; 36; 10:7; 16(3); 25(2); 11:7; 12:13; 40; 13:40; 43; 14:5; 36(2); 15:28; 33; 17:2(2); 9; 20; 18:3; 4; 17; 19; 25; 33; 19:19; 20:14; 28; 29; 21:6; 18; 23; 26; 22:9(2); 10(2); 30; 31; 39; 23:37; 24:3; 21; 27; 37; 38; 44; 25:14; 32; 40; 45; 26:7; 19; 21; 24; 26; 39(2); 55; 27:10; 32; 65(2); 28:1; 3; 4; 6; 9; 15; **Mk** 1:2; 16; 22(2); 42(2); 2:2; 14; 15; 19(2); 23; 3:5; 10(2); 20; 4:4; 18; 20; 26; 33; 36; 5:36(2); 6:15; 31; 34; 56(2); 7:4; 6; 8; 8:24; 9:3(2); 9; 13; 26; 10:1; 15; 32; 46; 11:2(2); 6; 20; 27; 12:25; 26; 31; 33; 13:1; 3; 19; 34; 14:3; 16; 18; 21; 22; 45(2); 48; 66; 15:8; 16:7; 10; 12; 14; **Lk** 1:1; 2; 23(2); 44(2); 55; 70; 2:15; 20; 23; 43; 3:4; 15; 23; 4:16; 5:1; 14; 17; 6:3; 10; 22; 31; 34; 36; 40; 8:5; 6(2); 23; 42; 9:18; 29; 33; 34; 42; 53; 54; 57; 10:3; 7; 8; 18; 27; 33; 38; 11:1(2); 2; 8(2); 27; 30; 36; 37; 41; 44; 53; 12:58; 13:34; 14:1; 22; 15:19; 25; 30(2); 17:6; 11; 12; 14; 24; 26; 28; 18:11(2); 13; 17; 35; 19:9; 11; 32; 33; 36; 20:1; 21:5; 6; 35; 22:13; 22; 26(2); 27; 29; 31; 39; 44; 52; 56; 66(2); 23:7(2); 14; 24; 26; 24:4; 5; 11; 17; 24; 28; 30; 36; 39; 50(2); **Jn** 1:12(2); 14; 23; 36; 3:14; 4:51; 5:21; 23; 26; 30; 6:11(2); 31; 57; 58; 59; 7:10; 28; 38; 8:6; 20; 28; 30; 9:1; 5(2); 29; 10:15; 26; 11:20(2); 29(2); 56; 12:14; 50; 13:15; 33; 34; 14:27; 31; 15:4; 6; 9; 10; 12; 16:21(2); 17:2(3); 11; 14; 16; 18; 21; 22; 23; 18:6(2); 19:40; 20:9; 11; 21; 21:8; 9(2); **Acts** 1:10; 11; 19; 2:2; 3; 4; 15; 22; 39(2); 45; 47; 3:6; 11; 12; 17; 24(2); 4:1; 6(2); 34(2); 35; 5:11(2); 35; 36(2); 37(2); 6:15; 7:5(2); 26; 28; 31; 40; 42; 44; 48; 51; 8:3; 16; 32; 36; 9:3; 17; 18; 32; 38; 10:9; 11; 25; 27; 29(2); 45(2); 47(2); 11:5; 15(2); 17(2); 19(2); 22(2); 12:13; 18(2); 13:1; 2; 17; 25; 33; 34; 48(2); 14:20; 15:8; 11; 15; 24; 16:4; 16; 17:2; 14; 23; 25; 28; 29; 19:2; 20:3; 9; 21:10; 25; 31; 37; 22:3; 5; 6; 23; 25; 23:11; 15; 20; 31; 24:10; 25; 25:10; 18; 26:12; 24; 29; 27:25; 27; 30(2); 28:10; 15(2); 22; **Rom** 1:13; 15(2); 17; 21; 28; 2:12(4); 24; 3:4; 5; 7; 8(2); 10; 4:1; 6; 17(2); 5:12; 15; 16; 18; 19; 21; 6:3; 4; 13(3); 19; 7:1(2); 2; 8:14(2); 26; 36(2); 9:5; 6; 13; 25; 27; 29(2); 32; 33; 10:15; 11:8; 13; 26; 28(2); 30; 12:3; 4; 18(2); 13:9; 13; 14:11; 15:3; 7; 9; 15; 21; 16:2; **1Cor** 1:6; 31; 2:9; 3:1(3); 3; 5; 10; 15; 4:1; 7; 8; 9; 13; 14; 17; 18; 5:1(2); 3(2); 7; 7:7; 8; 17(2); 25; 29; 30(3); 31; 39(2); 8:1; 2; 4; 5; 7; 9:5(3); 8; 20(2); 21; 22; 26(2); 10:6; 7(2); 8; 9; 10; 13; 15; 33; 11:1; 2; 5; 7; 12; 25(2); 26(2); 12:2; 11; 12; 18; 13:1; 11(3); 12; 14:12; 33; 34; 15:8; 22; 38; 48(2); 49; 58; 16:1; 2; 10; 12; **2Cor** 1:5; 7; 14(2); 18; 23; 2:17(3); 3:1; 3; 5; 13; 18(2); 4:1; 13; 5:20; 6:1; 4; 8; 9(3); 10(3); 13; 16; 7:14; 8:5; 6; 7; 11; 15; 9:1; 3; 5(2); 7; 9; 10:2; 7; 9; 11; 14(3); 11:2; 3; 10; 12; 15; 16; 17; 21(2); 23; 12:20(2); 13:2; 7; **Gal** 1:9; 2:7; 14(2); 3:6; 10(2); 16(2); 27(2); 4:1(2); 12(2); 14(2); 28; 29; 5:14; 21; 6:10; 12(2); 16(2); **Eph** 1:4; 2:3; 3:3; 5; 4:4; 17; 21; 32; 5:1; 2; 3; 8; 15(2); 22; 23; 24; 25; 28; 29; 33; 6:5; 6(2); 7; 20; **Phil** 1:7(2); 20; 27; 2:8; 12(2); 15; 22; 23; 3:5; 12; 15(2); 17; 4:15; **Col** 1:6(2); 7; 2:1(2); 6; 7; 20; 3:12; 13; 18; 22; 23; 4:4; **1Th** 1:5; 2:2; 4(2); 5; 6; 7; 11(2); 13(2); 14; 3:4; 6; 12; 4:1; 5; 6; 9; 11; 13; 5:2; 3; 4; 6; 11; **2Th** 1:3; 2:2(2); 4; 3:1; 15(2); **1Ti** 1:3; 5:1(2); 2(2); 6:1(2); **2Ti** 2:3; 9; 17; 3:8; 9; **Titus** 1:5; 7; 9; 2:3; **Philem** 1:9; 14; 16; 17; **Heb** 1:4; 11; 12; 2:14; 3:2; 3; 5; 6; 7; 8; 15; 4:2(2); 3(2); 7; 10; 15; 5:3; 4; 6; 12; 6:19; 7:9; 20; 27; 8:5; 9:8; 9; 25; 27; 10:25(2); 11:7; 9; 12(4); 27; 29; 12:5; 7; 16; 20; 27; 13:3(2); 5; 17; **Jas** 1:10; 2:8; 9; 12; 26; 5:3; 5; 17; **1Pet** 1:14; 15; 18(2); 19; 24(2); 2:2; 4; 5; 11; 12; 13; 14; 16(2); 25; 3:6(3); 7(2); 8; 16; 4:1; 10(2); 11(2); 12; 13; 15(4); 16; 19; 5:3; 8; 12; **2Pet** 1:3; 13(2); 14; 19; 21; 2:1; 12; 13; 3:4; 8(2); 9; 10; 15; 16(2); **1Jn** 1:7; 2:6; 18; 27(2); 3:2; 3; 7; 12; 23; 4:17; **2Jn** 4; 5; 6; **3Jn** 2; 3; **Jude** 7; 10; **Rev** 1:10; 14(3); 15(2); 16; 17; 2:24(3); 27(2); 3:3; 19(2); 21; 4:1; 7; 5:6; 13; 6:1; 11; 12(2); 13; 14; 8:8; 10; 12; 9:2; 3; 5; 7(2); 8(2); 9(2); 17; 10:1(2); 3; 7; 9; 10(3); 11:6(2); 12:4(2); 15; 13:2(2); 3; 11; 15(2); 14:2(2); 3; 15:2; 16:3; 15; 18; 17:12(2); 18:6; 17(2); 19:6(3); 12; 20:8; 21:2; 11; 16(2); 21; 22:1; 12

ASIDE

Ex 3:3; 4; 32:8; **Num** 5:12; 19; 20; 29; 22:23; **Deut** 5:32; 9:12; 16; 11:16; 28; 17:20; 28:14; 31:29; **Josh** 23:6; **Judg** 14:8; 19:12; 15; **Ruth** 4:1(2); **1Sa** 6:12; 8:3; 12:20; 21; **2Sa** 2:21(2); 22; 23; 3:27; 6:10; 18:30(2); **1Kin** 15:5; 20:39; 22:32; 43; **2Kin** 4:4; 22:2; **1Chr** 13:13; **Job** 6:18; **Ps** 14:3; 40:4; 78:57; 101:3; 125:5; **Song** 1:7; 6:1; **Is** 10:2; 29:21; 30:11; 44:20; **Jer** 14:8; 15:5; **Lam** 3:11; 35; **Amos** 2:7; 5:12; **Mal** 3:5; **Mt** 2:22; **Mk** 7:8; 33; **Lk** 9:10; **Jn** 13:4; **Acts** 4:15; 23:19; 26:31; **1Ti** 1:6; 5:15; **Heb** 12:1; **1Pet** 2:1

AT

Gen 3:24; 4:7; 6:6; 8:6; 9:5(3); 13:3; 4; 14:17; 17:21; 18:14; 19:1; 6; 11; 20:13; 21:2; 22; 32; 22:19; 23:10; 18; 24:11; 21; 30; 55; 57; 63; 25:32; 26:8; 27:41; 28:19; 31:10; 33:10; 19; 38:1; 5; 11; 41:1; 21; 43:16; 18; 19; 20; 25; 33; 44:12(2); 45:3; 48:3; 49:13; 19; 23; 27; **Ex** 2:5; 4:25; 5:23; 8:32; 9:14; 12:9; 18(2); 22; 29; 41; 16:6; 12; 13; 18:5; 22; 26; 19:15; 17; 22:23; 26; 28:7; 14; 22; 29:39; 41; 42; 30:8; 32:4; 33:8; 9; 10; 34:22; 35:15; 36:29; 38:8; 39:15; 40:8; 28; **Lev** 1:3; 15; 3:2; 4:7(2); 18(2); 25; 30; 34; 5:9; 6:20; 7:18; 8:15; 31; 33; 35; 9:9; 13:5; 37; 14:11; 15:24; 16:2; 7; 29; 17:6; 18:9; 19:5; 7; 20; 22:19; 29; 23:5; 32; 25:32; 26:32; 27:10; 13; 16; 31; 33; **Num** 3:39; 4:27; 6:6; 18; 9:2; 3; 5; 11; 15; 18(2); 23(3); 10:3; 11:6; 20; 35; 13:30; 16:34; 19:19; 20:24; 21:11; 15; 30; 33; 34; 22:4; 20; 38; 23:25(2); 24:1; 27:14; 21(2); 28:4; 8; 30:4; 6; 7; 11; 14(2); 31:12; 33:14; 16; 17; 19; 21; 26; 27; 30; 32; 34; 35; 38; 34:5; 9; 12; 35:11; 20; 26; **Deut** 1:4; 9; 16; 18; 2:32; 34; 3:1; 2; 4; 8; 12; 18; 21; 23; 4:14; 46; 5:5; 6:24; 7:21; 22; 8:16; 19; 9:11; 18; 19; 22(3); 25; 10:1; 8; 10; 14:28; 15:1; 9; 16:4; 6(4); 17:6(2); 19:15(2); 21:14; 23:24; 24:5; 15; 28:29; 67; 31:10; 32:35; 51; 33:3; 8(2); **Josh** 5:2; 3; 10; 6:16; 26; 7:7; 8:5; 6; 14; 29; 9:6; 10; 14; 16; 10:10; 16; 17; 21; 27; 42; 11:5; 10; 21; 12:4(2); 15:4; 5; 7; 8; 11; 63; 16:3; 7; 8; 17:9; 18:1; 9; 12; 14; 19(2); 19:22; 29; 33; 51; 20:4; 9; 21:2; 3; 22:11; 12; **Judg** 3:2; 29; 4:4; 10; 5:27(2); 28; 7:25; 8:18; 9:5; 41; 11:39; 12:2; 6(2); 10; 13:23(2); 25; 14:4; 16:3; 20; 28; 30; 18:27; 29; 19:16; 22; 26; 27; 20:15; 16; 20; 30; 31; 32; 33; 21:14; 22; 24; **Ruth** 2:14; 3:7; 8(2); 10; 14; **1Sa** 2:22; 29(2); 3:2; 10; 11; 6:10; 9:8; 10:2; 13:11; 14:18; 16:4; 17:1; 15; 18:10; 19; 19:19; 22; 20:5(2); 6; 16; 20; 25; 33; 35; 21:1; 4; 22:8; 13; 14; 23:29; 25:1; 24; 26:7; 8; 11; 16; 27:3; 28:7; 30:8; 21; 31:13; **2Sa** 2:32; 3:30; 32; 4:5; 6:4; 8:3; 9:7; 10; 11; 13; 10:5; 8; 11:1(2); 9; 13; 13:5; 6; 14:26(2); 15:8; 14; 16:3; 6(2); 13; 23; 17:7; 9; 19:9; 28; 32; 42; 20:3; 8; 18; 21:18; 22:16(2); 23:8; 24:8; 24; **1Kin** 1:6; 2:7; 8; 26; 39; 3:20; 5:14; 7:30; 8:2; 9; 59; 61; 65; 9:2; 6; 8; 10; 10:22; 26; 28; 11:29; 12:27; 13:20; 14:1; 6; 15:18; 27; 18:19; 27; 36(2); 44; 19:6; 20:9; 16; 22; 26; 22:5; 20; 28; 34; 35; 48; **2Kin** 2:3; 5; 15; 18; 4:17; 37; 5:9; 20; 6:32; 7:3; 8:3; 22; 29; 9:7; 24; 27; 30; 31; 10:8; 12; 14; 11:6(2); 12:4; 13:20; 14:10; 11; 13; 20; 16:6; 10; 17:25; 18:10; 16; 33; 19:21; 36; 20:12; 23:6; 8; 11; 15; 29; 33; 24:3; 10; 25:21; 25; **1Chr** 2:55; 4:28; 29(3); 30(3); 31(3); 8:29; 9:34; 38; 11:11; 13; 16; 17; 12:22; 32; 13:3; 14:3; 15:13; 29; 16:33; 39; 17:9; 19:5; 20:1(2); 4(2); 6; 21:19; 28; 29(2); 23:30; 26:18(3); 31; 28:7; 21; **2Chr** 1:3; 4; 6; 13; 14; 15; 16; 3:1; 5:10; 12; 7:8; 8:1; 14; 17; 9:1; 25; 13:18; 14:10; 15:10; 15; 16; 16:2; 7; 18:4; 9; 19; 33; 19:4; 20:16; 22:5; 6(2); 23:5(2); 13(2); 19; 24:8(2); 11; 21; 23; 25:19; 21; 23; 26:9(3); 28:16; 30:1; 3; 5; 13; 21; 31:13; 32:9; 33; 33:14; 35:15; 17; 23; 36:3; 7; **Ezr** 1:2; 2:68; 3:8; 4:10; 11; 17; 24; 5:2; 3; 17(2); 6:2; 3; 5(2); 9; 12; 17; 18; 7:12; 8:17(2); 21; 29; 34; 9:4; 5; 10:3; 14; **Neh** 2:12; 3:19; 4:22; 5:17; 6:1; 7; 7:5; 9:37; 10:34; 11:1; 2; 4; 6; 22; 24; 25(3); 26(3); 27(2); 28(2); 29(3); 30(2); 31; 32; 12:25; 27; 37(2); 44; 13:6; 19; 31; **Est** 1:12; 4:8; 14; 5:6; 13; 6:10; 7:2; 3(2); 8:3; 9; 14; 9:14; 15; 18; **Job** 2:10; 3:13; 17; 5:22; 23; 9:23; 12:5; 15:12; 23; 16:4; 12; 17:8; 18:12; 20; 19:25; 21:12; 23; 22:21; 23:15; 26:11; 27:23; 29:21; 31:9; 29; 34:20; 37:1; 39:22; 27; 41:9; 26; 29; **Ps** 7:4; 9:3; 10:5; 11:2; 12:5; 16:8; 11; 18:12; 15(2); 25:13; 30:t, 4; 34:1; 35:8; 26; 37:13; 39:5; 12; 42:7; 52:6; 55:6; 17; 20; 59:6; 8; 14; 62:8; 64:4(2); 7; 65:8; 68:2; 8(2); 12; 29; 73:3; 74:6; 76:6; 80:16; 81:7; 83:9; 10; 91:6; 7(2); 97:5(2); 12; 99:5; 9; 104:7(2); 105:22; 106:3; 7(2); 32; 107:27; 109:6; 31; 110:1; 5; 114:7(2); 118:13; 119:20; 45; 62; 162; 123:4; 132:6; 7; 135:21; 141:7; **Prov** 1:23; 25; 26; 4:19; 5:11; 19; 7:6; 12; 19; 20; 8:3(4); 34(2); 9:14; 14:9; 19; 16:7; 17:5; 17; 20:21; 21:13; 23:30; 32; 24:19; 28:18; 29:21; 30:17; **Eccl** 5:6; 8; 10:2(2); 12:4; 6(2); **Song** 1:7; 12; 2:9; 7:13; 8:11; **Is** 1:12; 26(2); 6:4; 7:3; 23; 9:1; 10:26; 28; 29; 32; 13:6; 8; 14:7; 8; 9; 16:2; 4; 17:7; 14; 19:1; 19; 20:2; 21:3(2); 22:7; 23:5(2); 26:11; 27:13; 28:15; 29:5; 30:2; 4; 13; 17(2); 19(2); 32:9; 11; 33:3(2); 37:22; 37; 39:1; 42:14; 47:14; 50:2(2); 51:17; 20; 52:14; 15; 59:10; 60:4; 14; 64:1; 2; 3;

66:2; 5; 8; **Jer** 1:15; 17; 2:12; 24; 3:17; 4:9; 11; 19; 26; 5:22; 6:4; 15(2); 7:2; 12; 8:1; 12; 16; 10:2(2); 10; 18; 11:12; 15:8; 17:11; 27; 18:7; 9; 20:16; 23:23; 32; 25:15; 17; 28; 33; 26:19; 27:18; 29:10; 25; 31:1; 12; 32:20; 33:7; 11; 15; 34:8; 14; 16(2); 35:11; 36:10; 17; 27; 39:10; 40:10; 41:3; 43:9; 44:1(3); 6; 22; 23; 45:1; 46:27; 47:3(3); 48:11; 41; 49:17; 21(2); 22; 50:11; 13; 14; 46; 51:31; 49; **Lam** 1:7; 20; 2:15(2); 3:56(2); **Eze** 2:6; 3:9; 15; 16; 17; 18; 20; 8:5; 16; 9:6(2); 10:19; 11:1; 12:4; 23; 14:3; 16:4(2); 25; 46(2); 57; 18:23; 20:32; 21:19; 21(2); 22; 22:13(2); 23:42; 24:18; 26:10; 15; 16(2); 18; 27:3; 28; 35; 36; 28:19; 29:7; 13; 30:18; 31:16; 32:10(2); 33:6; 7; 8; 34:10; 35:15; 36:8; 11; 37:22; 38:10; 11; 18; 20; 39:20; 40:40(2); 44(2); 41:12; 44:11; 17; 25; 46:2; 3; 19; 47:1; 7; 48:28; 32; 33; 34; **Dan** 1:5; 15; 18; 2:10; 3:5; 7; 8; 15; 4:4; 8; 29; 34; 36; 5:3; 6:24; 8:1; 2; 17; 19; 27; 9:7; 15; 21; 23; 10:3; 11:27(2); 29; 40(2); 43; 12:1(2); 13; **Hos** 1:5; 2:16; 4:12; 5:8; 9:10; 11:7; **Joel** 1:15; 2:1; 9; **Amos** 3:5; 9; 4:3(2); 4; 6:1; 7:13; 8:9; **Obad** 7; **Mic** 1:10(2); 3:4; 7:16; **Nah** 1:3; 5(2); 3:10; **Hab** 1:10; 2:3; 5; 19; 3:5; 11(2); 16; **Zeph** 1:7(2); 12; 2:4; 3:19; 20; **Zec** 1:11; 15; 3:1; 8; 7:5; 11:13; 12:8; 14:7; 14; **Mal** 1:10; 13; 2:7; 8; 13; **Mt** 3:2; 4:6; 17; 5:25; 34; 40; 7:13; 28; 8:6; 9:9; 10; 10:7; 35; 11:22; 25; 12:1; 41; 13:15; 49; 14:1; 9; 15:17; 30; 18:1; 29; 19:4; 22:33; 23:6; 24; 24:33; 41; 25:6; 27; 26:7; 18(2); 45; 46; 60; 27:15; **Mk** 1:15; 22; 32; 33; 2:14; 15; 4:12; 5:22; 23; 6:3; 7:25; 9:12; 10:22; 24; 11:1; 18; 12:2; 4; 17; 39; 13:29; 35(3); 14:3; 42; 54; 15:6; 34; 16:2; 14; **Lk** 1:10; 14; 29; 2:18; 33; 41; 47; 4:11; 18; 22; 32; 5:5; 8; 9; 27; 7:9; 37; 38; 49; 8:19; 26; 35; 41; 9:31; 43(2); 61(2); 10:14; 32; 39; 11:5; 32; 12:40; 46; 13:1; 24; 25; 14:10; 14; 15; 17; 15:29; 16:20; 17:16; 19:5; 23; 29; 30; 37; 42; 20:10; 26; 37; 40; 46; 21:30; 31; 34; 37; 22:27(2); 30; 40; 23:7(2); 11; 12; 17; 18; 24:12; 22; 27; 30; 47; **Jn** 1:18; 2:10; 13; 23; 4:21; 45(2); 46; 47; 52; 53; 5:2; 4; 28; 37; 6:21; 39; 40; 41; 44; 54; 61; 7:2; 11; 23; 8:7; 9; 59; 10:22; 40; 11:24; 32; 49; 55; 12:2; 16; 20; 13:28; 14:20; 16:4; 26; 18:16; 38; 39; 19:11; 39; 42; 20:11; 12(2); 19; 21:1; 20; **Acts** 1:6; 19; 2:5; 14; 3:1; 2; 10(2); 12; 4:6; 11; 18; 35; 37; 5:2; 9; 10; 15; 7:13; 26; 29; 31; 58; 8:1(2); 14; 35; 40; 9:10; 13; 19; 22; 27; 28; 32; 35; 36; 10:11; 25; 30; 11:8; 15; 12:13; 13:1; 5; 12; 27; 14:8; 15:14; 16:2; 4; 25; 17:13; 16; 30; 18:22; 24; 19:1; 17; 26; 27; 20:5; 14; 15(2); 16; 18; 21:3; 11; 13; 24; 22:3; 23:11; 23; 25:4; 8; 10; 15; 23; 24; 26:4(2); 13; 20; 32; 27:3; 28:12; **Rom** 1:10; 15; 3:26; 4:20; 8:34; 9:9; 32; 11:5; 13:12; 14:10; 15:26; 16:1; S:1; **1Cor** 1:2; 7:39; 8:10; 9:7; 13; 11:34; 14:16; 27; 35; 15:6; 23; 29; 32; 52; 16:8; 12(2); **2Cor** 1:1; 4:18(2); 5:6; 8:14; **Gal** 4:12; 13; **Eph** 1:1; 20; 2:12; 3:13; **Phil** 1:1; 2:10; 4:5; 10; **Col** 1:2; 2:1; **1Th** 2:2; 5; 19; 3:1; 13; 5:13; **2Th** 2:2; 3:11; **1Ti** 1:3; 5:4; **2Ti** 1:18; 2:26; 3:11(3); 4:1; 6; 8; 13; 16; 20(2); **Titus** 2:5; **Heb** 1:1; 5; 13; 2:1; 3; 7:13; 9:17; 12:2; 13:23; **Jas** 3:11; **1Pet** 1:7; 13; 2:8; 4:7; 17(2); 5:13; **1Jn** 1:5; 2:28; 4:12; **Rev** 1:3; 17; 3:20; 8:3; 18:14; 21; 22(2); 23(2); 19:2; 10; 21:12; 25; 22:10

AWAY

Gen 12:20; 15:11; 18:3; 21:14; 25; 24:54; 56; 59; 25:6; 26:27; 29; 31; 27:35; 36(2); 44; 45; 28:5; 6; 30:15; 23; 25; 31:1; 9; 18; 20; 26(2); 27(3); 42; 35:2; 38:19; 40:15; 42:36; 43:14; 44:3; 45:24; **Ex** 2:9; 17; 8:8; 28; 10:17; 19; 12:15; 28; 13:19; 22; 14:11; 15:15; 18:18; 19:24; 22:10; 23:25; 33:23; **Lev** 1:16; 3:4; 10; 15; 4:9; 31(2); 35(2); 6:2; 4; 7:4; 14:40; 43; 16:21; 21:7; 25:25; 26:39(2); 44; **Num** 4:13; 11:6; 14:43; 17:10; 20:21; 21:7; 24:22; 25:4; 11; 27:4; 32:15; 36:4; **Deut** 7:4; 15; 13:5(2); 10; 15:13; 16; 18; 17:7; 12; 17; 19:13; 19; 21:9; 21; 22:19; 21; 22; 24; 29; 23:14; 24:4; 7; 26:13; 14; 28:26; 31; 29:18; 30:17(2); **Josh** 2:21; 5:9; 7:13; 8:3; 16; 18:8; 22:6; 7; 16; 18; 24:14; 23; **Judg** 3:18; 4:15; 17; 5:21; 8:21; 9:21; 10:16; 11:13; 15; 38; 15:17; 16:3; 14; 18:24(2); 19:2; 20:13; 31; **1Sa** 1:14; 5:11; 6:3; 8; 7:3; 4; 9:26; 10:25; 14:16; 15:27; 17:26; 19:10; 17; 20:13; 22; 29; 21:6; 23:5; 26; 24:19; 25:10; 26:12; 27:9; 28:3; 25; 30:2; 18; 22; **2Sa** 1:21; 3:21; 22; 23; 24; 4:7; 11; 5:6; 7:15(2); 10:4; 12:13; 13:16; 17:18; 18:3; 9; 19:3; 41; 22:46; 23:6; 9; 24:10; **1Kin** 2:31; 39; 8:46; 48; 66; 11:2; 3; 4; 13; 14:8; 10(2); 26(3); 15:12; 22; 16:3; 19:4; 10; 14; 20:6; 24; 34(2); 41; 21:4; 21; 22:43; **2Kin** 2:3; 5; 9; 3:2; 4:27; 5:2; 11; 12; 6:23; 32; 7:15; 12:3; 18; 14:4; 17:6; 11; 23; 28; 33; 18:11; 22; 24; 32; 20:18; 23:11; 19; 24; 34; 24:14; 15; 25:11(2); 14; 15; 21; **1Chr** 5:6; 21; 26; 6:15; 7:21; 8:8; 13; 9:1; 10:12; 12:19; 14:14; 17:13; 19:4; 21:8; **2Chr** 6:36; 42; 7:10; 19; 9:12; 12:9(2); 14:3; 5; 13; 15; 15:8; 17; 16:6; 17:6; 19:3; 20:25(2); 33; 21:17; 25:12; 27; 28:5; 8(2); 17; 21; 29:6; 10; 19; 30:8; 9; 14(2); 32:12; 33:15; 34:33; 35:23; 36:20; **Ezr** 2:1(2); 5:12; 8:35; 9:4; 10:3; 6; 8; 19; **Neh** 7:6(2); **Est** 2:6(3); 4:4; 8:3; **Job** 1:15; 17; 21; 4:21; 6:15; 7:9; 21; 8:4; 20; 9:12; 25; 26; 34; 11:14; 16; 12:17; 19; 20(2); 24; 14:10; 19; 20; 15:12; 30; 20:8(2); 19; 28; 21:18; 22:9; 23; 24:2; 3; 10; 27:2; 8; 20; 21; 28:4; 30:12; 15; 32:22; 33:21; 34:5; 20(2); 36:18; **Ps** 1:4; 2:3; 18:22; 45; 27:9; 28:3; 31:13; 34:t, 37:20; 36; 39:10; 11; 48:5; 49:17; 51:11; 52:5; 55:6; 58:7; 8; 9; 64:8; 65:3; 66:20; 68:2(2); 69:4; 78:38; 39; 79:9; 85:3; 88:8; 90:5; 9; 10; 102:24; 104:7; 29; 106:23; 112:10; 119:37; 39; 119; 132:10; 137:3; 144:4; **Prov** 1:19; 32; 4:15; 16; 24; 6:33; 10:3; 14:32; 15:1; 19:26; 20:8; 30; 22:27; 23:5; 24:18; 25:4; 5; 10; 20; 23; 28:9; 29:8; 30:30; **Eccl** 1:4; 3:5; 6; 5:15; 11:10; **Song** 2:10; 13; 17; 4:6; 5:7; 6:5; **Is** 1:4; 13; 16; 25(2); 3:1; 18; 4:1; 4; 5:5; 23; 24; 25; 29; 6:7; 12; 8:4; 9:12; 17; 21; 10:2; 4; 27; 12:1; 15:6; 7; 16:10; 17:1; 18:5; 19:6; 7; 20:4; 22:4; 17; 24:4(2); 25:8(2); 27:9; 28:17; 29:5; 30:22; 31:7; 35:10; 36:7; 9; 17; 39:7; 40:24; 41:9; 16; 49:19; 25; 50:1(2); 5; 51:6; 11; 52:5; 57:1(2); 13; 58:9; 13; 59:13; 14; 64:6; **Jer** 1:3; 2:24; 3:1; 8; 19; 4:1; 4; 5:10; 25; 6:4; 29; 7:29; 33; 8:4; 13; 13:17; 19(2); 24; 15:15; 16:5; 18:20; 22:10; 23:2; 24:1; 5; 27:20; 28:3; 6; 29:1(2); 4(2); 7; 14(2); 32:40; 33:26; 37:13; 14; 38:22; 39:9(2); 40:1(2); 7; 41:10(2); 14; 43:3; 12; 46:5; 6; 15; 21; 48:9; 49:19; 29; 50:6; 17; 44; 51:50; 52:15(2); 18; 19; 27; 28; 29; 30; **Lam** 2:6; 14; 4:9; 15; 22; **Eze** 3:14; 4:17; 11:18; 14:6; 16:9; 50; 18:24; 26; 27; 28; 31; 20:7; 8; 23:25; 26; 29; 24:16; 23; 26:16; 30:4; 33:4; 6; 10; 34:4; 16; 36:26; 38:13(2); 43:9; 44:10(2); 22; 45:9; **Dan** 1:16; 2:35; 4:14; 7:12; 14; 26; 8:11; 9:16; 11:12; 31; 44; 12:11; **Hos** 1:6; 2:2; 9; 17; 4:3; 11; 5:14(2); 6:4; 9:11; 17; 13:3; 11; 14:2; 4; **Joel** 1:7; 12; **Amos** 1:3; 6(2); 9; 11; 13; 2:1; 4; 6; 16; 4:2; 10; 5:23; 6:3; 7:11; 12; 9:1; **Obad** 11; **Jonah** 3:9; **Mic** 1:11; 2:2; 4; 9; **Nah** 2:2; 7; 8; 3:10; 16; 17; **Zeph** 2:7; 3:11; 15; **Zec** 3:4; 7:11; 9:7; 10:11; 14:12(3); **Mal** 2:3; 6; 16; 3:7; **Mt** 1:11; 17(2); 19; 5:31; 32; 40; 42; 8:31; 13:6; 12; 19; 36; 48; 14:15; 22; 23; 15:23; 32; 39; 19:3; 7; 8; 9(2); 22; 21:19; 20; 22:13; 24:35(2); 39; 25:29; 46; 26:42(2); 44; 57; 27:2; 31; 64; 28:13; 16; **Mk** 1:43; 2:20; 21; 4:6; 15; 36; 5:10; 6:36; 45; 46; 8:3; 9; 26; 9:18; 10:2; 4; 11; 12; 22; 50; 11:21; 12:3; 4; 13:31(2); 14:36; 39; 44; 53; 15:1; 16; 16:3; 4; **Lk** 1:25; 53; 2:15; 5:35; 6:29; 30; 8:6; 12; 13; 38; 9:12(2); 25; 10:42; 11:52; 13:15; 16:3; 18(2); 17:31; 19:26; 20:10; 11; 21:24; 32; 33(2); 23:18; 26; 24:2; **Jn** 1:29; 4:8; 5:13; 6:22; 67; 10:40; 11:39; 41; 48; 12:11; 14:28; 15:2; 16:7(2); 18:13; 19:15(2); 16; 31; 38; 20:1; 2; 10; 13; 15; **Acts** 3:26; 5:37; 7:27; 43; 8:33; 39; 10:23; 13:3; 8; 17:10; 14; 19:26; 20:6; 30; 21:36; 22:16; 22; 24:7; 27:20; **Rom** 11:1; 2; 15; 26; 27; **1Cor** 5:2; 13; 7:11; 12; 31; 12:2; 13:8; 10; 11; **2Cor** 3:7; 11; 14(2); 16; 5:17; **Gal** 2:13; **Eph** 4:25; 31; **Col** 1:23; **2Th** 2:3; **1Ti** 1:19; **2Ti** 1:15; 3:5; 6; 4:4; **Heb** 6:6; 8:13; 9:26; 10:4; 9; 11; 35; 12:25; **Jas** 1:10; 11; 14; 4:14; **1Pet** 1:4; 24; 3:21; 5:4; **2Pet** 3:10; 17; **1Jn** 2:17; 3:5; **Rev** 7:17; 12:15; 16:20; 17:3; 20:11; 21:1; 4(2); 10; 22:19(2)

BACK

Gen 14:16; 19:9; 26; 38:29; 39:9; **Ex** 14:21; 18:2; 23:4; 33:23; **Num** 9:7; 13:26; 22:34; 24:11; **Deut** 23:13; **Josh** 8:20; 26; 11:10; 23:12; **Judg** 11:35; 18:26; **Ruth** 1:15; 2:6; **1Sa** 10:9; 15:11; 25:34; **2Sa** 1:22; 12:23; 15:20; 25; 17:3; 18:16; 19:10; 11; 12; 37; 43; **1Kin** 13:18; 19; 20; 22; 23; 26; 29; 14:9; 28; 18:37; 19:20; 21; 22:26; 33; **2Kin** 1:5(2); 2:13; 24; 8:29; 15:20; 19:28; 20:9; **1Chr** 21:20; **2Chr** 13:14; 18:25; 32; 19:4; 25:13; 34:16; **Neh** 2:15; **Job** 23:12; 26:9; 33:18; 30; 34:27; 39:22; **Ps** 9:3; 14:7; 19:13; 21:12; 35:4; 44:10; 18; 53:3; 6; 56:9; 70:3; 78:9; 41; 57; 80:18; 85:1; 114:3; 5; 129:3; 5; **Prov** 10:13; 19:29; 26:3; **Is** 14:27; 31:2; 37:29; 38:17; 42:17; 43:6; 50:5; 6; **Jer** 2:27; 4:8; 28; 6:9; 8:5; 11:10; 18:17; 21:4; 32:33; 38:22; 40:5(2); 42:4; 46:5(2); 21; 47:3; 48:10; 39; 49:8; **Lam** 1:13; 2:3; **Eze** 23:35; 24:14; 38:4; 8; 39:2; 44:1; **Dan** 7:6; **Hos** 4:16; **Nah** 2:8; **Zeph** 1:6; 3:20; **Mt** 24:18; 28:2; **Mk** 13:16; **Lk** 2:45; 8:37; 9:62; 17:15; 31; **Jn** 6:66; 20:14; **Acts** 5:2; 3; 7:39; 20:20; **Rom** 11:10; **Heb** 10:38; 39; **Jas** 5:4

BE

Gen 1:3; 6; 9; 14(2); 15; 22; 28; 29; 2:18; 23; 24; 3:5(2); 6; 12; 16; 4:7(2); 12; 14(2); 15; 24; 6:3; 15; 19; 21; 8:17; 9:1; 2; 3; 6; 7; 11(2); 13; 14; 16; 20; 25(2); 26(2); 27; 10:8; 11:4; 6; 12:2; 3; 13; 13:8(2); 16; 14:19; 20; 15:4(2); 5(2); 13; 15; 16:2; 3; 5; 10; 12(2); 17:1; 4; 5(2); 7; 8; 10; 11; 12; 13(2); 14; 15; 16(2); 17; 18:4; 11; 18; 24; 25(3); 29; 30(2); 31; 32(2); 19:9; 15; 17; 22; 20:9; 21:10; 12(2); 30; 22:14; 18; 23:8; 24:5; 8(2); 14; 27; 41(2); 44; 51; 60; 25:22; 23(2); 24; 26:3; 4; 11; 22; 28; 27:13; 21; 29(3); 33; 39; 45; 28:3; 9; 14(2); 20; 21; 22; 29:4; 7; 8; 15; 26; 29; 34; 30:32; 33; 34; 31:3; 8(2); 30; 44; 52(2); 32:12; 18; 28; 33:14; 34:7; 10; 15(3); 17(2); 22(2); 23; 30; 35:2; 10(2); 11(2); 36:43; 37:14; 27; 32; 35; 38:9; 11; 15; 23; 24; 29; 39:10; 40:14; 41:21; 27; 30; 31(2); 36(2); 40(3); 52; 42:15; 16(3); 19(2); 20; 32; 33; 43:3; 5; 9; 11; 14; 23; 29; 44:9(2); 10(3); 17; 26(2); 30; 34; 45:5; 6; 10; 46:15; 47:19(2); 24; 25; 48:5; 6(2); 16; 19(2); 21; 49:6; 7; 8; 10; 12; 13(2); 17; 20; 26; 29; 50:18; **Ex** 1:16(2); 2:4; 3:12(2); 4:12; 14; 15; 16(4); 18; 5:8; 9; 11; 18; 21; 6:7; 14(2); 7:1; 17; 19; 8:10; 21; 22; 23; 9:3; 9; 15; 16; 19(2); 22; 28; 29; 10:5; 7; 10; 14; 21(2); 24; 26; 11:6(2); 9; 12:2(2); 4; 5; 13(2); 14; 15; 16(4); 19(3); 25; 32; 33; 42(2); 46; 48(2); 49; 13:3; 5; 6; 7(3); 9(2); 11; 12; 14; 16; 14:4; 15:9; 14; 15; 16; 16:5; 8; 12; 23; 26; 32; 33; 34; 17:4; 18:10; 19(2); 21; 22(2); 23; 19:5; 6; 11; 12; 13(2); 15; 20:12; 20; 26; 21:4; 7; 8; 12; 15; 16(2); 17; 19(2); 20; 21; 22; 28(3); 29(2); 30; 31; 32; 34; 36(2); 22:2(3); 3(3); 4(2); 5; 6; 7(2); 8(2); 9(2); 10; 11; 12; 13; 14; 15(2); 16; 19; 20; 24; 25; 30; 31; 23:1; 12; 13(2); 22; 26; 30; 33; 24:7; 12; 25:7; 10; 12; 14; 15(2); 17; 20; 23; 27; 28; 31(2); 34; 35; 36(2); 38; 26:2; 3(2); 6; 7; 8(2); 11; 16(2); 17; 20; 24(4); 25; 31; 32; 37; 27:1(2); 2; 5; 7(2); 9; 10(2); 11; 12; 13; 14; 15; 16(2); 17(2); 18; 19; 21; 28:7; 8; 11; 16(3); 17(2); 18; 20; 21(2); 28(2); 30; 32(2); 35(2); 37(2); 38(3); 43(2); 29:9; 10; 21; 26; 28(2); 29(3); 34; 37(2); 42; 43; 45; 30:2(4); 4; 12; 13; 16; 21; 25; 29(2); 31; 32(2); 33; 34; 36; 37; 38; 31:14(2); 15(2); 32:4; 8; 33:16(2); 19(2); 23; 34:2; 3; 12; 25; 35:2(3); 9; 27; 29; 36:6; 18; 34; 37:3; 27; 38:5; 26; 39:7; 21(2); 37; 40:4; 9; 10; 15; **Lev** 1:3; 4; 9; 10; 14; 15; 2:1; 2; 3; 4; 5(2); 7(2); 10; 11; 12; 13; 3:1(2); 6; 12; 17; 4:2; 12; 13(2); 15; 20; 22; 26; 27(2); 31; 35; 5:2(2); 3(4); 4(2); 5(2); 7; 9; 10; 11; 13(2); 16; 17; 18; 6:4; 7; 9; 12(2); 13; 16; 17; 18(2); 21; 22; 23(2); 25; 26; 27; 28(3); 30(2); 7:6; 9; 14; 15; 16(3); 17; 18(4); 19(3); 20; 21; 24; 25; 26; 27(2); 30; 31; 36; 8:5; 33; 10:3(2); 9; 14; 15; 11:7; 10; 11; 12; 13; 20; 23; 24(2); 25; 26; 27; 28; 29; 31(2); 32(6); 33; 34(4); 35(4); 36(2); 37(2); 38(2); 39; 40(2); 41(2); 43; 44; 45(2); 47(2); 12:2(2); 3; 4; 5; 7; 8(2); 13:2(2); 3; 4(3); 5; 6(2); 7; 9; 10(2); 14; 15; 16; 17; 19(2); 20(2); 21(3); 24; 25(2); 26(3); 27; 28; 30(2); 31; 32(2); 33; 34(3); 36; 37; 39; 42; 43; 45; 46(3); 47; 48; 49(2); 51; 52; 53; 55(2); 56; 58(4); 14:2(2); 3; 4; 5; 7; 8(2); 9(2); 11; 14; 17; 18; 19; 20; 21(2); 22; 25; 28; 29; 31; 34; 36; 37; 39; 41; 44; 46; 53; 15:3(2); 4; 5; 6; 7; 8; 9; 10(2); 11; 12(2); 13; 16; 17(2); 18; 19(3); 20(2); 21; 22; 23(2); 24(3); 25(2); 26(2); 27(2); 28(2); 16:4(2); 10(2); 17; 29(2); 30; 31; 34; 17:3; 4(2); 7; 8; 9; 10; 13(2); 14; 15(3); 18:9; 29; 19:2; 6(2); 7(2); 8; 20(2); 22; 23(2); 24; 29; 31; 34; 20:2(2); 7; 9(2); 10; 11(2); 12(2); 13(2); 14(2); 15; 16(2); 17; 18; 21; 26(2); 27(2); 21:1; 3; 6(2); 8; 9; 17; 18; 20; 22:3(2); 4; 5; 6; 7; 12; 13; 18; 20; 21(3); 23; 25(2); 27(2); 28; 30; 32; 33; 23:2; 3; 10; 11; 13(2); 14; 15; 17(2); 18; 20; 21(2); 27(2); 29(3); 30; 31; 32; 34; 35; 36; 37; 39(2); 41; 24:3; 5; 7; 9; 12; 16(2); 17; 19; 20; 21; 25:4; 6; 7; 8; 10; 11; 12; 23; 25; 26; 28; 30(2); 31(2); 34; 35(2); 38; 39(2); 40; 42; 44; 45; 46; 48; 49; 50(2); 51; 53; 54; 26:12(2); 13; 17; 20; 22; 23; 25; 26; 32; 33; 34; 41; 43; 44; 45; 27:2; 3(2); 4(2); 5(2); 6(3); 7(3); 8; 9(2); 10; 11; 12(2); 14(2); 15; 16(2); 18; 19; 20; 21(2); 25(2); 26(2); 27(3); 28; 29(3); 32; 33(3); **Num** 1:4; 51(2); 53; 2:3; 5(2); 7; 10(2); 12(2); 14; 18(2); 20(2); 22; 25(2); 27(2); 29; 3:10; 12; 13; 24; 25; 30; 31; 32; 36; 38(2); 45; 46; 48; 4:4; 7; 27; 28; 45; 5:6; 8(2); 9; 10(2); 13(5); 14(4); 19; 20; 27(2); 28(3); 30; 31; 6:5(2); 12; 13; 25; 7:5; 8:14; 19; 9:10(2); 13; 10:7; 8; 9(2); 10; 31; 32(2); 35; 11:16; 20; 22(2); 12:6; 12; 14(3); 13:18; 19(2); 20(3); 28; 31; 14:3; 11; 17; 21; 31; 33; 35; 40; 42; 43; 15:2; 11; 14; 15(2); 16; 19; 24(2); 25; 26; 28; 30(2); 31(2); 34; 35; 39; 40; 41; 16:7(2); 16; 22; 26; 29; 38; 40(2); 17:3; 10; 13; 18:2; 4; 5; 7; 9(2); 10; 13; 14; 15(2); 16; 18; 23; 27; 30; 19:7; 8; 9; 10(2); 11; 12(2); 13(2); 14; 16; 17; 19; 20(2); 21(2); 22(2); 20:24; 26; 21:22; 27; 22:11; 23:9; 10; 23; 24:7(3); 18(2); 20; 22; 25:4; 26:53; 54; 55; 56; 27:4; 11; 13; 17; 20; 28:7(2); 14; 15; 17; 18; 19; 20; 24; 26; 31; 29:3; 8; 9; 13; 14; 18; 21; 24; 27; 30; 33; 37; 31:2; 23(2); 24; 32:5; 22(3); 23; 26; 29; 32; 33:54; 55; 34:3(2); 4; 5; 6; 7; 8; 9(2); 12(2); 35:3; 5(2); 6; 7; 8; 10; 11; 12; 14; 15; 16; 17; 18; 21; 27; 29; 30; 31; 33; 36:3(4); 4(3); 8; **Deut** 1:1; 17; 21; 29; 39; 42; 2:4; 25; 4:19; 20; 26; 27; 30; 5:16; 29; 33; 6:2; 3; 6; 8; 10; 11; 15; 18; 25; 7:4; 6; 10; 14(2); 16; 18; 20; 21; 23; 24; 25; 26; 8:14; 19; 20; 10:5; 16; 11:8; 15; 16; 17(2); 18; 21; 24(2); 25; 12:11; 21; 23; 27; 30(2); 13:5; 9; 14; 16(2); 14:2; 19; 24(2); 29; 15:4; 7; 9(3); 10; 12; 16; 17; 21(2); 16:4; 8; 17:2; 4(2); 6(2); 7; 9; 18; 19; 20; 18:3(2); 10; 13; 22; 19:10(2); 15; 17; 18; 20:1; 2; 3; 9; 11(3); 20(2); 21:1(2); 3; 5; 8(2); 13(2); 14; 15; 16; 22(2); 23; 22:2(2); 6(2); 7; 9; 19; 20(2); 22; 23; 28; 29; 23:10; 11; 13; 14; 17; 21; 22; 24:2; 3; 4; 5(2); 7; 12; 13; 14; 15; 16(3); 19; 20; 21; 25:1; 2(4); 6(2); 9; 10; 15; 19; 26:1; 3; 12; 17; 18; 19; 27:2; 4(2); 15; 16; 17; 18; 19; 20; 21; 22; 23; 24; 25; 26; 28:3(2); 4; 5; 6(2); 7; 10; 13(2); 16(2); 17; 18; 19(2); 20; 23(2); 24; 25(2); 26; 27; 29; 31(4); 32(2); 33; 34; 35; 44(2); 45; 46; 51; 54; 56; 61; 62; 63; 68; 29:13; 18(2); 30:4; 17; 31:6(2); 7; 8(2); 16; 17(2); 19; 21; 23(2); 26; 32:20; 24; 38; 43; 50; 33:6; 7(2); 8; 13; 20; 24(2); 25(2); 28; 29; **Josh** 1:4; 5(2); 6; 7; 9(3); 17; 18(3); 2:3; 14; 16; 17; 19(6); 20; 21; 3:4; 7; 13; 4:6; 7; 6:17; 26; 7:12; 14(2); 15(2); 8:1; 4; 8; 9:6; 13; 20; 21; 23; 10:25(2); 11:6; 13:1; 14:9; 12(3); 15:4; 17:15(2); 18(3); 20:3; 6; 21:13; 21; 27; 32; 38; 22:18(2); 19; 22; 27; 28; 34; 23:4; 6; 13; 16; 24:27(2); **Judg** 2:3(2); 3:6; 4:9; 20; 5:24(2); 31; 6:13(2); 16; 23; 31(2); 37(2); 39(3); 7:4; 11; 17; 8:5; 9:9; 11; 13; 24; 31; 33; 10:18; 11:6; 8; 9; 10; 26; 27; 31(2); 37; 13:5; 7; 8; 14:11; 15:3; 7; 16:6; 7(2); 9; 10; 11(2); 12; 13; 14; 17(2); 20; 28; 17:2; 10; 18:5; 9; 19(3); 25; 19:6(2); 9; 20; 28; 20:9; 21:3; 5; 17(3); 18; 22(3); **Ruth** 1:11; 16; 17; 2:4; 9; 12; 13; 19; 20; 3:1; 4; 10; 13; 14; 18; 4:10(2); 11; 12; 14(2); 15; **1Sa** 1:14; 22; 28; 2:9; 10; 28; 30(2); 31; 32; 33; 34; 3:9; 14; 20; 4:9(2); 19; 5:8; 6:3(2); 4; 8:11(2); 13(3); 17; 20; 9:13(2); 16; 10:1; 6; 7; 21; 11:3; 7; 9; 13; 12:15; 25; 13:14; 14:6; 10; 21; 24(2); 28; 39; 40(2); 15:1; 11; 13; 18; 33; 16:16; 17:9(3); 25; 26; 27; 36; 37; 18:17(3); 18; 21(3); 22; 23; 25; 26; 27; 19:6; 11; 22; 20:3; 7(2); 8; 9; 12; 13; 18(2); 23; 29; 31; 32; 42; 22:3; 15; 23; 23:3; 17(2); 20; 21; 23; 24:12; 13; 15; 20(2); 25:6(3); 10; 11; 24; 26; 27; 29; 31; 32; 33(2); 39; 41; 26:9; 19(2); 24; 25; 27:11; 12; 28:13; 19; 29:4(2); 10; 30:24; **2Sa** 1:5; 16; 21(2); 2:5; 7(2); 26(2); 3:12; 17; 35; 39; 5:2; 8; 14; 24; 6:22(3); 7:8; 11; 12; 14(2); 16(2); 24; 26(2); 28; 29; 10:5; 11(2); 12; 11:15; 20; 24; 12:9; 10; 22; 28; 13:12; 13; 15; 25; 28(2); 14:2(2); 9(2); 14(2); 15; 17(2); 25; 32; 15:20; 21(2); 33; 34(2); 35; 16:2(2); 12; 18; 19; 21; 17:3; 8(2); 9; 10; 11; 12(2); 13(2); 16; 17; 20; 18:25; 28; 32; 19:7; 13; 21; 22(2); 35; 37; 42; 43; 20:1; 4; 20(2); 21; 21:5; 6; 22:4(2); 44; 45; 46; 47(2); 23:1; 3; 4; 5; 6(2); 7(2); 8; 17; 24:3; 13; 17; 21; 22; **1Kin** 1:2; 5; 21; 35(2); 37; 48; 52; 2:2; 7; 19; 21; 24; 33; 37(2); 39; 45(2); 3:8; 13; 26; 5:6; 7; 9; 6:6; 8:5; 15; 16(2); 26; 29(2); 31; 33; 37(4); 38; 46; 51; 52; 53; 56; 57; 59; 61; 9:3; 7; 8; 10:9; 27(2); 11:37; 38(2); 12:7(2); 10; 13:2(2); 3(2); 6; 14:2(3); 5(2); 6; 10; 17:1; 4; 18:21; 24; 27; 31; 36; 19:15; 16(2); 20:6; 18(2); 23; 25; 39(2); 40; 21:7; 22:3; 13; 22; **2Kin** 1:10; 12; 13; 14; 15; 2:9(2); 10(2); 16; 21; 3:17; 4:1; 10; 13(2); 14; 23; 5:10; 12; 13; 17; 22; 23; 6:3; 8; 16(2); 7:1; 2; 12; 18; 19; 8:13; 29; 9:10; 15(2); 37; 10:6; 9; 15; 19(2); 23; 24; 11:5; 6(2); 8(2); 15; 17; 12:5; 15; 14:6(3); 15:19; 16:15; 18:23; 29; 30; 19:4; 6; 10; 11; 25; 26; 29; 20:8; 17(2); 18; 19; 22:17(2); 20; 23:27; 25:12; 24(2); **1Chr** 1:10; 4:10; 5:1; 6:17; 9:22; 11:2; 6; 12:17(3); 18(2); 13:2; 14:15; 15:16; 16:15; 25(2); 30(2); 31; 36; 38; 17:7; 9; 10; 11(3); 13(2); 14; 21; 23; 24(3); 27(2); 19:5; 12(2); 13; 21:3(2); 12; 17(3); 22; 22:5(2); 9(3); 10(2); 11; 13(2); 16(2); 19; 28:4(2); 6(2); 7; 9; 10; 20(3); 21(3); 29:2(2); 5; 10; 14; 22(2); **2Chr** 1:9; 2:8; 9; 12; 14; 18(2); 4:18; 5:6; 13; 6:4; 5(2); 6(2); 17; 20; 22; 24; 28(4); 29; 36; 40(2); 41; 7:13; 15; 16(2); 18; 20; 21; 22; 9:8(2); 10:7(2); 10; 11:22; 12:7; 8; 13:8; 9; 15:2(2); 7(3); 13; 18:3; 10; 12; 14; 21; 19:7; 11(2); 20:2; 15; 17(2); 20; 22:6; 23:4; 5(2); 7(2); 14; 16; 25:8; 14; 16; 26:15; 18; 29:11; 24; 30:7; 8; 19; 31:4; 32:7(3); 14; 33:4; 34:25(2); 28; 35:3; 36:22; 23; **Ezr** 1:1; 3; 4:12; 13(2); 15; 16; 21(2); 5:8; 15; 17(2); 6:3(2); 4; 5; 6; 8(2); 9; 11(3); 12; 7:20; 21; 23(2); 24; 26(2); 27; 9:12; 14(2); 10:3; 4(2); 8; 14; **Neh** 1:6; 11; 2:3; 6; 7; 17; 4:5; 7; 12; 14; 22; 5:5; 8; 13; 14; 6:6; 7; 9(2); 13; 7:3(3); 5; 8:10; 11; 9:5; 10:38; 11:23; 13:5; 19(4); **Est** 1:17(2); 19(2); 20; 22; 2:2; 3; 4; 9; 3:9(2); 14(2); 4:14; 5:3; 6(2); 14(3); 6:6; 8; 9(2); 11; 13; 7:2(2); 3; 4(2); 8:5(2); 13(2); 9:1; 12(2); 13(2); 14; 25; 28; **Job** 1:5; 21; 3:4; 6; 7; 9; 17; 4:2; 17(2); 5:1; 11(2); 21(2); 22; 23(2); 24; 25; 6:3; 6; 14; 28; 29; 7:4; 21; 8:2; 14(2); 22; 9:2; 29; 10:15(2); 11:2(2); 12(2); 14; 15; 17(2); 18; 20; 12:14(2); 13:5; 16; 18; 14:7; 12(2); 13; 15:14(2); 29; 31; 32(2); 34; 17:8; 9; 18:2; 4(2); 5; 6(2); 7; 12(2); 14; 15; 16(2); 18; 20; 19:4; 27; 29; 20:8(2); 12; 18; 21; 22; 26; 21:2; 4; 5; 30; 32; 33; 22:2(2); 21; 23; 25; 28; 23:7; 24:20(2); 23(2); 25; 25:4(2); 27:7; 14(2); 15; 19; 28:12; 15(2); 16; 17; 18; 19; 31:6; 8; 11; 22; 28; 31; 32:20; 33:3; 7; 21; 23; 25; 26; 30; 34:10; 20(2); 29; 30; 31; 33; 36; 35:2; 3(2); 6; 7; 36:4; 8(2); 16(2); 26; 37:6; 20(2); 38:11; 13; 15; 39:9; 40:8; 41:9; 17; 23; 32; 42:2; **Ps** 1:3; 2:10(2); 12; 3:2; 6; 4:4; 6; 5:11; 6:10(2); 7:3; 9:2; 9; 17; 18; 19; 20; 10:2; 6(2); 11:3; 6; 13:2; 14:7; 15:5; 16:4; 8; 17:15; 18:3(2); 45; 46(2); 19:10; 13(2); 14; 21:7; 13; 22:11; 19; 25; 26; 29; 30; 31; 24:7; 25:2; 3(2); 20; 26:11; 27:1; 3; 6; 14; 28:1(2); 6; 30:6; 10; 12; 31:1; 2; 7; 17(3); 18; 21; 24; 32:6; 9(2); 10; 11; 33:22; 34:1; 2; 18; 21; 22; 35:4(2); 5; 6; 9; 22; 26(2); 27(2); 36:2(2); 3; 8; 12; 37:1; 2; 3; 9; 10(2); 14; 15; 17; 18; 19(2); 20; 22(3); 24; 28; 36; 38(2); 38:18; 21; 39:13; 40:5(2); 13; 14(2); 15; 16(2); 41:2; 4; 10; 13; 42:8; 45:12; 14(2); 15; 16; 17; 46:2(2); 3; 5; 10(3); 48:1; 11; 14; 49:3; 16; 50:3; 22;

51:4(2); 7(2); 13; 19; 53:6; 55:6; 20; 22; 56:1; 2; 11; 57:1(3); 5(2); 11(2); 58:3; 7; 59:5; 12; 13; 15; 60:4; 5; 62:2; 3(2); 6; 9; 63:5; 10; 11; 64:7; 10; 65:1; 4; 66:8; 9; 20; 67:1; 2; 4; 68:1; 3; 13; 19; 23; 35; 69:6(2); 14; 23; 25; 28(2); 32; 70:2(2); 3; 4(2); 71:1; 3; 6; 8; 12; 13(2); 72:14; 15(3); 16; 17(2); 18; 19(2); 74:14; 75:10; 76:7; 8; 11(2); 77:2; 7; 9; 78:6; 8; 79:2; 5; 10; 80:3; 4; 7; 17; 19; 81:9; 83:1; 4; 17(2); 84:4; 10; 85:5; 86:3; 17; 87:5; 7; 88:11; 12; 89:2; 6(2); 7(2); 16; 17; 21; 24(2); 37; 52; 90:10; 14; 17; 91:4; 5; 15; 92:7; 9; 10; 13; 14; 93:1; 94:8; 13; 96:4(2); 10(2); 11; 12; 97:1; 7; 98:8; 99:1; 100:4; 101:6; 102:18(2); 26; 28; 104:5; 34(2); 35(2); 106:8; 46; 48; 107:30; 108:5; 6; 109:7(2); 8; 9; 10; 12(2); 13(2); 14(2); 15; 17; 19; 20; 28; 29; 110:3; 111:4; 5; 112:2(2); 3; 6(2); 7; 8; 9; 10; 113:2; 3; 9; 118:24; 26; 119:6; 46; 58; 74; 76; 78; 80(2); 116; 117; 122; 128; 132; 120:3(2); 121:3; 122:7; 8; 124:6; 125:1(2); 4; 5; 127:5; 128:2(2); 3; 4; 129:5; 6; 8; 130:2; 4; 132:9; 135:21; 137:8(2); 9; 138:6; 139:11; 24; 140:10; 11; 141:2; 5(3); 143:2; 7; 144:1; 12(2); 13; 14(3); 145:3; 14; 148:4; 149:2; 5; 6; **Prov** 1:9; 31; 33; 2:22(2); 3:7; 8; 10; 11; 15; 22; 24(2); 25; 26; 35; 4:10; 12; 26; 5:10(2); 16; 17; 18; 19(2); 20; 22; 6:1; 6; 15; 18; 27; 28; 29; 31; 33; 8:5; 6; 11(2); 33; 9:9; 11(2); 12(2); 10:9; 24; 27; 28; 29; 30; 31; 11:6; 9; 18; 21(2); 25(2); 26; 29; 31; 12:3(2); 8(2); 11; 14(2); 19; 21; 24; 13:4; 9; 11; 13(2); 18(2); 20(2); 21; 14:11; 14(2); 22; 16:3; 5; 7; 16; 19; 21; 31; 17:5; 11; 14; 18:19; 20(2); 19:2; 5; 9; 20; 23; 20:3; 11(2); 13; 17; 20; 21(2); 21:13; 15; 17(2); 18; 20; 22:1; 5; 9; 11; 13; 18; 19; 26; 23:2; 3; 4; 15; 17; 18; 19; 20; 25; 34; 24:1(2); 4; 8; 11; 14(3); 17; 19; 20(2); 25; 28; 25:5; 7(2); 16; 17; 21(2); 26:4; 5; 26; 27:11; 14; 18; 23; 28:2; 6; 9; 18; 20(2); 22; 25; 26; 29:1; 14; 19; 25; 30:6; 9(2); 10; 18; 24; 29; 31:6; 30; **Eccl** 1:9(2); 10; 11; 13; 15(2); 2:16; 18; 19; 3:2; 10; 14(2); 15; 22; 4:11; 13; 5:1; 2(3); 6; 8; 10; 6:3(2); 4; 11; 12; 7:9(2); 14; 16; 17(2); 23; 26; 8:1; 3; 7(2); 12(2); 13; 14(2); 15; 17; 9:8; 10:9(2); 10; 14(2); 11:2; 3(2); 6; 8; 12:2; 3; 4(2); 5(3); 6(3); 12; 14(2); **Song** 1:4; 7; 2:17; 7:8; 8:1; 3; 7; 8; 9(2); 14; **Is** 1:5; 18(4); 19; 20; 26; 27; 28(2); 29(2); 30; 31; 2:2(2); 6; 11(3); 12(2); 17(3); 22; 3:4; 5; 6(2); 7; 10; 11(2); 24; 4:1; 2(2); 3; 5; 6; 5:5(2); 6; 8(2); 9; 15(3); 16(2); 24; 27(3); 28; 29; 6:10; 11(2); 12; 13(3); 7:4(2); 8(2); 9; 16; 23(2); 25(2); 8:4; 9(3); 12; 13(2); 14; 15(3); 21; 22; 9:1; 5; 6(2); 7; 19; 20(2); 21; 10:2; 17; 18; 19; 22; 24; 27(2); 30; 33(2); 11:5; 9; 10(2); 11; 13; 16(2); 12:2; 13:7; 8(4); 10; 14; 15; 16(2); 19; 20(2); 21; 22; 14:1; 14; 15; 20(2); 29; 31; 15:2; 4(2); 6; 9; 16:2(2); 4; 5; 6; 10(2); 14(2); 17:1; 2; 3; 4; 5(2); 6; 9(2); 11; 13; 18:6; 7; 19:1; 5; 6; 7(2); 9; 10; 15; 16(2); 17(2); 18; 19; 20; 21; 22; 23; 24; 25; 20:5; 6; 21:17; 22:7; 14; 18; 21; 23; 25(3); 23:2; 4; 5; 15; 16; 18(3); 24:2; 3; 9; 13(2); 18; 20(2); 22(3); 23; 25:2(2); 5; 9(2); 10; 26:1; 10; 11; 20; 27:9; 10; 11; 12; 13; 28:3; 4; 5; 10; 13; 18(2); 19; 21; 22(2); 28; 29:2(2); 4(3); 5(3); 6; 7; 8(2); 14; 16; 17(2); 22; 30:3; 5; 8; 13; 14; 15(2); 16; 17; 18(2); 19; 20; 23; 25; 26(2); 28; 30; 31; 32; 31:4; 8; 9; 32:2; 3; 4; 5(2); 10; 11; 14(3); 15(3); 17; 19; 33:1; 2(2); 4; 6; 10; 12(2); 16(3); 20(3); 21; 24; 34:3(2); 4(2); 5; 7; 9; 10; 12(2); 13; 15; 35:1; 2; 4; 5(2); 7; 8(3); 9(2); 36:8; 14; 15; 37:4; 6; 10; 11; 26; 27; 30; 38:7; 39:6(2); 7; 8; 40:4(3); 5; 9; 20; 24(2); 25; 30; 31; 41:6; 7; 10; 11(2); 12; 22; 23; 42:2; 4; 17(2); 43:2(2); 9(3); 10; 26; 44:8; 9; 11(3); 15; 21; 26(2); 27; 28(2); 45:1; 14; 16; 17(2); 18; 22; 24; 25; 46:5; 13; 47:1; 3(2); 5; 7; 11; 12(3); 14(2); 15; 48:11; 14; 49:3; 5(4); 6(2); 9; 11; 13; 19(2); 22; 23(2); 24; 25(2); 26; 50:7(2); 51:3; 6(2); 7; 8; 11; 12(2); 14; 19; 52:3; 11; 12; 13(2); 53:11; 54:3; 4(3); 5; 9; 10(2); 13(2); 14(2); 55:6; 11; 12; 13(2); 56:1; 5; 6; 7(2); 12; 57:16; 58:4; 8; 10; 11; 12(2); 60:2; 4; 5(2); 7; 11(3); 12; 18; 19(2); 20(2); 21(2); 61:3(2); 5; 6; 7; 9; 10; 62:2; 3; 4(4); 8; 12; 63:3; 10; 16; 64:5; 9; 65:10; 13(3); 17; 18; 19; 20(2); 25; 66:5(2); 8(2); 10; 11(2); 12(2); 13; 14; 16; 17; 24(2); **Jer** 1:8; 17; 2:10; 12(3); 36; 3:1; 3; 16(2); 17; 4:7; 9; 11; 13; 14; 27; 28; 29; 5:1; 6; 9; 13; 29; 6:6; 8; 11; 12; 15; 22; 7:20(2); 23(3); 32(2); 33; 34; 8:2(3); 3; 12; 13; 14; 17; 9:2; 9; 10:2; 5(2); 10; 21; 11:3; 4(2); 5; 11; 19; 23; 12:13; 16; 13:10; 11; 12(2); 15; 19(3); 21; 27(2); 14:8; 9; 15(2); 16; 15:1; 4; 11; 18(2); 19; 16:4(5); 6; 14; 17:5; 6; 8(3); 11; 13(2); 14(2); 17; 18(4); 27; 18:14; 16; 20; 21(4); 22; 23; 19:6; 7; 8; 11(2); 13; 20:6; 10; 11(2); 14(2); 15; 16; 17; 18; 21:2; 9; 10; 22:19; 22; 23; 23:1; 3; 4(2); 6(2); 12(2); 26; 36; 40; 24:2; 3; 7(2); 8; 9(2); 10; 25:11; 16(2); 27; 28; 29(2); 32; 33(3); 36; 26:3; 9(2); 18; 27:16; 17; 18(2); 22(2); 28:9; 29:4; 6; 7; 8(2); 10; 14(2); 17; 18(2); 22; 26; 30:7; 10(3); 13; 16(2); 18; 19(2); 20(2); 21; 22(2); 31:1(2); 4(2); 6; 12; 14; 15; 16; 18; 30; 33(3); 37; 38; 40(2); 32:4; 5; 15; 36; 38(2); 43; 33:9; 10(2); 12; 16(2); 20; 21; 22; 24; 25; 26; 34:3; 16; 17; 20; 35:7; 36:3; 7; 19; 30; 37:17; 20; 38:3; 4; 17; 18; 20; 22; 23(2); 39:16; 17; 18; 40:9; 15; 42:2; 5; 6(3); 11(2); 17; 18(2); 44:8(2); 12(3); 26; 27(2); 29; 46:10; 11; 19; 23; 24(2); 26; 27(2); 47:2; 6(3); 7; 48:2(2); 3; 4; 6; 7; 8; 9; 10(2); 13; 26; 28; 30; 33; 34; 37(2); 38; 39; 41; 42; 43; 44; 46; 49:2(4); 5(2); 10; 13; 17(2); 22; 23; 26; 32; 33; 36; 37; 50:5; 8; 9(2); 10(2); 12(3); 13(3); 19; 20(3); 26; 30; 36; 37; 38; 39(2); 41; 51:2; 6; 8(2); 26; 29; 35; 46; 47; 58(3); 62; 63; 64; **Lam** 1:12; 17; 21; 2:6; 20; 3:6; 29(2); 4:9(2); 21(2); 5:6; 21; **Eze** 2:6(6); 8; 3:9(2); 12; 20; 26(2); 4:3(2); 7; 10; 17; 5:12; 13(2); 15; 16; 6:4(2); 6(6); 8; 9; 13; 7:4; 11; 16; 17(2); 18; 19(2); 24; 25; 26; 27(2); 9:4; 11:3; 11(2); 16; 20(2); 12:3(2); 11; 13; 19; 20(2); 24; 25; 28(2); 13:9(3); 11; 12; 13; 14(2); 21(2); 14:3; 9; 10; 11(3); 15; 16(2); 18; 22(3); 15:3; 5; 16:16; 20; 25; 28; 42(2); 52; 54; 61; 63; 17:8; 14; 15; 20; 21; 23; 18:5; 13; 20(2); 22; 24; 30; 19:9; 14(2); 20:3; 9; 12; 14; 20; 22; 31(2); 32(2); 41; 47(2); 48; 21:7(4); 11(2); 12(3); 13; 14; 15; 23(2); 24(2); 26; 27; 32(3); 22:5(2); 14; 21; 22; 23:25; 29; 32; 33; 46; 48; 24:8; 10; 11(3); 12; 13; 23; 25; 27(3); 25:10; 26:2; 5; 6; 13; 14(2); 16; 17; 18; 20; 21(3); 27:7; 30; 34; 35(3); 36(2); 28:9; 19(3); 22(2); 23; 24; 25; 29:5; 7; 9; 11; 12; 14; 15; 16; 19; 30:3; 4(2); 7(2); 8; 11; 13; 16; 18; 21(2); 31:13; 16; 17; 18(2); 32:6; 10; 12; 15; 19; 25; 27; 28; 30(2); 31; 32; 33:4; 5; 6; 10; 12; 13; 16; 27(2); 28; 34:2; 10; 14; 22; 23; 24; 26; 27; 28; 29; 35:4; 10; 15; 36:3; 9; 10(2); 12; 23; 25; 28(2); 32(2); 33; 34; 37; 38; 37:19; 20; 21; 22(3); 23(2); 24; 25; 26; 27(3); 28; 38:7(2); 8; 9; 16(2); 19; 20; 21; 23; 39:4; 12; 13(2); 16; 19(2); 20; 25; 28; 42:13; 43:10; 11; 12; 13(3); 14(2); 15(2); 16; 17(3); 19; 27; 44:2(3); 7; 11; 14; 17; 28; 29; 30; 31; 45:1(3); 2; 3; 4(2); 6; 7(2); 8; 11(2); 12(2); 17; 21; 46:1(3); 2; 4; 5(2); 6(2); 11; 16(2); 17(2); 18; 47:5; 8; 9(2); 10(2); 11(2); 12(2); 13; 15; 17; 20; 22; 48:8(2); 9; 10(2); 11; 12; 13; 15(2); 16; 17; 18(3); 20; 21(3); 22; 28; 31; 35; **Dan** 1:13; 2:5(2); 9; 13(2); 20; 28; 40; 41(2); 42; 44(2); 3:6; 11; 15(2); 17; 18; 19; 28; 29(2); 4:1; 15(2); 16(2); 19; 23(2); 25; 26; 27(2); 32; 5:7(2); 10; 12; 16(2); 17; 29; 6:1; 7; 8; 12; 15; 17; 25; 26(2); 7:14; 23(2); 24; 25; 27; 8:13(2); 14; 17; 19(2); 24; 25; 26; 9:16; 25(2); 26(2); 27; 10:19(3); 11:2; 4(3); 5(3); 6; 10(2); 11(2); 12(2); 15; 16; 17; 19; 20; 22(2); 25; 27(2); 28; 29; 30; 32; 34; 36(2); 41; 43; 12:1(3); 3; 4; 6; 7(2); 8; 10; 11(2); 13; **Hos** 1:9; 10(3); 11(2); 2:4; 16; 17; 3:3(2); 4:3; 6; 9; 19; 5:9(2); 12; 14; 7:4; 16; 8:4; 5; 6; 7; 8; 11; 9:4(3); 6; 12; 17; 10:2; 6(2); 8; 10; 14; 15; 11:5; 13:3; 7; 10; 14(3); 15(2); 16(2); 14:5; 6; 7; **Joel** 1:11; 2:2; 6; 8; 10; 18; 19; 21; 22; 23; 24; 26(2); 27; 31; 32(2); 3:12; 15; 16; 17; 19(2); **Amos** 3:3; 6(3); 11(2); 12; 14; 5:6; 14; 15(2); 16; 17; 20; 6:2; 7; 7:3; 6; 9(2); 11; 17(2); 8:3(2); 5; 8; 9:1; 3; 5; 15; **Obad** 9(2); 10; 15; 16; 17(2); 18(2); 21; **Jonah** 1:4; 6; 11; 12; 3:4; 7; 8; 4:4; 6; 9(2); **Mic** 1:2; 4(2); 7(2); 14; 2:4; 11; 3:6(3); 7; 12; 4:1(2); 10(2); 11; 5:2(2); 4; 5; 7; 8; 9(2); 6:7; 14(2); 7:4; 8; 10; 11(2); 13; 16(2); 17; **Nah** 1:10(2); 12(2); 14; 2:3(2); 5; 6(2); 7(2); 13; 3:11(2); 12(2); 13; **Hab** 1:5; 10; 2:5; 7; 9; 14; 16(3); 3:17(3); **Zeph** 1:10; 17; 18(2); 2:3(2); 4(2); 5; 6; 7; 9; 11; 12; 14; 3:7; 8; 11(2); 13; 14; 16(2); **Hag** 1:2; 8; 2:4(3); 9; 12; 13(2); **Zec** 1:4; 9; 16(2); 17; 19; 2:4; 5(2); 9; 11(2); 13; 3:9; 4:5; 12; 13; 5:3(2); 11; 6:13(2); 14; 8:3; 5; 6(2); 8(2); 9(2); 11; 12; 13(2); 19; 9:1(2); 2; 4; 5(3); 7(2); 10(2); 14; 15; 16; 10:5(2); 6; 7(2); 10; 11; 11:5; 9(2); 16; 17(3); 12:2; 3(2); 5; 6; 8(2); 10; 11; 13:1; 2; 4; 7; 8(2); 14:1; 2(2); 4; 6; 7(3); 8(2); 9(2); 10(2); 11(2); 12; 13; 14; 15(2); 17(2); 18; 19; 20(2); 21(2); **Mal** 1:5; 6(2); 8; 9; 11(3); 14; 2:4; 3:4; 5; 10(2); 12; 17; 4:1; 3; **Mt** 1:22; 23; 2:4; 13; 15; 18; 23(2); 3:13; 14; 15; 4:1; 3(2); 6; 14; 5:4; 6; 9; 12; 13(3); 14; 18; 19(2); 21; 22(3); 24; 25; 29; 30; 37; 45; 48; 6:1; 4; 5(2); 7; 8; 9; 10; 16; 21; 22(2); 23(3); 31; 33; 7:1; 2(2); 7(2); 8; 13; 14; 26; 8:3; 8; 12(2); 13; 17; 9:2(2); 5; 12; 15; 21; 22; 29; 10:13(2); 15; 16; 18; 19; 21; 22(2); 23; 25; 26(2); 36; 11:6; 22; 23; 24; 12:11; 17; 27; 31(2); 32(2); 37(2); 39; 40; 45; 13:12(2); 15; 35; 40; 42; 49; 50; 14:9; 27(2); 28; 15:5; 6; 13; 14; 28; 31; 16:2; 3; 4; 19(2); 21(2); 22(2); 23(2); 28; 17:4; 7; 9; 17; 20; 22; 23; 18:3; 7; 8; 9; 12; 13; 16; 17; 18(2); 19; 25(2); 19:5; 9; 10; 12; 21; 25; 30(2); 20:16(2); 18; 22; 23(2); 26(3); 27(2); 28; 33; 21:4; 13; 21(3); 43; 44; 22:13; 28; 23:4; 5; 7; 8; 10; 11; 12(2); 26; 31; 24:2(2); 3(2); 6; 7; 9(2); 10; 13; 14; 16; 20; 21(2); 22(3); 27; 28; 29(2); 34; 37; 39; 40(2); 41(2); 43; 44; 51; 25:1; 9; 29(2); 30; 32; 26:2; 5; 13(2); 31(2); 33(2); 37; 39; 42; 46; 54(2); 56; 63; 27:22; 23; 25; 26; 35; 40; 42; 49; 58; 64(2); 28:10; **Mk** 1:41; 2:5; 9; 20; 22(2); 3:14; 24; 25; 26; 28; 4:12(2); 21(2); 22; 24(2); 25(2); 31; 39; 5:18; 23; 28; 34; 36; 43; 6:9; 11; 27; 50(2); 7:4; 11(2); 24; 27; 34; 8:12; 31(2); 33(2); 38(2); 9:1; 5; 12; 19; 34; 35(2); 43; 45(2); 47; 49(2); 10:8; 12; 26; 31; 33; 38; 39; 40; 41; 43(3); 44(2); 45; 49(2); 11:2; 10; 17; 23(2); 12:7; 23; 13:2(2); 4(3); 7(3); 8(2); 9(2); 10; 11; 12; 13(2); 14; 18; 19(2); 20; 24; 25; 30; 14:2; 9(2); 19; 27(2); 29; 33(2); 49; 64; 15:15; 16:6; 16(2); **Lk** 1:15(2); 20(3); 29; 32(2); 33; 34; 35(2); 37; 38; 45; 57; 60; 66; 68; 71; 76; 2:1; 3; 5; 6; 10; 12; 23; 34; 35; 49; 3:5(4); 7; 12; 14; 23; 4:3(2); 7; 9; 5:13; 15; 23; 35; 37; 38; 6:17; 20; 21; 35(2); 36; 37(3); 38(2); 40; 7:7; 23; 8:9; 12; 17(2); 18(2); 38; 43; 48; 50; 9:22(3); 25; 26(2); 27; 33; 41; 44; 46; 48; 51; 10:5; 6; 11; 12; 14; 15; 42; 11:2(2); 9(2); 10; 18; 19; 29; 30; 35; 36(2); 46; 50; 51; 12:2(2); 3(2); 4; 9; 10(2); 19; 20(2); 26; 29; 31; 34; 35; 39; 40; 45; 47; 48(2); 49; 50(2); 52; 53; 55; 58; 13:14; 16; 23; 24; 28; 30(2); 32; 33; 14:8; 11(2); 12; 14(2); 23; 26; 27; 31; 33(2); 34; 15:7; 14; 19; 21; 23; 24; 32; 16:2; 21; 31; 17:6(2); 24; 25; 26; 30; 31; 34(3); 35(2); 36(2); 37; 18:13; 14(2); 26; 31; 32(2); 40; 19:7; 15; 19; 26(2); 38; 20:6; 13; 14; 18; 25(2); 35; 21:6(2); 7(2); 8; 9; 11(2); 15; 16(2); 17; 22(2); 23; 24(3); 25; 26; 32; 34; 36; 22:7; 16; 24; 26(2); 37; 42(2); 52; 23:23; 24; 31; 32; 35; 37; 39; 43; 24:7(2); 20; 36; 44; 47; 49; **Jn** 1:25; 31; 42; 3:2; 3; 4(2); 5; 7; 9; 14; 17; 20; 21; 27; 4:14; 5:6; 34; 6:12; 20; 45; 7:4; 17; 23; 8:5; 33(2); 36; 41; 55; 9:3; 22; 25; 27; 31; 39; 10:9; 16; 24; 35; 11:4; 12:23; 26; 31; 32; 34; 36; 38; 40; 42; 13:18; 24; 32; 14:1; 3; 13; 17; 21; 27(2); 15:7; 8; 11; 25; 16:1; 20(2); 24; 32; 33; 17:11; 12; 19; 21(2); 22; 23; 24; 26; 18:9; 28; 32; 36; 19:16; 24(2); 28; 31(2); 36(2); 20:15; 19; 21; 26; 27; 21:18; 25(2); **Acts** 1:5; 8; 20; 22(2); 2:14; 20; 21; 24; 25; 38; 47; 3:14; 19(2); 23; 25; 4:9; 10; 12; 19; 28; 30; 5:31; 36; 38; 39(2); 7:7; 35; 8:20; 22; 36; 9:6; 17; 10:42; 47; 48; 11:14; 16; 28; 12:19; 13:11; 22; 28; 38; 39; 42; 47(2); 14:3; 9; 15:1(2); 11; 24; 16:13; 15; 30; 31; 17:18; 27; 18:6; 9; 15(2); 19:2; 26; 27(3); 36(2); 39; 40; 20:16; 21:13; 14(2); 24; 26; 33; 34; 37; 22:5; 10; 15; 16; 24(2); 23:3; 11; 29; 35; 24:4; 15; 21; 25:4; 5; 6; 9; 10; 11(2); 17; 19; 20; 21(2); 26:3; 8; 23; 28; 27:10; 20; 22(2); 24; 25(2); 26; 31; 28:27; 28; **Rom** 1:1; 4; 7(2); 11; 12; 19; 22; 2:12; 13; 25; 26; 3:4(2); 8; 19; 20; 25; 26; 4:11(3); 13; 14; 16(2); 17; 18; 24; 5:9; 10; 15; 19; 6:5; 6; 8; 11; 17; 7:2; 3(4); 4; 10; 8:4; 6(2); 7; 9; 10; 17(2); 18(2); 21; 26; 29(2); 31(2); 39; 9:7; 17; 26; 27(2); 33; 10:1; 9; 11; 13; 15; 11:6; 9; 10; 12; 15(2); 16(2); 17; 19; 20; 22; 23; 24(2); 25(3); 26; 35; 36; 12:2(2); 9; 10; 16(2); 18; 21; 13:1(2); 3; 4; 5; 9; 14:4; 5; 9; 14; 15; 16; 15:5; 12; 16(2); 24(2); 31(2); 32; 33; 16:11; 20; 24; 27; **1Cor** 1:1; 2; 3; 8; 10(2); 17; 3:13(2); 15(2); 18(2); 4:2; 3; 6; 16; 17; 5:2; 5; 7; 11; 6:2; 5; 7; 9; 12; 16; 7:5; 11; 12; 13; 18; 21; 23; 25; 26; 27; 29; 34; 39(2); 8:5(2); 10; 9:2; 10; 12; 15; 19; 23; 27; 10:1; 7; 13(2); 21; 27; 30; 33; 11:1; 6(5); 16; 18; 19(2); 27; 31; 32; 12:13(2); 22; 23; 25; 26; 13:3; 8(3); 10; 14:7; 9(2); 10; 11(2); 20(3); 23; 26; 27; 28; 30; 31; 34; 37; 38(2); 40; 15:9; 12; 13; 14; 15; 17; 22; 26; 28(3); 33; 37; 51; 52(2); 54; 57; 58; 16:2; 4; 6; 10; 13; 14; 22; 23; 24; **2Cor** 1:2; 3; 4; 6(2); 7; 11; 16; 17; 2:4; 7; 9; 14; 3:3; 7; 8; 9; 16; 4:3; 7; 10; 11; 5:2; 3(2); 4(2); 8(2); 9; 10; 13(2); 17; 20; 21(2); 6:3; 13; 14; 16(2); 17; 18(2); 7:10; 11; 8:9; 10; 11; 12; 13; 14(3); 16; 23; 9:3(2); 4; 5; 15; 10:2(2); 8; 11; 15; 11:3; 6; 7; 12; 15(2); 12:6(2); 7(2); 11; 13; 14; 15(2); 16; 20(2); 13:1; 5(2); 7; 11(4); 14; **Gal** 1:3; 5; 7; 8; 9; 10; 2:3; 6(2); 9; 11; 16(2); 17; 3:4; 8; 9; 15(2); 18; 22; 23; 24; 29; 4:1; 9; 12; 18; 19; 20; 21; 30; 5:1; 2; 10(2); 15; 18; 26; 6:1(2); 3; 7; 9; 12; 16; 18; **Eph** 1:2; 3; 4; 12; 22; 3:6; 10; 16; 18; 19; 21; 4:14; 21; 23; 26; 31; 32; 5:1; 3; 7; 17; 18(2); 24; 27; 31(2); 6:3; 5; 8; 10; 11; 13; 16; 19; 23; 24; **Phil** 1:2; 10; 20(3); 23; 26; 27(2); 30; 2:1; 2; 3; 5; 6; 15; 17; 19; 28; 3:9; 15(3); 17; 21; 4:2; 5; 6(2); 8(2); 9; 11; 12(3); 20; 23; **Col** 1:2; 9; 12; 16; 20; 23; 2:2; 5; 20; 3:1; 15; 19; 21; 4:6; 16; 18; **1Th** 1:1; 2:4; 9; 16; 3:1; 3; 5; 4:11; 13; 17(2); 5:6; 7; 8; 13; 14; 23; 27; 28; **2Th** 1:5; 7; 9; 10(2); 12; 2:2(2); 3; 6; 7; 8; 10; 12; 3:1; 2; 8; 13; 14; 16; 18; **1Ti** 1:7; 10; 17; 2:1; 4; 6; 12; 15; 3:2; 8; 10; 11; 12; 4:3; 4(2); 6; 12; 5:7; 9; 13; 16; 17; 22; 25; 6:1; 8; 9; 16; 17; 18; 21; **2Ti** 1:4; 8(2); 15; 2:1; 2; 4; 6; 11; 15; 21; 24; 3:2; 9; 17; 4:2; 4; 6; 15; 16; 17; 18; 22(2); **Titus** 1:6; 7; 9; 11; 13; 2:2; 3; 4; 5(2); 6; 8(2); 9; 3:1(2); 2; 7; 8; 12; 13; 14; 15; **Philem** 1:8; 14; 22; 25; **Heb** 1:5(2); 12; 14; 2:3; 17(2); 3:5; 12; 13; 4:15; 5:5; 11; 12(2); 6:8; 12; 7:11; 8:4; 10(2); 12; 9:16; 23; 10:2; 13; 29; 11:16; 18; 24; 40; 12:3; 8; 9; 10; 11; 13(2); 15; 16; 18; 19; 20; 27; 28; 13:2; 5(2); 9(2); 19; 21; 25; **Jas** 1:4; 5; 13; 18; 19; 22; 23; 25; 26; 2:12; 15; 16; 3:1; 4; 10; 17; 4:4; 9(2); 14; 5:3; 7; 8; 9; 12; 15; 16; **1Pet** 1:2; 3; 5; 6; 7(2); 13(2); 15; 16; 21; 2:3; 6; 7; 13; 18; 20; 3:1(2); 3; 4; 7; 8(3); 13; 14(2); 15; 16; 17; 4:6; 7; 11(2); 13(2); 14; 16; 17; 18; 5:1; 5(2); 8(2); 11; 14; **2Pet** 1:2; 4; 8(2); 11; 12(2); 15; 2:1; 2; 4; 9; 12; 3:2; 8; 10; 11(2); 12; 14(2); 16; 18; **1Jn** 1:4; 2:19; 28; 3:1; 2(2); 4:10; 14; **2Jn** 2; 3; 12; **3Jn** 2; 8; 14; **Jude** 2; 18; 19; 25; **Rev** 1:4; 6; 19; 2:10(2); 11; 19; 27; 3:2; 5; 18(2); 19; 4:1; 5:13; 6:11(2); 17; 7:12; 9:5; 10:6; 7; 9; 11:5; 9; 18; 12:2; 4; 15; 13:10; 15; 14:10; 16:5; 12; 17:17; 18:4; 8; 21(2); 22(4); 23; 19:7; 8; 20:3(2); 6; 7; 10; 21:3(3); 4(2); 7(2); 25(2); 22:3(2); 4; 5; 6; 11(4); 12; 21

BECAME

Gen 2:7; 10; 6:4; 19:26; 20:12; 21:20; 24:67; 26:13; 44:32; 47:20; 26; 49:15; **Ex** 2:10; 4:3; 4; 7:10; 12; 8:17(2); 9:10; 24; 36:13; **Num** 12:10; 26:10; **Deut** 26:5; **Josh** 7:5; 14:14; 24:32; **Judg** 1:30; 33; 35; 8:27; 15:14; 17:5; 12; **Ruth** 4:16; **1Sa** 10:12; 16:21; 18:29; 22:2; 25:37; 42; **2Sa** 2:25; 4:4; 8:2; 6; 14; 11:27; **1Kin** 11:24; 12:30; 13:6; 33; 34; **2Kin** 17:3; 15; 24:1; **1Chr** 18:2; 6; 13; 19:19; **2Chr** 27:6; **Neh** 9:25; **Est** 8:17; **Ps** 69:11; 83:10; 109:25; **Jer** 51:30; **Eze** 17:6(2); 19:3; 6; 23:10; 31:5; 34:5; 8(2); 36:4; **Dan** 2:35(2); 8:4; 10:15; **Obad** 12; **Mt** 28:4; **Mk** 9:3; **Acts** 10:10; **Rom** 1:21; 22; 6:18; **1Cor** 9:20; 22; 13:11; **2Cor** 8:9; **Phil** 2:8; **1Th** 1:6; 2:14; **Heb** 2:10; 5:9; 7:26; 10:33; 11:7; **Rev** 6:12(2); 8:8; 11; 16:3; 4

BECAUSE

Gen 2:3; 23; 3:10; 14; 17; 20; 5:29; 7:7; 11:9; 12:13; 17; 16:11; 18:20(2); 19:13; 20:11; 18; 21:11; 12(2); 13; 25; 31; 22:16; 18; 25:21; 28; 26:5; 7; 9; 20; 27:20; 23; 41; 46; 28:11; 29:15; 33; 34; 30:18; 20; 31:30; 31; 32:32; 33:11(2); 34:7; 13; 19; 27; 35:7; 36:7; 37:3; 38:15; 26; 39:9; 23; 41:32; 57; 43:18(2); 32; 46:30; 47:20; 49:4; **Ex** 1:12; 19; 21; 2:10; 4:26; 5:21; 8:12; 9:11; 12:39; 13:8; 14:11; 17:7(2); 16; 18:15; 19:18; 29:33; 34; 32:35; 40:35; **Lev** 6:4; 9; 10:13; 11:4; 5; 6; 14:48; 15:2; 16:16(2); 19:8; 20; 20:3; 21:23; 22:7; 25; 26:10; 35; 43(3); **Num** 3:13; 6:7; 12; 7:9; 9:13; 11:3; 14; 20; 34; 12:1; 13:24; 14:16; 22; 24; 43; 15:31; 34; 19:13; 20; 20:12; 13; 24; 21:4; 22:3(2); 22; 29; 32; 25:13; 26:62; 27:4; 30:5; 14; 32:11; 17; 19; 35:28; **Deut** 1:27; 36; 2:5; 9; 19; 25; 4:3; 37; 7:7; 8(2); 8:20; 9:18; 25; 28(2); 12:20; 13:5; 10; 14:8; 29; 15:2; 10; 16(2); 16:15; 18:12; 19:6; 20:3; 21:14; 22:19; 21; 24(2); 29; 23:4(2); 5; 7; 24:1; 27:20; 28:20; 45; 47; 55; 62; 29:25; 31:17; 29; 32:3; 19; 47; 51(2); 33:21; **Josh** 2:9; 11; 24; 5:1; 6; 7; 6:1; 17; 25; 7:12; 15(2); 9:9; 18; 20; 24(2); 10:2(2); 42; 11:6; 14:9; 14; 17:1; 6; 20:5; 22:31; 23:3; **Judg** 1:19; 2:18; 20; 3:12; 5:23; 6:2; 6; 7; 22; 27; 30(2); 31; 32; 8:20; 24; 9:18; 10:10; 11:13; 12:4; 13:22; 14:17; 15:6; 18:28; 20:36; 21:15; 22; **1Sa** 1:6; 20; 2:1; 25; 3:13; 4:21(2); 6:19(2); 8:18; 9:13; 16; 10:1; 12:10; 22; 13:11; 14; 14:29; 15:23; 24; 16:7; 17:32; 18:3; 12; 16; 19:4(2); 20:17; 18; 34; 21:8; 22:17(2); 24:5; 25:28; 26:12; 16; 21; 28:18; 20; 30:6; 13; 16; 22; **2Sa** 1:9; 10; 12; 2:6; 3:11; 30; 6:8; 12; 8:10; 10:5; 12:6(2); 10; 14; 25; 13:22; 14:15; 26; 16:8; 10; 18:20; 19:21; 26; 42; 21:1; 7; 22:8; 20; 23:6; **1Kin** 1:50; 2:7; 26(2); 3:2; 11; 19; 7:47; 8:11; 33; 35; 64; 9:9; 10:9; 11:9; 33; 34; 14:13; 15; 16; 15:5; 13; 30; 16:7; 17:7; 19:7; 14; 20:28; 36; 42; 21:2; 4; 6; 20; 29; **2Kin** 1:3; 6; 16; 17; 5:1; 8:12; 29; 9:14; 10:30; 13:4; 23; 15:16; 17:26; 18:12; 19:28; 21:11; 15; 22:7; 13; 17; 19; 23:26; **1Chr** 1:19; 4:9; 41; 5:9; 20; 22; 7:21; 23; 9:27; 12:1; 13:10; 11; 14:2; 15:13; 22; 16:33; 41; 18:10; 19:2; 21:8; 30; 22:8; 23:28; 27:23; 24; 28:3; 29:3; 9; **2Chr** 1:11; 2:11; 6:24; 26; 7:2; 6; 7; 22; 8:11; 9:8; 12:2; 5; 14; 13:18; 14:6; 7; 15:16; 16:7; 8; 10; 17:3; 20:37; 21:3; 7; 10; 12; 22:6(2); 9; 24:16; 20; 24; 25:16; 20; 26:20; 27:6; 28:6; 9; 19; 23; 30:3; 34:21; 25; 27; 35:14; 36:15; **Ezr** 3:3; 11(2); 4:14; 8:22; 9:4; 15; 10:6; 9; **Neh** 4:9; 5:3; 9; 15; 18; 6:18; 8:12; 9:37; 38; 13:2; 29; **Est** 1:15; 8:7; 9:3; 24; **Job** 3:10; 6:20; 8:9; 11:16; 18; 15:27; 17:12; 18:15; 20:19(2); 23:17; 29:12; 30:11; 31:25(2); 32:1; 2; 3; 4; 34:27; 36; 35:12; 15; 36:18; 38:21(2); 39:11; 17; **Ps** 5:8; 11; 6:7(2); 7:6; 8:2; 13:6; 14:6; 16:8; 18:7; 19; 27:11; 28:5; 6; 31:10; 33:21; 37:1; 7(2); 40; 38:3(2); 5; 20; 39:9; 41:11; 42:9; 43:2; 44:3; 45:4; 48:11; 52:9; 53:5; 55:3(2); 19; 59:9; 60:4; 8; 63:3; 7; 68:29; 69:7; 18; 78:22; 86:17; 91:9; 14(2); 97:8; 102:10; 106:33; 107:11; 17(2); 26; 30; 109:16; 21; 116:1; 2; 118:1; 119:53; 56; 62; 74; 100; 136; 139; 158; 164; 122:9; **Prov** 1:24; 21:7; 22:22; 24:13; 19; **Eccl** 2:17; 18; 4:9; 5:20; 8:6; 11; 13; 15; 17; 10:15; 12:3; 5; 9; **Song** 1:3; 6(2); 3:8; **Is** 2:6; 3:8; 16; 5:13; 24; 6:5; 7:5; 24; 8:20; 10:27; 14:20; 29; 15:1(2); 17:9; 10; 19:16; 17; 20; 22:4; 24:5; 26:3; 28:15; 28; 30:12; 31:1(2); 32:14; 37:29; 40:7; 43:20; 48:4; 49:7; 50:2; 51:13; 53:9; 12; 55:5; 60:5; 9; 61:1; 64:7; 65:12; 16(2); 66:4; **Jer** 2:35(2); 4:4; 17; 18(2); 19; 28; 31; 5:6; 14; 6:19; 30; 7:13; 8:14; 19; 9:10; 13; 19(2); 10:5; 12:4; 11; 13; 13:17; 25; 14:4; 5; 6; 16; 15:4; 17; 16:11; 18; 17:13; 18:15; 19:4; 8; 13; 15; 20:8; 17; 21:12; 22:9; 15; 23:9(3); 10; 38; 25:8; 16; 27; 37; 38(2); 26:3; 28:16; 29:15; 19; 23; 25; 31; 32; 30:14; 15; 17; 31:15; 19; 32:24; 32; 35:16; 17; 18; 39:18; 40:3; 41:9; 18(2); 44:3; 22(2); 23(2); 46:15; 21; 23; 47:4; 48:7; 36; 42; 45; 50:7; 11(3); 13; 24; 51:11; 51; 55; 56; **Lam** 1:3(2); 4; 8; 16(2); 2:11; 3:22; 28; 51; 5:9; 10; 18; **Eze** 3:20; 21; 5:7; 9; 11; 6:9; 7:19; 12:19; 13:8; 10(2); 22; 14:5; 15; 15:8; 16:15; 28; 36; 43; 63; 18:18; 28; 20:16; 24; 21:7; 13; 24(2); 28; 22:19; 23:30(2); 35; 45; 24:13; 25:3; 6; 8; 12; 15; 26:2; 28:2; 5; 6; 17; 29:6; 9; 20; 31:5; 10; 33:29; 34:5; 8(2); 21; 35:5; 10; 15; 36:2; 3; 6; 13; 39:23; 44:2; 7; 12; 47:9; 12; **Dan** 2:8; 3:22; 29; 4:9; 6:3; 23; 7:11; 9:7; 8; 11; 16; 11:35; **Hos** 4:1; 6; 10; 13; 19; 5:1; 11; 7:13; 8:1; 11; 9:6; 17; 10:3; 5(2); 13; 15; 11:5; 6; **Joel** 1:5; 11; 12; 18;

2:20; 3:5; 19; **Amos** 1:3; 6; 9; 11; 13; 2:1; 4; 6; 4:12; **Jonah** 1:10; **Mic** 2:1; 10; 6:13; 7:9; 13; 17; 18; **Nah** 3:4; 11; **Hab** 1:16; 2:3; 5; 8(2); 17; **Zeph** 1:17; 2:10; 3:11; **Hag** 1:9; **Zec** 8:10; 9:8(3); 10:2; 5; 11:2; **Mal** 2:2; 14; **Mt** 2:18; 5:36; 7:14; 9:36; 11:20; 25; 12:41; 13:5; 6; 11; 13; 21; 58; 14:5; 15:32; 16:7; 8; 17:20; 18:7; 32; 19:8; 20:7; 15; 31; 21:46; 23:29; 24:12; 26:31; 33; 27:6; 19; **Mk** 1:34; 3:9; 30; 4:5; 6; 29; 5:4; 6:6; 34; 7:19; 8:2; 16; 17; 9:38; 41; 11:18; 12:24; 14:27; 15:42; 16:14; **Lk** 1:7; 20; 2:4; 7; 4:18; 5:19; 8:6; 30; 9:7; 49; 53; 10:20; 11:8(2); 18; 12:17; 13:2; 14; 15:27; 16:8; 17:9; 18:5; 19:3; 11(2); 17; 21; 31; 44; 23:8; **Jn** 1:50; 2:24; 3:18; 19; 23; 29; 4:41; 42; 5:16; 18; 27; 30; 6:2; 26(2); 41; 7:1; 7; 22; 23; 30; 39; 43; 8:22; 37; 43; 44; 45; 47; 9:16; 22; 10:13; 17; 26; 33; 36; 11:9; 10; 42; 12:6; 11; 30; 39; 42; 13:29; 14:12; 17; 19; 28; 15:19; 21; 27; 16:3; 4; 6; 9; 10; 11; 16; 17; 21; 27; 32; 17:14; 19:7; 31; 42; 20:13; 29; 21:17; **Acts** 2:6; 24; 27; 4:21; 6:1; 8:11; 20; 10:45; 12:3; 20; 23; 13:27; 14:12; 16:3; 17:18; 31; 18:2; 3; 20:16; 22:29; 30; 24:11; 25:20; 26:2; 3; 27:4; 9; 12; 28:2(2); 18; 20; **Rom** 1:19; 21; 3:2; 4:15; 5:5; 6:15; 19; 8:7; 10(2); 21; 27; 9:7; 28; 32; 11:20; 14:23; 15:15; **1Cor** 1:25; 2:14; 3:13; 6:7; 11:10; 12:15; 16; 15:9; 15; **2Cor** 2:13; 5:14; 7:13; 11:7; 11; **Gal** 2:4; 11; 3:19; 4:6; 16; **Eph** 4:18; 5:6; 16; **Phil** 1:7; 2:26; 30; 4:17; **1Th** 2:8; 9; 13; 4:6; **2Th** 1:3; 10; 2:10; 13; 3:9; **1Ti** 1:13; 4:10; 5:12; 6:2(2); **Philem** 1:7; **Heb** 3:19; 4:6; 6:13; 7:23; 24; 8:9; 10:2; 11:5; 11; 23; **Jas** 1:10; 4:2; 3; **1Pet** 1:16; 2:21; 5:8; **1Jn** 2:8; 11; 12; 13(3); 14(2); 21(2); 3:1; 9; 12; 14; 16; 22; 4:1; 4; 9; 13; 17; 18; 19; 5:6; 10; **3Jn** 7; **Jude** 16; **Rev** 1:7; 2:4; 14; 20; 3:10; 16; 17; 5:4; 8:11; 11:10; 17; 12:12; 14:8; 16:5; 11; 21

BECOME

Gen 3:22; 9:15; 18:18; 24:35; 32:10; 34:16; 37:20; 48:19(2); **Ex** 4:9; 7:9; 19; 8:16; 9:9; 15:2; 6; 23:29; 32:1; 23; **Lev** 19:29; **Num** 5:24; 27; **Deut** 27:9; 28:37; **Josh** 9:13; **Judg** 16:17; **1Sa** 28:16; **2Sa** 7:24; **1Kin** 2:15; 14:3; **2Kin** 21:14; 22:19; **Est** 2:11; **Job** 7:5; 15:28; 21:7; 30:19; 21; **Ps** 14:3; 28:1; 53:3; 62:10; 69:8; 22(2); 79:4; 109:7; 118:14; 21; 22; 119:83; **Prov** 29:21; **Is** 1:21; 22; 7:24; 12:2; 14:10(2); 19:11; 13; 29:11; 34:9; 35:7; 59:6; 60:22; **Jer** 2:5; 3:1; 5:13; 27; 7:11; 10:21; 22:5; 26:18; 49:13; 50:23; 37; 51:37; 41; **Lam** 1:1(2); 2; 6; 11; 4:1; 3; 8; **Eze** 22:4; 18; 19; 26:5; 36:35(2); 37:17; **Dan** 4:22; 9:16; 11:23; **Hos** 12:8; 13:15; 16; **Jonah** 4:5; **Mic** 3:12; **Zeph** 1:13; 2:15; **Zec** 4:7; **Mt** 18:3; 21:42; **Mk** 1:17; 12:10; **Lk** 20:17; **Jn** 1:12; **Acts** 4:11; 7:40; 12:18; **Rom** 3:12; 19; 4:18; 6:22; 7:4; 13; **1Cor** 3:18; 7:18; 8:9; 13:1; 15:20; **2Cor** 5:17; 12:11; **Gal** 4:16; 5:4; **Titus** 2:1; **Philem** 1:6; **Heb** 5:12; **Jas** 2:4; 11; **Rev** 11:15; 18:2

BEEN

Gen 13:3; 26:8; 31:5; 38; 41; 42; 38:26; 45:6; 46:32; 34; 47:9; **Ex** 2:22; 9:18; 14:12; 18:3; 21:29; 34:10; **Lev** 10:19; 13:7; **Num** 19:20; **Deut** 2:7; 4:32(2); 9:7; 24; 15:18; 21:3; 31:27; **Josh** 7:7; 9:4; 10:27; 23:9; **Judg** 16:8; 17; **Ruth** 2:11; **1Sa** 1:13; 4:7; 9; 17; 9:24; 14:29; 30; 38; 15:21; 18:19; 19:4; 20:13; 21:5; 25:28; 34; 29:3; 6; 8; **2Sa** 1:21; 26; 12:8; 13:20; 32; 14:32(2); 15:34; **1Kin** 1:37; 2:26; 14:8; 16:31; 17:7; 19:10; 14; **2Kin** 4:13; 20:12; **1Chr** 17:8; 28:3; 29:25; **2Chr** 1:12; 15:3; 23:9; **Ezr** 2:1; 4:18; 19(2); 20; 5:16; 8:35; 9:2; 4; 7(2); 8; 10:6; 8; **Neh** 2:1; 5:15; 7:6; 13:10; **Est** 2:6(2); 12; 4:11; 6:3; 7:4; **Job** 3:13(2); 16; 10:19(3); 22:9; 31:9; 27; 38:17; 42:11; **Ps** 25:6; 27:9; 35:14; 37:25; 42:3; 50:8; 18; 59:16; 60:1; 61:3; 63:7; 69:22; 71:6; 73:14; 85:1; 89:38; 90:1; 94:17; 115:12; 119:54; 71; 92; 124:1; 2; 143:3; **Prov** 7:26; **Eccl** 1:9; 10; 16; 2:12; 3:15(2); 4:3; 16; 6:10; **Is** 1:6; 9(2); 5:4; 17:10; 23:16; 25:4; 26:17; 18(2); 30:24; 38:9; 39:1; 40:21; 42:14; 43:4; 22; 48:18; 19(2); 49:21; 52:15; 57:11; 60:15; 66:2; **Jer** 2:31; 3:2; 3(2); 4:17; 15:9; 20:17; 22:21; 28:8; 32:31; 34:14; 42:18; 43:5; 44:18; 48:11(2); 50:6; 29; 51:5; 7; **Eze** 2:5; 4:14; 10:10; 11:17; 16:31; 20:41; 43; 22:13; 28:13; 29:6; 33:33; 34:12; 38:8; **Dan** 5:15; 9:12(2); **Hos** 5:1; 2; **Joel** 1:2; 2:2; **Obad** 16; **Mic** 5:2; **Zeph** 3:19; **Zec** 1:2; **Mal** 1:9; 2:9; 14; 3:13; **Mt** 1:6; 5:31; 33; 38; 43; 11:21; 23(2); 13:35; 23:30(2); 25:21; 23; 26:9; 24(2); **Mk** 5:4(2); 18; 6:49; 8:2; 14:5(2); 21; 15:44; 16:10; 11; **Lk** 1:4; 70; 2:44; 4:16; 7:10; 8:2; 10:13(2); 16:11; 12; 19:17; 24:21; **Jn** 5:6; 9:18; 11:21; 32; 39; 12:1; 38; 14:9; 15:27; **Acts** 1:16; 4:13; 16; 5:26; 6:15; 7:52; 9:18; 10:11; 11:5; 13:1; 46; 14:19; 26; 15:7; 16:27; 19:21; 20:18; 23:10; 27; 24:10; 19; 26; 25:14; 26:32; **Rom** 6:5; 9:29(2); 11:34; 15:22; 27; 16:2; **1Cor** 1:11; 12:13; **2Cor** 11:6; 21; 25; 12:11; **Gal** 3:1; 21(2); 27; 4:15; 5:13; **Eph** 3:9; 4:21; **Phil** 2:26; **Col** 1:26; 2:7; 4:11; **1Th** 2:6; **2Th** 2:15; **1Ti** 5:9; **2Ti** 3:14; **Titus** 1:9; **Heb** 8:7(2); 11:15; 13:9; **Jas** 3:7; 5:5; **2Pet** 2:21; **1Jn** 2:19; **Rev** 5:6; 17:2

BEFORE

Gen 2:5(2); 6:11; 13; 7:1; 10:9(2); 11:28; 12:15; 13:9; 10; 13; 17:1; 18; 18:8; 22; 19:4; 13; 27; 20:15; 23:3; 12; 17; 18; 19; 24:7; 15; 33; 40; 45; 51; 25:9; 18; 27:4; 7(2); 10; 33; 29:26; 30:30; 33; 38; 39; 41; 31:2; 5; 32; 35; 37; 32:3; 16; 17; 20; 21; 33:3; 12; 14(2); 18; 34:10; 36:31; 37:18; 40:9; 41:43; 46; 50; 42:6; 24; 43:9; 14; 15; 33; 34; 44:14; 45:1; 5; 7; 28; 46:28; 47:6; 7; 10; 19; 48:5; 15; 20; 49:8; 30; 50:13; 16; 18; **Ex** 4:3; 21; 6:12; 30; 7:9; 10(2); 8:20; 26; 9:10; 11; 13; 10:1; 3; 10; 14; 11:10; 12:34; 13:21; 22; 14:2(2); 9; 19(2); 16:9; 33; 34; 17:5; 6; 18:12; 19:2; 7; 20:3; 20; 21:1; 22:9; 23:15; 17; 20; 23; 27; 28(2); 29; 30; 31; 25:30; 27:21(2); 28:12; 25; 29; 30(2); 35; 38; 29:10; 11; 23; 24; 25; 26; 42; 30:6(2); 8; 16; 36; 32:1; 5; 23; 34; 33:2; 19(2); 34:3; 6; 10; 11; 20; 23; 24(2); 34; 39:18; 40:5; 6; 23; 25; 26; **Lev** 1:3; 5; 11; 3:1; 7; 8; 12; 13; 4:4(2); 6(2); 7; 14; 15(2); 17(2); 18; 24; 6:7; 14(2); 25; 7:30; 8:26; 27; 29; 9:2; 4; 5(2); 21; 24; 10:1; 2; 3; 4; 15; 17; 19; 12:7; 14:11; 12; 16; 18; 23; 24; 27; 29; 31; 36; 15:14; 15; 30; 16:1; 2; 7; 10; 12; 13; 14; 15; 18; 30; 17:4; 18:23; 24; 27; 28; 30; 19:14; 22; 32; 20:23; 23:11; 20; 28; 40; 24:3; 4; 6; 8; 26:7; 8; 17; 37(2); 27:8; 11; **Num** 3:4(2); 6; 7; 38(2); 5:16; 18; 25; 30; 6:12; 16; 20; 7:3(2); 10; 8:9; 10; 11; 13(2); 21; 22(2); 9:6(2); 10:9; 10; 33; 35; 11:6; 20; 13:22; 30; 14:5; 10; 14; 37; 42; 43; 15:15; 25; 28; 16:2; 7; 9; 16; 17; 38; 40; 43; 17:4; 7; 9; 10; 18:2; 19; 19:3; 4; 20:3; 8; 9; 10; 20:11; 22:32; 25:4; 6; 26:61; 27:2(3); 5; 14; 17(2); 19(2); 21(2); 22(2); 31:50; 54; 32:4; 17; 20; 21(2); 22(4); 27; 29(2); 32; 33:7(2); 8; 47; 52; 55; 35:12; 36:1(2); **Deut** 1:8; 21; 22; 30(2); 33; 38; 42; 45; 2:12; 21; 22; 31; 33; 3:18; 28; 4:8; 10; 32; 34; 38; 44; 5:7; 6:19; 22; 25; 7:1; 2; 22; 24; 8:20; 9:2; 3(2); 4(2); 5; 17; 18; 25; 10:8; 11; 11:23; 25; 26; 32; 12:7; 12; 18(2); 29; 30; 14:23; 26; 15:20; 16:11; 16(2); 17:12; 18; 18:7; 12; 19:17(2); 21:16; 22:6; 17; 23:14; 24:4; 13; 25:2; 26:4; 5; 10(2); 13; 27:7; 28:7(2); 25(2); 31(2); 66; 29:2; 10; 15; 30:1; 15; 19; 31:3(3); 5; 8; 11(2); 21; 32:52; 33:1; 10; 27; **Josh** 1:5; 14; 2:8; 3:1; 6(2); 10; 11; 14; 4:5; 7; 12; 13; 18; 23(2); 5:1; 6:4; 5; 6; 7; 8; 9; 13(2); 20; 26; 7:4; 5; 6; 8; 12(2); 13; 23; 8:5; 6(2); 10; 11; 14; 15; 33(2); 35; 9:24; 10:5; 8; 10; 11; 12; 14; 11:6; 13:3; 6; 25; 14:15; 15:7; 8; 15; 17:4(3); 7; 18:1; 6; 8; 10; 14; 16; 19:11; 46; 51; 20:6; 9; 21:44; 22:27; 29; 23:5; 9(2); 13; 24:1; 8; 12(2); 18; **Judg** 1:10; 11; 23; 2:3; 14; 21; 3:2; 27; 4:14; 15; 23; 5:5(2); 6:9; 18; 7:24; 8:13; 28; 9:39; 40; 11:9; 11; 23; 24; 33; 12:5; 14:16; 17; 18; 16:3; 20; 18:6; 21; 20:23; 26(2); 28; 32; 35; 39; 42; 21:2; **Ruth** 3:14; 4:4(2); **1Sa** 1:12; 15; 19; 22; 2:11; 15; 17; 18; 21; 28; 30; 35; 3:1; 4:2; 3; 17; 5:3; 4; 6:20; 7:6; 10; 8:11; 20; 9:12; 13; 15; 19; 24(2); 27; 10:5; 8; 19; 25; 11:15(2); 12:2(2); 3(2); 7; 16; 14:13; 21; 15:30(2); 33; 16:6; 8; 10; 16; 21; 22; 17:7; 31; 41; 57; 18:13; 16; 19:24; 20:1(2); 21:6; 7; 13; 22:4; 23:18; 24; 25:19; 23; 26:1; 3; 19; 20; 28:22; 25(2); 30:20; 31:1; **2Sa** 2:14; 17; 24; 3:28; 31; 34; 5:3; 20; 24; 6:4; 5; 14; 16; 17; 21(4); 7:15; 16; 18; 23; 26; 29; 10:6; 9; 13; 14; 15; 16; 18; 19; 11:13; 12:11; 12(2); 20; 13:9; 14:33; 15:1; 18; 18:7; 28; 19:8; 13; 17; 18; 28; 20:8; 21:9; 22:13; 23; 24; 24:13; 20; **1Kin** 1:2; 5; 23(2); 25; 28; 32; 2:4; 26; 45; 3:6; 12; 15; 16; 22; 24; 6:3(2); 7; 17; 21; 7:6(2); 49; 8:5; 8; 22; 23; 25(2); 28; 31; 33; 50; 54; 59; 62; 64(2); 65; 9:3; 4; 6; 25; 10:8; 11:7; 36; 12:6; 8; 30; 13:6; 14:9; 24; 15:3; 16:25; 30; 33; 17:1; 3; 5; 18:15; 46; 19:11(2); 19; 20:27; 21:10; 13; 26; 29(2); 22:10; 21; **2Kin** 1:13; 2:9; 15; 3:14; 24; 4:12; 31; 38; 43; 44; 5:15; 16; 23; 25; 6:22; 32; 8:9; 10:4; 11:18; 14:12; 15:10; 16:3; 14; 17:2; 8; 11; 18:5; 22; 19:14; 15; 26; 32; 20:3; 21:2; 9; 11; 22:10; 19(2); 23:3; 13; 25; 25:7; 29; **1Chr** 1:43; 5:25; 6:32; 10:1; 11:3; 13; 13:8; 10; 14:15; 15:24; 16:1; 4; 6; 29; 30; 37(2); 39; 17:8; 13; 16; 21; 24; 25; 27; 19:7; 9; 10; 14(2); 15; 16(2); 18; 19; 21:12; 30; 22:5; 18(2); 23:13; 31; 24:2; 6(2); 28:4; 29:10; 15; 22; 25; **2Chr** 1:5; 6; 10; 12; 13; 2:4; 6; 3:15; 17; 4:20; 5:6; 9; 6:12; 13; 14; 16; 19; 22; 24(2); 36; 7:4; 6; 7; 17; 19; 8:12; 14; 9:7; 11; 10:6; 8; 13:13; 14; 15; 16; 14:5; 7; 12(2); 13(2); 15:8; 18:9; 20; 19:2; 11; 20:5; 7; 9; 13; 16; 18; 21; 23:17; 24:14; 25:8; 14; 22; 26:19; 27:6; 28:3; 9; 14; 29:11; 19; 23; 30:9; 31:20; 32:12; 33:2; 7; 9; 12; 19; 23; 34:18; 24; 27(3); 31; 36:12; **Ezr** 3:12; 4:18; 23; 7:19; 28(2); 8:21; 29; 9:15(2); 10:1; 6; **Neh** 1:4; 6; 2:1; 13; 4:2; 5(2); 5:15; 6:19; 8:1; 2; 3(3); 9:8; 11; 24; 28; 32; 35; 12:36; 13:4; 19; **Est** 1:3; 11; 16; 17; 19; 2:11; 23; 3:7; 4:2; 6; 8; 6:1; 9; 11; 13(2); 7:6; 8; 9; 8:1; 3; 4; 5; 9:11; 25; **Job** 1:6; 2:1(2); 3:24; 4:15; 16; 19; 8:12; 16; 10:21; 13:15; 16; 15:4; 7; 32; 18:20; 21:8; 18; 33; 23:4; 17; 26:6; 30:11; 33:5; 35:14; 41:10; 22; 42:10; 11; **Ps** 5:8; 16:8; 18:6; 12; 22; 23; 42; 22:25; 27; 29; 23:5; 26:3; 31:19; 22; 34:t; 35:5; 36:1; 38:9; 17; 39:1; 5; 13; 41:12; 42:2; 44:15; 50:3; 8; 21; 51:3; 52:9; 54:3; 56:13; 57:6; 58:9; 61:7; 62:8; 68:1; 2; 3; 4; 7; 25; 69:19; 22; 72:9; 11; 73:22; 78:55; 79:11; 80:2; 9; 83:13; 84:7; 85:13; 86:9; 14; 88:1; 2; 89:14; 23; 36; 90:2; 8; 95:2; 6; 96:6; 9; 13; 97:3; 98:6; 9; 100:2; 101:3; 102:t; 28; 105:17; 106:23; 109:15; 116:9; 119:30; 46; 67; 168; 169; 170; 138:1; 139:5; 141:2; 3; 142:2(2); 147:17; **Prov** 4:25; 5:21; 8:22; 25(2); 30; 14:19; 15:11; 33; 16:18(2); 17:14; 24; 18:12(2); 13; 16; 22:29(2); 23:1; 25:5; 26; 26:26; 27:4; 30:7; **Eccl** 1:10; 16; 2:7; 9; 26; 3:14; 4:16; 5:2; 6; 6:8; 7:17; 8:12; 13; 9:1; **Song** 8:12; **Is** 1:12; 16; 7:16; 8:4(2); 9:3; 12; 13:16; 17:13(2); 14; 23:18; 24:23; 28:4; 30:8; 11; 36:7; 37:14; 27; 33; 38:3; 40:10; 17; 41:1; 2; 42:9; 16; 43:10; 13; 45:1(2); 2; 47:14; 48:5; 7; 19; 49:16; 52:12; 53:2; 7; 55:12; 57:16; 58:8; 59:12; 61:11; 62:11; 63:12; 65:6; 12; 24; 66:4; 7(2); 22; 23; **Jer** 1:5(2); 17; 2:22; 6:7; 21; 7:10; 8:2; 9:13; 13:16(2); 15:1; 9; 19; 17:16; 18:17; 20; 23; 19:7; 21:8; 24:1; 26:4; 28:8(2); 29:21; 30:20; 31:36(2); 32:12; 13; 30; 31; 33:9; 18; 24; 34:5; 15; 18; 35:5; 19; 36:7; 9; 22; 37:20; 38:10; 26; 39:6; 16; 40:4; 42:2; 9; 44:10(2); 47:1; 49:19; 37(2); 50:8; 44; 52:10; 33; **Lam** 1:5; 6; 22; 2:3; 19; 3:35; **Eze** 2:10; 3:20; 4:1; 6:4; 5; 8:1; 11; 9:6; 14:1; 3; 4; 7; 16:18; 19; 50; 57; 20:1; 9; 14; 41; 21:6; 22:30; 23:24; 41; 28:9; 17; 30:24; 32:10; 33:31; 36:17; 23; 37:20; 38:16; 40:12; 22; 26; 47; 41:4; 12; 22; 42:1; 2; 4; 8; 11; 12; 13; 43:24; 44:3; 4; 11; 12; 15; 22; 45:7(2); 46:3; 9; **Dan** 1:5; 13; 18; 19; 2:2; 9; 10; 11; 24; 25; 31; 36; 3:3; 13; 4:6; 7; 8(2); 5:1; 13; 15; 17; 19; 23; 6:10; 11; 12; 13; 18; 22(2); 26; 7:7; 8; 10(2); 13; 20; 8:3; 4; 6; 7; 15; 9:10; 13; 18; 20; 10:12; 16; 11:16; 22; **Hos** 7:2; **Joel** 1:16; 2:3(2); 6; 10; 11; 31; **Amos** 1:1; 2:9; 4:3; 9:4; **Jonah** 1:2; 4:2; **Mic** 1:4; 2:13(2); 6:1; 4; 6(3); **Nah** 1:6; 2:1; **Hab** 1:3; 2:20; 3:5; **Zeph** 2:2(4); 3:20; **Hag** 1:12; 2:14; 15; **Zec** 2:13; 3:1; 3; 4; 8; 9; 4:7; 6:5; 7:2; 8:10; 21; 22; 12:8; 14:4; 5; 20; **Mal** 2:5; 9; 3:1; 11; 14; 16; 4:5; **Mt** 1:18; 2:9; 5:12; 16; 24; 6:1; 2; 8; 7:6; 8:29; 10:18; 32(2); 33(2); 11:10(2); 14:6; 8; 22; 17:2; 21:9; 31; 24:25; 38; 25:32; 26:32; 34; 70; 75; 27:11; 24; 29; 28:7; **Mk** 1:2(2); 35; 2:12; 3:11; 5:33; 6:41; 45; 8:6(2); 7; 9:2; 10:32; 11:9; 13:9; 14:28; 30; 72; 15:42; 16:7; **Lk** 1:6; 8; 17; 75; 76; 2:21; 26; 31; 5:18; 19; 25; 7:27(2); 8:28; 47(2); 9:16; 52; 10:1; 8; 11:6; 38; 12:6; 8(2); 9(2); 14:2; 15:18; 16:15; 18:39; 19:4; 27; 28; 20:26; 21:12(2); 14; 36; 22:15; 34; 47; 61; 23:12; 14; 53; 24:19; 43; **Jn** 1:15(2); 27; 30(2); 48; 3:28; 5:7; 6:62; 7:51; 8:58; 9:8; 10:4; 8; 11:55; 12:1; 37; 13:1; 19; 14:29; 15:18; 17:5; 24; **Acts** 1:16; 2:20; 25; 31; 3:18; 20; 4:10; 28; 5:23; 27; 36; 6:6; 7:2; 40; 45; 46; 52; 8:32; 9:15; 10:4; 17; 30; 33; 41; 12:6; 14; 13:24; 14:13; 16:29; 34; 17:26; 18:17; 19:9; 19; 20:5; 13; 21:29; 38; 22:30; 23:1; 30; 33; 24:19; 20; 25:9; 16; 26(2); 26:2; 26; 27:24; **Rom** 2:13; 3:9; 18; 19; 4:2; 17; 9:29; 14:10; 22; 16:7; **1Cor** 2:7; 4:5; 6:1(2); 6; 10:27; 11:21; **2Cor** 1:15; 5:10; 7:3; 14; 8:10; 24; 9:5(2); 12:19; 13:2; **Gal** 1:9; 17; 20; 2:12; 14; 3:1; 8; 17; 23; 5:21; **Eph** 1:4(2); 2:10; **Phil** 3:13; **Col** 1:5; 17; **1Th** 2:2; 3:4; 9; 13; **1Ti** 1:13; 18; 5:4; 19; 20; 21(2); 24; 6:12; 13(2); **2Ti** 1:9; 2:14; 4:1; 21; S:1; **Titus** 1:2; **Heb** 6:18; 7:18; 10:15; 11:5; 12:1; 2; **Jas** 1:27; 2:6; 5:9; **1Pet** 1:20; **2Pet** 2:11; 3:2; 17; **1Jn** 2:28; 3:19; **3Jn** 6; **Jude** 4; 17; 24; **Rev** 1:4; 2:14; 3:2; 5(2); 8; 9; 4:5; 6(2); 10(2); 5:8; 7:9(2); 11; 15; 8:2; 3; 4; 9:13; 10:11; 11:4; 16; 12:4; 10; 13:12; 14:3(2); 5; 15:4; 16:19; 19:20; 20:12; 22:8

BEFOREHAND

Mk 13:11; **2Cor** 9:5; **1Ti** 5:24; 25; **1Pet** 1:11

BEGAN

Gen 4:26; 6:1; 9:20; 10:8; 41:54; 44:12; **Num** 25:1; **Deut** 1:5; **Judg** 13:25; 16:19; 22; 19:25; 20:31; 39; 40; **1Sa** 3:2; **2Sa** 2:10; 5:4; **1Kin** 6:1; 14:21; 15:25; 33; 16:8; 11; 23; 29; 22:41; 42; 51; **2Kin** 3:1; 8:16; 17; 26; 9:29; 10:32; 11:21; 12:1; 13:1; 10; 14:2; 23; 15:1; 2; 13; 17; 23; 27; 32; 33; 37; 16:1; 2; 17:1; 18:1; 2; 21:1; 19; 22:1; 23:31; 36; 24:8; 18; 25:27; **1Chr** 1:10; 27:24; **2Chr** 3:1; 2; 12:13; 13:1; 20:22; 31; 21:5; 20; 22:2; 24:1; 25:1; 26:3; 27:1; 8; 28:1; 29:1; 17; 27(2); 31:7; 10; 21; 33:1; 21; 34:1; 3(2); 36:2; 5; 9; 11; **Ezr** 3:6; 8; 5:2; 7:9; **Neh** 4:7; 13:19; **Jer** 52:1; **Eze** 9:6; **Jonah** 3:4; **Mt** 4:17; 11:7; 20; 12:1; 16:21; 22; 26:22; 37; 74; 28:1; **Mk** 1:45; 2:23; 4:1; 5:17; 20; 6:2; 7; 34; 55; 8:11; 31; 32; 10:28; 32; 41; 47; 11:15; 12:1; 13:5; 14:19; 33; 65; 69; 71; 15:8; 18; **Lk** 1:70; 3:23; 4:21; 5:7; 21; 7:15; 24; 38; 49; 9:12; 11:29; 53; 12:1; 14:18; 30; 15:14; 24; 19:37; 45; 20:9; 22:23; 23:2; **Jn** 4:52; 9:32; 13:5; **Acts** 1:1; 2:4; 3:21; 8:35; 10:37; 11:15; 18:26; 24:2; 27:35; **Rom** 16:25; **2Ti** 1:9; **Titus** 1:2; **Heb** 2:3

BEGIN

Gen 11:6; **Deut** 2:24; 25; 31; 16:9; **Josh** 3:7; **Judg** 10:18; 13:5; **1Sa** 3:12; 22:15; **2Kin** 8:25; **Neh** 11:17; **Jer** 25:29; **Eze** 9:6; **Mt** 24:49; **Lk** 3:8; 12:45; 13:25; 26; 14:9; 29; 21:28; 23:30; **2Cor** 3:1; **1Pet** 4:17(2); **Rev** 10:7

BEGINNING

Gen 1:1; 10:10; 13:3; 41:21; 49:3; **Ex** 12:2; **Deut** 11:12; 21:17; 32:42; **Judg** 7:19; **Ruth** 1:22; 3:10; **2Sa** 21:9; 10; **2Kin** 17:25; **1Chr** 17:9; **Ezr** 4:6; **Job** 8:7; 42:12; **Ps** 111:10; 119:160; **Prov** 1:7; 8:22; 23; 9:10; 17:14; 20:21; **Eccl** 3:11; 7:8; 10:13; **Is** 1:26; 18:2; 7; 40:21; 41:4; 26; 46:10; 48:3; 5; 7; 16; 64:4; **Jer** 17:12; 26:1; 27:1; 28:1; 49:34; **Lam** 2:19; **Eze** 40:1; **Dan** 9:21; 23; **Hos** 1:2; **Amos** 7:1; **Mic** 1:13; **Mt** 14:30; 19:4; 8; 20:8; 24:8; 21; **Mk** 1:1; 10:6; 13:19; **Lk** 1:2; 23:5; 24:27; 47; **Jn** 1:1; 2; 2:10; 11; 6:64; 8:9; 25; 44; 15:27; 16:4; **Acts** 1:22; 11:4; 15; 15:18; 26:5; **Eph** 3:9; **Phil** 4:15; **Col** 1:18; **2Th** 2:13; **Heb** 1:10; 3:14; 7:3; **2Pet** 2:20; 3:4; **1Jn** 1:1; 2:7(2); 13; 14; 24(2); 3:8; 11; **2Jn** 5; 6; **Rev** 1:8; 3:14; 21:6; 22:13

BEGUN

Num 16:46; 47; **Deut** 2:31; 3:24; **Est** 6:13; 9:23; **Mt** 18:24; **2Cor** 8:6; 10; **Gal** 3:3; **Phil** 1:6; **1Ti** 5:11

BEHIND

Gen 18:10; 19:17; 26; 22:13; 32:18; 20; **Ex** 10:26; 11:5; 14:19(2); **Lev** 25:51; **Num** 3:23; **Deut** 25:18; **Josh** 8:2; 4; 14; 20; **Judg** 18:12; 20:40; **1Sa** 21:9; 24:8; 30:9; 10; **2Sa** 1:7; 2:20; 23; 3:16; 5:23; 10:9; 13:34; **1Kin** 10:19; 14:9; **2Kin** 6:32; 9:18; 19; 11:6; **1Chr** 19:10; **2Chr** 13:13(2); 14; **Neh** 4:13; 16; 9:26; **Ps** 50:17; 139:5; **Song** 2:9; **Is** 9:12; 30:21; 38:17; 57:8; 66:17; **Eze** 3:12; 23:35; 41:15; **Joel** 2:3(2); 14; **Zec** 1:8; **Mt** 9:20; 16:23; **Mk** 5:27; 8:33; 12:19; **Lk** 2:43; 4:8; 7:38; 8:44; **1Cor** 1:7; **2Cor** 11:5; 12:11; **Phil** 3:13; **Col** 1:24; **Rev** 1:10; 4:6

BEING

Gen 18:12; 19:16; 21:4; 24:27; 34:30; 35:29; 37:2; 50:26; **Ex** 12:34; 13:15; 22:14; 28:16; 32:18; 39:9; **Lev** 21:4; 24:8; **Num** 1:44; 22:24; 30:3; 16; 31:32; 32:38; **Deut** 3:13; 17:8; 22:24; 32:31; **Josh** 9:23; 21:10; 24:29; **Judg** 2:0; 9:5; **1Sa** 2:10; 15:23, 26; 26:13; **2Sa** 8:13; 13:4; 14; 19:3; 21:16; **1Kin** 1:41; 2:27; 11:17; 15:13; 16:7; 20:15; **2Kin** 8:16; 10:6; 12:11; **1Chr** 9:19; 24:6; **2Chr** 5:12; 13:3; 15:16; 21:20; 26:21; **Ezr** 6:11; 10:19; **Neh** 6:11; **Est** 1:3; 7; 3:15; 8:14; **Job** 4:7; 21:23; 42:17; **Ps** 49:12; 65:6; 69:4; 78:9; 38; 83:4; 104:33; 107:10; 139:16; 146:2; **Prov** 3:26; 29:1; **Song** 3:8; 10; **Is** 3:26; 17:1; 40:13; 65:20; **Jer** 2:25; 12:11; 17:16; 31:36; 34:9; 40:1; 48:2; 42; **Eze** 17:10; 23:42; 47:8; 48:22; **Dan** 3:27; 5:31; 6:10; 8:22; 9:21; **Mt** 1:19; 23; 24; 2:12; 22; 7:11; 12:34; 14:8; **Mk** 3:5; 5:41; 8:1; 9:33; 14:3; 15:22; 34; **Lk** 1:74; 2:5; 3:1(2); 2; 19; 21; 23; 4:1; 2; 15; 7:29; 30; 8:25; 11:13; 13:16; 14:21; 16:23; 20:36; 21:12; 22:3; 44; **Jn** 1:38; 41; 4:6; 9; 5:13; 6:71; 7:50; 8:9; 10:33; 11:49; 51; 13:2; 14:25; 18:26; 19:38; 20:19; 26; **Acts** 1:3; 4; 2:23; 30; 33; 3:1; 4:2; 23; 36; 5:2; 7:55; 13:4; 12; 14:8; 15:3; 21; 25; 32; 40; 16:18; 20; 21; 37; 17:28; 18:25; 19:40; 20:9; 22:11; 26:11; 27:2; 18; **Rom** 1:20; 29; 2:18; 3:21; 24; 4:11; 12; 19; 21; 5:1; 9; 10; 6:9; 18; 22; 7:6; 9:11; 10:3; 11:17; 12:5; 15:16; **1Cor** 4:12(2); 13; 7:18; 21; 22(2); 8:7; 9:21; 10:17; 12:12; **2Cor** 5:3; 4; 8:17; 9:11; 10:1; 11:9; 12:16; 13:2; 10(2); **Gal** 1:14; 2:3; 14; 3:13; **Eph** 1:11; 18; 2:11; 12; 20; 3:17; 4:18; 19; **Phil** 1:6; 11; 2:2; 6; 8; 3:10; **Col** 1:10; 2:2; 13; **1Th** 2:8; 17; **1Ti** 2:14; 3:6; 10; **2Ti** 1:4; 3:13; **Titus** 1:16; 3:7; 11; **Philem** 1:9; **Heb** 1:3; 4; 2:18; 4:1; 2; 5:9; 7:2; 12; 9:11; 11:4; 7; 37; 13:3; **Jas** 1:25; 2:17; **1Pet** 1:7; 23; 2:8; 24; 3:5; 7; 18; 22; 5:3(2); **2Pet** 3:6; 12; 17; **Rev** 1:12; 12:2; 14:4

BENEATH

Gen 35:8; Ex 20:4; 26:24; 27:5; 28:33; 32:19; 36:29; 38:4; Deut 4:18; 39; 5:8(2); 28:13; 33:13; Josh 2:11; Judg 7:8; 1Kin 4:12; 7:29; 8:23; Job 18:16; Prov 15:24; Is 14:9; 51:6; Jer 31:37; Amos 2:9; Mk 14:66; Jn 8:23; Acts 2:19

BESIDE

Gen 26:1; 31:50; Ex 12:37; 14:9; 29:12; Lev 1:16; 6:10; 9:17; 10:12; 18:18; 23:38(4); Num 5:8; 20; 6:21; 11:6; 16:49; 24:6; 28:10; 15; 23; 24; 31; 29:6; 11; 16; 19; 22; 25; 28; 31; 34; 38; 39; 31:8; Deut 3:5; 4:35; 11:30; 18:8; 19:9; 29:1; Josh 3:16; 7:2; 12:9; 13:4; 17:5; 22:19; 29; Judg 6:37; 7:1; 8:26(2); 11:34; 20:15; 17; 36; Ruth 2:14; 4:4; 1Sa 2:2; 4:1; 19:3; 2Sa 7:22; 13:23; 15:2; 18; 1Kin 3:20; 4:23; 5:16; 9:26; 10:13; 15; 19; 11:25; 13:31; 2Kin 11:20; 12:9; 21:16; 1Chr 3:9; 17:20; 2Chr 9:12; 14; 17:19; 20:1; 26:19; 31:16; Ezr 1:4; 6; 2:65; Neh 5:15; 17; 7:67; 8:4; Job 1:14; Ps 23:2; 73:25; Song 1:8; Is 32:20; 43:11; 44:6; 8; 45:5; 6; 21(2); 47:8; 10; 56:8; 64:4; Jer 36:21; Eze 9:2; 10:6; 16; 19; 11:22; 32:13; Dan 11:4; Hos 13:4; Zeph 2:15; Mt 14:21; 15:38; 25:20; 22; Mk 3:21; Lk 16:26; 24:21; Acts 26:24; 2Cor 5:13; 11:28; 2Pet 1:5

BESIDES

Gen 19:12; 46:26; Lev 7:13; 1Kin 22:7; 2Chr 18:6; Is 26:13; Jer 36:32; 1Cor 1:16; Philem 1:19

BETTER

Gen 29:19; Ex 14:12; Num 14:3; Judg 8:2; 9:2; 11:25; 18:19; Ruth 4:15; 1Sa 1:8; 15:22; 28; 27:1; 2Sa 17:14; 18:3; 1Kin 1:47; 2:32; 19:4; 21:2; 2Kin 5:12; 2Chr 21:13; Est 1:19; Ps 37:16; 63:3; 69:31; 84:10; 118:8; 9; 119:72; Prov 3:14; 8:11; 19; 12:9; 15:16; 17; 16:8; 16; 19; 32; 17:1; 19:1; 22; 21:9; 19; 25:7; 24; 27:5; 10; 28:6; Eccl 2:24; 3:22; 4:3; 6; 9; 13; 5:5; 6:3; 9; 11; 7:1; 2; 3(2); 5; 8(2); 10; 8:15; 9:4; 16; 18; 10:11; Song 1:2; 4:10; Is 56:5; Lam 4:9; Eze 36:11; Dan 1:20; Hos 2:7; Amos 6:2; Jonah 4:3; 8; Nah 3:8; Mt 6:26; 12:12; 18:6; 8; 9; Mk 9:42; 43; 45; 47; Lk 5:39; 12:24; 17:2; Rom 3:9; 1Cor 7:9; 38; 8:8; 9:15; 11:17; Phil 1:23; 2:3; Heb 1:4; 6:9; 7:7; 19; 22; 8:6(2); 9:23; 10:34; 11:16; 35; 40; 12:24; 1Pet 3:17; 2Pet 2:21

BETWEEN

Gen 3:15(2); 9:12; 13; 15; 16; 17; 10:12; 13:3; 7; 8(2); 15:17; 16:5; 14; 17:2; 7; 10; 20:1; 31:44; 48; 49; 48:12; 49:10; 14; Ex 8:23; 9:4; 11:7; 13:9; 16; 14:2; 20; 16:1; 18:16; 22:11; 25:22; 26:33; 28:33; 30:18; 31:13; 17; 39:25(2); 40:7; 30; Lev 10:10(2); 11:47(2); 20:25(2); 26:46; Num 7:89; 11:33; 13:23; 16:48; 21:13; 26:56; 30:16(2); 31:27(2); 35:24; Deut 1:1; 16(2); 39; 5:5; 6:8; 11:18; 14:1; 17:8(3); 19:17; 25:1; 28:57; 33:12; Josh 3:4; 8:9; 11; 12; 18:11; 22:25; 27; 28; 34; 24:7; Judg 4:5; 17; 9:23; 11:10; 27; 13:25; 15:4; 16:25; 31; 20:38; 1Sa 4:4; 7:12; 14; 14:4; 42; 17:1; 3; 6; 20:3; 23; 42(2); 24:12; 15; 26:13; 2Sa 3:1; 6; 6:2; 18:9; 24; 19:35; 21:7(2); 1Kin 3:9; 5:12; 7:28; 29; 46; 14:30; 15:6; 7; 16; 19(2); 32; 18:6; 21; 42; 22:1; 34; 2Kin 9:24; 11:17(2); 16:14; 19:15; 25:4; 1Chr 13:6; 21:16; 2Chr 4:17; 12:15; 13:2; 16:3(2); 18:33; 19:10(2); 23:16(3); Neh 3:32; Job 41:16; Ps 80:1; 99:1; Prov 18:18; Is 22:11; 37:16; 59:2; Jer 7:5; 34:18; 19; 42:5; 52:7; Lam 1:3; Eze 4:3; 8:3; 16; 10:2(2); 6(2); 7(2); 18:8; 20:12; 20; 22:26(2); 34:17(2); 20(2); 22; 40:7; 41:10; 18; 42:20; 43:8; 44:23(2); 47:16; 48:22; Dan 7:5; 8:5; 16; 21; 11:45; Hos 2:2; Joel 2:17; Jonah 4:11; Zec 5:9; 6:1; 13; 9:7; 11:14; Mal 2:14; 3:18(2); Mt 18:15; 23:35; Lk 11:51; 16:26; 23:12; Jn 3:25; Acts 12:6; 15:9; 39; 23:7; 26:31; Rom 1:24; 10:12; 1Cor 6:5; 7:34; Eph 2:14; 1Ti 2:5

BEYOND

Gen 35:21; 50:10; 11; Lev 15:25; Num 22:18; 24:13; Deut 3:20; 25; 30:13; Josh 9:10; 13:8; 18:7; Judg 3:26; 5:17; 1Sa 20:22; 36; 37; 2Sa 10:16; 1Kin 4:12; 14:15; 1Chr 19:16; 2Chr 20:2; Ezr 4:17; 20; 6:6(2); 8; 7:21; 25; Neh 2:7; 9; 12:38; Is 7:20; 9:1; 18:1; Jer 22:19; 25:22; Amos 5:27; Zeph 3:10; Mt 4:15; 25; 19:1; Mk 3:8; 6:51; 7:37; Jn 1:28; 3:26; 10:40; Acts 7:43; 2Cor 8:3; 10:14; 16; Gal 1:13; 1Th 4:6

BOTH

Gen 2:25; 3:7; 6:7; 7:21; 23; 8:17; 9:23; 19:4; 11; 36; 21:27; 31; 22:6; 8; 24:25; 44; 27:45; 31:37; 36:24; 40:5; 41:10; 42:35; 43:8; 44:9; 16; 46:34; 47:3; 19; 48:13; 50:9; Ex 5:14; 7:19; 8:4; 9:25; 12:12; 31; 13:2; 15; 18:18; 22:9; 11; 26:24; 29:44; 32:15; 35:22; 25; 34; 36:29(2); 37:26; Lev 6:28; 8:11; 9:3; 15:18; 16:21; 17:15; 20:11; 12; 13; 14; 18; 21:22; 22:28; 25:41; 44; 54; 27:28; 33; Num 3:13; 5:3; 7:1; 13; 19; 25; 31; 37; 43; 49; 55; 61; 67; 73; 79; 8:17; 9:14; 12:5; 15:15; 29; 16:11; 25:8; 27:21; 31:11; 19; 26; 28; 47; 35:15; Deut 19:17; 21:15; 22:22(2); 24; 23:18; 30:19; 32:25; Josh 6:21; 8:25; 14:11; 17:16; Judg 5:30; 6:5; 8:22; 10:10; 15:5; 19:6; 8; 19; Ruth 1:5; 1Sa 2:26; 34; 3:11; 5:4; 9; 6:18; 9:26; 12:14; 25; 14:11; 15:3; 17:36; 20:11; 42; 22:19; 25:6; 16; 43; 26:25; 2Sa 8:18; 9:13; 15:25; 16:23; 17:18; 1Kin 3:13; 6:5; 15; 16; 25; 7:12; 50; 2Kin 2:11; 3:17; 6:15; 17:41; 21:12; 23:2; 15; 25:26; 1Chr 12:2; 15; 15:12; 16:3; 23:29; 24:3; 28:15; 29:12; 2Chr 20:25; 24:16; 25:21; 26:10; 27:5; 31:17; 32:26; Ezr 3:5; 6:9; Neh 1:6; 4:16; 8:2; 10:9; 12:27; 28; 45; Est 1:5; 20; 2:23; 3:13; 8:11; 9:20; Job 9:33; 15:10; Ps 4:8; 49:2; 58:9; 64:6; 76:6; 104:25; 115:13; 135:8; 139:12; 148:12; Prov 17:15; 20:10; 12; 24:22; 26:10; 27:3; 29:13; Eccl 4:3; 6; 8:5; 11:6; Is 1:31; 7:16; 8:14; 10:18; 13:9; 18:5; 31:3; 38:15; 44:12; Jer 5:24; 9:10; 14:18; 16:6; 21:6; 23:11; 26:5; 28:8; 31:13; 32:11; 14; 36:16; 44:25; 46:12; 50:3; 51:12; 46; Lam 3:26; Eze 9:6; 14:22; 15:4; 21:19; 23:13; 29; 34:11; 39:9; 42:11; Dan 8:13; 11:27; Mic 5:8; 7:3; Nah 3:3; Zeph 2:14; Zec 6:13; 12:2; Mt 9:17; 10:28; 12:22; 13:30; 15:14; 22:10; Mk 6:30; 7:37; Lk 1:6; 7; 2:46; 5:7; 36; 38; 6:39; 7:42; 21:16; 22:33; Jn 2:2; 4:36; 7:28; 9:37; 11:48; 57; 12:28; 15:24(2); 20:4; Acts 1:1; 8; 13; 2:29; 36; 4:27; 5:14; 8:12; 38(2); 10:39; 14:1(2); 5; 19:10; 20:21; 21:12; 22:4; 23:8; 24:15; 25:24; 26:16; 22; 29; 28:23; Rom 1:12; 14(2); 3:9; 11:33; 14:9(2); 1Cor 1:2; 24; 4:5; 11; 6:13; 14; 7:29; 34; 2Cor 9:10; Eph 1:10; 2:14; 16; 18; Phil 1:7; 2:13; 4:9; 12(3); 1Th 2:15; 5:15; 2Th 3:4; 1Ti 4:10; 16; Titus 1:9; Philem 1:16; Heb 2:4; 11; 5:1; 14; 6:19; 9:9; 19; 21; 10:33; 11:21; Jas 3:12; 2Pet 3:1; 18; 2Jn 9; Jude 25; Rev 13:15; 16; 19:5; 18(2); 20

BRING

Gen 1:11; 20; 24; 3:16; 18; 6:17; 19; 8:17; 9:7; 14; 18:16; 19; 19:5; 8; 12; 24:5; 6; 8; 27:4; 5; 7; 10; 12; 25; 28:15; 37:14; 38:24; 40:14; 41:32; 42:20; 34; 37(2); 38; 43:7; 9; 16; 44:21; 29; 31; 32; 45:13; 19; 46:4; 48:9; 21; 50:20; 24; Ex 3:8; 10; 11; 17; 6:6; 8; 13; 26; 27; 7:4; 5; 8:3; 18; 10:4; 11:1; 12:51; 13:5; 11; 15:17; 16:5; 18:19; 22; 21:6(2); 22:13; 23:4; 19; 20; 23; 25:2; 26:33; 27:20; 29:3; 4; 8; 32:2; 12; 33:12; 34:26; 35:5; 29; 36:5; 40:4(2); 12; 14; Lev 1:2(2); 5; 10; 13; 14; 15; 2:2; 4; 8(2); 11; 4:3; 4; 5; 14; 16; 23; 28; 32(2); 5:6; 7(2); 8; 11(2); 12; 15; 18; 6:6; 21; 7:29; 30(2); 10:15; 12:6; 8(2); 14:23; 15:29; 16:9; 11; 12; 15; 20; 17:5(2); 18:3; 19:21; 20:22; 23:10; 17; 24:2; 14; 23; 25:21; 26:10; 21; 25; 31; 32; 27:9; Num 3:6; 5:9; 15(2); 16; 6:10; 12; 16; 8:9; 10; 11:16; 13:20; 14:8; 16; 24; 31; 37; 15:4; 9; 10; 18; 25; 27; 16:9; 17; 17:10; 18:2; 13; 15; 19:2; 3; 20:5; 8; 12; 25; 22:8; 23:27; 27:17; 28:26; 32:5; Deut 1:17; 22; 4:38; 6:23; 7:1; 26; 9:3; 28; 12:6; 11; 14:28; 17:5; 21:4; 12; 19; 22:1; 2; 8; 14; 15; 21; 24; 23:18; 24:11; 26:2; 28:36; 49; 60; 61; 63; 68; 29:27; 30:5; 12; 13; 31:23; 33:7; Josh 2:3; 18; 6:22; 10:22; 18:6; 23:15; Judg 6:13; 18; 30; 7:4; 11:9; 19:3; 22; 24; Ruth 3:15; 1Sa 1:22; 4:4; 6:7; 9:7(2); 23; 11:12; 13:9; 14:18; 34; 15:32; 16:17; 19:15; 20:8; 23:9; 27:11; 28:8; 11(2); 15; 30:7; 15(2); 2Sa 2:3; 3:12; 13; 6:2; 9:10; 12:23; 13:10; 14:10; 21; 15:8; 14; 25; 17:3; 13; 14; 19:11; 12; 22:28; 1Kin 1:33; 2:9; 3:24; 5:9; 8:1; 4; 32; 34; 10:29; 12:21; 13:18; 14:10; 17:11; 13; 20:33; 21:21; 29(2); 2Kin 2:20(2); 3:15; 4:6; 41; 6:19; 10:22; 12:4; 19:3; 22:16; 20; 23:4; 1Chr 9:28; 13:3; 5; 6; 12; 15:3; 12; 14; 25; 16:29; 21:2; 12; 22:19; 2Chr 2:16; 5:2; 5; 6:25; 11:1; 24:6; 9; 19; 28:13; 29:31; 31:10; 34:24; 28; Ezr 1:8; 11; 3:7; 8:17; 30; Neh 1:9; 5:5; 8:1; 9:29; 10:31; 34; 35; 36; 37; 38; 39; 11:1; 12:27; 13:18(2); Est 1:11; 3:9; 6:1; 9; 14; Job 6:22; 10:9; 14:4; 9; 15:35; 18:14; 30:23; 33:30; 38:32; 39:1; 2; 3; 12; 40:12; 20; Ps 18:27; 25:17; 37:5; 6; 38:t, 43:3; 55:23; 59:11; 60:9; 68:22(2); 29; 70:t, 71:20; 72:3; 10; 76:11; 81:2; 92:14; 94:23; 96:8; 104:14; 108:10; 142:7; 143:11; 144:13; Prov 4:8; 19:24; 26:15; 27:1; 29:8; 23; Eccl 3:22; 11:9; 12:14; Song 8:2; 11; Is 1:13; 5:2; 4; 7:17; 14:2; 15:9; 23:4(2); 9; 25:5; 11; 12(2); 28:21; 31:2; 33:11; 37:3; 38:8; 41:21; 22; 42:1; 3; 7; 16; 43:5; 6; 8; 9; 45:8; 21; 46:8; 11; 13; 49:5; 22; 52:8; 55:10; 56:7; 58:7; 59:4; 60:6; 9; 11; 17(2); 63:6; 65:9; 23; 66:4; 8; 9(3); 20(2); Jer 3:14; 4:6; 5:15; 6:19; 8:1; 10:24; 11:8; 11; 23; 12:2; 15; 15:19; 16:15; 17:18; 21; 24; 18:22; 19:3; 15; 23:3; 12; 40; 24:6; 25:9; 13; 29; 26:15; 27:11; 12; 22; 28:3; 4; 6; 29:14; 30:3; 18; 31:8; 23; 32; 32:37; 42; 33:6; 11; 35:2; 17; 36:31; 38:23; 39:16; 41:5; 42:17; 45:5; 48:44; 47; 49:5; 6; 8; 16; 32; 36; 37; 39; 50:19; 51:40; 44; 64; Lam 1:21; Eze 5:17; 6:3; 7:24; 11:7; 8; 9; 12:4; 13; 13:14; 14:17; 16:40; 53(2); 17:8; 20; 23; 20:6; 15; 34; 35; 37; 38; 41; 42; 21:29; 23:22; 46; 24:6; 26:7; 19; 20; 28:7; 8; 18(2); 29:4; 8; 14; 31:6; 32:3; 9; 33:2; 34:13(2); 16; 36:11; 24; 37:6; 12; 21; 38:4; 16; 17; 39:2; 25; 47:12; Dan 1:3; 18; 2:24; 3:13; 4:6; 5:2; 7; 9:24; Hos 2:14; 7:12; 9:12; 13; 16; Joel 3:1; 2; Amos 3:11; 4:1; 4; 6:10; 8:10; 9:2; 14; Obad 3; 4; Jonah 1:13; Mic 1:15; 4:10; 7:9; Zeph 1:17; 2:2; 3:5; 10; 20; Hag 1:6; 8; Zec 3:8; 4:7; 5:4; 8:8; 10:6; 10(2); 13:9; Mal 3:10; Mt 1:21; 23; 2:8; 13; 3:8; 5:23; 7:18(2); 14:18; 17:17; 21:2; 28:8; Mk 4:20; 7:32; 8:22; 9:19; 11:2; 12:15; 15:22; Lk 1:31; 2:10; 3:8; 5:18; 19; 6:43; 8:14; 15; 9:41; 12:11; 14:21; 15:22; 23; 19:27; 30; Jn 10:16; 14:26; 15:2; 16; 18:29; 19:4; 21:10; Acts 5:28; 7:6; 9:2; 21; 12:4; 17:5; 22:5; 23:10; 15; 17; 18; 20; 24; 24:17; Rom 7:4; 5; 10:6; 7; 15; 1Cor 1:19; 28; 4:5; 17; 9:27; 16:3; 6; 2Cor 11:20; Gal 2:4; 3:24; Eph 6:4; 1Th 4:14; 2Ti 4:11; 13; Titus 3:13; 1Pet 3:18; 2Pet 2:1(2); 11; 2Jn 10; 3Jn 6; Jude 9; Rev 21:24; 26

BRINGETH

Ex 6:7; Lev 11:45; 17:4; 9; Deut 8:7; 14:22; 1Sa 2:6(2); 7; 2Sa 18:26; 22:48; 49; Job 12:6; 22; 19:29; 28:11; Ps 1:3; 14:7; 33:10; 37:7; 53:6; 68:6; 107:28; 30; 135:7; Prov 10:31; 16:30; 18:16; 19:26; 20:26; 21:27; 29:15; 21; 25; 30:33(3); 31:14; Eccl 2:6; Is 8:7; 26:5(2); 40:23; 26; 41:27; 43:17; 52:7(2); 54:16; 61:11; Jer 4:31; 10:13; 51:16; Eze 29:16; Hos 10:1; Nah 1:15; Hag 1:11; Mt 3:10; 7:17(2); 19; 12:35(2); 13:23; 52; 17:1; Mk 4:28; Lk 3:9; 6:43; 45(2); Jn 12:24; 15:5; Col 1:6; Titus 2:11; Heb 1:6; 6:7; Jas 1:15(2)

BRINGING

Ex 12:42; 36:6; Num 5:15; 14:36; 2Sa 19:10; 43; 1Kin 10:22; 2Kin 21:12; 2Chr 9:21; Neh 13:15; Ps 126:6; Jer 17:26(2); Eze 20:9; Dan 9:12; Mt 21:43; Mk 2:3; Lk 24:1; Acts 5:16; Rom 7:23; 2Cor 10:5; Heb 2:10; 7:19; 2Pet 2:5

BROUGHT

Gen 1:12; 21; 2:19; 22; 4:3; 4; 14:16(2); 18; 15:5; 7; 19:16; 17; 20:9; 24:53; 67; 26:10; 27:14; 20; 25(2); 31; 33; 29:13; 23; 30:14; 39; 31:39; 33:11; 37:2; 28; 32; 38:25; 39:1(2); 14; 17; 40:10; 41:14; 47; 43:2; 12; 17; 18(2); 21; 22; 23; 24; 26; 44:8; 46:7; 32; 47:7; 14; 17; 48:10; 12; 13; 50:23; Ex 2:10; 3:12; 8:7; 12; 9:19; 10:8; 13(2); 12:17; 39; 13:3; 9; 14; 16; 15:19; 22; 26; 16:3; 6; 32; 17:3; 18:1; 26; 19:4; 17; 20:2; 22:8; 29:10; 46; 32:1; 3; 4; 6; 8; 11; 21; 23; 33:1; 35:21; 22; 23; 24(2); 25; 27; 29; 36:3(2); 39:33; 40:21; Lev 6:30; 8:6; 13; 14; 18; 22; 24; 9:5; 9; 15; 16; 17; 10:18; 13:2; 9; 14:2; 16:27; 19:36; 22:27; 33; 23:14; 15; 43; 24:11; 25:38; 42; 55; 26:13; 41; 45; Num 6:13; 7:3(2); 9:13; 11:31; 12:15; 13:23; 26; 32; 14:3; 15:33; 36; 41; 16:10; 13; 14; 17:8; 9; 20:4; 16; 21:5; 22:41; 23:7; 14; 22; 28; 24:8; 25:6; 27:5; 31:12; 50; 54; 32:17; Deut 1:25(2); 27; 4:20; 37; 5:6; 15; 6:10; 12; 21; 23; 7:8; 19; 8:14; 15; 9:4; 12; 26; 28; 11:29; 13:5; 10; 16:1; 20:1; 22:19; 26:8; 9; 10; 13; 29:25; 31:20; 21; 33:14; Josh 2:6; 6:23(2); 7:7; 14; 16; 17(2); 18; 23; 24; 8:23; 10:23; 24; 14:7; 22:32; 24:5; 6; 7; 8; 17; 32; Judg 1:7; 2:1; 12; 3:17; 5:25; 6:8(2); 19; 7:5; 25; 11:35; 14:11; 15:13; 16:8; 18; 21; 31; 18:3; 19:3; 21; 25; 21:12; Ruth 1:21; 2:18; 1Sa 1:24; 25; 2:14; 19; 5:1; 2; 10; 6:21; 7:1(2); 8:8; 9:22; 10:18; 27; 12:6; 8; 14:34; 15:15; 20; 16:12; 17:54; 57; 18:27; 19:7; 20:8; 21:8; 14; 15; 22:4; 23:5; 25:27; 35; 28:25; 30:7; 11; 16; 2Sa 1:10; 2:8; 3:22; 26; 4:8; 10; 6:3; 4; 12; 15; 17; 7:6; 18; 8:2; 6; 7; 10; 10:16; 12:30; 31; 13:10; 11; 18; 14:23; 17:28; 19:41; 21:8; 13; 22:20; 23:16; 1Kin 1:3; 38; 53; 2:30; 40; 3:1; 24; 4:21; 28; 5:17; 6:7; 7:51; 8:4; 6; 16; 21; 9:9(2); 28; 10:11(2); 25; 28; 12:28; 13:20; 23; 26; 29; 14:28; 15:15; 17:6; 20; 23; 18:40; 20:9; 39; 22:37; 2Kin 4:5; 20; 42; 5:2; 6; 20; 10:1; 6; 8; 22; 24; 26; 11:4; 12; 19; 12:4; 9; 13; 16; 14:20; 16:14; 17:4; 7; 24; 27; 36; 19:25; 20:11; 20; 22:4; 9; 20; 23:6; 8; 30; 24:16; 25:6; 20; 1Chr 5:26; 10:12; 11:18; 19; 12:40; 13:13; 14:17; 15:28; 16:1; 17:5; 16; 18:2; 6; 7; 8; 11; 20:2; 3; 22:4; 2Chr 1:4; 16; 17(2); 5:1; 5; 7; 6:5; 7:22(2); 8:11; 18; 9:10(2); 12; 14(2); 24; 28; 10:8; 10; 12:11; 13:18; 15:11; 18; 16:2; 17:5; 11(2); 19:4; 22:9; 23:11; 14; 20; 24:10; 11; 14; 25:12; 14; 23; 28; 28:5; 8; 15; 19; 27; 29:4; 16; 21; 23; 31; 32; 30:15; 31:5(2); 6; 12; 32:23; 30; 33:11; 13; 34:9; 14(2); 16; 28; 35:24; 36:10; 17; 18; Ezr 1:7(2); 11; 4:2; 10; 5:14; 6:5(2); 8:18; Neh 4:15; 5:5; 8:2; 16; 9:18; 33; 12:31; 13:9; 12; 15; 16; 19; Est 1:17; 2:7; 8; 20; 6:8; 11; 9:11; Job 4:12; 10:18; 14:21; 21:30; 32; 24:24; 31:18; 42:11; Ps 7:14; 18:19; 20:8; 22:15; 30:3; 35:4; 26; 40:2; 45:14(2); 15; 71:24; 73:19; 78:16; 26; 54; 71; 79:8; 80:8; 81:10; 85:1; 89:40; 90:2; 105:30; 37; 40; 43; 106:42; 43; 107:12; 14; 39; 116:6; 136:11; 142:6; Prov 6:26; 8:24; 25; 30; Eccl 12:4; Song 1:4; 2:4; 3:4; 8:5(2); Is 1:2; 2:12; 5:2; 4; 15; 14:11; 15; 15:1(2); 18:7; 21:14; 23:13; 25:5; 26:18; 29:4; 20; 37:26; 43:14; 23; 45:10; 48:15; 49:21; 51:18(2); 53:7; 59:16; 60:11; 62:9; 63:5; 11; 66:7; 8; Jer 2:6; 7; 27; 7:22; 10:9; 11:4; 7; 19; 15:8; 16:14; 15; 20:3; 15; 23:7; 8; 24:1; 26:23; 27:16; 32:21; 42; 34:11; 13; 16; 35:4; 37:14; 38:22; 39:5; 40:3; 41:16; 44:2; 50:25; 51:10; 52:26; 31; Lam 2:2; 22; 3:2; 4:5; Eze 8:3; 7; 14; 16; 11:1; 24; 12:7(2); 14:22(3); 17:6; 24; 19:3; 4; 9(2); 20:10; 14; 22; 28; 21:7; 23:8; 27; 42; 27:6; 15; 26; 29:5; 30:11; 31:18; 34:4; 37:13; 38:8(2); 39:27; 40:1; 2; 3; 4; 17; 24; 28; 32; 35; 48; 49; 41:1; 42:1(2); 15; 43:1; 5; 44:1; 4; 7; 46:19; 21; 47:1; 2; 3; 4(2); 6; 8; Dan 1:2; 9; 18; 2:25; 3:13; 5:3; 13(2); 15; 23; 6:16; 17; 18; 24; 7:13; 9:14; 15; 11:6; Hos 12:13; Amos 2:10; 3:1; 9:7; Obad 7; Jonah 2:6; Mic 5:3; 6:4; Nah 2:7; Hag 1:9; 2:19; Zec 10:11; Mal 1:13(2); Mt 1:12; 25; 4:24; 8:16; 9:2; 32; 10:18; 11:23; 12:22; 25; 13:8; 26; 14:11(2); 35; 16:8; 17:16; 18:24; 19:13; 21:7; 22:19; 25:20; 27:3; Mk 1:32; 4:8; 21; 29; 6:27; 28; 9:17; 20; 10:13(2); 11:7; 12:16; 13:9; Lk 1:57; 2:7; 22; 27; 3:5; 4:9; 16; 40; 5:11; 18; 7:37; 10:34; 11:17; 12:16; 18:15; 40; 19:35; 21:12; 22:54; 23:14; Jn 1:42; 4:33; 7:45; 8:3; 9:13; 18:16; 19:13; 39; Acts 4:34; 37; 5:2; 15; 19; 21; 26; 27; 36; 6:12; 7:36; 40; 45; 9:8; 27; 30; 39; 11:26; 12:6; 17; 13:1; 17; 14:13; 15:3; 16:16; 20; 30; 34; 39; 17:15; 19; 18:12; 19:12; 19; 24; 37; 20:12; 21:5; 16; 28; 29; 22:3; 24; 30; 23:18; 28; 31; 25:6; 17; 18; 23; 26; 27:24; Rom 15:24; 1Cor 6:12; 15:54; 2Cor 1:16; Gal 2:4; 1Th 3:6; 1Ti 5:10; 6:7; 2Ti 1:10; S:1; Heb 13:11; 20; Jas 5:18; 1Pet 1:13; 2Pet 2:19; Rev 12:5; 13

BROUGHTEST

Ex 32:7; Num 14:13; Deut 9:28; 29; 2Sa 5:2; 1Kin 8:51; 53; 1Chr 11:2; Neh 9:7; 15; 23; Ps 66:11; 12

BUT

Gen 2:6; 17; 20; 3:3; 4:2; 5; 6:8; 18; 8:9; 9:4; 11:30; 12:12; 13:13; 15:4; 10; 16; 16:6; 17:5; 15; 21; 18:15; 22; 27; 32; 19:2; 4; 10; 14; 26; 20:3(2); 4; 12; 21:23; 26; 22:7; 23:6; 13; 24:4; 33; 38; 25:6; 28; 26:29; 27:22; 38; 28:17; 19; 29:17; 20; 31; 30:42; 31:5; 7; 29; 33; 34; 35; 47; 32:28; 34:12; 15; 17; 35:8; 10; 16; 18; 37:11; 22; 35; 38:20; 39:8; 9; 21; 40:14; 22; 23; 41:8; 21; 24; 54; 42:4; 7; 8; 10; 12; 20; 34; 43:5; 34; 44:17; 45:8; 22; 46:12; 47:18; 30; 48:7; 19; 21; 49:19; 24; 50:20(2); Ex 1:12; 16; 17(2); 2:15; 17; 3:22; 4:1; 10; 21; 5:16; 17; 6:3; 9; 7:4; 12; 8:15; 18; 29; 9:6; 30; 32; 10:8; 20; 23; 27; 11:7; 12:9; 44; 13:15; 18; 14:9; 16; 20; 29; 15:19; 16:8; 20; 26; 17:12; 18:22; 26; 19:13; 24; 20:10; 19; 21:13; 14; 18; 28; 29(2); 22:15; 23:11; 22; 24; 24:2; 29:14; 33; 31:15; 32:18; 33:11; 23; 34:13; 20; 21; 34; 35:2; 36:38; 40:37; Lev 1:9; 13; 17; 2:12; 5:8; 11; 6:28; 7:16; 17; 20; 24; 31; 8:17; 9:10; 10:6; 11:4; 5; 6; 11; 23; 36; 38; 12:5; 13:6; 7; 14; 21(2); 23; 26(2); 28; 33; 35; 37; 14:9; 53; 15:28; 16:10; 17:16; 19:14; 15; 18; 24; 34; 20:24; 21:2; 4; 14; 22:11; 13(2); 20; 23; 32; 23:3; 8; 25; 25:4; 17; 28; 31; 34; 36; 40; 43; 46; 52; 26:14; 15; 23; 27; 45; 27:8; 13; 18; 21; 29; Num 1:47; 50; 53; 2:33; 3:38; 4:15; 19; 20; 5:8; 20; 28; 6:12; 7:9; 8:26; 9:13; 22; 10:4; 7(2); 30; 11:6; 20; 26(2); 12:14; 13:31; 14:10; 21; 24; 31; 32; 38; 41; 44; 15:30; 16:9; 30; 41; 18:2; 17; 23; 24; 19:12; 20; 21:22; 23; 22:20; 24; 35; 23:13; 26; 24:1; 4; 11; 13; 16; 17(2);

20; 26:33; 64; 27:3; 28:19; 27; 29:8; 36; 30:5; 8; 9; 12; 14; 15; 31:18; 32:17; 23; 27; 30; 33:55; 35:8; 20; 22; 26; 28; 30; 31; 33; 36:9; **Deut** 1:17; 26; 38; 40; 43; 45; 2:11; 12; 21; 30; 3:7; 19; 26; 28; 4:4; 9; 12; 20; 22(2); 26; 29; 5:3; 14; 31; 7:5; 8; 15; 18; 23; 26; 8:3; 18; 9:4; 5; 19; 10:12; 11:7; 11; 28; 12:5; 10; 14; 18; 13:9; 14:7; 12; 20; 15:3; 6(2); 8; 16:6; 17:6; 16; 18:14; 20; 22; 19:11; 13; 21; 20:12; 14; 16; 17; 21:14; 17; 23; 22:7; 20; 25; 26; 23:5; 11; 20; 22; 24; 25; 24:5; 18; 25:15; 26:14; 28:15; 38; 39; 40; 41; 65; 29:15; 20; 29; 30:14; 17(2); 32:15; 52; 34:4; 6; **Josh** 1:8; 14; 2:4; 6; 22; 5:5; 12; 14; 6:13; 19; 22; 7:1; 3(2); 12; 8:4; 9; 14; 9:12; 19; 21; 10:16; 19; 30; 37; 40; 11:13; 14; 20; 13:13; 33; 14:3; 8; 15:63; 16:10; 17:3(2); 8; 12; 13; 14; 18; 18:7; 21:12; 22:3; 5; 7; 18; 19; 27; 28; 23:8; 9; 13; 24:4; 10; 12; 15; 21; **Judg** 1:6; 19; 21; 25; 27; 29; 30; 32; 33; 35; 2:2; 3; 17(2); 3:15; 16; 19; 4:8; 16; 5:31; 6:10; 13; 34; 39(2); 7:6; 10; 19; 8:20; 9:9; 11; 20; 51; 11:16; 17(2); 18; 20(2); 27; 13:3; 6; 7; 9; 21; 23; 14:4; 6; 9; 13; 16; 20; 15:1(2); 13(2); 19; 16:21; 17:6; 19:10(2); 16; 18; 24; 25; 28; 20:9; 13; 14; 32; 34; 40; 42; 47; **Ruth** 1:14; 17; 2:8; 3:3; 13; 4:4; **1Sa** 1:2; 5(2); 11; 13; 15; 22; 2:15; 16; 18; 25; 30; 4:20; 5:6; 6:3; 9; 7:10; 8:3; 6; 7; 19; 9:4(2); 7; 27; 10:12; 16; 19; 27(2); 12:10; 12; 15(2); 20; 23; 25; 13:8; 14; 16; 20; 22; 14:1; 10; 26; 27; 37; 39; 41; 43; 15:3; 9(2); 19; 21; 16:7(2); 14; 17:9; 15; 33; 42; 45; 50; 54; 18:8(2); 16; 17; 19; 25(2); 19:2; 10; 20:2; 3(2); 5; 7; 13; 15; 22; 39; 21:4; 6; 22:17; 23; 23:14; 24; 27; 24:7; 10; 12; 13; 22; 25:3; 14; 15; 19; 25; 29; 31; 37; 44; 26:3; 7; 11; 19; 23; 28:23(2); 29:2; 8; 30:2; 6; 10; 24; 31:4; **2Sa** 2:8; 10; 21; 31; 3:1; 13; 22; 26; 4:12; 5:17; 23; 6:10; 7:2; 6; 15; 19; 8:4; 9:10; 10:11; 11:1; 9; 13; 27; 12:3; 4; 12; 17; 19; 21; 23(2); 13:3; 9; 14; 16; 20; 21; 25; 27; 34; 37; 14:2; 6; 25; 29; 15:3; 10; 20; 26; 34; 16:18; 17:16; 18; 18:3(2); 20(2); 22; 23; 29; 19:4; 21; 27; 28; 37; 20:2; 3; 5; 10; 21; 21:2; 7; 8; 17; 22:19; 28; 42(2); 23:6; 7; 12; 16; 21; 23; 24:3; 17; 24; **1Kin** 1:1; 4; 8; 10; 19; 26; 52; 2:7; 8; 9; 26; 30; 33; 3:7; 11; 21; 22(2); 23; 26(2); 5:4; 7:1; 31; 8:16; 19; 27; 41; 9:6(2); 22(2); 24; 11:1; 10; 12; 13; 22; 32; 34; 35; 39; 12:8; 10; 11; 14; 17; 20; 22; 13:18; 22; 33; 14:4; 9; 14; 15:14; 16:22; 25; 17:1; 12; 13; 18:12; 18; 21; 22; 25; 26; 19:4; 11(2); 12; 20:9; 16; 23; 27; 28; 30; 21:5; 15; 25; 29; 22:8(2); 16; 18; 24; 30; 31; 48; 49; **2Kin** 1:3; 4; 6; 16; 2:10; 17; 19; 3:2; 5; 11; 15; 18; 24; 26; 4:27; 31; 41; 5:1; 11; 15; 16(2); 17; 20(2); 25; 6:5; 12; 19; 32(2); 7:2; 4; 10; 19; 8:13; 9:15; 18; 27; 35; 10:4; 9; 18; 19; 23; 31; 11:2; 15; 12:3; 6; 7; 9; 14; 13:6; 7; 11; 19; 22; 14:6(2); 11; 19; 27; 15:25; 16:3; 5; 17:2; 14; 18; 19; 36; 39; 40; 18:6; 12; 20(2); 22; 27; 36; 19:18; 27; 20:10; 21:9; 22:10; 23:9; 29; 35; 25:12; 25; **1Chr** 2:30; 34; 4:27; 5:1; 2; 6:49; 56; 7:14; 10:4; 11:18(2); 25; 12:17; 19; 13:13; 15:2; 16:5; 19; 26; 17:1; 5; 14; 18:4; 19:3; 12; 18; 20:1; 7; 21:3; 6; 8; 13; 17(2); 24; 30; 22:8; 23:11; 17; 22; 24:2; 27:23; 24; 28:3; 9; 29:1; 14; **2Chr** 1:4; 11; 2:6; 4:6; 5:9; 6:2; 6; 8; 9; 18; 32; 7:19; 8:8; 9(2); 10:8; 10; 11; 14(2); 17; 18; 11:2; 12:7; 13:10; 11; 13; 21; 15:2; 4; 5; 17; 16:12; 17:4; 18:6; 7(2); 15; 17; 29; 31; 19:6; 20:10; 12; 15; 21:3; 13; 20; 22:10; 11; 23:6(2); 7; 24:15; 19; 22; 25; 25:2; 4(3); 7; 8; 9; 13; 20; 27; 26:16; 18; 28:1; 9; 10; 20; 21; 23; 27; 29:34; 30:8; 10; 18; 32:8; 9; 25; 33:2; 10; 22; 23; 25; 35:13; 21(2); 22; 36:13; 16; **Ezr** 2:59; 62; 3:6; 12; 4:3(2); 5:5; 12; 13; 8:22; 9:9; 10:13; **Neh** 1:9; 2:2; 14; 19; 20; 3:3; 5; 14; 15; 4:1; 7; 5:15(2); 6:2; 8; 12; 7:4; 61; 64; 9:16; 17(2); 28; 29; 33; 11:3; 21; 13:2; 6; 24; **Est** 1:12; 16; 17; 2:15; 3:2; 15; 4:4; 11; 14; 5:9; 12; 6:12; 13; 7:4; 9:10; 15; 16(2); 18; 25; **Job** 1:11; 2:5; 6; 10; 3:9; 21; 4:2; 5; 16; 5:3; 15; 6:1; 14; 25; 7:21; 8:9; 15(2); 9:2; 11; 15; 18; 35; 11:5; 20; 12:2; 3; 7; 13:4; 15; 14:10; 21; 22; 16:5; 7; 12; 20; 17:10; 19:7(2); 28; 20:5; 13; 21:1; 22:8; 18; 20; 23:6; 8(2); 9; 10; 13; 24:24; 26:1; 14(2); 27:17; 19; 28:12; 30:1; 31:32; 32:8; 16; 35:10; 12; 15; 36:6; 7; 12; 13; 17; 37:21; 38:11; 40:5(2); 42:5; **Ps** 1:2; 4; 6; 2:12; 3:3; 4:3; 5:7; 11; 6:3; 7:9; 9:7; 20; 11:5; 13:5; 15:4; 16:3; 18:18; 27; 41(2); 20:7; 8; 22:2; 3; 6; 9; 19; 24; 26:11; 28:3; 30:5(2); 31:6; 11; 14; 32:10; 34:10; 19; 35:13; 15; 20; 37:9; 11; 17; 20; 21; 28; 36; 38; 39; 38:13; 19; 40:17; 41:10; 44:3; 7; 9; 49:15; 50:16; 21; 52:7; 8; 55:13; 21; 23(2); 59:0; 16; 62:4; 63:9; 11(2); 64:7; 66:12; 19; 68:3; 6; 21; 69:13; 20(2); 29; 70:5; 71:7; 14; 73:2; 4; 25; 26; 28; 74:6; 75:7; 8; 9; 10; 77:10; 78:7; 30; 38; 39; 50; 52; 53; 57; 68; 81:11; 15; 82:7; 85:8; 86:15; 88:13; 89:24; 38; 90:4; 91:7; 92:8; 10; 94:15; 22; 96:5; 102:12; 26; 27; 103:17; 105:12; 106:7; 14; 15; 25; 35; 43; 109:4; 16; 21; 28(2); 115:1; 3; 5(2); 6(2); 7(2); 16; 18; 118:10; 11; 13; 17; 18; 119:23; 61; 67; 69; 70; 78; 81; 87; 95; 96; 113; 161; 163; 120:7; 125:1; 5; 127:1; 5; 130:4; 132:18; 135:16(2); 17; 136:15; 138:6; 139:4; 12; 141:8; 142:4; 145:20; 146:9; **Prov** 1:7; 25; 28(2); 33; 2:22; 3:1; 32; 33; 34; 35; 4:18; 5:4; 6:31; 32; 8:36; 9:12; 18; 10:1; 2; 3; 4; 5; 6; 7; 8; 9; 10; 11; 12; 13; 14; 17; 19; 21; 23; 24; 25; 27; 28; 29; 30; 31; 32; 11:1; 2; 3; 4; 5; 6; 9; 11; 12; 13; 14; 17; 18; 20; 21; 23; 24; 26; 27; 28; 12:1; 2; 3; 4; 5; 6; 7; 8; 10; 11; 12; 13; 15; 16; 17; 18; 19(2); 20; 21; 22; 23; 24; 25; 26; 27; 13:1; 2; 3; 4; 5; 6; 8; 9; 10; 11; 12; 13; 15; 16; 17; 18; 19; 20; 21; 23; 24; 25; 14:1; 2; 3; 4; 5; 6; 8; 9; 11; 12; 15; 16; 18; 20; 21; 22; 23; 24; 25; 28; 29; 30; 31; 32; 33; 34; 35; 15:1; 2; 4; 5; 6; 7; 8; 9; 13; 14; 15; 18; 19; 20; 21; 22; 25; 26; 27; 28; 29; 32; 16:2; 9; 14; 22; 25; 33; 17:3; 9; 22; 24; 18:2; 14; 17; 23; 19:4; 12; 16; 20:3; 5; 6; 14; 15; 17; 21; 22; 21:2; 5; 8; 12; 13; 15; 20; 26; 28; 29; 31; 22:3; 15; 23:7; 17; 24:16; 25; 25:2; 27:3; 4; 6; 7; 12; 28:1; 2; 4; 5; 7; 10; 11; 12; 13; 14; 16; 18; 19; 20; 25; 26; 27; 28; 29:2; 3; 4; 6; 7; 8; 10; 11; 15; 16; 18; 23; 25; 26; 30:24; 26; 31:29; 30; **Eccl** 1:4; 2:14; 26; 3:12; 4:1; 10; 11; 5:7; 12; 14; 6:2; 7:4; 12; 14; 23; 26; 28(2); 29; 8:13; 9:5; 11; 18; 10:2; 10; 12; 19; 11:8; 9; **Song** 1:5; 6; 3:1; 2; 4(2); 5:2; 6(3); 6:9; **Is** 1:3; 6; 20; 21; 5:6; 7(2); 12; 16; 25; 6:9(2); 13; 7:1; 12; 13; 25; 8:14; 9:5; 10(2); 12; 17; 21; 10:4; 7; 20; 11:4; 14; 13:21; 14:19; 16:6; 12; 14; 17:11; 13; 22:11; 24:16; 26:11; 13; 28:7; 13; 27; 29:8(2); 9(2); 13; 23; 30:1(2); 5; 16; 20; 31:1; 2; 8; 32:8; 33:21; 34:11; 12; 35:8; 9; 36:5(2); 7; 12; 21; 37:19; 28; 38:17; 40:8; 31; 41:8; 42:19; 20(2); 22; 43:1; 22(2); 24; 45:17; 46:2; 47:9; 48:1; 10; 49:14; 25; 51:6; 8; 15; 21; 23; 53:5; 54:7; 8; 10; 15; 55:10; 11; 57:3; 13(2); 20; 59:2; 9(2); 11(2); 60:2; 10; 18; 19; 61:6; 62:4; 9; 63:10; 18; 64:6; 8; 65:6; 11; 12; 13(3); 14; 18; 20; 66:2; 4; 5; **Jer** 1:7; 19; 2:7; 11; 25; 27; 28; 34; 3:1; 7; 8; 10; 19; 4:22; 5:3(2); 5; 10; 23; 6:16; 17; 19; 7:12; 13(2); 23; 24(2); 26; 27(2); 28; 32; 8:6; 7; 15; 9:3; 8; 14; 24; 10:5; 8; 10; 19; 24; 11:8(2); 12; 19; 20; 12:3; 13(2); 17; 13:11; 14; 17; 14:12; 13; 15:19; 20; 16:4; 15; 17:6; 8; 18(2); 22; 23(2); 24; 27; 18:12; 23; 19:6; 20:3; 9; 11; 12; 21:9; 14; 22:5; 10; 12; 17(2); 21; 27; 23:8; 22; 38; 25:3; 4; 26:5; 15; 21; 27:11; 18; 28:13; 15; 29:19; 30:7; 9; 11; 31:30; 33; 32:4; 23; 34; 40; 33:5; 34:3; 5; 11; 14; 16; 35:6; 7; 10; 11; 14(2); 15; 16; 17(2); 36:20; 25; 26(2); 31; 37:2; 10; 14; 38:2; 4; 6; 18; 20; 21; 23; 25; 39:5; 10; 12; 17; 18; 40:4; 10; 14; 16; 41:8; 11; 15; 42:2; 13; 14; 21; 43:3; 5; 44:5; 14; 17; 18; 45:5; 46:17; 20; 27; 28(2); 48:30; 45; 49:10; 12; 19; 39; 50:13; 44; 51:9; 26; 62; 52:8; 16; **Lam** 1:19; 2:14; 3:2; 32; 5:22; **Eze** 2:8; 3:5; 7; 14; 18; 19; 20; 25; 27; 7:4; 14; 16; 20; 26; 8:6; 9:6; 10; 10:11; 11:7; 11; 12; 21; 12:16; 23; 28; 14:11; 14; 16; 18; 20; 16:5; 15; 32; 33; 43; 47; 51; 61; 17:14; 15; 18:5; 7; 11; 16; 21; 24; 19:12; 20:8; 9; 13; 14; 16; 18; 24; 39; 21:23; 22:30; 24:23; 28:9; 29:4; 16; 30:24; 25; 32:27; 33:5; 6(2); 8; 9; 11; 13; 17; 19; 24; 31(2); 32; 34:3; 4; 8; 16; 18(2); 28; 36:8; 21; 22; 37:8; 23; 38:8; 39:2; 28; 41:6; 42:6; 14; 44:8; 13; 14; 15; 22; 25; 46:1; 2; 9(2); 17(2); 18; 47:11; **Dan** 1:4; 8; 2:6; 9(2); 28; 30(2); 41; 43; 44; 49; 3:15; 18; 4:7; 8; 18; 5:8; 15; 20; 23; 6:4; 13; 7:18; 26; 28; 8:3; 4; 7; 17; 18; 22; 24; 25; 27; 9:7; 18; 26; 10:1; 7; 13(2); 21(2); 11:6(2); 7; 10; 11; 12; 14; 16; 17; 18; 19; 20; 21; 25; 27; 29; 32; 34; 38; 41; 43; 44; 12:4; 8; 10(2); 13; **Hos** 1:6; 7; 2:7(2); 5:6; 6:7; 7:16; 8:4; 6; 12; 13; 14; 9:3; 8; 10; 13; 10:11; 11:3; 5; 12; 13:1; 4; 9; 14:9; **Joel** 2:20; 3:16; 20; **Amos** 1:4; 7; 10; 12; 14; 2:2; 5; 12; 3:7; 8; 4:8; 5:5; 11(2); 24; 26; 6:6; 14; 7:13; 14; 8:11; **Obad** 12; 17; **Jonah** 1:3; 4; 5; 13; 2:9; 3:8; 4:1; 7; **Mic** 1:12; 3:4; 8; 4:1; 4; 12; 5:2; 6:8; 14(2); 15(3); **Nah** 1:8; 2:8(2); 3:17; **Hab** 2:3; 4; 5; 20; **Zeph** 1:13(2); 18; 3:5; 7; **Hag** 1:6(3); 2:16(2); **Zec** 1:4; 6; 15; 21; 4:6; 7:11; 14; 8:11; 13; 9:7; 11:6; 16; 13:5; 8; 14:7(2); 11; **Mal** 1:4(2); 12; 14; 2:8; 9; 3:2; 7; 8; 4:2; **Mt** 1:20; 2:19; 22; 3:7; 11; 12; 14; 4:4(2); 5:13(2); 15; 17; 19; 22(2); 28; 32; 33; 34; 37; 39(2); 44; 6:3; 6; 7; 13; 15; 17; 18; 20; 23; 33; 7:3; 15; 17; 21; 8:4; 8; 12; 20; 22; 24; 27; 9:6; 8; 12(2); 13(2); 14; 15; 17; 18; 21; 22; 24; 25; 31; 34; 36; 37; 10:6; 13; 17; 19; 20; 22; 23; 28(2); 30; 33; 34; 11:8; 9; 16; 19; 22; 24; 27; 12:2; 3; 4; 6; 7; 15; 24(2); 28; 31; 32; 36; 39(2); 48; 13:8; 11; 12; 16; 20; 21; 23; 25; 26; 29; 30; 32; 38; 48; 57; 14:6; 16; 17; 24; 27; 30; 15:3; 5; 8; 9; 11; 13; 18; 20; 23; 24(2); 26; 16:3; 4; 12; 15; 17; 23(2); 17:12(2); 21; 18:6; 7; 16; 17; 22; 25; 28; 30; 19:6; 8; 11; 14; 17(2); 22; 26(2); 30; 20:10; 12; 13; 16; 22; 23(2); 25; 26(2); 28; 31; 21:13; 19; 21; 26; 28; 29; 32; 37; 38; 44; 46; 22:5; 7; 8; 14; 18; 30; 31; 32; 34; 23:3; 4; 5; 8; 11; 13; 16; 18; 25; 27; 28; 24:6; 13; 20; 22; 35; 36(2); 37; 43; 48; 25:4; 9(2); 12; 18; 29; 33; 46; 26:5; 8; 11; 24; 29; 32; 39; 41; 54; 56; 58; 60; 63; 70; 27:20; 23; 24; 28:17; **Mk** 1:8; 30; 44; 45(2); 2:6; 7; 10; 17(2); 18; 20; 22; 26; 3:4; 7; 20; 29(2); 4:6; 11; 15; 17; 22; 29; 32; 34; 5:6; 19; 26; 28; 33; 39; 40; 6:4(2); 9; 16; 19; 49; 56; 7:5; 6; 11; 15; 19; 24; 27; 36; 8:28; 29; 33(2); 35; 9:13; 22; 27; 29; 32; 34; 37; 39; 50; 10:6; 8; 14; 18; 24; 27; 30; 31; 38; 40(2); 42; 43(2); 45; 48; 11:13; 17; 23; 26; 32; 12:7; 12; 14; 15; 25; 27; 32; 44; 13:7; 9; 11(3); 13; 14; 17; 20; 23; 24; 31; 32(2); 14:2; 7; 21; 28; 29; 31; 36; 38; 49; 56; 59; 61; 68; 71; 15:3; 5; 9; 11; 23; 16:7; 16; **Lk** 1:13; 60; 2:19; 37; 44; 51; 3:16; 17; 19; 4:4; 25; 26; 30; 5:2; 14; 15; 21; 22; 24; 30; 31; 32; 33; 35; 38; 6:4; 8; 24; 27; 35; 40; 41; 49; 7:7; 25; 26; 28; 30; 35; 44; 45; 46; 47; 8:10; 15; 16; 23; 27; 38; 42; 50; 52(2); 56; 9:9; 13(2); 19; 20; 24; 27; 32; 43; 45; 55; 56; 58; 59; 60; 61; 10:2; 10; 12; 14; 20; 22(2); 29; 33; 40; 42; 11:4; 15; 17; 20; 22; 28; 29; 33; 34; 39; 41; 42; 12:5; 7; 9; 10; 20; 31; 45; 48; 50; 51; 56; 13:3; 5; 27; 14:10; 13; 34; 35; 15:20; 22; 30; 16:15; 25(2); 30; 17:1(2); 7; 17; 25; 29; 18:4; 13; 15; 16; 39; 19:14; 27; 42; 46; 47; 20:6; 10; 14; 18; 21; 23; 35; 38; 21:4; 7; 9(2); 12; 18; 23; 33; 22:21; 22; 26(2); 27; 32; 36; 42; 48; 53; 56; 23:9; 21; 25; 28(2); 40; 41; 24:6; 16; 21; 24; 29; 37; 49; **Jn** 1:8; 12; 13; 17; 20; 26; 31; 33; 2:9; 10; 21; 24; 3:8; 13; 15; 16; 17; 18; 21; 28; 29; 30; 36; 4:2; 14(2); 23; 32; 5:7; 17; 18; 19; 22; 24; 30; 34(2); 36; 42; 47; 6:9; 20; 22; 26; 27; 32; 36; 38; 39; 64; 7:6; 7; 10(2); 12; 16; 18; 22; 24; 26; 27; 28; 29; 30; 39; 41; 44; 49; 8:5; 6; 10; 12; 14; 16; 26; 28; 35; 37; 40; 42; 49; 55(2); 59; 9:3; 9; 18; 21; 28; 31; 41; 10:1; 2; 5; 6; 8; 10; 12; 18; 26; 33; 38; 39; 41; 11:4; 10; 11; 13; 20; 22; 30; 42; 46; 51; 52; 54; 12:2; 6; 8; 9; 10; 16; 24; 27; 30; 37; 42; 44; 47; 49; 13:7; 9; 10(2); 18; 36; 14:6; 10; 17; 19; 24; 26; 31; 15:15; 16; 19(2); 21; 22; 24; 25; 26; 16:4; 5; 6; 7; 12; 13; 20(2); 21; 22; 25(2); 33; 17:9; 11; 12; 15; 20; 25; 18:16; 23; 28; 36; 39; 40; 19:9; 12; 13; 15(2); 21; 24; 33; 34; 38; 20:7; 11; 17; 24; 25; 27; 31; 21:4(2); 8; 18; 23; **Acts** 1:4; 5; 8; 2:14; 15; 16; 34; 3:6; 14; 18; 4:15; 17; 19; 20; 32; 5:1; 3; 4; 13; 19; 21; 22; 23; 39; 6:4; 7:9; 12; 17; 25; 27; 39; 47; 55; 8:9; 12; 20; 40; 9:7; 8; 15; 21; 22; 24; 26; 27; 29; 40; 10:10; 14; 26; 28; 35; 41; 11:4; 8; 9; 16; 19; 12:5; 9; 14; 15; 16; 17; 20; 24; 13:8; 14; 25; 30; 37; 45; 46; 50; 51; 14:2; 4; 15:5; 11; 20; 38; 16:1; 7; 18; 28; 37(2); 17:5; 13; 14; 21; 30; 18:9; 15; 19; 21(2); 19:9(2); 15; 22; 26; 27; 34; 39; 20:20; 24; 21:13; 24; 39; 22:9; 28; 23:6; 8; 9; 21; 29; 24:7; 11; 14; 27; 25:4; 9; 11; 19; 21; 25; 26:16; 20; 25(2); 29; 27:10; 14; 21; 22; 27; 39; 41; 43; 28:6; 16; 19; 22; **Rom** 1:13; 21; 32; 2:2; 5; 8(2); 10; 13; 25; 29(2); 3:4; 5; 21; 27; 4:2; 4; 5(2); 10; 12; 13; 16; 20; 24; 5:3; 8; 11; 13; 15; 16; 20; 6:10; 11; 13; 14; 15; 17(2); 22; 23; 7:2; 3; 6; 7; 8; 9; 13; 14; 15; 17; 18; 19; 20; 23; 25; 8:1; 4; 5; 6; 9(2); 10; 11; 13; 15; 20; 23; 24; 25; 26; 32; 9:7; 8; 10; 11; 13; 16; 20; 24; 31; 32; 10:2; 6; 8; 16; 18; 19; 20; 21; 11:4; 6; 7; 11; 15; 18(2); 20; 22; 28; 12:2; 3; 16; 19; 21; 13:1; 3; 4; 5; 8; 14; 14:1; 10; 13; 14; 15; 17; 20; 15:3; 21; 23; 25; 16:4; 18; 19; 26; **1Cor** 1:10; 14; 17; 18; 23; 24; 27; 30; 2:4; 5; 7; 9; 10; 11; 12; 13; 14; 15; 16; 3:1; 5; 6; 7; 10; 15; 4:3; 4; 10(3); 14; 19(2); 20; 5:3; 8; 11; 13; 6:6; 11(3); 12(2); 13(2); 17; 18; 7:4(2); 6; 7; 9; 10; 11; 12; 14; 15(2); 17; 19; 21; 28(2); 29; 32; 33; 34; 35; 36; 37; 38; 39; 40; 8:1; 3; 4; 6(2); 8; 9; 12; 9:12; 15; 17; 21; 24; 25; 27; 10:5; 13(3); 20; 23(2); 24; 28; 29; 33; 11:3; 5; 6; 7; 8; 9; 12; 15; 16; 17; 28; 32; 12:3; 4; 5; 6; 7; 11; 14; 18; 20(2); 24; 25; 31; 13:6; 8; 10; 11; 12(2); 13; 14:1; 2; 3; 4; 5; 14; 17; 20; 22(3); 24; 28; 33; 34; 38; 15:6; 10(3); 13; 20; 23; 27; 35; 37; 38; 39; 40; 46; 51; 57; 16:7; 8; 11; 12(2); **2Cor** 1:9(2); 12; 18; 19; 24; 2:1; 2; 4; 5(2); 13; 17(2); 3:3(2); 5; 6(2); 7; 14; 15; 18; 4:2(2); 3; 5; 7; 8; 9(2); 12; 16; 17; 18(2); 5:4; 11; 12; 15; 6:4; 12; 7:5; 7; 8; 9; 10; 12; 14; 8:5; 8; 10; 14; 16; 17; 19; 21; 22; 9:6; 12; 10:1; 2; 4; 10; 12; 13(2); 15; 17; 18; 11:3; 6(2); 12; 17; 12:5; 6; 14(2); 16; 19; 13:3; 4; 6; 7; 8; **Gal** 1:1; 7; 8; 11; 12; 15; 17; 19; 23; 2:2; 3; 6; 7; 11; 12; 14; 16; 17; 20; 3:11; 12; 15; 16; 18; 20; 22; 23; 25; 4:2; 4; 7; 9; 14; 17; 18; 23(2); 26; 29; 31; 5:6; 10; 13; 15; 18; 22; 6:4; 8; 13; 14; 15; **Eph** 1:21; 2:4; 13; 19; 4:7; 9; 15; 20; 28; 29; 5:3; 4; 8; 11; 13; 15; 17; 18; 27; 29; 32; 6:4; 6; 12; 21; **Phil** 1:12; 17; 20; 22; 28; 29; 2:3; 4; 7; 12; 19; 22; 24; 25; 27(2); 3:1; 7; 8(2); 9; 12; 13; 4:6; 10(2); 15; 17; 18; 19; **Col** 1:26; 2:17; 3:8; 11; 22; 25; **1Th** 1:5; 8; 2:2; 4(2); 7; 8; 13; 17; 18; 3:6; 4:7; 8; 9; 10; 13; 5:1; 4; 6; 8; 9; 15; **2Th** 2:12; 13; 3:3; 8; 9; 11; 13; 15; **1Ti** 1:8; 9; 13; 2:10; 12(2); 14; 3:3; 15; 4:7; 8; 12; 5:1; 4; 6; 8; 11; 13; 19; 23; 6:2; 4; 6; 9; 11; 17; **2Ti** 1:7; 8; 9; 10; 17; 2:9; 14; 16; 20(2); 22; 23; 24; 3:5; 9; 10; 11; 13; 14; 4:3; 5; 8; 13; 16; 20; **Titus** 1:3; 8; 15(2); 16; 2:1; 10; 3:2; 4; 5; 9; **Philem** 1:11; 14(2); 16(2); 22; **Heb** 1:8; 11; 12; 13; 2:6; 8; 9; 16; 3:4; 6; 13; 17; 18; 4:2; 13; 15; 5:4; 5; 14; 6:8; 9; 12; 7:3; 6; 8; 16; 19; 21; 24; 28; 8:6; 9:7; 11; 12; 23; 24; 26; 27; 10:3; 5; 12; 25; 27; 32; 38; 39(2); 11:6; 13; 16; 12:8; 10; 11; 13; 22; 26(2); 13:4; 14; 16; 19; **Jas** 1:4; 6; 10; 11; 14; 22; 25(2); 26; 2:6; 9; 20; 3:8; 14; 15; 17; 4:6(2); 11(2); 16; 5:12(2); **1Pet** 1:12; 15; 19; 20; 23; 25; 2:4; 7; 9; 10(2); 16; 18; 20; 23; 25; 3:4; 9; 12; 14; 15; 18; 21; 4:2; 6; 7; 13; 14; 15; 16; 5:2(2); 3; 10; **2Pet** 1:9; 16; 21; 2:1; 4; 5; 10; 12; 16; 22; 3:7; 8; 9(2); 10; 18; **1Jn** 1:7; 2:2; 5; 7; 11; 16; 17; 19(2); 20; 21; 22; 23; 27(2); 3:2; 17; 18; 4:1; 10; 18; 5:5; 6; 18; **2Jn** 1; 5; 8; 12; **3Jn** 9; 11(2); 13; 14; **Jude** 6; 9; 10(2); 17; 20; **Rev** 2:6; 9(2); 14; 24; 25; 3:5; 9; 9:4; 5; 11; 10:7; 9; 11:2; 12:12; 14:3; 17:12; 19:12; 20:5; 6; 21:8; 27; 22:3

BY

Gen 7:2(2); 3; 9:6; 11; 10:5; 32; 14:6; 15; 16:2; 7(2); 18:2; 8; 19:36; 20:3; 21:23; 28; 29; 22:13; 16; 23:20; 24:3; 11; 13; 30; 43; 25:11; 13; 16(2); 26:18; 27:40; 29:2; 30:3; 27; 40; 31:24; 31; 39(2); 40; 53; 32:16; 33:8; 35:4; 36:37; 40; 37:28; 38:14; 16; 18; 19; 20; 21; 24; 25; 39:10(2); 12; 16; 41:1; 3; 31; 32; 47; 42:15; 16; 23; 38; 43:32(3); 45:1; 7; 23; 24; 47:13; 48:7; 49:17; 22; 24; 25(2); **Ex** 2:3; 5; 15; 23(2); 3:7; 19; 4:4; 13; 24; 6:3(2); 7:4; 15; 8:24; 9:35; 12:14; 17; 26; 31; 51; 13:3; 14; 16; 21(3); 22(2); 14:2; 9; 20; 21; 15:16; 27; 16:3(2); 18:8; 13; 14; 19:19; 20:26; 21:3(2); 4; 22:25; 26; 23:30; 25:14; 26:9(2); 28:28; 29:11; 18; 25; 28; 32; 38; 41; 43; 30:4; 6; 20; 31:2; 32:13; 27; 33:6; 12; 17; 21; 22(2); 34:6; 7; 35:29; 30; 36:16(2); 37:3; 5; 27; 38:21; 39:4; 21; 40:29; 38(2); **Lev** 1:5; 9; 13; 16; 17; 2:2; 3; 9; 10; 11; 14; 16; 3:3; 4; 5; 9(2); 10; 11; 14; 15; 16; 4:9; 35; 5:12; 15; 17; 6:2; 17; 18; 7:4; 5; 25; 30; 34; 35; 36; 8:21; 28; 36; 10:11; 12; 13; 15(2); 16:21; 31; 19:12; 31; 20:25(3); 21:6; 9; 21; 22:4; 22; 27; 23:8; 13; 18; 25; 27; 36(2); 37; 24:7; 8; 9(2); 25:39; 47(3); 26:7; 8; 23(2); 26; 46; 27:2; **Num** 1:2(2); 3; 17; 18(2); 20(3); 22(3); 24(2); 26(2); 28(2); 30(2); 32(2); 34(2); 36(2); 38(2); 40(2); 42; 45; 52(2); 2:2; 12; 17; 20; 25; 27; 32; 34; 3:15; 17; 18; 19; 20; 26(2); 43; 47; 49; 4:2; 22; 26(2); 29; 32; 36; 37; 38; 40; 42; 45; 49; 5:2; 19; 6:9; 11; 7:84; 9:6; 7; 10; 16(2); 21(2); 23; 10:13; 34; 11:31; 12:2(2); 13:3; 22; 29(2); 14:3; 14(2); 18; 25; 36; 37; 43; 15:3; 10; 13; 14; 23; 24; 25; 28; 16:40; 18:8(2); 11; 17; 19; 32; 20:17; 18; 19; 23; 21:1; 4; 18; 22; 33; 22:1; 5; 23:3; 6; 15; 17; 24:6; 26:3; 55; 63(2); 27:2; 23; 28:2; 3(2); 6; 8; 13; 19; 24; 29:6; 13; 36; 30:3; 10; 31:12; 17; 18; 35; 33:2; 10; 48; 49; 50; 54; 34:3; 13; 18; 35:1; 20; 30; 33; 36:2(2); 13(2); **Deut** 1:2; 7; 19; 22; 33(3); 40; 2:1; 8(2); 27; 30; 36(2); 3:12; 4:34(7); 48; 5:5; 15; 31; 6:7; 13; 7:22; 8:3(2); 9:29(2); 10:20; 11:19; 30; 12:30; 14:22; 15:20; 16:1; 18:1; 20:19; 21:5; 17; 22:4; 23:10(2); 24:9; 25:2; 11; 17; 18; 27:16; 28:10; 68; 29:16; 33:12; 14(2); 29; **Josh** 2:12; 15; 18; 3:4(2); 4:6; 5:1; 4; 5; 7; 13; 7:14(2); 16; 17; 18; 8:3; 15; 9:13; 18; 19; 10:18; 11:7; 23; 13:6; 14; 16; 22; 29; 31; 32; 14:2(2); 15:1; 6; 8; 16:1; 6; 8; 17:2(2); 18:9; 20; 19:49; 51; 20:2; 8; 9; 21:2; 4; 5; 6; 7; 8(2); 9; 40(2); 22:9; 10; 23:4; 7; 24:26; **Judg** 2:18; 3:1; 4(2); 15; 19(2); 4:11; 5:10; 19; 22; 6:11; 25; 27(2); 28; 30; 36; 37; 7:1; 5; 7; 12; 8:11; 9:6; 9; 25; 32; 34; 37(2); 11:18; 26; 16:5; 26; 17:10; 18:3; 16; 28; 19:11; 14; 20:5; 9; 21:7; 11; 12; **Ruth** 2:8; 21; 23; 4:1; **1Sa** 1:7; 9; 26; 2:3; 9; 16; 23; 28; 3:21; 4:13; 18; 20; 5:2; 6:8; 9; 9:23; 10:2; 19(2); 21; 11:7; 9; 14:4; 6(2); 36; 16:9; 20; 17:2; 23; 26; 35; 43; 52; 18:25; 30; 20:7; 9; 19; 25(2); 23:7; 24:3; 21; 25:13; 16; 20; 22; 34; 26:3; 7; 24(2); 27:1; 28:6(3); 8(2); 10; 15(2); 17; 29:1; 2(2); 30:15; 24; **2Sa** 1:6; 12; 2:13; 15; 16; 24; 3:5; 18; 6:2; 7; 10:2; 8; 11:14; 12:14; 25; 13:31; 32; 34; 15:30; 36; 16:2; 13; 17:11; 17; 22; 18:4(3); 23; 19:3; 7; 37; 20:9; 11; 12; 21; 21:10(2); 22(2); 22:9; 30(2); 35; 23:2; 4; 15; 16; 24:16; **1Kin** 1:9(2); 17; 27; 30; 2:8; 23; 25; 29; 42; 3:5; 4:12; 20; 5:9; 11; 14; 6:21; 22; 7:20; 8:38(2); 43; 53; 56; 9:8; 10:5; 25; 29; 12:15; 13:1(2); 2; 5; 9(2); 10; 17(2); 18; 24(3); 25(2); 28; 32; 14:4; 18; 15:13; 29; 30; 16:7; 12; 13(2); 34; 17:3; 5; 16; 20; 24; 18:4; 6(2); 13; 24; 19:2; 11; 19; 20:14(2); 38; 39(2); 21:1; 23; 22:8; 19; 28; **2Kin** 2:1; 7; 11; 13; 23; 3:11; 20; 4:8; 9; 27; 5:1; 2; 6:14; 26; 30; 8:8; 21; 9:27(2); 36; 10:6; 10; 33; 11:11; 14(2); 16(2); 19; 13:7; 25; 14:7; 9; 25; 27; 16:15; 17:4; 6; 13(3); 23; 18:11; 17; 31; 19:7; 11; 23; 28(2); 33(2); 20:11; 21:10; 23:3; 7; 11; 24:2; 25:4(3); **1Chr** 1:48; 3:3; 4:38; 41; 5:7; 10; 17; 6:15; 61; 63; 65(2); 78; 7:4; 5; 7; 9; 11; 29; 8:28; 9:1; 22; 23; 28; 11:3; 11; 14; 18; 12:22; 31; 14:11; 15:16; 16:41; 17:21; 18:3; 19:4; 9; 20:8(2); 21:15; 25; 26; 23:3(2); 24(2); 27; 31; 24:5; 27; 26:16; 25; 27:1; 28:1; 12; 14(2); 15(2); 16; 17(2); 18; 19; 29:5; 8; **2Chr** 1:17; 2:16; 3:3; 5:11; 14; 6:23(4); 33; 34; 7:6; 12; 14; 20; 21; 8:14; 18; 9:4; 18; 24; 10:15; 12:7; 13:5; 16:14; 18:7; 27; 19:5; 20:15; 16; 21:9; 15(3); 19; 22:7; 23:10(2); 13; 15; 18(2); 24:11(2); 13; 25:18; 26:11(2); 15; 28:15; 29:9; 15; 25; 27; 30:12; 21; 31:6; 15; 17(2); 19(2); 32:11(2); 33:8; 34:14; 35:4; 6; 20; 36:13; 15; 21; 22; **Ezr** 1:1; 8; 2:62; 3:4; 11; 4:16; 23; 5:5; 6:9; 7:23; 8:3; 18; 20; 31; 33; 34(2); 9:11; 10:16; 17; 44; **Neh** 1:10(2); 2:6; 13(2); 15(2); 3:15; 23; 25; 4:3; 12; 18(2); 7:3; 5; 64; 8:14; 18; 9:9; 12(2); 14; 19(2); 30; 10:29; 34; 35; 12:37; 13:18; 25; 26; **Est** 1:12; 15; 2:14; 3:13; 15; 7:7; 8:5; 10; 14; 9:25; **Job** 4:9(2); 6:16; 9:11; 11:7; 15:30; 16:12; 17:7; 18:8; 9; 20:29; 21:29; 22:30; 26:12; 13; 27:11; 28:8; 9; 25; 29:3; 19; 30:4; 18; 31:9; 11; 23; 28; 30; 33; 33:18; 35:9(2); 36:12; 22; 31; 32; 37:10; 11; 12; 17; 19; 38:2; 24; 39:9; 26; 41:18; 25; 42:5; **Ps** 1:3; 5:10; 9:16; 10:10; 17:4; 7; 18:8; 29(2); 34; 19:11; 30:7; 33:6(2); 16(2); 17; 37:23; 38:8; 39:10; 41:11; 44:3; 12; 16; 48:4; 49:7; 50:5; 54:1(2); 56:7; 59:11; 63:10; 11; 65:5; 6; 66:7; 68:4; 71:6; 72:3; 73:23; 74:7; 13; 77:20; 78:17; 18; 26; 49; 55; 64; 65; 72; 79:10; 80:12; 88:9; 89:35; 39; 41; 90:7(2); 10; 91:5(2); 94:20; 102:5;

104:8(2); 12; 106:22; 107:7; 119:9; 121:6(2); 128:3; 129:8; 134:1; 136:5; 8; 9; 137:1; 140:5; 147:4; **Prov** 3:19(2); 20; 28; 29; 4:15; 6:26; 7:26; 8:2; 15; 16; 30; 9:11; 11:5; 11(2); 12:3; 13; 14; 13:2; 10; 11(2); 14:4; 15:13; 23; 16:6(2); 12; 20:4; 11; 18; 28; 21:6; 22:4; 24:3; 4; 6; 30(2); 25:15; 26:2(2); 6; 17(2); 26; 28; 27:9; 28:2; 8; 29:4; 19; 30:27; 31:18; **Eccl** 1:13; 5:3; 9; 14; 7:3; 11; 23; 26; 27; 9:1; 15; 10:3; 18; 12:11; 12; **Song** 1:7; 8; 2:7(2); 3:1; 5(2); 5:4; 12; 7:4; **Is** 1:7; 3:5(2); 25; 4:1; 4(2); 5(2); 7:20(2); 9:1; 10:13(2); 34; 13:15; 15:5; 18:2; 19:7(3); 20:2; 22:3; 5; 14; 23:3; 26:13; 27:7; 9; 12; 28:18; 19(3); 29:13; 32:8; 34:17; 36:2; 16; 37:7; 11; 24(2); 29(2); 34(2); 38:8; 16; 40:26(3); 41:3; 42:16; 43:1; 7; 44:4; 5(2); 24; 45:3; 4; 23; 46:3; 48:1(2); 17; 49:10; 19; 50:4; 51:18; 19; 52:12; 53:11; 54:15; 60:19; 62:2; 8(2); 63:12; 19; 64:4; 65:1; 5; 15; 16; 66:16(2); **Jer** 2:8; 17; 34; 4:26; 5:7(2); 22; 31; 6:5; 25; 7:10; 11; 14; 30; 8:3; 5; 10:12(3); 14; 11:21; 22(2); 12:16(2); 13:5; 24; 14:9; 12(3); 15; 15:16; 16:4(2); 17:2; 8(2); 11; 19; 20; 21; 18:21(2); 19:2; 7(2); 20:2; 4; 21:9(3); 22:2; 4; 5; 8; 13(2); 23:27; 32(2); 25:29; 27:3; 5(2); 8; 13(3); 29:3; 19; 22; 31:9; 32; 35(2); 32:17; 34; 36(3); 33:4(2); 34:4; 15; 35:4; 37:2; 38:2(3); 11; 23; 39:4(3); 18; 41:12; 17; 42:17(3); 22(3); 44:12(4); 13(3); 15; 18(2); 26; 27(2); 46:2; 6; 10; 18; 48:19; 49:3; 9; 13; 17; 50:1; 13; 51:14; 15(3); 17(2); 52:7(5); **Lam** 1:12; 14; 2:15; 21; 3:1; 5:12; **Eze** 1:1; 3; 15; 19; 3:15; 23; 4:10; 11; 16(2); 5:12; 14; 6:11(3); 12(2); 8:3; 9:2; 3; 11; 10:9(3); 15; 16; 20; 22; 11:10; 24; 12:3; 4; 7; 13:19; 22; 14:3; 7; 13; 14; 20; 16:6; 8; 15; 25; 36; 56; 61; 17:5; 7; 8; 9; 14; 17; 18; 21; 18:7; 12; 16; 18; 19:7; 10(2); 20:3; 31(2); 21:12; 22:7(2); 12; 23:21; 25(2); 24:6; 21; 25:12; 13; 14; 15; 26:6; 10; 11; 27:12; 16; 34; 28:5(2); 10; 16; 17; 18(2); 23; 29:7; 30:5; 6; 10; 12; 17; 31:7; 9; 12; 14; 18; 32:12; 20; 21; 22; 23; 24; 25; 26; 29(2); 30; 31; 33:27; 30; 34:13; 35:5; 36:17(2); 34; 37; 37:2; 18; 38:17; 39:15; 23; 40:2; 5; 7; 18; 22; 28; 38; 41; 49(2); 41:7; 17(2); 42:20; 43:3; 4; 6; 7(2); 8(3); 13; 44:2(2); 3(2); 45:1; 46:2(2); 8(2); 9(5); 14; 16; 18; 21; 47:2; 12; 16; 18; 22; 48:2; 3; 4; 5; 6; 7; 8; 12; 20; 24; 25; 26; 27; 28; 29; **Dan** 4:17(2); 27(2); 30; 5:10; 7:2; 8; 16; 8:2; 11; 12; 24; 25; 9:2; 3; 5; 10; 11; 12; 18; 19; 10:4; 16; 11:2; 12; 16; 18; 21; 32; 33(4); 12:7; **Hos** 1:2; 7(6); 2:17; 4:2; 6:5(2); 9; 7:4; 16; 8:4; 9; 11:3; 12:3(2); 10(2); 13(2); 13:7; 16; 14:1; **Amos** 2:8; 4:2; 5:3(2); 6:8; 10; 13; 7:2; 4; 5; 7; 8; 11; 17(2); 8:2; 5; 7; 8; 14; 9:5; 10; 12; **Obad** 5; 9; **Jonah** 2:2; 3:7; **Mic** 2:2; 5; 8; 12; 13; 3:8; 7:18; **Nah** 1:6; **Hab** 1:16; 2:4; 5; 10; 12; 3:10; 13; **Zeph** 1:5(2); 18; 2:12; 15; 3:6; **Hag** 1:1; 3; 2:1; 10; 13; 22; **Zec** 1:8; 3:5; 7; 4:3; 6(3); 14; 5:4; 7:7; 12; 8:9; 9:8; 11; **Mal** 1:1; 9; 2:10; **Mt** 1:22; 2:5; 14; 15; 17; 23; 3:3; 4:4(2); 14; 15; 18; 5:21; 26; 27; 33; 34; 35(2); 36; 6:27; 7:16; 20; 8:17; 28; 9:25; 11:12; 12:17; 24; 27(2); 28; 33; 37(2); 13:1; 4; 14; 19; 21(2); 35; 14:13; 15:3; 5(2); 6; 17:21; 18:7; 28; 20:30(2); 21:4; 23; 24; 27; 22:1; 31; 23:16(2); 18(2); 20(3); 21(3); 22(3); 24:15; 26:4; 24; 63; 73; 27:9; 32; 35; 39; 64; 28:9; 13; **Mk** 1:16; 31; 2:13; 14; 3:22; 4:1(2); 2; 4; 15; 5:4; 7; 21; 22; 41; 6:2; 7; 25(2); 32; 39; 40(2); 48; 7:11(2); 26; 8:3; 23; 27; 9:2; 27; 29(2); 33; 34; 10:1; 46; 11:4; 20; 28; 29; 33; 12:1; 36; 13:14; 14:1; 19; 21; 47; 69; 70; 15:21; 29; 35; **Lk** 1:61; 70; 77; 2:8; 18; 26; 27; 3:19; 4:1; 4(2); 5:1; 2; 15; 17; 19; 6:44; 8:4; 5; 12; 20; 36; 54; 9:7; 14; 47; 10:4; 19; 31(2); 32; 11:3; 19(2); 13:17; 16:22; 17:6; 7(2); 18:5; 31; 35; 36; 37; 19:8; 15; 24; 20:2; 8; 21:9(2); 16; 24; 22:22; 56; 23:8; 24:4; 12; 32; **Jn** 1:3; 10; 17(2); 42; 3:2; 34; 5:2; 6:15; 18; 57(2); 7:50; 8:9(2); 59; 9:1; 7; 21; 10:1; 2; 3; 9; 11:39; 42; 12:11; 29; 13:35; 14:6; 16:30; 18:22; 19:7; 25; 26; 39; 20:7; 21:19; **Acts** 1:3; 10; 16; 25; 2:16; 22(2); 23(2); 33; 43; 3:7; 12; 16; 18; 21; 4:7(2); 9; 10(2); 16; 25; 30(2); 36; 5:10; 12; 15; 19; 6:10; 7:25; 35; 42; 53; 9:8; 13; 25(2); 36; 39; 10:6; 22; 32; 36; 11:4; 5; 28; 30; 12:9; 20; 13:4; 8; 11; 19; 21; 36; 39(2); 45; 14:3; 15:3; 7; 9; 12; 23; 27; 40; 16:2; 8; 13; 16; 17:10; 23; 29; 31; 18:3; 9; 21; 28; 19:10; 11; 13; 25; 20:16; 19; 31; 21:19; 22:11; 20; 24; 25; 23:2; 4; 10; 11; 19; 31; 24:2(2); 8; 21; 25:14; 26:18; 27:2; 11; 12; 13; 16; 23; 28:16; 25; **Rom** 1:2; 4; 5; 10(2); 12; 17; 20; 2:7; 12; 14; 16; 27(2); 3:20(2); 21; 22; 24; 27(2); 28; 30; 4:2; 16; 5:1; 2(2); 5; 9; 10(2); 11; 12(2); 15(2); 16(2); 17(3); 18(2); 19(2); 21; 6:4(2); 7:2; 4; 5; 7; 8; 11(2); 13(2); 8:11; 14; 20; 24; 9:10(2); 32(2); 10:5; 17(2); 19(2); 11:6; 14; 20; 24; 12:1; 2; 14:14; 15:16; 18(2); 19; 24; 28; 32; 16:18; 26; S:1; **1Cor** 1:4; 5; 9; 10; 11; 21(2); 2:10; 3:5; 13; 15; 4:4; 6:2; 11; 14; 7:6; 14(2); 39; 8:6(2); 9; 9:22; 27; 10:30; 11:12; 12:3(2); 8(2); 9(2); 13; 14:6(4); 9; 19; 27(3); 30; 31; 15:2; 10; 21(2); 31; 16:2; 3; 7; S:1; **2Cor** 1:1; 4; 5; 11(3); 12; 16; 19(2); 20; 24; 2:2; 14; 3:3; 10; 18; 4:2; 14; 16; 5:7(2); 18; 20; 6:6(6); 7(3); 8(2); 7:6; 7(2); 9; 13; 8:5; 8(2); 14; 19; 20; 9:12; 13; 14; 10:1; 9; 11; 12; 15; 11:3; 26(2); 33; 12:17; 13:4(2); S:1; **Gal** 1:1(2); 12; 15; 22; 2:2(2); 5; 15; 16(5); 17; 20; 21; 3:2(2); 3; 5(2); 11(2); 18; 19; 21; 22; 24; 26; 4:8; 22(2); 23; 5:4; 5; 6; 13; 6:14; **Eph** 1:1; 5; 2:3; 5; 8; 11(2); 13; 16; 18; 3:3; 5; 6; 7; 9; 10; 12; 16; 17; 21; 4:14; 16; 21; 5:13; 26; S:1; **Phil** 1:11; 14; 20(2); 26; 28; 3:9; 11; 16; 4:6; 19; S:1; **Col** 1:1; 16(2); 17; 20(2); 21; 2:11; 18; 19; 3:17; 4:18; S:1; **1Th** 3:3; 5; 7; 4:1; 2; 15; 5:9; 27; **2Th** 2:1(2); 2(3); 3; 14; 15; 3:12; 14; 16; **1Ti** 1:1; 18; 4:5; 14; 5:21; **2Ti** 1:1; 6; 10; 14; 2:26; 3:16; 4:17; **Titus** 1:9; 3:5(2); 7; **Philem** 1:6; 7; S:1; **Heb** 1:1; 2(2); 3(2); 4; 2:2; 3(2); 9; 10; 3:4; 16; 5:3; 8; 14; 6:7; 13(2); 16; 17; 18; 7:2; 11; 19; 21; 22; 23; 25; 8:6; 9; 9:11; 12(2); 15; 22; 26; 10:1; 8; 10; 14; 19; 20; 33; 38; 11:2; 3; 4(3); 5; 7(3); 8; 9; 12; 17; 20; 21; 22; 23; 24; 27; 29(2); 30; 31; 13:11; 15; S:1; **Jas** 2:7; 12; 18; 21; 22; 24(2); 25; 5:4; 12(3); 17; **1Pet** 1:3; 5; 12; 18; 21; 23; 25; 2:5; 12; 14; 24; 3:1; 18; 19; 20; 21; 5:2; 10; 12; **2Pet** 1:4; 13; 21(2); 2:2; 3:1; 2; 5; 7; **1Jn** 3:24; 5:2; 6(3); **3Jn** 14; **Jude** 1; 12; 23; **Rev** 1:1; 5:9; 8:13; 9:2; 18(4); 20; 10:6; 12:11(2); 13:14(2); 14:20; 18:15; 17; 19; 23; 21:25

CAME

Gen 4:3; 8; 6:1; 4; 7:10; 8:6; 11; 13; 10:14; 11:2; 5; 31; 12:5; 11; 14; 13:18; 14:1; 5; 7; 13; 15:1; 4; 11; 17; 19:1; 5; 8; 9(2); 17; 29; 34; 20:3; 13; 21:22; 22:1; 9; 20; 23:2; 24:15(2); 16; 22; 30(2); 32; 42; 45; 52; 62; 25:11; 25; 26; 29; 26:8; 32(2); 27:1; 18; 27; 30(2); 35; 29:1; 9; 10; 13; 23; 25; 30:16; 25; 30; 38(2); 41; 31:10; 24; 32:6; 13; 33:1; 3; 6; 7(2); 18(2); 34:7; 20; 25(2); 27; 35:6; 9; 17; 18; 22; 27; 36:16; 17; 18; 29; 30; 40; 37:14; 18; 23; 25; 38:1; 9; 18; 24; 27; 28(2); 29(2); 30; 39:5; 7; 10; 11; 13; 14; 15; 16; 17; 18; 19; 40:1; 6; 20; 41:1; 2; 3; 5; 8; 13; 14; 18; 19; 22; 27; 50; 57; 42:5(2); 6; 29; 35; 43:2; 19; 20; 21(2); 25; 26; 44:14; 18; 24(2); 45:4; 25; 46:1; 6; 8; 26(2); 27; 28; 47:1; 15; 18; 48:1; 5; 7; 50:10; **Ex** 1:1(2); 5; 21; 2:5; 11; 16; 17; 18; 23(2); 3:1; 4:24; 5:15; 20; 23; 6:28; 8:6; 24; 10:3; 12:29; 41(2); 51; 13:3; 4; 8; 15; 17; 14:20(2); 24; 28; 15:23; 27; 16:1; 10; 13(2); 22(2); 27; 35(2); 17:8; 11; 18:5; 7; 12; 13; 19:1; 7; 16; 20; 21:3; 22:15; 24:3; 32:19(2); 24; 30; 33:7; 8; 9; 34:29(3); 32; 34(2); 35:21; 22; 36:4; 40:17; 32; **Lev** 9:1; 22; 23; 24; **Num** 4:47; 7:1; 9:6; 10:11; 21; 35; 11:20; 25(2); 12:4; 5(2); 13:22; 23; 26; 27; 14:45; 16:27; 31; 35; 42; 43; 17:8; 19:2; 20:1; 11; 20; 22; 28; 21:1; 7; 9; 23; 22:7; 9; 16; 20; 39; 41; 23:17; 24:2; 25:6; 26:1; 27:1; 31:14; 48; 32:2; 11; 16; 33:9; 36:1; **Deut** 1:3; 19; 22; 24; 31; 44; 2:14; 16; 23; 32; 3:1; 4:11; 45; 5:23(2); 9:7; 11; 15; 10:5; 11:5; 10; 22:14; 23:4; 29:7(2); 16; 31:24; 32:17; 44; 33:2(2); 21; **Josh** 1:1; 2:1; 2; 4; 5; 8; 10; 22; 23; 3:1; 2; 14; 16(2); 4:1; 11; 18; 19; 22; 5:1; 4(2); 5(2); 6; 8; 13; 6:1; 8; 9; 11; 13; 15; 16; 20; 8:11; 14; 24; 9:1; 12; 16; 17; 10:1; 9; 11; 20; 24(2); 27; 33; 11:1; 5; 7; 21; 14:6; 15:18(2); 16:7; 17:4; 13; 18:9; 11(2); 16; 19:1; 10; 17; 24; 32; 40; 21:1; 4; 45; 22:10; 15; 23:1; 24:6; 11; 29; **Judg** 1:1; 14(2); 28; 2:1; 4; 19; 3:10; 20; 22; 24; 27; 4:5; 22(2); 5:14; 19; 23; 6:3(2); 5(2); 7; 11; 25; 34; 35; 7:9; 13; 19; 8:4; 15; 33; 9:25; 26; 42; 52; 57; 11:4; 13; 16(2); 18(2); 29; 34(2); 35; 39; 13:6(2); 9; 10; 11; 20; 14:2; 5; 6; 9; 11; 14(2); 15; 17; 19; 15:1; 6; 14(2); 17; 19(2); 16:4; 5; 16; 18; 25; 31; 17:8; 18:2; 7; 8; 13; 15; 17; 27; 19:1; 5; 10; 16; 22; 26; 30; 20:4; 21; 24; 26; 33; 34; 42; 48(2); 21:2; 4; 5(2); 8(2); 14; **Ruth** 1:1; 2; 19(2); 22; 2:3; 4; 6; 7; 3:7; 8; 14; 16; 4:1; **1Sa** 1:12; 19; 20; 2:13; 14; 15; 19; 27; 3:2; 10; 4:1; 5; 12; 13(2); 14; 16; 18; 19; 5:10(2); 6:14; 7:1; 2; 11; 13; 8:1; 4; 9:12; 14; 15; 26; 10:9; 10(2); 11; 13; 14; 11:1; 4; 5; 6; 7; 9(2); 11(2); 12:12; 13:5; 8; 10(2); 17; 22; 14:1; 19; 20; 25; 15:2; 5; 6; 10; 12; 13; 32; 35; 16:4; 6; 13; 21; 23; 17:20; 22; 23; 34; 41; 48(2); 18:1; 6(3); 10(2); 13; 16; 19; 30; 19:18; 22; 23; 20:1; 27; 35; 38; 21:1; 5; 22:5; 11; 23:6(2); 19; 25; 27; 24:1; 3; 5; 16; 25:9; 12; 20(2); 36; 37; 38; 26:1; 3; 5; 7; 15; 27:9; 28:1; 4; 8; 21; 30:1; 3; 9; 12; 21(2); 23; 26; 31:7; 8(2); 12; **2Sa** 1:1; 2(3); 2:1; 4; 23(3); 29; 32; 3:6; 20; 22; 23; 24(2); 25; 35; 4:4(2); 5; 6; 7; 5:1; 3; 17; 18; 20; 22; 6:6; 16; 20; 7:1; 4(2); 8:1; 5; 10:1; 2; 8; 14; 16; 17; 11:1; 2; 4; 14; 16; 22; 23; 12:1; 4; 18; 20(2); 13:1; 23; 24; 30(2); 34; 36(2); 14:31; 33(2); 15:1; 2; 5; 6; 7; 13; 18; 32(2); 37(2); 16:5(4); 11; 14; 15; 16; 17:18; 20; 21(2); 24; 27; 18:4; 25; 31; 19:5; 8; 15(2); 16; 24(2); 25; 31; 41; 20:3; 12; 15; 21:18; 22:10; 23:13; 24:6(2); 7; 8; 11; 13; 18; **1Kin** 1:22; 28; 32; 40; 42; 47; 53; 2:7; 8; 13; 28; 30; 39; 3:15; 16; 18; 4:27; 34; 5:7; 6:1; 11; 7:14; 8:3; 9; 10; 9:1; 10; 12; 24; 28; 10:1; 2; 7; 10; 12; 14; 22; 29; 11:4; 15; 18(2); 29; 12:2; 3; 12; 20; 22; 13:1; 4; 10; 11; 12; 20(2); 21; 23; 25; 29; 31; 14:4; 6; 17(2); 25(2); 15:21; 29; 16:1; 7; 11; 18; 31; 17:2; 7; 8; 10; 17; 22; 18:1(2); 17; 21; 27; 29; 30; 31; 36(2); 44; 45; 19:3; 4; 7; 9(2); 13; 20:5; 12; 13; 19; 22; 26; 28; 30; 32; 33; 43; 21:1; 4; 5; 13; 15; 16; 17; 27; 28; 22:2(2); 15; 21; 32; 33; **2Kin** 1:6; 7; 10; 12; 13; 14; 2:1; 3; 4; 5; 9; 11; 15; 18; 23; 24; 3:5; 15(2); 20(2); 24; 4:6; 7; 11; 25(2); 27(2); 38; 39; 40; 42; 5:7; 9; 13; 14; 15; 24; 6:4; 14; 18; 20; 23; 24; 30; 32; 33; 7:8(2); 10(2); 17; 18; 8:3; 5; 7; 9; 14; 15; 9:5; 11(2); 17; 18; 19; 20; 22; 36; 10:7(2); 8; 9; 12; 17; 21(3); 25; 11:9; 13; 16; 19; 12:10; 13:14; 21; 14:5; 13; 15:12; 14; 19; 29; 16:5; 6; 11; 17:3; 5; 28; 18:1; 9(2); 17(2); 18; 37; 19:1; 5; 33; 35; 37; 20:1; 4(2); 14(2); 21:15; 22:3; 9; 11; 23:9; 17; 18; 34; 24:1; 3; 7; 10; 11; 20; 25:1(2); 8; 23; 25(2); 26; 27; **1Chr** 1:12; 2:53; 55; 4:41; 5:2; 7:21; 22; 10:7; 8(2); 11:3; 12:1; 16; 18; 19; 22; 23; 38; 13:9; 14:9; 11; 15:26; 29(2); 17:1; 3(2); 16; 18:1; 5; 19:1; 2; 7(2); 9; 15; 17; 20:1(2); 4; 21:4; 11; 21; 22:8; 24:7; 28; 25:9; 26:14; 16; 27:1; **2Chr** 1:13; 5:4; 10; 11; 13; 7:1; 3; 11; 8:1; 9:1; 6; 13; 21; 10:2; 3; 12; 11:2; 14; 16; 12:1; 2(2); 3; 4; 5; 7; 9; 11; 13:15; 14:9(2); 14; 15:1; 5; 16:1; 5; 7; 18:20; 23; 31; 32; 20:1(2); 2; 4; 10; 14; 24; 25; 28; 21:12; 17; 19; 22:1; 8; 23:2; 12; 20; 24:4; 11(2); 17; 18; 20; 23(3); 24; 25:3; 7; 14; 16; 20; 28:9; 12; 20; 29:15; 17; 30:11; 25(2); 27; 31:5; 8; 32:1; 21; 26; 34:9; 19; 35:20; 22; 36:6; **Ezr** 2:1; 2; 68; 4:2; 12; 5:3; 5; 16; 7:8; 9; 8:32; 9:1; 10:6; **Neh** 1:1; 2; 4; 2:1; 9; 11; 4:1; 7; 12(2); 15; 16; 5:17; 6:1; 10; 16; 17; 7:1; 5; 6; 7; 73; 13:3; 6; 7; 19; 21; **Est** 1:1; 17; 2:8; 13; 14; 3:4; 4:2; 3; 4; 9; 5:1; 5; 10; 6:6; 12; 14; 7:1; 8:1; 17; 9:25; **Job** 1:6(2); 14; 16; 17; 18; 19; 21; 2:1(2); 11; 3:11; 26; 4:14; 6:20; 26:4; 29:13; 30:14; 26(2); 38:29; 42:11; **Ps** 18:6; 9; 27:2; 51:t; 52:t; 54:t, 78:21; 31; 88:17; 105:19; 23; 31; 34; **Prov** 7:15; **Eccl** 5:15(2); 16; 9:14; **Song** 4:2; **Is** 7:1; 11:16; 20:1; 30:4; 36:1(2); 3; 22; 37:1; 5; 34; 38; 38:1; 4; 39:3(2); 41:5; 48:3; 5; 50:2; 66:7; **Jer** 1:2; 3; 4; 11; 13; 2:1; 3:9; 7:1; 25; 31; 8:15; 11:1; 13:3; 6; 8; 14:1; 3; 16:1; 17:16; 18:1; 5; 19:5; 14; 20:3; 18; 21:1; 24:4; 25:1; 26:1; 8; 10; 27:1; 28:1; 12; 29:30; 30:1; 32:1; 6; 8; 23; 26; 35; 33:1; 19; 23; 34:1; 8; 12; 35:1; 11(2); 12; 36:1(2); 9(2); 14; 16; 23; 27; 37:4; 6; 11; 38:27; 39:1; 3; 4; 15; 40:1; 8; 12; 13; 41:1(2); 4; 5; 6; 7; 13; 42:1; 7(2); 43:1; 7(2); 8; 44:1; 21; 46:1; 47:1; 49:34; 52:3; 4(2); 12; 31; **Lam** 1:9; **Eze** 1:1; 3; 4; 5; 3:15; 16(2); 4:14; 6:1; 7:1; 8:1; 9:2; 8; 10:6; 11:13; 14; 12:1; 8; 17; 21; 26; 13:1; 14:1; 2; 12; 15:1; 16:1; 23; 17:1; 3; 11; 18:1; 20:1(2); 2; 45; 21:1; 8; 18; 22:1; 17; 23; 23:1; 17; 39; 40; 24:1; 15; 20; 25:1; 26:1(2); 27:1; 28:1; 11; 20; 29:1; 17(2); 30:1; 20(2); 31:1(2); 32:1(2); 17(2); 33:1; 21(2); 22(2); 23; 34:1; 35:1; 36:16; 37:7; 8; 10; 15; 38:1; 40:6; 43:2; 3; 4; 46:9; 47:1; **Dan** 1:1; 2:2; 29; 3:8; 26(2); 4:7; 8; 13; 28; 5:5; 8; 10; 6:12; 20; 24; 7:3; 8; 10; 13(2); 16; 20; 22(2); 8:2; 3; 5; 6; 8; 9; 15; 17(2); 9:2; 23; 10:3; 13; 18; **Hos** 1:1; 2:15; **Joel** 1:1; **Amos** 6:1; 7:2; **Obad** 5(2); **Jonah** 1:1; 6; 2:7; 3:1; 6; 4:8; 10; **Mic** 1:1; 11; 12; **Hab** 3:3; 14; **Zeph** 1:1; **Hag** 1:1; 3; 9; 14; 2:1; 5; 10; 16(2); 20; **Zec** 1:1; 7; 4:1; 8; 5:9; 6:1; 9; 7:1(2); 4; 8; 12; 8:1; 10; 18; 10:4; 14:16; **Mt** 1:18; 2:1; 9; 21; 23; 3:1; 4:3; 11; 13; 5:1; 7:25; 27; 28; 8:2; 5; 19; 25; 34; 9:1; 10(2); 14; 18; 20; 23; 28; 10:34; 11:1; 18; 19; 12:42; 44; 13:4; 10; 25; 27; 36; 53; 14:12; 15; 33; 34; 15:1; 12; 22; 23; 25; 29; 30; 39; 16:1; 13; 17:7; 9; 14; 19; 24; 18:1; 21; 31; 19:1(2); 3; 16; 20:9; 10; 20; 28; 21:14; 19; 23; 28; 30; 32; 22:11; 23; 24:1; 3; 39; 25:10; 11; 20; 22; 24; 36; 39; 26:1; 7; 17; 43; 47; 49; 50; 60(2); 69; 73; 27:32; 53; 57; 62; 28:1; 2; 9; 11; 13; 18; **Mk** 1:9(2); 11; 14; 26; 31; 38; 40; 45; 2:15; 17; 23; 3:8; 13; 22; 31; 4:4(2); 5:1; 27; 33; 35; 6:1; 22; 25; 29; 33; 34; 35; 53; 7:1(2); 25; 31; 8:3; 10; 11; 9:7; 9; 14; 21; 25; 26; 33; 10:2; 17; 45; 46; 50; 11:1; 13(2); 12:28; 42; 14:3; 16; 32; 15:41; 43; 16:2; **Lk** 1:8; 22; 23; 28; 41; 57; 59(2); 65; 2:1; 9; 15; 16; 27; 46; 51; 3:2; 3; 7; 12; 21; 22; 4:16; 31; 35; 41; 42; 5:1; 7; 12; 15; 17; 32; 6:1; 6; 12; 17(2); 7:4; 11; 12; 14; 16; 33; 45; 8:1; 19; 22; 23; 24; 35; 40; 41; 44; 47; 51; 55; 9:12; 18; 28; 33; 34; 35; 37; 51; 57; 10:31; 32; 33; 38; 40; 11:1; 14; 24; 27; 31; 13:6; 31; 14:1; 21; 15:17; 20; 25; 28; 16:21; 22; 17:11; 14; 27; 18:3; 35; 19:5; 6; 15; 16; 18; 20; 29; 20:1(2); 27; 21:38; 22:7; 39; 66; 23:48; 55; 24:1; 4; 15; 23; 30; 51; **Jn** 1:7; 11; 17; 39; 3:2; 13; 22; 23; 26; 4:27; 30; 46; 6:23; 24; 38; 41; 42; 51; 58; 7:45; 50; 8:1; 2(2); 14; 42(2); 9:7; 10:8; 24; 35; 11:17; 19; 29; 33; 44; 45; 12:1; 9; 20; 21; 27; 28; 30; 47; 16:27; 28; 17:8; 18:37; 19:5; 32; 33; 34; 38; 39(2); 20:3; 4; 8; 18; 19; 24; 26; 21:8; **Acts** 2:2; 6; 43; 4:1; 5; 5:5; 7; 10; 11; 16; 21; 22; 25; 6:12; 7:4; 11; 23; 31; 45; 8:7; 36; 40; 9:3; 21; 32(2); 37; 43; 10:13; 29; 45; 11:5; 22; 23; 26; 27; 28; 12:7; 10; 12; 13; 20; 13:13; 14; 31; 44; 51; 14:1; 19; 20; 24; 15:1; 6; 30; 16:1; 8; 11; 16; 18; 29; 39; 17:1; 13; 18:1; 2; 19; 24; 19:1(2); 6; 18; 20:2; 6; 7; 14; 15(2); 18; 21:1(2); 7; 8; 10; 31; 33; 35; 22:6; 11; 13; 17; 27; 23:14; 27; 33; 24:7; 17; 24; 27; 25:7; 13; 27:5; 8; 44; 28:3; 8; 9; 13(2); 15; 16; 17; 21; 23; 30; **Rom** 5:18(2); 7:9; 9:5; **1Cor** 2:1(2); 14:36(2); 15:21(2); **2Cor** 1:8; 23; 2:3; 12; 11:9; **Gal** 1:21; 2:4; 12; 3:23; **Eph** 2:17; **1Th** 1:5; 3:4; 6; **1Ti** 1:15; **2Ti** 3:11; **Heb** 3:16; 11:15; **2Pet** 1:17; 18; 21; **1Jn** 5:6; **3Jn** 3; **Rev** 5:7; 7:13; 14; 8:3; 4; 9:3; 14:15; 17; 18; 20; 15:6; 16:17; 19; 17:1; 19:5; 20:9; 21:9

CAMEST

Gen 16:8; 24:5; 27:33; **Ex** 23:15; 34:18; **Num** 22:37; **Deut** 2:37; 16:3(2); 6; **1Sa** 13:11; 17:28; **2Sa** 11:10; 15:20; **1Kin** 13:9; 14; 17; 22; **2Kin** 19:28; **Neh** 9:13; **Is** 37:29; 64:3; **Jer** 1:5; **Eze** 32:2; **Mt** 22:12; **Jn** 6:25; 16:30; **Acts** 9:17

CAN

Gen 4:13; 13:16; 31:43; 39:9; 41:15; 38; 44:1; 15; **Ex** 4:14; 5:11; **Lev** 14:30; **Num** 23:10; **Deut** 1:12; 3:24; 7:17; 9:2; 31:2; 32:39; **Judg** 14:12; **1Sa** 9:6; 16:2; 17; 18:8; 26:9; 28:2; **2Sa** 7:20; 12:22; 23; 14:19; 15:36; 19:35(3); **1Kin** 5:6; **1Chr** 17:18; **2Chr** 1:10; 2:7; 8; **Est** 8:6(2); **Job** 3:22; 4:2; 6:6; 8:11(2); 9:12; 10:7; 11:10; 12:14; 14:4; 15:3; 22:2; 13; 17; 23:13; 25:4(2); 26:14; 34:29(2); 36:23; 26; 29; 38:37(2); 40:14; 19; 23; 41:13(2); 14; 16; 42:2; **Ps** 11:3; 19:12; 22:29; 40:5; 49:7; 56:4; 11; 58:9; 78:19; 20(2); 89:6(2); 106:2(2); 118:6; 147:17; **Prov** 6:27; 28; 18:14; 20:6; 9; 24; 26:16; 31:10; **Eccl** 2:12; 25(2); 3:11; 14; 4:11; 6:12; 7:13; 24; 8:7; 10:14; **Song** 8:7; **Is** 28:20(2); 38:18; 43:9; 13; 46:7; 49:15; 56:11; **Jer** 2:13; 24; 28; 32; 4:4; 5:1; 22(2); 9:10(2); 13:23; 14:22(2); 17:9; 21:12; 23:24; 31:37; 33:20; 38:5; 47:7; **Lam** 2:13; **Eze** 22:14(2); 28:3; 33:32; 37:3; **Dan** 2:9; 10; 11; 3:29; 4:35; 10:17; **Joel** 2:11; **Amos** 3:3; 5; 8; **Jonah** 3:9; **Mic** 3:11; 5:8; **Nah** 1:6(2); **Mt** 6:24; 27; 7:18; 9:15; 12:29; 34; 16:3(2); 19:25; 23:33; 27:65; **Mk** 2:7; 19; 3:23; 27; 7:15; 8:4; 9:3; 29; 39; 10:26; 38; 39; **Lk** 5:21; 34; 6:39; 12:4; 25; 56; 16:13; 26; 18:26; 20:36; **Jn** 1:46; 3:2; 4(2); 9; 27; 5:19; 30; 44; 6:44; 52; 60; 65; 9:4; 16; 10:21; 14:5; 15:4; 5; **Acts** 8:31; 10:47; 24:13; **Rom** 8:7; 31; **1Cor** 2:14; 3:11; 12:3; **2Cor** 13:8; **Phil** 4:13; **1Th** 3:9; **1Ti** 6:7; 16(2); **Heb** 5:2; 10:1; 11; **Jas** 2:14; 3:8; 12(2); **1Jn** 4:20; **Rev** 3:8; 9:20

CANNOT

Gen 19:19; 22; 24:50; 29:8; 31:35; 32:12; 34:14; 38:22; 43:22; 44:22; 26; **Ex** 10:5; 19:23; **Lev** 14:21; **Num** 22:18; 23:20; 24:13; 35:33; **Deut** 28:35; **Josh** 24:19; **Judg** 11:35; 14:13; **Ruth** 4:6(2); **1Sa** 12:21; 17:39; 55; 25:17; **2Sa** 5:6; 14:14; 23:6; **1Kin** 3:8; 8:27; 18:12; **2Chr** 2:6; 6:18; 24:20; **Ezr** 9:15; **Neh** 6:3; **Job** 5:12; 6:30; 9:3; 12:14; 14:5; 17:10; 19:8; 23:8; 9(2); 28:15; 16; 17; 31:31; 33:21; 36:18; 37:5; 19; 23; 41:17; 23; 26; 28; **Ps** 40:5; 77:4; 88:8; 93:1; 125:1; 139:6; **Prov** 30:21; **Eccl** 1:8; 15(2); 8:17; 10:14; **Song** 8:7; **Is** 1:13; 29:11; 38:18(2); 44:18(2); 20; 45:20; 50:2; 56:10; 11; 57:20; 59:1(2); 14; **Jer** 1:6; 4:19; 5:22; 6:10; 7:8; 10:5(2); 14:9; 18:6; 19:11; 24:3; 8; 29:17; 33:22; 36:5; 46:23; 49:23; **Lam** 3:7; 4:18; **Dan** 2:27; **Hos** 1:10; **Jonah** 4:11; **Hab** 2:5; **Mt** 5:14; 6:24; 7:18; 19:11; 21:27; 26:53; 27:42; **Mk** 2:19; 3:24; 25; 26; 7:18; 11:33; 15:31; **Lk** 11:7; 13:33; 14:14; 20; 26; 27; 33; 16:3; 13; 26; **Jn** 3:3; 5; 7:7; 34; 36; 8:14; 21; 22; 43; 10:35; 13:33; 37; 14:17; 15:4; 16:12; 18; **Acts** 4:16; 20; 5:39; 15:1; 19:36; 27:31; **Rom** 8:8; 26; **1Cor** 7:9; 10:21(2); 12:21; 15:50; **2Cor** 12:2(2); 3; **Gal** 3:17; 5:17; **1Ti** 5:25; **2Ti** 2:13; **Titus** 1:2; 2:8; **Heb** 4:15; 9:5; 12:27; 28; **Jas** 1:13; 4:2; **2Pet** 1:9; 2:14; **1Jn** 3:9

CANST

Gen 41:15; **Ex** 33:20; **Deut** 28:27; **Josh** 7:13; **Judg** 16:15; **1Sa** 30:15; **2Kin** 8:1; **Ezr** 7:16; **Job** 11:7(2); 8(2); 22:11; 33:5; 38:31; 32(2); 33; 34; 35; 39:1; 2; 10; 20; 40:9; 41:1; 2; 7; 42:2; **Prov** 3:15; 5:6; 30:4; **Is** 33:19(2); **Jer** 2:23; 12:5; **Eze** 3:6; **Dan** 5:16(2); **Hab** 1:13; **Mt** 5:36; 8:2; **Mk** 1:40; 9:22; 23; **Lk** 5:12; 6:42; **Jn** 3:8; 13:36; **Acts** 21:37; **Rev** 2:2

CHILDREN'S

Gen 31:16; 45:10; **Ex** 9:4; 34:7; **Deut** 4:25; **Josh** 14:9; **2Kin** 17:41; **Job** 19:17; **Ps** 103:17; 128:6; **Prov** 13:22; 17:6; **Jer** 2:9; 31:29; **Eze** 18:2; 37:25; **Mt** 15:26; **Mk** 7:27; 28

CITIES

Gen 13:12; 19:25(2); 29(2); 35:5; 41:35; 48; 47:21; **Ex** 1:11; **Lev** 25:32(2); 33; 34; 26:25; 31; 33; **Num** 13:19; 28; 21:2; 3; 25(2); 31:10; 32:16; 17; 24; 26; 33(2); 36; 38; 35:2(2); 3; 4; 5; 6(3); 7(2); 8(2); 11(2); 12; 13(2); 14(3); 15; **Deut** 1:22; 28; 2:34; 35; 37; 3:4(2); 5; 7; 10(2); 12; 19; 4:41; 42; 6:10; 9:1; 13:12; 19:1; 2; 5; 7; 9; 11; 20:15(2); 16; 21:2; **Josh** 9:17(2); 10:2; 19; 20; 37; 39; 11:12; 13; 14; 21; 13:10; 17; 21; 23; 25; 28; 30; 31; 14:4; 12; 15:9; 21; 32; 36; 41; 44; 51; 54; 57; 59; 60; 62; 16:9(2); 17:9(2); 12; 18:9; 21; 24; 28; 19:6; 7; 8; 15; 16; 22; 23; 30; 31; 35; 38; 39; 48; 20:2; 4; 9; 21:2; 3; 4; 5; 6; 7; 8; 9; 16; 18; 19(2); 20; 22; 24; 25; 26; 27; 29; 31; 32; 33(2); 35; 37; 39; 40(2); 41(2); 42(2); 24:13; **Judg** 10:4; 11:26; 33; 12:7; 20:14; 15; 42; 48; 21:23; **1Sa** 6:18(2); 7:14; 18:6; 30:29(2); 31:7; **2Sa** 2:1; 3; 8:8; 10:12; 12:31; 20:6; 24:7; **1Kin** 4:13; 8:37; 9:11; 12; 13; 19(3); 10:26; 12:17; 13:32; 15:20; 23; 20:34; 22:39; **2Kin** 3:25; 13:25(2); 17:6; 9; 24(2); 26; 29; 18:11; 13; 19:25; 23:5; 8; 19; **1Chr** 2:22; 23; 4:31; 32; 33; 6:57; 60(2); 61(2); 62; 63; 64; 65; 66; 67; 9:2; 10:7; 13:2; 18:8; 19:7; 13; 20:3; 27:25; **2Chr** 1:14; 6:28; 8:2; 4; 5; 6(3); 9:25; 10:17; 11:5; 10; 12:4; 13:19; 14:5; 6; 7; 14(2); 15:8; 16:4(2); 17:2(2); 7; 9; 12; 13; 19; 19:5; 10; 20:4; 21:3; 23:2; 24:5; 25:13; 26:6; 27:4; 28:18; 31:1(2); 6; 15; 19; 32:1; 29; 33:14; 34:6; **Ezr** 2:70(2); 3:1; 4:10; 10:14; **Neh** 7:73(2); 8:15; 9:25; 10:37; 11:1; 3(2); 20; 12:44; **Est** 9:2; **Job** 15:28; **Ps** 9:6; 69:35; **Is** 1:7; 6:11; 14:17; 21; 17:2; 9; 19:18; 33:8; 36:1; 37:26; 40:9; 42:11; 44:26; 54:3; 61:4; 64:10; **Jer** 1:15; 2:15; 28; 4:5; 7; 16; 26; 5:6; 17; 7:17; 34; 8:14; 9:11; 10:22; 11:6; 12; 13; 13:19; 17:26; 20:16; 22:6; 25:18; 26:2; 31:21; 23; 24; 32:44(4); 33:10; 12; 13(4); 34:1; 7(3); 22; 36:6; 9; 40:5; 10; 44:2; 6; 17; 21; 48:9; 15; 24; 28; 49:1; 13; 18; 50:32; 40; 51:43; **Lam** 5:11; **Eze** 6:6; 12:20; 19:7; 25:9(2); 26:19; 29:12(2); 30:7(2); 17; 35:4; 9; 36:4; 10; 33; 35; 38; 39:9; **Dan** 11:15; **Hos** 8:14(2); 11:6; 13:10; **Amos** 4:6; 8; 9:14; **Obad** 20; **Mic** 5:11; 14; 7:12; **Zeph** 1:16; 3:6; **Zec** 1:12; 17; 7:7; 8:20; **Mt** 9:35; 10:23; 11:1; 20; 14:13; **Mk** 6:33; 56; **Lk** 4:43; 13:22; 19:17; 19; **Acts** 5:16; 8:40; 14:6; 16:4; 26:11; **2Pet** 2:6; **Jude** 7; **Rev** 16:19

CONCERNING

Gen 5:29; 12:20; 19:21; 24:9; 26:32; 42:21; **Ex** 6:8; 24:8; **Lev** 4:2; 13; 22; 26; 27; 5:6; 18; 6:3; 18; 23:2; 27:32; **Num** 8:20; 22; 9:8; 10:29; 14:30; 30:1; 12(2); 32:28; 36:6; **Josh** 14:6; 23:14; **Judg** 15:3; 21:5; **Ruth** 4:7(2); **1Sa** 3:12; 25:30; **2Sa** 3:8; 7:25(2); 11:18; 13:39; 14:8; 18:5; **1Kin** 2:4; 27; 5:8(2); 6:12; 8:41; 10:1; 11:2; 10; 22:8; 18; 23; **2Kin** 10:10; 17:15; 19:21; 32; 22:13(2); **1Chr** 11:10; 17:23(2); 19:2; 22:12; 13; 23:14; 24:21; 29; 26:1; 21; **2Chr** 6:32; 8:15(2); 12:15; 15:16; 24:27; 31:6; 9; 34:21; 26; **Ezr** 5:5; 17; 6:3; 7:14; 10:2; **Neh** 1:2(2); 9:23; 11:23; 24; 13:14; 22; **Est** 3:2; 9:26; **Job** 36:33(2); **Ps** 7:t, 17:4; 73:8; 90:13; 106:34; 119:128; 152; 135:14; **Eccl** 1:13; 3:18; 7:10; **Is** 1:1; 2:1; 8:1; 16:13; 23:5; 29:22; 30:7; 37:9; 22; 33; 45:11(2); **Jer** 7:22; 14:1; 15; 16:3(4); 18:7(2); 9(2); 22:18; 23:15; 25:1; 27:19(4); 21; 29:31; 30:4(2); 32:36; 33:4(2); 39:11; 42:19; 44:1; 49:1; 7; 23; 28(2); 52:21; **Lam** 1:17; **Eze** 13:16; 14:7; 22(2); 18:2; 21:28(2); 36:6; 44:5; 45:14; 47:14; **Dan** 2:18; 5:29; 6:4; 5; 12; 17; 7:12; 8:13; **Amos** 1:1; **Obad** 1; **Mic** 1:1; 3:5; **Nah** 1:14; **Hag** 2:11; **Mt** 4:6; 11:7; 16:11; **Mk** 5:16; 7:17; **Lk** 2:17; 7:24; 18:31; 22:37; 24:19; 27; 44; **Jn** 7:12; 32; 9:18; 11:19; **Acts** 1:16; 2:25; 8:12; 13:34; 19:8; 39; 21:24; 22:18; 23:15; 24:24; 25:16; 28:21; 22; 23; **Rom** 1:3; 9:5; 27; 11:28; 16:19; **1Cor** 5:3; 7:1; 25; 8:4; 12:1; 16:1; **2Cor** 8:23; 11:21; **Eph** 4:22; 5:32; **Phil** 3:6; 4:15; **1Th** 3:2; 4:13; 5:18; **1Ti** 1:19; 6:21; **2Ti** 2:18; 3:8; **Heb** 7:14; 11:20; 22; **1Pet** 4:12; **2Pet** 3:9; **1Jn** 2:26

COULD

Gen 13:6; 27:1; 36:7; 37:4; 41:8; 21; 24; 43:7; 45:1; 3; 48:10; **Ex** 2:3; 7:21; 24; 8:18; 9:11; 12:39; 15:23; **Num** 9:6; **Josh** 7:12; 15:63; 17:12; **Judg** 1:19; 2:14; 3:22; 6:27; 12:6; 14:14; 17:8; 20:16; **Ruth** 3:14; **1Sa** 3:2; 4:15; 10:21; 23:13; 30:10; 21; **2Sa** 1:10; 3:11; 17:20; 22:39; **1Kin** 5:3; 8:5; 11; 13:4; 14:4; **2Kin** 3:26; 4:40; 16:5; **1Chr** 12:2; 8; 33; 38; 21:30; **2Chr** 4:18; 5:6; 14; 7:2; 13:7; 14:13; 20:25; 25:5; 15; 29:34; 30:3; 32:14; 34:12; **Ezr** 2:59; 3:13; 5:5; **Neh** 7:61; 8:2; 3; 13:24; **Est** 6:1; 7:4; 9:2; **Job** 4:16; 16:4(2); 31:23; **Ps** 37:36; 55:12; 73:7; 78:44; **Song** 5:6; **Is** 5:4; 7:1; 30:5; 33:23(2); 41:28; 46:2; **Jer** 6:15; 8:12; 15:1; 20:9; 24:2; 44:22; **Lam** 4:14; 17; **Eze** 31:8; 47:5(2); **Dan** 5:8; 15; 6:4; 8:4; 7; **Hos** 5:13; **Jonah** 1:13; **Mt** 17:16; 19; 26:40; 27:24; **Mk** 1:45; 2:4; 3:20; 5:3; 4; 6:5; 19; 7:24; 9:18; 28; 14:8; **Lk** 1:22; 5:19; 6:40; 8:19; 43; 9:40; 13:11; 14:6; 19:3; 48; 20:7; 26; **Jn** 9:33; 11:37; 12:39; 21:25; **Acts** 4:14; 11:17; 13:39; 21:34; 22:11; 25:7; 27:15; 43; **Rom** 8:3; 9:3; **1Cor** 3:1; 13:2; **2Cor** 3:7; 13; 11:1; **Gal** 3:21; **1Th** 3:1; 5; **Heb** 3:19; 6:13; 9:9; 12:20; **Rev** 7:9; 14:3

DAY'S

Num 11:31(2); **1Kin** 19:4; **1Chr** 16:37; **Est** 9:13; **Jonah** 3:4; **Lk** 2:44; **Acts** 1:12; 19:40

DAYS

Gen 1:14; 3:14; 17; 5:4; 5; 8; 11; 14; 17; 20; 23; 27; 31; 6:3; 4; 7:4(2); 10; 12; 17; 24; 8:3; 6; 10; 12; 9:29; 10:25; 11:32; 14:1; 17:12; 21:4; 34; 24:55; 25:7; 24; 26:1; 15; 18; 27:41; 44; 29:20; 21; 30:14; 35:28; 29; 37:34; 40:12; 13; 18; 19; 42:17; 47:9(4); 49:1; 50:3(3); 4; 10; **Ex** 2:11; 7:25; 10:22; 23; 12:15; 19; 13:6; 7; 15:22; 16:26; 20:9; 11; 12; 22:30; 23:12; 15; 26; 24:16; 18; 29:30; 35; 37; 31:15; 17; 34:18; 21; 28; 35:2; **Lev** 8:33(3); 35; 12:2(2); 4(2); 5; 6; 13:4; 5; 21; 26; 31; 33; 46; 50; 54; 14:8; 38; 15:13; 19; 24; 25(3); 26; 28; 22:27; 23:3; 6; 8; 16; 34; 36; 39; 40; 41; 42; **Num** 6:4; 5(2); 6; 8; 12(2); 13; 9:19; 20; 22; 10:10; 11:19(4); 12:14(2); 15; 13:25; 14:34(2); 19:11; 14; 16; 20:29; 24:14; 28:17; 24; 29:12; 31:19; **Deut** 1:46(2); 2:1; 4:9; 10; 26; 30; 32; 40; 5:13; 16; 33; 6:2(2); 9:9; 11; 18; 25; 10:10; 11:9; 21(3); 12:1; 16:3(2); 4; 8; 13; 15; 17:9; 19; 20; 19:17; 22:7; 19; 29; 23:6; 25:15; 26:3; 30:18; 20; 31:14; 29; 32:7; 47; 33:25; 34:8(2); **Josh** 1:5; 11; 2:16; 22; 3:2; 4:14; 6:3; 14; 9:16; 20:6; 22:3; 24:31(2); **Judg** 2:7(2); 18; 5:6(2); 8:28; 11:40; 14:12; 14; 17; 15:20; 17:6; 18:1(2); 19:1; 4; 20:27; 28; 21:25; **Ruth** 1:1; **1Sa** 1:11; 2:31; 3:1; 7:13; 15; 9:20; 10:8; 13:8; 11; 14:52; 17:12; 16; 18:26; 20:19; 21:5; 25:10; 28; 38; 28:1; 29:3; 30:12; 13; 31:13; **2Sa** 1:1; 7:12; 16:23; 20:4; 21:1; 9(2); 24:8; **1Kin** 2:1; 11; 38; 3:2; 13; 14; 4:21; 25; 8:40; 65(3); 10:21; 11:12; 25; 34; 12:5; 14:20; 30; 15:5; 6; 14; 16; 32; 16:15; 34; 17:15; 18:1; 19:8; 20:29; 21:29(2); 22:46; **2Kin** 2:17; 8:20; 10:32; 12:2; 13:3; 22; 15:18; 29; 37; 18:4; 20:1; 6; 17; 19; 23:22(2); 20; 24:1; 25:30; 30; **1Chr** 1:19; 4:41; 5:10; 17(2); 7:2; 22; 9:25; 10:12; 12:39; 13:3; 17:11; 21:12; 22:9; 23:1; 29:15; 28; **2Chr** 7:8; 9(2); 9:20; 10:5; 13:20; 14:1; 15:17; 20:25; 21:8; 24:2; 14; 15; 26:5; 29:17; 30:21; 22; 23(2); 32:24; 26; 34:33; 35:17; 18; 36:9; **Ezr** 4:2; 5; 7; 6:22; 8:15; 32; 9:7; 10:8; 9; **Neh** 1:4; 2:11; 5:18; 6:15; 17; 8:17; 18; 12:7; 12; 22; 23; 26(2); 46; 47(2); 13:6; 15; 23; **Est** 1:1; 2; 4(2); 5(2); 2:12; 21; 4:11; 16; 9:22(2); 26; 27; 28(2); 31; **Job** 1:5; 2:13; 3:6; 7:1(2); 6; 16; 8:9; 9:25; 10:5(3); 20; 12:12; 14:1; 5; 14; 15:20; 17:1; 11; 21:13; 24:1; 29:2; 4; 18; 30:16; 27; 32:7; 33:25; 36:11; 38:12; 21; 42:17; **Ps** 21:4; 23:6; 27:4; 34:12; 37:18; 19; 39:4; 5; 44:1; 49:5; 55:23; 72:7; 77:5; 78:33; 89:29; 45; 90:9; 10; 12; 14; 15; 94:13; 102:3; 11; 23; 24; 103:15; 109:8; 119:84; 128:5; 143:5; 144:4; **Prov** 3:2; 16; 9:11; 10:27; 15:15; 28:16; 31:12; **Eccl** 2:3; 16; 23; 5:17; 18; 20; 6:3; 12; 7:10; 15; 8:12; 13; 15; 9:9(2); 11:1; 8; 9; 12:1(2); **Is** 1:1; 2:2; 7:1; 17; 13:22; 23:7; 15; 24:22; 30:26; 32:10; 38:1; 5; 10; 20; 39:6; 8; 51:9; 53:10; 60:20; 63:9; 11; 65:20(2); 22(2); **Jer** 1:2; 3; 2:32; 3:6; 16; 18; 5:18; 6:11; 7:32; 9:25; 13:6; 16:9; 14; 17:11; 19:6; 20:18; 22:30; 23:5; 6; 7; 20; 25:34; 26:18; 30:3; 24; 31:27; 29; 31; 33; 38; 32:14; 33:14; 15; 16; 35:1; 7(2); 8; 36:2; 37:16; 42:7; 46:26; 48:12; 47; 49:2; 39; 50:4; 20; 51:47; 52; 52:33; 34; **Lam** 1:7(2); 2:17; 4:18; 5:21; **Eze** 3:15; 16; 4:4; 5(2); 6; 8; 9(2); 5:2; 12:22; 23; 25; 27; 16:22; 43; 60; 22:4; 14; 23:19; 38:8; 16; 17; 43:25; 26; 27; 44:26; 45:21; 23(2); 25; 46:1; **Dan** 1:12; 14; 15; 18; 2:28; 44; 4:34; 5:11; 6:7; 12; 7:9; 13; 22; 8:14; 26; 27; 10:2; 13; 14(2); 11:20; 33; 12:11; 12; 13; **Hos** 1:1(2); 2:11; 13; 15; 3:3; 4; 5; 6:2; 9:7(2); 9; 10:9; 12:9; **Joel** 1:2(2); 2:29; 3:1; **Amos** 1:1(2); 4:2; 5:21; 8:11; 9:11; 13; **Jonah** 1:17; 3:4; **Mic** 1:1; 4:1; 7:14; 15; 20; **Hab** 1:5; **Zeph** 1:1; **Hag** 2:16; **Zec** 8:6; 9; 10; 11; 15; 23; 14:5; **Mal** 3:4; 7; **Mt** 2:1; 3:1; 4:2; 9:15; 11:12; 12:5; 10; 12; 40(2); 15:32; 17:1; 23:30; 24:19; 22(2); 29; 37; 38; 26:2; 61; 27:40; 63; **Mk** 1:9; 13; 2:1; 20(2); 26; 3:4; 8:1; 2; 31; 9:2; 13:17; 19; 20(2); 24; 14:1; 58; 15:29; **Lk** 1:5; 23; 24; 25; 39; 75; 2:1; 6; 21; 22; 43; 46; 4:2(2); 25; 31; 5:35(2); 6:2; 9; 12; 9:28; 36; 13:14; 15:13; 17:22(2); 26(2); 28; 19:43; 20:1; 21:6; 22; 23; 23:29; 24:18; **Jn** 2:12; 19; 20; 4:40; 43; 11:6; 17; 39; 12:1; 20:26; **Acts** 1:3; 5; 15; 2:17; 18; 3:24; 5:36; 37; 6:1; 7:41; 45; 9:9; 19; 23; 37; 43; 10:30; 48; 11:27; 28; 12:3; 13:31; 41; 15:36; 16:12; 18; 17:2; 20:6(3); 21:4; 5; 10; 15; 26; 27; 38; 24:1; 11; 24; 25:1; 6; 13; 14; 27:7; 20; 28:7; 12; 14; 17; **Gal** 1:18; 4:10; **Eph** 5:16; **Col** 2:16; **2Ti** 3:1; **Heb** 1:2; 5:7; 7:3; 8:8; 10; 10:16; 32; 11:30; 12:10; **Jas** 5:3; **1Pet** 3:10; 20; **2Pet** 3:3; **Rev** 2:10; 13; 9:6; 10:7; 11:3; 6; 9; 11; 12:6

DAYS'

Gen 30:36; 31:23; **Ex** 3:18; 5:3; 8:27; **Num** 10:33(2); 33:8; **Deut** 1:2; **1Sa** 11:3; **2Sa** 24:13; **2Kin** 3:9; **Jonah** 3:3

DOWN

Gen 11:5; 7; 12:10; 15:11; 12; 17; 18:21; 19:4; 33; 35; 21:16; 23:12; 24:11; 14; 16; 18; 26; 45; 46; 48; 26:2; 27:29(2); 28:11; 37:10; 25(2); 35; 38:1; 39:1(2); 42:2; 3; 6; 38(2); 43:4; 5; 7; 11; 15; 20; 22; 28; 44:11; 21; 23; 26(2); 29; 31; 45:9; 13; 46:3; 4; 49:6; 8; 9; 14; 50:18; **Ex** 2:5; 15; 3:8; 7:10; 12; 9:19; 11:8(2); 17:11; 12; 19:11; 14; 20; 21; 24; 25; 20:5; 22:26; 23:24(2); 32:1; 6; 7; 15; 34:13; 29(2); **Lev** 9:22; 11:35; 14:45; 18:23; 19:16; 20:16; 22:7; 26:1; 6; 30; **Num** 1:51; 4:5; 10:17; 11:17; 25; 12:5; 13:23; 24; 14:45; 16:30; 33; 20:15; 28; 21:15; 22:27; 31; 23:24; 24:9; 25:2; 33:52; 34:11; 12; **Deut** 1:25; 5:9; 6:7; 7:5(2); 9:3; 12; 15; 18; 25(2); 10:5; 22; 11:19; 30; 12:3; 16:6; 19:5; 20:19; 20; 21:4; 22:4; 23:11; 24:13; 15; 19; 25:2; 26:4; 5; 15; 28:24; 43; 52; 33:3; 28; **Josh** 1:4; 2:8; 15; 18; 3:13; 16(2); 4:8; 6:5; 20; 7:5; 8:29(2); 10:11(2); 13; 27(2); 15:10; 16:3; 7; 17:15; 18; 18:16; 18; 24:4; **Judg** 1:9; 34; 2:2; 19; 3:25; 27; 28; 4:14; 15; 5:11; 14; 21; 27(2); 6:25(2); 26; 28(2); 30(2); 31; 32; 7:4; 5(2); 6; 9; 10(2); 11(2); 24; 8:9; 17; 9:36; 37; 45; 48; 49; 11:37; 14:1; 5; 7; 10; 18; 19; 15:8; 12; 16:21; 31; 19:6; 14; 15; 26; 27; 20:21; 25; 32; 39; 43; **Ruth** 3:3; 4(2); 6; 7(2); 13; 4:1(3); 2(2); **1Sa** 2:6; 3:2; 3; 5(2); 6; 9(2); 6:15; 18; 21; 9:25; 27; 10:5; 8(2); 13:12; 20; 14:16; 36; 37; 15:6; 12; 16:11; 17:8; 28(2); 52; 19:12; 24; 20:19; 24; 21:13; 22:1; 23:4; 6; 8; 11(2); 20(2); 25; 25:1; 20(2); 26:2; 6(2); 29:4; 30:15(2); 16; 24; 31:1; **2Sa** 2:13; 16; 23(2); 24; 3:35; 5:17; 8:2; 11:8; 9; 10(2); 13; 13:5; 6; 8; 15:20; 24; 17:18; 18:28; 19:16; 18; 20; 24; 31; 20:15; 21:15; 22:10; 28; 48; 23:13; 20; 21; **1Kin** 1:25; 33; 38; 53; 2:6; 8; 9; 19; 5:9; 8:33; 17:23; 18:30; 40; 42; 44; 19:4; 6; 10; 14; 21:4; 16; 18(2); 22:2; 36; **2Kin** 1:2; 4; 6; 9; 10(2); 11; 12(2); 14; 15(2); 16; 2:2; 3:12; 25; 5:14; 18; 21; 6:4; 6; 9; 18; 33; 7:17; 8:29; 9:16; 24; 33(2); 10:13; 27(2); 11:6; 18; 19; 12:20; 13:14; 21; 14:9; 13; 16:17; 18:4; 19:16; 23; 20:10; 11; 21:13; 23:5; 7; 8; 12(2); 14; 15; 25:10; **1Chr** 5:22; 7:21; 10:1; 11:15; 22; 23; 29:20; **2Chr** 6:13; 7:1; 3; 13:17; 14:3(2); 15:16; 18:2; 34; 20:16; 22:6; 23:17; 20; 25:8; 12; 14; 18; 23; 26:6; 31:1(2); 32:30; 33:3; 34:4(2); 7(2); 36:3; 19; **Ezr** 6:11; 9:3; 10:1; 16; **Neh** 1:3; 4; 2:13; 3:15; 4:3; 6:3(2); 16; 9:13; **Est** 3:15; 8:3; **Job** 1:7; 20; 2:2; 8; 13; 6:21; 7:4; 9; 19; 8:12; 11:19; 12:14; 14:2; 7; 12; 17:3; 16; 18:7; 20:11; 15; 18; 21:13; 26; 22:16; 20; 29; 27:19; 29:24; 31:10; 32:13; 33:24; 36:27; 40:12; 41:1; 9; **Ps** 3:5; 4:8; 7:5; 16; 9:15; 14:2; 17:11; 13; 18:9; 27; 20:8; 22:29; 23:2; 28:1; 30:3; 9; 31:2; 35:14; 36:12; 37:2; 14; 24; 38:6; 42:5; 6; 11; 43:5; 44:5; 25; 50:1; 53:2; 55:15; 23; 56:7; 57:6; 59:11; 15; 60:12; 62:4; 72:6; 11; 73:18; 74:6; 7; 75:7; 78:16; 24; 31; 80:12; 14; 16; 85:11; 86:1; 88:4; 89:23; 40; 44; 90:6; 95:6; 102:10; 19; 104:8; 19; 22; 107:12(2); 23; 26; 108:13; 109:23; 113:3; 115:17; 119:118; 136; 133:2(2); 137:1; 139:3; 143:3; 7; 144:5; 145:14; 146:8; 9; 147:6; **Prov** 1:12; 3:20; 24(2); 5:5; 7:26; 27; 14:1; 18:8; 21:22; 22:17; 23:34; 24:31; 25:26; 28; 26:22; **Eccl** 1:5; 3:3; **Song** 2:3; 6:2; 11; 7:9; **Is** 2:9; 11; 17; 5:5(2); 15; 9:10(2); 10:4; 6; 13; 33; 34; 11:6; 7; 14:8; 11; 12; 15; 19; 30; 16:8; 17:2; 18:2; 5; 21:3; 22:5(2); 10; 19; 25; 24:1; 10; 19; 25:5; 10(2); 11; 12; 26:5; 6; 27:10; 28:2; 18; 29:4; 16; 30:2; 30; 31; 31:1; 3; 4; 32:19; 33:9; 20; 34:4; 5; 7; 37:24; 38:8(2); 18; 42:10; 43:14; 17; 44:14; 15; 17; 19; 45:8(2); 14; 46:1; 2; 6; 47:1; 49:23; 50:11; 51:23; 52:2; 4; 55:10; 56:10; 59:5; 60:14; 20; 63:6(2); 14; 15; 18; 64:1(2); 3(2); 65:10; 12; **Jer** 1:10(2); 3:25; 4:26; 6:6; 15; 8:12; 9:18; 13:17; 18(2); 14:17; 15:9; 18:2; 3; 7; 21:13; 22:1; 7; 24:6; 25:37; 26:10; 31:28(2); 40; 33:4; 12; 36:12; 15; 38:6; 11; 39:8; 42:10; 45:4; 46:5; 23; 48:2; 5; 15; 18; 20; 39; 49:16; 50:15; 27; 51:25; 40; 52:14; **Lam** 1:9; 16; 2:1; 2(2); 10; 17; 18; 3:48; 49; 50; 63; **Eze** 1:13; 24; 25; 6:4; 6; 11:13; 13:14(2); 16:39(2); 17:24; 19:2; 6; 12; 24:16; 26:4; 9; 11(2); 12; 16; 20(2); 27:29; 28:8; 14; 30:4; 6; 25; 31:12; 14; 15; 16; 17; 18; 32:18(2); 19; 21; 24(2); 25; 27; 29; 30(2); 34:15; 18; 26; 37:1; 38:20; 39:10; 47:1; 8; **Dan** 3:5; 6; 7; 10; 11; 15; 23; 4:13; 14; 23(2); 5:19; 6:14; 7:9; 23; 8:7; 10; 11; 12; 11:12; 26; **Hos** 2:18; 7:12; 10:2; **Joel** 1:17; 2:23; 3:2; 11; 13; 18; **Amos** 2:8; 3:11; 5:24; 6:2; 8:9; 9:2; **Obad** 3; 4; 16; **Jonah** 1:3(2); 5; 2:6; **Mic** 1:3; 4; 6; 12; 3:6; 5:8; 11; 6:14; 7:10; **Nah** 1:6; 12; **Zeph** 1:11; 2:7; 14; 15; 3:13; **Hag** 2:22; **Zec** 10:5; 11; 12; 11:2; **Mal** 1:4; 11; 4:3; **Mt** 2:11; 3:10; 4:6; 9; 7:19; 8:1; 11; 32; 9:10; 11:23; 13:48; 14:19; 29; 15:29; 30; 35; 17:9; 14; 18:26; 29; 21:8; 24:2; 17; 26:20; 27:5; 19; 36; 40; 42; **Mk** 1:7; 40; 2:4; 3:11; 22; 5:13; 33; 6:39; 40; 8:6; 9:9; 35; 11:8; 13:2; 15; 15:30; 36; 46; **Lk** 1:52; 2:51; 3:9; 4:9; 20; 29; 31; 5:3; 4; 5; 8; 19; 29; 6:17; 38; 7:36; 8:5; 23; 28; 33; 41; 47; 9:14; 15; 37; 42; 44; 54; 10:15; 30; 31; 11:37; 12:18; 37; 13:7; 9; 29; 14:8; 10; 28; 31; 16:6; 17:7; 16; 31; 18:14; 19:5; 6; 21; 22; 21:6; 24; 22:14; 41; 44; 55(2); 23:53; 24:5; 12; **Jn** 2:12; 3:13; 4:47; 49; 51; 5:4; 7; 6:10(2); 11; 16; 33; 38; 41; 42; 50; 51; 58; 8:2; 6; 8; 10:15; 17; 18(2); 11:32; 13:12; 37; 38; 15:13; 19:13; 20:5; 11; **Acts** 4:35; 5:5; 10; 7:15; 34; 58; 60; 8:5; 15; 26; 38; 9:25; 30; 32; 40; 10:11; 20; 21; 25; 11:5; 12:19; 13:14; 29; 14:11; 25; 15:1; 16; 16:8; 13; 29; 17:6; 18:22; 19:35; 20:9(2); 10; 36; 21:5; 10; 32; 22:30; 23:10; 15; 20; 24:22; 25:5; 6; 7; 27:27; 30; 28:6; **Rom** 10:6; 11:3; 10; 16:4; **1Cor** 10:7; 14:25; 15:24; **2Cor** 4:9; 7:6; 10:4; 5; 11:33; **Eph** 2:14; 4:26; **Heb** 1:3; 10:12; 11:30; 12:2; 12; **Jas** 1:17; 5:4; **1Pet** 1:12; **2Pet** 2:4; **1Jn** 3:16(2); **Rev** 1:13; 3:12; 21; 4:10; 5:8; 14; 10:1; 12:10; 12; 13:13; 18:1; 21; 19:4; 20:1; 9; 21:2; 22:8

EACH

Gen 15:10; 34:25; 40:5(2); 41:11; 12; 45:22; **Ex** 18:7; 30:34; **Lev** 24:7; **Num** 1:44; 7:3; 11; 85(2); 14:34; 16:17; 17:6; 29:14; 15; **Josh** 18:4; 22:14(2); **Judg** 8:18; 21:22; **Ruth** 1:8; 9; **1Kin** 4:7; 6:23; 22:10; **2Kin** 9:21; 15:20; **1Chr** 20:6(2); **2Chr** 3:15; 4:13; 9:18; **Neh** 13:24; **Ps** 85:10; **Is** 2:20; 6:2; 35:7; 57:2; **Eze** 4:6; 40:16; 48; **Lk** 13:15; **Acts** 2:3; **Phil** 2:3; **2Th** 1:3; **Rev** 4:8

EITHER

Gen 31:24; 29; **Lev** 10:1; 13:49; 51; 53; 57; 58; 59; 22:23; 25:49; **Num** 6:2; 22:26; 24:13; **Deut** 17:3; 28:51; **Judg** 9:2; **1Sa** 20:2; 25:31; 30:2; **1Kin** 7:15; 10:19; 18:27; **1Chr** 21:12; **2Chr** 18:9; **Eccl** 9:1; 11:6; **Is** 7:11; 17:8; **Eze** 21:16; **Mt** 6:24; 12:33; **Lk** 6:42; 15:8; 16:13; **Jn** 19:18; **Acts** 17:21; **1Cor** 14:6; **Phil** 3:12; **Jas** 3:12; **Rev** 22:2

ELSE

Gen 30:1; 42:16; **Ex** 8:21; 10:4; **Num** 20:19; **Deut** 4:35; 39; **Josh** 23:12; **Judg** 7:14; **2Sa** 3:35; 15:14; **1Kin** 8:60; 20:39; 21:6; **1Chr** 21:12; **2Chr** 23:7; **Neh** 2:2; **Ps** 51:16; **Eccl** 2:25; **Is** 45:5; 6; 14; 18; 21; 22; 46:9; 47:8; 10; **Joel** 2:27; **Mt** 6:24; 9:17; 12:29; 33; **Mk** 2:21; 22; **Lk** 5:37; 14:32; 16:13; **Jn** 14:11; **Acts** 17:21; 24:20; **Rom** 2:15; **1Cor** 7:14; 14:16; 15:29; **Phil** 1:27; **Rev** 2:5; 16

ENOUGH

Gen 24:25; 33:9; 11; 34:21; 45:28; **Ex** 2:19; 9:28; 36:5; **Deut** 1:6; 2:3; **Josh** 17:16; **2Sa** 24:16; **1Kin** 19:4; **1Chr** 21:15; **2Chr** 31:10; **Prov** 27:27; 28:19; 30:15; 16; **Is** 56:11; **Jer** 49:9; **Hos** 4:10; **Obad** 5; **Nah** 2:12; **Hag** 1:6; **Mal** 3:10; **Mt** 10:25; 25:9; **Mk** 14:41; **Lk** 15:17; 22:38; **Acts** 27:38

EVEN

Gen 6:17; 9:3; 10:9; 19; 21; 13:3; 10; 14:23; 19:1; 4; 9; 20:5; 21:10; 23:7; 10; 24:11; 26:28; 27:34; 38; 34:29; 35:14; 37:18; 42:28; 44:18; 46:18; 34; 47:2; 21; 49:22; 25; **Ex** 3:1; 4:16; 22; 23; 9:18; 10:12; 21; 11:5; 12:15; 18(2); 19; 38; 41; 14:23; 16:6; 12; 13; 18:14; 23:31; 25:9; 19; 27:5; 28:1; 8; 17; 42; 29:27; 28; 39; 41; 30:8; 21; 23; 33; 38; 32:29; 35:35; 36:2; 37:3; 9; 38:21; 24; 39:37; 43; **Lev** 1:2; 2:14; 3:14; 4:12; 17; 5:12; 6:5; 15; 7:8; 20; 21; 25; 27; 8:9; 11:11; 22; 24; 25; 27; 28; 31; 32; 39; 40(2); 13:12; 18; 30; 38; 14:9; 31; 46; 15:5; 6; 7; 8; 10(2); 11; 16; 17; 18; 19; 21; 22; 23; 27; 16:32; 17:5; 9; 10; 13; 15; 18:9; 10; 29; 19:21; 20:6; 10; 22:6; 23:2; 4; 5; 16; 18; 32(3); 24:7; 26:16; 28; 34; 43; 27:3(2); 5; 6; 18; 23; 24; 32; **Num** 1:21; 23; 25; 27; 29; 31; 33; 35; 37; 39; 41; 43; 46; 3:22; 38; 47; 4:3; 14; 30; 35; 39;

40; 43; 44; 47; 48; 5:8; 26; 6:4; 7:10; 8:8; 16; 9:3; 5; 11; 13; 15; 21; 11:20; 12:8; 14:19; 34(2); 37; 45; 15:23; 16:5(2); 17:6; 18:21; 26; 29; 19:7; 8; 10; 19; 21; 22; 20:1; 22; 29; 21:24; 26; 30(2); 25:13; 14; 27:21; 28:4; 8; 31:47; 51; 32:4; 33(2); 33:49; 34:2; 6; 36:10; **Deut** 1:44; 2:22; 23; 36; 3:16(2); 17(2); 4:5; 13; 19; 20; 24; 30; 48; 49; 5:3; 23; 9:9; 11; 21; 10:15; 11:12; 24; 12:5; 22; 30; 31; 13:7; 16:3; 4; 6; 17:5; 12; 18:20; 20:14; 21:3; 22:26; 23:2; 3; 16; 18; 23; 25:18; 26:9; 28:59; 64(2); 67(2); 29:24; 31:21; 32:31; 39; 33:4; **Josh** 1:2; 4; 2:1; 24; 3:16; 5:4; 10; 6:17; 25; 7:5; 11(2); 8:4; 11; 13; 25; 28; 9:20; 27; 10:41(2); 11:4; 17(2); 12:2; 3; 7; 13:3; 8; 24; 27; 31; 14:10; 11; 15:1; 5; 13; 46; 16:5; 17:11; 17; 19:1; 28; 32; 50; 21:20; 23:4; 12; 24:2; 12; 18; **Judg** 3:1; 9; 4:13; 5:3; 5; 11; 15; 6:3; 25; 7:22; 8:14; 19; 27; 9:40; 11:13; 22(2); 33(2); 36; 18:15; 19:16; 20:1; 2; 23; 26; 33; 21:2; **Ruth** 2:7; 15; 17; **1Sa** 3:20; 5:6; 6:18; 19; 7:14; 8:8; 14; 14:21; 22; 17:40; 52; 18:4; 11; 19:10; 20:4; 5; 16; 25; 25:25; 27; 26:8; 27:3; 8; 28:3; 17; 30:17; 26; **2Sa** 1:2; 12; 2:5; 3:9; 10; 15; 6:5; 19; 7:6; 23; 8:2; 10:4; 11:13; 23; 14:25; 15:12; 21; 17:11; 18:5; 19:11; 14; 32; 20:2; 21; 22:42; 23:4; 24:2; 7; 15(2); **1Kin** 1:26; 30(2); 37; 48; 2:22; 4:12; 24; 25; 29; 33; 6:16(3); 7:7; 9; 10; 42; 51; 8:4; 6; 29; 39; 65; 11:26; 35; 12:27; 30; 33; 13:34; 14:14; 26; 15:13; 28; 16:7; 18:22; 26; 19:10; 14; 20:3; 14; 15; 21:11; 13; 19; 22:35; **2Kin** 3:24; 26; 4:3; 5:22; 7:6; 7; 13; 8:6; 9; 9:4; 6; 20; 10:3; 14; 33; 11:2; 5; 7; 12:4; 14:10; 29; 15:20; 17:16; 18:8; 10; 21; 19:15; 19; 22; 20:14; 21:15; 22:16; 24:14; 16(2); 25:22; 23; **1Chr** 2:23; 4:15; 39; 42; 5:8; 24; 26; 6:39; 10:13; 11:2; 8; 12:2; 40; 13:5; 14:16; 16:16; 19; 17:7; 24(2); 20:3; 21:2; 12; 17; 23:24; 30; 24:31; 25:7; 26:12; 21; 31; 28:15; 19; 20; 21; 29:4; 21; **2Chr** 2:3; 9; 5:7; 13(2); 6:21; 33; 39; 8:10; 13(2); 9:26; 11:6; 13:3; 5; 17:7; 8; 18:13; 21; 34; 19:10; 20:4; 24:14; 25:13; 19; 26:8; 19; 28:10; 27; 30:5; 10; 18; 27; 31:16; 33:14; 34:6; 11; 24; 27; 33; **Ezr** 1:8; 3:3; 4:5; 11; 5:1; 16; 6:8; 7:11; 21; 8:25; 26; 9:1; **Neh** 2:13; 3:1; 10; 21; 24; 27; 4:3(2); 13; 5:8; 11; 13; 14; 15; 8:13; 9:6; 12:23; 37; 38; 39; 43; 13:26; **Est** 1:1; 4; 2:18; 3:6; 13; 4:2; 5:3; 6; 6:10; 7:2; **Job** 4:8; 21; 5:5; 6:9; 10:21; 15:26; 17:5; 11; 18:13; 21:6; 23:2; 3; 13; 24:17; 25:5; 28:4; 31:6; 34:17; 36:16; 41:9; 42:16; **Ps** 18:6; 41; 21:4; 24:9; 26:12; 27:2; 35:23; 39:t, 2; 40:3; 45:12; 47:9; 48:14; 50:1; 7; 55:19; 57:4(2); 59:12; 64:3; 65:4; 67:6; 68:8; 17; 19; 24; 26; 71:16; 22; 73:1; 74:3; 11; 76:7; 77:1; 78:6; 54; 84:2; 3; 90:2; 11; 91:9; 105:17; 20; 106:7; 38; 107:43; 108:1; 109:16; 113:8; 115:16; 118:27; 119:41; 112; 121:8; 125:2; 131:2; 133:2; 3; 136:22; 137:7; 139:10; 11; 146:10; 148:14; **Prov** 2:16; 3:12; 8:16; 14:13; 20; 16:4; 7; 15; 28; 20:11; 12; 22:19; 23:15; 28:9; 30:1(2); **Eccl** 2:12; 15; 3:19; 4:16; 7:25; 9:1; 11:5; 12:10; **Song** 4:2; **Is** 1:6; 13; 4:3; 5:9; 7:6; 17; 23; 8:7; 8; 9:7; 9; 10:21; 23; 13:3; 5; 12; 14:9; 18; 15:4; 16:6; 8; 18:2; 19:13; 22; 24; 20:4; 22:15; 24; 23:4; 24:15; 16; 25:5; 10; 12; 26:5(2); 6; 27:1; 28:22; 29:7; 8; 14; 32:7; 35:2; 4; 37:16; 20; 23; 38:11; 12; 13; 39:3; 40:30; 41:3; 12; 28; 43:7; 11; 19; 25; 44:8; 17; 28; 45:4; 12; 24; 46:4(3); 47:15; 48:5; 6; 7; 11; 15; 20; 49:10; 19; 25; 51:12; 22; 55:3; 56:5; 7; 57:6; 7; 9; 11; 65:6; 66:2; **Jer** 3:25; 4:12; 6:11; 13(2); 19; 7:11; 15; 25; 8:10(2); 9:15; 22; 10:11; 11:7; 13; 23; 12:6(2); 12; 13:10; 13; 14; 18; 15:13; 16:5; 17:4; 10; 27; 19:11; 12; 21:5; 22:25; 23:12; 19; 33; 34; 39; 24:2; 25:3; 13; 31; 33; 28:6; 11; 29:23; 30:7; 31:2; 19; 21; 32:9; 20; 31; 33:10; 24; 34:20; 36:2; 12; 39:3; 12; 14; 40:7; 8; 12; 41:1; 3; 5; 10; 16; 42:1; 2; 5; 8; 43:1; 6; 7; 44:10; 12(2); 15; 45:4; 46:25; 48:32; 34(3); 44; 49:37; 50:7; 21; 51:9; 56; 60; **Lam** 4:3; **Eze** 1:27(2); 2:3; 4:1; 13; 14; 5:8; 6:3; 7:14; 8:2(2); 6; 9:1; 10:2; 5; 12; 11:15; 17; 12:4; 7; 13:10; 13; 20; 14:10; 22; 16:19; 37; 59; 17:9; 16; 19; 18:11; 18; 20:11; 13; 21; 31; 21:13; 28; 22:4; 18; 23:34; 24:2; 4; 9; 18; 29:10; 30:3; 32:6; 16; 18; 31; 32; 33:18; 34:11; 20; 23; 30; 35:6; 11; 15; 36:2; 10; 12; 37:19; 25; 38:4; 39:17; 40:14; 41:17; 42:12; 43:1; 3; 8; 13; 14(2); 44:6; 7; 10; 19; 47:10; 19; 48:3; 6; 10; 28; **Dan** 1:21; 2:43; 4:15; 23; 5:14; 6:26; 7:11; 18; 20; 8:1; 10; 11; 15; 9:5; 11; 21; 25; 27; 11:1; 4; 10; 11; 24(2); 30; 35; 41; 12:1; 4; **Hos** 2:20; 5:14; 9:16; 12:5; **Joel** 1:2; 12; 2:2; 12; 14; **Amos** 2:11; 3:11; 5:1; 20; 8:4; 12; 14; **Obad** 7; 8; 11; 20; **Jonah** 2:5; 3:5; 4:9; **Mic** 1:9; 2:2; 8; 10; 11; 3:4; 5; 4:7; 8; 10; 7:12(2); **Nah** 2:11; 3:12; **Hab** 1:2; 3:9; 13; **Zeph** 1:14; 18; 2:5; 9; 11; 3:8; 10; 15; 20; **Hag** 2:18; **Zec** 3:2; 6:10; 13; 7:1; 5(2); 8:23; 9:7; 10(2); 12; 11:7; 10; 14; 12:6; 14:16; 17; **Mal** 1:10; 11; 12; 2:2; 3; 3:1; 7; 9; 15; **Mt** 5:46; 47; 48; 6:29; 7:12; 17; 8:16; 27; 9:18; 11:26; 12:8; 45; 13:12; 15:28; 18:14; 33; 20:8; 14; 28; 23:8; 10; 28; 37; 24:27; 33; 25:29; 26:20; 38; 27:57; 28:20; **Mk** 1:27; 32; 4:25; 35; 36; 41; 6:2; 47; 10:45; 11:6; 19; 12:44; 13:22; 29; 35; 14:30; 54; 15:42; **Lk** 1:2; 15; 2:15; 6:33; 8:18; 25; 9:54; 10:11; 17; 21; 12:7; 41; 57; 17:30; 18:11; 19:26; 32; 37; 42; 44; 20:37; 24:24; **Jn** 1:12; 3:13; 14; 5:21; 23; 45; 6:16; 57; 8:9; 25; 41; 43; 10:15; 11:22; 37; 12:50; 14:17; 31; 15:10; 26; 17:14; 16; 18; 22; 20:21; 21:25; **Acts** 2:39; 4:10; 5:37; 39; 9:17; 10:41; 11:5; 12:15; 15:8; 11; 20:11; 22:17; 26:11; 27:25; **Rom** 1:13; 20; 26; 28; 3:22; 4:6; 17; 5:7; 14; 18; 21; 6:4; 19; 7:4; 8:23; 34; 9:10; 17; 24; 30; 10:8; 11:5; 31; 15:3; 6; **1Cor** 1:6; 2:7; 11; 3:1; 5; 4:11; 5:7; 7:7; 8; 9:14; 10:33; 11:1; 5; 12; 14; 12:2; 13:12; 14:7; 12; 15:22; 24; 16:1; **2Cor** 1:3; 8; 13; 14; 19; 3:10; 15; 18; 7:14; 10:7; 13; 11:12; 13:9; **Gal** 2:16; 3:6; 4:3; 14; 29; 5:12; 14; **Eph** 1:10; 2:3; 5; 15; 4:4; 15; 32; 5:12; 23; 25; 29; 33; **Phil** 1:7; 15; 2:8; 3:15; 18; 21; 4:16; **Col** 1:14; 26; 3:13; **1Th** 1:10; 2:2; 4; 7; 14; 18; 19; 3:4; 12; 13; 4:3; 5; 13; 14; 5:11; **2Th** 2:9; 16; 3:1; 10; **1Ti** 3:11; 6:3; **2Ti** 2:9; **Titus** 1:12; 15; **Philem** 1:19; **Heb** 1:9; 4:12; 5:14; 6:20; 7:4; 11:12; 19; **Jas** 2:17; 3:5; 9; 4:1; 14; **1Pet** 1:9; 2:8; 21; 3:4; 6; 21; 4:10; **2Pet** 1:14; 2:1(2); 3:15; **1Jn** 2:6; 9; 18; 25; 27; 3:3; 7; 4:3; 5:4; 6; 20; **3Jn** 2; 3; **Jude** 7; 23; **Rev** 1:7; 2:13(2); 27; 3:4; 21; 6:13; 14:20; 16:7; 17:11; 18:6; 21:11; 22:20

EVERY

Gen 1:21(2); 25; 26; 28; 29(2); 30(4); 31; 2:5(2); 9; 16; 19(3); 20; 3:1; 14; 24; 4:14; 22; 6:5; 17; 19(2); 20(2); 7:2; 4; 8; 14(5); 21(2); 23; 8:1; 17(2); 19(3); 20(2); 21; 9:2(2); 3; 5(2); 10(3); 12; 15; 16; 10:5; 13:10; 16:12(2); 17:10; 12; 23; 19:4; 20:13; 27:29; 30:33; 35; 32:16; 34:15; 22; 23; 24; 41:48; 42:25; 35; 43:21; 44:1; 11(2); 13; 45:1; 46:34; 47:20; 49:28; **Ex** 1:1; 22(2); 3:22; 7:12; 9:19; 22; 25(2); 10:5; 12; 15; 11:2(2); 12:3; 4; 16; 44; 13:12; 13; 14:7; 16:4; 16(3); 18; 21(2); 29; 18:22(2); 26; 25:2; 26:2; 27:18; 28:21; 29:36; 30:7; 12; 13; 14; 31:14; 32:27(4); 29; 33:7; 8; 10; 34:19; 35:10; 21(2); 22; 23; 24(2); 29; 36:1; 2(2); 3; 4; 8; 30; 38:26(2); 39:14; **Lev** 2:13; 6:12; 18; 23; 7:6; 10; 11:15; 21; 26(2); 33; 34; 35; 41; 46(2); 15:4(2); 12; 17(2); 20(2); 26; 17:15; 19:3; 8; 10; 20:9; 23:37; 24:8; 25:10(2); 13; 27:28; **Num** 1:2; 4(2); 20; 22; 52(2); 2:2; 17; 34; 3:15; 4:19; 30; 35; 39; 43; 47; 49; 5:2(2); 9; 10; 7:5; 8:16; 17; 11:10; 13:2(2); 15:12; 16:3; 17:2(2); 18; 27; 17:2(2); 6; 9; 18:7; 9(4); 10; 11; 13; 14; 15; 29; 31; 19:15; 21:8; 23:2; 4; 14; 30; 25:5; 26:54; 28:10; 14; 21; 29:14; 30:4; 9; 11; 13(2); 31:4; 5; 6; 17(2); 23; 50; 53; 32:18; 27; 29; 33:54; 34:18; 35:8; 15; 36:7; 8(2); 9; **Deut** 1:16; 22; 41; 2:34; 3:6; 20; 4:4; 8:3; 11:24; 12:2; 8; 13; 31; 13:16; 14:6; 14; 19; 15:1; 2; 16:17; 19:3; 20:13; 21:5(2); 23:9; 24:16; 26:11; 28:61(2); 30:9; 31:10; 33:3; **Josh** 1:3; 3:12; 4:2; 4; 5; 10; 6:5; 20; 11:14; 21:42; 24:28; **Judg** 2:6; 5:30; 7:5(2); 7; 8; 16; 18; 21; 22; 8:24; 25; 34; 9:49; 55; 16:5; 17:6; 20:16; 48; 21:11(2); 21; 24(2); 25; **1Sa** 2:36; 3:11; 18; 4:10; 8:22; 10:25; 12:11; 13:2; 20; 14:20; 34(3); 47; 15:9; 20:15; 22:2(3); 7; 23:14; 25:10; 13(2); 26:23; 27:3; 30:6; 22; **2Sa** 2:3; 16; 27; 6:19(2); 13:9; 29; 37; 14:26; 15:4; 30; 36; 18:17; 19:8; 20:1; 2; 12; 22; 21:20(2); **1Kin** 1:49; 4:25; 27; 28; 5:3; 4; 7:30(2); 36; 38(2); 8:38; 39; 9:8; 10:25; 11:15; 16; 12:24; 14:23(2); 19:18; 20:20; 24; 22:17; 28; 36(2); **2Kin** 3:19(4); 25(2); 6:2; 8:9; 9:13; 11:8; 9; 11; 12:4(2); 5; 14:6; 12; 16:4; 17:10(2); 29(2); 18:31(3); 23:35; 25:9; 30; **1Chr** 9:27; 32; 13:1; 2; 16:3(2); 37; 43; 22:15; 18; 23:30; 26:13; 32; 27:1; 28:14; 15(2); 16; 17(2); 21; **2Chr** 1:2; 2:14; 6:29; 30; 7:21; 8:13; 14(2); 9:21; 24; 10:16; 11:4; 12; 23; 13:11(3); 14:7; 18:16; 20:23; 27; 23:7; 8; 10; 25:4; 22; 28:4; 24; 25; 29:35; 30:17; 18; 31:1; 2; 16; 19; 21; 32:22; 35:15; **Ezr** 2:1; 3:4; 5; 6:5; 8:34; 9:4; 10:14; **Neh** 3:28; 4:15; 17; 18; 22; 23; 5:7; 13; 7:3(2); 6; 8:16; 10:28; 31; 11:3; 20; 23; 12:47; 13:10; 30; **Est** 1:8; 22(4); 2:11; 12; 13; 3:12(4); 14; 4:3; 6:13; 8:9(2); 11; 13; 17(2); 9:27; 28(4); **Job** 1:4; 10; 2:11; 12; 7:18(2); 12:10; 18:11; 19:10; 20:22; 21:33; 24:6; 28:10; 34:11; 36:25; 37:7; 39:8; 40:11; 12; 42:2; 11(2); **Ps** 7:11; 12:2; 8; 29:9; 31:13; 32:6; 39:5; 6; 11; 50:10; 53:3; 56:5; 58:8; 62:12; 63:11; 64:6; 65:12; 68:30; 69:34; 71:18; 21; 73:14; 84:7; 92:2; 104:11; 115:8; 119:101; 104; 128; 160; 128:1; 135:18; 145:2; 16; 150:6; **Prov** 1:19; 2:9; 3:18; 7:12; 13:16; 14:1; 15; 15:3; 16:5; 19:6; 20:3; 6; 18; 21:2; 5; 24:12; 26; 27:7; 24; 29:26; 30:5; **Eccl** 3:1(2); 11; 13; 17(2); 4:4; 5:19; 8:6; 9; 10:3; 15; 12:14(2); **Song** 3:8; 4:2; 6:6; 8:11; **Is** 1:23; 2:12(2); 15(2); 3:5(2); 4:3; 5; 7:22; 23; 9:5; 17(2); 20; 13:7; 14(2); 15(2); 14:18; 15:2; 3; 16:7; 19:2(2); 7; 14; 17; 24:10; 27:3; 30:25(2); 32; 31:7; 33:2; 34:15; 36:16(3); 40:4(2); 41:6(2); 43:7; 44:23; 45:23(2); 47:15; 51:13; 52:5; 53:6; 54:17; 55:1; 56:6; 11; 57:5; 58:6; **Jer** 1:15; 2:20(2); 3:6(2); 13; 4:29; 5:6; 8; 6:3; 13(2); 25; 8:6; 10(2); 9:4(3); 5; 20; 10:14(2); 11:8; 12:4; 15(2); 13:12(2); 15:10; 16:12; 16(2); 17:10; 18:11; 12; 16; 19:8; 9; 20:7; 10; 22:7; 8; 23:17; 27; 30; 35(2); 36; 25:5; 26:3; 29:26; 30:6; 16; 31:25; 30(2); 34(2); 32:19; 34:9(2); 10(2); 14; 15; 16(2); 17(2); 35:15; 36:3; 7; 37:10; 43:6; 47:4; 48:8; 37(2); 49:5; 17; 29; 50:13; 16(2); 42; 51:6; 9; 17(2); 29; 45; 56; 52:34; **Lam** 2:19; 3:23; 4:1; **Eze** 1:6(2); 9; 11; 12; 23(2); 6:13(3); 7:16; 8:10; 11; 12; 9:1; 2; 10:14; 19; 21(2); 22; 11:5; 12:14; 22; 23; 13:18; 14:4; 7; 16:15; 24; 25(2); 31(2); 33; 44; 17:23; 18:30; 19:8; 20:7; 8; 28; 39; 47(2); 21:7(2); 10; 22:6; 23:22; 24:4; 26:16; 28:13; 23; 29:18(2); 32:10(2); 33:20; 26; 30; 34:6; 8; 36:3; 37:21; 38:20; 21; 39:4; 17(3); 40:7; 41:5(2); 10; 18; 43:25; 44:5; 29; 30(2); 45:20; 46:13; 14; 15; 18; 21; 47:9(2); **Dan** 3:10; 29; 6:12; 26; 11:36; 12:1; **Hos** 4:3; 9:1; **Joel** 2:7; 8; **Amos** 2:8; 4:3; 4; 8:3; 8; 10; **Obad** 9; **Jonah** 1:5; 7; 3:8; **Mic** 4:4; 5; 7:2; **Hab** 1:10; **Zeph** 2:11; 15; 3:5; 19; **Hag** 1:9; 2:14; 22; **Zec** 3:10; 5:3(2); 7:9; 8:4; 10; 16; 10:1; 4; 11:6; 9; 12:4(2); 12; 14; 13:4; 14:13; 16; 21; **Mal** 1:11; 2:10; 17; **Mt** 3:10; 4:4; 7:8; 17; 19; 21; 26; 8:33; 9:35(2); 12:25(2); 36; 13:47; 52; 15:13; 16:27; 18:16; 35; 19:3; 29; 20:9; 10; 25:15; 29; 26:22; **Mk** 1:45; 7:14; 8:25; 9:49(2); 13:34; 15:24; 16:15; 20; **Lk** 2:3; 23; 41; 3:5(2); 9; 4:4; 37; 40; 5:17; 6:30; 40; 44; 8:1; 4; 9:6; 43; 10:1; 11:4; 10; 17; 16:5; 16; 19; 18:14; 19:15; 26; 43; **Jn** 1:9; 2:10; 3:8; 20; 6:7; 40; 45; 7:53; 53:13:10; 15:2(2); 16:32; 18:37; 19:23; 21:25; **Acts** 2:5; 6; 8; 38; 43; 45; 3:23; 26; 4:35; 5:16; 42; 8:3; 4; 10:35; 11:29; 13:27; 14:23; 15:21(2); 36; 16:26; 17:27; 30; 18:4; 20:23; 31; 21:26; 28; 22:19; 26:11; 28:2; 22; **Rom** 1:16; 2:6; 9; 10; 3:2; 4; 19; 10:4; 12:3(2); 5; 13:1; 14:5(2); 11(2); 12; 15:2; **1Cor** 1:2; 5; 12; 3:5; 8; 10; 13(2); 4:5; 17(2); 6:18; 7:2(2); 7; 17(2); 20; 24; 8:7; 9:25; 10:24; 11:3; 4; 5; 21; 12:7; 11; 18; 14:26; 15:23; 30; 38; 16:2; 16; **2Cor** 2:14; 4:2; 8; 5:10; 7:5; 8:7; 9:7; 8; 11; 10:5(2); 13:1; **Gal** 3:10; 13; 5:3; 6:4; 5; **Eph** 1:21; 4:7; 14; 16(2); 25; 5:24; 33; **Phil** 1:3; 4; 18; 2:4(2); 9; 10; 11; 4:6; 12; 21; **Col** 1:10; 15; 23; 28(3); 4:6; **1Th** 1:8; 2:11; 4:4; 5:18; **2Th** 1:3; 2:17; 3:6; 17; **1Ti** 2:8; 4:4; 5:10; **2Ti** 2:19; 21; 4:18; **Titus** 1:5; 16; 3:1; **Philem** 1:6; **Heb** 2:2; 9; 3:4; 5:1; 13; 6:11; 8:3; 11(2); 9:7; 19; 25; 10:3; 11; 12:1; 6; 13:21; **Jas** 1:14; 17(2); 19; 3:7; 16; **1Pet** 1:17; 2:13; 3:15; 4:10; **1Jn** 2:29; 3:3; 4:1; 2; 3; 7; 5:1; **Rev** 1:7; 2:23; 5:8; 9; 13; 6:11; 14; 15(2); 14:6; 16:3; 20; 21; 18:2(2); 17; 20:13; 21:21; 22:2; 12; 18

EXCEPT

Gen 31:42; 32:26; 42:15; 43:3; 5; 10; 44:23; 26; 47:26; **Num** 16:13; **Deut** 32:30; **Josh** 7:12; **1Sa** 25:34; **2Sa** 3:9; 13; 5:6; **2Kin** 4:24; **Est** 2:14; 4:11; **Ps** 127:1(2); **Prov** 4:16; **Is** 1:9; **Dan** 2:11; 3:28; 6:5; **Amos** 3:3; **Mt** 5:20; 12:29; 18:3; 19:9; 24:22; 26:42; **Mk** 3:27; 7:3; 4; 13:20; **Lk** 9:13; 13:3; 5; **Jn** 3:2; 3; 5; 27; 4:48; 6:44; 53; 65; 12:24; 15:4(2); 19:11; 20:25; **Acts** 8:1; 31; 15:1; 24:21; 26:29; 27:31; **Rom** 7:7; 9:29; 10:15; **1Cor** 7:5; 14:5; 6; 7; 9; 15:36; **2Cor** 12:13; 13:5; **2Th** 2:3; **2Ti** 2:5; **Rev** 2:5; 22

EXCEPTED

1Cor 15:27

FAR

Gen 18:25(2); 44:4; **Ex** 8:28; 23:7; **Num** 2:2; **Deut** 12:21; 13:7; 14:24; 20:15; 28:49; 29:22; 30:11; **Josh** 3:16; 8:4; 9:6; 9; 22; **Judg** 9:17; 18:7; 28; 19:11; **1Sa** 2:30; 20:9; 22:15; **2Sa** 15:17; 20:20(2); 23:17; **1Kin** 8:41; 46; **2Kin** 20:14; **2Chr** 6:32; 36; 26:15; **Ezr** 6:6; **Neh** 4:19; **Est** 9:20; **Job** 5:4; 11:14; 13:21; 19:13; 21:16; 22:18; 23; 30:10; 34:10; **Ps** 10:5; 22:1; 11; 19; 27:9; 35:22; 38:21; 55:7; 71:12; 73:27; 88:8; 18; 97:9; 103:12(2); 109:17; 119:150; 155; **Prov** 4:24; 5:8; 15:29; 19:7; 22:5; 15; 25:25; 27:10; 30:8; 31:10; **Eccl** 2:13; 7:23; 24; **Is** 5:26; 6:12; 8:9; 10:3; 13:5; 17:13; 19:6; 22:3; 26:15; 29:13; 30:27; 33:13; 17; 39:3; 43:6; 46:11; 12; 13; 49:1; 12; 19; 54:14; 57:9; 19; 59:9; 11; 60:4; 9; **Jer** 2:5; 4:16; 5:15; 6:20; 8:19; 12:2; 25:26; 27:10; 48:24; 47; 49:30; 51:64; **Lam** 1:16; 3:17; **Eze** 6:12; 7:20; 8:6; 11:15; 16; 12:27; 22:5; 23:40; 43:9; 44:10; **Dan** 9:7; 11:2; **Joel** 2:20; 3:6; 8; **Amos** 6:3; **Mic** 4:7; 7:11; **Hab** 1:8; **Zec** 6:15; 10:9; **Mt** 15:8; 16:22; 21:33; 25:14; **Mk** 6:35(2); 7:6; 8:3; 12:1; 34; 13:34; **Lk** 7:6; 15:13; 19:12; 20:9; 22:51; 24:29; 50; **Jn** 21:8; **Acts** 11:19; 22; 17:27; 22:21; 28:15; **Rom** 13:12; **2Cor** 4:17; 10:14; **Eph** 1:21; 2:13; 4:10; **Phil** 1:23; **Heb** 7:15

FARTHER

Mt 26:39; **Mk** 1:19; 10:1

FEW

Gen 24:55; 27:44; 29:20; 34:30; 47:9; **Lev** 25:52; 26:22; **Num** 9:20; 13:18; 26:54; 56; 35:8(2); **Deut** 4:27; 26:5; 28:62; 33:6; **Josh** 7:3; **1Sa** 14:6; 17:28; **2Kin** 4:3; **1Chr** 16:19(2); **2Chr** 29:34; **Neh** 2:12; 7:4; **Job** 10:20; 14:1; 16:22; **Ps** 105:12(2); 109:8; **Eccl** 5:2; 9:14; 12:3; **Is** 10:7; 19; 24:6; **Jer** 30:19; 42:2; **Eze** 5:3; 12:16; **Dan** 11:20; **Mt** 7:14; 9:37; 15:34; 20:16; 22:14; 25:21; 23; **Mk** 6:5; 8:7; **Lk** 10:2; 12:48; 13:23; **Acts** 17:4; 12; 24:4; **Eph** 3:3; **Heb** 12:10; 13:22; **1Pet** 3:20; **Rev** 2:14; 20; 3:4

FEWER

Num 33:54

FOR

Gen 1:14(3); 15; 29; 30; 2:5; 9; 17; 18; 20(2); 3:5; 6; 17; 19(2); 22; 4:23; 25; 5:24; 6:3; 7; 12; 13; 21(3); 7:1; 4; 8:9(2); 21(2); 9:3; 6; 12; 13; 10:25; 11:3(2); 12:10; 13; 16; 13:6; 8; 15(2); 17; 14:13; 15:6; 16; 16:10; 13; 17:4; 5; 7; 8; 13; 15; 19; 20; 18:5; 14; 15; 19; 24; 26; 28; 29; 31; 32; 19:8; 13; 14; 17; 21; 22; 30; 20:3(2); 6; 7(2); 11; 18; 21:2; 7; 10; 12; 16; 17; 18; 30; 22:2; 3; 7; 8; 12; 13; 16; 23:2(2); 8; 9(2); 13; 18; 20; 24:10; 14; 19; 20; 22; 23; 31(2); 32; 40; 44(2); 62; 65; 25:21; 30; 26:3; 7(2); 9; 14; 15; 16; 18; 21; 22(3); 24(2); 27:5; 9; 36(2); 37; 41; 28:11; 15; 18(2); 22; 29:2; 9; 15; 18; 20(2); 21; 24; 25; 27; 32; 30:13; 15; 16; 26(2); 27(2); 30(2); 31; 33(2); 31:12; 14; 15; 16; 18; 31; 32; 35; 41(2); 44; 45; 49; 52; 32:10; 11; 12; 13; 20; 26; 28; 30; 33:10; 17; 19; 34:8; 14; 21(3); 22; 35:18; 36:7; 37:7; 8(2); 17; 27; 28; 34; 35(2); 38:6; 11; 14; 16; 39:5; 40:15; 17; 41:8; 19; 31; 32; 36; 49; 51; 52; 55; 57; 42:2; 4; 5; 18; 19; 23; 25; 27; 30; 33; 38; 43:5; 9(2); 10; 16; 18; 25; 30; 32(4); 44:4; 14; 17; 18; 22; 26; 32(3); 34; 45:3; 5; 6; 11; 19(2); 20; 21; 23; 26; 46:3; 32; 34; 47:4(4); 13; 14; 15(2); 16; 17(6); 19; 20(2); 21; 22; 23(2); 24(5); 48:4; 7; 10; 14; 18; 49:6; 7(2); 13; 18; 30; 50:3(3); 5; 10; 13(2); 17; 19; 20; **Ex** 1:5; 11; 18; 19; 2:3; 7; 9; 19; 22; 3:5; 6; 7; 15; 4:1; 19; 5:7; 8; 18; 23; 6:1; 7; 8; 9(2); 7:9; 12; 24(2); 8:8; 9(3); 17; 25(2); 26; 28; 9:2; 11; 14; 15; 16(2); 19; 27; 28; 30; 31; 32; 10:1; 5; 9; 10; 11; 12; 15; 16; 23; 26; 28; 12:3; 4(2); 12; 13; 14(2); 15; 17(2); 19; 21; 23; 24(2); 30; 31; 33; 39(2); 42; 44; 48; 13:3; 9(3); 16(3); 17; 19; 14:3; 12(2); 13(2); 14; 25(2); 15:1; 17; 18; 19; 21; 23; 25; 26; 16:3; 4; 7; 8; 9; 15; 16(2); 22; 23; 25; 27; 29; 32; 33; 17:1; 3; 14(2); 16; 18:1(2); 3; 4; 8; 9; 11; 12; 18(2); 19; 22; 19:2; 5; 7; 9; 11; 23; 20:5; 7; 11; 20; 25; 21:2; 6; 19; 21; 23; 24(4); 25(3); 26; 27; 30; 36; 22:1(2); 2; 3(3); 9(6); 13; 15; 21; 27(3); 23:7; 8; 9; 15; 21(2); 23; 31; 33; 24:14; 25:6(3); 12; 26; 27; 26:14; 15; 17; 18; 19(2); 20; 22; 23; 24(2); 26; 27(3); 29(2); 36; 37(2); 27:4; 6; 9(3); 11; 12; 16; 20; 21; 28:2(3); 4; 12(2); 29; 40(5); 43; 29:9; 22; 24; 25(2); 26; 27(2); 28(2); 36(3); 37; 40; 41; 30:4(2); 12; 15; 16(2); 19; 21; 37(2); 31:10; 11; 13; 14(2); 16; 17(2); 32:1(2); 7; 12; 13; 18(2); 23(3); 25; 29; 30; 33:3(2); 5; 16; 17; 20; 34:7; 9(2); 10; 12; 14(2); 18; 24; 27; 35:8(3); 9(2); 14(2); 15; 17; 19; 21(2); 24; 27(2); 28(3); 29; 36:1; 3; 5; 6; 7(2); 14; 19; 20; 22; 23(2); 24(2); 25; 27; 28; 31; 32(3); 34; 36; 37; 37:3; 12; 13; 14; 27(2); 38:4; 5(2); 11; 12; 13; 15; 17; 18; 21; 24; 26(3); 27; 28; 30; 39:1; 4; 7; 27(2); 37; 38; 40(2); 41; 40:5; 15; 38; **Lev** 1:4(2); 10; 14; 2:11; 12(2); 14; 3:6; 7; 16; 17; 4:3(2); 8; 14; 20(2); 21; 26; 28; 31(2); 32; 33; 35; 5:6(3); 7(3); 8; 10(3); 11(3); 13; 15(2); 16(2); 18(2); 6:6; 7(2); 15; 17; 18; 20; 21; 22; 23(2); 26; 7:5; 7; 12; 13; 14; 15; 19; 25; 30; 32; 33; 34(2); 36; 8:2; 14(2); 18; 21; 27; 28; 29(2); 33; 34; 35; 9:2(2); 3(2); 4(2); 7(3); 8; 15(2); 18(2); 21; 10:7; 9; 12; 13; 14; 15(2); 17; 11:24; 35(2); 42; 44(2); 45(2); 12:2; 6(4); 7(2); 8(3); 13:7; 11; 15; 28; 36; 52; 14:4; 6; 10; 12(2); 13; 18; 19; 20; 21(3); 23; 24; 29; 31(3); 34; 53; 54; 55; 56(3); 15:13; 15(4); 30(4); 16:2; 3(2); 5(2); 6(3); 8(2); 9; 10; 11(4); 15; 16(2); 17(3); 18; 24(2); 26; 27(2); 29; 30(2); 31; 33(5); 34(2); 17:5; 6; 7; 11(4); 14(3); 18:10; 13; 17; 19; 24; 27; 29; 19:2; 10; 21; 22(2); 23; 28; 34; 20:7; 9; 19; 23; 26; 21:1; 2(6); 3(2); 6; 7; 8(2); 11(2); 12; 15; 18; 23; 22:9; 16; 18(3); 20(2); 23(2); 25; 27; 23:11; 12; 13; 14; 18; 19(2); 20(2); 21; 28(2); 29; 31; 34; 41; 24:2; 3; 7; 9; 18; 20(3); 22(3); 25:4; 5; 6(6); 7(2); 12; 16; 17; 21; 23(3); 24; 30; 33; 34; 37; 42; 46(3); 51; 55; 26:1; 9; 16; 18(2); 20; 24; 27; 28; 44(2); 45; 27:2; 5; 6; 7; 10(3); 34; **Num** 1:44; 48; 3:13; 25; 26(2); 38; 41; 46; 4:16; 24; 25; 26(2); 29; 35; 39; 43; 5:8; 15(2); 6:7(4);

11(4); 12; 14(3); 17; 20(2); 21; 7:3(2); 10; 11; 13; 15; 16; 17; 19(2); 21; 22; 23; 25; 27; 28; 29; 31; 33; 34; 35; 37; 39; 40; 41; 43; 45; 46; 47; 49; 51; 52; 53; 55; 57; 58; 59; 61; 63; 64; 65; 67; 69; 70; 71; 73; 75; 76; 77; 79; 81; 82; 83; 87(2); 88; 8:8; 11; 12(3); 13; 15; 16; 17(2); 18; 19; 21; 9:14(2); 10:2(2); 6; 8(2); 10; 29; 33; 11:13; 14; 18(2); 22(2); 29; 32; 12:1; 13:30; 31; 14:3; 9(2); 11; 13; 14; 32; 34; 40; 42; 43; 15:5(2); 6(2); 7(2); 8(2); 10(2); 11(3); 15(3); 16(2); 20; 24(3); 25(3); 27; 28(2); 29(3); 39; 16:11; 28; 34; 37; 38(2); 39; 46(2); 47; 17:3(2); 6; 8; 10; 18:4; 6; 7; 8; 9(2); 11; 16; 17(2); 19(2); 21(2); 23; 26(2); 31(2); 19:9(3); 10(2); 17(2); 20:2; 19; 24; 29; 21:5; 7(2); 13; 24; 26; 28; 34; 22:6(3); 12; 13; 17; 22; 29; 34; 23:9; 24:1; 18; 20; 24; 25:11; 13(2); 18(2); 26:53; 62; 65; 27:14; 21; 28:2(2); 3; 5; 6; 7(2); 9; 12(4); 13(2); 15; 19; 20(2); 21; 22(2); 23; 27; 30; 29:2; 3(2); 4; 5(2); 6; 8; 10; 11; 16; 18(3); 19; 21(3); 22; 24(3); 25; 27(3); 28; 30(3); 31; 33(3); 34; 37(3); 38; 39(4); 31:5; 18; 29; 50(2); 53(2); 54(2); 32:1; 4; 5; 9; 12; 15; 16(2); 19; 24(2); 27; 30; 33:4; 11; 50; 51; 34:2; 6(2); 7; 14; 23; 35:2; 3(3); 6(2); 11; 12; 13; 15(3); 21; 29; 31; 32; 33; 34; 36:2; 7; 11; **Deut** 1:10; 14; 17(2); 30(2); 37; 38; 40; 42; 2:5(2); 6(2); 7; 9(3); 15; 19(2); 28(2); 30; 35; 36; 3:2; 7; 11; 18; 19; 22(2); 24; 26; 27; 28; 4:1; 3; 6; 7(2); 15; 21(2); 24; 31; 32; 34; 38; 40; 5:5; 9; 11; 23; 25; 26; 29; 31; 6:8; 15; 24; 7:4; 6; 7; 16; 21; 25; 26; 8:7; 10; 18; 9:4(2); 5(3); 6(2); 12; 19; 20; 10:13; 17; 19; 21; 22; 11:2; 10; 12; 15; 18; 22; 25; 31; 12:9; 23; 28; 31(2); 13:3; 16(2); 14:1; 2; 7; 21; 24; 26(6); 27; 15:4(2); 6; 8; 10; 11; 17; 18; 16:1; 3; 19; 17:1; 8; 18:5(2); 12; 14(2); 19:2; 7; 9; 10; 11; 15(2); 21(5); 20:1; 4(2); 16; 19(2); 20; 21:5; 14; 17(2); 23(2); 22:5; 8; 20; 26; 27; 23:3; 6; 7; 14; 18(2); 21; 24:4(2); 6; 15; 16(3); 19(3); 20(3); 21(3); 25:11; 16; 19; 26:1; 3; 14(2); 28:20; 32; 34; 38; 39; 40; 41; 46(3); 47; 56; 57(2); 62; 67(2); 68; 29:8; 13; 16; 26; 29; 30:9(3); 11; 12; 13; 20; 31:6; 7; 18; 19(2); 20; 21(2); 23; 26; 27; 29; 32:4; 9; 20; 22; 28; 31; 32; 35; 36(2); 40(2); 43; 47(2); 49; 33:2; 7; 9; 13(3); 14(2); 15(2); 16(2); 19; 21; 34:8(2); 9; **Josh** 1:6(2); 8; 9; 11; 2:3; 5; 10(2); 11; 14; 15; 24; 3:4; 5; 15; 4:7(2); 10; 13; 23; 24; 5:6; 7; 13(2); 15; 6:16; 7:1; 3; 5; 9; 11; 13; 8:2(2); 6(2); 7; 18; 26; 27; 28; 9:9; 11; 12; 22; 23; 27(2); 10:4; 6; 8; 14(2); 18; 19; 24; 25; 42; 11:6; 10; 13; 14; 20; 23; 12:6; 7; 13:6; 7; 12; 32; 14:1; 2(2); 3; 4(3); 9; 11; 12; 13; 15:19; 63; 16:9; 17:1(3); 2(7); 15(2); 16; 18(2); 18:4; 6; 7; 8; 10; 19:1; 9(2); 10; 17; 24; 32; 40; 47; 49; 51; 20:2; 6; 9(2); 21:2; 4; 10; 12; 13; 21(2); 26; 27; 32; 38; 40; 22:17; 24; 25; 26(2); 28(2); 29(3); 34; 23:2(5); 3(2); 4; 9(2); 10(2); 13; 24:1(4); 13; 15; 17; 18; 19; 27; 31; 32; **Judg** 1:1; 15; 32; 34; 2:7; 10; 15; 18; 3:20; 28; 4:3; 5; 9(2); 14; 17; 19; 21; 5:2; 15; 16; 30; 6:4; 5(3); 22; 31(3); 38; 40; 7:2; 4; 9; 12(2); 14; 15; 8:5; 10; 11; 20; 21; 22; 24; 30; 9:2; 3; 5; 17(2); 21; 25; 28; 10:16; 11:2; 18; 31; 35; 36; 37; 38; 12:6; 9; 13:5(2); 7; 15; 16; 20; 14:2; 3(2); 4; 10; 15:18; 16:2; 17; 18(2); 19; 23(2); 24; 25(2); 28; 17:3; 18:1; 9; 10; 19; 26; 19:6; 15; 19(4); 20:6; 10; 27; 28; 36; 39; 41; 21:5; 6; 7(2); 9; 15; 16(2); 17; 18; 22(2); **Ruth** 1:6; 12; 13(4); 16; 20; 2:13(2); 16; 3:1; 9; 10; 11; 17; 18; 4:4; 6(2); 7; 8; 15; **1Sa** 1:5; 6; 16(2); 22(2); 27; 2:2; 3; 5; 8; 9; 14; 15(2); 17; 20; 23; 24; 25; 30(2); 32; 35; 36; 3:5; 6; 8; 9; 10; 13(3); 14; 21; 4:7(2); 10; 13(2); 18; 19; 20; 22; 5:7; 11; 6:2; 4; 8; 17(6); 7:2; 5; 8; 9(2); 17; 8:7; 11(2); 9:5(2); 7; 9; 12(2); 13(2); 14; 16; 19; 20(2); 24(2); 10:2(2); 7; 11:2; 13; 12:19(2); 21(2); 22(2); 23(2); 24(2); 13:6; 7; 13(2); 19; 21(4); 14:6(2); 10; 12; 18; 24; 26; 30; 39; 44; 45; 15:2; 6; 11; 15; 23; 24; 26; 29; 35; 16:1(2); 7(2); 11; 12; 22; 17:8; 12; 17; 20; 21; 26; 28; 31; 33; 39(2); 42; 47; 18:11; 17(2); 19:5(2); 13; 16; 20:4; 6(2); 8(2); 9; 15; 17; 21; 22; 23; 26; 29; 31(2); 34(2); 42; 21:6; 8; 9; 10; 22:3; 8; 10; 13; 15(2); 23; 23:4; 7; 10; 17; 21; 22; 26(2); 27; 24:10; 11; 17; 19(2); 25:8; 11; 17(2); 21; 25; 28; 34; 36; 39; 26:9; 12; 15; 18; 19; 20; 21; 23; 27:1; 4; 5; 8; 12; 28:1; 2; 9; 10; 12; 13; 15; 17; 20; 29:4; 6; 30:6(3); 8; 10; 12; 24; 25; 26; 31:4; **2Sa** 1:9; 12(4); 16; 21; 26; 2:7; 26; 3:6; 8; 14; 17; 18; 22; 27; 28; 37; 39; 4:2; 7; 10; 5:12; 19; 24; 6:6; 7; 17; 7:3; 5; 10; 13(2); 16(2); 19; 20; 21; 22; 23(3); 24(2); 25; 26; 27; 29(3); 8:4; 10; 9:1; 7(2); 10; 11; 13; 10:2; 11(2); 12(2); 11:4; 22; 25; 26; 12:4(2); 12; 16; 18; 21; 22; 13:2(3); 12; 13(2); 18; 22; 32(2); 33; 37; 39; 14:2; 7; 13; 14; 16; 17; 19; 25; 26; 29; 32; 33; 15:2; 6; 8; 12(2); 14; 19; 34; 16:2(2); 3; 11; 12; 17:8; 10; 11; 14; 17; 21; 29(3); 18:3(3); 5; 8; 12; 13; 16; 18(2); 31; 33; 19:1; 2(2); 6(2); 7; 8; 9; 20; 21; 22; 26; 28; 32; 38; 42; 20:11; 21:1(2); 3; 4(2); 8; 10; 14; 22:18(2); 22; 23(2); 29; 30; 31; 32; 40; 51(2); 23:5; 24:2; 10; 11; 14; 22(2); 24; 25; **1Kin** 1:2; 3; 25; 31; 35; 42; 51; 2:7; 9; 15; 17; 18; 19(2); 20; 22(6); 26; 28; 33(2); 36; 37(2); 42(2); 45; 3:4; 6; 8; 9; 11(3); 26; 28; 4:7; 22; 24; 26; 27(2); 28; 31; 5:1(2); 3; 6(2); 8; 9; 11; 6:2; 4; 6; 8; 16(3); 31; 33; 7:7; 8; 12(2); 15; 17(3); 18; 36; 40; 42(2); 45; 50(2); 51; 8:5; 7; 11; 13(2); 17; 20; 21; 36; 39; 41; 42; 43; 44; 46; 48; 51; 52; 53; 64; 66(3); 9:3; 5; 7; 15; 16(2); 19(2); 24; 10:9; 12(3); 22; 23(2); 26; 27; 29(4); 11:2; 4; 5; 7(2); 8; 12; 13(2); 15; 16; 31; 32(2); 34; 38; 39(2); 12:1; 2; 5; 7; 15; 17; 24; 28; 30; 13:6; 9; 12; 17; 23(2); 32; 14:4; 5(3); 6; 9; 11; 13(2); 15; 18; 23; 15:4; 27; 16:7; 13; 19; 24; 26; 31; 32; 17:5; 12; 13(2); 14; 18:4; 23; 25(2); 27; 41; 19:3; 4(2); 7; 10(2); 14; 20; 20:7(5); 9; 10(2); 18(2); 22; 25(2); 34; 38; 39; 42(2); 21:2(2); 4; 6(2); 15(2); 22; 22:6; 8; 12; 15; 34; 43; 48(2); 53; **2Kin** 2:2; 4; 6; 9; 18; 3:2; 9(2); 13; 17; 26; 27; 4:2; 10; 13(3); 14; 24; 27; 38; 39; 40; 41; 43; 5:3; 17; 27; 6:1; 5; 9; 11(2); 16; 23; 25(2); 33; 7:1(2); 6; 7; 16(2); 18(2); 20; 8:1(2); 3(2); 5(2); 18; 19; 27; 9:8; 16; 20; 25; 34; 10:3; 10; 16; 19; 20; 22; 24; 31; 11:15; 12:7(2); 12(2); 13; 15; 21; 13:4; 7; 17; 14:6(3); 10; 26(3); 28; 15:14; 16:8; 9; 15; 18(2); 17:4; 7; 12; 21; 22; 32; 37(2); 18:4; 6; 20; 24(2); 26; 29; 31; 36; 19:3; 4; 8; 18; 31; 34(3); 20:1; 6(2); 10; 12; 21:3(2); 5; 7; 22:13(4); 23:4(3); 7; 13(3); 24:3; 4(2); 7; 16; 20; 25:3; 16; 22; 26; 30; **1Chr** 4:14; 23; 39; 40; 41; 42; 5:1; 2; 20; 22; 6:26; 49(2); 54; 70; 7:4(2); 11; 9:1; 13; 26; 33; 10:4; 13(2); 11:9; 19; 20; 21; 12:8; 18; 19; 21; 22; 25; 29; 37; 39(2); 40; 13:3; 4; 9; 14:2; 10; 15; 15:1(2); 2(2); 3; 11(3); 12; 13(2); 22; 23; 24; 16:1; 17(2); 21; 25; 26; 34(3); 36; 41; 42; 17:2; 5; 9; 12; 14(2); 17(2); 18(2); 19; 22(2); 23; 24; 25; 27(3); 18:10; 19:3; 5; 12(2); 13(2); 21:6; 8; 13; 17; 22; 23(3); 24(3); 25; 29; 30; 22:1; 3(3); 4; 5(2); 6(2); 7; 9; 10(2); 14(2); 15; 18; 23:13(2); 24; 25(2); 26; 27; 28; 29(7); 24:5; 6(2); 25:6(2); 9; 26:5; 6; 8(2); 10; 13; 14; 29(2); 31; 32; 27:2; 3; 5; 7; 8; 9; 10; 11; 12; 13; 14; 15; 24; 26; 27; 28:2(4); 3; 4(2); 5; 6; 7; 8(4); 9(2); 10(2); 13(3); 14(4); 15(7); 16(3); 17(4); 18(2); 20(2); 21(3); 29:1(3); 2(6); 3; 5(3); 7; 9; 10; 11; 14; 15; 16; 17; 18; 19; 21; **2Chr** 1:3; 4(3); 9; 10; 11; 15; 17(4); 2:1(2); 4(3); 5; 8; 9; 12(2); 3:3; 6; 4:6(2); 9; 11(2); 16; 18; 19; 22; 5:1; 6; 8; 11; 13(3); 14; 6:2(3); 7; 8; 9; 10(2); 13; 27; 30; 32; 33; 34; 36; 38; 7:3(3); 6; 7; 9; 10; 12; 16(2); 17; 20; 8:7; 9; 11(2); 14; 9:6; 8(2); 11; 21; 25; 10:1; 7; 10; 11; 15; 17; 11:4; 5; 14(2); 15(3); 17; 21; 22; 12:13; 13:5; 8; 10; 11; 12(2); 14:3; 6; 11; 13; 14(2); 15:3; 6; 7; 9; 15; 16:9; 10; 14(2); 17:18; 18:2(2); 5; 7; 8; 11; 32; 33; 19:6(3); 7; 8(2); 11; 20:7; 8; 9; 12; 15; 17; 21(2); 23; 25; 26; 27; 30; 33; 21:6; 7; 19; 22:1; 3; 4; 7; 9; 11; 23:6; 8; 14; 24:3; 6(2); 7; 14; 18; 24; 25(2); 25:4(3); 6; 7; 8(2); 9; 20; 26:8; 10(2); 14; 15; 16; 18(2); 21; 23; 28:2(2); 6; 10; 11; 13(2); 17; 19(2); 21; 23; 29:6; 9(2); 11; 21(4); 23; 24(3); 25; 32; 34; 35; 36; 30:2; 3; 5; 8; 9(2); 14; 17(2); 18(2); 24; 26; 31:2(2); 3(5); 10; 16; 18; 32:1; 7(3); 15; 20; 25; 26; 27(6); 28(3); 29; 33:3(2); 4; 5; 7; 8; 22; 34:3; 11; 21(3); 26; 35:7(2); 8; 9; 14(4); 15(2); 21; 23; 24; 25; 36:17; 21; **Ezr** 1:4; 2:68; 3:3; 11(2); 12; 13; 4:2; 14; 15; 6:8; 9; 10; 11; 17(2); 19; 20(4); 22; 7:9; 10; 16; 18; 20; 23(2); 8:16(11); 17; 20; 21(3); 22(2); 23; 35(2); 9:2(3); 6; 7; 8; 9; 10; 12(3); 13(2); 15(2); 10:1; 4; 6; 9; 13; 14; 19; **Neh** 1:5; 6; 11; 2:3; 4; 6; 8(3); 14; 18; 4:4(2); 5; 6; 14; 18; 20; 23; 5:2(2); 4; 5; 18(3); 19(2); 6:6; 9; 10; 12; 13; 16; 18; 7:2; 8:4; 5; 9; 10(3); 11; 17; 9:5; 8; 10; 15(3); 20; 31(2); 33; 35; 36; 10:30; 32(2); 33(8); 34; 39; 11:23(3); 25; 12:29; 43; 44(8); 46; 13:1; 5; 6; 7; 10; 13; 14(2); 25; 31(3); **Est** 1:8; 9; 11; 13; 17; 20; 22; 2:2; 3; 7(2); 9; 10; 12(2); 15; 20; 3:2; 4; 6; 8; 13; 14; 4:2; 5; 7; 8; 14(2); 16; 5:4; 8; 9; 10; 6:3(2); 4; 7; 7:4(2); 7(2); 9(2); 10; 8:1; 6; 8(2); 11(2); 13; 17; 9:2; 4(2); 15; 16; 26; 31(2); 10:3; **Job** 1:4; 5; 9; 2:4(2); 11; 13; 3:6; 9; 13; 14; 21(3); 24; 25; 4:11; 20; 5:2; 18; 23; 27; 6:3; 4; 8; 10; 19; 21; 22; 27; 28; 7:2; 16; 21; 8:4; 6; 8; 9; 9:17; 32; 10:16; 11:4; 11; 12; 15; 13:7(2); 8; 16; 19; 24; 26; 14:7; 16; 20; 15:5; 22; 23; 25; 31; 34; 16:12; 17; 21(2); 17:1; 4; 10(2); 15; 18:4; 8; 10(2); 19:15; 17; 21; 24; 25; 27; 29; 20:2; 5; 7; 18; 21; 21:4; 14; 19; 21; 28; 22:4; 6(2); 8; 17; 26; 23:7; 14(2); 16; 24:3; 5(3); 8; 15; 16; 17; 24; 27:8; 14; 22; 28:1(2); 5; 15(2); 17; 18; 24; 25; 26(2); 29:13; 23(3); 30:3; 4; 23(2); 25(2); 26(2); 31:2; 11; 12; 18; 19; 23; 28; 32:11; 16; 18; 22; 33:10; 13; 14; 26; 32; 34:3; 5; 9; 11; 19; 21; 23; 36; 37; 35:3; 36:4; 7; 21; 27; 31; 37:6; 13(3); 19; 38:3; 7; 9; 10; 19; 25(2); 39; 41(2); 41:4(2); 5; 42:3; 7; 8(3); 10; 12; **Ps** 1:6; 2:8(2); 3:2; 3; 5; 7; 4:3; 8; 5:2; 4; 7; 9; 10; 11; 12; 6:2(2); 4; 5; 8; 7:6; 7; 9; 13; 8:5; 9:4; 5; 7(2); 9; 10; 12; 18(2); 10:3; 5; 6; 14; 16; 11:2; 7; 12:1(2); 5(2); 7; 13:1; 14:5; 16:1; 10; 11; 17:6; 15; 18:17(2); 21; 22; 27; 28; 29; 30; 31; 39; 50; 19:4; 9; 21:3; 4; 6(2); 7; 11; 22:11(2); 16; 21; 24; 26; 28; 30; 23:3; 4; 6; 24:2; 25:5; 6; 7; 11(2); 15; 16; 19; 20; 21; 26:1; 3; 11; 27:5; 12; 28:9; 29:10; 30:1; 5(2); 11; 12; 31:2; 3(2); 4(2); 7; 9; 10; 13; 16; 17; 19(2); 21; 22; 23; 32:4; 6; 11; 33:1(2); 4; 9; 11; 12; 17; 20; 21; 34:9; 35:2; 7(3); 10; 12; 13; 14; 20; 27; 36:2; 9; 37:2; 7; 9; 10; 13; 17; 18; 22; 24; 27; 28(2); 29; 37; 38:2; 4(2); 7; 10; 12; 15; 16; 17; 18(2); 20; 39:7; 11; 12; 40:1; 12; 15; 41:4; 12(2); 42:t, 2(2); 4; 5(2); 11; 43:2; 5; 44:t, 3; 4; 6; 8; 10; 11; 12; 16; 21; 22(2); 23; 25; 26(2); 45:t, 2; 6; 11; 17; 46:t; 47:t, 2; 4; 7; 9; 48:t, 2; 3; 4; 8; 14(2); 49:t, 7; 8(2); 9; 10; 11; 15; 17; 50:6; 8; 10; 12; 51:3; 16; 52:5; 8; 9(2); 53:5; 54:3; 6; 7; 55:3; 6; 9; 12; 15; 16; 18; 56:1; 2; 5; 6; 9(2); 13; 57:1; 2; 6; 10; 58:11; 59:3(4); 7; 9; 12(2); 15; 16; 17; 60:2; 11; 12; 61:3(2); 4; 5; 7; 8; 62:5; 8; 12; 63:1(2); 10; 64:9; 65:1; 3; 9; 13; 66:7; 10; 16; 67:4(2); 68:10; 16; 18(2); 28; 69:1; 3; 6(2); 7; 9; 13; 16; 17; 20(2); 21; 22; 26; 33; 35; 70:3; 71:3; 5; 10(2); 11; 12; 15; 24(2); 72:t, 12; 15; 17; 19; 73:2; 3; 4; 14; 16; 26; 27; 28; 74:1; 4; 10; 12; 19; 20; 75:1; 6; 8; 9; 77:7; 8(2); 78:5; 18; 20; 29; 32(2); 37; 39; 58; 69; 79:5; 7; 8; 9(2); 13; 80:15; 17; 81:4(2); 5; 15; 82:8; 83:2; 5; 10; 17; 84:t, 2(2); 3; 10; 11; 85:t, 5; 8; 86:1; 2; 3; 4; 5; 7; 10; 12; 13; 17; 87:t; 88:t, 3; 89:1; 2(2); 4; 6; 11; 17; 18; 28(2); 29; 36; 37; 46; 52; 90:4; 7; 9; 10; 91:5(2); 6(2); 11; 92:t, 4; 7; 8; 9(2); 93:5; 94:13; 14; 16(2); 95:3; 7; 96:4; 5; 13(2); 97:9; 11(2); 98:1; 9; 99:3; 5; 9; 100:5; 102:3; 9; 10; 12; 13; 14; 18; 19; 103:6; 9; 11; 14; 15; 16; 104:5; 8; 14(2); 17; 18(2); 19; 31; 105:8; 10(2); 14; 16; 17; 32; 38; 39; 42; 106:1(3); 8; 13; 31(2); 32; 43; 45; 107:1(3); 8(2); 9; 15(2); 16; 21(2); 25; 31(2); 34; 36; 108:4; 12; 13; 109:2; 4; 5(2); 19; 21(2); 22; 31; 110:4; 111:3; 8; 9; 10; 112:3; 6; 9; 113:2; 115:1(2); 18; 116:7; 8; 12; 117:2(2); 118:1(2); 2; 3; 4; 12; 21; 29(3); 119:20; 22; 28; 35; 39; 42; 43; 44; 45; 50; 66; 71; 76; 77; 78; 81; 82; 83; 85; 89; 91; 93; 94; 95; 98; 99; 102; 110; 111(2); 115; 118; 120; 122(2); 123(2); 126(2); 131(2); 152; 153; 155; 160; 166; 168; 172; 173; 174; 176; 120:7(2); 121:8; 122:5; 6; 8; 123:3; 125:1; 2; 3; 5; 126:2; 3; 127:t, 2(2); 128:2; 130:5; 6(3); 7; 131:1; 3; 132:5(2); 9; 10; 12; 13(2); 14(2); 16; 17; 133:1; 3(2); 135:3(2); 4(2); 5; 7; 12; 13; 14; 136:1(3); 2(2); 3(2); 4(2); 5(2); 6(2); 7(2); 8(2); 9(2); 10(2); 11(2); 12(2); 13(2); 14(2); 15(2); 16(2); 17(2); 18(2); 19(2); 20(2); 21(3); 22(2); 23(2); 24(2); 25(2); 26(2); 137:3; 138:2(3); 5; 8; 139:4; 6; 13; 14; 20; 140:2; 5(2); 9; 141:5; 6; 9; 142:3; 4; 6(2); 7; 143:2; 3; 8(2); 10; 11(2); 12; 145:1; 2; 21; 146:5; 6; 7; 10; 147:1(2); 8; 13; 20; 148:5; 6; 13; 149:4; 150:2; **Prov** 1:9; 11(2); 16; 18(2); 29; 32; 2:3; 4(2); 6; 7; 18; 21; 3:2; 12; 14; 26; 32; 4:2; 3; 13; 16; 17; 22; 23; 5:3; 21; 6:1; 23; 26(2); 34; 7:6; 19; 23; 26; 8:6; 7; 11; 32; 35; 9:4; 11; 12; 14; 16; 10:13; 21; 11:15(2); 12:6; 19(2); 13:22; 23; 16:4(2); 12; 26(2); 17:3(2); 13; 17; 26; 18:6; 16; 19:10(2); 18; 19; 29(2); 20:3; 16(2); 21:8; 12; 18(2); 25; 29; 22:9; 11; 18; 23; 26; 23:3; 5; 7; 9; 11; 13; 18; 21; 27; 28; 24:2; 6; 7; 16; 20; 22; 27; 25:3(2); 4; 7; 13; 16; 22; 27; 26:1; 3(3); 25; 27:1; 10; 13(2); 21(2); 24(2); 26; 27(4); 28:2; 8; 21(2); 29:5; 14; 19; 30:8; 18; 21(2); 22; 23; 30; 31:4(3); 8; 10; 21(2); **Eccl** 1:4; 18; 2:3; 10; 12; 16(2); 17; 21(2); 22; 23; 24; 25; 26; 3:12; 14; 17(3); 19(2); 22(2); 4:4; 8; 9; 10(2); 14; 5:1; 2; 3; 4; 7; 8; 9; 13; 16; 18(2); 20; 6:2; 4; 7; 8; 12(3); 7:2; 3; 5; 6; 9; 10; 12; 13; 18; 20; 22; 8:3; 7(2); 15; 16; 9:1; 4(2); 5(2); 6; 7; 9; 10; 12; 10:1; 4; 17(2); 19; 20; 11:1; 2; 6; 7; 8; 9; 10; 12:13; 14; **Song** 1:2; 7; 2:5; 11; 14; 15; 3:10; 4:4; 5:2; 4; 6:5; 7:6; 9; 13; 8:6; 7; 8(2); 11; **Is** 1:2; 17; 20; 29(2); 30; 2:3; 10(2); 12; 19(2); 20; 21(2); 22; 3:1; 7; 8; 9; 10; 11; 12; 14; 4:2; 5; 6(3); 5:7(3); 20(4); 23; 25; 6:5(2); 8; 7:4(2); 6; 8; 13; 16; 18(2); 22(2); 23; 25(2); 8:4; 10; 11; 14(5); 17; 18(2); 19; 9:4; 5; 6; 7; 12; 13; 16; 17(2); 18; 21; 10:3; 4; 8; 13(2); 17(2); 22; 23; 25; 26; 11:4; 9; 10; 12; 16; 12:2; 5; 6; 13:3; 6; 10; 11(2); 17; 14:1; 2; 9(2); 13; 21(2); 22; 23; 27; 29; 31; 15:5(3); 6(2); 8; 9(2); 16:2; 4; 7(2); 8; 9(3); 11(2); 17:2; 18:4; 5; 19:10; 15; 20(3); 20:3; 6; 21:6; 15; 16; 17; 22:5; 11; 13; 16; 23; 25; 23:1; 4; 13; 14; 18(3); 24:3; 11; 14; 18; 25:1; 2; 4; 8; 9(2); 10(2); 26:1; 4(2); 5; 8; 9; 11; 12(2); 19; 20; 21(2); 27:11; 28:5(2); 6(2); 8; 10; 11; 15; 16; 19; 20; 21; 22; 26; 27; 29:10; 11; 14; 16; 20(2); 21(3); 30:4; 7; 8(2); 15; 16; 18(2); 19; 31; 33(2); 31:1; 4(4); 7(2); 9; 32:6; 10; 12(3); 14(2); 15; 17; 33:2; 5; 22; 34:2; 5; 6; 8(2); 10(2); 13; 14; 16; 17(2); 35:1; 6; 8; 36:5; 9(2); 11; 14; 16; 21; 37:3; 4; 8; 19; 32; 35(3); 38:1; 14; 17(2); 18(2); 21(2); 39:1; 8; 40:2(2); 3; 5; 8; 10; 16; 26; 41:7; 10(2); 13; 17; 22; 28; 42:4; 6(2); 21; 22(2); 23; 24(2); 43:1; 3(3); 4(2); 5; 7(2); 14; 21; 25; 44:3; 7; 10; 14; 15(2); 17; 18; 21; 22; 23(2); 45:4; 13; 18; 22; 46:9; 13; 47:1; 4; 5; 7; 9(2); 10; 48:2; 8; 9(3); 11(3); 21; 49:4; 6; 8; 10; 13; 19; 20; 23(2); 25; 50:1(2); 2; 7; 51:2; 3; 4(2); 6(2); 8(2); 10; 19; 52:1; 3(2); 4; 5; 8; 9; 12(2); 15; 53:2; 5(2); 8(2); 10; 11; 12; 54:1; 3; 4(3); 5; 6; 7; 8; 9(2); 10; 14(2); 15; 16; 55:2(2); 4; 5(2); 7; 8; 9; 10; 12; 13(2); 56:1; 4; 7(2); 11; 57:8; 12; 15; 16(3); 17; 58:4; 5; 14; 59:3; 4(2); 9(2); 10; 11(2); 12(3); 14; 17(2); 21(2); 60:1; 2; 9; 10; 12; 17(4); 19; 20; 21; 61:3(3); 7(2); 8(2); 10; 11; 62:1(2); 4; 5; 8(2); 10; 63:3; 4; 8; 17; 64:3; 4(3); 5; 7; 9; 12; 65:1; 5; 8(2); 10(2); 11; 14(3); 15(2); 17; 18(2); 20; 22; 23(2); 66:2; 5; 8; 10(2); 12; 15; 16; 18; 20; 21(2); 22; 24; **Jer** 1:6; 7; 8; 12; 15; 18; 19; 2:10; 11; 13; 20; 22; 25; 27; 28; 37; 3:2; 5; 8; 10; 12(2); 14; 18; 21; 22; 23; 24; 25; 4:3; 6; 8(2); 13; 15; 20; 22; 27; 28; 29; 31(2); 5:4; 5; 7; 9; 10; 11; 22; 26; 29; 6:1; 4(2); 6; 11; 12; 13; 16(2); 23; 25; 26(2); 27; 29; 7:5; 7; 12; 16(3); 22; 29; 30; 32; 33(2); 34; 8:2; 10; 11; 14; 15(2); 16; 17; 21; 9:1; 2; 3(3); 4; 7(2); 9; 10(2); 12; 17(2); 18; 19; 21; 24; 26; 10:2; 3(2); 5; 7; 14; 16; 18; 19; 21; 25; 11:7; 13; 14(4); 17(2); 20; 23; 12:3(2); 4; 6; 12; 13:7; 10; 11(5); 15; 16; 17; 18; 21; 22; 14:4; 7(2); 8; 11(2); 16; 17; 19(3); 20; 21; 22; 15:2(4); 4; 5; 13; 14; 15; 16; 17; 20; 16:3; 4(2); 5(2); 6(2); 7(4); 9; 12; 16(2); 17; 17:3; 4(2); 6; 8; 14; 16; 25; 18:18; 20(4); 22(2); 19:5; 7(2); 20:4; 8; 10(2); 11; 12; 13; 21:2(2); 9; 10(3); 22:4; 6; 10(3); 11; 13; 17(4); 18(2); 20; 22; 30; 23:10(2); 11; 12; 15; 18; 27; 34; 36(2); 24:5; 6(2); 7; 9; 25:5; 12; 14; 15; 29(3); 31; 34; 36; 38; 26:11; 14; 15(2); 16; 27:10; 14; 15; 16; 19; 28:4; 13; 14; 29:6; 7(2); 8; 9; 10; 11; 13; 26; 28; 32; 30:3; 5; 7; 8; 10; 11; 12; 14(2); 15(2); 16; 17; 21; 31:6; 7(2); 9; 11; 12(4); 13; 15(2); 16; 18; 20(2); 22; 25; 30; 34(2); 35(2); 36; 37; 40; 32:2; 3; 7; 8(2); 15; 17; 19; 25(2); 27; 30(2); 31; 39(2); 42; 44(2); 33:4; 5; 9(2); 11(4); 17; 26; 34:5(2); 7; 11(2); 16(2); 17; 20; 35:6(2); 9; 11(2); 14; 19; 36:7; 31; 37:3; 4; 9; 10; 11; 15; 17; 38:2(2); 4(2); 5; 9(2); 27; 39:16(2); 18(2); 40:4; 10; 16; 41:8; 9; 18; 42:2(3); 5; 10; 11; 18; 20(2); 21; 43:1; 3; 7; 11(3); 44:11; 13; 14; 16; 17; 27(2); 29; 45:3; 5(3); 46:5; 10(2); 11; 12; 14; 19; 21; 22; 27; 28(2); 47:3; 4; 48:1; 5(2); 7; 9; 14; 18; 20; 26; 27(3); 31(3); 32; 34; 36(2); 37; 38; 40; 44; 46; 49:3(2); 8; 12; 13; 15; 19; 23; 30; 33(2); 37; 50:3; 9; 14; 15; 16; 20(2); 24; 25; 27; 29; 31; 38; 39; 44; 51:2; 5; 6; 8(2); 9; 11; 12; 17; 19; 20; 26(3); 29; 33; 36; 37; 46; 48(2); 51; 56; 62; 52:3; 6; 16(2); 34; **Lam** 1:5(2); 9; 10; 11(2); 13; 16; 18; 19; 20(2); 22(2); 2:11; 13(2); 14(2); 16; 19(2); 3:12; 25; 26; 27; 31(2); 33; 39; 48; 4:4; 6; 9(2); 13; 17(3); 18; 19; 5:4; 17(2); 19; 20; **Eze** 1:10; 13; 18; 20; 21; 2:4; 5; 7; 3:3; 5; 7(2); 26; 27; 4:3; 5; 6; 14; 15; 17; 5:4; 6; 16; 6:9; 11(2); 7:6; 8; 11; 12; 13(2); 14; 16; 20; 21(2); 22; 23; 8:12; 14; 17; 9:4; 9; 10; 10:10; 13; 17; 11:5; 12; 21; 12:2; 3; 4; 6(2); 7; 24; 25(2); 27; 13:5; 16; 19(2); 23; 14:7; 21; 15:4(2); 5(2); 6; 16:4; 14(2); 19; 21; 33; 52; 56; 59; 61; 63; 17:17; 20; 18:17; 18; 26; 31; 32; 19:1; 11; 14; 20:6; 9; 14; 16; 22; 28(2); 31; 39; 40; 42; 43; 44; 21:7; 12; 15; 21; 22; 28; 32(2); 22:10; 30(2); 23:8; 10; 14; 20; 21; 28; 34; 37; 39; 40(2); 46; 24:7; 9; 17; 23; 25:4; 5(2); 6; 7; 15; 26:5(2); 7; 14; 17; 19; 21; 27:2; 3; 5; 15; 18; 20; 31(2); 32; 28:10; 23; 29:3; 5; 15; 18(2); 19; 20(2); 30:3; 9; 18; 31:7; 11; 14(2); 15(3); 32:2; 10(2); 11; 16(3); 18; 32; 33:2; 11; 12(2); 13(2); 17; 24; 28; 31; 32; 34:8; 10(2); 11; 17; 19; 29; 36:5; 8; 9(2); 18(2); 21; 22(2); 24; 29; 31(2); 32(2); 37(2); 37:11; 16(4); 25(2); 26; 28; 38:7; 19; 21; 39:5; 10; 17; 19; 23; 25; 29; 40:4; 17; 42; 45; 46; 41:6; 7; 9; 24(2); 42:3(2); 5; 6; 8; 13; 14(2); 43:7; 9; 19; 22; 24; 25; 44:3; 8; 11; 14(2); 22; 25(6); 28; 45:1; 2(2); 4(3); 5(3); 6; 7; 14; 15(4); 16; 17; 20(2); 22(3); 23; 24(3); 46:5(2); 7(3); 14; 15; 17; 47:1; 5; 9; 12(3); 14; 22; 48:1(2); 2; 3; 4; 5; 6; 7; 10(2); 11; 14; 15(3); 18; 21(2); 22; 23; 29; **Dan** 1:7; 10; 17; 2:2; 4; 9(2); 12; 20(2); 23; 29; 30(3); 35; 37; 44; 3:9; 4:12; 18; 19; 21; 22; 30(2); 34; 36; 5:10; 19; 6:6; 7; 21; 23; 26(2); 7:12; 18(2); 28; 8:8; 15; 17; 19; 22; 26(2); 9:12; 14(2); 16(2); 17; 18(3); 19(2); 20; 23; 24; 26; 27(2); 10:7; 8; 11; 12(2); 14(2); 17(3); 19; 11:4(2); 6; 13; 17; 18; 23; 24; 25; 27; 30; 35; 36; 37; 39; 12:1; 3; 7(2); 9; 13; **Hos** 1:2; 4; 6; 9; 11; 2:2; 4; 5(2); 7; 8(2); 15; 17; 18; 19; 3:2(2); 3(3); 4; 4:1; 4; 6; 9; 10; 12; 14; 16; 5:1; 3; 4; 7; 14; 6:1; 4; 6; 9(2); 11; 7:1; 6; 10; 13; 14; 16; 8:6; 7; 9; 10; 13; 14; 9:1(2); 4(2); 6(2); 7; 11; 15(2); 10:3; 5(2); 6; 7; 12; 11:9; 12:12(2); 13:4; 13; 16; 14:1; 3; 4; 9; **Joel** 1:5; 6; 8; 10; 11(2); 13; 15(2); 17; 19; 20; 2:1(2); 11(3); 13; 18; 21; 22(2); 23(2); 32; 3:1; 2(2); 3(3); 8; 12; 13(3); 14; 19; 20; 21(2); **Amos** 1:3(2); 6(2); 9(2); 11(3); 13(2); 2:1(2); 4(2); 6(4); 11(2); 3:2; 5; 10; 4:5; 13; 5:3; 4; 5; 8; 12; 13; 17; 18; 23; 6:6; 10; 11; 12; 7:2; 3; 5; 6; 11; 13; 8:6(2); 8; 11; 13; 9:4(2); 6; 9; **Obad** 10(2); 15; 16; 18(2); **Jonah** 1:2; 7; 8; 10; 11; 12(2); 13; 14(2); 2:3; 6; 3:6; 4:2; 3(2); 8; 9; 10; **Mic** 1:3; 5(2); 7; 9(2); 12(2); 13; 16(2); 2:3; 9; 10; 3:1; 3; 7; 11(3); 12; 4:2; 4; 5(2); 7; 9; 10; 12; 13; 5:4; 7(2); 6:2; 4; 7(2); 12; 16; 7:1; 2; 3; 6; 7; 9; 13; 18; **Nah** 1:2; 10; 13; 14; 15; 2:2(2); 9; 12(2); 3:7; 10; 14; 19; **Hab** 1:3; 4; 5; 6; 9; 10; 12(2); 2:3(3); 7; 8; 11; 13; 14; 16; 17(2); 3:13(2); **Zeph** 1:6; 7(2); 11; 18; 2:4; 6(2); 7(2); 10; 11; 14; 15; 3:8(2); 9; 11(2); 13; 18; 20; **Hag** 1:4; 9; 11; 2:4; 6; 16; 23; **Zec** 1:5; 14(2); 15; 2:4; 5; 6; 8(2); 9; 10; 13; 3:8(2); 9; 4:10(2); 5:3; 9; 6:14; 7:6(2); 14; 8:2(2); 4; 10(4); 12; 14; 17; 23; 9:5; 7; 8; 11; 13; 16; 17; 10:2; 3; 6(2); 8(2); 10; 11:2(2); 3(2); 5; 6; 12; 16; 12:1; 3; 10(4); 13:1(2); 3; 5; 14:2; 5; **Mal** 1:3; 4; 8; 10(2); 11(2); 14; 2:1; 5; 7(2); 11; 16(2); 3:2; 6; 9; 11; 12; 16; 4:1; 3; 4; **Mt** 1:20; 21; 2:2; 5; 6; 8; 13; 18; 20; 3:2; 3; 8; 9; 15; 4:6; 10; 17; 18; 5:3; 4; 5; 6; 7; 8; 9; 10(2); 11; 12(2); 13; 18; 20; 29(2); 30(2); 32; 34; 35(2); 37; 38(2); 44; 45; 46; 6:5; 7(2); 8; 13(2); 14; 16; 19; 20; 21; 24; 25(2); 26; 28; 32(2); 34(3); 7:2; 8; 12; 13; 25; 29; 8:4; 9; 9:5; 13; 16; 21; 24; 10:10(2); 15(2); 17; 18(2); 19; 20; 22; 23; 25; 26; 29; 35; 39; 11:3; 8; 9; 10; 13; 14; 18; 21; 22(2); 23; 24(2); 26; 29; 30; 12:4(3); 8; 33; 34; 37; 40; 42; 50; 13:12; 15; 16(2); 17; 21(2); 44; 14:3(2); 4(2); 9; 24; 26; 15:2; 4; 9; 19; 23; 16:2; 3; 17; 23; 25(2); 26(2); 27; 17:4(4); 15(2); 20; 27; 18:6; 7; 8; 9; 10; 11; 19; 20; 19:3(2); 5; 9; 12(2); 14; 22; 24(2); 29; 20:1; 2; 13; 15; 16; 23; 28; 21:19; 26; 32; 46; 22:2; 14; 16(2); 28; 30; 23:3; 4; 5; 8; 9; 10; 13(2); 14(2); 15; 17; 19; 23; 25; 27; 39; 24:1;

5; 6; 7; 9; 14; 21; 22; 24; 27; 28; 38; 42; 44; 50; 25:8; 9(2); 13; 14; 29; 34; 35; 41; 42; 26:9(2); 10; 11; 12(2); 13; 15; 17; 24; 28(3); 31; 43; 52; 55; 73; 27:6; 10; 18(2); 19; 43; 47; 28:2; 4; 5; 6; **Mk** 1:4; 16; 22; 27; 37; 38; 44(2); 2:4; 15; 26; 27(2); 3:5; 10(2); 21; 32; 35; 4:17(2); 22; 25; 28; 5:8; 9; 19; 20; 28; 42; 6:8; 11(3); 14; 17(3); 18(2); 20; 26(2); 31; 36; 48; 50; 52(2); 7:3; 7; 8; 10; 12; 21; 25; 27; 29; 8:3; 33; 35(2); 36; 37; 9:5(4); 6(2); 31; 34; 39; 40; 41; 42; 43; 45; 47; 49; 10:2; 5; 7; 14; 22; 24; 25(2); 27; 29; 35; 36; 40; 45(2); 11:13; 14; 18; 23; 32; 12:1; 12; 14(2); 23; 25; 32; 36; 40; 44; 13:6; 7; 8; 9(3); 11; 13; 16; 19; 20; 22; 33; 34; 35; 14:5(2); 7; 9; 15; 21; 24; 27; 40; 55; 56; 70; 15:10(2); 43; 16:4; 8; 8<VM>; **Lk** 1:13; 15; 17; 18; 21; 22; 30; 33; 37; 44(2); 45; 48(2); 49; 55; 63; 68; 69; 76; 2:7; 10; 11; 20; 21; 25; 27; 30; 34(2); 38; 3:3; 8; 19(2); 4:6; 8; 10; 13; 16; 32; 36; 38; 41; 43; 5:4; 8; 9; 14(2); 39; 6:4; 19; 20; 21(2); 22; 23(3); 24; 25(2); 26; 28; 32(2); 33; 34; 35(2); 38; 43; 44(2); 45; 48; 7:4; 5; 6; 8; 19; 20; 24; 25; 26; 28; 33; 39; 44; 47; 8:13; 17; 18; 19; 25; 29(2); 37; 40(2); 42; 46; 47; 9:3; 5; 12; 13; 14; 24(2); 25; 26; 33(4); 38; 44; 48; 50(2); 52; 56; 62; 10:7; 12(2); 13; 14(2); 21; 24; 11:4; 6; 10; 11; 30; 31; 32; 42; 43; 44; 46; 47; 48; 52; 54; 12:2; 6; 12; 15; 19; 21; 22(2); 24; 26; 30; 32; 34; 36; 40; 46; 48; 52; 13:17; 24; 31; 33; 14:11; 14(2); 17; 24; 28; 35(2); 15:1; 6; 9; 24; 30; 32; 16:2; 3; 8; 13; 15; 17; 24; 28; 17:2; 21; 24; 18:4; 14; 16; 23; 25(3); 29; 32; 19:3; 4; 5; 10; 12; 21; 26; 37; 43; 48; 20:6; 9; 19; 22; 33; 36; 38(2); 47; 21:4; 6; 8; 9; 12; 13; 15; 17; 22; 23; 26(3); 28; 35; 38; 22:2; 16; 18; 19; 20; 27; 32; 37(2); 45; 59; 71; 23:8; 12; 15; 17; 19(2); 25; 28(3); 29; 31; 34; 41; 51; 24:29; 39; 41; **Jn** 1:7; 15; 16; 17; 30; 39; 2:25; 3:2; 16; 17; 20; 24; 34(2); 4:8; 9; 18; 22; 23; 35; 39; 42; 44; 45; 47; 5:3; 4; 10; 13; 19; 20; 21; 22; 26; 28; 35; 36; 38; 39; 46(2); 6:6; 7; 24; 27(3); 33; 38; 51(2); 55; 58; 64; 71; 7:1; 4; 5; 8; 12; 13; 29; 39; 52; 8:14; 16; 20; 24; 29; 35; 42; 44; 9:21; 22; 29; 39; 10:4; 5; 10; 11; 13; 15; 19; 32; 33(2); 11:4; 15; 28; 39; 47; 50(2); 51; 52; 53; 56; 12:5; 6; 8; 9; 18(2); 27; 30; 34; 35; 43; 47; 49; 13:11; 13; 15; 28; 29; 37; 38; 14:2; 3; 11; 16; 17; 28; 30; 15:5; 13; 15(2); 21; 22; 16:7(2); 13; 14; 21; 26; 27; 17:8; 9(4); 19; 20(2); 24; 18:2; 13; 14; 18; 31; 37; 19:6; 20; 24(2); 31; 36; 38; 42; 20:9; 17; 19; 21:6; 7; 8; 11; **Acts** 1:4; 5; 7; 17; 20; 2:15; 25(2); 34; 38; 39; 3:10; 22; 4:3; 12; 16; 20; 21(2); 22; 27; 28; 34; 5:8(2); 26; 31; 36; 38; 41; 6:14; 7:5; 16; 21; 25; 33; 40(2); 46; 8:3; 7; 15; 16; 21; 23; 24; 27; 33; 9:5; 11(2); 15; 16(2); 21; 10:4; 5; 14; 17; 20; 22; 24; 28; 29(3); 38; 46; 11:8; 13; 24; 25; 12:5; 14; 19; 13:2; 7; 8; 11; 15; 27; 36; 41; 47(2); 14:26; 15:6; 14; 21; 26; 28; 31; 16:3; 4; 10; 21; 28; 29; 17:15; 16; 20; 21; 23; 26; 28(2); 18:3; 10(2); 15; 17; 18; 28; 19:8; 22; 24(2); 32; 37; 40(2); 20:1; 3; 5; 10; 13; 16(3); 27; 29; 38; 21:3; 13(2); 22; 26; 29; 34; 35; 36; 22:5; 10; 11; 15; 18; 21; 22; 25; 26; 23:3; 5; 8; 11; 17; 21(3); 30; 24:5; 10; 11; 21; 24; 25(2); 26; 25:3; 8; 11; 16; 27; 26:1(2); 2; 6; 7; 14; 16(2); 20; 21; 24; 26(3); 27:22; 23; 25; 29; 34(3); 28:2; 20(3); 22; 27; **Rom** 1:5(2); 8; 9; 11; 16(2); 17; 18; 19; 20; 25; 26(2); 2:1(2); 7; 11; 12; 13; 14; 24; 25; 26; 28; 3:3; 6; 7; 9; 20; 22; 23; 25; 4:2; 3(2); 5; 9(2); 13; 14; 15; 22; 23; 24; 25(2); 5:6(2); 7(3); 8; 10; 12; 13; 15; 16; 17; 19; 6:5; 7; 10; 14(2); 19; 20; 21; 23; 7:1; 2; 5; 7; 8; 9; 11; 14; 15(2); 18(2); 19; 22; 8:2; 3(2); 5; 6; 7; 13; 14; 15; 18; 19(2); 20; 22; 23; 24(3); 25(2); 26(3); 27; 28; 29; 31; 32; 34; 36(2); 38; 9:3(2); 5; 6; 8; 9; 11; 15; 17(2); 19; 28; 32; 10:1; 2; 3; 4(2); 5; 10; 11; 12(2); 13; 16; 11:1; 7; 11; 13; 15; 16; 21; 23; 24; 25; 27; 28(2); 29; 30; 32; 34; 36(2); 12:3; 4; 17; 19; 20; 13:1; 3; 4(4); 5(2); 6(3); 8; 9; 11; 14; 14:2; 3; 4; 6; 7; 8; 9; 10; 11; 15; 17; 18; 19; 20(2); 23; 15:2; 3; 4(2); 8; 9(2); 18; 22; 24; 26(2); 27; 30(3); 31; 16:2; 4; 18; 19; 26; 27; **1Cor** 1:4; 7; 11; 13; 17; 18; 19; 21; 22; 26; 2:2; 8; 9; 10; 11; 14; 16; 3:2; 3(2); 4; 9; 11; 13; 17; 19(2); 21; 4:4; 6(2); 7; 9(2); 10; 15(2); 17; 20; 5:3; 5; 7(2); 10; 12; 6:12; 13(5); 16; 20; 7:1; 5(2); 7; 8; 9; 14; 16; 21; 22; 26(2); 31; 32; 33; 34(2); 35(2); 8:5; 7; 8; 10; 11; 9:2; 9(2); 10(2); 15(2); 16(2); 17; 19; 23; 25; 10:4; 5; 11(2); 17(2); 23(2); 25; 26; 27; 28(3); 29; 30(3); 11:5; 6(2); 7; 8; 9(2); 10; 12; 15(2); 17(2); 18; 19; 21; 23; 24; 26; 29; 30; 31; 33; 12:8; 12; 13; 14; 24; 25; 13:9; 12; 14:2(2); 5; 8; 9; 14; 17; 21; 22(3); 31; 33; 34; 35(2); 15:3(2); 9; 16; 21; 22; 25; 27; 29(2); 32; 34; 41; 52; 53; 16:1; 5; 7; 9; 10; 11(2); 17; 18; **2Cor** 1:5; 6(2); 8; 11(2); 12; 13; 19; 20; 23; 24(2); 2:2; 4; 9; 10(2); 11; 15; 16; 17; 3:6; 7; 9; 10; 11; 14; 4:5(2); 6; 11(2); 15(2); 16; 17(3); 18; 5:1; 2; 4(2); 5; 7; 10; 12; 13(2); 14(2); 15(2); 20; 21(2); 6:2; 13; 14; 16; 7:3; 5; 8(3); 9; 10; 11; 12(3); 13; 14; 8:3; 9(2); 10(2); 12; 13; 14(2); 16; 17; 21; 9:1(2); 2(2); 7; 9; 10; 12; 13(2); 14(2); 15; 10:3; 4; 8(3); 10; 12; 14(2); 18; 11:2(2); 4; 5; 9; 13; 14; 19; 20; 31; 12:1; 4; 6(2); 8; 9(2); 10(2); 11(2); 13; 14(4); 15; 19; 20; 13:4(2); 8(2); 9; **Gal** 1:4; 5; 10(2); 12; 13; 2:5; 6; 8; 12; 16; 18; 19; 20; 21; 3:6; 10(2); 11; 13(2); 18; 21; 26; 27; 28; 4:12; 15; 20; 22; 24; 25; 27(2); 30; 5:3; 5(2); 6; 13(2); 14; 17; 6:3; 5; 7; 8; 9; 12; 13; 15; 17; **Eph** 1:16; 2:4; 8; 10; 14; 15; 18; 22; 3:1(2); 13; 14; 4:12(3); 25; 32; 5:2(2); 5; 6; 8; 9; 12; 13; 20; 23; 25; 29; 30; 31; 6:1; 12; 18; 19; 20; 22; **Phil** 1:4; 5; 7; 8; 17; 19; 21; 23; 24; 25; 26; 27; 29(2); 2:13; 18; 20(2); 21; 26; 27; 30; 3:1; 3; 7; 8(2); 12; 14; 17; 18; 20(2); 4:1; 6; 11; 16; 20; **Col** 1:3; 5(2); 7; 9(2); 16(2); 19; 24(2); 25; 2:1(4); 5; 9; 3:3; 6; 20; 24; 25; 4:3(2); 8; 12; 13(2); **1Th** 1:2; 5(2); 8; 9; 10; 2:1; 3; 5; 9(2); 13; 14(2); 16; 17; 19; 20; 3:3; 4; 5; 8; 9(4); 4:2; 3; 7; 9; 14; 15; 16; 5:2; 3; 7; 8; 9; 10; 13; 15; 18; 25; **2Th** 1:3; 4; 5; 11; 2:3; 7; 11; 13; 3:1; 2; 5; 7(2); 8; 10; 11; **1Ti** 1:9(7); 10(5); 12; 16(2); 17; 2:1; 2(2); 3; 5; 6; 13; 3:5; 13; 4:4; 5; 8; 10; 16; 5:4; 8(2); 10; 11; 15; 18; 23; 6:7; 10; 19; **2Ti** 1:7; 12(2); 16; 2:5; 10; 11; 16; 21; 3:2; 6; 9; 16(4); 4:3; 6; 8; 10; 11(2); 15; 18; **Titus** 1:5; 7; 10; 11; 2:11; 13; 14; 3:3; 9; 12; 14; **Philem** 1:7; 9; 10; 15(3); 22; **Heb** 1:5; 8; 14; 2:2; 5; 8; 9(2); 10(2); 11(2); 16; 17; 18; 3:3; 4; 5; 14; 16; 4:2; 3; 4; 8; 10; 12; 15; 5:1(3); 2; 3(3); 6; 12(2); 13(2); 6:4(2); 7(2); 10; 13; 16(2); 18(2); 20(2); 7:1; 10; 11; 12; 13; 14; 15; 17(2); 18(2); 19; 21(2); 25; 26; 27(3); 28(2); 8:3; 4; 5; 7(2); 8; 10; 11; 12; 9:2; 7(2); 9; 12; 13; 15(2); 16; 17; 19; 24(2); 26; 28; 10:1; 2; 4; 6; 8; 10; 12(2); 14(2); 15; 18; 20; 23; 26(2); 27; 30; 34; 36; 37; 11:1; 2; 5; 6; 8; 10(2); 14; 16(2); 25; 26; 27; 32; 40; 12:2; 3; 6; 7; 10(3); 11; 13; 16; 17(2); 18; 20; 25; 29; 13:2; 5; 8; 9; 11(2); 14; 16; 17(4); 18(2); 21; 22; **Jas** 1:6; 7; 11; 12; 13; 20; 23; 24; 2:2; 10; 11; 13; 23; 26; 3:2; 7; 16; 4:14(2); 15; 5:1; 3; 7(2); 8; 10; 14; 16; **1Pet** 1:4; 6; 13; 16; 20; 23; 24; 25; 2:13; 14(2); 15; 16; 19(2); 20(3); 21(2); 25; 3:5; 9(2); 10; 12; 14; 17(3); 18(3); 4:1(2); 3; 6(2); 8; 11; 14(2); 17; 5:2; 5; 7(2); 11; **2Pet** 1:8; 10; 11; 16; 17; 21; 2:4; 8; 16; 17; 18; 19; 20; 21(2); 3:4; 5; 12; 13; 14; 18; **1Jn** 1:2; 2:2(3); 12; 16; 17; 19; 3:2; 4; 8(2); 9; 11; 16(2); 20; 4:7; 8; 10; 20; 5:3; 4; 7; 9; 16(2); **2Jn** 2(2); 7; 11; **3Jn** 3; 7; **Jude** 3(2); 4; 7; 11(2); 13; 21; **Rev** 1:3; 6; 9(2); 18; 2:3; 3:2; 4; 8; 4:9; 10; 11(2); 5:9; 13; 14; 6:6(2); 9(2); 11; 17; 7:12; 17; 8:12; 9:15(2); 19(2); 10:6; 11:2; 15; 12:4; 10; 12; 14; 13:18; 14:4; 5; 7; 11; 15(3); 18; 15:1; 4(3); 7; 16:6(2); 10; 14; 21; 17:14; 17; 18:3; 5; 7; 8; 9; 10(2); 11; 15; 17; 19; 20; 23(2); 19:2(2); 3; 6; 7; 8; 10; 20:4(2); 10; 11; 21:1; 2; 4; 5; 22; 23; 25; 22:2; 5(2); 9; 10; 15; 18

FOREMOST

Gen 32:17; 33:2; **2Sa** 18:27

FORTH

Gen 1:11; 12; 20; 21; 24; 3:16; 18; 22; 23; 8:7(2); 8; 9; 10; 12; 16; 17; 18; 19; 9:7; 18; 10:11; 11:31; 12:5; 14:18; 15:4; 5; 19:10; 16; 17; 22:10; 24:43; 45; 53; 30:39; 38:24; 25; 29; 39:13; 40:10(2); 41:47; 42:15; **Ex** 3:10; 11; 12; 4:4(2); 14; 5:20; 7:4; 5; 8:3; 5; 18; 20; 9:9; 10; 22; 23; 10:13; 22; 12:31; 39; 46; 13:8; 16; 14:11; 27; 15:7; 13; 16:3; 32; 19:1; 17; 22; 24; 25:20; 29:46; 32:11; **Lev** 4:12; 21; 6:11; 14:3; 45; 16:24; 27; 22:27; 24:14; 23; 25:21; 38; 42; 55; 26:10; 13; 45; **Num** 1:3; 20; 22; 24; 26; 28; 30; 32; 34; 36; 38; 40; 42; 45; 2:9; 16; 11:20; 31; 12:5; 17:8; 19:3; 20:8(2); 16; 24:6; 8; 26:4; 31:13; 33:1; 34:4; 8; **Deut** 1:27; 2:23; 4:20; 45; 46; 6:12; 8:14; 15; 9:12; 26; 14:22; 28; 16:1; 3(2); 6; 17:5; 21:2; 10; 22:15; 23:4; 9; 12; 24:9; 25:11; 17; 26:8; 29:25; 33:2; 14(2); **Josh** 2:3; 5:5; 8:9; 9:12; 10:23; 18:11; 17(2); 19:1; **Judg** 1:24; 3:21; 23; 5:25; 31; 6:8; 18; 21; 9:8; 43; 11:31; 14:12; 13; 14(2); 16; 15:15; 19:22; 25; 20:21; 25; 33; **Ruth** 1:7; 2:18; **1Sa** 11:7; 12:8; 14:11; 27; 17:20; 55; 18:30(2); 22:3; 17; 23:13; 24:6; 10; 26:9; 11; 23; 30:21; **2Sa** 1:14; 5:20; 6:6; 11:1; 12:30; 31; 13:39; 15:5; 16; 17; 16:5; 11; 18:2(2); 3; 12; 19:7(2); 20:8; 22:20; 49; **1Kin** 2:30; 36; 6:27; 8:7; 16; 19; 22; 38; 51; 9:9; 13:4(2); 19:11; 20:33; 21:13; 22:21; 22(2); **2Kin** 2:3; 21; 23; 24; 6:15; 8:3; 9:11; 15; 10:22(2); 25; 26; 11:7; 12; 15; 18:7; 19:3; 31; 21:15; 23:4; **1Chr** 12:33; 36; 13:9; 14:11; 15; 16:23; 19:16; 20:1; 24:7; 25:9; 26:16; **2Chr** 1:17; 3:13; 5:8; 6:5; 9; 12; 13; 29; 7:22; 20:20(2); 21:9; 23:14; 25:5; 11; 26:6; 29:5; 23; 32:21; **Ezr** 1:7(2); 8; 6:5; **Neh** 4:16; 8:15; 16; 9:7; 15; 13:8; 21; **Est** 4:6; 5:9; **Job** 1:11; 12(2); 2:5; 7; 5:6; 8:16; 10:18; 11:17; 14:2; 9; 15:35; 21:11; 30; 23:10; 24:5; 28:9; 11; 30:5; 38:8; 27; 32; 39:1; 2; 3; 4; 40:20; **Ps** 1:3; 7:14; 9:1; 14; 17:2; 18:19; 19:6; 37:6; 44:9; 51:15; 55:20; 57:3; 66:2; 68:7; 71:15; 78:52; 79:13; 80:1; 88:8; 90:2; 92:2; 14; 96:2; 104:14; 20; 23; 30; 105:30; 37; 43; 106:2; 107:7; 108:11; 113:2; 115:18; 121:8; 125:3; 5; 126:6; 138:7; 141:2; 143:6; 144:6; 13; 146:4; 147:15; 17; **Prov** 7:15; 8:1; 24; 25; 9:3; 10:31; 12:17; 25:4; 6; 8; 27:1; 30:27; 33(3); 31:20; **Eccl** 2:6; 5:15; 7:18; 10:1; **Song** 1:3; 8; 12; 2:9; 13; 3:11; 6:10; 7:11; 12; 8:5(2); **Is** 1:15; 2:3; 3:16; 5:2(2); 4(2); 25; 7:3; 25; 11:1; 13:10; 14:7; 29; 23:4; 25:11(2); 26:18; 27:8; 28:19; 29; 31:4; 32:20; 33:11; 34:1; 36:3; 37:3; 9; 32; 36; 41:21; 22; 42:1; 3; 5; 9; 13; 43:8; 9; 17; 19; 21; 44:23; 24; 45:8; 10; 48:1; 3; 20; 49:9; 13; 17; 51:5; 13; 18; 52:9; 54:1; 2; 3; 16; 55:10; 11; 12(2); 58:8(2); 9; 59:4; 60:6; 61:11(3); 62:1; 65:9; 23; 66:7; 8(2); 9(2); 24; **Jer** 1:5; 9; 14; 2:27; 37; 4:4; 7; 31; 6:25; 7:25; 10:13; 20(2); 11:4; 12:2; 14:18; 15:1; 2; 19; 17:22; 19:2; 20:3; 18; 22:11; 19; 23:15; 19; 25:32; 26:23; 29:16; 30:23; 31:4; 24; 39; 32:21; 34:13; 37:5; 7; 12; 38:2; 8; 17; 18; 21; 22; 39:4; 41:6; 42:18(2); 43:12; 44:6; 17; 46:4; 9; 48:7; 45; 49:5; 50:8; 25; 51:10; 16; 44; 52:7; 31; **Lam** 1:17; **Eze** 1:13; 22; 3:22; 23; 5:4; 7:10; 8:3; 9:7(2); 10:7; 11:7; 12:4(3); 6; 7(2); 12; 14:22(2); 16:14; 17:2; 6(2); 7; 8; 23; 18:8; 13; 20:6; 9; 10; 22; 38; 21:3; 4; 5; 19; 24:12; 27:7; 10; 33; 28:18; 29:21; 30:9; 31:5; 6; 32:2; 4; 33:30; 36:8; 20; 38:4; 8; 39:9; 42:1; 15; 44:5; 19; 46:2; 8; 9(2); 10(2); 12(2); 21; 47:3; 8; 10; 12; **Dan** 2:13; 14; 3:26(2); 5:5; 7:10; 8:9; 9:15; 22; 23; 25; 10:20; 11:11(2); 13; 42; 44; **Hos** 6:3; 5; 9:13; 16; 10:1; 13:13; 14:5; **Joel** 2:16; 3:18; **Amos** 5:3; 7:17; 8:3; 5; **Jonah** 1:5; 12; 15; **Mic** 1:3; 11; 4:2; 10(2); 5:2(2); 3; 7:9; **Hab** 1:4; 3:5; 13; **Zeph** 2:2; **Hag** 1:11; 2:19; **Zec** 1:16; 2:3; 6; 3:8; 4:7; 5:3; 4; 5(2); 6; 6:5; 6(3); 7; 9:11; 14; 10:4; 12:1; 14:2; 3; **Mal** 4:2; **Mt** 1:21; 23; 25; 2:16; 3:8; 10; 7:17(2); 18(2); 19; 8:3; 9:9; 25; 38; 10:5; 16; 12:13(2); 20; 35(2); 49; 13:3; 8; 23; 24; 26; 31; 41; 43; 49; 52; 14:2; 14; 31; 15:18; 16:21; 21:43; 22:3; 4; 7; 46; 24:26; 32; 25:1; **Mk** 1:38; 41; 2:12; 13; 3:3; 5; 6; 14; 4:8; 20; 28; 29; 6:7; 14; 17; 24; 7:26; 8:11; 9:29; 10:17; 11:1; 13:28; 14:13; 16; 16:20; **Lk** 1:1; 31; 57; 2:7; 3:7; 8; 9; 5:13; 27; 6:8(2); 10; 43(2); 45(2); 7:17; 8:14; 15; 22; 27; 10:2; 3; 12:16; 37; 14:7; 15:22; 20:9; 20; 21:30; 22:53; **Jn** 1:43; 2:10; 11; 5:29; 8:42; 10:4; 11:43; 44; 53; 12:13; 24; 15:2; 5; 6; 16; 16:28; 30; 18:1; 4; 19:4(2); 5; 13; 17; 20:3; 21:3; 18; **Acts** 1:26; 2:33; 4:30; 5:10; 15; 19; 34; 7:7; 9:30; 40; 11:22; 12:1; 4; 6; 13:4; 16:3; 17:18; 21:2; 23:28; 24:2; 25:17; 23; 26; 26:1; 25; 27:21; **Rom** 3:25; 7:4; 5; 10:21; **1Cor** 4:9; 16:11; **Gal** 3:1; 4:4; 6; 27; **Phil** 2:16; 3:13; **Col** 1:6; **1Ti** 1:16; **Heb** 1:14; 6:7; 13:13; **Jas** 1:15(2); 3:11; 5:18; **1Pet** 2:9; **3Jn** 7; **Jude** 7; **Rev** 5:6; 6:2; 12:5; 13; 16:14

FRO

Gen 8:7; **2Kin** 4:35; **2Chr** 16:9; **Job** 1:7; 2:2; 7:4; 13:25; **Ps** 107:27; **Prov** 21:6; **Is** 24:20; 33:4; 49:21; **Jer** 5:1; 49:3; **Eze** 27:19; **Dan** 12:4; **Joel** 2:9; **Amos** 8:12; **Zec** 1:10; 11; 4:10; 6:7(3); **Eph** 4:14

FROM

Gen 1:4; 6; 7; 14; 18; 2:2; 3; 6; 10; 22; 3:8; 23(2); 4:1; 10; 11(2); 14(2); 16; 6:7; 17; 7:4; 23; 8:2; 3; 7; 8(2); 11; 13; 21; 9:10; 24; 10:19; 30; 11:2; 6; 8; 9; 31; 12:1(2); 8; 13:3; 9; 11; 14(2); 14:17; 23; 15:18; 16:2; 6; 8; 17:14; 22; 18:2; 3; 16; 17; 22; 25(2); 19:4; 24; 26; 20:1; 6; 13; 22:12; 23:3; 6; 24:5; 7(3); 8; 41(2); 46; 50; 62; 25:6; 18; 23; 29; 26:16; 22; 23; 26; 27; 31; 27:9; 30(2); 39; 40; 45(2); 28:2; 6; 10; 29:3; 8; 10; 30:2; 32; 31:13; 16; 27; 31; 40; 49; 32:11(2); 33:18; 35:1; 7; 13; 16; 36:6; 37:25; 38:1; 14; 17; 19; 20; 39:5; 9; 40:19(2); 41:42; 46; 42:2; 7; 24(2); 43:34; 44:28; 29; 45:1; 46:5; 34; 47:10; 18; 21; 48:7; 12; 16; 17; 49:9; 10(2); 24; 26; 32; 50:25; **Ex** 2:15; 3:5; 4:3; 5:4; 5; 19; 20; 6:6; 7; 26; 27; 7:5; 8:8(2); 9; 11(4); 12; 29(4); 30; 31(3); 9:15; 33; 10:5; 6; 11; 17; 18; 23; 28; 11:5; 8; 12:5(2); 15(2); 19; 29; 31; 37; 41; 42; 13:3(2); 10; 14(2); 20; 22; 14:5; 19; 25; 15:22; 16:1; 4; 6; 32; 17:1; 14; 16; 18:4; 10; 13; 14; 19:2; 14; 20:22; 21:14; 22; 22:12; 23:7; 15; 25; 28; 29; 30; 31(2); 25:15; 22(2); 26:4; 28; 27:21; 28:1; 28; 42; 29:28(2); 30:14; 33; 38; 31:14; 32:12(2); 15; 27; 33:5; 7; 16; 34:18; 29(2); 35:5; 20; 36:4; 6; 11; 22; 33; 38:26; 39:21; 40:36; **Lev** 2:9; 13; 4:8; 10; 13; 19; 31; 35; 5:2; 3; 4; 6; 8; 7:20; 21; 25; 27; 34(2); 8:28; 9:22; 24; 10:2; 4; 7; 12:7; 13:12; 41; 58; 14:7; 19; 15:3; 16; 31; 32; 16:12; 19; 30; 17:4; 9; 10; 18:29; 19:8; 20:3; 4; 5; 6; 18; 24; 25; 26; 21:7; 22:2; 3; 4; 25; 27; 23:15(2); 29; 30; 32; 24:3; 8; 25:41; 50; 26:36; 27:3; 5; 6; 7; 17; 18; **Num** 1:3; 18; 20; 22; 24; 26; 28; 30; 32; 34; 36; 38; 40; 42; 45; 3:12; 15; 22; 28; 34; 39; 40; 43; 4:2; 3; 13; 18; 23; 30; 35; 39; 43; 47; 5:13; 19; 31; 6:3; 4; 7:89(2); 8:6; 14; 16; 19; 24; 25; 9:13; 17; 21; 10:9; 11; 33; 11:31(2); 35; 12:10; 14; 15; 16; 13:3; 21; 23; 24; 25; 14:9; 13; 19; 29; 43; 15:23; 30; 16:9; 15; 21; 24; 26; 27; 33; 35; 45; 46(2); 17:5; 9; 10; 18:6; 9; 16; 26; 30; 32; 19:13; 20; 20:6; 9; 14; 21; 22; 28; 21:4; 7; 11; 12; 13; 16; 18; 19(2); 20; 24; 28; 22:5; 16; 33(2); 23:7; 9(2); 13(2); 27; 24:11; 24; 25:4; 7; 8; 11; 26:2; 4; 62; 27:4; 30:14; 31:14; 42; 32:7; 8; 11; 15; 21; 33:3; 5; 6; 7; 8; 9; 10; 11; 13; 14; 15; 16; 17; 18; 19; 20; 21; 22; 23; 24; 25; 26; 27; 28; 29; 30; 31; 32; 33; 34; 35; 36; 37; 41; 42; 43; 44; 45; 46; 47; 48; 49; 52; 55; 34:3; 4(2); 5; 7; 8; 10; 11; 35:4; 5; 8(2); 12; 36:3(2); 4; 7; 9; **Deut** 1:2; 19; 2:8(3); 12; 14(2); 15; 16; 22; 36(2); 3:4; 8; 12; 16; 17; 4:2; 3; 9; 26; 29; 32; 34; 38; 48; 5:6; 6:12; 15; 19; 23; 7:4; 8; 15; 20; 24; 8:14; 9:4(2); 5; 7; 12; 14; 15; 23; 24; 10:5; 6; 7(2); 11:10; 12; 17; 23; 24(2); 12:10; 21; 29; 30; 32; 13:5(2); 7(2); 10(2); 13; 17; 14:24; 15:7; 12; 13; 16; 18; 16:9; 17:7; 11; 12; 15; 20; 18:3(2); 6; 12; 15; 18; 19:5; 13; 19; 20:15; 21:9; 13; 21; 22:1; 4; 8; 21; 22; 24; 23:9; 13; 14; 15; 24:7; 25:9; 19(2); 26:15(2); 28:14; 21; 24; 31; 35; 49(2); 57; 63; 64; 29:11; 18; 20; 22; 30:3; 4(2); 11; 31:3; 17; 29; 32:20; 26; 42; 33:2(4); 7; 16; 22; 27; 34:1; **Josh** 1:4; 7; 2:13; 23; 3:1; 3; 10; 13(2); 14; 16(2); 4:23(2); 5:1; 9; 15; 6:18; 7:2; 5; 9; 12; 13; 19; 26; 8:4; 6; 7; 16; 29; 9:6; 8; 9; 22; 23; 24; 10:6; 7; 9; 11(2); 29; 31; 34; 36; 41; 11:17; 21(6); 23; 12:1; 2(3); 3(2); 7; 13:3; 4; 5; 6(2); 9; 16; 26(2); 30; 14:7; 15; 15:2(2); 4; 5; 7; 9; 10; 46; 16:1(2); 2; 7; 8; 17:7; 18:4; 12; 13; 14; 15; 17; 19:12; 13; 29; 33(2); 34; 20:3; 6; 22:9; 16; 17; 18; 23; 25; 29; 32(2); 23:1; 4; 5(2); 9; 13(2); 15; 16; 24:3; 8; 12; 17; 18; **Judg** 1:11; 14; 36(2); 2:1; 3; 19(2); 21; 3:3; 19(2); 20; 21; 27; 4:11; 13; 14; 5:5(2); 11; 20; 6:8; 9; 11; 13; 14; 7:3; 8:13; 22; 9:20(3); 35; 36; 48; 10:11(4); 16; 11:3; 13; 16; 22(2); 23; 24; 29; 31; 33; 12:9; 13:5; 7; 20; 15:13; 14; 16:12; 17(2); 19; 20; 17:2; 3; 8; 18:2(3); 7; 11; 22; 28; 19:2; 16; 18(2); 30; 20:1; 13; 31; 32; 21:6; 8; 19; 24; **Ruth** 1:6; 13; 16; 2:4; 7; 8; 4:10(2); **1Sa** 1:14; 2:8; 19; 30; 33; 3:17(2); 18; 20; 4:4; 18; 21; 22; 5:1; 6:3; 5(3); 7; 20; 7:3; 14(2); 16; 9:2; 25; 10:2; 3; 5; 9; 23; 12:2; 20; 13:5; 8; 11; 15; 14:17; 21; 31; 46; 15:2; 6(2); 7; 11; 15; 23; 26; 28; 16:1; 13; 14(2); 15; 16; 23(2); 17:15; 24; 26; 30; 33; 46; 53; 57; 18:6; 9; 10; 12; 13; 19:8; 9; 20:1; 2; 9; 15(2); 34; 21:4; 5; 6; 22:15; 23:13; 28; 29; 24:1; 13; 25:10; 26(2); 33(2); 34; 39(2); 26:12(2); 19; 28:15; 16; 23; 30:17; 25; 31:1; 12; **2Sa** 1:1; 2; 3; 4; 22(2); 2:12; 19; 21; 22; 26; 27; 30; 3:10(2); 15(2); 22; 26(2); 28; 29; 4:11; 5:9; 13; 25; 6:2(2); 12; 7:1; 8(2); 11; 15(2); 23(2); 8:4; 8(2); 13; 9:5; 10:14; 11:2(2); 4; 8; 10; 15; 20; 21; 24; 12:10; 17; 20; 30; 13:4; 9(2); 13; 17; 32; 14:14; 18; 19; 25; 32; 15:12(2); 14; 18; 28; 17:11; 18:13; 16; 19:7; 24; 31; 20:2(2); 20; 21; 22; 21:5; 10; 12(2); 13; 22:3; 4; 14; 17; 18(2); 22; 23; 24; 44; 49(2); 23:11; 17; 24:2; 4; 15(2); 21; 25; **1Kin** 1:45; 53; 2:15; 27; 31(2); 33; 40; 41; 3:20; 4:12; 21; 24; 25; 33; 34; 5:9; 6:24; 7:7; 9; 23; 8:35; 51; 53; 54(2); 65; 9:6; 12; 28; 10:3; 11(2); 11:9; 11; 23; 12:2; 15; 24; 25; 13:4; 5; 12; 14; 21; 26; 33; 34; 14:7; 8; 10; 15:5; 13; 19; 16:17; 18:12(2); 26; 19:17; 21; 20:33; 34; 36(2); 41; 21:21; 22:24; 33; 43; **2Kin** 1:4; 6; 10(2); 12(2); 14; 2:1; 3; 5; 9; 10; 13; 14; 21; 23; 25(2); 3:27; 4:5; 27; 42; 5:19; 21; 22; 24; 26; 27; 6:32; 8:14; 20; 22; 9:2; 8; 10:21; 29(2); 31; 33(2); 11:2(2); 11; 19; 12:18; 13:5; 6; 11; 17; 23; 14:13; 24; 25; 27; 15:9; 14; 16; 18; 24; 28; 16:3; 6; 11(2); 12; 14(2); 17(2); 18; 17:7; 8; 9; 13; 21(2); 22; 24(5); 27; 28; 33; 18:6; 8; 14; 16(2); 17; 19:8; 20:14(3); 18; 21:16; 23:6; 8; 12; 17; 22; 26; 30; 24:7; 15; 20; 25:5; **1Chr** 2:23; 4:10; 5:9; 23; 9:25; 10:1; 11:8; 13; 13:5(2); 14:14; 16; 16:20(2); 23; 35; 17:5(2); 7(2); 8; 13(2); 21; 18:4; 8(2); 11(6); 19:7; 20:2; 21:2; 22; 26; 22:9; 23:3; 24; 27; 27:23; **2Chr** 1:4; 13(2); 4:2; 5:9; 6:21(2); 23; 25; 26; 27; 30; 32; 33(2); 35; 39(2); 7:1; 8; 14(2); 8:15; 9:2; 10; 26; 10:2; 11:4; 14; 12:12; 13:19; 15:8; 16; 16:3; 9; 18:23; 31; 32; 19:2; 4; 20:2; 10; 32; 21:8; 10(2); 12; 22:11(2); 23:10; 20; 24:5; 23; 25; 25:5; 12; 13; 14; 23; 27; 26:18; 19; 20; 21; 28:8; 12; 29:6; 10; 30:5; 6; 8; 9; 10; 31:16; 17; 32:22(2); 23; 33:8; 34:3; 33; 35:11; 15; 18; 21; 22(2); 36:12; 13; 20; **Ezr** 1:11; 2:59; 62; 3:6; 7; 8; 13; 4:12; 14; 21; 6:6; 11; 21; 7:6; 9; 8:1; 31(2); 9:1; 5; 8; 11; 10:6; 8; 11(2); 14; **Neh** 1:9; 3:15; 20; 21; 24; 25; 28; 4:5; 12; 16; 19; 21; 5:13(2); 14(2); 17; 6:9; 7:61; 64; 8:3; 18; 9:2; 13; 15; 19; 20; 27; 28; 35; 10:28; 11:30; 31; 12:28; 29; 38; 39; 13:3; 21; 28; 30; **Est** 1:1; 7; 19; 2:6; 3:7(2); 8; 10; 4:4; 14; 7:7; 8:2; 9; 15; 9:16; 22(3); 28(2); **Job** 1:7(2); 12; 16; 19; 2:2(3); 7(2); 11; 3:4; 10; 11; 17; 19; 4:2; 13; 20; 5:4; 15(3); 20(2); 21; 6:13; 14; 23(2); 7:19; 8:18; 9:34; 10:14; 19; 13:20; 21; 14:6; 11; 15:18; 17:4; 18:17; 18; 19:9; 13(2); 20:24; 29; 21:9; 14; 16; 22:6; 7; 17; 18; 22; 23; 23:7; 12; 17; 24:1; 9; 10; 12; 26:4; 5; 27:5; 28:4(2); 11; 21(2); 28; 30:5; 10; 31:2(2); 16; 18(2); 22(2); 23; 33:17(2); 18(2);

24; 28; 30; 34:10(2); 27; 35:3; 36:3; 7; 10; 38:15; 39:22; 29; 42:2; **Ps** 2:3; 12; 3:t, 6:8; 7:1; 9:13; 12:1; 5; 7; 13:1; 14:2; 17:2; 4; 7; 9(2); 13; 14(2); 18:(2); 3; 16; 17(2); 21; 22; 23; 43; 48(2); 19:6(2); 12; 13(2); 20:2; 6; 21:10(2); 22:1(2); 10(2); 11; 19; 20(2); 21(2); 24; 24:5(2); 27:9; 30:3; 31:11; 15(2); 20(2); 22; 32:7; 33:13; 14; 19; 34:4; 13(2); 14; 16; 35:10(2); 17(2); 22; 37:8; 27; 40; 38:9; 10; 11; 21; 39:2; 8; 10; 40:10; 11; 41:13; 42:6(2); 43:1; 44:7; 10; 18; 49:14; 15; 50:1; 4; 51:2(2); 9; 11(2); 14; 53:2; 55:1; 8; 11; 12; 18; 56:13(2); 57:t, 3(2); 58:3; 59:1(2); 2(2); 60:11; 61:2; 3; 62:1; 4; 5; 64:1; 2(2); 66:20; 68:20; 22(2); 26; 69:5; 14; 17; 71:5; 6; 12; 17; 20; 72:8(2); 14; 73:27(2); 75:6(3); 76:8; 78:4; 23; 30; 42; 50; 70; 71; 80:14; 18; 81:6(2); 83:4; 84:7; 11; 85:3; 11; 86:13; 88:5; 8; 14; 15; 18; 89:33; 48; 90:2; 91:3(2); 93:2; 94:13; 96:2; 101:4; 8; 102:2; 19(2); 103:4; 12(2); 17; 104:13; 21; 105:13(2); 106:10(2); 47; 48; 107:2; 3(4); 20; 41; 108:12; 109:15; 17; 20; 31; 110:3; 113:2; 3; 114:1; 115:18; 116:8(3); 119:10; 19; 21; 22; 29; 37; 51; 101; 102; 110; 115; 118; 134; 150; 155; 157; 160; 120:2(2); 121:1; 2; 7; 8; 125:2; 129:1; 2; 130:8; 131:3; 132:11; 135:7; 136:11; 24; 139:7(2); 12; 15; 19; 140:1(2); 4(2); 141:9; 142:6; 143:7; 9; 144:7(2); 10; 11; 148:1; 7; **Prov** 1:15; 33; 2:12(2); 16(2); 22; 3:7; 21; 26; 27; 4:5; 15; 21; 24(2); 27; 5:7; 8; 6:5(2); 24(2); 7:5(2); 8:23(2); 10:2; 11:4; 13:14; 19; 14:7; 14; 16; 27; 15:24; 29; 16:1; 6; 17; 17:13; 19:4; 7; 14; 27; 20:3; 9; 21:23; 22:5; 6; 15; 27; 23:4; 13; 14; 24:18; 25:4; 5; 17; 25; 27:8(2); 22; 28:9; 29:21; 26; 30:8; 12; 14(2); 31:14; **Eccl** 1:7; 2:10(2); 24; 3:5; 11; 14; 7:18; 23; 26; 8:10; 10:5; 11:10(2); 12:11; **Song** 3:4; 4:1; 2; 8(6); 15; 5:7; 6:5(2); 6; 8:5; **Is** 1:6; 15; 16; 2:3; 6; 22; 3:1(2); 4:4; 6(3); 5:23; 26(2); 6:6; 7:17(2); 8:17; 18; 9:7; 14; 10:2(2); 3; 27(2); 11:11(8); 12; 16; 13:5(2); 6; 20; 14:3(3); 9(2); 12; 22; 25(2); 31; 16:1; 4; 17:1; 3(2); 18:2; 7(2); 19:5; 20:2(2); 6; 21:1(2); 15(4); 22:3; 4; 14; 19(2); 24; 23:1; 24:14; 16; 18(2); 25:4(2); 8(2); 27:12; 28:9(2); 19; 22; 29; 29:13; 15; 30:6; 11; 14; 27; 31:6; 8; 32:2(2); 15; 33:15(3); 34:4(2); 10; 17; 36:2; 37:8; 14; 20; 38:7; 12(2); 13; 17; 39:3(3); 7; 40:21(2); 27(2); 41:2; 4; 9(2); 25(2); 26; 42:7; 10; 11; 43:5(2); 6(2); 44:2; 8; 24; 45:6(2); 8; 21(2); 46:3(2); 7; 10(2); 11(2); 12; 47:11; 12; 13; 14; 15; 48:3; 5; 6; 7; 8(2); 16(2); 19; 20; 49:1(3); 5; 12(4); 24; 50:6; 51:4; 8; 52:2(2); 11; 53:3; 8(2); 54:8; 10; 14(2); 55:10; 56:2(2); 3; 6; 11; 57:1; 58:7; 9; 13(2); 59:2; 9; 11; 13(2); 15; 19(2); 20; 21; 60:4; 6; 9; 63:1(2); 15(2); 16; 17(2); 64:7; 65:16; 66:6(2); 23(2); **Jer** 2:5; 25(2); 35; 37; 3:1; 4; 19; 20; 23(2); 24; 25; 4:6; 7(2); 8; 12; 14; 15(2); 16; 28; 5:15; 25; 6:8; 13(2); 20(2); 22(2); 7:1; 28; 34(2); 8:10(2); 13; 16; 9:2; 3; 21(2); 10:9(2); 11(2); 13; 11:1; 4; 15; 19; 12:2; 12; 14; 13:6; 7; 20; 25; 15:7; 19; 16:5; 15(2); 16(2); 17(2); 19; 17:4; 5; 8; 12; 13; 16; 26(6); 18:1; 8; 11; 14(2); 15; 18(3); 20; 22; 23; 19:14; 20:13; 17; 21:1; 2; 7(3); 22:20; 21; 23:8; 14; 15; 22(2); 30; 24:1; 10; 25:3; 5(2); 10; 30(2); 32(2); 33; 26:1; 3; 10; 27:1; 10; 16; 20; 28:3; 6; 10; 11; 12; 16; 29:1(2); 2; 4; 14(2); 20; 30:1; 8; 10(2); 21; 31:8(2); 11; 13; 16(3); 34; 36(2); 38; 32:1; 30; 31(2); 40(2); 33:5; 8; 34:1; 8; 12; 14; 21; 35:1; 15; 36:1; 2(3); 3; 4; 6; 7; 9; 29; 32; 37:5; 9; 11; 17; 38:10; 14; 25; 40:1(2); 4; 41:5(3); 6; 14; 15; 16(3); 42:1; 4; 8; 11; 17; 43:5; 12; 44:5; 7; 12; 46:16; 27(2); 47:4; 48:2; 3; 10; 11(2); 18; 33(3); 34(2); 42; 44; 45; 49:5; 7; 14; 16; 19(2); 32; 36; 38; 50:6; 9(2); 16; 26; 39; 41(2); 44(2); 51:16; 25; 45; 48; 53; 54(2); 64; 52:3; 8; 29; **Lam** 1:6; 13; 14; 16; 2:1; 3; 8; 9; 3:17; 18; 50; 66; 5:14(2); 16; 19; **Eze** 1:19; 21; 25; 27(2); 3:12; 17; 18; 19(2); 20; 4:8; 10; 11; 14; 6:9; 7:20; 22; 26(2); 8:2(2); 6; 9:2; 3; 10:2; 4; 6(2); 7; 16(2); 18; 19; 11:15; 17; 18; 23; 24; 12:3; 16(3); 19; 13:20; 22; 14:5; 6(2); 7; 8; 9; 11; 13; 17; 19; 21; 15:7; 16:9; 34; 41; 42; 17:22; 18:8; 17; 21; 23; 24; 26; 27; 28; 30; 31; 19:8; 20:17; 34; 38; 41; 47; 21:3; 4(2); 22:5; 26; 23:8; 17; 18(2); 22; 27(2); 28; 40; 42; 24:13; 16; 25; 25:7; 9(2); 13(2); 26:4; 7; 16; 27:5; 7(2); 29; 28:3; 15; 16; 18; 25; 29:10; 13; 30:6; 9; 31:12; 32:13; 33:6; 7; 8; 9(2); 11(2); 12; 14; 18; 19; 30; 34:10(2); 13(2); 35:7; 36:24; 25(2); 29; 33; 37:9; 21; 38:8; 15; 39:2; 22; 23; 24; 27; 29; 40:13; 15; 19; 23; 27; 41:7; 16; 20; 42:6; 9(2); 43:2; 9; 14(2); 15; 44:10(2); 15; 45:7(3); 9; 46:18; 47:1(3); 10; 15; 17; 18(5); 19; 20; 48:1; 2; 3; 4; 5; 6; 7; 8(2); 22(2); 23; 24; 25; 26; 27; 28; 35; **Dan** 2:1; 5; 8; 15; 3:17; 4:3; 13; 14(2); 16; 23; 25; 31(2); 32; 33; 34; 5:20(2); 21; 24; 6:18; 20; 27; 7:3(2); 4; 7; 10; 19; 23; 24; 8:5; 9:5(2); 13; 16; 25; 10:12; 11:22; 12:11; **Hos** 1:2; 2:2; 15; 4:12; 5:3; 6; 7:4; 13; 8:6; 9:1; 11(3); 12; 10:5; 9; 11:2; 7; 10; 12:9; 13:4; 14(3); 15; 14:4; 8; **Joel** 1:5; 9; 12; 13; 15; 16; 2:20; 3:6; 16; 20; **Amos** 1:2(2); 5(2); 8(2); 2:3; 9(2); 10; 14; 3:1; 5; 11; 4:7; 5:11; 12; 19; 23; 6:2; 14; 8:12(2); 9:3; 7(2); 8; **Obad** 1; **Jonah** 1:3(2); 10; 15; 2:6; 3:5; 6(2); 8(2); 9; 10; 4:3; 6; **Mic** 1:2; 12; 16; 2:3; 4; 8(2); 9(2); 3:2(2); 3; 4; 4:2; 7; 10; 5:2(2); 6; 7; 6:5; 7:5; 12(5); 20; **Nah** 1:13; 2:13; 3:7; 8; **Hab** 1:8; 12; 2:9; 3:3(2); 17; **Zeph** 1:2; 3; 4; 6; 10(3); 2:11; 3:10; **Hag** 1:10(2); 2:15(2); 18(3); 19; **Zec** 1:4(2); 2:6; 3:4(2); 6:1; 5; 10; 7:12; 8:7(2); 9:5; 7; 10(4); 13:5; 14:2; 5; 8; 10(3); 13; 16; **Mal** 1:5; 11; 2:6; 3:5; 7(2); **Mt** 1:17(3); 21; 24; 2:1; 16; 3:7; 13; 17; 4:17; 21; 25(5); 5:18; 29; 30; 42; 6:13; 7:23; 8:1; 11; 30; 9:9; 15; 16; 22; 11:12; 25; 12:15; 38; 42; 44; 13:12; 27; 35; 49; 14:2; 15:8; 18; 27; 28; 29; 16:1; 21; 22; 17:9(2); 18; 18:8; 9; 35; 19:1; 8; 12; 20; 20:8; 29; 21:8; 25(2); 43; 22:46; 23:34; 35; 24:1; 29; 31(2); 25:28; 29; 32(2); 34; 41; 26:16; 39; 42; 47; 27:31; 40; 42; 45; 51; 55; 64; 28:2(2); 7; 8; **Mk** 1:9; 11; 42; 45; 2:20; 21; 3:7(2); 8(3); 22; 4:25; 5:35; 6:1; 2; 10; 14; 16; 7:1; 4; 6; 15; 17; 18; 21; 23; 24; 31; 33; 8:3; 4; 11; 9:9(2); 10; 10:1; 6; 20; 11:12; 20; 30; 31; 12:2; 25; 34; 13:19; 27(2); 14:35; 36; 43; 52; 15:20; 30; 32; 38; 16:3; 8; **Lk** 1:2; 3; 15; 26; 38; 45; 48; 50; 52; 71(2); 78; 2:1; 4; 15; 36; 37; 3:7; 22; 4:1; 9; 13; 42; 5:3; 8; 10; 13; 35; 6:17; 22; 7:6; 8:18; 37; 49; 9:5; 7; 33; 37; 39; 45; 54; 10:7; 18; 21; 30; 42; 11:4; 7; 16; 22; 31; 50; 51; 12:36; 52; 58; 13:12; 15; 16; 27; 29(4); 16:3; 18; 21; 26(2); 30; 31; 17:7; 29; 18:21; 34; 19:8; 24; 26(2); 39; 42; 20:4; 5; 35; 21:11; 22:41; 42; 43; 45; 23:5; 49; 55; 24:2; 9; 13; 46; 49; 51; **Jn** 1:6; 19; 32; 2:22; 3:2; 13; 27; 31(2); 4:11; 5:24; 34; 41; 44; 6:23; 31; 32(2); 33; 38; 41; 42; 50; 51; 58; 64; 66; 7:29; 8:23(2); 25; 42; 44; 9:1; 29; 30; 10:5; 18; 32; 11:41; 53; 12:1; 9; 17; 27; 28; 32; 36; 13:3; 4; 14:7; 15:26(2); 27; 16:22; 27; 28; 30; 17:8; 15; 18:3; 28; 36; 19:11; 12; 23; 27; 20:1; 9; 21:8; 14; **Acts** 1:4; 11; 12(2); 22(2); 25; 2:2; 40; 46; 3:2; 15; 19; 23; 24; 26; 4:2; 10; 5:38; 41; 7:3; 4; 33; 39; 8:10; 26; 33; 9:3; 8; 14; 18; 10:17; 21; 22; 23; 37; 41; 11:4; 5; 9; 11; 27; 12:7; 10; 11; 19; 25; 13:4; 8; 13(2); 14; 29; 30; 31; 34; 39(2); 46; 14:8; 15; 17; 19; 26; 15:1; 18; 19; 20(4); 24; 29(5); 33; 38(2); 39; 16:11; 12; 17:3; 27; 31; 33; 18:1; 2(2); 5; 6; 16; 21; 19:9; 12(2); 35; 20:6; 9; 17; 18; 20; 26; 21:1(2); 7; 10; 25(4); 22:5; 6; 22; 29; 30; 23:10; 21; 24:18; 25:1; 7; 26:4; 5; 10; 12; 13; 17(2); 18(2); 23; 26; 27:4; 21; 34; 43; 28:13; 15; 17; 23; **Rom** 1:4; 7; 17; 18; 20; 4:24; 5:9; 14; 6:4; 7; 9; 13; 17; 18; 20; 22; 7:2; 3; 4; 6; 24; 8:2; 11(2); 21; 35; 39; 9:3; 10:6; 7; 9; 11:15; 26; 15:19; 22; 31; S:1; **1Cor** 1:3(2); 4:7; 5:2; 13; 7:10; 27; 9:19; 10:14; 14:36; 15:12; 20; 41; 47; S:1; **2Cor** 1:2(2); 10; 2:3; 13; 3:1; 18; 5:2; 6; 8; 6:17; 7:1; 11:3; 9(2); 12; 12:8; S:1; **Gal** 1:1; 3(2); 4; 6; 8; 15; 2:12; 3:13; 4:1; 24; 5:4; 6:17; S:1; **Eph** 1:2(2); 20; 2:12(2); 3:9; 4:16; 18; 31; 5:14; 6:6; 23; S:1; **Phil** 1:2(2); 5; 3:20; 4:15; 18; S:1; **Col** 1:2; 13; 18; 23; 26(2); 2:12; 19; 20; 4:16; S:1; **1Th** 1:1; 8; 9; 10(3); 2:17; 3:6; 4:3; 16; 5:22; S:1; **2Th** 1:2; 7; 9(2); 2:2; 13; 3:2; 3; 6; S:1; **1Ti** 1:2; 6; 4:1; 3; 5:13; 6:5; 10; S:1; **2Ti** 1:2; 3; 15; 2:8; 19; 21; 3:5; 15; 4:4; 18; S:1; **Titus** 1:4; 14; 3:14; S:1; **Philem** 1:3; S:1; **Heb** 3:12; 4:3; 4; 10(2); 5:1; 7; 6:1; 7; 7:1; 6; 26; 8:11; 9:14; 10:13; 22; 11:15; 19(2); 12:25(2); 13:20; S:1; **Jas** 1:17(2); 27; 3:15; 17; 4:1; 7; 5:19; 20(2); **1Pet** 1:3; 12; 18(2); 21; 2:11; 3:10; 4:1; **2Pet** 1:9; 17(2); 18; 2:8; 14; 18; 21; 3:4; 17; **1Jn** 1:1; 7; 9; 2:7(2); 13; 14; 19; 20; 24(2); 3:8; 11; 14; 17; 4:21; 5:21; **2Jn** 3(2); 4; 5; 6; **Jude** 14; 24; **Rev** 1:4(2); 5(2); 2:5; 3:10; 12; 6:4; 16(2); 7:2; 17; 8:10; 9:1; 6; 13; 10:1; 4; 8; 11:11; 12; 12:14; 13:8; 13; 14:2; 3; 4; 13(3); 18; 15:8(2); 16:17; 17:8; 18:1; 4; 14(2); 20:1; 9; 11; 21:2; 4; 10; 22:19(2)

FRONT

2Sa 10:9; **2Chr** 3:4

FURTHER

Num 22:26; **Deut** 20:8; **1Sa** 10:22; **Est** 9:12; **Job** 38:11; 40:5; **Ps** 140:8; **Eccl** 8:17; 12:12; **Mt** 26:65; **Mk** 5:35; 14:63; **Lk** 22:71; 24:28; **Acts** 4:17; 21; 12:3; 21:28; 24:4; 27:28; **2Ti** 3:9; **Heb** 7:11

FURTHERMORE

Ex 4:6; **Deut** 4:21; 9:13; **1Sa** 26:10; **1Chr** 17:10; 27:16; 29:1; **2Chr** 4:9; **Job** 34:1; **Eze** 8:6; 23:40; **2Cor** 2:12; **1Th** 4:1; **Heb** 12:9

GOODLY

Gen 27:15; 39:6; 49:21; **Ex** 2:2; 39:28; **Lev** 23:40; **Num** 24:5; 31:10; **Deut** 3:25; 6:10; 8:12; **Josh** 7:21; **1Sa** 9:2; 16:12; **2Sa** 23:21; **1Kin** 1:6; **2Chr** 36:10; 19; **Job** 39:13; **Ps** 16:6; 80:10; **Jer** 3:19; 11:16; **Eze** 17:8; 23; **Hos** 10:1; **Joel** 3:5; **Zec** 10:3; 11:13; **Mt** 13:45; **Lk** 21:5; **Jas** 2:2; **Rev** 18:14

GOODNESS

Ex 18:9; 33:19; 34:6; **Num** 10:32; **Judg** 8:35; **2Sa** 7:28; **1Kin** 8:66; **1Chr** 17:26; **2Chr** 6:41; 7:10; 32:32; 35:26; **Neh** 9:25; 35; **Ps** 16:2; 21:3; 23:6; 27:13; 31:19; 33:5; 52:1; 65:4; 11; 68:10; 107:8; 9; 15; 21; 31; 144:2; 145:7; **Prov** 20:6; **Is** 63:7; **Jer** 2:7; 31:12; 14; 33:9; **Hos** 3:5; 6:4; 10:1; **Zec** 9:17; **Rom** 2:4(2); 11:22(3); 15:14; **Gal** 5:22; **Eph** 5:9; **2Th** 1:11

GOTTEN

Gen 4:1; 12:5; 31:1; 18(2); 46:6; **Ex** 14:18; **Lev** 6:4; **Num** 31:50; **Deut** 8:17; **2Sa** 17:13; **Job** 28:15; 31:25; **Ps** 98:1; **Prov** 13:11; 20:21; **Eccl** 1:16; **Is** 15:7; **Jer** 48:36; **Eze** 28:4(2); 38:12; **Dan** 9:15; **Acts** 21:1; **Rev** 15:2

GREATER

Gen 1:16; 4:13; 39:9; 41:40; 48:19; **Ex** 18:11; **Num** 14:12; **Deut** 1:28; 4:38; 7:1; 9:1; 14; 11:23; **Josh** 10:2; **1Sa** 14:30; **2Sa** 13:15; 16; **1Kin** 1:37; 47; **1Chr** 11:9(2); **2Chr** 3:5; **Est** 9:4(2); **Job** 33:12; **Lam** 4:6; **Eze** 8:6; 13; 15; 43:14; **Dan** 11:13; **Amos** 6:2; **Hag** 2:9; **Mt** 11:11(2); 12:6; 41; 42; 23:14; 17; 19; **Mk** 4:32; 12:31; 40; **Lk** 7:28(2); 11:31; 32; 12:18; 20:47; 22:27; **Jn** 1:50; 4:12; 5:20; 36; 8:53; 10:29; 13:16(2); 14:12; 28; 15:13; 20; 19:11; **Acts** 15:28; **1Cor** 14:5; 15:6; **Heb** 6:13; 16; 9:11; 11:26; **Jas** 3:1; **2Pet** 2:11; **1Jn** 3:20; 4:4; 5:9; **3Jn** 4

GREATEST

1Chr 12:14; 29; **Job** 1:3; **Jer** 6:13; 8:10; 31:34; 42:1; 8; 44:12; **Jonah** 3:5; **Mt** 13:32; 18:1; 4; 23:11; **Mk** 9:34; **Lk** 9:46; 22:24; 26; **Acts** 8:10; **1Cor** 13:13; **Heb** 8:11

GREATNESS

Ex 15:7; 16; **Num** 14:19; **Deut** 3:24; 5:24; 9:26; 11:2; 32:3; **1Chr** 17:19; 21; 29:11; **2Chr** 9:6; 24:27; **Neh** 13:22; **Est** 10:2; **Ps** 66:3; 71:21; 79:11; 145:3; 6; 150:2; **Prov** 5:23; **Is** 40:26; 57:10; 63:1; **Jer** 13:22; **Eze** 31:2; 7; 18; **Dan** 4:22; 7:27; **Eph** 1:19

HAD

Gen 1:31; 2:2(2); 3; 5; 8; 22; 3:1; 4:4; 5; 5:4; 6:6; 12; 7:9; 16; 8:6; 9:24; 11:3(2); 30; 12:1; 4; 5(2); 16; 20; 13:1; 3; 4; 5; 14:13; 16:1; 3; 4; 5; 17:23; 18:8; 33; 19:17; 20:4; 18; 21:1(2); 2; 4; 9; 25; 22:3; 9; 23:16; 24:1; 2; 15; 16; 19; 21; 22; 29; 45; 48; 65(2); 66; 25:5; 6; 26:8; 14; 15(2); 18(3); 32; 27:17; 30; 31; 28:6; 9; 18; 29:16; 20; 30:9; 25; 35; 38; 43; 31:18(2); 19; 21; 25; 32; 34; 42; 32:23; 33:10; 19; 34:5; 7; 13; 19; 27; 35:16; 36:6; 38:15; 30; 39:1; 4; 5(3); 6(2); 13; 40:1; 16; 22; 41:21(2); 43; 54; 43:2(2); 6; 10(2); 23; 44:2; 45:27(2); 46:1; 5; 6; 47:11; 22; 27; 48:11; 49:33; 50:14; **Ex** 2:6(2); 16; 25; 4:28(2); 30; 31(2); 5:14; 7:10; 13; 22; 25; 8:12; 15; 19; 9:12; 35; 10:15; 23; 12:28; 39; 13:17; 19; 14:12; 15:25; 16:3; 18(2); 17:10; 18:1(2); 2; 8(2); 9(2); 24; 19:2; 31:18; 32:4; 20; 25; 29; 33:5; 34:4; 32; 33; 35:25; 29; 36:1; 2; 3; 7; 22; 39:43(3); 40:23; **Lev** 10:5; 19; 21:3; 24:23; **Num** 1:48; 3:4; 7:1(3); 8:4; 22; 12:1(2); 14; 13:32; 14:2(2); 24; 16:31; 39; 20:3; 21:9; 26; 22:2; 33(2); 23:2; 30; 26:33; 65; 27:3; 30:6; 31:32; 35; 53; 32:1; 9; 13; 33:4; **Deut** 1:3; 4; 39; 41; 2:12; 7:8; 9:16(4); 21; 25; 10:5; 15; 19:19; 29:26; 31:24; 32:30(2); 34:9; **Josh** 2:6(2); 11; 4:4; 5:1; 5; 7; 8; 12(2); 6:8; 10; 22(2); 23; 25; 7:7; 24; 25; 8:13; 18; 19; 20; 21; 24; 26; 33; 9:3; 4; 16; 18; 21; 10:1(6); 13; 20; 27; 32; 33; 35; 37; 39(2); 11:1; 14; 14:3; 15; 17:1; 3; 6(2); 8; 11; 18:2; 19:2; 9; 49; 21:4; 5; 6; 7; 10; 20; 45; 22:7; 23:1; 24:31(2); **Judg** 1:8(2); 19; 2:6; 7; 10; 15(2); 3:1; 11; 12; 16; 18; 20; 30; 4:3; 11; 18; 24; 5:26; 31; 6:3; 27; 7:19; 8:3; 8; 19; 24; 30(2); 34; 35; 9:22; 10:4(2); 11:34; 39; 12:9; 14; 14:4; 6(2); 9; 18(2); 20; 15:5; 6; 17; 19; 16:8; 18; 17:3(2); 5; 18:1; 7; 27(2); 28; 19:6; 17; 20:36; 21:1; 5; 12; 14; 15; **Ruth** 1:6(2); 2:1; 17; 18(2); 19; 3:7; 16; **1Sa** 1:2(3); 5; 6; 9(2); 13; 20; 24; 3:8; 4:18; 5:9(2); 6:6; 16; 19(2); 7:14; 9:2; 15; 10:9; 13; 20; 21; 26; 13:1; 4(2); 8; 10; 21; 14:11; 17; 22; 24; 30(2); 15:35; 17:5; 6; 12; 20; 21; 39; 40; 18:1; 19:18; 20:34; 37; 22:21; 24:5; 10; 16; 18; 25:2; 21; 34; 35; 37; 44; 26:5; 28:3(3); 20; 24; 30:1; 2; 4; 12(2); 16(2); 18; 19; 21; 31:11; **2Sa** 1:1; 21; 2:27; 30; 31; 3:7; 17; 22; 30; 4:2; 4; 5:12(2); 17; 25; 6:8; 13; 17; 18; 22; 23; 7:1; 8:9; 10(2); 11; 9:2; 10; 12; 11:10; 13; 22; 27; 12:2; 3(2); 6; 8; 13:1; 3; 10; 11; 15; 18; 22; 23; 28; 29; 36; 14:2; 6; 32; 33; 15:2; 24; 30; 16:23; 17:14; 18; 20; 18:18; 33; 19:6(3); 8; 24; 32; 43; 20:3; 5; 8; 21:2; 11; 12(3); 15; 20; 22:1; 38; 23:8; 18; 20; 21; 22; 24:8; 10; **1Kin** 1:6; 41; 2:28; 41; 3:1; 10; 21; 28; 4:2; 7; 11; 14; 24(2); 26; 34; 5:1(2); 15; 6:22; 7:8(2); 20; 28; 30(2); 37; 51; 8:11; 54; 66; 9:1; 2; 10; 11; 12; 16; 19; 34; 37; 10:4(3); 7; 15; 19; 22; 24; 26; 29; 11:3; 9; 10; 15; 16; 29; 12:8; 12; 32(2); 33(2); 13:4; 5; 11(2); 12; 23(3); 28; 31; 14:22(2); 26; 15:3; 12; 13; 15(2); 20; 22; 29; 16:31; 32; 17:7; 19:1(2); 21:1; 4(2); 11(2); 22:31; 53; **2Kin** 1:17(2); 2:14; 3:2; 4:12; 15; 17; 20; 5:1; 2(2); 7; 8(2); 13; 6:23; 30; 7:6; 15; 17; 18; 8:1; 5(2); 29; 9:14; 15; 31; 10:1; 17; 25; 11:15; 12:6; 11; 18; 13:7(2); 23(2); 25; 14:5; 15:3; 9; 34; 16:11; 18; 17:4(2); 7(3); 8; 12; 15; 20; 23; 28; 29; 35; 18:4; 16; 18; 19:8; 20:11; 12(2); 21:3; 7; 16; 24; 22:11; 23:5; 8; 11; 12(2); 13; 15; 19(2); 26; 29; 32; 37; 24:7; 9; 13(2); 19; 20; 25:16; 17; 22; 23; **1Chr** 2:22; 26; 34(2); 52; 4:5; 22; 27(2); 40; 6:31; 32; 49; 66; 7:4; 15; 8:8; 38; 40; 9:23; 28; 31; 44; 10:9; 11; 13; 11:10; 11; 20; 22; 24; 12:15; 29; 32; 39; 13:11; 14; 14:2; 4; 12; 15:3; 27; 16:1; 2; 18:9; 10(2); 19:6; 17; 21:28; 23:11; 17; 22; 24:2; 19; 28; 26:9; 10; 26; 28(2); 27:23; 28:2(2); 12; 29:25; **2Chr** 1:3; 4(3); 5; 12; 14; 16; 2:17; 3:1; 5:1; 14; 6:13(2); 7:1; 2; 6; 7; 10; 8:1; 2; 6; 11; 12; 14; 18; 9:3(2); 6; 12; 23; 25; 10:2; 6; 11:14; 15; 12:1(2); 2; 9; 13; 14:6(3); 8; 15:8; 11; 15; 16; 18(2); 16:14; 17:2; 5; 9; 13; 18:1; 2; 10; 30; 20:21; 23; 27; 29; 33; 21:2; 6; 7; 10; 22:1; 7; 9(2); 23:8; 9; 18; 21; 24:7; 10; 14; 16; 22; 24; 25:3; 26:5; 10; 11; 19; 20; 28:3; 6; 17; 18(2); 29:19; 22; 29; 34; 36; 30:2; 3(2); 5; 17; 18; 31:1; 10; 32:27; 29; 33:2; 3; 4; 7(2); 9; 15; 22; 23; 25; 34:4; 7(2); 8; 9; 10; 11; 19; 22; 35:20; 24; 36:13; 14; 15; 17; 20; 21; **Ezr** 1:5; 7(2); 2:1(2); 3:7; 12; 5:12; 14; 6:13; 21; 22; 7:6; 10; 8:20; 22; 25; 35; 9:4; 10:1(2); 6; 8; 17; 18; 44(3); **Neh** 1:2; 2:1; 9; 12; 16; 18; 4:6; 15; 18; 5:15(2); 6:1(2); 12(2); 18; 7:1; 6(2); 67; 8:1; 4; 12; 14; 17; 9:18(2); 28(2); 10:28; 11:16; 12:29; 43; 13:3; 5; 10; 23; **Est** 1:8; 2:1; 6(3); 7; 10(2); 12; 15; 20(2); 3:2; 4; 6; 12; 4:5; 7(2); 17; 5:5; 11(2); 12; 6:2; 4; 13; 14; 7:4(2); 9(2); 10; 8:1; 2; 3; 16; 17; 9:1; 16; 23(2); 24(2); 26(2); 31(2); **Job** 2:11; 3:13; 15; 16; 26; 6:20; 9:16(3); 10:18(2); 19; 22:8; 24:16; 29:12; 31:25; 31; 35; 32:3(2); 4(2); 16; 38:8; 42:7; 10; 11(2); 12; 13; **Ps** 27:13(2); 35:14; 42:4; 51:t, 55:6; 73:2; 74:5; 78:11; 23; 24(2); 43; 44; 54; 81:13(2); 84:10; 89:7; 94:17(2); 105:26; 106:21; 23; 119:51; 56; 87; 92; 124:1; 2; 3; 4(2); 5; **Prov** 8:26; 24:31; **Eccl** 1:16; 2:7(2); 11(2); 18; 4:1(2); 8:10(2); **Song** 3:4; 5:6; 8:11; **Is** 1:9; 6:2; 6; 22:11; 26:13; 29:16; 37:8; 38:9; 17; 21; 22; 39:1(2); 41:3; 48:18; 19; 49:21; 52:15(2); 53:9; 59:10; 60:10; **Jer** 2:21; 3:7; 8; 4:23; 5:7; 6:15; 8:12; 9:2; 11:19; 13:7; 16:15; 19:14; 23:8; 22(2); 24:1(2); 2(2); 25:17; 26:8(2); 19; 28:12; 29:1; 32:3; 16; 34:8; 10; 11; 15(2); 16; 18; 36:4; 11; 13; 16; 23; 25; 27; 32; 37:4; 10; 15; 16; 38:1; 7; 27; 39:5; 10; 40:1(2); 7(2); 11(2); 41:2; 4; 9(3); 10; 11; 14; 16(3); 18; 43:1(2); 5; 6; 44:15; 17; 20; 45:1; 52:2; 3; 20; 25; **Lam** 1:7; 9; 2:17(2); **Eze** 1:5; 6(2); 8(2); 10(3); 16; 23(2); 25; 27; 3:6; 8:8; 9:3; 11; 10:6; 10(2); 12; 14; 21; 11:24; 25; 16:14; 17; 17:3; 18; 19:5; 11; 20:6; 15; 24(3); 28; 23:10; 19; 32; 39; 29:18(2); 33:15; 21; 22; 35:5(2); 36:18(2); 21(2); 40:10; 26; 31; 34; 37; 41:6; 18; 23; 24; 42:6; 15; 20; 44:22; 25; 47:3; 7; **Dan** 1:4; 9; 11; 17; 18; 2:24; 3:2; 3(2); 7; 27(2); 4:12; 21; 5:2; 6:24(2); 7:1; 4; 5; 6(2); 7(2); 12; 20; 8:3; 5; 6(2); 15; 9:21; 10:1; 11; 15; 19; **Hos** 1:8; 2:23; 12:3; 4; **Amos** 7:2; **Obad** 5; 16; **Jonah** 1:10; 17; 3:10; 4:10; **Nah** 3:8; **Hab** 3:4; **Hag** 1:12; **Zec** 1:12; 5:9; 7:2; 10:6; 11:10; **Mal** 2:15; **Mt** 1:6; 24; 25; 2:3; 4; 7; 9; 11; 16; 3:4; 4:2; 12; 24; 7:28; 9:8; 10:1; 11:1; 2; 21; 23; 12:7; 10; 13:5(2); 6; 46(2); 53; 14:3; 13; 21; 23; 35; 16:5; 17:8; 18:24; 25(2); 32; 33(2); 19:1; 22; 20:2; 11; 34; 21:28; 32; 45; 22:11; 22; 25; 28; 34(2); 23:30; 24:43; 25:16; 17; 18; 20; 22; 24; 26:1; 8; 19; 24(2); 30; 57; 27:2; 3; 16; 18; 26; 29; 31; 34; 50; 59; 60; 28:12; 16; **Mk** 1:19; 22; 26; 37; 42; 2:4; 25; 3:1; 3; 5; 8; 10(2); 4:5(2); 6; 36; 5:3; 4(2); 15; 18; 19; 20; 25; 26(3); 27; 30; 32; 40; 6:17(2); 18; 19; 30(2); 31; 41; 46; 49; 53; 7:14; 25; 32; 8:7; 9; 14(2); 23; 33; 34; 9:8; 9; 34; 36; 10:22; 11:6; 11; 12:12; 22; 23; 28; 44; 13:20; 14:4; 16; 21; 23; 26; 44; 15:7(2); 8; 10; 15; 20; 24; 44; 16:1; 9; 10; 11(2); 14; 19; **Lk** 1:3; 7; 22; 58; 2:17; 20;

26; 36; 39; 43; 3:19; 4:13; 16; 17; 33; 35; 40; 5:4; 6; 9; 11; 6:8; 7:1; 10; 13; 39; 41; 42; 8:2; 8; 27; 29(2); 39; 42; 43; 47; 9:8; 10; 11; 36; 10:13(2); 33; 39; 11:38; 12:39; 13:1; 6; 11; 14; 17; 14:2; 15:9; 11; 14; 20; 16:1(2); 8; 17:6; 19:15(2); 28; 32; 37; 20:19; 33; 21:4; 22:13; 55; 61; 64; 23:8; 13; 25; 46; 51; 24:1; 14; 21; 23; 24; 37; 40; **Jn** 2:9; 15; 22(2); 4:1; 18; 50; 5:4; 5; 6; 13; 15; 16; 18; 46; 6:11; 13; 14; 19; 23; 25; 60; 7:9; 8:3; 10; 19; 9:6; 8; 15; 18(2); 22; 35(2); 11:6; 13; 17; 21; 28; 32; 43; 45; 46; 57; 12:1; 6; 9; 14; 16; 18; 37; 13:3; 12(2); 21; 26; 29(2); 14:7; 15:22(3); 24(3); 17:5; 18:1; 6; 18; 22; 24; 38; 19:23; 30; 20:12; 14; 18(2); 20; 22; 21:15; 19; **Acts** 1:2(2); 9; 17; 2:30; 44; 45; 3:10; 12; 18; 4:7; 13; 15; 21; 23; 31; 32; 35; 5:23; 27; 34; 40; 6:6; 15; 7:5; 17; 36; 44(3); 60; 8:11(2); 14; 25; 27(2); 9:18; 19; 27(3); 31; 33; 37; 38; 41; 10:8; 11; 17(2); 24; 31; 11:1; 5; 6; 13; 23; 26; 12:4; 12; 16; 17; 19; 25; 13:1; 3; 5; 6; 19; 22; 24; 29; 36; 14:8; 9; 11; 18; 19; 21(2); 23(2); 24; 25; 26; 27(3); 15:2; 4; 7; 12; 13; 30; 31; 34; 33; 16:6; 10(2); 23; 27; 34; 40; 17:1; 9; 13; 18:2; 18; 22; 23; 26; 27; 19:6; 13; 21; 35; 41; 20:2(2); 11; 13; 16; 36; 21:1; 3; 5; 6; 7; 9; 19(2); 29(2); 33; 40; 22:29; 23:7; 12; 13; 30; 34; 24:10; 19; 25:6; 12; 14; 19; 21; 25; 26; 26:30; 32; 27:4; 5; 7; 13; 16; 17; 28; 30; 35(2); 38; 40; 28:3; 6; 9; 11; 18; 19; 23; 25; 29(2); **Rom** 1:2; 4:11; 12; 21; 5:14; 6:21; 7:7(3); 9:10; 23; 29(2); **1Cor** 1:15; 2:8; 7:29; 11:24; 25; 14:19; **2Cor** 1:9; 12; 2:13; 3:10; 7:5; 12; 8:6; 15(4); 9:5; 11:21; **Gal** 1:23; 2:2; 3:21; 4:15; 22; **Eph** 2:3; **Phil** 2:26(2); 27; 3:12; **1Th** 1:9; 2:2; **2Th** 2:12; **Titus** 1:5; **Heb** 1:3; 2:14; 3:16; 17; 4:8; 5:7; 6:15; 7:6; 8:7; 9:1; 4(2); 19; 10:2; 6; 12; 15; 34; 11:5(2); 11; 15(2); 17; 26; 31; 36; 12:9; **Jas** 2:21; 25(2); **1Pet** 2:10; **2Pet** 2:21; **1Jn** 2:7; 19; **2Jn** 5; **3Jn** 13; **Rev** 1:16; 4:4; 7; 8; 5:6; 8; 6:2; 3; 5(2); 7; 9; 12; 8:1; 6; 9; 9:8; 9; 10; 11; 14; 19; 10:2; 3; 4; 10; 13:11; 14(2); 15; 17; 14:18(2); 15:2; 16:2; 17:1; 18:19; 19:12; 20; 20:4(2); 21:9; 12(2); 14; 15; 23; 22:8

HAPPEN

1Sa 28:10; **Prov** 12:21; **Is** 41:22; **Mk** 10:32

HAPPENED

1Sa 6:9; **2Sa** 1:6; 20:1; **Est** 4:7; **Jer** 44:23; **Lk** 24:14; **Acts** 3:10; **Rom** 11:25; **1Cor** 10:11; **Phil** 1:12; **1Pet** 4:12; **2Pet** 2:22

HE

Gen 1:5; 10; 16; 27(2); 31; 2:2(3); 3; 8(2); 19; 21(2); 22; 3:1; 6; 10; 11; 16(2); 17; 22; 23; 24(2); 4:4; 5; 9; 10; 17; 20; 21; 26; 5:1; 2; 4(2); 5; 7; 8; 10; 11; 13; 14; 16; 17; 18; 19; 20; 22; 24; 26; 27; 29; 30; 31; 6:3; 6; 22; 8:6; 7; 8; 9; 10(2); 12; 9:6; 20; 21(2); 25(2); 26; 27; 29; 10:8; 9; 11:11; 13; 15; 17; 19; 21; 23; 25; 12:4; 7; 8(2); 11(2); 16(3); 20; 13:1(2); 3; 4; 14:13; 14; 15(2); 16; 18; 19; 20; 15:4; 5(2); 6(2); 7; 8; 9; 10(2); 13; 16:4; 8; 12(2); 17:12(2); 13(2); 14; 20; 22; 24; 25; 18:1; 2(3); 7; 8(3); 9; 10; 15; 19(2); 28; 29(2); 30(2); 31(2); 32(2); 33; 19:1; 2; 3(2); 9; 14; 16; 17; 21; 25; 27; 28; 29; 30(3); 33; 35; 20:4; 5(2); 7(2); 13; 16(2); 21:1(2); 13; 17; 20; 21; 30; 31; 22:1; 2; 6; 7(2); 11; 12; 23:8; 9(3); 13; 16; 24:2; 7; 10; 11; 12; 15; 27; 30(4); 31; 32; 33(2); 34; 35(2); 36(2); 40; 52; 53; 54(2); 56; 62; 63; 66; 67; 25:5; 6; 7; 17; 18; 20; 28; 29; 33(2); 34; 26:7(3); 8; 11; 13; 14; 18; 20; 21; 22(3); 23; 25; 30; 33; 34; 27:1(3); 2; 9; 10(2); 14; 18(2); 20; 22; 23(2); 24(2); 25(5); 27(2); 29; 31; 32; 33(2); 34; 35; 36(6); 45; 28:5; 6(2); 9; 11(2); 12; 16; 17; 18; 19; 29:2; 5; 6(3); 7; 9; 12(2); 13(2); 14; 20; 23(2); 25; 28; 30(2); 31; 33; 30:2; 15; 16; 28; 29; 31; 35(2); 36; 38(2); 40; 42; 31:1(2); 8(2); 12; 15; 18(3); 20(2); 21(3); 23; 33(2); 35; 49; 32:2(2); 4; 6; 7; 11; 13; 14; 16; 17; 18; 19; 20(2); 22; 23(2); 25(4); 26(2); 27(2); 28; 29(2); 31(2); 32; 33:1; 2; 3(2); 5(2); 8(2); 11(2); 12; 13; 15; 18; 19(2); 20; 34:2; 3; 5; 7; 13; 19(2); 31; 35:6; 7(2); 9; 10; 13; 14(3); 36:6; 24; 43; 37:3(2); 5; 6; 9; 10; 13; 14(3); 15; 16; 18; 21; 22; 27; 29; 30; 33; 35(2); 38:2; 3; 5; 9(3); 10(2); 11(2); 12; 15; 16(2); 17; 18(2); 20; 21; 22; 26; 29; 39:2(2); 3; 4(4); 5(3); 6(5); 8(3); 9; 10; 12; 13; 14(2); 15(2); 18; 20; 22; 23; 40:3; 4; 7; 16; 20(2); 21(2); 22; 41:1; 5; 8; 11; 12(2); 13(3); 14; 25; 28; 43(3); 45; 46; 48(2); 49; 51; 52; 55; 42:2; 4; 6; 7(2); 9; 12; 17; 21; 23; 24; 25; 27; 28; 38(2); 43:7; 14; 16; 18; 23(2); 24; 27(2); 28; 29(2); 30(2); 31; 34; 44:1; 2; 5; 6(2); 10(2); 12; 14; 16; 17(2); 20; 22; 28; 31(2); 45:1; 2; 4; 8; 14; 15; 22(2); 23; 24(2); 26(2); 27(2); 46:1; 2; 3; 7; 28; 29; 47:2; 17; 21; 22; 29; 30; 31(2); 48:1; 9; 10(3); 12; 15; 17; 19(3); 20(2); 49:4; 8; 9(2); 11; 13; 15; 19; 20; 21; 27(2); 28; 29; 33; 50:6; 10; 12; 14(2); 16; 21; 22; 24; 26; **Ex** 1:9; 16; 21; 2:2; 10; 11(2); 12(3); 13(2); 14; 15(2); 18; 20(3); 21; 22(2); 3:1; 2; 4(2); 5; 6(2); 12; 14; 20; 4:2; 3(2); 4; 6(2); 7(2); 13; 14(5); 16(3); 20; 21; 23; 26; 27; 28; 31; 5:3; 17; 23; 6:1(2); 11; 7:2; 13(2); 14; 15(2); 20; 22; 23; 8:8; 10(2); 12; 15; 19; 20; 27; 31; 32; 9:7; 12; 20; 21; 34(2); 35; 10:6; 8; 10; 16; 17; 18; 20; 27; 11:1(3); 8; 10; 12:19; 23; 25; 27; 30; 31; 44; 48; 13:5; 11; 19; 22; 14:4; 6; 7; 8; 13; 15:1(2); 2(2); 4; 21(2); 25(4); 16:7; 9; 18(2); 23; 29; 17:7; 11; 12; 16; 18:2; 3; 4; 5; 6; 9; 11; 14(2); 24; 27; 19:13; 15; 24; 21:2(2); 3(3); 4; 6(2); 8(3); 9(2); 10(2); 11; 12(2); 13; 14; 15; 16(3); 17; 18; 19(3); 20(2); 21(3); 22(2); 26; 27(2); 29(2); 30; 31; 32; 35; 36; 22:1; 2; 3(3); 4; 5; 6; 8; 9; 11(2); 12; 13; 14; 15; 16; 17; 20(2); 27(2); 23:21; 25; 24:1; 5; 6; 7; 11; 14; 16; 25:39; 28:1; 3; 4; 29; 30; 35(3); 29:21; 30; 30:7(2); 8; 10; 31:15; 17; 18(2); 32:4(2); 5; 12; 14; 17; 18; 19(3); 20; 27; 29; 33:8; 11; 14; 15; 18; 19; 20; 34:4; 9; 10; 28(3); 29(2); 32; 33; 34(4); 35; 35:31; 34(3); 35; 36:8; 10(2); 11(2); 12(2); 13; 14(2); 16; 17(2); 18; 19; 20; 22; 23; 24; 25; 27; 28; 29; 31; 33; 34; 35(2); 36(2); 37; 38; 37:2; 3; 4; 5; 6; 7(2); 8; 10; 11; 12; 13; 15; 16; 17(2); 23; 24; 25; 26(2); 27; 28; 29; 38:1; 2(2); 3(2); 4; 5; 6; 7(2); 8; 9; 28; 30; 39:2; 7; 8; 22; 40:13; 16; 19; 20; 21; 22; 23; 24; 25; 26; 27; 28; 29; 30; 33; **Lev** 1:3; 4; 5; 6; 9; 10; 11; 12; 13; 14; 16; 17; 2:1; 2(2); 8; 3:1(2); 2; 3; 4; 6; 7(2); 8; 9(2); 10; 12; 13; 14; 15; 4:3; 4; 8; 9; 12(2); 18; 19; 20(3); 21(2); 23(2); 24; 26; 27; 28(3); 29; 31; 32(2); 33; 35(2); 5:1(3); 2; 3(3); 4(2); 5(3); 6(2); 7(3); 8; 9; 10(2); 11(4); 12; 13; 15; 16(2); 17(2); 18(2); 19; 6:4(5); 5(2); 6; 7; 10(2); 11; 12; 15; 20; 7:2; 3; 4; 8; 11; 12(2); 13; 14; 15; 16; 29; 30; 33; 35; 36; 38; 8:7(2); 8(2); 9(2); 11; 12; 14; 15; 16; 17; 18; 19; 20; 21; 22; 23; 24; 25; 26; 27; 33; 34; 9:2; 9; 10; 11; 12(2); 13; 14; 15; 16; 17; 18(2); 20; 10:1; 16; 20; 11:4(2); 5(2); 6(2); 7(3); 28; 39; 40(2); 13:2; 6; 7(2); 9; 11; 13(2); 14; 16; 17; 33(2); 34; 36; 37; 39; 40(2); 41(3); 44(2); 45; 46(3); 51; 52; 54; 56; 14:2; 6; 7; 8(3); 9(5); 10(2); 12; 13(2); 18; 19; 20; 21(2); 22; 23; 25; 29; 30(2); 31; 35; 37; 41; 42; 43(2); 45(2); 46; 47(2); 49; 50; 51; 52; 53; 15:2; 4(2); 6(2); 7; 8(2); 9; 10; 11(2); 12; 13(2); 14; 16; 23(2); 24(2); 16:2(2); 4(4); 5; 7; 12; 13(2); 14(2); 15(2); 16(2); 17(2); 18; 19; 20(2); 22; 23(2); 24; 25; 26; 28(2); 32(2); 33(3); 34; 17:4; 13; 15(2); 16(2); 18:5; 19:8; 21; 22(2); 20:2(2); 3; 4; 9; 10; 13; 14; 15; 17(2); 18; 19; 20; 21; 21:3; 4; 7; 8(2); 10; 11; 12; 13; 14(2); 15; 17; 18(3); 21(2); 22; 23(3); 22:3; 4(2); 5(3); 6; 7; 8; 11(2); 14; 18; 23:11; 12; 29; 24:4; 8; 16(4); 17; 18; 19; 20; 21(4); 25:15; 16; 25; 27(2); 28(2); 29(2); 35(2); 40; 41(3); 48(2); 49(2); 50(2); 51(2); 52(2); 53; 54(3); 27:8(2); 10(2); 11; 13(2); 15(2); 17; 18; 19(2); 20(2); 22; 23; 27; 28; 31; 33(3); **Num** 1:19; 3:3; 16; 50; 5:7(2); 14(2); 15(2); 23; 24; 27; 30; 6:3(2); 4; 5(2); 6(2); 7; 8; 9(3); 10; 11; 12; 13; 14(2); 17; 21(2); 7:7; 8; 9; 12; 17; 19; 23; 29; 35; 41; 47; 53; 59; 65; 71; 77; 83; 88; 89(2); 8:3; 4; 9:10; 13; 14; 10:30; 31; 36; 11:3; 30; 32; 34; 12:1(2); 2; 6; 8; 9; 12; 14:8; 16(2); 24(2); 15:4; 9; 14; 27; 28; 30; 31; 36; 16:4; 5(3); 7; 10; 26; 31; 37; 40; 47; 48; 17:11; 19:3; 5; 7(2); 8; 10; 11; 12(4); 13; 19; 20(2); 21(2); 20:9; 10; 11; 13; 16; 20; 24; 21:1; 3; 7; 8; 9(2); 14; 23; 29; 33; 22:5; 6(2); 8; 22(2); 25; 27; 30; 31(2); 36; 41; 23:3(2); 4; 6(3); 7; 12; 14; 15; 17(2); 18; 19(6); 20; 21(2); 22; 24(2); 24:1(2); 2; 3; 4; 7; 8(2); 9(4); 10; 15; 16; 19; 20(3); 21; 23; 24; 25:7; 8; 11; 13(2); 15; 27:3; 4; 9; 10; 11; 21(2); 22; 23; 30:2(2); 5; 7; 8(2); 12; 14(4); 15(3); 32:10; 13; 15; 21; 40; 33:39; 35:6; 8; 12; 16(3); 17(4); 18(4); 19(2); 20(2); 21(4); 22; 23; 25(2); 26; 27; 28; 31; 32; **Deut** 1:4; 11; 27; 30(2); 36(3); 38(2); 2:7; 22(2); 30; 32; 3:1; 22; 28(2); 4:13(3); 23; 31(2); 35; 36(3); 37(2); 39; 42; 5:22(2); 24; 6:10; 17; 23(3); 24; 25; 7:8(2); 9; 10(2); 12; 13(3); 24; 8:3(2); 10; 16(2); 18(3); 9:3(3); 5; 25; 28(3); 10:4; 6; 15; 18; 21(2); 11:3; 4(2); 5; 6; 7; 17; 25; 12:10; 12; 15; 20; 31; 13:2; 5; 10(2); 17; 14:21; 23; 27; 29; 15:2; 6; 8; 9; 16(3); 17; 18; 16:16; 17(2); 17:6(2); 16(2); 17(2); 18(2); 19(2); 20(3); 18:2; 6; 7; 18; 19; 19:4(2); 5(2); 6(2); 8(2); 11; 12; 15; 19; 20:4; 5; 6(2); 7; 21:16(3); 17(3); 20(2); 21; 22; 23; 22:3; 16; 17; 19(2); 24; 27; 29(2); 23:1; 2; 7; 10(2); 11(2); 14; 16(2); 24:1; 5(4); 6; 13; 14; 15(2); 25:3(2); 4; 7; 8; 18(2); 26:5; 9; 18; 19(2); 27:16; 17; 18; 19; 20(2); 21; 22; 23; 24; 25; 26; 28:8; 9; 21; 44(2); 45; 48(2); 51(2); 52(2); 54; 55(3); 60; 29:1; 13(4); 19(2); 25(2); 26; 30:4; 5; 9; 20; 31:2; 3(3); 4(2); 6(2); 8(3); 11; 23; 32:4(2); 6(2); 7; 8(2); 10(4); 13(3); 15; 19; 20; 36; 37; 39; 43; 44; 46; 33:2(3); 3; 5; 7; 8; 9; 12(2); 13; 17; 18; 20(3); 21(4); 22(2); 23; 24; 27; 34:6; 7; **Josh** 1:15; 17; 18(2); 2:11; 3:1; 10; 4:4; 21; 23; 5:6(2); 7; 13; 14; 6:7; 26(2); 7:6; 15(5); 17(3); 18; 24; 8:4; 10; 12; 14(2); 18; 19; 26(2); 27; 29; 32(2); 33; 34; 9:9; 10; 22; 26; 27; 10:1(2); 7; 12; 28(4); 30(3); 32; 33; 35(2); 37(2); 39(5); 40; 11:1; 9; 11; 12; 15; 17; 20(2); 13:14(2); 33; 14:3; 10; 14; 15:13; 15; 16; 17; 19; 17:1(3); 4; 19:50(2); 20:4(2); 5; 6(3); 9; 21:43; 44; 22:4; 7; 8; 18; 22(2); 23:3; 5; 10(2); 15; 16(2); 24:7; 10; 17; 18; 19(3); 20(2); 23; 27; 31; **Judg** 1:7; 11; 12; 13; 19; 20; 25; 33; 2:7; 10; 14(2); 20; 21; 23; 3:4; 8; 10; 13; 16; 17; 18(2); 19; 20(3); 22; 24(2); 25; 27(3); 28; 31; 4:3(2); 10; 18; 19; 20; 21(2); 22; 5:13; 15; 25; 27(7); 31; 6:15; 17; 18; 19(2); 20; 22; 27(3); 30(3); 31(2); 32(2); 34; 35(2); 38; 7:5; 8; 11; 15; 16(2); 17; 8:2; 3; 4; 5; 8; 9; 12; 14; 15; 16(2); 17; 18; 19; 20(3); 26; 30; 31; 35; 9:3; 5(2); 7; 18; 28; 29; 31; 33; 36; 40; 43(2); 45; 48; 54(2); 56; 10:1; 2; 4; 7; 18(2); 11:1; 17; 25(2); 28; 29(2); 33; 34; 35(2); 38(2); 39; 12:5; 6(2); 9(3); 11; 14(2); 13:5; 6(2); 7; 11; 16; 21; 23(2); 14:2; 4; 6(5); 7; 8(2); 9(3); 14; 15; 16; 17; 18; 19(2); 20; 15:1; 5(2); 6; 8(2); 10; 11; 14; 15; 17(2); 18; 19(3); 20; 16:4; 9; 11; 12; 13; 14; 17; 18(2); 20(2); 21; 22; 25(2); 30(3); 31; 17:2; 3; 4; 7; 8(3); 9; 18:4; 20; 24; 26; 27; 30; 31; 19:3; 4; 5; 7; 8; 9; 10; 13; 15(2); 16; 17(2); 18; 21; 28; 29(2); 21:5; 18; **Ruth** 1:1; 2:14; 19; 20; 21; 3:2; 3; 4(3); 7; 9; 10; 13(2); 14; 15(2); 17(2); 18; 4:1(2); 2; 3; 4; 8; 13; 15; 17; **1Sa** 1:2; 4; 5(2); 7; 22; 28(3); 2:6; 7; 8(2); 9; 10(2); 14; 15; 16; 23; 35; 3:2; 4; 5(3); 6; 8; 9; 13(2); 16; 17(2); 18; 4:13; 14; 15; 16(2); 18(5); 5:6; 9; 6:5; 6; 9; 19(2); 20; 7:3; 8; 16; 17(2); 8:1; 11(2); 12; 13; 14; 15; 16; 17; 21; 9:2(3); 4(2); 6(4); 9(2); 12(3); 13(3); 16; 26; 27; 10:9; 10; 11; 13(2); 14; 16(2); 21(2); 22; 23(2); 27; 11:6; 7; 8; 12; 12:5(2); 7; 9; 17; 24; 13:1; 2; 7; 8; 9; 10(2); 13; 14:1; 27; 33; 35; 37; 39; 40; 45(2); 47(2); 48; 52; 15:2(2); 8; 11(2); 12; 16; 23; 27; 29(2); 30; 35; 16:2; 5(2); 6; 8; 9; 11(3); 12(3); 16; 21(2); 22; 17:5(2); 6; 8; 9; 12; 20; 23; 25; 26; 28(2); 30; 31; 33; 35; 36; 37; 38(2); 39(2); 40(3); 42(2); 47; 49; 54; 55; 18:1; 3; 5; 8(2); 10; 11; 13; 15(2); 16; 27(2); 19:4; 5; 6; 7; 9; 10(2); 12; 14; 17(2); 18; 21; 22(2); 23(3); 24; 20:1; 2(2); 3(2); 6; 7(2); 13; 17(3); 26(3); 29(3); 30; 31; 32(2); 34; 36(2); 42; 21:13; 22:2; 3; 4; 10; 12; 13; 17; 18; 19; 22; 23; 23:6; 7; 9; 11; 13; 17; 22; 23(2); 25(2); 24:3; 5; 6(2); 10; 17; 19; 25:2(2); 3; 14; 17; 21; 25; 29; 30; 36(2); 37; 38; 39; 26:3; 10; 18; 27:2; 3; 4; 11; 12(2); 28:5; 8(2); 9; 11; 14(4); 17; 20; 21; 23(3); 29:3; 4(3); 9; 30:8; 9; 10; 11; 12(2); 13; 15; 16; 21; 25; 26; 31:3; 4; 5; **2Sa** 1:2(2); 3; 4; 7(2); 8; 9; 10(2); 13; 15(2); 18; 21; 2:1; 10; 19; 20; 23(2); 30; 3:11(2); 13; 16; 21; 22(2); 23(2); 24; 25; 26; 27; 28; 30; 4:4(2); 7; 5:2; 4(2); 5(2); 8; 12; 13; 20; 23; 6:7; 8; 13; 18; 19; 7:11; 13; 14(2); 18; 8:2(2); 3; 6; 10; 11(2); 13; 14(3); 9:2(2); 4(2); 6(2); 8; 11; 13; 10:3; 5; 7; 9; 10(2); 11; 17; 11:2; 4; 13(3); 15(2); 16(2); 20; 21; 12:1; 3; 4; 5; 6(3); 11; 17(2); 18(2); 19; 20(3); 22; 23(2); 24; 25(2); 30(2); 31(2); 13:2; 4; 8; 9; 11; 13; 14; 15(2); 16; 17; 20; 21; 22; 25(2); 26; 27; 32; 36; 39(2); 14:7; 10; 11; 12; 14; 19(2); 26(4); 29(3); 30(2); 33(2); 15:2; 5; 9; 12; 14; 25; 26; 30(2); 32; 16:3(2); 5(2); 6; 7; 13; 21; 23; 17:2; 5; 9; 10; 12; 13; 23; 24; 18:9; 14(2); 18(2); 23(2); 25(2); 26; 27; 28; 30; 33(2); 19:9(2); 14; 18(2); 21; 24; 25; 26; 27; 32(3); 39; 42; 20:1; 3; 5(2); 6; 8(2); 10(2); 11(2); 12(2); 13; 14; 17(4); 22; 21:1; 4; 9; 13; 16; 20; 21; 22:2; 3; 7; 8; 10; 11(2); 12; 15; 17(3); 18; 20(3); 21; 31; 33; 34; 35; 42; 51; 23:3; 4; 5(2); 8(2); 10; 12; 16; 17(2); 18; 19(3); 20(2); 21(2); 23(2); 24:1; 10; 17; **1Kin** 1:1; 5; 6; 7; 10; 13; 17; 19(2); 23(2); 24; 25; 26; 30; 35(2); 37; 41; 42; 51(2); 52(2); 53; 2:1(2); 4(2); 5(2); 8; 11(2); 13; 14; 15; 17(3); 22; 24; 25(2); 27(2); 28; 29; 30(2); 31; 32; 34; 46; 3:1; 3; 6; 15; 4:2; 15; 19; 24(2); 31; 32; 33(2); 5:1; 5; 7; 12; 14; 6:1; 4; 5(2); 6; 9; 10; 15(2); 16(2); 19; 20; 21(2); 22(3); 23; 27; 28; 29; 30; 31; 32; 33; 35; 36; 38; 7:1; 2; 6; 7(2); 8(2); 14(3); 15; 16; 18(2); 21(3); 23; 27; 36; 37; 38; 39(2); 40; 51; 8:12; 15; 19; 20; 21(2); 23; 42; 54; 55; 56(2); 57; 58(2); 59; 63; 64; 66; 9:1; 2; 13(2); 24; 25(3); 10:3; 4; 5; 9; 15; 17; 26(2); 27; 11:3; 8; 10(2); 14; 15; 16; 17; 19; 22; 24; 25(2); 26; 27; 28(2); 29; 31; 32; 34; 41; 12:2; 4; 5; 6; 8; 9; 15; 18; 21; 29(2); 31; 32(5); 33(4); 13:2(2); 3; 4(3); 10(2); 11; 12; 13(2); 14(2); 15; 16; 18(3); 19; 21; 23(4); 24; 26(2); 27; 28; 30; 31(2); 32; 33(2); 14:3; 5; 6; 13; 15(2); 16; 18; 19(2); 20; 21(2); 26(3); 29; 15:2; 3(2); 5; 7; 10; 12; 13; 15; 17; 19; 20; 21; 23(3); 26(2); 29(5); 30(3); 31; 34(2); 16:5; 7(2); 9; 11(4); 12; 14; 18; 19(2); 20; 23; 24(2); 26(2); 27(2); 31; 32(2); 34(2); 17:5(2); 6; 10(3); 11; 15; 16; 19(3); 20; 21; 22; 18:7; 8; 9; 10(2); 12(2); 14; 17; 18; 27(5); 30; 32(2); 33; 34(2); 35; 39(2); 42; 43(2); 44(2); 46; 19:1; 3(2); 4(3); 5; 6(2); 8; 9(2); 10; 11; 13; 14; 19(2); 20(2); 21(2); 20:1; 2; 7; 9; 11; 12(3); 14(3); 15(2); 16; 18; 25; 28; 31; 32(3); 33(2); 34; 36(2); 37(2); 39(3); 40; 41(2); 42; 21:4(2); 6(2); 10; 13; 15; 18(2); 20; 26; 27; 29; 22:4; 8; 11; 15(2); 17; 18; 19; 20; 22(2); 28; 34; 38; 39(3); 42(2); 43(2); 45(2); 46; 52; 53; **2Kin** 1:2; 5; 7(2); 8(2); 9(3); 11(2); 13; 15; 16; 17(2); 18; 2:3; 4; 5; 6; 10; 12(3); 13; 14(2); 16; 17(2); 18(2); 20; 21; 22; 23(2); 24; 25(2); 3:2(2); 3(2); 7(2); 8(2); 16; 18; 26; 27; 4:3; 6; 7; 8(2); 10(2); 11(2); 12(2); 13; 14; 15(2); 16; 18; 19(2); 20(2); 23; 25; 29; 30; 31; 33; 34(2); 35; 36(3); 38; 41(3); 42; 43; 44; 5:1(2); 3; 5; 6; 7(2); 8(2); 11; 12; 13; 14(2); 15(3); 16(3); 18; 19(2); 20; 21; 22; 23; 24(3); 25(2); 26; 27; 6:2; 3; 4; 5; 6(2); 7(2); 11; 13(3); 14; 16; 17(2); 18; 19; 21; 22; 23(2); 27; 30(3); 31; 32; 33(2); 7:2; 11; 17(2); 19; 20; 8:1; 5(3); 10; 11(2); 12; 13; 14(3); 15(2); 17(3); 18(2); 19; 21; 23; 26(2); 27(2); 28; 29(2); 9:5(3); 6(2); 10; 11; 12(2); 14; 15; 17(2); 18; 19; 20(2); 22(2); 24; 27(2); 32; 33(2); 34(2); 36(2); 10:5(2); 6; 8; 9; 10; 11; 12(2); 14(2); 15(5); 16; 17(4); 19(2); 22(2); 24; 25; 31; 34; 11:2; 3; 5; 8(3); 12; 19(2); 21; 12:1; 18; 19; 21; 13:2(2); 3; 4; 7; 8; 11(3); 12(2); 14; 15; 16(2); 17(4); 18(4); 21; 23; 25; 14:2(2); 3(2); 5; 6; 7; 11; 14; 15(2); 19; 20; 22; 24(2); 25(2); 27(2); 28(3); 15:2(3); 3; 5; 6; 9(2); 12; 13; 15; 16(2); 18(2); 21; 24(2); 25; 26; 28(2); 31; 33(3); 34(2); 35; 36; 16:2; 3; 4; 13; 14; 18; 19; 17:2; 4(2); 15(2); 20; 21; 22; 23; 26; 34; 37; 39; 18:2(3); 3; 4(2); 5; 6; 7(3); 8; 22; 27; 29; 32; 19:1; 2; 7; 8(2); 9(3); 32; 33(2); 37; 20:2; 7; 9; 11; 12; 15; 19; 20; 21:1; 2; 3(2); 4; 5; 6(2); 7(2); 16(2); 17(2); 19(2); 20; 21; 22; 25; 26; 22:1(2); 2; 4; 8; 11; 23:2; 4; 5; 6; 7; 8; 10; 11; 14; 15; 16; 17; 18; 19; 20; 24; 28; 29(2); 31(2); 32; 33; 34; 35(2); 36(2); 37; 24:1; 2; 3; 4(2); 5; 6(2); 9; 12; 13; 14; 15(2); 18(2); 19; 20; 25:1; 9(2); 19; 22; 25; 27; 28; 29; **1Chr** 1:10; 2:3; 21(2); 23; 3:4(2); 4:10; 5:1(2); 6; 9; 20; 26; 6:10; 7:23(2); 8:7; 8; 9; 11; 10:3; 4; 5; 13(2); 14; 11:2; 8; 11; 13; 19; 20(2); 21(3); 22(2); 23(2); 25; 12:1; 18; 19(2); 20; 13:10(3); 14; 14:4; 15:3; 22(2); 16:2; 3; 4; 12; 14; 15; 16; 21(2); 25; 33; 34; 37; 40; 17:12; 13; 18:2; 3; 6; 10(2); 11; 13(2); 19:3; 5; 8; 10; 11; 12; 17; 20:2; 3; 6; 7; 21:3; 6; 7; 15(2); 19; 26; 27; 28; 30; 22:2; 6; 10(2); 11; 18(2); 23:1; 2; 13(2); 25:10; 11; 12; 13; 14; 15; 16; 17; 18; 19; 20; 21; 22; 23; 24; 25; 26; 27; 28; 29; 30; 31; 26:10; 27:23; 24; 28:4(2); 5; 6(2); 7; 9(2); 12; 14; 16; 17; 20; 29:27(3); 28; **2Chr** 1:4; 5; 14(2); 15; 2:11(2); 18; 3:2; 4; 5(2); 6; 7; 8(2); 9; 10; 14; 15; 16; 17; 4:1; 2; 6; 7; 8(2); 9; 10; 11; 14(2); 21; 5:1; 13; 6:1; 4(2); 9; 10; 11; 12; 13; 7:3; 7; 10; 11; 21; 22; 8:4(2); 5; 11(2); 12; 14; 9:2; 3; 4; 8; 16; 25; 26; 27; 31; 10:2; 4; 5; 6; 8; 9; 15; 18; 11:1(2); 6; 11; 12; 15(2); 20; 21; 22; 23(3); 12:1; 4; 9(2); 12(2); 13(2); 14(2); 13:2; 20; 14:3; 5; 6(2); 7(2); 15:2(3); 4; 8(2); 9; 15; 16; 18(2); 16:1; 3; 5; 6; 8; 10; 12; 14; 17:2; 3; 5; 6; 7; 8; 11; 12; 13; 18:2(2); 3; 7; 14(2); 16; 17; 18; 19; 21; 27; 33; 34; 19:4; 5; 9; 20:15; 21(2); 31(3); 32; 36; 21:2; 3(2); 4; 5(2); 6(3); 7(2); 9; 10; 11; 19; 20(3); 22:2(2); 3; 4; 5; 6(3); 7(2); 8; 9(3); 12; 23:3; 7(3); 10; 19; 20; 24:1(2); 3; 5; 15(3); 16; 19; 20; 22(2); 25; 25:1(2); 2; 3; 4; 5; 6; 14; 15; 16; 20; 21; 24; 27; 26:2; 3(2); 4; 5(2); 6; 8; 10(3); 15(3); 16(2); 19; 20; 21; 23; 27:1(2); 2(2); 3(2); 4(2); 5; 6; 8(2); 28:1(3); 2; 3; 4; 5; 9(2); 19; 21; 22; 23(2); 24; 25; 29:1(2); 2; 3; 4; 8; 21(2); 23; 25; 30:6; 8; 19; 31:3; 4; 21(2); 32:2; 3; 5; 6; 9; 17; 21(2); 23; 24(2); 26; 27; 29; 31; 33:1(2); 3(2); 4; 5; 6(3); 7(2); 12(2); 13(2); 14; 15(2); 16; 19(2); 21; 22; 34:1(2); 2; 3(3); 4(2); 5; 6; 7(2); 8(2); 19; 30; 32; 35:2; 21(2); 22; 24(2); 36:2(2); 5(3); 8; 9(3); 11; 12; 13(2); 14; 15; 17(2); 18; 20; 22; 23; **Ezr** 1:1; 2; 3; 4; 3:11; 5:12; 14; 6:17; 7:6; 8; 9(2); 8:23; 31; 35; 10:1; 6(3); **Neh** 1:2; 2:8; 18; 20; 3:12; 14; 15; 4:1; 2; 3(2); 18; 5:13; 6:10; 12; 13; 18; 7:2; 8:3; 5(2); 10; 18; 9:29; 12:8; 13:2; 5; **Est** 1:3; 4; 10; 20; 22; 2:1; 4; 7; 9(2); 17; 18; 3:4(3); 6; 4:4; 5; 8; 11; 5:5; 9(2); 10(2); 11; 14; 6:1; 4; 7:5(2); 7; 8; 10; 8:1; 2; 3; 5; 7; 10; 9:25(3); 30; **Job** 1:10; 11(2); 12; 16; 17; 18; 2:3; 4; 5; 6; 8(2); 10; 4:18(2); 5:12; 13; 15; 18(2); 19; 20; 6:5; 9; 14; 7:9; 10; 8:4; 6; 15(2); 16; 18; 20; 21; 9:3(2); 4; 11(2); 12; 16(2); 17; 18; 19; 22; 23; 24(2); 32; 11:6; 10; 11(3); 12:4; 5; 13; 14(2); 15(2); 17; 18; 19; 20; 21; 22; 23(2); 24; 25; 13:9; 10; 15; 16; 19; 28; 14:2(2); 5; 6(2); 10; 14; 20; 21(2); 15:3(2); 14(3); 15; 22(3); 23(2); 25; 26; 27; 28; 29(2); 30(2); 33; 16:7; 9(2); 12(2); 13(2); 14(2); 17:3; 5; 6; 9; 18:4; 8(2); 17; 18; 19; 19:8(2); 9; 10(2); 11(2); 13; 16; 25; 20:7(2); 8(2); 12; 13; 15(2); 16; 17; 18(3); 19(3); 20(3); 22; 23(2); 24; 21:19(2); 20; 21; 22; 31; 32; 22:2; 4(2); 8; 13; 14(2); 18; 27; 29; 30; 23:5(2); 6(2); 8; 9(2); 10(2); 13(2); 14; 17; 24:18(2); 20; 21; 22(2); 23; 25:2; 4; 26:7; 8; 9; 10; 12(2); 13; 27:7; 8; 10(2); 16; 17; 18; 19(3); 21; 22; 28:3; 9(2); 10; 11(2); 23; 24; 25; 26; 27(2); 28; 30:11; 19; 24; 31:4; 14; 15; 18; 20; 32:1; 2; 4; 14; 33:10(2); 11(2); 13; 16; 17; 18; 19; 24; 25; 26(4); 27; 28; 34:9(2); 10(2); 11; 14(2); 17; 21; 23(2); 24; 25(2); 26; 28; 29(2); 33; 37(2); 35:7; 15(2); 16; 36:4; 5; 6; 7(2); 9; 10; 13; 15; 16; 18; 19; 27; 30; 31(2); 32; 37:3; 4(2); 5; 6; 7; 11(2); 12; 13; 17; 20; 23(2); 24; 39:7(2); 8; 10; 12; 17; 21(2); 22(2); 24(2); 25(2); 40:2(2); 15; 17; 19(2); 21; 23(3); 24; 41:3(2); 4; 25; 27; 29; 30; 31(2); 32; 34(2); 42:3; 10(2); 12; 13; 14; **Ps** 1:2; 3(2); 2:4; 5; 12; 3:t, 4; 7:t, 2; 12(3); 13(2); 14; 15(2); 9:7; 8(2); 12(3); 16; 10:5; 6; 8(2); 9(4); 10; 11(3); 13; 11:6; 13:6; 15:2; 3; 4(2); 5(2); 16:8; 18:t, 6; 7; 9; 10(2); 11; 14(2); 16(3); 17; 19(3); 20; 30; 33; 34; 41; 48; 50; 19:4; 20:6; 21:1; 4; 7; 22:8(3); 9; 24(4); 28; 31; 23:2(2); 3(2); 24:2; 4; 5; 10; 25:8; 9(2); 12(3); 14; 15; 27:5(3); 14; 28:5; 6; 8; 29:6; 31:21; 24; 32:1; 10; 33:5; 7(2); 9(2); 10; 12; 13; 14; 15(2); 17; 20; 34:2(2); 4; 12(2); 20; 35:8; 14; 36:2; 3; 4(3); 37:4; 5; 6; 13; 23; 24(2); 26; 33; 34; 36(3); 39; 40; 39:6; 40:1; 2; 3; 41:1; 2; 5; 6(4); 8(2); 44:21; 45:11; 46:6; 8; 9(3); 47:2; 3; 4(2); 9; 48:14; 49:9; 10; 12; 15; 17(2);

18(2); 19; 50:4(2); 9; 51:t, 52:5; 54:5; 7; 55:12; 17; 18; 19; 20(2); 22(2); 56:1; 57:t, 3; 58:7; 9; 10(2); 11; 60:t, 12; 61:7; 62:2(2); 6(2); 63:t, 65:4; 66:5; 6; 7; 16; 17; 19; 68:6; 20; 33; 35; 71:6; 72:2; 4(2); 6; 8; 12(2); 13; 14; 15(2); 74:5; 75:7; 8; 76:3; 12(2); 77:1; 7; 9; 78:4; 5(2); 11; 12; 13(2); 14; 15; 16; 20(3); 23; 25; 26(2); 27; 28; 29; 33; 34; 38(2); 39; 42; 43; 45; 46; 47; 48; 49; 50(2); 53; 54; 55; 59; 60(2); 62; 66(2); 67; 68; 69(2); 70; 71; 72; 81:5(2); 16; 82:1; 84:11; 85:8; 87:6; 89:26; 41; 48(2); 91:1; 2; 3; 4; 11; 14(2); 15; 92:12; 15; 93:1(2); 94:9(4); 10(4); 14; 23; 95:5; 7; 96:4; 10; 13(3); 97:10(2); 98:1; 2; 3; 9(2); 99:1; 2; 5; 6; 7(2); 100:3(2); 101:6(2); 7(2); 102:t, 16; 17; 19; 23(2); 103:7; 9(2); 10; 12; 14(2); 15; 104:10; 13; 14(2); 16; 19; 32(2); 105:5; 7; 8(2); 9; 14(2); 16(2); 17; 18; 21; 24; 25; 26(2); 28; 29; 31; 32; 33; 34; 36; 37; 39; 40; 41; 42; 43; 106:1; 3; 8(2); 9(2); 10; 15; 23(3); 26; 33; 40; 41; 43; 44(2); 45; 46; 107:1; 2; 6; 7; 9; 12; 13; 14; 16; 19; 20; 25; 28; 29; 30; 33; 35; 36; 38; 40; 41; 108:13; 109:7; 11; 15; 16(2); 17(2); 18; 19; 31; 110:6(3); 7(2); 111:4; 5(2); 6(2); 9(2); 112:4; 5; 6; 7; 8(2); 9(2); 10; 113:7; 8; 9; 115:3(2); 9; 10; 11; 12(3); 13; 16; 116:1; 2; 6; 118:1; 18; 26; 29; 120:1; 121:3(2); 4; 7; 123:2; 126:6; 127:2; 129:4; 7; 130:8; 132:2; 11; 13; 135:6; 7(3); 14; 136:1; 137:8; 9; 138:6(2); 142:t, 143:3(2); 144:2; 10; 145:19(2); 20; 146:4; 5; 9(2); 147:2; 3; 4(2); 6; 9; 10(2); 13(2); 14; 15; 16(2); 17; 18(2); 19; 20; 148:5; 6(2); 14; 149:4; **Prov** 2:7(2); 8; 3:6; 12(2); 19; 29; 30; 33; 34(2); 4:4; 5:21; 22; 23(2); 6:13(3); 14(2); 15; 19; 29; 30(2); 31(3); 32; 33; 34; 35(2); 7:8; 19; 20; 22; 8:26; 27(2); 28(2); 29(2); 36; 9:7(2); 8(2); 9(2); 18; 10:3; 4; 5(2); 9(2); 10; 17(2); 18(2); 19; 22; 11:12; 13; 15(2); 17; 19; 25; 26; 27(2); 28; 29; 30; 12:1; 2; 8; 9(2); 11(2); 15; 17; 27; 13:3(2); 11; 13; 18; 20; 24(2); 14:2(2); 17; 21(3); 29(2); 31(2); 15:5; 9; 10; 12; 15; 18; 24; 25; 27(2); 29; 32(2); 16:5; 7; 17; 20(2); 26; 30(2); 32(3); 17:5; 9(2); 15(2); 16; 19(2); 20(2); 21; 27; 28(2); 18:9; 13(2); 17; 20; 19:1; 2; 5; 7; 8(2); 9; 16(2); 17(3); 23(2); 25; 26; 20:4; 14(2); 19; 22; 21:1(2); 11; 13; 17(2); 21; 26; 27; 29; 22:5; 6(3); 8; 9(2); 11; 12; 14; 16(2); 22; 27; 29(2); 23:7(3); 9; 11; 13; 24; 34(2); 24:7; 8; 12(4); 17; 18; 24; 29; 25:10; 13; 17; 20(2); 21; 28; 26:5; 6; 8(2); 17; 24; 25; 27; 27:14; 18; 28:6(2); 7; 8(2); 9; 10; 13; 14; 16; 18; 19(2); 20; 22; 23(2); 25(2); 26(2); 27(2); 29:1; 3; 4; 9; 17(2); 18(2); 19(2); 21; 24; 27; 30:5; 6; 10; 22(2); 31; 31:11; 23; 28; **Eccl** 1:3; 5; 18; 2:19(2); 21; 22; 24(2); 26(2); 3:9(2); 11(2); 4:3; 8(2); 10(2); 14(2); 5:4; 8; 10(2); 12; 14; 15(4); 16(3); 17(2); 18; 20; 6:2(2); 3(2); 4; 5; 6(2); 10(2); 12; 7:13; 18; 8:3; 7; 8; 13(2); 17(2); 9:2(2); 9; 15; 10:3(3); 8; 9; 10(2); 15; 11:4(2); 12:4; 9(2); **Song** 1:13; 2:4; 7; 8; 9(2); 16; 3:5; 10; 5:6(2); 16; 6:3; 8:4; 11; **Is** 1:1; 11; 2:3; 4; 12; 18; 19; 21; 22; 3:7; 4:3(2); 5:2(2); 7; 14; 25; 26; 6:3(3); 6; 7; 9; 11; 7:13; 15(2); 22; 8:7; 8(3); 14; 9:1; 15(2); 20(2); 10:7; 8; 13; 16; 24; 26; 28(3); 32(2); 34; 11:3; 4(3); 12; 15; 16; 12:2; 5; 13:9; 14:6(2); 30; 15:2; 16:5; 6; 12(2); 17:5; 8; 14; 18:3(2); 5; 19:16; 17; 20(2); 22(2); 20:2; 21:4; 6; 7(2); 8; 9(2); 11; 22:8; 16; 18; 19; 21; 22(2); 23; 23:11(2); 12; 13; 24:18(2); 25:7; 8(2); 9; 11(3); 12; 26:3; 5(4); 10(2); 27:1; 5(2); 6; 7(3); 8; 9; 10; 11(2); 28:4(2); 9(2); 11; 12; 16; 20; 21(2); 24; 25(2); 28; 29:8(5); 10; 11; 12; 16(2); 23; 30:14(2); 18(3); 19(3); 23; 32; 33; 31:2; 3(2); 4; 5(2); 8; 9; 32:6; 7; 8; 33:4; 5(2); 8(3); 15(2); 16; 18; 22; 34:2(2); 11; 17; 35:4; 36:2; 7; 12; 14; 37:1; 2; 7; 8(2); 9(4); 33; 34(2); 38; 38:7; 9; 12; 13; 15; 19; 21; 39:1(2); 4; 8; 40:6; 11(2); 14; 15; 20(3); 22; 23; 24; 26(2); 29(2); 41:2; 3(2); 4; 7(2); 24; 25(3); 26; 42:1; 2; 3(3); 4(2); 5(3); 13(3); 19; 20; 21; 24; 25(3); 43:1; 10; 13; 25; 44:12(2); 13(3); 14(3); 15(4); 16(4); 17(2); 18; 20(2); 24; 28; 45:9; 13(2); 18(3); 46:4; 6; 7(3); 48:12; 14; 15; 21(3); 49:1; 2(3); 6; 7; 10(2); 50:4(2); 8; 9; 51:3(2); 12; 13; 14(2); 52:6; 9; 13; 15; 53:2(2); 3(2); 4; 5(2); 7(5); 8(3); 9(2); 10(3); 11(2); 12(4); 54:5; 55:1; 5; 6(2); 7(2); 57:2; 13; 17; 58:9; 59:2; 5; 15; 16; 17(2); 18(2); 60:9; 61:1; 3; 10(2); 62:7(2); 63:7; 8(2); 9(3); 10(2); 11(3); 64:4; 65:16(2); 66:3(8); 5; **Jer** 2:14(2); 17; 26; 3:1; 5(2); 4:7; 13; 5:12; 24; 26; 8:4; 8; 9:8; 12(2); 24; 10:10; 12(2); 13(3); 16; 11:16; 12:4; 13:16(2); 21; 14:10; 22; 15:4; 16:15; 17:6; 8; 11; 18:3; 4(2); 19:14; 20:4; 10; 13; 17; 21:2; 7(2); 9(3); 10; 22:4; 10; 11; 12; 16; 19; 28(2); 23:6; 20(2); 28; 31; 25:30(2); 31(2); 38; 26:11; 13; 16; 19(2); 21; 27:20; 29:21; 28; 31; 32(3); 30:7; 21; 24(2); 31:10; 11; 20; 32:3; 5(2); 28; 33:1; 15; 21; 24; 34:2; 3; 14; 16; 35:8; 14; 16; 18; 36:4; 12; 13; 18; 21; 23; 25(2); 30; 37:2(2); 13(2); 14; 17; 38:2(3); 4; 5(2); 9(2); 10; 26; 27; 28; 39:4; 5; 7; 12; 14(2); 15; 40:1; 3; 5(2); 11; 15; 41:4; 6(3); 7; 8; 9; 16(3); 42:8; 12; 21; 43:10; 11(2); 12(3); 13(2); 45:1; 46:8; 10; 16; 17; 18; 47:7; 48:10(2); 11(2); 18; 26(2); 27; 29; 36; 40; 42; 44(2); 49:1; 10(2); 12; 19; 20(3); 22; 50:8; 19; 34(2); 44; 45(3); 51:6; 12; 15(2); 16(3); 19; 34(5); 40; 44; 59; 52:1(2); 2; 3; 4; 9; 10; 11; 13; 25; 29; 33; **Lam** 1:13(4); 14; 15; 2:2(3); 3(3); 4(3); 5(3); 6(2); 7(2); 8(3); 9; 17(6); 3:2; 3(2); 4(2); 5; 6; 7(2); 8; 9(2); 10; 11(2); 12; 13; 15(2); 16(2); 27; 28(2); 29; 30(2); 32(2); 33; 37; 4:11; 16; 22(3); **Eze** 2:1; 2; 3; 10; 3:1; 2; 3; 4; 10; 19(2); 20(3); 21(3); 22; 27(2); 4:15; 16; 6:12(3); 7:15(2); 20; 8:3; 5; 6; 7; 8; 9; 12; 13; 14; 15; 16; 17; 9:1; 3(2); 5; 7; 9; 10:2(2); 5; 6(2); 11:2; 12:12(2); 13(3); 27(2); 13:22; 14:9; 17:1(2); 6(2); 7; 9; 13; 15(4); 16(3); 18(3); 19(2); 20(2); 18:8; 9(2); 10; 13(4); 14(2); 17(2); 18(2); 19; 21(3); 22(3); 23; 24(5); 26(2); 27(2); 28(4); 19:4; 6(2); 7(2); 8; 20:11; 13; 21; 49; 21:11; 21(3); 23; 27; 24:24; 26; 26:8(2); 9(2); 10; 11(2); 29:9; 18(2); 19; 20; 30:11; 24; 25; 31:5; 7; 10; 11; 15; 32:25; 32; 33:3(2); 5(2); 6; 9(2); 12(3); 13(4); 14; 15(3); 16(3); 18; 19; 22(2); 24; 34:12; 17; 23(3); 37:3; 4; 9; 10; 11; 38:17; 39:15; 40:2; 3(2); 5; 6; 8; 9; 11; 13; 14; 17; 19; 20; 23; 24(2); 27; 28(2); 32(2); 35; 45; 47; 48; 49; 41:1; 2; 3; 4(2); 5; 13; 15; 22; 42:1(2); 13; 15(2); 16; 17; 18; 19; 20; 43:1; 7; 18; 21; 44:1; 3(2); 4; 26; 27(2); 30; 45:17; 23; 24; 25; 46:2(2); 5; 7; 8(2); 9(4); 11; 17; 18; 19; 20; 21; 24; 47:1; 2; 3(2); 4(2); 5; 6(2); 8; **Dan** 1:2(2); 3; 5; 7; 8(4); 10; 14; 18; 20; 2:15; 16(2); 21(3); 22(2); 24; 29; 38; 49; 3:1; 11; 17; 19; 20; 25; 4:14; 17; 25; 29; 32; 33; 35; 37; 5:2; 12; 19(9); 20; 21(4); 29; 6:4; 7; 10(3); 14(2); 16; 20(2); 23; 26; 27(2); 7:1; 16; 23; 24(2); 25; 8:4; 5; 6; 7(2); 8(2); 11; 14; 17(3); 18(2); 19; 24; 25(4); 9:2; 10; 12(2); 14; 22; 27(3); 10:1; 11(2); 12; 15; 18; 19; 20; 11:2; 4(2); 5; 6(3); 8; 10; 11; 12(3); 16(2); 17(3); 18(2); 19(2); 20; 21; 23(2); 24(4); 25(2); 28(2); 29; 30(3); 32; 36; 37(2); 38(2); 39(3); 40; 41; 42; 43; 44; 45(2); 12:7(2); 9; 12; **Hos** 1:3; 5:6; 11; 13; 6:1(4); 2(2); 3; 11; 7:4; 5; 8; 9(2); 8:1; 13; 9:9(2); 10:1(2); 2(2); 12; 11:5; 10(2); 12:1; 2; 3(2); 4(4); 7(2); 12; 13; 14; 13:1(3); 13(2); 15(2); 14:5; 9(2); **Joel** 1:6; 7(2); 2:11; 13; 14; 20; 23(2); **Amos** 1:1; 2; 11(2); 15; 2:1; 9; 15(3); 16; 3:4(2); 7; 11; 4:2; 13; 5:6; 6:10(3); 11; 7:1; 2; 5; 7; 8:2; 9:1(3); 3; 5; 6(2); **Obad** 12; **Jonah** 1:3(2); 5; 9; 10(2); 12; 2:2; 3:4; 6(2); 7; 10(3); 4:1; 2; 5; 8; 9; **Mic** 1:1; 9; 11; 15; 2:4(3); 11; 3:4(2); 5; 4:2; 3; 12; 5:1; 2; 3; 4(2); 5; 6(3); 8; 6:2; 8; 7:3; 9(2); 12; 18(2); 19(3); **Nah** 1:2; 4; 7; 8; 9; 12; 15; 2:1; 5; **Hab** 1:11; 13; 2:1; 2; 5(2); 9(2); 3:4; 6(2); 16(2); 19(2); **Zeph** 1:7; 12; 18; 2:11; 13; 14; 3:5(3); 15; 17(4); **Hag** 1:6; **Zec** 1:6; 8; 19; 21; 2:2; 8(2); 13; 3:1; 4(2); 4:6; 7; 13; 14; 5:2; 3; 6(2); 8(3); 11; 6:7; 8; 12(2); 13(3); 7:13; 9:4; 7(3); 9; 10; 10:11; 11:16; 12:8; 13:3; 4; 5; 6; 14:3; **Mal** 1:8; 9(2); 2:5; 6; 7; 11; 13; 15(3); 16; 17; 3:1(2); 2(2); 3(2); 11; 4:6; **Mt** 1:20; 21; 25; 2:2; 3; 4(2); 7; 8; 14(2); 16(3); 21; 22(3); 23(2); 3:3; 7(2); 11(2); 12(2); 15; 16(2); 4:2(2); 3; 4; 6; 12; 13; 19; 21(2); 24; 5:1(2); 2; 19; 45; 6:24(2); 30; 7:8; 9; 10(2); 21; 29; 8:1; 9(3); 10; 14; 15; 16; 18; 23; 24; 26(2); 28; 32; 34; 9:1; 6; 7; 9(3); 12; 18; 22(2); 24; 25; 28; 29; 34; 36(2); 37; 38; 10:1(2); 22; 25; 37(2); 38; 30(2); 40(2); 41(2); 42; 11:1; 2; 3; 6; 10; 11(2); 15; 18; 20; 27; 12:3(2); 4; 9(2); 11(2); 13(2); 15(2); 18; 19; 20(3); 22; 26; 29(2); 30(2); 39; 43; 44(3); 45; 46; 48; 49; 13:2; 3; 4; 11; 12(2); 19; 20(2); 21(2); 22(3); 23(2); 24; 28; 29; 31; 33; 34; 37(2); 44(2); 46(2); 52; 53; 54(2); 58; 14:2; 5(2); 7; 9; 10; 13; 14; 18; 19(2); 22; 23(3); 29(2); 30(3); 15:3; 4; 6; 10; 13; 23; 24; 26; 30; 35; 36; 39; 16:1; 2; 4; 8; 12; 13; 15; 20(2); 21; 23; 26; 27; 17:5; 13; 15(2); 18; 23; 25(2); 18:6; 12; 13(2); 15; 16; 17(2); 24; 25(2); 28; 30(2); 32; 34; 19:1; 2; 4(2); 8; 11; 12; 13; 15; 17; 18; 22(2); 20:2(2); 3; 5; 6; 7; 13; 19; 21; 23; 21:3; 9; 10; 14; 15; 17(2); 18(2); 19(2); 23(2); 25; 27; 28; 29(2); 30(2); 34; 36; 37; 40; 41; 45; 22:4; 7(2); 8; 11; 12(2); 20; 21; 25; 34; 42; 43; 45; 23:11; 12; 15; 16; 18; 22; 39; 24:3; 13; 26(2); 31; 43; 46; 47; 50(2); 25:12; 15; 16; 17(2); 18; 20; 22; 24; 29(2); 31; 32; 33; 41; 45; 26:1; 7; 10; 16; 18; 20; 21; 23(2); 24; 25; 27; 37; 38; 39; 40; 42; 43; 44; 45; 46; 47; 48(2); 49; 53; 65; 66; 68; 70; 71; 72; 74; 75; 27:3(2); 5; 12(2); 14; 18; 19; 23; 24(2); 26(3); 34(2); 42(3); 43(3); 50; 58; 59; 60(2); 63; 64; 28:6(3); 7(2); **Mk** 1:6; 8; 10; 13; 16(2); 19(2); 20; 21; 22; 23; 26; 27; 31; 34; 35; 38; 39; 42(2); 43; 45; 2:1(2); 2; 4; 5; 8; 10; 12; 13(2); 14(3); 16; 17; 23; 25(3); 26; 27; 3:1; 2; 3; 4; 5(3); 8; 9; 10; 12; 13(2); 14(2); 16; 17; 21; 22(2); 23; 26; 27(2); 29; 30; 33; 34; 4:1(2); 2; 4; 9(2); 10; 11; 13; 21; 24; 25(3); 26; 27; 29; 30; 33; 34(2); 35; 36; 38; 39; 40; 5:2; 4; 5; 6(2); 8; 9(2); 10(2); 18(3); 20; 21; 22(2); 32; 34; 35; 36; 37; 38; 39(2); 40(2); 41; 43; 6:1; 2; 5(2); 6(2); 7; 10; 14; 16(2); 17; 20(3); 23; 26; 27; 31; 34(2); 37; 38; 39; 41(3); 45(2); 46(2); 47; 48(2); 50; 51; 55; 56; 7:6; 9; 11; 14(2); 17; 18; 20; 24(2); 26; 29; 31; 33(2); 34; 35; 36(2); 37(2); 8:5; 6(2); 7; 9; 10; 12; 13; 15; 17; 21; 22; 23(4); 24; 25(2); 26; 27; 29; 30; 31; 32; 33(2); 34(2); 36; 38; 9:1; 2; 6; 9; 12(2); 14(2); 16; 18(3); 19; 20(2); 21(2); 25; 26(2); 27; 28; 29; 30; 31(3); 33(2); 35; 36(3); 38(2); 40; 41; 42; 10:1(3); 3; 5; 11; 13; 14; 15; 16; 17; 20; 22(2); 30; 32; 34; 36; 46; 47(2); 48(2); 49; 50; 52; 11:1; 3; 7; 9; 11(2); 12; 13(4); 17; 19; 23(3); 27; 31; 32; 12:1; 2(2); 4; 5; 6; 9; 12; 15; 16; 21; 27; 28; 32; 34(2); 35; 37; 38; 43; 13:1; 3; 13; 20(2); 21; 27; 36; 14:3; 11(2); 13; 14; 15; 16; 17; 20; 21; 23(3); 24; 31; 32; 33; 35; 36; 37; 39; 40(2); 41; 42; 43; 44(2); 45(2); 52; 54; 61; 68(2); 70; 71; 72(2); 15:2; 3; 6; 8; 10; 11; 14; 15; 23; 28; 31(2); 35; 39(2); 41; 44(3); 45(2); 46; 47; 16:6(3); 7(2); 9(2); 11; 12; 14(2); 15; 16(2); 19; **Lk** 1:8; 9; 12; 15(2); 16; 17; 21; 22(4); 23; 25; 32; 33; 48; 49; 51(2); 52; 53(2); 54; 55; 60; 62; 63; 64; 68; 70; 73; 74; 2:4; 21; 26(2); 27; 28; 42; 49; 50; 51; 3:3; 7; 11(3); 13; 14; 15; 16; 17(2); 18; 20; 4:2(2); 9; 10; 13; 15; 16(3); 17(2); 18(2); 20(2); 21; 23; 24; 30; 35; 36; 38; 39; 40; 41(2); 42(2); 43; 44; 5:1; 3(3); 4(2); 8; 9; 12; 13; 14; 16; 17; 20(2); 22; 24; 25(2); 27(2); 28; 34; 36; 39; 6:1; 4; 5; 6; 7; 8(2); 10(2); 12; 13(3); 14; 17; 20; 35; 39; 47; 48; 49; 7:1(2); 3(3); 4(2); 5(2); 6; 8(3); 9; 11; 12; 13; 14(2); 15(2); 19; 20; 21(2); 23; 24; 27; 28(2); 33; 36(2); 39(2); 40; 42; 43(3); 44; 48; 50; 8:1; 4; 5; 8(3); 10; 16; 18; 21; 22(2); 23; 24; 25(2); 27; 28(2); 29(3); 30; 31; 32(2); 36; 37; 38; 39; 41(3); 42(2); 48; 49; 50; 51(2); 52; 54; 55; 56; 9:1; 2; 3; 7; 9; 10; 11; 13; 14; 16(2); 18(2); 20; 21; 23; 25; 26; 28; 29; 31; 33; 34; 38; 39(2); 42; 43; 48; 49; 50; 51(2); 53; 55; 59(2); 10:1; 2(2); 16(3); 18; 22; 23; 26; 27; 28; 29; 31(2); 32; 33(4); 35(2); 37(2); 38; 11:1(2); 2; 5; 7; 8(4); 10; 11(3); 12(2); 14; 15; 17; 22(3); 23(2); 24(2); 25(2); 26; 27; 28; 29; 33; 37(2); 38(2); 40; 46; 53; 12:1; 5; 9; 13; 14; 15(2); 16; 17; 18; 21; 22; 28; 36(2); 37(2); 38; 39; 43; 44(2); 46(2); 48; 54; 58; 13:6(2); 7; 8; 10; 12; 13; 17; 18; 20; 22; 23; 25; 27; 32; 35; 14:1; 4; 7(2); 9; 10(2); 11; 12; 15(2); 16; 25; 26; 28; 29; 31; 32; 33(3); 35; 15:3; 4(2); 5(2); 6(2); 11; 12; 14(2); 15(2); 16; 17(2); 20(2); 24; 25(2); 26; 27(2); 28; 29; 31; 16:1(2); 2; 5; 6(2); 7(3); 8; 10(2); 13(2); 15; 23; 24(2); 25; 27; 28; 30; 31; 17:1; 2(2); 3; 4; 7; 9(2); 11(2); 12; 14(2); 15(2); 16; 19; 20(2); 22; 25; 31(2); 37; 18:1; 4(2); 7; 8(2); 9; 14; 15; 21; 22; 23(3); 24(2); 27; 29; 31; 32; 33; 35; 36; 38; 39(2); 40(2); 41; 43; 19:2; 3(3); 4(2); 5; 6; 7; 9; 11(2); 12; 13; 15(4); 17; 19; 22; 24; 25; 26; 28(2); 29(2); 32; 36; 37; 40; 41(2); 45; 47; 20:1; 2; 3; 5; 9; 10; 11; 12; 16; 17; 19; 23; 25; 28; 30; 37; 38; 41; 44; 45; 21:1; 2; 3; 5; 8; 10; 29; 37(2); 22:4(2); 6; 8; 10(2); 12; 13; 14; 15; 17; 19; 22; 25; 26(3); 27(4); 31; 33; 34; 35; 36(3); 37; 38; 39(2); 40(2); 41; 44; 45(2); 47(2); 51; 56; 57; 59; 60; 61; 67; 70; 23:2; 3; 5; 6; 7(3); 8(4); 9(2); 13; 17; 22(2); 23; 25(2); 26; 35(2); 42; 46(2); 47; 50; 51; 53; 24:6(3); 12; 17; 19; 21; 23; 25; 27; 28(2); 29; 30(2); 31; 32(2); 35; 38; 40(2); 41; 43; 44; 45; 50(2); 51(2); **Jn** 1:8; 10; 11; 12; 15(3); 18; 20; 21(2); 23; 27; 30(2); 31; 33(2); 36(2); 39(2); 41; 42(2); 51; 2:5; 8; 12(2); 15(2); 21; 22(2); 23(2); 24; 25; 3:3; 4(2); 5; 13; 16; 18(3); 21; 22; 26; 29; 30; 31(3); 32(2); 33; 34; 36(2); 4:3; 4; 5; 10; 18; 25(2); 26; 27; 32; 36(3); 39; 40(2); 43; 45(2); 46; 47(4); 50; 51; 52(2); 54; 5:4; 6(2); 11(2); 13; 16; 18; 19(2); 20; 21; 23; 24; 26; 27; 32; 33; 35; 38; 46; 6:2; 3; 5; 6(3); 11(2); 12; 15; 20; 29; 31; 33; 35(2); 39; 41; 42; 46(2); 47; 51; 56; 57(2); 58; 59(2); 61; 62; 65; 71(2); 7:1; 4; 9(2); 10; 11; 12(2); 17; 18(2); 25; 26; 27(2); 28(2); 29; 31; 35(2); 36; 38; 39; 50; 51; 8:1; 2(2); 6; 7(2); 8; 10; 12; 20; 22(2); 23; 24; 26; 27; 28; 29; 30; 42; 44(4); 47; 51; 52; 54; 56; 9:1; 2; 6(3); 7; 8(2); 9(4); 11; 12(2); 15(3); 16; 17(3); 18; 19; 20; 21(3); 22(2); 23; 25(2); 26(2); 27; 29; 30(2); 31; 33; 35(2); 36(2); 37; 38(2); 10:1; 2; 3; 4(2); 6; 9; 12; 13; 20; 35; 39; 40; 11:3; 4; 6(4); 7; 9(2); 10; 11(2); 12(2); 13; 17(2); 24; 25(3); 33; 36; 39(2); 43(2); 44; 51(2); 52; 56; 57(2); 12:1; 6(3); 9(2); 14; 17; 18; 25(2); 33(2); 35(2); 37; 38; 40; 41; 44; 45; 48; 49; 13:1(2); 3; 4; 5(2); 6; 10; 11(2); 12(2); 16(2); 18; 19; 20(2); 21; 22; 24(2); 25; 26(3); 28; 29; 30; 31; 14:9; 10; 12(3); 16(2); 17; 21(3); 23; 24; 26; 15:2(2); 5; 6; 16; 23; 26; 16:2; 8(2); 13(6); 14(2); 15; 17; 18(2); 23; 17:2; 18:1(2); 5; 6(2); 7; 8; 9; 13; 14; 17; 22; 25; 30; 32(2); 38(2); 19:7(2); 8; 11; 13; 14; 16; 17; 21; 26(2); 27; 30(2); 33; 35(3); 38(2); 41; 20:5(2); 8; 9; 18; 20(2); 22(2); 25; 27; 21:1; 6; 7(2); 14; 15(2); 16(3); 17(3); 19(4); 20; 22; 23(2); **Acts** 1:2(3); 3; 4; 7; 9(2); 10; 17; 18; 22; 25(2); 26; 2:24; 25; 29; 30; 31; 33; 34; 40; 3:5; 7; 8; 10; 12; 13; 18; 20; 22; 4:9; 32; 35; 5:37; 6:10; 7:2(3); 4(2); 5(4); 8; 10; 12; 15; 21; 23; 24; 25; 26; 27; 29; 31(2); 36(2); 38; 44(3); 55; 60(3); 8:3; 6; 11; 13(2); 16; 18; 19; 27; 31(3); 32(3); 37; 38(2); 39; 40(2); 9:2(2); 3(2); 4; 5; 6; 8; 9; 10; 11; 12; 13; 14; 15; 16; 18; 19(2); 20(2); 21(2); 26(2); 27(3); 28; 29; 32; 33; 34; 38; 39; 41(2); 43; 10:3; 4(3); 6(2); 7; 8(2); 10(2); 17; 21; 23; 27(2); 28; 32(2); 35; 36; 39; 41; 42(2); 48; 11:13(2); 16; 17; 22; 23; 24; 26(2); 12:2; 3(2); 4(2); 7; 8(2); 9(2); 11; 12(2); 17(3); 19(2); 23(2); 13:11; 12; 17; 18; 19(2); 20; 22(3); 25(2); 28; 31; 33; 34(2); 35; 36; 37; 14:9; 10; 12; 17(2); 19; 20(2); 27; 15:8; 41; 16:1; 10; 18; 27; 29; 33(2); 34(2); 17:16; 17; 18(2); 24; 25(2); 27; 31(5); 18:3(2); 4; 6; 7; 11; 16; 18; 19(2); 20; 21; 22(2); 23(2); 25; 26; 27(2); 28; 19:2; 3; 8; 9; 21; 22(2); 25; 31; 34; 35; 41(2); 20:2(2); 3(2); 9; 11(2); 13; 14; 16(2); 17; 18; 28; 35; 36(2); 38; 21:4; 11(2); 14; 19(2); 33(2); 34(2); 35(2); 37; 40(2); 22:2(2); 8; 14; 21; 22; 24(2); 26; 27; 29(3); 30(3); 23:5; 6; 7; 15(2); 16; 17; 18; 20; 23; 25; 27; 34(4); 35(2); 24:2; 22; 23(2); 24; 25; 26(3); 25:1; 3; 4; 5; 6(2); 7; 8; 12; 16; 20; 22; 24; 25(2); 26:15; 23; 24; 25; 30; 32; 27:6; 35(4); 28:4; 5; 6(2); 15; 17; 23; 29; **Rom** 1:2; 28; 29; 3:26; 29(2); 4:2; 10; 11(3); 12; 13; 17; 18; 19(2); 20; 21(2); 6:7; 10(4); 7:1; 2; 8:9; 11; 24; 27(2); 29(3); 30(6); 32(2); 34; 9:15; 18(4); 19; 23(2); 24; 25; 28; 10:21; 11:2(2); 7; 21; 32; 12:3; 7; 8(4); 20; 13:4(3); 8; 14:2; 4; 5(2); 6(7); 9; 18; 22(2); 23(3); 15:10; 12; 21; **1Cor** 1:31; 2:14; 15(2); 16; 3:7(2); 8(2); 10; 14(2); 15(2); 18; 19; 4:4; 5:2; 6:16(2); 17; 18; 7:13; 20; 22(2); 24; 32(2); 33(2); 36(3); 37(2); 38(2); 8:2(3); 9:10(3); 10:12(2); 22; 11:7; 23; 24(2); 25(2); 26; 29; 12:11; 14:2(2); 3; 4(2); 5(3); 11; 13; 16(2); 24(2); 25; 15:4(2); 5; 6; 7; 8; 12; 15(2); 24(2); 25(2); 27(3); 16:10(2); 11; 12(2); **2Cor** 1:10; 21; 2:2; 5; 4:14; 5:5; 10; 15; 17; 21; 6:2; 15; 7:7(2); 15; 8:6(2); 9(2); 12; 15(2); 17(2); 23; 9:6(2); 7; 9(2); 10; 10:7(2); 17; 18; 11:4; 12:4; 6(2); 9; 13:4(2); **Gal** 1:4; 23(2); 2:8; 11; 12(2); 3:5(2); 16; 4:1(2); 23(2); 29; 5:3; 10(2); 6:3(2); 4; 7; 8(2); **Eph** 1:4; 6; 8; 9; 10; 20(2); 2:1; 4; 7; 14; 16; 3:3; 11; 16; 4:8(3); 9(2); 10(2); 11; 28; 5:14; 23; 26; 27; 28; 6:8(2); 22; **Phil** 1:6; 2:8; 22; 25; 26(2); 27; 30; 3:4(2); 21; **Col** 1:17; 18(2); 21; 2:13; 15; 18; 3:25(2); 4:8; 10; 13; **1Th** 1:10; 3:13; 4:8; 5:24; **2Th** 1:10; 2:4(2); 6; 7(2); 14; 3:6; 10; 14; **1Ti** 1:12; 3:1; 5; 6; 7(2); 5:8; 6:4; 15; **2Ti** 1:12; 16; 17(2); 18(2); 2:4; 5(2); 12; 13(2); 21; 4:11; 15; **Titus** 1:9(2); 2:8; 14; 3:5; 6; 11; **Philem** 1:13; 15; 18; **Heb** 1:2(2); 3; 4; 5(2); 6(2); 7; 8; 13; 2:5; 8(2); 9; 11(2); 14(2); 16(2); 17; 18(2); 3:3; 4; 17; 18; 4:3; 4; 7; 8; 10(2); 5:1; 2; 3; 4; 5; 6; 7(2); 8(3); 9; 13; 6:13(2); 15(2); 7:6; 8(2); 10; 13; 17; 20; 24; 25(2); 27(2); 8:4(2); 5(2); 6(2); 8; 13(2); 9:7; 12; 15; 19; 21; 25; 26(2); 28; 10:5(2); 8; 9(3); 12; 14; 15; 20; 23; 28; 29(2); 37; 11:4(3); 5(3); 6(3); 7; 8(4); 9; 10; 16; 17(2); 19; 21; 22; 23(2); 24; 26; 27(2); 28(2); 12:6(2); 7; 10; 17(4); 26; 13:5; 12; 23; **Jas** 1:6; 7; 9; 10(2); 12(2); 13(2); 14; 18; 23; 24(2); 25; 2:5; 10; 11; 13; 14; 21; 23; 4:6(2); 7; 8; 10; 11; 5:6; 7; 15; 17; 18; 20; **1Pet** 1:15; 2:6; 7; 23(3); 3:10; 13; 18; 19; 4:1; 2; 14(2); 5:6; 7; 8; **2Pet** 1:9(2); 17; 2:19; **1Jn** 1:7; 9; 2:2; 4; 6(3); 9(2); 10; 11(2); 17; 22(2); 23; 25; 28; 29; 3:2(2); 3; 5; 7(2); 8(2); 9(2); 10; 12; 14; 16; 23; 24(4); 4:4(2); 6(2); 8; 10; 13(2); 15; 16; 17; 18; 19; 20(5); 21; 5:5(2); 6; 9; 10(3); 12(2); 14; 15; 16(3); 18; **2Jn** 9(2); 11; **3Jn** 10(2); 11(2); **Jude** 6; 9; **Rev** 1:1; 2; 3; 7; 16; 17; 18; 2:1; 7; 11(2); 12; 17(2); 23; 26; 27; 29; 3:1; 5; 6; 7(4); 12; 13; 20; 22; 4:3; 5:7; 8; 6:2(2); 3; 9; 12; 7:2; 14; 15; 8:1; 3; 9:2; 5; 10:2(2); 3; 7(2); 9; 11; 11:5; 15; 12:9; 12(2); 13(2); 15; 13:6; 10(2); 11(2); 12; 13(2); 14; 15; 16; 17; 14:4; 10; 16; 17; 16:15(2); 16; 17:3; 10(2); 11; 14; 15; 18:2; 22; 19:2; 9(2); 10; 11(2); 12(2); 13; 15(3); 16; 17; 20; 20:2; 3(2); 6; 21:3; 5(2); 6; 7(2); 10; 15; 16; 17; 22:1; 6; 7; 9; 10; 11(4); 20

HER

Gen 2:22; 3:6(2); 15; 4:11; 12; 8:9(3); 11; 12:15(2); 16; 19(2); 16:2; 3(3); 4(2); 5; 6(3); 7; 9(2); 10; 11; 13; 17:15(2); 16(4); 19:33; 20:4; 6; 7; 13; 21:10; 12; 14(2); 16(2); 17; 19; 23:2; 24:15(2); 16(2); 17; 18(2); 20; 21; 22; 28; 43; 45(3); 46(2); 47(3); 51(2); 53(2); 55(2); 57; 58; 59; 60; 61; 64; 67(2); 25:1; 22; 23; 24(2); 26:9; 27:6; 15(3); 17; 42(2); 29:9; 12(2); 19(2); 20; 21; 23(2); 27; 28; 29; 31; 30:1; 3(2); 4(2); 9(2); 15; 16; 21; 22(2); 31:19; 35; 33:2; 7; 34:2(4); 8; 11(2); 35:17; 18; 20; 38:2(2); 8; 11; 14(3); 15(3); 16; 18(2); 19(3); 20; 22; 23(3); 24(2); 25; 26(2); 27(2); 39:7; 10(3); 12; 13; 14; 16; 40:10; 48:7; **Ex** 2:5(2); 8; 9; 10; 3:22(3); 4:25; 11:2; 15:20(2); 18:2; 3; 6(2); 21:4(2); 8(5); 9(2); 10(3); 11; 22(2); 22:16(2); 17(2); **Lev** 11:19; 12:2; 4(2); 5(2); 6; 7(3); 8; 15:19(3); 20; 21; 23; 24(2); 25(5); 26(4); 28; 29; 30(2); 33(3); 18:7; 11; 15; 17(5); 18(4); 19(2); 20; 25; 19:20; 29; 20:14; 17; 18(4); 21:3; 7; 9; 13; 22:13(3); 28; 25:19; 22; 26:4; 20; 34(2); 43; **Num** 5:13(3); 15(2); 16(2); 18; 19; 24; 27(6); 29; 30; 31; 12:12; 13; 14(4); 16:30; 32; 19:3(3); 4(2); 5(4); 8; 22:23; 25; 33; 25:8; 26:10; 59; 30:3(2); 4(8); 5(8); 6(2); 7(5); 8(6); 9(2); 10(2); 11(5); 12(6); 13(2); 14(6); 15; 16(2); 36:8; **Deut** 11:6; 17; 14:18; 20:7(2); 21:11(2); 12(3); 13(6); 14(5); 22:13(2); 14(4); 15; 16; 17; 19; 21(4); 23(2); 25(3); 27(2); 28(2); 29(3); 24:1(5); 3(5); 4(3); 25:5(4); 8; 11(2); 12(2); 28:30; 56(5); 57(3); 32:11(4); 22; **Josh** 2:14; 15; 17; 6:17; 22; 23(4); 25; 8:2(2); 10:1(2); 39; 13:17; 15:18(3); 19; 45(2); 47(4); 17:11(6); 16; 21:13(2); 14(2); 15(2); 16(3); 17(2); 18(2); 21(2); 22(2); 23(2); 24(2); 25(2); 27(2); 28(2); 29(2); 30(2); 31(2); 32(3); 34(2); 35(2); 36(2); 37(2); 38(2); 39(2); **Judg** 1:14(3); 15; 27(5); 4:5; 8; 18; 19; 20; 21; 22; 5:26(2); 27(2); 29(2); 11:26(2); 34; 35; 37; 38(3); 39(2); 13:3; 6; 9(2); 10; 13; 14(3); 14:2; 3; 8; 16; 17(2); 15:1; 2(6); 6(3); 16:1; 5(2); 7; 8; 9; 11; 13; 16; 17(2); 18(2); 19; 19:2; 3(5); 25(4); 26; 27(2); 28(2); 29(3); 20:6(2); **Ruth** 1:3; 5(2); 6; 7(2); 8(2); 9; 10; 14(2); 15(2); 18(2); 22(2); 2:1; 2; 3; 10; 11; 14(2); 15(2); 16(2); 18(2); 19(3); 20(2); 22; 23; 3:1(2); 5; 6(2); 7; 15; 16(3); 4:13(2); 16; 17; **1Sa** 1:4(2); 5; 6(4); 7; 8(2); 12; 13(3); 14; 18(2); 19; 22; 23(3); 24; 2:19; 4:19(4); 20(3); 21(2); 18:17; 21; 25:19(2); 20; 23; 35(2);

39; 40; 41; 42; 28:7(2); 10; 13; 14; **2Sa** 3:15(2); 16(3); 6:16; 23; 11:4(4); 26(2); 27; 12:24(2); 13:1; 2; 5; 6; 8; 10; 11(2); 14(3); 15(4); 16; 17; 18(3); 19(5); 20(3); 14:2; 3; 4; 5; 17:8; 20:17; 22; 21:10; **1Kin** 1:2(3); 3; 4; 31; 2:19(2); 20; 3:1; 17; 20(2); 26(3); 27; 9:24(2); 10:2; 3(3); 5; 13(4); 14:5(2); 6; 15:13(2); 17:10; 11; 13; 15; 19(2); 20; 21:6; **2Kin** 4:2; 5(3); 6(2); 9; 12; 13; 14(2); 15(2); 17; 20; 22; 24; 25; 26(2); 27(4); 30; 36; 37; 5:3; 6:28; 29(2); 8:2; 3(2); 5(3); 6; 9:10; 22; 30(2); 33(4); 34; 35(3); 11:1; 3; 14; 15(3); 16; 19:21; 22:14; **1Chr** 2:18; 5:16; 6:57; 58(2); 59(2); 60(3); 67(2); 68(2); 69(2); 70(2); 71(2); 72(2); 73(2); 74(2); 75(2); 76(3); 77(2); 78(2); 79(2); 80(2); 81(2); 7:29(4); 15:29; 18:1; **2Chr** 8:11; 9:1; 2(3); 4; 12(3); 11:20; 15:16(2); 22:10; 23:13; 14(3); 15(2); 34:22; 36:21; **Est** 1:11; 19; 2:1; 7; 9(6); 10(3); 11; 13(2); 14; 15(2); 17(2); 20(3); 4:4(2); 5; 8(3); 5:1; 3; 12; 8:1; **Job** 2:10; 5:16; 9:6; 21:10; 31:10; 18; 39:14; 16(2); 17(2); 26; 27; 29; 30; **Ps** 34:2; 45:13; 14(2); 46:5(2); 48:3; 12; 13(2); 55:11; 58:4; 67:6; 68:13; 31; 69:15; 80:11(2); 12(2); 84:3; 85:12; 87:5(2); 102:13; 14; 104:17; 107:42; 123:2; 132:15(2); 16(2); 137:5; **Prov** 1:20; 21; 2:4(2); 16; 17(2); 18(2); 19; 3:15; 16(2); 17(2); 18(2); 4:6(2); 8(2); 13(2); 5:3; 4; 5(2); 6; 8(2); 19(3); 6:6; 8(2); 25(3); 29; 7:5; 8(2); 11(2); 21(2); 22; 25(2); 26; 27; 8:1; 9:1(2); 2(3); 3; 14; 18; 12:4; 14:1(2); 17:12; 25; 27:8; 16; 30:20; 23; 28; 31:10; 11(2); 12; 13; 14; 15(2); 16; 17(2); 18(2); 19(2); 20(2); 21(2); 22; 23; 25; 26(2); 27; 28(4); 31(4); **Eccl** 7:26(3); 11:5; **Song** 2:13; 3:4; 6:9(6); 8:5; 9(2); **Is** 1:27; 3:26; 4:5; 5:14; 7:16; 9:1(2); 10:11(2); 13:10; 13; 22(2); 16:8; 21:9; 23:3; 7(2); 17; 18(3); 24:2; 26:17(2); 21(2); 27:2; 29:7(3); 34:12; 13; 15(3); 16; 37:22; 40:2(4); 49:15(2); 51:3(3); 18(2); 52:11; 53:7; 61:10; 11; 65:18; 19; 66:7; 8; 10(4); 11(2); 12(3); **Jer** 2:23; 24(6); 32(2); 3:1; 7; 8(3); 9; 10(2); 20; 4:17; 31(3); 5:10(2); 6:3(2); 4; 5; 6; 7(3); 8:7; 19(2); 9:20; 12:7; 9; 15:9; 17:8(2); 19:15; 20:17; 30:18; 31:8; 15(2); 44:17; 18; 19(4); 25; 46:21(2); 22; 23; 48:4; 15; 19; 28; 41; 49:2; 4; 14; 19(2); 22; 24(2); 26(2); 50:2(2); 3(2); 9; 10; 13; 14; 15(6); 26(5); 27; 29(3); 30(2); 35(2); 36; 37(2); 38; 44(2); 51:2(3); 3(2); 4; 6(2); 7; 8(2); 9(2); 27(3); 28; 30(2); 33(2); 36(2); 43; 45; 47(3); 48; 52(2); 53(2); 55(2); 56(2); 57(5); 58; 64; **Lam** 1:2(7); 3(2); 4(3); 5(5); 6(2); 7(7); 8(3); 9(3); 10(2); 11; 17(2); 2:5; 7; 9(5); 16; 4:6; 7; 13(3); **Eze** 5:5; 6; 12:19; 13:16; 16:2; 32; 44; 45(2); 46(2); 48; 49(2); 53(2); 55(2); 57; 17:7(3); 9; 19:2; 3; 5(2); 11(3); 12(2); 14(2); 22:2(2); 3; 10; 24; 25(2); 26; 27; 28; 23:4; 5(2); 7; 8(5); 9(2); 10(5); 11(5); 12; 14; 16; 17(3); 18(4); 19(2); 31; 42; 43(2); 44; 24:7(2); 8; 12(3); 26:4(4); 6; 17; 28:22(2); 23(4); 29:12; 19(3); 30:4(2); 6; 7; 8; 18(5); 31:4(2); 32:7; 16(4); 18; 20(2); 22; 23(2); 24(2); 25(3); 26(2); 29(2); 33:28; 34:27(2); 36:38; 44:22; **Dan** 11:6(3); 7; 17; **Hos** 1:6; 2:2(6); 3(5); 4; 6; 7; 8(2); 9; 10(3); 11(5); 12(2); 13(4); 14(3); 15(3); 17; 23(2); 3:1; 2; 3; 4:18; 19(2); 9:2; 10; 10:7; 11; 14; 13:8; 16; **Joel** 1:8; 2:16; 22; 3:17; **Amos** 4:3; 5:2(2); **Obad** 1; **Jonah** 1:15; 2:6; **Mic** 1:9; 4:6(3); 7(2); 11; 7:5; 6(2); 10(2); **Nah** 2:7(2); 13; 3:4(2); 7; 8; 9; 10(3); **Zeph** 2:14; 15(2); 3:1; 2; 3(3); 4(2); 19(2); **Hag** 1:10; 2:3; **Zec** 2:5(2); 5:11; 7:7; 8:2; 12(2); 9:4(2); 5; 12:6; 14:10; **Mal** 3:11; **Mt** 1:6; 19(3); 20; 25(2); 2:18; 5:28(2); 31; 32(2); 8:15(2); 9:18; 22; 25; 10:35(2); 11:19; 14:4; 7; 8; 9; 11; 15:23(2); 28(2); 19:7; 9; 20:20; 21; 21:2; 22:28; 23:37(2); 24:29; 26:13; **Mk** 1:30; 31(3); 5:23; 29(2); 32; 33; 34; 41; 43; 6:17; 23; 24; 26; 28; 7:26; 27; 29; 30(2); 10:4; 11; 12; 12:21; 22; 23; 44(2); 13:24; 28; 14:5; 6(2); 9; 16:11; **Lk** 1:5; 28; 29; 30; 35; 36(2); 38; 41; 45; 56(2); 58(4); 61; 2:7; 19; 22; 36; 51; 4:38; 39(2); 7:12; 13(3); 35; 38; 44; 47; 48; 8:43; 44; 48; 52; 54; 55(2); 56; 10:38; 40; 41; 42; 11:27; 12:53(2); 13:12(3); 13; 34(2); 15:9(2); 16:18(2); 18:5(2); 20:30; 31; 33; 21:4; **Jn** 2:4; 4:7; 10; 13; 16; 17; 21; 26; 27; 28(2); 8:3; 7; 10; 11; 11:1; 2; 5; 23; 25; 28(2); 31(3); 33(2); 40; 12:3; 7; 16:21; 18:16; 19:27; 20:13; 15; 16; 17; 18; **Acts** 5:8; 9; 10(4); 7:21; 8:27; 9:37; 40; 41(3); 12:15; 16:15; 16; 18; 19; 19:27; 21:3; 27:15; 32; **Rom** 7:2(2); 3(2); 9:12; 25; 16:2(2); **1Cor** 7:2; 4; 10; 11(2); 12; 13(2); 34; 36; 38(2); 39(2); 11:5(2); 6(2); 10; 15(3); 13:5; **Gal** 4:25; 30; **Eph** 5:33; **1Th** 2:7; **Jas** 1:4; 5:18; **2Pet** 2:22; **2Jn** 1; **Rev** 2:21(2); 22(2); 23; 6:13; 12:1(2); 4; 5; 6; 14; 15; 16; 17; 14:8; 18; 16:19; 17:2; 4(2); 5; 6; 7; 16(3); 18:3(3); 4(3); 5(2); 6(4); 7(2); 8(2); 9(4); 10; 11; 15(2); 18; 19; 20(2); 24; 19:2(2); 3; 8; 21:2; 11; 22:2

HERE

Gen 16:13; 19:12; 15; 21:23; 22:1; 5; 7; 11; 24:13; 27:1; 18; 31:11; 37; 37:13; 40:15; 42:33; 46:2; 47:23; **Ex** 3:4; 24:14; 33:16; **Num** 14:40; 22:8; 19; 23:1(2); 15; 29(2); 32:6; 16; **Deut** 5:3; 31; 12:8; 29:15(2); **Josh** 18:6; 8; 21:9; **Judg** 4:20; 18:3; 19:9; 24; 20:7; **Ruth** 2:8; 4:1; 2; **1Sa** 1:26; 3:4; 5; 6; 8; 16; 9:8; 11; 12:3; 14:34; 16:11; 21:8; 9(2); 22:12; 23:3; 29:3; **2Sa** 1:7; 11:12; 15:26; 18:30; 20:4; 24:22; **1Kin** 2:30; 18:8; 11; 14; 19:9; 13; 20:40; 22:7; **2Kin** 2:2; 4; 6; 3:11(2); 7:3; 4; 10:23; **1Chr** 29:17; **2Chr** 18:6; **Job** 38:11; 35; **Ps** 132:14; **Is** 6:8; 21:9; 22:16(3); 28:10; 13; 52:5; 58:9; **Eze** 8:6; 9; 17; **Hos** 7:9; **Mt** 12:41; 42; 14:8; 17; 16:28; 17:4(2); 20:6; 24:2; 23; 26:36; 38; 28:6; **Mk** 6:3; 8:4; 9:1; 5; 13:1; 21; 14:32; 34; 16:6; **Lk** 4:23; 9:12; 27; 33; 11:31; 32; 17:21; 23; 19:20; 22:38; 24:6; 41; **Jn** 6:9; 11:21; 32; **Acts** 4:10; 8:36; 9:10; 14; 10:33; 16:28; 24:19; 20; 25:24(2); **Col** 4:9; **Heb** 7:8; 13:14; **Jas** 2:3(2); **1Pet** 1:17; **Rev** 13:10; 18; 14:12(2); 17:9

HEREAFTER

Is 41:23; **Eze** 20:39; **Dan** 2:29; 45; **Mt** 26:64; **Mk** 11:14; **Lk** 22:69; **Jn** 1:51; 13:7; 14:30; **1Ti** 1:16; **Rev** 1:19; 4:1; 9:12

HERS

Deut 21:15; **1Sa** 25:42; **2Kin** 8:6; **Job** 39:16

HERSELF

Gen 18:12; 20:5; 24:65; 38:14; **Ex** 2:5; **Lev** 15:28; 21:9; **Num** 22:25; 30:3; **Judg** 5:29; **Ruth** 2:10; **1Sa** 4:19; 25:23; 41; **2Sa** 11:2; **1Kin** 14:5; **2Kin** 4:37; **Job** 39:18; **Ps** 84:3; **Prov** 31:22; **Is** 5:14; 34:14; 61:10; **Jer** 3:11; 4:31; 49:24; **Eze** 22:3(2); 23:7; 24:12; **Hos** 2:13; **Zec** 9:3; **Mt** 9:21; **Mk** 4:28; **Lk** 1:24; 13:11; **Jn** 20:14; 16; **Heb** 11:11; **Rev** 2:20; 18:7; 19:7

HIGH

Gen 7:19; 14:18; 19; 20; 22; 29:7; **Ex** 14:8; 25:20; 37:9; 39:31; **Lev** 21:10; 26:22; 30; **Num** 11:31; 20:17; 19; 21:22; 28; 22:41; 23:3; 24:16; 33:3; 52; 35:25; 28(2); **Deut** 2:27; 3:5; 12:2; 26:19; 28:1; 43; 52; 32:8; 13; 27; 33:29; **Josh** 20:6; **Judg** 5:18; **1Sa** 9:12; 13; 14; 19; 25; 10:5; 13; 13:6; **2Sa** 1:19; 25; 22:3; 14; 34; 49; 23:1; **1Kin** 3:2; 3; 4; 6:10; 23; 7:15; 35; 9:8; 11:7; 12:31; 32; 13:2; 32; 33(2); 14:23(2); 15:14; 21:9; 12; 22:43(2); **2Kin** 12:3(2); 10; 14:4(2); 15:4(2); 35(2); 16:4; 17:9; 10; 11; 29; 32(2); 18:4; 22; 19:22; 21:3; 22:4; 8; 23:4; 5; 8(2); 9; 13; 15(3); 19; 20; **1Chr** 11:23; 14:2; 16:39; 17:17; 21:29; **2Chr** 1:3; 13; 3:15; 6:13; 7:21; 11:15; 14:3; 5; 15:17; 17:6; 20:19; 33; 21:11; 23:20; 24:11; 27:3; 28:4; 25; 31:1; 32:12; 33:3; 17; 19; 34:3; 4; 9; **Neh** 3:1; 20; 25; 13:28; **Est** 5:14; 7:9; **Job** 5:11; 11:8; 16:19; 21:22; 22:12; 25:2; 31:2; 38:15; 39:18; 27; 41:34; **Ps** 7:7; 17; 9:2; 18:2; 27; 33; 21:7; 46:4; 47:2; 49:2; 50:14; 56:2; 57:2; 62:9; 68:15; 16; 18; 69:29; 71:19; 73:11; 75:5; 77:10; 78:17; 35; 56; 58; 69; 82:6; 83:18; 89:13; 91:1; 9; 14; 92:1; 8; 93:4; 97:9; 99:2; 101:5; 103:11; 104:18; 107:11; 41; 113:4; 5; 131:1; 138:6; 139:6; 144:2; 149:6; 150:5; **Prov** 8:2; 9:14; 18:11; 21:4; 24:7; **Eccl** 12:5; **Is** 2:13; 14; 15; 6:1; 10:12; 33; 13:2; 14:14; 15:2; 16:12; 22:16; 24:18; 21(2); 25:12; 26:5; 30:13; 25(2); 32:15; 33:5; 16; 36:7; 37:23; 40:9; 26; 41:18; 49:9; 52:13; 57:7; 15(2); 58:4; 14; **Jer** 2:20; 3:2; 6; 21; 4:11; 7:29; 31; 12:12; 14:6; 17:2; 3; 12; 19:5; 20:2; 25:30; 26:18; 31:21; 32:35; 48:35; 49:16; 51:58; **Lam** 3:35; 38; **Eze** 1:18; 6:3; 6; 13; 16:16; 24; 25; 31; 39; 17:22(2); 24; 20:28; 29; 21:26; 31:3; 4; 34:6; 14; 36:2; 40:2; 42; 41:22; 43:7; **Dan** 3:26; 4:2; 17; 24; 25; 32; 34; 5:18; 21; 7:18; 22; 25(2); 27; 8:3; **Hos** 7:16; 10:8; 11:7; **Amos** 4:13; 7:9; **Obad** 3; **Mic** 1:3; 5; 3:12; 6:6; **Hab** 2:9; 3:10; 19; **Zeph** 1:16; **Hag** 1:1; 12; 14; 2:2; 4; **Zec** 3:1; 8; 6:11; **Mt** 4:8; 17:1; 26:3; 51; 57; 58; 62; 63; 65; **Mk** 2:26; 5:7; 6:21; 9:2; 14:47; 53; 54; 60; 61; 63; 66; **Lk** 1:78; 3:2; 4:5; 8:28; 22:50; 54; 24:49; **Jn** 11:49; 51; 18:10; 13; 15(2); 16; 19; 22; 24; 26; 19:31; **Acts** 4:6(2); 5:17; 21; 24; 27; 7:1; 48; 9:1; 13:17; 16:17; 22:5; 23:2; 4; 5; 24:1; 25:2; **Rom** 12:16; 13:11; **2Cor** 10:5; **Eph** 4:8; 6:12; **Phil** 3:14; **Heb** 1:3; 2:17; 3:1; 4:14; 15; 5:1; 5; 10; 6:20; 7:1; 26; 27; 28; 8:1; 3; 9:7; 11; 25; 10:21; 13:11; **Rev** 21:10; 12

HIM

Gen 1:27; 2:15; 18(2); 20; 3:9; 23; 4:7; 8; 15(4); 19; 26; 5:1; 24; 6:6; 22; 7:5; 7; 16(2); 23; 8:1; 8; 9(2); 11; 12; 18; 9:8; 24; 10:21; 12:3; 4(2); 7; 20(2); 13:1; 11; 14; 14:5; 17(2); 19; 20; 15:4; 5(2); 6; 7; 9; 10; 12; 16:1; 12; 13; 17:1; 3; 17; 19(2); 20(4); 22; 23; 27; 18:1; 2; 9; 10; 18; 19(3); 29; 30; 19:3; 5; 6; 16(3); 21; 26; 30; 32; 34(2); 35; 20:3; 6; 9; 14; 21:2; 3(2); 4; 5; 7; 16(2); 18(2); 21; 22:1; 2; 3(2); 9(2); 11; 12; 13(2); 23:5; 14; 24:5; 6; 9; 18; 19; 24; 25; 32; 33; 35; 36; 47; 54; 25:2; 9; 21; 33; 26:2; 7; 9; 12; 14; 20; 24; 26; 31; 32(2); 27:1(2); 12; 13; 22; 23(2); 25(2); 26; 27(2); 32; 33; 37(3); 39; 41; 42; 44; 45; 28:1(3); 6(4); 29:5; 13(4); 14(2); 20; 23; 28; 30; 34; 30:4; 16; 20; 27; 29; 37; 31:2; 7; 14; 15; 20; 23(3); 24; 32; 32:1; 3; 6; 7; 11; 19; 20; 21; 24; 25(2); 27; 29(2); 31; 33:1; 4(3); 11; 13; 17; 34:6; 8; 35:2; 6; 7; 9; 10; 11; 13(2); 14; 15; 18; 26; 29; 36:5; 37:3; 4(3); 5; 8(2); 10(2); 11; 13; 14(2); 15(2); 18(3); 20(3); 21(2); 22(4); 23; 24(2); 27(2); 33; 35(2); 36; 38:5; 7; 10; 14; 18; 39:1(2); 3; 4(2); 5; 12(2); 15; 17; 19; 20(2); 21(2); 23; 40:7; 8; 9; 12; 23; 41:12; 13; 14; 33; 34; 42; 43(3); 45; 50; 42:4; 6; 8; 10; 16; 24; 29; 31; 37(3); 38; 43:3; 5; 7; 9(4); 19; 26(2); 32(2); 33; 34(2); 44:7; 9; 14; 18; 20; 21(2); 24; 28; 29; 32; 45:1(2); 3; 9; 15; 26; 27(2); 28; 46:5; 6; 7(2); 20; 27; 28; 29; 31; 47:7; 18(2); 29; 31; 48:1; 10; 13; 17; 49:9; 10; 19; 23(3); 26; 50:1(2); 3(2); 7; 9; 12; 13(2); 14; 15; 17; 26; **Ex** 1:16; 2:2(2); 3(2); 4; 6; 10(2); 12; 13; 20; 22; 3:2; 4; 18; 4:2; 6; 11; 13; 15; 16; 18; 23; 24(2); 26; 27(2); 28(2); 6:2; 20(2); 23(2); 25(2); 7:16; 8:1; 20; 9:1; 13; 29; 10:1; 3; 7; 28; 12:4; 44; 48; 49; 13:14; 19; 14:6; 15:2(2); 25; 16:8; 17:10; 12; 18:7; 17; 19:3; 7; 19; 24; 20:7; 21:3; 4(2); 6(3); 10; 13; 14(2); 16; 19(2); 22; 26; 27; 29; 30(2); 31; 36; 22:2; 3(2); 7; 12; 13; 17; 21; 25(2); 26; 23:4; 5(3); 21(3); 24:2; 14; 18; 28:1; 3; 41; 43(2); 29:5; 7; 17; 21(2); 29; 30:21; 31:3; 6; 18; 32:1(2); 23; 26(2); 33; 33:4; 15; 34:4; 5; 6; 20; 29; 30; 31; 32; 34; 35; 35:5; 21; 31; 36:2; 3; 38:23; 40:13(2); 16; **Lev** 1:1; 3; 4(2); 4:3; 12; 14; 19; 21; 26(2); 31(2); 35; 5:2; 3; 4; 6; 10(2); 13(2); 16(2); 18(2); 6:2; 4; 5; 7(2); 7:18; 20; 8:2; 4; 7(6); 8; 12(2); 30(2); 9:9; 12; 13; 18; 13:3(2); 4; 5(2); 6(2); 8; 10; 11(2); 12; 13; 14; 15; 17(2); 20; 21; 22; 23; 25; 26; 27(2); 28; 30; 31; 33; 34; 36; 37; 44; 46; 14:4; 7(2); 11; 12; 14; 17; 18(2); 19; 20; 21; 25; 28; 29(2); 31; 32; 15:7; 8; 10; 14; 15; 16; 24; 32(3); 33(2); 16:9; 10(2); 21(2); 22; 17:10; 18:6; 19:13(2); 17; 22(2); 33; 34; 20:2; 3; 4; 5(2); 6; 9; 21:2; 3; 8; 12; 15; 17; 22:3; 4; 24:9; 11; 12; 14(3); 16; 19; 20; 23(2); 25:27; 28(2); 30; 35; 36; 37(2); 39; 41; 43; 47; 48; 49(3); 50(4); 52(2); 53(2); 54; 26:46; 27:8(2); 18; 19; 23; 24(2); **Num** 2:5; 12; 20; 27; 3:6; 9; 42; 4:49; 5:7; 8; 12; 14(2); 30; 6:9; 11; 7:89(3); 8:2; 9:7; 14; 10:30; 11:20; 25(2); 29; 30; 12:6(2); 8; 13:27; 31; 14:24(2); 36; 15:28(2); 29(2); 31; 33(2); 34(2); 35; 36(2); 16:5(4); 10; 11; 25; 40; 17:6; 11; 19:13(2); 18; 20; 20:9; 18; 19; 20; 21; 21:24; 34(3); 35(2); 22:5; 7; 16; 20; 22(2); 32; 36; 40; 41; 23:4; 6; 9(2); 13; 14; 17(3); 21; 24:2; 8; 9; 17(2); 19; 25:12; 13; 26:54; 27:11; 18; 19(2); 20; 21(2); 22(2); 23(2); 31:17; 18; 35; 32:15; 16; 21; 35:16; 17; 18; 19(2); 20(2); 21(3); 22(2); 23(2); 25; 27; 30; 32; 33; **Deut** 1:3; 16; 36; 38; 2:24; 30(2); 33(2); 3:2(3); 3(2); 28(2); 4:7; 20; 25; 29(2); 34; 35; 42; 5:11; 6:13; 16; 7:9; 10(4); 8:6; 9:18; 20; 23; 10:8; 9; 12; 18; 20(2); 11:13; 22; 13:4(3); 8(4); 9(3); 10; 14:27; 15:8(2); 9; 10(2); 12; 13(2); 14(2); 18; 17:7(2); 15; 18; 19; 18:4; 5(2); 15; 18; 19; 20; 22; 19:6(3); 11(3); 12(2); 13; 16; 19; 20:5; 6; 7; 8; 21:1; 2; 5; 15; 17; 18; 19(2); 21; 22; 23; 22:2(2); 4; 18; 19; 26; 23:10; 16(2); 24:1; 7(2); 13; 15; 25:2; 3(2); 5; 8(2); 9; 10; 11(3); 26:3; 28:44; 55; 29:15(2); 20(2); 21; 30:20; 31:7; 14; 29; 32:10(4); 12(2); 13(2); 15; 16(2); 33:7(3); 9; 11(2); 12(2); 16(2); 24(2); 34:1; 4; 6; 9(2); 11; **Josh** 1:18; 2:19; 23; 4:14; 5:3; 13(3); 14; 6:5; 7; 20; 7:3; 19; 24; 25; 26; 8:11; 14; 23; 9:6; 9(2); 10:7; 15; 23; 24; 29; 31; 33(2); 34; 36; 38; 43; 11:7; 9; 13:1; 14:6; 7; 13; 15:16; 17; 18(2); 19:50; 20:4(2); 5(2); 22:5(2); 14; 27; 30; 24:3(2); 14; 22; 30; 33(2); **Judg** 1:3; 5; 6(2); 7; 12; 13; 14(2); 15; 24; 2:9; 3:10; 13; 15; 16; 19(2); 20; 23; 27; 28; 31; 4:6; 7; 10; 13; 14; 18(2); 19(2); 21; 22(2); 5:13; 25; 31; 6:12(2); 13; 14; 15; 16; 17; 19; 20; 23; 25; 27; 31(5); 32(2); 34; 35; 7:1; 3; 5; 8; 9; 19; 8:1(2); 3; 4; 8(2); 14(2); 31; 9:3; 4(2); 16; 19; 24; 25; 26; 28(2); 33; 34; 35; 36; 38(2); 40(2); 44; 48(3); 54(3); 10:3; 6; 11:2(2); 3; 11; 15; 19; 28; 34; 36; 12:5; 6(3); 8; 11; 13; 13:6; 10; 11; 12; 18; 23; 24; 25; 14:3; 5; 6(2); 11(2); 13; 16; 17(2); 18; 19; 15:1; 10; 12; 13(3); 14(2); 16:2(3); 5(4); 8; 9; 12(2); 14; 15; 16(2); 19(4); 20; 21(3); 24; 25; 26; 31(3); 17:9(2); 10; 11; 18:3; 5; 15; 19; 25; 26; 19:1; 2(2); 3(4); 4(2); 7; 9; 10(2); 12; 15; 18; 21; 22; 25; 28; 20:23; 21:5; **Ruth** 2:2; 4; 10; 3:13; 4:1; 15; **1Sa** 1:11; 17; 20; 22; 23(2); 24(3); 27; 28; 2:3; 16(2); 19(2); 25(2); 27; 28; 35; 36; 3:7; 13; 18(4); 19; 5:3; 4; 6:3; 4; 8; 7:3; 9; 8:5; 10; 12; 9:5; 6; 13(2); 16; 17; 10:1; 9; 10(2); 11; 14; 16; 19; 21; 23; 24(2); 26; 27(2); 11:3; 5; 12:14; 24; 13:2; 7; 8; 10(2); 14(2); 15(2); 14:2; 7; 13(2); 17; 20; 34; 37; 39; 43; 52(2); 15:2; 12; 13; 16; 28; 32; 16:1; 3; 6; 7; 8; 11; 12(2); 13; 14; 15; 17; 18; 21(2); 23; 17:7; 8; 9(2); 13; 20; 24; 25(3); 26; 27(2); 30(2); 31; 32; 33; 35(5); 38; 39; 40; 41; 42; 50; 51; 57(2); 58; 18:1; 2(2); 3; 4; 5(2); 8; 12; 13(3); 14; 15; 17(2); 20; 21(3); 24; 27; 28; 19:4; 7; 8; 11(3); 15(2); 18(2); 23; 20:2; 7; 17(2); 24; 26; 30; 31; 32; 33(2); 34; 35; 36; 40; 21:1; 5; 6; 11(2); 14; 22:1; 2(2); 4; 6(2); 7; 10(3); 13(3); 15; 17; 23:3; 4; 7; 9; 14(2); 17; 20; 22; 23; 25; 24:1; 4(2); 5; 6; 8; 19; 25:1(2); 5; 6; 12; 17; 21; 22; 25; 35; 36(2); 37(2); 39; 40; 26:2; 3; 5; 7; 8(2); 9; 10; 19; 24; 27:2; 4; 6; 12; 28:3(2); 6; 7; 8(2); 9; 17; 20; 21; 23; 29:3; 4(4); 6; 30:4; 6; 8; 9; 11(3); 12(2); 13; 15; 16; 21; 31:3; 5; **2Sa** 1:3(2); 4; 5; 6(2); 7; 8; 10(2); 11; 13; 14; 15(2); 16; 2:1; 3; 5; 8; 9; 20; 21(2); 23(2); 32; 3:9; 11; 16; 20(2); 22; 23(2); 24; 26; 27(3); 31; 34; 4:4; 6; 7(3); 10(3); 5:10; 12; 13; 14; 25; 6:2; 7; 10; 12; 16; 7:1; 14; 15; 23; 8:4; 10(4); 13; 9:1; 2(2); 3; 4; 5; 7; 9; 10; 10:2; 9; 12; 13(2); 17; 11:1; 4; 7(2); 8; 13(3); 15; 21; 22; 25; 27; 12:1(2); 3(2); 4(2); 9; 17(2); 18(3); 20; 21; 23(2); 24; 13:2; 4(2); 5(2); 6; 7; 9(2); 11; 12; 16; 17; 25(2); 26; 27(2); 28; 29; 34; 14:3; 6; 7(2); 10; 14; 24(2); 25; 26; 29(2); 31; 32; 33; 15:1(2); 2; 3; 4; 5(4); 9; 14; 16; 17; 18(2); 22; 24; 26(2); 30; 32; 16:1; 10(2); 11(3); 13(2); 14; 15; 18; 17:2(3); 6; 10; 12(4); 16; 22; 23; 24; 29; 18:1; 9; 11(3); 15; 17(2); 19; 20; 23; 30; 19:17(2); 23; 25; 29; 30; 31; 37(2); 38; 39; 40; 41; 20:5; 6(2); 7; 8; 9; 10(2); 11(2); 12(2); 14; 15; 17; 21; 21:4; 15; 17(3); 21; 22:1; 3; 12; 13; 24; 31; 23:9; 10; 11; 21(2); 23; 24:2; 10; 13(3); 16; 18; 20; 22; **1Kin** 1:1; 2(2); 4; 5(2); 6(2); 7; 13; 17; 20; 25; 27; 33; 34; 35(2); 38; 40; 41; 42; 44(2); 45; 52(2); 53(2); 2:8; 9(2); 16; 19; 22(2); 25; 29; 30; 31(3); 34(2); 36; 42; 46; 3:6(2); 11; 16; 28; 4:10; 12; 13(2); 24; 5:1; 3; 12; 8:5(2); 24; 25; 31(2); 32; 57; 58; 62; 65; 9:2; 3; 12(2); 10:1; 2; 11:9; 10; 17; 18(3); 19; 20; 22; 23; 24; 28; 29; 30; 34; 12:1; 3; 7; 8(3); 10(2); 13; 18(2); 20(2); 13:4(3); 6; 11; 13; 14(2); 15; 18(3); 19; 20; 23; 24(2); 26(5); 27; 29; 30; 31; 33; 14:3; 10(2); 11(2); 13(3); 14; 18(2); 22; 15:3; 4(2); 5; 8; 27(2); 28; 29; 16:4(2); 7(2); 9; 10(2); 11; 17; 18; 21; 25; 30; 31(2); 33; 17:2; 6; 8; 17; 19(3); 21; 22; 23(2); 18:7(2); 8; 15; 16; 17; 21(3); 24; 30; 33; 19:5(2); 6; 7; 9(2); 13; 15; 17(2); 18; 19(3); 20; 21(2); 20:1; 2; 7; 8(2); 9; 10; 11(2); 16; 17; 22; 23; 31; 33(4); 34(3); 35; 36(4); 37(2); 40; 41; 42; 21:4(2); 5(2); 6; 7; 10(4); 13(4); 19(2); 21(2); 24(2); 22:7; 8; 11; 13; 15(2); 16; 19; 21; 22(2); 26; 27; 32; 33; 53; **2Kin** 1:5; 6(2); 8; 9(3); 10; 11(2); 12; 13(2); 15(3); 16; 2:2; 3; 4; 5; 6; 12; 13; 14; 15(3); 16(3); 17(2); 18; 20; 23(2); 3:11; 12(2); 13; 15; 26(2); 27(2); 4:1; 5; 8; 10; 12; 13; 19; 20(2); 21(2); 23; 27; 29(2); 31(2); 35; 36; 38; 5:1; 3; 5; 6; 8; 10; 13; 15; 16; 19(2); 20(2); 21(3); 23(2); 25; 26; 6:6; 10(2); 13(2); 15; 18; 26; 28; 29(2); 31; 32(5); 33; 7:17(2); 20(2); 8:6; 7; 8; 9(3); 10(2); 14; 19(2); 21(2); 29; 9:1; 2(2); 6; 8(2); 11; 13; 15; 17; 18; 21; 25(2); 26; 27(2); 28(2); 32; 36; 10:3; 4; 7; 8; 9; 11; 15(6); 16; 17; 18; 22; 24(2); 35; 11:2(3); 4; 8; 12(4); 15; 12:2; 21(2); 13:4; 9; 14; 15(2); 19; 20; 25; 14:19(3); 20; 21; 15:7; 10(3); 14; 16; 19; 25(4); 30(2); 16:5; 9; 17:2; 3(2); 4(2); 17; 27; 36(3); 18:5(3); 6; 7(2); 15; 21; 36(2); 37; 19:3; 7(2); 16; 21; 37; 20:1(2); 4; 14; 21:6; 11; 23; 22:18; 23:1; 2; 17; 18; 25(4); 26; 29(3); 30(5); 33; 24:1; 2; 12; 25:5(2); 6(2); 7(2); 25(2); 28(2); 29; 30; **1Chr** 2:3(2); 4; 9; 19(2); 21; 24; 29; 35; 3:1; 4; 5; 4:6; 9; 10; 5:2; 20; 7:22; 9:20; 10:3; 9; 14; 11:9; 10(2); 11; 12; 23(2); 25; 42; 12:19; 20; 22; 23; 27; 13:10; 14:1; 2; 10; 14; 16; 17; 15:1; 2; 13; 27; 29; 16:5; 9(2); 29; 30; 17:13(2); 14; 25; 18:4; 10(3); 19:2(2); 10; 14(2); 17; 20:7; 21:11; 12; 15; 20; 26; 28; 22:6; 9; 23:13; 24:19; 26:5; 10; 27:7; 28:6; 9(3); 29:22; 23; 25(2); 30; **2Chr** 1:1(2); 3; 7; 2:3(2); 4(2); 6(4); 14; 15; 5:6; 6:15; 16; 22(2); 23; 7:8; 12; 8:18; 9:1; 10:1; 3; 7; 8(3); 10(2); 18(2); 11:13; 15; 18; 19; 20; 22; 12:1; 3; 12(2); 13:3; 5; 7; 10; 11; 19; 20; 14:1; 5; 6; 7; 10; 13; 15:2(4); 4; 5(2); 9(2); 15; 16:7; 9; 10(2); 14(3); 17:11; 14; 15(2); 16(2); 17; 18(2); 18:2(4); 3; 6; 7; 10; 12; 14; 15; 20(2); 21; 25; 26; 30; 31(3); 32; 19:2; 20:30; 36; 21:7; 9(2); 12; 17; 18; 19; 20; 22:6; 9(4); 11(4); 23:1; 11(4); 14; 16; 24:3; 6; 16; 21(2); 22; 23; 25(6); 26; 27; 25:3; 7; 10; 13; 15(2); 16(2); 23; 27(3); 28(2); 26:1; 5; 7; 17(2); 18; 20(3); 23; 27:5(2); 9; 28:5(3); 16; 20(3); 21; 23(2); 24; 27(2); 29:6; 11(3); 29; 30:9; 31:10; 15; 32:3; 6; 7(2); 9; 15; 17; 21; 24(2); 25(2); 29(2); 31(3); 33(2); 33:6; 11(2); 13(3); 18; 19; 20; 24(2); 34:26; 35:20; 21; 22(2); 24(3); 36:1; 3; 4; 6(3); 8; 10; 13; 17; 20; 23(3); **Ezr** 1:2; 3(2); 4; 4:2; 6; 11; 5:7; 15; 6:11; 7:6(2); 9; 26; 8:3; 4; 5; 6; 7; 8; 9; 10; 11; 12; 19; 21; 22(2); 33; 10:1; **Neh** 1:5; 11; 2:1; 6(2); 3:2; 8(2); 10; 12; 16; 17(2); 18; 19; 20; 21; 22; 23(2); 24; 25; 29; 30(2); 31; 4:3; 6:8; 12(2); 18; 19; 8:4; 9:7(2); 8; 11:8; 13:5; 7; 26(3); 28; **Est** 1:3; 12; 14; 17; 19; 2:2; 9(2); 20; 3:1(2); 2(2); 4; 5; 6; 4:4; 5; 7(2); 8(3); 10; 11; 17; 5:4; 9; 11(2); 14; 6:3(2); 4; 5(2); 6; 9(2); 11(2); 13(4); 14; 7:7; 9; 8:3; 7; 10:2; **Job** 1:2; 8; 10; 2:3(3); 8; 9; 11(3); 12; 13(2); 3:20; 4:4; 6:10; 14; 7:8; 10; 17(2); 18(2); 8:4; 18(2); 9:3(2); 4; 11(2); 12(2); 13; 14(2); 32; 34; 35; 11:10; 13; 12:4; 5; 13; 16; 13:7; 9; 15(2);

16; 14:6; 20(2); 22(2); 15:21; 24(2); 26; 31; 18:6; 7; 9(2); 10(2); 11(2); 14; 20; 21; 19:11; 16; 28; 20:7; 9(3); 11; 14; 16; 22; 23(2); 24; 25; 26(2); 27; 29; 21:15(2); 19; 21; 31; 33(3); 22:3; 14; 21; 27; 23:3; 4; 7; 8; 9(2); 13; 14; 15; 24:1; 10; 20(2); 23; 25:2; 26:2; 3; 6; 14; 27:9; 15; 20(2); 21(2); 22; 23(2); 29:12(2); 13; 30:25; 31:14; 15; 29(2); 37(2); 32:13; 14; 33:13; 23; 24(2); 26; 34:11; 13; 17; 19; 27; 28; 29; 35:6(2); 7; 14(3); 36:11; 22; 23; 26; 37:16; 18; 19; 20; 23; 24; 39:11(2); 12; 20; 23; 40:2(2); 9; 11; 12; 19(2); 20; 22(2); 41:4; 5(2); 6(2); 8; 9(2); 10; 11; 13; 22; 26(2); 28(2); 30; 32; 42:8; 11(6); **Ps** 2:12; 3:2; 4:3(2); 5:12; 7:4(2); 5; 13; 8:4(2); 5(2); 6; 10:9; 11:5; 12:5(3); 13:4; 17:13(2); 18:t, 6; 11; 12; 23; 30; 20:6; 21:2; 3; 4; 5; 6(2); 22:8(4); 23(3); 24(2); 25; 26; 29; 30; 24:6; 25:12; 14; 28:7(2); 32:6; 10; 33:2; 3; 8; 18; 21; 34:t, 5; 6(2); 7; 8; 9; 19; 22; 35:8(2); 10(4); 25; 37:5; 7(2); 12; 13; 22(2); 24; 32; 33(2); 36; 40; 41:1; 2(3); 3; 8; 42:5; 11; 43:5; 44:16; 45:11; 49:7; 17; 50:3(2); 18; 23; 51:t; 52:t, 6; 53:5; 55:12; 20; 56:t, 57:3; 59:t, 61:7; 62:1; 4; 5; 8(2); 63:11; 64:4; 10; 66:6; 17; 67:7; 68:1(2); 4(2); 33; 69:26; 30; 34; 71:11(3); 72:9; 11(2); 12; 15(2); 17(2); 74:14; 76:11(2); 78:17; 34; 36(2); 37; 40(2); 58(2); 70; 71; 79:10; 81:15; 85:9; 13; 89:7; 20; 21; 22(2); 23; 24; 27; 28(2); 33; 41; 43; 45; 91:2; 14(2); 15(4); 16(2); 92:15; 94:12; 13; 95:2; 96:6; 9; 97:2; 3; 7; 98:1; 100:4; 101:5(2); 103:11; 13; 17; 104:34; 105:2(2); 19; 20(2); 21; 106:7; 10; 23; 29; 31; 32; 43; 107:32(2); 41; 109:6; 7; 12; 17(2); 19(2); 30; 31; 111:5; 113:8; 116:2; 117:1; 119:2; 42; 120:6; 126:6; 130:7; 135:1; 136:4; 5; 6; 7; 10; 13; 16; 17; 140:11; 141:5; 142:2(2); 144:3(2); 145:18(2); 19; 20; 147:11; 148:1; 2(2); 3(2); 4; 14; 149:2(2); 3; 150:1; 2(2); 3(2); 4(2); 5(2); **Prov** 3:6; 6:16; 7:10; 13(3); 20; 21(2); 8:9; 30(3); 9:4(3); 16(3); 10:13(2); 24; 26; 11:18; 26(2); 27; 12:14; 13:6; 18; 24(2); 14:2; 6; 7; 31; 33; 35; 15:9; 10; 12; 14; 21; 16:7; 13; 22; 26; 29; 17:8; 11; 24; 25, 18.9; 13; 16(2); 17; 19:6; 7(3); 17; 19; 20:2; 7; 16; 19; 21:25; 22:15; 23:6; 13; 14; 24; 24:18(2); 24(2); 25; 29; 25:13; 21(2); 26:4; 12; 15; 17; 24; 25; 27; 27:11; 13; 14; 22; 28:8; 11; 17; 22; 29:20; 21; 23; 30:5; 31:1; 6; 7; 12; **Eccl** 2:26; 3:14; 22(2); 4:10(2); 12(2); 16; 5:12; 18; 19; 20; 6:2; 10; 12; 7:14; 8:3; 4; 6; 7; 12; 15(2); 9:2(2); 4; 17; 10:1; 3; 8; 14(2); 11:8; **Song** 1:2; 3:1(3); 2(3); 3; 4(4); 11; 5:4; 6(3); 8; 6:1; **Is** 3:10; 11(2); 5:19; 23; 6:4; 7:4; 8:13(2); 17; 9:11; 13; 10:6(2); 15(2); 20; 26; 11:2; 3; 14:25; 29; 15:4; 9; 16:3; 20:1; 21:6; 14(2); 22:11; 16; 21(2); 23; 24; 24:2; 25:9(2); 10; 26:3; 27:5; 7(3); 28:6; 26(2); 29:12; 16(2); 21; 23; 30:18; 32; 31:4; 6; 8; 33:16; 36:3; 6; 21(2); 22; 37:3; 7(2); 22; 38; 38:1(2); 39:3; 40:3; 10(3); 13; 14(4); 17(2); 18; 20; 41:2(3); 7; 42:1; 25(3); 43:7(3); 44:3; 14; 20; 45:1(2); 9(2); 10; 13; 24(2); 46:7(5); 48:14; 15(2); 49:5; 7(3); 25; 50:4; 8; 10; 51:2(3); 52:7; 15; 53:2(3); 3(2); 4; 5; 6; 10(2); 12; 55:4; 6; 7(2); 56:6; 8(2); 57:15; 17; 18(3); 19(3); 58:5; 7; 13; 59:15; 16(2); 19; 62:7; 11(2); 63:2; 11; 14; 64:4(2); 5; 66:2; **Jer** 2:3; 15; 37; 3:1; 4:2(2); 6:11; 8:6; 9:24; 10:25(2); 11:19; 15:8; 18:18; 19:14; 20:2; 3; 9; 10(2); 15; 16; 21:1; 9; 12; 22:10(2); 12; 13(2), 14; 15; 16; 18(2); 23:24; 28(2); 26:8(2); 13; 19(2); 21; 22; 23(2); 24(2); 27:6; 7(2); 11; 12; 28:9; 14(2); 29:26; 31; 30:8; 10; 21; 31:2; 10(2); 11(2); 20(4); 32:3; 4; 5; 9; 10; 33:13; 34:2; 14; 36:4; 8; 15; 22; 31; 37:4; 14(2); 15(2); 17(2); 21; 38:6; 11; 13; 14; 27(2); 39:5(3); 7(2); 9; 12(4); 14(2); 40:1(2); 2; 5(3); 6; 7; 14; 41:1; 2(2); 3; 7; 11; 12; 13; 16; 42:8; 9; 11; 43:1; 44:20; 45:4; 46:10; 25; 27; 48:11; 12(2); 17(2); 19; 26; 27; 35(2); 39; 49:5; 8(2); 19; 50:16; 17(2); 32(2); 43; 51:3(2); 44; 52:8; 9(2); 11(3); 31; 32(2); 33; 34; **Lam** 1:17; 2:19; 3:24; 25(2); 28; 30(2); **Eze** 1:3; 2:2; 3:18; 20(2); 27(2); 7:15; 9:4; 5; 10:7; 12:13(2); 14(2); 13:22; 14:4; 7(2); 8(2); 9(2); 10(2); 17:6(2); 7(2); 12; 13(2); 15(2); 16(2); 17; 20(3); 18:13; 20(2); 22; 32; 19:4(2); 5; 8(2); 9(3); 21:26(2); 27; 24:27; 28:9(2); 12; 29:2; 20; 30:11; 24; 31:4(2); 8(2); 9(2); 11(3); 12(3); 15(3); 16; 17; 32:2; 21(2); 22; 25; 26; 33:2; 4; 5; 12; 16; 27; 35:7(2); 37:19; 38:2; 21; 22(3); 40:46; 43:6; 44:26; 45:20; 46:12; 47:23; **Dan** 2:1; 16; 22; 24; 25; 46; 48(2); 3:28; 4:8; 16(2); 19; 23; 34; 35; 5:6; 9; 11; 17; 19(2); 20; 21; 24; 29; 6:3(2); 4; 5; 6; 14(2); 16; 18(2); 22; 23(2); 7:10(3); 13(2); 14(2); 16; 27; 8:4; 6; 7(5); 11; 12; 9:4; 9; 11; 10:16; 11:1; 5; 11; 16(2); 17(3); 18(2); 22; 23; 25; 26; 30; 40(2); 44; 45; 12:7; **Hos** 1:3; 4; 6; 4.17; 5:6; 14; 7:5; 9; 10; 8:3; 11; 12; 9:4; 17; 11:1; 7; 12:2; 4(2); 14(3); 13:11; 13; 14:2; 4; 8(2); **Joel** 2:13; 14; 20; **Amos** 1:5; 8; 2:3; 3:5; 14; 5:8; 10(2); 11; 19(2); 6:10(3); 9:13; **Obad** 7; **Jonah** 1:6(2); 8; 10; 11; 15; 3:6(2); 4:5; 6; **Mic** 1:4; 2:7; 3:5; 5:5; 6:5; 6; 7:9; 15; **Nah** 1:5; 6; 7; 15; **Hab** 2:4; 5(2); 6(4); 9; 12; 15(3); 19; 20; 3:5; **Zeph** 1:6; 2:11; 3:9; **Hag** 1:12; **Zec** 1:8; 2:3; 4; 3:1; 4(3); 5; 4:11; 12; 5:4; 6:12; 8:10; 23; 9:8(2); 10:4(4); 12:1; 10(2); 13:3(4); 6; **Mal** 2:5(2); 12; 17; 3:16; 17; 18(3); 4:4; **Mt** 1:20; 24(2); 2:2; 3; 5; 8(2); 11(2); 13; 3:5; 6; 13; 14; 15(2); 16(2); 4:3; 5(2); 6; 7; 8(2); 9; 10(2); 11(2); 20; 22; 24; 25; 5:1; 25; 31; 39; 40; 41; 42(2); 6:8; 7:8; 9; 10; 11; 24; 8:1; 2; 3; 4; 5(2); 7(2); 16; 18; 19; 20; 21; 22; 23; 25(2); 27; 28; 31; 34(2); 9:2; 9(2); 10; 14; 18; 19; 20; 22; 24; 27; 28(2); 32; 10:1; 4; 28; 32; 33; 40; 11:3; 15; 27; 12:2; 3; 4(2); 10(2); 14(2); 15; 16; 18; 22(2); 32(2); 46; 47; 48(2); 13:2; 9; 10; 12(2); 27; 28; 36; 43; 51; 57; 14:2; 3(2); 4; 5(2); 9; 13; 15; 17; 22; 26; 28; 31(2); 33; 35(2); 36; 15:4; 12; 15; 22; 23; 25; 30; 32; 33; 16:1; 17; 22(2); 24; 17:3; 5; 10; 12(2); 14(2); 16(2); 17; 18; 19; 23; 25; 26(2); 18:2(2); 6; 15(2); 17; 21(2); 22; 24(2); 25; 26; 27(2); 28(3); 29; 30; 32(2); 34(2); 19:2; 3(3); 7; 10; 12; 13; 16; 17; 18; 20; 21; 27; 20:7; 18; 19(2); 20(3); 21; 22; 25; 26; 27; 29; 33; 34; 21:7; 14; 16; 23; 25; 31; 32(3); 38; 39(3); 41(2); 44; 46(2); 22:12; 13(3); 15; 16; 19; 21; 22; 23(2); 35(2); 37; 42; 43; 45; 46(2); 23:15; 21; 22; 24:1(2); 3; 15; 17; 18; 47; 50; 51(2); 25:6; 10; 21; 23; 26; 28(2); 29; 31; 32; 37; 44; 26:4; 7; 15(2); 16; 17; 18; 22; 24; 25(2); 33; 34; 35; 37; 47; 48(2); 49; 50(2); 52; 56; 57; 58; 59; 62; 63; 64; 67(2); 69; 71; 73; 75; 27:1; 2(3); 3; 9; 11(2); 13; 14; 18; 19(2); 22(2); 23; 26; 27; 28(2); 29(2); 30(2); 31(5); 32; 34; 35; 36; 38; 39; 41; 42(2); 43(3); 44; 48; 49; 54; 55; 64; 28:4; 7; 9(2); 13; 14; 17(2); **Mk** 1:5(2); 10; 12; 13; 18; 20; 25(2); 26(2); 27; 30; 32; 34; 36(2); 37(2); 40(4); 41(2); 42; 43(2); 44; 45; 2:3; 4; 13; 14(2); 15; 16; 18; 24; 25; 26; 3:2(3); 6(2); 7; 8; 9(2); 10(2); 11(2); 12; 13(2); 14; 19; 21; 23; 31(2); 32(2); 34; 4:1; 9; 10(2); 23; 25(2); 36(2); 38(2); 41; 5:2; 3; 4(2); 6; 8; 9; 10; 12; 15; 16; 17; 18(2); 19(2); 20; 21; 22; 23; 24(3); 30(2); 31; 33(2); 37; 40(2); 6:1; 2(2); 3; 7; 14(2); 17; 19(2); 20(3); 22; 26; 27; 30; 33(2); 35; 37; 49; 50; 54; 56(2); 7:1; 5; 10; 12; 14; 15(3); 16; 17; 18; 25; 26; 28; 32(3); 33; 34; 8:1; 4; 11(3); 19; 22(3); 23(3); 25; 26; 29; 30; 32(2); 34(2); 38; 9:2; 7; 11;

13(2); 15(3); 18(3); 19(2); 20(4); 21; 22(2); 23(2); 25(3); 26(2); 27(2); 28(2); 31; 32; 36(2); 37; 38(2); 39; 42; 10:1; 2(3); 10; 13; 17(2); 18; 20; 21(3); 28; 32; 33(2); 34(4); 35; 37; 39; 42; 48; 49(2); 51(2); 52; 11:2(2); 3(2); 4; 7(2); 18(2); 21; 27; 28; 31; 12:3(3); 4(3); 5; 6; 7; 8(3); 12(2); 13(2); 14; 16; 17; 18(2); 19; 26; 28; 29; 32; 33; 34(2); 37(2); 43; 13:1; 2; 3; 14; 15; 16; 21; 14:1(2); 10; 11(2); 12; 13; 19; 21; 29; 30; 33; 35; 40; 43; 44(3); 45(2); 46(2); 50; 51(2); 53; 54; 55; 56; 57; 58; 61(2); 64; 65(4); 67; 69; 72; 15:1(2); 2(2); 3; 4; 7; 8; 10; 12; 13; 14; 15; 16; 17; 18; 19(3); 20(5); 22; 23; 24; 25; 27; 29; 32(2); 36(2); 39; 41(3); 44(2); 46(3); 16:1; 6; 7; 10; 14; **Lk** 1:11; 12(2); 13; 17; 19; 29; 32; 50; 59; 62; 66; 74; 75; 2:7(2); 22(2); 25; 26; 27; 28; 33; 38; 40; 44(2); 45(2); 46; 47; 48(2); 3:7; 10; 11(3); 12; 14; 19; 22; 4:3; 4; 5(2); 6; 8(2); 9(3); 12; 13; 14; 17; 20; 22; 29(3); 35(5); 37; 38; 40; 42(3); 5:1; 3; 5; 9; 11; 12; 13(2); 14; 15(2); 18(3); 19(2); 20; 27; 28; 29; 33; 6:3; 4; 7(2); 13; 17; 19(2); 29(2); 30; 7:2; 3(2); 4; 6(2); 9(3); 11; 14; 15; 17; 18; 19; 20; 29; 30; 36(2); 38; 39(2); 40; 42; 43; 49; 8:1; 3; 4; 8; 9; 18(2); 19(2); 20; 24(2); 25; 27; 28; 29; 30(2); 31; 32; 37; 38(3); 39; 40(2); 41; 42; 44; 45; 47(3); 49; 50; 53; 9:7; 9; 10; 11; 12; 18; 23; 26; 30; 32(2); 33; 35; 37; 39(4); 40; 42(3); 45; 47(2); 48; 49; 50(2); 52; 53; 57; 58; 60; 62; 10:16; 22; 23; 25; 26; 28; 30(3); 31; 32; 33(2); 34(4); 35(2); 36; 37(2); 38; 40; 11:1; 5(2); 6; 8(2); 10; 11(2); 12; 13; 16(2); 22(3); 26; 27; 37(2); 39; 45; 53(2); 54(2); 12:5(2); 8; 10(2); 13; 14; 20; 36; 41; 44; 46(3); 48(2); 58; 13:1; 8; 12; 15(2); 17; 23; 31; 14:1; 2; 4(3); 5; 6; 8; 9; 12(2); 15(2); 16; 18; 25; 29; 31(2); 35; 15:1(2); 15; 16; 18; 20(2); 21; 22; 27(2); 28; 30; 31; 16:1; 2(2); 5; 6; 7; 14; 27; 29; 31; 17:1; 2; 3(2); 4; 7; 8; 9; 12; 16; 19; 31(2); 37; 18:3; 7; 15; 16; 18; 19; 22; 31; 33(2); 37; 39; 40(3); 42; 43; 19:4; 5(2); 6; 8; 9; 14(2); 15, 17, 19; 22; 24(2); 25; 26(2); 30(2); 31(3); 34; 35; 39; 47; 48; 20:1; 2; 5; 10(3); 11(3); 12(2); 13(2); 14(2); 15(2); 18; 19; 20(2); 21; 27(2); 38; 40; 44; 21:7; 38(2); 22:2; 4; 5; 6; 9; 10; 14; 21; 26; 33; 36(2); 39; 43(2); 47; 48; 49(2); 51; 52; 54(3); 56(3); 57(2); 58; 59; 61; 63(2); 64(3); 65; 66; 23:1; 2; 3(2); 7; 8(3); 9(2); 10; 11(4); 14(2); 15(2); 16(2); 21(2); 22(3); 25; 26(2); 27(2); 32; 33; 35(2); 36(3); 38; 39; 40; 43; 49; 55; 24:16; 18; 19; 20(2); 24; 29; 31; 42; 52; **Jn** 1:3(2); 4; 7; 10(2); 11; 12; 15; 18; 19; 21; 22; 25(2); 29; 31; 32; 33(2); 37; 38; 39; 40; 41; 42(2); 43; 45(2); 46(2); 47(2); 48(2); 49; 50; 51; 2:3; 10; 11; 18; 3:2(2); 3; 4; 9; 10; 15; 16; 17; 18; 26(2); 27; 28; 29; 34; 36; 4:9; 10; 11; 14(3); 15; 19; 23; 24(2); 25; 30; 31; 33; 34; 39; 40(2); 42; 45; 47(2); 48; 49; 50(2); 51(2); 52(2); 53; 5:6(2); 7; 8; 10; 12; 14(2); 15; 16; 18; 20(2); 23; 24; 27; 38; 43; 6:2; 5; 6; 7; 8; 15(2); 21; 25(2); 27; 28; 29; 30; 34; 37; 38; 40(3); 41; 44(2); 54; 56; 64; 65; 66; 68; 71; 7:1; 3; 5; 11; 12; 13; 18(2); 26; 29(2); 30(2); 31; 32(2); 33; 35; 37; 39; 43; 44(2); 45; 48; 51; 52; 8:2; 3; 4; 6(2); 7(2); 13; 19; 20; 25; 26; 29; 30; 31; 33; 39; 41; 44; 48; 52; 55(4); 57; 59; 9:2; 3; 4; 7; 8; 9; 10; 12; 13; 15; 17; 18(2); 21; 23; 24; 26; 28; 31; 34(2); 35(3); 36; 37(2); 38; 40(2); 10:3; 4; 5; 20; 21; 24(2); 31; 33; 36; 38; 39; 41; 42; 11:3; 8; 10; 11; 15; 16; 20; 24; 27; 29; 30; 32(2); 34(2); 36; 39(2); 44(2); 45; 48(2); 53; 57; 12:2(2); 4; 11; 13; 16(2); 17(2); 18; 19; 21; 26(2); 29; 34; 37; 41; 42(2); 44; 45; 47; 48(2); 13:2; 6; 7; 8(2); 9; 10; 11; 16; 20; 24; 25; 27(2); 28; 29; 31; 32(3); 36(2); 37; 38; 14:5; 6; 7(2); 8; 9; 17(3); 21(2); 22; 23(4); 15:5; 21; 16:5; 7; 19; 29; 17:2(2); 18:2; 4; 5(2); 12; 13; 20; 23; 24; 25; 26; 30(2); 31(3); 33; 34; 37; 38(2); 19:1; 2; 3; 4(2); 6(6); 7; 9; 10; 12; 15(3); 16(2); 18(2); 32; 36; 37; 38; 20:2; 6; 13; 15(5); 16; 25; 28; 29; 21:3; 5; 7; 12; 15(2); 16(3); 17(4); 19; 21; 22; 23; **Acts** 1:6; 9; 11; 2:22; 23; 25; 30; 3:4; 7(2); 9; 10; 13(2); 16(2); 22; 26; 4:10; 5:6(3); 17; 21; 31; 32; 36; 37(2); 40; 6:11; 12(3); 14; 15; 7:3; 4; 5(3); 8(2); 9; 10(3); 14; 21(2); 24(2); 27; 30; 31; 33; 35; 37; 38; 39; 40; 47; 54; 57; 58(2); 8:2; 11; 20; 30(2); 31; 35; 38; 39; 9:2; 3; 4; 6; 7; 8(2); 10; 11; 12; 15; 16; 17; 21; 23; 24; 25(2); 26; 27(3); 29; 30(2); 34; 35; 38(2); 39(2); 40; 10:3(2); 4(2); 7; 11; 13; 15; 19; 21; 23; 25(2); 26; 27; 35(2); 38; 40(2); 41; 43(2); 48; 11:2; 13; 26(2); 12:4(5); 5; 6; 7(2); 8(2); 9; 10; 16; 17; 19(2); 20; 23; 13:9; 11(2); 22; 27(2); 28; 29(3); 30; 31; 34; 39; 14:9; 19; 20; 15:21; 38; 16:3(3); 9; 32; 17:15(2); 16; 17; 18; 19(2); 23; 27(2); 28; 31; 34; 18:12; 17; 18; 20; 26(2); 27; 19:2; 4(2); 22; 30; 31(2); 33; 38; 20:1; 3; 4; 10(3); 14; 16; 18; 37; 38; 21:8; 11; 12; 20; 27(2); 29; 30; 31; 33(2); 34; 36; 40; 22:9; 13; 18; 20; 22; 24(2); 25; 27; 29(3); 30(2); 23:2(2); 3; 9; 10(2); 11; 15(3); 17(2); 18(3); 19(3); 20; 21(2); 22; 23; 24; 27; 28(2); 30; 31; 32; 33; 35; 24:2; 7; 8; 10; 23(2); 24; 26(4); 25:2(2); 3(3); 5; 15; 16; 19; 20; 21(2); 22; 25; 26; 27; 26:26; 27:3; 28:6; 8(2); 16; 21; 23(2); 30; 31; **Rom** 1:20; 21; 3:26; 4:3; 4; 5(2); 17; 22; 23; 24; 5:9; 14; 6:4; 6; 8; 9; 7:4; 8:11; 17; 20; 32(2); 37; 9:11; 16(2); 20; 33; 10:9; 11; 12; 14(2); 11:4; 35(2); 36(3); 12:8; 20(2); 13:4; 14:1; 3(5); 4; 14(2); 15; 15:11; 12; 16:25; **1Cor** 1:5; 30; 31; 2:2; 9; 11; 14; 16; 3:17; 18; 5:3; 7:12(2); 13; 15; 17; 18(2); 36; 8:3; 6(2); 10; 10:12; 11:14; 28; 34; 12:18; 14:2; 11; 13; 28(2); 37; 38; 15:27(2); 28(3); 38; 16:2(2); 11(3); 12; 22; **2Cor** 1:19; 20(2); 2:7(2); 8; 5:9; 15; 16; 21(2); 6:1; 7:14; 15; 8:18; 9:7; 10:7; 17; 11:4; 12:18; 13:4(2); **Gal** 1:1; 6; 8; 9; 16; 18; 2:11; 13; 3:6; 4:29; 5:8; 6:6(2); **Eph** 1:4(2); 10; 11; 17; 20(2); 22; 23; 2:18; 3:12; 20; 21; 4:15; 21(2); 28(3); 6:9; **Phil** 1:29; 2:7; 9(2); 22; 23; 27(2); 28(2); 29; 3:9; 10; **Col** 1:16(3); 17; 19; 20(2); 2:6; 7; 9; 10; 12(3); 13; 3:4; 10(2); 17; 4:10; 13; **1Th** 4:14; 5:10; **2Th** 1:12; 2:1; 9; 3:14; 15(2); **1Ti** 1:16; 5:1; **2Ti** 1:12; 18; 2:4(2); 11(2); 12(2); 26; 4:11; 14; **Titus** 1:16; **Philem** 1:12; 15; 17; **Heb** 1:5; 6; 2:3; 6(2); 7(3); 8(3); 10; 13; 14; 16(2); 17; 3:2(2); 4:13; 5:5; 7(2); 9; 6:6; 7:1; 6; 10; 21(2); 25; 9:9; 28; 10:30; 38; 11:5; 6(2); 9; 11; 12; 19(2); 27; 12:2; 3; 5; 25(3); 13:13; 15; **Jas** 1:5(2); 6; 12; 2:3(2); 5; 14; 23; 3:13; 4:17(2); 5:13(2); 14(3); 15(2); 19; 20; **1Pet** 1:8; 21(3); 2:6; 9; 14; 23; 3:6; 10; 11(2); 22; 4:5; 11(2); 16(2); 19; 5:7; 11; **2Pet** 1:3; 17; 18; 3:14; 15; 18; **1Jn** 1:5(2); 6; 10; 2:3; 4(2); 5(2); 6; 8; 10; 13; 14; 15; 27(2); 28(2); 29; 3:1; 2(2); 3; 5; 6(3); 9; 12; 15; 17(2); 19; 22; 24(2); 4:9; 13; 15; 16; 19; 21; 5:1(3); 10; 14; 15; 16; 18; 20(2); **2Jn** 10(2); 11; **Jude** 9; 15; 24; **Rev** 1:1; 4; 5; 6; 7(3); 17; 2:7(2); 11; 17(3); 26; 28; 29; 3:6; 12(3); 13; 20(2); 21; 22; 4:8; 9; 10(2); 5:1; 7; 13; 14; 6:2(2); 4(2); 5; 8(2); 16; 7:14; 15; 8:3; 9:1; 10:6; 9; 12:9; 11; 13:2; 4; 5(2); 7(2); 8; 9; 12; 18; 14:1; 7(2); 15; 18; 16:8; 9; 17:14; 19:5; 7; 10; 11; 14; 19; 20(2); 21; 20:2; 3(3); 6; 11; 21:6; 22:3; 11(4); 17(3); 18

HIMSELF

Gen 14:15; 18:2; 19:1; 22:8; 23:7; 12; 24:52; 27:42; 30:36; 32:21; 33:3; 41:14; 42:7; 24; 43:31; 32; 45:1(2); 46:29; 47:31; 48:2; 12; **Ex** 10:6; 21:3(2); 4; 8; **Lev** 7:8; 9:8; 14:8; 15:5; 6; 7; 8; 10; 11; 13; 21; 22; 27; 16:6(2); 11(3); 17; 24; 17:15; 21:4(2); 11; 22:8; 25:26; 47; 49; 27:8; **Num** 6:3; 5; 6; 7; 16:9; 19:12(2); 13; 19(2); 20; 23:24; 25:3; 31:53; 35:19; 36:7; 9; **Deut** 7:6; 14:2; 17:16; 17(2); 23:11; 28:9; 29:13; 19; 32:36; 33:21; **Josh** 22:23; **Judg** 3:19; 20; 4:11; 6:31; 7:5; 9:5; 16:30; **Ruth** 3:8; **1Sa** 2:14; 3:21; 8:11; 10:19; 22; 14:47; 17:16; 18:4; 5; 14; 15; 30; 20:24; 41; 21:13; 23:19; 23; 24:8; 25:31; 26:1; 28:8; 14; 29:4; 30:6; 31; **2Sa** 3:6; 31; 6:20(2); 7:23; 9:8; 12:18; 20; 13:6; 14:22; 33; 15:23; 17:23; 18:18; 21; 24:20; **1Kin** 1:5; 23; 47; 52; 53; 2:19; 11:29; 15:15; 16:9, 17.21; 18:2; 6(2); 42; 19:4(2); 20:11; 16; 38; 21:25; 29(2); 22:30; **2Kin** 4:34; 35; 5:14; 6:10; 19:1; 23:16; **1Chr** 12:1; 13:13; 21:21; **2Chr** 12:1; 12; 13; 13:9; 12; 15:18; 16:9; 14; 17:1; 16; 18:29; 34; 20:3; 35; 36; 21:4; 23:1; 25:11; 14; 26:8; 20; 32:1; 5; 9; 26; 27; 33:12; 23(2); 35:22; 36:12; **Ezr** 10:1; 8; **Est** 5:10; **Job** 1:12; 2:1; 8; 4:2; 9:4; 15:25; 17:8; 18:4; 22:2; 23:9; 27:10; 32:2; 34:9; 14; 41:25; **Ps** 4:3; 10:10; 14; 35:8; 36:2; 4; 37:35; 50:6; 52:7; 54:t, 55:12; 68:30; 87:5; 93:1; 109:18; 113:6; 132:18; 135:4; 14; **Prov** 5:22; 9:7(2); 11:25; 12:9; 13:7(2); 14:14; 16:4; 26; 18:1; 24; 21:13; 22:3; 25:9; 14; 27:12; 28:10; 29:15; **Eccl** 5:9; 10:12; **Song** 2:9; 3:9; 5:6; **Is** 2:9; 20; 3:5; 7:14; 8:13; 19:17; 22:16; 28:20(2); 31:4; 37:1; 38:15; 44:5(2); 14; 15; 16; 23; 45:18; 56:3; 59:15; 61:10; 63:12; 64:7; 65:16(2); **Jer** 10:23; 16:20; 23:24; 29:26; 27; 31:18; 34:9; 37:12; 43:12; 48:26; 42; 49:10; 51:3; 14; **Lam** 1:9; **Eze** 7:13; 14:7; 24:2; 25:12; 45:22; **Dan** 1:8(2); 6:14; 8:11; 25; 9:26; 11:36(2); 37; **Hos** 5:6; 7:8; 8:9; 10:1; 13:1; **Amos** 2:14; 15(2); 6:8; **Jonah** 4:8; **Hab** 2:6; **Mt** 6:4; 8:17; 12:15; 26; 45(2); 13:21; 16:24; 18:4; 23:12(2); 27:3; 5; 42; 57; **Mk** 3:7; 21; 26; 5:5; 30; 6:17; 8:34; 12:33; 36; 37; 14:54; 67; 15:31; **Lk** 3:23; 5:16; 6:3; 7:39; 9:23; 25; 10:1; 29; 11:18; 26; 12:17; 21; 37; 47; 14:11(2); 15:15; 17; 16:3; 18:4; 11; 14(2); 19:12; 20:42; 23:2; 7; 35; 51; 24:12; 15; 27; 36; **Jn** 2:24; 4:2; 12; 44; 53; 5:13; 18; 19; 20; 26(2); 37; 6:6; 15; 61; 7:4; 18; 8:7; 10; 22; 59; 9:21; 11:38; 51; 12:36; 13:4; 32; 16:13; 27; 18:18; 25; 19:7; 12; 21:1(2); 7; 14; **Acts** 1:3; 2:34; 5:13; 36; 7:26; 8:9; 13; 34; 9:26; 10:17; 12:11; 14:17; 16:27; 18:19; 19:22; 31; 20:13; 21:26; 25:4; 8; 16; 25; 26:1; 24; 27:3; 28:16; **Rom** 12:3; 14:7(2); 12; 22; 15:3; **1Cor** 2:15; 3:15; 18; 7:36; 11:28; 29; 14:4; 8; 28; 37; 15:28; **2Cor** 5:18; 19; 10:7(2); 18; 11:14; 20; **Gal** 1:4; 2:12; 20; 6:3(2); 4; **Eph** 1:5; 9; 2:15; 20; 5:2; 25; 27; 28; 33; **Phil** 2:7; 8; 3:21; **Col** 1:20; **1Th** 3:11; 4:16; **2Th** 2:4(2); 16; 3:16; **1Ti** 2:6; **2Ti** 2:4; 13; 21; **Titus** 2:14(2); 3:11; **Heb** 1:3; 2:14; 18; 5:2; 3; 4; 5; 6:13; 7:27; 9:7; 14; 25; 26; 12:3; **Jas** 1:24; 27; **1Pet** 2:23; **1Jn** 2:6; 3:3; 5:10; 18; **3Jn** 10; **Rev** 19:12; 21:3

HIS

Gen 1:11; 12(2); 21; 24(2); 25(2); 27; 2:2(2); 3; 7; 21; 24(3); 25; 3:8; 15; 20; 21; 22; 4:1; 2; 4(2); 5(2); 7; 8(2); 17(2); 21; 23; 25(2); 26; 5:3(3); 29; 6:3; 5; 6; 9; 12; 20; 7:2(2); 7(3); 13; 14(3); 8:9; 18(3); 21(2); 9:1; 6; 8; 21; 22(2); 24(2); 25; 26; 27; 10:5; 10; 15; 25(2); 11:28(2); 31(4); 12:5(2); 8; 11; 12; 17; 20(2); 13:1; 3(2); 10; 12; 18; 14:12; 14(3); 15; 16(2); 17; 16:3; 11; 12(2); 15; 17:3; 14(2); 17(2); 19(2); 23(3); 24; 25(2); 26; 27; 18:2; 19(2); 33(2); 19:1; 3; 14(3); 16(3); 26; 30(2); 37; 38; 20:2; 7; 8; 14; 17(2); 21:2; 3; 4; 5; 7; 11; 21; 22; 32; 22:3(3); 4; 5; 6(2); 7; 9; 10(2); 13(3); 17; 19; 21(2); 24; 23:3; 6; 9; 10; 18; 19; 24:2(2); 7; 9(2); 10(3); 11; 20; 21(2); 26; 27(2); 29; 30(2); 32(2); 40; 48; 59; 61; 63; 67(3); 25:6; 8; 9; 10; 11; 17; 18; 21(2); 25; 26(3); 28; 30; 33; 34(2); 26:7; 8; 11(2); 15(2); 17; 18(2); 25; 26(2); 27:1(2); 5; 10; 11; 13; 14(3); 16(2); 18; 19; 20; 22; 23(2); 26; 27; 30(3); 31(3); 32; 34(2); 37; 38(2); 39; 40; 41(2); 28:7(2); 8; 9; 11; 16, 18; 29:1; 3; 6; 10(3); 11; 13(2); 23; 24(2); 28; 29(2); 32; 33; 34; 35; 30:6; 8; 11; 13; 14; 18; 20; 24; 35; 40; 31:4; 17(2); 18(4); 19; 21; 23; 25(2); 46; 53; 54; 55(3); 32:1; 3; 13(2); 16(2); 20; 22(3); 25; 31; 33:1; 3; 4; 5; 14; 16; 17; 18; 19; 34:3; 4; 5(4); 13; 19; 20; 24(3); 25; 26; 35:2; 7; 10; 18(2); 21; 22; 27; 29(2); 36:2; 6(8); 24; 32; 33; 34; 35(2); 36; 37; 38; 39(3); 37:1; 2(3); 3(2); 4(2); 5; 8(3); 9; 10(3); 11(2); 12; 17; 20; 22; 23(3); 26(2); 27; 29; 30; 34(3); 35(3); 38:1; 3; 4; 5; 6; 9(3); 11(2); 12(2); 13; 16; 20(2); 28(2); 29(3); 30(3); 39:2; 3(2); 4(3); 5; 7; 8; 9; 11; 12(2); 13; 15; 16(2); 18; 19(3); 23; 40:1; 2; 5(2); 7; 9; 13(2); 20(2); 21; 41:8(2); 10; 11; 12; 14; 37; 38; 42(3); 44; 42:1; 4; 7; 8; 21; 22; 25; 27(4); 28; 35; 37; 38; 43:8; 16; 21; 29(3); 30(3); 31; 33(2); 44:1(2); 2; 4; 11(2); 13; 14; 19; 20(4); 22(3); 30; 33; 45:1; 3(3); 4; 8; 14(2); 15(2); 16; 23(2); 24; 46:1(2); 4; 6; 7(5); 8; 15(3); 18; 25; 26; 28; 29(4); 31(2); 47:2; 3; 7; 11(2), 12(3); 20; 29; 48:1; 9; 12(2); 13(2); 14(3); 17(3); 18(2); 19(3); 49:1; 10; 11(4); 12(2); 13; 15; 16; 17; 20; 24(2); 26; 28; 31(2); 33(3); 50:1; 2(2); 4; 7(2); 8(2); 10; 12; 13; 14(3); 18(2); 22; 24; **Ex** 1:1; 6; 9; 22; 2:4; 7; 10; 11(2); 20; 21; 22; 24; 3:1; 6; 13; 4:4(2); 6(3); 7(4); 14; 15(2); 18; 20(3); 21; 25; 5:2; 21; 6:1; 11; 20; 7:2; 10(2); 12; 20; 23(2); 8:6; 15; 17(2); 24; 29(2); 31(2); 32; 9:20(2); 21(2); 23; 33; 34(2); 10:1(2); 13; 22; 23; 11:2; 5; 7; 10; 12:4(3); 9(2); 22; 29; 30; 48; 13:10; 13; 14:4; 5; 6(2); 9(2); 17(3); 18(2); 21; 23(2); 27(2); 31; 15:1; 3; 4(2); 19(2); 21; 26(3); 16:16(2); 18; 21; 29(2); 17:11(2); 12(2); 13; 18:1; 5(2); 7; 8; 15; 16; 24; 27(3); 20:7; 17(4); 20; 21:3; 4; 6(3); 7; 9; 13; 14; 15(2); 16; 17(2); 18(2); 19(2); 20(3); 21; 26(3); 27(3); 28; 29(3); 30; 34; 36(2); 22:3; 4; 5(3); 7; 8(2); 9(2); 10; 11(2); 14; 15; 16; 27(3); 30; 23:3; 4; 5; 6; 19; 21; 22; 24:10(2); 11; 13; 25:2; 31(5); 26:19(2); 27:2; 3(6); 11; 21; 28:1; 4; 12; 21; 29; 30; 35; 38; 41; 43(2); 29:4; 6; 7; 8; 9(2); 10; 14(2); 15; 16; 17(3); 19; 20(2); 21(6); 24; 27; 28; 29; 30; 31; 32; 35; 44; 30:12; 18; 19; 21; 27(2); 28(2); 30; 33; 38; 31:8(2); 9(2); 10; 14; 32:11; 14; 15; 19; 27(5); 29(2); 33:4; 8; 10; 11(2); 34:4; 8; 15; 20; 26; 29; 30; 33; 35; 35:11(7); 13(2); 14(2); 15; 16(4); 17; 19; 21(2); 34; 36:4; 24(2); 37:16(4); 17(5); 20(2); 23(3); 39:5; 14; 21; 27; 33(6); 39(4); 40(4); 41; 40:10; 11; 12; 14; 18(2); 31; **Lev** 1:3(2); 4; 6; 9(2); 10; 11; 12(3); 14(2); 15; 16(2); 2:1; 2; 3; 10; 3:1; 2(2); 6; 7; 8(2); 12; 13; 14; 4:3; 4; 6; 11(5); 17; 19; 22; 23(3); 24; 25(2); 26(2); 28(4); 29; 30; 33; 34; 35; 5:1; 4; 6(3); 7;

8(2); 10; 11; 12; 13; 15; 17; 18; 6:2(2); 5; 6; 9; 10(3); 11; 15; 16; 20; 22(2); 25; 7:13(2); 15; 16(2); 18(2); 20(2); 21; 25; 27; 29(3); 30; 31; 33; 34; 35; 8:2; 6; 9(2); 11(2); 14; 15; 17(3); 18; 22; 23(2); 27; 30(6); 31(2); 36; 9:1; 9; 22; 10:1; 3; 6; 12; 11:14; 15; 16; 22(4); 25; 27; 28; 29; 40(2); 12:3; 13:2(3); 3; 4; 5; 6; 7; 11; 12(2); 13; 23; 28; 34; 35; 37; 40; 41(3); 42(2); 43(2); 44(2); 45(3); 46; 55; 14:2; 8(3); 9(7); 14(2); 15; 16(3); 17(3); 19; 23; 25(2); 26; 27(2); 28(3); 32; 47(2); 15:2(2); 3(7); 5(2); 6; 7; 8; 10; 11(2); 13(4); 15; 16; 21; 22; 27; 16:4(2); 6(2); 11; 12; 14(2); 15; 17; 19; 21; 24(3); 26(2); 28(2); 32; 17:2; 4; 9; 10; 15; 16(2); 18:14; 19:3(2); 8(2); 21; 22; 20:2; 3(2); 4; 5; 6; 9(5); 10; 11(2); 12; 17(6); 19; 20(2); 21(2); 21:1; 2(6); 3; 4; 7; 10(3); 11(2); 12(2); 14; 15(2); 17; 20(2); 21; 22; 24; 22:2; 3; 6; 7; 11(3); 18(4); 21; 23; 23:29; 30; 37; 24:9; 11; 14; 15(2); 19; 25:10(2); 13; 25(3); 27; 28; 30; 33; 41(3); 48; 49(3); 50; 51; 52(2); 54; 27:8; 14; 15(2); 16; 17; 18; 21; 28; 31; **Num** 1:4; 44; 52(2); 2:2; 4; 6; 8; 11; 13; 15; 17; 19; 21; 23; 26; 28; 30; 3:7; 9; 10; 38; 48; 51; 4:5; 9(3); 15; 19(3); 25; 27; 49(2); 5:7; 9; 10(2); 14(2); 15; 18; 30; 6:4; 5(3); 7(6); 8; 9(3); 11; 12(2); 13; 14; 16(2); 17(2); 18(2); 19; 21(4); 23; 25; 26; 7:5; 11; 12; 13; 19; 25; 31; 37; 43; 49; 55; 61; 67; 73; 79; 8:8; 13; 19; 22; 9:2; 3; 7; 13(3); 10:14; 18; 22; 25; 11:1; 10; 28; 29; 12:12; 14:24; 15:4; 24(2); 30; 31(2); 16:4; 5(2); 6; 17(3); 18; 40; 17:2; 9; 19:3; 4; 5; 7(2); 8(2); 10; 13; 19; 21; 20:8; 11(2); 21; 24; 25; 26(3); 28(2); 21:23(2); 24; 26(2); 29(2); 33; 34(2); 35(3); 22:5; 18; 21; 22(2); 23(2); 31(4); 23:6; 7; 10; 16; 17; 18; 21; 24:1; 2(2); 3; 4; 7(4); 8(2); 10; 13; 15; 16; 18; 20(2); 21; 23; 25(2); 25:5; 6; 7; 13(2); 26:54; 27:1; 3; 4; 8(2); 9(2); 10(2); 11(4); 21(2); 23; 28:10; 15; 24; 31; 29:6(2); 16(2); 22(2); 25(2); 28(2); 31(2); 34(2); 38(2); 30:2(3); 4; 7; 11; 14(2); 16(2); 31:6; 32:18; 21; 42; 33:54; 35:8(2); 21; 23(2); 25; 26; 27; 28(2); 32; 36:2; 7; 8; 9; **Deut** 1:16; 31; 36; 41; 2:12; 24; 30(2); 31(2); 32; 33(2); 34; 3:1; 2(2); 3; 4; 11; 14; 20; 4:13; 30; 36(3); 37(2); 40(2); 42; 47; 5:11; 21(5); 24(3); 6:2(2); 13; 17(2); 22; 7:3(2); 7; 9; 10; 8:2; 5; 6; 11(3); 18; 9:23; 10:6(2); 8; 9(2); 12; 13; 20; 11:1(4); 2(3); 3(3); 14; 22; 12:5(2); 8; 11; 21; 13:4(2); 17; 18; 14:13; 14; 15; 21; 23; 24; 15:2(3); 8; 17; 16:2; 6; 11; 17:2; 17; 18; 19(2); 20(5); 18:1; 5; 6; 7(2); 8; 10(2); 18; 19:4; 5(3); 6; 9; 11; 12; 18; 19; 20:5; 6; 7; 8(3); 21:16; 17(2); 18(2); 19(4); 20; 21; 23; 22:1; 3(2); 4; 19(2); 24; 26; 29(2); 30(2); 23:1; 2; 7; 15(2); 24:1(2); 2; 3(2); 4; 5; 7; 10(2); 12; 13; 15(3); 16; 25:2(2); 6(2); 7(3); 8; 9(5); 10(2); 26:2; 17(5); 18(2); 27:10(2); 16(2); 17; 20(2); 22(3); 23; 24; 28:1; 9; 12(2); 15(2); 40; 45(2); 54(4); 55; 29:2(2); 12; 19; 20(2); 23(2); 30:2; 8; 10(2); 16(4); 20; 32:4(2); 5; 9(2); 10; 15; 19(2); 36(2); 43(5); 50; 33:1; 2; 3; 6; 7(3); 9(4); 11(2); 12; 13; 16; 17(3); 21; 24(2); 26; 28; 34:6; 7(2); 9; 11(2); **Josh** 2:19(3); 3:15; 4:5; 14; 18; 5:13(3); 14(2); 6:26(2); 27; 7:6(2); 18; 22; 24(6); 26; 8:1(3); 14; 18; 19; 26; 29; 9:24; 10:21; 33; 11:15; 13:27; 15:17; 17:3; 6; 10; 20:4; 5(2); 6(2); 21:12; 22:5(2); 20; 29; 24:3; 4; 10; 24; 28; 30; 33; **Judg** 1:2; 3; 6(2); 13; 17; 25; 2:6; 9; 3:10(2); 16(2); 20; 21(3); 22; 24(3); 4:7(2); 10; 11; 13; 15(4); 17; 21; 22; 5:11; 17; 26(2); 28(2); 31; 6:11; 13; 21(2); 27(2); 31; 32; 7:5(2); 7; 8; 11; 13; 14(2); 21; 22; 8:20(2); 21; 24; 25; 27(2); 29; 30; 31; 32; 9:1(2); 3; 5(2); 7; 16(2); 17; 18(2); 19; 21; 24; 26; 28; 30; 31; 41; 48(2); 49; 53; 54(2); 55; 56(2); 10:16; 11:2; 3; 11; 20(2); 21; 23; 32; 34(3); 35; 39; 12:9; 13:2; 5; 6(2); 7; 11; 19; 20; 21; 22; 23; 24; 14:2(2); 3(3); 4(2); 5(2); 6(3); 9(2); 10; 19(2); 20(2); 15:1; 6(2); 14(3); 15; 17; 19; 16:3; 5; 9; 12; 14; 16; 17; 18(2); 19(2); 20; 21; 22; 29(2); 30(3); 31(3); 17:2(2); 3(2); 4(2); 5(2); 6; 11; 12; 18:4; 26; 30; 19:2; 3; 4; 5; 7; 9(3); 10; 11; 12; 13; 15; 16; 17; 21; 24; 25; 27(2); 28; 29(2); 20:8(2); 21:1; 21; 22; 24(3); 25; **Ruth** 1:1(2); 2(2); 6; 2:1; 5; 15; 20; 22; 3:4; 7(2); 8; 14; 4:5; 7(2); 8; 10(3); 13; 14; 17; **1Sa** 1:1; 3; 4; 11(2); 19; 20; 21(2); 23; 2:9; 10(2); 11; 13; 19; 20; 22; 3:2(2); 9; 12; 13(2); 19; 4:10; 12(2); 13; 15; 18; 19; 5:3(2); 4(2); 7; 11; 6:2; 3; 5; 9(2); 7:1; 15; 17(2); 8:1; 2(2); 3(2); 11(3); 12(4); 14; 15(2); 16; 17; 22; 9:2; 3; 5; 7; 10; 15; 22; 10:1(2); 9; 14; 16; 23; 25; 27; 11:6; 7; 12:3; 5; 14; 22(3); 13:2; 14(2); 16; 20(4); 22; 14:1(2); 6; 7; 12(2); 13(4); 14; 17; 20; 26(2); 27(5); 34(3); 45; 47; 49; 50; 15:1; 27; 34; 35; 16:1; 4; 5; 7(2); 10; 13; 16; 17; 20; 21; 23; 17:5; 6(2); 7(2); 13; 15; 17; 22(2); 25(2); 28; 33; 34; 35(2); 38(2); 39(2); 40(4); 43; 49(5); 51(2); 54(2); 57; 18:1; 2; 3; 4(4); 7(2); 10; 11; 13; 14; 22(2); 26; 27(2); 30; 19:1(2); 4(3); 5(2); 7; 9(4); 13; 16; 24; 20:6; 17; 25; 27; 32; 33; 34; 36; 38; 40(2); 41; 21:7; 11(2); 12; 13(3); 14; 22:1(2); 6(3); 7; 11; 15; 23:5; 6; 8; 11; 13; 14; 15; 16; 18; 22(2); 24; 25; 26(3); 24:2; 3(2); 6; 7(2); 8; 16; 19; 22; 25:1; 2; 3(2); 4; 10; 13(4); 17; 20; 24; 25(2); 36; 37(2); 39(2); 42; 43; 44; 26:5; 7(2); 9; 10; 11; 16; 18; 19; 23(2); 25(2); 27:1(2); 3(3); 8; 11; 12; 28:3; 5; 7(2); 14; 18; 23; 25; 29:2; 4(2); 5(2); 11; 30:1; 3; 6(3); 12; 18; 22(2); 24(2); 26; 31; 31:2; 4(2); 5(2); 6(3); 7; 8; 9(2); 10(2); 12; **2Sa** 1:2(2); 4; 5; 6; 10(2); 11; 12; 17; 2:2; 3(2); 16(3); 21; 27; 29; 32(2); 3:2; 3; 8(2); 12; 27; 29; 30; 32; 38; 39; 4:1; 4(3); 6; 7(3); 8; 9; 10; 11(3); 12; 5:6; 12(2); 21; 6:6; 7; 11; 14; 17; 19; 20(2); 21; 7:1(2); 12; 13; 14; 25; 27; 8:3; 10; 15; 9:3; 6; 9; 11; 13; 10:1(2); 2(3); 3; 10; 11:1; 2; 9(2); 10; 13(3); 27(2); 12:3(4); 4(2); 9(2); 15; 17; 19(2); 20(2); 21; 24(2); 25; 30; 13:2; 8; 17; 18; 22(2); 24; 28; 29; 31(2); 32; 33; 34; 36; 37; 14:7(2); 9; 13; 14; 15; 16; 22(2); 24(2); 25(3); 26(2); 30; 31; 33; 15:5; 12; 14; 16; 18; 22; 25; 30(2); 32(2); 16:6(2); 9; 11; 12; 13; 18; 19; 22; 17:6; 8; 18; 23(6); 18:9; 14; 17; 18(2); 19; 24; 25; 28; 19:2; 4; 8; 11(2); 17(2); 19; 24(3); 30; 39; 41; 20:1; 3(2); 8; 10(2); 21(2); 22; 21:1; 2; 4; 6; 12; 13; 14(2); 15; 22; 22:1; 7(2); 9(2); 10; 14; 16; 23(2); 25; 31; 51(3); 23:2; 8; 10(2); 18; 21(2); 23; 24:14; 16; 20(2); 21; **1Kin** 1:2; 6(2); 9; 10; 21; 23; 37; 47; 49; 51; 2:1; 3(5); 4; 5(4); 6; 9; 10; 12(2); 15; 19(2); 22; 23; 32(2); 33(4); 34; 35; 40(3); 3:1; 3; 6; 15; 4:7(2); 21; 25(2); 26; 27; 28; 31; 32; 34; 5:1(2); 3(2); 10; 11; 7:1(2); 8; 14(2); 23; 51; 8:6; 14; 15(2); 20; 22; 28; 31; 32(3); 38(2); 39; 54(2); 56(3); 58(4); 59(2); 61(2); 66(2); 9:11; 15; 16; 19(3); 22(5); 27; 10:5(5); 13; 24(2); 25; 11:3(2); 4(5); 6; 8; 9; 17; 19; 20; 21; 23; 26; 27(2); 33; 34(2); 35; 36; 41; 43(4); 12:4; 6; 15; 18; 24; 26; 33; 13:4(2); 11; 12; 13; 19; 24; 27; 28; 30(2); 31(2); 33; 14:2; 4(2); 8; 18; 20(3); 21(2); 31(5); 15:2; 3(4); 4(2); 5; 6; 8(3); 10; 11; 12; 13; 14; 15; 18; 23(3); 24(5), 26(2); 20; 29; 30; 34; 16:3; 4; 5; 6(3); 7(2); 9(3); 10; 11(3); 13; 19(2); 20; 26; 27; 28(3); 34(3); 17:17; 19; 23; 18:3; 7; 42(2); 43; 46; 19:3(2); 6; 13(2); 19; 20:1; 11; 12; 20; 24; 31; 35; 38; 39; 41; 42(2); 43; 21:4(3); 5; 7; 8(2); 11(2); 25; 27(2); 29(3); 22:3; 10; 17; 19(3); 22; 31(2); 34; 35; 36(2); 38(2); 40(3); 42; 43; 45; 46; 50(5); 52(2); 53; **2Kin** 1:2; 8; 9; 10; 11; 12; 13(2); 16; 17; 2:8; 12; 3:2(3); 25; 27(2); 4:12; 18; 19(2); 20; 25; 32; 34(6); 35; 37; 38; 39; 43; 5:1; 3; 4; 6; 7(2); 8; 9(2); 11(2); 13; 14; 15; 20; 23; 25; 26; 27; 6:7; 8; 11; 12; 15; 17; 24; 30(2); 32(2); 7:12; 13; 8:11; 14; 15(2); 18; 19(2); 20; 24(4); 26; 9:2; 3; 6; 11(2); 13; 21(2); 23; 24(4); 25(2); 26; 28(3); 31; 32; 36; 10:3; 10; 11(3); 15; 16; 19(2); 24; 31; 34; 35(3); 11:2; 8(2); 9; 11(2); 18(2); 12:1; 2; 5; 17; 18(2); 20; 21(4); 13:8; 9(3); 12; 13(2); 14(2); 16(2); 21; 23(2); 24(2); 25; 14:2; 3(2); 5(3); 6; 15; 16(3); 20; 21; 22; 25; 28; 29(3); 15:2; 3; 5; 7(4); 9; 10; 14; 15; 18; 19(2); 22(3); 25(2); 30; 33; 34; 38(5); 16:2(2); 3; 13(4); 15; 20(4); 17:3; 15(3); 18; 20; 23(2); 18:2; 3; 6; 12; 21; 29; 31(3); 33; 19:1; 4; 7(2); 19; 23(2); 37(4); 20:2; 13(5); 20; 21(3); 21:1; 3; 6; 7; 10; 11; 12; 16; 17; 18(4); 19; 20; 21(2); 22; 23; 24(2); 26(3); 22:1; 2; 11; 23:3(3); 10(2); 18(2); 25(3); 26(2); 29; 30(3); 31; 32; 34(2); 35; 36; 37; 24:1(2); 2; 3; 6(3); 7; 8; 9; 11; 12(5); 15; 17(3); 18; 20; 25:1(2); 5; 7; 28; 29(2); 30(2); **1Chr** 1:13; 19(2); 43; 44; 45; 46(2); 47; 48; 49; 50(3); 2:4; 13; 18; 35(2); 42; 3:3; 10(3); 11(3); 12(3); 13(3); 14(2); 16(2); 17; 4:9(3); 18; 19; 25(3); 26(3); 27; 5:1(2); 2; 4(3); 5(3); 6; 7; 6:20(3); 21(4); 22(3); 23(3); 24(4); 26(2); 27(3); 29(3); 30(3); 39(2); 49; 50(3); 51(3); 52(3); 53(2); 7:14; 16(3); 18; 20(4); 21(2); 22; 23(3); 24; 25(3); 26(3); 27(2); 35; 8:1; 8; 9; 10; 30; 37(3); 39(2); 9:5; 19(2); 36; 43(3); 10:2; 4(2); 5; 6(2); 7; 8; 9(2); 10(2); 12; 13; 11:10; 11; 20; 23; 25; 45; 12:15; 19; 28; 13:9; 10; 14; 14:2(2); 4; 15:3; 5; 6; 7; 8; 9; 10; 17; 16:7; 8(2); 9; 10; 11(2); 12(3); 13(2); 14; 15; 16; 23; 24(2); 27(2); 29; 34; 37; 39; 41; 43(2); 17:1; 11; 12; 13; 14; 21; 23; 25; 18:3; 10(2); 14; 19:1(2); 2(2); 3; 7; 11; 13; 15; 19; 20:2; 8; 21:3; 13; 16(2); 20; 21; 23; 27; 22:5; 6; 9(3); 10(2); 17; 18; 23:1; 13(2); 14; 25; 25:9; 10(2); 11(2); 12(2); 13(2); 14(2); 15(2); 16(2); 17(2); 18(2); 19(2); 20(2); 21(2); 22(2); 23(2); 24(2); 25(2); 26(2); 27(2); 28(2); 29(2); 30(2); 31(2); 26:6; 10; 14(2); 15; 22; 25(6); 26; 28; 29; 30; 31; 32; 27:2; 4(2); 5; 6(2); 7(2); 8; 9; 10; 11; 12; 13; 14; 15; 28:1; 2; 6; 7; 11; 19; 20; 29:5; 23; 28(2); 30(2); **2Chr** 1:1(2); 8; 13; 2:1; 11; 12; 14; 15; 17; 3:1; 2; 4:16; 5:1; 7; 13; 6:3; 4(2); 10; 12; 13(2); 19; 22; 23(3); 29(3); 30; 7:3; 6; 10; 11; 8:1; 6; 9(3); 14; 18; 9:4(5); 8; 23(2); 24; 31(4); 10:4; 6; 15; 18; 11:4; 12; 14; 21(2); 22; 23; 12:8; 13(2); 14; 16(3); 13:2; 5; 6; 12; 17; 22(2); 14:1(4); 2; 11; 13; 15:9; 17; 18; 16:4; 5; 12(4); 13(2); 14; 17:1(2); 2; 3; 4(2); 5; 6; 7(2); 18:8; 9; 16; 18(3); 21; 33; 34; 19:1; 20:18(2); 20; 21; 25; 30; 31; 32; 21:1(4); 4(2); 7; 8; 9(2); 10(2); 17(3); 18; 19(4); 22:1(2); 2; 3(2); 4(3); 9; 11; 23:7(2); 8; 10(2); 11; 13; 17(2); 24:1; 11; 13; 16; 22(2); 25(2); 27(3); 25:1; 3(2); 4; 11; 14; 22; 28; 26:1; 2; 3; 4; 8; 15; 16(3); 19(2); 20; 21(2); 23(4); 27:1; 2; 6(2); 7(2); 9(3); 28:1; 3; 5; 22; 25; 26(2); 27(3); 29:1; 2; 3; 10; 19(2); 25; 30:2; 6; 8(2); 9; 19(2); 27; 31:1; 2; 3; 8; 10; 12; 13; 16; 20; 21(2); 32:3(2); 8; 9(2); 12(2); 14; 15; 16(2); 17; 21(3); 25; 26; 30; 31; 32; 33(4); 33:3; 6; 7; 10; 12(2); 13(2); 18(2); 19(3); 20(4); 22(2); 23; 24(2); 25(2); 34:2; 3(2); 4; 8(2); 19; 27; 31(6); 33; 35:3; 4; 8; 9; 22; 23; 24(2); 26; 27; 36:1; 4(3); 5; 7; 8(3); 10; 12; 13(2); 15(3); 16(3); 17; 18; 20; 22; 23(2); **Ezr** 1:1; 3(2); 4; 7; 2:1; 68; 3:2(2); 3; 9(3); 11; 4:6; 5:6; 15; 17; 6:5; 7; 10; 11(2); 12; 7:6(2); 9; 10; 11; 13; 14; 15; 23; 28; 8:17; 18(2); 19; 22(2); 25(2); 9:8; 10:8; 11; 18; **Neh** 1:5; 2:1; 20; 3:1; 10; 12; 17; 23; 28; 29; 30; 4:2; 15; 17; 18(2); 22; 5:7; 13(2); 6:5(2); 11; 18; 19; 7:3(2); 6; 8:4(2); 16; 9:8(2); 10(2); 10:29(2); 11:3; 13; 17; 20; 12:8; 36; 45; 47; 13:10; 26; 30; **Est** 1:2; 3(3); 4(2); 8; 12(2); 20; 22; 2:3; 7(2); 8; 15; 16(2); 17; 18(2); 3:1; 10(2); 4:1; 3; 4; 11; 17; 5:1; 2(2); 10(2); 11(2); 14(2); 6:6; 8; 12(2); 13(4); 7:5; 7(2); 8:2; 3(2); 5(2); 7; 17; 9:1; 4; 25(3); 10:2(2); 3(3); **Job** 1:3; 4(2); 10(3); 13(2); 20(2); 2:3; 4; 5(2); 6; 7(2); 9; 10; 11; 12; 13; 3:1(2); 19; 4:9; 17; 18(2); 5:3; 4; 18; 26; 6:5; 9; 14; 7:1; 2; 10(2); 8:12; 15; 16(2); 17; 18; 19; 9:5; 13; 33; 34(2); 11:5; 12:4; 5; 11; 16; 13:8; 11(2); 14:5(3); 6; 18; 20; 21; 22(2); 15:2; 15(2); 20; 21; 23; 25; 26(2); 27(3); 29; 30(2); 31; 32(2); 33(2); 16:9(3); 12; 13; 21; 17:5(2); 9; 18:4(2); 5; 6(2); 7(2); 8; 11; 12(2); 13(2); 14(2); 15(3); 16(2); 17; 19(2); 20; 19:6; 11(2); 12; 20:6(2); 7; 9; 10(2); 11(2); 12(2); 13; 14(2); 15; 18; 20; 21(2); 22; 23(2); 25; 26(2); 27; 28(3); 21:17; 19(2); 20(2); 21(2); 23; 24(2); 25; 31(2); 22:22(2); 23:3; 6; 11(2); 12(2); 13; 15; 24:1; 6; 15; 22; 23; 25:2; 3(2); 5; 26:8; 9(2); 11; 12(2); 13(2); 14(2); 27:1; 8; 9; 14(2); 15; 18; 19; 21; 22; 23; 28:9; 10; 29:1; 3(2); 17; 30:24(2); 31:20; 23; 30; 31; 32:1; 2; 3(2); 5; 12; 14; 33:10; 13; 17; 18(2); 19(2); 20(2); 21(2); 22(2); 23; 25(2); 26(2); 28(2); 30; 34:11; 14(3); 19; 21(2); 27; 29; 35; 36; 37(3); 35:15; 16; 36:7; 15; 18; 22; 23; 24; 26; 29; 30; 37:1; 2(2); 3; 4(2); 5; 6; 7; 11; 12; 13; 15; 38:12; 32(2); 41(2); 39:6; 8; 10; 11; 18; 19; 20; 21; 40:16(4); 17(2); 18(2); 19; 23; 24(2); 41:1; 2(2); 7(2); 12(3); 13(2); 14(2); 15(2); 18(2); 19; 20; 21(2); 22; 23; 24; 33; 42:10; 11(4); 12; 16(2); **Ps** 1:2(2); 3(3); 2:2; 5(2); 12; 3:t, 4; 7:12(2); 13; 16(4); 17; 8:6; 9:7; 11; 16; 10:2; 3; 4(2); 5(3); 6; 7(2); 8; 9(2); 10; 11(2); 13; 15; 16; 11:4(3); 5; 7; 12:2; 14:1; 6; 7; 15:2; 3(3); 4; 5; 17:12; 18:t, 6(2); 8(2); 9; 11(2); 12; 13; 14; 22(2); 24; 30; 50(3); 19:1; 5; 6(2); 12; 20:6(3); 21:2(2); 3; 5; 9; 22:24; 29; 31; 23:3; 24:3; 4; 5; 25:9; 10(2); 13(2); 14; 22; 27:4; 5(2); 6; 28:5; 8; 29:2; 9(2); 11(2); 30:4(2); 5(2); 31:21; 23; 33:4; 6; 11; 12; 14; 17; 18; 21; 34:t, 1; 3; 6; 9; 15; 20; 22; 35:8; 9; 14; 27; 36:1; 2(2); 3; 4; 37:7; 10; 12; 13; 23; 24; 25; 26; 28; 30; 31(3); 33; 34; 38:13; 39:5; 11; 40:4; 41:2; 3(2); 5; 6; 9; 42:5; 8(2); 46:6; 47:8; 48:1; 49:7; 16; 17; 18; 19; 50:4; 6; 23; 52:7(3); 53:1; 6; 54:7; 55:20(2); 21(3); 56:4; 10(2); 57:3(2); 58:7(2); 9; 10; 59:9; 60:6; 61:6; 62:4; 12; 64:9; 65:6; 66:2(2); 5; 7(2); 8; 20; 67:1; 68:1; 4(2); 5; 21(2); 33; 34(2); 35; 69:33; 36(2); 72:7; 9; 14; 17(2); 19(2); 73:10; 76:1; 2(2); 77:8(2); 9; 78:4(2); 7; 10; 11(2); 20; 22; 26; 32; 37; 38(2); 42; 43(2); 49; 50; 52; 54(2); 56; 61(2); 62(2); 66; 69; 70; 71(2); 72(2); 79:7; 81:6(2); 85:8(2); 9; 13; 87:1; 89:23(2); 24; 25(2); 29(2); 30; 36(2); 39; 40(2); 41; 42(2); 43; 44(2); 45; 48; 91:4(3); 11; 14; 94:14(2); 95:2; 4(2); 5(2); 7(3); 96:2(2); 3(2); 6; 8(2); 13; 97:2; 3; 4; 6(2); 10; 12; 98:1(2); 2(2); 3(2); 99:5; 6(2); 7; 9; 100:2; 3(2); 4(3); 5(2); 101:5; 102:t, 16; 19; 21; 103:1; 2; 7(2); 9; 11; 13; 15; 17; 18(2); 19(2); 20(3); 21(3); 22(2); 104:3(2); 4(2); 13; 15; 19; 23(2); 31; 105:1(2); 2; 3; 4(2); 5(3); 6(2); 7; 8; 9; 19; 21(2); 22(3); 24; 25(2); 26; 27; 28; 42(2); 43(2); 45(2); 106:1; 2; 8(2); 12(2); 13(2); 23(2); 24; 26; 33(2); 40(2); 45(2); 107:1; 8(2); 15(2); 20; 21(2); 22; 24; 31(2); 108:7; 109:6; 7; 8(2); 9(2); 10; 11; 12; 13; 14(2); 18(3); 31; 110:5; 111:3(2); 4; 5; 6(2); 7(2); 9(3); 10(2); 112:1; 2; 3(2); 5; 7; 8(3); 9(2); 10; 113:4; 8; 114:2(2); 116:2; 12; 14; 15; 18; 117:2; 118:1; 2; 3; 4; 29; 119:2; 3; 9; 125:2; 126:6; 127:2; 3; 5; 128:1; 129:7(2); 130:5; 8; 131:2; 132:1; 7(2); 13; 18(2); 133:2; 135:3; 4; 7; 9; 12; 14(2); 136:1; 2; 3; 4; 5; 6; 7; 8; 9; 10; 11; 12; 13; 14; 15(2); 16(2); 17; 18; 19; 20; 21; 22(2); 23; 24; 25; 26; 140:8; 144:4; 10; 145:3; 9(2); 12(2); 17(2); 21; 146:4(3); 5(2); 147:5; 9; 11; 15(2); 17(2); 18(2); 19(3); 20; 148:2(2); 8; 13(2); 14(2); 149:1; 3; 4; 9; 150:1(2); 2(2); **Prov** 2:6; 8; 3:11; 20; 31; 32; 5:21; 22(2); 23; 6:13(3); 14; 15; 27(2); 28; 29; 30; 31; 32; 33; 7:23(2); 8:22(2); 29(2); 30; 31; 36; 10:1; 9; 15; 19; 11:1; 5(2); 7; 8; 9(2); 12(2); 17(2); 19; 20; 28; 29; 12:4; 8; 10; 11; 13; 14; 15; 22; 26; 13:1; 2; 3(3); 8; 16; 22; 24(2); 25; 14:2(2); 8; 10(2); 14; 15; 20; 21; 26; 31; 32(2); 35; 15:5; 8; 20; 23; 27; 32; 16:2; 7; 9(2); 10; 11; 15; 17(2); 23(2); 26; 27; 29; 30(2); 32; 17:5; 12; 13; 18; 19; 21; 25; 27; 28(2); 18:2; 6; 7(3); 9; 11(2); 14; 17(2); 20(2); 19:1(2); 2; 3(2); 4; 7; 8; 11(2); 12; 13; 16(2); 18; 22; 24(3); 26(2); 20:2; 6; 7(2); 8; 11(2); 14; 16; 17; 19; 20(3); 24; 28; 21:2; 8; 10(2); 13; 23(3); 24; 25; 29(2); 22:5; 8; 9; 11(2); 16; 25; 29; 23:3; 6; 7(2); 14; 31; 24:7; 12; 15; 18; 26; 29; 25:5; 13; 18; 22; 28; 26:4; 5(2); 11(2); 12; 14(2); 15(3); 16; 19; 24; 25; 26; 27:8; 13; 14; 16; 17; 18; 21; 22; 28:6(2); 7; 8; 9(2); 10; 11; 13; 14; 16; 18; 19; 24(2); 25; 26; 27; 29:1; 3(2); 5(2); 10; 11; 12; 14; 15; 20; 21(2); 24; 25; 30:4(3); 6; 10; 17(2); 31:1; 7(2); **Eccl** 1:3; 5; 6; 2:14; 21; 22(2); 23(3); 24(2); 26; 3:11; 12; 13; 22(2); 4:4; 5(2); 8(2); 10; 14; 15; 5:14; 15(3); 17(2); 18(3); 19(2); 20(2); 6:2; 3(2); 4; 7; 12; 7:2; 15(3); 8:1(2); 3; 9; 12; 13; 15(2); 16; 9:12; 15; 16; 10:2(2); 3; 13(2); 12:5; 13; **Song** 1:2; 4; 12; 2:3(2); 4; 6(2); 16; 3:7; 8(2); 11(3); 4:16(2); 5:4; 11(2); 12; 13(2); 14(2); 15(2); 16; 6:2; 7:10; 8:3(2); 7; 10; **Is** 1:3(2); 2:3(2); 10; 19; 20(2); 21; 22; 3:5; 6(2); 8; 11; 14; 5:1; 7; 12; 19; 25(4); 6:1; 2(2); 3; 6; 7:2(2); 14; 8:3; 7(3); 8; 17; 9:4(3); 6(2); 7(2); 11; 12(2); 17(2); 19; 20; 21(2); 10:4(2); 7(2); 12(2); 16(2); 17(3); 18(2); 19; 24; 26; 27(2); 28; 32; 11:1; 3(2); 4(2); 5(2); 8; 10; 11(2); 15(2); 16; 12:4(3); 13:5; 10; 13; 14(2); 14:17; 18; 21; 25(2); 27; 29; 31; 32; 15:4; 5; 16:6(4); 12; 17:4; 5; 7(2); 8(2); 9; 19:1; 2(2); 14; 22:21; 22; 23; 24; 23:11; 24:2; 23; 25:4; 8; 9; 11(2); 26:21; 27:1; 8; 9; 28:4; 5; 21(4); 24; 26; 28(2); 29:8(2); 22; 23; 30:4(2); 26; 27(3); 28; 30(3); 31:2; 3; 4; 7(2); 8; 9(3); 32:6; 33:6; 15(3); 16(2); 17; 34:2; 14; 16; 17; 36:6; 16(3); 18; 37:1; 4; 7(2); 20; 24(2); 38(4); 38:2; 9; 39:2(5); 40:10(3); 11(3); 12; 13; 26; 28; 41:2(3); 3; 6(2); 42:2; 4; 10; 12; 13; 21; 24(2); 25; 44:5; 6; 11; 12(2); 13; 17; 19; 20; 26(2); 45:1; 9; 10; 11; 13; 46:7(3); 47:4; 15; 48:2; 14(2); 15; 16; 19; 20; 49:2(2); 5; 7; 13(2); 50:10(2); 51:14; 15; 17; 22; 52:9; 10; 14(2); 53:5; 6; 7(2); 8; 9(3); 10(4); 11(2); 12; 54:5; 16; 55:7(2); 56:2; 3; 6; 10; 11(2); 57:2; 13; 17(2); 18(2); 58:5(2); 13(2); 59:2; 16(2); 17; 18(2); 19; 60:2; 22; 62:8(2); 11(2); 63:1(2); 7(2); 9(3); 10; 11(3); 12; 65:15; 20; 66:5; 6; 13; 14(3); 15(3); 16; **Jer** 1:2; 9; 15; 2:3; 15(2); 35; 3:1; 5; 4:7(3); 13(2); 26; 5:8; 24; 6:3; 21; 7:5; 29; 8:1; 6(2); 16(2); 9:4; 5; 8(3); 20; 23(3); 10:10(2); 12(3); 13(2); 14(2); 16(2); 23; 25; 11:19; 12:15(2); 13:23(2); 16:12; 17:5; 10(2); 11(2); 18:11; 12; 16; 18; 19:3; 9; 20:9(2); 21:2; 7; 9; 22:4(2); 7; 8; 10; 11; 13(4); 18; 28; 30(2); 23:6(2); 9; 14; 17; 18(2); 20; 27; 30; 34; 35(2); 36; 24:8; 25:4; 5; 19(3); 30(3); 38(2); 26:3; 21(2); 23; 27:7(3); 8; 12; 28:11; 29:32; 30:6(2); 8; 18; 21; 24; 31:10; 30(2); 34(2); 35; 32:4(2); 18; 19(2); 33:2; 11; 21; 26; 34:1(2); 3(2); 9(3); 10(2); 14; 15; 16(2); 17(2); 21; 35:3(2); 14; 15; 18; 36:3; 7; 14; 17; 18; 24; 30; 31(2); 37:2; 10; 17; 38:2; 39:1; 6; 40:3; 42:11; 43:10(2); 12; 44:21; 23(3); 30(4); 46:8; 10; 26; 47:3(3); 48:7(2); 10; 11(4); 12; 15; 16; 17; 25; 26; 29(4); 30(2); 35; 40; 49:1(2); 2; 3(2); 10(4); 20; 22; 50:16(2); 17; 18; 19(2); 25(2); 28; 32; 34; 43; 45; 51:3(2); 5; 6; 9; 11(2); 15(3); 16(2); 17(2); 19(2); 21(2); 23(2); 28; 31; 34; 44; 45; 59; 52:1; 3; 4(2); 8; 10; 11; 27; 31; 32; 33(2); 34(3); **Lam** 1:10; 12; 14; 17; 18; 2:1(3); 2; 3(2); 4(3); 5; 6(3); 7(2); 8; 17; 3:1; 3; 12; 13; 22; 27; 29; 30; 32; 34; 36; 39; 4:4; 11(2); 20; **Eze** 1:15; 27(2); 3:12; 18(4); 19(3); 20(4); 7:13; 16; 20; 8:2(2); 11(2); 12; 9:1(2); 2(2); 3; 11; 10:7; 12:12(3); 14; 13:22; 14:4(5); 7(4); 16:15; 17:4; 14; 15; 17; 18; 19; 20; 21(2); 22; 18:6(2); 7(2); 8; 11; 12; 13; 14; 15(2); 16; 17(2); 18(4); 21; 22(2); 23; 24(4); 26(2); 27(2); 28; 30; 19:7; 9; 20:7; 39; 21:3; 4; 5; 21; 22; 30; 22:11(4); 25:9(2); 26:3; 9; 10; 11; 29:3; 18(2); 19; 20; 30:11; 22(2); 24; 31:3; 4; 5(3); 6(3); 7(3); 8(3); 9; 10(3); 11; 12(3); 13(2); 16; 17(2); 18; 32:10; 22; 31(2); 32; 33:4(2); 5(2); 6(2); 8(3); 9(3); 11; 12(3); 13(3); 14; 16; 18; 19; 20; 26; 30; 34:12(2); 26; 35:8(2); 36:20; 37:7; 16(2); 19; 38:6(2); 21; 22; 39:11; 40:3; 43:2(2); 17; 44:27; 45:8; 46:2(2); 7; 12(3); 16(2); 17(5); 18(3); 47:3; 12; 23; 48:1; **Dan** 1:2(3); 3; 8; 20; 2:1(2); 2; 7; 13; 17(2); 18; 20; 32(4); 33(2); 34; 46; 3:13; 19; 20; 24; 28(2); 4:3(4); 14(4); 15(2); 16; 19; 23; 33(3); 34; 35(2); 37; 5:1; 2(4); 3(3); 6(3); 7; 9(2); 10; 20(4); 21(3); 22; 23; 29; 6:5; 10(5); 11; 13; 14; 17(2); 18(2); 22; 23; 26(2); 7:1(2); 9(3); 11; 14(2); 19(2); 20(2); 25; 26; 8:4(2); 5; 6; 7(2); 11; 21; 22; 24(2); 25(3); 9:2; 4; 10(2); 12; 14(2); 17; 10:6(6); 9(2); 11:2(2); 3; 4(4); 5(2); 6; 7; 9(2); 10(2); 11; 12; 15; 16(2); 17(3); 18(3); 19(2); 20; 21; 24(3); 25(2); 26(2); 28(3); 31; 36; 37; 38(2); 41; 42; 43; 45(2); 12:7(2); **Hos** 1:4; 9; 3:5; 5:5; 13(2); 6:2; 3; 7:5; 9; 10; 8:14(2); 9:8(2); 13; 10:1(2); 6; 11; 11:5; 6(2); 12:2(2); 3(2); 5; 7; 14(3); 13:12; 15(3); 14:5; 6(3); 7; **Joel** 2:7; 8; 11(4); 16; 18(2); 19; 20(4); 3:16(2); **Amos** 1:2; 11(3); 15; 2:4; 7; 9(2); 14; 3:4; 7(2); 4:2; 13(2); 5:8; 19; 6:8; 7:7; 10; 17; 9:6(3); 11; **Obad** 3; 6; 11(2); 14(2); **Jonah** 1:5; 7; 2:1; 3:6(2); 7; 8; 9; 4:6(2); **Mic** 1:2; 3; 11; 2:2(2); 7; 3:4; 8(2); 4:2(2); 4(2); 5; 12; 5:3; 4; 6:2; 7:2; 3; 6; 9; 18(2); **Nah** 1:2(2); 3(2); 5; 6(3); 8; 13; 2:3(2); 5; 12(4); **Hab** 1:11(3); 2:4(2); 5; 6; 9(2); 15; 18; 20; 3:3(2); 4(3); 5; 6; 10(2); 14(2); 16; **Zeph** 1:7; 18; 2:3; 11; 13; 15; 3:5; 17; **Hag** 1:9; 2:12(2); 22; **Zec** 1:21; 2:1; 8; 12; 13; 3:1; 5(2); 10; 4:1; 2; 9; 5:4; 6:12; 13(2); 7:9; 10; 12; 8:4(2); 10; 16; 17; 9:7(4); 10; 14; 16(2); 17(2); 10:3(2); 12; 11:6(2); 17(4); 12:4; 10(2); 13:3(4); 4; 14:4; 9; 13(3); **Mal** 1:3(2); 6(2); 12; 14; 2:6(2); 7; 10; 15; 16; 3:1; 2; 5(2); 14; 16; 17; 4:2; **Mt** 1:2; 11; 18; 21(2); 23; 24; 25; 2:2; 11; 13; 14; 20; 21; 22; 3:3; 4(3); 7; 12(3); 4:6; 18; 21; 24; 5:1; 2; 13; 22(2); 28; 31; 32; 35; 45; 6:27; 29; 33; 7:9; 24; 26; 28; 8:3(2); 13; 14; 16; 20; 21; 23; 25; 9:1; 7; 10; 11; 19; 20; 21; 31; 37; 38; 10:1; 2(2); 10; 24(2); 25(3); 35; 36; 38; 39(2); 42; 11:1; 2; 20; 12:1; 10; 19; 21; 26; 29(2); 33(3); 46(2); 49(2); 13:19; 24; 25(2); 31; 36; 41(2); 52; 54; 55(2); 56; 57(2); 14:2; 3; 11; 12; 15; 19; 22; 31; 36; 15:5(2); 6(2); 12; 23; 32; 33; 36; 16:5; 13; 20; 21; 24(2); 25(2); 26(2); 27(3); 28; 17:1; 2(2); 10; 27; 18:6; 15; 23; 25(2); 28; 29(2); 31; 32; 34; 35; 19:3; 5; 9; 10(2); 13; 15; 23; 25; 28; 20:1; 2; 8; 28; 21:31; 34; 35; 37; 38; 41; 45; 22:3; 5(2); 6; 7; 8; 15; 24(3); 25(2); 33; 45; 23:1;

24:1; 17; 18; 31(2); 32; 43; 45(2); 46; 47; 48(2); 49; 51; 25:14(2); 15(2); 18; 21; 23; 26; 31(2); 32; 33; 34; 41; 26:1; 7; 8; 23; 39; 45; 51(3); 52; 63; 65(2); 67; 27:19; 24; 25; 29(2); 31; 32; 35; 37(2); 44; 53; 60; 64; 28:3(2); 7; 8; 9; 13; **Mk** 1:3; 6; 16; 19; 22; 28; 41; 2:8; 15(2); 16; 23; 3:5; 7; 9; 21; 27(2); 31(2); 4:2; 34; 5:3; 15; 22; 27; 28; 31; 6:1(2); 2; 3; 4(3); 5; 14; 17; 21(2); 26; 27; 28; 29(2); 35; 41; 45; 56; 7:2; 11; 12(2); 17; 19; 25; 32(2); 33(3); 35(2); 8:1; 4; 6; 10; 12; 23(2); 25(2); 26; 27(2); 33; 34(2); 35(2); 36; 37; 38; 9:3; 14; 18; 21; 28; 31; 36; 41; 42; 50; 10:2; 7(2); 10; 11; 13; 16(2); 23; 24; 45; 46; 48; 50; 52; 11:1; 14; 18; 23; 12:6; 13; 19(4); 33; 37; 38; 43; 13:1; 15; 16; 27(2); 34(3); 14:3; 12; 13; 16; 32; 47; 51; 61; 63; 65; 15:17; 20; 21; 24; 26; 27(2); 16:7; **Lk** 1:5; 8; 9; 13; 14; 15; 23(2); 24; 29; 31; 32; 33; 48; 49; 50; 51; 54(2); 55; 59; 60; 62; 63; 64(2); 67; 68; 69; 70; 72; 76; 77; 80; 2:3; 5; 21; 28; 33; 34; 41; 43; 47; 48; 51; 3:1; 4; 17(3); 18; 19; 4:10; 16; 22; 24; 30; 32(2); 40; 5:12; 13; 19; 25; 29; 30; 6:1; 10; 13; 14; 17; 20(2); 40(2); 44; 45(3); 7:1; 3; 11; 12; 15; 16; 19; 38(3); 8:5; 9; 19(2); 22; 35; 39; 41; 44; 9:1; 14; 18; 23; 24(2); 26(2); 29(2); 31; 32; 42; 43; 51; 52; 53; 54; 58; 62; 10:1; 2; 7; 23; 30; 34(2); 39; 11:1(2); 6; 8(2); 18; 21(2); 22(2); 54; 12:1; 22; 25; 27; 39; 42(2); 43; 45(2); 46; 47(2); 13:6; 7; 13; 15(2); 17; 19; 14:17; 21(2); 26(2); 27; 34; 15:5; 6; 12(2); 13(2); 15; 16; 20(3); 22(3); 25; 28; 29; 16:1(2); 5; 18; 20; 21; 23(2); 24; 17:2; 16(2); 24; 31; 33(2); 18:7; 13(2); 14; 15; 39; 43; 19:13; 14; 29; 20:20; 26(2); 28(3); 44; 45; 22:4; 36(2); 39; 44; 45; 50; 51; 71; 23:11; 34; 49; 55; 24:8; 23; 26; 40(2); 47; 50; **Jn** 1:11(2); 12; 14; 16; 35; 41; 2:2; 5; 11(2); 12(3); 17; 21; 22; 23; 3:4; 16; 17; 20; 21; 22; 32; 33(2); 35; 4:2; 5; 6; 8; 12(2); 27; 31; 34; 41; 44; 47; 50; 51; 53; 5:9; 18; 28; 35; 37(2); 38; 43; 47; 6:2; 3; 5; 8; 12; 16; 22(3); 24; 52; 53; 60; 61; 66; 7:3; 5; 10; 16; 17; 18(2); 30; 38; 53; 8:6; 20; 44; 55; 9:1; 2(2); 3; 7; 14; 15; 18(2); 20; 21; 22; 23; 27; 28; 31; 10:3(2); 4(2); 11; 11:2; 3; 7; 8; 12; 13; 16; 32; 41; 44; 54; 12:3; 4; 16; 17; 25(2); 41; 50; 13:1(2); 3; 4; 10; 12; 16; 18; 23; 15:10; 13(2); 15; 19; 20; 16:17; 29; 32; 17:1; 18:1(2); 2; 10; 19(2); 22; 25; 26; 19:2; 17; 23(2); 25(2); 26(2); 27; 29; 30; 33; 34; 35; 20:7; 20(2); 25(2); 26; 30; 31; 21:2; 7; 14; 20; 24; **Acts** 1:3; 7; 14; 18; 20(2); 22; 25; 2:6; 14; 29; 30(2); 31(2); 41; 3:2; 4; 7; 13; 16(2); 18; 21; 26(2); 4:26; 32; 5:1; 2; 7; 10; 31; 32; 41; 6:15; 7:4; 5(2); 6; 10(2); 13; 14(2); 20; 23(2); 25(2); 27; 8:1; 2; 28; 32(2); 33(4); 35; 39; 9:8; 12(2); 17(2); 18; 33; 41; 10:2; 7; 22; 24; 25; 34; 43; 11:13; 29; 12:1; 7(2); 10; 11; 15; 21; 13:8; 9; 13; 16; 23; 24; 25(2); 31; 36(2); 14:3; 8(2); 15:14; 18; 16:1; 3; 27(2); 32; 33; 34(2); 17:2; 16; 28; 18:2; 6; 8; 14; 18(2); 19:6; 12; 31; 33; 20:7; 10; 28; 32; 38; 21:11; 19; 22:14(2); 15; 20; 30; 23:29; 30; 24:8; 23; 24; 27:3; 28:3; 4; 8; 23; 30; **Rom** 1:2; 3; 5; 9; 20; 2:4; 6; 18; 26; 3:7; 20; 24; 25(2); 26; 4:5; 13; 19; 23; 5:8; 9; 10(2); 6:3; 5(2); 16; 8:3; 9; 11; 28; 29; 32; 9:19; 22(2); 23; 11:1; 2; 22; 33(2); 34; 12:20; 13:10; 14:4; 5; 13; 15:2(2); 9; 10; 16:13; 15; **1Cor** 1:9; 29; 2:10; 3:8(2); 5:1; 6:5; 14; 18; 7:2; 4; 7; 11; 33; 36; 37(4); 9:7; 10; 10:24; 28; 11:4(2); 7; 21; 14:25(2); 30; 15:10; 23(2); 25; 27; 38; 16:12; **2Cor** 2:11; 14; 3:7; 13; 5:10; 7:7; 12(2); 13; 15; 8:9; 17; 9:7; 9; 15; 10:10(3); 11:3; 15; 33; **Gal** 1:15; 16; 3:16; 4:4; 6; 5:10; 6:4; 5; 8; **Eph** 1:5; 6; 7(2); 9(2); 11; 12; 14; 18(2); 19(2); 20; 22; 23; 2:4; 7(2); 10; 15; 3:5; 6; 7; 16(2); 4:25; 28; 5:28; 29; 30(3); 31(2); 33; 6:10; **Phil** 1:29; 2:4; 13; 30; 3:10(3); 21; 4:19; **Col** 1:9; 11; 13; 14; 20; 22(2); 24; 26; 29; 2:14; 18; 3:9; 4:15; **1Th** 1:10; 2:11; 12; 19; 3:13; 4:4; 6; 8; **2Th** 1:7; 9; 10; 11; 2:6; 8(2); **1Ti** 3:4(2); 5; 5:8(2); 18; 6:1; 15; **2Ti** 1:8; 9; 2:19; 26; 4:1(2); 8; 14; 18; **Titus** 1:3; 3:5; 7; **Heb** 1:2; 3(3); 7(2); 2:4; 8; 17; 3:2; 5; 6; 7; 15; 18; 4:1; 4; 7; 10(3); 13; 5:7; 6:10; 17; 7:10; 27; 8:11(2); 9:12; 10:13(2); 20; 30; 11:4; 5; 7; 17; 21; 22; 23; 12:10; 16; 13:12; 13; 15; 21(2); **Jas** 1:8; 11; 14; 18(2); 23; 24; 25; 26(2); 2:21; 22; 3:13; 4:11(2); 5:20; **1Pet** 1:3; 2:9; 21; 22; 24(2); 3:10(2); 12; 4:2; 13; 5:10; **2Pet** 1:3; 9; 16; 2:8; 16; 22; 3:4; 9; 13; 16; **1Jn** 1:3; 7; 10; 2:3; 4; 5; 9; 10; 11(2); 12; 28; 3:9; 10; 12(3); 14; 15; 16; 17(2); 22(2); 23(2); 24; 4:9; 10; 12; 13; 20(2); 21; 5:2; 3(2); 9; 10; 11; 14; 16; 20; **2Jn** 6; 11; **3Jn** 7; 10; **Jude** 14; 24; **Rev** 1:1(3); 4; 5; 6; 14(3); 15(2); 16(4); 17(2); 2:1; 5; 18(2); 3:5(3); 21; 6:5; 8; 17; 7:15; 9:11; 10:1(3); 2(3); 5; 7; 11:15; 19(2); 12:3; 4; 5; 7(2); 9; 10; 15; 16; 13:1(2); 2(4); 3(2); 6(3); 17; 18; 14:1; 7; 9(4); 10; 11(2); 14(2); 16; 19; 15:2(3); 8; 16:2(2); 3; 4; 8; 10(2); 12; 15(2); 17; 19; 17:17; 18:1; 19:2(2); 5; 7; 10; 12(2); 13; 15; 16(2); 19; 20; 21; 20:1; 4(2); 7; 21:3; 7; 22:3; 4(2); 6(2); 12; 14; 19

HOW

Gen 26:9; 27:20; 28:17; 30:29(2); 38:29; 39:9; 44:8; 16; 34; 47:8; 18; **Ex** 2:18; 6:12; 30; 9:29; 10:2; 3; 7; 11:7; 16:28; 18:8; 19:4; 36:1; **Num** 10:31; 14:11(2); 27; 20:15; 23:8(2); 24:5; **Deut** 1:12; 31; 7:17; 9:7; 11:4(2); 6; 12:30; 18:21; 25:18; 29:16(2); 31:27; 32:30; **Josh** 2:10; 9:7; 24; 10:1(2); 14:12; 18:3; **Judg** 13:12(2); 16:15; 18:7; 20:3; 21:7; 16; **Ruth** 1:6; 2:11; 3:18; **1Sa** 1:14; 2:22; 10:27; 12:24; 14:29; 30; 15:2; 16:1; 2; 17:18; 23:3; 24:10; 18; 28:9; **2Sa** 1:4; 5; 14; 19; 25; 27; 2:22; 26; 4:11; 6:9; 20; 11:7(3); 12:18; 16:11; 18:19; 19:2; 34; 24:3; **1Kin** 3:7; 5:3; 8:27; 12:6; 14:19(2); 18:13; 21; 19:1; 20:7; 21:29; 22:16; 45; **2Kin** 5:7; 13; 6:15; 32; 8:5; 9:25; 10:4; 14:15; 28(2); 17:28; 18:24; 19:25; 20:3; 20; **1Chr** 13:12; 18:9; 19:5; **2Chr** 6:18; 7:3; 18:15; 20:11; 32:15; 33:19; **Ezr** 7:22; **Neh** 2:6; 17; **Est** 2:11; 5:11; 8:6(2); **Job** 4:19; 6:25; 7:19; 8:2(2); 9:2; 14; 13:23; 15:16; 18:2; 19:2; 21:17(2); 34; 22:12; 13; 25:4(2); 6; 26:2(2); 3(2); 14; 34:19; 37:17; **Ps** 3:1; 4:2(2); 6:3; 8:1; 9; 11:1; 13:1(2); 2(2); 21:1; 31:19; 35:17; 36:7; 39:4; 44:2(2); 62:3; 66:3; 73:11; 19; 74:9; 10; 22; 78:40; 43; 79:5; 80:4; 82:2; 84:1; 89:46; 47; 50; 90:13; 92:5; 94:3(2); 4; 104:24; 119:84; 97; 103; 159; 132:2; 133:1(2); 137:4; 139:17(2); **Prov** 1:22; 5:12; 6:9; 15:11; 23; 16:16; 19:7; 20:24; 21:27; 30:13; **Eccl** 2:16; 4:11; 10:15; 11:5; **Song** 4:10(2); 5:3(2); 7:1; 6(2); **Is** 1:21; 6:11; 14:4; 12(2); 19:11; 20:6; 36:9; 37:26; 38:3; 48:11; 50:4; 52:7; **Jer** 2:21; 23; 3:19; 4:14; 21; 5:7; 8:8; 9:7; 19; 12:4; 5(2); 15:5; 22:23; 23:26; 31:22; 36:17; 46:13; 47:5; 6; 7; 48:14; 17; 39(2); 49:25; 50:23(2); 51:41(3); **Lam** 1:1(3); 2:1; 4:1(2); 2; **Eze** 14:21; 15:5; 16:30; 26:17; 33:10; **Dan** 4:3(2); 8:13; 10:17; 12:6; **Hos** 8:5; 11:8(4); **Joel** 1:18; **Obad** 5; 6(2); **Mic** 2:4; **Hab** 1:2; 2:6; **Zeph** 2:15; **Hag** 2:3; **Zec** 1:12; 9:17(2); **Mt** 6:23; 28; 7:4; 11(2); 10:19; 25; 12:4; 5; 12; 14; 26; 29; 34; 15:34; 16:9; 10; 11; 12; 21; 17:17(2); 18:12; 21; 21:20; 22:12; 15; 43; 45; 23:33; 37; 26:54; 27:13; **Mk** 2:16; 26; 3:6; 23; 4:13; 27; 40; 5:16; 19; 20; 6:38; 8:5; 19; 20; 21; 9:12; 19(2); 21; 10:23; 24; 11:18; 12:26; 35; 41; 14:1; 11; 15:4; **Lk** 1:34; 58; 62; 2:49; 6:4; 42; 7:22; 8:18; 39(2); 47; 9:41; 10:26; 11:13(2); 18; 12:11; 24; 27; 28; 50; 56; 13:34; 14:7; 15:17; 16:2; 5; 7; 18:24; 19:15; 20:41; 44; 21:5; 22:2; 4; 61; 23:55; 24:6; 20; 35; **Jn** 3:4; 9; 12; 4:1; 9; 5:44; 47; 6:42; 52; 7:15; 8:33; 9:10; 15; 16; 19; 26; 10:24; 11:36; 12:19; 34; 14:5; 9; 22; 28; **Acts** 2:8; 4:21; 5:9; 7:25; 8:31; 9:13; 16; 27(2); 10:28; 38; 11:13; 16; 12:14; 17; 13:32; 14:27; 15:7; 14; 36; 19:35; 20:20; 35(2); 21:20; 23:30; **Rom** 3:6; 4:10; 6:2; 7:1; 18; 8:32; 10:14(3); 15(2); 11:2; 12; 24; 33; **1Cor** 1:26; 3:10; 6:3; 7:16; 32; 33; 34; 10:1; 14:7; 9; 16; 26; 15:3; 12; 35; **2Cor** 3:8; 7:15; 8:2; 12:4; 13:5; **Gal** 1:13; 4:9; 13; 6:11; **Eph** 3:3; 6:21; **Phil** 1:8; 2:23; 4:12(2); **Col** 4:6; **1Th** 1:9; 2:10; 11; 4:1; 4; **2Th** 3:7; **1Ti** 3:5(2); 15; **2Ti** 1:18; **Philem** 1:16; 19; **Heb** 2:3; 7:4; 8:6; 9:14; 10:29; 12:17; **Jas** 2:22; 24; 3:5; **2Pet** 2:9; **1Jn** 3:17; 4:20; **Jude** 5; 18; **Rev** 2:2; 3:3; 6:10; 18:7

HUNDRED

Gen 5:3; 4; 5; 6; 7; 8; 10; 11; 13; 14; 16; 17; 18; 19; 20; 22; 23; 25; 26; 27; 28; 30; 31; 32; 6:3; 15; 7:6; 24; 8:3; 9:28; 29; 11:10; 11; 13; 15; 17; 19; 21; 23; 25; 32; 14:14; 15:13; 17:17; 21:5; 23:1; 15; 16; 25:7; 17; 32:6; 14(2); 33:1; 19; 35:28; 45:22; 47:9; 28; 50:22; 26; **Ex** 6:16; 18; 20; 12:37; 40; 41; 14:7; 27:9; 11; 18; 30:23(3); 24; 38:9; 11; 24; 25(2); 26(2); 27(3); 28; 29; **Lev** 26:8(2); **Num** 1:21; 23; 25; 27; 29; 31; 33; 35; 37; 39; 41; 43; 46(2); 2:4; 6; 8; 9(2); 11; 13; 15; 16(2); 19; 21; 23; 24(2); 26; 28; 30; 31(2); 32(2); 3:22; 28; 34; 43; 46; 50; 4:36; 40; 44; 48; 7:13; 19; 25; 31; 37; 43; 49; 55; 61; 67; 73; 79; 85(2); 86; 11:21; 16:2; 17; 35; 49; 26:7; 10; 14; 18; 22; 25; 27; 34; 37; 41; 43; 47; 50; 51(2); 31:28; 32; 36(2); 37; 39; 43(2); 45; 52; 33:39; **Deut** 22:19; 31:2; 34:7; **Josh** 7:21; 24:29; 32; **Judg** 2:8; 3:31; 4:3; 13; 7:6; 7; 8; 16; 19; 22; 8:4; 10; 26; 11:26; 15:4; 16:5; 17:2; 3; 4; 18:11; 16; 17; 20:2; 10(2); 15; 16; 17; 35; 47; 21:12; **1Sa** 11:8; 13:15; 14:2; 15:4; 17:7; 18:25; 27; 22:2; 23:13; 25:13(2); 18(3); 27:2; 30:9; 10(2); 17; 21; **2Sa** 2:31; 3:14; 8:4(2); 10:18; 14:26; 15:11; 18; 16:1(3); 21:16; 23:8; 18; 24:9(2); **1Kin** 4:23; 5:16; 6:1; 7:2; 20; 42; 8:63; 9:23; 28; 10:10; 14; 16(2); 17; 26; 29(2); 11:3(2); 12:21; 18:4; 13; 19(2); 22; 20:15; 29; 22:6; **2Kin** 3:4(2); 26; 4:43; 14:13; 18:14; 19:35; 23:33; **1Chr** 4:42; 5:18; 21(2); 7:3; 9; 11; 8:40; 9:6; 9; 13; 22; 11:11; 20; 12:14; 24; 25; 26; 27; 30; 32; 35; 37; 15:5; 6; 7; 8; 10; 18:4; 21:3; 5(2); 25; 22:14; 25:7; 26:30; 32; 29:7; **2Chr** 1:14; 17(2); 2:2; 17(2); 18; 3:4; 8; 16; 4:8; 13; 5:12; 7:5; 8:10; 18; 9:9; 13; 15(2); 16(2); 11:1; 12:3; 13:3(2); 17; 14:8(2); 9; 15:11; 17:11(2); 14; 15; 16; 17; 18; 18:5; 24:15; 25:5; 6(2); 9; 23; 26:12; 13(2); 27:5; 28:6; 8; 29:32(2); 33; 35:8(2); 9; 36:3; **Ezr** 1:10; 11; 2:3; 4; 5; 6; 7; 8; 9; 10; 11; 12; 13; 15; 17; 18; 19; 21; 23; 25; 26; 27; 28; 30; 31; 32; 33; 34; 35; 36; 38; 41; 42; 58; 60; 64; 65(2); 66(2); 67(2); 69; 6:17(3); 7:22(4); 8:3; 4; 5; 9; 10; 12; 20; 26(3); **Neh** 5:17; 7:8; 9; 10; 11; 12; 13; 14; 15; 16; 17; 18; 20; 22; 23; 24; 26; 27; 29; 30; 31; 32; 34; 35; 36; 37; 38; 39; 41; 44; 45; 60; 62; 66; 67(2); 68(2); 69(2); 70; 71; 11:6; 8; 12; 13; 14; 18; 19; **Est** 1:1; 4; 8:9; 9:6; 12; 15; 30; **Job** 1:3(2); 42:16; **Prov** 17:10; **Eccl** 6:3; 8:12; **Song** 8:12; **Is** 37:36; 65:20(2); **Jer** 52:23; 29; 30(2); **Eze** 4:5; 9; 40:19; 23; 27; 47(2); 41:13(2); 14; 15; 42:2; 8; 16; 17; 18; 19; 20(2); 45:2(2); 15; 48:16(4); 17(4); 30; 32; 33; 34; **Dan** 6:1; 8:14; 12:11; 12; **Amos** 5:3(2); **Mt** 18:12; 28; **Mk** 4:8; 20; 6:37; 14:5; **Lk** 7:41; 15:4; 16:6; 7; **Jn** 6:7; 12:5; 19:39; 21:8; 11; **Acts** 1:15; 5:36; 7:6; 13:20; 23:23(2); 27:37; **Rom** 4:19; **1Cor** 15:6; **Gal** 3:17; **Rev** 7:4; 9:16; 11:3; 12:6; 13:18; 14:1; 3; 20; 21:17

I

Gen 1:29; 30; 2:18; 3:10(4); 11; 12; 13; 15; 16; 17; 4:1; 9(2); 13; 14(2); 23; 6:7(3); 13; 17(2); 18; 7:1; 4(3); 8:21(3); 9:3; 5(3); 9(2); 11; 12; 13; 14; 15; 16(2); 17; 12:1; 2(2); 3; 7; 11; 13; 19; 13:8; 9(3); 15; 16; 17; 14:22; 23(3); 15:1; 2; 7; 8(2); 14; 18; 16:2(2); 5(2); 8; 10; 13; 17:1; 2; 5; 6(2); 7; 8(2); 16(2); 19; 20(3); 21; 18:3(2); 4; 5; 10; 12(2); 13; 14; 15; 17(2); 19; 21(2); 26(2); 27; 28(2); 29; 30(3); 31(2); 32(2); 19:2; 7; 8(2); 19(2); 21(2); 22; 34; 20:5; 6(3); 9; 11; 13; 16; 21:7; 13; 18; 23; 24; 26(2); 30; 22:1; 2; 5; 7; 11; 12; 16; 17(2); 23:4(2); 8; 11(3); 13(3); 24:2; 3(2); 5; 7; 12; 13; 14(5); 17; 19; 23; 24; 27; 31; 33(2); 34; 37; 39; 40; 42(2); 43(3); 44; 45(3); 46(2); 47(2); 48; 49; 56; 58; 25:22; 30(2); 32; 26:2; 3(4); 4; 9(2); 24(2); 27:1; 2(2); 3; 4(3); 6; 7; 8; 9; 11; 12(2); 18; 19(3); 21(2); 24; 25; 32; 33; 37(4); 41; 45(2); 46; 28:13(2); 15(4); 16; 20; 21; 22(2); 29:18; 19(2); 21; 25; 33; 34; 35; 30:1; 2; 3; 8(2); 13; 14; 16; 18; 20; 25; 26(2); 27(3); 28; 29; 30(2); 31(2); 32; 34; 31:3; 5; 6; 10; 11(2); 12; 13; 27; 31(2); 35; 38(2); 39(2); 40; 41(2); 43; 44; 51; 52; 32:4; 5(3); 9; 10(3); 11(2); 12; 20(2); 26; 29; 30; 33:8; 9; 10(4); 11(2); 12; 14(3); 34:8; 11; 12; 30(3); 35:3(2); 11; 12(3); 37:6(2); 9; 10; 13(2); 14; 16(2); 17; 30(2); 35; 38:16; 17; 18; 22; 23; 25(2); 26(2); 39:9(2); 14; 15; 18; 40:8; 11(2); 14; 15(2); 16(2); 41:9; 11; 15(2); 17; 19; 21; 22; 24; 28; 40; 41; 44; 42:2; 14; 18; 22; 33; 34(2); 37(2); 43:9(2); 14(2); 23; 44:15; 17; 18; 21; 28(2); 30; 32(2); 33; 34(2); 45:3; 4(2); 11; 18; 28(2); 46:2; 3(2); 4(2); 30; 31; 47:16; 23; 29(3); 30(2); 48:4(2); 5; 7(2); 9(2); 11; 19(2); 21; 22(2); 49:1; 7; 18; 29; 31; 50:4(2); 5(4); 17; 19; 21; 24; **Ex** 2:7; 9; 10; 22; 3:3; 4; 6; 7(2); 8; 9; 10; 11(3); 12(2); 13(2); 14(3); 16; 17(2); 19; 20(2); 21; 4:10(2); 11; 12; 13; 14; 15; 18; 21(2); 23(2); 5:2(3); 10; 23; 6:1; 2; 3(2); 4; 5(2); 6(4); 7(3); 8(4); 29(2); 30; 7:1; 2; 3; 4; 5(2); 17(2); 8:2; 8; 9; 21; 22(2); 23; 28; 29(2); 9:14; 15(2); 16; 18; 27(2); 28; 29(2); 30; 10:1(2); 2(3); 4; 10; 16; 17; 29; 11:1; 4; 8; 12:12(3); 13(3); 17; 13:8; 15(2); 14:4(3); 17(3); 18(2); 15:1; 2(2); 9(4); 26(3); 16:4(2); 12(2); 32(2); 17:4; 6; 9; 14; 18:3; 6; 11; 16(2); 19; 19:4(2); 9(2); 20:2; 5; 22; 24(3); 21:5(2); 13; 22:23; 24; 27(2); 23:7; 13; 15; 20(2); 22(2); 23; 25; 26; 27(2); 28; 29; 30; 31(2); 24:12(2); 25:8; 9; 16; 21; 22(3); 28:3; 29:35; 42; 43; 44(2); 45; 46(3); 30:6; 36; 31:2; 3; 6(4); 11; 13; 32:8; 9; 10(2); 13(3); 18; 24(2); 30(2); 32; 33; 34(3); 33:1(2); 2(2); 3(2); 5(2); 12; 13(4); 14; 16(2); 17(2); 18; 19(4); 22(2); 23; 34:1; 9(2); 10(3); 11(2); 18; 24; 27; **Lev** 6:17; 7:34; 8:31; 35; 10:3(2); 13; 18; 19; 11:44(2); 45(2); 14:34(2); 16:2; 17:10; 11; 12; 14; 18:2; 3; 4; 5; 6; 21; 24; 25; 30; 19:2; 3; 4; 10; 12; 14; 16; 18; 25; 28; 30; 31; 32; 34; 36; 37; 20:3; 5; 6; 7; 8; 22; 23(2); 24(3); 25; 26; 21:8; 12; 15; 23; 22:2; 3; 8; 9; 16; 30; 31; 32(2); 33; 23:10; 22; 30; 43(3); 24:22; 25:2; 17; 21; 38; 42; 55(2); 26:1; 2; 4; 6(2); 9; 11; 12; 13(2); 16(2); 17; 18; 19(2); 21; 22; 24; 25(2); 26; 28(3); 30; 31(2); 32; 33; 36; 41; 42(3); 44(3); 45(4); **Num** 3:12(2); 13(3); 41; 45; 5:3; 6:27; 8:16; 17(2); 18; 19; 9:8; 10:10; 29; 30(2); 31; 11:11; 12(2); 13; 14; 15(2); 17(2); 21(2); 12:6; 8; 11; 13; 13:2; 14:11; 12; 17; 19; 20; 21; 22; 23; 24; 27(2); 28(2); 30; 31; 35(2); 15:2; 18; 41(2); 16:8; 15(2); 21; 26; 28; 45; 17:4; 5(2); 18:6(2); 7; 8(2); 11; 12; 19; 20; 21; 24(2); 26; 20:12; 17; 18; 19(3); 24; 21:2; 16; 34; 22:6(4); 8; 11; 16; 17(3); 18; 19(2); 20; 28; 29(2); 30(3); 32; 33; 34(3); 35; 37(2); 38(3); 23:3(2); 4(2); 8(2); 9(2); 11; 12; 13; 15; 20(2); 26(2); 27(2); 24:10; 11; 12; 13(2); 14(2); 17(2); 25:11; 12; 27:12; 32:8; 11; 33:53; 56(2); 35:34(2); **Deut** 1:8; 9(2); 12; 13; 15; 16; 17; 18; 20; 23; 29; 35; 36; 39; 42; 43; 2:5(2); 9(2); 13; 19(2); 24; 25; 26; 27(2); 28(3); 29; 31; 3:2; 12; 13; 15; 16; 18; 19(2); 20; 21; 23; 25; 4:1; 2(2); 5; 8; 10; 21(2); 22(2); 26; 40; 5:1; 5; 6; 9; 28; 31(2); 6:2; 6; 7:11; 17(2); 8:1; 11; 19; 9:9(3); 12; 13; 14(2); 15; 16; 17; 18(2); 19; 20; 21(2); 23; 24; 25(2); 26; 10:2; 3; 5(2); 10; 11; 13; 11:2; 8; 13; 14; 15; 22; 26; 27; 28; 32; 12:11; 14; 20; 21; 28; 30; 32; 13:18; 15:5; 11; 15; 16; 17:3; 14; 18:16; 18(2); 19; 20; 19:7; 9; 22:14(3); 16; 17; 24:8; 18; 22; 25:8; 26:3(2); 10; 13(3); 14(3); 27:1; 4; 10; 28:1; 13; 14; 15; 68; 29:5; 6; 14; 19(2); 30:1; 2; 8; 11; 15; 16; 18; 19(2); 31:2(2); 5; 14; 16; 17(2); 18; 20(2); 21(3); 23(2); 27(2); 28; 29(2); 32:1; 3; 20(2); 21(2); 23(2); 24; 26(3); 27; 39(6); 40(2); 41(2); 42; 46; 49; 52; 33:9; 34:4(3); **Josh** 1:2; 3(2); 5(3); 6; 9; 2:4; 5; 9; 12(2); 3:7(3); 5:9; 14; 6:2; 10; 7:8; 11; 12; 19; 20(2); 21(2); 8:1; 5; 8; 18; 10:8; 11:6; 13:6(2); 14:7(2); 8; 10; 11(2); 12; 15:16; 17:14; 18:4; 6; 8; 20:2; 22:2; 23:2; 4(2); 14; 24:3; 4(2); 5(4); 6; 7; 8(3); 10(2); 11; 12; 13; **Judg** 1:2; 3; 7; 12; 2:1(4); 3(2); 20; 21; 22; 3:19; 20; 4:7(2); 8(2); 9; 19(2); 22; 5:3(3); 7(2); 6:8; 9; 10(2); 14; 15(2); 16; 17; 18(3); 22; 37(2); 39(2); 7:4(3); 7; 9; 13; 17(2); 18(2); 8:2; 3; 5(2); 7; 9(2); 19; 23; 24; 9:2(2); 9; 11; 13; 29; 38; 48; 10:11; 12; 13; 11:9; 17; 27; 31(2); 35(2); 37(2); 12:2(2); 3(2); 13:4; 6; 11; 13; 14; 15; 16; 14:2; 12(2); 16(2); 15:1; 2(3); 3(2); 7(2); 11; 16; 18; 16:6; 7; 10; 11; 15; 17(3); 20; 26(2); 28(3); 17:2; 3(2); 9(3); 10; 13(2); 18:4; 24(2); 19:6; 8; 9; 11; 18(3); 23; 24; 20:4(2); 6; 23; 28(3); **Ruth** 1:12(4); 16(2); 17(2); 21; 2:2; 7; 9; 10(2); 13; 19; 3:1; 5; 9; 11; 12(2); 13; 4:4(4); 6(3); 9; 10; **1Sa** 1:8; 11; 15(2); 16; 20; 22(2); 26; 27(2); 28; 2:1; 16; 23; 24; 27; 28(2); 29; 30(2); 31; 33; 35(2); 36(2); 3:4; 5(2); 6(2); 8; 11; 12(4); 13(2); 14; 16; 17; 4:16(2); 7:5; 8:7; 8; 9:8(2); 16(2); 17; 18; 19(2); 21; 23(2); 24(2); 26; 27; 10:2; 8(2); 15; 18; 11:2(2); 12:1; 2(2); 3(7); 7; 17; 23(2); 13:11; 12(3); 14:7; 24; 29(2); 37; 40; 43(2); 15:2; 6; 11; 13; 14; 16; 20; 24(3); 25(2); 26; 30(3); 16:1(3); 2(2); 3(2); 5; 7; 18; 22; 17:8; 9; 10; 28; 29; 35(2); 39(2); 43; 44; 45; 46(2); 55; 58; 18:11; 17; 18(2); 21; 23; 19:2; 3(4); 15; 17; 20:1; 3; 4; 5(2); 9(2); 12(2); 13; 14(2); 20(2); 21(2); 22; 23; 29(3); 30; 36; 21:2(3); 5; 8; 15; 22:3(2); 9; 12; 15; 22(2); 23:2; 4; 11; 17; 22; 23(2); 24:4; 6; 10(2); 11(2); 17(2); 20; 25:7; 8; 11(3); 19; 21; 22; 24; 25(2); 28; 35; 26:6; 8(2); 11(2); 18; 19; 21(3); 23; 27:1(3); 5(2); 28:2; 7; 8(2); 11; 13; 15(3); 21; 22; 23; 29:3; 6; 8(3); 9; 30:7; 8(2); 13(2); 15; **2Sa** 1:3; 4; 6; 7(2); 8(2); 9; 10(3); 13; 16; 26; 2:1(2); 6; 20; 22(2); 3:8; 9; 13(2); 14; 18; 21; 28; 35; 39; 4:10(2); 11; 5:19(2); 6:21; 22(2); 7:2; 6(2); 7(3); 8; 9; 10; 11; 12(2); 13; 14(2); 15(2); 18; 27; 9:1; 3; 7; 8; 9; 10:2; 11; 11:5; 11(2); 12; 12:7(2); 8(2); 11(2); 12; 13; 22(2); 23(3); 27; 28; 13:4; 5(2); 6(2); 10; 13(3); 24; 26; 28(2); 14:2; 5; 8; 11; 12; 15(2); 18(2); 21; 22; 32(3); 15:4(2); 7(2); 8(2); 20(3); 25; 26(2); 28; 31; 34(3); 16:4(2); 9; 10; 18(2); 19(4); 17:1; 2(2); 3; 11; 15; 18:2; 4; 10; 11; 12(2); 13; 14; 18; 22; 29(2); 33; 19:6; 7; 20(2); 22(3); 26(2); 28; 29; 33; 34(2); 35(5); 37(2); 38(2); 20:16(2); 17(2); 19; 20; 21; 21:3(2); 4; 6; 22:3; 4(2); 7; 22; 23; 24; 30(2); 38(2); 39; 41; 43(2); 44; 50(2); 23:17; 24:2; 10(4); 12(2); 13; 14; 17(3); 24(2); **1Kin** 1:5; 12; 14; 21; 30(2); 35; 2:2; 7; 8(3); 14; 15; 16; 17; 18; 20(3); 26; 30; 42(2); 43; 3:5; 7(2); 9; 12(2); 13; 14; 17(2); 18; 21(3); 5:5(2); 6; 8(2); 9; 6:12(2); 13; 8:13; 16(3); 20; 21; 26; 27; 43; 44; 48; 59; 9:3(2); 4; 5(2); 6; 7(4); 10:6; 7(3); 11:11(2); 12(2); 13(2); 21; 31; 32; 34(3); 35; 36(2); 37; 38(3); 39; 12:6; 11(2); 14(2); 13:7; 8(2); 14; 16(2); 18; 31; 14:2(2); 6; 7; 10; 15:19; 16:2; 3; 17:1; 4; 9; 10(2); 11; 12(3); 18; 20; 21; 24; 18:1; 8; 9; 12(4); 13(2); 15(2); 18; 22(2); 23; 24; 36(2); 19:2; 4; 10(3); 14(3); 18; 20(3); 20:4(2); 5; 6; 7(2); 9(2); 13(2); 28(2); 31; 32; 34(2); 35; 37; 42; 21:2(3); 3; 4; 6(3); 7; 20; 21; 29(2); 22:4; 5; 6(2); 8; 13; 14; 16; 17; 18; 19; 21; 22(2); 27; 30; 34; **2Kin** 1:2; 10; 12; 13; 2:2(2); 3; 4(2); 5; 6(2); 9(3); 10; 18; 19; 21; 3:7(2); 13; 14(3); 4:2; 9; 10; 13; 22(2); 24; 26; 28(2); 30; 43; 5:5; 6; 7(2); 11; 12; 15(2); 16(2); 17; 18(2); 20; 22; 6:3(2); 13; 17; 18; 19; 21(2); 27; 29; 33; 7:12; 13(2); 8:4; 8; 9; 12; 9:3; 5; 6; 7; 8; 9; 12; 17; 25; 26(2); 10:9; 19; 24; 16:7; 17:13(2); 38; 18:14(2); 20; 23(2); 25; 26; 32; 19:7(2); 19; 20; 23(2); 24(2); 25(3); 27; 28(2); 34; 20:3(2); 5(3); 6(3); 8; 15; 21:4; 7(2); 8(3); 12; 13(2); 14; 22:8; 16; 19(2); 20(2); 23:17; 27(4); **1Chr** 4:9; 5:3; 11:19(2); 13:12; 14:10(2); 15:12; 16:18; 17:1; 5(2); 6(3); 7; 8; 9; 10(3); 11(2); 12; 13(3); 14; 16; 19:2; 12; 21:2; 8(4); 10(2); 12; 13; 17(3); 22; 23(2); 24(2); 22:5; 9(2); 10(2); 14(2); 23:5; 28:2; 6(2); 7; 29:2; 3(4); 14; 17(3); 19; **2Chr** 1:7; 10; 11; 12; 2:4; 5; 6(2); 8; 9; 10; 13; 6:2; 5(3); 6; 10; 11; 18; 33; 34; 38; 40; 7:12; 13(3); 14; 16; 17; 18(2); 19; 20(4); 9:5; 6(3); 10:11(2); 14(2); 12:5; 7(2); 16:3; 18:3; 4; 5; 7; 12; 13; 14; 15; 16; 17; 18; 20; 21; 26; 29; 33; 20:11; 25:9; 16; 28:23; 32:13; 33:7(2); 8(3); 34:15; 24; 27; 28(2); 35:21(3); 23; **Ezr** 4:19; 6:8; 11; 12; 7:13; 21(2); 28(2); 8:15(2); 16; 17(2); 21; 22; 24; 26; 28; 9:3(2); 4; 5(2); 6; **Neh** 1:1; 2; 4(2); 5; 6(2); 8(2); 9(2); 11(3); 2:1(2); 2; 4; 5(2); 6; 7(2); 8; 9; 11; 12(4); 13; 14; 15; 16(3); 17; 18; 20; 4:13(2); 14; 19; 22; 23; 5:6(2); 7(3); 8; 9; 10(2); 11; 12; 13; 14(2); 15; 16; 18; 19; 6:1(2); 3(4); 4; 8; 10; 11(4); 12; 13; 7:1; 2; 3; 5; 7; 9:8; 12:31; 38; 40; 13:6(3); 7; 8; 9(2); 10; 11(2); 13; 14; 15(2); 17; 19(2); 21(2); 22; 23; 25; 28; 30; **Est** 3:9; 4:11; 16(4); 5:4; 8(3); 12; 13; 7:3; 4(2); 8:5(2); 6(2); 7; **Job** 1:15; 16; 17; 19; 21(2); 3:3; 11(3); 12; 13(3); 16; 24; 25(2); 26(3); 4:7; 8; 16(2); 5:3(2); 8(2); 6:8(2); 10(3); 11(2); 22; 24(2); 28; 29; 7:3; 4(4); 8; 11(3); 12; 13; 16(2); 19; 20(3); 21(2); 8:8; 18; 9:2; 11(2); 14; 15(3); 16(2); 19; 20(3); 21(3); 22; 27(3); 28(2); 29(2); 30;

32(2); 35; 10:1(2); 2; 7; 9; 13; 14; 15(4); 18; 19(3); 20; 21(2); 11:4; 12:3(2); 4; 13:2(2); 3(2); 13; 14; 15(2); 18(3); 19(2); 20; 22; 14:14; 15; 15:6; 17(3); 16:2; 4(2); 5; 6(3); 12; 15; 22(2); 17:6; 10; 13(2); 14; 19:4; 7(3); 8; 10; 15; 16(2); 17; 18; 19; 20; 25; 26; 27; 20:2; 3; 21:3(2); 6(2); 27; 22:22; 23:3(3); 4; 5; 7; 8(2); 9(2); 10(2); 11; 12(2); 15(3); 17; 27:5(3); 6(2); 11(2); 29:2; 3; 4; 6; 7(2); 12; 13; 14; 15(2); 16(3); 17; 18(3); 24; 25; 30:1(2); 9(2); 19; 20(2); 23; 25; 26(2); 28(3); 29; 31:1(2); 5; 9; 13; 14(2); 16; 18; 19; 21(2); 23; 24; 25; 26; 28; 29; 30; 32; 33; 34(2); 36; 37(2); 39; 32:6(2); 7; 10(2); 11(2); 12; 14; 16; 17(3); 18; 20(3); 21; 22; 33:1; 2; 6(2); 8; 9(2); 12; 24; 27; 31; 32; 33; 34:5; 6; 31(2); 32(3); 33; 35:3(2); 4; 36:2(2); 3; 37:20; 38:3; 4; 9; 23; 39:6; 40:4(3); 5(3); 7; 14; 15; 41:11; 12; 42:2; 3(3); 4(3); 5; 6; 8(2); **Ps** 2:6; 7(2); 8; 3:4; 5(2); 6; 4:1(2); 3; 8; 5:2; 3; 7(2); 6:2; 6(3); 7:1; 3; 4(2); 17; 8:3; 9:1(2); 2(2); 13; 14(2); 10:6(2); 11:1; 12:5(2); 13:2; 3; 4(2); 5; 6; 16:1; 4; 6; 7; 8(2); 17:3; 4; 6; 15(3); 18:1; 2; 3(2); 6; 21; 22; 23(2); 29(2); 37(2); 38; 40; 42(2); 43; 49; 19:13(2); 20:6; 22:2; 6; 9; 10; 14; 17; 22(2); 25; 23:1; 4(2); 6; 25:1; 2; 5; 16; 20; 21; 26:1(3); 3; 4(2); 5; 6(2); 7; 8; 11; 12; 27:1(2); 3; 4(3); 6(3); 7; 8; 13(2); 14; 28:1(2); 2(2); 7(2); 30:1; 2; 3; 6(2); 7; 8(2); 9; 12; 31:1; 5; 6(2); 7; 9; 11; 12(2); 13; 14(2); 17; 22(3); 32:3; 5(4); 8(2); 34:1; 4; 11; 35:3; 11; 13; 14(2); 15; 18(2); 37:25(2); 35; 36; 38:6(3); 8(2); 13(2); 14; 15; 16; 17; 18(2); 20; 39:1(4); 2(2); 3(2); 4(2); 7; 9(2); 10; 12; 13(2); 40:1; 5; 7(2); 8; 9(2); 10(3); 12; 17; 41:4(2); 9; 10; 11; 42:2; 4(4); 5; 6; 9(2); 11; 43:2; 4(2); 5; 44:6; 45:1(2); 17; 46:10(3); 49:4(2); 5; 50:7(3); 8; 9; 11; 12(2); 13; 15; 21(3); 22; 23; 51:3; 4; 5; 7(2); 13; 16; 52:8(2); 9(2); 54:6(2); 55:2; 6(3); 7; 8; 9; 12(2); 16; 17; 23; 56:3(2); 4(3); 9(2); 10(2); 11(2); 12; 13; 57:1; 2; 4; 7; 8; 9(2); 59:9; 16(2); 17; 60:6(2); 8; 61:2(2); 4(2); 8(2); 62:2; 6; 11; 63:1; 2; 4(3); 6; 7; 66:13(2); 14; 15(2); 16; 17; 18; 68:22(2); 69:2(2); 3(2); 4(2); 7; 8; 10; 11(2); 12; 17; 20(3); 29; 30; 70:5; 71:1; 3; 6; 7; 14; 15; 16(2); 17; 18(2); 22(2); 23; 73:3(2); 13; 14; 15(3); 16; 17(2); 21; 22(2); 23; 25(2); 28(2); 75:2(2); 3; 4; 9(2); 10; 77:1; 2; 3(2); 4(2); 5; 6(2); 10(2); 11(2); 12; 78:2(2); 81:5(2); 6; 7(3); 8; 10(2); 12; 14; 16; 82:6; 84:10; 85:8; 86:1; 2; 3; 4; 7; 11; 12(2); 87:4; 88:1; 4(2); 8(2); 9(2); 13; 15(3); 89:1(2); 2; 3(2); 4; 19(2); 20(2); 23; 25; 27; 28; 29; 32; 33; 34; 35(2); 50; 91:2(2); 14(2); 15(3); 16; 92:4; 10; 94:18; 95:10; 11; 101:1(2); 2(2); 3(2); 4; 5(2); 8(2); 102:2(2); 4; 6(2); 7; 9; 11; 24; 104:33(4); 34; 105:11; 106:5(3); 108:1; 2; 3(2); 7(2); 9(2); 109:4; 22; 23(2); 25; 30(2); 110:1; 111:1; 116:1; 2(2); 3; 4(2); 6; 9; 10(3); 11; 12; 13; 14; 16(2); 17; 18; 118:5; 6; 7; 10; 11; 12; 13; 17; 19(2); 21; 25(2); 28(2); 119:6(2); 7(2); 8; 10; 11(2); 13; 14; 15; 16(2); 17; 18; 19; 22; 26; 27; 30(2); 31; 32; 33; 34(2); 35; 39; 40; 42(2); 43; 44; 45(2); 46; 47(2); 48(3); 51; 52; 55; 56(2); 57(2); 58; 59; 60; 61; 62; 63; 66; 67(3); 69; 70; 71(2); 73; 74; 75; 76; 77; 78; 80; 81; 83(2); 87; 88; 92; 93; 94(2); 95; 96; 97; 99; 100(2); 101(2); 102; 104(2); 106(3); 107; 108; 109; 110; 111; 112; 113(2); 114; 115; 116; 117(2); 119; 120; 121; 125(2); 127; 128(2); 131(2); 134; 141(2); 144; 145(2); 146(2); 147(2); 148; 152; 153; 157; 158; 159; 162; 163(2); 164; 166; 167; 168; 173; 174; 176(2); 120:1; 5(2); 7(2); 121:1; 122:1; 8; 9; 123:1; 130:1; 5(2); 6; 131:1; 2; 132:3; 4; 5; 11; 12; 14(2); 15(2); 16; 17(2); 18; 135:5; 137:5; 6(2); 138:1(2); 2; 3; 7; 139:6; 7(2); 8(2); 9; 11; 14(2); 15; 18(3); 21(2); 22(2); 140:6; 12; 141:1(2); 10; 142:1(2); 2(2); 3; 4; 5(2); 6(2); 7; 143:5(3); 6; 7; 8(3); 9; 12; 144:2; 9(2); 145:1(2); 2(2); 5; 6; 146:2(4); **Prov** 1:23(2); 24(2); 26(2); 28; 3:28; 4:2; 3; 11(2); 5:12; 14; 7:6; 7; 14(2); 15(2); 16; 17; 8:4; 6; 12; 13; 14(2); 17; 20; 21(2); 23; 24; 25; 27; 30(2); 9:5; 20:9(2); 22; 22:13; 19; 20; 21; 23:35(4); 24:29(2); 30; 32(2); 26:19; 27:11; 30:2; 3; 7(2); 9(2); 18; 20; **Eccl** 1:12; 13; 14; 16(2); 17(2); 2:1(2); 2; 3(2); 4(3); 5(2); 6; 7(2); 8(2); 9; 10(2); 11(2); 12; 13; 14; 15(3); 17; 18(3); 19(2); 20(2); 24; 25; 3:10; 12; 14; 16; 17; 18; 22; 4:1; 2; 4; 7(2); 8; 15; 5:13; 18; 6:1; 3; 7:15; 23(3); 25; 26; 27; 28(3); 29; 8:2; 9; 10; 12; 14; 15; 16; 17; 9:1; 11; 13; 16; 10:5; 7; 12:1; **Song** 1:5; 6(2); 7; 9; 2:1; 3; 5; 7; 16; 3:1(3); 2(4); 3; 4(4); 5; 4:6; 5:1(4); 2; 3(4); 5; 6(4); 8(2); 6:3; 11; 12; 7:8(3); 10; 12; 13; 8:1(3); 2(2); 4; 5; 10(2); **Is** 1:2; 11(2); 13; 14; 15(2); 24; 25; 26; 3:4; 7; 5:1; 3; 4(2); 5(3); 6(2); 6:1; 5(4); 8(4); 11; 7:12(2); 8:2; 3; 11; 17(2); 18; 10:6(2); 11(2); 12; 13(4); 14; 12:1; 2; 13:3(2); 11(2); 12; 13; 17; 14:13(3); 14(2); 22; 23(2); 24(2); 25; 30; 15:9; 16:9(2); 10; 18:4(2); 19:2; 3; 4; 11; 21:2; 3(2); 8(2); 10(2); 22:4(2); 19; 20; 21(2); 22; 23; 23:4(2); 24:16; 25:1(2); 26:9(2); 27:3(3); 4(2); 28:16; 17; 22; 29:2; 3(2); 11(2); 12(2); 14; 30:7; 33:10(3); 13; 24; 36:5(2); 8(2); 10; 11; 17; 37:7(2); 24(3); 25(2); 26(3); 28; 29(2); 35; 38:3(2); 5(3); 6(2); 8; 10(3); 11(3); 12; 13; 14(3); 15(2); 17; 19; 22; 39:4; 40:6; 25; 41:4(2); 8; 9(2); 10(5); 13(2); 14; 15; 17(2); 18(2); 19(2); 25; 27; 28(2); 42:1(2); 6; 8(2); 9(2); 14(4); 15(3); 16(4); 19; 43:1(2); 2; 3(2); 4(2); 5(2); 6; 7(3); 10(2); 11(2); 12(3); 13(2); 14; 15; 19(2); 20; 21; 23; 25(2); 28; 44:1; 2; 3(2); 5; 6(2); 7(2); 8(2); 16(2); 19(5); 21; 22(2); 24; 26; 27; 45:1(2); 2(2); 3(2); 4(2); 5(2); 6; 7(3); 8; 12(3); 13(2); 18; 19(4); 21; 22; 23; 24; 46:4(5); 9(2); 10; 11(4); 13(2); 47:3(2); 6(2); 7; 8(3); 10; 48:3(3); 4; 5(2); 6; 7; 8; 9(3); 10(2); 11(2); 12(3); 13; 15(4); 16(2); 17; 49:3; 4(3); 5; 6; 8(3); 11; 15; 16; 18; 20; 21(2); 22; 23; 25(2); 26(2); 50:1(2); 2(5); 3(2); 4; 5; 6(2); 7(4); 51:2; 4; 12(2); 15; 16(3); 19; 22; 23; 52:5; 6(2); 53:12; 54:7(2); 8(2); 9(3); 11; 12; 16(2); 55:3; 4; 11(2); 56:3; 5(2); 7; 8; 12; 57:6; 11; 12; 15; 16(3); 17(2); 18(2); 19(2); 58:5; 6; 9; 14; 59:21; 60:7; 10(2); 13; 15; 16; 17(3); 21; 22; 61:8(4); 10; 62:1(2); 6; 8; 63:1; 3(3); 5(2); 6(2); 7; 65:1(3); 2; 5; 6; 7; 8(2); 9; 12(4); 17; 18(2); 19; 24(2); 66:2; 4(4); 9(2); 12; 13; 18(2); 19(2); 21; 22; **Jer** 1:5(4); 6(3); 7(3); 8; 9; 10; 11(2); 12; 13(2); 15; 16; 17(2); 18; 19; 2:2; 7; 9(2); 20(2); 21; 23(2); 25(2); 30; 31; 34; 35(3); 3:7; 8(2); 12(3); 14(3); 15; 18; 19(3); 22; 4:6; 10; 12; 19(2); 21; 23; 24; 25; 26; 27; 28(3); 31; 5:1; 4; 5; 7(2); 9; 14; 15; 18; 29; 6:2; 8; 10; 11(3); 12; 15; 17; 19; 21; 27; 7:3; 7(2); 11; 12(2); 13(2); 14(3); 15(2); 16; 22(2); 23(3); 25; 31; 34; 8:3; 6(2); 10; 13(2); 17; 18; 21(2); 9:1; 2(2); 7(2); 9; 10; 11(2); 13; 15; 16(3); 24(2); 25; 10:18; 19(2); 23; 11:4(4); 5(3); 7(2); 8(2); 10; 11(2); 14; 18; 19(2); 20; 22; 23; 12:1; 7(3); 8; 14(2); 15(2); 17; 13:2; 5; 6; 7(2); 9; 11; 13; 14(2); 24; 26; 27; 14:12(3); 13(2); 14(2); 15; 16; 18(2); 15:3; 4; 6(2); 7(3); 8(2); 9; 10; 11; 13; 14; 15; 16(2); 17(2); 19; 20(2); 21(2); 16:5; 9; 13(2); 15(2); 16(2); 18; 21(2); 17:3; 4(2); 10(2); 14(2); 16(2); 22; 27; 18:2; 3; 6; 7; 8(3); 9; 10(3); 11; 17(2); 20; 19:2; 3; 5; 7(3); 8; 9; 11; 12; 15(2); 20:4(2); 5(2); 7(3); 8(3); 9(4); 10; 12; 14; 18; 21:2; 4(2); 5; 6; 7; 8; 10; 13; 14(2); 22:5; 6; 7; 14; 21(2); 24(2); 25; 26; 23:2; 3(2); 4; 5; 8; 9; 11; 12; 13; 14; 15; 21(2); 23; 24(2); 25(3); 30; 31; 32(2); 33; 34; 38; 39(4); 40; 24:3; 5(2); 6(4); 7(3); 8; 9(2); 10(2); 25:3; 6; 9; 10; 12; 13(2); 14; 15; 16; 17; 27; 29(2); 26:2; 3(2); 4; 5; 6; 14; 27:5; 6(2); 8(2); 10; 11; 12; 15(2); 16; 22(2); 28:2; 3; 4(2); 7; 11; 14(2); 16; 29:4; 7; 9; 10; 11(2); 12; 14(6); 17; 18(2); 19; 20; 21; 23(2); 31; 32(2); 30:2; 3(3); 6; 8; 9; 10; 11(5); 14; 15; 16; 17(2); 18; 19(2); 20; 21; 22; 31:1; 2; 3(2); 4; 8; 9(3); 13; 14; 18(3); 19(6); 20(3); 23; 25(2); 26; 27; 28(2); 31; 32(3); 33(2); 34(2); 37; 32:3; 5; 8(2); 9; 10; 11; 12; 13; 16(2); 27; 28; 31; 33; 35; 37(4); 38; 39; 40(3); 41(2); 42(3); 44; 33:3; 5(2); 6(2); 7; 8(2); 9(2); 11; 14(2); 15; 22; 25; 26(3); 34:2; 5; 13(2); 17(2); 18; 20; 21; 22(2); 35:3; 4; 5(2); 14; 15(2); 17(4); 36:2(2); 3(2); 5(2); 18; 31(3); 37:14; 18; 20(3); 38:14; 15(2); 16(2); 19; 20(2); 25; 26; 39:16; 17; 18; 40:4(2); 10; 15(2); 42:4(4); 10(4); 11; 12; 17; 19; 21; 43:10(2); 12; 44:2; 4(2); 10; 11; 12; 13(2); 26; 27; 29; 30(2); 45:3(2); 4(4); 5(2); 46:5; 8(2); 18; 25; 26; 27; 28(5); 48:12; 30; 31(2); 32; 33; 35; 38; 44; 47; 49:2; 5; 6; 8(2); 10(2); 11; 13; 14; 15; 16; 19(2); 27; 32(2); 35; 36; 37(4); 38; 39; 50:9; 18(2); 19; 20(2); 21; 24; 31(2); 32; 44(2); 51:1; 14; 20(2); 21(2); 22(3); 23(3); 24; 25(2); 36(2); 39(2); 40; 44(2); 47; 52; 57; 64; **Lam** 1:11; 14; 16; 18(2); 19; 20(2); 21; 2:13(4); 22; 3:1; 7; 8; 14; 17; 18; 21(2); 24; 54(2); 55; 57; 63; **Eze** 1:1(2); 4; 15; 24; 27(2); 28(3); 2:1; 2; 3; 4; 8(2); 9; 3:2; 3(2); 6; 8; 9; 10; 12; 13; 14; 15(2); 17; 18(2); 20(2); 22; 23(3); 26; 27(2); 4:5; 6; 8; 13; 14(2); 15; 16; 5:2; 5; 8(2); 9(3); 10(2); 11(3); 12(2); 13(4); 14; 15(2); 16(3); 17(3); 6:3(3); 4; 5(2); 7; 8; 9; 10(3); 12; 13; 14(2); 7:3; 4(3); 8(2); 9(3); 20; 21; 22; 24(2); 27(3); 8:1; 2; 4; 5; 6; 7; 8; 10; 18(3); 9:8(2); 10(2); 11; 10:1; 9; 15; 20(2); 22; 11:1; 5; 7; 8; 9; 10(2); 11; 12; 13(2); 16(3); 17(2); 19(3); 20; 21; 24; 25; 12:6; 7(6); 11(2); 13(2); 14(2); 15(2); 16(2); 20; 23; 25(4); 28; 13:7; 8; 9; 13; 14(2); 15; 20(2); 21(2); 22; 23(2); 14:3; 4; 5; 7; 8(3); 9(2); 11; 13; 15; 16; 17(2); 18; 19; 20; 21; 22(2); 23(2); 15:6(2); 7(3); 8; 16:6(3); 7; 8(3); 9(3); 10(3); 11(2); 12; 14; 17; 19(2); 27; 37(2); 38(2); 39; 41; 42(2); 43; 48; 50(2); 53(2); 59; 60(2); 61; 62(2); 63; 17:16; 19(2); 20(2); 21; 22(2); 23; 24(2); 18:3; 23; 30; 32; 20:3(2); 5(3); 6(2); 7(2); 8(2); 9(2); 10; 11; 12(2); 13(2); 14(2); 15(3); 17; 18; 19; 20; 21(2); 22(2); 23(2); 25; 26(3); 28(2); 29; 31(3); 33(2); 34; 35(2); 36(2); 37(2); 38(3); 40(2); 41(3); 42(3); 44(2); 47; 48; 49; 21:3; 4; 5; 15; 17(3); 24; 27(2); 30(2); 31(2); 32; 22:4; 13; 14(2); 15; 16; 19; 20(2); 21; 22; 26; 30(3); 31(3); 23:9; 13; 22(2); 24; 25; 27; 28; 30; 31; 34; 43; 46; 48; 49; 24:8; 9; 13(2); 14(5); 16; 18(3); 20; 21; 22; 24; 25; 27; 25:4; 5(2); 7(5); 9; 11(2); 13(2); 14; 16(2); 17(3); 26:2; 3; 4; 5; 6; 7; 13; 14(2); 19(2); 20(2); 21; 27:3; 28:2(2); 7; 9; 10; 14; 16(2); 17(2); 18(2); 22(4); 23(2); 24; 25(2); 26(2); 29:3(2); 4(3); 5(2); 6; 8; 9(2); 10(2); 12(2); 13; 14; 15; 16; 19; 20; 21(3); 30:8(2); 10; 12(3); 13(3); 14; 15(2); 16; 18; 19(2); 21; 22(2); 23; 24(2); 25(3); 26(2); 31:9; 11(2); 15(4); 16(2); 32:3; 4(3); 5; 6; 7(3); 8; 9(2); 10(2); 12; 13; 14; 15(3); 32; 33:2; 6; 7; 8(2); 11(2); 13; 14; 20; 22; 27(2); 28; 29(2); 30; 34:8; 10(3); 11(2); 12; 13; 14; 15(2); 16(3); 17; 20(2); 22(2); 23; 24(2); 25; 26(2); 27(2); 29; 30; 31; 35:3(3); 4(2); 6(2); 7; 8; 9(2); 11(4); 12(2); 13; 14; 15(2); 36:5; 6; 7; 9(2); 10; 11(3); 12; 15; 18; 19(2); 21; 22; 23(3); 24; 25(2); 26(4); 27; 28(2); 29(2); 30; 32; 33(2); 36(3); 37(2); 38; 37:3; 5; 6(2); 7(3); 8; 10; 12; 13(2); 14(2); 19; 21; 22; 23(2); 25; 26(2); 27; 28; 38:3; 4(2); 11(2); 16(2); 17(2); 19; 21; 22(2); 23(3); 39:1; 2; 3; 4; 5; 6(2); 7(3); 8; 11; 13; 17; 19; 21(3); 22; 23; 24; 25; 27; 28(2); 29(2); 40:4(2); 41:8; 43:3(5); 6; 7; 8; 9; 27; 44:4(2); 5; 12; 14; 28(2); 47:5; 7; 14; **Dan** 1:10; 12; 2:3; 8; 9; 23; 24; 25; 26; 30; 3:14; 15; 25; 29; 4:2; 4; 5; 6; 7; 8; 9(2); 10; 13; 18; 30; 34(3); 36; 37; 5:11; 14; 16; 17; 6:22; 26; 7:2; 4; 6; 7; 8; 9; 11(2); 13; 15; 16; 19; 21; 28; 8:2(5); 3; 4; 5; 6; 7; 13; 15(2); 16; 17(2); 18; 19; 27(3); 9:2; 3; 4; 16; 20; 21(2); 22; 23; 10:2; 3(2); 4; 5; 7; 8(2); 9(3); 11(3); 12; 13; 14; 15(2); 16(2); 19; 20(3); 21; 11:1(2); 2; 12:5; 7; 8(3); **Hos** 1:4; 5; 6(2); 7; 9; 2:2; 3; 4; 5; 6; 7; 8; 9; 10; 11; 12(2); 13; 14; 15; 17; 18(2); 19(2); 20; 21(2); 23(3); 3:2; 3(2); 4:5; 6(2); 7; 9; 14; 5:2; 3; 9; 10; 12; 14(4); 15; 6:4(2); 5(2); 6; 10; 11; 7:1; 2; 12(3); 13; 15; 8:4; 10; 12; 14; 9:10(2); 12(2); 13; 15(3); 16; 10:10; 11(2); 11:1; 3(2); 4(3); 8(4); 9(4); 11; 12:8(2); 9; 10(2); 13:4; 5; 7(2); 8(2); 10; 11; 14(4); 14:4(2); 5; 8(3); **Joel** 1:19; 2:19(2); 20; 25(2); 27(2); 28; 29; 30; 3:1; 2; 4; 7; 8; 10; 12; 17; 21(2); **Amos** 1:3; 4; 5; 6; 7; 8(2); 9; 10; 11; 12; 13; 14; 2:1; 2; 3; 4; 5; 6; 9(2); 10; 11; 13; 3:1; 2(2); 14(2); 15; 4:6; 7(2); 9; 10(3); 11; 12(2); 5:1; 12; 17; 21(3); 22(2); 23; 27; 6:8(2); 14; 7:2(2); 5(2); 8(3); 9; 14(3); 15; 8:2(2); 7; 9(2); 10(3); 11; 9:1(2); 2; 3(2); 4(2); 7; 8(2); 9(2); 11(3); 14; 15(2); **Obad** 2; 4; 8; **Jonah** 1:9(2); 12; 2:2(2); 4(3); 6; 7; 9(3); 3:2; 4:2(4); 3; 9; 11; **Mic** 1:6(3); 7; 8(3); 15; 2:3; 11; 12(3); 3:1(2); 8; 9; 4:6(3); 7; 13(3); 5:10(2); 11; 12; 13; 14(2); 15; 6:3(2); 4(2); 6(2); 7; 11; 13; 14; 16; 7:1; 7(2); 8(3); 9(3); 15; **Nah** 1:12(2); 13; 14(2); 2:13(3); 3:5(3); 6; 7; **Hab** 1:2; 5; 6; 2:1(3); 3:2; 7; 16(3); 18(2); **Zeph** 1:2; 3(3); 4(2); 8; 9; 12; 17; 2:5; 8; 9; 15; 3:6(2); 7(2); 8(2); 9; 11; 12; 18; 19(3); 20(4); **Hag** 1:8(2); 9; 11; 13; 2:4; 5; 6; 7(2); 9; 15; 17; 19; 21; 22(3); 23(2); **Zec** 1:3; 6; 8; 9(2); 14; 15(2); 16; 18; 19; 21; 2:1; 2; 5; 6; 9; 10(2); 11; 3:4(2); 5; 7; 8; 9(3); 4:2(2); 4; 5; 11; 12; 13; 5:1; 2(2); 4; 6; 9; 10; 6:1; 4; 7:3(2); 13; 14; 8:2(2); 3; 7; 8(2); 10; 11; 12; 13; 14(2); 15; 17; 21; 9:6; 7; 8(2); 10; 11; 12(2); 13; 10:3; 6(6); 8(2); 9; 10(2); 12; 11:5; 6(3); 7(5); 8; 9(2); 10(3); 12; 13(2); 14(2); 16; 12:2; 3; 4(2); 6; 9; 10; 13:2(2); 5(2); 6; 7; 9(3); 14:2; **Mal** 1:2(2); 3; 4; 6(2); 9; 10(2); 13; 14; 2:2(3); 3; 4; 5; 9; 3:1; 5(2); 6(2); 7; 10; 11; 17(2); 4:3; 4; 5; 6; **Mt** 2:8; 13; 15; 3:9; 11(3); 14; 17; 4:9; 19; 5:17(2); 18; 20; 22; 26; 28; 32; 34; 39; 44; 6:2; 5; 16; 25; 29; 7:23(2); 24; 8:3; 7; 8; 9(2); 10(2); 11; 19; 9:13(2); 21(2); 28; 10:15; 16; 23; 27; 32; 33; 34(2); 35; 42; 11:9; 10; 11; 16; 22; 24; 25; 28; 29; 12:6; 7; 18(2); 27; 28; 31; 36; 44(2); 13:13; 15; 17; 30; 35(2); 14:27; 15:24; 32(2); 16:11; 13; 15; 18(2); 19; 28; 17:5; 12; 16; 17(2); 20; 18:3; 10; 13; 18; 19; 20; 21; 22; 26; 29; 32; 33; 19:9; 16(2); 20(2); 23; 24; 28; 20:4; 13; 14; 15(2); 22(2); 23; 32; 21:21; 24(3); 27(2); 29; 30; 31; 43; 22:4; 32; 44; 23:34; 36; 37; 39; 24:2; 5; 25; 34; 47; 25:12(2); 20; 21; 22; 23; 24; 25; 26(3); 27; 35(3); 36(2); 40; 42(2); 43; 45; 26:13; 15; 18; 21; 22; 25; 29(3); 31; 32(2); 33; 34; 35(2); 36; 39; 42; 48; 53; 55; 61; 63; 64; 70; 72; 74; 27:4(2); 17; 19; 21; 22; 24; 43; 63; 28:5; 7; 20(2); **Mk** 1:2; 7(2); 8; 11; 17; 24; 38(2); 41; 2:11; 17; 3:28; 5:7(2); 23; 28(2); 41; 6:11; 16; 22; 23; 24; 25; 50; 8:2; 3; 12; 19; 24; 27; 29; 9:1; 13; 17; 18; 19(2); 24; 25; 41; 10:15; 17(2); 20; 29; 36; 38(2); 39(2); 51(2); 11:23; 24; 29(3); 33(2); 12:15; 26; 36; 43; 13:6; 23; 30; 37(2); 14:9; 14; 18; 19(2); 25(3); 27; 28(2); 29; 30; 31(2); 32; 36; 44; 49; 58(2); 62; 68(2); 71; 15:9; 12; **Lk** 1:18(2); 19; 34; 2:10; 48; 49; 3:8; 16(3); 22; 4:6(3); 24; 25; 34; 43(2); 5:5; 8; 13; 24; 32; 6:9; 27; 46; 47; 7:6; 7; 8(2); 9(2); 14; 26; 27; 28; 31; 40; 43; 44; 45; 47; 8:28(2); 46; 9:9(2); 18; 20; 27; 38; 40; 41; 57; 61; 10:3; 12; 18; 19; 21; 24; 25; 35(2); 11:6; 7; 8; 9; 18; 19; 20; 24(2); 49; 51; 12:4; 5(2); 8; 17(2); 18(3); 19; 22; 27; 37; 44; 49(2); 50(2); 51(2); 59; 13:3; 5; 7; 8; 18; 20; 24; 25; 27(2); 32(3); 33; 34; 35; 14:18(3); 19(3); 20(2); 24; 15:6; 7; 9(2); 10; 17; 18(2); 21; 29(3); 31; 16:2; 3(3); 4(2); 9; 24; 27; 28; 17:4; 8(2); 9; 34; 18:4; 5; 8; 11(2); 12(3); 14; 17; 18; 21; 29; 41(2); 19:5; 8(3); 13; 20; 21; 22(4); 23; 26; 27; 40; 20:3; 8(2); 13(2); 43; 21:3; 8; 15; 32; 22:11; 15(2); 16(2); 18(2); 27; 29; 32; 33; 34; 35; 37; 53; 57; 58; 60; 67; 68; 70; 23:4; 14; 15; 16; 22(2); 43; 46; 24:39; 44(2); 49; **Jn** 1:15; 20; 21; 23; 26; 27; 30; 31(2); 32; 33; 34; 48; 50(2); 51; 2:4; 19; 3:3; 5; 7; 11; 12(2); 28(3); 30; 4:14(2); 15; 17(2); 19; 25; 26; 29; 32; 35; 38; 39; 5:7(2); 17; 19; 24; 25; 30(4); 31; 32; 34(2); 36(2); 41; 42; 43; 45; 6:20; 26; 32; 35; 36; 37; 38; 39; 40; 41; 42; 44; 47; 48; 51(3); 53; 54; 56; 57; 63; 65; 70; 7:7; 8; 17; 21; 23; 28(2); 29(2); 33(2); 34; 36; 8:11; 12; 14(6); 15; 16(3); 18; 21(2); 22; 23(2); 24(2); 25; 26(3); 28(3); 29; 34; 37; 38(2); 40; 42(2); 45; 46; 49(2); 50; 51; 54; 55(5); 58(2); 9:4; 5(2); 9; 11(2); 12; 15; 25(4); 27; 36; 38; 39; 10:1; 7(2); 9; 10; 11; 14; 15(2); 16(2); 17(2); 18(4); 25(2); 26; 27; 28; 30; 32; 34; 36(2); 37; 38(2); 11:11(2); 15(2); 22; 24; 25; 27; 40; 41; 42(2); 12:24; 26; 27(2); 28; 32(2); 40; 46; 47(2); 48; 49(3); 50(3); 13:7; 8; 12; 13; 14; 15(2); 16; 18(3); 19(2); 20(2); 21; 26(2); 33(4); 34(2); 36; 37(2); 38; 14:2(2); 3(3); 4; 6; 9; 10(3); 11; 12(3); 13; 14; 16; 18(2); 19; 20(2); 21; 25; 26; 27(3); 28(5); 29; 30; 31(2); 15:1; 3; 4; 5(2); 9; 10; 11; 12; 14; 15(4); 16; 17; 19; 20; 22; 24; 26; 16:1; 4(4); 5; 6; 7(5); 10; 12; 15; 16; 17; 19; 20; 22; 23; 25(3); 26(2); 27; 28(2); 32; 33(2); 17:4(2); 5; 6; 8(2); 9(2); 10; 11(2); 12(3); 13(2); 14(2); 15; 16; 18; 19; 20; 21; 22; 23; 24(2); 25; 26(2); 18:5; 6; 8(2); 9; 11; 17; 20(3); 21(2); 23; 25; 26; 35; 36; 37(4); 38; 39(2); 19:4(2); 6; 10; 15; 21; 22(2); 28; 20:13; 15; 17(2); 21; 25(2); 21:3; 15; 16; 17; 18; 22(2); 23(2); 25; **Acts** 1:1; 2:17; 18; 19; 25(2); 35; 3:6(3); 17; 5:38; 7:3; 7; 32; 34(4); 43; 56; 8:19; 23; 31; 34; 37; 9:5; 10; 13; 16; 10:14; 20; 21; 26; 28; 29(3); 30(2); 33; 34; 37; 11:5(2); 6(2); 7; 8; 11; 15; 16; 17(2); 12:11; 13:2; 22; 25(3); 33; 34; 41; 47; 15:16(3); 16:18; 30; 17:3; 22; 23(3); 18:6(2); 10(2); 14; 15; 21(2); 19:15(2); 21(2); 20:18(2); 20; 22; 24(3); 25(2); 26(2); 27; 29; 31; 32; 33; 35; 21:13; 37; 39(2); 22:1; 3; 4; 5; 6; 7; 8(2); 10(2); 11(2); 13; 17(3); 19(2); 20; 21; 28(2); 23:1; 5; 6(2); 27; 28(2); 29; 30; 35; 24:4(2); 10(2); 11; 14(2); 16; 17; 20; 21(2); 22; 25(2); 25:8; 10(3); 11(3); 15; 16; 17; 18; 20(2); 21(2); 22; 25(2); 26(3); 26:2(3); 3(2); 5; 6; 7; 9(2); 10(3); 11(2); 12; 13; 14; 15(2); 16(2); 17; 19; 22; 25; 26(2); 27; 29(2); 27:10; 22; 23(2); 25; 34; 28:17(2); 19(2); 20(2); 27; **Rom** 1:8; 9(2); 10; 11(2); 12; 13(3); 14; 15; 16; 3:5; 7; 26; 4:17; 6:19; 7:1; 7(2); 9(2); 10; 14; 15(6); 16(3); 17; 18(2); 19(4); 20(3); 21(2); 22; 23; 24; 25(2); 8:18; 38; 9:1(2); 2; 3; 9; 13(2); 15(4); 17(2); 25; 33; 10:2; 18; 19(3); 20(2); 21; 11:1(2); 3; 4; 11; 13(3); 14; 19; 25; 27; 12:1; 3; 19; 14:11; 14; 15:8; 9; 14; 15; 16; 17(2); 18; 19; 20(2); 22; 24(4); 25; 28(2); 29(3); 30; 31(2); 32; 16:1; 4; 17; 19(2); 22; **1Cor** 1:4; 10; 12(5); 14(2); 15; 16(3); 19; 2:1(2); 2; 3; 3:1; 2; 4(2); 6; 10; 4:3(2); 4(2); 6; 8; 9; 14(2); 15; 16; 17(2); 18; 19; 21; 5:3(2); 9; 11; 12; 6:5; 12; 15; 7:6; 7(2); 8(2); 10(2); 12; 17; 25(2); 26(2); 28; 29; 32; 35(2); 40(2); 8:13(2); 9:1(3); 2(2); 6; 8; 15(2); 16(3); 17(2); 18(3); 19(3); 20(3); 21; 22(4); 23(2); 26(2); 27(3); 10:1; 15(2); 19; 20(2); 29; 30(3); 33; 11:1; 2(2); 3; 17(2); 18(2); 22(3); 23(2); 34(2); 12:1; 3; 15(2); 16(2); 21(2); 31; 13:1(2); 2(4); 3(2); 11(6); 12(3); 14:5; 6(3); 11(2); 14; 15(4); 18(2); 19(2); 21; 37; 15:1(2); 2; 3(2); 9(2); 10(4); 11; 31(3); 32; 34; 50; 51; 16:1; 2; 3(2); 4; 5(3); 6(2); 7(2); 8; 10; 11; 12; 15; 17; **2Cor** 1:13; 15; 17(4); 23(2); 2:1(2); 2; 3(4); 4(2); 5; 8; 9(2); 10(4); 12; 13(3); 4:13(2); 5:8; 11; 6:2(2); 13; 16(2); 17; 7:3(2); 4(2); 7; 8(4); 9; 12(2); 14(3); 16(2); 8:3; 8; 10; 13; 22; 9:2(2); 3(2); 5; 6; 10:1; 2(4); 8(2); 9(2); 11:2(3); 3; 5(2); 6; 7(2); 8; 9(4); 11; 12(3); 16(2); 17(2); 18; 21(3); 22(3); 23(2); 24; 25(4); 29(2); 30(2); 31; 33; 12:1; 2(3); 3(2); 5(2); 6(4); 7(2); 8; 9; 10(3); 11(4); 13; 14(3); 15(3); 16(2); 17(2); 18(2); 20(5); 21(2); 13:1; 2(5); 6; 7; 10(2); **Gal** 1:6; 9; 10(4); 11; 12(2); 13; 16(2); 17(2); 18; 19; 20(2); 21; 2:1; 2(3); 10; 11; 14(2); 18(3); 19(2); 20(5); 21; 3:2; 15; 17; 4:1; 11(2); 12(3); 13; 15; 16(2); 18; 19; 20(2); 5:2; 3; 10; 11(3); 12; 16; 21(2); 6:11; 14(2); 17; **Eph** 1:15(2); 3:1; 3; 7; 8; 13; 14; 4:1; 17; 5:32; 6:19; 20(3); 21; 22; **Phil** 1:3; 7; 8; 9; 12; 17; 18; 19; 20; 22(3); 23; 25(2); 27(2); 2:16(2); 17(2); 19(3); 20; 23(2); 24(2); 25; 27; 28(2); 3:4(2); 7; 8(3); 10; 11; 12(4); 13(2); 14; 18; 4:2; 3; 4; 10; 11(3); 12(3); 13; 15; 17(2); 18(2); **Col** 1:20; 23; 25; 29; 2:1(2); 4; 5(2); 4:3; 4(2); 8; 13; **1Th** 2:18; 3:5(2); 4:9; 13; 5:1; 23; 27; **2Th** 2:5(2); 3:17; **1Ti** 1:3(2); 12; 13(2); 15; 16; 18; 20; 2:1; 7(2); 8; 12; 3:14; 15; 4:13; 5:14; 21; 6:13; **2Ti** 1:3(3); 4; 5(2); 6; 11; 12(5); 2:7; 9; 10; 3:11; 4:1; 6; 7(3); 12; 13; 16; 17; 20; **Titus** 1:5(2); 3:8; 12(2); **Philem** 1:4; 8; 9; 10(2); 12; 13; 14; 19(3); 21(2); 22(2); **Heb** 1:5(2); 13; 2:12(2); 13(2); 3:10; 11; 4:3; 5:5; 6:14(2); 7:9; 8:8; 9(3); 10(3); 12(2); 10:7(2); 9; 16(3); 17; 30; 11:32; 12:21; 26; 13:5; 6; 19(2); 22(2); 23; **Jas** 1:13; 2:18(2); **1Pet** 1:16; 2:6; 11; 5:1; 12(2); **2Pet** 1:12; 13(2); 14; 15; 17; 3:1(2); **1Jn** 2:1; 4; 7; 8; 12; 13(3); 14(2); 21; 26; 4:20; 5:13; 16; **2Jn** 1(2); 4(2); 5(2); 12(2); **3Jn** 1; 2; 3; 4; 9; 10(2); 13(2); 14(2); **Jude** 3; 5; **Rev** 1:8; 9; 10; 11; 12(2); 17(3); 18(2); 2:2; 4; 5; 6; 7; 9(2); 10; 13; 14; 15; 16; 17; 19; 20; 21; 22; 23(3); 24(2); 25; 26; 27; 28; 3:1; 2; 3(2); 5(2); 8(2); 9(3); 10; 11; 12(3); 15(2); 16; 17; 18; 19(2); 20(2); 21(2); 4:1(3); 2; 4; 5:1; 2; 4; 6; 11(2); 13; 6:1(2); 2; 3; 5(2); 6; 7; 8; 9; 12; 7:1; 2; 4; 9; 14; 8:2; 13; 9:1; 13; 16; 17; 10:1; 4(2); 5; 8; 9; 10(2); 11:3; 12:10; 13:1; 2; 3; 11; 14:1; 2(2); 6; 13; 14; 15:1; 2; 5; 16:1; 5; 7; 13; 15; 17:1; 3; 6(3); 7; 18:1; 4; 7; 19:1; 6; 10(2); 11; 17; 19; 20:1; 4(2); 11; 12; 21:1; 2; 3; 5; 6(2); 7; 9; 22; 22:7; 8(3); 9; 12; 13; 16(2); 18; 20

IF

Gen 4:7(2); 24; 8:8; 13:9(2); 16; 15:5; 18:3; 21; 26; 28; 30; 20:7; 23:8; 13; 24:8; 41; 42; 49(2); 25:22; 27:46; 28:20; 30:27; 31; 31:8(2); 50(2); 32:8; 33:10; 13; 34:15; 17; 22; 37:26; 42:19; 37; 38; 43:4; 5; 9; 11; 14; 44:22; 26; 29; 32; 47:6; 16; 29; 50:4; **Ex** 1:16(2); 4:8; 9; 23; 8:2; 21; 9:2; 10:4; 12:4; 13:13; 15:26; 18:23; 19:5; 20:25(2); 21:2; 3(2); 4; 5; 7; 8; 9; 10; 11; 13; 14; 16; 18; 19; 20; 21; 22; 23; 26; 27; 28; 29; 30; 32; 33(2); 35; 36; 22:1; 2; 3(2); 4; 5; 6; 7(2); 8; 10; 12; 13; 14; 15(2); 16; 17; 23; 25; 26; 23:4; 5; 22; 33; 24:14; 29:34; 32:32(2); 33:13; 15; 34:9; 20; 40:37; **Lev** 1:2; 3; 10; 14; 2:4; 5; 7; 14; 3:1(2); 6; 7; 12; 4:2; 3; 13; 23; 27; 28; 32; 5:1(2); 2(2); 3; 4; 7; 11; 15; 17; 6:2; 28; 7:12; 16; 18; 10:19; 11:37; 38; 39; 12:2; 5; 8; 13:4; 5; 6; 7; 8; 10; 12; 13; 16; 17; 20; 21(2); 22; 23; 24; 25; 26; 27; 28; 29; 30; 31; 32; 34; 35; 36; 37; 38; 39; 42; 43; 49; 51; 53; 55; 56; 57; 58; 14:3; 21; 37; 39; 43; 44; 48; 15:8; 10; 19; 23; 24; 25(2); 28; 17:10; 18:5; 19:5; 6; 7; 33; 20:4; 12; 13; 14; 15; 16; 17; 18; 20; 21; 21:9; 22:9; 11; 12; 13; 14; 24:19; 25:14; 20; 25(2); 26; 28; 29; 30; 33; 35; 39; 47; 49; 51; 52; 54; 26:3; 14; 15(2); 18; 21; 23; 27; 40; 41; 27:4; 5; 6; 7(2); 8; 9; 10; 11; 13; 15; 16; 17; 18; 19; 20(2); 22; 27(2); 31; 33; **Num** 5:8; 12; 14; 19(2); 20(2); 27; 28; 6:9; 9:10; 14; 10:4; 9; 32; 11:15(2); 12:6; 14; 14:8; 15; 15:14; 22; 24; 27; 16:29(2); 30; 19:12; 20:19; 21:2; 9; 22:18; 20; 34; 24:13; 27:8; 9; 10; 11; 30:2; 3; 5; 6; 8; 10; 12; 14; 15; 32:5; 15; 20(2); 23; 29; 30; 33:55; 35:16; 17; 18; 20; 22; 26; 36:3; **Deut** 4:29(2); 30; 5:25; 6:25; 7:12; 17; 8:19; 11:13; 22; 27; 28; 12:21; 13:1; 6; 12; 14; 14:24(2); 15:5; 7; 12; 16; 21(2); 17:2; 8; 18:6; 21; 22; 19:8; 9; 11; 16; 18; 20:11; 12; 21:1; 14; 15(2); 18; 22; 22:2(2); 6; 8; 13; 20; 22; 23; 25; 28; 23:10; 22; 24:3(2); 7; 12; 25:1; 2; 3; 5; 7; 8; 28:1; 2; 9; 13; 15; 58; 30:4; 10(2); 17; 32:41; **Josh** 2:14; 19; 20; 8:15; 9:4; 14:12; 17:15(2); 20:5; 22:19; 22(2); 23(2); 24; 23:12; 24:15; 20; **Judg** 4:8(2); 6:13; 17; 31; 36; 37; 7:10; 8:19; 9:15(2); 16(2); 19; 20; 36; 11:9; 10; 30; 36; 12:5; 13:16; 23; 14:12; 13; 18; 16:7; 11; 13; 17; 21:21; **Ruth** 1:12(2); 17; 3:13(2); 4:4(2); **1Sa** 1:11; 2:16(2); 25(2); 3:9; 17; 6:3; 9(2); 7:3; 9:7; 10:22; 11:3; 12:14; 15; 25; 14:9; 10; 30; 16:2; 17:9(2); 19:11; 20:6; 7(2); 8; 9; 10; 12; 13; 21; 22; 29; 21:4; 9; 23:3; 23; 24:19; 25:22; 26:19(2); 27:5; **2Sa** 3:35; 7:14; 10:11(2); 11:20; 12:8; 18; 13:26; 14:32; 15:8; 25; 26; 33; 34; 16:23; 17:3; 6; 13; 18:3(2); 25; 19:6; 7; 13; **1Kin** 1:52(2); 2:4; 23; 3:14; 6:12; 8:31; 35; 37(4); 44; 46; 47; 9:4; 6; 11:38; 12:7; 27; 13:8; 16:31; 18:21(2); 19:2; 20:10; 39; 21:2; 6; 22:28; **2Kin** 1:10; 12; 2:10(2); 4:29(2); 5:13; 6:27; 31; 7:2; 4(4); 9; 19; 9:15; 10:6(2); 15; 24; 18:21; 22; 23; 20:19; 21:8; **1Chr** 12:17(2); 13:2; 19:12(2); 22:13; 28:7; 9(2); **2Chr** 6:22; 24; 26; 28(4); 32; 34; 36; 37; 38; 7:13(3); 14; 17; 19; 10:7; 15:2(2); 18:27; 20:9; 25:8; 30:9(2); **Ezr** 4:13; 16; 5:17; **Neh** 1:8; 9; 2:5(2); 7; 4:3; 9:29; 10:31; 13:21; **Est** 1:19; 3:9; 4:14; 16; 5:4; 8(2); 6:13; 7:3(2); 4; 8:5(2); 9:13; **Job** 4:2; 5:1; 6:28; 8:4; 5; 6; 18; 9:3; 13; 16; 19(2); 20(2); 23; 24; 27; 29; 30; 10:14; 15(2); 11:10; 13; 14; 13:10; 19; 14:7; 14; 16:4; 17:13; 19:5; 21:4; 15; 22:23; 24:17; 25; 27:14; 29:24; 31:5(2); 7(2); 9(2); 13; 16; 19; 20(2); 21; 24; 25; 26; 29; 31; 33; 38; 39; 33:5; 23; 27; 32; 33; 34:14(2); 16; 32; 35:3; 6(2); 7; 36:8; 11; 12; 37:20; 38:4; 5; 8; 18; **Ps** 7:3(2); 4; 12; 11:3; 14:2; 28:1; 40:5; 41:6; 44:20; 50:12; 53:2; 59:15; 62:10; 66:18; 73:15; 81:8; 89:30; 31; 90:10; 95:7; 124:1; 2; 130:3; 132:12; 137:5; 6(2); 139:8(2); 9; 11; 18; 24; **Prov** 1:10; 11; 2:1; 3; 4; 3:30; 6:1(2); 30; 31; 9:12(2); 16:31; 19:19; 22:18; 27; 23:2; 13; 15; 24:10; 11; 12; 25:21(2); 29:9; 12; 30:4; 32(2); **Eccl** 4:10; 11; 12; 5:8; 6:3; 10:4; 10; 11:3(2); 8; **Song** 1:8; 5:8; 7:12; 8:7; 9(2); **Is** 1:19; 20; 5:30; 7:9; 8:20; 10:15(3); 21:12; 36:6; 7; 8; 47:11; 12(2); 51:13; 58:9; 10; 13; 59:10; 66:3(4); **Jer** 2:10; 28; 3:1; 4:1(2); 5:1(2); 7:5(2); 6; 12:5(2); 16; 17; 13:17; 22; 14:18(2); 15:2; 19(2); 17:24; 27; 18:8; 10; 21:2; 22:4; 5; 23:22; 25:28; 26:3; 4; 15; 27:18(2); 31:36; 37; 33:20; 25(2); 38:15(2); 17; 18; 21; 25; 40:4(2); 42:5; 10; 13; 15; 49:9(2); 51:8; **Lam** 1:12; 2:6; 3:29; **Eze** 3:19; 21; 10:10; 14:9; 15; 17; 19; 16:47; 18:5; 10; 14; 21; 20:11; 13; 21; 39; 21:13; 33:2; 3; 4; 6(2); 8; 9(2); 10; 13; 14; 15; 19; 43:11; 46:16; 17; **Dan** 2:5; 6; 9; 3:15(2); 17; 18; 4:27; 5:16; **Hos** 6:3; 8:7; **Joel** 2:14; 3:4; **Amos** 3:4; 5:19; 6:9; **Obad** 5(3); **Jonah** 1:6; 3:9; **Mic** 2:11; 5:8; **Nah** 3:12; **Hag** 2:12; 13; **Zec** 3:7(2); 6:15; 8:6; 11:12(2); 14:18; **Mal** 1:6(2); 8(2); 2:2(2); 3:10; **Mt** 4:3; 6; 9; 5:13; 23; 29; 30; 40; 46; 47; 6:14; 15; 22; 23(2); 30; 7:9; 10; 11; 8:2; 31; 9:21; 10:13(2); 25; 11:14; 21; 23; 12:7; 11; 26; 27; 28; 14:28; 15:14; 16:24; 26; 17:4; 20; 18:8; 9; 12; 13; 15(2); 16; 17(2); 19; 35; 19:10; 17; 21; 21:3; 21(2); 24; 25; 26; 22:24; 45; 23:30; 24:23; 24; 26; 43; 48; 26:24; 39; 42; 27:40; 42; 43; 28:14; **Mk** 1:40; 3:24; 25; 26; 4:23; 26; 5:28; 6:56; 7:11; 16; 8:3; 23; 36; 9:22; 23; 35; 43; 45; 47; 50; 10:12; 11:3; 13; 25; 26; 31; 32; 12:19; 13:21; 22; 14:21; 31; 35; 15:44; 16:18; **Lk** 4:3; 7; 9; 5:12; 36; 6:32; 33; 34; 7:39; 9:23; 25; 10:6(2); 13; 11:11(2); 12; 13; 18; 19; 20; 36; 12:26; 28; 38; 39; 45; 49; 13:9(2); 14:26; 34; 15:4; 8; 16:11; 12; 30; 31; 17:3(2); 4; 6; 19:8; 31; 40; 42; 20:5; 6; 28; 22:42; 67; 68; 23:31; 35; 37; 39; **Jn** 1:25; 3:12(2); 4:10; 5:31; 43; 47; 6:51; 62; 7:4; 17; 23; 37; 8:16; 19; 24; 31; 36; 39; 42; 46; 51; 52; 54; 55; 9:22; 31; 33; 41; 10:9; 24; 35; 37; 38; 11:9; 10; 12; 21; 32; 40; 48; 57; 12:24; 26(2); 32; 47; 13:8; 14; 17(2); 32; 35; 14:2; 3; 7; 14; 15; 23; 28; 15:6; 7; 10; 14; 18; 19; 20(2); 22; 24; 16:7(2); 18:8; 23(2); 30; 36; 19:12; 20:15; 21:22; 23; 25; **Acts** 4:9; 5:38; 39; 8:22; 37; 9:2; 13:15; 15:29; 16:15; 17:27; 18:14; 15; 21; 19:38; 39; 20:16; 23:9; 24:19; 20; 25:5; 11(2); 26:5; 32; 27:12; 39; **Rom** 1:10; 2:25(2); 26; 27; 3:3; 5; 7; 4:2; 14; 24; 5:10; 15; 17; 6:5; 8; 7:2; 3(2); 16; 20; 8:9(2); 10; 11; 13(2); 17(2); 25; 31; 9:22; 10:9; 11:6(2); 12; 14; 15; 16(2); 17; 18; 21; 22; 23; 24; 12:18; 20(2); 13:4; 9; 14:15; 23; 15:24; 27; **1Cor** 3:12; 14; 15; 17; 18; 4:7(2); 19; 5:11; 6:2; 4; 7:8; 9; 11; 12; 13; 15; 21; 28(2); 36(2); 39; 40; 8:2; 3; 8(2); 10; 13; 9:2; 11(2); 12; 16; 17(2); 10:27; 28; 30; 11:5; 6(2); 14; 15; 16; 31; 34; 12:15; 16; 17(2); 19; 14:6; 8; 11; 14; 23; 24; 27; 28; 30; 35; 37; 38; 15:2; 12; 13; 14; 15; 16; 17; 19; 29; 32(2); 16:4; 7; 10; 22; **2Cor** 2:2; 5; 10; 3:7; 9; 11; 4:3; 5:1; 3; 14; 17; 7:14; 8:12; 9:4; 10:2; 7; 9; 11:4(2); 15; 16; 20(5); 30; 13:2(2); **Gal** 1:9; 10; 2:14; 17; 18; 21; 3:4; 15; 18; 21; 29; 4:7; 15; 5:2; 11; 15; 18; 25; 6:1; 3; 9; **Eph** 3:2; 4:21; **Phil** 1:22; 2:1(4); 17; 3:4; 11; 12; 15; 4:8(2); **Col** 1:23; 2:20; 3:1; 13; 4:10; **1Th** 3:8; 4:14; **2Th** 3:10; 14; **1Ti** 1:8; 10; 2:15; 3:1; 5; 15; 4:4; 6; 5:4; 8; 10(5); 16; 6:3; **2Ti** 2:5; 11; 12(2); 13; 21; 25; **Titus** 1:6; **Philem** 1:17; 18; **Heb** 2:2; 3; 3:6; 7; 14; 15; 4:3; 5; 7; 8; 6:3; 6; 7:11; 8:4; 7; 9:13; 10:26; 38; 11:15; 12:7; 8; 20; 25(2); 13:23; **Jas** 1:5; 23; 26; 2:2; 8; 9; 11(2); 15; 17; 3:2; 14; 4:11; 15; 5:15; 19; **1Pet** 1:6; 17; 2:3; 19; 20(2); 3:1; 13; 14; 17; 4:11(2); 14; 16; 17; 18; **2Pet** 1:8; 10; 2:4; 20; **1Jn** 1:6; 7; 8; 9; 10; 2:1; 3; 15; 19; 24; 29; 3:13; 20; 21; 4:11; 12; 20; 5:9; 14; 15; 16; **2Jn** 10; **3Jn** 6; 10; **Rev** 1:15; 3:3; 20; 11:5(2); 13:9; 14:9; 22:18; 19

IN

Gen 1:1; 6; 11; 12; 14; 15; 17; 20; 22(2); 26; 27(2); 29; 2:3; 4; 5; 8; 9; 17; 3:3; 5; 8(2); 10; 16; 17; 19; 4:3; 8; 12; 14; 16; 20; 22; 5:1(2); 2; 3; 6:4(3); 5; 8; 9; 14; 16(2); 17; 7:1; 7; 9; 11(2); 13; 15; 16(3); 22(2); 23; 8:1; 4; 5; 9; 11(3); 13(2); 14; 17; 21; 9:6; 7; 13; 14; 16; 27; 10:5(2); 8; 10; 20(2); 25; 31; 32(2); 11:2; 28(2); 31; 32; 12:3; 5; 6; 10(2); 13:2(3); 7; 12(2); 17(2); 18(2); 14:1; 3; 4; 5(4); 6; 7; 8; 12; 13; 14; 15:1; 3; 6; 10; 13; 15(2); 16; 18; 16:2; 3; 4(2); 5; 6; 7(2); 12; 17:7; 9; 12(2); 13(2); 17; 21; 23(2); 24; 25; 26; 27; 18:1(3); 3; 9; 10; 11; 18; 26; 19:1; 2(2); 3; 5; 8; 9; 12(2); 14(2); 15; 17; 19(2); 27; 29; 30(3); 31(2); 33; 34; 20:1; 3; 5; 6(2); 8(2); 11; 21:2; 7; 11; 12(3); 14(2); 15; 18; 20; 21; 22; 33; 34; 22:3; 6; 9; 13(2); 14; 17(2); 18; 23:2(2); 6; 9; 10(2); 11; 13; 16; 17(3); 18(2); 19(2); 24:1(2); 10; 23(2); 25; 27; 31; 37; 45; 48; 54; 62; 63; 65; 25:8; 9(2); 18; 23; 24; 27; 26:1(2); 2; 3; 4; 6; 12(2); 15; 17; 18; 19; 22; 29; 31(2); 27:15; 30; 41; 45; 28:11; 14(2); 15; 16; 18; 20; 21; 29:2; 3; 21; 23(2); 25; 26; 30; 30:2; 3; 4; 14(2); 16(2); 27; 33; 35; 37(2); 38(2); 40; 41; 42; 31:10; 11; 14; 18(2); 20; 23; 24; 25(2); 28; 29; 34; 40; 41; 54; 55; 32:5; 21; 32; 33:8; 10; 15; 18; 34:5; 7(2); 11; 15; 19; 21; 28(2); 29; 30; 35:3(2); 4(2); 6; 13; 14; 17; 18; 19; 22; 26; 36:5; 6; 8; 9; 16; 17; 21; 24; 30; 31; 32; 33; 34; 35(2); 36; 37; 38; 39; 43; 37:1(2); 7; 12; 13; 15; 17; 22; 24; 29; 31; 33; 38:1; 2; 7; 8; 9; 11(2); 12; 13; 14; 16(3); 18(2); 21; 22; 24; 25; 27(2); 39:2; 3; 4; 5(3); 6; 8; 9; 12; 13; 14(2); 17; 20; 21; 22; 40:3(2); 4; 5(2); 6(2); 7; 9; 10; 11; 16; 17; 41:2; 8; 10(2); 11; 14; 16; 17; 18; 19; 22(2); 30; 31; 34; 35; 36; 37(2); 38; 40; 42; 43; 44; 47; 48(3); 52; 53; 54(2); 56; 57; 42:1; 2; 3; 5; 13; 16(2); 19; 21; 27(2); 28; 32; 34; 35; 38; 43:1; 11(2); 12(3); 15; 18(2); 21(3); 22(2); 23; 26; 28; 44:1; 2; 5(2); 8; 12; 17(2); 18; 28; 30; 45:6(2); 7; 10; 13; 16; 46:2; 5; 6; 12; 15; 20; 27; 31; 34; 47:1; 4(3); 6(2); 7; 9; 11(3); 13; 14(2); 15(3); 17; 18; 24; 25; 27(2); 28; 29(2); 30; 48:3; 5; 6; 7(3); 9; 13(2); 16; 20; 49:1; 5; 6(2); 7(2); 8; 11(2); 17; 24; 27; 29(2); 30(3); 50:4(2); 5(2); 8; 11; 13; 19; 22; 26(2); **Ex** 1:5; 14(4); 19; 2:3; 11; 12; 15; 22; 23; 3:1; 2; 7; 16; 20; 21; 22; 4:2; 4; 14; 15; 17; 18(3); 19; 20; 21; 24; 27; 30; 5:1(2); 14; 16; 19; 20; 21(3); 23; 6:5; 8; 11; 28; 7:3; 10; 11; 15(2); 16; 17(3); 18; 19(2); 20(4); 21; 8:9; 11; 17(2); 20; 22(3); 25; 28; 29; 9:1; 3; 5; 8; 9; 13; 14; 16(2); 18; 19(2); 21; 22; 24; 25; 26; 31; 10:1; 2(2); 3; 14; 15(2); 16; 19; 22; 23; 28; 11:2; 3(4); 5; 8; 9; 12:1; 3; 6; 8; 11(2); 12; 16(3); 17(2); 18; 19(2); 20; 22(3); 23; 27; 29(2); 30(2); 33; 34; 36; 40; 42; 46; 48; 13:3; 4; 5; 6; 7; 8; 9; 10; 14; 15; 20(2); 21(2); 14:3(2); 11(2); 12(2); 23; 24; 27; 29; 15:4; 6(2); 7; 8; 10; 11(2); 13(2); 17(5); 19(2); 20; 22; 26; 16:2; 3; 4; 5; 7; 8(2); 10; 12; 13; 16; 25; 26; 29; 32; 17:1; 5; 6(2); 8; 9; 14(2); 18:1; 2; 3; 5; 6; 7; 8; 11; 12(2); 14; 15; 17; 23; 24; 27; 19:1; 2; 9; 11; 16(2); 18; 20:4(3); 7(2); 10; 11(2); 24; 21:2; 3; 13; 16; 29(2); 36(2); 22:4; 5(2); 6; 13; 21; 23; 31; 23:2; 3; 6; 9; 10; 11; 13; 14; 15(2); 16(3); 17; 19; 20; 21; 23; 26; 29; 33; 24:4; 6; 7; 10; 17; 18; 25:7(2); 12(3); 15; 18; 21; 22; 26; 33(3); 34; 40; 26:4(3); 5(3); 9; 10(2); 13; 17(2); 23; 28; 30; 33; 34; 27:4; 8; 11; 19; 21; 28:1; 3; 4; 11(2); 17; 20(2); 24; 25; 26(2); 29(2); 30(2); 32(2); 35; 38; 41; 43(2); 29:1; 3; 17; 24(2); 29; 30(2); 31; 32; 39; 44; 30:10(2); 30; 36; 31:3(4); 4(3); 5(3); 6; 10; 15(2); 17; 32:2; 3; 12; 15; 17; 20; 26; 27; 34; 33:3(2); 5; 10; 12; 13(2); 16(2); 17; 22; 34:1; 2(3); 4(2); 5; 6; 9; 10(2); 12; 18(2); 21(2); 23; 24; 26; 29; 32(2); 34; 35; 35:15; 19(2); 26; 31(4); 32(3); 33(2); 34; 35(4); 36:1; 2; 11(3); 12(3); 17; 28; 29; 37:13; 19(2); 20; 38:18; 23(3); 24; 39:1; 3(4); 6; 10; 13(2); 16; 17; 18; 23; 26; 37; 41(2); 40:4(4); 13; 15; 17(2); 18; 22; 23; 24; 26; 36; 38; **Lev** 1:7; 8; 9; 12; 2:4; 5; 6; 7; 11; 4:6; 7; 17; 18; 24; 29; 33; 5:4; 5(2); 13; 15; 16; 6:2(3); 3; 5(2); 7; 9; 12(2); 16(2); 18; 20(2); 21(2); 22; 25; 26(2); 27; 28(2); 30(2); 7:2; 6; 9(3); 24(2); 26; 35(2); 36; 38(3); 8:8; 21; 31; 33; 9:9; 10:3; 5; 13; 14; 17; 18(2); 19; 11:9(4); 10(4); 11; 12; 13; 33; 34; 46; 12:3; 4; 5(2); 13:2(2); 3(3); 4(2); 5(2); 6; 7; 8; 9; 10(2); 11; 12; 14; 18(2); 19; 20; 22; 23; 24; 25(2); 26; 27; 28(2); 30(2); 31(2); 32(3); 34(3); 35; 36; 37; 38; 39(2); 42(2); 43(3); 44; 45; 46; 47; 48(3); 49(5); 51(5); 52(3); 53(4); 55; 57(4); 59(2); 14:2; 3; 5; 6; 8; 9; 13(2); 16(2); 17; 18; 27; 28; 29; 32; 34; 35; 36(2); 37(2); 39; 40; 42; 43; 44(2); 47(2); 48(2); 50; 51(2); 15:3; 5; 6; 7; 8; 10; 11(2); 12; 13; 16; 18; 19; 20; 21; 22; 27; 31; 16:2; 4; 16(2); 17(3); 21; 22; 24; 26; 27(3); 28; 29; 32(2); 17:3; 5; 11; 15; 18:3; 5; 15; 18; 24(2); 19:6; 15(2); 17(2); 24; 25; 28; 33; 34; 35(4); 20:2; 12; 17; 23; 21:5; 11; 13; 17; 20; 23; 22:2; 11; 13; 18; 21; 23; 24; 25(2); 28; 23:3; 4; 5; 7; 8; 14; 21; 24(2); 28; 29; 30; 31; 32; 39(2); 41(3); 42(2); 43; 24:3(2); 5; 6; 8; 9; 10; 12; 16; 19; 20; 25:1; 3; 4; 7; 9; 11(2); 13; 18(2); 19; 20; 21; 22; 24; 28(2); 29; 30(2); 31; 33; 35; 45; 53; 54(2); 26:1; 3; 4; 5; 6; 16; 20; 22; 26; 28; 34; 35; 36; 39(3); 44; 45; 46; 27:19; 21; 23; 24; 34; **Num** 1:1(3); 3; 16; 19; 45; 2:9; 16(2); 17(2); 24; 31; 3:1(2); 3; 4(3); 13(2); 14; 25; 28; 4:3; 4; 6; 8; 12(2); 15; 16(2); 19; 20; 23(2); 27(3); 28; 31; 33; 35; 37; 39; 41; 43; 47; 5:3; 17(2); 18(2); 23; 6:5; 9; 18; 7:10; 84; 8:15; 17; 19; 22(2); 24; 26; 9:1(2); 3(2); 5; 7; 10; 13(2); 14; 17; 18; 20; 21; 22; 23; 10:9; 10(3); 11; 12; 14; 29; 31; 33; 11:1; 5; 8(3); 9; 10; 11; 12; 15; 18(2); 25; 26(2); 27; 12:5(2); 6(2); 7; 8; 14(2); 15; 16; 13:19(4); 22; 28; 29(2); 32; 33(2); 14:2(2); 8; 10; 13; 14(2); 16; 22(2); 25; 28; 29; 31; 32; 33(2); 34; 35; 40; 45; 15:3(3); 8; 13; 14; 15; 21; 26; 30; 32; 34; 38; 16:2; 7; 13; 17; 18(2); 21; 26; 27; 45; 49; 17:4; 7; 18:10; 11; 13(2); 14; 15; 20; 21; 31(2); 19:5; 7; 8(2); 9; 14(2); 16; 17; 18; 19; 20:1(2); 5; 12; 13; 15; 16(2); 23; 27; 28; 21:1; 5; 10; 11; 12; 13; 14(3); 20(2); 25(3); 27; 31; 22:1; 7; 13; 21; 22; 23(2); 24; 26; 29; 31(2); 34; 36(2); 38; 23:5; 12; 16; 21(2); 24:2; 7; 14; 21; 25:1; 6(2); 7; 9; 11; 15; 18(3); 26:2; 3; 9(2); 19; 59; 63; 64; 65; 27:3(4); 14(4); 17(2); 18; 19; 21; 28:2; 4; 6; 7; 11; 16; 17; 18; 23; 26; 29:1; 39; 30:3(2); 5; 7; 10; 14; 16(2); 31:6; 16; 35; 36; 32:5; 13(2); 14; 15; 17; 26; 30; 33; 39; 33:3(2); 5; 6(2); 8(2); 9; 11; 12; 13; 15; 18; 20; 22; 23; 24; 25; 28; 29; 31; 33; 36; 37(2); 38(2); 39; 40(2); 41; 42; 43; 44(2); 45; 46; 47; 48; 49; 50; 54; 55(3); 34:29; 35:1; 2; 3; 5; 12; 14; 21; 25; 28; 29; 32; 36:8; 12; 13; **Deut** 1:1(2); 3(3); 4(2); 5; 6(2); 7(4); 8; 17; 25; 27; 30; 31(2); 32; 33(4); 37; 38; 39(2); 44(2); 46; 2:4; 7; 8; 9; 10; 12(2); 14; 20; 21; 22(2); 23(2); 24; 25; 29(2); 37; 3:4; 10; 11; 19; 24(2); 29; 4:1; 5; 6; 7; 10; 14; 15; 17; 18; 21; 22; 25(2); 27; 30(2); 34; 37; 38; 39(2); 42; 43(4); 46(2); 5:1; 2; 4; 8(3); 11(2); 14; 15; 16; 22(2); 29; 31; 33(2); 6:1; 3; 6; 7; 16; 18(2); 20; 21; 23; 7:7; 13; 17; 8:1; 2(2); 5; 6; 9; 11; 16; 17; 9:1; 4(2); 7; 8; 9; 10(2); 15; 18(2); 28; 10:2(2); 3; 4(2); 5; 6(2); 8; 10; 11; 12; 15; 18; 19; 11:3; 5; 6(2); 8; 9; 10; 14(2); 15; 18(2); 19; 21; 22; 29; 30(2); 31; 12:1; 7; 8; 10(2); 13; 14(2); 15; 18(2); 21; 25; 28; 29; 31; 13:5; 12; 18; 14:9; 21(2); 23; 25; 29; 15:4; 7; 8; 9; 10(2); 11; 12; 15; 18(2); 20; 16:1; 2; 3; 4; 6; 7(2); 11; 12; 13; 14; 15(3); 16(5); 18; 17:2(2); 4; 8; 9; 15; 18; 20(2); 18:5; 7; 16(2); 18; 19; 20(2); 21; 22; 19:1(2); 2; 4; 6; 9; 10; 11; 14(2); 15; 17; 20:5; 6; 7; 14; 19(2); 21:1(2); 3; 4; 5; 6; 9; 13(2); 14; 23; 22:1; 3; 6(2); 7; 13; 15; 19; 21(2); 23; 24; 25; 26; 27; 23:1; 4; 7; 8; 14(2); 16(2); 20(2); 21; 22; 24; 24:1(3); 3; 8; 13(2); 14; 18; 19(3); 22; 25:5; 6; 7; 9(2); 10; 13; 14; 15; 19; 26:1; 2; 3; 11; 14; 17; 19(3); 27:3; 4; 15; 23; 28:3(2); 6; 8(3); 9; 11(5); 12; 16(2); 19; 20; 29(2); 32; 35(2); 38; 48(4); 52(2); 53(2); 55(3); 57(2); 58; 61; 62; 66; 67; 29:1(2); 2; 5; 9; 11; 16; 19(2); 20; 21; 23(2); 27; 28(3); 30:9(4); 10; 12; 14(2); 16(3); 20; 31:2; 7; 10(2); 11(2); 13; 14(2); 15(2); 17(2); 18(2); 19; 24; 26; 28; 29(2); 30; 32:10(2); 20; 22; 28; 34; 35; 37; 44; 47; 49; 50(2); 51(2); 33:3; 5; 12; 16; 18(2); 19; 21; 24; 26(2); 28; 34:5; 6(2); 8; 10; 11(2); 12(3); **Josh** 1:11; 14; 17; 18; 2:2; 6; 11(3); 18; 19; 21; 3:1; 7; 8; 13; 15; 17; 4:3; 6; 9(2); 10; 11; 14; 19(2); 20; 21; 5:1; 4; 5; 6; 7; 8(2); 10(2); 11; 13; 6:1; 11; 12; 17; 18; 21; 23; 25; 26(2); 7:1; 5; 13; 14; 15; 16; 21(2); 22; 8:4; 9; 10; 12; 13; 14; 16; 17; 18(2); 22; 24(2); 30; 31; 32; 34; 9:1(3); 9; 25; 27; 10:6; 11; 12(3); 13(2); 16; 17; 21; 27; 30; 11:2(2); 3(2); 4; 13; 17; 19; 20; 22(4); 12:2; 5(3); 7; 8(6); 23; 13:1(2); 9; 10; 12(3); 16; 17; 19; 21(2); 27; 30; 31; 32; 14:1; 4(2); 6(2); 7; 10; 11(2); 12(2); 15:5; 33; 48; 61; 16:10; 17:10(2); 11(2); 12; 15; 16; 18:5(2); 8; 9; 10; 16; 19:2; 14; 50; 51; 20:4; 6(2); 7(4); 8(3); 21:2(2); 6; 11; 21; 27; 32; 38; 39; 22:2; 5; 7; 9; 10; 11; 16; 17; 19; 20(2); 22(2); 24; 25; 27(2); 28; 33; 23:1; 2; 6; 12(2); 13(2); 14(2); 24:2; 7(2); 13; 14(3); 15; 17(2); 18; 25; 26; 30(3); 32(2); 33(2); **Judg** 1:4; 5; 9(3); 10; 16(2); 21; 27; 29(2); 35(3); 2:3; 9(3); 11; 17; 19; 3:3(2); 7; 12(2); 20; 22; 24; 27; 4:1; 2(2); 5; 11; 14; 18(3); 20; 21; 22; 5:6(2); 7(2); 8(2); 10; 11(2); 17(2); 18; 19; 20; 24; 25; 28; 31; 6:1; 2; 10; 11; 14; 15(2); 17; 19(3); 21; 24; 26; 28; 33; 37; 7:1; 3; 8(2); 11; 12; 16; 19(2); 20(2); 21; 22; 8:2; 3; 6; 9; 10; 11; 15; 27(2); 28(2); 29; 31; 32(3); 9:2; 3; 6; 7; 15(2); 16; 19(2); 24; 25(2); 26; 32(2); 33; 34; 35(2); 41; 43; 44(2); 48; 56; 10:1(2); 2; 4; 5; 6; 8(2); 14; 17(2); 11:2; 3; 4; 7; 11; 12; 17(2); 20; 26(3); 31; 39; 40; 12:3; 7; 9; 12(2); 15(3); 13:1; 9; 20; 25; 14:1; 2; 6; 8; 9; 14; 15:1(3); 4; 6; 8; 9(2); 19(2); 20; 16:1; 2(3); 4; 9(2); 12(2); 18; 21; 30; 31; 17:2; 4; 6(3); 10; 12; 18:1(4); 3(2); 6; 7(2); 10; 12(2); 14; 17(2); 19; 20; 22; 28; 31; 19:1(2); 4; 5(2); 7; 8; 9; 11(2); 13(2); 15(4); 16; 17; 20; 26; 27; 20:1; 2; 6(2); 10; 13; 19; 20; 22(3); 27; 28; 29; 30; 31(2); 33(2); 36; 37(2); 38; 39(2); 42; 45; 47; 21:1; 3(2); 12; 13; 15; 19(2); 20(2); 21; 22; 23; 25(3); **Ruth** 1:1(3); 6(3); 7; 8; 9; 11; 14; 15(2); 22(2); 2:2; 3; 7; 8; 10; 11; 13; 14; 17; 18; 19(2); 20; 22(2); 23; 3:1; 2; 4; 6; 10; 13; 16; 17; 18; 4:7(3); 11(3); 13; 14; 15; 16; **1Sa** 1:3; 9; 10; 13; 17; 18; 19; 24; 2:1(3); 9; 13(2); 14; 26; 27(2); 29; 31; 32(3); 33; 34; 35(2); 36; 3:1; 2; 3; 9; 11; 12; 21(2); 4:1; 2(2); 6; 8; 14; 19(2); 21; 5:3; 5; 9; 6:1; 3; 8; 13; 18; 7:1; 2; 6; 16(2); 8:2; 3; 5; 7; 18(2); 21; 9:6; 7; 9; 12; 15; 18; 19; 22; 10:2; 25; 11:4; 7; 8; 11(2); 13; 15; 12:1; 5; 8; 17(2); 23; 24; 13:2(3); 3; 4; 5(2); 6(6); 7; 16(2); 17; 22(2); 14:2(2); 3; 7; 9; 15(2); 16; 19; 22(2); 27(2); 33; 34; 39; 43; 45; 15:2; 4; 5; 12; 14; 17; 19; 21; 22(2); 33(2); 16:12; 13; 18(2); 22; 17:1; 2; 8; 12; 19; 20; 21; 22; 25; 28; 40(4); 45; 46; 49(2); 50; 54; 57; 18:5(2); 10(2); 13; 14; 16; 18(2); 21(2); 22(2); 23(2); 26; 27(2); 19:2(2); 3; 5; 7(2); 9(2); 11; 13; 15; 16(2); 18; 19; 22(2); 23(2); 24; 20:1; 3; 5; 8; 13; 19; 24; 29(2); 34; 35; 42(2); 21:3; 5(2); 6; 9(2); 11; 12; 13; 15; 22:2(2); 4; 5; 6(3); 8; 11; 13(2); 14(2); 23; 23:3; 6; 7; 14(4); 15(2); 16; 18; 19(3); 23; 24(2); 25(2); 29; 24:1; 3(2); 10; 11(3); 20; 25:1; 2(3); 3; 4; 5; 6; 7; 8(2); 9; 15; 21(2); 24; 28; 29; 34; 35; 36; 37; 26:1; 2; 3(2); 4; 5; 7; 15(2); 18; 19; 20; 21; 24(2); 27:1(2); 5(4); 7; 11; 28:1; 3(2); 4(2); 20; 21; 24; 29:1; 2; 3; 4; 5; 6(4); 7; 8; 9; 10(2); 11; 30:6; 11; 24; 27(3); 28(3); 29(3); 30(3); 31; 31:1; 7; 8; 9; 10; **2Sa** 1:1; 9; 18; 20(2); 23(2); 24; 25(2); 2:3; 11; 16(2); 19; 23; 26; 27; 32(2); 3:2; 5; 7; 17; 19(3); 21; 22(3); 23; 25; 27; 30; 32; 38; 4:1; 7; 10; 11; 12(3); 5:2(2); 3; 5(2); 6(2); 9; 14; 18; 22; 24; 6:3; 11; 16; 17(3); 18; 20; 22(2); 7:1; 2; 3; 5; 6(3); 7; 9; 10; 18; 19; 23; 27; 8:6; 13; 14; 9:4(2); 10; 12; 13; 10:1; 4; 8(3); 9; 10; 17; 11:2; 4; 11(2); 12; 14; 15(2); 21; 12:1; 3; 9; 11; 16; 24; 30; 13:5; 6; 8; 12; 13; 16; 20; 23; 30; 14:3; 6; 13; 19(2); 20; 22(2); 25(2); 28; 32; 15:4; 7; 8; 9; 10; 11; 17; 21(2); 25; 26; 27; 28; 16:2; 4; 8(2); 19(3); 21; 22(2); 23; 17:3; 8(2); 9(2); 11; 12; 16; 18(2); 23(2); 25; 26; 29; 18:6; 10; 12(2); 14(2); 17; 18(3); 25; 19:3; 6; 8(2); 10; 13; 22; 24; 27; 30; 33; 37; 43(3); 20:1(2); 3(3); 8(2); 9; 10(2); 12(2); 15(2); 18; 19(2); 22; 21:1; 2; 4; 5; 6; 9(4); 12; 14(3); 16; 19; 20(2); 22; 22:1; 3; 7; 19; 20; 25; 31; 23:2; 3; 5; 7; 8; 12; 13(2); 14(2); 17; 20(2); 21; 39; 24:3; 5(2); 9; 10; 11; 13(2); 14; 18; **1Kin** 1:1; 2; 6; 13; 14; 15; 19; 22; 23; 25; 30; 35; 41; 42; 45; 52; 2:3(3); 4; 5(2); 6; 8; 10; 11(2); 26; 27; 34(2); 35(2); 36; 38; 39; 46; 3:2; 3(2); 5(2); 6(3); 7; 8; 14; 17(2); 18(2); 19; 20(2); 21(2); 25; 26; 27; 28; 4:7; 8; 9(2); 10; 11; 13(3); 15; 16(2); 17; 18; 19(3); 20; 27; 31; 33; 5:1; 5; 9(2); 14; 15; 16; 6:1(3); 6(2); 7(3); 8; 12(3); 19; 20(4); 27; 37(2); 38(3); 7:3; 4(2); 5; 14(2); 19; 20; 21; 24(2); 35; 46(2); 51; 8:1; 2; 4; 6; 8; 9; 12; 13(2); 17; 18(2); 20; 22; 23; 25; 30; 31; 32; 33; 34; 36; 37(2); 39; 40; 43; 45; 47(2); 48; 49; 52; 58; 61; 65; 9:4(2); 11; 16; 18(2); 19(3); 21; 23; 25; 26(2); 27; 10:2; 5; 6; 9; 11; 14; 17; 20; 21; 22; 24; 26; 27(2); 11:2(3); 6; 7; 12; 14; 15(2); 16; 19; 20(2); 21; 22; 24; 29(2); 30; 33(2); 36; 38(2); 40; 41; 42; 43(2); 12:2(2); 16(2); 17; 25; 26; 27; 29(2); 32(4); 33(2); 13:2; 4(2); 8(2); 11(2); 16(2); 19; 22; 24; 25(2); 28; 30; 31; 32(2); 14:5; 6(2); 8; 10; 11(2); 13(2); 15; 19; 20; 21(2); 22; 24; 25; 27; 29; 31(2); 15:1; 2; 3; 4; 5(2); 7; 8(2); 9; 10; 11; 13; 15; 17; 18; 21;

23(3); 24(2); 25; 26(3); 28(2); 31; 33(2); 34(3); 16:2; 4(2); 5; 6(2); 7(3); 8(2); 9(3); 10(3); 13; 14; 15(2); 16; 19(5); 20; 23(2); 25; 26(2); 27; 28(2); 29(2); 30; 31; 32(2); 34(3); 17:6(2); 7; 10; 11; 12(3); 17; 24; 18:1; 2; 4; 7; 13; 18; 23; 27; 32; 33(2); 36; 38; 45; 19:8; 11(3); 12; 13(3); 16; 18; 20:6(2); 12(3); 16; 23; 24; 25; 29(2); 34(2); 35; 37; 21:1; 2; 8(2); 9; 11(2); 13(2); 18(2); 19; 20; 21; 24(2); 25; 26; 27; 29(2); 22:2; 3; 10(2); 16; 17; 22; 23; 25; 27(2); 28; 35; 37; 38; 39; 40; 41; 42; 43(3); 45; 46; 47; 49; 50(2); 51; 52(4); **2Kin** 1:2(2); 3; 6; 13; 14; 16; 17(2); 18; 2:12; 21; 24; 3:1; 2; 18; 20; 21; 22; 24; 25; 27; 4:2(2); 4; 8; 10; 15; 29; 33; 35; 36; 37; 38; 40; 41; 42; 5:1; 3; 4; 8; 10; 12(2); 14; 15(2); 18(4); 19; 20; 23; 24; 25; 6:6; 8; 12(2); 13; 20; 25; 32; 7:1; 2; 3; 4; 5; 7; 12(2); 13(2); 15; 17; 18; 19; 20; 8:2; 8; 15(2); 16; 17; 18(2); 20; 23; 24(2); 25; 26; 27(3); 28; 29(2); 9:1; 2; 8; 10; 15(2); 16; 17; 21(2); 24; 25; 26; 27; 28(3); 29; 31; 34; 36; 37; 10:1; 5; 7; 8(2); 9; 11; 12; 16; 17; 19; 24; 25; 29(2); 30(3); 31; 32(2); 34; 35(2); 36; 11:2; 3; 4; 5; 8(2); 9; 10; 11; 15; 18; 20; 12:1(2); 2; 3; 6; 9; 10(3); 18(2); 19; 20; 21(2); 13:1(2); 2; 5; 6; 8; 9(2); 10(2); 11; 12; 13; 17; 20; 24; 14:1; 2; 3; 5; 6; 7; 8; 9(3); 11; 14(2); 15; 16(2); 18; 19; 20; 23(2); 24; 28; 29; 15:1; 2; 3; 5; 6; 7(2); 8(2); 9; 10; 11; 13(2); 14(2); 15; 17(2); 18; 19; 20; 21; 22; 23(2); 24; 25(3); 26; 27(2); 28; 29; 30(2); 31; 32; 33; 34; 35; 36; 37; 38(2); 16:1; 2(2); 3; 4; 8(2); 18; 19; 20(2); 17:1(2); 2; 4(2); 6(4); 8; 9; 10; 11; 14; 17; 19; 22; 24(2); 26; 28; 29(2); 31; 32; 18:1; 2; 3; 4; 5; 9; 10; 11(3); 13; 15(2); 17; 22(2); 26(3); 28; 30; 19:7; 10; 12; 27; 28(2); 29(2); 35(2); 37(2); 20:1(2); 3(2); 11; 13(3); 15(2); 17(2); 18; 19; 20; 21; 21:1; 2; 4(2); 5; 6; 7(3); 15; 16(2); 17; 18(3); 19; 20; 21(2); 22; 23; 24; 25; 26(3); 22:1; 2(2); 3; 5; 8; 9; 14(2); 20; 23:2(2); 3; 4; 5(3); 8(2); 9; 10; 11(2); 12; 14; 16; 19(2); 21; 22; 23(2); 24(4); 28; 29; 30(3); 31; 32; 33(3); 34; 36; 37; 24:1; 5; 6; 8; 9; 12; 13(2); 17; 18; 19; 20; 25:1(3); 3; 5; 8; 11; 13(3); 15(2); 19(3); 21; 22; 24; 25; 27(3); 28; **1Chr** 1:19; 43; 44; 45; 46(2); 47; 48; 49; 50; 2:3; 4; 6; 7; 21; 22; 24; 3:1; 4(2); 5; 4:22; 38; 41(2); 5:8; 9(2); 10(2); 11; 12; 16(4); 17(2); 18; 20(2); 22; 23; 6:10(2); 31; 32; 54; 55; 62; 67; 71; 76; 78; 80; 7:2(2); 5; 21; 23; 29; 8:8; 28; 32; 9:1; 2(2); 3; 9; 16; 18(2); 20; 22(3); 24; 25; 26; 28; 31; 33(2); 35; 10:1; 7(2); 8; 10(2); 12; 11:2(2); 3; 7; 10; 14; 15; 16; 19; 22(2); 23; 12:2; 15; 17; 21; 33; 35; 36; 40; 13:2(2); 3; 4; 7; 14; 14:4; 9; 11; 13; 15; 15:1; 29; 16:1; 2; 10; 14; 19; 27(2); 29; 35; 39; 40; 17:1(2); 2; 4; 5; 8; 9; 14(2); 17; 19; 21; 25; 18:6; 12; 13; 19:1; 4; 9(2); 10; 11; 13; 17(2); 18; 20:2; 3; 8; 21:12; 13; 16(2); 18; 19; 23; 28; 29(2); 22:2; 3(2); 4; 7; 8; 9; 14(2); 15; 23:11; 13; 25; 28(3); 29; 31(2); 32; 24:3; 19; 31; 25:5; 6; 7; 26:12; 27; 30(2); 31; 27:1(2); 2; 4; 5; 6; 7; 8; 9; 10; 11; 12; 13; 14; 15; 21; 24; 25(4); 28; 29(2); 28:2; 8(2); 13; 19; 29:2; 11(2); 12(2); 17(2); 18; 21; 25(2); 27(2); 28(2); 29(3); **2Chr** 1:1; 2; 3; 7; 8; 9; 10; 11; 14; 15; 2:2; 7(7); 8; 9; 11; 14(10); 16; 17; 18; 3:1(3); 2(2); 4; 10; 16; 4:2; 3; 6(3); 7; 8; 17(2); 18; 5:1; 3(2); 5; 7; 10; 12; 13; 6:1; 5; 7; 8(3); 10; 11; 12; 13; 14(2); 16(2); 18; 22; 24; 28(2); 29; 31(2); 32; 37(2); 38; 40; 41; 7:8; 9; 10; 11(2); 15; 18; 8:4(2); 6(2); 8; 11; 13(4); 17; 9:1(2); 4; 5; 8; 11; 13; 16; 19; 20; 22; 23; 25; 27(3); 29(3); 30; 31(2); 10:2; 16(2); 17; 11:3; 5(2); 10(2); 11; 12; 13; 17; 23; 12:2; 5; 12; 13(2); 15; 16(2); 13:1; 2; 3(2); 4; 8; 11; 20; 22; 14:1(3); 2; 6(2); 10(2); 11; 14; 15; 15:4; 5(2); 9; 10(2); 16; 16:1(2); 9; 10(2); 11; 12(3); 13; 14(3); 17:1; 2(3); 3; 4; 5(2); 6; 7(2); 9; 12; 13(2); 19; 18:1; 2; 3; 9(3); 15; 16; 21; 22; 26(2); 27; 34; 19:1; 3(2); 5; 6; 8; 9; 10; 11; 20:2; 5(2); 6(2); 9(3); 14; 17; 20(2); 24; 25(2); 26; 27; 31; 32(2); 34(2); 36; 21:1(2); 3; 5; 6(2); 8; 9; 11; 12(2); 13; 17; 18; 19; 20(3); 22:1; 2; 3; 4; 6; 9; 11; 12; 23:1; 2; 3; 5; 6; 7(2); 8; 9; 10; 13; 14; 17; 18(2); 19(2); 24:1; 2; 6; 9(2); 10; 11; 13; 14; 16(2); 21; 25(3); 27(2); 25:1; 2; 4(2); 10; 12; 17; 18(3); 21; 24; 26; 27; 28; 26:1; 3; 4; 5(2); 7; 8; 9; 10(5); 15; 17; 19(3); 20; 21; 23(2); 27:1; 2; 4(2); 7; 8; 9(2); 28:1(2); 2; 3(2); 4; 6(2); 9; 13; 22; 24(2); 25; 26; 27(3); 29:1; 2; 3(2); 4; 6; 7; 9; 10; 16; 17(2); 18; 19(2); 25; 31; 34; 35(2); 30:2(2); 5; 12; 13; 14; 15; 16; 17; 25; 26(2); 31:1(2); 2; 3; 4(2); 5(2); 6(2); 7(2); 11; 12; 15(2); 16; 17; 18(2); 19(2); 21(4); 32:5(2); 6; 10(2); 18; 21; 23; 24; 26; 29; 30; 31(3); 32(2); 33(2); 33:1; 2; 4(2); 5; 6(2); 7(3); 12; 14(3); 15(2); 17; 18(2); 20(2); 21; 22; 24; 25; 34:1; 2(2); 3(2); 4(2); 6; 8; 10(2); 13; 15; 17; 21(3); 22(2); 24; 28; 30(2); 31(2); 32; 33; 35:1; 2; 3; 5; 10(2); 12; 13(3); 14; 15; 18; 19; 22; 24(2); 25(3); 26; 27; 36:1(2); 2; 3; 5(2); 6; 7; 8(3); 9(2); 11; 12; 14; 17; 22(2); 23(2); **Ezr** 1:1(2); 2; 3(2); 4(2); 5; 7; 2:42; 68; 70(2); 3:1; 2; 8(2); 9; 10; 11; 4:4; 6(2); 7(3); 8; 10; 15(2); 17; 23; 5:1(2); 8(2); 13; 14; 15(2); 16(2); 17; 6:1(2); 2(3); 5; 7; 15; 18(3); 22; 7:1; 6; 7; 8(2); 10; 13; 14; 15; 16(2); 17; 25; 27(2); 8:1; 15; 22; 29; 31; 33; 9:2; 7; 8(2); 9(4); 14; 15; 10:2; 9; 13; 14; 16; **Neh** 1:1(3); 3(2); 11; 2:1(3); 5; 12(2); 15; 17; 20; 3:17; 26; 4:2; 4; 11; 13; 16; 17; 20; 21; 22; 5:5; 9; 14; 16; 18; 6:2(2); 5(2); 7; 10(2); 11; 14; 15(2); 16; 17; 18(2); 19; 7:3; 73(2); 8:5; 7; 8(2); 14(3); 15(2); 16(4); 18; 9:1; 3(2); 9; 12(3); 15; 17; 19(3); 21; 23; 24; 25(2); 27; 28; 29; 30; 33; 35(3); 36; 37; 10:29; 34; 36(2); 37; 11:1(2); 3(4); 17; 18; 20(2); 21; 24; 25(3); 27; 28; 30(2); 31; 36(2); 12:7; 9; 12; 22; 23; 26(2); 39; 40; 46; 47(2); 13:1(2); 6(2); 7(2); 11; 15(4); 16; 19; 23; 24(2); 27; 28; 30; **Est** 1:1; 2(2); 3; 5(2); 7(2); 9; 10; 12; 14; 16; 17(2); 22; 2:3; 5; 12; 14(3); 15(2); 16(2); 17; 19; 21(2); 22; 23; 3:2; 3; 7(2); 8; 12; 13; 14; 15; 4:3(2); 8; 11; 13; 16(2); 5:1(2); 2(3); 8; 9; 12; 14; 6:4; 5(2); 6(2); 7:3; 5; 7; 8; 9; 8:5(3); 8(2); 9; 10; 11; 12; 13; 15; 17(2); 9:1(3); 2; 4; 6; 11; 12(2); 13; 15; 16; 19; 20; 31; 32; 10:2; **Job** 1:1; 4; 5(2); 7(2); 8; 10; 12; 13; 18; 22; 2:2(2); 3; 6; 10; 3:3; 20(2); 23; 26; 4:13; 18; 19(3); 21; 5:4; 13; 14(3); 19(2); 20(2); 23; 24; 26(3); 6:2; 4; 6; 10; 13; 29; 30; 7:11(2); 21(2); 8:12; 16; 9:4(2); 5; 29; 31; 32; 10:1; 13; 11:4; 14(2); 18; 12:5; 9; 10; 12; 24; 25; 13:14(2); 15; 27; 14:8(2); 13; 17; 15:9; 15(2); 21(2); 28(2); 31; 16:4; 8; 9; 15; 17; 19; 17:2; 3; 13; 16; 18:3; 4; 6; 10(2); 15; 17; 19; 19:2; 8; 15(2); 23; 24; 26; 28; 20:11; 12; 14; 20; 22(2); 26(2); 28; 21:7; 8; 13(2); 16; 17; 21(2); 23; 25; 26; 32; 34(2); 22:8; 12; 14; 22; 26; 23:6; 13; 24:5; 6; 7; 13; 14; 16(2); 17; 18; 23; 25:2; 5; 26:8; 27:3(2); 10; 15; 20; 28:13; 14; 29:2(2); 4; 7; 18; 20(2); 25; 30:1; 2; 3; 6(3); 10; 14(2); 17(2); 24; 25; 28; 31:6; 15(2); 21; 26; 32; 33; 32:1; 5; 8; 22; 33:2; 5; 6; 8; 9; 11; 12; 15(3); 34:8; 20; 24(2); 25; 26; 35:10; 14; 15(2); 16; 36:4; 5; 8(2); 11(2); 13; 14; 15(2); 20; 31; 37:8; 12; 16; 21; 23(3); 38:16; 32; 33; 36; 37; 40(3); 39:4; 10; 14(2); 16; 21(2); 40:12; 13(2); 16(2); 21; 41:9; 22; 23; 42:6; 8; 11; 15; **Ps** 1:1(3); 2(2); 3; 5(2); 2:4(2); 5(2); 9; 12; 3:2; 4:1; 4; 5; 7(2); 8(2); 5:3(2); 4; 5; 7(2); 8; 9; 10; 11(2); 6:1(2); 5(2); 7:1; 2; 3; 5; 6; 8; 10; 8:1; 9; 9:2; 4; 8(2); 9; 10; 11; 14(2); 15(2); 16; 19; 20; 10:1; 2(2); 4; 6(2); 8(2); 9(3); 11; 13; 11:1; 2; 4(2); 12:5; 6; 13:2(2); 5(2); 14:1; 5(2); 15:1(2); 2; 4; 16:1; 3(2); 6; 7; 9; 10; 11; 17:3; 5; 7; 10; 11; 12; 14; 15; 18:t; 2; 6; 13; 18; 19; 24; 30; 42; 19:4; 11; 14; 20:1; 5(2); 7(2); 21:1(2); 5; 7; 9(2); 13; 22:2(2); 4; 5; 8; 14; 22; 25; 23:2; 3; 5; 6; 24:3; 7; 8; 9; 25:2; 5; 8; 9; 12; 20; 26:1(2); 3; 4; 6; 10; 11; 12(2); 27:3; 4(2); 5(3); 6; 9; 11; 13; 28:3; 7; 29:2; 9; 30:5(2); 6; 9; 31:1(2); 6; 7(2); 8; 9; 14; 15; 17; 19; 20(2); 21; 22; 24; 32:2; 6(2); 8; 9; 10; 11(2); 33:1; 4; 7; 8; 18; 19; 21(2); 22; 34:1; 2; 8; 22; 35:7; 9(2); 15; 16; 18; 20; 25; 27; 36:2; 4; 5; 9; 10; 37:3(2); 4; 5; 7(2); 8; 11; 19(2); 23; 31; 33; 35; 39; 40; 38:1(2); 2; 3(2); 7; 14; 15; 39:6(2); 7; 40:3(2); 5; 7; 9; 16; 41:1; 3; 9; 12; 42:4; 5(2); 8(2); 10; 11; 43:5; 44:1(2); 3; 6; 8; 17; 19; 45:4; 5; 9; 14; 16; 17; 46:1; 5; 8; 9(2); 10; 48:1(2); 3; 6; 8(2); 9; 49:5; 6(2); 12; 14(3); 20; 50:15; 16; 21; 22; 51:t; 4; 5(2); 6(2); 10; 16; 18; 52:1; 7(2); 8(2); 53:1; 5; 54:5; 55:2; 3; 7; 9; 10; 11; 14; 15; 18; 21; 23; 56:t; 3; 4(2); 7; 8; 10(2); 11; 13; 57:t; 1(2); 58:2(2); 6; 7; 9; 10; 11; 59:3; 7; 8; 12; 13(2); 16(2); 60:t; 6; 61:4(2); 62:4; 7(2); 8; 9; 10(2); 63:t; 1; 2; 4; 6; 7; 11; 64:1; 4; 5; 10(3); 65:1; 4; 5; 8; 66:3; 5; 6; 9; 14; 18; 68:5; 6(2); 14(2); 16(2); 17(2); 21; 23(2); 24; 26; 30; 34; 69:1; 2; 12; 13(3); 17; 21; 25; 35; 70:4; 71:1; 2; 9; 16; 72:4; 7; 9; 14; 16; 17; 73:4; 5; 11; 12(2); 13(2); 18; 19; 21; 25; 28; 74:3; 4; 8(2); 12; 13; 14; 75:8; 76:1(2); 2(2); 7; 77:2(2); 6; 9; 13; 18; 19(2); 78:2; 5(2); 7; 9; 10; 12(3); 14; 15; 17; 18; 19; 22; 26(2); 28; 30; 33(2); 37; 40(2); 43(2); 51(2); 52; 55; 66; 79:10; 80:5; 81:3(2); 5; 7(2); 9; 12; 13; 82:1; 5; 83:4; 12; 84:4; 5(2); 7; 10(3); 12; 85:6; 9; 13; 86:2; 5; 7; 11; 15; 87:1; 5; 7; 88:5; 6(3); 11(2); 12(2); 13; 89:2; 5; 6; 7(2); 10; 12; 15; 16(2); 17; 19; 24; 25(2); 30; 37; 43; 47; 49; 50; 90:1; 4(2); 5; 6(2); 8; 9; 91:1; 2; 6; 11; 12; 15; 92:2; 4; 12; 13(2); 14; 15; 94:5; 15; 17; 19; 23; 95:4; 8(3); 10; 11; 96:6; 9; 97:11; 12; 98:2; 99:2; 4; 7; 101:2; 6; 7; 102:2(3); 14; 16; 21(2); 23; 24; 103:8; 19; 20; 22; 104:3; 22; 24; 27; 31; 34; 105:3; 7; 12(2); 18; 23; 27; 30(2); 31; 32; 35; 36; 39; 41; 106:5; 7; 14(2); 16; 18; 19; 21; 22; 23; 25; 26; 27; 29; 47; 107:4(3); 5; 6; 10(3); 13; 14; 16; 19; 23(2); 24; 28; 32(2); 40; 108:7; 109:13; 16; 17; 110:2; 3(2); 5; 7; 111:1(2); 8; 112:1; 3; 4; 6; 7; 113:6(2); 115:3; 8; 9; 10; 11; 116:9; 11; 14; 15; 18; 19(2); 118:5(2); 8(2); 9(2); 10; 11; 12; 15; 23; 24; 26; 119:1(2); 3; 11; 14(2); 15; 16; 19; 23; 35; 37; 40; 42; 43; 47; 48; 50; 51; 54; 55; 70; 74; 75; 78; 80; 81; 83; 89; 92; 109; 114; 133; 147; 148; 161; 120:1; 5(2); 121:8; 123:1; 124:8; 125:1; 4; 126:4; 5(2); 127:1(2); 4; 5; 128:1; 129:8; 130:5; 7; 131:1(2); 3; 132:6; 11; 133:1; 134:1; 2; 135:2(2); 6(3); 17; 18; 136:10; 15; 23; 137:2; 4; 7; 138:3(2); 5; 7; 139:4; 8; 9; 13; 15(2); 16(2); 18; 20; 24(2); 140:2; 7; 11; 13; 141:5; 6; 8; 142:t; 3; 5; 143:1(2); 2; 3; 8(2); 144:2; 12; 13; 14(2); 15; 145:15; 17(2); 18; 146:3(3); 4; 5; 147:3; 10(2); 11(3); 14; 148:1; 149:1; 2(2); 3; 4; 5; 6(2); 150:1(2); **Prov** 1:14; 15; 17(2); 20; 21(3); 22; 2:13; 14; 15; 20; 21(2); 3:4; 5; 6; 7; 12; 16(2); 23; 27; 33; 4:3; 11(2); 14; 21; 5:10; 14(2); 16; 23; 6:8(2); 14; 18; 25; 27; 29; 34; 7:9(3); 11; 12(2); 25; 8:2(2); 3; 8(2); 20(2); 22; 31; 9:4; 6; 9; 14; 17; 18; 10:5(2); 8; 13; 17; 19; 11:4; 6; 8; 14; 20; 21; 22; 28; 31; 12:4; 6; 15; 20; 25; 27; 28(2); 13:6; 23; 14:2(2); 3; 7; 13; 14; 23; 26; 28(2); 32(2); 33(2); 15:3; 4; 6(2); 22; 23; 16:1; 2; 5(2); 10(2); 15; 20; 21; 27; 31; 17:8; 12; 16; 18; 24; 18:2; 5; 9; 11; 17; 21; 19:1(2); 20; 21; 24; 20:4; 5; 7; 8; 20; 21:1; 2; 4; 9(2); 10; 14(2); 16; 19; 20; 24; 22:5; 6; 13; 15; 18; 19; 20; 22; 29; 23:7; 9; 17; 19; 28; 31; 34; 24:6; 7; 10; 23; 27; 25:5; 6(2); 7; 8; 11; 13; 19(2); 20; 24(2); 26:1(2); 5; 7; 8; 9; 12; 13(2); 15; 16; 19; 25; 27:10; 14; 15; 19; 22; 28:6(2); 10(2); 11; 18; 25; 26; 29:2; 6; 11; 20; 22; 23; 25; 27; 30:4(2); 5; 9; 12; 19(2); 25; 26; 28; 29; 32; 31:8; 11; 23; 25; 26; 31; **Eccl** 1:1; 12; 16; 18; 2:1; 3; 5; 7(2); 9; 10; 14(2); 15(2); 16; 21(3); 23; 24; 26; 3:9; 10; 11(2); 12(2); 17; 18; 22; 4:14; 15; 16; 5:2; 4; 7; 8; 14; 15; 16; 17; 19; 20; 6:4(2); 12; 7:4(2); 8(2); 9(2); 14(2); 15(3); 19; 8:2; 3; 8(2); 10; 11; 9:1(2); 3; 6; 9(2); 10; 12(3); 15; 17; 10:1; 6(2); 16; 17; 20(2); 11:3; 5; 6(2); 8; 9(4); 12:1(2); 3; 4; 5; 9; **Song** 1:4; 9; 14; 2:12; 14(2); 3:2(2); 8(2); 11(2); 4:7; 5:4; 6:2; 13; 7:4; 5; 11; 8:8; 10; 13; **Is** 1:1; 6; 7; 8(2); 11; 21; 2:2(2); 3; 5; 6; 10; 11; 17; 20; 22; 3:7(2); 14; 18; 25; 4:1; 2; 3(3); 6; 5:1; 2; 4; 8; 9; 11; 12; 16(2); 21(2); 25; 30(2); 6:1; 5; 6; 12; 13(2); 7:1; 3; 6; 11(2); 18(3); 19(2); 20; 21; 22; 23; 8:1; 6; 9(3); 11; 18(2); 20; 9:1(2); 2(2); 3; 4; 5; 9; 14; 17; 18; 10:3(2); 5; 7; 17; 20(2); 23; 24; 25; 27; 11:3; 9; 10; 11; 15; 16; 12:1; 4; 5; 6; 13:3; 4; 8; 10; 13(2); 17; 20; 22(2); 14:1; 2; 3; 6(2); 13(2); 18(2); 20; 25; 28; 30; 31; 32; 15:1(2); 3(2); 5; 16:3; 5(3); 10(2); 17:4; 5; 6(3); 9; 11(3); 18:2; 4(2); 5; 7; 19:1; 3; 9; 10; 14(3); 16; 17; 18(2); 19(2); 20; 21; 23; 24(2); 20:1; 6; 21:1; 5; 8(2); 13(2); 22:2; 3; 5; 7; 8; 12; 14; 16; 20; 23; 25(2); 23:1; 13; 15; 24:10; 11; 12; 13; 15(2); 18; 21; 22(2); 23(2); 25:4; 5; 6; 7; 8; 9(2); 10; 11; 26:1(2); 2; 3(2); 4(2); 8; 9(2); 10; 12; 16; 17(3); 18(2); 19; 27:1(2); 2; 4(2); 8(2); 9; 12; 13(4); 28:4; 5; 6; 7(2); 14; 16; 20; 21(2); 25(2); 29(2); 29:15; 18; 19(2); 21; 23; 24; 30:2(2); 3; 7; 8(2); 12; 13; 14(2); 15(3); 19; 21; 23(2); 25; 26; 28; 29; 32(2); 31:1(2); 7; 9(2); 32:1(2); 2(2); 13; 16(2); 18(3); 19; 33:2; 12; 14; 17; 34:5; 6(2); 11; 13(2); 35:6(2); 7; 36:1; 2; 6(2); 7; 11(3); 13; 15; 37:7; 10; 12; 28; 29(2); 30; 36(2); 38(2); 38:1(2); 3(2); 8; 10; 11; 15; 16; 17; 20; 39:2(3); 4(2); 6(2); 7; 8; 40:3(2); 11; 12(4); 14; 22; 24; 26; 41:16(2); 18(2); 19(2); 42:1; 2; 4; 6; 7; 12; 16; 17; 22(2); 24; 43:4; 14; 16(2); 19(2); 20(2); 26; 44:7; 12; 13; 16; 19(2); 20; 23; 45:2(2); 13; 14(2); 17; 18; 19(3); 23; 24; 25; 46:6; 7; 13; 47:1; 8; 9(3); 10(2); 13; 48:1(2); 10; 16; 49:2(2); 3; 4(2); 5; 8(2); 9(3); 20; 21; 22; 50:4; 10(2); 11(3); 51:6; 7; 9(2); 14; 16(2); 20; 52:6; 10; 53:9(2); 10; 54:6; 8; 14; 16; 17; 55:2; 11; 56:5; 7; 9; 57:2(2); 5; 6; 10; 13; 15; 17; 58:2; 3; 10; 11; 12; 14; 59:4; 6; 7; 8; 9; 10(2); 13; 14; 19; 20; 21; 60:10(2); 18; 22; 61:3; 6; 7(2); 8; 10(2); 11; 62:3(2); 4; 7; 9; 63:1(3); 2(2); 3(2); 4; 6(2); 9(3); 13; 64:5(2); 65:2; 3; 4(2); 5; 8(2); 10; 16(3); 18; 19(3); 23; 25; 66:3; 4; 8; 13; 17(2); 20(3); **Jer** 1:1(2); 2(2); 3(2); 5; 9; 2:2(3); 5; 7; 17; 18(2); 19; 23; 24(2); 27; 28; 30; 34; 37; 3:2(2); 6; 16(2); 18; 23(2); 25; 4:2(5); 5(3); 11; 19; 20; 30; 31; 5:1; 6; 7; 8; 13; 14; 18; 19(2); 20(2); 24(2); 30; 31; 6:1(2); 3; 6; 7; 10; 11; 16; 23; 24; 26; 29; 7:2(2); 3; 4; 6; 7(2); 8; 10; 11; 12; 17(2); 22; 23; 24(2); 30(2); 31(2); 32; 8:3; 7; 8(2); 9; 12; 16; 18; 19(3); 22; 9:2; 4; 6; 8; 23(3); 24(3); 26(3); 10:5; 6; 7; 13; 14(2); 15; 23(2); 24; 11:4; 6(2); 7; 8; 12; 14; 15; 17; 21; 12:2; 5(2); 8; 16; 13:1; 4; 10; 17; 21; 22; 25; 27; 14:4; 5; 6; 8(2); 9; 13; 14; 15(2); 16; 15:4; 7; 11(2); 13; 14; 15; 17; 16:2; 3(2); 6; 7; 9(2); 19; 17:3; 4(2); 5; 6(3); 7; 8; 11; 13; 17; 19(3); 20; 21; 24; 25; 27(2); 18:4; 6(2); 10; 15(3); 17; 21; 23; 19:4; 7; 9; 10; 11; 14; 20:1; 2(2); 6; 7; 9(3); 16; 21:4; 5(3); 7; 9; 12; 14; 22:2; 3; 4(2); 12; 15; 20; 21; 23(2); 30(2); 23:5; 6; 8; 11; 12; 13(2); 14(2); 18; 19; 20; 22; 24; 25; 26; 29; 24:8(2); 9; 25:1; 5; 13; 23; 24; 34; 26:1; 2(2); 4; 7; 9(2); 10; 14; 15; 16; 18; 20; 27:1; 11; 15; 18(2); 19; 21(2); 28:1(5); 5(3); 7(2); 11; 15; 17; 29:5; 7; 8; 9; 10; 15; 16; 21; 22(2); 23(2); 25; 26(4); 28(2); 29; 31; 30:2; 6; 8; 10; 11; 24; 31:2; 4; 9; 10; 12; 13; 15; 17; 22; 23(2); 24(2); 29; 32; 33(2); 32:1; 2(2); 7; 8(3); 9; 10; 12(3); 14; 15; 19(2); 20(2); 23(2); 34; 35; 37(3); 40; 41; 43; 44(6); 33:1; 5(2); 10(3); 12(2); 13(6); 15(2); 16; 20; 34:5; 6; 13; 15(3); 17; 18; 35:1; 7(2); 8; 9; 10; 15; 36:1; 6(4); 8(2); 9(3); 10(5); 13; 14(3); 15(2); 18; 20(3); 21(2); 22(2); 23; 28(2); 30(2); 32; 37:1; 4; 10; 12; 13; 15(2); 17; 18; 21(2); 38:2; 4(2); 5; 6(3); 7(3); 9(3); 13; 14; 22(2); 28; 39:1(2); 2(2); 3(2); 5(2); 6; 9; 10; 15; 16; 17; 18; 40:1; 6; 7(2); 9; 10(2); 11(3); 13; 15(2); 41:1(2); 5; 8; 10(2); 12; 17; 18; 42:10; 13; 16(2); 20; 22; 43:4; 5; 8; 9(5); 12(2); 13; 44:1(2); 3; 6(2); 8(2); 9(2); 10(2); 12; 13; 15(2); 16; 17(2); 21(2); 23(3); 24; 26(3); 27; 29; 45:1(2); 3; 5; 46:2(2); 10; 11; 14(4); 19; 21; 25; 26; 27; 28; 48:2; 5(2); 6; 7(2); 11; 18; 20; 26(2); 28(3); 35(2); 38; 41(2); 44; 47; 49:1; 2; 4(2); 7; 11; 16; 18(2); 21; 22; 24; 26(2); 27; 32; 33; 34; 38; 39; 50:2(2); 4(2); 5; 9(2); 14; 16; 20(2); 22; 25; 28; 30(2); 32; 37; 39; 42; 43; 51:1; 2; 3; 4(2); 6; 7; 10; 13; 16; 17; 18; 20; 21(2); 22(3); 23(3); 24(2); 27; 30; 39; 44; 46(3); 47; 58(2); 59; 60; 62; 52:1; 2; 3; 4(3); 6(3); 8; 9; 10; 11(2); 12(2); 15; 17(2); 19(2); 20; 25(2); 27(2); 28; 29; 30; 31(4); 32; **Lam** 1:2; 4; 7(2); 9; 12; 15(2); 19; 20; 2:1(2); 2; 3; 4; 5; 6(2); 7(2); 11; 12; 17; 19(3); 20; 21(2); 22(2); 3:6; 10(2); 11; 20(2); 24; 27; 29; 36; 41; 45; 53; 57; 66; 4:1; 3; 5(2); 6; 7; 8; 10; 11; 13; 14; 17; 18; 19; 20; 21; 5:11(2); **Eze** 1:1(3); 2; 3; 16; 20; 21; 28(2); 3:3; 10; 14(2); 18; 19; 20; 4:9; 12; 14; 16; 5:2(2); 3(2); 4; 5; 6; 7; 8(2); 9; 10(2); 12; 13(2); 14; 15(4); 6:6; 7; 9; 10; 13; 14; 7:4; 7; 9; 13; 15(2); 19(2); 20; 8:1(4); 3; 4; 5; 7; 8(2); 9; 10; 11(2); 12(2); 18(2); 9:1(2); 2(2); 4; 5; 7; 8; 10:1; 2(3); 3; 6; 8; 10; 13; 17; 19; 11:2; 6; 7; 10; 11(2); 12; 15; 16; 20; 24; 12:2; 3(2); 4(2); 5; 6(2); 7(3); 8; 10; 12; 13; 15; 22; 23; 25; 13:4; 5(2); 9(2); 13(3); 14; 21; 14:3; 4; 5; 7(2); 14; 16; 18; 19; 20; 23; 16:4(2); 5(2); 6(3); 12; 15; 22(2); 24; 29; 31(4); 34(3); 38; 41; 43; 47; 49(2); 51; 52; 53; 54(2); 56; 59; 60; 17:4; 5; 8; 9; 10; 15; 16(2); 17; 20; 23(2); 18:3; 9; 17; 18; 22; 24(3); 26; 32; 19:4; 8; 9(2); 10; 11; 12; 13(2); 20:1(2); 5(2); 6; 8; 9(2); 11; 13(4); 14; 15; 16; 17; 18(2); 19; 21(3); 22(2); 23; 26(2); 27(2); 36; 40(3); 41; 43; 47(2); 21:20; 21; 22; 23; 24(2); 30(2); 31; 32; 22:3; 4(2); 6; 7(3); 9(3); 10(2); 11(2); 12; 13; 14; 15; 16(2); 18; 20(2); 21(2); 22(2); 24; 25(2); 27; 30; 23:3(2); 8; 11(3); 15; 19(2); 21; 31; 32; 37; 38; 39; 43; 44(3); 45; 24:1(3); 7; 11; 12; 13; 18(2); 25; 26; 27; 25:4(2); 6; 10; 14; 26:1(2); 5; 6; 8; 12; 15; 17; 18(2); 20(3); 27:4; 8; 9(2); 10(2); 11; 12; 13; 14; 16; 17; 18(2); 19(2); 20; 21(2); 22; 24(3); 25(2); 26; 27(4); 30; 32(2); 34(3); 35; 28:2(2); 8; 9; 12; 13(3); 14; 15(2); 18; 22(3); 23; 25(3); 29:1(3); 3; 4; 12; 17(3); 21(2); 30:4(2); 5; 6; 7(2); 8; 9(3); 13; 14(2); 16; 18; 19; 20(3); 24; 31:1(3); 2; 3; 6; 7(2); 8(3); 9; 10(2); 12; 14(2); 15; 16; 17; 18(3); 32:1(3); 2; 3; 10; 17(2); 19; 20; 23(2); 24; 25(3); 26; 27; 28; 32(2); 33:6; 8; 9; 10; 11; 12(3); 15; 21(3); 22(2); 27(4); 30; 34:12(2); 13; 14(3); 25(2); 26; 27; 29; 35:5(2); 8(3); 36:2; 3; 5; 6(2); 15; 17; 23(2); 27; 28; 31; 33(2); 34; 38; 37:1(2); 2; 6; 8; 14(2); 17; 19(2); 20; 22; 24; 25; 26; 28; 38:8; 12; 14; 16(2); 17(2); 18; 19(4); 23; 39:6; 7(2); 9; 11(2); 15; 26; 27(2); 40:1(5); 2; 3(2); 5; 25(2); 27; 29(2); 33; 39; 44; 41:6(2); 42:3; 6; 8; 10; 12; 43:7(2); 8(2); 9; 11(2); 16; 17; 18; 21; 44:2(2); 3; 5; 7(4); 8; 9(2); 11; 13; 17(2); 19; 24(3); 27(2); 28; 29; 30; 45:1; 2(2); 3; 8(2); 16; 17(4); 18(2); 21(2); 25(3); 46:1; 3(2); 4; 6; 8; 9(3); 10(3); 11(2); 21; 22; 23; 47:3; 5; 19; 22; 23; 48:8(3); 9(2); 10(5); 13(2); 15(2); 18; 21; 22; 28; **Dan** 1:1; 4(5); 8; 14; 15; 17(2); 18(2); 20(2); 2:1; 4; 5; 16; 19; 22; 24(2); 25(2); 27; 28(2); 40(2); 41; 44(2); 45; 49; 3:1(2); 13; 16; 20; 21; 24; 25; 28; 29; 30; 4:1; 4(2); 6; 7; 8(2); 9; 10(2); 12(2); 13; 15(3); 17; 18; 21; 23(2); 25; 29; 31; 32; 35; 36; 37; 5:2; 3; 5; 7(2); 8; 9; 11(4); 12; 13; 14(2); 15; 16; 20; 21; 23(2); 27; 29; 30; 6:3; 4; 10; 19(2); 22; 23; 24; 25; 26; 27(2); 28(2); 7:1; 2; 5; 7(2); 8; 13; 15(2); 19; 20; 23; 28(2); 8:1; 2(4); 6; 7; 18; 19; 22; 23; 25(2); 9:1; 2(2); 6; 10; 11; 13; 14; 21(2); 24; 25; 27; 10:1; 2; 3; 4; 5; 6; 8(2); 9; 14; 17(2); 21(2); 11:1; 2; 6(2); 7; 14; 16; 20(4); 21(2); 38; 39; 45; 12:1; 2; 6; 7; 13; **Hos** 1:1(2); 5; 10; 2:3; 9(2); 10; 15(2); 18; 19(4); 20; 21; 23; 3:5; 4:1; 5(2); 16; 19; 5:4; 5; 8(2); 9; 11; 15; 6:2(2); 9; 10; 7:1; 2; 5; 6(2); 16; 8:6; 9:2; 3(2); 5(2); 6; 8(2); 9; 10(2); 13; 15; 10:4(2); 9; 10(2); 12(2); 13(2); 14(2); 15; 11:9; 11; 12:3; 4; 7; 8(2); 9(2); 11(3); 13:1(2); 5(2); 9; 10; 11(2); 13; 16; 14:3; 9; **Joel** 1:2(2); 13; 2:1(2); 5; 8; 9(2); 15; 23(2); 26; 27; 29; 30(2); 32(3); 3:1(2); 13; 14(2); 17; 18; 19; 21; **Amos** 1:1(2); 14(3); 2:7; 8; 16; 3:4; 5; 6(2); 9(5); 10; 12(4); 13; 14; 4:1; 6(2); 5:6(2); 7; 10; 11; 12; 13; 15; 16(2); 17; 20; 21; 25; 6:1(2); 6; 9; 13; 14; 7:1; 7; 8; 10; 17(2); 8:3(2); 9(2); 11; 13; 9:1; 3(2); 6(2); 9; 11(2); **Obad** 1; 3(2); 7; 8; 11(2); 12(3); 13(3); 14(2); 18; 20; **Jonah** 1:4; 5; 17; 2:3; 7; 3:6; 8; 4:2; 5; 8; 10(2); **Mic** 1:1; 10(2); 11; 13; 2:1; 4; 5; 11; 12; 3:3; 4; 4:1(2); 2; 5(2); 6; 7; 9(2); 10(3); 13; 5:1; 2; 4(2); 5; 6; 7; 8(2); 10; 15; 6:10; 12; 13(2); 14; 16; 7:2; 5(3); 6(2); 8; 11(2); 12; 14(4); 18; **Nah** 1:3(3); 6; 7(2); 13; 2:1; 3(2); 4(2); 5; 10; 12; 13; 3:10(2); 13; 17(2); 18; **Hab** 1:5; 15(2); 2:4; 13; 19; 20; 3:2(3); 7; 11; 12(2); 16(2); 17(2); 18(2); **Zeph** 1:1; 8; 9; 10; 12; 18(2); 2:3; 7(2); 14(4); 15(2); 3:2; 5; 11(2); 12(2); 13; 15; 16; 17(2); 19; 20; **Hag** 1:1(3); 4; 6; 8; 13; 14; 15(2); 2:1(2); 3(3); 9; 10(2); 12; 15; 17; 19; 20; 22; 23; **Zec** 1:1(2); 7; 8; 16; 2:1; 5; 10; 11(2); 12; 3:7; 9; 10; 4:10; 5:4; 7; 9; 11; 6:2(2); 3(2); 8; 14; 15; 7:1(3); 3(2); 5; 7; 10; 12; 8:3; 4(2); 5; 6(3); 8(3); 9(2); 10; 11; 15; 16; 17; 22; 23; 9:1; 4; 6; 7; 16; 10:1(2); 2; 3; 5(2); 7; 9; 11; 12(2); 11:8; 11; 13; 16(2); 12:2; 3(2); 4; 5; 6(4); 8; 9; 10(2); 11(3); 13:1; 2; 3; 4; 6(2); 8; 14:1; 3; 4(2); 5; 6; 8(3); 9; 10; 11; 12(2); 13; 14; 15; 20(2); 21(4); **Mal** 1:7; 10; 11; 12; 14; 2:6(3); 9; 11(2); 17(2); 3:1; 3; 4(2); 5; 8; 10; 11; 17; 4:2; 3; 4; **Mt** 1:20(2); 2:1(2); 2; 5; 6; 9; 12; 13; 16(2); 18; 19(2); 22(3); 23; 3:1(2); 3; 6; 12; 17; 4:6; 13(2); 16(2); 21; 23; 5:3; 8; 12; 15; 16; 18; 19(2); 20; 21; 22(3); 25; 28; 45; 48; 6:1; 2(2); 4(2); 5(2); 6(2); 9; 10(2); 18(2); 20; 23; 29; 7:3(2); 4; 11; 13(2); 15; 21; 22(4); 8:10; 11; 13; 24; 32; 9:4; 10; 16; 25; 31; 33; 35; 10:9; 11; 15; 16; 17; 19; 20; 23; 27(3); 28; 32; 33; 35(2); 41(2); 42(2); 11:1; 2; 6; 8(2); 11; 16; 21(3); 23(2); 24; 26; 29; 12:5(2); 6; 18; 19; 21; 32(2); 36; 40(2); 41; 42; 45; 50; 13:3; 10;

13; 14; 19; 21; 24; 27; 30(2); 31; 32; 33; 34; 35; 40(2); 43; 44; 54; 57(3); 14:2; 3; 8; 10; 11; 24; 25; 33; 15:9; 17; 32; 33; 16:3; 17; 19(2); 26; 27; 28; 17:5; 22; 18:1; 2; 4; 5; 6(2); 10(2); 14; 16; 18(2); 19; 20(2); 19:21; 28(2); 20:1; 3; 17; 21; 21:8(2); 9(2); 12; 14; 15; 18; 19; 22; 24; 28; 32; 33; 41; 42(2); 22:11; 12; 15; 16; 28; 30(3); 36; 43; 23:2; 6; 7; 9; 13(2); 30(2); 34; 39; 24:5; 7; 14; 15; 16; 18; 19; 20; 26(2); 30(2); 38(2); 40; 43; 44; 45; 48; 50(2); 25:4; 10; 18; 25; 31; 35; 36; 38; 39; 43(2); 44; 26:6(2); 12; 13; 23; 29; 55(2); 58; 61; 64; 67; 69; 27:4; 5; 7; 19; 29; 40; 43; 44; 51; 59; 60(2); 28:1; 18(2); 19; **Mk** 1:2; 3; 4; 5; 9(2); 11; 13; 14; 19; 20; 23; 35; 39; 45; 2:1; 6; 8(2); 15; 20; 26; 3:23; 29; 4:1; 2; 11; 15; 17; 19; 28; 29; 31(2); 36; 38; 5:4; 5(2); 13; 14(2); 15; 20; 27; 29; 30(2); 33; 34; 39; 40; 6:2; 4(2); 8; 10; 11; 14; 17; 22; 25(2); 27; 28; 29; 40; 47; 48; 51; 55; 56; 7:7; 32; 8:1; 4; 12; 14; 26; 37; 38(2); 9:33; 36(2); 37; 38; 39; 41; 42; 50; 10:10; 16; 21; 24; 30(2); 32; 37; 52; 11:4; 8(2); 9; 10(2); 15; 20; 22; 23; 25; 26; 27; 12:4; 11; 13; 14; 23; 25(2); 26(2); 35; 38(3); 39; 41; 42; 43; 44(2); 13:6; 8; 9; 11; 14; 16; 17; 18; 19; 24; 25; 26; 28; 32; 35; 14:3(2); 14; 17; 20; 25; 30; 31; 49; 60; 62; 66; 15:1; 7; 29; 38; 41; 43; 46(2); 16:2; 5; 12; 17; **Lk** 1:1(2); 3; 5; 6; 7; 8; 15; 17; 18; 19; 20; 21; 22; 25; 26; 28; 29; 31; 36; 39; 41; 44(2); 47; 51; 54; 66; 69; 75; 79(2); 80(2); 2:1; 7(3); 8(2); 11; 12(2); 14; 16; 19; 21; 23; 24; 25; 27; 28; 29; 34; 38(2); 40; 43; 44; 46(2); 51; 52(2); 3:1; 2; 4(2); 15(2); 17; 18; 20; 22(2); 4:2; 5; 11; 14; 15; 20; 21; 23(2); 24; 25(2); 27(2); 28; 33; 35; 44; 5:7; 12; 18(2); 19; 22; 29; 35; 6:1; 8; 12(2); 17; 23(3); 41(2); 42(3); 7:1; 7; 9; 21; 23; 25(2); 28; 32; 37(2); 45; 50; 8:10; 13; 15; 16; 23; 27(2); 29; 34(2); 35; 48; 51; 9:12; 14; 26(2); 31; 36; 48; 49; 57; 10:7; 12; 13(3); 20(2); 21(3); 26; 34; 11:1; 2(3); 6; 7; 21; 26; 31; 32; 33(2); 35; 37; 43(2); 52(2); 12:1; 3(4); 12; 15; 27; 28; 33; 38(2); 42; 45; 46(2); 52; 53(4); 58; 13:4(2); 6; 10; 11; 14(2); 19; 21; 24(2); 26(2); 28; 29; 35; 14:8; 10(2); 15; 21; 23; 15:4; 7; 10; 14(2); 21; 25; 28; 16:8; 10(4); 11; 12; 15; 19; 23(3); 24(2); 25; 17:4(2); 6; 24; 26(2); 27; 28; 30; 31(3); 34(2); 36; 18:2; 3; 9; 12; 17; 22; 30(2); 19:17; 20; 30; 36; 38(3); 42; 43; 44; 47; 20:1; 31; 33; 34; 35; 42; 45; 46(3); 21:2; 3; 4(2); 6; 8; 11; 14; 19; 21(3); 23(2); 25(3); 27; 37(3); 38(2); 22:6; 10; 16; 19; 20; 28; 30; 37; 44; 53; 55; 23:4; 9; 11; 14; 19; 22; 29; 31(2); 38; 40; 43; 45; 53(3); 24:1; 3; 4; 6; 12; 18(2); 19; 27; 29; 35(2); 36; 38; 44(3); 47; 49; 53; **Jn** 1:1; 2; 4; 5; 10; 18; 23; 28; 45; 47; 2:1; 11; 14; 19; 20(2); 23(3); 25; 3:13; 14; 15; 16; 18; 21; 23; 4:14; 18; 20(2); 21; 23(2); 24(2); 31; 44; 53; 5:2; 3; 4; 6; 13; 14; 26(2); 28(2); 35; 38; 39; 42; 43(2); 45; 6:10(2); 31; 37; 45; 49; 53; 56(2); 59(2); 61; 7:1(2); 4; 5; 9; 10; 18; 28; 37; 8:1; 2; 3(2); 4(2); 5; 9; 12; 17; 20(2); 21; 24(2); 31; 33; 35; 37; 44(2); 9:3; 5; 7; 34; 10:2; 9(2); 23(2); 25; 34; 38(2); 11:6; 9(3); 10(2); 13; 17; 20; 24; 25; 26; 30; 31; 33; 38; 52; 56; 12:13; 25; 35; 36; 46; 48; 13:1; 21; 31; 32(2); 14:1(2); 2; 10(3); 11(2); 13(2); 14; 17; 20(3); 26; 30; 15:2; 4(4); 5(2); 6; 7(2); 9; 10(2); 11; 16; 25; 16:21; 23(2); 24; 25(2); 26; 33(2); 17:10; 11(2); 12(2); 13(2); 21(3); 23(3); 26(2); 18:13; 15; 16; 20(3); 26; 38; 19:4; 6; 13(3); 17; 18; 20; 40; 41(2); 20:5(2); 7; 8; 12; 19; 25; 26; 30(2); 21:2; 8; **Acts** 1:2; 7; 8(3); 10; 11; 13; 14; 15(2); 18; 19; 20; 21; 2:1; 6; 8; 9(3); 10(2); 11; 12; 17; 18; 19(2); 22; 26; 27; 31; 37; 38; 42(3); 46; 3:6; 11; 13; 16(2); 22; 25; 26; 4:3; 7; 12; 16; 17; 18; 19; 24; 5:4(2); 7; 10; 12; 18; 20; 21; 22; 25(2); 28; 34(2); 37; 40; 42(2); 6:1(2); 7; 15; 7:2(2); 4; 5; 6; 7(2); 10; 12; 16; 17; 20(2); 22(3); 29; 30(3); 34; 35; 36(3); 38(3); 39; 41(2); 42(2); 44; 45; 48; 51; 8:8; 9; 16; 21(2); 23(2); 25; 28; 33; 40; 9:10; 11; 12(2); 17; 20; 21; 22; 25; 27(2); 28; 29; 31(2); 37(2); 42; 43; 10:1; 3(2); 17; 23; 25; 27; 30(2); 31(2); 32; 35; 39(2); 43; 48; 11:1; 3; 5(2); 13; 22; 26; 27; 28; 29; 12:4; 5; 7; 14; 21; 13:1; 5; 13; 14; 17; 18; 19; 27; 28; 29; 33(2); 35; 40; 41(2); 43; 14:1; 3; 8; 11(2); 14; 16(2); 17; 22; 23; 25; 15:21(2); 23; 33; 35; 36; 39; 16:3; 5(2); 6; 9; 12; 18; 24; 29; 32; 34; 36; 17:2; 11(2); 16; 17(2); 21; 22(2); 24; 28; 31(3); 18:2; 4; 5; 9; 10; 18; 21; 23; 24; 25(2); 26; 19:5; 9; 10; 16; 21; 22; 27; 29; 30; 39; 40(2); 20:6; 8; 9; 10; 13; 14; 16; 19; 22; 23; 29; 21:18; 27; 29; 31; 39; 40; 22:2; 3(3); 17(2); 19; 23:1; 6(2); 9; 10; 11; 16; 21; 35; 24:3; 12(3); 14(2); 18; 20; 21; 24; 25:3; 5; 14; 26:3; 10(2); 11; 13; 14; 16; 18; 21; 26; 27:12; 20; 21; 27; 31; 35; 37(2); 39; 28:7; 8; 9; 11(2); 18; 30(2); **Rom** 1:2; 7; 9(2); 15; 18; 19; 21; 27(2); 28; 32; 2:7; 12; 14; 15; 16; 17; 19; 20; 28; 29(2); 3:4; 9; 16; 20; 24; 25; 26; 4:10(4); 12; 18; 19; 20; 5:2; 3; 5; 6; 8; 11; 13; 17; 6:1; 4; 5(2); 10(2); 12(2); 21; 7:5(2); 6(2); 8; 13; 17; 18(2); 20; 22; 23(2); 8:1; 2; 3(3); 4; 8; 9(3); 10; 11(2); 18; 20; 22; 37; 39; 9:1(2); 2; 7; 17; 25; 26; 28; 33; 10:6; 8(2); 9; 14(2); 11:17; 19; 22; 23(3); 25(3); 30; 32; 12:4; 5; 10; 11(2); 12(3); 16; 17; 18; 20; 13:4; 9; 13(4); 14:1; 5; 13; 17; 18; 22; 15:12; 13(2); 15(2); 17; 23; 24; 27; 29; 30; 31; 16:2(2); 3; 5; 7; 8; 9; 10; 11; 12(2); 13; 22; **1Cor** 1:2(2); 5(3); 6; 7; 8; 10(2); 13; 15; 21; 29; 30; 31; 2:3(3); 4; 5(2); 7; 11; 13; 3:1; 16; 18; 19; 21; 4:2; 6(2); 10; 15(2); 17(3); 20(2); 21(2); 5:3(2); 4; 5; 9; 6:4; 11; 19; 20(2); 7:15; 17; 18; 20; 22; 28; 34(2); 37(2); 38(2); 39; 8:4(2); 5(2); 6; 7; 10; 9:1; 2; 9; 10(2); 18; 24; 25; 10:2(2); 5; 8; 19; 25; 28; 33; 11:2; 11; 13; 17; 18; 21; 22(2); 23; 24; 25(2); 34; 12:6; 18; 25; 27; 28; 13:6(2); 9(2); 10; 12; 14:2(2); 4; 7; 10; 13; 14; 19(2); 20(3); 21; 23; 24; 25; 27; 28; 33; 34; 35; 40; 15:2(2); 10; 17; 18; 19(2); 22(2); 23; 28; 30; 31; 41; 42(2); 43(4); 52(2); 54; 58(3); 16:2; 11; 13; 19(2); 24; **2Cor** 1:1; 4(2); 5; 6; 8; 9(3); 10; 12(2); 14(2); 15; 19; 20(2); 21; 22; 2:1; 3; 5; 9; 10; 13; 14(2); 15(2); 17(2); 3:2; 3(2); 7; 9; 10; 14(2); 18; 4:2(2); 4; 6(2); 7; 8; 10(2); 11; 12(2); 5:1; 2; 4; 6; 10; 11; 12(2); 17; 19; 20; 21; 6:1; 2(2); 3; 4(5); 5(6); 12(2); 13; 16(2); 7:1; 3; 4; 7; 9; 11(3); 12; 13; 14; 16(2); 8:2; 6; 7(5); 18; 20; 21(2); 22(2); 9:3(2); 4; 7; 8; 11; 14; 10:1; 3; 6; 11(2); 14; 16(2); 17; 11:1; 3; 6(3); 7; 9; 10(2); 17; 23(4); 25; 26(12); 27(5); 32; 33; 12:2(2); 3; 5; 7; 9(2); 10(5); 11(2); 12(2); 18(2); 19; 13:1; 3(2); 4; 5(2); 11; **Gal** 1:13(2); 14(2); 16; 22; 23; 24; 2:2; 4(3); 6; 8(2); 16; 20(2); 21; 3:3; 4(2); 8; 10(2); 11; 12; 17; 19; 26; 28; 4:3; 9; 11; 14; 18; 19(2); 20; 25(2); 5:1; 6; 10; 14(2); 16; 21; 25(2); 6:1(2); 4(2); 6(2); 9(2); 12; 13; 14; 15; 17; **Eph** 1:1; 3(2); 4(2); 6; 7; 8; 9; 10(5); 11; 12; 13(2); 15; 16; 17; 18; 20(2); 21(2); 23; 2:1; 2(2); 3(2); 4; 5; 6(2); 7(2); 10(2); 11(3); 12; 13; 15(3); 16; 21(2); 22; 3:3; 4; 5; 6; 9; 10; 11; 12; 15; 16; 17(2); 20; 21; 4:2; 3; 4; 6; 13; 14; 15(2); 16(2); 17(2); 18; 21; 23; 24; 5:2; 5; 8; 9; 12; 19(2); 20; 21; 24; 33; 6:1; 4; 5; 9; 10(2); 12; 13; 18; 20; 21; 24; **Phil** 1:1; 4; 5; 6; 7(3); 8; 9(2); 13(3); 14; 18(2); 20(2); 22; 23; 24; 26; 27; 28; 29; 30(2); 2:1; 3; 5(2); 6; 7; 8; 10(2); 12(2); 13; 15(2); 16(3); 19; 22; 24; 25; 29(2); 3:1; 3(3); 4(2); 6; 9; 14; 15; 19; 20; 4:1; 2; 3(2); 4; 6; 9; 10; 11(2); 12; 15; 16; 19; 21; **Col** 1:2; 4; 5(2); 6(3); 8; 9; 10(2); 12; 14; 16(2); 18; 19; 20(2); 21; 22(2); 23; 24(2); 27; 28(2); 29; 2:1; 2; 3; 5(3); 6; 7(2); 9; 10; 11(2); 12; 13; 15; 16(3); 18; 20; 23(2); 3:3; 4; 7(2); 10; 11; 15(2); 16(4); 17(2); 18; 20; 22(2); 4:1; 2(2); 3; 5; 7; 12(2); 13(2); 15(2); 16; 17; **1Th** 1:1(2); 2; 3(2); 5(4); 6; 7; 8(2); 9; 2:1(2); 2; 3; 4; 13(2); 14(2); 17(2); 19; 3:2; 5; 7; 8; 10; 12; 13; 4:4; 5; 6; 10; 14; 16; 17(2); 5:2; 4; 7(2); 12; 13; 18(2); **2Th** 1:1; 4(3); 8; 10(3); 12(2); 2:2; 4; 6; 10; 12; 17; 3:4; 6; 13; 17; **1Ti** 1:2; 4; 13; 14; 16; 2:2(2); 3; 6; 7(2); 9(2); 11; 12; 14; 15(2); 3:4; 9; 11; 13(2); 15; 16(3); 4:1; 2; 6(2); 10; 12(6); 14; 16(2); 5:5(2); 6; 7; 17; 6:9; 13; 15; 16; 17(3); 18; 19; **2Ti** 1:1; 3; 5(3); 6(2); 9; 13(2); 14; 15; 17; 18(2); 2:1(2); 7; 10; 14; 20; 25; 3:1; 12; 14; 15; 16; 4:2; 5; **Titus** 1:2; 3; 5(3); 13; 16; 2:2(3); 3; 7(2); 9; 10; 12; 3:1; 3; 8; 15; **Philem** 1:2; 4; 6(2); 7; 8; 10; 11; 13(2); 16(2); 20(2); 21; 23; **Heb** 1:1(2); 2; 6; 10; 2:5; 6; 8(3); 10; 12; 13; 17(2); 18; 3:2; 5; 8(3); 10; 11; 12(2); 15; 17; 19; 4:1; 3; 5; 6; 7; 13; 15; 16; 5:1; 6; 7(2); 13; 6:7; 10; 18; 7:9; 10; 19; 8:1; 5; 9(2); 10; 13; 9:9; 10; 12; 23; 24; 26; 10:3; 6; 7; 16; 22; 32; 34(3); 38; 11:9(3); 12; 13; 18; 19; 26; 34; 37; 38(3); 12:3; 9; 23; 13:3(2); 4; 18; 21(3); 22; **Jas** 1:6; 8; 9; 10; 11; 23; 25; 27; 2:2(3); 3; 4; 5; 10; 16; 3:2(2); 3; 7; 14; 18; 4:1; 5(2); 10; 16; 5:5(2); 10; 14; **1Pet** 1:4; 5; 6; 8; 11; 14; 15; 17; 20; 21(2); 22; 2:6(2); 10; 12; 22; 24; 3:1; 4(2); 5(3); 15(2); 16; 18; 19; 20; 4:1(2); 2; 3; 6(2); 11; 15; 19; 5:6; 9(3); 14; **2Pet** 1:4; 8(2); 12(2); 13(2); 15; 17; 18; 19(2); 21; 2:1; 5; 8; 10; 11; 12; 13; 18; 19; 22; 3:1; 3; 5; 7; 10(2); 11; 14; 16(3); 18(2); **1Jn** 1:5; 6; 7(2); 8; 10; 2:4; 5(2); 6; 8(2); 9(2); 10(2); 11(2); 14; 15(2); 16; 24(4); 27(2); 28; 3:3; 5; 6; 9; 10; 14; 15; 17; 18(4); 22; 24(3); 4:2; 3(2); 4(2); 9; 12(2); 13(2); 15(2); 16(3); 17(2); 18(2); 5:7; 8(2); 10; 11; 14; 19; 20(2); **2Jn** 1; 2; 3; 4; 6; 7; 9(2); **3Jn** 1; 2; 3(2); 4; **Jude** 1; 4; 5; 6; 7; 10; 11(2); 12; 16; 18; 20; 21; **Rev** 1:4; 5; 9(3); 10; 11(2); 13; 15; 16(2); 20; 2:1(2); 7; 8; 12; 13; 17; 18; 24; 3:1; 4(2); 5; 7; 12; 18; 20; 21(2); 4:1; 2(2); 3; 4; 6; 5:1; 3(2); 6(2); 13(3); 6:5; 6; 15(2); 7:3; 9; 13; 14; 15; 17; 8:1; 9; 9:4; 6; 10; 11(2); 14; 17; 19(2); 10:2; 7; 8; 9; 10; 11:3; 5; 6; 8; 9; 12; 13; 15; 19(2); 12:1; 2; 3; 7; 8; 10; 12; 13:6(2); 8; 13; 14; 16(2); 14:1; 5; 6; 9(2); 10(2); 13; 14; 15; 16; 17; 18; 19; 15:1(2); 5; 6; 16:3; 16; 19; 17:3; 4(2); 8; 17; 18:6; 7; 8; 10; 16; 17(2); 19(2); 22(3); 23(2); 24; 19:1; 8; 11; 13; 14(2); 17(2); 20:1; 4; 6; 8; 12; 13(2); 15; 21:8; 10; 14; 23; 24; 27(2); 22:2; 3; 4; 14; 16; 18; 19

INASMUCH

Deut 19:6; **Ruth** 3:10; **Mt** 25:40; 45; **Rom** 11:13; **Phil** 1:7; **Heb** 3:3; 7:20; **1Pet** 4:13

INDEED

Gen 17:19; 20:12; 37:8(2); 10; 40:15; 43:20; 44:5; **Ex** 19:5; 23:22; **Lev** 10:18; **Num** 12:2; 21:2; 22:37; **Deut** 2:15; 21:16; **Josh** 7:20; **1Sa** 1:11; 2:30; **2Sa** 14:5; 15:8; **1Kin** 8:27; **2Kin** 14:10; **1Chr** 4:10; 21:17; **Job** 19:4; 5; **Ps** 58:1; **Is** 6:9(2); **Jer** 22:4; **Mt** 3:11; 13:32; 20:23; 23:27; 26:41; **Mk** 1:8; 9:13; 10:39; 11:32; 14:21; **Lk** 3:16; 11:48; 23:41; 24:34; **Jn** 1:47; 4:42; 6:55(2); 7:26; 8:31; 36; **Acts** 4:16; 11:16; 22:9; **Rom** 6:11; 8:7; 14:20; **1Cor** 11:7; **2Cor** 8:17; 11:1; **Phil** 1:15; 2:27; 3:1; **Col** 2:23; **1Th** 4:10; **1Ti** 5:3; 5; 16; **1Pet** 2:4

INSIDE

1Kin 6:15

INSOMUCH

Ps 106:40; **Mal** 2:13; **Mt** 8:24; 12:22; 13:54; 15:31; 24:24; 27:14; **Mk** 1:27; 45; 2:2; 12; 3:10; 9:26; **Lk** 12:1; **Acts** 1:19; 5:15; **2Cor** 1:8; 8:6; **Gal** 2:13

INSTEAD

Gen 2:21; 4:25; 44:33; **Ex** 4:16(2); 5:12; **Num** 3:12; 41(2); 45(2); 5:19; 20; 29; 8:16(2); 10:31; **Judg** 15:2; **2Sa** 17:25; **1Kin** 3:7; **2Kin** 14:21; 17:24; **1Chr** 29:23; **2Chr** 12:10; **Est** 2:4; 17; **Job** 31:40(2); **Ps** 45:16; **Is** 3:24(5); 55:13(2); **Jer** 22:11; 37:1; **Eze** 16:32

INTO

Gen 2:7; 10; 15; 6:10; 19; 7:1; 7; 9; 13; 15; 8:9(2); 9:2; 11:31; 12:5(2); 10; 11; 14; 15; 13:1; 14:20; 16:5; 18:6; 19:2; 3; 10; 23; 21:32; 22:2; 24:20; 32; 67; 26:2; 27:17; 28:15; 29:1; 30:35; 31:33(4); 32:7; 16; 36:6; 37:20; 22; 24; 28; 35; 36; 39:4; 11; 20; 40:3; 11(2); 13; 15; 21; 41:57; 42:17; 25; 37; 43:17; 18; 24; 26; 30; 45:4; 25; 46:3; 4; 6; 7; 8; 26; 27; 28; 47:14; 48:5; 16; 49:6; 33; 50:13; 14; **Ex** 1:1; 22; 3:18; 4:6(2); 7(2); 19; 21; 27; 5:3; 7:23; 8:3(5); 21; 24(3); 27; 9:20; 10:4; 19; 11:4; 13:5; 11; 14:22; 28; 15:1; 4; 5; 19; 21; 22; 25; 16:3; 18:5; 7; 27; 19:1; 12; 21:13; 23:19; 20; 31; 24:12; 13; 15; 18(2); 25:14; 16; 26:11; 27:7; 29:3; 30; 30:20; 32:24; 33:5; 8; 9; 11; 37:5; 38:7; 39:3(2); 40:20; 21; 32; 35; **Lev** 1:6; 12; 6:30; 8:20; 9:23; 10:9; 11:32; 12:4; 13:17; 14:7; 8; 15; 26; 34; 36; 40; 41; 45; 46; 53; 16:2; 3; 10; 21; 23(2); 26; 28; 19:23; 23:10; 25:2; 26:25; 32; 36; 41; **Num** 4:3; 30; 35; 39; 43; 5:17; 22; 24; 27; 7:89; 11:30; 13:17; 14:3; 4; 8; 16; 24; 25; 30; 40; 15:2; 18; 16:14; 30; 33; 47; 17:8; 19:6; 7; 14; 20:1; 4; 12; 15; 24; 27; 21:2; 22(2); 23; 27; 29; 34; 22:13; 23(2); 41; 23:14; 24:4; 16; 25:8; 27:12; 31:24; 27; 54; 32:7; 9; 32; 33:8; 38; 51; 34:2; 35:10; 28; 36:12; **Deut** 1:22; 24; 27; 31; 40; 41; 43; 2:1; 24; 29; 30; 3:2; 3; 27; 5:5; 30; 6:10; 7:1; 24; 26; 8:7; 9:9; 21; 28; 10:1; 3; 22; 11:5; 13:16; 14:6; 25; 17:8; 18:9; 19:3; 5; 11; 12; 20:13; 21:10; 23:1; 2(2); 3(2); 5; 8; 11; 18; 24; 25; 24:10; 26:5; 9; 28:25; 38; 41; 68; 29:12(2); 28; 30:5; 31:20; 21; 23; 32:26; 49; **Josh** 2:1; 3; 18; 19; 24; 3:11; 4:5; 6:2; 11; 14; 19; 20; 22; 24; 7:7; 8:1; 7; 13; 18; 19; 10:8; 19(2); 20; 27; 30; 32; 11:8; 13:5; 18:5; 6; 9; 20:4; 5; 21:44; 22:13; 24:4; 8(2); 11; **Judg** 1:2; 3(2); 4; 16; 24; 25; 26; 34; 2:14(2); 23; 3:8; 10; 21; 28; 4:2; 7; 9; 14; 18; 21(2); 22; 5:15; 6:1; 5; 13; 7:2; 7; 9; 13; 14; 15(2); 16; 8:3; 7; 9:27(2); 42; 43; 46; 10:7(2); 11:19; 21; 30; 32; 12:3; 13:1; 15:1; 5; 12; 13; 18(2); 16:23; 24; 18:10; 18; 19:3; 11; 12; 15; 21; 22; 23; 29(3); 20:4; 8; 28; **Ruth** 1:2; 2:18; 3:14; 15; 4:11; **1Sa** 2:14; 36; 4:3; 5; 6; 7; 10; 13; 5:2; 5; 6:14; 19; 7:1; 13; 9:13; 14(2); 22; 25; 10:6; 11:11; 12:8; 9(3); 14:10; 12; 21; 26; 37; 17:22; 46; 47; 49; 19:10; 20:8; 11(2); 35; 42; 21:15; 22:5(2); 23:4; 7(2); 11; 12; 14; 16; 20; 25; 24:4; 10; 18; 26:3; 8; 10; 23; 27:1; 28:19(2); 29:11; 30:15; 23; 31:9; **2Sa** 2:1; 3:8; 34; 4:6; 7; 5:8; 19(2); 6:10(2); 12; 16; 10:2; 10; 14; 11:11; 23; 12:8; 20; 13:10(2); 15:25; 27; 31; 37(2); 16:8; 17:13(2); 17; 18:6; 17; 19:3; 8; 15; 20:12; 21:9; 22:7; 20; 23:11; 24:14(2); **1Kin** 1:15; 28; 3:1; 6:8(2); 8:6; 11:17; 40; 13:18; 14:12; 28(2); 15:15; 18; 16:18; 21; 17:19; 21; 22; 23; 18:5; 9; 19:4; 20:2; 13; 28; 30(3); 33; 39; 21:4; 22:6; 12; 15; 25; 30(2); 35; **2Kin** 2:1; 11; 16; 3:10; 13; 18; 4:4; 11; 32; 39(2); 41; 5:18; 6:5; 20; 23; 7:4; 8(2); 12; 8:21; 9:6; 26; 10:15; 21; 23; 24; 11:4; 13; 16; 18; 12:4(3); 9(2); 11; 13; 15; 16; 13:3(2); 21; 17:6; 20; 18:21; 30; 19:1; 10; 14; 18; 23(2); 25; 28; 32; 33; 37; 20:4; 8; 17; 20; 21:14; 22:4; 5; 7; 9; 20; 23:2; 12; 24:15; **1Chr** 5:20; 6:15; 10:9; 11:15; 12:8; 13:13; 14:10(2); 17; 16:7; 19:2; 15; 21:13(2); 27; 22:18; 19; 23:6; 24:19; **2Chr** 5:7; 6:41; 7:2; 10; 11; 9:4; 12:11(2); 13:16; 15:12; 18; 16:8; 18:5; 11; 14; 24; 20:20; 21:17(2); 23:1; 6; 7; 12; 20; 24:10; 24; 25:20; 26:16; 27:2; 28:5(2); 9; 27; 29:4; 16(3); 31; 30:8; 9; 14; 15; 31:1; 10; 16; 32:1; 21; 33:13; 34:7; 9; 14; 17; 30; 36:17; **Ezr** 5:8; 12(2); 14; 15; 9:7; 10:6; **Neh** 2:7; 8; 5:5; 6:11; 7:5; 8:1; 9:11(2); 22; 23; 24; 27; 30; 10:29(2); 34; 38; 12:44; 13:1; 2; 15; **Est** 1:22(2); 2:14; 16; 3:9; 13; 4:1; 2; 11; 6:4; 7:7; 8; 9:22; **Job** 3:6; 9:24; 10:9; 12:6; 14:3; 16:11; 17:12; 18:8; 18; 22:4; 30:3; 19; 31; 33:28; 34:23; 36:16; 37:8; 38:16; 22; 38; 39:12; 40:23; 41:2; 22; 28; **Ps** 4:2; 5:7; 7:15; 9:17; 10:9; 16:4; 18:6; 19; 22:15; 24:3; 28:1; 30:11; 31:5; 8; 32:4; 35:8; 13; 37:15; 20; 45:2; 15; 46:2; 55:15; 23; 56:8; 57:6; 60:9(2); 63:9; 66:6; 11; 12; 13; 69:2; 27; 73:17; 18; 19; 74:7; 76:6; 78:44; 61(2); 79:1; 12; 88:4; 18; 95:11; 96:8; 100:4(2); 104:10; 105:23; 29; 106:15; 20; 41; 42; 107:33(2); 34; 35(2); 108:10(2); 109:18(2); 114:8(2); 115:17; 118:19; 20; 122:1; 132:3(2); 7; 8; 135:9; 136:13; 139:8; 140:10(2); 141:10; 143:2; 7; 10; **Prov** 1:12; 2:10; 4:14; 6:3; 13:17; 16:29; 33; 17:10(2); 20; 18:6; 8; 10; 19:15; 23:10; 24:16; 26:9; 22; 27:10; 28:10; 14; 29:8; 30:4; **Eccl** 1:7; 10:8; 11:9; 12:14; **Song** 1:4; 3:4(2); 4:16; 5:1; 6:2; 11; 7:11; 8:2; **Is** 2:4(2); 10; 19(2); 21(2); 3:14; 5:13; 14; 9:8; 10; 13:2; 14; 14:7; 13; 19:1; 4; 8; 23(2); 21:4; 22:18; 21; 23:9; 24:18; 26:20; 29:17; 30:2; 6; 20; 29; 34:9(2); 36:6; 15; 37:1; 10; 19; 24; 26; 29; 33; 34; 38; 38:18; 40:9; 44:23; 46:2; 47:5; 6; 49:13; 51:23; 52:1; 4; 9; 54:1; 55:12; 57:2; 59:5; 63:14; 65:6; 7; 17; 66:20; **Jer** 2:7; 21; 4:5; 29; 6:9; 25; 7:31; 8:6; 14; 9:21(2); 10:9; 12:7; 13:16; 14:18(3); 15:4; 14; 16:5; 8; 13; 15; 17:25; 19:5; 20:4(2); 5; 6; 21:4; 7(3); 10; 13; 22:7; 22; 25(4); 26; 28; 23:15; 24:5; 9; 26:21; 22(2); 23; 24; 27:6; 28:3; 4; 6; 29:14; 16; 21; 30:6; 16; 31:13; 32:3; 4; 18; 24; 25; 28(2); 35; 36; 43; 33:11; 34:2; 3; 10; 11; 16; 17; 20(2); 21(3); 35:2(2); 4(2); 11; 36:2; 5; 12(2); 20; 23; 37:4; 7; 12; 16(2); 17; 21; 38:3; 6; 9; 11(2); 14; 16; 18; 19; 39:9; 17; 40:4(2); 41:7(2); 17; 42:14; 15; 17; 18; 19; 43:2; 3(2); 7; 44:12; 14(2); 21; 28(2); 30(3); 46:11; 19; 24; 26(3); 47:6; 48:7; 11; 44; 49:3; 32; 51:9; 50; 51; 59; 63; 52:12; **Lam** 1:3; 5; 7; 10(2); 13; 14; 18; 2:7; 9; 12; 3:2(2); 13; 4:12; 22; 5:15; **Eze** 2:2; 3:22; 23; 24; 4:14; 5:4(2); 6; 10; 12; 7:11; 21; 22; 8:16; 10:7; 11:5; 9; 24; 12:4; 11; 13:5; 9; 14:19; 15:4; 16:8; 13; 39; 17:4; 15; 19:9; 20:6; 10; 15; 28; 32; 35; 37; 38; 42(2); 21:11; 14; 30; 31; 22:19; 20; 23:9(2); 16; 17; 28(2); 31; 39; 24:3; 4; 25:3; 26:10(2); 20; 27:26; 27; 28:4; 23(2); 29:5; 14(2); 30:12; 17; 18; 25; 31:11; 16; 17; 32:9; 18; 24; 36:5; 24; 37:5; 10; 12; 17; 21; 22; 38:4; 8; 10; 39:23(2); 28; 40:2; 17; 32; 41:6; 42:1(2); 9; 12; 14; 43:4; 5; 44:7; 9; 12; 16; 19(2); 21; 27; 46:19; 20; 21; 47:8(3); **Dan** 1:2(3); 9; 2:29; 38; 3:6; 11; 15; 20; 21; 23; 24; 5:10; 6:7; 10; 12; 16; 24; 7:25; 10:8; 11:7; 8; 9(2); 11; 28; 40; 41; **Hos** 2:14; 4:7; 9:4; 11:5; 9; 12:1; 12; **Joel** 1:14; 2:20; 31(2); 3:2; 5; 8; 10(2); **Amos** 1:4; 5; 15; 2:1; 4:3; 5:5(2); 8; 19; 27; 6:12(2); 7:12; 17; 8:10(2); 9:2; 4; **Obad** 11; 13; **Jonah** 1:3; 4; 5(2); 12; 15; 2:3; 7; 3:4; **Mic** 1:6; 16; 3:5; 4:3(2); 12; 5:5; 6; 7:19; **Nah** 3:10; 12; 14; **Hab** 3:16; **Hag** 1:6; **Zec** 5:4(2); 8; 6:6; 10; 10:10; 11:6(2); 14:2; **Mal** 3:10; **Mt** 1:17(2); 2:11; 12; 13; 14; 20; 21; 22; 3:10; 12; 4:1; 5; 8; 12(2); 18; 5:1; 20; 25; 29; 30; 6:6; 13; 26; 30; 7:19; 21; 8:5; 12; 14; 23; 28; 31; 32(2); 33; 9:1(2); 17(2); 23; 26; 28; 38; 10:5(2); 11; 12; 23; 11:7; 12:4; 9; 11; 29; 44; 13:2; 8; 20; 23; 30; 36; 42; 47; 48; 50; 54; 14:13; 15; 22; 23; 32; 34; 35; 15:11; 14; 17(2); 21; 29; 39; 16:13; 17:1; 15(2); 22; 25; 18:3; 8(2); 9(2); 12; 30; 19:1; 17; 23; 24; 20:1; 2; 4; 7; 21:2; 10; 12; 17; 18; 21; 23; 31; 33; 22:9; 10; 13; 24:16; 38; 25:14; 21; 23; 30; 41; 46(2); 26:18; 30; 32; 41; 45; 52; 71; 27:6; 27; 53; 28:7; 10; 11; 16(2); **Mk** 1:12; 14; 16; 21(2); 29; 35; 38; 45; 2:1; 11; 22(2); 26; 3:1; 13; 19; 27; 4:1; 26; 37; 5:1; 12(2); 13(2); 18; 6:1; 10; 31; 32; 36(2); 45; 46; 51; 53; 56; 7:15; 17; 18; 19(3); 24(2); 33; 8:10(2); 13; 26; 27; 9:2; 22(2); 25; 28; 31; 42; 43(3); 45(3); 47(2); 10:1; 17; 23; 24; 25; 11:2(2); 11(2); 15; 23; 12:1; 41; 43; 13:15; 14:13; 16; 26; 28; 38; 41; 54; 68; 15:16; 16:5; 7; 12; 15; 19; **Lk** 1:9; 39(2); 40; 79; 2:3; 4; 15; 27; 39; 3:3; 9; 17; 4:1; 5; 14; 16; 37; 38; 42; 5:3; 4; 16; 19; 24; 37; 38; 6:4; 6; 12; 38; 39; 7:1; 11; 24; 36; 44; 8:22; 29; 30; 31; 32; 33(2); 37; 41; 51; 9:4; 10; 12; 28; 34; 44(2); 52; 10:1; 2; 5; 8; 10(2); 38(2); 11:4; 12:5; 28; 58; 13:19; 14:1; 5; 21; 23; 15:13; 15; 16:4; 9; 16; 22; 28; 17:2; 12; 27; 18:10; 24; 25; 19:4; 12; 23; 30; 45; 20:9; 21:1; 12; 24; 22:3; 10(2); 33; 40; 46; 54; 66; 23:19; 25; 42; 46; 24:7; 26; 51; **Jn** 1:9; 43; 3:4; 5; 17; 19; 22; 24; 35; 4:3; 14; 28; 38; 43; 45; 46; 47; 54; 5:4; 7; 24; 6:3; 14; 15; 17; 21; 22; 7:3; 14; 8:2; 9:39; 10:1; 36; 40; 11:7; 27; 30; 54; 12:24; 46; 13:2; 3; 5; 27; 15:6; 16:13; 20; 21; 28; 17:18(2); 18:1; 11; 15; 28; 33; 37; 19:9; 17; 20:6; 11; 25(2); 27; 21:3; 7; **Acts** 1:11(3); 13; 2:20(2); 34; 3:1; 2; 3; 8; 5:15; 21; 7:3; 4; 6; 9; 15; 16; 23; 34; 39; 45; 55; 8:3; 38; 9:6; 8; 11; 17; 39; 10:10; 16; 22; 24; 11:8; 10; 12; 12:17; 13:14; 14:1; 20; 22; 25; 16:7; 9; 10; 15; 19; 23; 24; 34; 37; 40; 17:10; 18:7; 18; 19; 27; 19:8; 22; 29; 31; 20:1; 2; 3; 4; 9; 18; 21:3; 8; 11; 26; 28; 29; 34; 37; 38; 22:4; 10;

11; 23; 24; 23:10; 16; 20; 28; 24:27; 25:1; 23; 27:1; 2; 6; 15; 17; 30; 38; 39; 41; 43; 28:5; 17; 23; **Rom** 1:23; 25; 26; 5:2; 12; 6:3(2); 4; 7:23; 8:21; 10:6; 7; 18; 11:24(2); 15:24; 28; **1Cor** 2:9; 4:17; 9:27; 11:20; 12:13(2); 14:9; 23; **2Cor** 1:16; 2:13; 3:18; 7:5; 8:16; 9:13; 10:5; 11:13; 14; 20; 12:4; **Gal** 1:6; 17; 21; 2:4; 3:27; 4:6; **Eph** 4:9; 15; **Col** 1:13; 2:18; **2Th** 3:5(2); **1Ti** 1:3; 12; 15; 3:6; 7; 16; 5:9; 6:7; 9(2); **2Ti** 3:6; **Heb** 1:6; 3:11; 18; 4:1; 3(2); 5; 10; 11; 14; 6:19; 8:10; 9:6; 7; 8; 12; 24(2); 25; 10:5; 16; 19; 31; 11:8; 13:11; **Jas** 1:2; 25; 4:13; 5:4; 12; **1Pet** 1:12; 2:9; 3:22; **2Pet** 1:11; 2:4; 6; **1Jn** 4:1; 9; **2Jn** 7; 10; **Jude** 4; **Rev** 2:10; 22(2); 5:6; 8:5; 8; 11:11; 12:6; 9; 14(2); 13:10(2); 14:10; 19(2); 15:8; 16:16; 17; 19; 17:3; 8; 11; 18:21; 19:20; 20:3; 10; 14; 15; 21:24; 26; 27; 22:14

IS

Gen 1:11; 29(2); 30; 2:9; 11(3); 12(2); 13(2); 14(3); 18; 23; 3:3; 13; 17; 22; 4:6; 9; 13; 5:1; 6:3; 13(2); 15; 17(2); 21; 7:15; 8:17; 21; 9:4; 10; 12(2); 15; 16; 17(2); 18; 10:9; 12; 11:6; 9; 12:12; 18; 19; 13:9; 18; 14:2; 3; 6; 7; 8; 15; 17; 23; 15:2; 3; 13; 16; 16:6; 14; 17:4; 10; 12(3); 13(2); 14; 17(2); 18:9; 14; 20(2); 21; 19:8; 13; 20(3); 31(2); 37; 38; 20:2; 3; 5(2); 7; 11; 12(2); 13(2); 15; 16; 21:13; 17; 22; 22:7; 14; 17; 23:2; 9(2); 11; 15(2); 19; 20; 24:23; 35; 51; 65(2); 25:9; 18; 26:7(2); 9(2); 10; 20; 33; 27:11; 20; 22; 27; 33; 36; 28:16; 17(3); 29:6(2); 7(2); 19; 25; 30:15; 30; 33; 31:5; 14; 16; 29; 32; 35; 36(2); 43; 48; 50(2); 32:2; 8; 18(2); 20; 27; 29; 30; 32; 33:11; 17; 18; 34:14; 21; 35:6(2); 10; 19; 20; 27; 36:1; 8; 19; 43; 37:10; 22; 26; 27; 30; 33(2); 38:14; 18; 21; 24; 39:8; 9; 40:8; 12; 18; 41:15; 16; 25(2); 26; 28(2); 32(2); 38(2); 39; 42:2; 13(2); 14; 21; 22; 28(3); 30; 32(2); 36(2); 38(2); 43:7; 27(2); 28(2); 29; 32; 44:5; 10; 15; 16; 17; 20(2); 28; 30; 31; 45:12; 20; 26(2); 28(2); 46:33; 34; 47:3; 4; 6; 18(2); 23; 48:1; 7; 18; 49:9; 14; 21; 22; 24; 28; 29; 30(2); 32; 50:10; 11(2); 20; **Ex** 1:22; 2:6; 14; 18; 20(2); 3:3; 5; 9; 13; 15(2); 16; 4:2; 14; 22; 5:2; 16(2); 22; 7:14; 17; 18; 8:10; 19; 26; 9:3(2); 4; 14; 27; 28; 29; 10:5; 7; 10; 11:5; 12:11; 19; 22(2); 27; 42(2); 43; 44; 48; 49; 13:2; 8; 14; 14:12; 15:2(3); 3(2); 6; 11(2); 26; 16:1; 15(2); 16; 23(2); 25; 26; 32; 36; 17:3; 7; 18:11; 14; 17; 18(2); 19:5; 20:4(3); 10(2); 11; 17; 20; 21:21; 30; 22:16; 25; 27(2); 31; 23:16; 21; 25:3; 26:5; 10; 27:21; 28:8; 26; 29:1; 13(2); 14; 18(2); 21; 22(2); 23; 25; 27(4); 28; 30; 32; 34; 38; 30:6(2); 10; 13; 32; 31:7; 13; 14; 15; 17; 32:1; 5; 9; 17; 18(2); 23; 26; 33:13; 16; 21; 34:9; 10; 14(2); 19(2); 35:4; 5; 36:25; 38:21; 26; 40:9; **Lev** 1:5; 8(2); 12(2); 13; 17(2); 2:3; 6; 8(2); 9; 10(2); 15; 16; 3:3; 4(2); 5(3); 9; 10(2); 11; 14; 15(2); 16(2); 4:3; 5; 7(2); 8; 9(2); 14; 16; 18(3); 21; 22; 24; 31; 35; 5:1; 8; 9; 11; 12; 17; 19; 6:4; 9(2); 14; 15; 17(2); 20(2); 21; 22(2); 25(3); 27; 28; 29; 30; 7:1(2); 4(3); 5; 6; 7(3); 9(2); 11; 15; 24; 35; 37; 8:5; 28; 31; 9:6; 10:3; 7; 12; 13; 17; 11:3; 4; 5; 6; 7; 10; 26; 32; 33; 36; 37; 46; 12:7; 13:3(2); 6; 8; 9; 11(2); 13(2); 15(2); 17; 18; 20; 22; 23; 24; 25(2); 27; 28(2); 30; 31; 36; 37(3); 39(2); 40(3); 41(2); 42; 44(3); 45; 46; 47; 49; 51(3); 52(2); 54; 55(3); 57(2); 59; 14:4; 7; 8; 11; 13(3); 14; 16; 17(2); 18(2); 19; 22; 25; 27; 28(2); 29(2); 31(2); 32(3); 35; 36; 40; 43; 44(2); 46; 48; 54; 57(3); 15:2; 3; 4; 8; 13; 17; 31; 32(2); 33(2); 16:2; 6; 11(2); 13; 15; 18; 17:2; 11(2); 14(3); 18:6; 7; 8; 10; 11; 12; 13; 14; 15; 16; 17; 19; 22; 23; 25; 27; 19:7; 13; 20; 20:14; 17; 21; 27; 21:2(2); 3; 7(2); 10(2); 12; 19; 22:4(2); 7(2); 8; 11; 13; 24; 25; 27; 23:3(2); 5; 6; 8; 28; 36; 24:9; 16; 25:5; 12; 23; 28; 29; 30; 34; 48; 49; 27:22; 26; 28; 30(2); **Num** 1:51; 3:26; 47; 48; 4:15; 16; 24; 25; 26(2); 28; 31; 33; 5:2; 15; 17; 18; 29(2); 6:4; 7; 8; 13; 18; 19; 20; 21; 8:24; 9:13(2); 10:7; 11:6(2); 14; 17; 20; 23; 12:7(2); 12; 13:18; 19; 20; 27; 32; 14:7; 9(2); 18; 42; 15:25; 29; 16:3; 5; 11; 13; 40; 46(2); 18:11(2); 13(2); 16; 19; 31; 19:2(2); 9(2); 13(2); 14(2); 15; 16; 20; 20:5(2); 13; 21:5(2); 8; 11; 13(2); 14; 16; 20; 28; 30; 22:5(2); 6(2); 11; 32; 36(2); 23:19; 21(2); 23(2); 24:9(2); 21; 26:9; 27:11; 14; 18; 28:3; 6; 10; 14; 16; 17; 23; 29:1; 30:1; 9; 31:20; 21; 32:4; 19; 33:6; 7; 36; 34:2; 13; 35:16; 17; 18; 21; 31; 32; 33; 36:6; **Deut** 1:14; 16; 17(2); 25; 28; 2:36(2); 3:11; 12; 16; 24; 25; 4:6(2); 7(2); 8; 17; 18; 24; 31; 32; 35(2); 38; 39(2); 44; 48(2); 5:8(3); 14(2); 21; 26; 6:4; 15; 18; 24; 7:9; 21; 25(2); 26; 8:13(2); 18(2); 9:3; 13; 10:9; 14(2); 15; 17; 21(2); 11:10; 11; 12:8; 12; 18; 22; 23; 25; 28; 13:6; 11; 14; 15; 18; 14:8; 10; 19; 21; 27; 15:2(2); 3; 9; 16; 16:11; 17; 20; 17:1(2); 4; 6; 15; 18; 18:2; 22; 19:4; 6(2); 16; 17; 20:1; 4; 5; 6; 7; 8(2); 11; 14; 19; 21:2; 3; 4; 6; 9; 16; 17(2); 20(2); 23(2); 22:23; 26(2); 28(2); 23:1; 7; 10; 11; 15; 19; 23; 24:2; 4(2); 14; 15; 25:6; 26:11; 12; 28:23(2); 43; 54; 61; 29:5; 11; 15; 23(2); 28; 30:11(2); 12; 13; 14; 20; 31:6; 8; 11; 12; 17; 32:4(3); 5; 6; 9(2); 20; 21; 22; 27; 28; 31; 32; 33; 34; 35; 36(2); 39(2); 47(2); 49(2); 33:1; 7; 17; 22; 26; 27; 29(2); 34:1; 4; **Josh** 1:2; 8; 9; 2:9; 11; 3:10; 16; 4:24; 5:4; 9; 15; 6:7; 7:2; 13; 15; 8:18; 31; 34; 9:12(2); 10:13; 11:4; 12:2(2); 9; 13:2; 3(2); 4; 9(2); 16(2); 25; 28; 14:11; 15:7(2); 8(2); 9; 10; 12; 13; 20; 25; 49; 54; 60; 16:8; 17:10; 16; 18; 18:7; 13; 14; 16; 17; 28(2); 19:8; 11; 16; 23; 31; 39; 48; 20:7; 21:11; 22:9; 16; 17; 28; 29; 31; 34; 23:3; 6; 10; 24:17; 18; 19(2); 30; **Judg** 1:26; 4:11; 14(2); 20; 5:9; 28; 6:12; 13; 15; 24; 25; 31; 7:1; 3; 14; 8:2; 21(2); 9:2; 3; 18; 28(3); 32; 33(2); 38(3); 10:8; 18; 13:17; 18; 14:3; 15; 18(2); 15:2; 11; 19; 16:2(2); 3; 9; 15; 17:2; 18:6; 9; 10(2); 12; 14; 19; 24; 19:10; 12; 18; 19(4); 23; 24; 20:5; 12(2); 21:3; 5; 6; 8; 11; 12; 19(2); **Ruth** 1:13; 15; 19; 2:5; 6; 19; 20; 22; 3:2; 12(2); 4:3; 4; 11; 15; 17(2); **1Sa** 1:8; 2:1(2); 2(3); 3; 5; 20; 24; 35; 36; 3:17; 18; 4:7; 16; 17(2); 21; 22(2); 5:7; 6:3; 9; 20; 9:6(2); 7(2); 9; 11; 12(3); 16; 18; 19; 20(2); 24; 10:1; 5; 7; 11(3); 12(2); 24; 11:12; 12:5(3); 6; 17(2); 13:5; 14:1; 2; 6; 7; 17; 15:7; 11; 12; 22; 23(2); 28; 29; 32; 16:6; 12; 16(2); 18(2); 19; 17:25(2); 26; 29; 46; 47; 55; 56; 18:18; 19:14; 17; 19; 22; 24; 20:1(2); 2; 3; 5; 6; 7(2); 18; 21; 26(2); 37; 21:3(2); 4(2); 5; 8; 9(3); 11; 14; 22:8(3); 14(3); 17; 23:7; 19; 22(2); 24:1; 6; 10; 11; 14; 16; 25:10(2); 17(2); 25(4); 29; 26:1; 3; 11; 15; 16(2); 17(2); 18; 20; 27:1; 28:7; 14(2); 15; 16(2); 29:1; 3; 5; 6; 30:20; 24; **2Sa** 1:9(2); 18; 19; 21; 2:7; 16; 3:12; 13; 23; 24(2); 29; 38; 4:10; 5:7; 6:2; 7:3(2); 18; 19; 22(2); 23; 26; 9:1(2); 2; 3(2); 4(2); 8; 11:3; 21; 24; 12:14; 18; 19(2); 21; 23; 13:16(2); 20; 23; 28; 30; 32; 33; 35; 14:5; 7(2); 13; 15; 17; 19; 20; 30; 15:2; 3; 31; 16:3; 17; 17:2; 3; 7; 8; 9(2); 10(3); 11; 14; 20; 29; 18:3; 13; 18(2); 20; 25; 27(2); 28; 29; 32(2); 19:9; 10; 11; 26; 27(2); 30; 42; 20:8; 11; 21; 21:1; 22:2; 3; 4; 31(3); 32(2); 33; 35; 48; 51; 23:5; 15; 17; 24:16; 21; **1Kin** 1:9; 25; 27; 41; 45; 2:3; 15(2); 22; 29; 38; 42; 44; 3:6; 8; 9; 22(4); 23(4); 27; 4:12(2); 13; 20; 29; 33; 5:4; 6; 6:1; 17; 38; 8:1; 2; 21; 23; 24; 35(2); 41; 43; 46; 60(2); 9:8; 15; 26; 11:7; 11; 33; 38; 12:24; 28; 32; 13:3; 26; 31; 14:2; 5; 10; 13; 15; 15:19; 17:3; 5; 24; 18:8; 10(2); 11; 14; 24; 27(4); 39(2); 41; 43; 19:4; 7; 20:3; 6; 28(2); 32(2); 21:2; 5; 14(2); 15; 18(3); 21; 22:3; 7; 8; 13; 16; 32; **2Kin** 1:3(2); 6(2); 8; 16(2); 2:14; 19(2); 3:11(2); 12; 18; 23; 4:1(2); 4; 6; 9; 13; 14(2); 23; 25; 26(4); 27; 31; 40; 5:3; 4; 6; 8; 15; 21; 22; 26; 6:1; 11; 12; 13(2); 19(2); 32; 33; 7:4; 9; 8:5(2); 7; 13; 9:8; 11; 12; 13; 17; 18; 19; 20; 22; 23; 27; 32; 34; 36; 37; 10:5; 15(3); 30; 33; 11:5; 12:4(2); 14:6; 18:10; 17; 19; 21; 22; 19:3(2); 9; 13; 21; 28; 30; 20:3; 10; 15; 17; 19(2); 22:4; 5; 13(4); 23:10; 17(2); 21; 25:4; 8; **1Chr** 1:27; 5:1; 6:10; 7:31; 11:4; 5; 11; 17; 12:17; 13:6(2); 11; 14:15; 16:14; 25(2); 32; 34; 40; 17:2(2); 16; 20(2); 21; 24; 19:13; 21:15; 17(2); 23; 24; 22:1(2); 5(2); 14; 16; 18(2); 19; 23:29(2); 27:6; 29:1(3); 5; 11(4); 12(2); 14; 15; 16; **2Chr** 1:10; 12; 2:4; 5(2); 6; 5:2; 9; 13; 6:11; 14; 15; 26(2); 32(2); 33; 36; 40; 7:3; 15; 21; 11:4; 12:6; 13:4; 6; 10; 12; 14:7; 11; 15:2; 16:3; 7; 9; 18:6; 7(2); 31; 19:2; 6; 7; 11; 20:2; 6(2); 9; 15; 34; 22:9; 23:4; 18; 25:4; 7; 9; 26:23; 28:11; 13(2); 22; 29:10; 30:9; 31:3; 10(2); 32:7; 8(2); 34:21(4); 35:12; 21; 36:23(2); **Ezr** 1:2; 3(4); 4; 5; 9; 2:68; 3:2; 4; 11; 4:11; 15; 19; 24; 5:2; 8(2); 15; 16(2); 17; 6:2; 5(2); 12; 18(2); 7:11; 14; 15; 16; 17; 23; 25; 27; 8:1; 22(2); 9:6; 7; 11; 13; 15; 10:2; 13(2); 23; **Neh** 1:3; 2:2(2); 19; 4:10(2); 14; 19; 5:5(2); 9; 14; 6:6; 7; 11; 8:9(2); 10(3); 11; 15; 9:5; 6; 10; 18; 33; 10:34; 36; 13:11; 17; **Est** 1:1; 19; 20; 2:7; 16; 3:7(3); 8(2); 11; 13; 4:11(2); 16; 5:3; 6(2); 7; 6:3; 4; 8; 7:2(2); 5(2); 6; 8:8; 9; 12; 9:1; 12(2); 24; **Job** 1:8; 10; 12; 16; 2:3; 6; 3:3; 19; 20(2); 23(2); 25(2); 4:5; 6; 19; 21; 5:4; 7; 13; 17; 27; 6:6(2); 11(2); 12(2); 13(2); 14; 16; 17; 26; 28; 29; 30; 7:1; 5(2); 7; 9; 17; 8:12; 16; 19; 9:2; 4; 19; 22; 24(2); 32; 33; 35; 10:1; 3; 7; 13; 22; 11:4; 6; 8; 9; 18; 12:4; 5(3); 10; 12; 13; 16; 24; 13:9; 19; 28; 14:1(2); 2; 7; 10; 17; 18; 15:9; 11; 14(2); 16; 20; 21; 22; 23(2); 31; 16:6; 8; 16(2); 17; 19(2); 17:1; 3; 7; 12; 13; 15; 16; 18:8; 10; 15; 21; 19:7; 17; 28; 29; 20:5; 7; 14(2); 23(2); 25; 26; 29; 21:4; 8; 9; 15; 16(2); 17; 21; 28; 30; 22:2; 3(2); 5; 12; 18; 20; 29; 30; 23:2(2); 8; 13; 14; 24:14; 17; 18(2); 22; 25:3; 4; 6(2); 26:2; 3; 6; 8; 14; 27:3(2); 8; 11; 13; 14; 19; 28:1; 2(2); 5; 7; 11; 12; 13; 14(2); 18; 20; 21; 28(2); 30:16; 18; 30; 31; 31:2; 3; 11(2); 12; 28; 35; 32:8; 19(2); 33:9; 12; 19; 21; 24; 34:4; 6; 7; 17; 18; 22; 31; 36; 35:2; 10; 14; 15; 36:4(2); 5(2); 14; 16; 18; 26; 37:1; 4; 10(2); 12; 16; 18; 21; 22; 23; 38:2; 14; 15; 19(2); 21; 24; 26(2); 30; 39:8; 11; 16(2); 20; 22; 24; 30; 40:11; 12; 16(2); 19; 41:9; 10(2); 11(2); 16; 22; 24; 33(2); 34; 42:3; 7(2); 8; **Ps** 1:1; 2; 2:12; 3:2; 8; 4:3; 5:9(3); 6:3; 5; 7; 7:2; 4; 8; 10; 11; 15; 8:1; 4; 9; 9:6; 15; 16(2); 10:4; 7(2); 16; 11:4(2); 12:4; 14:1(2); 3; 5; 6; 15:4; 16:3; 5; 8; 9; 11; 17:12; 13; 18:2; 3; 30(3); 31(2); 32; 34; 47; 19:3(2); 4; 5; 6(2); 7(2); 8; 9; 11(2); 21:5; 22:11(2); 14(2); 15; 28(2); 23:1; 24:1; 6; 8; 10(2); 25:8; 11; 12; 14; 26:3; 10(2); 27:1(2); 28:3; 7; 8(2); 29:3(2); 4(2); 30:5; 9; 31:9; 10; 19; 32:1(3); 2(2); 4; 6; 33:1; 4; 5; 12(2); 16(2); 17; 18; 20; 34:8(2); 9; 12; 16; 18; 20; 35:10(2); 36:1; 4; 5; 6; 7; 9; 37:13; 16; 26(2); 31; 33; 37; 39(2); 38:3(2); 7; 9(2); 10; 17; 20; 39:1; 4; 5(2); 7; 11; 40:4; 7; 8; 41:1; 42:3; 6; 10; 11; 43:5; 44:15; 17; 18; 25; 45:1(2); 2; 6(2); 11; 13(2); 46:1; 4; 5; 7(2); 11(2); 47:2(2); 5; 7; 9; 48:1; 2; 3; 10(2); 14; 49:8; 11; 12; 13; 16(2); 20(2); 50:6; 10; 12; 51:3; 52:t, 7; 9; 53:1(2); 3(2); 54:4(2); 6; 55:4; 11; 15; 56:9; 57:4; 6; 7(2); 10; 58:4; 11(2); 59:9; 17; 60:7(4); 8; 11; 12; 61:2(2); 62:2(2); 5; 6(2); 7(2); 8; 63:1; 3; 64:6; 65:4; 9; 66:5; 10; 68:2; 5; 15; 16; 17; 20(2); 27; 34(2); 35; 69:2; 3; 13; 16; 71:11; 18; 19(2); 73:1; 4; 11; 25; 26; 28; 74:9(2); 12; 16(2); 75:1; 7; 8(3); 76:1(2); 2; 12; 77:8; 10; 13(2); 19; 79:10(2); 80:16(2); 83:8; 18; 84:5(2); 10; 11; 12; 85:9; 12; 86:8; 13; 87:1; 88:3; 89:7; 8; 10; 11; 13(2); 15; 18(2); 19; 34; 41; 47; 48; 90:4; 6; 9; 10(2); 11; 91:2; 9; 92:1; 7; 15(3); 93:1(3); 2; 4; 94:12; 22(2); 95:3; 4; 5; 7; 10; 96:4(2); 12; 97:11; 99:2(2); 3; 5; 9; 100:3(2); 5(2); 102:t, 4; 13; 103:1; 5; 8; 11(2); 12; 16; 17; 104:13; 20; 24; 25; 26; 105:7; 106:1; 107:1; 26; 40; 43; 108:1; 4; 8(4); 9; 12; 13; 109:19; 21; 22; 27; 111:3; 4; 9; 10; 112:1; 4; 7; 8; 113:3; 4; 5; 115:2; 3; 8; 9; 10; 11; 116:5(2); 15; 117:2; 118:1; 6; 8; 9; 14(2); 15; 16; 22; 23(2); 24; 27; 29; 119:38; 50; 64; 70; 71; 72; 77; 89; 90; 96; 97; 105; 109; 118; 126; 140; 142(2); 144; 155; 160; 174; 120:5; 121:5(2); 122:3(2); 123:4; 124:7(2); 8; 125:2; 127:2; 3; 5; 128:1; 129:4; 130:4; 7(2); 131:1; 2(2); 132:14; 133:1; 2; 135:3(2); 5(2); 17; 18; 136:1; 138:5; 139:4; 6(2); 17; 140:3; 141:8; 143:4(2); 10; 144:3; 4; 8; 10; 11; 15(4); 145:3(2); 8; 9; 13; 17; 18; 146:3; 5(2); 6; 147:1(3); 5(2); 148:13(2); **Prov** 1:7; 17; 19; 2:7; 10; 3:13; 14; 15; 16; 18(2); 27(2); 32(2); 33; 4:7; 13; 16; 18; 19; 5:3; 4; 6:14; 23(2); 26; 30; 34; 7:11; 12; 19(2); 23; 27; 8:4; 7; 8; 11; 13; 14; 19; 34; 9:4; 10(2); 13(2); 16; 17; 10:1; 5(2); 7; 11; 13(3); 14; 15(2); 17; 18; 19; 20(2); 23; 25(2); 26; 29; 32; 11:1(2); 2; 8; 10; 11(2); 12; 13; 14(2); 15(2); 17; 22(2); 23(2); 24(3); 30(2); 12:1; 4(2); 8; 9(2); 11; 13; 15(2); 16; 18(2); 19; 20(2); 26; 27; 28(2); 13:5; 6; 7(2); 10; 12; 14; 15; 17; 19(2); 22; 23(3); 14:2; 3; 4(2); 6; 8(2); 9; 12; 13(2); 16; 17(2); 20; 21; 23; 24(2); 26; 27; 28(2); 29(3); 30; 32; 33(2); 34; 35(2); 15:4(2); 5; 6(2); 8(2); 9; 10; 13; 15; 16; 17(2); 18; 19(2); 21(2); 23; 24; 27; 29; 33(2); 16:1; 5(2); 6; 8; 10; 12(2); 14; 15(2); 16; 17; 19; 20; 22(2); 25; 27; 29; 31; 32(2); 33(2); 17:1; 3; 5; 8; 14; 16; 17; 24; 25; 26; 27; 28(2); 18:5; 7; 9(3); 10(2); 11; 12(2); 13; 17; 19; 24; 19:1(3); 2; 4; 6; 10; 11; 12(2); 13; 14; 18; 22(2); 26; 20:1(4); 2; 3; 5; 11; 14(3); 15; 16; 17; 18; 23; 25(2); 27; 28; 29(2); 21:1; 2; 3; 4; 5; 6; 8(2); 9; 11(3); 15; 19; 20; 24; 27; 30; 31(2); 22:1; 2; 6; 7; 13; 14(2); 15; 18; 22; 23:1; 5; 7(2); 11; 18; 22; 27(2); 31; 24:3(2); 5; 6; 7; 9(2); 10; 13(2); 23; 25:2(2); 3; 7; 11; 12; 13; 14; 15; 16; 18; 19; 20; 24; 25; 26; 27(2); 28(2); 26:1; 7; 8; 9; 12; 13(2); 16; 17; 19; 20(2); 21; 26; 27:3(2); 4(3); 5; 7; 8; 10(2); 13; 21; 28:3; 6(2); 7(2); 11; 12(2); 14; 15; 16; 18; 21; 24(2); 25; 26; 29:6; 9; 18(2); 20(2); 24; 27(3); 30:4(2); 5(2); 9; 11; 12(2); 13; 14; 15; 16(2); 20; 21; 22; 23(2); 28; 30; 31; 31:4(2); 6; 10; 14; 15; 18; 21; 22; 23; 26; 30(2); **Eccl** 1:2; 7; 8; 9(4); 10(2); 11; 14; 15(2); 17; 18; 2:1; 2; 15; 16(2); 17(3); 19; 21(3); 23; 24; 26(3); 3:1; 2; 12; 13; 15(3); 17; 19; 22(2); 4:3(2); 4(2); 6; 8(6); 10; 12; 13; 14; 16(2); 5:2; 3; 5; 8; 9(2); 10; 11; 12; 13; 14; 16; 18(2); 19; 6:1(2); 2(2); 3; 7(2); 9(2); 10(4); 11; 12; 7:1; 2(2); 3(2); 4(2); 5; 6(2); 8(2); 10; 11(2); 12(3); 15(2); 18; 20; 24; 26; 8:1; 4(2); 6(2); 8(2); 9(2); 10; 11(2); 14(3); 16(2); 17; 9:1; 2(3); 3(4); 4(3); 5; 6(2); 9; 10; 11; 16(2); 18; 10:1; 2; 3(2); 5; 6; 10; 11; 13(2); 14; 16; 17; 19; 11:5(2); 7(2); 8; 12:4; 5; 8; 12(2); 13; **Song** 1:1; 2; 3; 13; 14; 16; 2:2; 3; 6; 9; 11(2); 12(2); 14(2); 16; 3:6; 7; 4:1; 2; 3; 4; 7; 10(2); 11; 12; 5:2(2); 9(2); 10; 11; 14; 15; 16(4); 6:1(2); 2; 3; 5; 6; 9(3); 10; 7:2(2); 4(2); 5(2); 7; 10; 8:5; 6(2); 12(2); **Is** 1:5; 6; 7(2); 8; 11; 13(2); 21; 22; 2:7(4); 8; 12(2); 22(2); 3:7; 8(2); 14; 4:3(2); 5:7; 16; 25(3); 30; 6:3(2); 5; 7; 13; 7:2; 8(2); 9(2); 13; 18(2); 20; 22; 8:10; 20(2); 9:5; 6(2); 12(2); 15(2); 17(3); 19; 21(2); 10:4(2); 5; 7; 9(3); 28(2); 29(2); 31; 12:1; 2(3); 4; 5; 6; 13:6; 15(2); 22; 14:6; 7(2); 8; 9; 11(2); 16; 26(4); 27; 29; 15:1(2); 2; 6(2); 8; 16:4; 6; 9; 10; 12(2); 13; 17:1; 14(2); 18:1; 5(2); 19:11; 20:6; 21:2; 9(2); 22:5; 15; 25; 23:1(3); 3(2); 7(2); 10; 14; 24:5; 10(2); 11(3); 12(2); 13; 19(3); 25:4; 7; 9(2); 10; 26:3; 4; 7; 8; 11; 17; 19; 27:1; 4; 7; 9; 11; 28:1; 4(2); 8; 12(2); 14; 20; 27; 28; 29; 29:8(2); 11(4); 12(2); 13; 17; 20(2); 30:7; 9; 14; 18; 21; 27; 29; 33(3); 31:2; 3; 4; 9; 33:5; 6; 9(2); 17; 18(3); 22(3); 23; 34:1; 2; 6(2); 8; 36:4; 6; 7; 37:3(2); 4; 9; 13; 22; 29; 31; 38:3; 8; 12(2); 16; 22; 39:4(2); 6; 8; 40:2(2); 6(2); 7; 10; 16; 20; 22; 26; 27(2); 28(2); 41:7; 17; 24; 26(4); 42:8; 10; 19(3); 21; 22; 43:7; 9; 11; 13; 14; 44:3; 6; 8(2); 10; 12(2); 16; 19; 20; 28; 45:5(2); 6(2); 14(3); 18; 21(2); 22; 23; 46:9(2); 47:1; 4; 48:2; 4; 22; 49:4; 6; 7; 20; 50:1(3); 2(2); 4; 8(2); 9; 10; 51:5(2); 7; 13; 15; 18(2); 52:5(2); 6; 53:1; 2; 3; 7(2); 54:5(2); 9; 17(3); 55:2(2); 6; 56:1; 2; 57:1; 6; 10; 15(2); 19(2); 21; 58:5(2); 6; 7; 59:1; 5; 6; 8; 9; 11(2); 14(2); 21(2); 60:1(2); 61:1; 62:11; 63:1(2); 4(2); 11(2); 15; 16; 64:5; 7; 10; 11; 65:4; 6; 8(2); 66:1(4); 2; 3; **Jer** 1:13; 2:6; 8; 14(3); 19(2); 22; 25; 26(3); 34; 3:6; 23(2); 4:7(3); 8; 18(2); 20(2); 22; 31(2); 5:12; 13; 15(2); 16; 19; 27; 30; 6:6(2); 7(2); 10(2); 11; 13; 14; 16; 18; 25; 29; 7:10; 11(2); 14; 28(3); 30; 31; 8:5; 8(2); 9; 10; 11; 16; 18; 19(2); 20(2); 22(3); 9:6; 8; 12(3); 19; 21(2); 10:5; 6(2); 7; 8; 9(2); 10(2); 13; 14(4); 16(4); 19(3); 20(2); 22; 23(2); 11:5; 9; 15; 19; 12:8; 9; 11; 13:4; 10; 17; 20; 25; 14:2; 4; 17; 19(2); 15:9; 10; 14; 18; 16:10(2); 17; 19; 21; 17:1(2); 7(2); 9; 12; 15; 18:6; 12; 19:2; 20:11; 15; 21:12; 22:14; 28(3); 23:6; 9; 10(3); 15; 19; 28; 29; 33; 25:3; 13; 18; 29; 38; 26:11; 16; 28:6; 29:26; 28; 30:7(3); 12(2); 13; 15; 17; 21; 31:9; 17; 20(2); 35; 32:7(2); 8(4); 14(2); 17; 18; 24(2); 25; 27; 34; 43(2); 33:2; 5; 11; 12; 16; 34:8; 15; 36:7; 37:7; 14; 17(2); 38:5(2); 9(3); 14; 21; 40:3; 4; 41:17; 43:9; 13; 44:22; 23; 45:3; 46:7; 10; 17; 18(2); 20; 47:2; 5(2); 48:1(3); 4; 11; 15(2); 16; 17; 19; 20(3); 21; 25(2); 29; 32; 33; 38; 39; 41; 47; 49:3; 7(3); 10(2); 14; 19(3); 21; 23(2); 24; 25; 29; 50:2(3); 15; 17; 22; 23(2); 25; 27; 31; 34(2); 35; 36(2); 37(2); 38(2); 44(3); 46(2); 51:6; 8; 9(2); 11(2); 13; 16; 17(4); 19(4); 31; 33(2); 41(3); 42(2); 48; 55; 56(2); 57; 52:28; **Lam** 1:1(2); 3; 4; 6; 8; 9; 12(2); 14; 16; 17(2); 18; 20(2); 21; 22; 2:9; 11; 12; 13; 15; 16; 3:3; 18; 20; 22; 23; 24; 25; 26; 27; 30; 37; 47; 4:1(2); 3; 6; 8(3); 15; 18(2); 22; 5:1; 2; 4; 8; 15(2); 16; 17; 18; **Eze** 1:28; 3:21; 4:14; 5:5; 6:12(3); 7:2; 3; 5; 6(3); 7(3); 10(2); 11; 12(2); 13(2); 14; 15(3); 19; 23(2); 8:17; 9:6; 9(2); 10:15; 20; 11:3(2); 7; 15; 23; 12:12; 19; 22; 27; 13:12(2); 15; 16; 15:2(2); 4(3); 5; 16:3; 7; 20; 30; 34(2); 44(2); 46(2); 17:12; 18:4; 5; 9; 10; 18; 19; 21; 25(2); 27; 29; 19:2; 10; 13; 14(2); 20:6; 15; 29(2); 21:9; 10(2); 11(2); 13; 14; 15(2); 16; 25; 26(2); 27; 28(2); 29; 22:18; 22; 24; 25; 23:4; 20(2); 22; 28; 37; 45; 24:6(2); 7; 13; 24; 27; 25:8; 26:2(3); 10; 15; 27:27; 32; 28:2; 3; 5; 29:3; 9; 30:3(2); 5; 12; 31:10; 18; 32:16; 20; 22; 23; 24; 25; 26; 29; 33:6; 14; 16; 17(2); 19; 20; 21; 24; 27; 30; 34:5; 12; 36:35; 37:11; 19; 38:8(3); 39:4; 8(3); 40:45(2); 46(2); 41:4; 22(2); 42:13; 15; 43:4; 12(2); 13; 44:3; 9; 22; 26; 31; 45:13; 14; 20; 46:11; 20; 47:16(2); 17; 18; 19; 20; 48:12; 14; 22; 29; 35; **Dan** 2:5; 8; 9; 10(2); 11(3); 15; 22; 28; 30; 36; 43; 45; 47(2); 3:4; 14; 15; 17; 25; 29; 4:3(2); 8; 9; 17; 18; 22(2); 24(3); 30; 31(2); 34(2); 37; 5:11(2); 14(2); 23; 25; 26; 28; 6:12; 13; 15; 20; 26; 7:14; 27; 28; 8:2; 21(3); 26; 9:11(2); 13(2); 14; 17; 18; 10:4; 14; 17; 21(2); 11:35; 36; 12:12; **Hos** 2:2; 4:1; 13; 17; 18; 5:1; 3(2); 4; 11; 6:3; 4; 8(2); 10(2); 7:7; 8; 11; 8:3; 5; 6; 8(2); 9:7(2); 8; 13; 15; 16(2); 10:1; 2; 5; 7; 10; 11(2); 12; 11:8; 12; 12:1; 5; 7; 11; 13:3; 4; 8; 9; 10; 12(2); 13; 14:4; 8; 9; **Joel** 1:5; 6; 9; 10(3); 11; 12(2); 13; 15; 16; 17(2); 2:1; 3; 4; 11(3); 13; 17; 3:13(3); 14; **Amos** 2:11; 13(2); 15; 16; 3:5; 4:3; 13(2); 5:2(3); 8; 11; 13; 18(2); 27; 6:8; 10(2); 7:2; 5; 10; 13(2); 8:2; 9:5; 6(2); 9; 11; **Obad** 1; 3; 7; 15; 20; **Jonah** 1:2; 7; 8(3); 12; 2:9; 3:8; 4:3; 8; **Mic** 1:2; 5(3); 9(3); 13; 2:1(2); 3; 7; 8; 10(2); 13; 3:1; 7; 11; 4:6; 9(2); 5:2; 6:8; 10; 12; 7:1(2); 2(2); 4(2); 10(2); 18; **Nah** 1:2(2); 3; 5; 6; 7; 11; 15; 2:1; 3; 8; 9; 10(2); 11; 3:1; 3(2); 7; 17; 18; 19(2); **Hab** 1:4; 13; 16; 2:3; 4(2); 5(2); 6; 13; 19(2); 20; 3:19; **Zeph** 1:7; 14(2); 15; 2:5; 15(3); 3:1; 5; 6(2); 8; 15; 17; **Hag** 1:2; 4; 6; 9; 10(2); 2:3(2); 6; 8(2); 13; 14(4); 19; **Zec** 1:7; 11; 2:2(2); 13; 3:2; 4:1; 6; 5:2; 3; 5; 6(3); 7; 8; 6:12; 7:13; 8:23(2); 9:9; 11; 17(2); 10:5; 11:2(2); 3(3); 9; 16; 12:8; 10; 13:7; 9(4); 14:4; 16; **Mal** 1:6(2); 7; 8(2); 10; 12(2); 13; 14; 2:1; 7; 11; 14; 17(2); 3:2; 14(2); **Mt** 1:16; 20(2); 23; 2:2(2); 5; 3:2; 3; 9; 10(2); 11; 12; 17; 4:4; 6; 7; 10; 13; 16; 17; 5:3; 10; 12; 13; 14; 16; 22; 29; 30; 32; 34; 35(2); 37; 45; 48(2); 6:1; 6; 10; 13; 18; 21; 22; 23(2); 25; 30(2); 34; 7:3(2); 4; 6; 9; 11; 12; 13(2); 14(2); 19; 21; 8:27; 9:5; 15; 16(2); 18; 24; 37; 10:2; 7; 10; 11; 20; 24; 25; 26; 28; 32; 33; 37(2); 38; 11:6; 10(2); 11(2); 14; 16; 19; 30(2); 12:2; 6; 8; 10; 12(2); 18; 23; 25; 26; 28; 30(2); 33; 41; 42; 43; 44; 45; 48; 50(2); 13:11(2); 14; 15; 19; 20; 21; 22; 23; 24; 31; 32(3); 33; 37; 38; 39(2); 44; 45; 47; 52(3); 55(2); 57; 14:2(2); 4; 15(2); 26; 27; 15:5; 8; 17; 22; 26; 28; 16:2(2); 3; 7; 11; 17; 26; 17:4; 5; 12; 15; 18:1; 4; 8; 9; 10; 11; 12; 14(2); 19; 23; 19:3; 9; 10; 11; 12; 14; 17(2); 24; 26; 20:1(2); 4; 7; 14; 15(2); 23(2); 21:9; 10; 11; 13; 20; 21; 38; 42(3); 22:2; 8; 17; 20; 23; 32; 36; 38; 39; 42; 45; 23:8; 9(2); 10; 11; 15; 16(2); 17; 18(3); 19; 26; 38; 39; 24:6; 17; 18; 23; 26(2); 28; 32(2); 33; 45; 46; 50; 25:14; 25; 26:2(2); 8; 18; 22; 24(2); 25; 26; 28(2); 31; 38; 41(2); 45(2); 46; 48; 62; 66; 68; 27:4; 6(2); 17; 22; 33; 37; 46; 64; 28:6(2); 7; 15; 18; **Mk** 1:2; 15(2); 27(2); 2:9; 16; 19; 21; 22; 24; 26; 28; 3:4; 17; 21; 29; 33; 35; 4:11; 15; 21; 22; 26; 29(2); 31(3); 32; 40; 41; 5:9(2); 35; 39; 41; 6:2(2); 3; 4; 15(2); 16(2); 18; 35(2); 50; 7:2; 6(2); 11(2); 15; 27; 29; 34; 8:16; 21; 9:5; 7; 12; 13(2); 21; 26; 31(2); 39; 40(2); 42; 43; 44; 45; 46; 47; 48; 50; 10:2; 14; 18(2); 24; 25; 27; 29; 40(2); 11:9; 17; 21; 25; 26; 12:7; 10; 11; 14; 16; 18; 27; 28; 29(2); 30; 31(2); 32(2); 33; 35; 37; 13:11; 15; 16; 21(2); 28(2); 29; 33; 34; 14:8; 14; 19(2); 20; 21(2); 22; 24(2); 27; 34; 38(2); 41(3); 42; 44; 58; 60; 69; 15:22; 34; 42; 16:6(2); 16; **Lk** 1:13; 28; 36; 42; 43; 45; 49(2); 50; 61(2); 63; 2:4; 11(2); 15; 23; 24; 34; 49; 3:4; 8; 9(2); 13; 17; 4:4; 6; 8; 10; 12; 18; 21;

IT

ITS

ITSELF

LARGE

LARGENESS

LEAST

LESS

LESSER

LEST

LET

LETTING

LIKE

Gen 13:10; 25:25; **Ex** 7:11; 8:10; 9:14; 24; 11:6(2); 15:11(2); 16:31(2); 23:11; 24:17; 25:33(2); 34; 28:11; 21; 36; 30:32; 33; 34; 38; 34:1; 4; 37:19; 20; 39:8; 14; 30; **Lev** 13:2; **Num** 23:10; **Deut** 4:32; 7:26; 10:1; 3; 17:14; 18:8; 15; 18; 22:3; 25:7; 8; 29:23; 33:17(2); 26; 29; 34:10; **Josh** 10:14; **Judg** 7:12; 11:17; 13:6; 16:12; 17; **Ruth** 2:13; 4:11(2); 12; **1Sa** 2:2; 4:9(2); 8:5; 20; 10:24; 17:7; 19:24; 21:9; 25:36; 26:15; **2Sa** 7:9; 22; 23(2); 18:27; 21:19; 22:34; **1Kin** 3:12(2); 13; 5:6; 7:8(2); 26; 33; 8:23; 10:20; 12:32; 16:3; 7; 18:44; 20:25; 27; 21:22(2); 25; 22:13; **2Kin** 3:2(2); 5:14; 9:9(2); 20; 13:7; 14:3; 16:2; 17:14; 15; 18:5; 32; 23:25(2); 25:17; **1Chr** 4:27; 11:23; 12:8; 22; 14:11; 17:8; 20; 21; 20:5; 27:23; **2Chr** 1:9; 12; 4:5; 6:14; 9:19; 18:12; 21:6; 13; 19; 22:4; 28:1; 30:7(2); 26; 33:2; 35:18; **Neh** 6:5; 13:26; **Est** 2:20; **Job** 1:8; 2:3; 3:24; 5:26; 7:1; 8:2; 10:10; 11:12; 12:25; 13:12; 14:2; 9; 15:16; 16:14; 19:10; 20:7; 21:11; 30:19; 32:19; 34:7(2); 36:22; 38:3; 40:7; 9(2); 17; 18; 41:18; 31(2); 33; 42:8; **Ps** 1:3; 4; 2:9; 7:2; 17:12; 18:33; 22:14(2); 15; 28:1; 29:6(2); 31:12; 35:10; 36:6; 37:2; 35; 39:11; 44:11; 49:12; 14; 20; 52:2; 8; 55:6; 58:4(2); 8; 59:6; 14; 64:3; 71:19; 72:6; 16(2); 73:5; 77:20; 78:16; 27; 52(2); 57(2); 65; 69(2); 79:3; 5; 80:1; 10; 82:7(2); 83:11(2); 13; 86:8(2); 88:5; 17; 89:8; 46; 90:5; 92:10; 12(2); 97:5; 102:3; 4; 6(2); 9; 11(2); 26; 103:5; 13; 104:2; 105:41; 107:27; 41; 109:18(3); 23; 113:5; 114:4(2); 6(2); 115:8; 118:12; 119:83; 119; 176; 126:1; 128:3; 133:2; 135:18; 140:3; 143:7; 144:4; 147:16(2); 17; **Prov** 12:18; 17:22; 18:19; 20:5; 23:32(2); 25:11; 14; 19; 28; 26:4; 17; 23; 28:3; 31:14; **Song** 2:9; 17; 3:6; 4:2; 3(2); 4; 5; 11; 5:13; 6:12; 7:1; 2(2); 3; 4; 5(2); 7; 8; 9; 8:10; 14; **Is** 1:9; 18; 2:6; 3:18; 5:28(2); 29(2); 30; 9:18; 10:6; 13; 16; 11:7; 16; 13:4; 14:10; 14; 19; 16:11; 17:12(2); 13(2); 18:4(2); 19:16; 20:3; 22:18; 24:20(2); 26:17; 27:10; 29:5; 30:33; 31:4; 33:4; 9; 36:17; 38:12; 14; 40:11; 42:13; 14; 46:5; 9; 48:19; 49:2; 50:7; 51:3(2); 6(3); 8(2); 53:6; 57:20; 58:1; 11(2); 59:10; 11(2); 19; 63:2; 64:6; 65:25; 66:12(2); 14; 15; **Jer** 2:30; 4:4; 5:19; 6:23; 9:3; 12; 10:6; 7; 16; 11:19; 12:3; 14:6; 17:6; 21:12; 23:9(2); 29(2); 24:2; 5; 25:34; 26:6; 9; 18; 29:17; 22(2); 30:7; 31:28; 32:42; 36:32; 38:9; 46:8(2); 20; 21; 22; 48:6; 28; 36(2); 38; 49:19(2); 50:42(2); 44(2); 51:19; 33; 34; 38; 40(2); 55; 52:22; **Lam** 1:6; 12; 21; 2:3; 4(2); 13; 18; 19; 3:52; 4:3; 8; 5:10; **Eze** 1:7(2); 13(2); 16; 24; 2:8; 5:9; 7:16; 12:11; 13:4; 16:16; 18:10; 14; 19:10; 20:36; 22:25; 27; 23:18; 20; 25:8; 26:4; 14; 19; 27:32(2); 31:2; 8(3); 18; 32:2; 14; 36:35; 37; 38:9(2); 40:3; 25; 41:25; 42:11; 43:2; 3; 45:25; **Dan** 1:19; 2:35; 3:25; 4:33(2); 5:11; 21(2); 7:4; 5; 6; 8; 9(2); 13; 10:6(3); 16; 18; 11:40; **Hos** 2:3; 4:9(2); 5:10(2); 6:7; 7:6; 11; 16; 9:10; 11; 11:10; 13:8; 14:8; **Joel** 1:8; 2:2; 5(2); 7(2); 9; **Amos** 2:9; 5:6; 6:5; 9:5; 9; **Jonah** 1:4; **Mic** 1:8; 4:10; 7:17(2); 18; **Nah** 1:6; 2:4(2); 8; 3:12; 15; **Hab** 3:19; **Zeph** 1:17; 2:13; **Zec** 1:6; 5:9; 9:15; 10:7; 12:6(2); 14:5; 20; **Mal** 3:2(2); **Mt** 3:16; 6:8, 29, 11:16; 12:13; 13:31; 33; 44; 45; 47; 52; 20:1; 21:24; 22:2; 39; 23:27; 28:3; **Mk** 1:10; 4:31; 7:8; 13; 12:31; 13:29; **Lk** 3:22; 6:23; 47; 48; 49; 7:31; 32; 12:27; 36; 13:18; 19; 21; 20:31; **Jn** 1:32; 7:46; 8:55; 9:9; **Acts** 1:11; 2:3; 3:22; 7:37; 8:32; 11:17; 14:15; 17:29; 19:25; **Rom** 1:23; 28; 6:4; 9:29; **1Cor** 16:13; **Gal** 5:21; **Phil** 3:21; **1Th** 2:14; **1Ti** 2:9; **Heb** 2:17; 4:15; 7:3; **Jas** 1:6; 23; 5:17; **1Pet** 3:21; **2Pet** 1:1; **1Jn** 3:2; **Jude** 7; **Rev** 1:13; 14; 15; 2:18(2); 4:3(2); 6; 7(3); 9:7(2); 10; 19; 11:1; 13:2; 4; 11; 14:14; 16:13; 18:18; 21; 21:11(2); 18

LIKEWISE

Ex 22:30; 26:4; 27:11; 36:11; **Lev** 7:1; **Deut** 9:23; 12:30; 15:17; 22:3; **Judg** 1:3; 7:5; 17; 8:8; 9:49; **1Sa** 14:22; 19:21; 31:5; **2Sa** 1:11; 17:5; **1Kin** 11:8; **1Chr** 10:5; 18:8; 19:15; 23:30; 24:31; 27:4; 28:16; 17; 29:24; **2Chr** 3:11; 29:22; **Neh** 4:22; 5:10; **Est** 1:18; 4:16; **Job** 31:38; 37:6; **Ps** 49:10; 52:5; **Eccl** 7:22; **Is** 30:24; **Jer** 40:11; **Eze** 13:17; 40:16; 46:3; **Nah** 1:12; **Mt** 17:12; 18:35; 20:5; 10; 21:30; 36; 22:26; 24:33; 25:17; 26:35; 27:41; **Mk** 4:16; 12:21; 14:31; 15:31; **Lk** 2:38; 3:11; 14; 5:33; 6:31; 10:32; 37; 13:3; 5; 14:33; 15:7; 10; 16:25; 17:10; 28; 31; 19:19; 21:31; 22:20; 36; **Jn** 5:19; 6:11; 21:13; **Acts** 3:24; **Rom** 1:27; 6:11; 8:26; 16:5; **1Cor** 7:3; 4; 22; 14:9; **Gal** 2:13; **Col** 4:16; **1Ti** 3:8; 5:25; **Titus** 2:3; 6; **Heb** 2:14; **Jas** 2:25; **1Pet** 3:1; 7; 4:1; 5:5; **Jude** 8; **Rev** 8:12

LOW

Deut 28:43; **Judg** 11:35; **1Sa** 2:7; **1Chr** 27:28; **2Chr** 9:27; 26:10; 28:18; 19; **Job** 5:11; 14:21; 24:24; 40:12; **Ps** 49:2; 62:9; 79:8; 106:43; 107:39; 116:6; 136:23; 142:6; **Prov** 29:23; **Eccl** 10:6; 12:4(2); **Is** 2:12; 17; 13:11; 25:5; 12; 26:5(2); 29:4; 32:19(2); 40:4; **Lam** 3:55; **Eze** 17:6; 24; 21:26; 26:20; **Lk** 1:48; 52; 3:5; **Rom** 12:16; **Jas** 1:9; 10

LOWER

Gen 6:16; **Lev** 13:20; 21; 26; 14:37; **Neh** 4:13; **Ps** 8:5; 63:9; **Prov** 25:7; **Is** 22:9; 44:23; **Eze** 40:18; 19; 42:5; 43:14; **Eph** 4:9; **Heb** 2:7; 9

LOWEST

Deut 32:22; **1Kin** 12:31; 13:33; **2Kin** 17:32; **Ps** 86:13; 88:6; 139:15; **Eze** 41:7; 42:6; **Lk** 14:9; 10

MAN'S

Gen 8:21(2); 9:5; 6; 16:12; 20:3; 42:11; 25; 35; 43:21; 44:1; 26; **Ex** 4:11; 12:44; 21:35; 22:5; 7; 30:32; **Lev** 7:8; 15:16; 20:10; **Num** 5:10; 12; 17:2; 5; 33:54; **Deut** 20:19; 24:2; 6; **Judg** 7:16; 22; 19:26; **Ruth** 2:19; **1Sa** 12:4; 14:20; 17:32; **2Sa** 12:4; 17:18; 25; **1Kin** 18:44; **2Kin** 12:4; 23:8; 25:9; **Est** 1:8; **Job** 10:5; 32:21; **Ps** 104:15; **Prov** 10:15; 12:14; 13:8; 16:7; 9; 18:4; 11; 16; 20; 19:21; 20:24; 27:9; 29:23; 26; **Eccl** 2:14; 8:1; 5; 9:16; 10:2; 12; **Is** 8:1; 13:7; **Jer** 3:1; 23:36; **Eze** 4:15; 10:8; 38:21; 39:15; 40:5; **Dan** 4:16; 5:5; 7:4; 8:16; **Amos** 6:10; **Jonah** 1:14; **Mic** 7:6; **Mt** 10:36; 41; 12:29; **Mk** 3:27; 12:19; **Lk** 6:22; 12:15; 16:12; 21; 20:28; **Jn** 18:17; **Acts** 5:28; 7:58; 11:12; 13:23; 17:29; 18:7; 20:33; 27:22; **Rom** 5:17; 19; 14:4; 15:20; **1Cor** 2:4; 13; 3:13(2); 14; 15; 4:3; 10:29; **2Cor** 4:2; 10:16; **Gal** 2:6; 3:15; **2Th** 3:8; **Jas** 1:26; **1Pet** 1:17; **2Pet** 2:16

MANY

Gen 17:4; 5; 21:34; 37:3; 23; 32; 34; **Ex** 5:5; 19:21; 23:2; 35:22; **Lev** 15:25; 25:51; **Num** 9:19; 10:36; 13:18; 22:3; 24:7; 26:54; 56; 35:8(2); **Deut** 1:11; 46; 2:1; 10; 21; 3:5; 7:1; 15:6(2); 25:3; 28:12; 31:17; 21; 32:7; **Josh** 11:4; 22:3; **Judg** 3:1; 7:2; 4; 8:30; 9:40; 16:24; **1Sa** 2:5; 6:19; 14:6; 25:10; **2Sa** 1:4; 2:23; 12:2; 22:17; 23:20; 24:3; **1Kin** 2:38; 4:20; 7:47; 11:1; 17:15; 18:1; 25; 22:16; **2Kin** 9:22; **1Chr** 4:27; 5:22; 7:4; 22; 8:40; 11:22; 21:3; 23:11; 17; 28:5; **2Chr** 11:23; 14:11; 16:8; 18:15; 26:10; 29:31; 30:17; 18; 32:23; **Ezr** 3:12(2); 5:11; 10:13(2); **Neh** 5:2; 6:17; 18; 7:2; 9:28; 30; 13:26; **Est** 1:4; 2:8; 4:3; 8:17; **Job** 4:3; 11:19; 13:23; 16:2; 23:14; 41:3; **Ps** 3:1; 2; 4:6; 18:16; 22:12; 25:19; 29:3; 31:13; 32:10; 34:12; 19; 37:16; 40:3; 5; 55:18; 56:2; 61:6; 71:7; 78:38; 93:4; 106:43; 110:6; 119:84; 157; 129:1; 2; **Prov** 4:10; 6:35; 7:26(2); 10:21; 14:20; 19:4; 6; 21; 28:2; 27; 29:26; 31:29; **Eccl** 5:7; 6:3(2); 11; 7:29; 11:1; 8(2); 12:9; 12; **Song** 8:7; **Is** 1:15; 2:3; 4; 5:9; 8:7; 15; 17:12; 13; 22:9; 23:16; 24:22; 31:1; 32:10; 42:20; 52:14; 15; 53:11; 12; 58:12; 60:15; 61:4; 66:16; **Jer** 3:1; 5:6; 11:15; 12:10; 13:6; 14:7; 16:16(2); 20:10; 22:8; 25:14; 27:7; 28:8; 32:14; 35:7; 36:32; 37:16; 42:2; 46:11; 16; 50:41; 51:13; **Lam** 1:22; **Eze** 3:6; 12:27; 16:41; 17:7; 9; 17; 19:10; 22:25; 26:3; 27:3; 15; 33; 32:3; 9; 10; 33:24; 37:2; 38:6; 8(2); 9; 15; 17; 22; 23; 39:27; 43:2; 47:7; 10; **Dan** 2:48; 8:25; 26; 9:27; 10:14; 11:12; 14; 18; 26; 33(2); 34; 39; 40; 41; 44; 12:2; 3; 4; 10; **Hos** 3:3; 4; 8:11; **Joel** 2:2; **Amos** 8:3; **Mic** 4:2; 3; 11; 13; 5:7; 8; **Nah** 1:12; 3:15(2); **Hab** 2:8; 10; **Zec** 2:11; 7:3; 8:20; 22; **Mal** 2:6; 8; **Mt** 3:7; 7:13; 22(2); 8:11; 16; 30; 9:10; 10:31; 13:3; 17; 58; 14:36; 15:30; 34; 16:9; 10; 21; 19:30; 20:16; 28; 22:9; 10; 14; 24:5(2); 10; 11(2); 12; 25:21; 23; 26:28; 60; 27:19; 52; 53; 55; **Mk** 1:34(2); 2:2; 15(2); 3:10(2); 4:2; 33; 5:9; 26(2); 6:2; 13(2); 20; 31; 33; 34; 38; 56; 7:4; 8; 13; 8:5; 19; 20; 31; 9:12; 26; 10:31; 45; 48; 11:8; 12:5; 41; 13:6(2); 14:24; 56; 15:3; 4; 41; **Lk** 1:1; 14; 16; 2:34; 35; 3:18; 4:25; 27; 41; 7:11; 21(2); 47; 8:3; 30; 32; 9:22; 10:24; 41; 11:8; 53; 12:7; 19; 47; 13:24; 14:16; 15:13; 17; 29; 17:25; 21:8; 22:65; 23:8; 9; **Jn** 1:12; 2:12; 23; 4:39; 41; 6:9; 60; 66; 7:31; 40; 8:26; 30; 10:20; 32; 41; 42; 11:19; 45; 47; 55; 12:11; 37; 42; 14:2; 16:12; 17:2; 19:20; 20:30; 21:11; 25; **Acts** 1:3; 5; 2:39; 40; 43; 3:24; 4:4; 6; 34; 5:11; 12; 36; 37; 8:7(2); 25; 9:13; 23; 42; 43; 10:27; 45; 12:12; 13:31; 43; 48; 14:21; 15:32; 35; 16:18; 23; 17:12; 18:8; 19:18; 19; 20:8; 19; 21:10; 20; 24:10; 17; 25:7; 14; 26:9; 10; 27:7; 20; 28:10; 23; **Rom** 2:12(2); 4:17; 18; 5:15(2); 16; 19(2); 6:3; 8:14; 29; 12:4; 5; 15:23; 16:2; **1Cor** 1:26(3); 4:15; 8:5(2); 10:5; 17; 33; 11:30(2); 12:12(2); 14; 20; 14:10; 16:9; **2Cor** 1:11(2); 2:4; 6; 17; 4:15; 6:10; 8:22; 9:2; 12; 11:18; 12:21; **Gal** 1:14; 3:4; 10; 16; 27; 4:27; 6:12; 16; **Phil** 1:14; 3:15; 18; **Col** 2:1; **1Ti** 6:1; 9; 10; 12; **2Ti** 1:18; 2:2; **Titus** 1:10; **Heb** 2:10; 5:11; 7:23; 9:28; 11:12; 12:15; **Jas** 3:1; 2; **2Pet** 2:2; **1Jn** 2:18; 4:1; **2Jn** 7; 12; **3Jn** 13; **Rev** 1:15; 2:24; 3:19; 5:11; 8:11; 9:9; 10:11; 13:15; 14:2; 17:1; 18:17; 19:6; 12

MATTER

Gen 24:9; 30:15; **Ex** 18:16; 22(2); 26; 23:7; **Num** 16:49; 25:18(2); 31:16; **Deut** 3:26; 17:8; 19:15; 22:26; **Ruth** 3:18; **1Sa** 10:16; 20:23; 39; 30:24; **2Sa** 1:4; 18:13; 19:42; 20:18; 21; **1Kin** 8:59; 15:5; **1Chr** 26:32; 27:1; **2Chr** 8:15; 24:5; **Ezr** 5:5(2); 17; 10:4; 9; 14; 15; 16; **Neh** 6:13; **Est** 2:23; 9:26; **Job** 19:28; 32:18; **Ps** 45:1; 64:5; **Prov** 11:13; 16:20; 17:9; 18:13; 25:2; **Eccl** 5:8; 10:20; 12:13; **Jer** 38:27; **Eze** 9:11; 16:20; **Dan** 1:14; 2:10; 23; 3:16; 4:17; 7:28(2); 9:23; **Mk** 1:45; 10:10; **Acts** 8:21; 11:4; 15:6; 17:32; 18:14; 19:38; 24:22; **1Cor** 6:1; **2Cor** 7:11; 9:5; **Gal** 2:6; **1Th** 4:6; **Jas** 3:5

MATTERS

Ex 24:14; **Deut** 17:8; **1Sa** 16:18; **2Sa** 11:19; 15:3; 19:29; **2Chr** 19:11(2); **Neh** 11:24; **Est** 3:4; 9:31; 32; **Job** 33:13; **Ps** 35:20; 131:1; **Dan** 1:20; 7:1; **Mt** 23:23; **Acts** 18:15; 19:39; 25:20; **1Cor** 6:2; **1Pet** 4:15

ME

Gen 3:12(2); 13; 4:10; 14(3); 25; 6:7; 13; 7:1; 9:12; 13; 15; 17; 12:12; 13; 18(2); 19; 13:8; 9; 14:21; 24; 15:2; 3; 9; 16:2; 5; 13(2); 17:1; 2; 4; 7; 10; 11; 18:21; 27; 31; 19:8; 19(2); 20; 20:5; 6; 9(2); 11; 13(3); 21:6(2); 16; 23(3); 26; 30; 22:12; 23:4; 8(2); 9(2); 11; 13(2); 15(2); 24:5; 7(3); 12; 17; 23; 27; 30; 37; 39; 40; 43; 44; 45; 48; 49(2); 54; 56(2); 25:30; 31; 32; 33; 26:7; 27(3); 27:3; 4(2); 7(2); 9; 12(2); 13(2); 19(2); 20; 25; 26; 31; 33; 34(2); 36(2); 38(2); 46; 28:20(3); 22; 29:15(2); 19; 21; 25(2); 27; 32; 33; 34; 30:1; 6(2); 13; 14; 16; 18; 20(2); 24; 25; 26(2); 27; 28; 29; 31(2); 33(2); 31:5(2); 7(2); 9; 11; 13; 26; 27(2); 28; 29; 31; 32; 35; 36; 40; 42(2); 44; 48; 49; 50; 51; 52; 32:9; 11(2); 16; 20(2); 26(2); 29; 33:10; 11; 13; 14; 15(3); 34:4; 11(2); 12(3); 30(4); 35:3(2); 37:9; 14; 16; 38:16(3); 17; 39:7; 8; 9; 12; 14(2); 15; 17(2); 18; 19; 40:8; 9; 14(4); 15; 41:10(2); 13; 16; 24; 51; 52; 42:20; 33; 34; 36(2); 43:6; 8; 9; 16; 29; 44:21; 27; 28; 29; 34; 45:1; 4; 5(2); 7; 8(2); 9(2); 10; 18; 46:30; 31; 47:29(2); 30(2); 31; 48:3(2); 4; 7(2); 9(2); 11; 15; 16; 49:29; 50:5(4); 20; **Ex** 2:9; 14; 3:9; 13(2); 14; 15; 16; 4:1; 18; 23; 25; 5:1; 22; 6:7; 12(2); 30; 7:16(2); 8:1; 8; 9; 20; 28; 9:1; 13; 14; 10:3(2); 17; 28; 11:8(2); 12:32; 13:2; 8; 14:15; 17; 18; 17:2; 4; 18:4; 15; 16; 19:5; 6; 20:3; 5; 6; 23; 24; 25; 22:23; 27; 29; 30; 31; 23:14; 15; 33; 24:12; 25:2; 8; 30; 28:1; 3; 4; 41; 29:1; 44; 30:30; 31; 31:13; 17; 32:2; 10; 23; 24; 26; 32; 33; 33:12(3); 13; 15; 18; 20; 21; 34:2; 20; 40:13; 15; **Lev** 10:3; 19; 14:35; 20:26; 22:2; 25:23; 55; 26:14; 18; 21(2); 23(2); 27(2); 40(2); **Num** 3:13; 41; 8:16(2); 11:11; 12; 13; 14; 15(3); 16; 14:11(2); 22; 23; 24; 27(2); 29; 35; 16:28; 29; 17:5; 10; 18:9; 20:12(2); 18; 21:22; 22:5; 6(2); 8; 10; 11; 13; 16; 17(2); 18; 19; 28; 29; 32; 33(3); 34(2); 37; 23:1(2); 3(2); 7(2); 10; 11; 13(2); 18; 27; 29(2); 24:12; 13; 27:14; 28:2(2); 32:11; **Deut** 1:14; 17; 22; 23; 37; 41; 42; 2:1; 2; 9; 17; 27; 28(2); 29; 31; 3:2; 25; 26(4); 4:5; 10(3); 14; 21; 5:7; 9; 10; 22; 23; 28(2); 29; 31; 7:4; 8:17; 9:4; 10; 11; 12; 13; 14; 19; 10:1(2); 4; 5; 10; 11; 17:14(2); 18:15; 16(2); 17; 26:10; 13; 14; 28:20; 31:2; 16; 19; 20; 28; 32:21(2); 34; 35; 39; 41; 51(2); **Josh** 2:4; 12(2); 7:19(2); 8:5; 10:4(2); 22; 14:6; 7; 8; 10; 11; 12(2); 15:19(3); 17:14(2); 18:4; 6; 8; 24:15; **Judg** 1:3; 7; 15(3); 3:28; 4:8(2); 18; 19; 5:13; 6:17(2); 39(2); 7:2(3); 17; 18; 8:5; 15; 24; 9:7; 9; 15; 48; 54(2); 10:12; 13; 11:7(3); 9(2); 12(2); 17; 27(2); 31; 35(2); 36; 37(2); 12:2; 3(3); 5; 13:6(2); 7; 10(2); 16; 14:2; 3(2); 12; 13(2); 16(3); 15:11; 12(2); 16:6; 7; 10(3); 11; 13(3); 15(3); 17; 18; 26; 28(2); 30; 17:2; 10(2); 13; 18:4(2); 24; 19:18; 19; 20; 20:5(3); **Ruth** 1:8; 11; 13(2); 16; 17(2); 20(3); 21(4); 2:2; 7; 10; 11; 13(2); 21; 3:5; 17(2); 4:4; **1Sa** 1:11; 27; 2:16; 28; 29; 30(4); 35; 36; 3:5; 6; 8; 17(2); 8:7; 8; 9:16; 18; 19(2); 21; 10:2; 8; 15; 12:1; 3; 12; 23; 13:9; 11; 12; 14:12; 33; 34; 42; 43; 15:1; 11(2); 16; 20; 25; 30(2); 32; 16:1; 2; 3; 5; 17(2); 19; 22; 17:8; 9(2); 10; 35; 37(2); 43; 44; 45; 18:8; 17; 19:15; 17(3); 20:2(2); 3; 5; 6(2); 8(3); 10; 14; 23; 28; 29(3); 31; 42; 21:2(2); 3; 8; 9; 14; 22:3; 8(5); 13(2); 15; 17; 23(2); 23:11; 12; 21; 22; 23; 24:10; 12(2); 15(2); 17; 18(3); 19; 21(2); 25:19; 21; 24(2); 32; 33; 34(2); 26:6; 8; 19(2); 24; 27:1(3); 5; 28:1; 7; 8(2); 9; 11; 12; 15(6); 16; 17; 19; 21; 22; 29:3(2); 6(2); 30:7; 13; 15(4); 31:4(3); **2Sa** 1:4; 7(2); 8; 9(5); 26(2); 2:7; 22; 3:8; 12; 14(2); 35; 39; 4:10; 5:20; 6:9; 21(2); 7:5(2); 7; 18; 10:2; 11(2); 11:6; 12:10; 22; 23; 13:4; 5; 6; 9; 11; 12; 13; 16(2); 17; 14:0; 10; 15; 10, 10, 10, 32(4); 15:4; 7; 8; 25(2); 26; 28; 33(2); 34; 36; 16:3; 9; 12; 17:1; 18:13; 19; 22; 23; 27; 29; 19:13(2); 19; 22; 25; 26(2); 33(2); 36; 38(2); 20:4; 20; 22:3; 5(2); 6(2); 17(2); 18(3); 19; 20(3); 21(2); 23; 25; 34; 36(2); 37; 40(3); 41(2); 44(3); 45(2); 48(2); 49(4); 23:2; 3; 5; 15; 17; 24:13; 14; 17; 24; **1Kin** 1:12; 13; 17; 24; 26(2); 28; 30; 32; 51; 2:4(2); 5; 7; 8(2); 15; 16; 17; 20; 23; 24(3); 30; 31; 42; 3:20; 24; 5:4; 6; 8; 9; 8:25(2); 9:3; 4; 6; 13; 10:7; 11:21; 22(2); 33; 36(2); 12:5; 9; 12; 24; 27; 13:6(2); 7; 8; 9; 13; 15; 17; 18; 27; 31; 14:2; 8; 9(2); 15:19(2); 16:2; 17:10; 11; 12; 13(2); 18; 19; 18:9; 12; 14; 19; 30; 37(2); 19:2; 18; 20; 20:5; 7; 10(2); 32; 35; 36; 37; 39; 21:2; 3; 6; 20; 22; 29(2); 22:4; 8; 14; 16; 18; 24; 28; 34; **2Kin** 2:2; 4; 6; 9; 10; 20; 3:7(2); 15; 4:2; 6; 22; 24; 27(2); 28; 5:7(2); 8; 11; 22(2); 6:11; 19; 28; 31; 8:4; 9; 10; 13; 14; 9:12; 18; 19; 10:6; 15; 16; 19; 16:7(2); 15; 18:14(2); 20; 22; 25; 27(2); 31(2); 19:6; 20; 27; 28; 20:8; 21:15; 22:10; 13; 15; 17(2); 19; **1Chr** 4:10(4); 10:4(2); 11:17; 19; 12:17(3); 13:12; 17:4; 6; 12; 16; 17; 19:2; 12(2); 21:2; 12; 13(2); 17; 22(2); 22:7; 8; 28:2(2); 3; 4(3); 5; 6; 19(2); 29:17; **2Chr** 1:8; 9; 10; 2:3; 7(2); 8; 9; 6:16; 7:17; 9:6; 10:5; 6; 9; 12; 11:4; 12:5; 13:4; 15:2; 16:3(2); 18:3; 7; 15; 17; 23; 27; 33; 20:20; 28:11; 23; 29:5; 34:18; 21; 23; 25(2); 27(2); 35:21(2); 23; 36:23(2); **Ezr** 1:2(2); 4:18; 21; 7:28(3); 8:1; 9:1; 4; **Neh** 1:3; 9; 2:2; 4; 5; 6(2); 7(2); 8(3); 9; 12(2); 14; 18(2); 4:18; 23; 5:15; 18(2); 19; 6:2(2); 4; 5; 12; 13; 14; 19(2); 12:40; 13:8; 14; 22(2); 28; 31; **Est** 4:16; 5:13; 7:3; 8; **Job** 2:3; 3:12; 25(2); 4:12; 14; 6:4(2); 8; 9(2); 13(2); 22(2); 23(2); 24(2); 28; 7:3; 8(3); 12; 13; 14(2); 16; 19(2); 20; 21; 9:11; 16; 17; 18(2); 19; 20(2); 28; 31(2); 34(2); 35; 10:2(3); 8(3); 9(2); 10(2); 11(2); 12; 14(2); 15; 16(2); 17(3); 18(2); 20; 13:13(2); 15; 19; 20; 21(2); 22(2); 23; 24; 26(2); 14:3; 13(4); 15:17; 16:7; 8(3); 9(4); 10(3); 11(2); 12(4); 13; 14(2); 20; 17:1; 2; 3(2); 6; 19:2; 3(2); 5(2); 6(2); 9; 10; 11(2); 12; 13(2); 14; 15; 16; 18(2); 19(2); 21(3); 22; 27; 28; 20:2; 3; 21:3; 4; 5; 16; 27; 34; 22:18; 23:5(2); 6(2); 10; 14; 16; 24:15; 25; 27:3; 5; 6; 7; 28:14(2); 29:2; 5(2); 6; 8; 11(4); 13; 14; 20; 21; 23; 30:1; 2; 10(2); 11(2); 12; 14(2); 15; 16(2); 17; 18; 19; 20(2); 21(2); 22(2); 23; 26; 27; 30; 31:6; 8; 13; 15; 18; 20; 23; 29; 34; 35(2); 36; 38; 32:10; 14; 18(2); 21(2); 22; 33:4(2); 5(2); 9; 10(2); 27; 31; 32; 33; 34:2; 10; 32; 34(2); 36:2; 38:3; 40:7; 8; 41:10; 11; 42:3; 4; 7; 8; **Ps** 2:7; 8; 3:1(2); 3; 4; 5(2); 6; 7; 4:1(3); 8(2); 5:7; 8; 6:1(2); 2(2); 4; 8; 7:1(3); 4; 6; 8(2); 9:13(3); 13:1(2); 2; 3; 4; 6; 16:1, 0, 7(2); 8; 11; 17:3(2); 4; 6(2); 8(2); 9(2); 15; 18:4(2); 5(2); 16(2); 17(3); 18; 19(3); 20(2); 22(2); 24; 32; 33; 35(3); 36; 39(3); 40(2); 43(3); 44(3); 47(2); 48(4); 19:12; 13; 22:1(2); 7(2); 9(2); 11; 12(2); 13; 15; 16(2); 17; 19(2); 21(2); 23:2(2); 3; 4(2); 5; 6; 25:2(2); 4(2); 5(2); 7; 16(2); 17; 19; 20(2); 21; 26:1; 2(2); 11(3); 27:2; 3(2); 5(3); 6; 7(2); 9(3); 10(2); 11(2); 12(2); 28:1(2); 3; 30:1(2); 2; 3; 10; 11(2); 31:1(2); 2(3); 3(2); 4(2); 5; 8; 9; 11(2); 13; 15(2); 16; 17; 21; 32:4; 7(2); 34:3; 4(2); 11; 35:1(2); 3; 7; 12; 13; 15(2); 16; 19(2); 21; 22; 24(2); 26; 36:11(2); 38:1(2); 2(2); 4; 10(2); 12; 16(3); 17; 19; 21(2); 22; 39:1; 3; 4; 8(2); 10; 13; 40:1; 2; 7; 11(2); 12(3); 13(2); 14; 15; 17; 41:4; 5; 6; 7(3); 9; 10(2); 11(2); 12(3); 42:3; 4; 5; 6; 7; 8; 9; 10(2); 11; 43:1(2); 2; 3(2); 5; 44:6; 15(2); 49:5; 15; 50:5(2); 8; 15(2); 23; 51:1; 2(2); 3; 5; 6; 7(2); 8; 10(2); 11(2); 12(2); 14; 54:1(2); 3; 7; 55:2(2); 3(2); 4(2); 5(2); 12(3); 16(2); 18(2); 56:1(3); 2(2); 4; 5; 9; 11; 12; 57:1(2); 2; 3(2); 6; 59:1(3); 2(2); 3; 4; 10(2); 60:5; 8; 9(2); 61:2; 3; 5; 63:8; 64:2; 65:3; 66:18; 19; 20; 69:1; 2; 4(2); 9(2); 12; 13(2); 14(4); 15(3); 16(2); 17; 18; 21(2); 29; 70:1(2); 5; 71:1; 2(4); 3; 4; 6; 9(2); 10; 12; 17; 18; 20(3); 21; 73:2; 16; 23; 24(2); 28; 77:1; 81:8; 11; 13; 86:1; 3; 7; 11; 13; 14; 16(2); 17(4); 87:4; 88:6; 7(2); 8(2); 14; 16(2); 17(2); 18; 89:26; 36; 91:14; 15; 92:4; 11; 94:16(2); 18; 19; 95:9(2); 101:2; 3; 4; 6(2); 102:2(3); 8(3); 10(2); 24; 103:1; 106:4(2); 108:6; 10(2); 109:2(2); 3(2); 5; 21(2); 22; 25; 26(2); 116:2; 3(2); 6; 12; 118:5(2); 6; 7(2); 10; 11(2); 12; 13(2); 18(2); 19; 21; 119:8; 10; 12; 19; 22; 23; 25;

26(2); 27; 28; 29(2); 30; 31; 33; 34; 35; 37; 40; 41; 42; 49; 50; 51; 53; 58; 61; 64; 66; 68; 69; 71; 72; 73(3); 74; 75; 77; 78; 79; 82; 84; 85; 86(2); 87; 88; 93; 94; 95(2); 98(2); 102; 107; 108; 110; 115; 116(2); 117; 121; 122; 124; 125; 132(2); 133; 134; 135; 139; 143; 144; 145; 146; 149; 153; 154(2); 156; 159; 161; 169; 170; 171; 173; 175; 120:1; 5; 122:1; 129:1; 2(2); 131:1; 138:3(2); 7(2); 8; 139:1(2); 5(2); 6; 10(2); 11(2); 13; 17; 19; 23(2); 24(2); 140:1(2); 4(2); 5(2); 9; 141:1; 4; 5(2); 9(2); 142:3(2); 4(2); 6; 7(2); 143:1; 3; 4(2); 7(2); 8(2); 9(2); 10(2); 11; 144:2; 7(2); 11(2); **Prov** 1:28(3); 33; 4:4(2); 5:7; 13; 7:14; 24; 8:15; 16; 17(3); 18; 21; 22; 32; 34; 35; 36(2); 9:11; 23:26; 35(2); 24:29; 27:11; 30:7; 8(4); 18; **Eccl** 1:16; 2:4(3); 5; 6; 7(2); 8(2); 9(2); 15; 17; 18; 7:23; 9:13; **Song** 1:2; 4(2); 6(4); 7; 13; 14; 2:4(2); 5(2); 6; 10; 14(2); 3:3; 4; 4:6; 8(2); 5:2; 6; 7(4); 6:5(2); 12; 7:10; 8:2; 3; 6; 12; 13; **Is** 1:2; 11; 12; 13; 14; 24(2); 3:7; 5:3; 6:5; 6; 8; 8:1; 2; 3; 5; 11(2); 18; 10:4; 12:1(2); 18:4; 21:2; 3; 4(2); 6; 11; 16; 22:4(2); 24:16; 26:9; 27:4(2); 5(2); 29:2; 13(4); 16; 30:1; 31:4; 36:5; 7; 10; 12(2); 16(2); 37:6; 21; 28; 29; 38:12(3); 13; 14; 15; 16(2); 20; 39:3; 40:25; 41:1; 43:10(3); 11; 20; 22(2); 23(2); 24(4); 26; 27; 44:6; 7; 8; 17; 21; 22; 45:4; 5(2); 6; 11(2); 19; 21(2); 22; 23; 46:3(2); 5(3); 9; 12; 47:8; 10(2); 48:12; 16(2); 19; 49:1(2); 2(3); 3; 5; 14(2); 16; 20(2); 21; 23; 50:4; 7; 8(3); 9(2); 51:1; 4(3); 5; 7; 54:9; 15; 17; 55:2; 3; 11; 56:3; 4; 57:8; 11(2); 13; 16; 17; 58:2(2); 59:21; 60:9; 61:1(3); 10(2); 63:3; 5(2); 15; 65:1(4); 3; 5; 6; 7; 10; 66:1; 22; 23; 24; **Jer** 1:4; 7; 9; 11; 12; 13; 14; 16; 2:1; 2; 5(2); 8(2); 13; 21; 22; 27(2); 29(2); 32; 35; 3:1; 4; 6; 7; 10; 11; 19(2); 20; 4:1; 12; 17; 19; 22; 31; 5:5; 7; 11; 19; 22; 6:7; 20(2); 7:10; 16; 18; 19; 26; 8:18; 19; 21; 9:3; 6; 24; 10:19; 20; 24(2); 11:6; 9; 11; 14; 17; 18(2); 19; 20; 12:1; 3(2); 8(2); 9; 11; 13:1; 3; 5; 6; 8; 11(2); 22; 25(2); 14:11; 14; 15:1(2); 6; 8; 10(4); 15(4); 16; 17; 18; 19; 16:1; 11(2); 12; 17:13; 14(2); 15; 16; 17; 18(3); 19; 24; 27; 18:5; 15; 19(2); 22; 23(2); 19:4; 20:7(2); 8; 11; 12; 14; 17(2); 22:6; 14; 16; 23:9; 14; 17; 24:1; 3; 4; 7(2); 25:3; 6; 7(2); 15; 17; 26:3; 4; 12; 14(2); 15(2); 27:2; 5; 28:1; 8; 29:12(2); 13(3); 30:20; 21(2); 31:3; 18(2); 26; 34; 36(2); 32:6; 8(2); 25; 27; 29; 30(2); 31; 32; 33; 39; 40; 33:3; 8(2); 9; 18; 22; 34:14; 15; 17; 18; 35:14; 15; 16; 19; 36:18; 37:7(2); 18; 20; 38:14; 15(2); 19(2); 21; 26; 39:18; 40:4(2); 10; 15; 42:9; 10; 20; 21; 44:3; 8; 45:3; 49:4; 11; 19(3); 50:44(3); 51:1; 34(5); 35; 53; **Lam** 1:12(2); 13(2); 14; 15(2); 16; 19; 20; 21(2); 22; 3:2(2); 3(2); 5(2); 6; 7; 10; 11(2); 12; 15(2); 16; 20; 52; 53; 60; 61; 62(2); **Eze** 2:1; 2(4); 3(3); 9; 10; 3:1; 2; 3; 4; 7; 10; 12(2); 14(3); 16; 17; 22(2); 24(4); 4:15; 16; 6:1; 9(2); 7:1; 8:1(2); 3(3); 5; 6; 7; 8; 9; 12; 13; 14; 15; 16; 17(2); 9:9; 10; 11; 11:1(2); 2; 5(2); 14; 24(3); 25; 12:1; 8; 17; 21; 26; 13:1; 19; 14:1(2); 2; 5; 7(2); 11; 12; 13; 15:1; 16:1; 20; 26; 43; 50; 17:1; 11; 20; 18:1; 20:1; 2; 3; 8(2); 12; 13; 20; 21; 27(2); 38; 39; 40; 45; 49; 21:1; 8; 18; 22:1; 12; 17; 18; 23; 30; 23:1; 35(2); 36; 37; 38; 24:1; 15; 19; 20; 25:1; 26:1; 2; 27:1; 28:1; 11; 20; 29:1; 17; 20; 30:1; 9; 20; 31:1; 32:1; 17; 33:1; 7; 21; 22(2); 23; 34:1; 35:1; 13(2); 36:16; 17; 37:1(3); 2; 3; 4; 9; 10; 11; 15; 38:1; 16; 39:23; 26; 40:1(2); 2(2); 3; 4; 17; 24; 28; 32; 35; 45; 48; 49; 41:1; 4; 22; 42:1(2); 13; 15; 43:1; 5(2); 6(2); 7; 8; 9; 18; 19(2); 44:1; 2; 4; 5; 10(2); 13(2); 15(5); 16; 46:19; 20; 21(2); 24; 47:1; 2(2); 3; 4(2); 6(3); 8; **Dan** 1:10; 2:5(2); 6(2); 8; 9(4); 23(2); 24; 26; 30(2); 4:2; 5(2); 6(2); 7; 8; 9; 18; 34; 36(4); 5:7; 15(2); 16; 6:22(2); 7:15; 16(2); 28(3); 8:1(3); 14; 15; 17; 18(3); 9:21; 22(2); 10:7; 8(2); 10(2); 11(2); 12; 13(2); 15; 16(2); 17(3); 18(2); 19(2); 21; **Hos** 2:5; 7; 12; 13; 16(2); 19(2); 20; 23; 3:1; 2; 3; 4:6; 7; 5:3; 15; 6:7; 7:7; 13(3); 14(2); 15; 8:2; 4; 11:7; 8; 12; 12:8(2); 13:4(2); 6; 9; 10; 14:8; **Joel** 2:12; 3:4(3); **Amos** 4:6; 8; 9; 10; 11; 5:4; 22; 23; 25; 7:1; 4; 7; 8; 15(2); 8:1; 2; 9:7; **Obad** 3; **Jonah** 1:2; 12(2); 2:2; 3(3); 5(2); 6; 7; 4:3(2); 8; **Mic** 2:4; 5:2; 6:3; 7:1; 7; 8(2); 9(2); 10; **Hab** 1:3(3); 2:1(2); 2; 3:14; 19; **Zeph** 2:15; 3:7; 8; 11; **Hag** 2:14; 17; **Zec** 1:3; 4; 9(2); 13; 14(2); 19(2); 20; 2:2; 3; 8; 9; 11; 3:1; 4:1(2); 2; 4; 5(2); 6; 8; 9; 13; 5:2; 3; 5(2); 10; 11; 6:4; 5; 8(2); 9; 15; 7:4; 5(2); 8:1; 14; 18; 9:13; 10:9; 11:7; 8; 11; 12; 13; 15; 12:10; 13:5; **Mal** 2:5; 6; 3:1; 5; 7; 8; 9; 10; 13; **Mt** 2:8; 3:11; 14; 4:9; 19; 7:4; 21; 22; 23; 8:2; 9; 21; 22; 9:9; 10:32; 33; 37(4); 38(2); 40(3); 11:6; 27; 28; 29; 12:30(3); 14:8; 18; 28; 30; 15:5; 8(3); 9; 22; 25; 32; 16:23(2); 24(2); 17:17; 27; 18:5; 6; 21; 26; 28; 29; 32; 19:14; 17; 21; 28; 20:13; 15; 21:2; 24; 22:18; 19; 23:39; 25:20; 22; 35(3); 36(3); 40; 41; 42(2); 43(3); 45; 26:10; 11; 15; 21; 23(2); 31; 34; 38; 39; 40; 42; 46; 53; 55(2); 75; 27:10; 46; 28:10; 18; **Mk** 1:7; 17; 40; 2:14; 5:7; 31; 6:22; 23; 25; 7:6(2); 7; 11; 14; 8:2; 33; 34(2); 38; 9:19; 37(4); 39; 42; 10:14; 18; 21; 47; 48; 11:29; 30; 12:15(2); 14:6; 7; 18(2); 20; 27; 30; 36; 42; 48; 49; 72; 15:34; **Lk** 1:3; 25(2); 38; 43(2); 48; 49; 2:49; 4:6; 7; 8; 18(3); 23; 5:8; 12; 27; 6:42; 46; 47; 7:8; 23; 42; 44; 45; 8:28; 45(2); 46(2); 9:23(2); 26; 48(3); 59(2); 61; 10:16(4); 22; 40(2); 11:5; 6; 7(2); 23(3); 12:8; 9; 13; 14; 13:27; 35; 14:18; 19; 26; 27; 15:6; 9; 12(2); 19; 29; 31; 16:3; 4; 24; 17:8; 18:3; 5(2); 13; 16; 19; 22; 38; 39; 19:27; 20:3; 23; 24; 22:19; 21(2); 28; 29; 34; 37(2); 42; 53; 61; 68(2); 23:14; 28; 42; 43; 24:39(2); 44; **Jn** 1:15(3); 27(2); 30(3); 33(2); 43; 48; 2:17; 3:28; 4:7; 9; 10; 15; 21; 29; 34; 39; 5:7(2); 11(2); 24; 30; 32(2); 36(3); 37(2); 39; 40; 43; 46(2); 6:26; 35(2); 36; 37(3); 38; 39(2); 40; 44(2); 45; 47; 56; 57(3); 65; 7:7; 16; 19; 23; 28(2); 29; 33; 34(2); 36(2); 37; 38; 8:12; 16; 18(2); 19(2); 21; 26; 28; 29(3); 37; 40; 42(2); 45; 46(2); 49; 54; 9:4; 11; 10:8; 9; 15; 17; 18; 25; 27; 29; 32; 37; 38(2); 11:25; 26; 41; 42(2); 12:8; 26(3); 27; 30; 32; 44(3); 45(2); 46; 48; 49(2); 50; 13:8; 13; 18(2); 20(3); 21; 33; 36(2); 38; 14:1; 6; 7; 9(2); 10(2); 11(3); 12; 15; 19(2); 20; 21(2); 23; 24(2); 28; 30; 31; 15:2; 4(2); 5(2); 6; 7; 9; 16; 18; 20; 21; 23; 24; 25; 26; 27; 16:3; 5(2); 9; 10; 14; 16(2); 17(2); 19(2); 23; 27; 32(2); 33; 17:4; 5; 6(2); 7; 8(2); 9; 11; 12; 18; 20; 21(2); 22; 23(3); 24(4); 25; 26; 18:8; 9; 11; 21(2); 23; 34; 35; 19:10; 11(2); 20:15; 17; 21; 29; 21:15; 16; 17(2); 19; 22; **Acts** 1:4; 8; 2:28(2); 29; 3:22; 5:8; 7:7; 28; 37; 42; 49; 8:19; 24(2); 31; 36; 9:4; 6; 15; 17; 10:28; 29; 30; 11:5; 7; 9; 11; 12(2); 12:8; 11; 13:2; 25; 15:13; 16:15; 20:19; 22; 23; 24; 34; 21:39; 22:5; 6; 7(2); 8; 9(2); 10; 11; 13(2); 18(2); 21; 27; 23:3(2); 11; 18(2); 19; 22; 30; 24:12; 13; 18; 19; 20; 25:5; 9; 11(2); 15; 24; 27; 26:3; 5; 13(2); 14(2); 18; 21(2); 28; 29; 27:21; 23; 25; 28:18(3); **Rom** 1:12; 15; 7:8; 11(2); 13(2); 17; 18(2); 20; 21; 23; 24; 8:2; 9:1; 19; 20; 10:20(2); 12:3; 14:11; 15:3; 15; 18; 30(2); 16:7; **1Cor** 1:11; 17; 3:10; 4:3; 4; 16; 6:12(2); 7:1; 9:3; 15(2); 16(2); 17; 10:23(2); 11:1; 2; 24; 25; 13:3; 14:11; 21; 15:8; 10(2); 32; 16:4; 6; 9; 11; 21; **2Cor** 1:17; 19; 2:2(2); 5; 12; 7:7; 9:1; 4; 11:1(2); 9; 10(2); 16(2); 28; 32; 12:1; 6(3); 7(2); 8; 9(2); 11; 13; 21; 13:3; 10; **Gal** 1:2; 11; 15(2); 16; 17; 24; 2:1; 3; 6(2); 7; 8; 9(2); 20(3); 4:12; 14; 15; 21; 6:14; 17; **Eph** 3:2; 3; 7; 8; 6:19(2); **Phil** 1:7; 12; 21; 26; 30(2); 2:18; 22; 23; 27; 30; 3:1; 7; 17; 4:3; 9; 10; 13; 15; 21; **Col** 1:25; 29; 4:11; 18; **1Ti** 1:12(3); 16; **2Ti** 1:8; 13; 15; 16; 17(2); 18; 2:2; 3:11(2); 4:8(3); 9; 10; 11(2); 14; 16(2); 17(3); 18(2); **Titus** 1:3; 3:12; 15; **Philem** 1:11; 13(2); 16; 17; 19; 20; 22; **Heb** 1:5; 2:13; 3:9(2); 8:10; 11; 10:5; 7; 30; 34; 11:32; 13:6; **Jas** 2:18; **2Pet** 1:14; **Jude** 3; **Rev** 1:10; 12; 17(2); 3:4; 18; 20; 21; 4:1; 5:5; 7:13; 14; 10:4; 8; 9(2); 11; 11:1; 14:13; 17:1(2); 3; 7; 15; 19:9(2); 10; 21:5; 6; 9(2); 10(2); 15; 22:1; 6; 8; 9; 10; 12

MIDST

Gen 1:6; 2:9; 3:3; 15:10; 19:29; 48:16; **Ex** 3:2; 4; 20; 8:22; 11:4; 14:16; 22; 23; 27; 29; 15:19; 23:25; 24:16; 18; 26:28; 27:5; 28:32; 33:3; 5; 34:12; 38:4; 39:23; **Lev** 16:16; **Num** 2:17; 5:3; 16:47; 19:6; 33:8; 35:5; **Deut** 4:11; 12; 15; 33; 34; 36; 5:4; 22; 23; 24; 26; 9:10; 10:4; 11:3; 6; 13:5; 16; 17:20; 18:15; 19:2; 23:14; 32:51; **Josh** 3:17; 4:3; 5; 8; 9; 10; 18; 7:13; 21; 23; 8:13; 22; 10:13; 13:9; 16; **Judg** 15:4; 18:20; 20:42; **1Sa** 11:11; 16:13; 18:10; **2Sa** 1:25; 4:6; 6:17; 18:14; 20:12; 23:12; 20; 24:5; **1Kin** 3:8; 6:27; 8:51; 20:39; 22:35; **2Kin** 6:20; **1Chr** 11:14; 16:1; 19:4; **2Chr** 6:13; 20:14; 32:4; **Neh** 4:11; 9:11; **Est** 4:1; **Job** 21:21; **Ps** 22:14; 22; 46:2; 5; 48:9; 55:10; 11; 57:6; 74:4; 12; 78:28; 102:24; 110:2; 116:19; 135:9; 136:14; 137:2; 138:7; **Prov** 4:21; 5:14; 8:20; 14:33; 23:34; 30:19; **Song** 3:10; **Is** 4:4; 5:2; 8; 25; 6:5; 12; 7:6; 10:23; 12:6; 16:3; 19:1; 3; 14; 19; 24; 24:13; 18; 25:11; 29:23; 30:28; 41:18; 52:11; 58:9; 66:17; **Jer** 6:1; 6; 9:6; 12:16; 14:9; 17:11; 21:4; 29:8; 30:21; 37:12; 41:7(2); 46:21; 48:45; 50:8; 37; 51:1; 6; 45; 47; 63; 52:25; **Lam** 1:15; 3:45; 4:13; **Eze** 1:4(2); 5; 5:2; 4; 5; 8; 10; 12; 6:7; 7:4; 9; 8:11; 9:4(3); 10:10; 11:7(2); 9; 11; 23; 12:2; 13:14; 14:8; 9; 15:4; 16:53; 17:16; 20:8; 21:32; 22:3; 7; 9; 13; 18; 19; 20; 21; 22(2); 25(2); 27; 23:39; 24:7; 26:5; 12; 15; 27:4; 25; 26; 27(2); 32; 34; 28:2; 8; 14; 16(2); 18; 22; 23; 29:3; 4; 12; 21; 30:7(2); 31:14; 17; 18; 32:20; 21; 25(2); 28; 32; 36:23; 37:1; 26; 28; 38:12; 39:7; 41:7; 43:7; 9; 46:10; 48:8; 10; 15; 21; 22; **Dan** 3:6; 11; 15; 21; 23; 24; 25; 26; 4:10; 7:15; 9:27; **Hos** 5:4; 11:9; **Joel** 2:27; **Amos** 2:3; 3:9(2); 6:4; 7:8; 10; **Jonah** 2:3; **Mic** 2:12; 5:7; 8; 10; 13; 14; 6:14; 7:14; **Nah** 3:13; **Hab** 2:19; 3:2(2); **Zeph** 2:14; 3:5; 11; 12; 15; 17; **Zec** 2:5; 10; 11; 5:4; 7; 8; 8:3; 8; 14:1; 4; **Mt** 10:16; 14:24; 18:2; 20; **Mk** 6:47; 7:31; 9:36; 14:60; **Lk** 2:46; 4:30; 35; 5:19; 6:8; 17:11; 21:21; 22:55; 23:45; 24:36; **Jn** 7:14; 8:3; 9; 59; 19:18; 20:19; 26; **Acts** 1:15; 18; 2:22; 4:7; 17:22; 27:21; **Phil** 2:15; **Heb** 2:12; **Rev** 1:13; 2:1; 7; 4:6; 5:6(2); 6:6; 7:17; 8:13; 14:6; 19:17; 22:2

MINE

Gen 14:22; 15:3; 24:33; 45; 30:25; 30; 31:10; 40; 42; 43; 41:13; 44:21; 48:5(2); 49:6; **Ex** 7:4; 5; 17; 13:2; 17:9; 18:4; 19:5; 20:26; 21:14; 23:23; 32:34; 33:23; 34:19; **Lev** 18:4; 30; 20:26; 22:9; 25:23; **Num** 3:12; 13(2); 45; 8:14; 17; 10:30; 12:7; 14:28; 16:28; 18:8; 22:29; 23:11; 24:10; 13; **Deut** 8:17; 10:3; 26:13; 29:19; 32:22; 23; 41(2); 42; **Josh** 14:7; **Judg** 6:36; 37; 7:2; 8:7; 11:30; 16:17; 17:2; 19:23; **Ruth** 4:6; **1Sa** 2:1(2); 28; 29; 33; 35(2); 12:3; 14:24; 29; 43; 15:14; 17:46; 18:17; 19:17; 20:1; 21:3; 4; 23:7; 24:6; 10(3); 11; 12; 13; 25:33; 26:11; 18; 23; 24; 28:2; **2Sa** 5:19; 20; 6:22; 11:11; 14:5; 30; 16:12; 18:12(2); 13; 19:37; 22:4; 24; 35; 38; 41; 49; **1Kin** 1:33; 48; 2:15; 22; 3:26; 9:3(2); 10:6; 7; 11:21; 33; 14:8; 20:3(2); 21:20; **2Kin** 4:13; 5:26; 6:32; 10:6; 30(2); 18:34; 35(2); 19:28; 34; 20:6; 15; 21:14; **1Chr** 12:17(3); 14:10; 11(2); 16:22; 17:14; 16; 22:18; 28:2; 29:3; 17; **2Chr** 7:15(2); 16(2); 9:5; 6; 29:10; 32:13; 14(2); 15(2); 17(2); **Neh** 7:5; **Job** 3:10; 4:12; 16; 6:11; 7:7; 21; 9:20; 31; 10:6; 14; 15; 13:1(2); 14; 15; 23; 14:17; 16:4; 9; 17; 20; 17:2; 7; 13; 19:4; 10; 13; 15; 17; 27; 27:5; 7; 31:1; 6; 7(3); 9; 12; 22(2); 25; 33; 35; 32:6; 10; 17; 33:8; 40:4; 41:11; 42:5; **Ps** 3:3; 7; 5:8; 6:7(2); 10; 7:4; 5; 6; 8; 9:3; 13:2; 3; 4; 16:5; 17:3; 18:3; 23; 34; 37; 40; 48; 23:5; 25:2; 11; 15; 18; 19; 26:1; 3; 6; 11; 27:2; 6(2); 11; 12; 31:9; 10; 11(2); 15; 32:5; 8; 35:2; 13; 15; 19; 26; 38:4(2); 10; 18; 19; 20; 39:4; 5; 40:6; 12(2); 41:5; 9; 11; 12; 42:10; 49:4; 50:10; 11; 12; 51:2; 9; 54:4; 5; 7(2); 55:13(2); 56:2; 9; 59:1; 10; 60:7(3); 69:3; 4(2); 18; 19; 71:10; 77:4; 6; 88:8; 9; 18; 89:21; 92:11(3); 101:3; 6; 102:8; 105:15; 108:8(3); 109:20; 29; 116:8; 119:11; 18; 37; 82; 92; 98; 112; 121; 123; 136; 139; 148; 153; 157; 121:1; 123:1; 131:1; 132:4(2); 17; 138:7; 139:2; 22; 141:8; 143:9; 12; **Prov** 5:13; 8:14; 23:15; **Eccl** 1:16; 2:1; 3(2); 10; 3:17; 18; 7:25; 8:16; **Song** 1:6; 2:16; 6:3; 8:12; **Is** 1:15; 16; 24(2); 5:9; 6:5; 10:5(2); 25; 13:3; 16:4; 11; 19:25; 22:14; 29:23; 37:29; 35; 38:12; 14; 39:4; 42:1; 43:1; 25; 45:4; 47:6; 48:5; 9; 11(2); 13; 49:22; 50:4; 5; 8; 11; 51:5(2); 16; 56:5; 7(2); 60:7; 63:3; 4; 5; 6; 65:9; 12; 16; 22; 66:2; 4; **Jer** 2:7; 3:12; 15; 7:20; 9:1; 11:15; 12:3; 7(2); 8; 9; 14; 13:17; 14:17; 15:14; 16; 16:17(2); 18; 21; 17:4; 18:6; 20:9; 23:9; 24:6; 32:8; 12; 31; 37; 33:5; 42:18; 44:6; 28; 48:31; 36(2); 50:11; 51:25; **Lam** 1:16(2); 19; 20; 21; 2:11; 22; 3:19; 48; 49; 51(2); 52; 54; **Eze** 5:11; 13; 7:3; 4; 8; 9; 8:1; 3; 5; 18(2); 9:1; 5; 10; 11:20; 12:7; 13:9; 13; 14:13; 16:8; 18(2); 17:19; 18:4(2); 20:5(2); 6; 17; 22; 23; 28; 40; 42; 21:17; 31; 22:8; 13; 20; 26; 31; 23:4; 5; 39; 41(2); 25:7; 13; 14; 16; 29:3; 9; 35:3; 10; 36:7; 21; 22; 37:19; 43:8; 44:8; 12; 24; 47:14; **Dan** 4:4; 10; 34(2); 36; 8:3; 10:5; **Hos** 2:5; 10; 8:5; 13; 9:15; 11:8; 9; 13:11; 14; 14:4; **Amos** 1:8; 9:2; 4; **Jonah** 2:2; **Mic** 7:8; 10(2); **Hab** 1:12; 3:19; **Zeph** 1:4; 3:8; 10; **Hag** 1:9; 2:8(2); **Zec** 1:18; 2:1; 9; 5:1; 9; 6:1; 8:6; 9:8(2); 10:3; 11:14; 12:4; 13:7; **Mal** 1:6; 7; 10; 3:7; 10; 17; **Mt** 7:24; 26; 20:15; 23; 25:27; **Mk** 9:24; 10:40; **Lk** 1:44; 2:30; 9:38; 11:6; 18:3; 19:23; 27; **Jn** 2:4; 5:30(2); 6:38; 7:16; 8:50; 9:11; 15; 30; 10:14; 14:24; 16:14; 15(2); 17:10(2); **Acts** 11:6; 13:22; 21:13; 26:4; **Rom** 11:13; 12:19; 16:13; 23; **1Cor** 1:15; 4:3; 9:2; 3; 10:33; 16:21; **2Cor** 11:26; 30; 12:5; **Gal** 1:14; 6:11; **Phil** 1:4; 3:9; **2Th** 3:17; **Titus** 1:4; **Philem** 1:12; 18; 19; **Rev** 22:16

MORE

Gen 3:1; 8:12; 21(2); 9:11(2); 15; 17:5; 29:30; 32:28; 34:19; 35:10; 36:7; 37:3; 4; 5; 8; 9; 38:26(2); 44:23; **Ex** 1:9; 12(2); 5:7; 9; 8:29; 9:28; 29; 34; 10:28; 29; 11:1; 6; 14:13; 16:17; 30:15; 36:5; 6; **Lev** 6:5; 11:42; 13:5; 33; 54; 17:7; 26:18; 21; 27:20; **Num** 3:46; 8:25; 18:5; 22:15(2); 18; 19; 26:54; 33:54(2); **Deut** 1:11; 3:26; 5:22; 25; 7:7; 17; 10:16; 13:11; 17:13; 16; 18:16; 19:9; 20; 20:1; 28:68; 31:2; 27; **Josh** 2:11; 5:1; 12; 7:12; 10:11; 23:13; **Judg** 2:19; 8:28; 10:13; 13:21; 15:3; 16:30; 18:24; **Ruth** 1:11; 17; 3:10; **1Sa** 1:18; 2:3; 3:17; 7:13; 14:30; 44; 15:35; 18:2; 8; 29; 30; 20:13; 22:15; 23:3; 24:17; 25:22; 36; 26:21; 27:1; 4; 28:15; 30:4; **2Sa** 2:28(2); 3:9; 35; 4:11; 5:13; 6:22; 7:10(2); 20; 10:19; 11:25; 14:10; 11; 16:11; 18:8; 19:13; 28; 29; 35; 43; 20:6; 21:17; 23:23; **1Kin** 2:23; 32; 10:5; 10; 16:33; 19:2; 20:10; **2Kin** 2:12; 21; 4:6; 6:16; 23; 31; 9:35; 12:7; 8; 21:8; 9; 24:7; **1Chr** 4:9; 11:21; 14:3(2); 17:9(2); 18; 19:19; 21:3; 23:26; 24:4; **2Chr** 9:4; 10:11; 15:19; 20:25; 25:9; 28:13; 22; 29:34; 32:7; 16; 33:8; 23(2); **Ezr** 7:20; **Neh** 2:17; 13:18; 21; **Est** 1:19; 2:14; 17; 4:13; 6:6; **Job** 3:21; 4:17(2); 7:7; 8; 9; 10(2); 14:12; 15:16; 20:9(2); 23:12; 24:20; 32:15; 16; 34:19; 23; 31; 32; 35:2; 11; 41:8; 42:12; **Ps** 4:7; 10:18; 19:10; 39:13; 40:5; 12; 41:8; 52:3; 69:4; 71:14(2); 73:7; 74:9; 76:4; 77:7; 78:17; 83:4; 87:2; 88:5; 103:16; 104:35; 115:14(2); 119:99; 100; 130:6(2); 139:18; **Prov** 3:15; 4:18(2); 10:25; 11:24; 31; 12:26; 15:11; 17:10; 19:7; 21:3; 27; 26:12; 28:23; 29:20; 30:2; 31:7; **Eccl** 1:16; 2:9; 15; 16; 25; 4:2; 13; 5:1; 6:5; 8; 7:19; 26; 9:5; 6; 17; 10:10; **Song** 1:4; 5:9(2); **Is** 1:5(3); 13; 2:4; 5:4; 9:1; 10:20; 13:12; 15:9; 19:7; 23:10; 12; 26:21; 30:19; 20; 32:5; 38:11; 47:1; 5; 51:22; 52:1; 14(2); 54:1; 4; 9; 56:12; 60:18; 19; 20; 62:4(2); 8; 65:19; 20; **Jer** 2:31; 3:11; 16(2); 17; 7:32; 10:20; 11:19; 16:14; 19:6; 20:9; 22:10; 11; 12; 30; 23:4; 7; 36; 25:27; 30:8; 31:12; 29; 34(2); 40; 33:24; 34:10; 38:9; 42:18; 44:26; 46:23; 48:2; 49:7; 50:39; 51:44; **Lam** 2:9; 4:7; 15; 16; 22; **Eze** 5:6(2); 7; 9; 6:14; 12:23; 24; 25; 28; 13:15; 21; 23; 14:11(2); 21; 15:2; 16:41; 42; 47; 51; 52(2); 63; 18:3; 19:9; 20:39; 21:5; 13; 27; 32; 23:11(2); 27; 24:13; 27; 26:13; 14; 21; 27:36; 28:19; 24; 29:15(2); 16; 30:13; 32:13; 33:22; 34:10; 22; 28; 29(2); 36:12; 14(2); 15(3); 30; 37:22(2); 23; 39:7; 28; 29; 42:6; 43:7; 45:8; **Dan** 2:30; 3:19; 7:20; 11:8; **Hos** 1:6; 2:16; 17; 6:6; 9:15; 13:2(2); 14:3; 8; **Joel** 2:2; 19; 3:17; **Amos** 5:2; 7:8; 13; 8:2; 9:15; **Jonah** 4:11; **Mic** 4:3; 5:12; 13; **Nah** 1:12; 14; 15; 2:13; **Hab** 1:8; 13; **Zeph** 3:11; 15; **Zec** 9:8; 11:6; 13:2; 14:11; 21; **Mal** 2:13; **Mt** 5:37; 47; 6:25; 30; 7:11; 10:15; 25; 31; 37(2); 11:9; 22; 24; 12:45; 13:12; 18:13; 16; 19:6; 20:10; 31; 21:36; 22:46; 23:15; 25:20; 26:53; 27:23; **Mk** 1:45; 4:24; 6:11; 7:12; 36(2); 8:14; 9:8; 25; 10:8; 48; 12:33; 43; 14:5; 25; 31; 15:14; **Lk** 3:13; 5:15; 7:26; 9:13; 10:12; 14; 35; 11:13; 26; 12:4; 7; 23(2); 24; 28; 48; 14:8; 15:7; 19; 21; 18:30; 39; 20:36; 21:3; 22:16; 44; 23:5; **Jn** 4:1; 41; 5:14; 18; 6:66; 7:31; 8:11; 10:10; 11:54; 12:43; 14:19; 15:2; 4; 16:10; 21; 25; 17:11; 19:8; 21:15; **Acts** 4:19; 5:14; 8:39; 9:22; 13:34; 17:11; 18:26; 19:32; 20:25; 35; 38; 22:2; 23:13; 15; 20; 21; 24:10; 22; 25:6; 27:11; 12; **Rom** 1:25; 2:18; 3:7; 5:9; 10; 15; 17; 20; 6:9(2); 7:17; 20; 8:37; 11:6(4); 12; 24; 12:3; 14:13; 15:15; 23; **1Cor** 6:3; 9:19; 12:22(2); 23(2); 24; 31; 14:18; 15:10; **2Cor** 1:12; 2:4; 3:9; 11; 4:17; 5:16; 7:7; 13; 15; 8:17; 22; 10:8; 11:23(3); 12:15; **Gal** 1:14; 3:18; 4:7; 27; **Eph** 2:19; 4:14; 28; **Phil** 1:9(2); 14; 24; 26; 2;12; 28; 3:4; **1Th** 2:17; 4:1(2); 10(2); **2Ti** 2:16; 3:4; **Philem** 1:16; 21; **Heb** 1:4; 2:1; 3:3(2); 6:17; 7:15; 8:6; 12; 9:11; 14; 10:2; 17; 18; 25; 26; 11:4; 32; 12:19; 25; 26; 27; **Jas** 4:6; **1Pet** 1:7; **2Pet** 1:19; **Rev** 2:19; 3:12; 7:16(2); 9:12; 12:8; 18:11; 14; 21; 22(3); 23(2); 20:3; 21:1; 4(2); 22:3

MOREOVER

Gen 24:25; 32:20; 45:15; 47:4; 48:22; **Ex** 3:6; 15; 11:3; 18:21; 26:1; 30:22; **Lev** 7:21; 26; 14:46; 18:20; 25:45; **Num** 13:28; 16:14; 33:56; 35:31; **Deut** 1:28; 39; 7:20; 28:45; 60; **Judg** 10:9; **Ruth** 4:10; **1Sa** 2:19; 12:23; 14:21; 17:37; 20:3; 24:11; 28:19; **2Sa** 7:10; 12:8; 15:4; 17:1; 13; 21:15; **1Kin** 1:47; 2:5; 14; 44; 8:41; 10:18; 14:14; **2Kin** 12:15; 21:16; 23:15; 24; **1Chr** 11:2; 12:40; 17:10; 18:12; 22:15; 23:5; 25:1; 26:4; 28:7; 29:3; **2Chr** 1:5; 2:12; 4:1; 20; 6:32; 7:7; 9:17; 17:6; 19:8; 21:11; 16; 23:9; 25:5; 26:9; 11; 27:4; 28:3; 29:19; 30; 31:4; 32:29; 35:1; 36:14; **Ezr** 6:8; 10:25; **Neh** 2:7; 3:6; 26; 5:14; 17; 6:17; 9:12; 22; 11:19; 12:8; **Est** 5:12; **Job** 27:1; 29:1; 35:1; 40:1; **Ps** 19:11; 78:67; 105:16; **Eccl** 3:16; 5:9; 6:5; 12:9; **Is** 3:16; 7:10; 8:1; 19:9; 29:5; 30:26; 39:8; **Jer** 1:11; 2:1; 8:4; 20:5; 25:10; 33:1; 23; 37:18; 39:7; 40:13; 44:24; 48:35; **Eze** 3:1; 10; 4:3; 16; 5:14; 7:1; 11:1; 12:17; 16:20; 29; 17:11; 19:1; 20:12; 45; 22:1; 23:36; 38; 28:11; 35:1; 36:16; 37:16; 26; 45:1; 46:18; 48:22; **Zec** 4:8; 5:6; **Mt** 6:16; 18:15; **Lk** 16:21; **Acts** 2:26; 11:12; 19:26; **Rom** 5:20; 8:30; **1Cor** 4:2; 10:1; 15:1; **2Cor** 1:23; 8:1; **1Ti** 3:7; **Heb** 9:21; 11:36; **2Pet** 1:15

MOST

Gen 14:18; 19; 20; 22; **Ex** 26:33; 34; 29:37; 30:10; 29; 36; 40:10; **Lev** 2:3; 10; 6:17; 25; 29; 7:1; 6; 10:12; 17; 14:13; 21:22; 24:9; 27:28; **Num** 4:4; 19; 18:9(2); 10; 24:16; **Deut** 32:8; **2Sa** 22:14; 23:19; **1Kin** 6:16; 7:50; 8:6; **1Chr** 6:49; 23:13; **2Chr** 3:8; 10; 4:22; 5:7; 31:14; **Ezr** 2:63; **Neh** 7:65; **Est** 6:9; **Job** 34:17; **Ps** 7:17; 9:2; 21:6; 7; 45:3; 46:4; 47:2; 50:14; 56:2; 57:2; 73:11; 77:10; 78:17; 56; 82:6; 83:18; 91:1; 9; 92:1; 8; 107:11; **Prov** 20:6; **Song** 5:11; 16; 8:6; **Is** 14:14; 26:7; **Jer** 6:26; 50:31; 32; **Lam** 3:35; 38; 4:1; **Eze** 2:7; 23:12; 33:28; 29; 35:3; 7; 41:4; 42:13(2); 43:12; 44:13; 45:3; 48:12; **Dan** 3:20; 26; 4:17; 24; 25; 32; 34; 5:18; 21; 7:18; 22; 25(2); 27; 9:24; 11:15; 39; **Hos** 7:16; 11:7; 12:14; **Mic** 7:4; **Mt** 11:20; **Mk** 5:7; **Lk** 1:1; 3; 7:42; 43; 8:28; **Acts** 7:48; 16:17; 20:38; 23:26; 24:3; 26:5; 25; **1Cor** 14:27; 15:19; **2Cor** 12:9; **Heb** 7:1; **Jude** 20; **Rev** 18:12; 21:11

MUCH

Gen 23:9; 26:16; 30:43; 34:12; 41:49; 43:34; 44:1; 50:20; **Ex** 12:38; 42; 14:28; 16:5; 18; 22; 30:23; 36:5; 7; **Lev** 7:10; 13:7; 22; 27; 35; 14:21; **Num** 16:3; 7; 20:20; 21:4; 6; **Deut** 2:5; 3:19; 28:38; 31:27; **Josh** 11:4; 13:1; 19:9; 22:8(3); **Ruth** 1:13; **1Sa** 2:16; 14:30(2); 18:30; 19:2; 20:13; 23:3; 26:24(2); **2Sa** 4:11; 8:8; 13:34; 14:25; 16:11; 17:12; 18:33; **1Kin** 4:29; 8:27; 10:2; 12:28; **2Kin** 5:13; 10:18; 12:10; 21:6; 16; **1Chr** 18:8; 20:2; 22:4; 8; **2Chr** 2:16; 6:18; 14:13; 14; 17:13; 20:25; 24:11; 25:9; 13; 26:10; 27:3; 5; 28:8; 30:13; 32:4(2); 15; 27; 29; 33:6; 36:14; **Ezr** 7:22; 10:13; **Neh** 4:10; 6:16; 9:37; **Est** 1:18; **Job** 4:19; 9:14; 15:10; 16; 25:6; 31:25; 34:19; 42:10; **Ps** 19:10; 33:16; 35:18; 119:14; 107; **Prov** 7:21; 11:31; 13:23; 14:4; 15:6; 11; 16:16; 17:7; 19:7; 10; 24; 21:27; 25:16; 27; **Eccl** 1:18(2); 5:12; 17; 20; 7:16; 17; 9:18; 10:18; 12:12; **Song** 4:10; **Is** 21:7; 30:33; 56:12; **Jer** 2:22; 36; 40:12; **Eze** 14:21; 15:5; 17:15; 22:5; 23:32; 26:7; 33:31; **Dan** 4:12; 21; 7:5; 28; 11:13; **Joel** 2:6; **Jonah** 4:11; **Nah** 2:10; **Hag** 1:6; 9; **Mal** 3:13; **Mt** 6:7; 26; 30; 7:11; 10:25; 12:12; 13:5; 15:33; 26:9; **Mk** 1:45; 2:2; 3:20; 4:5; 5:10; 21; 24; 6:31; 34; 7:36; 10:14; 41; 12:41; **Lk** 5:15; 6:3; 34; 7:11; 12; 26; 47; 8:4; 9:37; 10:40; 11:13; 12:19; 24; 28; 48(3); 16:5; 7; 10(2); 18:13; 39; 19:15; 24:4; **Jn** 3:23; 6:10; 11; 7:12; 12:9; 12; 24; 14:30; 15:5; 8; **Acts** 5:8(2); 37; 7:5; 9:13; 10:2; 11:24; 26; 14:22; 15:7; 16:16; 18:10; 27; 19:2; 26; 20:2; 26:24; 27:9; 10; 16; **Rom** 1:15; 3:2; 5:9; 10; 15; 17; 20; 9:22; 11:12; 24; 12:18; 15:22; 16:6; 12; **1Cor** 2:3; 5:1; 6:3; 12:22; 16:19; **2Cor** 2:4; 3:9; 11; 6:4; 8:4; 15; 22; **Phil** 1:14; 2:12; **1Th** 1:5; 6; 2:2; **1Ti** 3:8; **2Ti** 4:14; **Titus** 2:3; **Philem** 1:8; 16; **Heb** 1:4; 7:22; 8:6; 9:14; 10:25; 29; 12:9; 20; 25; **Jas** 5:16; **1Pet** 1:7; **2Pet** 2:18; **Rev** 5:4; 8:3; 18:7(2); 19:1

MY

Gen 2:23(2); 4:9; 13; 23(4); 6:3; 18; 9:9; 11; 13; 15; 12:13(2); 19; 13:8; 15:2; 3; 16:2; 5(2); 8; 17:2; 4; 7; 9; 10; 13; 14; 19; 21; 18:3; 12; 19:2; 8; 18; 19; 20; 34; 20:2; 5(4); 9; 11; 12(4); 13(2); 15; 21:10; 23(2); 30; 22:7(2); 8; 18; 23:4(2); 6; 8(2); 11(2); 13; 15; 24:2; 3; 4(3); 6; 7(3); 8(2); 12(2); 14; 18; 27(3); 35; 36(2); 37(2); 38(3); 39; 40(3); 41(3); 42(2); 44; 48(3); 49; 54; 56(2); 65; 26:5(5); 7(2); 9; 24; 27:1; 2; 4; 7; 8(2); 11; 12; 13(2); 18(2); 19; 20; 21(2); 24; 25(2); 26; 27; 31; 34; 36(2); 37; 38(2); 41(2); 43(3); 46(2); 28:21(2); 29:4; 14(2); 15; 21(2); 32(2); 34; 30:3(2); 6; 8; 15(2); 16; 18(3); 20; 25; 26(3); 30; 32; 33(2); 31:5; 6; 7; 26; 28(2); 29; 30; 35; 36(2); 37(2); 39; 40; 41; 42(2); 43(4); 50(2); 32:4; 5; 9(2); 10; 11; 17; 18; 29; 30; 33:8; 9; 10(2); 11; 13; 14(2); 15; 34:8; 30; 35:3; 37:7(2); 16; 33; 35; 38:11; 26; 39:8(2); 15; 18; 40:9; 11; 16(2); 17; 41:9; 17; 22; 40(2); 51(2); 52; 42:10; 28(2); 36; 37(2); 38(2); 43:3; 5; 9; 14; 29; 44:2; 5; 7; 9; 10; 16(2); 17; 18(2); 19; 20; 22; 23; 24(2); 27(2); 29; 30; 32(2); 33; 34(2); 45:3; 9; 12(2); 13(3); 28; 46:31(2); 47:1(2); 6; 9(3); 18(3); 25; 29; 30; 48:9; 15(2); 16(2); 18; 19; 22(2); 49:3(3); 4; 6; 9; 26; 29(2); 50:5(3); 25; **Ex** 3:7; 10; 15(2); 20(2); 4:1; 10; 13; 18; 22(2); 23; 5:1; 6:3; 4; 5; 7:3(2); 4(2); 16; 8:1; 8; 20; 21; 22; 23; 9:1; 13; 14; 15; 16(2); 17; 27; 29; 10:1; 2; 3; 4; 17; 28(2); 11:9; 12:31; 13:15; 19; 15:2(4); 9(3); 16:4; 28(2); 18:4; 19; 19:5(2); 20:6; 24; 21:5(3); 22:24; 25; 23:18(2); 21; 27; 25:2; 29:43; 31:13; 32:10; 22; 33; 33:12; 14; 17; 19; 20; 22(2); 23(2); 34:9; 25; **Lev** 6:17; 15:31; 17:10; 18:4; 5(2); 26(2); 19:3; 12; 19; 30(2); 37(2); 20:3(3); 5; 6; 8; 22(2); 21:23; 22:2; 3; 31; 32; 23:2; 25:18(2); 21; 42; 55; 26:2(2); 3(2); 9; 11(2); 12; 15(4); 17; 25; 30; 42(3); 43(2); 44; **Num** 6:27; 10:30; 11:15; 23; 28; 29; 12:6; 7; 8; 11; 14:17; 22(3); 24; 34; 15:40; 20:19(2); 24; 21:2; 22:18; 38; 23:10; 12; 24:14; 25:11(3); 12; 27:14; 28:2(3); 32:25; 27; 36:2(2); **Deut** 2:28; 4:5; 10; 5:10; 29; 8:17; 9:4; 15; 17; 11:13; 18; 18:16; 18; 19(2); 20; 22:16; 17; 25:7(2); 26:5; 14(2); 31:16; 17(2); 18; 20; 27; 29; 32:1; 2(2); 20; 34; 39; 40; 41; 42; **Josh** 1:2; 7; 2:12; 13(4); 5:14; 7:11; 19; 21; 9:23; 14:8(2); 9; 11(2); 15:16; 22:2; 24:15; **Judg** 1:3; 7; 12; 2:1; 2; 20(2); 4:18; 5:9; 21; 6:10; 13; 15(3); 18; 8:19(2); 23; 9:9; 11(2); 13; 15; 17; 18; 29; 11:7; 12; 13; 19; 31; 35(2); 36; 37(2); 12:2; 3(3); 13:8; 18; 14:3; 16(3); 18(2); 15:1; 16:13; 17(2); 28; 17:2; 3(2); 13; 18:24; 19:23; 24; 20:4; 5; 6; 23; 28; **Ruth** 1:11(2); 12; 13; 16(2); 2:2; 8(2); 13; 21(2); 22; 3:1; 10; 11(2); 16; 18; 4:4; 6; 10; **1Sa** 1:15(2); 16; 26(2); 27; 2:1(2); 24; 28; 29(3); 32; 35; 3:6; 16; 4:16; 9:5; 16(3); 17; 21; 10:2; 12:2(2); 5; 14:29; 39; 40; 42; 15:11; 25; 30; 16:22; 18:17; 18(2); 21; 19:2; 3(2); 20:1(2); 2(2); 9; 12; 13(2); 15; 29(2); 42; 21:2; 8(2); 15(2); 22:3(2); 8(3); 12; 15; 23; 23:10; 12; 17(2); 24:6; 8; 10; 11(3); 15; 16; 21(3); 25:5; 11(4); 24; 25(2); 26(2); 27(2); 28(2); 29; 30; 31(3); 39; 41; 26:17(3); 18; 19; 20; 21(2); 23; 24; 25; 27:12; 28:9; 21(2); 29:6; 8; 9; 30:13; 15; 23; **2Sa** 1:9; 10; 26; 2:22; 3:7; 12; 13(2); 14; 18(2); 21; 28; 4:8; 9; 5:2; 7:5; 7; 8(2); 10; 11; 13; 14; 15; 18; 9:7; 10; 11(2); 11:11(3); 12:28; 13:4; 5(2); 6(2); 11; 12; 13; 20; 25; 26; 32; 33; 14:7(2); 9(2); 11; 12; 15; 16; 17(2); 18; 19(2); 20; 22; 24; 31; 15:7; 15; 21(2); 16:3; 4; 9; 11(3); 18:5; 18; 22; 28; 31; 32; 33(5); 19:4(3); 12(3); 13(2); 19(2); 20; 26(2); 27(2); 28(2); 30; 35; 37(3); 20:9; 22:2(3); 3(6); 7(4); 18; 19(2); 21(2); 22; 25(2); 29(2); 30; 33(2); 34(2); 35; 37(2); 39; 44; 47(2); 23:2; 5(3); 24:3(2); 17; 21; 22; 24; **1Kin** 1:2(2); 13(2); 17(2); 18; 20(2); 21(2); 24(2); 27(2); 29; 30(2); 31; 33; 35(2); 36; 37(2); 48; 2:15; 20; 24; 26(2); 31; 32; 38; 44; 3:6; 7(2); 14(3); 17; 20(2); 21(2); 22(2); 23(2); 26; 5:3; 4; 5(3); 6; 9(3); 6:12(4); 13; 8:15; 16(3); 17; 18(2); 19; 20; 24; 25(2); 26; 28; 29; 59; 9:3; 4(2); 6(2); 7(2); 13; 11:11(2); 13; 32; 33(3); 34(3); 36(2); 38(5); 12:10(2); 11(2); 14(2); 13:6; 30; 31; 14:7; 8(2); 15:19; 16:2(2); 17:1; 12; 18(2); 20; 21; 18:7; 10; 12; 13; 19:4(2); 10; 14; 20(2); 20:4; 6; 7(4); 9; 32; 34(2); 21:2; 3; 4; 6; 22:4(2); 49; **2Kin** 1:13; 14; 2:12(2); 19; 3:7(2); 4:1(2); 16; 19(2); 28; 29(2); 5:3; 6; 13; 18(2); 20; 22; 6:8; 12; 15; 21; 26; 28; 29; 8:5; 12; 9:7; 32; 10:6; 9; 15; 16; 13:14(2); 14:9; 17:13(3); 18:23; 24; 27; 19:12; 23; 24; 28(2); 34; 20:5; 6; 15; 19; 21:4; 7; 8; 15; 22:17; 23:27(2); **1Chr** 4:10; 11:2(2); 19; 16:22; 17:4; 6; 7(2); 9; 10; 13(2); 14; 25; 21:3(3); 17(2); 23; 22:5; 7(3); 8(2); 10(2); 11; 14; 28:2(2); 3; 4(3); 5(2); 6(3); 7(2); 9; 20; 29:1; 2(2); 3(3); 14; 17; 19; **2Chr** 1:8; 9; 11; 2:3; 4; 7; 8; 13; 14; 15; 6:4; 5(3); 6(2); 7; 8(2); 9; 10; 15; 16(3); 19; 40; 7:13; 14(3); 16; 17(2); 19(2); 20(3); 8:11; 10:10(2); 11(2); 14(2); 12:7; 8; 16:3; 18:3; 13; 25:16; 18; 29:11; 32:13; 14; 15; 33:4; 7; 34:25; **Ezr** 7:13; 28; 9:3(4); 5(6); 6(3); 10:3; **Neh** 1:2; 6; 9(2); 2:3(2); 5; 8; 12(2); 18; 4:16; 23(2); 5:10(2); 13; 14; 16; 17; 19; 6:9; 14; 19; 7:2; 5; 13:14(3); 19; 22; 29; 31; **Est** 4:16; 5:7(2); 8(2); 7:3(4); 4(2); 8:6(2); **Job** 1:5; 8; 21; 2:3; 3:10; 24(2); 4:14; 15(2); 5:8; 6:2(2); 3; 4; 7(2); 8; 11(2); 12(2); 13; 15; 21; 24; 29; 30(2); 7:5(2); 6; 7; 11(3); 13(3); 15(2); 16; 19; 21; 9:14; 15; 16; 17; 18; 21(2); 25; 27(2); 28; 30; 10:1(4); 6; 12; 15; 20; 11:4; 13:6(2); 14(3); 16; 17(2); 18; 19; 23(2); 26; 27(3); 14:14(2); 16(2); 17; 16:4; 5(2); 6; 7; 8(2); 12; 13(2); 15(2); 16(2); 17; 18(2); 19(2); 20; 17:1(2); 7; 11(3); 13; 14(3); 15(2); 19:2; 5; 8(2); 9(2); 12; 13; 14(2); 15; 16(2); 17(2); 19; 20(4); 21; 22; 23; 25; 26(2); 27; 20:2; 3(2); 21:2; 4(2); 6; 23:2(3); 4(2); 7; 11; 12; 16; 17; 24:25; 27:2(2); 3(2); 4(2); 6(2); 29:3; 4(2); 5; 6; 7; 14; 18(2); 19(2); 20(3); 21; 22(2); 24; 30:1; 10; 11; 12(2); 13(2); 15(2); 16; 17(2); 18(3); 22; 26; 27; 30(2); 31(2); 31:4(2); 5; 7; 8; 9; 10; 13(2); 17; 18(2); 20; 21(2); 22; 24(2); 25; 27(3); 30; 31; 32; 33(2); 35; 36; 37; 38; 32:17; 19; 20; 22; 33:1(2); 2(3); 3(3); 7(2); 11(2); 34:2; 5; 6(2); 16; 36; 35:2; 3; 10; 36:3(2); 4; 37:1; 38:10; 40:4; 8; 42:7(2); 8(3); **Ps** 2:6(2); 7; 3:2; 3; 4; 7; 4:1(2); 2; 7; 5:1(2); 2(3); 3(2); 8; 6:2; 3; 4; 6(4); 8; 9(2); 7:1(2); 2; 3(2); 5(2); 8; 10; 9:1; 4(2); 13; 11:1(2); 13:2(2); 3; 5; 14:4; 16:1; 2(3); 3; 4; 5(2); 7; 8; 9(3); 10; 17:1(2); 2; 3; 5(2); 6; 9; 13; 18:1; 2(8); 6(4); 17; 18(2); 20(2); 21; 24(2); 28(3); 29; 32; 33(2); 34; 36(2); 38; 46(2); 19:14(4); 22:1(3); 2; 9; 10(2); 14(3); 15(3); 16(2); 17; 18(2); 19; 20(2); 22; 25(2); 23:1; 3; 5(2); 6; 25:1; 2; 5; 7(2); 15; 17(2); 18(2); 20(2); 26:2(2); 9(2); 12; 27:1(3); 2(2); 3; 4; 7; 8(2); 9(2); 10(2); 28:1; 2(2); 6; 7(5); 30:1; 2; 3; 6; 7; 9; 10; 11(2); 12(2); 31:1; 2; 3(2); 4; 5; 7(2); 8; 9(2); 10(4); 11; 13; 14; 15; 22(2); 32:3(2); 4; 5(3); 7; 34:1; 2; 4; 35:1; 3; 4(2); 7; 9; 10; 11; 12; 13(3); 14; 17(2); 23(4); 24; 27; 28; 36:1; 38:3(3); 5(2); 7(2); 8; 9(2); 10(2); 11(4); 12(2); 15; 16; 17; 18; 21; 22; 39:1(3); 2(2); 3(2); 4; 5; 7; 8; 9; 12(4); 40:1; 2(2); 3; 5; 8(2); 9; 10; 12; 14; 17(3); 41:4; 7; 9; 42:1; 2; 3(2); 4; 5; 6(2); 8(2); 9; 10; 11(3); 43:1; 2; 4(2); 5(3); 44:4; 6(2); 15(2); 45:1(2); 49:3(2); 4; 5; 15; 50:5; 7; 16(2); 17; 51:1; 2; 3(2); 5; 9; 14(2); 15(2); 53:4; 54:2(2); 3; 4; 55:1(2); 2; 4; 8; 13; 17; 18; 56:4; 5; 6(2); 8(2); 11; 13(2); 57:1(2); 4; 6(2); 7(2); 8; 59:1; 3(3); 4; 9; 10(2); 11; 16(2); 17(3); 60:7; 8(2); 61:1(2); 2; 5; 8; 62:1(2); 2(3); 5(2); 6(3); 7(4); 63:1(3); 3; 4; 5(2); 6; 7; 8; 9; 64:1(3); 66:13; 14(2); 16; 17(2); 18; 19; 20; 68:22; 24(2); 69:1; 3(3); 5(2); 6(2); 7; 8(2); 10(2); 11; 13; 18; 19(3); 20; 21(2); 70:2(2); 5(2); 71:1; 3(3); 4; 5(3); 6(2); 7; 8; 9; 10; 12(2); 13(2); 15; 17; 21; 22; 23(2); 24(2); 73:2(2); 13(2); 21(2); 23; 26(4); 28; 74:12; 77:1(2); 2(3); 3; 6(2); 10; 78:1(3); 2; 81:8; 11(2); 13(2); 14; 83:13; 84:2(3); 3(2); 8; 10; 86:2(2); 4; 6(2); 7; 11; 12(2); 13; 14; 87:7; 88:1; 2(2); 3(2); 9; 13; 14; 15; 89:1; 3(2); 20(2); 21; 24(3); 26(3); 27; 28(2); 30(2); 31(2); 33(2); 34(2); 35; 47; 50; 91:2(3); 9; 14; 16; 92:10; 11(2); 15; 94:17(2); 18; 19(2); 22(3); 95:9; 10; 11(2); 101:2; 7(2); 102:1(2); 3(2); 4(2); 5(3); 9; 11; 23(2); 24(2); 103:1; 2; 22; 104:1(2); 33(2); 34; 35; 105:15; 108:1(2); 8; 9(2); 109:1; 4(2); 5; 20; 22; 24(2); 26; 30; 110:1(2); 111:1; 116:1(2); 4; 7; 8(2); 11; 14; 16; 18; 118:6; 7(2); 14(2); 21; 28(2); 119:5; 10; 13; 20; 24(2); 25; 26; 28; 32; 34; 36; 39; 43; 48; 50(2); 54(2); 57; 58; 59(2); 69; 76; 77; 80; 81; 92; 97; 99(2); 101; 103(2); 105(2); 108; 109(2); 111; 114(2); 115; 116; 120; 129; 131; 133; 139; 143; 145; 149; 154; 157; 161; 167; 168; 169; 170; 171; 172; 174; 175; 120:1; 2; 6; 121:1; 2; 122:8; 129:1; 2; 3; 130:2(2); 5; 6; 131:1; 2; 132:3(2); 12(2); 14; 137:5; 6(3); 138:1; 3; 139:2(2); 3(3); 4; 8; 13(2); 14; 15; 16(2); 23(2); 140:4; 6(2); 7(2); 141:1; 2(2); 3(2); 4; 5(2); 6; 8(2); 142:1(3); 2(2); 3(2); 4(2); 5(2); 6(2); 7; 143:1(2); 3(2); 4(2); 6(2); 7; 8; 10; 11; 12; 144:1(3); 2(6); 145:1; 21; 146:1; 2; **Prov** 1:8; 10; 15; 23(3); 24; 25(2); 30(2); 2:1(3); 3:1(3); 11; 21; 4:2; 3(2); 4(2); 5; 10(2); 20(3); 5:1(3); 7; 12; 13; 20; 6:1; 3; 20; 7:1(3); 2(2); 4; 6(2); 14; 16; 17; 24; 8:4; 6; 7(2); 8; 10; 19(2); 31; 32; 34(2); 9:5; 19:27; 20:9(2); 22:17; 23:15(2); 16; 19; 26(2); 24:13; 21; 27:11(2); 30:9; 31:2(3); **Eccl** 1:13; 16; 17; 2:7; 9; 10(5); 11; 15(2); 18; 19; 20; 4:8; 7:15; 28; 8:9; 9:1; 12:12; **Song** 1:6; 7; 9; 12; 13(2); 14; 15; 16; 2:2; 3(2); 6; 7; 8; 9; 10(3); 13(2); 14; 16; 17; 3:1(2); 2; 3; 4(2); 5; 4:1; 7; 8; 9(4); 10(2); 11; 12(2); 16(2); 5:1(9); 2(8); 3(2); 4(2); 5(3); 6(3); 7; 8; 10; 16(2); 6:2; 3(2); 4; 9(2); 12; 7:9; 10; 11; 12; 13; 8:1(2); 2(2); 3; 4; 10; 12; 14; **Is** 1:3; 12; 14; 25; 3:7; 12(2); 15; 5:1(3); 3; 4; 5; 13; 6:7; 7:13; 8:4(2); 16; 10:2; 6; 8; 10; 13(2); 14; 24; 11:9; 12:2(4); 13:3(3); 14:13; 25(2); 15:5; 16:9; 11; 18:4(2); 19:25(2); 20:3; 21:3; 4(2); 8(2); 10(2); 22:4; 20; 24:16(2); 25:1; 26:9(2); 19; 20; 27:5; 28:23(2); 29:23; 30:1; 2; 32:9(2); 13; 18; 33:13; 34:5(2); 16; 36:8; 9; 12; 19; 20(2); 37:12; 24; 25; 29(2); 35; 38:10(2); 12; 13; 15(2); 16; 17(2); 20; 39:4; 8; 40:1; 27(3); 41:8(2); 9; 10; 25; 42:1(3); 8(3); 14; 19(2); 43:4; 6(2); 7(2); 10(2); 12; 13; 20(2); 21; 44:1; 2; 3(2); 8; 17; 20; 21(2); 28(2); 45:4; 11(2); 12; 13(2); 23; 46:10(2); 11; 13(3); 47:6; 48:3; 5(2); 9(2); 11(2); 12; 13; 18; 49:1(2); 2; 3; 4(4); 5(2); 6(2); 11(2); 14; 16; 21; 22; 50:1; 2(2); 6(3); 7; 51:4(3); 5(2); 6(2); 7; 8(2); 16(2); 22; 52:4; 5(2); 6(2); 13; 53:8; 11; 54:8; 10(2); 55:8(2); 9(2); 11(2); 56:1(2); 4(2); 5; 6; 7(2); 57:11; 13; 14; 21; 58:1; 2; 13; 59:21(3); 60:7; 10(2); 13(2); 21(2); 61:10(2); 62:1; 9; 63:3(3); 4; 5; 6; 8; 65:1; 2; 3; 5; 8; 9(2); 10; 11; 13(3); 14; 15; 19; 22; 25; 66:1(3); 2; 5; 18; 19(3); 20; **Jer** 1:9(2); 12; 16; 2:7; 11; 13; 19; 27; 31; 32; 3:4(2); 13; 19; 4:1; 4; 11; 19(6); 20(2); 22; 31; 5:9; 14; 22; 26; 29; 31; 6:8; 12; 14; 19(2); 26; 27; 7:10; 11; 12(3); 14; 15; 20; 23(2); 25; 30(2); 31; 8:7; 11; 18; 19; 21; 22; 9:1(2); 2; 7; 9; 13(2); 10:19(2); 20(5); 11:4(2); 7; 10(2); 15; 20; 12:7; 10(3); 14; 16(4); 13:2; 10; 17; 14:14; 15; 17; 15:1(2); 6; 7; 10; 15; 18(2); 19; 16:5; 11; 17; 18; 19(3); 21(2); 17:3; 14; 16; 17; 18:2; 10(2); 15; 20; 22; 19:5; 15; 20:9; 10(2); 11; 12; 14; 15; 17(2); 18; 21:10; 12; 22:18; 21; 24; 23:1; 2(2); 3; 9; 11; 13; 22(3); 25; 27(3); 28(2); 29; 30; 32; 39; 24:7; 25:8; 9; 13; 15; 29; 26:4; 5; 27:5(2); 6; 15; 29:9; 10; 19(2); 21; 23; 32; 30:3; 10; 22; 31:1; 9; 14(2); 18; 19(2); 20(2); 26; 32; 33(2); 32:7; 8; 9; 31(2); 34; 35; 37; 38; 40; 41(2); 33:5(2); 20(2); 21(3); 22; 24; 25; 26; 34:15(2); 16; 18; 35:13; 15; 36:6; 37:20(2); 38:9; 26; 39:16; 42:18(2); 43:10; 44:4; 6; 10(2); 11; 26(2); 29; 45:3(2); 46:27; 28; 49:25; 37; 38; 50:6; 51:20; 34; 35(2); 45; **Lam** 1:9; 12; 13(2); 14(3); 15(2); 16(2); 18(3); 19(2); 20; 21; 22(3); 2:11(3); 21(2); 22; 3:4(3); 7; 8; 9(2); 11; 13; 14; 16; 17; 18(2); 19; 20; 21; 24(2); 48; 51; 53; 56(3); 58(2); 59(2); 4:3; 6; 10; **Eze** 1:28; 2:2; 7; 3:2; 3; 4; 10; 14; 17; 23; 24; 4:14(3); 5:6(4); 7(2); 11; 13(3); 6:12; 14; 7:8; 14; 22(2); 8:6; 9:6; 8; 10:2; 13; 19; 11:12(2); 13; 20(2); 12:7(2); 13(2); 28; 13:9; 10; 13(2); 15; 18; 19(2); 21; 23; 14:8(2); 9(2); 11; 19; 21; 15:7(2); 16:8; 14; 17(2); 19; 21; 27; 42(2); 60; 62; 17:19; 20(2); 18:9(2); 17(2); 19; 21; 25; 29; 20:8(2); 9; 11(2); 12; 13(4); 14; 15; 16(3); 19(2); 20; 21(5); 22; 24(3); 39; 44; 21:3; 4; 5; 10; 12(2); 17; 31; 22:8; 20; 21; 22; 26(2); 31; 23:18(2); 25; 38(2); 39; 24:13; 18; 21; 25:3; 14(4); 17; 28:25; 29:3; 30:15; 24; 25; 32:3(2); 10; 32; 33:7; 22(2); 31; 34:6(2); 8(5); 10(2); 11; 12; 15; 17; 19; 22; 23; 24; 26; 30; 31(2); 36:5(2); 6(2); 8; 12; 18; 20; 23; 27(3); 28; 37:12; 13; 14; 23; 24(3); 25(2); 26; 27(2); 28; 38:14; 16(2); 17; 18(2); 19(2); 20; 21; 39:7(3); 17; 19; 20; 21(3); 23; 24; 25; 29(2); 43:3; 7(3); 8(3); 44:4; 7(5); 8(2); 9; 11; 13; 15; 16(3); 23; 24(4); 45:8(2); 9; 46:18; 48:11; **Dan** 1:10(2); 2:3; 23; 3:14; 15; 4:4; 5(2); 8; 9; 10; 13(2); 18; 19; 24; 27; 30(2); 36(5); 5:13; 6:22; 26; 7:2; 15(3); 28(3); 8:17; 18; 9:3; 4(2); 18; 19; 20(5); 10:3; 8; 9(2); 10(2); 15; 16(4); 17(2); 19; 12:8; **Hos** 1:9; 10; 2:2; 5(6); 7; 9(4); 12(2); 23(3); 4:6; 8; 12; 5:10; 15(2); 6:5; 11; 7:2; 12; 8:1(2); 2; 12; 9:8; 17; 10:10; 11:1; 7; 8; 12:8; 13:11; **Joel** 1:6; 7(2); 13; 2:1; 25; 26; 27; 28; 29; 3:2(3); 3; 5(3); 17; **Amos** 2:7; 7:8; 15; 8:2; 9:3; 10; 12; 14; **Obad** 13; 16; **Jonah** 1:12; 2:2; 5; 6(2); 7(2); 4:2(2); 3; **Mic** 1:9; 2:4; 7; 8; 9(2); 3:3; 5; 6:3; 5; 7(4); 16; 7:1; 7(2); 9; **Hab** 1:12; 2:1; 3:16(3); 18; 19(3); **Zeph** 2:8; 9(2); 12; 3:8(3); 10(2); 11; **Hag** 2:5; 23; **Zec** 1:6(3); 9; 16; 17; 2:11; 3:7(4); 8; 4:4; 5; 6; 13; 5:4; 6:4; 8; 8:7; 8; 11:4; 8; 10(2); 12(2); 12:5; 13:5; 6; 7(2); 9(3); 14:5; **Mal** 1:6(2); 11(3); 14; 2:2; 4; 5(2); 9; 3:1; 17; 4:2; 4; **Mt** 2:6; 15; 3:17; 5:11; 7:21; 8:6; 8(2); 9; 21; 9:18; 10:18; 22; 32; 33; 39; 11:10; 27; 29; 30(2); 12:18(4); 44; 48(2); 49(2); 50(2); 13:30; 35; 15:13; 22; 16:17; 18; 25; 17:5; 15; 18:5; 10; 19; 20; 21; 35; 19:20; 29; 20:21; 23(4); 21:13; 28; 37; 22:4(3); 44(2); 24:5; 9; 35; 36; 48; 25:27(2); 34; 40; 26:12(2); 18(2); 26; 28; 29; 38; 39; 42; 53; 27:35(2); 46(2); 28:10; **Mk** 1:2; 11; 3:33(2); 34(2); 35(2); 5:9; 23; 30; 6:23; 8:35; 38; 9:7; 17; 37; 39; 41; 10:20; 29; 40(2); 51; 11:17; 12:6; 36(2); 13:6; 9; 13; 31; 14:8; 14; 22; 24; 34; 15:34(2); 16:17; **Lk** 1:18; 20; 25; 43; 44; 46; 47(2); 2:49; 3:22; 6:47; 7:6; 7; 8; 27; 44(2); 45; 46(2); 8:21(2); 9:24; 26; 35; 38; 48; 59; 61; 10:22; 29; 40; 11:7; 24; 12:4; 13; 17; 18(3); 19; 45; 14:23; 24; 26; 27; 33; 15:6; 17; 18; 24; 29; 16:3; 5; 24; 27; 18:21; 41; 19:8; 23(2); 46; 20:13; 42(2); 21:8; 12; 17; 33; 22:11; 19; 20; 28; 29; 30(2); 42; 23:46; 24:39(2); 49; **Jn** 2:16; 3:29; 4:34; 49; 5:17; 24; 30; 31; 43; 47; 6:32; 51; 54(2); 55(2); 56(2); 65; 7:6; 8; 16; 8:14; 16; 19(2); 21; 28; 31(2); 37; 38; 43(2); 49; 51; 52; 54(2); 56; 10:14; 15; 16; 17(2); 18; 25; 26; 27(2); 28; 29(2); 30; 32; 37; 11:21; 32; 12:7; 20(2); 27; 47; 48; 13:6; 8; 9(3); 35; 37; 38; 14:2; 7; 12; 13; 14; 15; 20; 21(2); 23(2); 24; 26; 27; 28; 15:1; 7; 8(2); 9; 10(3); 11; 12; 14; 15; 16; 20; 21; 23; 24; 16:5; 10; 23; 24; 26; 17:13; 24; 18:11; 36(4); 37; 19:24(2); 20:13; 17(4); 21; 25(2); 27(2); 28(2); 21:15; 16; 17; **Acts** 2:14; 17; 18(3); 25(2); 26(3); 27; 34(2); 7:34; 49(3); 50; 59; 9:15; 16; 10:30; 11:8; 13:22; 33; 15:7; 17; 19; 16:15; 20:24(2); 25; 29; 34; 22:1; 6; 24:14; 17; 25:26; 26:4(2); 10; 28:19; **Rom** 1:8; 9(3); 2:16; 3:7; 7:4; 18; 23(3); 9:1; 2; 3(2); 17(2); 25(2); 26; 10:1; 21; 11:3; 14; 27; 15:14; 24(3); 31; 16:3; 4; 5; 7(2); 8; 9; 11; 21(2); 25; **1Cor** 1:4; 11; 2:4(2); 4:14; 17(2); 5:4; 7:25; 40; 8:13(2); 9:1; 15; 17; 18(2); 27; 10:14; 29; 11:24; 25; 33; 13:3(2); 14:14(2); 18; 19(2); 15:58; 16:6; 18; 24; **2Cor** 1:16; 23; 2:3; 13(3); 6:13; 16; 18; 7:4(2); 8:10; 23; 11:1; 12:9(3); 21; **Gal** 1:13; 14(2); 15; 4:14(2); 19; 20; 6:17; **Eph** 1:16; 3:4; 13; 14; 6:10; 19; 21; **Phil** 1:3; 7(3); 8; 13; 14; 16; 19; 20(3); 22; 26; 2:2; 12(3); 25(2); 3:1; 8; 4:1(3); 3; 14; 16; 19; **Col** 1:24(2); 2:1; 4:7; 10; 11; 18; **1Ti** 1:2; 11; **2Ti** 1:2; 3(2); 6; 16; 2:1; 8; 3:10; 4:6; 7; 16; **Philem** 1:4(2); 10(2); 20; 23; 24; **Heb** 1:5; 13; 2:12; 13; 3:9; 10; 11(2); 4:3(2); 5; 5:5; 8:9; 10; 10:16; 34; 38; 12:5; 13:6; **Jas** 1:2; 16; 19; 2:1; 3; 5; 14; 18(2); 3:1; 10; 12; 5:10; 12; **1Pet** 5:13; **2Pet** 1:14; 15; 17; **1Jn** 2:1; 3:13; 18; **3Jn** 4; **Rev** 1:20; 2:3; 13(3); 16; 20; 26; 27; 3:5; 8(2); 10; 12(5); 16; 20; 21(2); 10:10(2); 11:3; 18:4; 21:7; 22:12

MYSELF

Gen 3:10; 22:16; **Ex** 19:4; **Num** 8:17; 12:6; **Deut** 1:9; 12; 10:5; **Judg** 16:20; **Ruth** 4:6; **1Sa** 13:12; 20:5; 25:33; **2Sa** 18:2; 22:24; **1Kin** 18:15; 22:30; **2Kin** 5:18(2); **2Chr** 7:12; 18:29; **Neh** 5:7; **Est** 5:12; 6:6; **Job** 6:10; 7:20; 9:20; 27; 30; 10:1; 13:20; 19:4; 27; 31:17; 29; 42:6; **Ps** 18:23; 35:14; 55:12; 57:8; 101:2; 108:2; 109:4; 119:16; 47; 52; 131:1; 2; **Eccl** 2:3; 12; 14; 19; **Is** 33:10; 42:14; 43:21; 44:24; 45:23; **Jer** 8:18; 21:5; 22:5; 49:13; **Eze** 14:7; 20:5; 9; 29:3; 35:11; 38:23(2); **Dan** 10:3; **Mic** 6:6; **Hab** 3:16; **Zec** 7:3; **Lk** 7:7; 24:39; **Jn** 5:31; 7:17; 28; 8:14; 18; 28; 42; 54; 10:18; 12:49; 14:3; 10; 21; 17:19; **Acts** 10:26; 20:24; 24:10; 16; 25:22; 26:2(2); 9; **Rom** 7:25; 9:3; 11:4; 15:14; 16:2; **1Cor** 4:4; 6; 7:7; 9:19; 27; **2Cor** 2:1; 10:1; 11:7; 9(2); 16; 12:5; 13; **Gal** 2:18; **Phil** 2:24; 3:13; **Philem** 1:17

NAMELY

Lev 1:10; **Num** 1:32; 9:15; 13:11; 31:8; **Deut** 4:43; 13:7; 20:17; **Judg** 3:3; 8:35; **1Chr** 6:57; 61; 9:23; 23:6; **Ezr** 10:18; **Neh** 12:35; **Est** 8:12; **Eccl** 5:13; **Is** 7:20; **Jer** 26:22; **Mk** 12:31; **Acts** 15:22; **Rom** 13:9

NEAR

Gen 12:11; 18:23; 19:9; 20; 20:4; 27:21; 22; 25(2); 26; 27; 29:10; 33:3; 6; 7(2); 37:18; 43:19; 44:18; 45:4(2); 10; 48:10; 13; **Ex** 12:48; 13:17; 14:20; 16:9; 19:22; 20:21; 24:2; 28:43; 30:20; 40:32; **Lev** 9:5; 10:4; 5; 18:6; 12; 13; 17; 20:19; 21:2; **Num** 3:6; 5:16; 16:5(2); 9; 10; 40; 17:13; 26:3; 63; 31:12; 48; 32:16; 33:48; 50; 34:15; 35:1; 36:1; 13; **Deut** 1:22; 4:11; 5:23; 27; 16:21; 21:5; 25:11; **Josh** 3:4; 10:24(2); 15:46; 17:4; 18:13; 21:1; **Judg** 18:22; 19:13; 20:24; 34; **Ruth** 2:20; 3:9; 12; **1Sa** 4:19; 7:10; 9:18; 10:20; 21; 14:36; 38; 17:16; 40; 41; 30:21; **2Sa** 1:15; 14:30; 18:25; 19:42; 20:16; 17; **1Kin** 8:46; 18:30(2); 36; 21:2; 22:24; **2Kin** 4:27; 5:13; **2Chr** 6:36; 18:23; 21:16; 29:31; **Est** 5:2; 9:1; **Job** 31:37; 33:22; 41:16; **Ps** 22:11; 32:9; 73:28; 75:1; 107:18;

119:151; 169; 148:14; **Prov** 7:8; 10:14; 27:10; **Is** 13:22; 26:17; 29:13; 33:13; 34:1; 41:1(2); 5; 45:20; 21; 46:13; 48:16; 50:8(2); 51:5; 54:14; 55:6; 56:1; 57:3; 19; 65:5; **Jer** 12:2; 25:26; 30:21; 42:1; 46:3; 48:16; 24; 52:25; **Lam** 3:57; 4:18; **Eze** 6:12; 7:7; 12; 9:1; 6; 11:3; 18:6; 22:4; 5; 30:3(2); 40:46; 44:13(2); 15; 16; 45:4; **Dan** 3:8; 26; 6:12; 7:13; 16; 8:17; 9:7; **Joel** 3:9; 14; **Amos** 6:3; **Obad** 15; **Zeph** 1:14(2); 3:2; **Mal** 3:5; **Mt** 21:34; 24:33; **Mk** 13:28; **Lk** 15:1; 18:40; 19:41; 21:8; 22:47; 24:15; **Jn** 3:23; 4:5; 11:54; **Acts** 7:31; 8:29; 9:3; 10:24; 21:33; 23:15; 27:27; **Heb** 10:22

NEARER

Ruth 3:12; **Rom** 13:11

NEITHER

Gen 3:3; 8:21; 9:11(2); 17:5; 19:17; 21:26(2); 22:12; 24:16; 29:7; 39:9; 45:6; **Ex** 4:8; 9; 10; 5:2; 23; 7:22; 23; 8:32; 9:29; 35; 10:6; 14; 23; 12:39; 46; 13:7; 16:24; 20:23; 26; 22:21; 25; 31; 23:2; 3; 13; 18; 24:2; 30:9; 32; 32:18; 34:3(2); 24; 25; 28; 36:6; **Lev** 2:13; 3:17; 5:11; 7:18; 10:6; 11:43; 44; 17:12; 18:3; 17; 18; 21; 23(2); 26; 19:9; 10; 11(2); 12; 13; 16; 19; 26; 27; 31; 21:5; 7; 11; 12; 15; 22:24; 25; 32; 23:14; 22; 25:4; 5; 11; 26:1(2); 6; 20; 44; 27:33; **Num** 1:49; 5:13; 6:3; 11:19; 14:9; 23; 16:15; 18:3; 20; 22; 32; 20:5; 17; 21:5; 23:19; 21; 23; 25; 35:23; 36:9; **Deut** 1:21; 29; 42; 2:9; 27; 4:2; 28; 31; 5:18; 19; 20; 21(2); 7:3; 16; 26; 8:3; 4; 9:9; 18; 13:8(3); 16:4; 19; 22; 17:17(2); 18:16; 20:3; 21:4; 7; 22:5; 24:5; 15; 16; 26:13; 14; 28:36; 39; 64; 65; 29:6; 14; 30:11; 13; 31:8(2); 32:28; 39; 33:9; **Josh** 1:9; 2:11; 5:1; 12; 6:10; 7:12; 8:1; 11:14; 23:7(2); **Judg** 1:27; 29; 30; 31; 33; 2:23; 6:4; 8:23; 35; 11:34; 13:6; 7; 14; 23; 20:8; **Ruth** 2:8; **1Sa** 1:15; 2:2; 3:7; 4:20; 5:5; 12:4; 13:22; 16:8; 9; 20:27; 21:8; 24:11; 25:7; 15; 26:12; 27:9; 11; 28:6; 15; 30:15; 19(3); **2Sa** 1:21; 2:28; 7:10; 22; 12:17; 13:22; 14:7; 14; 18:3; 19:6; 19; 24; 20:1; 21:4; 10; 24:24; **1Kin** 3:11; 12; 26; 5:4; 6:7; 7:47; 11:2; 12:16; 13:8; 16; 16:11; 17:14; 16; 18:29; 22:31; **2Kin** 3:17; 4:23; 31; 5:17; 6:19; 7:10; 10:14; 12:8; 13:7; 23; 17:34; 38; 18:30; 21:8; 23:25; **1Chr** 4:27; 17:9; 20; 19:19; 27:24; **2Chr** 1:11; 12; 6:5; 9:9; 13:20; 20:12; 25:4; 26:18; 30:3; 32:15; 33:8; 34:2; 28; 35:18; **Ezr** 9:12; 10:13; **Neh** 2:12(2); 16; 4:11; 23; 5:5; 16; 8:10; 11; 9:17; 19; 34; 35; **Est** 2:7; 3:8; 4:16; **Job** 3:4; 9; 26(2); 5:4; 6; 21; 22; 7:10; 8:20; 9:33; 15:29(2); 18:19; 20:9; 21:9; 23:12; 17; 28:13; 15; 19; 31:30; 32:9; 14; 21; 33:7; 9; 34:12; 35:13; 36:26; 39:7; 17; 22; 24; **Ps** 5:4; 6:1; 16:10; 18:37; 22:24; 26:4; 27:9; 33:17; 35:19; 37:1; 38:1; 3; 44:3; 6; 17; 18; 55:12; 69:15; 73:5; 74:9; 75:6; 78:37; 81:9; 82:5; 86:8; 91:10; 92:6; 94:7; 14; 103:9; 109:12; 115:7; 17; 121:4; 129:8; 131:1; 135:17; **Prov** 2:19; 3:11; 25; 4:5; 6:25; 35; 15:12; 22:22; 23:6; 24:1; 19; 27:10; 30:3; 8; **Eccl** 1:11; 4:8(3); 5:6; 6:10; 7:16; 17; 8:8(2); 13; 16; 9:5; 6; 11; **Song** 8:7; **Is** 1:6(2); 23; 2:4; 7(2); 3:7; 5:12; 27; 7:4; 7; 12; 8:12; 9:13; 17; 10:7; 11:3; 13:20(3); 16:10; 17:8; 19:15; 22:11; 23:4; 26:18; 28:27; 29:22; 31:1; 33:20; 21; 36:15; 40:28; 42:8; 24; 43:2; 10; 18; 23; 24; 44:8; 19; 47:7; 8; 49:10; 50:5; 51:7; 18; 53:9; 54:4; 10; 55:8; 56:3(2); 57:16; 59:1; 6; 9; 60:19; 20; 62:4; 64:4; 9; 66:19; 24; **Jer** 2:6; 3:16(4); 17; 4:28; 5:12(2); 15; 24; 6:15; 7:6; 16(2); 31; 8:12; 9:10; 13; 16; 23; 10:5; 11:14; 14:13; 14(2); 15:10; 16:2; 4; 5; 6; 7(2); 13; 17; 17:8; 16; 22(2); 23; 18:23; 19:4; 5; 21:7; 22:3; 10; 23:4; 25:33; 29:8; 32; 30:10; 32:23; 35; 33:18; 22; 34:14; 35:6; 7; 9; 36:24; 37:2; 38:16; 42:13; 44:3; 10; 48:11; 49:18; 31; 50:39; 40; 51:43; 62; **Eze** 2:6; 3:9; 4:14; 5:7(2); 11(2); 7:4; 9; 11; 13; 19; 8:18; 9:5; 10; 11:11; 12; 13:5; 9(2); 15; 14:11; 16; 18; 20; 16:4; 16; 49; 51; 17:17; 18:6(3); 8; 15; 16(2); 20; 20:8; 17; 18; 21; 22:26; 23:8; 24:14(2); 16(2); 29:11; 15; 31:14(2); 32:13; 33:12; 34:4(4); 8; 10; 28; 29; 36:14; 15(3); 37:22; 23; 38:11; 39:10; 29; 43:7; 44:20; 21; 22; 47:12; 48:14; **Dan** 3:27; 6:4; 18; 8:4; 9:6; 10; 10:3(2); 17; 11:6; 15(2); 17; 20; 37; **Hos** 2:2; 4:15; 9:4; 14:3; **Joel** 2:2; 8; **Amos** 2:14; 15(2); 5:22; 7:14; **Obad** 12(2); 14(2); **Jonah** 3:7; 4:10; **Mic** 2:3; 4:3; 12; **Hab** 2:5; 3:17; **Zeph** 1:12; 18; 3:13; **Zec** 8:10; 11:16; 13:4; **Mal** 1:10(2); 3:11; 4:1; **Mt** 5:15; 34; 35; 36; 6:15; 20; 26; 28; 7:6; 18; 9:17; 10:9; 10(2); 11:18; 27; 12:4; 19; 32(2); 13:13; 16:9; 10; 21:27; 22:16; 30; 46; 23:10; 13(2); 24:18; 20; 25:13; **Mk** 4:22; 5:4; 8:14; 17; 26; 11:26; 33; 12:21; 24; 25; 13:11; 15; 19; 32; 14:40; 59; 68; 16:8; 13; **Lk** 1:15; 3:14; 6:43; 7:7; 33; 8:17; 27; 43; 9:3(4); 10:4; 11:33; 12:2; 22; 24(2); 29; 33; 47; 14:12; 35; 15:29; 16:26; 31; 17:21; 18:2; 34; 20:8; 21; 35; 36; **Jn** 1:25; 3:20; 4:15; 21; 5:37; 6:24; 7:5; 8:11; 19; 42; 9:3; 10:28; 13:16; 14:17; 27; 17:20; **Acts** 2:27; 31; 4:12; 32; 34; 8:21; 9:9; 15:10; 16:21; 17:25; 19:37; 20:24; 21:21; 23:8; 12; 21; 24:12(3); 13; 18; 25:8(2); 27:20; 28:21(2); **Rom** 1:21; 2:28; 4:19; 6:13; 8:7; 38; 9:7; 11; 14:21; **1Cor** 2:9; 14; 3:2; 7(2); 5:8; 6:9; 8:8(2); 9:15; 10:7; 8; 9; 10; 32; 11:9; 11(2); 16; 15:50; **Gal** 1:1; 12(2); 17; 2:3; 3:28(3); 5:6; 6:13; 15; **Eph** 4:27; 5:4; 6:9; **Phil** 2:16; **Col** 3:11; **1Th** 2:5; 6; **2Th** 2:2; 3:8; 10; **1Ti** 1:4; 7; 5:22; **Heb** 4:13; 7:3; 9:12; 18; 10:8; **Jas** 1:13; 17; 5:12(3); **1Pet** 2:22; 3:14; 5:3; **2Pet** 1:8; **1Jn** 2:15; 3:6; 10; 18; **2Jn** 10; **3Jn** 10; **Rev** 3:15; 16; 5:3(2); 4; 7:3; 16(2); 9:4(2); 20; 21; 12:8; 20:4(2); 21:4(2); 23; 27; 22:5

NEVER

Gen 34:12; 41:19; **Lev** 6:13; **Num** 19:2; **Deut** 15:11; **Judg** 2:1; 14:3; 16:7; 11; **2Sa** 12:10; **2Chr** 18:7; 21:17; **Job** 3:16; 9:30; 21:25; **Ps** 10:6; 11; 15:5; 30:6; 31:1; 49:19; 55:22; 58:5; 71:1; 119:93; **Prov** 10:30; 27:20(2); 30:15; **Is** 13:20; 14:20; 25:2; 56:11; 62:6; 63:19; **Jer** 20:11; 33:17; **Eze** 16:63; 26:21; 27:36; 28:19; **Dan** 2:44; 12:1; **Joel** 2:26; 27; **Amos** 8:7; 14; **Hab** 1:4; **Mt** 7:23; 9:33; 21:16; 42; 26:33; 27:14; **Mk** 2:12; 25; 3:29; 9:43; 45; 11:2; 14:21; **Lk** 15:29; 19:30; 23:29(2); 53; **Jn** 4:14; 6:35(2); 7:15; 46; 8:33; 51; 52; 10:28; 11:26; 13:8; 19:41; **Acts** 10:14; 14:8; **1Cor** 13:8; **2Ti** 3:7; **Heb** 10:1; 11; 13:5; **2Pet** 1:10

NEVERTHELESS

Ex 32:34; **Lev** 11:4; 36; **Num** 13:28; 14:44; 18:15; 24:22; 31:23; **Deut** 14:7; 23:5; **Josh** 13:13; 14:8; **Judg** 1:33; 2:16; **1Sa** 8:19; 15:35; 20:26; 29:6; **2Sa** 5:7; 17:18; 23:16; **1Kin** 8:19; 15:4; 14; 23; 22:43; **2Kin** 2:10; 3:3; 13:6; 23:9; **1Chr** 11:5; 21:4; **2Chr** 12:8; 15:17; 19:3; 30:11; 33:17; 35:22; **Neh** 4:9; 9:26; 31; 13:26; **Est** 5:10; **Ps** 31:22; 49:12; 73:23; 78:36; 89:33; 106:8; 44; **Prov** 19:21; **Eccl** 9:16; **Is** 9:1; **Jer** 5:18; 26:24; 28:7; 36:25; **Eze** 3:21; 16:60; 20:17; 22; 33:9; **Dan** 4:15; **Jonah** 1:13; **Mt** 14:9; 26:39; 64; **Mk** 14:36; **Lk** 5:5; 13:33; 18:8; 22:42; **Jn** 11:15; 12:42; 16:7; **Acts** 14:17; 27:11; **Rom** 5:14; 15:15; **1Cor** 7:2; 28; 37; 9:12; 11:11; **2Cor** 3:16; 7:6; 12:16; **Gal** 2:20; 4:30; **Eph** 5:33; **Phil** 1:24; 3:16; **2Ti** 1:12; 2:19; **Heb** 12:11; **2Pet** 3:13; **Rev** 2:4

NEXT

Gen 17:21; **Ex** 12:4; **Num** 2:5; 11:32; 27:11; **Deut** 21:3; 6; **Ruth** 2:20; **1Sa** 17:13; 23:17; 30:17; **2Kin** 6:29; **1Chr** 5:12; 16:5; **2Chr** 17:15; 16; 18; 28:7; 31:12; 15; **Neh** 3:2(2); 4(3); 5; 7; 8(2); 9; 10(2); 12; 17; 19; 13:13; **Est** 1:14; 10:3; **Jonah** 4:7; **Mt** 27:62; **Mk** 14:38; **Lk** 9:37; **Jn** 1:29; 35; 12:12; **Acts** 4:3; 7:26; 13:42; 44; 14:20; 16:11; 20:15(3); 21:8; 26; 25:6; 27:3; 18; 28:13

NO

Gen 8:9; 9:15; 11:30; 13:8; 15:3; 16:1; 26:29; 30:1; 31:50; 32:28; 37:22(2); 24; 32; 38:21; 22; 26; 40:8; 41:44; 42:11; 31; 34; 44:23; 45:1; 47:4; 13; **Ex** 2:12; 3:19; 5:7; 16; 18; 8:22; 9:26; 28(2); 10:14; 28; 29; 12:16; 19; 43; 48; 13:3; 7; 14:11; 13; 15:22; 16:4; 18; 19; 29; 17:1; 20:3; 21:8; 22; 22:2; 10; 23:8; 13; 32; 30:9; 12; 33:4; 20; 34:3; 7; 14; 17; 35:3; **Lev** 2:11(2); 5:11; 6:30; 7:23; 24; 26; 11:12; 12:4; 13:21; 26(2); 31; 32; 16:17; 29; 17:7; 12; 14; 19:15; 35; 20:14; 21:3; 21; 22:10; 13(2); 21; 23:3; 7; 8; 21; 25; 28; 31; 35; 36; 25:31; 36; 26:1; 37; 27:26; 28; **Num** 1:53; 3:4; 5:8; 13; 15; 19; 6:3; 5; 6; 8:19; 25; 26; 14:18; 16:40; 18:5; 20; 23; 24; 32; 19:2; 15; 20:2; 5; 21:5; 22:26; 23:23; 26:33; 62; 27:3; 4; 8; 9; 10; 11; 17; 28:18; 25; 26; 29:1; 12; 35; 33:14; 35:31; 32; **Deut** 1:39; 2:5; 3:26; 4:12; 15; 5:22; 7:2; 16; 24; 8:2; 15; 10:9; 16; 11:17; 25; 12:12; 13:11; 14:27; 29; 15:4; 19; 16:3; 4; 8; 17:13; 16; 18:1; 2; 19:20; 20:12; 21:14; 22:26; 23:14; 17; 22; 24:1; 6; 25:5; 28:26; 29; 32; 65; 68(2); 31:2; 32:12; 20; 39; 34:6; **Josh** 8:20; 31; 10:14; 11:20; 14:4; 17:3; 18:7; 22:25; 27; 23:9; 13; **Judg** 2:2; 4:20; 5:19; 6:4; 8:28; 10:13; 11:39; 13:5; 7; 21; 15:13; 17:6; 18:1; 7(2); 10; 28(2); 19:1; 15; 18; 19; 30; 21:12; 25; **1Sa** 1:2; 11; 15; 18; 2:3; 9; 24; 3:1; 6:7; 7:13; 10:14; 27; 11:3; 13:19; 14:6; 26; 15:35; 17:32; 50; 18:2; 20:15; 21; 34; 21:1; 2; 4; 6; 9; 25:31; 26:12; 21; 27:4; 28:10; 15; 20(2); 29:3; 30:4; 12; **2Sa** 1:21; 2:28; 6:23; 7:10; 12:6; 13:12; 16; 14:25; 15:3; 26; 18:13; 18; 20; 22; 20:1; 10; 21:4; 17; **1Kin** 1:1; 3:2; 18; 22; 26; 27; 6:18; 8:16; 23; 35; 46; 9:22; 10:5; 10; 12; 13:9; 17; 22(2); 17:7; 17; 18:10; 23(2); 25; 26; 21:4; 5; 22:17; 18; 47; **2Kin** 1:16; 17; 2:12; 3:9; 4:14; 41; 5:15; 25; 6:23; 7:5; 10; 9:35; 10:31; 12:7; 8; 17:4; 19:18; 22:7; 23:10; 18; 25; 25:3; **1Chr** 2:34; 12:17; 16:21; 22; 17:9; 22:16; 23:22; 26; 24:2; 28; **2Chr** 6:5; 14; 26; 36; 7:13; 8:9; 9:4; 13:9; 14:6; 11; 15:5; 19; 17:10; 18:16(2); 19:7; 20:12; 21:19; 22:9; 32:15; 35:18; 36:16; 17; **Ezr** 4:16; 9:14; 10:6; **Neh** 2:14; 17; 20; 6:1; 8; 13:19; 21; 26; **Est** 1:19; 2:14; 5:12; 8:8; 9:2; **Job** 3:7; 4:18; 5:19; 6:21; 7:7; 8; 9; 10; 9:25; 10:18; 11:3; 12:2; 14; 24; 13:4; 14:12; 15:3; 15; 19; 28; 16:18; 18:17; 19:7; 16; 20:9; 21; 23:6; 24:7; 15; 20; 22; 26:2; 3; 6; 28:7; 18; 30:13; 17; 32:3; 5; 15; 16; 19; 34:22; 32; 36:16; 19; 38:11; 26(2); 40:5; 41:8; 16; 42:2; 15; **Ps** 3:2; 5:9; 6:5; 10:18; 14:1; 3; 4; 19:3; 22:6; 23:4; 32:2; 9; 33:16; 34:9; 36:1; 38:3; 7; 14; 39:13; 40:17; 41:8; 50:9; 53:1; 3; 4; 5; 55:19; 63:1; 69:2; 70:5; 72:12; 73:4; 74:9; 77:7; 78:64; 81:9; 83:4; 84:11; 88:4; 5; 91:10; 92:15; 101:3; 102:27; 103:16; 104:35; 105:14; 15; 107:4; 40; 119:3; 142:4(2); 143:2; 144:14(2); 146:3; **Prov** 1:24; 3:30; 6:7; 8:24(2); 10:22; 25; 11:14; 12:21; 28; 14:4; 17:16; 20; 21; 18:2; 21:10; 30; 22:24; 24:20; 25:28; 26:20(2); 28:1; 3; 17; 24; 29:9; 18; 30:20; 27; 31; 31:7; 11; **Eccl** 1:9; 11; 2:11; 16; 3:11; 12; 19; 4:1(2); 8; 13; 16; 5:4; 6:3; 7:21; 8:5; 8(2); 15; 9:1; 8; 10; 15; 10:11; 20; 12:1; 12; **Song** 4:7; 5:6; 8:8; **Is** 1:6; 13; 30; 5:6; 8; 13; 8:20; 9:7; 17; 19; 10:15; 20; 13:14; 18; 14:8; 15:6; 16:10(2); 19:7; 23:1(2); 10; 12(2); 24:10; 25:2; 26:21; 27:11(2); 28:8; 29:16; 30:7; 16; 19; 32:5; 33:8; 21; 34:16; 35:9; 37:19; 38:11; 40:20; 28; 29; 41:28(2); 43:10; 11; 12; 24; 44:6; 8; 12; 45:5; 9; 14; 20; 21; 47:1(2); 5; 6; 48:22; 50:2(3); 10; 51:22; 52:1; 11; 53:2(2); 9; 54:9; 17; 55:1; 57:1; 10; 21; 58:3; 59:8; 10; 15; 16(2); 60:15; 18; 19; 20; 62:4; 7; 8; 65:19; 20; **Jer** 2:6(2); 11; 13; 25(2); 30; 31; 3:3; 16; 4:22; 23; 25; 5:7; 6:10; 14; 23; 7:32(2); 8:6; 11; 13; 15; 22(2); 10:14; 11:19; 23; 12:11; 12; 14:3; 4; 5; 6; 19(2); 16:14; 19; 20; 17:21; 24(2); 18:12; 19:6; 11; 22:3(2); 10; 12; 28; 30; 23:4; 7; 17; 36; 25:6; 27; 35; 30:8; 13; 17; 31:29; 34(2); 33:24; 35:6(2); 8; 36:19; 38:6; 9; 24; 39:12; 40:15; 41:4; 42:14(2); 18; 44:2; 5; 17; 22; 26; 45:3; 46:25; 48:2; 8; 33; 38; 49:1(2); 7; 18; 33; 36; 50:14; 39; 40; 51:17; 43; 52:6; **Lam** 1:3; 6; 9; 2:9(2); 18; 4:4; 6; 15; 16; 22; 5:5; **Eze** 12:23; 24; 25; 13:10; 15; 16; 21; 23; 14:11; 15; 15:5; 16:34; 41; 42; 18:32; 19:9; 14; 20:39; 21:13; 27; 32; 22:26; 24:6; 17; 27; 26:13; 14; 21; 28:3; 9; 24; 29:11; 15; 16; 18; 30:13; 14; 15; 16; 33:11; 22; 34:5; 8; 22; 28; 29; 36:12; 14; 29; 30; 37:8; 22; 39:10; 43:7; 44:2; 9; 17; 25(2); 28; 45:8; **Dan** 1:4; 2:10; 35; 3:25; 27; 29; 4:9; 6:2; 15; 22; 23; 8:4; 7; 10:3; 8(2); 16; 17; **Hos** 1:6; 2:16; 17; 4:1; 4; 6; 8:7(2); 8; 9:15; 16; 10:3; 13:4(2); **Joel** 1:18; 2:19; 3:17; **Amos** 3:4; 5; 5:2; 20; 6:10; 7:14; 9:15; **Mic** 3:7; 4:9; 5:12; 13; 7:1; **Nah** 1:12; 14; 15; 2:13; 3:8; 18; 19; **Hab** 1:14; 2:19; 3:17(2); **Zeph** 2:5; 3:5; 6; 11; **Hag** 2:12; **Zec** 1:21; 4:5; 13; 7:14; 8:10; 17; 9:8; 11; 10:2; 11:6; 13:2; 5; 14:11; 17; 18; 21; **Mal** 1:10; **Mt** 5:18; 20; 26; 6:1; 24; 25; 31; 34; 8:4; 10; 28; 9:16; 30; 36; 10:19; 42; 11:27; 12:39; 13:5; 6; 16:4; 7; 8; 20; 17:8; 9; 19:6; 18; 20:7; 13; 21:19; 22:23; 24; 25; 46; 23:9; 24:4; 21; 22; 36(2); 25:3; 42(2); 26:55; **Mk** 1:45; 2:2(2); 17; 21; 22; 3:27; 4:5; 6; 7; 17; 40; 5:3(2); 37; 43; 6:5; 8(3); 31; 7:12; 24; 36; 8:12; 16; 17; 30; 9:3; 8; 9; 25; 39; 10:8; 29; 11:14; 12:14; 18; 19; 20; 22; 34; 13:11; 20; 32(2); 14:25; **Lk** 1:7; 33; 2:7; 3:13; 14; 4:24; 5:14; 36; 37; 39; 7:9; 44; 45; 8:13; 14; 16; 27; 51; 56; 9:13; 21; 36; 62; 10:4; 22; 11:20; 29; 33; 36; 12:4; 11; 17; 22; 33; 13:11; 15:7; 16; 19; 21; 16:2; 13; 18:17; 29; 20:22; 31; 22:36; 53; 23:4; 14; 15; 22; **Jn** 1:18; 21; 47; 2:3; 3:2; 13; 32; 4:9; 17(2); 27; 38; 44; 5:7; 14; 22; 6:37; 44; 53; 65; 66; 7:4; 13; 18; 27; 30; 44; 52; 8:10; 11(2); 15; 20; 37; 44; 9:4; 25; 41; 10:18; 29; 41; 11:10; 54; 13:8; 28; 14:6; 19; 15:4; 13; 22; 16:10; 21; 22; 25; 29; 17:11; 18:38; 19:4; 6; 9; 11; 15; 21:5; **Acts** 1:20; 4:17(2); 5:13; 23; 7:5(2); 11; 8:39; 9:7; 8; 10:34; 12:18; 13:28; 34; 37; 41; 15:2; 9; 24; 28; 16:28; 18:10; 15; 19:23; 24; 26; 40; 20:25; 33; 38; 21:25; 39; 23:8; 9; 22; 25:10; 11; 26; 27:20; 22; 28:2; 4; 5; 6; 18; 31; **Rom** 2:11; 3:9(2); 10; 12; 18; 20; 22; 4:15(2); 5:13; 6:9(2); 7:3; 17; 18; 20; 8:1; 10:12; 19; 11:6(4); 12:17; 13:1; 8; 10; 14:7; 13; 15:23; **1Cor** 1:7; 10; 29; 2:11; 15; 3:11; 18; 21; 4:6; 11; 5:11; 6:5; 7:25; 37; 8:13; 9:10; 10:13; 24; 25; 27; 11:16; 12:3(2); 21(2); 24; 25; 13:5; 14:2; 28; 15:12; 13; 16:2; 11; **2Cor** 2:13; 3:10; 5:16(2); 21; 6:3; 7:2(3); 5; 8:15; 20; 11:9; 10; 14; 15; 16; 13:7; **Gal** 2:5; 6(2); 16; 3:11; 15; 18; 25; 4:7; 8; 5:4; 23; 6:17; **Eph** 2:12; 19; 4:14; 28; 29; 5:5; 6; 11; 29; **Phil** 2:7; 20; 3:3; 4:15; **Col** 2:16; 18; 3:25; **1Th** 3:1; 3; 5; 4:6; 13; 5:1; **2Th** 2:3; 3:14; **1Ti** 1:3; 3:3; 4:12; 5:22; 23; 6:16(2); **2Ti** 2:4; 14; 3:9; 4:16; **Titus** 1:7; 2:8; 15; 3:2(2); **Heb** 5:4; 6:13; 7:13; 8:7; 12; 9:17; 22; 10:2; 6; 17; 18; 26; 38; 12:11; 14; 17; 13:10; 14; **Jas** 1:11; 13; 17; 2:11; 13; 3:8; 12; **1Pet** 2:22; 3:10; 4:2; **2Pet** 1:20; **1Jn** 1:5; 8; 2:7; 19; 21; 27; 3:5; 7; 15; 4:12; 18; **3Jn** 4; **Rev** 2:17; 3:7(2); 8; 11; 12; 5:3; 4; 7:9; 16; 10:6; 13:17; 14:3; 5; 11; 15:8; 17:12; 18:7(2); 11; 14; 21; 22(3); 23(2); 19:12; 20:3; 6; 11; 21:1; 4; 22; 23; 25; 27; 22:3; 5(2)

NOR

Gen 19:33; 35; 21:23(2); 45:5; 6; 49:10; **Ex** 4:1; 10; 10:6; 11:6; 12:9; 13:22; 20:5; 10(5); 17(5); 22:21; 28; 23:24(2); 26; 32; 30:9(2); 34:3; 10; 28; 36:6; **Lev** 2:11; 3:17; 10:9(2); 11:12; 26; 12:4; 13:34; 17:16; 18:26; 19:4; 14; 15; 18; 20; 26; 28; 20:19; 21:5; 10; 11; 12; 23; 22:22; 23:14(2); 25:4; 11; 20; 37; 26:1; 27:10; **Num** 5:15; 6:3; 9:12; 11:19(3); 18:3; 20:17; 23:25; **Deut** 1:45; 2:19; 27; 37(3); 4:28(3); 31; 5:9; 14(8); 7:2; 3; 7; 25; 9:9; 18; 23; 27(2); 10:9; 17; 12:12; 17(2); 32; 13:6; 8; 14:1; 8; 27; 29; 15:7; 19; 17:11; 16; 18:1; 22; 21:4; 22:30; 23:6; 17; 24:17(2); 26:14; 28:36; 39; 50; 64; 29:23(2); 31:6(2); 33:9; 34:7; **Josh** 1:5; 6:10; 10:25; 13:13; 22:19; 26; 28; 23:7(2); 24:12; 19; **Judg** 1:27(4); 30; 31(6); 33; 2:10; 19; 6:4(2); 11:15; 34; 13:4; 7; 14; 23; 14:16; 19:30; **1Sa** 1:15; 3:14; 5:5; 12:4; 21; 13:22; 15:29; 20:27; 31; 21:8; 22:15; 24:11; 25:31; 26:12; 27:9; 11; 28:6(2); 15; 18; 20; 30:12; 15; 19(3); **2Sa** 1:21; 2:19; 3:34; 13:22; 14:7; 19:6; 24(2); 21:4(2); 10; **1Kin** 3:8; 11; 26; 5:4; 6:7; 8:5; 57; 10:12; 12:24; 13:8; 9(2); 16(2); 17(2); 28; 16:11; 17:1; 18:26; 29(2); 20:8; 22:31; **2Kin** 3:14; 4:23; 31; 5:17; 6:10; 9:15; 14:6; 26(2); 17:35(3); 18:5; 12; 19:32(3); 20:13; 23:22(2); **1Chr** 21:24; 22:13; 23:26; 28:20(2); **2Chr** 1:11; 5:6; 6:14; 11:4; 15:5; 19:7(2); 20:15; 17; 21:12; 29:7; 32:7(2); 15; 34:2; **Ezr** 9:12; 14; 10:6; **Neh** 1:7(2); 2:16(4); 20(2); 4:23(3); 7:61; 8:9; 9:31; 34(2); 10:30; 13:25; **Est** 2:7; 10; 20; 3:2; 5; 4:16; 5:9; 9:28; **Job** 1:22; 3:10; 7:19; 14:12; 18:19(2); 24:13; 27:4; 28:8; 34:19; 22; 36:19; 41:12(2); 26; **Ps** 1:1(2); 5; 15:3(2); 5; 16:4; 19:3; 22:24; 24:4; 25:7; 26:9; 28:5; 37:25; 33; 40:4; 49:7; 50:9; 59:3; 66:20; 75:6(2); 78:42; 89:22; 33; 34; 91:5; 6(2); 103:10; 121:4; 6; 129:7; 131:1; 132:3; 144:14; 146:3; **Prov** 4:27; 5:13; 6:4; 8:26(2); 17:26; 21:30(2); 30:3; 8; 31:3; 4; **Eccl** 1:8; 3:14; 4:8; 5:10; 6:5; 8:16; 9:10(3); 11(3); 11:5; 12:1; 2; **Song** 2:7; 3:5; 8:4; **Is** 3:7; 5:6; 27(3); 8:12; 11:9; 14:21(2); 22:2; 23:4(2); 18; 28:28(2); 30:5(2); 31:4; 32:5; 34:10; 35:9; 37:33(3); 39:2; 40:16; 42:2(2); 4; 43:23; 44:9; 18; 19; 20; 45:13; 17; 46:7; 47:14; 48:1; 19; 49:10(2); 51:14; 52:12; 53:2; 54:9; 57:11; 58:13(2); 59:4; 21(2); 60:11; 18; 62:6; 64:4; 65:17; 19; 20; 23; 25; **Jer** 4:11; 5:4; 12; 6:19; 20; 25; 7:16; 22; 24; 26; 28; 32; 8:2; 13; 9:16; 11:8; 13:14(2); 14:16(2); 15:10; 17; 16:5; 6(2); 13; 17:21; 23; 18:18(2); 19:4(2); 5; 6; 20:9; 21:7; 22:3; 10; 23:4; 32; 25:4; 33; 35; 27:9(4); 31:40; 35:6; 7(3); 8; 9(3); 15; 36:24(2); 37:2(2); 19; 42:14(2); 21; 44:3; 5; 10(2); 23(3); 46:6; 49:31; 33; 51:5; 26; 62; **Lam** 2:22; 3:33; **Eze** 2:6; 3:18; 19; 7:11(2); 12; 12:24; 13:23; 14:16; 18; 20; 16:4; 47; 48; 18:17; 20:18; 44; 22:24; 23:27; 24:16; 22; 23; 28:24; 29:5; 11; 18; 31:8; 32:13; 37:23(2); 38:11; 43:7(2); 44:9; 13; 20; 22; 48:14; **Dan** 1:8; 2:10; 3:12; 14; 18; 27(2); 28; 5:8; 10; 23(2); 6:4; 13; 15; 10:3; 11:4; 6; 20; 24; 37(2); **Hos** 1:7(3); 10; 4:1(2); 4; 14; 15; 5:13; 7:10; **Amos** 5:5; 8:11; 9:10; **Obad** 13; **Jonah** 3:7(3); **Mic** 5:7; **Zeph** 1:6; 18; 3:13; **Zec** 1:4; 4:6; 7:10(2); 14; 8:10; 11:16(2); 14:6; 7; **Mal** 4:1; **Mt** 5:35; 6:20(2); 25; 26; 10:9(2); 10(2); 14; 24; 11:18; 12:19; 22:29; 30; 24:21; 25:13; **Mk** 6:11; 8:26; 12:25; **Lk** 1:15; 6:44; 7:33; 9:3; 10:4(2); 12:24(2); 14:12(2); 35; 17:23; 18:4; 20:35; 21:15; 22:68; 23:15; **Jn** 1:13(2); 25; 4:21; 5:37; 8:19; 9:3; 11:50; 12:40; 16:3; **Acts** 4:18; 8:21; 9:9; 13:27; 15:10; 19:37; 23:8; 12; 21; 24:12; 18; 25:8; 27:20; **Rom** 8:38(6); 39(3); 9:16; 14:21(2); **1Cor** 2:6; 9; 6:9(4); 10(5); 10:32(2); 12:21; **2Cor** 4:2; 7:12; **Gal** 3:28(3); 4:14; 5:6; 6:15; **Eph** 5:4(2); 5(2); **Col** 3:11(3); **1Th** 2:3(2); 5; 6(2); 5:5; **2Th** 2:2(2); **1Ti** 1:7; 2:12; 6:16; 17; **2Ti** 1:8; **Heb** 7:3; 9:25; 12:5; 18; 13:5; **2Pet** 1:8; **Rev** 3:15; 16; 5:3; 7:1(2); 3; 16; 9:20(2); 21(3); 14:11; 21:4

NOT

Gen 2:5(2); 17; 18; 20; 25; 3:1; 3; 4; 11; 17; 4:5; 7(2); 9; 12; 5:24; 6:3; 7:2; 8; 8:12; 21; 22; 9:4; 23; 11:7; 12:18; 13:6(2); 9; 14:23(2); 15:1; 4; 10; 13; 16; 16:10; 17:12; 14; 15; 18:3; 15; 21; 24; 25; 28; 29; 30(2); 31; 32(2); 19:7; 8; 17; 18; 20; 21; 31; 33; 35; 20:4; 5; 6; 7; 9; 11; 12; 21:10; 12; 16; 17; 23; 26; 22:12(2); 16; 24:3; 5; 6; 8(2); 21; 27; 33; 37; 39; 41; 49; 56; 26:2; 22; 24; 29; 27:1; 2; 12; 21; 23; 36(2); 28:1; 6; 8; 15; 16; 29:25; 26; 30:31; 33; 40; 42; 31:2; 5; 7; 15; 20; 24; 27; 28; 29; 32(2); 33; 34; 35(2); 38(2); 39; 52(2); 32:10; 25; 26; 32; 34:7; 17; 19; 23; 35:5; 10; 17; 36:7; 37:4; 13; 21; 27; 29; 30; 38:9; 14; 16; 20; 23; 26; 39:6; 8; 10; 23; 40:8; 23; 41:16; 21; 31; 36; 42:2; 4; 8; 13;

15; 20; 21; 22(3); 23; 32; 36(2); 37; 38; 43:3; 5(3); 8; 9; 23; 32; 44:4; 5; 15; 18; 26; 28; 30; 31; 32; 34; 45:1; 3; 5; 8; 9; 20; 24; 26; 46:3; 47:9; 18(2); 19(2); 22(2); 26; 29; 48:10; 11; 18; 49:4; 6(2); 10; 50:19; 21; **Ex** 1:8; 17; 19; 2:3; 3:2; 3; 5; 19(2); 21; 4:1(2); 8; 9; 10; 11; 14; 21; 5:2; 8; 9; 10; 11; 14; 19; 6:3; 9; 12; 7:4; 13; 16; 21; 24; 8:15; 18; 19; 21; 26(2); 28; 29(2); 31; 9:6; 7(2); 11; 12; 17; 18; 19; 21; 30; 32(2); 33; 10:7; 11; 15; 19; 20; 23; 26(2); 27; 11:7; 9; 10; 12:9; 13; 23; 30(2); 39(2); 45; 46; 13:13; 17; 22; 14:12; 13; 20; 28; 15:23; 16:8; 15; 20; 24; 25; 17:7; 18:17; 18; 19:12; 13(2); 15; 24; 20:4; 5; 7(2); 10; 13; 14; 15; 16; 17(2); 19; 20(2); 23; 25; 26; 21:5; 7; 8; 10; 11; 13; 18; 21; 28; 29; 33; 36; 22:8; 11(2); 13; 14; 15; 16; 18; 22; 25; 28; 29; 23:1(2); 2; 6; 7(2); 9; 18; 19; 21(2); 24; 29; 33; 24:2; 11; 25:15; 28:28; 32; 35; 43; 29:33; 34; 30:15(2); 20; 21; 32; 37; 32:1; 18; 22; 23; 32; 33:3; 11; 12; 15(2); 16; 20; 23; 34:10; 20; 25; 26; 29; 39:21; 23; 40:35; 37(2); **Lev** 1:17; 2:12; 4:2; 13; 22; 27; 5:1; 7; 8; 11; 17; 18; 6:12; 17; 23; 7:15; 18; 19; 8:33; 35; 10:1; 6; 7; 9; 17; 18; 11:4(2); 5; 6; 7; 8(2); 10; 11; 13; 26; 41; 42; 43; 47; 12:8; 13:4(2); 5; 6; 11; 21; 23; 28; 31; 32(2); 33; 34; 36; 53; 55(2); 14:32; 36; 48; 15:11; 31; 16:2(2); 13; 22; 17:4; 9; 16; 18:3(2); 7(2); 8; 9; 10; 11; 12; 13; 14(2); 15(2); 16; 17; 19; 20; 21; 22; 24; 26; 28; 30(2); 19:4; 7; 9; 10; 11; 12; 13(2); 14; 15; 16; 17(2); 18; 19(2); 20(3); 23; 26; 27; 28; 29; 31; 33; 20:4; 19; 22; 23; 25; 21:4; 5; 6; 7; 10; 14; 17; 18; 21; 23(2); 22:2; 4; 6; 8; 10; 12; 15; 20(2); 22; 23; 24; 25; 28; 23:22; 29; 25:5; 11; 14; 17; 20; 23; 28; 30(2); 34; 37; 39; 42; 43; 46; 53; 54; 26:11; 13; 14(2); 15; 18; 20; 21; 23; 26; 27; 31; 35; 44; 27:10; 11; 20(2); 22; 27; 33(2); **Num** 1:47; 49; 2:33; 4:15; 18; 19; 20; 5:3; 14; 19; 28; 6:7; 9:6; 7; 13(2); 19; 22; 10:7; 30; 31; 11:11; 14; 15; 17; 19; 23; 25; 26; 12:2; 7; 8(2); 11; 12; 14; 15; 13:20; 31; 14:3; 9(2); 16; 22; 23; 30; 41; 42(3); 43; 44; 15:22; 34; 39; 16:12; 14(2); 15(2); 28; 29; 40(2); 17:10; 18:3; 4; 17; 19:12(2); 13(2); 20(2); 20:12(2); 17(2); 18; 20; 24; 21:22(2); 23; 34; 22:12(2); 30; 34; 37(3); 23:8(2); 9; 12; 13; 19(3); 21; 24; 26; 24:1; 12; 17(2); 25:11; 26:11; 62; 64; 65; 27:3; 17; 29:7; 30:2; 5; 11; 12; 31:18; 23; 35; 49; 32:5; 9; 11; 18; 19; 23; 30; 33:55; 35:12; 23(2); 27; 30; 33; 34; 36:7; **Deut** 1:9; 17(2); 21; 26; 29; 32; 35; 37; 42(2); 43; 45; 2:5(3); 9(2); 19(2); 30; 36; 37; 3:2; 4(2); 11; 22; 26; 27; 4:2; 21(2); 22; 26; 31; 42; 5:3; 5; 8; 9; 11(2); 14; 17; 32; 6:10; 11(3); 14; 16; 7:3; 7; 10; 14; 18; 21; 22; 25; 8:3(2); 4; 9; 11(2); 16; 20; 9:4; 5; 6; 7; 23; 26; 27; 28; 10:10; 17; 11:2(3); 10; 16; 17; 28(2); 30; 12:4; 8; 9; 13; 16; 17; 19; 23(2); 24; 25; 30(2); 31; 32; 13:2; 3; 6; 8; 13; 16; 14:1; 3; 7(2); 8(2); 10(2); 12; 19; 21(2); 24; 27; 15:2; 6(2); 7; 9; 10; 13; 16; 18; 21; 23; 16:5; 16; 19(2); 21; 17:1; 3; 6; 11; 12; 15(2); 16; 17; 20(2); 18:9; 10; 14; 16(2); 19; 20; 21; 22(3); 19:4; 6(2); 10; 13; 14; 15; 21; 20:1; 3(3); 5; 6; 7; 15; 18; 19(2); 20; 21:1; 3(2); 7; 8; 14(2); 16; 18(2); 20; 23(2); 22:1; 2(2); 3; 4; 5; 6; 8; 9; 10; 11; 14; 17; 19; 20; 24; 28; 29; 30; 23:1; 2(2); 3(2); 4; 5; 6; 7(2); 10(2); 15; 16; 18; 19; 20; 21; 24; 25; 24:4(2); 5; 10; 12; 14; 16; 17; 19; 20; 21; 25:3; 4; 5; 6; 7(2); 8; 9; 12; 13; 14; 18; 19; 26:13; 14; 27:5; 26; 28:12; 13(2); 14; 15; 27; 29; 30(2); 31(2); 33; 40; 41; 44; 45; 47; 49; 50; 51; 55; 56; 58; 61; 62; 29:4; 5(2); 6; 15; 20; 23; 26(2); 30:11; 12; 17; 18; 31:2; 6(2); 8(2); 13; 17(2); 21; 32:5; 6(2); 17(3); 21(2); 27(2); 31; 34; 47; 51; 52; 33:6(2); 9; 11; 34:4; 7; 10; **Josh** 1:5(2); 7; 8; 9(2); 18; 2:4; 5; 14; 22; 3:4(2); 5:5; 6(2); 7; 6:10; 7:3(2); 12; 13; 19; 8:1; 4; 14; 17(2); 26; 35(2); 9:14; 18; 19; 26; 10:6; 8(2); 13(2); 19(2); 25; 11:6; 11; 19; 13:13; 33; 15:63; 16:10; 17:12; 13; 16; 17; 18:2; 20:5(2); 9; 21:44; 45; 22:3; 17; 19; 20(2); 22; 24; 26; 27; 28; 31; 33; 23:6; 7; 14(2); 24:10; 12; 13(3); 19; **Judg** 1:19; 21; 28; 32; 34; 2:2; 3; 10; 14; 17(2); 19; 20; 21; 22; 3:1; 22; 25; 28; 29; 4:6; 8(2); 9; 14; 16; 18; 5:23; 30(2); 6:10(2); 13; 14; 18; 23(2); 27; 39; 7:4(2); 8:1; 2; 19; 20; 23; 34; 9:15; 20; 28; 38; 41; 54; 10:6; 11; 11:2; 7; 10; 15; 17(2); 18; 20; 24; 26; 27; 28; 12:1; 2; 3; 6; 13:2; 3; 4(2); 6; 9; 14; 16(2); 23; 14:4; 6; 9; 14; 15; 16(3); 18(2); 15:1; 2; 11; 12; 13; 16:8; 9; 15(2); 17; 20; 18:1; 9; 25; 19:10; 12(2); 20; 23(2); 24; 25; 20:8; 13; 16; 34; 21:1; 5(2); 7; 8; 14; 17; 18; 22(2); **Ruth** 1:16; 20; 2:8(2); 9(2); 11; 13; 15; 16; 20; 22; 3:1; 2; 3; 10; 11; 13; 14; 17; 18; 4:4; 10; 14; **1Sa** 1:7; 8(2); 11; 13; 16; 22(2); 2:3; 12; 15; 16(2); 25; 31; 32; 33; 3:2; 5; 6; 7; 13; 14; 17; 4:7; 9; 15; 20(2); 5:7; 11; 12; 6:3(2); 6; 9(2); 12; 7:8; 8:3; 5; 7(2); 18; 9:2; 4(3); 7; 13; 20(2); 21; 10:1; 16; 21; 11:7; 11; 13; 12:4; 5; 14; 15; 17; 19; 20(2); 21; 22; 13:8; 11; 12; 13; 14(2); 14:1; 3; 9; 17; 27; 30; 34; 36; 37; 39; 45(2); 15:3; 9; 11; 17; 19; 26; 29(2); 16:7(2); 10; 11; 17:8; 29; 33; 39(2); 47; 18:17; 25; 26; 19:4(2); 6; 11; 20:2(2); 3; 5; 9; 12; 14(2); 15(2); 26(3); 27; 29; 30; 31; 37; 38; 39; 21:8; 11(2); 22:5; 15; 17(2); 23; 23:14; 17(2); 19; 24:7; 10; 11(2); 12; 13; 18; 21(2); 25:7; 11; 15; 19; 25(2); 28; 34; 26:1; 8; 9; 14; 15(2); 16(2); 20; 23; 28:6; 13; 18; 23; 29:3; 4(2); 5; 6(2); 7; 8; 9; 30:2; 10; 17; 21; 22(2); 23; 31:4; **2Sa** 1:10; 14; 20(2); 21; 22(2); 23; 2:19; 21; 26; 3:8; 11; 13; 22; 26; 29; 34; 37; 38; 4:11; 5:6; 8; 23; 6:10; 7:6; 7; 15; 9:3; 7; 10:3; 11:3; 9; 10(3); 11; 13; 20; 21; 25; 12:13; 17; 18; 23; 13:4; 12(2); 13; 14; 16; 20; 25(2); 26; 28(2); 30; 32; 33; 14:2; 7; 10; 11(2); 13; 14; 18; 19; 24(2); 28; 29(2); 15:11; 14; 27; 35; 16:17; 19; 17:6; 7; 8; 12; 13; 16; 17; 19; 20; 22(2); 23; 18:3(2); 11; 12; 14; 20; 29; 19:7(2); 10; 13(2); 19; 21; 22; 23; 25; 43; 20:3; 10; 21; 21:2; 17; 22:22; 23; 37; 38; 39; 42; 44; 23:5(2); 16; 17(2); 19(2); 23; 24:14; **1Kin** 1:4; 6; 8; 10; 11(2); 13; 18; 19; 26; 27; 51; 52; 2:4; 6; 8; 9; 16; 17; 20(2); 23; 26; 28; 32; 36; 42; 43; 3:7; 11; 13(2); 21; 5:3; 6; 6:6; 13; 7:31; 8:5; 8; 11; 19; 25; 41; 46; 56; 57; 9:5; 6; 12; 20; 21; 10:3(2); 7(2); 20; 11:2; 4; 6; 10(2); 11; 12; 13; 33; 34; 39; 41; 12:15; 16; 24; 31; 13:4; 8; 10; 16; 21; 22; 28; 33; 14:2; 4; 8; 29; 15:3; 5; 7; 14; 17; 23; 29; 31; 16:5; 11; 14; 20; 27; 17:1; 12; 13; 14; 16; 18:5; 10(3); 12; 13; 18; 21; 40; 44; 19:2; 4; 11(2); 12; 18(2); 20:7; 8; 9; 11; 28; 36; 21:4; 6; 15; 29; 22:3; 7; 8(2); 17; 18; 28; 33; 39; 43(2); 45; 48; 49; **2Kin** 1:3(2); 4; 6(3); 15; 16(2); 18; 2:2; 4; 6; 10(2); 16; 17; 18(2); 21; 3:2; 3; 11; 14(2); 17; 26; 4:2; 3; 6; 16; 24; 27; 28(2); 29(2); 30; 31; 39; 40; 5:12(2); 13; 17; 20; 26; 6:9; 10; 11; 16; 19; 22; 27; 32; 7:2; 9; 19; 8:19; 23; 9:3; 18; 20; 37; 10:4; 5; 19; 21(2); 29; 31; 34; 11:2; 6; 15; 12:3; 6; 7; 13; 15; 16; 19; 13:2; 6; 8; 11; 12; 23; 14:3; 4; 6(2); 11; 15; 18; 24; 26; 27; 28; 15:4; 6; 9; 16; 18; 20; 21; 24; 28; 35; 36; 16:2; 5; 19; 17:2; 9; 12; 14(2); 15; 19; 22; 25; 26(2); 34; 35; 37; 38; 40; 18:6; 7; 12(2); 22; 26; 27; 29(2); 30; 31; 32(2); 36(2); 19:3; 6; 10(2); 25; 32; 33; 20:1; 13; 15; 19; 20; 21:9; 17; 22; 25; 22:2; 13; 17; 20; 23:9; 22; 26; 28; 33; 24:4; 5; 7; 25:24; **1Chr** 4:10; 27; 5:1; 10:4; 13; 14; 11:5; 18; 19; 21; 25; 12:19; 33; 13:3; 13; 14:14; 15:13(2); 16:22; 30; 17:4; 5; 6; 13; 19:3; 21:3; 6; 13; 17(2); 24; 30; 22:8; 13; 18(2); 23:11; 26:10; 27:23; 24; 28:3; 20(2); 29:1; 25; **2Chr** 1:11; 4:18; 5:6; 9; 11; 14; 6:9; 16; 32; 36; 42; 7:2; 7; 18; 8:7; 8; 11; 15; 9:2; 6(2); 19; 20; 29; 10:15; 16; 11:4; 12:7(2); 12; 14; 15; 13:5; 7; 9; 10; 12(2); 14:11; 13; 15:7; 13; 17; 16:7; 8; 12; 17:3; 4; 18:6; 7; 17(2); 27; 30; 32; 19:6; 10(2); 20:6(3); 7; 10(2); 12; 15(2); 17(2); 32; 33(2); 37; 21:7; 12; 20; 22:11; 23:8; 14; 24:5; 6; 19; 22; 25; 25:2; 4(2); 7(2); 13; 15; 16; 20; 26; 26:18; 27:2; 28:1; 10; 13; 20; 21; 27; 29:7; 11; 34; 30:3(2); 5; 7; 8; 9; 17(2); 18; 19; 26; 32:7; 11; 12; 13; 15; 17(2); 25; 26; 33:10; 23; 34:21; 25; 33; 35:3; 15; 21(2); 22(2); 36:12; **Ezr** 2:59; 62; 63; 3:6; 13; 4:13; 14; 21; 22; 5:5; 16; 6:8; 7:24; 25; 26; 9:1; 9; 12; 14; 10:8; 13; **Neh** 1:7; 2:1; 2; 3; 16; 3:5; 4:5(2); 10; 11; 14; 5:9(2); 13; 14; 15; 18; 6:1; 9; 11; 12; 7:3; 4; 61; 64; 65; 8:9; 17; 9:16; 17; 19(2); 20; 21(2); 29(2); 30; 31; 32; 35; 10:30; 31; 39; 13:1; 2; 6; 10; 14; 18(2); 19; 24; 25; 26; **Est** 1:15; 16; 17; 19; 2:10(2); 20; 3:2; 4; 5; 8; 4:4; 11(2); 13; 16; 5:9; 6:1; 13; 7:4; 9:10; 15; 16; 27; 28; 10:2; **Job** 1:10; 12; 22; 2:10(2); 12; 3:4; 6(2); 10; 11(2); 16; 18; 21; 26; 4:6; 16; 21; 5:6; 17; 24; 6:10(2); 13; 29; 7:1(2); 8; 11; 16; 19; 21(2); 8:10; 12; 15(2); 18; 20; 9:5; 7; 11(2); 13; 15; 16; 18; 21; 24; 28; 32; 34; 35(2); 10:2; 7; 10; 14; 15; 19; 20; 21; 11:2; 11; 14; 15; 20; 12:3(2); 9; 11; 13:2; 11; 16; 20(2); 21; 14:2; 4; 7; 12(2); 16; 21(2); 15:6; 9(2); 15; 18; 22; 29; 30; 31; 32; 16:6; 13; 17; 18; 22; 17:2(2); 4; 18:5; 21; 19:3; 7; 22; 27; 20:4; 8; 13; 17; 18(2); 19; 20(2); 26; 21:4; 10(2); 14; 16; 29(2); 22:5; 7; 11; 12; 14; 20; 23:8; 11; 17; 24:1(2); 12; 13; 16; 18; 21(2); 25; 25:3; 5(2); 26:8; 27:4; 5; 6(2); 11; 14; 15; 19(2); 22; 28:7; 8; 13; 14(2); 17; 19; 29:16; 22; 24(2); 30:10; 20(2); 24; 25(2); 27; 31:3; 4; 15(2); 17; 20(2); 23; 31; 32; 34; 32:6; 9; 13; 14; 16; 21; 22; 33:7; 12; 13; 14; 21; 27; 33; 34:12; 19; 23; 27; 30; 31; 32; 33; 35:13; 14; 15(2); 36:4; 5; 6; 7; 12; 13; 19; 20; 21; 26; 32; 37:4; 21; 23; 24; 39:4; 16; 22; 40:5; 23; 41:9; 12; 33; 42:3(2); 7; 8; **Ps** 1:1; 3; 4; 5; 3:6; 4:4; 5:4; 5; 6:1; 7:12; 9:10; 12; 18(2); 19; 10:4(2); 6; 12; 13; 14:3; 4; 15:3; 4; 5; 16:2; 4; 8; 10; 17:1; 3; 5; 18:21; 22; 36; 38; 41; 43; 19:3; 13; 21:2; 7; 11; 22:2(2); 5; 11; 19; 24; 23:1; 24:4; 25:2(2); 7; 20; 26:1; 4; 5; 9; 27:3; 9(3); 12; 28:1; 3; 5(2); 30:1; 3; 12; 31:8; 17; 32:2; 5; 6; 9; 33:16; 34:5; 10; 20; 35:11; 15(2); 19; 20; 22(2); 24; 25(2); 36:4(2); 11(2); 12; 37:1; 7; 8; 10(2); 19; 21; 24; 25; 28; 33; 36(2); 38:1; 9; 13(2); 14; 21(2); 39:1; 6; 8; 9; 12; 40:4; 6(2); 9; 10(2); 11; 12; 41:2; 11; 44:3; 6; 9; 12; 17; 18; 21; 23; 46:2; 5; 49:9; 12; 16; 17; 20; 50:3; 8; 12; 51:11(2); 16(2); 17; 52:7; 53:3; 4; 54:t; 3; 55:1; 11; 12; 19; 23; 56:4; 8; 11; 13; 58:5; 6; 59:3; 5; 11; 13; 15; 60:10(2); 62:2; 6; 10(3); 64:4; 66:7; 9; 18; 20; 69:4; 5; 6(2); 14; 15(2); 17; 23; 27; 28; 33; 71:9(2); 12; 15; 18; 73:5; 74:9; 19(2); 21; 23; 75:4(2); 5(2); 77:2; 19; 78:4; 7; 8(3); 10; 22(2); 30; 32; 37; 38(2); 39; 42; 44; 50; 53; 56; 63; 67; 79:6(2); 8; 80:18; 81:5; 11; 82:5; 83:1(3); 85:6; 8; 86:14; 89:22; 30; 31; 33; 34; 35; 43; 48; 91:5; 7; 92:6; 94:7; 9(2); 10(2); 14; 95:8; 10; 11; 96:10; 100:3; 101:3; 4; 5; 7(2); 102:2; 17; 24; 103:2; 9; 10; 104:5; 9(2); 105:15; 28; 37; 106:7(2); 11; 13; 23; 24; 25; 34; 107:38; 108:11(2); 109:1; 14; 16; 17; 110:4; 112:6; 7; 8; 115:1(2); 5(2); 6(2); 7(2); 17; 118:6; 17; 18; 119:6; 8; 10; 11; 16; 19; 31; 36; 43; 46; 51; 60; 61; 80; 83; 85; 87; 102; 109; 110; 116; 121; 122; 133; 136; 141; 153; 155; 157; 158; 176; 121:3(2); 6; 124:1; 2; 6; 125:3; 127:5; 129:2; 7; 131:1; 132:3; 4; 10; 11; 135:16(2); 17; 137:6(2); 138:8; 139:4; 12; 15; 21(2); 140:8(2); 10; 11; 141:4(2); 5; 8; 143:2; 7; 146:3; 147:10(2); 20(2); 148:6; **Prov** 1:8; 10; 15; 28(2); 29; 3:1; 3; 5; 7; 11; 15; 21; 23; 24; 25; 27; 28; 29; 30; 31; 4:2; 5; 6; 12(2); 13; 14(2); 15; 16; 19; 21; 27; 5:6; 7; 8; 13; 17; 6:4; 20; 25; 27; 28; 29; 30; 33; 34; 35; 7:11; 19; 23; 25(2); 8:1; 10; 11; 26; 29; 33; 9:8; 18; 10:3; 19; 30; 11:4; 21; 12:3(2); 7; 27; 13:1; 8; 14:5; 6; 7; 10; 22; 15:7; 12; 16:5; 10; 29; 17:5; 7; 13; 26; 18:5; 19:2; 5(2); 9; 10; 18; 23; 24; 20:1; 4; 13; 19; 21; 22; 23; 21:13; 17; 26; 22:6; 20; 22; 24; 26; 28; 29; 23:3; 4; 5; 6; 7; 9; 10(2); 13(2); 17; 18; 20; 22; 23; 31; 35(2); 24:1; 7; 12(4); 14; 15(2); 17(2); 19; 21; 23; 28(2); 29; 25:6(2); 8(2); 9; 10; 27(2); 26:1; 2; 4; 7; 17; 19; 25; 27:1(2); 2(2); 10; 22; 24; 28:5; 13; 20; 21; 22; 27; 29:7; 19(2); 24; 30:2; 6; 7; 10; 11; 12; 15; 16(2); 18; 25; 30; 31:3; 4(2); 12; 18; 21; 27; **Eccl** 1:7; 8; 2:10(2); 21; 23; 4:3(2); 8; 10; 12; 16; 5:1; 2(2); 4; 5(2); 6; 8; 10; 12; 20; 6:2; 3; 5; 6; 7; 7:9; 10(2); 16; 17; 18; 20(2); 28(2); 8:3(2); 7; 11; 13(2); 17(2); 9:2; 5; 11; 12; 16; 10:4; 10; 15; 17; 20(3); 11:2; 4(2); 5(2); 6(2); 12:1; 2; **Song** 1:6(2); 8; 2:7; 3:1; 2; 4; 5; 5:6; 6:6; 7:2; 8:1; 4; **Is** 1:3(2); 6; 11; 15; 23; 2:4; 9; 3:7(2); 9; 5:4; 6; 12; 25; 6:9(2); 7:1; 4; 7; 8; 9(2); 12; 17; 25; 8:10; 11; 12; 19; 20; 9:1; 3; 12; 13; 17; 20; 21; 10:4; 7(2); 8; 9(3); 11; 24; 11:3; 9; 13(2); 12:2; 13:10(2); 17(2); 18; 22; 14:17; 20; 21; 29; 16:3; 6; 12; 17:8; 10; 14; 22:2; 4; 11; 14; 23:4; 13; 18; 24:9; 20; 26:10(2); 11; 14(2); 18; 27:4; 9; 11; 28:12; 15; 16; 18; 22; 25; 27; 28; 29:9(2); 12(2); 16; 17; 22; 30:1(2); 2; 5; 6; 9; 10(2); 14(2); 15; 20; 31:1; 2; 3(2); 4; 8(2); 32:3; 10; 33:1(2); 19(2); 20(2); 23(2); 24; 34:10; 35:4; 8(2); 9; 36:7; 11; 12; 14(2); 15; 16; 21(2); 37:3; 6; 10(2); 26; 33; 34; 38:1; 11; 18; 39:2; 4; 40:9; 16; 20(2); 21(4); 24(3); 26; 28(3); 31(2); 41:3; 7; 9; 10(2); 12; 13; 14; 17; 42:2; 3(2); 4; 8; 16(3); 20(2); 24(2); 25(2); 43:1; 2(2); 5; 6; 17; 18; 19; 22; 23(2); 25; 44:2; 8(3); 9(2); 18; 20; 21; 45:1; 4; 5; 13; 17; 18; 19(2); 21; 23; 46:2; 7(2); 10; 13(2); 47:3; 7; 8; 11(3); 14(2); 48:1; 6(2); 7(2); 8(3); 9; 10; 11; 16; 19; 21; 49:5; 10; 15(2); 23; 50:5; 6; 7(2); 51:6; 7; 9; 10; 14; 21; 52:12; 15(2); 53:3; 7(2); 54:1(2); 2; 4(4); 9; 10; 11; 14(2); 15; 55:2(2); 5(2); 8; 10; 11; 13; 56:5; 57:4; 10(2); 11(3); 12; 16; 58:1; 2; 3; 4; 6; 7(2); 11; 13; 59:1; 2; 6; 8(2); 21; 60:11; 12; 62:1(2); 6; 8; 12; 63:8; 13; 16; 19; 64:3; 4; 9; 65:1(3); 2; 5; 6; 8(2); 12(3); 17; 20; 22(2); 23; 25; 66:4(2); 9; 19; 24; **Jer** 1:7; 8; 17; 19; 2:2; 8(3); 11; 17; 19; 20; 23(2); 24; 27; 34; 35; 37; 3:1; 2; 4; 7; 8; 10; 12(2); 13; 19; 25; 4:1; 3; 6; 8; 11; 22; 27; 28; 29; 5:3(2); 4; 9(2); 10(2); 12; 13; 15; 18; 19; 21(2); 22(4); 28(2); 29(2); 6:8; 15; 16; 17; 19; 20; 25; 29; 7:4; 6(2); 9; 13(2); 16(2); 17; 19; 20; 22; 24(2); 26; 27(2); 28; 31; 8:2; 4(2); 6; 7; 12; 17; 19(2); 20; 22; 9:3(2); 4; 5; 9(2); 13; 23(2); 10:2(2); 4; 5(2); 7; 10; 11; 16; 20; 21(2); 23(2); 24; 25(2); 11:3; 8(2); 11(2); 12; 14(2); 19; 21(2); 12:4; 6; 13; 17; 13:1; 11; 12; 14; 15; 17; 21; 27; 14:9; 10(2); 11; 12(2); 13; 14; 15(2); 17; 18; 21(3); 22; 15:1; 7; 14; 15; 17; 19; 20; 16:2; 4; 5; 6; 8; 11; 12; 13(2); 17; 17:4; 6(2); 8(2); 11(2); 16; 17; 18(2); 23(2); 27(3); 18:10; 15; 17; 18(2); 23; 19:5; 15; 20:3; 9(2); 11(2); 14; 16; 17; 21:7; 10; 22:5; 6; 10; 11; 13; 15; 16; 17; 18(2); 21(2); 26; 27; 28; 30; 23:2; 10; 16(2); 20; 21(2); 23; 24(2); 29; 32(2); 38; 40; 24:2; 6(2); 25:3; 4; 6(2); 7; 8; 29; 33; 26:2; 4; 5; 16; 19; 24; 27:8(2); 9(2); 13; 14(2); 15; 16; 17; 18; 20; 28:15; 29:6; 8; 9; 11; 16; 19(2); 23; 27; 31; 32; 30:5; 10; 11(2); 14; 19(2); 24; 31:9; 12; 15; 32; 40; 32:4; 5; 23; 33(2); 35; 40(2); 33:3; 20; 21; 24; 25(2); 26; 34:3; 4; 14; 17; 18; 35:13; 14(2); 15(2); 16; 17(2); 19; 36:24; 25(2); 31; 37:4; 9(2); 14(2); 19; 20; 38:4; 5; 15(2); 16; 17; 18(2); 20; 23; 24; 25(2); 26; 27; 39:16; 17; 18; 40:3; 5; 7; 9; 14; 16; 41:8(2); 42:5; 10(2); 11(2); 13; 19; 21; 43:2(2); 4; 7; 44:3; 4; 5; 10; 16; 21(2); 23; 27; 45:5; 46:5; 6; 11; 15; 21; 27(2); 28(3); 47:3; 48:11(2); 27; 30(2); 49:9; 10(2); 12(2); 25; 36; 50:2; 5; 7; 13; 20; 24; 42; 51:3; 5; 6; 9; 19; 26; 39; 44; 50; 57; 64; **Lam** 1:9; 10; 14; 2:1; 2; 8; 14; 17; 18; 21; 3:2; 22(2); 31; 33; 36; 37; 38; 42; 43; 44; 49; 56; 57; 4:8; 12; 14; 15; 16(2); 17; 5:7; 12; **Eze** 1:9; 12; 17; 2:6(2); 8; 3:5; 6(2); 7(2); 9; 18; 19; 20(2); 21(2); 25; 26; 4:8; 14(2); 5:6; 7; 9(2); 6:10; 7:4; 7; 9; 12; 13(2); 19(2); 8:12; 18(2); 9:5; 6; 9; 10; 10:11(2); 16; 11:3; 11; 12; 12:2(2); 6; 9; 12; 13; 13:5; 6; 7(3); 9; 12; 19(2); 22(2); 14:23; 16:4(2); 16; 22; 28; 29; 31; 43(2); 47; 48; 56; 61; 17:9; 10; 12; 14; 18; 18:3; 6; 7; 8; 11; 12; 13; 14; 15(2); 16; 17(2); 18; 19; 20; 21; 22; 23; 24; 25(3); 28; 29(3); 30; 20:3; 7; 8(2); 9; 13; 14; 15; 16; 18; 21; 22; 24; 25(2); 31; 32; 38; 39; 44; 47; 48; 49; 21:5; 26; 22:24; 28; 30; 23:27; 48; 24:6; 7; 8; 12; 13(2); 14; 17(2); 19; 22; 23; 25; 25:10; 26:15; 19; 20; 28:2; 29:5; 30:21; 31:8(3); 32:7; 9; 27; 33:4; 5; 6(2); 8; 9; 12(2); 13; 15; 17(2); 20; 31; 32; 34:2; 3; 4; 8; 10; 35:6; 9; 36:22; 31; 32; 37:18; 38:14; 39:7; 41:6; 42:6; 14; 44:2; 8; 13; 18; 19; 31; 46:2; 9; 18(2); 20; 47:5(2); 11; 12; 48:11; 14; **Dan** 1:8(2); 2:5; 9; 10; 11; 18; 24; 30; 43(2); 44; 3:6; 11; 12(2); 14; 15; 16; 18(2); 24; 28; 4:7; 18; 19; 30; 5:8; 10; 15; 22; 23(2); 6:5; 8(2); 12(2); 13; 17; 22; 26; 7:14(2); 8:5; 22; 24; 9:11; 12; 13; 14; 18; 19; 26; 10:7; 12; 19; 11:4; 6; 12; 15; 17; 19; 21; 24; 25; 27; 29; 38; 42; 12:8; **Hos** 1:7; 9(2); 10; 2:2; 4; 6; 7(2); 8; 23(2); 3:3(2); 4:10(2); 14(2); 15(2); 5:3; 4(2); 6; 13; 6:6; 7:2; 8; 9(2); 10; 14; 16; 8:4(2); 6; 13; 9:1; 2; 3; 4(2); 12; 17; 10:3; 9; 11:3; 5; 9(4); 13:13; 14:3(2); **Joel** 1:16; 2:2; 7; 8; 13; 17; 21; 22; 3:21; **Amos** 1:3; 6; 9(2); 11; 13; 2:1; 4(2); 6; 11; 12; 14; 15; 3:6(2); 8; 10; 4:6; 7(2); 8(2); 9; 10; 11; 5:5(2); 11(2); 14; 18; 20(2); 21; 22; 23; 6:6; 10; 13; 7:3; 6; 8; 10; 13; 16(2); 8:2; 8; 11; 12; 9:1(2); 4; 7(2); 8; 9; 10; **Obad** 5(2); 8; 12; 13(2); 16; 18; **Jonah** 1:6; 13; 14(2); 3:7; 9; 10; 4:2; 10; 11; **Mic** 1:5(2); 10(2); 11; 2:3; 6(3); 7; 10; 3:1; 4; 5; 6(2); 11; 4:3; 12; 5:7; 15; 6:14(2); 15(3); 7:5(2); 8; 18; **Nah** 1:3; 9; 3:1; 17; 19; **Hab** 1:2(2); 5; 6; 12(2); 13; 17; 2:3(2); 4; 6(2); 7; 13; 3:17; **Zeph** 1:6; 12; 13(2); 2:1; 3:2(4); 3; 5(2); 7; 11; 13; 15; 16(2); **Hag** 1:2; 6(2); 2:3; 5; 17; 19; **Zec** 1:4(2); 6; 12; 3:2; 4:5; 6; 13; 7:6; 7; 10; 11; 13(2); 14; 8:11; 13; 14; 15; 9:5; 10:6; 10; 11:5(2); 6; 9; 12; 16; 12:7; 13:3; 14:2; 6; 7; 17; 18(3); 19; **Mal** 1:2; 8(2); 2:2(3); 6; 9; 10(2); 13; 15; 16; 3:5; 6(2); 7; 10(2); 11; 18; **Mt** 1:19; 20; 25; 2:6; 12; 18(2); 3:9; 10; 11; 4:4; 7; 5:17(2); 21; 27; 29; 30; 33; 34; 36; 39; 42; 46; 47; 6:1; 2; 3; 5; 7; 8; 13; 15; 16; 18; 19; 20; 25; 26(2); 28; 29; 30; 7:1(2); 3; 6; 19; 21; 22; 25; 26; 29; 8:8; 10(2); 20; 9:12; 13(2); 14; 24; 10:5(2); 13; 14; 20; 23; 24; 26(3); 28(2); 29(2); 31; 34(2); 37(2); 38(2); 11:6; 11; 17(2); 20; 12:2; 3; 4; 5; 7(2); 11; 16; 19; 20(2); 23; 24; 25; 30(2); 31; 32; 13:5; 11; 12; 13(2); 14(2); 17(2); 19; 21; 27; 34; 55(2); 56; 57; 58; 14:4; 16; 27; 15:2; 6; 11; 13; 17; 20; 23; 24; 26; 32; 16:3; 9; 11(2); 12; 17; 18; 22; 23; 28; 17:7; 12; 16; 19; 21; 24; 18:3; 10; 12; 13; 14; 16; 22; 25; 30; 33; 35; 19:4; 6; 8; 10; 14; 18(3); 20:13; 15; 22; 23; 26; 28; 21:21(2); 25; 29; 30; 32(2); 22:3; 8; 11; 12; 16; 17; 29; 31; 32; 23:3(2); 4; 8; 23; 30; 37; 39; 24:2(3); 6(2); 17; 20; 21; 23; 26(2); 29; 34; 35; 36; 39; 42; 43; 44; 50(2); 25:9(2); 12; 24(2); 26(2); 29; 43(3); 44; 45(2); 26:5; 11; 24; 29; 35; 39; 40; 41; 42; 70; 72; 74; 27:6; 13; 34; 28:5; 6; 10; **Mk** 1:7; 22; 34; 2:2; 4; 17; 18; 24; 26; 27; 3:12; 20; 4:5; 12(2); 13; 21; 22; 25; 27; 34; 38; 5:3; 7; 10; 19; 36; 39; 6:3(2); 4; 9; 11; 18; 19; 26; 34; 50; 52; 7:3; 4; 5; 18; 19; 24; 27; 8:17; 18(3); 21; 33; 9:1; 6; 18; 28; 30; 32; 37; 38(2); 39; 40; 41; 44(2); 46(2); 48(2); 10:9; 14; 15(2); 19(5); 27; 38; 40; 43; 45; 11:13; 16; 17; 23; 26; 31; 12:10; 14(2); 15; 24(2); 26; 27; 34; 13:2(2); 7(2); 11; 14; 15; 16; 18; 19; 21; 24; 30; 31; 32; 33; 35; 14:2; 7; 29; 31; 36; 37; 49; 56; 68; 71; 15:23; 16:6(2); 11; 14; 16; 18; **Lk** 1:13; 20(2); 22; 30; 34; 60; 2:10; 26; 37; 43; 45; 49; 50; 3:8; 9; 15; 16; 4:4; 12; 22; 35; 41; 42; 5:10; 19; 31; 32; 36; 6:2; 3; 4; 29; 30; 37(4); 39; 40; 41; 42; 43; 44; 46; 48; 49; 7:6(3); 9(2); 13; 23; 28; 30; 32(2); 45; 46; 8:10(2); 17(2); 18; 19; 28; 31; 47; 49; 50; 52(2); 9:5; 27; 33; 40; 45(2); 49; 50(2); 53; 55; 56; 58; 10:6; 7; 10; 20; 24(2); 40; 42; 11:4; 7; 8; 23(2); 35; 38; 40; 42; 44(2); 46; 52; 12:2(2); 4; 6(2); 7; 10; 15; 21; 26; 27(3); 29; 32; 33(2); 39; 40; 46(2); 47; 48; 56; 57; 59; 13:9; 14; 15; 16; 24; 25; 27; 34; 35; 14:5; 6; 8; 12; 26; 27; 28; 29; 30; 31; 33; 15:4; 8; 13; 28; 16:11; 12; 31; 17:8; 9; 17; 18; 20; 22; 23; 31(2); 18:1; 2; 4(2); 7; 11; 13; 16; 17; 20(4); 30; 19:3; 14; 21(2); 22(2); 23; 26; 27; 44(2); 48; 20:5; 7; 26; 38; 40; 21:6(2); 8(2); 9(2); 14; 15; 18; 21; 32; 33; 22:16; 10; 20; 27; 32; 34; 40; 42; 57; 58; 60; 67; 68; 23:28; 34; 40; 51; 24:3; 6; 11; 16; 18; 23; 24; 26; 32; 39; 41; **Jn** 1:3; 5; 8; 10; 11; 13; 20(2); 21; 25; 26; 27; 31; 33; 2:4; 9; 12; 16; 24; 25; 3:7; 8; 10; 11; 12; 15; 16; 17; 18(3); 24; 28; 34; 36(2); 4:2; 15; 18; 22; 29; 32; 35; 42; 48; 5:10; 13; 18; 23(2); 24; 28; 30; 31; 34; 38(2); 40; 41; 42; 43; 44; 45; 47; 6:7; 17; 20; 22; 24; 26; 27; 32; 36; 38; 42; 43; 46; 50; 58; 64(2); 70; 7:1; 6; 8(2); 10; 16; 19; 22; 23; 24; 25; 28(2); 30; 34; 35; 36; 39(2); 42; 45; 49; 8:6; 12; 13; 16; 20; 23; 24; 27; 29; 35; 40; 41; 43; 44; 45; 46; 47(2); 48; 49; 50; 55(2); 57; 9:8; 12; 16(2); 18; 21(2); 25; 27; 29; 30; 31; 32; 33; 39; 10:1; 5(2); 6; 8; 10; 12(2); 13; 16; 21; 25; 26(2); 33; 34; 37(2); 38; 11:4; 9(2); 15; 21; 30; 32; 37(2); 40; 50; 51; 52; 56; 12:5; 6; 8; 9; 15; 16; 30; 35; 37; 39; 40; 42; 44; 46; 47(3); 48; 49; 13:7; 8; 9; 10(2); 11; 16; 18; 36; 38; 14:1; 2; 5; 9; 10(2); 17; 18; 22(2); 24(3); 27(2); 30; 15:2; 6; 15(2); 16; 19; 20; 21; 22(2); 24(2); 16:1; 3; 4; 7(2); 9; 13; 16; 17; 19; 26; 30; 32; 17:9; 14(2); 15; 16(2); 25; 18:11; 17(2); 25(2); 26; 28; 30(2); 31; 36(3); 40; 19:10(2); 12; 21; 24; 31; 33; 36; 20:2; 5; 7; 9; 13; 14; 17(2); 24; 25; 27; 29; 30; 21:4; 6; 8; 11; 18; 23(3); 25; **Acts** 1:4; 5; 7; 2:7; 15; 24; 25; 27; 31; 34; 3:23; 4:18; 5:4(3); 7; 22; 28(2); 40; 42; 6:2; 10; 13; 7:5; 18; 19; 25; 32; 39; 40; 48; 50; 52; 53; 60; 8:21; 32; 9:21; 26; 38; 10:14; 15; 28; 41; 47; 11:8; 9; 12:9; 14; 19; 22; 23; 13:10; 11; 25(2); 27; 35; 39; 14:17; 18; 15:19; 38(2); 16:7; 21; 17:4; 5; 6; 12; 24; 27; 29; 18:9(2); 20; 19:2; 9; 26; 27; 30; 31; 32; 35; 20:10; 12; 16; 22; 27; 29; 31; 21:4; 12; 13; 14; 21;

34; 38; 22:9; 11; 18; 22; 23:5(2); 9; 21; 24:4; 25:7; 11; 16; 24; 27; 26:19; 25; 26; 29; 32; 27:7; 10; 12; 14; 15; 21; 24; 34; 39; 28:4; 19; 24; 25; 26(2); **Rom** 1:13; 16; 21; 28(2); 32; 2:4; 8; 13; 14(2); 21(2); 22; 26; 27; 28; 29(2); 3:3; 8; 10; 12; 17; 29; 4:2; 4; 5; 8; 10; 11; 12; 13; 16; 17; 19(2); 20; 23; 5:3; 5; 11; 13; 14; 15; 16; 6:3; 6; 12; 14(2); 15; 16; 7:1; 6; 7(3); 15(2); 16; 18; 19(2); 20; 8:1; 3; 4; 7; 9(2); 12; 15; 18; 20; 23; 24; 25; 26; 32(2); 9:1; 6(2); 8; 10; 11(2); 16; 21; 24; 25(2); 26; 30; 31; 32; 33; 10:2; 3; 6; 11; 14(2); 16; 18; 19; 20(2); 11:2(2); 4; 7; 8(2); 10; 18(2); 20; 21(2); 23; 25; 30; 31; 12:2; 3; 4; 11; 14; 16(2); 19; 21; 13:3(2); 4; 5; 9(5); 13(3); 14; 14:1; 3(4); 6(4); 13; 15(2); 16; 17; 20; 22; 23(2); 15:1; 3; 18(2); 20; 21(2); 31; 16:4; 18; **1Cor** 1:16; 17(2); 20; 21; 26(3); 28; 2:1; 2; 4; 5; 6; 8; 9; 12; 13; 14; 3:1; 2(2); 3; 4; 16; 4:3; 4; 6; 7(2); 14; 15; 18; 19; 20; 5:1; 2; 6(2); 8; 9; 10; 11(2); 12; 6:1; 2; 3; 5(2); 7(2); 9(3); 12(2); 13; 15; 16; 19(2); 7:1; 4(2); 5(2); 6; 10(2); 11; 12(3); 13(2); 15; 18(2); 21; 23; 27(2); 28(2); 30(3); 31; 35; 36; 38; 8:7; 8(2); 10; 9:1(4); 2; 4; 5; 6; 7(2); 8; 9; 12(2); 13; 16; 18; 21; 24; 26(2); 10:1; 5; 6; 13; 16(2); 18; 20(2); 23(2); 27; 28; 29; 33; 11:6; 7; 8; 14; 17(2); 20; 22(3); 29; 31; 32; 34; 12:1; 14; 15(3); 16(3); 13:1; 2; 3; 4(3); 5(3); 6; 14:2; 11; 16; 17; 20; 21; 22(4); 23; 24; 33; 34; 39; 15:9; 10(2); 13; 14; 15(2); 16(2); 17; 29; 32; 33; 34(2); 36; 37; 39; 46; 51; 58; 16:7; 12; 22; **2Cor** 1:8; 9; 12; 18; 19; 23; 24; 2:1; 4; 5(2); 11; 13; 17; 3:3(2); 5; 6; 7; 8; 13(2); 4:1; 2; 4; 5; 7; 8(2); 9(2); 16; 18(3); 5:1; 3; 4; 7; 12(2); 15; 19; 6:1; 3; 9; 12; 14; 17; 7:3; 7; 8; 9; 10; 12; 14; 8:5; 8; 10; 12(2); 13; 19; 21; 9:4; 5; 7; 12; 10:2; 3; 4; 8(2); 9; 12(2); 13; 14(2); 15; 16; 18; 11:4(3); 5; 6; 11; 17; 29(2); 31; 12:1; 4; 5; 6; 13; 14(3); 16; 18(2); 20(2); 21; 13:2; 3; 5; 6; 7; 10; **Gal** 1:1; 7; 10; 11; 16; 20; 2:5; 14(2); 15; 16(2); 20; 21; 3:1; 10; 12; 16; 20; 4:8; 12; 14; 17; 18; 21; 27(2); 30; 31; 5:1; 7; 8; 13; 15; 16; 18; 21; 26; 6:4; 7(2); 9(2); **Eph** 1:16; 21; 2:8; 9; 3:5; 13; 4:17; 20; 26(2); 30; 5:3; 4; 7; 15; 17; 18; 27; 6:4; 6; 7; 12; **Phil** 1:16; 22; 29; 2:4; 6; 12; 16; 21; 27; 30; 3:1; 9; 12; 13; 4:11; 17; **Col** 1:9; 23; 2:1; 8; 18; 19; 21(3); 23; 3:2; 9; 19; 21; 22; 23; **1Th** 1:5; 8(2); 2:1; 3; 4; 8; 9; 13; 15; 17; 19; 4:5(2); 7; 8; 9; 13(2); 15; 5:3; 4; 5; 6; 9; 19; 20; **2Th** 1:8(2); 2:2; 3; 5; 10; 12; 3:2; 6; 7; 8; 9(2); 10; 11; 13; 14; 15; **1Ti** 1:9; 20; 2:7; 9; 12; 14; 3:3(4); 5; 6; 8(3); 11; 4:14; 5:1; 8; 9; 13(2); 16; 18; 19; 6:1; 2; 3; 4; 17; **2Ti** 1:7; 8; 9; 12; 16; 2:5; 9; 13; 14; 15; 20; 24; 4:3; 8; 16; **Titus** 1:6; 7(4); 11; 14; 2:3(2); 5; 9; 10; 3:5; 14; **Philem** 1:14; 16; 19; **Heb** 1:12; 14; 2:5; 8(2); 11; 16; 3:8; 10; 11; 15; 16; 17; 18(2); 19; 4:2(2); 6; 7; 8; 13; 15; 5:5; 12; 6:1; 10; 12; 7:6; 11; 16; 20; 21; 23; 27; 8:2; 4; 9(3); 11; 9:7; 8; 9; 11(2); 24; 10:1; 2; 4; 5; 8; 25; 35; 37; 39; 11:1; 3; 5(2); 7; 8; 13; 16; 23; 27; 31(2); 35; 38; 39; 40; 12:4; 5; 7; 8; 9; 18; 19; 20; 25(3); 26; 13:2; 6; 9(3); 16; 17; **Jas** 1:5; 7; 16; 20; 22; 23; 25; 26; 2:1; 4; 5; 6; 7; 11(2); 14; 16; 17; 21; 24; 25; 3:1; 2; 10; 14(2); 15; 4:1; 2(3); 3; 4; 11(2); 14; 17; 5:6; 9; 12; 17(2); **1Pet** 1:4; 8(2); 12; 14; 18; 23; 2:6; 10(2); 16; 18; 23(2); 3:1; 3; 4; 6; 7; 9; 14; 21; 24(2); 4:4; 12; 16; 17; 5:2(2); 4; **2Pet** 1:12; 16; 21; 2:3(2); 4; 5; 10; 11; 12; 21; 3:8; 9(2); **1Jn** 1:6; 8; 10(2); 2:1; 2; 4(2); 11; 15(2); 16; 19(2); 21(2); 23; 27; 28; 3:1(2); 2; 6(2); 9; 10(3); 12; 13; 14; 18; 21; 4:1; 3(2); 6(2); 8(2); 10; 18; 20(2); 5:3; 6; 10(2); 12(2); 16(3); 17; 18(2); **2Jn** 1; 5; 7; 8; 9(2); 10(2); 12; **3Jn** 9; 10; 11(2); 13; **Jude** 5; 6; 9; 10; 19; **Rev** 1:17; 2:2(2); 3; 9; 11; 13; 21; 24(2); 3:2; 3(2); 4; 5; 8; 9; 17; 18; 4:8; 5:5; 6:6; 10; 7:1; 3; 8:12; 9:4(2); 5; 6; 20(3); 10:4; 11:2; 6; 9; 12:8; 11; 13:8; 15; 14:4; 15:4; 16:9; 11; 18; 20; 17:8(3); 10; 11; 18:4(2); 19:10; 20:4; 5; 15; 21:25; 22:9; 10

NOTHING

Gen 11:6; 19:8; 26:29; 40:15; **Ex** 9:4; 12:10; 20; 16:18; 21:2; 22:3; 23:26; **Num** 6:4; 11:6; 16:26; 22:16; **Deut** 2:7; 20:16; 22:26; 28:55; **Josh** 11:15; **Judg** 3:2; 7:14; 14:6; **1Sa** 3:18; 20:2; 22:15; 25:21; 36; 27:1; 30:19; **2Sa** 12:3; 24:24; **1Kin** 4:27; 8:9; 10:21; 11:22; 18:43; 22:16; **2Kin** 10:10; 20:13; 15; 17; **2Chr** 5:10; 9:2; 14:11; 18:15; **Ezr** 4:3; **Neh** 2:2; 5:8; 12; 8:10; 9:21; **Est** 2:15; 5:13; 6:3; 10; **Job** 6:18; 8:9; 24:25; 26:7; 34:9; **Ps** 17:3; 19:6; 39:5; 49:17; 119:165; **Prov** 8:8; 9:13; 10:2; 13:4; 7; 20:4; 22:27; **Eccl** 2:24; 3:14; 22; 5:14; 15; 6:2; 7:14; **Is** 34:12; 39:2; 4; 6; 40:17(2); 23; 41:11; 12; 24; 29; 44:10; **Jer** 10:24; 13:7; 10; 32:17; 23; 38:14; 39:10; 42:4; 50:26; **Lam** 1:12; **Eze** 13:3; **Dan** 4:35; **Joel** 2:3; **Amos** 3:4; 5; 7; **Hag** 2:3; **Mt** 5:13; 10:26; 15:32; 17:20; 21:19; 23:16; 18; 26:62; 27:12; 19; 24; **Mk** 1:44; 4:22; 5:26; 6:8; 36; 7:15; 8:1; 2; 9:29; 11:13; 14:60; 61; 15:3; 4; 5; **Lk** 1:37; 4:2; 5:5; 6:35; 7:42; 8:17; 9:3; 10:19; 11:6; 12:2; 22:35; 23:9; 15; 41; **Jn** 3:27; 4:11; 5:19; 30; 6:12; 39; 63; 7:26; 8:28; 54; 9:33; 11:49; 12:19; 14:30; 15:5; 16:23; 24; 18:20; 21:3; **Acts** 4:14; 21; 10:20; 11:8; 12; 17:21; 19:36; 20:20; 21:24; 23:14; 29; 25:25; 26:31; 27:33; 28:17; **Rom** 14:14; **1Cor** 1:19; 4:4; 5; 7:19(2); 8:2; 4; 9:16; 13:2; 3; **2Cor** 6:10; 7:9; 8:15; 12:11(2); 13:8; **Gal** 2:6; 4:1; 5:2; 6:3; **Phil** 1:20; 28; 2:3; 4:6; **1Th** 4:12; **1Ti** 4:4; 5:21; 6:4; 7(2); **Titus** 1:15; 3:13; **Philem** 1:14; **Heb** 2:8; 7:14; 19; **Jas** 1:4; 6; **3Jn** 7; **Rev** 3:17

NOW

Gen 2:23; 3:1; 22; 4:11; 10:1; 11:6; 27; 12:1; 11; 19; 13:14; 15:5; 16:1; 2; 18:3; 11; 21; 27; 31; 19:2; 8; 9; 19; 20; 20:7; 21:23; 22:2; 12; 24:42; 49; 25:12; 26:22; 28; 29; 27:2; 3; 8; 9; 26; 36; 37; 43; 29:32; 34; 35; 30:20; 30(2); 31:12; 13; 16; 25; 28; 30; 34; 42; 44; 32:4; 10; 33:10; 15; 34:5; 35:22; 36:1; 37:3; 20; 32; 41:33; 42:1; 43:10; 11; 44:10; 30; 33; 45:5; 8; 19; 46:30; 34; 47:4; 29; 48:5; 10; 50:4; 5; 17(2); 21; **Ex** 1:1; 8; 2:15; 16; 3:1; 3; 9; 10; 18; 4:6; 12; 5:5; 18; 6:1; 7:11; 9:15; 18; 19; 10:11; 17; 11:2; 12:40; 16:36; 18:11; 19; 19:5; 21:1; 29:38; 32:10; 30; 32; 34; 33:5; 13(2); 34:9; **Num** 11:6; 23; 12:3; 6; 13; 13:20; 22; 14:15; 17; 19; 22; 25; 41; 16:1; 49; 20:10; 22:4; 6; 11; 19; 22; 29; 33; 34; 38; 24:11; 14; 17; 25:14; 31:17; 43; 32:1; **Deut** 2:13; 4:1; 32; 5:25; 6:1; 10:12; 22; 26:10; 31:19; 21; 32:39; **Josh** 1:1; 2; 2:12; 3:12; 5:5; 14; 6:1; 7:19; 8:11; 9:6; 11; 12; 17; 19; 23; 25; 10:1; 12:1; 13:1; 7; 14:10(2); 11; 12; 17:8; 18:21; 22:4(2); 7; 26; 31; 24:14; 23; **Judg** 1:1; 8; 10; 23; 3:1; 4:11; 6:13; 17; 39; 7:3; 8:2; 6; 10; 15; 9:16; 32; 38(2); 11:1; 7; 8; 13; 23; 25; 12:6; 13:3; 4; 7; 12; 14:2; 12; 15:3; 18; 16:9; 10; 27; 17:3; 13; 18:14; 19:9; 18; 22; 24; 20:3; 9; 13; 38; 21:1; **Ruth** 1:1; 2:2; 7; 3:2; 11; 12; 4:7; 18; **1Sa** 1:1; 9; 13; 2:12; 16; 22; 30; 3:7; 4:1; 15; 6:7; 8:2; 5; 9; 9:1; 3; 6(2); 9; 12; 13; 15; 10:19; 12:2; 7; 10; 13; 16; 13:12; 13; 14; 19; 14:1; 17; 30; 49; 15:1; 3; 25; 30; 16:12; 15; 16; 17; 17:1; 12; 17; 19; 29; 18:22; 19:2; 20:29; 31; 36; 21:3; 7; 22:6; 7; 12; 23:20; 24:20; 21; 25:3; 7(2); 10; 17; 21; 26(2); 27; 26:8; 11; 16; 19; 20; 27:1; 5; 28:3; 22; 29:1; 7; 10; 31:1; **2Sa** 1:1; 2:6; 7; 14; 3:1; 18; 4:11; 7:2; 8; 25; 28; 29; 9:6; 10; 12:10; 23; 28; 13:7; 13; 17; 20; 24; 25; 28(2); 33; 14:1; 2; 15(2); 17; 18; 21; 32; 15:34; 16:11; 17:1; 5; 9; 16; 17; 18:3(2); 18; 19; 19:7(2); 9; 10; 32; 20:6; 23; 21:2; 23:1; 24:2; 3; 10; 13; 14; 16; **1Kin** 1:1; 12; 18(2); 2:1; 9; 16; 24; 3:7; 5:4; 6; 8:25; 26; 9:11; 10:14; 12:4; 11; 16; 26; 13:6; 11; 14:14; 29; 15:1; 7; 31; 16:5; 14; 20; 27; 17:24; 18:3; 11; 14; 19; 43; 19:4; 20:31; 33; 21:7; 22:13; 23; 39; 45; **2Kin** 1:4; 5; 14; 18; 2:16; 3:1; 15; 23; 4:1; 9; 13; 26; 5:1; 6; 8; 15(2); 22; 6:1; 7:4; 9; 12; 19; 8:6; 9:12; 14; 26; 34; 10:2; 6; 10; 19; 34; 12:7; 13:8; 14; 19; 14:15; 19; 28; 15:36; 16:19; 18:1; 13; 19; 20; 21; 23; 25; 19:19; 25; 20:3; 21:17; 25; 22:14; 23:28; 24:5; 25:4; 11; **1Chr** 1:32; 43; 2:34; 42; 3:1; 5:1; 6:54; 7:1; 8:1; 9:2; 10:1; 11:15; 12:1; 14:1; 4; 17:1; 7; 23; 26; 27; 18:1; 9; 19:1; 10; 21:8; 12; 13; 15; 20; 22:5; 11; 14; 19; 23:3; 14; 24:1; 7; 25:9; 27:1; 28:8; 10; 29:2; 13; 17; 20; 29; **2Chr** 1:9; 10; 2:7; 13; 15; 3:3; 6:7; 16; 17; 40; 41; 7:1; 15; 16; 8:16; 9:13; 29; 10:4; 16; 12:15; 13:1; 8; 15:3; 18:1; 22; 30; 19:7; 20:10; 34; 21:1; 4; 23:12; 24:11; 17; 27; 25:3; 14; 19; 26; 27; 26:22; 27:7; 28:10; 11; 26; 29:5; 10; 11; 17; 31; 30:8; 31:1; 32:15; 32; 33:14; 18; 34:8; 22; 35:3; 26; 36:8; 22; **Ezr** 1:1; 2:1; 3:8; 4:1; 13; 14; 21; 22; 23; 5:16; 17; 6:6; 7:1; 11; 8:1; 33; 9:1; 8; 10; 12; 10:1; 2; 3; 11; 14; **Neh** 1:6(2); 10; 11; 2:1; 9; 4:3; 5:5; 18; 6:1; 7(2); 9; 7:1; 4; 9:1; 32; 10:1; 11:3; 12:1; 13:3; **Est** 1:1; 2:5; 12; 15; 3:4; 5:1; 6:4; 6; 9:1; 12; **Job** 1:6; 11; 2:5; 11; 3:13; 4:5; 12; 5:1; 6:3; 21; 28; 7:21; 8:6; 9:25; 12:7; 13:6; 18; 19; 14:16; 16:7; 19; 17:3; 10; 15; 19:6; 23; 22:21; 24:25; 30:1; 9; 16; 32:4; 14; 33:2; 34:16; 35:15; 37:21; 38:3; 40:7; 10; 15; 16; 42:5; 8; **Ps** 2:10; 12:5; 17:11; 20:6; 27:6; 37:25; 39:7; 41:8; 50:22; 71:18; 74:6; 115:2; 116:14; 18; 118:2; 3; 4; 25(2); 119:67; 122:8; 124:1; 129:1; **Prov** 5:7; 6:3; 7:12(2); 24; 8:32; **Eccl** 2:1; 16; 3:15; 9:6; 7; 15; 12:1; **Song** 3:2; 7:8; **Is** 1:18; 21; 5:1; 3; 5; 7:3; 13; 8:7; 16:14; 19:12; 22:1; 28:22; 29:22(2); 30:8; 31:3; 33:10(3); 36:1; 4; 5; 8; 10; 37:20; 26; 38:3; 42:14; 43:1(2); 19; 44:1; 47:8; 12; 13; 48:7; 16; 49:5; 19; 51:21; 52:5; 64:8; **Jer** 2:18; 4:12; 31; 5:1; 21; 24; 7:12; 13; 14:10; 17:15; 18:11(2); 13; 20:1; 25:5; 26:8; 13; 27:6; 16; 18; 28:7; 15; 29:1; 27; 30:6; 32:16; 36; 34:10; 15; 35:15; 36:15; 16; 17; 22; 37:3; 4; 19; 20; 38:7; 12; 25; 39:11; 15; 40:3; 4; 5; 7; 41:1; 9; 13; 42:15; 21; 22; 44:7; 45:3; 52:7; 12; **Eze** 1:1; 15; 4:14; 7:3; 8; 8:5; 8; 10:3; 16:8; 17:12; 18:14; 25; 19:5; 13; 22:2; 23:43; 26:2; 18; 27:2; 32:32; 38:12; 39:25; 41:12; 42:5; 15; 43:9; 46:12; 47:7; 48:1; **Dan** 1:6; 9; 18; 2:23(2); 3:15; 4:18; 37; 5:10; 12; 15; 16; 6:8; 10; 16; 8:18; 22; 9:15; 17; 22; 10:11; 14; 20; 11:2; 34; **Hos** 1:8; 2:7; 10; 4:16; 5:3; 7; 7:2; 8:8; 10; 13; 10:2; 3; 13:2; **Joel** 2:12; **Amos** 6:7; 7:16; **Jonah** 1:1; 17; 3:3; 4:3; **Mic** 4:9; 10; 11; 5:1; 4; 6:1; 5; 7:4; 10; **Nah** 1:13; **Hag** 1:5; 2:2; 3; 4; 11; 15; 18; **Zec** 1:4; 3:3; 8; 5:5; 8:11; 9:8; **Mal** 1:8; 9; 2:1; 3:10; 15; **Mt** 1:18; 22; 2:1; 3:10; 15; 4:12; 8:18; 9:18; 10:2; 11:2; 12; 14:15; 24; 15:32; 21:18; 22:25; 24:32; 26:6; 17; 20; 45; 48; 53; 59; 65; 69; 27:15; 42; 43; 45; 54; 62; 28:11; **Mk** 1:14; 16; 4:37; 5:11; 6:35(2); 8:2; 14; 10:30; 11:11; 12:20; 13:12; 28; 14:41; 15:6; 32; 42; 16:9; **Lk** 1:7; 57; 2:15; 29; 41; 3:1; 9; 21; 4:40; 5:4; 6:21(2); 25; 7:1; 6; 12; 39; 8:11; 22; 38; 9:7; 10:36; 38; 11:7; 39; 14:17; 15:25; 16:25; 18:22; 19:37; 42; 20:37; 21:30(2); 22:1; 36; 23:47; 24:1; **Jn** 1:44; 2:8; 10; 23; 4:6; 18; 23; 42; 43; 51; 5:2; 6; 25; 6:10; 16; 17; 7:2; 14; 8:5; 40; 52; 9:19; 21; 25; 31; 41; 11:1; 5; 18; 22; 30; 57; 12:27; 31(2); 13:1; 2; 7; 19; 23; 28; 31; 33; 36; 37; 14:29; 15:3; 22; 24; 16:5; 12; 19; 22; 29; 30; 31; 32; 17:5; 7; 11; 13; 18:14; 24; 36; 40; 19:23; 25; 28; 29; 41; 21:4; 6; 7; 10; 14; **Acts** 1:18; 2:6; 33; 37; 3:1; 17; 4:3; 13; 29; 5:24; 38; 7:4; 11; 34; 52; 8:14; 9:36; 10:5; 17; 33; 11:19; 12:1; 11; 18; 13:1; 11; 13; 34; 43; 15:10; 16:6; 36; 37; 17:1; 16; 30; 18:14; 20:22; 25; 32; 21:3; 22:1; 16; 23:15; 21; 24:13; 17; 25:1; 26:6; 17; 27:9(3); 22; **Rom** 1:10; 13; 3:19; 21; 4:4; 19; 23; 5:9; 11; 6:8; 19; 21; 22; 7:6; 17; 20; 8:1; 9; 22; 11:12; 30; 31; 13:11(2); 14:15; 15:5; 8; 13; 23; 25; 30; 33; 16:17; 25; 26; **1Cor** 1:10; 12; 2:12; 3:2; 8; 12; 4:7; 8(2); 18; 5:11; 6:7; 13; 7:1; 14; 25; 8:1; 9:25; 10:6; 11; 11:2; 17; 12:1; 4; 18; 20; 27; 13:12(2); 13; 14:6; 15:12; 20; 50; 16:1; 5; 7; 10; **2Cor** 1:21; 2:14; 3:17; 5:5; 16; 20; 6:2(2); 13; 7:9; 8:11; 14; 22; 9:10; 10:1; 12:6; 13:2; 7; **Gal** 1:9; 10; 20; 23; 2:20; 3:3; 16; 20; 4:1; 9; 20; 25; 28; 29; 5:19; **Eph** 2:2; 13; 19; 3:5; 10; 20; 4:9; 5:8; **Phil** 1:5; 20; 30; 2:12; 3:18; 4:10; 15; 20; **Col** 1:21; 24; 26; 3:8; **1Th** 3:6; 8; 11; 5:14; **2Th** 2:1; 6; 7; 16; 3:6; 12; 16; **1Ti** 1:5; 17; 4:1; 8; 5:5; **2Ti** 1:10; 3:8; 4:6; **Philem** 1:9; 11; 16; **Heb** 2:8; 7:4; 8:1; 6; 13; 9:5; 6; 24; 26; 10:18; 38; 11:1; 16; 12:11; 26; 13:20; **Jas** 2:11; 4:13; 16; 5:1; **1Pet** 1:6; 8; 12; 2:10(2); 25; 3:21; **2Pet** 2:3; 3:1; 7; 18; **1Jn** 2:8; 9; 18; 28; 3:2; 4:3; **2Jn** 5; **Jude** 24; 25; **Rev** 12:10

O

Gen 17:18; 24:12; 42; 27:34; 38; 32:9; 43:20; 49:6; 18; **Ex** 4:10; 13; 15:6(2); 11; 16; 17(2); 32:4; 8; 34:9; **Num** 10:36; 12:13; 16:22; 21:17; 29; 24:5(2); **Deut** 3:24; 4:1; 5:1; 29; 6:3; 4; 9:1; 26; 20:3; 21:8; 26:10; 27:9; 32:1(2); 6; 29; 43; 33:23; 29(2); **Josh** 7:7; 8; 13; **Judg** 3:19; 5:3(2); 21; 31; 6:22; 13:8; 16:28(2); 21:3; **1Sa** 1:11; 4:9; 17:55; 20:12; 23:10; 11; 20; 26:17; **2Sa** 1:25; 7:18; 19(2); 22; 25; 27; 28; 29; 14:4; 9; 22; 15:31; 34; 16:4; 18:33(2); 19:4(2); 26; 20:1; 22:29; 50; 23:17; 24:10; **1Kin** 1:13; 20; 24; 3:7; 17; 26; 8:26; 28; 53; 12:16; 28; 13:2; 17:18; 20; 21; 18:26; 37; 19:4; 20:4; 21:20; 22:28; **2Kin** 1:11; 13; 4:40; 6:12; 26; 8:5; 9:5(2); 23; 13:14; 19:15; 19; 20:3; **1Chr** 16:13; 34; 35; 17:16; 17(2); 19; 20; 25; 27; 21:17; 29:11(2); 16; 18; **2Chr** 1:9; 6:14; 16; 17; 19; 41(2); 42; 10:16; 13:12; 14:11(2); 20:6; 12; 17; 20; 25:7; **Ezr** 9:6; 10; 15; **Neh** 1:5; 11; 4:4; 6:9; 13:14; 22; 29; 31; **Est** 7:3; **Job** 6:2; 7:7; 20; 16:18; 19:21; 33:31; 34:2; 37:14; **Ps** 2:10; 3:3; 7(2); 4:1; 2; 5:1; 3; 8; 10; 6:1; 2(2); 3; 4; 7:1; 3; 6; 8; 8:1; 9; 9:1; 2; 6; 13; 19; 20; 10:1; 12(2); 12:7; 13:1; 3; 16:1; 2; 17:1; 6; 7; 13; 14; 18:1; 15; 49; 19:14; 21:1; 22:2; 3; 19(2); 24:6; 7; 9; 25:1; 2; 4; 6; 7; 11; 17; 20; 22; 26:1; 2; 6; 27:7; 9; 11; 28:1; 29:1; 30:1; 2; 3; 4; 8; 10; 12; 31:1; 5; 9; 14; 17; 23; 33:1; 22; 34:3; 8; 9; 35:1; 22(2); 24; 36:5; 6; 7; 10; 38:1; 15(2); 21(2); 22; 39:12; 13; 40:5; 8; 9; 11; 13(2); 17; 41:10; 42:1; 5; 6; 11; 43:1(2); 3; 4; 5; 44:1; 4; 23; 45:3; 6; 10; 47:1; 48:9; 10; 50:7(2); 51:1; 10; 14; 15; 17; 52:1; 4; 54:1; 2; 6; 55:1; 9; 23; 56:1; 2; 7; 12; 57:1; 5; 7; 9; 11; 58:1(2); 6(2); 59:1; 3; 5; 8; 11; 17; 60:1(2); 10(2); 61:1; 5; 7; 62:12; 63:1; 64:1; 65:1; 2; 5; 66:8; 10; 67:3; 4; 5; 68:7; 9; 10; 24; 28; 32; 35; 69:1; 5; 6(2); 13(2); 16; 29; 70:1(2); 5(2); 71:1; 4; 5; 12(2); 17; 18; 19(2); 22(2); 72:1; 73:20; 74:1; 10; 18; 19; 21; 22; 75:1; 76:6; 77:13; 16; 78:1; 79:1; 8; 9; 12; 80:1; 3; 4; 7; 14; 19; 81:8(2); 82:8; 83:1(2); 13; 16; 84:1; 3; 8(2); 9; 12; 85:4; 7; 86:1; 2; 3; 4; 6; 8; 9; 11; 12; 14; 15; 16; 87:3; 88:1; 13; 89:5; 8; 15; 51; 90:13; 14; 92:1; 5; 9; 93:3; 5; 94:1(2); 5; 12; 18; 95:1; 6; 96:1; 7; 9; 97:8; 98:1; 99:8; 101:1; 2; 102:1; 12; 24; 103:1; 2; 22; 104:1(2); 24; 35; 105:1; 6; 106:1; 4(2); 47; 107:1; 108:1; 3; 5; 11(2); 109:1; 21; 26(2); 113:1; 114:5; 115:1; 9; 10; 116:4; 7; 16; 19; 117:1; 118:1; 25(2); 29; 119:5; 8; 10; 12; 31; 33; 41; 52; 55; 57; 64; 65; 75; 89; 97; 107; 108; 137; 145; 149; 151; 156; 159; 169; 174; 120:2; 122:2; 123:1; 3; 125:4; 126:4; 130:1; 3; 132:8; 135:1; 9; 13(2); 19(2); 20; 136:1; 2; 3; 26; 137:5; 7; 8; 138:4; 8; 139:1; 4; 17; 19; 21; 23; 140:1; 4; 6; 7; 8; 141:3; 8; 142:5; 143:1; 7; 9; 11; 144:5; 9; 145:1; 10; 146:1; 10; 147:12(2); **Prov** 4:10; 5:7; 6:9; 7:24; 8:4; 5; 32; 24:15; 30:13; 31:4; **Eccl** 10:16; 17; 11:9; **Song** 1:5; 7; 8; 9; 2:7; 14; 3:5; 11; 4:11; 16; 5:1(2); 8; 9; 16; 6:1; 4; 13; 7:1; 6; 13; 8:1; 4; 12; **Is** 1:2(2); 2:5; 3:12; 5:3; 7:13; 8:8; 9; 10:5; 24; 30(2); 12:1; 14:12; 31(2); 16:9; 21:2(2); 10; 13; 23:4; 10; 12; 24:17; 25:1; 26:8; 13; 15; 17; 27:12; 33:2; 37:16; 17(2); 20; 38:3; 14; 16; 40:9(2); 27(2); 41:1; 43:1(2); 22(2); 44:1; 2; 21(2); 23(2); 45:15; 46:3; 8; 47:1(2); 5; 48:1; 12; 18; 49:1; 3; 13(3); 51:4; 9; 17; 52:1(2); 2(2); 54:1; 11; 62:6; 63:16; 17; 64:4; 8; 9; 12; **Jer** 2:4; 12; 28; 31; 3:14; 20; 4:1; 14; 19; 5:3; 15; 21; 6:1; 8; 18; 19; 23; 26; 7:29; 9:20; 10:1; 6; 7; 17; 23; 24; 11:5; 13; 20; 12:1; 3; 13:27; 14:7; 8; 9; 20; 22; 15:5; 15; 16; 16:19; 17:3; 13; 14; 18:6(2); 19; 19:3; 20:7; 12; 21:12; 13; 22:2; 23; 29; 30:10(2); 31:4; 7; 10; 21; 22; 23; 32:25; 34:4; 37:20; 42:19; 45:2; 46:11; 19; 27(2); 28; 47:6; 48:2; 19; 28; 32; 43; 46; 49:3; 4; 8; 16; 30; 50:11; 24; 31; 42; 51:13; 25; 62; **Lam** 1:9; 11; 20; 2:13(2); 18; 20; 3:55; 58; 59; 61; 64; 4:21; 22(2); 5:1; 19; 21; **Eze** 3:25; 7:7; 8:15; 17; 10:13; 11:4; 5; 12:25; 13:4; 11; 16:35; 18:25; 29; 30; 31; 20:31; 39; 44; 23:22; 26:3; 27:3(2); 8; 28:16; 22; 33:7; 8; 10; 11; 20; 34:9; 17; 35:3; 15; 36:8; 22; 32; 37:3; 4; 9; 12; 13; 38:3; 16; 39:1; 44:6; 45:9; **Dan** 2:4; 23; 29; 31; 37; 3:4; 9; 10; 12; 14; 16; 17; 18; 24; 4:9; 18; 22; 24; 27; 31; 5:10; 18; 22; 6:7; 8; 12; 13; 15; 20; 21; 22; 8:17; 9:4; 7; 8; 15; 16; 17; 18; 19(4); 22; 10:11; 16; 19; 12:4; 8; **Hos** 5:1(2); 3; 8; 6:4(2); 11; 8:5; 9:1; 14; 10:9; 13:9; 14(2); 14:1; **Joel** 1:11(2); 19; 2:17; 21; 3:4; 11; **Amos** 2:11; 3:1; 4:5; 12(2); 5:1; 25; 6:14; 7:2; 5; 12; 8:4; 14; 9:7; **Obad** 9; **Jonah** 1:6; 14(2); 2:6; 4:2; 3; **Mic** 1:2; 13; 15; 2:7; 12; 3:1; 4:8; 10; 13; 5:1; 6:2; 3; 5; 8; 7:8; **Nah** 1:15; 3:18; **Hab** 1:2; 12(3); 3:2(2); **Zeph** 2:1; 5; 3:14(3); **Hag** 1:4; 2:4(2); 23; **Zec** 1:9; 12; 2:7; 10; 13; 3:2; 8; 4:7; 8:13; 9:9(2); 13(2); 11:1; 2; 7; 13:7; **Mal** 1:6; 2:1; **Mt** 3:7; 6:30; 8:26; 11:25; 12:34; 14:31; 15:22; 28; 16:3; 8; 17:17; 18:32; 20:30; 31; 23:37; 26:39; 42; **Mk** 9:19; 12:29; **Lk** 3:7; 5:8; 9:41; 10:21; 12:28; 13:34; 24:25; **Jn** 17:5; 25; **Acts** 1:1; 7:42; 13:10; 18:14; 25:26; 26:13; 19; **Rom** 2:1; 3; 7:24; 9:20; 11:33; **1Cor** 7:16(2); 15:55(2); **2Cor** 6:11; **Gal** 3:1; **1Ti** 6:11; 20; **Heb** 1:8; 10:7; 9; **Jas** 2:20; **Rev** 4:11; 6:10; 11:17; 15:4; 16:5

OF

Gen 1:2(3); 6; 10; 14; 15; 17; 20; 24; 25; 26(2); 27; 28(2); 29(2); 30(2); 2:1; 4(2); 5(2); 6; 7(3); 9(5); 10; 11(2); 12; 13(2); 14(2); 15; 16(2); 17(4); 19(3); 20(2); 21; 23(3); 3:1(3); 2(3); 3(4); 6; 7; 8(4); 11; 12; 14(2); 17(6); 18; 19(2); 20; 21; 22(3); 23; 24(4); 4:2(2); 3(3); 4(3); 10; 14; 16(3); 17(2); 19(2); 20(2); 21; 22(2); 23; 25; 26; 5:1(3); 4; 8; 11; 14; 17; 20; 23; 27; 29(2); 31; 6:1; 2(3); 4(4); 5(3); 7(2); 8; 9; 13; 14; 15(4); 16; 17(2); 19(3); 20(5); 21; 7:2(2); 3(3); 4; 6; 7(2); 8(4); 10; 11(4); 13(2); 14; 15(2); 16; 18; 21(4); 22(2); 23(2); 8:2(2); 3; 4(2); 5(2); 6(2); 8; 9(2); 10; 13(3); 14; 16; 17(4); 19; 20(2); 21; 9:2(5); 5(5); 6; 10(6); 11; 12; 13; 15; 16; 17; 18(3); 19(2); 21; 22(2); 23; 25; 26; 27; 29; 10:1(2); 2; 3; 4; 5; 6; 7(2); 10(2); 11; 14; 18; 19; 20; 21(3); 22; 23; 25; 29; 30; 31; 32(2); 11:1(2); 2; 4; 5; 8; 9(3); 10; 27; 28(2); 29(5); 31(3); 32; 12:1; 2; 3; 4; 5(2); 6(2); 8(2); 13; 15; 17; 13:1; 4(2); 7(2); 10(3); 11; 12(2); 13; 16(2); 17(2); 18; 14:1(5); 2(5); 3; 7; 8(6); 9(4); 10(3); 11; 13(3); 15; 17(4); 18(2); 19(2); 20; 21; 22(2); 24; 15:1; 2(2); 4(2); 7(2); 9(3); 12; 13; 16; 18; 16:2; 3; 7(2); 8; 9; 10; 11; 12; 13; 17:4; 5; 6(2); 8; 11(2); 12(2); 14; 16(4); 23(2); 24; 25; 27(2); 18:1(2); 5; 6; 10; 11; 13; 14; 18; 19(2); 20; 21; 25; 28(2); 19:1; 4(2); 8; 11; 12; 13(2); 14; 15; 16(2); 22; 24; 25; 26; 28(3); 29(3); 30; 31; 32; 34; 36; 37; 38(2); 20:2(2); 5(2); 6; 11; 12(2); 13; 16(2); 18(3); 21:2; 3; 9; 10; 11; 12(2); 13(2); 14(2); 15; 16; 17(4); 19; 21(3); 22; 25(2); 26; 27; 28; 30; 31; 32(2); 33; 22:2(3); 3(2); 6(2); 8; 9; 11(2); 13; 14(2); 15(2); 17(2); 18; 21; 23:1(2); 2; 3; 4(2); 5; 6(2); 7(2); 8(2); 9(3); 10(5); 11(2); 12; 13(3); 15; 16(3); 17; 18(3); 19(3); 20(2); 24:2; 3(4); 7(2); 9; 10(4); 11(2); 12; 13; 13(3); 15; 17; 22(3); 24(2); 27(3); 28; 30; 31; 37(2); 40(2); 42; 43(2); 47; 48; 53(2); 60(3); 62; 25:3; 4(2); 6; 7(2); 8; 9(3); 10(2); 11; 12; 13(3); 16; 17(2); 18; 19; 20(2); 21; 22; 23; 27; 28; 34; 26:1(2); 2; 4(2); 7(3); 8; 9; 10; 14(3); 15; 17; 18(3); 19; 20(2); 21; 22; 24; 25; 26(2); 29; 33; 34(2); 35; 27:2; 9; 15; 16(3); 17; 19; 22; 25; 27(3); 28(4); 30(2); 31; 33; 34; 39(3); 41(2); 42; 45; 46(7); 28:1(2); 2(3); 3; 4; 5(2); 6(2); 8; 9(2); 11(2); 12(2); 13(2); 14(2); 15; 16; 17(2); 18; 19(2); 22; 29:1(2); 2(2); 4; 5; 10(3); 13; 14; 16(2); 22; 30:2; 14(2); 16; 32; 35; 36; 37(2); 40(2); 41; 31:1(2); 2; 3; 5; 9; 11; 13(2); 15; 18(2); 25; 29(2); 33; 35; 37; 38; 39(3); 42(4); 48; 53(4); 32:1; 2; 3(2); 9(2); 10(3); 11(2); 12; 13; 16; 20; 24; 25(3); 30; 32(4); 33:8; 10; 15(2); 17; 18(2); 19(4); 34:1(2); 2(2); 3; 6; 7(2); 8; 13; 15; 19; 20(2); 23; 24(4); 25(2); 26(2); 27; 30; 35:1; 3; 5(2); 6; 7; 8; 9; 11(3); 14; 15; 20; 21; 22; 23; 24; 25; 26(2); 27; 28; 29; 36:1; 2(5); 3; 5(2); 6(3); 7; 9(2); 10(5); 11; 12; 13(2); 14(3); 15(4); 16(3); 17(4); 18(3); 19; 20; 21(3); 22; 23; 24(2); 25(2); 26; 27; 28; 29; 30(2); 31(2); 32(2); 33(2); 34(2); 35(3); 36; 37; 38; 39(4); 40(2); 43(3); 37:1; 2(3); 3(2); 14(2); 20; 21; 22; 23(2); 25; 28(2); 31; 32; 36(2);

38:2; 7; 12(2); 19; 20; 21; 22; 27; 39:1(4); 2; 5; 11(2); 14; 19; 21(2); 22(2); 23; 40:1(3); 2(3); 3(2); 4; 5(4); 7; 8; 12; 14(2); 15(2); 17(3); 20(2); 41:1; 2; 3(2); 5; 8; 10; 11; 12; 14; 15; 16; 17; 18; 19; 25; 27; 29(2); 30(2); 31; 33; 34(2); 35(2); 36(2); 37(2); 38; 41; 42; 43; 44; 45(3); 46(3); 48(3); 49; 50(3); 51; 52(2); 53(2); 54(2); 55; 56(2); 42:5(2); 6; 7; 9(2); 12; 13(2); 15; 16(2); 19(3); 21; 27; 29; 30(2); 32(2); 33(3); 35(2); 36; 43:2; 7(3); 9; 11; 12; 14; 16; 18; 19(2); 21; 23; 27(2); 29; 34; 44:1; 2; 4; 8(3); 9; 16; 20(2); 24; 31; 33; 45:2; 8(2); 9; 10; 11; 12; 13(2); 17; 18(3); 19(2); 20(2); 21(2); 22(4); 23; 25(2); 26; 27(2); 46:1; 2; 3(2); 5; 6; 8(2); 9; 10(2); 11; 12(3); 13; 14; 15(2); 16; 17(2); 18; 19; 20(3); 21; 22; 23; 24; 25; 26; 27(3); 28; 31; 34; 47:1(3); 2; 4(2); 6(4); 9(8); 11(3); 13(3); 14(2); 15(2); 17; 18(2); 20; 21(2); 22(2); 24(2); 25; 26(2); 27(2); 28(2); 30; 48:3; 4(2); 5; 6; 7(2); 10; 16(2); 17; 19; 21; 22(2); 49:2; 3(3); 5; 8; 10; 11; 13(2); 16(2); 20; 24(4); 25(5); 26(6); 28; 29; 30(4); 32(3); 33; 50:3; 4(3); 5; 7(4); 8(2); 10; 11(3); 13(5); 17(4); 19; 23(3); 24; 25(2); **Ex** 1:1(2); 5(2); 7; 9(2); 10; 12(2); 13; 14; 15(4); 16; 17; 18; 2:1(3); 3; 5; 6; 7; 10; 11; 13; 15(2); 16; 19(2); 23(5); 25; 3:1(4); 2(4); 4(2); 6(4); 7(2); 8(4); 9(2); 10(2); 11(2); 12; 13(2); 14; 15(5); 16(5); 17(3); 18(3); 19; 21; 22(4); 4:5(4); 7; 8(2); 9(3); 10(2); 13; 14; 16(2); 20(2); 25; 26; 27; 28; 29(2); 30; 31; 5:1; 3; 4; 5; 6; 8; 10; 11; 12(2); 14(2); 15(2); 18; 19(3); 21(2); 6:1; 3; 4(2); 5(2); 6(3); 7; 9(2); 11(3); 12(2); 13(5); 14(4); 15(3); 16(4); 17; 18(3); 19(2); 20(2); 21; 22; 23(2); 24(2); 25(4); 26(2); 27(2); 28; 29; 30; 7:2(2); 3; 4(3); 5; 11; 16; 18(2); 19(5); 20(2); 21(3); 22; 24(2); 8:3; 5; 6(2); 7; 12; 13(4); 16(2); 17(3); 19; 21(4); 22(3); 24(5); 26(2); 29; 31(2); 9:1; 3; 4(4); 6(4); 7(3); 8(3); 9(2); 10; 11; 12; 13; 20(2); 21; 22(3); 23; 24; 25(3); 26(2); 29; 33; 35(2); 10:1; 2(2); 3; 5(3); 6(2); 12(3); 13; 14(2); 15(5); 19; 20; 21; 22; 23; 11:2(5); 3(4); 4; 5(4); 6; 7(2); 9; 10(2); 12:1; 2(2); 3(3); 4; 5; 6(3); 7(2); 9; 10(2); 12(3); 13; 15; 16(2); 17(3); 18(2); 19; 21; 22(3); 27(3); 28; 29(4); 31; 33; 35(5); 36; 37; 39(3); 40(2); 41(3); 42(4); 43; 46(2); 47; 50; 51(3); 13:2(3); 3(3); 5; 8(2); 9; 11; 12; 13(2); 14(2); 15(4); 16(2); 17(2); 18(5); 19(2); 20; 21(2); 22(2); 14:2; 3(2); 5(3); 7(2); 8(4); 9; 10(2); 11; 13; 15; 16(2); 17; 19(3); 20(2); 22(2); 23; 24(4); 25; 27; 28(2); 29(2); 30(2); 15:1; 3; 7; 8(2); 14; 15(3); 16; 17; 19(4); 20; 22; 23(3); 26(2); 27; 16:1(6); 2(2); 3(3); 6(2); 7; 9(2); 10(3); 12(2); 14; 15; 16(2); 17; 19; 20(2); 22; 23; 27; 29(2); 31(2); 32(2); 33; 35(3); 36; 17:1(4); 3; 5(2); 6(3); 7(4); 9(2); 10; 12; 13; 14(2); 15; 18:1(3); 3(2); 4(3); 5; 7; 9(2); 10(5); 12; 15; 16; 21(6); 24; 25(5); 19:1(4); 2; 3(3); 6(2); 7; 8; 9; 11; 12; 16; 17(2); 18; 19; 20(2); 21; 20:2(4); 4; 5(2); 6; 7; 10; 18; 22; 23(2); 24; 25(2); 21:9; 10; 19; 26(2); 28; 30(2); 32; 34(2); 35; 22:5(4); 6; 7; 8; 9(3); 11(2); 14; 17; 21; 25; 28; 29(3); 31; 23:5; 6; 8; 9(3); 11(2); 12; 13(3); 15(2); 16(5); 18(2); 19(3); 21; 25; 26; 29; 31(2); 24:1(2); 3; 4(2); 5(3); 6(2); 7(2); 8; 9(2); 10(3); 11(2); 12; 13; 16(3); 17(5); 18; 25:2(2); 3; 9(2); 10; 11; 12(3); 13; 14; 15; 17; 18(3); 19; 20; 22(3); 23; 24; 25; 26; 27; 28; 29; 31(3); 32(6); 33; 35(4); 36(2); 38; 39(2); 26:1(2); 2(3); 4(4); 5(3); 6; 7; 8(3); 9; 10(2); 11; 12(3); 13(4); 14(2); 15; 16(2); 17; 19; 20; 21; 22; 23; 24; 25; 26(3); 27(4); 28; 29; 31(2); 32(3); 33; 34; 35; 36(2); 37(3); 27:1; 2(2); 3; 4(2); 5(2); 6; 7; 9(3); 10(3); 11(4); 12(2); 13; 14(2); 16(3); 17(2); 18(3); 19(3); 20; 21(3); 28:1; 3; 6(4); 8(4); 9(2); 10(2); 11(5); 12(3); 13; 14(2); 15(7); 17(2); 21(3); 22(2); 23(2); 24(2); 25(2); 26(3); 27(3); 28(3); 29(3); 30(3); 31(2); 32(4); 33(5); 34; 36(2); 37; 38(2); 39(3); 43; 29:2; 4(2); 5(2); 10(2); 11(2); 12(4); 14; 15; 17; 19; 20(7); 21(3); 22(2); 23(4); 24(2); 25; 26(2); 27(6); 28(4); 29; 30; 31; 32(3); 34(3); 38; 40(5); 41; 42(2); 43; 44; 45; 46(2); 30:1; 2; 3; 4(2); 5; 6; 10(3); 12(2); 13(2); 16(5); 18(3); 20; 23(3); 24(3); 25(2); 26(2); 27; 28; 31; 32; 33; 34; 35; 36(3); 31:2(4); 3(2); 5(3); 6(4); 7(3); 8; 9; 10(2); 13; 15; 16; 17; 18(4); 32:1(4); 2(3); 4(2); 7(2); 8(3); 10; 11(2); 12(2); 13(2); 14; 15; 16(2); 17(2); 18(3); 19; 20(2); 22; 23(3); 26(2); 27; 28(3); 31; 32; 33; 34; 33:1(2); 3; 5(2); 6(2); 7(2); 9; 11(2); 16; 19; 22; 34:1; 2; 4(2); 5; 7; 10; 12(2); 15(2); 16; 18(2); 20(2); 22(4); 23; 25(3); 26(3); 27; 28; 29(2); 30(2); 31; 32; 34; 35(3); 35:1(2); 2; 4(2); 5(2); 12; 15; 16; 17(2); 18(2); 19(2); 20(3); 21(2); 22(2); 23; 24(2); 25(4); 29(3); 30(5); 31(2); 33(3); 34(3); 35(8); 36:1(2); 3(4); 4; 5; 6; 8(3); 9(3); 11(4); 12(2); 13; 14; 15(3); 17(2); 18; 19(2); 20; 21(2); 22; 24; 25; 26; 27; 28; 29; 30; 31(3); 32(3); 34; 35(2); 36(3); 37(2); 38(2); 37:1(4); 2; 3(4); 4; 5; 6; 7(3); 8; 9; 10; 11; 12(2); 13; 15; 16; 17(3); 18(5); 19(2); 21(4); 22(3); 23; 24(2); 25(5); 26(3); 27(2); 28; 29(2); 38:1(2); 2(2); 3(2); 4(2); 5(2); 6; 7; 8(7); 9(2); 10(2); 11(3); 12(3); 14(2); 15(2); 16(2); 17(6); 18(3); 19(4); 20(3); 21(6); 22(4); 23(3); 24(3); 25(3); 26; 27(5); 28; 29; 30(3); 31(4); 39:1(2); 2; 5(3); 6(3); 7(2); 8(3); 10; 13; 14(3); 15(2); 16(2); 17(2); 18(2); 19(4); 20(3); 21(3); 22(3); 23(2); 24(2); 25(2); 26; 27(2); 28(3); 29(2); 30(3); 31; 32(4); 34(3); 35; 39; 40(4); 41; 42; 40:2(3); 3; 5(3); 6(4); 7; 10; 12(2); 17; 19; 21(2); 22(2); 24(2); 26; 28; 29(4); 30; 32; 33; 34(2); 35(2); 36; 38(3); **Lev** 1:1(2); 2(5); 3(4); 4; 5(2); 7; 9; 10(3); 11; 13; 14(3); 15; 16; 17; 2:1; 2(4); 3(3); 4(2); 5; 7; 8; 9; 10(3); 11; 12; 13(3); 14(4); 16(3); 3:1(2); 2(3); 3(2); 5; 6(2); 8(2); 9(2); 11; 13(3); 16; 4:2(4); 3; 4(2); 5(2); 6(2); 7(9); 8; 10(3); 11; 13(4); 14; 15(2); 16(2); 17; 18(7); 22(2); 23; 24; 25(6); 26(2); 27(3); 28; 29(2); 30(4); 31; 33; 34(5); 35(2); 5:1(2); 2(3); 3(2); 4(2); 5; 6; 9(5); 11(2); 12; 13; 15(4); 16; 17(2); 18; 6:3; 5; 6; 7; 9(3); 12; 14(2); 15(5); 16(2); 17; 18(3); 20(5); 21; 22; 25; 26(2); 27; 30(2); 7:1; 3; 8; 10; 11(2); 12(2); 13(2); 14(3); 15(3); 16(2); 17(2); 18(4); 20(3); 21(4); 23(5); 24(4); 25(2); 26(4); 27; 29(4); 30; 32(2); 33(2); 34(4); 35(6); 36(2); 37(7); 38(2); 8:2; 3(2); 4(2); 7; 12; 14; 15(2); 18; 22(2); 23(5); 24(4); 26(3); 29(2); 30(2); 31(3); 32(2); 33(4); 35(3); 36; 9:1; 3(3); 5; 6; 7; 8; 9(3); 10; 17; 18; 19(2); 22; 23(2); 10:1(2); 4(3); 5; 6; 7(4); 9; 11(2); 12(2); 13(2); 14(4); 15; 16(2); 17; 18; 19; 11:2; 4(2); 8; 9; 10(2); 11; 21; 22; 24; 25(2); 26; 27; 28; 32(2); 33; 34; 35; 36; 37; 38; 39; 40(3); 44; 45(2); 46(4); 12:2(2); 3; 4(2); 5; 6(4); 7; 13:2(4); 3(3); 4; 7(2); 9; 11; 12; 19; 20(2); 25(2); 27; 28(2); 31(2); 38; 39; 41; 43(2); 47; 48(3); 49(2); 51; 52; 53; 56(5); 57; 58; 59(4); 14:2(2); 3(2); 5; 6; 8; 10(3); 11(2); 12; 14(6); 15(3); 16; 17(7); 18(2); 21(2); 23(2); 24(2); 25(7); 26(2); 27; 28(7); 29(2); 30(2); 32(2); 34(4); 37; 38(2); 39; 42; 45(3); 50; 51; 52; 53; 54(2); 55(2); 57; 15:2(3); 7; 10; 12(2); 13; 14(2); 16; 17; 18; 25(7); 26(3); 28; 29(2); 30; 31; 32(2); 33(6); 16:1(2); 5(4); 6; 7(2); 11(2); 12(3); 13; 14(3); 15(2); 16(6); 17(2); 18(5); 19(3); 20(2); 21(5); 23; 24; 25; 29(2); 31; 33(2); 34; 17:2; 3(3); 4(3); 5(3); 6(3); 8(3); 9(2); 10(4); 11; 12(2); 13(3); 14(6); 15(2); 18:2; 3(4); 6(2); 7(2); 8; 9(3); 10(2); 11(2);

12; 13; 14; 15; 16; 17; 21(2); 24; 26(2); 27; 29; 30; 19:2(2); 5; 8; 9(3); 10; 12; 13; 15(2); 16; 18; 19; 21(2); 22; 23(2); 25; 27(2); 29; 32; 34; 36(2); 20:2(6); 3; 4(2); 11; 12; 13; 17; 18(2); 19(2); 23; 25; 21:1; 5; 6(3); 8; 9; 12(4); 14; 17(2); 21(4); 22(3); 24; 22:2(2); 3(2); 4(3); 5; 6; 7; 8; 10(3); 11(2); 12(2); 13; 14; 15(2); 16; 18(4); 19(3); 21; 22; 25(3); 29; 30; 32; 33(2); 23:2(2); 3(2); 4; 5; 6(2); 10(3); 12; 13(3); 15; 17(3); 18(2); 19(3); 20; 22(4); 24(4); 27(2); 28; 31; 32(2); 34(3); 37; 38; 39(2); 40(4); 43(3); 44(2); 24:2; 3(2); 8; 9(2); 10(4); 11(4); 12; 15; 16(2); 22(2); 23(3); 25:2; 4; 5(4); 6; 8(3); 9(3); 11(2); 12; 13; 14; 15(4); 16(5); 22(2); 24; 25(2); 27; 28(2); 30; 31(2); 32(3); 33(6); 34(2); 36; 38(3); 40; 41; 42(2); 44(2); 45(4); 46; 47; 48; 49(2); 50(4); 51(2); 52(2); 54; 55(3); 26:1; 4; 6; 8(2); 10; 13(3); 16; 19; 20; 22; 25(2); 26; 29(2); 30; 31; 36(3); 38; 39(2); 40; 41(3); 43(3); 44; 45(4); 46(2); 27:2; 3(3); 5; 6(3); 9; 11; 15(2); 16(4); 17; 18; 19(2); 22(2); 23(2); 24(3); 25; 26; 27(2); 28(4); 29; 30(5); 31; 32(3); 34; **Num** 1:1(5); 2(5); 4(3); 5(4); 6(2); 7(2); 8(2); 9(2); 10(6); 11(2); 12(2); 13(2); 14(2); 15(2); 16(4); 18(3); 19; 20(3); 21(3); 22(5); 23(3); 24(4); 25(3); 26(4); 27(3); 28(4); 29(3); 30(4); 31(3); 32(6); 33(3); 34(4); 35(3); 36(4); 37(3); 38(4); 39(3); 40(4); 41(3); 42(4); 43(3); 44(2); 45(3); 47; 49(3); 50; 52; 53(5); 54; 2:2(4); 3(7); 4; 5(4); 7(4); 9; 10(5); 12(4); 13; 14(4); 15; 16; 17(3); 18(5); 19; 20(4); 21; 22(4); 23; 24(2); 25(5); 26; 27(4); 28; 29(4); 30; 31; 32(4); 33; 34(2); 3:1; 2(2); 3(2); 4(2); 6; 7(3); 8(5); 9(2); 12(3); 13; 14; 15(2); 16; 17; 18(2); 19; 20(3); 21(4); 22(3); 23; 24(4); 25(5); 26(3); 27(6); 28(2); 29(3); 30(5); 31; 32(4); 33(4); 34(2); 35(6); 36(3); 37; 38(4); 39(2); 40(4); 41(6); 42; 43(3); 45(4); 46(4); 47; 48; 49; 50(4); 51(2); 4:2(4); 3; 4(3); 5; 6(2); 7(2); 8(2); 9(2); 10; 11(2); 12(3); 14(3); 15(6); 16(4); 18(2); 22(3); 23; 24(2); 25(5); 26(4); 27(3); 28(6); 29(2); 30(2); 31(3); 32(3); 33(6); 34(3); 35; 36; 37(5); 38(3); 39; 40(2); 41(6); 42(4); 43; 44; 45(5); 46(3); 47(3); 48; 49(3); 5:2(2); 4(2); 6; 8; 9(3); 12; 13; 14(4); 15(4); 17(2); 18; 19; 20; 21; 25; 26; 29(2); 30; 6:2(2); 3(3); 4(2); 5(4); 7; 8; 9(2); 10(2); 12(2); 13(4); 14(2); 15(3); 17(2); 18(6); 19(4); 21(3); 23; 27; 7:2(4); 3; 5(3); 7; 8(3); 9(2); 10; 11; 12(3); 13(4); 14(3); 15; 16; 17(4); 18(2); 19(4); 20(3); 21; 22; 23(4); 24(3); 25(4); 26(2); 27; 28; 29(4); 30(3); 31(6); 32(2); 33; 34; 35(4); 36(3); 37(4); 38(2); 39; 40; 41(4); 42(3); 43(6); 44(2); 45; 46; 47(4); 48(3); 49(4); 50(2); 51; 52; 53(4); 54(3); 55(6); 56(2); 57; 58; 59(4); 60(3); 61(4); 62(2); 63; 64; 65(4); 66(3); 67(4); 68(2); 69; 70; 71(4); 72(3); 73(4); 74(2); 75; 76; 77(4); 78(3); 79(4); 80(2); 81; 82; 83(4); 84(4); 85(2); 86(3); 87(2); 88(3); 89(3); 8:4(2); 6; 7; 9(3); 10; 11(3); 12; 14; 15(2); 16(5); 17(3); 18(2); 19(7); 20(3); 22; 24(2); 25; 26; 9:1(4); 2; 3(2); 4; 5(3); 6; 7(3); 10(4); 11; 12(3); 13; 14; 15(2); 16; 17(2); 18(3); 19(2); 20(2); 22; 23(5); 10:2(4); 3(2); 4(2); 8; 10(3); 11(2); 12(4); 13(2); 14(4); 15(4); 16(4); 17(2); 18(3); 19(4); 20(4); 22(4); 23(4); 24(4); 25(5); 26(4); 27(4); 28(2); 29(2); 31; 33(3); 34(2); 36; 11:1(2); 3(2); 4; 7; 8(3); 10(2); 11; 15; 16(4); 17(2); 18; 20; 22; 24(3); 25; 26(4); 28(3); 30; 31; 33; 34; 12:1; 3; 4; 5(2); 8; 9; 12(2); 16; 13:2(4); 3(4); 4(3); 5(3); 6(3); 7(3); 8(3); 9(3); 10(3); 11(5); 12(3); 13(3); 14(3); 15(3); 16(2); 17; 20(4); 21; 22; 23(4); 24(3); 25; 26(4); 27; 28; 29(2); 32(3); 33(2); 14:2(2); 5(3); 6(3); 7(2); 9; 10(3); 12; 14(3); 15; 17; 18(2); 19(2); 21; 23; 25; 27(2); 29; 30(2); 34(2); 38(3); 39; 40; 41; 44(3); 15:2(2); 3(2); 4(4); 5(2); 6(3); 7(2); 9(3); 10(2); 13(2); 14; 15; 18; 19(2); 20(3); 21(2); 23; 24(2); 25(2); 26(2); 27; 29; 31; 32; 38(4); 39; 41(2); 16:1(6); 2(4); 3(2); 7; 8; 9(4); 10; 12; 13; 14(2); 15; 17; 18(2); 19(3); 22(2); 24; 25; 26(2); 27(2); 28; 29(2); 31; 34; 37(2); 38(3); 39; 40(4); 41(3); 42(2); 43; 47; 49; 50(2); 17:2(6); 3(3); 4; 5(2); 6(3); 7; 8(3); 9; 12; 13; 18:1(2); 2(4); 3(2); 4(3); 5(3); 6(3); 7(2); 8(5); 9(5); 11(4); 12(4); 13; 15(3); 16(2); 17(3); 18; 19(3); 20; 21(3); 22(2); 23(3); 24(3); 26(4); 27(2); 28(3); 29(4); 30(2); 31; 32(4); 19:2(2); 4(3); 6(2); 9(4); 10(2); 11; 13(3); 16; 17(3); 20(2); 21(2); 20:1(2); 4; 5(5); 6(4); 8; 10; 12(2); 13(2); 14; 16(2); 17(2); 19(2); 22; 23(2); 24(2); 26; 27; 28(2); 29; 21:1(2); 3(2); 4(4); 5; 6; 9(2); 10; 12; 13(4); 14(3); 15(3); 18(2); 20(2); 21; 22(2); 24(4); 25; 26(4); 27; 28(5); 29(2); 31; 33(2); 34; 22:1(2); 2; 3(3); 4(4); 5(5); 6; 7(4); 8; 10(2); 11(2); 13; 14; 16; 18(3); 21; 22; 23(2); 24(2); 25; 26; 27; 28; 31(2); 32; 34; 35(2); 36(2); 41(2); 23:6; 7(3); 9; 10(4); 13; 14(2); 17; 18; 19; 21; 22(2); 23(2); 24(2); 28; 24:2; 3; 4(2); 6; 7; 8(2); 13(3); 15; 16(3); 17(4); 19(2); 20; 24; 25:1; 2; 3; 4(2); 5; 6(8); 7(2); 8(4); 11(4); 12; 13(2); 14(3); 15(3); 18(5); 26:1; 2(3); 3; 4(4); 5(6); 6(4); 7(2); 8; 9(2); 11; 12(7); 13(4); 14; 15(7); 16(4); 17(4); 18(3); 19(2); 20(7); 21(5); 22(2); 23(6); 24(4); 25(2); 26(8); 27(2); 28; 29(6); 30(5); 31(4); 32(4); 33(3); 34(2); 35(7); 36(3); 37(4); 38(7); 39(4); 40(5); 41(2); 42(4); 43(2); 44(8); 45(6); 46(2); 47(3); 48(6); 49(4); 50(2); 51(2); 53; 54; 55(2); 57(7); 58(6); 59(2); 62(3); 63(2); 64(3); 65(4); 27:1(9); 2(2); 3(2); 4(2); 7(3); 8; 11(3); 12; 14(4); 16(2); 17; 18; 20(3); 21(2); 23; 28:2; 3; 5(4); 7; 8(2); 9(2); 10; 11(2); 12(2); 13(2); 14(5); 15; 16(2); 17; 18; 19; 20; 24(2); 26; 27; 28; 30; 29:1(2); 2; 3; 5; 6; 7; 8; 9; 11(3); 12; 13(2); 14(3); 15; 16; 17; 19; 20; 23; 25; 26; 29; 32; 36(2); 40; 30:1(2); 2; 5(2); 6; 8; 9(2); 12(2); 31:2(2); 3(2); 4(2); 5(3); 6(2); 8(4); 9(3); 11(2); 12(3); 13; 14; 16(4); 20(3); 21(2); 23; 26(4); 28(7); 29(2); 30(11); 32(2); 35; 36; 37; 38; 39; 40; 42(2); 47(7); 48(3); 49(3); 50(2); 51; 52(5); 53; 54(5); 32:1(5); 2(3); 4; 6(2); 7(2); 9(3); 11(2); 12(2); 13; 14(2); 17(3); 18; 21; 24; 25(2); 26; 28(4); 29(3); 30; 31(2); 32(2); 33(9); 34; 36; 37; 39(2); 40; 41; 33:1(5); 2; 3(3); 5; 6; 8(2); 9; 11; 12(2); 15; 16; 36; 37(2); 38(5); 40(4); 44; 47; 48(2); 49; 50; 51(2); 52; 53; 54; 55(2); 34:2(3); 3(3); 4; 5(2); 8(2); 9; 11(3); 12; 13; 14(7); 17(2); 18; 19(4); 20(4); 21(3); 22(4); 23(5); 24(4); 25(4); 26(4); 27(4); 28(4); 29(2); 35:1; 2(3); 3; 4(2); 5; 8(4); 10(2); 11; 13; 14(2); 15; 16; 18; 19; 20(2); 21; 22; 24; 25(5); 26(2); 27(5); 28(4); 29; 30; 31(2); 32(2); 33(2); 34; 36:1(10); 2(2); 3(7); 4(5); 5(4); 6(3); 7(6); 8(7); 9(3); 10; 11; 12(5); 13(3); **Deut** 1:2; 3(2); 4(2); 5; 7(2); 10; 11; 15; 17(2); 19(2); 20; 21; 22; 23(2); 24; 25(2); 26; 27(3); 28; 29; 34; 35(2); 36; 38; 40; 41; 43; 2:1; 4(3); 5; 6(2); 7; 8(4); 9(2); 12(2); 14(2); 15; 16; 18; 19(5); 20; 22; 23; 24; 25(4); 26(4); 29; 30; 34; 35; 36(2); 37(3); 3:1; 2; 3; 4(2); 6(2); 7; 8(4); 10(3); 11(8); 13(5); 14(3); 16(2); 17; 18; 26; 27; 4:1; 2; 3; 4; 6; 9; 11; 12(3); 13; 15(3); 16(2); 17(2); 18(2); 19; 20(3); 23(2); 25(2); 28; 31; 32(2); 33(3); 34; 36(3); 37; 42; 43(3); 44; 45(2); 46(4); 47(3); 48; 49(2); 5:3; 4(2); 5(2); 6(3); 8; 9(2); 10; 11; 14(2); 15; 22(5); 23(3); 24(2); 25; 26(4); 28(3); 6:2; 3; 7; 9; 11; 12(3); 14(2); 15(2); 17; 18; 21; 7:4; 6; 7; 8(4); 13(4); 15(2); 18; 19; 22; 25; 8:3(2); 6; 7(4); 8(2); 9; 14(3); 15(2); 17; 20; 9:2(3); 4; 5(2); 7(2); 9(2); 10(5); 11(3);

12(2); 14; 15; 16; 17; 18(2); 19; 21; 23; 26; 27; 10:1(2); 3(2); 4(3); 6(3); 7(2); 8(3); 12; 13; 14; 16; 17(2); 18; 19; 22; 11:2; 3(2); 4(2); 6(3); 7; 10(2); 11(3); 12(3); 14; 19; 20; 21(2); 24; 25(2); 27; 28(2); 30(2); 12:1; 3(3); 5; 6(3); 11; 14; 15(3); 17(7); 21(2); 22; 25; 27(3); 28; 13:1; 3(2); 5(7); 6(2); 7(4); 9; 10(3); 12; 13(2); 15(3); 16(2); 17(2); 18(2); 14:1; 7(2); 8; 9; 11; 12; 20; 21(2); 22; 23(5); 28(2); 29; 15:1; 2(3); 3; 5; 7(3); 9; 11; 14(4); 15; 19(4); 16:1(3); 2; 3(6); 4; 5; 6(2); 10(3); 13; 15; 16(3); 17; 19(2); 21(2); 17:2(2); 3(2); 4; 6(3); 7(2); 8; 9; 10; 11; 18(3); 19(2); 20; 18:1(2); 4(5); 5(2); 6(3); 7; 8(2); 9; 10; 12; 14; 15(2); 16(3); 19; 20; 22(2); 19:2; 3; 4; 5; 6(2); 11; 12(3); 13; 14; 15(2); 20:1(3); 3; 6(2); 9(2); 11; 13; 14; 15(2); 16(2); 19(2); 21:3; 4; 5(2); 6; 8; 9(2); 13; 14; 16(2); 17(4); 18(2); 19(2); 20; 21; 22; 23; 22:3; 9(2); 11(2); 12; 14; 15(3); 17(3); 18; 19(3); 20; 21(2); 22; 24; 26; 29; 23:1; 2(2); 3(2); 4(4); 8(2); 10(2); 14; 16; 17(4); 18(3); 19(3); 21; 23; 25; 24:1(3); 2; 3(2); 7(4); 8; 9; 14(2); 17(2); 19; 21; 22; 25:5(3); 6(2); 7; 8; 9; 10; 11(3); 17; 18; 19; 26:2(4); 4(2); 7; 8; 10; 12(3); 13; 14; 27:1; 3(2); 5; 6(2); 8; 9; 10; 14; 15(2); 18; 19; 21; 22(2); 26; 28:1(2); 2; 4(5); 9; 10(3); 11(3); 12; 13; 14; 15; 18(4); 20(2); 24; 25; 26(2); 27; 28; 33; 34; 35(2); 39; 42; 45; 47(2); 48(2); 49; 50(2); 51(4); 53(3); 54(2); 55(3); 56(2); 57; 58; 59(3); 60(2); 61; 62(2); 64; 65(3); 66; 67(2); 29:1(3); 2; 7(2); 8; 9; 10(3); 11(2); 16; 18; 19(2); 20; 21(4); 22(2); 23; 24; 25(4); 27; 28; 29; 30:4(2); 6; 8; 9(4); 10(2); 20; 31:4(2); 6(2); 7(2); 9(4); 10(4); 12; 14(2); 15(3); 16(2); 19(2); 21(2); 22; 23(3); 24(2); 25(2); 26(4); 28; 29(2); 30(3); 32:1; 3; 4; 5; 7(2); 8(4); 9; 10; 13(4); 14(8); 15; 18; 19(3); 22; 24(3); 25; 26; 27; 28; 32(5); 33(2); 35; 38(2); 39; 42(3); 43; 44(3); 45; 46; 49(3); 51(5); 52; 33:1(2); 2; 3; 4(2); 5(2); 7(2); 8(2); 11(3); 12(2); 13(3); 15(2); 16(5); 17(5); 18; 19(4); 20(2); 21(3); 22; 23(2); 24; 26; 28(2); 29(2); 34:1(4); 2(2); 3(3); 5(3); 6(2); 8(3); 9(4); 11; 12; **Josh** 1:1(3); 2; 3; 4(2); 5; 6; 8(2); 9; 10; 12; 13; 14; 15; 18; 2:1(2); 2(3); 3; 5(2); 6(2); 9(2); 10(3); 11; 17; 18; 19(2); 20; 23; 24(2); 3:1; 3(2); 6(2); 7; 8(3); 9(2); 11(3); 12(3); 13(6); 14; 15(3); 16; 17(3); 4:2(2); 3(3); 4(3); 5(6); 7(5); 8(6); 9(3); 10; 11(2); 12(4); 13; 14(2); 16(2); 17; 18(6); 19(3); 20; 21; 23; 24(2); 5:1(7); 2; 3(2); 4(3); 5; 6(4); 9(2); 10(3); 11(2); 12(6); 14(2); 15; 6:1(2); 2; 3; 4; 5(2); 6(4); 7; 8(3); 10; 11; 12; 13(3); 15; 18(2); 19(2); 20; 21; 23; 24(4); 26; 7:1(9); 2; 4(2); 5(3); 6(2); 7; 9(2); 11; 12; 13(2); 15; 16; 17(3); 18(5); 19; 20; 21(4); 23(3); 24(3); 26(4); 8:1(2); 3(2); 8; 9; 10; 11(2); 12; 13(3); 14(2); 15; 19; 20(2); 21(2); 22(3); 23; 24(4); 25(2); 26; 27(2); 29(4); 30; 31(5); 32(4); 33(6); 34(2); 35(2); 9:1; 3; 5; 6; 7; 9(3); 10(3); 11; 12; 13(2); 14(2); 15; 16; 17; 18(3); 19; 20; 21(2); 23(4); 24(3); 26(3); 27(3); 10:1(2); 2; 3(5); 4; 5(6); 6(2); 7(2); 8; 11; 12(3); 13(2); 14; 18; 19; 20(3); 21(2); 22(2); 23(6); 24(5); 25; 27(2); 28(3); 30(3); 32(2); 33; 35; 37; 39; 40(5); 41; 42; 11:1(4); 2(4); 3; 5; 6; 7(2); 8(2); 10; 11; 12(4); 13; 14(3); 15; 16(3); 17; 19(2); 20; 21(2); 22(3); 12:1(3); 2(5); 3(2); 4(4); 5(3); 6(4); 7(4); 9(2); 10(2); 11(2); 12(2); 13(2); 14(2); 15(2); 16(2); 17(2); 18(2); 19(2); 20(2); 21(2); 22(3); 23(4); 24; 13:2; 3(2); 4(2); 5; 6(2); 7; 8; 9(3); 10(4); 11; 12(3); 13; 14(3); 15(2); 16(2); 19; 21(5); 22(2); 23(4); 24(2); 25(3); 26; 27(5); 28(2); 29(4); 30(3); 31(6); 32; 33(2); 14:1(7); 2; 3; 4; 5; 6(3); 7; 8; 10; 13; 14(3); 15; 15:1(6); 2; 4(2); 5(3); 6(3); 7(3); 8(7); 9(4); 10; 11(2); 12(2); 13(5); 14(2); 15(2); 17(2); 18; 19; 20(3); 21(4); 47; 62; 63(3); 16:1(3); 2; 3(2); 4; 5(3); 8(3); 9(3); 17:1(5); 2(10); 3(5); 4(3); 5; 6(3); 7(2); 8(3); 9(6); 11(4); 12(2); 13; 14; 15(2); 16(6); 17; 18; 18:1(3); 2; 3(2); 4; 5; 7(3); 10; 11(6); 12(2); 13(2); 14(3); 15(3); 16(6); 17(3); 19(4); 20(3); 21(4); 28(2); 19:1(4); 8(4); 9(9); 10(2); 12; 14; 16(2); 17; 22; 23(3); 24(2); 27(2); 31(3); 32(2); 39(3); 40(2); 41; 47(5); 48(3); 49(3); 50; 51(8); 20:2(3); 3; 4(5); 5; 6; 7; 8(6); 9(3); 21:1(7); 2(2); 3(3); 4(9); 5(9); 6(10); 7(7); 8(2); 9(6); 10(5); 11(3); 12(2); 13(2); 16; 17(2); 19(2); 20(7); 21; 23(2); 25(2); 26(2); 27(6); 28(2); 30(2); 32(3); 33; 34(5); 36(2); 38(3); 40(3); 41(3); 44; 45(2); 22:1; 2; 3(2); 4(2); 5; 7(2); 8; 9(10); 10(5); 11(8); 12(4); 13(6); 14(5); 15(4); 16(2); 17(2); 18; 19(4); 20(2); 21(5); 22(2); 24(2); 25(2); 27; 28(2); 29; 30(6); 31(7); 32(7); 33(3); 34(2); 23:3; 5; 6(2); 7(2); 10; 12; 13; 14(2); 16(2); 24:1(2); 2(4); 3(2); 6; 8; 9(3); 10; 11; 12; 13; 14; 15(2); 17(3); 23; 26(3); 27; 29(2); 30(3); 31(3); 32(10); 33; **Judg** 1:1(2); 4; 8(2); 9; 10; 11(2); 13; 14; 15; 16(6); 17; 19(3); 20; 21(2); 22; 23(2); 24; 25; 26; 27(4); 30(2); 31(7); 32; 33(5); 34; 35(2); 36; 2:1(2); 2; 4(2); 5; 6; 7(3); 8(2); 9(3); 11(2); 12(5); 14(3); 15; 16(2); 17(2); 18(5); 20; 21; 22; 23; 3:1(2); 2(2); 3(2); 4(2); 5; 7(2); 8(4); 9(3); 10(2); 11; 12(4); 13(2); 14(2); 15(4); 16; 17; 20; 22; 23; 24; 25; 27(2); 28; 29(2); 30; 31(2); 4:1(2); 2(4); 3(3); 4; 5(2); 6(7); 7; 9; 11(4); 12; 13(3); 15; 16(3); 17(4); 19; 20(2); 21; 23(2); 24(4); 5:1; 2; 3; 4(3); 5; 6(3); 7; 9; 11(5); 12; 14(5); 15(3); 16(3); 18; 19(3); 21; 22(2); 23(3); 24; 28(2); 30(6); 6:1(3); 2(3); 3; 4; 6(2); 7(2); 8(4); 9(4); 10; 11; 12(2); 13(2); 14; 19(2); 20; 21(5); 22(2); 24; 25(2); 26(2); 27(2); 28(2); 29; 30(2); 33(2); 34; 37; 38(2); 7:1(4); 3(2); 4(2); 5; 6(2); 8(2); 11; 12; 13(2); 14(3); 15(3); 17; 18(3); 19(2); 20(2); 22; 23(4); 24; 25(3); 8:1; 2(4); 3(2); 5(3); 6(2); 7; 8(2); 9; 10(3); 11(2); 12; 13; 14(4); 15(2); 16(3); 17(2); 18(2); 19; 22(2); 24(2); 25; 26(3); 28(2); 29; 30; 32(3); 33; 34(3); 35; 9:1(3); 2(3); 3(3); 4(3); 5(2); 6(3); 7(2); 15(2); 16; 17(2); 18(2); 20(4); 21; 23(2); 24(3); 25(2); 26(2); 27; 28(4); 30(3); 31; 35(3); 36(2); 37(2); 39; 40; 43; 44(2); 46(4); 47(2); 49(2); 51(2); 52; 53; 54; 55; 56; 57(4); 10:1(3); 4; 6(8); 7(4); 8(3); 9(2); 10; 11(2); 12; 14; 15; 16; 17(2); 18(3); 11:1(2); 2; 3; 4(2); 5(4); 6; 7(2); 8(3); 9(2); 10; 11; 12(2); 13(4); 14(2); 15(3); 17(3); 18(7); 19(2); 21(4); 22; 23; 25(2); 26; 27(2); 28(3); 29(4); 30; 31(3); 32; 33(3); 35; 36(4); 39; 40(2); 12:1(2); 2(2); 3; 4(3); 5(2); 6(2); 7(2); 8; 12; 13; 15(3); 13:1(3); 2(3); 3; 5(2); 6(3); 7; 8; 9(2); 13(2); 14(2); 15; 16(3); 17; 18; 20(2); 21(2); 25(2); 14:1(2); 2(2); 3(2); 4; 5; 6; 8(3); 9(2); 12(2); 13; 14(2); 16; 17; 18; 19(3); 15:1; 2; 5; 6; 7; 8; 10; 11(2); 12; 14; 15; 16(2); 17(2); 18(2); 20; 16:2; 3(3); 4; 5(3); 8; 9; 13; 14(2); 18(2); 19; 20; 21; 22; 23; 24(2); 25; 27(2); 28; 29(3); 31(2); 17:1; 2(3); 3; 4(2); 5(2); 7(3); 8(2); 9; 10(2); 11; 12; 18:1(2); 2(4); 3(2); 5; 7; 10; 11(5); 13; 14; 15(2); 16(4); 17(2); 19; 20; 22(2); 23; 25(2); 26; 27; 29(3); 30(6); 31; 19:1(2); 3(2); 5; 6; 8; 11; 12(3); 13; 15; 16(3); 17; 18(2); 19; 22(3); 23; 26(2); 27(2); 29; 30(4); 20:1(2); 2(5); 3(3); 4; 5; 6(2); 7; 8(2); 10(5); 11; 12(2); 13(4); 14(3); 15(3); 17(2); 18(5); 19; 20(2); 21(3); 22; 23(3); 24(2); 25(3); 26(2); 27(4); 28(3); 30(2); 31(5); 32(2); 33(6); 34; 35(2); 36(2); 37; 38(2); 39(3); 40(3); 41(2); 42(4); 44(2); 45(3); 46(2); 48(4); 21:1(2); 2; 3; 5(2); 6; 7; 8(2); 9(2); 10(3); 12(2); 13; 14(2); 15;

16(2); 17(2); 18(2); 19(4); 20; 21(5); 23(2); 24; **Ruth** 1:1(2); 2(5);
4(4); 5(2); 6(2); 7(2); 9(2); 13; 22(3); 2:1(4); 2; 3(3); 6(2); 9; 10;
11(2); 12(2); 13; 14; 16(2); 17; 19; 20(3); 23(3); 3:2; 7(2); 10;
11; 13(3); 15; 17; 4:1; 2(2); 3(3); 4; 5(5); 9(2); 10(4); 11; 12(3);
15(2); 17(2); 18; **1Sa** 1:1(6); 2(2); 3(4); 7; 9(2); 10; 11(3); 15;
16(3); 17(2); 20; 24(3); 27; 2:3(2); 4; 8(3); 9; 10(4); 12(2); 13;
15; 17(2); 20; 22(2); 23; 25; 27(2); 28(5); 29(2); 30(2); 31; 33(3);
34; 36(4); 3:1; 3(3); 7; 11; 14(2); 15(2); 17; 19; 20; 21; 4:1; 2;
3(6); 4(6); 5(2); 6(4); 8(2); 10; 11(2); 12(2); 13; 14(2); 16(2); 17;
18(3); 19; 20; 21(2); 22; 5:1; 2(2); 3(2); 4(4); 5(2); 6(2); 7(3);
8(7); 9(2); 10(4); 11(4); 12; 6:1(2); 2; 3(2); 4(2); 5(3); 8(2); 9;
11(3); 12(3); 13; 14(2); 15(3); 16; 18(7); 19(4); 20; 21(2); 7:1(4);
2; 3(3); 4; 6; 7(4); 8(3); 11(2); 12; 13(3); 14(2); 15; 8:2(2); 4; 7;
8; 9; 10(2); 11; 12(2); 14; 15(2); 17; 18; 19; 21(2); 22; 9:1(6);
2(2); 3(2); 4(3); 5; 6; 7; 8(3); 9; 10; 12; 16(4); 17; 20; 21(6); 23;
25; 26(3); 27(2); 10:1; 2(2); 3(3); 4(2); 5(3); 6; 8; 10(2); 11; 12;
13; 16(2); 18(8); 19; 20(2); 21(3); 22; 23; 25; 26; 27; 11:1; 3(2);
4(2); 5(3); 6; 7(4); 8(2); 9(2); 10; 11(3); 15(2); 12:3; 4; 6(2); 7(2);
8; 9(6); 10(2); 11(2); 12(2); 14; 15(3); 17; 13:2(3); 3(2); 4; 6;
7(2); 10; 13; 15; 16; 17(3); 18(2); 19; 22(3); 23(2); 14:1; 2; 3(3);
4(2); 5; 6; 11(3); 12(2); 14(2); 16(2); 18(3); 19; 22; 24(2); 25;
27; 28; 29; 30(2); 36; 37(2); 38; 41; 43; 45; 47(2); 48(2); 49(4);
50(5); 51(3); 52; 15:1(2); 2; 4; 5; 6(2); 8(2); 9(3); 10; 13(2); 14(2);
15(2); 17(2); 19(2); 20(2); 21(2); 22(2); 23(2); 24; 26; 27; 28(2);
29; 30; 32(2); 34; 35; 16:4; 7; 10; 12; 13(3); 14; 18(3); 20;
17:2(2); 4(3); 5(4); 6(2); 7(2); 8; 10; 11; 12(3); 13(2); 17; 18;
19(2); 22(2); 23(3); 24; 25; 26; 28; 32; 33; 34; 35; 36(2); 37(6);
38(2); 40; 42; 44(2); 45(4); 46(4); 50; 51; 52(4); 53; 54; 55; 57(2);
58; 18:1(3); 4; 5(3); 6(4); 10; 11; 12; 15; 17; 21(2); 23; 24; 25(3);
27; 29; 30(2); 19:3; 4; 6; 10; 13; 16; 20(3); 23; 20:6; 8; 11; 12;
14; 15(2); 16(2); 21; 23; 27(2); 28; 30(3); 31; 33; 34; 37; 41;
42(2); 21:1; 2; 3; 5(2); 7(3); 9(2); 10(2); 11(3); 12(2); 13; 15;
22:3(2); 4; 5(2); 7(4); 8(3); 9(3); 10(2); 11(2); 12; 13(2); 15(3);
17(3); 19(3); 20(3); 22(2); 23:2; 3; 4; 5; 6; 10; 11(2); 12(2); 13;
14; 15; 17; 19(2); 20; 21; 23(2); 24(2); 25(2); 26(3); 24:1; 2(2);
3; 4(3); 6; 7; 8; 11(2); 12; 13; 14; 15; 16; 20; 21; 25:1; 3(6); 9;
10; 14(2); 17; 18(4); 20; 21; 22(2); 24; 25(2); 28(2); 29(5); 31;
32; 34; 35; 36; 37; 39(3); 40; 41(2); 42(2); 43(2); 44(2); 26:1;
2(3); 3; 5(2); 6; 11; 12; 13; 14; 15; 16; 19(3); 20(2); 22; 24(2);
27:1(5); 2(2); 6; 7; 8(3); 10(3); 11; 28:2; 3; 5; 6; 7; 9; 13; 14; 16;
17; 18; 19(3); 20(2); 22(2); 29:2; 3(4); 4(3); 5; 6; 7; 8; 9(2); 11;
30:5; 6(2); 12(3); 13; 14(2); 15; 16(5); 17(2); 22(3); 26(5); 29(2);
31:1; 3; 7(3); 9(2); 10(2); 11(2); 12(3); **2Sa** 1:1(2); 2; 3(2); 4;
12(2); 13; 15; 18(3); 19; 20(3); 21(4); 22(4); 24(2); 25; 26; 27;
2:1(3); 3; 4(3); 5(2); 7; 8(3); 10; 11; 12(3); 13(5); 15(4); 17(2);
18(2); 21(2); 23; 24(3); 25(2); 30; 31(3); 32(2); 3:1(3); 2; 3(5);
4(2); 6(3); 7; 8(3); 10(2); 13; 14; 15; 17; 18(6); 19(3); 22; 23; 25;
26; 27; 28(2); 29(2); 32; 36; 37(2); 39(2); 4:2(6); 4(3); 5(3); 6;
8(5); 9(2); 10; 11; 12(2); 5:1; 3; 6; 7(2); 8; 9; 10; 11; 13; 14; 17;
18; 19; 20(2); 22; 23; 24(3); 6:1; 2(4); 3(4); 4(3); 5(3); 6(2); 7(2);
8; 9(2); 10(3); 11(2); 12(6); 13; 15(3); 16(2); 17(2); 18(3); 19(4);
20(5); 21; 22(3); 23(2); 7:2(2); 4; 6(2); 7(4); 8; 9(2); 10(2); 12;
13; 14(3); 19(2); 26(2); 27(2); 29(2); 8:1(2); 3(2); 4; 5(3); 6; 7(2);
8; 9(2); 10(3); 11; 12(10); 13(2); 14; 16(2); 17(2); 18; 9:1(2);
2(2); 3(3); 4(2); 5(3); 6(2); 7; 11; 12; 10:1(2); 2(4); 3(2); 4; 6(6);
7(2); 8(4); 9(3); 10(3); 11; 12(2); 14(2); 16(2); 18(3); 19; 11:1;
2; 3(2); 7; 8(2); 9(2); 11; 13; 14; 15; 17(4); 19(2); 21(2); 23; 24;
26; 12:3(2); 4(2); 7(3); 8(2); 9(3); 10; 11(2); 14; 17; 18; 20; 25(2);
26(2); 27; 28; 30(2); 31(4); 13:1(2); 3; 6; 10; 11; 13; 18; 19; 21;
29; 30; 32(2); 34; 36; 37(2); 39; 14:1; 4; 7; 9; 11(2); 13; 15(2);
16(4); 17(2); 19(2); 20(3); 22; 25(2); 26; 27; 15:2(5); 3; 6(2);
10(2); 11; 13(2); 14; 23; 24(4); 25(2); 27; 28; 29; 30; 31; 32; 34;
35; 16:1(7); 3(2); 5(4); 6; 7; 8(3); 9; 10; 11; 15; 18; 19; 21(2);
22(2); 23(3); 17:4; 8(2); 9; 10; 12(2); 14(4); 15; 16; 18; 20; 21;
22; 23; 24; 25(3); 26; 27(7); 29; 18:1(2); 2(5); 3(3); 6; 7(3); 8;
9(3); 11; 12; 14(2); 17; 19(2); 22; 23; 27(3); 31; 32; 19:5(5); 9(6);
10; 11(2); 13(4); 14(3); 16(3); 17(3); 18; 19; 20(2); 21; 22; 24;
27; 28; 29; 32; 35; 37(2); 38; 40(2); 41(2); 42(4); 43(6); 20:1(3);
2(3); 3; 4; 5; 6; 7(2); 10; 11; 12(2); 13(2); 14; 15; 16; 17; 19(2);
21(2); 22(2); 23(2); 24; 21:1(2); 2(6); 3; 4(2); 5(2); 6(2); 7(4);
8(5); 9(3); 10(5); 11(2); 12(4); 13(3); 14(3); 16(4); 17(3); 18(2);
19(3); 20; 21(2); 22(2); 22:1(5); 3(2); 5(2); 6(2); 7; 8; 9(2); 11;
12; 13; 16(5); 17; 19; 21; 22; 31; 35; 36; 41; 43(2); 44(2); 46;
47(2); 51; 23:1(5); 2; 3(3); 4(2); 6(2); 7; 8; 9(3); 11(3); 12; 13(4);
14; 15(3); 16(3); 17(2); 18(2); 19; 20(6); 21; 22; 24(4); 26; 29(5);
30(2); 32(2); 33; 34(3); 36(2); 37; 24:1; 2(3); 3; 4(4); 5(3); 6;
7(4); 8; 9(3); 10; 11; 12; 13; 14(2); 15; 16(3); 18; 19; 21; 22;
24(3); **1Kin** 1:3; 5; 7; 8; 9(2); 11(2); 12; 19(2); 20(2); 25; 26; 27;
29; 30; 32; 33; 36(2); 37; 38; 39(2); 40; 41(3); 42; 44; 46; 47;
48; 50(2); 51; 52; 2:1; 2; 3(2); 4; 5(7); 7(3); 8(2); 10; 12; 13(2);
16; 20; 22; 24; 25(2); 26(2); 27(2); 28(2); 29(2); 30; 31; 32(6);
33(2); 34; 35(2); 39(5); 43; 45; 46(2); 3:1(5); 2; 3; 6; 7; 8; 11;
15(2); 17; 28(2); 4:2; 3(2); 4; 5(2); 6; 8; 9; 10(2); 11(3); 12; 13(4);
14; 15; 16; 17; 18; 19(6); 21(3); 22(2); 23; 25; 26; 29; 30(3); 31;
33(6); 34(4); 5:1(3); 3(2); 5; 6; 7; 8(2); 11(2); 13; 16; 17; 6:1(5);
3(2); 4; 5(4); 6(2); 7(2); 8(2); 9; 10; 11; 13; 15(6); 16(2); 18;
19(2); 20; 21; 23; 24(4); 25; 26(2); 27(4); 29(2); 30; 31(3); 32(2);
33(3); 34(3); 36(2); 37(2); 38; 7:2(3); 6; 7(2); 8; 9(2); 10(3); 11;
12(5); 13; 14(3); 15(4); 16(4); 17(3); 19(2); 21; 22(2); 23; 24;
26(2); 27(3); 28; 29; 30(2); 31(3); 32(2); 33(2); 34(2); 35(4);
36(2); 37; 38(2); 39(3); 40(2); 41(4); 42(2); 45(2); 46; 47; 48(3);
49(2); 50(5); 51(3); 8:1(9); 2; 3; 4(2); 5; 6(4); 7; 8; 9(4); 10(2);
11(3); 14(2); 15; 16(3); 17(3); 19; 20(4); 21(3); 22(3); 23; 25(2);
26; 27; 28; 29; 30(2); 34; 36(2); 37; 38; 39(2); 41(2); 42(3); 43;
46; 47; 48; 51(3); 52(2); 53(3); 54(2); 55; 56(2); 59(2); 60; 63(3);
64(4); 65(2); 66; 9:1(2); 4; 5(2); 7(2); 9(2); 10(2); 11(2); 13; 14;
15(3); 16; 19(2); 20(3); 21(2); 22(4); 23; 24(2); 26(3); 27(2);
10:1(4); 2; 4; 5(4); 6(2); 9; 10(4); 11(2); 12(2); 13(2); 14(2);
15(7); 16(2); 17(4); 18; 19(2); 21(8); 22(3); 23; 25(2); 28; 29(4);
11:1(2); 2(2); 4; 5(2); 6; 7(3); 9; 11; 12(2); 14; 15; 17; 18(3);
19(3); 20(2); 21; 23(2); 24; 25; 26(2); 27(2); 28(3); 29; 31(3);
32(2); 33(4); 34(2); 35; 39; 40(2); 41(4); 43; 12:2(3); 3; 4; 8; 14;
15; 16; 17(2); 19; 20(2); 21(4); 22(2); 23(4); 24(3); 26; 27(4);
28(3); 31(5); 32(2); 33(3); 13:1(3); 2(3); 4(2); 5(2); 6(3); 7; 8; 9;
11; 12; 14(2); 17; 18; 20; 21(2); 22(2); 26(3); 29(2); 31; 32(3);
33(5); 34(2); 14:1; 2; 3(2); 4(2); 5(2); 6(2); 7; 8; 10(3); 11(2);
13(3); 14; 15; 16(2); 17; 18(2); 19(5); 21(3); 22; 24(2); 25(2);
26(4); 27(3); 28; 29(5); 31; 15:1(2); 2; 3(2); 5(3); 6; 7(5); 8; 9(2);
10; 11; 12; 15; 16; 17(2); 18(7); 19(2); 20(3); 21; 22(2); 23(6);
24; 25(3); 26(2); 27(3); 28(2); 29(2); 30(3); 31(5); 32; 33(3);
34(2); 16:1(2); 2(2); 3(4); 4(3); 5(5); 7(6); 8(3); 9(3); 10(2); 11(3);
12(2); 13(3); 14(5); 15(2); 16; 18; 19(2); 20(5); 21(3); 22; 23(2);
24(5); 25; 26(3); 27(5); 29(4); 30(2); 31(4); 32; 33(2); 34(2);
17:1(3); 2; 4; 5; 6; 8; 10(2); 11; 12; 14(3); 15; 16(3); 17(2); 18;
19; 22(2); 23; 24(2); 18:1; 3; 4; 5; 9; 10; 12; 13(2); 15; 18; 19(2);
20; 22; 24(2); 25(2); 26; 29(2); 30; 31(4); 32(2); 36(4); 38; 40(2);
41(2); 42; 44; 46(2); 19:2(2); 6; 7; 8(2); 9; 10(2); 13; 14(2); 15;
16(3); 17(2); 19(2); 21(2); 20:1; 2; 4; 6; 7(2); 9; 10; 11; 13; 14(2);
15(3); 17(3); 19(3); 20; 21; 22(3); 23(3); 24; 26; 27(3); 28(4);
29(2); 30; 31(3); 32; 35(3); 36; 39(2); 40; 41(2); 42; 43; 21:1(2);
2(2); 3; 4(2); 7(2); 10; 11; 13(4); 15(2); 16(2); 17; 18(2); 19; 20;
22(4); 23(2); 24(2); 25; 26; 28; 22:2(2); 3(4); 4; 5(2); 6(2); 7(2);
8(3); 9(2); 10(4); 11(2); 13(3); 15; 16; 18; 19(2); 22; 23; 24(2);
26(2); 27(2); 28; 29(2); 30(2); 31(2); 32(2); 33(2); 34(4); 35(2);
36; 38(2); 39(5); 41(3); 42; 43(2); 44; 45(5); 46(3); 48; 49; 50;
51(3); 52(5); 53; **2Kin** 1:1; 2(3); 3(5); 6(2); 7; 8; 9(3); 10(2);
11(2); 12(2); 13(4); 14; 15(2); 16(3); 17(4); 18(5); 2:3; 5; 7(2);
9; 11(2); 12(2); 13(2); 14(2); 15(2); 16; 19(2); 21; 22; 23; 24(3);
3:1(3); 2(2); 3(2); 4(2); 5(2); 6; 7(2); 8; 9(4); 10(2); 11(6);
12(3); 13(5); 14(3); 15; 16; 18; 19(2); 20; 24; 25(2); 26(2); 4:1(3);
2; 3; 7(2); 9; 13; 16(2); 17; 21(2); 22(3); 25(2); 27(2); 28; 29; 30;
31; 34; 38(2); 39; 40(2); 42(4); 44; 5:1(3); 2(2); 3; 4(2); 5(5);
6(2); 7(2); 8(2); 9(2); 11; 12(2); 14(3); 15(2); 17; 18(3); 20(3);
22(4); 23(3); 27; 6:1; 6; 8; 9(2); 10(3); 11(4); 12(2); 15(2); 17(3);
18; 20(2); 21; 23(2); 24; 25(4); 26; 27(2); 30; 31(2); 32(2); 33;
7:1(4); 2; 3; 4; 5(3); 6(7); 8; 9; 10(3); 12(2); 13(4); 14; 15; 16(4);
17(2); 18(4); 19; 8:2(3); 3(2); 4(2); 6; 7(2); 8(3); 9(4); 11; 12;
16(6); 18(5); 20; 21; 22; 23(5); 24; 25(5); 26(2); 27(6); 28(2);
29(5); 9:1(3); 2(2); 3; 5(2); 6(2); 7(5); 8; 9(5); 10; 11; 13; 14(4);
15(3); 16; 17; 20(2); 21(3); 22; 25(2); 26(4); 27(2); 28; 29(2);
30; 33; 35(2); 36(3); 37(3); 10:1; 3; 5; 6(2); 8(2); 10(3); 11(2);
13(5); 14(2); 15; 17; 19(2); 21(3); 22; 23(6); 24(2); 25(4); 26(2);
27(2); 28; 29(2); 30(3); 31(3); 32; 33; 34(5); 11:1; 2(3); 3; 4(3);
5(3); 6(2); 7(3); 10; 11(2); 13(3); 14; 15(3); 18(4); 19(5); 20;
12:1(2); 2; 4(4); 5(2); 6(2); 7(3); 8(2); 9(3); 10; 11(4); 12(3);
13(6); 14; 16; 17; 18(5); 19(5); 20; 21(3); 13:1(4); 2(3); 3(5);
4(2); 5(2); 6(2); 7(2); 8(5); 10(3); 11(3); 12(6); 13; 14(3); 16;
17(2); 18; 19; 20(2); 21(3); 22(2); 23; 24; 25(7); 14:1(5); 2; 3;
6(3); 7(3); 8(3); 9(2); 10; 11(2); 13(6); 14(2); 15(6); 16; 17(5);
18(5); 20; 21(2); 23(5); 24(3); 25(8); 26; 27(3); 28(5); 29; 15:1(4);
2; 3; 5(2); 6(5); 7; 8(3); 9(3); 10; 11(5); 12(2); 13(3); 14(2); 15(5);
17(3); 18(3); 19(2); 20(7); 21(5); 23(3); 24(3); 25(4); 26(5); 27(3);
28(3); 29(4); 30(4); 31(5); 32(5); 33; 34; 35(2); 36(5); 37(2); 38;
16:1(4); 2; 3(4); 5(3); 6; 7(7); 8(3); 9(3); 10(3); 13; 14(3); 15(4);
17(2); 18(2); 19(5); 20; 17:1(3); 2(2); 3; 4(4); 5; 6(4); 7(5); 8(4);
9(2); 14; 16(2); 17; 18(2); 19(2); 20(3); 21(2); 22(2); 23(2); 24(4);
25(2); 26(6); 27(4); 28; 29(2); 30(3); 31; 32(4); 33; 34; 36(2);
39(2); 18:1(5); 2; 3; 4; 5(2); 7; 8; 9(5); 10(4); 11(3); 12(2); 13(3);
14(6); 15(2); 16(4); 17(3); 18(2); 19; 21(2); 23; 24(3); 26(2);
28(2); 29; 30(2); 31(4); 32(4); 33(5); 34(4); 35(3); 37(3); 19:1;
2(2); 3(2); 4(2); 5; 6(3); 8; 9(2); 10(3); 11; 12(2); 13(5); 14(3);
15(3); 16; 17(2); 18; 19(2); 20(3); 21(2); 22; 23(5); 24(2); 25;
26(2); 29(2); 30(2); 31(4); 32; 35(2); 36; 37(2); 20:1; 4; 5(3);
6(3); 7; 8; 9; 11; 12(2); 13(2); 16; 18(3); 19; 20(5); 21:2(3); 3(2);
4(2); 5(3); 6; 7(4); 8(2); 9; 11; 12(2); 13(3); 14(2); 15; 16; 17(5);
18(2); 19(2); 20; 22(2); 23; 24(2); 25(5); 26; 22:1(2); 2(2); 3(4);
4(3); 5(7); 7; 8(2); 9(3); 11(2); 12(3); 13(4); 14(4); 15; 16(2); 17;
18(3); 23:1(2); 2(6); 3; 4(7); 5(3); 6(3); 7(2); 8(7); 9(3); 10(2);
11(5); 12(6); 13(7); 14; 15; 16(3); 17(4); 18(2); 19(3); 20; 21;
22(5); 23; 24(3); 25; 26(2); 27(2); 28(5); 29(2); 30(2); 31(2); 32;
33(4); 34(2); 35(4); 36(2); 37; 24:1; 2(6); 3(3); 5(5); 7(5); 8(2);
9; 10(2); 11; 12(4); 13(6); 14(3); 15; 16(2); 17; 18(2); 19; 20(2);
25:1(3); 2; 3(2); 4(2); 5(2); 6; 7(3); 8(6); 9(2); 10(3); 11(4); 12(3);
13(4); 14; 15(3); 16(2); 17(3); 18(2); 19(7); 20(2); 21(3); 22(4);
23(6); 24(2); 25(3); 26(2); 27(8); 28; 29; 30(2); **1Chr** 1:5; 6; 7;
8; 9(2); 12; 17; 19; 23; 28; 29; 31; 32(2); 33(2); 34; 35; 36; 37;
38; 39; 40(2); 41(2); 42(2); 43(4); 44(2); 45(2); 46(3); 47; 48;
49; 50(3); 51; 54; 2:1; 3(5); 4; 5; 6(2); 7(2); 8; 9; 10(2); 16; 17;
18(3); 21(2); 22; 23(3); 24; 25(2); 26; 27(2); 28(2); 29(2); 30;
31(3); 32(2); 33(2); 42(5); 43; 44; 45(2); 47; 49(4); 50(4); 51(2);
52(2); 53(2); 54(3); 55(4); 3:1(3); 2(4); 3; 5(2); 9(2); 15; 16; 17;
19(2); 21(5); 22(2); 23; 24; 4:1; 2(2); 3(3); 4(5); 5; 6; 7; 8(2); 10;
11(2); 12(2); 13(2); 14(2); 15(3); 16; 17(2); 18(5); 19(3); 20(2);
21(8); 22; 24; 26; 27; 31; 34; 35(3); 37(5); 38; 39(2); 40(2);
41(2); 42(4); 43; 5:1(4); 2; 3(2); 4; 6(2); 7; 8(3); 9(2); 10(2); 11(2);
13(2); 14(8); 15(4); 16; 17(4); 18(3); 20; 21(4); 22; 23(2); 24(5);
25(3); 26(6); 6:1; 2; 3(2); 15; 16; 17(2); 18; 19(2); 20; 22; 25;
26; 28; 29; 31(2); 32(3); 33(4); 34(4); 35(4); 36(4); 37(4); 38(4);
39(2); 40(3); 41(3); 42(3); 43(3); 44(4); 45(3); 46(3); 47(4); 48(4);
49(4); 50; 54(4); 55; 56(2); 57(3); 60(2); 61(6); 62(9); 63(7); 64;
65(9); 66(6); 67(2); 70(5); 71(4); 72(2); 74(2); 76(2); 77(4); 78(3);
80(2); 7:1; 2(5); 3(3); 4(2); 5(2); 6; 7(4); 8(2); 9(4); 10(2); 11(3);
12(2); 13(2); 14(2); 15(2); 16(2); 17(4); 19; 20; 21; 29(4); 30;
31(2); 33(2); 34; 35; 36; 38; 39; 40(5); 8:3; 6(4); 8; 9; 10; 11;
12; 13(4); 16; 18; 21; 25; 27; 28; 29; 34; 35; 38; 39; 40(4); 9:1(2);
3(6); 4(7); 5; 6(2); 7(5); 8(6); 9(2); 10; 11(7); 12(8); 13(5); 14(6);
15(3); 16(6); 18(2); 19(10); 20; 21(4); 23(4); 26(2); 27; 28(2);
29(2); 30(3); 31(2); 32(3); 33(2); 34; 35; 40; 41; 44; 10:1; 2; 3;
7; 9; 10(2); 12(2); 13(3); 14(2); 11:3(2); 4; 5(3); 6; 7; 8; 9; 10(2);
11(2); 12(2); 13(2); 14; 15(4); 17(3); 18(4); 19(2); 20(2); 21;
22(4); 23(2); 24; 26(4); 28; 30; 31(3); 32(2); 34(2); 35(2); 37;
38(2); 39(2); 41; 42(2); 43; 44; 45; 46; 12:1(3); 2(3); 3(2); 7(2);
8(4); 14(4); 15; 16(2); 17; 18(3); 19(3); 20(3); 21(2); 22; 23(3);
24; 25(3); 26(2); 27; 28(2); 29(6); 30(4); 31(2); 32(4); 33(3); 34;
35; 36; 37(6); 38(3); 40(2); 13:1; 2(3); 3(2); 4; 5(3); 6; 7(3); 9;
10; 12(2); 13(2); 14(3); 14:1(2); 2; 4; 8; 9; 10; 11(2); 14; 15(3);
16; 17(2); 15:1(2); 2(2); 3; 4; 5(2); 6(2); 7(2); 8(2); 9(2); 10(2);
12(4); 14(2); 15(3); 16(2); 17(6); 18; 19; 22; 24; 25(5); 26(2);
27(3); 28(3); 29(4); 16:1(2); 2(2); 3(4); 4(3); 6(2); 7; 9; 10; 12;
13(2); 15; 16(2); 18(2); 26; 28; 29; 33(2); 35; 36; 37(2); 38; 39;
40(2); 42(2); 17:1(3); 3; 6(3); 7; 8; 9; 11; 17(3); 18; 21(2); 24(3);
27; 18:1(2); 3; 4; 5(3); 7(2); 8(2); 9(3); 10(3); 11; 12(2); 15(2);
16(2); 17(2); 19:1(2); 2(4); 3(2); 6(6); 7(2); 8(2); 9(2); 10(2);
11(3); 12; 13(2); 15; 16(2); 18(2); 19(2); 20:1(3); 2(3); 3(3); 4(2);
5(2); 6(2); 7; 8(2); 21:2(2); 3; 5(3); 8; 10; 12(4); 13(2); 14; 15(3);
16(2); 18(2); 19(2); 21; 22; 25; 26; 28; 29(2); 30(4); 22:1(2);
2(2); 3; 4; 5(2); 6; 7; 8; 9; 10; 11(2); 12; 13; 14(4); 15(3); 16; 17;
18; 19(5); 23:1; 2; 3; 4(3); 6; 7; 8; 9(3); 10(2); 12; 13; 14(3); 15;
16(2); 17(2); 18(2); 19(2); 20(2); 21(2); 22; 23; 24(7); 25; 26;
27; 28(7); 29; 32(7); 24:1(3); 3(4); 4(9); 5(7); 6(5); 19(3); 20(6);
21(2); 22(3); 23; 24(4); 25(3); 26(2); 27; 28; 29; 30(3); 31(4);
25:1(6); 2(5); 3(3); 4(2); 5(2); 6(4); 7(2); 26:1(5); 2; 4; 6(2); 7;
8(3); 10(2); 11; 12(2); 13; 15; 16; 19(3); 20(4); 21(3); 22(3); 23;
24(3); 26(2); 27(2); 28(5); 29; 30(5); 31(5); 32(3); 27:1(5); 2;
3(4); 4(2); 5(2); 7; 9; 10(2); 11; 12; 13; 14(2); 15; 16(5); 17(3);
18(5); 19(4); 20(6); 21(5); 22(4); 23(2); 24(3); 25(2); 26(3); 27;
28; 29; 31; 32; 34(2); 28:1(5); 2(4); 3; 4(6); 5(3); 8(4); 9(3); 11(7);
12(10); 13(6); 14(7); 15(4); 16(2); 17; 18(5); 19; 20(3); 21(5);
29:2(8); 3(4); 4(5); 5(4); 6(6); 7(6); 8(3); 10; 12; 14(2); 16; 17;
18(5); 20; 22; 23(2); 24; 25; 26; 28; 29(4); 30; **2Chr** 1:1; 2(3);
3(3); 4; 5(3); 6; 9; 11; 12; 13; 16; 17(4); 2:1; 3; 4(2); 6; 8; 10(4);
11; 12; 13; 14(6); 15; 16; 17; 18(2); 3:1(2); 2(2); 3(2); 4(3); 6; 8;
9(2); 10; 11(4); 12(3); 13; 14; 15(3); 16; 17(2); 4:1; 2(2); 3(2);
5(5); 7; 8; 9(2); 10; 11; 12(3); 13(2); 16(2); 17; 18; 19; 20; 21;
22(5); 5:1(3); 2(9); 3; 4; 5; 6; 7(4); 8; 9(2); 10(2); 11; 12(5); 13(2);
14(3); 6:2; 3(2); 4; 5(3); 7(3); 9; 10(4); 11(2); 12(3); 13(3); 14;
16(2); 17; 18; 19; 21(2); 25; 27(2); 28; 29(2); 30(2); 32; 33; 37;
38; 41; 42(2); 7:1(2); 2(2); 3(2); 5(2); 6(2); 7(3); 8(2); 9; 10;
11(2); 12; 18; 20(2); 22(3); 8:1(2); 2; 6(2); 7(2); 8(2); 9(5); 10;
11(6); 12; 13(4); 14(4); 15; 16(5); 17; 18(4); 9:1(4); 3(2); 4(4);
5(2); 6(2); 9(3); 10(2); 11(3); 12; 13(2); 14(2); 15(2); 16(4); 17;
18(2); 20(9); 21(2); 22; 23(2); 24(2); 26(2); 28(2); 29(6); 31;
10:2(3); 4; 13; 14; 15(3); 16; 17(2); 18; 19; 11:1(2); 2(2); 3(2);
4(2); 11(2); 13; 16(4); 17(3); 18(4); 20; 21; 22; 23(2); 12:1; 2(2);
3; 5(3); 6; 7(2); 8(2); 9(5); 10(5); 11; 12; 13(2); 15(3); 16; 13:1;
2(2); 3(3); 5(2); 6(3); 7(2); 8(3); 9(5); 10; 11(2); 12(2); 15(2); 16;
17; 18(3); 20; 22(3); 14:1; 2; 3; 4; 5(2); 8(4); 9; 10; 14; 15;
15:1(2); 2; 4(2); 5; 6(2); 8(6); 9(3); 10(2); 11; 12; 13; 15; 16;
17(2); 18; 19(2); 16:1(4); 2(5); 3; 4(3); 5; 6; 7(5); 9(2); 10(2);
11(3); 12; 13; 14(2); 17:2(3); 3; 4(2); 6(2); 7(2); 9(3); 10(2); 11;
12; 13(3); 14(5); 16(2); 17(2); 18:3(2); 4(2); 5(2); 6(2); 7(3); 8(3);
9(5); 10(2); 11; 12(2); 15; 17; 18(2); 19; 21; 22; 23(2); 25(2);
26(2); 28(2); 29(2); 30(3); 31(2); 32(2); 33(3); 34(2); 19:1; 2; 3;
4; 5; 7(3); 8(6); 9; 10; 11(4); 20:1(2); 4(3); 5(2); 6(2); 7(2); 10(3);
11; 14(8); 15(2); 16(3); 17; 18; 19(5); 20(2); 21; 22; 23(4); 25(2);
26(3); 27(2); 28; 29(3); 30; 31; 32(2); 33; 34(6); 35(2); 37(2);
21:1; 2(3); 3(3); 4(3); 6(5); 7(2); 8; 9; 10(2); 11(2); 12(4); 13(6);
15(2); 16(2); 17; 19(5); 20(2); 22:1(4); 2; 3(2); 4(3); 5(3); 6(5);
7(4); 8(4); 9(2); 10(3); 11(5); 12; 23:1(6); 2(4); 3(3); 4(4); 5(3);
6(3); 9(2); 10(2); 12(2); 13(2); 14(3); 15; 17(2); 18(6); 19(2);
20(5); 21; 24:1; 2(2); 4; 5(3); 6(8); 7(4); 8(2); 9; 11; 12(5); 13;
14(5); 15; 16; 17(2); 18(2); 20(3); 21(3); 23(5); 24(3); 25(4);
26(2); 27(5); 25:1; 2; 4; 5; 6(3); 7(3); 9(3); 10; 11(3); 12(3); 13(3);
14(3); 15(3); 16; 17(4); 18(2); 20(3); 21(2); 23(6); 24(2); 25(5);
26(4); 28; 26:1(2); 3; 4; 5(2); 6(3); 8; 9; 11(5); 12(4); 16(2); 17;
18(2); 19; 21(3); 22(3); 23; 27:1; 2(2); 3(3); 4; 5(6); 7(4); 9; 28:1;
2(2); 3(4); 5(5); 6(2); 7(2); 8(2); 9(2); 10; 11(2); 12(7); 15(2); 16;
18(3); 19(2); 20; 21(6); 22; 23(5); 24(7); 25(2); 26(4); 27(2);
29:1; 2; 3(3); 5(3); 6(2); 7(2); 8; 10; 12(11); 13(4); 14(4); 15(3);
16(5); 17(5); 18(2); 19; 20(2); 21(2); 25(4); 26; 27(2); 29; 30(2);
31(2); 32; 35(3); 30:1(2); 5(2); 6(7); 7; 8; 10; 11(2); 12(4); 13;
15(2); 16(4); 17(2); 18(2); 19(2); 21(2); 22(2); 24(2); 25(4); 26(3);
31:1(3); 2(3); 3(2); 4(2); 5(5); 6(4); 7; 10(3); 11; 13(4); 14(3); 15;
16(2); 17(2); 18; 19(4); 21(2); 32:1; 3; 4(2); 5; 6(3); 7; 8(3); 9(2);
10; 11(3); 13(4); 14(3); 15(5); 17(6); 18; 19(5); 20; 21(6); 22(4);
23(2); 26(4); 27; 28(2); 29; 30(3); 31(4); 32(6); 33(4); 33:2(3);
3; 4; 5(3); 6(3); 7(3); 8(3); 9(2); 11(3); 12; 13; 14(4); 15(5); 16(2);
18(7); 19(2); 22; 25(2); 34:2(2); 3(2); 4(3); 5; 6; 7; 8(5); 9(6);
10(4); 11; 12(8); 13(4); 14(3); 15(2); 17(3); 19; 20(3); 21(4);
22(4); 23; 24; 25; 26(3); 28; 29; 30(6); 31; 32(3); 33(3); 35:1;
2(2); 3(2); 4(4); 5(5); 6(2); 7(3); 8(2); 9; 12(3); 14(3); 15(2); 16(3);
17(2); 18(3); 19(2); 20; 21; 22(3); 24(3); 25; 26(3); 27(2); 36:1(2);
3(3); 4; 5; 6; 7(3); 8(4); 9; 10(2); 12(2); 13; 14(3); 15; 16(2);
17(2); 18(6); 19(2); 20(2); 21(2); 22(6); 23(4); **Ezr** 1:1(6); 2(3);
3(3); 4(2); 5(3); 6; 7(4); 8(3); 9(3); 10(2); 11(3); 2:1(4); 2(3); 3;
4; 5; 6(3); 7; 8; 9; 10; 11; 12; 13; 14; 15; 16(2); 17; 18; 19; 20;
21; 22; 23; 24; 25; 26; 27; 28; 29; 30; 31; 32; 33; 34; 35; 36(3);
37; 38; 39; 40(3); 41; 42(7); 43(3); 44(3); 45(3); 46(3); 47(3);
48(3); 49(3); 50(3); 51(3); 52(3); 53(3); 54(2); 55(4); 56(3); 57(5);
58; 59; 60(3); 61(7); 63; 65; 68(4); 69(3); 70; 3:1; 2(6); 3(2);
4(2); 5(4); 6(3); 7(5); 8(8); 9(3); 10(5); 11(2); 12(3); 13(4); 4:1(3);
2(3); 3(5); 4(3); 5(4); 6(3); 7(4); 9; 10(2); 11; 13; 15(4); 17; 19;
22; 23; 24(5); 5:1(3); 2(4); 4; 5(2); 6; 8(2); 10(2); 11(3); 12(3);
13(3); 14(7); 15; 16(2); 17(2); 6:1; 2; 3(2); 4(3); 5(4); 7(5); 8(5);
9(4); 10(4); 12; 14(7); 15(3); 16(5); 17(4); 18(2); 19(2); 20(2);
21(5); 22(6); 7:1(5); 2(3); 3(3); 4(3); 5(4); 6(3); 7(4); 8; 9(3); 10;
11(5); 12(4); 13(4); 14(3); 15; 16(4); 17(2); 18(2); 19(3); 20(2);
21(4); 22(4); 23(4); 24(3); 25(2); 26(3); 27(2); 28(2); 8:1(3); 2(6);
3(5); 4(3); 5(3); 6(3); 7(3); 8(3); 9(3); 10(3); 11(3); 12(3); 13(2);
14(2); 15(2); 16; 17; 18(6); 19(2); 20(3); 21(2); 22(3); 23; 24(3);
25(2); 26(2); 27(3); 28; 29(5); 30(2); 31(5); 33(6); 34; 35(3); 36;
9:1(3); 2(3); 3(2); 4(4); 7(4); 9(3); 11(2); 12; 14; 15(2); 10:1(3);
2(5); 3(4); 4; 6(5); 7; 8(2); 9(5); 10; 11(2); 13(2); 14(3); 15(2);
16(5); 17; 18(4); 19; 20(2); 21(2); 22(2); 23; 24(2); 25(3); 26(2);
27(2); 28(2); 29(2); 30(2); 31(2); 33(2); 34(2); 43(2); 44; **Neh**
1:1(2); 2(3); 3(2); 4; 5; 6(4); 9(2); 11(3); 2:1; 2; 3; 4; 5; 8(4); 9;
10(3); 13(2); 14; 15; 17; 18(2); 20; 3:1(3); 2(2); 3; 4(5); 5; 6(2);
7(3); 8(4); 9(3); 10(2); 11(3); 12(3); 13; 14(3); 15(7); 16(5); 17(3);
18(3); 19(3); 20(4); 21(6); 22; 23(2); 24(3); 25(4); 27; 29(3);
30(3); 31(3); 32; 4:2(3); 4; 7; 8; 9; 10(2); 14(2); 15; 16(3); 17;
19; 20; 21(2); 23(2); 5:1(2); 3; 5(2); 7; 9(3); 10; 11(3); 12(2);
14(3); 15(4); 16; 17; 18(3); 6:1; 2(2); 7; 8; 10(5); 14; 15; 16;
17(2); 18(4); 7:2; 3(3); 5(2); 6(4); 7(3); 8; 9; 10; 11(3); 12; 13;
14; 15; 16; 17; 18; 19; 20; 21(2); 22; 23; 24; 25; 26; 27; 28; 29;
30; 31; 32; 33; 34; 35; 36; 37; 38; 39(3); 40; 41; 42; 43(4); 44;
45(6); 46(3); 47(3); 48(3); 49(3); 50(3); 51(3); 52(3); 53(3); 54(3);
55(3); 56(2); 57(4); 58(3); 59(5); 60; 61; 62(3); 63(6); 65; 67;
70(3); 71(5); 72(3); 73(2); 8:1(2); 2(2); 3(2); 4; 5; 8; 9; 10; 13(3);
14(2); 15; 16(6); 17(5); 18(2); 9:1(2); 2(2); 3(3); 4; 6(2); 7(3); 8;
9; 10; 11; 12; 14; 15; 17(2); 18; 19(2); 22(5); 23; 24(2); 25; 27(4);
28; 30(2); 32(2); 37; 38; 10:1; 9(3); 14; 28(3); 29(2); 30; 31(3);
32(3); 33(4); 34(3); 35(4); 36(6); 37(9); 38(3); 39(6); 11:1(3);
3(3); 4(13); 5(7); 6; 7(8); 9(2); 10(2); 11(7); 12(7); 13(5); 14(3);
15(5); 16(5); 17(6); 20(3); 22(9); 24(4); 25(2); 30; 31; 35; 36;

12:1; 7(3); 12(4); 13(2); 14(2); 15(2); 16(2); 17(3); 18(2); 19(2); 20(2); 21(2); 22(3); 23(5); 24(4); 25; 26(5); 27(3); 28(3); 29(3); 31(2); 32(2); 35(7); 36(2); 37(4); 38(3); 39(3); 40(3); 43; 44(3); 45(4); 46(4); 47(4); 13:1(3); 2; 4(3); 5(2); 6(3); 7(3); 8(2); 9(2); 10; 11; 12; 13(3); 14; 15; 16(3); 17; 19(2); 20(2); 22; 23(3); 24(2); 25; 26(2); 28(3); 29(2); 30; **Est** 1:1; 2; 3(3); 4(2); 5(2); 6(4); 7(2); 8; 10(2); 14; 15; 16; 17; 18(3); 19; 21; 22; 2:1; 3(4); 4; 5(3); 6(2); 8(3); 9(4); 11(2); 12(4); 13(2); 14(2); 15(5); 16; 17; 18; 20; 21(2); 23(2); 3:1; 5; 6(3); 7; 8; 9(3); 10; 12(4); 13(2); 14; 4:1; 5; 6; 7(3); 8(2); 9; 11(2); 5:1(2); 2; 3; 6(2); 8; 9; 11(4); 14; 6:1(2); 2(3); 4; 9(3); 10; 11; 13(2); 7:2(2); 7; 8(4); 9(2); 8:1; 2; 3; 5; 6; 7; 9; 11(2); 12(2); 13; 15(5); 17(3); 9:1(2); 2(2); 3(3); 5; 10(3); 11; 12(2); 15; 16; 17(3); 18(2); 19(4); 20; 21(2); 22(2); 24(2); 26(3); 28(2); 29(2); 30(3); 31(2); 32(2); 10:1; 2(7); 3(3); **Job** 1:1; 3(3); 5(2); 6; 10; 12; 15; 16; 17; 19; 21(2); 2:1; 7(2); 10(2); 11; 3:5(2); 6(2); 9(2); 10; 11; 14; 18; 25; 4:6; 9(2); 10(3); 11; 13; 15; 19; 5:1; 5; 6(2); 12; 13; 15; 17; 20; 21(2); 22(2); 23(2); 25; 26; 6:3; 4(2); 6; 10; 12(2); 14; 15; 16; 17; 18; 19(2); 22; 23; 26; 7:1; 2; 3; 4(2); 5; 8; 11(2); 20; 8:2; 6; 8(2); 9; 10; 13; 17; 19(2); 22; 9:2; 3; 6; 8; 9; 19(2); 23; 24(2); 28; 10:1(2); 3(2); 4; 5; 7; 15; 18; 21(2); 22(3); 11:2(2); 6(2); 20(2); 12:4; 5; 6; 7; 8; 9; 10(2); 12; 18; 20(2); 21; 22(2); 24(3); 13:4(2); 6; 12; 26; 27; 14:1(3); 4; 5; 7; 9; 12; 14; 15; 18; 19(3); 21; 15:5; 8; 11; 13; 14; 20; 22(2); 23; 26; 27; 30(2); 34(2); 16:5; 11; 16; 17:5; 6; 7; 11; 12; 16; 18:2; 4; 5(2); 7; 13(2); 14(2); 15; 18; 21(2); 19:7; 9; 11; 17; 20; 21; 28; 29(2); 20:3(2); 4; 5(2); 8; 11(2); 14; 15; 16; 17; 20; 21; 22(2); 23; 24; 25(2); 28(2); 29; 21:9; 12; 14; 16; 17; 20(2); 21; 24; 25; 28(2); 30(2); 33; 22:4; 6; 9; 11; 12(2); 14; 16; 18; 20; 24(2); 25; 30(2); 23:12(2); 15; 24:3; 4(2); 6; 8(2); 9; 12(2); 13; 15; 17(3); 18; 22; 24(3); 25:3; 4; 6; 26:9; 11; 14(3); 27:3; 8; 11; 13(3); 15; 21; 22; 23; 28:2(2); 3(2); 4; 5; 6(3); 12; 13; 16; 17(2); 18(3); 19; 20; 21(2); 24; 26; 28; 29:4(2); 6; 10; 13; 17(2); 24; 30:1; 2; 6(2); 8(2); 12; 14; 16; 18(2); 27; 31; 31:2(2); 3; 7; 13(2); 16; 19; 20; 23; 29; 31(2); 34(2); 37; 40(3); 32:2(4); 5; 6; 7; 8; 12; 18; 33:3(2); 4(2); 6; 8; 13(2); 15; 16; 19; 25; 30; 34:8; 10; 11; 16; 19(2); 21; 22(2); 26; 27; 28(2); 34; 36; 35:7; 8; 9(4); 11(2); 12(2); 36:6; 8; 16(2); 17; 19; 26; 27; 29(2); 30; 37:1; 2(2); 3; 4; 6; 7; 9(2); 10(2); 12; 14; 15; 16(2); 19; 22; 23; 24; 38:1; 3; 4; 7; 8; 13(3); 16(2); 17(3); 18; 21; 22(2); 23(2); 25(2); 27; 28; 29(2); 30; 31(2); 33; 34; 37; 39; 41; 39:1; 5; 7(2); 8; 17; 20; 24; 25; 28; 40:6; 7; 11; 16; 17; 18(2); 19(2); 20; 21; 22; 41:6; 9(2); 13; 14; 18; 19(2); 20(2); 21; 23; 24; 25; 26; 29; 31; 34; 42:4; 5(2); 7; 8; 10; 11(3); 12(2); 14(3); 15; 17; **Ps** 1:1(3); 2; 3; 5; 6(2); 2:2; 6; 8(2); 9; 10; 3:t, 2; 3; 4; 6(2); 7; 4:t, 1; 2; 5; 6; 5:t, 2; 5; 7; 8; 10; 6:t, 5; 7(2); 8(2); 7:(2); 6(2); 7; 9; 10; 13; 17; 8:t, 2(3); 3; 4(2); 6; 7; 8(3); 9:t, 9; 12; 13(2); 14(2); 16; 18; 10:1; 3; 4; 5; 7; 8; 14; 15; 16; 17; 18; 11:t, 4; 6; 12:t, 1; 5(2); 6(2); 13:t, 3; 14:t, 2; 4; 5; 6; 7(3); 15:t; 16:t, 4; 5(2); 11(2); 17:t, 1; 4(3); 8(2); 12; 14(3); 18:(5); 2; 4(2); 5(2); 6; 7; 8(2); 10; 11; 12; 13; 15(4); 16; 18; 20; 21; 24; 30; 34; 35; 40; 43(2); 44; 45; 46; 19:t, 1; 4; 5; 6(2); 7(2); 8(2); 9(2); 11; 14(2); 20:t, 1(3); 2; 5; 6; 7; 21:t, 2; 3(2); 4(2); 7; 9; 10; 12; 22:t, 1; 3; 6(2); 9; 12; 14(2); 15; 16; 20; 21; 22; 23(2); 24; 25; 27(2); 23:t, 3; 4(2); 5; 6(2); 24:t, 3; 5; 6; 7; 8; 9; 10(3); 25:t, 5; 6; 7; 10; 14; 15; 17(2); 22; 26:t, 5; 7(2); 8; 10; 27:t, 1(2); 4(4); 5(2); 6; 9; 11; 12; 13(2); 14; 28:t, 2; 3; 4(2); 5(2); 6; 8; 29:t, 2; 3(2); 4(3); 5(2); 7(2); 8(2); 9(2); 30:(2); 4(2); 31:t, 2; 4; 5; 8; 10; 12; 13; 15; 19; 20(3); 22; 24; 32:t, 4; 5; 6; 7; 33:2; 4; 5(2); 6(3); 7; 8(2); 10(3); 11(2); 13; 14(2); 16; 18; 34:t, 6; 7; 11; 15; 16(2); 17; 18(2); 19(2); 20; 22(2); 35:t, 2; 5; 6; 12; 27; 28(2); 36:(2); 1(2); 3; 7(2); 8(3); 9; 11(2); 12; 37:t, 1(2); 4; 7(2); 11; 14; 16; 17; 18; 19; 20(2); 22(2); 23; 28; 30(2); 31(2); 37; 38; 39(3); 38:t, 3(2); 5; 8(2); 10; 39:t, 4; 8; 10; 40:t, 2(2); 5; 7(2); 12; 15; 41:t, 1; 2; 3; 5; 9; 13; 42:t, 4(2); 5; 6(2); 7; 8; 9(2); 11; 43:2(3); 4; 5; 44:t, 1; 3; 14; 15; 16(2); 19(2); 20; 21; 45:(2); 1(2); 2; 4; 5; 6; 7; 8(2); 9; 12; 13; 14; 16; 46:t, 2; 4(3); 5; 7(2); 8; 9; 11(2); 47:t, 1; 4; 5; 7; 8; 9(4); 48:t, 1(2); 2(3); 6; 7; 8(3); 9(2); 10(2); 11(2); 49:t, 1; 3(3); 5(2); 6; 7; 8; 15; 16; 19; 50:t, 1; 2(2); 9(2); 10; 11(2); 13(2); 15; 23; 51:t, 1; 12; 14(2); 17; 18; 19; 52:(2); 1; 5(3); 7; 8(2); 53:t, 2; 3; 4; 5; 6(3); 54:t, 2; 7; 55:t, 3(4); 4; 10; 14; 19; 21; 23; 56:t, 13; 57:t, 1; 3; 4; 58:t, 1; 2; 4; 5; 6; 8(2); 10; 59:t, 2; 5(2); 9; 10; 12(2); 13; 16(3); 17; 60:(3); 3; 4; 6; 7; 8; 11; 61:t, 2; 4; 5; 62:t, 3; 7; 9(2); 63:(2); 7; 9; 11; 64:t, 1; 2(3); 5; 6(2); 9(2); 65:t, 4(2); 5(4); 7(3); 8; 9(2); 12; 66:2; 3; 5(2); 8; 15(2); 19; 67:7; 68:t, 2; 5(2); 8(3); 10; 11; 12; 13; 15(3); 17(2); 19; 20; 21(2); 22; 23(2); 24; 26; 27(3); 29; 30(4); 31; 32; 33(2); 35(2); 69:t, 3; 4; 6(2); 9(2); 12; 13(2); 14(2); 16; 18; 20; 24; 26; 28(2); 30; 35; 36; 70:t, 3; 71:4(4); 6(2); 9; 16(3); 20; 22; 24; 72:4(2); 7; 8; 10(3); 13; 15(2); 16(4); 18; 20(2); 73:t, 1; 3; 10; 15; 17; 26; 74:t, 1; 2(2); 4; 7; 8; 11; 12(2); 13; 14; 17; 19(3); 20(3); 23(2); 75:t, 3; 8(4); 9; 10(2); 76:t, 3; 4; 5(2); 6; 9; 10(2); 12(2); 77:t, 2; 5(2); 10(2); 11(2); 12(2); 15; 18; 20; 78:t, 1; 2; 4; 7; 9(2); 10; 12(3); 14; 15; 16; 23; 24(2); 27; 28; 31(3); 38; 41; 43; 45; 49; 51(2); 54; 55; 60; 65(2); 67(2); 68; 72(2); 79:t, 2(4); 9(2); 10(2); 11(2); 13; 80:t, 1; 4(2); 5; 7; 8; 10; 13(2); 14; 16; 17(2); 19; 81:t, 1; 4(2); 5; 7(2); 10(2); 11; 15; 16(2); 82:t, 1; 2; 4(2); 5(2); 6(2); 7; 83:t, 4; 6(2); 7; 8; 9; 12; 84:t, 1; 2; 3; 5; 6; 7; 8(2); 9; 10(2); 12; 85:t, 1; 2; 3; 4; 11; 13; 86:t, 4; 6; 7; 14; 15; 16; 87:t, 2(2); 3(2); 4; 5; 88:(2); 1; 3; 9; 12; 89:t, 1(2); 5; 6; 7(2); 8; 9; 14; 15; 17; 18; 19; 22; 26; 27; 29; 34; 39; 42; 43; 45; 48; 50(2); 51; 90:(2); 3; 8; 10(2); 11; 17(3); 91:1(2); 2; 3; 8; 92:3; 4; 7; 9; 10; 11; 13(2); 93:2; 4(2); 94:2; 4; 7; 11; 12; 13; 16; 19; 20; 21; 22; 95:1; 4(2); 7(2); 8; 96:5; 7; 9; 12; 97:1; 2; 5(3); 7; 8(2); 10(3); 12; 98:2; 3(3); 5; 6; 99:8; 100:t, 3; 101:t, 1; 3; 6; 8(2); 102:t, 5(2); 6(2); 10; 15(2); 17; 19; 20; 21; 24; 25(3); 26; 28; 103:t, 7; 15; 17; 20; 21; 22; 104:3(2); 5; 7; 11; 12; 13; 14(2); 15; 16(3); 20; 24; 30; 31; 34; 35; 105:2; 3; 5; 6(2); 11(2); 16; 19; 20; 21(2); 23; 27; 30; 31; 33; 35; 36; 38; 40; 44(2); 106:2; 5(2); 7; 10(2); 11; 16; 17; 20; 22; 25; 28; 32; 38(3); 40; 41; 45; 46; 48; 107:2(2); 3; 6; 7; 8; 10; 11(2); 13; 14(2); 15; 16(2); 17(2); 18(2); 19; 21; 22; 24; 26; 28; 31; 32(2); 34; 37; 43; 108:t, 7; 8; 12; 109:t, 1; 2(2); 3; 10; 14(2); 15; 20(2); 24; 31; 110:t, 2(3); 3(4); 4; 5; 7; 111:1; 2(2); 4; 5; 6(2); 7; 10(2); 112:2; 4; 7; 10; 113:1(2); 2; 3(2); 7(2); 8; 9; 114:1(3); 7(3); 8; 115:4; 10; 12(3); 15; 16; 116:3(2); 4; 9; 13(2); 14; 15(2); 16; 17(2); 18; 19(2); 117:2; 118:3; 10; 11; 12(2); 15(3); 16(2); 17; 19; 20; 22; 26(3); 27; 119:1; 7; 13; 14; 18; 27(2); 29; 30; 32; 33; 35; 43(2); 46; 52; 53; 54; 61; 62; 63(2); 64; 72(2); 84; 88; 96; 108; 111; 115; 116; 119; 120(2); 123; 130; 134; 136; 144; 147;

152; 160; 161; 164; 172; 120:t, 4(2); 5; 121:t, 122:(2); 1; 4(3); 5(3); 6; 9(2); 123:t, 2(4); 4(2); 124:(2); 7(2); 8; 125:t, 3(2); 5; 126:t, 1; 127:t, 2; 3(2); 4(2); 5; 128:t, 2; 3; 5(3); 129:t, 4; 8(2); 130:t, 1; 2; 131:(2); 2; 132:t, 2; 3; 5; 6(2); 8; 10; 11(2); 17; 133:(2); 2; 3(2); 134:t, 1(2); 3; 135:1(2); 2(3); 7(2); 8(2); 9; 11(3); 15(2); 19(2); 20; 21; 136:2; 3; 14; 19; 20; 26; 137:1; 3(4); 6; 7(2); 8; 138:t, 4(2); 5(2); 7(2); 8; 139:t, 9(2); 15; 16; 17; 140:t, 4; 6; 7(2); 8; 9(2); 12(2); 141:t, 2; 3; 4; 9(2); 142:t, 5; 7; 143:t, 5(2); 10; 11; 12; 144:t, 3(3); 7(2); 8; 9; 11(2); 12; 13; 145:t, 5(3); 6(2); 7(2); 8(2); 11(3); 12(2); 15; 16; 19; 21; 146:3; 5; 8; 9; 147:2; 4; 5; 10(2); 13; 14; 148:3; 4; 5; 11(2); 13; 14(4); 149:1; 2; 6; 8; 150:1; 3; **Prov** 1:1(3); 2; 3; 5; 6; 7(2); 8(2); 9; 17; 19(3); 21(2); 25; 29; 30; 31(2); 32(2); 33; 2:5(2); 6; 8(2); 12; 13(2); 14; 17(2); 19(2); 20(2); 22; 3:2; 3; 4; 9; 11(2); 14(2); 16; 17; 18; 25(3); 27; 31; 33(3); 35; 4:1; 3; 5; 9(2); 10; 11; 13; 14(2); 17(2); 18; 19; 21; 23(2); 26; 5:3; 6; 7; 8; 10; 13; 14; 15(2); 16; 18; 20; 21(2); 22; 23; 6:2(2); 3; 5(2); 9; 10; 20; 23(2); 24(2); 26(2); 31; 34(2); 7:2; 3; 6; 7; 10(2); 16(2); 18; 20; 21; 22; 24; 27; 8:2(2); 3; 4; 5; 6(2); 8; 12; 13; 16; 20(3); 22(2); 26(2); 27; 28; 29; 31(2); 34; 35; 9:3; 5(2); 6; 10(3); 11; 14(2); 18; 10:1(2); 2; 3(2); 4; 6(2); 7(2); 11(3); 13(3); 14; 15; 16(2); 17; 19; 20(2); 21(2); 22; 23; 24(2); 27(2); 28(2); 29(2); 31; 32(2); 11:3(2); 4; 5; 6; 7; 8; 11(2); 12(2); 13; 14; 20; 21; 22; 23(2); 26; 29; 30(2); 12:2(2); 3; 5(2); 6(2); 7; 8; 10(2); 11; 12(2); 13(2); 14(2); 15; 18(2); 19; 20(2); 23; 24; 25; 26; 27; 28; 13:2(2); 4(2); 8; 9(2); 12; 14(3); 15; 20; 22; 23(2); 25(2); 14:3(3); 4; 7(2); 8(2); 11(2); 12; 13; 17; 19; 20; 23; 24(2); 26(2); 27(3); 28(3); 29(2); 30(2); 33(2); 15:2(2); 3; 4; 6(2); 7(2); 8(2); 9; 11(2); 13; 14(2); 15(2); 16; 17; 19(3); 21(2); 22; 23; 24; 25(2); 26(2); 27; 28(2); 29; 30; 31; 33(2); 16:1(2); 2; 4; 6; 10; 11; 13; 14(2); 15(2); 17; 19; 21; 22(2); 23; 25; 26; 31(2); 33; 17:1; 2; 6(2); 8; 12; 14; 16; 18(2); 21; 23(2); 24(2); 27(2); 28; 18:4(2); 5; 7; 8(2); 10; 12; 14; 15(2); 19; 20(2); 21; 22; 19:3; 6; 7; 11; 12; 13(2); 14; 19; 21; 22; 23; 27; 28; 29; 20:2(2); 4; 5(2); 8; 10; 12; 15(2); 16; 17; 24; 27(3); 29(2); 30(2); 21:1(2); 2; 4; 5(2); 6(2); 7; 8; 9; 10; 12; 13; 15; 16(3); 20; 22(2); 25; 27; 31(2); 22:2; 4; 5; 8; 9; 11(2); 12(2); 14(2); 15(2); 17; 21(3); 23; 26(2); 23:3; 6; 9(2); 10; 12; 17; 20; 24(2); 29; 34(2); 24:2; 5; 6; 9; 10; 14; 15; 19; 20; 22; 23; 30(3); 33; 25:1(3); 2(2); 3; 6(2); 7; 11(2); 12(2); 13(3); 14; 17; 19(2); 22; 24; 26:6; 7(2); 9(2); 12(2); 22(2); 27:1; 6(2); 9; 10; 13; 16; 17; 19; 20; 23; 25; 26; 27; 28:2(2); 7; 17; 19; 21(2); 24; 25; 29:6; 7; 20(2); 25; 30:1(2); 2; 3; 4; 5; 7; 9; 17; 19(5); 20; 27; 33(3); 31:1; 2(2); 5(2); 6; 8; 9; 11(2); 12; 16; 21; 22; 23; 26; 27(2); 31(2); **Eccl** 1:1(2); 2(2); 3; 8; 10; 11(2); 13; 14; 16; 17; 2:2(2); 3(2); 5(2); 6; 7; 8(5); 10; 11; 16(2); 17; 20; 22(3); 24; 26; 3:6(2); 10; 13(2); 16(2); 18(2); 19; 20; 21(2); 4:1(2); 4(2); 6; 8(2); 14; 16(3); 5:1(2); 3(2); 6; 7; 8(2); 9; 11; 12(2); 15(2); 18(2); 19; 20(2); 6:2; 3; 7; 9(3); 12; 7:1(2); 2(3); 3; 4(4); 5(2); 6(2); 8; 9; 12; 13; 14(2); 15; 18(2); 25(3); 8:1(2); 2(2); 3; 4; 6; 8; 10; 11(2); 14(2); 15(2); 17; 9:1; 3(3); 5; 9(3); 11(2); 12; 17(2); 18; 10:1; 4; 12(2); 13(3); 14; 15(2); 17; 18; 20; 11:3; 5(3); 8; 9(3); 12:1; 3(2); 4(3); 5; 8; 10; 11(2); 12(2); 13(2); **Song** 1:1; 2; 3(2); 5(3); 6; 7; 8; 9; 10(2); 11(2); 13; 14(2); 17(2); 2:1(2); 3; 5; 7(2); 8; 12(3); 14(2); 17; 3:4; 5(2); 6(3); 7(2); 8; 9(2); 10(5); 11(4); 4:1; 2; 3(2); 4(2); 6(2); 8(3); 9(2); 10; 11(2); 13; 14; 15(2); 5:2(2); 4; 5; 7; 8(2); 12(2); 13; 15(2); 16; 6:2; 5; 6; 7; 9(2); 11(2); 12; 13; 7:1(3); 2; 4(3); 5; 7; 8(3); 9(2); 13; 8:1; 2(3); 4; 6; 7; 9(2); 11; 14; **Is** 1:1(4); 4(2); 6; 8(2); 9; 10(4); 11(7); 13; 15; 16; 19; 20; 21; 23(2); 24(4); 26; 28(2); 29; 31; 2:1; 2(2); 3(6); 5(2); 6(2); 7(4); 8(2); 10(2); 11(2); 12(2); 13(2); 16; 17(2); 19(4); 20(2); 21(4); 22; 3:1(3); 2; 3; 6(3); 7; 8; 9; 10; 11; 12; 14(2); 15(2); 16; 17(3); 18; 20; 22; 24(6); 4:1; 2(3); 4(5); 5(2); 6; 5:1; 2; 3(2); 7(4); 8; 9(2); 10(2); 12(2); 15; 16; 17; 18; 19(2); 22; 23; 24(4); 25(2); 26; 27(2); 29; 30; 6:3(2); 4(2); 5(4); 6; 8; 10; 12; 7:1(7); 2(3); 3(3); 4(4); 5; 6(2); 8(2); 9(2); 11; 13; 16; 17; 18(3); 19(2); 20(2); 22; 25(3); 8:2; 4(3); 6; 7(2); 8(2); 9; 11; 13; 14(4); 17; 18; 22; 9:1(4); 2(2); 4(4); 5(2); 6; 7(5); 9(2); 11; 13; 16(2); 18(2); 19(3); 20; 10:2; 3; 5; 6(2); 10(3); 12(4); 13(2); 14; 16(2); 17; 18(2); 19(2); 20(4); 21; 22(2); 23(2); 24(3); 26(4); 27; 29; 30; 31; 32(3); 33(2); 34; 11:1(3); 2(6); 3(4); 4(3); 5(2); 8; 9(2); 10(2); 11(2); 12(3); 13(2); 14(3); 15; 16(3); 12:3(2); 6(3); 13:1(2); 2; 4(6); 5(2); 6; 8; 9(2); 10; 11(2); 12; 13(4); 18; 19(2); 21(2); 22; 14:1; 2(2); 4; 5(2); 8; 9(2); 11; 12; 13(3); 14; 15; 17; 18(2); 19(3); 20; 21(2); 22; 23(3); 24; 27; 29(2); 30; 32(2); 15:1(3); 3; 4; 5(4); 6; 7; 8; 9(4); 16:1(3); 2(3); 3; 4(2); 5; 6(3); 7; 8(3); 9(2); 10; 14(2); 17:1; 2; 3(4); 4(2); 5; 6(3); 7; 8; 9(2); 10(3); 11(2); 12(4); 13(2); 14(2); 18:1; 2; 3; 4(2); 6(3); 7(5); 19:1(4); 3; 4(2); 6; 7; 11(5); 12; 13(3); 16(4); 17(4); 18(4); 19(2); 20(3); 22; 23; 24; 25(2); 20:1; 2; 4(2); 5(2); 6(2); 21:1(2); 3(3); 4; 7(3); 9(3); 10(4); 11(4); 13; 14(2); 15; 16(2); 17(5); 22:1(2); 2; 4(3); 5(6); 6; 7; 8(3); 9(3); 10; 11; 12; 14(2); 15; 18(2); 20; 21(2); 22(2); 24(4); 25; 23:1(3); 2(2); 3(3); 4; 5; 6; 7; 8; 9(3); 10; 12; 13; 14; 15(2); 17(3); 24:2(2); 4; 6; 8(3); 10; 11; 13(2); 14; 15(3); 16; 17; 18(4); 21(2); 23; 25:1; 2(3); 3; 4; 5(3); 6(6); 7; 8; 10; 11(2); 12(2); 26:1; 6(2); 7(2); 8(3); 9; 10(2); 11; 13; 15; 17; 18; 19; 21(2); 27:2; 5; 6(2); 7; 8; 9(2); 11; 12(3); 13(2); 28:1(4); 2(2); 3(2); 4; 5(4); 6; 7(3); 8; 13; 14; 17; 21; 22; 24; 28; 29; 29:4(5); 5(2); 6(3); 7(2); 8; 10; 11(2); 13; 14(2); 16(3); 18(4); 19; 21; 22; 23(4); 30:1(2); 2(2); 3(2); 5; 6(5); 9; 11(3); 12; 14(3); 15; 17(3); 18; 19; 20(2); 22(4); 23(3); 25(2); 26(6); 27(2); 28(3); 29(3); 30(3); 31; 32; 33(3); 31:1; 2(2); 4(4); 5; 6; 7(2); 8(2); 9; 32:2(2); 3(2); 4(2); 6(2); 7; 13(2); 14(3); 17(2); 20; 33:2; 3(2); 4(2); 6(3); 7; 12; 15(3); 16(2); 19(2); 20(3); 21; 23; 34:1; 2; 3; 4; 5; 6(5); 8(3); 11(2); 13; 14(3); 16(3); 35:2(4); 4; 5(2); 6; 7(2); 8; 10; 36:1(3); 2(3); 4; 6(2); 8; 9(3); 11; 13(2); 15(2); 16(4); 17(2); 18(5); 19(3); 20(3); 22(3); 37:1; 2(2); 3(3); 4(2); 5; 6(3); 8; 9; 10(3); 11; 12(2); 13(4); 14(2); 16(4); 17; 18(2); 19; 20; 21(3); 22(2); 23; 24(5); 25(2); 26; 27(2); 30(2); 31(2); 32(4); 33; 36(2); 37; 38(2); 38:1; 4; 5; 6(3); 8(2); 9(3); 10(4); 11(2); 12; 13; 15; 16; 17; 20(2); 21; 22; 39:1(2); 2(3); 5(2); 7(3); 8; 40:2; 3(2); 5(2); 6; 7; 8; 9; 12(2); 13; 14(2); 15(2); 21; 22; 23; 26; 28(3); 41:5; 6; 8; 9; 10; 12; 14(2); 16; 17; 18(3); 20(2); 21; 22; 24(2); 25; 28; 42:5; 6(2); 7; 9; 10; 11(2); 13; 22; 25(2); 43:3; 6; 13; 14; 15; 18; 20; 22; 23; 24; 28; 44:5(2); 6(2); 9; 11; 12; 13(2); 14; 19(2); 21; 23; 25; 26(3); 28; 45:1; 2(2); 3(3); 6; 9; 11(3); 13; 14(4); 15; 16(2); 19(2); 20(2); 22; 23; 25; 46:3(3); 6; 7; 9; 47:1(2); 4(2); 5(2); 7; 8; 9(3); 12; 13; 14; 48:1(7); 2(3); 3; 10; 13; 17; 18; 19; 20(3); 21; 49:1(2); 2; 5; 6(3); 7(4); 8(2); 10; 12; 15; 16; 17; 19(2); 23; 25(2); 26; 50:1(2); 4; 10(2); 11(2); 51:1; 3(2); 4; 7(2); 9(2); 10(2); 11; 12(3); 13(4); 15; 16(2); 17(4);

18; 20(4); 22(5); 23; 52:2(2); 7(2); 9; 10(3); 11(3); 12; 14; 53:1; 2; 3(2); 4; 5; 6; 8(3); 10; 11(2); 12; 54:1(2); 2(2); 4(2); 5(3); 6; 9(2); 10; 12(3); 13(2); 17(3); 55:3; 5(2); 11; 12; 13(2); 56:2; 3; 4; 5(2); 6(3); 7(2); 8; 9; 57:3(2); 4(2); 5; 6; 10(2); 11(2); 14(2); 15(3); 17(2); 19; 58:1; 2(3); 3; 4; 6; 8; 9(2); 11; 12(4); 13; 14(3); 59:5; 6(2); 7; 8; 13; 17(2); 19(3); 21(5); 60:1; 3; 5(2); 6(3); 7(3); 9(3); 10; 11; 13(3); 14(5); 15; 16(3); 20; 21(2); 61:1(2); 2(3); 3(5); 4; 5; 6(3); 10(2); 62:2; 3(3); 6; 8(2); 9; 10; 11(2); 12; 63:1; 3; 4(2); 7(4); 9(2); 11(3); 12; 14; 15(4); 16; 17; 18; 64:4; 7(2); 8; 65:1(2); 3; 4; 7; 9(3); 10(2); 14(3); 16(2); 19(2); 20; 21; 22(3); 23(2); 66:1; 2; 5; 6(2); 7; 11(2); 12; 14; 15; 16; 19; 20(3); 21; 24; **Jer** 1:1(4); 2(5); 3(8); 4; 5; 8; 11(2); 13; 14(2); 15(5); 16; 18(2); 2:1; 2(3); 3; 4(4); 6(7); 10; 13; 16(2); 18(4); 19; 20; 21; 26; 27; 28(2); 31(2); 34(2); 36(2); 3:4; 6; 8; 9; 14(2); 16(2); 17(3); 18(4); 19(2); 20; 21(2); 23(2); 24; 25; 4:1; 3; 4(5); 7; 8; 9(2); 11(2); 16; 17; 19(2); 21; 25; 26; 29; 30; 31(5); 5:1; 4(2); 5(2); 6(2); 11(2); 14; 15; 20; 22; 24; 27(2); 28(3); 6:1(5); 2; 4; 6(2); 9(2); 10; 11(4); 12; 13(2); 14(2); 17; 19; 22; 23; 24(2); 25; 26; 29; 7:2(3); 3(2); 4(3); 11; 12; 15(2); 17(2); 18; 19; 20(2); 21(2); 22(2); 24; 25(2); 28; 29; 30; 31(3); 32(3); 33(3); 34(6); 8:1(8); 2(2); 3(3); 5; 6; 7(2); 8(2); 9; 11(2); 12; 14; 15; 16(3); 19(4); 21(2); 22(2); 9:1(3); 2(2); 4; 6; 7(2); 10(3); 11(2); 12; 14; 15(3); 17; 19(2); 20(2); 22; 26(2); 10:1; 2(2); 3(4); 5; 7(2); 8; 9(4); 13(3); 15(2); 16(4); 17(2); 18; 20; 22(4); 23; 11:2(3); 3(2); 4(2); 6(3); 7(2); 8(2); 9(2); 10(3); 12(3); 13(3); 16(3); 17(5); 18; 19; 20; 21(3); 22; 23(3); 12:1(2); 3; 4(2); 5(2); 6; 7(2); 9; 12(3); 13(3); 14(2); 16(2); 13:2; 3; 4; 8; 9(2); 10; 11(3); 12; 13(2); 16; 18; 19(2); 22; 24; 25; 27; 14:1; 2; 8(2); 9; 14(2); 16(2); 17; 19; 20; 21; 22; 15:1; 3(2); 4(4); 7(2); 8(2); 9; 10(3); 11(2); 15; 16(2); 17(2); 21(4); 16:1; 4(4); 5; 7; 8; 9(7); 12; 13; 14(3); 15(2); 16(2); 18; 19(2); 17:1(5); 8; 10; 11; 12; 13(2); 15; 16; 17; 18; 19(4); 20(3); 21; 22; 24; 25(4); 26(4); 27(2); 18:4(2); 5; 6(2); 8; 10; 11(2); 12; 13; 14(2); 17; 18; 19; 21(2); 23; 19:1(4); 2(3); 3(5); 4(2); 5; 6(3); 7(4); 8; 9(3); 10; 11; 13(6); 14; 15(2); 20:1(2); 2(2); 3; 4(3); 5(4); 8; 9; 10; 12; 13(2); 18; 21:1(2); 2(2); 4(4); 6(2); 7(6); 8(2); 10(2); 11(3); 12(5); 13(2); 14; 22:1(2); 2(3); 3(2); 4(2); 6(2); 9; 11(4); 16; 18(2); 19(2); 23(2); 24(2); 25(5); 29; 30(2); 23:1; 2(2); 3(2); 7(3); 8(3); 9(4); 10(3); 12; 13; 14(3); 15(3); 16(5); 17; 18; 19(2); 20(2); 22; 26(3); 33; 34; 36(4); 38(3); 39; 24:1(6); 4; 5(4); 8(3); 9; 25:1(6); 2(2); 3(4); 5; 6; 7; 8; 9(2); 10(6); 11; 12(2); 14(2); 15(2); 16; 18; 19; 20(5); 21; 22(3); 24(2); 25(3); 26(4); 27(3); 28; 29(2); 30; 31; 32(2); 33(3); 34(3); 35; 36(4); 37(2); 38(3); 26:1(4); 2(2); 3(3); 5; 6; 7; 8; 9(2); 10(4); 13(2); 15; 16; 17(3); 18(3); 19(2); 20(4); 22; 23(2); 24(3); 27:1(4); 3(7); 4(2); 6(3); 7(2); 8(3); 9; 11(2); 12(3); 13; 14(2); 16(2); 17; 18(5); 19(2); 20(4); 21(6); 28:1(8); 2(4); 3(2); 4(5); 5(3); 6; 7; 8(4); 9(2); 11(5); 12(2); 13(2); 14(6); 16; 29:1(2); 2; 3(5); 4(2); 5; 7; 8(3); 11(2); 14; 16(4); 17; 18; 20(2); 21(8); 22(3); 25(3); 26(2); 27; 28; 29; 30; 31; 30:2; 3; 5(3); 7(2); 8(2); 10; 11(2); 14(3); 15; 16; 17; 18; 19(2); 21(2); 23(2); 24(2); 31:1(2); 2; 3; 4(2); 5; 7(2); 8; 9; 10; 11; 12(4); 14; 16; 19; 21; 23(5); 27(4); 31(2); 32(2); 33; 34(2); 35(3); 36; 37(2); 38(2); 40(4); 32:1(3); 2(3); 3(3); 4(5); 6; 7(2); 8(5); 9(2); 11; 12(7); 14(3); 15(2); 16(2); 18(3); 19(3); 20; 21(2); 23; 24(4); 25; 26; 27; 28(3); 30(4); 31(2); 32(7); 35(3); 36(3); 37; 39(2); 43; 44(5); 33:1(2); 4(4); 5; 6; 7(2); 9(2); 10(2); 11(10); 12(2); 13(6); 14(2); 15; 17(2); 19; 20(2); 22(3); 23; 25; 26(3); 34:1(3); 2(4); 3(3); 4(3); 5; 6; 7(4); 9(2); 10; 12; 13(5); 14; 17; 18; 19(4); 20(4); 21(5); 22; 35:1(3); 2(3); 3(3); 4(9); 5(3); 6; 8(2); 11(5); 12; 13(4); 14(2); 16(3); 17(3); 18(4); 19(3); 36:1(3); 2(2); 3; 4(4); 5; 6(4); 8(2); 9(4); 10(7); 11(4); 12(4); 13; 14(5); 16; 20(2); 21(3); 24; 26(3); 27(2); 28; 29(2); 30(3); 31(2); 32(4); 37:1(5); 2(2); 3(2); 5(2); 6; 7(3); 10; 11(2); 12(3); 13(4); 15; 17(2); 19; 20; 21(4); 38:1(4); 3(2); 4(4); 6(3); 7(2); 8; 10; 11; 13(2); 14; 16; 17(3); 18(3); 19; 20; 22(2); 23(3); 24; 28; 39:1(3); 2(2); 3(5); 4(5); 5(3); 6(4); 8(2); 9(3); 10(4); 11(2); 13(2); 14(4); 15(2); 16(2); 17(2); 40:1(2); 2; 5(5); 6; 7(6); 8(5); 9(3); 11(4); 12(2); 13(2); 14(3); 15(2); 16(3); 41:1(5); 2(4); 3; 5; 6(2); 7(3); 8(4); 9(5); 10(4); 11(4); 12; 13(2); 14; 15; 16(6); 17; 18(5); 42:1(3); 2; 6(2); 7; 8(2); 9; 10; 11(4); 13; 14(3); 15(4); 16; 17; 18(3); 19; 21; 43:1(2); 2(2); 3(2); 4(4); 5(4); 6(4); 7(2); 8; 9(3); 10(3); 11; 12(3); 13(4); 44:1(2); 2(3); 3; 6(2); 7(3); 8(3); 9(7); 11(2); 12(3); 13; 14(4); 15; 16; 17(5); 18; 19; 21(3); 22(3); 23; 24(2); 25(3); 26(5); 27(3); 28(5); 30(6); 45:1(5); 2; 46:1; 2(6); 10(5); 11; 12; 13(2); 16; 17; 18; 20; 21(3); 22; 24(3); 25(3); 26(5); 27; 28(2); 47:1; 2(2); 3(6); 4(3); 5; 6; 48:1(2); 2; 3; 5(3); 10; 13(3); 15(2); 16; 18; 19; 24(2); 25; 27; 28; 29(2); 31; 32(3); 33; 34(3); 36; 38; 41; 43; 44(2); 45(7); 46; 47(2); 49:2(2); 3; 5; 6(2); 7; 8(2); 12(2); 16(3); 18(2); 19(2); 20(3); 21; 22(3); 25(2); 26(2); 27(2); 28(3); 30(2); 32; 33; 34(4); 35(3); 36(2); 39; 50:1; 3; 4(2); 7(2); 8(4); 9(2); 11; 12; 13(2); 15; 16(2); 17(2); 18(4); 20(2); 21(2); 22(2); 23; 25(4); 26; 27; 28(5); 29; 30; 31; 33(3); 34(2); 35; 37; 38; 39(2); 40; 41; 42; 43(4); 44(2); 45(3); 46(2); 51:1; 2; 4; 5(4); 6(3); 7; 10; 11(4); 12(2); 13; 14; 16(3); 18(2); 19(4); 20; 23; 24; 26; 27; 28(2); 29(2); 30; 31; 32; 33(4); 34; 35(2); 41; 42; 43; 44(2); 45(3); 47(2); 49(2); 51; 53; 54(2); 55(2); 56(2); 57; 58(2); 59(4); 63(2); 64; 52:1(2); 2; 3(2); 4(3); 5; 6(2); 7(4); 8(2); 9(2); 10(3); 11(3); 12(5); 13(3); 14(3); 15(6); 16(3); 17(4); 18; 19(3); 20(2); 21(2); 22(3); 24(2); 25(9); 26(2); 27(3); 29; 30(3); 31(9); 32; 33; 34(4); **Lam** 1:1; 3(2); 4; 5; 6; 7(4); 12; 14; 15(2); 21; 2:1(3); 2(3); 3; 4(2); 5; 6(3); 7(4); 8(2); 10(3); 11(3); 12; 13(2); 14; 15(3); 17(2); 18(3); 19(4); 20(2); 21; 22; 3:1; 6; 13; 22; 26; 32; 33; 34; 35(2); 38(2); 39; 45; 48(3); 51(2); 55; 58; 62; 64; 65; 66; 4:1(2); 2(3); 3; 4(2); 6(5); 7; 9(2); 10(3); 12(3); 13(4); 16(2); 19; 20(3); 21(2); 22(3); 5:8; 9(3); 10; 11; 12; 15; 18(2); 21; **Eze** 1:1(3); 2(2); 3(4); 4(5); 5(3); 7(3); 8; 10(5); 11; 13(4); 14(2); 16(3); 18; 20; 21; 22(3); 24(5); 26(4); 27(5); 28(7); 2:1; 3(2); 6(4); 8; 9; 3:1(2); 3; 4(2); 5(3); 6(2); 7(2); 10; 11(2); 12(2); 13(4); 14(2); 15(2); 16(2); 17(2); 22; 23(2); 25; 26; 4:1; 3(2); 4(3); 5(4); 6(2); 7; 8; 9; 11; 12; 13; 14(2); 16(2); 5:1; 2(2); 4(3); 5; 7; 8(2); 9; 10(2); 12(2); 14; 16(2); 6:1; 2(2); 3(2); 5(2); 7; 9; 11(2); 12; 13; 7:1; 2(3); 4; 7(2); 9; 11(5); 13; 16(3); 19(3); 20(3); 21(2); 23(2); 24(2); 26; 27(2); 8:1(3); 2(4); 3(6); 4(2); 5(3); 6(2); 7; 8; 10(3); 11(6); 12(4); 14(2); 15; 16(4); 17(2); 9:2; 3(3); 4(3); 8(2); 9(4); 10:1(3); 2; 3; 4(4); 5(2); 7; 8; 9(2); 10; 12; 14(4); 15; 17; 18(2); 19(4); 20(2); 21(2); 22(2); 11:1(5); 2; 4; 5(3); 7(3); 9(2); 10; 11; 12; 13(3); 14; 15(4); 17(2); 19(2); 21; 22(2); 23(3); 24(2); 25; 12:1; 2(2); 3; 6; 8; 9(2); 10; 13; 16; 17; 18; 19(7); 21; 22(2); 23; 24; 26; 27(4); 28; 13:1; 2(4); 5(2); 9(4);

16(2); 17(3); 18(2); 19(2); 21; 22(2); 23; 14:1(2); 2; 3(3); 4(4); 5; 6; 7(5); 8; 9; 10(3); 11; 12; 13(2); 15; 15:1; 2(2); 3; 4(2); 6(2); 16:1; 2; 3(2); 5(2); 7; 8; 13; 15; 16; 17(3); 20; 22; 25; 26; 27(3); 29; 30; 31; 32; 35; 36(2); 39; 41; 43; 45; 49(4); 51; 53(4); 56; 57(4); 60; 63; 17:1; 2(2); 3(2); 4(3); 5(2); 6; 7; 9; 11; 12; 13(3); 14; 16; 22(3); 23(4); 24; 18:1; 2; 4(2); 6(2); 10(2); 11; 15(2); 17; 19; 20(4); 25(2); 29(3); 30; 31; 32; 19:1; 3; 4(2); 5; 7; 9(2); 10(2); 11(2); 14(2); 20:1(4); 2; 3(4); 4(2); 5(3); 6(3); 7(2); 8(4); 9(2); 10(2); 13; 15; 17; 18; 22; 27(2); 28; 30(2); 31(3); 32; 34; 35; 36(2); 37; 38(2); 39; 40(5); 41; 42; 44; 45; 46(2); 47(2); 49; 21:1; 2(2); 3(2); 4; 5; 6(2); 8; 9; 10; 11; 12(3); 14(3); 15; 18; 19(5); 20; 21(3); 25; 28(2); 29(2); 30; 31(2); 32; 22:1; 2; 3; 6; 7; 9; 12; 13; 15; 16; 17; 18(4); 19; 20; 21; 22; 23; 24(2); 25; 29; 31; 23:1; 2(2); 3; 4; 6; 7; 8; 9(2); 12; 14; 15(4); 17; 19(2); 20(2); 21(2); 23(2); 24; 26; 27; 28(2); 29; 31; 32; 33(2); 36; 39; 42(2); 45(2); 48; 49; 24:1(2); 2(4); 5(2); 6; 7(2); 8; 11(3); 12; 15; 16(2); 17(2); 20; 21(3); 22; 25(3); 25:1; 2; 3(3); 4; 6; 7; 8; 9(2); 10; 12; 13; 14; 16; 26:1(2); 2(2); 4(2); 5(2); 7(2); 9; 10(5); 11; 12(3); 13(2); 14; 15(2); 16; 17; 18; 20(4); 27:1; 2; 3(3); 4; 5(2); 6(6); 7; 8; 9(2); 10(4); 11; 12(3); 13(2); 14(2); 15(3); 16(3); 17(2); 18(4); 21; 22(2); 23; 24(3); 25(3); 26; 27(5); 28(2); 29; 31; 32; 33(4); 34(2); 35; 28:1; 2(5); 5; 6; 7(2); 8(2); 9; 10(2); 11; 12(3); 13(3); 14(3); 16(6); 17(2); 18(4); 20; 21; 22; 23; 24(2); 25(2); 29:1(2); 2(2); 3(2); 4(4); 5(3); 6(3); 7; 8; 9; 10(3); 11(2); 12(2); 13; 14(3); 15; 16(2); 17(2); 18(2); 19(2); 20; 21(4); 30:1; 2; 3(2); 5; 6(2); 7(2); 9; 10(3); 11; 12(2); 13(4); 15(2); 17(2); 18(2); 20(2); 21(3); 22(2); 24(3); 25(6); 31:1(2); 2(2); 3; 4; 5(3); 6(2); 7; 8(2); 9(3); 11(2); 12(3); 13(2); 14(4); 15; 16(4); 17; 18(4); 32:1(2); 2(3); 3; 4(2); 6; 8; 9; 10; 11(2); 12(4); 13(2); 15(2); 16; 17(2); 18(4); 20; 21(2); 22; 23(3); 24(3); 25(4); 26(2); 27(4); 28; 30(3); 32(2); 33:1; 2(4); 4; 5; 7(2); 9; 10(2); 11(2); 12(5); 15; 16; 17(2); 20(2); 21(3); 22; 23; 24(3); 27; 28(2); 29; 30(3); 32; 34:1; 2(3); 5; 6; 7; 8; 9; 12; 13(2); 14(2); 18(2); 25(2); 26; 27(5); 28; 29(2); 30; 31; 35:1; 2; 5(4); 11; 12; 15(3); 36:1(4); 3(3); 4(3); 5(3); 6(2); 8(2); 10(2); 12; 15(2); 16; 17(3); 20(2); 21; 22(2); 23; 24; 26(2); 30(3); 32; 34; 35; 37(2); 38(2); 37:1(4); 3; 4; 9; 11(2); 12(2); 13; 15; 16(4); 18; 19(4); 21; 22; 23(2); 26(2); 28; 38:1; 2(3); 3; 4(3); 5; 6(2); 8(4); 11(2); 12(2); 13; 14(2); 15(2); 16; 17(2); 18; 19(2); 20(4); 23; 39:1(2); 2(2); 3(2); 4(3); 7; 9; 10(2); 11(5); 12(2); 13; 14(3); 15; 16; 17(3); 18(9); 19; 20; 22; 23(2); 25(2); 27(2); 28; 29; 40:1(4); 2(3); 3(2); 4(2); 5(3); 6(2); 7(2); 8; 9(2); 10(2); 11(3); 13(2); 14(2); 15(4); 18(2); 19(2); 20; 21; 22; 23; 38; 39; 40(2); 41; 42(2); 43; 44(3); 45(2); 46(4); 48(3); 49; 41:1; 2(2); 3(2); 5(2); 6(2); 7(2); 8(3); 9(2); 10; 11(2); 12; 14(3); 15(2); 19(2); 20; 21(4); 22(2); 25(2); 26(2); 42:2; 4(2); 5; 6; 7; 8; 10(2); 11; 12(2); 14; 15; 43:2(4); 3; 4(2); 5; 6; 7(8); 8; 9(2); 10(3); 11(2); 12(3); 13(2); 18(2); 19(2); 20(3); 21(2); 22; 23(2); 25; 44:1(2); 2; 3(3); 4(3); 5(5); 6(3); 7; 8(2); 9(2); 11; 12; 13(2); 14(2); 15(3); 17(2); 22(3); 30(6); 31(2); 45:1(2); 2; 3(3); 4(2); 5(3); 6(3); 7(7); 8(2); 9; 11(3); 13(6); 14(5); 15(4); 16; 17(3); 18; 19(7); 20; 21(2); 22; 23(2); 24(2); 25(2); 46:1(2); 2(4); 3(2); 5; 6; 7; 8(2); 9(6); 10; 11; 13(2); 14(3); 16; 17(3); 18(3); 19(2); 21(2); 22(3); 23; 24(3); 47:1(5); 2(2); 6(2); 7; 9; 10; 12; 13; 15(2); 16(3); 17(2); 18; 19; 21; 22(2); 48:1(5); 2; 3; 4; 5; 6; 7; 8(4); 9(2); 10; 11(3); 12(2); 13; 14(2); 17; 18(2); 19(2); 20; 21(5); 22(5); 23; 24; 25; 26; 27; 28(2); 29; 30; 31(6); 32(3); 33(3); 34(3); 35; **Dan** 1:1(4); 2(7); 3(5); 4; 5(2); 6(2); 7(5); 8(3); 9; 10(2); 11; 13(3); 15(2); 16; 18(2); 20(2); 21; 2:1(2); 6; 7; 8; 12; 14(2); 16; 18(4); 19; 20; 23(2); 24(2); 25(2); 27; 28; 30; 32(3); 33(3); 34; 35; 37(2); 38(4); 39; 41(4); 42(3); 43; 44(2); 45; 47(4); 48(3); 49(4); 3:1(3); 2(2); 3(2); 5(2); 6; 7(2); 10(2); 11; 12(2); 15(4); 17; 19(2); 21; 22; 23; 24; 25(3); 26(4); 27(2); 28; 29; 30; 4:5; 6(2); 8(2); 9(3); 10(2); 11; 12(3); 13; 15(5); 17(4); 18(2); 21(2); 22; 23(5); 24; 25(3); 26; 27; 29(3); 30(3); 32(2); 33; 34; 35(3); 36; 37; 5:1; 2; 3(3); 4(6); 5(4); 6; 7(2); 10(2); 11(4); 12(3); 13(4); 14(2); 15; 16(2); 21(3); 23(4); 24; 26; 29; 30; 6:2; 5; 7(4); 8; 12(4); 13(3); 14; 15; 16; 17(2); 18; 19; 20; 23(3); 24(3); 26(2); 27; 28(2); 7:1(4); 2; 5(2); 6(2); 7; 8(2); 9(2); 11(2); 12; 13(3); 15(2); 16(3); 17; 18; 19(3); 20(3); 22(2); 24; 25(2); 27(3); 28; 8:1(2); 2(2); 4; 5; 6; 7; 8; 9(2); 10(3); 11(2); 12; 13; 15; 16; 17(2); 19; 20; 21; 22; 23(2); 25; 26; 9:1(5); 2(4); 6; 7(4); 8; 10; 11(2); 13; 15(2); 16; 17; 20(2); 21; 23; 24; 25; 26(2); 27(2); 10:1(3); 4(2); 5; 6(4); 9(2); 10; 13(4); 16(2); 17; 18; 20(2); 21; 11:1; 2; 4; 5(2); 6(4); 7(4); 8(3); 9; 10; 11(2); 13; 14(2); 15(2); 17(2); 19; 20(2); 21; 22(2); 24; 25(2); 26(2); 30; 31; 35(3); 36; 37(2); 38; 40(3); 41(3); 42; 43(3); 44(2); 45; 12:1(2); 2(2); 3; 4; 5(4); 6(2); 7(2); 8; 9; 10; 13; **Hos** 1:1(7); 2(4); 3; 4(4); 5(2); 6; 7; 10(4); 11(4); 2:2; 4; 10(2); 12; 13; 15(5); 17(2); 18(4); 3:1(4); 2(3); 4; 5; 4:1(4); 3(3); 6(2); 8; 12; 13; 19; 5:1(2); 2; 4(2); 5; 9(2); 10; 12; 13; 14; 6:5; 6; 8; 9(2); 10(2); 11; 7:1(3); 5(2); 10; 12; 16(2); 8:1; 4; 6; 10(2); 12; 13; 9:4(2); 5(2); 6; 7(3); 8(3); 9; 15(2); 16; 10:1(2); 4; 5(3); 6; 8(2); 9(2); 13(2); 14; 15(2); 11:1; 4(2); 5; 6; 9(2); 11(3); 12; 12:5; 7; 9(2); 10; 11; 12; 13; 13:2(4); 3(2); 4; 5; 8(2); 10; 12; 13(3); 14; 15(2); 14:2; 3; 7; 9; **Joel** 1:1(2); 2(2); 3; 5(2); 6(2); 8; 9; 11; 12(2); 13(3); 14(2); 15; 16; 18(2); 19(2); 20(3); 2:1(2); 2(5); 3; 4(2); 5(4); 7; 11; 13(2); 16(2); 17; 22(2); 23; 24; 26; 27; 30; 31; 32; 3:1; 2; 4; 6(2); 7; 8(2); 9; 12; 14(3); 16(4); 18(4); 19; **Amos** 1:1(7); 2(2); 3(2); 4(2); 5(4); 6; 7; 8; 9; 10; 11; 12; 13(3); 14(3); 2:1(3); 2(2); 4(2); 5; 6(2); 7(3); 8(2); 9; 10(2); 11(3); 13; 15; 3:1(2); 2(2); 4; 9(2); 12(5); 13(2); 14(3); 15; 4:1(2); 5(2); 6(2); 10(2); 11(2); 13(2); 5:1; 2; 3; 4; 6; 8(3); 11(3); 14; 15(2); 16(2); 18(2); 20; 22; 23(2); 25; 26(2); 27; 6:1(3); 2; 3; 4(4); 5(2); 6; 7; 8(2); 10(4); 12; 13; 14(4); 7:1(2); 2(2); 8; 9(3); 10(4); 11; 12; 14; 16(2); 17; 8:1; 2(2); 3; 4; 6(2); 7(2); 8; 10; 11(3); 12; 14(2); 9:1(5); 3(2); 5(2); 6(2); 7(4); 8(3); 9; 10; 11(2); 12(2); 13; 14(3); 15; **Obad** 1; 3(2); 6; 7; 8(3); 9(2); 11; 12(4); 13(4); 14(3); 15; 17; 18(5); 19(5); 20(6); 21; **Jonah** 1:1(2); 3(2); 5(2); 8; 9; 10; 17; 2:1; 2(3); 3; 4; 6; 9(2); 3:1; 3(2); 5(3); 6; 7; 10; 4:2(2); 5(3); 6; 8; **Mic** 1:1(3); 3(2); 5(5); 6(2); 7(3); 9; 10; 11(4); 12(2); 13(4); 14(2); 15(2); 2:1; 4; 5; 7(2); 8; 9; 11(3); 12(6); 13; 3:1(3); 3; 7; 8(4); 9(4); 12(2); 4:1(3); 2(6); 4(2); 5(2); 8(4); 10(3); 12; 13(2); 5:1(2); 2(3); 3(2); 4(4); 6(2); 7(3); 8(4); 10(2); 11; 12; 13(3); 14(2); 6:2; 4(4); 5(3); 6; 7(5); 8; 9; 10(2); 11; 12; 13; 14; 16(4); 7:1; 2; 4(2); 5; 6; 7; 9; 10; 13(2); 14(3); 15(3); 17(4); 18(2); 19; 20; **Nah** 1:1(3); 3; 4; 6; 7; 8; 11; 14(3); 15; 2:2(2); 3(2); 6; 7; 8(2); 9(4); 10; 11(2); 13(2); 3:1; 2(5); 3(3); 4(4); 5; 10; 11; 12; 13(2); 16; 18; 19(2); **Hab** 1:2; 6; 7; 13; 14; 15; 2:8(5); 9; 11(2); 13(2); 14(2); 16; 17(6); 18(2); 19; 3:1; 2(2); 3; 4(2); 7(3); 8; 9; 10; 11(2); 13(3); 14; 15; 16; 17; 18; **Zeph** 1:1(8); 3(2); 4(3); 5; 7(2); 8; 10; 11; 14(3); 15(5); 16; 18(3); 2:2(2); 3(2); 5(4); 7(3); 8(3); 9(6); 10(2); 11(2); 14(3); 3:8; 9; 10(2); 11(3); 12(2); 13; 14(2); 15(2); 17; 18(2); 20; **Hag** 1:1(6); 2; 3; 5; 7; 9(2); 11; 12(5); 14(9); 15(2); 2:1(2); 2(4); 3; 4(3); 5; 6; 7(2); 8; 9(4); 10(3); 11; 12; 13; 14; 15; 16(2); 17; 18(2); 20(2); 21; 22(4); 23(3); **Zec** 1:1(4); 3(3); 4; 6(2); 7(5); 11; 12(3); 14; 16; 17; 21(2); 2:4; 5(2); 6(2); 7; 8(2); 9; 10(2); 11(2); 13; 3:1; 2; 4; 5; 6; 7; 9(2); 10; 4:1; 2(2); 3; 6(2); 8; 9(3); 10(3); 11; 12; 14; 5:3; 4(4); 7(2); 8(2); 9; 11; 6:1; 5(2); 9; 10(7); 11(2); 12(3); 13(2); 14(2); 15(3); 7:1(3); 2; 3(2); 4(2); 5; 8; 9; 10; 12(2); 13; 8:1(2); 2; 3(4); 4(2); 5(2); 6(4); 7; 8; 9(5); 10; 11(2); 12; 13(2); 14(2); 15; 16; 17; 18(2); 19(6); 20(2); 21(2); 22; 23(5); 9:1(6); 3; 6; 7; 8(3); 9(3); 10; 11(2); 12; 13; 14; 15(2); 16(2); 10:1(3); 3(2); 4(4); 5; 6(2); 7; 10(4); 11(3); 11:2(2); 3(5); 4; 6(3); 7(2); 9; 11(2); 12; 13(3); 15; 16; 12:1(4); 2; 3; 4(2); 5(3); 6(3); 7(5); 8(3); 10(4); 11(2); 12(4); 13(3); 13:1(2); 2(4); 3; 4; 6; 7; 14:1(2); 2(2); 3; 4(4); 5(4); 8(2); 10(3); 13(2); 14; 15(5); 16(3); 17(3); 18(2); 19(3); 20; 21(4); **Mal** 1:1(2); 3; 4(2); 5; 6; 7; 8; 9; 10; 11(3); 12; 13(2); 14; 2:2; 3; 4; 5; 6; 7(2); 8(3); 10; 11(2); 12(3); 13; 14(2); 15(2); 16(2); 17(2); 3:1(2); 2; 3(2); 4(2); 5; 6; 7(2); 10(2); 11(2); 12; 14; 16; 17; 4:1; 2(2); 3(2); 4; 5(2); 6(2); **Mt** 1:1(4); 3; 5(2); 6(2); 16(2); 18(2); 20(3); 22; 24; 2:1(2); 2; 4(2); 5; 6(3); 7; 12; 13; 15(3); 16(2); 19; 20; 21; 22(3); 3:1; 2; 3(3); 4; 6; 7(2); 9; 10; 13; 14; 16(2); 4:1(2); 3; 4(2); 5; 6; 8(2); 13; 15(4); 16; 17; 18; 19; 21; 23(3); 25; 5:3; 9; 10; 11; 13(2); 14; 19(3); 20(2); 21(2); 22(3); 27; 29; 30; 31; 32; 33; 35; 37; 42; 45; 6:1(2); 2; 5(2); 8; 16; 22(2); 23; 26; 27; 28; 29; 30(2); 32; 33; 34; 7:4; 5(2); 9; 15; 16(2); 21(2); 24; 26; 27; 8:6; 11; 12(2); 14; 20(2); 21; 26; 27; 28(2); 29; 30; 31; 32(2); 33; 34; 9:2(3); 3; 6(2); 9; 14; 15; 16; 20(2); 22; 27; 34; 35; 38; 10:1(2); 2(2); 3; 5(2); 6(2); 7; 10; 14(2); 15(2); 16; 17; 20; 22; 23(2); 25(2); 29; 30; 31; 36; 37(2); 38; 41(2); 42(3); 11:1; 2(2); 10; 11(2); 12(2); 19(3); 20; 22; 24(2); 25; 27; 29; 12:1; 4; 8(2); 23; 24; 28(2); 31; 32; 34(3); 35(3); 36; 38(2); 39; 40(2); 41(2); 42(3); 43; 45; 50; 13:1; 5; 11(2); 14; 15; 18; 19; 21; 22(2); 24; 27; 30; 31(2); 32(2); 33(2); 35; 36(2); 37; 38(2); 39; 40; 41(2); 42(2); 43; 44; 45; 46; 47(2); 49; 50(2); 52(2); 58; 14:1(2); 6; 8; 13(2); 20; 24; 25; 27; 29; 31; 33(2); 34; 35(2); 36; 15:1; 2; 3; 6(2); 7; 9; 11; 14; 18; 19; 21; 22(3); 24(2); 27; 29; 31; 37; 39; 16:3(2); 4; 6(3); 8; 9; 10; 11(3); 12(5); 13(2); 14; 16; 18; 19(2); 21; 23(2); 27(2); 28(2); 17:5; 9; 12(2); 13; 18; 20(2); 22(2); 25(4); 26; 27; 18:1; 2; 3; 4; 6(2); 7; 10(2); 11; 12; 13(2); 14(2); 16; 19(2); 20; 23(2); 27; 28; 19:1; 7; 8(2); 10; 12(2); 14(2); 23; 24(2); 28(3); 20:1; 8; 11; 12; 13; 18; 20(2); 22(2); 23(2); 25; 28; 30; 31; 21:1; 3; 5(2); 9(2); 11(2); 12(3); 13(2); 15; 16(2); 17; 23; 25(2); 26; 31(3); 32; 34(2); 37; 39; 40; 42; 43; 45; 22:2; 5; 13; 16(2); 27; 28; 29; 30; 31; 32(5); 35; 42(2); 23:4; 5(2); 7; 13; 15; 16; 22; 23(2); 25(3); 26; 27(2); 28; 29(2); 30(2); 31; 32; 33(2); 34(2); 35(3); 39; 24:1; 3(4); 6(2); 8; 9; 12; 14; 15(2); 17; 21; 27(3); 29(2); 30(5); 31(2); 32; 36(2); 37(3); 39(2); 43; 44; 50(2); 51; 25:1; 2; 8; 13; 14; 19; 21; 23; 30; 31(2); 34(2); 40(2); 45(2); 26:2(2); 3(2); 6; 7; 13; 14; 15; 17(2); 21; 22; 24(3); 27; 28(2); 29(2); 30; 31(2); 33; 37; 45(2); 47(2); 51(2); 53; 56; 61; 63; 64(3); 65; 66; 67; 69; 71; 73; 75; 27:1; 3; 5; 6; 8; 9(4); 11; 12; 19; 21; 24(2); 27(2); 29(2); 32; 33; 37; 40; 42; 43; 47; 48; 51; 52; 53; 54; 56(2); 57; 58; 60; 62; 28:1(2); 2; 4; 11; 19(3); 20; **Mk** 1:1(3); 3(2); 4(2); 5(4); 6; 7; 9(2); 10; 13; 14(2); 15; 16; 17; 19; 24(2); 25; 26; 29(2); 30(2); 34; 2:3(2); 4; 5; 6; 9; 10(2); 14(2); 17; 18(4); 19; 21; 23; 26(2); 28(2); 3:5; 9; 11; 17(3); 18; 21; 22; 28; 29; 35; 4:4; 5; 10; 11(2); 19(3); 26; 28; 30; 31; 32(2); 37; 38; 41; 5:1(2); 2(2); 7; 8; 10; 11; 17; 22(2); 23; 25; 26; 27; 29(2); 30; 34; 35; 36; 37; 38(2); 40; 42(2); 6:3(3); 6; 11; 14; 15; 21; 22(2); 23(2); 24; 25; 29; 33; 37; 43(2); 44; 47; 48; 50; 52; 53; 54; 56; 7:1; 2; 3; 4(2); 5; 6; 7; 8(3); 9; 13(2); 14; 15; 20; 21(2); 24; 25; 26; 28; 29; 31(4); 35; 8:3; 8; 10; 11; 15(4); 19; 20; 23; 27; 28; 30; 31(3); 33(2); 38(5); 9:1(3); 7; 9; 12(2); 13; 17; 21; 24; 25; 26; 31(2); 35(2); 36; 37; 39; 41; 42; 47; 10:1(2); 4; 5; 6; 10; 14(2); 15; 23; 24; 25(2); 26; 33; 35; 38(2); 39(2); 44(2); 45; 46(3); 47(2); 48; 49; 11:1(2); 3; 5; 9; 10(2); 13; 14; 15(2); 17(3); 19; 29; 30(2); 32; 12:2(2); 8; 9; 10; 13(2); 14(2); 22; 23; 24; 26(4); 27(2); 28(2); 29; 34; 35; 38; 44(2); 13:1(3); 3; 7(2); 8; 13; 14(2); 15; 19; 25; 26; 27(2); 28; 32; 34; 35; 14:1(2); 2; 3(3); 4; 9(2); 10; 12; 13(2); 14; 18; 20; 21(3); 23; 24; 25(3); 26; 27; 41(2); 43; 47(2); 54; 61; 62(3); 64; 65; 66(2); 67; 69; 70; 71; 15:2; 3; 9; 12; 17; 18; 21(2); 22; 26(2); 32; 35; 36; 38; 39; 40(2); 43(3); 45; 46(2); 47; 16:1; 2(2); 3; 6; 9(2); 11; 12; 14; 19; **Lk** 1:1; 2; 3; 4; 5(6); 6; 8; 9(2); 10(2); 11(3); 15; 16(2); 17(3); 19; 23; 26; 27(2); 29; 32(2); 33(2); 35(3); 38; 39; 40; 41; 42; 43; 44; 45; 48; 51; 52; 54; 59; 61; 65; 66(2); 68; 69(2); 70; 71; 74(2); 75; 76(2); 77(2); 78; 79(2); 80; 2:2; 4(5); 9(2); 10; 11; 13; 21(2); 22(2); 23; 24(2); 25; 27; 31; 32; 33; 34; 35; 36(4); 37; 38; 39; 40; 41; 42; 43; 46; 3:1(8); 2(2); 3(2); 4(4); 6; 7(2); 8(2); 9; 14; 15; 16; 23(3); 24(5); 25(5); 26(5); 27(5); 28(5); 29(5); 30(5); 31(5); 32(5); 33(5); 34(5); 35(5); 36(5); 37(5); 38(4); 4:1; 2; 3; 4; 5(2); 6; 9(2); 14(2); 15; 17; 18(2); 19; 20; 22; 25(2); 26(2); 27(2); 29(2); 30; 31; 33; 34(2); 35(2); 37(2); 38; 40; 41(2); 43; 44; 5:1(2); 2; 3(2); 6; 9; 10; 12; 15(2); 17(4); 19; 24(2); 27; 29(2); 33(2); 34; 36(2); 6:1; 2; 4; 5(2); 13; 15; 16; 17(5); 19; 20; 22; 26; 30(2); 34; 35; 42; 44(2); 45(6); 49; 7:1; 3(2); 11; 12(3); 17; 18(2); 19; 21(2); 24; 27; 28(2); 29; 30(2); 31; 34(2); 35; 36; 37; 38; 39; 42; 44; 8:1(2); 2(2); 3(2); 4; 5; 10(2); 11; 12; 13; 14; 21; 22; 23; 24; 25; 26; 27; 28; 29(2); 32; 33; 35(2); 36; 37(2); 38; 41; 42; 43(2); 44(2); 46; 48; 49; 51; 9:2; 5; 7(2); 8(3); 9; 11(3); 17; 19; 20; 22(2); 26(5); 27(3); 29; 31; 35; 36; 38; 43; 44(2); 45; 46; 47; 52; 55(2); 56; 58(2); 60; 62; 10:2; 6; 7; 9; 10; 11(3); 19; 21; 22; 30; 34; 35; 36; 11:1; 5; 6; 8; 11(2); 15(2); 16; 20(2); 24; 26; 27; 28; 29; 30; 31(4); 32(2); 34(3); 36(3); 39(2); 41; 42(2); 44; 45; 46; 47; 48; 49(2); 50(3); 51(3); 52; 53; 54; 12:1(4); 4; 6; 7(2); 8(2); 9; 10; 13; 15(2); 16; 20; 25; 27; 28; 29; 30(2); 31; 39; 40; 42; 44; 46; 48(3); 54; 56(2); 57; 13:1; 7; 10; 11; 14; 15; 16; 18; 19(3); 20; 21; 25; 27; 28(2); 29; 31; 33; 35; 14:1(2); 5; 8(2); 10; 14; 15(2); 18; 19; 21(2); 24(2); 28; 32; 33; 15:4(2); 8; 10(2); 12(2); 15; 17; 19; 26; 16:2(2); 4; 5; 6; 7; 8(2); 9(2); 15; 16; 17; 20; 24; 28; 17:2; 6; 7; 11; 15; 20(3); 21; 22(3); 24(2); 25; 26(3); 28; 29; 30; 18:3; 8; 12; 16(2); 17; 24; 25; 29; 31; 34; 37; 38; 39; 19:3; 8; 9; 10; 11; 22; 29(2); 31; 34; 37(3); 38; 39; 44; 46(2); 47; 20:1; 4(2); 6; 10(2); 13; 15(2); 17; 20(2); 21(2); 26; 27; 32; 33; 34; 36(2); 37(3); 38(2); 39; 42; 45; 46; 21:3; 4(3); 5; 9; 16; 17; 18; 21; 22; 24(3); 25; 26; 27; 30; 31; 34; 35; 36; 37; 22:1; 3(2); 6; 7; 10; 11; 16; 18(3); 19; 21; 22; 23; 24; 25; 30; 39; 44; 47; 48; 50(2); 52; 53; 55; 58; 59(2); 61; 66; 69(3); 70; 71; 23:1; 3; 6; 8(2); 11; 15; 17; 22; 23(2); 26; 27(2); 28; 35; 37; 38(2); 39; 41; 45; 51(4); 52; 24:1; 3; 7(2); 10; 13; 14; 17; 18; 19; 22; 23; 24; 25; 31; 35(2); 36; 42(2); 44; 47; 48; 49(2); **Jn** 1:4; 7; 8; 12; 13(6); 14(3); 15(2); 16; 18; 19; 22; 23(2); 24; 29(2); 30; 34; 35; 36; 40; 42; 44(2); 45(3); 46; 47; 49(2); 51(2); 2:1(2); 3; 6(3); 8; 9(2); 11(2); 14; 15(2); 16; 17; 21(2); 25; 3:1(2); 3; 5(3); 6(2); 8; 10; 12; 13; 14; 18(2); 22; 25; 29(2); 31(2); 34; 36; 4:5(2); 7; 9(3); 10(2); 13; 14(2); 22; 30; 32; 34; 39(3); 41; 42(2); 46; 47(2); 52; 54; 5:1; 3(3); 4(2); 19; 25(2); 27; 29(2); 30(2); 31; 32(2); 36(2); 37; 39; 42; 44; 46; 6:1(2); 4; 7(2); 8; 11; 13; 14; 18; 22; 25; 26; 27; 28; 29; 33; 35; 38; 39; 40; 42; 45(2); 46; 48; 51(2); 53(2); 58; 60; 62; 64; 65; 66; 68; 69; 70; 71(3); 7:2; 7; 13(2); 14; 17(3); 18; 19; 22(2); 23; 25(2); 28; 31; 36; 37; 38(2); 39; 40(2); 41; 42(4); 43; 44; 48(2); 50; 52(2); 8:1; 12(2); 13; 14; 17; 18(2); 23(2); 26(2); 27; 28(2); 34; 39; 40; 41(2); 42; 44(4); 46(2); 47(2); 52; 54; 59(2); 9:3; 4; 5; 6(2); 7; 11; 16(2); 17; 18; 21; 22; 23; 31; 32; 33; 35; 40; 10:2; 5; 7; 14; 16; 18(2); 20; 21(2); 22; 25; 26; 28; 29; 32; 35; 36(2); 37; 39; 41; 11:1(2); 4(2); 8; 9; 11; 13(3); 19; 22; 27; 37(2); 39; 40; 42; 45; 46; 49; 51; 52; 55; 12:2; 3(4); 4; 7; 9; 11(2); 13(3); 15; 16; 17; 21(2); 23; 24; 30; 31(2); 34(3); 36; 38(2); 41; 42(2); 43(2); 49; 13:1(2); 2; 18; 21; 22; 23; 24; 26; 29(2); 31; 14:10; 17; 21; 30; 15:4; 15; 16; 19(3); 26(2); 16:2; 4; 5; 8(3); 9; 10; 11(2); 13(2); 14; 15; 17; 19; 21; 25; 33; 17:6; 7; 12(2); 14(2); 15; 16(2); 24; 18:3; 5; 7; 9; 12; 15; 17; 18; 19(2); 22(2); 23; 25; 26(2); 28; 32; 33; 34(2); 36(2); 37; 39; 19:2; 3; 5; 7; 14; 17; 19(2); 20; 21(3); 25(2); 29; 32(2); 34; 36; 38(5); 39; 40(2); 42; 20:1; 2; 12; 19(2); 24; 25(2); 30; 31; 21:1; 2(3); 6(2); 9; 10; 11; 12; 15; 16; 17; 24; **Acts** 1:1; 3(3); 4(2); 6; 8; 9; 11; 13(2); 14; 15(2); 16; 17; 18; 19; 20; 21; 22(2); 24(2); 25; 2:1; 2; 3(2); 5; 10(2); 11; 13; 14; 15; 17; 18; 19; 20; 21; 22(4); 23; 24(2); 28(2); 29; 30(2); 31(2); 33(3); 36; 37; 38(4); 42; 46; 3:1; 2(2); 5; 6(2); 10; 12; 13(5); 15; 16; 18; 19(2); 21(3); 22; 24; 25(3); 26; 4:1; 4(2); 6(2); 8(2); 9; 10(3); 11(2); 13(2); 15; 18; 19; 21; 22; 25; 26; 27(2); 30; 31; 32(5); 33(2); 34(2); 36(3); 5:2; 3(2); 7; 9(2); 12; 13; 14; 15(2); 16; 17; 19; 20; 21(2); 24(2); 30; 31; 32; 34; 35; 36; 37(2); 38; 39; 40; 41; 6:1(2); 2(2); 3(2); 4; 5(3); 7(3); 8; 9(5); 14; 15; 7:2; 3; 4(2); 8; 10(3); 11; 16(4); 17; 22; 23; 24; 29; 30(3); 31; 32(4); 34; 35; 36; 37(2); 40(3); 41; 42(4); 43(2); 44; 45(3); 46; 49; 52(4); 53; 55(3); 56(2); 58; 8:1; 3; 5; 7; 9; 10; 11; 12(2); 14; 16(2); 18; 20; 21; 22(2); 23(2); 24; 25(2); 26; 27(4); 32; 34(3); 37; 39(2); 9:1; 2(2); 11(2); 13; 15; 20; 24; 26; 27; 29; 31(2); 33; 36; 10:1; 3(2); 7(2); 12(3); 22(3); 28; 31; 32; 33; 34(2); 36(2); 38(2); 39(2); 41; 42(2); 43; 45(2); 48; 11:1; 2; 5; 6(2); 16; 20(2); 21; 22(2); 23(2); 24(2); 28(2); 30; 12:1; 2; 3; 4; 5; 7; 10; 11(5); 12(2); 13; 17; 18; 20; 22(2); 23(2); 24; 13:1; 5(2); 7(2); 10(4); 11; 12; 15(3); 16; 17(4); 18; 19; 20; 21(4); 22; 23; 24(2); 25; 26(3); 27; 28; 29; 31; 34; 36; 38; 39; 40; 42; 43(2); 44; 46(2); 47(2); 48; 49; 50(2); 51; 14:1(3); 3; 4; 5(2); 6(2); 11(2); 13; 14; 15; 19; 22(2); 26; 27; 15:1; 2; 3; 4(2); 5(3); 6; 7; 10; 11; 14; 15; 16; 17; 18; 20; 21; 22; 23; 26; 35; 36; 40; 16:1; 2; 3; 4; 6(2); 9; 12(2); 13; 14(4); 16; 17(2); 18(2); 19; 26; 27(2); 32; 33; 36; 39; 40(2); 17:1; 2; 4(3); 5(2); 6; 7; 8; 9(2); 10; 11; 12(3); 13(3); 18(3); 22(2); 24; 26(4); 27; 28; 29; 30; 32(3); 18:3; 8(2); 11; 12; 14; 15(3); 17(2); 18; 23; 25(3); 26; 19:4; 5; 8(2); 9(2); 10(2); 11; 12; 13(2); 14(2); 16; 17; 19(3); 20; 22; 25; 27; 28(2); 29; 31(2); 33; 34(2); 35(4); 37(2); 40; 20:4(4); 6; 7; 11; 16; 17; 19(2); 24(4); 25; 26; 27; 28; 30; 31; 32; 35; 38; 21:5; 6; 8(3); 11; 12; 13; 14; 16(3); 20(2); 21; 26(3); 27; 28; 30; 31; 32; 35(2); 36; 39(2); 22:3(3); 5; 8; 9; 10; 11(2); 12; 14(2); 15; 16; 18; 20(2); 30; 23:5(2); 6(3); 9; 10; 11(2); 12; 16; 17; 20; 21; 23; 27(2); 29(4); 34(2); 24:4; 5(3); 7; 8(2); 10; 14; 15(2); 16; 21; 22(2); 23; 25; 26; 25:2; 8; 9; 11(2); 15; 16; 18; 19(2); 20(3); 21; 23(2); 24; 25; 26; 26:2; 4; 5; 6(2); 7; 9(2); 10; 13; 16(2); 18(2); 20(2); 22; 25; 26(2); 31(2); 27:1; 2(3); 5(2); 6; 8; 10(2); 11; 12; 19; 21; 22(3); 23; 25; 29; 30(2); 32; 34(2); 35; 36; 41; 42; 44; 28:2(2); 3(2); 7(2); 8(3); 11; 15; 16; 17(3); 18; 19; 20; 21(3); 22; 23(4); 27(2); 28; 31; **Rom** 1:1(2); 3(2); 4(2); 6; 7; 8; 9(2); 10; 12; 16(3); 17; 18(2); 19; 20(2); 23; 24; 25; 27(2); 29; 30(2); 32(2); 2:2; 3; 4(2); 5(3); 9(3); 11; 13(2); 15; 16; 17; 18; 19(2); 20(4); 23; 24; 25; 26; 29(3); 3:1; 2; 3; 5; 7; 12; 13; 14; 17; 18; 20(2); 21; 22(2); 23(2); 25(2); 26; 27(2); 28; 29(3); 4:4(2); 6; 11(4); 12(4); 13(2); 14(2); 16(5); 17; 18; 19; 20; 5:2(2); 5; 10; 14(2); 15(2); 16; 17(3); 18(3); 19; 6:3; 4(2); 5(2); 6; 13(2); 16(2); 17(2); 18; 19(3); 20; 21; 23(2); 7:2; 4; 5; 6(2); 8; 22; 23(2); 24; 25(2); 8:2(3); 3; 4; 5(2); 7; 9(3); 10(2); 11; 13; 14(2); 15(2); 16; 17; 18; 19(3); 20; 21(3); 23(2); 27(2); 29; 33; 34; 35; 39; 9:4(2); 5; 6(2); 7; 8(3); 9; 11(3); 16(3); 21; 22; 23(2); 24(2); 26; 27(3); 29; 30; 31(2); 32; 33; 10:2; 3(2); 4; 5; 6; 8; 13; 14; 15(3); 17; 18; 20; 11:1(4); 2; 4(2); 5; 6(2); 8; 12(4); 13; 14; 15(3); 17(3); 20; 22; 24; 25(2); 26; 29; 33(3); 34; 36; 12:1; 2(2); 3(2); 5; 6; 13; 16(2); 17; 20; 21; 13:1(2); 2; 3(2); 4(2); 10; 11; 12(2); 14:7; 9; 10; 12(2); 14; 16; 17; 18; 20; 23(2); 15:1; 2; 3; 4; 5; 6; 7; 8(2); 12; 13(2); 14(2); 15(2); 16(3); 18(2); 19(3); 21; 26; 27; 29(3); 30; 31; 32; 33; 16:1; 2(3); 4; 5; 7; 10; 11(2); 16; 18; 20(2); 23(2); 24; 25(3); 26(3); S:1; **1Cor** 1:1(2); 2(2); 4; 6; 7; 8; 9; 10; 11(3); 12(5); 13; 14; 16; 17(3); 18(2); 19(2); 20(2); 21(2); 24(2); 25(2); 27(2); 28; 30(2); 2:1(3); 4(3); 5(2); 6(3); 7; 8(3); 9; 10; 11(4); 12(3); 14(2); 15; 16(2); 3:4(2); 10; 13; 16(2); 17(2); 19; 20; 4:1(5); 3(2); 5(3); 6(2); 13(2); 16; 17; 19; 20; 21; 5:4(2); 5(2); 8(2); 10(2); 6:1; 4; 9(2); 10; 11(3); 12; 15(3); 19(2); 7:4(2); 6; 7; 19(2); 23; 25(2); 31; 33; 34(2); 36; 40; 8:3; 4; 6; 7; 9; 10; 9:2; 5; 7(3); 9(2); 10; 12(2); 13(2); 14; 15; 16; 17; 18; 10:4; 5; 7; 8; 9(2); 10(2); 11; 16(5); 17; 18(2); 21(5); 27; 29(2); 30; 31; 32; 33; 11:1(2); 3(3); 7(2); 8(2); 10; 12(2); 16; 18; 22; 23; 24; 25; 27(3); 28(2); 32; 12:3; 4; 5; 6; 7; 8(2); 9; 10(4); 12; 15(2); 16(2); 18; 21(2); 22; 23; 27; 28(2); 29; 30; 13:1(2); 2; 13; 14:10(2); 11; 12(2); 16(2); 21; 24(2); 25(2); 26; 32; 33(3); 36; 37; 15:3; 5(2); 6(2); 7(2); 8(4); 9(2); 10(2); 12; 13; 15(2); 19; 20; 21; 32; 34; 37(2); 39(5); 40(2); 41(3); 42; 47; 49(2); 50; 52; 56(2); 58; 16:1; 2(2); 10; 15(3); 17(2); 19; 21; 23; **2Cor** 1:1(3); 3(3); 4; 5; 6; 7(3); 8(3); 9; 11; 12(2); 14; 16(2); 19; 20(2); 22; 24; 2:3(2); 4(2); 6; 9; 10; 11(2); 12; 13; 14; 15; 16(2); 17(4); 3:1(2); 2; 3(4); 5(3); 6(3); 7(4); 8; 9(2); 10; 12; 13(2); 14; 17; 18(2); 4:2(4); 4(5); 6(5); 7(3); 10(2); 11; 13; 15(2); 17; 5:1(2); 4; 5; 9; 10; 11; 14; 18(2); 19; 21; 6:1; 2(2); 4; 7(3); 16(2); 7:1(2); 4(2); 6; 10(2); 11; 12; 13; 14; 15; 8:1(3); 2(3); 3; 4; 5; 8(3); 9; 11(2); 16; 17; 19(3); 21(2); 23(4);

24(2); 9:2(3); 3; 4; 5(2); 7; 10; 12(2); 13(2); 14; 10:1; 2; 4(2); 5(2); 7; 8; 12; 13(2); 14; 15(2); 16; 11:7; 8; 10(3); 13; 14; 15; 17; 20; 22; 23; 24; 26(2); 28; 30; 31; 32; 12:1; 2; 3; 5(2); 6(2); 7(2); 9; 11; 12; 17(2); 18; 21; 13:1; 3; 4(2); 11(3); 14(3); S:1; **Gal** 1:1; 2; 4; 6; 7; 10; 11; 12(2); 13(2); 14(2); 19; 21; 22; 2:2; 4; 5; 6; 7(2); 8; 9; 12; 14(2); 15; 16(5); 17; 20(2); 21; 3:2(3); 5(2); 7(2); 9; 10(3); 11; 12; 13; 14(2); 15; 16(2); 17(2); 18(2); 19(2); 20; 21; 22; 26; 27; 4:1; 2; 3; 4(2); 5; 6; 7; 9; 11; 13; 14; 15; 19; 20; 23(2); 26; 28; 30(2); 31(2); 5:1; 4(2); 5; 8; 11; 15; 16; 18; 19; 21(2); 22; 26; 6:1; 2; 8(2); 10(2); 12; 14; 16; 17; 18; **Eph** 1:1(2); 3; 4; 5(2); 6(2); 7(2); 9; 10(2); 11(2); 12; 13(3); 14(3); 15; 16; 17(4); 18(4); 19(2); 23; 2:2(4); 3(4); 7; 8(2); 9; 12(2); 13; 14; 15(2); 19(2); 20; 22; 3:1; 2(3); 4; 5; 6(2); 7(3); 8(2); 9(2); 10; 12; 14; 15; 16; 19(2); 4:1(2); 3(2); 4; 6; 7(3); 9; 12(4); 13(7); 14(2); 16(3); 17; 18(3); 23; 25; 29(2); 30(2); 5:1; 4; 5(2); 6(3); 8; 9; 11; 12(2); 17; 20; 21; 23(3); 26; 30(3); 33; 6:4; 5; 6(2); 8; 9; 10; 11(2); 12(2); 13; 14; 15(2); 16(2); 17(3); 19; **Phil** 1:1; 3; 4; 6(2); 7(3); 8; 10; 11(2); 12; 14; 15(2); 16; 17(2); 19(2); 22; 25; 27(3); 28(3); 29; 2:1(2); 2(2); 3; 4; 6; 7(3); 8; 10(2); 11; 13; 15(2); 16(2); 17; 19; 22; 26; 30(2); 3:2(3); 5(5); 8(3); 9(3); 10(2); 11; 12; 14(2); 17; 18(3); 4:2; 3; 7; 8; 9; 10; 11; 15; 18(2); 22; 23; **Col** 1:1(2); 3; 4(2); 5(2); 6(2); 7(2); 9; 10(2); 12(2); 13(2); 14; 15(2); 18; 20; 22; 23; 24(2); 25(2); 27(3); 2:2(6); 3; 5; 8(2); 9; 10; 11(3); 12(2); 13; 14(2); 15; 16(3); 17(2); 18(2); 19; 20; 22; 23(3); 3:1; 6(2); 8; 10; 12(3); 14; 15; 16; 17; 22; 24(2); 25; 4:3(2); 9; 11(2); 12(3); 16; 18; **1Th** 1:1; 2; 3(4); 4; 5; 6(3); 8; 9(2); 2:2; 3(2); 4; 5; 6(4); 8(2); 9(2); 11; 12; 13(4); 14(4); 19(2); 3:2(2); 6(2); 13; 4:1; 3; 4; 5; 6; 9; 12; 15(2); 16(2); 5:1; 2; 5(4); 8(3); 18; 22; 23(2); 28; **2Th** 1:1; 3(2); 4; 5(4); 8; 9(2); 11(3); 12(2); 2:1; 2; 3(2); 4; 7(2); 8(2); 9; 10(2); 13(3); 14(2); 3:1; 5; 6(2); 8; 16; 17; 18; **1Ti** 1:1(2); 5(4); 7; 9(2); 11; 14; 15(2); 20; 2:1(2); 3; 4; 7; 3:1; 2(2); 3; 5(2); 6; 7(2); 8; 9; 10; 12; 13; 15(3); 16(2); 4:1; 3; 4; 5; 6(4); 8(2); 9; 10(2); 12; 14(2); 5:8; 9; 10; 17; 18; 22; 25; 6:1(2); 2; 3; 4; 5(3); 10(2); 11; 12; 13; 14; 15(2); 20; S:1; **2Ti** 1:1(3); 3; 4; 6(2); 7(4); 8(6); 10; 11; 13(2); 15; 16(2); 18; 2:2; 3; 4; 6; 8(2); 9; 14(2); 15; 17; 18; 19(2); 20(4); 22; 24; 25; 26(2); 3:2; 3; 4(2); 5; 6; 7; 8; 10; 11; 14(2); 16; 17; 4:2; 5(2); 6; 8; 15; 17(2); 19; S:1(2); **Titus** 1:1(4); 2; 3; 6(2); 7; 8(2); 10; 12(2); 14; 2:3; 5; 7; 8(2); 10; 11; 13; 14; 3:2; 4; 5(3); 7; 11; S:1(3); **Philem** 1:1; 4; 5; 6(2); 7; 9; 13; 14; 20; 25; **Heb** 1:2; 3(4); 5; 6; 7(2); 8(2); 9; 10(2); 13; 14; 2:2; 4; 6(2); 7; 9(2); 10; 11; 12; 14(3); 15; 16(2); 17; 3:1(2); 3; 5; 6; 8; 12(2); 13(2); 14(2); 16; 19; 4:1(3); 3; 4; 6; 8; 9; 11; 12(5); 13; 14; 15; 16(2); 5:2; 4; 6; 7; 9; 10(2); 11(2); 12(4); 13; 14(2); 6:1(4); 2(7); 4(2); 5(2); 6; 9; 10; 11(2); 12; 16; 17(2); 19; 20; 7:1(3); 2(4); 3(3); 4; 5(7); 6; 7; 8; 10; 11(2); 12(2); 13(2); 14(2); 15; 16(2); 17; 18; 19; 21; 22; 23; 28; 8:1(3); 2(2); 3; 5(2); 6; 8(2); 9(2); 10; 9:1; 3; 4(2); 5(2); 6; 7; 8; 10; 11(2); 12; 13(4); 14; 15(4); 16(2); 17(2); 19(2); 20; 21; 22; 23; 24(2); 25; 26(3); 28; 10:1(2); 2; 3; 4(2); 7(2); 10(2); 12; 18; 19; 21; 22; 23; 25(2); 26; 27; 29(4); 31; 32; 33; 34(2); 35; 36(2); 39(3); 11:1(2); 3(2); 4; 6; 7(4); 9(2); 11; 12(2); 13; 15; 18; 21(2); 22(3); 23(2); 24; 25(2); 26(2); 27; 28; 30; 32(6); 33; 34(4); 36(2); 38(2); 12:1; 2(3); 3; 5(2); 9(2); 10; 11; 13; 15(3); 16; 17; 19(2); 22(2); 23(3); 24(3); 27(2); 13:7(2); 11; 15(2); 20(3); 22; 24; **Jas** 1:1(2); 3; 5(2); 6; 7; 9; 10; 11(2); 12; 13; 14; 17(2); 18(4); 20(2), 21; 22; 23; 24; 25(2); 2:1(3); 4; 5(2); 9; 10; 11; 12; 15; 16; 23; 3:4; 6(3); 7(5); 8; 9; 10; 13(2); 17; 18(2); 4:1; 4(3); 10; 11(4); 5:3; 4(5); 5; 7(2); 8; 10(3); 11(4); 14(2); 15; 16; 17; 19; 20(2); **1Pet** 1:1; 2(4); 3(2); 5; 7(3); 8; 9(2); 10(2); 11(3); 13(2); 15; 17(2); 19(2); 20; 22; 23(3); 24(2); 25; 2:2; 4(2); 7; 8(2); 9(2); 10; 12; 13; 14(2); 15(2); 16(2); 25; 3:1; 3(5); 4(4); 7(2); 8(2); 12(2); 13; 14; 15; 16(2); 17; 20(2); 21(4); 22; 4:2(3); 3(3); 4(2); 7; 8; 10(2); 11(2); 13; 14(4); 15; 17(3); 19(2); 5:1(3); 2(2); 4; 5; 6; 10; 12; 14; **2Pet** 1:1(2); 2(2); 3; 4; 8; 11; 12; 16(2); 19; 20(2); 21(2); 2:2(3); 3(2); 4; 5(2); 6; 7; 9(2); 10(2); 12; 13; 14; 15(3); 16; 17; 18(2); 19(3); 20(2); 21; 3:1; 2(4); 4(2); 5(4); 7(2); 8; 10; 11; 12(2); 14; 15; 16; 17; 18; **1Jn** 1:1(2); 5; 7; 2:2; 5; 10; 14; 15; 16(5); 17; 19(3); 21; 27(2); 29; 3:1(2); 2; 4; 8(3); 9(2); 10(3); 12; 16; 17(2); 19; 22; 23; 4:1; 2(2); 3(2); 4; 5(2); 6(4); 7(2); 9; 13; 14; 15; 17; 5:1(2); 2; 3; 4; 5; 9(4); 10(2); 12; 13(4); 15; 18(2); 19; 20; **2Jn** 3; 4; 9(2); 11; 13; **3Jn** 3; 6; 7; 10; 11; 12(2); **Jude** 1(2); 3; 4(2); 5(2); 6; 7; 8; 9; 10; 11(3); 12(2); 13(2); 14(2); 15(2); 16; 17(2); 21(2); 22; 23; 24; **Rev** 1:1; 2(5); 3; 5(3); 7(2); 9(3); 10; 13(2); 14; 15; 16; 18(2); 20(2); 2:1(3); 5; 6; 7(4); 8; 9(2); 10(3); 11; 12; 14(2); 15; 16; 17; 18(3); 21; 22; 23; 24; 27(3); 3:1(2); 5(2); 7(2); 9(2); 10(2); 12(5); 14(4); 16; 17; 18(2); 4:1; 4; 5(3); 6(3); 8(2); 5:1; 5(4); 6(4); 7(2); 8(3); 9; 11(3); 6:1(3); 5; 6(3); 7; 8(2); 9(2); 11; 12; 13(2); 14; 15(2); 16(2); 17; 7:1(2); 2; 3; 4(4); 5(6); 6(6); 7(6); 8(6); 9; 13; 14(2); 15; 17(2); 8:1; 3; 4(3); 5; 7; 8; 9(2); 10(2); 11(3); 12(5); 13(5); 9:1; 2(4); 3(2); 4(2); 5; 7(2); 8(2); 9(4); 11; 13; 15; 16(3); 17(5); 18(2); 20(5); 21(4); 10:1; 7(3); 8; 10; 11:1; 4; 5; 6; 7; 8; 9; 11; 13(3); 15(3); 18; 19(2); 12:1; 4(2); 5; 6; 10(3); 11(2); 12(2); 14(2); 15(2); 16; 17(3); 13:1(3); 2(2); 3; 8(3); 10; 11; 12; 13; 14(2); 15(3); 17(2); 18(2); 14:2(3); 5; 6; 7(2); 8(3); 10(6), 11(2); 12(3); 14; 15(2); 17; 18(2); 19(3); 20(2); 15:1; 2(4); 3(4); 5(2); 6; 7(3); 8(2); 16:1(3); 2; 3; 4; 5; 6; 7; 9; 10(2); 11(3); 12(2); 13(6); 14(5); 17(2); 19(4); 21(4); 17:1(2); 2(3); 3(2); 4(2); 5(2); 6(3); 7(2); 8(3); 11; 14(2); 17; 18; 18:2(3); 3(6); 4(3); 9(2); 10; 11; 12(5); 13; 15(2); 18; 19; 22(4); 23(4); 24(3); 19:1; 2; 5; 6(3); 7; 8; 9(2); 10(4); 12; 13; 15(4); 16(2); 17(2); 18(6); 19; 20(2); 21(2); 20:1; 4(3); 5; 6(2); 7; 8(3); 9(3); 10; 12(2); 14; 15(2); 21:2; 3(2); 6(3); 9(2); 10; 11; 12(3); 14(3); 16; 17(2); 18(3); 19(3); 21(2); 22; 23(3); 24(3); 25; 26; 27; 22:1(5); 2(7); 3(2); 5; 6; 7(2); 8; 9(3); 10(2); 14; 16; 17; 18(2); 19(5); 21

OFF

Gen 7:4; 8:3; 7; 8; 11(2); 13; 9:11; 11:8; 17:14; 22; 21:16; 22:4; 24:64; 27:40; 37:18; 38:14; 40:19(2); 41:42; 44:4; **Ex** 2:4; 3:5(2); 4:25; 9:15; 12:15; 19; 14:25; 20:18; 21; 23:23; 24:1; 30:33; 38; 31:14; 32:2; 3; 24; 33:5; 7; 34:34; **Lev** 1:15; 3:9; 4:8; 10; 31; 5:8; 6:11; 7:20; 21; 25; 27; 34; 8:28; 13:40; 41; 14:8; 9(2); 41; 16:12; 23; 17:4; 9; 10; 14; 18:29; 19:8; 20:3; 5; 6; 17; 18; 21:5; 22:3; 23:29; **Num** 2:2; 4:18; 7:89; 9:10; 13; 10:11; 12:10; 15:30; 31; 16:46; 19:13; 20; **Deut** 4:26; 6:15; 11:17; 12:29; 13:7; 19:1; 20:15; 21:4; 13; 23:1; 25:9; 12; 28:21; 63; 30:11; **Josh** 3:13; 16; 4:7(2); 5:9; 15; 7:9; 10:27; 11:21; 15:18; 23:4; 13; 15; 16; **Judg** 1:6; 7; 14; 4:15; 5:26; 13:20; 15:14; 16:12; 19; 21:6; **Ruth** 2:20; 4:7; 8; 10; **1Sa** 2:31; 33; 4:18; 5:4; 6:5(3); 17:39; 51; 19:24; 20:15(2); 24:4; 5; 11; 21; 25:23; 26:13; 28:9; 31:9(2); **2Sa** 4:12; 7:9; 10:4(2); 11:2; 24; 12:30; 15:17; 16:9; 20:22; **1Kin** 9:7; 11:16; 13:34(2); 14:10; 14; 15:21; 18:4; 20:11; 21:21; **2Kin** 1:16; 2:7; 4:25; 9:8; 16:17(3); 18:16; 23:27; **1Chr** 17:8; 19:4; 20:2; 28:9; **2Chr** 6:36; 11:14; 16:5; 20:25; 22:7; 26:21; 32:21; **Ezr** 3:13; 9:3; **Neh** 4:23(2); 5:10; 12:43; 13:25; **Est** 8:2; **Job** 2:12; 4:7; 6:9; 8:14; 9:27; 11:10; 15:4; 33(2); 17:11; 18:16; 21:21; 23:17; 24:24; 32:15; 36:20; 25; 39:25; 29; **Ps** 10:1; 12:3; 30:11; 31:22; 34:16; 36:3; 37:9; 22; 28; 34; 38; 38:11; 43:2; 44:9; 23; 54:5; 55:7; 60:1; 10; 65:5; 71:9; 74:1; 75:10; 76:12; 77:7; 83:4; 88:5; 14; 16; 89:38; 90:10; 94:14; 23(2); 101:5; 8; 108:11; 109:13; 15; 138:6; 139:2; 143:12; **Prov** 2:22; 17:14; 23:18; 24:14; 26:6; 27:10; 30:14; **Eccl** 7:24; **Song** 5:3; **Is** 6:6; 9:14; 10:7; 27(2); 11:13; 14:22; 25(2); 15:2; 17:13; 18:5; 20:2(2); 22:25; 23:7; 25:8(2); 27:11; 12; 29:20; 33:9; 13; 17; 34:4; 38:10; 12(2); 46:13; 47:11; 48:9; 19; 50:6; 53:8; 55:13; 56:5; 57:9; 19; 59:11; 14; 66:3; 19; **Jer** 7:28; 29; 9:21; 11:19; 23:23; 24:10; 28:10; 12; 16; 30:8; 31:10; 37; 33:24; 38:27; 44:7; 8; 11; 18; 46:27; 47:4; 5; 48:2; 25; 49:26; 30; 50:16; 30; 51:6; 50; 62; **Lam** 2:3; 7; 3:17; 31; 53; 54; **Eze** 6:12; 8:6; 10:18; 11:16; 12:27; 14:8; 13; 17; 19; 21; 17:4; 9; 17; 22; 18:17; 21:3; 4; 26; 23:34; 25:7; 13; 16; 26:16; 29:8; 30:15; 31:12; 35:7; 37:11; 44:19; **Dan** 4:14(2); 27; 9:7; 26; **Hos** 4:10; 8:3; 4; 5; 10:7; 15; 11:4; **Joel** 1:5; 9; 16; 2:20; 3:8; **Amos** 1:5; 8; 11; 2:3; 3:14; 5:7; 9:8; **Obad** 5; 9; 10; 14; **Mic** 2:8; 3:2(3); 3; 4:3; 7; 5:9; 10; 11; 12; 13; **Nah** 1:13; 14; 15; 2:13; 3:15; **Hab** 2:10; 3:17; **Zeph** 1:2; 3(2); 4; 11; 3:6; 7; **Zec** 5:3(2); 6:15; 9:6; 10(2); 10:6; 11:8; 9(2); 16; 13:2; 8; 14:2; **Mal** 2:12; **Mt** 5:30; 8:30; 10:14; 18:8; 26:51; 58; 27:31; 55; **Mk** 5:6; 6:11; 9:43; 45; 11:8; 13; 14:47; 54; 15:20; 40; **Lk** 9:5; 10:11; 14:32; 15:20; 16:23; 17:12; 18:13; 22:50; 54; 23:49; **Jn** 11:18; 18:10; 26; **Acts** 2:39; 7:33; 12:7; 13:51; 16:22; 22:23; 27:32(2); 28:5; **Rom** 11:17; 19; 20; 22; 13:12; **2Cor** 11:12; **Gal** 5:12; **Eph** 2:13; 17; 4:22; **Col** 2:11; 3:8; 9; **1Ti** 5:12; **Heb** 11:13; **2Pet** 1:9; 14; **Rev** 18:10; 15; 17

OFTEN

Prov 29:1; **Mal** 3:16; **Mt** 23:37; **Mk** 5:4; **Lk** 5:33; 13:34; **1Cor** 11:26; **2Cor** 11:26; 27(2); **Phil** 3:18; **1Ti** 5:23; **Heb** 9:25; 26; **Rev** 11:6

OH

Gen 18:30; 32; 19:18; 20; 44:18; **Ex** 32:31; **Judg** 6:13; 15; **1Sa** 1:26; **2Sa** 15:4; 23:15; **1Chr** 4:10; 11:17; **Job** 6:8; 10:18; 11:5; 13:5; 14:13; 16:21; 19:23(2); 23:3; 29:2; 31:31; 35; **Ps** 6:4; 7:9; 14:7; 31:19; 53:6; 55:6; 81:13; 107:8; 15; 21; 31; **Is** 64:1; **Jer** 9:1; 2; 44:4

ON

Gen 2:2(2); 4:15; 16; 6:1; 6; 8:4; 5; 9; 14; 20; 12:8(3); 9; 13:3; 4; 14:15; 17:3; 18:5; 16; 19:2; 34; 20:9(2); 21:14; 33; 22:4; 9; 24:33; 45; 25:26; 28:12(2); 20; 29:1; 31:22; 32:1; 19; 33:4; 14; 16; 34:25; 37:23; 38:9; 19; 40:14; 16; 19; 41:45; 50; 43:31; 32; 44:14; 34; 46:20; 29(2); 48:16; 49:26(2); **Ex** 1:10; 2:6; 11; 4:3(2); 6:28; 8:4; 9:6; 12:7(2); 11; 18; 23; 29; 37; 14:16; 22(2); 29(2); 15:14; 19; 16:1; 5; 14; 22; 26; 27; 29(2); 30; 17:5; 9; 12(2); 18:13; 19:4; 16; 18; 20; 21:30; 22:30; 23:12; 24:6; 8; 17; 25:19(3); 20; 26; 26:10; 13(4); 18; 20; 35(2); 27:12; 13; 15; 21; 28:9; 10(2); 23; 24; 25; 27; 37; 29:9; 30; 31:17; 32:6; 15(3); 22; 26; 30; 33:4; 19; 34:21; 33; 35:2; 36:11; 37:7; 8(5); 9; 38:2; 7; 9; 15; 39:7; 17; 18; 19(2); 20; 31; 40:2; 17; 20; 24; 38; **Lev** 1:8; 9; 11; 12(2); 15; 16; 2:12; 3:4; 5(2); 4:12; 5:12; 6:10(2); 11; 12; 7:4; 16; 17; 18; 8:26; 28; 9:1; 14; 24; 11:2; 27; 34; 13:3(2); 5; 6; 21; 26; 31; 32; 34; 36; 51(2); 55; 14:9; 10; 23; 37; 15:6; 14; 23(2); 29; 16:4(2); 10; 23; 24; 29; 30; 32; 19:6; 7; 20:25; 21:10; 22:30; 23:6; 11; 21; 27; 35; 36; 39(2); 40; 24:6; 7; 25:9; **Num** 1:1; 18; 2:3; 10; 18; 25; 3:10; 13; 29; 35; 4:12; 6:9; 10; 23; 7:1; 11; 18; 24; 30; 36; 42; 48; 54; 60; 66; 72; 78; 8:17; 9:5; 6(2); 15; 10:5; 6; 11; 11:31(2); 14:5; 16:1; 27; 41; 46; 47; 17:8; 19:12(2); 19(3); 20:19; 21:13; 22:1; 24(2); 31; 41; 23:2; 14; 30; 24:20; 21; 28:9; 25; 29:1; 7; 12; 17; 20; 23; 26; 29; 32; 35; 30:8; 12; 31:19(2); 24; 32:19(2); 32; 33:3(2); 34:4(3); 9; 11; 15; 35:5(4); 14; **Deut** 1:1; 3; 5; 41; 2:28; 3:8; 4:15; 17; 18; 41; 46; 47; 49; 6:9; 7:25; 9:10; 10:2; 4; 11:30; 16:8; 21:19; 22; 22:5; 6; 28; 23:11; 26:7; 27:2; 28:1; 2; 30:7; 32:11, 13, 22; 41; 33:26; **Josh** 1:14; 15; 2:10; 19; 3:17(2); 4:14; 19; 22; 5:1; 10; 11; 12; 14; 6:7(2); 8; 9; 13(2); 15(2); 7:2; 7; 8:8; 9; 11; 12; 13(2); 19; 22(2); 24; 29; 33(2); 9:1; 12; 17; 10:26; 32; 35; 11:2(2); 3(2); 12:1(2); 3(2); 7(2); 13:16; 27; 32; 14:3; 9; 15:3; 7; 10(2); 16:1; 5; 6(2); 17:5; 7; 8; 9; 10(2); 18:5(2); 7; 12(2); 13; 15; 16(2); 20; 19:13(2); 14; 27; 34(2); 20:8; 22:4; 7; 20; 24:2; 8; 14; 15; 30; **Judg** 1:8; 2:9; 3:25; 4:15; 17; 23; 5:1; 10; 15; 17; 30; 6:32; 37; 38; 40; 7:1; 17; 18; 25; 8:11; 21; 26; 34; 9:8; 42; 48; 49; 10:4; 8; 11:18; 12:14; 13:5; 19; 20(2); 14:9; 15; 17; 18; 15:5; 18; 16:29; 19:1; 5; 8; 9; 14; 29; 20:30; 48; 21:4; 19(3); **Ruth** 1:7; 2:3; 9; 10; 3:15; **1Sa** 1:11; 2:26; 34; 5:3; 4; 5; 6:4(2); 7; 15; 7:6; 10; 9:20(4); 27(2); 10:3; 11:2; 7; 11; 12:11; 13:5; 14:1; 4(2); 16; 19; 24; 32; 40(2); 47; 15:12; 16; 18; 16:6; 7(4); 16; 17:3(4); 41; 18:10; 24; 19:23; 20:20; 21; 27; 41; 21:13; 22:18; 23:19; 21; 24; 26(2); 24:7; 25:13(3); 14; 18; 19; 20; 23; 41; 26:13; 25; 27:11; 28:8; 20; 22; 29:2(2); 30:1; 2; 31:7(2); 8; **2Sa** 1:2; 10; 11; 24; 2:13(2); 21; 25; 3:12; 29(4); 4:5; 7; 5:8; 10; 6:5(6); 8:7; 9:3; 6; 13; 11:13; 12:18; 30; 13:5; 19(4); 31; 14:2; 3; 4; 9(2); 12; 14; 22; 26; 30(2); 31; 33; 15:6; 18(2); 33; 16:2; 6(2); 12; 13; 17:12; 19:40(2); 20:8; 13; 21:10; 20(2); 22:4; 49; 23:1; 24:5; 20(2); **1Kin** 1:20; 27; 46; 48; 50; 51; 2:4; 5; 14; 15; 16; 19(2); 20; 24; 28; 37; 42; 3:6; 4:24(3); 29; 5:3; 4; 6:10; 15; 16; 7:3; 9; 28; 29; 35; 36(2); 39(3); 41; 43; 49(2); 8:20; 23; 25; 27; 50; 54; 66; 9:26; 10:9; 19(2); 20(2); 11:30; 12:32; 13:4; 14:23; 16:11; 24; 18:7; 23(2); 24(2); 25; 26; 33(3); 39; 46; 19:6; 15; 20:11; 20; 31; 32(2); 21:9; 12; 22:10(2); 19(3); 20(2); 24; 30; **2Kin** 1:4; 6; 9; 13; 16; 2:6; 8; 11; 15; 24; 3:11; 21; 22; 25; 4:8; 10; 11; 18; 20; 21; 31; 38; 5:2; 11; 18; 6:29; 31; 7:2; 17; 8:12; 15(2); 9:3; 6; 13; 17; 18; 19; 32; 33(2); 10:3; 15; 30; 11:5; 7; 9(2); 16; 19; 12:9; 15; 13:21; 23; 14:4; 20; 15:4; 12; 16:4; 14; 18:14; 20; 21(2); 23; 24; 26; 27; 19:22; 26; 20:5; 7; 23:8; 12; 13; 25:3; 8; 27; **1Chr** 4:10; 6:32; 39; 44; 49; 78(2); 10:5; 8; 12:18; 37; 40(4); 13:6; 14:2; 15:20; 21; 16:7; 18:7; 20:6(2); 21:17(3); 22:18; 23:28; 31; 26:30; 29:15; 21; 22; 23; 25; **2Chr** 2:4(3); 3:7; 13; 15; 16(2); 17(4); 4:6(2); 7(2); 8(2); 10; 12(2); 13(2); 6:10; 18; 7:6; 10; 22; 8:12; 13(3); 9:8; 18; 19(2); 10:12(2); 11:12; 14:7; 11; 16:7(2); 8; 17:19; 18:9; 18(2); 24; 29; 20:2; 19; 26; 29; 23:4; 8(2); 15; 24:25; 26:15; 27:3; 28:4; 29:17(2); 21; 22; 30:15; 32:15; 17; 18; 22; 33:14; 34:4; 35:1; 36:15(2); **Ezr** 4:10, 11, 16; 5:3; 6(2); 8; 6:13, 15, 7:9; 8:31; 33; 36; 10:9; **Neh** 2:14; 3:7; 13; 4:13; 17; 22; 6:14; 8:4(2); 13; 18; 9:10(2); 11; 32(6); 10:31(3); 12:31; 13:1; 15(2); 16; 19; 21(2); **Est** 1:2; 10; 11; 2:14; 21; 23; 3:6; 12; 4:1; 5:1(2); 6:1; 2; 4; 9; 11; 7:2; 10; 8:1; 9; 10(2); 13; 14; 9:1; 2; 10; 11; 15(2); 16; 17(2); 18(3); 25; **Job** 1:10; 4:13; 5:11; 9:11; 13:13; 15:26; 27; 16:16; 19; 17:9; 18:11; 19:10; 21:3; 6; 23:9(2); 24:20; 27:17; 20; 29:9; 14; 24; 31:2; 36:2; 7; 16; 17; 37:6; 38:26(2); 39:18; 21; 27; 28; 40:12; **Ps** 4:t; 6:t, 7:7; 12:8; 21:3; 22:8; 25:3; 5; 21; 27:14(2); 31:13; 35:17; 37:34; 48:2; 49:14; 52:9; 54:t; 55:t, 57:4; 63:6; 65:12; 66:6; 67:t, 68:18; 21; 25; 69:6; 29; 71:21; 75:5; 76:t, 78:53; 79:1; 81:3; 82:5; 83:14; 87:7; 91:14; 92:11; 93:4; 104:32; 107:41; 113:5; 118:6; 119:59; 84; 143; 124:1; 2; 142:4; 143:5(2); **Prov** 4:25; 5:5; 9:14; 15; 14:21; 31; 15:14; 20:22; 22:3; 27:12; 18; **Eccl** 2:3; 11(2); 4:1; **Song** 2:12; 3:1; 5:3; **Is** 7:25; 9:17; 20(2); 10:12; 11:8(2); 13:18; 14:1; 15:2; 3; 16:12; 18:3(2); 22:16; 24:18; 21; 25:6(2); 26:3; 5; 27:11(2); 28:1; 4; 20; 30:17; 31:1; 4; 32:15; 19; 33:5; 16; 36:5; 6; 8; 9; 11; 37:23; 27; 40:26; 42:25; 44:20; 47:1; 48:14(2); 49:10; 15; 18; 51:5; 9; 52:1(2); 53:6; 54:3(2); 8; 10; 56:2; 57:17; 58:4; 13; 59:17(2); 60:7; 10; 63:7(2); **Jer** 4:7; 5:9; 29; 6:23; 25; 7:29; 8:13(2); 21; 9:9; 10:25; 11:20; 12:15; 13:2; 27; 15:10(2); 17:11; 21; 22; 24; 25; 27; 18:3; 20:3; 10(2); 12; 22:4; 23:12; 25:29; 30; 30:6; 18; 31:29; 30; 32:29; 33:26; 36:22; 23(2); 38:22; 43:3; 12; 46:4; 48:11; 49:23; 24; 29; 50:6; 19; 52:23; **Lam** 1:2; 2:21; 4:6; **Eze** 1:8; 10(2); 23(2); 3:23; 4:6; 7:16; 10:3; 11:23; 16:11; 12; 15; 33; 18:2; 19:8; 21:16(2); 23:5(2); 7; 22; 24:3(2); 10; 17; 25:9; 26:17; 28:23; 31:4; 33:32; 36:3; 37:21; 39:6; 9; 11; 17; 40:2; 5; 10(4); 12(4); 21(2); 26(2); 34(3); 37(2); 39(2), 40, 41(2); 40(4); 49(2); 41:1(2); 2(2); 5; 10; 15(2); 16; 19(2); 20; 25(2); 26(3); 42:7; 9; 14; 43:20(2); 22; 44:19; 45:7(2); 46:1; 12; 19; 47:2; 7(2); 12(2); 48:16; 21(2); 30; **Dan** 3:27; 6:14; 7:5; 8:5; 18; 10:9; 11:17; 31; 12:5(2); **Hos** 4:8; 5:1; 6:3; 10:5; 8(2), 11:4, 6; 12:1; 6; **Joel** 2:5; 7; 32; **Amos** 1:7; 10; 2:7; 5:19, **Obad** 11; 12; 13(2); 21; **Jonah** 3:5; 4:5; 10; **Mic** 2:13; **Nah** 1:2; **Hab** 1:13; 2:9; 15; 16; 3:10; 19; **Zeph** 1:9; 12; **Zec** 1:12(2); 5:3(2); 10:5; 12:6(2); 13:9; 14:4; 13; **Mal** 1:10; **Mt** 1:18; 20; 4:5; 21; 5:14; 15; 28; 39; 45(4); 6:25; 9:2; 6; 27; 36; 10:29; 34; 12:1; 5; 10; 11(2); 12; 13:2; 14:3; 13; 19; 25; 26; 28; 29; 15:22, 32; 35; 16:19(2); 17:6; 15; 18:18(2); 19; 28; 33(2); 19:13; 15; 20:21(2); 23(2); 30; 31; 34; 21:7; 19; 38; 44(2); 46; 22:11; 40; 44; 23:4; 24:17; 20; 25:33(2); 34; 41; 26:5; 7; 12; 39; 45; 50; 55; 57; 64; 27:19; 25(2); 28; 30; 31; 38(2); 48; **Mk** 1:21; 2:10; 12; 21; 23; 24; 3:2; 4; 5; 9; 21; 34; 4:1; 5; 8; 16; 20; 21; 38; 5:19; 23; 6:9; 21; 47; 8:2; 6; 23; 33; 9:3; 20; 22; 40; 10:37(2); 40(2); 47; 48; 11:7; 12; 12:12; 36; 13:15; 14:2; 3; 6; 35; 41; 46; 51; 62; 65; 15:19; 20; 27(2); 29; 36; 40; 16:5; 18; 19; **Lk** 1:11; 25; 50; 59; 65; 78; 2:14; 4:9; 16; 20; 31; 40; 5:12; 17; 6:1; 2; 6; 7; 9; 20; 29; 48; 7:13; 16; 40; 8:8; 13; 15; 16; 22; 23; 32; 9:37; 10:11; 19; 31; 32(2); 33; 34; 35; 37; 11:33; 12:22; 49; 51; 13:7; 10; 13; 14(2); 15; 16; 14:1; 3; 5; 15:5; 20; 22(3); 16:24; 17:13; 16; 18:8; 32; 38; 39; 19:43; 20:1; 18; 19; 42; 21:12; 26; 35(2); 22:21; 30; 64; 69; 23:26; 30; 33(2); 39; 54; 24:49; **Jn** 1:12; 33; 2:11; 3:18; 36(2); 4:6; 35; 39; 5:9; 16; 24; 6:2; 19; 22; 25; 29; 35; 40; 47; 7:22; 23(2); 30; 31; 38; 39; 44; 48; 8:6; 8; 20; 30; 31; 9:6; 35; 36; 10:42; 11:45; 48; 12:11; 12; 15; 37; 42; 44(3); 46; 13:22; 23; 25; 14:12; 16:9; 17:4; 20; 19:2(2); 18; 19; 31; 37; 20:22; 21:1; 4; 6; 20; **Acts** 2:18(2); 21; 25; 30; 34; 3:4; 12; 4:3; 5; 22; 5:5; 15; 18; 30; 6:6; 15; 7:5; 6; 54; 55; 56; 8:17; 18; 19; 36; 39; 9:12; 14; 17; 21; 10:4; 7; 9(2); 19; 23; 39; 44; 45; 11:15(2); 17; 12:7; 8; 10; 13:3; 9; 11; 14; 15; 34; 36; 14:10; 23; 15:3; 16:13; 31; 17:5; 26; 18:8; 10; 19:4(2); 6; 16; 17; 20:7; 10; 37; 21:3; 5(2); 23; 27; 40; 22:16; 19; 30; 23:2; 24; 32; 25:6; 17(2); 23; 27:20; 33; 44(2); 28:3(2); 4; 8; **Rom** 4:5; 24; 9:15(2); 18; 23; 33; 10:6; 11; 14; 11:22; 12:7(2); 8; 20; 13:12; 14; 15:3; 24; 16:6; 19; **1Cor** 1:4; 11:10; 14:25; 15:53(2); 54(2); 16:6; 17; **2Cor** 1:11; 16; 4:8; 5:12; 6:7(2); 7:5; 8:1; 24; 10:7; 11:20; **Gal** 3:13; 14; 27; 6:16; **Eph** 1:10; 4:8; 24; 6:3; 11; 14; **Phil** 1:29; 2:4(2); 27(3); 4:8; **Col** 3:1; 2(3); 6; 10; 12, 14, **1Th** 5:8; **2Th** 1:8; **1Ti** 1:16; 18; 3:16; 4:14; 5:22; 6:12; 19; **2Ti** 1:6; 2:22; **Titus** 3:6; 13; **Philem** 1:18; **Heb** 1:3(2); 13; 2:16(2); 4:4; 5:2(2); 6:1; 2; 8:1; 4; 9:10; 10:12; 11:13; 12:25; **Jas** 3:6(2); 4:14; 5:5; 17; **1Pet** 1:17; 2:6; 24; 3:3; 22; 4:14(2); 16; **2Pet** 3:12; **1Jn** 3:23; 5:10; 13(2); **3Jn** 6; **Jude** 20; **Rev** 1:10; 3:3; 4:2; 4; 9; 10; 5:1(2); 10; 13; 6:2; 5; 8; 10(2); 16(2); 7:1(4); 11; 15; 16; 9:7; 17; 10:2; 11:10; 16; 13:13; 14(2); 14:1; 6; 14; 15; 16(2); 15:2; 17:8; 9; 18:19; 20; 19:4; 12; 16(2); 18; 19; 20:2; 6; 9; 11; 21:13(4); 22:2

ONE

Gen 1:9; 2:21; 24; 3:6; 22; 4:14; 19; 10:5; 8; 25; 11:1(2); 3; 6(2); 7; 13:11; 14:13; 15:3; 10; 19:9; 14; 20(2); 21:15; 22:2; 24:41; 25:23; 26:10; 26; 31; 27:29; 38; 45; 30:33; 35; 31:49; 32:8; 33:13; 34:14; 16; 22; 37:19; 38:28; 40:5; 41:5; 11; 22; 25; 26; 38; 42:1; 11; 13(2); 16; 19; 21; 27; 28; 32; 33; 43:33; 44:20; 28; 47:21; 48:1; 2; 22; 49:16; 28; **Ex** 1:15; 2:6; 11; 6:25; 8:31; 9:6; 7; 10:5; 19; 23; 11:1; 12:18; 30; 46; 48; 49; 14:7; 20; 28; 16:15; 22; 17:12(2); 18:3; 16; 21:18; 35; 23:29; 24:3; 25:12; 19(2); 20; 32; 33; 36; 26:2(4); 3(2); 4; 5(2); 6; 8(3); 10; 11; 13; 16; 17(2); 19; 21; 24; 25; 26; 27:9; 14; 28:10; 21; 29:1; 3; 15; 23(3); 39; 40; 30:13; 14; 31:14; 32:15; 33:7; 34:15; 35:21(2); 24; 36:2; 9(3); 10(2); 11; 12(2); 13(2); 15(3); 18; 21; 22(2); 24; 26; 29; 31; 33;

37:3; 6; 7; 8; 9; 18; 19; 22; 38:14; 26; 39:14; **Lev** 4:27; 5:4; 5; 7; 13; 6:18; 7:7; 10; 14; 8:26(2); 11:26; 12:8; 13:2; 14:5; 10(2); 12; 21(2); 22; 30; 31; 50; 15:15; 30; 16:5; 8; 27; 29; 17:15; 18:30; 19:8; 11; 34; 20:9; 22:28; 23:18; 19; 24:5; 22(2); 25:14; 17; 46; 48; 26:26; 37; **Num** 1:4; 41; 44; 2:16; 28; 34; 4:19; 30; 35; 39; 43; 47; 49; 5:2; 6:11; 14(3); 19(2); 7:3; 13(2); 14; 15(3); 16; 19(2); 20; 21(3); 22; 25(2); 26; 27(3); 28; 31(2); 32; 33(3); 34; 37(2); 38; 39(3); 40; 43; 44; 45(3); 46; 49(2); 50; 51(3); 52; 55(2); 56; 57(3); 58; 61(2); 62; 63(3); 64; 67(2); 68; 69(3); 70; 73(2); 74; 75(3); 76; 79(2); 80; 81(3); 82; 89; 8:12; 9:14; 10:4; 11:19; 26; 28; 12:12; 13:2; 23; 14:4; 15; 15:5; 11(2); 12; 15; 16(2); 24(2); 29; 16:3; 15(2); 22; 17:2; 3; 6(2); 18:11; 13; 19:3; 5; 16; 18(2); 21:8; 25:5; 6; 26:54; 28:4; 7; 11; 12(2); 13; 15; 19; 22; 27; 28(2); 29; 30; 29:2(2); 4(2); 5; 8(2); 9; 10; 11; 16; 19; 22; 25; 28; 31; 34; 36(2); 38; 31:28; 30; 34; 39; 47; 49; 34:18; 35:8; 15; 30; 36:7; 8; 9(2); **Deut** 1:22; 23; 35; 2:36; 4:4; 32; 42; 6:4; 12:14; 13:7; 12; 15:7; 17:6; 15; 18:10; 19:5; 11; 15; 21:1; 15; 23:16; 24:5; 25:5; 11(2); 28:7; 25; 57; 64; 32:30; 33:3; 8; **Josh** 9:2; 10:2; 42; 12:9(2); 10(2); 11(2); 12(2); 13(2); 14(2); 15(2); 16(2); 17(2); 18(2); 19(2); 20(2); 21(2); 22(2); 23(2); 24(2); 13:31; 17:14(2); 17; 20:4; 21:42; 22:7; 14; 23:10; 14(2); **Judg** 6:16; 29; 31; 7:5(2); 8:18; 9:2; 5; 18; 10:18; 11:35; 12:7; 16:5; 29; 17:5; 11; 18:19; 19:13; 20:1; 8; 11; 16; 31; 21:3; 6; 8; **Ruth** 1:4; 2:13; 20; 3:14; 4:1; **1Sa** 1:2; 24; 2:25; 34; 36(2); 3:11; 6:4; 17(5); 9:3; 10:3; 11; 12; 11:7; 13:1; 17; 14:4(2); 5; 16; 28; 40; 45; 16:18; 17:3; 7; 36; 18:7; 21; 19:22; 20:15; 41(2); 21:11; 22:2(3); 7; 20; 25:14; 26:15; 20; 22; 27:1; 29:5; **2Sa** 1:15; 2:13(2); 16; 21; 25; 27; 3:13; 29; 4:2; 10; 6:19(2); 20; 7:23; 8:2; 9:11; 10:4; 11:3; 25; 12:1(2); 3; 13:13; 30; 14:6; 11; 12; 13; 27; 15:2; 31; 17:12; 13; 22; 18:17; 19:7; 14; 20:11; 12; 19; 23:8; 9; 15; 24; 24:12; **1Kin** 1:48; 2:16; 20; 3:17(2); 23; 25; 4:22; 6:24(2); 25(2); 26; 27(3); 34; 7:7; 16; 17; 18; 23; 27; 34; 36; 37(3); 38(3); 42; 44; 8:56; 9:8; 10:14; 16; 17; 20; 11:13; 32; 36; 12:29; 30; 13:33; 14:21; 15:10; 16:11; 18:6; 23; 25; 40; 19:2; 20:20; 29(2); 22:8; 13(2); 20; 28; 38; **2Kin** 3:11; 23; 4:22(2); 39; 5:4; 6:3; 5; 12; 7:3; 6; 8; 9; 13; 8:26; 9:1; 11; 18; 10:21; 12:4; 9; 14:8; 11; 23; 17:27; 28; 18:24; 31(2); 19:22; 21:16; 22:1; 23:35; 24:18; 25:16; 17; **1Chr** 1:19; 9:31; 10:13; 11:11; 12; 17; 12:14; 25; 38; 16:3(2); 20; 17:5; 21; 21:10; 23:11; 24:5; 6(3); 17; 25:28; 26:12; 27:18; 29:7; **2Chr** 3:11(2); 12; 17; 4:15; 5:13(2); 6:29; 7:21; 9:6; 13; 15; 16; 19; 12:13; 16:13; 18:7; 8; 12(2); 19; 20:23; 22:2; 25:17; 21; 26:11; 28:6; 30:12; 17; 18; 31:16; 32:12; 34:1; 35:24; 36:11; **Ezr** 2:1; 26; 69(2); 3:1; 5; 5:14; 6:5; 8:34; 9:4; 11; 10:2; 13; **Neh** 1:2; 3:8; 28; 4:15; 17(2); 18; 19; 22; 23; 5:7; 18; 6:2; 7:3(2); 6; 30; 37; 63; 8:1; 16; 9:3; 10:28; 11:1; 3; 14; 20; 12:31; 13:10; 28; 30; **Est** 1:7; 3:13; 4:5; 11; 6:9; 7:9; 8:12; 9:19; 22; **Job** 1:1; 4; 8; 2:3; 10; 11; 12; 5:2; 6:10; 26; 9:3; 22; 12:4; 13:9; 14:3; 4; 16:21; 17:10; 19:11; 21:23; 23:13; 24:6; 17; 29:25; 31:15; 35; 33:23; 40:11; 12; 41:9; 16; 17; 32; 42:11; **Ps** 12:2; 14:3; 16:10; 27:4; 29:9; 32:6; 34:20; 35:14; 49:16; 50:21; 53:3(2); 58:8; 63:11; 64:6; 68:21; 30; 71:18; 22; 73:20; 75:7; 78:41; 65; 82:7; 83:5; 84:7; 89:10; 18; 19(3); 105:13(2); 37; 106:11; 115:8; 119:160; 162; 128:1; 135:18; 137:3; 141:7; 145:4; **Prov** 1:14; 19; 3:18; 6:11; 28; 8:30; 15:12; 16:5; 17:14; 19:25; 20:6; 21:5; 22:26; 24:34; 26:17; **Eccl** 1:4; 2:14; 3:19(3); 20; 4:8; 9; 10; 11; 12; 5:18; 6:6; 7:14; 27(2); 28; 8:9; 9:2; 3; 18; 10:3; 15; 12:11; **Song** 1:7; 2:10; 13; 4:2; 9(2); 6:6(2); 9(3); 8:10; 11; **Is** 1:4; 23; 24; 2:12(2); 20; 3:5(2); 4:1; 3; 5:10; 19; 24; 30; 6:2; 3; 6; 7:22; 9:14; 17; 10:14; 17(2); 20; 34; 12:6; 13:8; 14; 15(2); 14:18; 32; 15:3; 16:7; 17:7; 19:2(2); 17; 18; 20; 23:15; 27:12(2); 28:2; 29:4; 11; 19; 20; 23; 30:11; 12; 15; 17(2); 29(2); 31:1; 33:20; 34:15; 16; 36:9; 16(3); 37:23; 40:25; 26; 41:6(2); 14; 16; 20; 25; 27; 43:3; 7; 14; 15; 44:5; 45:11; 24; 46:7; 47:4; 9; 15; 48:17; 49:7(2); 26; 53:6; 54:5; 55:1; 5; 56:6; 11; 57:2; 15; 60:9; 14; 16; 22(2); 65:8; 66:8; 13; 17; 23(2); **Jer** 1:15; 3:14; 5:6; 8; 6:3; 13(2); 8:6; 10(2); 9:4; 5; 8; 20; 10:3; 11:8; 12:12; 13:14; 15:10; 16:12; 18:11; 12; 16; 19:8; 9; 11; 20:7; 11; 22:7; 23:17; 30; 35(2); 24:2; 25:5; 26; 33; 30:14; 16; 31:30; 32:19; 39(2); 34:10(2); 17; 35:2; 36:7; 16; 38:7; 46:16; 49:17; 50:13; 16(2); 29; 42; 51:5; 9; 31(3); 46; 56; 52:1; 20; 21; 22; **Eze** 1:6(2); 9(2); 11(2); 12; 15; 16; 23(3); 28; 3:13; 4:8; 9; 17; 7:16; 9:2; 10:7; 9(2); 10; 14; 19; 21(2); 22; 11:5; 19; 13:10; 14:7; 15:7; 16:15; 25; 44; 17:22; 18:10; 30; 19:3; 20:39; 21:16; 19; 22:6; 11; 23:2; 13; 24:23; 31:11; 33:20; 21; 24; 26; 30(2); 32; 34:23; 37:16; 17(3); 19(2); 22(2); 24; 39:7; 40:5(2); 6(2); 7(3); 8; 10(2); 12(2); 13; 26; 40; 42; 44; 49; 41:1; 2; 6; 11; 15; 19; 21; 24; 26; 42:4; 9; 12; 43:14(2); 45:7(2); 11; 15; 20; 46:12(2); 17; 22; 47:7; 14; 48:1; 8; 21; 31(3); 32(3); 33(3); 34(3); **Dan** 2:9; 43; 3:19; 4:13; 19; 23; 5:6; 7:3; 5; 13; 16; 8:3; 9; 13; 9:27; 10:13(2); 16; 18; 11:5; 7; 10; 27; 12:1; 5; 6; **Hos** 1:11; 4:3; 11:9; **Joel** 2:7; 8(2); **Amos** 3:5; 4:7(2); 8; 6:9; 12; 8:8; **Obad** 9; 11; **Jonah** 1:7; 3:8; **Mic** 2:4; 4:5; **Nah** 1:11; 2:4; **Hab** 1:12; 3:3; **Zeph** 2:11; 15; 3:9; **Hag** 2:1; 12; 13; 16(2); 22; **Zec** 3:9(2); 4:3; 5:3(2); 8:10; 21; 10:1; 11:6; 7; 8; 9; 16; 12:10(2); 13:4; 6; 14:7; 9(2); 13; 16; **Mal** 2:3; 10(2); 15(2); 16; 17; 3:16; **Mt** 3:3; 5:18(2); 19; 29; 30; 36; 6:24(2); 27; 29; 7:8; 21; 26; 29; 10:29; 42; 12:6; 11; 22; 29; 47; 13:19(2); 38; 46; 16:14; 17:4(3); 18:5; 6; 9; 10; 12; 14; 16; 24; 28; 35; 19:5; 6; 16; 17; 29; 20:12; 13; 21; 21:24; 35; 22:5; 35; 23:4; 8; 9; 10; 15; 24:2; 10(2); 31; 40; 41; 25:15(2); 18; 24; 29; 32; 40; 45; 26:14; 21; 22; 40; 47; 51; 73; 27:38; 48; **Mk** 1:3; 7; 22; 24; 2:3; 4:41; 5:22; 6:15; 7:14; 32; 8:14; 28; 9:5(3); 10; 17; 26; 37; 38; 42; 47; 49; 50; 10:8(2); 17; 18; 21; 37; 11:29; 12:6; 28; 29; 32; 13:1; 2; 14:10; 18; 19(2); 20; 37; 43; 47; 66; 69; 70; 15:6; 7; 21; 27; 36; **Lk** 2:3; 15; 36; 3:4; 16; 4:34; 40; 5:3; 6:9; 11; 29; 40; 7:8; 32; 36; 41; 8:25; 42; 49; 9:8; 19; 33(3); 43; 49; 10:42; 11:1; 4; 10; 45; 46; 12:1; 6; 13; 25; 27; 52; 13:10; 15; 23; 14:1; 15; 18; 15:4; 7; 8; 10; 19; 26; 16:5; 13(2); 17; 30; 31; 17:2; 15; 22; 24; 34(2); 35; 36; 18:10; 14; 19; 22; 19:26; 44; 20:1; 3; 21:6; 22:36; 47; 50; 59; 23:14; 17; 26; 33; 39; 24:17; 18; 32; **Jn** 1:23; 26; 40; 3:8; 20; 4:33; 37; 5:44; 45; 6:7; 8; 22; 40; 70; 71; 7:21; 50; 8:9(2); 18; 41; 50; 9:25; 32; 10:16(2); 30; 11:49; 50; 52; 12:2; 4; 48; 13:14; 21; 22; 23; 34(2); 35; 15:12; 17; 17:11; 21(2); 22(2); 23; 18:14; 17; 22; 25; 26; 37; 39; 19:18; 34; 20:12; 24; 21:25; **Acts** 1:14; 22; 2:1(2); 7; 12; 27; 38; 46; 3:14; 26; 4:24; 32(2); 5:12; 16; 25; 34; 7:24; 26(2); 52; 57; 8:6; 9; 9:11; 43; 10:2; 5; 6; 22; 28; 32; 11:28; 12:10; 20; 13:25; 35; 15:25; 39; 17:7; 26; 27; 18:7; 12; 19:9; 14; 29; 32; 34; 38; 20:31; 21:6; 7; 8; 16; 26; 34; 22:12; 14; 23:6; 17; 24:21; 25:19; 27:1; 2; 28:2; 13; 25; **Rom** 1:16; 27; 2:15; 28; 29; 3:10; 12; 30; 5:7; 12; 15(2); 16(2); 17(3); 18(2); 19(2); 9:10; 21; 10:4; 12:4; 5(3); 10(2); 16; 13:8; 14:2; 5(2); 12; 13; 19; 15:2; 5; 6(2); 7; 14; 16:16; **1Cor** 1:12; 3:4; 8; 4:6(2); 5:1; 5; 11; 6:5; 7; 16(2); 17; 7:5; 7; 17; 25; 8:4; 6(2); 9:24; 26; 10:8; 17(3); 11:5; 20; 21(2); 33; 12:8; 11; 12(3); 13(3); 14; 18; 19; 20; 25; 26(2); 14:23; 24(2); 26; 27; 31(2); 15:8; 39; 40; 41(2); 16:2; 16; 20; **2Cor** 2:7; 16; 5:10; 14; 10:11; 11:2; 24; 12:2; 5; 13:11; 12; **Gal** 3:10; 13; 16; 20(2); 28; 4:22; 24; 5:13; 14; 15(2); 17; 26(2); 6:1; 2; **Eph** 1:10; 2:14; 15; 16; 18; 4:2; 4(3); 5(3); 6; 7; 25; 32(2); 5:21; 31; 33; **Phil** 1:16; 27(2); 2:2(2); 3:13; **Col** 3:9; 13(2); 15; 16; 4:9; 12; **1Th** 2:11; 3:12; 4:4; 9; 18; 5:11; **2Th** 1:3; **1Ti** 2:5(2); 3:2; 4; 12; 5:9; 21; **2Ti** 2:19; **Titus** 1:6; 12; 3:3; **Philem** 1:9; **Heb** 2:6; 11; 3:13; 5:12; 13; 6:11; 10:12; 14; 24; 25; 11:12; 12:16; 13:14; **Jas** 2:10; 16; 19; 4:11; 12; 5:9; 16(2); 19; **1Pet** 1:22; 3:8(2); 4:9; 10; 5:5; 14; **2Pet** 3:8(3); **1Jn** 1:7; 2:13; 14; 20; 29; 3:11; 12; 23; 4:7(2); 11; 12; 5:1; 7; 8; 18; **2Jn** 5; **Rev** 1:13; 2:23; 4:2; 5:5; 8; 6:1(2); 4; 11; 7:13; 9:12; 11:10; 13:3; 14:14; 15:7; 17:1; 10; 12; 13; 18:8; 10; 17; 19; 21:9; 21

ONE'S

Eccl 7:1; **Acts** 16:26

ONES

Gen 34:29; 43:8; 45:19; 46:5; 47:24; 50:8; 21; **Ex** 10:10; 24; **Num** 14:31; 31:9; 17; 32:16; 17; 24; 26; **Deut** 1:39; 2:34; 3:19; 20:14; 22:6; 29:11; **Josh** 1:14; 8:35; **Judg** 5:22; 18:21; **2Sa** 15:22; **1Chr** 16:13; **2Chr** 20:13; 31:18; **Ezr** 8:21; **Est** 8:11; **Job** 21:11; 38:41; 39:3; 4; 16; 30; **Ps** 10:10; 83:3; 137:9; **Prov** 1:22; 7:7; **Is** 5:17; 10:16; 33; 11:7; 13:3(2); 14:9; 24:21; 25:4; 5; 29:5; 32:11; 33:7; 57:15; **Jer** 2:33; 8:16; 14:3; 46:5; 48:4; 45; **Lam** 4:3; **Dan** 4:17; 8:8; 11:17; **Joel** 3:11; **Zec** 4:14; 13:7; **Mt** 10:42; 18:6; 10; 14; **Mk** 9:42; 10:42; **Lk** 17:2

ONLY

Gen 6:5; 7:23; 14:24; 19:8; 22:2; 12; 16; 24:8; 27:13; 34:22; 23; 41:40; 47:22; 26; 50:8; **Ex** 8:9; 11; 28; 9:26; 10:17(2); 24; 12:16; 21:19; 22:20; 27; **Lev** 21:23; 27:26; **Num** 1:49; 12:2; 14:9; 18:3; 20:19; 22:35; 31:22; 36:6; **Deut** 2:28; 35; 37; 3:11; 4:9; 12; 8:3; 10:15; 12:16; 23; 26; 15:5; 23; 20:20; 22:25; 28:13; 29; 33; 29:14; **Josh** 1:7; 17; 18; 6:15; 17; 24; 8:2; 27; 11:13; 22; 13:6; 14; 17:17; **Judg** 3:2; 6:37; 39; 40; 10:15; 11:34; 16:28; 19:20; **1Sa** 1:13; 23; 5:4; 7:3; 4; 12:24; 18:17; 20:14; 39; **2Sa** 13:32; 33; 17:2; 20:21; 23:10; **1Kin** 3:2; 3; 4:19; 8:39; 12:20; 14:8; 13; 15:5; 18:22; 19:10; 14; 22:31; **2Kin** 3:25; 10:23; 17:18; 19:19; 21:8; **1Chr** 22:12; **2Chr** 2:6; 6:30; 18:30; 33:17; **Ezr** 10:15; **Est** 1:16; **Job** 1:12; 15; 16; 17; 19; 13:20; 34:29; **Ps** 4:8; 51:4; 62:2; 4; 5; 6; 71:16; 72:18; 91:8; **Prov** 4:3; 5:17; 11:23; 13:10; 14:23; 17:11; 21:5(2); **Eccl** 7:29; **Song** 6:9; **Is** 4:1; 26:13; 28:19; 37:20; **Jer** 3:13; 6:26; 32:30(2); **Eze** 7:5; 14:16; 18; 44:20; **Amos** 3:2; 8:10; **Zec** 12:10; **Mt** 4:10; 5:47; 8:8; 10:42; 12:4; 14:36; 17:8; 21:19; 21; 24:36; **Mk** 2:7; 5:36; 6:8; 9:8; **Lk** 4:8; 7:12; 8:42; 50; 9:38; 24:18; **Jn** 1:14; 18; 3:16; 18; 5:18; 44; 11:52; 12:9; 13:9; 17:3; **Acts** 8:16; 11:19; 18:25; 19:27; 21:13; 25; 26:29; 27:10; **Rom** 1:32; 3:29; 4:9; 12; 16; 5:3; 11; 8:23; 9:10; 24; 13:5; 16:4; 27; **1Cor** 7:39; 9:6; 14:36; 15:19; **2Cor** 7:7; 8:10; 19; 21; 9:12; **Gal** 1:23; 2:10; 3:2; 4:18; 5:13; 6:12; **Eph** 1:21; **Phil** 1:27; 29; 2:12; 27; 4:15; **Col** 4:11; **1Th** 1:5; 8; 2:8; **2Th** 2:7; **1Ti** 1:17; 5:13; 6:15; 16; **2Ti** 2:20; 4:8; 11; **Heb** 9:10; 11:17; 12:26; **Jas** 1:22; 2:24; **1Pet** 2:18; **1Jn** 2:2; 4:9; 5:6; **2Jn** 1; **Jude** 4; 25; **Rev** 9:4; 15:4

OR

Gen 13:9; 17:12; 24:21; 49; 50; 26:11; 27:21; 30:1; 31:14; 24; 29; 39; 43; 50; 37:8; 32; 39:10; 41:44; 42:16; 44:8; 16; 19; **Ex** 4:11(4); 5:3; 10:15; 11:7; 12:5; 19; 16:4; 17:7; 19:12; 13(2); 20:4(3); 21:4; 6; 15; 16; 17; 18; 20; 21; 26; 27; 28; 29; 31; 32; 33(2); 36; 22:1(2); 4(2); 5; 6(2); 7; 9; 10(5); 14; 22; 23:4; 28:43; 29:34; 30:20; 33; 34:19; **Lev** 1:10; 14; 2:4; 3:1; 6; 4:23; 28; 5:1; 2(3); 3; 4(2); 6; 7; 11; 6:2(3); 3; 4(3); 5; 7:16; 21(2); 23(2); 26; 11:4; 32(3); 35; 36; 42; 12:6(2); 7; 8; 13:2(2); 16; 19; 24(2); 29(2); 30; 38; 42(2); 43; 47; 48(3); 49(4); 51(3); 52(3); 53(2); 55; 56(3); 57(2); 58(2); 59(4); 14:22; 30; 37; 15:3; 14; 23; 25; 29; 16:29; 17:3(3); 8(2); 10; 13(2); 15(2); 18:7; 9(2); 10; 17; 19:35; 20:2; 9(2); 17; 25(2); 27(2); 21:7; 11; 14(3); 18(3); 19(2); 20(6); 22:4(2); 5(2); 8; 10; 13; 16; 18; 19; 21(2); 22(5); 23(2); 24(3); 27(2); 28; 25:14; 35; 36; 47(3); 49(3); 26:15; 27:10; 12; 14; 20; 26; 27; 28; 30; 32; 33; **Num** 5:6; 14; 30; 6:2; 3(2); 7(2); 10; 9:10(2); 21; 22(3); 11:8; 22; 23; 13:18(2); 19(2); 20(2); 14:2; 15:3(4); 5; 6; 8(2); 11(3); 14; 30; 16:14; 29; 18:15; 17(2); 19:16(3); 18(3); 20:5(3); 17; 21:22; 22:18; 26; 23:8; 19; 24:13; 30:2; 5; 6; 10; 12; 13; 14; 32:19; 35:18; 20; 21; 22; 23; **Deut** 3:24; 4:16; 23; 25; 32; 34; 5:8(3); 21(4); 32; 7:14(2); 25; 8:2; 9:5; 12:17(5); 13:1(2); 2; 3; 5; 6(4); 7; 14:7; 21; 24; 26(4); 15:2; 12; 21(2); 17:1(2); 2; 3(2); 5(2); 6; 12; 20; 18:3; 10(5); 11(4); 20; 19:15(2); 21:18; 22:1; 2; 4; 6(3); 23:1; 3; 18; 24:3; 6; 7; 14; 27:15; 16; 22; 28:14; 51(3); 29:6; 18(3); 32:36; **Josh** 1:7; 5:13; 7:3; 8:17; 20; 22; 10:14; 19:2; 22:22; 23(3); 28; 29; 23:6; 24:15; **Judg** 2:22; 5:8; 30; 9:2; 11:25; 13:14; 14:3; 6; 18:19; 19:13; 20:28; 21:22; **Ruth** 1:16; 3:10; **1Sa** 2:14(3); 6:12; 12:3(3); 13:19; 14:6; 52; 16:7; 18:18; 20:2; 10; 12; 21:3; 8; 22:8; 15; 25:31; 36; 26:10(2); 18; 29:3; 30:2; **2Sa** 2:21; 3:29(4); 35; 14:19; 15:4; 21; 17:9; 19:35; 42; 20:20; 24:13(2); **1Kin** 3:7; 8:23; 37; 38; 46; 9:6; 15:17; 18:10; 27(3); 20:18; 39; 21:2; 6; 22:6; 15; **2Kin** 2:16; 21; 4:13; 6:27; 9:32; 12:13; 13:19; 17:34(2); 20:9; 22:2; 23:10; **1Chr** 21:12(2); **2Chr** 1:11; 6:28(3); 29(2); 36; 7:13(2); 8:15; 14:11; 15:13(2); 16:1; 18:5; 14; 30; 20:9(2); 32:15; 36:17(2); **Ezr** 7:24(2); 26(3); 9:12; 10:13; **Neh** 2:16; 5:8; 10:31(2); 13:20; 25; **Est** 4:11; 16; 8:6; 9:12; **Job** 3:12; 15; 16; 4:7; 6:5; 6; 12; 22; 23(2); 7:12; 8:3; 10:4; 11:10; 12:8; 13:9; 22; 15:3; 7; 16:3; 22:3; 11; 25:4; 28:16; 18; 31:5; 9; 13; 16; 17; 19; 24; 26; 27; 29; 34; 38; 39; 32:12; 34:13; 29; 33; 35:6; 7; 36:23; 29; 37:13(2); 38:5; 6; 8; 16; 17; 21; 22; 25; 28; 31; 32; 36; 37; 39; 39:1; 2; 5; 9; 10; 11; 13; 15; 40:9; 41:1; 2; 5; 7; 13; 20; **Ps** 18:31; 24:3; 32:9; 35:14; 44:20; 50:8; 13; 16; 66:t; 67:t; 68:t, 69:31; 75:t; 76:t; 83:t; 87:t, 88:t, 11; 89:8; 90:2; 92:t, 94:16; 108:t, 120:3; 131:1; 132:4; 139:7; 144:3; **Prov** 6:7; 7:22; 8:8; 23; 20:20; 22:26; 23:34; 28:24; 29:9; 30:4; 9; 32; **Eccl** 2:19; 25; 5:12; 9:1; 11:3; 6(2); 12:2(3); 6(4); 14; **Song** 2:9; 17; 6:12; 8:14; **Is** 1:11(2); 7:11; 10:14(2); 15(2); 17:6(2); 8; 19:15(2); 27:5; 7; 29:8; 16; 30:14; 38:14; 40:13; 18; 25; 41:22; 23; 42:19; 43:9; 44:10; 45:9; 10; 49:24; 50:1; 2; 57:11; 66:8; **Jer** 2:18; 32; 7:22; 11:14; 19; 13:23; 14:22; 15:5(2); 16:2; 7; 10(2); 18:14; 20:17; 21:13; 22:18(2); 23:33(2); 32:43; 34:9; 36:23; 37:18(2); 40:5; 42:6; 17; 44:14; 28; 48:24; **Eze** 2:5; 7; 3:11; 4:14; 14:7; 17; 19; 15:2; 3; 17:9; 15; 21:16(2); 22:14; 34:6; 44:22; 25(4); 31(2); 46:12; **Dan** 2:10(2); 4:19; 35; 6:4; 7; 12; 24; 11:29; **Joel** 1:2; **Amos** 3:12; 4:8; 5:19; 6:2; **Mic** 6:7; **Hag** 2:12(4); **Zec** 8:10; **Mal** 1:8; 2:13; 17; **Mt** 5:17; 18; 36; 6:24; 25; 31(2); 7:4; 9; 10; 16; 9:5; 10:11; 14; 19; 37(2); 11:3; 12:5; 25; 29; 33; 13:21; 15:4; 5; 6; 16:14; 26; 17:25(2); 18:8(3); 16(2); 20; 19:29(7); 21:25; 22:17; 23:17; 19; 24:23; 25:37; 38; 39(2); 44(5); 27:17; **Mk** 2:9; 3:4(2); 33; 4:17; 21; 30; 6:15; 56(2); 7:10; 11; 12; 8:37; 10:29(7); 11:30; 12:14; 15; 13:21; 35(3); **Lk** 2:24; 3:15; 5:23; 6:9(2); 7:19; 20; 8:16; 9:25; 11:11; 12; 12:11(2); 14; 29; 38; 41; 13:4; 15; 14:5; 12; 31; 32; 16:13; 17:7; 21; 23; 18:11; 29(4); 20:2; 4; 22; 22:27; **Jn** 2:6; 4:27; 6:19; 7:17; 48; 9:2; 21; 25; 13:29; 14:11; 18:34; **Acts** 1:7; 3:12(2); 4:7; 34; 5:38; 7:49; 8:34; 9:2; 10:14; 28(2); 11:8; 17:21; 29(2); 18:14; 19:12; 20:33(2); 23:9; 15; 29; 24:20; 23; 25:11; 26:31; 28:6; 17; 21; **Rom** 2:4; 15; 3:1; 4:9; 10; 13; 6:16; 8:35(6); 9:11; 10:7; 11:34; 35; 12:7(2); 8; 14:4; 8; 10; 13; 21(2); **1Cor** 1:13; 2:1; 3:22(7); 4:3; 21; 5:10(3); 11(5); 7:11; 15; 16; 8:5; 9:6; 7; 8; 10; 10:19; 31(2); 11:4; 5; 6; 22; 12:13(2); 26; 13:1; 14:6(3); 7(2); 23; 24; 27; 29; 36; 37; 15:11; 37; **2Cor** 1:6; 13; 17; 3:1(2); 5:9; 10; 13; 6:15; 8:23; 9:7; 10:12; 11:4(2); 12:2; 3; 6; 13:1; **Gal** 1:8; 10(2); 2:2; 3:2; 5; 15; 4:9; **Eph** 3:20; 5:3; 27(2); 6:8; **Phil** 1:18; 20; 27; 2:3; **Col** 1:16(3); 20; 2:16(4); 3:17; **1Th** 2:19(2); 5:10; **2Th** 2:2; 4; 15; **1Ti** 2:9(3); 5:4; 16; 19; **Titus** 1:6; 3:12; **Philem** 1:18; **Heb** 2:6; 10:28; 12:16; 20; **Jas** 2:3; 15; 4:13; 15; **1Pet** 1:11; 2:14; 3:3; 9; 4:15(3); **Rev** 2:5; 16; 3:15; 13:16; 17(3); 14:9; 20:4; 21:27

OTHER

Gen 4:19; 8:10; 12; 13:11; 20:16; 25:23; 28:17; 29:27; 30; 31:50; 32:8; 41:3(2); 19; 43:14; 22; 47:21; **Ex** 1:15; 4:7; 14:20; 17:12(2); 18:4; 7; 20:3; 23:13; 25:12; 19(2); 32; 33; 26:3; 13; 27; 27:15; 28:10(2); 25; 27(2); 29:19; 39; 41; 30:32; 32:15; 34:14; 36:10; 25; 32; 33; 37:3; 8; 18; 38:15; 39:20(2); **Lev** 5:7; 6:11; 7:24; 8:22; 11:23; 12:8; 13:26; 14:22; 31; 42(2); 15:15; 30; 16:8; 18:18; 20:24; 26; 25:53; **Num** 6:11; 8:12; 10:21; 11:26; 31; 21:13; 24:1; 28:4; 8; 32:38; 36:3; **Deut** 4:32; 5:7; 6:14; 7:4; 8:19; 11:16; 28; 30; 13:2; 6; 7; 13; 17:3; 18:20; 28:14; 36; 64(2); 29:26; 30:17; 31:18; 20; **Josh** 2:10; 7:7; 8:22; 11:19; 12:1; 13:27; 32; 14:3; 17:5; 20:8; 21:27; 22:4; 7; 23:16; 24:2(2); 3; 8; 14; 15; 16; **Judg** 2:12; 17; 19; 7:7; 25; 9:44; 10:8; 13; 11:18; 13:10; 16:17; 20; 29; 20:30; 31(2); **Ruth** 1:4; 2:22; **1Sa** 1:2; 3:10; 8:8; 14:1; 4(2); 5; 40; 17:3; 18:10; 19:21; 20:25; 21:9; 26:13; 19; 28:8; 30:20; 31:7(2); **2Sa** 1:24; 2:13(2); 4:2; 12:1; 13:16; 14:6; 17:9; 24:22; **1Kin** 3:22; 23; 25; 26; 6:24(2); 25; 26; 27(2); 34; 7:6; 7; 16; 17; 18; 20; 23; 9:6; 9; 10:20; 11:4; 10; 12:29; 14:9; 18:23; 20:29; **2Kin** 3:22; 5:17; 12:7; 17:7; 35; 37; 38; 22:17; **1Chr** 6:78; 9:32; 12:37; 23:17; **2Chr** 3:11(2); 12(3); 17; 7:19; 22; 9:19; 13:9; 20:1; 25:12; 28:25; 29:34; 30:23(2); 32:13; 17; 22; 34:12; 25; 35:13; **Ezr** 1:10; 2:31; **Neh** 3:11; 20; 4:16; 17; 5:5; 7:33; 34; 11:1; 12:38; **Est** 2:12; 9:16; **Job** 8:12; 24:24; **Ps** 73:5(2); 85:10; **Eccl** 3:19; 6:5; 7:14; **Is** 26:13; 49:20; **Jer** 1:16; 7:6; 9; 18; 11:10; 12:12; 13:10; 16:11; 13; 19:4; 13; 22:9; 24:2; 25:6; 33; 32:20; 29; 35:15; 36:16; 44:3; 5; 8; 15; **Eze** 1:23; 16:34; 21:16; 40:6; 40; 41:1; 2; 15; 19; 21; 24; 26; 42:14; 44:19; 45:7; 47:7; 48:8; 21; **Dan** 2:11; 44; 3:21; 29; 7:20; 8:3; 12:5(2); **Hos** 3:1; 9:1; 13:10; **Obad** 11; **Zec** 4:3; 11:7; 14; **Mt** 4:21; 5:39; 6:24(2); 8:18; 28; 12:13; 45; 13:8; 14:22; 16:5; 20:21; 21:36; 41; 22:4; 23:23; 24:31; 40; 41; 25:11; 16; 17; 20; 22; 27:61; 28:1; **Mk** 3:5; 4:8; 19; 35; 36; 5:1; 21; 6:45; 7:4; 8; 8:13; 10:37; 12:31; 32; 15:27; 41; **Lk** 3:18; 4:43; 5:7; 6:10; 29; 7:41; 8:8; 22; 10:1; 31; 32; 11:26; 42; 14:32; 16:13(2); 17:24; 34; 35; 36; 18:10; 11; 14; 22:65; 23:33; 40; 24:10; **Jn** 4:38; 6:22(2); 23; 25; 10:1; 16; 15:24; 18:16; 19:32; 20:2; 3; 4; 8; 12; 25; 30; 21:2; 8; 25; **Acts** 2:4; 40; 4:12(2); 5:29; 8:34; 15:2; 39; 17:9; 18; 19:39; 23:6; 26:22; 27:1; **Rom** 1:13; 8:39; 13:9; **1Cor** 1:16; 3:11; 7:5; 8:4; 9:5; 10:29; 11:21; 14:17; 21(2); 29; 15:37; **2Cor** 1:13; 2:16; 8:13; 10:15; 11:8; 12:13; 13:2; **Gal** 1:8; 9; 19; 2:13; 4:22; 5:17; **Eph** 3:5; 4:17; **Phil** 1:13; 17; 2:3; 3:4; 4:3; **2Th** 1:3; **1Ti** 1:3; 10; 5:22; **Jas** 5:12; **1Pet** 4:15; **2Pet** 3:16; **Rev** 2:24; 8:13; 17:10

OTHERS

Job 8:19; 31:10; 34:24; 26; **Ps** 49:10; **Prov** 5:9; **Eccl** 7:22; **Is** 56:8; **Jer** 6:12; 8:10; **Eze** 9:5; 13:6; 10; **Dan** 7:19; 11:4; **Mt** 5:47; 15:30; 16:14; 20:3; 6; 21:8; 26:67; 27:42; **Mk** 6:15(2); 8:28; 11:8; 12:5; 9; 15:31; **Lk** 5:29; 8:3; 10; 9:8; 19; 11:16; 18:9; 20:16; 23:32; 35; 24:1; **Jn** 7:12; 41; 9:9; 16; 10:21; 12:29; 18:34; 19:18; **Acts** 2:13; 15:35; 17:32; 34; 28:9; **1Cor** 9:2; 12; 27; 14:19; **2Cor** 3:1; 8:8; **Eph** 2:3; **Phil** 2:4; **1Th** 2:6; 4:13; 5:6; **1Ti** 5:20; **2Ti** 2:2; **Heb** 9:25; 11:35; 36; **Jude** 23

OTHERWISE

2Sa 18:13; **1Kin** 1:21; **2Chr** 30:18; **Ps** 38:16; **Mt** 6:1; **Lk** 5:36; **Rom** 11:6(2); 22; **2Cor** 11:16; **Gal** 5:10; **Phil** 3:15; **1Ti** 5:25; 6:3; **Heb** 9:17

OUGHT

Gen 20:9; 34:7; 39:6; 47:18; **Ex** 5:8; 11; 19; 12:46; 22:14; 29:34; **Lev** 4:2; 27; 11:25; 19:6; 25:14(2); 27:31; **Num** 15:24; 30; 30:6; **Deut** 4:2; 15:2; 26:14(2); **Josh** 21:45; **Ruth** 1:17; **1Sa** 12:4; 5; 25:7; 30:22; **2Sa** 3:35; 13:12; 14:10; 19; **1Chr** 12:32; 15:2; **2Chr** 13:5; **Neh** 5:9; **Ps** 76:11; **Mt** 5:23; 21:3; 23:23; **Mk** 7:12; 8:23; 11:25; 13:14; **Lk** 11:42; 12:12; 13:14; 16; 18:1; 24:26; **Jn** 4:20; 33; 13:14; 19:7; **Acts** 4:32; 5:29; 17:29; 19:36; 20:35; 21:21; 24:19(2); 25:10; 24; 26:9; 28:19; **Rom** 8:26; 12:3; 15:1; **1Cor** 8:2; 11:7; 10; **2Cor** 2:3; 7; 12:11; 14; **Eph** 5:28; 6:20; **Col** 4:4; 6; **1Th** 4:1; **2Th** 3:7; **1Ti** 5:13; **Titus** 1:11; **Philem** 1:18; **Heb** 2:1; 5:3; 12; **Jas** 3:10; 4:15; **2Pet** 3:11; **1Jn** 2:6; 3:16; 4:11; **3Jn** 8

OUR

Gen 1:26(2); 5:29(2); 19:31; 32(2); 34; 23:6; 24:60; 29:26; 31:1(2); 14; 15; 16(2); 32; 33:12; 34:9; 14; 16; 17; 21; 31; 37:26; 27(3); 41:12; 42:13; 21; 32(2); 43:4; 7(2); 8; 18(2); 21(3); 22(3); 28; 44:8; 25; 26(2); 31; 46:34(2); 47:3; 18(4); 19(3); 25; **Ex** 1:10; 3:18; 5:3; 8; 21; 8:10; 26; 27; 10:9(6); 25; 26(2); 12:27; 17:3(2); 34:9(2); **Lev** 25:20; **Num** 11:6(2); 13:33; 14:3(2); 20:3; 4; 15(2); 16; 21:5; 27:3; 4(2); 31:49; 50; 32:16(2); 17; 18; 19; 26(4); 32; 36:2; 3(2); 4; **Deut** 1:6; 19; 20; 25; 28(2); 41; 2:1; 8; 29; 33; 36; 37; 3:3(2); 4:7; 5:2; 3; 24; 25; 27(2); 6:4; 20; 22; 23; 24(2); 25(2); 21:7(2); 20(2); 26:3; 7(5); 15; 29:15; 18; 29(2); 31:17; 32:3; 27; 31(2); **Josh** 2:11; 13; 14(2); 19; 20; 24; 5:13; 7:9; 9:11(2); 12(3); 13(2); 24; 17:4; 18:6; 21:2; 22:19; 24; 25; 27(5); 28(2); 29; 24:17(3); 18; 24; **Judg** 6:13; 9:3; 10:10; 11:2; 6; 8; 24; 13:23; 16:23(3); 24(4); 18:5; 19:19; 21:7; 18; 22; **Ruth** 2:20; 3:2; 4:3; **1Sa** 2:2; 4:3; 5:7; 10; 11; 7:8; 8:20(2); 9:6; 7; 8; 12:10; 19; 14:9; 10; 16:16; 17:9; 47; 20:29; 23:20; 25:14; 17; 30:23; **2Sa** 7:22; 10:12(2); 12:18; 18:12; 19:9; 41; 43(2); 22:32; **1Kin** 1:11; 43; 47; 8:21; 40; 53; 57(2); 58(2); 59; 61; 65; 12:4; 10; 20:31(2); **2Kin** 7:9; 18:22; 19:19; 22:13; **1Chr** 12:17; 19; 13:2(2); 3; 15:13; 16:14; 35; 17:20; 19:13(2); 28:2; 8; 29:10; 13; 15(2); 16; 18; **2Chr** 2:4; 5; 6:31; 10:4; 10; 13:10; 11; 12; 14:7; 11(2); 19:7; 20:6; 7; 9; 12(2); 28:13(3); 29:6(2); 9(4); 32:8(2); 11; 34:21; **Ezr** 4:3; 5:12; 7:27; 8:17; 18; 21(3); 22; 23; 25; 30; 31; 33; 9:6(3); 7(4); 8(4); 9(3); 10; 13(4); 15; 10:2; 3(2); 14(3); **Neh** 4:4; 9(2); 11; 15; 20; 23; 5:2(2); 3; 4; 5(8); 8(2); 9(2); 6:1; 16(2); 8:10; 9:9; 16; 32(6); 34(4); 36; 37(3); 38; 10:29; 30(2); 32; 33; 34(3); 35; 36(6); 37(5); 38; 39; 13:2; 4; 18; 27; **Job** 8:9; 17:16; 22:20; 28:22; 37:19; **Ps** 8:1; 9; 12:4(3); 17:11; 18:31; 20:5(2); 7; 22:4; 33:20(3); 21; 35:21; 40:3; 44:1(2); 5; 7; 9; 13; 18(2); 20(2); 24(2); 25(2); 26; 46:1; 7; 11; 47:3; 4; 6; 48:1; 8; 14(2); 50:3; 59:11; 60:10; 12; 65:3; 5; 66:8; 9(2); 11; 12; 67:6; 68:19; 20; 74:9; 77:13; 78:3; 5; 79:4; 9(2); 10; 12; 80:6(2); 81:1; 3; 84:9; 85:4; 9; 12; 89:17; 18(2); 90:1; 8(2); 9(2); 10; 12(2); 14; 17(3); 92:13; 94:23; 95:1; 6; 7; 98:3; 99:5; 8; 9(2); 103:10(2); 12; 14; 105:7; 106:6; 7; 47; 108:11; 13; 113:5; 115:3; 116:5; 118:23; 122:2; 9; 123:2(2); 4; 124:1; 2; 4; 5; 7; 8; 126:2(2); 4; 135:2; 5; 136:23; 24; 137:2; 141:7; 144:12(2); 13(3); 14(2); 147:1; 5; 7; **Prov** 1:13; 7:18; **Song** 1:16; 17(2); 2:9; 12; 15; 7:13; 8:8; **Is** 1:10; 3:6; 4:1(3); 20:6; 25:9; 26:8; 12; 13; 28:15; 33:2; 20; 22(3); 35:2; 36:7; 37:20; 38:20; 40:3; 8; 42:17; 47:4; 52:10; 53:1; 3; 4(2); 5(3); 55:7; 58:3; 59:12(4); 13; 61:2; 6; 63:16(3); 17; 18; 64:6(2); 7; 8(2); 11(4); **Jer** 3:22; 23; 24(2); 25(6); 5:19; 24; 6:24; 8:14; 9:18(2); 19; 21(2); 11:21; 12:4; 14:7(2); 20(2); 22; 16:10(3); 19; 17:12; 18:12; 20:10; 21:13; 23:6; 36; 26:16; 19; 31:6; 33:16; 35:6; 8(5); 10; 36:15; 37:3; 42:2; 6(2); 20(2); 43:2; 44:17(4); 19; 25; 46:16(2); 50:28; 51:10(2); 51; **Lam** 3:40; 41(2); 44; 46; 4:17(3); 18(5); 19; 20; 5:1; 2(2); 3; 4(2); 5; 7; 9(2); 10; 15(2); 16; 17(2); 21; **Eze** 33:10(2); 21; 37:11(3); 40:1; **Dan** 1:13; 3:17; 9:6(3); 8(3); 9; 10; 12; 13(3); 14; 15; 16(2); 17; 18(3); **Hos** 7:5; 14:2; 3(2); **Joel** 1:16(2); **Amos** 6:13; **Mic** 2:4; 4:5; 11; 5:5(2); 6(2); 7:17; 19; 20; **Zec** 1:6(2); 9:7; **Mal** 2:10; **Mt** 3:9; 6:9; 11; 12(2); 8:17(2); 20:33; 21:42; 23:30; 25:8; 27:25; **Mk** 9:40; 11:10; 12:11; 29; **Lk** 1:55; 71; 72; 73; 74; 75; 78; 79; 3:8; 7:5; 11:2; 3; 4; 13:26; 17:5; 10; 23:41; 24:20; 22; 32; **Jn** 3:11; 4:12; 20; 6:31; 7:51; 8:39; 53; 9:20; 11:11; 48; 12:38; 14:23; 19:7; **Acts** 2:8; 11; 39; 3:12; 13; 25; 5:30; 7:2; 11; 12; 15; 19(2); 38; 39; 44; 45(2); 13:17; 14:17; 15:10; 25; 26; 36; 16:20; 17:20; 28; 19:25; 27; 20:21; 21:5(2); 6; 7; 15; 22:14; 24:6; 7; 26:5; 6; 7; 27:10; 19; 28:17; 25; **Rom** 1:3; 7; 3:5; 4:1; 12; 24; 25(2); 5:1; 5; 11; 21; 6:6; 11; 23; 7:5; 25; 8:16; 23; 26; 39; 9:10; 10:16; 12:7; 13:11; 15:4; 6; 16:1; 9; 18; 20; 24; **1Cor** 1:1; 2; 3; 7; 8; 9; 10; 2:7; 4:12; 5:4(2); 7; 6:11; 9:1; 10(2); 10:1; 6; 11; 12:23; 24; 15:3; 14; 31; 57; 16:12; 23; **2Cor** 1:1; 2; 3; 4; 5; 7; 8; 11; 12(3); 18; 22; 3:2(2); 5; 4:3; 6; 10; 11; 16; 17; 5:1; 2; 12; 6:11(2); 7:3; 4; 5; 12; 14; 8:9; 22; 23; 24; 9:3; 10:4; 8; 13; 14; 15(2); 16; 11:31; **Gal** 1:3; 4(2); 2:4; 3:24; 6:14; 18; **Eph** 1:2; 3; 14; 17; 2:3(2); 14; 3:11; 14; 5:20; 6:22; 24; **Phil** 1:2; 3:20; 21; 4:20; 23; **Col** 1:1; 2; 3; 7; 3:4; **1Th** 1:1; 2; 3(2); 5; 2:1; 2; 3; 4; 8; 9; 19(2); 20; 3:2(2); 5; 7; 9; 11(3); 13(2); 5:9; 23; 28; **2Th** 1:1; 2; 8; 10; 11; 12(2); 2:1(2); 14(2); 15; 16(2); 3:6; 12; 14; 18; **1Ti** 1:1(2); 2(2); 12; 14; 2:3; 6:3; 14; **2Ti** 1:2; 8; 9; 10; 4:15; **Titus** 1:3; 4; 2:10; 13; 3:4; 6; **Philem** 1:1(2); 2(2); 3; 25; **Heb** 1:3; 3:1; 14; 4:14; 15; 7:14; 10:22(2); 23; 12:2; 9; 10; 29; 13:15; 20; 23; **Jas** 2:1; 21; 3:6; **1Pet** 1:3; 2:24; 4:3; **2Pet** 1:1; 2; 8; 11; 14; 16; 3:15(2); 18; **1Jn** 1:1(2); 3; 9(2); 2:2; 3:5; 16; 19; 20(2); 21; 4:10; 17; 5:4; **2Jn** 12; **3Jn** 12; 14; **Jude** 4(2); 17; 21; 25; **Rev** 1:5; 5:10; 6:10; 7:3; 10; 12; 11:8; 15; 12:10(3); 19:1; 5; 22:21

OURS

Gen 26:20; 31:16; 34:23; **Num** 32:32; **1Kin** 22:3; **Eze** 36:2; **Mk** 12:7; **Lk** 20:14; **1Cor** 1:2; **2Cor** 1:14; **Titus** 3:14; **1Jn** 2:2

OURSELVES

Gen 37:10; 44:16; **Num** 32:17; **Deut** 2:35; 3:7; **1Sa** 14:8; **1Chr** 19:13; **Ezr** 4:3; 8:21; **Neh** 10:32; **Job** 34:4; **Ps** 83:12; 100:3; **Prov** 7:18; **Is** 28:15; 56:12; **Jer** 50:5; **Lk** 22:71; **Jn** 4:42; **Acts** 6:4; 23:14; **Rom** 8:23(3); 15:1; **1Cor** 11:31; **2Cor** 1:4; 9(2); 3:1; 5(2); 4:2; 5(2); 5:12; 13; 6:4; 7:1; 10:12(2); 14; 12:19; **Gal** 2:17; **1Th** 2:10; **2Th** 1:4; 3:7; 9; **Titus** 3:3; **Heb** 10:25; **1Jn** 1:8

OUT

Gen 2:9; 10; 19; 23; 3:19; 24; 4:14; 16; 8:10; 19; 9:10; 10:11; 14; 12:1; 4; 13:1; 14:8; 17; 15:4; 7; 14; 17:6; 19:5; 6; 8; 12; 14(2); 24; 29; 30; 21:10; 17; 21; 22:11; 15; 23:4; 8; 24:11; 13; 15; 20; 44; 63; 25:25; 26; 26:8; 27:3; 30; 28:10; 16; 29:2; 30:16(2); 31:13; 33; 32:25; 34:1; 6; 7; 24(2); 26(2); 35:9; 11; 37:14; 21; 22; 23; 28; 38:28(2); 29; 30; 39:12; 15; 18; 40:14; 15; 17; 41:2; 3; 14; 18; 33; 45; 46; 43:2; 23; 31; 44:4; 8(2); 16; 28; 45:1; 19; 24; 25; 46:26; 47:1; 10; 30; 48:12; 14; 22; 49:20; 50:24; **Ex** 1:5; 10(2); 2:10; 11; 13; 19; 3:2; 4; 8(2); 10; 11; 12; 17; 20; 4:6; 7; 9; 5:10; 6:1; 6(3); 7; 11; 13; 26; 27; 7:2; 4; 5; 15; 19; 8:6; 12; 13(3); 16; 17; 29; 30; 9:15; 29; 33; 10:5; 6; 11; 12; 18; 21; 11:1; 4; 8(3); 10; 12:5; 15; 17; 21; 22; 33; 39(2); 41; 42; 46; 51; 13:3(3); 4; 8; 9; 14; 16; 18; 14:8; 10; 11; 16; 21; 26; 30; 15:12; 20; 22; 16:1; 4; 6; 27; 29; 17:3; 6; 9(2); 14; 18:1; 7; 9; 10(2); 21; 25; 19:1; 3; 17; 20:2(2); 21:2; 3(2); 4; 5; 7; 11; 27; 22:6; 7; 23:13; 15; 16; 28; 29; 30; 31; 24:16; 25:32(3); 33; 35; 28:35; 29:23; 46; 32:1(2); 4; 7; 8(2); 11; 12; 19; 23; 24; 27; 32; 33; 33:1; 2; 7; 8; 11; 34:11; 18; 24; 34(2); 37:7; 8; 9; 18(3); 19; 21; **Lev** 1:1; 15; 2:14; 4:12(2); 18; 25; 30; 34; 5:9; 15; 18; 6:6; 12; 13; 7:14; 35; 8:26; 33; 9:9; 23; 24; 10:2; 4; 5; 7; 14; 11:45; 13:12; 20; 25; 56(4); 14:3; 8; 38; 41; 43; 45; 53; 15:2; 16; 25; 16:17; 18; 17:3; 13; 18:24; 25; 28(2); 19:36; 20:22; 23; 21:12; 22:33; 23:17; 43; 24:10; 23; 25:12; 28; 30; 31; 33; 38; 42; 51; 54; 55; 26:6; 13; 33; 45; 27:21; **Num** 1:1; 3:9; 5:2; 3; 4; 23; 25; 6:19; 9:1; 10:12; 33; 34; 11:15; 20(2); 24; 26; 12:4(2); 12; 14; 15; 13:16; 17; 14:44; 15:41; 16:13; 14; 27; 35; 37; 46; 17:9; 18:29(2); 20:5; 8; 10; 11; 16; 18; 20; 21:5; 13; 23; 26; 28; 32(2); 33; 22:5; 6; 11(2); 23; 32; 36; 23:7; 22; 24:7; 8; 17(2); 19; 26:4; 27:17(2); 21; 28:26; 30:2; 6; 12; 31:5; 27; 28; 36; 32:11; 21; 23; 24; 33:1; 2(2); 3; 12; 38; 52; 55; 34:5; 7; 8; 9; 10; 12; 35:25; **Deut** 1:22; 24; 27; 33; 44; 2:14; 23; 26; 32; 3:1; 8; 4:12; 15; 20(2); 33; 34; 36(2); 37(2); 38; 45; 46; 5:4; 6; 15(2); 22; 23; 24; 26; 6:12; 19; 21; 23; 7:1; 8(2); 19(2); 22; 8:3; 7; 9; 14; 15; 9:3; 4(2); 5; 7; 10; 12(2); 14; 16; 17; 21; 26; 28(2); 29(2); 10:4; 11:2; 10; 23; 28; 12:3; 5; 27; 13:5(3); 10; 13; 15:11; 13; 14(3); 16:1; 3(2); 6; 17:18; 18:5; 6; 12; 20:1(2); 21:19; 22:21; 24; 23:4; 10; 23; 24:1; 2; 3; 5; 9; 11; 25:4; 6; 11; 17; 19; 26:4; 8; 13; 27:18; 28:6; 7; 19; 25; 38; 57; 29:7; 20; 21; 25; 28; 30:4; 31:2; 21; 32:13(2); 39; 33:18; 27; **Josh** 1:8; 2:1; 2; 3; 5; 7; 10; 19; 3:10; 12(2); 4:2(2); 3(2); 4; 8; 16; 17; 18; 19; 20; 5:4(2); 5(2); 6; 6:1; 10; 22(2); 23(2); 25; 7:23(2); 8:3; 5; 6; 14; 17; 18(2); 19(2); 22; 26; 9:12; 26; 10:22(2); 23; 24; 11:4; 13:6; 12; 14:7; 11; 12; 15:3; 4(2); 7; 9; 11(3); 63; 16:2; 3; 6; 7; 8(2); 10; 17:12; 13; 18; 18:4; 12; 14; 15(2); 19:9; 12; 13; 17; 24; 27; 32; 34; 40; 47; 20:2; 8(3); 21:3; 4(4); 5(3); 6(4); 7(3); 9(2); 16; 17; 20; 23; 25; 27; 28; 30; 32; 34; 36; 38; 22:9; 31; 32; 23:5; 9; 13; 24:5; 6; 10; 12; 17; 18; 32; **Judg** 1:16; 19(2); 21; 24; 27; 28; 29; 30; 31; 32; 33; 2:1; 3; 12; 15; 16; 17; 18; 21; 23; 3:10; 19; 20; 22(2); 24; 4:6; 14; 18; 22; 5:4(2); 14(3); 28; 6:8; 9(3); 19; 20; 21(2); 30; 38; 7:23(3); 8:34; 9:4; 15; 17; 20(2); 27; 29; 33; 35; 38; 39; 41; 42; 43; 10:12; 11:2; 3; 5; 7; 13; 24; 34; 36; 12:2; 13:5; 14:9; 12; 14(2); 18; 15:17; 16:14; 20(2); 21; 25; 17:7; 8; 18:2; 11(2); 14; 17; 19:1; 16; 23; 24; 27; 30; 20:1; 10; 14(2); 15; 20; 21; 25; 28; 31; 33(3); 34; 38; 40; 42; 21:16; 17; 21(2); 24; **Ruth** 1:7; 13; 21; 22; 2:6; 17; 22; 4:3; **1Sa** 1:3; 15; 16; 2:3; 5; 8; 10; 28; 3:3; 4:1; 3(2); 8; 12; 13; 16(2); 5:10; 7:3; 6; 8; 11; 14; 8:8; 18; 20; 9:11; 14; 16(2); 26; 10:18(3); 19; 11:2; 3; 5; 7; 10; 12:6; 8; 10; 11; 13:10; 17; 23; 14:11; 48; 15:6; 16:16; 17:4(2); 8; 23; 34; 35(2); 37(3); 40; 51; 18:5; 6; 11; 13; 16; 19:3; 8; 10; 20:11(2); 21; 35; 36; 41; 21:5; 23:13; 15; 23; 24:2; 7; 8; 14; 15; 21; 25:5; 14; 29(2); 37; 26:4; 19; 20; 24; 27:1; 28:1; 3; 9; 13; 17; 29:6; 30:16(2); **2Sa** 1:2; 3; 2:12; 13; 23; 3:18(2); 25; 26; 4:4; 9; 5:2; 13; 24; 6:3; 4; 20; 7:6; 9; 12; 8:1; 9:5; 10:3; 8; 16; 11:8; 13; 17; 23; 12:7; 11; 13:9(3); 17; 18; 14:16(2); 15:11; 24; 35; 16:5; 7(2); 17:1; 21; 18:3; 4; 6; 19:9(3); 19; 20:7(2); 8; 10; 12; 13; 16; 22; 21:10; 17; 22:1(2); 7; 9(2); 15; 17; 46; 23:4; 16(2); 21; 29; 24:4; 7; 16; 20; **1Kin** 1:29; 39; 2:27; 37; 42; 46; 3:7; 4:23; 33; 5:6; 13; 6:1; 8; 7:13; 47; 8:1; 8(2); 9; 10; 16(2); 19; 21; 41; 42; 44; 51; 53; 9:7(2); 9; 12; 24; 10:28; 29(2); 11:12; 18(2); 29; 31; 32; 34; 35; 12:25; 28; 13:1; 3; 5; 14:15; 21; 24; 15:12; 17; 16:2; 17:19; 23; 18:28; 44; 19:13; 20:16; 17(3); 18(2); 19; 21; 24; 31; 39; 42; 21:10; 13; 26; 22:3; 32; 34; 35; 46; **2Kin** 2:23; 24; 3:6; 4:4; 5; 18; 21; 37; 39; 40(2); 41; 5:2(2); 11; 27; 6:7; 27(2); 7:12(2); 16; 20; 8:3; 9:2; 15; 19; 21(2); 24; 30; 32; 10:3; 9; 25; 26; 28; 11:8; 9; 12:11; 12; 13:5; 25(2); 14:27; 16:3; 7(2); 17:7; 8; 18; 20; 23(2); 36(2); 39; 18:18; 29; 31; 33; 34; 35(2); 19:9; 19; 27; 31(2); 35; 20:4; 6; 21:2; 7; 8; 15; 23:4; 6; 8; 16; 18; 27; 24:3; 7; 12; 13; 20; 25:7; 19; 21; 27; **1Chr** 5:18; 6:60; 61(2); 62(4); 63(3); 65(3); 66; 70; 71; 72; 74; 76; 77; 78; 80; 7:11; 9:28; 11:2; 18(2); 23; 12:2; 17; 13:7; 14:8; 15; 17; 15:25; 29; 16:33; 17:21(2); 18:1; 19:3; 6(3); 9; 10; 20:1; 2; 3; 21:16; 21; 26:14; 27; 27:1; 28:18; **2Chr** 1:10; 16; 17(2); 2:2; 8; 14; 16; 4:18; 5:2; 9; 10; 11; 6:5; 9; 32; 34; 7:20(2); 22; 8:11; 9:28(2); 10:2; 11:13; 16; 12:3; 7; 13; 13:9; 14:5; 8(2); 9; 10; 15:2; 5; 8(2); 9(3); 17; 16:1; 2(2); 7; 17:6; 18:20; 21(2); 31; 33; 19:2; 3; 4; 20:4; 7; 10; 11; 17; 21; 21:15; 19; 22:7; 23:2; 7; 8; 11; 14; 24:5; 6(2); 25:6; 10; 15; 26:11; 18; 20(2); 28:3; 9; 21(2); 29:5; 7; 16(2); 30:6; 25(2); 31:1(2); 32:11; 13; 14(2); 15(3); 17(2); 33:2; 8; 15(2); 34:14; 21; 25; 33; 35:20; 24; **Ezr** 1:7; 2:1; 3:8; 5:14(2); 6:4; 5; 21; 7:20; 28; 8:35; 9:5; 10:1; **Neh** 1:9; 2:13; 3:25; 26; 27; 4:2; 5; 5:13(2); 6:8; 7:6; 8:17; 9:7; 15; 18; 27; 12:27; 28; 29; 44; 13:8; 14; **Est** 2:9; 13; 23; 3:15; 4:1; 11; 5:2; 7:8(2); 8:4; 14; 15; 9:4; **Job** 1:17; 21; 3:11; 24; 5:5; 6; 6:17; 8:10; 19; 9:6; 8; 10; 14; 10:7; 10; 18; 11:7(2); 13; 12:15; 22(2); 13:9; 14:4; 12; 18; 19; 15:13; 22; 25; 30; 16:13; 20; 18:4; 5; 6; 14; 18; 19:7; 20:15; 25(2); 21:17; 22:16; 24:4; 12(2); 24; 26:7; 27:21; 22; 23; 28:2(2); 3; 4; 5; 10; 27; 29:6; 7; 16; 17; 19; 25; 30:16; 24; 31:7; 8; 12; 34; 32:11; 13; 33:6; 21; 35:9; 36:16; 26; 37:1; 2; 9(2); 18; 22; 23; 38:1; 8; 13; 29; 39:3; 5; 40:6; 41:1; 19(2); 20(2); 21; **Ps** 3:4; 5:10; 8:2; 9:5; 10:5; 15; 16; 14:7; 15:5; 17:1; 18:6; 8(2); 14(2); 16; 42; 45; 19:4; 5; 20:2; 21:8(2); 22:7; 9; 14(2); 25:15; 17; 22; 27:12; 31:4; 12; 34:6; 17; 19; 35:3; 37:14; 40:2(2); 42:4; 43:3; 44:2(2); 20; 21; 45:8; 50:2; 9(2); 51:1; 9; 52:5(2); 53:6; 54:7; 55:23; 58:6; 59:7; 60:6; 8; 10; 62:8; 64:6; 66:12; 68:6; 31(2); 33; 35; 69:14(2); 24; 28; 71:4(2); 6; 73:7; 10; 74:11; 75:8(2); 77:17(2); 78:15; 16; 20; 55; 65; 79:6; 80:8(2); 11; 13; 81:5; 10; 16; 82:4; 5; 84:2; 85:5; 11; 88:9; 89:19; 34; 94:12; 97:10; 102:t; 104:2; 14; 35; 105:41; 107:3; 6; 13; 14; 19; 28; 108:7; 9; 109:10; 13; 14; 110:2; 111:2; 113:7(2); 114:1; 118:26; 119:10; 43; 121:8; 124:7; 128:5; 130:1; 132:5; 134:3; 135:7; 21; 136:6; 11; 12; 142:2; 7; 143:11; 144:6; 7; 14; 147:18; **Prov** 1:23; 24; 2:6; 22; 3:10; 4:23; 5:15(2); 6:9; 8:12; 9:1; 10:31; 11:8; 12:13; 13:9; 15:2; 28; 17:14; 23; 20:5; 20; 21:16; 22:10(2); 24:20; 25:1; 2; 19; 26:20; 28:11; 30:17; 31:18; 20; **Eccl** 1:13; 3:11; 4:14; 7:24; 25; 27; 29; 8:3; 17(2); 12:3; 9; 10; **Song** 3:6; 4:16; 8:11; **Is** 2:3; 5:2; 25; 8:8; 9:12; 17; 21; 10:4; 11:1(2); 16; 12:3; 6; 13:9; 13; 14:19; 26; 27; 29; 15:4; 5; 16:2; 4; 8; 10(2); 18:2; 7; 19:23; 21:11; 22:16(2); 23:11; 24:18; 26:16; 17; 19; 21; 28:7(2); 27; 29:4(4); 9; 10; 18(2); 30:11(2); 13; 14; 31:3; 34:3(2); 11; 16; 35:6; 36:16; 18; 19; 20(2); 37:28; 32(2); 38:6; 40:12; 22(2); 26; 42:5(2); 7(2); 43:13; 25; 44:13(3); 22; 45:12; 23; 46:6; 7; 48:1; 3; 21(2); 51:17; 22; 52:11(2); 12; 53:2; 8; 12; 55:11; 12; 57:4; 14; 58:7; 10; 59:5; 21(3); 62:10; 12; 63:11; 65:2; 9(2); 66:5; 11; 20; **Jer** 1:5; 10; 14; 2:6; 13; 3:18; 4:1; 16; 5:6(2); 6:1(2); 4; 7(2); 11; 12; 7:15(2); 18; 20; 22; 25; 8:1(2); 9:8; 18; 19(2); 10:3; 12; 13; 17; 18; 22; 25; 11:4; 7; 12:3; 8; 14(2); 15; 14:16; 15:1; 6; 21(2); 16:9; 13; 14; 16; 17:8; 16; 19; 22; 18:21; 23; 19:13; 20:3; 8; 18; 21:9; 12(2); 22:3; 11; 14; 26; 28; 23:3; 7; 8; 16; 39; 24:5; 26:23; 27:10; 15; 30:7; 19; 31:32; 37; 32:4; 17; 21(2); 29; 37; 34:3; 13(2); 36:6; 11; 21; 30; 37:4; 5; 12; 17; 21; 38:8; 10; 13; 18; 23(2); 39:4(2); 7; 14; 40:12; 44:7; 17(2); 18; 19(2); 25; 28; 46:20; 47:2; 48:15; 31; 44; 45; 49:5; 20; 50:3; 8(2); 28; 45; 51:6; 15; 16; 25; 34; 44; 45; 55; 52:3; 7; 11; 25; 27; 31; **Lam** 1:10; 2:4; 8; 12; 19(2); 3:7; 8; 38; 55; 4:1; 3; 11; 5:8; **Eze** 1:4(3); 5; 13; 3:25; 4:12; 5:2; 12; 6:14; 7:8; 9:8; 10:7; 19; 11:7; 9; 17; 19; 12:5; 12; 14; 13:2; 17; 21; 23; 14:9; 13; 19; 15:7; 16:5; 15; 27; 36; 19:14; 20:8; 9; 10; 13; 14; 21; 28; 33(2); 34(4); 38(2); 41(2); 21:3; 4; 5; 19; 31; 22:15; 22; 31; 23:26; 34; 48; 24:6(2); 12; 25:7(2); 13; 16; 27:6; 33; 28:16; 29:4; 8; 30:13; 22; 25; 31:4; 11; 32:3; 7; 21; 33:21; 34:11; 12(3); 13; 25; 27; 35:3; 7; 11; 36:5; 20; 24; 26; 37:1; 12; 13; 23; 38:8(2); 12; 15; 39:3(2); 10(2); 14; 27; 29; 42:11; 14; 43:6; 11; 23; 25; 44:3; 45:14; 15(3); 46:9; 18(2); 20; 47:1; 2(2); 8; 12; 48:19; 30; **Dan** 2:34; 45; 3:15; 17; 5:2; 3; 13; 6:23(2); 7:17; 24; 25; 8:4; 7; 9; 22; 9:15; 11:7; 41; 44(2); **Hos** 1:11; 2:2; 10; 15; 17; 18; 4:2; 5:10; 7:5; 9:15; 10:11; 11:1; 11(2); 12:8; 13; 13:3(2); **Joel** 2:16; 28; 29; 3:7; 16; **Amos** 3:4; 12(2); 4:3; 11; 5:3; 6; 8; 6:4(2); 10(2); 7:11; 8:8; 9:3; 6; 7; 15; **Obad** 6; 8(2); **Jonah** 1:4; 2:1; 2; 4; 10; 4:5; **Mic** 1:3; 2:9; 13; 4:6; 9; 10; 5:2; 10; 12; 13; 14; 6:4(2); 7:2; 15; 17; **Nah** 1:6; 11; 14; 2:2; 9; **Hab** 1:2; 2:11(2); 3:4; 13; 14; **Zeph** 1:4; 17; 2:4; 13; 3:11; 15; 19; **Hag** 2:5; 16(2); **Zec** 1:21; 2:3; 13; 3:2; 4:1; 12; 5:9; 6:1; 12; 8:10; 23; 9:4; 7; 11; 10:4(4); 10(2); 11:6; 13:2(2); 14:8; **Mal** 2:8; 12; 13; 3:10; **Mt** 2:6; 15; 3:5; 16; 4:4; 5:13; 26; 29; 7:4(2); 5(4); 22; 8:12; 16; 28; 29; 31; 32; 34(2); 9:17; 32; 33; 34; 10:1; 8; 14; 11:7; 8; 9; 12:11; 14; 24; 26; 27(2); 28; 34; 35(2); 43; 44; 13:1; 41; 52; 14:13; 26; 29; 35; 15:11; 17; 18; 19; 22; 17:5; 18; 19; 21; 18:9; 28; 20:1; 3; 5; 6; 30; 21:12; 16; 17; 33; 39; 41; 22:10; 16; 24:1; 17; 27; 25:6; 8; 26:30; 51; 55; 71; 75; 27:23; 32; 53; 60; **Mk** 1:5; 10; 23; 25; 26; 29; 34; 35; 39; 45; 3:5; 15; 21; 22; 23; 4:3; 32; 5:2(2); 8; 10; 13; 14; 17; 30; 40; 6:1; 12; 13; 33; 34; 49; 54; 7:15; 19; 20; 21; 26; 29; 30; 8:23; 27; 9:7; 18; 24; 25; 26; 28; 38; 47; 10:26; 46; 47; 11:11; 15; 19; 12:1; 8; 13:1; 15; 14:26; 48; 68; 15:13; 14; 20; 21; 39; 46; 16:8; 9; 17; **Lk** 1:22; 42; 74; 2:1; 4; 4:14; 22; 29; 33; 35(2); 36; 37; 38; 41(2); 5:2; 3(2); 4; 17; 36; 6:12; 17; 19; 22; 42(4); 45(2); 7:12; 24; 25; 26; 8:2; 4; 5; 12; 27; 28; 29; 31; 33; 35(2); 38; 46; 54; 9:5; 35; 38; 39; 40; 49; 10:10; 35; 11:14(2); 15; 18; 19(2); 20; 24(2); 54; 12:54; 13:28; 31; 32; 33; 14:5; 7; 21; 23; 35; 15:28; 16:4; 17:24; 29; 19:22; 40; 45; 20:12; 15; 21:21; 37; 22:39; 52; 62; 23:18; 26; 24:31; 50; **Jn** 1:46; 2:8; 15(2); 4:30; 47; 54; 6:37; 7:38; 41; 42; 52; 8:9; 59; 9:22; 34; 35; 10:3; 9; 28; 29; 39; 11:11; 31; 55; 12:17; 31; 34; 42; 13:1; 30; 31; 15:19; 16:2; 27; 17:6; 8; 15; 18:16; 29; 38; 19:6; 12; 15; 34; 20:2; **Acts** 1:9; 18; 21; 2:5; 17; 18; 3:19; 4:15; 5:6; 9; 16; 6:3; 7:3; 4; 10; 12; 19; 21; 36; 40; 45; 57; 58; 8:7; 9; 39; 9:1; 28; 10:45; 12:9; 10; 11; 17; 13:17; 42; 50; 14:14; 19; 15:14; 24; 16:13; 18(2); 27(2); 30; 37(2); 39(2); 40; 17:2; 5; 19:12; 16; 28; 33; 34; 21:5; 28; 30; 38; 22:18; 23; 23:6; 24:7; 27:19; 29; 30(2); 38; 42; 28:3; 21; 23(2); **Rom** 2:18; 3:12; 11:24; 26; 33; 13:11; **1Cor** 5:7; 10; 9:9; 14:36; 15:8; **2Cor** 1:8; 16; 2:4; 4:6; 6:17; 8:11; 12:2; 3; **Gal** 2:4; 4:15; 30; **Eph** 4:29; **Phil** 1:12; 2:12; **Col** 2:14(2); 3:8; **1Th** 1:8; **2Th** 2:7; **1Ti** 1:5; 5:18; 6:7; **2Ti** 1:17; 2:22; 26; 3:11; 4:2; 17; **Heb** 3:16; 5:2; 7:5; 14; 8:9; 11:8(2); 15; 34; 12:13; **Jas** 2:25; 3:10; 13; **1Pet** 2:9; **2Pet** 2:9; 3:5; **1Jn** 2:19(2); 4:1; 18; **3Jn** 10; **Jude** 5; 13; 23; **Rev** 1:16; 2:5; 3:5(2); 12(2); 16; 4:5; 5:7; 9; 6:4; 14; 7:14; 8:4; 9:2; 3; 17; 18; 10:10; 11:2; 5; 7; 12:9(3); 15; 16; 13:1; 11; 14:10; 15; 17; 18; 20; 15:6; 16:1(2); 2; 3; 4; 7; 8; 10; 12; 13(3); 17(2); 21; 17:8; 18:4; 19:5; 15; 21; 20:7; 8; 9; 12; 21:2; 3; 10; 22:1; 19(2)

OUTSIDE

Judg 7:11; 17; 19; **1Kin** 7:9; **Eze** 40:5; **Mt** 23:25; 26; **Lk** 11:39

OVER

Gen 1:18(2); 26(5); 28(3); 3:16; 4:7; 8:1; 9:14; 21:16(2); 24:2; 25:25; 27:29; 31:21; 52(2); 32:10; 16; 21; 22; 23(2); 31; 33:3; 14; 36:31; 37:8(2); 39:4; 5; 41:33; 34; 40; 41; 43; 45; 56; 42:6; 45:26; 47:6; 20; 26; 49:22; **Ex** 1:8; 11; 2:14; 5:14; 8:5(3); 6; 9; 10:12; 13; 14; 21; 12:13; 23; 27; 14:2; 7; 16; 21; 26; 27; 15:16(2); 16:18; 23; 18:21; 25; 25:27; 37; 26:12; 13; 35; 28:27; 30:6; 36:14; 37:9; 14; 39:20; 40:19; 24; 36; **Lev** 14:5; 6; 50; 16:21; 25:43; 46(2); 53; 26:16; 17; **Num** 1:50(3); 3:32; 49; 4:6; 5:30; 7:2; 8:2; 3; 10:10(2); 14; 15; 16; 18; 19; 20; 22; 23; 24; 25; 26; 27; 11:16; 14:14; 16:13; 22:5; 25:15; 27:16; 31:14(2); 48; 32:5; 7; 21; 27; 29; 30; 32; 33:51; 35:10; **Deut** 1:1; 13; 15(5); 2:13(2); 14; 18; 19; 24; 29; 3:18; 25; 27; 28; 29; 4:14; 21; 22(2); 26; 46; 9:1; 3; 11:30; 31; 12:10; 15:6(2); 17:14; 15(3); 21:6; 24:20; 27:2; 3; 4; 12; 28:23; 36; 63(2); 30:9(2); 13; 18; 31:2; 3(2); 13; 15; 32:11; 47; 49; 34:1; 4; 6; **Josh** 1:2; 11; 2:23; 3:1; 6; 11; 14; 16; 17(2); 4:1; 3; 5; 7; 8; 10; 11(2); 12; 13; 18; 22; 23(2); 5:1; 13; 7:7; 26; 8:31; 33(2); 9:1; 18:13; 17; 18; 22:11; 19; 24:11; **Judg** 3:28; 5:13(2); 6:33; 8:4; 22; 23(3); 9:2(2); 8(2); 9; 10; 11; 12; 13; 14; 15; 18; 22; 26; 10:9; 18; 11:8; 11; 29(3); 32; 12:1; 3; 5; 14:4; 15:11; 19:10; 12; 20:43; **Ruth** 2:5; 6; 3:9; **1Sa** 2:1; 8:1; 7; 9; 11; 12(2); 19; 9:16; 17; 10:1; 19; 11:12; 12:1; 12; 13; 14; 13:1; 7; 14; 14:1; 4; 5(2); 6; 8; 23; 47; 15:1(2); 7; 17; 26; 35; 16:1; 17:50; 18:5; 13; 19:20; 22:2; 9; 23:17; 25:30; 26:13; 22; 27:2; 30:10; **2Sa** 1:17(2); 24; 2:4; 7; 8; 9(6); 10; 11; 15; 29; 3:10(2); 17; 21; 33; 34; 4:12; 5:2(2); 3; 5(2); 12; 17; 23; 6:21(2); 7:8(2); 11; 26; 8:15; 16; 18; 10:17; 12:7; 15:22(2); 23(3); 16:9; 13; 17:16; 19; 20; 21; 22(2); 24; 18:1; 8; 24; 33; 19:10; 15; 17; 18(3); 22; 31(2); 33; 36; 37; 38; 39(2); 41; 20:21; 23(3); 24; 22:30; 23:3; 23; 24:5; **1Kin** 1:34; 35(2); 2:11; 35; 37; 4:1; 4; 5; 6(2); 7; 21; 24(2); 5:7; 14; 16(2); 6:1; 7:20; 39; 8:7; 16; 9:23(2); 11:24; 25; 28; 37; 42; 12:17; 18; 20; 13:30; 14:2; 7; 14; 15:1; 9; 25(2); 33; 16:2; 8; 16; 18; 23; 29(2); 19:15; 16; 20:29; 22:31; 41; 51(2); **2Kin** 2:8; 9; 14; 3:1; 5:11; 8:13; 20; 21; 9:3; 6(2); 12; 29; 10:5(2); 22; 36; 11:3; 4; 9; 10; 18; 19; 13:1; 10; 14; 15:5; 8; 17; 23; 27; 17:1; 18:18; 37; 19:2; 21:13; 25:19; 22; **1Chr** 1:43; 5:11; 6:31; 8:32; 9:19(2); 20; 26; 31; 32; 38; 11:2; 3; 25; 12:4; 14(2); 15; 38; 14:2; 8; 14; 15:25; 17:7; 10; 18:14; 15; 17; 19:17; 21:16; 22:10; 23:1; 24:31(2); 26:20(2); 22; 26(2); 29; 32; 27:2; 4; 16; 25(2); 26; 27(2); 28(2); 29(2); 30(2); 31; 28:1(3); 4(2); 5; 29:3; 12; 26; 27; 30(3); **2Chr** 1:9; 11; 13; 2:11; 4:10; 5:8; 6:5; 6; 36; 8:10; 9:8; 26; 30; 10:17; 18; 13:1; 5; 19:11; 20:6; 27; 31; 22:12; 23:14; 25:5(2); 26:21; 31:12; 14; 32:6; 11; 34:13; 36:4; 10; **Ezr** 4:10; 20(2); 9:6; **Neh** 2:7; 3:10; 16; 19; 23; 25; 26; 27; 28; 29; 30; 31; 5:15; 7:2; 3; 9:28; 37(3); 11:9; 21; 22; 12:8; 9; 24(2); 37; 38; 44; 13:13; 26; **Est** 1:1; 3:12; 5:1(2); 8:2; 9:1(2); **Job** 6:5; 7:12; 14:16; 16:11; 26:7; 34:13; 41:34; 42:11; **Ps** 8:6; 12:4; 13:2; 18:29; 19:13; 23:5; 25:2; 27:12; 30:1; 35:19; 24; 38:4; 16; 41:11; 42:7; 47:2; 8; 49:14; 60:8; 65:13; 66:12; 68:34; 78:50; 62; 83:18; 88:16; 91:11; 103:16; 19; 104:9; 106:41; 108:9(2); 109:6; 110:6; 118:18; 119:133; 124:4; 5; 145:9; **Prov** 17:2; 19:10; 11; 20:26; 22:7; 24:31; 25:28; 28:15; **Eccl** 1:12; 2:19; 7:14; 16(2); 17; 8:8; 9; **Song** 2:4; 11; **Is** 3:4; 12; 8:7(2); 8; 10:29; 11:15(2); 14:2; 15:2(2); 16:8; 19:4(2); 16; 22:15; 23:2; 6; 11; 12; 25:7(2); 26:13; 28:19; 31:5; 9; 35:8; 36:3; 22; 37:2; 40:19; 27; 41:2; 45:14(2); 47:2; 51:10; 23(2); 52:5; 54:9; 62:5(2); 63:19; **Jer** 1:10(2); 2:10; 5:6; 22; 6:17; 13:21; 15:3; 23:4; 31:28(2); 39; 32:41; 33:26; 40:5; 11; 41:2; 10; 43:10; 44:27; 48:32; 40; 49:19; 22; 50:44; **Lam** 2:17; 3:54; 5:8; **Eze** 1:20; 21; 22; 25; 26; 3:13; 9:1; 10:1; 2; 4; 18; 19; 11:22; 16:8; 27; 19:8; 20:33; 27:32; 29:15; 32:3; 8; 31; 34:23; 37:24; 40:18; 23; 41:6; 15; 16; 42:1; 3(2); 7; 10(2); 45:6; 7; 46:9; 47:5(2); 20; 48:13; 15; 18(2); 21(3); **Dan** 1:11; 2:38; 39; 48(2); 49; 3:12; 4:16; 17; 23; 25; 32; 5:5; 21; 6:1(2); 2; 3; 9:1; 11:39; 40; 43(2); **Hos** 10:5; 11; 12:4; **Joel** 2:17; **Obad** 12; **Jonah** 2:3; 4:6(2); **Mic** 3:6(2); 4:7; **Nah** 3:19; **Hab** 1:11; 14; 2:19; **Zeph** 3:17(2); **Hag** 1:10; **Zec** 1:21; 5:3; 9:14; 14:9; **Mt** 2:9; 9:1; 10:23; 14:34; 20:25; 21:2; 24:45; 47; 25:21(2); 23(2); 27:37; 45; 61; **Mk** 4:35; 5:1; 21; 6:7; 53; 10:42(2); 11:2; 12:41; 13:3; 15:26; 33; 39; **Lk** 1:33; 2:8; 4:10; 39; 6:38; 8:22; 26; 9:1; 10:19; 11:42; 44; 12:14; 42; 44; 15:7(2); 10; 19:14; 17; 19; 27; 30; 41; 22:25; 23:38; 44; **Jn** 6:1; 13; 17; 17:2; 18:1; **Acts** 6:3; 7:10; 11; 16; 27; 8:2; 16:9; 18:23; 19:13; 20:2; 15; 28; 21:2; 27:5; 7(2); **Rom** 1:28; 5:14; 6:9; 14; 7:1; 9:5; 21; 10:12; 15:12; **1Cor** 7:37; 9:12; **2Cor** 1:24; 3:13; 8:15; 11:2; **Eph** 1:22; 4:19; **Col** 2:15; **1Th** 3:7; 5:12; **1Ti** 2:12; **Heb** 2:7; 3:6; 9:5; 10:21; 13:7; 17; 24; **Jas** 5:14; **1Pet** 3:12; 5:3; **Jude** 7; **Rev** 2:26; 6:8; 9:11; 11:6; 10; 13:7; 14:18; 15:2(4); 16:9; 17:18; 18:11; 20

PART

Gen 41:34; 47:24; 26; **Ex** 16:36; 19:17; 29:26; 40(2); **Lev** 1:16; 2:6; 16(2); 5:11; 16; 6:5; 20; 7:33; 8:29; 11:35; 37; 38; 13:41; 22:14; 23:13; 27:13; 15; 16; 19; 27; 31; **Num** 5:7; 15; 15:4; 5; 6; 7; 18:20(2); 26; 29; 22:41; 23:10; 13; 28:5(2); 7; 14(2); **Deut** 10:9; 12:12; 14:27; 29; 18:1; 33:21; **Josh** 14:4; 15:1; 5; 13; 18:7; 19:9; 22:25; 27; **Ruth** 1:17; 2:3; 3:13(4); **1Sa** 9:8; 14:2; 23:20; 30:24(3); **2Sa** 14:6; 18:2(3); 20:1; **1Kin** 6:24(2); 31; 33; **2Kin** 6:25; 7:5; 8; 11:5; 6(2); 18:23; **1Chr** 12:29; **2Chr** 23:4; 5(2); 29:16; **Neh** 1:9; 3:9; 12; 14; 15; 16; 17(2); 18; 5:11; 9:3(2); 10:32; **Job** 32:17; 41:6; **Ps** 5:9; 22:18; 51:6; 118:7; **Prov** 8:26; 31; 17:2; **Is** 7:18; 24:16; 36:8; 44:16(2); 19; **Eze** 4:11; 5:2(3); 12(3); 39:2; 45:11(2); 13(2); 14; 17; 46:14(2); **Dan** 1:2; 2:33(2); 41(2); 42(2); 5:5; 24; 11:31; **Joel** 2:20; **Amos** 7:4; **Zec** 13:9; **Mk** 4:38; 9:40; 13:27(2); **Lk** 10:42; 11:36; 39; 17:24(2); **Jn** 13:8; 19:23; **Acts** 1:8; 17; 25; 5:2(2); 3; 8:21; 14:4(2); 16:12; 19:32; 23:6; 9; 27:12; 41; **Rom** 11:25; **1Cor** 12:24; 13:9(2); 10; 12; 15:6; 16:17; **2Cor** 1:14; 2:5; 6:15; **Eph** 4:16; **Titus** 2:8; **Heb** 2:14; 7:2; **1Pet** 4:14(2); **Rev** 6:8; 8:7; 8; 9(2); 10; 11; 12(5); 9:15; 18; 11:13; 12:4; 20:6; 21:8; 22:19

PARTS

Gen 47:24; **Ex** 33:23; **Lev** 1:8; 22:23; **Num** 10:5; 11:1; 31:27; **Deut** 19:3; 30:4; **Josh** 18:5; 6; 9; **1Sa** 5:9; **2Sa** 19:43; **1Kin** 6:38; 7:25; 16:21; **2Kin** 11:7; **2Chr** 4:4; **Neh** 11:1; **Job** 26:14; 38:36; 41:12; **Ps** 2:8; 51:6; 63:9; 65:8; 78:66; 136:13; 139:9; 15; **Prov** 18:8; 20:27; 30; 26:22; **Is** 3:17; 16:11; 44:23; **Jer** 31:33; 34:18; 19; **Eze** 26:20; 31:14; 16; 18; 32:18; 24; 37:11; 38:15; 39:2; 48:8; **Zec** 13:8; **Mt** 2:22; 12:42; **Mk** 8:10; **Lk** 11:31; **Jn** 19:23; **Acts** 2:10; 20:2; **Rom** 15:23; **1Cor** 12:23; 24; **Eph** 4:9; **Rev** 16:19

PEOPLE'S

Lev 9:15; **Eze** 46:18; **Mt** 13:15; **Heb** 7:27

PEOPLES

Rev 10:11; 17:15

PERHAPS

Acts 8:22; **2Cor** 2:7; **Philem** 1:15

RATHER

Josh 22:24; **2Sa** 10:3; **2Kin** 5:13; **Job** 7:15; 32:2; 36:21; **Ps** 52:3; 84:10; **Prov** 8:10; 16:16; 17:12; 22:1(2); **Jer** 8:3; **Mt** 10:6; 28; 18:8; 9; 25:9; 27:24; **Mk** 5:26; 15:11; **Lk** 10:20; 11:28; 41; 12:31; 51; 17:8; 18:14; **Jn** 3:19; **Acts** 5:29; **Rom** 3:8; 8:34; 11:11; 12:19; 14:13; **1Cor** 5:2; 6:7(2); 7:21; 9:12; 14:1; 5; 19; **2Cor** 2:7; 3:8; 5:8; 12:9; **Gal** 4:9; **Eph** 4:28; 5:4; 11; **Phil** 1:12; **1Ti** 1:4; 4:7; 6:2; **Philem** 1:9; **Heb** 11:25; 12:9; 13; 13:19; **2Pet** 1:10

REACH

Gen 11:4; **Ex** 26:28; 28:42; **Lev** 26:5(2); **Num** 34:11; 35:4; **Job** 20:6; **Is** 8:8; 30:28; **Jer** 48:32; **Zec** 14:5; **Jn** 20:27(2); **2Cor** 10:13

REACHED

Gen 28:12; **Josh** 19:11(2); **Ruth** 2:14; **Dan** 4:11; 20; **2Cor** 10:14; **Rev** 18:5

REACHETH

Num 21:30; **Josh** 19:22; 26; 27; 34(2); **2Chr** 28:9; **Ps** 36:5; 108:4; **Prov** 31:20; **Jer** 4:10; 18; 51:9; **Dan** 4:22

REACHING

2Chr 3:11(2); 12; **Phil** 3:13

SEEMED

Gen 19:14; 29:20; **2Sa** 3:19(2); **Eccl** 9:13; **Jer** 18:4; 27:5; **Mt** 11:26; **Lk** 1:3; 10:21; 24:11; **Acts** 15:25; 28; **Gal** 2:6(2); 9

SEEMLY

Prov 19:10; 26:1

SELF

Ex 32:13; **Jn** 5:30; 17:5; **1Cor** 4:3; **Philem** 1:19; **1Pet** 2:24

SEVERAL

Num 28:13; 21; 29; 29:10; 15; **2Kin** 15:5; **2Chr** 11:12; 26:21; 28:25; 31:19; **Mt** 25:15; **Rev** 21:21

SHALL

Gen 1:29; 2:23; 24(3); 3:1; 3(2); 4; 5(2); 15; 16(2); 18; 4:7; 12; 14(4); 15; 24; 5:29; 6:3(2); 15; 17; 19; 20; 21; 8:22; 9:2; 3; 4; 6; 11(2); 13; 14(2); 15; 16; 25; 26; 27(3); 12:3; 12(3); 13; 13:16; 15:4(3); 5; 8(2); 13(3); 14(2); 16; 16:10; 12; 17:5(2); 6; 10(2); 11(2); 12; 13; 14; 15; 16(2); 17(2); 19; 20; 21; 18:5; 10; 12; 13; 14; 17; 18(2); 19; 25; 28; 29; 30; 31; 32; 19:2; 20; 20:7; 13; 21:10; 12; 22:14; 17; 18; 23:6; 9; 24:7; 14(3); 43; 55; 25:23(3); 32; 26:2; 4; 11; 22; 27:12(2); 33; 37; 39; 40; 46; 28:14(2); 21; 22; 29:15; 30:3; 15; 24; 30; 31; 32; 33(3); 31:8(2); 32:4; 8; 19; 28; 34:10(2); 11; 12; 23; 30(2); 35:10(2); 11(2); 37:10; 20; 30; 38:18; 40:13; 14; 19(3); 41:16; 27; 30(3); 31(2); 36(2); 40; 44; 42:15(2); 16; 20(2); 33; 34(2); 38(2); 43:3; 5; 16; 44:10(2); 16(3); 17; 23; 29; 31(2); 32; 34(2); 45:6; 13(2); 18; 46:4; 33(3); 34; 47:19; 23; 24(3); 48:5; 6(2); 19(4); 20; 21; 49:1; 8(3); 9; 10(2); 12; 13(3); 16; 17(2); 19(2); 20(2); 25(2); 26; 27(3); 50:17; 25; **Ex** 1:16(2); 22(2); 2:7; 3:12(2); 13(3); 18(2); 21(2); 22(3); 4:8; 9(2); 15; 16(3); 21; 5:7; 8(2); 11; 18(2); 19; 6:1(2); 7; 12; 30; 7:1; 2; 4; 5; 9(2); 17; 18(3); 8:3(2); 4; 9; 11(2); 21; 22; 23; 26(2); 27; 28; 9:3; 4(2); 5; 9(2); 19(4); 28; 29(2); 10:5(3); 6; 7; 8; 14; 26(2); 11:1(2); 5; 6(2); 7; 8; 9; 12:2(2); 3; 4; 5(2); 6(2); 7(2); 8(2); 10(2); 11(2); 13(2); 14(3); 15(3); 16(3); 17(2); 18; 19(2); 20(2); 22(2); 24; 25(2); 26(2); 27; 43; 44; 45; 46(2); 47; 48(3); 49; 13:3; 5(2); 6; 7(3); 9; 11(3); 12; 14; 16; 19; 14:2; 4; 13; 14(2); 16; 17; 18; 15:9(2); 14(2); 15(3); 16(2); 18; 24; 16:4; 5(3); 6; 7; 8(2); 12(3); 25; 26(2); 17:4; 6; 18:19; 22(5); 23; 19:5; 6; 12; 13(4); 20:23(2); 21:2(2); 3(2); 4(2); 5; 6(4); 7; 8(2); 9; 10; 11; 12; 13; 15; 16; 17; 19(3); 20; 21; 22(2); 26; 27; 28(3); 29(2); 30; 31; 32(3); 33(2); 34(2); 35(2); 36(2); 22:1(2); 2; 3(2); 4; 5(4); 6; 7; 8; 9(3); 11(3); 12; 13; 14; 15; 16; 17; 19; 20; 22; 24(2); 27(2); 30; 31(3); 23:11; 15; 17; 18; 23; 25(2); 26; 28; 33; 24:2(3); 25:2; 3; 9; 10(2); 12; 15(2); 16; 17; 19; 20(3); 21; 23; 27; 31(2); 32; 34; 35; 36(2); 37; 38; 39; 26:2(2); 3(2); 6; 8(2); 12; 13; 16(2); 17; 20; 24(4); 25; 28; 31; 32; 33; 37; 27:1(2); 2; 7(2); 8; 9; 10(2); 11; 12; 13; 14; 15; 16(2); 17(2); 18; 19; 21(2); 28:4(2); 5; 6; 7(2); 8; 12; 16(3); 17(2); 18; 20; 21(2); 28; 29; 30(2); 32(2); 35(2); 37; 38(3); 42; 43(2); 29:9; 10; 15; 19; 21; 26; 28(2); 29; 30; 32; 33(2); 34; 37(2); 42; 43; 46; 30:2(4); 4; 7(2); 8; 9(2); 10(2); 12; 13(2); 14; 15(2); 19; 20; 21(2); 25; 29; 31; 32(3); 33; 34; 36; 37(2); 38(2); 31:11; 13; 14(3); 15; 16; 32:1; 13; 23; 30; 34; 33:14; 16(2); 20; 22; 23; 34:3; 10; 13; 20; 23; 24; 25; 35:2(3); 3; 10; 40:9; 10; 15; **Lev** 1:2; 3; 4(2); 5(2); 6; 7; 8; 9(2); 10; 11(2); 12(2); 13(2); 14; 15(2); 16; 17(3); 2:1(2); 2(3); 3; 4; 5; 7; 8; 9(2); 10; 11(3); 12(2); 16; 3:1; 2(2); 3; 4; 5; 6; 7; 8(2); 9(2); 10; 11; 12; 13(2); 14; 15; 16; 17; 4:2(2); 4(2); 5; 6; 7(2); 8; 9; 10; 12(2); 14; 15(2); 16; 17; 18(2); 19; 20(4); 21; 23; 24; 25(2); 26(3); 28; 29; 30(2); 31(4); 32; 33; 34(2); 35(4); 5:1; 2; 3(2); 4(2); 5(3); 6(2); 7; 8(3); 9(2); 10(3); 11(3); 12(2); 13(3); 15; 16(4); 17; 18(3); 6:4(2); 5(2); 6; 7(2); 9; 10(3); 11; 12(4); 13(2); 14; 15(2); 16(3); 17; 18(3); 20; 21; 22(2); 23(2); 25; 26(2); 27(2); 28(2); 29; 30(2); 7:2(2); 3; 4; 5; 6(2); 7; 8; 9; 10; 11; 12; 13; 14(2); 15(2); 16(2); 17; 18(4); 19(3); 20; 21(2); 23; 24; 25; 26; 27; 29; 30(2); 31(2); 32; 33; 8:31; 32; 33(2); 35; 9:6; 10:7; 9; 13; 14; 15(2); 11:2; 3; 4; 8(2); 9(2); 10; 11(3); 12; 13(2); 20; 23; 24(2); 25; 26; 27; 28; 29; 31; 32(3); 33(2); 34(2); 35(3); 36(2); 37; 38; 39; 40(2); 41(2); 42; 43(2); 44(3); 45; 12:2(2); 3; 4(2); 5(2); 6; 7(2); 8(3); 13:2(2); 3(2); 4; 5(2); 6(3); 7; 8; 9; 10; 11(2); 13(2); 14; 15; 16; 17(2); 20; 21; 22; 23; 25(2); 26; 27(2); 28; 30(2); 31; 32; 33(3); 34(3); 36(2); 37; 39; 43; 44; 45(3); 46(4); 49; 50; 51; 52(2); 53; 54(2); 55; 56; 58(2); 14:2(2); 3(2); 4; 5; 6(2); 7(3); 8(3); 9(6); 10; 11; 12; 13(2); 14(2); 15; 16(2); 17; 18(2); 19(2); 20(3); 21; 22; 23; 24(2); 25(2); 26; 27; 28; 29; 30; 31; 35; 36(2); 37; 38; 39(2); 40(2); 41(2); 42(3); 44; 45(2); 46; 47(2); 48(2); 49; 50; 51; 52; 53(2); 15:3; 4; 5; 6; 7; 8; 9; 10(2); 11; 12(2); 13(2); 14; 15(2); 16; 17; 18(2); 19(2); 20(2); 21; 22; 23; 24(2); 25(2); 26(2); 27(2); 28(2); 29; 30(2); 31; 16:3; 4(5); 5; 6; 7; 8; 9; 10; 11(3); 12; 13; 14(2); 15; 16(2); 17; 18(2); 19; 20; 21(2); 22(2); 23(3); 24; 25; 26; 27(2); 28(2); 29(2); 30; 31(2); 32(4); 33(3); 34; 17:4(2); 6; 7(2); 9; 12(2); 13; 14(2); 15(2); 16; 18:3(3); 4; 5(2); 6; 23; 26(2); 29(2); 30; 19:2; 3; 5; 6(2); 7; 8(2); 11; 12; 13; 15; 19(2); 20(2); 21; 22(2); 23(5); 24; 25; 26(2); 27; 28; 30; 33; 34; 35; 36; 37; 20:2(2); 8; 9(2); 10; 11(2); 12(2); 13(2); 14; 15(2); 16(2); 17(3); 18(3); 19; 20(3); 21(2); 22; 23; 24; 25(2); 26; 27(3); 21:1; 4; 5(2); 6(2); 7(2); 8; 9; 10; 11; 12; 13; 14(2); 15; 18; 21(2); 22; 23; 22:3; 4; 6(2); 7(2); 8; 9; 10(2); 11(2); 13(2); 14(2); 15; 19; 20(2); 21(2); 22; 23; 24(2); 25(2); 27(2); 28; 30(2); 31; 32; 23:2; 3(2); 4; 7(2); 8(2); 10(2); 11(2); 12; 13(2); 14(2); 15(2); 16(2); 17(3); 18(2); 19; 20(2); 21(3); 24; 25(2); 27(3); 28; 29(2); 31(2); 32(3); 34; 35(2); 36(4); 37; 39(3); 40(2); 41(3); 42(2); 24:3(2); 4; 5; 8; 9(2); 15; 16(3); 17; 18; 19; 20; 21(2); 22; 25:2; 4; 6; 7; 8; 9; 10(4); 11(2); 12(2); 13; 14; 15; 17; 18(2); 19(2); 20(3); 21; 22(2); 23; 24; 25; 28(3); 30(2); 31(2); 33; 40(2); 41(3); 42; 44(2); 45(2); 46(3); 50(3); 51; 52(2); 53(2); 54; 26:1(2); 2; 4(2); 5(3); 6(3); 7(2); 8(3); 10; 11; 12; 15; 16(3); 17(3); 20(3); 22(2); 25(2); 26(3); 29(2); 30; 32; 33; 34(2); 35; 36(3); 37(2); 38(2); 39(2); 40; 43(3); 27:2(2); 3(2); 4; 5; 6(2); 7; 8(3); 9; 10(3); 11; 12(2); 13; 14(4); 15(2); 16(3); 17; 18(2); 19(2); 20; 21(2); 23(2); 24; 25(2); 26; 27(3); 28(2); 29(3); 31; 32; 33(4); **Num** 1:3; 4; 5; 50(3); 51(3); 52; 53(2); 2:2(2); 3(2); 5(2); 7; 9; 10(2); 12(2); 14; 16; 17(2); 18(2); 20(2); 22; 24; 25(2); 27(2); 29; 31; 3:7; 8; 10(2); 12; 13; 23; 24; 25; 29; 30; 31; 32; 35; 36; 38(2); 45; 4:4; 5(2); 6(3); 7(2); 8(2); 9; 10(2); 11(2); 12(2); 13; 14(2); 15(2); 19; 20; 25; 26; 27(2); 28; 32; 5:3(2); 6; 7(2); 8; 9; 10(2); 15(3); 16; 17(2); 18(2); 19; 21(2); 22(2); 23(2); 24(2); 25(2); 26(2); 27(5); 28(2); 30(2); 31(2); 6:2; 3(3); 4; 5(3); 6; 7; 9(2); 10; 11(2); 12(3); 13; 14; 16(2); 17(2); 18(2); 19(2); 20; 21; 23; 27; 7:11; 8:2; 10; 11; 12; 14; 15; 24; 25(2); 26(2); 9:3(2); 10(2); 11; 12(2); 13(2); 14(3); 10:3(2); 4; 5; 6(2); 7(2); 8(2); 9(3); 10; 32(3); 11:4; 17; 18(3); 19; 22(2); 23; 12:8; 13:2; 14:13; 21; 23(2); 24; 27; 29; 30; 31; 32; 33; 34(2); 35(2); 41; 43; 15:4; 9; 11; 12(2); 13; 14; 15(2); 16; 19(2); 20(2); 21; 24(2); 25(3); 26; 27; 28(2); 29; 30; 31(2); 35(2); 39; 16:7(2); 22; 28; 30; 38; 17:3; 5(3); 13(2); 18:1(2); 2; 3(2); 4(2); 5; 7(3); 9(3); 10(2); 11; 12; 13(3); 14; 15; 18; 23(3); 24; 26; 27; 28(2); 29; 30; 31; 32(2); 19:3(2); 4; 5(2); 6; 7(4); 8(2); 9(2); 10(2); 11; 12(3); 13(2); 14; 16; 17(2); 18; 19(3); 20(3); 21(3); 22(2); 20:8; 12; 24(2); 26(2); 21:8(2); 22:4; 6; 8; 11; 20; 35; 38; 23:8(2); 9(2); 19(2); 23; 24(2); 24:7(4); 8(2); 9; 14; 17(5); 18(3); 19(3); 20; 22(2); 23; 24(4); 25:13; 26:53; 54; 55(2); 56; 65; 27:8; 9; 10; 11(3); 21(4); 28:2; 3; 7; 11; 14; 15; 17; 18(2); 19(2); 20(2); 23; 24(2); 25(2); 26(2); 27; 31(2); 29:1(2); 2; 3; 7(3); 8(2); 9; 12(3); 13(2); 14; 17; 18; 21; 24; 27; 30; 33; 35(2); 36; 37; 39; 30:2(2); 4(3); 5(2); 7(2); 8(2); 9; 11(2); 12(2); 15(2); 31:4; 23(4); 24(3); 32:6(2); 11; 15; 17; 22(2); 26; 29(2); 30; 33:52; 53; 54(5); 55(3); 56(2); 34:2; 3(2); 4(3); 5(2); 6(2); 7(2); 8(2); 9(3); 10; 11(3); 12(3); 13; 17; 18; 35:2; 3(2); 4(2); 5(3); 6(4); 7(3); 8(5); 11; 12; 13(2); 14(3); 15; 16; 17; 18; 19(2); 21(2); 24; 25(3); 26; 27; 28; 29; 30(2); 31(2); 32; 33; 34; 36:3(3); 4(3); 6; 7(2); 8; 9(2); **Deut** 1:17(3); 22(2); 28; 30; 35; 36; 38(2); 39(2); 2:4; 6(2); 25(2); 29; 3:18; 19; 20; 21; 22(2); 28(2); 4:2(2); 6; 10; 22; 25(3); 26(3); 27(3); 28; 5:25; 27(2); 32(2); 33(2); 6:6; 8; 10(2); 14; 16; 17; 25; 7:1; 2; 5(2); 12(2); 14; 16(2); 19; 23(2); 24(2); 25; 8:1; 19(2); 20; 9:3(2); 11:8; 13(2); 18; 19; 22; 23; 24(3); 25(3); 29; 31(2); 32; 12:1; 2(2); 3(2); 4; 5(2); 6; 7(2); 8; 11(3); 12; 14; 16(2); 18; 20; 22; 26; 27; 29; 13:4(2); 5; 8; 9; 11(2); 16(2); 17; 14:1; 4; 6; 7; 8; 9(2); 11; 12; 19; 21; 23; 24; 25; 29(2); 15:2(2); 3; 4(2); 6; 10(2); 11; 16; 17; 18(2); 20; 22; 16:2; 4(2); 6; 7; 8; 15(2); 16(3); 17; 18; 17:6(2); 7; 8; 9(2); 10(2); 11(3); 12; 13; 15; 16(2); 17(2); 18(2); 19(2); 18:1(2); 2; 3(2); 6; 7; 8; 10; 15; 18(2); 19(2); 20(3);

21; 19:4; 5; 12; 13; 15(2); 17(2); 18; 19; 20(2); 21(2); 20:2(2); 3; 5; 8(2); 9(2); 11(4); 21:2(2); 3(2); 4(2); 5(2); 6; 7; 8; 12; 13(3); 14; 16; 17; 19; 20; 21(2); 23; 22:2; 5(2); 15; 16; 17; 18; 19(2); 21(2); 22; 24(2); 25; 29(2); 30; 23:1; 2(2); 3(2); 8; 10(2); 11(3); 13; 14; 16(2); 17; 22; 24:5(4); 6; 7; 8(2); 11; 13; 15; 16(3); 19; 20; 21; 25:1; 2(2); 5(2); 6(2); 8; 9(3); 10; 12; 19; 26:1; 2; 3; 4; 27:2(2); 4(2); 12; 13; 14; 15; 16; 17; 18; 19; 20; 21; 22; 23; 24; 25; 26; 28:1; 2; 4; 5; 7(2); 8(2); 9; 10(2); 11; 12; 13; 15(2); 17; 18; 20; 21; 22(2); 23(2); 24(2); 25; 26(2); 28; 29; 30; 31(4); 32(3); 33; 35; 36; 37; 38; 39; 40; 41; 42; 43; 44(2); 45(2); 46; 48(2); 49; 50; 51(2); 52(2); 53; 54(2); 55(2); 56; 57(3); 60; 62; 63(2); 64; 65(2); 66; 68(3); 29:19; 20(3); 21; 22(3); 24; 25; 30:1; 12; 13; 16; 18(2); 31:3; 4; 5; 11; 17(3); 18; 20(2); 21(3); 32:2(2); 20; 22(2); 24; 25; 35(2); 36; 37; 42; 46; 47; 33:3; 10(2); 12(3); 17; 19(3); 22; 25(2); 27(2); 28(3); 29; **Josh** 1:3; 4; 5; 8; 11; 14(2); 15; 18; 2:5; 14; 19(5); 3:3; 4; 8; 10; 13(4); 4:3(2); 7(2); 21; 22; 6:3; 4(3); 5(4); 10(3); 17(2); 19; 26(2); 7:8; 9(2); 14(7); 15(2); 25; 8:2; 4; 5; 7; 8(3); 9:7; 23; 10:8; 25; 14:9; 12; 15:4; 17:18(2); 18:4(2); 5(3); 6; 20:3; 4(3); 5; 6(3); 22:22; 25; 28; 34; 23:5(2); 10; 12; 13; 15(2); 16(2); 24:27(2); **Judg** 1:1; 2; 2:2(2); 3(2); 4:9(2); 20; 5:11(2); 24(2); 6:15; 37; 7:4(5); 11; 17(2); 8:23(2); 9:33; 10:18; 11:9; 24; 31(2); 13:5(3); 7; 8(2); 12(2); 15; 22; 14:13; 16; 15:3; 18; 16:2; 7; 11; 17; 18:5; 10; 20:9; 18(2); 23; 28(2); 21:1; 5; 7; 11(2); 16; 22; **Ruth** 1:16; 2:2; 9; 3:1; 3; 4(2); 13; 4:12; 15; **1Sa** 1:11; 28; 2:9(2); 10(4); 25(2); 30; 31; 32(2); 33(3); 34(3); 35(2); 36(3); 3:9; 11; 14; 4:8; 5:7; 8; 6:2(2); 3(2); 4(2); 5(2); 9; 20; 8:9; 11(2); 17; 18(2); 9:7; 13(2); 17; 19; 10:2; 3; 5(2); 27; 11:7; 9(2); 10; 12; 13; 12:12; 14; 15; 17; 25(2); 13:14; 14:10; 37; 39; 45(2); 15:33; 16:16(2); 17:9; 25; 26; 27; 36; 47; 18:25; 19:6; 20:7; 10; 31; 32; 21:15; 23:2; 17(2); 20; 23; 24:4; 12; 13; 20; 25:6; 11; 29(2); 30(3); 31(2); 26:10(3); 27:1(3); 12; 28:8; 10; 11; 15; 19; 29:9; 30:8(2); 23; 24(2); **2Sa** 2:1(2); 26(2); 3:12; 39; 4:11; 5:8(2); 19; 24; 6:9; 22; 7:10; 12; 13; 14; 15; 16(2); 9:10(2); 11(2); 11:11; 12:5; 6; 10; 11; 14; 23(2); 13:13; 14:7(2); 10; 11; 17; 18; 15:8; 10; 14; 15; 21; 25; 35; 36; 16:3; 10; 20; 21(2); 17:2; 3; 6; 10; 12(3); 13; 19:21; 22; 37; 38(2); 20:6; 18; 21; 21:3(2); 4; 22:4; 44; 45(2); 46(2); 23:4; 6; 7(2); 24:13(2); **1Kin** 1:13(2); 17(2); 20; 21(3); 24(2); 30(2); 35(2); 52(3); 2:4; 24; 32; 33(2); 37(2); 44; 45(2); 3:5; 12; 13; 5:5; 6; 9; 8:19(2); 25; 29(2); 30; 33; 38; 42(2); 44; 47; 59; 9:3; 5; 6; 7; 8(3); 9; 11:2(2); 32; 38; 12:10; 24; 26; 27(2); 13:2(3); 3(2); 22; 32; 14:3(2); 5(2); 11(2); 12; 13(2); 14(2); 15(3); 16; 16:4(2); 17:1; 4; 14(2); 18:12(3); 14; 31; 19:17(3); 20:6(3); 10; 14; 23; 25; 28; 36; 39; 40; 42; 21:19; 23; 24(2); 22:6(3); 12; 15(3); 16; 20; **2Kin** 1:2; 2:9; 10(2); 16; 21; 3:8; 17(3); 19(2); 4:2; 10(2); 23; 43(2); 5:8; 10; 17; 27; 6:8; 15; 21(2); 27; 31; 7:1; 4(3); 12; 18; 8:1; 8; 9; 10; 9:8; 10(2); 36; 37(2); 10:4; 10; 18; 19(2); 24; 30; 11:5(2); 6(2); 7; 8; 12:5; 14:6(2); 15:12; 16:15; 17:12; 35; 36(3); 37(2); 38(2); 39(2); 18:22; 29; 30; 19:6; 7(2); 10(2); 29(2); 30; 31(2); 32; 33(2); 20:8(2); 9; 17(2); 18(3); 21:12; 14; 22:17(2); 18; 20; 23:27; 25:24; **1Chr** 11:6; 19; 12:17; 13:12; 14:10; 15; 16:30; 33; 17:9(3); 11(2); 12; 13; 14; 27; 21:12; 22:9(3); 10(2); 23:26; 28:6; 21(2); **2Chr** 1:7; 12; 2:8; 9; 14; 6:9(2); 16; 21; 24; 29(3); 7:14; 15; 16; 18; 19; 21(2); 22; 8:11; 10:10; 11:4; 12:7; 8; 13:12; 15:7; 18:5(2); 11; 14(3); 15; 19; 19:9; 10(3); 11(2); 20:16; 17; 20(2); 23:3; 4(2); 5(2); 6(2); 7(2); 25:4(3); 8; 9; 26:18; 28:13; 30:9(2); 32:11; 12; 15; 17; 33:4; 34:25(2); 26; 28; 35:3; **Ezr** 4:21; 6:8; 11; 12; 7:18; 20; 21; 24; 9:10; **Neh** 2:6; 8; 4:3; 11; 12; 20; 5:8; 6:7; 9; 9:29; 10:38(2); 39; 13:25; 27; **Est** 1:15; 17(3); 18(2); 20(3); 4:11(2); 14(2); 5:3; 6(2); 8; 6:6; 9; 11; 7:2(2); 8:6; 9:12(2); **Job** 1:21; 2:10(2); 4:17(2); 5:19(2); 20; 23; 24; 25; 7:4; 7; 8; 9; 10(2); 13(2); 20; 21(2); 8:2; 10; 13; 14(2); 15(4); 18; 19; 22(2); 9:14; 19; 20(2); 31; 10:21; 11:3; 17; 19(2); 20(3); 12:2; 7(2); 8(2); 13:11; 16(2); 18; 19; 14:6; 12; 14; 22(2); 15:21; 22; 24(2); 29(3); 30(3); 31; 32(2); 33(2); 34(2); 16:3; 22(2); 17:5; 8(2); 9(2); 15; 16; 18:4(2); 5(2); 6(2); 7(2); 9(2); 11(2); 12(2); 13(2); 14(2); 15(2); 16(2); 17(2); 18; 19; 20; 19:25; 26; 27(2); 20:7(2); 8(3); 9(2); 10(2); 11; 15(2); 16(2); 17; 18(4); 20(2); 21(2); 22(2); 23(2); 24(2); 26(3); 27(2); 28(2); 21:19; 20(2); 22; 26(2); 30; 31(2); 32(2); 33(2); 22:21; 25; 27; 28(2); 29; 30; 23:10; 24:15; 20(4); 27:4; 6; 13; 14; 15(2); 17(2); 19(2); 22; 23(2); 28:12; 15; 17; 18; 19(2); 29:18(2); 31:14(2); 33:3(2); 7(2); 25(2); 26(2); 28; 33; 34:11; 15(2); 17; 20(3); 24; 35:3; 36:4; 11; 12(2); 37:19; 20(2); 38:11; 15; 40:2; 4; 41:6(2); 9; 42:8; **Ps** 1:3(3); 5; 6; 2:4(2); 5; 8; 5:4; 5; 6:5; 7:7; 8; 16(2); 9:3; 7; 8(2); 17; 18(2); 10:6(2); 11:6(2); 12:3; 13:2(2); 5; 14:7(2); 15:1(2); 5; 16:4; 8; 9; 17:3; 15; 18:3; 43; 44(2); 45; 19:13(2); 21:1(2); 7; 8(2); 9(2); 22:25; 26(3); 27(2); 29(2); 30(2); 31(3); 23:1; 6; 24:3(2); 5; 7; 9; 25:12(2); 13(2); 15; 26:1; 27:1(2); 3; 5(3); 6; 14; 28:5; 30:6; 9(2); 31:24; 32:6(2); 10(2); 33:17; 21; 34:1; 2(2); 10; 21(2); 22; 35:9(2); 10; 28; 36:8; 9; 12; 37:2; 4; 5; 6; 9(2); 10(2); 11(2); 13; 15(2); 17; 18; 19(2); 20(4); 22(2); 24; 28; 29; 31; 34; 38(2); 40(2); 39:6; 40:3(2); 41:2; 5; 8; 42:2; 5; 8; 11; 43:5; 44:6; 21; 45:4; 11; 12(2); 14(2); 15(2); 16; 17; 46:4; 5(2); 47:3; 4; 49:3(2); 5; 11; 14(3); 15; 17(2); 19(2); 50:3(4); 4; 6; 51:7(2); 13; 14; 15; 19; 52:5(2); 6(2); 53:6(2); 54:5; 55:16; 17; 19; 22(2); 23; 56:7; 9; 57:3(2); 58:9; 10(2); 11; 59:10(2); 60:12(2); 61:7; 62:2; 3(2); 6; 63:3; 5(2); 9; 10(2); 11(3); 64:5; 7(2); 8(2); 9(3); 10(3); 65:1; 2; 4; 66:3; 4(3); 67:6(2); 7(2); 68:13; 21; 29; 31(2); 69:31; 32(2); 36(2); 71:6; 15; 23; 24; 72:2; 3; 4(3); 5; 6; 7; 8; 9(2); 10(2); 11(2); 12; 13(2); 14(2); 15(4); 16(3); 17(4); 73:27; 74:10(2); 75:2; 8; 10; 76:10; 12; 79:5; 80:3; 7; 19; 81:9; 82:7; 85:11(2); 12(2); 13(2); 86:9(2); 87:5(2); 6; 7; 88:10; 11; 12; 13; 89:2; 5; 12; 14; 15; 16(2); 17; 21(2); 22; 24(2); 26; 28; 36; 37; 46; 48(2); 91:1; 3; 4(2); 7(2); 10(2); 11; 12; 15; 92:7; 9(2); 10; 11(2); 12(2); 13; 14(2); 94:3(2); 4; 7(2); 9(2); 10(2); 15(2); 20; 23(3); 96:10(3); 12; 13; 98:9; 101:3; 4; 6(2); 7(2); 102:15; 16(2); 18(3); 26(3); 27; 28(2); 103:16; 104:12; 31(2); 34; 107:42(2); 43; 108:13(2); 109:7; 31; 110:2; 3; 5; 6(3); 7(2); 112:2(2); 3; 6(2); 7; 8; 9; 10(3); 115:14; 116:12; 118:7; 17; 20; 119:6; 7; 9; 27; 33; 34(2); 42; 44; 88; 117; 144; 146; 165; 171; 172; 175; 120:3(2); 121:4; 6; 7(2); 8; 122:2; 6; 125:1; 3; 5(2); 126:5; 6; 127:5(2); 128:2; 3; 4; 5; 130:3; 8; 132:12(2); 16; 18; 137:4; 8; 9; 138:4; 5; 7; 139:7(2); 10(2); 11(2); 140:11; 13(2); 141:5(4); 6; 142:7; 143:2; 144:5; 145:4(2); 6; 7(2); 10(2); 11; 21; 146:10; 148:6; **Prov** 1:5; 9; 13(2); 28(3); 31; 32(2); 33(2); 2:11(2); 21(2); 22(2); 3:2; 6; 8; 10(2); 22; 23; 24; 26(2); 35(2); 4:6(2); 8(2); 9(2); 10; 5:22(2); 23(2); 6:11; 15(2); 22(3); 29; 31(2); 33(2); 8:6; 7; 17; 35; 9:11(2); 10:7; 8; 9; 10; 24(2); 27; 28(2); 29; 30(2); 31; 11:3(2); 5(2); 6(2); 7; 9; 15; 18; 21(2); 25(2); 26(2); 27; 28(2); 29(2); 31; 12:3(2); 6; 7; 8(2); 11; 13; 14(2); 19; 21(2); 24(2); 13:2(2); 3; 4; 9; 11(2); 13(2); 18(2); 20(2); 21; 25; 14:3; 11(2); 14(2); 22; 26; 15:10; 27; 16:3; 5; 20; 21; 17:2(2); 5; 11; 13; 18:20(2); 21; 19:5(2); 8; 9(2); 15; 16; 19; 21; 23(2); 20:4; 17; 20; 21; 22; 21:7; 13(2); 15; 16; 17(2); 18; 28; 22:5; 8(2); 9; 10(2); 11; 13; 14; 15; 16; 18; 29(2); 23:11; 13; 15; 16; 18; 21(2); 24(2); 25(2); 33(2); 35; 24:4; 8; 12; 14(3); 16; 20(2); 22; 24(2); 25(2); 26; 34; 25:4; 5; 22; 26:2; 26; 27; 27:14; 18(2); 28:2; 8; 9; 10(2); 13(2); 14; 16; 17; 18(2); 19(2); 20(2); 22; 23; 25; 26; 27(2); 29:1; 14; 16; 17(2); 21; 23(2); 25; 30:17(2); 31:11; 25; 30; **Eccl** 1:9(2); 11(2); 2:16; 18; 19(2); 21; 3:14; 17; 22(2); 4:12; 15; 16; 5:10; 15(2); 16; 20; 6:4; 12; 7:18; 26(2); 8:1; 5; 7(2); 8; 12; 13(2); 15; 17(2); 9:5; 10:8(2); 9(2); 14(2); 20(2); 11:2; 3; 4(2); 6(2); 8; 12:3(2); 4(3); 5(5); 7(2); 14; **Song** 1:13; 5:3(2); 7:8; 8:8(2); **Is** 1:18(2); 19; 20; 27; 28(2); 29(2); 30; 31(3); 2:2(4); 3(2); 4(5); 11(3); 12(2); 17(3); 18; 19; 20; 3:4; 5(2); 6; 7; 10(2); 11(2); 24(2); 25; 26(2); 4:1; 2(2); 3(2); 4(2); 5; 6; 5:5(2); 6(2); 9; 10(2); 14; 15(3); 16(2); 17(2); 24(2); 26; 27(3); 28; 29(5); 30; 6:8; 13(4); 7:7(2); 8; 9; 14(3); 15; 16(2); 17; 18(2); 19(2); 20(2); 21(2); 22(4); 23(3); 24(2); 25(3); 8:4(2); 7; 8(4); 9(3); 10(2); 12; 14; 15; 19; 21(4); 22(2); 9:1; 5; 6(2); 7; 9; 11; 12; 17(2); 18(3); 19(2); 20(4); 21; 10:3; 4(2); 11; 12; 15(2); 16(2); 17(2); 18(2); 19; 20(3); 21; 22(2); 23; 24(2); 25; 26(2); 27(3); 32(2); 33(3); 34(2); 11:1(2); 2; 3(2); 4(3); 5; 6(3); 7(3); 8(2); 9(2); 10(4); 11(3); 12(2); 13(4); 14(4); 15(3); 16(2); 12:3; 4; 13:6; 7(2); 8(5); 9; 10(3); 13; 14(2); 15(2); 16(2); 17(2); 18(3); 19; 20(4); 21(4); 22(2); 14:1(2); 2(4); 3(2); 10; 16; 20; 24(2); 25; 27(2); 29(2); 30(3); 31(2); 32(2); 15:2(2); 3(2); 4(4); 5(4); 6; 7; 9; 16:2(2); 5(2); 6; 7(3); 10(3); 11; 12(3); 14(2); 17:1; 2(3); 3(2); 4(3); 5(2); 6; 7(2); 8(2); 9(2); 11; 13(4); 18:5; 6(3); 7; 19:1(3); 2; 3(2); 4; 5(2); 6(3); 7; 8(3); 9; 10; 15; 16(2); 17(2); 18(2); 19; 20(4); 21(4); 22(5); 23(3); 24; 25; 20:4; 5; 6(2); 21:13; 16; 17; 22:7(3); 13; 14; 18; 19; 20; 21; 22(4); 23; 24; 25(2); 23:5; 7; 15(3); 17(3); 18(3); 24:2; 3; 9(2); 13(2); 14(3); 18(3); 20(4); 21(2); 22(3); 23(2); 25:2; 3(2); 5; 6; 8; 9; 10(2); 11(2); 12; 26:1; 6; 11(2); 14(2); 19(3); 21(2); 27:1(2); 5; 6(2); 9(2); 10(3); 11; 12(3); 13(4); 28:2; 3; 4; 5; 9(2); 15(2); 16; 17(2); 18(4); 19(3); 21(2); 29:2(2); 4(3); 5(3); 7; 8(2); 14(2); 16(3); 17(2); 18(2); 19(2); 22(2); 23(2); 24(2); 30:3; 6; 7; 13; 14(3); 15(2); 16(2); 17(2); 19(2); 20(2); 21; 22; 23(3); 24; 25; 26(2); 28(2); 29; 30(2); 31; 32(3); 31:3(4); 4; 7; 8(4); 9(2); 32:1(2); 2; 3(2); 4(2); 5; 8; 10(3); 12; 13; 14(3); 16; 17; 18; 19(2); 33:1; 4(2); 6; 7(2); 11(3); 12(2); 14(2); 16(4); 17(2); 18; 20(4); 21(2); 24(2); 34:3(3); 4(3); 5(2); 7(2); 9(3); 10(4); 11(3); 12(3); 13(2); 14(3); 15(2); 16(2); 17(2); 35:1(2); 2(3); 5(2); 6(2); 7(2); 8(5); 9(4); 10(3); 36:7; 14; 15; 37:6; 7; 10(2); 30(2); 31; 32(2); 33; 34(2); 38:7; 10; 11(2); 15(2); 19(2); 21; 22; 39:6(2); 7(3); 8; 40:4(3); 5(2); 6; 8; 10; 11(3); 20; 24(6); 25; 30(2); 31(4); 41:11(3); 12; 16(2); 22; 25(3); 27; 42:1; 2; 3(3); 4(2); 13(4); 17(2); 43:2(2); 10; 13; 17(2); 19(2); 20; 21; 44:4; 5(3); 7(3); 9; 11(3); 15; 19(2); 26; 28(2); 45:1; 9; 13(2); 14(6); 16(2); 17(2); 23(3); 24(3); 25(2); 46:7(2); 10; 13(2); 47:3(2); 7; 8(2); 9(2); 11(3); 13; 14(4); 15(3); 48:14; 15; 49:5(2); 7(3); 9(2); 10(4); 11; 12; 17(2); 19(2); 20; 22(2); 23(3); 24; 25(2); 26(2); 50:7(2); 9(3); 11(2); 51:3(2); 4; 5(3); 6(5); 8(3); 11(4); 12(2); 19(2); 52:1; 3; 6(2); 8(4); 10; 12; 13(2); 15(4); 53:2(2); 8; 10(3); 11(4); 12; 54:3; 5; 10(3); 13(2); 14; 15(3); 17(2); 55:3; 5; 11(4); 12(3); 13(4); 56:5; 7(2); 12; 57:2(2); 12; 13(4); 14; 58:4; 8(4); 9(2); 10; 11; 12(2); 59:6(2); 8; 19(3); 20; 21; 60:2(3); 3; 4(2); 5(3); 6(4); 7(3); 9; 10(2); 11(2); 12(2); 13; 14(3); 18; 19(3); 20(4); 21(2); 22; 61:4(3); 5(2); 6(4); 7(4); 9(2); 10; 62:2(2); 4(2); 5(2); 6; 8; 9(2); 12; 63:3; 64:5; 65:9(2); 10; 12; 13(6); 14(3); 15(2); 16(2); 17; 19; 20(3); 21(2); 22(3); 23; 24; 25(4); 66:5(2); 8(2); 9(2); 12(2); 13; 14(3); 16; 17; 18(2); 19; 20; 22(2); 23(2); 24(4); **Jer** 1:7; 14; 15(2); 19(2); 2:3(2); 19(2); 24; 35; 3:1(2); 15; 16(6); 17(3); 18(2); 19; 4:2(2); 7; 9(4); 10; 11; 12; 13(2); 14; 21; 27; 28; 29(3); 5:6(4); 7; 9(2); 12(2); 13(2); 14; 17(4); 19(3); 29(2); 6:3(3); 9; 10; 11; 12; 15(2); 16; 21(2); 22; 23; 26; 30; 7:20(3); 23; 32(2); 33(2); 34; 8:1; 2(3); 3; 4(2); 10; 12(2); 13(3); 17; 9:7; 9(2); 22(2); 10:10(2); 11(2); 15; 21(2); 11:4; 11(2); 12(2); 22(2); 23; 12:4(2); 12(2); 13(3); 15; 16(2); 13:10; 12(3); 17(2); 18; 19(4); 21(2); 27; 14:13(2); 15(2); 16(2); 15:2(2); 5(3); 11; 12; 14; 20(2); 16:4(6); 7(2); 10(2); 13; 14; 16(2); 19(2); 20; 21; 17:4; 6(3); 8(5); 11(2); 13(2); 14(2); 24; 25(2); 26; 27(2); 18:7; 9; 14; 16; 18; 20; 19:2; 3; 6; 8; 9(2); 11; 13; 20:4(4); 5; 6; 10(2); 11(5); 21:3; 6; 7(2); 9(3); 10(2); 13(2); 14; 22:4; 5; 7; 8(2); 9; 10; 11; 12(2); 18(2); 19; 22(2); 26; 27; 30(2); 23:3; 4(3); 5(2); 6(3); 7; 8; 12(2); 17(2); 19; 20(2); 24; 26; 32; 33; 34; 35; 36(2); 38; 40; 24:7(2); 9; 25:11(2); 12; 14; 16; 26; 28(2); 29; 30(3); 31; 32(2); 33(3); 34; 35; 36; 26:9(2); 15; 18(2); 27:4; 7(2); 8; 9; 11; 14; 16; 22(2); 28:9(2); 14; 29:7; 12(2); 13(2); 21; 22; 32(2); 30:3; 7; 8(2); 9; 10(3); 16(3); 18(2); 19(3); 20(2); 21(3); 22; 23; 24(2); 31:1; 5(2); 6(2); 8; 9(2); 12(4); 13; 14; 16(2); 17; 18; 22; 23(2); 24; 28; 29; 30; 31; 32(2); 33; 34(2); 36; 38; 39(2); 40(2); 32:3; 4(4); 5(3); 7; 15; 20; 29; 30; 38; 40; 43; 44; 33:9(3); 10(2); 11(2); 12; 13; 15; 16(3); 17; 18; 34:2; 3(2); 5; 20; 22; 35:6; 7(2); 15; 19; 36:29(2); 30(2); 37:7(2); 8; 9(2); 19; 38:2(4); 3(2); 17(2); 18(2); 20(3); 22(2); 23; 39:12; 16; 18; 40:9; 15; 42:4(2); 5; 14; 16(4); 17(3); 18(4); 20; 22; 43:10; 11; 12(3); 13(2); 44:12(4); 14(3); 26; 27; 28(3); 29(2); 46:6; 10(2); 14; 18; 19; 22(2); 23; 24(2); 26; 27(2); 47:2(4); 3; 48:2(2); 3; 5; 7; 8(4); 9; 12(2); 13; 18(2); 26(2); 30(2); 31; 33(2); 34; 36(2); 37(2); 38; 39(2); 40(2); 41; 42; 43; 44(2); 45(2); 49:2(3); 3; 4; 5(2); 10; 12; 13(2); 17(3); 18(2); 19; 20(2); 22(2); 26(2); 27; 28; 29(3); 32; 33(2); 36(2); 39; 50:3(4); 4(2); 5(2); 9(4); 10(2); 12(3); 13(3); 16(2); 19(2); 20(3); 30(2); 32(3); 34; 36(2); 37(2); 38; 39(4); 40(2); 41(2); 42(3); 44; 45(2); 51:2(3); 4; 14; 18; 26; 29(2); 31; 33; 35(2); 37; 38(2); 44(2); 46(3); 47(2); 48(2); 49; 52; 53; 56; 57; 58(4); 62(2); 63; 64(3); **Lam** 1:21; 2:13(3); 20(2); 4:15; 20; 21; 5:21; **Eze** 2:5; 3:10; 18; 19; 20(3); 21; 25(2); 4:3(2); 7; 10; 13; 16(2); 5:4; 10(2); 11; 12(3); 13(2); 15(2); 16(2); 17(2); 6:4(2); 6(2); 7(2); 8(2); 9(3); 10; 11; 12(3); 13(2); 14; 7:4(3); 9(2); 11(2); 13(3); 15(2); 16(2); 17(2); 18(3); 19(4); 21; 22(2); 24(2); 25(2); 26(4); 27(4); 8:18; 9:10; 11:10(2); 11(2); 12; 16; 18(2); 20; 12:11(2); 12(4); 13(3); 15(2); 16; 19; 20(3); 23; 24; 25(3); 28(2); 13:9(5); 11(4); 12; 13; 14(4); 21(2); 23(2); 14:8; 10(2); 16(3); 18(2); 20(2); 22(5); 23(2); 15:3; 5; 7(3); 16:16(2); 39(4); 40(2); 41; 42; 44; 53; 55(3); 17:9(3); 10(3); 15(3); 16; 17; 18; 20; 21(3); 23(3); 24; 18:3; 4; 9; 13(4); 17(2); 18; 19; 20(5); 21(2); 22(2); 24(3); 26; 27; 28(2); 30; 19:14; 20:11; 13; 20; 21; 31; 32; 38(2); 40; 42(2); 43(2); 44; 47(3); 48(2); 21:4; 5; 7(6); 12(3); 13; 19; 23; 24; 25; 26; 27; 29; 30; 32; 22:5; 14; 21; 22(2); 23:24(3); 25(5); 26; 29(4); 45; 47(2); 49(3); 24:12; 14(2); 16; 21; 22(2); 23(3); 24(2); 25; 26; 27(2); 25:4(3); 5; 11; 13; 14(2); 17(2); 26:2; 4; 5(2); 6(2); 8(2); 9(2); 10(3); 11(3); 12(3); 13; 15; 16(4); 17; 18(2); 19(3); 20(3); 27:27; 28; 29(2); 30(4); 31(2); 32; 34; 35(3); 36; 28:7(2); 8; 18; 19; 22(3); 23(2); 24(2); 25(3); 26(4); 29:4; 6; 9(2); 11(3); 12; 14; 15(3); 16(3); 19(2); 21; 30:3; 4(5); 5; 6(3); 7(2); 8(2); 9(2); 11(2); 13; 14(3); 17(2); 18(5); 19; 21; 24; 25(4); 26; 31:11; 13(2); 16; 32:3; 6; 7(2); 9; 10(3); 11; 12(2); 13; 15(4); 16(3); 20; 21; 27(2); 29; 31(2); 32; 33:4; 5(2); 8; 9; 12(3); 13(4); 15(2); 16(2); 18; 19; 25; 26; 27(2); 28(3); 29; 33; 34:10; 14(3); 22; 23(3); 25; 26; 27(4); 28(4); 29; 30; 35:6(2); 8; 9(2); 10; 15; 36:7; 8; 9; 10(2); 11(2); 12; 23(2); 25; 27; 28(2); 30; 31(2); 33(2); 34; 35; 36; 38(2); 37:5; 6(2); 13; 14(4); 17; 18; 19; 20; 22(3); 23(2); 24(3); 25(3); 26; 27(2); 28(2); 38:8; 10(2); 13; 16(2); 18(3); 19; 20(4); 21; 23; 39:6; 7; 9(3); 10(3); 11(4); 12; 13(3); 14(2); 15; 16(2); 18; 19; 20; 21; 22; 23; 28; 40:4; 42:13(2); 14(4); 43:7; 12; 13(3); 14(2); 15(2); 16; 17(4); 18; 21; 22; 24(2); 25; 26(2); 27(2); 44:2(4); 3(3); 9; 10; 11(3); 12; 13(2); 14; 15(2); 16(3); 17(3); 18(3); 19(3); 20(2); 21; 22(2); 23; 24(4); 25; 26; 27; 28(2); 29(2); 30(2); 31; 45:1(5); 2; 3; 4(3); 5; 6(2); 7(2); 8(3); 10; 11(2); 12(2); 13(2); 14; 16; 17(2); 19; 20; 21(2); 22; 23; 24; 25; 46:1(3); 2(6); 3; 4(2); 5(2); 6(2); 7(2); 8(3); 9(5); 10(2); 11; 12(5); 15; 16(2); 17(3); 18(2); 20(2); 24; 47:8; 9(7); 10(4); 11(2); 12(5); 13(3); 14(2); 15; 17; 18; 20; 21; 22(5); 23(2); 48:8(3); 9(2); 10(2); 11; 12; 13(2); 14; 15(2); 16; 17; 18(3); 19; 20(2); 21(3); 22; 23; 24; 28; 29; 31; 35; **Dan** 1:10; 2:5(2); 6; 9; 28; 29; 30; 39(2); 40(2); 41(2); 42; 43(2); 44(5); 45; 3:6; 10(2); 15(2); 29(2); 4:25(5); 26; 32(4); 5:7(3); 6:5; 7(2); 12(2); 26(2); 7:14(2); 17; 18; 23(4); 24(4); 25(3); 26(2); 27(2); 8:13; 14; 17; 19(2); 22; 23; 24(4); 25(5); 26; 9:25(2); 26(4); 27(4); 10:14; 20; 11:2(3); 3(2); 4(4); 5(3); 6(5); 7(5); 8(2); 9(2); 10(4); 11(4); 12(3); 13(3); 14(3); 15(3); 16(4); 17(4); 18(4); 19(2); 20(2); 21(3); 22(2); 23(3); 24(4); 25(4); 26(3); 27(4); 28(3); 29(2); 30(4); 31(4); 32(2); 33(2); 34(3); 35; 36(5); 37(2); 38(2); 39(4); 40(4); 41(3); 42(2); 43(2); 44(2); 45(3); 12:1(4); 2; 3; 4(2); 6; 7(3); 8; 10(4); 11(2); **Hos** 1:5; 10(3); 11(3); 2:6; 7(5); 10; 12; 15; 16; 17; 21(2); 22(2); 23; 3:4; 5(2); 4:3(3); 5; 9; 10(3); 13(2); 14; 19; 5:5(2); 6(2); 7; 9(2); 14; 6:2; 3(2); 4(2); 7:12; 16(2); 8:1; 2; 3; 6; 7(3); 8; 10; 11; 13; 14; 9:2(2); 3(3); 4(5); 6(4); 7; 11; 12; 13; 16; 17; 10:2(3); 3; 5(2); 6(3); 8(3); 10(2); 11(2); 14(2); 15(2); 11:5(2); 6(2); 8(4); 10(4); 11; 12:8; 14(2); 13:3; 8; 13; 14; 15(5); 16(4); 14:3; 5; 6(2); 7(3); 8; 9(4); **Joel** 1:15; 2:2; 3; 4; 5; 6(2); 7(4); 8(3); 9(4); 10(4); 11; 19; 20(2); 24(2); 26(2); 27(2); 28(4); 31; 32(5); 3:1; 8; 15(2); 16(2); 17(3); 18(6); 19(2); 20; **Amos** 1:2(2); 4; 5; 7; 8; 10; 12; 14; 15; 2:2(2); 5; 14(3); 15(3); 16; 3:5; 6(2); 11(3); 12; 14(2); 15(2); 4:2; 3(2); 5:2; 3(2); 4; 5(2); 6; 9; 11(2); 13; 14; 16(3); 17; 20; 6:7(2); 9(2); 10(4); 12; 14; 7:2; 3; 5; 6; 9(2); 11(2); 17(4); 8:3(3); 8(3); 9; 12(3); 13; 14; 9:1(2); 2; 3; 4; 5(4); 9; 10(2); 13(3); 14(3); 15; **Obad** 3; 8; 9; 10; 15(2); 16(4); 17(3); 18(3); 19(3); 20(2); 21(2); **Jonah** 1:11; 12; 3:4; **Mic** 1:4(2); 7(3); 11; 14; 15; 2:3(2); 4; 5; 6(2); 10; 11; 12; 13; 3:4; 6(6); 7(2); 12(2); 4:1(4); 2(2); 3(4); 4(2); 7; 8(2); 10; 12; 5:1; 2; 3; 4(3); 5(4); 6(2); 7; 8; 9(2); 10; 6:6(2); 7; 9; 11; 14; 16; 7:4; 8(2); 9; 10(4); 11; 12; 13; 16(3); 17(4); **Nah** 1:8; 9; 10; 12(2); 15; 2:3(2); 4(4); 5(4); 6(2); 7(3); 8(3); 13(2); 3:7(3); 12(2); 13(2); 15(3); 18; 19; **Hab** 1:2; 6; 7; 8(3); 9(3); 10(4); 11(2); 12; 17; 2:1; 3; 4; 6; 7(3); 8; 11(2); 13(2); 14; 16(2); 17; 19; 3:17(6); **Zeph** 1:8; 10(2); 12; 13(3); 14; 17(2); 18(3); 2:3; 4(3); 5; 6; 7(4); 9(3); 10; 11; 12; 14(5); 15; 3:8; 10; 12; 13(4); 16; **Hag** 2:7; 9; 12; 13(2); 22; **Zec** 1:16(2); 17(3); 2:4; 9(2); 11(2); 12(2); 3:9; 10; 4:7; 9; 10(2); 5:3(2); 4(3); 11; 6:12(2); 13(5); 14; 15(3); 8:3; 4; 5; 8(2); 12(4); 13(2); 16; 19; 20(2); 21; 22; 23(3); 9:1(2); 2; 4; 5(5); 6; 7(2); 8; 10(3); 14(4); 15(4); 16(2); 17; 10:1; 5(3); 6; 7(4); 8; 9(2); 10; 11(5); 12; 11:6; 16(3); 17(3); 12:2; 3; 5(2); 6(2); 7; 8(3); 9; 10(3); 11; 12; 13:1; 2(2); 3(4); 4(3); 5; 6(2); 7; 8(3); 9(2); 14:1; 2(3); 3; 4(4); 5(4); 6(2); 7(4); 8(3); 9(2); 10(2); 11(3); 12(4); 13(4); 14(2); 15(2); 16(2); 17(2); 18; 19; 20(2); 21(3); **Mal** 1:4(2); 5(2); 11(3); 2:3; 4; 3:1(3); 2; 3(2); 4; 7; 10; 11(2); 12(2); 17; 18; 4:1(4); 2(3); 3(3); 6; **Mt** 1:21(2); 23(3); 2:6(2); 23; 3:11; 4:4; 6(2); 5:4; 5; 6; 7; 8; 9; 11(2); 13; 18; 19(5); 20(2); 21(2); 22(5); 31; 32(2); 39; 41; 6:4; 6; 7; 18; 22; 23; 25(3); 30; 31(3); 33; 34; 7:2(2); 7(3); 8; 11; 16; 20; 21; 26; 8:8; 11(2); 12(2); 9:15(2); 18; 21; 10:11; 14; 15; 18; 19(3); 21(2); 22(2); 23; 25; 26(2); 29; 32; 33; 36; 39(2); 41(2); 42(2); 11:6; 10; 16; 22; 24; 29; 12:11(2); 18; 19(2); 20(2); 21; 25; 26; 27; 31(2); 32(2); 36(2); 39; 40; 41(2); 42(2); 45; 50; 13:12(3); 14(4); 40; 41(2); 42(2); 43; 49(2); 50(2); 15:5; 6; 13; 14; 16:4; 18; 19(2); 22; 25(2); 26(2); 27(2); 28; 17:11; 12; 17(2); 20(3); 22; 23(2); 18:3; 4; 5; 6; 15(2); 17; 18(4); 19(3); 21; 35; 19:5(3); 9(2); 16; 23; 27; 28(2); 29(2); 30(2); 20:7; 16; 18(2); 19(2); 22; 23(2); 26; 32; 21:2; 3; 13; 21(3); 22(2); 25; 26; 41; 43; 44(3); 22:9; 13; 24; 28; 23:11; 12(4); 14; 16(2); 18; 20; 21; 22; 34(2); 36; 39(2); 24:2(2); 3(2); 5(2); 6; 7(2); 9(3); 10(3); 11(2); 12(2); 13(2); 14(2); 15; 21(2); 22; 23; 24(3); 26; 27; 28; 29(4); 30(3); 31(2); 33; 34; 35(2); 37; 39; 40(2); 41(2); 46; 47; 48; 49; 50; 51(2); 25:1; 29(3); 30; 31(2); 32(2); 33; 34; 37; 40; 41; 44; 45; 46; 26:13(2); 21; 23; 31(2); 33; 48; 52; 53; 54; 64; 27:22; 64; 28:7; 10; **Mk** 1:2; 8; 2:20(2); 3:28(2); 29; 35; 4:22; 24(2); 25(2); 30(2); 5:23; 28; 6:11(2); 24; 37; 7:11(2); 8:12; 35(3); 36(2); 37; 38(2); 9:1; 19(2); 31(2); 35; 37(2); 39; 41(2); 42; 43; 45; 49(2); 10:7; 8; 11; 12; 15(2); 17; 23; 30; 31; 33(3); 34(5); 35; 39(2); 40; 43(2); 44; 11:2; 17; 23(5); 24; 31; 32; 12:7; 9; 15(2); 23(2); 25; 40; 13:2(2); 4(3); 6(2); 7(2); 8(3); 9(3); 11(3); 12(3); 13(3); 14; 19(2); 21; 22(2); 24(2); 25(2); 26; 27(2); 29; 30; 31(2); 14:9(2); 13; 14(2); 18; 27(2); 29; 32; 44; 62; 15:12; 16:3; 7; 16(2); 17(3); 18(4); **Lk** 1:13; 14; 15(3); 16; 17; 18; 20(2); 32(3); 33(2); 34; 35(4); 37; 45; 48; 60; 66; 2:10; 12(2); 23; 34; 35; 3:5(4); 6; 10; 12; 14; 16; 4:4; 7; 10; 11; 5:35(2); 37; 6:21(2); 22(3); 25(2); 26; 35(2); 37(3); 38(3); 39; 40; 7:7; 23; 27; 31; 8:17(2); 18(2); 50; 9:24(2); 26(3); 27; 41; 44; 48(3); 10:6(2); 12; 14; 19; 25; 42; 11:5(2); 7; 9(3); 10; 11; 12; 13; 18; 19; 22; 29; 30; 31; 32(2); 36; 49; 51; 12:2(2); 3(2); 5; 8(2); 9; 10(3); 11(2); 12; 17; 20(2); 22(2); 29(2); 31; 37(2); 38; 42; 43; 45; 47; 48(2); 52; 53; 13:3; 5; 8; 18; 20; 24; 25; 26; 27; 28(2); 29(2); 30(2); 32; 35(2); 14:5; 11(2); 15; 24; 34; 15:7; 16:3; 12; 17:10; 21; 22(2); 23; 24; 26; 30; 31; 33(4); 34(3); 35(2);

36(2); 18:7; 8; 14(2); 17(2); 18; 24; 30; 31; 32(2); 33(2); 41; 19:26(2); 30; 31; 43(2); 44(2); 20:5; 13; 15; 16(2); 18(3); 35; 47; 21:6(2); 7(2); 8; 9; 10; 11(2); 12; 13; 14; 15; 16(2); 17; 18; 20; 23; 24(3); 25; 26; 27; 32; 33(2); 35; 36; 22:10; 11(2); 12; 18; 26; 34; 49; 69; 23:29; 30; 31; **Jn** 1:51; 3:12; 36; 4:13; 14(4); 21; 23; 5:24; 25(2); 28; 29; 43; 47; 6:5; 27; 28; 35(2); 37; 45; 51; 57; 58; 62; 68; 7:17; 34(2); 35; 36(2); 38; 41; 8:12(2); 21(2); 24(2); 28; 32(2); 33; 36(2); 51; 52; 55; 9:21; 10:9(2); 16(2); 28(2); 11:12; 23; 24; 25; 26; 48; 12:25(2); 26; 27; 31; 48; 13:21; 26; 32(2); 33; 35; 38; 14:12(2); 13; 14; 16; 17; 19; 20; 21; 26; 15:7(2); 8; 10; 16; 26; 27; 16:2; 4; 13(3); 14(3); 15(2); 16(2); 17(2); 19(2); 20(4); 22; 23(2); 24; 25(2); 26; 32(2); 33; 17:20; 18:11; 19:15; 24; 36; 37; 20:25; 21:6; 18; 21; 23; **Acts** 1:5; 8(2); 11; 2:17(4); 18; 20; 21(3); 26; 37; 38; 39; 3:19; 20; 22(3); 23(2); 25; 4:16; 5:9; 6:14(2); 7:3; 7(2); 37(2); 8:33; 9:6; 10:6; 32; 43; 11:14(2); 16; 13:22; 41; 15:11; 27; 29; 18:10; 19:39; 20:22; 25; 29; 30; 21:11(2); 22:10(2); 23:3; 24:15; 22; 26:2; 27:22; 25; 34; 28:26(3); **Rom** 1:17; 2:12(2); 13; 16; 26; 27; 3:3; 5; 6; 20; 30; 4:1; 18; 24; 5:9; 10; 17; 19; 6:1(2); 2; 5; 8; 14; 15; 7:3; 7; 24; 8:11; 13(2); 18; 21; 31; 32; 33; 35(2); 39; 9:7; 9; 12; 14; 20; 26(2); 27; 30; 33; 10:5; 6; 7; 11; 13(2); 14(3); 15; 11:15; 23; 24; 26(3); 27; 35; 13:2; 14:4; 10; 11(2); 12; 15:12(3); 21(2); 29; 16:20; **1Cor** 1:8; 3:8; 13(4); 14; 15(3); 17; 4:5; 17; 21; 6:2(2); 3; 5; 9; 10; 13; 15; 16; 7:28; 8:10; 11; 9:11; 11:22(2); 27(2); 12:15; 16; 13:8(3); 10; 12; 14:6(2); 7; 8; 9(2); 11(2); 16; 15:22; 24(2); 26; 28(2); 29; 37; 49; 51(2); 52(3); 54(3); 16:3; 4; 5; 12; **2Cor** 1:7; 13; 3:8; 16(2); 4:14(2); 5:3; 6:16; 18; 9:6(2); 10:15; 11:10; 15; 12:6; 20(2); 21; 13:1; 4; 6; 11; **Gal** 2:16; 3:8; 11; 12; 4:30; 5:2; 10; 16; 21; 6:4; 5; 7; 8(2); 9; **Eph** 5:14; 31(3); 6:8; 16; 21; **Phil** 1:19; 20(2); 22; 25; 2:23; 24; 3:15; 21; 4:7; 9; 19; **Col** 3:4(2); 24; 25; 4:7; 9; **1Th** 4:15; 16(2); 17(2); 5:3(2); **2Th** 1:7; 9; 10; 2:3; 8(3); 11; 3:3; **1Ti** 2:15; 3:5; 4:1; 6:15; **2Ti** 2:2; 11; 12; 21; 3:1; 2; 9(2); 12; 13; 4:1; 3; 4(2); 8; 18; **Titus** 3:12; **Philem** 1:22; **Heb** 1:5; 11(2); 12(2); 14; 2:3; 3:11; 4:3; 5; 6:6; 8:10; 11(2); 9:14; 28; 10:27; 29; 30; 37; 38(2); 11:18; 32; 12:9; 14; 20; 25; 13:6; **Jas** 1:5; 7; 10; 11; 12; 25; 2:10; 12; 13; 3:1; 4:10; 14; 15; 5:1; 3(2); 15(3); 20(2); **1Pet** 2:6; 12; 20; 4:5; 8; 13; 17; 18; 5:1; 4(2); **2Pet** 1:8; 10; 11; 2:1(2); 2(2); 3; 12; 13; 3:3; 10(3); 11; 12(2); **1Jn** 2:18; 24(2); 27; 28; 3:2(4); 19; 4:15; 5:16(3); **2Jn** 2; **3Jn** 14(2); **Rev** 1:7(2); 19; 2:10(2); 11; 23; 27(2); 3:4; 5; 10; 12; 5:10; 6:17; 7:15; 16(2); 17(3); 9:6(4); 10:7; 9(2); 11:2; 3; 7(3); 8; 9(2); 10(2); 15; 13:8; 14; 14:10(2); 15:4(2); 17:8(2); 13; 14(2); 16(3); 17; 18:7; 8(2); 9(2); 11; 15; 21(2); 22(3); 23(2); 19:15; 20:6(2); 7; 8; 10; 21:3(2); 4(3); 7(2); 8; 24; 25(2); 26; 27; 22:3(3); 4(2); 5(2); 12; 18(2); 19(2)

SHALT

Gen 2:17(2); 3:14(2); 15; 16; 17(2); 18; 19(2); 4:7(2); 12; 6:14(2); 15; 16(4); 18; 19; 21; 7:2; 12:2; 15:15(2); 16:11(2); 17:4; 9; 15; 19; 20:7(2); 13; 21:23; 30; 24:3; 4; 7; 8; 37; 38; 40; 41(2); 27:10; 40(4); 28:1; 6; 14; 22; 29:27; 30:31; 31:50(2); 52; 32:18; 35:17; 37:8(2); 40:13; 41:40; 43:9; 45:10(2); 47:30; 49:4; 50:5; **Ex** 3:14; 15; 18; 4:9; 12; 15; 16; 17(2); 22; 6:1; 7:2; 9; 15(2); 16; 17; 9:15; 10:28; 12:46; 13:5; 6; 8; 10; 12; 13(3); 14; 15:17; 17:6; 18:20(2); 21; 23(2); 19:3; 6; 12; 24; 20:3; 4; 5; 7; 9; 10; 13; 14; 15; 16; 17(2); 22; 24(2); 25; 26; 21:1; 14; 23; 22:18; 21; 25(2); 26; 28; 29(2); 30(2); 23:1; 2(2); 3; 4; 5; 6; 8; 9; 10(2); 11(2); 12(2); 14; 15(2); 18; 19(2); 22; 24(2); 27; 31; 32; 25:11(3); 12; 13; 14; 16; 17; 18(2); 21(2); 23; 24; 25(2); 26; 28; 29(2); 30; 31; 37; 26:1(2); 4(2); 5(2); 6; 7(2); 9(2); 10; 11; 14; 15; 17; 18; 19; 22; 23; 26; 29(2); 30; 31; 32; 33; 34; 35(2); 36; 37(2); 27:1; 2(2); 3(2); 4(2); 5; 6; 8; 9; 20; 28:2; 3; 9; 11(2); 12; 13; 14; 15(3); 17; 22; 23(2); 24; 25; 26(2); 27(2); 30; 31; 33; 36; 37; 39(3); 40(3); 41(2); 42; 29:1; 2; 3; 4(2); 5; 6; 7; 8; 9(2); 10; 11; 12; 13; 14; 15; 16(2); 17; 18; 19; 20; 21; 22; 24(2); 25; 26; 27; 31; 34; 35(2); 36(3); 37; 38; 39(2); 41(2); 30:1(2); 3(2); 4(2); 5; 6; 16(2); 18(3); 25; 26; 29; 30; 31; 35; 36; 37; 33:21; 23; 34:14; 17; 18(2); 20(3); 21(3); 22; 24; 25; 26(2); 40:2; 3; 4(2); 5; 6; 7(2); 8; 9(2); 10; 11; 12; 13; 14; 15; **Lev** 2:6; 8; 13(3); 14; 15; 6:21(2); 27; 9:3; 13:55; 57; 58; 17:8; 18:7(2); 8; 9; 10; 11; 12; 13; 14(2); 15(2); 16; 17(2); 18; 19; 20; 21(2); 22; 23; 19:9(2); 10(3); 12; 13; 14(2); 15(2); 16(2); 17(2); 18(2); 19(2); 27; 32; 34; 20:2; 16; 19; 21:8; 23:22(3); 24:5; 6; 7; 15; 25:3(2); 4; 5; 8; 9; 15; 16(2); 17; 35; 37; 39; 43(2); 44; **Num** 1:49; 50; 3:9; 10; 15; 41; 47(2); 48; 4:23; 29; 30; 7:5; 8:7; 8; 9(2); 10; 12; 13; 14; 15; 26; 10:2; 11:23; 14:15; 15:5; 6; 7; 10; 17:3; 4; 10; 18:10; 15(2); 16; 17(3); 20(2); 30; 20:8(2); 18; 20; 21:34; 22:12(2); 20; 35; 23:5; 13(2); 26:54(2); 27:7(2); 8; 13; 20; 28:3; 4(2); 7; 8(2); 21; 31:2; 30; **Deut** 1:37; 2:28; 3:2; 27; 28; 4:25; 29(2); 30; 40; 5:7; 8; 9; 11; 13; 14; 17; 18; 19; 20; 21(2); 31; 6:5; 7(2); 8; 9; 11; 13(2); 18; 21; 7:2(2); 3(3); 11; 14; 16(2); 17; 18(2); 21; 24; 25; 26(3); 8:2; 5; 6; 9(2); 10; 18; 9:3; 10:2; 20(3); 11:1; 20; 29; 12:5; 14(2); 18; 20; 21(2); 22; 24(2); 25(2); 26; 27(2); 31; 32; 13:3; 5; 8(3); 9; 10; 12; 14; 15; 16(2); 18; 14:3; 21(2); 22; 23; 25(2); 26(3); 27; 28(2); 15:1; 6(3); 7; 8(2); 10; 11; 12; 13; 14(2); 15; 17(2); 19(2); 20; 21; 22; 23(2); 16:2; 3(2); 6; 7(2); 8(2); 9; 10(2); 11; 12(2); 13; 14; 15(2); 18; 19(2); 20; 21(2); 22; 17:1; 5(2); 7; 8; 9; 10(2); 11(2); 12; 14(3); 15(2); 18:4; 9; 13; 14; 22; 19:2; 3; 7; 9(2); 13; 14(2); 19; 20:12; 13; 14(2); 15; 16; 17; 19(3); 20(2); 21:9(2); 12; 13; 14(3); 21; 23; 22:1(2); 2(2); 3(3); 4(2); 6; 7; 8; 9; 10; 11; 12; 21; 22; 24; 26; 23:6; 7(2); 12(2); 13(3); 15; 16; 18; 19; 20; 21(2); 22; 23; 24; 25; 24:4; 7; 10; 11; 12; 13; 14; 15; 17; 18; 19; 20; 21; 22; 25:4; 12; 13; 14; 15(2); 19(2); 26:2(4); 3; 5; 10; 11; 13; 16; 27:2; 3; 4; 5(2); 6(2); 7(2); 8; 10; 28:1; 2; 3(2); 6(2); 9; 12(2); 13(2); 14; 16(2); 19(2); 25(2); 29(3); 30(5); 31(2); 33; 34(2); 36(2); 37; 38(2); 39(2); 40(2); 41(2); 43; 44(2); 48; 49; 53; 64; 65; 66(2); 67(4); 68; 30:1; 2(2); 5; 8; 10; 17; 31:2; 3; 7; 11; 16; 23; 32:52(2); 33:29; 34:4; **Josh** 1:6; 8(3); 2:18(2); 3:8; 6:3; 8:2; 11:6; 17:17; 18(2); **Judg** 4:20; 6:14; 16; 23; 26; 7:5; 11; 9:33(2); 11:2; 30; 13:3; 5; 7; **Ruth** 2:21; 3:4(3); **1Sa** 2:16; 32; 3:9; 9:16; 10:2; 3(2); 4; 5(2); 6(2); 8(3); 8; 14:44; 16:3(2); 16; 18:21; 19:11; 20:2; 8; 14; 15; 18; 19(2); 31; 22:16; 23; 23:17; 24:20; 26:25(2); 28:1; 2; 19; 30:8; **2Sa** 3:13; 5:2(2); 6; 23; 24; 7:5; 8; 12; 9:7; 10; 10:11; 11:25; 12:13; 13:13; 15:33; 35(2); 18:3; 20(3); 19:23; 38; 21:4; 17; **1Kin** 2:37(2); 42; 5:6; 9(3); 8:19; 44; 11:37(2); 12:10(2); 13:17; 14:5; 17:4; 19:16(2); 20:5; 13; 34; 39; 21:19(2); 22:11; 22; 25(2); **2Kin** 1:4(2); 6(2); 16(2); 4:4(3); 16; 5:10; 6:22; 7:2(2); 19(2); 8:13; 9:7; 10:5; 13:17; 19; 19:11; 20:1; 5; 9; 18; 22:20; **1Chr** 11:2(2); 5; 14:15(2); 17:4; 7; 19:12; 21:22; 22:8; 13; 28:3; **2Chr** 2:16(2); 6:9; 34; 7:17; 10:10(2); 16:9; 18:10; 21(2); 24(2); 21:15; 34:28; **Ezr** 4:13; 15; 16; 7:20; **Est** 4:13; 6:13(2); **Job** 5:21(2); 22(2); 23; 24(3); 25; 26; 7:21; 9:31; 11:15(3); 16; 17(2); 18(3); 19; 14:15; 17:4; 22:23(2); 24; 25; 26(2); 27(2); 28; 29; 35:14; 38:11; **Ps** 2:9(2); 5:3; 6; 12:7(2); 17:3; 21:9; 10; 12(2); 31:20(2); 32:7(2); 8; 36:8; 37:3(2); 10; 34; 50:15; 51:6; 19; 55:23; 59:8(2); 65:3; 67:4; 71:20(2); 21; 73:20; 24; 76:10; 81:9; 82:8; 89:2; 91:4; 5; 8; 13(2); 92:10; 102:12; 13; 26(2); 119:32; 128:2(2); 5; 6; 138:7; 142:7; **Prov** 2:5; 9; 3:4; 23; 24(2); 4:12; 9:12(2); 20:13; 22:24; 23:8; 14(2); 34; 35; 24:6; 25:22; 27:27; **Eccl** 11:1; 12:1; **Is** 1:26; 12:1; 14:4; 15; 20; 17:10(2); 11(2); 22:18; 23:12(2); 25:5; 29:4(2); 6; 30:19; 22(2); 23; 33:1(3); 19; 37:11; 38:1; 39:7; 41:12(2); 15(2); 16(3); 43:2; 44:21; 26; 28; 47:1; 5; 11(3); 12; 49:18; 20; 21; 23; 51:22; 53:10; 54:3; 4(4); 14(3); 17; 55:5; 58:9(2); 11; 12(2); 13; 14; 60:5; 16(3); 18; 62:2; 3; 4(2); 12; **Jer** 1:7(2); 2:36; 37(2); 3:19(2); 4:1; 2; 30; 5:19; 7:27(2); 28; 8:4; 13:12; 13; 14:17; 15:2; 19(2); 16:2(2); 8; 10; 11; 17:4; 18:22; 19:10; 11; 20:6(3); 21:8; 22:15; 22; 23; 23:33; 37; 25:27; 28; 26:4; 8; 28:13; 16; 29:24; 31:4(3); 5; 34:3(3); 4; 5; 14; 36:6; 29; 37:17; 38:17; 18; 23(3); 24; 26; 39:17; 18; 40:16; 45:4; 46:11(2); 48:2; 7; 49:12(2); 51:26; 61(2); 62; 63; 64; **Lam** 4:21(2); **Eze** 2:4; 7; 3:18; 25; 26(2); 27; 4:3; 4(2); 5; 6; 7(2); 8; 9(2); 10(2); 11(2); 12(2); 15; 5:2(3); 3; 8:6; 13; 15; 12:3; 4(2); 6(2); 16:41; 43; 61(2); 62; 21:7; 32(2); 22:2; 16(2); 23:27; 32(2); 33; 34(2); 24:13; 16; 27(2); 25:7; 26:14(2); 21(2); 27:34; 36(2); 28:8; 9; 10; 19(2); 29:5(2); 31:18(2); 32:28(2); 33:7; 8; 14; 35:4(2); 12; 15; 36:12(2); 14; 15(2); 38:8(2); 9(2); 10; 11; 14; 15; 16; 39:4; 5; 43:19; 20(2); 21; 22; 23; 24; 25; 44:6; 45:3; 18; 20; 46:13(2); 14; **Dan** 4:26; 5:16(2); 12:13; **Hos** 2:16(2); 20; 3:3(3); 4:5; 6; 13:4; **Amos** 7:17; **Obad** 10; **Mic** 1:14; 2:5; 4:10(4); 13; 5:12; 13; 6:14(3); 15(5); **Nah** 3:11(3); **Hab** 2:7; **Zeph** 3:11(2); 15; **Zec** 2:11; 3:7(2); 4:7; 9; 13:3; **Mt** 1:21; 4:7; 10(2); 5:21; 26; 27; 33(2); 36; 43; 6:5; 7:5; 11:23; 12:37(2); 16:19(2); 17:27; 19:18(4); 19; 21; 22:37; 39; 26:34; 75; **Mk** 6:23; 10:21; 12:30; 31; 14:30; 72; **Lk** 1:13; 14; 20; 31(2); 76(2); 4:8(2); 12; 5:10; 6:42; 10:15; 27; 28; 12:59; 13:9; 14:10; 14(2); 17:4; 8; 18:22; 22:34; 61; 23:43; **Jn** 1:33; 42; 50; 13:7; 8; 36; 21:18(2); **Acts** 2:28; 13:11; 35; 16:31; 22:15; 23:5; 25:12; 22; **Rom** 2:3; 7:7; 10:9(3); 11:22; 12:20; 13:3; 9(6); **1Cor** 7:16(2); 9:9; 14:16; **Gal** 5:14; **1Ti** 4:6; 16; 5:18; **Heb** 1:12; **Jas** 2:8; **3Jn** 6; **Rev** 2:10; 3:3(2); 16:5; 18:14

SHE

Gen 2:23(2); 3:6; 12; 20; 4:1; 2; 17; 22; 25(2); 8:9; 11:30; 12:14; 16; 18; 19; 15:9; 16:1; 4(3); 5(2); 6; 8; 13(2); 17:16; 18:15; 19:26; 33(2); 35(2); 38; 20:2; 3; 5(3); 12(3); 16; 21:7; 9; 10; 14; 15; 16(3); 19(2); 22:20; 24; 24:14(2); 16; 18(2); 19(2); 20; 24(2); 25; 36; 44; 45; 46(2); 47; 55; 58; 64(2); 65(2); 67; 25:2; 21; 22(2); 26; 26:7(3); 9(2); 27:16; 17(2); 42; 29:9; 12; 32(2); 33(2); 34; 35(3); 30:1; 3(2); 4; 6; 8; 9(2); 11; 13; 15; 17; 18; 20; 21; 23; 24; 35; 31:35; 38; 32:14; 15; 34:1; 35:8; 16; 17; 18(2); 36:12; 14; 38:3; 4(2); 5(2); 14(3); 15; 16(2); 17; 18(2); 19; 24; 25(3); 26; 28; 29; 39:7; 10; 12; 13; 14; 16; 17; 19; 45:23; 46:15; 18; 25; **Ex** 1:16; 2:2(2); 3(3); 5(2); 6(3); 7; 10(3); 22; 4:26; 6:20; 23; 25; 21:4; 7; 8; 11; **Lev** 12:2(2); 4(2); 5(3); 6; 7; 8(3); 15:19; 20(2); 22; 23; 25; 26(2); 28(3); 29; 18:7; 9; 11; 12; 13; 14; 15; 19; 19:20(2); 20:17; 18; 21:9(3); 22:12; 13; 26:43; **Num** 5:13(2); 14(2); 27; 28; 12:10; 14; 15:27; 22:25; 27; 28; 33; 26:59; 30:4(2); 5; 6(3); 7; 8(3); 10; 11; **Deut** 21:12; 13(2); 14; 22:19; 21(2); 24; 29; 24:1; 2(2); 4; 25:6; 28:57(2); **Josh** 2:6(2); 8; 9; 15(2); 16; 21(3); 6:17(2); 22; 23; 25(3); 15:18(3); **Judg** 1:14(3); 15; 4:4; 5; 6; 9; 18; 19; 5:24; 25(2); 26(4); 29; 8:31; 11:34; 36; 37; 38; 39(2); 13:9; 14; 14:3; 7; 17(3); 15:2; 16:8; 9; 14; 15; 16; 18; 19(4); 20; 19:3; 20:5; **Ruth** 1:3; 6(3); 7(2); 9; 15; 18(3); 20; 2:2; 3; 7(3); 10; 13; 14(2); 15; 16; 17(2); 18(5); 19(2); 23; 3:5; 6; 7; 9; 14(2); 15(2); 16(3); 17; 18; 4:13(2); **1Sa** 1:7(3); 10; 11; 12; 13(2); 18; 20; 22; 23; 24(2); 26; 2:5; 19; 21; 4:19(2); 20(2); 21; 22; 18:19; 21; 19:14; 25:3; 19(2); 20(3); 23; 35; 36; 41; 42; 28:12; 14; 24; 25; **2Sa** 4:4; 6:16; 11:4(3); 26; 27; 12:24; 13:2; 8; 9; 10; 11; 12; 14; 16; 18; 14:4; 5; 11; 27; 20:17; 18; 21:8(2); **1Kin** 1:17; 22; 28; 2:13; 14; 16; 19; 20; 21; 3:19; 20; 26; 27; 10:1; 2(3); 6; 10; 13(3); 14:5(2); 6; 17; 15:13; 17:11; 12; 15(2); 18; 21:8; 9; 11; **2Kin** 2:24; 4:2; 5(2); 6; 7; 8; 9; 12; 13; 14; 15; 16; 21; 22; 23; 24; 25; 26; 27(2); 28; 36; 37; 5:2; 3; 6:28; 29; 8:2; 3; 6(2); 9:30; 31; 34; 11:1; 13; 14; 16(2); 22:14; 15; **1Chr** 1:32; 2:21; 26; 29; 35; 49; 4:17; 7:14; 16; 23; 15:29; **2Chr** 9:1(3); 5; 9; 12(4); 15:16; 22:10; 11(2); 23:12; 13; 15; 34:22; 23; 36:21(2); **Est** 1:11; 15; 17; 19; 2:1; 7; 9; 10; 12; 13; 14(4); 15; 17; 20; 4:4; 8; 5:2; 12; **Job** 1:3; 39:16; 18(2); 28; 29; 30; 42:12; **Ps** 45:14; 46:5; 68:12; 80:11; 84:3; **Prov** 1:20; 21(2); 3:15; 18; 4:6(2); 8(2); 9(2); 13; 7:11; 12; 13; 21(2); 26; 8:2; 3; 9:1; 2(3); 3(2); 4; 13; 14; 16; 12:4; 23:22; 25; 28; 30:20; 23; 31:12; 13; 14(2); 15; 16(2); 17; 18; 19; 20(2); 21; 22; 24; 25; 26; 27; 30; **Song** 6:9(2); 10; 8:5; 8(2); 9(2); **Is** 3:26; 8:3; 23:3; 17; 40:2; 49:15; 51:18(2); 66:7(3); 8; **Jer** 3:1; 6; 7(2); 9; 4:17; 6:6; 7; 11:15; 15:9(3); 33:16; 46:24; 50:9; 12; 14; 15(2); 29(2); 51:8; 9; 42; 53; **Lam** 1:1(3); 2(2); 3(2); 4; 7; 8(2); 9(3); 10; **Eze** 5:6; 16:46; 48; 49; 19:2(2); 3; 5(3); 10; 11(2); 12(2); 13; 14; 23:5(2); 7(3); 8; 9; 10; 11(2); 12; 13; 14(2); 16(2); 17; 18; 19(2); 20; 43; 24:7(2); 12; 26:2(3); 17; 32:20; **Dan** 11:6(2); 17; **Hos** 1:6; 8(2); 2:2; 3; 5(2); 6; 7(4); 8; 12; 13(3); 15(2); 13:16; **Amos** 5:2(2); **Mic** 1:7; 13; 5:3; 7:10(2); **Nah** 2:7; 10; 3:10(2); **Zeph** 2:15; 3:2(4); **Zec** 9:4; **Mal** 2:14; **Mt** 1:18; 21; 25; 8:15; 9:18; 21; 12:42; 14:7; 8; 11; 15:23; 25; 27; 20:21; 22:28; 26:10; 12(2); **Mk** 1:31; 5:23(2); 26; 27; 28; 29(2); 42; 6:19; 24(2); 25; 7:26; 28; 30(2); 10:12; 12:23; 42; 44(2); 14:3; 6; 8(3); 9; 67(2); 16:10; **Lk** 1:29(2); 36; 42; 45; 57(2); 2:6; 7; 36; 37; 38; 4:39; 7:12; 37; 39; 44; 47; 8:42; 47(5); 50; 52; 53; 55; 10:39; 40; 11:31; 13:13; 15:8(2); 9(2); 18:3; 5; 20:33; 21:4(2); **Jn** 8:11; 11:20; 27; 28(2); 29(2); 31(2); 32; 12:7; 16:21(3); 20:2; 11(2); 13; 14(2); 15; 16; 18; **Acts** 5:8; 10; 9:36; 37; 39; 40(3); 12:14(2); 15; 16:14; 15(3); 18; **Rom** 7:2; 3(5); 16:2(2); **1Cor** 7:11; 12; 28; 34(3); 36; 39(2); 40(2); 11:5; **Gal** 4:27; **Eph** 5:33; **1Ti** 2:15; 5:5; 6(2); 10(5); **Heb** 11:11(2); 31; **Jas** 2:25; **Rev** 2:21; 6:13; 12:2; 5; 6; 14(2); 14:8; 18:6(2); 7(2); 8; 19; 19:8

SO

Gen 1:7; 9; 11; 15; 24; 27; 30; 3:24; 6:22; 8:11; 11:8; 12:4; 19; 13:6; 16; 15:5; 18:5; 19:7; 11; 18; 20:17; 21:6; 22:8; 19; 24:46; 25:22; 27:1; 20; 23; 28:21; 29:26; 28; 30:33; 42; 31:21; 28; 36; 32:19; 21; 33:16; 34:12; 35:6; 37:14; 40:7; 41:4; 13; 21; 39; 57; 42:20(2); 34; 43:6; 11; 34; 44:5; 17; 45:8; 21; 24; 47:13; 20; 28; 48:10; 18; 49:17; 50:3; 17; 26; **Ex** 1:10; 2:18; 4:26; 5:12; 22; 6:9; 7:6; 10; 20; 22; 8:7; 17; 18(2); 24; 26; 9:24; 10:10; 11; 15; 20; 11:10; 12:28; 36; 50; 14:4; 20; 25; 28; 15:22; 16:17; 30; 34; 17:6; 10; 18:22; 23; 24; 19:16; 25; 21:12; 22; 22:6; 25:9; 33; 27:8; 28:7; 30:21; 23; 32:21; 24; 33:16; 36:6; 13; 37:19; 39:32; 42; 43; 40:16; 33; **Lev** 4:20; 7:7; 8:34; 35; 36; 10:5; 13; 11:32; 14:13; 21; 16:4; 16; 24:19; 20; 26:15; 27:12; 14; **Num** 1:19; 45; 54; 2:17; 34(2); 4:26; 5:4(2); 6:21; 8:3; 4; 7; 20; 22; 9:5; 14; 16; 20; 21; 12:7; 13:21; 33; 14:28; 15:12; 14; 15; 20; 16:27; 17:11(2); 20:8; 21:35; 22:30; 35; 25:8; 31:5; 32:23; 28; 31; 35:7; 16; 29; 33; 36:3; 4; 7; 10; **Deut** 1:11; 15; 43; 46; 2:5; 16; 3:3; 21; 29; 4:5; 7(2); 8(2); 7:4; 19; 8:5; 20; 9:3; 8; 15; 12:4; 10; 22; 30; 31; 13:5; 14:24; 17:7; 18:14; 19:10; 19; 20:18; 21:9; 21; 22:3; 5; 21; 22; 24; 26; 24:8; 25:9; 28:34; 54; 55; 63; 29:22; 30:17; 31:17; 32:12; 33:25; 34:5; 8; **Josh** 1:5; 17; 2:21; 23; 3:7; 4:8; 5:15; 6:11; 14; 20(2); 27; 7:4; 16; 22; 26; 8:3; 22(2); 25; 9:26; 10:1; 7; 13; 23; 39; 40; 11:7; 15(2); 16; 23; 14:5; 11; 12; 15:7; 16:4; 19:51; 21:40; 22:6; 25; 28; 23:15; 24:10; 25; 28; **Judg** 1:3; 7; 35; 2:14; 17; 3:14; 22; 30; 4:14; 15; 21; 23; 5:28; 31; 6:3; 20; 27; 38; 40; 7:1; 5; 8; 15; 17; 19; 8:18; 21; 28; 9:49; 10:9; 11:5; 10; 21; 23; 24; 32; 12:5; 13:19; 14:10(2); 15; 15:11; 16:9; 16; 30; 17:10; 18:21; 19:4; 21; 23; 24; 25; 30; 20:11; 36; 46; 21:14; 23; **Ruth** 1:17; 19; 22; 2:7; 17; 23; 4:8; 13; **1Sa** 1:7(2); 9; 18; 23; 2:3; 5; 14; 21; 3:9; 17; 4:4; 5; 5:7; 9; 11; 6:10; 7:13; 8:8; 9:10; 21; 24; 10:9; 11:7; 11(2); 12:18; 13:22; 14:15; 23; 24; 44; 45; 47; 15:6; 31; 33; 16:13; 23; 17:27; 50; 18:30; 19:12; 17; 18; 20:2; 13; 16; 24; 34; 21:6; 22:14; 23:5(2); 24:7; 25:12; 20; 21; 22; 25; 35; 26:7; 12; 24; 25; 27:1; 11(2); 28:23; 29:8; 11; 30:3; 9; 10; 21; 23; 24; 25; 31:6; **2Sa** 1:2; 10; 2:2; 16; 28; 31; 3:9(2); 20; 30; 34; 35; 5:3; 9; 25; 6:10; 12; 13; 15; 19; 7:8; 17; 8:2; 9:11; 13; 10:14; 19; 11:12; 20(2); 22; 12:31; 13:2; 6; 8; 15; 20; 35; 38; 14:3; 7; 17; 23; 24; 25; 28; 33; 15:2; 5; 6; 9; 34; 37; 16:10(2); 19; 22; 23; 17:3; 12(2); 26; 18:6; 19:13; 14; 15; 20:2; 3; 5; 10(2); 18; 21; 22:4; 35; 37; 23:5; 24:8; 13; 15; 24; 25; **1Kin** 1:3; 6; 30; 36; 37; 38; 40; 45; 53; 2:7; 10; 23; 27; 34; 38; 46; 3:9; 12; 13; 4:1; 5:4; 10; 18; 6:7; 9; 14; 20; 21; 26; 27; 33; 38; 7:9; 18; 22; 40; 51; 8:11; 25; 46; 48; 54; 63; 9:25; 10:13; 23; 29; 11:19; 12:12; 16(2); 19; 32; 33; 13:4; 9; 10; 13; 19; 14:4; 6; 28; 15:20; 16:6; 22; 28; 17:5; 10; 17; 18:4; 6; 12; 16; 20; 42; 19:2; 13; 19; 20:10; 19; 25; 29; 32; 34; 37; 38; 40; 21:5; 8; 22:8; 12; 15; 22; 29; 37; 40; **2Kin** 1:17; 2:2; 4; 8; 10(2); 22; 3:9; 12; 24; 4:5; 8; 25; 36; 40; 44; 5:8; 9; 12; 19; 21; 6:4; 23; 29; 31; 7:10; 16; 20; 8:6; 9; 14; 15; 21; 9:4; 14; 16; 18; 22(2); 27; 33; 37; 10:11; 16; 21; 11:2; 6; 12:6; 10; 13:5; 24; 15:5; 7; 12; 20; 16:7; 11; 17:4; 7; 23; 25; 32; 41(2); 18:5; 21; 19:5; 8; 36; 22:14; 23:18; 24:6; 25:6; 21; **1Chr** 9:1; 23; 10:4; 6; 13; 11:6; 9; 13:4; 5; 13; 14:11; 15:14; 17; 19; 25; 16:1; 37; 17:15; 18:14; 19:2; 7; 14; 17; 20:3; 21:3; 11; 14; 25; 22:5; 23:1; 25:7; 29:14; **2Chr** 1:3; 10; 17; 2:3; 5:14; 6:16; 31; 7:5; 21; 8:14; 16; 9:12; 10:3; 12; 15; 16; 11:17; 12:9; 13; 13:9; 13; 17; 14:1; 7; 12; 15:10; 17:10; 18:7; 11; 21; 28; 29; 19:10; 20:6; 20(2); 25; 30; 21:10; 17; 19; 22:1; 9; 11(2); 23:8; 15; 24:13; 24; 25:21; 26:23; 27:5; 6; 28:14; 29:17; 22; 25; 34; 35; 30:5; 6; 9; 10; 26; 32:4; 17; 21; 23; 26; 33:8; 9; 20; 34:6; 26; 28; 35:6; 10; 12; 16; **Ezr** 2:70; 3:13; 4:13; 15; 24; 5:17; 6:13; 8:23; 30; 9:2; 14; 10:12; 16; **Neh** 2:4; 6; 11; 15; 18; 4:6; 10; 18; 21; 23; 5:12; 13; 15; 6:3; 13; 15; 7:73; 8:8; 11; 16; 17; 9:10; 11; 21; 22; 24; 25; 28; 12:40; 43; 13:20; 21; **Est** 1:8; 13; 17; 2:4; 8; 12; 16; 17; 3:2; 4:4; 6; 16; 17; 5:2(2); 5; 13; 6:6; 10; 7:1; 5; 10; 8:4; 14; 9:14; 27; **Job** 1:3; 5; 12; 2:7; 13; 5:12; 16; 27; 7:3; 9; 15; 20; 8:13; 9:2; 30; 35; 13:9; 14:12; 21:4; 23:7; 24:19; 25; 27:6; 32:1; 22; 33:20; 34:25; 28; 35:15; 36:16; 41:10; 16; 42:7; 9; 12; 15; 17; **Ps** 1:4; 7:7; 18:3; 34; 21:13; 22:1; 26:6; 35:25; 37:3; 40:12; 42:1; 45:11; 48:5; 8; 10; 58:5; 11; 61:8; 63:2; 64:8; 65:9; 68:2(2); 72:7; 73:20; 22; 77:4; 13; 78:21; 29; 53; 60; 72; 79:13; 80:12; 18; 81:12; 83:15; 90:11; 12; 102:4; 15; 103:5; 11; 12; 13; 15; 104:25; 106:9; 30; 32; 33; 107:2; 29; 30; 38; 109:17(2); 18; 115:8; 119:27; 42; 44; 88; 134; 123:2; 125:2; 127:2; 4; 135:18; 147:20; **Prov** 1:19; 2:2; 3:4; 10; 22; 6:11; 29; 7:13; 10:25; 26; 11:19; 22; 15:7; 19:24; 20:30; 23:7; 24:14; 29; 34; 25:12; 13; 16; 17; 20; 23; 25; 27; 26:1; 2; 7; 8; 9; 11; 14; 19; 20; 21; 27:8; 9; 17; 18; 19; 20; 21; 28:15; 30:33; 31:11; **Eccl** 2:9; 15; 3:11; 19(2); 4:1; 5:16; 6:2; 3; 7:6; 8:10(2); 9:2; 12; 10:1; 11:5; **Song** 2:2; 3; 5:9; **Is** 5:24; 6:13; 10:7(2); 11; 26; 14:24(2); 16:2; 6; 18:4; 20:2; 4; 21:1; 22:22; 23:1; 5; 24:2(6); 26:17; 28:8; 29:8; 30:14; 31:4; 5; 36:6; 37:5; 8; 37; 38:8; 13; 14; 16; 40:20; 41:7; 47:7; 12(2); 52:14; 15; 53:7; 54:9; 55:9; 11; 59:19; 60:15; 61:11; 62:5(2); 63:8; 14; 65:8; 66:13; 22; **Jer** 2:26; 36; 3:20; 5:19; 27; 31; 6:7; 9:10; 10:18; 11:4; 5; 13:2; 5; 11; 17:11; 18:4; 6; 19:11; 21:2; 24:2; 3; 5; 8(2); 26:3; 7; 28:6; 11; 17; 29:17; 30:7; 31:28; 32:8; 11; 42; 33:22; 26; 34:5; 35:11; 36:14; 15; 21; 37:14; 38:6; 11; 12; 13; 16; 20; 23; 27; 28; 39:13; 14; 40:5; 41:7; 8; 14; 42:17; 18; 20; 43:4; 7; 44:14; 22; 46:18; 48:30(2); 39; 50:40; 51:8; 49; 60; 52:5; 6; 26; **Lam** 2:22; 3:29; 4:14; 5:20; **Eze** 1:18; 28; 3:2; 14; 4:5; 5:15; 17; 6:14; 8:5; 10; 11:24; 12:7; 11; 13:14(2); 14:15; 17; 15:6; 16:16; 42; 44; 17:6; 18:4; 30; 19:14; 20:36; 21:24; 22:20; 22; 23:18; 27; 44; 24:18; 19; 28:14; 31:9; 33:7; 34:12; 35:15; 36:38; 37:7; 10; 23; 38:20; 39:7; 10; 22; 23; 40:5; 47; 41:4; 7; 13; 18; 19; 43:5; 15; 27; 45:20(2); 47:21; **Dan** 1:5; 14; 2:2; 15; 42; 3:17; 5:6; 6:23; 28; 7:16; 8:4; 17; 10:7; 11:9; 15;

30; **Hos** 1:3; 3:2; 3; 4:7; 6:9; 8:7; 10:15; 11:2; 13:6; 14:2; **Joel** 2:4; 3:17; **Amos** 3:12; 4:8; 5:9; 14; **Obad** 16; **Jonah** 1:3; 4; 6(2); 7; 12; 15; 3:3; 5; 4:5; 6; **Mic** 2:2; 5:14; 7:3; **Zeph** 3:6; 7; **Hag** 2:5; 14(3); **Zec** 1:6; 14; 21; 3:5; 4:4; 6:7; 7:3; 13; 8:13; 15; 10:1; 11:11; 12; 14:15; **Mal** 3:13; **Mt** 1:17; 3:15; 5:12; 16; 19; 47; 6:30; 7:12; 17; 8:10; 13; 28; 31; 9:19; 33; 11:26(2); 12:40; 45; 13:2; 27; 32; 40; 49; 15:33(2); 18:13; 14; 31; 35; 19:8; 10; 12; 20:8; 16; 26; 34; 22:10; 23:28; 24:27; 33; 37; 39; 46; 25:9; 20; 27:64; 66; 28:15; **Mk** 2:2; 8; 3:20(2); 4:1; 17; 26; 32; 37; 40; 6:31; 7:18; 36; 8:8; 9:3; 10:8; 43; 13:29; 14:59; 15:5; 15; 39; 16:19; **Lk** 1:21; 60; 2:6; 21; 5:7; 10; 15; 6:3; 10; 26; 7:9; 9:15; 10:21(2); 11:2; 30; 12:21; 28; 38; 43; 54; 14:21; 33; 16:5; 26; 17:10; 24; 26; 18:13; 39; 20:15; 20; 21:31; 34; 22:26; 24:24; **Jn** 3:8; 14; 16; 4:40; 46; 53; 5:21; 26; 6:9; 10; 19; 57; 7:43; 8:7; 59; 10:15; 11:28; 12:37; 50; 13:12; 13; 33; 14:2; 9; 31; 15:8; 9; 17:18; 18:15; 22; 20:4; 20; 21; 21:11; 15; **Acts** 1:11; 3:12; 18; 4:21; 5:8(2); 32; 7:1; 5; 8; 15; 19; 51; 8:32; 10:14; 11:8; 12:8; 15; 13:4; 8; 47; 14:1; 15:30; 39(2); 16:5; 26; 17:11; 33; 19:2; 10; 12; 14; 16; 20; 22; 27; 20:11; 13; 24; 35; 21:11; 35; 22:24; 23:7; 11; 18; 22; 24:9; 14; 27:17; 44; 28:9; 14; **Rom** 1:15; 20; 4:18; 5:3; 11; 12; 15; 16; 18; 19; 21; 6:3; 4; 19; 7:2; 3(2); 25; 8:8; 9; 17; 9:16; 10:17; 11:5; 16; 26; 31; 12:5; 20; 14:12; 15:19; 20; **1Cor** 1:7; 2:11; 3:7; 15; 4:1; 5:1; 3; 6:5; 7:17(2); 26; 36; 37; 38; 40; 8:12; 9:14; 15; 24; 26(2); 11:12; 28; 12:12; 13:2; 14:9; 10; 12; 25; 15:11(2); 15; 22; 42; 45; 54; 16:1; **2Cor** 1:5; 7; 10; 2:7; 3:7; 4:12; 5:3; 7:7; 14; 8:6; 11; 9:7; 10:7; 11:3; 9; 22(3); 12:16; **Gal** 1:6; 9; 3:3; 4; 9; 4:3; 29; 31; 5:17; 6:2; **Eph** 2:15; 4:20; 21; 5:24; 28; 33; **Phil** 1:13; 20; 2:23; 3:17; 4:1; **Col** 2:6; 3:13; **1Th** 1:7; 8; 2:4; 8; 4:1; 14; 17; 5:2; **2Th** 1:4; 2:4; 3:17; **1Ti** 1:4; 3:11; 6:20; **2Ti** 3:8; **Heb** 1:4; 2:3; 3:11; 19; 4:7; 5:3; 5; 6:15; 7:9; 22; 9:28; 10:25; 33; 11:3; 12; 12:1(2); 20; 21; 13:6; **Jas** 1:11; 2:12(2); 17; 26; 3:4; 5; 6; 10; 12; **1Pet** 1:15; 2:3; 15; 3:17; 4:10; 5:13; **2Pet** 1:11; **1Jn** 2:6; 4:11; 17; **Rev** 1:7; 2:15; 3:16; 8:12; 13:13; 16:7; 18(2); 17:3; 18:7; 17; 22:20

SOME

Gen 19:19; 27:3; 30:35; 33:15; 37:20(2); 47:2; **Ex** 16:17(2); 20; 27; 30:36; **Lev** 4:7; 17; 18; 14:14; 15; 25; 27; 25:25; 27:16; **Num** 5:20; 21:1; 27:20; 31:3; **Deut** 24:1; **Josh** 8:22(2); **Judg** 21:13; **Ruth** 2:16; **1Sa** 8:11; 13:7; 24:10; 27:5; **2Sa** 11:17; 24; 17:9(3); 12; **1Kin** 14:13; **2Kin** 2:16(2); 5:13; 7:9; 13; 9:33; 17:25; **1Chr** 4:42; 9:29; 30; 12:19; **2Chr** 12:7; 16:10; 17:11; 20:2; **Ezr** 2:68; 70; 7:7; 10:44; **Neh** 2:12; 5:3; 5; 6:2; 7:70; 71; 73; 11:25; 12:44; 13:15; 19; **Job** 24:2; **Ps** 20:7(2); 69:20; **Prov** 4:16; **Jer** 49:9; **Eze** 6:8; **Dan** 8:10; 11:35; 12:2(2); **Amos** 4:11; **Obad** 5; **Mt** 13:4; 5; 7; 8(3); 23(3); 16:14(2); 28; 19:12(2); 23:34(2); 27:47; 28:11; 17; **Mk** 2:1; 4:4; 5; 7; 8(3); 20(3); 7:2; 8:28; 9:1; 12:5(2); 14:4; 65; 15:35; **Lk** 8:5; 6; 7; 9:7; 8; 19; 27; 11:15; 49; 13:1; 19:39; 21:5; 16; 23:8; **Jn** 3:25; 6:64; 7:12; 25; 41; 44; 9:9; 16; 40; 10:1; 11:37; 46; 13:29; 16:17; **Acts** 5:15; 8:9; 31; 34; 11:20; 13:11; 15:36; 17:4; 18(2); 21; 32; 18:23; 19:32(2); 21:34(2); 27:27; 34; 36; 44(2); 28:24(2); **Rom** 1:11; 13; 3:3; 8; 5:7; 11:14; 17; 15:15; **1Cor** 4:18; 6:11; 8:7; 9:22; 10:7; 8; 9; 10; 12:28; 15:6; 12; 34; 35; 37; **2Cor** 3:1; 10:2; 12; **Gal** 1:7; **Eph** 4:11(4); **Phil** 1:15(2); **Col** 3:7; **1Th** 3:5; **2Th** 3:11; **1Ti** 1:3; 6; 19; 4:1; 5:15; 24(2); 25; 6:10; 21; **2Ti** 2:18; 20(2); **Heb** 3:4; 16; 4:6; 10:25; 11:40; 13:2; **1Pet** 4:12; **2Pet** 3:9; 16; **Jude** 22; **Rev** 2:10

SOMEBODY

Lk 8:46; **Acts** 5:36

SOMETHING

1Sa 20:26; **Mk** 5:43; **Lk** 11:54; **Jn** 13:29; **Acts** 3:5; 23:15; 18; **Gal** 6:3

SOMETIME

Col 1:21; **1Pet** 3:20

SOMEWHAT

Lev 4:13; 22; 27; 13:6; 19; 21; 24; 26; 28; 56; **1Kin** 2:14; **2Kin** 5:20; **2Chr** 10:4; 0; 10; **Lk** 7:40; **Acts** 23:20; 25:26; **Rom** 15:24; **2Cor** 5:12; 10:8; **Gal** 2:6(2); **Heb** 8:3; **Rev** 2:4

STAY

Gen 19:17; **Ex** 9:28; **Lev** 13:5; 23; 28; 37; **Josh** 10:19; **Ruth** 1:13; **1Sa** 15:16; 20:38; **2Sa** 22:19; 24:16; **1Chr** 21:15; **Job** 37:4; 38:37; **Ps** 18:18; **Prov** 28:17; **Song** 2:5; **Is** 3:1(3); 10:20(2); 19:13; 29:9; 30:12; 31:1; 48:2; 50:10; **Jer** 4:6; 20:9; **Dan** 4:35; **Hos** 13:13

STAYED

Gen 8:10; 12; 32:4; **Ex** 10:24; 17:12; **Num** 16:48; 50; 25:8; **Deut** 10:10; **Josh** 10:13; **1Sa** 20:19; 24:7; 30:9; **2Sa** 17:17; 24:21; 25; **1Kin** 22:35; **2Kin** 4:6; 13:18; 15:20; **1Chr** 21:22; **2Chr** 18:34; **Job** 38:11; **Ps** 106:30; **Is** 26:3; **Lam** 4:6; **Eze** 31:15; **Hag** 1:10(2); **Lk** 4:42; **Acts** 19:22

STEAD

Gen 22:13; 30:2; 36:33; 34; 35; 36; 37; 38; 39; **Ex** 29:30; **Lev** 6:22; 16:32; **Num** 32:14; **Deut** 2:12; 21; 22; 23; 10:6; **Josh** 5:7; **2Sa** 10:1; 16:8; **1Kin** 1:30; 35; 11:43; 14:20; 27; 31; 15:8; 24; 28; 16:6; 10; 28; 22:40; 50; **2Kin** 1:17; 3:27; 8:15; 24; 10:35; 12:21; 13:9; 24; 14:16; 29; 15:7; 10; 14; 22; 30; 38; 16:20; 19:37; 20:21; 21:18; 24; 26; 23:30; 24:6; 17; **1Chr** 1:44; 45; 46; 47; 48; 49; 50; 19:1; 29:28; **2Chr** 1:8; 9:31; 12:16; 14:1; 17:1; 21:1; 22:1; 24:27; 26:23; 27:9; 28:27; 32:33; 33:20; 25; 36:1; 8; **Job** 16:4; 33:6; 34:24; **Prov** 11:8; **Eccl** 4:15; **Is** 37:38; **Jer** 29:26; **2Cor** 5:20; **Philem** 1:13

SUCH

Gen 4:20(2); 21; 27:4; 9; 14; 46; 30:32; 41:19; 38; 44:15; **Ex** 9:18; 24; 10:14(2); 11:6; 12:36; 18:21(2); 34:10; **Lev** 10:19; 11:34(2); 14:22; 30; 31; 20:6; 22:6; 27:9; **Num** 8:16; **Deut** 4:32; 5:29; 13:11; 14; 16:9; 17:4; 19:20; 25:16; **Judg** 3:2; 13:23; 18:23; 19:30; **Ruth** 4:1; **1Sa** 2:23; 4:7; 21:2(2); 25:17; **2Sa** 9:8; 12:8(2); 13:12; 18; 14:13; 16:2; 19:36; **1Kin** 10:10; 12; **2Kin** 6:8(2); 9; 7:19; 19:29; 21:12; 23:22; 25:15; **1Chr** 12:33; 36; 29:25; **2Chr** 1:12; 4:6; 9:9; 11; 11:16; 23:13; 24:12(2); 30:5; 35:18; **Ezr** 4:10; 11; 17; 6:21; 7:12; 25; 27; 8:31; 9:13; 10:3; **Neh** 6:8; 11; **Est** 2:9; 4:11; 14; 9:2; 27; **Job** 12:3; 14:3; 15:13; 16:2; 18:21; 23:14; **Ps** 25:10; 27:12; 34:18; 37:14; 22; 40:4; 16; 50:21; 55:20; 68:21; 70:4; 73:1; 103:18; 107:10; 125:5; 139:6; 144:15; **Prov** 11:20; 28:4; 30:20; 31:8; **Eccl** 4:1; **Is** 9:1; 10:20; 20:6; 37:30; 58:5; 66:8(2); **Jer** 2:10; 5:9; 29; 9:9; 15:2(4); 18:13; 21:7; 38:4; 43:11(3); 44:14; **Eze** 17:15; 18:14; **Dan** 1:4; 2:10; 10:15; 11:32; 12:1; **Amos** 5:16; **Mic** 5:15; **Zeph** 1:8; **Mt** 9:8; 18:5; 19:14; 24:21; 44; 26:18; **Mk** 4:18; 20; 33; 6:2; 7:8; 13; 9:37; 10:14; 13:7; 19; **Lk** 9:9; 10:7; 8; 11:41; 13:2; 18:16; **Jn** 4:23; 7:32; 8:5; 9:16; **Acts** 2:47; 3:6; 15:24; 16:24; 18:15; 21:25; 22:22; 25:18; 20; 26:29; 28:10; **Rom** 1:32; 2:2; 3; 16:18; **1Cor** 5:1; 5; 11; 6:11; 7:15; 28; 10:13; 11:16; 15:48(2); 16:16; 18; **2Cor** 2:6; 7; 3:4; 12; 10:11(3); 11:13; 12:2; 3; 5; 20(2); **Gal** 5:21(2); 23; 6:1; **Eph** 5:27; **Phil** 2:29; **1Th** 4:6; **2Th** 3:12; **1Ti** 6:5; **2Ti** 3:5; **Titus** 3:11; **Philem** 1:9; **Heb** 5:12; 7:26; 8:1; 11:14; 12:3; 13:5; 16; **Jas** 4:13; 16; **2Pet** 1:17; 3:14; **3Jn** 8; **Rev** 5:13; 16:18; 20:6

SURELY

Gen 2:17; 3:4; 9:5; 18:18; 20:7; 11; 26:11; 28:16; 22; 29:14; 32; 30:16; 31:42; 32:12; 42:16; 43:10; 44:28; 46:4; 50:24; 25; **Ex** 2:14; 3:7; 16; 4:25; 11:1; 13:19; 18:18; 19:12; 13; 21:12; 15; 16; 17; 20; 22; 28; 36; 22:6; 14; 16; 19; 23; 23:4; 5; 33; 31:14; 15; 40:15; **Lev** 20:2; 9; 10; 11; 12; 13; 15; 16; 27; 24:16; 17; 27:29; **Num** 13:27; 14:23; 35; 15:35; 18:15; 22:33; 23:23; 26:65; 27:7; 32:11; 35:16; 17; 18; 21; 31; **Deut** 1:35; 4:6; 8:19; 13:9; 15; 15:8; 10; 16:15; 22:4; 23:21; 30:18; 31:18; **Josh** 14:9; **Judg** 3:24; 4:9; 6:16; 11:31; 13:22; 15:13; 20:39; 21:5; **Ruth** 1:10; **1Sa** 9:6; 14:39; 44; 15:32; 16:6; 17:25; 20:26; 31; 22:16; 22; 24:20; 25:21; 34; 28:2; 29:6; 30:8; **2Sa** 2:27; 9:7; 11:23; 12:5; 14; 15:21; 18:2; 20:18; 24:24; **1Kin** 2:37; 42; 8:13; 11:2; 11; 13:32; 18:15; 20:23; 25; 22:32; **2Kin** 1:4; 6; 16; 3:14; 23; 5:11; 8:10; 14; 9:26; 18:30; 23:22; 24:3; **Est** 6:13; **Job** 8:6; 13:3; 10; 14:18; 18:21; 20:20; 28:1; 31:36; 33:8; 34:12; 31; 35:13; 37:20; 40:20; **Ps** 23:6; 32:6; 39:6(2); 11; 62:9; 73:18; 76:10; 77:11; 85:9; 91:3; 112:6; 131:2; 132:3; 139:11; 19; 140:13; **Prov** 1:17; 3:34; 10:9; 22:16; 23:18; 30:2; 33; **Eccl** 4:16; 7:7; 8:12; 10:11; **Is** 7:9; 14:24; 16:7; 19:11; 22:14; 17; 18; 29:16; 36:15; 40:7; 45:14; 24; 49:4; 18; 53:4; 54:15; 60:9; 62:8; 63:8; **Jer** 2:35; 3:20; 4:10; 5:2; 4; 8:13; 16:19; 22:6; 22; 24:8; 26:8; 15; 31:18; 19; 20; 32:4; 34:3; 36:16; 37:9; 38:3; 15; 39:18; 44:25(3); 29; 46:18; 49:12; 20(2); 50:45(2); 51:14; 56; **Lam** 3:3; **Eze** 3:6; 18; 21; 5:11; 17:16; 19; 18:9; 13; 17; 19; 21; 28; 20:33; 31:11; 33:8; 13; 14; 15; 16; 27; 34:8; 36:5; 7; 38:19; **Hos** 5:9; 12:11; **Amos** 3:7; 5:5; 7:11; 17; 8:7; **Mic** 2:12(2); **Hab** 2:3; **Zeph** 2:9; 3:7; **Mt** 26:73; **Mk** 14:70; **Lk** 1:1; 4:23; **Jn** 17:8; **Heb** 6:14; **Rev** 22:20

THAN

Gen 3:1; 4:13; 19:9; 25:23; 26:16; 29:19; 30; 34:19; 36:7; 37:3; 4; 38:26; 39:9; 41:40; 48:19; **Ex** 1:9; 14:12; 18:11; 30:15; 36:5; **Lev** 13:3; 4; 20; 21; 25; 26; 30; 31; 32; 34; 14:37; 27:8; **Num** 3:46; 13:31; 14:12; 22:15; 24:7; **Deut** 1:28; 4:38; 7:1; 7; 17; 9:1; 14; 11:23; 20:1; **Josh** 10:2; 11; **Judg** 2:19; 8:2; 11:25; 14:18(2); 15:2; 3; 16:30; **Ruth** 3:10; 12; 4:15; **1Sa** 1:8; 9:2(2); 10:23; 15:22(2); 28; 18:30; 24:17; 27:1; **2Sa** 1:23(2); 6:22; 13:14; 15; 16; 17:14; 18:8; 19:7; 43(2); 20:5; 6; 23:23; **1Kin** 1:37; 47(2); 2:32; 4:31(2); 12:10; 16:25; 33; 19:4; 20:23(2); 25; 21:2; **2Kin** 5:12; 6:16; 9:35; 21:9; **1Chr** 4:9; 11:21; 24:4; **2Chr** 10:10; 20:25; 21:13; 25:9; 29:34; 30:18; 32:7; 33:9; **Ezr** 8:15; 9:13; **Est** 1:19; 2:17; 4:13; 6:6; **Job** 3:21; 4:17(2); 6:3; 7:6; 15; 9:25; 11:6; 8; 9(2); 17; 15:10; 23:2; 12; 30:1; 8; 32:2; 4; 33:12; 25; 34:19; 23; 35:2; 5; 11(2); 36:21; 42:12; **Ps** 4:7; 8:5; 19:10(3); 37:16; 40:5; 12; 45:2; 51:7; 52:3(2); 55:21(2); 61:2; 62:9; 63:3; 69:4; 31; 73:7; 76:4; 84:10(2); 87:2; 89:27; 93:4(2); 105:24; 118:8; 9; 119:72; 98; 99; 100; 103; 130:6(2); 139:18; 142:6; **Prov** 3:14(2); 15; 5:3; 8:10; 11; 19(3); 11:24; 12:9; 26; 15:16; 17; 16:8; 16(2); 19; 32(2); 17:1; 10; 12; 18:19; 24; 19:1; 22; 21:3; 9; 19; 22:1(2); 25:7; 24; 26:12; 16; 27:3; 5; 10; 28:6; 23; 29:20; 30:2; **Eccl** 1:16; 2:9; 16; 24; 25; 3:22; 4:2; 3; 6; 9; 13; 5:1; 5; 8(2); 6:3; 5; 8; 9; 10; 7:1(2); 2; 3; 5; 8(2); 10; 19; 26; 8:15; 9:4; 16; 17; 18; **Song** 1:2; 4; 4:10(2); 5:9(2); **Is** 13:12(2); 28:20(2); 33:19; 40:17; 52:14(2); 54:1; 55:9(3); 56:5; 57:8; 65:5; **Jer** 3:11; 4:13; 5:3; 7:26; 8:3; 16:12; 20:7; 31:11; 46:23; **Lam** 4:6; 7(3); 8; 9; 19; **Eze** 3:9; 5:6(2); 7; 6:14; 8:15; 15:2(2); 16:47; 51; 52(2); 23:11(2); 28:3; 36:11; 42:5(3); 6; **Dan** 1:10; 15; 20; 2:30; 3:19; 7:20; 8:3; 11:2; 8; 13; **Hos** 2:7; 6:6; **Amos** 6:2(2); **Jonah** 4:3; 8; 11; **Mic** 7:4; **Nah** 3:8; **Hab** 1:8(2); 13(2); **Hag** 2:9; **Mt** 3:11; 5:37; 47; 6:25(2); 26; 10:15; 31; 37(2); 11:9; 11(2); 22; 24; 12:6; 12; 41; 42; 45(2); 18:8; 9; 13; 19:24; 21:36; 23:15; 26:53; 27:64; **Mk** 1:7; 4:31; 32; 6:11; 8:14; 9:43; 45; 47; 10:25; 12:31; 33; 43; 14:5; **Lk** 3:13; 16; 7:26; 28(2); 10:12; 14; 11:22; 26(2); 31; 32; 12:7; 23(2); 24; 14:8; 15:7; 16:8; 17; 17:2; 18:14; 25; 21:3; **Jn** 1:50; 3:19; 4:1; 12; 5:20; 36; 7:31; 8:53; 10:29; 12:43; 13:16(2); 14:12; 28; 15:13; 20; 21:15; **Acts** 4:19; 5:29; 15:28; 17:11; 20:35; 23:13; 21; 25:6; 26:22; 27:11; **Rom** 1:25; 3:9; 8:37; 12:3; 13:11; **1Cor** 1:25(2); 3:11; 7:9; 9:15; 10:22; 14:5; 18; 19; 15:10; **2Cor** 1:13; **Gal** 1:8; 9; 4:27; **Eph** 3:8; **Phil** 2:3; **1Ti** 1:4; 5:8; **2Ti** 3:4; **Philem** 1:21; **Heb** 1:4(2); 2:7; 9; 3:3(2); 4:12; 7:26; 9:23; 11:4; 25; 26; 12:24; **1Pet** 1:7; 3:17; **2Pet** 2:20; 21; **1Jn** 3:20; 4:4; **3Jn** 4; **Rev** 2:19

THAT

Gen 1:4; 10; 12; 18; 20(2); 21(2); 25(2); 26; 28; 30; 31; 2:3; 4; 9; 11; 12; 13; 14; 17; 18; 19; 3:5; 6(2); 7; 11(2); 13; 4:3; 8; 14(2); 5:1; 5; 6:2(2); 3; 4; 5(2); 6; 7; 17; 21; 22; 7:2; 4; 5; 8(2); 10; 14; 16; 19; 21(2); 22; 23; 8:1; 6; 11; 17(3); 9:2; 3; 10(2); 12; 14; 16(2); 17; 18; 10:11; 11:2; 7; 12:1; 3(2); 5(2); 11(2); 12; 13; 14(2); 18(2); 20; 13:1; 6(2); 10; 14; 16; 14:2; 5; 7; 10; 13; 14; 17; 23(3); 24; 15:4; 7; 8; 13(2); 14; 17(2); 16:2; 4; 5; 10; 13(2); 17:12(2); 13(2); 14; 17(2); 18; 23(2); 18:5; 17; 18; 19(3); 24; 25(3); 19:5; 11(2); 14; 17; 21; 25; 29; 32; 33; 34(2); 35; 20:6; 7(2); 9(2); 10; 13; 16; 21:3; 6(2); 7; 8; 12; 22(3); 23(2); 30(2); 31; 22:1; 12; 14; 17; 20; 23:4; 6; 8; 9; 10; 11; 15; 17(2); 18; 20; 24:2(2); 3; 6; 7; 9; 11; 14(4); 15; 22; 30; 32; 36; 43; 49; 52; 54; 55; 56; 65; 66; 25:5; 11; 18; 26; 30; 26:1; 5; 8; 11; 12; 21; 22; 28; 29; 32; 27:1(2); 4(2); 7; 8; 10(2); 19; 20; 21; 25; 29(2); 30; 31; 33; 40; 45; 28:3; 4; 6(2); 7; 8; 11(2); 15; 18; 19(2); 20; 21; 22; 29:2; 7; 10; 12(2); 13; 19(2); 21; 23; 25; 31; 33; 30:1; 3; 9; 15; 16; 25(2); 27; 33(2); 35(4); 38; 41(2); 31:1(2); 5; 6; 10(2); 12; 16; 19; 20(2); 21; 22; 24; 26; 27; 29; 32; 35; 36; 37; 39; 43; 52(2); 32:2; 5; 7; 13(2); 19; 20; 21; 22; 23; 25; 29; 32; 33:9; 11; 13; 14; 15; 16; 34:5; 14(2); 15; 24(2); 25; 28(2); 29; 35:1; 2(2); 5; 6(2); 17; 18; 20; 22(2); 36:7; 16; 17; 18; 24(2); 29; 30; 31; 40; 37:4; 10; 22(2); 23(2); 38:1(2); 9(3); 14; 16(2); 18; 21(2); 22; 24; 26; 27; 28; 29; 30; 39:3(3); 4; 5(4); 6; 7; 8; 10; 11; 13; 14; 15(2); 18; 19; 22; 23(2); 40:1; 7; 15; 16; 20; 41:1; 8(2); 15(2); 21; 24; 27; 31; 32; 35; 36(2); 53; 57; 42:1; 2(2); 5; 6; 14(2); 16; 21; 23; 28; 29; 33; 34(2); 35; 43:7; 8; 12; 14; 15; 18(2); 21; 25; 32; 44:2; 7; 15(2); 17; 21; 27; 30; 31(2); 34; 45:1; 5; 8; 10; 11; 12(2); 13; 15; 24; 46:1; 26; 32; 34(2); 47:1; 13; 14; 17; 18(2); 19(2); 24; 26; 29; 48:1; 10; 17; 20; 49:1(2); 15(2); 17(2); 25; 26; 28; 29; 30; 32; 50:14; 15; **Ex** 1:5; 6; 10; 21; 22; 2:2; 7; 11; 13(3); 13; 18; 20(2); 23; 3:4; 8; 10; 11(2); 12; 14; 16; 18; 19; 20; 21; 22; 4:2; 5(2); 8; 9; 14; 21(2); 23; 24; 31(2); 5:1; 2; 9; 19; 22; 6:7; 11; 26; 27; 29(2); 7:2(2); 4; 5; 13; 16; 17(2); 18; 19(2); 20(2); 21; 25; 8:1; 8(2); 9; 10(2); 15; 16; 20; 22(3); 28; 29; 9:1; 4; 6; 13; 14(2); 15; 16; 17; 19; 20; 21; 22; 25; 28; 29(2); 30; 34; 10:1; 2(3); 3; 5(2); 6; 7(2); 8; 11(2); 12(2); 13(2); 15; 17; 20; 21; 25; 28; 11:5(2); 7(2); 8(2); 9; 10; 12:8; 10; 15; 16(2); 19(2); 22(2); 25; 27; 29(3); 33; 36; 37; 41; 42; 44; 48; 49(2); 51; 13:5; 8(2); 9; 12(3); 14; 15(2); 17(2); 14:2; 4(3); 5(2); 12(3); 15; 18; 20; 21; 24; 25(2); 26; 28; 30; 31; 15:7; 26(2); 16:4; 5(2); 6; 7(2); 8; 10; 12; 13; 14; 18(2); 22; 23(4); 25; 27; 29; 32; 17:2; 3; 6; 11; 16; 18:1(2); 8(2); 11; 13; 14(2); 17; 18; 19; 20; 22; 24; 19:8; 9; 12; 16(3); 20:4(3); 5; 6; 7; 10; 11; 12; 17; 20(2); 22; 26; 21:12(2); 14; 15; 16; 17; 19; 22; 26; 28; 29; 35; 36; 22:2; 6(2); 11; 13; 16; 20; 25; 26; 27(2); 31; 23:5; 11; 12; 13; 22; 24:7; 12; 25:2(2); 8; 9; 14; 21; 26; 28; 33; 35; 37; 40; 26:5(2); 10; 11; 12(2); 13(2); 33; 27:5; 20; 28:1; 3(3); 4; 28(2); 32; 35; 37; 38(2); 41; 43; 29:1; 13(3); 21; 22(2); 23; 27(2); 30(2); 32; 38; 46(3); 30:6(2); 12; 13(2); 14(2); 16; 20; 21; 29; 30; 38; 31:6(3); 7; 11; 13(3); 14(2); 32:1(2); 10(2); 13; 18(3); 19; 21; 22; 23; 25; 28; 29; 30; 33:5; 7; 8; 13(3); 16(3); 17; 22; 34:1; 3; 7; 10; 11; 19(2); 29(2); 32; 34; 35; 35:1; 10; 22; 24; 25(2); 34; 35(2); 36:1; 4; 8; 18; 19; 37:8; 13; 38:15; 22; 24; 25; 26(2); 39:5; 7; 21(2); 23; 32; 42; 40:4; 9; 13; 15; 16; 17; 37; **Lev** 1:5; 8; 12; 17; 2:8; 10; 3:3(2); 4; 5; 9(2); 10; 14(2); 15; 17; 4:3; 5; 8(2); 9; 16; 18; 35; 5:3; 4; 5(3); 8; 11; 13; 16; 6:2; 3(2); 4(3); 5; 7; 18; 22; 26; 27; 7:3; 4(2); 7; 8; 9(3); 14; 15; 16; 18(2); 19(2); 20(3); 21(2); 24(2); 25; 27(2); 29; 30; 33; 36; 38; 8:10; 16; 25; 26; 31; 32; 35; 9:1; 5; 6; 19; 10:3(2); 10; 11; 12(2); 20; 11:2; 3; 4(2); 9; 10(2); 12; 20; 21; 26; 27; 28; 29; 31; 34(2); 36; 39; 40(2); 41; 42; 43(2); 44; 45; 46(2); 47(2); 12:7; 13:4; 7; 8; 12; 13; 17; 24; 31(2); 33; 37; 39; 41; 47; 50; 51; 52; 54; 55; 57; 14:4; 5; 6; 7; 8(3); 9; 11(2); 14; 16; 17(2); 18(2); 19; 25; 27; 28(2); 29(2); 31; 32; 35; 36(3); 40; 41; 43; 46(2); 47(2); 15:4; 6(2); 7(2); 8(2); 9; 10(2); 11; 12; 13; 20(2); 22; 28; 31(2); 32; 33(4); 16:2(2); 13(3); 15(2); 16; 18; 26; 28; 29(2); 30(2); 17:3(2); 4(2); 5(2); 8; 9; 10(4); 11; 12; 13(2); 15(3); 18:6; 26; 28(2); 29; 30(2); 19:8(2); 13; 20; 25; 31; 34; 20:2(2); 3; 5(2); 6(2); 9; 10(2); 11; 14; 22; 24; 25; 26; 27(2); 21:2(2); 3; 7; 10(2); 17; 18(2); 19; 20; 21; 23; 22:2(2); 3(2); 4; 8; 11; 18; 20; 23(2); 24; 33; 23:12; 14; 15; 21; 28; 29(2); 30(2); 42; 43(2); 24:2; 7; 12; 14(2); 16(2); 17; 18; 21(2); 23(2); 25:5; 6; 7; 11(2); 25; 27; 28(2); 30(2); 33; 35; 36; 39; 44; 45(2); 47; 48; 49; 50(2); 51; 26:13; 15(2); 16; 17; 25; 36; 39; 40; 41; 44; 45; 27:8; 9; 15; 18; 19; 23; 28(2); **Num** 1:3; 5; 20; 21; 22(2); 23; 24; 25; 26; 27; 28; 29; 30; 31; 32; 33; 34; 35; 36; 37; 38; 39; 40; 41; 42; 43; 44; 45(2); 46; 50; 51; 53; 54; 2:4; 5; 6; 8; 9; 11; 13; 15; 16; 19; 21; 23; 24; 26; 27; 28; 30; 31; 32; 34; 3:1; 6; 10; 12; 13; 22(2); 32; 34; 36; 38(2); 39; 43; 46; 49(2); 51; 4:3; 15; 16; 19; 23; 25; 26; 30; 35; 36; 37(2); 38; 39; 40; 41(2); 42; 43; 44; 45; 46; 47; 48; 5:2(2); 3; 6(2); 17; 18; 19; 22; 24(2); 27(3); 6:4; 6; 11(2); 12; 20; 21(2); 7:1; 2(2); 5; 9; 10; 12; 88; 89; 8:11; 15; 17; 19; 20; 22; 24; 9:4; 5; 6(3); 7; 13(2); 14; 15; 17; 21(2); 22; 10:2; 5; 6; 9; 10; 11; 32; 35(2); 11:1; 4; 11; 12; 13; 16; 17; 20; 21; 25(2); 26; 29(2); 32(3); 34(2); 12:14; 13:2; 18; 19(2); 28; 31; 32(2); 14:1; 2; 3; 6; 14(4); 23; 29; 35; 37; 38; 42; 45; 15:4; 12; 13; 15; 16; 19; 23(2); 24; 26; 28; 29(3); 30(2); 31; 32; 33; 38(2); 39(2); 40; 16:7; 9; 11; 13(2); 14; 21; 28; 30(2); 31(2); 32; 33; 34; 35; 37; 39; 40(2); 42; 45; 49(2); 17:5; 8; 10; 18:2; 3; 5; 7; 11; 13; 15; 16; 23; 19:2; 3; 8; 9; 10(2); 11; 13(2); 14(2); 16; 18(2); 20(2); 21(3); 22; 20:3; 4; 14; 29; 21:1; 7; 8(2); 9; 13; 15; 16; 20; 27; 29; 32; 22:2; 4(2); 6(3); 19; 20; 24; 28; 34; 35(2); 36; 38(2); 40; 41(2); 23:12; 19(2); 26(2); 27; 28; 24:1; 9(2); 13; 19(2); 20; 25:4;

5; 9; 11; 14(2); 15; 26:1; 2; 7; 9; 10; 18; 22; 25; 27; 34; 37; 41; 43; 47; 50; 54; 57; 62; 63; 27:3; 11; 14; 17; 20; 29:40; 30:2; 5; 7; 8(2); 9; 14; 15; 31:8; 17; 18; 20; 23(2); 26; 27; 35; 36; 42; 43; 52; 32:1; 9; 11; 13; 24; 32; 33:55; 56; 34:2; 35:2; 6; 8(2); 11; 12; 15(2); 16; 20; 21(2); 23; 32(2); 33(2); 36:8(2); **Deut** 1:3(2); 9; 16(2); 17; 18; 19; 30; 31(2); 35; 36; 39; 41; 44; 46; 2:6(2); 17; 20; 25; 28(2); 30; 31; 34; 36; 3:4; 8(2); 12; 18(2); 19; 21(2); 23; 24; 25(2); 4:1; 2; 3; 4; 5; 7; 8; 10(4); 14(2); 15; 17(2); 18(2); 21(3); 22; 26; 32(2); 34; 35(2); 36; 39; 40(2); 42(2); 5:1; 5; 8(3); 9; 10; 11; 14(2); 15(2); 16(2); 21; 23; 24; 26; 27(2); 28; 29(3); 31; 33(3); 6:1; 2(2); 3(3); 18(3); 23; 24; 7:4; 6; 9(2); 10(2); 12; 15; 16; 20; 25; 8:1; 3(3); 5; 7; 11; 13; 15; 16(2); 18(2); 19; 9:3; 4; 5; 6; 7; 8; 11; 14; 19; 21; 24; 10:1; 2; 8; 10; 11; 14; 21; 11:6; 8; 9(2); 14(2); 15; 16; 17(2); 18; 21; 25; 29; 12:1; 3; 7; 8; 10; 11; 12; 13(2); 14; 18(2); 19; 23; 25(2); 28(2); 30(3); 13:3(2); 5(2); 10; 14; 15(2); 17; 18; 14:2; 6(2); 7(2); 9(2); 19; 21(3); 22; 23; 24; 26; 27; 29; 15:2; 3; 8; 9; 10(2); 14; 15; 18; 19; 16:3; 6; 11(2); 12; 13; 14; 20(2); 17:1; 2; 4; 5(5); 6; 9; 10(2); 12(3); 14; 16(2); 17; 18(2); 19; 20(3); 18:3; 8; 10(2); 12; 16(2); 17; 18; 19; 20(2); 22; 19:3; 4; 5; 10; 11; 12; 13; 14; 15; 16; 20:2; 4; 5; 6; 7; 8; 9; 11(2); 14; 16; 18; 20(2); 21:2; 3(2); 4; 6(3); 9; 11; 13; 15; 16(2); 17; 18; 21; 23(3); 22:5(2); 7(2); 8; 18(2); 21; 22; 23; 24(2); 25; 28; 29; 23:1; 8; 10(2); 13; 14; 16; 19; 20(2); 23; 24:1; 4(2); 7; 8(2); 9; 13; 14(2); 18; 19; 22; 25:1; 2; 6(2); 9(2); 10; 11; 15; 16(2); 18; 19; 26:2(2); 3(2); 9; 11; 12; 14; 15; 18; 19; 27:2; 3(2); 4; 15; 16; 17; 18; 19; 20; 21; 22; 23; 24; 25; 26; 28:1; 7; 8; 10; 13; 15; 20; 23(2); 34; 35; 43; 54(2); 55; 57; 58(2); 63; 29:2; 6(2); 9(2); 11; 12; 13(2); 15(2); 18; 19; 20(2); 21; 22(4); 23(2); 27; 29; 30:2; 3; 6; 7; 12(2); 13(2); 14; 16(2); 17; 18(2); 19(2); 20(4); 31:5; 6; 8; 12(3); 13; 14(2); 17(3); 18(2); 19; 20; 21; 25; 26; 28; 29; 32:6; 13; 17; 18(2); 21; 27; 29(3); 35; 36; 39(2); 41; 42; 48; 49; 33:11(3); 13; 16(2); 20; 34:1; 12; **Josh** 1:1; 3(2); 7(2); 8(2); 16; 18(2); 2:3; 5; 9(3); 10; 12; 13(2); 14; 19; 23; 3:2; 4; 7(2); 8; 10(2); 13(3); 15(2); 16(3); 17; 4:1; 6(2); 7; 10(2); 11; 14; 16(2); 18(2); 24(3); 5:1(2); 2; 4(2); 5(2); 6(4); 8; 12; 13; 6:5; 7; 8; 9; 15(2); 17(3); 20(2); 21; 22(2); 23(2); 24; 25; 26(2); 7:14; 15(3); 24; 26; 8:5(2); 8; 9; 11; 13(2); 14(2); 16; 17; 18(2); 20(2); 21(2); 22(2); 24; 25(3); 27; 29(2); 33(2); 34; 35(2); 9:2; 9; 10(2); 16(3); 24; 26; 27; 10:2; 4; 6; 10; 11; 14(2); 20; 24; 27; 28(2); 30; 32(2); 35(4); 37(3); 39; 40; 11:1; 2; 4; 10; 11; 13(2); 15; 16; 17; 19; 20(4); 21; 23; 12:4; 7; 13:2; 4; 9(2); 16(2); 17; 22; 25; 14:6; 8; 9; 11; 12(3); 14; 15:2; 4; 7; 8; 16; 18; 46; 16:1; 10; 17:7; 12; 13; 16; 18:6; 8(2); 13; 14; 16; 19:8; 11; 20:3(2); 4(3); 6(2); 9(2); 21:26; 44; 22:2(2); 10; 16(3); 18(2); 20; 23; 27(3); 28(2); 29(2); 30; 31; 34; 23:1(2); 3(2); 4(2); 6(2); 7(2); 10; 11; 12; 13; 14; 15; 24:5; 8; 15; 16; 17; 20; 22; 25; 26; 29; 31(2); 33; **Judg** 1:1; 3; 9; 10; 12; 14; 17; 21; 27; 28; 29; 35; 2:4; 5; 7(2); 10; 12; 14(2); 16; 18; 19; 20; 22; 3:2; 3; 18; 19(2); 22; 24; 27; 29; 30; 4:2; 4; 9; 12; 13; 15; 20; 23; 5:1; 5; 7(2); 9; 10(2); 11; 13; 14; 18; 21; 30; 31; 6:3; 8; 9; 11; 17; 21; 22; 25(3); 27(2); 28(2); 30(2); 31(2); 32; 37; 40; 7:1(2); 2; 4; 5(2); 6; 7; 9; 11; 13(3); 15; 17; 18; 19(2); 8:1; 3; 4; 5; 6; 10(2); 11; 15(2); 21; 24; 26(3); 28; 31; 33; 9:2(3); 6; 7; 16; 24; 25(2); 28; 32; 33(2); 34; 35; 38(2); 41; 42; 44(2); 45(2); 46; 47; 48(2); 49; 54; 55; 10:4; 8(2); 9; 18; 11:4; 5; 6; 8; 12; 21; 24; 26(2); 31; 35(2); 36; 37; 39; 40; 12:3; 5(2); 6; 14; 13:8; 10; 11; 13; 14(2); 16; 17; 20; 21; 14:3; 4(3); 9; 11; 13; 15(3); 17; 15:1; 2; 7; 11(2); 12(2); 14(2); 17(2); 19; 16:3; 4; 5; 7; 11; 16; 17; 18; 20; 25(2); 26(3); 27; 28; 30; 17:2; 6; 13; 18:1; 5; 7(2); 9; 10; 12; 14(2); 17(2); 19; 22; 23; 24; 26; 27; 28; 31; 19:1; 5; 9(2); 10; 12; 15; 18; 22(2); 23; 30(3); 20:2; 3; 4(2); 5; 10(2); 12; 13; 15(2); 17; 21; 26; 34; 35; 36; 38; 41; 46(3); 48(2); 21:3; 4; 5(2); 7(2); 8; 11(2); 12; 13; 14; 15; 16; 17(2); 18; 19; 22(2); 23; 24; 25; **Ruth** 1:1; 6(2); 9; 11; 13; 18; 19; 2:5; 6(2); 7; 9(3); 10; 11; 13(2); 16; 17; 18; 19; 22(2); 3:1; 4; 5; 6; 8; 11(2); 12; 13; 14; 15; 16; 4:3; 4; 9(3); 10; 11(2); 14; **1Sa** 1:4; 12; 17; 20; 22; 26; 2:4; 5(4); 13; 14(2); 15; 21; 22(2); 24; 30(3); 31(2); 34; 35(2); 36(3); 3:2(2); 4; 8; 9; 11; 12; 13; 14; 17(2); 20; 4:3; 4; 5; 6; 8; 9; 15; 16; 18; 19(2); 20; 5:5; 7; 9; 10; 11; 12; 6:5; 8; 9(3); 15; 7:2; 6; 7; 8; 10; 8:1; 7(2); 8; 9; 10; 11; 18(2); 20(2); 9:5; 6(2); 8; 9; 13; 16; 19; 20; 22; 24(3); 26(2); 27; 10:5(2); 7; 9(2); 11(3); 14; 16; 18; 24; 11:2; 3; 5; 9(2); 10; 11(3); 12(2); 12:1; 5; 6(2); 7; 12; 14; 17(2); 18; 19; 23; 13:3; 4(2); 6; 8; 10(2); 11(3); 14; 15; 16; 17; 18; 22(2); 14:1(3); 2; 3; 6(2); 7; 14; 17; 18; 19(2); 20; 21(3); 22; 23; 24(3); 27; 28; 31; 33; 34; 35; 37; 39; 43; 45; 48; 15:2; 3; 7; 9(3); 11; 25; 28; 29; 30; 35; 16:4; 6; 13; 16; 17; 18; 23; 17:10; 12; 13; 25(2); 26(3); 27; 28; 37; 41; 43; 46(2); 47; 48; 49; 18:1; 2; 4; 6; 9; 10; 15; 18; 19; 21(2); 23; 27; 28(2); 30(2); 19:1; 3; 10; 15; 17; 18; 22; 24(2); 20:1; 2; 3; 5; 6; 7; 9; 13; 14; 26; 27; 30; 33; 35; 21:6; 7(2); 9(3); 10; 15; 22:2(3); 4; 6(2); 7; 8(5); 11; 13(2); 17; 18(2); 21; 22(2); 23; 23:6; 7(2); 9; 10; 13; 15; 17; 22; 23; 25; 26; 28; 24:1; 4; 5; 6; 10; 11(2); 16; 18; 19; 20(2); 21(2); 25:4; 6(2); 7; 10; 11; 17; 20; 21(3); 22(2); 26; 27; 30; 31(3); 34; 35; 37; 38(2); 39(2); 42; 26:3; 4; 11(2); 14; 16(2); 27:1; 2; 4; 5; 6; 7; 28:1(2); 3; 7(3); 9; 14; 15; 21; 22; 25; 29:4; 7; 8; 9; 10; 30:1; 2; 4; 9(2); 10; 15; 16; 18; 19; 21(2); 22(3); 23(2); 24(2); 25(2); 31:5; 6; 7(4); 8; 11; **2Sa** 1:2(2); 4; 5(2); 6; 10(4); 11; 13; 15; 2:1; 3; 4(2); 5; 11; 16; 17; 23(2); 24; 26; 29; 31; 3:6; 8; 13; 19(2); 20; 21(3); 23; 24; 25(2); 27; 29(5); 31; 37(2); 38; 4:1; 2; 4(2); 10; 5:2; 8(2); 12(2); 14; 17; 20; 24; 6:2(2); 3; 9; 12; 13(2); 17; 7:2; 3; 4(2); 6; 9; 10; 11(2); 18; 22; 25; 28; 29; 8:1; 7; 9; 11; 9:1(2); 3; 8; 9; 10; 11; 12; 10:1; 3(2); 6; 9; 10; 12; 13; 14; 15; 16; 19(2); 11:1; 2; 12; 14; 15; 16(2); 20(2); 21; 22; 26; 27; 12:4(2); 5; 8; 14; 15; 18(3); 19(2); 21; 22; 31; 13:1; 2; 5; 6; 10; 15; 16; 17; 18; 19; 23; 27; 30; 32(2); 33; 34; 36; 14:1; 2; 7(2); 11; 13; 14; 15(2); 16; 18; 19; 20; 22(2); 26; 32; 15:1; 2(2); 4(2); 5; 6; 7; 11; 14; 17; 22; 30; 32; 35; 36; 16:2; 4(2); 12(2); 14; 16; 21(2); 17:2; 7; 8; 9(2); 10(2); 11(3); 12; 13; 14; 16; 21; 22(2); 23; 25; 27; 29; 18:1; 3; 7; 8; 9; 11; 12; 15; 19; 22; 28; 31; 32(2); 19:2(2); 3; 6(3); 7(2); 14; 19(3); 20; 22(2); 25; 26; 28; 34; 37; 38(2); 43; 20:8; 10; 11(2); 12(3); 15; 16; 19; 20; 21:3; 4; 5(3); 7; 13; 14(2); 17; 18; 20; 22:1; 18; 28; 31; 35; 37; 39; 40; 41(2); 48(2); 49(2); 23:3; 7; 8; 9; 10; 15; 16; 17(2); 24:2; 3; 5; 9; 10(2); 12; 13(2); 16; 17; 18; 21; 24; **1Kin** 1:2; 11; 12; 20; 21; 29; 30; 35; 40; 41; 45(2); 49; 51; 2:1; 3(2); 4; 5(2); 7; 11; 15(3); 17; 25; 27; 29; 31; 37(2); 39; 41; 42(2); 43; 44; 46; 3:4(2); 6; 8; 9; 10; 12; 13(2); 16; 18(2); 23; 28; 4:12; 27; 29; 33(2); 5:1; 3; 4; 6(4); 7; 9; 15; 16; 6:1; 6; 7; 17; 22; 27; 7:3; 18; 19; 29; 40; 41; 42; 48; 51; 8:1; 4; 5(2); 8; 10; 11; 12; 16(2); 18;

19; 20; 23; 24; 25(3); 27; 29(2); 36; 40(2); 41; 43(4); 44; 46(2); 47; 50(2); 52(2); 54; 56(2); 58; 59; 60(3); 64(2); 65; 66; 9:2; 3; 4; 8; 11; 16; 19(2); 20; 21; 23(2); 25; 27; 10:2(2); 4; 6; 8; 11; 13; 14; 15; 27; 11:4; 7; 10(2); 17; 19; 21(3); 22; 25; 27; 28; 29(2); 30; 33(2); 36; 37; 38(3); 41; 42; 12:3; 6(2); 8; 9; 10(2); 13; 15; 16; 18; 20(3); 32(2); 13:2; 3; 4(2); 6; 9; 10; 11(2); 14; 17; 18; 20(2); 21; 23; 26; 31; 14:1; 2(2); 5; 6; 8; 9; 10(2); 11(2); 14; 22; 25; 28; 29; 15:5(2); 7; 11; 12; 17; 18(2); 19; 21; 23; 29(2); 31; 16:4(2); 7; 11(2); 14; 16(2); 18(2); 20; 22(2); 25; 27; 30; 31; 33; 17:3; 4; 5; 7; 10; 12(2); 14; 17(2); 24(2); 18:1; 4; 5; 7; 9; 10; 12; 17(2); 18; 24; 26; 27; 29(2); 30; 36(4); 37(3); 38; 44(2); 45; 19:1; 3; 4; 8; 13; 17(3); 20:4; 6; 9; 10; 11(2); 12; 13; 16; 25; 26; 28; 29; 30; 31; 37; 41; 21:1; 2; 3; 5; 8; 10; 13; 15(2); 16(2); 21(2); 24(2); 27; 22:2; 3; 7; 13(2); 14; 16(2); 17; 18; 20(2); 25; 31; 32; 33(2); 35; 39(2); 43; 45; 53; **2Kin** 1:2; 3; 4; 6(3); 16; 2:1; 3(2); 5(2); 8; 9; 11; 13; 14; 3:2; 5; 9; 10; 11; 14; 15; 17(2); 20; 21(2); 24; 26(2); 27; 4:1; 4; 6; 8(2); 9; 10; 11; 17(2); 18; 22; 25(2); 40; 41; 42; 43; 5:3; 4; 6; 7(2); 8(3); 15; 18; 20; 6:9; 12(2); 13; 16(2); 17; 20(2); 22; 24; 28; 29; 30; 7:9; 12; 13(3); 19; 8:3; 4; 5; 6(2); 10; 12; 13(2); 14; 15(2); 23; 9:7; 8(2); 22; 25; 37; 10:1; 5(4); 7; 9; 10(2); 11; 17; 19; 21(2); 22; 23; 24; 25; 29(2); 30(2); 34; 36; 11:1; 2; 5(2); 6; 7; 8; 9(3); 10; 15; 17; 12:2; 4(4); 6; 9(2); 10(3); 11(3); 12; 13; 14; 18(2); 19; 13:2; 5; 8; 11; 12; 21; 14:3; 5; 6; 9(3); 10; 14; 22; 24; 26; 27; 28; 15:3(2); 4; 5; 6; 9; 16(2); 18; 19; 21; 24; 26; 28; 31; 34(2); 36; 16:2; 6; 8; 10; 11; 16; 17; 18; 17:2(2); 7; 9; 14; 15(3); 25; 38; 18:1; 3(2); 4; 5(2); 9; 10; 12; 14; 15; 16; 20; 21; 22; 26; 27; 32; 35(2); 19:1; 4; 8; 19(2); 20; 21; 25(2); 29; 30; 31; 33; 35(2); 37; 20:3; 4; 8(2); 9(2); 12(2); 13(2); 15(2); 17(3); 18; 21:2; 7; 8(2); 11; 12; 15; 16; 17(2); 20; 21(2); 24; 22:2; 3; 4; 5; 7; 9(3); 11; 13(3); 15; 17; 19; 23:3; 4; 5; 7; 8; 10; 11; 12; 13; 15(2); 16; 17(3); 18; 19(2); 20; 22; 24(3); 25; 26; 28; 32(2); 33; 37(2); 24:3; 4; 5; 7; 9(2); 10; 16; 19(2); 20; 25:1; 10; 11(2); 13(2); 19(3); 22; 23; 25(3); 27(2); 28; **1Chr** 1:43; 2:9; 24; 55; 4:10(5); 21; 23; 33; 41; 43; 5:18; 20; 6:10(2); 31; 33; 49; 61; 7:21(2); 40; 9:2; 16; 28; 31; 33; 10:5; 7(3); 8; 11; 13; 11:2; 14; 17(2); 18; 19(2); 31; 12:1; 8; 15; 20; 22; 23; 24; 32; 38; 40; 13:2(3); 4; 6(2); 11; 12; 14; 14:2; 8; 11; 15; 15:12(2); 13; 26(2); 27; 29; 16:1; 7; 10; 12; 30; 32; 35; 39; 40; 41; 42; 17:1; 2; 3; 5; 7; 8; 10(2); 11(2); 13; 16; 20; 23; 24; 25; 27; 18:1; 7; 11; 19:1; 3(2); 6; 9; 10; 13; 14; 15; 16(2); 19; 20:1(2); 3; 4(2); 21:2; 5(2); 10; 12(2); 15; 17(3); 18; 22(2); 23; 24; 28(2); 29; 22:2; 5; 12; 19; 23:13; 24; 25; 29(2); 32; 25:7(2); 26:6; 28; 27:1; 26; 29(2); 28:1; 8; 12; 18; 29:3; 9; 11; 14; 16; 17; 21; 22; 27; 30; **2Chr** 1:3; 5; 7; 10(2); 11; 12; 13; 15; 2:6; 7(2); 8; 10; 12(2); 17; 3:1; 4; 15; 17(2); 4:11; 19; 20; 21; 5:1(2); 5; 6; 9; 11; 13; 14; 6:1; 4; 5(2); 6; 8; 10; 11; 14; 15; 16(2); 20(2); 31; 33(3); 34; 40; 7:7; 10; 11; 13; 15; 16; 17; 21(2); 8:2; 6(2); 7; 10; 11; 18; 9:1(2); 3; 6; 12; 13; 14; 23; 27; 10:2; 4; 6; 8(2); 9(2); 10(2); 15; 16; 17; 18(2); 11:1; 13; 12:2; 3; 5; 7; 8; 10; 12; 13:5; 9(2); 15; 18; 14:2; 8(2); 11; 13(2); 15:5(2); 8; 9; 13; 18(2); 16:1; 2; 3; 5; 7; 17:10(2); 18:2; 6; 12; 13; 15; 16; 17; 19(2); 24; 30; 31; 32(2); 33; 34; 19:2; 3; 10(2); 20:1; 2; 6; 12; 21; 29; 32; 37; 21:6; 7; 16; 17(2); 19; 22:1; 8(2); 10; 11(2); 23:4; 6; 8(3); 9; 14; 16; 19; 21; 24:2; 4; 5; 7; 9; 11(2); 20; 23; 26; 25:2; 3(2); 5; 10; 12; 13; 14(2); 16(2); 18(3); 19; 20; 24; 27; 26:2; 4(2); 7; 11; 13; 17; 18; 27:2(2); 28:1; 7; 9(2); 12; 15; 16; 22; 23; 29:2(2); 6; 10; 11; 16; 24; 29; 34; 36; 30:1; 3; 5; 6; 8; 9(2); 14; 17(2); 19; 21; 22; 25(3); 31:1; 4(2); 6; 10; 16; 19(2); 20; 21; 32:2(2); 4; 5; 7; 9; 10; 14(3); 18(2); 21; 23; 26; 31(3); 33:2; 8(2); 13; 15; 18; 22; 25; 34:2; 4(2); 9(2); 10(2); 12; 13; 14; 16; 17; 19; 21(4); 22(2); 23; 24; 25; 28; 30; 32; 33(2); 35:3; 6; 7; 12; 17(2); 18(2); 21; 22; 24(2); 26; 36:5; 8; 9; 12; 17; 20; 22(2); **Ezr** 1:1(2); 4; 6(2); 11; 2:1; 62; 63; 3:5(2); 7; 8; 12; 13; 4:1; 10; 11; 12; 13; 15(3); 16; 17; 19(2); 21; 22; 5:1; 4; 5; 6; 8; 10(2); 11; 12; 14; 15; 16; 17; 6:2; 8(2); 9; 10; 11; 12(2); 13; 7:11; 13; 16; 17; 18; 19; 21; 24; 25(3); 8:1; 17; 21; 22(2); 34; 35; 9:2; 4(2); 8; 12; 13(2); 14; 10:3; 5; 6; 7; 8(2); 13; 17; 18; 19; **Neh** 1:2(2); 3; 4; 5(2); 6; 8; 9; 2:1; 5(2); 7; 8(2); 10; 11; 12; 14; 16; 17(2); 18; 19; 3:15; 16; 25; 26; 27; 4:1(2); 3; 7(3); 10; 12; 15(2); 16(2); 17(2); 18; 22; 23; 5:2(2); 3(2); 4(2); 9; 11; 12; 13; 14(2); 15; 17(2); 18; 19; 6:1(3); 2; 3; 6(2); 9; 11; 12(2); 13(3); 14; 16(3); 7:2; 5; 6(2); 64; 65; 72; 8:1; 2; 3(2); 9; 12; 14; 15; 17(2); 9:6(2); 10; 11; 15; 17; 18; 21; 23; 24; 28; 29; 32; 33; 35; 36; 10:1; 28; 30; 31(2); 36; 37(2); 39; 11:2; 3; 6; 12; 19; 23; 12:1; 31; 38; 40; 43(2); 44(2); 13:1(2); 2; 3; 7; 10(2); 14; 17; 19(4); 21; 22(2); 23; **Est** 1:2; 5; 8; 10; 13; 16; 17; 19(3); 22(2); 2:2; 3; 7; 8; 10; 12; 14; 15; 17; 3:1; 2; 4(2); 5; 6; 7(3); 9(2); 12(2); 14(2); 4:1; 7(2); 8(2); 11(2); 13; 16; 17; 5:1; 2(2); 4; 5(2); 8; 9(2); 12; 14; 6:1; 2; 3; 4; 8; 9; 10(2); 13; 14; 7:5; 7; 10; 8:1; 3; 6; 9(3); 11; 13(2); 14; 9:1(4); 5; 11(2); 15; 16; 18; 19; 20; 21; 22; 24; 25(2); 26; 27; 28(2); **Job** 1:1(2); 3; 5(2); 8(2); 10; 11; 12; 2:3(2); 4; 11; 13; 3:4; 6; 7; 8; 12; 15; 20; 25; 4:4; 8; 19; 5:1; 11(2); 12; 24; 25; 6:2; 6; 7; 8(3); 9(2); 11(2); 14; 26; 7:7; 8; 9; 12; 15; 17(2); 18; 20; 8:13; 22; 9:16; 26; 28; 32; 33; 10:3(2); 6; 7(2); 9; 13; 18; 20; 11:5; 6(4); 16; 12:5(2); 6; 9; 13:5; 9; 13; 18; 19; 28; 14:1; 5; 6; 7(2); 13(3); 15:7; 9; 13; 14(2); 17; 22; 23; 31; 16:3; 21; 17:3; 5; 9; 18:20(2); 21; 19:3; 4; 6; 8; 15; 23(2); 24; 25(2); 29; 20:5; 18; 20; 26; 21:3(2); 15; 18; 22; 29; 30; 22:3(2); 11; 14; 23:3(2); 9; 10; 13; 14; 24:1; 7; 13; 21; 25:4; 6; 26:2(2); 3; 27:5; 7; 11; 15; 18; 28:11; 28; 29:2; 12(2); 13; 25; 30:1; 23; 25; 31; 31:6; 12; 15; 28; 29; 31; 34; 35(3); 38; 32:5; 12(2); 20; 33:12; 17; 20; 21(2); 27; 34:2; 9; 10(2); 17(2); 19; 23; 25; 28; 30; 32; 36; 35:2; 36:2; 4; 9; 10; 16; 24; 32; 37:2; 7; 12; 20; 24; 38:2; 13(2); 20(2); 34; 35; 39:2; 12; 15(2); 24; 40:2(2); 8; 11; 12; 14; 19; 23; 41:10; 11; 16; 17; 26; 42:2(2); 3(2); 7(2); 8; 11(2); **Ps** 1:1; 3; 2:4; 12; 3:1(2); 6; 4:3(2); 6; 7; 5:4; 6; 11(2); 7:1; 4(2); 6; 8; 8:2; 4(2); 9:10(2); 13(2); 14; 15; 17; 20; 10:2; 10; 18; 11:2; 5; 12:3; 5; 13:4; 14:1; 2; 3; 7; 15:2; 3; 4(2); 5(2); 16:3; 4; 17:1; 2; 3; 5; 7(2); 9; 12; 18:t; 12; 30; 32; 34; 36; 38; 39; 40(2); 47; 48; 20:6; 21:8; 22:3; 7; 8; 9; 23; 25; 26; 29(2); 31(2); 24:1; 4; 6(2); 25:3; 12(2); 14; 26:7; 27:4(2); 28:1; 30:3; 12; 31:4; 6; 11; 15; 19(2); 24; 32:6; 10; 11; 33:18(2); 34:7; 8(2); 9; 10; 12(2); 16; 18; 21; 22; 35:1(2); 3; 4(2); 8(2); 10(2); 11; 14; 19(2); 20; 26(2); 27; 36:1; 4; 10; 37:9; 13; 16; 22; 37; 38:12(2); 13; 14; 19; 20(2); 39:1; 4; 13; 40:4(2); 12; 14(2); 15; 16; 41:1; 7; 8; 10; 11; 42:4; 44:5; 7; 13; 16; 45:14; 46:5; 10; 48:13; 49:6; 9; 10; 11; 12; 20(2); 50:4; 5; 16; 21; 22; 23; 51:4; 8; 52:7; 53:1; 2(2); 3; 5; 6; 54:4; 55:6; 12(3); 18; 19; 56:2; 13; 57:2; 3; 4; 58:4; 8; 11(2); 59:1; 13(2); 60:4(2); 5; 12; 61:2; 5; 8; 62:11; 63:9;

11(2); 64:4; 8; 65:2; 4; 5; 8; 66:16; 67:2; 68:1; 4; 11; 12; 18; 20; 23; 28; 30; 33(2); 35; 69:4(3); 6(2); 9; 10; 12; 14; 22; 23; 31; 32; 34; 35; 36; 70:2(2); 3; 4; 71:6; 10; 13(2); 18; 24; 72:6; 9; 12; 73:25; 27(2); 28; 74:3; 9; 18(2); 23; 75:1; 76:11(2); 77:4; 14; 78:4; 5; 6; 7; 8; 11; 20; 35; 39(2); 44; 53; 60; 65; 79:4; 6(2); 11; 80:1(2); 12; 15; 81:5; 13; 83:2; 4; 16; 18(2); 84:4; 11; 12; 85:6; 9(2); 12; 86:2; 5; 17; 87:4; 5; 6; 88:4(2); 5; 89:7; 10; 15; 19; 23; 34; 35; 41; 48; 90:9; 12; 14; 91:1; 5; 6(2); 92:7; 11; 13; 15; 93:1; 94:9(2); 10(2); 11; 13; 95:10; 11; 96:10(2); 12; 97:7(2); 10; 98:7; 99:6; 7; 8; 100:3(2); 101:3; 5; 6(2); 7(2); 8; 102:4; 8; 11; 20; 103:1; 5; 6; 11; 13; 14; 17; 18; 20(2); 21; 104:5; 9(2); 14; 15; 26; 27; 28; 105:3; 5; 19; 34; 45; 106:3(2); 4; 5(3); 8; 10; 20; 23; 31; 32; 33; 40; 41; 46; 107:7; 8; 15; 21; 23(2); 29; 31; 34; 36; 38; 108:6; 13; 109:11; 15; 16(2); 20; 27(3); 31; 111:2; 5; 6; 10; 112:1(2); 113:6; 8; 114:5(2); 6; 115:8(2); 11; 13; 17; 118:2; 3; 4(2); 7(2); 13; 26; 119:2(2); 5; 11; 17; 18; 20; 21; 42; 53; 57; 63(2); 71(2); 73; 74; 75(2); 77; 79(2); 80; 84; 101; 106; 116; 118; 125; 132; 138; 148; 150; 152; 162; 120:5(2); 6; 121:3; 4; 122:3; 6; 123:1; 2; 4; 125:1; 4(2); 126:1; 5; 6; 127:1; 5; 128:1(2); 4(2); 129:5; 7; 130:4; 6(2); 131:2; 132:12; 133:2(2); 3; 134:3; 135:2; 5(2); 6; 18(2); 20; 136:5; 6; 7; 10; 137:3(2); 8; 9; 138:8; 139:14; 21(2); 140:9; 10; 12; 141:4; 10; 142:4; 7; 143:3; 7; 12; 144:3(2); 4; 10; 12(2); 13(2); 14(3); 15(3); 145:14(2); 18(2); 19; 20; 146:4; 5; 6; 8; 147:11(2); 148:4; 149:2; 150:6; **Prov** 1:12; 19; 29; 2:2; 7; 12; 19; 20; 3:13(2); 18(2); 4:18; 22; 5:2(2); 6; 13; 6:11; 17; 18(2); 19(2); 29; 32; 7:5; 23; 8:9(2); 11; 17(2); 21(2); 29; 32; 34; 36(2); 9:4; 7(2); 16; 18(2); 10:4; 5(3); 9(2); 10; 13(2); 17(2); 18(2); 19; 26; 11:12; 13; 15(2); 17; 18; 19; 20; 24(2); 25; 26(2); 27(2); 28; 29; 30; 12:1; 4; 8; 9(2); 11(2); 15; 17; 18; 20; 22; 27; 13:3(2); 6; 7(2); 11; 13; 18(2); 20; 23; 24(2); 14:2(2); 6; 13; 17; 21(2); 22(2); 29(2); 31(2); 33(2); 35; 15:5; 9; 10(2); 12; 14; 15; 18; 21; 24; 27(2); 31; 32(2); 16:5; 13; 17; 20; 22; 25; 26; 29; 32(3); 17:2; 5; 8; 9(2); 15(2); 19(2); 20(2); 21; 24; 25; 27; 28; 18:2; 9(2); 13; 17; 21; 24(2); 19:1(2); 2(2); 5; 6; 8(2); 9; 16(2); 17(2); 20; 21; 23; 25; 26(2); 27; 20:8; 16; 19(2); 25; 21:5; 6; 16; 17(2); 21; 28; 22:5; 8; 9; 11; 14; 16(2); 19; 21(3); 23; 26(2); 23:5; 6; 22; 24; 25; 30(2); 34(2); 24:8; 11(2); 12(2); 21; 24; 25; 26; 34; 25:7(2); 10; 13; 18; 20(2); 28(2); 26:6; 8(2); 10; 16; 17(2); 19; 24; 27; 28; 27:8(2); 10; 11(2); 13; 14; 18; 28:3; 4; 5; 6(2); 7; 8(2); 9; 11; 13; 14(2); 16(2); 17; 18; 19(2); 20; 21; 22(2); 23(2); 25(2); 26; 27(2); 29:1(2); 3; 4; 5; 14; 18; 20; 21; 27; 30:5; 11; 12; 15; 16(2); 17; 23; 31:1; 3; 6(2); 11; 18; 30; **Eccl** 1:9(4); 11(2); 13; 14; 15(2); 16; 17; 18; 2:3; 6; 7; 8; 9; 11(2); 12(2); 13; 14; 15; 16; 17; 18; 21; 24(3); 26(3); 3:2; 9(2); 11(2); 12; 13; 14(2); 15(3); 16(2); 18(3); 19(2); 21(2); 22(3); 4:1; 3; 4; 10; 14; 15; 16(2); 5:1; 4; 5(2); 6; 8; 10(2); 11; 16(2); 18(2); 6:2(2); 3(3); 8; 10(3); 11; 7:2; 10; 11; 12(2); 13; 14; 15(2); 18(2); 20; 21; 22; 24; 29; 8:2; 7; 8(3); 9; 12(2); 14(2); 15; 16(2); 17(2); 9:1(2); 2(4); 3(3); 4; 5; 6; 9; 11; 12(2); 15; 17; 10:1; 3(2); 8; 9; 20; 11:4(2); 5; 6; 8; 9; 12:3; 5; 10; **Song** 1:7; 2:7; 14; 15; 3:3; 4(2); 5; 6; 4:1; 2; 5; 16; 5:2; 7; 8(2); 9; 6:1; 5; 9; 10; 13; 7:3; 9(2); 8:1(2); 4; 5(2); 10; 12; 13; **Is** 1:4; 28; 29; 30; 2:1; 2; 8; 11; 12(2); 13; 14; 17; 20; 3:7; 10; 15; 18; 24; 4:1; 2(2); 3(4); 5:2; 4(2); 6; 8(3); 11(3); 14; 16; 18; 19(3); 20(3); 21; 22; 30; 6:1; 4; 7:1; 8; 15; 16; 17(2); 18(4); 20; 21(2); 22(2); 23(2); 25; 8:6; 11; 17; 19(3); 21; 9:2(2); 9; 13; 15; 16; 10:1(2); 2(2); 12; 14(2); 15(3); 19; 20(3); 24; 27(2); 32; 11:10; 11(2); 16; 12:1; 4(2); 13:2; 3; 8; 14; 15(2); 14:3; 4; 6; 16(3); 17(2); 19(2); 21; 25; 26(2); 28; 29; 32; 15:7; 9; 16:2; 3; 12(2); 13(2); 14; 17:4(2); 5; 7; 8; 9; 12; 14(2); 18:2; 7; 19:3; 8(2); 9(2); 10; 13; 16; 17; 18; 19; 21; 23; 24; 20:1; 6; 21:3; 10; 14(2); 22:1; 2; 3; 7; 8; 9; 11; 12; 16(3); 20(2); 25(3); 23:1; 2; 13; 15(2); 16(2); 17; 18; 24:6; 8; 9; 10; 18(2); 21(3); 25:7; 9; 11; 26:1; 2; 5; 17; 19; 27:1(3); 2; 5; 6; 7(2); 9; 11(2); 12(2); 13(2); 28:1; 4; 5; 6(2); 8; 9; 13; 14; 16; 19; 20(2); 21; 29:4; 5; 7(3); 8; 11(2); 12; 15; 16(2); 18; 20; 21(2); 24(2); 30:1(3); 2; 5; 6; 8; 9(2); 14(2); 16; 18(3); 23(2); 24; 26; 31:1; 2; 3(2); 7; 32:3(2); 9; 11; 20(2); 33:1; 13(2); 15(4); 17; 18; 19; 20; 24; 34:1(2); 35:4; 36:1; 5; 6; 11; 12(2); 20(2); 22; 37:1; 4; 6; 8; 16; 20(2); 26(2); 30; 31; 32; 34; 38; 38:3; 7(2); 13; 18; 22; 39:1(2); 2(2); 4(2); 6(3); 7; 40:2(2); 3; 9(2); 11; 20(4); 22(2); 23; 26(2); 28; 29; 31; 41:3; 7(3); 11(2); 12(2); 20(2); 22; 23(4); 24; 26(5); 27; 28; 42:5(5); 7; 8; 10(2); 11; 16(2); 17(2); 18; 19(2); 43:1(2); 7; 8(2); 9; 10(2); 12; 13; 25; 26; 44:2; 3; 7; 8; 9(2); 10; 13; 18(2); 20; 24(4); 25(2); 26(2); 27; 28; 45:3(2); 6(2); 9(2); 10; 15; 16; 18(2); 19; 20(3); 21; 23; 24; 46:5; 10; 11; 12; 47:7; 8(3); 13; 48:4; 8(3); 9; 16; 17; 18; 49:5; 6(2); 7; 9(2); 10; 15; 17; 19; 20; 23(2); 25; 26(2); 50:2; 4(2); 6; 7; 8; 9; 10(3); 11(3); 51:1(2); 2; 6; 7; 9; 10; 12(3); 13; 14(3); 15; 16; 18(2); 22; 23(3); 52:5(2); 6(3); 7(5); 11; 15(2); 53:2; 54:1(2); 9(2); 10; 16(2); 17(2); 55:1(2); 2(3); 5(2); 10; 11(2); 13; 56:2(3); 3; 4(2); 5; 6(2); 8; 11; 57:1; 11; 13; 15(2); 19(2); 58:2; 5; 6(2); 7(4); 12; 59:1(2); 2; 5(2); 15(2); 16(2); 20; 21; 60:8; 11(2); 12; 14(2); 15; 16; 21; 61:1; 2; 3(3); 9(2); 11; 62:1; 6; 9(2); 63:1(3); 2; 5; 7; 8; 11(2); 12; 13(2); 64:1(3); 2; 4; 5(2); 7(2); 65:1(3); 2; 3(2); 5; 8; 10; 11(6); 12; 16(2); 18; 20; 24; 66:1; 2; 3(4); 4; 5(3); 6; 10(2); 11(2); 17; 18; 19(3); 23; 24; **Jer** 1:1; 7; 17; 2:2; 3; 5; 6(3); 8(2); 11; 13; 17; 19(3); 24(2); 28; 3:1; 6; 9; 13; 16; 17; 18; 4:4; 9(2); 11; 14; 16; 31(3); 5:1(2); 6; 7; 19; 22; 24; 26; 6:10; 11; 15(2); 27; 7:1; 2; 7; 8; 18; 22; 23(2); 25; 28; 32; 8:1; 3; 10; 12; 13; 16(2); 19; 9:1(2); 2(2); 10; 12(3); 17(2); 18; 24(3); 25; 26(2); 10:4; 11; 18; 23(2); 25(2); 11:1; 3; 4; 5; 7; 13; 14; 17; 19(3); 20(2); 21(2); 12:1; 4; 14; 15; 17; 13:4; 6; 11; 12; 13; 20(2); 23; 24; 26; 14:1; 8; 9; 15; 18(2); 22; 15:4; 9; 10; 13; 15; 18; 16:3(3); 10; 12; 13; 14(2); 15(2); 21; 17:4; 5; 7; 8; 11; 13(2); 16; 18; 20; 23; 18:4; 8(2); 10; 14; 16; 19; 20; 19:2; 6; 7; 8; 9; 10; 11; 15(2); 20:1; 2; 3; 6; 12; 16; 17; 18; 21:2(2); 4; 7; 9(3); 12(2); 22:2(2); 5; 10; 13(2); 14; 21; 23; 25; 26; 30; 23:1; 2; 5; 7; 14; 16; 17(2); 24; 25; 26; 28(2); 29; 30; 31; 32; 34(2); 39; 24:1; 2; 3; 5; 7; 8(2); 10; 25:1(2); 3; 5; 7; 12(2); 13(2); 16; 23; 24; 30; 31; 33; 26:2; 3; 8(2); 12; 13; 15; 20; 24; 27:5; 8(3); 10; 11; 13; 14; 15(3); 16; 18; 19; 21; 22; 28:1; 3; 4; 5; 6; 7; 8; 9; 12; 14; 29:1; 2; 4; 6(2); 8; 10; 11; 16(4); 17; 25; 26(3); 31; 32; 30:1; 2; 3(2); 4; 7(2); 8(2); 13; 16(3); 19; 20; 21; 31:4; 6; 8; 10; 11; 17; 19(2); 24; 27; 28; 30; 31; 32(2); 33; 37; 38; 32:1; 7; 8(2); 9; 11(2); 12(2); 14; 23; 24; 29; 31(2); 35; 39; 40(2); 42; 33:2; 9(2); 10; 11(2); 13; 14(2); 15; 20; 21; 22; 24; 26; 34:7; 8(2); 9(2); 10(2); 13; 18; 20; 21; 35:7; 8; 10; 11; 14; 17; 18; 36:1; 2; 3(3); 6; 7; 8; 9(2); 13; 23(3); 24; 25; 27; 28; 31; 37:5; 7; 10; 11; 15; 18; 20; 21(2); 38:1; 2(2); 4; 5; 6; 7; 9;

THE

33(3); 34; 22:2(2); 3(4); 4(2); 5(2); 6(3); 7(3); 9(4); 10; 11(2); 12; 13(2); 14(3); 15(3); 16; 17(5); 18(2); 21; 23:1(2); 2(2); 3; 5; 6; 7(3); 8; 9(2); 10(5); 11(4); 12(2); 13(4); 15; 16(4); 17(6); 18(3); 19(4); 20(3); 24:1; 3(6); 5(3); 7(2); 8; 9(2); 10(4); 11(4); 13(4); 14(2); 15; 16(2); 17; 20(2); 21(2); 22(2); 24(2); 26(2); 27(4); 28; 29(2); 30(6); 31(3); 32(4); 35; 37(2); 39; 40; 42; 43(2); 44(3); 45; 46; 47(3); 48(3); 49(2); 50(2); 51; 52(2); 53; 54(2); 55(2); 56; 57; 60(2); 61(3); 62(3); 63(3); 64; 65(3); 66; 25:3; 4(2); 6(3); 7(2); 8; 9(4); 10(2); 11(2); 12(2); 13(3); 16; 17(3); 18; 19; 20(4); 21(2); 22(2); 23(5); 25; 27(2); 29; 32; 26:1(4); 2(2); 3; 4(3); 7(4); 8; 10; 12(2); 13; 14; 15(3); 17; 18(5); 19; 20(4); 21; 22(3); 24(3); 25(2); 26; 28; 29(2); 31; 32(2); 33(2); 34(4); 27:2; 3; 5; 7; 9(2); 15; 16(4); 17(3); 20; 22(3); 27(4); 28(3); 30; 34; 39(3); 40; 41(2); 46(4); 28:1; 2(2); 4(2); 5(2); 6; 8; 9(3); 11(2); 12(3); 13(4); 14(8); 16; 17(2); 18(3); 19(3); 21; 22; 29:1(3); 2(3); 3(6); 5; 6; 7(2); 8(4); 10(5); 13; 14; 16(4); 20; 22(2); 23; 25; 26(2); 27; 31; 32; 33; 35; 30:2(2); 13; 14(2); 16(2); 17; 19; 24; 27; 30; 32(5); 33(2); 35(5); 36; 37(3); 38(5); 39(2); 40(6); 41(6); 42(3); 43; 31:1; 2; 3(2); 4; 5; 8(4); 9; 10(4); 11; 12(2); 13(3); 16; 18(2); 19; 20; 21(2); 22; 23; 24; 25(2); 26; 29(2); 33; 34(3); 35(2); 38; 39; 40(3); 42(4); 46; 48; 49; 53(4); 54(2); 55; 32:1; 2; 3(2); 6; 7(3); 8(2); 9; 10(3); 11(4); 12(2); 16; 17; 19(3); 20; 21(2); 22; 23; 24(2); 25(2); 26; 30(2); 31; 32(6); 33:1(2); 2; 3; 5(3); 6; 8; 10; 13(3); 14(2); 15(2); 17(2); 18(2); 19(2); 34:1(3); 2(3); 3(3); 5; 6; 7(3); 8; 10; 12; 13; 19(3); 20(2); 21(2); 22; 24(2); 25(4); 26(2); 27(3); 28(2); 29; 30(4); 35:1; 2; 3(2); 4(2); 5(3); 6(2); 7(2); 8; 12(2); 13; 14; 15(2); 17; 19; 20; 21; 22; 23; 24; 25; 26(2); 27; 28; 29; 36:1; 2(6); 5(2); 6(4); 7; 9(3); 10(5); 11; 12; 13(2); 14(3); 15(3); 16(3); 17(4); 18(3); 19; 20(3); 21(4); 22; 23; 24(4); 25(2); 26; 27; 28; 29(2); 30(2); 31(3); 32(2); 33; 34; 35(3); 37; 38; 39(4); 40(2); 43(4); 37:1(2); 2(5); 3; 5; 7; 8; 9(3); 10; 11; 13; 14(2); 15(2); 17; 22; 24; 27; 28(2); 29(2); 30; 31(3); 32; 35; 36(2); 38:7(3); 9(2); 10(2); 12(2); 14; 16; 17; 19; 20(4); 21(3); 22(2); 24; 25(2); 27; 28(2); 30; 39:1(3); 2(3); 3(2); 5(7); 6; 8; 11(3); 14; 17; 19; 20(3); 21(4); 22(5); 23(4); 40:1(3); 2(4); 3(5); 4(2); 5(5); 6; 7; 9; 10(2); 11(2); 12(2); 13; 15(3); 16(2); 17(3); 18(2); 19; 20(4); 21(2); 22; 23; 41:1(2); 2; 3(4); 4(2); 5; 6; 7(2); 8(3); 9; 10(3); 11; 12(2); 14; 17(2); 18; 19; 20(3); 21; 23; 24(3); 25; 26(3); 27(3); 28; 29; 30(4); 31(2); 32(2); 33; 34(4); 35(3); 36(5); 37(3); 38; 40; 41; 43(3); 44; 45(2); 46(2); 47(2); 48(8); 49(2); 50(2); 51(2); 52(3); 53(2); 54(3); 55(3); 56(7); 57; 42:5(3); 6(5); 7; 9(3); 12(2); 13(3); 15; 16; 18; 19(2); 21; 22; 25; 26; 27; 29; 30(4); 32(2); 33(4); 34; 35; 38(3); 43:1(2); 2; 3; 5; 6; 7(2); 8; 9; 11(3); 12(2); 13; 14; 15; 16; 17(3); 18(3); 19(3); 20; 21(2); 23; 24(2); 25; 26(3); 27; 32(4); 33(3); 44:1(2); 2(4); 3(2); 4(2); 8(2); 11; 12(3); 13; 14; 16(2); 17(2); 22; 24; 26; 28; 29; 30(2); 31(3); 32(2); 33(2); 34(2); 45:2(2); 6(3); 7; 8; 10; 12; 16; 17; 18(4); 19; 20(2); 21(3); 23(2); 24; 25; 26; 27(3); 46:1; 2(2); 3; 5(2); 6; 8(2); 9; 10(2); 11; 12(3); 13; 14; 15(2); 16; 17(2); 18; 19; 20(2); 21; 22(2); 23; 24; 25(2); 26(2); 27(3); 28; 31; 32; 34(2); 47:1(2); 4(4); 6(4); 9(8); 11(4); 13(5); 14(5); 15(4); 17(4); 18(2); 19; 20(4); 21(3); 22(3); 23(2); 24(3); 25; 26(4); 27(2); 28(2); 29; 31; 48:2; 3; 5; 6; 7(4); 10; 12; 14(2); 15; 16(5); 17; 18; 21; 22(2); 49:1; 3(3); 8; 9; 10(3); 11(3); 13(2); 15; 16; 17(3); 19; 22; 23; 24(5); 25(5); 26(7); 27(3); 28; 29(3); 30(5); 32(4); 33(2); 50:2(2); 3(2); 4(3); 5; 7(4); 8(2); 10; 11(7); 13(5); 15; 17(4); 19; 23(3); 24; 25; **Ex** 1:1(2); 5(2); 7(2); 9(2); 10; 12(3); 13(2); 14; 15(6); 16(3); 17(3); 18(3); 19(4); 20(2); 21; 22; 2:1; 2; 3(3); 5(5); 6(3); 7(2); 8(2); 9(2); 10(2); 12(2); 13(3); 14; 15(2); 16(2); 17; 19(3); 20; 21; 23(4); 25; 3:1(6); 2(5); 3; 4(3); 5; 6(4); 7(2); 8(9); 9(4); 10; 11; 12; 13(2); 14; 15(5); 16(3); 17(8); 18(6); 19; 20; 21(2); 22; 4:1; 2; 3(2); 4(2); 5(4); 6; 8(4); 9(6); 10; 11(5); 13; 14(3); 16; 19(2); 20(2); 21(2); 22; 24(3); 25; 26; 27(3); 28(3); 29(2); 30(5); 31(3); 5:1(2); 2(2); 3(5); 4(2); 5(2); 6(3); 7; 8(2); 9; 10(3); 12(2); 13; 14(2); 15(2); 16; 17; 18; 19(2); 20; 21(3); 22; 6:1; 2; 3; 4(2); 5(3); 6(4); 7(3); 8(3); 9; 10; 11; 12(2); 13(4); 14(4); 15(3); 16(4); 17; 18(3); 19(2); 20(2); 21; 22; 24(3); 25(4); 26(3); 27; 28(3); 29(2); 30; 7:1; 2; 3; 4(2); 5(3); 6; 8; 10; 11(3); 13; 14(2); 15(4); 16(3); 17(5); 18(6); 19(3); 20(8); 21(7); 22(2); 24(4); 25(2); 8:1(2); 3(2); 4; 5(5); 6(3); 7(2); 8(4); 9(2); 10; 11(2); 12(2); 13(6); 14; 15; 16(4); 17(5); 18; 19(3); 20(4); 21(3); 22(5); 24(5); 25; 26(5); 27(2); 28(2); 29(4); 30; 31(3); 32; 9:1(3); 3(8); 4(4); 5(3); 6(5); 7(4); 8(4); 9(2); 10; 11(5); 12(3); 13(4); 14; 15; 16; 18; 19(3); 20(4); 21(3); 22(4); 23(5); 24(2); 25(6); 26(2); 27; 28; 29(5); 30; 31(5); 32(2); 33(5); 34(3); 35(3); 10:1(2); 2(2); 3(2); 4; 5(6); 6(5); 7(2); 8; 9; 10; 11; 12(6); 13(5); 14(3); 15(11); 16; 17; 18; 19(4); 20(2); 21(2); 22; 23; 24; 25; 26(2); 27; 11:1; 2(2); 3(9); 4(2); 5(7); 6; 7(3); 8; 9(2); 10(2); 12:1(2); 2(3); 3(3); 4(5); 5(3); 6(5); 7(4); 8; 9; 10(2); 11; 12(5); 13(5); 14; 15(3); 16(2); 17(2); 18(5); 19(2); 21(2); 22(8); 23(8); 25(2); 27(7); 28(2); 29(8); 30(2); 31(2); 33(3); 34; 35(3); 36(5); 37; 39; 40(2); 41(6); 42(4); 43(3); 46(2); 47; 48(3); 49; 50(2); 51(4); 13:1; 2(3); 3(3); 4; 5(7); 6(2); 8; 9(2); 11(3); 12(4); 13; 14(2); 15(8); 16; 17(5); 18(6); 19(2); 20(2); 21(2); 22(4); 14:1; 2(3); 3(3); 4(2); 5(4); 7; 8(4); 9(3); 10(4); 11; 12(4); 13(4); 14; 15(2); 16(4); 17(2); 18(2); 19(4); 20(6); 21(5); 22(5); 23(3); 24(8); 25(4); 26(4); 27(8); 28(5); 29(4); 30(5); 31(5); 15:1(5); 2; 3(2); 4(2); 5(2); 6; 7; 8(6); 9(2); 10(2); 11; 12; 13; 14(2); 15(3); 16(2); 17(3); 18; 19(8); 20(3); 21(3); 22(3); 23(2); 24; 25(4); 26(4); 27; 16:1(6); 2(3); 3(6); 4(2); 5; 6(3); 7(4); 8(6); 9(3); 10(6); 11; 12(4); 13(5); 14(5); 15(3); 16(3); 17; 19; 20; 21; 22(3); 23(5); 24; 25(2); 26(2); 27(2); 28; 29(5); 30(2); 31(3); 32(5); 33; 34(2); 35(3); 36; 17:1(6); 2(2); 3(2); 4; 5(4); 6(5); 7(6); 9(3); 10(2); 12(6); 13(2); 14(3); 15; 16(2); 18:1(2); 3(2); 4(4); 5(2); 7; 8(5); 9(4); 10(7); 11(2); 12; 13(5); 14(3); 15; 16; 17; 19(2); 20(2); 21; 22(2); 24; 25; 26(2); 19:1(5); 2(3); 3(4); 4; 5; 6(2); 7(3); 8(5); 9(5); 10(2); 11(5); 12(4); 13(2); 14(3); 15(2); 16(7); 17(4); 18(4); 19(2); 20(6); 21(3); 22(3); 23(3); 24(4); 25; 20:2(3); 4(3); 5(5); 7(3); 8; 10(3); 11(5); 12(2); 18(7); 20; 21(2); 22(2); 21:1; 2; 4; 5; 6(3); 7; 9; 19; 22(2); 26(2); 28(3); 29(2); 30; 32(2); 34(4); 35(3); 36(2); 22:3; 4; 5(2); 6(4); 7(2); 8(4); 9(3); 11(2); 12; 14; 15; 17; 20; 21; 24; 26; 28(2); 29(2); 30; 31(2); 23:1; 5; 6; 7(2); 8(4); 9(2); 10; 11(4); 12(3); 13; 14; 15(3); 16(7); 17(2); 18(3); 19(4); 20(2); 23(6); 25(2); 26; 27; 28(3); 29(3); 30; 31(7); 24:1(2); 2(2); 3(7); 4(5); 5(2); 6(3); 7(5); 8(5); 9; 10(2); 11(2); 12(2); 13; 14; 15(2); 16(6); 17(7); 18(4); 25:1; 2; 3; 6; 7(2); 9(4); 10(3); 12(3); 14(5); 15(3); 16(2); 17(2); 18(2); 19(6); 20(5); 21(4); 22(5); 23(3); 25; 26(3); 27(4); 28(2); 29; 30; 31(2); 32(5); 33(3); 34; 35(5); 36; 37(2); 38(2); 40; 26:1; 2(3); 3;

4(7); 5(6); 6(2); 7; 8(3); 9(3); 10(6); 11(3); 12(6); 13(7); 14; 15; 16(2); 17(2); 18(3); 19; 20(3); 22(2); 23(3); 24(2); 26(3); 27(7); 28(3); 29(3); 30(3); 32; 33(8); 34(4); 35(9); 36(2); 37; 27:1(2); 2(3); 3; 4(2); 5(5); 6; 7(5); 8; 9(4); 10(3); 11(3); 12(3); 13(3); 14(2); 15; 16(2); 17(2); 18(4); 19(6); 20(3); 21(7); 28:1(2); 3(2); 4(2); 6; 7(2); 8(4); 9(2); 10(3); 11(5); 12(5); 14(3); 15(3); 16(2); 17(2); 18; 19; 20; 21(5); 22(2); 23(4); 24(4); 25(5); 26(5); 27(6); 28(8); 29(5); 30(7); 31(2); 32(4); 33(2); 34(2); 35(2); 36(2); 37(3); 38(4); 39(3); 41; 42(2); 43(4); 29:1(2); 3(3); 4(3); 5(8); 6(3); 7; 9(2); 10(4); 11(5); 12(7); 13(7); 14(3); 15(2); 16(2); 17(2); 18(4); 19(3); 20(9); 21(4); 22(10); 23(3); 24(3); 25(3); 26(3); 27(6); 28(4); 29; 30(3); 31(3); 32(7); 33; 34(5); 36; 37(2); 38(2); 39(3); 40(3); 41(5); 42(4); 43(2); 44(4); 45; 46(3); 30:2(5); 3(3); 4(4); 5; 6(5); 7; 8(2); 10(5); 11; 12(3); 13(4); 14; 15(3); 16(7); 17; 18(3); 20(4); 22; 24(2); 25(2); 26(4); 27(3); 28(2); 30; 31; 32; 34; 35(2); 36(3); 37(3); 31:1; 2(3); 3; 6(3); 7(7); 8(3); 9(2); 10(5); 11(2); 12; 13(2); 14; 15(4); 16(3); 17(3); 18; 32:1(5); 2(2); 3(2); 4; 5; 6(2); 7(2); 8(2); 9; 11(2); 12(4); 13; 14(2); 15(6); 16(5); 17(3); 18(3); 19(5); 20(4); 22(2); 23(2); 24; 25; 26(4); 27(2); 28(3); 29; 30(3); 31; 33; 34(3); 35(3); 33:1(4); 2(6); 3(2); 4; 5(3); 6(2); 7(9); 8(3); 9(5); 10(4); 11(4); 12; 16(3); 17; 19(2); 21; 22; 34:1(4); 2(4); 3(2); 4(4); 5(4); 6(3); 7(7); 8; 10(4); 11(6); 12(3); 14; 15(2); 18(4); 19; 20(2); 21; 22(4); 23(3); 24(3); 25(5); 26(4); 27(2); 28(5); 29(3); 30(2); 31(2); 32(2); 34(3); 35(4); 35:1(4); 2(2); 3; 4(4); 5(2); 8(2); 9(2); 10; 11; 12(5); 13(2); 14(4); 15(7); 16(2); 17(5); 18(4); 19(6); 20(3); 21(5); 22; 24(2); 25; 26; 27(3); 28(3); 29(4); 30(5); 31; 33; 34(2); 35(4); 36:1(4); 2(2); 3(5); 4(3); 5(4); 6(4); 7(2); 8(2); 9(3); 10(2); 11(6); 12(5); 13(2); 14(2); 15(3); 17(6); 18; 19; 20; 21(2); 22(2); 23(2); 24; 25(3); 27(2); 28(3); 29(2); 31(3); 32(6); 33(4); 34(3); 37; 38; 37:1(4); 3(3); 5(5); 6(3); 7(2); 8(5); 9(5); 10(4); 12; 13(3); 14(5); 15(2); 16(2); 17(3); 18(5); 19(3); 20; 21(4); 22; 24; 25(6); 26(3); 27(4); 28; 29(4); 38:1(4); 2(4); 3(8); 4(3); 5(3); 6; 7(5); 8(7); 9(4); 10(2); 11(4); 12(3); 13; 14(3); 15(2); 16(2); 17(7); 18(8); 19; 20(3); 21(8); 22(4); 23; 24(8); 25(4); 26(2); 27(6); 28(2); 29(2); 30(8); 31(8); 39:1(4); 2; 3(5); 4; 5(4); 6(2); 7(4); 8(3); 9(3); 10(2); 11; 12; 13; 14(5); 15(2); 16(3); 17(4); 18(5); 19(5); 20(6); 21(8); 22(2); 23(4); 24(2); 25(5); 26(3); 29; 30(4); 31(2); 32(6); 33(2); 34(4); 35(4); 36(3); 37(5); 38(5); 39(2); 40(9); 41(5); 42(3); 43(2); 40:1; 2(5); 3(4); 4(4); 5(7); 6(6); 7(4); 8(3); 9(3); 10(3); 11; 12(3); 13(2); 15; 16; 17(5); 18(3); 19(5); 20(6); 21(7); 22(6); 23(3); 24(6); 25(3); 26(4); 27; 28(3); 29(8); 30(4); 32(4); 33(6); 34(5); 35(6); 36(3); 37(2); 38(5); **Lev** 1:1(3); 2(5); 3(5); 4(2); 5(9); 6; 7(5); 8(7); 9(3); 10(3); 11(5); 12(4); 13(5); 14(2); 15(6); 16(4); 17(6); 2:1; 2(8); 3(4); 4; 7; 8(4); 9(4); 10(3); 11(2); 12(4); 13(2); 14(3); 16(6); 3:1(2); 2(7); 3(7); 4(6); 5(5); 6(2); 7; 8(5); 9(10); 10(6); 11(5); 12; 13(6); 14(5); 15(6); 16(6); 4:1; 2(3); 3(4); 4(8); 5(4); 6(6); 7(15); 8(7); 9(6); 10(5); 11(2); 12(5); 13(6); 14(5); 15(7); 16(4); 17(4); 18(13); 19; 20(3); 21(4); 22(2); 23; 24(5); 25(7); 26(4); 27(3); 28; 29(5); 30(7); 31(7); 33(4); 34(8); 35(10); 5:1; 2; 3; 6(4); 7(2); 8(2); 9(8); 10(3); 11; 12(5); 13(3); 14; 15(6); 16(7); 17(2); 18(3); 19; 6:1; 2; 4(2); 5(3); 6(3); 7(2); 8; 9(8); 10(6); 11(2); 12(6); 13(2); 14(5); 15(8); 16(5); 17(2); 18(4); 19; 20(5); 21(3); 22(2); 23; 24; 25(6); 26(5); 27(3); 28; 29(2); 30(5); 7:1(2); 2(5); 3(4); 4(6); 5(3); 6(2); 7(3); 8(4); 9(5); 10; 11(3); 12; 13(2); 14(5); 15(4); 16(4); 17(4); 18(4); 19(2); 20(4); 21(5); 22; 23; 24(3); 25(4); 28; 29(5); 30(6); 31(4); 32(3); 33(5); 34(6); 35(8); 36(3); 37(8); 38(5); 8:1; 2(3); 3(4); 4(5); 5(3); 7(6); 8(4); 9(5); 10(2); 11(3); 12; 13; 14(5); 15(7); 16(6); 17(3); 18(4); 19(2); 20(4); 21(6); 22(4); 23(4); 24(6); 25(8); 26(4); 27; 28(3); 29(4); 30(3); 31(6); 32(2); 33(4); 34; 35(5); 36(2); 9:1(2); 2; 3(3); 4(2); 5(4); 6(4); 7(5); 8(3); 9(8); 10(7); 11(3); 12(3); 13(4); 14(4); 15(5); 16(2); 17(4); 18(5); 19(8); 20(4); 21(3); 22(3); 23(6); 24(5); 10:1(2); 2(2); 3(2); 4(4); 5; 6(4); 7(6); 8; 9(2); 11(4); 12(4); 13(3); 14(3); 15(6); 16(3); 17(5); 18(3); 19(4); 11:1; 2(4); 3(3); 4(5); 5(3); 6(3); 7(3); 9(4); 10(4); 12; 13(4); 14(2); 16(4); 17(3); 18(3); 19(4); 21; 22(4); 24(2); 25(2); 26(3); 27; 28(2); 29(5); 30(5); 31; 32; 38; 39(2); 40(4); 41; 42(2); 44(2); 45(2); 46(5); 47(4); 12:1; 2(3); 3(2); 4(3); 5; 6(6); 7(3); 8(4); 13:1; 2(5); 3(9); 4(6); 5(6); 6(6); 7(4); 8(4); 9(2); 10(5); 11(2); 12(5); 13(3); 15(3); 16(2); 17(4); 18(2); 19(3); 20(5); 21(3); 22(2); 23(2); 24(2); 25(7); 26(4); 27(5); 28(5); 29(2); 30(5); 31(7); 32(6); 33(3); 34(7); 35(2); 36(4); 37(3); 38; 39(4); 40; 41; 42; 43(6); 44; 45(2); 46(3); 47(2); 48; 49(6); 50(3); 51(7); 52(2); 53(5); 54(3); 55(5); 56(7); 57(4); 58(3); 59(3); 14:1; 2(4); 3(5); 4; 5(2); 6(8); 7(3); 8; 9; 10(2); 11(6); 12(3); 13(8); 14(8); 15(3); 16(4); 17(9); 18(6); 19(3); 20(5); 22(2); 23(6); 24(6); 25(9); 26(3); 27(3); 28(9); 29(5); 30(3); 31(5); 32(2); 33; 34(3); 35(3); 36(7); 37(5); 38(5); 39(5); 40(4); 41(3); 42(2); 43(4); 44(4); 45(6); 46(3); 47(2); 48(7); 49; 50(2); 51(8); 52(8); 53(4); 54; 55; 57; 15:1; 2; 4; 5; 6(2); 7(3); 8(2); 9; 10(2); 11(2); 12(2); 14(6); 15(5); 16; 17(2); 18(2); 19; 21; 22; 23; 24; 25(5); 26(3); 27; 29(5); 30(6); 31; 32; 33(2); 16:1(4); 2(7); 3; 4(3); 5(3); 6; 7(5); 8(4); 9(2); 10(5); 11(4); 12(3); 13(7); 14(5); 15(8); 16(6); 17(4); 18(8); 19(3); 20(5); 21(8); 22(3); 23(4); 24(4); 25(3); 26(3); 27(7); 28; 29(3); 30(2); 32(5); 33(7); 34(2); 17:1; 2(3); 3(3); 4(6); 5(9); 6(9); 8(2); 9(4); 10(2); 11(6); 12; 13(3); 14(7); 15; 18:1; 2(2); 3(4); 4; 5; 6; 7(2); 8; 9(2); 10; 11; 12; 13; 14; 15; 16; 17; 18; 21(3); 24; 25(3); 27(3); 28(2); 29; 30; 19:1; 2(3); 3; 4; 5; 6(4); 7; 8(2); 9(3); 10(2); 12(2); 13(2); 14(3); 15(4); 16(2); 18(2); 21(4); 22(5); 23(2); 24(3); 25(4); 26; 27(2); 28(2); 29(2); 30; 31; 32(4); 34(3); 36(2); 37; 20:1; 2(5); 4(3); 6; 7; 8; 10(3); 11; 15; 16(2); 17; 18; 19; 22; 23(2); 24; 25; 26; 21:1(4); 5; 6(4); 8(2); 9(2); 10(3); 12(5); 15; 16; 17; 21(5); 22(3); 23(3); 24; 22:1; 2(3); 3(4); 4(3); 6(2); 7(2); 8; 9; 10(3); 11; 12(2); 13; 14(4); 15(3); 16(2); 17; 18(4); 19(3); 21; 22(3); 24; 25; 26; 27(3); 29; 30(3); 31; 32(2); 33(2); 23:1; 2(3); 3(4); 4(2); 5(3); 6(4); 7; 8(2); 9; 10(5); 11(5); 12(3); 13(4); 14; 15(5); 16(3); 17(2); 18(4); 19(2); 20(7); 21; 22(5); 23; 24(4); 25; 26; 27(2); 28; 30; 32(2); 33; 34(4); 35; 36(3); 37(3); 38(3); 39(7); 40(5); 41(3); 43(3); 44(3); 24:1; 2(3); 3(7); 4(3); 6(2); 7(2); 8(2); 9(3); 10(4); 11(5); 12(2); 13; 14(2); 15; 16(7); 22(2); 23(4); 25:1; 2(4); 3; 4(3); 5(2); 6(2); 7(2); 8(2); 9(6); 10(3); 11; 12(3); 13; 15(4); 16(7); 17; 18; 19; 20; 21; 22(3); 23(2); 24(2); 26; 27(4); 28(3); 30(4); 31(5); 32(5); 33(8); 34(2); 38(3); 40; 41; 42; 44; 45(2); 46; 47(3); 50(5); 51(2); 52(2); 53; 54; 55(3); 26:1; 2; 4(3); 5(4); 6(3); 7; 8; 10(2); 13(3); 16(2); 19; 20(2); 25(4); 26; 29(2); 30; 31; 32; 33; 34(2); 36(2); 38(2); 39; 40; 41(2); 42; 43(2); 44(2); 45(5); 46(4); 27:1; 2(3); 3(3); 5(2); 6(2); 7; 8(3); 9(2); 10; 11(3); 12(2); 14(3); 15(2); 16(2); 17; 18(6);

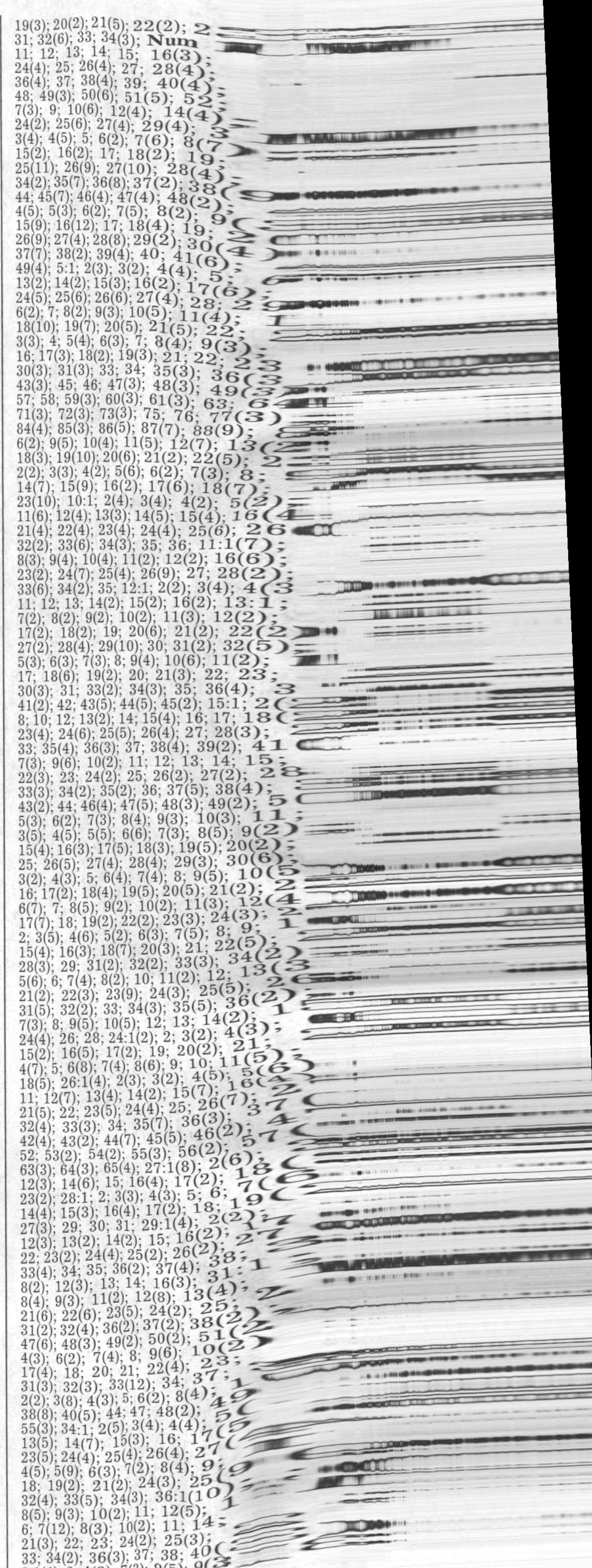

15(3); 16(2); 17; 18; 19(4); 20; 21(2); 22(2); 23(2); 24(2); 25(4);
26; 27(3); 29(4); 30; 31; 33; 34(3); 35(3); 36(5); 37(6); 3:1(2);
2(2); 3(2); 4(2); 6; 7(3); 8(5); 9(2); 10(3); 11(5); 12(4); 13(5);
14(3); 16(8); 17(5); 18(3); 20(3); 21(3); 22; 23; 25; 26(2); 27;
28; 29; 4:1(4); 2(3); 3(3); 4; 5(2); 6(2); 7; 9(2); 10(6); 11(3);
12(5); 14(2); 15(4); 16(2); 17(4); 18(5); 19(6); 20(2); 21(2); 23(4);
24; 25(4); 26; 27(4); 28; 29; 30(2); 31(2); 32(5); 33(3); 34(2);
35; 36(2); 39(2); 40(2); 41; 42; 43(5); 44(2); 45(4); 46(4); 47(3);
48(2); 49(4); 5:1; 2; 3; 4(4); 5(5); 6(3); 8(3); 9(5); 11(3); 12(2);
14(3); 15(4); 16(3); 22(6); 23(5); 24(3); 25(2); 26(4); 27(2); 28(5);
31(4); 32(3); 33(3); 6:1(5); 2(2); 3(2); 4; 5; 7; 9; 10(2); 12(3); 13;
14(2); 15(5); 16; 17(2); 18(4); 19; 20(4); 21; 22; 23; 24(2); 25;
7:1(9); 2; 4(2); 6(4); 7(2); 8(5); 9(2); 11(3); 12(3); 13(5); 15(2);
16(2); 18; 19(8); 20(2); 21; 22(3); 23; 25(3); 8:1(3); 2(3); 3(2);
5; 6(2); 7; 10(2); 11; 14(3); 15; 16; 17; 18; 19; 20(4); 9:2(3);
3(2); 4(4); 5(5); 6; 7(5); 8(2); 9(6); 10(9); 11(5); 12(2); 13; 15(4);
16(3); 17; 18(4); 19(3); 20(2); 21(4); 22; 23(4); 24(2); 25(3); 26;
27; 28(4); 10:1(3); 2(4); 3(3); 4(10); 5(4); 6(3); 8(6); 9(2); 10(4);
11(3); 12(3); 13(2); 14(4); 15; 16; 17; 18(3); 19(2); 20; 22(2);
11:1; 2(2); 3(2); 4(4); 5; 6(5); 7(2); 8(2); 9(2); 10(2); 11(2); 12(7);
13; 14(3); 17(5); 19; 20; 21(5); 22; 23; 24(5); 25(4); 27(2); 28(3);
29(4); 30(7); 31(2); 32; 12:1(5); 2(4); 3(2); 4; 5(2); 6; 7(2); 8;
9(3); 10(2); 11(3); 12(2); 14(2); 15(6); 16(2); 17(2); 18(5); 19(2);
20; 21(3); 22(4); 23(5); 24; 25(2); 26(2); 27(8); 28(2); 29(2);
31(3); 13:2(2); 3(3); 4; 5(7); 6(2); 7(6); 9(2); 10(3); 12; 13(2); 14;
15(6); 16(6); 17(3); 18(4); 14:1(3); 2(4); 4(4); 5(7); 6(4); 7(7);
8(3); 9; 12(3); 13(3); 15(4); 16(3); 17(3); 18(4); 21(2); 22(2);
23(5); 24(4); 25(3); 26; 27; 28(3); 29(6); 15:1; 2(3); 4(3); 5(2);
6; 7; 9(3); 10; 11(2); 12; 14; 15(2); 17; 18; 19(4); 20(3); 21;
22(4); 23(2); 16:1(5); 2(6); 3(5); 4(3); 5(2); 6(6); 7(3); 8(2); 9(3);
10(4); 11(7); 13; 14(4); 15(5); 16(6); 17(2); 18(2); 19(4); 20(2);
21(2); 22; 17:1(2); 2(3); 3(2); 4; 6(2); 7(5); 8(2); 9(4); 10(2);
11(6); 12(5); 13; 14(3); 15; 16(3); 18(3); 19(3); 20(5); 18:1(5);
2; 3(6); 4(3); 5(3); 6(3); 7(4); 8; 9(3); 10; 12(2); 13; 14; 15(2);
16(5); 17; 20(2); 21(2); 22(6); 19:1(3); 2(2); 3(2); 4(2); 5(5); 6(4);
8(2); 9; 10; 12(3); 13; 14(2); 15(3); 17(5); 18(2); 19; 20:1(2);
2(3); 4; 5(3); 6; 7; 8(2); 9(4); 11; 13(3); 14(7); 15(2); 16(2); 17(7);
18; 19(4); 20(2); 21:1(3); 2; 3(4); 4(4); 5(5); 6(4); 8; 9(3); 10; 11;
13; 15(3); 16(5); 17(6); 18(2); 19(2); 20; 21; 23(2); 22:4; 5(2);
6(7); 7(2); 9(2); 12; 15(7); 16(2); 17(4); 18; 19(2); 20(2); 21(4);
22(3); 23; 24(4); 25(3); 26(2); 27(2); 29(2); 23:1(3); 2(4); 3(4);
4(2); 5(4); 8(3); 9; 10(2); 11(2); 12; 14(2); 15; 17(2); 18(5); 20(2);
21(2); 23; 25(2); 24:3(2); 4(3); 6(2); 7; 8(3); 9(2); 11(2); 12;
13(3); 15(2); 16(4); 17(3); 18; 19(6); 20(4); 21(4); 22; 25:1(3);
2(2); 4(2); 5(3); 6(3); 7(4); 8; 9(2); 10; 11(4); 15(2); 16; 17; 18(2);
19(4); 26:1(2); 2(6); 3(4); 4(4); 5; 6; 7(2); 8; 10(4); 11(3); 12(7);
13(6); 14(3); 15; 16; 17; 18; 19; 27:1(3); 2(3); 3(4); 5; 6(3); 7;
8(2); 9(4); 10(2); 11(2); 12; 14(2); 15(6); 16; 17; 18(3); 19(3);
20; 21; 22(3); 23; 24; 25; 26(2); 28:1(4); 2(2); 3(2); 4(5); 7; 8(4);
9(3); 10(3); 11(6); 12(4); 13(5); 14(3); 15(2); 16(2); 18(4); 20(2);
21(3); 22(2); 23; 24(2); 25(3); 26(3); 27(5); 28; 29; 30; 32; 33;
34; 35(5); 36; 37; 38(2); 39(3); 40; 42; 43; 44(2); 45(2); 47(2);
48; 49(4); 50(3); 51(3); 52; 53(5); 54(3); 55(3); 56(4); 57; 58(2);
59(2); 60; 61(2); 62(3); 63(3); 64(4); 65(2); 67(3); 68(2); 29:1(6);
2(2); 3(2); 4; 5; 6; 7(2); 8(3); 9; 10(2); 11(2); 12(2); 15; 16(2);
18(2); 19(2); 20(5); 21(5); 22(5); 23(3); 24(2); 25(3); 27(3); 28;
29(3); 30:1(4); 2; 3(3); 4(2); 5(2); 6(3); 7; 8(2); 9(5); 10(4); 13(2);
14; 16(3); 18; 20(4); 31:2; 3(2); 4(3); 5(2); 6; 7(3); 8; 9(6); 10(4);
11(2); 12(3); 13(2); 14(5); 15(6); 16(4); 18; 19(2); 20; 21(2);
22(2); 23(3); 24; 25(4); 26(5); 27; 28; 29(5); 30(3); 32:1; 2(6);
3(2); 4; 5; 6; 7(2); 8(7); 9(2); 10(2); 12; 13(6); 14(4); 15; 18;
19(2); 22(4); 24(3); 25(5); 26; 27(3); 30; 32(2); 33(2); 35(2); 36;
38(2); 42(5); 43; 44(4); 46(2); 47; 48; 49(3); 50; 51(5); 52(3);
33:1(3); 2; 3; 4(2); 5(3); 7(2); 8; 11(2); 12(4); 13(4); 14(4); 15(4);
16(8); 17(7); 19(5); 20(3); 21(6); 23(4); 26(3); 27(3); 28; 29(3);
34:1(5); 2(3); 3(4); 4(2); 5(5); 6; 8(3); 9(4); 10; 11(4); 12(2); **Josh**
1:1(5); 2(2); 3; 4(8); 5; 6; 7(3); 8; 9; 10(2); 11(4); 12(3); 13(4);
14(2); 15(6); 17; 2:1(2); 2(3); 3(3); 4(2); 5(4); 6(4); 7(4); 8; 9(5);
10(6); 11; 12; 14(3); 15(3); 16(3); 17; 18(2); 19(3); 21(2); 22(4);
23(3); 24(4); 3:1(2); 2(2); 3(6); 4; 5(2); 6(7); 7(2); 8(5); 9(3);
10(8); 11(4); 12; 13(10); 14(5); 15(7); 16(6); 17(7); 4:1(2); 2;
3(4); 4(2); 5(6); 7(6); 8(7); 9(6); 10(6); 11(6); 12(4); 13(2); 14(3);
15; 16(3); 17; 18(9); 19(4); 21; 23(4); 24(5); 5:1(10); 2(3); 3(3);
4(5); 5(4); 6(8); 7; 8(2); 9(4); 10(5); 11(5); 12(7); 14(3); 15(3);
6:1; 2(3); 3(2); 4(5); 5(7); 6(6); 7(4); 8(8); 9(7); 10(2); 11(5);
12(4); 13(9); 14(3); 15(6); 16(6); 17(5); 18(3); 19(4); 20(11);
21(3); 22(4); 23(2); 24(7); 25(2); 26(4); 27(2); 7:1(10); 2(3); 3(2);
4(2); 5(5); 6(5); 7(3); 9(4); 10; 11; 12(2); 13(4); 14(8); 15(3);
16(2); 17(5); 18(4); 19; 20; 21(4); 22(2); 23(4); 24(5); 25; 26(4);
8:1(3); 2(3); 3; 4(3); 5(3); 6(2); 7(3); 8(4); 9(2); 10(4); 11(4);
12(2); 13(8); 14(5); 15(2); 16(2); 17; 18(4); 19(3); 20(6); 21(5);
22(3); 23; 24(8); 25; 26(2); 27(4); 29(6); 30; 31(6); 32(4); 33(10);
34(5); 35(4); 9:1(11); 3; 5; 6(2); 7(2); 9(3); 10(2); 11(2); 12; 13;
14(3); 15(2); 16; 17(2); 18(6); 19(3); 20; 21(3); 23; 24(4); 26(2);
27(4); 10:1; 2(2); 4; 5(7); 6(5); 7(2); 8; 10(2); 11(4); 12(7); 13(6);
14(3); 15; 17; 18(2); 19(2); 20(2); 21(3); 22(3); 23(6); 24(5); 25;
26(2); 27(6); 28(6); 30(8); 32(6); 35(3); 37(6); 39(6); 40(6); 41;
42; 43; 11:1(2); 2(7); 3(10); 4(2); 5; 6; 7(2); 8(3); 9; 10(3); 11(3);
12(6); 13; 14(5); 15(2); 16(8); 17(2); 19(3); 20(2); 21(4); 22(3);
23(3); 12:1(9); 2(8); 3(9); 4(3); 5(4); 6(8); 7(7); 8(12); 9(2); 10(2);
11(2); 12(2); 13(2); 14(2); 15(2); 16(2); 17(2); 18(2); 19(2);
20(2); 21(2); 22(2); 23(4); 24(2); 13:1; 2(3); 3(9); 4(6); 5(4); 6(5);
7(2); 8(4); 9(6); 10(4); 11(2); 12(3); 13(6); 14(3); 15(2); 16(6);
17; 19(2); 21(6); 22(4); 23(7); 24(2); 25(3); 26; 27(6); 28(3);
29(4); 30(2); 31(5); 32(3); 33(2); 14:1(9); 2(4); 3(3); 4(3); 5(3);
6(6); 7(3); 8(3); 9(2); 10(4); 11; 12(5); 13; 14(4); 15(3); 15:1(7);
2(3); 3(2); 4(3); 5(7); 6(5); 7(8); 8(13); 9(7); 10(3); 11(6); 12(5);
13(6); 14(2); 15(2); 17(2); 19(2); 20(3); 21(4); 32; 33; 46; 47(3);
48; 61; 62; 63(5); 16:1(5); 2; 3(5); 4; 5(5); 6(5); 8(7); 9(5); 10(3);
17:1(4); 2(10); 3(5); 4(7); 5(2); 6(3); 7(4); 8(3); 9(9); 10(3); 11(4);
12(3); 13(2); 14(2); 15(4); 16(6); 17; 18(3); 18:1(5); 2; 3(3); 4(2);
5(3); 6(3); 7(7); 8(4); 9(3); 10(3); 11(6); 12(7); 13(6); 14(7); 15(5);
16(11); 17(4); 18; 19(8); 20(5); 21(4); 28(2); 19:1(5); 8(5); 9(8);
10(3); 11(2); 12(2); 13; 14(4); 16(2); 17(2); 22(2); 23(4); 24(3);
27(4); 29(6); 31(3); 32(3); 33; 34(4); 35; 39(4); 40(3); 41; 46;
47(6); 48(3); 49(3); 50(4); 51(12); 20:1; 2(2); 3(2); 4(6); 5(2);
6(5); 7; 8(6); 9(6); 21:1(9); 2(4); 3(4); 4(9); 5(6); 6(6); 7(4); 8(4);
9(4); 10(5); 11(4); 12(4); 13(3); 17; 19(3); 20(6); 21; 23; 25;
26(3); 27(5); 28; 30; 32(2); 33(2); 34(5); 36; 38(2); 40(4); 41(4);
43(2); 44(2); 45(2); 22:1(3); 2(2); 3(3); 4(5); 5(5); 7(3); 8; 9(10);
10(5); 11(8); 12(3); 13(7); 14(3); 15(4); 16(5); 17(3); 18(3); 19(8);
20(3); 21(5); 22(3); 23(2); 24; 25(3); 27(3); 28(3); 29(4); 30(8);
31(10); 32(8); 33(5); 34(4); 23:1; 3(2); 4(2); 5(2); 6(4); 7; 8; 9;
10; 11; 12; 13(2); 14(4); 15(3); 16(5); 24:1(2); 2(6); 3(3); 6(3);
7(4); 8(3); 9(2); 11(8); 12(3); 13; 14(5); 15(7); 16(2); 17(5); 18(5);
19(2); 20; 21(2); 22(2); 23(2); 24(2); 25; 26(4); 27(3); 28; 29(3);
30(3); 31(6); 32(6); 33; **Judg** 1:1(4); 2(2); 3; 4(3); 5(2); 8(4);
9(5); 10(2); 11(2); 13; 15(2); 16(7); 17(3); 18(3); 19(5); 20; 21(4);
22(2); 23(3); 24(4); 25(6); 26(5); 27(5); 28; 29(2); 30(3); 31(2);
32(4); 33(6); 34(4); 35(3); 36(4); 2:1(2); 2; 4(4); 5(2); 6(3); 7(7);
8(3); 9(4); 10(2); 11(3); 12(5); 13; 14(4); 15(4); 16(2); 17(3);
18(7); 19; 20(2); 21; 22(2); 23(2); 3:1(3); 2(3); 3(5); 4(3); 5(2);
7(5); 8(4); 9(5); 10(3); 11(2); 12(7); 13(2); 14(2); 15(6); 17; 18(3);
19; 21; 22(6); 23(3); 24(2); 25(3); 26; 27(3); 28(3); 30(2); 31(2);
4:1(3); 2(4); 3(3); 4; 5(2); 6(4); 7(2); 9(3); 11(5); 12; 13(3); 14(3);
15(3); 16(6); 17(6); 18; 20(2); 21(3); 22(2); 23(2); 24(3); 5:1;
2(3); 3(2); 4(4); 5(3); 6(5); 7(2); 8; 9(3); 10; 11(9); 13(4); 14(2);
15(3); 16(4); 17; 18(3); 19(3); 20; 21(2); 22(4); 23(8); 24(3);
26(3); 28(3); 30(3); 31(2); 6:1(5); 2(5); 3(4); 4(2); 5; 6(3); 7(3);
8(4); 9(3); 10(3); 11(4); 12(3); 13(5); 14(3); 15; 16(2); 19(3);
20(4); 21(11); 22(2); 23; 24(2); 25(5); 26(6); 27(3); 28(7); 29;
30(4); 33(5); 34(2); 37(4); 38(4); 39(3); 40(2); 7:1(7); 2(3); 3(3);
4(5); 5(4); 6(3); 7(4); 8(4); 9(3); 10; 11(4); 12(7); 13(2); 14(3);
15(6); 16(2); 17(2); 18(4); 19(8); 20(7); 21(2); 22(6); 23(2); 24(4);
25(5); 8:1(2); 2(3); 3; 4; 5(2); 6(2); 7(3); 8(2); 9; 10(3); 11(4);
12(2); 13(2); 14(3); 15(2); 16(4); 17(3); 18; 19(2); 20; 21(2);
22(2); 23; 24; 25; 26(4); 28(3); 29; 32(3); 33; 34(3); 35(2); 9:1(3);
2(3); 3(2); 4; 5(2); 6(4); 7; 8(2); 9(2); 10(2); 11(2); 12(2); 13(2);
14(2); 15(4); 16; 17; 18(2); 20(4); 23(2); 24(4); 25(3); 26(2);
27(3); 28(4); 30(4); 31(2); 32(2); 33(4); 34; 35(5); 36(5); 37(3);
38; 39; 40(2); 42(3); 43(4); 44(7); 45(4); 46(4); 47(2); 48(3);
49(5); 51(5); 52(3); 54; 55; 56; 57(4); 10:1(2); 4; 6(11); 7(6);
8(5); 9(2); 10(2); 11(6); 12(3); 14(2); 15(2); 16(3); 17(2); 18(3);
11:1(2); 2; 3; 4; 5(3); 6; 7; 8(3); 9(3); 10(2); 11(3); 12(2); 13(3);
14(2); 15(3); 16(2); 17(3); 18(8); 19(2); 21(5); 22(3); 23(2); 24;
25; 26(2); 27(4); 28(3); 29(3); 30(2); 31(3); 32(2); 33(4); 35;
36(3); 37; 38; 39; 40(3); 12:1(2); 2; 3(2); 4(4); 5(4); 6(2); 7(2);
12(2); 13; 15(5); 13:1(6); 2(2); 3(3); 5(4); 6(2); 7(3); 8(3); 9(4);
10(3); 11(3); 12; 13(3); 14; 15(2); 16(4); 17(2); 18(2); 19(2);
20(7); 21(3); 23; 24(3); 25(3); 14:1(2); 2(2); 3(2); 4(3); 5; 6(2);
7; 8(4); 9(3); 10(2); 12(2); 14(3); 15(2); 16; 17(4); 18(4); 19(3);
15:1(2); 3; 4; 5(6); 6(4); 8(2); 9; 10; 11(3); 12(2); 13; 14(4); 16(2);
17; 18(4); 19(2); 20(2); 16:2(5); 3(5); 4; 5(2); 8(2); 9(4); 12(2);
13(2); 14(5); 18(4); 19; 20(2); 21(2); 22; 23(2); 24(2); 25(2);
26(4); 27(4); 28(2); 29(4); 30(5); 31(2); 17:2(3); 3(3); 4(3); 5; 7;
8(3); 10(2); 11(3); 12(3); 13; 18:1(3); 2(4); 3(4); 6(2); 7(6); 9(2);
10; 11(2); 13; 14(2); 15(4); 16(4); 17(10); 18(5); 19; 20(6); 21(3);
22(4); 23; 24; 25(2); 26; 27(5); 28; 29(6); 30(8); 31(2); 19:1; 2;
3(2); 4; 5(3); 6(2); 7; 8(3); 9(4); 10; 11(3); 12(2); 14; 15; 16(3);
17(3); 18(3); 19; 20(2); 21; 22(8); 23(3); 25(5); 26(5); 27(7);
28(2); 29; 30(3); 20:1(4); 2(5); 3(3); 4(3); 5(2); 6(2); 8; 9; 10(3);
11(2); 12(2); 13(5); 14(3); 15(3); 17; 18(5); 19(2); 20(2); 21(3);
22(4); 23(5); 24(3); 25(4); 26(5); 27(4); 28(4); 30(3); 31(8); 32(5);
33(3); 34; 35(4); 36(4); 37(5); 38(3); 39(4); 40(5); 41(2); 42(6);
43(2); 45(3); 46; 47(3); 48(7); 21:1; 2(2); 4(2); 5(5); 6; 7; 8(4);
9(2); 10(7); 11; 12(3); 13(3); 14; 15(3); 16(3); 18; 19(5); 20(2);
21(4); 22; 23(2); 24; **Ruth** 1:1(4); 2(5); 4(5); 5; 6(3); 7(3); 8(2);
9(2); 13(2); 17; 19; 20; 21(3); 22(3); 2:1; 2(2); 3(4); 4(3); 5; 6(4);
7(4); 9(4); 10; 11(2); 12(2); 14(3); 15; 16; 17; 18; 19; 20(4); 21;
23(2); 3:2; 3(2); 4; 6; 7(2); 8; 10(3); 11; 13(7); 14(2); 15(2); 16;
18(3); 4:1(2); 2(2); 3(2); 4(2); 5(7); 6; 7; 8; 9(3); 10(7); 11(6);
12(3); 13; 14(2); 16; 17(3); 18; **1Sa** 1:1(4); 2(4); 3(4); 4; 5; 6;
7(2); 9(3); 10; 11(3); 12; 15; 16; 17; 18; 19(3); 20(2); 21(3);
22(2); 23(2); 24(3); 25; 26(2); 27; 28(3); 2:1(2); 2; 3; 4(2); 5;
6(2); 7; 8(9); 9(2); 10(6); 11(3); 12(2); 13(4); 14(4); 15(4); 16;
17(5); 18; 19; 20(3); 21(3); 22(4); 24; 25(4); 26(2); 27(2); 28(4);
29(2); 30(3); 31(2); 32; 33(3); 36; 3:1(4); 3(4); 4; 6; 7(3); 8(4);
10; 11(2); 13; 14(2); 15(5); 17(3); 18; 19(2); 20; 21(4); 4:1(3);
2(4); 3(9); 4(8); 5(5); 6(9); 7(2); 8(5); 9; 10; 11(2); 12(2); 13(5);
14(4); 16(3); 17(4); 18(4); 19(2); 20(2); 21(3); 22(2); 5:1(2); 2(3);
3(4); 4(8); 5(2); 6(3); 7(3); 8(8); 9(5); 10(5); 11(6); 12(4); 6:1(4);
2(5); 3(2); 4(4); 5(2); 6(2); 7(2); 8(5); 9; 10(2); 11(6); 12(9); 13(2);
14(6); 15(9); 16(3); 17(3); 18(10); 19(7); 20; 21(4); 7:1(7); 2(4);
3(6); 4(2); 5; 6(3); 7(6); 8(4); 9(3); 10(4); 11(2); 12(2); 13(6);
14(6); 15; 17; 8:2(2); 4; 5; 6(2); 7(3); 8(2); 9(2); 10(3); 11(2); 14;
15; 17; 18; 19(2); 20; 21(4); 22(2); 9:1(4); 2(2); 3(3); 4(4); 5(2);
7(3); 8(3); 9; 10(2); 11(3); 12(3); 13(4); 14(3); 15; 16(3); 17(2);
18(2); 19(2); 20; 21(5); 22(2); 23(2); 24(3); 25(4); 26(4); 27(4);
10:1; 2(4); 3; 5(5); 6(2); 10(2); 11(4); 12(2); 13; 14; 16(3); 17(2);
18(5); 19; 20(2); 21(3); 22(4); 23(2); 24(5); 25(5); 27; 11:1(2);
2; 3(2); 4(5); 5(5); 6; 7(5); 8(2); 9(5); 10; 11(8); 12(2); 13; 14(2);
15(4); 12:2; 3; 5; 6(3); 7(3); 8(2); 9(7); 10(3); 11(2); 12(3);
13(2); 14(5); 15(6); 16; 17(3); 18(4); 19(2); 20(3); 22(2); 23(3);
24; 13:2(2); 3(6); 4(3); 5(3); 6(3); 7(3); 8(2); 9; 10; 11(3); 12(2);
13(3); 14(3); 15; 16(2); 17(5); 18(5); 19(3); 20(2); 21(5); 22(3);
23(3); 14:1(4); 2(2); 3(5); 4(8); 5(3); 6(4); 10; 11(5); 12(4); 15(6);
16(2); 17; 18(3); 19(5); 20(2); 21(5); 22(3); 23(2); 24(4); 25(2);
26(5); 27(4); 28(4); 29; 30(3); 31(2); 32(5); 33(3); 34(4); 35(4);
36(3); 37(2); 38(2); 39(2); 40(2); 41(2); 43(2); 45(4); 46(2); 47(4);
48(2); 49(6); 50(5); 51(3); 52(2); 15:1(4); 2(2); 4; 5; 6(5); 7;
8(5); 9(6); 10(2); 11; 12; 13(3); 14(3); 15(7); 16; 17(3); 18(3);
19(5); 20(6); 21(5); 22(4); 23(3); 24(3); 25; 26(3); 27; 28(2); 29;
30(2); 31; 32(3); 33; 35(2); 16:1(2); 2(2); 3; 4(3); 5(3); 6; 7(6);
8; 9; 10; 11(2); 12; 13(4); 14(3); 16; 18(3); 19; 23(2); 17:1; 2(4);
3(3); 4(2); 5(2); 7; 8; 10(2); 11; 12(3); 13(6); 14(2); 16; 17; 18;
19(3); 20(6); 21(2); 22(4); 23(5); 24(2); 25(3); 26(5); 27(2); 28(4);
30(3); 31; 34; 36(4); 37(7); 40(2); 41(3); 42; 43(2); 44(5); 45(5);
46(9); 47(3); 48(3); 49(3); 50(3); 51(3); 52(7); 53(2); 54(2); 55(3);
56(2); 57(4); 58(2); 18:1(2); 4; 5(4); 6(3); 7; 8(2); 10(4); 11(2);
12; 13; 14; 17(3); 18; 19(2); 20; 21(4); 22(2); 23; 24; 25(5);
26(2); 27(3); 28; 29; 30(3); 19:2; 3; 4; 5(2); 6(2); 8; 9(2); 10(4);
11; 13; 15(2); 16(2); 20(4); 21; 23; 24; 20:3; 5(4); 6; 8; 11(2);
12; 13(2); 14(2); 15(4); 16(3); 18; 19(3); 20; 21(4); 22(3); 23(2);
24(3); 25(2); 27(4); 29(2); 30(3); 31(2); 34(3); 35(3); 36(2); 37(5);
38(2); 39(2); 40; 41(3); 42(4); 21:1(2); 2(3); 4(2); 5(5); 6(4); 7(4);
8; 9(5); 10; 11(3); 12; 13(2); 14; 15; 22:1; 3; 4(3); 5(4); 6; 7; 8;
9(4); 10(3); 11(5); 13; 14(2); 15(2); 16; 17(8); 18(4); 19(6); 20(2);
21; 22(3); 23:1(2); 2(3); 3(2); 4(3); 5(2); 6; 8; 9(2); 10; 11(2);
12(3); 14(2); 15; 16; 17; 18(2); 19(4); 20(2); 21; 23(4); 24(3);
25(2); 26(2); 27(2); 28; 24:1(2); 2(2); 3(4); 4(4); 6(4); 7; 8(3);
10(3); 11(2); 12(2); 13(3); 14; 15; 18; 19; 20; 21; 22; 25:1(2); 2;
3(5); 4; 5; 7; 8; 9; 10; 13; 14(2); 15(2); 16(2); 20(3); 21; 22(3);
23(2); 24; 25; 26(2); 27; 28(4); 29(5); 30(2); 31; 32; 34(3); 36(2);
37(2); 38; 39(5); 40; 41(3); 42; 44; 26:1(2); 2(2); 3(4); 5(6); 6(3);
7(4); 8(3); 9; 10(2); 11(4); 12(3); 13(2); 14(3); 15(3); 16(4); 19(7);
20(5); 21; 22(2); 23(3); 24(2); 27:1(3); 2(2); 3(2); 5(2); 6; 7(3);
8(6); 9(6); 10(5); 11(3); 28:1; 3(2); 4; 5(2); 6(2); 8(2); 9(3); 10(2);
11; 12(2); 13(3); 14; 15; 16; 17(3); 18(3); 19(7); 20(4); 21; 22;
23(3); 24(2); 29:1(2); 2(3); 3(6); 4(6); 6(4); 7(2); 8(2); 9(3); 10(2);
11(4); 30:1(3); 2; 3; 4; 5(3); 6(4); 7(3); 8; 9(2); 10; 11; 14(4); 15;
16(5); 17(3); 18; 20(2); 21(4); 22(2); 23(2); 24(2); 26(5); 29(4);
31; 31:1(3); 2(2); 3(3); 7(7); 8(3); 9(4); 10(2); 11(2); 12(4); **2Sa**
1:1(3); 2(3); 3; 4(4); 5; 6(2); 10(2); 11; 12(4); 13(2); 14; 15; 16;
18(4); 19(2); 20(5); 21(3); 22(6); 25(3); 26; 27(2); 2:1(3); 2(2);
3; 4(3); 5(2); 6; 7; 8(2); 9; 10; 11(2); 12(3); 13(9); 14; 15(2); 16;
17(2); 19(2); 21; 22; 23(6); 24(4); 25(2); 26(3); 27(2); 28; 29;
30; 31; 32; 3:1(3); 2; 3(5); 4(4); 5; 6(3); 7; 8(3); 9; 10(3); 12; 14;
15; 17; 18(5); 19(3); 20; 21; 22; 23(3); 24; 25; 26; 27(3); 28(3);
29(3); 30; 31(2); 32(3); 33; 34; 35(2); 36(3); 37(3); 38; 39(3);
4:1; 2(6); 3; 4; 5(5); 6(3); 7(2); 8(6); 9(3); 11; 12(3); 5:1; 2; 3(3);
6(6); 7(3); 8(7); 9(2); 10; 12; 14; 17(3); 18(2); 19(4); 20(3); 22(2);
23(2); 24(6); 25(2); 6:1; 2(5); 3(4); 4(3); 5(2); 6(2); 7(3); 8(3);
9(3); 10(5); 11(5); 12(6); 13(2); 14; 15(5); 16(4); 17(5); 18(3);
19(4); 20(5); 21(4); 22; 23(2); 7:1(2); 2(3); 3(2); 4(2); 5; 6(2);
7(3); 8(3); 9(3); 10; 11(2); 13; 14(3); 18; 19; 23(2); 25; 26(3);
29(2); 8:1(3); 2(2); 3(2); 4; 5(2); 6(2); 7(2); 9; 11(2); 12(3); 13(2);
14; 16(3); 17(4); 18(3); 9:1; 2(2); 3(4); 4(4); 5(2); 6(2); 7; 9;
10(2); 11(4); 12; 13; 10:1(2); 2(4); 3(3); 4(2); 5(2); 6(4); 7(2);
8(6); 9(4); 10(4); 11(2); 12(3); 13(3); 14(4); 15; 16(4); 17; 18(4);
19(3); 11:1(3); 2(4); 3(4); 5; 6; 7(2); 8(2); 9(3); 11(3); 12; 13;
14(2); 15(3); 16; 17(5); 18(2); 19(4); 20(3); 21(4); 22; 23(5);
24(4); 25(3); 26; 27(3); 12:1(3); 2; 3; 4(4); 5(3); 6; 7(3); 8; 9(6);
10(3); 11(2); 12; 13(2); 14(3); 15(2); 16(2); 17(2); 18(6); 19(2);
20(3); 21(2); 22(2); 24; 25(3); 26(2); 27; 28(4); 29; 30(4); 31(5);
13:1(2); 3; 4; 5; 6(2); 8; 10(4); 13(2); 15(2); 16; 17; 18(2); 23;
24(2); 25; 26; 27; 29(2); 30(2); 31(2); 32(5); 33(3); 34(4); 35(2);
36(2); 37; 39; 14:1(2); 2; 3(2); 4(3); 5; 6(3); 7(4); 8(2); 9(4); 10;
11(5); 12(2); 13(4); 14; 15(5); 16(4); 17(4); 18(5); 19(8); 20(2);
21(2); 22(4); 24(2); 25(2); 26(3); 28; 29(2); 30; 32(2); 33(5);
15:2(4); 3; 4; 6(3); 7(2); 8(2); 9; 10(3); 12(3); 13(2); 14(3); 15(3);
16(3); 17(2); 18(4); 19(3); 21(4); 22(2); 23(7); 24(6); 25(5); 27(4);
28(2); 29; 30(2); 31(2); 32(3); 34(2); 35(3); 37; 16:1(3); 2(7);
3(4); 4; 5(3); 6(3); 8(6); 9(3); 10(2); 11; 12(2); 13(2); 14(2); 15(2);
16(3); 18(2); 19; 21(2); 22(3); 23(3); 17:2(2); 3(3); 4(2); 5; 7;
8(2); 9(2); 10; 11(2); 12(3); 13; 14(8); 15(2); 16(4); 17; 19(3);
20(4); 21(2); 22(2); 23; 24; 25(2); 26; 27(4); 29(3); 18:1; 2(8);
3(2); 4(4); 5(5); 6(4); 7(2); 8(5); 9(7); 11(2); 12(4); 13; 14(3);
16(3); 17; 18(2); 19(3); 20; 21; 22; 23(2); 24(5); 25(3); 26(4);
27(6); 28(6); 29(3); 30; 31(2); 32(4); 33(3); 19:1; 2(4); 3(2); 4(2);
5(6); 7(2); 8(7); 9(7); 10; 11(6); 12(2); 13(2); 14(4); 15(3); 16(2);
17(3); 18(3); 19(4); 20(3); 21(2); 23(2); 24(5); 25(2); 26; 27(2);
28(2); 29(2); 30(2); 31(2); 32; 33; 34(2); 35(2); 36(2); 37(2); 38;
39(3); 40(4); 41(5); 42(4); 43(7); 20:1(2); 2(2); 3(4); 4(2); 5(2);
6; 7(4); 8(2); 9(2); 10(4); 12(6); 13(3); 14(2); 15(4); 16; 17(2);
18; 19(2); 21(6); 22(6); 23(4); 24(2); 25; 26; 21:1(4); 2(8); 3(4);
4; 5(3); 6(3); 7(5); 8(7); 9(7); 10(7); 11(2); 12(6); 13(3); 14(5);
15(2); 16(3); 17(4); 18(4); 19(5); 20; 21(2); 22(3); 22:1(6); 2;
3(2); 4; 5(2); 6(2); 7; 8(2); 10; 11(2); 12; 13; 14(2); 16(8); 19(2);
21(2); 22(2); 25; 26(2); 27(2); 28(2); 29; 31(2); 32; 36; 41; 42;
43(4); 44(2); 47(3); 48; 49; 50; 51; 23:1(6); 2(2); 3(3); 4(5); 6;
7(3); 8(7); 9(5); 10(4); 11(5); 12(4); 13(6); 14(2); 15(3); 16(6);
17(2); 18(3); 19; 20(3); 21(3); 22(2); 23(2); 24(3); 25(2); 26(3);
27(2); 28(2); 29(3); 30(2); 31(2); 32(2); 33(3); 34(5); 35(2); 36(2);
37(3); 39; 24:1(2); 2(7); 3(6); 4(8); 5(4); 6; 7(5); 8(2); 9(6); 10(3);
11(4); 12; 14(3); 15(4); 16(9); 17(3); 18(3); 19(2); 20(3); 21(5);
22(2); 23(3); 24(4); 25(4); **1Kin** 1:2(3); 3(2); 4(3); 5; 7(2); 8(4);
9(4); 10(2); 11(2); 12; 14; 15(5); 16(2); 17; 18; 19(5); 20(3); 21;
22(2); 23(5); 25(4); 26(2); 27(3); 28(2); 29(2); 30; 31(2); 32(4);
33(2); 34(3); 36(4); 37(3); 38(5); 39(4); 40(4); 41(4); 42(2); 44(7);
45(4); 46(2); 47(4); 48(2); 49; 50(2); 51(3); 52; 53; 2:1; 2(2);
3(3); 4(2); 5(7); 6; 7(2); 8(4); 9; 10; 11; 12; 13(2); 15(3); 17(2);
18; 19(2); 20; 21; 22(4); 23; 24(2); 25(2); 26(4); 27(4); 28(4);
29(4); 30(4); 31(3); 32(6); 33(3); 34(2); 35(6); 36; 37(2); 38(3);
39(2); 42(4); 43(3); 44(3); 45(2); 46(4); 3:1(4); 2(3); 3(2); 4(2);
5; 8; 10(2); 11; 13; 15(3); 16; 17(2); 18(3); 19; 21(2); 22(6);
23(6); 24(2); 25(4); 26(5); 27(3); 28(4); 4:2(3); 3(3); 4(3); 5(4);
6(3); 7; 8; 9; 10(2); 11(3); 12(2); 13(4); 14; 15; 16; 17; 18; 19(6);
20(2); 21(5); 23; 24(4); 25; 28(3); 29(2); 30(4); 31(2); 33(3);
34(2); 5:1; 3(5); 4; 5(3); 6; 7(2); 8; 9(2); 12; 13; 14; 15; 16(4);
17(3); 18(2); 6:1(8); 2(5); 3(8); 4; 5(6); 6(8); 7(2); 8(7); 9(2);
10(2); 11(2); 13; 14; 15(9); 16(6); 17(2); 18(2); 19(5); 20(4);
21(3); 22(4); 23; 24(8); 25(2); 26(3); 27(12); 28; 29(2); 30(2);
31(4); 32(3); 33(3); 34(5); 35; 36; 37(5); 38(6); 7:2(6); 3; 5(2);
6(5); 7(4); 8(2); 9(5); 10; 11; 12(6); 14; 16(6); 17(5); 18(5);
19(4); 20(6); 21(7); 22(4); 23(2); 24(3); 25(5); 26(2); 27(3); 28(4);
29(4); 30(3); 31(6); 32(5); 33(3); 34(3); 35(7); 36(4); 37; 38;
39(8); 40(6); 41(10); 42(4); 43(2); 44; 45(5); 46(3); 47(3); 48(6);
49(7); 50(12); 51(10); 8:1(10); 2(4); 3(3); 4(8); 5(2); 6(9); 7(6);
8(5); 9(5); 10(5); 11(6); 12(2); 14(3); 15; 16(2); 17(3); 18; 19(2);
20(6); 21(4); 22(4); 25; 27(2); 28(3); 29(2); 30; 31; 32(2); 33;
34(2); 36(2); 37(2); 38; 39(2); 40(2); 43(2); 44(3); 46(3); 47(2);
48(3); 51(2); 52(2); 53(3); 54(3); 55; 56(2); 57; 59(5); 60(3); 61;
62(2); 63(5); 64(13); 65(3); 66(5); 9:1(4); 2(2); 3; 5(2); 7; 8; 9(3);
10(5); 11(2); 12; 13; 14; 15(5); 16(2); 17; 18(2); 19(2); 20(3);
21(2); 22; 23(4); 24; 25(5); 26(3); 27(3); 10:1(4); 3; 4(2); 5(5);
6; 7(3); 9(3); 10(2); 11; 12(5); 13; 14; 15(6); 17(3); 18(2); 19(6);
20(4); 21(4); 22(3); 23(2); 24; 26(2); 27(3); 28(2); 29(3); 11:1(2);
2(3); 4(2); 5(4); 6(3); 7(4); 9(2); 10; 11(2); 12; 13; 14(3); 15(3);
19(4); 20(2); 21(2); 23; 25(2); 26(2); 27(4); 28(4); 29(4); 30;
31(4); 32(2); 33(6); 34(2); 35; 36; 39; 40; 41(4); 42; 43; 12:2(2);
3; 4; 5; 6; 8(3); 9; 10; 12(4); 13(3); 14(2); 15(7); 16(4); 17(2);
18; 19; 20(3); 21(5); 22(2); 23(4); 24(6); 26(2); 27(3); 28(2);
29(2); 30(2); 31(3); 32(8); 33(6); 13:1(3); 2(7); 3(5); 4(4); 5(7);
6(7); 7(2); 8(2); 9(3); 10; 11(4); 12; 13(2); 14(2); 17(3); 18(2);

20(4); 21(6); 22(4); 23(2); 24(5); 25(6); 26(9); 27; 28(7); 29(6); 31(2); 32(7); 33(5); 34(3); 14:1; 2(2); 3; 4; 5(2); 6(2); 7(2); 8(2); 10(4); 11(6); 12(2); 13(3); 14(2); 15(4); 16; 17(3); 18(4); 19(5); 20; 21(4); 22(2); 24(5); 25; 26(6); 27(5); 28(5); 29(5); 31; 15:1(2); 2; 3(3); 4; 5(5); 6; 7(5); 8; 9; 10; 11(2); 12(3); 13; 14(2); 15(4); 18(10); 20(4); 22(2); 23(7); 24; 25(2); 26(3); 27(3); 28; 29(4); 30(2); 31(5); 33(2); 34(3); 16:1(3); 2(2); 3(4); 4(5); 5(5); 7(10); 8(2); 9; 10; 11; 12(4); 13(3); 14(5); 15(3); 16(5); 18(4); 19(3); 20(5); 21(3); 22(3); 23; 24(6); 25(2); 26(3); 27(5); 29(3); 30(3); 31(4); 32; 33(2); 34(6); 17:1(3); 2(2); 3; 4(2); 5(3); 6(4); 7(2); 8(2); 10(3); 12; 14(6); 15; 16(4); 17(4); 20(2); 21(2); 22(4); 23(3); 24(3); 18:1(4); 3(2); 4(2); 5(3); 6; 7; 9; 10(2); 12(3); 13(3); 15; 18(2); 19(3); 20(2); 21(3); 22(2); 23; 24(5); 25(2); 26(3); 28; 29(3); 30(4); 31(5); 32(4); 33(5); 34(4); 35(3); 36(4); 37; 38(8); 39(5); 40(2); 42(2); 43; 44(3); 45(2); 46(3); 19:1(2); 2(2); 4; 6; 7(4); 8(2); 9(2); 10(3); 11(11); 12(4); 13(2); 14(3); 15(2); 16(2); 17(2); 18; 19(2); 20; 21(3); 20:1; 2; 3; 4; 5; 6; 7(3); 8(2); 9(4); 10(3); 11; 12(3); 13(2); 14(5); 15(5); 16(3); 17(3); 19(4); 20(3); 21(3); 22(5); 23(4); 24; 25(2); 26(3); 27(4); 28(7); 29(5); 30(4); 31(3); 32; 33(2); 34; 35(5); 36(2); 37; 38(3); 39(4); 40; 41(3); 42; 43; 21:1(2); 2; 3(2); 4(3); 6; 7(3); 8(3); 9(2); 10; 11(5); 12; 13(5); 15(2); 16(2); 17(3); 18; 19(4); 20(2); 21; 22(5); 23(3); 24(5); 25(2); 26(3); 28(3); 29(2); 22:2(3); 3(3); 4; 5(3); 6(5); 7; 8(4); 9(2); 10(5); 11(3); 12(3); 13(5); 14(2); 15(5); 16(3); 17(2); 18; 19(4); 20; 21; 22(2); 23(3); 24(4); 26(4); 27(2); 28; 29(2); 30(4); 31(2); 32(3); 33(3); 34(5); 35(7); 36(3); 37(2); 38(5); 39(7); 41(2); 42; 43(6); 44; 45(5); 46(4); 48; 49(2); 50; 51(2); 52(6); 53; **2Kin** 1:1; 2; 3(6); 4; 5; 6(3); 8; 9(3); 10; 11; 12; 13(3); 14(2); 15(3); 16(2); 17(4); 18(5); 2:1; 2(2); 3(3); 4(2); 5(3); 6(2); 7(2); 8; 12(2); 13(2); 14(4); 15(4); 16(2); 19(5); 21(4); 22(2); 23(2); 24(3); 3:1(2); 2(3); 3(2); 4(2); 5(2); 6; 7(2); 8(2); 9(5); 10(3); 11(5); 12(4); 13(6); 14(3); 15(3); 16; 17; 18(3); 20(4); 21(3); 22(6); 23(2); 24(4); 25(5); 26(3); 27; 4:1(5); 2(2); 4; 5(2); 6(2); 7(3); 10; 11; 13(3); 15; 16; 17(2); 18(2); 21(3); 22(3); 25(2); 26; 27(5); 29(2); 30(3); 31(4); 32(2); 33(2); 34(4); 35(3); 37; 38(6); 39(2); 40(3); 41(3); 42(4); 43(2); 44(2); 5:1(3); 2(2); 3; 4(2); 5(2); 6(2); 7(2); 8(3); 9(2); 11(4); 12; 13; 14(3); 15(2); 16; 17; 18(5); 20(3); 21; 22(2); 24(3); 26; 27; 6:1(3); 5(2); 6(3); 8; 9(3); 10(3); 11(3); 12(3); 14; 15(3); 17(4); 18(2); 19(3); 20(3); 21; 23(2); 25; 26(2); 27(3); 28; 29; 30(5); 31(2); 32(8); 33(3); 7:1(4); 2(3); 3(2); 4(5); 5(5); 6(9); 7(2); 8(2); 9(2); 10(5); 11(2); 12(7); 13(5); 14(3); 15(4); 16(5); 17(8); 18(3); 19(2); 20(2); 8:1(3); 2(5); 3(5); 4(4); 5(4); 6(7); 7(2); 8(3); 10; 11; 12(3); 13; 15; 16(3); 18(6); 19; 20; 21(5); 22(2); 23(5); 24; 25(3); 26; 27(7); 28(3); 29(4); 9:1(3); 2(2); 3(3); 4(3); 5(2); 6(5); 7(7); 8(2); 9(5); 10(3); 11(2); 12; 13(2); 14(2); 15(3); 17(2); 18(3); 19; 20(4); 21(2); 22; 24; 25(4); 26(7); 27(5); 28; 29(2); 31; 32; 33(2); 35(3); 36(5); 37(4); 10:1(2); 3; 5(5); 6(6); 7(2); 8(5); 9(2); 10(6); 11; 12(2); 13(6); 14(2); 15(2); 16; 17(2); 18; 19(3); 21(3); 22(2); 23(6); 24(2); 25(9); 26(2); 27(2); 29(3); 30(4); 31(3); 32(2); 33(5); 34(5); 36; 11:1(2); 2(4); 3(3); 4(9); 5(4); 6(5); 7(5); 8(3); 9(6); 10(4); 11(8); 12(4); 13(6); 14(7); 15(10); 16(4); 17(6); 18(8); 19(14); 20(5); 12:1; 2(3); 3(3); 4(11); 5(3); 6(4); 7(6); 8(4); 9(11); 10(6); 11(9); 12(4); 13(5); 14(3); 15(2); 16(4); 18(6); 19(5); 20; 21(3); 13:1(3); 2(4); 3(5); 4(4); 5(4); 6(3); 7(3); 8(5); 10(2); 11(4); 12(5); 13; 14(3); 16(3); 17(5); 18(3); 19; 20(5); 21(4); 22; 23; 25(6); 14:1(2); 3(2); 4(3); 5(2); 6(9); 7(2); 8(2); 9(4); 11; 12; 13(5); 14(6); 15(5); 16; 17(2); 18(5); 20; 21; 22; 23(3); 24(4); 25(9); 26(2); 27(4); 28(5); 29; 15:1; 3(2); 4(3); 5(7); 6(5); 7; 8(2); 9(4); 10(2); 11(5); 12(4); 13(2); 14(2); 15(5); 16(2); 17(2); 18(4); 19(3); 20(5); 21(5); 23(2); 24(4); 25(4); 26(5); 27(2); 28(4); 29(2); 30(4); 31(5); 32(3); 33; 34(2); 35(6); 36(5); 37(3); 38; 16:1(3); 2(2); 3(7); 4(2); 6(2); 7(4); 8(6); 9(3); 10(5); 11(2); 12(5); 13(2); 14(9); 15(13); 16; 17(5); 18(7); 19(5); 20; 17:1(2); 2(3); 4(3); 5(2); 6(5); 7(4); 8(5); 9(5); 11(4); 12; 13(5); 14(2); 15(2); 16(3); 17(3); 18(2); 19(3); 20(3); 21(3); 22(2); 23(2); 24(4); 25(3); 26(9); 27(5); 28(2); 29(3); 30(3); 31(3); 32(5); 33(3); 34(5); 35; 36(2); 37(4); 38; 39(2); 41; 18:1(2); 2; 3(2); 4(5); 5(2); 6(2); 7(2); 8(5); 9(2); 10(3); 11(4); 12(4); 13(2); 14(2); 15(5); 16(6); 17(5); 18(6); 19(2); 20; 21; 22; 23; 24(2); 25(2); 26(6); 27(2); 28(4); 29; 30(4); 31(2); 32; 33(4); 34(2); 35(3); 36(2); 37(6); 19:1(2); 2(6); 3(2); 4(7); 5; 6(4); 7; 8; 10(2); 11; 12(3); 13(4); 14(6); 15(5); 16(2); 17(2); 18(2); 19(3); 20(2); 21(5); 22; 23(9); 24(2); 26(5); 28; 29(4); 30(2); 31(2); 32(2); 33(3); 35(5); 37(3); 20:1(3); 2(2); 4(3); 5(6); 6(2); 7; 8(5); 9(4); 10(2); 11(4); 12; 13(6); 14; 15; 16(2); 17(2); 18(2); 19(2); 20(6); 21:2(6); 3(2); 4(3); 5(4); 6(3); 7(3); 8(3); 9(3); 10(2); 11; 12; 13(3); 14(2); 15; 16(2); 17(5); 18(2); 19; 20(2); 21(2); 22(3); 23(2); 24(4); 25(5); 26; 22:1; 2(5); 3(7); 4(7); 5(12); 6; 7; 8(7); 9(10); 10(4); 11(4); 12(6); 13(6); 14(7); 15(2); 16(5); 17; 18(4); 19(3); 20(2); 23:1(2); 2(13); 3(6); 4(13); 5(9); 6(9); 7(6); 8(12); 9(5); 10(3); 11(11); 12(11); 13(11); 14(3); 15(6); 16(8); 17(5); 18(2); 19(6); 20(3); 21(5); 22(5); 23(2); 24(12); 25(2); 26(3); 27(2); 28(5); 29(2); 30(3); 31; 32(2); 33(2); 34(2); 35(9); 36; 37(2); 24:2(8); 3(3); 4(2); 5(5); 7(5); 8; 9(2); 10(2); 11; 12(4); 13(9); 14(6); 15(4); 16(2); 17; 18; 19(2); 20(3); 25:1(4); 2(2); 3(6); 4(10); 5(4); 6(2); 7(2); 8(6); 9(4); 10(5); 11(9); 12(4); 13(9); 14(5); 15(4); 16(5); 17(8); 18(6); 19(11); 20(2); 21(2); 22(4); 23(8); 24(4); 25(6); 26(4); 27(7); 28(2); 29; 30(2); **1Chr** 1:5; 6; 7; 8; 9(2); 10; 12; 14(3); 15(3); 16(3); 17; 19(3); 23; 27; 28; 29; 31; 32(2); 33(2); 34; 35; 36; 37; 38; 39; 40(2); 41(2); 42(2); 43(5); 44; 45(2); 46(3); 48; 49; 50(3); 51; 54; 2:1; 3(6); 4; 5; 6; 7(3); 8; 9; 10; 13(2); 14(2); 15(2); 16; 17(2); 18; 21(2); 22; 23(4); 24; 25(3); 26; 27(2); 28(2); 29(2); 30; 31(3); 32(2); 33(2); 42(5); 43; 44; 45(2); 47; 49(4); 50(4); 51(2); 52(2); 53(7); 54(5); 55(7); 3:1(5); 2(5); 3(2); 5; 9(3); 15(5); 16; 17; 19(2); 21(5); 22(2); 23; 24; 4:1; 2(3); 3(2); 4(5); 5; 6; 7; 8(2); 10; 11(2); 12(2); 13(2); 14(2); 15(3); 16; 17(2); 18(5); 19(5); 20(2); 21(7); 22(2); 23(2); 24; 26; 27; 31; 33; 34; 35(3); 37(5); 38; 39(3); 40; 41(2); 42(2); 43(2); 5:1(7); 2(2); 3(2); 4; 6; 7(2); 8(3); 9(4); 10(3); 11(2); 12(2); 13; 14(8); 15(3); 16; 17(2); 18(4); 19; 20(2); 22(2); 23(3); 24(3); 25(4); 26(7); 6:1; 2; 3(2); 10(2); 15(2); 16; 17(2); 18; 19(3); 22; 25; 26; 28(2); 29; 31(4); 32(5); 33(4); 34(4); 35(4); 36(4); 37(4); 38(4); 39(2); 40(3); 41(3); 42(3); 43(3); 44(5); 45(3); 46(3); 47(4); 48(3); 49(6); 50; 54(4); 55(2); 56(4); 57(3); 60; 61(4); 62(5); 63(4); 64(2); 65(6); 66(4); 67; 70(4); 71(3); 72; 74; 76; 77(3); 78(4); 80; 7:1; 2(2); 3(2); 4; 5; 6; 7(2); 8(2); 9(2); 10(2); 11(2); 12(2); 13(2); 14(3); 15(3); 16(2); 17(4); 19; 20; 21; 24(2); 28(4); 29(4); 30; 31(2); 33(2); 34; 35; 36; 38; 39; 40(5); 8:1(2); 2(2); 3; 6(4); 8; 10; 12(2); 13(3); 16; 18; 21; 25; 27; 28; 29; 34; 35; 38; 39(3); 40(2); 9:1(2); 2(4); 3(3); 4(6); 5(2); 6; 7(4); 8(6); 9(2); 10; 11(7); 12(8); 13(4); 14(5); 15(3); 16(7); 17(2); 18(3); 19(12); 20(3); 21(4); 22(2); 23(6); 24(2); 26(3); 27(3); 28(2); 29(8); 30(4); 31(6); 32(3); 33(4); 34; 35; 40; 41; 44; 10:1(3); 2(3); 3(3); 5; 7(3); 8(3); 9(3); 10(2); 11; 12(4); 13(3); 14(3); 11:2; 3(5); 4(3); 5(3); 6(2); 7(2); 8(3); 9; 10(4); 11(4); 12(3); 13(3); 14(3); 15(6); 16(2); 17(3); 18(6); 19(2); 20(3); 21(3); 22(2); 23(3); 24(3); 25(2); 26(4); 27(2); 28(3); 29(2); 30(3); 31(3); 32(2); 33(2); 34(4); 35(3); 36(2); 37(2); 38(2); 39(4); 40(2); 41(2); 42(3); 43(2); 44(3); 45(2); 46(3); 47; 12:1(3); 2(2); 3(5); 4(4); 5; 6; 7; 8(7); 9(3); 10(2); 11(2); 12(2); 13(2); 14(4); 15(4); 16(2); 17; 18(3); 19(4); 20; 21(3); 22; 23(6); 24(2); 25(2); 26; 27(2); 29(5); 30(2); 31; 32(3); 35; 37(5); 38; 13:1; 2(4); 3(2); 4(4); 5(2); 6(3); 7(3); 9(3); 10(3); 11; 12; 13(4); 14(4); 14:2; 4; 8(2); 9(2); 10(2); 11(2); 13(2); 14; 15(4); 16(2); 17(3); 15:1(2); 2(4); 3(2); 4(2); 5(2); 6(2); 7(2); 8(2); 9(2); 10(2); 11(2); 12(6); 13(3); 14(4); 15(6); 16(4); 17(5); 18(2); 19; 21; 22(2); 23; 24(4); 25(6); 26(4); 27(6); 28(4); 29(5); 16:1(3); 2(5); 4(4); 5; 6(3); 7(2); 8(2); 10(2); 11; 12; 14(2); 15; 16; 17; 18(2); 23(2); 24; 25; 26(4); 28(3); 29(4); 30(2); 31(4); 32(3); 33(5); 34; 35; 36(3); 37(4); 38; 39(5); 40(5); 41(2); 42; 43; 17:1(4); 3(2); 4; 5; 6; 7(3); 8(3); 9(2); 10(2); 16(2); 17; 18; 21; 23; 24(3); 27; 18:1(3); 2; 3; 4; 5(2); 6(2); 7(2); 8(3); 9; 11(5); 12(3); 13(2); 15(3); 16(3); 17(5); 19:1(2); 2(4); 3(3); 4; 5(3); 6(2); 7(2); 8(2); 9(6); 10(3); 11(4); 12(2); 13(2); 14(3); 15(3); 16(6); 17(3); 18(4); 19(4); 20:1(6); 2(2); 3(4); 4(4); 5(4); 6(2); 7; 8(3); 21:2(3); 3(2); 4; 5(3); 6; 8; 9; 10; 11; 12(8); 13(3); 14; 15(7); 16(5); 17; 18(5); 19(3); 20; 21(2); 22(5); 23(5); 24(2); 25; 26(3); 27(3); 28(3); 29(6); 30(3); 22:1(4); 2(3); 3(4); 4; 5(2); 6; 7(2); 8(3); 10; 11(3); 12(3); 13(2); 14(2); 16(5); 17; 18(5); 19(10); 23:2(3); 3(2); 4(3); 5(2); 6; 7; 8(2); 9(3); 10(2); 11(2); 12; 13(3); 14(2); 15; 16(2); 17(3); 18(2); 19(5); 20(3); 21(2); 22; 23; 24(9); 25; 26(3); 27(2); 28(10); 29(4); 30; 31(6); 32(10); 24:1(3); 2; 3(2); 4(6); 5(5); 6(10); 7(2); 8(2); 9(2); 10(2); 11(2); 12(2); 13(2); 14(2); 15(2); 16(2); 17(2); 18(2); 19(4); 20(4); 21(2); 22(2); 23(5); 24(2); 25(2); 26(2); 27; 29; 30(4); 31(7); 25:1(6); 2(5); 3(3); 4; 5(4); 6(6); 7(3); 8(4); 9(2); 10; 11; 12; 13; 14; 15; 16; 17; 18; 19; 20; 21; 22; 23; 24; 25; 26; 27; 28; 29; 30; 31; 26:1(5); 2(5); 3(3); 4(6); 5(3); 6; 7; 8(2); 10(4); 11(4); 12(5); 13(3); 14; 15; 16(4); 18; 19(4); 20(5); 21(4); 22(4); 23(4); 24(3); 26(7); 27(3); 28(5); 29(2); 30(5); 31(6); 32(4); 27:1(6); 2(3); 3(5); 4(3); 5(4); 6(2); 7(3); 8(3); 9(4); 10(4); 11(4); 12(4); 13(4); 14(4); 15(3); 16(6); 17(3); 18(2); 19(2); 20(4); 21(3); 22(3); 23(4); 24(4); 25(8); 26(4); 27(6); 28(5); 29(5); 30(4); 31(4); 32(2); 33(3); 34(3); 28:1(15); 2(6); 4(6); 5(4); 8(6); 9(4); 10(2); 11(8); 12(10); 13(10); 15(7); 16(2); 17(4); 18(7); 19(2); 20(5); 21(7); 29:1(5); 2(5); 3(3); 4(3); 5(4); 6(6); 7(2); 8(5); 9(3); 10(2); 11(8); 15; 17(2); 18(3); 19(2); 20(6); 21(3); 22(5); 23(2); 24(4); 25(2); 26; 27; 29(8); 30(3); **2Chr** 1:1(2); 2(4); 3(7); 4(2); 5(6); 6(4); 9(2); 11; 12(2); 13(3); 14(2); 15(3); 16(2); 17(3); 2:1(2); 2; 3; 4(8); 5; 6; 7; 9; 10; 11(2); 12(3); 14(3); 15(4); 17(3); 18(2); 3:1(6); 2(3); 3(6); 4(7); 5; 6(2); 7(6); 8(5); 9(3); 10; 11(8); 12(6); 13; 14; 15(3); 16(4); 17(9); 4:1(3); 2; 3(2); 4(5); 5(4); 6(5); 7(3); 8(3); 9(5); 10(4); 11(5); 12(10); 13(4); 14; 16(5); 17(3); 18(2); 19(5); 20(3); 21(3); 22(11); 5:1(9); 2(10); 3(4); 4(3); 5(7); 6(2); 7(9); 8(6); 9(6); 10(4); 11(3); 12(4); 13(7); 14(5); 6:1(2); 3(3); 4; 5(3); 7(3); 8; 9(2); 10(7); 11(4); 12(4); 13(3); 14(2); 16; 18(2); 19(3); 20(2); 21; 22; 23(2); 24(2); 25(3); 26; 27(2); 28(2); 30(2); 31; 32; 33(3); 34(2); 35; 37(2); 38(3); 39; 40; 41; 42(2); 7:1(6); 2(6); 3(8); 4(3); 5(3); 6(6); 7(10); 8(4); 9(4); 10(5); 11(5); 12; 13(2); 15; 18; 20; 21; 22(2); 8:1(3); 2(2); 4(2); 5(2); 6(5); 7(6); 8(2); 9; 10(2); 11(7); 12(4); 13(8); 14(8); 15(4); 16(7); 17(2); 18(3); 9:1(2); 3(3); 4(5); 5; 6(3); 8(2); 9(2); 10(2); 11(6); 12(2); 13; 14(2); 16(3); 17; 18(4); 19(4); 20(5); 21(3); 22(2); 23(3); 25(2); 26(5); 27(3); 29(9); 31; 10:2(3); 4; 5; 6; 8(3); 9; 10(2); 12(4); 13(3); 14(2); 15(7); 16(4); 17(2); 18(2); 19; 11:1(2); 2(3); 3; 4(3); 11; 13(2); 14(3); 15(3); 16(3); 17(3); 18(4); 20; 21; 22(2); 23; 12:1(3); 2(2); 3(4); 4; 5(4); 6(3); 7(4); 8(3); 9(6); 10(5); 11(5); 12(2); 13(3); 14; 15(4); 16; 13:1; 2; 3(2); 5(2); 6(3); 7(2); 8(4); 9(7); 10(5); 11(7); 12; 13; 14(4); 15(2); 16; 18(3); 19(3); 20(2); 22(4); 14:1(2); 2(2); 3(5); 4(3); 5(4); 6(2); 7(2); 9; 10(2); 11; 12(3); 13(3); 14(4); 15; 15:1(2); 2; 3; 4; 5(2); 8(9); 9(2); 10(3); 11(3); 12; 13; 14; 15(2); 16(3); 17(2); 18(2); 19(2); 16:1(3); 2(4); 4(3); 6(3); 7(5); 8(3); 9(4); 10(3); 11(3); 12(3); 13; 14(3); 17:2(3); 3(2); 4(2); 5(2); 6(3); 7(2); 9(5); 10(4); 11(2); 13(2); 14(4); 15; 16(2); 18; 19(3); 18:2; 3; 4(3); 5(2); 6; 7(5); 8(2); 9(4); 10(2); 11(4); 12(4); 13; 14(2); 15(4); 16(2); 17; 18(4); 19; 20(2); 21(2); 22(3); 23(4); 25(4); 26(2); 27; 28(2); 29(4); 30(4); 31(4); 32(3); 33(4); 34(6); 19:1; 2(5); 3(2); 4(2); 5(2); 6(3); 7(3); 8(6); 9(2); 10; 11(9); 20:1(3); 2; 3; 4(3); 5(4); 6(2); 7(2); 9; 10(2); 13; 14(9); 15(2); 16(4); 17(3); 18(4); 19(6); 20(3); 21(5); 22(2); 23(3); 24(4); 25(3); 26(6); 27(2); 28(2); 29(4); 30; 31; 32(3); 33(3); 34(6); 36; 37(3); 21:1; 2(2); 3(2); 4(3); 6(6); 7(3); 8(2); 9(3); 10(4); 11(2); 12(4); 13(5); 14; 15; 16(5); 17(3); 18; 19(2); 20(3); 22:1(6); 2; 3(2); 4(4); 5(2); 6(3); 7(4); 8(4); 9(4); 10(3); 11(8); 12(2); 23:1(7); 2(4); 3(6); 4(5); 5(7); 6(7); 7(4); 8(6); 9(3); 10(8); 11(4); 12(6); 13(8); 14(8); 15(3); 16(3); 17(4); 18(11); 19(4); 20(14); 21(4); 24:2(4); 4(2); 5(6); 6(9); 7(5); 8(4); 9(4); 10(3); 11(7); 12(9); 13(3); 14(8); 16(2); 17(4); 18(2); 19; 20(7); 21(5); 22(3); 23(8); 24(4); 25(6); 26(2); 27(7); 25:2(2); 3(2); 4(7); 5; 7(3); 8(2); 9(5); 10; 11(2); 12(5); 13(3); 14(4); 15(4); 16(3); 17(3); 18(3); 19; 20(2); 21(2); 22; 23(6); 24(7); 25(2); 26(4); 27(2); 28; 26:1(2); 2; 4(2); 5(3); 6(5); 7(3); 8(2); 9(4); 10(4); 11(6); 12(4); 13(2); 14; 15(2); 16(4); 17(2); 18(6); 19(6); 20(3); 21(7); 22(4); 23(3); 27:1; 2(5); 3(4); 4(2); 5(7); 6; 7(4); 9; 28:1(2); 2(2); 3(7); 4(2); 5(5); 6(2); 7(4); 8(2); 9(3); 10(2); 11(3); 12(7); 13(2); 14(5); 15(5); 16; 17; 18(7); 19(2); 21(6); 22(2); 23(4); 24(7); 25; 26(3); 27(3); 29:1; 2(2); 3(5); 4(3); 5(4); 6(4); 7(5); 8(2); 9; 10; 11; 12(11); 13(2); 14(2); 15(6); 16(12); 17(10); 18(7); 19(3); 20(5); 21(6); 22(10); 23(4); 24(5); 25(8); 26(4); 27(7); 28(4); 29; 30(6); 31(4); 32(4); 33; 34(7); 35(7); 36(3); 30:1(4); 2(4); 3(2); 4(3); 5(2); 6(9); 7; 8(3); 9(2); 10(2); 12(6); 13(2); 14(3); 15(8); 16(6); 17(6); 18(3); 19(3); 20(2); 21(6); 22(5); 23; 24(3); 25(6); 26(3); 27(3); 31:1(6); 2(7); 3(9); 4(6); 5(6); 6(5); 7(4); 8(3); 9(3); 10(7); 11(2); 12(5); 13(5); 14(8); 15(4); 16(2); 17(4); 18(2); 19(8); 20; 21(4); 32:1(2); 3(3); 4(5); 5(3); 6(4); 7(2); 8(3); 10; 11(3); 12; 13(3); 14; 15; 16; 17(4); 18(4); 19(6); 20(3); 21(7); 22(5); 23(2); 24(2); 25; 26(5); 28; 30(3); 31(5); 32(7); 33(4); 33:2(6); 3(2); 4(3); 5(4); 6(5); 7(3); 8(6); 9(4); 10; 11(5); 12(2); 13; 14(6); 15(9); 16(3); 17(3); 18(8); 19(3); 22(3); 23; 25(4); 34:2(5); 3(7); 4(6); 5(2); 6; 7(5); 8(10); 9(7); 10(9); 11(3); 12(8); 13(3); 14(6); 15(6); 16(3); 17(7); 18(4); 19(3); 20(5); 21(7); 22(7); 23(2); 24(5); 25; 26(4); 27(2); 28(4); 29(2); 30(13); 31(5); 32(3); 33(6); 35:1(4); 2(4); 3(6); 4(3); 5(8); 6(4); 7(5); 8(6); 9(2); 10(4); 11(4); 12(7); 13(4); 14(7); 15(6); 16(7); 17(3); 18(6); 19(2); 20; 21; 22(3); 23(2); 24(2); 25(3); 26(4); 27(2); 36:1(3); 3(2); 4; 5(2); 7(3); 8(4); 9(2); 10(4); 12(5); 13; 14(7); 15; 16(3); 17(4); 18(7); 19(4); 20(3); 21(4); 22(6); 23(4); **Ezr** 1:1(6); 2(3); 3(3); 4(3); 5(6); 7(5); 8(3); 9; 11(2); 2:1(4); 2(3); 3; 4; 5; 6(2); 7; 8; 9; 10; 11; 12; 13; 14; 15; 16; 17; 18; 19; 20; 21; 22; 23; 24; 25; 26; 27; 28; 29; 30; 31(2); 32; 33; 34; 35; 36(3); 37; 38; 39; 40(3); 41(2); 42(8); 43(4); 44(3); 45(3); 46(3); 47(3); 48(3); 49(3); 50(3); 51(3); 52(3); 53(3); 54(2); 55(4); 56(3); 57(4); 58(2); 60(3); 61(7); 62; 63(2); 64; 68(5); 69(2); 70(6); 3:1(4); 2(7); 3(3); 4(4); 5(5); 6(6); 7(4); 8(13); 9(5); 10(9); 11(6); 12(4); 13(8); 4:1(5); 2(3); 3(5); 4(4); 5(2); 6(3); 7(6); 8(3); 9(12); 10(6); 11(5); 12(6); 13(4); 14(3); 15(5); 16(3); 17(6); 18; 20; 22(2); 23(3); 24(4); 5:1(6); 2(4); 3(2); 4(2); 5(4); 6(6); 7; 8(5); 10(3); 11(3); 12(5); 13(3); 14(6); 15(2); 16(3); 17(4); 6:1(4); 2(3); 3(10); 4(2); 5(5); 6(3); 7(5); 8(5); 9(4); 10(3); 12; 13(2); 14(8); 15(5); 16(7); 17(3); 18(4); 19(5); 20(6); 21(5); 22(7); 7:1(4); 2(3); 3(3); 4(3); 5(5); 6(5); 7(8); 8(3); 9(5); 10(2); 11(8); 12(3); 13; 14(2); 15(3); 16(6); 17(2); 18(4); 19(4); 20(2); 21(7); 23(5); 24; 25(4); 26(3); 27(4); 28(4); 8:1(4); 2(3); 3(3); 4(2); 5(2); 6(2); 7(2); 8(2); 9(2); 10(2); 11(2); 12(2); 13; 14; 15(4); 17(5); 18(4); 19; 20(4); 21; 22(5); 24(2); 25(6); 28(5); 29(7); 30(7); 31(7); 33(11); 34; 35(4); 36(6); 9:1(14); 2(4); 3; 4(4); 5(2); 6; 7(5); 8; 9(4); 11(5); 12(2); 14; 10:1(2); 2(4); 3(4); 5(2); 6(4); 7(2); 8(4); 9(8); 10(2); 11(4); 12; 13; 14(4); 15(3); 16(8); 17(3); 18(4); 19; 20; 21; 22; 23(2); 24(2); 25; 26; 27; 28; 29; 30; 31; 33; 34; 43; **Neh** 1:1(5); 2(2); 3(5); 4; 5; 6(4); 7(3); 8(2); 9(3); 11(4); 2:1(5); 2; 3(5); 4(2); 5(3); 6(3); 7(4); 8(10); 9(5); 10(5); 12(2); 13(6); 14(4); 15(5); 16(7); 17(3); 18(2); 19(5); 20; 3:1(6); 2(2); 3(6); 4(5); 5(2); 6(7); 7(6); 8(5); 9(3); 10(2); 11(5); 12(3); 13(7); 14(6); 15(12); 16(8); 17(4); 18(3); 19(6); 20(7); 21(6); 22(3); 23(2); 24(5); 25(8); 26(5); 27(3); 28(2); 29(4); 30(3); 31(7); 32(5); 4:1(2); 2(4); 3; 4; 5; 6(4); 7(5); 10(3); 11(2); 12; 13(4); 14(5); 15; 16(9); 17(3); 18(2); 19(6); 20(2); 21(5); 22(4); 23(2); 5:1(2); 3; 4; 5; 7(2); 8(2); 9(3); 11(5); 12; 13(3); 14(7); 15(4); 16(2); 17(2); 18(3); 6:1(5); 2(2); 3; 4; 5; 6(3); 7; 9; 10(8); 11; 14(3); 15(3); 16; 17(2); 18(4); 7:1(5); 2(2); 3(4); 4(3); 5(5); 6(4); 7(3); 8; 9; 10; 11(2); 12; 13; 14; 15; 16; 17; 18; 19; 20; 21; 22; 23; 24; 25; 26; 27; 28; 29; 30; 31; 32; 33(2); 34(2); 35; 36; 37; 38; 39(3); 40; 41; 42; 43(3); 44(2); 45(7); 46(4); 47(3); 48(3); 49(3); 50(3); 51(3); 52(3); 53(3); 54(3); 55(3); 56(2); 57(4); 58(3); 59(4); 60(2); 62(3); 63(6); 64; 65(2); 66; 70(5); 71(4); 72(2); 73(8); 8:1(7); 2(5); 3(9); 4(2); 5(4); 6(5); 7(4); 8(4); 9(10); 10(4); 11(3); 12(2); 13(9); 14(5); 15; 16(8); 17(6); 18(7); 9:1(2); 2(2); 3(5); 4(3); 5(2); 6(4); 7(4); 8(7); 9(2); 10; 11(6); 12(3); 14; 15(2); 19(6); 21; 22(4); 23(2); 24(7); 27(3); 28(2); 29; 30(3); 32(6); 35; 36(3); 37; 10:1(2); 8; 9(3); 14(2); 28(10); 29(3); 30(2); 31(7); 32(3); 33(10); 34(10); 35(4); 36(6); 37(10); 38(10); 39(13); 11:1(5); 2(2); 3(7); 4(9); 5(7); 6; 7(8); 9(3); 10(2); 11(7); 12(8); 13(5); 14(2); 15(5); 16(5); 17(9); 18(2); 19(2); 20(4); 21(2); 22(10); 23(2); 24(5); 25(5); 27; 28; 30(3); 31; 35; 36; 12:1(3); 7(3); 8(2); 9; 12(3); 22(6); 23(7); 24(5); 25(3); 26(7); 27(4); 28(4); 29(3); 30(5); 31(5); 32; 35(7); 36(3); 37(7); 38(7); 39(7); 40(4); 41; 42; 43(3); 44(12); 45(6); 46(2); 47(8); 13:1(6); 2(2); 3(2); 4(4); 5(12); 6(3); 7(3); 8(2); 9(5); 10(5); 11(2); 12(5); 13(6); 14(2); 15(3); 16(2); 17(2); 18; 19(6); 20; 21(2); 22(4); 24(3); 28(4); 29(4); 30(3); 31(2); **Est** 1:1; 2(3); 3(4); 4(2); 5(6); 6; 7(3); 8(4); 9(3); 10(6); 11(5); 12(3); 13(4); 14(5); 15(4); 16(8); 17(3); 18(4); 19(5); 20(2); 21(5); 22(3); 2:1; 2(2); 3(9); 4(4); 5(4); 6(2); 7; 8(6); 9(5); 11(2); 12(5); 13(4); 14(9); 15(8); 16(3); 17(4); 18(4); 19(3); 20; 21(4); 22(3); 23(4); 3:1(3); 2(3); 3(3); 6(4); 7(6); 8(4); 9(5); 10(4); 11(3); 12(9); 13(6); 14(2); 15(6); 4:1(2); 2(2); 3(2); 4; 5; 6(3); 7(4); 8(4); 9; 11(8); 13(2); 14(2); 16(3); 5:1(8); 2(7); 3(3); 4(3); 5(3); 6(4); 8(6); 9; 11(6); 12(4); 13(2); 14(5); 6:1(4); 2(4); 3(2); 4(6); 5(3); 6(4); 7(3); 8(5); 9(8); 10(5); 11(6); 12; 13(2); 14(2); 7:1(2); 2(5); 3(2); 4(2); 5(2); 6(3); 7(5); 8(10); 9(6); 10(2); 8:1(5); 2(2); 3(4); 4(3); 5(8); 6(2); 7(6); 8(6); 9(10); 10(2); 11(5); 12(4); 13(3); 14(4); 15(3); 16; 17(6); 9:1(10); 2(4); 3(7); 4(2); 5(3); 6(2); 10(5); 11(3); 12(7); 13(3); 14(2); 15(4); 16(3); 17(4); 18(5); 19(5); 20(3); 21(4); 22(4); 23; 24(6); 25(3); 26(2); 27; 28(2); 29(3); 30(4); 31(4); 32(2); 10:1(4); 2(7); 3(4); **Job** 1:1; 3(3); 5(3); 6(2); 7(3); 8(2); 9; 10(2); 12(3); 14(2); 15(4); 16(3); 17(5); 19(4); 20; 21(4); 2:1(3); 2(3); 3(2); 4; 6; 7(3); 8; 10(2); 11(3); 13; 3:3(2); 4; 5(3); 6(4); 8; 9(4); 10; 11(3); 12(2); 14; 17(2); 18(3); 19(2); 20; 22; 24; 25; 4:1; 3; 4; 6; 7; 8; 9(2); 10(6); 11(2); 13(2); 15; 16; 19(2); 5:1; 2(2); 3; 4; 5(3); 6(2); 7; 10(2); 12(2); 13(3); 14(3); 15(4); 16; 17(3); 20(2); 21(2); 22(2); 23(4); 25(2); 6:2; 3(2); 4(4); 5(2); 6; 7; 8; 10(2); 12; 14(2); 15; 16(2); 18; 19(2); 23(3); 26; 27; 7:1; 2(2); 4(3); 8; 9(2); 11(2); 21(2); 8:1; 2; 3; 5; 6; 8(2); 11(2); 13(2); 16; 17(2); 19(2); 20; 22(2); 9:5; 6(2); 7(2); 8(3); 9(2); 13; 22(2); 23(3); 24(5); 26(3); 31; 10:1; 3(3); 5; 9; 18(2); 19(2); 21(2); 22(2); 11:1; 2; 6; 7; 9(3); 17(2); 20(4); 12:2; 4; 5; 6; 7(3); 8(3); 9(2); 10(2); 11(2); 12; 15(2); 16(2); 17; 18; 19; 20(4); 21(2); 22; 23(2); 24(4); 25; 13:2; 3; 6; 19; 25; 26; 27(2); 14:5; 7; 8(4); 9; 10; 11(3); 12; 13; 14; 15; 18(2); 19(6); 15:1; 2; 5(2); 7(2); 8; 10; 11; 15; 19; 20(3); 21; 22; 23; 24; 25; 26; 29(2); 30(2); 33(2); 34(2); 16:5; 10; 11(3); 13; 15; 16; 22; 17:1; 5; 6; 8(2); 9; 11; 12(2); 13(2); 14; 16(3); 18:1; 4(2); 5(3); 6; 7; 9(3); 10(3); 13(2); 14; 17(2); 18; 21(3); 19:9; 17; 20; 21; 24; 25(2); 28(2); 29(3); 20:1; 3(2); 5(4); 6(2); 8; 9; 10; 11(2); 14; 16(2); 17(3); 18; 19; 22(2); 23; 24(2); 25(2); 27(2); 28(2); 29(2); 21:7; 9; 12(3); 13; 14; 15; 16(2); 17(2); 18(2); 20(2); 21(2); 25; 26(2); 27; 28(4); 29; 30(3); 32(2); 33(2); 22:1; 3; 6; 7(2); 8(3); 9(2); 12(3); 13; 14; 15; 17; 18(2); 19(2); 20(2); 22; 23; 24(3); 25; 26; 28; 29; 30(3); 23:5; 7; 9(2); 10; 12(2); 14; 16; 17(2); 24:1; 2; 3(3); 4(4); 5(2); 6(3); 7(2); 8(3); 9(3); 10(2); 12(3); 13(3); 14(4); 15(3); 16(3); 17(4); 18(4); 19(2); 20(2); 21(2); 22; 24(3); 25:1; 5(2); 6; 26:2; 3; 5(2); 7(3); 8(2); 9; 10(2); 11; 12(2); 13(2); 14; 27:2; 3(2); 7(2); 8(2); 10; 11(2); 13(3); 14; 16(2); 17(3); 18; 19; 20; 21; 28:1; 2(2); 3(2); 4(4); 5; 6(2); 7; 8(2); 9(3); 10; 11(2); 12; 13(3); 14(2); 15; 16(3); 17(3); 18; 19; 20; 21(3); 22; 23(2); 24(3); 25(3); 26(3); 28(2); 29:2; 4(2); 5; 6; 7(3); 8(2); 9; 10(2); 11(2); 12(2); 13(2); 15(2); 16(2); 17(3); 18; 19(2); 23(2); 24; 25(2); 30:1; 2; 3; 4; 6(4); 7(2); 8; 11; 12(2); 14; 15; 16; 17;

10(3); 11; 12(3); 13(3); 14; 15; 16(3); 17(4); 18; 19(5); 20(2); 21(4); 22(3); 23(2); 12:1(2); 3(2); 4(5); 5(3); 6; 7(2); 8; 9(3); 11; 12(8); 13(2); 14(3); 16(3); 17; 13:1; 2(2); 3(3); 4(2); 5; 6(2); 7(3); 8(2); 9(3); 10; 11(5); 12; 13(6); 14(3); 15; 16(3); 17; 18(3); 19(2); 20(2); 22; 23(2); 24(3); 25(2); 27(3); 14:1(3); 2(3); 3(2); 4(3); 5(2); 6(3); 8(3); 9; 10(2); 11; 12(3); 13(2); 14(3); 15(2); 16(4); 17; 18(6); 19; 20; 21; 22(3); 15:1; 2(7); 3(7); 4(2); 6; 7(2); 8(5); 9(4); 10; 11(4); 12(2); 13; 16; 17(2); 19(3); 20; 21(4); 16:1(2); 3(3); 4(6); 5(3); 6(2); 7(2); 8; 9(8); 10(2); 11; 12; 14(5); 15(5); 16(3); 18; 19(4); 21; 17:1(4); 2(2); 3(2); 4; 5(3); 6(4); 7(3); 8(3); 9; 10(4); 11(2); 12(2); 13(4); 15(2); 16; 17; 18; 19(7); 20(3); 21(3); 22(2); 24(4); 25(4); 26(8); 27(5); 18:1(2); 2; 3(2); 4(4); 5(2); 6(3); 8; 10; 11(3); 12; 13(3); 14(4); 15; 17(4); 18(6); 19; 21(4); 23; 19:1(5); 2(5); 3(5); 4(2); 5; 6(5); 7(7); 8; 9(4); 10(3); 11; 12(2); 13(6); 14(4); 15(3); 20:1(4); 2(5); 3(3); 4(5); 5(6); 8(2); 10; 11; 12(3); 13(5); 14(2); 15; 16(5); 17; 18; 21:1(5); 2(2); 4(6); 6; 7(10); 8(3); 9(4); 10(3); 11(4); 12(5); 13(3); 14(3); 22:1(3); 2(3); 3(7); 4(2); 5; 6(3); 7; 8; 9(2); 10; 11(2); 12; 16(3); 18(2); 19(2); 20; 22; 23(2); 24(3); 25(5); 27; 29(2); 30(2); 23:1(3); 2(4); 3; 4; 5(3); 6; 7(5); 8(4); 9(3); 10(4); 11; 12(3); 13; 14(3); 15(5); 16(5); 17(2); 18(2); 19(3); 20(4); 22; 23; 24(2); 25; 26(3); 28(4); 29(2); 30(2); 31(2); 32(2); 33(4); 34(5); 35(2); 36(5); 37(3); 38(7); 39; 24:1(6); 2(2); 3(3); 4(2); 5(4); 7; 8(5); 9(2); 10(4); 25:1(5); 2(4); 3(5); 4(2); 5(3); 6; 7(2); 8; 9(5); 10(10); 11; 12(4); 13; 14; 15(3); 16; 17(4); 18(3); 20(7); 21; 22(5); 23; 24(4); 25(4); 26(7); 27(3); 28(2); 29(4); 30(4); 31(6); 32(3); 33(6); 34(3); 35(3); 36(5); 37(3); 38(3); 26:1(4); 2(6); 3(2); 4; 5(2); 6(2); 7(5); 8(5); 9(5); 10(7); 11(4); 12(4); 13(4); 15(2); 16(6); 17(4); 18(7); 19(4); 20(4); 21(3); 22(2); 23(4); 24(4); 27:1(4); 2; 3(8); 4(2); 5(4); 6(4); 7; 8(9); 9; 11(4); 12(2); 13(6); 14(3); 15(2); 16(5); 17; 18(8); 19(6); 20(2); 21(7); 22(2); 28:1(12); 2(4); 3(2); 4(5); 5(8); 6(5); 7(2); 8; 9(5); 10(3); 11(7); 12(7); 13(2); 14(5); 15(3); 16(4); 17(3); 29:1(8); 2(6); 3(3); 4(2); 5; 7(4); 8(3); 9; 10; 11(2); 14(5); 15; 16(4); 17(4); 18(6); 19(3); 20(3); 21(5); 22(4); 23; 24; 25(6); 26(6); 28; 29(3); 30(2); 31(3); 32(5); 30:1(2); 2(2); 3(5); 4(2); 5; 7; 8; 9; 10(2); 11; 12; 14(3); 15; 17; 18(5); 19; 21(2); 23(4); 24(4); 31:1(4); 2(4); 3; 4; 5(2); 6(3); 7(4); 8(6); 9; 10(3); 11(2); 12(6); 13(2); 14(3); 15; 16(4); 17; 18(2); 19; 20; 21(2); 22(2); 23(5); 24; 25; 27(6); 28; 29(2); 30; 31(4); 32(5); 33(3); 34(4); 35(8); 36(2); 37(5); 38(7); 39(2); 40(9); 32:1(4); 2(5); 3(3); 4(4); 5(2); 6(2); 7(2); 8(9); 9(2); 10(3); 11(3); 12(12); 14(3); 15(2); 16(4); 17(2); 18(6); 19(3); 20; 21; 24(8); 25(4); 26(2); 27(2); 28(4); 29(2); 30(5); 31; 32(5); 33(2); 34; 35(4); 36(7); 39; 42(2); 43(2); 44(10); 33:1(5); 2(4); 4(7); 5(2); 6; 7(3); 9(5); 10(3); 11(16); 12(2); 13(12); 14(4); 15(2); 16(2); 17(3); 18(2); 19(2); 20(3); 21(2); 22(5); 23(2); 24(2); 25(2); 26(2); 34:1(6); 2(5); 3(2); 4(4); 5(4); 6; 7(3); 8(4); 10(3); 11(2); 12(3); 13(5); 14; 15; 17(7); 18(5); 19(8); 20(6); 21(4); 22(2); 35:1(4); 2(5); 3(4); 4(11); 5(3); 6; 7; 8(2); 11(5); 12(2); 13(5); 14(2); 15(2); 16(3); 17(4); 18(5); 19(3); 36:1(3); 2(4); 3(2); 4(4); 5(2); 6(8); 7(4); 8(6); 9(7); 10(13); 11(5); 12(9); 13(4); 14(9); 16(2); 18; 19; 20(8); 21(8); 22(4); 23(6); 24; 25(2); 26(7); 27(6); 28(3); 29(2); 30(6); 31(3); 32(6); 37:1(3); 2(5); 3(6); 4; 5; 6(3); 7(3); 8; 9(2); 10(2); 11(2); 12(3); 13(6); 14(2); 15(4); 16(2); 17(5); 19; 20(3); 21(8); 38:1(6); 2(5); 3(3); 4(8); 5(2); 6(6); 7(6); 8(2); 9(5); 10(4); 11(5); 12(2); 13(3); 14(6); 16(3); 17(4); 18(3); 19(3); 20(2); 21(2); 22(4); 23(3); 25(3); 26; 27(3); 28(3); 39:1(2); 2(5); 3(6); 4(9); 5(3); 6(4); 8(5); 9(7); 10(6); 11(2); 13(3); 14(5); 15(4); 16(3); 17(3); 18(2); 40:1(4); 2(3); 3(2); 4(2); 5(7); 6(3); 7(8); 8(6); 9(5); 10; 11(6); 12(2); 13(4); 14(4); 15(4); 16(2); 41:1(7); 2(7); 3(3); 4; 5(2); 6(2); 7(6); 8; 9(5); 10(9); 11(5); 12(3); 13(4); 14(2); 15(2); 16(10); 17; 18(5); 42:1(7); 2(2); 3(3); 4(3); 5(3); 6(4); 7(2); 8(6); 9(2); 10; 11(2); 13(2); 14(3); 15(4); 16(3); 17(5); 18(3); 19; 20(3); 21(3); 22(4); 43:1(4); 2(4); 3(3); 4(7); 5(5); 6(7); 7(3); 8(2); 9(5); 10(3); 11(3); 12(3); 13(5); 44:1(4); 2(4); 4; 6(2); 7(3); 8(4); 9(7); 11(2); 12(9); 13(4); 14(4); 15(4); 16(3); 17(3); 18(3); 19; 20(4); 21(6); 22(3); 23(3); 24(5); 25(3); 26(7); 27(4); 28(5); 29; 30(4); 45:1(6); 2(2); 3; 4; 5; 46:1(4); 2(4); 3; 4(3); 5; 6(4); 7; 8(4); 9(6); 10(6); 11; 12(4); 13(4); 14; 15; 16(2); 17; 18(4); 20; 21(3); 22; 23(2); 24(4); 25(3); 26(5); 27; 28(2); 47:1(4); 2(7); 3(6); 4(6); 5; 6; 7(2); 48:1(2); 2; 5(3); 6(2); 8(4); 9; 10(2); 12(2); 13; 14; 15(3); 16; 17(2); 18; 19; 21; 24(2); 25(2); 26; 28(5); 29(2); 30; 31; 32(4); 33(3); 34(2); 35(2); 36(2); 37(2); 38(3); 39; 40; 41(3); 42; 43(3); 44(6); 45(7); 46; 47(4); 49:1(2); 2(4); 3; 4; 5; 6(3); 7(2); 8(2); 12(2); 13(2); 14(3); 15; 16(7); 17; 18(3); 19(4); 20(5); 21(5); 22(4); 23; 25(2); 26(2); 27(2); 28(4); 30; 31(2); 32(3); 34(5); 35(3); 36(3); 37(2); 38(3); 39(3); 50:1(5); 2; 3; 4(4); 5(2); 6; 7(4); 8(5); 9; 10; 11; 12(2); 13(2); 14(2); 15(2); 16(4); 17(2); 18(4); 20(3); 21(3); 22; 23(3); 24; 25(6); 26; 27(2); 28(5); 29(4); 30(2); 31(2); 32; 33(3); 34(3); 35(3); 36; 37(2); 38; 39(5); 40(2); 41(3); 42(4); 43(2); 44(4); 45(6); 46(5); 51:1(2); 2; 3; 4(3); 5(2); 6(3); 7(4); 9; 10(3); 11(9); 12(7); 13; 14; 15(3); 16(5); 17; 18(2); 19(4); 20; 21(2); 22(2); 23(2); 24(2); 25(3); 26; 27(7); 28(6); 29(3); 30; 31; 32(3); 33(4); 34; 35(3); 36; 39; 40; 41(3); 42(3); 44(2); 45(3); 46(3); 47(3); 48(5); 49(3); 50(2); 51(2); 52(3); 53(2); 54(2); 55(2); 56(2); 57(2); 58(5); 59(6); 60; 63; 64(2); 52:1; 2(2); 3(3); 4(4); 5(2); 6(7); 7(11); 8(4); 9(3); 10(3); 11(3); 12(6); 13(6); 14(5); 15(10); 16(4); 17(9); 18(6); 19(9); 20(5); 21(3); 22(4); 23(2); 24(6); 25(13); 26(3); 27(2); 28(2); 29; 30(5); 31(7); 32(2); 33; 34(3); **Lam** 1:1(3); 2; 3(2); 4(2); 5(4); 6(2); 7(5); 9; 10(2); 11; 12(2); 13; 14(2); 15(5); 16(2); 17; 18; 19(2); 20; 21; 2:1(5); 2(7); 3(2); 4(3); 5(2); 6(6); 7(7); 8(5); 9(4); 10(5); 11(7); 12(3); 13; 15(5); 16(2); 17(3); 18(3); 19(7); 20(5); 21(6); 22(2); 3:1(2); 3; 12; 13; 14; 18; 19(2); 22; 24; 25(2); 26(2); 27; 29; 31; 32; 33; 34(2); 35(3); 36; 37; 38(2); 39; 40; 41; 45(3); 48(2); 50; 51; 53; 55; 57; 58; 62(2); 64; 66(2); 4:1(5); 2(4); 3(5); 4(4); 5; 6(5); 8; 9(3); 10(4); 11(2); 12(7); 13(5); 14; 15; 16(5); 19(4); 20(4); 21(2); 22; 5:6(3); 9(3); 10; 11(3); 12; 13(3); 14(3); 15; 16; 18(2); **Eze** 1:1(7); 2(3); 3(9); 4(5); 5(3); 7(3); 8; 10(7); 12; 13(6); 14(2); 15(3); 16(4); 19(5); 20(5); 21(5); 22(6); 23(3); 24(6); 25; 26(7); 27(5); 28(10); 2:2; 3; 4; 3:1; 4; 5; 7(2); 11(3); 12(3); 13(5); 14(4); 15(2); 16(3); 17(2); 18(3); 19; 21(2); 22(3); 23(5); 24; 26; 27; 4:1; 2; 3(2); 4(4); 5(5); 6(2); 7; 8; 9(2); 11; 13(3); 16; 5:1; 2(5); 4(4); 5(3); 6(2); 7(4); 8(4); 9; 10(6); 11; 12(4); 13; 14(2); 15(2); 16(2); 17(2); 6:1(2); 2; 3(7); 5(2); 6(2); 7(3); 8(3); 9(2); 10; 11(6); 12(3); 13(4); 14(3); 7:1(2); 2(5); 3; 4(2); 5; 6; 7(6); 9(2); 10(3); 12(5); 13(4); 14(3); 15(6); 16(2); 19(5); 20(2); 21(4); 22; 23(2); 24(4); 26(4); 27(6); 8:1(7); 2(4); 3(10); 4(4); 5(7); 6(2); 7(3); 8(2); 9; 10(3); 11(4); 12(7); 14(4); 16(12); 17(4); 9:1; 2(4); 3(7); 4(8); 5(2); 6(3); 7(4); 8; 9(7); 11(3); 10:1(5); 2(5); 3(6); 4(10); 5(5); 6(4); 7(4); 8(2); 9(5); 10; 11(2); 12(2); 13; 14(8); 15(3); 16(5); 17(2); 18(5); 19(8); 20(4); 21(2); 22(3); 11:1(8); 2; 3(2); 5(4); 6(2); 7(5); 8(2); 9(2); 10(3); 11(3); 12(3); 13(2); 14(2); 15(4); 16(4); 17(4); 18(2); 19; 21(2); 22(4); 23(7); 24(4); 25(3); 12:1(2); 2; 5; 6(3); 7(3); 8(3); 9(2); 10(3); 12(4); 13(2); 14; 15(3); 16(5); 17(2); 19(6); 20(3); 21(2); 22(2); 23(3); 24; 25(4); 26(2); 27(3); 28(3); 13:1(2); 2(3); 3(2); 4(2); 5(6); 6(3); 7; 8(2); 9(6); 12(2); 13; 14(5); 15(2); 16(2); 17; 18(5); 19(2); 20(4); 21; 22(4); 23; 14:1; 2(2); 3; 4(6); 5; 6(2); 7(4); 8(2); 9(3); 10(4); 11(2); 12(2); 13(3); 14; 15(2); 16(2); 17; 18; 20; 21(5); 22; 23; 15:1(2); 2(3); 4(4); 5; 6(6); 7; 8(2); 16:1(2); 3(2); 4; 5(3); 7(2); 8(2); 14(2); 15; 16(2); 19; 21; 22; 23; 25; 26; 27(3); 28(3); 29; 30(2); 31; 34; 35(2); 36(3); 41(2); 43(2); 44; 45; 48; 49(3); 53(4); 56; 57(4); 58; 59(3); 60; 62; 63; 17:1(2); 2; 3(3); 4; 5(2); 6; 7; 9(5); 10(2); 11(2); 12(4); 13(3); 14; 15; 16(4); 17; 18(2); 19; 21(2); 22(4); 23(4); 24(8); 18:1(2); 2(3); 3; 4(5); 6(3); 7(3); 9; 10; 11; 12(3); 15(3); 16(3); 17(2); 19(4); 20(11); 21; 23(2); 24(3); 25(2); 27; 29(3); 30; 32(2); 19:1; 3; 4(2); 6(2); 7(3); 8(2); 9(2); 10; 11(3); 12(3); 13; 20:1(6); 2(2); 3(3); 4; 5(6); 6(3); 7(3); 8(4); 9(2); 10(2); 12; 13(3); 14; 15(3); 17; 18(2); 19; 20; 21(2); 22(2); 23(3); 26(4); 27(2); 28(4); 29(2); 30(3); 31(2); 32(3); 33; 34(2); 35(2); 36(3); 37(3); 38(4); 39; 40(6); 41(3); 42(4); 44(2); 45(2); 46(4); 47(8); 48; 21:1(2); 2(2); 3(4); 4(4); 5; 6; 7(2); 8(2); 9; 10; 11(2); 12(2); 13(3); 14(6); 15(3); 16(2); 17; 18(2); 19(5); 20(3); 21(6); 22(5); 23; 24(2); 26(4); 28(6); 29(2); 30(2); 31(2); 32(4); 22:1(2); 2; 3(3); 4; 6; 7(4); 9(2); 12; 13; 14(2); 15(2); 16(3); 17(2); 18(4); 19(2); 20(3); 21(2); 22(4); 23(2); 24(2); 25(4); 26(3); 27(2); 28(2); 29(4); 30(3); 31(2); 23:1(2); 2; 3; 4(2); 5(2); 7; 8; 9(3); 10; 12; 14(3); 15(3); 17(2); 19(3); 20(2); 21(3); 22; 23(3); 25(2); 27; 28(3); 29; 30; 31; 32; 33(2); 34(2); 35; 36; 37; 38; 39(2); 42(3); 44(2); 45(3); 46; 47; 48; 49(2); 24:1(6); 2(3); 3(2); 4(4); 5(4); 6(3); 7(3); 8; 9(3); 10(3); 11(4); 12; 14(2); 15(2); 16; 17(3); 18(3); 19; 20(2); 21(5); 22; 24; 25(3); 27; 25:1(2); 2; 3(6); 4(2); 5(2); 6(3); 7(4); 8(3); 9(4); 10(5); 11; 12(2); 13(2); 14(2); 15(3); 16(5); 17; 26:1(5); 2(2); 3(2); 4(2); 5(5); 6(3); 7(2); 8(3); 10(5); 11(3); 12(2); 13(2); 14(3); 15(6); 16(3); 17(2); 18(4); 19(3); 20(7); 21; 27:1(2); 3(4); 4(2); 6(4); 7; 8; 9(4); 10; 11(2); 12; 13; 14; 15(2); 16(2); 17; 18(4); 21; 22; 23; 25(3); 26(3); 27(5); 28(3); 29(5); 30; 32(3); 33(4); 34(5); 35(2); 36(2); 28:1(2); 2(6); 6(2); 7(3); 8(4); 9; 10(4); 11(2); 12(3); 13(11); 14(4); 15; 16(5); 17; 18(5); 19; 20(2); 22(3); 23(4); 24(2); 25(5); 26; 29:1(6); 3(3); 4(3); 5(7); 6(3); 8; 9(3); 10(3); 12(7); 13(4); 14(3); 15(4); 16(3); 17(6); 18; 19(3); 20(2); 21(6); 30:1(2); 2(2); 3(5); 4(2); 5(4); 6(5); 7(4); 8; 9(2); 10(3); 11(5); 12(7); 13(4); 15(2); 17(2); 18(3); 19; 20(6); 21(2); 22(3); 23(3); 24(3); 25(7); 26(4); 31:1(6); 3(2); 4(4); 5(3); 6(3); 7; 8(5); 9(3); 10(2); 11(3); 12(8); 13(4); 14(9); 15(8); 16(7); 17(3); 18(8); 32:1(6); 2(3); 3; 4(6); 5(2); 6(3); 7(4); 8(2); 9(3); 10; 11(3); 12(6); 13(4); 14; 15(3); 16(4); 17(5); 18(6); 19; 20(3); 21(4); 22; 23(5); 24(6); 25(7); 26(3); 27(6); 28(3); 29(3); 30(6); 31(2); 32(6); 33:1(2); 2(4); 3(4); 4(3); 5(2); 6(6); 7(2); 8(2); 9; 10; 11(4); 12(9); 13; 14; 15(3); 17(3); 18; 19; 20(2); 21(5); 22(4); 23(2); 24(3); 25(3); 26; 27(8); 28(3); 29(2); 30(6); 31; 34:1(2); 2(6); 3(3); 4; 5(2); 6(3); 7(2); 8(3); 9(2); 10(4); 11; 12(2); 13(6); 14(2); 15; 16(2); 17(3); 18(4); 20(3); 21; 24(2); 25(4); 26(2); 27(6); 28(3); 29(3); 30(3); 31(2); 35:1(2); 3; 4; 5(6); 6; 8; 9; 10; 11; 12(2); 14(2); 15(3); 36:1(3); 2(3); 3(5); 4(11); 5(5); 6(8); 7(2); 10(3); 11; 13; 14; 15(5); 16(2); 17(2); 18(2); 19(2); 20(3); 21(2); 22(3); 23(5); 24; 26; 28; 29; 30(5); 32; 33(4); 34(2); 35(2); 36(4); 37(2); 38(4); 37:1(6); 2; 4(2); 5; 6; 7; 8(3); 9(4); 10; 11; 12(2); 13; 14(2); 15(2); 16(3); 18; 19(5); 20; 21(3); 22(2); 25; 26; 28(3); 38:1(2); 2(2); 3(2); 6(2); 8(5); 9; 10(2); 11; 12(5); 13(2); 14; 15; 16(3); 17(2); 18(3); 19(2); 20(13); 21; 22; 23(2); 39:1(2); 2(3); 4(5); 5(2); 6(2); 7(4); 8(2); 9(8); 10(4); 11(7); 12(2); 13(4); 14(5); 15(4); 16(3); 17(3); 18(5); 20; 21(2); 22(2); 23(4); 25(3); 27(2); 28(2); 29(2); 40:1(10); 2(4); 3(2); 4(3); 5(7); 6(7); 7(5); 8(2); 9(5); 10(3); 11(5); 12(4); 13(4); 14(3); 15(6); 16(3); 17(3); 18(6); 19(5); 20(5); 21(7); 22(4); 23(5); 24(4); 25(3); 26(2); 27(3); 28(3); 29(4); 30; 31(4); 32(3); 33(4); 34(4); 35; 36(6); 37(4); 38(5); 39(5); 40(6); 41(2); 42(5); 43(3); 44(11); 45(5); 46(9); 47(3); 48(5); 49(5); 41:1(6); 2(8); 3(5); 4(4); 5(4); 6(6); 7(9); 8(4); 9(5); 10(3); 11(7); 12(7); 13(4); 14(5); 15(9); 16(7); 17(3); 19(7); 20(4); 21(8); 22(7); 23(2); 24(3); 25(5); 26(6); 42:1(7); 2(3); 3(4); 4(2); 5(5); 6(6); 7(6); 8(4); 9(3); 10(7); 11(4); 12(8); 13(11); 14(4); 15(3); 16(3); 17(2); 18(2); 19(2); 20(3); 43:1(3); 2(5); 3(7); 4(6); 5(5); 6(2); 7(7); 8; 9(2); 10(3); 11(11); 12(7); 13(10); 14(7); 15(2); 16(2); 17(5); 18(4); 19(4); 20(5); 21(5); 22(4); 23; 24(3); 25; 26; 27(4); 44:1(4); 2(3); 3(7); 4(7); 5(8); 6(3); 7(2); 8; 9(2); 10; 11(6); 12(2); 13(2); 14(3); 15(8); 17(4); 19(5); 21; 22(2); 23(4); 27(5); 29(3); 30(6); 31; 45:1(7); 2(2); 3(4); 4(7); 5(5); 6(5); 7(17); 8(4); 9(2); 11(8); 12; 13(3); 14(4); 15(3); 16(3); 17(10); 18(5); 19(11); 20(3); 21(4); 22(3); 23(4); 25(10); 46:1(8); 2(10); 3(6); 4(4); 5(3); 6(2); 7; 8(4); 9(14); 10(2); 11(4); 12(6); 13(2); 14(4); 15(3); 16(3); 17(2); 18(2); 19(7); 20(7); 21(4); 22(2); 23; 24(5); 47:1(12); 2(6); 3(5); 4(5); 5; 6(2); 7(4); 8(5); 9(2); 10(3); 11(2); 12(6); 13(4); 14; 15(5); 16(3); 17(6); 18(5); 19(5); 20(4); 21; 22(4); 23(2); 48:1(7); 2(3); 3(3); 4(3); 5(3); 6(3); 7(3); 8(9); 9(2); 10(8); 11(4); 12(3); 13(5); 14(3); 15(6); 16(5); 17(6); 18(7); 19(2); 20(4); 21(18); 22(9); 23(4); 24(3); 25(3); 26(3); 27(3); 28(6); 29(3); 30(3); 31(4); 32; 33; 34; 35(3); **Dan** 1:1(2); 2(7); 3(5); 4(4); 5(5); 6; 7(3); 8(5); 9(2); 10(5); 11(2); 13(4); 15(4); 16(2); 18(5); 19(2); 20(2); 21; 2:1(2); 2(7); 3(2); 4(4); 5(5); 6(4); 7(3); 8(3); 9(4); 10(4); 11(3); 12(2); 13(2); 14(3); 15(4); 16(3); 17; 18(3); 19(2); 20; 21(3); 22(3); 23; 24(6); 25(4); 26(3); 27(9); 28(3); 30(3); 31; 34; 35(11); 36(3); 37; 38(5); 39; 40; 41(5); 42(3); 43; 44(3); 45(11); 46; 47; 48(4); 49(5); 3:1(4); 2(13); 3(12); 5(4); 6(2); 7(8); 8; 9; 10(3); 11; 12(3); 13; 14; 15(5); 16; 17; 18; 19(2); 20(2); 21(2); 22(4); 23(2); 24(4); 25(5); 26(5); 27(4); 28(2); 29; 30(2); 4:1(2); 2(2); 5(2); 6(3); 7(6); 8(5); 9(5); 10(4); 11(5); 12(7); 13; 14(3); 15(8); 17(10); 18(5); 19(5); 20(4); 21(5); 22(2); 23(10); 24(4); 25(5); 26(3); 27; 28; 29(3); 30(5); 31(3); 32(4); 33(3); 34(3); 35(5); 36(2); 37; 5:1(2); 2(4); 3(4); 4; 5(8); 6(2); 7(9); 8(4); 10(5); 11(8); 12(3); 13(5); 14(2); 15(5); 16(4); 17(4); 18; 19; 21(6); 23(4); 24(2); 25; 26(2); 27; 28; 29(2); 30(2); 31(2); 6:1(2); 2(2); 3(3); 4(2); 5; 6; 7(7); 8(4); 9(2); 10; 12(7); 13(4); 14(3); 15(5); 16(3); 17(5); 18(2); 19(3); 20(4); 21; 22; 23(3); 24(6); 25; 26(3); 27(2); 28(3); 7:1(4); 2(3); 3; 4(4); 5(2); 6(2); 7(4); 8(4); 9(5); 10(2); 11(5); 12(2); 13(4); 15(2); 16(3); 17; 18(4); 19(4); 20(2); 21(2); 22(6); 23(3); 24(2); 25(4); 26(2); 27(7); 28(3); 8:1(3); 2(3); 3(4); 4; 5(5); 6(3); 7(5); 8(3); 9(3); 10(4); 11(4); 12(3); 13(5); 14; 15(3); 16(2); 17(3); 18; 19(4); 20(2); 21(4); 22; 23(3); 24(2); 25; 26(4); 27(2); 9:1(6); 2(7); 3; 4(3); 6(3); 7(3); 9; 10(3); 11(4); 12; 13(2); 14(3); 15; 16; 17(2); 18; 20(3); 21(5); 23(4); 24(3); 25(6); 26(7); 27(8); 10:1(5); 4(4); 6(4); 7(3); 9(3); 10; 11; 12; 13(4); 14(2); 15; 16(3); 17; 18; 20(2); 21; 11:1(2); 2(3); 4; 5(2); 6(7); 7(3); 8(2); 9(2); 11(5); 12; 13(3); 14(4); 15(5); 16; 17(2); 18(2); 19; 20(2); 21(3); 22(3); 23; 24(4); 25(4); 26; 27(2); 28; 29(4); 30(3); 31(3); 32(2); 33(2); 35(2); 36(3); 37(2); 38; 39(2); 40(7); 41(3); 42(2); 43(4); 44(2); 45(3); 12:1(3); 2(2); 3(3); 4(4); 5(6); 6(4); 7(5); 8; 9(3); 10(3); 11(3); 12; 13(3); **Hos** 1:1(6); 2(6); 3; 4(5); 5(2); 6; 7(2); 10(7); 11(4); 2:3; 4; 5; 9(2); 10; 12(2); 13(2); 14; 15(4); 16; 17; 18(9); 20; 21(3); 22(4); 23; 3:1(4); 3; 4; 5(4); 4:1(6); 3(6); 4; 5(3); 6; 8; 10; 11; 12; 13(4); 14; 15(2); 16; 19; 5:1; 2; 4(3); 5; 6; 7; 8(2); 9(2); 10(2); 11; 12; 13; 14; 6:1; 2; 3(5); 4; 5(3); 6; 7; 9(2); 10(2); 11; 7:1(4); 3(2); 4(2); 5(2); 6(2); 8; 10(2); 12(2); 16(4); 8:1(3); 3(2); 6(2); 7(4); 8; 10(3); 12; 13(2); 14; 9:2(3); 3; 4(4); 5(4); 6; 7(6); 8(3); 9; 10(3); 11(3); 13; 15; 16; 17; 10:1(3); 3; 4(2); 5(5); 7(2); 8(6); 9(3); 10; 11; 12; 13(2); 14(2); 15; 11:4; 5(2); 6; 7; 9(4); 10(3); 11(2); 12(2); 12:1(2); 2; 3(2); 4; 5(2); 7; 9(4); 10(3); 11(2); 12; 13; 13:2(4); 3(7); 4(2); 5(2); 7; 8(2); 12; 13(3); 14(2); 15(4); 16; 14:1; 2(2); 3(2); 5(2); 6; 7(4); 9(4); **Joel** 1:1(3); 2(2); 4(6); 5; 6(2); 7; 8; 9(6); 10(5); 11(4); 12(8); 13(4); 14(6); 15(4); 16(2); 17(4); 18(3); 19(6); 20(6); 2:1(5); 2(4); 3(2); 4(2); 5(4); 6; 7; 8; 9(4); 10(5); 11(3); 12; 13(2); 14; 15; 16(7); 17(7); 18; 19(2); 20(3); 21; 22(6); 23(6); 24(2); 25(5); 26(2); 27(2); 29(2); 30(2); 31(5); 32(5); 3:1; 2(2); 4; 6(3); 7; 8(4); 9(3); 10; 12(3); 13(4); 14(4); 15(3); 16(7); 17; 18(6); 19(2); 21; **Amos** 1:1(6); 2(4); 3(2); 4(2); 5(7); 6(3); 7(2); 8(5); 9(4); 10(2); 11(3); 12; 13(4); 14(5); 15; 2:1(4); 2(3); 3(4); 4(5); 5; 6(4); 7(7); 8(3); 9(4); 10(4); 11; 12(2); 14(4); 15(2); 16(2); 3:1(3); 2(2); 4; 5(2); 6(3); 7(2); 8(2); 9(8); 10; 11(2); 12(6); 13(3); 14(6); 15(5); 4:1(3); 2(2); 3(3); 5(2); 6; 7(3); 8; 9(2); 10(5); 11(2); 13(7); 5:2; 3(3); 4(2); 6(2); 7; 8(9); 9(4); 10; 11; 12(3); 13; 14(2); 15(5); 16(5); 17; 18(4); 19(2); 20(2); 22; 23(2); 25; 26(2); 27(2); 6:1(3); 2(2); 3(2); 4(5); 5(2); 6(2); 7(2); 8(5); 10(6); 11(3); 12(2); 14(5); 7:1(6); 2(2); 3(2); 4(3); 6(2); 7; 8(3); 9(4); 10(4); 11; 12; 13(2); 15(3); 16(3); 17(3); 8:1; 2(2); 3(3); 4(3); 5(5); 6(4); 7(2); 8(2); 9(4); 10(2); 11(5); 12(4); 13; 14(2); 9:1(8); 3(4); 4; 5(3); 6(7); 7(5); 8(7); 9(3); 10(3); 11(3); 12(3); 13(7); 14(4); 15; **Obad** 1(4); 2; 3(4); 4(3); 5; 6; 7(3); 8(3); 9(2); 11(4); 12(5); 13(4); 14(2); 15(3); 16; 17; 18(5); 19(6); 20(6); 21(3); **Jonah** 1:1(3); 3(5); 4(4); 5(6); 6; 7; 9(4); 10(4); 11(2); 12(2); 13(3); 14; 15(2); 16(3); 17(3); 2:1(2); 2(2); 3(4); 5(4); 6(3); 7; 9(2); 10(3); 3:1(3); 2; 3(2); 4; 5(3); 6; 7(2); 8; 10; 4:2(2); 4; 5(5); 6(2); 7(3); 8(3); 9; 10(3); **Mic** 1:1(4); 2(2); 3(3); 4(4); 5(5); 6(4); 7(6); 8(2); 9; 10(2); 11(2); 12(3); 13(6); 14(2); 15; 16; 2:1(2); 3; 4; 5(2); 7(3); 8(2); 9; 11(2); 12(5); 13(4); 3:1; 2(2); 3(3); 4; 5(2); 6(3); 7(2); 8(2); 9(2); 11(5); 12(4); 4:1(7); 2(7); 4(2); 5(3); 6; 7; 8(6); 10(4); 12(4); 13(3); 5:1(2); 2; 3(3); 4(7); 5(2); 6(5); 7(6); 8(6); 10(2); 11; 13(2); 14; 15; 6:1(3); 2(3); 4(2); 5(3); 6(2); 7(3); 8; 9(4); 10(4); 11(2); 12(2); 14(2); 15; 16(5); 7:1(4); 2(2); 3(3); 4(3); 5; 6(5); 7(2); 8; 9(3); 10(3); 11(2); 12(3); 13(2); 14(4); 15(2); 16; 17(3); 18(2); 19(2); 20(3); **Nah** 1:1(4); 2(3); 3(7); 4(3); 5(4); 6(2); 7(2); 8; 9(2); 11; 12; 14(4); 15(3); 2:1(2); 2(4); 3(5); 4(4); 5(2); 6(3); 7; 9(4); 10(3); 11(7); 12; 13(5); 3:1(2); 2(6); 3(3); 4(4); 5(3); 8(4); 10(2); 11; 12(3); 13(3); 14(3); 15(5); 16(2); 17(5); 18(2); 19(2); **Hab** 1:1(2); 4(3); 5; 6(4); 8(3); 9(3); 10(2); 13(2); 14(3); 15; 17; 2:1; 2(2); 3(2); 4; 8(5); 9; 11(4); 13(4); 14(6); 16(2); 17(5); 18(4); 19(3); 20(2); 3:1; 2(4); 3(3); 4(2); 5; 6(4); 7(3); 8(4); 9(3); 10(4); 11(3); 12(2); 13(6); 14(2); 15(2); 16(3); 17(8); 18(2); 19(2); **Zeph** 1:1(8); 2(2); 3(8); 4(5); 5(3); 6(2); 7(5); 8(4); 9(2); 10(5); 11; 12(2); 13; 14(6); 16(3); 17(2); 18(5); 2:2(7); 3(4); 4; 5(8); 6; 7(6); 8(3); 9(6); 10(2); 11(5); 13; 14(9); 15; 3:1; 2(2); 3(2); 4(2); 5(3); 6; 8(7); 9(3); 10(2); 11; 12(3); 13; 14; 15(4); 17(2); 18(2); 20(3); **Hag** 1:1(11); 2(4); 3(3); 5; 7; 8(3); 9; 10(2); 11(8); 12(12); 13(4); 14(11); 15(4); 2:1(6); 2(5); 4(5); 5; 6(5); 7(2); 8(3); 9(4); 10(6); 11(3); 12(2); 13; 14; 15(2); 16(2); 17(2); 18(5); 19(6); 20(4); 21(2); 22(7); 23(4); **Zec** 1:1(7); 2; 3(3); 4(3); 5; 6(2); 7(9); 8(2); 9; 10(4); 11(5); 12(3); 13(2); 14(2); 15(2); 16(2); 17(2); 19(2); 20; 21(4); 2:2(2); 3; 4; 5(3); 6(6); 7; 8(4); 9; 10(2); 11(3); 12(2); 13; 3:1(3); 2(4); 3; 4; 5(2); 6(2); 7; 8(2); 9(4); 10(3); 4:1; 2(3); 3(4); 4; 5; 6(3); 7; 8(2); 9(3); 10(6); 11(3); 12(2); 14(3); 5:2(2); 3(3); 4(7); 5; 6; 7(2); 8(4); 9(5); 10(2); 11; 6:1; 2(2); 3(2); 4; 5(5); 6(5); 7(4); 8(2); 9(2); 10(4); 11(3); 12(5); 13(4); 14(4); 15(5); 7:1(5); 2(2); 3(5); 4(2); 5(4); 7(6); 8(2); 9; 10(4); 11; 12(5); 13; 14(3); 8:1(2); 2; 3(5); 4(2); 5(3); 6(4); 7(3); 8; 9(8); 10; 11(3); 12(5); 13; 14(2); 15; 16(3); 17; 18(2); 19(11); 20(2); 21(3); 22(2); 23(3); 9:1(8); 3(3); 4(2); 5; 6(2); 8; 9; 10(7); 11(2); 12; 13(2); 14(5); 15(3); 16(3); 17(2); 10:1(5); 2(2); 3(5); 4(3); 5(5); 6(3); 7; 9; 10(2); 11(7); 12(2); 11:1; 2(4); 3(4); 4(3); 5; 6(6); 7(5); 9(2); 10; 11(4); 13(6); 14; 15(2); 16(4); 17(3); 12:1(8); 2(2); 3(2); 4(3); 5(3); 6(5); 7(6); 8(5); 9; 10(3); 11(2); 12(5); 13(3); 14; 13:1(2); 2(7); 3(2); 4; 6; 7(5); 8(3); 9(3); 14:1(3); 2(7); 3(2); 4(9); 5(8); 6; 7; 8(2); 9(2); 10(6); 12(3); 13(3); 14(2); 15(6); 16(4); 17(4); 18(5); 19(3); 20(7); 21(4); **Mal** 1:1(3); 2(2); 3(2); 4(5); 5(2); 6; 7(2); 8(3); 9; 10(2); 11(7); 12(3); 13(4); 14(4); 2:2; 3; 4; 5; 6; 7(4); 8(4); 9(2); 10; 11(3); 12(6); 13(3); 14(3); 15(3); 16(3); 17(4); 3:1(5); 2; 3(2); 4(3); 5(7); 6; 7(2); 10(4); 11(5); 12; 13; 14; 15; 16(3); 17; 18(2); 4:1(4); 2(2); 3(4); 4(2); 5(4); 6(6); **Mt** 1:1(4); 6(3); 11; 16; 17(3); 18(2); 20(3); 22(2); 24(2); 2:1(3); 2(2); 3; 4(2); 5; 6(3); 7(2); 8; 9(4); 10; 11(2); 13(4); 14; 15(3); 16(5); 17; 19; 20(3); 21(2); 22(2); 23; 3:1(2); 2; 3(5); 4; 5; 7(2); 10(4); 11; 12(2); 16(3); 4:1(3); 3(2); 4; 5(3); 6; 7; 8(4); 10; 11; 13(2); 14; 15(5); 16(2); 17; 18(2); 21; 22; 23(3); 24; 5:1; 3(2); 5(2); 7; 8; 9(2); 10; 12; 13(3); 14(2); 15; 17(2); 18; 19(4); 20(3); 21; 22(2); 23; 24; 25(5); 26; 32; 33; 35(3); 39; 40; 45(5); 46(2); 47; 6:2(3); 5(4); 7; 13(3); 16; 22(3); 23; 24(4); 25(2); 26(2); 28(2); 30(3); 32; 33; 34(5); 7:3(2); 4; 5(2); 6; 12(2); 13(3); 14(2); 19; 21(2); 25(3); 26; 27(4); 28; 29; 8:1; 4(2); 6; 8(2); 11(2); 12(2); 13(2); 15; 16(2); 17; 18; 20(4); 22; 24(3); 26(2); 27(3); 28(4); 29; 31(2); 32(4); 33(3); 34; 9:2(3); 3; 6(3); 8; 9; 10; 11; 13; 14(2); 15(5); 16(2); 17(3); 20; 22; 23(3); 24; 25(3); 26; 28(2); 33(3); 34(3); 35(4); 36; 37(2); 38(2); 10:2(4); 3(2); 4; 5(3); 6(2); 7; 8(3); 10; 13; 14; 15(2); 16; 17; 18; 20; 21(5); 22; 23(2); 24(2); 25(4); 27(2); 28(2); 29; 30; 35(2); 41(2); 42; 11:2(2); 5(7); 7(3); 11(2); 12(4); 13(2); 16; 19;

20; 21; 22; 23; 24(2); 25; 27(5); 12:1(3); 2(2); 4(3); 5(5); 6; 7;
8(2); 10; 11; 12; 13(2); 14; 17; 18; 19; 21; 22; 23(2); 24(3); 28(2);
29; 31(2); 32(3); 33(3); 34(3); 35(3); 36; 38(2); 39(2); 40(4);
41(2); 42(6); 43; 45(2); 46; 50(2); 13:1(3); 2(2); 4(2); 6; 7; 10;
11(2); 14; 18(2); 19(4); 20(3); 21; 22(5); 23(2); 24; 25; 26(2);
27(2); 28; 29(2); 30(5); 31; 32(5); 33(2); 34; 35(3); 36(5); 37(2);
38(8); 39(7); 40(3); 41; 43(3); 44(2); 45; 47(2); 48(2); 49(5); 50;
52; 55; 14:1(2); 2(2); 5; 6; 9(2); 10; 11; 12; 13(2); 15(3); 19(7);
20; 22(2); 23(2); 24(4); 25(3); 26(2); 28; 29(2); 30; 32(2); 33(2);
34; 35; 36; 15:2(2); 3; 4; 6; 9; 10; 11(2); 12; 14(4); 17(3); 18(3);
19; 20; 21; 22; 24(2); 26; 27(2); 29; 31(6); 32(2); 33; 35(2);
36(4); 37; 39(2); 16:1(2); 2; 3(6); 4(2); 5; 6(3); 9(2); 10(2); 11(3);
12(4); 13(2); 14(2); 16(3); 18; 19(2); 20; 21(2); 23; 26; 27(2);
28; 17:2(2); 5; 6; 9(4); 10; 12; 13(2); 14; 15(2); 18(2); 19; 22(2);
23; 25(3); 26; 27(2); 18:1(4); 2; 3; 4(2); 6(2); 7(2); 10; 11; 12(2);
13; 14; 16; 17(2); 20; 23; 26; 27(2); 28(2); 30; 34; 19:1; 3; 4;
8(2); 10(2); 12; 13; 14; 17; 20; 21; 22; 23; 24(2); 28(4); 30;
20:1(2); 2; 3(2); 4; 5; 6(2); 7; 8(5); 9; 10; 11(2); 12(2); 16(2);
17(2); 18(3); 19(2); 20; 21(3); 22(2); 23; 24(2); 25(2); 28; 30;
31(2); 21:1; 2; 3; 4; 5(2); 6; 7(2); 8(3); 9(5); 10; 11(2); 12(5); 13;
14(3); 15(5); 16; 17; 18(2); 19(2); 20(2); 21(2); 23(4); 25; 26;
28; 30; 31(5); 32(3); 34(4); 35; 36; 38(3); 39; 40(2); 41; 42(7);
43(2); 45; 46; 22:2; 3; 4; 6; 7; 8; 9(2); 10(2); 11(2); 13(2); 15;
16(3); 19; 21(2); 23(2); 25; 26(3); 27; 28(2); 29(2); 30(2); 31(2);
32(6); 33; 34(2); 36(2); 37; 38; 39; 40(2); 41; 42; 44; 23:1; 2(2);
5; 6(3); 7; 9; 13; 14; 15; 16(3); 17(3); 18(2); 19(3); 20; 21; 22;
23(3); 25(3); 26(2); 29(4); 30(3); 31(2); 32; 33; 35(6); 37; 39(2);
24:1(3); 3(5); 6; 8; 12; 13(2); 14(3); 15(3); 16; 17; 18; 20(2);
21(2); 22; 24; 26(2); 27(5); 28(2); 29(6); 30(6); 31(2); 32; 33; 36;
37(3); 38(4); 39(3); 40(3); 41(3); 43(3); 44; 49; 50; 51; 25:1(2); 4;
5; 6; 8(2); 9; 10(3); 11; 13(3); 14; 16(2); 18; 19; 21; 23; 24; 25;
27; 28; 30; 31(3); 32; 33(3); 34(4); 37; 40(2); 41(2); 45; 46;
26:2(3); 3(6); 5(2); 6(2); 9; 10; 11; 13; 14(2); 17(4); 18(3); 19(2);
20(2); 23(2); 24(2); 26; 27; 28(2); 29; 30; 31(3); 34; 35; 36; 37;
40; 41(2); 42; 44(2); 45(3); 47(3); 51; 52(2); 54; 55(2); 56(3);
57(3); 58(3); 59(2); 60; 61; 62; 63(4); 64(3); 65; 67; 69; 71; 72;
74(2); 75(2); 27:1(3); 2; 3(2); 4; 5(2); 6(4); 7; 8; 9(4); 10(2);
11(4); 12; 14; 15(2); 19; 20(2); 21(2); 23(2); 24(2); 25; 27(4);
29(2); 30(2); 31; 35; 37(2); 38(2); 40(3); 41(2); 42(2); 43; 44(2);
45(3); 46; 49; 50; 51(6); 52(2); 53(2); 54(3); 56(2); 57; 58(2);
59; 60(3); 61(2); 62(4); 64(6); 66(2); 28:1(6); 2(4); 4; 5(2); 6(2);
7; 8; 9; 11(4); 12(2); 14; 15(2); 16; 19(4); 20(2); **Mk** 1:1(3); 2;
3(4); 4(3); 5(2); 7; 8; 10(3); 12(2); 13(3); 14(2); 15(3); 16(2);
19(2); 20(2); 21(2); 22; 24; 26; 27; 28; 29(2); 31(2); 32; 33(2);
34; 35; 38; 42; 44; 45(2); 2:1; 2(2); 3; 4(5); 5(2); 6; 9(2); 10(3);
12; 13(2); 14(2); 16; 17(2); 18(4); 19(4); 20(2); 21(3); 22(4);
23(3); 24(2); 26(5); 27(2); 28(2); 3:1; 2; 3(2); 4; 5(3); 6(2); 7; 9;
11; 17(3); 18(2); 20; 22(3); 27; 28; 29; 32; 35(2); 4:1(5); 4(3); 6;
7; 10(2); 11(2); 14(2); 15(3); 16; 17; 18; 19(4); 20; 26(2); 27;
28(5); 29(3); 30; 31(3); 32(3); 33; 35(3); 36(2); 37(2); 38(2);
39(3); 41(2); 5:1(4); 2(2); 3; 4(2); 5(2); 7; 8; 10; 11; 12(2); 13(5);
14(3); 15(2); 16(2); 18(2); 19; 21(2); 22(2); 23; 27; 29; 30; 31;
33(2); 35(3); 36(3); 37; 38(4); 39; 40(4); 41(2); 42(2); 6:2(2);
3(3); 6; 7; 11(2); 14(2); 15; 16; 22(4); 23; 24(2); 25(3); 26; 27(2);
28(2); 30; 33; 35(2); 36(2); 39; 41(4); 43(2); 44; 45(3); 47(4);
48(4); 49; 51(2); 52(2); 53(2); 54; 56(3); 7:1(2); 3(4); 4(2); 5(3);
7; 8(3); 9; 10; 13; 14; 15(2); 17(3); 18; 19(2); 20(2); 21; 23; 24;
26(2); 27(3); 28(3); 29; 30(2); 31(4); 33; 35; 36(2); 37(2); 8:1; 2;
3; 4; 6(4); 8; 10; 11; 13(2); 14(2); 15(3); 19; 20; 23(3); 26(2);
27(2); 28(2); 29; 31(3); 33(2); 34; 35(2); 36; 38(3); 9:1; 7; 9(3);
10(2); 11; 12; 14; 15; 16; 17; 20(2); 22(2); 24(2); 25(2); 26; 27;
28; 31(3); 33(2); 34(2); 35(2); 36; 42; 43; 44; 45; 46; 47; 48; 50;
10:1(3); 2; 5; 6(2); 10(2); 14(2); 15; 17; 19; 21(2); 23; 24(2);
25(2); 29; 30; 31; 32(2); 33(4); 34; 35; 37; 38(2); 39(2); 41; 42;
44; 45; 46(2); 48; 49; 51; 52; 11:1; 2; 3; 4(2); 5; 7; 8(3); 9(2);
10(4); 11(3); 12; 13; 15(5); 16; 17; 18(2); 19; 20(3); 21; 23;
27(4); 30; 32; 12:1; 2(5); 4; 7(2); 8; 9(4); 10(4); 11; 12(2); 13(2);
14(2); 17(2); 18; 20; 21(2); 22(2); 23(2); 24(2); 25(2); 26(6);
27(4); 28(2); 29(3); 30(2); 31; 32(2); 33(4); 34; 35(3); 36(2); 37;
38(2); 39(3); 41(3); 43; 13:1; 3(2); 4; 7; 8; 9; 10; 11; 12(4); 13(2);
14(3); 15(2); 16; 18; 19(2); 20(3); 22; 24(2); 25(2); 26(2); 27(4);
28; 29; 32(3); 33; 34(2); 35(4); 14:1(4); 2(2); 3(3); 4; 5; 7; 8; 9;
10(2); 12(3); 13; 14(5); 16(2); 17(2); 20(2); 21(2); 23; 24; 25(3);
26; 27(2); 30; 31; 35(2); 38(2); 39; 41(4); 43(4); 47; 49(2); 51;
52; 53(4); 54(4); 55(2); 60(2); 61(4); 62(3); 63; 64; 65(2); 66(3);
68(2); 72(4); 15:1(4); 2(2); 3; 7; 8; 9(2); 10; 11(2); 12(2); 14; 15;
16(3); 18; 19; 20; 21(2); 22(2); 25; 26(3); 27(2); 28(2); 29; 30;
31(2); 32(2); 33(3); 34; 37; 38(4); 39(3); 40(2); 42(4); 43(2); 44;
45(2); 46(3); 47; 16:1(2); 2(6); 3(3); 4; 5(2); 6; 8; 9(2); 12; 13;
14; 15(2); 18; 19(2); 20(2); **Lk** 1:2(2); 3; 4; 5(4); 6(2); 8(2); 9(4);
10(3); 11(3); 13; 15(3); 16(2); 17(8); 18; 19(2); 20; 21(2); 22;
23; 25(2); 26(2); 27(2); 28(2); 30; 32(4); 33; 34; 35(5); 36; 38(3);
39; 40; 41(3); 42; 43; 44(2); 45; 46; 48; 51(2); 52; 53(2); 58;
59(3); 65; 66(2); 67; 68; 69; 70(2); 71; 72; 73; 74; 75; 76(4); 77;
78(2); 79(2); 80(3); 2:1; 4(3); 6; 7; 8(2); 9(4); 10; 11(2); 12; 13(2);
14; 15(3); 16; 17; 18; 20(2); 21(4); 22(3); 23(4); 24(2); 25(3);
26(2); 27(6); 31; 32(2); 34; 35; 36(2); 37; 38; 39(2); 40(2); 41(2);
42(2); 43(2); 44; 46(3); 50; 3:1(4); 2(4); 3(3); 4(7); 5(2); 6; 7(2);
9(4); 10; 14; 15(2); 16(2); 17(2); 18; 19(2); 21(2); 22; 23(2);
24(5); 25(5); 26(5); 27(5); 28(5); 29(5); 30(5); 31(5); 32(5); 33(5);
34(5); 35(5); 36(5); 37(5); 38(4); 4:1(3); 2; 3(2); 5(3); 6(2); 8;
9(2); 12; 13(2); 14(3); 16(2); 17(4); 18(7); 19(2); 20(4); 22; 25(3);
27(3); 28; 29(3); 30; 31; 33; 34; 35(2); 36; 37(2); 38; 39; 40; 41;
42; 43; 44; 5:1(3); 2(2); 3(4); 4; 5(2); 7(2); 9(2); 10; 13; 14; 15;
16; 17(3); 19(4); 21(2); 24(3); 27; 32; 33(3); 34(3); 35(2); 36(4);
37(3); 39; 6:1(4); 2(2); 4(3); 5(2); 6; 7(2); 8(3); 9; 10(2); 15;
16(2); 17(3); 19; 20; 22; 23(2); 26; 29(2); 33; 35(4); 38; 39(3);
40; 41(2); 42(4); 45(4); 46; 48(3); 49(3); 7:1(2); 3(2); 6(2); 9;
10(2); 11; 12(4); 13; 14; 17; 18; 20; 22(7); 24(4); 28(2); 29(3);
30(2); 31(2); 32; 33; 34; 36(2); 37(2); 38(2); 39; 41(2); 44(2);
45; 47; 50; 8:1(3); 3; 5(3); 7; 10(2); 11(3); 12(3); 13(2); 15(2);
16; 19; 21; 22(2); 23; 24(3); 25; 26(2); 27(2); 29(5); 31; 32;
33(5); 34(2); 35(3); 36; 37(4); 38(2); 39; 40; 41; 42; 44; 45;
47(2); 49(3); 51(4); 54; 9:2(2); 5; 6(2); 7(2); 8; 10(2); 11(2);
12(4); 16(4); 18; 19(2); 20; 22(3); 24; 25; 26(2); 27; 29; 32; 34;
35; 36; 37(2); 38; 42(3); 43; 44(2); 47; 48; 51; 52; 56; 57; 58(2);
60(2); 62(2); 10:1; 2(4); 4; 6; 7(2); 9(2); 10(2); 11(2); 13; 14;
17(2); 19(2); 20; 21; 22(5); 23(2); 26; 27; 31; 32(2); 35(2); 36;

11:7; 13; 14(3); 15(2); 20(2); 24; 26(2); 27(3); 28; 29(3); 30(2);
31(7); 32(3); 33; 34(3); 35; 36(2); 38; 39(4); 42(2); 43(3); 44;
45; 46; 47(2); 48; 49; 50(4); 51(4); 52; 53(2); 12:1(3); 3(3); 4; 7;
8(2); 9; 10(2); 11; 12(2); 13(2); 15(2); 16; 22; 23(2); 24(2); 26;
27; 28(3); 30(2); 31; 32; 33; 36; 37; 38(2); 39(3); 40; 42; 45;
46(2); 48; 49; 53(10); 54(2); 55; 56(3); 58(6); 59; 13:1; 2; 4; 7(2);
10(2); 14(5); 15(3); 16; 17(2); 18; 19(3); 20; 21; 22; 24; 25(4);
28(2); 29(5); 31(2); 32; 33; 34; 35(3); 14:1(3); 2; 3(2); 5; 7; 8; 9;
10(2); 13(4); 14(2); 15; 18; 21(8); 22; 23(3); 28; 29; 32; 34;
35(2); 15:1; 2; 4(2); 8; 9; 10(2); 12(2); 13; 16(2); 21; 22(2); 23;
25(2); 26; 27; 30; 16:1; 3(2); 4; 5; 8(4); 9; 10; 11(2); 13(4); 14;
15; 16(3); 17; 21(3); 22(3); 24; 29; 30; 31(2); 17:1; 2; 5(2); 6(3);
7; 9; 11; 14; 17; 20(3); 21; 22(4); 24(4); 26(3); 27(3); 28; 29;
30(2); 31(3); 34(2); 35(2); 36(3); 37(2); 18:6(2); 8(2); 10(3); 11;
12; 13; 14; 16; 17; 20; 22; 24; 25; 27; 29; 30; 31(3); 32; 33; 34;
35; 36; 39; 43; 19:2(2); 3; 5; 8(3); 10; 11; 15(2); 16; 18; 23; 24;
29(2); 30(2); 31; 33(3); 34; 35; 36; 37(5); 38(4); 39(2); 40; 41;
42; 43; 44(2); 45; 46; 47(5); 48; 20:1(6); 4; 6; 9; 10(5); 13(2);
14(3); 15(3); 16; 17(5); 19(4); 20(2); 21(2); 25(2); 26; 27; 29;
30; 31(2); 32; 33; 34; 35(2); 36(4); 37(6); 38(2); 39; 42(2); 45(2);
46(5); 47; 21:1(2); 4(2); 5; 6(2); 8; 9; 12; 20; 21(3); 22; 23; 24(5);
25(6); 26(2); 27; 29(2); 31; 35(2); 36; 37(4); 38(3); 22:1(2); 2(2);
3(2); 4; 6(2); 7(2); 8; 10(2); 11(5); 13; 14(2); 16; 17; 18(3); 20(2);
21(2); 22; 24; 25(2); 26; 30; 31; 34; 37(2); 39; 40; 44; 47; 48;
49; 50(2); 52(3); 53(2); 54; 55(2); 56; 59; 60; 61(4); 63; 64;
66(4); 67; 69(3); 70; 23:1; 2; 3(2); 4(2); 5(2); 6; 10; 12; 13(3);
14; 17; 19; 22; 23(2); 26(2); 29(5); 30(2); 31; 33(5); 35(3); 36;
37(2); 38(2); 39; 40(2); 41; 44(3); 45(4); 46; 47; 48(2); 49; 51(4);
52; 54(2); 55(2); 56(2); 24:1(5); 2(2); 3(2); 5(3); 7(3); 9(3); 10(2);
12(2); 18(2); 19; 20; 21; 22; 24(2); 25; 27(3); 28; 29; 32(2); 33(2);
34; 35; 36; 44(4); 45; 46(2); 49(2); 53; **Jn** 1:1(4); 2(2); 4(2); 5(2);
7(2); 9(2); 10(3); 12; 13(3); 14(4); 17; 18(3); 19(2); 20; 23(5);
24; 29(4); 32; 33(4); 34; 35; 36; 37; 39; 40; 41(2); 42; 43; 44;
45(3); 48; 49(2); 50; 51(2); 2:1(2); 2; 3; 5; 6(3); 7(2); 8(2); 9(8);
10(2); 13; 14(2); 15(5); 17; 18; 20; 21; 22(3); 23(3); 3:1(2); 2; 3;
4; 5(2); 6(2); 8(3); 13; 14(3); 16; 17(3); 18(2); 19(2); 20(2); 21;
22; 25; 26; 28; 29(5); 31(2); 34(2); 35(2); 36(3); 4:1(2); 5; 6(2);
8; 9(3); 10; 11(2); 12; 14(2); 15; 17; 19; 20; 21(2); 22; 23(4); 25;
27; 28(3); 29; 30; 31; 33; 34; 35; 39(3); 40; 42(4); 45(4); 46; 47;
49; 50(2); 52(3); 53(3); 54; 5:1; 2(2); 3(2); 4(4); 7(3); 9(3); 10(2);
11; 14; 15(2); 16(2); 18(3); 19(3); 20(2); 21(3); 22(2); 23(4);
25(4); 26(2); 27; 28(3); 29(2); 30(2); 32; 33; 36(4); 37; 39; 42;
44; 45; 6:1(2); 4(2); 10(3); 11(4); 12; 13(2); 14(2); 16; 17; 18;
19(2); 21(3); 22(5); 23(2); 24; 25(2); 26(2); 27(3); 28; 29; 31;
32; 33(2); 35; 37; 38; 39(2); 40(3); 41(2); 42; 44(2); 45(2); 46(2);
49; 50; 51(4); 52; 53(2); 54; 57(2); 59; 62; 63(3); 64; 67; 68;
69(2); 71(2); 7:1; 2; 3; 4; 7(2); 10; 11(2); 12(2); 13; 14(3); 15;
17; 18; 19(2); 20; 22(2); 23(3); 24; 26(2); 28; 31; 32(4); 35(4);
37(2); 38; 39(2); 40(2); 41; 42(3); 43; 45(2); 46; 47; 48(2); 49;
8:1(2); 2(3); 3(2); 4; 5; 6; 8; 9(4); 10; 12(3); 13; 15; 16; 17; 18;
20(2); 22; 25(2); 26; 27; 28; 29; 32(2); 34; 35(3); 36; 39; 40; 41;
44(5); 45; 46; 48; 52(2); 53; 57; 59(2); 9:3; 4(2); 5(3); 6(5); 7; 8;
11; 13; 14(2); 15; 16(2); 17; 18(2); 22(3); 24(2); 30; 32(2); 35;
40; 10:1(3); 2(3); 3(2); 4; 5; 7(2); 8; 9; 10; 11(3); 12(6); 13(2);
14; 15(3); 19; 21(3); 22(2); 23; 24(2); 25; 31; 33; 35(2); 36(3);
37; 38(2); 40; 11:1; 2; 4(2); 6; 8; 9(3); 10; 15; 17; 19; 20; 24(2);
25(2); 27(3); 28; 30; 31(3); 33(2); 36; 37(2); 38; 39(2); 40; 41(3);
42; 45(2); 46; 47(2); 48; 49; 50(2); 52; 54(2); 55(3); 56(2); 57(2);
12:1(2); 2; 3(4); 5; 6(2); 7; 8; 9(2); 10; 11; 12(2); 13(3); 16; 17(2);
18; 19(2); 20; 21; 23(2); 24; 29; 31(2); 32; 34(3); 35(2); 36(2);
38(4); 42(3); 43(2); 46; 47(2); 48(3); 49; 50; 13:1(5); 2(2); 3;
5(2); 16; 18; 22; 26(2); 27; 28; 29(3); 30; 31; 33; 38; 14:4; 5;
6(4); 8; 9(2); 10(5); 11(3); 12; 13(2); 16; 17(2); 19; 22; 24(2);
26(3); 27; 28; 30; 31(3); 15:1(2); 3; 4(2); 5(3); 6; 9; 15; 16; 18;
19(5); 20(2); 24; 25; 26(4); 27; 16:2(2); 3; 4(2); 7(2); 8; 11; 13;
15; 16; 17; 20; 21(3); 23; 25(2); 26; 27; 28(4); 32(2); 33(2); 17:1;
3; 4(2); 5(2); 6(2); 8; 9; 11(2); 12(3); 13; 14(3); 15(2); 16(2);
18(2); 19; 21; 22; 23; 24(2); 25; 26; 18:1(2); 2; 3; 6; 9; 10(2);
11(2); 12(3); 13; 14(2); 15(3); 16(3); 17(2); 18; 19; 20(4); 22(3);
23; 24; 26(3); 27; 28(3); 31; 32; 33(3); 35; 36; 37(3); 38; 39(3);
19:2; 3; 5(3); 6; 7(2); 8; 9; 11; 12; 13(3); 14(4); 15; 17(2); 18;
19(4); 20(3); 21(5); 23(3); 24(2); 25(2); 26; 27; 28; 30(2); 31(5);
32(4); 34; 36; 38(3); 39; 40(4); 41(2); 42(2); 20:1(5); 2(3); 3;
4(2); 5; 6(2); 7(2); 8; 9(2); 10; 11(2); 12(5); 15; 18(2); 19(7);
20(2); 22; 24; 25(6); 26(2); 30; 31(2); 21:1(2); 2; 4(3); 6(4); 7(3);
8(2); 10; 11(2); 12(2); 14(2); 16; 17(2); 20; 23; 24; 25(3); **Acts**
1:1; 2(3); 3(2); 4(2); 5; 6; 7(3); 8(3); 12; 13(2); 14(2); 15(3);
16(2); 18(2); 19(2); 20; 21(2); 22; 24; 26(2); 2:1; 2; 4(2); 6; 9;
10; 11; 14; 15(2); 16; 17; 19; 20(3); 21(2); 22; 23; 24; 25; 28;
29; 30(2); 31; 33(4); 34(2); 36; 37(2); 38(4); 39(2); 41; 42; 43;
46; 47(3); 3:1(3); 2(3); 3; 6; 7; 8; 9; 10(2); 11(3); 12; 13(3); 14(2);
15(2); 16(2); 18; 19(3); 21(4); 22(2); 23; 24; 25(5); 4:1(5); 2(3);
3; 4(3); 5; 6(3); 7; 8(2); 9(2); 10(3); 11(3); 13; 14; 15; 17; 18;
19; 20; 21; 22; 23; 24; 25(3); 26(4); 27(2); 30; 31(3); 32(2);
33(3); 34(2); 35; 36(3); 37(2); 5:2(2); 3(3); 5; 6; 7; 8; 9(4); 10(2);
11; 12(3); 13(2); 14(2); 15(4); 16; 17(3); 18(2); 19(3); 20(3);
21(7); 22(2); 23(3); 24(4); 25(3); 26(3); 27(2); 29; 30; 32; 33;
34(4); 37(2); 40(2); 41(2); 42; 6:1(5); 2(4); 3; 4(2); 5(3); 6; 7(5);
8; 9(3); 10(2); 12(4); 13; 14; 15(2); 7:1; 2; 3; 4(2); 7; 8(3); 9; 10;
11; 13; 16(3); 17(3); 19(2); 22(2); 23; 24; 26; 28; 29; 30(2); 31(3);
32(4); 33(2); 34; 35(4); 36(3); 37(2); 38(5); 40; 41(2); 42(5);
43(2); 44(3); 45(4); 46; 48(2); 49(2); 51; 52(4); 53(2); 54; 55(3);
56(3); 58(2); 8:1(3); 3; 4; 5; 6(2); 9(2); 10(3); 12(3); 13; 14(2);
15; 16(2); 17; 18(2); 19; 20; 21; 22; 23(2); 24; 25(4); 26(4);
27(2); 28; 29; 30; 32(3); 33; 34(2); 35; 36; 37; 38(3); 39(4); 40;
9:1(3); 2; 4; 5(2); 6(2); 7; 8(2); 10; 11(3); 14; 15(3); 17(4); 19;
20(2); 21; 22(2); 23; 24; 25(2); 26; 27(4); 29(3); 30; 31(5); 32;
33; 35; 38; 39(3); 40; 41; 42; 10:1(2); 2; 3(2); 6; 7; 9(4); 11(2);
12(2); 15(2); 16; 17(2); 19(2); 21(2); 22(3); 23; 24; 30; 31; 32(2);
36(2); 37; 38(2); 39(2); 40; 41(2); 42(2); 43; 44(2); 45(4); 47;
48(2); 11:1(3); 2; 4(2); 5; 6(3); 9; 11; 12(2); 15(2); 16(3); 17(2);
18; 19(3); 20(2); 21(3); 22(2); 23(2); 24(2); 26(2); 28(3); 29(2);
30(2); 12:1(2); 2(2); 3(2); 4; 5; 6(4); 7(4); 8; 9; 10(5); 11(5);
12(3); 13(2); 14(2); 16; 17(4); 18; 19; 20(2); 22(2); 23(4); 24;
13:1(2); 2(3); 4; 5(3); 6; 7(3); 8(3); 9; 10(3); 11(4); 12(3); 14(2);
15(6); 17(3); 18(2); 19; 20(2); 21(3); 22; 24(2); 26(2); 27(2); 29;
30; 31; 32(2); 33(2); 34(2); 36; 38; 39; 40; 42(4); 43(3); 44(3);
45(2); 46(2); 47(4); 48(3); 49(3); 50(4); 51; 52(2); 14:1(4); 2(3);

3(2); 4(4); 5(2); 6; 7; 9; 11(4); 12; 13(3); 14(2); 15(2); 18; 19(2);
20(3); 21; 22(4); 23; 25; 26(2); 27(3); 28; 15:1(2); 2; 3(4); 4(2);
5(3); 6; 7(3); 8(2); 10(2); 11(2); 12(2); 14(2); 15(2); 16(2); 17(4);
18(2); 19; 21; 22(3); 23(3); 24; 26; 27; 28; 30(2); 31; 32; 33(2);
35(2); 36(2); 38; 39(2); 40(2); 41; 16:1; 2; 3; 4(3); 5(2); 6(3); 7;
9; 10(3); 11; 12; 13(3); 14(3); 15; 17(4); 18(3); 19(3); 20; 22(2);
23; 24(2); 25; 26(3); 27(4); 31; 32(2); 33(2); 35(2); 36(3); 38(2);
39; 40(3); 17:1; 2; 3; 4(2); 5(5); 6(3); 7; 8(3); 9; 10(3); 11(2);
13(3); 14(2); 16; 17(4); 18(3); 21; 22; 23; 24; 26(4); 27; 29(2); 30;
31(3); 32(2); 34(2); 18:3; 4(3); 5(2); 6; 7; 8(4); 9(2); 11; 12(3);
13; 14; 16; 17(4); 18; 19(2); 22; 23(2); 24; 25(6); 26(2); 27(2);
28(2); 19:1; 2; 4(2); 5(2); 6; 7; 8(4); 9(3); 10(3); 11; 12(3); 13(3);
14; 15; 16(2); 17(3); 19; 20; 21; 23; 24; 25; 27(3); 28; 29(2);
30(2); 31(2); 32(2); 33(4); 34(2); 35(6); 38(2); 41; 20:1(2); 3; 4;
6; 7(4); 8; 9; 12; 15(3); 16(2); 17(2); 18; 19(3); 21(2); 22(2); 23;
24(4); 25; 26; 27; 28(4); 29; 31; 32; 35(3); 38(2); 21:1; 3(2); 4;
5(2); 7; 8(4); 9; 11(5); 13(2); 14(2); 16; 17; 18(2); 19; 20(2);
21(3); 22; 24; 25; 26(5); 27(4); 28(4); 29(2); 30(4); 31(2); 32(2);
33; 34(4); 35(4); 36(2); 37(2); 38; 39; 40(4); 22:2(2); 3(4); 4;
5(4); 7; 9(2); 10; 11(2); 12(2); 13; 14(2); 16(2); 17; 20(2); 21;
22; 23; 24(2); 25; 26(2); 27; 28; 29; 30(4); 23:1; 2(2); 3(2); 5(2);
6(6); 7(3); 8(2); 9(2); 10(3); 11(2); 12; 14; 15(2); 16; 17(2); 18(2);
19(2); 20(2); 22(2); 23(2); 24; 26; 27; 28; 30(2); 31; 32(3); 33(2);
34(2); 24:1(3); 5(4); 6; 7; 9; 10(2); 12(4); 13; 14(4); 15(2); 18;
20; 21(2); 22(2); 24; 26; 27; 25:1; 2(3); 3; 6(2); 7; 8(3); 9; 10;
12; 14; 15(3); 16(4); 17(3); 18; 21; 22; 23(4); 24(2); 27; 26:1;
2(2); 3; 4(2); 5(2); 6(2); 7; 8; 9; 10(2); 12; 13(3); 14(3); 16; 17(2);
18; 19; 20(2); 21(2); 22; 23(4); 25; 26; 27; 30(2); 27:2; 3; 4; 5;
6; 7; 8(2); 9; 10; 11(4); 12(3); 13; 15(2); 16; 17(2); 18(2); 19(3);
21; 22; 23; 27(2); 29(2); 30(5); 31(3); 32(3); 33(2); 34; 37; 38(3);
39(3); 40(5); 41(5); 42(2); 43(2); 44(2); 28:1; 2(3); 3(2); 4(3); 5(2);
7(3); 8; 9; 11; 13(2); 15(2); 16(4); 17(5); 19; 20; 21; 23(3); 24;
25(2); 27; 28(2); 29; 31(2); **Rom** 1:1; 2; 3(2); 4(4); 5; 6; 7; 8; 9;
10; 11; 12; 14(4); 15; 16(4); 17(2); 18(2); 20(4); 23(2); 24; 25(3);
26; 27(3); 32(2); 2:1; 2; 3(2); 4(2); 5(2); 8; 9(2); 10(2); 12(2);
13(4); 14(5); 15(3); 16(2); 17; 18(2); 19; 20(4); 23(2); 24(2);
25(2); 26(3); 27(3); 28; 29(3); 3:1; 2; 3; 5; 6; 7; 12; 13; 17; 19(3);
20(4); 21(4); 22; 23; 24; 25(2); 26; 27; 28(2); 29(4); 30; 31(2);
4:1; 3; 4; 5; 6(2); 8(2); 9(2); 11(4); 12(3); 13(5); 14(2); 15; 16(6);
17; 18; 19; 20; 24; 5:2; 5(2); 6; 10; 11; 12; 13(2); 14(2); 15(5);
16(3); 17; 18(3); 19; 20(2); 6:4(3); 5(2); 6; 9; 12; 13; 14; 15;
17(2); 18; 19(2); 20; 21; 22; 23(2); 7:1(2); 2(4); 4(3); 5(3); 6(3);
7(3); 8(2); 9(2); 10; 11; 12(2); 13; 14; 16; 19(2); 22(2); 23(2);
24; 25(4); 8:1(2); 2(4); 3(4); 4(4); 5(6); 7(2); 8; 9(4); 10(2); 11(3);
12(2); 13(4); 14(2); 15(2); 16(2); 18(2); 19(4); 20(3); 21(4); 22;
23(4); 26(2); 27(5); 28; 29(2); 33; 34; 35; 36(2); 39; 9:1(2); 3;
4(7); 5(2); 6; 7; 8(6); 9; 11(2); 12(2); 17(2); 20; 21(3); 22; 23(2);
24(2); 26(3); 27(4); 28(3); 29; 30(2); 31(2); 32(2); 10:3; 4(2);
5(3); 6; 7(2); 8(2); 9(2); 10(2); 11; 12(3); 13(2); 15(2); 16; 17;
18(3); 11:1(2); 2; 4(3); 5; 7(2); 8; 11; 12(6); 13(2); 15(5); 16(4);
17(3); 18(3); 19; 21; 22; 24(2); 25(2); 26; 28(3); 29; 33(3); 34(2);
12:1; 2; 3(2); 4; 6(2); 11; 13; 16; 17; 19; 13:1(2); 2(2); 3(3); 4(3);
8; 10(2); 11; 12(4); 13; 14(3); 14:1; 6(6); 8(3); 9; 10; 11; 14;
17(2); 19; 20; 15:1(2); 3; 4; 5; 6; 7; 8(4); 9(2); 11; 12(2); 13(3);
15(2); 16(6); 18; 19(3); 20; 25; 26; 27; 29(3); 30(3); 31; 32; 33;
16:1; 2; 4(2); 5(2); 7; 8; 11(2); 12(3); 13; 14; 15; 16; 17; 18(2);
20(2); 22; 23(3); 24; 25(4); 26(5); S:1(2); **1Cor** 1:1; 2(2); 3; 4;
6; 7; 8(2); 9; 10(4); 11; 13; 16; 17(2); 18(3); 19(4); 20(4); 21(3);
22(2); 23(2); 24(2); 25(2); 26; 27(6); 28; 31; 2:1; 4; 5(2); 6(2);
7(3); 8(2); 9(2); 10(2); 11(4); 12(4); 13(2); 14(3); 16(3); 3:5; 6;
7; 10(2); 13(2); 16(2); 17(2); 19(2); 20(3); 22; 4:1(2); 4; 5(5);
9(2); 13(3); 15; 17; 19(3); 20; 21; 5:1; 4(2); 5(5); 6; 7; 8(3); 10(3);
6:1(2); 2(4); 4; 6; 9(2); 10; 11(3); 12; 13(6); 14; 15(3); 17; 18;
19(2); 7:1; 3(4); 4(4); 5; 8; 10(3); 11; 12(2); 13; 14(4); 15; 17;
19(2); 20; 22(2); 23; 25(2); 26; 28; 29; 31; 32(3); 33(2); 34(5);
35; 36; 39(3); 40; 8:3; 4(2); 6; 7; 8(2); 10(2); 11; 12; 13; 9:1;
2(2); 5(2); 7(3); 8(2); 9(4); 12; 13(4); 14(3); 16(2); 17; 18(3); 19;
20(5); 21; 22(2); 23; 24; 25; 26; 10:1(2); 2(2); 3; 4; 5; 6; 7; 10;
11(2); 13; 16(6); 18(3); 19; 20(2); 21(5); 22; 25; 26(3); 28(3);
29; 31; 32(3); 33; 11:2; 3(5); 6; 7(4); 8(4); 9(4); 10(2); 11(5);
12(4); 16; 17(2); 18; 20; 22; 23(3); 25(3); 26; 27(3); 29; 32(2);
34; 12:3(3); 4; 5; 6; 7(2); 8(4); 9(3); 10(2); 11; 12(2); 14; 15(4);
16(4); 17(4); 18(2); 19; 21(4); 22; 23; 24; 25(3); 26(2); 27; 28;
30; 31; 13:1; 2; 3; 6; 13; 14:2; 4; 5; 7; 8(2); 9(2); 10; 11(2); 12(2);
15(4); 16(3); 17; 19; 21(2); 23; 25; 27; 28; 29(2); 30; 32(3); 33(2);
34(2); 35; 36; 37(3); 15:1; 3; 4(2); 5; 6; 7; 9(3); 10(2); 12(2); 13;
15; 16; 20(2); 21(2); 23; 24(3); 26; 28; 29(3); 32(2); 34; 35; 39;
40(4); 41(3); 42(2); 45(2); 47(4); 48(2); 49(4); 50; 52(4); 54;
56(3); 57; 58(3); 16:1(3); 2(2); 7(2); 10(2); 11; 12; 13; 15(4); 17;
19(3); 20; 21; 22; 23; S:1(2); **2Cor** 1:1(3); 2; 3(3); 4; 5; 6(2);
7(2); 9(2); 11(2); 12(3); 13; 14(2); 17(2); 19; 20(2); 22(2); 2:2;
3; 4; 9; 10; 12; 14; 16(4); 17(2); 3:3(4); 6(5); 7(4); 8(2); 9(2); 10;
13(2); 14(3); 15; 16(2); 17(3); 18(5); 4:2(4); 4(5); 5; 6(5); 7(2);
10(4); 11; 13; 14; 15(3); 16; 18(4); 5:1; 5(3); 6(2); 8(2); 10(2);
11(2); 14; 16(2); 18; 19(2); 21; 6:1; 2(3); 3; 4; 6; 7(5); 13; 16(3);
17(2); 18; 7:1(2); 6; 7(2); 8; 10(2); 12(2); 13(2); 15; 8:1(2); 2(2);
4(4); 5(2); 6; 8(2); 9; 11; 16(2); 17; 18(3); 19(3); 21(3); 22; 23(3);
24(2); 9:1(2); 2; 3; 5(2); 9; 10(2); 12(3); 13(2); 14; 10:1; 2; 3(2);
4(2); 5(2); 7; 8; 12; 13(2); 14; 16(2); 17; 18; 11:3(2); 5; 7; 9;
10(2); 13; 15; 17; 18; 20; 22; 24; 25; 26(4); 28(2); 30; 31; 32(4);
33; 12:1; 2(3); 3(2); 6; 7(4); 8; 9; 11; 12; 14(5); 15(2); 18(2); 21;
13:1(2); 2; 4(2); 5; 8(2); 10(2); 11; 13; 14(5); S:1(2); **Gal** 1:1(2);
2(2); 3; 4; 6; 7; 10; 11; 12; 13(2); 14(2); 16; 19(2); 20; 21; 22;
23; 2:2; 5(2); 7(4); 8(4); 9(4); 10(2); 11; 12(2); 13; 14(6); 15;
16(8); 17; 18; 19(2); 20(4); 21(2); 3:1; 2(4); 3(2); 5(4); 7(2); 8(3);
10(5); 11(3); 12(2); 13(2); 14(4); 15; 16; 17(3); 18(2); 19(4);
21(3); 22(2); 23(2); 24; 26; 29; 4:1; 2(2); 3(2); 4(3); 5(2); 6; 9;
13(3); 15; 16; 21(2); 22(2); 23(3); 24(3); 26; 27; 28; 29(2); 30(6);
31(2); 5:1(2); 3; 4; 5(2); 7; 9; 10; 11(2); 13; 14; 16(3); 17(7);
18(2); 19(2); 21(2); 22(2); 24(2); 25(2); 6:1; 2; 6; 8(3); 10; 12(2);
13; 14(3); 16; 17(2); 18; S:1; **Eph** 1:1(3); 2; 3; 4(2); 5(2); 6(3);
7(2); 9; 10(2); 11(2); 12; 13(2); 14(4); 15(2); 17(4); 18(5); 19(2);
20(2); 22(2); 23; 2:2(6); 3(5); 7(2); 8; 11(3); 12(3); 13; 14; 15(2);
16(2); 18; 19(2); 20(3); 21(2); 22; 3:1; 2(2); 3; 4; 5(2); 6(3);
7(3); 8(3); 9(4); 10(4); 11; 12; 14; 15; 16(2); 18; 19(2); 20;
21; 4:1(3); 3(3); 7(2); 9(2); 10; 12(6); 13(7); 14; 15(2); 16(5);
17(2); 18(4); 21; 22(3); 23; 24; 26; 27; 28; 29(2); 30(2); 5:5; 6(2);
8; 9(2); 10; 11; 13; 14; 16(2); 17(2); 18; 19; 20(2); 21; 22; 23(7);

24(2); 25; 26(2); 29(2); 32; 33; 6:1; 2; 3; 4(2); 5; 6(3); 7; 8(2); 9; 10(2); 11(3); 12(2); 13(2); 14; 15(2); 16(3); 17(4); 18; 19(2); 21; 22; 23(3); S:1; **Phil** 1:1(3); 2; 5(2); 6; 7(2); 8; 10; 11(2); 12(3); 13; 14(3); 16; 17(3); 19(2); 22(2); 24; 27(3); 29; 30; 2:1; 2; 4; 6; 7(2); 8(2); 10(2); 11(2); 15(3); 16(2); 17; 18; 19; 21; 22(3); 24; 28(2); 29; 30; 3:1(2); 2; 3(3); 4(2); 5(5); 6(3); 8(3); 9(3); 10(2); 11(2); 14(3); 16(2); 18(2); 20(2); 21; 4:1; 2(2); 3(2); 4; 5; 7; 9; 10(2); 15(2); 18; 21; 22; 23; S:1; **Col** 1:1; 2(2); 3; 4(2); 5(4); 6(3); 8; 9(2); 10(2); 12(3); 13(2); 14; 15(3); 18(7); 19; 20; 22; 23(3); 24(2); 25(2); 26; 27(4); 2:1; 2(4); 3; 5(3); 6; 7; 8(3); 9(2); 10; 11(5); 12(3); 13; 14(2); 16(2); 17; 19(3); 20(3); 22(2); 23(3); 3:1; 2; 5; 6(2); 7; 9; 10(2); 12; 14; 15(2); 16(2); 17(3); 18; 20; 22; 23; 24(4); 25; 4:2; 3; 5; 7; 8; 11(2); 12; 14; 15(2); 16(3); 17(2); 18(2); S:1; **1Th** 1:1(5); 3; 5; 6(3); 8(2); 9; 10(2); 2:2; 4; 6; 8; 9; 13(3); 14(2); 15; 16(3); 17; 19; 3:2; 5; 8; 9; 12; 13(2); 4:1; 2; 3; 5(2); 6(2); 10; 15(4); 16(5); 17(4); 5:1(2); 2(3); 5(4); 7(2); 8(3); 12; 14(2); 18; 19; 23(2); 26; 27(2); 28; S:1(2); **2Th** 1:1(3); 2; 3; 4; 5(2); 7; 8; 9(3); 11(2); 12(3); 2:1; 2; 3; 4; 7(2); 8(3); 9; 10(2); 12; 13(4); 14(2); 15; 3:1(2); 3; 4(2); 5(3); 6(2); 16(2); 17(2); 18; S:1(2); **1Ti** 1:1; 2; 5(2); 7; 8; 9(3); 11(2); 12; 14; 15; 17(2); 18; 2:3; 4(2); 5; 7(2); 11; 12; 14(2); 3:1; 2; 5; 6(2); 7(2); 8; 9(2); 10; 12(2); 13(2); 15(5); 16(5); 4:1(3); 3; 5; 6(2); 8; 10(2); 12; 14(4); 16; 5:1; 2(2); 8; 9(2); 10(2); 11; 14(3); 16; 17(2); 18(4); 21(2); 25; 6:1(2); 2; 3(2); 5; 10(3); 12; 13; 14; 15(2); 16; 17; 19; 21; S:1(2); **2Ti** 1:1(2); 2; 5; 6(2); 7; 8(4); 9; 10(2); 11; 12; 13; 14; 16(2); 18(2); 2:1; 2(2); 4; 6(2); 7; 8(2); 9; 10(2); 14(3); 15; 18(3); 19(3); 21; 22; 24(2); 25(2); 26(2); 3:1; 5; 7(2); 8(2); 11; 14; 15; 17; 4:1(3); 2; 3; 4; 5; 6; 7; 8(2); 11; 13(3); 14(2); 17(5); 18; 19; 21; 22; S:1(5); **Titus** 1:1(3); 2; 3; 4(3); 5; 6; 7; 9(2); 10; 12; 13; 14; 15; 2:1; 2; 3; 4; 5; 8; 10; 11; 13(2); 3:4; 5(2); 7; 9; 10; 13; 15; S:1(3); **Philem** 1:2; 3; 5; 6(2); 7(2); 9; 13(2); 16(2); 20(2); 25; **Heb** 1:1(2); 2; 3(5); 4; 5; 6(3); 7; 8(2); 9; 10(5); 12; 13; 2:1(2); 2; 3(2); 4; 5(2); 6; 7(2); 9(3); 10; 12(2); 13; 14(4); 16(2); 17(2); 3:1(2); 3(2); 6(4); 7; 8(3); 12; 13; 14(2); 15; 17; 4:2(2); 3(3); 4(2); 9; 11; 12(5); 13; 14(2); 15; 16; 5:2(2); 3; 6; 7; 8; 9; 10; 12(3); 13; 6:1(3); 2(2); 4(2); 5(3); 6; 7(2); 10; 11(3); 12; 15; 16; 17(2); 18; 19(2); 20(2); 7:1(3); 3; 4(3); 5(6); 6; 7(2); 10; 11(5); 12(2); 13; 15; 16(2); 17; 18(2); 19(3); 21(2); 25; 26; 27; 28(5); 8:1(6); 2(3); 4; 5(4); 6; 7; 8(4); 9(5); 10(3); 11(3); 13; 9:1; 2(5); 3(3); 4(6); 5(2); 6(3); 7(4); 8(4); 9(3); 10; 12(2); 13(5); 14(3); 15(6); 16(2); 17; 18; 19(5); 20(2); 21(3); 22; 23(3); 24(4); 25(2); 26(5); 27; 28(2); 10:1(4); 2; 4; 5; 7(2); 8; 9(2); 10(3); 11; 12; 15; 16(2); 19(2); 20; 21; 23; 25(4); 26(2); 27; 29(4); 30(2); 31(2); 32; 34; 36(2); 38; 39(2); 11:1(2); 2; 3(2); 7(4); 9(3); 12(4); 13(2); 17; 19; 21(2); 22(2); 23; 24; 25(2); 26(4); 27(2); 28(3); 29(2); 30; 31(2); 32(2); 33; 34(5); 37; 38(2); 39; 12:1(2); 2(6); 5(3); 6; 7; 9; 11(2); 12(2); 13; 14; 15; 17; 18; 19(3); 20; 21; 22(3); 23(4); 24(3); 26(2); 27; 13:3; 4; 6; 7(3); 8; 9; 10; 11(4); 12(2); 13; 15(2); 17; 19(2); 20(5); 22; 24(2); S:1; **Jas** 1:1(2); 3; 6(2); 7; 9; 10(3); 11(6); 12(3); 17; 18; 20(2); 21; 22; 23; 25(2); 27(3); 2:1(2); 3(2); 5(2); 6(2); 7; 8(2); 9; 10; 11; 12; 16; 19; 21; 23(2); 25(2); 26(2); 3:1; 2(2); 3; 4(2); 5; 6(4); 7; 8; 9(2); 10; 11; 12; 14; 17; 18; 4:4(4); 5(2); 6(2); 7; 10(2); 11(4); 14; 15; 5:3(2); 4(5); 5; 6; 7(6); 8(2); 9(2); 10(3); 11(4); 12; 14(4); 15(3); 16; 17(2); 18(2); 19; 20(2); **1Pet** 1:1; 2(4); 3(3); 5(2); 7(2); 9(2); 10(2); 11(3); 12(4); 13(4); 14; 17(2); 19; 20(2); 21; 22(3); 23; 24(4); 25(4); 2:2(2); 3; 6; 7(5); 8; 9; 10; 11; 12(2); 13(2); 14(2); 15(2); 16; 17(2); 18(2); 24; 25; 3:1(4); 3; 4(4); 5(2); 7(3); 12(5); 15(2); 17; 18(4); 19; 20(3); 21(6); 22; 4:1(3); 2(4); 3(3); 4; 5(2); 6(3); 7; 8; 10(3); 11(2); 12; 14(2); 17(4); 18(3); 19(2); 5:1(3); 2(2); 3; 4; 5(3); 6; 8; 9(3); 10; 12; 13; **2Pet** 1:1; 2; 3; 4(3); 8; 10; 11; 12; 16; 17(2); 18; 19(2); 20; 21(3); 2:1(2); 2; 4; 5(5); 6; 7(2); 9(4); 10(2); 11; 12; 13(2); 15(4); 16(3); 17; 18(2); 19(2); 20(6); 21(2); 22(4); 3:2(5); 3; 4(4); 5(5); 6; 7(4); 8; 9; 10(8); 12(4); 15(2); 16; 17(2); 18; **1Jn** 1:1(2); 2(2); 3; 5; 6; 7(3); 8; 2:1(2); 2(3); 4; 5; 7(4); 8(2); 9; 10; 13(3); 14(3); 15(6); 16(8); 17(3); 18(2); 20; 21(2); 22(3); 23(5); 24(4); 25; 27(2); 3:1(3); 2; 4(3); 8(6); 10(3); 11(2); 13; 14; 16(2); 17; 19; 23; 24; 4:1(2); 2(2); 3(2); 4; 5(3); 6(2); 9(2); 10; 14(4); 15; 16; 17; 5:1; 2; 3; 4(3); 5(2); 6(2); 7(3); 8(3); 9(3); 10(3); 11; 12(2); 13(4); 14; 15; 19; 20(2); **2Jn** 1(4); 2; 3(4); 4; 5; 6(2); 7(2); 9(4); 13; **3Jn** 1(3); 3(3); 5; 6; 7; 8; 9(2); 10(2); 12; 14; **Jude** 1(2); 3(3); 4(2); 5(3); 6(3); 7(2); 8; 9(4); 11(3); 12; 13(2); 14(2); 17(2); 18; 19; 20; 21(2); 23(3); 24; 25; **Rev** 1:1; 2(2); 3(2); 4(2); 5(6); 7; 8(4); 9(4); 10(2); 11(3); 12; 13(5); 15; 16; 17(2); 18; 19(3); 20(8); 2:1(5); 5; 6(2); 7(5); 8(4); 9(2); 10; 11(3); 12(3); 14(2); 15(2); 16; 17(4); 18(3); 19(2); 23(2); 24(2); 26(2); 27; 28; 29(2); 3:1(4); 2; 5(2); 6(2); 7(3); 9; 10(4); 12(4); 13(2); 14(7); 18(2); 20(2); 22(2); 4:1; 2(2); 3; 4(2); 5(3); 6(4); 7(4); 8; 9; 10(3); 5:1(3); 2(2); 3(2); 4; 5(6); 6(7); 7(3); 8(4); 9(2); 10; 11(5); 12; 13(5); 14(2); 6:1(4); 3(2); 4; 5(2); 6(4); 7(3); 8(4); 9(5); 10; 12(3); 13(2); 14; 15(9); 16(5); 17; 7:1(7); 2(6); 3(4); 4(3); 5(3); 6(3); 7(3); 8(3); 9(2); 10(2); 11(5); 13; 14(2); 15(2); 16; 17(3); 8:1(2); 2; 3(4); 4(5); 5(4); 6(2); 7(3); 8(4); 9(5); 10(4); 11(5); 12(10); 13(6); 9:1(4); 2(7); 3(4); 4(3); 5; 7(3); 8(2); 9(2); 11(4); 13(3); 14(4); 15(2); 16(4); 17(5); 18(4); 20(3); 10:1; 2(2); 4(2); 5(3); 6(5); 7(5); 8(6); 9(2); 10(2); 11:1(3); 2(4); 4(4); 6(2); 7(2); 8(2); 9; 10(2); 11; 13(6); 14(2); 15(3); 16; 18(6); 19(2); 12:1(2); 4(5); 6(2); 7(2); 9(4); 10(3); 11(4); 12(4); 13(4); 14(4); 15(3); 16(5); 17(5); 13:1(4); 2(4); 3(2); 4(4); 7; 8(5); 10(5); 11; 12(4); 13(2); 14(7); 15(6); 17(4); 18(3); 14:1; 2(3); 3(5); 4(3); 5; 6(3); 7(3); 8(2); 9(2); 10(8); 11(3); 12(4); 13(3); 14(2); 15(5); 16(3); 17; 18(5); 19(6); 20(5); 15:1(2); 2(5); 3(4); 5(3); 6(3); 7(3); 8(5); 16:1(5); 2(5); 3(4); 4(2); 5(2); 6; 7; 8(2); 9; 10(3); 11; 12(6); 13(6); 14(5); 16; 17(4); 18; 19(6); 20; 21(4); 17:1(4); 2(5); 3(2); 4; 5(3); 6(5); 7(5); 8(7); 9(3); 10; 11(3); 12(2); 13; 14(2); 15(2); 16(3); 17(2); 18(3); 18:1; 2(3); 3(7); 6; 8; 9(3); 10; 11(2); 12; 14; 15(2); 17; 18; 19; 21; 22(2); 23(6); 24(2); 19:1; 2(3); 4(3); 5; 6(4); 7(2); 8(2); 9(3); 10(3); 13; 14; 15(3); 17(5); 18(5); 19(4); 20(4); 21(4); 20:1(2); 2(2); 3(3); 4(4); 5(4); 6(2); 7; 8(6); 9(5); 10(4); 11(2); 12(5); 13(3); 14(2); 15(2); 21:1(2); 2; 3; 4; 5; 6(4); 8(4); 9(5); 10(2); 11; 12(4); 13(4); 14(5); 15(3); 16(8); 17(3); 18(3); 19(7); 20(8); 21(3); 22(3); 23(6); 24(4); 25; 26(2); 27; 22:1(2); 2(8); 3(2); 5(2); 6(3); 7(2); 8(2); 9(2); 10(3); 13(4); 14(3); 16(4); 17(3); 18(3); 19(5); 21

THEE

Gen 3:11(2); 15; 16; 17; 18; 4:7; 12; 6:14; 18(2); 19; 20; 21(3); 7:1; 2; 8:16; 17(2); 12:1(2); 2(2); 3(3); 12(2); 13(2); 13:8(2); 9(2); 15; 17; 15:7(2); 16:2; 5(2); 6; 17:2(2); 4; 5; 6(3); 7(4); 8(2); 9; 10; 16; 18; 19; 20; 21; 18:3; 10; 14; 25(2); 19:5; 9; 17; 21; 22; 20:6(2); 7; 9; 15(2); 16(2); 21:12; 17; 22; 23; 22:2(2); 17; 23:6; 11(3); 13(2); 15; 24:2; 3; 7; 8; 12; 14; 17; 23; 40; 41; 43; 45; 50; 51; 25:30; 26:2; 3(3); 24(2); 28(3); 29(3); 27:3; 4; 7; 8; 10; 19; 21(2); 25; 28; 29(5); 37; 42(2); 45(2); 28:2; 3(3); 4(3); 13; 14; 15(5); 22; 29:18; 19; 25; 27; 30:2; 14; 15; 16; 26(2); 27; 29; 30; 31; 31:3; 12; 13; 16; 27; 32; 35; 38; 39; 41; 42; 44; 48; 49; 50; 51; 52; 32:6; 9; 11; 12; 17(3); 26; 29; 33:5; 10; 11(2); 12; 14; 15; 35:1; 11; 12(2); 37:10; 13; 14; 16; 38:16(2); 17; 18; 25; 29; 39:9; 40:13; 14(2); 19(3); 41:15; 39; 41; 44; 42:37(2); 43:4; 9(2); 29; 44:8; 18; 32; 33; 45:11; 46:3; 4(2); 47:4; 5; 6; 29(2); 48:2; 4(4); 5(2); 9; 20(2); 22; 49:8; 25(2); 50:5; 6; 17(3); **Ex** 2:7(2); 9; 14; 3:10; 12(3); 18; 4:1; 5; 8; 12; 13; 14(2); 16; 18; 23; 5:3; 6:29; 7:1; 2; 15; 16; 8:4; 9(2); 11; 21; 29; 9:15; 16(2); 30; 10:17; 28; 11:8(2); 12:24; 48; 13:5(2); 7(2); 9(2); 11(3); 14; 14:12; 15:7; 11(2); 17; 26(2); 17:5; 6; 18:6; 14; 18(2); 19(2); 22(2); 23; 19:9(3); 24(2); 20:2; 4; 12; 24(2); 21:13; 22:25; 23:5; 7; 15; 20(3); 23(2); 25; 27(2); 28(2); 29(2); 30; 31; 33(2); 24:12; 25:9; 16; 21; 22(3); 40; 26:30; 27:8; 20; 28:1; 29:35; 42; 30:6; 23; 34; 36; 37; 31:6; 11; 32:4; 7; 8; 10; 21; 32; 34(2); 33:2; 3(2); 5(4); 12; 13(2); 14(2); 17; 18; 19(2); 22(2); 34:1; 3; 9; 10; 11(2); 12; 15; 17; 18; 24; 27; **Lev** 9:2; 10:9; 14; 15; 19:13; 19; 33; 21:8; 24:2; 25:6(2); 8(2); 15; 16; 35(2); 36; 39(2); 40(2); 41; 47(2); **Num** 5:19; 20; 21; 6:24(2); 25(2); 26(2); 10:2; 3; 4; 29; 31; 32; 35(2); 11:15; 16; 17(3); 23; 12:11; 13; 14:12; 15; 17; 19; 16:10(2); 18:1(2); 2(4); 4; 7; 8(2); 9; 10; 11(2); 12; 19(4); 19:2; 20:17; 18; 21:7; 8; 29; 22:6; 9; 16(2); 17(2); 20(2); 28; 29; 30; 32; 33; 34; 35; 37(3); 38; 23:3; 11; 13; 26; 27(2); 24:9(2); 10; 11(2); 14; 22; 27:12; 18; **Deut** 1:21(2); 31; 38; 2:7(2); 9; 19; 25(4); 31; 3:25; 26; 27; 4:21; 23; 30; 31(2); 32; 35; 36(3); 37; 38(3); 40(4); 5:6; 8; 12; 15(2); 16(3); 27; 28; 31(2); 6:2; 3(2); 6; 10(2); 12; 15(2); 17; 18; 19; 20; 7:1(2); 2; 4; 6; 11; 12; 13(4); 15(3); 16(2); 19; 20; 22(2); 23; 24; 25; 8:1; 2(3); 3(4); 4; 5; 7; 10; 11; 14; 15(2); 16(4); 18; 9:3(2); 4(2); 5; 6; 12; 14; 10:1(2); 10; 12; 13; 21; 22; 11:29; 12:1; 7; 14; 15; 20; 21(3); 25(2); 28(3); 29; 30; 13:1; 2; 5(3); 6; 7(2); 10(2); 12; 17(3); 18; 14:2; 24(3); 27; 29(2); 15:4(2); 5; 6(3); 7; 9(2); 10; 11; 12(3); 13; 14; 15(2); 16(4); 18(5); 16:1; 4; 5; 9; 10; 15; 17; 18(2); 20; 21(2); 22; 17:2; 4; 8(2); 9; 10(2); 11(3); 14; 15(3); 18:9; 12; 14(2); 15(2); 18; 19:1; 2(2); 3(2); 7(2); 8; 9(2); 10(2); 13; 14; 20:1(2); 11(4); 12(2); 14; 15; 16; 17; 20; 21:1; 23; 22:2(2); 6; 7(2); 12; 23:4(2); 5(2); 9; 13; 14(4); 15; 16; 20; 21(2); 22; 24:4; 11; 13(2); 15(2); 18(2); 19; 22; 25:3; 15; 17; 18(3); 19(2); 26:1; 2; 11; 16; 18(2); 19; 27:2(2); 3(2); 10; 28:1(2); 2(2); 7(3); 8(3); 9(2); 10; 11(2); 12; 13(2); 14; 15(3); 20; 21(2); 22(2); 23; 24; 25; 27; 28; 29; 31; 35; 36(2); 37; 43(2); 44; 45(4); 46; 48(2); 49; 51(2); 52(3); 53(2); 55; 57; 60(2); 61; 64; 65; 66; 68(2); 29:12; 13(3); 30:1(3); 2; 3(3); 4(2); 5(3); 7(2); 8; 9(2); 11(2); 14; 15; 16(2); 31:3(3); 6(3); 8(4); 23; 26; 32:6(3); 7(2); 18(2); 49; 52; 33:10; 27; 29(2); 34:4; **Josh** 1:5(4); 7; 9(2); 17(2); 2:3; 14; 18; 19; 3:7(2); 5:2; 7:10; 13; 19; 25; 8:1; 2; 9:25; 10:8; 13:6; 14:6; 17:15(2); **Judg** 1:3; 24(2); 3:19; 20; 4:6; 7; 9; 14; 19; 20; 22; 5:14; 6:12; 14; 16; 18(3); 23; 39; 7:2; 4(6); 9; 9:31; 32; 33; 10:10; 15(2); 11:8; 17; 19; 24; 27; 36; 12:1(2); 13:4; 15(3); 17; 14:15; 16; 15:2; 12(2); 13(3); 16:5; 6(2); 9; 10; 12; 14; 15; 20; 28(2); 17:2; 3; 10; 18:3; 5; 19; 23; 24; 25; 19:6; 8; 11; 20; **Ruth** 1:10; 16(2); 17; 2:4; 9; 12; 19; 22; 3:1(2); 3(3); 4(2); 11; 13(3); 15; 4:4(3); 8; 12; 14; 15(3); **1Sa** 1:8; 14; 17; 23; 26; 2:2; 15; 20; 34; 36; 3:9; 17(4); 8:7(2); 8; 9:3; 16; 17; 18; 19(2); 20; 23(3); 24(2); 26; 27; 10:1; 2; 3; 4(2); 6; 7(3); 8(3); 15; 11:1; 3; 12:10; 13:13; 14; 14:7(2); 36; 40; 15:1; 16; 17; 18; 23; 25; 26(2); 28; 30; 16:1; 2; 3(2); 15; 16(2); 22; 17:37; 45; 46(3); 18:17; 22(2); 19:2(2); 3(2); 4; 17; 20:4; 8; 9(3); 10; 12(2); 13(4); 21(2); 22(2); 23; 29(2); 37; 42; 21:1; 2(2); 22:3; 5; 23:11; 12; 17(2); 27; 24:4(2); 10(3); 11(2); 12(3); 13; 15; 17; 19; 25:6; 8(2); 24; 25; 26; 28(2); 29; 30(2); 31; 32; 34; 40(2); 26:6; 8; 11; 15; 19(2); 21; 23; 27:5; 28:2; 8(2); 10; 11; 15; 16; 18; 19; 22(2); 29:6(2); 8; 10; 30:7; 15; **2Sa** 1:4; 9; 16; 26; 2:21(3); 22(2); 3:8; 12(2); 13(2); 21; 24; 25; 5:2; 24; 7:3; 8; 9(2); 11(3); 12; 15; 16; 20; 22(2); 23; 24; 26; 27(2); 29(2); 9:7(2); 10:3(2); 11(2); 11:12; 20; 25; 12:7(2); 8(3); 11; 14; 13:5(3); 6; 13(3); 20; 24; 25; 26(2); 14:2; 5; 8; 10(2); 11; 12; 17; 18(2); 19; 32(2); 15:3; 7; 20(2); 26; 31; 35; 16:4; 8; 9; 21; 17:3; 11; 18:11; 12; 14; 22; 31(2); 32(2); 33; 19:6; 7(3); 33; 37(2); 38(2); 41; 20:16; 21; 22:30; 50; 24:10; 12(3); 13(2); 17; 21; 23; 24; **1Kin** 1:12(2); 13; 14; 20; 30; 2:4; 8(2); 14; 16; 17(2); 18; 20(3); 26(2); 36; 42(2); 43; 3:5; 6(2); 12(5); 13(2); 5:6; 6:12; 8:13(2); 23(2); 25; 26; 27; 28; 33(3); 35; 40; 43(2); 46; 47; 48(2); 50(2); 52; 9:4; 5; 10:8; 9(3); 11:11(3); 31(2); 35; 37; 38(4); 12:4; 10; 28; 13:2(3); 7; 8; 16(3); 18; 21; 22; 14:2(2); 3(2); 5; 6; 7(2); 8; 9(2); 12; 15:19(2); 16:2(2); 17:3(2); 4; 9(2); 10; 11; 13; 18; 21; 18:10(2); 12(3); 41; 44(2); 19:7; 20(3); 20:5; 6; 22; 25; 31; 32; 34(2); 35; 36; 37; 21:2(3); 3; 4; 6(3); 7; 15; 20; 21; 22:5; 13; 16; 18; 23; 24; **2Kin** 1:10; 12; 13; 2:2(2); 4(2); 6(2); 9(3); 10(2); 16; 19; 3:13(2); 14(2); 4:2; 3; 4; 10; 13; 22; 24; 26(2); 29; 30; 5:6(2); 10; 13(2); 15; 17; 22; 26(2); 27; 6:1; 2; 3; 7; 17; 18; 27(2); 28; 7:13; 8:4; 9; 14; 9:3; 5(2); 6; 11; 12; 18; 19; 26; 14:10(2); 18:23(2); 26; 27; 19:9; 10; 19; 21(3); 28; 29; 20:3(2); 5; 6; 14; 18; 22:19; 20; **1Chr** 11:2; 12:18(2); 14:15; 16:18; 17:2; 7; 8(3); 10(2); 11; 13; 18; 20(2); 21; 24; 25; 27(2); 19:3(2); 12(2); 21:8; 10(3); 11; 12; 17; 23(2); 22:9; 11(2); 12(2); 15; 16; 28:9(2); 10; 20(3); 21(2); 29:12; 13; 14(2); 15; 16; 17; 18; **2Chr** 1:7; 11; 12(4); 2:11; 16; 6:2; 14(2); 16; 18; 19; 24(2); 26; 31; 33(2); 34; 36; 37; 38; 39; 40; 7:17(2); 18; 9:7; 8(3); 10:4; 10; 14:11(3); 16:3(2); 18:3; 4; 12; 15; 17; 22; 23; 19:2; 3; 20:2; 6; 8; 9; 12; 25:7; 8; 9; 16; 19(2); 26:18; 34:27; 28; 35:21(4); **Ezr** 4:12; 5:10; 7:13; 18; 19; 9:6; 15(2); 10:4(2); **Neh** 1:5; 6(2); 7; 8; 11(2); 4:5(2); 6:7; 10(2); 9:6; 8; 10; 18; 26(2); 27; 28(2); 32; 35; **Est** 3:11(2); 5:3; 6; 7:2; 9:12; **Job** 1:11; 15; 16; 17; 19; 2:5; 4:2; 5(2); 7; 5:1; 19(2); 20; 23; 7:20(2); 8:6; 8; 10(2); 18; 22; 10:3; 9; 13; 11:3; 5; 6(2); 18; 19(2); 12:7(2); 8(2); 13:20; 14:3; 5; 15; 15:6(2); 11(2); 12; 17; 16:3; 17:3; 18:4; 22:4(3); 10(2); 11; 21; 22; 27; 28; 26:4; 30:20; 33:1; 7(2); 12; 32; 33; 35:3; 4(2); 36:2; 4; 16; 17; 18(2); 38:3; 17; 34; 35; 39:9; 10; 40:4; 7; 14(2); 15; 41:3(2); 4; 42:2; 4(2); 5(2); 7; **Ps** 2:7; 8; 5:2; 3; 4; 10; 11(2); 6:5(2); 7:1; 7; 9:1; 2; 10(2); 10:14; 16:1; 2; 17:6; 7; 18:1; 29; 49; 20:1(2); 2(2); 4; 21:4; 8; 11; 22:4; 5(2); 10; 19; 22; 25; 27; 25:1; 2; 3; 5; 16; 20; 21; 27:8; 28:1; 2; 30:1; 2; 8; 9; 12(2); 31:1; 14; 17; 19(2); 22; 32:5; 6; 8(3); 9; 33:22; 35:10; 18(2); 36:9; 10; 37:4; 34; 38:9(2); 15; 39:5; 7; 12; 40:5; 16(2); 41:4; 42:1; 6; 43:4; 44:5; 17; 45:2; 4; 5; 7; 8; 14; 17; 49:18; 50:7; 8; 12; 15; 17; 21; 51:4(2); 13; 52:5(4); 9; 53:5; 54:6; 55:22; 23; 56:3; 9; 12; 57:1; 9(2); 59:9; 17; 60:4; 61:2; 62:12; 63:1(3); 2; 3; 4; 5; 6(2); 8; 65:1(2); 2; 4; 66:3; 4(2); 13; 15; 67:3(2); 5(2); 68:29; 69:5; 6(2); 9; 13; 19; 70:4(2); 71:1; 6(2); 14; 19; 22(2); 23; 72:5; 73:22; 23; 25(2); 27(2); 74:22; 23; 75:1(2); 76:10; 77:16(2); 79:6; 11; 12; 13; 80:14; 18; 81:7(3); 8; 9; 10; 16; 83:2; 5; 84:4; 5; 12; 85:6; 86:2; 3; 4; 5; 7; 8; 9; 12; 14; 87:3; 7; 88:1; 2; 9(2); 10; 13(2); 89:8(2); 90:8; 13; 91:3; 4; 7; 10; 11(2); 12; 94:20; 101:1; 102:1; 28; 103:4; 104:27; 105:11; 108:3(2); 114:5; 116:4; 7; 17; 19; 118:21; 25(2); 28(2); 119:7; 10; 11; 62; 63; 74; 76; 79; 108; 120; 126; 146; 164; 168; 169; 170; 175; 120:3(2); 121:3; 6; 7; 122:6; 8; 123:1; 128:2; 5; 130:1; 4; 134:3; 135:9; 137:5; 6; 8; 138:1(2); 4; 139:12(2); 14; 15; 18; 20; 21(2); 141:1(2); 2; 8(2); 142:5; 143:6(2); 8(2); 9; 144:9(2); 145:1; 2; 10(2); 15; 147:13; 14; **Prov** 1:10; 2:1; 11(2); 12; 16; 3:2; 3; 28; 29; 30; 4:6(2); 8(2); 9; 11(2); 24(2); 25; 5:17; 19; 6:22(3); 24; 25; 7:1; 5; 15(2); 9:8(2); 20:22; 22:18; 19(2); 20; 21(2); 27; 23:1; 7(2); 11; 22; 25; 25:7; 8; 10; 16; 17(2); 22; 27:2; 29:17; 30:6; 7; 9; 10; **Eccl** 2:1; 7:21; 8:2; 9:9; 10:4; 16; 11:9(2); **Song** 1:3; 4(3); 9; 11; 4:7; 6:1; 13; 7:5; 12; 13; 8:1(2); 2(3); 5(4); **Is** 1:25; 2:10; 3:12(2); 7:5; 11; 17; 8:1; 9:3; 10:24(2); 12:1; 6; 14:3; 8; 9(3); 10; 11(2); 16(3); 29; 16:4; 9; 19:12; 22:1; 3; 15; 16; 17(2); 18; 19(2); 24:17; 25:1; 3(2); 26:3(2); 8(2); 9(2); 13(2); 16; 20; 29:3(3); 11; 12; 30:19(2); 21; 22; 33:1(3); 2; 36:8(2); 11; 12; 37:9; 10; 22(3); 29; 30; 38:3(2); 6; 7; 18(2); 19; 39:3; 7; 40:9; 41:9(4); 10(4); 11(2); 12(2); 13(2); 14; 15; 42:6(3); 43:1(4); 2(3); 3; 4(2); 5(2); 23(2); 44:2(3); 8; 21; 22; 24; 45:2; 3(2); 4(2); 5; 14(5); 47:3; 5; 9(2); 10; 11(3); 13(2); 15(2); 48:5(2); 6; 9(2); 10(2); 17(2); 49:6; 7; 8(4); 15; 16; 17(2); 18(3); 19; 23; 25; 26; 51:16; 19(3); 23; 52:1; 14; 54:6; 7(2); 8(2); 9(2); 10(2); 14; 15; 17(2); 55:5(3); 57:8; 12; 13; 58:8; 9; 11; 12; 14(2); 59:12; 21; 60:1; 2(2); 4; 5(2); 6; 7(2); 9; 10(3); 11; 12; 13; 14(4); 15(2); 19(2); 62:4; 5(2); 64:4; 5; 7; 9; 11; 65:15; **Jer** 1:5(4); 7(2); 8(2); 10; 17(2); 18; 19(4); 2:2; 17; 19(3); 21; 22(2); 28(2); 31; 35; 3:19(2); 22; 4:14; 18; 30(2); 5:7; 6:8(2); 23; 26(2); 27; 7:16; 27(2); 10:6; 7(3); 25; 11:15; 17(2); 20; 12:1(2); 3; 5(2); 6(3); 13:1; 6; 12; 20; 21(3); 27; 14:7; 20; 22; 15:2; 5(2); 6(2); 11; 14; 19(2); 20(6); 21(2); 16:2; 10; 19; 17:4(2); 13; 16(2); 18:2; 20; 23; 19:2; 10; 20:4; 12; 15; 21:2; 13; 22:6; 7; 21; 23; 24; 25; 26(2); 23:33; 37; 25:15; 26:2; 27:2; 28:8; 15; 16; 29:22; 26; 30:2(2); 10; 11(6); 14(3); 15; 16(3); 17(3); 31:3(2); 4; 21(2); 23; 32:7(2); 8; 17; 20; 25; 33:3(2); 34:3; 4; 5(3); 14(3); 36:2(3); 19; 28; 37:18; 20(3); 38:4; 10; 14; 15(2); 16(2); 20(4); 22(2); 25(5); 39:12; 16; 17; 18(2); 40:4(6); 5; 14; 15(3); 42:2(2); 5; 6; 43:2; 3; 44:16; 45:2; 5; 46:14(2); 27; 28(5); 48:2; 18; 27; 32; 43; 46; 49:5(2); 9; 15; 16(2); 50:21; 24; 31(2); 42; 51:14(2); 20(2); 21(2); 22(3); 23(3); 25(4); 26; 36; **Lam** 1:22; 2:13(5); 14(2); 15; 16; 17; 3:57; 4:21; 22; 5:21; **Eze** 2:1; 3; 4; 6; 8(2); 3:3; 4; 6(2); 7; 10; 11; 17; 22; 25(2); 27; 4:1(2); 3(2); 5; 6; 8(2); 9(2); 15; 5:1(3); 8(2); 9; 10(3); 11; 12(3); 14(2); 15(2); 17(3); 7:3(4); 4(3); 6; 7; 8(4); 9(2); 8:6; 13; 15; 12:3; 6; 9; 16:4; 5(3); 6(4); 7; 8(5); 9(3); 10(4); 11; 14; 17; 19(2); 23; 24(2); 27(3); 33; 34(3); 37; 38(2); 39(3); 40(3); 41(2); 42(2); 44; 57; 59; 60(2); 61; 62; 63; 20:47(2); 21:3(2); 4; 7; 16; 19; 29(3); 30; 31(3); 22:4; 5(2); 6; 7(3); 9(3); 10(2); 11; 12; 13; 14; 15(3); 23:22(2); 24(3); 25(2); 26; 27; 28; 29(2); 30; 24:2; 13(2); 14; 16; 17; 26(2); 25:4(3); 7(5); 26:3(2); 8(3); 10; 14; 15; 16; 17(2); 19(3); 20(2); 21; 27:5; 7; 8; 9(2); 10; 15; 21; 25; 26(2); 27(2); 30; 31(2); 32(2); 34; 35; 36; 28:3; 4; 7; 8; 9(2); 13; 14; 15; 16(3); 17(3); 18(4); 19(2); 22(2); 29:3; 4; 5(3); 7(2); 8(2); 10; 21; 32:3(2); 4(4); 6; 7; 8; 10(2); 11; 33:7; 30; 31(2); 35:3(3); 6(3); 9; 11; 14; 15; 36:12; 15; 37:16; 18; 38:3; 4(2); 6; 7; 9; 13; 15; 16(2); 17; 39:1; 2(4); 4(2); 40:4(2); 44:5; **Dan** 1:12; 13; 2:23(3); 29(2); 31; 37; 38; 39(2); 3:12; 16; 18; 4:9(2); 18; 19(2); 25(4); 26; 27; 31(2); 32(3); 5:10; 14(3); 16; 23; 6:7; 12; 13; 16; 20; 22; 8:19; 9:7(2); 8; 15; 16; 18; 22; 23; 10:11(2); 14; 19; 20; 21; 11:2; **Hos** 1:2; 2:19(2); 20; 3:3; 4:5; 6; 5:8; 6:4(2); 11; 8:2; 5; 11:8(4); 9; 12:9; 13:5; 10; 11; 14:3; **Joel** 1:19; 20; **Amos** 3:11; 4:12(2); 5:17; 6:10; 7:2; 5; 10; 12; **Obad** 2; 3; 4; 5(2); 7(5); 10; 15; **Jonah** 1:8; 11; 14(3); 2:7; 9; 3:2; 4:2(2); 3; **Mic** 1:13; 15; 16(3); 2:11; 12; 4:8; 9(2); 10; 11; 5:2; 10; 13; 14; 6:3(2); 4(3); 8(2); 13(3); 14; 15; 16; 7:12; 17; 18; **Nah** 1:11; 12(2); 13; 14; 15; 2:13; 3:5; 6(3); 7(3); 13; 14; 15(3); 19(2); **Hab** 1:2; 2:7(2); 8; 16; 17; 3:10; **Zeph** 2:5; 3:11; 12; 15; 17(3); 18; 19; **Hag** 2:23(3); **Zec** 1:9; 2:10; 11(2); 3:2(2); 4(2); 7; 8; 9:9; 11; 12; 13; 11:15; 14:1; 5; **Mal** 1:7; 8; 2:14; 3:8; 13; **Mt** 1:20; 2:6; 13; 3:14; 4:6(2); 9; 10; 5:23; 25(2); 26; 29(3); 30(3); 39; 40; 41; 42(2); 6:2; 4; 6; 18; 23; 8:13; 19; 29; 9:2; 5; 22; 11:10; 21(2); 23; 24; 25; 12:38; 47; 14:4; 28; 15:28; 16:17; 18; 19; 22(2); 23; 17:4; 27; 18:8(3); 9(3); 15(3); 16(2); 17; 22; 26; 29; 32; 33; 19:27; 20:13; 14; 21:5; 19; 23; 23:37; 25:21; 23; 24; 37(3); 38(3); 39(2); 44(2); 26:17; 33; 34; 35(2); 62; 63; 68; 73; 27:13; **Mk** 1:2; 24(2); 37; 2:5; 9; 11; 3:32; 5:7(2); 19(2); 23; 31; 34; 41; 6:18; 22; 23; 8:33; 9:5; 17; 25; 43(2); 45(2); 47(2); 10:28; 49; 51; 52; 11:14; 28; 14:30; 31(2); 36; 60; 15:4; **Lk** 1:3; 13; 19(2); 28; 35(3); 2:48; 3:22; 4:6; 8; 10(2); 11; 34(2); 5:20; 23; 24; 6:29; 30; 7:7; 14; 20; 27; 40; 47; 50; 8:20; 28(2); 39; 45(2); 48; 9:33; 38; 57; 61; 10:13(2); 21; 35; 11:7; 27; 35; 36; 12:20; 58(3); 59; 13:31(2); 34; 14:9(2); 10(3); 12(2); 14; 18; 19; 15:18; 29; 16:2; 27; 17:3; 4(2); 19; 18:11; 28; 41; 42; 19:21; 22; 43(4); 44(3); 20:2; 22:11; 32; 33; 34; 64; 23:43; **Jn** 1:48(2); 50(2); 2:4; 3:3; 5; 7; 11; 26; 4:10(2); 26; 5:10; 12; 14; 6:30; 7:20; 8:10; 11; 9:26; 37; 10:33; 11:8; 22; 28; 40; 41; 13:8; 37; 38; 16:30; 17:1; 3; 4; 5; 7; 8; 11; 13; 21; 25(2); 18:26; 30; 34; 35; 19:10(2); 11(2); 21:3; 15; 16; 17; 18(3); 20; 22; 23; **Acts** 3:6; 5:9; 7:3(2); 27; 34; 35; 8:20; 22; 34; 9:5; 6; 17; 34; 10:6; 19; 20; 22(2); 32; 33(2); 11:14; 12:8; 13:11; 33; 47; 16:18; 17:32; 18:10(3); 21:21; 23; 24; 37; 39; 22:10(2); 14; 18; 19; 21; 23:3; 18(2); 20; 21; 30(2); 35; 24:2; 4(2); 8; 14; 19; 25; 25:26; 26:2; 3(2); 14; 16(3); 17(2); 24; 27:24(2); 28:21(2); 22; **Rom** 2:4; 27; 4:17; 9:17(2); 10:8; 11:18; 21; 22; 13:4; 15:3; 9; **1Cor** 4:7; 8:10; 12:21; **2Cor** 6:2(2); 12:9; **Gal** 3:8; **Eph** 5:14; 6:3; **Phil** 4:3; **1Ti**

1:3; 18(2); 3:14(2); 4:14(2); 16; 5:21; 6:13; 21; **2Ti** 1:3; 4; 5(2); 6(2); 14; 2:7; 3:15; 4:1; 11; 13; 21; **Titus** 1:5(2); 2:15; 3:12; 15; **Philem** 1:4; 7; 8; 9; 10; 11(2); 16; 18(2); 19; 20; 21; 23; **Heb** 1:5; 9; 2:12; 5:5; 6:14(2); 8:5; 13:5(2); **Jas** 2:18; **2Jn** 5(2); 13; **3Jn** 3; 13; 14(3); **Jude** 9; **Rev** 2:4; 5; 10; 14; 16; 20; 3:3(2); 8; 9; 10; 16; 18; 4:1; 11:17(2); 14:15; 15:4(2); 17:1; 7; 18:14(2); 22(3); 23(2); 21:9

THEIR

Gen 1:21; 25; 5:2; 6:20(2); 7:14; 8:19; 9:23(4); 10:5(3); 20(4); 30; 31(4); 32(2); 11:7; 12:5; 13:6; 14:6; 11(2); 24; 17:7; 8; 9; 23; 18:20; 22; 26; 19:10; 33; 35; 36; 20:8; 24:52; 59; 25:13(2); 16(4); 26:18; 31:38; 43; 53; 32:15; 33:2; 6; 34:13; 18; 20(2); 21; 23(2); 27; 28(3); 29(3); 35:4(3); 36:7(2); 19; 30; 40(3); 43(2); 37:2; 4; 12; 16; 21; 22; 25(2); 32; 40:1; 42:6; 24; 25; 26; 28; 29; 35(2); 36; 43:2; 11; 15; 24(2); 26; 27; 28; 44:3; 13; 45:25; 27; 46:5(3); 6(2); 17; 32(3); 47:1(2); 4; 9; 12; 17(2); 22(2); 30; 48:6(2); 49:5; 6(4); 7(2); 28; 50:8(3); 15; 17; **Ex** 1:11; 14(2); 2:11; 16; 17; 18; 23; 24; 3:7(3); 4:5; 31(2); 5:4; 5; 6; 10; 21; 6:4; 6; 14; 16; 17; 19; 25; 26; 7:11; 12; 19(4); 22; 8:7; 18; 26; 10:7; 23; 12:3; 34(4); 42; 51; 13:20; 14:10; 19; 22(2); 25; 26(2); 29(2); 16:1(2); 17:1; 18:7; 23; 19:7; 10; 14; 21:32; 22:23; 23:24(3); 26; 27; 32; 33; 25:20(3); 34(2); 36(2); 40; 26:21; 25; 29; 32; 37; 27:10(2); 11(2); 12(2); 14(2); 15(2); 16(2); 17(2); 18; 21; 28:10(2); 12; 20; 21; 38; 42; 29:10; 15; 19; 20(2); 25; 28(2); 45; 46(2); 30:12; 19(2); 21(3); 31:16; 32:3; 4; 15; 25(2); 32; 34; 33:6; 34:13(3); 15(2); 16(4); 35:17; 18; 25; 36:26; 30; 34; 36; 38(4); 37:9(3); 22(2); 38:10(3); 11(3); 12(3); 14(2); 15(2); 17(2); 19(5); 28; 39:13; 14; 40:15(3); 31(2); 36; 38; **Lev** 4:15; 6:17; 7:34; 36; 38; 8:14; 16; 18; 22; 24(3); 25; 28; 9:24; 10:5; 19(2); 11:8(2); 11(2); 21; 27; 35; 36; 37; 38; 13:38; 39; 15:31(2); 16:16(3); 21(2); 22; 27(3); 34; 17:5; 7(2); 18:3; 6; 9; 10; 29; 20:4; 5; 11; 12; 13; 16; 17; 18; 19; 20; 24; 27; 21:5(3); 6(3); 17; 22:16; 25; 23:4; 18(2); 24:14; 25:32; 33; 34(2); 45; 26:4; 13; 20; 36(2); 39(2); 40(3); 41(3); 43(2); 44(2); 45(3); **Num** 1:2(4); 3; 16; 17; 18(4); 20(4); 22(4); 24(3); 26(3); 28(3); 30(3); 32(3); 34(3); 36(3); 38(3); 40(3); 42(3); 45; 47; 52(2); 2:2; 3; 9; 10; 16; 17; 18; 24; 25; 31; 32(2); 34(3); 3:4; 10; 15(2); 17; 18; 19; 20(2); 31; 37(3); 39; 40; 45; 4:2(2); 22(2); 26(2); 27(3); 28; 29(2); 31(2); 32(6); 33; 34(2); 36; 38(2); 40(2); 42(2); 44; 46(2); 5:3; 7; 6:15(2); 7:2; 3; 7; 8; 9; 10; 11; 87; 8:7(2); 10; 12; 21; 22; 26(2); 9:17; 18; 20; 22; 10:6(2); 12; 13; 14; 18; 22; 25; 28; 11:10; 12; 33; 13:2; 4; 33; 14:1; 5; 6; 9; 23; 15:12; 25(3); 38(2); 16:15; 22; 26; 27(4); 32(2); 38; 45; 17:2(3); 3; 6(3); 10; 18:11; 17(2); 20; 21; 23; 20:6; 8(2); 11; 21:2; 3; 18; 22:7; 24:2; 8; 25:2(2); 18(2); 26:2; 12; 15; 20; 23; 26; 28; 35; 37; 38; 41; 42(2); 44; 48; 50; 55; 57; 59; 27:5; 7(2); 14; 19; 28:2; 14; 20; 28; 31; 29:3; 6(2); 9; 11; 14; 18(3); 19; 21(3); 24(3); 27(3); 30(3); 33(3); 37(3); 30:9; 31:9(4); 10(2); 29; 32:17; 38; 33:1; 2(4); 4(2); 12; 52(3); 34:14(4); 15; 35:2; 3(3); 7; 36:3; 4(2); 6; 11; 12(2); **Deut** 1:8; 25; 2:5; 9; 12; 21; 22; 23; 4:10; 37; 38; 5:29; 7:5(4); 10; 16; 24(2); 25; 9:5; 14; 27(2); 10:6; 11; 15; 11:4(2); 6(3); 9; 12:2; 3(4); 29; 30(2); 31(4); 13:13; 14:8(2); 18:2(2); 18; 19:1(2); 20:18(2); 21:5; 6; 23:3; 6(2); 8; 29:8; 17(2); 25; 28; 31:7; 11; 13; 19; 20; 21(2); 28; 32:5; 8; 20; 21; 27; 29; 30; 31; 32(3); 33; 35(2); 36; 37(2); 38(2); 33:29; **Josh** 1:6; 3:14; 4:6; 18; 21; 5:1; 6; 7(2); 8; 7:6; 8(2); 11; 12(3); 16; 8:13; 19; 33(2); 9:4; 5(2); 14; 16; 17(2); 10:5; 13; 19; 24; 40; 42; 11:4; 6(2); 9(2); 13; 17; 20; 21; 23(2); 12:1; 7; 13:8; 14; 15; 16; 23; 24; 25; 28(2); 29; 30; 31; 33; 14:2; 4(3); 15:1; 2; 5; 12; 20; 32; 36; 41; 44; 46; 51; 54; 57; 59; 60; 62; 16:4; 5(2); 8; 9; 17:2(2); 4; 18:2; 5(2); 7(2); 10; 11(2); 12; 20; 21; 24; 28(2); 19:1(2); 2; 6; 7; 8; 9; 10(2); 11; 15; 16(2); 17; 18; 22(2); 23(2); 24; 25; 30; 31(2); 32; 33; 38; 39(2); 40; 41; 47; 48(2); 49; 21:3(2); 7; 8; 19; 20; 26; 33(2); 40(2); 41; 42; 43; 44(4); 22:6; 7(2); 9; 14; 23:1; 2(4); 5; 7; 24:1(3); 8; **Judg** 1:4; 7(3); 2:2; 3; 4; 10; 12; 14(2); 17(2); 18(2); 19(3); 20; 22; 3:4; 6(5); 7; 25; 5:18; 20; 22; 6:5(3); 9; 7:2; 6(3); 8(2); 12; 19; 20(2); 8:3; 10; 21; 26; 28; 33; 34(2); 9:3; 24(2); 26; 27(2); 57; 10:12; 12:2; 13:20; 14:17; 19; 15:13; 16:18; 23; 24; 25; 18:1; 2(2); 8(2); 14; 16; 23; 26; 29; 19:14; 21; 22; 20:13; 22; 33(2); 42; 21:2; 6; 22(2); 23(2); **Ruth** 1:9; 14; **1Sa** 1:19; 2:20; 25; 33; 5:9; 6:6; 7; 10; 11; 13(2); 8:9; 22; 9:16; 10:4; 12; 21; 11:4; 12:9; 14:30; 46; 15:24; 17:1; 18(2); 51; 53; 18:27; 21:13; 22:17(2); 23:5; 25:12; 28:1; 23; 29:1; 30:2; 3(3); 4; 31:9; 13; **2Sa** 1:23(2); 2:26; 3:18; 30; 4:12(2); 5:21; 7:10; 23; 24; 10:3; 4(3); 18; 12:30; 13:31; 36; 15:11; 36; 17:8; 18:28; 20:2; 3; 22:46; 23:17; 19; **1Kin** 2:4(3); 15; 33; 4:8; 6:27; 7:25; 31; 33(4); 8:7; 23; 25; 34; 35; 37(2); 44; 45(3); 48(5); 49(3); 50; 66; 9:9(2); 21; 10:5; 29; 11:2; 8; 12:16; 27; 13:11; 12; 14:15(2); 22(2); 27; 30; 15:16; 32; 16:2; 13; 26; 18:28; 37; 39; 19:21; 20:6; 23; 24; 25; 32(2); 22:10; **2Kin** 1:14; 3:24; 27; 5:24; 6:20; 22; 23; 7:7(4); 15; 8:12(4); 21; 10:7; 11:12; 13:3; 5; 14:12; 16:15(2); 17:7; 9(2); 14(3); 15; 16; 17(2); 19; 23; 25; 29(2); 31; 33; 34(2); 40; 41(4); 18:12; 27(2); 35; 36; 37; 19:17; 18; 26; 21:8; 14(2); 15; 22:7; 17; 23:2; 3(2); 9; 14; 25:21; 23(2); 24; **1Chr** 1:29; 3:9; 19; 4:3; 27; 31; 32; 33(3); 38(3); 39; 41(3); 42; 5:7(2); 9; 10(2); 13(2); 15; 16; 20(2); 21(2); 22; 24(2); 25; 6:19; 32(2); 33; 44; 48; 54(3); 57; 60(2); 62; 63; 64; 65; 66; 7:2(2); 4(2); 5(2); 7(2); 9(3); 11; 21; 22; 28; 30; 32; 40; 8:28; 32; 9:1; 2(2); 6; 9(3); 13(2); 17; 19; 22(3); 23; 25(2); 26; 32; 34; 38(2); 10:7; 9; 10; 12; 11:19(2); 21; 12:30; 32(2); 39; 13:2; 8; 14:12; 15:15; 16; 17; 18; 16:21; 38; 17:9; 22; 19:4(2); 7; 20:2; 21:16; 23:3(2); 11; 22; 24(2); 28; 32; 24:2; 3(2); 4(2); 19(3); 30; 31(2); 25:1; 3; 6; 7; 26:6; 8(2); 13; 27:1(2); 28:15; 18; 29:18; 20(2); 21; **2Chr** 1:17; 3:13(2); 4:4; 7; 16; 20; 5:8; 12(2); 13; 6:14; 16; 25; 26; 28(2); 34; 35(3); 36; 37; 38(5); 39(3); 7:3; 6(2); 10; 14(3); 22; 8:8; 14(3); 9:4(2); 6; 10:16; 11:13; 14(2); 16(2); 13:10; 16; 18; 14:4; 15:4; 12(3); 15(2); 17:14; 18:9; 19:4; 10; 20:13(3); 27; 33(2); 21:3; 22:5; 24:18(2); 24(2); 25:4; 5; 10; 15; 20; 26:11; 13; 28:6; 8; 15; 29:6(2); 15; 23; 24; 30; 34; 30:7; 16(2); 22; 27(2); 31:1; 2; 6; 15(2); 16(4); 17(3); 18(5); 19; 32:13; 17; 33:17; 34:5; 6; 25; 30; 32; 33(2); 35:2; 10(2); 11; 15(3); 25; 36:15; 17(2); **Ezr** 1:6; 2:59(2); 61; 62; 65(2); 66(2); 67(2); 69; 70(2); 3:8(2); 9(2); 10; 12; 4:5; 7; 9; 17; 23; 5:3; 5; 8; 10; 6:12; 13; 18(2); 20; 22; 7:13; 16; 17(2); 8:1; 19; 24; 26; 9:1; 2(2); 11(2); 12(4); 10:16(2); 19(3); **Neh** 2:18; 3:5(3); 18; 23; 4:3; 4(2); 5(2); 13(4); 15; 5:1(2); 5; 6; 8; 11(4); 14; 15; 6:6; 9; 14; 16; 7:61(2); 63; 64; 67(2); 68(2); 69; 73(2); 8:6(3); 7; 12; 15; 16; 9:2(2); 3(3); 4; 6; 9; 11; 15(2); 16; 17(3); 20(2); 21(2); 23(2); 24(2); 26; 27(3); 28; 29; 35(2); 37; 10:10; 28(3); 29(2); 30; 11:3; 9; 12; 14(2); 19; 25; 30; 31; 12:7; 9; 24; 27; 42; 45; 13:11; 13(2); 24; 25(3); **Est** 1:17(2); 20; 22; 2:3; 12; 3:8; 12; 8:9(3); 11; 13; 9:2(2); 5; 10; 15; 16(4); 22; 27(3); 28; 31(3); **Job** 1:4(2); 5(2); 13; 18; 2:12(3); 3:8; 15; 4:21; 5:5; 12(2); 13; 15; 6:17; 18; 8:4; 8; 10; 11:3; 20; 12:18; 14:12; 15:18; 35; 16:10; 17:2; 4; 19:12; 15; 20:10; 21:8(4); 9; 10(2); 11(2); 13; 16(2); 17; 29; 22:6; 18; 24:5(2); 11(2); 18; 23; 27:23; 29:9(2); 10(3); 23; 25; 30:2; 4; 9(2); 12; 31:16; 39; 33:16; 34:24; 25; 36:9(2); 10; 11(2); 14; 15; 20; 37:8; 38:15; 40; 39:3(2); 4; 40:12; 13; 22; 42:15(2); **Ps** 2:3(2); 12; 4:7(2); 5:9(4); 10(2); 11; 7:7; 9:5; 6; 10; 15; 10:17; 11:2(2); 6; 16:4(3); 17:7; 10(2); 11; 14(3); 18:45; 19:3; 4(2); 21:10(2); 12; 22:13; 26:10; 28:3(2); 4(4); 8; 33:15(2); 19; 34:5; 15; 17; 35:6; 7; 16; 17; 21; 25; 36:7; 37:14; 15(3); 18; 30; 40:16; 44:1; 3(2); 12; 49:6(2); 9; 10; 11(5); 13(4); 14(2); 55:9; 15; 23; 56:5; 57:4; 58:4; 6(2); 59:7(2); 12(3); 62:4; 64:3(3); 8; 65:7; 68:27(2); 69:22(2); 23(2); 25(2); 27; 70:3; 72:14(2); 73:4(2); 7; 9(2); 17; 20; 74:4; 8; 76:5(2); 78:4; 5; 6; 7; 8(2); 12; 18(2); 28(2); 29; 30(3); 33(2); 35(2); 36(2); 37; 38; 44(2); 46(2); 47(2); 48(2); 50(2); 51; 53; 55; 57; 58(2); 63(2); 64(2); 79:3; 10; 12(2); 81:12(2); 14(2); 15; 83:11(2); 16; 85:2; 89:17; 32(2); 90:10; 16; 91:12; 93:3(2); 94:23(2); 95:10; 98:8; 99:8; 102:17; 28; 104:11; 12; 17; 21(2); 22; 27; 29(2); 105:14; 24; 25; 29(2); 30(2); 31; 32; 33(3); 35(2); 36(2); 37; 106:11; 15(2); 18; 20; 21; 25; 27; 29; 32; 35; 36; 37(2); 38(2); 39(2); 42(2); 43(2); 44(2); 107:5; 6(2); 12; 13(2); 14; 17(2); 18; 19(2); 20; 26; 27; 28(2); 30; 38; 109:10(2); 13; 25; 29; 115:2; 4; 7; 9(2); 10(2); 11(2); 119:70; 118; 123:2; 124:3; 6; 125:3; 4; 5; 129:3; 132:12; 135:12; 17; 136:10; 21; 140:2; 3(2); 9; 141:4; 5; 6; 10; 144:8; 11; 12; 145:15; 19; 147:3; 4; 149:2; 5; 6(2); 8(2); **Prov** 1:6; 15; 16; 18(2); 22; 31(2); 2:15; 4:16; 22; 8:21; 9:15; 10:15; 11:6; 20; 14:24; 17:6; 18:19; 20:29; 21:12; 22:23; 23:11(2); 24:2(2); 22; 25:27; 29:13; 16; 30:5; 11(2); 12(2); 13(2); 14; 25; 26; **Eccl** 2:3; 3:11; 4:1; 9; 5:11; 13; 9:1; 3; 6(3); **Is** 2:4(2); 7(4); 8(3); 3:4; 8(2); 9(3); 10; 12; 16; 17; 18(4); 5:12; 13(2); 14(3); 17; 21(2); 24(2); 25; 27(2); 28(3); 29; 6:10(5); 13; 8:12; 19; 21(2); 9:17(2); 10:2; 5; 13; 25; 29; 11:7; 14; 13:8; 10; 11(2); 16(4); 18(2); 20; 21; 22(2); 14:1; 2(2); 9; 21; 25; 15:2; 3(3); 4; 16:10(2); 18:2; 7; 20:4; 5(2); 21:14; 24:14; 25:11(2); 26:11; 14; 21; 28:25; 29:13(4); 14(2); 15(2); 19; 30:6(2); 7; 26; 31:3; 4; 33:2; 7; 9; 23; 24; 34:2; 3(4); 4; 7(2); 35:10; 36:12(2); 20; 21; 22; 37:18; 19; 27; 40:24; 26; 31; 41:1; 17; 29(2); 42:11; 15; 43:9; 14; 44:9(2); 18(2); 25; 45:12; 20; 46:1; 47:9; 49:9; 22(2); 23(2); 26(2); 50:2; 3; 51:7; 11; 52:15; 53:11; 54:17; 55:12; 56:7(2); 11; 57:2; 8; 58:1(2); 2; 59:5; 6(4); 7(3); 8; 18; 60:8; 9(2); 10; 11; 61:6; 7(2); 8; 9(2); 62:6; 63:3; 6; 8; 9; 10; 65:2; 4; 6; 7(2); 22; 23; 66:3(3); 4(2); 18(2); 24(2); **Jer** 1:8; 16(2); 17; 2:11(2); 26(4); 27(3); 3:17; 21(2); 24(4); 4:16; 5:3; 4; 5; 6(3); 16; 24; 27; 31; 6:3(2); 10; 12(2); 19; 23; 27; 7:18; 19; 24(2); 26(3); 28(2); 30; 31(2); 8:1; 7; 10(2); 12; 19; 9:3(2); 5; 8; 14(2); 16; 10:7; 9; 15; 21; 11:8(2); 10(2); 12; 14; 18; 22(2); 23; 12:2(2); 14; 13:10; 14:3(4); 4; 6; 10(3); 11; 12; 14; 16(4); 15:7; 8; 9; 16:3(2); 4; 7(2); 15(2); 17(2); 18(3); 17:1; 2(3); 23(2); 25; 18:8; 15; 16; 17; 21(6); 22; 23(3); 19:4; 5; 7(3); 9(4); 15; 20:4; 5; 11; 21:7(2); 22:9; 23:3; 8; 10(2); 11; 12(2); 16; 22(2); 26; 27(2); 31; 32(2); 24:5; 7(2); 9; 10; 25:12; 14(2); 36; 38; 26:3; 27:4; 8; 11(2); 29:23; 30:3; 9(2); 10; 20(2); 21(2); 31:12; 13(2); 17; 23; 32; 33(3); 34(2); 32:18; 22; 30(2); 32(4); 34; 35(2); 38; 39; 40; 44; 33:8(2); 12; 20; 26; 34:14; 16; 20(3); 21(2); 35:14; 16; 36:3(2); 6; 7; 15; 24; 31; 37:7; 38:18; 19; 23; 40:7; 8; 9; 41:5(3); 8; 42:17; 43:1(2); 44:3; 5(2); 9; 12; 15; 46:5; 10; 21(2); 25(2); 26; 27; 47:3; 5; 48:12; 13; 33; 34; 44; 49:1; 3; 7; 20; 21; 29(5); 32(3); 35; 37(2); 50:4; 5; 6(2); 7(2); 9; 27(2); 34(2); 37(2); 38; 42; 45; 51:5; 18; 24; 30(2); 39(2); 55; 56; **Lam** 1:11; 14; 19(2); 22; 2:10(2); 12(3); 15(2); 16; 18; 20; 3:14; 46; 60(2); 61(2); 62; 63(3); 64; 4:3; 7; 8(3); 10(2); 14; 20; 5:7; 8; 12; 14; **Eze** 1:5; 7(2); 8(4); 9; 10; 11(3); 13; 16(3); 17; 18(2); 20; 22; 23(2); 24(2); 25(2); 26; 2:3; 6(3); 3:8(2); 9; 4:4; 5; 12; 13; 17; 5:10; 16; 6:5; 9(4); 13(4); 14; 7:11; 18; 19(7); 20(2); 24(2); 27(2); 8:16(2); 17; 9:10(2); 10:8; 10; 11; 12(4); 16; 19; 21; 22(2); 11:19; 20; 21(4); 22; 12:3(2); 4(2); 5; 6; 7; 16; 19(2); 13:2; 3; 17; 14:3(4); 5(2); 10; 11(2); 14(2); 20(2); 22(2); 23(2); 16:39; 40; 45(2); 47(2); 53; 55(2); 19:4; 7(2); 8(2); 20:4; 8; 16(2); 18(3); 24(2); 26; 28(4); 30; 21:6; 14; 15(3); 23; 28; 29; 22:6; 10; 26; 31(2); 23:3(3); 4; 7; 8; 15(3); 17; 20; 24; 30; 36; 37(3); 39(2); 42(2); 45; 47(4); 24:25(6); 25:4(2); 26:10; 16(3); 17; 27:9; 11; 29; 30(2); 32; 35(2); 28:7; 25; 26; 29:7(2); 14; 16; 30:11; 13; 31:6(2); 14(4); 32:2; 10; 14(2); 24(2); 25(2); 26; 27(5); 29; 30(3); 33:2(2); 17; 29; 31(3); 34:10(2); 13; 14; 23; 24; 27(2); 30; 35:5(2); 36:5(2); 7; 12; 17(4); 18; 19(2); 23; 37:10; 20; 21; 23(5); 25(3); 27; 38:16; 39:22; 23(2); 24(2); 26(3); 27; 28(2); 40:16; 22(3); 41; 44; 41:16; 42:4; 11(3); 14; 43:7(4); 8(4); 9(2); 10; 11; 44:10(2); 12(2); 13(2); 18(2); 19(2); 20(3); 22; 28(2); 45:4; 8; 46:16; 18; 47:10(2); 12; 48:29; 34; **Dan** 1:15; 16; 2:30; 3:21(4); 27(2); 28(2); 29; 4:21; 6:24(3); 7:12(2); 8:23; 9:7; 11:8(3); 32; **Hos** 1:7; 2:5; 17; 3:5(2); 4:7; 8(2); 9(2); 12(3); 18; 19; 5:4(2); 5; 6(2); 7; 15(2); 7:2(3); 3(2); 6(2); 7(2); 10; 12; 14(2); 15; 16(3); 8:4(2); 13(2); 9:4(3); 6(2); 9(2); 10; 11; 12; 15(3); 16(2); 10:2(3); 8; 10; 11:3; 4; 6; 11; 12:11; 13:2(2); 6(2); 8; 16(2); 14:4; **Joel** 1:3(2); 17; 2:6; 7; 10; 17; 22; 3:6; 13; 15; 19; 21; **Amos** 1:13; 15; 2:4(2); 8; 3:10; 4:1; 5:12; 6:2; 4; 7:11; 8:7; 9:4; 15(2); **Obad** 12; 13(5); 17; **Jonah** 1:2; 2:8; 3:8; 10(2); 4:11(2); **Mic** 2:1(2); 9(2); 12; 13; 3:2(3); 3(2); 4; 5(2); 7; 4:3(2); 13(2); 6:12(2); 16; 7:4; 13; 16(4); 17; 19; **Nah** 2:2; 5; 7; 3:3(2); 17; **Hab** 1:7(2); 8(3); 9; 15(2); 16(4); 17; 2:15; 3:11; 14; **Zeph** 1:9; 12(2); 13(2); 17(2); 18(2); 2:7(2); 8; 10; 14; 3:6(3); 7(2); 13; **Hag** 1:12(2); 14; 2:14; 22; **Zec** 1:21; 2:9; 5:6; 9; 7:2; 11; 12; 8:8; 12; 9:16; 10:2; 5; 6; 7(3); 9; 11:3; 5; 6; 8; 16; 12:5(2); 12(2); 13(2); 14; 14:12(6); **Mal** 4:6; **Mt** 1:21; 2:11; 12; 3:6; 4:6; 20; 21(2); 22; 23; 6:2; 5; 7; 14; 15; 16(2); 7:6; 16; 20; 8:22; 33; 34; 9:2; 4; 29; 30; 35; 10:17; 21; 11:1; 5; 16; 12:9; 25; 13:15(5); 43; 54; 58; 14:14; 15:2; 8(3); 27; 17:6; 8; 25; 18:10; 31; 35; 19:12; 20:4; 8; 31; 34(2); 21:7; 8; 41; 22:5; 7; 16; 18; 22; 23:3; 4; 5(3); 25:1; 3; 4(2); 7; 26:43; 67; 27:39; **Mk** 1:5; 18; 19; 20; 23; 39; 2:5; 6; 3:4; 5; 4:12; 15; 5:17; 6:6; 8(2); 26; 52; 7:3; 6(2); 8:3; 9:34; 44; 46; 48; 10:42; 11:4; 7; 8; 12:12; 15; 44; 13:12; 14:40; 46; 56; 59; 65; 15:19; 29; 16:14; **Lk** 1:16; 20; 51; 52; 66; 77; 2:8; 39; 44; 3:15; 4:11; 15; 29; 5:2; 6; 7; 11; 15; 20; 22; 30; 6:1; 8; 17; 22; 23; 26; 7:21; 8:3; 12; 9:47; 60; 11:17; 48; 12:36; 42; 13:1; 14:4; 16:4; 8; 17:13; 19:32; 35; 36; 40; 20:23; 26; 21:1; 4; 12; 22:66; 23:25; 48; 24:5; 11; 16; 31(2); 45; **Jn** 3:19; 4:38; 8:9; 10:39; 11:19; 46; 12:40(4); 13:12; 15:22; 25; 17:19; 20; 18:8; 19:3; 31; 20:10; **Acts** 1:9; 19; 26; 2:37; 45; 46; 4:5; 23; 24; 29; 5:18; 6:1; 6; 7:19; 34; 39; 41; 54; 57; 58; 60; 8:17; 36; 9:24; 10:9; 11:18; 12:17; 20(2); 25; 13:3; 5; 18; 19; 22; 27; 33; 50; 51; 14:2; 3; 5; 11; 13; 14; 16; 15:3; 9; 13; 22; 26; 16:19; 22; 24; 33; 17:21; 26; 18:3; 19:18; 19; 21:21; 24; 22:22; 23; 30; 23:16; 28; 29; 25:19; 26:18; 27:13; 43; 28:6; 27(5); **Rom** 1:21(2); 24(2); 26; 27(2); 28; 2:15(3); 3:3; 13(3); 15; 16; 18; 10:3; 18(2); 11:9; 10(2); 11; 12; 24; 27; 30; 13:7; 15:27(3); 16:4; 5; 18; **1Cor** 3:19; 8:7; 12; 14:35; 16:19; **2Cor** 3:14; 15; 5:19; 6:16; 8:2(3); 3(2); 5; 14(2); 9:14; 11:15; **Gal** 2:13; **Eph** 4:17; 18; 5:24; 28(2); **Phil** 2:21; 3:19(2); **Col** 2:2; **1Th** 2:15; 16; 5:13; **2Th** 3:12; **1Ti** 3:11; 12(2); 4:2; 5:4; 12; 6:1; **2Ti** 2:17; 3:2; 9; 4:3; 4; 16; **Titus** 1:12; 15; 2:4(2); 5; 9; 3:13; **Heb** 2:10; 15; 3:10; 5:14; 7:5; 8:9; 10(2); 12(3); 10:16(2); 17; 11:16; 35; 12:10; 13:7; **Jas** 1:27; 3:3; **1Pet** 3:5; 12; 14; 4:14; 19; **2Pet** 2:2; 3; 8; 12; 13; 3:3; 16; **3Jn** 6; **Jude** 6(2); 13; 15(2); 16(2); 18; **Rev** 2:22; 3:4; 4:4; 10; 6:11(2); 14; 7:3; 9; 11; 14; 17; 9:4; 5; 7(2); 8; 9; 10(2); 17; 18; 19(4); 20; 21(4); 10:3; 4; 11:5(2); 6; 7; 8; 9(2); 11; 12; 16(2); 12:8; 11(2); 13:16(2); 14:1; 2; 5; 11; 13(2); 15:6; 16:10; 11(3); 17:13; 17(2); 18:11; 19; 19:19; 21; 20:4(2); 12; 13; 21:3; 4; 8; 24; 22:4

THEIRS

Gen 15:13; 34:23; 43:34; **Ex** 29:9; **Lev** 18:10; **Num** 16:26; 18:9(4); **Josh** 21:10; **1Chr** 6:54; **2Chr** 18:12; **Jer** 44:28; **Eze** 7:11; **Hab** 1:6; **Mt** 5:3; 10; **1Cor** 1:2; **2Ti** 3:9

THEM

Gen 1:14; 15; 17; 22; 26; 27; 28(2); 2:1; 19(2); 3:7; 21; 5:2(2); 6:1; 2; 4; 7; 13(2); 19; 20; 21; 7:13; 9:1; 19; 10:1; 11:3; 6; 8; 9; 29; 31; 12:3; 13:6; 14:8; 14; 15(3); 24; 15:5; 10; 11; 13(2); 18:2(2); 8(2); 16(2); 19:1(2); 3(2); 5(2); 6; 8(2); 9; 10; 12; 13; 17; 18; 20:14; 21:27(2); 31; 22:6; 8; 23:8; 24:28; 53; 56; 60; 25:6; 26; 26:15(2); 18(2); 27; 30; 31; 27:9; 13; 14; 15; 28:11; 29:4; 5; 6; 7; 9(2); 30:14; 35; 37; 40; 42; 31:5; 9; 32; 33; 34(3); 55; 32:2; 4; 16; 23(2); 33:3; 13; 34:8; 14; 21(3); 23; 35:4; 5; 36:7; 37:6; 13; 17(2); 18; 22; 38:26; 39:14; 40:3; 4(2); 5; 6(2); 8(2); 11; 17; 22; 41:3; 6; 8(2); 19; 21(2); 23; 27; 30; 35(2); 42:7(4); 9(2); 12; 14; 17; 18; 22; 23(2); 24(4); 25(2); 27; 28; 29; 36; 43:2; 11; 16; 23; 24; 27; 32; 34; 44:4(2); 6(2); 15; 45:1; 15; 21(2); 22; 24; 26; 27; 47:2; 6(3); 11; 17(2); 20; 21; 22(2); 24; 48:6; 9(2); 10(3); 12; 13(2); 16(2); 20; 49:7(2); 28(3); 29(2); 50:12; 19; 21(2); **Ex** 1:7; 10(2); 11(2); 12; 14; 16; 17; 18; 19; 21; 2:17(2); 25; 3:8(2); 9; 13(2); 16; 22; 4:20; 5:4; 5; 7; 8; 9; 13; 14; 21; 6:1(2); 3; 4(2); 13; 7:5; 6; 13; 22; 8:2; 14; 15; 19; 9:2(2); 12; 17; 19; 27; 10:2; 8; 10; 14(2); 19; 27; 12:3; 16; 21; 33; 36; 38; 42; 13:17; 21(3); 14:3; 4; 7; 9(2); 10; 13; 17; 19(2); 20; 22; 23; 25(2); 28(2); 29; 15:5; 7(2); 9(2); 10; 12; 13; 15; 16; 17(2); 19; 21; 25(2); 16:3; 4; 12; 15; 16; 20(2); 23; 17:2; 18:8(2); 11; 16; 20(2); 21; 22; 25; 19:10(2); 21; 22; 24; 25; 20:5(3); 6; 11; 21:1; 34; 22:11; 23; 23:23; 24(2); 29; 30; 31; 32; 24:12; 14; 25:3; 8(2); 12; 13; 14; 18; 28(2); 29; 40; 26:1; 24; 37(2); 27:6; 28:9; 11; 14; 25; 26; 27; 33; 40(2); 41(4); 42; 29:1(2); 2; 3(2); 4; 8; 9(2); 13(2); 17; 22; 24; 25(2); 29; 30; 33; 35; 46(2); 30:5; 12(3); 13; 14; 21; 29(2); 30; 31:5; 32:2(2); 3; 4; 8(2); 10(2); 12(3); 13; 18(3); 19; 21; 24(2); 25; 27; 31; 34; 34:31(2); 32; 33; 35:1(2); 23; 26; 29; 33; 35(2); 36:8(2); 14; 29; 36(2); 37:4; 7; 15; 28; 38:6; 25; 28; 39:7; 18; 19; 20; 43; 40:12; 14; 15; **Lev** 1:2; 12; 2:12; 3:4; 10; 15; 16; 4:2; 9; 10; 20(2); 35; 5:8; 6:10; 17; 18; 7:4; 5; 7; 34; 35; 36(2); 8:6; 10; 11; 13(3); 26; 27; 28(2); 9:2; 7; 13; 14; 22; 10:1(2); 2; 3; 4; 5; 11; 17; 11:1; 4(2); 9; 22; 24; 25; 26; 28; 31; 32; 33; 42; 43; 13:58; 14:6; 12; 23; 24; 40; 42; 45; 51; 15:2; 14; 15; 29; 31; 16:4; 7; 16; 21; 23; 28; 17:2; 5(2); 7; 8; 16; 18:2; 5; 29; 19:2; 10; 31(2); 37; 20:6; 8; 11(2); 12(2); 13(2); 16; 18; 22; 23; 27(2); 21:1; 23; 22:3; 9; 16(2); 18; 22; 25(2); 31; 23:2; 10; 20; 22; 43; 24:6; 12; 25:2; 18; 31; 44; 45; 46(2); 51; 26:3; 36(2); 39; 41(2); 43(2); 44(4); 27:2; **Num** 1:3; 19; 21; 22; 23; 25; 27; 29; 31; 33; 35; 37; 39; 41; 43; 47; 49; 2:4; 13; 15; 19; 21; 23; 26; 28; 30; 3:6; 15; 16; 22(2); 32; 34; 43; 47; 48; 49(2); 51; 4:8; 12(3); 19(2); 23; 26; 27; 29; 30; 36; 40; 44; 48; 5:3; 4; 12; 23; 6:2; 16; 19; 20; 23; 27; 7:1(2); 2; 3; 5(2); 6; 9; 13; 19; 25; 31; 37; 43; 49; 55; 61; 67; 73; 79; 8:6; 7(5); 8; 13; 15(2); 16; 17; 20; 21(3); 22; 9:8; 10:2(2); 3; 33(2); 34; 35; 11:1(2); 3; 4; 12(2); 16(2); 17; 21; 22(4); 24; 25; 26(2); 28; 29; 31; 32; 12:9; 13:2; 3; 17(2); 26(2); 14:2; 6; 9(2); 10; 11; 12(2); 13; 14(2); 16(2); 23; 28; 31; 40; 45(2); 15:2; 18; 25; 26; 29; 38(2); 39; 16:3(3); 7; 9; 15(2); 17; 18; 19; 21; 28; 30(2); 31; 32; 33(2); 34(2); 38(3); 45; 46; 49; 17:2; 4; 18:8; 11; 12(2); 18; 20; 24; 26(2); 30; 19:9; 10; 21; 20:6; 8; 10; 12; 13; 25; 26; 28; 21:1; 3; 16; 30(2); 33; 22:6(2); 8; 11(3); 12; 20; 23:11; 13(4); 21; 22; 25(2); 27; 24:8; 10; 25:4; 8; 11; 17; 26:3; 7; 10; 18; 22; 25; 27; 34; 37; 41; 43; 47; 50; 62(2); 64; 65(2); 27:3; 7(2); 17(4); 28:2; 3; 31; 30:12(3); 14(2); 15(2); 31:3; 6(2); 8; 13; 15; 27(2); 30; 36; 47; 51; 32:7; 8; 9; 13; 15; 17; 19; 20; 28; 29(2); 33; 41; 33:4; 51; 55; 56; 34:2; 35:2; 3; 5; 6; 7; 8(2); 10; 15; 36:6; **Deut** 1:3; 8(2); 13; 15; 29; 39; 42; 2:5; 6(2); 9; 11; 12(4); 14; 15(2); 19(2); 20; 21(3); 22(2); 23; 3:4; 6; 14; 20; 22; 28; 4:1; 3; 6; 7; 9; 10; 13; 14; 19(2); 31; 37; 5:1(3); 9(3); 10; 22(2); 29(2); 30; 31(3); 6:1; 7(2); 8; 9; 7:2(5); 3; 5; 9; 10(2); 11; 12; 15(2); 16; 17; 18; 20; 21; 22; 23(2); 24; 25; 8:19(2); 9:3(4); 4(2); 5; 10; 12(2); 14; 17(2); 28(5); 10:2; 4; 11; 15(2); 11:4(2); 6; 9; 16; 18; 19(2); 20; 21; 22; 12:3; 18; 22(2); 29(2); 30; 13:2; 14:7(2); 17:3; 5; 19; 18:2; 3; 12; 18(2); 19:1; 9; 20:1; 3(2); 17; 19(4); 20; 21:5; 8; 10(2); 18; 22:1(2); 4(2); 19; 22; 24(2); 23:8; 24:8; 25:1; 5; 26:13(2); 16; 27:2; 3; 4; 5; 26; 28:13; 14; 25(2); 26; 31; 32; 39(2); 41; 55; 57; 61; 29:1; 2; 7; 9; 17; 25(2); 26(2); 28(2); 30:1; 7; 17; 20; 31:2; 3; 4(2); 5(2); 6; 7(2); 10; 16(2); 17(4); 20(2); 21(3); 23; 28; 32:11(2); 19; 20; 21(2); 23(2); 24; 26(2); 28; 30(2); 35; 38; 41; 46; 33:2(2); 11(2); 17; 27; **Josh** 1:2; 6; 14; 15; 2:4;

5(2); 6(2); 7(2); 8; 15; 16; 21; 22(2); 23; 4:3(3); 5; 7; 8(3); 12; 5:1; 5; 6; 7(2); 6:6; 8; 13; 23; 26; 7:2; 5(3); 11; 21(2); 23(3); 24; 25(2); 8:3; 4; 5; 6(2); 9; 11; 12; 15; 16; 20; 22(3); 24; 33(3); 35; 9:5; 8; 11(2); 15(4); 16(2); 18(2); 19(2); 20(3); 21(4); 22(2); 26(3); 27; 10:1; 8(3); 9; 10(4); 11; 18; 19(3); 20(2); 24; 25; 26(3); 27(2); 28; 39; 41; 11:4; 6(2); 7(2); 8(5); 9; 11; 12(3); 13; 14; 17(2); 20(2); 21; 12:6; 13:6; 8(2); 12; 14; 22(2); 33; 14:1; 3; 12; 15:63; 17:4; 13; 15; 18:1; 4(2); 7; 8; 10; 19:9(2); 47; 49; 20:4(2); 9; 21:2; 11; 21; 42; 44(2); 22:2; 4; 6(2); 7(2); 8; 12; 15; 30; 32; 33; 23:2; 5(2); 7(3); 12(2); 16; 24:5; 7(2); 8(2); 11; 12; 13; 25; **Judg** 1:1; 4; 22; 25; 28; 29; 30; 32; 33; 34; 2:3; 10; 12(3); 14(3); 15(2); 16(2); 17; 18(5); 19(2); 21; 22; 23(2); 3:1; 2; 4; 8; 9; 15; 23; 25; 27; 28; 4:2; 5:14; 21; 30; 31; 6:1; 2; 3; 4; 8; 9; 20; 35; 7:1; 4(2); 6; 17; 24; 8:2; 4; 8; 10; 11; 12; 16; 19; 20; 23; 24; 25; 34; 9:1; 7; 8; 9; 11; 13; 24; 25; 33; 38; 43(3); 44; 49(2); 51(2); 57; 10:7; 14; 16; 11:9; 11; 21; 24; 25; 26; 32(2); 33; 35; 12:2; 3; 13:1; 14:9(2); 12; 14; 18; 19(2); 15:3(2); 5; 7; 8; 11(2); 12; 16:3(3); 8; 12; 23; 25; 26; 17:4; 18:1(2); 2; 4; 6; 7; 8; 9; 18; 21; 27; 31; 19:6; 8; 14; 15; 23(2); 24(3); 25; 20:13; 20; 25; 28; 32; 34; 40; 41; 42(3); 43(2); 45(3); 48; 21:6; 7(2); 10; 12; 13; 14(2); 15; 16; 17; 18; 22(3); 23(3); **Ruth** 1:4; 5; 6; 9; 13(2); 19; 20; 2:9; 16(2); **1Sa** 2:8(3); 10; 16; 23; 25; 30; 34; 3:13; 5:6(3); 8; 6:6; 7; 10; 12; 15; 7:10; 11; 8:7; 8; 9(3); 11; 12; 14(2); 16; 21; 22; 9:4(2); 11; 12; 14; 20; 22(3); 26; 10:5; 6; 10; 18; 11:2; 7(2); 8; 11; 12; 12:5; 8; 9(2); 13:16; 19; 14:8; 9; 10; 11; 12; 21; 22; 32(2); 34(3); 36(2); 37; 47; 48(2); 15:3; 4; 6; 9; 15; 18; 16:5; 20; 17:3; 8; 23(2); 31; 36; 39(2); 40; 18:16; 27; 19:8; 20; 20:11; 21; 40; 21:13; 22:2; 4; 11; 23:5; 26; 24:7; 22; 25:7(2); 14; 15; 16; 18; 20; 29; 43; 26:12(2); 13; 27:5; 30:2; 8(2); 17(2); 19(2); 21; 22(2); 27(3); 28(3); 29(3); 30(3); 31; 31:7; 12; 13; **2Sa** 1:10; 11; 18; 2:5; 7; 14; 3:22; 36; 4:7; 9; 12(2); 5:3; 19; 20; 21; 23(2); 6:22; 7:10(2); 21; 8:1; 2(2); 4; 7; 10:4; 5; 9; 10; 16; 19; 11:23; 12:11; 17; 31(2); 13:9; 10; 11; 30; 14:6; 15:36(2); 16:1; 17:9; 17; 18(2); 20(2); 22; 18:1; 4; 14; 31; 19:3; 28; 20:3(3); 8; 19; 21:2(3); 6(2); 7; 9(2); 10(2); 12(2); 13; 22:15(2); 18; 23; 28; 31; 38(2); 39(2); 40; 41; 42; 43(3); 49; 23:6; 7; 18; 24:1; 12; **1Kin** 1:20; 33; 40; 2:7; 32; 5:3; 9(4); 14; 18; 6:12; 15; 16; 32(2); 35; 7:6(2); 15; 25; 37; 46; 8:21; 34; 35; 36; 37; 44; 46(3); 47(2); 48; 50(4); 52; 53; 9:6; 7; 9(3); 13; 21; 10:17; 29; 11:2; 18; 24; 12:5; 7(3); 9; 10; 14; 16; 17; 28; 13:11; 12; 14:15; 23; 27; 28(2); 15:18(2); 22; 18:4(2); 6; 13; 23(2); 26; 27; 28; 40(5); 19:2; 21; 20:15; 18(2); 19; 20; 23; 25; 27(2); 21:8; 11(2); 22:6; 10; 11; 13; 17; **2Kin** 1:2; 3; 5; 7; 12; 2:11; 12; 16; 18; 24(3); 3:9; 10; 13; 21; 24; 4:31; 33; 39(2); 44; 5:12; 22; 23(2); 24(2); 6:4; 11; 16; 18; 19(2); 21(3); 22(2); 23(2); 33; 7:10; 12; 15; 9:11; 17; 18; 19; 20; 10:1; 6(2); 7(2); 8; 14(4); 18; 22; 25(3); 26; 29; 32; 11:4(4); 5; 9; 15; 12:5(2); 7; 11; 13:3; 4; 7(2); 17; 18; 23(5); 14:27; 15:29; 16:17; 17:6; 7; 9; 10; 11; 12; 15(4); 16; 18; 20(3); 21; 22; 24; 25(2); 26(2); 27(2); 28; 29; 32(2); 35(4); 18:11; 12(2); 13; 18; 19; 23; 27; 19:6; 11; 12; 18; 20:13(3); 15; 21:3; 8(2); 9; 14; 21; 24; 22:5(2); 7; 9; 15; 23:4(2); 5; 12(2); 16; 19; 20; 24:2; 3; 16; 20; 25:13; 19; 20; 21(2); 22; 24(2); **1Chr** 2:6; 23; 53; 4:21; 41; 42; 5:11; 20(3); 25; 26(2); 6:55; 67; 78; 7:3; 4; 9; 40; 8:6; 7; 8; 32; 9:20; 25; 27(2); 28(2); 29; 10:7; 12; 11:3; 14; 20; 12:15; 17(2); 18(2); 19; 29; 32; 34; 39; 40; 13:2; 14:8; 10(2); 11; 14(3); 15:2; 12; 14; 16; 18:10; 21; 41; 42; 17:9(2); 18:1; 4; 7; 11; 19:4(2); 5; 6; 10; 16; 17(2); 20:3; 21:2; 6; 10; 23:6; 22; 31; 24:3; 6; 19; 25:7; 26:30; 31; 27:23; 26; 29:8; **2Chr** 2:2; 11; 17; 18; 3:10; 15; 16(2); 4:4; 6(2); 7; 8; 9; 17; 5:12(2); 6:25(2); 26; 27; 28; 34; 36(3); 38; 7:6; 19; 20(2); 22(4); 8:2; 8(2); 18; 9:8(2); 16; 10:5; 7(2); 9; 10; 13; 14; 16; 17; 11:11; 12; 14; 16; 23; 12:5; 7(2); 10; 11(2); 13:7; 9; 13(2); 16; 17; 14:7; 9; 11; 13; 14(2); 15:4; 6; 9; 15(2); 16:8; 9; 17:8(2); 9; 14; 18:5; 9(2); 16; 31; 19:2; 4; 9; 10; 20:1; 10(2); 12; 16(2); 17; 23; 25(2); 27(2); 21:3; 22:8; 12; 23:3; 8; 14; 24:5; 13; 17; 19(3); 20; 23; 25:5(3); 10; 12(2); 13; 14(3); 20; 26:9; 14; 27:5; 28:5(2); 8; 9(3); 12; 13; 15(7); 23(2); 29:3; 4; 5; 8; 21; 23; 24; 34; 30:7; 9(2); 10(2); 12; 14; 17; 18; 31:1; 6; 7; 11; 32:1; 6(2); 18(2); 22; 26; 33:3; 8; 11; 15; 22; 25; 34:4(4); 12; 21; 23; 35:2; 11; 13; 15; 25; 36:7; 15; 17(2); 20; **Ezr** 1:5; 6; 7; 8; 9; 11; 2:63; 65; 3:3; 7(2); 4:2; 3; 4; 5; 20; 23; 5:1; 2(2); 3(2); 4; 5; 9; 10; 12; 14; 15; 6:5; 9; 20; 21; 22(2); 7:17; 24; 25(2); 8:1; 13; 14; 15; 17(2); 20; 22(2); 24; 25; 28; 29(2); 30; 33; 10:3; 6; 10; 14(2); 15; 16; 44; **Neh** 1:2; 5; 9(3); 2:9; 10; 17; 18; 20(2); 3:2; 4(3); 5; 7; 9; 10; 27; 29; 4:4; 8; 9(2); 11(2); 12; 14; 16; 21; 23; 5:2; 5; 7(2); 8; 10; 11(2); 12(3); 15; 6:3; 4; 8; 17; 7:3(3); 5; 65; 8:8; 10(2); 12; 16; 17; 9:1; 6; 10; 11; 12(2); 13(2); 14(2); 15(4); 17(2); 18; 19(4); 20(2); 21; 22(2); 23; 24(3); 26(2); 27(5); 28(4); 29(3); 30(3); 31(2); 34; 35(2); 10:31; 11:23; 12:9; 24; 27; 29; 31; 32; 36; 37; 38(3); 40; 43; 44; 47; 13:2(2); 10; 11(2); 13; 15; 17; 21(2); 25(4); 29; 30; **Est** 1:7; 2:3; 15; 3:4(2); 8; 11; 13; 4:7; 8; 15; 5:8; 11; 8:11(2); 17; 9:1(3); 2(2); 3; 5; 21; 22(2); 23; 24(3); 26; 27(2); 28; 31; **Job** 1:4; 5(2); 6; 14; 15(2); 16; 17; 2:1; 3:8; 4:19; 21; 5:4; 6:19; 8:4; 9:5; 12:15; 23(2); 24; 25; 14:21; 15:19; 17:4; 20:15(2); 21:8; 9; 17; 26; 29; 22:17; 19; 20; 24:5; 12; 17(2); 26:8; 29:22; 24; 30:5; 31; 32:8; 34:25; 26; 36:7; 9; 13; 31; 37:4; 12; 15; 21; 39:4; 14; 15(2); 40:13; 41:16; 42:9; 15; **Ps** 2:4; 5(2); 9(2); 5:6; 10(3); 11(3); 6:10; 7:1; 9:6; 10; 12; 13; 20; 10:2; 5; 12:7(2); 15:4; 17:7(2); 18:14(2); 17; 37; 38; 40; 41(2); 42(2); 19:4; 11(2); 13; 21:9(3); 12(2); 22:4; 18; 25; 24:6; 9; 25:3; 14(2); 28:1; 4(3); 5(2); 9(2); 29:6; 31:6; 15; 17; 19(2); 20(2); 33:6; 18(2); 19; 34:7(2); 9; 16(2); 17; 18; 19; 20; 22; 35:1(2); 3; 4(2); 5(2); 6; 19(2); 20; 24; 25(2); 26(2); 27(2); 36:8; 10; 37:40(4); 39:6; 40:5; 14(2); 15; 41:10; 42:4; 43:3(2); 44:2(2); 3(2); 5; 7; 13; 48:6; 49:7; 14(2); 50:21; 53:3; 5(2); 54:3; 4; 5; 55:15(3); 19; 23; 57:4; 58:7(2); 8; 9; 59:1; 8; 11(3); 12; 13(3); 14(2); 15; 60:4; 62:10; 63:11; 64:5; 6; 7; 8; 65:3; 5; 9; 68:1; 2; 3(2); 17; 18; 25; 69:6; 9; 11; 14; 22; 24(2); 27; 28; 70:2(2); 3; 71:13(2); 73:6(2); 10; 18(2); 27; 74:8; 75:8(2); 78:4; 5; 6(2); 11; 13; 14; 15; 24(2); 25; 27; 29; 31(2); 34; 38; 42; 45(3); 49(2); 52; 53; 54; 55(2); 66; 72(2); 79:3; 4; 80:5(2); 81:12; 16; 82:4; 83:4; 8; 9; 13; 15(2); 17(2); 84:5; 7; 11; 85:8; 9; 86:5; 14; 87:4; 88:4; 8; 89:7; 9; 11; 12; 23; 90:5; 94:23(3); 97:10; 99:3; 6(2); 7(2); 8(2); 101:3; 102:26(2); 103:11; 13; 17; 18; 104:8; 12; 22; 24; 27; 28; 105:3; 14; 17; 24; 27; 32; 37; 38(2); 40; 44; 106:8; 9; 10(3); 11; 15; 23(2); 26(2); 27; 29; 34; 36; 41(3); 42; 43; 45; 46(2); 107:3; 5; 6; 7; 13; 14; 19; 20(2); 22; 28; 30; 32; 34; 38; 40; 109:10; 15(2); 20; 25; 28(2); 29; 111:2; 5; 6; 115:8(3); 13; 118:4; 7(2); 10; 11; 12; 19; 119:63(2); 84; 93; 118; 129; 152; 165; 167; 125:4; 5; 126:1; 2; 127:5; 129:5; 6; 132:12; 135:18(3); 136:11; 139:16; 17; 18; 21; 22(2); 140:9; 10(2); 143:7; 12; 144:6(2); 145:15; 18; 19(2); 20; 146:8; 147:4; 11; 18; 20; 148:5; 6; 13; 149:3(2); 5; 9; **Prov** 1:12; 15; 32(2); 2:7; 3:3(2); 18; 21; 27; 4:21(2); 22; 5:6; 13; 17; 6:21(2); 7:3(2); 8:8; 9; 17; 10:26; 11:3(2); 6; 12:6; 20; 26; 14:3; 22; 19:7; 20:10; 12; 26; 21:6; 7; 22:2; 5; 18; 21; 23; 26(2); 24:1; 11; 21; 22; 25(2); 25:13; 27:3; 28:4; 13; 30:5; 7; 27; 31:29; **Eccl** 2:5; 10; 14; 3:12; 18; 19; 4:16; 5:11(2); 7:11; 12; 18; 8:11; 12; 9:1; 5; 11; 12; 10:15; 11:8; 12:1; **Song** 3:4; 4:2; 5:3; 6:6; **Is** 1:14; 23; 31; 2:9; 3:4; 9; 12; 4:2; 5:8; 11(2); 18; 20; 21; 22; 25(2); 26; 27; 30; 6:13; 7:19; 20; 8:7; 12; 15; 19; 20; 9:2; 10; 13; 16(2); 10:1; 6; 10; 15; 19; 20; 22; 11:6; 14(2); 13:2; 3; 8; 15; 17; 14:1(2); 2(4); 18; 20; 22; 25; 16:4; 17:2; 13; 14(2); 18:6(2); 19:3; 4; 12(2); 20(2); 22(2); 23:1; 13; 18; 24:8; 9; 25:11; 26:5; 11; 14; 16; 27:4(2); 6; 7; 11(5); 28:1; 6; 9; 13; 29:1; 15; 30:5; 6; 8; 22; 28; 31:1; 2; 4; 32:3(2); 33:4; 34:2(2); 7; 16; 17(2); 35:1; 4; 36:1; 4; 8; 37:6; 11; 12; 19; 38:21; 39:2(3); 4; 40:11; 22; 24(2); 26; 29; 41:1(2); 2; 3; 12(3); 15; 16(3); 17(2); 22(5); 27; 28(2); 42:5(2); 7; 9; 11; 12; 16(4); 22; 43:9(3); 44:7(2); 9; 11(2); 45:8; 16; 21(2); 47:6(2); 14; 48:3(2); 5(2); 6; 7(2); 13; 14; 21(2); 49:9; 10(4); 18(2); 26; 50:6; 9; 51:8(2); 17; 23(2); 52:4; 5(2); 15; 54:2; 56:5(2); 7(2); 57:6; 8; 13(2); 59:8; 12; 20; 21; 60:9; 14; 61:1; 3(2); 7; 8; 9(2); 62:12; 63:3(2); 6; 7; 9(4); 10; 11; 12(2); 13; 19; 65:1(2); 8; 21(2); 23; 66:4; 19(2); 21; **Jer** 1:16; 17(2); 2:3; 13; 25; 28; 37; 3:2; 4:12; 5:3(2); 5; 6(2); 7(2); 13(2); 14; 19; 6:10; 13(2); 15(2); 18; 21; 30(2); 7:16; 22(2); 23; 25; 27(2); 28; 31; 33; 8:2; 3(2); 4; 9; 10(2); 12; 13(3); 19; 9:2; 7(2); 9; 10; 13; 14; 15(2); 16(3); 18; 22; 25; 10:2; 5(2); 11; 14; 16; 18; 11:3; 4(2); 5; 6; 7; 8(3); 10; 11(2); 12; 14(2); 20; 22; 23; 12:2; 3(2); 4; 6; 14(2); 15(3); 13:10(2); 12; 13; 14(2); 19; 20; 21; 24; 14:10; 12(2); 13; 14(3); 15; 16(3); 17(2); 18; 15:1(2); 2; 3; 4; 7(2); 8; 9; 10; 16; 19(2); 16:3(2); 5; 6(2); 7(3); 8; 11(3); 15(2); 16(2); 21(2); 17:11(2); 18(4); 20; 18:8; 10; 15; 17(2); 19; 20(2); 22; 23(2); 19:7(2); 9(2); 11(2); 20:4(2); 5(3); 12; 21:3; 4; 7(2); 22:7; 9; 25(2); 23:2(2); 3(2); 4(2); 8; 12(2); 14; 15(2); 17; 21; 22; 32(4); 33; 24:1; 5; 6(6); 7; 8; 9(2); 10(2); 25:4; 6(2); 9(3); 10; 14(2); 16; 18; 26; 27; 28; 30(2); 31; 26:2; 3; 4; 5; 19; 27:2; 3; 4; 8; 15; 17; 18(2); 22(3); 28:3; 13; 29:5(2); 9; 17(2); 18(3); 19(2); 21(2); 22; 23; 28(2); 31; 30:3; 9; 16; 19(4); 20; 21; 31:4; 5; 8(3); 9(2); 13(2); 28(2); 32(3); 34(2); 32:13; 14; 18; 22(2); 23(2); 33(2); 35; 37(4); 39(3); 40(3); 41(3); 42(2); 44; 33:5; 6(2); 7; 8; 9; 11(2); 13; 24(2); 26; 34:8; 9; 10(2); 11; 13; 16; 20(2); 21; 22; 35:2(3); 4; 5; 15(2); 16; 17(3); 36:3; 6; 13; 14; 18(2); 25; 26; 31(2); 32; 37:5; 10; 38:4; 11; 26; 27; 39:4; 5; 10; 40:7; 9; 10; 11; 14; 41:5; 6(3); 7(2); 8(2); 9; 10; 18; 42:4; 9; 17(2); 43:1; 9; 10(2); 12(2); 44:4; 13; 21; 27(2); 30; 45:5; 46:5; 15; 21; 25; 26; 47:2; 48:39; 49:2; 11; 20(2); 29; 32; 36; 37(4); 50:6(2); 7(2); 20; 21; 27(2); 28; 33(3); 43; 44; 45(2); 51:1(2); 17; 19; 39; 40; 52:3; 17; 25; 26(2); 27(2); **Lam** 1:13; 17; 22; 2:2; 21; 3:20; 25; 64; 65(2); 66; 4:4; 15; 16(2); **Eze** 1:18; 19; 20; 21; 2:4(2); 5; 6; 7; 3:4; 6; 9; 11(3); 13; 15(2); 17; 25(2); 26; 27; 4:6; 9; 13; 5:2; 3; 4(3); 6; 12; 13(2); 16; 6:2; 10; 12; 14; 7:11(2); 16(2); 18; 19; 20; 22; 27(2); 8:11(2); 18; 9:1; 2; 7; 8; 10:1; 2; 13; 16(2); 17; 19(2); 11:4; 5; 16(3); 19(2); 20; 21; 22(2); 24; 25; 12:10(2); 11; 12; 14; 15(2); 16; 19; 23(2); 28; 13:2; 6; 11; 15; 17; 20(3); 14:3; 4(2); 15:7(3); 16:17; 18(2); 19; 20; 21(3); 27; 28; 33; 36; 37(4); 50; 53; 54; 61; 17:12(2); 18:19; 24; 26; 19:11; 12; 20:3; 4(3); 5(3); 6(3); 7; 8(2); 9(2); 10(2); 11(3); 12(3); 13(3); 14; 15(3); 17(3); 19; 21(4); 22; 23(3); 25; 26(2); 27; 28(2); 29; 38(2); 40(2); 21:23(2); 29; 22:26; 28(2); 30; 31(2); 23:4; 6; 7(2); 12; 15; 16(3); 17(2); 22; 23(3); 24; 27; 28(2); 36; 37(2); 43; 45; 46(2); 47(2); 24:3; 5; 20; 25; 27; 25:2; 10; 12; 17(2); 26:20(2); 27:31; 28:8; 18; 24(2); 25; 26(2); 29:12; 14; 15; 16; 21; 30:5; 9; 23; 26; 31:14; 16; 17; 18; 32:10; 12; 13(2); 15; 18(2); 20; 21; 22; 23; 24(2); 25(3); 26; 28; 29(2); 30(3); 31; 32; 33:2; 6; 7; 10; 11; 17; 25; 27; 31; 32(2); 33; 34:2; 3; 4; 6; 10(2); 11; 12; 13(4); 14; 15; 16; 20; 21; 23(3); 24; 25; 26; 27(2); 28(2); 29; 30; 35:11(2); 13; 36:12; 18; 19(2); 20; 23; 27; 37(2); 37:2; 4; 8(3); 10; 12; 17; 19(3); 21(3); 22(2); 23(2); 24(2); 26(5); 27; 28; 38:4(2); 5(2); 7; 8; 11(2); 15; 17; 39:6; 7; 9; 10(2); 12; 13(2); 18; 21; 23(2); 24(2); 26; 27(3); 28(3); 29; 40:4; 22; 26; 41:25; 42:9; 11; 12; 43:8(2); 9(2); 10; 11(2); 24(3); 44:11(2); 12(2); 14; 17; 19; 23; 28(2); 45:15; 46:10; 17; 18; 20; 23(2); 24; 48:10; 12; 18; **Dan** 1:4; 5(2); 12; 14(2); 16; 17; 18(2); 19(2); 20(2); 2:3; 21; 34; 35(2); 38; 3:14; 20; 27; 4:7; 19; 5:3; 23; 6:2; 24(3); 7:8; 16; 21; 24; 8:9; 10; 9:4(2); 7; 10:7; 11:7; 24; 30; 34; 35(3); 39; 12:2; **Hos** 1:6; 7(2); 10(2); 2:5; 7(3); 12(2); 13; 18(2); 23; 4:9(2); 12(2); 16; 5:2; 4; 5; 6; 7; 10(2); 6:5(2); 8; 7:2; 7; 12(3); 13(3); 8:4; 5; 10; 13; 9:2; 4; 6(3); 12(3); 14(2); 15(3); 17; 10:9; 10(2); 11:2(2); 3(2); 4(3); 6; 7; 11; 13:2(2); 7(2); 8(3); 14(2); 14:4; 9(2); **Joel** 2:3(5); 4; 10; 17(2); 3:2(2); 6; 7(2); 8; 9; **Amos** 1:6; 2:4; 9; 4:3; 9; 5:8; 11(2); 22; 6:1; 7; 7:8; 8:2; 3; 9:1(5); 2(2); 3(2); 4(2); 6; 14(2); 15(2); **Obad** 11; 18(2); **Jonah** 1:3; 5; 9; 10; 12; 13; 3:5(2); 7; 8; 10; **Mic** 2:1; 2(2); 6(2); 8; 12; 13(3); 3:2; 3(2); 4(2); 6; 4:4; 7; 12; 5:3; 6:11; 7:4; 13; 14; **Nah** 1:7; 2:2; 10; 11; 3:18; **Hab** 1:10; 12(2); 13; 14; 15(3); 16; 2:7; 17; 3:16; **Zeph** 1:5(2); 6; 13; 18(2); 2:7; 9(2); 11; 3:7; 8; 11; 13; 18; 19; **Hag** 2:22; **Zec** 1:3; 21; 2:9; 3:5; 6:6; 10; 11; 13; 7:14(2); 8:8; 9:8; 14; 15; 16; 10:1; 3; 5; 6(5); 8(3); 9; 10(4); 12; 11:5(3); 6; 8; 12; 13(2); 12:8(2); 13:9(3); 14:8(2); 13; 17; 21; **Mal** 1:4; 2:2; 5; 17; 3:3; 7; 16; 17; 4:1(2); **Mt** 2:4; 7; 8; 9; 3:7; 4:8; 16; 19; 21; 24; 5:2; 19; 21; 27; 33; 44(3); 46; 6:1; 8; 26; 7:6; 11; 12; 16; 20; 23; 24; 26; 29; 8:4; 10; 15; 26; 30; 32; 33; 9:12; 15(3); 18; 24; 28; 30; 36; 10:1(2); 5; 16; 18; 21; 25; 26; 28; 29; 11:4; 5; 11; 25; 12:3; 4; 11; 15; 16; 25; 27; 39; 13:3; 4; 7; 10; 11(2); 13; 14; 15; 17(2); 24; 28(2); 29; 30(2); 31; 33; 34; 37; 39; 41; 42; 50; 51; 52; 54; 57; 14:6; 9; 14; 16(2); 18; 25; 27; 15:3; 10; 14; 30(3); 32; 34; 36; 16:1; 2; 4; 6; 8; 12; 15; 17:1; 2; 3; 5; 7; 9; 11; 12; 13; 20; 22; 27(2); 18:2; 8(2); 12; 17; 19; 20; 19:2; 4(3); 8; 11; 13(2); 14; 15; 26(2); 28; 20:2; 4; 6; 7; 8; 12; 13; 17; 23(2); 25(3); 31; 32; 34; 21:2(3); 3(2); 6; 7; 8; 12(2); 13; 14; 16; 17; 21; 24; 27; 31(2); 36; 37; 42; 45; 22:1; 3; 4; 6(2); 20; 21; 29; 35; 41; 43; 23:4(2); 13; 26; 30; 31; 34(3); 37; 24:2; 4; 16; 19(2); 39; 45; 25:2; 3; 9; 14; 16; 19; 20; 22; 32; 34; 40; 41; 45; 26:10; 15; 19; 22; 27; 31; 36; 38; 40; 43; 44; 45; 48; 51; 70; 71; 73; 27:6; 7; 10; 17; 21; 22; 26; 35; 47; 48; 65; 28:9; 10; 16; 18; 19; 20; **Mk** 1:17; 20; 22; 31; 32; 38; 44; 2:2(2); 8; 12; 13; 17; 19(3); 20; 25; 26; 27; 3:4; 5; 12; 14; 17; 23(2); 33; 34; 4:2(2); 9; 11(2); 12; 13; 21; 24; 33; 34; 35; 40; 5:10; 12; 13; 16; 19; 38; 39; 40(2); 43; 6:4; 5; 7(2); 8; 10; 11; 13; 22; 31; 33(2); 34(2); 36; 37(3); 38; 39; 41(3); 46; 48(4); 50(2); 51; 7:6; 9; 14; 18; 36(2); 8:1; 3(2); 5; 6(2); 7(2); 9; 13; 14; 15; 17; 21; 27; 29; 30; 31; 34; 9:1(2); 2(2); 3; 4; 7; 9; 12; 14(2); 16; 29; 31; 33; 35; 36(2); 10:1; 3; 5; 6; 11; 13(2); 14(2); 16(3); 24(2); 27; 32(2); 36; 38; 39; 40; 42(4); 11:2; 5(2); 6(2); 8; 15(2); 17; 22; 24(2); 29; 33; 12:1; 4; 6; 12; 15; 16; 17; 23; 24; 28(2); 38; 43; 13:5; 9; 12; 14; 17(2); 14:7; 10; 13; 16; 20; 22; 23; 24; 27; 34; 37; 40; 41; 44; 47; 48; 52; 69(2); 70; 15:6; 7; 8; 9; 11; 12; 14; 15; 24; 35; 16:6; 10; 12; 13; 14(2); 15; 17; 18; 19; 20; **Lk** 1:2; 22(2); 50; 52; 65; 66(2); 79; 2:7; 9(2); 10; 15; 17; 18; 19; 20; 34; 38; 46(2); 49; 50; 51(2); 3:11; 13; 14; 16; 4:6; 18; 20; 21; 23; 26; 27; 30; 31; 39; 40(3); 41(2); 42; 43; 5:2; 7; 14; 17; 22; 25; 29; 31; 34(2); 35; 36; 6:1; 2; 3; 4; 5; 9; 10; 13; 17; 19; 27; 28(2); 30; 31; 32(2); 33; 34; 39; 47; 7:6; 19; 22; 38(2); 42(2); 44; 8:21; 22; 25; 31; 32(3); 34; 36; 37; 54; 56; 9:1; 2; 3; 5; 10; 11(3); 13(2); 14; 15; 16; 17; 18; 20; 21(2); 23; 34; 45; 46(2); 48; 54; 55; 56; 61; 10:1; 2; 9; 18; 21; 24(2); 35; 11:2; 5; 13; 15; 17; 19; 31; 44(2); 47; 48; 49(2); 52; 53; 12:4; 6; 15; 16; 24; 37(2); 38; 42; 13:2; 4; 14; 23; 32; 34; 14:5; 7; 10; 15; 17; 19; 23; 25; 15:2; 3; 4; 6; 12(2); 16:15; 28; 29(2); 30; 17:14(2); 15; 20; 23(2); 27; 29; 37; 18:1; 7; 8; 15(2); 16(2); 29; 31; 34; 19:13(2); 24; 27(2); 32; 33; 40; 45(2); 46; 20:3; 8; 15; 17; 19; 23; 25; 33; 34; 41; 21:8; 10; 21(3); 23(2); 26; 29; 35; 22:4; 6; 10; 13; 15; 19; 23; 24(2); 25(3); 35; 36; 38; 40; 41; 45; 46; 47; 50; 55; 58; 67; 70; 23:1; 14; 17; 20; 22; 23; 25; 28; 34; 35; 51; 24:1; 4; 5; 10; 11(2); 13; 15; 17; 18; 19; 24; 25; 27; 29; 30(2); 33(2); 35; 36(2); 38; 40; 41; 43; 44; 46; 50(2); 51(2); **Jn** 1:12(2); 22; 26; 38(2); 39; 2:7(2); 8; 15; 16; 19; 22; 24; 3:22; 4:32; 34; 40; 52; 5:11; 17; 19; 21; 39; 6:2; 7(2); 11; 13(2); 17; 20; 26; 29; 31; 32; 35; 43; 53; 61; 70; 7:6; 9; 16; 21; 25; 33; 44; 45; 47; 50(2); 8:2; 6; 7; 12; 14; 21; 23; 25; 27; 28; 34; 39; 42; 47; 58; 59; 9:15; 16; 19; 20; 27; 30; 41; 10:3; 4; 6(2); 7; 8; 12; 16; 20; 25; 27; 28(2); 29(2); 32; 34; 35; 11:11; 14; 19; 37; 44; 46(2); 49(2); 12:2; 20; 23; 35; 36; 37; 40; 13:1; 5; 12; 17; 29; 14:21; 15:6(2); 22; 24; 16:4; 12; 19; 31; 17:6; 8(2); 9(2); 10; 12(3); 14(2); 15(2); 17; 18; 20; 22; 23(2); 26(3); 18:4; 5(2); 6; 7; 9; 18; 21(2); 29; 31; 38; 19:4; 5; 6; 15; 16; 24; 20:2; 13; 17; 19; 20; 21; 22(2); 23; 24; 25; 26; 21:3; 5; 6; 10; 12; 13; **Acts** 1:3; 4(2); 7; 10; 16; 2:3(2); 4; 6; 11; 14; 38; 41; 45; 3:2; 5(2); 8; 11; 4:1; 3(2); 4; 7; 8; 13; 14; 15; 16(2); 17; 18(2); 19; 21(3); 23; 24; 32(2); 33; 34(2); 35; 5:5; 9; 13(2); 15(2); 16; 18; 19; 21; 22; 24; 25; 26; 27(3); 32; 33; 35; 38; 40(2); 6:2; 6; 9; 7:6(2); 24; 25; 26(2); 34; 36; 39; 42; 43; 52; 8:3; 5; 7; 11; 14; 15; 16; 17; 18; 9:2; 21(2); 27; 28; 38; 39(2); 40; 10:7; 8(2); 20(2); 23(3); 24; 28; 44; 46; 48; 11:3; 4; 12; 15; 17; 20; 21; 23; 28; 12:10; 17(2); 20; 21; 25; 13:2; 3(2); 8; 13; 15; 17; 19; 20; 21; 22; 27; 31; 42; 43(2); 50; 51; 14:5(2); 18; 22; 23(2); 27; 15:2(2); 4; 5(2); 7; 8(2); 9; 12; 14; 19; 20; 21; 23; 32; 37; 38(3); 39; 16:4; 7; 10; 19; 20; 22(2); 23(3); 24; 25; 30; 33; 34(2); 37(2); 39(3); 40; 17:2(2); 4; 5(2); 6; 9; 12; 16; 18; 33; 34; 18:2; 3; 6; 11; 16; 19; 20; 21; 26; 27; 19:2; 3; 6(2); 9; 12(2); 13(2); 16(3); 17; 19(3); 22; 38; 20:1; 2; 6; 7; 18; 30; 32; 34; 36; 21:1; 7; 16; 19; 23; 24(3); 26(2); 32; 40; 22:2; 5; 11; 19; 20; 30; 23:2; 10(2); 21(2); 24; 27; 31; 24:21; 22; 25:5; 6; 11; 26:10; 11(4); 13; 18(2); 20; 30; 27:9; 10; 21; 24; 33; 35; 42; 43; 28:3; 14; 17; 23; 27; **Rom** 1:19(2); 24; 26; 28; 32(2); 2:2; 3; 7; 8; 19; 3:2; 19; 22; 4:11(2); 12; 5:14; 7:1; 8:1; 28(2); 30(3); 9:25; 26; 10:2; 5; 15; 19; 20(2); 11:8; 9; 11; 12(2); 14(2); 15(2); 17(2); 22; 23; 27; 32; 12:14; 15(2); 15:3; 26; 27(2); 28; 31; 16:10; 11; 14; 15; 17(2); **1Cor** 1:2; 11; 18; 21; 24; 2:6; 9; 10; 14; 4:19; 5:12(2); 13; 6:4; 13; 15; 7:8; 9; 36; 8:9; 9:3; 20(2); 21(2); 10:4; 5; 7; 8; 9; 10; 11; 27; 11:2; 22; 12:18; 14:10; 22(4); 34; 35; 15:20; 16:3; 18; **2Cor** 1:4; 2:3; 13; 15(2); 4:3; 4(2); 5:12; 15; 19; 6:16(2); 17; 8:22; 24; 9:2; 13; 11:8; 12; 12:17; 13:2; **Gal** 1:17; 2:2(2); 12; 14; 3:10; 12(2); 22; 4:5; 8; 15; 17; 6:10; 16; **Eph** 2:10; 17; 4:18; 5:7; 11; 12; 6:4; 5; 9; 24; **Phil** 1:28; 3:8; 17; **Col** 2:1; 15(2); 3:7; 19; 4:5; 13(2); **1Th** 2:16; 4:12; 13; 14; 15; 17; 5:3; 12; 13; 14; **2Th** 1:6; 8; 10; 2:10; 11; 3:12; **1Ti** 1:10; 16; 18; 3:7; 10; 4:3; 15; 16(2); 5:4; 16(3); 20; 6:2(3); 17; **2Ti** 2:14(2); 19; 22; 25; 3:11; 14; 4:8; **Titus** 1:13; 15; 2:9; 3:1; 13; 15; **Heb** 1:12; 14; 2:1; 3; 4; 11; 15; 18; 3:17; 18; 4:2(3); 8; 5:2; 9; 14; 6:6; 7; 12; 16; 7:6; 8; 25(2); 8:8; 9(3); 10(2); 9:10; 28; 10:14; 16(2); 33; 39(2); 11:6; 13(3); 16; 28; 31; 12:9; 11; 19; 13:3(3); 7; 9; 17; 24; **Jas** 1:12; 2:5; 16(2); 25; 3:18; 5:3; 4; 11; 14; **1Pet** 1:11; 12; 2:7; 8; 14(2); 3:7; 12; 4:4; 6; 17; 19; **2Pet** 1:1; 12; 2:1; 4(2); 6(2); 8; 10; 11; 18; 19; 20; 21(2); 22; 3:16; **1Jn** 2:26; 4:4; 5; 5:16; **3Jn** 9; 10(2); **Jude** 1; 5; 7; 11; 15; 23; **Rev** 2:2(3); 9; 14; 15; 16; 22; 27; 3:9(2); 10; 4:8; 5:8; 11; 13; 6:8; 9; 10; 11(2); 7:4; 14; 15; 16; 17(2); 8:2; 12; 9:3; 4; 5(2); 6; 11; 16; 17(2); 19; 10:4; 11:1; 5(2); 6; 7(3); 10(2); 11(3); 12(2); 18(2); 12:4; 10; 12; 13:6; 7; 12; 14(2); 14:6; 9; 13; 15:1; 2; 16:2; 6; 14; 16; 17:14; 18:14; 19:15; 18(2); 20(2); 20:4(3); 8; 9; 10; 11; 13; 21:3(2); 14; 24; 22:5; 8; 9

THEMSELVES

Gen 3:7; 8; 13:11; 19:11; 21:28; 29; 30:40; 32:16; 33:6; 7(2); 34:30; 42:6; 43:26; 32(2); **Ex** 5:7; 11:8; 12:39; 18:26; 19:22; 26:9(2); 32:1; 7; 26; 33:6; 36:16(2); **Lev** 15:18; 22:2; **Num** 6:2(2); 8:7; 10:3; 4; 11:32; 16:3; 20:2; 27:3; **Deut** 7:20; 9:12; 31:14; 20; 32:5; 27; 31; **Josh** 8:27; 9:2; 10:5; 13; 16; 11:14; 22:12; 24:1; **Judg** 2:12; 17; 19; 5:2; 9; 7:2; 23; 24; 10:17; 12:1; 15:9; 20:2; 14; 20; 22(2); 30; 33; 37; **1Sa** 2:5; 3:13; 4:2; 8:4; 13:5; 6; 11; 14:11(2); 20; 22; 21:4; 22:2; 28:4; **2Sa** 2:25; 5:18; 22; 10:8; 15; 17; 16:14; 22:45; **1Kin** 8:2; 47; 18:23; 28; 20:12; **2Kin** 2:15; 7:12; 8:20; 17:17; 32; 19:29; **1Chr** 11:1; 10; 14; 12:8; 13:2; 14:9; 13; 15:14; 19:6; 7; 9; 11; 21:20; 29:24; **2Chr** 3:13; 5:3; 6:37; 7:3; 14; 12:6; 7(2); 13:7; 14:13; 15:10; 20:4; 25; 26; 21:8; 29:15; 29; 34(2); 30:3(2); 11; 15; 18; 24; 31:18; 32:8; 35:14(2); **Ezr** 3:1; 6:20; 21; 9:1; 2(2); 10:7; 9; **Neh** 4:2; 8:1; 16; 9:2; 25; 10:28; 11:2; 12:28; 30; 13:22; **Est** 8:11; 13; 9:2; 15; 16; 27; 31; **Job** 1:6; 2:1; 3:14; 6:4; 16:10; 24:4; 16; 29:8; 30:14; 34:22; 39:3; 41:23; 25; **Ps** 2:2; 3:6; 9:20; 18:44; 35:15(2); 26; 37:11; 38:16; 44:10; 49:6; 56:6(2); 57:6; 59:4; 64:5; 8; 66:3; 7; 80:6; 81:15; 94:4; 21; 97:7; 104:22; 106:28; 109:29; 140:8; **Prov** 23:5; 28:28; **Eccl** 3:18; 11:3; 12:3; **Is** 2:6; 3:9; 8:21; 10:31; 15:3; 22:7; 30:2; 46:2; 47:14; 48:2(2); 49:18; 56:6; 59:6; 60:4; 14;

66:17(2); **Jer** 2:24; 4:2; 5:7; 22; 7:19; 9:5; 11:17; 12:13; 16:6(2); 7; 25:14; 27:7; 30:8; 21; 34:10; 41:5; 49:29; 50:9; **Lam** 2:10; 4:14; **Eze** 6:9; 7:18; 10:17; 22; 14:18; 26:16; 27:30; 31; 31:14; 34:2; 8; 10; 27; 37:23; 43:26; 44:18; 25(2); 45:5; **Dan** 2:43; 10:7; 11:6; 14; **Hos** 1:11; 4:14; 7:14; 9:9; 10; 10:10; **Amos** 2:8; 6:4; 5; 6; 7; 9:3; **Mic** 3:4; **Hab** 1:7; 8; 2:13; **Zeph** 2:8; 10; **Zec** 4:12; 11:5; 12:3; 7; **Mt** 9:3; 14:2; 15; 16:7; 19:12; 21:25; 38; 23:4; **Mk** 1:27; 2:8; 4:17; 6:14; 30; 36; 51; 8:16; 9:2; 8; 10; 34; 10:26; 11:31; 12:7; 14:4; 15:31; 16:3; **Lk** 4:36; 7:30; 49; 18:9; 20:5; 14; 20; 22:23; 23:12; 24:12; **Jn** 6:52; 7:35; 11:55; 56; 12:19; 16:17; 17:13; 18:18; 28; 19:24; **Acts** 4:15; 5:36; 11:26; 15:32; 16:37; 18:6; 21:25; 23:12; 21; 24:15; 26:31; 27:40; 43; 28:4; 25; 29; **Rom** 1:22; 24; 27; 2:14; 10:3; 13:2; **1Cor** 6:9; 16:15; **2Cor** 5:15; 8:3; 10:12(5); 11:13; **Gal** 6:13; **Eph** 4:19; **Phil** 2:3; **1Th** 1:9; **1Ti** 1:10; 2:9; 3:13; 6:10; 19; **2Ti** 2:25; 26; 4:3; **Titus** 1:12; **Heb** 6:6; 9:23; **1Pet** 1:12; 3:5; **2Pet** 2:1; 13; 19; **Jude** 7; 10; 12; 19; **Rev** 6:15; 8:6

THEN

Gen 3:5; 4:26; 8:9; 12:6; 13:7; 9(2); 11; 16; 18; 17:17; 18:15; 26; 19:15; 24; 20:9; 21:32; 22:4; 24:8; 41; 50; 25:1; 8; 34; 26:12; 26; 27:41; 45; 28:9; 21; 29:1; 8; 25; 30:14; 31:8(2); 16; 17; 25; 33; 54; 32:7; 8; 18; 33:6; 10; 34:16; 17; 35:2; 37:28; 38:11; 21; 39:9; 41:9; 14; 42:25; 34; 38; 43:9; 44:8; 11; 13; 18; 26; 32; 45:1; 47:1; 6; 23; 49:4; **Ex** 1:16(2); 2:7; 4:25; 26; 31; 5:15; 6:1; 12; 7:9; 11; 8:8; 19; 9:1; 10:16; 12:21; 44; 48; 13:13; 15:1; 15; 16:4; 6; 7; 17:8; 18:2; 23; 19:5; 21:3; 6; 8; 11; 13; 19; 23; 28; 30; 35; 22:3; 8; 11; 13; 23:22; 24:9; 29:7; 20; 34; 30:12; 32:24; 26; 34:20; 36:1; 40:34; 37; **Lev** 1:14; 3:7; 12; 4:3; 14; 28; 5:1; 3; 4; 7; 11; 12; 15; 6:4; 7:12; 10:3; 12:2; 4; 5; 8; 13:2; 4; 5; 8; 9; 13; 17; 21; 22; 25; 26; 27; 30(2); 31; 34; 36; 39; 43; 54; 56; 58; 14:4; 21; 36; 38; 40; 44; 48; 15:8; 13; 16; 28; 16:15; 17:15; 16; 19:23; 20:5; 22:14; 27; 23:10; 19; 25:2; 9; 21; 25; 27; 28; 29; 30; 33; 35; 41; 52; 54; 26:4; 18; 24; 28; 34(2); 41(2); 42; 27:4; 5; 6; 7; 8; 10; 11; 13; 14; 15; 16; 18; 19; 23; 27(2); 33; **Num** 2:7; 14; 17; 22; 29; 5:7; 15; 21; 25; 27; 28; 31; 6:9; 7:89; 8:8; 9:17; 19; 21; 10:4; 5; 6; 9; 11:10; 12:8; 14:5; 8; 13; 15; 45; 15:4; 9; 19; 24; 27; 16:3; 29; 30; 18:26; 30; 19:7; 12; 20:1; 19; 21:1; 2; 17; 22:31; 27:1; 8; 9; 10; 11; 30:4; 7; 8; 11; 12; 14; 15; 32:22; 29; 33:52; 55; 34:3; 35:11; 24; 36:3; 4; **Deut** 1:29; 41; 2:1; 32; 3:1; 20; 4:41; 5:25; 6:12; 21; 8:10; 14; 9:9; 23; 11:17; 23; 12:11; 21; 13:14; 14:25; 15:12; 17; 17:5; 8; 18:7; 19:9; 12; 17; 19; 20:10; 11; 12; 21:2; 12; 14; 16; 19; 22:2; 8; 15; 21; 22; 24; 25; 29; 23:9; 10; 24; 25; 24:1; 7; 25:1; 3; 7; 8; 9; 12; 26:13; 28:59; 29:20; 25; 30:3; 31:17; 20; 32:15; 33:28; **Josh** 1:8(2); 10; 15; 2:15; 20; 3:3; 4:4; 7; 22; 6:10; 7:21; 8:7; 21; 30; 10:12; 22; 29; 33; 14:6; 11; 12; 15:1; 17:15; 19:12; 29; 34; 20:5; 6; 21:1; 22:1; 7; 19; 21; 23:16; 24:9; 20; **Judg** 2:18; 3:23; 4:8(2); 21; 5:1; 8; 11; 13; 19; 22; 6:13; 17; 21(2); 24; 27; 30; 33; 37; 7:1; 11; 18; 24; 8:3; 7; 18; 21; 22; 9:12; 14; 15; 19(2); 23; 29; 33; 38; 50; 54; 10:17; 11:3; 11; 17; 18; 29; 31; 12:3; 4; 6(2); 7; 10; 13:6; 8; 21; 14:3; 5; 12; 13; 15:6; 9; 11; 16:1; 7; 8; 11; 17; 18; 23; 31; 17:13; 18:7; 14; 18; 19:26; 28; 20:1; 3; 26; 21:16; 19; 21; **Ruth** 1:6; 9; 18; 21; 2:5; 8; 10; 13; 3:1; 13; 18; 4:1; 4; 5; **1Sa** 1:8; 11; 17; 22; 2:16(2); 3:10; 16; 6:3; 4; 6; 9(2); 7:3; 4; 12; 8:4; 9:4; 7; 10; 18; 21; 10:1; 2; 3; 11; 25; 11:1; 3; 4; 14; 12:8; 14; 15; 21; 13:6; 14:8; 9; 10; 17; 28; 29; 33; 36; 40; 43; 46; 15:10; 14; 16; 19; 30; 32; 34; 16:8; 9; 13; 18; 17:9(2); 45; 18:3; 30; 19:5; 22; 20:4; 6; 7; 9; 10; 12; 13; 18; 19; 21; 30; 21:1; 14(2); 22:5; 7; 9; 11; 14; 15; 23:1; 3; 4; 10; 12; 13; 19; 24:2; 4; 25:11; 18; 31; 26:2; 6; 8; 13; 14; 15; 21; 25; 27:6; 28:7; 9; 11; 16(2); 20; 25; 29:3; 6; 30:4; 22; 23; 31:4; **2Sa** 1:11; 2:15; 20; 22; 26(2); 27; 3:8; 16; 18; 24; 5:1; 24(2); 6:20; 7:18; 8:6; 10; 9:5; 9; 11; 10:2; 5; 11(2); 14; 11:10; 11; 18; 21; 25; 12:18; 20(2); 21; 13:7; 15; 17; 18; 26; 28; 29; 31; 14:11; 12; 13; 17; 18; 31; 15:2; 8; 10; 19; 33; 34; 16:4; 9; 10; 20; 21; 17:5; 13; 15; 22; 24; 18:14; 19; 21; 22; 23; 19:6; 8; 12; 35; 40; 42; 43; 20:4; 16; 17; 18; 22; 21:1; 17; 18; 22:8; 43; 23:14(2); 24:6; **1Kin** 1:5; 13; 28; 31; 35; 2:12; 20; 23; 28; 29; 43; 3:14; 16; 23; 26; 27; 6:10; 12; 7:7; 38; 8:1; 12; 32; 34; 36; 39; 45; 49; 9:5; 7; 11; 24; 11:7; 22; 12:5; 7; 18; 25; 27; 13:15; 31; 15:18; 22; 16:1; 21; 18:21; 22; 38; 19:2; 5; 20; 21; 20:7; 14; 15; 33(2); 34; 36; 37; 39; 21:10; 13; 14; 22:6; 9; 47; 49; **2Kin** 1:1; 9; 10; 3:27; 4:3; 7; 14; 20; 24; 28; 29; 35; 37; 41; 5:13; 14; 17; 6:8; 31; 7:1; 2; 4; 9; 8:1; 16; 22; 9:3(2); 11; 13; 15; 19; 25; 10:4; 6; 12:7; 17; 13:17; 19; 14:8; 15:16; 16:5; 17:5; 27; 28; 18:24; 26; 28; 31; 37; 19:20; 20:2; 14; 19; 23:17; 24:1; **1Chr** 1:29; 2:24; 6:32; 9:36; 10:4; 7; 11:1; 16(2); 12:3; 18(2); 14:11; 15; 15:2; 16:7; 33; 17:2; 18:6; 19:5(2); 12(2); 15; 21:3; 16; 18; 22; 28; 22:1; 6; 13; 26:14; 28:2; 11; 29:5; 6; 9; 23; **2Chr** 1:2; 13; 2:6; 11; 3:1; 5:2; 11; 13; 6:1; 17; 23; 25; 27; 29; 30; 33; 35; 39; 7:4; 14; 18; 20; 8:12; 17; 10:18; 12:5; 13:15; 14:10; 16:2; 6; 10; 18:16; 20; 23; 25; 27; 20:2; 9; 14; 27; 37; 21:9; 23:11; 13; 14; 17; 24:17; 25:10; 16; 17; 26:1; 19; 28:12; 15; 29:12; 18; 20; 31; 30:15; 27; 31:1; 9; 11; 32:18; 33:13; 34:18; 29; 36:1; **Ezr** 1:5; 3:2; 9; 4:2; 4; 9; 13; 17; 24; 5:1; 2; 4; 5; 9; 16; 6:1; 13; 8:16; 21; 24; 31; 9:4; 10:5; 6; 9; 12; **Neh** 2:2; 4; 9; 14; 15; 17; 18; 20; 3:1; 4:7; 5:7; 8; 12(2); 6:5; 8; 8:10; 9:4; 5; 12:31; 13:9; 11; 12; 17; 21; 27; **Est** 1:13; 2:2; 13; 18; 19; 3:3; 5; 12; 4:4; 5; 13; 14; 15; 5:3; 5; 7; 9; 14(2); 6:3; 10; 11; 13; 7:3; 5; 6; 8(2); 9; 10; 8:4; 7; 9; 9:13; 29; **Job** 1:7; 9; 20; 2:9; 3:13; 4:1; 15; 6:10; 7:14; 8:1; 18; 9:1; 29; 35; 10:14; 18; 20; 11:1; 10; 11; 15; 13:20; 22; 15:1; 16:1; 22; 18:1; 19:1; 20:1; 21:34; 22:1; 24; 26; 29; 23:1; 25:1; 4; 27:12; 28:20; 27; 29:11; 18; 30:26; 31:1; 8; 10; 14; 22; 32:2; 5; 33:16; 24; 34:29(2); 36:9; 18; 37:8; 38:1; 21; 40:3; 6; 14; 41:10; 42:1; 11; **Ps** 2:5; 18:7; 15; 42; 19:13; 27:10; 39:3; 40:7; 43:4; 50:18; 51:13; 19(2); 55:6; 7; 12(2); 56:9; 67:6; 69:4; 73:17; 78:34; 65; 80:12; 89:19; 32; 96:12; 106:12; 30; 107:6; 13; 19; 28; 30; 116:4; 119:6; 92; 124:3; 4; 5; 126:2(2); 142:3; **Prov** 1:28; 2:5; 9; 3:23; 8:30; 11:2; 15:11; 18:3; 20:14; 24; 24:14; 32; **Eccl** 2:11; 13; 15(3); 4:7; 11; 8:15; 17; 9:16; 10:10; 12:7; **Song** 8:10; **Is** 5:17; 6:5; 6; 8; 11; 7:3; 8:3; 14:25; 32; 24:23; 28:18; 30:23; 31:8; 32:16; 33:23; 35:5; 6; 36:3; 9; 11; 13; 22; 37:21; 36; 38:2; 4; 39:3; 4; 5; 8; 40:18; 25; 41:1; 44:15; 48:18; 49:4; 21; 58:8; 9; 10; 14; 60:5; 63:11; 66:12; **Jer** 1:4; 6; 9; 12; 14; 2:21; 4:1; 10; 5:7; 19; 7:7; 34; 8:5; 22; 11:5; 6; 12; 15; 18; 12:5(2); 16; 13:7; 8; 13; 23; 14:11; 13; 14; 18(2); 15:1; 2; 19; 16:11; 17:25; 27; 18:3; 5; 10; 18; 19:10; 14; 20:2; 3; 9; 21:3; 22:4; 9; 15; 16; 22; 23:22; 33; 24:3; 25:17; 28; 26:6; 10; 11; 12; 16; 17; 27:7; 22; 28:5; 9; 10; 12; 15; 29:12; 30; 31:13; 36; 32:2; 8; 26; 33:21; 26; 34:6; 10; 35:3; 12; 36:4; 10; 12; 13; 18; 19; 27; 32; 37:5; 6; 12; 14; 17; 21; 38:1; 5; 6; 7; 10; 14; 15; 17(2); 18; 24; 26; 27; 39:4; 6; 9; 40:6; 8; 15; 41:2; 10; 12; 13; 16; 42:1; 4; 5; 8; 10; 16; 43:2; 8; 44:15; 17; 20; 47:2; 49:1; 2; 51:48; 62; 52:7; 9; 11; 15; **Lam** 3:54; **Eze** 3:3; 12; 15; 23; 24; 4:14; 15; 5:1; 4; 6:13; 7:26; 8:2; 5; 8; 12; 14; 15; 17; 9:6; 9; 10:1; 4; 6; 18; 11:2; 13; 22; 25; 12:4; 14:1; 13; 16:9; 53; 55; 61; 18:13; 19:5; 8; 20:2; 7; 8; 13; 21; 28; 29; 49; 21:4; 10; 22:3; 23:13; 18; 39; 43; 24:11; 20; 26:16; 28:25; 32:4; 14; 15; 33:4; 10; 23; 29; 33; 36:25; 31; 36; 37:9; 11; 14; 16; 39:15; 28; 40:6; 9; 13; 17; 19; 41:3; 42:1; 13; 14; 44:1; 2; 4; 46:2; 12(2); 17; 20; 21; 24; 47:2; 6; 8; **Dan** 1:10; 11; 13; 18; 2:2; 4; 14; 15; 16; 17; 19(2); 25; 35; 46; 48; 49; 3:2; 3; 4; 13(2); 19; 21; 24; 26(2); 28; 30; 4:7; 19; 5:3; 6; 8; 9; 13; 17; 24; 29; 6:3; 4; 5; 6; 11; 12; 13; 14; 15; 16; 18; 19; 21; 23; 25; 7:1; 11; 19; 8:3; 13; 14; 15; 10:5; 9; 12; 16; 18; 20; 11:10; 19; 20; 28; 12:5; 8; **Hos** 1:9; 11; 2:7(2); 3:1; 5:13; 6:3; 7:1; 10:3; 11:1; 10; **Joel** 2:18; 23; 3:17; **Amos** 6:2; 10; 7:2; 5; 8; 10; 14; 8:2; **Jonah** 1:5; 8; 10; 11; 16; 2:1; 4; 4:4; 10; **Mic** 3:4; 7; 5:3; 5; 7:10; **Hab** 1:11; **Zeph** 3:9; 11; **Hag** 1:3; 12; 13; 2:13; 14; **Zec** 1:9; 12; 18; 21; 2:2; 3:7; 4:5; 6; 11; 14; 5:1; 3; 5; 9; 10; 6:4; 8; 11; 7:4; 11:9; 14; 13:3; 6; 14:3; **Mal** 1:6; 3:4; 16; 18; **Mt** 1:19; 24; 2:7; 16; 17; 3:5; 13; 15; 4:1; 5; 10; 11; 5:24; 7:5; 11; 23; 8:26; 9:6; 14; 15; 29; 37; 11:20; 12:12; 13; 14; 22; 26; 28; 29; 38; 44; 45; 47; 13:19; 26; 27; 28; 36; 43; 52; 56; 14:33; 15:1; 12; 15; 21; 25; 28; 32; 16:6; 12; 20; 22; 24; 27; 17:4; 10; 13; 17; 19; 26; 18:16; 21; 27; 32; 19:7; 13; 23; 25; 27; 20:20; 21:1; 25; 22:8; 13; 15; 21; 35; 43; 45; 23:1; 32; 24:9; 10; 14; 16; 21; 23; 30(2); 40; 45; 25:1; 7; 16; 24; 27; 31; 34; 37; 41; 44; 45; 26:3; 14; 25; 31; 36; 38; 45; 50; 52; 54; 56; 65; 67; 74; 27:3; 9; 13; 16; 22; 25; 26; 27; 38; 58; 28:10; 16; **Mk** 2:20; 3:27; 31; 4:13; 28; 7:1; 5; 10:8; 21; 26; 28; 11:31; 12:18; 37; 13:14; 21; 26; 27; 14:63; 15:12; 14; 16:19; **Lk** 1:34; 2:28; 3:7; 10; 12; 5:35; 36; 6:9; 42; 7:6; 22; 31; 8:12; 19; 24; 33; 35; 37; 9:1; 12; 16; 46; 10:37; 11:13; 26; 45; 12:20; 26; 28; 41; 42; 13:7; 9; 15; 18; 23; 26; 14:10; 12; 16; 21; 15:1; 16:3; 7; 27; 17:1; 18:26; 28; 31; 19:15; 16; 23; 20:5; 9; 13; 17; 27; 39; 44; 45; 21:10; 20; 21; 27; 28; 22:3; 7; 36; 52; 54; 70(2); 23:4; 9; 30; 34; 24:12; 25; 45; **Jn** 1:21; 22; 25; 38; 2:10; 18; 20; 3:25; 4:5; 9; 11; 28; 30; 35; 45; 48; 52; 5:4; 12; 19; 6:5; 14; 21; 28; 30; 32; 34; 41; 42; 53; 67; 68; 7:6; 10; 11; 25; 28; 30; 33(2); 35; 45; 47; 8:12; 19; 21; 22; 25; 28(2); 31(2); 41; 48; 52; 57; 59; 9:12; 15; 19; 24; 26; 28; 10:7; 24; 31; 11:7; 12; 14; 16; 17; 20; 21; 31; 32; 36; 41; 45; 47; 53; 56; 12:1; 3; 4; 7; 16; 28; 35; 13:6; 14; 22; 25; 27; 30; 14:9; 16:17; 18:3; 6; 7; 10; 11; 12; 16; 17; 19; 27; 28; 29; 31; 33; 36; 37; 40; 19:1; 5; 10; 16; 20; 21; 23; 27; 32; 40; 20:2; 6; 8; 10; 19; 20; 21; 26; 27; 21:5; 9; 13; 20; 23; **Acts** 1:12; 2:38; 41; 3:6; 4:8; 5:9; 10; 17; 25; 26; 29; 34; 6:2; 9; 11; 7:1; 4; 14; 29; 32; 33; 42; 57; 8:5; 13; 17; 24; 29; 35; 9:13; 19; 25; 31; 39; 10:21; 23; 34; 46; 48; 11:16; 17; 18; 22; 25; 29; 12:3; 15; 13:9; 12; 16; 46; 14:13; 15:12; 22; 16:1; 29; 17:14; 18; 22; 29; 18:9; 17; 18; 19:3; 4; 13; 36; 21:13; 26; 33; 22:22; 27; 29; 23:3; 5; 17; 19; 22; 27; 31; 24:10; 25:2; 10; 12; 22; 26:1(2); 20; 28; 32; 27:20; 29; 32; 36; 28:1; **Rom** 3:1; 6; 9; 27; 31; 4:1; 9; 10; 5:9; 6:1; 15; 18; 21; 7:3; 7; 13; 16; 17; 21; 25; 8:8; 17; 25; 31; 9:14; 16; 19; 30; 10:14; 17; 11:1; 5; 6(2); 7; 11; 19; 12:6; 13:3; 14:12; 16; 15:1; **1Cor** 3:5; 7; 4:5; 5:10; 6:4; 15; 7:38; 9:18; 10:19; 12:28; 13:10; 12(2); 14:15; 26; 15:5; 7; 13; 14; 16; 18; 24; 28; 29; 54; **2Cor** 2:2; 3:12; 4:12; 5:14; 20; 6:1; 12:10; **Gal** 1:18; 2:1; 21; 3:9; 19; 21; 29; 4:7; 8; 15; 29; 31; 5:11; 16; 6:4; **Eph** 5:15; **Phil** 1:18; **Col** 3:1; 4; **1Th** 4:1; 17; 5:3; **2Th** 2:8; **1Ti** 2:13; 3:2; 10; **Heb** 2:14; 4:8; 14; 7:27; 8:7; 9:1; 9; 26; 10:2; 7; 9; 12:8; 26; **Jas** 1:15; 2:4; 24; 3:17; 4:14; **1Pet** 4:1; **2Pet** 3:6; 11; **1Jn** 1:5; 3:21; **Rev** 3:16; 22:9

THERE

Gen 1:3(2); 6; 14; 30; 2:5; 6; 8; 11; 12; 20; 4:26; 6:4; 7:9; 9:11; 11:2; 7; 9; 31; 12:7; 8; 10(2); 13:4(2); 7; 8; 18; 14:8; 10; 13; 18:24; 28(2); 29(2); 30(3); 31(2); 32; 19:1; 31; 21:31; 33; 22:2; 9; 23:13; 24:23; 33; 25:10; 24; 26:1; 8; 17; 19; 25(3); 28; 28:11; 29:2; 31:14; 46; 32:4; 13; 24; 29; 33:20; 35:1(2); 3; 7(2); 16; 36:31; 37:24; 28; 38:2; 21; 22; 39:9; 11(2); 20; 22; 40:8; 17; 41:2; 8; 12(2); 15; 18; 24; 29; 30; 39; 54; 42:1; 2; 16; 43:25; 30; 44:14; 45:1; 6(2); 11(2); 46:3; 47:13; 18; 48:7(2); 49:31(3); 50:5; 9; 10; **Ex** 1:8; 10; 2:1; 12; 5:9; 13; 16; 18; 7:19; 21; 8:10; 15; 18; 22; 24; 31; 9:3; 4; 7; 14; 22; 24(2); 26; 28; 29; 10:14; 15; 19; 21; 22; 26; 11:6(2); 12:16(2); 19; 30(3); 43; 13:3; 7(2); 14:11; 28; 15:25(2); 27; 16:14; 24; 26; 27; 17:1; 3; 6(2); 19:2; 13; 16; 21:30; 22:2; 3; 23:26; 24:10; 12; 25:22; 35; 26:17; 20; 27:9; 11; 28:32; 29:42; 43; 30:12; 34; 32:17; 24; 28; 33:20; 21; 34:2; 5; 28; 35:2; 36:30; 39:23; 40:30; **Lev** 6:27; 7:7; 8:31; 9:24; 10:2; 11:36; 13:10; 19; 21; 24(2); 26; 30; 31; 32; 37; 42; 14:35; 16:17; 23; 17:3; 8; 10; 13; 20:14; 21:1; 22:10; 13; 21; 23:27; 25:51; 52; **Num** 1:4; 53; 5:13; 6:5; 8:19; 9:6; 15; 17; 11:6; 16; 17; 26; 27; 31; 34; 12:6; 13:20; 28; 33; 14:35; 43; 16:35; 46; 18:5; 19:18; 20:1(2); 2; 4; 5; 26; 28; 21:5(2); 28; 32; 35; 22:5; 11; 29; 23:23(2); 24:17; 26:62; 64; 65; 31:5; 16; 49; 32:26; 33:9; 38; 35:6; **Deut** 1:2; 28; 35; 46; 2:36; 3:4; 24; 4:7; 8; 28; 32; 35; 39; 5:26; 29; 7:14; 24; 8:15; 10:5; 6(2); 11:17; 25; 12:5; 7; 11(2); 14(2); 21; 13:1; 12; 17; 14:23; 24; 26; 15:4; 7; 9; 21; 16:2; 4(2); 6; 11; 17:2; 8; 12; 18:7; 10; 20:5; 7; 8; 21:4; 22:26; 27; 23:10; 17; 25:1; 26:2; 5(2); 27:5; 7; 28:32; 36; 64; 65; 68; 29:18(2); 31:26; 32:12; 28; 36; 39(2); 33:19; 21; 26; 34:5; 10; **Josh** 1:5; 2:1; 2; 4; 11; 16; 22; 3:1; 4; 4:8; 9; 5:1; 13; 7:4; 13; 8:11; 14; 17; 32; 35; 9:23; 10:8; 14; 11:11; 19; 22(2); 13:1; 14:12; 17:1; 2; 5; 15; 18:1; 2; 10; 21:44; 45; 22:10; 17; 24:26; **Judg** 1:7; 2:5; 10; 3:29; 4:16; 17; 20; 5:8; 11; 14; 15; 16; 27; 6:11; 21; 24; 39; 40; 7:3(2); 4; 13; 8:10; 9:21; 36; 37; 51; 10:1; 11:3; 12:6; 13:2; 14:3; 8; 10; 15:19; 16:1; 9; 12; 17; 27(2); 17:1; 6; 7(2); 18:1; 2; 7; 10; 11; 14; 28; 19:1(2); 2; 4; 7; 10; 15; 16; 18; 19(3); 30; 20:16; 26; 27; 34; 38; 44; 21:1; 2; 3; 4; 5; 6; 8(2); 9(2); 17; 19; 25; **Ruth** 1:1; 2; 4; 11; 17; 3:12; 4:1; 4; 17; **1Sa** 1:1; 3; 11; 22; 28; 2:2(3); 27; 31; 32; 3:1; 4:4; 7; 10(2); 12; 16; 17; 5:11(2); 6:7; 14(2); 7:6; 14; 17(3); 9:1; 2; 4; 6; 7; 12; 10:3; 24; 26; 11:3; 13; 14; 15(3); 13:19; 22(2); 14:4; 6; 15; 17; 20; 25; 30; 34; 39; 45; 52; 16:11; 17:3; 4; 23; 29; 34; 46; 50; 18:10; 19:8; 16; 20:3; 6(2); 8; 12; 21; 29; 21:3; 4(2); 6(2); 7; 8; 9(2); 22:2; 8(2); 22; 23:22; 27; 24:11; 25:2; 7; 10; 13; 34; 26:15; 27:1; 5; 28:7; 10; 20; 30:17; 19; 31:12; **2Sa** 1:21(3); 2:4; 15; 17; 18(2); 23; 30; 3:1; 6; 27; 29; 38; 4:3; 5:13; 20; 21; 6:7(2); 7:22(2); 9:1; 2; 3; 10:18; 11:8; 17; 12:1; 4; 13:16; 30; 34; 38; 14:6; 11; 25(2); 27; 30; 32(2); 15:3; 13; 21; 28; 29; 35; 36; 16:14; 17:9; 12; 13(2); 22; 18:7(2); 8; 11; 13; 25; 19:7; 17; 18; 22; 20:1(2); 7; 21:1; 18; 19; 20; 22:9; 42; 23:9; 24:9; 13; 15; 25; **1Kin** 1:2; 14; 34; 52; 2:4; 33; 36; 3:2; 4; 12; 13; 16; 18; 4:34; 5:4; 6; 9; 12; 6:7; 18; 19; 7:4; 24; 29; 34; 35; 8:8; 9(2); 21; 23; 25; 29; 35; 37(4); 46; 56; 60; 64; 9:3(2); 5; 10:3; 5; 10; 12; 19; 20(2); 11:16; 36; 12:20; 13:1; 11; 17; 14:2; 13; 21; 24; 30; 15:6; 7; 16; 19; 32; 17:1; 4; 7; 9(2); 10; 17; 18:2; 10(2); 26; 29; 40; 41; 43; 44; 45; 19:3; 6; 9; 13; 20:1; 13; 17; 28; 30; 40; 21:13; 25; 22:7; 8; 21; 36; 47; **2Kin** 1:3; 6(2); 10; 14; 16; 2:11; 16; 21(2); 23; 24; 3:9; 11; 20; 27; 4:1; 6; 10; 11; 31; 38; 40; 41; 42; 5:8; 15; 17; 18; 22; 6:2; 10; 25; 26; 7:3; 4; 5(2); 10(2); 9:2; 10; 16; 17; 18; 23; 27; 32; 10:2; 8; 10; 21; 23; 11:16; 12:10; 13; 13:6; 14:9; 19; 26; 15:20; 16:6; 17:11; 18; 25; 27; 18:18; 19:3; 32; 20:13; 15; 22:7; 23:16; 20; 22; 25(2); 27; 34; 25:3; 23; **1Chr** 3:4; 4:23; 40; 41(3); 43; 5:22; 11:13; 12:8; 16; 17; 19; 20; 22; 39; 40; 13:10; 14:11; 12; 16:37; 17:20(2); 19:5; 20:2; 4; 5; 6; 21:14; 26; 28; 22:15; 16; 24:4(2); 26:31; 27:24; 28:21; 29:15; **2Chr** 1:3; 12; 5:9; 10; 6:5; 6; 14; 16; 20; 26; 28(4); 36; 7:7; 13; 16(2); 18; 8:2; 9:2; 4; 9; 11; 18; 19(2); 12:13; 15; 13:2; 7; 8; 17; 14:9; 14; 15:5; 19; 16:3(2); 18:6; 7; 20; 19:3; 7; 20:2(2); 6; 26; 21:12; 17; 23:15; 24:11; 25:7; 18; 27; 28:9; 10; 13; 18; 30:13; 17; 26(2); 32:4; 7; 14; 21; 25; 34:13; 35:18; 36:16; 23; **Ezr** 1:3; 2:63; 65(2); 4:20; 5:17(2); 6:2; 12; 7:7; 23; 8:15(2); 21; 25; 32; 9:14; 10:1; 2; 18; **Neh** 1:3; 9(2); 2:10; 11; 12; 14; 4:10; 5:1; 2; 3; 4; 17; 6:1; 7; 8; 11; 18; 7:65; 67; 8:17; 12:46; 13:16; 19; 26; **Est** 1:18; 19; 2:2; 5; 3:8; 12; 4:3; 11; 14; 6:3; 7:7; **Job** 1:1; 2; 6; 8; 13; 14; 16; 17; 18; 19; 2:1; 3; 3:3; 17(2); 18; 19; 4:16; 5:1; 4; 19; 6:6; 30; 7:1; 9:33; 10:7; 11:18; 12:14; 24; 14:7; 15:11; 17:2; 19:7; 29; 20:21; 21:33; 34; 22:29; 23:7; 8; 25:3; 28:1; 7; 30:26; 31:2; 32:5; 8; 12; 33:9; 23; 34:22; 35:12; 36:16; 18; 38:26; 39:30; 41:33; 42:11; **Ps** 3:2(2); 4:6; 5:9; 6:5; 7:2; 3; 14:1(2); 2; 3; 5; 16:11; 18:8; 41; 19:3; 6; 11; 22:11; 30:9; 32:2; 33:16; 34:9; 36:1; 12; 38:3(2); 7; 45:12; 46:4; 48:6; 50:22; 53:1(2); 2; 3; 5; 55:18; 58:11; 66:6; 68:27; 69:2; 20; 35; 71:11; 72:16; 73:4; 11; 25; 74:9(2); 75:8; 76:3; 79:3; 81:9; 86:8(2); 87:4; 6; 7; 91:10; 92:15; 104:26(2); 105:31; 37; 106:11; 107:12; 36; 40; 109:12(2); 112:4; 122:5; 130:4; 7; 132:17; 133:3; 135:17; 137:1; 3; 139:4; 8(2); 10; 16; 24; 142:4; 144:14(2); 146:3; **Prov** 7:10; 8:8; 24(2); 27; 9:18; 10:19; 11:10; 14; 24(2); 12:18; 21; 28; 13:7(2); 23; 14:9; 12; 23; 16:25; 27; 17:16; 18:24; 19:18; 21; 20:15; 21:20; 30; 22:13; 23:18; 24:6; 14; 20; 25:4; 26:12; 13; 20(2); 25; 28:12; 29:6; 9; 18; 20; 30:11; 12; 13; 14; 15; 18; 24; 29; 31; **Eccl** 1:9; 10; 11(2); 2:11; 16; 21; 24; 3:1; 12; 16(2); 17(2); 22; 4:1; 8(3); 16; 5:7; 8; 11; 13; 14; 6:1; 11; 7:11; 15(2); 20; 8:4; 6; 8(2); 9; 14(3); 16; 9:2; 3; 4; 10; 14(2); 15; 10:5; 11:3; 12:12; **Song** 4:4; 7; 6:6; 8; 7:12; 8:5(2); **Is** 1:6; 2:7(2); 3:24; 4:6; 5:6; 8; 6:12; 7:23; 25; 8:20; 9:7; 10:14; 11:1; 10; 16; 13:20(2); 21(3); 14:31; 15:6; 16:10(2); 17:9; 19:15; 19; 23; 22:18(2); 23:1; 10; 12; 24:11; 13; 27:10(2); 28:8; 10; 13; 29:2; 30:14; 25; 28; 33:21; 34:12; 14; 15(2); 35:8; 9(3); 37:3; 33; 39:2; 4; 8; 40:28; 41:17; 26(3); 28(2); 43:10(2); 11; 12; 13; 44:6; 8(2); 19; 20; 45:5(2); 6(2); 14(2); 18; 21(2); 22; 46:9(2); 47:1; 14; 48:16; 22; 50:2(3); 51:18(2); 52:1; 4; 53:2; 57:10; 21; 59:8; 11; 15; 16(2); 63:3; 5(2); 64:7; 65:9; 20; **Jer** 2:10; 25; 3:3; 6; 4:25; 5:1; 6:14; 20; 7:2; 32; 8:11; 13; 14; 22(3); 10:6; 7; 13; 14; 20; 11:23; 13:4; 6; 14:4; 5; 6; 19(2); 22; 16:13; 19; 17:25; 18:2; 12; 19:2; 11; 20:6(2); 22:1; 4; 26; 26:20; 27:22; 29:6; 30:13; 31:6; 17; 24; 32:5; 17; 27; 33:10; 20; 36:12; 22; 32; 37:10; 13; 16; 17(2); 20; 38:6; 9; 26; 28; 41:1; 3; 5; 42:14; 15; 16(3); 17; 43:2; 44:12; 14(2); 27; 28; 46:17; 47:7; 48:2; 38; 49:18; 23; 33(2); 36; 50:3; 20; 39; 40; 51:16; 17; 52:6; 23; 34; **Lam** 1:12; 17; 20; 21; 3:29; 4:15; 5:8; **Eze** 1:3; 25; 2:5; 10; 3:15; 22(2); 23; 4:14; 7:11; 25; 8:1; 4; 11; 14; 10:1; 8; 12:13; 24; 28; 13:10; 11; 13; 16; 20; 17:7; 20; 20:28(4); 35; 40(3); 43; 22:20; 25; 23:2; 3(2); 28:3; 24; 29:14; 30:13; 18; 32:22; 24; 26; 29; 30; 34:5; 8; 14; 26; 35:10; 37:2; 7; 8; 38:19; 39:11(2); 28; 40:3; 16; 17; 25; 26; 27; 29; 33; 49; 41:7; 25(2); 26; 42:13; 14; 45:2; 46:19; 21; 22; 23; 47:2; 9; 23; 48:35; **Dan** 2:9; 10(2); 11; 28; 41; 3:12; 29; 4:31; 5:11; 6:4; 7:8(2); 14; 8:3; 4; 7(2); 15; 10:8; 13; 17(2); 18; 21; 11:2; 14; 15; 12:1(2); 5; 11; **Hos** 1:10; 2:15; 4:1; 9; 6:7; 10; 7:7; 9; 9:12; 15; 10:9; 12:4; 11; 13:4; 8; **Joel** 2:2; 3:2; 12; 17; **Amos** 3:6; 11; 4:7; 5:2; 6; 6:9; 10; 12; 7:12(2); 8:3; **Obad** 7; 17; 18; **Jonah** 1:4; 4:5; **Mic** 3:7; 4:9; 10(2); 6:10; 7:1; 2; **Nah** 1:11; 2:9; 3:3(2); 15; 19; **Hab** 1:3; 2:19; 3:4; 17; **Zeph** 1:10; 14; 2:5; 15; 3:6(2); **Hag** 1:6; 2:14; 16(2); **Zec** 1:8; 5:7; 9; 11; 6:1; 8:4; 10(2); 20; 10:2; 11:3; 12:11; 13:1; 14:4; 9; 11; 18; 20; 21; **Mal** 1:10; 3:10(2); **Mt** 2:1; 13; 15; 18; 4:25; 5:23; 24; 6:21; 7:9; 13; 14; 8:2; 5; 12; 24; 26; 28; 30; 9:18; 10:11; 26; 11:11; 12:10; 11; 39; 45; 13:42; 50; 58; 14:23; 15:29; 16:4; 28; 17:3; 14; 18:20; 19:2; 12(3); 13; 17; 21:17; 33; 22:11; 13; 23; 25; 24:2; 7; 22; 23; 24; 28; 51; 25:6; 9; 25; 30; 26:5; 7; 13; 71; 27:36; 38; 45; 47; 55; 57; 61; 28:2; 7; 10; **Mk** 1:5; 7; 11; 13; 23; 35; 38; 40; 2:2; 6(2); 15; 3:1(2); 31; 4:1; 3; 22; 36; 37; 39; 5:2; 11(2); 22; 35; 6:5; 10; 31; 7:4; 15; 8:12; 9:1; 4; 7; 39; 10:17; 18; 29; 11:5; 27; 12:18; 20; 31; 32(2); 42; 13:2; 8(2); 21; 14:2; 3; 4; 13; 15; 51; 57; 66; 15:7; 33; 40; 16:7; **Lk** 1:5; 11; 33; 45; 61; 2:1; 6; 7; 8; 13; 25; 36; 4:14; 17; 33; 5:15; 17; 29; 6:6; 19; 7:12; 16; 28; 41; 8:23; 24; 27; 32(2); 41; 49; 9:4; 17; 27; 30; 34; 35; 46; 10:6; 31; 11:26; 29; 12:1; 2; 18; 34; 52; 54; 55; 13:1; 11; 14; 23; 28; 30(2); 31; 14:2; 22; 25; 15:10; 13; 14; 16:1; 19; 20; 26; 17:12; 17; 18; 21; 23; 34; 18:2; 3; 29; 19:2; 20:27; 29; 21:6; 7; 11; 18; 23; 25; 22:10; 12; 24; 43; 23:27; 32; 33; 44; 50; 24:18; **Jn** 1:6; 26; 46; 2:1(2); 6(2); 12; 3:1; 22; 23(2); 25; 4:6; 7; 35; 40; 46; 5:1; 2; 5; 32; 45; 6:3; 9; 10; 22(2); 23; 24; 64; 7:4; 12; 43; 8:44; 50; 9:16; 10:16; 19; 40; 42; 11:9; 10; 15; 31; 54; 12:2; 9; 20; 26; 28; 13:23; 14:3; 18:18; 19:25; 29; 34; 39; 41; 42; 21:2; 9; 11; 25; **Acts** 2:2; 3; 5; 41; 4:12(2); 34; 5:16; 34; 6:1; 9; 7:11; 12; 30; 8:1; 8; 9; 9:3; 10; 18; 33; 36; 38; 10:1; 13; 18; 11:11; 28(2); 12:18; 19; 13:1; 11; 25; 14:5; 7; 8; 19; 28; 15:5; 7; 33; 34; 16:1; 9; 15; 26; 17:7; 14; 21; 18:11; 18; 19; 23; 19:2; 14; 21;

23; 35; 38; 40; 20:3; 4; 8; 9; 13; 22; 21:3; 4; 10(2); 16; 20; 40; 22:5; 6; 10; 12; 23:7; 8; 9; 10; 21; 24:11; 15; 25:5; 9; 11; 14(2); 20; 27:6; 12; 14; 22; 23; 34; 28:3; 12; 18; 23; **Rom** 2:11; 3:1; 10; 11(2); 12; 18; 20; 22; 4:15; 5:13; 8:1; 9:14; 26; 10:12; 11:5; 26; 13:1; 9; 14:14; 15:12; **1Cor** 1:10; 11; 3:3; 5:1; 6:5; 7; 7:34; 8:4; 5(2); 6; 7; 10:13; 11:18; 19; 12:4; 5; 6; 25; 13:8(3); 14:10; 23; 24; 28; 15:12; 13; 39; 40; 41; 44(2); 16:2; 9; **2Cor** 1:17; 3:17; 8:11(2); 12; 14; 12:7; 20; **Gal** 1:7; 3:21; 28(3); 5:23; **Eph** 4:4; 6:9; **Phil** 2:1; 4:8(2); **Col** 3:11; 25; **2Th** 2:3; 3:11; **1Ti** 1:10; 2:5; **2Ti** 2:20; 4:8; **Titus** 1:10; 3:12; **Philem** 1:23; **Heb** 3:12; 4:9; 13; 7:8; 11; 12; 15; 18; 8:4; 9:2; 16; 10:3; 18; 26; 11:12; 12:16; **Jas** 2:2(2); 3; 19; 3:16; 4:12; 13; **2Pet** 1:17; 2:1(2); 3:3; **1Jn** 2:10; 18; 4:18; 5:7; 8; 16; 17; **2Jn** 10; **Jude** 4; 18; **Rev** 2:14; 4:3; 5; 6; 6:4(2); 12; 7:4; 8:1; 3; 5; 7; 10; 9:2; 3; 10; 12; 10:6; 11:1; 13; 15; 19(2); 12:1; 3; 6; 7; 13:5; 14:8; 16:2; 17; 18(2); 21; 17:1; 10; 20:11; 21:1; 4(2); 9; 25(2); 27; 22:2; 3; 5(2)

THEREBY

Gen 24:14; **Lev** 11:43; **Job** 22:21; **Prov** 20:1; **Eccl** 10:9; **Is** 33:21; **Jer** 18:16; 19:8; 51:43; **Eze** 12:5; 12; 33:12; 18; 19; **Zec** 9:2; **Jn** 11:4; **Eph** 2:16; **Heb** 12:11; 15; 13:2; **1Pet** 2:2

THEREFORE

Gen 2:24; 3:23; 4:15; 11:9; 12:12; 19; 17:9; 18:5; 12; 19:8; 22; 20:6; 7; 8; 21:23; 23:15; 24:65; 25:30; 26:33; 27:3; 8; 28; 43; 29:15; 32; 33; 34; 35; 30:6; 15; 31:44; 48; 32:32; 33:10; 17; 34:21; 37:20; 38:29; 41:33; 42:21; 22; 44:30; 33; 45:5; 47:4; 50:5; 21; **Ex** 1:11; 20; 3:9; 10; 4:12; 5:8; 17; 18; 9:19; 10:17; 12:17; 13:10; 15; 15:23; 16:29; 19:5; 31:14; 32:10; 34; 33:5; 13; **Lev** 8:35; 9:8; 11:44; 45; 13:52; 16:4; 17:12; 14; 18:5; 25; 26; 30; 19:8; 37; 20:7; 22; 23; 25; 21:6; 8; 22:9(2); 31; 25:17; **Num** 3:12; 11:18; 14:16; 43; 16:38; 18:7; 24; 30; 20:12; 21:7; 22:5; 6; 17; 19; 34; 24:11; 14; 27:4; 31:17; 50; 35:34; **Deut** 2:4; 4:1; 6; 15; 37; 39; 40; 5:15; 25; 32; 6:3; 7:9; 11; 8:6; 9:3; 6; 26; 10:16; 19; 11:1; 8; 18; 14:7; 15:11; 15; 16:2; 15; 18:2; 23:14; 24:18; 22; 25:19; 26:16; 27:4; 10; 28:48; 29:9; 30:19; 31:19; 22; **Josh** 1:2; 2:12; 3:12; 4:17; 7:12; 14; 8:6; 9; 9:6; 11; 19; 23; 24; 10:5; 9; 13:7; 14:4; 12; 14; 17:1; 4; 18:6; 19:9; 47; 22:4; 26; 28; 23:6; 11; 15; 24:10; 14; 18; 23; 27; **Judg** 2:23; 3:8; 25; 6:32; 7:3; 8:7; 9:16; 32; 11:8; 13; 26; 13:4; 14:2; 15:2; 16:12; 17:3; 18:14; 19:7; 20:13; 42; 21:20; **Ruth** 3:3; 9; 4:8; **1Sa** 1:7; 13; 28; 3:9; 14; 5:5; 8; 10; 6:7; 8:9; 9:13; 10:12; 19; 22; 11:10; 12:7; 13; 16; 13:12(2); 14:41; 15:1; 25; 17:51; 18:13; 22; 19:2; 20:8; 29; 21:3; 22:1; 23:2; 20; 23; 28; 24:15; 21; 25:17; 26; 26:4; 8; 19; 20; 27:12; 28:2; 15; 18; 22; 31:4; **2Sa** 2:7; 4:11; 5:20; 6:21; 23; 7:8; 27; 29; 9:10; 12:10; 16; 19; 28; 13:13; 33; 14:15; 17; 21; 26; 29; 30; 32; 15:29; 35; 17:11; 16; 18:3; 19:7; 10; 20; 23; 27; 28; 22:25; 50; 23:17; 19; **1Kin** 1:12; 2:2; 6; 9; 19; 24; 33; 44; 3:9; 5:6; 8:25; 61; 9:9; 10:9; 11:40; 12:4; 18; 24; 13:26; 14:10; 12; 18:19; 23; 20:23; 28; 42; 22:19; 23; **2Kin** 1:4; 6; 14; 16; 2:17; 3:23; 4:33; 5:15; 27; 6:7; 11; 14; 7:4; 9; 12; 14; 9:26; 10:19; 12:7; 14:11; 15:16; 17:4; 18; 25; 26; 18:23; 19:18; 19; 26; 28; 32; 21:12; 22:17; 20; **1Chr** 10:14; 11:3; 7; 19; 14:11; 14; 16; 17:7; 23; 25; 27; 21:7; 12; 22:5; 16; 19; 23:11; 24:2; 28:8; 29:13; **2Chr** 2:7; 15; 6:10; 16; 19; 21; 41; 7:22; 9:8; 10:4; 12:5; 7; 14:7; 15:7; 16:7; 9; 17:5; 18:5; 12; 16; 18; 22; 31; 33; 19:2; 20:26; 28:11; 23; 30:7; 17; 32:15; 25; 34:25; 35:14; 24; 36:17; **Ezr** 2:62; 4:14; 5:17; 6:6; 9:12; 10:3; 11; **Neh** 2:20; 4:13; 20; 5:2; 6:7; 9; 13; 7:64; 9:27; 28; 30; 32; 13:8; 28; **Est** 1:12; 2:23; 3:8; 9:19; 26; **Job** 5:17; 6:3; 28; 7:11; 9:22; 10:15; 11:6; 17:4; 20:2; 21; 21:14; 22:10; 23:15; 32:10; 34:10; 25; 33; 35:14; 16; 37:24; 42:3; 8; **Ps** 1:5; 2:10; 7:7; 16:9; 18:24; 49; 21:12; 25:8; 26:1; 27:6; 28:7; 31:3; 36:7; 40:12; 42:6; 45:2; 7; 17; 46:2; 55:19; 59:5; 63:7; 73:6; 10; 78:21; 33; 91:14; 106:23; 26; 40; 107:12; 110:7; 116:2; 10; 118:7; 119:104; 119; 127; 128; 129; 140; 139:19; 143:4; **Prov** 1:31; 4:7; 5:7; 6:15; 34; 7:15; 24; 8:32; 17:11; 14; 20:4; 19; **Eccl** 2:1; 17; 20; 5:2; 8:6; 11; 11:10; **Song** 1:3; **Is** 1:24; 2:6; 9; 3:17; 5:13; 14; 24; 25; 7:14; 8:7; 9:11; 14; 17; 10:16; 24; 12:3; 13:7; 13; 15:4; 7; 16:7; 9; 17:10; 21:3; 22:4; 24:6(2); 25:3; 26:14; 27:9; 11; 28:16; 22; 29:14; 22; 30:3; 7; 13; 16(2); 18(2); 36:8; 37:19; 20; 27; 29; 33; 38:20; 42:25; 43:4; 12; 28; 47:8; 11; 50:7(2); 51:11; 21; 52:5; 6(2); 53:12; 57:10; 59:9; 16; 60:11; 61:7; 63:5; 10; 65:7; 12; 13; **Jer** 1:17; 2:19; 33; 3:3; 5:4; 27; 6:11; 15; 18; 21; 7:14; 16; 20; 27; 32; 8:10; 12; 9:7; 15; 10:21; 11:8; 11; 14; 21; 22; 12:8; 13:12; 24; 26; 14:10; 15; 17; 22; 15:6; 19; 16:13; 14; 21; 18:11; 13; 21; 19:6; 20:11; 22:18; 23:2; 7; 15; 30; 32; 38; 39; 25:8; 27; 30; 26:13; 27:9; 14; 28:16; 29:20; 27; 28; 32; 30:10; 16; 31:3; 12; 20; 32:23; 28; 36; 34:12; 17; 35:17; 19; 36:6; 14; 30; 37:20; 38:4; 40:3; 42:15; 22; 44:7; 11; 22; 23; 26; 48:11; 12; 31; 36; 49:2; 20; 26; 50:18; 30; 39; 45; 51:7; 36; 47; **Lam** 1:8; 9; 2:8; 3:21; 24; **Eze** 3:17; 4:7; 5:7; 8; 10; 11; 7:20; 8:18; 11:4; 7; 16; 17; 12:3; 23; 28; 13:8(2); 13; 23; 14:4; 6; 15:6; 16:27; 34; 37; 43; 50; 17:19; 18:30; 20:27; 21:4; 6; 12; 14; 24; 22:4; 13; 19(2); 31; 23:22; 31; 35(2); 24:9; 25:4; 7; 9; 13; 16; 26:3; 28:6; 7; 16; 18; 29:8; 10; 19; 30:22; 31:5; 10; 11; 32:3; 33:7; 10; 12; 34:7; 9; 20; 22; 35:6; 11; 36:3; 4; 5; 6; 7; 14; 22; 37:12; 38:14; 39:1; 23; 25; 41:7; 42:6; 44:2; 12; **Dan** 1:8; 19; 2:6; 9; 10; 24; 3:7; 19; 22; 29; 4:6; 8:8; 9:11; 14; 17; 23; 25; 10:8; 11:30; 44; **Hos** 2:2; 6; 9; 14; 4:3; 5; 7; 13; 14; 5:5; 10; 12; 6:5; 8:6; 9:9; 10:14; 12:6; 14; 13:3; 6; 7; **Joel** 2:12; **Amos** 2:14; 3:2; 11; 4:12; 5:11; 13; 16; 27; 6:7; 8; 7:16; 17; **Jonah** 4:2; 3; **Mic** 1:6; 8; 14; 2:3; 5; 3:6; 12; 5:3; 6:13; 16; 7:7; **Hab** 1:4(2); 15; 16; 17; **Zeph** 1:13; 2:9; 3:8; **Hag** 1:5; 10; **Zec** 1:3; 16; 7:12; 13; 8:19; 10:2; **Mal** 2:9; 15; 16; 3:6; **Mt** 3:8; 10; 5:19; 23; 48; 6:2; 8; 9; 22; 23; 25; 31; 34; 7:12; 24; 9:38; 10:16; 26; 31; 32; 12:27; 13:13; 18; 40; 52; 14:2; 18:4; 23; 26; 19:6; 27; 21:40; 43; 22:9; 17; 21; 28; 23:3; 14; 20; 24:15; 42; 44; 25:13; 27; 28; 27:17; 64; 28:19; **Mk** 1:38; 2:28; 6:14; 19; 8:38; 10:9; 11:24; 12:6; 9; 23; 24; 27; 37; 13:35; **Lk** 1:35; 3:8; 9; 4:7; 43; 6:36; 7:42; 8:18; 10:2(2); 40; 11:19; 34; 35; 36; 49; 12:3; 7; 22; 40; 13:14; 14:20; 15:28; 16:11; 27; 19:12; 20:15; 25; 29; 33; 44; 21:8; 14; 36; 23:16; 20; 22; **Jn** 1:31; 2:22; 3:29; 4:1; 6; 33; 5:10; 16; 18; 6:13; 15; 24; 30; 43; 45; 52; 60; 65; 7:3; 22; 40; 8:13; 24; 36; 47; 9:7; 8; 10; 16; 23; 41; 10:17; 19; 39; 11:3; 6; 33; 38; 54; 12:9; 17; 19; 21; 29; 39; 50; 13:11; 24; 31; 15:19; 16:15; 18; 22; 18:4; 8; 25; 31; 37; 39; 19:1; 4; 6; 8; 11; 13; 16; 24(2); 26; 30; 31; 38; 42; 20:3; 25; 21:6; 7; **Acts** 1:6; 2:26; 30; 33; 36; 3:19; 8:4; 22; 10:20; 29(2); 32; 33(2); 12:5; 13:38; 40; 14:3; 15:2; 10; 27; 16:11; 36; 17:12; 17; 20; 23; 19:32; 20:11; 28; 31; 21:22; 23; 23:15; 25:5; 17; 26:22; 28:20; 28; **Rom** 2:1; 21; 26; 3:20; 28; 4:16; 22; 5:1; 18; 6:4; 12; 8:1; 12; 9:18; 11:22; 12:1; 20; 13:2; 7; 10; 12; 14:8; 13; 19; 15:17; 28; 16:19; **1Cor** 3:21; 4:5; 5:7; 8; 13; 6:7; 20; 7:8; 26; 8:4; 9:26; 10:31; 11:20; 12:15; 16; 14:11; 23; 15:11; 58; 16:11; 18; **2Cor** 1:17; 4:1; 13(2); 5:6; 11; 17; 7:1; 13; 16; 8:7; 11; 9:5; 11:15; 12:9; 10; 13:10; **Gal** 2:17; 3:5; 7; 4:16; 5:1; 6:10; **Eph** 2:19; 4:1; 17; 5:1; 7; 24; 6:14; **Phil** 2:1; 23; 28; 29; 3:15; 4:1; **Col** 2:6; 16; 3:5; 12; **1Th** 3:7; 4:8; 5:6; **2Th** 2:15; **1Ti** 2:1; 8; 4:10; 5:14; **2Ti** 1:8; 2:1; 3; 10; 21; 4:1; **Philem** 1:12; 15; 17; **Heb** 1:9; 2:1; 4:1; 6; 9; 11; 16; 6:1; 7:11; 9:23; 10:19; 35; 11:12; 13:13; 15; **Jas** 4:4; 7; 17; 5:7; **1Pet** 2:7; 4:7; 5:6; **2Pet** 3:17; **1Jn** 2:24; 3:1; 4:5; **3Jn** 8; **Jude** 5; **Rev** 2:5; 3:3(2); 19; 7:15; 12:12; 18:8

THEREIN

Gen 9:7; 18:24; 23:11; 17; 20; 34:10(2); 21; 47:27; 49:32; **Ex** 2:3; 5:9; 16:24; 33; 21:33; 29:29; 30:18; 31:14; 35:2; 40:3; 7; 9; **Lev** 6:3; 7; 8:10; 10:1; 13:21; 37; 18:4; 30; 20:22; 22:21; 23:3; 7; 8; 21; 25; 35; 36; 25:19; 26:32; **Num** 4:16; 13:18; 20; 14:30; 16:7; 46; 28:18; 29:7; 35; 32:40; 33:53; 35:33; **Deut** 2:10; 20; 7:25; 8:12; 10:14; 11:31; 13:15; 15:21; 16:8; 17:14; 19; 20:11; 26:1; 28:30; 29:23; **Josh** 1:8(2); 6:17; 24; 10:28; 30; 32; 35; 37(2); 39; 11:11; 19:47; 50; 21:43; **Judg** 2:22; 8:25; 9:45; 16:30; 18:7; 28; **1Sa** 30:2; **2Sa** 12:31; **1Kin** 8:16; 11:24; 12:25; **2Kin** 2:20; 12:9; 13:6; 11; 15:16(2); **1Chr** 16:32; 21:22; **2Chr** 2:3; 5:10; 20:8(2); **Ezr** 4:19; 6:2; **Neh** 6:1; 7:4; 5; 8:3; 9:6(2); 13:1; 16; **Job** 3:7; 20:18; **Ps** 24:1; 37:29; 68:10; 69:34; 36; 96:12; 98:7; 104:26; 107:34; 111:2; 119:35; 146:6; **Prov** 15:4; 22:14; 26:27; **Eccl** 2:21; **Is** 5:2; 7:6; 24:6; 33:24; 34:1; 17; 35:8; 42:5; 10; 44:23; 51:3; 6; 59:8; **Jer** 4:29; 6:16(2); 8:16; 9:13; 12:4; 17:24; 23:12; 27:11; 36:2; 29; 32; 44:2; 47:2(2); 48:9; 50:3; 39; 40; 51:48; **Eze** 2:9; 10; 7:20; 12:19(2); 14:22; 20:47; 24:5; 6; 28:26; 30:12; 32:15; 37:25; 40:33; 42:14; 44:14; **Dan** 5:2; **Hos** 4:3; 14:9; **Amos** 6:8; 8:8; 9:5; **Mic** 1:2; 7:13; **Nah** 1:5; **Hab** 2:8; 17; 18; **Zec** 2:4; 6:6; 13:8(2); 14:21; **Mt** 23:21; **Mk** 10:15; 13:15; **Lk** 10:9; 18:17; 19:45; **Jn** 12:6; **Acts** 1:20; 14:15; 17:24; 27:6; **Rom** 1:17; 6:2; **1Cor** 7:24; **Eph** 6:20; **Phil** 1:18; **Col** 2:7; **Heb** 4:6; 10:8; 13:9; **Jas** 1:25; **2Pet** 2:20; 3:10; **Rev** 1:3; 10:6(3); 11:1; 13:12; 21:22

THEREOF

Gen 2:17; 19; 21; 3:5; 6; 4:4; 6:16; 9:4(2); 40:10; 18; 41:8; 45:16; 47:21; **Ex** 3:20; 5:8; 9:18; 10:26; 12:9; 43; 44; 45; 46; 48; 16:31; 19:18; 22:11; 12; 14; 15; 23:10; 25:9; 10(3); 12; 17(2); 19; 23(3); 25; 26; 29(4); 37(2); 38(2); 26:30; 27:1; 2; 3; 4; 10; 19(2); 28:7(2); 8; 16(2); 26; 27(2); 28; 32; 33; 29:33; 41; 30:2(4); 3(3); 4; 37; 35:12; 36:29; 37:6(2); 8; 10(3); 12; 13; 18(3); 24; 25; 26; 27(2); 38:1(3); 2(2); 3; 4; 39:5; 9(2); 20; 35; 36; 37(2); 40:4; 9; 18(2); **Lev** 1:15; 17; 2:2(3); 9; 16(3); 3:8; 9; 13; 14; 4:30(2); 31; 34; 35; 5:12; 6:15; 16; 20; 27(2); 29; 7:2; 3; 6; 19; 8:11; 9:13; 17; 11:39; 13:4; 18; 20; 14:45; 17:13; 14(2); 18:25; 19:23; 24; 25(2); 22:13; 14; 24; 23:10; 13(2); 24:5; 25:3; 7; 10; 12; 16; 27; 27:10; 13; 16; 21; 31; 33; **Num** 1:50(2); 2:6; 8; 11; 3:25; 26; 31; 36(4); 4:6; 8; 9; 10; 11; 14; 16; 31(3); 5:7(2); 26; 7:1(2); 13; 8:3; 4(2); 25; 9:3; 14; 11:7; 13:32; 18:28; 29(2); 30; 21:25; 32; 26:56; 28:7; 8; 9; 29:19; 32:33; 41; 42; 34:2; 4; 12; **Deut** 3:11; 12; 17; 9:21; 12:15; 13:15; 16(2); 15:23; 20:13; 14; 19; 26:14(3); 28:30; 31; 29:23; 33:16; **Josh** 6:2; 26; 7:14; 8:2(2); 9:1; 10:2; 28; 30(2); 37(2); 39(3); 11:10; 13:23(2); 15:7; 12; 47; 16:3; 8; 18:12; 14; 20; 19:14; 29; 33; 21:2; 11; 12; 22:7; 23:14; **Judg** 1:18(3); 26(2); 3:2; 5:23; 7:15; 8:14; 27; 14:9; 15:19; 17:4; **1Sa** 5:6; 6:8; 7:14; 17:51; 20:20; 28:24; **2Sa** 20:8; 23:16; **1Kin** 2:32; 3:27; 6:2(3); 3(2); 20; 38; 7:2(3); 6(2); 21(2); 26; 27; 30; 31; 35(2); 36(2); 8:7; 13:26; 15:21; 22; 16:34(2); 17:13; **2Kin** 2:12; 3:25; 4:39; 40; 42; 43; 44; 7:2; 19; 13:14; 15:16; 16:10; 17:24; 18:8; 19:23(2); 29; 22:16; 19; 23:6; **1Chr** 2:23; 6:55; 56; 7:28(4); 8:12; 9:27; 16:32; 21:27; 23:26; 28:11(4); 15(2); **2Chr** 3:7(2); 8; 4:1(3); 2; 22; 5:8; 13:11; 19(3); 16:6; 28:18(3); 29:18(2); 32:1; 34:24; 27; 36:19(2); **Ezr** 4:12; 16; 6:3(3); 9:9; 10:14; **Neh** 1:3; 2:3; 13; 17; 3:3(4); 6(4); 13(3); 14(3); 15(3); 4:6; 6:16; 9:36(2); 11:25(3); 27; 28; 30(2); 13:14; **Est** 1:22; 2:22; 3:12; 8:9(2); 9:18(2); **Job** 3:9; 4:12; 16; 9:6; 24; 11:9; 14:7; 8(2); 15:29; 24:2; 13(2); 26:5; 28:13; 15; 22; 23(2); 31:17; 38; 39(2); 36:27; 33; 38:5; 6(2); 9; 19; 20(2); 33; **Ps** 19:6; 24:1; 34:2; 46:3(2); 48:12; 50:1; 12; 55:10; 11; 60:2; 65:10(3); 71:15; 72:16; 74:6; 75:3; 8; 80:10; 89:9; 11; 96:11; 97:1; 98:7; 102:14; 103:16; 107:25; 29; 137:2; 7; **Prov** 1:19; 3:14; 12:28; 14:12; 16:25; 33; 18:21; 20:21; 21:22; 24:31(2); 25:8; 27:18; 28:2(2); **Eccl** 5:11; 13; 19; 6:2; 7:8; **Song** 1:12; 3:10(3); 4:16; 7:8; 8:6; 11; 12; **Is** 3:14; 4:4; 5:2; 5(2); 30; 6:13; 13:9; 10; 14:17; 15:8(2); 16:8; 17:6; 19:3(2); 10; 13; 14(2); 17; 19; 21:2; 22:11; 23:11; 13(2); 24:1; 5; 20; 27:10; 11; 28:25; 30:27; 33; 31:4; 33:20(2); 34:9(3); 10; 12; 13; 37:24(2); 30; 40:6; 16; 22; 41:9; 42:10; 11; 44:15; 16(2); 17; 19(2); 26; 48:19; 62:1(2); **Jer** 1:13; 15; 18(2); 2:7(2); 4:26; 5:1; 22; 31; 6:24; 11:19; 14:2; 8; 17:27; 19:8; 12; 20:5(2); 21:14; 23:14; 25:9; 18(2); 26:15; 29:7; 30:18; 31:23; 24; 35; 33:2; 12; 34:1; 18; 46:8; 22; 48:9; 38; 49:13; 17; 18; 21; 32; 50:29; 40; 51:28(2); 42; 52:21; **Lam** 2:2; 4:11; **Eze** 1:4; 5; 4:9(2); 5:3; 4; 7:12; 13; 14; 9:4; 10:7; 11:6; 9; 11; 18(2); 13:14(2); 14:13; 15:3; 17:6; 9(3); 12(2); 23; 19:7; 20:29; 22:21; 22; 25(2); 27; 23:34; 24:4; 11; 27:9; 31:15; 32:7; 12; 13; 38:13; 40:6; 9; 20(2); 21(4); 22; 24(2); 25; 26(2); 29(4); 31(2); 33(4); 34(2); 36(3); 37(2); 38; 41:2; 4; 12; 13; 15; 22(4); 42:7; 43:11(9); 12; 13(2); 16; 17(2); 20; 44:5; 14; 45:1; 2; 11; 46:8; 16; 47:11(2); 12(4); 48:10; 15; 16; 18; 21; **Dan** 1:5; 2:5; 6(2); 9; 26; 31; 36; 45; 3:1; 4:7; 9; 10; 11(2); 12(3); 18; 19(2); 20; 21; 23; 5:7; 8; 15; 16; 7:4; 9:26; **Hos** 2:9(2); 4:13; 8:14; 9:4; 10:5(3); 14:7; **Joel** 1:7; **Amos** 1:3; 6; 7; 9; 10; 11; 13; 14; 2:1; 3(2); 4; 6; 3:9(2); 8:10; 9:11; 14; **Jonah** 1:3; **Mic** 1:6(2); 7(3); 3:11(3); 5:6; 6:12(2); 16; **Nah** 1:8; 2:5; **Hab** 2:18; **Zeph** 1:13; 3:5; **Zec** 2:2(2); 3:9; 4:2; 3; 7; 11; 5:2(2); 4(2); 8; 7:7; 8:5; 9:1; 14:4; **Mal** 1:12; **Mt** 2:16; 6:34; 12:36; 13:32; 44; 14:13; 21:43; 22:7; 27:34; **Mk** 6:16; **Lk** 19:33; 21:20; 22:16; **Jn** 3:8; 4:12; 6:50; 7:7; **Acts** 15:16; **Rom** 6:12; 13:14; **1Cor** 9:7; 23; 10:26; 28; **2Ti** 3:5; **Heb** 7:18; **Jas** 1:11; **1Pet** 1:24; 5:2; **1Jn** 2:17; **Rev** 5:2; 5; 9; 16:12; 21; 21:15(2); 17; 23

THEREON

Gen 35:14(2); **Ex** 17:12; 20:24; 26; 30:7; 9(2); 40:27; 35; **Lev** 2:1; 6; 15; 5:11; 6:12; 10:1; 11:38; **Num** 4:6; 7(2); 13; 5:15; 9:22; 16:18; **Deut** 27:6; **Josh** 8:29; 31; 22:23(2); **2Sa** 17:19; 19:26; **1Kin** 6:35; 13:13; **2Kin** 16:12; **1Chr** 12:17; 15:15; **2Chr** 3:5; 14; 33:16; **Ezr** 3:2; 3; 6:11; **Est** 5:14; 7:9; **Is** 30:12; 35:9; **Eze** 15:3; 40:39; 43:18(2); **Zec** 4:2; **Mt** 21:7; 19; 23:20; 22; **Mk** 11:13; 14:72; **Lk** 13:6; 19:35; **Jn** 12:14; 21:9; **1Cor** 3:10; **Rev** 5:3; 4; 6:4; 21:12

THERETO

Ex 25:24; 29:41; 30:38; **Lev** 5:16; 6:5; 18:23; 20:16; 27:27; 31; **Num** 3:36; 19:17; **Deut** 12:32; **Judg** 11:17; **1Chr** 22:14; **2Chr** 10:14; 21:11; **Ps** 119:9; **Is** 44:15; **Mk** 14:70; **Gal** 3:15

THEREUPON

Ex 31:7; **Eze** 16:16; **Zeph** 2:7; **1Cor** 3:10; 14

THESE

Gen 2:4; 6:9; 9:19; 10:1; 5; 20; 29; 31; 32(2); 11:10; 27; 14:2; 3; 13; 15:1; 10; 19:8; 20:8; 21:29; 30; 22:1; 20; 23; 23:1; 24:28; 25:4; 7; 12; 13; 16(2); 17; 19; 26:3; 4; 27:36; 42; 46; 29:13; 31:43(4); 32:17; 33:8; 34:21; 35:26; 36:1; 5; 9; 10; 12; 13(2); 14; 15; 16(2); 17(3); 18(2); 19(2); 20; 21; 23; 24; 25; 26; 27; 28; 29; 30; 31; 40; 43; 37:2; 38:25(2); 39:7; 17; 40:1; 42:36; 43:7; 16(2); 44:6; 7; 45:6; 46:8; 15; 18(2); 22; 25(2); 48:1; 8; 49:28; **Ex** 1:1; 4:9; 6:14(2); 15; 16; 19; 24; 25; 26; 27(2); 10:1; 11:8; 10; 14:20; 15:26; 19:6; 7; 20:1; 21:1; 11; 24:8; 25:39; 28:4; 30:34; 32:4; 8; 33:4; 34:1; 27(2); 35:1; **Lev** 2:8; 5:4; 5; 13; 17; 6:3; 11:2; 4; 9; 13; 21; 22; 24; 29; 31; 16:4; 18:24(2); 26; 27; 29; 30; 20:23; 21:14; 22:22; 25; 23:2; 4; 37; 25:54; 26:14; 23; 46; 27:34; **Num** 1:5; 16; 17; 44; 2:9; 32; 3:1; 2; 3; 17; 18; 20; 21; 27; 33; 35; 4:15; 37; 41; 45; 5:23; 13:4; 16; 14:22; 39; 15:13; 22; 16:14; 26; 28; 29; 30; 31; 38; 21:25; 22:9; 28; 32; 33; 24:10; 26:7; 14; 18; 22; 25; 27; 30; 34; 35; 36; 37(2); 41; 42(2); 47; 50; 51; 53; 57; 58; 63; 64; 27:1; 28:23; 29:39; 30:16; 31:16; 33:1; 2; 34:17; 19; 29; 35:13; 15; 24; 29; 36:13; **Deut** 1:1; 35; 2:7; 3:5; 21; 4:6; 30; 42; 45; 5:22; 6:1; 6; 24; 25; 7:12; 17; 8:2; 4; 9:4; 5; 10:21; 11:18; 22; 23; 12:1; 28; 30; 14:4; 7; 9; 12; 15:5; 16:12; 17:19; 18:12(2); 14; 19:9(2); 11; 20:15; 16; 22:17; 23:18; 25:3; 26:16; 27:4; 12; 13; 28:2; 15; 45; 65; 29:1; 18; 30:1; 7; 31:1; 3; 17; 28; 32:45; **Josh** 2:11; 4:6; 7; 21; 9:13(2); 10:16; 24; 42; 11:5; 14; 12:1; 7; 13:12; 32; 14:1; 10; 17:2; 3; 9; 19:8; 16; 31; 48; 51; 20:9; 21:3; 8; 9; 42(2); 22:3; 23:3; 4; 7(2); 12(2); 13; 24:26; 29; **Judg** 2:4; 3:1; 9:3; 13:23(2); 16:15; 18:14; 18; 19:13; 20:17; 25; 35; 44; 46; **Ruth** 3:17; 4:18; **1Sa** 4:8(2); 6:17; 10:7; 14:6; 8; 49; 16:10; 17:17; 18; 39; 18:26; 21:5; 12; 23:2; 24:7; 16; 25:37; 29:3(3); 4; 31:4; **2Sa** 3:5; 39; 5:14; 7:17; 21; 13:21; 14:19; 16:2; 21:22; 23:1; 8; 17(2); 22; 24:17; 23; **1Kin** 4:2; 8; 7:9; 45; 8:59; 9:13; 23; 10:8; 10; 11:2; 17:1; 17; 18:36; 20:19; 21:1; 22:11; 17; 23; **2Kin** 1:7; 13; 2:21; 3:10; 13; 6:20; 7:8; 10:9; 17:41; 18:27; 20:14; 21:11; 23:16; 17; 25:16; 17; 20; **1Chr** 1:23; 29; 31; 33; 43; 54; 2:1; 18; 23; 33; 50; 55; 3:1; 4; 5; 9; 4:2; 3; 4; 6; 12; 18; 22; 23; 31; 33; 38; 41; 5:14; 17; 24; 6:17; 19; 31; 33; 50; 54; 64; 65; 7:8; 11; 17; 29; 33; 40; 8:6(2); 10; 28(2); 32; 38(2); 40; 9:9; 22(2); 26; 33; 34(2); 44(2); 10:4; 11:10; 19(3); 24; 12:1; 14; 15; 23; 38; 14:4; 17:15; 19; 18:11; 20:8; 21:17; 23:9; 10; 24; 24:1; 19; 20; 30; 31; 25:5; 6; 26:8; 12; 19; 27:22; 31; 29:17; 19; **2Chr** 3:3; 13; 4:18; 5:5; 8:10; 9:7; 14:7; 8; 15:8; 17:14; 19; 18:10; 16; 22; 21:2; 24:26; 29:32; 32:1; 35:7; 36:18; **Ezr** 1:11; 2:1; 59; 62; 4:21; 5:9; 11; 15; 6:8(2); 7:1; 8:1; 13; 9:1; 14; 10:44; **Neh** 1:4; 10; 4:2; 5:6; 6:6; 7; 14; 16; 7:6; 61; 64; 10:8; 11:3; 7; 12:1; 7; 26; 13:26; **Est** 1:5; 2:1; 3:1; 4:11; 9:20; 26; 27; 28(2); 31; 32; **Job** 8:2; 10:13; 12:3; 9; 19:3; 26:14; 32:1; 5; 33:29; 42:7; **Ps** 15:5; 42:4; 50:21; 57:1; 73:12; 104:27; 107:24; 43; **Prov** 6:16; 24:23; 25:1; **Eccl** 7:10; 11:9; 12:12; **Is** 7:4; 34:16; 36:12; 20; 38:16(2); 39:3; 40:26; 42:16; 44:21; 45:7; 47:7; 9; 13; 48:14; 49:12(3); 18; 21(3); 51:19; 57:6; 60:8; 64:12; 65:5; **Jer** 2:34; 3:7; 12; 4:18; 5:4; 5; 9; 19; 25; 29; 7:2; 4; 10; 13; 27; 9:9; 24; 26; 10:11; 11:6; 13:22; 14:22; 16:10; 17:20; 20:1; 22:2; 5; 23:21; 24:5; 25:9; 11; 30; 26:7; 10; 15; 27:6; 12; 28:14; 29:1; 30:4; 15; 31:21; 32:14; 34:6; 7; 36:16; 17; 18; 24; 38:9; 12; 16; 24; 27; 43:1; 10; 45:1; 51:60; 61; 52:20; 22; **Lam** 1:16; 4:9; 5:17; **Eze** 1:21(2); 8:15; 10:17(2); 11:2; 14:3; 14; 16; 18; 16:5; 20; 30; 43; 17:12; 18; 18:10; 13; 23:10; 30; 24:19; 27:21; 24; 30:17; 35:10(2); 36:20; 37:3; 4; 5; 9; 11; 18; 40:24; 28; 29; 32; 33; 35; 46; 42:5; 9; 43:13; 18; 27; 46:22; 24; 47:8; 9; 48:1(2); 16; 29; 30; **Dan** 1:6; 17; 2:28; 40; 44(2); 3:12; 13; 21; 23; 27; 6:2; 5; 6; 11; 14; 15; 7:17; 10:21; 11:6; 27; 41; 12:6; 7; 8; **Hos** 2:12; 14:9; **Amos** 6:2; **Mic** 2:7; **Hab** 2:6; **Hag** 2:13; **Zec** 1:9(2); 10; 12; 19(2); 21(3); 3:7; 4:4; 5; 11; 12; 13; 14; 5:10; 6:4; 5; 8; 7:3; 8:6; 9(2); 10; 12; 15; 16; 17; 13:6; 14:15; **Mt** 1:20; 2:3; 3:9; 4:3; 9; 5:19; 37; 6:29; 32(2); 33; 7:24; 26; 28; 9:18; 10:2; 5; 42; 11:25; 13:34; 51; 53; 54; 56; 15:20; 18:6; 10; 14; 19:1; 20; 20:12; 21; 21:16; 23; 24; 27; 22:22; 40; 23:23; 36; 24:2; 3; 6; 8; 33; 34; 25:40; 45; 46; 26:1; 62; **Mk** 2:8; 4:11; 15; 16; 18; 20; 6:2; 7:23; 8:4; 9:42; 10:20; 11:28(2); 29; 33; 12:31; 40; 13:2; 4(2); 8; 29; 30; 14:60; 16:17; **Lk** 1:19; 20; 65; 2:19; 51; 3:8; 4:28; 5:27; 7:9; 18; 8:8; 13; 21; 9:28; 44; 10:1; 21; 36; 11:27; 42; 53; 12:27; 30(2); 31; 13:2; 7; 16; 17; 14:6; 15; 21; 15:26; 29; 16:14; 17:2;

18:21; 22; 34; 19:11; 15; 40; 20:2; 8; 16; 21:4; 6; 7(2); 9; 12; 22; 28; 31; 36; 23:31; 49; 24:9; 10; 14; 17; 18; 21; 26; 44; 48; **Jn** 1:28; 50; 2:16; 18; 3:2; 9; 10; 22; 5:3; 16; 19; 20; 34; 6:1; 5; 59; 7:1; 4; 9; 31; 8:20; 28; 30; 9:22; 40; 10:19; 21; 11:11; 12:16(3); 36; 41; 13:17; 14:12; 25; 15:11; 17; 21; 16:1; 3; 4(2); 6; 25; 33; 17:1; 11; 13; 20; 25; 18:1; 8; 19:24; 36; 20:18; 31; 21:1; 15; 24(2); **Acts** 1:9; 14; 21; 24; 2:7; 13; 15; 22; 3:24; 4:16; 5:5(2); 11; 24; 32; 35; 36; 38; 7:1; 50; 54; 8:24; 10:8; 44; 47; 11:12; 18; 22; 27; 12:17; 13:42; 14:15(2); 18; 15:17; 28; 16:17; 20; 38; 17:6; 7; 8; 11; 20; 18:1; 19:21; 28; 36; 37; 20:5; 24; 34; 21:12; 38; 23:22; 24:8; 9; 20; 22; 25:9; 11(2); 20; 26:16; 21; 26(2); 29; 27:31; 28:29; **Rom** 2:14; 8:31; 37; 9:8; 11:24; 31; 14:18; 15:23(2); **1Cor** 4:6; 14; 9:8; 15(2); 10:6; 11; 12:2; 11; 23; 13:13(2); **2Cor** 2:16; 7:1; 13:10; **Gal** 2:6; 4:24; 5:17; 19; **Eph** 5:6; **Phil** 4:8; **Col** 3:8; 14; 4:11; **1Th** 3:3; 4:18; **2Th** 2:5; **1Ti** 3:10; 14; 4:6; 11; 15; 5:7; 21; 6:2; 11; **2Ti** 1:12; 2:14; 21; 3:8; **Titus** 2:15; 3:8(2); **Heb** 1:2; 7:13; 9:6; 23(2); 10:18; 11:13; 39; **Jas** 3:10; **1Pet** 1:20; **2Pet** 1:4; 8; 9; 10; 12; 15; 2:12; 17; 3:11; 16; 17; **1Jn** 1:4; 2:1; 26; 5:7; 8; 13; **Jude** 8; 10; 12; 14; 16; 19; **Rev** 2:1; 8; 12; 18; 3:1; 7; 14; 7:1; 13; 14; 9:18; 20; 11:4; 6; 10; 14:4(3); 16:9; 17:13; 14; 16; 18:1; 15; 19:1; 9; 20; 21:5; 22:6; 8(2); 16; 18; 20

THEY

Gen 2:4; 24; 25; 3:7(3); 8; 4:8; 5:2; 6:2(3); 4; 19; 7:14; 15; 16; 23(2); 8:17; 9:2; 23; 11:2(3); 3(3); 4; 6(3); 7; 8; 31(2); 12:5(4); 12(3); 20; 13:6(2); 11; 14:4(2); 7; 8; 10; 11; 12; 15:13; 14(2); 16; 18:5; 8; 9; 19; 21; 19:2; 3(2); 4; 5; 8; 9(3); 11(2); 16; 17; 33; 35; 20:11; 17; 21:30; 31; 32(2); 22:6; 8; 9; 19; 24:19; 41; 54(2); 57; 58; 59; 60; 61; 25:18; 25; 26:18; 20; 21; 22; 28; 30; 31(2); 32; 29:2; 3; 4; 5; 6; 8(2); 20; 30:38(2); 41; 31:23; 37; 43; 46(2); 54; 32:18; 33:4; 6(2); 7; 34:5; 7(2); 14; 22; 23; 25; 26; 27; 28; 29; 30; 31; 35:4; 5(2); 16; 36:7(2); 37:4; 5; 8; 16; 17; 18(2); 19; 23; 24; 25(2); 28(2); 31; 32(2); 38:21; 39:22; 40:4; 5; 6; 8; 15; 41:2; 14; 18; 21(3); 43; 42:7; 8; 10; 13; 20; 21; 23; 26; 28; 29; 35(3); 43:2(2); 7; 15; 18(2); 19(2); 24; 25(3); 26; 28(2); 32; 33; 34; 44:1; 3; 4; 7; 11; 13; 14; 45:3; 4; 24; 25; 27; 46:6(2); 28; 32(2); 47:1(2); 3; 4; 14; 17; 18; 22; 25; 27; 48:5; 9; 49:6(2); 26; 31(2); 50:8; 10(2); 11; 15; 16; 17(2); 18; 26; **Ex** 1:10(2); 11(2); 12(3); 14(2); 19; 2:16; 18; 19; 23; 3:13; 18; 4:1(2); 5; 8(2); 9; 18; 31(2); 5:1; 3; 8(3); 9; 10; 16; 19; 20(2); 21; 6:4; 9; 27; 7:6; 7; 10; 11; 12(2); 16; 17; 19; 24; 8:1; 8; 9; 11; 14; 17; 18; 20; 21; 26; 9:1; 10; 13; 19; 32; 10:3; 5(2); 6(2); 7; 8; 11; 12; 14(2); 15(2); 23; 12:3; 7(2); 8(2); 28; 33(2); 35; 36(3); 39(4); 50; 13:17(2); 20; 14:2; 3; 4; 5; 10; 11; 15; 17; 25; 15:5; 10; 16; 22(2); 23(3); 27(2); 16:1; 4; 5(3); 10; 15(2); 18(2); 20; 21; 22; 24; 27; 32; 35(3); 17:4; 7; 12; 18:7(2); 11; 16(2); 20(2); 22(3); 26(3); 19:1; 2; 13; 14; 17; 21; 20:18; 19; 21:28; 35(2); 22:23; 23:11; 33(2); 24:2; 7; 10; 11; 25:2; 10; 15; 37(2); 26:24(3); 25; 27:8; 20; 28:3; 4(2); 5; 6; 20; 21; 28; 30; 38; 41; 42; 43(4); 29:33(2); 46; 30:4; 12; 13; 15; 20(4); 21(2); 29; 30; 31:6; 11; 32:4; 6; 8(2); 13; 15; 17; 20; 22; 23; 24; 35; 33:4; 34:15; 30; 35:21(2); 22; 25; 36:3(2); 4; 5; 6; 7; 29; 39:1; 3; 4; 6; 7; 9; 10; 13; 15; 16; 17; 18; 19; 20; 21; 24; 25; 27; 30; 31; 32; 33; 43(2); 40:15; 32(3); 37; **Lev** 2:12; 4:13; 14; 24; 33; 6:16; 20; 7:2(2); 8:28; 9:5; 13; 20; 24; 10:2; 5; 7; 14; 15; 19; 11:8; 10; 11; 13(3); 28; 31; 32; 35(2); 42; 13:54; 14:36; 40(2); 41(2); 42; 15:18; 31(2); 16:1; 27; 17:5(2); 7(2); 18:17; 19:20; 20:12; 13; 14(2); 16; 17; 19; 20(2); 21; 23; 27; 21:5(2); 6(3); 7(2); 22:2(3); 9(3); 11; 15(2); 16; 18; 25; 23:17(3); 18; 20; 24:2; 9; 11; 12; 23; 25:31(2); 42(2); 45(2); 46; 55; 26:7; 17; 26; 36(2); 37; 39(2); 40(3); 41; 43(2); 44; 27:11; **Num** 1:1; 18(2); 46; 50(2); 54; 2:2; 3; 16; 17(2); 24; 31(2); 34(2); 3:4(2); 6; 7; 8; 9; 10; 13; 31; 4:5; 7; 8; 9(2); 10; 11; 12(2); 13; 14(3); 15(2); 19(2); 20(2); 25; 26; 37; 41; 49(2); 5:2; 3; 7(2); 9; 6:7; 27; 7:3(2); 5; 9; 11; 8:11; 16; 21; 22; 24; 25; 9:1; 4; 5; 6(2); 11; 12(2); 18(2); 20(2); 21(2); 22; 23(3); 10:3; 4; 6; 8; 10; 13; 21; 28; 33; 34; 11:13; 16; 17; 21; 25; 26(2); 32(2); 34; 12:2; 4; 5; 13:2; 18; 19(3); 21; 22; 23(3); 25; 26; 27; 31; 32(2); 14:4; 7; 9; 11; 12; 14(2); 23; 27; 31; 32; 35(2); 40; 44; 15:25; 32; 33; 34; 38(2); 16:2; 3; 16; 18; 22; 27; 29; 30; 33(2); 34; 37; 38(3); 39(2); 42; 45; 49; 17:5; 9; 10; 18:2; 3(3); 4; 6; 9; 12; 13; 15; 17; 21; 22; 23(2); 24(2); 19:2; 17; 20:2; 6; 27; 29; 21:3; 4; 6; 11; 12; 13; 16; 18; 27; 32; 33; 35(2); 22:3; 5(2); 6; 7; 12; 14; 15; 16; 39; 24:6; 25:2; 18(2); 26:7; 9; 10; 41; 50; 55; 57; 61; 62; 63; 64; 65; 27:2; 21(2); 28:19; 31; 29:8; 13; 30:9; 31:7(2); 8(2); 10(2); 11; 12; 49; 52; 32:1; 5; 9(3); 11; 12; 16; 30(2); 38; 33:3; 6; 7(2); 8; 9(2); 10; 11; 12; 13; 14; 15; 16; 17; 18; 19; 20; 21; 22; 23; 24; 25; 26; 27; 28; 29; 30; 31; 32; 33; 34; 35; 36; 37; 41; 42; 43; 44; 45; 46; 47; 48; 49; 34:29; 35:2; 3; 12; 36:2; 3(2); 4; 6(2); 12; **Deut** 1:22; 24; 25; 39(2); 2:4; 12; 15; 21; 22; 3:20; 4:9; 10(3); 45; 46; 47; 5:28(3); 29; 31; 6:8; 7:4(2); 20; 23; 9:12(2); 14; 29; 10:5; 7; 11; 11:4; 18; 30; 12:30; 31(2); 14:7(2); 12; 10; 15:6; 16:16; 18; 17:5; 9; 10(2); 11(3); 18:1; 2; 3; 8; 17(2); 19:14; 20:8; 9; 11; 18(2); 20; 21:2; 7; 15; 18; 20; 22:6; 17; 19; 21; 22; 24; 28; 23:3; 4(2); 25:1(2); 26:12; 28:7; 10; 22; 41; 46; 60; 29:22; 25; 26(2); 31:12(2); 16; 17(2); 18(2); 20(2); 21; 24; 30; 32:5(2); 7; 16(2); 17(2); 20; 21(2); 24; 27; 28; 29(3); 37; 33:3; 9; 10(2); 11; 17(2); 19(3); **Josh** 1:15; 16; 2:1; 3; 4; 7(2); 8; 13; 21; 22; 24; 3:1(2); 3; 6; 7; 13; 15; 4:8; 9; 14(2); 16; 18; 20; 5:4; 5(2); 6; 7(2); 8(3); 11; 12(2); 6:5; 11; 14(2); 15(2); 19; 20; 21; 23; 24(2); 7:3(2); 4; 5; 11(3); 12; 21; 22; 23; 24; 25; 26; 8:5; 6(3); 9; 13; 14; 15; 16; 17; 19(2); 20(2); 21; 22(3); 23; 24(3); 29; 31; 33; 9:2; 4(2); 6; 8; 9; 13; 16(4); 24; 26; 10:2; 5; 11(4); 20; 23; 24(2); 26; 27(2); 34; 35; 36; 37; 39; 11:4(2); 5; 7; 8(2); 11; 14(3); 19; 20(2); 14:4; 5; 16:10; 17:4; 10; 13; 16(2); 18(2); 18:4(2); 5; 19:2; 49; 50; 51; 20:3; 4; 5; 7; 8; 21:2; 9; 11; 12; 13; 20; 21; 27; 43; 22:6; 9; 10; 15(2); 28; 23:12; 13; 24:1; 2; 7; 8; 22; 30; 32; 33; **Judg** 1:4; 5(3); 6; 7; 10; 16; 17; 19; 20; 22; 24; 25(2); 28; 32; 34; 35; 2:3; 5(2); 9; 12; 13; 14; 15(2); 17(4); 19(2); 22; 3:4(2); 6; 12; 24(2); 25(3); 26; 28; 29; 4:12; 24; 5:7; 8; 11(2); 14; 19; 20; 23; 30(2); 6:3; 4; 5(4); 29(3); 35; 7:11; 19(2); 20; 21; 25(3); 8:1; 5; 18(3); 19; 24(2); 25(2); 28; 35; 9:3; 4; 7; 8; 9; 25; 27; 31; 34; 36; 41; 42; 46; 51; 55; 10:4; 8; 16; 11:2; 6; 13; 17; 18; 21; 22; 12:4; 6(2); 14:9; 11(2); 13; 14; 15; 15:6; 10; 11; 12; 13(2); 16:2; 7; 11; 23; 24(2); 25(3); 30; 17:4; 18:2(3); 3(3); 5; 7(2); 8; 9; 12(2); 13; 15; 19; 21; 22; 23(2); 26; 27(2); 28(2); 29; 31; 19:4; 5; 6; 8(2); 11; 14(2); 15; 21; 22; 25(2); 20:5; 6; 10(3); 22; 31; 32; 34; 36(3); 38; 39(2); 41; 42(2); 43; 45(2); 48(2); 21:5; 8; 12(2); 14(3); 17; 19; 20; 23(2); 24; **Ruth** 1:2; 4(2); 7; 9; 10; 11; 13; 14; 19(4); 22; 2:4; 9(2); 21; 22; 4:2; 17; **1Sa** 1:9(2); 19; 25; 2:4; 5(2); 12; 14; 15; 20; 22; 25; 27; 30; 34; 4:2(2); 4; 6(2); 7(2); 9; 10; 5:2; 3(2); 4; 7; 8(3); 9(2); 10(2); 11; 6:3; 4(2); 6(2); 11; 12; 13(2); 14; 16; 18; 19; 21; 7:6; 7; 10; 11; 13; 8:2; 6; 7(3); 8(3); 19; 9:4(4); 5; 10; 11(2); 12; 13; 14(2); 20; 25; 26(2); 27; 10:2; 4; 5; 10; 14; 21; 22; 23; 27; 11:5(2); 7; 9(2); 11(2); 15(2); 12:4; 5; 9(2); 10; 21; 13:5; 6; 21; 14:9; 10; 11; 13; 15; 16; 17; 20; 21; 22(2); 25; 30; 31; 33(2); 36; 15:3; 6; 9; 15; 18; 16:6; 17:11; 19; 24; 31; 51; 53; 18:6; 7; 8(2); 20; 27; 30; 19:1; 8; 20(2); 21(2); 22; 24; 20:11; 41; 21:11; 22:1; 4; 11; 17; 23:1(2); 12; 13; 18; 24; 25; 28; 25:7; 8; 9; 11; 13; 16; 26; 40; 43; 26:12(2); 19(3); 27:11; 28:4; 8; 25(2); 29:5; 30:2; 4; 10; 11(2); 12; 16(2); 19; 20; 21(3); 22(2); 24; 31:7(2); 8; 9; 10(2); 13; **2Sa** 1:12(2); 23(3); 2:3; 4(3); 13; 16(2); 24; 28; 29; 32(2); 3:21; 23; 32; 4:6(3); 7(2); 8; 12(2); 5:3; 8; 11; 17; 21; 6:3; 4; 6; 13; 17; 7:10; 8:14; 9:2; 10:5; 6; 13; 14; 15(2); 16; 19(2); 11:1; 10; 20; 12:18; 19; 20; 13:9; 30; 32; 14:6; 7(2); 11; 15:11(2); 24; 29; 30(2); 36; 16:22; 17:8(2); 10; 17(2); 18(2); 20(4); 21(2); 22; 29; 18:3(2); 17; 19:3; 8; 14; 17; 20:3; 7; 8; 14; 15(2); 18(3); 22(2); 21:5; 9(2); 13; 14(2); 22:18; 19; 39(2); 42; 45(2); 46; 23:6; 7; 9; 24:3; 5; 6(2); 7; 8(2); 13; 17; **1Kin** 1:1; 3; 7; 23; 25; 32; 39; 41; 44; 45; 53; 2:7; 39; 3:22; 24; 28(2); 4:21; 27; 28; 5:1; 6; 12; 14; 17; 18; 6:8; 10; 27; 7:28; 47; 8:1; 4; 8(3); 9; 25; 30; 33; 35(2); 36; 40(2); 42; 43; 46(2); 47(2); 50(2); 51; 52; 66; 9:8; 9(2); 12; 22; 28; 10:25; 29; 11:2(2); 18(3); 24; 29; 33; 41; 12:3; 7(2); 8; 13; 20; 24; 27; 13:11; 13; 20; 25; 27; 30; 14:15; 18; 19; 22(2); 23; 24; 29; 15:7; 8; 22; 23; 31; 16:5; 13(2); 14; 17; 20; 27; 18:6; 10(2); 26(3); 28; 29; 34(2); 39(2); 40; 19:10; 14; 21; 20:6(2); 12; 15; 16; 17; 18(2); 20; 23(2); 25; 29; 32; 33; 21:12; 13; 14; 22:1; 6; 32(2); 33; 37; 38; 39; 45; 48; **2Kin** 1:6; 8; 18; 2:2; 4; 6; 7; 8(2); 9; 11; 14; 15(2); 16; 17(3); 18; 20; 3:9; 21; 22; 23(2); 24(3); 25(3); 26; 27; 4:39; 40(4); 41; 42; 43(2); 44; 5:23; 24; 6:4(2); 14; 16(2); 18; 20(4); 22; 23(2); 25; 7:3; 4(2); 5(2); 6; 7; 8; 9; 10(3); 11; 12(3); 13(2); 14; 15; 8:23; 9:12; 13; 21; 27; 33; 35(2); 36; 37; 10:4; 7; 8; 13; 14; 16; 20; 21; 24; 25; 26; 27; 34; 35; 11:2; 7; 9; 12(2); 16; 17; 18; 19; 20; 12:10(2); 11(2); 14; 15(3); 19; 21; 13:5; 6; 8; 9; 12; 20; 21(3); 14:12; 15; 18; 19(2); 20; 28; 15:6; 7; 11; 15; 16; 21; 26; 31; 36; 16:5; 18; 19; 17:8; 9; 10; 11; 12; 14; 15(3); 16; 17; 19; 21; 22; 24; 25; 26(3); 28(2); 29; 32; 33(2); 34(3); 40(2); 41; 18:10; 12; 17(3); 18; 20; 27; 34; 35; 19:3; 18(2); 26(2); 31; 35(2); 37; 20:7; 14(2); 15(2); 18(2); 20; 21:8; 9; 14; 15; 17; 25; 22:7; 14; 17(2); 19; 20; 23:1; 9; 18; 28; 24:5; 25:1; 6(2); 7; 14(2); 23(2); 26; **1Chr** 4:14; 23; 28; 39; 40(2); 43; 5:10(2); 16; 19; 20(3); 21; 22; 23; 25; 6:31; 32(2); 33; 55; 56; 57; 65; 67(2); 7:2; 4; 21; 8:6; 9:1; 18; 23; 27; 28; 33; 38; 10:7(2); 8; 9(2); 10; 12; 11:3; 7; 14; 19; 12:1(2); 2; 15(2); 19; 21(2); 33; 39; 40; 13:2; 4; 7; 9; 14:11(2); 12(2); 16; 15:26; 16:1(2); 20; 17:9; 19:6; 7; 11; 14; 15; 16(2); 17; 19(2); 20:4; 8; 21:3(2); 5; 17(2); 22:4; 23:11; 24; 25; 26; 32; 24:4; 5; 25:8; 26:6; 8; 13; 14; 27; 31; 28:21; 29:8; 9(2); 21; 22; 29; **2Chr** 1:17(2); 2:17; 3:13; 4:6(2); 20; 5:5; 9(2); 10; 13; 6:21; 24; 26(2); 27; 31(2); 32; 34; 36(2); 37(2); 38(2); 7:3; 9(2); 22; 8:9; 15; 18; 9:24; 28; 29; 10:3; 7(2); 11:4; 17(2); 12:2; 6; 7(2); 8(2); 15; 13:11(2); 13; 14; 18; 14:1; 7; 10; 13(3); 14(2); 15; 15:4; 9(2); 10; 11(2); 12; 14; 15; 16:4; 6; 11; 14(2); 17:9; 10; 18:5; 9; 10; 14; 29; 31(2); 32; 19:8; 10; 20:2; 4; 8; 10(2); 11; 16; 20(2); 21; 22(2); 23; 24(2); 25(4); 26(2); 27; 28; 29; 34; 36; 37; 21:17; 20; 22:4; 9(4); 23:2(2); 6(3); 11; 15(2); 16; 20; 21; 24:7; 8; 9; 10; 11(2); 13; 14(3); 16; 18; 19(2); 21; 23; 24(2); 25(4); 26; 27; 25:10; 12; 13; 20; 21; 22; 26; 27(2); 28; 26:18; 20; 23(2); 27:7; 9; 28:5; 6; 15; 18; 23(2); 26; 27(2); 29:7; 15; 16; 17(4); 18; 19; 21; 22(5); 23(2); 24; 29; 30(2); 34; 30:1; 3; 5(3); 9; 10; 14(2); 15; 16(2); 18; 22; 23; 31:1; 4; 5; 6; 7; 8; 11; 18; 32:3; 18(2); 19; 21; 32; 33; 33:8; 10; 18; 19; 20; 34:4; 9(3); 10(2); 11; 13; 14; 16; 17; 22(2); 24; 25(2); 28; 33; 35:1; 6; 11; 12(3); 13(2); 14; 15; 24; 25; 27; 36:8; 16; 19; 20; **Ezr** 1:6; 2:59(3); 62(2); 63; 68; 69; 3:3(2); 4; 6; 7(2); 8; 10; 11(2); 4:2; 6; 11; 13; 15; 23; 5:5(2); 7; 11; 14; 6:3; 8; 9; 10; 13; 14(2); 18; 7:13; 8:17(2); 18; 36(2); 9:2; 10:5(2); 7(2); 17; 19(3); 44; **Neh** 1:3; 2:7; 18(2); 19; 3:1(3); 6; 8; 13; 4:2(4); 3; 5; 7; 11; 12(2); 17(2); 22; 5:8(2); 12(2); 6:2; 4; 9; 10(2); 13(2); 16(2); 19; 7:3; 5; 61(3); 64; 65; 67; 8:1; 4; 6; 8; 9; 12; 14; 15; 18; 9:3(2); 10; 11; 12; 15; 16; 18; 19; 21; 22; 23; 24(2); 25(2); 26(2); 27; 28(4); 29; 30; 35(2); 37; 10:28; 29; 11:30; 12:27; 37; 39; 43; 47; 13:1; 2; 3(2); 5; 9; 13; 15(2); 19; 21; 22(2); 29; **Est** 1:7; 8; 17; 2:3; 23; 3:4(2); 6; 7; 8; 9; 14; 4:12; 6:1; 9; 14; 7:8; 10; 8:7; 9:5; 10(2); 12; 14; 15; 16; 17; 18; 21; 22; 23; 26(2); 27; 31; 10:2; **Job** 1:15; 19; 2:11(2); 12(3); 13(2); 3:18; 22; 4:8; 9(2); 20(2); 21; 5:4; 14; 6:15; 17(3); 18; 20(3); 8:10; 22; 9:5; 25(2); 26; 11:6; 20; 12:6; 7(2); 15(2); 25; 14:12; 21; 15:24; 35; 16:10(3); 17:12; 16; 18:20(2); 19:15; 18; 19; 23; 24; 20:7; 21:11; 12; 13; 14; 18; 26; 30; 22:12; 24:1; 2; 3(2); 4; 5; 6(2); 7(2); 8; 9; 10(2); 13(2); 16(3); 17; 24(2); 27:13; 28:1; 4(2); 29:22; 23(2); 24(2); 30:1; 3; 5(2); 7(2); 8(2); 10(2); 11; 12(2); 13(3); 14(2); 15; 24; 31:13; 32:3; 4; 15(3); 16; 34:19; 20; 25; 27; 28; 35:9(2); 12; 36:7(2); 8; 9; 10; 11(2); 12(3); 13; 14; 27; 37:12; 38:14; 35; 40; 41; 39:2(2); 3(3); 4(2); 16; 41:6; 17(3); 23(2); 25; 42:11(2); **Ps** 2:12; 3:1(2); 5:9; 10; 9:3; 10; 15(2); 10:2; 11:2(2); 12:2(2); 14:1(2); 3(2); 4; 5; 17:10(2); 11(2); 14; 18:17; 18; 37; 38(2); 41; 44(2); 19:10; 20:8; 21:11(3); 22:4; 5(2); 7(3); 13; 16; 17; 18; 26; 29(2); 31; 23:4; 24:1; 25:6; 19(2); 27:2; 28:5; 31:4; 11; 13(2); 32:6; 9; 34:5; 10; 21; 35:7(2); 11; 12; 13; 15(2); 16; 20(2); 21; 36:8; 12; 37:2; 9; 19(2); 20(2); 22; 28; 40; 38:4; 12(2); 16(2); 19(2); 20; 39:6; 40:5(2); 12; 41:7; 8; 42:3; 10; 44:3; 10; 45:8; 15(2); 48:4; 5(3); 49:6; 11; 14; 19; 51:19; 53:1; 3; 4(2); 5; 54:3; 55:3(2); 10; 19(2); 21; 56:2; 5; 6(4); 7; 8; 57:6(3); 58:3(2); 4; 8; 59:t, 3; 4; 6(2); 7(2); 12; 13; 15; 62:4(4); 9; 63:10(2); 64:4(2); 5(3); 6(2); 7; 8; 9; 65:8; 12; 13(2); 66:4; 6; 68:24; 69:4(2); 12; 21(2); 23; 26(2); 35; 36; 71:10; 24(2); 72:5; 9; 16; 73:5(2); 7; 8(2); 9; 11; 12; 19(2); 27; 74:4; 6; 7(2); 8(2); 76:5; 77:16; 78:5; 7; 10; 17; 18; 19(2); 22; 29; 30; 32; 34(2); 35; 36(2); 37; 39; 40; 41; 42; 44; 53; 56; 57; 58; 79:1(2); 2; 3; 7; 12; 80:12; 16; 81:12; 82:5(3); 83:2; 3; 4; 5(2); 8; 10; 16; 84:4(2); 7; 86:17; 88:5; 17(2); 89:15; 16(2); 31; 51; 90:5(2); 10; 91:12; 92:7; 14(2); 94:4; 5; 6; 7; 11; 21; 95:10; 11; 97:7; 98:7; 99:6; 7; 101:6; 102:8; 26(2); 104:7(2); 8(2); 9(2); 11; 22; 28(2); 29(2); 30; 32; 105:12; 13; 18; 27; 28; 38; 41; 44; 45; 106:3; 7; 12(2); 13(2); 16; 19; 20; 21; 24(2); 28; 29; 32; 33; 34; 36; 37; 38; 39; 41; 42; 43; 107:4(2); 6; 7; 11; 12; 13; 18; 19; 23; 26(2); 27; 28; 30(2); 36; 38; 39; 43; 109:2; 3; 4; 5; 25(2); 27; 28; 111:8; 10; 115:5(4); 6(4); 7(5); 8; 118:11(2); 12(2); 119:2; 3(2); 74(2); 78; 86; 87; 91; 98; 111; 126; 136; 150(2); 155; 158; 165; 120:7; 122:1; 6; 124:3; 125:1; 126:2; 5; 127:1; 5(2); 129:1; 2(2); 3; 8; 130:6(2); 135:16(4); 17(2); 18; 137:3(2); 138:4; 5; 139:18; 20; 140:2; 3; 5(2); 8; 10; 141:6(2); 9; 142:3; 6; 144:5; 145:7; 11; 147:20; 148:5; **Prov** 1:9; 11; 18(2); 28(3); 29; 30(2); 31; 2:15; 19; 3:2; 22; 4:16(3); 17; 19(2); 22; 7:5; 8:9; 32; 36; 11:20; 12:22; 14:22; 15:22; 16:13; 17:15; 18:8; 21; 19:7; 21:7; 22:18; 23:3; 5; 30(2); 35(2); 26:22; 28:4; 5; 28; 30:24; 25; 26; 27; 31:5; **Eccl** 1:7; 16; 2:3; 3:18(2); 19; 4:1(2); 3; 9; 10; 11; 16; 5:1(2); 8; 11; 7:29; 8:10(2); 9:3(2); 5(2); 6; 11:3; 6; 8; 12:3; 5; **Song** 1:6; 3:8; 5:7(2); 6:5; 9; **Is** 1:2; 4(3); 6; 14; 18(3); 23; 28; 29; 31; 2:4(2); 6(2); 8; 19; 20; 3:9(3); 10; 12; 16; 5:6; 8; 11; 12; 13; 24; 26; 29(2); 30; 6:10; 13; 7:19; 22; 8:19; 20; 21(3); 22(2); 9:2; 3(2); 12; 13; 16; 18; 20(2); 21; 10:1; 2; 4(2); 18; 29(2); 11:9; 14(3); 13:2; 5; 8(3); 14; 17; 18; 14:1; 2(3); 7; 10; 16; 21; 15:3; 5(2); 7(3); 16:7; 8(3); 17:2; 3; 9; 13; 18:6; 19:2; 3; 6; 8(2); 9(2); 10; 12; 13(2); 14; 20; 21; 22; 20:5; 21:14; 15; 22:3; 9; 24; 23:5; 13(2); 24:5; 6; 9; 14(3); 22(2); 26:11(2); 14(4); 16(2); 19; 27:11; 13; 28:7(5); 12; 13; 29:9(2); 15; 23; 24(2); 30:1; 5; 6; 16; 18; 31:1(3); 3; 32:12; 33:1(2); 12; 17; 23(2); 34:12; 17(2); 35:2; 10; 36:5; 12; 19; 20; 21; 37:3; 19(2); 27(2); 32; 36(2); 38; 38:18; 39:3(2); 4(2); 7(2); 40:17; 24(3); 31(4); 41:6; 11(3); 12; 20; 22; 29; 42:9; 16(2); 17(2); 22(3); 24(2); 43:2; 9; 17(4); 21; 44:4; 9(4); 11(3); 18(3); 45:6; 14(5); 16(2); 20; 46:1; 2(3); 6(3); 7(2); 47:9; 14(2); 15(2); 48:2; 3(2); 7; 13; 21; 49:9; 10; 15; 17; 19; 21; 22; 23(2); 26; 50:9; 51:5; 6; 11; 20(2); 52:5; 6; 8(2); 15(3); 54:15; 56:10(3); 11(3); 12; 57:2; 6(2); 12; 58:2(3); 3; 12; 59:4(2); 5; 6; 7; 8(2); 19; 60:4(2); 6(3); 7; 11; 14(2); 21; 61:3; 4(3); 7(2); 9; 62:9(2); 12; 63:8; 10; 13; 15; 19; 65:11; 16; 21(2); 22(2); 23(2); 24(2); 25; 66:3; 4(2); 5; 17; 18; 19; 20; 24(2); **Jer** 1:15(2); 19(2); 2:5; 6; 8; 13; 15; 24(2); 26; 27(2); 28; 30; 3:1; 16(3); 17(2); 18; 21(2); 4:2; 17; 22(5); 23; 24; 29; 30; 5:2(2); 3(4); 4(2); 5; 7; 8; 10; 12; 15; 16; 17(4); 22(3); 23; 24; 26(3); 27; 28(6); 6:3(2); 9; 10(3); 14; 15(6); 16; 17; 19; 23(3); 28(3); 7:17; 18; 19(2); 24; 26(2); 27(2); 30; 31; 32; 8:1; 2(8); 4; 5(2); 6; 9(2); 11; 12(6); 16; 17; 19; 9:2; 3(4); 5(2); 6; 10(2); 13; 16; 17(2); 10:4(2); 5(4); 8; 9; 11; 15(2); 18; 20; 21; 25; 11:8(2); 10(2); 11(2); 12(2); 14; 17; 19; 12:1; 2(3); 4; 5(2); 6(3); 10(2); 11; 13(3); 16(3); 17; 13:11(2); 12; 14:2; 3(3); 4; 6; 10(2); 12(2); 14; 15; 16(2); 18; 15:2; 7; 20(2); 16:4(5); 6; 10; 12; 16(2); 17; 18(2); 20; 21; 17:13(2); 15; 19; 23(2); 25; 26; 18:12; 15(2); 18; 20; 22; 19:4(2); 5; 9(2); 11; 13; 15(2); 20:4; 10; 11(3); 21:6; 22:7; 8; 9(2); 12; 18(2); 27(2); 28(2); 23:3; 4(2); 7; 8; 12; 13; 14(3); 16(2); 17(2); 21(2); 22(2); 26; 27; 32; 24:2; 3; 7(2); 8; 10; 25:5; 16; 28; 30; 33(2); 26:3; 10; 23; 24; 27:10; 11; 14; 15; 16; 18; 22(2); 28:14(2); 29:6; 9; 17; 19; 23; 30:3; 9; 14; 16(2); 17; 19(2); 31:1; 9(2); 12(2); 15; 16; 23; 24; 29; 32; 33; 34(2); 37; 32:14; 23(3); 24; 29; 31; 32(2); 33(2); 34; 35(2); 38; 39; 40; 33:5; 8(3); 9; 24(2); 34:5(2); 10; 11(2); 18(2); 22; 35:6; 14; 17(2); 36:3; 7; 9; 15; 16(2); 17; 20(2); 24; 31; 37:4; 5; 9; 10; 15; 21(2); 38:6(2); 7; 9(2); 13; 18; 19(2); 20; 22; 23; 25; 27; 39:1; 4; 5(2); 14; 16; 40:7; 8(2); 12; 41:1; 7; 12; 13; 17; 18; 42:5; 17; 43:3; 5; 7(3); 44:2; 3(4); 5; 6; 9; 10(2); 12(4); 14(2); 46:6; 12; 15; 16; 17; 21(2); 22; 23(2); 48:2; 32; 34; 39; 45; 49:9(3); 12; 23(2); 29(3); 50:3(2); 4(2); 5; 6(3); 7; 9; 16(2); 20; 33; 36(2); 37(2); 38(2); 42(3); 51:2; 4; 14; 18(2); 24; 26; 30(3); 32; 38(2); 39; 57; 58; 64; 52:7; 9; 18(2); **Lam** 1:2; 6; 8; 10; 11(2); 14; 19(2); 21(3); 2:7; 8; 10(2); 12(2); 14; 15; 16(2); 3:6; 23; 53; 4:2; 3; 5(2); 7(2); 8; 9(2); 10; 14(2); 15(4); 16(2); 18; 19(2); 5:11; 13; **Eze** 1:5; 7; 8(2); 9(3); 10(3); 12(4); 16; 17(4); 18(2); 20; 24(3); 25; 2:3; 4; 5(4); 6; 7(3); 3:6; 7; 9; 11(2); 15; 25; 26; 27; 4:16(2); 17; 5:6(2); 12; 13; 17; 6:9(4); 10; 11; 13; 14; 7:13; 14; 16; 18; 19(2); 20; 21; 22; 24; 25; 26; 27; 8:6; 9; 12; 13; 16; 17(4); 18; 9:2; 6; 7; 8; 9; 10:10; 11(7); 12; 17(2); 19; 20; 22; 11:7; 15; 16; 18(2); 20(2); 12:2(2); 3(2); 4; 11; 12; 15; 16(3); 19; 23; 27; 13:6(3); 9(3); 10; 15; 21; 14:5; 10; 11; 14; 15; 16(2); 18(2); 20(2); 22; 23; 15:7; 8; 16:33(2); 37; 39(2); 40(2); 41; 47; 50; 51; 52(2); 17:15; 21; 23; 18:22; 19:4; 9(2); 20:8(3); 9; 12; 13(3); 16; 20; 21(2); 24; 25; 26(2); 27; 28(4); 38(2); 49; 21:7; 23; 29(2); 22:7(3); 9(2); 10(2); 12; 18(2); 20; 25(3); 26(2); 29; 23:3(3); 4(2); 8(2); 10(2); 13; 17; 24(2); 25(3); 26; 29; 37(3); 38(2); 39(3); 40; 43; 44(3); 45(2); 47; 49; 24:14; 25; 27; 25:3; 4(3); 11; 13; 14(2); 17; 26:4; 6; 12(3); 16(2); 17; 27:5(2); 6; 10(3); 11(2); 12; 13(2); 14; 15; 16; 17(2); 21(2); 22(2); 29; 30; 31(2); 32; 35; 28:3; 7(2); 8; 16; 17; 19; 22; 23; 24; 25(2); 26(3); 29:6; 7(2); 9; 13; 14; 15; 16(2); 20; 21; 30:4; 6(2); 7; 8; 11; 19; 25; 26; 31:14; 17(2); 32:3; 10; 12; 15; 16(2); 20; 21(2); 24; 25(2); 26; 27(3); 29; 30(2); 33:24; 27(2); 29(2); 31(5); 32(2); 33; 34:5(3); 10; 12; 14(2); 19(2); 22; 25; 27; 28(2); 29; 30(2); 35:8; 12(2); 15; 36:3; 7; 8; 11; 12; 13; 17; 18(2); 19; 20(4); 21; 35; 38; 37:2; 9; 10; 11; 17; 19; 21; 22(2); 23(3); 24(2); 25(3); 27; 38:8; 23; 39:6; 9(2); 10(3); 11(2); 12; 14(2); 16; 23(2); 26(3); 28; 40:10; 22; 38; 41; 42(2); 49; 41:6(3); 42:6; 11(2); 13(2); 14(4); 43:7; 8(2); 10; 11(3); 18; 22(2); 24; 25; 26(2); 44:7; 10; 11(3); 12(2); 13(3); 15(2); 16(3); 17(3); 18(2); 19(5); 20(2); 21; 22(2); 23; 24(4); 25(2); 26; 29; 45:8; 46:6; 10(2); 15; 20(2); 47:9; 10; 11; 12(2); 22(2); 48:14; 19; **Dan** 1:4; 5; 16; 19; 2:2; 7; 13; 18; 43(2); 46; 3:3; 9; 12; 13; 19; 24; 25; 28; 4:6; 7; 25(3); 26; 32(2); 5:3; 4; 8; 15(2); 20; 21; 23; 29; 6:4; 12; 13; 16; 22; 23; 24(3); 7:5; 12; 13; 25; 26; 9:7; 11; 10:7; 11:2; 6(2); 14; 21; 22; 25; 26; 27; 31(2); 33(2); 34(2); 12:3(2); **Hos** 1:11; 2:4; 8; 17; 21; 22; 23; 4:2; 4; 7(2); 8(2); 10(3); 12; 13; 14(3); 18; 19; 5:4(2); 6(2); 7(2); 15(2); 6:7(2); 9; 7:1; 2(2); 3; 4; 6(2); 7; 10; 11(2); 12; 13(3); 14(4); 15; 16(2); 8:1; 4(4); 5; 7(2); 8; 9; 10(2); 12; 13(2); 9:3(2); 4(2); 6; 9; 10(2); 12; 16(2); 17(2); 10:1; 2; 3; 4; 8; 9; 10; 11:2(3); 3; 4; 5; 7; 10; 11; 12:1; 8; 11(2); 13:2(2); 3; 6(3); 16; 14:7(2); **Joel** 1:18; 2:4; 5; 7(4); 8(3); 9(4); 17; 3:2; 3(2); 8; 19; **Amos** 1:3; 6; 9; 13(2); 2:4; 6; 8(2); 3:3; 10; 4:8; 5:10(2); 12(3); 16(2); 6:2; 6; 7; 9; 14; 7:2; 8:3; 12(2); 14(2); 9:2(2); 3(2); 4; 12; 14(3); 15; **Obad** 5(3); 7; 16(4); 18; 19(3); **Jonah** 1:7(2); 8; 11; 13; 14; 15; 2:8; 3:10; **Mic** 1:5; 7; 16; 2:1; 2(2); 6(3); 12; 13; 3:3; 4(2); 5; 7; 10; 11; 4:3(2); 4; 12(2); 5:1; 4; 6; 15; 7:1; 2(2); 3(2); 16; 17(3); **Nah** 1:10(3); 12(2); 2:4(3); 5(2); 8(2); 3:3; 7; 10; 12(2); 17(2); **Hab** 1:7; 8; 9(2); 10(3); 15(3); 16; 17; 2:7; 3:10; 11; 14; **Zeph** 1:11; 13(2); 17(2); 2:4; 7(2); 8; 10(2); 3:3; 4; 7; 9; 12; 13;

19; **Hag** 1:14; 2:14; **Zec** 1:4; 5(2); 6(2); 10; 11; 15; 2:9; 3:5; 8; 4:10(2); 5:9(2); 6:7(2); 15; 7:2; 11(2); 12(2); 13(2); 14(2); 8:8(2); 9:15(3); 16; 10:2(3); 5(2); 6; 7; 8(2); 9(2); 12; 11:5; 6; 12; 12:2; 6; 10(3); 13:2; 4; 9(2); 14:12; 13; 21; **Mal** 1:4(2); 2:7; 3:3; 15(2); 16; 17; 4:3; **Mt** 1:11; 12; 18; 23; 2:5; 9(3); 10(2); 11(4); 12(2); 13; 18; 20; 4:6; 18; 20; 22; 24; 5:4(2); 5; 6(2); 7; 8; 9; 10; 12; 16; 6:2(2); 5(3); 7(2); 16(3); 26(3); 28(3); 7:6; 15; 8:16; 29; 32(2); 33; 34(2); 9:2; 8; 11; 12(2); 15; 17; 24; 28; 31(2); 32(2); 36; 10:17(2); 19; 23; 25(2); 36; 11:7; 8; 18; 19; 20; 21; 12:2; 3; 10(2); 14; 16; 24; 27; 36; 41; 45; 13:5(3); 6(3); 13(3); 15(2); 16(2); 41; 48; 51; 54; 56; 57; 14:5; 13; 15; 16; 17; 20(2); 21; 26(2); 32; 33; 34(2); 35; 36; 15:2(2); 9; 12; 14; 18; 31(2); 32(2); 34; 37(2); 38; 16:5; 7; 12; 14; 20; 28; 17:6; 8(2); 9; 12(2); 14; 16; 22; 23(2); 24(2); 18:19; 31; 19:5; 6; 7; 11; 25; 20:4; 7; 9(2); 10(3); 11(2); 18; 22; 24; 25; 29; 30; 31(2); 33; 34; 21:1; 7; 15; 20; 25; 27; 31; 34; 36; 37; 38; 39; 41; 45; 46(3); 22:3; 5; 8; 10; 15; 16; 19; 21; 22(2); 28; 30; 33; 34; 42; 23:3(2); 4(2); 5(2); 25; 24:9; 24; 26; 30; 31; 38; 25:3; 5; 10(2); 44; 26:4; 5; 8; 15; 19; 21; 22; 26; 30(2); 50; 52; 57; 60; 66; 67; 73; 27:2(2); 4; 7; 9(2); 13; 15; 16; 17; 18; 20; 21; 22; 23; 28; 29(3); 30; 31(2); 32(3); 33; 34; 35(3); 36; 39; 47; 54(2); 66; 28:8; 9(2); 10(2); 11; 12(2); 15(2); 17(2); **Mk** 1:5; 16; 18; 20; 21; 22; 27(3); 29(2); 30; 32; 34; 36; 37(2); 45; 2:3; 4(4); 8; 12; 15; 16; 17(2); 18; 19(2); 20; 23; 24; 25; 3:2(2); 4; 6; 8(2); 9; 10; 11; 12; 13; 14; 19; 20; 21(2); 28; 30; 32; 4:10; 12(3); 15(2); 16(2); 17; 18; 20; 33; 34; 36(2); 38; 41; 5:1; 13; 14(2); 15(2); 16; 17; 40; 42; 6:3; 8; 12; 13; 29; 30(2); 31; 32; 34; 36(2); 37; 38(2); 40; 42; 43; 44; 49(2); 50; 51; 52; 53(2); 54(2); 55; 56(2); 7:2(2); 3; 4(4); 7; 15; 32(2); 36(2); 8:2; 3; 5; 6; 7; 8(2); 9; 14; 16; 19; 20; 22; 28; 30; 9:1; 4; 6; 8(2); 9(3); 10; 11; 13(2); 15; 18(2); 20; 30; 31; 32; 34(2); 10:4; 8(2); 13; 23; 26; 32(4); 33; 34; 37; 39; 41; 42; 46; 49; 11:1; 4(2); 6(2); 7; 9(2); 12; 15; 18(2); 20(2); 27; 31; 32; 33; 12:3; 4; 5; 6; 8; 12(3); 13; 14(2); 16(2); 17; 18; 23; 25(2); 26; 43; 44; 13:9; 11; 26; 14:1; 2; 5; 11(2); 12; 16; 18; 19; 22; 23; 26(2); 31; 32; 40; 46; 50; 53; 64; 70; 15:4; 6; 13; 14; 16; 17; 19; 20(2); 21; 22; 23; 24(2); 25; 27; 29; 32; 35; 16:1; 2; 3; 4(2); 5(2); 6; 8(3); 8<VM>; 10; 11(2); 12; 13(2); 14(2); 17(2); 18(4); 20; **Lk** 1:2; 6; 7(2); 22; 58; 59(2); 61; 62; 63; 66; 2:6; 9; 16; 17(2); 18; 20; 22; 39(2); 42; 43(2); 44(2); 45(2); 46; 48(2); 50; 4:2; 11; 22; 28(2); 29; 32; 36(2); 38; 40; 41; 5:6(2); 7(4); 9; 11(2); 18; 19(3); 26(2); 31(2); 33; 35; 6:3; 7; 11(2); 18(2); 22; 39; 44; 7:4(2); 10; 14; 16; 20; 25; 31; 32; 42; 49; 8:10(2); 12(2); 13(3); 14(2); 15; 16; 22; 23(2); 24(2); 25(2); 26; 31; 32; 34(2); 35(2); 36; 37; 40; 45; 53; 56; 9:6; 10(2); 11; 12; 13; 14; 15; 17; 19; 27; 32(3); 33; 34(2); 36(2); 37; 40; 43(2); 45(3); 52; 53; 54; 56; 57; 10:7; 8; 10; 13; 38; 11:19; 26; 28; 29; 32; 33; 48; 49; 54; 12:1; 4; 11; 24; 27(3); 36; 48; 13:2; 4; 29; 14:1; 4; 6; 7; 12; 14; 18; 15:24; 16:4; 9; 14; 15; 26(2); 28; 29; 30; 31(2); 17:1; 13; 14(2); 21; 23; 27(4); 28(6); 37; 18:9; 15(2); 24; 26; 33; 34(2); 37; 39; 43; 19:7(2); 11(2); 25; 32; 33; 34; 35(3); 36; 37; 42; 44; 48; 20:5; 6; 7(2); 10; 11; 12; 13(2); 14; 15; 16(2); 19(2); 20(3); 21; 24; 26(2); 27; 31; 35; 36(2); 40; 41; 21:3; 7; 12; 16; 24; 27; 30; 22:2(2); 5; 9; 13(2); 23; 25; 28; 35; 38; 49(2); 54; 55; 64(2); 65; 70; 71; 23:2; 5; 12; 18; 21; 23; 24; 25; 26(3); 29; 30; 31; 33(2); 34(3); 56; 24:1(2); 2; 3; 4; 5(2); 8; 11; 14; 15; 16; 19; 23(3); 24; 28(2); 29; 31; 32; 33; 35; 36; 37(2); 41; 42; 45; 52; **Jn** 1:21; 22; 24; 25; 37; 38; 39; 2:3(2); 7; 8; 12; 22; 23; 3:21; 23; 26; 4:24; 30; 35; 40; 45; 52; 5:12; 23; 25; 29(2); 39(2); 6:2; 9; 11; 12; 13; 14; 15; 19(3); 21(2); 23; 24; 25(2); 28; 30; 34; 42; 45; 60; 63(2); 64; 7:25; 26; 30; 39; 40; 45; 52; 8:3; 4; 6(2); 7; 9; 19; 25; 27; 33; 39; 41; 59; 9:8; 10; 12; 13; 17; 18; 19; 22; 24; 26; 28; 34(2); 35; 39(2); 10:4; 5(2); 6(2); 10(2); 16; 25; 27; 28; 39; 11:13; 31; 34; 41; 42; 53; 56(2); 57; 12:2; 9(2); 10; 12; 16(2); 18; 37; 39; 40; 42(2); 43; 15:6; 20(4); 21(2); 22(2); 24(2); 25; 16:2; 3(2); 9; 18; 19; 17:3; 6(2); 7; 8(2); 9; 11; 13; 14; 16; 19; 21(2); 22; 23; 24(2); 18:5; 6; 7; 18; 21; 25; 28(4); 30; 40; 19:2; 3; 6; 15; 16; 18; 23; 24(3); 29; 31; 33(2); 37(2); 40; 42; 20:2(2); 4; 9; 13(3); 20; 23(2); 29; 21:3(3); 5; 6(2); 8; 9(2); 15; 25; **Acts** 1:4; 6(2); 9; 10; 12; 13(2); 23; 24; 26; 2:1; 2; 4; 7; 12; 18; 37(2); 41; 42; 46; 3:2; 10(2); 4:1; 2; 3; 7(2); 13(5); 14; 15(2); 17; 18; 21(3); 23; 24(2); 29; 31(4); 32; 5:12; 15; 16; 17; 21(3); 22; 24; 26(2); 27(2); 33(2); 40(4); 41(2); 42; 6:5; 6(3); 10; 11; 12; 7:6; 7(2); 19(2); 25; 26; 35; 41; 52; 54(3); 57; 59; 8:1; 4; 10; 11; 12(2); 14; 15(2); 16; 17(2); 25(2); 36(2); 38; 39; 9:2; 8; 24; 26; 29; 30; 37(2); 38; 39; 10:9; 10; 22; 24; 39; 45; 46; 48; 11:2; 18(2); 19; 20; 22; 23; 26; 30; 12:10(3); 15(2); 16(2); 19; 20; 25; 13:2; 3(2); 4(2); 5(3); 6(2); 13; 14(2); 17; 21; 27(3); 28(2); 29(2); 45; 48; 51; 14:1; 3; 6; 7; 11; 12; 14; 18(2); 21(2); 23(3); 24(2); 25(2); 26(2); 27(2); 28; 15:2; 3(2); 4(3); 11; 13; 20; 23; 30(4); 31(2); 33(2); 36; 39; 16:3; 4(2); 6; 7(2); 8; 19; 23(2); 31; 32; 37(2); 38(3); 39; 40(3); 17:1(2); 6(2); 8(2); 9(2); 11; 13; 15(2); 19; 27(2); 32; 18:3; 6; 20; 26; 19:2; 3; 4; 5(2); 6; 10; 16; 19; 26; 28(2); 29; 32; 33; 34; 20:8; 12; 18; 37; 38(2); 21:5; 6; 12; 20(3); 21(2); 22; 24(2); 25(2); 27; 29(2); 30; 31; 32(2); 22:2(2); 9(2); 18; 19; 22; 23; 24; 25; 29; 23:4; 12(2); 13; 14; 20; 21(3); 24; 28; 30; 32; 33; 24:12; 13(2); 14; 15; 19; 20; 25:7; 14; 17; 18; 26:5; 10; 18; 20; 30; 31(2); 27:1; 12; 13(2); 17(3); 18; 27; 28(2); 29; 30(2); 36(2); 38(2); 39(3); 40(2); 41; 43; 44; 28:1(2); 2; 4; 6(3); 10; 15; 17; 18; 21; 23; 25(2); 27(2); 28; **Rom** 1:20; 21(2); 22; 28; 32; 3:9(2); 12(2); 13; 17; 4:7; 11; 14; 17; 5:17; 8:5(2); 8; 14; 23; 9:6; 7(2); 8; 26; 32(2); 10:1; 2; 3; 14(5); 15(2); 16; 18; 11:3(2); 8(2); 10; 11(2); 20; 23(2); 28(2); 31; 13:2; 6; 15:21(2); 27; 16:18; **1Cor** 2:8(2); 14(2); 3:20; 7:8; 9; 14; 29(2); 30(6); 31; 9:13(2); 14; 24; 25; 10:4; 5; 6; 11; 18; 20; 33; 11:19; 12:19; 20; 13:8(2); 14:7; 21; 23; 34; 35; 15:10; 11; 18; 23; 29(2); 35; 48(2); 16:4; 15; 17; 18; **2Cor** 5:15; 6:16; 8:3; 5; 23; 9:4; 5; 13; 10:10; 12; 11:12(2); 22(3); 23; 12:21; **Gal** 1:23; 24; 2:4; 6(2); 7; 9(2); 10; 12; 14; 3:7; 9; 4:17(2); 5:12; 21; 24; 6:12(2); 13(2); **Eph** 4:14; 5:31; **Phil** 3:18; 4:2; 22; **Col** 1:16; 20; 3:21; 4:9; **1Th** 1:9; 2:14; 15; 16; 5:3(2); 7(2); **2Th** 2:10(2); 11; 12; 3:12; **1Ti** 1:3; 7(2); 20; 2:15; 3:13; 5:7; 11(2); 12; 13(2); 17; 24; 25; 6:2(3); 9; 10; 17; 18(2); 19; **2Ti** 1:15; 2:10; 14; 16; 23; 26; 3:6; 9; 4:3(2); 4; **Titus** 1:10; 11; 13; 16(3); 2:3; 4; 10; 3:8; 9; 14; **Heb** 1:4; 11(2); 12; 14; 2:11; 3:10(2); 11; 16; 18; 19; 4:3; 5; 6; 6:6(2); 7:5(2); 23(2); 8:9; 10; 11; 9:15; 10:1; 2; 11:13; 14(2); 15(3); 16; 23(2); 29; 30; 35; 37(3); 38; 40; 12:10; 19; 20; 25; 13:10; 17(3); 24; **Jas** 2:7; 12; 3:3; 4(2); 4:1; 5:15; **1Pet** 1:12; 2:8; 12(3); 3:1; 2; 10; 16(2); 4:4; 6; **2Pet** 1:8; 21; 2:3; 10(2); 12; 13(3); 14; 18(2); 19(2); 20(2); 21; 3:4; 5; 16(2); **1Jn** 2:19(7); 4:1; 5(2); **2Jn** 1; **3Jn** 7; **Jude** 10(3); 11; 12(2); 15; 18; 19; **Rev** 1:3; 7; 15; 2:2; 9; 22; 24; 27; 3:4(2); 9; 4:4; 8(2); 11; 5:9; 6:4; 9; 10; 11(2); 7:13; 14; 15; 16; 8:7; 11; 9:4; 5(2); 8; 9; 10; 11; 19; 20; 21; 11:2; 3; 6; 7; 9; 10; 11; 12(2); 18; 12:6; 11(2); 13:4(2); 14; 14:3; 4(3); 5; 11; 12; 13; 15:3; 16:4; 6(2); 9; 10; 14; 15; 17:8(2); 14; 18:9; 18; 19; 19:3; 9; 20:4(2); 6; 9; 13; 21:3; 26; 27; 22:4; 5(2); 14(2)

THINE

Gen 13:14; 14:20; 23; 15:4(3); 20:7; 21:18; 22:2; 12(2); 16; 30:27; 31:12; 32; 38:18; 40:13; 44:18; 46:4; 47:19; 48:6; 49:8; **Ex** 4:2; 4; 6; 7; 17; 21; 5:16; 7:15; 19; 8:3(2); 5; 9:14; 22; 10:12; 21; 13:9(2); 16(2); 14:16; 26; 15:7; 16; 17; 17:5; 20:24; 22:30; 23:1; 4; 12(2); 22(2); 27; 32:13; 34:9; **Lev** 2:13; 10:15; 18:10; 14; 19:17; 27:23; 27; **Num** 5:20; 10:35; 18:9; 11; 13(2); 14; 15; 16; 18(2); 20; 22:30(2); 32; 27:18; 20; **Deut** 2:24; 3:21; 27(2); 4:9; 19; 39; 5:14(2); 6:5; 6; 7; 8(2); 19; 7:13; 16; 17; 19; 24; 26; 8:2; 5; 14; 17; 9:4; 5; 26; 29; 10:21; 11:14; 19; 20; 12:17; 18; 13:6; 8; 9; 17; 14:23; 25; 26; 28; 29; 15:3(2); 7(2); 8; 9; 10(2); 11; 16; 16:10; 15(2); 18:4; 21; 19:13; 14; 21; 20:1; 13; 14; 21:10(2); 12; 13; 22:2; 8; 23:9; 14; 20; 24; 25; 24:19(2); 20; 25:12; 14; 19; 26:4; 11; 12; 16; 28:7; 8; 12; 20; 25; 31(4); 32(2); 34; 40; 48; 53(2); 55; 57; 67(2); 29:3; 30:2; 4; 6(2); 7; 9; 10; 17; 33:10; 29; 34:4; **Josh** 2:3; 17; 20; 6:2; 7:13; 8:18; 9:25; 10:8; 14:9; 17:18(2); **Judg** 4:7; 9; 14; 5:31; 6:39; 7:7; 9; 11; 8:6(2); 15; 9:29; 11:36; 12:1; 16:15; 18:19; 19:5; 6; 8; 9; 22; 20:28; **Ruth** 2:9; 10; 11; 13(2); 3:9(2); 4:11; 15; **1Sa** 1:11(3); 16; 18; 2:31(2); 32; 33(4); 36; 9:19; 20; 14:7; 19; 15:17; 28; 16:1; 17:28; 46; 20:3; 29; 30; 21:3; 8; 22:14; 23:4; 24:4(2); 10; 15; 18; 20; 25:6; 8(2); 24(3); 25; 26(2); 27; 28; 29; 31; 35; 41; 26:8(2); 21; 27:5; 28:16; 17; 21; 22; **2Sa** 1:14; 25; 3:21; 4:8; 5:19; 7:3; 9; 11; 16; 21; 11:10; 12:10; 11(2); 13:10; 14:7; 8; 12; 17; 19; 16:4; 17:11; 19:6; 27; 28; 20:17; 22:28; 24:13; 16; 17; **1Kin** 1:12; 13; 17; 53; 2:26; 37; 44(2); 3:11; 20; 26; 8:18(2); 24; 29; 31; 51; 52; 53; 11:22; 12:16; 13:8; 18; 14:12; 17:11; 19:10; 14; 20:4; 6(2); 13; 28; 21:7; 19; 22; 22:34; **2Kin** 4:2; 16; 29; 7:2; 19; 8:1; 8; 9:1; 10:5; 15(2); 13:16; 14:10; 19:16(2); 22; 20:1; 15; 17; 22:19; 20; **1Chr** 4:10; 12:18(2); 14:10; 17:2; 8; 10; 17; 19; 22; 21:12; 15; 17; 24; 29:11(3); 12(2); 14; 16(3); **2Chr** 1:11(2); 6:8(2); 15; 20; 22; 40(2); 42; 9:5; 10:16; 16:7; 8; 18:33; 19:3; 20:6; 25:15; 19(2); 26:18; 34:27; 28; **Ezr** 7:14; 25; **Neh** 1:6(2); 11; 6:8; **Job** 1:11; 12; 2:5; 6; 9; 5:25; 7:8; 17; 10:3; 7; 8; 13; 17; 11:4; 6; 13(2); 14; 17; 13:21; 24; 14:3; 15; 15:5; 6(2); 12; 22:5; 22; 30; 35:7; 40:14; 41:8; **Ps** 2:8; 6:1; 7:6; 8:2; 10:12; 17; 16:10; 17:2; 6; 20:4; 21:8(2); 9; 12; 13; 26:6; 8; 27:14; 28:9; 31:2; 5; 22; 37:4; 38:2; 3; 39:10; 44:3; 45:5; 10(2); 50:20; 21; 51:19; 56:7; 66:3; 68:9; 23; 69:9; 24; 71:2; 16; 74:1; 2; 4; 16(2); 22; 23; 77:15; 17; 79:1; 83:2; 84:3; 9; 85:3; 4; 5; 86:1; 16; 88:2; 89:10; 11(2); 38; 51(2); 90:7; 11; 91:8; 92:9(2); 93:5; 94:5; 102:2; 10; 103:3; 104:28; 106:5; 110:1; 2; 116:16; 119:91; 94; 173; 128:2; 3; 130:2; 132:10; 138:7; 8; 139:5; 16; 20; 144:6; 7; 145:16; **Prov** 2:2(2); 10; 3:1; 3; 5(2); 7; 9; 21; 27; 4:4; 9; 20; 21(2); 25(2); 5:1; 9; 15(2); 17; 6:4(2); 21; 25; 7:2; 3; 25; 20:13; 22:17(2); 23:4; 5; 12(2); 15; 17; 18; 19; 26(2); 33(2); 24:17(2); 27; 25:7; 10; 21; 27:2(2); 10; 30:32; **Eccl** 5:2; 6; 7:18; 22; 11:6; 9(2); **Song** 4:9; 10; 6:5; 7:4; 5(2); 8:6(2); **Is** 6:7; 12:1; 14:13; 26:11; 30:20; 21; 33:17; 18; 20; 37:17(2); 23; 38:1; 39:4; 6; 42:6; 43:24; 44:3; 45:14; 47:6; 8; 9; 10; 12; 48:8; 49:18; 20; 21; 51:22; 54:2; 5; 57:10; 58:7; 8; 13(3); 60:4; 5; 17; 20; 62:8; 63:2; 17; 19; 64:2; **Jer** 2:2; 19; 22; 37(2); 3:2; 13; 4:1; 14; 18; 5:3; 17(2); 6:9; 7:29; 9:6; 10:24; 13:22(2); 27(2); 15:14; 17:4(2); 18:23; 20:4; 6; 22:17(2); 25:28; 28:7; 30:14; 15(2); 16; 31:16; 17; 21; 32:7(2); 8(2); 19; 34:3; 36:14; 38:12; 17; 40:4; 42:2; 43:9; 49:16; 51:13; **Lam** 2:14; 16; 17(2); 18; 19; 21; 3:56; 4:22(2); **Eze** 3:10(2); 18; 20; 24; 4:7; 5:1; 9; 11; 6:11; 7:3; 4; 8; 9; 8:5; 10:2; 16:6; 7; 12(2); 15; 22; 27; 30; 31(2); 39; 41; 43(2); 46; 51(2); 52; 54; 58; 61; 21:14; 22:4; 14(2); 16; 23:25; 27; 31; 34; 24:16; 17; 26; 25:6; 27:6; 10; 11; 15; 28:2(2); 4; 5; 6; 17; 18; 33:8; 35:11(2); 37:17; 20; 38:4; 12; 39:3; 40:4(3); 44:5(2); 30; **Dan** 2:38; 3:17; 4:19; 27; 5:22; 9:16; 18(2); 19; 10:12; **Hos** 9:7; 13:9; 14:1; **Joel** 2:17; **Obad** 3; 15; **Jonah** 1:8; 2:7; **Mic** 4:10; 13; 5:9(3); 12; 13; 7:14; **Nah** 3:13; **Hab** 3:8(2); 11; 13; 15; **Zeph** 3:15; 16; **Zec** 3:4; 5:5; 13:6; **Mt** 5:25; 33; 43; 6:2; 4; 13; 17; 22; 23; 7:3; 4(2); 5; 9:6; 12:13; 18:9; 20:14; 15; 22:44; 25:25; **Mk** 2:11; 3:5; 9:47; 12:36; **Lk** 4:7; 5:24; 33; 6:41; 42(3); 7:44; 8:39; 11:34(2); 12:19; 58; 13:12; 15:31; 19:22; 42; 43; 20:43; 22:42; **Jn** 2:17; 8:10; 9:10; 17; 26; 17:5; 6; 9; 10(2); 11; 18:35; **Acts** 2:27; 4:30; 5:3; 4(3); 8:22; 37; 10:4; 31; 13:35; 23:35; **Rom** 10:6; 9; 11:3; 12:20; **1Cor** 10:29; **1Ti** 5:23; **Philem** 1:19; **Heb** 1:10; 13; **Rev** 3:18

THING

Gen 1:24; 25; 26; 28; 30; 31; 6:7; 17; 19; 20; 7:8; 14; 21; 8:1; 17(2); 19; 21; 9:3; 14:23; 18:14; 17; 19:21; 22; 20:10; 21:11; 26; 22:12; 16; 24:50; 30:31(2); 34:7; 14; 19; 38:10; 39:9; 23; 41:28; 32; 37; 44:7; **Ex** 1:18; 2:14; 15; 9:5; 6; 10:15; 12:24; 16:14; 16; 32; 18:11; 14; 17; 18; 23; 20:4; 17; 22:9; 15; 29:1; 33:17; 34:10; 35:4; **Lev** 2:3; 10; 4:13; 5:2; 5; 16; 6:2; 4(2); 7; 7:19; 21(2); 8:5; 9:6; 11:10; 21; 35; 41; 43; 44; 12:4; 13:48; 49; 52; 53; 54; 57; 58; 59; 15:4; 6; 10; 20(2); 22; 23; 17:2; 19:8; 26; 20:17; 21; 25; 21:18; 22:4; 5; 10(2); 14(2); 23; 23:37; 27:23; 28(2); **Num** 4:15; 16:9; 13; 30; 17:13; 18:7; 14; 15; 20:19; 22:38; 30:1; 31:23; 32:20; 35:22; 36:6; **Deut** 1:14; 32; 4:18; 23; 25; 32(2); 5:8; 21; 7:26(2); 8:9; 12:32; 13:14; 17; 14:3; 19; 21; 15:10; 15; 16:4; 17:4; 5; 18:22(2); 22:20; 23:9; 14; 19; 24:10; 18; 22; 26:11; 31:13; 32:47(2); **Josh** 4:10; 6:18(2); 7:1(2); 11; 13(2); 15; 9:24; 14:6; 21:45; 22:20; 24; 33; 23:14(2); **Judg** 6:29(2); 8:27; 11:25; 37; 13:4; 7; 14(2); 18:7; 10; 19:19; 24; 20:9; 21:11; **Ruth** 3:18; **1Sa** 3:11; 17(2); 4:7; 8:6; 12:16; 14:12; 15:9; 18:20; 23; 20:2; 26; 39; 21:2; 22:15; 24:6; 25:15; 26:16; 28:10; 18; 30:19; **2Sa** 2:6; 3:13; 7:19; 11:11; 25; 27; 12:5; 6; 12; 21; 13:2; 12; 20; 33; 14:13(2); 15; 18; 20; 21; 15:11; 35; 36; 17:19; 24:3; **1Kin** 1:27; 3:10; 11; 10:3; 11:10; 12:24; 30; 13:33; 34; 14:5; 13; 15:5; 16:31; 20:9; 24; 33; **2Kin** 2:10; 3:18; 4:2; 5:13; 18(2); 6:11; 7:2; 19; 8:9; 13; 11:5; 17:12; 20:9; 10; **1Chr** 2:7; 11:19; 13:4; 17:17; 23; 21:3; 7; 8; 26:28; **2Chr** 9:20; 11:4; 16:10; 23:4; 19; 29:36; 30:4; **Ezr** 7:27; 9:3; 10:2; 13; **Neh** 2:19; 13:17; **Est** 2:4; 22; 5:14; 6:13; 8:5; **Job** 3:25; 4:12; 6:8; 21; 9:22; 12:10; 13:28; 14:4; 15:11; 22:28; 23:14; 26:3; 28:10; 11; 33:32; 39:8; 42:2; 7; 8; **Ps** 2:1; 27:4; 33:17; 34:10; 38:20; 69:34; 84:11; 89:34; 92:1; 101:3; 141:4; 145:16; 150:6; **Prov** 4:7; 18:22; 22:18; 25:2; 27:7; **Eccl** 1:9(2); 10; 3:1; 11; 14; 19; 5:2; 6:5; 7:8; 8:1; 3; 5; 15; 9:5; 6; 11:7; 12:14; **Is** 7:13; 15:6; 17:13; 19:7; 29:16; 21; 38:7; 40:15; 41:12; 43:19; 49:6; 52:11; 55:11; 64:6; 66:8; **Jer** 2:10; 19; 5:30; 7:23; 11:13; 14:14; 18:13; 22:4; 23:14; 31:22; 32:27; 33:14; 38:5; 14; 40:3; 16; 42:3; 4; 21; 44:4; 17; **Lam** 2:13(2); **Eze** 8:17; 14:9; 16:47; 34:18; 44:18; 29; 31; 47:9(2); 48:12; **Dan** 2:5; 8; 11; 15; 17; 3:29; 4:33; 5:15; 26; 6:12; 10:1(3); **Hos** 6:10; 8:3; 12; **Amos** 6:13; **Jonah** 3:7; **Mal** 1:14; **Mt** 8:33; 18:19; 19:16; 20:20; 21:24; 24:17; **Mk** 1:27; 4:22; 5:32; 7:18; 9:22; 10:21; 11:13; 13:15; 16:8; 18; **Lk** 1:35; 2:15; 6:9; 8:17; 9:21; 10:42; 12:11; 26; 18:22; 19:8; 20:3; 22:23; 35; **Jn** 1:3; 46; 5:14; 7:4; 9:25; 30; 14:14; 18:34; **Acts** 5:4; 10:14; 28; 12:12; 17:21; 25; 19:32; 39; 21:25; 34; 23:17; 25:8; 11; 26; 26:8; 10; 26; **Rom** 7:18; 8:33; 9:20; 13:6; 8; 14:14; 21; 22; **1Cor** 1:5; 10; 2:2; 3:7; 4:3; 8:2; 7; 9:11; 17; 10:19(2); 14:30; 35; **2Cor** 2:10(2); 3:5; 5:5; 6:3; 17; 7:11; 14; 8:7; 9:11; 10:5; 11:15; 12:8; **Gal** 4:18; 5:6; 6:15; **Eph** 4:28; 5:24; 27; 6:8; **Phil** 1:6; 3:13; 15; 16; 4:6; **1Th** 1:8; 5:18; **2Th** 1:6; **1Ti** 1:10; **2Ti** 1:14; **Titus** 2:8; **Philem** 1:6; **Heb** 10:29; 31; 11:40; 13:9; **Jas** 1:7; **1Pet** 4:12; **2Pet** 3:8; **1Jn** 2:8; 5:14; **Rev** 2:15; 9:4; 21:27

THINGS

Gen 7:23; 9:3; 15:1; 20:8; 22:1; 20; 24:1; 28; 53; 66; 29:13; 39:7; 40:1; 42:36; 45:23; 48:1; **Ex** 10:2; 12:36; 23:13; 25:22; 28:38; 29:33; 35; 40:4; **Lev** 2:8; 4:2; 13; 22; 27; 5:2; 5; 15; 17; 8:36; 10:19; 11:23; 29; 42; 14:11; 15:10; 27; 18:24; 20:23; 22:2(2); 3; 4; 6; 7; 12; 15; 16; 26:23; **Num** 1:50; 4:4; 15; 19; 20; 5:9; 10; 15:13; 18:8; 9; 19; 32; 29:39; 31:20; 35:29; **Deut** 1:18; 4:7; 9; 30; 6:11; 10:21; 12:8; 26; 18:12; 22:3; 25:16; 26:13; 28:47; 48; 57; 29:29(2); 30:1; 32:35; 33:13; 14; 15(2); 16; **Josh** 1:17; 2:11; 23; 11:1; 23:14; 15(2); 24:29; **Judg** 13:23(2); 18:27; **Ruth** 4:7; **1Sa** 2:23; 3:12; 17; 12:21; 24; 15:21; 19:7; 25:37; 26:25; **2Sa** 7:21; 23; 11:18; 12:8; 13:21; 14:20; 23:5; 17; 22; 24:12; 23; **1Kin** 4:33; 5:8; 7:51; 15:15(2); 17:17; 18:36; 21:1; 26; **2Kin** 8:4; 11:9; 12:4; 18(2); 14:3; 17:9; 11; 19:29; 20:13; 15; 23:17; 25:15; **1Chr** 4:22; 9:31; 11:19; 24; 17:19; 21:10; 23:13; 28; 26:20; 26; 28:12; 14; 29:2(5); 5(2); 14; 17; 19; **2Chr** 3:3; 4:6; 5:1; 12:12; 15:18; 19:3; 21:3; 23:8; 24:7; 29:33; 31:5; 6; 12; 14; 32:1; **Ezr** 1:6; 2:63; 7:1; 9:1; **Neh** 6:8; 16; 7:65; 9:6; 10:33; 12:47; 13:26; **Est** 2:1; 3; 9(2); 12; 3:1; 5:11; 9:20; **Job** 5:9(2); 6:7; 30; 8:2; 9:10; 10:13; 12:3; 22; 13:20; 26; 14:19; 16:2; 22:18; 23:14; 26:5; 33:29; 37:5; 41:30; 34; 42:3; **Ps** 8:6; 12:3; 15:5; 17:2; 31:18; 35:11; 38:12; 42:4; 45:1; 4; 50:21; 57:2; 60:3; 65:5; 71:19; 72:18; 78:12; 86:10; 87:3; 94:4; 98:1; 103:5; 104:25; 106:21; 22; 107:43; 113:6; 119:18; 128; 126:2; 3; 131:1; 148:10; **Prov** 2:12; 3:15; 6:16; 8:6(2); 11; 15:28; 16:4; 30; 22:20; 23:16; 33; 24:23; 26:10; 28:5; 10; 30:7; 15(2); 18; 21; 24; 29; **Eccl** 1:8; 11(2); 13; 6:11; 7:15; 25; 9:2; 3; 10:19; 11:9; **Is** 12:5; 25:1; 6(2); 29:16; 30:10(2); 32:8(2); 34:1; 38:16(2); 39:2; 40:26; 41:22(2); 23; 42:9(2); 16(2); 20; 43:9; 18(2); 44:7; 9; 24; 45:7; 11; 19; 46:9; 10; 47:7; 9; 13; 48:3; 6(2); 14; 51:19; 56:4; 61:11; 64:3; 11; 12; 65:4; 66:2(2); 8; **Jer** 2:8; 3:5; 7; 4:18; 5:9; 19; 25(2); 29; 8:13; 9:9; 24; 10:16; 13:22; 14:22; 16:18; 19; 17:9; 18:13; 20:1; 5; 21:14; 26:10; 30:15; 31:5; 33:3; 42:5; 44:18; 45:5; 51:19; **Lam** 1:7; 10; 11; 16; 2:14; 5:17; **Eze** 5:11; 7:20; 8:10; 11:5; 18; 21; 25; 16:16; 30; 43; 17:12; 15; 18; 18:10; 20:40; 22:8; 25; 26; 23:30; 24:19; 27:24; 37:23; 38:10; 20; 42:13(2); 14; 44:8; 13; 30; **Dan** 2:10; 22; 40; 7:8; 16; 20; 10:21; 11:36; 38; 43; 12:7; 8; **Hos** 2:18; 8:12; 9:3; 14:9; **Joel** 2:20; 21; 3:5; **Obad** 6(2); **Mic** 7:15; **Hab** 1:14; **Zeph** 1:2; **Zec** 4:10; 8:12; 16; 17; **Mt** 1:20; 2:3; 4:9; 6:8; 32(2); 33; 34; 7:11; 12; 9:18; 11:4; 25; 27; 12:34; 35(2); 13:3; 17(2); 34; 35; 41; 51; 52; 56; 15:18; 20; 16:21; 23; 17:11; 19:20; 26; 21:15; 22; 23; 24; 27; 22:4; 21(2); 23:20; 36; 24:2; 3; 6; 33; 34; 25:21(2); 23(2); 27:13; 19; 54; 28:11; 20; **Mk** 1:44; 2:8; 3:8; 4:2; 11; 19; 34; 5:19; 20; 26; 6:2; 20; 30; 34; 7:4; 8; 13; 15; 23; 37; 8:31; 33(2); 9:9; 12(2); 23; 10:27; 32; 11:11; 23; 24; 28(2); 29; 33; 12:17(2); 13:4(2); 7; 23; 29; 30; 14:36; 15:3; 4; **Lk** 1:1; 3; 4; 20; 45; 49; 53; 2:18; 19; 20; 33; 39; 3:18; 4:28; 5:26; 27; 6:46; 7:9; 18; 22; 8:8; 39(2); 9:9; 22; 36; 43; 10:1; 7; 8; 21; 22; 23; 24(2); 41; 11:27; 41(2); 53(2); 12:15; 20; 30(2); 31; 48; 13:2; 17(2); 14:6; 15; 17; 21; 15:26; 16:14; 25(2); 17:9; 10; 25; 18:22; 27; 31; 34(2); 19:11; 42; 20:2; 8; 25(2); 21:6; 7(2); 9; 22; 26; 28; 31; 36; 22:37; 65; 23:8; 14; 31; 48; 49; 24:9; 10; 14; 18; 19; 21; 26; 27; 35; 44; 48; **Jn** 1:3; 28; 50; 2:16; 18; 3:9; 10; 12(2); 22; 35; 4:25; 29; 45; 5:16; 19; 20; 34; 6:1; 59; 7:1; 4; 32; 8:26(2); 28; 29; 10:6; 41; 11:11; 45; 46; 12:16(3); 36; 41; 13:3; 17; 29; 14:25; 26(2); 15:11; 15; 17; 21; 16:1; 3; 4(2); 6; 12; 13; 15; 25; 30; 33; 17:7; 13; 18:4; 19:24; 28; 36; 20:18; 21:1; 17; 24(2); 25; **Acts** 1:3; 9; 2:44; 3:18; 21; 22; 4:20; 25; 32(2); 34; 5:5; 11; 24; 32; 7:1; 50; 54; 8:6; 12; 24; 9:16; 10:8; 12; 33; 39; 11:6; 18; 22; 12:17; 13:39; 45; 14:15(2); 15:4; 17; 20; 27; 28; 29; 16:14; 17:8; 11; 20(2); 22; 24; 25; 18:1; 17; 25; 19:8; 21; 36; 20:22; 24; 30; 35; 21:12; 19; 24; 25; 22:10; 23:22; 24:8; 9; 13; 14; 22; 25:9; 11; 18; 26:2; 9; 16(2); 22; 26(2); 27:11; 28:10; 24; 31; **Rom** 1:20(2); 23; 28; 30; 32; 2:1; 2; 3; 14; 18; 3:19; 4:17; 6:21(2); 8:5(2); 28; 31; 32; 37; 38(2); 10:5; 15; 11:36; 12:16; 17; 14:2; 18; 19(2); 20; 15:4; 17; 18; 27(2); **1Cor** 1:27(3); 28(4); 2:9; 10(2); 11(2); 12; 13(2); 14; 15; 3:21; 22(2); 4:5; 6; 13; 14; 6:3; 4; 12(3); 7:1; 32; 33; 34(2); 8:1; 4; 6(2); 10; 9:8; 11(2); 12; 13(2); 15(2); 22; 25; 10:6(2); 11; 20; 23(4); 33; 11:2; 12; 13:7(4); 11; 14:7; 26; 37; 40; 15:27(3); 28(2); 16:14; **2Cor** 1:13; 17; 2:9; 16; 4:2; 15; 18(4); 5:10; 17(2); 18; 6:4; 10; 7:11; 14; 16; 8:21; 22; 9:8; 10:7; 13; 15; 16; 11:6; 9; 28; 30; 12:19; 13:10; **Gal** 1:20; 2:18; 3:4; 10; 4:24; 5:17; 21; 6:6; **Eph** 1:10; 11; 22(2); 3:9; 4:10; 15; 5:6; 12; 13; 20; 6:9; 21; **Phil** 1:10; 12; 2:4(2); 10(3); 14; 21; 3:1; 7; 8(2); 13(2); 19; 21; 4:8(7); 9; 12; 13; 18; **Col** 1:16(2); 17(2); 18; 20(3); 2:17; 18; 23; 3:1; 2(2); 14; 20; 22; 4:9; **1Th** 2:14; 5:21; **2Th** 2:5; 3:4; **1Ti** 3:11; 14; 4:6; 8; 11; 15; 5:7; 13; 21; 6:2; 11; 13; 17; **2Ti** 1:12; 18; 2:2; 7; 10; 14; 3:14; 4:5; **Titus**

1:5; 11; 15; 2:1; 3; 7; 9; 10; 15; 3:8(2); **Heb** 1:2; 3; 2:1; 8(2); 10(2); 17(2); 3:4; 5; 4:13; 5:1; 8; 11; 6:9(2); 18; 7:13; 8:1; 5(2); 9:6; 11; 22; 23(2); 10:1(2); 11:1(2); 3(2); 7; 14; 20; 12:24; 27(3); 13:5; 18; **Jas** 2:16; 3:2; 5; 7; 10; 5:12; **1Pet** 1:12(2); 18; 4:7; 8; 11; **2Pet** 1:3; 8; 9; 10; 12; 15; 2:12; 3:4; 11; 14; 16(2); 17; **1Jn** 1:4; 2:1; 15; 20; 26; 27; 3:20; 22; 5:13; **2Jn** 8; 12; **3Jn** 2; 13; **Jude** 10(2); **Rev** 1:1; 2; 3; 19(3); 2:1; 8; 10; 12; 14(2); 18; 20(2); 3:1; 2; 7; 14; 4:1; 11; 7:1; 10:4; 6(3); 13:5; 18:1; 14; 15; 19:1; 20:12; 21:4; 5; 7; 22:6; 8(2); 16; 18; 19; 20

THIS

Gen 2:23; 3:13; 14; 4:14; 5:1; 29; 6:15; 7:1; 9:12; 17; 11:6; 12:7; 12; 18; 15:2; 4; 7; 18; 17:10; 21; 18:25; 32; 19:5; 9; 12; 13; 14(2); 20; 21(2); 34; 37; 38; 20:5; 6; 10; 11; 13; 21:10(2); 26; 30; 22:14; 16; 23:19; 24:5; 7; 8; 12; 41; 42; 58; 65; 25:31; 32; 33; 26:3; 10; 11; 33; 28:15; 16; 17(3); 20; 22; 29:25; 27; 33; 34; 30:31; 31:1; 13; 38; 43; 48(2); 51(2); 52(5); 32:2; 10; 19; 32; 33:8; 34:4; 14; 15; 35:17; 20; 36:24; 37:6; 10; 19; 22; 32; 38:21; 22; 23; 28; 29; 39:9(2); 11; 19; 40:12; 14; 18; 41:9; 24; 28; 34; 38; 39; 42:13; 18; 21; 28; 32; 43:10; 11; 29; 44:5; 7; 15; 29; 45:17; 19; 23; 47:23; 26; 48:4; 9; 15; 18; 49:28; 50:11; 20; 24; **Ex** 1:18; 2:6; 9; 12; 14; 15; 3:3; 12(2); 15(2); 21; 4:17; 5:22; 23; 7:17; 23; 8:19; 23; 32; 9:5; 14; 16; 18; 27; 10:6; 7; 17(2); 12:2; 3; 12; 14; 17(2); 24; 25; 26; 42; 43; 13:3(2); 4; 5(2); 8; 10; 14; 14:5; 12; 15:1; 16:3(2); 8; 15; 16; 23; 32; 17:3; 4; 14; 18:14; 18(2); 23(2); 21:31; 25:3; 26:13; 28:17; 29:1; 38; 42; 30:13; 31; 32:1; 9; 12; 13; 21; 23; 24; 29; 31; 33:12; 13; 17; 34:11; 35:4; 37:8; 38:15; 21; 39:10; **Lev** 4:20; 6:9; 14; 20; 25; 7:1; 11; 35; 37; 8:5; 34; 9:6; 10:3; 19; 11:46; 12:7; 13:59; 14:2; 32; 54; 57; 15:3; 32; 16:29; 34; 17:2; 7; 23:27; 34; 24:10; 25:13; 26:16; 18; 27; **Num** 4:4; 24; 28; 31; 33; 5:19; 22; 29; 30; 31; 6:13; 20; 21; 23; 7:17; 23; 29; 35; 41; 47; 53; 59; 65; 71; 77; 83; 84; 88; 8:4; 24; 9:3; 11:6; 11; 12; 13; 14; 31; 13:17; 27; 14:2; 3; 8; 11; 13; 14(2); 15; 16; 19(2); 27; 29; 32; 35(2); 15:13; 16:6; 21; 45; 18:9; 11; 27; 19:2; 14; 20:4; 5; 10; 12; 13; 21:2; 5; 17; 22:1; 4; 6; 8; 17; 19; 24; 30; 23:23; 24:14; 23; 26:9; 27:12; 28:3; 10; 14; 17; 24; 29:7; 30:1; 31:21; 32:5; 15; 19; 20; 22; 32; 34:2; 6; 7; 9; 12; 13; 15; 35:5; 14; 36:6; **Deut** 1:1; 5(2); 6; 10; 31; 32; 35; 2:3; 7; 18; 22; 25; 30; 3:8; 12; 14; 18; 26; 27; 28; 4:4; 6(2); 8(2); 20; 22; 26; 32; 38; 39; 40; 41; 44; 46; 47; 49; 5:1; 3(2); 24; 25; 28; 6:6; 24; 7:11; 8:1; 11; 17; 18; 19; 9:1; 3; 4; 6; 7; 13; 27; 10:8; 13; 15; 11:2; 4; 5; 8; 13; 26; 27; 28; 32; 12:8; 13:11; 18; 15:2; 5; 10; 15; 17:18; 19; 18:3; 16; 19:4; 9; 20:3; 21:7; 20; 22:14; 16; 20; 26; 24:18; 22; 26:3; 9(2); 16; 17; 18; 27:1; 3; 4; 8; 9; 10; 26; 28:1; 13; 14; 15; 58(3); 61; 29:4; 7; 9; 10; 12; 14(2); 15(2); 18; 19; 20; 21; 24(2); 27(2); 28; 29; 30:2; 8; 10; 11(2); 15; 16; 18; 19; 31:2(2); 7; 9; 11; 12; 16; 19(2); 21; 22; 24; 26; 27; 30; 32:27; 29; 34; 44; 46(2); 47; 49; 33:1; 7; 34:4; 6; **Josh** 1:2(2); 4; 6; 8; 11; 13; 14; 15; 2:14; 17; 18; 20; 3:4; 7; 4:3; 6; 9; 22; 5:4; 9(2); 6:25; 26; 7:7; 25; 26(2); 8:20; 22; 28; 29; 33; 9:1; 12; 20; 24; 27; 10:13; 27; 11:6; 12:7; 13:2; 7; 13; 23; 28; 29; 14:10(2); 11; 12; 14; 15:1; 4; 12; 20; 63; 16:8; 10; 18:14; 19; 20; 28; 19:8; 16; 23; 31; 39; 48; 22:3; 7; 16(3); 17; 18; 22; 24; 29; 31(2); 23:8; 9; 13; 14; 15; 24:15; 27; **Judg** 1:21; 26; 2:2(2); 20; 4:14; 6:13; 14; 20; 24; 26; 29(2); 39(2); 7:4(2); 14; 8:9; 9:18; 19; 29; 38; 10:4; 15; 11:27; 37; 12:3; 13:23; 15:6; 7; 11; 18; 19; 16:18; 28; 18:3; 12; 24; 19:11; 23(2); 24; 30; 20:3; 9; 12; 16; 21:3; 6; 11; 22; **Ruth** 1:19; 2:5; 3:13; 18; 4:7(2); 9; 10; 12; 14; **1Sa** 1:3; 27; 2:20; 23; 34; 4:6; 14; 5:5; 6:9; 18; 20; 8:8; 11; 9:6; 13; 16; 17; 24; 10:11; 19; 27; 11:2; 13; 12:2; 5; 8; 16; 19; 20; 14:10; 28; 29; 33; 38(2); 45(2); 15:14; 16; 28; 16:8; 9; 12; 17:10; 17; 25; 26(2); 27; 32; 33; 36; 37; 46(2); 47; 55; 18:21; 24; 20:2; 3; 21; 21:5; 11; 15(2); 22:8; 13; 15; 23:26; 24:6; 10; 16; 18; 19; 25:21; 24; 25; 27; 31; 32; 33; 26:8; 16; 17; 19; 21; 24; 27:6; 28:10; 18(2); 29:3(2); 4; 5; 6; 8; 30:8; 15(2); 20; 24; 25; **2Sa** 1:17; 2:1; 5; 6(2); 3:8(2); 38; 39; 4:3; 8; 6:8; 7:6; 17; 19(2); 27; 28; 8:1; 10:1; 11:3; 11; 25; 12:5; 6; 11; 12; 14; 21; 13:1; 12; 16; 17; 20; 32; 14:3; 13; 15; 19; 20(2); 21; 15:1; 6; 20; 16:9; 11; 12; 17; 18; 17:1; 6; 7; 16; 18:18; 20(2); 31; 19:5(2); 6(3); 7; 14; 20; 21; 22(3); 35; 42; 21:18; 22:1; 23:5; 17(2); 24:3; **1Kin** 1:25; 27; 30; 41; 45; 48; 2:23; 24; 26; 3:6(2); 9; 10; 11; 17; 18; 19; 22; 23; 4:24(2); 5:7(2); 6:12; 7:8; 28; 37; 8:8; 24; 27; 29(2); 30; 31; 33; 35; 38; 42; 43; 54; 61; 9:3; 7; 8(3); 9; 13; 15; 21; 10:12; 11:10; 11; 27; 39; 12:6; 7(2); 9; 10; 19; 24; 27(2); 30; 13:3; 8; 16; 33; 34; 14:2; 15; 17:21; 24; 18:36; 37; 19:2; 20:6; 7; 9; 12; 13(2); 24; 28; 34; 39; 22:20; 27; **2Kin** 1:2; 2:19; 22; 3:16; 18; 23; 4:9; 12; 13; 16; 36; 43; 5:6; 7; 18(2); 20; 6:11; 18; 19(2); 24; 28; 31; 32; 33; 7:1; 2; 9; 18; 8:5(2); 8; 9; 13; 22; 9:1; 11; 25; 26; 27; 34; 36; 37; 10:2; 6; 27; 11:5; 14:7; 10; 15:12; 16:6; 17:12; 23; 34; 41; 18:19; 21; 22; 25(2); 30; 19:3; 21; 29(2); 31; 32; 33; 34; 20:6(2); 9; 17; 21:7; 15; 22:13(2); 16; 17; 19; 20; 23:3(2); 21; 23; 27; 24:3; **1Chr** 4:41; 43; 5:26; 11:11; 19; 13:11; 16:7; 17:5; 15; 17; 19; 26; 18:1; 19:1; 20:4; 21:3; 7; 8; 22; 22:1(2); 26:30; 27:6; 28:7; 8; 19(2); 29:5; 14; 16; 18; **2Chr** 1:10(2); 11; 2:4; 5:9; 6:15; 18; 20(2); 21; 22; 24; 26; 29; 32; 33; 34; 40; 7:12; 15; 16; 20; 21(3); 22; 8:8; 10:6; 7; 9; 19; 11:4; 14:11; 16:10; 18:19; 26; 19:10; 20:1; 2; 7; 9(2); 12; 15; 17; 26; 35; 21:10; 18; 23:4; 24:4; 18; 25:9; 16; 28:22; 29:9; 28; 30:9; 31:1; 10; 32:9; 15; 20; 30; 33:7; 14; 34:21; 24; 25; 27; 28; 31; 35:19; 20; 21; 25; **Ezr** 1:9; 3:12; 4:8; 10; 11(2); 13; 15(2); 16(3); 19; 21; 22; 5:3(3); 4(2); 5; 6(2); 8; 9; 12; 13; 17(2); 6:7(2); 8; 11(2); 12; 13; 15; 16; 17; 7:6; 11; 17; 24; 27; 8:1; 23; 35; 36; 9:2; 3; 7(2); 10; 13; 15(2); 10:2; 4; 5; 9; 13(2); 14; 15; **Neh** 1:11(2); 2:2; 18; 19; 3:7; 5:10; 11; 12; 13(2); 16; 18(2); 19; 6:4; 12; 16; 7:7; 8:9; 10; 9:1; 10; 18; 32; 36; 38; 13:4; 6; 14; 17; 18(2); 22; 27; **Est** 1:1; 17; 18; 4:14(2); 15; 5:4; 13; 6:3; 9; 7:6; 9:4; 13; 21; 26(2); 29; **Job** 1:3; 22; 2:10; 11; 3:1; 4:6; 5:27; 8:19; 9:22; 10:13; 12:9; 13:1; 17:8; 18:21; 19:26; 20:2; 4; 29; 21:2; 27:13; 31:11; 28; 33:12; 34:16; 35:2; 36:21; 37:1; 14; 38:2; 42:16; **Ps** 2:7; 7:3; 11:6; 12:7; 17:14; 18:t; 22:31; 24:6; 8; 10; 27:3; 32:6; 34:6; 35:22; 41:11; 44:17; 21; 48:14; 49:1; 13; 50:22; 51:4; 52:7; 56:9; 62:11; 68:16; 69:31; 32; 71:18; 73:16; 74:2; 18; 77:10; 78:21; 32; 54; 59; 80:14; 81:4; 5; 87:4; 5; 6; 92:6; 95:10; 102:18; 104:25; 109:20; 27; 113:2; 115:18; 118:20; 23; 24; 119:50; 56; 91; 121:8; 132:14; 149:9; **Prov** 6:3; 7:14; 22:19; **Eccl** 1:10; 13; 17; 2:1; 10; 15; 19; 21; 23; 24; 26; 4:4(2); 8; 16; 5:10; 16; 19; 6:2; 5; 9; 12; 7:6; 10; 18(2); 23; 27; 29; 8:9; 10; 14; 9:1(2); 3; 9; 13; 11:6; 12:13; **Song** 3:6; 5:16(2); 7:7; 8:5; **Is** 1:12; 3:6; 5:25; 6:7; 9; 10; 8:6; 11; 12; 20; 9:5; 7; 12; 16; 17; 21; 10:4; 12:5; 14:4; 16; 26(2); 28; 16:13; 17:14; 20:6; 22:14; 15; 23:7; 8; 13; 24:3; 25:6; 7; 9(2); 10; 26:1; 27:9(2); 28:11; 12(2); 14; 29; 29:11; 12; 13; 14; 30:7; 9; 12; 13; 21; 36:4; 6; 7; 10(2); 15; 37:3; 22; 30(2); 32; 33; 34; 35; 38:6(2); 7(2); 19; 39:6; 41:20; 42:22; 23; 43:9; 21; 45:21; 46:8; 47:8; 48:1; 6(2); 16; 20; 50:11; 51:21; 54:9; 17; 56:2; 12; 58:4; 5; 6; 59:21; 63:1(2); 66:2; 14; **Jer** 1:10; 18; 2:12; 17; 3:4; 10; 25; 4:8; 10; 11; 18; 28; 5:7; 9; 14(2); 20; 21; 23; 29; 6:6; 19; 21; 7:2; 3; 6; 7; 10; 11; 14; 16; 20; 23; 25; 28; 33; 8:3; 5; 9:9; 12; 15; 24; 10:18; 19; 11:2; 3; 5; 6; 7; 8; 14; 13:9; 10(2); 12; 13; 25; 14:10; 11; 13; 15; 17; 15:1; 20; 16:2; 3(2); 5; 6; 9; 10(2); 13; 21; 17:24; 25(2); 18:6; 19:3; 4(2); 6; 7; 8; 11(2); 12(2); 15; 20:5; 21:4; 6; 7; 8; 9; 10; 22:1; 3; 4(2); 5; 8(2); 11; 12; 16; 21; 28; 30; 23:6; 26; 32; 33; 38; 24:5; 6; 8; 25:3; 9; 11; 13; 15; 18; 26:1; 6(2); 9(2); 11(2); 12(2); 15; 16; 20(2); 27:1; 16; 17; 19; 22; 28:3(2); 4; 6; 7; 15; 16; 29:10; 16; 28; 29; 32; 30:17; 21; 31:23; 26; 33; 32:3; 8; 14(2); 15; 20(2); 22; 23; 28; 29(2); 31(2); 35; 36; 37; 41; 42(2); 43; 33:4; 5; 10; 12; 16; 24; 34:2; 8; 22; 35:14; 16; 36:1; 2; 7; 29(2); 37:8; 10; 18; 19; 38:2; 3; 4(4); 16; 17; 18; 21; 23; 39:16; 40:2(2); 3; 4; 16; 42:2; 10; 13; 18; 19; 21; 44:2; 4; 6; 7; 10; 22; 23(2); 29(2); 45:4; 46:7; 10; 50:17; 25; 51:6; 59; 62; 63; 52:28; **Lam** 2:15; 16; 20; 3:21; 5:17; **Eze** 1:5; 23; 28; 2:3; 3:1; 3; 4:3; 5:5; 6:10; 8:5; 15; 17; 10:15; 20; 11:2; 3; 6; 7; 11; 15; 12:10; 23; 16:20; 43; 44; 49; 17:7; 18:2; 3; 19:14; 20:27; 29; 31; 21:11; 26; 23:11; 38; 24:2(2); 24; 31:18; 32:16; 33:33; 36:22; 32; 35; 37; 39:8; 40:10(2); 12(2); 21; 26; 34; 37; 39; 41; 45; 48(2); 49; 41:4; 22; 43:12(2); 13; 44:2; 45:1; 2; 3; 13; 16; 46:3; 20; 47:6; 12; 13; 14; 15; 17; 18; 19; 20; 21; 48:10; 12; 29; **Dan** 1:14; 2:12; 18; 30; 31; 32; 36; 38; 47; 3:16; 29; 4:17; 18; 24(2); 28; 30; 5:7; 15; 22; 24; 25; 26; 6:3; 5; 28; 7:6; 7; 8; 16; 24; 8:16; 9:7; 13; 15; 10:8; 11; 17(2); 11:18; 12:5; **Hos** 5:1; 7:10; 16; **Joel** 1:2(2); 3:9; **Amos** 3:1; 4:1; 5; 5:1; 7:3; 6(2); 8:4; 8; 9:12; **Obad** 20; **Jonah** 1:7; 8; 10; 12; 14; 4:2; **Mic** 1:5; 2:3(2); 10; 11; 3:9; 5:5; **Hab** 1:11; **Zeph** 1:4; 2:10; 15; **Hag** 1:2; 4; 2:3; 7; 9(2); 14(2); 15; 18; 19; **Zec** 2:4; 3:2; 4:6; 9; 5:3(2); 5; 6(2); 7; 8; 6:15; 8:6; 11; 12; 14:12; 15; 19; **Mal** 1:9; 13; 2:1; 4; 12; 13; 3:9; 4:3; **Mt** 1:18; 22; 3:3; 17; 6:9; 11; 7:12; 8:9(2); 27; 9:3; 28; 10:23; 11:10; 14; 16; 23; 12:6; 7; 23; 24; 32; 41; 42; 45; 13:15; 19; 22; 28; 40; 54(2); 55; 56; 14:2; 15; 15:8; 11; 12; 15; 16:18; 22; 17:5; 20; 21; 18:4; 19:5; 11; 26; 20:14; 21:4; 10; 11; 21(2); 23; 38; 42; 44; 22:20; 33; 38; 23:36; 24:14; 21; 34; 43; 26:8; 9; 12; 13(3); 26; 28; 29; 31; 34; 39; 42; 56; 61; 71; 27:8; 19; 24; 37; 47; 54; 28:14; 15(2); **Mk** 1:27(2); 2:7; 12; 4:13; 19; 41; 5:32; 39; 6:2(2); 3; 35; 7:6; 29; 8:12(2); 38; 9:7; 21; 29; 10:5; 7; 30; 11:3; 23; 28; 12:7; 10; 11; 16; 30; 31; 43; 13:19; 30; 14:4; 9(2); 22; 24; 27; 30(2); 36; 58; 69; 71; 15:39; **Lk** 1:18; 29; 34; 36; 43; 61; 66; 2:2; 11; 12; 15; 17; 34; 3:20; 4:3; 6; 21(2); 22; 23; 36; 5:6; 21; 6:3; 7:4; 8; 17; 27; 31; 39(2); 44; 45; 46; 49; 8:9; 11; 14; 25; 9:9; 13; 35; 45; 48; 54; 10:5; 11; 20; 28; 11:29; 30; 31; 32; 50; 51; 12:18; 20; 39; 41; 56; 13:6; 7; 8; 16(2); 14:9; 30; 15:2; 3; 24; 30; 32; 16:2; 8; 24; 26; 28; 17:6; 18; 25; 18:1; 5; 9; 11; 14; 23; 30; 34; 19:9(2); 14; 42; 20:2; 9; 14; 17; 19; 34; 21:3; 23; 32; 34; 22:15; 17; 19(2); 20; 23; 34; 37; 42; 53; 56; 59; 23:2; 4; 5; 14(2); 18; 38; 41; 47; 52; 24:21; **Jn** 1:15; 19; 30; 34; 2:11; 12; 19; 20; 22; 3:19; 29; 4:13; 15; 20; 21; 27; 29; 42; 54; 5:1; 28; 6:6; 14; 29; 34; 39; 40; 42; 50; 51; 52; 58(2); 60(2); 61; 7:8(2); 15; 25; 26; 27; 31; 36; 39; 40(2); 41; 46; 49; 8:4; 6; 23(2); 40; 9:2; 3; 8; 9; 16; 19; 20; 24; 29; 33; 39; 10:6; 16; 18; 41; 11:4; 9; 26; 37(2); 39; 47; 51; 12:5; 6; 7; 18(2); 25; 27(3); 30; 31(2); 33; 34; 13:1; 28; 35; 14:30; 15:12; 13; 25; 16:11; 17; 18; 30; 17:3; 18:17; 29; 34; 36(2); 37(2); 38; 40; 19:12; 20; 28; 38; 20:22; 30; 21:1; 14; 19(2); 21; 23; 24; **Acts** 1:6; 11; 16; 17; 18; 25; 2:6; 12; 14; 16; 29; 31; 32; 33; 37; 40; 3:12(2); 16(2); 4:7; 9; 10; 11; 17; 22; 5:4; 20; 24; 28(2); 37; 38(2); 6:3; 13(2); 14(2); 7:4; 6; 7; 29; 35; 37; 38; 40; 60(2); 8:10; 19; 21; 22; 29; 32; 34; 9:2; 13; 21(2); 22; 36; 10:16; 17; 30; 11:10; 13:17; 23; 26; 33; 34; 38; 48; 15:2; 6; 15; 16; 23; 16:18; 36; 17:3; 18; 19; 23; 30; 32; 18:10; 13; 18; 21; 25; 19:5; 10; 17; 25; 26; 27; 40(2); 20:26; 29; 21:11; 23; 28(3); 22:3(2); 4; 22; 26; 28; 23:1; 9; 13; 17; 18; 25; 27; 24:2; 5; 10; 14; 21(2); 25; 25:5; 24; 26:2; 16; 22; 26; 29; 31; 32; 27:10; 21; 23; 33; 34; 28:4; 9; 20(2); 22; 26; 27; **Rom** 1:26; 2:3; 3:26; 4:9; 5:2; 6:6; 7:24; 8:18; 9:9(2); 10; 17; 10:6; 11:5; 8; 25; 27; 12:2; 13:6(2); 9(2); 14:9; 13; 15:9; 28(2); 16:22; **1Cor** 1:12; 20(2); 2:6(2); 8; 3:12; 18; 19; 4:11; 13; 17; 5:2; 3; 10; 6:3; 4; 7:6; 7; 26; 29; 31(2); 35; 8:7; 9; 9:3; 10; 12(2); 17; 23; 10:28; 11:10; 17; 20; 22; 24(2); 25(2); 26(2); 27(2); 30; 14:21; 15:6; 19; 34; 50; 53(2); 54(2); 16:12; **2Cor** 1:12; 15; 2:1; 3; 6; 9; 3:10; 14; 15; 4:1; 4; 7; 5:1; 2; 4; 7:3; 11(2); 8:5; 7; 10; 14; 19; 20(2); 9:3; 4; 6; 12; 13; 10:7; 11; 11:10; 17; 12:8; 13; 13:1; 9; **Gal** 1:4; 3:2; 17; 4:25; 5:8; 14; 16; 6:16; **Eph** 1:21; 2:2; 3:1; 8; 14; 4:17; 5:5; 31; 32; 6:1; 12; **Phil** 1:6; 7; 9; 19; 22; 25; 2:5; 3:13; 15; **Col** 1:9; 27; 2:4; 3:20; 4:16; **1Th** 2:13; 3:5; 4:3; 15; 5:18; 27; **2Th** 1:11; 2:11; 3:10; 14; **1Ti** 1:9; 15; 16; 18; 2:3; 3:1; 4:9; 16; 6:7; 14; 17; **2Ti** 1:15; 2:4; 19; 3:1; 6; 4:10; **Titus** 1:5; 13; 2:12; 3:8; **Heb** 1:5; 3:3; 4:4; 5; 5:4; 6:3; 7:1; 4; 21; 24; 27; 8:1; 3; 10; 9:8; 11; 15; 20; 27; 10:12; 16; 11:5; 12:27; 13:19; **Jas** 1:3; 25; 26; 27; 2:5; 3:15; 4:15; **1Pet** 1:25; 2:19; 20; 3:5; 4:6; 16; 5:12; **2Pet** 1:5; 13; 14; 17; 18; 20; 3:1; 3; 5; 8; **1Jn** 1:5; 2:25; 3:3; 8; 10; 11; 17; 23; 4:3; 9; 17; 21; 5:2; 3; 4; 6; 9; 11(2); 14; 20; **2Jn** 6(2); 7; 10; **Jude** 4; 5; **Rev** 1:3; 2:6; 24; 4:1; 7:9; 11:5; 15; 18:18; 20:5; 14; 22:7; 9; 10; 18(2); 19(2)

THOSE

Gen 6:4; 15:17; 19:25; 24:60; 33:5; 41:35; 42:5; 50:3; **Ex** 2:11; 4:21; 29:33; 35:35; **Lev** 11:27; 14:11; 42; 15:10; 27; 22:2; **Num** 1:21; 22; 23; 25; 27; 29; 31; 33; 35; 37; 39; 41; 43; 44; 45; 2:4; 5; 6; 8; 11; 12; 13; 15; 19; 21; 23; 26; 27; 28; 30; 32(2); 3:22(2); 34; 38; 43; 46; 4:36; 38; 40; 42; 44; 45; 46; 48; 9:7; 13:3; 14:22; 37; 18:16; 25:9; 26:18; 22; 25; 27; 34; 37; 43; 47; 54; 62; 33:55; **Deut** 7:22; 17:9; 18:9; 19:5; 17; 20; 26:3; 29:3; 29; 32:21; **Josh** 3:16; 4:20; 10:22; 23; 24; 11:1; 10; 12; 18; 17:12; 20:4; 6; 21:16; 24:17; **Judg** 2:16; 23; 7:8; 11:13; 12:5; 17:6; 18:1(2); 19:1; 20:27; 28; 21:25; **1Sa** 3:1; 7:16; 10:9; 11:6; 17:11; 28; 18:23; 19:7; 25:9; 12; 27:8; 28:1; 3; 9; 30:9; 20; 22; **2Sa** 5:14; 16:23; **1Kin** 2:7; 3:2; 4:27; 8:4; 9:21; 21:27; **2Kin** 4:4; 6:22; 10:32; 15:37; 17:9; 18:4; 20:1; 24:15; **1Chr** 4:23; 16:42; **2Chr** 14:6; 15:5; 17:19; 20:29; 32:13; 14; 24; **Ezr** 1:8; 2:1; 62; 3:3; 5:9; 14; 7:19; 8:35; 9:2; 4; 10:3; 8; **Neh** 4:17; 5:17; 6:17; 7:6; 64; 8:3; 10:1; 13:15; 23; **Est** 1:2; 2:21(2); 3:9; 9:5; 11; **Job** 5:11(2); 21:22; 24:13; 19; 27:15; **Ps** 5:11; 13:4; 17:7; 18:30; 39; 48; 21:8; 37:9; 40:16; 50:5; 61:5; 63:9; 68:6; 11; 69:6; 26; 70:4; 74:23; 79:11; 92:13; 102:20; 103:18; 106:46; 109:31; 119:79(2); 132; 123:4; 125:4; 139:21; 140:9; 143:3; 145:14; 147:11; **Prov** 1:12; 4:22; 8:17; 21; 22:23; 24:11; 26:28; 31:6; **Eccl** 1:11; 5:14; 7:28; 8:8; 12:3; **Song** 7:9; 8:12; **Is** 14:19; 27:7; 35:8; 38:1; 40:11; 56:8; 60:12; 64:5(2); 66:2(2); 19; **Jer** 3:16; 18; 4:12; 5:18; 8:16; 14:15; 21:7; 27:11; 31:29; 33; 36; 33:15; 16; 38:22; 39:9; 46:26; 49:5; 36; 50:4; 20; 52:15; **Lam** 2:22; 3:62; **Eze** 1:21(3); 18:11; 22:5(2); 28:26; 33:24; 34:27; 38:17; 39:10(2); 14; 40:25; 42:14; **Dan** 3:22; 4:37; 6:24; 10:2; 11:4; 14; **Joel** 2:16; 29; 3:1; **Obad** 14(2); **Zeph** 1:6; 9; **Hag** 2:16; 22; **Zec** 3:4; 4:10; 7:5; 8:23; 11:16; 13:6; 14:3; **Mal** 3:5; **Mt** 3:1; 4:24(3); 11:4; 13:17(2); 15:18; 30; 16:23; 21:40; 41; 22:7; 10; 24:19; 22(2); 29; 25:7; 19; 27:54; **Mk** 1:9; 44; 2:20; 6:55; 7:15; 8:1; 10:13; 11:23; 12:7; 13:17; 19; 20; 24; **Lk** 1:1; 4; 24; 39; 45; 2:1; 18; 33; 4:2; 5:35; 6:12; 32; 7:28; 8:12; 9:36(2); 10:24(2); 12:20; 37; 38; 13:4; 14:7; 24; 17:10; 19:27; 20:1; 21:23; 26; 23:14; **Jn** 2:14; 6:14; 8:10; 26; 29; 31; 10:32; 13:29; 17:11; 12; **Acts** 1:15; 2:18; 3:18; 24; 6:1; 7:41; 8:6; 9:37; 13:45; 16:3; 35; 17:11(2); 18:17; 20:2; 21:5; 15; 24; 26:16; 22; 27:11; 28:31; **Rom** 1:28; 4:17; 6:13; 21(2); 10:5; 15:17; 18; **1Cor** 8:4; 10; 12:22; 23; 14:23; **2Cor** 7:6; 11:28; **Eph** 5:12; **Phil** 3:7; 13(2); 4:3; 9; **Col** 2:18; 3:1; **1Ti** 4:10; 5:8; **2Ti** 2:25; 3:3; **Heb** 3:5; 5:14; 6:4; 7:21; 27; 8:10; 10:1; 3; 16; 12:27(2); 13:11; **Jas** 2:16; **2Pet** 2:6; 18; **1Jn** 3:22; **2Jn** 8; **Jude** 10(2); **Rev** 1:3; 2:10; 13; 4:9; 9:4; 6; 10:4; 13:14; 20:12

THOU

Gen 2:16; 17(3); 3:9; 11(3); 12; 13; 14(4); 15; 16; 17(3); 18; 19(5); 4:6; 7(4); 10; 11; 12(2); 14; 6:14; 15; 16(4); 18(2); 19; 21(2); 7:1; 2; 8:16; 10:19(2); 30; 12:2; 11; 13; 18(2); 19; 13:9(2); 10; 14; 15; 14:23; 15:2; 3; 5; 15(2); 16:8(2); 11; 13; 17:1; 4; 8; 9(2); 15; 19; 18:5; 15; 23; 24; 28; 19:12(2); 15; 17(2); 19(2); 21; 22; 34; 20:3(2); 4; 6; 7(5); 9(3); 10(2); 13; 21:22; 23(3); 26; 29; 30; 22:2; 12(3); 16; 18; 23:6(2); 13; 24:3; 4; 5; 6(2); 7; 8; 14(2); 23; 31(2); 37; 38; 40; 41(3); 42; 44; 47; 58; 60(2); 25:18; 26:9; 10(2); 16; 29(2); 27:10; 18; 19; 20; 21; 24; 32; 33; 36; 38; 40(3); 43; 45; 28:1; 3; 4(2); 6; 13; 14; 15; 22; 29:14; 15(2); 25(2); 27; 30:15(2); 16; 26; 29; 30; 31(2); 31:13(2); 24; 26(2); 27; 28; 29(2); 30(3); 31; 32(2); 36; 37(2); 39; 41; 42; 43; 44(2); 50(2); 52; 32:10; 12; 17(2); 18; 26; 28; 29; 33:8; 9; 10; 35:1; 17; 37:8(2); 10; 15; 38:16(2); 17(2); 23; 29; 39:9; 17; 40:13(2); 41:15; 39; 40(2); 43:4; 5; 8; 9; 44:4; 18; 21; 23; 45:10(4); 11(2); 19; 46:30; 47:6; 8; 25; 30(2); 48:6; 49:3; 4(3); 6(2); 8; 9; 10; 50:5; **Ex** 2:13; 14(2); 3:5; 10; 12; 14; 15; 18(2); 4:9(2); 10; 12; 13; 15; 16; 17(2); 21(2); 22; 23; 25; 26; 5:15; 22(2); 23; 6:1; 29; 7:2; 9; 15(2); 16(2); 17; 8:2; 10; 21; 22; 9:2; 4; 14; 15; 17(2); 19; 29; 30; 3; 4; 7; 25; 28(2); 29; 12:44; 46; 13:5; 6; 8; 10; 12(2); 13(4); 14; 14:11(2); 15; 16; 15:7(2); 10; 12; 13(3); 16; 17(2); 26; 17:3; 5; 6; 18:14(2); 17; 18(3); 19(2); 20; 21; 23(2); 19:3; 6; 12; 23; 24(2); 20:3; 4; 5; 7; 9; 10(2); 13; 14; 15; 16; 17(2); 19; 22; 24; 25(4); 26; 21:1; 2; 14; 23; 22:18; 21; 23; 25(3); 26(2); 28; 29(2); 30(2); 23:1; 2(2); 3; 4(2); 5(2); 6; 7; 8; 9; 10; 11(2); 12(2); 14; 15(3); 16(2); 18; 19(2); 22; 24(2); 27; 30; 31; 32; 33; 24:1; 12; 25:11(2); 12; 13; 14; 16; 17; 18(2); 21(2); 23; 24; 25(2); 26; 28; 29(2); 30; 31; 37; 40; 26:1(2); 4(2); 5(2); 6; 7(2); 9; 10; 11; 14; 15; 17; 18; 19; 22; 23; 26; 29(2); 30; 31; 32; 33(2); 34; 35(2); 36; 37(2); 27:1; 2(2); 3(2); 4(2); 5; 6; 8; 9; 20; 28:1; 2; 3; 9; 11(2); 12; 13; 14; 15(3); 17; 22; 23; 24; 25; 26(2); 27; 30; 31; 33; 36; 37; 39(3); 40(3); 41; 42; 29:1; 2; 3; 4; 5; 6; 7; 8; 9(2); 10; 11; 12; 13; 14; 15; 16(2); 17; 18; 19; 20; 21; 22; 24; 25; 26; 27; 31; 34; 35(2); 36(4); 37; 38; 39(2); 41; 30:1(2); 3(2); 4(2); 5; 6; 12(3); 16; 18(3); 23; 25; 26; 29; 30; 31; 35; 36; 37; 31:13; 32:7; 11; 13; 21; 22; 32(2); 33:1(2); 3; 12(5); 16; 17(2); 20; 21; 23; 34:1; 10; 11; 12(2); 14; 15(2); 16; 17; 18(3); 20(4); 21(3); 22; 24; 25; 26(2); 27; 40:2; 3; 4(2); 5; 6; 7; 8; 9; 10; 11; 12; 13; 14; 15(2); **Lev** 2:4; 6; 8; 13(3); 14(2); 15; 6:21(2); 27; 8:3; 9:3; 10:9; 14; 13:55; 57; 58; 17:8; 18:7(2); 8; 9; 10; 11; 12; 13; 14(2); 15(2); 16; 17(2); 18; 19; 20; 21(2); 22; 23; 19:9(2); 10(3); 12; 13; 14; 15(2); 16(2); 17(2); 18(2); 19(2); 27; 32; 34; 20:2; 16; 19; 21:8; 22:23; 23:22(4); 24:5; 6; 7; 15; 25:3(2); 4; 5; 8; 9; 14; 15; 16(2); 17; 35; 36; 37; 39; 43; 44; 27:12; **Num** 1:3; 49; 50; 3:9; 10; 15; 41; 47(2); 48; 4:23; 29; 30; 5:19(2); 20(2); 7:5; 8:2; 7; 8; 9(2); 10; 12; 13; 14; 15; 26; 10:2(2); 29; 31(2); 32; 11:11(2); 12(2); 15; 16; 17; 18; 21; 23; 29; 13:2; 27; 14:13; 14(3); 15; 17; 19; 15:5; 6; 7; 8; 10; 16:11; 13(2); 14(2); 15; 16(2); 17; 22; 37; 17:2; 3; 4; 10; 18:1(2); 2(2); 7; 10; 15(2); 16; 17(2); 20(2); 30; 20:8(4); 14; 18; 20; 21:2; 29; 34(2); 22:6(2); 12(2); 17; 20; 28; 29; 30; 32; 34; 35; 37; 23:5; 11(2); 13(2); 18; 27; 24:10; 11; 12; 21; 26:54(2); 27:7(2); 8; 13(2); 20; 28:3; 4(2); 7; 8(2); 21; 31:2; 26; 30; **Deut** 1:14; 31; 37; 2:4; 7; 18; 19; 28; 31; 37; 3:2(2); 21; 24; 27; 28; 4:9; 10; 19(2); 25; 29(3); 30(2); 33; 35; 36; 38; 40(2); 5:7; 8; 9; 11; 13; 14(3); 15; 17; 18; 19; 20; 21(2); 27(2); 31(2); 6:2(2); 5; 7(5); 8; 9; 10; 11(4); 12; 13; 18(2); 21; 7:1(2); 2(2); 3(3); 6; 11; 14; 15; 16(2); 17; 18; 19; 21; 22; 24(2); 25(2); 26(4); 8:2(2); 3; 5; 6; 9(3); 10(2); 11; 12; 13; 14; 17; 18; 19; 9:1; 2(2); 3; 4; 5; 6; 7(2); 12; 26(2); 28; 29; 10:2(2); 20(3); 11:1; 10(2); 14; 15; 19(4); 20; 29(2); 12:5; 13(2); 14(2); 15; 17(2); 18(4); 19(2); 20(2); 21(2); 22; 23(2); 24(2); 25(2); 26(2); 27(2); 28; 29(2); 30(2); 31; 32; 13:2; 3; 5; 6(2); 8(3); 9; 10; 12; 14; 15; 16; 18; 14:2; 3; 21(4); 22; 23(2); 24; 25; 26(4); 27; 28; 29; 15:1; 3; 5; 6(3); 7; 8; 9; 10(3); 11; 12; 13(2); 14(2); 15(2); 17(2); 18(2); 19(2); 20(2); 21; 22; 23(2); 16:2; 3(5); 4; 5; 6(2); 7(2); 8(2); 9(2); 10(2); 11(2); 12(3); 13(2); 14(2); 15(2); 18; 19(2); 20(2); 21(2); 22; 17:1; 4; 5; 7; 8; 9; 10(2); 11(2); 12; 14; 15(3); 18:4; 9(2); 13; 14; 16; 21; 22; 19:1; 2; 3; 7; 9(2); 13; 14(2); 19; 20:1(2); 10; 12; 13; 14(2); 15; 16; 17; 19(4); 20(3); 21:8; 9(2); 10(2); 11; 12; 13; 14(5); 21; 22; 23; 22:1(2); 2(3); 3(5); 4(2); 6; 7(2); 8(3); 9(2); 10; 11; 12(2);

21; 22; 24; 26; 23:6; 7(3); 12(2); 13(3); 15; 16; 18; 19; 20(4); 21(2); 22; 23(3); 24(3); 25(3); 24:4; 7; 8; 10(2); 11(2); 12; 13; 14; 15; 17; 18(2); 19(2); 20(2); 21(2); 22(2); 25:4; 12; 13; 14; 15(2); 18; 19(2); 26:1; 2(2); 3; 5; 10(2); 11(2); 12; 13(2); 14; 15(2); 16; 17; 18; 19; 27:2; 3(3); 4; 5(2); 6(2); 7; 8; 9; 10; 28:1; 2; 3(2); 6(4); 8; 9; 10; 12(2); 13(3); 14; 15; 16(2); 19(4); 20(4); 21; 22; 24; 25; 27; 29(3); 30(4); 31(2); 33(2); 34(2); 36(3); 37; 38; 39; 40(2); 41(2); 43; 44(2); 45(2); 47; 48; 49; 51; 52; 53; 58(2); 60; 61; 62; 63; 64(2); 65; 66; 67(4); 68; 29:12; 30:1; 2; 5; 6; 8; 10(2); 12; 13; 14; 16(2); 17; 18; 19; 20(4); 31:2; 3; 7(2); 11; 14; 16; 23; 32:14; 15(3); 18; 50; 52(2); 33:7; 8(2); 23; 29(2); 34:4; **Josh** 1:2; 6; 7(4); 8(4); 9(2); 16(2); 18; 2:17; 18(3); 20(2); 3:8; 5:13; 15; 6:3; 7:7; 9; 10; 13; 19; 25; 8:1; 2(2); 10:12(2); 11:6; 13:1; 6; 14:6; 9; 12; 15:18; 19; 17:14; 15; 17(2); 18(2); **Judg** 1:14; 15; 4:8(2); 9; 20; 22; 5:4(2); 12; 16; 21; 6:4; 12; 14; 16; 17; 18; 23; 26; 36(2); 37(2); 7:5; 10(2); 11; 8:1(3); 18; 21; 22(3); 9:8; 10; 12; 14; 32; 33(3); 36; 38(2); 10:15; 11:2(2); 8; 12(2); 23; 24; 25; 27; 30; 33; 35(2); 36; 12:1; 5; 13:3(2); 5; 7; 8; 11; 16(3); 18; 14:3; 16(2); 15:2; 11(2); 18; 16:6; 10(2); 13(3); 15(2); 17:2(2); 9; 18:3(2); 19; 23; 25; 19:9; 17(2); **Ruth** 1:15; 16(2); 17; 2:8; 9(2); 10; 11(3); 12; 13(2); 14; 19(2); 21; 22; 3:2; 4(3); 5; 9(2); 10(3); 11(2); 15; 16; 18; 4:4(2); 5(2); 6; 11; **1Sa** 1:8(2); 11; 14; 17; 23; 2:16; 32; 3:5; 6; 8; 9; 17; 4:20; 8:5; 9:16; 21; 27; 10:2(3); 3(2); 4; 5(3); 6; 7; 8(3); 12:4(2); 13:11(2); 13(2); 14; 14:37; 43; 44; 15:1; 7; 13; 17(2); 19; 23; 26; 28; 16:1; 3(2); 4; 16; 17:28(4); 33(2); 43; 45(2); 52; 56; 58(2); 18:17; 21; 19:3; 5(2); 11(2); 17; 20:2; 8(3); 13; 14; 15; 18; 19(3); 21; 23; 30(2); 31; 21:1; 9(2); 22:12; 13(2); 16(2); 18; 23(2); 23:17; 24:4; 9; 11(2); 14; 17(2); 18(3); 19; 20; 21(2); 25:6; 7; 17; 25; 31; 33; 34; 26:11; 14(2); 15(2); 16; 25(2); 27:8; 28:1(3); 2; 9(2); 12(2); 13; 15(2); 16; 18; 19; 21; 22(3); 29:4; 6; 7; 8; 9; 30:8; 13(2); 15(2); **2Sa** 1:3; 5; 8; 13; 14; 25; 26; 2:20; 26(2); 27; 3:7; 8; 13(3); 21; 24(2); 25(2); 34; 5:2(3); 6(2); 19; 23; 24(2); 25; 6:22; 7:5; 8; 9; 12; 18; 19; 20; 21; 22; 23; 24(2); 25(2); 27; 28(2); 29; 9:2; 7; 8; 10(2); 10:3; 11; 11:10(2); 11; 19; 21; 25(2); 12:7; 9(2); 10; 12; 13; 14; 21(3); 13:4(2); 12; 13; 16; 14:11; 13; 15:2; 19(2); 20(2); 27; 33(2); 34(2); 35(3); 16:2; 7(2); 8(3); 10; 17; 21; 17:3; 6; 8; 11; 18:3(3); 11(2); 13; 20(3); 21; 22(2); 19:5; 6(3); 7; 13(2); 14; 19; 23; 25; 28; 29(2); 33; 38; 20:4; 6; 9; 17; 19(2); 21:4; 17(2); 22:3; 26(2); 27(2); 28(2); 29; 36; 37; 40(2); 41; 44(2); 49(2); 24:13; **1Kin** 1:6; 11; 12; 13; 14; 16; 17; 18; 20(2); 24; 27; 42; 2:2; 3(3); 5; 8; 9(3); 13; 15; 22; 26(3); 31; 37(3); 42(3); 43; 44(2); 3:6(3); 7; 8; 11; 13; 14; 5:3; 6(3); 8; 9(3); 6:12(2); 8:18; 19; 24(2); 25(2); 26; 28; 29(2); 30(3); 32; 34(2); 35; 36(3); 39(4); 40; 43; 44(2); 45; 46; 48(2); 49; 51; 53(3); 9:3(2); 4; 13; 11:11; 22(2); 37; 38; 12:4; 7; 10(3); 13:8; 9; 14; 17(2); 18; 21; 14:2; 5; 6(2); 8; 9; 12; 16:2; 17:4; 13; 18(2); 20; 24; 18:7; 9; 11; 14; 17; 18(2); 36; 37(2); 19:9; 13; 15; 16(2); 20:5; 9; 13(2); 14; 22; 25; 34; 36(2); 39; 42; 21:5; 7; 10; 19(3); 20(2); 22; 29; 22:4(2); 11(2); 16; 19; 22; 25(2); 28; 30; **2Kin** 1:4(2); 6(3); 9; 16(3); 2:3; 5; 10(2); 23(2); 3:7(2); 4:1; 2; 4(3); 7; 13(2); 16(2); 23; 29; 40; 5:6; 8; 10; 13; 25; 6:9; 12; 22(3); 7:2; 19; 8:1(2); 10; 12(3); 13; 14; 9:2; 7; 18; 19; 25; 10:5(2); 30; 13:17(2); 19(4); 14:10(4); 17:26; 18:14; 19; 20(3); 21; 23; 24; 19:6; 10; 11(2); 15(3); 19(3); 20; 22(2); 23; 25(2); 28; 20:1; 5; 9; 18; 19; 22:18; 19(2); 20; 23:17; **1Chr** 4:10(2); 11:2(3); 5; 12:18; 14:10; 15(2); 17:4; 7(2); 8; 11; 16; 17; 18; 19; 21; 22(2); 23(2); 25(2); 26; 27; 19:3; 12; 21:22; 22:8(3); 11; 12; 13(2); 14; 28:3(2); 9(4); 20; 29:10; 11; 12; 17; **2Chr** 1:8; 9; 11(2); 2:3; 16(2); 6:8; 9; 15(2); 16(2); 17; 20(2); 21(2); 23; 25(2); 26; 27(3); 30(3); 31; 33; 34(2); 35; 36; 38(2); 39; 41; 7:17; 9:6; 10:4; 7; 10(3); 13:4; 14:11; 16:7; 8; 9(2); 18:3(2); 10; 12; 15; 21(2); 24(2); 27; 29; 33; 19:2; 3; 20:6(2); 7; 9; 10; 11; 12; 15; 37; 21:12; 15; 24:6; 25:8; 15; 16(3); 19(5); 26:18; 34:26; 27(2); 28; 35:21; **Ezr** 4:13; 15; 16; 7:14; 16; 17; 19; 20; 25; 9:11; 13; 14(2); 15; 10:12; **Neh** 1:6; 7; 8; 10; 2:2; 4; 5; 6; 5:12; 6:6(3); 7; 8(2); 14; 9:6(4); 7; 8; 10(2); 11(2); 12; 13; 15; 17(2); 19; 20; 21; 22; 23(2); 24; 27(3); 28(3); 29; 30(2); 31(2); 33(2); 34; 35(2); 36; 37; **Est** 3:3; 4:13; 14(3); 5:3; 14(2); 6:10(2); 13(2); **Job** 1:7; 8; 10(2); 2:2; 3(2); 9; 10; 4:2; 3(2); 4; 5(2); 5:1; 17; 21(2); 22(2); 23; 24(2); 25; 26; 27; 7:12; 14; 17(2); 18; 19; 20(2); 21(2); 8:2; 5; 6; 9:12; 28; 31; 10:2; 3(2); 4(2); 6; 7; 8; 9(2); 10; 11; 12; 13; 14(2); 15; 16(2); 17; 18; 11:3; 4; 7(2); 8(2); 13; 15(2); 16; 17(2); 18(3); 19; 13:22(2); 24; 25(2); 26; 27(2); 14:3; 5; 13(3); 15(2); 16(2); 17; 19(2); 20(2); 15:4; 5; 7(2); 8(2); 9(2); 13; 16:3; 7; 8; 18; 17:4(2); 14(2); 20:4; 22:3(2); 6; 7(2); 9; 11; 13; 15; 23(3); 24; 25; 26; 27(2); 28; 29; 26:2(2); 3(2); 4; 30:20(2); 21(2); 22(2); 23; 31:24; 33:5; 8; 12; 13; 32; 34:16; 17; 18; 32; 33(3); 35:2(2); 3; 5; 6(3); 7(2); 8; 14(3); 36:17; 21; 23; 24; 37:6; 15; 16; 18; 38:3; 4(2); 5; 11; 12; 16(2); 17; 18(2); 20(2); 21(2); 22(2); 31; 32(2); 33(2); 34; 35; 39; 39:1(2); 2(2); 10; 11(2); 12; 13; 19(2); 20; 40:7; 8(3); 9(2); 41:1(2); 2; 4; 5(2); 7; 42:2; 4; **Ps** 2:7; 9(2); 3:3; 7(2); 4:1; 6; 7; 8; 5:3; 4; 5; 6; 10; 11; 12(2); 6:3; 7:6; 7; 8:2(2); 3; 4(2); 5; 6(2); 9:2; 4(2); 5(3); 6(2); 10; 13; 10:1(2); 13; 14(3); 15(2); 17(3); 12:7(2); 13:1(2); 16:2(2); 5; 10(2); 11; 17:3(3); 6; 7; 14; 18:25(2); 26(2); 27; 28; 35; 36; 39(2); 40; 43(2); 48(2); 19:12; 21:2; 3(2); 4; 5; 6(2); 9; 10; 12(2); 13; 22:1(2); 2; 3(2); 4; 9(2); 10; 15; 19; 21; 23:4; 5(2); 25:5; 7; 17; 27:8; 9; 28:1; 30:1; 2; 3(2); 7(2); 10; 11(2); 31:2; 3; 4; 5; 7(2); 8; 14; 19(2); 20(2); 22; 32:5; 6; 7(3); 8; 35:17; 22; 36:6; 8; 37:1; 3(2); 10; 34; 38:15; 39:5; 9; 11(2); 40:5; 6(3); 9; 11; 17; 41:2; 3; 10; 11; 12; 42:5(3); 9; 11(3); 43:2(2); 5(2); 44:1; 2(2); 3; 4; 7; 9; 10; 11; 12; 13; 14; 19; 23; 24; 45:2; 7; 11; 16; 48:7; 49:16; 18; 50:15; 16(2); 17; 18(2); 19; 20(2); 21(2); 51:4(3); 6(2); 8; 14; 15; 16(2); 17; 18; 19; 52:1; 3; 4(2); 9; 53:5; 55:13; 23; 56:2; 8(2); 13(2); 57:5; 11; 59:5; 8(2); 16; 60:1(3); 2(2); 3(2); 4; 8; 10(2); 61:3; 5(2); 6; 62:5; 12; 63:1; 7; 65:2; 3; 4; 5; 8; 9(4); 10(4); 11; 66:3; 10(2); 11(2); 12(2); 67:4; 68:7(2); 9(2); 10; 18(3); 28; 30; 35; 69:5; 19; 26(2); 70:5; 71:3(3); 5(2); 6; 7; 17; 20; 21; 22; 23; 73:18(2); 20(2); 23; 24; 27; 74:1; 2(3); 11; 13(2); 14; 15(2); 16; 17(2); 76:4; 7(3); 8; 10; 77:4; 14(2); 15; 20; 79:5; 11; 80:1(2); 4; 5; 6; 8(2); 9; 12; 15; 17; 81:7; 8; 9; 82:8; 83:1; 18; 85:1(2); 2(2); 3(2); 5(2); 6; 86:2; 5; 7; 9; 10(2); 13; 15; 17; 88:5; 6; 7; 8(2); 10; 14(2); 18; 89:2; 9(2); 10(2); 11; 12; 13; 17; 19; 26; 38(2); 39(2); 40(2); 42(2); 43; 44; 45(2); 46; 47; 49; 90:1; 2(2); 3; 5; 8; 15; 17(2); 91:4; 5; 8; 9; 12; 13(2); 92:4; 8; 10; 93:2; 94:2; 12; 13; 97:9(2); 99:4(2); 8(3); 101:2; 102:10; 12; 13; 25; 26(2); 27; 104:1(2); 6; 8; 9; 20; 24; 26; 27; 28(2); 29(2); 30(2); 35; 106:4; 108:5; 11(2); 109:6; 21(2); 27; 28; 110:1; 2; 3; 4; 114:5(4); 7; 115:9; 116:8; 16; 118:13; 21; 28(2); 119:4; 12; 18; 21; 25; 26; 28; 32; 37; 49; 57; 65; 68; 75; 82; 84; 86; 90; 93; 98; 102; 114; 117; 118; 119; 132(2); 137; 138; 151; 152; 171; 120:3; 123:1; 128:2(2); 5; 6; 130:3; 4; 132:8; 137:8; 138:2; 3; 7(2); 139:1; 2(2); 3; 4; 5; 8(2); 13(2); 19; 140:6; 7; 142:3; 5; 7; 143:10; 144:3(2); 145:15; 16; **Prov** 1:10; 15; 2:1; 2; 3; 4; 5; 9; 20; 3:4; 15; 23; 24(3); 28; 31; 4:8; 12(3); 5:2; 6(2); 9; 11; 19; 20; 6:1(2); 2(2); 3; 6; 9(2); 22(3); 35; 7:4; 9:12(4); 14:7; 19:19(2); 20; 20:13(2); 22; 22:18; 21; 24; 25; 26; 27; 29; 23:1; 2; 5; 6(2); 8(2); 13; 14; 17; 19; 31; 34; 35; 24:1; 6; 10; 11; 12; 13; 14; 19; 21; 24; 25:7; 8; 16(2); 22; 26:4; 12; 27:1; 22; 23; 27; 29:20; 30:4; 6(2); 10; 32(2); 31:29; **Eccl** 5:1; 2; 4(2); 5(2); 6; 7; 8; 7:10(2); 16; 17(2); 18; 21; 22; 8:4; 9:9(2); 10; 10:17; 11:1; 2; 5(2); 6; 9; 12:1; **Song** 1:7(3); 8(2); 15(3); 16; 2:17; 4:1(3); 7; 9(2); 16; 5:9(2); 6:1; 4; 7:6; 8:1; 12; 13; 14; **Is** 1:26; 2:6; 3:6(2); 7:3; 16; 9:3; 4; 12:1(3); 6; 14:3; 4; 8; 10(2); 12(2); 13; 15; 19; 20(2); 29; 31; 16:4; 17:10(2); 11(2); 22:1; 2; 8; 16(3); 18; 23:2; 4; 12(3); 16(2); 25:1(2); 2; 4; 5; 26:3; 7; 12(2); 14; 15(4); 20; 27:8; 29:4; 6; 30:19; 22(2); 23; 33:1(4); 2; 19(3); 36:4; 5(3); 6; 7; 8; 9; 37:6; 10; 11(2); 16(3); 20(2); 21; 23(2); 24; 26(2); 29; 38:1; 12; 13; 16; 17(2); 39:7; 8; 40:27; 28(2); 41:8; 9(2); 10; 12; 14; 15; 16(2); 42:20; 43:1; 2(3); 4(2); 22(2); 23(2); 24(4); 26(2); 44:2; 17; 21(3); 26; 28; 45:3; 4; 5; 9; 10(2); 15; 47:1; 5(2); 6(2); 7(2); 8; 10(3); 11(3); 12(3); 13; 15; 48:4; 5; 6(2); 7(2); 8(3); 17; 18; 49:3; 6(2); 9; 18; 20(2); 21; 23; 51:9; 10; 12(2); 16; 17; 21; 22; 23; 53:10; 54:1(2); 3; 4(4); 6; 11; 14(3); 17; 55:5(2); 57:6(2); 7(2); 8(5); 9; 10(4); 11(3); 13; 58:3(2); 5; 7(4); 9(3); 10; 11; 12(2); 13; 14; 60:5; 15; 16(2); 18; 62:2; 3; 4(2); 8; 12; 63:2; 14; 16(2); 17; 19; 64:1(2); 3(2); 5(2); 7; 8(2); 12(2); 65:5; **Jer** 1:5; 7(2); 11; 12; 13; 17; 2:2; 17(2); 18(2); 19; 20(2); 21; 22; 23(3); 25; 27(2); 28; 33(2); 35(2); 36(3); 37(2); 3:1; 2(3); 3(2); 4(2); 5(2); 6; 7; 12; 13; 19; 22; 4:1(3); 2; 10; 14; 19; 30(6); 5:3(2); 15; 17; 19; 6:8; 27; 7:16; 17; 27(2); 28; 8:4; 10:6; 24; 11:3; 14; 15(2); 18; 21; 12:1; 2(2); 3(2); 5(4); 13:4; 12; 13; 21(2); 22; 25; 27; 14:7; 8; 9(2); 17; 19(2); 22(2); 15:2; 5; 6(2); 10; 14; 15; 17; 18; 19(5); 16:2(2); 8; 10; 11; 17:4(2); 14; 16; 17; 18:22; 23; 19:10; 20:6(5); 7(2); 21:8; 22:2; 6; 15(2); 21(2); 22; 23; 25; 23:33; 37; 24:3; 25:27; 28; 30; 26:4; 8; 9; 27:13; 28:6; 7; 13(2); 15; 16(2); 29:24; 25; 26; 27; 30:10; 13(2); 15; 31:4(2); 5; 18(3); 21; 22(2); 32:3; 17; 18; 22; 23(2); 24(2); 25; 33:3; 24; 34:3(2); 4; 5; 14; 36:6(3); 14; 17; 19; 29(3); 37:13; 17; 20; 38:15(2); 17(2); 18(2); 21; 23(2); 24; 25; 26; 39:17(2); 18(2); 40:14; 16(2); 43:2; 44:16; 45:3; 4; 5(2); 46:11(2); 19; 27; 28; 47:5; 6(2); 48:2; 7(2); 18; 27(2); 49:4; 12(3); 16(2); 50:24(4); 31; 51:13; 20; 26; 61; 62(2); 63(2); 64; **Lam** 1:10; 21(3); 22; 2:20; 21(2); 22; 3:17; 42; 43(3); 44; 45; 56; 57(2); 58(2); 59(2); 60; 61; 4:21; 5:19; 20; 21; 22(2); **Eze** 2:4; 6(2); 7; 8(2); 3:1; 5; 6; 18(2); 19(2); 20; 21(2); 25(2); 26; 27; 4:1; 3(2); 4(3); 5; 6(2); 7(2); 8(2); 9(3); 10(2); 11(2); 12(2); 15; 5:1; 2(3); 3; 11; 7:2; 7; 8:6(2); 12; 13; 15(2); 17; 9:8; 11; 11:13; 12:2; 3(2); 4(2); 5; 6(3); 9; 10; 13:2; 17(2); 16:4(3); 5(2); 6(2); 7(3); 8; 13(4); 15; 16; 17; 18; 19; 20(3); 21; 22(2); 24; 25; 26; 28(3); 29(2); 30; 31(2); 33; 34(2); 36; 37(3); 41; 43(2); 45(2); 47(2); 48(2); 51(2); 52(5); 54(3); 55; 58; 59; 61(2); 62; 63(2); 17:9; 19:1; 20:4(2); 21:6; 7(2); 14; 19(2); 25; 28(2); 30; 32(2); 22:2(4); 3; 4(4); 8; 12(2); 13; 16(2); 24; 23:21; 27; 28; 30(2); 31; 32(2); 33; 34(2); 35(2); 36; 40; 41; 24:13(2); 16; 19(2); 25; 27(2); 25:3; 6; 7; 26:14(2); 17; 20; 21(3); 27:2; 3(2); 7; 25; 33(2); 34; 36; 28:2(3); 3; 4; 5; 6; 8; 9(2); 10; 12; 13(2); 14(3); 15(2); 16; 17; 18; 19(2); 29:5(2); 7(2); 31:2; 10; 18(3); 32:2(3); 6; 9; 19(2); 28; 33:7(2); 8(2); 9(2); 10; 12; 14; 27; 30; 32; 35:4(2); 5; 6; 10; 11; 12(2); 15(2); 36:1; 12(2); 13; 14; 15(2); 37:3; 16; 18(2); 20; 38:7(3); 8(2); 9(3); 10; 11; 13(2); 14; 15(2); 16; 17; 39:1; 4(2); 5; 17; 40:4(2); 43:10; 19; 20(2); 21; 22; 23(2); 24; 25; 44:6; 45:3; 18; 20; 46:13(2); 14; 47:6; **Dan** 1:13; 2:23(2); 26; 30; 31; 34; 37; 38; 41(2); 43; 45; 47; 3:10; 12(2); 18; 4:18(2); 20; 22; 25; 26; 32; 35; 5:13; 16(3); 18; 22(2); 23(3); 27; 6:12; 13; 16; 20; 8:20; 26; 9:7; 23; 10:12; 19; 20; 12:4; 13(2); **Hos** 2:16; 20; 23(2); 3:3(3); 4:5; 6(3); 15; 5:3; 9:1(2); 14; 10:9; 13; 12:6; 13:4; 9; 10; 14:1; **Amos** 5:23; 7:8; 12; 16(2); 17; 8:2; **Obad** 2; 3; 4(2); 5; 10; 11(2); 12(3); 13(2); 14(2); 15; **Jonah** 1:6; 8(2); 10; 14; 2:2; 3; 6; 4:2; 4; 9; 10(2); **Mic** 1:11; 13; 14; 2:5; 7; 4:8; 9; 10(4); 13; 5:2(2); 12; 13; 6:1; 14(3); 15(4); 7:19; 20(2); **Nah** 1:14; 3:8; 11(3); 16; **Hab** 1:2(2); 3; 12(3); 13(2); 2:7; 8; 10; 15; 16(2); 3:8; 9; 12(2); 13(2); 14; 15; **Zeph** 3:7(2); 11(3); 15; 16; **Zec** 1:3; 12(2); 14; 2:2; 11; 3:7(3); 8; 4:2; 5; 7(2); 9; 13; 5:2; 6:10; 13:3(2); **Mal** 1:2; 2:14; **Mt** 1:20; 21; 2:6; 13; 3:14; 4:3; 6(2); 7; 9; 10(2); 5:21; 22; 23; 25(2); 26(2); 27; 33; 36(2); 42; 43; 6:2; 3; 5(2); 6(3); 17(2); 18; 7:3; 4; 5(2); 8:2(2); 3; 4; 8; 13; 19; 29(2); 31; 9:27; 11:3; 23; 25; 12:37(2); 13:10; 27; 28; 14:28; 31(2); 33; 15:5; 12; 22; 28; 16:14; 16; 17; 18; 19(2); 23(2); 17:4; 25; 27(3); 18:15; 28; 32(2); 33; 19:17(2); 18(4); 19; 21(3); 20:12; 13; 21; 30; 31; 21:16(2); 21(2); 23; 22:12; 16(3); 17; 37; 39; 44; 23:26; 37; 25:20; 21(3); 22; 23(2); 24(3); 25; 26(2); 27; 26:17; 25; 34; 39; 50; 53; 62; 63(2); 64; 68; 69; 70; 73; 75; 27:4; 11(2); 13; 19; 40(2); 46; **Mk** 1:11; 24(3); 40(2); 41; 44; 3:11; 4:38; 5:7(2); 8; 31(2); 35; 6:22; 23; 25; 7:11; 8:29; 33; 9:22; 23; 24; 25; 10:18; 19; 21(3); 35; 47; 48; 51; 11:21; 23(2); 28; 12:14(2); 30; 31; 32; 34; 36; 13:2; 14:12(2); 30; 36; 37(2); 60; 61; 67; 68; 70(2); 72; 15:2(2); 4; 29; 34; **Lk** 1:4(2); 13; 14; 20(2); 28(2); 30; 31; 42; 76(2); 2:29; 31; 48; 3:22; 4:3; 7; 8(2); 9; 11; 12; 34(3); 41; 5:10; 12(2); 13; 6:41; 42(4); 7:6; 19; 20; 43; 44(2); 45; 46; 8:28; 45; 9:54; 57; 60; 10:15; 21; 26; 27; 28(2); 35; 36; 37; 40; 41; 11:27; 45; 12:19; 20(2); 41; 58(3); 59(2); 13:9; 12; 15; 26; 14:8(2); 9; 10(2); 12; 13; 14(2); 22; 15:29; 30; 31; 16:2; 5; 7; 25(2); 27; 17:4; 6(2); 8; 18:19; 20; 22(3); 38; 39; 41; 19:17(3); 19; 21(4); 22(2); 23; 42(2); 44; 20:2; 21(2); 39; 42; 22:9; 32; 34(2); 42; 48; 58; 60; 61; 67; 70; 23:3(2); 37; 39; 40(2); 42; 43; 24:18; **Jn** 1:19; 21(2); 22(2); 25(2); 33; 38; 42(2); 48(2); 49(2); 50(2); 2:10; 18(2); 20; 3:2(2); 8; 10; 26; 4:9; 10(2); 11(2); 12; 17; 18(3); 19; 27(2); 5:6; 14; 6:25; 30(2); 68; 69; 7:3; 4; 20; 52; 8:5; 13; 25; 33; 48; 52(2); 53(2); 57(2); 9:17; 28; 34(2); 35; 37; 10:24(2); 33; 36; 11:3; 8; 21; 22; 26; 27; 32; 40(2); 41; 42(2); 12:34; 13:6; 7(2); 8(2); 27; 36(3); 38(2); 14:5; 9(2); 10; 22; 16:5; 29; 30(2); 17:2(2); 3; 4; 5; 6(2); 7; 8(2); 9; 11; 12; 15(2); 18; 21(2); 22; 23(3); 24(3); 25; 26; 18:9; 17; 21; 22; 23; 25; 33; 34; 35; 37(2); 19:9; 10(2); 11; 12(2); 20:13; 15(4); 29(2); 21:12; 15(2); 16(2); 17(4); 18(6); 22; **Acts** 1:6; 24(2); 2:27(2); 28(2); 34; 4:24; 27; 5:4(2); 7:28(2); 33; 8:20; 21; 23; 30(2); 37(2); 9:4; 5(2); 6(2); 17(2); 10:6; 15; 33(2); 11:3; 9; 14; 12:15; 13:10(3); 11; 33; 35; 47; 16:31; 17:19; 20; 21:20; 21; 22; 24; 37; 38; 22:7; 8(2); 14; 15(2); 16; 26; 27; 23:3(2); 4; 5; 11(2); 19; 20; 21; 22(2); 24:4; 10; 11; 25:9; 10; 12(2); 22; 26:1; 14; 15(2); 16; 24; 27(2); 28; 29; 27:24; 28:22; **Rom** 2:1(5); 3(2); 4; 17; 19; 21(4); 22(4); 23(2); 25(2); 3:4(2); 7:7; 9:19; 20(2); 10:9(2); 11:17; 18(2); 19; 20; 22(2); 24; 12:20; 13:3(2); 4; 9(6); 14:4; 10(2); 15; 22; **1Cor** 4:7(5); 7:16(4); 21(2); 27(2); 28(2); 9:9; 14:16(2); 17; 15:36(2); 37(2); **Gal** 2:14(2); 4:7; 27(2); 5:14; 6:1; **Eph** 5:14; 6:3; **Col** 4:17(2); **1Ti** 1:3; 18; 3:15(2); 4:6(3); 12; 16; 5:18; 21; 6:11; 12; 14; **2Ti** 1:6; 8(2); 13; 15; 18; 2:1; 2(2); 3; 3:10; 14(3); 15; 4:5; 13; 15; **Titus** 1:5; 2:1; 3:8; **Philem** 1:5; 12; 15; 17; 19; 21; **Heb** 1:5; 9; 10; 11; 12(2); 2:6(2); 7(2); 8; 5:5; 6; 7:17; 21; 8:5; 10:5(2); 6; 8; 12:5(2); **Jas** 2:3(2); 8; 11(3); 18; 19(2); 20; 22; 4:11(2); 12; **3Jn** 2; 3; 5(2); 6(2); **Rev** 1:11; 19; 20(2); 2:2(2); 4; 5(2); 6(2); 9; 10(2); 13(2); 14; 15; 20; 3:1(2); 3(3); 4; 8; 10; 11; 15(2); 16; 17(2); 18(3); 4:11(2); 5:9(2); 6:6; 10; 7:14; 10:11; 11:17; 18; 15:3; 4; 16:5(2); 6; 17:7; 8; 12; 15; 16; 18; 18:14; 20; 19:10; 22:9

THOUGH

Gen 31:30; 33:10; 40:10; **Lev** 5:17; 11:7; 25:35; **Num** 18:27; **Deut** 29:19; **Josh** 17:18(2); **Judg** 13:16; 15:3; 7; **Ruth** 2:13; **1Sa** 14:39; 20:20; 21:5; **2Sa** 1:21; 3:39; 4:6; 18:12; **1Kin** 2:28; **1Chr** 26:10; **2Chr** 30:19; **Neh** 1:9; 6:1; **Est** 9:1; **Job** 8:7; 9:15; 21; 10:19; 11:12; 13:15; 14:8; 16:6(2); 19:17; 26; 27; 20:6; 12(2); 13; 24:23; 27:8; 16; 30:24; 39:16; **Ps** 23:4; 27:3(2); 35:14; 37:24; 44:19; 46:2(2); 3(2); 49:18; 68:13; 78:23; 99:8; 138:6; 7; **Prov** 6:35; 11:21; 16:5; 27:22; 28:6; 29:19; **Eccl** 6:6; 8:12; 17(2); **Is** 1:18(2); 10:22; 12:1; 30:20; 35:8; 45:4; 5; 49:5; 63:16; **Jer** 2:22; 4:30(3); 5:2; 22(2); 11:11; 12:6; 14:7; 15:1; 22:24; 30:11; 32:5; 33; 37:10; 46:23; 49:16; 51:5; 53(2); **Lam** 3:32; **Eze** 2:6(2); 3:9; 8:18; 12:3; 13; 14:14; 16; 18; 20; 26:21; 28:2; 32:25; 26; 27; **Dan** 5:22; 9:9; **Hos** 4:15; 5:2; 7:13; 15; 8:10; 9:12; 16; 11:7; 13:15; **Amos** 5:22; 9:2(2); 3(2); 4; **Obad** 4(2); 16; **Mic** 5:2; **Nah** 1:12(2); **Hab** 1:5; 2:3; **Zec** 9:2; 10:6; 12:3; **Mt** 26:33; 35; 60; **Lk** 9:53; 11:8; 16:31; 18:4; 7; 24:28; **Jn** 4:2; 8:6; 14; 10:38; 11:25; 12:37; **Acts** 3:12; 13:28; 41; 17:25; 27; 23:15; 20; 27:30; 28:4; 17; **Rom** 4:11; 17; 7:3; 9:6; 27; **1Cor** 4:15; 18; 5:3; 7:29; 30(3); 8:5; 9:16; 19; 13:1; 2(2); 3(2); **2Cor** 4:16; 5:16; 20; 7:8(3); 12; 8:9; 10:3; 8; 14; 11:6; 21; 12:6; 11; 15; 13:4; 7; **Gal** 1:8; 3:15; 4:1; **Phil** 3:4; 12; **Col** 2:5; 20; **Philem** 1:8; **Heb** 5:8; 6:9; 7:5; 12:17; **Jas** 2:14; 3:4; **1Pet** 1:6; 7; 8; 4:12; **2Pet** 1:12; **2Jn** 5; **Jude** 5

THROUGH

Gen 6:13; 12:6; 13:17; 30:32; 41:36; **Ex** 10:15; 12:12; 23; 13:17; 18; 14:16; 24; 19:13; 21; 24; 21:6; 36:33; **Lev** 4:2; 13; 22; 27; 5:15; 18:21; 26:6; **Num** 13:32; 14:7; 15:27; 29; 20:17(3); 19; 20; 21; 21:22; 23; 24:8; 25:8(2); 31:16; 23(2); 33:8; **Deut** 1:19; 2:4; 7; 8; 18; 27; 28; 5:15; 8:15; 9:26; 15:17; 18:10; 29:16; 31:29; 32:47; 33:11; **Josh** 1:11; 2:15; 3:2; 18:4; 8; 9; 12; 24:17; **Judg** 2:22; 3:23; 5:6; 26; 28; 9:54; 11:16; 17; 18; 19; 20; 20:12; **1Sa** 9:4(4); 19:12; 31:4(2); **2Sa** 2:29(2); 4:7; 6:16; 12:31; 18:14; 20:14; 22:13; 30; 23:16; 24:2; 8; **2Kin** 1:2; 3:8; 26; 10:21; 16:3; 17:17; 21:6; 23:10; 24:20; **1Chr** 10:4; 11:18; **2Chr** 19:4; 23:20; 24:9; 30:10; 31:18; 32:4; 33:6; **Ezr** 6:14; **Neh** 9:11; **Est** 6:9; 11; **Job** 7:14; 14:9; 20:24; 22:13; 24:16; 26:12; 29:3; 7; 40:24; 41:2; **Ps** 8:8; 10:4; 18:29; 19:4; 21:7; 23:4; 32:3; 44:5(2); 60:12; 66:3; 6; 12(2); 68:7; 73:9; 78:13; 81:5; 84:6; 92:4; 106:9(2); 107:39; 108:13; 109:24; 110:5; 115:7; 119:98; 104; 136:14; 16; **Prov** 7:6; 8; 23; 11:9; 18:1; 24:3; **Eccl** 5:3; 10:18(2); **Song** 2:9; **Is** 8:8; 21; 9:19; 13:15; 14:19; 16:8; 21:1; 23:10; 27:4; 28:7(4); 15; 18; 30:31; 34:10; 43:2(3); 48:21; 60:15; 62:10(2); 63:13; **Jer** 2:6(5); 3:9; 5:1; 9:6; 10; 12; 12:12; 17:24; 32:35; 51:4; 52; 52:3; **Lam** 3:44; 4:9; 21; **Eze** 5:17; 6:8; 9:4(2); 5; 12:5; 7; 12; 14:5; 15(2); 17; 16:14; 21; 36; 40; 20:23; 26; 31; 23:37; 29:11(2); 12; 30:23; 33:28; 34:6; 36:19; 39:14; 15; 41:19; 46:19; 47:3; 4(2); **Dan** 8:25; 9:7; 11:2; 10; **Joel** 3:17; **Amos** 2:10; 5:17; **Jonah** 3:7; **Mic** 2:13; 5:8; **Nah** 1:12; 15; 3:4(2); **Hab** 1:6; 3:12; 14; 15(2); **Zec** 1:10; 11; 17; 4:10; 12; 5:6; 6:7(3); 7:14; 9:8; 15; 10:7; 11; 13:3; 9; **Mt** 6:19; 20; 9:34; 12:1; 43; 19:24; **Mk** 2:23; 6:55; 7:13; 31; 9:30; 10:25; 11:16; **Lk** 1:78; 2:35; 4:14; 30; 5:19; 6:1; 9:6; 10:17; 11:15; 18; 24; 12:39; 13:22; 17:1; 11; 18:25; 19:1; **Jn** 1:7; 3:17; 4:4; 8:59; 15:3; 17:11; 17; 19; 20; 20:31; **Acts** 1:2; 3:16; 17; 4:2; 8:18; 40; 10:43; 12:10; 13:6; 38; 14:22; 15:3; 11; 41; 16:4; 17:1; 18:27; 19:1; 21; 20:3; 21:4; **Rom** 1:8; 24; 2:23; 24; 3:7; 24; 25(2); 30; 31; 4:13(2); 20; 5:1; 9; 11; 15; 21; 6:11; 23; 7:25; 8:3; 13; 37; 11:11; 30; 31; 36; 12:3; 15:4; 13; 17; 19; 16:27; **1Cor** 1:1; 4:15; 8:11; 10:1; 13:12; 15:57; 16:5(2); **2Cor** 3:4; 4:15; 8:9; 9:11; 10:4; 11:3; 33; 12:7; 13:4; **Gal** 2:19; 3:8; 14(2); 4:7; 13; 5:5; 10; **Eph** 1:7; 2:7; 8; 18; 22; 4:6; 18; **Phil** 1:19; 2:3; 3:9; 4:7; 13; **Col** 1:14; 20; 22; 2:8; 12; **2Th** 2:13; 16; **1Ti** 6:10; **2Ti** 1:10; 3:15; **Titus** 1:3; 3:6; **Philem** 1:22; **Heb** 2:10; 14; 15; 3:13; 6:12; 9:14; 10:10; 20; 11:3; 11; 28; 29; 33; 39; 12:20; 13:20; 21; **1Pet** 1:2; 5; 6; 22; 4:11; **2Pet** 1:1; 2; 3; 4; 2:3; 18(2); 20; **1Jn** 4:9; **Rev** 8:13; 18:3; 22:14

THROUGHOUT

Gen 41:29; 46; 45:8; **Ex** 5:12; 7:19; 21; 8:16; 17; 9:9; 16; 22; 25; 11:6; 12:14; 29:42; 30:8; 10; 21; 31; 31:13; 16; 32:27; 34:3; 35:3; 36:6; 37:19; 40:15; 38; **Lev** 3:17; 7:36; 10:9; 17:7; 23:14; 21; 31; 25:9; 10; 30; **Num** 1:42; 52; 2:3; 9; 16; 24; 32; 3:39; 4:22; 38; 40; 42; 10:8; 25; 11:10; 15:38; 18:23; 26:2; 28:14; 21; 24; 29; 29:4; 10; 31:4; 35:29; **Deut** 16:18; 28:40; 52(2); **Josh** 2:22; 6:27; 16:1; 22:14; 24:3; **Judg** 6:35; 7:22; 24; 20:6; 10; **1Sa** 5:11; 11:7; 13:3; 19; 23:23; **2Sa** 8:14; 15:10; 19:9; **1Kin** 1:3; 6:38; 15:22; 18:6; 22:36; **2Kin** 17:5; **1Chr** 5:10; 6:54; 60; 62; 63; 7:40; 9:34; 12:30; 21:4; 12; 22:5; 26:6; 27:1; **2Chr** 8:6; 11:23; 16:9; 17:9; 19; 19:5; 20:3; 25:5; 26:14; 30:5; 6; 22; 31:20; 34:7;

36:22; **Ezr** 1:1; 10:7; **Est** 1:20; 3:6; 9:2; 4; 28; **Ps** 72:5; 102:24; 135:13; 145:13; **Jer** 17:3; **Eze** 38:21; **Mt** 4:24; **Mk** 1:28; 39; 14:9; **Lk** 1:65; 4:25; 7:17(2); 8:1; 39; 23:5; **Jn** 19:23; **Acts** 8:1; 9:31; 32; 42; 10:37; 11:28; 13:49; 14:24; 16:6; 19:26; 24:5; 26:20; **Rom** 1:8; 9:17; **2Cor** 8:18; **Eph** 3:21; **1Pet** 1:1

THUS

Gen 2:1; 6:22; 19:36; 20:16; 21:32; 24:30; 25:22; 34; 31:8(2); 9; 40; 41; 32:4(2); 36:8; 37:35; 42:25; 45:9; **Ex** 3:14; 15; 4:22; 5:1; 10; 15; 7:17; 8:1; 20; 9:1; 13; 10:3; 11:4; 12:11; 50; 14:11; 30; 19:3; 20:22; 26:17; 24; 29:35; 32:27; 36:22; 29; 39:32; 40:16; **Lev** 15:31; 16:3; **Num** 4:19; 49; 8:7; 14; 26; 10:28; 11:15; 15:11; 18:26; 28; 20:14; 21; 21:31; 22:16; 23:5; 16; 32:8; **Deut** 7:5; 9:25; 20:15; 29:24; 32:6; **Josh** 2:4; 6:3; 7:10; 13; 20(2); 10:25; 16:5; 21:12; 43; 22:16; 24:2; **Judg** 6:8; 8:1; 28; 9:56; 11:15; 33; 13:18; 18:4(2); 20:43; **1Sa** 2:27; 9:9; 10:18; 11:9; 14:9; 10; 15:2; 18:25; 20:7; 22; 25:6; 26:18; **2Sa** 6:22; 7:5; 8; 11:25; 12:7; 11; 31; 15:26; 16:7; 17:15(4); 21; 18:14; 33; 24:12; **1Kin** 1:48; 2:30(3); 3:22; 5:11; 9:8; 11:31; 12:10(2); 24; 13:2; 21; 14:5(2); 7; 16:12; 17:14; 20:2; 5; 13; 14; 28; 42; 21:19(2); 22:11; 27; **2Kin** 1:4; 6; 11; 16; 2:21; 3:16; 17; 4:43; 5:4(2); 7:1; 9:3; 6; 12(3); 18; 19; 10:28; 16:16; 18:19; 29; 31; 19:3; 6(2); 10; 20; 32; 20:1; 5; 21:12; 22:15; 16; 18(2); **1Chr** 15:28; 17:4; 7(2); 18:6; 13; 21:10; 11; 24:4; 5; 29:26; **2Chr** 4:18; 5:1; 7:11; 21; 10:10(2); 11:4; 12:5; 13:18; 18:10; 26; 19:9; 20:15; 21:12; 24:11; 20; 22; 31:20; 32:10; 22; 34:23; 24; 26; 36:23; **Ezr** 1:2; 5:3; 7; 9; 11; 6:2; **Neh** 5:13; 13:18; 30; **Est** 1:18; 2:13; 6:9; 11; 9:5; **Job** 1:5; 27:12; **Ps** 38:14; 63:4; 73:15; 21; 106:20; 29; 39; 128:4; **Is** 7:7; 8:11; 10:24; 21:6; 16; 22:15; 24:13; 28:16; 29:22; 30:12; 15; 31:4; 36:4; 14; 16; 37:3; 6(2); 10; 21; 33; 38:1; 5; 42:5; 43:1; 14; 16; 44:2; 6; 24; 45:1; 11; 14; 18; 47:15; 48:17; 49:7; 8; 22; 25; 50:1; 51:22; 52:3; 4; 56:1; 4; 57:15; 65:8; 13; 66:1; 12; **Jer** 2:2; 5; 4:3; 27; 5:13; 14; 6:6; 9; 16; 21; 22; 7:3; 20; 21; 8:4; 9:7; 15; 17; 22; 23; 10:2; 11; 18; 11:3; 11; 21; 22; 12:14; 13:1; 9; 12; 13; 14:10(2); 15; 15:2; 19; 16:3; 5; 9; 17:5; 19; 21; 18:11; 13; 23; 19:1; 3; 11; 12; 15; 20:4; 21:3; 4; 8; 12; 22:1; 3; 6; 8; 11; 18; 30; 23:2; 15; 16; 35; 37; 38; 24:5; 8; 25:8; 15; 27; 28; 32; 26:2; 4; 18; 19; 27:2; 4(2); 16; 19; 21; 28:2; 11; 13; 14; 16; 29:4; 8; 10; 16; 17; 21; 24; 25; 31; 32; 30:2; 5; 12; 18; 31:2; 7; 15; 16; 18; 23; 35; 37; 32:3; 14; 15; 28; 36; 42; 33:2; 4; 10; 12; 17; 20; 24; 25; 34:2(2); 4; 13; 17; 35:8; 13; 17; 18; 19; 36:29; 30; 37:7(2); 9; 21; 38:2; 3; 4; 17; 39:16; 42:9; 15; 18; 43:7; 10; 44:2; 7; 11; 25; 30; 45:2; 4(2); 47:2; 48:1; 10; 47; 49:1; 7; 12; 20; 35; 50:18; 33; 51:1; 4; 33; 36; 58; 64(2); 52:27; **Eze** 1:11; 2:4; 3:11; 27; 4:13; 5:5; 7; 8; 13; 6:3; 11; 12; 7:2; 5; 11:5(2); 7; 16; 17; 12:10; 19; 23; 28; 13:3; 8; 13; 15; 18; 20; 14:4; 6; 21; 15:6; 16:3; 13; 19; 36; 59; 17:3; 9; 19; 22; 20:3; 5; 27; 30; 39; 47; 21:3; 9; 24; 26; 28; 22:3; 19; 28; 23:4; 7; 21; 22; 27; 28; 32; 35; 39; 46; 48; 24:3; 6; 9; 21; 24; 25:3; 6; 8; 12; 13; 15; 16; 26:3; 7; 15; 19; 27:3; 28:2; 6; 12; 22; 25; 29:3; 8; 13; 19; 30:2; 6; 10; 13; 19; 22; 31:7; 10; 15; 18; 32:3; 11; 33:10; 25; 27(2); 34:2; 10; 11; 17; 20; 30; 35:3; 7; 13; 14; 36:2; 3; 4; 5; 6; 7; 13; 22; 33; 37; 37:5; 9; 12; 19; 21; 38:3; 10; 14; 17; 23; 39:1; 16; 17; 20; 25; 43:18; 20; 44:6; 9; 45:9; 18; 46:1; 15; 16; 47:13; **Dan** 1:16; 2:24; 25; 4:10; 14; 6:6; 7:5; 23; 11:17; 39; **Hos** 10:4; **Amos** 1:3; 6; 9; 11; 13; 2:1; 4; 6; 11; 3:11; 12; 4:12; 5:3; 4; 16; 7:1; 4; 7; 11; 17; 8:1; **Obad** 1; **Mic** 2:3; 3:5; 5:6; **Nah** 1:12(2); **Hag** 1:2; 5; 7; 2:6; 11; **Zec** 1:3; 4; 14; 16; 17; 2:8; 3:7; 6:12; 7:9; 14; 8:2; 3; 4; 6; 7; 9; 14; 19; 20; 23; 11:4; **Mal** 1:4; 13; **Mt** 2:5; 3:15; 15:6; 26:54; **Mk** 2:7; **Lk** 1:25; 2:48; 9:34; 11:45; 17:30; 18:11; 19:28; 31; 22:51; 23:46; 24:36; 40; 46(2); **Jn** 4:6; 9:6; 11:43; 48; 13:21; 18:22; 20:14; **Acts** 19:41; 20:36; 21:11; 26:24; 30; 27:35; **Rom** 9:20; **1Cor** 14:25; **2Cor** 1:17; 5:14; **Phil** 3:15; **Heb** 6:9; 9:6; **Rev** 9:17; 16:5; 18:21

THY

Gen 3:10; 14(2); 15(2); 16(4); 17(3); 19; 4:6; 9; 10; 11(2); 14; 6:18(3); 7:1; 8:16(3); 12:1(3); 2; 7; 13; 18; 19(2); 13:8; 15; 16(2); 14:20; 15:1(2); 5; 13; 15; 18; 16:5; 6(2); 9; 10; 11; 17:5(2); 7(2); 8; 9; 10; 12; 13(2); 15; 19; 18:3(2); 9; 10; 19:12(2); 15(2); 17; 19(3); 20:6; 13; 16; 21:12(3); 13; 22:2; 12; 16; 17(2); 18; 20; 23:6(2); 11; 15; 24:2; 5; 7; 14(3); 17; 19; 23; 40; 43; 44; 46; 51; 60; 25:23(2); 31; 26:3(2); 4(3); 9; 10; 24(2); 27:3(3); 6(2); 9; 10; 13; 19(2); 20; 29(2); 31; 32(2); 35(2); 37; 39; 40(3); 42; 44; 45; 28:2(2); 4; 13(2); 14(2); 29:15; 18; 30:14; 15; 27; 28; 29; 31; 32; 33; 34; 31:3(2); 8(2); 13; 30; 31; 32; 37(2); 38(3); 41(3); 32:4; 5; 6; 9(2); 10; 12; 18; 20; 27; 28; 29; 33:5; 10(2); 35:1; 10(3); 11; 12; 37:10(2); 13; 14; 32; 38:8(2); 11; 13; 18(3); 24; 39:19; 40:13; 19(2); 41:40; 42:10; 11; 13; 43:28; 44:7; 8; 9; 16; 18(2); 21; 22; 24; 27; 30; 31(2); 32; 33; 45:9; 10(4); 11; 17; 46:3; 30; 34; 47:3; 4(2); 5(2); 6; 15; 29(2); 48:1; 2; 4; 5; 6; 11(2); 18; 22; 49:4; 8(3); 18; 25; 26; 50:6; 16; 17(2); 18; **Ex** 2:9; 13; 3:5(2); 6; 18; 4:6; 7; 9; 10; 12; 14; 15; 16; 19; 23(2); 5:15; 16(2); 23(2); 7:1(2); 2; 9; 19; 8:2; 3(5); 4(2); 5; 9(3); 10; 11(3); 16; 21(3); 23; 9:3; 14(2); 15; 19; 30; 10:2(2); 4; 6(4); 29; 11:8; 12:24; 13:5; 7; 8; 9; 11; 13; 14; 14:16; 15:6(2); 7; 8; 10; 12; 13(3); 16; 17; 26; 17:5; 18:6(2); 20:2; 5; 7; 9; 10(8); 12(4); 16; 17(3); 24(3); 25; 26; 22:26; 28; 29(3); 30; 23:6; 10; 11(3); 12(2); 13; 16(2); 17; 19(2); 25(2); 26(2); 31; 33; 28:1; 2; 4; 41; 29:12; 26; 32:4; 7; 8; 11(2); 12(2); 13; 32; 33:1; 5; 13(4); 15; 16(3); 18; 34:9; 10; 16(2); 19; 20; 24(3); 26(2); **Lev** 2:5; 7; 13(3); 14(2); 5:15; 18; 6:6; 9:7(2); 10:9; 13(2); 14(4); 15; 16:2; 18:7(3); 8(2); 9(3); 10(2); 11(3); 12(2); 13(2); 14; 15(2); 16(2); 20; 21(2); 19:9(2); 10(2); 12; 13; 14; 15; 16(2); 17(2); 18(2); 19(2); 27; 29; 32; 20:19(2); 21:8; 17; 23:22(2); 25:3(2); 4(2); 5(2); 6(4); 7(2); 11; 14(2); 15; 17; 25; 35; 36(2); 37(2); 39; 43; 44(2); 47; 53; 27:2; 3(2); 4; 5; 6(2); 7; 8; 13; 15; 16; 17; 18; 19; 23; 25; 27; **Num** 5:19; 20; 21(3); 22(3); 11:11(2); 12; 15; 14:13; 14; 19; 20; 16:10; 11; 16; 18:1(3); 2(3); 3; 7; 8; 9; 11(3); 19(3); 20; 20:8; 14; 16; 17(2); 19; 21:22(2); 34; 22:32; 23:3; 15; 24:5(2); 11; 12; 14; 21(2); 27:13(2); 31:2; 49; 32:4; 5(2); 25; 27; 31; **Deut** 1:21(2); 31; 2:7(4); 27; 30(2); 3:2; 24(5); 4:3; 9(5); 10; 19; 21; 23; 24; 25; 29(3); 30; 31(2); 37; 40(3); 5:6; 9; 11; 12; 13; 14(10); 15(2); 16(5); 20; 21(3); 6:2(5); 3; 5(3); 7; 9(2); 10(2); 13; 15(2); 18; 20; 21; 7:1; 2; 3(2); 4; 6(2); 9; 12(2); 13(7); 16; 18; 19(2); 20; 21; 22; 23; 25; 8:2; 3; 4(2); 5; 6; 7; 10; 11; 13(4); 14; 16(2); 18(2); 19; 9:3(2); 4; 5(3); 6(2); 7; 12; 26(2); 27; 29(3); 10:9; 11; 12(5); 13; 14; 15; 20; 21(2); 22(2); 11:1; 10(2); 12(2); 14(2); 15(2); 20; 29; 12:1; 7; 13; 14(2); 15(3); 17(8); 18(8); 20(4); 21(5); 25; 26(2); 27(4); 28(2); 29; 31; 13:5; 6(7); 10; 12(2); 16; 17; 18(2); 14:2; 21(2); 22; 23(6); 24(2); 25; 26(3); 27; 28; 29(2); 15:3; 4; 5; 6; 7(5); 9(2); 10(2); 11(4); 12; 14(4); 15; 17(2); 18; 19(5); 20(2); 21; 22; 16:1(2); 2; 3; 4; 5(2); 6; 7(2); 8; 10(3); 11(7); 13(2); 14(6); 15(2); 16(2); 17; 18(3); 20; 21; 22; 17:1(2); 2(3); 5; 8(2); 12; 14; 15(3); 18:4(3); 5(2); 6; 9; 12; 13; 14; 15(2); 16; 19:1(2); 2(2); 3(2); 8(4); 9; 10(2); 14(2); 20:1; 13; 14; 16; 17; 21:1; 2(2); 5; 8(2); 10; 11; 13; 23(2); 22:1(2); 2(2); 3; 4; 5; 7; 8; 9(3); 12; 17; 23:5(3); 6; 7; 13; 14(3); 16; 18(2); 19; 20(2); 21(2); 23(3); 24(3); 25(2); 24:4; 9; 10; 13; 14(4); 18; 19(2); 21; 25:3; 13; 15(2); 16; 19(2); 26:1; 2(3); 3; 4; 5; 10(2); 11; 12; 13(3); 15(2); 16(2); 17; 19; 27:2; 3(2); 5; 6(2); 7; 9; 10; 28:1(2); 2; 4(5); 5(2); 7; 8(2); 9; 11(4); 12; 13; 15; 17(2); 18(4); 20; 23(2); 24; 26; 29; 31(2); 32(2); 33(2); 35(2); 36(2); 40; 42(2); 45; 46; 47; 48; 51(4); 52(6); 53(3); 55; 57; 58; 59(2); 62; 64; 65; 66(2); 29:5(2); 11(4); 12(2); 13; 30:1; 2(3); 3(3); 4; 5(3); 6(4); 7; 9(5); 10(3); 14(2); 16(2); 19; 20(4); 31:3; 6; 11; 12(2); 14; 16; 27(2); 32:6; 7(2); 50(2); 33:3(3); 8(3); 9(2); 10(2); 18(2); 25(3); 26; 27; 29(2); 34:4; **Josh** 1:5; 8(2); 9; 17; 18(2); 2:18(4); 19; 5:15(2); 7:9; 10; 8:1; 18; 9:8; 9(2); 24(2); 10:6(2); 14:9(2); 24:12(2); **Judg** 1:3; 5:12; 14; 6:14; 17; 25(2); 26; 30; 7:10; 8:15; 22(2); 9:38; 54; 11:10; 17; 19; 24; 36(2); 13:12; 16; 17(2); 14:3; 13; 15(2); 15:2; 18; 16:6; 15; 17:10; 18:19(2); 25(3); 19:19(2); 20; **Ruth** 1:10; 15(2); 16(2); 2:11(4); 12; 13; 14; 3:3; 9; 12; 17; 4:12; 15(2); **1Sa** 1:8; 14; 17; 18; 26; 2:1; 16; 27; 28; 29; 30(2); 31; 34; 3:9; 10; 4:17; 8:5(2); 9:20(2); 10:2; 12:19(2); 13:13(2); 14; 14:7; 28; 15:15; 21; 24; 30; 33(2); 16:11; 16; 19; 17:17(2); 18; 28; 32; 34; 36; 44; 55; 58; 19:11; 20:1; 3(2); 4; 6; 7; 8(3); 10; 15; 18; 22; 30; 31; 42; 22:14(2); 15; 16; 22; 23; 23:10; 11(2); 20; 24:9; 11(2); 16; 25:7; 8(3); 26; 28; 29(2); 33; 35(2); 26:15(2); 17; 24; 27:5; 28:1; 2; 17; 19; 21(2); 22; 29:6(3); 8; 10; 31:4; **2Sa** 1:16(3); 19; 26; 2:21(2); 22; 3:8; 12; 25(2); 34(2); 4:8; 5:1(2); 6:21; 7:9; 12(4); 16(2); 19(2); 20; 21(2); 23(3); 24; 25; 26(2); 27(2); 28(2); 29(3); 9:2; 6; 7(2); 8; 9; 10(4); 11; 10:3; 11:8(2); 10; 11; 21; 24(2); 25; 12:8(3); 9; 10; 11(3); 13; 13:5(2); 7; 20(3); 24(2); 35; 14:6; 11(2); 15; 17; 19(2); 20; 22(2); 31; 15:2; 3; 8; 15; 19; 20; 21; 27; 34(3); 16:3; 4; 8(2); 17(3); 19(2); 21(2); 17:8(2); 10; 18:28; 29; 19:5(6); 6; 7(2); 14; 19; 20; 26(2); 27; 28; 29; 35(2); 36; 37(2); 20:6; 22:36(2); 24:3; 10; 13(2); 23; **1Kin** 1:2; 12; 13; 14; 17(2); 19; 26(2); 27; 30; 47(2); 2:3; 4; 6; 7(2); 21; 37; 38; 39; 44; 3:6; 7; 8(2); 9(3); 12; 13; 14(2); 22(2); 23(2); 5:5(3); 6(2); 8; 6:12; 8:19(2); 23; 24(2); 25(2); 26(2); 28(2); 29; 30(3); 32; 33(2); 34; 35; 36(4); 38; 39; 41(2); 42(3); 43(4); 44(2); 48; 49; 50; 51; 52(2); 53; 9:3(2); 4; 5(2); 10:6(2); 7; 8(3); 9; 11:11; 12(3); 13; 37; 12:4(2); 7; 9; 10; 28; 13:6; 21; 22(2); 14:9; 12; 15:19(2); 16:3; 17:12; 13; 19; 23; 24; 18:8; 9; 10; 11; 12; 14; 18; 31; 36(2); 44; 19:2; 10(2); 14(2); 15; 16; 20:3(4); 4; 5(4); 6; 9; 31; 32; 33; 34; 39(2); 40(2); 42(3); 21:2; 5; 6; 19; 21; 22:4(2); 13; 23; 30; 49; **2Kin** 1:10; 12; 13(2); 14; 2:2; 3(2); 4; 5(2); 6; 9; 16(2); 3:7(2); 13(2); 4:1(2); 3; 4; 7(2); 24; 26; 29(2); 30; 36; 5:8; 10; 15; 17(2); 18(2); 25; 27; 6:3; 12; 22(2); 28; 29; 8:9; 13; 9:1; 7; 22; 10:5; 15; 30; 14:9; 10; 15:12; 16:7(2); 18:23; 24; 26; 27; 19:4(3); 10; 22; 23; 27(4); 28(4); 20:3; 5(3); 6; 17; 18; 22:9; 19; 20(2); **1Chr** 10:4; 11:1(2); 2; 12:18(2); 16:35(2); 17:11(4); 17; 18(2); 19; 21(2); 22; 23; 24(2); 25(2); 26; 27; 19:3; 21:8; 12; 17; 22:11; 12; 28:6; 9; 21; 29:13; 17; 18; 19(3); **2Chr** 1:9; 10; 2:8(2); 10; 14(2); 6:2; 9(2); 14; 15(2); 16(2); 17(2); 19(2); 20(2); 21(3); 23; 24(2); 25; 26; 27(4); 29; 30; 31; 32(4); 33(4); 34(2); 38; 39(2); 41(4); 42; 7:12; 17; 18(2); 9:5; 6; 7(3); 8(3); 10:4(2); 7; 9; 10; 14:11; 16:3(2); 7; 18:3; 12; 22; 29; 20:7(2); 8; 9(2); 11; 37; 21:12(2); 13(2); 14(4); 15(2); 25:18; 34:16; 27; 28(2); **Ezr** 4:11; 15; 7:14; 18; 19; 20; 25(2); 26; 9:10; 11; 14; **Neh** 1:6(2); 7; 8; 10(4); 11(4); 2:2; 5(2); 6; 9:5; 8; 14(2); 16; 17; 18; 19; 20(2); 25; 26(2); 27; 28; 29(3); 30(2); 31; 32; 34(3); 35; 13:22; **Est** 3:8; 4:14(2); 5:3; 6(2); 7:2(2); 3; 9:12(2); **Job** 1:11; 12; 18(2); 2:5; 4:4; 6(4); 5:24(2); 25; 26; 27; 8:2; 4; 5; 6; 7(2); 21(2); 10:5(2); 12; 17; 11:3; 14; 15; 16; 18; 13:21; 24; 14:13; 15:5; 10; 12; 13(2); 21:14; 22:3; 5; 6; 23; 25; 26(2); 27(2); 28; 30:21; 33:5; 6; 8; 31; 33; 34:33; 35:4; 6; 8(2); 36:16; 19; 37:17; 38:3; 11; 12; 21; 34; 39:9; 11; 12(2); 26; 27; 40:7; 11; 41:5; 42:7; **Ps** 2:8; 3:8(2); 4:6; 5:5; 7(4); 8(2); 11; 6:1; 4; 8:1(2); 3(2); 6; 9; 9:1; 2; 3; 10; 14(2); 19; 10:5; 14; 13:1; 5(2); 15:1(2); 16:11(2); 17:2; 4; 5; 7(2); 8; 13; 14(2); 15(2); 18:15(2); 35(3); 49; 19:11; 13; 14; 20:3(2); 4; 5(2); 21:1(2); 5; 6; 8; 12; 13; 22:22; 23:4(2); 24:6; 25:4(2); 5; 6(2); 7(2); 11; 26:3(2); 7; 8; 27:8; 9(2); 11; 28:2; 9; 30:7(2); 9; 31:1; 3; 7; 15; 16(3); 19; 20; 32:4; 33:22; 34:13(2); 35:3; 24; 28(2); 36:5(2); 6(2); 7(2); 8(2); 9; 10(2); 37:5; 6(2); 38:1(2); 2; 39:10; 12; 40:5(2); 8(2); 10(5); 11(3); 16; 41:12; 42:3; 7(3); 10; 43:3(4); 44:2; 3(2); 5; 8; 12(2); 17; 18; 22; 24; 26; 45:2; 3(4); 4(2); 6(2); 7(2); 8; 9(2); 10; 11(2); 12; 16(2); 17; 48:9(2); 10(3); 11; 50:7; 8(2); 9(2); 14; 16; 19(2); 20; 51:1(2); 4; 9; 11(2); 12(2); 13; 14; 15; 18; 52:2; 5; 9(2); 54:1(2); 5; 6; 55:22; 56:8(2); 12; 57:1; 5; 10(2); 11; 59:11; 16(2); 60:3; 5(2); 61:4(2); 5; 8; 63:2(2); 3; 4; 7; 8; 65:4(3); 8; 11(2); 66:3(2); 4; 13; 67:2(2); 68:7; 10(2); 23(2); 24; 28(2); 29; 35; 69:7; 13(2); 16(2); 17(2); 24; 27; 29; 70:4; 71:2; 8(2); 15(2); 16; 17; 18(2); 19; 22; 24; 72:1(2); 2(2); 73:15; 24; 28; 74:1; 2; 3; 4; 7(2); 10; 11(3); 13; 18; 19(2); 21; 75:1(2); 76:6; 7; 77:11; 12(2); 13; 14; 15; 18; 19(3); 20; 79:1; 2(2); 5; 6(2); 8; 9(2); 10; 11; 13(3); 80:2; 3; 4; 7; 15; 16; 17(2); 18; 19; 81:10(2); 83:1; 3(2); 15(2); 16; 84:1; 4; 10; 85:1; 2; 3; 6; 7(2); 86:2; 4; 8; 9; 11(3); 12; 13; 16(2); 88:5; 7(2); 11(2); 12(2); 14; 15; 16(2); 89:1; 2; 4(2); 5(2); 8; 10; 12; 13(2); 14(2); 15; 16(2); 17; 19; 39; 46; 49(2); 50; 90:4; 7; 8; 9; 11(2); 13; 14; 16(3); 91:4; 7(2); 9; 10; 11; 12; 92:1; 2(2); 4(2); 5(2); 93:2; 5; 94:5; 12; 18; 19; 97:8; 99:3; 102:2; 10; 12; 14; 15; 24; 25; 27; 28; 103:3; 4; 5(2); 104:7(2); 13; 24(2); 29; 30; 106:4(2); 5(2); 7(2); 47(2); 108:4(2); 5; 6(2); 109:1; 21(2); 26; 27; 28; 110:1; 2; 3(3); 5; 115:1(3); 116:7; 16(2); 119:4; 5; 6; 7; 8; 9; 10; 11; 12; 13; 14; 15(2); 16(2); 17(2); 18; 19; 20; 21; 22; 23(2); 24; 25; 26; 27(2); 28; 29; 30; 31; 32; 33; 34; 35; 36; 37; 38(3); 39; 40(2); 41(3); 42; 43; 44; 45; 46; 47; 48(2); 49; 50; 51; 52; 53; 54; 55(2); 56; 57; 58(2); 59; 60; 61; 62; 63; 64(2); 65(2); 66; 67; 68; 69; 70; 71; 72; 73(2); 74; 75; 76(3); 77(2); 78; 79; 80; 81(2); 82; 83; 84; 85; 86; 87; 88(2); 89; 90; 91; 92; 93; 94; 95; 96; 97; 98; 99; 100; 101; 102; 103; 104; 105; 106; 107; 108; 109; 110; 111; 112; 113; 114; 116; 117; 118; 119; 120; 122; 123(2); 124(3); 125(2); 126; 127; 128; 129; 130; 131; 132; 133; 134; 135(3); 136; 137; 138; 139; 140(2); 141; 142(2); 143; 144; 145; 146; 147; 148; 149(2); 150; 151; 152; 153; 154; 155; 156(2); 157; 158; 159(2); 160(2); 161; 162; 163; 164; 165; 166(2); 167; 168(2); 169; 170; 171; 172(2); 173; 174(2); 175; 176(2); 121:3; 5(3); 7; 8(2); 122:2; 7(2); 9; 128:3(3); 5; 6; 132:8(2); 9(2); 10; 11(2); 12(2); 135:13(2); 137:9; 138:2(6); 4; 7; 8; 139:7(2); 10(2); 14; 16; 17; 20; 140:13(2); 142:7; 143:1(2); 2(2); 5(2); 7; 8; 10(2); 11(2); 12(2); 144:5; 145:1; 2; 4(2); 5(2); 6(2); 7(2); 10(2); 11(2); 13(2); 146:10; 147:12; 13(2); 14; **Prov** 1:8(2); 9(2); 14; 15; 2:3; 10; 3:3; 6(2); 8(2); 9; 10(2); 22(2); 23(2); 24; 26(2); 28; 29; 4:7; 10; 12; 13; 23; 26(2); 27; 5:2; 8; 9; 10(2); 11(2); 16; 18(2); 6:1(2); 2(2); 3(2); 9; 11(2); 20(2); 21; 7:3; 4; 15; 9:11(2); 16:3(2); 19:18(2); 20; 22:18; 19; 25; 27; 28; 23:2; 8; 9; 16; 22(2); 25(2); 24:6; 10; 12; 13; 14(2); 27; 28(2); 34(2); 25:8; 9(2); 17(2); 27:10(3); 23(2); 26; 27(3); 29:17(2); 30:32; 31:3(2); 8; 9; **Eccl** 5:1; 2(2); 6(3); 7:9; 17; 21; 9:7(4); 8(2); 9(4); 10(2); 10:4; 16(2); 17(2); 20(2); 11:1; 6; 9(3); 10(2); 12:1(2); **Song** 1:2; 3(2); 4; 7(2); 8(2); 10(2); 2:14(4); 4:1(2); 2; 3(4); 4; 5; 9; 10(2); 11(3); 13; 5:9(2); 6:1(2); 5; 6; 7(2); 7:1(2); 2(2); 3; 4(2); 7(2); 8(2); 9; 8:5; 13; **Is** 1:22(2); 23; 25(2); 26(2); 2:6; 3:6; 12; 25(2); 4:1; 6:7(2); 7:3; 11; 17(2); 8:8; 10:22; 27(2); 30; 14:3(2); 9; 11(2); 19; 20(2); 30(2); 16:3; 9(2); 17:10(2); 11(2); 19:12; 20:2(3); 22:2; 3; 7; 18(2); 19(2); 21(3); 23:10; 25:1(2); 12; 26:8(2); 9; 11; 13; 16; 17; 19(2); 20(2); 29:4(3); 5; 30:19; 20(2); 22(2); 23(2); 33:6; 23; 36:8; 9; 11; 12; 37:4(3); 10; 23; 24; 28(4); 29(4); 38:3; 5(4); 17; 18; 19; 39:6; 7; 40:9; 41:10; 13(2); 14; 43:1; 3(3); 4; 5; 23(2); 24(2); 25(2); 27(2); 44:3; 22(2); 24; 27; 28; 45:3; 4; 9; 47:2; 3(2); 6; 7; 9; 10(3); 12(2); 13; 15(2); 48:4(2); 17(2); 18(2); 19(2); 49:16; 17(2); 19(3); 22(2); 23(3); 25; 26(2); 51:13; 15; 16; 20(2); 22(2); 23(2); 52:1(2); 2; 7; 8; 54:2(3); 3; 4(2); 5(2); 6; 8; 11(2); 12(3); 13(2); 15; 55:5; 57:6(2); 7; 8(2); 9(2); 10; 11; 12(2); 13; 58:1; 7(2); 8(3); 10(3); 11(2); 13(2); 14; 59:21(4); 60:1; 3(2); 4(3); 9(2); 10; 11; 14; 16(2); 17; 18(4); 19(3); 20(3); 21; 62:2(2); 3; 4(3); 5(2); 6; 8(2); 11; 63:2; 14; 15(6); 16; 17(3); 18(2); 19; 64:1; 2(2); 3; 5; 7(2); 8; 9; 10; 12; 66:9; **Jer** 1:9; 17; 2:2; 16; 17; 19(2); 20(2); 23; 25(2); 28(4); 33(2); 34; 36; 37; 3:2(2); 13(2); 4:7(2); 14; 18(3); 30(3); 5:7; 14; 17(7); 10:6; 17; 25(2); 11:13(2); 16; 20; 21; 12:1; 6(2); 13:1; 4; 20; 22(2); 25(2); 26(3); 27(2); 14:7; 9; 19; 21(3); 15:11; 13(4); 15(2); 16(3); 17; 17:3(4); 18:20; 23; 20:3; 4; 6; 12; 22:2(2); 7; 15; 17; 20(2); 21(3); 22(3); 23; 25; 26; 27:2; 13; 28:6; 29:25; 30:8(2); 10; 12(2); 13; 14(2); 15(2); 17; 31:4; 7; 16(2); 17; 21; 32:17; 21; 23(2); 34:5; 37:18; 38:16; 17; 20; 22(2); 23(2); 39:18(2); 40:2; 42:2; 3; 5; 45:5; 46:12(2); 15; 27; 47:6; 48:7(2); 18(2); 32(3); 46(2); 49:4; 11(2); 16(2); 50:31; 51:13; 36; **Lam** 1:10; 2:13; 14(2); 19(2); 3:23; 55; 65; 4:22; 5:19; **Eze** 2:1; 8; 3:3(2); 8(2); 9; 11; 19; 21; 26(2); 27; 4:3; 4; 6; 7; 8; 9; 10; 15; 5:1; 3; 11; 6:2; 11; 7:3; 4; 8; 9; 9:8(2); 11:15(3); 12:3; 4; 6(2); 18(2); 13:4; 17(2); 16:3(4); 4(2); 5; 6(2); 7; 8(2); 9; 11(2); 12; 13; 14(2); 15(2); 16(2); 17; 18; 20(3); 22(3); 23; 25(4); 26(2); 27; 29; 33(3); 34; 36(6); 37(3); 39(3); 43(2); 45(2); 46(3); 47; 48(2); 49; 51(2); 52(4); 53; 55(2); 56(3); 57(2); 58; 60; 61(4); 63(2); 19:2; 10(2); 20:46(2); 21:2(2); 6; 12; 16; 30; 32; 22:4(3); 12; 13(2); 15; 23:21(3); 22(2); 25(5); 26(2); 27(2); 28; 29(4); 31; 32; 33; 35(3); 40; 24:13(2); 14(2); 16; 17(3); 27; 25:2; 4(2); 6; 26:8; 9(2); 10(2); 11(3); 12(7); 13(2); 15; 18(2); 27:4(3); 5; 6; 7; 8(3); 9(2); 10(2); 11(4); 12(2); 13(2); 14; 15; 16(3); 17(2); 18(2); 19(2); 20; 21; 22(2); 23; 24(2); 25; 26; 27(10); 28; 33(3); 34(2); 28:4(2); 5(4); 7(2); 13(3); 15; 16; 17(3); 18(2); 21; 29:2; 4(6); 5; 7; 10; 31:2; 32:2(2); 5(2); 6; 8; 9; 10; 12; 33:2; 9; 12; 17; 30; 31; 32; 35:2; 4; 8(3); 9; 11; 12; 36:13; 14; 15; 37:18; 38:2; 4; 7; 9; 10; 13; 15; 39:3(3); 4; **Dan** 1:12; 13; 2:4; 28(3); 29(3); 30; 3:12; 18; 4:22(2); 25; 26; 27(2); 32; 5:10(2); 11(4); 16; 17(2); 18; 23(5); 26; 28; 6:16; 20; 9:5(2); 6(2); 11(2); 13; 15; 16(5); 17(3); 18(2); 19(3); 23; 24(2); 10:12(3); 14; 11:14; 12:1(2); 9; 13(2); **Hos** 2:6; 4:4; 5; 6(2); 6:5; 8:1; 5; 9:1; 10:13(2); 14(2); 12:6(2); 9; 13:4; 10(3); 14(2); 14:1; 8; **Joel** 2:17; 3:11; **Amos** 3:11(2); 4:12; 5:23(2); 6:10; 7:16; 17(4); 8:14; 9:15; **Obad** 4; 7(2); 9; 10(2); 12; 15; **Jonah** 1:6; 8; 2:3(2); 4(2); **Mic** 1:11; 16(2); 4:9; 13; 5:10(2); 11(2); 13(2); 14(2); 6:1; 8; 9; 13; 14; 7:4(2); 5(2); 10; 11; 14(2); 15; **Nah** 1:13; 14(3); 15(2); 2:1(3); 13(3); 3:5(4); 9; 12; 13(3); 14; 16; 17(2); 18(3); 19(2); **Hab** 1:13; 2:10(2); 15; 16(2); 3:2(2); 8(2); 9(2); 11; 13; **Zeph** 1:7; 3:11(2); 15; 17; **Zec** 3:8; 9:9; 11(2); 13(2); 11:1(2); 14:1; **Mal** 1:6; 8(2); 2:14(3); **Mt** 1:20; 4:6; 7; 10; 5:23(2); 24(4); 29(3); 30(3); 36; 39; 40(2); 43; 6:3(2); 4; 6(4); 9; 10(2); 17; 18(2); 22; 23; 7:3; 4; 5; 22(3); 8:4; 13; 9:2; 5; 6; 14; 18; 22; 11:10(2); 26; 12:2; 37(2); 47(2); 13:27; 15:2; 4; 28; 17:16; 18:8(2); 15(2); 33; 19:19(3); 20:14; 21(2); 21:5; 22:37(4); 39; 44; 23:37; 24:3; 25:21; 23; 25; 26:18; 42; 52; 73; **Mk** 1:2(2); 25; 44(2); 2:5; 9(2); 11(2); 18; 3:32(2); 5:9; 19; 23; 34(2); 35; 6:18; 7:5; 10(2); 29(2); 9:18; 38; 43; 45; 10:19; 21; 37(3); 52(2); 12:30(5); 31; 36; 14:70; **Lk** 1:13(2); 31; 36; 38; 42; 44; 61; 2:29(2); 30; 32; 35; 48; 4:8; 11; 12; 23; 35; 5:5; 14; 20; 23; 24; 6:10; 29(2); 30; 41; 42(2); 7:27(2); 48; 50; 8:20(2); 30; 48; 49; 9:40; 41; 49; 10:17; 21; 27(6); 11:2(3); 34(2); 36; 12:20; 13:26; 34; 14:12(4); 15:19(2); 21(2); 27(2); 29; 30(2); 32; 16:2; 6; 7; 25(2); 17:3; 19(2); 18:20(2); 42(2); 19:5; 16; 18; 20; 39; 42(2); 44(2); 20:43; 22:32(2); 23:42; 46; **Jn** 4:16; 18; 42; 50(2); 51; 53; 5:8; 10; 11; 12; 7:3; 8:13; 19; 11:23; 12:15; 28; 13:37; 38; 17:1(2); 6(2); 12; 14; 17(2); 26; 18:11; 19:26; 27; 20:27(2); 21:18; **Acts** 2:28; 35(2); 3:25; 4:25; 27; 28(2); 29(2); 30; 5:9; 7:3(2); 32; 33(2); 8:20; 21; 22; 9:13; 14; 15; 17; 34; 10:4; 31; 11:14; 12:8(2); 14:10; 16:31; 18:9; 22:13; 16; 18; 20; 23:5; 24:2; 4; 25; 26:16; **Rom** 2:5; 17; 23; 25; 3:4; 4:18; 8:36; 9:7; 10:8(2); 9; 11:3; 13:9; 14:10(2); 15(3); 21; 15:9; **1Cor** 7:16(2); 8:11; 14:16; 15:55(2); **Gal** 3:16; 5:14; **Eph** 6:2; **1Ti** 4:12; 15; 5:23; 6:20; **2Ti** 1:4; 5(2); 4:5; 9; 21; 22; **Philem** 1:2; 5; 6; 7; 13; 14(2); 21; **Heb** 1:8(2); 9(2); 12; 13; 2:7; 12; 10:7; 9; 11:18; **Jas** 2:8; 18(2); **2Jn** 4; 13; **3Jn** 2; 6; **Rev** 2:2(3); 4; 5; 9; 13; 19(3); 3:1; 2; 8; 9; 11; 15; 18; 4:11; 5:9; 10:9(2); 11:17; 18(3); 14:15; 18; 15:3(2); 4(2); 16:7; 18:10; 14; 23(2); 19:10(2); 22:9(2)

TILL

Gen 2:5; 3:19; 23; 19:22; 29:8; 38:11; 17; **Ex** 15:16(2); 16:19; 24; 34:33; 40:37; **Num** 12:15; **Deut** 17:5; 28:45; **Josh** 5:6; 8; 8:6; 10:20; **Judg** 3:25; 6:4; 11:33; 16:3; 19:26; 21:2; **Ruth** 1:13; **1Sa** 10:8; 16:11; 22:3; **2Sa** 3:35; 9:10; **1Kin** 14:10; 18:28; **2Kin** 2:17; 4:20; 7:9; 10:17; 13:17; 19; 21:16; **2Chr** 26:15; 29:34; 36:16; **Ezr** 2:63; 5:5; 9:14; **Neh** 2:7; 4:11; 21; 7:65; 13:19; **Job** 7:19; 8:21; 14:6; 12; 14; 27:5; 32:4; **Ps** 10:15; 18:37; 68:30; **Prov** 7:23; 29:11; **Eccl** 2:3; **Song** 2:7; 3:5; **Is** 5:8; 11; 22:14; 30:17; 38:13; 42:4; 62:7(2); **Jer** 7:32; 9:16; 19:11; 23:20; 24:10; 27:11; 49:9; 37; 52:3; 11; **Lam** 3:50; **Eze** 4:8; 14; 24:13; 28:15; 34:21; 39:15; 19(2); 47:20; **Dan** 2:9; 34; 4:23; 25; 33; 5:21; 6:14; 7:4; 9; 11; 10:3; 11:36; 12:9; 13; **Hos** 5:15; 10:12; **Obad** 5; **Jonah** 4:5; **Zeph** 3:3; **Mt** 1:25; 2:9; 5:18(2); 26; 10:11; 23; 12:20; 13:33; 16:28; 18:21; 30; 34; 22:44; 23:39; 24:34; **Mk** 6:10; 9:1; 9; 12:36; 13:30; **Lk** 1:80; 9:27; 12:50; 59; 13:8; 21; 15:8; 17:8; 19:13; 20:43; 21:32; **Jn** 13:38; 21:22; 23; **Acts** 7:18; 8:40; 20:11; 21:5; 23:12; 21; 25:21; 28:23; **1Cor** 11:26; 15:25; **Gal** 3:19; **Eph** 4:13; **Phil** 1:10; **1Ti** 4:13; **Heb** 10:13; **Rev** 2:25; 7:3; 15:8; 20:3

TO

Gen 1:14; 15; 16(2); 17; 18(2); 29; 30(3); 2:5(2); 9(2); 10; 15(2); 19; 20(3); 21; 3:6(3); 12; 16; 18; 21; 22; 23; 24; 4:3; 4; 5; 8; 11; 14; 23(2); 26(3); 6:1(2); 4; 16; 17; 19; 20; 21; 22; 7:2; 3; 4; 10; 8:1; 6; 7; 8; 11; 13; 9:8; 10; 11; 14; 15; 20; 10:8; 19; 21; 11:2; 3(2); 4; 5; 6(2); 7; 8; 31; 12:5; 10; 11(3); 12; 14; 19(2); 13:3; 6; 9(3); 15(2); 14:1; 7; 10; 17; 21; 22; 23; 15:3; 5; 6; 7(2); 15; 17; 16:2; 3(2); 6; 7; 9; 16; 17:1; 7(2); 8; 18:2; 5; 7; 10; 11; 14; 16; 19; 21; 25(2); 27; 31; 19:1(2); 5; 8; 9(2); 10(2); 11; 13; 17(2); 19; 20; 27; 29; 30; 31; 34; 20:3(2); 6; 9; 13(2); 16; 21:2; 3; 6; 17; 22; 23(2); 26; 22:1; 5; 9; 10; 14; 19; 20; 23; 23:2(2); 7(2); 8; 16; 24:4; 5; 8; 9; 10; 11(2); 13; 14(2); 15(2); 16(2); 17; 20; 21; 22; 23; 25; 27; 30; 32; 33; 36; 37; 38; 41; 43(4); 44; 48; 49(2); 52(2); 53(3); 56; 63; 65; 25:8; 11; 13; 16; 20(2); 22; 24; 30; 32(2); 33; 26:4; 7(2); 8; 11; 23; 26; 27; 31; 32; 34; 35; 27:1; 3; 4; 5(4); 8; 9; 10; 11; 12; 14; 20; 25(2); 29(2); 30; 37; 40; 42(2); 43(2); 45; 46; 28:2(2); 4(2); 5; 6(2); 7; 9; 11; 12; 13(2); 14(4); 15; 20(2); 21; 29:10; 13(3); 14; 19(2); 20; 23(2); 25(2); 26; 28; 29(2); 30:4; 9; 14; 15; 16; 18; 22; 24; 25(2); 32; 33; 34; 38(2); 41; 31:3; 4; 7; 9; 10; 18(2); 19; 20; 24(2); 26(2); 28; 29(2); 31; 32; 35; 36; 51; 52; 54; 32:3; 5; 6(3); 8; 9; 13; 30; 33:3(2); 4; 8; 11; 14; 17; 18; 34:1; 4; 6; 7; 8; 12; 14(2); 16; 17; 19; 21; 22(2); 25; 30(3); 35:1; 2; 3; 6; 12(2); 16(2); 17; 18; 19; 22; 26; 36:4; 12(2); 14; 40; 43; 37:7; 8; 9; 10(5); 12; 13; 14(2); 17; 18; 19; 22(2); 23; 25(3); 27; 28; 32; 35(2); 38:1(2); 8; 9(2); 11; 12; 13(2); 14(2); 15; 16; 20; 22; 23; 24; 25; 26; 27; 28; 29; 39:1; 3; 5; 7; 8; 10(4); 11(2); 13; 14(2); 15; 17(2); 18; 19(2); 22; 23(2); 40:1; 5; 7; 8; 9(2); 20; 22; 41:1; 8; 11; 12(4); 13(2); 15; 24; 25; 28; 32; 36; 43; 45; 52; 54; 55(2); 57(2); 42:3; 5; 6(2); 7; 9; 10; 12; 21; 24; 25(3); 27; 28; 30; 35; 37(2); 38; 43:2; 6; 7; 15; 16; 19; 20; 21(2); 22; 23; 26(2); 30; 33(2); 44:2; 7; 11; 13; 14; 24; 29; 30; 31(2); 32; 33; 34; 45:1; 4; 5; 7(2); 8; 9; 11; 21; 22(2); 23; 27; 46:1; 3; 5; 18; 22; 28; 29(2); 32; 33; 47:4; 6; 12; 21(2); 24; 48:1; 4; 7; 11; 12; 17; 22; 49:4(2); 15; 28; 29; 50:2; 7; 10; 11; 14; 20(3); 24(3); **Ex** 1:10; 11; 13; 15; 16; 21; 2:1; 4(2); 5(2); 7(2); 8; 11; 13; 14; 15; 16; 18(2); 21; 23; 3:1(3); 4; 6; 8(2); 13; 16; 18(2); 21; 4:8(2); 9; 14; 16(2); 18(2); 20; 21; 23; 24(2); 25; 27(2); 5:2; 7; 8; 10; 12; 14; 16; 17; 21(3); 23(3); 6:1; 3; 4; 7(2); 8(4); 13; 16; 17; 19; 20; 23; 25(2); 26(2); 27(2); 28; 7:1; 14; 15; 17; 18; 20; 23; 24; 8:2; 5; 9; 10(2); 13; 18; 20; 22; 23; 25; 26(2); 27; 28; 29(3); 31; 9:2; 5; 8; 16; 18(2); 10:3; 4(2); 5; 10; 26; 28; 12:2; 3(2); 4(2); 13(2); 14; 16; 21; 23(3); 24(2); 25(2); 26; 29; 35; 37; 41(2); 42(2); 48; 49; 51; 13:5; 6; 10; 11; 14; 15(2); 17(2); 21(3); 14:11(2); 12; 13(3); 20(2); 21; 23; 24; 27; 15:17; 21; 23; 26(2); 27; 16:3(3); 5; 8(2); 10; 13; 15(2); 16(2); 18; 21; 22; 23(3); 25(3); 27(2); 28; 32; 33; 34; 35; 17:1(2); 3; 4; 9; 10(2); 11; 16; 18:7; 8; 9; 12; 13(2); 14(2); 15; 18; 19; 21; 23(2); 24; 19:2; 3; 10(2); 12(2); 13; 16; 17; 20; 21; 22; 23; 24; 20:5; 8; 20; 21:6; 7; 8(2); 12; 14; 15; 16; 17; 19; 29(3); 31; 36; 22:5; 7; 8; 9; 10; 16; 17(2); 18; 19; 25(2); 26; 27; 29; 31; 23:1; 2(3); 4; 5; 20(2); 24; 27; 24:4; 12; 14; 25:7; 9; 20; 25; 27; 29; 35; 26:3(2); 7; 13; 28; 30; 27:3; 5; 7; 20(2); 21; 28:3; 8; 10; 11; 14; 21(2); 35; 36; 42; 43; 29:1(2); 10; 29(2); 30; 33(2); 35(2); 36; 41(2); 42; 44(2); 30:1; 4(2); 15; 16; 18; 20(3); 21(3); 37(2); 38; 31:4(2); 5(2); 10; 11; 14; 15(2); 16; 32:1; 5(2); 6(3); 12(2); 13; 14; 19; 20; 27; 28; 29(2); 30; 33:1(2); 5; 7; 8; 9; 11; 19; 22; 34:2; 7; 12; 24; 29; 30; 34; 35; 35:2(3); 9; 19(2); 21; 27; 29(2); 32(2); 33(2); 35; 36:1(3); 2(2); 3; 5; 6; 7; 12; 18; 29(2); 33(2); 34; 37:2; 3; 5; 9(2); 14; 15; 16; 21; 27(2); 29; 38:5; 7; 18; 21(2); 26; 30; 39:1; 3; 4; 5; 7; 14(3); 26; 30(2); 31; 32; 37; 41(2); 42; 40:4; 5; 16; 17; 30; 35; **Lev** 1:4; 9; 14; 2:2(2); 13; 4:2; 3; 5; 16; 23; 27; 28; 35; 5:4(2); 7; 10; 11; 12(2); 17; 6:2; 4; 5; 25; 30; 7:8; 35; 36; 38; 8:5; 11; 12; 15; 31; 34(2); 9:1; 4(2); 16; 10:7; 15; 17(2); 19; 11:1; 7; 8; 21; 31; 37; 45; 47; 12:2; 8; 13:12; 15; 19; 59(2); 14:4(2); 7; 8; 11; 14; 17; 18; 19; 21(2); 22; 25; 28; 29(2); 31(2); 32(2); 34; 35; 36(2); 38; 41; 49; 57; 15:1; 13; 14; 28; 29; 16:10(3); 17; 27; 30; 32; 34; 17:4; 5; 9; 11(2); 18:4; 6(3); 14; 17; 18(3); 19; 20; 21; 23(2); 19:4; 11; 20(2); 24; 29(3); 31; 20:2(2); 3(2); 5; 6; 9; 10; 11; 12; 13; 15; 16; 22; 24; 27; 21:4; 10; 11; 14; 17; 21(2); 24; 22:2; 8; 16; 18; 21(2); 33; 23:2; 11; 20; 22; 28; 37(2); 43; 24:2(2); 16(2); 17; 19; 20; 21; 23; 25:9; 15; 16(3); 25; 26(2); 27; 28(2); 30; 38(2); 39; 46; 47; 50(2); 26:1; 5; 8; 21; 37; 44(2); 27:8; 14; 16; 17; 18; 19; 20; 24(2); 25; 27(2); 29; **Num** 1:3(2); 18; 20(3); 22(3); 24(3); 26(3); 28(3); 30(3); 32(3); 34(3); 36(3); 38(3); 40(3); 42(3); 45(2); 50; 51(2); 54; 2:10; 18; 34(2); 3:3; 7; 8; 9; 10; 16; 20; 22; 34; 38; 46; 48(2); 51(2); 4:3; 7; 11; 14; 15(2); 16; 19(2); 20; 23(2); 24; 30; 31; 33; 37; 41; 45; 47; 49(3); 5:6; 8(2); 15; 19; 20; 21(2); 22(3); 24; 26; 27(2); 29; 6:2(2); 4; 10(2); 21; 7:1; 5(3); 7; 89; 8:7; 12; 15; 19(4); 20; 21; 22; 24; 26; 9:3(2); 5; 12; 13; 14(2); 20(2); 10:3; 7; 8; 9; 10; 11; 13; 14; 18; 22; 28; 30(2); 31(2); 33; 35; 11:4; 13; 14; 16; 18(2); 22(2); 23; 25; 12:8(2); 13:16; 17; 21; 26(4); 30; 31; 32; 14:3(2); 4; 7; 14(2); 16; 20; 22; 25; 28; 29; 30; 36(2); 38; 44; 15:3; 12(3); 24; 28; 34; 35; 39; 41; 16:5(3); 7; 9(5); 10; 12; 13; 16; 28; 31; 33; 40(3); 42; 17:2(2); 5(2); 6; 8; 10; 18:6(2); 7; 8; 11(2); 16(2); 19; 24(2); 28; 20:5(3); 8; 12; 17(2); 21; 21:3; 4; 5; 7; 8; 9; 15; 16; 18; 19(2); 20; 23(2); 29; 32; 33; 34; 22:2; 5(2); 11; 13(2); 14; 16(2); 18; 20; 23; 26(3); 30; 32; 36; 37(3); 38; 40(2); 41; 23:3(2); 11; 12; 14; 17; 20; 23; 24:1(2); 2; 10; 11(2); 12; 13; 14; 25; 25:1; 2; 26:1; 2(2); 18; 22; 25; 27; 37; 43; 47; 50; 53; 54(4); 55; 56; 59; 27:7; 8; 11; 14; 28:2; 7; 22; 30; 29:5; 9(2); 14; 15; 18; 21; 24; 27; 30; 33; 37; 40; 30:2(2); 13; 14; 31:4; 6(3); 13; 16; 21; 27; 28; 36; 50; 52; 32:2; 6(2); 8; 14; 19; 20; 27; 29; 33(2); 39; 33:2(2); 14; 53; 54(3); 55; 56(2); 34:4(5); 8; 9; 10; 11; 12; 13(2); 14(2); 18; 29; 35:2; 3; 5; 6; 7; 8; 11; 16; 17; 18; 21; 24; 25; 30(3); 31; 32(2); 36:2(3); 3(2); 5; 6(2); 7(2); 9(2); **Deut** 1:3; 5; 7(2); 8(2); 9; 14; 19; 27(2); 28; 30; 33(3); 35; 36(2); 38; 41(2); 45; 2:4; 15; 16; 18; 22; 24; 25; 27; 31(2); 32; 34; 3:1(2); 3; 7; 12; 18; 24(3); 28; 4:1; 5; 9; 10; 13; 14(2); 19; 20; 25(2); 26(2); 30; 34(2); 36; 38(3); 5:4; 5; 12; 15; 23; 30; 31; 32(3); 6:1(2); 2; 3; 10(4); 19; 20; 23; 24(2); 25; 7:1; 6; 9; 10(4); 11; 12(2); 13; 24; 25; 8:1; 2(3); 3; 6(2); 16; 18; 9:1(4); 4; 5; 6; 7; 8(2); 9; 10; 11; 18(2); 19; 20; 22; 23; 27(2); 28(2); 10:4; 6; 7; 8(4); 10; 11; 12(4); 13; 15; 20; 11:4(2); 8; 9(2); 10; 11; 13(3); 16; 21; 22(4); 25; 28; 29(2); 31(2); 32; 12:1(2); 5; 9(2); 10; 11(2); 13; 15; 19; 20; 21; 29; 30; 31(2); 32; 13:2; 3; 5(4); 9(2); 10; 12; 17; 18(3); 14:2; 23(2); 24(2); 15:4; 5(2); 11(2); 15; 18; 16:2; 6; 8; 9(3); 11; 17; 17:6(2); 7(2); 10(3); 11(4); 12; 16(4); 17(2); 19(3); 20(3); 18:5(2); 8; 9; 10; 14; 16; 19; 20(2); 22; 19:2; 3; 5(2); 8; 9(3); 14; 16; 19; 20:1; 4(2); 5; 9; 10; 18; 19(2); 21:1; 5(2); 10; 11; 12; 16; 22(2); 22:2; 4; 6; 7; 14; 16; 21(2); 22; 23:2; 3; 4; 14(2); 19; 20(2); 21; 22; 24:1; 3; 4(2); 5; 6(2); 8(2); 10; 11; 16(3); 17; 18; 19; 22; 25:2(4); 5(2); 7(3); 8(2); 11; 19; 26:2; 3; 5; 13(3); 14(2); 16; 17(4); 18; 19; 27:12; 13; 18; 25; 26; 28:1(3); 7; 11; 12(2); 13(2); 14(4); 15(3); 20; 21; 25; 31(2); 44(2); 45; 50; 55; 56; 58; 63(7); 29:1; 4(3); 8(2); 13(4); 18; 19(3); 21; 22; 27; 29; 30:1(2); 2; 6; 10; 12; 16(4); 18(2); 19; 20(4); 31:4(2); 7(2); 11; 12; 13(2); 16; 21; 24; 28; 29(2); 32:8(2); 13; 16(2); 17(3); 21(4); 26; 30; 35; 40; 41; 43(2); 45; 46(2); 47; 33:7; 9; 17; 24; 34:1; 4; 5; 10; 11(4); **Josh** 1:1; 2(2); 5; 6; 7(4); 8(2); 11(3); 12(3); 18; 2:1; 2(2); 3(2); 5; 6; 7; 16; 20; 23; 3:1; 2; 5; 7; 8; 13; 14(2); 4:1; 6; 8; 10(2); 11; 13; 18; 21; 23; 5:1; 8; 13; 14; 6:5; 8; 15; 16; 17; 20; 25; 7:2; 3(2); 6; 7(3); 13; 14(2); 19; 8:1; 2; 3; 5; 8; 9; 10; 12; 14(2); 16; 20(3); 23; 24; 34; 9:1; 2; 3; 6(2); 10(3); 11(2); 12; 15; 16; 20; 24(2); 25; 10:1(3); 6(3); 10(2); 11(2); 12; 13; 15; 18; 19; 20; 21(2); 24; 25; 27; 28; 32(2); 33; 35(2); 37(2); 38; 39(5); 43; 11:1(4); 2; 3(3); 5; 6; 11; 14; 17; 20; 23(2); 12:3(2); 7(2); 13:1; 3; 4; 15; 31; 14:1; 4; 7; 11(2); 12; 15:1; 3(6); 6(2); 7; 8; 9(2); 10(2); 11(2); 12(2); 13(2); 15; 16(2); 17; 18(2); 20; 16:1; 2(2); 3(2); 5; 6(2); 7(3); 17:1; 4(2); 5; 7; 8; 13(2); 14; 15; 17(2); 18:3(2); 4(2); 6; 8(2); 9(2); 10; 11; 12; 13(2); 15; 16(4); 17(2); 19; 20; 21; 28; 19:1(2); 8(2); 10; 11(2); 12(2); 13(4); 14; 16; 17(2); 22; 23; 24; 26(2); 27(4); 29(4); 31; 32(2); 33; 34(5); 39; 40; 47; 48; 49; 50; 20:2; 21:2(2); 12; 13(2); 21; 27; 32; 33; 38; 43; 44; 45; 22:5(6); 7; 9(3); 10(2); 12(2); 13(2); 15(2); 16; 18(2); 23(3); 24(2); 26; 27(2); 28(3); 29; 31(2); 32; 33(2); 23:1; 4; 6(4); 7; 9; 12; 14; 15; 16; 24:1; 4; 5; 9; 15; 16; 22; 29; 33; **Judg** 1:1(2); 7; 9; 12(2); 13; 14(3); 23; 28(2); 34(2); 36; 2:1(2); 4; 6; 12; 19(3); 22; 3:1; 2; 4(2); 6(2); 9; 10; 18; 27; 28; 4:5; 7; 9; 10; 12; 17; 18(2); 19; 20; 21; 5:3; 11; 16; 23(2); 26(2); 29; 30(2); 6:5; 7; 11; 22; 25; 29; 31; 35; 7:2; 3; 5; 6(2); 9; 10(2); 11; 17; 20; 22(2); 25; 8:1; 3; 4; 8; 27; 33; 35(2); 9:1; 3; 7; 8; 9; 10; 11; 13; 16; 21; 24; 26; 29(2); 31; 33; 36; 42; 48; 49; 50; 51(2); 52; 53; 10:1; 9; 12; 18(2); 11:3; 4; 5; 8; 9; 10; 12(2); 16; 20; 24; 27; 31; 32; 33; 34(2); 35; 36(2); 39(2); 40; 12:1(2); 3; 6; 13:5; 7(2); 9; 11; 12; 17; 20(2); 21(2); 23; 25; 14:1; 2; 3; 5(2); 8(2); 9; 10; 11(2); 15(2); 17(2); 19(2); 20; 15:1(3); 2; 4; 6; 10(4); 11(2); 12; 17; 16:1; 3; 4; 5; 6(2); 8; 16; 19(2); 21; 22; 23(2); 25; 17:3(2); 4; 8(3); 9; 11; 13; 18:1; 2(4); 7(2); 8; 9(3); 10; 14(2); 15; 17; 19(2); 22; 30; 19:1(2); 2; 3(3); 5(2); 7; 8; 9(3); 12; 13(2); 14; 15(3); 18(3); 22; 25(2); 27; 20:1; 3; 4(2); 5; 8; 9; 10(3); 13(2); 14(2); 18(2); 20(2); 21; 23; 25; 28(2); 31(3); 36; 39; 40(2); 47; 48(2); 21:1; 2; 3(2); 4; 5(3); 7; 8(4); 12; 13(3); 18; 19; 21(2); 22(2); 23; 24(3); **Ruth** 1:1(2); 7; 8; 12(2); 16(2); 17; 18; 19(3); 22; 2:2; 3; 8; 10; 12; 15; 18; 19(2); 20(2); 23; 3:2; 3; 6; 7; 8; 11; 13(2); 16(2); 17; 4:1; 4(2); 5; 6; 7(2); 10(2); 15; 17; **1Sa** 1:3(2); 4(2); 6; 7; 8(2); 12; 19(2); 20; 21; 25; 28(2); 2:6; 8(2); 10; 11(2); 15(2); 16; 19(3); 20; 24; 28(4); 29; 33(2); 35; 36(2); 3:2(2); 3; 6; 8; 11; 15; 17; 19; 20(2); 21; 4:1(2); 3; 4; 9; 12; 16; 18; 19; 5:3; 4(2); 10(5); 11; 12; 6:2(2); 3; 4(2); 7; 9(2); 10; 12(3); 13; 16; 18(2); 20(2); 21(2); 7:1; 2; 5; 6; 7; 8(2); 10; 14; 16(2); 17; 8:1; 4; 5; 6; 8; 11; 12(3); 13(3); 14; 15(2); 16; 19; 22; 9:3; 5(2); 6; 7(3); 8(2); 9(2); 10; 11(2); 12(3); 13(2); 14(2); 16(2); 17; 18; 19(2); 21; 26(2); 27(2); 10:1; 2(2); 3(3); 5(3); 8(4); 9(2); 10; 11(2); 13; 14(3); 17; 20; 21; 24; 25; 26; 11:3(2); 4; 9(2); 10; 11; 12; 13(2); 14(2); 15; 12:3; 7(2); 17; 19; 22; 23; 13:2; 4; 5; 7; 8(2); 9; 10(2); 12; 13; 14; 17; 18(3); 20(2); 21; 22; 23; 14:1(2); 4; 6(3); 7; 9; 12; 19; 20; 21; 25; 26; 27; 30; 31; 43; 45; 46; 15:1(2); 2; 5; 6; 7; 11; 12(3); 13; 15; 16; 21; 22(2); 27; 28; 32; 34(3); 35; 16:1; 2(2); 3; 4; 5(3); 6; 9; 10; 12(2); 13; 16(2); 17; 21; 22; 23; 17:1(2); 8(3); 9(2); 13(2); 15; 17(2); 20(2); 23; 25; 26(2); 27; 32; 33(3); 39; 40; 43; 44(3); 45(3); 46; 48(3); 49; 52(3); 54; 58; 18:1; 2; 4(4); 6(2); 8; 10; 11; 17(2); 18; 19(3); 21(2); 23(2); 25(3); 26; 27(2); 30; 19:1(2); 2(2); 4; 5; 7; 10(2); 11(4); 14; 15(2); 18(3); 20; 22(2); 23(2); 20:5(2); 6; 8; 9; 10; 12; 13(2); 17; 18(2); 19; 21; 24; 27(3); 28(2); 29; 30; 33(2); 35; 37; 38; 40; 41; 42; 21:1(2); 2; 6; 7; 10; 11; 14; 15; 22:1(3); 3; 8; 9(2); 11(2); 13; 15(2); 17(2); 18; 23:3; 4; 5; 6(3); 7; 8(4); 9; 10(3); 13; 15; 16; 18; 19(2); 20(3); 23(2); 24; 25; 26(2); 24:1; 2; 3(2); 4; 5; 6; 7; 8; 9; 10; 11; 16; 17; 25:1; 5(2); 6(3); 8(2); 9(2); 14; 17; 22; 23; 26(2); 29(2); 30(3); 32(2); 33; 34; 35(2); 36; 37; 38; 39(3); 40(5); 41(2); 44; 26:1; 2(2); 5; 6(5); 7; 8(2); 9; 10; 13; 14(3); 15(3); 16; 20(2); 23(2); 25(2); 27:1; 4; 8; 9; 10; 11(2); 12; 28:1(3); 2(2); 7(2); 8; 9(2); 10(2); 12; 14; 15(2); 17(3); 19; 29:1; 4(3); 5; 9(2); 11(3); 30:1(2); 3; 4; 7(2); 9; 11; 12; 13(2); 14; 15(3); 19(2); 21(5); 22; 24; 26(2); 27(3); 28(3); 29(3); 30(3); 31(3); 31:8(2); 9; 10; 11; 12; **2Sa** 1:1; 2(3); 14(2); 26; 2:1; 8; 10; 12; 14; 15; 19(2); 21(3); 22(3); 23(3); 24; 26; 29; 32; 3:5; 6; 7; 8(3); 9(3); 10(3); 12(3); 13; 14(2); 16; 17; 19(3); 20(2); 23; 24; 25(3); 27(2); 31(2); 35(3); 37; 39; 4:2; 3; 4(2); 5; 8(2); 10; 5:1; 2; 3(2); 4; 6; 8; 11; 13; 17(2); 19; 20; 24; 25; 6:2; 6(2); 8; 9; 19(3); 20(3); 21; 7:1; 3; 4; 5; 6; 7; 8; 11(2); 17(2); 19; 21(2); 22; 23(5); 24(2); 27(2); 29; 8:1; 2(4); 3; 5; 6; 7; 10(2); 9:9(3); 10; 11; 10:1; 2; 3(3); 4; 5; 14; 16; 17; 19(2); 11:1(2); 2(2); 6(2); 8(2); 9; 11(3); 12(3); 13(2); 14(2); 16; 27; 12:4(3); 5; 7; 9(2); 10; 14(2); 17(2); 18(2); 20; 22; 23(2); 27; 29; 13:1; 2(2); 4; 5; 6; 7(2); 8; 9; 10; 11; 12; 13; 23; 24; 25; 30(2); 33(2); 36; 37; 38; 39; 14:2(2); 3; 4(2); 6; 7; 8; 10; 11(2); 15; 16; 17; 19(2); 20(3); 22; 23(2); 24(2); 25(2); 29(3); 31; 32(3); 33(3); 15:1(2); 2; 3; 5(2); 6(2); 7; 8; 9; 13; 14; 15; 16; 19(2); 22; 26; 28; 29; 32(3); 34; 35; 16:2(2); 4; 5; 10; 11(2); 15; 16; 17(2); 20; 21; 17:6; 9; 11(2); 13; 14(2); 15; 17; 18; 20(3); 21; 23(2); 24; 25(2); 27(2); 29; 18:11; 17; 18; 21; 22; 24; 28; 32; 33; 19:5; 8; 11(6); 12; 13(2); 15(5); 16; 18(2); 19; 20(2); 21; 22(2); 24; 25(3); 26; 28; 31; 34; 37; 38; 40; 41; 42; 20:1(2); 2; 3(2); 4; 5; 6; 7; 9(2); 10(2); 13; 14; 15; 18; 19; 21; 22(3); 21:2(2); 9; 10; 16; 17; 18; 20; 22; 22:4; 7; 21(2); 25(2); 31; 35; 40; 42; 44; 51(2); 23:3; 5; 9; 10; 13; 16; 21; 23; 37; 24:1; 2(2); 4; 6(4); 7(4); 8; 13(2); 15(2); 16(2); 18; 19; 21(3); **1Kin** 1:3; 4; 5; 8; 21; 23; 31(2); 33(2); 35; 38(2); 43; 44; 47; 48; 51; 52; 53(2); 2:3(2); 4(2); 5(2); 6(2); 7; 8(4); 9(2); 13; 14; 17; 19(3); 21(2); 23; 24; 26(2); 28; 30; 32; 39; 40(3); 41; 42; 44(3); 3:4(2); 5; 6; 7; 9(2); 11; 12; 14; 15(2); 18; 21; 25(2); 28; 4:10; 11; 12(2); 13(2); 15; 24; 25; 28; 34; 5:2; 5; 6(2); 7; 8(2); 9; 10; 11(2); 14; 17; 18; 6:1(2); 3; 11; 12; 19; 38; 7:7; 8; 9; 14(2); 16; 18; 23; 32; 34; 36; 41; 42; 45; 50; 8:6; 10; 11; 13(2); 16(2); 17; 18; 25(2); 28(4); 30; 31(2); 32(3); 33; 36; 39(2); 43(3); 44; 46; 52; 53; 54; 56; 58(2); 61(2); 64; 9:1(2); 2; 3; 4(2); 5; 8; 10; 11; 12; 14; 15; 19; 21; 28(2); 10:1; 2(2); 6; 9(2); 10; 13; 14; 16; 17; 24(2); 27(2); 11:2; 4; 11; 13; 15(2); 17; 18(2); 19; 21(2); 22(2); 24; 25; 29; 31(2); 33(2); 36; 37; 38; 40; 12:1(3); 2; 5; 7; 9; 11; 12(2); 14(2); 16(2); 18(4); 20; 21(4); 23; 24(4); 26; 27(2); 28(2); 30; 13:1; 4(2); 5; 10; 11; 17(2); 20; 22; 23(2); 26; 27; 29(3); 31(2); 32; 34(2); 14:2(3); 3; 4(2); 5(2); 6(2); 8; 9(2); 12; 13; 15(2); 16; 17(2); 18; 21(2); 22; 24; 25; 15:4(2); 17(2); 18; 21; 25; 26; 27(2); 29(2); 30; 33; 34; 16:1; 2(3); 7; 8; 11(2); 12; 13(2); 15; 18; 19(2); 21; 23; 26(3); 29; 31(3); 33(2); 34; 17:1; 4; 7; 9(3); 10(3); 11(2); 15; 16; 17; 18(4); 24; 18:1(2); 2; 5; 6; 9; 10; 12; 15; 16(2); 17; 19; 27; 29(2); 31; 36; 40; 42(3); 43; 44; 45(2); 46; 19:2(2); 3(2); 9; 10; 14; 15(2); 16(2); 17; 20; 20:2; 4; 6; 9; 12; 22; 26(3); 30; 31; 32; 33(2); 35; 42; 43(2); 21:1; 2; 3; 4; 5; 8; 10; 14; 15(3); 16(4); 17; 18(2); 20(2); 22(2); 25; 26; 27; 28; 22:2(2); 4(3); 5; 6; 12; 13; 15(2); 17; 24; 25; 26; 29; 32(2); 33; 36(2); 37; 41; 42; 48(2); 51; 52; 53(2); **2Kin** 1:3(3); 6(2); 7; 9; 10; 16(2); 17; 2:1; 2(2); 3(2); 4(2); 5(2); 6; 7; 9; 11; 15(3); 18; 20; 22; 25(2); 3:1; 3; 5; 7(2); 10; 12; 13(4); 15; 20; 21(2); 23; 24; 26; 27; 4:1(2); 5; 6; 8(3); 10; 12; 13(3); 14; 16; 17; 18(2); 19(2); 20; 22; 23(2); 24; 25(3); 26; 27(3); 29; 31; 35; 37; 38; 39; 40(2); 44; 5:5; 6(2); 7(4); 8(2); 10; 11; 13; 14; 15; 16; 17; 18; 21; 22; 24; 26(3); 6:4; 7; 10; 18(2); 19(2); 20; 22; 23; 24; 28(2); 30; 31; 32(3); 7:1; 3; 5(2); 6(3); 8; 9; 10; 11; 12(2); 16; 17(2); 18(3); 8:1; 3(2); 5(5); 7; 9(2); 14(3); 15; 16; 17; 19(2); 21; 25; 26; 28; 29(2); 9:1; 2; 4; 5(2); 10; 11(2); 12; 15(3); 16(2); 17; 18(3); 19(2); 22; 23; 25; 26; 27(2); 28; 29; 30; 32(2); 35; 10:1(3); 2; 5; 6(4); 7(3); 9(2); 12; 13; 15(3); 17(3); 19(3); 21; 24; 25(4); 29(2); 30; 31(2); 32; 11:4; 9(3); 10; 11; 13; 19; 21; 12:1; 4(2); 5; 8(2); 11; 12(4); 14; 15; 17(2); 18; 20; 13:1; 2; 7; 10; 16; 21; 14:2; 3; 5; 6(3); 8; 9(4); 10; 11; 12(2); 13; 14; 19(2); 22; 23; 24; 25; 28; 15:1; 2; 3; 9; 12; 13; 14; 16; 17; 18; 19; 20(2); 23; 24; 27; 28; 29; 32; 33; 34; 37; 16:1; 2; 3(2); 5(2); 6(2); 7; 8; 9; 10(4); 11; 12; 15; 16; 17:1; 4(2); 5; 9; 11(2); 13(2); 14; 17(4); 23; 26; 31; 35(2); 36; 37; 18:1(2); 2; 3; 4; 6; 8; 9; 14(2); 16; 17(2); 18(2); 19; 22; 23(2); 25(2); 26; 27(4); 29; 31(2); 32; 37; 19:1; 2; 3(2); 4; 5; 6; 7(2); 9; 10; 11; 16; 20(2); 21; 23(2); 25(2); 34; 35; 37; 20:1; 2; 4(2); 10; 21:1; 6(2); 7(2); 8(3); 9; 11; 14; 15; 16(2); 19; 22:1; 2(2); 3(2); 4; 5(2); 6(2); 8; 9; 11; 13; 15; 17; 18(3); 23:3(4); 4; 5(5); 6; 8; 9; 10(2); 11; 15(2); 16; 19(4); 20; 23; 25(2); 29; 30; 31; 32; 33; 34(2); 35(5); 36; 37; 24:2(2); 3(2); 7; 8; 9; 12; 15(2); 16; 17; 18; 19; 20; 25:1; 6(2); 7; 11; 12; 13; 20(2); 23(2); 24(3); 25; 26; 27(2); 28; **1Chr** 1:10; 2:21; 23; 35(2); 4:27; 39(2); 42; 5:1; 18(3); 20; 26; 6:19; 32; 49(2); 56; 57; 62; 64; 7:2; 11; 15; 21; 22; 23; 40(2); 8:6; 9:1; 9; 22; 25(2); 27; 29; 32; 10:4; 8(2); 9(2); 11; 12; 13; 11:1; 3(3); 4; 5; 10(2); 13; 15(2); 18(2); 21; 23; 25; 31; 12:1(2); 8; 15; 16; 17(4); 18; 19(4); 20(2); 22(2); 23(6); 24; 31; 32(2); 33; 36; 38(3); 13:2; 3; 5; 6(4); 9; 10; 11; 12; 13(2); 14:1(2); 8; 11; 15(2); 16; 15:2(3); 3(2); 14; 15; 16(3); 19; 21; 25; 26; 29(2); 16:3(2); 4(3); 5; 7; 15; 17(2); 20(2); 21; 23; 25(2); 33; 35; 37; 38; 40(3); 41(2); 43(2); 17:1(2); 3(2); 4; 5(2); 6(2); 10; 11(2); 15(2); 17(2); 18; 19; 20; 21(3); 24; 25; 27; 18:1; 3; 5; 7; 10(3); 19:1; 2(4); 3(4); 5; 6(2); 7; 15; 16; 19; 20:1(2); 2; 3; 4; 21:1; 2(4); 3; 4; 6; 11; 12(2); 15(2); 17; 18(2); 21(3); 22; 23; 24; 25; 30; 22:2(3); 4; 5; 6; 7(2); 8; 9; 13; 17; 19(4); 23:4; 5; 11; 13(3); 28; 30(2); 31(2); 24:3; 4; 7(2); 8(2); 9(2); 10(2); 11(2); 12(2); 13(2); 14(2); 15(2); 16(2); 17(2); 18(2); 19(2); 25:1(2); 2; 3(2); 5(2); 6(2); 9(2); 10; 11; 12; 13; 14; 15; 16; 17; 18; 19; 20; 21; 22; 23; 24; 25; 26; 27; 28; 29; 30; 31; 26:12; 13; 14; 15(2); 16; 27; 31; 32; 27:1; 23; 24; 28:1; 2; 4(3); 5; 6; 7; 10; 11; 15; 20; 29:2(2); 3(2); 4; 5(2); 8; 9; 12(2); 14; 16; 17; 19(3); 20; 22(2); **2Chr** 1:2(3); 3; 4; 6; 8; 11; 13(2); 2:1; 2(3); 3(3); 4(5); 6(2); 7(2); 8; 9(2); 10; 11; 12; 14(4); 16(3); 18(3); 3:1; 2; 4; 8(2); 11(2); 12(2); 4:2; 6(2); 7; 11; 12(2); 13; 16; 5:2; 7; 11; 13(3); 14; 6:4; 5(2); 6; 7; 8(2); 16(3); 19(3); 20; 22; 23; 24; 25(2); 31; 33(2); 34; 38; 7:3; 6; 7; 10(2); 11; 12(2); 13; 17; 18; 20; 21; 8:1; 2(2); 3; 6; 8; 13; 14(4); 17(2); 18(2); 9:1(2); 5; 8(4); 11(2); 12(2); 13; 14; 15; 16; 18(2); 21; 23; 26; 10:1(3); 2; 3; 6(2); 7(2); 9(2); 11; 12(2); 15; 16(3); 18(4); 11:1(3); 2; 3; 4; 13; 14; 16(3); 18; 22(2); 12:1; 2; 4(2); 5(3); 7; 10; 13(2); 14; 13:1; 5(4); 8; 9; 11; 12; 13; 15; 14:4(2); 11; 15; 15:2; 5(2); 9; 12; 13; 16:1(2); 2; 5; 7; 9(2); 12(2); 17:4; 5; 7(7); 14; 15; 18:2(4); 3; 4; 5(2); 11; 12(3); 14(3); 15(2); 16; 17; 23; 24; 25(2); 28; 29(2); 31(3); 32; 33; 19:1(2); 2(2); 3; 4; 6; 8; 10; 20:1(2); 3; 4(2); 6; 7; 11(3); 12; 16; 17(2); 18; 19; 21; 22(2); 23(2); 24; 25; 27(3); 28; 31; 36(3); 37(2); 21:3; 4; 5; 6; 7(3); 11; 12; 13(2); 19; 20; 22:1; 2; 3; 4; 5; 6(2); 7(2); 8(2); 9(2); 23:2; 7; 8(3); 9; 10; 12; 13; 15; 17; 18; 24:1; 4(2); 5(3); 6(2); 9(2); 11(2); 12(3); 14(2); 17; 19(2); 22; 23(2); 25:1; 3(2); 5(3); 7(2); 8(2); 9(3); 10(3); 11; 13; 14(2); 16(2); 17; 18(4); 19(2); 21; 22(2); 23(2); 24; 27(2); 26:2; 3; 4; 5; 8(2); 11(2); 13; 14; 15(2); 16(2); 18(3); 19; 20; 23; 27:1; 2; 8; 28:1; 5; 7; 8; 9; 10; 13(3); 15(5); 16; 23; 25(2); 29:1; 2; 8(3); 10; 11(2); 15(2); 16(2); 17(2); 18; 20; 21; 24; 25; 27; 30; 32; 34; 30:1(4); 2; 3; 5(3); 6(2); 7; 10(2); 11; 12(2); 13; 16; 17; 19(2); 20; 22; 23; 24(2); 27;

34; 37; 39; 22:2; 3; 5(3); 6; 9; 10; 12; 17(2); 24; 25; 30; 23:2; 3(3); 9; 10(3); 14; 15(3); 17; 18(3); 19; 20(2); 22; 23(2); 29(3); 30(3); 31; 32(2); 33(2); 35; 24:2; 6(2); 8; 10; 11(2); 16; 17(2); 19; 23(3); 25; 27; 25:1; 3(2); 6; 9(2); 10(2); 11; 13; 15; 16(5); 17; 19; 20; 21(3); 22; 24; 25(2); 26(2); 27(3); 26:1; 3(2); 7; 9(2); 10; 11; 12; 14(2); 16; 18(3); 20(2); 21; 22; 23; 28; 29; 27:2; 3(2); 5; 12(4); 16; 21; 22; 27; 30; 31(2); 33; 34; 35(2); 39; 40; 42; 43(2); 44(2); 28:4; 6; 8(2); 13(2); 14; 15; 16(3); 17; 19(2); 20(2); 22; 23(2); **Rom** 1:1; 3; 4(2); 5; 7(3); 10; 11(2); 13; 14(4); 15(2); 16(3); 17; 22; 23(2); 24(2); 28(3); 30; 2:2; 4; 6(2); 7; 10(3); 16; 3:15; 19; 25(2); 26; 4:1; 2; 4; 5; 8; 9; 12; 13(2); 16(4); 18; 20; 21; 22; 23; 24; 5:7; 10; 14(2); 16; 18; 6:2; 11; 16(3); 19(3); 22; 7:1; 2; 3(2); 3(2); 4(3); 5; 10(2); 18(2); 23; 8:1; 6(2); 7; 12(2); 15; 18; 20; 23; 27; 28(3); 29(2); 31; 33; 38; 39; 9:3; 4; 11; 15; 20; 21; 22(3); 26; 30; 31; 10:1; 2; 3; 4; 6; 7; 19; 21; 11:2; 4(2); 5; 11(2); 13; 14; 23; 24; 25; 35; 36(2); 12:2; 3(5); 6(3); 9; 10; 13(2); 16; 17; 13:2; 3(2); 4(2); 7(5); 8; 10; 11; 14; 14:1; 4(2); 6(3); 7(2); 9; 11(2); 12; 13; 14(3); 18; 21(2); 22; 15:1(2); 2; 5(2); 7; 8; 9; 12; 14; 15; 16; 17; 18(2); 20; 21; 22; 23; 24(3); 25; 26; 27; 28; 30; 16:17; 25(4); 26(2); 27; S:1; **1Cor** 1:1; 2(2); 17(2); 18; 19; 21; 27(2); 28(2); 2:1; 2; 6; 12; 3:2; 5; 8; 10; 18; 22; 4:5; 6(3); 7; 8; 9(3); 14; 18; 19; 5:5; 9; 11(2); 12(2); 6:1; 2; 3; 4(2); 5(2); 6; 7(2); 16; 7:1; 2; 5; 8; 9(2); 11; 12(2); 13; 15; 17; 25; 26; 27; 32; 39(2); 8:2; 6; 8; 9; 10(2); 13(2); 9:2; 3; 4(2); 5; 6; 15; 16; 20; 21(3); 22(2); 25; 27; 10:6; 7(2); 13(4); 15; 19; 20(2); 22; 27(2); 31; 32(3); 11:2; 6; 7; 10; 15; 16; 20; 22(3); 29; 33; 12:3; 7(2); 8(2); 9(2); 10(5); 11; 13; 21; 22; 23; 24; 13:3(2); 12; 14:3; 6; 8; 9; 12; 22(2); 28(2); 30; 32; 34(2); 35; 37; 39(2); 15:3; 4; 9; 24; 32; 34(2); 38; 54; 57; 16:1; 3; 7; 12(2); 15; 16; S:1; **2Cor** 1:2; 4; 8; 12; 13; 15; 16(3); 17; 23; 2:1; 3; 6; 7; 9; 10(2); 12(2); 14; 16(2); 3:1(2); 3; 4; 5; 7; 13; 16; 18; 4:2; 3; 6(2); 15; 5:2; 8(2); 10; 12(2); 13; 18(2); 19; 20; 21; 7:3(2); 9; 10(2); 11; 14(2); 8:1; 3; 4; 5; 7; 8; 10(2); 11; 12(2); 16; 19(2); 24; 9:1(3); 2; 5; 8(2); 9; 10; 11(2); 10:2(2); 4; 5; 6; 7; 13(3); 14; 15; 16(3); 11:1; 2(2); 7; 8; 9(2); 15; 32; 12:1(2); 2; 4; 6(2); 7(2); 11; 13(2); 14(4); 13:1; 2(2); 3; 7; 10(3); S:1; **Gal** 1:3; 4; 5; 10; 16; 17(2); 18(2); 2:1; 2; 3; 4; 5; 6(4); 8; 9(2); 10; 11(3); 14(3); 17; 19; 3:5; 6; 8; 10; 16(3); 18; 19; 22; 24; 29; 4:5; 9(2); 15; 18; 20(2); 21; 24; 25; 5:3(2); 13; 17; 6:3; 8(2); 12(2); 13; 16; **Eph** 1:1(2); 2; 5(2); 6; 7; 9; 11; 12; 16; 19(2); 21; 22(2); 2:2(2); 7; 15; 17(2); 3:2; 7; 9; 10; 11; 16(2); 18; 19; 20(2); 4:3; 7; 14(2); 16; 19; 22; 27; 28(2); 29; 32; 5:2; 12; 19(2); 21; 24; 27; 28; 6:4; 5(2); 7(2); 11; 13(2); 16; 19; 20; 21; 23; **Phil** 1:1; 7; 14; 16(2); 19; 20; 21(3); 23(2); 24; 26; 28(2); 29(2); 30; 2:6; 11; 13(2); 19; 23; 25(3); 30; 3:1(3); 7; 13; 21(2); 4:11; 12(6); 17; 18; 19; S:1; **Col** 1:2; 3; 4; 9(2); 11; 12; 20; 22; 23; 25(3); 26; 27; 29; 2:2; 14(2); 17; 20; 22; 23; 3:9; 15; 16; 17; 21; 22; 23; 4:3; 4; 6; 10; 17(2); S:1; **1Th** 1:2; 7; 8(2); 9(2); 10(2); 2:2; 4; 8; 15; 16(4); 17; 3:1; 2(2); 4; 5; 6(2); 9; 12; 13; 4:1(2); 4; 9; 11(3); 13; 17; 5:9(2); 12; 13; 15; **2Th** 1:3; 6(2); 7; 10(2); 12; 2:13(3); 14; 3:7; 8; 9(2); S:1; **1Ti** 1:3; 4; 7; 10; 11(2); 15; 16(2); 18; 20; 2:4(2); 6; 12(3); 3:2(2); 3; 5; 8; 13; 14; 15; 4:1; 3(3); 4; 8; 13(3); 15(2); 5:4(2); 11; 13(2); 14(2); 24; 6:3(3); 16; 17; 18(2); 19; 20; S:1; **2Ti** 1:1; 2; 4; 5; 8; 9(2); 10; 12; 2:2(2); 4; 8; 14(2); 15(2); 20(2); 24; 25; 3:2; 7(2); 15; 4:3; 6; 8; 9; 10; 11; 12; 14; 16; 18; 21; **Titus** 1:1; 3; 4; 7(2); 9(2); 14; 2:3; 4(3); 5(2); 6; 8; 9(2); 11; 3:1(5); 2(2); 5; 7; 8; 12(3); 14; S:1; **Philem** 1:2(2); 3; 8; 11(3); 16; 19; S:1; **Heb** 1:5(2); 13; 14; 2:1(2); 3; 4; 5; 10; 11; 15; 17(3); 18; 3:2; 5; 7; 13; 15; 18(2); 4:1; 6; 7(2); 9; 11; 12; 13; 16; 5:1; 3; 5(2); 7; 11(2); 12; 14(2); 6:5; 6(3); 8; 10(2); 11; 13; 16; 17; 18(2); 7:2; 5(2); 13; 23; 25(3); 27; 8:3(2); 4; 5(3); 9(2); 10(2); 11; 12; 13; 9:9; 11(2); 13; 14(2); 19(2); 24; 26; 27; 28; 10:1; 2; 7; 9; 15; 19; 20; 24(2); 31; 32; 39; 11:6(2); 7; 8; 11; 15; 16; 19; 20; 24(2); 25(2); 29; 32; 34; 35; 12:11; 19; 22; 23(3); 24(2); 13:2; 8; 10; 14; 15(2); 16(2); 18; 19(2); 21(2); S:1; **Jas** 1:1; 5; 12; 19(3); 21; 26; 27(2); 2:3(2); 5; 8; 9; 16; 3:2; 10; 17; 4:2; 5; 7; 8(2); 9(2); 12(2); 13(3); 15; 17(3); 5:1; 16; 17; **1Pet** 1:1; 2; 3; 4; 5; 12; 13(2); 14; 17; 2:4; 5(2); 8; 13(2); 15; 18(3); 23; 24; 3:1; 7; 15(2); 18(2); 4:2(2); 3; 4; 5(2); 6(3); 9; 10; 11; 12; 19(2); 5:3; 5(2); 11; **2Pet** 1:1; 3; 5(2); 6(3); 7(2); 10; 12; 13; 15; 17; 2:4(2); 8; 9(3); 10; 12; 13; 17; 21(2); 22(3); 3:9(2); 11; 13; 15; 16; 18; **1Jn** 1:9(2); 2:6; 3:5; 16; 4:10; 11; 14; 16; 5:11; 14; **2Jn** 8; 12(3); **3Jn** 4; 5(2); 8(2); 9; 13; 14(2); **Jude** 1; 3(2); 4; 7; 13; 15(2); 24(2); 25; **Rev** 1:1(2); 4(2); 6; 8; 12; 13; 2:7(2); 12; 14(3); 17(2); 19; 20(4); 21; 23; 26; 27; 3:2; 7; 9(2); 10; 18; 20; 21(2); 4:3; 8; 9; 11; 5:2(2); 3(2); 4(3); 5(2); 9(3); 12; 6:2; 4(2); 8; 16; 17; 7:2(3); 10; 14; 8:2; 6; 13(2); 9:1; 5; 6; 9; 10; 14; 15; 10:4; 5; 7(2); 11:6(4); 9; 10; 12; 13; 17(2); 18; 12:2; 4(3); 5(2); 12; 14; 15; 17; 13:3; 4; 5; 6; 7(2); 12; 14(3); 15; 16; 14:4; 6(2); 7; 15(2); 18; 15:8; 16:1; 6; 8; 9; 14(2); 19; 17:17(2); 18:6(2); 17; 19:7; 8; 10; 17; 19; 20:8(3); 12; 13; 21:10; 15; 17; 23; 22:6; 8; 12; 14; 16

TOGETHER

Gen 1:9; 10; 3:7; 13:6(2); 14:3; 22:6; 8; 19; 25:22; 29:7; 8; 22; 34:30; 36:7; 42:17; 49:1; 2; **Ex** 2:13; 3:16; 4:29; 8:14; 15:8; 19:8; 21:18; 26:3; 6; 11; 24(2); 28:7; 30:35; 32:1; 26; 35:1; 36:18; 29; 39:4(2); **Lev** 8:3; 4; 24:10; 26:25; **Num** 1:18; 8:9; 10:7; 11:22; 14:35; 16:3; 11; 20:2; 8; 10; 21:16; 23; 24:10; 26:10; 27:3; **Deut** 4:10; 22:10; 11; 25:5; 11; 31:12; 33:5; 17; **Josh** 8:16; 9:2; 10:5; 6; 11:5(2); 17:10; 18:1; 22:12; **Judg** 4:13; 6:33; 38; 7:23; 24; 9:6; 47; 10:17(2); 11:20; 12:1; 4; 16:23; 18:22; 19:6; 29; 20:1; 11; 14; **1Sa** 5:11; 7:6; 7; 8:4; 10:17; 11:11; 13:4; 5; 11; 15:4; 17:1(2); 2; 10; 23:8; 25:1; 28:1; 4(2); 29:1; 31:6; **2Sa** 2:13; 16; 25; 30; 6:1; 10:15; 17; 12:3; 28; 29; 14:6; 16; 20:14; 21:9; 23:9; 11; **1Kin** 3:18; 5:12; 10:26; 11:1; 18:20; 20:1; 22:6; **2Kin** 2:8; 3:10; 13; 9:25; 10:18; **1Chr** 10:6; 11:13; 13:5; 15:3; 16:35; 19:7; 22:2; 23:2; **2Chr** 12:5; 15:10; 18:5; 20:4; 24:5; 25:5; 28:24; 29:4; 30:3; 32:4; 6; 34:17; 29; **Ezr** 2:64; 3:1; 9; 11; 4:3; 6:20; 7:28; 8:15; 10:7; 9; **Neh** 4:6; 8; 6:2; 7; 10; 7:5; 66; 8:1; 13; 12:28; 13:11; **Est** 2:3; 8; 19; 4:16; 8:11; 9:2; 15; 16; 18; **Job** 2:11; 3:18; 6:2; 9:32; 10:8; 11:10; 16:10; 17:16; 19:12; 24:4; 30:7; 34:15; 38:7; 38; 40:13; 17; 41:15; 17; 23; **Ps** 2:2; 14:3; 31:13; 33:7; 34:3; 35:15(2); 26; 37:38; 40:14; 41:7; 47:9; 48:4; 49:2; 50:5; 55:14; 56:6; 71:10; 74:8; 83:5; 85:10; 88:17; 94:21; 98:8; 102:22; 104:22; 122:3; 133:1; 140:2; 147:2; **Prov** 22:2; 29:13; **Eccl** 3:5; 4:5; 11; **Is** 1:18; 28; 31; 8:10; 9:11; 21; 11:6; 7; 12; 14; 13:4; 18:6; 22:3(2); 9; 24:22; 25:11; 26:19; 27:4; 31:3; 34:4; 40:5; 41:1; 19; 20; 23; 43:9; 17; 26; 44:11(2); 45:8; 16; 20; 21; 46:2; 48:13; 49:18; 50:8; 52:8; 9; 54:15(2); 60:4; 5; 7; 13; 62:9; 65:7; 25; 66:17; **Jer** 3:18; 4:5; 6:11; 12; 21; 13:14; 31:8; 12; 13; 24; 41:1; 46:12; 21; 48:7; 49:3; 14; 50:4; 29; 33; 51:27; 38; 44; **Lam** 2:8; **Eze** 21:14; 17; 29:5; 37:7; **Dan** 2:35; 3:2; 3; 27; 6:6; 7; 11:6; **Hos** 1:11; 11:8; **Joel** 3:11; **Amos** 1:15; 3:3; **Mic** 2:12; **Nah** 1:10; 2:10; **Zeph** 2:1(2); **Zec** 10:4; 12:3; 14:14; **Mt** 1:18; 2:4; 13:2; 30(2); 18:20; 19:6; 22:10; 34; 41; 23:37; 24:28; 31; 26:3; 27:17; 62; **Mk** 1:33; 2:2; 15; 3:20; 6:30; 33; 7:1; 9:25; 10:9; 12:28; 13:27; 14:56; 59; 15:16; **Lk** 5:15; 6:38; 8:4; 9:1; 11:29; 12:1; 13:11; 34; 15:6; 9; 13; 17:35; 37; 22:55; 66; 23:12; 13; 48; 24:14; 15; 33; **Jn** 4:36; 6:13; 11:52; 53; 20:4; 7; 21:2; **Acts** 1:4; 6; 15; 2:6; 44; 3:1; 11; 4:6; 26; 27; 31; 5:9; 21; 10:24; 27; 12:12; 13:44; 14:1; 27; 15:6; 30; 16:22; 19:19; 25; 32; 20:7; 8; 21:22; 30; 23:12; 28:17(2); **Rom** 1:12; 3:12; 6:5; 8:17; 22; 28; 15:30; **1Cor** 1:10; 3:9; 5:4; 7:5; 11:17; 18; 20; 33; 34; 12:24; 14:23; 26; **2Cor** 1:11; 6:1; 14; **Eph** 1:10; 2:5; 6(2); 21; 22; 4:16; **Phil** 1:27; 3:17; **Col** 2:2; 13; 19; **1Th** 4:17; 5:10; 11; **2Th** 2:1; **Heb** 10:25; **Jas** 5:3; **1Pet** 3:7; 5:13; **Rev** 6:14; 16:16; 19:17; 19; 20:8

TOLD

Gen 3:11; 9:22; 14:13; 20:8; 22:3; 9; 20; 24:28; 33; 66; 26:32; 27:42; 29:12(2); 13; 31:20; 22; 37:5; 9; 10; 38:13; 24; 40:9; 41:8; 12; 24; 42:29; 43:7; 44:24; 45:26; 27; 47:1; 48:1; 2; **Ex** 4:28; 5:1; 14:5; 16:22; 18:8; 19:9; 24:3; **Lev** 21:24; **Num** 11:24; 27; 13:27; 14:39; 23:26; 29:40; **Deut** 17:4; **Josh** 2:2; 23; 9:24; 10:17; **Judg** 6:13; 7:13; 9:7; 25; 42; 47; 13:6(2); 23; 14:2; 6; 9; 16(2); 17(2); 16:2; 10; 13; 15; 17; 18; **Ruth** 3:16; **1Sa** 3:13; 18; 4:13; 14; 8:10; 9:15; 10:16(2); 25; 11:4; 5; 14:1; 33; 43; 15:12; 18:20; 24; 26; 19:2; 11; 18; 19; 21; 23:1; 7; 13; 22; 25; 24:1; 25:12; 14; 19; 36; 37; 27:4; **2Sa** 1:5; 6; 13; 2:4; 3:23; 4:10; 6:12; 10:5; 17; 11:5; 10; 18; 14:33; 15:31; 17:17(2); 18; 21; 18:10; 11; 25; 19:1; 8; 21:11; 24:13; **1Kin** 1:23; 51; 2:29; 39; 41; 8:5; 10:3(2); 7; 13:11(2); 25; 14:2; 18:13; 16; 19:1; 20:17; **2Kin** 1:7; 4:7; 27; 31; 5:4; 6:10; 13; 7:10; 11; 15; 8:6; 7; 14; 9:18; 20; 36; 10:8; 12:10; 11; 18:37; 23:17; **1Chr** 17:25; 19:5; 17; **2Chr** 2:2; 5:6; 9:2(2); 6; 20:2; 34:18; **Ezr** 8:17; **Neh** 2:12; 16; 18; **Est** 2:22; 3:4(2); 4:4; 7; 9; 12; 5:11; 6:2; 13; 8:1; **Job** 15:18; 37:20; **Ps** 44:1; 52:t; 78:3; 90:9; **Eccl** 6:6; **Is** 7:2; 36:22; 40:21; 44:8; 45:21; 52:15; **Jer** 36:20; 38:27; **Dan** 4:7; 8; 7:1; 16; 8:26; **Jonah** 1:10; **Hab** 1:5; **Zec** 10:2; **Mt** 8:33; 12:48; 14:12; 18:31; 24:25; 26:13; 28:7; **Mk** 5:14; 16; 33; 6:30; 9:12; 16:10; 13; **Lk** 1:45; 2:17; 18; 20; 8:20; 34; 36; 9:10; 36; 13:1; 18:37; 24:9; 10; 35; **Jn** 3:12; 4:29; 39; 51; 5:15; 8:40; 9:27; 10:25; 11:46; 14:2; 29; 16:4(2); 18:8; 20:18; **Acts** 5:22; 25; 9:6; 12:14; 16:36; 38; 22:10; 26; 23:16; 30; 27:25; **2Cor** 7:7; 13:2; **Gal** 5:21; **Phil** 3:18; **1Th** 3:4; **2Th** 2:5; **Jude** 18

TOO

Gen 18:14; **Ex** 12:4; 18:18; 36:7; **Num** 11:14; 16:3; 7; 22:6; **Deut** 1:17; 2:36; 12:21; 14:24(2); 17:8; **Josh** 17:15; 19:9; 47; 22:17; **Judg** 7:2; 4; 18:26; **Ruth** 1:12; **2Sa** 3:39; 10:11(2); 12:8; 22:18; **1Kin** 1:36; 8:64; 12:28; 19:7; **2Kin** 3:26; 6:1; **1Chr** 19:12(2); **2Chr** 29:34; **Est** 1:18; **Job** 42:3; **Ps** 18:17; 35:10; 38:4; 73:16; 131:1; 139:6; **Prov** 24:7; 30:18; **Is** 49:19; 20; **Jer** 32:17; 27; **Acts** 17:22

TOWARD

Gen 2:14; 12:9; 13:12; 15:5; 18:2; 16; 22; 19:1; 28(2); 20:1; 25:18; 28:10; 30:40; 31:2; 5; 21; 48:13(2); **Ex** 9:8; 10; 22; 23; 10:21; 22; 16:10; 25:20; 26:35; 28:27; 34:8; 36:25; 39:20; **Lev** 9:22; 13:41; **Num** 2:3; 3:38; 16:42; 21:11; 20; 23:28; 24:1; 32:14; 34:15; **Deut** 4:41; 47; 28:54(3); 56(3); 57(2); **Josh** 1:4; 15; 3:16; 8:18(2); 12:1; 13:5; 15:4; 7(3); 21; 16:6; 18:13; 17; 18; 19:11; 12; 18; 27(2); 34; **Judg** 3:28; 4:6; 5:9; 11; 8:3; 13:20; 19:9; 18; 20:43; 45; **1Sa** 13:18; 17:30; 48; 20:12; 41; **2Sa** 14:1; 15:23; 24:5; 20; **1Kin** 7:9; 25(4); 8:22; 29(3); 30; 35; 38; 42; 44(2); 48; 14:13; 18:43; **2Kin** 3:14; 25:4; **1Chr** 9:24; 12:15(2); 26:17; **2Chr** 4:4(4); 6:13; 20; 21; 26; 34; 38(3); 16:9; 20:24; 24:16(2); 31:14; **Ezr** 3:11; **Neh** 3:26; 12:31; **Est** 1:13; 8:4; **Job** 2:12; 11:13; 39:26; **Ps** 5:7; 25:15; 28:2; 66:5; 85:4; 86:13; 98:3; 103:11; 116:12; 117:2; 138:2; **Prov** 14:35; 23:5; **Eccl** 1:6; 11:3(2); **Song** 7:4; 10; **Is** 7:1; 11:14; 29:13; 38:2; 49:23; 63:7; 15; 66:14(2); **Jer** 1:13; 3:12; 4:6; 11; 12:3; 15:1; 29:10; 11; 31:21; 40; 46:6; 49:36; **Lam** 2:19; **Eze** 1:23; 4:7; 6:2; 14; 8:3; 5(2); 14; 16(3); 9:2; 12:14; 16:42; 63; 17:6; 7(2); 21; 20:46(2); 21:2(2); 24:23; 33:25; 40:6; 20; 22; 23(2); 24(2); 27(2); 31; 32; 34; 37; 44(2); 45; 46; 41:11(3); 12; 14; 19(2); 42:1(2); 4; 7; 10; 11; 12(2); 15(2); 43:1; 4; 17; 44:1; 46:1; 12; 19; 47:1; 8; 15; 48:10(4); 17(4); 21(2); 28; **Dan** 4:2; 6:10; 8:8; 9(3); 18; 10:9; 15; 11:4; 19; 29; **Hos** 3:1; 5:1; **Joel** 2:20(2); **Jonah** 2:4; **Zec** 6:6; 8; 9:1; 14:4(4); 8(2); **Mt** 12:49; 14:14; 28:1; **Mk** 6:34; **Lk** 2:14; 12:21; 13:22; 24:29; **Jn** 6:17; **Acts** 1:10; 8:26; 20:21(2); 22:3; 24:15; 16(2); 27:12; 40; 28:14; **Rom** 1:27; 5:8; 11:22; 12:16; 15:5; **1Cor** 7:36; **2Cor** 1:16; 18; 2:8; 7:4; 7; 15; 9:8; 10:1; 13:4; **Gal** 2:8; **Eph** 1:8; 2:7; **Phil** 2:30; 3:14; **Col** 4:5; **1Th** 3:12(3); 4:10; 12; 5:14; **2Th** 1:3; **Titus** 3:4; **Philem** 1:5(2); **Heb** 6:1; 10; **1Pet** 2:19; 3:21; **1Jn** 3:21; 4:9

TWO

Gen 1:16; 4:19; 5:18; 20; 26; 28; 6:19; 20; 7:2; 9(2); 15(2); 9:22; 10:25; 11:10; 19; 20; 21; 23; 32; 19:1; 8; 15; 16; 30(2); 22:3; 24:22; 25:23(2); 27:9; 36; 29:16; 31:33; 41; 32:7; 10; 14(2); 22(2); 33:1; 34:25; 40:2; 41:1; 50; 42:37; 44:27; 45:6; 46:27; 48:1; 5; 49:14; **Ex** 2:13; 4:9; 12:7; 22; 23; 16:22; 29; 18:3; 6; 21:21; 25:10; 12(2); 17; 18(2); 19; 22; 23; 35(3); 26:17; 19(4); 21(2); 23(2); 24; 25(2); 27; 27:7; 28:7(2); 9; 11; 12(2); 14; 23(3); 24(2); 25(3); 26(2); 27(2); 29:1; 3; 13; 22; 38; 30:2; 4(3); 23(2); 31:18; 32:15; 34:1; 4(2); 29; 36:22; 24(4); 26(2); 28(2); 30; 37:1; 3(2); 6; 7(2); 8; 10; 21(3); 25; 27(3); 38:29; 39:4; 16(4); 17(2); 18(3); 19(2); 20(2); **Lev** 3:4; 10; 15; 4:9; 5:7(2); 11(2); 7:4; 8:2; 16; 25; 12:5; 8(2); 14:4; 10; 22(2); 49; 15:14(2); 29(2); 16:1; 5; 7; 8; 23:13; 17(2); 18; 19; 20; 24:5; 6; **Num** 1:35(2); 39; 2:21(2); 26; 3:34; 39; 43(2); 46; 4:36; 40; 44; 6:10(2); 7:3; 7; 17; 23; 29; 35; 41; 47; 53; 59; 65; 71; 77; 83; 85; 89; 9:22; 10:2; 11:19; 26; 31; 13:23; 15:6; 16:2; 17; 35; 22:22; 26:10; 14(2); 34; 37; 28:3; 9(2); 11; 12; 19; 20; 27; 28; 29:3; 9; 13; 14(2); 17; 20; 23; 26; 29; 32; 31:27; 35; 40; 34:15; 35:5(4); 6; **Deut** 3:8; 21; 4:13; 47; 5:22; 9:10; 11; 15(2); 17(2); 10:1; 3(2); 14:6; 17:6; 18:3; 19:15; 21:15; 32:30; **Josh** 2:1; 4; 10; 23; 3:4; 6:22; 7:3; 21; 9:10; 14:3; 4; 15:60; 19:30; 21:16; 25; 27; 24:12; **Judg** 3:16; 5:30; 7:3; 25; 8:12; 9:44; 10:3; 11:37; 38; 39; 12:6; 15:4; 13; 16:3; 28; 29; 17:4; 19:10; 20:21; 45; **Ruth** 1:1; 2; 3; 5; 7; 8; 19; 4:11; **1Sa** 1:2; 3; 2:21; 34; 4:4; 11; 17; 6:7; 10; 10:2; 4; 11:11; 13:1; 2; 14:49; 15:4; 18:27; 23:18; 25:13; 18(3); 27:3; 28:8; 30:5; 10; 12; 18; 21; **2Sa** 1:1; 2:2; 10; 4:2; 8:2; 5; 12:1; 13:23; 14:6(2); 26; 28; 15:11; 27; 36; 16:1; 18:24; 21:8; 23:20; **1Kin** 2:5; 32; 39; 3:16; 18; 25; 5:12; 14; 6:23; 32; 34(3); 7:15; 16; 18; 20(2); 24; 26; 41(5); 42(3); 8:7; 9; 63; 9:10; 10:16; 19; 11:29; 12:28; 14:20; 15:25; 16:8; 21; 24; 29; 17:12; 18:21; 23; 32; 20:1; 15(2); 16; 27; 21:10; 13; 22:31; 51; **2Kin** 1:14; 2:6; 7; 8; 12; 24(2); 4:1; 5:17; 22(2); 23(5); 7:1; 14; 16; 18; 8:17; 26; 9:32; 10:4; 8; 14; 11:7; 15:2; 23; 27; 17:16; 18:23; 21:5; 19(2); 23:12; 25:4; 16; **1Chr** 1:19; 4:5; 5:21(2); 7:2; 7; 9; 11; 9:22; 11:21; 22; 12:28; 32; 15:6; 8; 18:5; 19:7; 24:17; 25:7; 29; 26:8; 17(2); 18; 32; **2Chr** 3:10; 15; 4:3; 12(4); 13(3); 5:10; 7:5; 8:10; 9:15; 18; 13:21; 14:8; 17:15; 16; 17; 21:5; 19; 20; 22:2; 24:3; 26:3; 12; 28:8; 29:32; 33:5; 21(2); 35:8; **Ezr** 2:3(2); 4; 6; 7; 10; 12(2); 14; 19; 24; 27; 28; 29; 31; 37; 38; 58; 60; 64; 65; 66; 6:17; 8:4; 9; 20; 27; 10:13; **Neh** 5:14; 6:15; 7:8(2); 9; 10; 11; 12; 17(2); 19; 28; 31; 33; 34; 40; 41; 60; 62; 66; 67; 68; 71(2); 72; 11:12; 13(2); 18; 19; 12:31; 40; 13:6; **Est** 2:21; 6:2; 9:27; **Job** 13:20; 42:7; **Prov** 30:7; 15; **Eccl** 4:9; 11; 12; **Song** 4:5(2); 6:13; 7:3(2); 8:12; **Is** 7:4; 21; 17:6; 22:11; 36:8; 45:1; 47:9; 51:19; **Jer** 2:13; 3:14; 24:1; 28:3; 11; 33:24; 39:4; 52:7; 20; 29; **Eze** 1:11(2); 23(2); 21:19; 21; 23:2; 35:10(2); 37:22(2); 40:9; 39(2); 40(2); 41:3; 18; 22; 23; 24(4); 43:14; 45:15; 46:19; 47:13; 48:17(4); **Dan** 5:31; 8:3(2); 6; 7; 14; 20; 9:25; 26; 12:5; 11; **Hos** 6:2; 10:10; **Amos** 1:1; 3:3; 12; 4:8; **Zec** 4:3; 11; 12(2); 14; 5:9; 6:1; 11:7; 13:8; **Mt** 2:16; 4:18; 21; 6:24; 8:28; 9:27; 10:10; 29; 11:2; 14:17; 19; 18:8(2); 9; 16(2); 19; 20; 20:21; 24; 30; 21:1; 28; 22:40; 24:40; 41; 25:15; 17(2); 22(3); 26:2; 37; 60; 27:38; **Mk** 5:13; 6:7(2); 9; 37; 38; 41(2); 9:43; 45; 47; 11:1; 4; 12:42; 14:1; 13; 15:27; 16:12; **Lk** 2:24; 3:11; 5:2; 7:19; 41; 9:3; 13; 16; 30; 32; 10:1(2); 35; 12:6; 52(2); 15:11; 16:13; 17:34; 35; 36; 18:10; 19:29; 21:2; 22:38; 23:32; 24:4; 13; **Jn** 1:35; 37; 40; 2:6; 4:40; 43; 6:7; 9; 8:17; 11:6; 19:18; 20:12; 21:2; 8; **Acts** 1:10; 23; 24; 7:29; 9:38; 10:7; 12:6(2); 19:10; 22; 34; 21:33; 23:23(3); 24:27; 27:37; 41; 28:30; **1Cor** 6:16; 14:27; 29; **2Cor** 13:1; **Gal** 4:22; 24; **Eph** 5:31; **Phil** 1:23; **1Ti** 5:19; **Heb** 6:18; 10:28; **Rev** 2:12; 9:12; 16; 11:2; 3(2); 4(2); 10; 12:6; 14; 13:5; 11

UNDER

Gen 1:7; 9; 6:17; 7:19; 16:9; 18:4; 8; 19:8; 21:15; 24:2; 9; 35:4; 8; 39:23; 41:35; 47:29; 49:25; **Ex** 6:6; 7; 17:12; 14; 18:10; 20:4; 21:20; 23:5; 24:4; 10; 25:35(3); 26:19(3); 21(2); 25(2); 33; 27:5; 30:4; 36:24(3); 26(2); 30; 37:21(3); 27; 38:4; **Lev** 15:10; 22:27; 27:32; **Num** 3:36; 4:28; 33; 6:18; 7:8; 16:31; 22:27; 31:49; 33:1; **Deut** 2:25; 3:17; 4:11; 19; 49; 7:24; 9:14; 12:2; 25:19; 28:23; 29:20; **Josh** 7:21; 22; 11:3; 17; 12:3; 13:5; 16:10; 24:26; **Judg** 1:7; 3:16; 30; 4:5; 6:11; 19; 9:29; **Ruth** 2:12; **1Sa** 7:11; 14:2; 21:3; 4; 8; 22:6; 31:13; **2Sa** 2:23; 3:27; 4:6; 12:31(3); 18:2(3); 9(2); 22:10; 37; 39; 40; 48; **1Kin** 4:25(2); 5:3; 7:24; 30; 32; 44; 8:6; 13:14; 14:23; 18:23(2); 25; 19:4; 5; **2Kin** 8:20; 22; 9:13; 33; 13:5; 14:27; 16:4; 17; 17:7; 10; **1Chr** 10:12; 17:1; 24:19; 25:2; 3; 6; 26:28; 27:23; **2Chr** 4:3; 15; 5:7; 13:18; 21:8; 10(2); 26:11; 13; 28:4; 10; 31:13; **Neh** 2:14; 8:17; **Job** 9:13; 20:12; 26:5; 8; 28:5; 24; 30:7; 37:3; 40:21; 41:11; 30; **Ps** 8:6; 10:7; 17:8; 18:9; 36; 38; 39; 47; 36:7; 44:5; 45:5; 47:3(2); 91:1; 4; 13; 106:42; 140:3; 144:2; **Prov** 12:24; 22:27; **Eccl** 1:3; 9; 13; 14; 2:3; 11; 17; 18; 19; 20; 22; 3:1; 16; 4:1; 3; 7; 15; 5:13; 18; 6:1; 12; 7:6; 8:9; 15(2); 17; 9:3; 6; 9(2); 11; 13; 10:5; **Song** 2:3; 6; 4:11; 8:3; 5; **Is** 3:6; 10:4(2); 16; 14:11; 19; 25; 18:7; 24:5; 25:10; 28:3; 15; 34:15; 57:5(2); 58:5; **Jer** 2:20; 3:6; 13; 10:11; 12:10; 27:8; 11; 12; 33:13; 38:11; 12(2); 48:45; 52:20; **Lam** 1:15; 3:34; 66; 4:20; 5:5; 13; **Eze** 1:8; 23; 6:13(2); 10:2; 8; 20; 21; 17:6; 23; 20:37; 24:5; 31:6(2); 17; 32:27; 42:9; 46:23; 47:1(2); **Dan** 4:12; 14; 21; 7:27; 8:13; 9:12; **Hos** 4:12; 13; 14:7; **Joel** 1:17; **Amos** 2:13; **Obad** 7; **Jonah** 4:5; **Mic** 1:4; 4:4(2); **Zec** 3:10(2); **Mal** 4:3; **Mt** 2:16; 5:13; 15; 7:6; 8:8; 9(2); 23:37; **Mk** 4:21(2); 32; 6:11; 7:28; **Lk** 7:6; 8(2); 8:16; 11:33; 13:34; 17:24(2); **Jn** 1:48; 50; **Acts** 2:5; 4:12; 8:27; 23:12; 14; 27:4; 7; 16; 30; **Rom** 3:9; 13; 19; 6:14(2); 15(2); 7:14; 16:20; **1Cor** 6:12; 7:15; 9:20(3); 21; 27; 10:1; 14:34; 15:25; 27(3); 28; **2Cor** 11:32; **Gal** 3:10; 22; 23; 25; 4:2; 3; 4; 5; 21; 5:18; **Eph** 1:22; **Phil** 2:10; **Col** 1:23; **1Ti** 5:9; 6:1; **Heb** 2:8(4); 7:11; 9:15; 10:28; 29; **Jas** 2:3; **1Pet** 5:6; **Jude** 6; **Rev** 5:3; 13; 6:9; 11:2; 12:1

UNDERNEATH

Ex 28:27; 39:20; **Deut** 33:27

UNLESS

Lev 22:6; **Num** 22:33; **2Sa** 2:27; **Ps** 27:13; 94:17; 119:92; **Prov** 4:16; **1Cor** 15:2

UNTIL

Gen 8:5; 7; 24:19; 33; 26:13; 27:44; 45; 28:15; 29:8; 32:4; 24; 33:3; 14; 34:5; 39:16; 41:49; 46:34; 49:10; **Ex** 9:18; 10:26; 12:6; 10(2); 15; 18; 22; 16:20; 23; 35(2); 17:12; 23:18; 30; 24:14; 33:8; 34:34; 35; **Lev** 7:15; 8:33; 11:24; 25; 27; 28; 31; 32; 39; 40(2); 12:4; 14:46; 15:5; 6; 7; 8; 10(2); 11; 16; 17; 18; 19; 21; 22; 23; 27; 16:17; 17:15; 19:6; 13; 22:4; 6; 30; 23:14; 25:22(2); 28; **Num** 4:3; 23; 6:5; 9:15; 11:20; 14:19; 33; 19:7; 8; 10; 21; 22; 20:17; 21:22; 35; 23:24; 24:22; 32:13; 17; 18; 21; 35:12; 28; 32; **Deut** 1:31; 2:14(2); 15; 29; 3:3; 20(2); 7:20; 23; 24; 9:7; 21; 11:5; 16:4; 20:20; 22:2; 28:20(2); 21; 22; 24; 48; 51(2); 52; 61; 31:24; 30; **Josh** 1:15; 2:16; 22; 3:17; 4:10; 23(2); 5:1; 6:10; 7:6; 13; 8:24; 26; 29; 10:13; 26; 27; 33; 11:8; 14; 13:13; 20:6(2); 9; 22:17; 23:13; 15; **Judg** 4:24; 5:7; 6:18(2); 13:15; 18:30; 19:8; 25; 20:23; 26; **Ruth** 1:19; 2:7; 17; 21; 3:3; 13; 14; 18(2); **1Sa** 1:22; 23(2); 3:15; 7:11; 9:13; 11:11; 14:9; 24; 36; 15:7; 18; 35; 17:52; 19:2; 23; 20:41; 25:36; 30:4; **2Sa** 1:12; 4:3; 5:25; 10:5; 15:24; 28; 17:13; 19:7; 24; 21:10; 22:38; 23:10; **1Kin** 3:1; 2; 5:3; 6:22; 10:7; 11:16; 40; 15:29; 17:14; 18:26; 29; 22:11; 27; **2Kin** 6:25; 7:3; 8:6; 11; 10:8; 11; 17:20; 23; 18:32; 24:20; **1Chr** 5:22; 6:32; 12:22; 19:5; 28:20; **2Chr** 8:8; 16; 9:6; 16:12; 18:10; 26; 34; 21:15; 24:10; 29:28; 34; 31:1; 35:14; 36:16; 20; 21; **Ezr** 4:5; 21; 5:16; 8:29; 9:4; 10:14; **Neh** 7:3; 8:3; 12:23; **Job** 14:13; 26:10; **Ps** 36:2; 57:1; 71:18; 73:17; 94:13; 104:23; 105:19; 110:1; 112:8; 123:2; 132:5; **Prov** 7:18; **Song** 2:17; 3:4; 4:6; 8:4; **Is** 5:11; 6:11; 26:20; 32:15; 36:17; 39:6; 62:1; **Jer** 23:20; 27:7; 8; 22; 30:24(2); 32:5; 36:23; 37:21; 38:28; 44:27; 52:34; **Eze** 21:27; 33:22; 46:2; **Dan** 4:32; 7:22; 25; 9:27; **Hos** 7:4; **Mic** 5:3; 7:9; **Zeph** 3:8; **Mt** 1:17; 2:13; 15; 11:12; 13; 23; 13:30; 17:9; 18:22(2); 24:38; 39; 26:29; 27:64; 28:15; **Mk** 14:25; 15:33; **Lk** 1:20; 13:35; 15:4; 16:16; 17:27; 21:24; 22:16; 18; 23:44; 24:49; **Jn** 2:10; 9:18; **Acts** 1:2; 2:35; 3:21; 10:30; 13:20; 20:7; 21:26; 23:1; 14; **Rom** 5:13; 8:22; 11:25; **1Cor** 4:5; 16:8; **2Cor** 3:14; **Gal** 4:2; 19; **Eph** 1:14; **Phil** 1:5; 6; **2Th** 2:7; **1Ti** 6:14; **Heb** 1:13; 9:10; **Jas** 5:7; **2Pet** 1:19; **1Jn** 2:9; **Rev** 6:11; 17:17; 20:5

UNTO

Gen 1:9; 28; 2:19; 22; 24; 3:1; 2; 4; 6; 9(2); 13; 14; 16; 17(2); 19(2); 21; 4:3; 4; 5; 6; 7; 9; 10; 12; 13; 15; 18; 19; 23(2); 6:1; 4; 13; 20; 21; 7:1; 5; 9; 15; 8:9(2); 12; 15; 20; 9:1; 8; 17; 24; 25; 10:1; 19(3); 21; 25; 30; 11:4; 31; 12:1(3); 4; 6(3); 7(4); 8(3); 11; 18; 13:3; 4; 8; 10; 14; 17; 18; 14:6; 14; 15; 21; 22; 15:1; 4; 5; 7; 9; 10; 13; 18(2); 16:2(2); 4; 5; 6; 9; 10; 11; 13; 17:1; 7; 8; 9; 15; 17; 18; 21; 23; 18:1; 6; 7(2); 9; 10; 13; 14; 21; 27; 29; 30; 31; 33; 19:3; 5(3); 6; 8(2); 12; 14(2); 16; 18; 19; 20; 21; 31(2); 34; 37; 38; 20:5; 6; 9(3); 10; 13(2); 14; 16(2); 17; 21:1; 3; 5; 7; 9; 10; 12(3); 14; 17; 22; 23(3); 27; 29; 30; 22:1; 3; 5; 7; 11; 12; 15; 19; 20; 23:3; 5; 13; 14; 15; 16; 18; 20; 24:2; 3; 4(2); 5(3); 6; 7(4); 10; 12; 14; 20; 24(2); 25; 29(2); 30(2); 36; 38(2); 39; 40; 42; 45(2); 47; 48; 50; 54; 56; 58; 60; 65; 25:5; 6(2); 12; 17; 18; 23; 33(2); 26:1(2); 2; 3(3); 4; 9; 10; 16; 24; 27; 29; 32; 33; 35; 27:1(2); 6(2); 13; 18; 19; 20; 21; 22; 26; 31(2); 32; 34; 37(2); 38; 39; 42; 28:1; 4; 5; 9(2); 22; 29:4; 5; 6; 15; 20; 21(2); 23; 24; 25; 30; 34; 30:1; 3; 4; 14; 15; 16; 17; 25(2); 27; 29; 30; 40; 31:3(2); 4; 5; 11; 12; 13(2); 14; 16; 24; 29; 39; 43(3); 46; 52; 55; 32:3; 4; 9(2); 10; 16; 18; 19; 27; 32; 33:1(3); 9; 13; 14(2); 16; 34:1; 3(2); 4; 6; 9(2); 11(3); 12; 14(2); 15; 16; 17; 20; 22; 23; 24(2); 35:1(3); 2; 3; 4; 7; 9; 10; 11; 17; 20; 27(3); 29; 36:5; 37:2; 4; 6; 10; 13(2); 18; 22; 23; 26; 29; 30; 35; 36; 38:2; 8(2); 9; 12; 14; 16(3); 18; 39:8; 10; 14(4); 17(3); 19; 40:6; 8(2); 12; 13; 14(2); 16; 20; 21; 41:8; 9; 13; 14; 15; 17; 24; 25; 28(2); 32; 38; 39; 40; 41; 44; 50(2); 55(2); 56; 42:1; 7(3); 9; 10; 12; 14(2); 18; 20; 22; 23; 25; 28(2); 29(3); 31; 33; 34; 36; 37; 43:2; 3(2); 5; 8; 9; 11; 13; 23; 29(2); 32; 34; 44:4(2); 6; 7; 8; 10; 15; 16; 17; 18; 20; 21(2); 22; 23; 24; 27; 32(2); 45:1; 3; 4; 9(2); 10; 12; 17(3); 18; 24; 25; 27; 46:1; 2; 15; 18; 20(2); 25(2); 28(2); 29; 30; 31(4); 34; 47:2; 3(2); 4; 5(2); 8; 9(2); 15; 17; 18(2); 19; 23; 24; 26; 29; 31(2); 48:2; 3(2); 4; 5(2); 7; 9(2); 10; 11; 13; 15; 17; 18; 21(2); 49:1; 2; 6; 10; 11(2); 13; 15; 26; 28; 29(2); 33; 50:4; 12; 15; 16; 17(3); 19; 20; 21; 24(2); **Ex** 1:9; 10; 18; 19(2); 2:9; 10; 11; 20; 23; 25; 3:2; 4; 8(3); 9; 10; 11(2); 12; 13(5); 14(3); 15(4); 16(2); 17(2); 18(2); 4:1(2); 2; 4; 5; 6; 9; 10(2); 11; 15; 16; 18(2); 19; 21; 22; 23; 30; 5:1; 3; 4(2); 15; 16; 21; 22; 6:1; 2(2); 3(3); 6; 8; 9(2); 10; 11; 12; 13(4); 28; 29(3); 30; 7:1; 2; 4; 7; 8(2); 9(2); 10; 13; 14; 15(2); 16(2); 19(2); 22; 8:1(3); 5(2); 8; 9; 10; 12; 15; 16(2); 19(2); 20(2); 9:1(2); 8(2); 12(2); 13(2); 22; 27; 29(2); 33; 10:1(2); 3(2); 5; 6; 7(2); 8(2); 9; 10; 12; 21; 24; 25; 28; 11:1; 5; 8(2); 9(2); 12:1; 2; 3; 4; 14; 21; 23; 26; 29; 36; 42; 43; 49; 13:1; 2; 3; 5; 8; 9; 11; 12; 14; 14:1; 2; 10; 11; 13; 15(3); 22; 24; 26; 29; 15:1(2); 11; 13; 25; 16:1; 3; 4; 6; 9(2); 10; 11; 12; 15; 20; 23(2); 25; 28; 33; 35; 17:2; 4(2); 5; 9; 14; 18:5; 6(2); 8; 13; 14; 15(2); 16; 17; 19(2); 22; 26; 19:3(2); 4(2); 5; 6(2); 8; 9(3); 10(2); 12; 14; 15; 21(2); 23; 24(2); 25(2); 20:4; 5; 6; 19; 20; 21; 22(2); 23; 24(2); 26; 21:6(2); 8; 9; 11; 31; 32; 34; 22:7; 8(2); 9; 10; 11; 12; 17; 20(2); 23; 26; 27; 29; 31; 23:13; 14; 22(2); 23; 27; 31(2); 33; 24:1(2); 5; 12; 14(3); 16; 25:1; 2; 22; 25; 33; 34; 26:24; 33; 27:21; 28:1(2); 3(2); 4; 12; 28; 29; 35; 41; 42; 43(3); 29:1(2); 4; 17(2); 18(2); 25; 28; 34; 35; 41; 42; 30:3; 10; 11; 12; 14; 15; 16; 17; 20; 22; 23; 30; 31(2); 32; 34(2); 36; 37; 38; 31:1; 12; 13; 14; 18; 32:1(2); 2(2); 3; 7; 9; 13(2); 14; 17; 19; 21(2); 23; 24; 25; 26(2); 27; 30(2); 31; 33; 34(2); 33:1(4); 3; 5(3); 7; 8; 11(2); 12(2); 15; 17; 34:1(2); 2; 4(2); 7; 15; 16; 25; 26; 27; 31(2); 34; 35:1; 4; 5; 22; 29; 30; 36:2; 3; 5; 10(2); 13; 37:26; 38:4; 39:21; 31; 33; 40:1; 12; 13; 15; 32; **Lev** 1:1(2); 2(3); 9; 13; 15; 17; 2:1; 2; 8(3); 9; 11; 12; 14; 16; 3:3; 5; 6; 9; 11; 14; 4:1; 2; 3; 4; 12; 31; 35; 5:6; 7; 8; 12; 14; 15; 16; 18; 6:1; 2; 5; 6(2); 8; 9; 11; 15; 17; 19; 20; 21; 22; 24; 25; 7:5; 11; 14; 18; 20; 21; 22; 23; 25; 28; 29(3); 32; 34(2); 35; 38; 8:1; 3; 4; 5; 7; 21; 28; 31; 9:2; 3; 4; 6; 7(2); 8; 9; 12; 13; 18; 23; 10:3; 4; 6(3); 8; 11; 12(3); 19; 11:1(2); 2; 4; 5; 6; 10; 11; 12; 20; 23; 26; 27; 28; 29; 35; 38; 12:1; 2; 6(2); 13:1; 2(2); 9; 16(2); 49; 14:1; 2; 23(2); 33(2); 15:1; 2(2); 14(2); 26; 29(2); 16:1; 2(2); 18; 22; 29; 31; 34; 17:1; 2(4); 4(3); 5(4); 6; 7(2); 8; 9(2); 12; 14; 18:1; 2(2); 19; 19:1; 2(2); 4; 5; 21(2); 23; 25; 34; 20:1; 2; 3; 4; 16; 24(2); 26; 21:1(3); 2; 3; 6; 7; 8; 16; 17; 23(2); 24(2); 22:1; 2(2); 3(3); 12; 13; 14(2); 15; 17; 18(4); 21; 22(2); 24; 26; 27; 29; 23:1; 2(2); 6; 8; 9; 10(4); 12; 13; 14; 15; 16(2); 17; 18(2); 21; 22; 23; 24; 25; 26; 27(2); 32(2); 33; 34(2); 36(3); 37; 38; 39; 41; 44; 24:1; 2; 3; 7; 9; 11; 13; 15; 25:1; 2(3); 4; 5; 8(2); 10(4); 11; 12; 13; 14; 15(2); 16; 27(2); 28; 39; 40; 41(2); 47; 49; 50(2); 51; 52(2); 55; 26:1; 5(2); 9; 14; 16; 18; 21(2); 23; 24; 27(2); 28; 31; 40; 41; 27:1; 2(2); 3; 5; 6; 9(2); 11; 13; 14; 15; 16; 18(2); 19; 21; 22; 23(3); 24; 28(2); 30; 32; **Num** 1:1; 48; 50; 2:1(2); 5; 3:5; 6; 9(2); 11; 13; 14; 40; 44; 48; 51; 4:1(2); 9; 17(2); 19(2); 21; 27; 30; 35; 39; 43; 47; 5:1; 4; 5; 6; 7(2); 8(2); 9; 11; 12(2); 15; 19; 21; 6:1; 2(3); 5; 6; 8; 12; 13; 14; 17; 21; 22; 23(3); 25; 7:4; 5; 6; 7; 8(2); 9(2); 11; 89(2); 8:1; 2(2); 4(3); 5; 7; 12; 13; 16(2); 19; 20(2); 22; 23; 24; 26; 9:1; 4; 7; 8; 9; 10(2); 12; 14; 21; 10:1; 4; 29(2); 30; 32(2); 36; 11:2(2); 11; 12(3); 13(2); 16(3); 18; 20; 23(2); 25(2); 26; 29; 35; 12:4(4); 6(2); 11; 13; 14; 13:1; 2; 17; 21; 22; 23; 26(3); 27; 32; 14:2; 3; 7; 11; 13; 16; 18; 19; 23; 26(2); 28; 35; 39; 40; 44; 45; 15:1; 2(3); 3(2); 4; 7; 8; 10; 13; 14; 17; 18(2); 19; 21; 22; 24; 25; 33(2); 35; 37; 38; 39; 40; 16:3; 5(4); 8; 9(2); 15; 16; 19(2); 20(2); 23; 24; 25; 26; 30; 32; 36; 37; 38; 40; 44; 46(2); 50(2); 17:1; 2; 6; 9; 10; 12; 13; 18:1; 2(2); 4(2); 7; 8(2); 9; 10; 11; 12; 13; 15; 17; 19(2); 20; 24(2); 25; 26(2); 27; 28; 30(2); 19:1(2); 2; 3; 10(2); 21; 20:5; 6(2); 7; 8; 10; 12; 14; 16; 18; 19; 22; 23; 24(2); 25; 26; 21:2; 7; 8; 16; 17; 21; 24(2); 26; 29; 30(3); 34(2); 22:4; 5; 7(2); 8(2); 9; 10(2); 12; 13; 14; 16; 17(2); 18; 19; 20(3); 25; 28(2); 29; 30(3); 32; 34; 35(2); 36; 37(3); 38(2); 39; 23:1; 3; 4; 5; 6; 11(2); 13(2); 15; 16; 17; 18; 25; 26; 27(2); 28; 29; 24:10; 11; 12(2); 14; 25:2; 3; 4; 5(2); 6; 10; 12; 16; 26:1(2); 52; 53; 59; 60; 27:4; 6; 7; 8(2); 9; 10; 11(2); 12(2); 13; 15; 18; 28:1; 2(3); 3(2); 6; 7; 8; 11; 13(2); 14(3); 15; 19(2); 24; 26; 27; 28(2); 29; 31; 29:1; 2; 6(2); 8(2); 12; 13; 14; 36; 39; 30:1; 2; 3; 31:1; 2; 3(2); 12(3); 15; 21; 25; 28; 29; 30; 41; 43; 47; 48; 49; 32:2(2); 5; 6; 9; 11(3); 16; 17; 18; 20; 25; 29; 31; 33(2); 38; 40; 33:7; 9; 49; 50; 51(2); 56(2); 34:1; 2(2); 5; 8; 11; 13; 16; 17; 29; 35:1; 2(2); 4; 6; 8; 9; 10(2); 12; 25; 29; 36:2; 4; 8; 11; 13; **Deut** 1:1; 2; 3(3); 6; 7(3); 8(2); 9; 17; 20(3); 21; 22; 24; 25; 29; 35; 39; 41; 42(2); 43; 44; 45; 46; 2:1; 2; 4; 5; 9(2); 12(2); 14; 17; 19; 22; 23; 26; 27; 29; 31; 35; 36(2); 37(4); 3:2(3); 6; 8; 10; 12; 13; 14(2); 15; 16(4); 17; 20(3); 21(2); 26(2); 4:1(2); 2; 4; 7; 10; 11; 12; 13; 15(2); 19(2); 20; 21; 23; 30; 31; 32; 35; 42; 45; 48; 49; 5:1; 9(2); 10; 22(2); 23; 27(2); 28(3); 31; 6:7; 10; 18; 21; 23; 7:2; 3(2); 6(2); 8; 12(2); 13; 16; 18(2); 19; 23; 25; 8:1; 18; 20; 9:3; 5; 7; 10; 12; 13; 19; 26; 27; 10:1(3); 3; 4(2); 7; 8(2); 10; 11(3); 11:3(2); 4(3); 5; 6; 9(2); 12; 13; 21; 22; 24; 25; 29; 12:4; 5(2); 7; 11; 18; 26; 31(2); 13:2; 3; 4; 7(2); 8(2); 17; 14:2(2); 7; 8; 10; 19; 21(3); 25; 15:2; 5; 6; 8; 9(2); 10(2); 11; 12; 14; 16; 17(2); 18; 19; 21; 16:1; 2; 7; 9; 10(2); 15; 21; 17:1(2); 5; 9(2); 12(2); 14; 16; 18:2; 3; 6; 12; 14(2); 15(3); 17; 18(2); 19; 19:5; 8(2); 19(2); 20:2(2); 3(2); 5; 6; 7; 8(2); 9; 10(2); 11(2); 14; 15; 18; 21:2; 3; 4; 5; 6; 8(2); 11; 13; 18; 19(2); 20; 22:1; 2(2); 5(2); 13; 15; 16(2); 19; 23; 24; 26; 29; 23:5(2); 15(2); 18; 20(2); 21; 23; 25; 24:9; 11; 13; 15(2); 25:1; 3; 5(3); 7(2); 8; 9(2); 16; 17; 26:1; 2; 3(5); 7; 11(2); 12; 13(2); 15; 17; 19; 27:2; 3; 5; 6; 9; 14; 15; 28:1; 2; 8; 9(2); 11; 12(3); 13; 15; 20; 21; 26(2); 31; 32; 35; 36; 45; 60; 64; 68(2); 29:2(5); 4; 7(2); 8; 11; 13(4); 21; 24; 26; 29(2); 30:2; 4; 10(2); 12; 13; 14; 18; 20(2); 31:1; 2(2); 4(2); 5(2); 7(4); 9(2); 14; 16; 18; 20(2); 23; 28; 32:3; 17; 22; 43; 46(2); 48; 49(2); 50(2); 52; 33:2; 7; 9; 19; 26; 29(2); 34:1(2); 2; 3; 4(5); 6; 9; 10; **Josh** 1:1; 2; 3(2); 4(2); 6(2); 15; 17(2); 18; 2:3; 4; 7; 8; 9; 10; 12(2); 16; 17; 18; 21; 22; 24; 3:4; 5; 6; 7; 9; 15; 4:1; 5(2); 7; 8(2); 9; 10; 12; 13; 15; 18(2); 21; 5:2; 6(2); 9(2); 13(2); 14(2); 15; 6:2; 6; 7; 8; 16; 19; 22(2); 25; 7:2; 3; 5; 9; 10; 19(2); 22; 23(2); 24; 26(2); 8:1; 2(2); 5; 18; 24; 27(2); 28; 29; 30; 31; 9:3; 6(2); 7; 8(2); 9; 11; 12; 15; 17; 18; 19(2); 20; 21(2); 22; 25(2); 26; 27; 10:3(4); 4; 6; 8; 9; 10; 11; 14; 15; 22; 23; 24(2); 25; 28; 29; 30(2); 31; 34; 36; 41(2); 43; 11:6; 8(3); 9; 14; 17; 23(2); 12:1; 2; 3; 5; 6; 7(2); 13:1; 3; 4; 5; 6(2); 7; 9; 10; 11; 14(2); 15; 24(2); 25; 26(2); 27; 29; 31; 33(2); 14:3; 4; 6(3); 10; 13; 14; 15:3; 4; 5; 8; 9; 10(2); 11(2); 13; 18(2); 46; 47; 63; 16:1; 2; 3; 5; 6; 8; 10; 17:7; 9; 14; 17; 18:3; 10; 18; 19:10; 12; 28; 33; 20:1; 2; 4(2); 6(3); 21:1(3); 2; 3; 8; 27; 34; 43(2); 44; 45; 22:2; 3; 4(3); 5; 6; 7(2); 8(2); 9; 10; 13; 15(2); 19; 21; 24; 31; 32; 23:1; 2; 3; 4(2); 5; 7; 8(2); 9; 11; 12(2); 13; 14; 16; 24:2; 4(2); 6(2); 7; 10; 11; 15; 19; 21; 22; 23; 24; 27(4); 28; **Judg** 1:3; 14; 15; 20; 21; 24; 26; 33; 2:1(2); 3; 4; 5; 6; 10; 12; 15; 17(2); 19; 20; 3:3; 4; 9; 13; 15(2); 17; 19; 20(2); 26; 28; 4:3; 6; 7; 8; 11; 13; 14; 16; 18(2); 19; 20; 21; 22; 5:3; 18; 6:4; 6; 7; 8(2); 10; 11; 12(2); 13; 15; 16; 17; 18; 19; 20; 23(2); 24(2); 25; 26; 27; 30; 31; 35(3); 36; 39; 7:2; 4(4); 5(2); 7(2); 8; 9(2); 11(2); 13(2); 17; 19; 22; 24(2); 8:1; 2; 5(2); 6; 8; 9; 14; 15(2); 18; 20; 22; 23; 24; 27; 35; 9:1; 5; 7(3); 8; 9; 11; 12; 13; 14; 15; 16; 31; 36; 38; 40; 48; 52(2); 54(2); 55; 56; 10:4; 10; 11; 14; 15(3); 11:2; 6; 7(2); 8; 9; 10; 12; 13(3); 14; 15; 16; 17(2); 19(2); 22(2); 28; 29; 30; 32; 33; 34; 35; 36(2); 37; 39; 12:1; 2; 3; 5; 6; 13:3(2); 5; 6; 7; 8(2); 9; 10(2); 11(2); 12; 13(2); 15; 16(2); 17; 18; 19; 22; 23; 14:3(2); 10; 12(2); 13; 14; 15(2); 16(2); 18(2); 19; 15:7; 11(4); 12(3); 13; 14; 19; 16:1; 5(2); 7; 9; 10; 11; 12; 13(2); 14; 15; 16; 17(2); 18; 23; 26; 28; 17:2; 3(2); 4; 9(2); 10(2); 11; 18:1(2); 2; 3; 4; 5; 6; 8(2); 10; 12; 13(2); 14; 15; 18; 19(3); 23(2); 24; 25; 26; 27(2); 29; 19:2; 3; 5; 6; 9; 11; 12; 13; 18; 21; 23(2); 24(2); 25; 28(2); 30; 20:1; 14; 26; 32; 36; 42; 45(2); 47; 21:1; 5; 12; 13; 22(4); 23; **Ruth** 1:7; 8; 10(2); 14; 15(2); 18; 20; 2:2(2); 3; 4; 5; 8; 9; 10; 11(3); 13(2); 14; 19; 20(3); 21; 22; 23; 3:1; 3; 5(2); 6; 13; 17; 4:1; 3; 8; 9(2); 12; 13; 14; 15; 16; **1Sa** 1:3; 5; 10; 11(2); 14; 21; 22; 23; 24; 26; 2:10; 11; 14; 16; 20; 22; 23; 25; 27(3); 28; 34; 3:1; 5; 7; 9; 14; 17(2); 4:3; 7; 8; 9; 16; 20; 5:1; 5; 8(2); 6:5; 12; 14; 15; 17; 18(2); 7:3(3); 5; 8; 9(2); 14; 17; 8:4; 5; 6; 7(3); 8(2); 9(2); 10; 22(3); 9:6; 10; 11; 16; 17; 19; 23(2); 24; 10:2; 7; 8; 11; 14; 15; 16; 17; 18; 19; 11:1; 3(2); 7; 9(2); 10(2); 12; 12:1(3); 2; 5; 6; 8; 10; 12; 17; 18; 19(3); 20; 13:12; 15; 17(2); 14:1; 4; 6; 7; 8(2); 9(2); 10(2); 11; 12; 17; 18; 19(2); 23; 33; 34; 35(2); 36(2); 40(3); 41; 45; 52; 15:1(2); 6; 10; 11; 13; 15; 16(2); 20; 21; 24; 26; 28; 32; 16:1; 3(2); 5; 7; 10; 11(2); 15; 17; 19; 20; 17:8(2); 13; 17; 18; 28; 34; 37; 39; 41; 43; 44; 46; 52(2); 55; 18:1; 8; 18; 19; 19:4(2); 6; 11; 17(2); 20:2; 4; 5(2); 11; 12(2); 21; 22; 27; 29; 30(2); 31; 32; 36; 40(2); 21:1; 2(2); 5; 8; 11; 14; 22:2; 3; 5; 7; 8; 13; 15; 17; 22; 23:2; 3; 17(2); 27; 24:4(3); 6(2); 16; 19; 21; 22(2); 25:5; 6; 7; 8; 11; 13; 15; 16; 19; 21; 22; 27(2); 31(2); 34; 35; 40(2); 26:1; 27:2; 5; 6(2); 8; 28:1; 7; 8(2); 9; 11; 13(2); 14; 15; 18; 21(4); 22; 23; 29:3(3); 4(2); 6(3); 8(2); 30:13; 15; 17; 24; 25; 26; 31:4; **2Sa** 1:3(2); 4; 5; 7; 8; 9; 10; 13; 14; 16; 26; 2:1(2); 5(4); 6; 3:2; 7; 8; 12; 16; 21(2); 24; 38; 4:8; 9; 5:1; 6(2); 14; 19; 6:10; 12; 21; 23; 7:2; 4; 8; 9; 17; 20; 24; 27; 28; 8:10; 11; 15; 9:2(2); 3(2); 4(2); 6; 7; 9(2); 11; 12; 10:2(2); 3(3); 5; 13; 11:4(2); 7; 10(3); 11; 16; 19; 20(2); 23(3); 25(2); 12:1(3); 3; 4(2); 8; 11; 13(2); 14; 15(2); 18(2); 19; 21; 24; 31(2); 13:4(2); 5(2); 6; 10; 11(2); 13; 14; 15; 16(3); 17; 20; 22; 25; 26; 28; 29; 35; 39; 14:2; 3; 5; 8; 9; 10; 12; 15(2); 18; 21; 27; 30; 31(2); 32; 15:2; 3; 4; 7(2); 9; 14; 15; 25; 26; 27; 33(2); 34; 36; 16:2; 3; 4; 9; 10; 16(2); 18; 21(2); 22; 17:1; 3; 6; 7; 11; 15; 20; 21; 18:2; 4; 11; 12; 18; 20; 21; 23; 24; 26; 28; 30; 32; 19:2; 7(2); 8; 11; 14; 19(2); 22; 23(2); 25; 27; 28; 29; 30(2); 33; 34(2); 35; 37; 38; 39; 41; 20:2; 3(2); 8; 14; 16; 17(2); 21; 22(2); 21:2(2); 3; 4; 6(2); 8; 17; 22:1; 42; 45(2); 50; 51; 23:10; 13; 16; 19; 24:3(2); 9; 10; 11; 12(2); 13(2); 14; 17; 18(2); 21; 22(2); 23(2); 24(2); 25; **1Kin** 1:2; 11; 13(3); 15(2); 16; 17(2); 27; 30; 33; 42; 51; 53; 2:5(2); 7; 9; 14; 16; 17; 18; 19(3); 20; 22; 26(2); 27; 28; 29; 30; 31; 36; 38; 39; 42(3); 3:2; 6; 11; 12; 13; 16; 26; 4:12; 21(2); 27; 28; 33; 5:1; 3; 5(3); 6(2); 7; 9(2); 6:12; 24; 7:8; 9; 48; 8:1; 2; 5; 6; 8; 15; 18(2); 19; 26; 28(2); 29; 33; 34(2); 40; 44; 46; 47; 48(3); 52(4); 54; 56; 58; 59; 63; 65; 66; 9:2; 3; 8; 13; 16; 21; 24; 25; 10:5; 12; 13; 11:2(3); 8; 9; 11; 14; 18; 22; 24; 35; 36; 38(2); 40; 12:3; 5; 7(2); 9; 10(5); 15(2); 16(2); 19; 20; 22; 23(2); 27(2); 28; 30; 32(2); 33; 13:1; 2; 6; 7; 8; 11; 12; 13; 14; 15; 18(3); 20; 21; 22; 26(3); 34; 14:5(2); 27; 15:19; 20; 29; 17:1; 2; 5; 8; 13(2); 18(2); 19; 20; 21; 23; 18:1; 2; 5(3); 15; 17; 19; 20(2); 21; 22; 25; 30(3); 31; 40; 41; 44; 19:2; 5; 8; 9(2); 13; 15; 18; 20; 21(2); 20:2; 5; 6; 7; 8(2); 9; 10(2); 12; 13; 22; 23; 25; 28; 31; 34; 35; 36; 39(2); 40; 42; 21:2(2); 3; 5; 6(3); 7; 8; 11(2); 19(2); 25; 22:3; 4; 5; 6; 8; 13(2); 14; 15; 16; 18; 22; 24; 26; 30; 34; 38; 49; **2Kin** 1:2; 3; 5(2); 6(4); 7; 9(2); 11(2); 12; 13; 15(2); 16; 2:2(2); 3; 4; 5; 6; 9; 10; 16; 18(2); 19; 21; 22; 23(2); 3:3; 4; 13(2); 26; 4:1(2); 2; 6(2); 9; 13(2); 16; 17; 19; 22; 25; 26; 33; 36; 38; 42; 5:1; 3; 5; 6; 7; 10; 13; 14; 17(2); 19; 25; 26; 27(2); 6:1; 2; 9; 11; 15; 18; 19; 21; 26; 28(2); 29; 33; 7:4; 5; 10; 12; 15; 20; 8:1; 3; 6; 8; 10(2); 12; 22; 9:1; 5; 6; 11(2); 20; 10:1; 6; 10; 17; 18; 19; 22; 23; 27; 30(2); 11:15; 12:7; 13:4; 14; 15(2); 18; 23(2); 14:6; 7; 13; 25; 15:5; 12(2); 16:6; 9; 17:12; 23; 32; 34; 41; 18:4; 8; 11; 14; 19; 21; 22; 26; 27; 32; 19:3; 6; 9; 29; 20:1(2); 2; 5; 6; 8; 11; 12; 13; 14(3); 16; 17; 19; 21:15; 22:6; 8; 13(2); 14; 15; 17; 20; 23:1; 4; 5; 6; 21; 25; 35; 24:7; 25:2; 8; 17; 24; **1Chr** 1:19; 2:3; 9; 19; 3:1; 4; 5; 4:31; 33; 39; 41; 43; 5:1; 8; 9; 11; 23(2); 26(3); 6:48; 61; 63; 67; 71; 77; 7:20; 10:9; 14; 11:1; 2; 12:8; 16; 17(3); 18; 40; 13:2(4); 5; 9; 14:10; 14; 15:2; 3; 12(2); 16:8; 9(2); 16; 18; 23; 28(2); 29(2); 34; 40; 17:2; 5; 7; 15; 26; 18:3; 11; 19:2; 3(2); 11; 14; 20:8; 21:5; 8; 9; 10; 11; 13; 15; 17; 18; 22; 23; 26; 22:7; 8; 9; 23:13; 25; 26; 31(2); 26:6; 28:1; 3; 6; 29:1; 5; 12; 17; 18; 19; 21(2); 22; 24; **2Chr** 1:2; 5; 7(2); 8(2); 9; 12; 2:15; 3:1; 5:2; 3; 6; 7; 9; 6:14; 17; 19; 20; 21; 25; 27; 30(2); 31; 34; 36; 37; 38; 40; 7:8; 10; 12; 15; 21(2); 8:11; 12; 15; 16; 9:12; 26; 28; 10:5(2); 7; 9; 10(3); 15; 16; 19; 11:3; 14; 16; 23; 12:5; 13:7; 10; 11; 14; 14:7; 9; 11; 13; 15:2; 4; 11; 14; 10; 16:4; 7; 17:3; 16; 18:3; 4; 5; 7(2); 14; 17; 20; 23; 29; 19:4; 20:9; 15; 21; 24; 26; 28; 33; 21:10; 23:3; 14; 24:5; 6; 11; 17; 19; 20; 23; 25:12; 13; 14; 15(2); 16(2); 26:18(3); 21; 27:5; 28:9(2); 10; 13; 16; 20; 21; 23; 25; 29:5; 7; 11; 30; 31; 30:1; 5; 6; 8; 9(2); 10; 17; 21; 22; 27; 31:6; 16; 32:9(2); 13; 18; 23; 24(2); 25; 31; 33:2; 13; 17; 18; 22; 34:4; 6; 25; 26; 35:1; 3(2); 8(2); 9; 12; 22; 36:13; **Ezr** 1:8; 11; 2:1(3); 63; 69; 3:3; 5; 6; 7(2); 8(2); 11; 4:1; 2(2); 3(3); 6; 7; 11(2); 12(2); 13; 15; 17(2); 18; 20; 23; 24; 5:1(2); 3; 4; 6; 7(2); 8; 9; 12; 14; 15; 6:5(2); 8; 10; 21; 22; 7:7; 11; 12; 15; 22; 26; 28; 8:17(3); 22; 25; 26; 28(3); 30; 31; 35(2); 36; 9:4; 5; 6; 7; 9; 11; 12(2); 10:1; 2; 4; 7(2); 9; 10; 11; **Neh** 1:3; 9(3); 2:1; 2; 3; 4; 5(3); 6; 7; 8; 17; 18; 20; 3:1(2); 2; 4(3); 5; 7(2); 8(3); 9; 10(2); 12; 13; 15; 16(2); 17; 20; 24(2); 26; 27; 31; 32; 4:6; 9; 12(2); 14; 15(2); 19; 20; 22; 5:5; 7; 8(3); 14; 15; 16; 17; 6:2; 3; 4; 5; 8; 10; 17(2); 18; 7:3; 6; 65; 70; 8:1; 3; 9(2); 10(3); 12; 13; 15; 17; 18(2); 9:4; 14; 27; 28; 29(2); 32; 34; 36; 37; 38; 10:28; 30; 35; 36; 37(2); 38; 39; 11:30; 12:37; 38; 39; 46; 47(2); 13:4; 6; 12; 13; 16; 17; 21; 25(2); 27; **Est** 1:1; 3; 5(2); 14; 15; 17; 18; 19; 2:2; 3(2); 8(2); 9; 13(2); 14; 15; 16; 18; 22; 3:3; 4(2); 8; 10; 11; 12; 14; 4:6; 7; 8(4); 10(2); 11(2); 16; 5:3; 4(2); 6; 12(2); 14(3); 6:3; 4; 5; 6(2); 11; 13; 14; 7:2; 5; 8:1(2); 2; 6; 7; 9(4); 13; 9:5; 12; 13; 20; 22; 23; 26; 27; 30; 10:3; **Job** 1:2; 7; 8; 12; 14; 2:2; 3; 6; 7; 9; 10; 13; 3:6; 20; 25; 5:7; 8(2); 6:22; 28; 7:4; 20; 8:5; 9:12; 16; 10:2; 3; 15; 11:7; 19; 12:8; 13:2; 12; 20; 27; 15:19; 16:20; 19:11; 20:6; 29; 21:14; 15; 33; 22:2(2); 17; 21; 26; 27; 28; 23:5; 28:28; 29:21; 30:20; 26; 31:10; 37(2); 32:12; 21; 33:22; 23; 24; 26(3); 31; 33; 34:2; 10; 11; 14; 15; 28; 31; 34; 36; 37; 35:3; 5; 6; 37:3; 14; 19; 38:17; 35; 41; 39:4; 13(2); 40:6; 7; 14; 19; 41:3(2); 42:4; 7; 8; 11; **Ps** 2:5; 7; 3:4; 8; 4:3; 5:2(2); 3; 7:t, 4; 10:14; 13:6; 16:2; 6; 17:1(2); 6; 18:t, 6; 39; 41; 44; 49(2); 19:2(2); 6; 22:5; 22; 24; 27; 31; 24:4; 25:1; 10; 16; 26:11; 27:6; 8; 12; 28:1; 2; 29:1(2); 2(2); 11; 30:2; 4; 8; 12; 31:22; 32:2; 5(2); 6(2); 9; 33:2; 3; 34:5; 11; 15; 18; 35:3; 10; 23; 36:5; 10; 37:5; 39:12; 40:1; 3; 5; 15; 41:2; 4; 8; 10; 42:3; 7; 8; 9; 10; 43:3; 4(2); 44:3; 25; 45:14(2); 46:9; 47:1; 6; 9; 48:10; 14; 50:1; 5; 14(2); 16; 51:t, 1; 12; 13; 18; 52:t, 54:5; 6; 55:2; 14; 56:1; 4; 9; 11; 12; 57:1(2); 2(2); 9; 10(2); 59:13; 17; 61:1; 2; 8; 62:11; 12; 65:1; 2; 4; 66:1; 3(2); 4; 15; 17; 67:1; 68:4; 20; 29; 31; 32(2); 34; 35; 69:1; 8(2); 13; 16; 18; 27; 70:5; 71:2; 7; 18; 19; 22; 23; 24; 72:1; 8; 74:3; 19; 20; 75:1(2); 4; 76:11(2); 77:1(3); 78:36; 46(2); 62; 79:2(2); 12; 80:6; 11(2); 81:1(2); 8(2); 12; 13; 15; 83:9(2); 85:1; 8; 86:3(2); 4; 5; 6; 8(2); 16(2); 88:2; 3; 8; 9; 13; 89:3; 6(2); 8; 26; 35; 49; 90:12; 16(2); 92:1(2); 94:15; 95:1; 2; 11; 96:1(2); 2; 7(2); 8(2); 98:1; 4; 5; 99:7; 100:1; 4; 101:1; 2; 102:1; 2; 12; 103:7(2); 17; 20; 104:8; 23; 33; 105:1; 2(2); 9; 10; 11; 106:1; 4; 25; 28; 31(2); 36; 37; 38; 47; 107:1; 6; 13; 18; 19; 28; 30; 108:3; 4; 109:4; 12; 17; 19; 25; 110:1; 111:5; 9; 112:4; 113:3; 5; 115:1(3); 8; 116:2; 7; 12; 14; 18; 118:1; 6; 18; 27; 29; 119:6; 15; 20; 25; 28; 31; 33; 36; 38; 41; 48; 49; 58; 59; 62; 65; 72; 76; 77; 79; 90; 103; 105(2); 107; 112; 116; 117; 124; 130; 132(2); 146; 149; 120:1; 3(2); 121:1; 122:1; 4(2); 123:1; 2(2); 125:3; 4; 5; 130:1; 132:2(2); 11; 135:3; 4; 12; 18; 136:1; 2; 22; 26; 138:1; 6; 139:6; 17; 140:6; 13; 141:1(4); 8; 142:1(2); 5; 6; 143:6; 7; 8; 9; 144:9(2); 10; 145:18; 146:2; 10; 147:1; 7(2); 19(2);

148:14; 149:1; 3; **Prov** 1:5; 9; 23(2); 33; 2:2; 10; 18(2); 19; 3:5; 15; 22; 28; 34; 4:4; 18; 20; 22; 5:1; 9(2); 6:16; 7:4; 13; 24; 8:4; 32; 11:27; 12:14; 15; 14:6; 12; 15:9; 10; 12; 16:3; 22; 25; 18:13; 19:17; 20:23; 22:17; 21; 23:12; 22; 24:11; 14; 24; 25:7; 26:4; 28:27; 29:17; 30:1(2); 5; 6; 10; 31:3; 6(2); 24; **Eccl** 1:6; 7; 2:3; 17; 18; 3:20; 5:4; 7:21; 8:4; 9; 14; 9:3; 13; 12:7; **Song** 1:13; 14; 2:10; 8:11; **Is** 1:4; 6; 9(2); 10; 11; 13; 14; 23; 2:2; 3:9(2); 11; 5:8; 11; 18; 20; 21; 22; 26; 30; 6:3; 6; 7:3; 4; 10; 8:1; 2; 3; 5; 19(4); 22; 9:6(2); 13; 10:1; 11; 21; 30; 12:5; 13:2; 15; 14:10(2); 15:4(2); 5; 8(2); 16:1; 8; 18:4; 6; 7; 19:11; 16; 17; 20(2); 21; 20:1; 21:2; 4; 6; 9; 10; 16; 22:11(2); 15(2); 24:16; 25:6; 26:15; 27:2; 12; 28:5; 13; 15; 29:2; 11; 15; 30:10(2); 18; 19; 22; 31:1; 4; 6; 7; 32:9; 33:2; 21; 34:17; 35:2; 36:2; 3; 4; 10; 11(2); 37:2; 3; 6(2); 14; 15; 21; 30; 38:1(3); 2; 5; 7; 15; 39:3(4); 40:2; 9; 18; 20; 41:9; 13; 42:3; 5; 10; 12; 16; 24; 44:5; 7; 17(2); 22; 45:9; 10(2); 14(3); 19; 20; 22; 23; 46:3; 7; 12; 47:15; 48:11; 12; 13; 16; 22; 49:1; 3; 6; 51:1; 2(2); 4(2); 7; 11; 16; 19; 52:7; 53:12; 54:9; 55:2; 3; 5; 7; 11; 56:4; 5; 8; 57:9; 18; 59:16; 20; 60:5(2); 7(2); 9; 10; 11; 13; 14; 19(2); 61:1; 3(2); 7; 62:11; 63:5; 65:1; 2; 11; 15; 66:1; 19; 20; 24; **Jer** 1:3(2); 4; 5; 7; 9; 11; 12; 13; 14; 16; 17; 2:3; 10; 17; 21; 27; 31(2); 3:1; 2; 4; 6; 7; 10; 11; 14; 17; 18; 22; 25; 4:1; 10; 12; 13; 18(2); 5:5(2); 13; 19; 24; 6:3; 4; 10; 12; 13(2); 19; 20; 7:9; 12; 13; 14(2); 18; 21; 22; 23; 25(2); 26; 27(2); 28; 8:4; 10(3); 10:1; 6; 7; 11; 11:2; 3; 5; 6; 7(2); 9; 11(2); 12(2); 13; 14; 17; 20; 12:6; 8; 9; 11; 13:1; 3; 6; 8; 11(2); 12(2); 13; 18; 27; 14:2; 10; 11; 13; 14(3); 17; 15:1; 2; 16; 18; 19(2); 20; 16:1; 10; 11; 12; 15; 19; 20; 17:15; 17; 19; 20; 24; 26; 27; 18:8; 19:2; 4; 5; 11; 12; 13(2); 20:3; 8; 12; 13; 15; 21:1(2); 3; 8; 9; 22:6(2); 8; 13; 21; 23:1; 5; 12; 14; 16(2); 17(2); 33; 38; 24:3; 4; 7; 10; 25:2; 3(3); 4; 5; 7; 15; 17; 27; 28; 30; 33; 26:2(2); 3; 4; 5; 8; 10; 11; 12; 14; 15; 16; 23; 27:1; 3; 4(2); 5(2); 9; 10; 14(3); 15; 16(2); 17; 28:1; 5; 12; 15; 29:1; 3; 4(2); 7; 9; 12(2); 19; 21; 25; 28; 30; 31; 30:2; 9; 15; 17; 21(2); 31:3; 6; 26; 32; 34; 38; 40(3); 32:6; 7; 8; 12; 16(2); 18; 20; 24; 25; 26; 29(2); 31; 33; 35; 37; 33:1; 3; 6; 9(2); 14; 15; 19; 22; 34:1; 6; 8(2); 14(2); 16; 17; 20; 35:1; 2(2); 5; 12; 14(3); 15(2); 16; 17(2); 18(2); 36:1; 2(2); 3; 4; 9; 13; 14(2); 15; 16; 18; 19; 32; 37:2; 3; 6; 7; 18; 19; 38:1; 4(2); 12; 14(2); 15(3); 16; 17(2); 19; 20(2); 24; 25(5); 26; 27; 39:12(2); 14; 15; 18; 40:1; 2; 4(3); 5; 6; 7; 9; 10; 12; 14; 15; 16; 41:1; 6; 8; 14; 42:1; 2(2); 4(3); 7; 9(2); 10; 12; 20(4); 21; 43:1; 2; 8; 10; 44:4; 5; 8(2); 10; 12; 15; 16(2); 17(2); 18; 19(2); 20; 23; 24; 25; 29; 45:1; 2; 4; 5; 48:1; 9; 12; 27; 34(3); 46; 49:2; 4; 14; 29; 31; 50:15; 27; 29; 44; 51:2; 6; 9; 24; 44; 48; 53; 52:5; 9; 22; 32; **Lam** 1:12(2); 21; 22(2); 2:1; 18; 3:10; 25; 41; 64; 65; 4:4; 15; 21; 5:4; 16; 21; **Eze** 1:3; 16; 2:1(2); 2(2); 3(2); 4(2); 7; 8; 9; 3:1(2); 3; 4(3); 6; 7(2); 10(2); 11(2); 16; 17; 18; 22; 24; 27; 4:3; 9; 15; 16; 5:15; 6:1; 10; 7:1; 2; 7; 27; 8:5; 6; 8; 9; 12; 13; 15; 17; 9:4; 7; 9; 10:2; 7; 13; 11:1; 2; 5; 14; 15(2); 25; 12:1; 6; 8; 9; 10; 11; 19; 21; 23; 28; 13:1; 2; 3; 11; 12; 15; 18; 14:1; 2; 4(2); 6; 10; 22; 15:1; 16:1; 3; 5; 6(2); 8; 20(2); 23; 24; 27; 29; 33; 34; 36; 37; 54; 60; 61; 17:1; 2; 3; 11; 18:1; 22; 19:4; 20:2; 3(2); 5(4); 6; 7; 8; 9; 15; 18; 23; 27(2); 29(2); 30; 31; 39; 45; 21:1; 7; 8; 18; 23; 29(2); 22:1; 4(2); 17; 23; 24; 28; 23:1; 16; 27; 30; 36(2); 37; 38; 40; 43; 44(4); 24:1; 3(2); 15; 18; 19; 20; 21; 24; 26; 27; 25:1; 3; 8; 10; 26:1; 2; 27:1; 3; 28:1; 2; 11; 12; 20; 24; 29:1; 4(2); 10; 17; 19; 30:1; 20; 31:1; 2; 4; 8; 14; 17; 18; 32:1; 2; 17; 18; 33:1; 2; 7; 8; 10; 11; 12; 14; 16; 21; 23; 25; 27; 31; 32; 34:1; 2(2); 18; 20; 35:1; 3; 6; 15; 36:1; 3; 6; 9; 11; 13; 16; 20; 22; 32; 37:3; 4(2); 5; 9(2); 11; 12; 15; 18; 19; 21; 25; 38:1; 7(2); 13; 14; 39:4; 11; 17; 24; 28; 40:4(2); 6; 14; 15; 19; 22; 45; 46; 41:4; 17; 20; 22; 42:13(2); 43:6; 7; 18; 19(2); 24; 44:2; 5(2); 11; 12; 13(2); 15(2); 16; 26; 27; 28; 30; 45:1; 4; 7; 46:4; 7; 12; 13; 14; 16; 20; 24; 47:1; 2; 6; 8; 10; 14(2); 18; 21; 22(2); 48:2; 3; 4; 5; 6; 7; 8(2); 9; 12; 14; 18; 23; 24; 25; 26; 27; 28; 29; **Dan** 1:1; 3; 7(2); 10; 21; 2:3; 5; 9; 19; 21; 23(2); 24(3); 25(2); 26; 27; 46; 47; 3:3; 14; 18; 24(2); 4:1(2); 6; 7; 11; 16; 18; 20; 22; 26; 27; 34(2); 35; 36(4); 5:13; 15; 17; 6:2; 6; 15(2); 16; 19; 20; 21; 25(2); 26; 7:5; 10; 16; 26; 8:1(3); 6; 7; 13; 14(2); 17; 9:3; 4; 6; 7(3); 25; 26; 10:1; 11(4); 12; 15; 16; 19(2); 20; 11:18; 12:7; **Hos** 1:1; 2; 4; 6; 10(2); 2:1; 14; 19(2); 20; 23; 3:1; 3; 4:12; 15; 5:4; 12; 14; 6:1; 3(2); 4(2); 7:7; 13(2); 14; 8:2; 11; 9:4(2); 10; 17; 10:1; 6; 15; 11:2; 4; 12:4; 14; 13:7; 14:1; 2; 5; **Joel** 1:14; 20; 2:13; 14; 19; 3:6; **Amos** 1:5; 2:7; 3:7; 4:6; 8(2); 9; 10(2); 11; 12(2); 13; 5:4; 15; 18; 25; 6:2; 10; 14; 7:1; 4; 8; 12; 15(2); 8:1; 2; 9:7; **Obad** 15; 20; **Jonah** 1:1; 3(2); 5; 6; 8; 9; 10; 11(3); 12(2); 14; 16; 2:1; 2; 7; 9; 10; 3:1; 2(2); 3; 6; 8; 10; 4:2(2); 9; **Mic** 1:9(2); 12; 15(2); 2:11; 3:4; 6(2); 8; 4:1; 8; 13(2); 5:2; 3; 4; 6:3; 5; 9; 7:7; 8; 10; 15; 18; 20; **Nah** 3:13; **Hab** 1:2; 10; 11; 16(2); 2:1; 5(2); 7; 15; 16; 19; 3:13; 16; **Zeph** 1:1; 2:5; 11; **Hag** 1:1; 9; 13; 2:20; **Zec** 1:1; 3(3); 4(2); 6; 7; 9; 14; 19; 2:2; 4; 5; 8; 11; 3:2; 4(2); 6; 4:2; 5; 6(2); 7; 8; 9; 11; 12; 5:2; 3; 5; 11; 6:4; 5; 8; 9; 12; 15; 7:1; 2; 3; 4; 5(2); 8; 8:3; 11; 15; 18; 9:9; 10; 12; 11:7; 12; 13(2); 15(2); 12:2; 13:3; 6; 14:5; 10(3); 17; 20; 21; **Mal** 1:6; 8; 9; 11(2); 14; 2:2; 4; 12; 3:3; 4; 7(2); 4:2; 4; **Mt** 1:17; 20(2); 24; 2:5; 11; 3:7; 9(2); 10; 11; 13; 15; 16; 4:6; 7; 9; 10; 11; 19; 24; 5:1; 15; 18; 20; 22; 26; 28; 32; 33; 34; 39; 44; 6:2; 5; 8; 16(2); 18(2); 25; 27; 29; 33; 34; 7:6; 7; 11; 14; 21; 23; 24; 26; 8:4(2); 5; 7; 10; 11; 13(2); 15; 16; 18; 19; 20; 21; 22; 26; 32; 9:2; 6; 8; 9; 11; 12; 15; 16; 18; 24; 28(2); 29; 37; 10:1; 15; 23; 42(2); 11:3; 4; 7; 9; 11; 16(2); 17(2); 21(2); 22; 23; 24; 25; 27; 28; 29; 12:2; 3; 6; 11; 20; 22; 25; 28; 31(3); 36; 39; 45; 47; 48; 13:2; 3; 10(2); 11(2); 17; 24(2); 27; 28(2); 31; 33(2); 34(2); 36(2); 37; 44; 45; 47; 51(2); 52(3); 57; 14:2; 4; 16; 17; 22; 25; 27; 28; 31; 35; 15:3; 8; 10; 12; 15(2); 22; 24; 28(2); 29; 30; 32; 33; 34; 16:2; 4; 6; 8; 15; 17(2); 18; 19; 21(2); 22; 23(2); 24; 28; 17:3; 4; 11; 12(2); 13; 20(4); 22; 26(2); 27; 18:1; 2; 3; 7; 10; 13; 17(2); 18; 19; 22(2); 23; 24; 31; 32; 34; 35; 19:3(2); 4; 7; 8; 9; 10; 11; 13; 14; 16; 17; 18; 20; 21; 23(2); 24; 26; 27; 28(2); 20:1; 4; 6; 7(2); 8(2); 12; 14(2); 17; 18(2); 21(2); 22; 23; 25; 28; 32; 33; 21:1(2); 2(2); 3; 5; 13; 16(2); 19; 21(3); 23; 24; 25; 27; 31(3); 32; 36; 37; 40; 41(2); 42; 43; 22:1; 2; 4; 12; 16; 17; 19; 20; 21(4); 24; 25; 26; 29; 31; 37; 39; 42; 43; 44; 23:13; 14; 15; 16; 23; 25; 27(2); 28; 29; 31; 34; 35; 36; 37; 38; 39; 24:2(2); 3; 4; 13; 14; 19; 23; 26; 27; 34; 47; 25:1; 8; 12; 14; 15; 20; 21; 22; 23; 26; 28; 29; 34; 36; 39; 40(4); 41; 44; 45; 26:1; 3; 7; 10; 13; 14; 15(2); 17; 18; 21; 22; 24; 25; 29; 31; 33; 34(2); 35; 36(2); 38(2); 40(2); 45; 50; 52; 58; 62; 63; 64(2); 68; 69; 71; 73; 75; 27:8; 11; 13; 15; 17(2); 19; 21(2); 22(2); 26; 27; 33; 45; 53; 55; 62; 64; 65; 28:5; 10; 11; 12; 18(2); 20; **Mk** 1:5; 13; 17; 31; 32; 37; 38; 40; 41; 44(2); 2:2; 3; 4; 5; 8; 11; 13; 14; 16; 17; 18; 19; 24; 25; 27; 3:3; 4; 5; 8; 13(2); 23(2); 28(2); 31; 32; 4:1; 2; 9; 11(3); 13; 21; 24(2); 33; 34; 35(2); 38; 39; 40; 5:1; 8; 11; 19; 21(3); 31; 34; 36; 39; 41(2); 6:2; 4; 7; 10; 11; 18; 22; 23(2); 24; 25; 30; 31; 33; 35; 37(2); 38; 45; 48(2); 50; 51; 7:1; 6; 9; 14(3); 18; 27(2); 28; 29; 31; 32; 34; 8:1(2); 12(2); 17; 19; 21; 22; 27; 29(2); 34(2); 9:1(2); 4; 13(2); 17; 19; 20; 21; 23; 25; 29; 31; 35; 36; 41; 10:1; 3; 5; 11; 14(2); 15; 18; 20; 21; 23; 24; 28; 29; 32; 33(2); 35; 36; 37(2); 38; 39(2); 42; 45; 49; 51(3); 52; 11:1; 2; 3; 5; 6; 11; 14; 17; 21; 22; 23(2); 24; 28; 29; 33(2); 12:1; 4; 6; 9; 13; 14; 15; 16(2); 17; 18; 19(2); 24; 26; 32; 34; 38; 43(3); 13:1; 2; 13; 19; 30; 37(2); 14:9; 10(2); 12; 13; 16; 18; 19; 20; 24; 25; 27; 29; 30(2); 34(2); 36; 37; 41; 48; 61; 65; 72; 15:2; 6; 8; 9; 11; 12(2); 14; 15; 22; 41(2); 43; 44; 46; 16:2; 6; 7; 12; 13; 14; 15; 19; **Lk** 1:2; 3; 11; 13; 18; 19(2); 22(2); 26; 28; 30; 32; 34; 35; 38; 61; 74; 77; 80; 2:4; 10; 11; 12; 15(2); 20; 26; 34; 38; 48; 49; 50; 51; 3:2; 8(2); 9; 11; 12; 13; 14; 16; 18; 4:3; 5; 6(2); 8; 9; 12; 17; 21; 23(2); 24; 26(3); 29; 39; 40; 42; 43; 5:4; 5; 7; 10; 14; 20; 22; 24(2); 27; 31; 33; 34; 36; 6:2; 5; 9; 10; 13; 23; 24; 25(2); 26; 27; 29; 35; 38; 39; 7:2; 3; 6; 7; 8; 9(2); 13; 14; 19; 20(2); 21; 22; 24; 26; 28; 32(2); 40(2); 43; 44; 47; 48; 8:3; 10; 21; 22(2); 25; 39(2); 47; 48; 9:3; 11; 12; 13; 20; 33; 43; 48; 50; 57; 58; 59; 60; 62; 10:2; 9(2); 11; 12; 13(2); 17; 18; 19; 20; 21; 23; 26; 28; 29; 35; 36; 37; 41; 11:1; 2; 5(3); 8; 9(2); 13; 17; 24; 27; 30; 39; 41; 42; 43; 44; 45; 46; 47; 51(2); 52; 53; 12:1; 4; 5; 8; 10; 11(2); 13; 14; 15; 16; 20; 22(2); 27; 31; 36(2); 37; 41(2); 44; 48; 13:2; 7; 8; 12; 14; 18; 23(2); 24; 25(2); 31; 32; 34; 35(2); 14:3; 7; 10; 15; 16; 18; 23; 24; 25; 15:1; 3; 6; 7; 10; 12; 16; 18; 21; 27; 31; 16:1(2); 2; 5(3); 6; 7; 9; 15; 28; 29; 30; 31; 17:1(2); 5; 6; 7; 8; 14(2); 19; 22; 24; 37(2); 18:1; 3; 7; 9; 13; 15; 16(2); 17; 19; 22(2); 29(2); 31(2); 32; 35; 40; 41; 42; 43; 19:5; 8; 9; 13; 15; 17; 22; 24; 25; 26(2); 31; 32; 33; 39; 40; 42; 46; 20:2; 3; 8; 15; 20; 22; 23; 25(3); 28(2); 34; 36; 38; 41; 42; 45; 21:3; 4; 10; 23; 32; 22:4; 6; 9; 10; 11(2); 13; 15; 16; 18; 19; 22; 25; 29(2); 33; 35; 36; 37; 38; 40; 43; 46; 47; 48; 49; 52; 61; 67; 70; 23:1; 7; 14(2); 15; 17; 18; 22; 25; 28; 42; 43(2); 52; 24:1; 5; 6; 9; 10; 12; 17; 18; 19(2); 25; 27; 28; 36(2); 38; 41; 44(2); 46; **Jn** 1:11; 22; 25; 29; 33; 38(2); 39; 41; 43; 45; 46(2); 48(2); 49; 50(2); 51(2); 2:3; 4; 5(2); 7; 8(2); 10; 16; 18(2); 19; 22; 24; 3:2; 3(2); 4; 5; 7; 9; 10; 11; 26(2); 34; 4:7; 8; 9; 10; 11; 13; 15; 16; 17; 19; 21; 25; 26(2); 30; 32; 34; 35; 36; 40; 42; 45; 47; 48; 49; 50(2); 52; 53; 5:6; 8; 10; 11; 12; 14(2); 19(2); 22; 24(2); 25; 29(2); 33(2); 6:5(2); 8; 12; 13; 16; 19; 20; 23; 25; 26; 27(2); 28; 29; 30; 32(2); 33; 34; 35; 36; 43; 45; 47; 53(2); 61; 63; 65(3); 67; 7:3; 6; 8(2); 9; 10; 21; 22; 26; 33(2); 35; 37; 45; 50; 52; 53; 8:1; 2; 3; 4; 7; 9; 10; 11; 12; 13; 14; 19; 21; 23; 24; 25(3); 28; 34; 39(2); 42; 48; 51; 52; 55; 57; 58(2); 9:7; 10; 11; 12; 15; 17; 24; 29; 30; 34; 35; 37; 40; 41; 10:1; 6(2); 7(2); 24; 26; 28; 35; 41; 11:3; 4; 8; 11; 14; 15; 16; 18; 21; 23; 24; 25; 27; 29; 31; 32; 34; 39; 40(2); 44; 49; 54; 12:16; 24; 25; 27; 32; 35; 50; 13:1(2); 6; 7; 8; 9; 12; 16; 20; 21; 25; 27; 28; 29; 33; 34; 36; 37; 38; 14:3; 5; 6(2); 8; 9; 10; 12(2); 22(3); 23(2); 25; 26; 27(2); 28(3); 15:3; 7; 11; 15; 20; 21; 22; 26; 16:1; 3; 4; 6; 7(2); 12; 14; 15; 17; 19; 20; 23; 25(2); 26; 29; 33; 17:6; 8; 26; 18:4; 5; 6; 11; 15; 16(2); 17; 21; 24; 25; 28; 29; 30(2); 31(2); 33; 35; 37(2); 38(3); 39(2); 19:4; 5; 6; 9; 10(2); 11; 14; 15; 16; 26; 27; 20:1; 2; 10; 13(2); 15(2); 16(2); 17(3); 18; 19(2); 20; 21; 22; 23; 25(2); 26; 28; 29; 21:3(2); 5; 6; 7(2); 10; 12; 15(2); 16(2); 17(4); 18; 19; 22; 23; **Acts** 1:2; 7; 8(2); 12; 19; 22; 2:3; 14(2); 29(2); 34; 37; 38; 39; 41; 3:5; 10; 11; 12; 14; 20; 22(4); 25; 26; 4:1; 3; 8; 10; 19(3); 23; 29; 35; 5:4(2); 8; 9; 16; 35; 38; 6:2; 7:2; 3; 13; 26; 31; 37(3); 38; 40; 41; 44; 45; 8:1; 5; 6; 14; 20; 26(3); 29; 35; 36; 9:1; 2; 4; 6; 11; 15(2); 17; 21; 27; 34; 38; 10:3; 4; 7; 8; 9; 11; 15; 19; 21; 28(2); 29; 32; 36; 41; 42; 11:4; 7; 11(2); 13; 17; 18; 19; 20; 21; 22; 23; 24; 26; 27; 29; 12:5; 8(2); 10(2); 15; 17(3); 21; 13:4; 6; 15; 20; 21; 22; 23; 31; 32(2); 33; 36; 38(2); 41; 47; 51; 14:3; 6(2); 13; 15(2); 18; 27; 15:2; 3; 7; 8; 13; 18; 20; 23; 25(2); 33; 36; 39; 40; 16:10; 13; 14; 17; 19; 25; 32; 37; 38; 17:2; 3; 5; 6; 10; 15(2); 18; 19; 23; 29; 31; 34; 18:2; 6(2); 14; 21; 26(2); 19:2(2); 3(3); 4; 12; 22; 24; 30; 31; 33; 20:1; 6; 7; 13; 18; 20; 22; 24; 27; 28; 34; 38; 21:1(3); 2; 8; 11; 18; 20; 31; 32; 37(2); 39; 40(2); 22:1; 4; 5(2); 6; 7(2); 8; 10; 13(2); 15; 18; 20; 21(2); 22; 25; 27; 23:3; 15; 17(2); 18(3); 21; 23; 24; 26; 24:2; 4; 8; 10(2); 14; 23; 25:6; 11(2); 12(2); 13; 14; 21; 22; 26; 26:1; 6; 7; 11; 14; 16(2); 17; 18; 19; 20; 22; 23; 28; 32(2); 27:1; 3; 8; 10; 21; 40; 28:17; 19; 21; 25; 26; 28(2); 30; **Rom** 1:1; 10; 11; 13; 16; 19; 26; 2:5; 8; 14; 3:2; 7; 22; 4:3; 6; 11; 5:5; 15; 16; 18; 21(2); 6:10(2); 11(2); 13(3); 16(2); 19(2); 22; 7:4; 5; 10; 13; 16; 9:12; 17; 19; 21(2); 23; 26; 29; 10:3; 10(2); 12; 18; 20; 21; 11:4; 8; 9; 11; 27; 35; 12:1; 3; 19; 13:1; 14:6; 8(2); 15:8; 9; 15; 19; 23; 25(2); 27; 29; 32; 16:1; 4; 5; 19(2); **1Cor** 1:2; 3; 8; 9; 11; 18; 23(2); 24; 30; 2:1; 7; 10; 14; 3:1(4); 10; 4:9; 11; 13; 17; 21; 5:5; 9; 11; 6:12; 17; 7:1; 3(2); 10; 27; 8:1; 4; 7(2); 9:2; 11; 15; 16; 17; 19; 20; 10:2; 11; 28(2); 11:13; 14; 17; 23; 34; 12:2; 21; 31; 14:2(2); 3; 6; 11(2); 21; 26; 34; 36; 37; 15:1(2); 2; 3; 6; 28(2); 16:3; 5; 9; 11; 12; 16; **2Cor** 1:1; 13; 15; 16; 20; 23; 2:3; 4(2); 12; 14; 15; 16(2); 3:15; 4:4; 11; 5:5; 11; 12; 15(2); 19(3); 6:11; 13; 18; 7:12(2); 8:2; 5; 17; 9:5; 12; 13(2); 15; 10:13; 14; 11:9; 12:9; 17; 19; 20; **Gal** 1:2; 6; 8(2); 9; 17; 20; 22; 2:2; 7(2); 9(3); 14; 19; 3:8; 23; 24; 4:8; 13; 5:2; 4; 13; 6:6; 10(2); 11; 14(2); S:1; **Eph** 1:5; 9; 14; 15; 17; 2:10; 16; 18; 21; 3:3; 5(2); 7; 8; 10; 14; 20; 21; 4:7; 8; 13(2); 16; 19; 29; 30; 5:10; 20; 22(2); 24; 31; 6:5; 9; 13; 19; 22; S:1; **Phil** 1:2; 11; 12(2); 29; 2:8; 19; 27; 30; 3:10; 11; 13; 15; 21(2); 4:5; 6; 16; 20; **Col** 1:2; 6; 8; 10; 11; 12; 20; 2:2; 3:18; 20; 23; 4:1; 3; 7; 8; 9; 10; 11(2); **1Th** 1:1(2); 5; 9; 2:1; 2; 8(2); 9(2); 12; 18; 3:6; 11; 4:7(2); 8; 9; 15(2); 5:1; 15; 23; 27; S:1; **2Th** 1:1; 2; 2:1; 3:9; **1Ti** 1:2; 6; 17; 18; 20; 2:4; 3:14(2); 16; 4:7; 8; 16(2); 6:16; **2Ti** 1:12; 14; 16; 18(2); 2:9; 15; 16; 21(2); 24; 3:9; 11; 15; 17; 4:4; 8; 9; 10(2); 18; S:1; **Titus** 1:3; 15(2); 16; 2:9; 14; 3:2; 8; 12(2); 13; **Philem** 1:1; 13; 16; 19; 21; 22; **Heb** 1:1; 2; 5; 8; 2:3; 5; 10; 12(2); 17; 3:6; 14; 4:2(2); 13; 16; 5:4; 5; 7; 9; 6:1; 6; 8; 11; 17; 7:3; 4; 19; 21; 25; 8:5; 9:20; 27; 28(2); 10:24; 29; 30; 39; 11:4; 26; 12:2; 4; 5(2); 9; 11; 18(2); 22(2); 13:6; 7; 13; 22; **Jas** 1:23; 2:2; 3; 16; 23; 4:6; 5:7; **1Pet** 1:2(2); 3; 5; 7; 10; 12(5); 13; 22; 25; 2:4; 7(2); 14(2); 24; 25; 3:5; 7(2); 12; 19; 22; 4:7; 12; 19; 5:5; 10; 12; **2Pet** 1:2; 3(2); 4; 11; 16; 19; 2:4; 6; 9; 21; 22; 3:1; 7; 12; 15(2); 16; **1Jn** 1:2(2); 3; 4; 5; 2:1; 7; 8; 12; 13(3); 14(2); 21; 26; 3:14; 5:13; 16(3); 17; **2Jn** 1; 5; 10; 12(2); **3Jn** 1; 9; 13; **Jude** 2; 3(3); 6; 11; 21; 24; **Rev** 1:1(3); 4; 5; 6; 11(8); 13; 15; 17; 2:1; 5; 7; 8; 10; 11; 14; 16; 17; 18(2); 20; 23; 24(2); 26; 29; 3:1; 6; 13; 14; 22; 4:3; 6; 5:5; 10; 13(2); 6:2; 4; 8; 11(2); 13; 7:10; 12; 13; 14; 17; 8:3; 9:1; 3; 7(2); 10; 19; 10:4; 8; 9(3); 11; 11:1; 2; 3; 12; 18; 12:5; 11; 12; 13; 13:2; 4(2); 5(2); 7; 15; 14:4; 6; 13; 14; 20; 15:7; 16:8; 14; 19; 17:1(2); 7; 13; 15; 17; 18:5; 6; 18; 19:1; 9(3); 10; 17; 20:4; 21:5; 6(2); 9; 11; 18; 22:6(2); 9; 10; 16; 18(3)

UP

Gen 2:6; 21; 4:8; 7:11; 17(2); 8:7; 13; 13:1; 10; 14; 14:22; 17:22; 18:2; 16; 19:1; 2; 14; 27; 28; 30; 20:18; 21:14; 16; 18; 32; 22:3(2); 4; 13(2); 19; 23:3; 7; 24:16; 54; 63; 64; 25:8; 17; 34; 26:23; 31; 27:38; 28:12; 18(2); 29:11; 31:10; 12; 17; 21; 35; 45; 55; 32:22; 33:1; 5; 35:1; 3; 13; 14; 29; 37:25; 28; 35; 38:8; 12; 13; 39:15; 16; 18; 40:13; 19; 20; 41:2; 3; 4; 5; 6; 18; 19; 20; 21; 22; 23; 27; 34; 35; 44; 48(3); 43:2; 15; 29; 44:4; 17; 24; 30; 33; 34; 45:9; 25; 46:4; 5; 29; 31; 47:14; 48:17; 49:4(2); 9(2); 33(2); 50:5; 6; 7(2); 9; 14; 23; 25; **Ex** 1:8; 10; 2:17; 23; 3:8; 17; 7:12; 20; 8:3; 4; 5; 6; 7; 20; 9:10; 13; 16; 32; 10:12; 14; 12:6; 30; 31; 34; 38; 13:18; 19; 14:10; 16; 15:7; 16:13; 14; 23; 24; 33; 34; 17:3; 10; 11; 12; 19:3; 12; 13; 20(2); 23; 24(2); 20:25; 26; 22:2; 24:1; 2; 4; 9; 12; 13(2); 15; 18; 26:15; 30; 33; 29:27; 32:1(2); 4; 6(2); 8; 23; 30; 33:1(2); 3; 5; 8; 10; 12; 15; 34:2; 3; 4(2); 24; 35:21; 26; 36:2; 20; 40:2; 8(2); 17; 18(3); 21; 28; 33(2); 36; 37(2); **Lev** 6:10; 9:22; 11:45; 13:4; 5; 11; 21; 26; 31; 33; 37; 42; 50; 54; 14:38; 46; 19:16; 32; 22:30; 26:1(2); 38; **Num** 1:51; 6:26; 7:1; 9:15; 17; 21(2); 22; 10:11; 21; 35; 11:32; 13:17(2); 21; 30; 31(2); 32(2); 14:1; 13; 36; 37; 40(3); 42; 44; 15:19; 20; 16:2; 3; 12; 13; 14; 24; 25; 27; 30; 32; 34; 37; 45; 17:4; 7; 18:26; 19:9(2); 20:4; 5; 11; 25; 27; 21:3; 5; 17; 33; 22:4(2); 13; 14; 20; 21; 41; 23:7; 18(2); 24(2); 24:2; 3; 8; 9; 15; 20; 21; 23; 25; 25:4; 7; 26:10; 27:12; 31:52; 32:9; 11; 14; 33:38; **Deut** 1:21; 22; 24; 26; 28(2); 41(2); 42; 43; 2:13; 24; 3:1; 27(2); 4:19; 5:5; 6:7; 8:14; 9:1; 9; 23; 10:1; 3; 11:6; 17; 18; 19; 14:25; 28; 16:22; 17:8; 20; 18:15; 18; 19:11; 15; 16; 20:1; 22:4; 14; 19; 23:14; 24:5; 25:7(2); 9; 27:2; 4; 5; 28:7; 33; 43; 29:22; 30:12; 31:5; 16; 32:11; 17; 30; 34(2); 36; 38; 40; 49; 50; 33:2; 34:1; **Josh** 2:6; 8; 10; 3:6(2); 16; 4:5; 8; 9; 16; 17; 18(2); 19; 23(2); 5:1; 7; 13; 6:1; 5; 6; 12; 20; 26(2); 7:2(2); 3(2); 4; 10; 13; 16; 8:1; 3; 7; 10(2); 11; 14; 20; 31; 9:4; 10:4; 5; 6; 9; 10; 12; 33; 36; 11:6; 17; 12:7; 14:8; 15:3(2); 6(2); 7(2); 8(2); 15; 16:1; 17:15; 18:1; 11; 12(2); 17; 19:10; 11; 12; 47; 20:5; 22:12; 33; 24:17; 26; 32; **Judg** 1:1; 2; 3; 4; 16; 22; 36; 2:1(2); 4; 16; 18; 3:9; 15; 4:5; 10(2); 12; 14; 6:3(2); 5; 8; 13; 21; 35; 38; 7:1; 8:8; 11; 13; 20; 28; 9:7; 18; 32; 33; 34; 35; 43; 48; 51; 11:2; 13; 16; 31; 37; 12:3; 13:20; 14:2; 19; 15:5; 6; 9; 10(2); 13; 16:3; 5; 8; 18(2); 29; 31; 18:9; 12; 17; 30; 31; 19:5; 7; 9; 10; 17; 27; 28(3); 30; 20:3; 9; 18(3); 19; 23(3); 26; 28; 30; 31; 33; 38; 40(2); 21:2; 5(2); 8; 19; **Ruth** 1:9; 14; 2:15; 18; 3:14; 4:1; 5; 10; **1Sa** 1:3; 5; 6; 7; 9; 19; 21; 22(2); 24; 2:6; 7; 8(2); 14; 19; 35; 5:12; 6:9; 10; 13; 20; 21; 7:1; 7; 10; 8:8; 9:11; 13(2); 14(2); 19; 24; 26; 10:3; 18; 25; 11:1; 4; 12:6; 13:5; 15; 14:9; 10(2); 12(2); 13; 21; 46; 15:2; 6; 11; 12; 34; 16:13; 17:20; 23; 25(2); 19:15; 20:38; 21:12; 22:8; 23:11; 12; 19; 29; 24:7; 16; 22; 25:5; 13; 35; 26:19; 27:8; 28:8; 11(2); 14; 15; 25; 29:9; 10(2); 11(2); 30:4; **2Sa** 2:1(3); 2; 3; 22; 27; 32; 3:10; 32; 4:4; 12; 5:8; 17; 19(2); 22; 23; 6:2; 12; 15; 7:6; 12; 12:3(2); 11; 17; 13:29; 34; 36; 14:14; 15:2; 20; 24; 30(4); 17:16; 21; 18:9; 18; 24(2); 28(2); 31; 33; 19:34; 20:2; 3; 15; 19; 20; 21; 21:6; 8; 13; 22:9; 40; 49(2); 23:1; 8; 18; 24:9; 11; 18; 19; 22; **1Kin** 1:35; 40; 45; 49; 2:19; 34; 3:15; 6:8; 7:21(3); 8:1; 3; 4(2); 20; 35; 54; 9:16; 24; 10:5; 29; 11:14; 15; 23; 26; 27; 12:8; 10; 18; 24; 27; 28(2); 13:4; 29; 14:10; 14; 15; 16; 25; 15:4; 17; 16:17; 32; 34; 17:7; 19; 18:38; 41; 42(2); 43(2); 44; 46; 20:1; 22; 26; 33; 21:16; 21; 25; 22:6; 12; 20; 29; 35; 38; **2Kin** 1:3; 4; 6(2); 7; 9; 13; 14; 16; 2:1; 11; 13; 16; 23(4); 3:7; 8; 21; 22; 24; 4:21; 29; 34; 35; 36; 37; 6:7; 24; 7:5; 8:12; 9:1; 2; 8; 25; 27; 32; 10:1; 5; 6; 15; 12:10(2); 17(2); 13:21; 14:10; 11; 26; 15:14; 16; 16:5; 7(2); 9; 17:3; 4; 5(2); 7; 10; 36; 18:9; 13; 17(2); 25(2); 19:4; 14; 22; 23; 24; 26; 28; 20:5; 8; 17; 21:3(2); 22:4; 23:2; 9; 29; 24:1; 10; 25:4; 6; 27; **1Chr** 5:26; 11:6; 11; 20; 13:6(2); 14:2; 8; 10(2); 11; 14; 15:3; 12; 14; 16; 25; 28; 17:5; 11; 21:1; 16; 18(2); 19; 27; 25:5; 26:16; 28:2; **2Chr** 1:4; 6; 17; 2:16; 3:17; 5:2; 4; 5(2); 13; 6:10; 26; 7:13; 20; 8:11; 9:4; 10:8; 10; 18; 11:4; 12:2; 9; 13:4; 6; 16:1; 17:6; 18:2; 5; 11; 14; 19; 28; 34; 20:16; 19; 23; 21:4; 9; 16; 17; 24:7; 23; 25:14; 19; 21; 26:16; 19; 28:9; 12; 15; 24; 29:7; 20; 30:7; 27; 32:5(2); 25; 33:3; 14; 19; 34:30; 35:20; 36:6; 15; 22; 23; **Ezr** 1:1; 3; 5(2); 11(2); 2:1; 59; 63; 68; 3:2; 4:2; 12(2); 13; 16; 23; 5:2; 3; 9; 11; 6:1; 11; 7:6; 7; 9; 13; 28; 8:1; 9:5; 6(2); 9; 10:6; 10; **Neh** 2:1; 15; 17; 18; 3:1(2); 3; 6; 13; 14; 15; 19; 31; 32; 4:3; 7; 14; 5:2; 6:1; 10; 7:1; 5; 6; 61; 65; 8:5; 6; 9:3; 4; 5; 18; 10:38; 12:1; 31; 37(2); **Est** 2:7; 20; 5:9; 7:7; **Job** 1:5; 7; 16; 2:2; 12(2); 3:8; 10; 11; 4:15; 5:5(2); 11; 18; 6:3; 4; 7:9; 8:11; 9:7; 10:15; 18; 11:10; 15; 20; 12:14; 15; 13:19; 14:10; 11; 17(2); 15:30; 16:4; 8; 12; 17:8; 18:16; 19:8; 12; 20:6; 15; 27; 21:19; 22:22; 23; 24; 26; 29; 24:22; 26:8; 27:7; 16; 28:4; 5; 29:8; 30:4; 12; 20; 22; 28; 31:14; 18; 21; 29; 33:5; 34:7; 36:13; 37:7; 20; 38:3; 8; 10; 34; 39:4; 18; 27; 30; 40:7; 23(2); 41:10; 15; 25; 42:8; **Ps** 3:1; 3; 4:6; 5:3; 7:6; 9:13; 10:12; 14:4; 15:3; 16:4; 17:5; 7; 18:8; 35; 39; 48(2); 20:5; 21:9; 22:15; 24:4; 7(2); 9(2); 25:1; 27:2; 5; 6; 10; 12; 28:2; 5; 9; 30:1; 3; 31:8; 19; 33:7; 35:2; 11; 23; 25; 39:6; 40:2; 5; 12; 41:8; 9; 10; 44:5; 47:5; 53:4; 54:3; 56:1; 2; 57:3; 8; 59:1; 15; 63:4; 69:9; 15; 29; 71:6; 20; 74:3; 4; 5; 8; 15; 23; 75:3; 4; 5; 7; 77:9; 78:21; 38; 48; 80:2; 81:3; 12; 83:2; 86:4; 87:6; 88:8; 15; 89:2; 4; 42; 90:5; 6; 91:12; 92:11; 93:3(3); 94:2; 16(2); 18; 97:3; 102:10; 16; 104:8; 105:35; 106:9; 17; 18; 26; 30; 107:25; 26; 109:23; 110:7; 113:7; 119:48; 117; 121:1; 122:4; 123:1; 124:2; 3; 127:2(2); 129:6; 132:3; 134:2; 139:8; 21; 140:10; 141:2; 143:8; 144:12; 145:14; 147:2; 3; 6; **Prov** 1:12; 2:3; 7; 3:20; 7:1; 8:23; 30; 10:12; 14; 13:22; 15:1; 18; 16:27; 21:20; 22:6; 23:8; 24:16; 25:7; 26:9; 24; 28:25; 29:21; 22; 30:4; 13; 31; 32; 31:28; **Eccl** 2:26; 3:2; 3; 4:10(2); 15; 10:4; 12; 12:4; **Song** 2:7; 10; 3:5; 4:2; 12; 5:5; 6:6; 7:8; 12; 13; 8:4; 5(2); **Is** 1:2; 6; 2:3; 4; 12; 13; 14; 3:13; 14; 5:5; 6; 11; 13; 24;

UPON

US

1:6(2); 8:21; **Mal** 1:2; 9; 2:10; **Mt** 1:23; 3:15; 6:11; 12; 13(2); 8:25; 29; 31(2); 9:27; 13:36; 56; 15:15; 23; 17:4(2); 20:7; 12; 30; 31; 21:25; 38(2); 22:17; 25; 24:3; 25:8; 9; 11; 26:46; 63; 68; 27:4; 25; 49; **Mk** 1:24(2); 38; 4:35; 5:12; 6:3; 9:5(2); 22(2); 38(2); 40; 10:35; 37; 12:7; 19; 13:4; 14:15; 42; 15:36; 16:3; **Lk** 1:1; 2; 69; 71; 74; 78; 2:15(2); 48; 4:34(2); 7:5; 16; 20; 8:22; 9:33(2); 49; 50(2); 10:11; 17; 11:1; 3; 4(4); 45; 12:41; 13:25; 15:23; 16:26(2); 17:13; 19:14; 20:2; 6; 14; 22; 28; 22:8; 67; 23:18; 30(2); 39; 24:22; 24; 29; 32(3); **Jn** 1:14; 22; 2:18; 4:12; 25; 6:34; 52; 8:5; 9:34; 10:24(2); 11:7; 15; 16; 50; 14:8(2); 9; 22; 31; 16:17; 17:21; 18:31; 19:24; **Acts** 1:17; 21(2); 22(2); 2:29; 3:4; 12; 4:17; 5:28; 6:14; 7:27; 38; 40(3); 10:41; 42; 11:13; 15; 17; 13:33; 47; 14:11; 17; 15:7; 8; 9; 24; 25; 28; 36; 16:9; 10; 14; 15(2); 16; 17(2); 21; 37(4); 17:27; 20:5; 14; 21:5; 11; 16; 17; 18; 23:9; 24:4; 7; 25:24; 27:2; 6; 7; 20; 28:2(2); 7(2); 10(2); 15(2); **Rom** 3:8; 4:16; 24; 5:5; 8(2); 6:3; 8:4; 18; 26; 31(2); 32(2); 34; 35; 37; 39; 9:24; 29; 12:6(2); 7; 13:12(2); 13; 14:7; 12; 13; 19; 15:2; 7; 16:6; **1Cor** 1:18; 30; 2:10; 12; 4:1; 6; 8; 9; 5:7; 8; 6:14; 7:15; 8:6; 8; 10:8; 9; 15:32; 57; 16:16; **2Cor** 1:4; 5; 8; 10(2); 11(2); 14; 19; 20; 21(2); 22; 2:11; 14(2); 3:3; 6; 4:7; 12; 14(2); 17; 5:5(2); 14; 18(2); 19; 20; 21; 6:12; 7:1; 2; 6; 7; 9; 8:4(2); 5; 7; 19(2); 20(2); 9:11; 10:2; 8; 13; **Gal** 1:4; 23; 2:4; 3:13(2); 24; 4:26; 5:1; 25; 26; 6:9; 10; **Eph** 1:3; 4; 5; 6; 8; 9; 2:4; 5; 6(2); 7; 14; 3:20; 4:7; 5:2(2); **Phil** 3:15; 16(2); 17; **Col** 1:8; 12; 13(2); 2:14(2); 4:3(2); **1Th** 1:6; 9; 10; 2:8; 13; 15; 16; 18; 3:6(4); 4:1; 7; 8; 5:6(2); 8; 9; 10; 25; **2Th** 1:7; 2:2; 16(2); 3:1; 6; 7; 9; **1Ti** 6:8; 17; **2Ti** 1:7; 9(3); 14; 2:12; **Titus** 2:12; 14(2); 3:5; 6; 15; **Heb** 1:2; 2:3; 4:1(2); 2; 11; 14; 16; 6:1; 18; 20; 7:26; 9:12; 24; 10:15; 20; 22; 23; 24; 11:40(2); 12:1(4); 9; 10; 28; 13:13; 15; 18; **Jas** 1:18; 3:3; 4:5; **1Pet** 1:3; 12; 2:21(2); 3:18; 21; 4:1; 3; 17; 5:10; **2Pet** 1:1; 3(2); 4; 3:2; **1Jn** 1:2; 3; 7; 8; 9(2); 10; 2:19(5); 25; 3:1(2); 16; 18; 20; 21; 23; 24(2); 4:6(2); 7; 9; 10; 11; 12(2); 13(2); 16; 19; 5:11; 14; 15; 20; **2Jn** 2(2); **3Jn** 9; 10; **Rev** 1:5(2); 6; 5:9; 10; 6:16(2); 19:7

USE

Lev 7:24; 19:26; **Num** 10:2; 15:39; **Deut** 26:14; **2Sa** 1:18; **1Chr** 12:2; 28:15; **Jer** 23:31; 31:23; 46:11; **Eze** 12:23; 16:44; 18:2; 3; 21:21; **Mt** 5:44; 6:7; **Lk** 6:28; **Acts** 14:5; **Rom** 1:26; 27; **1Cor** 7:21; 31; **2Cor** 1:17; 3:12; 13:10; **Gal** 5:13; **Eph** 4:29; **1Ti** 1:8; 3:10; 5:23; **2Ti** 2:21; **Heb** 5:14; **1Pet** 4:9

USED

Ex 21:36; **Lev** 7:24; **Judg** 14:10; 20; **2Kin** 17:17; 21:6; **2Chr** 33:6(2); **Jer** 2:24; **Eze** 22:29; 35:11; **Hos** 12:10; **Mk** 2:18; **Acts** 8:9; 19:19; 27:17; **Rom** 3:13; **1Cor** 9:12; 15; **1Th** 2:5; **1Ti** 3:13; **Heb** 10:33

USES

Titus 3:14

USING

Col 2:22; **1Pet** 2:16

VERY

Gen 1:31; 4:5; 12:14; 13:2; 18:20; 21:11; 24:16; 26:13; 27:21; 24; 33; 34:7; 41:19; 31; 49; 47:13; 50:9; 10; **Ex** 1:20; 8:28; 9:3; 16; 18; 24; 10:14; 11:3; 12:38; 30:36; **Num** 6:9; 11:33; 12:3; 13:28; 16:15; 22:17; 32:1; **Deut** 9:20; 21; 20:15; 27:8; 28:43(2); 54; 30:14; 32:20; **Josh** 1:7; 3:16; 8:4; 9:9; 13; 22; 10:20; 27; 11:4; 13:1; 22:8(2); 23:6; **Judg** 3:17; 11:33; 35; 13:6; 18:9; **Ruth** 1:20; **1Sa** 2:17; 22; 4:10; 5:9; 11; 14:15; 20; 31; 18:8; 15; 19:4; 20:7; 23:22; 25:2; 15; 34; 36; 26:4; **2Sa** 1:26; 2:17; 3:8; 11:2; 12:15; 13:3; 21; 36; 18:17; 19:32(2); 24:10; **1Kin** 1:4; 6; 15; 7:34; 10:2(2); 10; 19:10; 14; 21:26; **2Kin** 14:26; 17:18; 21:16; **1Chr** 9:13; 18:8; 21:8; 13; 23:17; **2Chr** 6:18; 7:8; 9:1; 14:13; 16:8; 14; 20:35; 24:24; 30:13; 32:29; 33:14; 36:14; **Ezr** 10:1(2); **Neh** 1:7; 2:2; 4:7; 5:6; 8:17; **Est** 1:12; **Job** 1:3; 2:13; 15:10; 32:6; **Ps** 5:9; 35:8; 46:1; 50:3; 71:19; 79:8; 89:2; 92:5; 93:5; 104:1; 105:12; 119:107; 138; 140; 142:6; 146:4; 147:15; **Prov** 17:9; 27:15; **Is** 1:9; 5:1; 10:25; 16:6; 14; 24:16; 29:17; 30:19; 31:1; 33:17; 40:15; 47:6; 48:8; 52:13; 64:9; 12; **Jer** 2:12; 4:19; 5:11; 12:1; 14:17; 18:13; 20:15; 24:2(2); 3(2); 27:7; 40:12; 46:20; **Lam** 5:22; **Eze** 2:3; 16:47; 27:25; 33:32; 37:2(2); 40:2; 47:7; 9; **Dan** 2:12; 6:19; 7:20; 8:8; 11:25; **Joel** 2:11(2); **Amos** 5:20; **Jonah** 4:1; **Hab** 2:13(2); **Zec** 1:15; 8:4; 9:2; 5; 14:4; **Mt** 10:30; 15:28; 17:18; 18:31; 21:8; 24:24; 26:7; 37; **Mk** 8:1; 14:3; 33; 16:2; 4; **Lk** 1:3; 9:5; 10:11; 12:7; 59; 18:23(2); 24; 19:17; 48; 24:1; **Jn** 7:26; 8:4; 12:3; 14:11; **Acts** 9:22; 10:10; 24:2; 25:10; **Rom** 10:20; 13:6; **1Cor** 4:3; **2Cor** 9:2; 11:5; 12:11; 15; **Phil** 1:6; **1Th** 5:13; 23; **2Ti** 1:17; 18; **Heb** 10:1; **Jas** 3:4; 5:11

WAS

Gen 1:2(2); 3; 4; 7; 9; 10; 11; 12(2); 15; 18; 21; 24; 25; 30; 31; 2:5(2); 10; 19; 20; 23; 3:1; 6(2); 10(2); 20; 23; 4:2(2); 5; 18; 19; 20; 21(2); 22; 26; 5:24; 32; 6:5(2); 9; 11(2); 12; 7:6(2); 12; 17(2); 22(2); 23(2); 8:1; 2; 11; 13; 14; 9:19; 21(2); 10:9; 10; 19; 25(3); 30; 11:1; 10; 29; 30; 12:4; 6; 10(2); 11; 14(2); 15; 18; 13:2; 6(2); 7; 10; 14; 14:10; 14; 18; 15:12; 17; 16:1; 4; 5; 14; 16; 17:1; 24(2); 25(2); 26; 18:10; 15; 19:22; 23; 20:16; 21:3; 5(2); 8(2); 11; 15; 20; 22:20; 24; 23:1; 17(3); 24:1; 15; 16; 29; 33; 36; 67; 25:1; 8; 10; 17; 20; 21(2); 26(2); 27(2); 29; 30; 26:1(2); 7; 8; 28; 34; 27:1; 30; 28:7; 11; 17; 19; 29:2; 12(2); 16(2); 17(2); 25; 31(2); 33; 34; 30:2; 29; 30; 37; 31:1(2); 2; 22(2); 31; 36; 39; 40; 48; 32:7(2); 24; 25; 34:19; 24; 28(2); 29; 35:3; 4; 5; 8(2); 16; 17; 18; 19; 29; 36:12; 22; 24; 32; 35; 39(2); 37:1; 2(2); 3; 15; 23(2); 24(2); 29; 38:1; 2; 5; 6; 7; 12; 13; 14(2); 16; 21(2); 22; 24; 25; 29; 30; 39:1; 2(3); 3; 5; 6; 11; 13; 19; 20; 21; 22; 23(2); 40:2; 3; 9; 10; 11; 15; 16(2); 17; 20; 41:7; 8(2); 10; 12; 13; 24; 32; 37; 46; 48; 49; 53; 54(2); 55; 56; 57; 42:1; 5; 6(2); 27; 35; 43:1; 12(2); 18; 21; 26; 34; 44:3; 12; 14; 45:8; 16; 47:13(2); 14; 18; 28; 48:7; 14(2); 49:7(2); 15(2); 26; 32; 33; 50:9; 11; 15; 26; **Ex** 1:5; 7; 14; 15; 2:2; 11; 12; 21; 3:2; 6; 4:6; 7; 14; 5:13; 19; 6:3; 7:7; 15; 21(2); 22; 8:15; 19; 24; 9:7(2); 11; 24(2); 25; 26; 31(3); 33; 35; 10:13; 15; 22; 11:3; 6; 12:29; 30(3); 34; 39; 40; 13:17; 14:5(2); 20; 15:23; 16:14; 15; 20; 24; 31(2); 17:1; 18:3; 4(2); 11; 19:16; 18; 20:21; 22:13; 24:10; 17; 18; 25:40; 26:30; 27:8; 29:33; 31:17; 32:16; 33:7; 8; 34:28; 34; 35:23; 24; 36:7; 9; 12; 15(2); 21; 37:1; 6; 10; 22; 25(3); 38:1(2); 18(3); 21; 23; 24(2); 25; 29; 39:4; 5(2); 9(2); 10(2); 19; 23; 32; 40:17; 35; 36; 37; 38(2); **Lev** 4:10; 6:2; 3; 4; 27; 8:4; 10; 16; 21; 25; 26; 29; 30; 9:8; 15; 18; 10:16(2); 18; 20; 13:18; 14:6; 48; 15:10; 16:27; 17:15; 19:20; 21:10; 24:10; 11; 25:33; 50; 51; 27:24; **Num** 1:44; 3:16; 21; 27; 33; 35; 6:12; 7:9; 10; 12; 13(2); 17; 19; 23; 25(2); 29; 31; 35; 37(2); 41; 43; 47; 49(2); 53; 55; 59; 61(2); 65; 67(2); 71; 73(2); 77; 79(2); 83; 84(2); 86; 88(2); 89(2); 8:4(2); 9:14; 15(2); 16; 17; 20(2); 21(4); 22; 10:11; 14; 15; 16; 17; 18; 19; 20; 22; 23; 24; 25(2); 26; 27; 34; 11:1; 2; 4; 7; 8; 10(2); 18; 25; 26; 33(3); 12:3; 9; 10; 15(2); 13:20; 22; 24; 14:16; 15:34; 16:15; 31; 42; 47; 48; 50; 17:6; 8; 19:13; 20:1; 2; 13; 29; 21:4; 24; 26; 35; 22:3(2); 4; 22(2); 26; 27; 30(2); 36; 24:10; 20; 25:3; 8; 11; 13; 14(3); 15(3); 18; 26:46; 59; 60; 62; 64; 65; 27:3; 13; 28:6; 31:14; 16; 26; 32; 36(2); 37; 38; 39; 40; 41; 43; 52; 32:1; 10; 13(2); 39; 33:14; 39; 35:23; 25(2); 26; 36:2; **Deut** 1:34; 37; 2:14; 15; 20; 36; 3:3; 4; 8; 11(2); 13; 26; 4:21; 35; 8:2; 15; 9:8; 9; 10; 19(2); 20; 21; 28; 10:6; 11:6; 19:6; 21:15; 22:27; 26:5; 29:27; 32:12; 50; 33:5; 16; 21; 34:7(2); 9; **Josh** 1:5; 17; 2:2; 5; 15; 3:7; 4:10; 5:1; 13; 6:1; 21; 24; 27(2); 7:1; 16; 17; 18; 22; 26; 8:11; 13; 17; 25; 29; 33; 35; 9:5; 10; 24; 10:2(2); 14; 17; 11:10; 11; 19; 20; 22; 12:4; 13:1; 16; 23(2); 25; 29; 30; 33; 14:2; 7(2); 11(2); 15(2); 15:1(2); 2; 5(2); 9(2); 11; 12; 15; 16:5(2); 17:1(3); 2; 7; 9; 10(2); 18:1; 12; 14(2); 15; 17; 19; 20(2); 19:1; 9(2); 10; 18; 25; 33; 41; 21:10; 22:14; 17; 24:26; 33; **Judg** 1:10; 11; 17; 19; 22; 23; 28; 36; 2:14; 15; 18; 19; 20; 3:8; 17; 20; 24; 25; 27; 30; 31; 4:1; 2; 11; 12; 16; 17; 21; 22; 5:8(2); 14; 15; 6:3; 6; 11; 21; 22; 27; 28(5); 30; 34; 35; 38; 40(2); 7:8; 13(2); 15; 8:3(2); 11; 13; 20; 26(2); 28(2); 31; 32; 33; 9:5; 6; 25; 30; 44; 45; 47; 51; 55; 10:2; 5; 7; 9; 16; 11:1(2); 5; 18; 34; 39; 12:5; 7; 10; 12; 15; 13:2(3); 6(2); 9; 16; 21; 14:4; 8; 19; 20; 15:14; 18; 19; 16:2; 4; 9; 16; 20; 22; 27; 29; 17:1(2); 6(2); 7(2); 11(2); 12; 18:1; 7; 20; 28(3); 29(2); 31; 19:1(2); 2; 10; 11; 15; 16; 26(2); 27; 29; 30(2); 20:1; 3; 4; 27; 34(2); 38; 41; 21:25(2); **Ruth** 1:1; 2; 3; 4; 5; 7; 18; 19; 2:1; 3(2); 5; 6; 14; 15; 17; 18; 3:7; 8; 4:3; 7(2); 9(2); 13; **1Sa** 1:1(2); 2; 4; 10; 13; 18; 20; 24; 2:13(2); 17; 22; 26; 3:1(2); 2; 3(2); 7; 19; 20; 4:2; 6; 10(2); 11; 15; 18; 19(2); 21; 5:3; 4(2); 6; 7; 9(2); 11(2); 6:1; 4; 9; 14; 15; 7:2(2); 10; 13; 14; 17(2); 8:1; 2; 9:1(2); 2(3); 5; 9; 10; 24; 10:9; 20; 21(2); 23; 11:6; 11; 12:8; 12; 15; 13:3; 4; 7; 19; 22(2); 14:3; 4(2); 5; 14; 15(2); 18; 19; 20(2); 25; 27; 35; 39; 42; 43; 50(2); 51(2); 52; 15:9(2); 12; 16:12; 23(3); 17:3; 4; 5(2); 7; 12(2); 14; 20; 28; 40; 42; 50; 51; 18:1; 4; 5; 6; 8; 10; 12(3); 14; 15; 19; 28; 29; 30; 19:7; 8; 9; 16; 19; 20; 21; 23; 20:19; 24; 25; 27(2); 30; 33; 34; 37; 41; 21:1; 6(3); 7(2); 12; 22:2(3); 4; 6; 9; 22; 23:7(2); 13(2); 15(2); 24:1(2); 3; 25:2(3); 3(4); 7; 20; 21; 36(2); 37; 39; 44; 26:4; 12; 16; 21; 24; 27:4(2); 7; 28:3; 5; 14; 20(2); 21; 30:3; 6(2); 19; 25; 31:3; 4; 5; **2Sa** 1:1; 2; 10(4); 26; 2:10; 11(2); 16; 17(2); 18; 32; 3:1; 2; 6; 7; 8; 22(2); 23; 26; 27; 35; 37; 4:1; 2(2); 4(3); 5:2; 4; 10; 13; 6:3; 4; 7; 8; 9; 12; 13; 14; 20; 21; 7:9; 19; 8:16(2); 17; 18; 9:2(2); 6; 12; 13; 10:9; 17; 11:1; 2; 4; 7; 26; 27; 12:3; 4(2); 5; 15; 18(2); 19; 21(2); 22; 30(2); 13:1; 2(2); 3(2); 6; 8; 15; 19; 21; 38; 39(2); 14:1; 6; 25(2); 26(2); 27(2); 15:2; 5; 12; 17; 30; 32; 16:1; 5; 16; 23(2); 17:6; 19; 22; 23(2); 25(2); 27; 18:6; 7; 8; 9(2); 14; 29; 33; 19:1; 2(2); 16; 18; 25; 32(2); 39; 20:1; 8; 10; 13; 17; 23(2); 24(2); 25; 26; 21:1; 7; 11; 14; 16; 18(2); 19(2); 20(3); 22:8; 10; 11; 19; 24; 42; 23:1; 2; 8; 9; 10; 11(2); 14(2); 16; 18; 19(2); 23; 24; 24:1; 2; 11; 16; 25(2); **1Kin** 1:1; 4; 6; 15; 23; 51; 2:5; 10; 12; 15(2); 26; 29(2); 34; 41(2); 46; 3:2; 4; 12; 15; 17; 18(3); 21(2); 26; 28; 4:1; 4; 5(2); 6(2); 15; 16; 19(3); 22; 31(2); 5:1; 12; 13; 14; 6:2; 3(2); 6(3); 7(5); 8; 17; 18(3); 20(2); 22; 24; 25; 26(2); 37; 38(2); 7:1; 2; 3; 4; 5; 6(2); 7; 8; 10; 12; 14(3); 16(2); 20; 22(2); 23(2); 24; 25; 26(2); 27; 28; 29; 31(2); 32; 33; 35; 38; 47; 48; 51; 8:9; 17; 18(2); 54; 57; 64(3); 9:1; 25; 10:2(2); 3; 5; 6; 7; 14; 19; 20; 21; 11:4(3); 9(2); 14; 15(2); 20; 21; 25; 26; 27; 28(2); 30; 40; 42; 43; 12:2(2); 15; 18; 20(2); 21; 13:5; 6(2); 9; 17; 24(2); 26; 14:6; 8; 21(2); 28; 30; 31(2); 15:2; 3; 5; 6; 7; 10; 11; 14; 16; 22; 23; 24; 32; 16:6; 9; 18; 28; 17:1; 10; 11; 17(2); 18:2; 3; 4; 7; 13; 26(3); 29(2); 30; 38; 45(2); 46; 19:6; 11(2); 12; 13; 19; 20:12; 16; 29(2); 36; 40(2); 41; 21:1; 11; 15(2); 16; 25; 22:13; 33; 35; 37; 42(2); 43; 47(2); 50; **2Kin** 1:2(2); 7; 8; 2:17; 23; 3:4; 5; 9; 20(2); 26; 27; 4:8(2); 18; 31; 32(2); 36; 38; 41; 5:1(3); 8; 11; 14; 6:5(2); 11; 13; 15; 17; 25(2); 26; 7:5; 7; 10; 15; 16; 8:5; 6; 7(2); 11; 17; 18; 24; 26(2); 27; 29; 9:15; 16; 21; 30; 33; 34; 10:5(2); 12; 15; 21(2); 22; 30; 36; 11:1; 2; 3; 14; 16; 20; 21; 12:1; 2; 6; 9; 10(3); 12; 13; 16(2); 18; 13:2; 3; 11; 13; 14; 19; 21; 23; 14:2(2); 3; 5; 9(3); 12; 16; 20; 21; 24; 25; 26(2); 15:2(2); 3; 5(2); 9; 12; 18; 24; 28; 33(2); 34; 38; 16:2(2); 8; 10; 12; 14; 20; 17:2; 7; 18(2); 23; 25; 18:2(2); 3; 5; 7; 9; 10; 15; 18; 36; 37; 19:2; 8; 37; 20:1; 4; 13(2); 21:1(2); 2; 15; 16; 18; 19(2); 20; 26; 22:1(2); 2; 7(2); 9; 19; 23:2; 11; 15; 22; 23; 25; 26; 31(2); 32; 36(2); 37; 24:8(2); 9; 10; 18(2); 19; 25:2; 3; 4; 13; 16; 17(2); 19; 21; 30; **1Chr** 1:19(3); 39; 43; 44; 45; 46(2); 47; 48; 49; 50(3); 2:3; 17; 19; 21; 24; 26(2); 29; 34; 42; 45(2); 49; 3:10; 4:3; 9; 11; 40; 41; 5:1(2); 2; 6; 7; 20; 22; 6:54; 7:2; 9; 15(2); 16; 24; 25; 40; 8:29; 34; 37; 9:17; 20(2); 21; 27; 31; 35; 40; 10:3; 4; 5; 11:2; 6; 9; 12(2); 13(2); 16(2); 18; 20; 21(2); 23; 25; 12:3; 14; 18; 22; 27; 40; 13:4; 10; 11; 12; 14:2; 8; 15:22(2); 27; 16:39; 17:13; 17; 18:15; 16; 17; 19:10; 17; 20:1; 2; 4; 5(2); 6(3); 21:5; 6; 7; 15; 20; 30; 22:7; 23:1; 3; 8; 11; 13; 16; 28; 24:21; 25; 29; 25:1; 7; 26:1; 10; 20; 24; 28; 31; 27:2; 3; 4(2); 5; 6(2); 7; 8; 9; 10; 11; 12; 13; 14; 15; 16; 24; 25(2); 26; 27(2); 28(2); 29(2); 30(2); 31(2); 32(2); 33(2); 34(2); 29:27; **2Chr** 1:1(2); 3(2); 6; 11; 13; 2:14; 3:3(2); 4(3); 6; 8; 9; 11(2); 12(2); 15(2); 4:3(2); 4; 5; 6; 11; 19; 5:1; 3; 10; 13; 6:7; 8(2); 7:7(2); 8:16(3); 9:1(2); 2; 4; 5; 6; 9; 13; 19; 20; 31; 10:2; 15; 18; 11:1; 12:13(2); 16; 13:2(2); 7; 13; 14; 14:1; 2; 5; 14; 15:4; 5; 6; 8; 9; 15; 17; 19; 16:3; 6; 10(2); 12(2); 14; 17:3; 6; 15; 16; 18; 18:14; 32; 20:25; 26; 29; 30; 31(2); 32; 21:1; 3; 4; 5; 6; 17(2); 20; 22:2(2); 3; 6; 7(2); 8; 9; 10; 11; 12; 23:15; 18; 19; 21; 24:1(2); 2; 4; 11(2); 13; 15(2); 25:1(2); 2; 3; 10(2); 14; 15; 18(3); 22; 26:1; 3(2); 4; 13; 15(2); 16(2); 19(2); 20; 21(3); 27:1(2); 2; 8; 28:1(2); 5; 7; 9(3); 29:1(2); 2; 6; 8; 25; 28; 32; 34; 35; 36; 30:5; 12; 17; 18; 26(2); 27; 31:1; 12(2); 14; 20; 32:2(2); 4; 5; 14; 15; 21; 23; 24; 25(2); 31(2); 33:1; 2; 12; 13(2); 19(2); 21; 22; 34:1; 2; 3; 9; 14; 16; 17; 27; 30; 35:10; 16; 18; 19; 24; 26; 36:2; 5(2); 8; 9(2); 10; 11; 12; 16; **Ezr** 1:6; 2:61; 64; 3:1; 3; 6; 11; 12; 13; 4:7; 14; 15; 20; 23; 5:5; 7; 11; 14(2); 17; 6:1; 2(2); 15(2); 7:6; 8; 28(2); 8:22; 23; 31; 33(3); 34; 35; 10:9; **Neh** 1:1; 11; 2:1; 2; 10; 11; 12; 14(2); 18; 3:16; 25; 4:1; 3; 6; 15; 18; 5:1; 6; 14; 18(3); 6:1; 6; 10; 13; 15; 16; 18; 7:1; 2; 4; 7; 63; 64; 66; 72; 8:1; 3; 5; 17; 18; 10:29; 11:9(2); 11; 14; 17; 22; 23; 24; 12:8; 37; 43; 13:1; 4; 5; 6; 13(2); 26(2); 28; **Est** 1:2; 8; 10; 11; 12; 13; 14; 2:1(2); 5(2); 7; 8(2); 12; 13; 15; 16; 20; 22; 23(3); 3:4; 5; 12(2); 14; 15(2); 4:1; 3; 4; 5(2); 6; 8; 5:2(2); 9; 6:2; 4; 7:6; 7; 8(2); 10; 8:1; 9; 13; 14; 15; 9:1; 4; 11; 14; 22; 32; 10:3; **Job** 1:1(3); 3(2); 5; 6; 13; 16; 17; 18; 2:1; 11; 13; 3:3(2); 25; 26(2); 4:4; 12; 16(2); 8:7; 15:7; 19; 16:12; 17:6; 20:4; 22:16; 23:17; 29:4(2); 5; 13; 14; 15(2); 16; 19; 20(2); 30:2; 25(2); 31:18; 23; 25; 32:1; 2(2); 3; 5(2); 6; 12; 33:27; 42:7; **Ps** 4:1; 7:4; 18:7; 9; 12; 18; 23; 41; 22:9; 10; 30:7; 31:11; 13; 32:4; 33:9; 35:13; 37:36; 38:13; 14; 39:2(2); 3(2); 9; 50:21; 51:5; 53:5; 55:12(2); 13; 18; 21; 63:t, 66:14; 17; 68:8; 9; 11; 14; 69:10; 12; 20; 73:3; 16; 21(2); 22(2); 74:5; 76:8; 77:3(2); 18; 78:8; 21(2); 30; 35; 37; 59; 62; 79:3; 81:4; 87:4; 5; 6; 95:10; 97:8; 105:17; 18; 37; 38; 106:9; 11; 18; 30; 31; 38; 40; 107:12; 114:2; 3; 116:6; 10; 119:67; 158; 122:1; 124:1; 2; 3; 126:2; 139:15(2); 16; 142:t, 3; 4; **Prov** 4:3; 5:14; 8:23(2); 24; 25; 27; 30(2); 23:35; 24:31(2); **Eccl** 1:10; 12; 2:3; 9; 10; 11(2); 15; 24; 3:16(2); 4:1; 5:6; 7:23; 9:14; 15; 12:7; 9; 10(2); **Song** 2:3; 4; 3:4; 5:6; 6:12; 8:10; 11; **Is** 1:21; 6:4; 7:2(2); 9:1; 10:14; 26; 11:16; 14:28; 21:3(2); 14; 22:14; 25; 23:13; 26:16; 28:13; 36:3; 21; 22; 37:2; 8; 38; 38:1; 8; 9; 20; 39:1; 2(3); 41:28(2); 43:10; 12; 13; 47:6; 48:8; 16; 49:21; 50:2(2); 5; 52:14; 53:3; 5(3); 7(2); 8(3); 9; 12; 57:17(2); 59:15; 16(2); 17; 63:3; 5(2); 8; 9; 10; 65:1; 2; 66:7; **Jer** 2:2; 3; 3:21; 4:23; 25; 26; 7:12; 8:16; 11:19; 13:7(2); 20; 14:4; 5; 6; 15:9; 16; 17:16; 18:4; 20:1; 2; 7; 8; 9(2); 14; 22:15; 16(2); 25:1; 26:20; 21; 24; 28:1; 31:11; 15; 18; 19(3); 26; 32; 32:1; 2(2); 8; 9; 11(2); 33:1; 35:4(2); 36:22; 23(3); 37:5; 11; 13(3); 16; 38:6(2); 7; 27; 28(3); 39:2; 15; 40:5; 41:7; 9; 44:6(2); 46:2; 5; 21; 48:13; 27(2); 49:12; 21; 51:5; 59; 52:1(2); 2; 5; 6(2); 7(2); 8; 12; 17; 19(2); 20; 21(3); 22(2); 27; 34; **Lam** 1:1(2); 2:5; 12; 3:10; 14; 4:6; 7; 20; 5:10; **Eze** 1:1; 2; 3; 4; 5; 7; 12; 13(2); 16(2); 20(3); 21; 22; 25(2); 26(3); 28(2); 2:9(2); 10(2); 3:3; 14; 22; 8:3; 4; 14; 9:2; 3(2); 8; 10:1; 4(2); 5; 7(2); 9; 13; 14(2); 17; 19; 21; 22; 11:22; 12:7; 13:10; 15:5(2); 16:3; 4; 8; 13; 14; 15; 19; 36; 45; 49(2); 56; 57; 17:7; 8; 19:4; 5; 7; 8; 10; 11; 12(2); 21:22; 22:10; 23:5; 11; 13; 17(2); 18(2); 40; 42; 43; 24:18; 25:3(2); 26:2; 27:7(2); 12; 16; 18; 20; 28:13(2); 15; 17; 29:18(2); 30:22; 31:3(2); 5; 7(2); 8; 32:15; 25; 33:22(4); 24; 34:4(4); 6; 8; 16(4); 35:10; 15; 36:17; 23; 35; 36; 37:1(2); 7(2); 8; 40:1(2); 2; 3(2); 6(2); 7(2); 9; 12(2); 13; 18; 21; 23; 25; 27; 29; 33; 36; 40; 43; 44(2); 47; 48; 49; 41:1; 2; 6; 7(2); 9(4); 10; 11(3); 12(3); 15; 18(2); 19(2); 22; 42:1(2); 2(2); 3(2); 4; 6; 7(2); 8; 9; 11; 12; 43:2; 3; 44:1; 46:19(2); 21; 23(2); 47:5; 48:35; **Dan** 1:4; 19; 2:1; 3; 12; 14; 19; 26; 31(2); 32; 34; 35(2); 45; 3:1; 19(3); 22; 24; 27; 4:4; 8; 10; 11; 12(2); 19(2); 20; 21; 31; 33(3); 36(2); 5:2; 3; 6; 9(2); 11; 13; 20(2); 21(4); 24(2); 25; 30; 6:2; 3(2); 4(2); 10; 14; 17; 22; 23(3); 7:4(3); 6; 7; 9(2); 10; 11; 14; 15; 19; 20; 22; 8:2(2); 3; 4; 5; 7(3); 8(2); 11(2); 12; 17; 18(2); 26; 27(2); 9:1; 20; 21; 10:1(4); 2; 4; 6; 8(2); 9; 19; 12:1(2); 6; 7; **Hos** 1:10; 2:3; 7; 7:1; 8:6; 9:8; 10:14; 11:1; 4; 12:13; 13:6; **Amos** 1:1; 2:9(2); 4:7; 7:1; 14(3); **Jonah** 1:4(2); 5(2); 11; 13; 17; 2:6; 3:3; 4:1; 2(2); 6; **Mic** 4:7; **Nah** 3:8(3); 9; 10; **Hab** 3:2; 3; 4(2); 8(3); 9; 14; **Zeph** 3:18; 19; **Hag** 2:15; 18; **Zec** 1:15; 3:3; 5:7; 9; 7:7; 14; 8:2(2); 9; 10(2); 10:2; 3; 11:11(2); 13; 13:6; **Mal** 1:2; 13; 2:5(2); 6(2); 3:16; **Mt** 1:16; 18(3); 19; 22(2); 2:1; 3; 9; 15(2); 16(2); 17(2); 18; 19; 22; 23; 3:3; 4; 16; 4:1; 2; 12; 14; 5:1; 21; 27; 6:29; 7:25; 27; 8:1; 3; 5; 13; 14; 16; 17; 23; 24(2); 26; 28; 30; 33; 9:20; 22; 28; 33(2); 36; 10:3; 11:14; 12:3; 4; 9; 10; 13; 17; 22; 40; 13:6; 19; 26; 33; 35; 47; 48; 54; 14:6; 9; 11; 14; 15; 23(2); 24(2); 29; 30; 15:28; 37; 16:20; 17:2(2); 18; 25; 18:11; 24; 27; 31(2); 34(2); 19:8; 20:8; 21:4(2); 10(2); 23(2); 25; 33; 22:7; 10; 12; 31; 35; 46; 24:21; 25:6; 10; 25; 35(3); 36(2); 42(2); 43; 26:3; 6; 20; 56; 71(2); 27:1; 3; 8; 9(3); 12; 15; 19; 24; 35; 45; 51; 54; 56; 57(2); 61; 63; 28:2; 3; 5; **Mk** 1:6; 9; 13(2); 14; 23; 33; 42; 45; 2:1(2); 2; 3; 4; 25; 27; 3:1; 5; 4:1(2); 6(2); 10; 15; 22; 35; 36; 37; 38; 39; 5:2; 5; 11; 14(2); 15; 16; 18; 21(2); 26; 29(2); 33; 36; 39; 40; 42; 6:2; 14(2); 20; 21; 26; 34; 35; 47(2); 48; 52; 55; 7:17; 26; 30; 32; 35; 8:8; 25; 9:2; 7; 26; 28; 33; 10:1; 14; 17; 22; 47; 11:11; 12; 13; 18; 19; 27; 30; 32; 12:11; 13:19; 14:1; 4; 32; 45; 49; 66; 15:7; 25; 26; 28(2); 33(2); 38; 39; 40; 41; 42(2); 46; 47; 16:1; 4(2); 6; 9; 11; 14; 19; **Lk** 1:5(3); 7; 9; 12; 26; 27(2); 29; 36; 41; 64; 66; 67; 80; 2:2(2); 4; 6; 7; 13; 17; 20; 21(3); 25(4); 26; 36(2); 37; 40; 42; 51; 3:21; 23(2); 24(5); 25(5); 26(5); 27(5); 28(5); 29(5); 30(5); 31(5); 32(5); 33(5); 34(5); 35(5); 36(5); 37(5); 38(4); 4:1; 16; 17(2); 25(2); 26(2); 27; 29; 32; 33; 38; 40; 41; 42; 5:3; 9; 10; 12; 17(2); 18; 29; 36; 6:3; 6(2); 10; 13; 16; 48; 49; 7:2(2); 4; 6; 12(3); 15; 37; 41; 8:5; 6; 20; 24; 29(2); 32; 34; 35; 36(2); 40; 41; 47(2); 53; 56; 9:7(4); 8; 17; 18; 29(2); 36(2); 42; 45; 51; 53; 10:32; 33; 36; 40; 11:1; 14(3); 30; 50; 12:27; 13:10; 11(2); 13; 21; 14:2; 30; 15:6; 20; 24(2); 25; 28; 30; 32(3); 16:1(2); 19(2); 20(2); 22(2); 17:10; 15; 16; 20; 26; 28; 18:2; 3; 23(2); 24; 34; 35; 40; 19:2(3); 3(2); 4; 7; 10; 11; 15; 22; 29; 37; 41; 20:4; 6; 7; 21:5; 37; 22:14; 22; 23; 24; 37; 39; 40; 41; 44; 45; 47; 53; 56; 59; 66; 23:7; 8(2); 19; 25; 38; 44(2); 45(2); 47(2); 50(2); 51; 53(2); 54; 55; 24:6; 10; 12; 13; 18; 19; 23; 35; 44; 51; **Jn** 1:1(3); 2; 3(2); 4(2); 6(2); 8(2); 9; 10(2); 14; 15(2); 17; 28; 30; 39; 40; 44; 2:1(2); 2; 9(2); 13; 17; 20; 22; 23; 25; 3:1; 23(2); 24; 26; 4:6(2); 45; 46(2); 47(2); 51; 53; 54; 5:1; 4; 5; 9(2); 10; 13(2); 15; 18; 35; 6:4; 10; 16; 17(2); 21; 22; 24; 62; 71; 7:2; 12; 30; 39(2); 42; 43; 8:4; 9; 20; 44; 56; 58; 9:1; 2;

8; 13; 14; 16; 19; 20; 22; 24; 25; 32(2); 10:19; 22(2); 11:1; 2(2); 6(2); 15; 18; 20; 30(2); 32(2); 33; 38; 39; 41; 44(2); 55; 12:1; 2; 3; 5; 6(2); 9; 12; 16; 17; 21; 13:1; 3; 5; 12; 21; 23; 30; 31; 16:4; 17:5; 12; 18:1; 10; 13(2); 14(2); 15; 16; 18; 28; 37; 40; 19:8; 14; 19; 20(3); 23; 29; 31(2); 32; 33; 41(3); 42; 20:1; 7; 14; 24; 21:4(2); 7(2); 11; 12; 14; 17; **Acts** 1:2; 9; 16; 17; 19; 22; 23; 26; 2:1; 6; 16; 24; 26; 31; 3:2; 10; 11; 13; 20; 4:3; 4; 11; 14; 21; 22(2); 31; 32; 33; 34; 35; 36; 5:4(3); 7(2); 36; 6:1; 7:2; 4; 9; 12; 13(2); 20(2); 21; 22(2); 23; 24; 29; 38; 58; 8:1(3); 8; 9(2); 13; 16; 18; 28; 32(2); 33; 40; 9:9; 10; 18; 19(2); 24; 26(2); 28; 33; 36(2); 37; 38(2); 39(2); 42; 10:1; 4; 7; 16(2); 18; 22; 25; 29; 30; 37; 38; 42; 45; 11:2; 5; 10; 11; 17; 21; 22; 23; 24(2); 12:5(2); 6; 9(2); 11; 12; 15; 18(3); 20(2); 23; 25; 13:1(2); 6; 7; 12; 29; 31; 32; 36; 43; 46; 49; 14:4; 5; 12; 13; 15:5; 37; 39; 16:1(3); 2; 3; 13; 15; 19; 26; 33; 35; 17:1; 2; 13; 16; 34; 18:3; 5(2); 12; 14; 25; 27(2); 28; 19:1; 16; 17(2); 29; 32; 34; 20:1; 3; 9(2); 11; 20; 21:3; 8; 11; 30; 31; 33; 35(2); 37; 40; 22:3; 6; 17(2); 20(2); 28; 29(2); 30; 23:5; 7; 12; 27(2); 30; 31; 34(2); 24:2; 24; 25:1; 7; 15; 19; 23(3); 26:4; 19; 26; 27:1; 8; 9(3); 12; 15; 20; 25; 27; 33; 39; 41; 42; 28:1; 6; 7; 9; 11; 16; 17; 18; 19; **Rom** 1:3; 13; 21; 27; 4:3; 9; 10(2); 13; 18; 19; 20; 21; 22; 23(2); 25(2); 5:13; 14; 16(2); 6:4; 17; 7:8; 9; 10; 13; 8:3; 20; 9:12; 25; 26; 10:20(2); 15:8; 20; 21; 16:25; **1Cor** 1:6; 13; 2:3; 4; 7:20; 10:4; 5; 11:9; 23; 13:11; 15:4; 5; 6; 7; 8; 10(3); 45(2); 46; 16:12; 17; S:1; **2Cor** 1:15; 17; 18; 19(3); 2:6; 12; 3:7(2); 10; 11; 5:19; 7:7; 13; 8:9; 11; 17; 9:2; 11:5; 9(3); 25(2); 33; 12:4; 7; 13; 13:4; S:1; **Gal** 1:11; 12; 22; 2:3(2); 7(2); 8; 9; 10; 11(2); 13; 3:6; 17(2); 19(3); 24; 4:4; 14; 23(3); 28; 29(2); **Eph** 3:5; 7; **Phil** 2:5; 7; 26; 27; 30; S:1; **Col** 1:23; 2:14(2); **1Th** 2:1; 3; S:1; **2Th** 1:10; 2:5; S:1; **1Ti** 1:11; 13; 14; 2:13; 14(2); 3:16; 4:14; S:1; **2Ti** 1:9; 14; 16; 17; 2:8; 3:9; 4:17; S:1(2); **Titus** 1; **Philem** 1:11; **Heb** 2:2; 3; 9; 3:2(2); 3; 5; 10; 17(2); 4:2; 6; 15; 5:4; 7(2); 6:18; 7:4; 10; 11; 20; 22; 28; 8:5(2); 6; 9:2(2); 4; 8(2); 9; 18; 23; 28; 10:29; 11:4; 5(2); 8; 11(2); 17; 18; 19; 21; 23(3); 24; 38; 12:2; 17; 20; 21; **Jas** 1:24; 2:21; 22; 23(3); 25; 5:17; **1Pet** 1:11; 12; 20(2); 2:22; 23; 3:20; 4:6; **2Pet** 1:9; 2:16; 22; 3:6; **1Jn** 1:1; 2(3); 3:5; 8; 12; 4:9; **Jude** 3(2); **Rev** 1:4; 8; 9; 10; 16; 18; 2:8; 13(2); 4:1(2); 2(2); 3(2); 6; 7(2); 8; 5:3; 4; 11; 12; 6:2; 4(3); 8(2); 11; 12; 7:2; 8:1; 3(2); 7(2); 8; 12(2); 9:1; 3; 4; 5(2); 9; 10; 18; 10:1(2); 4; 10(2); 11:1; 8; 13; 19(2); 12:4(2); 5(2); 7; 8; 9(2); 13; 17; 13:2; 3; 5(2); 7(2); 12; 14:5; 16; 20; 15:5; 8(2); 16:8; 10; 12; 18(2); 19; 21; 17:4; 5; 8(2); 11; 18:1; 16; 24; 19:8; 11; 13; 20; 20:4; 10; 11; 12; 15(2); 21:1; 11; 18(2); 19; 21(2); 22:2

WE

Gen 3:2; 11:4; 13:8; 19:2; 5; 9; 13; 32(2); 34; 20:13; 24:25; 50; 57; 26:16; 22; 28(2); 29(2); 32; 29:4; 5; 8(2); 27; 31:15; 49; 32:6; 34:14; 15(2); 16(4); 17(2); 37:7; 20(2); 26; 32; 38:23; 40:8; 41:11(2); 12; 38; 42:2; 11(2); 21(3); 31(3); 32; 43:4; 5; 7(2); 8(3); 10(2); 18; 20; 21(3); 22(2); 44:8(3); 9; 16(5); 20(2); 22; 24(2); 26(4); 46:34; 47:3; 4(2); 15; 18; 19(4); 25; 50:15; 17; 18; **Ex** 1:9; 3:18(2); 5:3; 8:26(2); 27; 10:9(3); 25; 26(4); 12:33; 14:5(2); 12(3); 15:24; 16:3(3); 7; 8; 17:2; 19:8; 20:19(2); 24:3; 7; 14; 32:1; 23; 33:16; **Lev** 25:20(2); **Num** 9:7(3); 10:29(2); 31; 32; 11:5(2); 13; 20; 12:11(2); 13:27; 28; 30; 31(2); 32(2); 33(3); 14:2(2); 7; 40(2); 16:12; 14; 17:12(3); 13; 20:3; 4; 10; 15; 16(2); 17(5); 19; 21:7(2); 22(4); 30(2); 22:6; 31:50; 32:5; 16; 17(2); 18; 19; 31; 32; **Deut** 1:19(3); 22(3); 28(3); 41(2); 2:1(2); 8(2); 13; 14(2); 33; 34(2); 35(2); 3:1; 3; 4(2); 6(2); 7; 8; 12; 29; 4:7; 5:24(2); 25(3); 26; 27; 6:21; 25; 12:8; 18:21; 26:7; 29:7; 8; 16(2); 29; 30:12; 13; **Josh** 1:16(2); 17(2); 2:10; 11; 14; 17; 18; 19; 20; 4:23; 5:1; 6:17; 7:7; 8:5; 6(2); 9:6; 7; 8; 9; 11; 12(2); 13; 19(2); 20(3); 22; 24; 25; 10:4; 22:17; 23; 24; 26; 27; 28(2); 29; 31; 24:15; 16; 17(2); 18; 21; 22; 24(2); **Judg** 1:3; 24(2); 8:6; 15; 25; 9:28(2); 38; 10:10(2); 15(2); 11:6; 8; 10; 19; 24; 12:1; 13:8; 12(2); 15; 17; 22(2); 14:13; 15(2); 15:10; 12(2); 13(2); 16:2; 5(3); 18:5(3); 9(2); 19:12(2); 18; 22; 20:8(2); 9(2); 10; 13; 21:7(3); 16; 18; 22(2); **Ruth** 1:10; 4:11; **1Sa** 5:8; 6:2(2); 4; 9; 7:6; 8:19; 20; 9:6; 7(3); 10:14(2); 11:1; 3(2); 10; 12; 12:10(3); 19(2); 14:8(2); 9(2); 10; 12; 15:15; 16:11; 17:9; 10; 20:42; 23:3(2); 25:7; 8; 15(4); 16; 30:14(2); 22(2); **2Sa** 5:1; 7:22; 11:23; 12:18(2); 13:25; 14:7(2); 14; 15:14; 16:20; 17:6; 12(2); 13; 18:3; 19:6; 10; 42; 43(2); 20:1(2); 21:4; 5; 6; **1Kin** 3:18(2); 8:47(2); 12:4; 9; 16(2); 17:12; 18:5(2); 20:23(2); 25(2); 31; 22:3; 7; 8; 15(2); **2Kin** 2:16; 3:8; 11; 6:1; 2(2); 15; 28(2); 29(2); 7:3(2); 4(7); 9(4); 10; 12(2); 10:4; 5(2); 13(2); 18:22; 26; **1Chr** 11:1; 12:18; 13:3; 15:13; 16:35; 17:20; 29:13; 14(2); 15; 16; **2Chr** 2:16(2); 6:37(2); 10:4; 9; 16(2); 13:10; 11; 14:7(2); 11(2); 18:3; 5; 6; 7; 14; 20:9; 12(2); 25:9; 28:13; 29:18; 19; 31:10; **Ezr** 4:2(2); 3; 14(2); 16; 5:4; 8; 9; 10(2); 11; 7:24; 8:15; 21; 22; 23; 31; 32; 9:7(2); 9; 10(2); 14; 15(3); 10:2; 4; 12; 13(2); **Neh** 1:6; 7; 2:17(2); 20; 4:1; 4; 6; 9; 10, 11, 15, 19, 21, 5:2(3); 3(2); 4; 5; 8; 12(2); 16; 9:33; 36(2); 37; 38; 10:30; 31(2); 32; 34; 37; 39; 13:27; **Est** 1:15; 7:4(2); **Job** 2:10(2); 4:2; 5:27; 8:9; 9:32; 15:9; 18:2; 3; 19:28; 21:14; 15(3); 28:22; 31:31(2); 32:13; 36:26; 37:5; 19(2); 23; 38:35; **Ps** 12:4; 20:5(2); 7; 8; 9; 21:13; 33:21; 22; 35:25(2); 36:9; 44:1; 5(2); 8; 17(2); 20; 22(2); 46:2; 48:8(2); 9; 55:14; 60:12; 65:4; 66:6; 12; 74:9; 75:1(2); 78:3; 4; 79:4; 8; 13(2); 80:3; 7; 14; 18(2); 19; 90:7(2); 9; 10; 12; 14; 15; 95:7; 100:3(2); 103:14; 106:6(3); 108:13; 115:18; 118:24; 26; 123:3; 124:7; 126:1; 3; 129:8; 132:6(2); 7(2); 137:1(3); 2; 4; **Prov** 1:13(2); 24:12; **Song** 1:4(3); 11; 6:1; 13; 8:8(2); 9(2); **Is** 1:9(2); 2:3; 4:1; 5:19(2); 9:10(2); 14:10; 16:6; 20:6(2); 22:13; 24:16; 25:9(3); 26:1; 8; 13; 17; 18(4); 28:15(4); 30:16(2); 33:2; 36:7; 11; 38:20; 41:22; 23(2); 26(2); 42:24; 46:5; 51:23; 53:2(2); 3(2); 4; 5; 6(2); 56:12; 58:3(2); 59:9(2); 10(5); 11(2); 12; 63:19; 64:3; 5(2); 6(2); 8(2); 9(2); **Jer** 2:31(2); 3:22; 25(3); 4:13; 5:12; 6:16; 17; 24; 7:10; 8:8; 14(2); 15; 20; 9:19(3); 13:12; 14:7; 9; 19; 20(2); 22; 15:2; 16:10; 18:12(2); 20:10(3); 26:19; 30:5; 35:6; 8(2); 9; 10; 11(2); 36:16; 38:4; 25; 41:8; 42:2(2); 3(2); 5; 6(3); 13; 14(3); 20; 44:16; 17(4); 18(2); 19(2); 25(2); 48:14; 29; 50:7; 51:9; 51(2); **Lam** 2:16(4); 3:22; 42; 4:17; 18; 20(2); 5:3; 4; 5; 6; 7; 9; 16; 21; **Eze** 11:3; 20:32; 21:10; 33:10(2); 24; 35:10; 37:11; **Dan** 2:4; 7; 23; 36; 3:16; 17; 18; 24; 6:5(2); 9:5; 6; 8; 9; 10; 11; 13(2); 14; 15(2); 18; **Hos** 6:2; 3(2); 8:2; 10:3(2); 14:2; 3(2); **Amos** 6:10; 13; 8:5(2); 6; **Obad** 1; **Jonah** 1:6; 7; 8; 11; 14(2); 3:9; **Mic** 2:4; 4:2; 5; 5:5; **Hab** 1:12; **Zec** 1:11; 8:23(2); **Mal** 1:4(2); 6; 7; 2:10(2); 17; 3:7; 8; 13; 14(2); 15; **Mt** 2:2; 3:9; 6:12; 31(3); 7:22; 8:25; 29; 9:14; 11:3; 17(2); 12:38; 13:28; 14:17; 15:33; 16:7; 17:19; 27; 19:27(2); 20:18; 22; 21:25; 26(2); 27; 22:16; 23:30(2); 25:37; 38; 39; 44; 26:17; 65; 27:42; 63; 28:13; 14; **Mk** 1:24; 2:12; 4:30(2); 38; 5:9; 12; 6:37; 8:16; 9:28; 38(2); 10:28; 33; 35(2); 37; 39; 11:31; 32; 33; 12:14; 15(2); 14:12; 58; 63; 15:32; **Lk** 1:71; 74; 3:8; 10; 12; 14; 4:23; 34; 5:5; 26; 7:19; 20; 32(2); 8:24; 9:12; 13(2); 49(2); 54; 10:11; 11:4; 13:26; 15:32; 17:10(2); 18:28; 31; 19:14; 20:5; 6; 21; 22:8; 9; 49; 71(2); 23:2; 41(2); 24:21; **Jn** 1:14; 16; 22; 41; 45; 3:2; 11(3); 4:22(2); 42(2); 6:5; 28(2); 30; 42; 68; 69; 7:27; 35; 8:33; 41(2); 48; 52; 9:20; 21(2); 24; 28; 29(2); 31; 40; 41; 10:33; 11:16; 47; 48; 12:21; 34; 13:29; 14:5(2); 23; 16:18; 30(2); 17:11; 22; 18:30; 19:7; 15; 20:2; 25; 21:3; 24; **Acts** 2:8(2); 11; 32; 37; 3:12; 15; 4:9; 12; 10(2); 20(2); 5:23(3); 28; 29; 32; 6:2; 3; 4; 11; 14; 7:40; 10:33; 39; 47; 11:12; 13:32; 46; 14:15; 22; 15:10; 11(2); 19; 20; 24(2); 27; 36; 16:10; 11; 12; 13(2); 16; 28; 17:19; 20; 28(2); 29(2); 32; 19:2; 13; 25; 40(2); 20:6(2); 13; 14; 15(3); 21:1(2); 2; 3(2); 4; 5(4); 6(2); 7(2); 8(2); 10; 12(2); 14; 15; 16; 17; 23(2); 25; 23:9; 14(3); 15; 24:2; 3; 5; 6; 8; 26:14; 27:1; 2; 3; 4(2); 5(2); 7(2); 15; 16; 18; 19; 20; 26; 27; 29; 37; 28:10; 11; 12; 13(2); 14(2); 16; 21; 22(2); **Rom** 1:5; 2:2; 3:5; 8(2); 9(2); 19; 28; 31(2); 4:1; 9; 24; 5:1; 2(2); 3; 6; 8; 9; 10(3); 11(2); 6:1(2); 2; 4(2); 5(2); 6; 8(3); 15(2); 7:4; 5; 6(3); 7; 14; 8:12; 15; 16; 17(2); 22; 23; 24; 25(3); 26(3); 28; 31; 36(2); 37; 9:14; 29; 30; 10:8; 12:4; 5; 13:11; 14:8(6); 10; 15:1; 4; **1Cor** 1:23; 2:6; 7; 12(2); 13; 16; 3:9; 4:8; 9; 10(3); 11; 12(2); 13(2); 6:3; 8:1(2); 4; 6(2); 8(4); 9:4; 5; 6; 11(2); 12(3); 25; 10:6; 16(2); 17(2); 22(2); 11:16; 31(2); 32(3); 12:13(3); 23(2); 13:9(2); 12; 15:11; 15(2); 19(2); 30; 32; 49(2); 51(2); 52; **2Cor** 1:4(2); 6(3); 8(3); 9(2); 10; 12; 13; 14; 24; 2:11; 15; 16; 17(2); 3:1(2); 4; 5; 12(2); 18; 4:1(3); 5; 7; 8(2); 11; 13(2); 16; 18; 5:1(2); 2; 3; 4(2); 6(3); 7; 8; 9(2); 10; 11(2); 12; 13(2); 14; 16(3); 20(2); 21; 6:1; 9; 7:2(3); 5(2); 13(2); 14; 8:1; 4; 5; 6; 18; 22(2); 9:4(2); 10:2; 3(2); 7; 11(4); 12; 13; 14(3); 15; 11:4; 6; 12; 21; 12:18(2); 19(3); 13:4(2); 6; 7(2); 8; 9(3); **Gal** 1:8(2); 9; 2:4; 5; 9; 10; 15; 16(2); 17(2); 3:14; 23; 24; 25; 4:3(2); 5; 28; 31; 5:5; 25; 6:9(2); 10; **Eph** 1:4; 7; 11; 12; 2:3; 5; 10(2); 18; 3:12; 20; 4:13; 14; 25; 5:30; 6:12; **Phil** 3:3; 16; 20; **Col** 1:3; 4; 9(2); 14; 28(2); **1Th** 1:2; 5; 7; 8; 9; 2:2(2); 4(2); 5; 6(2); 7; 8; 9(2); 10; 11; 13; 17; 18; 3:1(2); 3; 4(3); 6; 7; 8; 9(2); 10; 12; 4:1; 2; 6; 10; 11; 14; 15(2); 17(2); 5:5; 10(2); 12; 14; **2Th** 1:3; 4; 11; 2:1; 13; 3:2; 4(2); 6; 7; 8(2); 9; 10(2); 11; 12; **1Ti** 1:8; 2:2; 4:10(2); 6:7(2); **2Ti** 2:11(2); 12(3); 13; **Titus** 2:12; 3:3; 5; 7; **Philem** 1:7; **Heb** 2:1(3); 3(2); 5; 8; 9; 3:6(2); 14(2); 19; 4:3; 13; 14; 15(2); 16; 5:11; 6:3; 9(2); 11; 18; 19; 7:19; 8:1(2); 9:5; 10:10; 26(2); 30; 39; 11:3; 12:1; 9(3); 10; 25(2); 28(2); 13:6; 10; 14(2); 18(2); **Jas** 1:18; 3:1; 2; 3(2); 9(2); 4:13; 15; 5:11; 17; **1Pet** 2:24; 4:3; **2Pet** 1:16(2); 18(2); 19; 3:13; **1Jn** 1:1(3); 2; 3(2); 4; 5; 6(3); 7(2); 8(3); 9; 10(3); 2:1; 3(3); 5(2); 18; 28; 3:1; 2(5); 11; 14(3); 16(2); 19(2); 21; 22(3); 23; 24; 4:6(2); 9; 10; 11; 12; 13(2); 14; 16; 17(2); 19; 21; 5:2(3); 3; 9; 14(2); 15(5); 18; 19(2); 20(3); **2Jn** 4; 5(2); 6; 8(3); **3Jn** 8(2); 12; 14; **Rev** 5:10; 7:3; 11:17

WENT

Gen 2:6; 10; 4:16; 7:7; 9; 15; 16(2); 18; 8:7; 18; 19; 9:18; 23; 10:11; 11:31; 12:4; 5; 10; 13:1; 3; 5; 14:8; 11; 17; 24; 15:17; 16:4; 17:22; 18:16; 22; 33; 19:6; 14; 28; 30; 33; 21:16; 19; 22:3; 6; 8; 13; 19; 23:10; 18; 24:10; 16; 45; 61; 63; 25:22; 34; 26:1; 13; 23; 26; 27:5; 14; 22; 28:5; 9; 10(2); 29:1; 10; 23; 30; 30:4; 14; 16; 31:19; 33(2); 32:1; 21; 34:1; 6; 24(2); 26; 35:3; 13; 22; 36:6; 37:12; 17; 38:1; 2; 9; 11; 12; 19; 39:11; 41:45; 46(2); 42:3; 43:15; 31; 44:28; 45:25; 46:29; 47:10; 49:4; 50:7(2); 9; 14; 18; **Ex** 2:1; 8; 11; 13; 4:18; 27; 29; 5:1; 10; 7:10; 23; 8:12; 30; 9:33; 10:6; 14; 18; 11:8; 12:28; 38; 41; 13:18; 21; 14:8; 19(3); 22; 23; 15:19(2); 20; 22(2); 16:27; 17:10; 18:7; 27; 19:3; 14; 20; 25; 24:9; 13; 15; 18; 32:15; 33:7; 8; 34:4; 34; 35; 38:26; 40:32; 36; **Lev** 9:8; 23; 10:2; 5; 16:23; 24:10; **Num** 8:22; 10:14; 33; 34; 11:8; 24; 26; 31; 13:21; 26; 31; 14:24; 38; 16:25; 33; 17:8; 20:6; 15; 27; 21:16; 18; 23; 33(2); 22:14; 21; 22; 23; 26; 32; 35; 36; 39; 23:3; 24:1; 25(2); 25:8; 26:4; 31:13; 21; 27; 28; 36; 32:9; 39; 41; 42; 33:1; 3; 8; 23; 29; 33; 38; **Deut** 1:19; 24; 31; 33; 43; 2:13; 3:1; 5:5; 10:3; 22; 26:5; 29:26; 31:1; 14; 33:2; 34:1; **Josh** 2:1; 5(2); 22; 3:2; 6; 5:13; 6:1; 9; 13(2); 20; 23; 7:2; 4; 8:9; 10; 11; 13; 14; 17; 9:4; 6; 10:5; 9; 24; 36; 11:4; 14:8; 15:3(2); 4; 6(2); 7; 8(2); 9; 10; 11(2); 15; 16:6(2); 7(2); 8; 17:7; 18:8(2); 9; 12(2); 13; 15(2); 17(2); 18; 19:11; 47(2); 22:6; 24:4; 11; 17; **Judg** 1:3; 4; 9; 10; 11; 16(2); 17; 22; 26; 2:6; 15; 17; 3:10; 13; 19; 22; 23; 27; 28; 4:9; 10(2); 14; 18; 21; 6:19; 33; 7:11; 8:8; 11; 27; 29; 33; 9:1; 5; 6; 7; 8; 21; 26; 27(2); 35; 39; 42; 50; 52; 11:3; 5; 11; 18; 38; 40; 12:1; 13:11; 20; 14:1; 5; 7; 9; 10; 18; 19(2); 15:4; 8; 9; 11; 16:1(2); 3; 14; 19; 17:10; 18:11; 12; 14; 17(2); 18; 20; 26(2); 19:2; 3; 14(2); 15; 18; 23; 27; 20:1; 18; 20; 23; 25; 26; 30; 31; 21:23; 24; **Ruth** 1:1; 7(2); 19; 21; 2:3; 18; 3:6; 7; 15; 4:1; 13; **1Sa** 1:3; 7; 18; 21; 22; 2:11; 20; 3:3; 5; 6; 8; 9; 4:1; 5:12; 6:12(3); 7:7; 11; 16; 9:9; 10; 11; 14; 26; 10:14; 26(2); 11:15; 13:7; 10; 20; 23; 14:16; 19; 21; 46(2); 15:34(2); 16:13; 17:4; 7; 12; 13(2); 15; 20; 35; 41; 18:5; 13; 16; 27; 30(2); 19:8; 12; 18; 22; 23(2); 20:11; 35; 42; 21:10; 22:1; 3; 23:5; 13; 16; 18; 24; 25; 26; 28; 29; 24:2; 3; 7; 8; 22; 25:1; 12; 13; 42(2); 26:2; 13; 25; 27:8; 28:8; 25; 29:11; 30:2; 9; 21; 22(2); 31:3; 12; **2Sa** 1:4; 2:2; 12; 13; 15; 24; 29; 32; 3:16; 19; 21; 4:5; 5:6; 10; 17; 6:2; 4; 12; 7:18; 23; 8:3; 6; 14; 10:16; 11:9; 10; 13(2); 17; 21; 22; 12:16; 17; 24; 29; 13:8; 9; 19; 37; 38; 14:23; 15:9; 11(2); 16; 17; 24; 30(5); 16:13(3); 22; 17:17(2); 18(2); 21; 25; 18:6; 9(2); 24; 33(2); 19:17; 18; 19; 31; 39; 40(2); 20:2; 3; 5; 7(2); 8(2); 13; 14(2); 22; 21:12; 15; 22:9; 23:13; 17; 20; 21; 24:4; 7; 19; 20; **1Kin** 1:15; 38; 49; 50; 2:8; 19; 34; 40(2); 46; 3:4; 6:8; 8:66; 10:5; 13; 16; 17; 29; 11:5; 6; 24; 29; 12:1; 25; 30; 13:10; 12(2); 14; 19; 28; 14:4; 28; 15:17; 16:10; 17; 18; 31; 17:5(2); 10; 15; 18:2; 6(2); 16(2); 42(2); 43; 45; 19:3; 4; 8; 13; 21; 20:1; 16; 17; 21; 26; 27; 39; 43; 21:27; 22:24(2); 29; 30; 36; 48; **2Kin** 1:9; 13; 15; 2:1; 2; 6; 7; 8; 11(2); 13; 14; 21; 23; 25; 3:6; 7; 9; 12; 24; 25; 4:5; 18; 21(2); 25; 31; 33; 34; 35; 37(2); 39; 5:4; 11; 12; 14; 25(2); 26; 27; 6:4; 23; 24; 7:8(3); 15; 16; 8:2; 3; 9; 21; 28; 29(2); 9:4; 6; 16; 18; 21(2); 24; 35; 10:9; 23; 24; 25; 11:16; 18; 12:17; 18; 13:5; 14:11; 15:14; 16:9; 10; 17:5; 15; 18:7; 17; 19:1; 14; 35; 36; 22:14; 23:2; 29(2); 24:12; 25:4; **1Chr** 2:21; 4:39; 42; 5:18; 25; 6:15; 7:23(2); 10:3; 11:4; 6; 15; 22; 23; 12:15; 17; 20; 33; 36; 13:6; 14:8(2); 17; 15:25; 16:20; 17:21; 18:3; 6; 13; 19:5; 16; 21:4; 19; 21; 27:1; 29:30; **2Chr** 1:3; 6; 8:3; 17; 18; 9:4; 12; 15; 16; 21; 10:1; 16; 12:12; 14:10; 15:2; 5; 17:9; 18:2; 12; 23; 28; 29; 19:2; 4; 20:20(2); 21; 21:9; 22:5; 6; 7; 23:2; 17; 25:11; 21; 26:6; 11; 16; 17; 28:9; 29:16; 18; 20; 30:6; 31:1; 34:22; 30; 35:20; **Ezr** 2:1; 59; 4:23; 5:8; 7:6; 7; 8:1; 10:6; **Neh** 2:13; 14; 15; 16; 7:6; 61; 8:12; 16; 9:11; 24; 12:1; 31; 32; 37; 38; **Est** 2:14; 3:15; 4:1; 6; 17; 5:9; 7:7; 8; 8:14; 15; 9:4; **Job** 1:4; 12; 2:7; 18:20; 29:7; 30:28; 31:34; 42:9; **Ps** 18:8; 42:4; 66:6; 12; 68:25; 73:17; 77:17; 81:5; 105:13; 106:32; 39; 114:1; 119:67; 176; **Prov** 7:8; 24:30; **Eccl** 8:10; **Song** 5:7; 6:11; **Is** 7:1; 8:3; 37:1; 14; 36; 37; 48:3; 51:23; 52:4; 57:17; 60:15; **Jer** 3:8; 7:24; 11:10; 13:5; 7; 18:3; 22:11; 26:21; 28:4; 11; 31:2; 36:12; 20; 37:4; 12; 38:8; 11; 39:4(2); 40:6; 41:6(2); 12; 14; 15; 44:3; 51:59; 52:7(2); **Eze** 1:9(2); 12(3); 13(2); 17(3); 19(2); 20; 21(2); 24; 3:14; 23; 8:10; 11; 9:2; 7; 10:2; 3; 4; 6; 7; 11(4); 16(2); 19; 22; 11:23; 24; 16:14; 19:6; 20:16; 23:44(2); 24:12; 25:3; 27:33; 31:15; 17; 36:20; 21; 22; 39:23; 40:6; 22; 49; 41:3; 7; 44:10(2); 15; 47:3; 48:11(3); **Dan** 2:13; 16; 17; 24(2); 6:10; 18(2); 19; **Hos** 1:3; 2:13; 5:13; 9:10; 11:2; **Amos** 5:3(2); 19; **Jonah** 1:3(2); 2:6; 3:3; 4:5; **Nah** 3:10; **Hab** 3:5(2); 11; **Zec** 2:3(2); 5:5; 6:7; 8:10; 10:2; **Mt** 2:9; 3:5; 16; 4:23; 24; 5:1; 8:32; 33; 9:25; 26; 32; 35; 11:7; 8; 9; 12:1; 9; 14; 13:1; 2; 3; 25; 36; 46; 14:12; 14; 23; 25; 15:21; 29; 18:13; 28; 30; 19:22; 20:1; 3; 4; 5; 6; 21:6; 9; 12; 17; 29; 30; 33; 22:5; 10; 15; 22; 24:1; 25:1; 10(2); 16; 18; 25; 26:14; 30; 39; 42; 44; 58; 75; 27:5; 53; 58; 66; 28:9; 16; **Mk** 1:5; 20; 21; 35; 45; 2:12; 13; 23(2); 26; 3:6; 19; 21; 4:3; 5:13; 14; 24; 6:1; 6; 12; 24; 27; 51; 7:24; 8:27; 10:22; 32; 46; 11:4; 9; 11; 15; 19; 12:1; 12; 13:1; 14:10; 16; 26; 35; 39; 68; 15:43; 16:8; 10; 12; 13; 20; **Lk** 1:9; 39; 2:1; 3; 4; 41; 42; 44; 51; 4:14; 16; 30; 37; 42; 5:15; 19; 27; 6:1; 4; 12; 19; 7:6; 11(2); 17; 24; 25; 26; 36; 8:1; 2; 5; 22; 27; 33; 34; 35; 37; 39; 42; 9:6; 10; 28; 52; 56; 57; 10:30; 34; 38; 11:37; 13:22; 14:1; 25; 15:15; 16:30; 17:11; 14; 29; 18:10; 14; 39; 19:12; 28; 32; 36; 45; 20:9; 21:37; 22:4; 13; 39; 47; 62; 23:52; 24:13; 15; 24; 28; 29; **Jn** 2:12; 13; 4:28; 30; 43; 45; 47; 50; 5:1; 4; 6:1; 3; 16; 17; 21; 22; 66; 7:10; 14; 53; 8:1; 9; 59; 9:7; 11; 10:40; 11:20; 28; 31; 46; 54; 55; 12:11; 13; 13:3; 30; 18:1; 4; 6; 15; 16; 28; 29; 38; 19:4; 9; 17; 20:3; 5; 6; 8; 10; 21:3; 11; 23; **Acts** 1:10; 13; 21; 3:1; 4:23; 5:26; 7:15; 8:4; 5; 27; 36; 38; 39; 9:1; 17; 29; 39; 10:9(2); 21; 23; 27; 38; 12:9; 10; 17; 19; 13:11; 14; 14:1; 25; 15:24; 38; 41; 16:4; 13; 16; 40; 17:2; 10; 18:22; 23; 19:8; 12; 20:10; 13; 21:2; 5; 15; 16; 18; 31; 22:5; 26; 23:16; 19; 24:11; 25:6; 26:12; 21; 28:14; **Rom** 10:18; **2Cor** 2:13; 8:17; **Gal** 1:17(2); 18; 2:1; 2; **1Ti** 1:3; 18; **Heb** 9:6; 7; 11:8(2); **1Pet** 3:19; **1Jn** 2:19(2); **3Jn** 7; **Rev** 1:16; 6:2; 4; 10:9; 12:17; 16:2; 20:9

WERE

Gen 1:5; 7(2); 8; 13; 19; 23; 31; 2:1; 4; 25(2); 3:7(2); 4:8; 5:2; 4; 5; 8; 11; 14; 17; 20; 23; 27; 31; 6:1; 2; 4(2); 7:10; 11(2); 18; 19(2); 20; 23(2); 8:2; 3; 5; 7; 8; 9; 11; 13; 9:18; 23; 29; 10:1; 5; 18; 21; 25; 29; 32; 11:32; 13:13; 14:3; 5; 13; 17; 17:23(2); 27; 18:11; 19:11; 36; 20:8; 21:16; 23:1; 17(3); 20; 24:10; 32; 54; 63; 25:3; 4; 24(2); 26:35; 27:1; 15; 23; 42; 29:2; 3; 30:35(2); 42(2); 31:10; 19; 34:5(2); 7(2); 14; 25; 35:2; 4(2); 5; 6; 22; 26; 28; 36:5; 7(2); 11; 12; 13; 14; 15; 16; 18; 22; 23; 25; 37:7; 27; 38:27; 39:20; 22; 40:5; 6; 7; 10; 41:21; 48; 50; 53; 42:28; 35; 43:18(2); 34; 44:3; 4; 45:3; 46:12; 15; 20; 21; 22(2); 25; 26; 27(3); 31; 48:5; 10; 49:24; 50:3; 4; 23; **Ex** 1:5; 7; 12; 5:12; 14; 19; 6:4; 16; 18; 20; 7:20(3); 25; 8:18; 9:26; 32(2); 34; 10:6; 8; 11; 14(2); 12:33; 37; 39; 14:10; 11; 21; 22; 29; 15:8(2); 23; 25; 27; 17:12(2); 19:1; 2(2); 16; 21:3; 29; 22:21; 23:9; 24:10(2); 28:32; 32:3; 15(3); 16; 25; 34:1; 30; 35:22; 25; 36:6; 9; 15; 29; 30(2); 36; 38; 37:9; 13; 14; 16; 17; 20; 22; 25; 38:2; 9; 10(2); 11(2); 12; 14; 15; 16; 17(2); 19; 20; 25; 27; 39:13; 14; 40:37; **Lev** 8:28; 10:12; 16; 14:35; 18:27; 28; 30; 19:34; 26:37; **Num** 1:1; 16; 20; 21(2); 22(2); 23(2); 24; 25(2); 26; 27(2); 28; 29(2); 30; 31(2); 32; 33(2); 34; 35(2); 36; 37(2); 38; 39(2); 40; 41(2); 42; 43(2); 44; 45(3); 46(2); 47; 2:4(2); 6(2); 8(2); 9(2); 11(2); 13(2); 15(2); 16(2); 19(2); 21(2); 23(2); 24(2); 26(2); 28(2); 30(2); 31(2); 32(3); 33; 3:3; 17; 22(3); 28; 34(2); 39(2); 43(2); 49(2); 51; 4:36(2); 37(2); 38; 40(2); 41; 42; 44(2); 45; 46; 48(2); 49(2); 6:12; 7:2(3); 13; 86; 87; 88; 8:21; 9:1; 6(2); 15; 22; 10:28; 11:1; 26(2); 29; 31(3); 12:3; 8; 13:3; 4; 22; 33(2); 14:3; 6; 29; 38; 15:26; 32; 16:34; 39(2); 49; 18:27; 19:18; 21:32; 22:3; 22; 29; 40; 23:22; 24:8; 25:5; 6; 9; 26:7(2); 9; 18; 19; 20; 21; 22; 25; 27; 28; 33; 34; 37; 40; 41(2); 43(2); 47(2); 50(2); 51; 54; 57; 62(3); 63; 31:5; 8; 38; 39; 40; 48; 33:9; 38; 36:11; 12; **Deut** 1:41; 2:11; 14(2); 15; 16; 3:5; 4:32; 46; 47; 5:5; 29; 6:21; 7:7(2); 8:15; 9:15; 10:2; 19; 24:9; 25:17; 18; 28:62; 67(2); 29:17; 31:24; 30; 32:27; 29; 33:5; 34:8; **Josh** 2:4; 7; 8; 10; 22; 3:15(2); 16; 17; 4:1; 7(2); 11; 18(2); 23(2); 5:1(3); 4; 5(2); 6(2); 7; 8; 6:23; 7:12; 8:11; 14; 15; 16(3); 22; 24(2); 25; 35; 9:1; 10; 13; 16; 17; 24; 10:1; 2; 11(2); 20; 26; 28; 30; 32; 35; 37(2); 39; 11:2; 5; 11; 13:21; 22; 31; 14:4; 12(2); 15:4; 7; 11; 21; 16:8; 9; 17:2; 5; 9; 13; 18:12; 14; 19; 21; 19:8; 22; 33; 20:9; 21:4; 10; 19; 26; 33; 40(2); 41; 42(2); 22:9; 30; 24:15; **Judg** 2:10; 12; 15; 3:4; 19; 24; 25; 4:13; 5:6; 15(2); 16; 18; 22; 6:5; 33; 7:1(2); 6; 11; 12; 19(2); 8:4; 10(2); 18(2); 19; 21; 24; 26; 9:29; 34; 35; 36; 40; 43; 44; 47; 48(2); 10:8; 17; 11:3; 33; 12:2; 5; 13:23; 15:14; 16:2; 7; 9; 11; 12; 25; 27(2); 30(2); 17:2; 4; 18:3; 7(2); 16; 17; 22(3); 26; 27; 30; 19:10; 11; 14; 16; 22; 27; 20:3; 11; 15(2); 16; 17(2); 31; 36; 41; 44; 46(2); 21:9(2); 13; **Ruth** 1:13; 19; 4:11; **1Sa** 1:3; 2:5(2); 12; 27; 4:3; 4; 7; 11; 15; 19; 5:4; 12; 6:13; 15; 7:7(2); 10; 13; 14; 8:2; 9:3; 4; 5; 14; 20; 22(2); 25; 27; 10:14; 16; 11:8; 9; 11(2); 13:2(2); 4; 6(2); 8; 11; 15; 16; 22; 14:2(2); 14; 17(2); 20; 21(2); 24; 26; 27; 28; 31; 41; 49(2); 16:6; 17:1; 2; 11; 13; 19; 24; 31; 18:26; 19:16; 20:9; 21:5; 22:2; 6(2); 11; 23:13; 24; 25:1; 2; 7(2); 15(4); 16(2);

40; 43; 26:12; 27:2; 8; 29:4; 30:1; 2; 3; 4; 5; 9(2); 10; 16; 21(2); 27(3); 28(3); 29(3); 30(3); 31(2); 31:7(3); **2Sa** 1:11; 12; 23(4); 2:3; 4; 18; 24; 3:2; 5; 20; 23; 31; 34; 4:1(2); 2; 3; 5:13; 14; 6:2; 8:7; 17; 18; 9:12; 10:5; 8; 13; 14; 15; 16; 19(2); 11:16; 23; 12:1; 31; 13:18(2); 30; 14:27; 15:4; 11; 14; 16; 22; 24; 16:6; 14; 17:21; 22; 29; 18:1; 7; 19:9; 17; 28; 43; 20:3; 8; 14; 15; 18; 25; 21:2; 9; 13; 22; 22:9; 13; 16; 18; 23; 23:9(2); 11; 24:9(2); **1Kin** 1:8; 41; 49(2); 2:5; 11; 3:16; 18; 4:2; 4; 20; 28; 32; 5:3; 14; 16; 6:1; 24; 25; 31; 32; 34(3); 7:4; 5; 6; 9; 11; 17; 18; 19(2); 20; 24(2); 25; 28; 29(3); 30; 31; 32(2); 33; 34(2); 35; 41(2); 42; 45; 47; 8:4; 5(2); 8(2); 10; 47; 9:20(2); 21(2); 22; 23(2); 10:12; 19; 21(3); 11:29; 12:1; 8; 10; 21; 31; 14:4; 9; 20; 24; 15:14; 18; 16:15; 16; 21; 25; 30; 33; 20:1; 15; 23; 27(2); 30; 21:8; 11; 22:43; 48; **2Kin** 2:3; 5; 8; 9; 15; 22; 3:14; 21(2); 4:6; 38; 40; 5:3; 6:20(2); 7:3; 5; 10; 9:5; 10:4; 6; 29(2); 11:2; 9; 10; 12:3; 13; 13:21; 14:4; 14; 15:4; 16(2); 35; 16:17; 17:2; 9; 15; 18:5; 17; 19:12; 18; 26(3); 35; 21:11; 23:3; 4; 7; 8(2); 12; 13(2); 16; 19; 20; 24(2); 24:16; 25:4; 5; 10; 11; 13; 15; 19(3); 25; 26; 28; **1Chr** 1:19; 23; 51; 2:3; 4; 9; 16; 25; 27; 28; 33; 42; 50; 3:1(2); 4; 5; 9; 15; 19; 24; 4:3; 6; 7; 14; 17; 20(2); 21; 23; 24; 31; 32; 33(2); 38; 41; 43; 5:3; 7; 9; 13; 17; 18; 20(3); 24; 6:18; 48; 49; 60; 61(2); 63; 71; 77; 78; 7:1; 2; 4; 5; 7; 11; 16; 17; 19; 21; 28; 40(2); 8:3; 8; 10; 13; 28; 35; 38; 39; 40; 9:1(3); 2; 9; 17; 18; 19(2); 22(3); 24; 25(2); 26(2); 29; 31; 32; 33(2); 34; 41; 44; 10:7(2); 11:4; 13; 26; 12:1; 2; 8(2); 14; 20; 21(2); 23; 24; 27; 31; 32(3); 33; 38; 39; 40; 14:12; 15:19; 23; 24; 16:19; 41(2); 42; 18:7; 16; 17; 19:5(2); 9(2); 14; 15; 16(2); 19; 20:2; 3; 4; 6; 8; 21:5; 16; 29; 22:2; 23:3; 4(2); 5; 7; 9; 10(2); 11; 14; 15; 17(2); 24(2); 27; 24:4(3); 5(2); 19; 20; 26; 30; 25:5; 6; 7(2); 9; 10; 11; 12; 13; 14; 15; 16; 17; 18; 19; 20; 21; 22; 23; 24; 25; 26; 27; 28; 29; 30; 31; 26:2; 4; 6(2); 7; 8; 11; 12; 17; 21; 22; 26; 29; 30; 31(2); 32; 27:1; 2; 4; 5; 7; 8; 9; 10; 11; 12; 13; 14; 15; 22; 28; 29; 31; 29:8; 15; **2Chr** 2:17(2); 3:11; 13; 4:3; 4; 12(2); 13; 19; 22; 5:5; 6; 9(2); 11(3); 12; 13; 8:7(2); 8; 9; 10; 9:11; 18(2); 20(3); 10:1; 8; 10; 11:1; 13; 12:3; 5; 15; 13:13; 18; 14:8; 13(3); 15:5; 17; 16:8; 17:10; 13; 18:30; 20:22(2); 24; 25; 33; 37(2); 21:2; 13; 16; 22:4; 6; 11; 23:8(2); 9; 14; 24:14; 25; 25:12; 24; 26:12; 17; 28:6; 15(2); 23; 29:29; 31; 32; 33; 34(2); 35; 30:8; 14; 15; 17(2); 21; 31:1; 6; 13; 15; 19(3); 32:3; 9; 13; 18; 19; 34:4; 12; 13(3); 32; 33; 35:3; 7(2); 14; 15; 17; 18; 36:20; **Ezr** 1:6; 11(2); 2:58; 59(2); 62(3); 65(2); 66; 3:1; 5; 8; 12; 5:1; 2; 6; 10; 14; 6:1; 20(2); 21; 8:3; 20; 35; 9:1; 4; 9; 10:15; 16; 18; **Neh** 1:2; 9; 2:13(2); 4:7(2); 16; 5:2; 3; 4; 8; 15; 16; 17; 18; 6:16(2); 18; 7:1; 4(2); 60; 61(2); 64(2); 67; 73; 8:3; 12; 13; 17; 9:1; 17; 25; 26; 10:1; 8; 11:6; 12; 18; 19; 20; 21; 22; 36; 12:7; 9; 12; 22; 23; 25; 26; 44; 46; 13:10; 13; **Est** 1:5(2); 6(2); 2:7; 8; 9; 12; 14; 19; 21; 23; 3:1; 2; 3; 6; 12(2); 13; 6:1; 14; 8:9; 11; 9:11; 15; 16; 18; 20; **Job** 1:2; 5; 13; 14; 18; 4:7; 6:2; 20(2); 9:15; 21; 16:4; 18:20; 19:23(2); 24; 21:4; 22:16; 28:5; 29:2; 5; 30:3; 5; 7; 8(2); 31:20; 28; 32:4; 15; 33:21; 34:35; 39:16; 42:15; **Ps** 14:2; 5; 7; 17:12; 18:7; 8; 11; 15(2); 17; 22; 37; 38; 22:5(2); 33:6; 34:5(2); 35:13; 39:12; 45:9; 46:6; 48:4; 5; 50:12; 53:2; 5; 6; 55:18; 21(3); 68:25; 33; 73:2; 77:16(2); 78:29; 30; 37; 39; 57; 63; 80:10(2); 81:6; 90:2; 105:12; 106:35; 36; 39; 42; 43; 119:5; 126:1; 139:16(2); 148:5; **Prov** 8:24(2); 25; 31; **Eccl** 2:7; 9; 4:1; 7:10; 8:10; **Song** 1:6; 5:4; 6:13; **Is** 5:18; 25; 7:23; 10:15; 14:2; 26:18; 20; 27:13; 30:4; 5; 33:3; 37:12; 19; 27(3); 36; 41:5; 11; 42:24; 46:1(2); 51:13; 52:14; 53:3; 63:19; **Jer** 1:1; 4:25; 26; 5:8; 6:15(2); 8:12(2); 9:1; 11:13; 14:3; 4; 15:16; 20:2; 22:24; 26; 24:1; 2; 26:9; 29:1; 2; 30:14; 15; 31:2; 15; 34:5; 7; 8; 15; 36:16; 24; 28; 32; 37:15; 21; 40:1(2); 4; 6; 7(2); 11(2); 12; 13; 41:2; 3(2); 7; 8; 9; 10; 11; 13(3); 16; 18; 42:8; 16; 43:5; 44:17; 49:2; 50:11; 33; 52:7; 14; 17; 20; 22; 23(2); 25(3); 30; 32; **Lam** 2:4; 6; 4:5; 7(3); 10; 5:12; **Eze** 1:1; 7; 9; 11(3); 16; 18(3); 19(2); 20; 21(2); 23; 27; 7:13; 8:16; 9:6; 8; 10:1; 12; 15; 17; 19; 20; 14:14; 16; 18; 20; 16:47; 50; 17:6; 19:12; 20:9; 24; 25; 22:6; 23:2; 3; 4(3); 6; 7; 42; 27:8(3); 9(2); 10; 11(2); 13; 15(2); 17; 19; 21; 22; 23; 24; 29:13; 31:5; 8(2); 9; 15; 17; 32:27; 29; 34:5(2); 36:19; 31; 37:2(2); 40:7; 10(2); 12; 15; 16(3); 17(2); 21(2); 22(2); 25; 26(2); 29; 30; 31(2); 33(2); 34(2); 37(2); 38; 39; 40(2); 41; 42; 43; 44; 49; 41:2; 6; 8; 9; 11; 16; 20; 21; 22; 25(3); 26; 42:3; 5(2); 6; 8(2); 10; 11(2); 12; 43:3; 46:22(2); 47:3; 4(2); 5; 7; **Dan** 1:6; 20; 2:34; 42; 3:3; 20; 21(2); 27; 4:10; 12; 21; 33; 5:3; 6; 9; 12; 6:18; 7:4; 7; 8(2); 9; 10; 12; 19; 20; 8:3; 10:3; 5; 7; 12; **Hos** 2:23; 4:7; 5:10; 8:12; 9:10; 12:8; 13:6(2); **Amos** 4:7; 8; 11; **Obad** 7; **Jonah** 1:5(2); 10; 2:5; **Mic** 1:13; **Nah** 3:9(2); 10(2); **Hab** 3:6; **Hag** 2:16(3); **Zec** 1:8(2); 6:1; 2; 7:3; 8:9; 13; 10:2; **Mt** 1:11; 12; 2:11; 13; 16; 3:6; 16; 4:18; 24(3); 5:12; 7:28; 8:16(2); 32; 9:25; 30; 31; 36; 11:20; 21; 12:1; 3; 4; 23; 13:2; 6; 54; 57; 14:20; 21; 26; 32; 33; 34; 35; 36; 15:1; 12; 30; 37; 38; 16:5; 17:6; 14; 23; 24; 18:6(3); 31; 19:12(2); 13; 25; 20:9; 24; 21:1; 15; 22:3; 8(2); 25; 33; 34; 41; 24:24; 37; 38(2); 25:2(2); 3; 10; 26:22; 26; 43; 51; 57; 71; 27:17; 33; 38; 44; 52; 54(2); 55; 28:11(2); 12; 15; **Mk** 1:5; 16; 19; 22; 27; 29; 32(2); 34; 36; 2:2; 6; 12; 15; 25; 26; 4:10; 33; 34; 36; 5:13(2); 15; 40; 42; 6:2; 3; 13; 31; 34; 42; 44; 50; 51; 54; 55; 56(2); 7:35; 37; 8:8; 9; 9:4; 6; 9; 15; 32; 42(2); 10:24; 26; 32(3); 11:12; 12:14; 20; 41; 13:22; 14:4; 11; 21; 35; 40; 53; 15:32; 40; 44; 16:5; 8; 8<VM>; **Lk** 1:2; 6; 7; 10; 23; 45; 65; 2:6(2); 8; 9; 15; 18; 21; 22; 33; 47; 48; 3:15(2); 21; 4:2; 20(2); 25; 27; 28; 32; 36; 5:2(2); 7; 9; 10; 17(2); 26(2); 6:3; 4; 11; 18(2); 7:10; 20; 21; 24; 39; 8:1; 4(2); 23(2); 30; 33; 35(2); 37; 38; 40; 45; 56; 9:10; 14; 17; 18; 30; 32(3); 37; 43; 11:29; 52; 12:1; 13:1; 2; 4; 17(2); 14:7; 17; 24; 16:14; 16; 17:2(2); 9; 12; 14; 17; 27; 18:9; 34; 19:32; 33; 48; 20:29; 22:5; 44; 49; 52; 55; 23:5; 6; 12(2); 23; 32; 33; 39; 48; 24:4; 5; 10; 16; 21; 22; 24; 31; 33; 35; 37; 44; 53; **Jn** 1:3; 13; 24(2); 28; 2:6; 3:19; 23; 4:8; 40; 5:35; 6:2; 11; 12; 19; 22(2); 26; 64; 65; 7:10(2); 8:33; 39; 42; 9:10; 33; 40; 41; 10:6; 41; 11:25; 31; 52; 57; 12:12; 16; 20; 13:1; 14:2; 15:19; 16:19; 17:6; 18:30; 36; 19:11; 28; 36; 20:19(2); 20; 26; 21:2; 6; 8(2); 9; 11; **Acts** 1:6; 13; 15; 2:1; 2; 4; 5; 6; 7; 8; 12(2); 37; 41(2); 43; 44; 3:10; 4:6(2); 13; 26; 27; 31(2); 32; 34(2); 5:12(2); 14; 16(2); 17(2); 21; 33; 36; 37; 41; 6:1; 7; 10; 7:16; 30; 54; 8:1; 4; 7(3); 12; 13; 14; 15; 16; 39; 9:2; 8; 19; 21; 23; 26; 31(2); 10:12; 17; 18; 21; 27; 38; 45; 11:1; 2; 10; 11; 19; 20(2); 26; 12:3; 10; 12; 16; 13:1; 5; 42; 45(2); 48(2); 52; 14:6; 27; 15:4(2); 10; 30; 33; 16:2; 3; 4(2); 5; 6; 7; 12; 14; 26(3); 32; 38; 17:11(2); 12; 14; 21; 18:3; 5; 8; 14; 19:3; 5; 7; 9; 12; 14; 21; 28; 31; 32; 20:8(2); 12; 16; 18; 34; 21:1; 5; 8; 17; 18; 24; 27(2); 30; 38; 22:5; 9(2); 11; 23:6; 9; 13; 24:9; 25:17; 26:10; 14; 29; 31; 27:4; 7; 11; 17; 27; 30; 36; 37; 39(2); 28:1; 7; 9; 10; 14; 17; 24; **Rom** 1:21; 3:2; 4:2; 17; 5:6; 8; 10(2); 19; 6:3(2); 17; 20(2); 7:5(2); 6; 9:3; 25; 32; 11:7; 19; 20; 15:4(2); 16:7; **1Cor** 1:9; 13; 3:2; 4:9; 5:3; 6:11; 7:7; 14; 9:15; 10:1; 2; 5; 6; 7; 9; 10; 11:5; 12:2(2); 17(4); 19(2); 15:11; **2Cor** 1:8; 3:14; 5:1; 14; 7:5(4); 8; 9(2); 13; 8:3; 11:17; 12:12; 13; 13:2; **Gal** 1:17; 22; 2:2; 6; 12(2); 3:16; 23; 4:3(2); 5; 5:12; **Eph** 1:13; 2:1; 3; 5; 12; 13; 17(2); 5:8; **Phil** 3:7; 12; 4:10; 18; **Col** 1:16(2); 21; **1Th** 1:5; 7; 2:2(2); 4; 7; 8(2); 3:4; 7; **2Th** 3:10; **Titus** 3:3; **Philem** 1:14; **Heb** 2:15; 3:5; 4:3; 5:8; 6:4(2); 7:11; 21; 23(2); 8:4; 9:6; 9; 15; 10:32; 33(2); 11:3(2); 13(2); 23; 29; 30; 34; 35; 37(4); **Jas** 5:3; **1Pet** 1:18; 2:8; 10; 21; 24; 25; 3:20(2); **2Pet** 1:16; 18; 21; 2:1; 18; 3:2; 4; 5; **1Jn** 2:19(2); 3:12; **Jude** 4; 17; **Rev** 1:14(2); 4:1; 4; 5; 6; 8; 11; 6:1; 9; 11(2); 14; 7:4(2); 5(3); 6(3); 7(3); 8(3); 8:2; 5; 7; 8; 9(2); 10; 11; 9:2; 7(4); 8; 9; 10; 15(2); 16; 17; 19; 20; 10:1; 11:13(2); 15; 18; 19; 12:9; 14; 13:2; 3; 14:3(2); 4(2); 15:2; 8; 16:9; 18(2); 20; 17:8; 18:14; 15; 19; 23(2); 24; 19:6; 12(2); 14; 20; 21(2); 20:4; 5; 12(3); 13(3); 14; 21:1; 19; 21(2); 22:2

WHAT

Gen 2:19; 3:13; 4:10; 9:24; 12:18; 15:2; 20:9(2); 10; 21:17; 29; 23:15; 24:65; 25:32; 26:10; 27:37; 46; 29:15; 25; 30:31; 31:26; 32; 36(2); 37; 43; 32:27; 33:8; 15; 34:11; 37:10; 15; 20; 26; 38:16; 18; 39:8; 41:25; 28; 55; 42:28; 44:15; 16(2); 46:33; 47:3; **Ex** 2:4; 3:13(2); 4:2; 12; 15; 6:1; 10:2; 26; 12:26; 13:14; 15:24; 16:7; 8; 15; 17:4; 18:14; 19:4; 23:11; 32:1; 21; 23; 33:5; **Lev** 15:9; 17:3; 22:4; 25:20; **Num** 9:8; 10:32; 13:18; 19(2); 20; 15:34; 16:11; 21:14; 22:9; 19; 28; 23:11; 17; 23; 24:13; 14; 26:10; 31:50; **Deut** 1:22(2); 33; 3:24; 4:3; 7; 8; 6:20; 7:18; 8:2; 10:12; 11:4; 5; 6; 12:32; 20:5; 6; 7; 8; 24:9; 25:17; 29:24; 32:20; **Josh** 2:10; 4:6; 21; 5:14; 7:8; 9; 19; 9:3; 15:18; 22:16; 24; 24:7; **Judg** 1:14; 7:11; 8:2; 3; 18; 9:48; 10:18; 11:12; 13:8; 17; 14:6; 18(2); 15:11; 16:5; 18:3(2); 8; 14; 18; 23; 24(3); 19:24; 20:12; 21:8; **Ruth** 2:18; 3:4; 4:5; **1Sa** 1:23; 3:17; 18; 4:6; 14; 16; 5:8; 6:2; 4; 9:7(2); 10:2; 8; 11; 15; 11:5; 13:11; 14:40; 43; 15:14; 16; 16:3; 17:26; 29; 18:8; 18; 19:3; 20:1(3); 10; 32; 21:2; 3(2); 22:3; 25:17; 26:18(2); 28:2; 9; 13; 14; 15; 29:3; 8(2); **2Sa** 3:24; 7:18; 20; 23; 9:8; 12:21; 14:5; 15:2; 21; 35; 16:2; 10; 20; 17:5; 18:4; 21; 29; 19:18; 22; 27; 28; 35(2); 37; 21:3; 4; 11; 24:13; 17; 22; **1Kin** 1:16; 2:5(2); 9; 3:5; 8:38; 9:13; 11:22; 12:9; 16; 13:12(2); 14:3; 14; 16:5; 17:18; 18:9; 13; 19:9; 13; 20; 20:22; 22:14; **2Kin** 1:7; 2:9; 3:13; 4:2(2); 13; 14; 43; 6:28; 33; 7:12; 8:13; 14; 9:18; 19; 22; 18:19; 19:11; 20:8; 14; 15; 22:19; 23:17; **1Chr** 12:32; 17:16; 18; 21; 21:12; 17; 29:14; **2Chr** 1:7; 6:29(2); 10:6; 9; 16; 18:13; 19:6; 10; 20:12; 24:11; 25:9; 32:13; 35:21; **Ezr** 5:4; 6:8; 8:17; 9:10; **Neh** 2:4; 12; 16; 19; 4:2; 20; 13:17; **Est** 1:15; 2:1(2); 11; 15; 4:5; 5:3(2); 6(2); 6:3; 6; 7:2(2); 8:1; 9:5; 12(3); **Job** 2:10; 6:11(2); 17; 25; 7:17; 20; 9:12; 11:8(2); 13:2; 13; 15:9(2); 12; 14; 16:3; 6; 21:15(2); 21; 31; 22:17; 23:5; 13; 27:8; 31:2(2); 14(2); 32:11; 34:4; 7; 33; 35:3(2); 6(2); 7(2); 37:19; 38:24; 39:18; 40:4; **Ps** 8:4; 11:3; 25:12; 30:9; 34:12; 39:4; 7; 44:1; 46:8; 50:16; 56:3; 4; 11; 66:16; 85:8; 89:48; 114:5; 116:12; 118:6; 120:3(2); 144:3; **Prov** 4:19; 10:32; 23:1; 25:8; 27:1; 30:4(2); 31:2(3); **Eccl** 1:3; 2:2; 3; 12; 22; 3:9; 22; 5:11; 16; 6:8(2); 11; 12(2); 7:10; 8:4; 10:14(2); 11:2; 5; **Song** 5:9(2); 6:13; 8:8; **Is** 1:11; 3:15; 5:4; 5; 10:3; 14:32; 19:12; 21:6; 11(2); 22:1; 16; 33:13; 36:4; 37:11; 38:15; 22; 39:3; 4; 40:6; 18; 41:22(2); 45:9; 10(2); 52:5; 64:4; **Jer** 1:11; 13; 2:5; 18(2); 23; 4:30; 5:15; 31; 6:18; 20; 7:12; 17; 8:6; 9; 9:12; 11:15; 13:21; 16:10(2); 18:7; 9; 23:25; 28; 33(2); 35(2); 37(2); 24:3; 32:24; 33:24; 37:18; 38:25(2); 48:19; **Lam** 2:13(3); 5:1; **Eze** 2:8; 8:6; 12; 12:9; 22; 15:2; 17:12; 18:2; 19:2; 20:29; 21:13; 24:19; 27:32; 33:30; 37:18; 47:23; **Dan** 2:22; 23; 28; 29(2); 45; 3:5; 15; 4:35; 8:19; 10:14; 12:8; **Hos** 6:4(2); 9:5; 14; 10:3; 14:8; **Joel** 3:4; **Amos** 4:13; 5:18; 7:8; 8:2; **Jonah** 1:6; 8(3); 11; 4:5; **Mic** 1:5(2); 6:1; 3; 5(2); 8(2); **Nah** 1:9; **Hab** 2:1(2); 18; **Zec** 1:9(2); 19; 21; 2:2(2); 4:2; 4; 5; 11; 12; 13; 5:2; 5; 6; 6:4; 13:6; **Mal** 1:13; 3:13; 14; **Mt** 2:7; 5:46; 47; 6:3; 8; 25(3); 31(2); 7:2(2); 9; 8:27; 29; 33; 9:13; 10:19(2); 27(2); 11:7; 8; 9; 12:3; 7; 11; 16:26(2); 17:25; 18:31; 19:6; 16; 20; 27; 20:15; 21; 22; 32; 21:16; 23; 24; 27; 28; 40; 22:17; 42; 24:3; 42; 43; 26:8; 15; 40; 62; 65; 66; 70; 27:4; 22; 23; **Mk** 1:24; 27(2); 2:25; 3:8; 4:24(2); 30; 41; 5:7; 9; 14; 33; 6:2; 10; 24; 30(2); 8:36; 37; 9:6; 9; 10; 16; 33; 10:3; 9; 17; 32; 36; 38; 51; 11:5; 24; 28; 29; 33; 12:9; 13:1(2); 4; 11; 37; 14:8; 36(2); 40; 60; 63; 64; 68; 15:12; 14; 24; **Lk** 1:29; 66; 3:10; 12; 14; 4:34; 36; 5:19; 22; 6:3; 11; 32; 33; 34; 7:22; 24; 25; 26; 31; 39; 8:9; 25; 28; 30; 34; 35; 36; 47; 56; 9:25; 33; 55; 10:25; 26; 12:11(2); 12; 17; 22(2); 29(2); 39; 49; 57; 13:18; 14:31; 15:4; 8; 26; 16:3; 4; 18:6; 18; 36; 41; 19:48; 20:2; 8; 13; 15; 17; 21:7; 14; 22:49; 60; 71; 23:22; 31; 34; 47; 24:17; 19; 35; **Jn** 1:21; 22; 38; 2:4; 18; 25; 3:32; 4:22(2); 27; 5:12; 19(2); 6:6; 9; 28; 30(2); 62; 7:36; 51; 8:5; 9:17; 21; 26; 10:6; 11:46; 47; 56; 12:6; 27; 33; 49(2); 13:7; 12; 28; 15:7; 15; 16:17; 18(2); 18:21(2); 29; 32; 35; 38; 19:22; 21:19; 21; 22; 23; **Acts** 2:12; 37; 4:7(2); 9; 16; 5:7; 35; 7:40; 49(2); 8:30; 36; 9:6(2); 10:4; 6; 15; 17; 21; 29; 11:9; 17; 12:18; 13:12; 14:11; 15:12; 16:30; 17:18; 19; 20; 19:3; 35; 20:18; 21:13; 19; 22; 33; 22:10; 15; 26; 23:19; 30; 34; 28:22; **Rom** 3:1(2); 3; 5; 9; 19; 27; 4:1; 3; 21; 6:1; 15; 21; 7:7; 15(2); 8:3; 24; 26; 27; 31; 9:14; 22; 30; 10:8; 11:2; 4; 7; 15; 12:2; **1Cor** 2:11; 3:13; 4:7; 21; 5:12; 6:16; 19; 7:16; 36; 9:18; 10:15; 19; 11:22(2); 14:6; 7; 9; 15; 16; 36; 15:2; 10; 29; 32; 35; **2Cor** 1:13; 6:14(2); 15(2); 16; 7:11(7); 11:12; 12:13; **Gal** 4:30; **Eph** 1:18(2); 19; 3:9; 18; 4:9; 5:10; 17; **Phil** 1:18; 22; 3:7; **Col** 1:27; 2:1; **1Th** 1:5; 9; 2:19; 3:9; 4:2; **2Th** 2:6; **1Ti** 1:7; **2Ti** 2:7; 3:11; **Heb** 2:6; 7:11; 11:32; 12:7; 13:6; **Jas** 1:24; 2:14; 16; 4:14(2); **1Pet** 1:11(2); 2:20; 4:17; **2Pet** 3:11; **1Jn** 3:1; 2; **Jude** 10; **Rev** 1:11; 2:7; 11; 17; 29; 3:3; 6; 13; 22; 7:13; 18:18

WHATSOEVER

Gen 2:19; 8:19; 19:12; 31:16; 39:22; **Ex** 13:2; 21:30; 29:37; 30:29; **Lev** 5:3; 4; 6:27; 7:27; 11:3; 9; 12; 27; 32(2); 33; 42(3); 13:58; 15:26; 17:8; 10; 13; 21:18; 22:5; 18; 20; 23:29; 30; 27:32; **Num** 5:10; 18:13; 19:22; 22:17; 23:3; 30:12; **Deut** 2:37; 12:8; 15; 20; 21; 14:10; 26(2); **Judg** 10:15; 11:31; **1Sa** 14:36; 20:4; 25:8; **2Sa** 3:36; 15:15; 19:38; **1Kin** 8:37(2); 10:13; 20:6; **2Chr** 6:28(2); 9:12; **Ezr** 7:18; 20; 21; 23; **Est** 2:13; **Job** 37:12; 41:11; **Ps** 1:3; 8:8; 115:3; 135:6; **Eccl** 2:10; 3:14; 8:3; 9:10; **Jer** 1:7; 42:4; 44:17; **Mt** 5:37; 7:12; 10:11; 14:7; 15:5; 17; 16:19(2); 17:12; 18:18(2); 20:4; 7; 21:22; 23:3; 28:20; **Mk** 6:22; 23; 7:11; 18; 9:13; 10:21; 35; 11:23; 13:11; **Lk** 4:23; 9:4; 10:5; 8; 10; 35; 12:3; **Jn** 2:5; 5:4; 11:22; 12:50; 14:13; 26; 15:14; 16; 16:13; 23; 17:7; **Acts** 3:22; 4:28; **Rom** 14:23; 15:4; 16:2; **1Cor** 10:25; 27; 31; **Gal** 2:6; 6:7; **Eph** 5:13; 6:8; **Phil** 4:8(6); 11; **Col** 3:17; 23; **1Jn** 3:22; 5:4; 15; **3Jn** 5; **Rev** 18:22; 21:27

WHEN

Gen 2:4; 3:6; 4:8; 12; 5:2; 6:1; 4; 7:6; 9:14; 12:4; 11; 12; 14; 14:14; 15:11; 12; 17; 16:4; 5; 6; 16; 17:1; 24; 25; 18:2; 19:15; 17; 23; 29(2); 33(2); 35(2); 20:13; 21:5; 24:19; 30(2); 36; 41; 43; 52; 64; 25:20; 24; 26; 26:8; 34; 27:1; 5; 34; 40; 28:6; 29:10; 13; 31; 30:1; 9; 25; 30; 33; 38(2); 42; 31:49; 32:2; 17; 19; 25; 33:18; 34:2; 7; 25; 35:1; 7; 9; 17; 22; 37:4; 18; 23; 38:5; 9; 15; 25; 28; 39:13; 15; 19; 40:13; 14; 16; 41:21; 46; 55; 42:1; 21; 35; 43:2; 16; 21; 26; 44:4(2); 24; 30; 31; 45:27; 46:33; 47:15; 18; 48:7(2); 17; 49:33; 50:4; 11; 15; 17; **Ex** 1:10; 16; 2:2; 3; 5; 6; 11; 12; 13; 15; 18; 3:4; 12; 13; 21; 4:6; 14; 21; 31; 5:13; 6:28; 7:5; 7; 9; 8:9; 15; 9:34; 10:13; 11:1; 12:13(2); 23; 25; 26; 27; 44; 48; 13:5; 8; 11; 14; 15; 17(2); 14:10; 18; 27; 15:23; 25; 16:3(2); 8; 14; 15; 18; 21; 32; 17:11(2); 18:1; 14; 16; 19:1; 9; 13; 19; 20:18; 22:27; 23:16; 28:29; 30; 35(2); 43(2); 29:30; 36; 30:7; 8; 12(3); 15; 20(2); 31:18; 32:1; 5; 17; 25; 34; 33:4; 8; 34:24; 29(2); 30; 34; 40:32(2); 36; **Lev** 2:1; 8; 4:14; 22; 5:3; 4; 5; 6:20; 21; 27; 7:35; 9:24; 10:9; 20; 11:31; 32; 12:6; 13:2; 3; 9; 14; 20; 14:34; 57(2); 15:2; 13; 23; 31; 16:1; 17; 20; 23; 18:28; 19:9; 23; 20:4; 22:7; 16; 27; 29; 23:10; 12; 22(2); 39; 43; 24:16; 25:2; 26:17; 25; 26; 35; 36; 37; 44; 27:2; 14; 21; **Num** 1:51(2); 3:4; 4:5; 15; 19; 20; 5:6; 21; 27; 29; 30; 6:2; 7; 13; 7:84; 89; 8:2; 19; 9:17; 19; 20; 21; 22; 10:3; 5; 6; 7; 28; 34; 35; 36; 11:1; 2; 9; 25; 12:12; 15:2; 8; 18; 19; 28; 16:4; 42; 18:26; 30; 32; 19:14; 20:3; 16; 29; 21:1; 8; 9; 22:25; 27; 36; 23:17; 24:1; 20; 23; 25:7; 26:9; 10; 61; 64; 27:13; 28:26; 30:6; 32:1; 8; 9; 33:39; 51; 34:2; 35:10; 19; 21; 36:4; **Deut** 1:19; 41; 2:8; 12; 16; 19; 22; 4:10; 19; 25; 30; 5:23; 28; 6:7(4); 10; 11; 20; 7:1; 2; 8:10; 12; 13; 9:9; 23; 11:19(4); 29; 12:10(2); 20; 25; 28; 29; 13:18; 14:24; 15:4; 10; 13; 18; 16:3; 17:14; 18:9; 22; 19:1; 5; 20:1; 2; 9; 10; 13; 19; 21:9; 10; 16; 18; 22:8; 14; 26; 23:4; 9; 11(2); 13; 21; 24; 25; 24:1; 2; 5; 10; 13; 19; 20; 21; 25:4; 11; 17; 18; 19; 26:1; 7; 12; 27:2; 3; 4; 12; 28:6(2); 19(2); 29:7; 19; 22; 25; 30:1; 31:11; 20; 21; 24; 32:8(2); 19; 36; 33:5; 34:7; **Josh** 2:5; 10; 14; 18; 3:3; 8; 14; 4:1; 6; 7; 11; 18; 21; 5:1; 8; 13; 6:5(2); 8; 16; 18; 20(2); 7:8; 21; 8:5; 8; 13; 14; 20; 21; 24(2); 9:1; 3; 22; 10:1; 12; 20; 24; 11:1; 5; 14:7; 17:13; 19:49; 20:4; 22:7; 10; 12; 28; 30; 23:16; 24:7; **Judg** 1:14; 25; 28; 2:4; 6; 18; 19; 21; 3:9; 15; 18; 24(2); 27; 4:1; 18; 20; 22; 5:2; 4(2); 26; 31; 6:3; 7; 22; 28; 29; 7:13; 15; 17; 18; 8:1; 3; 7; 9; 12; 9:7; 22; 30; 33; 36; 46; 55; 11:5; 7; 13; 16; 31; 35; 12:2; 3; 5; 13:17; 20; 14:11; 15:5; 14; 17; 19; 16:2; 9; 15; 16; 18; 24; 25; 17:3; 18:2; 3; 10; 22; 26; 19:1; 3; 5; 7; 9; 11; 14; 15; 17; 25; 29; 20:10; 39; 40; 41; 21:22; **Ruth** 1:1; 18; 19; 2:9; 15; 3:4; 7; 15; 16; 4:13; **1Sa** 1:4; 7; 20; 24; 2:13; 19; 27; 3:2; 12; 4:2; 3(2); 5; 6; 13(2); 14; 18; 19; 5:2; 3; 4; 7; 6:6; 16; 7:7(2); 8:1; 6; 9:5; 9; 14; 17; 25; 10:2; 5; 7; 9; 10; 11; 13; 14; 20; 21(2); 23; 11:6; 8; 12:8; 9; 12(2); 13:1; 6; 14:17; 22; 26; 27; 52; 15:2; 6; 12; 17; 16:6; 16; 23; 17:11; 24; 28; 31; 35; 42; 48; 51; 55; 18:1; 6; 15; 19; 26; 19:14; 16; 20; 21; 20:12; 15; 19(2); 24; 37; 21:6; 22:1; 6; 17; 22; 23:6; 25; 24:1; 8; 16; 25:9; 15; 23; 30; 31; 37; 39; 40; 26:20; 28:5; 6; 12; 22; 30:1; 12; 16; 21; 26; 31:5; 7; 8; 11; **2Sa** 1:1; 2; 7; 2:10; 24; 30; 3:13; 23; 26; 27; 28; 35; 4:1; 4; 7; 10; 11; 5:2; 4; 17; 23; 24; 6:6; 13; 7:1; 12; 8:5; 9; 13; 9:2; 6; 10:5; 6; 7; 9; 14; 15; 17; 19; 11:1; 7; 10; 13; 16; 19; 20; 26; 27; 12:19; 20; 21; 13:5; 6; 11; 21; 28(2); 14:4; 26; 29; 33; 15:2; 5; 32; 16:1; 5; 7; 16; 17:6; 9; 20(2); 23; 27; 18:5; 29; 19:3; 25; 39; 20:8; 12(2); 13; 17; 21:12; 21; 22:5; 23:4; 9; 24:8; 11; 16; 17; **1Kin** 1:21; 23; 41; 2:7; 8; 3:21(2); 5:7; 6:7; 7:24; 8:9(2); 10; 21; 30(2); 33; 35(2); 42; 53; 54; 9:1; 10; 10:1; 2; 4; 11:4; 15; 21; 24; 29; 12:2; 16; 20; 21; 13:4; 24; 26; 31; 14:5; 6; 12; 17; 21; 28; 15:21; 29; 16:11; 18; 17:10; 18:4; 10; 12; 13; 17; 29; 39; 19:3; 13; 15; 20:12; 21:15; 16; 27; 22:25; 32; 33; 42; **2Kin** 1:5; 2:1; 9; 10; 14; 15; 17; 18; 3:5; 15; 20; 21; 24; 26; 4:4; 6; 10; 12; 15; 18; 20; 25; 27; 32; 36; 5:6; 7; 8; 13; 18(2); 21; 24; 26; 6:4; 15; 18; 20; 21; 23; 30; 32; 7:5; 8; 12; 17; 8:6; 17; 26; 29; 9:2; 5; 15; 22; 25; 27; 30; 34; 10:7; 15; 17; 24; 11:1; 13; 14; 21; 12:10; 13:21; 14:2; 15:2; 33; 16:2; 12; 18:2; 17; 18; 32; 19:1; 9; 35; 21:1; 19; 22:1; 11; 19; 23:29; 31; 36; 24:8; 18; 25:23; **1Chr** 1:44; 45; 46; 47; 48; 49; 50; 2:19; 21; 5:7; 6:15; 7:23; 10:5; 7; 8; 9; 11; 11:2; 12:15; 19; 13:9; 14:8; 12; 15; 15:26; 16:2; 19; 20; 17:11; 18:5; 9; 19:6; 8; 10; 15; 16; 17; 19; 20:7; 21:28; 23:1; **2Chr** 4:3; 5:10(2); 11; 13; 6:21; 26(2); 27; 29; 7:1; 3; 6; 9:1(2); 3; 10:2; 16; 11:1; 12:1; 7; 11; 12; 13; 13:7; 14; 15:4; 8; 9; 16:5; 18:14; 24; 31; 32; 19:8; 20:9; 10; 21; 22; 23; 24; 25; 29; 31; 21:4; 5; 20; 22:2; 6; 7; 8; 9; 10; 23:7(2); 12; 15; 24:1; 11; 14; 15(2); 22; 25; 25:1; 3; 26:3; 16; 27:1; 8; 28:1; 29:1; 22; 27; 29; 31:1; 8; 32:2; 21; 33:1; 12; 21; 34:1; 7; 8; 9; 14; 19; 27; 35:20; 36:2; 5; 9; 10; 11; **Ezr** 2:68; 3:1; 10; 11; 12; 4:1; 23; 9:1; 3; 10:1(2); 6; **Neh** 1:4; 2:3; 6; 10; 19; 4:1; 7; 12; 15; 5:6; 6:1; 16; 7:1; 73; 8:5; 9; 9:18; 27; 28; 10:38; 13:3; 19; **Est** 1:2; 4; 5; 10; 17; 20; 2:1; 7; 8(2); 12; 15; 19; 20; 23; 3:4; 5; 4:1; 5:2; 9; 10; 9:1; 25; **Job** 1:5; 6; 13; 2:1; 11; 12; 3:11; 22; 4:13; 5:21; 6:5; 17; 7:4(2); 13; 11:3; 16:22; 17:16; 20:23; 21:6; 21; 22:29; 23:10; 15; 27:8; 9; 28:26; 29:2; 3(2); 4; 5(2); 6; 7(2); 11(2); 30:26(2); 31:13; 14(2); 21; 26; 29; 32:5; 16; 33:15; 34:29(2); 36:13; 20; 37:4; 15;

17; 38:4; 7; 8; 9; 38; 40; 41; 39:1(2); 2; 41:25; 42:10; **Ps** 2:12; 3:t, 4:1(2); 3; 8:3; 9:3; 12; 10:9; 12:8; 13:4; 14:7; 17:15; 20:9; 21:12; 22:9; 24; 27:2; 7; 8; 10; 28:2(2); 30:9; 31:22; 32:3; 6; 34:t, 35:13; 37:33; 34; 38:16; 39:11; 41:5; 6; 42:2; 4; 49:5; 16(2); 17; 18; 50:16; 51:t, 4(2); 52:t, 53:6; 54:t; 56:t, 6; 9; 57:t, 58:7; 10; 59:t, 60:(2); 61:2; 63:t, 6; 65:9; 66:14; 68:7(2); 9; 14; 69:10; 71:9; 18; 23; 72:12; 73:3; 16; 20(2); 75:2; 76:7; 9; 78:34; 42; 59; 81:5; 87:6; 89:9; 90:4; 92:7(2); 94:8; 18; 95:9; 101:2; 102:t, 2(2); 16; 22; 105:12; 13; 38; 106:44; 109:7; 23; 25; 28; 114:1; 119:6; 7; 32; 74; 82; 84; 171; 120:7; 122:1; 124:2; 3; 126:1; 137:1; 138:3; 4; 139:15; 16; 18; 141:1; 6; 7; 142:t, 3; **Prov** 1:26; 27(2); 2:10; 3:24; 25; 27; 28; 4:8; 12(2); 5:11; 6:3; 9; 22(3); 30; 8:24(2); 27(2); 28(2); 29(2); 11:2; 7; 10(2); 13:12; 14:7; 16:7; 17:14; 28; 18:3; 20:14; 21:11(2); 27; 22:6; 23:1; 16; 22; 31(3); 35; 24:14; 17(2); 25:8; 26:25; 28:1; 12(2); 28(2); 29:2(2); 16; 30:22(2); 23; 31:23; **Eccl** 4:10; 5:1; 4; 11; 8:7; 16; 9:12; 10:3; 16; 17; 12:1; 3; 4; 5; **Song** 5:6; 8:1; 8; **Is** 1:12; 15(2); 2:19; 21; 3:6; 4:4; 5:4; 6:13; 8:10; 21; 9:1; 3; 10:12; 18; 13:19; 16:12; 17:5; 18:3(2); 5; 20:1; 24:13(2); 23; 25:4; 26:9; 11; 16; 27:8; 9; 11; 28:4; 15; 18; 25; 29:8(2); 23; 30:19; 21(2); 25; 29(2); 31:3; 4; 32:7; 19; 33:1(2); 37:1; 9; 36; 38:9; 41:17; 28; 43:2(2); 12; 48:7; 13; 21; 50:2(2); 52:8; 53:2; 10; 54:6; 57:13; 20; 58:7; 59:19; 64:2; 3; 65:12(2); 66:4(2); 14; **Jer** 2:2; 7; 17; 20; 26; 3:8; 16; 4:30; 5:7; 19; 6:14; 15; 8:11; 12; 18; 10:13; 11:15; 12:1; 13:21; 27; 14:12(2); 16:10; 17:6; 8; 18:22; 21:1; 22:23; 23:33; 25:12; 26:8; 10; 21(2); 27:20; 28:9; 29:13; 31:2; 23; 35; 32:16; 34:1; 7; 10; 14; 18; 35:11; 36:11; 13; 16; 23; 37:5; 11; 13; 16; 38:7; 28; 39:4; 5; 40:1; 7; 11; 41:7; 11; 13; 42:6; 18; 20; 43:1; 11; 44:19; 45:1; 51:16; 55; 59; 61; 63; 52:1; **Lam** 1:7; 2:12(2); 3:8; 37; 4:15; **Eze** 1:9; 12; 17(2); 19(2); 21(3); 24(2); 25; 28; 2:2; 9; 3:18; 20; 27; 4:6; 5:2; 13; 15; 16; 6:8; 13; 8:7; 8; 10:3; 5; 6; 9; 11; 16(2); 17(2); 19; 11:13; 12:15; 13:12; 14:9; 13; 21; 23; 15:5(2); 7; 16:6(3); 8; 22; 53; 55; 61; 63; 17:10; 18; 18:19; 24; 26; 27; 19:5; 20:5(2); 28; 31(2); 41; 42; 44; 21:7; 25; 29; 22:28; 23:5; 11; 14; 39; 24:24; 25; 25:3(3); 17; 26:10; 15(2); 19(2); 20; 27:33; 34; 28:22; 25; 26; 29:7(2); 16; 30:4; 8(2); 18; 25; 31:5; 15; 16; 32:7; 9; 10; 15(2); 33:2; 3; 8; 13; 14; 18; 29; 33; 34:5; 27; 35:11; 14; 36:17; 20(2); 23; 37:8; 13; 18; 28; 38:14; 16; 18; 39:15; 26; 27; 42:14; 15; 43:3; 18; 23; 27; 44:7; 10; 15; 17; 19; 21; 45:1; 46:8; 9; 10(2); 12; 47:3; 7; 48:11; **Dan** 3:7; 5:20; 6:10; 14; 20; 8:2; 8; 15; 17; 23; 10:9; 11; 15; 19; 20; 11:4; 12; 34; 12:7(2); **Hos** 1:8; 2:15; 4:14(2); 5:13; 6:11; 7:1; 12; 14; 9:12; 10:10; 11:1; 10; 13:1(2); **Joel** 2:8; 3:1; **Amos** 3:4; 4:7; 9; 7:2; 8:5; **Jonah** 2:7; 4:2; 7; 8; **Mic** 2:1; 5:5(2); 6(2); 7:1; 8(2); **Nah** 1:12; 3:17; **Hab** 1:13; 2:1; 3:10(2); **Zeph** 3:20; **Hag** 1:9; 2:5; 16(2); **Zec** 7:2; 5; 6(2); 7(2); 8:14; 9:1; 13; 12:2; 13:3(2); 4; 14:3; **Mal** 2:17; 3:2; 17; **Mt** 1:18; 2:1; 3; 4; 7; 8; 9; 10; 11(2); 13; 14; 16; 19; 22; 3:7; 16; 4:2; 3; 12; 5:1; 11; 6:2; 3; 5; 6(2); 7; 16; 17; 7:28; 8:1; 5; 10; 14; 16; 18; 23; 28; 32; 34; 9:8; 11; 12; 15; 22; 23; 25; 27; 28; 31; 33; 36; 10:1; 12; 14; 19; 23; 11:1; 2; 12:2; 3; 9; 15; 24; 43; 44; 13:4; 6; 19; 21; 26; 32; 44; 46; 48; 53; 54; 14:5; 6; 13(2); 15; 23(2); 26; 29; 30; 32; 34; 35; 15:2; 31; 16:2; 5; 8; 13; 17:6; 8; 14; 24; 25; 27; 18:24; 31; 19:1; 22; 25; 28; 20:2; 8; 9; 10; 11; 24; 30; 21:1; 10; 15; 19; 20; 23; 32; 34; 38; 40; 45; 46; 22:7; 11; 22; 25; 33; 34; 23:15; 24:3; 15; 32; 33; 46; 50; 25:31; 37; 38; 39; 44; 26:1; 6; 8; 10; 20; 29; 30; 71; 27:1; 2; 3; 12; 17; 19; 24; 26; 29; 33; 34; 47; 50; 54; 57; 59; 28:11; 12; 17; **Mk** 1:19; 26; 29; 32; 37; 2:4(2); 5; 8; 16; 17; 20; 25; 3:5; 8; 11; 21; 4:6; 10; 15; 16; 17; 29; 31; 32; 34; 35; 36; 5:2; 6; 18; 21; 22; 27; 39; 40; 6:2; 11; 16; 20; 21; 22; 29; 34; 35; 38; 41; 46; 47; 49; 53; 54; 7:2; 4; 14; 17; 30; 8:17; 19; 20; 23; 33; 34; 38; 9:8; 14; 15; 20; 25; 28; 36; 10:14; 17; 41; 47; 11:1; 11; 12; 13; 19; 24; 25; 12:14; 23; 25; 34; 13:4(2); 7; 11; 14; 28; 29; 33; 35; 14:11; 12; 23; 26; 40; 67; 72; 15:15; 20; 24; 33; 35; 39; 41; 42; 45; 16:1; 4; 9; 11; **Lk** 1:9; 12; 22; 29; 41; 2:2; 17; 21; 22; 27; 39; 42; 43; 45; 48; 3:21; 4:2; 13; 17; 25(2); 28; 35; 40; 42; 5:4; 6; 8; 11; 12; 19; 20; 22; 35; 6:3; 13; 22(2); 26; 42; 48; 7:1; 3; 4; 6; 9; 12; 13; 20; 24; 37; 39; 42; 8:4; 8; 13; 14; 16; 27; 28; 34; 40; 45; 47; 50; 51; 9:5; 10; 11; 12; 26; 32; 36; 37; 51; 54; 10:31; 32; 33; 35(2); 11:1; 2; 14; 21; 22; 24; 25; 29; 33; 34(2); 36; 38; 12:1; 11; 36(2); 37; 40; 43; 46(2); 54; 55; 58; 13:12; 17; 25; 28; 35; 14:7; 8; 10(2); 12; 13; 15; 15:5; 6; 9; 14; 17; 20; 16:4; 9; 17:7; 10; 14; 15; 20(2); 22; 30; 18:8; 15; 22; 23; 24; 40; 43; 19:5; 7; 15; 28; 29; 37; 41; 20:13; 14; 16; 37; 21:7(2); 9; 20; 28; 30; 31; 22:7; 10; 14; 32; 35; 40; 45; 49; 53; 55; 64; 23:6; 8; 13; 33; 42; 46; 47; 24:6; 23; 40; **Jn** 1:19; 42; 48; 2:3; 9; 10; 15; 22; 23(2); 3:4; 4:1; 21; 23; 25; 40; 45; 47; 52; 54; 5:6; 7; 25; 6:5; 11; 12; 14; 15; 16; 19; 22; 24; 25(2); 60; 61; 7:9; 10; 27; 31; 40; 8:3; 7; 10; 28; 44; 9:4; 6; 14; 35; 10:4; 11:4; 6; 17; 28; 31; 32; 33; 43; 12:12; 14; 16; 17; 41; 13:1; 19; 21; 26(2); 31; 14:29; 15:26; 16:4; 8; 13; 21; 25; 18:1; 22; 38; 19:6; 8; 13; 23; 26; 30; 33; 20:1; 14; 19; 20(2); 22; 24; 21:4; 7; 15; 18(2); 19; **Acts** 1:6; 9; 13; 2:1; 6; 37; 3:12; 13; 10; 4:7; 13; 15; 21; 24; 31; 5:7; 21; 22; 23; 24; 27; 33; 40; 6:1; 6; 7:2; 4; 5; 12; 17; 21; 23; 30; 31; 54; 60; 8:12; 13; 14; 15; 18; 25; 39; 9:8; 19; 26; 30; 37; 39; 40; 41; 10:4; 7; 8; 32; 11:2; 6; 18; 20; 23; 26; 12:4; 6; 10; 11; 12; 14; 16; 19; 25; 13:3; 5; 6; 12; 13; 14; 17; 19; 22; 24; 29; 42; 43; 45; 48; 14:5; 11; 14; 21; 23; 25; 27; 15:2; 4; 7; 30(2); 31; 16:6; 15; 19; 23; 34; 35; 38; 40; 17:1; 6; 8; 9; 13; 16; 32; 18:5; 6; 12; 14; 20; 22; 26; 27(2); 19:5; 6; 9; 21; 28; 30; 34; 35; 41; 20:2; 3; 7; 11; 14; 18; 36; 21:3; 5; 6; 7; 11; 12; 14; 17; 19; 20; 27(2); 32; 34; 35; 40(2); 22:2; 11; 17; 20; 26; 23:6; 7; 10; 12; 16; 28; 30; 33; 34(2); 35; 24:2; 22(2); 24; 25; 25:1; 6; 7; 12; 14; 15; 17; 18; 21; 23; 25; 26:10; 14; 30; 31; 27:1; 4; 5; 7; 9(2); 13; 15; 17; 20; 27; 28; 30; 35(2); 38; 39; 40; 28:1; 3; 4; 6; 9; 10; 15(2); 16; 17; 18; 19; 23; 25; 29; **Rom** 1:21; 2:14; 16; 3:4; 4:10; 19; 5:6; 10; 13; 6:20; 7:5; 9; 21; 9:10; 11:27; 13:11; 15:28; 29; **1Cor** 2:1; 5:4; 8:12; 9:18; 27; 11:18; 20; 24; 25; 32; 33; 34; 13:10; 11(2); 14:16; 26; 15:24(2); 27; 28; 54; 16:2; 3; 5; 12; **2Cor** 1:17; 2:3; 12; 3:15; 16; 7:5; 7; 10:2; 6; 11(2); 15; 11:9; 12:10; 20; 21; 13:9; **Gal** 1:15; 2:7; 9; 11; 12; 14; 4:3; 4; 8; 18; 6:3; **Eph** 1:20; 2:5; 3:4; 4:8; **Phil** 2:19; 28; 4:15; **Col** 3:4; 7; 4:16; **1Th** 2:6; 13; 3:1; 4; 5; 6; 5:3; **2Th** 1:7; 10; 2:5; 3:10; **1Ti** 1:3; 5:11; **2Ti** 1:5; 17; 4:3; 13; S:1; **Titus** 3:12; **Heb** 1:3; 6; 3:9; 16; 5:7; 12; 6:13; 7:10; 27; 8:5; 8; 9; 9:6; 19; 10:5; 8; 11:8; 11; 17; 21; 22; 23; 24; 31; 12:5; 17; **Jas** 1:2; 12; 13; 14; 15(2); 2:21; 25; **1Pet** 1:11; 2:20(2); 23(2); 3:20; 4:3; 13; 5:4; **2Pet** 1:16; 17; 18; 2:18; **1Jn** 2:28; 3:2; 5:2; **3Jn** 3; **Jude** 3; 9; 12; **Rev** 1:17; 4:9; 5:8; 6:1; 3; 5; 7; 9; 12; 13; 14; 8:1; 9:5; 10:3(2); 4; 7; 11:7; 12:13; 17:6; 8; 10; 18:9; 18; 20:7; 22:8

WHENCE

Gen 3:23; 16:8; 24:5; 29:4; 42:7; **Num** 11:13; 23:13; **Deut** 9:28; 11:10; **Josh** 2:4; 9:8; 20:6; **Judg** 13:6; 17:9; 19:17; **1Sa** 25:11; 30:13; **2Sa** 1:3; 13; **2Kin** 5:25; 6:27; 20:14; **Neh** 4:12; **Job** 1:7; 2:2; 10:21; 16:22; 28:20; **Ps** 121:1; **Eccl** 1:7; **Is** 30:6; 39:3; 47:11; 51:1(2); **Jer** 29:14; **Jonah** 1:8; **Nah** 3:7; **Mt** 12:44; 13:27; 54; 56; 15:33; 21:25; **Mk** 6:2; 8:4; 12:37; **Lk** 1:43; 11:24; 13:25; 27; 20:7; **Jn** 1:48; 2:9; 3:8; 4:11; 6:5; 7:27(2); 28; 8:14(2); 9:29; 30; 19:9; **Acts** 14:26; **Phil** 3:20; **Heb** 11:15; 19; **Jas** 4:1; **Rev** 2:5; 7:13

WHERE

Gen 2:11; 3:9; 4:9; 13:3; 10; 14; 18:9; 19:5; 27; 20:15; 21:17; 22:7; 27:33; 31:13(2); 33:19; 35:13; 14; 15; 27; 37:16; 38:21; 39:20; 40:3; 43:30; **Ex** 2:20; 5:11; 9:26; 12:13; 30; 15:27; 18:5; 20:21; 24; 27:18; 29:42; 30:6; 36; **Lev** 4:12(2); 24; 33; 6:25; 7:2; 14:13; **Num** 9:17; 13:22; 17:4; 22:26; 33:14; 54; **Deut** 1:31; 8:15; 11:10; 30; 18:6; 23:16; 32:37; **Josh** 4:3(2); 8; 9; **Judg** 5:27; 6:13; 9:38; 17:8; 9; 18:10; 19:26; 20:22; **Ruth** 1:7; 16; 17; 2:19(2); 3:4; **1Sa** 3:3; 6:14; 9:10; 18; 10:5; 14; 14:11; 19:3; 22; 20:19; 23:22; 23; 24:3; 26:5(2); 16; 30:9; 31; **2Sa** 2:23; 9:4; 11:16; 15:32; 16:3; 17:12; 20; 18:7; 21:12; 19; 20; 23:11; **1Kin** 4:28; 7:7; 8; 13:25; 17:19; 21:19; **2Kin** 2:14; 4:8; 6:1; 2; 6; 13; 18:34(2); 19:13; 23:7; 8; **1Chr** 11:4; 13; 13:2; 20:6; **2Chr** 3:1; 25:4; 36:20; **Ezr** 1:4; 6:1; 3; **Neh** 10:39; 13:5; **Est** 1:6; 7:5; **Job** 4:7; 9:24; 10:22; 12:24; 14:10; 15:23; 17:15; 20:7; 21:28(2); 23:3; 9; 28:1; 12(2); 20; 34:22; 35:10; 36:16; 38:4; 19(3); 26; 39:30; 40:20; **Ps** 19:3; 26:8; 42:3; 10; 53:5; 63:1; 69:2(2); 79:10; 81:5; 84:3; 89:49; 104:17; 107:40; 115:2; **Prov** 11:14; 14:4; 15:17; 26:20(2); 29:18; **Eccl** 1:5; 8:4; 10; 11:3; **Song** 1:7(2); **Is** 7:23; 10:3; 19:12(2); 29:1; 30:32; 33:18(3); 35:7; 36:19(2); 37:13; 49:21; 50:1; 51:13; 57:8; 63:11(2); 15; 64:11; 66:1(2); **Jer** 2:6(2); 8; 28; 3:2; 6:16; 7:12; 13:7; 20; 16:13; 17:15; 22:26; 35:7; 36:19; 37:19; 38:9; 39:5; 42:14; 52:9; **Lam** 2:12; **Eze** 3:15; 6:13; 8:3; 11:16; 17; 13:12; 17:10; 16; 20:38; 21:30; 34:12; 40:38; 42:13; 43:7; 46:20(2); 24; **Dan** 8:17; **Hos** 1:10; 13:10; **Joel** 2:17; **Amos** 3:5; **Mic** 7:10; **Nah** 2:11(2); 3:17; **Zeph** 3:19; **Zec** 1:5; **Mal** 1:6(2); 2:17; **Mt** 2:2; 4; 9; 6:19(2); 20(2); 21; 8:20; 13:5; 18:20; 25:24(2); 26(2); 26:17; 57; 28:6; 16; **Mk** 2:4; 4:5; 15; 5:40; 6:55; 9:44; 46; 48; 11:4; 13:14; 14:12; 14(2); 15:47; 16:6; 20; **Lk** 4:16; 17; 8:25; 9:6; 58; 10:33; 12:17; 33; 34; 17:17; 37; 22:9; 10; 11(2); **Jn** 1:28; 38; 39; 3:8; 4:20; 46; 6:23; 62; 7:11; 34; 36; 42; 8:10; 19; 9:12; 10:40; 11:6; 30; 32; 34; 41; 57; 12:1; 26; 14:3; 17:24; 18:1; 19:18; 20; 41; 20:2; 12; 13; 15; 19; **Acts** 1:13; 2:2; 4:31; 7:29; 33; 8:4; 11:11; 12:12; 15:36; 16:13; 17:1; 30; 20:6; 8; 21:28; 25:10; 27:41; 28:14; 22; **Rom** 3:27; 4:15; 5:20; 9:26; 15:20; **1Cor** 1:20(3); 4:17; 12:17(2); 19; 15:55(2); **2Cor** 3:17; **Gal** 4:15; **Phil** 4:12; **Col** 3:1; 11; **1Ti** 2:8; **Heb** 9:16; 10:18; **Jas** 3:16; **1Pet** 4:18; **2Pet** 3:4; **Rev** 2:13(3); 11:8; 12:6; 14; 17:15; 20:10

WHEREAS

Gen 31:37; **Deut** 19:6; 28:62; **1Sa** 24:17; **2Sa** 7:6; 15:20; **1Kin** 8:18; 12:11; **2Kin** 13:19; **2Chr** 10:11; 28:13; **Job** 22:20; **Eccl** 4:14; **Is** 37:21; 60:15; **Jer** 4:10; **Eze** 13:7; 16:7; 34; 35:10; 36:34; **Dan** 2:41; 43; 4:23; 26; 8:22; **Mal** 1:4; **Jn** 9:25; **1Cor** 3:3; **Jas** 4:14; **1Pet** 2:12; 3:16; **2Pet** 2:11

WHEREBY

Gen 15:8; 44:5; **Lev** 22:5; **Num** 5:8; 17:5; **Deut** 7:19; 28:20; **1Sa** 20:33; **Ps** 45:5; 8; 68:9; **Jer** 3:8; 17:19; 23:6; 33:8(3); **Eze** 18:31; 20:25; 39:26; 40:49; 46:9; 47:13; **Zeph** 2:8; **Lk** 1:18; 78; **Acts** 4:12; 11:14; 19:40; **Rom** 8:15; 14:21; **Eph** 3:4; 4:14; 30; **Phil** 3:21; **Heb** 12:28; **2Pet** 1:4; 3:6; **1Jn** 2:18

WHEREFORE

Gen 10:9; 16:14; 18:13; 21:10; 31; 24:31; 26:27; 29:25; 31:27; 30; 32:29; 38:10; 40:7; 43:6; 44:4; 7; 47:19; 22; 50:11; **Ex** 2:13; 5:4, 14, 15, 22; 6:6; 14:11; 15; 17:2(2); 3; 20:11; 31:16; 32:12; **Lev** 10:17; 13:25; 25:18; **Num** 9:7; 11:11(2); 12:8; 14:3; 41; 16:3; 20:5; 21; 21:5; 14; 27; 22:32; 37; 25:12; 32:5; 7; **Deut** 7:12; 10:9; 19:7; 29:24; **Josh** 5:9; 7:5; 7; 10; 26; 9:11; 22; 10:3; **Judg** 2:3; 10:13; 11:27; 12:1; 3; 15:19; 18:12; **Ruth** 1:17; **1Sa** 1:20; 2:17; 29; 30; 4:3; 6:5; 6; 9:21; 14:27; 15:19; 16:19; 18:15; 21; 27; 19:5; 24; 20:27; 31; 32; 21:14; 23:25; 28; 24:9; 19; 25:8; 36; 26:15; 18; 27:6; 28:9; 16; 29:7; 10; **2Sa** 2:16; 22; 23; 3:7; 5:8; 7:22; 10:4; 11:20; 12:9; 23; 14:13; 31; 32; 15:19; 16:10; 18:22; 19:12; 25; 35; 42; 21:3; 24:21; **1Kin** 1:2; 11; 41; 11:11; 12:15; 16:16; 20:9; 22:34; **2Kin** 4:23; 31; 5:7; 8; 7:7; 9:11; 36; 17:26; 19:4; **1Chr** 13:11; 19:4; 21:4; 29:10; **2Chr** 5:3; 19:7; 22:4; 25:10; 15; 28:5; 29:8; 34; 33:11; **Neh** 2:2; **Est** 3:6; 9:26; **Job** 3:20; 10:2; 18; 13:14; 24; 18:3; 21:7; 32:6; 33:1; 42:6; **Ps** 10:13; 44:24; 49:5; 79:10; 89:47; 115:2; **Prov** 17:16; **Eccl** 3:22; 4:2; 5:6; **Is** 5:4; 10:12; 16:11; 24:15; 28:14; 29:13; 30:12; 37:4; 50:2; 55:2; 58:3(2); 63:2; **Jer** 2:9; 29; 31; 5:6; 14; 19; 12:1(2); 13:22; 16:10; 20:18; 22:8; 28; 23:12; 27:17; 30:6; 32:3; 37:15; 40:15; 44:6; 7; 46:5; 49:4; 51:52; **Lam** 3:39; 5:20; **Eze** 5:11; 7:24; 13:20; 16:35; 18:32; 20:10; 25; 30; 21:7; 23:9; 24:6; 33:25; 36:18; 43:8; **Dan** 3:8; 4:27; 6:9; 8:26; 10:20; **Joel** 2:17; **Jonah** 1:14; **Hab** 1:13; **Mal** 2:14; 15; **Mt** 6:30; 7:20; 9:4; 12:12; 31; 14:31; 18:8; 19:6; 23:31; 34; 24:26; 26:50; 27:8; **Lk** 7:7; 47; 19:23; **Jn** 9:27; **Acts** 1:21; 6:3; 10:21; 13:35; 15:19; 19:32; 38; 20:26; 22:24; 30; 23:28; 24:26; 25:26; 26:3; 27:25; 34; **Rom** 1:24; 5:12; 7:4; 12; 9:32; 13:5; 15:7; **1Cor** 4:16; 8:13; 10:12; 14; 11:27; 33; 12:3; 14:13; 22; 39; **2Cor** 2:8; 5:9; 16; 6:17; 7:12; 8:24; 11:11; **Gal** 3:19; 24; 4:7; **Eph** 1:15; 2:11; 3:13; 4:8; 25; 5:14; 17; 6:13; **Phil** 2:9; 12; **Col** 2:20; **1Th** 2:18; 3:1; 4:18; 5:11; **2Th** 1:11; **2Ti** 1:6; **Titus** 1:13; **Philem** 1:8; **Heb** 2:17; 3:1; 7; 10; 7:25; 8:3; 10:5; 11:16; 12:1; 12; 28; 13:12; **Jas** 1:19; 21; 4:6; **1Pet** 1:13; 2:1; 6; 4:19; **2Pet** 1:10; 12; 3:14; **1Jn** 3:12; **3Jn** 10; **Rev** 17:7

WHEREIN

Gen 1:30; 6:17; 7:15; 17:8; 21:23; 28:4; 36:7; 37:1; **Ex** 1:14; 6:4; 12:7; 18:11; 20; 22:27; 33:16; **Lev** 4:23; 5:18; 6:28; 11:32; 36; 13:46; 52; 54; 57; 18:3; **Num** 12:11(2); 10:2; 31:10; 33:55; 35:33; 34; **Deut** 8:9; 15; 12:2; 7; 17:1; 28:52; **Josh** 8:24; 10:27; 22:19; 33; 24:17; **Judg** 16:5; 6; 15; 18:6; **1Sa** 6:15; 14:38; **2Sa** 7:7; **1Kin** 2:26; 8:21; 36; 50; 13:31; **2Kin** 12:2; 14:6; 17:29; 18:19; 23:23; **2Chr** 3:3; 6:11; 27; 8:1; 33:19; **Ezr** 5:7; **Neh** 6:6; 9:12; 19; 13:15; **Est** 5:11; 8:11; 9:22; **Job** 3:3; 6:16; 24; 38:26; **Ps** 74:2; 90:15(2); 104:20; 25; 142:3; 143:8; **Eccl** 2:19(2); 22; 3:9; 8:9; **Is** 2:22; 14:3; 33:21; 36:4; 47:12; 65:12; **Jer** 5:17; 7:14; 12:5; 16:19; 20:14(2); 22:28; 31:9; 36:14; 41:9; 42:3; 48:38; 51:43; **Eze** 20:34; 41; 43; 23:19; 26:10; 32:6; 37:23; 25; 42:14; 44:19; **Hos** 2:13; 8:8; **Jonah** 4:11; **Mic** 6:3; **Zeph** 3:11; **Zec** 9:11; **Mal** 1:2; 6; 7; 2:17; 3:7; 8; **Mt** 11:20; 25:13; **Mk** 2:4; **Lk** 1:4; 25; 11:22; 23:53; **Jn** 19:41; **Acts** 2:8; 7:4; 10:12; **Rom** 2:1; 5:2; 7:6; **1Cor** 7:20; 24; 15:1; **2Cor** 11:12; 12:13; **Eph** 1:6; 8; 2:2; 5:18; **Phil** 4:10; **Col** 2:12; **2Ti** 2:9; **Heb** 6:17; 9:2; 4; **1Pet** 1:6; 3:20; 4:4; 5:12; **2Pet** 3:12; 13; **Rev** 2:13; 18:19

WHEREOF

Gen 3:11; **Lev** 6:30; 13:24; 27:9; **Num** 5:3; 7:19; 25; 37; 49; 61; 67; 73; 79; 21:16; **Deut** 13:2; 28:27; 68; **Josh** 14:12; 20:2; 22:9; **1Sa** 10:16; 13:2; **2Sa** 12:30; **2Kin** 13:14; 17:12; **2Chr** 3:8; 6:20; 24:14; 33:4; **Neh** 12:31; **Job** 6:4; **Ps** 46:4; 57:6; 126:3; **Eccl** 1:10; **Song** 4:2; 6:6; **Jer** 32:36; 43; 42:16; **Eze** 32:15; 39:8; **Dan** 9:2; **Hos** 2:12; **Lk** 23:14; **Acts** 2:32; 3:15; 17:19; 31; 21:24; 24:8; 13; 25:11; 26:2; **Rom** 4:2; 6:21; 15:17; **1Cor** 7:1; **2Cor** 9:5; **Eph** 3:7; **Phil** 3:4; **Col** 1:5; 23; 25; **1Ti** 1:7; 6:4; **Heb** 2:5; 10:15; 12:8; 13:10; **1Jn** 1:3

WHERESOEVER

Lev 13:12; **2Kin** 8:1; 12:5; **1Chr** 17:6; **Jer** 40:5; **Dan** 2:38; **Mt** 24:28; 26:13; **Mk** 9:18; 14:9; 14; **Lk** 17:37

WHEREUNTO

Num 36:3; 4; **Deut** 4:26; **2Chr** 8:11; **Est** 10:2; **Ps** 71:3; **Jer** 22:27; **Eze** 5:9; 20:29; **Mt** 11:16; **Mk** 4:30; **Lk** 7:31; 13:18; 20; **Acts** 5:24; 13:2; 27:8; **Gal** 4:9; **Col** 1:29; **2Th** 2:14; **1Ti** 2:7; 4:6; 6:12; **2Ti** 1:11; **1Pet** 2:8; 3:21; **2Pet** 1:19

WHEREUPON

Lev 11:35; **Judg** 16:26; **1Kin** 7:48; 12:28; **2Chr** 12:6; **Job** 38:6; **Eze** 9:3; 23:41; 24:25; 40:41; 42; **Amos** 4:7; **Mt** 14:7; **Acts** 24:18; 26:12; 19; **Heb** 9:18

WHETHER

Gen 18:21; 24:21; 27:21; 31:39; 37:14; 32; 42:16; 43:6; **Ex** 4:18; 12:19; 16:4; 19:13; 21:31; 22:4; 8; 9; 34:19; **Lev** 3:1; 5:1; 2; 7:26; 11:32; 35; 13:47; 48(2); 52; 55; 15:3; 16:29; 17:15; 18:9; 22:28; 27:12; 14; 26; 30; 33; **Num** 9:21; 22; 11:23; 13:18; 19(2); 20(2); 15:30; 18:15; **Deut** 4:32; 8:2; 13:3; 18:3; 22:6; 24:14; **Josh** 24:15; **Judg** 2:22; 3:4; 9:2; 18:5; **Ruth** 3:10; **2Sa** 12:22; 15:21; **1Kin** 20:18(2); 33; **2Kin** 1:2; **2Chr** 14:11; 15:13(2); **Ezr** 2:59; 5:17; 7:26; **Neh** 7:61; **Est** 3:4; 4:11; 14; **Job** 34:29; 33(2); 37:13; **Prov** 20:11(2); 29:9; **Eccl** 2:19; 5:12; 11:6(2); 12:14(2); **Song** 6:11; 7:12; **Jer** 30:6; 42:6(2); **Eze** 2:5(2); 7(2); 3:11(2); 44:31; **Mt** 9:5; 21:31; 23:17; 19; 26:63; 27:21; 49; **Mk** 2:9; 3:2; 15:36; 44; **Lk** 3:15; 5:23; 6:7; 14:28; 31; 22:27; 23:6; **Jn** 7:17(2); 9:25; **Acts** 1:24; 4:19; 5:8; 9:2; 10:18; 17:11; 19:2; 25:20; **Rom** 6:16; 12:6; 14:8(3); **1Cor** 1:16; 3:22; 7:16(2); 8:5; 10:31; 12:13(2); 26; 13:8(3); 14:7; 15:11; **2Cor** 1:6(2); 2:9; 5:9; 10; 13(2); 8:23; 12:2(2); 3; 13:5; **Eph** 6:8; **Phil** 1:18; 20; 27; **Col** 1:16; 20; **1Th** 5:10; **2Th** 2:15; **1Pet** 2:13; **1Jn** 4:1

WHICH

Gen 1:7(2); 21; 29(2); 2:2(2); 3; 11; 14; 22; 3:1; 3; 17; 24; 4:11; 5:29; 6:2; 4; 15; 7:23; 8:6; 7; 12; 9:4; 12; 15; 17; 11:5; 6; 13:4; 5; 15; 18; 14:2; 3; 6; 7; 15; 17; 20; 24(2); 16:15; 17:10; 12; 21; 18:8; 10; 13; 17; 19; 21; 27; 19:5; 8; 14; 15; 19; 21; 25; 29; 20:3; 13; 21:2; 9; 25; 29; 22:2; 3; 9; 17; 23:9(2); 16; 17(3); 24:7(2); 24; 42; 48; 60; 25:6; 7; 9; 10; 26:2; 3; 15; 18(2); 32; 35; 27:8; 15; 17; 27; 45; 46; 28:4; 9; 15; 22; 29:27; 30:26; 30; 37; 38; 31:1; 10; 12; 16; 18(2); 39; 43; 51; 32:8; 9; 10; 12; 13; 32(2); 33:5; 8; 18; 34:1; 7; 28(2); 35:3; 4(3); 6; 12; 19; 26; 27; 36:5; 6; 37:6; 38:10; 14; 39:1; 6; 17; 19; 23; 40:5; 20; 41:28; 36; 43; 48(2); 50; 42:9; 38; 43:2; 26; 32; 44:5; 8; 45:6; 27(2); 46:5; 6; 8; 15; 20; 22; 25; 26; 27(2); 31; 47:14; 22; 26; 48:5; 6; 15; 16; 22; 49:1; 30(2); 50:3; 5; 10; 11; 13; 15; 24; **Ex** 1:1; 8; 15; 3:7; 16; 20; 4:9; 18; 19; 21; 28; 30; 5:8; 14; 6:7; 8; 27; 7:15; 17; 8:3; 12; 22; 9:3; 19; 10:2; 5(3); 6; 15; 19; 21; 12:10; 16; 19; 25; 39; 13:3; 5; 8; 12; 14:13; 19; 31; 15:7; 13; 16; 17; 16:17(2); 25; 26(2); 16:1;

5; 8; 15; 16(2); 23(3); 26; 32; 18:3; 9; 19:6; 7; 22; 20:2; 12; 21:1; 22:9; 13; 23:16(2); 20; 28; 24:3; 5; 8; 12; 25:3; 16; 22(2); 40; 26:10; 13; 30; 27:21; 28:4; 8; 24; 26; 38; 29:27(4); 35; 38; 30:37; 32:1; 2; 3; 4; 7; 8(2); 11; 14; 20; 23; 32; 34; 35; 33:1(2); 7(2); 34:1; 10; 11; 34; 35:1; 4; 25; 29; 36:3; 4; 5; 12; 17; 25; 37:16; 38:8; 39:19; **Lev** 1:8; 12; 2:10; 11; 3:4; 5; 10; 15; 4:2; 3; 7(2); 9; 13; 14; 18(2); 22; 27; 28(2); 5:6; 7; 8; 10; 17; 6:2; 3; 4(4); 5; 10; 15; 20; 7:4; 8; 11; 21; 24; 25; 36; 38; 8:5; 30; 32; 36; 9:5; 6; 8; 12; 15; 18(2); 19; 24; 10:1; 6; 11; 14; 16; 11:2; 10; 13; 21; 23; 26; 34(2); 36; 37; 39; 13:18; 58; 14:32; 34; 37; 40; 15:12; 16:2; 6; 9; 10; 11(2); 23; 17:2; 5; 8; 13; 15(2); 18:5; 24; 27; 30; 19:22(2); 36; 20:8; 23; 24; 25; 21:3; 8; 22:2; 3; 6; 8; 15; 18; 24; 32; 23:2; 4; 10; 37; 38; 25:2; 5; 11; 25; 28; 31; 38; 42; 44; 45; 26:13; 22; 32; 40; 46; 27:11; 22(2); 26; 29; 34; **Num** 1:17; 44; 2:12; 32; 3:3; 26; 39; 46; 4:26; 37; 5:7; 9; 18; 6:5; 18; 21; 8:4; 10:4; 25; 29; 11:5; 12; 17; 20; 12:3; 13:2; 16; 24; 32(2); 33; 14:6; 7; 8; 11; 15; 16; 22(2); 23; 27(2); 29; 30; 31(2); 34; 36; 38; 40; 45; 15:2; 22; 39; 41; 16:11; 12; 40; 18:9; 12; 13; 15; 16; 19; 21; 24; 26; 28; 19:2(2); 15; 20:12; 24; 21:1; 11; 13; 20; 30; 34; 22:5; 11; 20; 30; 36(2); 23:12; 24:4(2); 6; 12; 16(2); 25:18; 26:4; 9; 27:12; 17(5); 28:3; 6; 23; 30:1; 8(2); 14; 16; 31:12; 14; 21(2); 28; 30; 32; 36; 38; 39; 40; 41; 42; 47; 48; 49; 32:4; 7; 9; 11; 24; 38; 39; 33:1; 4; 6; 7; 36; 40; 55; 34:13(2); 17; 35:4; 6(2); 7; 8(2); 11; 13; 14; 25; 31; 34; 36:6; 13; **Deut** 1:1; 4(2); 8; 14; 18; 19; 20; 25; 30; 35; 38; 39(2); 44; 2:4; 8; 11; 12; 14; 22; 23(2); 29(3); 35; 36; 3:2; 4; 9; 12(2); 13; 16; 19; 20(2); 28; 4:1(2); 2(2); 6; 8; 9; 13; 19; 21; 23(2); 28; 31; 32; 40(2); 42; 44; 45; 47; 48(2); 5:1; 6; 16; 28; 31(2); 33(2); 6:1; 2; 6; 10(2); 11(3); 12; 14; 17; 18(2); 20; 23; 7:8; 9; 11; 12; 13; 15; 16; 19; 8:1(2); 2; 3; 10; 11; 14; 16; 18; 20; 9:3; 5; 9; 10; 12(2); 16; 18; 21; 23; 26(2); 28; 29; 10:2; 4; 5; 11; 13; 17; 21; 11:2(2); 3; 7; 8; 9; 12; 13; 17; 21; 22; 27; 28(2); 30; 31; 32; 12:1(2); 2; 5; 9; 10; 11(2); 14; 15; 17; 18; 21(2); 25; 26(2); 28(2); 31; 13:2; 5(2); 6(2); 7; 10; 12; 13; 18(2); 14:4; 12; 23; 24; 25; 29(2); 15:3; 4; 5; 7; 8; 20; 16:2; 4; 5; 6; 7; 10; 11; 15; 16; 17; 18; 20(2); 21; 22; 17:2; 3; 5; 8; 10(2); 11(3); 14; 15; 18; 18:6; 7; 8; 9; 14; 17; 19; 20(2); 21; 22; 19:2; 3; 4; 8; 9; 10; 14(2); 16; 17; 20; 20:1; 14; 15(2); 16; 18; 20; 21:1; 2; 3(3); 4; 9; 16(2); 18; 23; 22:3; 5; 9; 28; 23:13; 15; 16; 23(2); 24:3; 4(2); 5; 25:6(2); 15; 19; 26:1; 2(2); 3; 10; 11; 12; 13; 15; 19; 27:1; 2; 3; 4; 10; 26; 28:1; 8; 11; 13; 14; 15; 33; 34; 36(2); 45; 48; 50; 51; 52; 53; 54; 56; 57; 60; 61; 64; 67; 29:1(2); 3; 12; 16; 17; 22; 23; 25; 29; 30:1; 5; 7; 8; 10; 11; 20; 31:5; 7; 9; 11; 13; 16; 18; 20; 21(2); 23; 25; 29; 32:15; 21(2); 38; 46(2); 49(2); 52; 34:4; 11; 12; **Josh** 1:2; 6; 7; 11; 13; 14; 15(2); 2:3; 6; 7; 17; 18; 20; 3:4; 16; 4:9; 10; 20; 23; 5:1(2); 6(2); 6:25; 7:2; 11; 14(3); 8:27; 31; 32; 33; 35; 9:1; 10; 13; 20; 27; 10:11; 20; 24; 27; 32; 12:1; 2(2); 4; 7(2); 9; 13:3(2); 8; 10; 12; 21(2); 30; 32; 14:1(2); 15; 15:7; 8; 9; 10; 13; 25; 49; 54; 60; 17:5; 18:2; 3; 7; 13; 14; 16; 17; 28; 19:50; 51; 20:7; 21:4; 9; 10; 11; 20; 40; 43; 45; 22:4; 5; 9; 17; 28; 30; 23:13; 14; 15(2); 16(2); 24:5; 8; 12; 13(3); 14; 15; 17; 18; 23; 27; 30; 31; 32(2); 33; **Judg** 1:16; 26; 2:1; 10(2); 12; 16; 17; 20; 21; 3:1; 4; 16; 20; 31; 4:2; 11(2); 14; 6:2; 8; 11; 13; 26; 8:27; 35; 9:2; 4; 13; 24(2); 56; 10:4(2); 8; 14; 11:24; 28; 36; 39; 12:5; 13:8; 14:19; 15:19; 16:8; 24; 29(2); 30(2); 17:2; 6; 18:5; 16; 24; 27(2); 31; 19:10; 14; 16; 19; 20:9; 13; 15; 18; 31; 36; 42; 46; 21:12; 14; 19; 25; **Ruth** 1:22; 2:9; 11; 4:3; 11; 12; 14; 15(2); **1Sa** 1:27; 2:20; 29; 32; 35; 3:11; 12; 13; 4:4; 6:4; 7; 8; 17; 18; 7:14; 8:8; 18; 9:22; 23(2); 24(2); 10:2; 4; 11:11; 12:7; 8; 16; 17; 21; 13:5; 13; 14; 14:2; 4; 14(2); 21; 22; 30; 39; 15:2; 14; 20; 21; 16:4; 16; 19; 17:1; 31; 40; 20:23; 27; 36; 37; 22:9; 14; 23:13; 19; 24:4; 25:7; 27; 32; 33; 34; 35; 44; 26:1; 3; 28:21; 29:1; 3; 4; 30:10; 14; 17; 20; 21; 23; 27(3); 28(3); 29(3); 30(3); 31; 31:11; **2Sa** 2:15; 16; 32; 3:8; 14; 26; 4:8; 5:6; 6:4; 21; 22; 7:12; 23; 8:11(2); 9:3; 10:12; 12:3; 13:10; 23; 14:7; 13; 14; 15:4; 7; 16; 18; 16:11; 21; 23; 17:10; 18; 25; 18:18; 28; 19:5; 16; 19; 38; 20:5; 8; 21:12; 16; 18; 22:44; 23:15; 24:2; 24; **1Kin** 1:8; 9; 48; 2:4; 8; 24; 27; 31; 44; 46; 3:8; 13; 21; 28; 4:2; 7; 11; 12; 13(2); 19; 20; 34; 5:3; 7; 8; 16(2); 6:1; 2; 12(2); 20; 38; 7:8; 17; 20; 41; 45; 51; 8:1; 2; 9; 15; 21; 26; 28; 29(2); 34; 36; 38; 40; 43; 44; 48(4); 51; 56; 58; 63; 9:1; 3; 6; 7(2); 8; 12; 13; 15; 19; 20; 23; 24; 25; 26; 10:3; 5; 7; 8; 9; 10; 13; 24; 11:2; 8; 9; 10; 11; 13; 18; 23; 32; 33; 36; 12:4; 8(2); 9; 15; 17; 21; 28; 31; 32; 33(2); 13:3; 4(2); 5; 11; 12; 21; 22; 26(2); 32(2); 14:2; 8; 15; 18; 20; 21; 22; 24; 26; 27; 15:3; 5; 11; 15(2); 20; 23; 27; 29; 30(2); 16:12; 13(2); 15; 19(2); 24; 27; 32; 34; 17:9; 16; 18:3; 19; 26(2); 19:3; 18(2); 20:19; 34; 21:1; 4; 11; 15; 18; 25; 22:13; 16; 24; 38; 39; 43; 46; **2Kin** 1:4; 6; 7; 16; 17; 18; 2:15; 22; 3:3; 8; 11; 4:4; 9; 5:20; 6:10; 11; 7:13; 15; 8:21; 29; 9:5; 15; 19; 27; 36; 10:5; 6; 10(2); 17; 30; 31; 33; 11:2; 16; 12:2; 20; 13:2(2); 11; 25; 14:3; 5; 6; 11; 15; 21; 24; 25(2); 28; 15:3; 9; 12; 15; 18; 24; 28; 34; 16:3; 7; 14; 19; 17:2; 7; 8; 13(2); 15; 19; 22; 25; 26; 29; 32; 34; 37; 18:3; 6; 9; 14; 16; 17; 18; 21; 27; 37; 19:2; 4; 6(2); 12(2); 15; 16; 20; 28; 29; 20:3; 11; 17; 18; 19; 21:2; 3; 4; 7(2); 8; 11; 15; 16; 20; 25; 22:2; 4(2); 5; 13; 16; 18(2); 20; 23:2; 8; 10; 11; 12(2); 13(2); 15; 16; 17; 19; 24; 27(2); 32; 37; 24:2; 4; 9; 13; 19; 25:4; 8; 16; 19(2); **1Chr** 1:46; 2:3; 19; 42; 55; 3:1; 4:10; 11; 18; 6:61; 65; 9:22; 25; 10:13(2); 11:4; 5; 12:31; 32; 33; 13:2; 6; 14:4; 15:3; 16:15; 16; 40; 17:11; 19:13; 18; 20:4; 21:19; 23; 24; 29; 22:13; 23:4; 5; 29(2); 25:2; 26:22; 26(2); 27:1; 31; 29:3; 17; 19; **2Chr** 1:3; 4; 6; 14; 2:5; 9; 11; 14; 15; 3:5; 4:3; 12(2); 13; 5:2; 3; 6; 10; 12; 6:4; 9; 14; 15(2); 16; 17; 18; 19; 20; 21; 25; 27; 31; 32; 33; 34(2); 36; 38(3); 39; 7:6; 7; 14; 19; 20(2); 21; 22; 8:2; 4; 7; 12; 9:2; 4; 5; 7; 8; 10; 12; 14; 18; 10:8; 9; 15; 11:1; 10; 15; 19; 20; 12:4; 9; 10; 13; 13:4; 8; 10; 14:2; 15:8; 11; 16:14(2); 17:2; 18:23; 20:2; 11; 22; 25; 32; 21:6; 9; 13; 22:6; 23:9; 19; 24:2; 20; 22; 25:2; 9; 13; 15(2); 21; 26:4; 23; 27:2; 28:1; 6; 11; 15; 23; 29:2; 6; 19; 32; 30:7; 8; 16; 31:6; 10; 12; 19; 20; 32:3; 19; 21; 33:2; 3; 7(3); 8; 11; 22(2); 34:2; 9; 11; 24; 26; 31; 35:3(2); 26; 36:5; 8(2); 9; 12; 14; 23; **Ezr** 1:2; 3(2); 5; 7; 2:1; 2; 59; 61; 68; 4:2; 12; 15; 18; 20; 24; 5:2; 6; 8; 11; 14; 16; 17; 6:5(3); 6; 9(2); 12; 13; 15; 18; 21; 7:6; 8; 13; 14; 15; 16; 17; 20; 21; 25; 27(2); 8:25; 35; 9:11(3); 10:14; **Neh** 1:2; 6(2); 7; 2:8; 13; 18; 3:25; 4:2; 3; 12; 14; 17; 23; 5:8; 18; 6:6; 7:5; 61; 63; 72; 8:1; 4; 9; 14; 9:5; 15; 23; 26; 29; 35; 10:29; 12:8; 37; 13:5; 15; 16; **Est** 1:1; 2; 9; 13; 14(2); 18; 20; 2:4; 6; 9; 14; 16; 21; 3:3; 13; 4:6; 16; 6:8(2); 7:9; 8:2; 5(2); 8; 9; 11; 12; 9:13; 22; 25; 26(2); **Job** 3:3; 14; 16; 21; 22; 25(2); 4:14; 19; 21; 5:1; 9; 11; 6:6; 16; 26; 9:5(2); 6; 7; 8; 9; 10; 11:6; 14:19; 15:9; 14; 16; 17; 18; 28(2); 16:8; 20:7; 9; 11; 18; 19; 20; 21:27; 22:15; 16; 17; 23:5; 24:11; 16; 19; 25:6; 27:11; 13; 28:7(2); 29:16; 32:19; 33:27; 34:8; 32; 35:5; 36:16; 24; 28; 37:5; 16; 18; 21; 38:23; 24; 39:14; 40:15; 41:1; 42:3; 8; **Ps** 1:4; 3:2; 7:t, 10; 15; 8:3; 9:11; 13; 15; 16; 17:7; 13; 14(2); 18:17; 19:5; 21:11; 25:3; 28:3; 31:18; 19(2); 32:8; 9; 35:7; 10; 27; 40:5(2); 41:9; 44:10; 45:1; 51:8; 58:5; 7; 8; 59:12; 60:10(2); 61:7; 65:6; 7; 9; 66:9; 14; 20; 68:6; 16; 28; 33; 69:4; 22; 71:20; 23; 74:2(2); 78:3; 5; 6; 45(2); 54; 60; 68; 69; 79:10; 80:12; 15; 81:10; 83:10; 85:12; 86:17; 89:49; 90:5; 91:9; 94:20; 102:18; 104:8; 10; 12; 15; 16; 105:8; 9; 106:21; 36; 107:25; 37; 109:19; 114:8; 115:15; 118:20; 22; 24; 27; 119:21; 39; 47; 48; 49; 85; 165; 121:2; 125:1; 129:6; 8; 134:1; 135:21; 136:13; 16; 17; 138:8; 139:16; 140:2; 141:5; 9; 144:1; 146:6(2); 7(2); 147:9; 148:6; **Prov** 1:19; 2:16; 17; 6:7; 7:5; 9:5; 11:22; 12:27; 14:12; 33; 19:17; 20:25; 22:28; 23:5; 8; 24:13; 25:1; 27:16; 28:3; 30:18(2); 21; 24; 29; 30; 31:3; **Eccl** 1:3; 9(3); 10; 15(2); 2:3; 12; 16; 18; 20; 3:2; 10; 15(3); 19; 4:2(2); 3; 15; 5:4; 13; 15; 18(2); 6:1; 10; 12; 7:13; 19; 24; 28; 8:7; 12; 13; 14; 15; 9:9(2); 10:5(2); 20; 12:5; 10; 11; **Song** 1:1; 3:7; 4:2; 5; 6:6; 7:2; 4; 13; 8:6; 12; **Is** 1:1; 29; 2:8; 20; 3:12; 5:23; 6:6; 8:18; 10:1; 3; 11:10; 11; 16; 13:1; 17; 14:12; 15:7; 17:2; 8; 9; 12; 18:1; 19:15; 16; 17; 21:10; 22:3; 15; 26:2; 27:13; 28:1; 2; 4(2); 14; 29; 29:11; 30:10; 24; 31; 32; 31:7; 36:3; 37:4; 12(2); 17; 22; 29; 30; 38:3; 8(2); 39:6; 7; 8; 42:5; 43:16; 17; 44:2; 14; 45:3; 46:3(2); 47:11; 48:1(2); 14; 17(2); 49:20; 50:1; 51:10; 12; 17; 23; 52:15(2); 55:2(3); 11; 56:8; 11; 57:16; 59:5; 21; 61:9; 62:2; 6; 8; 63:7; 64:3; 65:2; 4(2); 5; 7; 18; 66:4; 22; **Jer** 2:11(2); 3:6; 15; 5:17; 21(2); 22; 7:10; 11; 12; 14(2); 10; 31(2); 8:3; 17; 9:13; 14; 24; 25; 10:1; 11:4(2); 5; 8; 10(2); 11; 17; 12:14; 13:4; 6; 10(3); 15:4; 14(2); 18; 17:4(2); 16; 19; 18:1; 14; 19:2; 3; 5; 20:2; 5; 16; 21:1; 4; 13; 22:6; 11(2); 28; 23:4; 7; 8(2); 27(2); 40; 24:2; 8; 25:2; 13(2); 22; 26; 27; 29; 26:2; 3; 4; 19; 27:3; 8; 9; 18; 20; 28:1; 6; 9; 29:1; 8; 19; 21; 22; 23; 27; 31:2; 21; 32; 35(2); 32:1; 2; 8; 11(2); 14(2); 20; 22; 32; 34; 35(2); 33:3; 4; 9; 10; 12; 14; 24; 34:1; 5; 8; 10; 14; 15; 18(2); 19; 21; 35:1; 4(2); 15; 16; 36:3; 4; 6; 21; 27; 28; 32; 37:2; 7; 19; 38:3; 7; 20; 39:10; 40:1; 4; 7; 10; 15; 41:9; 13; 17; 42:5; 8; 16; 21; 43:1; 9; 44:1(2); 3; 9; 14(2); 15; 20; 22; 45:4(2); 46:1; 2(2); 49:28; 31(2); 50:3; 51:12; 25; 44; 59; 52:2; 7; 12(2); 19(2); 20; 25(2); **Lam** 1:12; 2:3; 17; 5:18; **Eze** 1:2; 23(2); 3:20; 23; 4:10; 14; 5:9; 16(2); 6:9(3); 7:13(2); 8:3; 14; 17; 9:2; 3; 6; 11; 10:22; 11:1; 3; 23; 12:2; 28; 13:11; 16(2); 17; 14:7; 15:2; 6; 16:14; 17; 19; 27; 32; 36; 45; 51; 52; 57; 59; 17:3; 18:5; 14; 18; 19; 21; 27; 19:14; 20:6; 11; 13; 15(2); 21; 28; 32; 42; 21:14; 22:4; 5; 13(2); 23:6; 24; 42; 24:21; 27; 25:9; 26:6; 17(2); 27:3; 7(2); 27; 29:3; 16; 30:22; 32:9; 23; 24(2); 27; 29; 30; 33:14; 16; 19; 29; 34:4(4); 16(4); 19(2); 35:11; 12; 36:4; 5; 21; 22; 23(2); 37:1; 19; 38:8; 12; 17; 39:19; 28; 40:2; 6(3); 40; 44; 46; 41:1; 6; 9(2); 15; 42:1; 3(2); 11; 13; 14; 43:3; 19; 44:1; 10; 13; 45:4; 14; 46:19(2); 47:8; 9; 14; 16(2); 22; 48:8; 11(2); 22; 29; **Dan** 1:2; 5; 8; 10; 15; 2:14; 26; 27; 34; 39; 44; 3:2; 12; 14; 15; 18; 29; 4:5; 20; 21; 24; 5:2(2); 3; 13; 23; 6:1; 8; 12; 13; 15; 24; 26; 7:6; 11; 14(2); 17(2); 19(2); 20; 23; 8:1; 2; 3; 6; 9; 13; 16; 20; 26; 9:1; 6; 10; 12; 14; 18; 10:4; 10; 21; 11:4; 7; 16; 24; 12:1; 6; 7; **Hos** 1:3; 10; 2:8; 23; 5:9; **Joel** 1:4(3); 2:25; **Amos** 1:1; 4; 7; 10; 12; 2:4; 3:1; 4:1(3); 3; 5:1; 3; 26; 6:1; 13(2); 9:10; 12; 15; **Obad** 20; **Jonah** 1:9; 4:10(2); **Mic** 1:1; 2:3; 5:3; 6:14; 7:10; 14; 20; **Nah** 3:17; **Hab** 1:1; 5; 6; 2:4; 6; 17; **Zeph** 1:1; 9; 2:3; **Hag** 1:11; 2:14; **Zec** 1:6; 7; 12; 19; 21(2); 2:8; 4:2; 10; 12; 6:5; 6; 10; 7:3; 7; 12; 8:9; 10:5; 11:10; 16; 12:1; 13:6; 14:4; 7; 16; **Mal** 1:13; 14; 2:11; 4:4; **Mt** 1:20; 22; 23; 2:9; 15; 16; 17; 20; 23; 3:10; 4:13; 14; 16(2); 24(2); 5:6; 10; 12; 16; 44; 45; 46; 48; 6:1; 4; 6(2); 9; 18(2); 27; 30; 7:6; 11; 13; 14; 15; 21; 24; 26; 8:17; 9:8; 16; 20; 10:20; 28(2); 32; 33; 11:4; 10; 14; 21; 23(2); 12:2; 4(2); 10; 17; 50; 13:14; 17(2); 19(2); 23; 24; 31; 32; 33; 35(2); 41; 44; 48; 52(2); 14:9; 15:1; 11(2); 13; 18; 20; 27; 16:8; 17; 28; 17:5; 18:6; 10; 11; 12; 13; 14; 19; 23; 24; 28; 19:4; 9; 12(3); 18; 28; 20:1; 12; 21:4; 21; 24; 33; 41; 42; 22:2; 4; 8; 11; 21; 23; 31; 35; 36; 23:9; 16; 24; 26; 27; 31; 37; 24:16; 17; 18; 25:1; 24; 28; 29; 26:25; 28; 51; 62; 75; 27:3; 9; 17; 22; 35; 44; 52; 55; 56; 60; 28:5; **Mk** 1:2; 44; 2:3; 24; 26(2); 3:1; 3; 17; 19; 22; 34; 4:16; 18; 20; 22; 25; 31; 5:25; 35; 41; 6:2; 26; 7:1; 4; 13; 15; 20; 9:1; 17; 39; 10:42; 11:21; 23; 25; 26; 12:10; 18; 25; 28; 38; 40; 42; 43; 13:19; 32; 14:18; 24; 32; 60; 15:7; 22; 28; 34; 39; 41; 43; 46; 16:6; 14; **Lk** 1:1; 2; 20; 35; 45; 70; 73; 2:4; 10; 11; 15(2); 17; 18; 21; 24; 31; 33; 34; 37; 50; 3:9; 13; 19; 22; 23; 24(5); 25(5); 26(5); 27(5); 28(5); 29(5); 30(5); 31(5); 32(5); 33(5); 34(5); 35(5); 36(5); 37(5); 38(4); 4:22; 33; 5:3; 7; 9; 10; 17; 18; 21; 6:2; 3; 4; 8; 16; 17; 27(2); 28; 32; 33; 45(2); 46; 48; 49; 7:25; 27; 37; 39; 41; 42; 47; 8:2; 3; 13(2); 14(2); 15; 16; 18; 20; 21; 26; 27; 36; 43; 9:27; 30; 31; 36; 43; 46; 61; 10:11; 13; 15; 23; 24(2); 30; 36; 39; 42; 11:2; 5; 27; 33; 35; 40(2); 44; 50; 51; 12:1; 3; 5; 15; 20; 24; 25; 26; 28; 33; 47; 13:11; 14; 19; 21; 30(2); 34; 14:2; 5; 7; 24; 28; 15:4; 6; 7; 9; 30; 16:1; 10; 12(2); 15(2); 19; 20; 21; 26; 17:7; 10(2); 12; 31; 18:2; 7; 9; 27; 34; 39; 19:2; 10; 20; 26; 27; 30; 42; 20:17; 20; 25(2); 27; 35; 46; 47; 21:6(2); 15; 21(2); 22; 26; 22:1; 19; 20; 23; 24; 28; 49; 52; 23:27; 29(2); 33; 39; 48; 55; 24:1; 10; 12; 13; 14; 18; 19; 21; 22; 23; 24; 44(2); **Jn** 1:9; 13; 18; 24; 29; 30; 33; 38; 40; 41; 42; 2:9; 10; 22; 23; 3:6(2); 13; 29; 4:5; 9; 12; 25; 29; 39; 53; 5:2; 5; 12; 15; 23; 28; 30; 32; 36; 37; 39; 44; 6:1; 2; 9; 13; 22; 27(3); 33; 39(2); 40; 41; 44; 46; 50; 51(2); 58; 7:31; 39; 8:9; 26; 31; 38(2); 40; 46; 53; 9:1; 7; 8; 39(2); 40; 10:6; 16; 29; 32; 11:2; 16; 27; 31; 33; 37; 42; 45(2); 12:1; 4; 21; 38; 49; 13:1; 14:24(2); 26; 15:3; 24; 26; 17:4; 5; 6; 8; 9; 20; 22; 24; 18:1; 2; 5; 9(2); 11; 13; 14; 16; 21; 22; 32; 19:17; 24; 32; 39; 20:8; 16; 30; 21:10; 20(2); 24; 25(2); **Acts** 1:2; 4; 7; 11(2); 12; 16(2); 21; 24; 25; 2:7; 16; 22; 33; 3:2; 10(2); 11; 16; 18; 20; 21; 23; 25; 4:4; 11(2); 14; 20; 21; 24; 32; 36; 5:9; 16; 17; 6:9; 10; 11; 13; 14; 7:3; 17; 18; 20; 34; 35; 37; 38; 40; 43; 45; 52(2); 8:1; 6(2); 9; 13; 14; 24; 26; 32; 9:7; 11; 19; 21; 22; 30; 32; 33; 36(2); 39; 10:2; 7; 17(2); 18; 21; 36; 37(2); 39; 42; 44; 45; 47; 11:6; 13; 19; 20; 22; 28; 29; 30; 12:9; 10; 13:1; 7; 22; 27; 31; 32; 39; 40; 41; 45; 14:3; 13; 14; 15; 26; 15:1; 5; 8; 10; 16; 19; 23; 24; 29; 31; 16:1; 2; 3; 4; 12; 13; 14(2); 16; 17; 21; 17:5; 12; 21; 31; 34; 18:27; 19:4; 10; 13; 14; 19; 24; 26; 31; 35; 37; 38; 20:19; 24; 28(2); 32(2); 38; 21:8; 9; 20; 21; 23; 25; 27; 38; 39; 22:1; 3; 5; 10; 12; 29; 23:13; 21; 24:14(2); 15; 24; 25:5; 7(2); 16; 19; 24; 26:3; 4; 5; 7(2); 10; 13; 16(2); 18; 22; 27:8; 11; 12; 16; 17; 39; 43; 28:9; 11; 24; 31; **Rom** 1:2; 3; 19; 26; 27(2); 28; 32; 2:2; 3; 14; 15; 19; 20; 21; 27; 28(2); 29; 3:22; 26; 30; 4:11; 12; 14; 16(2); 17; 18; 5:5; 15; 17; 6:17; 7:2; 5; 10; 13(2); 15; 16; 18; 19; 23; 8:1; 18; 23; 26; 39; 9:6; 8; 23; 25(2); 30(2); 31; 10:5(2); 6; 8; 11:2; 7; 14; 22; 24(2); 12:1; 9(2); 14; 13:3; 4; 14:3; 19; 22; 15:17; 18; 22; 26; 31; 16:1(2); 10; 11; 12; 14; 15; 17(2); 19; 25; **1Cor** 1:2; 4; 11; 18; 24; 27; 28(2); 2:7; 8; 9; 11; 12; 13(3); 3:10; 11; 14; 17; 4:6; 17; 19; 6:16; 19(2); 20; 7:13; 35; 8:10(3); 9:13(2); 14; 24; 10:16(2); 18; 19; 20; 30; 11:19; 23(2); 24; 12:6; 22; 23; 24; 13:10(2); 14:22; 15:1(2); 2; 3; 10(2); 18; 27; 29; 31; 36; 37; 46(3); 57; 16:17; **2Cor** 1:1(2); 4; 6(2); 8; 9; 21; 2:2; 4; 6; 14; 17; 3:7; 10; 11(2); 13(2); 14; 4:4; 11; 14; 16; 17; 18(4); 5:2; 12; 15(2); 7:14; 8:11; 16; 19; 20; 22; 9:2; 6(2); 11; 14; 10:2; 8; 13; 11:4(2); 9(2); 12; 17; 28; 30; 31; 12:4; 6; 21(2); 13:2; 3; 7; 10; **Gal** 1:2; 7; 8; 11; 17; 20; 22; 23(2); 2:2(2); 4; 10; 12; 18; 20; 3:7; 9; 10; 16; 17; 21; 23; 4:8; 14; 24(3); 25; 26(2); 27; 5:6; 12; 19; 21(2); 6:1; **Eph** 1:1; 9; 10(2); 14; 20; 21; 23; 2:10; 11; 17; 3:2; 5; 9; 11; 13; 19; 4:15; 16; 22; 24; 28; 29; 5:4; 12; 6:2; 17; 20; **Phil** 1:1; 6; 11; 12; 23; 28; 30; 2:5; 9; 13; 21; 3:3; 6; 9(3); 12; 13(2); 17; 4:3; 7; 9; 13; 18; 21; **Col** 1:2; 4; 5; 6; 12; 23(3); 24(2); 25; 26; 27; 29; 2:10; 14; 17; 18; 19; 22; 23; 3:1; 5(2); 6; 7; 10; 14; 15; 25; 4:1; 3; 9; 11(2); 15(2); 17; **1Th** 1:1; 10; 2:4; 13(2); 14; 3:10; 4:5; 10; 13(2); 14; 15(2); 17; 5:12; 15; 21; **2Th** 1:5(2); 2:15; 16; 3:4; 6; 11; 17; **1Ti** 1:1; 4(2); 6; 11; 14; 16; 18; 19; 2:10; 3:7; 13; 15; 4:3(2); 8; 14; 5:13; 6:3; 9; 10; 15; 16; 20; 21; S:1; **2Ti** 1:1; 5; 6; 9; 12(2); 13(2); 14(2); 15; 2:10; 3:6; 11; 14; 15(2); 4:8; **Titus** 1:1; 2; 3; 11; 2:1; 3:5; 6; 8; **Philem** 1:5; 6; 8; 11; **Heb** 1:5; 13; 2:1; 3; 11; 13; 3:5; 4:3; 15; 5:8; 12; 6:7; 8; 10; 18; 19(2); 7:2; 13; 14; 19; 28(2); 8:1; 2; 6; 13; 9:2; 3; 4; 5; 7; 9(2); 10; 15; 20; 24; 10:1; 8; 10; 11; 20; 27; 32; 35; 11:3(2); 4; 7(2); 8; 10; 12; 29; 12:1; 5; 9; 11; 12; 13; 14; 19; 20; 23; 27; 28; 13:3; 7; 9; 10; 21; **Jas** 1:1; 12; 21; 2:5; 7; 16; 23; 3:4; 9; 5:4(2); 11; 20; **1Pet** 1:3; 10; 11; 12(2); 15; 23; 25; 2:7(3); 8; 10(2); 11; 12; 3:4(2); 13; 19; 20; 4:11; 12; 5:1; 2; **2Pet** 1:18; 2:11; 15; 3:1; 2; 7; 10; 16(2); **1Jn** 1:1(4); 2; 3; 5; 2:7(2); 8; 24(2); 27; 3:24; 5:9; 16; **2Jn** 2; 5; 8; **3Jn** 6; 10; 11(2); **Jude** 3; 6; 10; 15(2); 17; **Rev** 1:1(2); 3; 4(5); 7; 8(3); 11; 19(3); 20(2); 2:2(2); 6; 7; 8; 9; 10; 12; 15; 17; 20; 23; 24; 25; 3:2; 4; 9; 10; 11; 12(2); 4:1(3); 5; 8; 5:6; 8; 13; 6:9; 7:4; 9; 10; 13; 14; 17; 8:2; 3; 4; 6; 9; 13; 9:4; 11; 13; 14(2); 15; 18; 20(2); 10:4; 5; 6; 8(3); 11:2; 8; 11; 16; 17; 18; 12:4; 9; 10; 13; 16; 17; 13:2; 4; 12; 14(2); 14:3; 4(2); 10; 13; 17; 18; 16:2(2); 5; 9; 14; 17:1; 7; 9(2); 12(2); 15; 16; 18(2); 18:6; 14; 15; 19:2; 9; 14; 20; 21; 20:2; 4; 8; 12(2); 13(2); 21:8(2); 9; 12; 24; 27; 22:2; 6; 8; 9; 11; 19; 20

WHILE

Gen 8:22; 19:16; 25:6; 29:9; 45:1; 46:29; **Ex** 33:22(2); 34:29; **Lev** 4:27; 14:46; 26:43; **Num** 11:33; 15:32; 23:15; 25:11; **Deut** 19:6; 31:27; **Josh** 14:10; **Judg** 3:26; 11:26; 14:17; 15:1; 16:27; **1Sa** 2:13; 7:2; 9:27; 14:19; 20:14; 22:4; 25:7; 16; 27:11; **2Sa** 3:6; 35; 7:19; 12:18; 21; 22; 13:30; 15:8; 12; 17:2; 18:14; 19:32; 24:13; **1Kin** 1:14; 22; 42; 3:20; 6:7; 12:6; 17:7; 18:45; **2Kin** 6:33; **1Chr** 12:1; 17:17; 21:12; **2Chr** 10:6; 14:7; 15:2; 26:19; 34:3; **Neh** 7:3; **Est** 2:21; 6:14; **Job** 1:16; 17; 18; 20:23; 24:24; 27:3; **Ps** 7:2; 31:13; 37:10; 39:1; 3; 42:3; 10; 49:18; 63:4; 69:3; 78:30; 88:15; 104:33; 146:2(2); **Prov** 8:26; 19:18; 31:15; **Eccl** 9:3; 12:1; 2; **Song** 1:12; **Is** 10:25; 28:4; 29:17; 55:6(2); 63:18; 65:24; **Jer** 13:16; 15:9; 33:1; 39:15; 40:5; 51:33; **Lam** 1:19; **Eze** 9:8; **Dan** 4:31; **Hos** 1:4; **Nah** 1:10(2); **Hag** 2:6; **Zec** 14:12; **Mt** 1:20; 9:18; 12:46; 13:21; 25; 29; 14:22; 17:5; 22; 22:41; 25:5; 10; 26:36; 47; 73; 27:63; 28:13; **Mk** 1:35; 2:19; 5:35; 6:31; 45; 12:35; 14:32; 43; 15:44; **Lk** 1:8; 2:6; 5:34; 8:13; 49; 9:34; 43; 10:13; 14:32; 18:4; 22:47; 58; 60; 24:15; 32(2); 41; 44; 51; **Jn** 4:31; 5:7; 7:33; 9:4; 12:35(2); 36; 13:33; 14:19; 16:16(2); 17(2); 18; 19(2); 17:12; **Acts** 1:9; 10; 9:39; 10:10; 17; 19; 44; 15:7; 17:16; 18:18; 19:1; 20:11; 22:17; 24:20; 25:8; 27:33; 28:6; **Rom** 2:15; 5:8; 7:3; **1Cor** 3:4; 8:13; 16:7; **2Cor** 4:18; **Gal** 2:17; **1Ti** 5:6; 6:10; **Heb** 3:13; 15; 9:8; 17; 10:37; **1Pet** 3:2; 20; 5:10; **2Pet** 2:13; 19

WHITHER

Gen 16:8; 20:13; 28:15; 32:17; 37:30; **Ex** 21:13; 34:12; **Lev** 18:3; 20:22; **Num** 13:27; 15:18; 35:25; 26; **Deut** 1:28; 3:21; 4:5; 14; 27; 6:1; 7:1; 11:8; 10; 11; 29; 12:29; 21:14; 23:12; 20; 28:21; 37; 63; 30:1; 3; 16; 18; 31:13; 16; 32:47; 50; **Josh** 2:5; **Judg** 19:17; **Ruth** 1:16; **1Sa** 10:14; 27:10; **2Sa** 2:1; 13:13; 15:20; 17:18; **1Kin** 2:36; 42; 8:47; 18:10; 12; 21:18; **2Kin** 5:25; **2Chr** 6:37; 38; 10:2; **Neh** 2:16; **Ps** 122:4; 139:7(2); **Eccl** 9:10; **Song** 6:1(2); **Is** 20:6; **Jer** 8:3; 15:2; 16:15; 19:14; 22:12; 23:3; 8; 24:9; 29:7; 14; 18; 30:11; 32:37; 40:4; 12; 42:22; 43:5; 44:8; 45:5; 46:28; 49:36; **Eze** 1:12; 4:13; 6:9; 10:11; 12:16; 29:13; 36:20; 21; 22; 37:21; 47:9; **Dan** 9:7; **Joel** 3:7; **Zec** 2:2; 5:10; **Lk** 10:1; 24:28; **Jn** 3:8; 6:21; 7:35; 8:14(2); 21; 22; 12:35; 13:33; 36(2); 14:4; 5; 16:5; 18:20; 21:18(2); **Heb** 6:20; 11:8; **1Jn** 2:11

WHO

Gen 3:11; 12:7; 14:12; 21:7; 26; 24:15; 27; 27:18; 32; 33; 30:2; 33:5; 35:3; 36:1; 19; 20; 35; 42:30; 43:22; 48:8; 14; 49:9; 25(2); **Ex** 2:14; 3:11; 4:11(2); 28; 5:2; 20; 6:12; 10:8; 12:27; 40; 15:11(2); 18:10(2); 21:8; 32:26; **Lev** 5:8; 12:7; 27:12; **Num** 6:21; 7:2; 9:6; 11:4; 18; 12:7; 14:36; 16:5(2); 21:26; 23:10; 24:9; 23; 25:6; 26:9; 47; 63; 27:21; 31:27; **Deut** 1:33; 2:25; 4:7; 46; 5:3; 26; 8:15(2); 16; 9:2; 21:1; 30:12; 13; 33:9; 26; 29(2); **Josh** 9:8; 11:8; 12:2; 13:12; 15:19; 17:16(2); 21:10; **Judg** 1:1; 2:7; 3:9; 19; 6:29; 35; 7:1; 8:34; 9:28(2); 38; 11:39; 15:6; 17:4; 5; 7; 18:2; 3; 29; 19:1; 21:5; **Ruth** 2:3; 20; 3:9; 16; **1Sa** 2:25; 4:8; 6:20; 10:12; 19; 11:12; 14:17; 45; 16:16; 17:25; 26; 18:18; 20:10; 22:14; 23:22; 25:10(2); 26:6; 9; 14; 15; 30:23; 24; **2Sa** 1:8; 24(2); 4:5; 9; 10; 6:20; 7:18; 10:18; 11:21; 12:22; 16:10; 22:4; 32(2); 23:1; 20; **1Kin** 1:20; 27; 2:24; 32; 3:9; 8:23; 24; 50; 9:9; 12:2; 9; 18;

13:26; 14:8(2); 14; 16(2); 17:1; 19:19; 20:14; 21:11; 22:20; 52; **2Kin** 4:5; 7:17; 8:14; 9:31; 32(2); 10:9; 13; 29; 13:6; 11; 14:24; 15:9; 18; 24; 28; 17:36; 18:35; 23:15; 16; **1Chr** 2:7; 22; 4:22; 5:8; 10; 6:39; 7:24; 31; 8:12; 13(2); 9:1; 18; 31; 33; 11:10; 12; 22; 12:18; 16:41; 17:16; 19:7; 21:16; 22:9; 24:28; 25:1; 3; 9; 27:6; 29:5; 14; **2Chr** 1:10; 2:6(2); 12; 6:4; 8:8; 10:2; 17:16; 18:19; 19:6; 20:7; 34; 35; 22:9; 26:1; 5; 28:5; 30:7; 32:4; 14; 31; 34:26; 35:21; 36:13; 17; 23; **Ezr** 1:3; 3:12; 5:3; 9; 12; **Neh** 1:11; 3:3; 6:10; 11; 7:7; 9:7; 27(2); 32; 13:26; **Est** 2:6; 15; 22; 4:11; 14; 6:2; 4; 7:5; 9; **Job** 3:8; 15; 4:2; 7; 5:10; 9:4; 12(2); 19; 24; 11:10; 12:3; 4; 9; 13:19; 14:4; 16:9; 17:3; 15; 21:31(2); 23:13; 24:25; 26:14; 27:2(2); 30:4; 34:7; 13(2); 29(2); 35:10; 11; 36:22; 23(2); 38:2; 5(2); 6; 8; 25; 28; 29; 36(2); 37(2); 41; 39:5(2); 41:10; 11; 13(2); 14; 33; 42:3; **Ps** 4:6; 6:5; 8:1; 12:4(2); 14:4; 15:1(2); 16:7; 17:9; 18:t, 3; 31(2); 19:12; 24:3(2); 4; 8; 10; 34:t, 35:10; 37:7(2); 39:6; 42:11; 43:5; 53:4; 59:7; 60:9(2); 64:3; 5; 65:5; 68:19; 71:19(2); 72:18; 73:12; 76:7; 77:13; 78:6; 83:12; 84:6; 86:6(2); 8; 90:11; 94:10(2); 103:3(2); 4(2); 5; 104:2(2); 3(3); 4; 5; 105:17; 106:2(2); 108:10(2); 11; 113:5(2); 6; 119:1; 38; 124:1; 2; 6; 8; 130:3; 135:8; 9; 10; 136:4; 23; 25; 137:7; 8; 140:4; 144:2; 10; 147:8(3); 17; **Prov** 2:13; 14; 9:15; 18:14; 20:6; 9; 25; 21:24; 23:29(6); 24:22; 26:18; 27:4; 30:4(4); 9; 31:10; **Eccl** 2:19; 25(2); 3:21; 22; 4:3; 13; 6:12(2); 7:13; 24; 8:1(2); 4; 7; 10; 10:14; 11:5; 12:7; **Song** 3:6; 6:10; 8:2; 5; **Is** 1:12; 6:8; 14:6; 27(2); 23:8; 24:18; 27:4; 29:15(2); 22; 33:14(2); 36:20; 37:2; 40:12; 13; 14; 26; 41:2; 4; 26; 42:19(2); 23(2); 24; 43:9; 13; 44:7; 10; 45:21(2); 49:21(2); 50:8(2); 9; 10; 51:12; 19; 53:1; 8; 60:8; 63:1; 65:16; 66:8(2); **Jer** 1:16; 2:24; 9:12(2); 10:7; 15:5(3); 17:9; 18:13; 20:1; 15; 21:13(2); 23:18(2); 26:20; 23; 30:21; 36:32; 46:7; 49:4; 19(4); 50:44(4); 52:25; **Lam** 2:13; 3:37; **Eze** 10:7; **Dan** 1:10; 2:23; 3:15; 28; 6:27; **Hos** 3:1; 7:4; 14:9; **Joel** 2:11; 14; **Amos** 1:1; 3:8(2); 10; 5:7; **Obad** 3; **Jonah** 3:9; **Mic** 3:2(2); 3; 5:8; 6:9; 7:18; **Nah** 1:6(2); 3:7; **Hab** 2:5; **Zeph** 3:18; **Hag** 2:3; **Zec** 4:7; 10; **Mal** 1:10; 3:2(2); **Mt** 1:16; 3:7; 10:2; 4; 11; 12:48(2); 13:9; 43; 46; 18:1; 19:25; 21:10; 23; 24:45; 25:14; 26:3; 68; 27:57; **Mk** 1:19; 24; 2:7; 3:33; 4:16; 5:3; 30; 31; 9:34; 10:26; 11:28; 13:34; 15:7; 21; 41; 16:3; **Lk** 1:36; 3:7; 4:34; 5:12; 21(2); 7:2; 39; 49; 8:45(2); 9:9; 31; 10:22(2); 29; 12:14; 42; 16:11; 12; 14; 18:26; 30; 19:3; 20:2; 22:64; 23:7; 19; 51; **Jn** 1:19; 22; 27; 4:10; 5:13; 6:60; 64(2); 7:20; 49; 8:25; 9:2; 19; 21; 36; 12:34; 38; 13:11; 24; 25; 18:18; 21:12; **Acts** 1:23; 3:3; 4:25; 36; 5:36; 7:27; 35; 38; 46; 53; 8:15; 27; 33; 9:5; 10:32; 38; 41; 11:14; 17; 23; 13:7; 9; 31; 43; 14:8; 9; 16; 19; 15:17; 27; 38; 16:24; 17:10; 18:27; 19:15; 21:4; 32; 33; 37; 22:8; 23:18; 33; 24:1; 6; 19; 26:15; 28:7; 10; 18; **Rom** 1:18; 25(3); 32; 2:6; 7; 27; 3:5; 19; 4:12(2); 16; 17; 18; 25; 5:14; 7:4; 24; 8:1; 4; 20; 28; 31; 33; 34(3); 35; 9:4; 5; 19; 20; 10:6; 7; 16; 11:4; 34(2); 35; 14:2; 4; 20; 16:4; 5; 6; 7(2); 12; 22; **1Cor** 1:8; 30; 2:16; 3:5(2); 4:5; 7; 17(2); 6:4; 9:7(3); 10:13; 14:8; **2Cor** 1:4; 10; 19; 22; 2:2; 16; 3:6; 4:4; 6; 5:5; 18; 21; 8:10; 19; 10:1; 11:29(2); **Gal** 1:1; 4; 15; 2:3; 4; 6(2); 9; 15; 20; 3:1; 4:23; 5:7; 6:10; 13; **Eph** 1:3; 11; 12; 19; 2:1; 4; 11; 13; 14; 3:8; 9; 4:6; 19; 5:5; **Phil** 2:6; 20; 3:19; 21; **Col** 1:7; 8; 13; 15; 18; 24; 2:12; 3:4; 4:7; 9; 11; 12; **1Th** 2:12; 15; 4:8; 5:8; 10; 24; **2Th** 1:7; 9; 2:4; 7; 12; 3:3; **1Ti** 1:12; 13; 2:4; 6; 4:10; 5:17; 6:13(2); 15; 16; 17; **2Ti** 1:9; 10; 2:2; 4; 18; 26; 4:1; **Titus** 1:11; 2:14; **Heb** 1:1; 3; 7; 14; 2:9; 11; 15; 3:2; 3; 5:2; 7; 14; 6:4; 12; 18; 7:1; 5; 9; 16; 26; 27; 28; 8:1; 5; 9:14; 10:29; 39; 11:11; 27; 33; 12:2; 16; 25; 13:7; **Jas** 3:13; 4:12(2); 5:4; 10; **1Pet** 1:5; 10; 17; 20; 21; 2:9; 22; 23; 24; 3:5; 13; 22; 4:5; 5:1; 10; **2Pet** 2:1; 15; 18; **1Jn** 2:22; 3:12; 4:21; 5:5; **2Jn** 7; **3Jn** 9; **Jude** 4; 18; 19; **Rev** 1:2; 5; 9; 2:1; 13; 14; 18; 4:9; 5:2; 6:17; 10:6; 12:5; 13:4(2); 14:11; 15:4; 7; 18:8; 9

WHOM

Gen 2:8; 3:12; 4:25; 6:7; 10:14; 15:14; 21:3; 22:2; 24:3; 14; 40; 44; 47; 25:12; 30:26; 41:38; 43:27; 29; 44:10; 16; 45:4; 46:18; 48:9; 15; 49:8; **Ex** 4:13; 6:5; 26; 14:13; 18:9; 22:9; 23:27; 28:3; 32:13; 33:12; 19(2); 35:21; 23; 24; 36:1; **Lev** 6:5; 13:45; 14:32; 15:18; 16:32(2); 17:7; 22:5; 25:27; 55; 26:45; 27:24(2); **Num** 3:3; 4:41; 45; 46; 5:7; 11:16; 21; 12:1; 12; 16:5; 7; 17:5; 22:6(2); 23:8(2); 26:5; 59; 64; 27:18; 34:29; 36:6; **Deut** 4:46; 7:19; 9:2(2); 17:15; 19:4; 17; 21:8; 24:11; 28:55; 29:26(2); 31:4; 32:17(2); 20; 37; 33:8(2); 34:10; **Josh** 2:10; 4:4; 5:6; 7; 10:11; 25; 13:8; 21; 24:15; 17; **Judg** 4:22; 7:4; 8:15; 18; 12:9; 14:20; 21:23; **Ruth** 2:19(2); 3:9(2); 16; **1Sa** 2:25; 6:20; 9:17; 20; 10:24; 12:3(2); 13(2); 16:3; 17:28; 45; 21:9; 24:14(2); 25:11; 25; 28:8; 11; 29:5; 30:13; 21; **2Sa** 7:7; 15; 23; 14:7; 15:33; 16:18; 19; 17:3; 19:10; 20:3; 21:6; 8(2); 23:8(2); **1Kin** 2:5; 5:5; 7:8; 9:21; 10:26; 11:20; 34; 13:23; 17:1; 20; 18:15; 31; 20:14; 42; 21:25; 26; 22:8; **2Kin** 3:14; 5:16; 6:19; 22; 8:5; 10:24; 16:3; 17:8; 11; 15; 27; 28; 33; 34; 35; 18:20; 19:4; 10; 22(2); 21:2; 9; 23:5; 25:22; **1Chr** 1:12; 2:21; 5:6; 25; 6:31; 7:14; 21; 9:22; 11:10; 11; 17:6; 21(2); 26:32; 29:1; 8; **2Chr** 1:11; 2:7; 8:8; 9:25; 17:19; 18:7; 20:10; 22:7; 23:18; 28:3; 33:2; 9; **Ezr** 2:1; 65; 4:10; 5:14; 8:20; 10:44; **Neh** 1:10; 7:6; 67; 8:10; 9:37; **Est** 2:6; 7; 4:5; 11; 6:6(2); 7; 9(2); 11; 13; **Job** 3:23; 5:17; 9:15; 15:19; 19:19; 27; 25:3; 26:4; 30:2; **Ps** 10:3; 16:3; 18:2; 43; 27:1(2); 32:2; 33:12; 41:9; 45:16; 47:4; 65:4; 69:26(2); 73:25; 80:17; 86:9; 88:5; 89:21; 94:1(2); 12; 95:11; 104:26; 105:26; 106:34; 38; 107:2; 144:2; 146:3; **Prov** 3:12(2); 27; 25:7; 30:31; **Eccl** 4:8; 5:19; 6:2; 8:14(2); 9:9; **Song** 1:7; 3:1; 2; 3(2); 4; **Is** 6:8; 8:12; 18; 10:3; 19:25; 22:16; 23:2; 28:9(2); 12; 31:6; 36:5; 37:4; 10; 23(2); 40:14; 18; 25; 41:8; 9; 42:1(2); 24; 43:10; 44:1; 2; 46:5; 47:15; 49:3; 7(2); 50:1(2); 51:18; 19; 53:1; 57:4(2); 11; 66:13; **Jer** 1:2; 6:10; 7:9; 8:2(5); 9:12; 16; 11:12; 14:16; 18:8; 19:4; 20:6; 23:9; 24:5; 25:15; 17; 26:5; 27:5; 29:1; 3; 4; 20; 22; 30:9; 17; 33:5; 34:11; 16; 37:1; 38:9; 39:17; 40:5; 41:2; 9; 10; 16(2); 18; 42:6; 9; 11; 44:3; 50:20; 52:28; **Lam** 1:10; 14; 2:20; 4:20; **Eze** 9:6; 11:1; 7; 15; 13:22; 16:20; 37; 20:9; 23:7; 9; 22; 28(2); 37; 40(2); 24:21; 28:25; 31:2; 18; 32:19; 38:17; **Dan** 1:4(2); 7; 11; 2:24; 3:12; 17; 4:8; 5:11(2); 12; 13; 19(4); 6:2; 16; 20; 7:8; 20; 9:21; 11:21; 38; 39; **Hos** 13:10; **Joel** 2:32; 3:2; **Amos** 6:1; 7:2; 5; **Nah** 3:19; **Zeph** 3:18; **Zec** 1:4; 10; 7:14; 12:10; **Mal** 1:4; 2:14; 3:1(2); **Mt** 1:16; 3:17; 7:9; 11:10; 12:18(2); 27; 16:13; 15; 17:5; 25; 18:7; 19:11; 20:23; 23:35; 24:45; 46; 26:24; 27:9; 15; 17; **Mk** 1:11; 3:13; 6:16; 8:27; 29; 10:40; 13:20; 14:21; 71; 15:12; 40; 16:9; **Lk** 6:13; 14; 34; 47; 7:4; 27; 43; 47; 8:2; 35; 38; 9:9; 18; 20; 10:22; 11:19; 12:5; 37; 42; 43; 48; 13:4; 16; 17:1; 19:15; 22:22; 23:25; **Jn** 1:15; 26; 30; 33; 45; 47; 3:26; 34; 4:18; 5:21; 38; 45; 6:29; 68; 7:25; 28; 8:53; 54; 10:35; 36; 11:3; 12:1; 9; 38; 13:18; 22; 23; 24; 26; 14:17; 26; 15:26; 17:3; 11; 24; 18:4; 7; 19:26; 37; 20:2; 15; 21:7; 20; **Acts** 1:2; 3; 2:24; 36; 3:2; 13; 15; 16; 21; 4:10(2); 22; 27; 5:25; 30; 32; 36; 6:3; 6; 7:7; 35; 39; 45; 52; 8:10; 34; 9:5; 37; 10:21; 39; 13:22; 25; 37; 14:23; 15:17; 24; 17:3; 7; 23; 31; 18:26; 19:13; 16; 25; 27; 20:25; 21:16; 29; 22:5; 8; 23:29; 24:6; 8; 25:15; 16; 18; 19; 24; 26; 26:15; 17; 26; 27:23; 28:4; 8; 15; 23; **Rom** 1:5; 6; 9; 3:25; 4:6; 8; 17; 24; 5:2; 11; 6:16(2); 8:29; 30(3); 9:4; 5; 15(2); 18(2); 24; 10:14(2); 11:36; 13:7(4); 14:15; 15:21; 16:4; **1Cor** 1:9; 3:5; 7:39; 8:6(2); 11; 10:11; 15:6; 15; **2Cor** 1:10; 2:3; 10(2); 4:4; 8:22; 10:18; 11:4; 12:17; **Gal** 1:5; 2:5; 3:19; 4:19; 6:14; **Eph** 1:7; 11; 13(2); 2:3; 21; 22; 3:12; 15; 4:16; 6:22; **Phil** 2:15; 3:8; 18; **Col** 1:14; 27; 28; 2:3; 11; 4:8; 10; **1Th** 1:10; **2Th** 2:8; **1Ti** 1:15; 20(2); 6:16(2); **2Ti** 1:3; 12; 15; 2:17; 3:14; 4:15; 18; **Philem** 1:10; 12; 13; **Heb** 1:2(2); 2:10(2); 3:17; 18; 4:6; 13; 5:11; 6:7; 7:2; 4; 8; 13; 11:18; 38; 12:6(2); 7; 13:21; 23; **Jas** 1:17; **1Pet** 1:8(2); 12; 2:4; 4:11; 5:8; 9; **2Pet** 1:17; 2:2; 17; 19; **1Jn** 4:20(2); **2Jn** 1; **3Jn** 1; 6; **Jude** 13; **Rev** 7:2; 17:2; 20:8

WHOSE

Gen 1:11; 12; 7:22; 11:4; 16:1; 17:14; 22:24; 24:23; 37; 47; 32:17(2); 38:1; 2; 6; 25(2); 44:17; 49:22; **Ex** 34:14; 35:21; 26; 29; 36:2(2); **Lev** 13:40; 14:32; 15:32; 16:27; 21:10; 22:4; 24:10; **Num** 24:3; 15; **Deut** 8:9(2); 19:1; 28:49; 29:18; **Josh** 24:15; **Judg** 4:2; 6:10; 8:31; 13:2; 16:4; 17:1; **Ruth** 2:2; 5; 12; 3:2; **1Sa** 9:1; 2; 10:26; 12:3(3); 17:4; 12; 55; 56; 58; 25:2; **2Sa** 3:7; 12; 6:2; 9:2; 12; 13:1; 3; 14:27; 16:5; 8; 17:10; 25; 20:1; 21:16; 19; **1Kin** 3:26; 8:39; 11:26; **2Kin** 7:2; 17; 8:1; 5; 12:15; 18:22(2); **1Chr** 2:16; 26; 34; 7:2; 15; 8:29; 38; 9:35; 44; 12:8; 13:6; 20:5; 6; 26:7; **2Chr** 6:30; 16:9; 28:9; **Ezr** 1:5; 5:14; 7:15; 8:13; **Est** 2:5; **Job** 1:1; 3:23; 4:19; 5:5; 8:14(2); 12:6; 10; 22:16; 26:4; 30:1; 38:29; 39:6; **Ps** 15:4; 17:14; 26:10; 32:1(2); 2; 9; 33:12; 38:14; 57:4; 78:8; 83:18; 84:5(2); 105:18; 144:8; 11; 15; 146:5; **Prov** 2:15; 26:26; 30:14; **Eccl** 2:21; 7:26; **Is** 1:30; 2:22; 5:28; 6:13; 10:10; 14:2; 18:2; 7; 23:7; 8(2); 26:3; 28:1; 30:13; 31:9; 36:7(2); 43:14; 45:1; 51:7; 15; 57:15; 20; 58:11; **Jer** 5:15; 17:5; 7; 19:13; 22:25; 32:29; 33:5; 37:13; 44:28; 46:7; 10; 48:15; 49:12; 51:57; **Eze** 3:6; 11:21; 17:6; 16(2); 20:9; 14; 22; 21:25; 27; 29; 23:20(2); 24:6(2); 32:23; 40:3; 45; 46; 42:15; 43:4; 47:12; **Dan** 2:11; 26; 31; 3:1; 27; 4:8; 19; 20; 21(2); 34; 37; 5:23(2); 7:9; 19; 20; 27; 10:1; 5; **Joel** 1:6; **Amos** 2:9; 5:27; **Obad** 3; **Jonah** 1:7; 8; **Mic** 5:2; **Nah** 3:8; **Zec** 6:12; 11:5; **Mt** 3:11; 12; 10:3; 22:20; 28; 42; **Mk** 1:7; 7:25; 12:16; 23; **Lk** 1:27; 2:25; 3:16; 17; 6:6; 12:20; 13:1; 20:24; 33; 24:18; **Jn** 1:6; 27; 4:46; 6:42; 10:12; 11:2; 18:26; 19:24; 20:23(2); **Acts** 7:58; 10:5; 6; 32; 11:13; 12:12; 25; 13:6; 25; 15:37; 16:14; 18:7; 27:23; 28:7; 11; **Rom** 2:29; 3:8; 14; 4:7(2); 9:5; **2Cor** 8:18; 11:15; **Gal** 3:1; **Phil** 3:19(3); 4:3; **2Th** 2:9; **Titus** 1:11; **Heb** 3:6; 17; 6:8; 7:6; 11:10; 12:26; 13:7; 11; **1Pet** 2:24; 3:3; 6; **2Pet** 2:3; **Jude** 12; **Rev** 9:11; 13:8; 12; 17:8; 20:11

WHOSO

Gen 9:6; **Lev** 11:27; 22:4; **Num** 35:30; **Deut** 19:4; **2Chr** 23:14; **Ps** 50:23; 101:5; 107:43; **Prov** 1:33; 6:32; 8:35; 9:4; 16; 12:1; 13:13; 16:20; 17:5; 13; 18:22; 20:2; 20; 21:13; 23; 25:14; 26:27; 27:18; 28:7; 10; 13; 18; 24; 26; 29:3; 24; 25; **Eccl** 7:26; 8:5; 10:8; 9; **Dan** 3:6; 11; **Zec** 14:17; **Mt** 18:5; 6; 19:9; 23:20; 21; 24:15; **Mk** 7:10; **Jn** 6:54; **Jas** 1:25; **1Jn** 2:5; 3:17

WHY

Gen 4:6(2); 12:18; 19; 25:22; 27:45; 42:1; 47:15; **Ex** 1:18; 2:20; 3:3; 5:22; 14:5; 17:2; 18:14; 32:11; **Num** 11:20; 20:4; 27:4; **Deut** 5:25; **Josh** 5:4; 7:25; 17:14; **Judg** 2:2; 5:16; 17; 28(2); 6:13; 8:1; 9:28; 11:7; 26; 13:18; 15:10; 21:3; **Ruth** 1:11; 21; 2:10; **1Sa** 1:8(3); 2:23; 6:6; 17:8; 28; 19:17(2); 20:2; 8; 21:1; 22:13; 27:5; 28:12; 15; **2Sa** 3:24; 7:7; 11:10; 21; 13:4; 26; 16:9; 17; 18:11; 19:10; 11; 29; 36; 41; 43; 20:19; 24:3; **1Kin** 1:6; 13; 2:22; 43; 9:8; 14:6; 21:5; **2Kin** 1:5; 7:3; 8:12; 12:7; 14:10; **1Chr** 17:6; 21:3(2); **2Chr** 7:21; 24:6; 20; 25:15; 16; 19; 32:4; **Ezr** 4:22; 7:23; **Neh** 2:2; 3; 6:3; 13:11; 21; **Est** 3:3; 4:5; **Job** 3:11(2); 12(2); 23; 7:20; 21; 9:29; 15:12; 19:22; 28; 21:4; 24:1; 27:12; 31:1; 33:13; **Ps** 2:1; 10:1(2); 22:1(2); 42:5(2); 9(2); 11(2); 43:2(2); 5(2); 44:23; 52:1; 68:16; 74:1(2); 11; 80:12; 88:14(2); **Prov** 5:20; 22:27; **Eccl** 2:15; 7:16; 17; **Song** 1:7; **Is** 1:5; 40:27; 63:17; **Jer** 2:14; 33; 36; 8:5; 14; 19; 22; 14:8; 9; 19; 15:18; 26:9; 27:13; 29:27; 30:15; 36:29; 46:15; 49:1; **Eze** 18:19; 31; 33:11; **Dan** 1:10; 2:15; **Jonah** 1:10; **Mic** 4:9; **Hab** 1:3; **Hag** 1:9; **Mal** 2:10; **Mt** 6:28; 7:3; 8:26; 9:11; 14; 13:10; 15:2; 3; 16:8; 17:10; 19; 19:7; 17; 20:6; 21:25; 22:18; 26:10; 27:23; 46; **Mk** 2:7; 8; 18; 24; 4:40; 5:35; 39; 7:5; 8:12; 17; 9:11; 28; 10:18; 11:3; 31; 12:15; 14:4; 6; 15:14; 34; **Lk** 2:48; 5:30; 33; 6:2; 41; 46; 12:26; 57; 13:7; 18:19; 19:31; 33; 20:5; 23; 22:46; 23:22; 24:5; 38(2); **Jn** 1:25; 4:27; 7:19; 45; 8:43; 46; 9:30; 10:20; 12:5; 13:37; 18:21; 23; 20:13; 15; **Acts** 1:11; 3:12(2); 4:25; 5:3; 4; 7:26; 9:4; 14:15; 15:10; 22:7; 16; 26:8; 14; **Rom** 3:7; 8:24; 9:19; 20; 14:10(2); **1Cor** 4:7; 6:7(2); 10:29; 30; 15:29; 30; **Gal** 2:14; 5:11; **Col** 2:20

WILLING

Gen 24:5; 8; **Ex** 35:5; 21; 22; 29(2); **1Chr** 28:9; 21; 29:5; **Job** 39:9; **Ps** 110:3; **Is** 1:19; **Mt** 1:19; 26:41; **Mk** 15:15; **Lk** 10:29; 22:42; 23:20; **Jn** 5:35; **Acts** 24:27; 25:9; 27:43; **Rom** 9:22; **2Cor** 5:8; 8:3; 12; **1Th** 2:8; **1Ti** 6:18; **Heb** 6:17; 13:18; **2Pet** 3:9

WILLINGLY

Ex 25:2; **Judg** 5:2; 9; 8:25; **1Chr** 29:6; 9(2); 14; 17(2); **2Chr** 17:16; 35:8; **Ezr** 1:6; 3:5; 7:16; **Neh** 11:2; **Prov** 31:13; **Lam** 3:33; **Hos** 5:11; **Jn** 6:21; **Rom** 8:20; **1Cor** 9:17; **Philem** 1:14; **1Pet** 5:2; **2Pet** 3:5

WITH

Gen 3:6; 12; 4:8; 5:22; 24; 6:3; 9; 11; 13(2); 14; 16; 18(2); 19; 7:7; 13; 23; 8:1; 16; 17(2); 18; 9:4; 8; 9(2); 10(3); 11; 12; 11:31; 12:4; 13; 17; 13:1; 5; 14:2(2); 5; 8; 9(3); 13; 17; 24; 15:14; 18; 16:6; 11; 17:3; 4; 12; 13; 19(2); 21; 22; 23; 27(2); 18:11; 16; 23; 25; 33; 19:1; 9(2); 11; 30; 32; 33; 34(2); 35; 36; 20:16(2); 21:6; 10(2); 19; 20; 22; 23(3); 22:3; 5; 23:4(2); 8; 16; 24:15; 32; 40; 45; 49; 54; 55; 58; 25:30; 26:3; 8; 10; 15; 20(2); 24; 28(2); 27:15; 34; 35; 37; 44; 28:4; 15; 20; 29:6; 9(2); 14; 19; 25; 27; 30; 30:8(2); 15; 16(2); 20(2); 29; 33; 31:3; 5; 6; 21; 23; 25; 26; 27(4); 32(2); 36; 38; 42; 50; 32:4; 6; 7; 9; 10; 11; 15; 20; 24; 25; 28(2); 33:1; 5; 7; 10; 11; 13(2); 15(2); 34:2; 5; 6; 7; 8; 9; 10; 16; 20; 21; 22; 23; 26; 31(2); 35:2; 3; 6; 13; 14; 15; 22; 37:2(3); 14(2); 25; 38:14; 24; 25; 39:2; 3; 7; 8; 10; 12; 14(2); 15; 18; 21; 23; 40:4; 7; 14; 41:6; 10; 12; 23; 27; 42:4; 6; 13; 24; 25; 26; 32; 33; 38(2); 43:3; 4; 5; 6; 8; 16(2); 19; 32(2); 34; 44:1; 9; 10; 16; 23; 26(2); 29; 30; 31(2); 33; 34; 45:1; 5; 15; 23(2); 46:1; 4; 6; 7(2); 15; 26; 47:12; 17; 29; 30; 48:1; 12; 21; 22(2); 49:12(2); 25; 29; 30; 50:7; 9; 10; 13; 14; **Ex** 1:1; 7; 10; 11; 13; 14(2); 20; 2:3(2); 21; 24(3); 3:2; 8; 12; 17; 18; 20; 4:12; 15(2); 5:3(3); 15; 6:1(2); 4; 6(2); 7:11; 17; 22; 8:2; 5; 7; 17; 18; 9:9; 10; 15; 24; 10:9(6); 10; 24; 26(2); 12:8(2); 9(4); 10; 11; 22; 38; 48; 13:5; 7(2); 9; 13; 19(2); 14:6; 8; 11; 15:8; 10; 19(2); 20(2); 16:3; 12; 18; 20; 31; 17:2(2); 3; 5; 8; 9(2); 10; 13; 16; 18:5; 6; 12; 18; 19; 22; 19:9; 17; 24; 20:19(2); 22; 23; 21:3; 6; 8; 9; 14; 18(2); 20; 22; 29; 22:14; 15; 16; 19; 24; 30(3); 23:1; 5; 11(2); 18; 32(2); 24:2; 3; 8; 14; 25:2; 11; 13; 14; 20; 22(2); 24; 28(2); 33(2); 34; 39; 26:1(2); 6; 29(2); 31; 32; 36; 37; 27:2; 6; 8; 16; 17; 28:1; 3; 6; 11(2); 15; 21(2); 28; 41; 29:2(2); 3; 4; 5; 9; 12; 14; 21(2); 34; 40(2); 43; 30:3; 5; 6; 10; 20; 28; 34; 36; 31:3; 6; 8; 9; 18(2); 32:4; 11(2); 33:3; 9; 12; 14; 15; 16; 22; 34:3; 5; 10; 12; 15; 20; 25; 27(2); 28; 29(2); 31; 32; 33; 34; 35; 35:12; 14; 16; 23; 24; 25; 31; 35; 36:8; 13; 34(2); 35; 36; 38(2); 37:2; 4; 9(2); 11; 15; 26; 28; 38:2; 6; 7; 17; 23; 39:3; 6; 14; 31; 33; 37(2); 40:3; 12; 14; **Lev** 1:12; 13; 16; 17; 2:2; 4(2); 5; 7; 11; 13(2); 16; 3:4; 10; 15; 4:9; 11(2); 12; 20(3); 25; 30; 34; 5:4(2); 15; 16; 18; 6:6; 10; 16; 17; 21; 7:4; 10; 12(4); 13; 17; 19; 24; 30; 8:2; 6; 7(3); 13; 15; 17; 30(2); 31; 32; 9:4; 11; 13; 10:9; 14; 15(2); 16; 11:43(2); 44; 13:57; 14:10; 16; 21; 27; 31; 37; 52(6); 15:3; 17; 18(2); 24; 33; 16:3; 4(2); 10; 14(2); 15(2); 19; 24; 17:13; 15; 18:20(2); 22(2); 23; 19:13; 19(2); 20; 22; 26; 33; 34; 20:2; 5; 10(2); 11; 12; 13(2); 14; 15; 18; 20; 24; 27; 21:9; 22:6; 8; 11; 14; 23:13; 17; 18(2); 20(2); 24:23; 25:6; 23; 35(2); 36; 40; 41; 43; 45; 46; 50(2); 52; 53(2); 54; 26:9; 39; 40; 42(3); 44; **Num** 1:2; 4; 5; 2:2; 17; 31; 3:1; 4:5; 8; 11; 12; 32(2); 5:7; 13(2); 19(2); 20; 21; 23; 6:15(2); 17; 20; 7:13; 19; 25; 31; 37; 43; 49; 55; 61; 67; 73; 79; 87; 89; 8:8(2); 26; 9:11; 10:3; 4; 8; 9; 10; 29; 32; 11:15; 16; 17(2); 18; 33; 12:8; 13:23; 27; 31; 14:8; 9; 10; 12; 21; 24; 27; 43; 15:4; 5; 6; 9(2); 14; 15; 16; 24; 35; 36; 16:2; 10; 13; 14; 18; 22; 30; 17:4; 13; 18:1(2); 2(2); 7; 11(2); 19(2); 19:4; 5; 12; 16; 20:3; 11; 13; 18; 20(2); 21:18; 24; 22:7; 8; 9; 12; 13; 14; 20; 21; 22; 27; 35(2); 39; 40; 23:13; 17; 21; 24:8; 25:1; 14; 18; 26:3; 10; 27:21; 28:5; 9; 12(2); 13; 20; 28; 29:3; 9; 14; 30:2; 8; 10; 31:6; 8; 10; 14(2); 17; 18; 23; 35; 32:19; 29; 30; 33; 33:1; 3; 34:2; 12; 35:7; 16; 17; 18; 21; 23; 25; **Deut** 1:16; 37; 2:5; 7; 9; 19; 24; 26; 3:5; 13; 26; 27; 4:11(2); 21; 23; 29(2); 37; 40(2); 5:2; 3(2); 4; 16; 22; 23; 24; 29(2); 33; 6:3(2); 5(3); 18; 21; 7:2; 3; 5(2); 8; 9; 23; 25; 8:3; 16; 9:8; 9; 10(2); 15; 20; 21; 26; 10:9; 12(2); 14; 22; 11:2; 9; 10; 13(2); 12:3; 12; 23; 25(2); 28(2); 13:3(2); 10; 15(2); 16; 14:27; 29; 15:3; 16; 19; 16:3; 4; 10; 18; 17:5; 19; 18:1; 6; 11; 13; 19:5(2); 13; 20:1; 4; 12; 13; 20; 21:3; 21; 22:2; 3(3); 6; 7; 9; 10; 21; 22(2); 23; 24; 25(2); 28; 29; 23:4(2); 11; 16; 23; 25; 24:5; 12; 25:3; 11; 26:5; 8(5); 9; 15; 16(2); 27:1; 2; 3; 4; 14; 20; 21; 22; 23; 28:22(7); 27(4); 28; 30; 32; 35; 40; 47(2); 68; 29:1(2); 10; 12(2); 14; 15(4); 25; 30:2(2); 6(2); 10(2); 31:6; 7; 8; 16(2); 20; 23; 27; 32:12; 14(2); 15; 16(2); 21(4); 22; 24(4); 25; 34; 39; 42(2); 43; 33:2; 8(2); 17; 20; 21(2); 23(2); 24; 34:4; **Josh** 1:5(2); 9; 17(2); 2:6; 14; 19; 3:7(2); 4:3; 8; 5:6; 13; 6:4; 5(2); 8; 9(2); 10; 13(2); 16; 17; 20(2); 21; 24; 27; 7:12; 15(2); 24; 25(3); 8:1; 5; 11; 24; 35; 9:2(3); 6; 7; 11(2); 15(2); 16; 10:1; 4(2); 7; 10; 11(2); 15; 20; 24; 28; 29; 30; 31; 32; 34; 35; 36; 37; 38; 39; 43; 11:4(2); 6; 7; 9; 10; 11(2); 12; 14; 18; 19; 21; 13:8; 21; 22; 14:4; 8; 12; 15:32; 36; 41; 44; 45; 46; 47(2); 51; 54; 57; 59; 60; 62; 63; 16:9; 18:24; 28; 19:15; 16; 22; 30; 31; 38; 46; 47; 48; 21:2; 8; 11; 13(2); 14(2); 15(2); 16(3); 17(2); 18(2); 19; 21(2); 22(2); 23(2); 24(2); 25(2); 26; 27(2); 28(2); 29(2); 30(2); 31(2); 32(3); 33; 34(2); 35(2); 36(2); 37(2); 38(2); 39(2); 41; 42; 22:5(2); 8(8); 14; 15; 18; 24; 27(3); 30; 23:4; 12; 24:6; 8; 12(2); 25; **Judg** 1:3(3); 8; 16; 17; 18(3); 19; 21; 22; 25; 2:1; 2; 18; 3:27; 31; 4:6; 7; 8(2); 9(2); 10(2); 13; 15; 18; 5:15; 26; 6:5; 12; 13; 16; 17; 26; 39; 7:1; 2; 4(3); 5; 10; 11; 16; 18(2); 19; 8:1(2); 4; 7(2); 10; 15; 16; 9:1(2); 16; 19(2); 23; 26; 32; 33; 34; 35; 38; 39; 44; 45; 48(2); 52; 11:3; 6; 8; 11; 12; 33; 34(2); 38; 39; 12:1(2); 2; 4; 13:9; 19; 14:7; 11; 15; 18; 15:1; 5; 6; 8; 13; 14; 16(2); 16:3; 7; 8; 9; 11; 13; 14(3); 15; 16; 21; 29(2); 30(2); 17:2; 10; 11; 18:4; 7; 11; 16; 17(2); 19; 23; 25; 27(2); 28; 19:3; 4; 5; 10(2); 19; 20; 24; 29; 20:1; 37; 38; 40; 43; 48; 21:5; 10(2); 12; **Ruth** 1:6; 7; 8(3); 10; 11; 18; 20; 22; 2:4; 6; 19(2); 22; 23; 3:1; 2; **1Sa** 1:24(2); 2:4; 13(2); 18; 19; 22; 26(2); 29; 3:14; 19; 4:4; 5; 8; 12(2); 19; 5:6; 7; 8; 9; 12; 6:11; 15; 19; 7:3; 10; 9:3; 5; 19; 24; 25; 10:5; 6; 7; 26; 11:1; 2; 7; 10; 12:2; 7; 20; 24; 13:2(2); 4; 5; 15; 16; 22(3); 14:2; 7; 17; 18; 20; 21(4); 27; 28; 32; 33; 34(2); 43; 45; 15:6; 8; 25; 26; 30; 16:1; 2; 5; 16; 18; 19; 20; 23; 17:5; 9; 19; 20; 23; 25; 28; 32; 33; 37; 38(2); 39; 43; 45(3); 47; 50(2); 57; 18:1; 6(3); 10; 11; 12; 14; 22; 28; 19:3;

8(2); 9(2); 10; 13; 16; 20:5; 8(2); 13(2); 16; 35(2); 41; 21:1; 8; 22:2; 3; 4; 6; 8; 17; 19(2); 23(2); 23:5(2); 6; 19; 23(2); 24:7; 8; 18; 25:7; 15; 16; 25; 26; 29; 31; 33; 39; 42; 26:2; 6(2); 8; 27:2(2); 3(3); 5; 28:1(2); 8; 12; 14(2); 19(2); 23; 29:2; 3; 4(3); 6; 8; 9; 10(2); 30:1; 3; 4; 9; 14; 21; 22(2); 23; 31:5; **2Sa** 1:2; 11; 17; 21; 24; 2:3(2); 23; 3:8; 12(2);.13; 16; 17; 20(2); 21; 22(2); 23; 27; 31(2); 5:3; 10; 6:2(2); 12; 14(2); 15(2); 7:3; 7(2); 9; 12; 14(2); 22; 29; 8:2(3); 10(2); 11; 10:13; 17; 19; 11:1; 4; 5; 9; 11; 13; 17; 12:3(2); 9(2); 11; 17; 24; 30; 13:11; 14; 18; 20; 24; 26(2); 27; 28; 31; 14:2; 17; 19; 15:11; 12; 14(2); 19(2); 20(2); 22; 23; 24; 27; 30; 31; 32; 33; 35; 36; 16:1; 10; 14; 15; 17; 18; 21; 23(2); 17:2; 8; 10; 12; 16; 22; 24; 29; 18:1; 2; 5(2); 14; 27; 19:4; 7; 16; 17(2); 22; 25; 31; 33(2); 34; 36(2); 37; 38; 40; 41; 20:8; 9; 15; 16; 21:15(2); 16; 17; 18; 19; 22:26(2); 27(2); 40; 23:5(2); 6; 7(2); 9; 21(2); 24:2; **1Kin** 1:1; 7(2); 8; 14; 21; 22; 23; 31; 33; 34; 37(2); 40(3); 41; 44; 49; 51; 2:4(2); 8(3); 9; 10; 32; 43; 3:1; 6; 17; 18; 4:13; 5:6; 6:8; 9; 10; 12; 15(3); 16; 18; 20; 21(2); 22(2); 28; 29; 30; 32; 35; 36; 7:2; 3; 5; 7; 9; 12; 14; 18; 26; 31; 49; 8:5; 9; 15(2); 21; 23(2); 24(3); 25; 46; 48(2); 54; 55; 57(2); 61; 62; 65; 9:11(2); 16; 27; 10:1; 2(3); 18; 22; 26; 11:1; 4; 9; 16; 17; 18; 21; 22; 29; 38; 43; 12:6; 8(2); 10; 11(3); 14(2); 18; 21; 13:7; 8; 15; 16(3); 18; 19; 14:3; 6; 8; 20; 22; 31(2); 15:3; 8; 14; 19; 20; 22; 24(2); 16:2; 6; 7; 13; 17; 18; 26; 28; 17:18; 20; 18:4; 13; 28; 32; 33; 35; 45; 19:1; 10; 14; 19(2); 21; 20:1; 20; 21; 34(2); 38; 21:8(2); 13; 22:4; 11; 13; 27(2); 31(2); 40; 44; 49; 50(2); **2Kin** 1:8; 9; 11; 13; 14; 15(2); 2:1; 16; 3:4; 7; 12; 13; 17; 19; 20; 26; 4:13; 26(3); 5:1; 3; 5; 9(2); 23; 26; 6:1; 3; 4; 8; 15; 16(2); 18(2); 22(2); 32; 33; 7:2; 19; 8:2; 4; 9; 12(2); 21; 24(2); 28; 9:13; 15; 18; 19; 24; 28; 10:2(2); 6; 13; 15; 16; 23; 25; 31; 35; 11:3; 4(2); 8(2); 9; 11; 14; 15; 20; 12:15; 21; 13:9; 13(2); 19; 23; 14:10; 15; 16(2); 20; 22; 29(2); 15:7(2); 16; 19; 22; 25(2); 38(2); 16:15; 20(2); 17:15; 18; 35; 36; 38; 18:7; 17; 26; 27; 28; 31; 37; 19:1; 2; 6; 23; 24; 32; 37; 20:3; 21; 21:6; 11; 18; 22:7; 14; 17; 23:2; 3; 11; 14; 18; 24; 25(3); 24:4; 6; 25:7; 9; 10; 11; 17; 24; 25(2); 28; **1Chr** 2:23(2); 4:9; 10; 23; 5:10; 18; 19(2); 20; 6:32; 33; 57(2); 58(2); 59(2); 60(3); 64; 67(2); 68(2); 69(2); 70(2); 71(2); 72(2); 73(2); 74(2); 75(2); 76(3); 77(2); 78(2); 79(2); 80(2); 81(2); 7:4; 23; 28; 8:12; 32; 9:20; 25; 38; 11:3; 9; 10(2); 13; 19; 23(2); 42; 12:2; 19; 27; 33; 34(2); 37; 38; 39; 13:1(2); 2; 8(7); 14; 14:1; 12; 15:15; 16(2); 18; 19; 20; 21; 24; 25; 27(2); 28(5); 16:5(3); 6; 16; 38; 41; 42(3); 17:2; 6; 8; 11; 20; 18:10(2); 11; 19:14; 17; 19; 20:3(4); 4; 5; 21:7; 20; 21; 22:11; 13; 15; 16; 18; 23:2; 5; 24:5; 25:1(3); 3; 6; 7; 9; 26:16; 27:32; 28:1(3); 9(2); 20; 21(2); 29:2; 6; 8; 9(2); 17; 21; 22; 30; **2Chr** 1:1; 3; 14; 2:3(2); 7(2); 8; 12; 13; 14(2); 3:4; 5(2); 6; 7; 8; 9; 10; 4:5; 9; 20; 5:10; 12(3); 13(2); 6:4(2); 11; 14; 15(3); 16; 18; 36; 38(2); 41; 7:3; 6; 8; 18; 8:5; 18; 9:1(3); 17; 18; 21; 25; 31; 10:6; 8(2); 10; 11(2); 14(2); 18; 12:1; 3(2); 16; 13:3(2); 8; 9; 11; 12(2); 14; 17; 19(3); 14:1; 9; 11(3); 13; 15:2(2); 6; 9(2); 12(2); 14(4); 15(2); 16:3; 8; 10(2); 13; 14; 17:3; 8(2); 9; 14; 15; 16; 17(2); 18; 18:1; 2(2); 3(2); 10; 12; 26(2); 30(3); 19:6; 7; 9; 11; 20:1; 13; 17(2); 18; 19; 21; 25; 27; 28; 35; 36; 37; 21:1(2); 3; 4; 7; 9(2); 14; 18; 22:1; 5; 6; 7; 9; 12; 23:1; 3; 7(2); 8; 13(2); 14; 18(2); 21; 24:21; 24; 25:2; 7(3); 13; 16; 19; 24; 28; 26:2; 13; 17; 19; 23(2); 27:5; 9; 28:5; 9; 10(2); 15; 18(2); 27; 29:8; 10; 18(2); 24; 25(3); 26(2); 27(2); 29; 30(2); 35; 30:6; 21(2); 23; 25; 31:9; 21; 32:3; 7(3); 8(2); 9; 18; 21(2); 33; 33:6(2); 11; 20; 34:6; 25; 31(2); 35:12; 13; 21(3); 22; 36:10; 17; 19; 23; **Ezr** 1:3; 4(4); 5; 6(5); 11; 2:2; 63(2); 3:9(2); 10(2); 11; 12; 13; 4:2; 3; 5:2; 8; 6:4; 12; 16; 22; 7:13; 16; 17(2); 18; 28; 8:1; 3; 4; 5; 6; 7; 8; 9; 10; 11; 12; 13; 14; 17; 18; 24; 33(2); 9:2; 11(3); 14(2); 10:3; 4; 12; 14; 16; 17; **Neh** 1:3; 2:3; 9; 12(2); 13; 17; 3:1; 4:13; 17(3); 22; 5:7; 6:5; 7:7; 65; 8:2; 6(2); 9:1(2); 4; 6; 8; 13; 24(2); 10:32; 38; 11:25; 12:1; 24; 27(5); 35; 36; 40; 41; 42; 43; 13:2(2); 9; 11; 17; 25; **Est** 1:6; 10; 11; 2:6(2); 9; 12(3); 13; 20; 3:1; 11; 12; 4:1(2); 2; 13; 5:9; 12(2); 14; 6:14; 7:1; 8:3; 8(2); 10; 15(2); 9:5; 29; 30; **Job** 1:4; 15; 17; 2:7; 10; 11; 13; 3:14; 15(2); 4:2; 18; 5:14; 23(2); 7:5; 14; 8:21(2); 22; 9:2; 3; 14; 17; 18; 30; 35; 10:2; 11(2); 13; 12:2; 5; 12; 13; 16; 18; 13:3; 17; 19; 14:3; 5; 15:2; 3(2); 10; 11(2); 20; 27; 16:5; 8; 9; 10; 14; 16; 21; 17:2; 3(2); 18:6; 19:2; 4; 6; 16; 20; 22; 24; 20:11; 26; 21:8; 24; 25; 22:4; 16; 18; 21; 23:4; 6; 7; 14; 24:8; 14; 22; 25:2; 4; 26:10; 12; 27:11; 13; 14; 28:14; 16(2); 19; 22; 29:5; 6; 30:1; 21; 30; 31:1; 5; 13; 18(2); 20; 32:14; 33:19(2); 23; 26; 29; 30; 34:8(2); 9; 23; 35:4; 36:4; 7; 18; 32; 37:4; 5; 18; 22; 38:8; 30; 32; 39:4; 10; 19; 24; 40:2; 9; 10(2); 15; 22; 24; 41:1(2); 2; 4; 5(2); 7(2); 13; 15; 28; 42:8; 11; **Ps** 2:9; 11(2); 3:4; 4:4; 5:4; 9; 12(2); 6:6(2); 7:4; 11; 14; 8:5; 9:1; 6; 10:14; 12:2(3); 4; 13:6; 15:3; 17:10; 14; 15; 18:25(2); 26(2); 32; 39; 20:6; 21:3; 6; 22:13; 23:4; 5; 25:14; 19; 26:4(2); 5; 7; 9(2); 27:7; 28:3(2); 7; 29:11; 30:11; 31:9; 10(2); 32:7; 8; 9; 33:2(2); 3; 34:3; 35:1(2); 13; 16(2); 19; 26; 36:8; 9; 37:12; 24; 38:7; 39:1(2); 2; 3; 11; 12; 42:4(4); 8; 10; 44:1; 2; 9; 19; 45:3; 7; 12; 15; 46:3; 7; 11; 47:1; 5(2); 7; 48:7; 50:5; 18(2); 51:7; 12; 19(2); 54:t, 4; 55:18; 20; 58:9; 59:7; 60:(2); 5; 10; 62:4; 63:5(2); 64:7; 65:4; 6; 9; 10; 11; 13(2); 66:13; 15(2); 17(2); 68:6; 13(2); 19; 25; 27; 30(2); 69:10; 28; 30(2); 71:8(2); 13; 22(2); 72:2(2); 19; 73:7; 19; 23; 24; 74:6; 75:5; 77:1(2); 6; 15; 78:8; 14(2); 36(2); 37; 47(2); 58(2); 62; 71; 80:5; 10; 16; 81:2; 16(2); 83:5; 7; 8; 15(2); 16; 85:5; 86:12; 87:4; 88:4; 7; 89:1; 3; 10; 20; 21; 24; 28; 32(2); 38; 45; 90:5; 14; 91:4; 8; 15; 16; 92:3; 10; 93:1(2); 94:20; 95:2(2); 10; 96:13(2); 98:5(2); 6; 9(2); 100:2(2); 4(2); 101:2; 6; 102:9; 103:4; 5; 10; 104:1; 2(2); 6(2); 13; 28; 105:9; 18; 25; 37; 40; 43(2); 106:4(2); 5; 6; 29; 32; 33; 38; 39(2); 43; 107:9; 12; 22; 108:1; 6; 11; 109:2; 3; 14; 18(2); 29(3); 30; 110:6; 111:1; 112:5; 9; 10; 113:8(2); 116:7; 118:7; 27; 119:2; 7; 10; 13; 17; 34; 58; 65; 69; 78; 93; 98; 124; 145; 120:4; 6; 123:3; 4(2); 125:5; 126:2(2); 6(2); 127:5; 128:2; 130:4; 7(2); 132:9; 15; 16; 18; 136:12(2); 138:1; 3; 139:3; 18; 21; 22; 141:4; 142:1(2); 7; 143:2; 147:7; 8; 14; 20; 149:3; 4; 8(2); 150:3(2); 4(2); **Prov** 1:11; 13; 15; 31; 2:1; 16; 3:5; 9(2); 10(2); 30; 32; 4:7; 23; 5:10; 17; 18; 19; 20; 22; 6:1; 2(2); 12; 13(3); 22; 25; 32; 7:1; 5; 10; 13; 14; 16(3); 17; 18; 20; 21(2); 8:12; 18; 24; 30; 31; 10:4; 10; 18; 22; 11:2; 9; 10; 12:11; 14; 21; 13:10; 16; 20; 14:1; 10; 14; 18; 15:16; 16:7; 8; 19(2); 17:1; 14; 18:1; 3; 20(2); 19:2; 7; 23; 20:8; 13; 17; 18; 19(2); 21:9; 19; 27; 22:24(2); 23:1; 7; 11; 13; 14; 21; 24:1; 4; 21; 28; 31; 25:9; 24; 26:17; 23; 24; 27:14; 22; 28:4; 20; 23; 29:3; 9; 24; 30:8; 16; 19; 22; 28; 31:13; 16; 17; 21; 26; **Eccl** 1:8(2); 11; 16; 2:1; 3; 9; 4:6(2); 8; 15; 5:2; 10(2); 11; 17; 6:3; 4(2); 10; 7:11; 8:12; 13; 15; 16; 9:7(2); 9; 10; 11:5; 12:14; **Song** 1:2; 6; 10(2); 11; 2:3; 5(2); 13; 3:6(2); 10; 11; 4:8(2); 9(2); 13(2); 14(2); 5:1(3); 2(2); 5(2); 12; 14(2); 6:1; 4; 10; 7:1; 2; 8:9; **Is** 1:4; 6; 7; 13; 20; 22; 27(2); 3:10; 11; 14; 16(2); 17; 5:2; 13; 18(2); 26; 6:2(3); 4; 6; 10(3); 7:2(2); 4; 20; 24(2); 25; 8:1; 10; 11; 9:5(2); 7(2); 10; 12; 10:22; 24; 33; 34; 11:4(4); 6(2); 15; 12:1; 3; 13:9; 14:1; 6; 19; 20; 21; 23; 30; 15:3; 5; 16:4; 9(2); 14; 17:5; 10; 18:1; 5; 19:23; 24(2); 20:4; 21:3; 7(2); 9; 14; 22:2; 6; 12; 17; 21(2); 23:17; 24:2(12); 9; 12; 25:5; 11; 26:9(2); 17; 18; 19; 27:1; 5(2); 6; 8; 28:1; 2; 11; 15(2); 18(2); 27(3); 28(2); 29:3; 6(3); 9(2); 13(2); 30:1; 24(2); 27; 28; 29; 30(3); 31; 32(2); 31:8; 32:7; 33:1(2); 5; 14(2); 21; 34:3; 6(4); 7(4); 14; 15; 35:2; 4(2); 7; 10; 36:2; 12; 13; 16; 22; 37:1; 2; 9; 25; 33; 38; 38:3; 11; 12; 14; 40:9; 10(2); 11(2); 12; 14; 19; 31; 41:3; 4; 7(2); 10(2); 11; 12; 43:2; 5; 23(3); 24(4); 44:5; 12(3); 13(3); 16; 45:9(2); 17; 47:6; 12(2); 15; 48:10; 20; 49:4(2); 18(2); 23; 25(2); 26(3); 50:3; 8; 11; 51:11; 21; 52:8; 12; 53:3; 5; 9(2); 12(3); 54:1; 7; 8; 9; 11(3); 55:3; 12(2); 56:12; 57:5; 8; 9; 15; 58:4; 14; 59:3(2); 6; 12; 17; 21; 60:7; 9; 61:8; 10(4); 62:11; 63:1; 3; 11; 12; 64:11; 65:23; 66:10(3); 11(2); 15(4); 16; **Jer** 1:8; 19; 2:9(2); 22; 29; 35; 3:1; 2(3); 9(2); 10; 15; 18; 20; 4:8; 30(3); 5:17; 18; 6:3; 11(3); 12; 26; 28; 8:8; 19(2); 9:4; 8; 15; 18(2); 25; 10:3; 4(4); 13; 24; 11:5; 10; 15; 16; 19; 12:1(2); 5(2); 6; 13:12(2); 13; 17; 14:3; 17(3); 18(2); 21; 15:6; 7; 11; 14; 17; 20; 16:8; 18; 17:1(2); 18; 18:6; 17; 18; 19; 23; 19:4; 5; 10; 20:4; 9; 11; 17; 18; 21:2; 5(2); 7; 10; 22:7; 14(2); 15; 16; 19; 23:15; 24:1; 7; 25:6; 7; 26; 31(2); 26:11; 14; 21; 22; 23; 24; 27:8(3); 18; 28:4; 29:13; 16; 18(3); 23; 30:6(2); 11; 14(2); 23(2); 31:3(2); 4; 7; 8(3); 9(2); 14(2); 24; 27(2); 31(2); 32; 33; 32:4; 5; 21(5); 22; 29; 30; 40; 41(2); 33:5(2); 21(2); 25; 34:2; 3; 5; 8; 13; 22; 36:18(2); 23; 37:8; 10; 15; 38:6; 10; 11; 13; 17; 18; 23; 25; 27; 39:3; 7; 8; 9; 40:4(2); 5; 6; 9; 41:1; 2(2); 3(2); 5; 7; 9; 11; 12; 13(2); 15; 16; 42:6; 8; 11; 17; 43:6; 12; 13; 44:8; 25(2); 46:4; 10; 22(2); 25; 28; 47:5; 48:7; 32; 33; 39; 49:2; 3; 20; 50:5; 39; 45; 51:5; 14(2); 16; 20(2); 21(2); 22(3); 23(3); 28; 32; 34; 40; 42; 58; 59; 52:13; 14; 22; 32; **Lam** 1:2; 16; 2:1; 4; 10; 11; 3:5; 9; 15(2); 16(2); 30; 41; 43; 44; 48; 4:9(2); 14; 5:6; 9; **Eze** 1:15; 2:6; 3:3; 4; 10; 22; 24; 25; 27; 4:12; 16(2); 17; 5:2(2); 11(2); 12(2); 6:9(2); 11(2); 7:15; 18; 27; 8:11; 16; 17; 18; 9:1(2); 2(2); 3; 7; 11; 10:2(2); 4; 6; 7; 11:6; 13; 12:7; 12; 18(3); 19(2); 13:10; 11; 13; 14; 15; 22; 14:11; 16:8; 9(2); 10(4); 11; 13; 16; 17; 26; 28(2); 36(2); 37(2); 40(2); 41; 59; 60; 62; 17:3; 7; 12; 13; 16; 17; 20; 21; 18:7; 16; 19:4; 11; 20:6; 7; 15; 18; 31; 33(3); 34(3); 35; 36(2); 39(2); 40; 41; 44; 21:6(2); 21; 22; 24; 22:7; 11; 14; 28; 31; 23:6; 7(4); 8; 10; 14; 15; 16; 17(2); 23; 24(2); 25; 29; 30; 33(3); 37; 40; 42(2); 43(2); 47(3); 24:4; 7; 12; 16; 26; 25:6(2); 10; 15; 17; 26:7(3); 8; 9; 11; 16; 20(3); 27:7; 9; 11; 12; 14; 16; 21; 22(2); 24; 31(2); 33; 28:4(2); 16; 26; 30:5; 11(2); 24; 31:3(2); 4; 11; 14; 16; 17(2); 18(2); 32:2(3); 3; 4; 5; 6; 7; 18; 19; 21; 24; 25(2); 27(2); 28(2); 29(3); 30(4); 32(2); 33:25; 31; 34:3; 4(2); 16; 18(2); 19(2); 21(3); 25; 29; 30; 35:8(2); 13; 36:5(2); 37; 38; 37:6; 19(2); 23(3); 26(2); 27; 38:4(2); 5(2); 6; 9; 13; 15; 22(3); 39:4; 9; 10; 14; 20(3); 40:3; 4(2); 41:13; 15; 16; 18; 42:16(2); 17; 18; 19; 43:2; 22; 44:5(3); 17; 18; 19; 45:2; 46:14; 23; 47:22; 48:20; 34; **Dan** 1:2; 8(2); 9; 13; 19; 2:5; 11; 14; 18; 22; 41; 43(3); 4:15(3); 23(3); 25(2); 32; 33; 5:7; 16; 21(3); 29; 6:14; 17(2); 20; 7:7; 13; 19; 21; 8:7; 18; 9:3; 15; 22; 26; 27; 10:5; 7; 13; 17; 20; 21; 11:3; 7; 8(2); 11(3); 13(2); 17(2); 22; 23(2); 25(2); 28; 30; 34(2); 38(2); 39(2); 40(3); 44; **Hos** 2:2; 3; 6; 7; 13; 18(3); 4:1; 3(2); 4; 5; 14(2); 18; 5:5; 6(2); 7; 6:8; 7:3(2); 5(2); 14; 9:8; 11:4(2); 12(4); 12:1; 2; 3; 4; 13:3; 16; 14:2; 8; **Joel** 1:8; 2:12(4); 20; 24; 26; 3:2; 4; 18(2); **Amos** 1:3; 11; 13; 14(2); 2:2(3); 3; 3:15; 4:2(2); 5; 9; 10; 5:8; 14; 6:6; 7; 8; 10; 11(2); 12; 7:7; 9; 8:3; 9:1; **Obad** 7; **Jonah** 1:3; 2:6; 9; 3:6; 8; **Mic** 1:7; 2:4; 8; 10; 3:5; 10(2); 5:1; 6; 6:2(2); 6(2); 7(2); 8; 11(2); 15; 7:2; 3; 14; **Nah** 1:8; 2:3; 7; 12(2); 3:12; **Hab** 1:15; 2:6; 12; 14; 16; 19; 3:9; 13; 14; 15; 16; **Zeph** 1:3; 4; 8; 9; 12; 3:8; 9; 14; 17(2); **Hag** 1:6(2); 12; 13; 2:4; 5; 7; 12; 17(3); **Zec** 1:2; 6; 9; 13(2); 14(2); 15; 16; 19; 2:1; 3; 7; 3:3; 4; 5; 4:1; 2; 4; 5; 7; 10; 5:4; 5; 10; 6:4; 7:14; 8:2(2); 4; 23(2); 9:4; 8; 13; 14; 15; 10:5; 9; 11; 11:10; 12:3; 4(3); 13:6; 14:5; **Mal** 1:8; 2:3; 4; 5; 6; 13(4); 16; 17; 3:9; 4:2; 4; 6; **Mt** 1:18; 23(2); 2:3; 10; 11; 3:11(3); 12; 4:21; 24(2); 5:22; 25(2); 28; 41; 7:2(2); 8:11; 16(2); 24; 28; 29; 9:10; 11; 15; 20; 32; 36; 11:7; 12:3; 4; 22; 30(2); 41; 42; 45; 46; 47; 13:15(3); 20; 29; 56; 14:7; 9; 14; 24; 15:8(2); 20; 22; 30; 32; 16:1; 27; 17:3; 17; 18:9; 16; 26; 27; 29; 19:10; 26(2); 20:2; 13; 15; 20; 22(2); 23(2); 24; 21:2; 25; 22:10; 16; 25; 37(3); 23:4; 30; 24:19; 30; 31; 49; 51; 25:3; 4; 10; 16; 19; 27; 31; 26:11; 15; 18; 20; 23; 29; 35; 36; 37; 38; 40; 47(2); 51; 52; 55(2); 58; 67; 69; 71; 72; 27:7; 19; 22; 34; 38; 41; 44; 46; 48; 50; 54; 28:8; 12; 20; **Mk** 1:6(2); 8(2); 13; 20; 23; 24; 26; 27; 29; 32; 36; 41; 2:15; 16(2); 19(2); 25; 26; 3:5; 6; 7; 14; 4:10; 16; 24; 30; 33; 36; 5:2; 3; 4; 5; 7(2); 15; 16; 18(2); 24; 40; 42; 6:3; 9; 13; 22; 25; 26; 34; 50; 7:2(2); 5; 6; 8:2; 4; 10; 11; 14; 34; 38; 9:1; 2; 4(2); 8; 10(2); 14; 16; 18; 19; 24; 47; 49(2); 50; 10:27(3); 30; 38(2); 39; 41; 46; 11:11; 31; 12:30(4); 33(4); 13:17; 26; 14:7; 14; 17; 18; 20; 31; 33; 43(2); 48(2); 49; 53; 54; 58; 65; 67; 15:1; 7(2); 17; 19; 23; 27; 28; 31; 32; 34; 37; 41; 16:10; 14; 17; 20(2); **Lk** 1:15; 25; 28; 30; 36; 37; 39; 41; 42; 51; 53; 56; 58; 66; 67; 2:5(2); 13; 16; 36; 37; 40; 48; 51; 52; 3:14; 16(3); 17; 4:28; 32; 33; 34; 36; 38; 40; 5:9; 10; 18; 19; 26; 29; 30; 34; 36; 6:3; 4; 11(2); 17; 18; 38; 7:6; 11; 12; 24; 29; 36; 38(3); 44(2); 46(2); 49; 8:1; 7; 13; 14; 15; 16; 22; 23; 28(2); 29; 37; 38; 45; 9:18; 30; 32(3); 41; 49; 10:17; 27(4); 11:7; 20; 23(2); 31; 32; 37; 46(2); 12:13; 25; 46; 47; 48; 50; 58; 13:1; 14; 14:9; 10; 15; 18; 25; 31(2); 15:2; 6; 9; 13; 16; 17; 29; 30; 31; 16:21; 17:15; 20; 18:7; 11; 27(2); 19:7; 23; 37; 44; 20:1; 5; 21:5; 20; 23; 25; 27; 34; 22:4; 11; 14; 15(2); 21; 28; 33; 48; 49; 52; 53; 56; 59; 23:9; 11; 18; 23; 32; 35; 43; 46; 55; 24:1; 10; 15; 24; 29(2); 30; 32; 33; 44; 49; 52; **Jn** 1:1; 2; 26; 31; 33(2); 39; 2:4; 7; 3:2; 22; 26; 4:6; 9; 11; 27(2); 40; 5:18; 6:3; 13; 22; 66; 7:33; 8:6; 29; 38(2); 9:6; 37; 40; 11:2(2); 16; 31; 33; 43; 44(2); 54; 12:2; 3(2); 8; 17; 35; 40(2); 13:5; 8; 18; 33; 14:9; 16; 17; 23; 25; 27; 30; 15:27; 16:4; 32; 17:5(3); 12; 24; 18:1; 2; 3; 5; 15; 18; 22; 26; 19:3; 15(2); 18; 29; 32; 34; 40; 20:7; 24; 26; 21:3; 8; **Acts** 1:4; 5(2); 14(3); 17; 18; 21; 22; 26; 2:1; 4(2); 14; 28; 29; 30; 40; 46(2); 47; 3:4; 8; 10; 25; 4:8; 13; 14; 24; 27; 29; 31(2); 33; 5:1; 12; 16; 17(2); 21; 23; 26; 28; 31; 6:9; 7:9(2); 19; 38(2); 45; 48; 54; 57(2); 60; 8:6; 7(3); 11; 13; 20(2); 31; 37; 9:7; 17; 19; 28; 39(2); 43; 10:2; 6; 20; 23; 27; 35; 38(3); 41; 45; 46; 11:2; 3; 12; 16(2); 21; 23; 26; 12:2; 6; 17; 20(2); 25; 13:1; 7; 9; 16; 17; 31; 45; 52(2); 14:4(2); 5; 10; 13; 15; 17; 18; 20; 23; 27; 28; 15:2; 4; 22(2); 24; 25(2); 32; 35; 37; 38(2); 16:3; 11; 16; 28; 34; 17:2; 4; 5; 11; 15; 17(4); 23; 24; 25; 34; 18:2; 3; 8; 10; 12; 14; 18; 19; 20; 19:4; 6; 25; 26; 29(2); 33; 34; 38; 20:9; 14; 18; 19(2); 24; 28; 31; 34; 36; 21:1; 5; 7; 8; 16(3); 18; 24(2); 26; 29; 33; 36; 40; 22:9; 11; 22; 25; 28; 23:15; 19; 21; 27; 32; 24:1(2); 3; 7; 12; 18(2); 24; 26; 25:5; 12; 23(2); 24(2); 26:8; 9; 12; 13; 24; 30; 27:2; 10; 18; 19; 24; 39; 41; 28:10(2); 14; 16; 20(2); 27(3); 31; **Rom** 1:4; 9; 12; 27; 29; 2:11; 3:13; 5:1; 6:4; 6; 8(2); 7:18; 21; 25(2); 8:16; 17(2); 18; 25; 26; 32; 9:14; 22; 10:9; 10(2); 11:17; 12:8(3); 10; 15(2); 18; 21; 14:15(2); 20; 15:6; 10; 13; 14; 24; 30; 32(2); 33; 16:14; 15; 16; 20; 24; **1Cor** 1:2; 17; 2:1; 3; 4; 13; 3:2(2); 9; 19; 4:3; 8; 12; 21; 5:4; 8(3); 9; 10(3); 11; 6:6; 7; 9; 20; 7:5; 12; 13; 23; 24; 8:7; 9:13; 23; 10:5; 13; 20; 11:5; 32; 12:26(2); 30; 13:1; 14:5(2); 6; 15(4); 16; 18; 19; 21; 23; 39; 15:10; 32; 35; 16:4; 6; 7; 10; 11; 12; 14; 16; 19; 20; 21; 23; 24; **2Cor** 1:1; 12; 17; 21; 2:1; 4; 7; 3:3(2); 18; 4:14; 5:1; 2; 8; 6:1; 14(3); 15(2); 16; 7:3; 4; 8; 15; 8:4; 18; 19(2); 22; 9:4; 10:2; 12; 11:1(2); 2; 4; 9; 25; 32; 12:16; 18; 13:4; 11; 12; 14; **Gal** 1:2; 16; 18; 2:1(2); 3; 5; 12; 13(2); 20; 3:9; 4:18; 20; 25; 30; 5:1; 24; 6:11; 18; **Eph** 1:3; 13; 2:5; 19; 3:12; 16; 18; 19; 4:2(2); 14; 19; 25; 28; 31; 5:6; 7; 11; 18(2); 26; 6:2; 3; 5; 6; 7; 9; 14; 15; 18(2); 23; 24; **Phil** 1:1; 4; 11; 20; 23; 25; 27; 2:6; 12; 17; 18; 22(2); 23; 29; 4:3(3); 6; 9; 14; 15; 21; 23; **Col** 1:9; 11(2); 2:4; 5; 7; 11; 12(2); 13; 19; 20; 22; 3:1; 3; 4; 9; 16; 22; 4:2; 6(2); 8; **1Th** 1:6; 2:2; 4; 17; 3:4; 13; 4:11; 14; 16(3); 17(2); 18; 5:3; 10; 26; 28; **2Th** 1:6; 7(2); 9; 11; 2:5; 8(2); 9; 10; 3:1; 8; 10; 12; 14; 16; 17; 18; **1Ti** 1:10; 14; 2:9(2); 10; 11; 15; 3:4; 6; 4:2; 3; 4; 14; 5:2; 6:6; 10; 21; **2Ti** 1:3; 4; 9; 2:4; 10; 11(2); 12; 22; 3:6(2); 4:2; 11(2); 13(2); 16; 17; 22(2); **Titus** 2:15; 3:15(2); **Philem** 1:13; 19; 25; **Heb** 1:9; 2:4(2); 7; 9; 3:10; 17(2); 4:2; 13; 15; 5:2; 7; 7:21; 8:8(3); 9; 10; 9:4; 11; 19; 21; 22; 23(2); 24; 25; 10:1; 16; 22(2); 11:7; 9(2); 25; 31(2); 37; 12:1(2); 7(2); 14; 17; 18; 20; 28; 13:3; 5; 9(3); 12; 16; 17(2); 23; 25; **Jas** 1:6; 11; 13; 17; 18; 21; 2:1; 2; 22; 3:4; 13(2); 4:4; 5:14; **1Pet** 1:7; 8; 12; 18; 19; 22; 2:15; 18; 20; 3:2; 6; 7; 15; 4:1; 4; 13; 5:5; 13; 14(2); **2Pet** 1:1; 18; 2:3; 6; 7; 8; 13(2); 14; 16; 17; 20; 3:6; 8; 10(2); 12; 17; **1Jn** 1:1; 2; 3(3); 6; 7; 2:1; 19; **2Jn** 2; 3; 12; **3Jn** 10; 13; **Jude** 9; 12; 14; 23; 24; **Rev** 1:7; 12; 13(2); 2:12; 16; 22; 23; 27; 3:4; 17; 18; 20(2); 21(2); 4:1; 5:1; 2; 12; 6:8(5); 10; 7:2; 9; 10; 8:3; 4; 5; 7; 8; 13; 9:19; 10:1; 3; 11:6; 12:1; 2; 5; 9; 17(2); 13:4; 7; 10(2); 14:1; 2; 4; 7; 9; 10; 15; 18; 15:2; 6; 8; 16:8; 9; 17:1; 2(2); 4; 6(3); 12; 14(2); 16; 18:1; 2; 3; 8; 9; 16; 21; 19:2; 13; 15(2); 17; 20(3); 21(2); 20:4; 6; 21:3(3); 8; 9; 15; 16; 19; 22:12; 21

WITHIN

Gen 6:14; 9:21; 18:12; 24; 26; 25:22; 39:11; 40:13; 19; **Ex** 20:10; 25:11; 26:33; 37:2; **Lev** 10:18; 13:55; 14:41; 16:2; 12; 15; 25:29(2); 30; 26:25; **Num** 4:10; 18:7; **Deut** 5:14; 12:12; 17; 18; 14:27; 28; 29; 15:7; 22; 16:5; 11; 14; 17:2; 8; 23:10; 24:14; 26:12; 28:43; 31:12; 32:25; **Josh** 1:11; 19:1; 9; 21:41; **Judg** 7:16; 9:51; 11:18; 26; 14:12; 15:1; **1Sa** 13:11; 14:14; 25:36; 37; 26:7; **2Sa** 7:2; 20:4; **1Kin** 6:15; 16; 18; 19; 21; 23; 27; 29; 30; 7:8; 9; 31; **2Kin** 4:27; 6:30; 7:11; 11:8; **2Chr** 3:4; **Ezr** 4:15; 10:8; 9; **Neh** 4:22; 6:10; **Job** 6:4; 14:22; 19:27; 20:13; 14; 24:11; 32:18; **Ps** 36:1; 39:3; 40:8; 10; 42:6; 11; 43:5; 45:13; 51:10; 55:4; 94:19; 101:2; 7; 103:1; 109:22; 122:2; 7(2); 8; 142:3; 143:4(2); 147:13; **Prov** 22:18; 26:24; **Eccl** 9:14; **Song** 4:1; 3; 6:7; **Is** 7:8; 16:14; 21:16; 26:9; 56:5; 60:18; 63:11; **Jer** 4:14; 23:9; 28:3; 11; **Lam** 1:20; **Eze** 1:27; 2:10; 3:24; 7:15; 11:19; 12:24; 36:26; 27; 40:7; 8; 16; 43; 41:9; 17; 44:17; **Dan** 6:12; 11:20; **Hos** 11:8; **Jonah** 2:7; **Mic** 3:3; 5:6; **Zeph** 3:3; **Zec** 12:1; **Mt** 3:9; 9:3; 21; 23:25; 26; 27; 28; **Mk** 2:8; 7:21; 23; 14:4; 58; **Lk** 3:8; 7:39; 49; 11:7; 40; 12:17; 16:3; 17:21; 18:4; 19:44; 24:32; **Jn** 20:26; **Acts** 5:23; **Rom** 8:23; **1Cor** 5:12; **2Cor** 7:5; **Heb** 6:19; **Rev** 4:8; 5:1

WITHOUT

Gen 1:2; 6:14; 9:22; 19:16; 24:11; 31; 37:33; 41:44; 49; **Ex** 12:5; 21:11; 25:11; 26:35; 27:21; 29:1; 14; 33:7(2); 37:2; 40:22; **Lev** 1:3; 10; 3:1; 6; 4:3; 12; 21; 23; 28; 32; 5:15; 18; 6:6; 11; 8:17; 9:2; 3; 11; 10:12; 13:46; 55; 14:10(2); 40; 41; 16:27; 22:19; 23:12; 18; 24:3; 14; 26:43; **Num** 5:3; 4; 6:14(3); 15:24; 35; 36; 19:2; 3; 9; 20:19; 28:3; 9; 11; 19; 31; 29:2; 8; 13; 17; 20; 23; 26; 29; 32; 36; 31:13; 19; 35:5; 22(2); 26; 27; **Deut** 8:9; 23:12; 25:5; 32:4; 25; **Josh** 3:10; 6:23; **Judg** 2:23; 6:5; 7:12; 11:30; **Ruth** 4:14; **1Sa** 19:5; 30:8; **2Sa** 23:4; **1Kin** 6:6; 29; 30; 7:9; 8:8; 22:1; **2Kin** 10:24; 11:15; 16:18; 18:25; 23:4; 6; 25:16; **1Chr** 2:30; 32; 21:24; 22:3; 14; **2Chr** 5:9; 12:3; 15:3(3); 21:20; 24:8; 32:3; 5; 33:14; **Ezr** 6:9; 7:22; 10:13; **Neh** 13:20; **Job** 2:3; 4:20; 21; 5:9; 6:6; 7:6; 8:11(2); 9:10; 17; 10:22; 11:15; 12:25; 24:7; 10; 26:2; 30:28; 31:19; 39; 33:9; 34:6; 20; 24; 35(2); 35:16; 36:12; 38:2; 39:16; 41:33; 42:3; **Ps** 7:4; 25:3; 31:11; 35:7(2); 19; 59:4; 69:4; 105:34; 109:3; 119:78; 161; **Prov** 1:11; 20; 3:30; 5:23; 6:15; 7:12; 11:22; 15:22; 16:8; 19:2; 22:13; 23:29; 24:27; 28; 25:14; 28; 29:1; **Eccl** 10:11; **Song** 6:8; 8:1; **Is** 5:9; 14; 6:11(2); 10:4; 33:7; 36:10; 45:17; 52:3; 4; 55:1(2); **Jer** 2:15; 32; 4:7; 23; 5:21; 9:11; 21; 15:13; 21:4; 22:13; 26:9; 32:43; 33:10(5); 12(2); 34:22; 44:19; 22; 46:19; 48:9; 49:31; 51:29; 37; 52:20; **Lam** 1:6; 3:49; 52; **Eze** 2:10; 7:15; 14:23; 17:9; 33:15; 38:11; 40:19; 40; 44; 41:9; 17(2); 25; 42:7; 43:21; 22; 23(2); 25; 45:18; 23; 46:2; 4(2); 6(2); 13; 47:2; **Dan** 2:34; 45; 8:25; 11:18; **Hos** 3:4(6); 7:1; 11; **Joel** 1:6; **Zec** 2:4; **Mt** 5:22; 10:29; 12:46; 47; 13:34; 57; 15:16; 26:69; **Mk** 1:45; 3:31; 32; 4:11; 34; 6:4; 7:15; 18(2); 11:4; 14:58; **Lk** 1:10; 74; 6:49; 8:20; 11:40; 13:25; 20:28; 29; 22:35; **Jn** 1:3; 8:7; 15:5; 25; 18:16; 19:23; 20:11; **Acts** 5:23; 26; 9:9; 10:29; 12:5; 14:17; 25:17; **Rom** 1:9; 20; 31(2); 2:12(2); 3:3; 21; 28; 4:6; 5:6; 7:8; 9; 10:14; 11:29; 12:9; **1Cor** 4:8; 5:12; 13; 6:18; 7:32; 35; 9:18; 21(4); 11:11(2); 14:7; 10; 16:10; **2Cor** 7:5; 10:13; 15; 11:28; **Eph** 1:4; 2:12(2); 3:21; 5:27; **Phil** 1:10; 14; 2:14; 15; **Col**

2:11; 4:5; **1Th** 1:3; 2:13; 4:12; 5:17; **1Ti** 2:8; 3:7; 16; 5:21; 6:14; **2Ti** 1:3; 3:3; **Philem** 1:14; **Heb** 4:15; 7:3(3); 7; 20; 21; 9:7; 14; 18; 22; 28; 10:23; 28; 11:6; 40; 12:8; 14; 13:5; 11; 12; 13; **Jas** 2:13; 18; 20; 26(2); 3:17(2); **1Pet** 1:17; 19(2); 3:1; 4:9; **2Pet** 2:17; 3:14; **Jude** 12(3); **Rev** 11:2; 14:5; 10; 20; 22:15

WORSE

Gen 19:9; **2Sa** 19:7; **1Kin** 16:25; **2Kin** 14:12; **1Chr** 19:16; 19; **2Chr** 6:24; 25:22; 33:9; **Jer** 7:26; 16:12; **Dan** 1:10; **Mt** 9:16; 12:45; 27:64; **Mk** 2:21; 5:26; **Lk** 11:26; **Jn** 2:10; 5:14; **1Cor** 8:8; 11:17; **1Ti** 5:8; **2Ti** 3:13(2); **2Pet** 2:20

WORST

Eze 7:24

WOULD

Gen 2:19; 21:7; 30:34; 42:21; 22; 43:7; 44:22; **Ex** 2:4; 8:32; 9:35; 10:20; 27; 11:10; 13:15; 16:3; **Num** 11:29(2); 14:2(2); 20:3; 21:23; 22:18; 29(2); 24:13; **Deut** 1:26; 43; 45; 2:30; 3:26; 5:29; 7:8; 8:20; 9:25; 10:10; 23:5; 21; 28:56; 67(2); 32:26(2); 29; **Josh** 5:6(2); 7:7; 17:12; 24:10; **Judg** 1:27; 34; 35; 2:17; 3:4; 8:19; 24(2); 9:29(2); 11:17(2); 13:23(3); 14:6; 15:1; 19:10; 25; 20:13; **Ruth** 1:13(2); **1Sa** 2:16; 25; 13:13; 15:9; 18:2; 20:9; 22:17; 22; 26:23; 31:4; **2Sa** 2:21; 4:6; 10; 6:10; 11:20; 12:8; 17; 18; 13:14; 16; 25; 14:16; 29(2); 15:4; 18:11; 12; 33; 23:15; 16; 17; **1Kin** 8:12; 13:33; 18:32; 20:33; 21:4; 22:18; 49; **2Kin** 2:1; 3:14; 5:3(2); 7:2; 8:19; 13:23; 14:11; 27; 17:14; 18:12; 24:4; **1Chr** 10:4; 11:17; 18; 19; 13:4; 19:19; 27:23; **2Chr** 6:1; 10:16; 12:12; 15:13; 18:17; 21:7; 24:19; 25:20; 33:10; 35:22; **Ezr** 10:8; 19; **Neh** 6:11; 14; 9:24; 29; 30; 10:30; 31(2); **Est** 3:4; 6:6; 8:11; 9:5; 27; **Job** 5:8(2); 6:3; 8; 9(2); 10; 7:16; 8:6; 9:15(2); 16; 21(2); 35; 11:5; 6; 12; 13:3; 5; 16:5; 23:4; 5(3); 6; 27:22; 30:1; 31:12; 35(2); 36; 37(2); 32:22; 34:27; 36:16; 41:32; **Ps** 22:8; 35:25; 40:5; 50:12; 51:16; 55:6; 7; 8; 12; 56:1; 2; 57:3; 69:4; 81:11(2); 106:23; 107:8; 15; 21; 31; 119:57; 142:4; **Prov** 1:25; 30; **Song** 3:4; 8:1; 2(3); 7(2); **Is** 27:4(3); 28:12; 30:15; 42:24; 54:9; **Jer** 8:18; 10:7; 13:11; 18:10; 22:24; 29:19; 36:25(2); 38:26; 49:9; 51:9; **Lam** 4:12; **Eze** 3:6; 6:10; 13:6; 20:8; 13; 15; 21; 23; 38:17; **Dan** 1:8; 2:8; 16(2); 18; 5:19(4); 7:19; 9:2; **Hos** 7:1; 11:7; **Obad** 5(2); **Jonah** 3:10; 4:5; **Zec** 7:13(2); **Mal** 1:10; **Mt** 2:18; 5:42; 7:12; 8:34; 11:21; 23; 12:7; 38; 14:5; 7; 16:1; 18:23; 30; 22:3; 23:30; 37(2); 24:43(3); 27:15; 34; **Mk** 3:2; 13; 5:10; 6:19; 26; 48; 7:24; 26; 9:30; 10:35; 36; 11:16; **Lk** 1:62; 74; 5:3; 6:7; 31; 7:3; 36; 39; 8:31; 32; 41; 9:53; 10:1; 2; 12:39(2); 13:34(2); 15:16; 28; 16:26(2); 18:4; 13; 15; 19:27; 40; 22:49; 24:28; **Jn** 1:43; 4:10; 40; 47; 5:46; 6:6; 11; 15; 7:1; 44; 8:39; 42; 9:27; 12:21; 14:2; 28; 15:19; 18:30; 36; **Acts** 2:30; 5:24; 7:5; 25(2); 26; 39; 8:31; 9:38; 10:10; 11:23; 12:6; 14:13; 16:3; 27; 17:20; 18:14; 19:30; 31; 33; 20:16; 21:14; 22:30; 23:12; 15; 20; 28; 24:6; 25:3; 4; 20; 22; 26:5; 29; 27:30; 28:18; **Rom** 1:13; 5:7; 7:15; 16; 19(2); 20; 21; 11:25; 16:19; **1Cor** 2:8; 4:8; 18; 7:7; 32; 10:1; 20; 11:3; 31; 12:1; 14:5; **2Cor** 1:8; 2:1; 8; 5:4; 8:4; 6; 9:5; 10:9; 11:1; 12:6; 20(2); **Gal** 1:7; 2:10; 3:2; 8; 4:15; 17; 5:12; 17; **Eph** 3:16; **Phil** 1:12; **Col** 1:27; 2:1; 4:3; **1Th** 2:9; 12; 18; 4:1; 13; **2Th** 1:11; 3:10; **Philem** 1:13; 14; **Heb** 4:8; 10:2; 11:32; 12:17; **1Jn** 2:19; **2Jn** 12; **3Jn** 10; **Rev** 3:15; 13:15

WOULDEST

Gen 30:15; 31:30; 31; **Ex** 7:16; 23:5; **Deut** 8:2; 21:11; 28:62; **Josh** 15:18; **2Sa** 14:11; 18:13; **1Kin** 1:16; 18:9; **2Kin** 4:13; 5:13; 6:22; **1Chr** 4:10(2); **2Chr** 6:20; 20:10; **Ezr** 9:14; **Neh** 2:5; **Job** 8:5; 14:13(3); **Is** 48:8; 64:1(2); **Lk** 16:27; **Jn** 4:10; 11:40; 21:18(2); **Acts** 23:20; 24:4; **Heb** 10:5; 8

YE

Gen 3:1; 3(3); 4; 5(2); 4:23; 9:4; 7; 17:10; 11; 18:5(3); 19:2; 8; 22:5; 24:49; 26:27(2); 29:4; 5; 7; 31:6; 32:4; 19(2); 20; 34:9; 10(2); 11; 12; 15; 17; 30; 40:7; 42:1; 7; 9(2); 12; 14; 15(2); 16(2); 19(2); 20; 22; 33; 34(3); 36(2); 38(2); 43:3; 5; 6(2); 7; 27; 29; 44:4; 5; 10; 15(2); 19; 23; 27; 29(2); 45:4; 5; 9; 13(3); 17; 18; 19; 24; 46:34(2); 47:23; 24; 49:2; 50:17; 20; 21; 25; **Ex** 1:16(2); 18; 22(2); 2:18; 20; 3:12; 18; 21(2); 22(2); 4:15; 5:4; 5; 7; 8(2); 11(2); 14; 17(3); 18; 19; 21; 6:7; 8:25; 28(2); 9:28; 30; 10:2; 11(2); 24; 11:7; 12:3; 5; 6; 10(2); 11(2); 13; 14(2); 15(2); 17(2); 18; 20(2); 22; 24; 25(2); 26; 27; 31(2); 32; 46; 13:3; 4; 19; 14:2; 13(3); 14; 15:21; 16:3; 6; 7(2); 8; 12(3); 16; 23(2); 25; 26; 28; 29; 17:2(2); 19:4; 5(2); 6; 12; 20:20; 22; 23(2); 22:21; 22; 31(3); 23:9(2); 25; 24:1; 14; 25:2; 3; 9; 19; 30:9(2); 32; 37; 31:13(2); 14; 32:30; 33:5; 34:13; 35:1; 3; 5; **Lev** 1:2; 2:11(2); 12; 3:17; 7:23; 24; 26; 32; 8:32; 33; 35(2); 9:3; 6; 10:6; 7(2); 9(2); 10; 11; 13; 14; 17; 18; 11:2; 3; 4; 8(2); 9(2); 11(2); 13; 21; 22; 24; 33; 39; 42; 43(3); 44(3); 45; 14:34; 15:31; 16:29; 30; 31; 17:14; 18:3(4); 4; 5; 24; 26; 28; 30(3); 19:2; 3; 4; 5(2); 6; 9; 11; 12; 15; 19; 23(2); 25; 26(2); 27; 28; 30; 33; 34; 35; 36; 37; 20:7; 8; 15; 22; 23; 24; 25(2); 26(2); 22:19; 20; 22; 24(2); 25; 28; 29; 30; 31; 32; 23:2; 3; 4; 6; 7(2); 8(2); 10(2); 12(2); 14(2); 15(2); 16(2); 17; 18; 19; 21(2); 22; 24; 25(2); 27; 28; 31; 32(2); 35; 36(3); 37; 38; 39(2); 40(2); 41(2); 42; 24:22; 25:2; 9; 10(3); 11; 12; 13; 14; 17; 18(2); 19; 20; 22(2); 23; 24; 44; 45; 46(2); 26:1(2); 2; 3; 5; 6; 7; 10; 12; 13; 14; 15(3); 16; 17(2); 18; 21; 23; 25(2); 26; 27; 29(2); 34; 35; 37; 38; **Num** 1:2; 4:18; 27; 32; 5:3(2); 6:23; 9:3(2); 14; 10:5; 6; 7(2); 9(4); 10; 11:18(3); 19; 20; 12:4; 8; 13:2; 20; 14:9(2); 28; 30; 31(2); 34(3); 41; 42; 43(2); 15:2; 12(2); 14; 15; 18; 19(2); 20(3); 21; 22; 29; 39(3); 40; 16:3(2); 7(2); 8; 10; 11; 17; 26; 28; 30; 41; 18:3; 5; 7; 26(2); 28(3); 29; 30; 31(2); 32(4); 19:3; 20:4; 5; 8; 10; 12(2); 24; 21:5; 17; 22:19; 25:5; 27:8; 9; 10; 11; 14; 28:2; 3; 11; 18; 19; 20; 23; 24; 25(2); 26(3); 27; 31; 29:1(2); 2; 7(3); 8; 12(3); 13; 17; 35(2); 36; 39; 31:4; 15; 19; 23(2); 24(3); 32:6; 7; 14; 15(2); 20(2); 22; 23(2); 29; 33:51; 52; 53; 54(4); 55(3); 34:2; 6; 7; 8; 10; 13; 18; 35:2; 4; 5; 6(3); 7(2); 8(3); 10; 11; 13(2); 14(2); 31; 32; 33(2); 34; **Deut** 1:6; 10; 11; 14; 17(3); 18; 19; 20; 22; 26; 27; 31(2); 32; 33; 39; 41(3); 42; 43; 45; 46(2); 2:3; 4(2); 6(4); 24; 3:18; 19; 20; 22; 4:1; 2(3); 4; 5(2); 11; 12(2); 14(2); 15(2); 16; 20; 22; 23; 25; 26(3); 27; 28; 5:1; 5; 23(2); 24; 28; 32(2); 33(4); 6:1(2); 3; 14; 16(2); 17; 7:5(2); 7(2); 12; 25; 8:1(2); 19; 20(2); 9:7(2); 8; 16(2); 18; 21; 22; 23(2); 24; 10:19(2); 11:2; 5; 8(3); 9; 10; 11; 13; 16; 17; 18; 19; 22; 23; 25; 27; 28(2); 31(2); 32; 12:1(2); 2(2); 3(2); 4; 5; 6; 7(4); 8; 9; 10(2); 11(2); 12(2); 16(2); 13:3; 4(2); 13; 14:1(2); 4; 6; 7; 8; 9(2); 10; 11; 12; 20; 21; 17:16; 18:15; 19:19; 20:2; 3(2); 18; 22:24(2); 23:4; 24:8; 9; 25:17; 27:2; 4(2); 12; 28:62(2); 63; 68; 29:2; 6(3); 7; 9(2); 10; 16(2); 17; 30:18(2); 31:5; 13(2); 19; 27; 29(2); 32:1; 3; 6; 43; 46; 47(2); 51(2); **Josh** 1:11; 14; 15; 2:5; 10(3); 12; 13; 14; 16; 3:3(2); 4(3); 8(2); 10; 4:3(3); 6; 7; 17; 22; 23; 24; 6:3(2); 4; 5; 10(2); 18(3); 22; 7:12; 13; 14; 8:2; 4(2); 7; 8(3); 9:6; 7; 8(2); 11; 22(2); 23; 10:19; 25; 18:3; 6; 22:2; 3; 4; 16(3); 18(2); 19; 24; 25(2); 27; 31(2); 23:3; 5; 6(2); 7; 8; 11; 12; 13; 14; 16(2); 24:6; 7; 8; 11; 13(5); 14; 15(2); 19; 20; 22(2); 27; **Judg** 2:2(4); 5:2; 3(2); 9; 10(2); 23(2); 6:10(2); 31(2); 7:17; 18; 8:15; 18; 19; 24; 9:7; 15; 16(3); 18; 19(2); 48; 10:12; 13; 14; 11:7(3); 9; 26; 12:2; 3(2); 4; 14:12; 13(2); 15; 18(2); 15:7; 10; 12; 18:6; 8; 9; 10(2); 14(2); 18; 24(3); 19:24; 20:7; 21:11(2); 21; 22(2); **Ruth** 1:8; 9; 11; 13(2); 21; 4:2; 9; 10; **1Sa** 2:23; 24; 29; 4:9(2); 6:3(2); 5(2); 6; 8; 21; 7:3; 8:17; 18(2); 22; 9:13(3); 19; 10:14; 19(2); 24; 11:9(2); 10; 12:1; 5; 11; 12(2); 13(2); 14(2); 15; 17(2); 20; 21(2); 25(3); 14:33; 38; 40; 15:6; 32; 17:8(2); 9; 25; 18:25; 21:14(2); 15; 22:7; 13; 23:21(2); 23; 25:6; 13; 26:16(2); 27:10; 29:10; 30:23; **2Sa** 1:21; 24; 2:5(2); 6; 7; 3:17; 38; 7:7; 11:15(2); 20(3); 21; 13:28; 15:10(2); 36(2); 16:10; 19:10; 11; 12(3); 13; 22(2); 42; 43(2); 21:3; 4; 24:2; **1Kin** 1:34; 35; 45; 9:6(2); 11:2; 12:6; 9; 24; 18:18; 21; 24; 25; 20:28; 33; 22:3; **2Kin** 1:3; 5; 2:3; 5; 16; 3:17(4); 19; 6:2; 11; 19; 32; 7:1; 9:11; 10:6(3); 8; 9; 13; 11:5; 6; 8(2); 12:7; 17:12; 13; 27; 35; 36(3); 37(2); 38(2); 39; 18:19; 22(2); 31(2); 32; 19:6; 10; 29(2); 22:13; 18; **1Chr** 12:17(2); 15:12(3); 13; 16:9; 10; 13(2); 15; 19; 28; 35; 17:6; 22:19; 28:8; **2Chr** 7:19; 10:6; 9; 11:4; 12:5; 13:5; 8(2); 9; 11; 12(2); 15:2(4); 7; 18:14; 25; 27; 30; 19:6(2); 9; 10(2); 20:15(2); 16(2); 17(2); 20(3); 23:4; 7; 24:5; 20(3); 28:9; 10; 11; 13(2); 29:5; 8; 11; 31; 30:6; 7(2); 8; 9(2); 32:10(2); 12; 13; 34:23; 26; **Ezr** 4:2; 3; 18; 21; 22; 6:6; 8; 7:25; 8:28; 29(2); 9:11; 12; 10:10; **Neh** 1:8; 9; 2:17; 19(2); 20; 4:12; 14; 20(2); 5:7; 8; 9(2); 11; 8:10; 11; 13:17; 18; 21(2); 25; **Est** 4:16; 8:8; **Job** 6:21(2); 26; 27(2); 12:2; 13:2; 4(3); 5; 7; 8(2); 9; 10; 16:2; 4; 17:10; 18:2; 19:2; 3(3); 5; 21; 22; 28; 29(2); 21:27; 28; 29(2); 34; 27:12(2); 32:6; 11; 13; 34:2(2); 10; 18; 42:7; 8; **Ps** 2:10(2); 12; 4:2(3); 6:8; 11:1; 14:6; 22:23(3); 24:7(3); 9(2); 27:8; 29:1; 30:4; 31:23; 24; 32:9; 11(2); 33:1; 34:9; 11; 47:1; 7; 48:13(2); 49:1(2); 50:22; 58:1(3); 2(2); 62:3(3); 8; 66:1; 8; 16; 68:13(2); 16(2); 26; 32; 34; 82:2; 6; 7; 90:3; 94:8(3); 95:7; 96:7; 97:7; 10; 12; 99:5; 100:1; 3; 103:20; 21(3); 104:35; 105:2; 3; 6(2); 45; 106:1; 48; 111:1; 112:1; 113:1(2); 9; 114:6(3); 115:11; 15; 116:19; 117:1(2); 2; 119:115; 134:1(2); 135:1(3); 2; 20; 21; 139:19; 146:1; 10; 147:1; 20; 148:1(2); 2(2); 3(2); 4(2); 7; 14; 149:1; 9; 150:1; 6; **Prov** 1:22(2); 24; 25; 4:1; 2; 5:7; 7:24; 8:5(3); 32; **Song** 1:5; 2:7(2); 3:3; 5(2); 11; 5:8(2); 6:13; 8:4; **Is** 1:5(2); 10(2); 12; 15(2); 19(2); 20(2); 29(3); 30; 2:3; 5; 22; 3:10; 14; 15(2); 6:9(2); 7:9(2); 13(2); 8:9(5); 12(2); 10:3(3); 12:3; 4; 13:2; 6; 16:1; 7; 18:2; 3(3); 19:11; 21:5; 12(2); 13(2); 22:9(2); 10(2); 11(2); 14; 23:1; 2; 6(2); 14; 24:15; 26:2; 4; 19; 27:2; 12(2); 28:12; 14; 15; 18; 22; 23; 29:1; 9; 30:12; 15(2); 16(2); 17(2); 21(3); 22; 29; 31:6; 32:9(2); 10(2); 11(2); 20; 33:11(2); 13(2); 34:1(2); 16; 35:3; 36:4; 7; 13; 16(2); 37:6; 10; 30(2); 40:1(2); 2; 3; 18(2); 21(3); 25; 41:14; 23; 24; 42:10; 17; 18(3); 43:10(2); 12; 18; 19; 44:8(2); 23(3); 26; 45:8; 11; 17; 19; 20; 21; 22; 46:5; 8; 12; 48:1; 6; 14; 16(2); 20(4); 49:1; 50:1; 11(4); 51:1(4); 7(3); 52:3(2); 9; 11(5); 12; 55:1(2); 2(2); 6(2); 12; 56:1; 9(2); 12; 57:3; 4(3); 14(2); 58:3; 4(3); 6; 61:6(3); 7; 62:6; 10; 11; 65:11; 12(3); 13(3); 14; 15; 18; 66:1; 5; 10(3); 11(2); 12(2); 13; 14; **Jer** 2:4; 7(2); 12(2); 29(2); 31; 3:13; 16; 20; 22; 4:4; 5(2); 10; 16; 5:1(2); 10; 14; 19(3); 22(2); 31; 6:1; 4; 6; 16(2); 18; 7:2; 4; 5(2); 6; 8; 9(2); 12; 13(3); 14; 23(2); 8:8; 9:4(2); 17; 20; 10:1; 11; 11:2; 4; 6; 13; 12:9; 13:15; 16; 17; 23; 14:13(2); 16:12(2); 13(3); 17:4; 20(2); 22(2); 24; 27; 18:6; 11; 13; 19:3; 20:13; 21:3; 4; 11; 22:3; 4; 5; 10; 26(2); 30; 23:2; 17; 20; 35; 36(2); 38(3); 25:3; 4; 5; 7(2); 8; 27; 28; 29(2); 34(3); 26:4; 5; 11; 12; 15(3); 27:4; 9(2); 10; 13; 14; 15(2); 29:5; 6(2); 7; 8; 12(2); 13(2); 15; 19; 20(2); 26; 28; 30:6; 22; 24; 31:6; 7(2); 10; 32:5(2); 36; 43; 33:10; 20; 34:14; 15(2); 16; 17; 35:5; 6(2); 7(4); 13; 14; 15(3); 18; 36:19; 37:7; 10; 18; 40:3; 10(3); 42:9; 10; 11; 13; 15(2); 16(3); 18(3); 19(2); 20(2); 21; 22(2); 44:2; 3; 7; 8(4); 9; 21(2); 22; 23(2); 25(2); 26; 29; 46:3; 4; 9(2); 14(2); 48:14; 17(2); 20; 26; 28; 49:3; 5; 8; 14; 28; 30; 50:2; 11(4); 14; 29; 45; 51:3(2); 27; 45(2); 46; 50; **Lam** 1:12; 4:15; **Eze** 5:7; 6:3; 7; 8(2); 13; 7:4; 9; 9:5(2); 7; 11:5; 6(2); 7; 8; 10(2); 11; 12(2); 17; 12:20; 22; 13:2; 5; 7(3); 8; 9; 11; 12; 14(3); 18(2); 19; 20(2); 21; 22; 23(2); 14:8; 22(2); 23(2); 15:7; 17:12; 21; 18:2(2); 3; 19; 25; 31(2); 32; 20:3; 7; 18; 20; 29; 30(2); 31(3); 32; 34; 38; 39(4); 41; 42; 43(4); 44(2); 21:24(3); 22:19; 21; 22(2); 23:40; 49(2); 24:21; 22(2); 23(2); 24(2); 25:5; 30:2; 33:10; 11(3); 20(2); 25(2); 26(4); 34:3(4); 4(6); 7; 9; 18(2); 19(2); 21(2); 31; 35:9; 13; 36:1; 3(2); 4; 6; 8(2); 9; 11; 22(2); 23; 25; 27; 28(2); 30; 31; 37:4; 5; 6(2); 13; 14(2); 39:17; 18; 19(3); 20; 44:6; 7(2); 8(2); 28; 30; 45:1(2); 6; 10; 13(2); 14; 20; 21; 47:13; 14; 18; 21; 22; 23; 48:8; 9; 20; 29; **Dan** 1:10; 2:5(2); 6(2); 8(2); 9(3); 3:5(2); 14; 15(5); 26; **Hos** 1:9; 10(2); 2:1; 4:1; 15(2); 18; 5:1(4); 8; 9:5; 10:13(3); 14:3; **Joel** 1:2(2); 3; 5(2); 11(3); 13(3); 14; 2:1; 12; 19; 22; 23; 26; 27; 3:4(3); 5; 6(2); 7; 9; 11; 13; 17; **Amos** 2:11; 12; 3:13; 4:1; 3(2); 5; 6; 8; 9; 10; 11(2); 5:1; 4(2); 6; 7; 11(5); 14(2); 22; 25; 26(2); 6:2(2); 3; 12; 13; 8:4; 9:7; **Obad** 1; 16; **Mic** 1:2; 10(2); 11; 2:3(2); 6; 8; 9(2); 10; 3:1; 6(2); 9; 6:1; 2(2); 5; 9; 16(2); 7:5(2); **Nah** 1:9; 2:9; **Hab** 1:5(2); **Zeph** 1:11; 2:3(3); 12(2); 3:8; **Hag** 1:4; 6(6); 9(3); 2:3; 4; 5(2); 17; **Zec** 1:3; 4(2); 2:9; 3:10; 6:15(2); 7:5(2); 6(3); 7; 8:9; 13(2); 15; 16(2); 9:12; 10:1; 11:2; 12; 14:5(3); **Mal** 1:2; 5; 6; 7(3); 8(2); 10; 12(2); 13(4); 2:1; 2(3); 4; 8(3); 9; 13; 14; 16; 17(3); 3:1(2); 6; 7(2); 8(2); 9(2); 10; 12; 13; 14; 18; 4:2; 3; 4; **Mt** 2:8; 3:2; 3; 5:11; 13; 14; 20; 21; 27; 33; 38; 39; 43; 45; 46(2); 47(2); 48; 6:1(2); 7; 8(3); 9; 14; 15; 16; 24; 25(3); 26; 28; 30; 32; 33; 7:1; 2(3); 6; 7; 11; 12(2); 13; 16; 20; 23; 8:26(2); 9:4; 6; 13; 28; 38; 10:5; 7; 8; 11(2); 12; 14; 16; 18; 19(2); 20; 22; 23(2); 27(3); 31(2); 11:4; 7; 8; 9; 14; 17(2); 28; 29; 12:3; 5; 7(2); 34; 13:14(2); 17(2); 18; 29(2); 30; 51; 14:16; 15:3; 5; 6; 7; 16; 17; 34; 16:2; 3(3); 8(3); 9(2); 10; 11(2); 15; 17:5; 20(2); 18:3(2); 10; 12; 18(2); 35; 19:4; 28(2); 20:4; 6; 7(2); 22(3); 23; 25; 32; 21:2; 3; 5; 13; 16; 21(3); 22(2); 24; 25; 28; 32(4); 42; 22:9(2); 18(2); 29; 31; 42; 23:3; 8(2); 10; 13(3); 14(2); 15(2); 16; 17; 19; 23(2); 24; 25; 27; 28(2); 29; 31(2); 32; 33(3); 34(2); 35; 37; 39(2); 24:2; 6(2); 9; 15; 20; 32; 33(2); 42; 44(2); 25:6; 9; 13; 30; 34; 35(3); 36(3); 40(2); 41; 42(2); 43(3); 45(2); 26:2; 10; 11(2); 15; 27; 31; 36; 38; 40; 41; 55(2); 64; 65; 66; 27:17; 21; 24; 65(2); 28:5(2); 7; 13; 19; **Mk** 1:3; 15; 17; 2:8; 10; 25; 4:13(2); 24(2); 40(2); 5:39; 6:10(2); 11; 31; 37; 38; 7:8(2); 9(2); 11; 12; 13(2); 18(2); 8:5; 17(4); 18(3); 19; 20; 21; 29; 9:16; 33; 41; 50; 10:36; 38(3); 39(2); 42; 11:2(2); 3(2); 5; 17; 24(4); 25(2); 26; 31; 12:10; 15; 24(2); 26; 27; 13:7(2); 9(2); 11(4); 13; 14; 18; 23; 28; 29(2); 33(2); 35(2); 14:6; 7(4); 13; 14; 27; 32; 34; 38(2); 48; 49; 62; 64(2); 71; 15:9; 12(2); 16:6; 7; 15; **Lk** 2:12; 49(2); 3:4; 4:23; 5:22; 24; 30; 34; 6:2; 3; 20; 21(4); 22; 23; 24; 25(2); 31(2); 32(2); 33(2); 34(3); 35(2); 36; 37(3); 38; 46; 7:22; 24; 25; 26; 32(2); 33; 34; 8:18; 9:4; 5; 13; 20; 55(2); 10:2; 5; 8; 10; 11; 23; 24(2); 11:2; 9; 13; 18; 39; 40; 41; 42(2); 43; 44; 46(3); 47; 48(3); 52(3); 12:1; 3(2); 5; 7; 11(3); 12; 22(2); 24; 26(2); 28; 29(4); 30; 31; 33; 36; 40(2); 51; 54(2); 55(2); 56(3); 57; 13:2; 3(2); 4; 5(2); 25(2); 26; 27(2); 28; 32; 34; 35(2); 16:9; 11; 12; 13; 15; 17:6(2); 10(2); 22(2); 19:30(2); 31(2); 33; 46; 20:5; 23; 21:6; 8(2); 9; 14; 16; 17; 19; 20; 30; 31(3); 36(2); 22:10; 11; 26; 28; 30; 35; 40; 46(2); 51; 52; 53; 67; 68; 70; 23:14(2); 24:5; 17(2); 38; 39; 41; 48; 49(2); **Jn** 1:26; 38; 51; 3:7; 11; 12(2); 28; 4:20; 21; 22(2); 32; 35; 38(2); 48(2); 5:20; 33; 34; 35; 37; 38(2); 39(2); 40(2); 42; 43(2); 44; 45; 46(2); 47(2); 6:26(3); 29; 36; 53(2); 62; 67; 7:8; 19; 21; 22; 23; 28(3); 34(2); 36(2); 45; 47; 8:14; 15; 19(3); 21(2); 22; 23(2); 24(3); 28(2); 31(2); 32; 33; 36; 37(2); 38(2); 39(2); 40; 41; 42; 43(2); 44(2); 45; 46; 47(2); 49; 54; 55; 9:19; 27(3); 30; 41(3); 10:20; 25; 26(2); 32; 34; 36; 38(2); 11:15; 34; 39; 49; 56; 12:8(2); 19(2); 35; 36(2); 13:10; 11; 12; 13(2); 14; 15; 17(3); 19; 33(2); 34(2); 35(2); 14:1; 3; 4(2); 7(3); 13; 14; 15; 17; 19(2); 20(2); 24; 28(3); 29; 15:3; 4(2); 5(2); 7(3); 8(2); 9; 10(2); 12; 14(2); 16(3); 17; 18; 19(2); 27(2); 16:1; 4; 10; 12; 16(2); 17(2); 19(3); 20(2); 22; 23(2); 24(2); 26; 27; 31; 32; 33(2); 18:4; 7; 8; 29; 31; 39(2); 19:4; 6; 35; 20:22; 23(2); 31(2); 21:5; 6; 10; **Acts** 1:4; 5; 8(2); 11(3); 2:14(2); 15; 22(2); 23; 33; 36; 38; 3:12(3); 13; 14; 16; 17; 19; 22; 25; 4:7; 8; 10; 19; 5:8; 9; 25; 28(3); 30; 35(2); 39(2); 6:3; 7:4; 26(2); 37; 42(2); 43(2); 49; 51(3); 52; 8:24(2); 10:21(2); 28; 29; 37; 11:16; 13:15(2); 16; 25; 39; 41(2); 46; 14:15(2); 15:1(2); 7; 10; 24; 29(4); 16:15; 17:22(2); 23; 18:14; 15; 19:2(2); 3; 15; 25; 26; 35; 36; 37; 39; 20:18; 25; 34; 35; 21:13; 22:1; 3; 23:15(2); 25:24; 27:21; 31; 33; 28:26(2); **Rom** 1:6; 11; 6:3; 11; 12; 13; 14; 16(4); 17(2); 18; 19; 20(2); 21(2); 22; 7:1; 4(2); 8:9; 13(4); 15(2); 9:26; 11:2; 25(2); 30; 12:1; 2(2); 13:5; 6; 14; 14:1; 15:6; 7; 10; 11(2); 13; 14; 30; 16:2(2); 17; **1Cor** 1:5; 7; 8; 9; 10(2); 13; 26; 30; 3:2(2); 3(2); 4; 5; 9(2); 16(2); 17; 23; 4:6; 8(4); 10(3); 15(2); 16; 21; 5:2; 4; 6; 7(2); 10; 12; 6:2(2); 3; 4; 7(3); 8; 9; 11(3); 15; 16; 19(3); 20; 7:1; 5(2); 23(2); 35; 8:12(2); 9:1; 2; 13; 24(2); 10:1; 7; 10; 13(2); 15; 20; 21(2); 27; 31(2); 11:1; 2; 17; 18; 20; 22(2); 25(2); 26(2); 33; 34; 12:2(3); 27; 14:1; 5(2); 9(3); 12(3); 18; 20; 23; 26; 31; 15:1(2); 2(3); 11; 17; 58(2); 16:1; 3; 6; 13; 15; 16; 18; 20; **2Cor** 1:7(2); 11; 13(2); 14(2); 15; 24; 2:4(2); 7; 8; 9; 10; 3:2; 3; 5:12; 20; 6:1; 11; 12(2); 13; 14; 16; 17; 18; 7:3; 9(4); 11(2); 15; 8:7(2); 9(2); 11; 13; 24; 9:3; 4; 5; 8; 10:7; 11:1; 4(4); 7; 19(2); 20; 12:11; 13; 19; 20; 13:3; 5(3); 6; 7(2); 9; **Gal** 1:6; 9; 13; 3:1; 2; 3(2); 4; 7; 26; 28; 29(2); 4:6; 8(2); 9(3); 10; 12(2); 13; 14; 15(2); 17; 21(2); 5:2; 4; 7(2); 10; 13; 15(2); 16; 17(2); 18(2); 6:1; 2; 11; **Eph** 1:13(4); 18; 2:2; 5; 8; 11; 12; 13; 19; 22; 3:2; 4(2); 13; 17; 19; 4:1(2); 4; 17; 20; 21; 22; 24; 26; 30; 32; 5:1; 5; 7; 8(2); 15; 17; 6:4; 9; 11; 13; 16; 21; 22; **Phil** 1:7; 10(2); 12; 27; 30; 2:2(2); 12; 15(2); 18; 22; 26; 28(2); 3:15; 17; 4:9; 10(2); 14(2); 15(2); 16; **Col** 1:4; 5; 6; 7; 9; 10; 23(2); 2:1; 6(2); 7; 10; 11; 12; 20(2); 3:1; 3; 4; 7(2); 8; 9; 13; 15(2); 17; 23; 24(2); 4:1; 6(2); 10; 12; 16; **1Th** 1:5; 6; 9; 2:2; 5; 8; 9; 10; 11; 12; 13(3); 14(2); 19; 20; 3:4; 6; 8; 4:1(3); 2; 3; 9(2); 10(2); 11; 12(2); 13; 5:1; 4; 5; 11; **2Th** 1:4; 5(2); 12; 2:2; 5; 6; 15; 3:4; 6; 7; 13; **Heb** 3:7; 15; 4:7; 5:11; 12(2); 6:10(2); 12; 10:25; 29; 32(2); 33(2); 34(2); 36(3); 12:3; 4; 5; 7; 8(2); 17; 18; 22; 25; 13:5; 23; **Jas** 1:2; 4; 22; 2:3; 4; 6; 7; 8(2); 9(2); 12; 16(2); 24; 3:14; 4:2(5); 3(3); 4(2); 5; 8(2); 13; 14; 15; 16; 5:1; 3; 5(2); 6; 8; 9; 11; 12; 16; **1Pet** 1:6(2); 8(3); 15; 16; 17; 18(2); 22(2); 2:2; 3; 5; 9(2); 15; 20(4); 21(2); 24; 25; 3:1; 6(2); 7; 8; 9(2); 13; 14(2); 17; 4:4; 7; 13(2); 14(2); 5:4; 5; 10; 12; 14; **2Pet** 1:4; 8; 10(2); 12; 15; 19(2); 3:2; 11; 14(2); 17(3); **1Jn** 1:3; 2:1; 7(2); 13(3); 14(3); 18; 20(2); 21(2); 24(3); 27(3); 29(2); 3:5; 11; 15; 4:2; 3; 4; 5:13(3); **2Jn** 6(2); **3Jn** 12; **Jude** 3; 5; 17; 20; **Rev** 2:10(2); 25; 12:12(2); 18:4(2); 20; 19:5(2); 18

YEA

Gen 3:1; 17:16; 20:6; 27:33; **Lev** 25:35; **Num** 10:32; **Deut** 33:3; **Judg** 5:29; **1Sa** 15:20; 21:5; 24:11; **2Sa** 19:30; 22:39; **2Kin** 2:3; 5; 16:3; **1Chr** 16:21; **2Chr** 26:20; **Ezr** 9:2; **Neh** 5:15; 16; 6:10; 9:18; 21; **Est** 5:12; **Job** 1:15; 17; 2:4; 5:19; 6:10; 27; 29; 9:10; 11:15; 18; 19; 12:3; 14:10; 15:4; 6; 15; 18:5; 19:18; 20:8; 25; 21:7; 22:25; 25:5; 28:27; 30:2; 8; 9; 31:8; 11; 32:12; 33:14; 22; 34:12; 36:7; 40:5; 41:24; **Ps** 7:4; 5; 8:7; 16:6; 18:10; 14; 48; 19:10; 23:4; 25:3; 27:6; 29:5; 10; 31:9; 35:10; 15; 21; 27; 37:10; 36; 40:8; 41:9; 43:4; 44:22; 57:1; 58:2; 59:16; 68:3; 16; 18; 72:11; 78:19; 38; 41; 83:11; 17; 84:2; 3; 85:12; 90:17; 93:4; 94:23; 102:13; 26; 105:12; 14; 106:24; 37; 109:30; 116:5; 118:11; 119:34; 103; 127; 128:6; 137:1; 138:5; 139:12; 144:15; **Prov** 2:3; 9; 3:24; 6:16; 7:26; 8:18; 19; 16:4; 22:10; 23:16; 34; 24:5; 29:17; 30:15; 18; 29; 31:20; **Eccl** 1:16; 2:18; 23; 3:19; 4:3; 8(2); 6:6; 7:18; 8:17; 9:3; 10:3; 12:9; **Song** 1:16; 5:1; 16; 6:9; 8:1; **Is** 1:15; 5:10; 29; 14:8; 19:21; 24:16; 26:8; 9; 11; 29:5; 30:33; 32:13; 40:24(3); 41:10(2); 23; 26(3); 42:13; 43:7; 13; 44:8; 12; 15(2); 16; 19; 45:21; 46:6; 7; 11; 47:3; 48:8(3); 15; 49:15;

55:1; 56:9; 11; 59:15; 60:12; 66:3; **Jer** 2:37; 5:28; 8:7; 12:2(2); 6; 14:5; 18; 23:11; 26; 27:21; 31:3; 19; 32:41; 46:16; 51:44; **Lam** 1:8; **Eze** 6:14; 16:6; 8; 9; 28; 52; 17:10; 22:2; 21; 29; 23:36; 26:18; 28:26; 32:10; 28; 34:6; 36:12; 37:27; 39:13; **Dan** 8:11; 9:11; 21; 10:19; 11:22; 24; 26; **Hos** 2:19; 4:3; 7:9; 8:10; 9:12; 16; 12:4; 11; **Joel** 1:16; 18; 2:3; 19; 3:4; **Amos** 8:6; **Obad** 13; 16; **Jonah** 3:8; **Mic** 3:7; **Nah** 1:5; **Hab** 2:5; **Zeph** 2:1; **Hag** 2:19; **Zec** 7:12; 8:22; 10:7; 14:5; 21; **Mal** 2:2; 3:15(2); 4:1; **Mt** 5:37(2); 9:28; 11:9; 13:51; 21:16; 26:60; **Lk** 2:35; 7:26; 11:28; 12:5; 57; 14:26; 24:22; **Jn** 11:27; 16:2; 32; 21:15; 16; **Acts** 3:16; 24; 5:8; 7:43; 20:34; 22:27; **Rom** 3:4; 31; 8:34; 14:4; 15:20; **1Cor** 1:28; 2:10; 4:3; 9:16; 15:15; 16:6; **2Cor** 1:17(2); 18; 19(2); 20; 5:16; 7:11(6); 13; 8:3; **Gal** 4:17; **Phil** 1:18; 2:17; 3:8; **2Ti** 3:12; **Philem** 1:20; **Heb** 11:36; **Jas** 2:18; 5:12(2); **1Pet** 5:5; **2Pet** 1:13; **3Jn** 12; **Rev** 14:13

YES

Mt 17:25; **Mk** 7:28; **Rom** 3:29; 10:18

YET

Gen 6:3; 7:4; 8:10; 12; 15:16; 18:22; 29; 32; 20:12; 21:26; 25:6; 27:30; 29:7; 9; 27; 30; 31:14; 30; 37:5; 8; 9; 38:5; 40:13; 19; 23; 43:6; 7; 27; 28; 44:4; 14; 45:3; 6; 11; 26; 28; 46:30; 48:7; **Ex** 4:18; 5:11; 18; 9:17; 30; 34; 10:7; 11:1; 21:22; 32:32; 33:12; 36:3; **Lev** 5:17; 11:7; 21; 13:40; 41; 25:22; 51; 26:18; 24; 44; **Num** 9:10; 11:33; 19:13; 22:15; 20; 30:16; 32:14; 15; **Deut** 1:32; 9:29; 12:9; 14:8; 20:6; 22:17; 29:4; 31:27; 32:52; **Josh** 3:4; 13:1; 2; 14:11; 17:12; 13; 18:2; **Judg** 1:35; 2:10; 17; 6:24; 31; 7:4; 8:4; 20; 9:5; 10:13; 15:7; 17:4; 19:19; 20:28; 21:14; **Ruth** 1:11; **1Sa** 3:6; 7(2); 8:9; 10:22; 12:20; 13:7; 21; 15:30; 16:11; 18:29; 20:14; 23:4; 22; 24:11; 25:29; **2Sa** 1:9; 3:35; 5:13; 22; 6:22; 7:19; 9:1; 3(2); 12:18; 22; 14:14; 18:12; 14; 22; 19:28(2); 35; 21:15; 20; 23:5; **1Kin** 1:14; 22; 42; 8:28; 47; 11:17; 12:2; 5; 6; 14:8; 19:18; 20:6; 32; 22:8; 43; **2Kin** 3:17; 4:6; 6:33; 8:19; 22; 13:23; 14:3; 4; 17:13; 19:30; **1Chr** 12:1; 14:13; 17:17; 20:6; 26:10; 29:1; **2Chr** 1:11; 6:16; 26; 37; 10:6; 13:6; 14:7; 16:8; 12; 18:7; 20:33; 24:19; 27:2; 28:22; 30:18; 32:15; 16; 33:17; 34:3; **Ezr** 3:6; 5:16; 9:9; 15; 10:2; **Neh** 1:9; 2:16; 5:5; 18; 6:4; 9:19; 28; 29; 30(2); 13:18; 26; **Est** 2:20; 5:13; 6:14; 8:3; **Job** 1:16; 17; 18; 3:26; 5:7; 6:10; 8:7; 12; 9:15; 16; 21; 31; 10:8; 15; 13:15; 14:9; 19:26; 20:7; 14; 21:32; 22:18; 24:12; 23; 29:5; 32:3; 33:14; 35:14; 15; 36:2; **Ps** 2:6; 37:10; 25; 36; 40:17; 42:5; 8; 11; 43:5; 44:17; 49:13; 55:21; 68:13; 71:14; 78:17; 30; 56; 90:10; 94:7; 107:41; 119:51; 83; 109; 110; 141; 143; 157; 129:2; 138:6; 139:16(2); 141:5; **Prov** 6:10; 8:26; 9:9; 11:24; 13:7(2); 19:7; 19; 23:35; 24:33; 27:22; 30:12; 25; 26; 27; 31:15; **Eccl** 1:7; 2:3; 19; 21; 4:2; 3; 8; 6:2; 6; 7; 7:28; 8:12; 17(2); 9:11(3); 15; 11:8; **Is** 6:13; 10:22; 25; 32; 14:1; 15; 17:6; 26:10; 27:10; 28:4; 12; 29:2; 17; 30:20; 31:2; 42:25(2); 44:1; 11; 46:7; 10; 49:4; 5; 15; 53:4; 7; 10; 56:8; 57:10; 58:2; 65:24; **Jer** 2:9; 11; 21; 22; 32; 35; 3:1; 8; 10; 4:27; 5:22(2); 28; 7:26; 9:20; 11:8; 12:1; 14:9; 15; 15:1; 9; 10; 18:23; 22:6; 24; 23:21(2); 32; 25:7; 27:15; 30:11; 31:5; 23; 39; 32:33; 33:1; 34:4; 36:24; 37:10; 40:5; 44:28; 46:28; 48:47; 51:33; 53; **Lam** 3:32; 4:17; **Eze** 2:5; 3:19; 6:8; 7:13; 8:6; 13; 15; 18; 11:16; 12:13; 14:22; 15:5; 16:28; 29; 47; 18:19; 25; 29; 20:15; 27; 23:19; 44; 24:16; 26:21; 28:2; 9; 29:13; 18; 31:18; 32:24; 25; 33:17; 20; 36:37; 44:11; **Dan** 4:23; 5:17; 7:12; 9:13; 10:9; 14; 11:2; 27; 33; 35; 45; **Hos** 1:4; 10; 3:1(2); 4:4; 15; 5:13; 7:9; 13; 15; 9:12; 16; 11:12; 12:8; 9; 13:4; **Amos** 2:9(2); 4:6; 7; 8; 9; 10; 11; 6:10; 9:9; **Jonah** 2:4; 6; 3:4; 4:2; **Mic** 1:15; 3:11; 5:2; 6:10; **Nah** 1:12; 2:8; 3:10; **Hab** 2:3; 3:18; **Hag** 2:4; 6; 17; 19(2); **Zec** 1:17(4); 8:4; 20; 11:15; 13:3; **Mal** 1:2(2); 2:14(2); 15; 17; 3:8; 13; **Mt** 6:25; 26; 29; 10:10; 12:46; 13:21; 15:16; 17; 27; 16:9; 17:5; 19:20; 24:6; 32; 26:33; 35; 47; 60; 27:63; **Mk** 5:35; 6:26; 7:28; 8:17(2); 11:13; 12:6; 13:7; 28; 14:29; 43; 15:5; **Lk** 3:20; 8:49; 9:42; 11:8; 12:27; 14:22; 32; 35; 15:20; 29; 18:5; 22; 19:30; 22:37; 47; 60; 23:15; 24:6; 41; 44; **Jn** 2:4; 3:24; 4:21; 27; 35; 7:6; 8(2); 19; 30; 33; 39(2); 8:14; 16; 20; 55; 57; 9:30; 11:25; 30; 12:35; 37; 13:33; 14:9; 19; 25; 16:12; 32; 19:41; 20:1; 5; 9; 17; 29; 21:11; 23; **Acts** 7:5(2); 8:16; 9:1; 10:44; 13:27; 28; 18:18; 19:37; 22:3; 24:11; 25:8; 28:4; 17; **Rom** 3:7; 4:11; 12; 19; 5:6; 7; 8; 8:24; 9:11; 19; 11:30; 16:19; **1Cor** 2:6; 15; 3:2; 3; 15; 4:4; 15; 5:10; 7:10; 25; 8:2; 9:2; 19; 12:20; 31; 14:19; 21; 15:10; 17; **2Cor** 1:10; 23; 4:8; 16; 5:16; 6:8; 9; 10(3); 8:9; 9:3; 11:6; 16; 12:5; 13:4; **Gal** 1:10; 2:20; 3:4; 15; 5:11(2); **Eph** 5:29; **Phil** 1:9; 22; 2:25; **Col** 1:21; 2:5; **1Th** 2:6; **2Th** 2:5; 3:15; **2Ti** 2:5; 13; **Philem** 1:9; **Heb** 2:8; 4:15; 5:8; 7:10; 15; 9:8(2); 25; 10:37; 11:4; 7; 12:4; 26; 27; **Jas** 2:10; 11; 3:4; 4:2; **1Pet** 1:8; 4:16; **1Jn** 3:2; **Jude** 9; **Rev** 6:11; 8:13; 9:20; 17:8; 10; 12

YOU

Gen 1:29(2); 9:2(2); 3(2); 7; 9(2); 10(2); 11; 12(2); 15; 17:10(2); 11; 12; 18:4; 19:2; 7; 8(2); 14; 22:5; 23:4(2); 9; 26:27; 27:45; 31:29; 34:8; 9; 10(2); 15(2); 16(2); 35:2; 37:6; 40:8; 41:55; 42:2; 14; 16(2); 22; 34; 38; 43:3; 5; 14; 23(2); 44:17(2); 23; 45:4; 5; 7(2); 8; 12; 17; 18; 19; 46:33; 47:16; 23(2); 48:21(2); 49:1(2); 50:4; 20; 21; 24(2); 25; **Ex** 3:13; 14; 15; 16(2); 17; 19; 20; 4:15; 5:4; 10; 11; 18; 21; 6:6(3); 7(3); 8(2); 7:4; 9(2); 8:28; 9:8; 28; 10:5(2); 10(3); 16; 24; 11:1(3); 9; 12:2(2); 13(4); 14; 16(2); 21; 22; 23; 25; 26; 31; 49; 13:3; 19(2); 14:13; 14; 16:4; 6; 8; 15; 23; 29(2); 32(2); 18:10; 19:4(2); 20:20; 22; 23; 22:24; 23:13; 24:8; 14(2); 26:33; 29:42; 30:32; 36; 31:13(2); 14; 32:29; 35:2; 5; 10; **Lev** 1:2; 8:33; 34; 9:4; 6; 10:7; 17; 11:4; 5; 6; 7; 8; 10; 11; 12; 20; 23; 26; 27; 28; 29; 31; 35; 38; 45; 14:34; 16:29(2); 30(2); 31; 34; 17:8; 10; 11; 12(2); 13; 18:3; 6; 24; 26; 27; 28(2); 30; 19:23; 25; 28; 34(3); 36; 20:8; 14; 22(2); 23; 24(3); 25; 26; 21:8; 22:20; 25; 32; 33; 23:10; 11; 15; 21; 27; 28; 32; 36; 40; 25:2; 6; 10; 11; 12; 21; 38(2); 44; 45(2); 46; 26:1(2); 4; 6; 7; 8(3); 9(4); 11(2); 12; 13(2); 16(2); 17(4); 18; 21; 22(3); 24(2); 25(2); 26; 28(2); 30; 33(2); 36; 38; 39; **Num** 1:4; 5; 9:8; 10; 14; 10:8; 9; 10; 29; 11:18; 20(2); 12:6; 13:17; 14:25(2); 28; 29; 30; 32; 42; 43(2); 15:2; 14(2); 15(2); 16(2); 18; 23; 39; 41; 16:3; 6; 7; 8; 9(3); 17; 24; 26; 45; 17:4; 5; 18:4; 6; 7; 26; 27; 20:10; 22:8; 13(2); 19; 25:18(2); 28:19; 22; 30; 31; 29:1; 5; 8; 32:21; 23; 24; 29(2); 30(2); 33:52; 53; 55(2); 56; 34:2; 7; 17; 35:11(2); 12; 29; **Deut** 1:7; 8; 9(2); 10; 11(3); 13(2); 15; 17; 18; 20; 22; 23; 29; 30(3); 33(3); 40(2); 42; 43; 44(3); 45; 2:3; 4; 5; 13; 3:18(2); 19; 20(2); 22; 4:1(2); 2(2); 3; 4; 5; 8; 12; 13(2); 14; 15; 16; 20(2); 23(2); 26; 27(2); 34; 5:4; 5(2); 30; 32; 33(2); 6:1; 14; 15; 20; 7:4; 7(2); 8(3); 14; 21; 8:19; 9:8(2); 9; 10; 16(2); 19(2); 23(2); 24; 25; 10:4; 15; 11:4; 5; 8; 13; 14; 17(2); 22; 23; 25(4); 26; 27; 28; 31; 32; 12:9; 10(2); 11; 12; 32; 13:1; 3; 5(3); 7; 11; 13; 14; 14:7; 8; 10; 19; 15:4; 7; 16:11; 17:2; 7; 16; 18:10; 19:19; 20; 20:4(3); 18; 21:9; 21; 22:21; 24; 23:4; 10; 16; 24:7; 8; 26:11; 27:1; 4; 28:54; 56; 63(6); 68; 29:4; 5(2); 10; 14; 18(2); 22; 30:18; 19(2); 31:5; 19; 27; 29(2); 32:38; 46; 47; **Josh** 1:3; 11(2); 13(3); 14; 15(2); 2:9(2); 10; 11; 12(2); 16(2); 3:4; 5; 10(2); 11; 12; 4:2; 3(2); 5(2); 6; 23; 5:9; 6:10; 16; 7:12(2); 13; 8:8; 9:7; 11; 12; 22; 23; 24(3); 18:3; 4; 6; 7; 8; 20:2(2); 22:2(2); 4(2); 5; 16; 19; 25; 27; 28; 23:3(2); 4; 5(2); 7; 9(3); 10(3); 12(2); 13(3); 14(2); 15(5); 16(3); 24:5; 7; 8(3); 9; 10(2); 11; 12(2); 13; 15(2); 20(3); 22; 23; 27; **Judg** 2:1(3); 3(2); 6:8(2); 9(4); 10; 7:7; 8:2; 3; 5; 19; 23(3); 24; 9:2(4); 7; 15; 17(2); 19; 10:11; 12(2); 13; 14; 12:2; 14:12(2); 15:7; 19:9(2); 23; 24; 20:12; 21:21; **Ruth** 1:8; 9(2); 2:4; 7; **1Sa** 4:9; 6:3(2); 4; 5; 21; 7:3(2); 5; 8:11; 18(2); 9:12; 13; 10:2; 15; 18(2); 19; 11:2; 10(2); 12:1; 2(3); 3; 5; 7(2); 11; 12; 13; 14; 15; 17; 22; 23(2); 24; 14:9; 12; 29; 15:6(2); 17:8(2); 47; 18:23; 22:3; 7(2); 8(2); 23:22; 23; 25:5; 19; 30:24; 26; **2Sa** 1:21; 24; 2:6(2); 3:17; 31; 4:11; 7:23; 13:28(2); 15:27; 28; 16:10; 20; 17:21; 18:2; 4; 19:22; 20:16; 21:3; 4; **1Kin** 1:33; 9:6; 11:2; 12:11(3); 14(2); 28; 18:25; 20:7; 22:28; **2Kin** 1:6; 7(2); 2:18; 5:7; 6:19; 7:12; 10:2(3); 23; 11:5; 7; 17:13; 36; 37; 38; 39; 18:27; 29(2); 30; 32(2); 22:15; 18; 25:24; **1Chr** 12:17; 13:2; 22:18(2); 28:8; **2Chr** 7:19; 10:11(3); 14(2); 12:5; 13:8(2); 9; 12; 15:2(3); 19:6; 7; 10(2); 11(2); 20:15; 17(2); 23:4; 24:20; 28:10(3); 11; 29:11; 30:6; 8; 9; 32:11; 14; 15(3); 34:23; 26; 36:23; **Ezr** 1:3; 4:2; 5:3; 9; 7:21; 24; **Neh** 1:8; 9; 4:12; 5:10; 11; 6:3; 13:21; 27; **Est** 8:8; **Job** 6:28; 29; 12:2; 3(2); 13:2; 9; 10; 11(2); 16:4(2); 5; 17:10(2); 27:5; 11; 32:6; 12(2); 21; 42:8(3); **Ps** 34:11; 50:22; 62:3; 82:6; 115:14(2); 118:26; 127:2; 129:8(2); **Prov** 1:23(3); 27; 4:2; 8:4; **Song** 2:7; 3:5; 5:8; 8:4; **Is** 1:15; 16(2); 5:3; 5; 7:13; 14; 8:19; 21:10; 22:14; 28:19; 29:10; 11; 30:11; 13; 16; 18(2); 20; 31:7; 32:11(2); 33:11; 35:4; 36:12; 14(2); 15; 17; 18; 40:21; 41:24; 42:9; 23; 43:12; 46:4(2); 50:1; 10; 51:2; 12; 52:12; 55:3; 12; 59:2(2); 61:6; 65:12; 66:5(2); 13; **Jer** 2:7; 9; 3:12; 14(3); 15(2); 4:8; 5:15; 18; 25; 6:17; 7:3; 7; 13(2); 14; 15; 23(2); 25; 8:17(2); 10:1; 11:4; 14:13; 14; 15:14; 16:13(2); 18:6; 11(2); 21:4; 5; 8; 9; 14; 23:2; 16(2); 17; 33; 38; 39(4); 40; 25:3; 4; 5; 6; 27; 26:4; 5; 13; 14; 15; 27:9; 10(3); 14(2); 15(2); 16(2); 29:7; 8(2); 9; 10(3); 11(2); 12; 14(5); 16; 21; 27; 31(2); 34:16; 17(2); 21; 35:14; 15(2); 18; 37:7(2); 10; 19(2); 38:5; 40:3; 9; 42:4(4); 10(5); 11(3); 12(3); 16(2); 18; 19(2); 21(2); 44:4; 7(2); 10; 11; 23; 29(3); 49:3; 30(3); 31; 50:12; **Lam** 1:12; 18; **Eze** 5:7(2); 16(2); 17; 6:3; 7; 9; 11:7; 8; 9(3); 10; 11; 12; 15; 17(3); 19; 13:8; 12; 15; 18; 14:22; 23; 18:30; 31(2); 20:3; 20; 31(2); 33; 34(2); 35(2); 36; 37(2); 38; 39; 41(4); 42; 44; 22:19; 20(3); 21(2); 22; 23:49; 24:24; 33:20; 30; 34:3; 17; 18; 36:2; 3(2); 7; 9(2); 10; 11(3); 12; 13; 23; 24(3); 25(2); 26(3); 27(2); 29(2); 32; 33(2); 36; 37:5; 6(4); 12(2); 13; 14(2); 39:17; 19; 43:27; 44:6; 45:9; 47:14; 21; 22(5); **Dan** 2:9; 3:4; 15; 4:1; 6:25; **Hos** 5:1; 13(2); 10:12; 15; 14:2; **Joel** 2:19(2); 20; 23(2); 25(2); 26; 3:13; **Amos** 2:10(2); 13; 3:1; 2(2); 4:2(2); 5; 6; 7; 9; 10; 11; 5:1; 14; 18(2); 27; 6:14(2); **Jonah** 1:12(2); **Mic** 1:2; 11; 2:4; 10; 3:1(2); 6(2); 9; **Hab** 1:5; **Zeph** 2:2(2); 5; 3:20(3); **Hag** 1:4; 6; 10; 13; 2:3; 4; 5(2); 15; 17; 19; **Zec** 1:3; 2:6; 8(2); 4:9; 6:7; 15; 7:10; 8:13; 14; 17; 23(2); 9:12; 11:7; 9; **Mal** 1:2; 6; 9; 10(2); 2:1; 2; 3; 4; 9; 3:5; 7; 10(2); 12; 4:2; 5; **Mt** 3:7; 9; 11(2); 4:19; 5:11(3); 12; 18; 20; 22; 28; 32; 34; 39; 44(5); 46; 6:2; 5; 14; 16; 25; 27; 29; 30; 33; 7:2; 6; 7(2); 9; 12; 15; 23; 8:10; 11; 9:29; 10:13; 14; 15; 16; 17(2); 19(2); 20; 23(2); 27; 40; 42; 11:9; 11; 17(2); 21; 22(2); 24; 28; 29; 12:6; 11; 28; 31; 36; 13:11; 17; 15:7; 16:11; 28; 17:12; 17(2); 20(2); 18:3; 10; 13; 18; 19(2); 35; 19:8; 9; 23; 24; 28; 20:4; 26(2); 27; 32; 21:2; 3; 21; 24(2); 27; 31(2); 32; 43(2); 22:31; 23:3; 11; 13; 14; 15; 16; 23; 25; 27; 29; 34; 35; 36; 38; 39; 24:2; 4; 9(2); 23; 25; 26; 34; 47; 25:9; 12(2); 34; 40; 45; 26:11; 13; 15; 21(2); 29(2); 32; 55; 64; 27:17; 21; 28:7(2); 14; 20(2); **Mk** 1:8(2); 17; 3:28; 4:11; 24(2); 6:11(3); 7:6; 14; 8:12; 9:1; 13; 19(2); 41(2); 10:3; 5; 15; 29; 36; 43(2); 44; 11:2; 3; 23; 24; 25; 29(2); 33; 12:43; 13:5; 9; 11(3); 21; 23; 30; 36; 37; 14:7; 9; 13; 15; 18(2); 25; 28; 49; 15:9; 16:7(2); **Lk** 2:10; 11; 12; 3:7; 8; 13; 16(2); 4:24; 25; 6:9; 22(3); 24; 25(2); 26(2); 27(2); 28(2); 31; 32; 33; 38(2); 47; 7:9; 26; 28; 32(2); 8:10; 9:5; 27; 41(2); 48; 10:3; 6; 8(2); 9; 10; 11(2); 12; 13; 14; 16(2); 19(2); 20; 24; 11:5; 8; 9(3); 11; 20; 41; 42; 43; 44; 46; 47; 51; 52; 12:4; 5(2); 8; 11; 12; 14; 22; 25; 27; 28; 31; 32; 37; 44; 51; 13:3; 5; 15; 24; 25(2); 27(2); 28; 35(2); 14:5; 24; 28; 33; 15:4; 7; 10; 16:9(2); 12; 26(2); 17:6; 7; 10; 21; 23; 34; 18:8; 14; 17; 29; 19:26; 30; 31; 40; 20:3; 8; 21:3; 12(3); 13; 15; 16; 32; 34; 22:10; 12; 15; 16; 18; 19; 20; 26; 27; 29; 31(2); 35; 37; 53; 67; 68; 23:14; 15; 24:6; 36; 44(2); 49; **Jn** 1:26; 51; 2:5; 3:12(2); 4:35; 38; 5:19; 24; 25; 38; 42(2); 45(2); 6:26; 27; 32(3); 36; 47; 53(2); 61; 63; 64; 65; 70(2); 7:7; 19(2); 22; 33; 8:7; 24; 25; 26; 32; 34; 36; 37; 40; 45; 46; 51; 55; 58; 9:27; 10:1; 7; 25; 26; 32; 12:8; 24; 35(2); 13:12; 15(2); 16; 18; 19; 20; 21(2); 33(2); 34(2); 14:2(2); 3(2); 9; 10; 12; 16(2); 17(2); 18(2); 20; 25(2); 26(2); 27(3); 28(2); 29; 30; 15:3; 4; 7(2); 9; 11(2); 12; 14; 15(3); 16(3); 17; 18(2); 19(2); 20(2); 21; 26; 16:1; 2(2); 3; 4(4); 5; 6; 7(4); 12; 13(2); 14; 15; 20; 22(2); 23(2); 25(3); 26(2); 27; 33; 18:8; 39(2); 19:4; 20:19; 21(2); 26; **Acts** 1:7; 8; 11; 2:14; 22(2); 29; 38; 39; 3:14; 16; 20; 22(2); 26(3); 4:10(2); 11; 19; 5:28; 38; 6:3; 7:37; 43; 10:29; 13:26(2); 32; 34; 38(2); 40; 41; 46(2); 14:15(2); 15:24; 25; 27; 28; 16:36; 17:3; 23; 18:14; 21; 19:13; 20:18; 20(3); 26; 27; 28; 29; 32(3); 35; 22:1; 25; 23:15; 24:21; 25:5; 26; 26:8; 27:22(2); 34(2); 28:20(3); 28; **Rom** 1:7; 8; 9; 10; 11(2); 12(2); 13(3); 15; 2:24; 6:14; 17; 8:9; 10; 11(2); 10:19(2); 11:13; 12:1; 3; 14; 18; 15:5; 13; 14; 15(2); 22; 23; 24(3); 28; 29; 30; 32(2); 33; 16:1; 2; 16; 17; 19; 20; 21; 22; 23(2); 24; 25; **1Cor** 1:3; 4; 6; 8; 10(2); 11(2); 12; 13; 14; 2:1(2); 2; 3; 3:1; 2; 3; 16; 18; 4:3; 6; 8; 14(2); 15; 16; 17(2); 18; 19; 21; 5:1; 2; 9; 11; 6:1; 2; 5; 7; 11; 19; 7:5; 28; 32; 35; 9:2; 11; 12; 23; 10:13(2); 27(2); 28; 11:2(2); 3; 14; 17(2); 18; 19(2); 22(3); 23; 24; 30; 12:1; 3; 21; 31; 14:6(3); 25; 26; 36(2); 37; 15:1(2); 2; 3; 12; 51; 16:2; 5; 6; 7(2); 10; 12; 13; 15; 19(2); 20; 23; 24; **2Cor** 1:2; 7; 8; 13; 15; 16(3); 18; 19; 21; 23; 2:1; 2; 3(3); 4(2); 5; 8; 9; 3:1(2); 4:12; 14; 5:12(2); 20(2); 6:1; 11; 17; 18; 7:3(2); 4(2); 7; 8(2); 11; 12(3); 13; 14(2); 15(2); 16; 8:1; 6; 10; 16; 17; 22; 23; 9:1; 2; 3; 4; 5; 8; 14(3); 10:1(3); 2; 9; 13; 14(2); 15; 16; 11:2(3); 6; 7; 8; 9(2); 11; 20(4); 12:11; 12; 13; 14(3); 15(2); 16(2); 17(2); 18; 19; 20(2); 21; 13:1; 2(2); 3; 4; 5; 11; 13; 14; **Gal** 1:3; 6; 7; 8(2); 9; 11; 20; 2:5; 3:1(2); 2; 5(2); 27; 4:11(2); 12; 13; 15; 16; 17(2); 18; 19; 20(2); 5:2(2); 4(2); 7; 8; 10(2); 12; 21(2); 6:11; 12; 13; **Eph** 1:2; 16(2); 17; 2:1; 17; 3:1; 13; 16; 4:1; 6; 31; 32; 5:3; 6; 33; 6:13; 21; 22; **Phil** 1:2; 3; 4; 6; 7(2); 8; 24; 25; 26; 27; 28; 29; 2:5; 13; 17; 19; 25; 26; 3:1(2); 15; 18(2); 4:9; 18; 21; 22; 23; **Col** 1:2; 3; 5; 6(2); 7; 9; 21; 22; 24; 25; 27; 2:1; 4; 5; 8; 13(2); 16; 18; 3:13; 16; 4:7; 8; 9(2); 10(2); 12(3); 13; 14; 16; 18; **1Th** 1:1; 2(2); 5(2); 8; 9; 2:1; 2; 6; 7; 8(2); 9(2); 10; 11; 12; 13; 17; 18; 3:2(2); 4(2); 5; 6(2); 7; 9; 11; 12(2); 4:1(2); 2; 4; 6; 9; 10; 11; 13; 15; 5:1; 4; 12(4); 14; 18; 23; 24; 27; 28; **2Th** 1:2; 3(2); 4; 6; 7; 10; 11(2); 12; 2:1; 3; 5(2); 13(2); 14; 17; 3:1; 3(2); 4(2); 6; 7; 8; 9; 10(2); 11; 16(2); 18; **2Ti** 4:22; **Titus** 2:8; 3:15; **Philem** 1:3; 6; 22; **Heb** 3:12; 13; 4:1; 5:12; 6:9; 11; 9:20; 12:5; 7; 15; 13:7(2); 17(2); 19(2); 21(2); 22(2); 23; 24(2); 25; **Jas** 1:5; 26; 2:6(2); 16; 3:13; 4:1; 7; 8; 10; 5:1; 3; 4; 6; 13; 14; 19; **1Pet** 1:2; 4; 10; 12(2); 13; 15; 20; 25; 2:7; 9; 11; 12; 3:13; 15(2); 16; 4:4; 12(2); 14; 15; 5:1; 2; 5; 6; 7; 10(2); 12; 13(2); 14; **2Pet** 1:2; 8(2); 11; 12; 13(2); 16; 2:1; 3; 13; 3:1; 15; **1Jn** 1:2; 3; 4; 5; 2:1; 7; 8(2); 12(2); 13(3); 14(3); 21; 24(2); 26(2); 27(4); 3:7; 13; 4:4; 5:13; **2Jn** 3; 10; 12(2); **Jude** 2; 3(3); 5; 12; 18; 24(2); **Rev** 1:4; 2:10; 13; 23; 24(2); 12:12; 18:6; 20; 22:16; 21

YOUR

Gen 3:5; 9:2; 5(2); 9; 17:11; 12; 13; 18:4; 5(2); 19:2(3); 8; 23:8; 31:5; 6; 7; 9; 29; 34:8; 9; 11; 16; 35:2; 37:7; 42:15; 16(2); 19(3); 20(2); 33(2); 34(2); 43:3; 5; 7(2); 11; 12(3); 13; 14; 23(4); 27; 29; 44:10; 17; 23; 45:4; 7; 12; 17; 18(2); 19(3); 20; 46:33; 47:3; 16(2); 23; 24(4); 48:21; 49:2; 50:4; 21; **Ex** 3:13; 15; 16; 22(2); 5:4; 11; 13(2); 14; 19(2); 6:7; 8:25; 28; 10:8; 10; 16; 17; 24(3); 12:4; 5; 11(5); 14; 15; 17(2); 19; 20; 21; 23; 26; 32(2); 14:14; 16:7; 8(2); 9; 12; 16; 32; 33; 19:15; 20:20; 22:24(2); 23:21; 25; 31; 29:42; 30:8; 10; 15; 16; 31; 31:13; 32:2(3); 13(2); 30; 34:23; 35:3; **Lev** 1:2; 3:17(2); 6:18; 7:26; 32; 8:33; 10:4; 6(3); 9; 11:44; 45; 14:34; 16:29(2); 30; 31; 17:11; 15; 18:2; 4; 26; 30; 19:2; 3; 4; 5; 9; 10; 25; 27; 28; 31; 33; 34; 36; 20:7; 24; 25; 22:3(2); 19; 24; 25; 29; 33; 23:3; 10; 14(3); 17; 21(2); 22(2); 27; 28; 31(2); 32(2); 38(3); 40; 41; 43(2); 24:3; 22(2); 25:9; 17; 19; 24; 38(2); 45(2); 46(3); 55; 26:1(2); 5(3); 6; 7; 8; 12; 13(2); 15; 16(2); 17; 18; 19(3); 20(2); 21; 22(3); 24; 25; 26(3); 28; 29(2); 30(4); 31(3); 32; 33(2); 34; 35; 37; 38; 39; **Num** 9:10; 10:8; 9(3); 10(7); 11:20; 14:29(2); 31; 32; 33(3); 34; 42; 15:2; 3; 14; 15; 20; 21(2); 23; 39(2); 40; 41(3); 18:1; 6; 7(2); 23; 26; 27; 28; 29; 31(3); 22:13; 28:11; 26; 29:7; 39(7); 31:19; 20; 24; 32:6; 8; 14; 22; 23; 24(3); 33:54(2); 55(2); 34:3(2); 4; 6; 7; 8; 9; 10; 12; 35:29(2); **Deut** 1:7; 8; 10; 11; 12(3); 13; 15(2); 16(2); 26; 27; 30(2); 32; 33; 34; 35; 37; 39(2); 40; 42; 45; 2:4; 24; 3:18(2); 19(4); 20(2); 21; 22; 26; 4:1; 2; 3; 4; 6(2); 21; 23; 26; 34(2); 5:1; 22; 23(2); 28; 30; 32; 33(2); 6:1; 16; 17; 7:8; 14; 8:1; 20(2); 9:16; 17; 18; 21; 23; 10:16; 17; 11:2(2); 7; 9(2); 13(3); 14; 16; 18(4); 19; 21(3); 22; 24(2); 25; 27; 28; 31; 12:4; 5(2); 6(8); 7(3); 9; 10(2); 11(6); 12(6); 13:3(4); 4; 5; 14:1(2); 20:3(2); 4(2); 18; 28:68; 29:2; 5; 6; 10(5); 11(2); 22; 30:18; 31:5; 12; 13; 26; 28(2); 29; 32:17; 38; 46(2); 47(2); **Josh** 1:3; 4; 11; 13; 14(4); 15(3); 2:9; 11; 16; 21; 3:3(2); 9; 4:5; 6; 21; 22; 23(2); 24; 6:10(2); 7:14; 8:7(2); 9:11; 10:19(3); 24; 25; 15:4; 18:3; 20:3; 22:3(2); 4(4); 5(3); 8(3); 19; 24; 25; 27; 23:3(2); 4; 5(3); 8; 10; 11; 13(4); 14(3); 15(2); 16; 24:2; 3; 6(2); 7; 8; 11; 14; 15; 19(2); 23; 27; **Judg** 2:1; 3; 3:28(2); 6:10; 7:15; 8:3; 7; 9:2(2); 15; 18; 10:14; 11:9; 18:6; 10; 19:5; 9; 30; 20:7; **Ruth** 1:11; 12; 13; **1Sa** 2:3; 23; 6:4; 5(4); 6; 7:3(2); 8:11; 13; 14(3); 15(2); 16(4); 17; 18; 10:19(5); 11:2; 12:1; 6; 7; 8(2); 11; 12(2); 14; 15; 16; 17; 20; 24; 25; 17:8; 9; 26:16; **2Sa** 1:24; 2:5; 7(2); 3:31; 4:11; 10:5; 15:27; **1Kin** 1:33; 8:61; 9:6; 11:2; 12:11; 14(2); 16; 24; 18:24; 25; **2Kin** 2:3; 5; 3:17(2); 18; 9:15; 10:2; 3(2); 6; 24; 12:7; 17:13(2); 39(2); 18:32; 19:6; 23:21; **1Chr** 15:12; 16:18; 19:5; 22:18; 19(3); 28:8(2); 29:20; **2Chr** 10:11; 14; 16; 11:4; 13:12; 15:7(2); 18:14; 19:10(2); 20:20; 24:5; 28:9(2); 10; 11; 29:5; 8; 30:7(2); 8(2); 9(3); 32:14; 15; 33:8; 35:3(2); 4(2); 5; 6; **Ezr** 4:2; 6:6; 7:17; 18; 8:28; 9:12(3); 10:11; **Neh** 4:14(5); 5:8; 8:9; 10(2); 11; 9:5; 13:18; 25(2); **Job** 6:22; 25; 27; 13:5(2); 12(2); 13; 17; 16:4; 5; 18:3; 21:2; 5(2); 27; 34; 32:11(2); 14; 42:8; **Ps** 4:4(2); 5; 11:1; 22:26; 24:7; 9; 31:24; 47:1; 58:2; 9; 62:8; 10; 69:32; 75:5; 76:11; 78:1; 95:8; 9; 105:11; 115:14; 134:2; 146:3; **Prov** 1:26(2); 27(2); **Is** 1:7(4); 11; 12; 14(2); 15(2); 16; 18; 3:14; 8:13(2); 10:3; 23:7; 14; 28:18(2); 22; 29:10(2); 16; 30:3(2); 15; 31:7; 32:11; 33:4; 11; 35:4; 36:17; 37:6; 40:1; 9; 26; 41:21(2); 24; 26; 43:14(2); 15(2); 46:1; 4; 50:1(4); 11; 51:2; 6; 52:12; 55:2(2); 3(2); 8(2); 9(2); 58:3(2); 4; 59:2(3); 3(4); 61:5(3); 7; 65:7(2); 15; 66:5(2); 14(2); 20; 22(2); **Jer** 2:5; 9; 30(3); 3:18; 22; 4:3; 4(2); 5:19; 25(2); 6:16; 20(2); 7:3(2); 5(2); 6; 7; 11; 14; 15; 21(2); 22; 23; 25; 9:20(2); 11:4(2); 5; 7; 12:13; 13:16(2); 17; 18(2); 20; 16:9(2); 11; 12; 13; 17:1; 22(2); 18:11(2); 21:4; 12; 14; 23:2; 39; 25:4; 5(2); 6; 7(2); 34(2); 26:11; 13(3); 14; 15; 27:4; 9(5); 10; 12; 16; 29:6(2); 8(3); 13; 14; 16; 21; 30:22; 34:13; 14; 35:6; 7; 15(3); 18; 37:19; 38:5; 40:10(2); 42:4(2); 9; 12; 13; 15; 20(2); 21; 44:3; 7; 8; 9(3); 10; 21(3); 22(2); 25(5); 46:4; 48:6; 50:12; 51:24; 46; 50; **Eze** 5:16; 6:3; 4(4); 5(2); 6(5); 9:5; 11:5; 6; 7; 11; 12:11; 25; 13:19(2); 20(2); 21(3); 23; 14:6(3); 16:45(2); 55; 18:25; 29; 30(2); 31; 20:5; 7; 18; 19; 20; 27; 30; 31(3); 32; 36; 39(2); 40(3); 41; 42; 43(4); 44(2); 21:24(4); 23:48; 49(2); 24:21(5); 22; 23(5); 33:11; 25(2); 26; 34:18(3); 19(2); 21; 31; 35:13(2); 36:8(2); 11(2); 22; 24; 25(2); 26; 28(2); 29; 31(5); 32(2); 33; 37:12(2); 13(2); 14; 25; 43:27(2); 44:6; 7; 30(2); 45:9; 12; 47:14; **Dan** 1:10(4); 2:5; 47; 10:21; **Hos** 1:9; 2:1(2); 2; 4:13(2); 14(2); 5:13; 6:4; 9:10; 10:12; 15; **Joel** 1:2(2); 3(2); 5; 13; 14; 2:12; 13(3); 14; 23; 26; 27; 28(4); 3:4(2); 5; 7(2); 8(2); 10(2); 17; **Amos** 2:11(2); 3:2; 4:2; 4(2); 6(2); 9(4); 10(4);

5:11; 12(2); 21(2); 22(2); 26(3); 6:2; 8:10(2); **Mic** 2:3; 10; 3:12; **Hab** 1:5; **Zeph** 3:20(2); **Hag** 1:4; 5; 7; 2:3; 17; **Zec** 1:2; 4(3); 5; 6; 6:15; 7:10; 8:9; 13; 14; 16; 17; **Mal** 1:5; 9(2); 10; 13; 2:2; 3(3); 13; 15; 16; 17; 3:7; 11(3); 13; 4:3; **Mt** 5:12; 16(3); 20; 37; 44; 45; 47; 48; 6:1(2); 8; 14; 15(2); 21(2); 25(2); 26; 32; 7:6; 11(2); 9:4; 11; 29; 10:9; 10; 13(2); 14(2); 20; 29; 30; 11:29; 12:27(2); 13:16(2); 15:3; 6; 17:20; 24; 18:14; 35; 19:8(2); 20:26; 27; 23:8; 9(2); 10; 11; 32; 34; 38; 24:20; 42; 25:8; 26:45; 27:65; **Mk** 2:8; 6:11; 7:9; 13; 8:17; 10:5; 43; 11:2; 25(2); 26(2); 13:18; 14:41; 16:7; **Lk** 3:14; 4:21; 5:4; 22; 6:22; 23; 24; 27; 35(2); 36; 38; 7:22; 8:25; 9:3; 5; 44; 10:3; 6; 10; 11; 20; 11:13(2); 19(2); 39; 46; 47; 48; 12:7; 22; 30; 32; 34(2); 35(2); 13:35; 16:11; 12; 15; 19:30; 21:14; 15; 18; 19(2); 28(2); 30; 34; 22:53; 23:28; 24:38; **Jn** 4:35; 6:49; 58; 7:6; 8:17; 21; 24(2); 38; 41; 42; 44(2); 54; 56; 9:19; 41; 10:34; 11:15; 12:30; 13:14(2); 14:1; 26; 27; 15:11; 16; 16:6; 20; 22(2); 24; 18:31; 19:14; 15; 20:17(2); **Acts** 2:17(4); 39; 3:17; 19; 22(2); 5:28; 7:37(2); 43; 51; 52; 13:41; 15:24; 17:23; 28; 18:6(2); 15; 19:37; 20:30; 24:22; 27:34; **Rom** 1:8; 6:12; 13(2); 19(3); 22; 8:11; 11:25; 28; 31; 12:1(2); 2; 16; 14:16; 15:24; 30; 16:19(2); 20; **1Cor** 1:4; 26; 2:5; 4:6; 5:6; 6:5; 8; 15; 19(2); 20(2); 7:5; 14; 35; 9:11; 14:34; 15:14; 17(2); 31; 34; 58; 16:3(2); 14; 17; **2Cor** 1:6(2); 14; 24(2); 2:8; 10; 4:5; 15; 5:11; 13; 6:12; 7:7(3); 13; 8:7; 8; 9; 14(2); 19; 24(2); 9:2(2); 5; 10(3); 13(2); 10:6; 8; 15; 11:3; 12:19; 13:5(2); 9; **Gal** 4:6; 15; 16; 6:13; 18; **Eph** 1:13; 15; 18; 3:13; 17; 4:4; 23; 26; 29; 5:19; 22; 25; 6:1; 4; 5(2); 9; 14; 15; 22; **Phil** 1:5; 9; 19; 25; 26; 27(2); 28; 2:12; 17; 19; 20; 25; 30; 4:5; 6; 7; 10; 17; 19; **Col** 1:4; 8; 21; 2:5(2); 13(2); 18; 3:2; 3; 5; 8; 15; 16; 18; 19; 20; 21; 22; 4:1; 6; 8(2); **1Th** 1:3; 4; 5; 8; 2:14; 17; 3:2; 5; 6; 7; 9; 10(2); 13; 4:3; 11(2); 5:23; **2Th** 1:3; 4(2); 2:17; 3:5; **Philem** 1:22; 25; **Heb** 3:8; 9; 15; 4:7; 6:10; 9:14; 10:34; 35; 12:3; 13; 13:5; 17; **Jas** 1:3; 21; 22; 2:2; 3:14; 4:1(2); 3; 8(2); 9(2); 14; 16; 5:1; 2(2); 3(2); 4; 5; 8; 12(2); 16; **1Pet** 1:7; 9(2); 13; 14; 17; 18(2); 21; 22; 2:12(2); 16; 18; 20; 25; 3:1; 2; 7; 15; 16; 4:14; 5:7; 8; 9; **2Pet** 1:5; 10; 19; 3:1; 17; **1Jn** 1:4; 2:12; **2Jn** 10; **Jude** 12; 20; **Rev** 1:9; 2:23; 16:1

YOURS

Gen 45:20; **Deut** 11:24; **Josh** 2:14; **2Chr** 20:15; **Jer** 5:19; **Lk** 6:20; **Jn** 15:20; **1Cor** 3:21; 22; 8:9; 16:18; **2Cor** 12:14

YOURSELVES

Gen 18:4; 45:5; 49:1; 2; **Ex** 19:12; 30:37; 32:29; **Lev** 11:43(2); 44(2); 18:24; 30; 19:4; 20:7; **Num** 11:18; 16:3; 21; 31:3; 18; 19; **Deut** 2:4; 4:15; 16; 23; 25; 11:16; 23; 14:1; 31:14; 29; **Josh** 2:16; 3:5; 6:18(2); 7:13; 8:2; 23:7; 11; 16; 24:22; **Judg** 15:12; **1Sa** 2:29; 4:9(2); 10:19; 14:34; 16:5; **1Kin** 18:25; 20:12; **2Kin** 17:35; **1Chr** 15:12; **2Chr** 20:17; 29:5; 31; 30:8; 32:11; 35:4; 6; **Ezr** 10:11; **Neh** 13:25; **Job** 19:3; 5; 27:12; 42:8; **Is** 8:9(3); 29:9; 45:20; 46:8; 48:14; 49:9; 50:1; 11; 52:3; 57:4; 5; 61:6; **Jer** 4:4; 5; 6:1; 8:14; 13:18; 17:21; 25:34; 26:15; 37:9; 44:8; 50:14; **Eze** 14:6; 18:30; 32; 20:7; 18; 31; 43; 36:31; 39:17(2); 44:8; **Hos** 10:12; **Joel** 1:13; 3:11(2); **Amos** 3:9; 5:26; **Zeph** 2:1; **Zec** 7:6(2); **Mt** 3:9; 6:19; 20; 16:8; 23:13; 15; 31; 25:9; **Mk** 6:31; 9:33; 50; 13:9; **Lk** 3:8; 11:46; 52; 12:33; 36; 57; 13:28; 16:9; 15; 17:3; 14; 21:34; 22:17; 23:28; **Jn** 3:28; 6:43; 16:19; **Acts** 2:22; 40; 5:35; 13:46; 15:29; 20:10; 28; 34; **Rom** 6:11; 13; 16; 12:19; **1Cor** 5:13; 6:7; 7:5; 11:13; 16:16; **2Cor** 7:11(2); 11:19; 13:5; **Eph** 2:8; 5:19; 21; 22; **Col** 3:18; **1Th** 2:1; 3:3; 4:9; 5:2; 11; 13; 15; **2Th** 3:6; 7; **Heb** 10:34; 13:3; 17; **Jas** 2:4; 4:7; 10; **1Pet** 1:14; 2:13; 4:1; 8; 5:5; 6; **1Jn** 5:21; **2Jn** 8; **Jude** 20; 21; **Rev** 19:17

The New Strong's®

Expanded Dictionary

of the Words in the

Hebrew Bible

with their Renderings in the
King James Version

and with Additional Definitions
Adapted from W. E. Vine
and Cross-references to Other
Word Study Resources

read this first!

How to Use the Hebrew and Aramaic Dictionary

For many people Strong's unique system of numbers continues to be *the* bridge between the original languages of the Bible and the English of the *King James Version* (AV). *Strong's Hebrew and Aramaic Dictionary* is a fully integrated companion to the main concordance, and its entries contain a wealth of information about the words of the Bible in their original language. In order to enhance the strategic importance of the *Dictionary* for Bible students, significant features have been added in this new, expanded edition.

New Features

The *Dictionary* is designed to provide maximum information so that your word studies are enriching and satisfying. The most significant enhancement is the expanded definitions, which come from the best of the standard word-study resources: *Vine's Complete Expository Dictionary of Old and New Testament Words, Brown-Driver-Briggs Hebrew and English Lexicon,* and *Girdlestone's Synonyms of the Old Testament.* The expanded definitions reveal the entire range of meanings so that the user can conduct more precise and accurate word studies. In addition, they help to convey the depth and richness of Hebrew and Aramaic words.

The second item that has been added is the frequency word counts, which appear in curly brackets {}. Frequency counts are provided for both the Hebrew words and the English words used in the AV. For example, the Hebrew word *ab* (entry #1) has {1211x} following it. This means that this word occurs 1211 times in the Hebrew text. Then after the :— symbol, a list of English translations and their occurrences are given. For example, "chief" {2x} means that this word is used twice in the AV as a translation of the Hebrew word *ab.*

For those wanting to conduct more advanced word studies, a cross-reference to other lexicons is given at the end of the definition. These lexicons are the *Theological Wordbook of the Old Testament,* by R. Laird Harris, Gleason L. Archer, Jr., and Bruce K. Waltke (Moody, 1980); and the *Brown-Driver-Briggs Hebrew and English Lexicon* (Hendrickson, 1999). These two lexicons are abbreviated in the definitions as TWOT and BDB.

Using the Dictionary with the Main Concordance

To use this *Dictionary,* locate the number given to the biblical reference for any particular entry in the main concordance. For example, under "abide" you find *Strong's* number 3427 next to the Bible reference 1 Sa 22:23. Since this reference is in the Old Testament, and since this numeral is set in regular type (and not in italic type), you know that it refers to the *Hebrew and Aramaic Dictionary.*

Using the Dictionary to Do Word Studies

Careful Bible students do word studies, and *The New Strong's® Expanded Exhaustive Concordance* with enhanced *Hebrew and Aramaic Dictionary* offers unique assistance. Consider the word "love" as found in the AV. By skimming the main concordance, you find these numbers for Hebrew and Aramaic words that the King James Bible translates with the English word "love": 157, 160, 2836, 7355, 1730, 7474, 5690, and 5691. Now for any one Bible reference in this entry there is only one Hebrew word cited and you may be interested only in establishing the precise meaning for just that word in that occurrence. If so, it will be very helpful for you to observe that same Hebrew word in *each* of its occurrences in the Bible. In that way, you develop an idea of its possible range of meanings, and you can help clarify what is most likely the precise meaning in the specific Bible reference you are studying.

But don't overlook exploring each Hebrew and Aramaic words translated as "love." You may wish to take notes as you look up each occurrence of the word that goes with 160, and so forth. This method gives you an excellent basis for understanding all that the Hebrew Bible signifies with the AV word "love."

Now see the *Dictionary* entry 157 itself, and notice that after the symbol :— all the words and word prefixes and suffixes are listed. These show you that this one Hebrew word, *'ahab,* is translated into several different but related words in the King James Bible: beloved, love, loved, lovely, lover, like, befriend. This list tells you the range of uses of the one Hebrew word in the AV. This information can help you distinguish between the nuances of the meaning found where this and the other Hebrew words are translated by these same words and similar ones in the King James Bible.

These three ways of using the *Dictionary* in conjunction with the main concordance show you only a sampling of the many ways *The New Strong's® Expanded Exhaustive Concordance of the Bible* can enrich your study of the Bible. (See also *Getting the Most from Your New Strong's® Exhaustive Bible Concordance,* Nelson, 2000.) They also show why it is important that you take the time to become familiar with each feature in the *Dictionary* as illustrated on the following page.

An Example from the Hebrew and Aramaic Dictionary

Strong's number, corresponding to the numbers at the ends of the context lines in the main concordance.

An unnumbered cross-reference entry.

The word as it appears in the original Hebrew (or Aramaic) spelling.

The degree symbol denotes the presence of a textual variation. (See "Special Symbols")

The Hebrew (or Aramaic) word represented in English letters in **bold** type (the transliteration).

Strong's syllable-by-syllable pronunciation in *italics,* with the emphasized syllable marked by the accent.

Information regarding relationship to other Hebrew (or Aramaic) words, usually cited by Strong's numbers. Sometimes a word may refer to a Greek entry (shown by *italic* numbers) or it may come from another language.

צְאוֹן° **tse'ôn**. See 6629.

6628. צֶאֶל **tse'el**, *tseh´-el;* from an unused root mean. to *be slender;* the *lotus* tree:— shady tree.

6629. צֹאן **tsô'n**, *tsone;* or

צְאוֹן° **tse'ôwn** (Psa. 144:13) *tseh-one´;* from an unused root mean. to *migrate;* a collect. name for a flock (of sheep or goats); also fig. (of men):— (small) cattle, flock (+ -s), lamb (+ s), sheep ([-cote, -fold, -shearer, -herds]).

See "Special Symbols."

Occasional, helpful Scripture references.

Improved, consistent abbreviations. All abbreviations occur with their full spelling in the list of abbreviations.

Brief English definitions (shown by italics).

After the long dash (—), there is a complete, alphabetical listing of all renderings of this Hebrew (or Aramaic) word in the KJV. (See also "Special Symbols").

Note that Hebrew (or Aramaic) spelling variations are conveniently indented for easy comparison.

Plan of the Hebrew and Aramaic Dictionary

1. All the original words are presented in their alphabetical order (according to Hebrew and Aramaic). They are numbered for easy matching between this Dictionary and the main part of the Concordance. Many reference books also use these same numbers created by Dr. Strong.

2. Immediately after each word, the exact equivalent of each sound (phoneme) is given in English characters, according to the transliteration system given below.

3. Next follows the precise pronunciation, with the proper stress mark.

4. Then comes the etymology, root meaning, and common uses of the word, along with any other important related details.

5. In the case of proper names, the normal English spelling is given, accompanied by a few words of explanation.

6. Finally, after the colon and the dash (:—), all the different ways that the word appears in the Authorized Version (KJV) are listed in alphabetical order. When the Hebrew or Aramaic word appears in English as a phrase, the main word of the phrase is used to alphabetize it.

By looking up these words in the main concordance and by noting the passages which display the same number in the right-hand column, the reader also possesses a complete *Hebrew Concordance*, expressed in the words of the Authorized Version.

Transliteration and Pronunciation of the Hebrew and Aramaic

The following shows how the Hebrew words are transliterated into English in this Dictionary.

1. The Hebrew and Aramaic read *from right to left*. Both alphabets consist of 22 letters (and their variations), which are all regarded as *consonants*, although four consonants (א ה ו י) sometimes indicate vowel sounds. To help enunciation, vowels are primarily indicated by certain "points" or marks, mostly beneath the letters. Hebrew and Aramaic do not use *capitals, italics,* etc.

2. The Hebrew and Aramaic characters are as follows:

No.	Form	Name	Transliteration and Pronunciation
1.	א	'Aleph (*aw´-lef*)	', silent
2.	ב	Bêyth (*bayth*)	**b**
3.	ג	Gîymel (*ghee´-mel*)	**g** hard = γ
4.	ד	Dâleth (*daw´-leth*)	**d**
5.	ה	Hê' (*hay*)	**h**, often quiescent
6.	ו	Vâv (*vawv*) or Wâw (*waw*)	**v** or **w**, quiescent
7.	ז	Zayin (*zah´-yin*)	**z**, as in *zeal*
8.	ח	Chêyth (*khayth*)	German **ch** = χ (nearly *kh*)
9.	ט	Têyth (*tayth*)	**ṭ** = T
10.	י	Yôwd (*yode*)	**y**, often quiescent
11.	כ final ך	Kaph (*caf*)	**k** = ק
12.	ל	Lâmed (*law´-med*)	**l**
13.	מ final ם	Mêm (*mame*)	**m**
14.	נ final ן	Nûwn (*noon*)	**n**
15.	ס	Çâmek (*saw´-mek*)	**ç** = *s* sharp = שׂ
16.	ע	'Ayin (*ah´-yin*)	ʻ peculiar [1]
17.	פ final ף	Phê' (*fay*)	**ph** = *f* = φ
	פּ	Pê' (*pay*)	**p**
18.	צ, final ץ	Tsâdêy (*tsaw-day´*)	**ts**
19.	ק	Qôwph (*cofe*)	**q** = *k* = כ
20.	ר	Rêysh (*raysh*)	**r**
21.	שׂ	Sîyn (*seen*)	**s** sharp = ס = σ
	שׁ	Shîyn (*sheen*)	**sh**
22.	ת	Thâv (*thawv*)	**th**, as in *THin* = θ
	תּ	Tâv (*tawv*)	**t** = ט = τ

[1] The letter *'Ayin*, because Westerners find it difficult to pronounce accurately (it is a deep guttural sound, like that made in *gargling*), is generally passed over silently in reading. We have represented it to the eye (but not exactly to the ear) by the Greek *rough breathing* mark (ʻ) in order to distinguish it from *'Âleph*, which is likewise treated as silent, being similarly represented by the Greek *smooth breathing* (').

3. The vowel points are as follows:

Form [2]	Name	Transliteration and Pronunciation
בָ	Qâmêts (*caw-mates´*)	**â**, as in *All*
בַ	Pattach (*pat´-takh*)	**a**, as in *mAn*
בֲ	Shᵉvâ'-Pattach (*she-vaw´ pat´-takh*)	**ă**, as in *hAt*
בֵ	Tsêrêy (*tsay-ray´*)	**ê**, as in *thEy* = η
בֶ	Çegôwl (*seg-ole´*)	**e**, as in *thEir*
		e, as in *mEn* = ε
בֱ	Shᵉvâ'-Çegôwl (*she-vaw´ seg-ole´*)	**ĕ**, as in *mEt*
בְ	Shᵉvâ' (*she-vaw´*) [3]	obscure, as in *avErage*
		silent, as *e* in *madE*
בִ	Chîyriq (*khee´-rik*)	**î**, as in *machIne* [4]
		i, as in *supplIant* (*misery, hit*)
בֹ	Chôwlem (*kho´-lem*) [5]	**ô**, as in *no* = ω
בָ	Short Qâmêts (*caw-mates´*) [6]	**o**, as in *nor* = o
בֳ	Shᵉvâ -Qâmêts (*she-vaw´ caw-mates´*)	**ŏ**, as in *not*
וּ	Shûwrêq * (*shoo-rake´*) [7]	**û**, as in *crUel*
בֻ	Qîbbûts * (*kib´-boots*) [7]	**u**, as in *fUll, rude*

4. A point in the heart of a letter is called *Dâgêsh´*, and is of two kinds, which must be carefully distinguished.

a. Dâgêsh *lenè* occurs only in the letters בּ, גּ, דּ, כּ, פּ, תּ (technically vocalized *Bᵉgad´-Kᵉphath´*), when they *begin* a clause or sentence, or are preceded by a consonant *sound;* and simply has the effect of removing their aspiration. [8]

b. Dâgêsh *fortè* may occur in any letter except א, ה, ח, ע or ר; it is equivalent to *doubling* the letter, and at the same time it removes the aspiration of a Bᵉgad-Kᵉphath letter. [9]

5. The *Maqqêph´* (־), like a *hyphen*, unites words only for purposes of pronunciation (by removing the primary accent from all except the last word), but it does not affect their meaning or grammatical construction.

Special Symbols

+ (*addition*) denotes a rendering in the A.V. of one or more Hebrew or Aramaic words in connection with the one under consideration. For example, in 2 Kgs. 4:41, No. 1697, דָּבָר (**dâbâr**) is translated as "harm," in connection with No. 7451. Literally, it is "bad thing."

× (*multiplication*) denotes a rendering in the A.V. that results from an idiom peculiar to the Hebrew or Aramaic. For example, in Psa. 132:15, the whole Hebrew phrase in which בָּרַךְ, **bârak** (1288) appears is a means of expressing a verb root emphatically, i. e. "blessing, I will bless" = "I will abundantly bless."

° (*degree*), attached to a Hebrew word, denotes a corrected vowel pointing which is different from the Biblical text. (This mark is set in Hebrew Bibles over syllables in which the vowels of the margin have been inserted instead of those which properly belong to the text.)

For example, see the difference between the Hebrew text and the scribes' marginal note in Ezek. 40:15 for No. 2978, translated "entrance."

( ) (*parentheses*), in the renderings from the A.V., denote a word or syllable which is sometimes given in connection with the principal word to which it is attached. In Num. 34:6, the only occurrence of "western" in the A. V., the underlying Hebrew word is יָם (**yâm**, No. 3220), which is usually translated "sea."

[ ] (*brackets*), in the rendering from the A.V., denote the inclusion of an additional word in the Hebrew or Aramaic. For example, No. 3117, יוֹם (**yôwm**), is translated as "birthday" in Gen. 40:20, along with No. 3205. So, two Hebrew words are translated by one English word.

Italics, at the end of a rendering from the A.V., denote an explanation of the variations from the usual form.

---

[2] The same Hebrew/Aramaic consonant (ב) is shown here in order to show the position of the vowel points, whether below, above, or in the middle of Hebrew or Aramaic consonants.

[3] *Silent Shᵉvâ'* is not represented by any mark in our method of transliteration, since it is understood whenever there is no other vowel point.

[4] *Chîyriq* is long only when it is followed by a quiescent *yôwd* (either expressed or implied).

[5] *Chôwlem* is written *fully* only over *Vâv* or *Wâw* (ו), which is then quiescent (*w*); but when used "defectively" (without the *Vâv* or *Wâw*) it may be written either over the left-hand corner of the letter to which it belongs, or over the right-hand corner of the following one.

[6] Short *Qâmêts* is found only in *unaccented syllables ending with a consonant sound.*

[7] *Shûwrêq* is written only in the heart of *Vâv* or *Wâw*. Sometimes it is said to be "defectively" written (without the *Vâv* or *Wâw*), and then takes the form of *Qibbûts*, which in such cases is called *vicarious*.

[8] In our system of transliteration Dâgêsh *lenè* is represented only in the letters פּ and תּ, because elsewhere it does not affect the pronunciation.

[9] A point in the heart of ה is called *Mappîyq* (*map-peek´*). It occurs only in the final vowel-less letter of a few words, and we have represented it by *hh*. A Dâgêsh *fortè* in the heart of ו may easily be distinguished from the vowel *Shûwrêq* by noticing that in the former case the letter has a proper vowel point accompanying it.

It should be noted that both kinds of Dâgêsh are often omitted in writing (being *implied*), but (in the case at least of Dâgêsh *fortè*) the word is usually pronounced the same as if it were present.

Abbreviations

abb. = abbreviated
abbreviation
abstr. = abstract
abstractly
act. = active (voice)
actively
acc. = accusative (case) [1]
adj. = adjective
adjectivally
adv. = adverb
adverbial
adverbially
aff. = affix [2]
affixed
affin. = affinity
alt. = alternate
alternately
anal. = analogy
appar. = apparent
apparently
arch. = architecture
architectural
architecturally
art. = article [3]
artif. = artificial
artificially
Ass. = Assyrian
A.V. = Authorized Version
(King James Version)
Bab. = Babylon
Babylonia
Babylonian
caus. = causative [4]
causatively
cerem. = ceremony
ceremonial
ceremonially
Chald. = Chaldee (Aramaic)
Chaldaism
(Aramaism)
Chr. = Christian
collat. = collateral
collaterally
collect. = collective
collectively
comp. = compare [5]
comparison
comparative
comparatively
concr. = concrete
concretely
conjec. = conjecture
conjectural
conjecturally
conjug. = conjugation [6]
conjugational
conjugationally
conjunc. = conjunction
conjunctional
conjunctionally
constr. = construct [7]
construction
constructive
constructively

contr. = contracted [8]
contraction
correl. = correlated
correlation
correlative
correlatively
corresp. = corresponding
correspondingly
dat. = dative (case) [9]
def. = definite [10]
definitely
demonstr. = demonstrative [11]
denom. = denominative [12]
denominatively
der. = derived
derivation
derivative
derivatively
desc. = descended
descendant
descendants
dimin. = diminutive [13]
dir. = direct
directly
E. = East
Eastern
eccl. = ecclesiastical
ecclesiastically
e.g. = for example
Eg. = Egypt
Egyptian
Egyptians
ellip. = ellipsis [14]
elliptical
elliptically
emphat. = emphatic
emphatically
equiv. = equivalent
equivalently
err. = error
erroneous
erroneously
espec. = especially
etym. = etymology [15]
etymological
etymologically
euphem. = euphemism [16]
euphemistic
euphemistically
euphon. = euphonious [17]
euphonically
extens. = extension [18]
extensive
extern. = external
externally
fem. = feminine (gender)
fig. = figurative
figuratively
for. = foreign
foreigner
freq. = frequentative
frequentatively
fut. = future

gen. = general
generally
generic
generical
generically
Gr. = Greek
Graecism
gut. = guttural [19]
Heb. = Hebrew
Hebraism
i.e. = that is
ident. = identical
identically
immed. = immediate
immediately
imper. = imperative [20]
imperatively
imperf. = imperfect [21]
impers. = impersonal
impersonally
impl. = implied
impliedly
implication
incept. = inceptive [22]
inceptively
incl. = including
inclusive
inclusively
indef. = indefinite
indefinitely
ind. = indicative [23]
indicatively
indiv. = individual
individually
infer. = inference
inferential
inferentially
infin. = infinitive
inhab. = inhabitant
inhabitants
ins. = inserted
intens. = intensive
intensively
interch. = interchangeable
intern. = internal
internally
interj. = interjection [24]
interjectional
interjectionally
interrog. = interrogative [25]
interrogatively
intr. = intransitive [26]
intransitively
invol. = involuntary
involuntarily
irreg. = irregular
irregularly
Isr. = Israelite
Israelites
Israelitish
Lat. = Latin
Levit. = Levitical
Levitically

lit. = literal
literally
marg. = margin
marginal reading
masc. = masculine (gender)
mean. = meaning
ment. = mental
mentally
metaph. = metaphorical
metaphorically
mid. = middle (voice) [27]
modif. = modified
modification
mor. = moral
morally
mult. = multiplicative [28]
nat. = natural
naturally
neg. = negative
negatively
neut. = neuter (gender)
obj. = object
objective
objectively
obs. = obsolete
ord. = ordinal [29]
or. = origin
orig. = original
originally
orth. = orthography [30]
orthographical
orthographically
Pal. = Palestine
part. = participle
pass. = passive (voice)
passively
patron. = patronymic [31]
patronymical
patronymically
perh. = perhaps
perm. = permutation [32] (of
adjacent letters)
pers. = person
personal
personally
Pers. = Persia
Persian
Persians
phys. = physical
physically
plur. = plural
poet. = poetry
poetical
poetically
pos. = positive
positively
pref. = prefix
prefixed
prep. = preposition
prepositional
prepositionally
prim. = primitive
prob. = probable
probably

prol. = prolonged [33]
prolongation
pron. = pronoun
pronominal
pronominally
prop. = properly
prox. = proximate
proximately
recip. = reciprocal
reciprocally
redupl. = reduplicated [34]
reduplication
refl. = reflexive [35]
reflexively
reg. = regular
rel. = relative
relatively
relig. = religion
religious
religiously
Rom. = Roman
second. = secondary
secondarily
signif. = signification
signifying
short. = shorter
shortened
sing. = singular
spec. = specific
specifically
streng. = strengthening
subdiv. = subdivision
subdivisional
subdivisionally
subj. = subjectively
subjective
subject
substit. = substituted
suff. = suffix
superl. = superlative [36]
superlatively
symb. = symbolic
symbolical
symbolically
tech. = technical
technically
term. = termination
tran. = transitive [37]
transitively
transc. = transcription
transm. = transmutation [38]
transp. = transposed [39]
transposition
typ. = typical
typically
uncert. = uncertain
uncertainly
var. = various
variation
voc. = vocative (case) [40]
vol. = voluntary
voluntarily

---

[1] often indicating the direct object of an action verb

[2] part of a word which, when attached to the beginning of the word is called a prefix; if attaching within a word, an infix; and if at the end, a suffix

[3] "the" is the definite article; "a" and "an" are indefinite articles

[4] expressing or denoting causation

[5] the comparative of an adjective or adverb expresses a greater degree of an attribute, e.g. "higher"; "more slowly"

[6] a systematic array of various verbal forms

[7] the condition in Hebrew and Aramaic when two adjacent nouns are combined semantically as follows, e.g."sword" + "king" = "(the) sword of (the) king" or "(the) king's sword". These languages tend to throw the stress of the entire noun phrase toward the end of the whole expression.

[8] a shortened form of a word. It is made by omitting or combining some elements or by reducing vowels or syllables, e.g. "is not" becomes "isn't".

[9] often the indirect object of an action verb

[10] the definite article ("the")

[11] demonstrative pronouns which point (show), e.g. "this," "that"

[12] derived from a noun

[13] a grammatical form which expresses smallness and/or endearment

[14] a construction which leaves out understood words

[15] the historical origin of a word

[16] the use of a pleasant, polite, or harmless-sounding word or phrase to hide harsh, rude, or infamous truths, e.g. "to pass away" = "to die"

[17] a linguistic mechanism to make pronunciation easier, e.g. "an" before "hour" instead of "a"

[18] when a general term can denote an entire class of things

[19] speech sounds which are produced deep in the throat

[20] the mood which expresses a command

[21] used of a tense which expresses a continuous but unfinished action or state

[22] used of a verbal aspect which denotes the beginning of an action

[23] used of the mood which expresses a verbal action as actually occurring (not hypothetical)

[24] an exclamation which expresses emotion

[25] indicating a question

[26] referring to verbs which do not govern direct objects

[27] reflexive

[28] capable of multiplying or tending to multiply

[29] This shows the position or the order within a series, e.g. "second"; the corresponding cardinal number is "two".

[30] the written system of spelling in a given language

[31] a name derived from that of a paternal ancestor, often created by an affix in various languages

[32] a rearrangement

[33] lengthening a pronunciation

[34] the repetition of a letter or syllable to form a new, inflected word

[35] denoting an action by the subject upon itself

[36] expressing the highest degree of comparison of the quality indicated by an adjective or an adverb, e.g. "highest"; "most timely"

[37] expressing an action directed toward a person or a thing (the direct object)

[38] the change of one grammatical element to another

[39] switching word order

[40] an inflection which is used when one is addressing a person or a thing directly, e.g. "John, come here!"

HEBREW AND ARAMAIC DICTIONARY

ACCOMPANYING

THE EXHAUSTIVE CONCORDANCE.

א

1. אָב {1211x} ʼâb, *awb;* a prim. word; *father* in a lit. and immed., or fig. and remote application:—chief {2x}, (fore-{1x}) father {1205x} ([-less] {1x}), × patrimony {1x}, principal {1x}. comp. names in "Abi-".

Ab means "father; grandfather; forefather; ancestor." **(1)** Basically, *ab* relates to the familial relationship represented by the word "father." This is the word's significance in its first biblical appearance: "Therefore shall a man leave his father and his mother, and shall cleave unto his wife . . ." (Gen 2:24). **(2)** In poetical passages, the word is sometimes paralleled to em, "mother": "I have said to corruption, Thou art my father: to the worm, Thou art my mother, and my sister" (Job 17:14). The word is also used in conjunction with "mother" to represent one's parents (Lev 19:3). But unlike the word em, *ab* is never used of animals. **(3)** *Ab* also means "grandfather" and/or "greatgrandfather," as in Gen 28:13: "I am the LORD God of Abraham thy [grand]father, and the God of Isaac. . . ." Such progenitors on one's mother's side were called "thy mother's father" (Gen 28:2).

(4) This noun may be used of any one of the entire line of men from whom a given individual is descended: "But he [Elijah] himself went a day's journey into the wilderness, and came and sat down under a juniper tree: and he requested for himself that he might die; and said, It is enough; now, O LORD, take away my life; for I am not better than my fathers" (1 Kin 19:4). In such use, the word may refer to the first man, a "forefather," **(4a)** a clan (Jer 35:6), **(4b)** a tribe (Josh. 19:47), **(4c)** a group with a special calling (1 Chr 24:19), **(4d)** a dynasty (1 Kin 15:3), or **(4e)** a nation (Josh 24:3). **(5)** Thus, "father" does not necessarily mean the man who directly sired a given individual. **(6)** This noun sometimes describes the adoptive relationship, especially when it is used of the "founder of a class or station," such as a trade: "And Adah bare Jabal: he was the father of such as dwell in tents, and of such as have cattle" (Gen 4:20). **(7)** *Ab* can be a title of respect, usually applied to an older person, as when David said to Saul: "Moreover, my father, see, yea, see the skirt of thy robe in my hand . . ." (1 Sa 24:11).

(8) The word is also applied to teachers: "And Elisha saw it, and he cried, My father, my father, the chariot of Israel, and the horsemen thereof . . ." (2 Kin 2:12). **(9)** In 2 Kin 6:21, the word is applied to the prophet Elisha. **(10)** In Judg 17:10 it is applied to a priest. **(11)** This word is also a title of respect when used of "one's husband": "Wilt thou not from this time cry unto me, My father, thou art the guide of my youth?" (Jer 3:4). **(12)** In Gen 45:8, the noun is used of an "advisor": "So now it was not you that sent me hither, but God: and he hath made me a father [advisor] to Pharaoh, and lord of all his house, and a ruler throughout all the land of Egypt." **(13)** In each case, the one described as "father" occupied a position or status and received the honor due to a "father." **(14)** In conjunction with bayit [1004 - "house"], the word *ab* may mean "family": "In the tenth day of this month they shall take to them every man a lamb, according to the house of their fathers . . ." (Ex 12:3). **(15)** Sometimes the plural of the word used by itself can represent "family": ". . . These are the heads of the fathers [households] of the Levites according to their families" (Ex 6:25).

(16) God is described as the "father" of Israel (Deut 32:6). **(16a)** He is the One who begot and protected them, the One they should revere and obey. **(16b)** Mal 2:10 tells us that God is the "father" of all people. **(16c)** He is especially the "protector" or "father" of the fatherless: "A father of the fatherless, and a judge of the widows, is God in his holy habitation" (Ps 68:5). **(17)** As the "father" of a king, God especially aligns Himself to that man and his kingdom: "I will be his father, and he shall be my son. If he commit iniquity, I will chasten him with the rod of men, and with the stripes of the children of men" (2 Sa 7:14). **(17a)** Not every king was a son of God—only those whom He adopted. **(17b)** In a special sense, the perfect King was God's adopted Son: "I will declare the decree: the LORD hath said unto me, Thou art my Son; this day have I begotten thee" (Ps 2:7). The extent, power, and duration of His kingdom are guaranteed by the Father's sovereignty (Ps 2:8–9). **(18)** On the other hand, one of the Messiah's enthronement names is "Eternal Father": ". . . And his name shall be called Wonderful, Counselor, The mighty God, The everlasting Father, The Prince of Peace" (Is 9:6). See: TWOT—4a; BDB—1a, 3a, 1078b.

2. אַב {9x} ʼab (Aram.), *ab;* corresp. to 1:—father {9x}. See: TWOT—2553; BDB—1078a, b.

3. אֵב {2x} ʼêb, *abe;* from the same as 24; a *green* plant:—greenness {1x}, fruit {1x}. See: TWOT—1a; BDB—1a, 1078a.

4. אֵב {3x} ʼêb (Aram.), *abe;* corresp. to 3:—fruit {3x}. See: TWOT—2554; BDB—1078a, 1081b.

5. אֲבַגְתָא {1x} ʼĂbagthâʼ, *ab-ag-thaw';* of for. or.; *Abagtha,* a eunuch of Xerxes:—*Abagtha.* BDB—1b.

6. אָבַד {184x} ʼâbad, *aw-bad';* a prim. root; prop. to *wander* away, i.e. *lose* oneself; by impl. to *perish* (caus. *destroy*); :—break {1x}, destroy {62x} (-uction {1x}), + not escape {1x}, fail {2x}, lose {10x}, (cause to, make) perish {98x}, spendeth {1x}, × and surely {2x}, take {1x}, be undone {1x}, × utterly {2x}, be void of {1x}, have no way to flee {1x}.

Basically *âbad* represents the disappearance of someone or something. **(1)** In its strongest sense the word means "to die or to cease to exist" (Lev 26:38). **(2)** bring to non-existence (Num 33:52; Deut 12:2–3). **(3)** to go to ruin or to be ruined (Ex 10:7; Num 21:29–30). **(4)** to succumb, focuses on the process rather than the conclusion (Num 17:12–13). **(5)** being carried off to death or destruction by some means (Num 6:33; Deut 4:26). **(6)** to disappear but not be destroyed, to be lost (Deut 22:3; Jer 50:6). **(7)** to go astray, in the sense of wandering (Deut 26:5). **(8)** human qualities which are lessening or have lessened (Deut 32:28; Ps 146:4). Syn.: 2763, 7843, 8045. Summary: This word refers to the death of the righteous or the wicked; to the downfall and dissolution of nations; to the desolation of countries; to the withering away of herbage and crops; to the fading away of strength, hope, wisdom, knowledge, and wealth. Syn: See: TWOT—2; BDB—1b, 1078b.

7. אֲבַד {7x} ʼăbad (Aram.), *ab-ad';* corresp. to 6:—to destroy {5x}, to perish {2x}.

Basically *abad* represents the disappearance of someone or something. **(1)** In its strongest sense the word means "to die or to cease to exist." The LORD warned Israel that disobedience and godlessness would be punished by their removal from the Promised Land and death in a foreign land: "And ye shall perish among the heathen, and the land of your enemies shall eat you up" (Lev 26:38). This sense may be further heightened by the use of the intensive stem so that the verb comes to mean "utterly destroy." The stem also changes the force of the verb from intransitive to transitive. So God told Israel "to utterly destroy" ("bring to non-existence") the false gods of Canaan: ". . . [Utterly] destroy all their pictures and [utterly] destroy all their molten images . . ." (Num 33:52). The force of this command was further heightened when He said: "Ye shall utterly destroy all the places, wherein the nations which ye shall possess served their gods . . . and destroy the names of them out of that place" (Deut 12:2–3). This intensified sense is used of the destruction of peoples (armies), too; as for Pharaoh's army, "the LORD hath destroyed them unto this day" (Deut 11:4).

(2) A somewhat different emphasis of *abad* is "to go to ruin" or "to be ruined." After the second plague Pharaoh's counsellors told him to grant Israel's request to leave because the nation was in ruins: ". . . knowest thou not yet that Egypt is destroyed [ruined]?" (Ex 10:7—the first biblical occurrence). In a similar sense Moab is said "to be ruined" or laid waste: "Woe to thee, Moab!

Thou art undone, O people of Chemosh. . . . We have shot at them; Heshbon is perished even unto Dibon, and we have laid them waste even unto Nophah . . ." (Num 21:29–30). **(3)** Closely related to the immediately preceding emphasis is that of "to succumb." This use of *abad* focuses on the process rather than the conclusion. The sons of Israel spoke to Moses about the disastrous effects of everyone drawing near to God. They needed some mediators (priests) who could focus on keeping ritualistically prepared so they would not die when they approached God. They used the verb, therefore, in the sense of the nation gradually perishing, or "succumbing" to death: "Behold, we die, we perish, we all perish. Whosoever cometh any thing near unto the tabernacle of the LORD shall die: shall we be consumed with dying?" (Num 17:12–13). God responds by establishing the priesthood so "that there be no wrath any more upon the children of Israel" (Num 18:5).

(4) *Abad* can also speak of being carried off to death or destruction by some means. The leaders of the rebellion against the Aaronic priesthood (Korah, Dathan, and Abiram) and their families were swallowed up by the ground: ". . . and the earth closed upon them: and they perished from among the congregation" (Num 16:33). This same nuance appears when God says the people will "perish" from off the land if they do not keep the covenant: ". . . Ye shall soon utterly perish from off the land whereunto ye go over Jordan to possess it; ye shall not prolong your days upon it, but shall utterly be destroyed" (Deut 4:26). As a nation they will be destroyed as far as the land is concerned. **(5)** The verb may mean to disappear but not be destroyed, in other words "to be lost." God instructs Israel concerning lost possessions: "In like manner shalt thou do with his ass; and so shalt thou do with his raiment; and with all lost things of thy brother's, which he hath lost, and thou hast found, shalt thou do likewise: thou mayest not hide thyself" (Deut 22:3). Israel is called "lost sheep" whose "shepherds have caused them to go astray" (Jer 50:6). **(6)** Another nuance of the verb is "to go astray" in the sense of wandering. At the dedication of the first fruits Israel is to recognize God's rights to the land, that He is the landowner and they are the temporary tenants, by confessing "a Syrian ready to perish was my father" (Deut 26:5).

(7) Finally, *abad* can be applied to human qualities which are lessening or have lessened: "For they are a nation void of counsel, neither is there any understanding in them" (Deut 32:28). The word can also be used of the failure of human wisdom as in Ps 146:4: as for men "his breath goeth forth, he returneth to his earth; in that very day his thoughts perish."

8. אֹבֵד {2x} **ʼôbêd**, *o-bade';* act. of part. of 6; (concr.) *wretched* or (abstr.) *destruction:*—perish {2x}. See: TWOT—2a; BDB—1b, 2b.

9. אֲבֵדָה {4x} **ʼăbêdâh**, *ab-ay-daw';* from 6; concr. something *lost;* abstr. *destruction,* i.e. Hades:—lost thing {3x}, that which was lost {1x}. *Abedah,* which is found 4 times, refers to a "thing which has been lost" (Exod 22:9). Syn.: comp. 10. See: TWOT—2b; BDB—2b.

10. אֲבַדֹּה {1x} **ʼăbaddôh**, *ab-ad-do';* the same as 9, miswritten for 11; a *perishing:*—destruction {1x}. See: TWOT—2b; BDB—2b, c.

11. אֲבַדּוֹן {6x} **ʼăbaddôwn**, *ab-ad-done';* intens. from 6; abstr. a *perishing;* concr. Hades:—destruction {6x}. The noun *abaddown* occurs 6 times and means "the place of destruction" (Job 26:6). See: TWOT—2d; BDB—2b.

12. אַבְדָן {1x} **ʼabdân**, *ab-dawn';* from 6; a *perishing:*—destruction {1x}. *Abdan* occurs once with the meaning "destruction" (Est 9:5). See: TWOT—2c; BDB—2b.

13. אָבְדָן {2x} **ʼobdân**, *ob-dawn';* from 6; a *perishing:*—destruction {2x}. A variant spelling *obdan* also occurs with the meaning "destruction" (Est 8:6; 9:5). See: TWOT—2c; BDB—2b.

14. אָבָה {54x} **ʼâbâh**, *aw-baw';* a prim. root; to *breathe* after, i.e. (fig.) to *be accquiescent:*—consent {3x}, rest content {1x}, will {4x}, be willing {4x}, would {42x}.

This verb, which occurs 54 times, is sometimes associated with the noun *'ebyon,* "needy (person)." **(1)** This verb means "to consent to" in Deut 13:8: "Thou shalt not consent unto him, nor hearken unto him. . . ." Basically represents the inclination which leads towards action, rather than the volition which immediately precedes it. See: TWOT—3; BDB—2c.

15. אָבֶה {1x} **ʼâbeh**, *aw-beh';* from 14; *longing:*—desire {1x}. See: TWOT—3; BDB—106b.

16. אֵבֶה {1x} **ʼêbeh**, *ay-beh';* from 14 (in the sense of *bending* toward); the *papyrus:*—swift {1x}. See: TWOT—3c; BDB—3a.

17. אֲבוֹי {1x} **ʼăbôwy**, *ab-o'ee;* from 14 (in the sense of *desiring*); *want:*—sorrow {1x}. See: TWOT—3d; BDB—5a.

18. אֵבוּס {3x} **ʼêbûwç**, *ay-booce';* from 75; a *manger* or *stall:*—crib {3x}. See: TWOT—10a; BDB—7b.

19. אִבְחָה {1x} **ʼibchâh**, *ib-khaw';* from an unused root (appar. mean. to *turn*); *brandishing* of a sword:—point (of the sword) {1x}. See: TWOT—786b; BDB—5b.

20. אֲבַטִּחַ {1x} **ʼăbaṭṭîyach**, *ab-at-tee'-akh;* of uncert. der.; a *melon* (only plur.):—melons {1x}. See: TWOT—234a; BDB—5b, 105c.

21. אֲבִי {1x} **ʼĂbîy**, *ab-ee';* from 1; *fatherly; Abi,* Hezekiah's mother:—Abi {1x}. See: BDB—4a, 5b.

22. אֲבִיאֵל {3x} **ʼĂbîyʼêl**, *ab-ee-ale';* from 1 and 410; *father* (i.e. *possessor*) *of God; Abiel,* the name of two Isr.:—Abiel {3x}. See: BDB—3d.

23. אֲבִיאָסָף {1x} **ʼĂbîyʼâçâph**, *ab-ee-aw-sawf';* from 1 and 622; *father of gathering* (i.e. *gatherer*); *Abiasaph,* an Isr.:—Abiasaph {1x}. See: BDB—4a.

24. אָבִיב {8x} **ʼâbîyb**, *aw-beeb';* from an unused root (mean. to *be tender*); *green,* i.e. a young *ear* of grain; hence, the name of the month *Abib* or Nisan:—Abib {6x}, in the ear {1x}, green ears of corn {1x}. See: TWOT—1b; BDB—1b.

25. אֲבִי גִבְעוֹן {2x} **ʼĂbîy Gibʻôwn**, *ab-ee' ghib-one';* from 1 and 1391; *father* (i.e. *founder*) *of Gibon; Abi-Gibon,* perh. an Isr.:—father of Gibeon {2x}. See: BDB—149c.

26. אֲבִיגַיִל {17x} **ʼĂbîygayil**, *ab-ee-gah'-yil,* or short.

אֲבִיגַל **ʼĂbîygal**, *ab-ee-gal';* from 1 and 1524; *father* (i.e. *source*) *of joy; Abigail* or *Abigal,* the name of two Israelitesses:—Abigal {17x}. See: BDB—1b, 4a, 5a.

27. אֲבִידָן {5x} **ʼĂbîydân**, *ab-ee-dawn';* from 1 and 1777; *father of judgment* (i.e. *judge*); *Abidan,* an Isr.:—Abidan {5x}. See: BDB—4a.

28. אֲבִידָע {2x} **ʼĂbîydâʻ**, *ab-ee-daw';* from 1 and 3045; *father of knowledge* (i.e. *knowing*); *Abida,* a son of Abraham by Keturah:—Abida, Abidah. {2x}. See: BDB—4a.

29. אֲבִיָּה {25x} **ʼĂbîyâh**, *ab-ee-yaw';* or prol.

אֲבִיָּהוּ **ʼĂbîyâhûw**, *ab-ee-yaw'-hoo;* from 1 and 3050; *father* (i.e. *worshipper*) *of Jah; Abijah,* the name of several Isr. men and two Israelitesses:—Abijah 20, Abiah 4, Abia 1; {25x}. See: BDB—4a, 5b.

30. אֲבִיהוּא {12x} **ʼĂbîyhûwʼ**, *ab-ee-hoo';* from 1 and 1931; *father* (i.e. *worshipper*) of *Him* (i.e. *God*); *Abihu,* a son of Aaron:—Abihu {12x}. See: BDB—4b.

31. אֲבִיהוּד {1x} **ʼĂbîyhûwd**, *ab-ee-hood';* from 1 and 1935; *father* (i.e. *possessor*) *of renown; Abihud,* the name of two Isr.:—Abihud {1x}. See: BDB—4b.

32. אֲבִיהַיִל {6x} **ʼĂbîyhayil**, *ab-ee-hah'-yil;* or (more correctly)

אֲבִיחַיִל **ʼĂbîychayil**, *ab-ee-khah'-yil;* from 1 and 2428; *father* (i.e. *possessor*) *of might; Abihail* or *Abichail,* the name of three Isr. and two Israelitesses:—Abihail {6x}. See: BDB—4b, 5b.

33. אֲבִי הָעֶזְרִי {3x} **ʼĂbîy hâ-ʻEzrîy**, *ab-ee'-haw-ez-ree';* from 44 with the art. ins.; *father of the Ezrite;* an *Abiezrite* or desc. of Abiezer:—Abiezrite {3x}. See: BDB—4c, 5b.

34. אֶבְיוֹן {35x} **ʼebyôwn**, *eb-yone';* from 14, in the sense of *want* (espec. in feeling); *destitute:*—beggar {1x}, needy {35x}, poor {24x}, poor man {1x}.

(1) This noun refers to someone who is poor in a material sense. Such a one may have lost the land of his inheritance: "But the seventh year thou shalt let it rest and lie still; that the poor of thy people may eat: and what they leave the beasts of the field shall eat" (Ex 23:11). He has come into difficult financial straits (Job 30:25) and perhaps lacks clothing (Job 31:19) or food (Ps 132:15). **(2)** Secondly *ebyown* may refer to the lack of social standing which causes a need for protection. The first biblical occurrence bears this emphasis. God guarantees protection for such a one: "Thou shalt not wrest the judgment of thy poor in his cause" (Ex 23:6). The godly man defends the needy and defenseless: "I was a father to the poor: and the cause which I knew not I searched out" (Job 29:16; cf. Pro 31:9; Rom 3:14–15). Divine provisions are encased in the Mosaic stipulations such as the seventh year reversion of ancestral hereditary lands (Ex 23:11), cancellation of loans (Deut 15:4), and special extension of loans (Deut 15:7, 9, 11).

(3) Thirdly, this noun sometimes describes one's spiritual condition before God: "Thus saith the LORD; For three transgressions of Israel, and for four, I will not turn away the punishment thereof; because they sold the righteous for silver, and the poor for a pair of shoes" (Amos 2:6). In this verse *ebyown* is in synonymous parallelism to "righteous," which means that it describes a moral quality. Syn.: 1800, 6041. See: TWOT—3a; BDB—2d, 5b.

35. אֲבִיּוֹנָה {1x} **ʼabîyôwnâh**, *ab-ee-yo-naw';* from 14; provocative of *desire;* the

caper berry (from its *stimulative* taste):—desire {1x}. See: TWOT—3b; BDB—2d.

36. אֲבִיטוּב {1x} **ʾĂbîytûwb**, *ab-ee-toob';* from 1 and 2898; *father of goodness* (i.e. *good*); *Abitub*, an Isr.:—Abitub {1x}. See: BDB—4b.

37. אֲבִיטַל {2x} **ʾĂbîytal**, *ab-ee-tal';* from 1 and 2919; *father of dew* (i.e. *fresh*); *Abital*, a wife of King David:—Abital {2x}. See: BDB—4b.

38. אֲבִיָּם {5x} **ʾĂbîyâm**, *ab-ee-yawm';* from 1 and 3220; *father of* (the) *sea* (i.e. *seaman*); *Abijam* (or Abijah), a king of Judah:—Abijam {5x}. See: BDB—4a, 5b.

39. אֲבִימָאֵל {2x} **ʾĂbîymâʾêl**, *ab-ee-maw-ale';* from 1 and an elsewhere unused (prob. for.) word; *father of Mael* (appar. some Arab tribe); *Abimael*, a son of Joktan:—Abimael {2x}. See: BDB—4b.

40. אֲבִימֶלֶךְ {67x} **ʾĂbîymelek**, *ab-ee-mel'-ek;* from 1 and 4428; *father of* (the) *king; Abimelek*, the name of two Philistine kings and of two Isr.:—Abimelech {67x}. See: BDB—4b.

41. אֲבִינָדָב {12x} **ʾĂbîynâdâb**, *ab-ee-naw-dawb';* from 1 and 5068; *father of generosity* (i.e. *liberal*); *Abinadab*, the name of four Isr.:—Abinadab {12x}. See: BDB—4c.

42. אֲבִינֹעַם {4x} **ʾĂbîynôʿam**, *ab-ee-no'-am;* from 1 and 5278; *father of pleasantness* (i.e. *gracious*); *Abinoam*, an Isr.:—Abinoam {4x}. See: BDB—4c.

אֲבִינֵר **ʾĂbîynêr**. See 74.

43. אֶבְיָסָף {3x} **ʾEbyâçâph**, *eb-yaw-sawf';* contr. from 23; *Ebjasaph*, an Isr.:—Ebiasaph {3x}. See: BDB—4a, 5b.

44. אֲבִיעֶזֶר {7x} **ʾĂbîyʿezer**, *ab-ee-ay'-zer;* from 1 and 5829; *father of help* (i.e. *helpful*); *Abiezer*, the name of two Isr.:—Abiezer {7x}. See: BDB—4c, 33b.

45. אֲבִי־עַלְבוֹן {1x} **ʾĂbîy-ʿalbôwn**, *ab-ee al-bone';* from 1 and an unused root of uncert. der.; prob. *father of strength* (i.e. *valiant*); *Abialbon*, an Isr.:—Abialbon {1x}. See: BDB—3d, 748a.

46. אֲבִיר {6x} **ʾâbîyr**, *aw-beer';* from 82; *mighty* (spoken only of God):—mighty (One) {6x}. See: TWOT—13c; BDB—7d.

47. אַבִּיר {17x} **ʾabbîyr**, *ab-beer';* from 46:—bulls {4x}, strong (ones) {4x}, mighty {3x}, stouthearted {2x}, valiant {2x}, angels {1x}, chiefest {1x}. See: TWOT—13d; BDB—7d.

48. אֲבִירָם {11x} **ʾĂbîyrâm**, *ab-ee-rawm';* from 1 and 7311; *father of height* (i.e. *lofty*); *Abiram*, the name of two Isr.:—Abiram {11x}. See: BDB—4d.

49. אֲבִישַׁג {5x} **ʾĂbîyshag**, *ab-ee-shag';* from 1 and 7686; *father of error* (i.e. *blundering*); *Abishag*, a concubine of David:—Abishag {5x}. See: BDB—4d.

50. אֲבִישׁוּעַ {5x} **ʾĂbîyshûwaʿ**, *ab-ee-shoo'-ah;* from 1 and 7771; *father of plenty* (i.e. *prosperous*); *Abishua*, the name of two Isr.:—Abishua {5x}. See: BDB—4d.

51. אֲבִישׁוּר {2x} **ʾĂbîyshûwr**, *ab-ee-shoor';* from 1 and 7791; *father of* (the) *wall* (i.e. perh. *mason*); *Abishur*, an Isr.:—Abishur {2x}. See: BDB—4d.

52. אֲבִישַׁי {25x} **ʾĂbîyshay**, *ab-ee-shah'ee;* or (short.)

אַבְשַׁי **ʾAbshay**, *ab-shah'ee;* from 1 and 7862; *father of a gift* (i.e. prob. *generous*); *Abishai*, an Isr.:—Abishai {25x}. See: BDB—5a, 8a.

53. אֲבִישָׁלוֹם {111x} **ʾĂbîyshâlôwm**, *ab-ee-shaw-lome';* or (short.)

אַבְשָׁלוֹם **ʾAbshâlôwm**, *ab-shaw-lome';* from 1 and 7965; *father of peace* (i.e. *friendly*); *Abshalom*, a son of David; also (the fuller form) a later Isr.:—Abishalom {2x} Absalom {109x}. See: BDB—5a, 8a.

54. אֶבְיָתָר {30x} **ʾEbyâthâr**, *eb-yaw-thawr';* contr. from 1 and 3498; *father of abundance* (i.e. *liberal*); *Ebjathar*, an Isr.:—Abiathar {30x}. See: BDB—5a.

55. אָבַךְ {1x} **ʾâbak**, *aw-bak';* a prim. root; prob. to *coil* upward:—mount up {1x}. See: TWOT—5; BDB—5b.

56. אָבַל {39x} **ʾâbal**, *aw-bal';* a prim. root; to *bewail:*—lament {3x}, mourn {36x}.

(1) *Abal* is used in the simple, active verbal form primarily in poetry, and usually in a figurative sense. When it is used of mourning for the dead in a literal sense, the word is found in prose sections and in the reflexive form, indicating action back on the subject. To mourn, lament for the dead **(1)** in a literal sense over the dead (Gen 37:34). **(2)** When used in the figurative sense, *abal* expresses "mourning" by gates (Is 3:26), by the land (Is 24:4), and by pastures (Amos 1:2). **(3)** In addition to mourning for the dead, "mourning" may be over Jerusalem (Is 66:10), over sin (Ezra 10:6), or over God's judgment (Ex 33:4). **(4)** One may pretend to be a mourner (2 Sa 14:2) simply by putting on mourning clothes. Syn: 5594 is more dramatic stressing wailing and tearing out the hair. See: TWOT—6; BDB—5b.

57. אָבֵל {8x} **ʾâbêl**, *aw-bale';* from 56; *lamenting:*—mourn {8x}. This word is usually mourning **(1)** for the dead or **(2)** because of calamity. See: TWOT—6b; BDB—5c.

58. אָבֵל {1x} **ʾâbêl**, *aw-bale';* from an unused root (mean. to *be grassy*); a *meadow:*—plain {1x}. See: TWOT—7a; BDB—5d.

59. אָבֵל {4x} **ʾÂbêl**, *aw-bale';* from 58; a *meadow; Abel*, the name of two places in Pal.:—*Abel* {4x}. BDB—5d.

60. אֵבֶל {24x} **ʾêbel**, *ay'-bel;* from 56; *lamentation:*—mourning. This may refer to the rites associated with mourning. See: TWOT—6a; BDB—5c.

61. אֲבָל {11x} **ʾăbâl**, *ab-awl';* appar. from 56 through the idea of *negation; nay* (i.e. *truly* or *yet*):—but {4x}, verily {3x}, indeed {2x}, nevertheless {2x}. See: TWOT—8; BDB—6a.

62. אָבֵל בֵּית־מַעֲכָה {2x} **ʾÂbêl Bêyth-Maʿakâh**, *aw-bale' bayth ma-a-kaw';* from 58 and 1004 and 4601; *meadow of Beth-Maakah; Abel of Beth-maakah*, a place in Pal.:—Abel-beth-maachah {2x}. See: BDB—6a.

63. אָבֵל הַשִּׁטִּים {1x} **ʾÂbêl hash-Shiṭṭîym**, *aw-bale' hash-shit-teem';* from 58 and the plur. of 7848, with the art. ins.; *meadow of the acacias; Abel hash-Shittim*, a place in Pal.:—Abel-shittim {1x}. See: BDB—6a, 1008d.

64. אָבֵל כְּרָמִים {1x} **ʾÂbêl Kᵉrâmîym**, *aw-bale' ker-aw-meem';* from 58 and the plur. of 3754; *meadow of vineyards; Abel-Keramim*, a place in Pal.:—plain of the vineyards {1x}. See: BDB—6a.

65. אָבֵל מְחוֹלָה {3x} **ʾÂbêl Mᵉchôwlâh**, *aw-bale' mekh-o-law';* from 58 and 4246; *meadow of dancing; Abel-Mecholah*, a place in Pal.:—Abel-meholah {3x}. See: BDB—6a, 562d, 563a.

66. אָבֵל מַיִם {1x} **ʾÂbêl Mayim**, *aw-bale' mah'-yim;* from 58 and 4325; *meadow of water; Abel-Majim*, a place in Pal.:—Abel-maim {1x}. See: BDB—6a.

67. אָבֵל מִצְרַיִם {1x} **ʾÂbêl Mitsrayim**, *aw-bale' mits-rah'-yim;* from 58 and 4714; *meadow of Egypt; Abel-Mitsrajim*, a place in Pal.:—Abel-mizraim {1x}. See: BDB—5c, 6a.

68. אֶבֶן {272x} **ʾeben**, *eh'-ben;* from the root of 1129 through the mean. to *build;* a *stone:*—+ carbuncle + 688 –{1x}, + mason + 7023 – {1x}, + plummet {1x}, [chalk-, hail- 5, head- {1x}, sling- {1x}] stone (-s {247x} – ny {2x}), (divers +68 – {3x}) weight (-s {7x}).

(1) Primarily, a construction material, **(2)** covers for wells (Gen 29:3ff.), **(3)** storage containers (Ex 7:19), **(4)** weights (Deut 25:13; Prov 11:1), **(5)** slingstones (1 Sa 17:49), **(6)** plumblines were suspended stones (Is 34:11), **(7)** pavement (2 Kin 16:17), **(8)** hailstones (Josh 10:11; Eze 13:11ff.), **(9)** tombs (Is 14:19), **(10)** bodies heaped with "stones" (Josh 7:26; 8:29; 2 Sa 18:17). **(11)** Worship of the carved "stone" figurines strictly forbidden to Israel (Lev 26:1). **(12)** Altars and memorials made of unhewn "stones" (Gen 28:18ff.; 31:45; Josh 4:5; 24:26–27). **(13)** Precious "stones" - onyx (Gen 2:12) and sapphire (Eze 1:26) **(14)** God is called the "stone of Israel" (Gen 49:24). **(15)** Viewed as messianic (Gen 28:18; Ps 118:22; Is 8:14; 28:16; Dan 2:34; Zec 4:7). Syn.: *Eben* is used almost exclusively for movable stone(s), sela (5553) a large immovable rock, and sur (6697), a cliff. See: TWOT—9; BDB—6b, 918d, 1078b.

69. אֶבֶן {8x} **ʾeben** (Aram.), *eh'-ben;* corresp. to 68:—stone(s) {8x}. See: TWOT—2556; BDB—1078b.

70. אֹבֶן {2x} **ʾôben**, *o'-ben;* from the same as 68; a *pair of stones* (only dual); a potter's *wheel* or a midwife's *stool* (consisting alike of two horizontal disks with a support between):—stools {1x}, wheels {1x}. See: TWOT—9a; BDB—7a.

71. אֲבָנָה {1x} **ʾĂbânâh**, *ab-aw-naw';* perh. fem. of 68; *stony; Abanah*, a river near Damascus:—Abana {1x}. See: BDB—7b. comp. 549.

72. אֶבֶן הָעֵזֶר {3x} **ʾEben hâ-ʿêzer**, *eh'-ben haw-e'-zer;* from 68 and 5828 with the art. ins.; *stone of the help; Eben ha-Ezer*, a place in Pal.:—Ebenezer {3x}. See: BDB—7a.

73. אַבְנֵט {9x} **ʾabnêṭ**, *ab-nate';* of uncert. der.; a *belt:*—girdle(s) {9x}. These are the sashes of the high priest or other priests. See: TWOT—256a; BDB—7b, 126a.

74. אַבְנֵר {63x} **ʾAbnêr**, *ab-nare';* or (fully)

אֲבִינֵר **ʾĂbîynêr**, *ab-ee-nare';* from 1 and 5216; *father of light* (i.e. *enlightening*); *Abner*, an Isr.:—Abner {63x}. BDB—4c, 7b.

75. אָבַס {2x} **ʾâbaç**, *aw-bas';* a prim. root; to *fodder:*—fatted {1x}, stalled {1x}. See: TWOT—10; BDB—7b.

76. אֲבַעְבֻּעָה {2x} **ʾăbaʿbûʿâh**, *ab-ah-boo-aw';* (by redupl.) from an unused root (mean. to *belch* forth); an inflammatory *pustule*

(as *eruption*):—blains {2x}. See: TWOT—217a; BDB—7b, 101b.

77. אֶבֶץ {1x} **ʼEbets**, *eh'-bets;* from an unused root prob. mean. to *gleam; conspicuous; Ebets,* a place in Pal.:—Abez {1x}. See: BDB—7b.

78. אִבְצָן {2x} **ʼIbtsân**, *ib-tsawn';* from the same as 76; *splendid; Ibtsan,* an Isr.:—Ibzan {2x}. See: BDB—7b.

79. אָבַק {2x} **ʼâbaq**, *aw-bak';* a prim. root, prob. to *float* away (as vapor), but used only as denom. from 80; to *bedust,* i.e. *grapple:*—wrestled {2x}. See: TWOT—12; BDB—7c.

80. אָבָק {6x} **ʼâbâq**, *aw-bawk';* from root of 79; light *particles* (as *volatile*):—dust {5x}, powder {1x}. See: TWOT—11a; BDB—7b.

81. אֲבָקָה {1x} **ʼăbâqâh**, *ab-aw-kaw';* fem. of 80:—powders {1x}. See: TWOT—11b; BDB—7c.

82. אָבַר {1x} **ʼâbar**, *aw-bar';* a prim. root; to *soar:*—fly {1x}. See: TWOT—13b; BDB—7c.

83. אֵבֶר {3x} **ʼêber**, *ay-ber';* from 82; a *pinion:*—wings {2x}, winged {1x}. See: TWOT—13a; BDB—7c.

84. אֶבְרָה {4x} **ʼebrâh**, *eb-raw';* fem. of 83:—feathers {2x}, wings {2x}. See: TWOT—13a; BDB—7c.

85. אַבְרָהָם {175x} **ʼAbrâhâm**, *ab-raw-hawm';* contr. from 1 and an unused root (prob. mean. to *be populous*); *father of a multitude; Abraham,* the later name of Abram:—*Abraham* {175x}. See: BDB—4d, 7d.

86. אַבְרֵךְ {1x} **ʼabrêk**, *ab-rake';* prob. an Eg. word mean. *kneel:*—bow the knee {1x}. See: TWOT—14; BDB—7d.

87. אַבְרָם {61x} **ʼAbrâm**, *ab-rawm';* contr. from 48; *high father; Abram,* the original name of Abraham:—*Abram* {61x}. See: BDB—4d, 8a.

אַבְשַׁי **ʼAbshay**. See 52.

אַבְשָׁלוֹם **ʼAbshâlôwm**. See 53.

88. אֹבֹת {4x} **ʼÔbôth**, *o-both';* plur. of 178; water- *skins; Oboth,* a place in the Desert:—*Oboth* {4x}. See: BDB—15c.

89. אָגֵא {1x} **ʼÂgê**, *aw-gay';* of uncert. der. [comp. 90]; *Agë,* an Isr.:—Agee {1x}. See: BDB—8a.

90. אֲגַג {8x} **ʼĂgag**, *ag-ag';* or

אֲגָג **ʼĂgâg**, *Ag-awg';* of uncert. der. [comp. 89]; *flame; Agag,* a title of Amalekitish kings:—*Agag* {8x}. See: BDB—8a.

91. אֲגָגִי {5x} **ʼĂgâgîy**, *ag-aw-ghee';* patrial or patron. from 90; an *Agagite* or descendent (subject) of Agag:—Agagite {5x}. See: BDB—8a.

92. אֲגֻדָּה {4x} **ʼăguddâh**, *ag-ood-daw';* fem. pass. part. of an unused root (mean. to *bind*); a *band, bundle, knot,* or *arch:*—troop {2x}, bunch {1x}, burdens {1x}. See: TWOT—15a; BDB—8a.

93. אֱגוֹז {1x} **ʼĕgôwz**, *eg-oze';* prob of Pers. or.; a *nut:*—nut {1x}. TWOT—16; BDB—8b.

94. אָגוּר {1x} **ʼÂgûwr**, *aw-goor';* pass. part. of 103; *gathered* (i.e. *received* among the sages); *Agur,* a fanciful name for Solomon:—Agur {1x}. See: BDB—8d.

95. אֲגוֹרָה {1x} **ʼăgôwrâh**, *ag-o-raw';* from the same as 94; prop. something *gathered,* i.e. perh. a *grain* or *berry;* used only of a small (silver) *coin:*—piece [of] silver {1x}. Payment. See: TWOT—23a; BDB—8d.

96. אֶגֶל {1x} **ʼegel**, *eh'-ghel;* from an unused root (mean. to *flow* down or together as drops); a *reservoir:*—drops {1x}. See: TWOT—17a; BDB—8b.

97. אֶגְלַיִם {1x} **ʼEglayim**, *eg-lah'-yim;* dual of 96; a *double pond; Eglajim,* a place in Moab:—Eglaim {1x}. See: BDB—8b.

98. אֲגַם {9x} **ʼăgam**, *ag-am';* from an unused root (mean. to *collect* as water); a *marsh;* hence, a *rush* (as growing in swamps); hence, a *stockade* of reeds:—pools {6x}, standing {2x}, reeds {1x}. See: TWOT—18a; BDB—8b.

99. אָגֵם {1x} **ʼâgêm**, *aw-game';* prob. from the same as 98 (in the sense of *stagnant* water); fig. *sad:*—pools {1x}. See: TWOT—18b; BDB—8c.

100. אַגְמוֹן {5x} **ʼagmôwn**, *ag-mone';* from the same as 98; a marshy *pool* [others from a different root, a *kettle*]; by impl. a *rush* (as growing there); collect. a rope of rushes:—rush {2x}, bulrush {1x}, caldron {1x}, hook {1x}. See: TWOT—19; BDB—8c.

101. אַגָּן {3x} **ʼaggân**, *ag-gawn';* prob. from 5059; a *bowl* (as *pounded* out hollow):—basins {1x}, cups {1x}, goblet {1x}. See: TWOT—20a; BDB—8c.

102. אַגָּף {7x} **ʼaggâph**, *ag-gawf';* prob. from 5062 (through the idea of *impending*); a *cover* or *heap;* i.e. (only plur.) *wings* of an army, or *crowds* of troops:—bands {7x}. See: TWOT—21a; BDB—8c, 1086d.

103. אָגַר {3} **ʼâgar**, *aw-gar';* a prim. root; to *harvest:*—gather {3x}. See: TWOT—22; BDB—8d.

104. אִגְּרָא {3x} **ʼiggᵉrâ** (Aram.), *ig-er-aw';* of Pers. or.; an *epistle* (as carried by a state courier or postman):—letter {3x}. See: TWOT—2557; BDB—1078b.

105. אֲגַרְטָל {2x} **ʼăgarṭâl**, *ag-ar-tawl';* of uncert. der.; a *basin:*—charger {1x}. See: TWOT—380a; BDB—8d, 173d.

106. אֶגְרֹף {2x} **ʼegrôph**, *eg-rofe';* from 1640 (in the sense of *grasping*); the *clenched* hand:—fist {2x}. See: TWOT—385a; BDB—8d, 175d.

107. אִגֶּרֶת {10x} **ʼiggereth**, *ig-eh'-reth;* fem. of 104; an *epistle:*—letter(s) {10x}. See: TWOT—23b; BDB—8d, 1078b.

108. אֵד {2x} **ʼêd**, *ade;* from the same as 181 (in the sense of *enveloping*); a *fog:*—mist {1x}, vapor {1x}. See: TWOT—38d; BDB—9a, 15d.

109. אָדַב {1x} **ʼâdab**, *aw-dab';* a prim. root; to *languish:*—grieve {1x}. See: TWOT—24; BDB—9a.

110. אַדְבְּאֵל {2x} **ʼAdbᵉʼêl**, *ad-beh-ale';* prob. from 109 (in the sense of *chastisement*) and 410; *disciplined of God; Adbeël,* a son of Ishmael:—*Adbeel* {2x}. See: BDB—9a.

111. אֲדַד {1x} **ʼĂdad**, *ad-ad';* prob. an orth. var. for 2301; *Adad* (or Hadad), an Edomite:—Hadad {1x}. See: BDB—9a, 212d.

112. אִדּוֹ {2x} **ʼIddôw**, *id-do';* of uncert. der.; *Iddo,* an Isr.:—Iddo {2x}. See: BDB—9a.

אֱדוֹם **ʼĔdôwm**. See 123.

אֱדוֹמִי **ʼĔdôwmîy**. See 30.

113. אָדוֹן {1x} **ʼâdôwn**, *aw-done';* or (short.)

אָדֹן {335x} **ʼâdôn**, *aw-done';* from an unused root (mean. to *rule*); *sovereign,* i.e. *controller* (human or divine):—Lord {31x}, lord {197x}, master(s) {105x}, owner {1x}, sir {1x};. comp. also names beginning with "Adoni-".

Adon (113), or adonay (136), "lord; master; Lord." The form *adon* appears 335 times, while the form adonay (used exclusively as a divine name) appears 439 times. **(1)** Basically, *adon* means "lord" or "master." It is distinguished from the Hebrew word ba'al, which signifies "possessor" or "owner." *Adon* basically describes the one who occupies the position of a "master" or "lord" over a slave or servant: "And the servant put his hand under the thigh of Abraham his master . . ." (Gen 24:9). It is used of kings and their most powerful aides. Joseph told his brothers: "So now it was not you that sent me hither, but God: and he hath made me a father [i.e., an adviser] to Pharaoh, and lord of all his house, and a ruler throughout all the land of Egypt" (Gen 45:8; cf. 42:30). Only once is this word used in the sense of "owner" or "possessor" (1 Kin 16:24). **(2)** *Adon* is often used as a term of polite address. In some cases, the one so named really occupies a position of authority. In Gen 18:12 (the first occurrence) Sarah called Abraham her "lord." On the other hand, this may be a purely honorary title by which the speaker intends to indicate his submission to the one so addressed. Jacob instructed his slaves to speak to "my lord Esau" (Gen 32:18); i.e., Jacob called his brother Esau "lord." In places where the speaker is addressing someone calling him "lord," the word virtually means "you."

(3) When applied to God, *adon* is used in several senses. **(3a)** It signifies His position as the one who has authority (like a master) over His people to reward the obedient and punish the disobedient: "Ephraim provoked him to anger most bitterly: therefore shall he leave his blood upon him, and his reproach shall his Lord return unto him" (Hos 12:14). In such contexts God is conceived as a Being who is sovereign ruler and almighty master. **(3b)** The word is often a title of respect, a term of direct address usually assuming a specific concrete lord-vassal or master-servant relationship (Ps 8:1). **(3c)** In some cases the word appears to be a title suggesting God's relationship to and position over Israel: "Three times in the year all thy males shall appear before the Lord God" (Ex 23:17). In such contexts *adon* is a formal divine name and should probably be transliterated if the proper emphasis is to be retained. Syn: YHWH (3068) sets forth His essential and unswerving principles of mercy and judgment, and presents Him as Father, a Friend, and a Moral Governor. Yahh (3050), the shortened form of YHWH, is usually used when Yah is stressed as the One accomplishing a deed in contrast to no other. See: TWOT—27b; BDB—10d.

114. אַדּוֹן {1x} **ʼAddôwn**, *ad-done';* prob. intens. for 113; *powerful; Addon,* appar. an Isr.:—Addon {1x}. See: BDB—11d.

115. אֲדוֹרַיִם {1x} **ʼĂdôwrayim**, *ad-o-rah'-yim;* dual from 142 (in the sense of

eminence); *double mound; Adorajim,* a place in Pal.:—Adoraim {1x}. See: BDB—12a.

116. אֱדַיִן {57x} **ʾêdayin** (Aram.), *ed-ah'-yin;* of uncert. der.; *then* (of time):—then {55x}, now {1x}, time {1x}. See: TWOT—2558; BDB—1078c.

117. אַדִּיר {27x} **ʾaddîyr**, *ad-deer';* from 142; *wide* or (Gen) *large;* fig. *powerful:*—excellent {4x}, famous {2x}, gallant {1x}, glorious {1x}, goodly {1x}, lordly {1x}, mighty (-ier, one {5x}), noble {1x}, nobles {7x}, principal {3x}, worthy {1x};

(1) As a noun, *ʾaddir* is **(1a)** paralleled to "mighty" in Judg 5:13: "Then he made him that remaineth have dominion over the nobles among the people: the LORD made me have dominion over the mighty." The word also occurs in Jer 14:3 and Jer 30:21. **(1b)** In 2 Chr 23:20 *ʾaddir* is paralleled to "captains and governors." **(1c)** The word is applied to the Messiah; the Messiah is none other than God Himself: "But there the glorious LORD will be unto us a place of broad rivers . . ." (Is 33:21). Syn.: *ʾAddîyr* stresses the might of the person; whereas chor (2715) stresses rank. See: TWOT—28b; BDB—12b.

118. אֲדַלְיָא {1x} **ʾĂdalyâʾ**, *ad-al-yaw';* of Pers. der.; *Adalja,* a son of Haman:—Adalia {1x}. See: BDB—9a.

119. אָדַם {10x} **ʾâdam**, *aw-dam';* of unknown derivation; to *show blood* (in the face), i.e. *flush* or turn rosy:—dyed red {5x}, red {4x}, ruddy {1x}. See: TWOT—26b; BDB—10a.

120. אָדָם {552x} **ʾâdâm**, *aw-dawm';* from 119; *ruddy,* i.e. a *human being* (an individual or the species, *mankind,* etc.):—Adam {13x}, + hypocrite {1x}, + common sort {1x}, × low, man {408x}, men {121x}, person(s) {8x}.

Adam means "man; mankind; people; someone (indefinite); *Adam* (the first man); or a city in the Jordan Valley (Josh 3:16)." **(1)** This noun is related to the verb adom, "to be red," and therefore probably relates to the original ruddiness of human skin. **(2)** The noun connotes "man" as the creature created in God's image, the crown of all creation. In its first appearance *adam* is used for mankind, or generic man: "And God said, Let us make man in our image, after our likeness . . ." (Gen 1:26). In Gen 2:7 the word refers to the first "man," *Adam:* "And the LORD God formed man of the dust of the ground, and breathed into his nostrils the breath of life; and man became a living soul."

(3) Throughout Gen 2:5—5:5 there is a constant shifting and interrelationship between the generic and the individual uses. **(3a)** "Man" is distinguished from the rest of the creation insofar as he was created by a special and immediate act of God: he alone was created in the image of God (Gen 1:27). **(3b)** He consisted of two elements, the material and the nonmaterial (Gen 2:7). **(3c)** From the outset he occupied an exalted position over the rest of the earthly creation and was promised an even higher position (eternal life) if he obeyed God: "And God blessed them, and God said unto them, Be fruitful, and multiply, and replenish the earth, and subdue it: and have dominion over the fish of the sea, and over the fowl of the air, and over every living thing that moveth upon the earth" (Gen 1:28; cf. 2:16–17). **(3d)** In Gen 1 "man" is depicted as the goal and crown of creation, while in Gen 2 the world is shown to have been created as the scene of human activity. **(3e)** "Man" was in God's image with reference to his soul and/or spirit. (He is essentially spiritual; he has an invisible and immortal aspect which is simple or indivisible.) Other elements of this image are his mind and will, intellectual and moral integrity (he was created with true knowledge, righteousness, and holiness), his body (this was seen as a fit organ to share immortality with man's soul and the means by which dominion over the creation was exercised), and dominion over the rest of the creation.

(4) The Fall greatly affected the nature of "man," but he did not cease to be in God's image (Gen 9:6). **(4a)** Fallen "man" occupies a new and lower position before God: "And God saw that the wickedness of man was great in the earth, and that every imagination of the thoughts of his heart was only evil continually" (Gen 6:5; cf. 8:21). **(4b)** No longer does "man" have perfect communion with the Creator; he is now under the curse of sin and death. **(4c)** Original knowledge, righteousness, and holiness are destroyed. **(4d)** Restoration to his proper place in the creation and relationship to the Creator comes only through spiritual union with the Christ, the second *Adam* (Rom 5:12–21). **(5)** In some later passages of Scripture *adam* is difficult to distinguish from ish (376) —man as the counterpart of woman and/or as distinguished in his maleness.

(6) Sometimes *adam* identifies a limited and particular "group of men": "Behold, waters rise up out of the north, and shall be an overflowing flood, and shall overflow the land [of the Philistines], and all that is therein; the city, and them that dwell therein: then the men [used in the singular] shall cry, and all the inhabitants of the land shall howl" (Jer 47:2). **(7)** When used of a particular group of individual "men," the noun appears in the phrase "sons of men": "And the LORD came down to see the city and the tower, which the children of men builded" (Gen 11:5). **(8)** The phrase "son of man" usually connotes a particular individual: "God is not a man [ish], that he should lie; neither the son of man, that he should repent . . ." (Num 23:19; cf. Eze 2:1). The one notable exception is the use of this term in Dan 7:13–14: "I saw in the night visions, and, behold, one like the Son of man [enos (582)] came with the clouds of heaven. . . . His dominion is an everlasting dominion, which shall not pass away . . ." Here the phrase represents a divine being.

(9) *Adam* is also used in reference to any given man, or to anyone male or female: "When a man [anyone] shall have in the skin of his flesh a rising, a scab, or bright spot, and it be in the skin of his flesh like the plague of leprosy; then he shall be brought unto Aaron . . ." (Lev 13:2). Syn.: Man is represented by four apparently inconsistent aspects: As *ʾâdâm,* he is of the earth, earthy; as Ish (376 – {967x}), he is endued with immaterial and personal existence, as bachur (970) he is the fully developed, vigorous, unmarried man in his prime; as Enosh (582 – {32x}), he is weak or incurable; and as Gibbor (1397 – {54x}), he is mighty and noble. Syn.: *ʾÂdâm* connotes man as the creature created in God's image, the crown of all creation. Ish (376) is used for man as the counterpart of woman and/or as distinguished in his maleness. Geber (1397) denotes a male as an antonym of a woman, many times suggesting strength, strong man. Enosh (582) sets forth a collective idea man suggesting the frailty, vulnerability, and finitude of man as contrasted to God. See also: 376, 582, 1167, 1397, 1400, 4962. See: TWOT—25a; BDB—9a.

121. אָדָם {9x} **ʾÂdâm**, *aw-dawm';* the same as 120; *Adam* the name of the first man, also of a place in Pal.:—*Adam* {9x}. See: BDB—9c.

122. אָדֹם {9x} **ʾâdôm**, *aw-dome';* from 119; *rosy:*—red {8x}, ruddy {1x}. See: TWOT—26b; BDB—10b.

123. אֱדֹם {100x} **ʾÊdôm**, *ed-ome';* or (fully)

אֱדוֹם **ʾÊdôwm**, *ed-ome';* from 122; *red* [see Gen 25:25]; *Edom,* the elder twin-brother of Jacob; hence, the region (Idumæa) occupied by him:—Edom {87x}, Edomites {9x}, Idumea {4x}. See: BDB—10b.

124. אֹדֶם {3x} **ʾôdem**, *o'-dem;* from 119; *redness,* i.e. the *ruby, garnet,* or some other red gem:—sardius {3x}. See: TWOT—26c; BDB—10b.

125. אֲדַמְדָּם {6x} **ʾădamdâm**, *ad-am-dawm';* redupl. from 119; *reddish:*—(somewhat) reddish {6x}. See: TWOT—26g; BDB—10c.

126. אַדְמָה {5x} **ʾAdmâh**, *ad-maw';* contr. for 127; *earthy; Admah,* a place near the Dead Sea:—*Admah* {5x}. See: BDB—10a.

127. אֲדָמָה {225x} **ʾădâmâh**, *ad-aw-maw';* from 119; *soil* (from its Gen *redness*) [the productive agent]:—country {1x}, earth {53x}, ground {43x}, husband [-man {2x}] (-ry {1x}), land(s) {125x}.

Initially this noun represents **(1)** arable "ground" (probably red in color) supporting water and plants (Gen 2:6); **(2)** source of Adam's body (Gen 2:7); **(3)** the actual soil itself (2 Kin 5:17), **(4)** ground (Ex 3:5), **(5)** property or possession (Zec 2:12); **(6)** a relationship exists between adam, "man," and the *ʾădâmâh.* If Adam were to remain obedient to God, the "ground" would give forth its fruit (Gen 2:6). Sin disrupted the harmony between man and the "ground," and the "ground" no longer responded to man's care. Increased human rebellion caused decreased fruitfulness of the "ground" (Gen 4:12, 14; cf. 8:21). In Abraham the promised redemption (Gen 3:15) took the form of the restoration of a proper relation between God and man and between man and the "ground" (Gen 28:14–15). Under Moses the fruitfulness of the "ground" depended on the obedience of God's people (cf. Deut 11:17). Syn.: *ʾĂdâmâh,* from its Gen redness is the productive agent; Erets (776 – {1505x}) a territory or even the whole earth; Sadeh (7704 – {7x}) a field, plot of land, or estate. See: TWOT—25b; BDB—9c.

128. אֲדָמָה {1x} **ʾĂdâmâh**, *ad-aw-maw';* the same as 127; *Adamah,* a place in Pal.:—*Adamah* {1x}. See: BDB—10a.

129. אֲדָמִי {1x} **ʾĂdâmîy**, *ad-aw-mee';* from 127; *earthy; Adami,* a place in Pal.:—Adami {1x}. See: BDB—10a.

130. אֱדֹמִי {12x} **ʾÊdômîy**, *ed-o-mee';* or (fully)

אֱדוֹמִי **ʾÊdôwmîy**, *ed-o-mee';* patron. from 123; an *Edomite,* or desc. from (or inhab. of) Edom:—Edomite(s) {11x}, Syria {1x}. Syn.: See 726. See: BDB—10c.

131. אֲדֻמִּים {2x} **ʾĂdummîym**, *ad-oom-meem';* plur. of 121; *red* spots; *Adummim,* a pass in Pal.:—Adummim {2x}. See: BDB—10c, 751c.

132. אַדְמֹנִי {3x} **ʾadmônîy**, *ad-mo-nee';* or (fully)

אַדְמוֹנִי **ʾadmôwnîy**, *ad-mo-nee';* from 119; *reddish* (of the hair or the complexion):—red {1x}, ruddy {2x}. See: TWOT—26h; BDB—10c.

133. אַדְמָתָא {1x} **ʾAdmâthâʾ**, *ad-maw-thaw';* prob. of Pers. der.; *Admatha,* a Pers. nobleman:—*Admatha* {1x}. See: BDB—10c.

134. אֶדֶן {57x} **ʼeden**, *eh'-den;* from the same as 113 (in the sense of *strength*); a *basis* (of a building, a column, etc.):—socket(s) {56x}, foundations {1x}. See: TWOT—27a; BDB—10d.

אָדֹן **ʼâdôn**. See 113.

135. אַדָּן {1x} **ʼAddân**, *ad-dawn';* intens. from the same as 134; *firm; Addan,* an Isr.:—*Addan* {1x}. See: BDB—11d.

136. אֲדֹנָי {434x} **ʼĂdônây**, *ad-o-noy';* an emphat. form of 113; the *Lord* (used as a proper name of God only):—(my) Lord {431x}, lord {2x}, God {1x}. Syn.: See 113. See: TWOT—27b; BDB—10d.

In the form *adonay* the word means "Lord" par excellence or "Lord over all," even as it sometimes does in the form adon (cf. Deut 10:17, where God is called the "God of gods, and Lord of lords"; Josh 3:11, where He is called the "Lord of all the earth"). The word *adonay* appears in Gen 15:2: "And Abram said, Lord God, what wilt thou give me, seeing I go childless, ..." This word frequently appears in Psalms (Ps 68:17; 86:3) and Isaiah (Isa. 29:13; 40:10).

137. אֲדֹנִי־בֶזֶק {3x} **ʼĂdônîy-Bezeq**, *ad-o"-nee-beh'-zek;* from 113 and 966; *lord of Bezek; Adoni-Bezek;* a Canaanitish king:—Adoni-bezek {1x}. See: BDB—11d.

138. אֲדֹנִיָּה {26x} **ʼĂdônîyâh**, *ad-o-nee-yaw';* or (prol.)

אֲדֹנִיָּהוּ **ʼĂdônîyâhûw**, *ad-o-nee-yaw'-hoo;* from 113 and 3050; *lord* (i.e. worshipper) of Jah; *Adonijah,* the name of three Isr.:—Adonijah {26x}. See: BDB—11d.

139. אֲדֹנִי־צֶדֶק {2x} **ʼĂdônîy-Tsedeq**, *ad-o"-nee-tseh'-dek;* from 113 and 6664; *lord of justice; Adoni-Tsedek,* a Canaanitish king:—Adonizedec {2x}. See: BDB—11d.

140. אֲדֹנִיקָם {3x} **ʼĂdônîyqâm**, *ad-o-nee-kawm';* from 113 and 6965; *lord of rising* (i.e. *high*); *Adonikam,* the name of one or two Isr.:—Adonikam {3x}. See: BDB—12a.

141. אֲדֹנִירָם {2x} **ʼĂdônîyrâm**, *ad-o-nee-rawm';* from 113 and 7311; *lord of height; Adoniram,* an Isr.:—Adoniram {2x}. See: BDB—12a.

142. אָדַר {3x} **ʼâdar**, *aw-dar';* a prim. root; to *expand,* i.e. *be great* or (fig.) *magnificent:*—glorious {2x}, honourable {1x}.

This verb occurs only twice and in a poetical usage. The word appears in Is 42:21: "The LORD is well pleased for his righteousness' sake; he will magnify the law, and make it honorable [ʼ*adar*]." The word also appears in Ex 15:6; 11. See: TWOT—28; BDB—12a.

143. אֲדָר {8x} **ʼĂdâr**, *ad-awr';* prob. of for. der.; perh. mean. *fire; Adar,* the 12th Heb. month:—*Adar* {8x}. See: BDB—12c, 1078d.

144. אֲדָר {1x} **ʼĂdâr** (Aram.), *ad-awr';* corresp. to 143:—*Adar* {1x}. See: BDB—1078d.

145. אֶדֶר {2x} **ʼeder**, *eh'-der;* from 142; *amplitude,* i.e. (concr.) a *mantle;* also (fig.) *splendor:*—goodly {1x}, robe {1x}. *ʼEder* may refer to a "luxurious outer garment" (Mic 2:8). See: TWOT—28a; BDB—12a.

146. אַדָּר {1x} **ʼAddâr**, *ad-dawr';* intens. from 142; *ample; Addar,* a place in Pal.; also an Isr.:—Adar {1x}, *Addar* {1x}. See: BDB—12a.

147. אִדַּר {1x} **ʼiddar** (Aram.), *id-dar';* intens. from a root corresp. to 142; *ample,* i.e. a threshing- *floor:*—threshing-floors {1x}. See: TWOT—2560; BDB—1078d.

148. אֲדַרְגָּזֵר {2x} **ʼădargâzêr** (Aram.), *ad-ar"-gaw-zare';* from the same as 147 and 1505; a *chief diviner,* or *astrologer:*—judge(s) {2x}. See: TWOT—2561; BDB—1078d.

149. אַדְרַזְדָּא {1x} **ʼadrazdâʼ** (Aram.), *ad-raz-daw';* prob. of Pers. or.; *quickly* or *carefully:*—diligently {1x}. Correctly, exactly. See: TWOT—2562; BDB—1079a.

150. אֲדַרְכֹּן {2x} **ʼădarkôn**, *ad-ar-kone';* of Pers. or.; a *daric* or Pers. coin:—drams {2x}. See: TWOT—28; BDB—12c, 204b.

151. אֲדֹרָם {2x} **ʼĂdôrâm**, *ad-o-rawm';* contr. for 141; *Adoram* (or Adoniram), an Isr.:—Adoram {2x}. See: BDB—12a, c.

152. אַדְרַמֶּלֶךְ {3x} **ʼAdrammelek**, *ad-ram-meh'-lek;* from 142 and 4428; *splendor of* (the) *king; Adrammelek,* the name of an Ass. idol, also of a son of Sennacherib:—Adrammelech {3x}. See: BDB—12c.

153. אֶדְרָע {1} **ʼedraʻ** (Aram.), *ed-raw';* an orth. var. for 1872; an *arm,* i.e. (fig.) *power:*—force {1x}. See: TWOT—2682b; BDB—1079a, 1089a.

154. אֶדְרֶעִי {8x} **ʼedreʻîy**, *ed-reh'-ee;* from the equiv. of 153; *mighty; Edrei,* the name of two places in Pal.:—Edrei {8x}. See: BDB—12c, 204c.

155. אַדֶּרֶת {12x} **ʼaddereth**, *ad-deh'-reth;* fem. of 117; something *ample* (as a *large* vine, a *wide* dress); also the same as 145:—mantle {5x}, garment {4x}, glory {1x}, goodly {1x}, robe {1x}.

ʼAddereth may mean "luxurious outer garment, mantle, cloak." This word appears in Gen 25:25 to mean "mantle." See: TWOT—28c; BDB—12b.

156. אָדַשׁ {1x} **ʼâdash**, *aw-dash';* a prim. root; to *tread* out (grain):—thresh {1x}. See: TWOT—419; BDB—12c, 190c.

157. אָהַב {208x} **ʼâhab**, *aw-hab';* or

אָהֵב **ʼâhêb**, *aw-habe';* a prim. root; to *have affection* for (sexually or otherwise):—(be-) love {169x} (-d {5x}, -ly {1x}, -r(s) {19x} -ing {1x}), like {1x}, friend(s) {12x}.

Ahab or *aheb* means "to love; like." Basically this verb is equivalent to the English "to love" in the sense of having a strong emotional attachment to and desire either to possess or to be in the presence of the object. **(1)** First, the word refers to the love a man has for a woman and a woman for a man. Such love is rooted in sexual desire, although as a rule it is desire within the bounds of lawful relationships: "And Isaac brought her into his mother Sarah's tent, and took Rebekah, and she became his wife; and he loved her . . ." (Gen 24:67). **(2)** This word may refer to an erotic but legal love outside marriage. Such an emotion may be a desire to marry and care for the object of that love, as in the case of Shechem's love for Dinah (Gen 34:3). **(3)** In a very few instances *ahab* (or *aheb*) may signify no more than pure lust—an inordinate desire to have sexual relations with its object (cf. 2 Sa 13:1). **(4)** Marriage may be consummated without the presence of love for one's marriage partner (Gen 29:30). **(5)** *Ahab* (or *aheb*) seldom refers to making love [usually this is represented yada (3045), "to know," or by shakab (7901), "to lie with"]. **(6)** The word does seem to have this added meaning, however, in 1 Kin 11:1: "But King Solomon loved many strange women, together with the daughter of Pharaoh . . ." (cf. Jer 2:25). Hosea appears to use this nuance when he writes that God told him to "go yet, love a woman beloved of her friend, yet an adulteress . . ." (3:1). **(7)** This is the predominant meaning of the verb when it appears in the causative stem (as a participle). **(8)** In every instance except one (Zec 13:6) *ahab* (or *aheb*) signifies those with whom one has made or intends to make love: "Go up to Lebanon, and cry; and lift up thy voice in Bashan, and cry from the passages: for all thy lovers are destroyed" (Jer 22:20; cf. Eze 16:33).

(9) *Ahab* (or *aheb*) is also used of the love between parents and their children. In its first biblical appearance, the word represents Abraham's special attachment to his son Isaac: "And he said, Take now thy son, thine only son Isaac, whom thou lovest . . ." (Gen 22:2). **(10)** *Ahab* (or *aheb*) may refer to the family love experienced by a daughter-in-law toward her mother-in-law (Ruth 4:15). This kind of love is also represented by the word racham (7356). **(11)** *Ahab* (or *aheb*) sometimes depicts a special strong attachment a servant may have toward a master under whose dominance he wishes to remain: "And if the servant shall plainly say, I love my master, my wife, and my children; I will not go out free . . ." (Ex 21:5). **(12)** Perhaps there is an overtone here of family love; he "loves" his master as a son "loves" his father (cf. Deut 15:16). This emphasis may be in 1 Sa 16:21, where we read that Saul "loved [David] greatly." Israel came "to love" and deeply admire David so that they watched his every move with admiration (1 Sa 18:16).

(13) A special use of this word relates to an especially close attachment of friends: ". . . The soul of Jonathan was knit with the soul of David, and Jonathan loved him as his own soul" (1 Sa 18:1). In Lev 19:18: ". . . Thou shalt love thy neighbor as thyself" (cf. Lev 19:34; Deut 10:19) *ahab* (or *aheb*) signifies this brotherly or friendly kind of love. **(14)** The word suggests, furthermore, that one seek to relate to his brother and all men according to what is specified in the law structure God gave to Israel. This was to be the normal state of affairs between men. **(15)** This verb is used politically to describe the loyalty of a vassal or a subordinate to his lord—so Hiram of Tyre "loved" David in the sense that he was completely loyal (1 Kin 5:1). **(16)** The strong emotional attachment and desire suggested by *ahab* (or *aheb*) may also be fixed on objects, circumstances, actions, and relationships. Syn.: 1730; 7453. See: TWOT—29; BDB—12c.

158. אַהַב {2x} **ʼahab**, *ah'-hab;* from 157; *affection* (in a good or a bad sense):—lovers {1x}, loving {1x}. See: TWOT—29a; BDB—13b.

159. אֹהַב {1x} **ʼôhab**, *o'-hab;* from 156; mean. the same as 158:—love {1x}. See: TWOT—29b; BDB—13b.

160. אַהֲבָה {40x} **ʼahăbâh**, *ă-hab-aw;* fem. of 158 and mean. the same:—love {40x}.

Ahabah means "love." This word represents several kinds of "love." **(1)** The first biblical occurrence of *ahabah* is in Gen 29:20; there the word deals with the "love" between man and wife as a general concept. **(2)** In Hos 3:1 the word is used of "love" as a sexual activity. **(3)** *Ahabah* means "love" between friends in 1 Sa 18:3: "Then Jonathan and David made a covenant because he loved him as his own soul." **(4)** The word refers to Solomon's "love" in 1 Kin

11:2 and **(5)** to God's "love" in Deut 7:8. Syn.: See 158. See: TWOT—29c; BDB—13b.

161. **אֹהַד** {2x} **ʼÔhad,** *o'-had;* from an unused root mean. to *be united; unity; Ohad,* an Isr.:—*Ohad* {2x}. See: BDB—13c.

162. **אֲהָהּ** {15x} **ʼâhâhh,** *ă-haw';* appar. a prim. word expressing *pain* exclamatorily; *Oh!:*—Ah {8x}, Alas {6x}, O {1x}. See: TWOT—30; BDB—13c.

163. **אַהֲוָא** {3x} **ʼAhăvâʼ,** *ă-hav-aw';* prob. of for. or.; *Ahava,* a river of Bab.:—Ahava {3x}. BDB—13c.

164. **אֵהוּד** {9x} **ʼÊhûwd,** *ay-hood';* from the same as 161; *united; Ehud,* the name of two or three Isr.:—Ehud {9x}. See: BDB—13c.

165. **אֱהִי** {3x} **ʼĕhîy,** *e-hee';* appar. an orth. var. for 346; *where:*—will {3x}. [*which is often the rendering of the same Heb. form from* 1961]. See: TWOT—31; BDB—13c.

166. **אָהַל** {1x} **ʼâhal,** *aw-hal';* a prim. root; to *be clear:*—shineth {1x}. See: TWOT—33; BDB—14c.

167. **אָהַל** {3x} **ʼâhal,** *aw-hal';* a denom. from 168; to *tent:*—pitch tent {2x} remove a tent {1x}. See: TWOT—32; BDB—14b.

168. **אֹהֶל** {345x} **ʼôhel,** *o'-hel;* from 166; a *tent* (as *clearly* conspicuous from a distance):—covering {1x}, (dwelling {2x}) (place [s] {2x}), home {1x}, tabernacle {198x}, tent(s) {141x}.

Ohel (168) means "tent; home; dwelling, habitation." **(1)** First, this word refers to the mobile structure called a "tent." This is its meaning in Gen 4:20: "And Adah bare Jabal: he was the father of such as dwell in tents, and of such as have cattle." These are what nomadic Bedouins normally live in. **(2)** "Tents" can also be used as housing for animals: "They smote also the tents of cattle and carried away sheep and camels in abundance . . ." (2 Chr 14:15). **(3)** Soldiers lived in "tents" during military campaigns (1 Sa 17:54). **(4)** A "tent" was pitched on top of a house so everyone could see that Absalom went in to his father's concubines (2 Sa 16:22). This constituted an open rejection of David's dominion and a declaration that he (Absalom) was claiming the throne. **(5)** The word is a synonym for "home, dwelling," and "habitation." This emphasis is especially evident in Judg 19:9: ". . . Behold, the day groweth to an end, lodge here, that thine heart may be merry; and tomorrow get you early on your way, that thou mayest go home." This meaning appears in the phrase "to your tents": "We have no part in David, neither have we inheritance in the son of Jesse: every man to his tents, O Israel" (2 Sa 20:1). The "tabernacle" ("tent") of David, therefore, is his dwelling place or palace (Is 16:5). **(6)** Similarly, the "tabernacle" ("tent") of the daughter of Zion is Israel's capital, or what Israel inhabits—Jerusalem (Lam 2:4).

(7) *Ohel* may represent those who dwell in the dwellings of a given area or who form a unit of people. Thus the "tents" of Judah are her inhabitants: "The LORD also shall save the tents of Judah first, that the glory of the house of David and the glory of the inhabitants of Jerusalem do not magnify themselves against Judah" (Zec 12:7; cf. Ps 83:6). **(8)** Bedouin "tents" today (as in the past) are constructed of strong black cloth of woven goat's hair. They are shaped variously. The women pitch them by stretching the cloth over poles and tying it down with cords of goat's hair or hemp. Wooden mallets are used to drive the tent pegs into the ground (Judg 4:21). Sometimes the structure is divided in order to separate families or to separate animals from people (2 Chr 14:15). The back of the "tent" is closed and the front open. The door is made by turning back the fold where the two ends of the cloth meet (Gen 18:1). The "tent" and all its contents are transported on the back of a single pack animal. Richer people cover the floor with mats of various materials. A chief or sheikh may have several "tents"—one for himself and his guest(s), another for his wives and other females in his immediate family, and still another for the animals (Gen 31:33).

(9) Before the construction of the tabernacle Moses pitched a "tent" outside the camp (Ex 33:7). There he met with God. The "tent" outside the camp persisted as a living institution for only a short period after the construction of the tabernacle and before the departure from Sinai (Num 11:16ff.; 12:4ff.). Eventually the ark of the covenant was moved into the tabernacle (Ex 40:21) where the LORD met with Moses and spoke to Israel (Ex 29:42). This structure is called the tent of meeting inasmuch as it contained the ark of the covenant and the tables of testimony (Num 9:15). As the tent of meeting it was the place where God met with His people through Moses (or the high priest) and revealed His will to them (1 Sa 2:22). Syn.: Mishkan (4908) stresses the dwelling place/residence; whereas *ʼôhel* stresses a specific dwelling place, a tent. See: TWOT—32a; BDB—13d.

169. **אֹהֶל** {1x} **ʼÔhel,** *o'-hel;* the same as 168; *Ohel,* an Isr.:—*Ohel* {1x}. See: BDB—13b.

170. **אָהֳלָה** {5x} **ʼOhŏlâh,** *ŏ-hol-aw';* in form a fem. of 168, but in fact for

אָהֳלָהּ **ʼOhŏlâhh,** *ŏ-hol-aw';* from 168; *her tent* (i.e. idolatrous *sanctuary*); *Oholah,* a symbol. name for Samaria:—Aholah {5x}. See: TWOT—32b; BDB—14b.

171. **אָהֳלִיאָב** {5x} **ʼOhŏlîyʼâb,** *ŏ″-hol-e-awb';* from 168 and 1; *tent of* (his) *father; Oholiab,* an Isr.:—Aholiab {5x}. See: BDB—14b, c.

172. **אָהֳלִיבָה** {6x} **ʼOhŏlîybâh,** *ŏ″-hol-ee-baw';* (similarly with 170) for

אָהֳלִיבָהּ **ʼOhŏlîybâhh,** *ŏ″-hol-e-baw';* from 168; *my tent* (is) *in her; Oholibah,* a symb. name for Judah:—Aholibah {6x}. See: BDB—14c.

173. **אָהֳלִיבָמָה** {8x} **ʼOhŏlîybâmâh,** *ŏ″-hol-ee-baw-maw';* from 168 and 1116; *tent of* (the) *height; Oholibamah,* a wife of Esau:—Aholibamah {8x}. See: BDB—14c.

174. **אֲהָלִים** {4x} **ʼăhâlîym,** *ă-haw-leem';* or (fem.)

אֲהָלוֹת **ʼăhâlôwth,** *ă-haw-loth'* (only used thus in the plur.); of for. or.; *aloe* wood (i.e. sticks):—aloes {3x}, trees of lign aloes {1x}. See: TWOT—34; BDB—14d.

175. **אַהֲרוֹן** {347x} **ʼAhărôwn,** *ă-har-one';* of uncert. der.; *Aharon,* the brother of Moses:—Aaron {345x}, Aaronites {2x}. See: BDB—14d.

176. **אוֹ** {21x} **ʼôw,** *o;* presumed to be the "constr." or genitival form of

אַו **ʼav,** *av;* short. for 185; *desire* (and so prob. in Prov 31:4); hence, (by way of alternative) *or,* also *if:*—also, and, either, if, at the least, × nor, or, otherwise, then, whether {21x}. See: TWOT—36; BDB—14d, 16b.

177. **אוּאֵל** {1x} **ʼÛwʼêl,** *oo-ale';* from 176 and 410; *wish of God; Uel,* an Isr.:—Uel {1x}. See: BDB—15a.

178. **אוֹב** {17x} **ʼôwb,** *obe;* from the same as 1 (appar. through the idea of *prattling* a father's name); prop. a *mumble,* i.e. a water-*skin* (from its hollow sound); hence, a *necromancer* (ventriloquist, as from a jar):—bottle(s) {1x}, familiar spirit(s) {16x}.

Owb means "spirit (of the dead); necromancer; pit." **(1)** The word usually represents the troubled spirit (or spirits) of the dead. This meaning appears unquestionably in Is 29:4: ". . . Thy voice shall be, as of one that hath a familiar spirit, out of the ground, and thy speech shall whisper out of the dust." **(2)** Its second meaning, "necromancer," refers to a professional who claims to summon forth such spirits when requested (or hired) to do so: "Regard not them that have familiar spirits, neither seek after wizards" (Lev 19:31—first occurrence). These mediums summoned their "guides" from a hole in the ground. Saul asked the medium (witch) of Endor (1 Sa 28:8). **(3)** God forbade Israel to seek information by this means, which was so common among the pagans (Lev 19:31; Deut 18:11). Perhaps the pagan belief in manipulating one's basic relationship to a god (or gods) explains the relative silence of the Old Testament regarding life after death. Yet God's people believed in life after death, from early times (e.g., Gen 37:35; Is 14:15ff.)

(4) Necromancy was so contrary to God's commands that its practitioners were under the death penalty (Deut 13). **(5)** Necromancers' unusual experiences do not prove that they truly had power to summon the dead. For example, the medium of Endor could not snatch Samuel out of God's hands against His wishes. But in this particular incident, it seems that God rebuked Saul's apostasy, either through a revived Samuel or through a vision of Samuel. Mediums do not have power to summon the spirits of the dead, since this is reprehensible to God and contrary to His will. Syn.: 7307. TWOT—37a; BDB—15a.

179. **אוֹבִיל** {1x} **ʼÔwbîyl,** *o-beel';* prob. from 56; *mournful; Obil,* an Ishmaelite:—Obil {1x}. See: BDB—6a.

180. **אוּבָל** {3x} **ʼûwbâl,** *oo-bawl';* or (short.)

אֻבָל **ʼûbâl,** *oo-bawl';* from 2986 (in the sense of 2988); a *stream:*—river {3x}. See: TWOT—835g; BDB—6b, 385c.

181. **אוּד** {3x} **ʼûwd,** *ood;* from an unused root mean. to *rake* together; a *poker* (for *turning* or *gathering* embers):—firebrand(s) {2x}, brand {1x}. See: TWOT—38a; BDB—15c.

182. **אוֹדוֹת** {11x} **ʼôwdôwth,** *o-dōth';* or (short.)

אֹדוֹת **ʼôdôwth,** *o-dōth'*(only thus in the plur.); from the same as 181; *turnings* (i.e. *occasions*); (adv.) on *account* of:—because {5x}, cause(s) {2x}, concerning {2x}, [concerning] thee {1x}, sake {1x}. See: TWOT—38b; BDB—15c.

183. **אָוָה** {26x} **ʼâvâh,** *aw-vaw';* a prim. root; to *wish* for:—desire {17x}, lust {4x}, longed {3x}, covet {2x}. See: TWOT—40; BDB—16a.

184. **אָוָה** {1x} ʾ**âvâh**, *aw-vaw';* a prim. root; to *extend* or *mark* out:—point out {1x}. See: TWOT—41; BDB—16c, 1060d, 1063b.

185. **אַוָּה** {7x} ʾ**avvâh**, *av-vaw';* from 183; *longing:*—desire {3x}, lust after {3x}, pleasure {1x}. See: TWOT—40b; BDB—16b.

186. **אוּזַי** {1x} ʾ**Ûwzay**, *oo-zah'-ee;* perh. by perm. for 5813, *strong; Uzai,* an Isr.:—Uzai {1x}. See: BDB—17a.

187. **אוּזָל** {2x} ʾ**Ûwzâl**, *oo-zâwl';* of uncert. der.; *Uzal,* a son of Joktan:—Uzal {2x}. See: BDB—23d.

188. **אוֹי** {24x} ʾ**ôwy**, *ō'-ee;* prob. from 183 (in the sense of *crying* out after); *lamentation;* also interj. *Oh!:*—woe {23x}, alas {1x}. See: TWOT—42; BDB—17a.

189. **אֱוִי** {2x} ʾ**Ĕvîy**, *ev-ee';* prob. from 183; *desirous; Evi,* a Midianitish chief:—Evi {2x}. See: BDB—16c.

אוֹיֵב ʾ**ôwyêb**. See 341.

190. **אוֹיָה** {1x} ʾ**ôwyâh**, *o-yaw';* fem. of 188:—woe {1x}. See: BDB—17a.

191. **אֱוִיל** ʾ**ĕvîyl**, *ev-eel';* from an unused root (mean. to *be perverse*); (fig.) *silly:*—fool(s) {20x}, (-ish) (man {6x}).

Primarily *ʾĕvîyl* describes one who **(1)** lacks wisdom (Prov 24:7); **(2)** is morally undesirable despising wisdom and discipline (Prov 1:7; 15:5); **(3)** mocks guilt (Prov 14:9), **(4)** is quarrelsome (Prov 20:3); **(5)** licentious (Prov 7:22); and **(6)** refuses instruction (Prov 16:22). Syn.: The fool's **(a)** only authority is himself (5034 - {94x}- Ps 14:1; 53:1); **(b)** twists God's ways into his own (191 - {18x}); **(c)** is insensitive to godly prodding (3688 -46x); and **(d)** lives by his own resources, deserving pity (5528 - 8x). See: TWOT—44a; 17b; BDB—17b.

192. **אֱוִיל מְרֹדַךְ** {2x} ʾ**Ĕvîyl Mᵉrôdak**, *ev-eel' mer-o-dak';* of Aram. der. and prob. mean. *soldier of Merodak; Evil-Merodak,* a Bab. king:—Evil-merodach {2x}. See: See: BDB—17b.

193. **אוּל** {2x} ʾ**ûwl**, *ool;* from an unused root mean. to *twist,* i.e. (by impl.) *be strong;* the *body* (as being *rolled* together); also *powerful:*—mighty {1x}, strength {1x}. See: TWOT—45a; BDB—17c.

194. **אוּלַי** {11x} ʾ**ûwlay**, *oo-lah'ee;* or (short.)

אֻלַי ʾ**ûlay**, *oo-lah'ee;* from 176; *if not;* hence, *perhaps:*—if (so be), may (be), peradventure, unless = {11x}.

Ulay (194) means "peradventure; perhaps; suppose; if; less." **(1)** This word meaning "peradventure or perhaps" usually expresses a hope: "Behold now, the LORD hath restrained me from bearing: I pray thee, go in unto my maid; it may be that I may obtain children by her" (Gen 16:2—the first occurrence). **(2)** Elsewhere *ulay* expresses fear or doubt: "Peradventure the woman will not be willing to follow me unto this land; must I needs bring thy son again unto the land from whence thou camest?" (Gen 24:5). **(3)** If followed by another clause the word almost functions to introduce a protasis: "Peradventure there be fifty righteous within the city: wilt thou also destroy . . ." (Gen 18:24). **(4)** In Num. 22:33 the word has a different force: "And the ass saw me, and turned from me these three times: unless she had turned from me, surely now also I had slain thee, and saved her alive." See: TWOT—46; BDB—19c.

195. **אוּלַי** {2x} ʾ**Ûwlay**, *oo-lah'ee;* of Pers. der.; the *Ulai* (or Eulæus), a river of Pers.:—Ulai {2x}. See: BDB—19c, 47a.

196. **אֱוִלִי** {1x} ʾ**ĕvîlîy**, *ev-ee-lee';* from 191; *silly, foolish;* hence, (mor.) *impious:*—foolish {1x}. See: TWOT—44b; BDB—17c.

197. **אוּלָם** {34x} ʾ**ûwlâm**, *oo-lawm';* or (short.)

אֻלָם ʾ**ûlâm**, *oo-lawm';* from 481 (in the sense of *tying*); a *vestibule* (as *bound* to the building):—porch (es) {34x}. See: TWOT—45c; BDB—17c, 19d.

198. **אוּלָם** {4x} ʾ**Ûwlâm**, *oo-lawm';* appar. from 481 (in the sense of *dumbness*); *solitary; Ulam,* the name of two Isr.:—Ulam {4x}. BDB—17d, 19d.

199. **אוּלָם** {19x} ʾ**ûwlâm**, *oo-lawm';* appar. a var. of 194; *however* or *on the contrary:*—but {8x}, but truly {3x}, surely {2x}, very deed {2x}, howbeit {1x}, wherefore {1x}, truly {1x}, not translated {1x}. See: TWOT—47; BDB—19d, 48a.

200. **אִוֶּלֶת** {25x} ʾ**ivveleth**, *iv-veh'-leth;* from the same as 191; *silliness:*—folly {13x}, foolishness {10x}, foolish {1x}, foolishly {1x}.

(1) This noun can mean "foolishness" in the sense of violating God's law, or "sin" (Ps 38:5). **(2)** The word also describes the activities and life-style of the man who ignores the instructions of wisdom (Prov 5:23). **(3)** In another nuance, the noun means "thoughtless." Hence *ivveleth* describes the way a young person is prone to act (Pro 22:15) and the way any fool or stupid person chatters (Prov 15:2). Syn.: 5039. See: TWOT—44c; BDB—17c.

201. **אוֹמָר** {3x} ʾ**Ôwmâr**, *o-mawr';* from 559; *talkative; Omar,* a grandson of Esau:—Omar {3x}. See: BDB—57b.

202. **אוֹן** {12x} ʾ**ôwn**, *ōne;* prob. from the same as 205 (in the sense of *effort,* but successful); *ability, power,* (fig.) *wealth:* —strength {7x}, might {2x}, force {1x}, goods {1x}, substance {1x}.

This noun generally means **(1)** vigour, generative power; **(2)** wealth; **(3)** physical strength (of men and behemoth). See: TWOT—49a; BDB—20b.

203. **אוֹן** {1x} ʾ**Ôwn**, *ōne;* the same as 202; *On,* an Isr.:—On {1x}. See: BDB—20b.

204. **אוֹן** {3x} ʾ**Ôwn**, *ōne;* or (short.);

אֹן ʾ**Ôn**, *ōne;* of Eg. der.; *On,* a city of Egypt:—*On* {3x}. See: BDB—20a, c, 58a.

205. **אָוֶן** {78x} , ʾ**âven**, *aw-ven';* from an unused root perh. mean. prop. to *pant* (hence, to *exert* oneself, usually in vain; to *come to naught*); strictly *nothingness;* also *trouble, vanity, wickedness;* spec. an *idol:*—affliction {3x}, evil {1x}, false {1x}, idol {1x}, iniquity {47x}, mischief {3x}, mourners {1x} (-ing {1x}), naught {1x}, sorrow {1x}, unjust {1x}, unrighteous {2x}, vain {1x}, vanity {6x}, wicked (-ness {8x}). comp. 369.

Aven (205) means "iniquity; misfortune." **(1)** This noun is derived from a root meaning "to be strong." The first occurrence is in Num 23:21: "He hath not beheld iniquity in Jacob, neither hath he seen perverseness in Israel: the LORD his God is with him, and the shout of a king is among them." **(2)** The meaning of "misfortune" comes to expression in the devices of the wicked against the righteous. The psalmist expected "misfortune" to come upon him: "And if he come to see me, he speaketh vanity: his heart gathereth iniquity to itself; when he goeth abroad, he telleth it" (Ps 41:6). **(3)** *Aven* in this sense is synonymous with ed (343), "disaster" (Job 18:12). **(4)** In a real sense *aven* is part of human existence, and as such the word is identical with 'amal (5999), "toil," as in Ps 90:10: "The days of our years are threescore years and ten; and if by reason of strength they be fourscore years, yet is their strength labor and sorrow; for it is soon cut off, and we fly away." **(5)** *Aven* in a deeper sense characterizes the way of life of those who are without God: "For the vile person will speak villany, and his heart will work iniquity, to practice hypocrisy, and to utter error against the LORD, to make empty the soul of the hungry, and he will cause the drink of the thirsty to fail" (Is 32:6).

(6) The being of man is corrupted by "iniquity." **(7)** Though all of mankind is subject to *aven* ("toil"), there are those who delight in causing difficulties and "misfortunes" for others by scheming, lying, and acting deceptively. The psalmist puts internalized wickedness this way: "Behold, he travaileth with iniquity, and hath conceived mischief, and brought forth falsehood" (Ps 7:14; cf. Job 15:35). **(8)** Those who are involved in the ways of darkness are the "workers of iniquity," the doers of evil or the creators of "misfortune" and disaster. **(9)** Synonyms for *aven* with this sense are ra, "evil," and rasha, "wicked," opposed to "righteousness" and "justice." They seek the downfall of the just (Ps 141:9). Between Ps 5:5 and 141:9 there are as many as 16 references to the workers of evil (cf. "The foolish shall not stand in thy sight: thou hatest all workers of iniquity"—Ps 5:5). In the context of Ps 5, the evil spoken of is falsehood, bloodshed, and deceit (v. 6).

(10) The qualitative aspect of the word comes to the best expression in the verbs with *aven.* The wicked work, speak, beget, think, devise, gather, reap, and plow *aven,* and it is revealed ("comes forth") by the misfortune that comes upon the righteous. **(11)** Ultimately when Israel's religious festivals (Is 1:13) and legislation (Is 10:1) were affected by their apostate way of life, they had reduced themselves to the Gentile practices and way of life. **(12)** The prophetic hope lay in the period after the purification of Israel, when the messianic king would introduce a period of justice and righteousness (Is 32) and the evil men would be shown up for their folly and ungodliness. Syn.: 2398, 5771, 7451, 7561. See: TWOT—48a; BDB—19d, 58a.

206. **אָוֶן** {3x} ʾ**Âven**, *aw'-ven;* the same as 205; *idolatry; Aven,* the contemptuous synonym of three places, one in Cæle-Syria, one in Egypt (On), and one in Pal. (Bethel):—*Aven* {3x}. See also 204, 1007. See: BDB—19d, 122b.

207. **אוֹנוֹ** {5x} ʾ**Ôwnôw**, *o-no';* or (short.)

אֹנוֹ ʾ**Ônôw**, *o-no';* prol. from 202; *strong; Ono,* a place in Pal.:—Ono {1x}. See: BDB—20c.

208. **אוֹנָם** {4x} ʾ**Ôwnâm**, *o-nawm';* a var. of 209; *strong; Onam,* the name of an Edomite and of an Isr.:—Onam {4x}. See: BDB—20c.

209. **אוֹנָן** {8x} ʾ**Ôwnân**, *o-nawn';* a var. of 207; *strong; Onan,* a son of Judah:—Onan {8x}. See: BDB—20c.

210. **אוּפָז** {2x} ʾ**Ûwphâz**, *oo-fawz';* perh. a corruption of 211; *Uphaz,* a famous gold region:—Uphaz {2x}. See: BDB—20c.

211. אוֹפִיר {13x} **ʾÔwphîyr**, *o-feer'*; or (short.)
אֹפִיר **ʾÔphîyr**, *o-feer'*; and
אוֹפִר **ʾÔwphîr**, *o-feer'*; of uncert. der.; *Ophir*, the name of a son of Joktan, and of a gold region in the East:—Ophir {13x}. See: TWOT—50; BDB—20c.

212. אוֹפָן {36x} **ʾôwphân**, *o-fawn'*; or (short.)
אֹפָן **ʾôphân**, *o-fawn'*; from an unused root mean. to *revolve*; a *wheel*:—wheel(s) {35x}, fitly {1x}. See: TWOT—146a; BDB—66d.

אוֹפִר **ʾÔwphîr**. See 211.

213. אוּץ {10x} **ʾûwts**, *oots*; a prim. root; to *press*; (by impl.) to *be close, hurry, withdraw*:—haste {8x}, labour {1x}, narrow {1x}. See: TWOT—51; BDB—21a.

214. אוֹצָר {79x} **ʾôwtsâr**, *o-tsawr'*; from 686; a *depository*:—treasure(s) {61x}, treasury {10x}, storehouse(s) {3x}, cellars {2x}, armoury {1x}, garners {1x}, store {1x}. See: TWOT—154a; BDB—69d.

215. אוֹר {43x} **ʾôwr**, *ore*; a prim. root; to *be* (caus. *make*) *luminous* (lit. and metaph.):—light {19x}, shine {14x}, enlighten {5x}, break of day {1x}, fire {1x}, give {1x}, glorious {1x}, kindle {1x}.

Owr (215) means **(1)** "to become light in Gen 44:3: "As soon as the morning was light, the men were sent away, they and their asses," **(2)** become lighted up (of daybreak), **(3)** to give light in Num 8:2: ". . . the seven lamps shall give light over against the candlestick," or **(4)** cause light to shine." See: TWOT—52; BDB—21a.

216. אוֹר {120x} **ʾôwr**, *ore*; from 215; *illumination* or (concr.) *luminary* (in every sense, incl. *lightning, happiness*, etc.):—bright {1x}, clear {1x}, + day {2x}, light(s) {114x} (-ning), morning {1x}, sun {1x}.

Owr (216), the noun, means "light." **(1)** The first occurrence of *owr* is in the Creation account: "And God said, Let there be light: and there was light" (Gen 1:3). Here "light" is the opposite of "darkness." **(2)** The opposition of "light" and "darkness" is not a unique phenomenon. **(2a)** It occurs frequently as a literary device: "Woe unto them that call evil good, and good evil; that put darkness for light, and light for darkness; that put bitter for sweet, and sweet for bitter!" (Is 5:20); and "In that day they shall roar against them like the roaring of the sea: and if one look unto the land, behold darkness and sorrow, and the light is darkened in the heavens thereof" (Is 5:30). **(3)** In Hebrew various antonyms of *owr* are used in parallel constructions: "The people that walked in darkness have seen a great light: they that dwell in the land of the shadow of death, upon them hath the light shined" (Is 9:2).

(4) The basic meaning of *owr* is "daylight" (Gen 1:3). **(5)** The "light" given by the heavenly bodies was also known as or: "Moreover the light of the moon shall be as the light of the sun, and the light of the sun shall be sevenfold, as the light of seven days, in the day that the LORD bindeth up the breach of his people, and healeth the stroke of their wound" (Is 30:26). **(6)** In the metaphorical use *owr* signifies life over against death: "For thou hast delivered my soul from death: wilt not thou deliver my feet from falling, that I may walk before God in the light of the living?" (Ps 56:13). **(7)** To walk in the "light" of the face of a superior (Prov 16:15), or of God (Ps 89:15), is an expression of a joyful, blessed life in which the quality of life is enhanced. **(8)** The believer is assured of God's "light," even in a period of difficulty; cf. "Rejoice not against me, O mine enemy: when I fall, I shall arise; when I sit in darkness, the LORD shall be a light unto me" (Mic 7:8; cf. Ps 23:4). Syn.: 3974; 7043. See: TWOT—52a; BDB—21c, 70b.

217. אוּר {6x} **ʾûwr**, *oor*; from 215; *flame*, hence, (in the plur.) the *East* (as being the region of light):—fire(s) {5x}, light {1x}. Syn.: See also 224. See: TWOT—52d; BDB—22a.

218. אוּר {5x} **ʾÛwr**, *oor*; the same as 217; *Ur*, a place in Chaldæa; also an Isr.:—Ur {5x}. See: BDB—22b, d.

219. אוֹרָה {4x} **ʾôwrâh**, *o-raw'*; fem. of 216; *luminousness*, i.e. (fig.) *prosperity*; also a plant (as being *bright*):—herbs {2x}, light {2x}. See: TWOT—52b; BDB—21d, 77a.

220. אֲוֵרָה {1x} **ʾăvêrâh**, *av-ay-raw'*; by transp. for 723; a *stall*:—cotes {1x}. See: TWOT—158b; BDB—22d, 71d.

221. אוּרִי {8x} **ʾÛwrîy**, *oo-ree'*; from 217; *fiery*; *Uri*, the name of three Isr.:—Uri {8x}. See: BDB—22b.

222. אוּרִיאֵל {4x} **ʾÛwrîyʾêl**, *oo-ree-ale'*; from 217 and 410; *flame of God*; *Uriel*, the name of two Isr.:—Uriel {4x}. See: BDB—22b.

223. אוּרִיָּה {39x} **ʾÛwrîyâh**, *oo-ree-yaw'*; or (prol.)
אוּרִיָּהוּ **ʾÛwrîyâhûw**, *oo-ree-yaw'-hoo*; from 217 and 3050; *flame of Jah*; *Urijah*, the name of one Hittite and five Isr.:—Uriah {39x}, Urijah {11x}. See: BDB—22c.

224. אוּרִים {7x} **ʾÛwrîym**, *oo-reem'*; plur. of 217; *lights*; *Urim*, the oracular brilliancy of the figures in the high-priest's breastplate:—Urim {7x}. See: BDB—22a, 1070d.

אוֹרְנָה **ʾOwrenâh**. See 728.

225. אוּת {4x} **ʾûwth**, *ooth*; a prim. root; prop. to *come*, i.e. (impl.) to *assent*:—consent {1x}. See: TWOT—53; BDB—22d.

226. אוֹת {79x} **ʾôwth**, *ōth*; prob. from 225 (in the sense of *appearing*); a *signal* (lit. or fig.), as a *flag, beacon, monument, omen, prodigy, evidence*, etc.:—mark {1x}, miracles {2x}, ensign(s) {2x}, sign(s) {60x}, token(s) {14x}.

Owth means "sign; mark." **(1)** This word represents something by which a person or group is characteristically marked. This is its emphasis in Gen 4:15: "And the LORD set a mark upon Cain, lest any finding him should kill him." **(2)** In Ex 8:23 God promises to "put a division between my people and thy people: tomorrow shall this sign be" (cf. Ex 12:13). **(3)** Num 2:2 uses owth to represent a military banner, while Job 21:29 uses the word of the identifying banners of nomadic tribes. **(4)** Rahab asked her Israelite guests for a trustworthy "mark" which they stipulated to be the scarlet cord by which she lowered them out of her window and outside Jericho's walls (Josh 2:12, 18).

(5) The word means "sign" as a reminder of one's duty. This usage first appears in Gen 9:12: "This [the rainbow] is the token of the covenant which I make between me and you and every living creature . . ." (cf. vv. 4–15). **(6)** A reminding token is represented by *owth*: "And it [the observance of the Feast of Unleavened Bread] shall be for a sign unto thee upon thine hand, and for a memorial between thine eyes, that the LORD's law may be in thy mouth . . ." (Ex 13:9). **(7)** A "sign" eventually showing the truth of a statement is indicated by *owth*: "Certainly I will be with thee; and this shall be a token unto thee, that I have sent thee: When thou hast brought forth the people out of Egypt, ye shall serve God upon this mountain (Ex 3:12). **(8)** In passages such as Ex 4:8 *owth* represents a miraculous "sign": "And it shall come to pass, if they will not believe thee, neither hearken to the voice of the first sign, that they will believe the voice of the latter sign." **(9)** "Signs" are attestations of the validity of a prophetic message, but they are not the highest or final test of a prophet; he must speak in conformity to past revelation (cf. Deut 13:1–5).

(10) Several passages use *owth* of omens and/or indications of future events: "But if they say thus, Come up unto us; then we will go up: for the LORD hath delivered them into our hand: and this shall be a sign unto us (1 Sa 14:10). **(11)** An *owth* can be a "warning sign": "The censers of these sinners against their own souls, let them make them broad plates for a covering of the altar: for they offered them before the LORD therefore they are hallowed: and they shall be a sign unto the children of Israel" (Num 16:38). **(12)** The first occurrence of *owth* is in Gen 1:14. Here it refers to the stars, indicators of the time of day and seasons. Syn.: 4159. See: TWOT—41a; BDB—16d, 23a.

227. אָז {22x} **ʾâz**, *awz*; a demonstr. adv.; *at that time* or *place*; also as a conjunc., *therefore*:—beginning, even, for, from, hitherto, now, old, since, then, time, when, yet = {22x}. See: TWOT—54; BDB—23a.

228. אֲזָא {3x} **ʾăzâʾ** (Aram.), *az-zaw'*; or
אֲזָה **ʾăzâh** (Aram.), *az-aw'*; to *kindle*; (by impl.) to *heat*:—heated {2x}, hot {1x}. See: TWOT—2563; BDB—1079a.

229. אֶזְבַּי {1x} **ʾEzbay**, *ez-bah'ee*; prob. from 231; *hyssop-like*; *Ezbai*, an Isr.:—Ezbai {1x}. See: BDB—23c.

230. אֲזַד {2x} **ʾăzad** (Aram.), *az-awd'*; of uncert. der.; *firm*:—gone {2x}. See: TWOT—2564; BDB—1079a.

231. אֵזוֹב {10x} **ʾêzôwb**, *ay-zobe'*; prob. of for. der.; *hyssop*:—hyssop {10x}. Hyssop is a plant used for religious and medicinal purposes. See: TWOT—55; BDB—23c.

232. אֵזוֹר {14x} **ʾêzôwr**, *ay-zore'*; from 246; something *girt*; a *belt*, also a *band*:—girdle(s) {14x}. A waistcloth. See: TWOT—59a; BDB—25b.

233. אֲזַי {3x} **ʾăzay**, *az-ah'ee*; prob. from 227; *at that time*:—then {3x}. TWOT—54; BDB—23b.

234 אַזְכָּרָה {7x} **ʾazkârâh**, *az-kaw-raw'*, from 2142; a *reminder*; spec. *remembrance-offering*:—memorial {7x}.

The noun *'azkarah* means "memorial offering" and **(1)** it occurs primarily in Leviticus. **(2)** "Memorials" were directed toward God. **(3)** A "memorial" portion of each meal offering was burnt on the altar (Lev 2:2, 9, 16), in other words a small portion in place of the whole amount. See: TWOT—551d; BDB—23c, 272b.

235. אָזַל {6x} **ʾâzal**, *aw-zal'*; a prim. root; to *go away*, hence, to *disappear*:—gone {2x}, fail {1x}, gaddest about {1x}, to and fro {1x}, spent {1x}. See: TWOT—56; BDB—23c, 1079b.

236. אֲזַל {7x} **ʾăzal** (Aram.), *az-al'*; the same as 235; to *depart*:—went (up) {6x}, go {1x}. See: TWOT—2565; BDB—1079b.

237. אֶזֶל {1x} **ʾezel**, *eh'-zel;* from 235; *departure; Ezel,* a memorial stone in Pal.:—*Ezel* {1x}. See: BDB—23d.

238. אָזַן {41x} **ʾâzan**, *aw-zan';* a prim. root; prob. to *expand;* but used only as a denom. from 241; to *broaden out the ear* (with the hand), i.e. (by impl.) to *listen:*—give ear {31x}, hearken {6x}, hear {3x}, perceived by the ear {1x}. Syn.: 241, 6030, 7181, 8085. See: TWOT—57; BDB—24b.

239. אָזַן {1x} **ʾâzan**, *aw-zan';* a prim. root [rather ident. with 238 through the idea of *scales* as if two ears]; to *weigh,* i.e. (fig.) *ponder:*—gave good heed {1x}. See: TWOT—58; BDB—24d, 1079b.

240. אָזֵן {1x} **ʾâzên**, *aw-zane';* from 238; a *spade* or *paddle* (as having a *broad* end):—weapon {1x}. See: TWOT—57b; BDB—24c.

241. אֹזֶן {187x} **ʾôzen**, *o'-zen;* from 238; *broadness,* i.e. (concr.) the *ear* (from its form in man):—advertise +1540 –{1x}, audience {7x}, + displeased {1x}, ear(s) {63x}, hear {1x}, hear + 8088 {1x}, hearing {5x}, reveal +1540 – {1x}, show +1540 –{6x}, tell + 1540 –{1x}.

Ozen means "ear, audience; hearing." **(1)** It mainly designates a part of the body. The first occurrence is in Gen 20:8: "Abimelech rose early in the morning, and called all his servants, and told all these things in their ears: and the men were sore afraid." **(2)** The "ear" was the place for earrings (Gen 35:4); thus it might be pierced as a token of perpetual servitude (Ex 21:6). **(3)** Several verbs are found in relation to "ear": **(3a) (3b)** "to inform" (Eze 24:26), **(3c)** "to pay attention" (Ps 10:17), **(3d)** "to listen" (Ps 78:1), **(3e)** "to stop up" (Is 33:15), **(3f)** "to make deaf" (Is 6:10), and **(3g)** "to tingle" (1 Sa 3:11). **(4)** Animals are also said to have "ears" (Prov 26:17).

(5) God is idiomatically said to have "ears": "Hide not thy face from me in the day when I am in trouble; incline thine ear unto me; . . . when I call answer me speedily" (Ps 102:2). Elsewhere, "And Samuel heard all the words of the people, and he rehearsed them in the ears of the LORD" (1 Sa 8:21). **(5a)** The LORD "pierces" (i.e., opens up) ears (Ps 40:6), **(5b)** implants ears (Ps 94:9), and **(5c)** fashions ears (Prov 20:12) in order to allow man to receive direction from his Creator. **(5d)** As the Creator, He also is able to hear and respond to the needs of His people (Ps 94:9). **(6)** The LORD reveals His words to the "ears" of his prophets: "Now the LORD had told Samuel in his ear a day before Saul came, saying . . ." (1 Sa 9:15).

(7) Since the Israelites had not responded to the prophetic message, they had made themselves spiritually deaf: "Hear now this, O foolish people, and without understanding; which have eyes, and see not; which have ears, and hear not" (Jer 5:21). **(8)** After the Exile, the people of God were to experience a spiritual awakening and new sensitivity to God's Word which, in the words of Isaiah, is to be compared to the opening of the "ears" (Is 50:5). Syn.: 238. See: TWOT—57a; BDB—23d.

242. אֻזֵּן שֶׁאֱרָה {1x} **ʾUzzên Sheʾĕrâh**, *ooz-zane' sheh-er-aw';* from 238 and 7609; *plat of Sheerah* (i.e. settled by him); *Uzzen-Sheërah,* a place in Pal.:—Uzzen-sherah {1x}. See: BDB—25a.

243. אַזְנוֹת תָּבוֹר {1x} **ʾAznôwth Tâbôwr**, *az-nōth' taw-bore';* from 238 and 8396; *flats* (i.e. *tops*) *of Tabor* (i.e. situated on it); *Aznoth-Tabor,* a place in Pal.:—Aznoth-tabor {1x}. See: BDB—24d.

244. אָזְנִי {2x} **ʾOznîy**, *oz-nee';* from 241; *having* (quick) *ears; Ozni,* an Isr.; also an *Oznite* (collect.), his desc.:—Ozni {1x}, Oznites {1x}. See: BDB—24c.

245. אֲזַנְיָה {1x} **ʾĂzanyâh**, *az-an-yaw';* from 238 and 3050; *heard by Jah; Azanjah,* an Isr.:—Azaniah {1x}. See: BDB—24c.

246. אֲזִקִּים {2x} **ʾăziqqîym**, *az-ik-keem';* a var. for 2131; *manacles:*—chains {2x}. See: TWOT—577b; BDB—25a, 279b.

247. אָזַר {16x} **ʾâzar**, *aw-zar';* a prim. root; to *belt:*—gird (up) {14x}, bind about {1x}, compass about {1x}. See: TWOT—59; BDB—25a.

248. אֶזְרוֹעַ {2x} **ʾezrôwaʿ**, *ez-ro'-ă;* a var. for 2220; the *arm:*—arm {2x}. See: TWOT—583b; BDB—25b, 284b, 1089b.

249. אֶזְרָח {18x} **ʾezrâch**, *ez-rawkh';* from 2224 (in the sense of *springing up*); a spontaneous *growth,* i.e. *native* (tree or persons):—born {8x}, country {5x}, land {1x}, homeborn {1x}, nation {1x}, bay tree {1x}.

A baytree is native to the land of Israel. See: TWOT—580b; BDB—25b, 280c.

250. אֶזְרָחִי {3x} **ʾEzrâchîy**, *ez-raw-khee';* patron. from 2246; an *Ezrachite* or desc. of Zerach:—Ezrahite {3x}. See: BDB—280d.

251. אָח {629x} **ʾâch**, *awkh;* a prim. word; a *brother* (used in the widest sense of lit. relationship and metaph. affinity or resemblance [like 1]):—another {24x}, brethren {332x}, brother {269x}(-ly {1x}), kindred {1x}, like {1x}, other {1x}. Compare also the proper names beginning with "Ah-" or "Ahi-".

Ach (251) means "brother." **(1)** In its basic meaning, *ach* represents a "male sibling," a "brother." This is its meaning in the first biblical appearance: "And she again bare his brother Abel" (Gen 4:2). This word represents a full brother or a half-brother: "And he said to him, Go, I pray thee, see whether it be well with thy brethren . . ." (Gen 37:14). **(2)** In another nuance, *ach* can represent a "blood relative." Abram's nephew is termed his "brother": "And he brought back all the goods, and also brought again his brother Lot, and his goods, and the women also, and the people" (Gen 14:16). This passage, however, might also reflect the covenantal use of the term whereby it connotes "ally" (cf. Gen 13:8). **(3)** In Gen 9:25, *ach* clearly signifies "relative": "Cursed be Canaan; a servant of servants shall he be unto his brethren." Laban called his cousin Jacob an *ʾach:* "And Laban said unto Jacob, Because thou art my brother, shouldest thou therefore serve me for nought?" (Gen 29:15). Just before this, Jacob described himself as an *ach* of Rachel's father (Gen 29:12).

(4) Tribes may be called achim: "And [the tribe of] Judah said unto [the tribe of] Simeon his brother, Come up with me into my lot . . ." (Judg 1:3). **(5)** The word *ach* is used of a fellow tribesman: "With whomsoever thou findest thy gods, let him not live: before our brethren discern thou what is thine . . ." (Gen 31:32). **(6)** Elsewhere it describes a fellow countryman: "And it came to pass in those days, when Moses was grown, that he went out unto his brethren, and looked on their burdens . . ." (Ex 2:11).

(7) In several passages, the word *ach* connotes "companion" or "colleague"—that is, a brother by choice. One example is found in 2 Kin 9:2: "And when thou comest thither, look out there Jehu the son of Jehoshaphat the son of Nimshi, and go in, and make him arise up from among his brethren, and carry him to an inner chamber" (cf. Is 41:6; Num 8:26). **(8)** Somewhat along this line is the covenantal use of the word as a synonym for "ally": "And Lot went out at the door unto them, and shut the door after him, and said, I pray you, brethren, do not so wickedly" (Gen 19:6–7). Notice this same use in Num 20:14 and 1 Kin 9:13. **(9)** *Ach* can be a term of polite address, as it appears to be in Gen 29:4: "And Jacob said unto them [shepherds whose identity he did not know], My brethren, whence be ye?" **(10)** The word *ach* sometimes represents someone or something that simply exists alongside a given person or thing: "And surely your blood of your lives will I require; at the hand of every beast will I require it, and at the hand of . . . every man's brother will I require the life of man" (Gen 9:5–6). See: TWOT—62a; BDB—25b, 26a, 1079c.

252. אַח {1x} **ʾach** (Aram.), *akh;* corresp. to 251:—brother 1. See: TWOT—2566; BDB—1079c.

253. אָח {2x} **ʾâch**, *awkh;* a var. for 162; *Oh!* (expressive of grief or surprise):—ah {1x}, alas {1x}. See: TWOT—60; BDB—25b.

254. אָח {3x} **ʾâch**, *awkh;* of uncert. der.; a fire-*pot* or chafing-dish:—hearth {3x}. See: TWOT—66a; BDB—25b, 28d.

255. אֹחַ {1x} **ʾôach**, *o'-akh;* prob. from 253; a *howler* or lonesome wild animal:—doleful creatures {1x}. *Oach* may be a jackal or hyena. See: TWOT—65a; BDB—25b, 28d.

256. אַחְאָב {93x} **ʾAchʾâb**, *akh-awb';* once (by contr.)

אֶחָב **ʾEchâb** (Jer 29:22), *ekh-awb';* from 251 and 1; *brother* [i.e. *friend*] *of* (his) *father; Achab,* the name of a king of Israel and of a prophet at Bab.:—Ahab {93x}. See: BDB—25b, 26c.

257. אַחְבָּן {1x} **ʾAchbân**, *akh-bawn';* from 251 and 995; *brother* (i.e. *possessor*) *of understanding; Achban,* an Isr.:—Ahban {1x}. See: BDB—25b, 26c.

258. אָחַד {1x} **ʾâchad**, *aw-khad';* perh. a prim. root; to *unify,* i.e. (fig.) *collect* (one's thoughts):—go thee one way or other {1x}. See: TWOT—605; BDB—25c.

259. אֶחָד {951x} **ʾechâd**, *ekh-awd';* a numeral from 258; prop. *united,* i.e. *one;* or (as an ord.) *first:*—an {7x}, another {35x}, any {18x}, a certain {9x}, eleven + 6240 –{13x}, every {10x}, first {36x}, once {13x}, one {687x}, other {30x}, some {7x}, together {1x},

Misc: a, alike, alone, altogether, anything, apiece, daily, each (one), few, + highway, a man, only, together = {86x}. Syn.: *ʾEchâd* stresses unity/oneness but recognizes diversity within that oneness; whereas pa'am (6471 – {12x}) stresses a single occurrence such as a step. See: TWOT—61; BDB—25c, 31c, 1079c.

260. אָחוּ {3x} **ʾâchûw**, *aw'-khoo;* of uncert. (perh. Egyp. der.); a *bulrush* or any marshy grass (particularly that along the Nile):—meadow {2x}, flag {1x}. See: TWOT—63; BDB—28a.

261. אֵחוּד {1x} **ʾÊchûwd**, *ay-khood';* from 258; *united; Echud,* the name of three Isr.:—Ehud {1x}. See: BDB—26a.

262. אַחְוָה {1x} **ᵓachvâh**, *akh-vaw';* from 2331 (in the sense of 2324); an *utterance:*—declaration {1x}. See: TWOT—618a; BDB—28a, 296a.

263. אַחֲוָה {1x} **ᵓachăvâh** (Aram.), *akh-av-aw';* corresp. to 262; *solution* (of riddles):—shewing {1x}. See: TWOT—2722a; BDB—1079c, 1092b.

264. אַחֲוָה {1x} **ᵓachăvâh**, *akh-av-aw';* from 251; *fraternity:*—brotherhood {1x}. See: TWOT—62b; BDB—27c.

265. אֲחוֹחַ {1x} **ᵓĂchôwach**, *akh-o'-akh;* by redupl. from 251; *brotherly; Achoach,* an Isr.:—Ahoah {1x}. See: BDB—29a.

266. אֲחוֹחִי {5x} **ᵓĂchôwchîy**, *akh-o-khee';* patron. from 264; an *Achochite* or desc. of Achoach:—Ahohite {5x}. See: BDB—29a.

267. אֲחוּמַי {1x} **ᵓĂchûwmay**, *akh-oo-mah'-ee;* perh. from 251 and 4325; *brother* (i.e. *neighbour*) *of water; Achumai,* an Isr.:—Ahumai {1x}. See: BDB—26c.

268. אָחוֹר {41x} **ᵓâchôwr**, *aw-khore';* or (short.) אָחֹר **ᵓâchôr**, *aw-khore';* from 299; the *hinder* part; hence, (adv.) *behind, backward;* also (as facing north) the *West:*—back(s) {16x}, backward {11x}, behind {5x}, hinder parts {3x}, afterwards {1x}, back parts {1x}, backside {1x}, hereafter {1x}, time to come {1x}, without {1x}. Syn.: 322. See: TWOT—68d; BDB—30d.

269. אָחוֹת {114x} **ᵓachôwth**, *aw-khōth';* irreg. fem. of 251; a *sister* (used very widely [like 250], lit. and fig.):—(an- {6x}) other {1x}, sister(s) {106x}, together with + 802 – {1x}.

Achowth (269) means "sister." **(1)** The first occurrence is in Gen 4:22: "And Zillah, she also bare Tubal-cain, an instructor of every artificer in brass and iron: and the sister of Tubal-cain was Naamah." **(2)** The translation of "sister" for *achowth* is only the beginning. **(2a)** In Hebrew custom the word was a term employed to refer to the daughter of one's father and mother (Gen 4:22) or **(2b)** one's half-sister (Gen 20:12). **(2c)** It may also refer to one's aunt on the father's side (Lev 18:12; 20:19) or **(2d)** on the mother's side (Lev 18:13; 20:19).

(3) The use of *achowth* more generally denotes female relatives: "And they blessed Rebekah, and said unto her, Thou art our sister, be thou the mother of thousands of millions, and let thy seed possess the gate of those which hate them" (Gen 24:60). **(4)** This meaning lies behind the metaphorical use, where two divisions of a nation (Judah and Israel; Jer 3:7) and two cities (Sodom and Samaria; Eze 16:46) are portrayed as sisters—Hebrew names of geographical entities are feminine. **(5)** The more specialized meaning "beloved" is found only in Song 4:9: "Thou hast ravished my heart, my sister [or beloved], my spouse; thou hast ravished my heart with one of thine eyes, with one chain of thy neck." Here *achowth* is used as a term of endearment rather than a term for a blood relative. See: TWOT—62c; BDB—27d.

270. אָחַז {67x} **ᵓâchaz**, *aw-khaz';* a prim. root; to *seize* (often with the accessory idea of holding in possession):—- hold {31x}, take {16x}, possess {5x}, caught {3x}, fastened {3x}, misc.: be affrighted, bar, come upon, fasten, handle, portion, (have or take) possess (-ion) = {9x}.

Achaz means to seize, grasp, hold fast, bolt (a door)." **(1)** The verb appears in Gen 25:26: ". . . And his hand took hold on Esau's heel. . . ." (cf. Gen 22:13). **(2)** The meaning of "to bolt" (a door) appears in Neh 7:3: ". . . Let them shut and bar the doors." **(3)** In 2 Chr 9:18, *ᵓachaz* means "fastened." **(4)** Metaphorical sense: **(4a)** God seized Job by the neck (Job 16:12); **(4b)** He holds the Psalmist's hand (Ps 73:23); **(4c)** pain seizes Isarel's enemies (Ex 15:14–15); **(4d)** horror seizes people of the east (Job 18:20). Syn.: 2388; 4686. See: TWOT—64; BDB—28a.

271. אָחָז {41x} **ᵓÂchâz**, *aw-khawz';* from 270; *possessor; Achaz,* the name of a Jewish king and of an Isr.:—Ahaz {41x}. See: BDB—28c.

272. אֲחֻזָּה {66x} **ᵓăchuzzâh**, *akh-ooz-zaw';* fem. pass. part. from 270; something *seized,* i.e. a *possession* (espec. of land):—possession(s) {66x}.

Achuzzah (272) means "property; possession." **(1)** Essentially *achuzzah* is a legal term usually used of land, especially family holdings to be passed down to one's heirs. **(1a)** In Gen 17:13 Abram is promised the territory of Palestine as a familial or tribal possession until the indiscriminate future. **(1b)** In Gen 23:20 (cf. vv. 4, 9) the word bears a similar meaning. The difference appears to be that here no feudal responsibilities were attached to this "possession." However, the rather small lot belonged to Abraham and his descendants as a burial site: "And the field, and the cave that is therein, were made sure unto Abraham for a possession of a burying place by the sons of Heth" (Gen 23:20). **(2)** In Lev 25:45–46 non-Israelites could also be inheritable property, but a fellow Israelite could not. **(3)** The "inheritable property" of the Levites was not fields but the Lord Himself (Eze 44:28). See: TWOT—64a; BDB—28c.

273. אַחְזַי {1x} **ᵓAchzay**, *akh-zah'ee;* from 270; *seizer; Achzai,* an Isr.:—Ahasai {1x}. BDB—28d, 403d.

274. אֲחַזְיָה {37x} **ᵓĂchazyâh**, *akh-az-yaw';* or (prol.) אֲחַזְיָהוּ **ᵓĂchazyâhûw**, *akh-az-yaw'-hoo;* from 270 and 3050; *Jah has seized; Achazjah,* the name of a Jewish and an Isr. king:—Ahaziah {37x}. See: BDB—28d, 306c.

275. אֲחֻזָּם {1x} **ᵓĂchuzzâm**, *akh-ooz-zawm';* from 270; *seizure; Achuzzam,* an Isr.:—Ahuzam {1x}. See: BDB—28d.

276. אֲחֻזַּת {1x} **ᵓĂchuzzath**, *akh-ooz-zath';* a var. of 272; *possession; Achuzzath,* a Philistine:—Ahuzzath {1x}. See: BDB—28d.

277. אֲחִי {2x} **ᵓĂchîy**, *akh-ee';* from 251; *brotherly; Achi,* the name of two Isr.:—Ahi {1x}. See: BDB—26c

278. אֵחִי {1x} **ᵓÊchîy**, *ay-khee';* prob. the same as 277; *Echi,* an Isr.:—Ehi {1x}. See: BDB—29a.

279. אֲחִיאָם {2x} **ᵓĂchîyᵓâm**, *akh-ee-awm';* from 251 and 517; *brother of* (the) *mother* (i.e. *uncle*); *Achiam,* an Isr.:—Ahiam {1x}. See: BDB—26c.

280. אֲחִידָה {1x} **ᵓăchîydâh** (Aram.), *akh-ee-daw';* corresp. to 2420, an *enigma:*—hard sentences {1x}. See: TWOT—2567; BDB—1079c, 1092a.

281. אֲחִיָּה {24x} **ᵓĂchiyâh**, *akh-ee-yaw;* or (prol.) אֲחִיָּהוּ **ᵓĂchîyâhûw**, *akh-ee-yaw'-hoo;* from 251 and 3050; *brother* (i.e. *worshipper*) *of Jah; Achijah,* the name of nine Isr.:—Ahiah {4x}, Ahijah {20x}. See: BDB—26c.

282. אֲחִיהוּד {1x} **ᵓĂchîyhûwd**, *akh-ee-hood';* from 251 and 1935; *brother* (i.e. *possessor*) *of renown; Achihud,* an Isr.:—Ahihud {1x}. See: BDB—26d.

283. אַחְיוֹ {6x} **ᵓAchyôw**, *akh-yo';* prol. from 251; *brotherly; Achio,* the name of three Isr.:—Ahio {6x}. See: BDB—26d.

284. אֲחִיחֻד {1x} **ᵓĂchîychûd**, *akh-ee-khood';* from 251 and 2330; *brother of a riddle* (i.e. *mysterious*); *Achichud,* an Isr.:—Ahihud {1x}. See: BDB—26d.

285. אֲחִיטוּב {15x} **ᵓĂchîytûwb**, *akh-ee-toob';* from 251 and 2898; *brother of goodness; Achitub,* the name of several priests:—Ahitub {15x}. See: BDB—26d.

286. אֲחִילוּד {5x} **ᵓĂchîylûwd**, *akh-ee-lood';* from 251 and 3205; *brother of* one *born; Achilud,* an Isr.:—Ahilud {5x}. See: BDB—27a.

287. אֲחִימוֹת {1x} **ᵓĂchîymôwth**, *akh-ee-mōth';* from 251 and 4191; *brother of death; Achimoth,* an Isr.:—Ahimoth {1x}. See: BDB—27a.

288. אֲחִימֶלֶךְ {17x} **ᵓĂchîymelek**, *akh-ee-meh'-lek;* from 251 and 4428; *brother of* (the) *king; Achimelek,* the name of an Isr. and of a Hittite:—Ahimelech {17x}. See: BDB—27a.

289. אֲחִימַן {4x} **ᵓĂchîyman**, *akh-ee-man';* or אֲחִימָן **ᵓĂchîymân**, *akh-ee-mawn';* from 251 and 4480; *brother of a portion* (i.e. *gift*); *Achiman,* the name of an Anakite and of an Isr.:—Ahiman {4x}. See: BDB—27a.

290. אֲחִימַעַץ {15x} **ᵓĂchîymaᶜats**, *akh-ee-mah'-ats;* from 251 and the equiv. of 4619; *brother of anger; Achimaats,* the name of three Isr.:—Ahimaaz {15x}. See: BDB—27a, 591d.

291. אַחְיָן {1x} **ᵓAchyân**, *akh-yawn';* from 251; *brotherly; Achjan,* an Isr.:—Ahian {1x}. See: BDB—27b.

292. אֲחִינָדָב {1x} **ᵓĂchîynâdâb**, *akh-ee-naw-dawb';* from 251 and 5068; *brother of liberality; Achinadab,* an Isr.:—Ahinadab {1x}. See: BDB—27b.

293. אֲחִינֹעַם {7x} **ᵓĂchîynôᶜam**, *akh-ee-no'-am;* from 251 and 5278; *brother of pleasantness; Achinoam,* the name of two Israelitesses:—Ahinoam {7x}. See: BDB—27b.

294. אֲחִיסָמָךְ {3x} **ᵓĂchîyçâmâk**, *akh-ee-saw-mawk';* from 251 and 5564; *brother of support; Achisamak,* an Isr.:—Ahisamach {3x}. See: BDB—27b.

295. אֲחִיעֶזֶר {6x} **ᵓĂchîyᶜezer**, *akh-ee-eh'-zer;* from 251 and 5828; *brother of help; Achiezer,* the name of two Isr.:—Ahiezer {6x}. See: BDB—27b.

296. אֲחִיקָם {20x} **ᵓĂchîyqâm**, *akh-ee-kawm';* from 251 and 6965; *brother of rising* (i.e. *high*); *Achikam,* an Isr.:—Ahikam {20x}. See: BDB—27b.

297. אֲחִירָם {1x} **ᵓĂchîyrâm**, *akh-ee-rawm';* from 251 and 7311; *brother of height* (i.e. *high*); *Achiram,* an Isr.:—Ahiram {1x}. See: BDB—27b.

298. אֲחִירָמִי {1x} **ᵓĂchîyrâmîy**, *akh-ee-raw-mee';* patron. from 297; an *Achiramite* or desc. (collect.) of Achiram:—Ahiramites {1x}. See: BDB—27c.

299. אֲחִירַע {5x} ʾĂchîyraʿ, *akh-ee-rah';* from 251 and 7451; *brother of wrong; Achira,* an Isr.:—Ahira {5x}. See: BDB—27c.

300. אֲחִישַׁחַר {1x} **ʾAchîyshachar**, *akh-ee-shakh'-ar;* from 251 and 7837; *brother of* (the) *dawn; Achishachar,* an Isr.:—Ahishar {1x}. See: BDB—27c.

301. אֲחִישָׁר {1x} **ʾĂchîyshâr**, *akh-ee-shawr';* from 251 and 7891; *brother of* (the) *singer; Achishar,* an Isr.:—Ahishar {1x}. See: BDB—27c.

302. אֲחִיתֹפֶל {20x} **ʾĂchîythôphel**, *akh-ee-tho'-fel;* from 251 and 8602; *brother of folly; Achithophel,* an Isr.:—Ahithophel {20x}. See: BDB—27c.

303. אַחְלָב {1x} **ʾAchlâb**, *akh-lawb';* from the same root as 2459; *fatness* (i.e. *fertile*); *Achlab,* a place in Pal.:—Ahlab {1x}. See: BDB—29a, 317b.

304. אַחְלַי {2x} **ʾAchlay**, *akh-lah'ee;* the same as 305; *wishful; Achlai,* the name of an Israelitess and of an Isr.:—Ahlai {2x}. See: BDB—29a.

305. אַחֲלַי {2x} **ʾachălay**, *akh-al-ah'ee;* or
אַחֲלֵי **ʾachălêy**, *akh-al-ay';* prob. from 253 and a var. of 3863; *would that!:*—O that {1x}, would God {1x}. See: TWOT—67a; BDB—25b.

306. אַחְלָמָה {2x} **ʾachlâmâh**, *akh-law'-maw;* perh. from 2492 (and thus *dream-stone*); a gem, prob. the *amethyst:*—amethyst {2x}.

The identification is not certain but is a purple stone or perhaps a corundum or red or brown jasper. See: TWOT—67b; BDB—29a.

307. אַחְמְתָא {1x} **ʾAchmᵉthâʾ**, *akh-me-thaw';* of Pers. der.; *Achmetha* (i.e. *Ecbatana*), the summer capital of Persia:—Achmetha {1x}. See: BDB—1079c.

308. אֲחַסְבַּי {1x} **ʾĂchaçbay**, *akh-as-bah'ee;* of uncert. der.; *Achasbai,* an Isr.:—Ahasbai {1x}. See: BDB—29b.

309. אָחַר {17x} **ʾâchar**, *aw-khar';* a prim. root; to *loiter* (i.e. *be behind*); by impl. to *procrastinate:*—continue {1x}, defer {3x}, delay {1x}, hinder {1x}, sit up late {1x}, slack {2x}, stayed there {1x}, tarry {7x}.

Achar means "to tarry (Judg 5:28), remain behind/stayed there (Gen 32:4), delay." Other words derived from this verb are: "other," "after (wards)," "backwards." *ʾAchar* appears in Ex 22:29 with the meaning "delay": "Thou shalt not delay to offer the first of thy ripe fruits, and of thy liquors: the firstborn of thy sons shalt thou give unto me." Syn.: 3427. See: TWOT—68; BDB—29b.

310. אַחַר {709x} **ʾachar**, *akh-ar';* from 309; prop. the *hind* part; Gen used as an adv. or conjunc., *after* (in various senses):—after {454x}, follow {78x}, afterward(s) {46x}, behind {44x}, misc. {87x} = again, at, away from, back (from, -side), beside, by, forasmuch, from, hereafter, hinder end, + out (over) live, + persecute, posterity, pursuing, remnant, seeing, since, thence [-forth], when, with.

(1) As an adverb *achar* means "behind; after-(wards)." **(1a)** One adverbial use of *achar* has a local-spatial emphasis that means "behind": "The singers went before, the players on instruments followed after . . ." (Ps 68:25). **(1b)** Another adverbial usage has a temporal emphasis that can mean "afterwards": "And I will fetch a morsel of bread, and comfort ye your hearts; after that ye shall pass on . . ." (Gen 18:5). **(2)** As a preposition *achar* means "behind; after." **(2a)** *Achar* as a preposition can have a local-spatial significance, such as "behind": "And the man said, They are departed hence; for I heard them say, Let us go to Dothan" (Gen 37:17). As such, it can mean "follow after": "And also the king that reigneth over you [will] continue following the LORD your God" (1 Sa 12:14). **(2b)** *Achar* can signify "after" with a temporal emphasis: "And Noah lived after the flood three hundred and fifty years" (Gen 9:28, the first biblical occurrence of the word). **(2c)** This same emphasis may occur when *achar* appears in the plural (cf. Gen 19:6—local-spatial; Gen 17:8—temporal). **(3)** As a conjunction *achar* can mean "after" with a temporal emphasis: "And the days of Adam after he had begotten Seth were eight hundred years . . ." (Gen 5:4). Syn.: see 309. See: TWOT—68b, 68c; BDB—29d, 30c, 405b, 1079d.

311. אַחַר {3x} **ʾachar** (Aram.), *akh-ar';* corresp. to 310; *after:*—hereafter {2x}, after {1x}. Ref. TWOT—2568; BDB—1079d.

312. אַחֵר {166x} **ʾachêr**, *akh-air';* from 309; prop. *hinder;* Gen *next, other,* etc.:—other(s) {105x}, another {55x}, next {2x}, following {1x}, man's {1x}, men {1x}, strange {1x}.

Acher (312) means "following; different; other." **(1)** The first meaning of this word is temporal, and is seen in Gen 17:21: "But my covenant will I establish with Isaac, which Sarah shall bear unto thee at this set time in the next year" (i.e., the year "following"). **(2)** The first biblical occurrence of the word is in Gen 4:25: "And Adam [had relations with] his wife again; and she bare a son, and called his name Seth: For God, said she, hath appointed me another seed instead of Abel. . . ." **(3)** This meaning of "different" or "another" also appears in Lev 27:20: "And if he will not redeem the field, or if he have sold the field to another man, it shall not be redeemed any more." **(4)** In Is 28:11, *acher* defines tongue or language; hence it should be understood as "foreign": "For with stammering lips and another tongue will he speak to this people." **(5)** Finally, *acher* can mean "other." In this usage, the word distinguishes one thing from another without emphasizing any contrast. This is its meaning in Ex 20:3: "Thou shalt have no other gods before me." Syn: 259, 310, 7453. See: TWOT—68a; BDB—29c.

313. אַחֵר {1x} **ʾAchêr**, *akh-air';* the same as 312; *Acher,* an Isr.:—Aher {1x}. See: BDB—31b.

314. אַחֲרוֹן {51x} **ʾachărôwn**, *akh-ar-one';* or (short.)
אַחֲרֹן **ʾachărôn**, *akh-ar-one';* from 309; *hinder;* Gen *late* or *last;* spec. (as facing the east) *western:*—last {20x}, after(-ward)(s) {15x}, latter {6x}, end {2x}, utmost {2x}, following {1x}, hinder {1x}, hindermost {1x}, hindmost {1x}, rereward {1x}, uttermost {1x}.

Acharon (314) means "at the back; western; later; last; future." **(1)** *Acharon* has a local-spatial meaning. Basically, it means "at the back": "And he put the handmaids and their children foremost, and Leah and her children after, and Rachel and Joseph hindermost" (Gen 33:2—the first biblical appearance). **(2)** When applied elsewhere, the word means "western": "Every place whereon the soles of your feet shall tread shall be yours: from the wilderness and Lebanon, from the river, the river Euphrates, even unto the uttermost [western] sea shall your coast be" (Deut 11:24).

(3) Used temporally, *acharon* has several nuances. **(3a)** First, it means "last" as contrasted to the first of two things: "And it shall come to pass, if they will not believe thee, neither hearken to the voice of the first sign, that they will believe the voice of the latter sign" (Ex 4:8). **(3b)** Second, it can represent the "last" in a series of things or people: "Ye are my brethren, ye are my bones and my flesh: wherefore then are ye the last to bring back the king?" (2 Sa 19:12). **(3c)** The word also connotes "later on" and/or "afterwards": "But thou shalt surely kill him; thine hand shall be first upon him to put him to death, and afterwards the hand of all the people" (Deut 13:9). **(4)** Next the emphasis can be on the finality or concluding characteristic of a given thing: "Now these be the last words of David" (2 Sa 23:1). **(5)** *Acharon* connotes "future," or something that is yet to come: ". . . So that the generation to come of your children that shall rise up after you, and the stranger that shall come from a far land, shall say, when they see the plagues of that land . . ." (Deut 29:22).

(6) The combination of "first" and "last" is **(6a)** an idiom of completeness: "Now the rest of the acts of Solomon, first and last, are they not written in the book of Nathan the prophet, and in the prophecy of Ahijah the Shilonite, and in the visions of Iddo the seer against Jeroboam the son of Nebat?" (2 Chr 9:29). **(6b)** Likewise the phrase expresses the sufficiency of the LORD, since He is said to include within Himself the "first" as well as the "last": "Thus saith the LORD the King of Israel, and his Redeemer the LORD of hosts; I am the first, and I am the last; and beside me there is no God" (Is 44:6; cf. 48:12). These verses affirm that there is no other God, because all exists in Him. See: TWOT—68e; BDB—30d.

315. אַחְרַח {1x} **ʾAchrach**, *akh-rakh';* from 310 and 251; *after* (his) *brother; Achrach,* an Isr.:—Aharah {1x}. See: BDB—31b.

316. אֲחַרְחֵל {1x} **ʾĂcharchêl**, *akh-ar-kale';* from 310 and 2426; *behind* (the) *intrenchment* (i.e. *safe*); *Acharchel,* an Isr.:—Aharhel {1x}. See: BDB—31c.

317. אָחֳרִי {6x} **ʾochŏrîy** (Aram.), *okh-or-ee';* from 311; *other:*—another {5x}, other {1x}. Syn.: 259, 312. See: TWOT—2568a; BDB—1079d.

318. אָחֳרֵין {1x} **ʾochŏrêyn** (Aram.), *okh-or-ane';* or (short.)
אָחֳרֵן **ʾochŏrên** (Aram.), *okh-or-ane';* from 317; *last:*—last one {1x}. See: TWOT—2568c; BDB—1079d.

319. אַחֲרִית {61x} **ʾachărîyth**, *akh-ar-eeth';* from 310; the *last* or *end,* hence, the *future;* also *posterity:*—end {31x}, latter {12x}, last {7x}, posterity {3x}, reward {2x}, hindermost {1x}, misc. {5x}.

Achariyth (319) means "hind-part; end; issue; outcome; posterity." **(1)** Used spatially, the word identifies the "remotest and most distant part of something": "If I take the wings of the morning, and dwell in the uttermost parts of the sea . . ." (Ps 139:9). **(2)** The most frequent emphasis of the word is "end," "issue," or "outcome." **(2a)** This nuance is applied to time in a superlative or final sense: ". . . The eyes of the LORD thy God are always upon it, from the beginning of the year even unto the end of the year" (Deut 11:12). **(2b)** A slight shift of meaning occurs in Dan 8:23, where *achariyth* is applied to time in a relative or comparative sense: "And in the latter time of their kingdom, when the transgressors are come to the full, a king of fierce countenance, and understanding dark sentences, shall stand up." Here the word refers to a "last period," but not necessarily the "end" of history.

(3) In a different nuance, the word can mean "latter" or "what comes afterward": "O that they were wise, that they understood this, that they would consider their latter end!" (Deut 32:29). **(4)** In some passages, *achariyth* represents the "ultimate outcome" of a person's life. Num 23:10 speaks thus of death: "Who can count the dust of Jacob, and the number of the fourth part of Israel? Let me die the death of the righteous, and let my last end be like his!" **(5)** In other passages, *achariyth* refers to "all that comes afterwards." Passages such as Jer 31:17 use the word of one's "descendants" or "posterity" (KJV, "children"). In view of the parallelism suggested in this passage, the first line should be translated "and there is hope for your posterity." **(6)** In Amos 9:1, *achariyth* is used of the "rest" (remainder) of one's fellows.

(7) Both conclusion and result are apparent in passages such as Is 41:22, where the word represents the "end" or "result" of a matter: "Let them bring them forth, and show us what shall happen: let them show the former things what they be, that we may consider them, and know the latter end of them; or declare us things for to come." **(8)** *Achariyth* indicates the "last" or the "least in importance": "Your mother shall be sore confounded; she that bare you shall be ashamed: behold, the hindermost of the nations shall be a wilderness, a dry land, and a desert" (Jer 50:12).

(9) The fact that *achariyth* used with "day" or "years" may signify either "a point at the end of time" or "a period of the end time" has created considerable debate on fourteen Old Testament passages. Some scholars view this use of the word as non-eschatological—that it merely means "in the day which follows" or "in the future." This seems to be its meaning in Gen 49:1 (its first occurrence in the Bible): "Gather yourselves together, that I may tell you that which shall befall you in the last days." Here the word refers to the entire period to follow. **(10)** On the other hand, Is 2:2 uses the word more absolutely of the "last period of time": "In the last days, . . . the mountain of the LORD's house shall be established [as the chief of the mountains]. . . ." **(11)** Some scholars believe the phrase sometimes is used of the "very end of time": "Now I am come to make thee understand what shall befall thy people in the latter days: for yet the vision is for many days" (Dan 10:14). This point, however, is much debated. Syn.: 3615; 7093; 7097. See: TWOT—68f; BDB—31a.

320. אַחֲרִית {1x} **ʼachărîyth** (Aram.), *akh-ar-eeth'*; from 311; the same as 319; *later:*—latter {1x}. See: TWOT—2568b; BDB—1079d.

321. אׇחֳרָן {5x} **ʼochŏrân** (Aram.), *okh-or-awn'*; from 311; the same as 317; *other:*—other {3x}, another {2x}. See: TWOT—2568c; BDB—1079d.

אׇחֳרֵן **ʼochŏrên.** See 318.

322. אֲחֹרַנִּית {7x} **ʼăchôrannîyth**, *akh-o-ran-neeth'*; prol. from 268; *backwards:*—backward {6x}, again {1x}. See: TWOT—68d; BDB—30d.

323. אֲחַשְׁדַּרְפַּן {4x} **ʼăchashdarpan**, *akh-ash-dar-pan'*; of Pers. der.; a *satrap* or governor of a main province (of Persia):—lieutenants {4x}. See: TWOT—69; BDB—31c.

324. אֲחַשְׁדַּרְפַּן {9x} **ăchashdarpan** (Aram.), *akh-ash-dar-pan'*; corresp. to 323:—princes {9x}. See: TWOT—2569; BDB—1080a.

325. אֲחַשְׁוֵרוֹשׁ {31x} **ʼĂchashvêrôwsh**, *akh-ash-vay-rōsh'*; or (short.)

אֲחַשְׁרֹשׁ **ʼAchashrôsh**, *akh-ash-rōsh'* (Esth. 10:1); of Pers. or.; *Achashverosh* (i.e. Ahasuerus or Artaxerxes, but in this case Xerxes), the title (rather than name) of a Pers. king:—Ahasuerus {31x}. See: BDB—31c.

326. אֲחַשְׁתָּרִי {1x} **ʼăchashtârîy**, *akh-ash-taw-ree'*; prob. of Pers. der.; an *achastarite* (i.e. courier); the designation (rather than name) of an Isr.:—Haakashtari [*includ. the art.*] {1x}. See: BDB—31c.

327. אֲחַשְׁתְּרָן {2x} **ʼăchastârân**, *akh-ash-taw-rawn'*; of Pers. or.; a *mule:*—camels {2x}. See: TWOT—70; BDB—31c.

328. אַט {6x} **ʼaṭ**, *at;* from an unused root perh. mean. to *move softly;* (as a noun) a *necromancer* (from their soft incantations), (as an adv.) *gently:*—softly {3x}, charmers {1x}, gently {1x}, secret {1x}.

Isaiah 19:3 speaks of charmers, those who speak with soft voices and perhaps charm serpents. See: TWOT—72b; BDB—31c, 31d, 521b.

329. אָטָד {6x} **ʼâṭâd**, *aw-tawd';* from an unused root prob. mean. to *pierce* or *make fast;* a *thorn*-tree (espec. the *buckthorn*):—bramble {3x}, *Atad* {2x}, thorns {1x}. See: TWOT—71a; BDB—31d.

330. אֵטוּן {1x} **ʼêṭûwn**, *ay-toon';* from an unused root (prob. mean. to *bind*); prop. *twisted* (yarn), i.e. *tapestry:*—fine linen {1x}. See: TWOT—73b; BDB—32a.

331. אָטַם {8x} **ʼâṭam**, *aw-tam';* a prim. root; to *close* (the lips or ears); by anal. to *contract* (a window by bevelled jambs):—narrow {4x}, stoppeth {3x}, shutteth {1x}. See: TWOT—73; BDB—31d.

332. אָטַר {1x} **ʼâṭar**, *aw-tar';* a prim. root; to *close* up:—shut {1x}. See: TWOT—74; BDB—32a.

333. אָטֵר {5x} **ʼÂṭêr**, *aw-tare';* from 332; *maimed; Ater,* the name of three Isr.:—*Ater* {5x}. See: BDB—32a.

334. אִטֵּר {2x} **ʼiṭṭêr**, *it-tare';* from 332; *shut* up, i.e. *impeded* (as to the use of the right hand):—lefthanded + 3025 {2x}. See: TWOT—74a; BDB—32a.

335. אַי {16x} **ʼay**, *ah'ee;* perh. from 370; *where?* hence, *how?:*—where {9x}, what {3x}, whence {4x}. See: TWOT—75; BDB—32a, 58b.

336. אִי {1x} **ʼîy**, *ee;* prob. ident. with 335 (through the idea of a *query*); *not:*—island {1x}. (Job 22:30). See: TWOT—77; BDB—33a.

337. אִי {2x} **ʼîy**, *ee;* short. from 188; *alas!:*—woe {2x}. See: TWOT—76; BDB—33a.

338. אִי {3x} **ʼîy**, *ee;* prob. ident. with 337 (through the idea of a *doleful* sound); a *howler* (used only in the plur.), i.e. any solitary wild creature:—wild beasts of the islands {3x}. See: TWOT—43a; BDB—17b.

339. אִי {36x} **ʼîy**, *ee;* from 183; prop. a *habitable* spot (as *desirable*); dry *land,* a *coast,* an *island:*—isle(s) {30x}, islands {5x}, country {1x}. See: TWOT—39a; BDB—15d, 33b.

340. אָיַב {1x} **ʼâyab**, *aw-yab';* a prim. root; to *hate* (as one of an opposite tribe or party); hence, to *be hostile:*—enemy {1x}. See: TWOT—78; BDB—33b.

341. אֹיֵב {282x} **ʼôyêb**, *o-yabe';* or (fully)

אוֹיֵב **ʼôwyêb**, *o-yabe';* act. part. of 340; *hating;* an *adversary:*—enemy(s) {280x}, foes {2x}.

Oyeb means "enemy." In form, the word is an active infinitive (or more precisely, a verbal noun). **(1)** This word means "enemy," and is used in at least one reference to both individuals and nations: ". . . In blessing I will bless thee, and in multiplying I will multiply thy seed as the stars of the heaven, and as the sand which is upon the sea shore; and thy seed shall possess the gate of his enemies" (Gen 22:17—the first occurrence). **(2)** "Personal foes" may be represented by this word: "If thou meet thine enemy's ox or his ass going astray, thou shalt surely bring it back to him again" (Ex 23:4). This idea includes "those who show hostility toward me": "But mine enemies are lively, and they are strong; and they that hate me wrongfully are multiplied" (Ps 38:19). **(3)** One might be an "enemy" of God: ". . . The LORD will take vengeance on his adversaries, and he reserveth wrath for his enemies" (Nah 1:2). **(4)** God is the "enemy" of all who refuse to submit to His lordship: "But they rebelled, and vexed his holy Spirit: therefore he was turned to be their enemy . . ." (Is 63:10). Syn.: Tsar (6862) is the general designation for enemy; ʼôwyêb is specific; sone (8130) stresses hatred; and rodep (7291) stresses persecution. Syn.: 6862, 6887, 8324. See: TWOT—78; BDB—33b.

342. אֵיבָה {5x} **ʼêybâh**, *ay-baw';* from 340; *hostility:*—enmity {3x}, hatred {2x}. See: TWOT—78a; BDB—33c.

343. אֵיד {24x} **ʼêyd**, *ade;* from the same as 181 (in the sense of *bending* down); *oppression;* by impl. *misfortune, ruin:*—calamity {17x}, destruction {7x}.

(1) This word signifies a "disaster" or "calamity" befalling a nation or individual. When used of a nation, it represents a "political or military event": "To me belongeth vengeance, and recompense; their foot shall slide in due time: for the day of their calamity is at hand, and the things that shall come upon them make haste" (Deut 32:35—first occurrence). The prophets tend to use *ʼed* in the sense of national "disaster," while Wisdom writers use it for "personal tragedy." Syn.: 3589, 4288, 7667, 7701. See: TWOT—38c; BDB—15c, 33d.

344. אַיָּה {3x} **ʼayâh**, *ah-yaw';* perh. from 337; the *screamer,* i.e. a *hawk:*—kite {2x}, vulture {1x}. See: TWOT—43b; BDB—17b, 33d.

345. אַיָּה {6x} **ʼAyâh**, *ah-yaw';* the same as 344; *Ajah,* the name of two Isr.:—Aiah {5x}, Ajah {1x}. See: BDB—17b.

346. אַיֵּה {2x} **ʼayêh**, *ah-yay';* prol. from 335; *where?:*—where {2x}. See: TWOT—75a; BDB—32c, 33d.

347. אִיּוֹב {58x} **ʼÎyôwb**, *ee-yobe';* from 340; *hated* (i.e. *persecuted*); *Ijob,* the patriarch famous for his patience:—Job {58x}. See: BDB—33c.

348. אִיזֶבֶל {22x} **ʼÎyzebel**, *ee-zeh'-bel;* from 336 and 2083; *chaste; Izebel,* the wife of king Ahab:—Jezebel {22x}. See: BDB—33b.

349. אֵיךְ {10x} ʾ**êyk**, *ake;* also

אֵיכָה ʾ**êykâh**, *ay-kaw';* and

אֵיכָכָה ʾ**êykâkâh**, *ay-kaw'-kah;* prol. from 335; *how?* or *how!;* also *where:*—how, what, where = {10x}. See: TWOT—75b, c, d, e; BDB—32c, 32d, 33d.

350. אִי־כָבוֹד {2x} **Îy-kâbôwd**, *ee-kaw-bode';* from 336 and 3519; (there is) *no glory,* i.e. *inglorious; Ikabod,* a son of Phineas:—I-chabod {2x}. See: BDB—33b.

351. אֵיכֹה {1x} ʾ**êykôh**, *ay-kō;* prob. a var. for 349, but not as an interrogative; *where:*—where {1x}. TWOT—75d; BDB—33d.

אֵיכָה ʾ**êykâh**;

אֵיכָכָה ʾ**êykâkâh**. See 349.

352. אַיִל {185x} ʾ**ayîl**, *ah'-yil;* from the same as 193; prop. *strength;* hence, anything *strong;* spec. a *chief* (politically); also a *ram* (from his strength); a *pilaster* (as a strong support); an *oak* or other strong tree:—ram(s) {156x}, post(s) {21x}, mighty (men) {4x}, trees {2x}, lintel {1x}, oaks {1x}.

The basic meaning of ʾ*ayîl* is strength; hence, also *ayil* means "ram." **(1)** *Ayil* represents a male sheep or "ram." The word first appears in Gen 15:9, where God told Abram: "Take me a heifer of three years old, and a she goat of three years old, and a ram of three years old, and a turtledove, and a young pigeon." **(2)** These animals were often used in sacrificing (cf. Gen 22:13). **(3)** They were eaten (Gen 31:38), and the wool used to make clothing (cf. 2 Kin 3:4). **(4)** Consequently, as highly valuable animals, such "rams" were selected by Jacob to be part of a peace present sent to Esau (Gen 32:14).

(5) Many passages use *ayil* as a figure of despots or mighty men: "Then the dukes of Edom shall be amazed; the mighty men of Moab, trembling shall take hold upon them . . ." (Ex 15:15). The king of Babylon deported Judah's kings, princes, and the "mighty of the land" (Eze 17:13). **(6)** In the first instance the word represents chiefs in the sense of head political figures, whereas in the second use it appears to signify lesser figures. An even more powerful figure is in view in Eze 31:11, where *ayil* represents a central, powerful, earthly figure who will ruthlessly destroy Assyria: "I have therefore delivered him into the hand of the mighty one of the heathen; he shall surely deal with him: I have driven him out for his wickedness." Syn.: ʾ*Ayîl* is the support upon which the rafters rest; whereas mashshebah (4676 – {32x}) refers to a "pillar" as **(1)** a personal memorial (2 Sa 18:18); **(2)** a monument (Gen 28:18); or **(3)** sacred stones or pillars (Ex 24:4). See also: 1368, 2389, 4676. See: TWOT d, e, f, g; BDB—17d, 18a, 18b, 33d.

353. אֱיָל {1x} ʾ**ěyâl**, *eh-yawl';* a var. of 352; *strength:*—strength {1x}. See: TWOT—79; BDB—33d.

354. אַיָּל {11x} ʾ**ayâl**, *ah-yawl';* an intens. form of 352 (in the sense of *ram*); a *stag* or male deer:—hart(s) {11x}. See: TWOT—45k; BDB—19d.

355. אַיָּלָה {8x} ʾ**ayâlâh**, *ah-yaw-law';* fem.of 354; a *doe* or female deer:—hind(s) {8x}. See: TWOT—45l; BDB—19b.

356. אֵילוֹן {7x} ʾ**Êylôwn**, *ay-lone';* or (short.)

אֵלוֹן ʾ**Êlôwn**, *ay-lone';* or

אֵילֹן ʾ**Êylôn**, *ay-lone';* from 352; *oak-grove; Elon,* the name of a place in Pal., and also of one Hittite, two Isr.:—Elon {7x}. See: BDB—19a.

357. אַיָּלוֹן {10x} ʾ**Ayâlôwn**, *ah-yaw-lone';* from 354; *deer-field; Ajalon,* the name of five places in Pal.:—Aijalon {7x}, Ajalon {3x}. See: BDB—19c.

358. אֵילוֹן בֵּית חָנָן {1x} ʾ**Êylôwn Bêyth Chânân**, *ay-lone' bayth chaw-nawn';* from 356, 1004, and 2603; *oak-grove of* (the) *house of favor; Elon of Beth-chanan,* a place in Pal.:—Elon-beth-hanan {1x}. See: BDB—19a, 111c.

359. אֵילוֹת {8x} ʾ**Êylôwth**, *ay-lōth';* or

אֵילַת ʾ**Êylath**, *ay-lath';* from 352; *trees* or a *grove* (i.e. palms); *Eloth* or *Elath,* a place on the Red Sea:—Elath {5x}, Eloth {3x}. See: BDB—19a.

360. אֱיָלוּת {1x} ʾ**ěyâlûwth**, *eh-yaw-looth';* fem. of 353; *power;* by impl. *protection:*—strength {1x}. See: TWOT—79a; BDB—33d.

361. אֵילָם {15x} ʾ**êylâm**, *ay-lawm';* or (short.)

אֵלָם ʾ**êlâm**, *ay-lawm';* or (fem.)

אֵלַמָּה ʾ**êlammâh**, *ay-lam-maw';* prob. from 352; a *pillar-space* (or colonnade), i.e. a *pale* (or portico):—arches {15x}. See: TWOT—45j; BDB—19a, 48a.

362. אֵילִם {6x} ʾ**Êylîm**, *ay-leem';* plur. of 352; palm- *trees; Elim,* a place in the Desert:—Elim {1x}. See: BDB—18c.

363. אִילָן {6x} ʾ**îylân** (Aram.), *ee-lawn';* corresp. to 356; a *tree:*—tree {6x}. See: TWOT—2570; BDB—1079a, 1080a.

364. אֵיל פָּארָן {1x} ʾ**Êyl Pâʾrân**, *ale paw-rawn';* from 352 and 6290; *oak of Paran; El-Paran,* a portion of the district of Paran:—El-paran {1x}. See: BDB—18c.

אֵילֹן ʾ**Êylôn**. See 356.

365. אַיֶּלֶת {3x} ʾ**ayeleth**, *ah-yeh'-leth;* the same as 355; a *doe:*—hind {2x}, Aijeleth {1x}. See: TWOT—45l; BDB—19b.

אַיִם ʾ**ayim**. See 368.

366. אָיֹם {3x} ʾ**âyôm**, *aw-yome';* from an unused root (mean. to *frighten*); *frightful:*—terrible {3x}. See: TWOT—80a; BDB—33d.

367. אֵימָה {17x} ʾ**êymâh**, *ay-maw';* or (short.)

אֵמָה ʾ**êmah**, *ay-maw';* from the same as 366; *fright;* concr. an *idol* (as a bugbear):—terror(s) {7x}, fear {5x}, terrible {2x}, dread {1x}, horror {1x}, idols {1x}.

The basic meaning is to be in the presence of an object (God, army) that causes a deep-seated terror; or dread. Syn.: 2851. See: TWOT—80b; BDB—33d, 1080a.

368. אֵימִים {3x} ʾ**Êymîym**, *ay-meem';* plur. of 367; *terrors; Emim,* an early Canaanitish (or Moabitish) tribe:—Emims {3x}. See: BDB—33d, 34a.

369. אַיִן {29x} ʾ**ayin**, *ah'-yin;* as if from a prim. root mean. to *be nothing* or *not exist;* a *non-entity;* Gen used as a neg. particle:—except {1x}, faileth {1x}, fatherless + 1 – {1x}, incurable + 4832 – {1x}, infinite {3x}, innumerable {4x}, neither {40x}, never {2x}, no {52x}, none {48x}, not {164x}, nothing {23x}, nought {1x}, without {42x}.

ʾ*Ayin* may be used **(1)** absolutely and signify nonexistence (Gen 2:5); **(2)** preceded by the particle im, the word may mean not (Ex 17:7) or because (Jer 7:32), **(3)** or else (Gen 30:1; Ps 39:5); **(4)** without (Prov 15:22); **(5)** simple negation (Ps 135:17); **(6)** With a suffixed pronoun ʾ*ayin* negates the existence of the one or thing so represented; with the suffixed pronoun "he," the word means he was no longer (Gen 5:24). Syn.: comp. 370, 1097, 3808. See: TWOT—81; BDB—33b, 34a.

370. אַיִן {17x} ʾ**ayin**, *ah'-yin;* prob. ident. with 369 in the sense of *query* (comp. 336); *where?* (only in connection with prep. pref., *whence*):—whence {16x}, where {1x}. See: TWOT—75f; BDB—32d, 34a.

371. אִין {1x} ʾ**îyn**, *een;* appar. a short. form of 369; but (like 370) interrog.; is it *not?:*—(is) there not {1x}. See: TWOT—81; BDB—35b.

372. אִיעֶזֶר {1x} ʾ**Îyʿezer**, *ee-eh'-zer;* from 336 and 5828; *helpless; Iezer,* an Isr.:—Jeezer {1x}. See: BDB—4c.

373. אִיעֶזְרִי {1x} ʾ**Îyʿezrîy**, *ee-ez-ree';* patron. from 372; an *Iezrite* or desc. of Iezer:—Jezerite {1x}. See: BDB—4d.

374. אֵיפָה {40x} ʾ**êyphâh**, *ay-faw';* or (short.)

אֵפָה ʾ**êphâh**, *ay-faw';* of Eg. der.; an *ephah* or measure for grain; hence, a *measure* in Gen:—*ephah* {34x}, measure(s) {6x}. See: TWOT—82; BDB—35b.

375. אֵיפֹה {10x} ʾ**êyphôh**, *ay-fō';* from 335 and 6311; *what place?;* also (of time) *when?;* or (of means) *how?:*—where {9x}, what {1x}. See: TWOT—75h; BDB—33a, 35c.

376. אִישׁ {1639x} ʾ**îysh**, *eesh;* contr. for 582 [or perh. rather from an unused root mean. to *be extant*]; a *man* as an individual or a male person; often used as an adjunct to a more def. term (and in such cases frequently not expressed in translation):—man {1002x}, men {210x}, one {188x}, husband {69x}, any {27x}, misc.: also, another, a certain, + champion, consent, each, every (one), fellow, he, high (degree), him (that is, man [-kind], + none, people, person, + steward, what (man) soever, whoso = {143x}.

Iysh means "man; husband; mate; human being; human; somebody; each; every." The plural of this noun is usually anashim (582). **(1)** Basically, this word signifies "man" in correspondence to woman; a "man" is a person who is distinguished by maleness. This emphasis is in Gen 2:24 (the first biblical occurrence): "Therefore shall a man leave his father and his mother, and shall cleave unto his wife. . . ." Sometimes the phrase "man and woman" signifies anyone whatsoever, including children: "If an ox gore a man or a woman, that they die: then the ox shall be surely stoned . . ." (Ex 21:28). **(2)** This phrase can also connote an inclusive group, including children: "And they utterly destroyed all that was in the city, both man and woman, young and old, and ox, and sheep, and ass, with the edge of the sword" (Josh 6:21). This idea is sometimes more explicitly expressed by the word series "men, women, and children": "Gather the people together, men, and women, and children, and thy stranger that is within thy gates . . ." (Deut 31:12).

(3) *Iysh* is often used in marriage contexts (cf. Gen 2:24) meaning "husband" or "mate": "Take ye wives, and beget sons and daughters; and take wives for your sons, and give your daughters to husbands, that they may bear sons and daughters . . ." (Jer 29:6). A virgin is described as a lass who has not known a "man" ("husband"): ". . . And she went with her companions, and bewailed her virginity upon the mountains. And it came to pass at the end of two months, that she returned unto her father, who did with her according to his vow which he had vowed: and she knew no man" (Judg 11:38–39). **(4)** The sense "mate" appears in Gen 7:2, where the word represents male animals: "Of every clean beast thou shalt take to thee by sevens, the male and his female. . . ."

(5) One special nuance of *iysh* appears in passages such as Gen 3:6, where it means "husband," or one responsible for a wife or woman and revered by her: "[And she] gave also unto her husband with her: and he did eat." This emphasis is in Hos 2:16 where it is applied to God. **(6)** Sometimes this word connotes that the one so identified is a "man" par excellence. As such he is strong, influential, and knowledgeable in battle: "Be strong, and quit yourselves like men, O ye Philistines, that ye be not servants unto the Hebrews . . ." (1 Sa 4:9). **(7)** In a few places *iysh* is used as a synonym of "father": "We are all sons of one man . . ." (Gen 42:11). **(8)** In other passages the word is applied to a son (cf. Gen 2:24). **(9)** In the plural the word can be applied to groups of men who serve or obey a superior. Pharaoh's men escorted Abraham: "And Pharaoh commanded his men concerning him: and they sent him away . . ." (Gen 12:20). **(10)** In a similar but more general sense, the word may identify people who belong to someone or something: "For all these abominations have the men of the land done, which were before you, and the land is defiled" (Lev 18:27). **(11)** Infrequently (and in later historical literature) this word is used as a collective noun referring to an entire group: "And his servant said, . . . Should I set this before a hundred men?" (2 Kin 4:43).

(12) Many passages use *iysh* in the more general or generic sense of "man," a human being: "He that smiteth a man, so that he die, shall be surely put to death" (Ex 21:12). Even if one strikes a woman or child and he or she dies, the attacker should be put to death. Again, notice Deut 27:15: "Cursed be the man that maketh any graven or molten image. . . ." **(12a)** This is the sense of the word when it is contrasted with animals: "But against any of the children of Israel shall not a dog move his tongue, against man or beast . . . ." (Ex 11:7). **(12b)** The same nuance appears when man over against God is in view: "God is not a man, that he should lie . . ." (Num 23:19).

(13) Sometimes *iysh* is indefinite, meaning "somebody" or "someone" ("they"): "And I will make thy seed as the dust of the earth: so that if a man can number the dust of the earth, then shall thy seed also be numbered" (Gen 13:16). **(14)** In other passages the word suggests the meaning "each" (Gen 40:5). **(15)** Closely related to the previous nuance is the connotation "every" (Jer 23:35). comp. 802. Syn.: 'Adam (120) connotes man as the creature created in God's image, the crown of all creation. *Iysh* (376) is used for man as the counterpart of woman and/or as distinguished in his maleness. Geber (1397) denotes a male as an antonym of a woman, many times suggesting strength, strong man. Enosh (582) sets forth a collective idea man suggesting the frailty, vulnerability, and finitude of man as contrasted to God. Bachur (970) signifies the fully developed, vigorous, unmarried man is in his prime. See also: 120, 582, 1167, 1397, 1400, 4962. See: TWOT—83a; BDB—35c.

377. **אִישׁ** {1x} **ʼîysh**, *eesh;* denom. from 376; to *be a man,* i.e. act in a manly way:—shew yourselves men {1x}. See: TWOT—83a; BDB—84a, 1083b.

378. **אִישׁ־בֹּשֶׁת** {11x} **ʼÎysh-Bôsheth**, *eesh-bō'-sheth;* from 376 and 1322; *man of shame; Ish-Bosheth,* a son of King Saul:—Ish-bosheth {11x}. See: BDB—36b.

379. **אִישְׁהוֹד** {1x} **ʼÎyshhôwd**, *eesh-hode';* from 376 and 1935; *man of renown; Ishod,* an Isr.:—Ishod {1x}. See: BDB—36b.

380. **אִישׁוֹן** {6x} **ʼîyshôwn**, *ee-shone';* dimin. from 376; the *little man* of the eye; the *pupil* or *ball;* hence, the *middle* (of night):—apple {3x}, obscure {2x}, black {1x}.

The word ishown means "little man," a diminutive form of the noun. Although it literally means "little man," it signifies the pupil of the eye and is so translated ("apple of his eye"). See: TWOT—83b; BDB—36b, 37c.

אִישׁ־חַי **ʼÎysh-Chay**. See 381.

381. **אִישׁ־חַיִל** **ʼÎysh-Chayil**, *eesh-khah'-yil;* from 376 and 2428; *man of might;* by defect. transc. (2 Sa 23:20)

אִישׁ־חַי {4x} **ʼÎysh-Chay**, *eesh-khah'ee;* as if from 376 and 2416; *living man; Ish-chail* (or *Ish-chai*), an Isr.:—a valiant man {1x}. See: BDB—35d.

382. **אִישׁ־טוֹב** {2x} **ʼÎysh-Ṭôwb**, *eesh-tobe';* from 376 and 2807; *man of Tob, Ish-Tob,* a place in Pal.:—Ish-tob {1x}. See: BDB—36a.

383. **אִיתַי** {17x} **ʼîythay** (Aram.), *ee-thah'ee;* corresp. to 3426; prop. *entity;* used only as a particle of affirmation, there *is:*—art thou, can, do ye, have, it be, there is (are), × we will not = {17x}. See: TWOT—2572; BDB—1080a, 1083c.

384. **אִיתִיאֵל** {3x} **ʼÎythîyʼêl**, *eeth-ee-ale';* perh. from 837 and 410; *God has arrived; Ithiel,* the name of an Isr., also of a symb. person:—Ithiel {3x}. See: BDB—36b, 87b.

385. **אִיתָמָר** {21x} **ʼÎythâmâr**, *eeth-aw-mawr';* from 339 and 8558; *coast of* the *palm*-tree; *Ithamar,* a son of Aaron:—Ithamar {21x}. BDB—16a, 33b, 36b.

386. **אֵיתָן** {13x} **ʼêythân**, *ay-thawn';* or (short.) **אֵתָן** **ʼêthân**, *ay-thawn';* from an unused root (mean. to *continue*); *permanence;* hence, (concr.) *permanent;* spec. a *chieftain:*—strong {5x}, mighty {4x}, strength {2x}, hard {1x}, rough {1x}. See: TWOT—935a; BDB—36b, 450d.

387. **אֵיתָן** {8x} **ʼÊythân**, *ay-thawn';* the same as 386; *permanent; Ethan,* the name of four Isr.:—Ethan {8x}. See: BDB—451a.

388. **אֵיתָנִים** {1x} **ʼÊythânîym**, *ay-thaw-neem';* plur. of 386; always with the art.; the *permanent* brooks; *Ethanim,* the name of a month:—Ethanim {1x}. See: BDB—450d.

389. **אַךְ** {22x} **ʼak**, *ak;* akin to 403; a particle of affirmation, *surely;* hence, (by limitation) *only:*—also, but, certainly, even, howbeit, least, nevertheless, notwithstanding, only, save, scarce, surely, surety, truly, verily, wherefore, yet = {22x}. See: TWOT—84; BDB—36c.

390. **אַכַּד** {1x} **ʼAkkad**, *ak-kad';* from an unused root prob. mean. to *strengthen;* a *fortress; Accad,* a place in Bab.:—Accad {1x}. See: BDB—37a.

391. **אַכְזָב** {2x} **ʼakzâb**, *ak-zawb';* from 3576; *falsehood;* by impl. *treachery:*—liar {1x}, lie {1x}. See: TWOT—970b; BDB—37a, 469d.

392. **אַכְזִיב** {4x} **ʼAkzîyb**, *ak-zeeb';* from 391; *deceitful* (in the sense of a winter-torrent which *fails* in summer); *Akzib,* the name of two places in Pal.:—Achzib {4x}. See: BDB—37a, 469d.

393. **אַכְזָר** {4x} **ʼakzâr**, *ak-zawr';* from an unused root (appar. mean. to *act harshly*); *violent;* by impl. *deadly,* also (in a good sense) *brave:*—cruel {3x}, fierce {1x}. See: TWOT—971a; BDB—37a, 470a.

394. **אַכְזָרִי** {8x} **ʼakzârîy**, *ak-zaw-ree';* from 393; *terrible:*—cruel {7x}, one {1x}. See: TWOT—971b; BDB—37a, 470a.

395. **אַכְזְרִיּוּת** {1x} **ʼakzᵉrîyûwth**, *ak-ze-ree-ooth';* from 394; *fierceness:*—cruel {1x}. See: TWOT—971c; BDB—37a, 470a.

396. **אֲכִילָה** {1x} **ʼăkîylâh**, *ak-ee-law';* fem. from 398; something *eatable,* i.e. *food:*—meat {1x}. See: TWOT—85c; BDB—38b.

397. **אָכִישׁ** {21x} **ʼÂkîysh**, *aw-keesh';* of uncert. der.; *Akish,* a Philistine king:—Achish {21x}. See: BDB—37a.

398. **אָכַל** {810} **ʼâkal**, *aw-kal';* a prim. root; to *eat* (lit. or fig.):—eat (-er, up) {604x}, devour (-er, up), {111x}, consume {32x}, misc. {63x}.

Akal means "to eat, feed, consume, devour." **(1)** Essentially, this root refers to the "consumption of food by man or animals." In Gen 3:6, we read that Eve took of the fruit of the tree of the knowledge of good and evil and "ate" it. **(2)** The function of eating is presented along with seeing, hearing, and smelling as one of the basic functions of living (Deut 4:28). **(3)** "Eating," as every other act of life, is under God's control; He stipulates what may or may not be eaten (Gen 1:29). **(3a)** After the Flood, man was allowed to "eat" meat (Gen 9:3). **(3b)** But under the Mosaic covenant, God stipulated that certain foods were not to be "eaten" (Lev 11; Deut 14) while others were permissible. This distinction is certainly not new, inasmuch as it is mentioned prior to the Flood (Gen 7:2; cf. Gen 6:19). A comparison of these two passages demonstrates how the Bible can speak in general terms, with the understanding that certain limitations are included. Hence, Noah was commanded to bring into the ark two of every kind (Gen 6:19), while the Bible tells us that this meant two of every unclean and fourteen of every clean animal (Gen 7:2). Thus, Gen 9:3 implies that man could "eat" only the clean animals.

(4) This verb is often used figuratively with overtones of destroying something or someone. **(4a)** So the sword, fire, and forest are said to "consume" men. **(4b)** The things "consumed" may include such various things as land (Gen 3:17), fields (Is 1:7), offerings (Deut 18:1), and a bride's purchase price (Gen 31:15). **(5)** *Akal* might also connote bearing the results of an action (Is 3:10). **(6)** The word can refer not only **(6a)** to "eating" but **(6b)** to the entire concept "room and board" (2 Sa 9:11, 13), **(6c)** the special act of "feasting" (Eccl 10:16), or **(6d)** the entire activity of "earning a living" (Amos 7:12; cf. Gen 3:19). **(7)** In Dan 3:8 and 6:24, "to eat one's pieces" is to charge someone maliciously. **(8)** "To eat another's flesh," used figuratively, **(8a)** refers to tearing him to pieces or "killing him" (Ps 27:2), although *akal* may also be used literally, **(8b)** as when one "eats" human beings in times of serious famine (Lev 26:29). **(9)** Eccl 4:5 uses the expression, "eat one's own flesh," for allowing oneself to waste away.

(10) Abstinence from eating may indicate deep emotional upset, like that which overcame Hannah before the birth of Samuel (1 Sa 1:7). **(11)** It may also indicate the religious self-denial seen in fasting. **(12)** Unlike the pagan deities (Deut 32:37–38) God "eats" no food (Ps 50:13); although as a "consuming" fire (Deut 4:24), He is ready to defend His own honor and glory. **(13)** He "consumes" evil and the sinner. **(14)** He will also "consume" the wicked like a lion (Hos 13:8). **(15)** There is one case in which God literally "consumed" food—when He appeared to Abraham in the form of three "strangers" (Gen 18:8). **(16)** God provides many good things to eat, **(16a)** such as manna to the Israelites (Ex 16:32) and **(16b)** all manner of food to those who delight in the LORD (Is 58:14), **(16c)** even the finest food (Ps 81:16). **(17)** He puts the Word of God into one's mouth; by "consuming" it, it is taken into one's very being (Eze 3:2). Syn.: 1104. See: TWOT—85; v. BDB—37a, 1080b.

399. אֲכַל {7x} **ʼăkal** (Aram.), *ak-al';* corresp. to 398:—devour {4x}, accused {2x}, eat {1x}. See: TWOT—2573; BDB—1080b.

400. אֹכֶל {44x} **ʼôkel**, *o'-kel;* from 398; *food:*—- meat {18x}, food {16x}, eating {4x}, victuals {3x}, prey {2x}, mealtime + 6256 –{1x}.

Okel means "food." **(1)** *Okel* appears twice in Gen 41:35 with the sense of "food supply": "And let them gather all the food of those good years that come, and lay up corn under the hand of Pharaoh, and let them keep food in the cities." **(2)** The word refers to the "food" of wild animals in Ps 104:21: "The young lions roar after their prey, and seek their meat from God." **(3)** *Okel* is used for "food" given by God in Ps 145:15. **(4)** The word may also be used for "food" as an offering, as in Mal 1:12. Syn.: 3899, 6720. See: TWOT—85a; BDB—38a.

401. אֻכָל {1x} **ʼÛkâl**, *oo-kawl';* or

אֻכָּל **ʼUkkâl**, *ook-kawl';* appar. from 398; *devoured; Ucal,* a fancy name:—Ucal {1x}. See: BDB—38b.

402. אָכְלָה {18x} **ʼoklâh**, *ok-law';* fem. of 401; *food:*—meat {8x}, devour {3x}, fuel {3x}, eat {2x}, consume {1x}, food {1x}. See: TWOT—85b; BDB—38a.

403. אָכֵן {18x} **ʼâkên**, *aw-kane';* from 3559 [comp. 3651]; *firmly; fig. surely;* also (advers.) *but:*—surely {9x}, but {3x}, verily {2x}, truly {2x}, certainly {1x}, nevertheless {1x}. See: TWOT—86; BDB—38c.

404. אָכַף {1x} **ʼâkaph**, *aw-kaf';* a prim. root; appar. mean. to *curve* (as with a burden); to *urge:*—craveth {1x}. See: TWOT—87; BDB—38c.

405. אֶכֶף {1x} **ʼekeph**, *eh'-kef;* from 404; a *load;* by impl. a *stroke* (others *dignity*):—hand {1x}. See: TWOT—87a; BDB—38d.

406. אִכָּר {7x} **ʼikkâr**, *ik-kawr';* from an unused root mean. to *dig;* a *farmer:*—husbandman {5x}, plowman {2x}. See: TWOT—88a; BDB—38d.

407. אַכְשָׁף {3x} **ʼAkshâph**, *ak-shawf';* from 3784; *fascination; Acshaph,* a place in Pal.:—Achshaph {3x}. See: BDB—38d, 506d.

408. אַל {12x} **ʼal**, *al;* a neg. particle [akin to 3808]; *not* (the qualified negation, used as a deprecative); once (Job 24:25) as a noun, *nothing:*—never {2x}, nay {1x}, neither {1x}, no {1x}, none {1x}, nor {1x}, not {1x}, nothing {1x}, rather than {1x}, whither {1x}, nothing worth {1x}. See: TWOT—90; BDB—39a, 1080b.

409. אַל {3x} **ʼal** (Aram.), *al;* corresp. to 408:—not 3. See: TWOT—2574; BDB—1080b.

410. אֵל {245x} **ʼêl**, *ale;* short. from 352; *strength;* as adj. *mighty;* espec. the *Almighty* (but used also of any *deity*):—God {213x}, god {16x}, power {4x}, mighty {5x}, goodly {1x}, great {1x}, idols {1x}, Immanuel + 6005 – {2x}, might {1x}, strong {1x}. comp. names in "*-el.*"

El (410) means "god." **(1)** This term was the most common general designation of deity in the ancient Near East. **(2)** While it frequently occurred alone, *el* was also combined with other words to constitute a compound term for deity, or to identify the nature and functions of the "god" in some manner. Thus the expression "God, the God of Israel" (Gen 33:20) identified the specific activities of Israel's God. **(3)** In the ancient world, knowledge of a person's name was believed to give one power over that person. A knowledge of the character and attributes of pagan "gods" was thought to enable the worshipers to manipulate or influence the deities in a more effective way than they could have if the deity's name remained unknown. To that extent, the vagueness of the term *el* frustrated persons who hoped to obtain some sort of power over the deity, since the name gave little or no indication of the god's character. This was particularly true for *El,* the chief Canaanite god. The ancient Semites stood in mortal dread of the superior powers exercised by the gods and attempted to propitiate them accordingly. They commonly associated deity with the manifestation and use of enormous power. Perhaps this is reflected in the curious Hebrew phrase, "the power [ʼ*el*] of my hand" (Gen 31:29; cf. Deut 28:32).

(4) Some Hebrew phrases in the Psalms associated *el* with impressive natural features, such as the cedar trees of Lebanon (Ps 80:10) or mountains (Ps 36:6). In these instances, *el* conveys a clear impression of grandeur or majesty. **(5)** Names with *el* as one of their components were common in the Near East in the second millennium B.C. The names Methusael (Gen 4:18) and Ishmael (Gen 16:11) come from a very early period. **(6)** In the Mosaic period, *el* was synonymous with the LORD who delivered the Israelites from bondage in Egypt and made them victorious in battle (Num 24:8). **(7)** This tradition of the Hebrew *el* as a "God" who revealed Himself in power and entered into a covenant relationship with His people was prominent in both poetry (Ps 7:11; 85:8) and prophecy (Is 43:12; 46:9). **(8)** The name of *el* was commonly used by the Israelites to denote supernatural provision or power. This was both normal and legitimate, since the covenant between "God" and Israel assured an obedient and holy people that the creative forces of the universe would sustain and protect at all times. Equally, if they became disobedient and apostate, these same forces would punish them severely. Syn.: 410 + 7706, 426, 430, 433, 3069. See: TWOT—93a; BDB—41d, 42b, 769b.

אֵל שַׁדַּי *El* shadday (410, 7706) means "God Almighty." **(1)** This combination of *el* with a qualifying term represents a religious tradition among the Israelites that was probably in existence by the third millennium B.C. **(2)** A few centuries later, shadday appeared in Hebrew personal names such as Zurishaddai (Num 1:6) and Ammishaddai (Num 1:12). **(3)** The earliest Old Testament appearance of the appellation as a title of deity ("God Almighty") is in Gen 17:1, where "God" identifies Himself in this way to Abraham. Unfortunately, the name is not explained in any manner; and even the directions "walk before me, and be thou perfect" throw no light on the meaning of shadday.

(4) Scholars have attempted to understand the word relating it to the Akkadian shadu ("mountain"), as though "God" had either revealed His mighty power in association with mountain phenomena such as volcanic eruptions or that He was regarded as strong and immutable, like the "everlasting hills" of the blessing of Jacob (Gen 49:26). **(5)** Certainly the associating of deity with mountains was an important part of Mesopotamian religion. The "gods" were believed to favor mountaintop dwellings, and the Sumerians constructed their staged temple-towers or ziggurats as artificial mountains for worship. It was customary to erect a small shrine on the uppermost stage of the ziggurat so that the patron deity could descend from heaven and inhabit the temple. The Hebrews began their own tradition of mountain revelation just after the Exodus, but by this time the name *el* shadday had been replaced by the tetragrammaton of Yahweh (Ex 3:15, 6:3). **(6)** *El* shadday served as the patriarchs' covenant name for "God," and continued as such until the time of Moses, when a further revelation took place (Ex 6:3). **(7)** The Abrahamic covenant was marked by a degree of closeness between "God" and the human participants that was distinctive in Hebrew history.

(8) "God Almighty" revealed Himself as a powerful deity who was able to perform whatever He asserted. But the degree of intimacy between *el* shadday and the patriarchs at various stages shows that the covenant involved God's care and love for this growing family that He had chosen, protected, and prospered. He led the covenant family from place to place, being obviously present with them at all times. His covenant formulations show that He was not preoccupied with cultic rites or orgiastic celebrations. Instead, He demanded a degree of obedience that would enable Abraham and his descendants to walk in His presence, and live blameless moral and spiritual lives (Gen 17:1). **(9)** The true covenantal service of *el* shadday, therefore, was not cultic or ritualistic, but moral and ethical in character. **(10)** In the early Mosaic era, the new redemptive name of "God" and the formulation of the Sinai covenant made *el* shadday largely obsolete as a designation of deity. Subsequently, the name occurs about 35 times in the Old Testament, most of which are in the Book of Job. **(11)** Occasionally, the name is used synonymously with the tetragrammaton of Yahweh (Ruth 1:21; Ps 91:1–2), to emphasize the power and might of "God" in characteristic fashion.

אֵל עוֹלָם *El* olam (410, 5769) means "God of eternity; God the everlasting; God for ever." **(1)** The word olam has related forms in various ancient Near Eastern languages, all of which describe lengthy duration or distant time. The idea seems to be quantitative rather than metaphysical, expressing a period of time that could not be measured other than as lengthy duration. **(2)** Only in rare poetic passages such as Ps 90:2 are temporal categories regarded inadequate to describe the nature of God's existence as *el* olam. In such an instance, the Creator is deemed to have been "from everlasting to everlasting"; but even this use of olam expresses the idea of continued, measurable existence rather than a state of being independent of temporal considerations.

(3) The name *el* olam was associated predominantly with Beer-sheba (Gen 21:25–34). The settlement of Beer-sheba means "well of the oath" (Gen 21:31). But it could also mean "well of the seven"—i.e., the seven lambs that were set apart as witnesses of the oath. Abraham planted a commemorative tree in Beer-sheba and invoked the name of the LORD as *el* olam. The fact that Abraham subsequently stayed many days in the land of the Philistines seems to imply that he associated continuity and stability with *el* olam, who was not touched by the vicissitudes of time. Although Beer-sheba may have been a place where the Canaanites worshiped originally, the area later became associated with the veneration of the God of Abraham. **(4)** At a subsequent period, Jacob journeyed to Beer-sheba and offered sacrifices to the God of Isaac his father. He did not offer sacrifices to *el* olam by name, however; and although he saw a visionary manifestation of God, he received no revelation that this was the God Abraham had venerated at Beer-sheba. Indeed, God omitted any mention of Abraham, stating that He was the God of Jacob's father. **(5)** Gen 21:33 is the only place in the Old Testament where the title *el* olam occurs. Is 40:28 is the only other instance where olam is used in conjunction with a noun meaning God.

411. אֵל {9x} **ʾêl**, *ale;* a demonstr. particle (but only in a plur. sense) *these* or *those:*—these {7x}, those {2x}. See: TWOT—92; BDB—41b.

412. אֵל {1x} **ʾêl** (Aram.), *ale;* corresp. to 411:—these {1x}. See: TWOT—2575; BDB—1080b.

413. אֵל {38x} **ʾêl**, *ale;* (but only used in the short. constr. form אֶל **ʾel**, *el*); a prim. particle; prop. denoting motion *towards,* but occasionally used of a quiescent position, i.e. *near, with* or *among;* often in general, *to:*—unto, with, against, at, into, in, before, to, of, upon, by, toward, hath, for, on, beside, from, where, after, within = {38x}. See: TWOT—91; BDB—39b.

414. אֵלָא {1x} **ʾÊlâʾ**, *ay-law';* a var. of 424; *oak; Ela,* an Isr.:—Elah {1x}. See: BDB—41d.

415. אֵל אֱלֹהֵי יִשְׂרָאֵל {1x} **ʾÊl ʾělôhêy Yisrâʾêl**, *ale el-o-hay' yis-raw-ale';* from 410, 430 and 3478; the *mighty God of Jisrael; El-Elohi-Jisrael,* the title given to a consecrated spot by Jacob:—El-elohe-israel {1x}. See: BDB—42d.

416. אֵל בֵּית־אֵל {1x} **ʾÊl Bêyth-ʾÊl**, *ale bayth-ale';* from 410 and 1008; the *God of Bethel; El-Bethel,* the title given to a consecrated spot by Jacob:—El-beth-el {1x}. See: BDB—42c.

417. אֶלְגָּבִישׁ {3x} **ʾelgâbîysh**, *el-gaw-beesh';* from 410 and 1378; *hail* (as if a *great pearl*):—hailstone + 68 {3x}. See: TWOT—89a; BDB—38d.

418. אַלְגּוּמִּים {3x} **ʾalgûwmmîym**, *al-goom-meem';* by transp. for 484; sticks of *algum* wood:—algum {2x}, algum tree {1x}. See: TWOT—89b; BDB—38d.

419. אֶלְדָּד {2x} **ʾEldâd**, *el-dâd';* from 410 and 1730; *God has loved; Eldad,* an Isr.:—*Eldad* {2x}. See: BDB—44d.

420. אֶלְדָּעָה {2x} **ʾEldâʿâh**, *el-daw-aw';* from 410 and 3045; *God of knowledge; Eldaah,* a son of Midian:—*Eldaah* {2x}. See: BDB—44d.

421. אָלָה {1x} **ʾâlâh**, *aw-law';* a prim. root [rather ident. with 422 through the idea of *invocation*]; to *bewail:*—lament {1x}. See: TWOT—95; BDB—46d, 1080c.

422. אָלָה {6x} **ʾâlâh**, *aw-law';* a prim. root; prop. to *adjure,* i.e. (usually in a bad sense) *imprecate:*—swear {4x}, curse {1x}, adjure {1x}. See: TWOT—94; BDB—46c, 1060d.

423. אָלָה {36x} **ʾâlâh**, *aw-law';* from 422; an *imprecation:*—curse {18x}, oath {14x}, execration {2x}, swearing {2x}.

Alah means "curse; oath." **(1)** In distinction from arar (779) ["to curse by laying an anathema on someone or something"] and qalal (7043) ["to curse by abusing or by belittling"], *alah* basically refers to "the execution of a proper oath to legalize a covenant or agreement." **(2)** As a noun, *alah* refers to the "oath" itself: "Then shalt thou be clear from this my oath, when thou comest to my kindred; and if they give not thee one, thou shalt be clear from my oath" (Gen 24:41—the first occurrence). **(3)** The "oath" was a "curse" on the head of the one who broke the agreement. **(4)** This same sense appears in Lev 5:1, referring to a general "curse" against anyone who would give false testimony in a court case. **(5)** So *alah* functions as a "curse" sanctioning a pledge or commission, and it can close an agreement or covenant. **(6)** On the other hand, the word sometimes represents a "curse" against someone else, whether his identity is known or not. Syn.: Arar (779 – {63x}) - to curse by laying an anathema on someone or something; qalal (7043 – {83x} and 7045 – {33x}) to curse by abusing or by belittling. See: TWOT—91a; BDB—46d.

424. אֵלָה {13x} **ʾêlâh**, *ay-law';* fem. of 352; an *oak* or other strong tree:—oak {11x}, elm {1x}, teil tree {1x}. See: TWOT—45h; BDB—18c.

425. אֵלָה {16x} **ʾÊlâh**, *ay-law';* the same as 424; *Elah,* the name of an Edomite, of four Isr., and also of a place in Pal.:—*Elah* {16x}. See: BDB—18d.

426. אֱלָהּ {95x} **ʾělâhh** (Aram.), *el-aw';* corresp. to 433; *God:*—God {79x}, god {16x}.

Elahh means "god." **(1)** This Aramaic word is the equivalent of the Hebrew eloah (433). It is a general term for "God" in the Aramaic passages of the Old Testament, and it is a cognate form of the word allah, the designation of deity used by the Arabs. The word was used widely in the Book of Ezra, occurring no fewer than 43 times between Ezra 4:24 and 7:26. On each occasion, the reference is to the "God" of the Jewish people, whether the speaker or writer was himself Jewish or not. Thus the governor of the province "Beyond the River" (i.e., west of the river Euphrates) spoke to king Darius of the "house of the great God" (Ezra 5:8). So also Cyrus instructed Sheshbazzar, the governor, that the "house of God be builded" in Jerusalem (Ezra 5:15). **(2)** While the Persians were certainly not worshipers of the "God" of Israel, they accorded Him the dignity that befitted a "God of heaven" (Ezra 6:10). This was done partly through superstition; but the pluralistic nature of the newly-won Persian empire also required them to honor the gods of conquered peoples, in the interests of peace and social harmony.

(3) When Ezra himself used the word *elahh,* he frequently specified the God of the Jews. Thus he spoke of the "God of Israel" (5:1; 6:14), the "God of heaven" (5:12; 6:9) and "God of Jerusalem" (7:19); he also associated "God" with His house in Jerusalem (5:17; 6:3). **(4)** In the decree of Artaxerxes, Ezra was described as "the priest, the scribe of the God of heaven" (7:12, 21). This designation would have sounded strange coming from a pagan Persian ruler, had it not been for the policy of religious toleration exercised by the Achaemenid regime. **(5)** Elsewhere in Ezra, *elahh* is associated with the temple, both when it was about to be rebuilt (5:2, 13) and as a finished edifice, consecrated for divine worship (6:16). **(6)** In the only verse in the Book of Jeremiah that was written in Aramaic (10:11), the word *elahh* appears in plural form to describe "gods" that had not participated in the creation of the universe. Although such false "gods" were being worshiped by pagan nations (and perhaps worshiped by some of the Hebrews who were in exile in Babylonia), these deities would ultimately perish because they were not eternal in nature.

(7) In the Book of Daniel, *elahh* was used both of heathen "gods" and the one true "God" of heaven. **(7a)** The Chaldean priests told Nebuchadnezzar: "And it is a rare thing that the king requireth, and there is none other that can show it before the king, except the gods, whose dwelling is not with flesh" (Dan 2:11). The Chaldeans referred to such "gods" when reporting that Shadrach, Meshach, and Abed-nego refused to participate in idol worship on the plain of Dura (Dan 3:12). The "gods" were enumerated by Daniel when he condemned Nebuchadnezzar's neglect of the worship of Israel's one true "God" (Dan 5:23). In Dan 3:25, the word refers to a divine being or messenger sent to protect the three Hebrews (Dan 3:28). In Dan 4:8–9, 18; and 5:11, the phrase "the spirit of the holy gods" appears. **(7b)** Elsewhere the references to *elahh* are to the living "God" whom Daniel worshiped. Syn.: 410 + 7706, 426, 430, 433, 3069. See: TWOT—2576; n.m. BDB—1080c.

427. אַלָּה {1x} **ʾallâh**, *al-law';* a var. of 424:—oak {1x}. See: TWOT—100a; BDB—47c.

428. אֵלֶּה {20x} **ʾêl-leh**, *ale'-leh;* prol. from 411; *these* or *those:*—these, those, this, thus, who, so, such, some, same, other, which, another, whom, they, them = {20x}. See: TWOT—92; BDB—41c, 1080d.

429. אֵלֶּה {1x} **ʾêlleh** (Aram.), *ale'-leh;* corresp. to 428:—these {1x}. See: TWOT—2577; BDB—1080c.

אֱלֹהַּ **ʾělôahh**. See 433.

430. אֱלֹהִים {2606x} **ʾělôhîym**, *el-o-heem';* plur. of 433; *gods* in the ordinary sense; but spec. used (in the plur. thus, espec. with the art.) of the supreme *God;* occasionally applied by way of deference to *magistrates;* and sometimes as a superlative:—God {2346x}, god {244x}, judge {5x}, GOD {1x}, goddess {2x}, great {2x}, mighty {2x}, angels {1x}, exceeding {1x}, Godward + 4136 –{1x}, godly {1x}.

Plural in number refers to **(1)** rulers, judges, either as divine, representatives at sacred places or as reflecting divine majesty and power; **(2)** divine, ones, superhuman beings including God and angels; **(3)** angels; cf. the sons of God, or sons of gods = angels; **(4)** gods, goddess. Syn.: See 410. See: TWOT—93c; BDB—43b, 218d, 238a.

431. אֲלוּ {5x} ʼ**ălûw** (Aram.), *al-oo';* prob. prol. from 412; *lo!:*—behold {5x}. See: TWOT—2578; BDB—1080d, 1082d.

432. אִלּוּ {2x} ʼ**illûw**, *il-loo';* prob. from 408; *nay,* i.e. (softened) *if:*—but if {1x}, yea though {1x}. See: TWOT—96; BDB—47a.

433. אֱלוֹהַּ {57x} ʼ**ĕlôwahh**, *el-o'-ah;* rarely (short.)

אֱלֹהַּ ʼ**ĕlôahh**, *el-o'-ah;* prob. prol. (emphat.) from 410; a *deity* or the *Deity:*—God {52x}, god {5x}.

Eloahh (433) means "god." **(1)** This Hebrew name for "God" corresponds to the Aramaic elahh (426). The origin of the term is unknown, and it is used rarely in Scripture as a designation of deity. **(2)** *Eloahh* occurs 40 times in the Book of Job between 3:4 and 40:2, while in the remainder of the Old Testament it is used no more than 15 times. **(3)** Certain scholars regard the word as being a singular version of the common plural form elohim (430), a plural of majesty. **(4)** *Eloahh* is commonly thought to be vocative in nature, meaning "O God." But it is not clear why a special form for the vocative in an address to God should be needed, since the plural elohim is frequently translated as a vocative when the worshiper is speaking directly to God, as in Ps 79:1. There is an obvious general linguistic relationship between *eloahh* and elohim, but determining its precise nature is difficult.

(5) The word *eloahh* is predominant in poetry rather than prose literature, and this is especially true of the Book of Job. Some scholars have suggested that the author of Job deliberately chose a description for godhead that avoided the historical associations found in a phrase such as "the God of Bethel" (Gen 31:13) or "God of Israel" (Ex 24:10). But even the Book of Job is by no means historically neutral, since places and peoples are mentioned in introducing the narrative (cf. Job 1:1, 15, 17). Perhaps the author considered *eloahh* a suitable term for poetry and used it accordingly with consistency. **(6)** This is also apparently the case in Ps 18:31, where *eloahh* is found instead of el, as in the parallel passage of 2 Sa 22:32. *Eloahh* also appears as a term for God in Ps 50:22; 139:19; and Prov 30:5. **(7)** Although *eloahh* as a divine name is rarely used outside Job, its literary history extends from at least the second millennium B.C. (as in Deut 32:15) to the fifth century B.C. (as in Neh 9:17). Syn.: See 430. See: TWOT—93b; BDB—43a, 1080c.

434. אֱלוּל {1x} ʼ**ĕlûwl**, *el-ool';* for 457; good for *nothing:*—thing of nought {1x}. See: TWOT—99a; BDB—47b.

435. אֱלוּל {1x} ʼ**Ĕlûwl**, *el-ool';* prob. of for. der.; *Elul,* the sixth Jewish month:—Elul {1x}. See: TWOT—97; BDB—47a.

436. אֵלוֹן {9x} ʼ**ēlôwn**, *ay-lone';* prol. from 352; an *oak* or other strong tree:—plain {9x}.

This word means "large tree," usually an isolated tree in relation to places of worship. It may well be that these were all ancient cultic sites. The word does not represent a particular genus or species of tree but, like the noun to which it is related, simply a "big tree": "Gaal spoke again and said, Look, men are coming down from the center of the land, and one company is coming from the direction of the Meonenim ["diviner's oak"]" (Judg 9:37). Judg 9:6 speaks of the "plain of the pillar" in Shechem where the men of Shechem and Beth-millo made Abimelech king. Syn.: See 356. See: TWOT—45i; BDB—18d.

437. אַלּוֹן {8x} ʼ**allôwn**, *al-lone';* a var. of 436:—oak {1x}. See: TWOT—100b; BDB—47c.

438. אַלּוֹן {2x} ʼ**Allôwn**, *al-lone';* the same as 437; *Allon,* an Isr., also a place in Pal.:—Allon {2x}. See: BDB—47d.

439. אַלּוֹן בָּכוּת {1x} ʼ**Allôwn Bâkûwth**, *al-lone' baw-kooth';* from 437 and a var. of 1068; *oak of weeping; Allon-Bakuth,* a monumental tree:—Allon-bachuth {1x}. See: BDB—18d, 47c, 113d.

440. אֵלוֹנִי {1x} ʼ**Êlôwnîy**, *ay-lo-nee';* or rather (short.)

אֵלֹנִי ʼ**Êlônîy**, *ay-lo-nee';* patron. from 438; an *Elonite* or desc. (collect.) of Elon:—Elonites {1x}. See: BDB—19a.

441. אַלּוּף {69x} ʼ**allûwph**, *al-loof';* or (short.)

אַלֻּף ʼ**allûph**, *al-loof';* from 502; *familiar;* a *friend,* also *gentle;* hence, a *bullock* (as being tame; applied, although masc., to a *cow*); and so, a *chieftain* (as notable, like neat cattle):—duke {57x}, guide {4x}, friends {2x}, governors {2x}, captains {1x}, governor {1x}, ox {2x}. See: TWOT—109b; BDB—48d, 49b.

442. אָלוּשׁ {2x} ʼ**Âlûwsh**, *aw-loosh';* of uncert. der.; *Alush,* a place in the Desert:—Alush {2x}. See: BDB—47a.

443. אֶלְזָבָד {2x} ʼ**Elzâbâd**, *el-zaw-bawd';* from 410 and 2064; *God has bestowed; Elzabad,* the name of two Isr.:—*Elzabad* {1x}. See: BDB—44d.

444. אָלַח {3x} ʼ**âlach**, *aw-lakh';* a prim. root; to *muddle,* i.e. (fig. and intr.) to *turn* (morally) *corrupt:*—become filthy {3x}. See: TWOT—98; BDB—47a.

445. אֶלְחָנָן {4x} ʼ**Elchânân**, *el-khaw-nawn';* from 410 and 2603; *God* (is) *gracious; Elchanan,* an Isr.:—Elkanan {4x}. See: BDB—44d.

אֵלִי ʼ**Êlîy**. See 1017.

446. אֱלִיאָב {21x} ʼ**Ĕlîyʼâb**, *el-ee-awb';* from 410 and 1; *God of* (his) *father; Eliab,* the name of six Isr.:—Eliab {21x}. See: BDB—45a.

447. אֱלִיאֵל {10x} ʼ**Ĕlîyʼêl**, *el-ee-ale';* from 410 repeated; *God of* (his) *God; Eliel,* the name of nine Isr.:—Eliel {10x}. See: BDB—45a.

448. אֱלִיאָתָה {2x} ʼ**Ĕlîyʼâthâh**, *el-ee-aw-thaw';* or (contr.)

אֱלִיָּתָה ʼ**Ĕlîyâthâh**, *el-ee-yaw-thaw';* from 410 and 225; *God of* (his) *consent; Eliathah,* an Isr.:—Eliathah {2x}. See: BDB—45a, 46a.

449. אֱלִידָד {1x} ʼ**Ĕlîydâd**, *el-ee-dawd';* from the same as 419; *God of* (his) *love; Elidad,* an Isr.:—Elidad {1x}. See: BDB—44d, 45a.

450. אֶלְיָדָע {4x} ʼ**Elyâdâʻ**, *el-yaw-daw';* from 410 and 3045; *God* (is) *knowing; Eljada,* the name of two Isr. and of an Aramaean leader:—Eliada {3x}, Eliadah {1x}. See: BDB—45a.

451. אַלְיָה {5x} ʼ**alyâh**, *al-yaw';* from 422 (in the orig. sense of *strength*); the *stout* part, i.e. the fat *tail* of the Oriental sheep:—rump {5x}. See: TWOT—95a; BDB—46d.

452. אֵלִיָּה {71x} ʼ**Êlîyâh**, *ay-lee-yaw';* or prol.

אֵלִיָּהוּ ʼ**Êlîyâhûw**, *ay-lee-yaw'-hoo;* from 410 and 3050; *God of Jehovah; Elijah,* the name of the famous prophet and of two other Isr.:—Elijah {69x}, Eliah {2x}. See: BDB—45b.

453. אֱלִיהוּ {11x} ʼ**Ĕlîyhûw**, *el-ee-hoo';* or (fully)

אֱלִיהוּא ʼ**Ĕlîyhûwʼ**, *el-ee-hoo';* from 410 and 1931; *God of him; Elihu,* the name of one of Job's friends, and of three Isr.:—Elihu {11x}. See: BDB—45b.

454. אֶלְיְהוֹעֵינַי {9x} ʼ**Elyᵉhôwʻêynay**, *el-ye-ho-ay-nah'ee;* or (short.)

אֶלְיוֹעֵינַי ʼ**Elyôwʻêynay**, *el-yo-ay-nah'ee;* from 413 and 3068 and 5869; *toward Jehovah* (are) *my eyes; Eljehoenai* or *Eljoenai,* the name of seven Isr.:—Elihoenai {1x}, Elionai {8x}. See: BDB—41b.

455. אֶלְיַחְבָּא {2x} ʼ**Elyachbâʼ**, *el-yakh-baw';* from 410 and 2244; *God will hide; Eljachba,* an Isr.:—Eliahbah {2x}. See: BDB—45b.

456. אֱלִיחֹרֶף {1x} ʼ**Ĕlîychôreph**, *el-ee-kho'-ref;* from 410 and 2779; *God of autumn; Elichoreph,* an Isr.:—Elihoreph {1x}. See: BDB—45b.

457. אֱלִיל {20x} ʼ**ĕlîyl**, *el-eel';* appar. from 408; good for *nothing,* by anal. *vain* or *vanity;* spec. an *idol:*—- idol {17x}, image {1x}, no value {1x}, things of nought {1x}.

Eliyl means "idol; gods; nought; vain." **(1)** This disdainful word signifies an "idol" or "false god." **(2)** *Eliyl* first appears in Lev 19:4: "Turn ye not unto idols, nor make to yourselves molten gods. . . ." **(3)** In Lev 26:1 the elilim are what Israel is forbidden to make: "Ye shall make you no idols. . . ." The irony of this is biting not only with respect to the usual meaning of this word but also in view of its similarity to the usual word for God (elohim; cf. Ps 96:5): "For all the gods [elohim] of the people are idols [elohim] . . ." (1 Chr 16:26). **(4)** This word can mean "nought" or "vain." 1 Chr 16:26 might well be rendered: "For all the gods of the people are nought." This nuance appears clearly in Job 13:4: "But ye are forgers of lies; ye are all physicians of no value [physicians of vanity]." Jeremiah told Israel that their prophets were "prophesy [ing] unto you a false vision and divination, and a thing of nought . . .". gillulim (1544), "idols."

(5) Of the 48 occurrences of this word, all but 9 appear in Ezekiel. This word for "idols" is a disdainful word and may originally have meant "dung pellets": "And I will destroy your high places, and cut down your images, and cast your carcases upon the carcases of your idols, and my soul shall abhor you" (Lev 26:30). Syn: This word and others for "idol" exhibit the horror and scorn that biblical writers felt toward them. In passages such as Is 66:3 the word for "idol," awen (205), means "uncanny or wickedness." Jer 50:38 evidences the word emim (367), which means "fright or horror." The word elil appears for "idol" in Lev 19:4; it means "nothingness or feeble." 1 Kin 15:13 uses the Hebrew word, mipletset (4656), meaning a "horrible thing, a cause of trembling." A root signifying to make an image or to shape something, tsb (6091)[a homonym of the root meaning "sorrow and grief"] is used in several passages (cf. 1Sa 31:9). See: TWOT—99a; BDB—47b.

458. אֱלִימֶלֶךְ {6x} **Ĕlîymelek**, *el-ee-meh'-lek;* from 410 and 4428; *God of* (the) *king; Elimelek,* an Isr.:—Elimelech {6x}. See: BDB—45b.

459. אִלֵּין {5x} **ʾillêyn** (Aram.), *il-lane';* or short.

אִלֵּן **ʾillên**, *il-lane';* prol. from 412; *these:*—these {4x}, the {1x}. See: TWOT—2579; BDB—1080c, 1080d, 1088d.

460. אֶלְיָסָף {6x} **ʾÊlyâçâph**, *el-yaw-sawf';* from 410 and 3254; *God* (is) *gatherer; Eljasaph,* the name of two Isr.:—Eliasaph {6x}. See: BDB—45b.

461. אֱלִיעֶזֶר {14x} **ʾÊlîyʿezer**, *el-ee-eh'-zer;* from 410 and 5828; *God of help; Eliezer,* the name of a Damascene and of ten Isr.:—Eliezer {14x}. See: BDB—45c.

462. אֱלִיעֵינַי {1x} **ʾÊlîyʿêynay**, *el-ee-ay-nah'ee;* prob. contr. for 454; *Elienai,* an Isr.:—Elienai {1x}. See: BDB—41b.

463. אֱלִיעָם {2x} **ʾÊlîyʿâm**, *el-ee-awm';* from 410 and 5971; *God of* (the) *people; Eliam,* an Isr.:—Eliam {2x}. See: BDB—45c.

464. אֱלִיפַז {15x} **ʾÊlîyphaz**, *el-ee-faz';* from 410 and 6337; *God of gold; Eliphaz,* the name of one of Job's friends, and of a son of Esau:—Eliphaz {15x}. See: BDB—45c.

465. אֱלִיפַל {1x} **ʾÊlîyphâl**, *el-ee-fawl';* from 410 and 6419; *God of judgment; Eliphal,* an Isr.: Eliphal {1x}. See: BDB—45c.

466. אֱלִיפְלֵהוּ {2x} **Ĕlîyphᵉlêhûw**, *el-ee-fe-lay'-hoo;* from 410 and 6395; *God of his distinction; Eliphelehu,* an Isr.:—Elipheleh {2x}. See: BDB—45c.

467. אֱלִיפֶלֶט {9x} **Ĕlîyphelet**, *el-ee-feh'-let;* or (short.)

אֶלְפֶּלֶט **ʾÊlpelet**, *el-peh'-let;* from 410 and 6405; *God of deliverance; Eliphelet* or *Elpelet,* the name of six Isr.:—Eliphalet {2x}, Eliphelet {6x}, Elpalet {1x}. See: BDB—45c, 46c.

468. אֱלִיצוּר {5x} **ʾÊlîytsûwr**, *el-ee-tsoor';* from 410 and 6697; *God of* (the) *rock; Elitsur,* an Isr.:—Elizur {5x}. See: BDB—45d.

469. אֱלִיצָפָן {6x} **ʾÊlîytsâphân**, *el-ee-tsaw-fawn';* or (short.)

אֶלְצָפָן **ʾEltsâphân**, *el-tsaw-fawn';* from 410 and 6845; *God of treasure; Elitsaphan* or *Eltsaphan,* an Isr.:—Elizaphan {4x}, Elzaphan {2x}. See: BDB—45d, 46c.

470. אֱלִיקָא {1x} **ʾÊlîyqâʾ**, *el-ee-kaw';* from 410 and 6958; *God of rejection; Elika,* an Isr.:—Elika {1x}. See: BDB—45d.

471. אֶלְיָקִים {12x} **ʾElyâqîym**, *el-yaw-keem';* from 410 and 6965; *God of raising; Eljakim,* the name of four Isr.:—Eliakim {12x}. See: BDB—45d.

472. אֱלִישֶׁבַע {1x} **ʾÊlîyshebaʿ**, *el-ee-sheh'-bah;* from 410 and 7651 (in the sense of 7650); *God of* (the) *oath; Elisheba,* the wife of Aaron:—Elisheba {1x}. See: BDB—45d, 989d.

473. אֱלִישָׁה {3x} **ʾÊlîyshâh**, *el-ee-shaw';* prob. of for. der.; *Elishah,* a son of Javan:—Elishah {3x}. See: BDB—47a.

474. אֱלִישׁוּעַ {2x} **ʾÊlîyshûwaʿ**, *el-ee-shoo'-ah;* from 410 and 7769; *God of supplication* (or *of riches*); *Elishua,* a son of King David:—Elishua {2x}. See: BDB—46a.

475. אֶלְיָשִׁיב {17x} **ʾElyâshîyb**, *el-yaw-sheeb';* from 410 and 7725; *God will restore; Eljashib,* the name of six Isr.:—Eliashib {17x}. See: BDB—46a.

476. אֱלִישָׁמָע {17x} **Ĕlîyshâmâʿ**, *el-ee-shaw-maw';* from 410 and 8085; *God of hearing; Elishama,* the name of seven Isr.:—Elishama {17x}. See: BDB—46a.

477. אֱלִישָׁע {58x} **ʾÊlîyshâʿ**, *el-ee-shaw';* contr. for 474; *Elisha,* the famous prophet:—Elisha {58x}. See: 46a.

478. אֱלִישָׁפָט {1x} **ʾÊlîyshâphâṭ**, *el-ee-shaw-fawt';* from 410 and 8199; *God of judgment; Elishaphat,* an Isr.:—Elishaphat {1x}. See: BDB—46a.

479. אִלֵּךְ {14x} **ʾillêk** (Aram.), *il-lake';* prol. from 412; *these:*—these {10x}, those {4x}. See: TWOT—2580; BDB—1080d, 1088c.

480. אַלְלַי {2x} **ʾalᵉlay**, *al-le-lah'ee;* by redupl. from 421; *alas!:*—woe {2x}. See: TWOT—101; BDB—47d.

481. אָלַם {9x} **ʾâlam**, *aw-lam';* a prim. root; to *tie* fast; hence, (of the mouth) to be *tongue-tied:*—dumb {7x}, put to silence {1x}, binding {1x}. See: TWOT—102; BDB—47d.

482. אֵלֶם {1x} **ʾêlem**, *ay'-lem;* from 481; *silence* (i.e. mute justice):—congregation {1x}.

In Ps 58:1 this word signifies either to bind into a sheaf or to be bound/dumb; a very suitable symbol of a congregation. Syn.: comp. 3128. See: TWOT—102b; BDB—48a.

אֵלָם **ʾêlâm**. See 361.

אֻלָם **ʾûlâm**. See 485.

483. אִלֵּם {6x} **ʾillêm**, *il-lame';* from 481; *speechless:*—dumb (man) {6x}. See: TWOT—102c; BDB—48a.

484. אַלְמֻגִּים {3x} **ʾalmuggiym**, *al-moog-gheem';* prob. of for. der. (used thus only in the plur.); *almug* (i.e. prob. sandal-wood) sticks:—almug trees {3x}. Syn.: comp. 418. See: TWOT—89c; BDB—38d.

485. אֲלֻמָּה {5x} **ʾălummâh**, *al-oom-maw';* or (masc.)

אָלֻם **ʾâlûm**, *aw-loom';* pass. part. of 481; something *bound;* a *sheaf:*—sheaf {5x}. See: TWOT—102a; BDB—48a.

486. אַלְמוֹדָד {2x} **ʾAlmôwdâd**, *al-mo-dawd';* prob. of for. der.; *Almodad,* a son of Joktan:—Almodad {2x}. See: BDB—38d, 46b.

487. אַלַּמֶּלֶךְ {1x} **ʾAllammelek**, *al-lam-meh'-lek;* from 427 and 4428; *oak of* (the) *king; Allammelek,* a place in Pal.:—Alammelech {1x}. See: BDB—47d.

488. אַלְמָן {1x} **ʾalmân**, *al-mawn';* prol. from 481 in the sense of *bereavement; discarded* (as a divorced person):—forsaken {1x}. See: TWOT—103; BDB—48a.

489. אַלְמֹן {1x} **ʾalmôn**, *al-mone';* from 481 as in 488; *bereavement:*—widowhood {1x}. See: TWOT—104; BDB—48a.

490. אַלְמָנָה {55x} **ʾalmânâh**, *al-maw-naw';* fem. of 488; a *widow;* also a *desolate* place:—widow {53x}, desolate house {1x}, desolate palace {1x}.

Almanah means "widow." **(1)** The word represents a woman who, because of the death of her husband, has lost her social and economic position. The gravity of her situation was increased if she had no children. In such a circumstance she returned to her father's home and was subjected to the Levirate rule whereby a close male relative surviving her husband was to produce a child through her in her husband's behalf: "Then said Judah to Tamar his daughter-in-law, Remain a widow at thy father's house, till Shelah my son be grown . . ." (Gen 38:11 the first occurrence of the word). These words constitute a promise to Tamar that the disgrace of being without both husband and child would be removed when Shelah was old enough to marry.

(2) Even if children had been born before her husband's death, a widow's lot was not a happy one (2 Sa 14:5). **(3)** Israel was admonished to treat "widows" and other socially disadvantaged people with justice, God Himself standing as their protector (Ex 22:21–24). **(4)** Wives whose husbands shut them away from themselves are sometimes called "widows": "And David came to his house at Jerusalem; and the king took the ten women his concubines, whom he had left to keep the house, and put them in ward, and fed them, but went not in unto them. So they were shut up unto the day of their death, living in widowhood" (2 Sa 20:3). **(5)** Destroyed, plundered Jerusalem is called a "widow" (Lam 1:1). Syn.: See also 489, 491. See: TWOT—105; BDB—48a.

491. אַלְמָנוּת {4x} **ʾalmânûwth**, *al-maw-nooth';* fem. of 488; concr. a *widow;* abstr. *widowhood:*—widow {1x}, widowhood {3x}. See: TWOT—106; BDB—48b.

492. אַלְמֹנִי {3x} **ʾalmônîy**, *al-mo-nee';* from 489 in the sense of *concealment; some* one (i.e. *so and so,* without giving the name of the person or place):—and such {2x}, a one {1x}. See: TWOT—107; BDB—48c.

493. אֶלְנַעַם {1x} **ʾElnaʿam**, *el-nah'-am;* from 410 and 5276; *God* (is his) *delight; Elnaam,* an Isr.:—*Elnaam* {1x}. See: BDB—46b.

494. אֶלְנָתָן {7x} **ʾElnâthân**, *el-naw-thawn';* from 410 and 5414; *God* (is the) *giver; Elnathan,* the name of four Isr.:—*Elnathan* {7x}. See: BDB—46b.

495. אֶלָּסָר {2x} **ʾEllâçâr**, *el-law-sawr';* prob. of for. der.; *Ellasar,* an early country of Asia:—Ellasar {2x}. See: BDB—48c.

496. אֶלְעָד {1x} **ʾElʿâd**, *el-awd';* from 410 and 5749; *God has testified; Elad,* an Isr.:—Elead {1x}. See: BDB—46b.

497. אֶלְעָדָה {1x} **ʾElʿâdâh**, *el-aw-daw';* from 410 and 5710; *God has decked; Eladah,* an Isr.:—*Eladah* {1x}. See: BDB—46b.

498. אֶלְעוּזַי {1x} **ʾElʿûwzay**, *el-oo-zah'ee;* from 410 and 5756 (in the sense of 5797); *God* (is) *defensive; Eluzai,* an Isr.:—Eluzai {1x}. See: BDB—46b.

499. אֶלְעָזָר {72x} **ʾElʿâzâr**, *el-aw-zawr';* from 410 and 5826; *God* (is) *helper; Elazar,* the name of seven Isr.:—Eleazar {72x}. See: BDB—46b.

500. אֶלְעָלֵא {5x} **ʾElʿâlêʾ**, *el-aw-lay';* or (more prop.)

אֶלְעָלֵה **ʾElʿâlêh**, *el-aw-lay';* from 410 and 5927; *God* (is) *going up; Elale* or *Elaleh,* a place east of the Jordan:—Elealeh {5x}. See: BDB—46c.

501. אֶלְעָשָׂה {6x} **ʾElʿâsâh**, *el-aw-saw';* from 410 and 6213; *God has made; Elasah,* the name of four Isr.:—*Elasah* {2x}, Eleasah {4x}. See: BDB—46c.

502. אָלַף {4x} **ᵓâlaph**, *aw-laf';* a prim. root, to *associate* with; hence, to *learn* (and caus. to *teach*):—teach {2x}, learn {1x}, utter {1x}. See: TWOT—108; BDB—48c.

503. אָלַף {1x} **ᵓâlaph**, *aw-laf';* denom. from 505; caus. to *make a thousandfold:*—bring forth thousands {1x}. See: TWOT—109; BDB—48d.

504. אֶלֶף {8x} **ᵓeleph**, *eh'-lef;* from 502; a *family;* also (from the sense of *yoking* or *taming*) an *ox* or *cow:*—kine {4x}, oxen {3x}, family {1x}.

Cattle signifies **(1)** the domesticated animal or the herd animal: oxen, sheep, goats, cows (Deut 7:13); **(2)** thousand (Gen 20:16); **(3)** group (Num 1:16); **(4)** leaders of a large group (Gen 36:15). Syn.: 1241, 6510. See: TWOT—108a; BDB—48c.

505. אֶלֶף {505x} **ᵓeleph**, *eh'-lef;* prop. the same as 504; hence, (the ox's head being the first letter of the alphabet, and this eventually used as a numeral) a *thousand:*—thousand {500x}, eleven hundred + 3967 {3x}, variant {1x}, twelve hundred + 3967 {1x}. See: TWOT—109a; BDB—48d, 1081a.

506. אֲלַף {4x} **ᵓălaph** (Aram.), *al-af';* or

אֶלֶף **ᵓeleph** (Aram.), *eh'-lef;* corresp. to 505:—thousand {4x}. See: TWOT—2581; BDB—1081a.

507. אֶלֶף {1x} **ᵓEleph**, *eh'-lef;* the same as 505; *Eleph*, a place in Pal.:—*Eleph* {1x}. See: BDB—49b.

508. אֶלְפַּעַל {3x} **ᵓElpaᶜal**, *el-pah'-al;* from 410 and 6466; *God* (is) *act; Elpaal*, an Isr.:—*Elpaal* {3x}. See: BDB—46c.

509. אָלַץ {1x} **ᵓâlats**, *aw-lats';* a prim. root; to *press:*—urge {1x}. See: TWOT—110; BDB—49b.

אֶלְצָפָן **ᵓEltsâphân**. See 469.

510. אַלְקוּם {1x} **ᵓalqûwm**, *al-koom';* prob. from 408 and 6965; a *non-rising* (i.e. *resistlessness*):—rising up {1x}. See: TWOT—90; BDB—39a, 49b, 879c.

511. אֶלְקָנָה {21x} **ᵓElqânâh**, *el-kaw-naw';* from 410 and 7069; *God has obtained; Elkanah*, the name of several Isr.:—Elkanah {21x}. See: BDB—46c.

512. אֶלְקֹשִׁי {1x} **ᵓElqôshîy**, *el-ko-shee';* patrial from a name of uncert. der.; an *Elkoshite* or native of Elkosh:—Elkoshite {1x}. See: BDB—49b.

513. אֶלְתּוֹלַד {2x} **ᵓEltôwlad**, *el-to-lad';* prob. from 410 and a masc. form of 8435 [comp. 8434]; *God* (is) *generator; Eltolad*, a place in Pal.:—Eltolad {2x} See: BDB—39a.

514. אֶלְתְּקֵא {2x} **ᵓEltᵉqêᵓ**, *el-te-kay';* or (more prop.)

אֶלְתְּקֵה **ᵓEltᵉqêh**, *el-te-kay';* of uncert. der.; *Eltekeh* or *Elteke*, a place in Pal.: Eltekeh {2x}. See: BDB—49c.

515. אֶלְתְּקֹן {1x} **ᵓEltᵉqôn**, *el-te-kone';* from 410 and 8626; *God* (is) *straight; Eltekon*, a place in Pal.:—Eltekon {1x}. See: BDB—49c.

516. אַל תַּשְׁחֵת {4x} **ᵓAl tashchêth**, *al tash-kayth';* from 408 and 7843; *Thou must not destroy;* prob. the opening words of a popular song:—Al-taschith {4x}. See: BDB—1008c.

517. אֵם {220x} **ᵓêm**, *ame;* a prim. word; a *mother* (as the *bond* of the family); in a wide sense (both lit. and fig. [like 1]:—mother {214x}, dam {5x}, parting {1x}.

Em (517) means "mother; grandmother; stepmother." **(1)** The basic meaning of the word has to do with the physical relationship of the individual called "mother." This emphasis of the word is in Gen 2:24 (the first biblical appearance): "Therefore shall a man leave his father and his mother, and shall cleave unto his wife. . . ." **(2)** *Em* sometimes represents an animal "mother": "Likewise shalt thou do with thine oxen, and with thy sheep: seven days it shall be with its [mother]; on the eighth day thou shalt give it me" (Ex 22:30). **(3)** The phrase "father and mother" is the biblical phrase for parents: "And he brought up Hadassah, that is, Esther, his uncle's daughter: for she had neither father nor mother [living]" (Est 2:7). **(4)** The "son of one's mother" is his brother (Gen 43:29), just as the "daughter of one's mother" is his sister (Gen 20:12). These phrases usually emphasize that the persons so represented are whole brothers or sisters, whereas the Hebrew words ach, (251- "brother") and achot, (269- "sister") meaning both whole and half siblings, leave the issue unclear.

(5) On the other hand, in Gen 27:29 this phrase appears to mean peoples more distantly related: "Let people serve thee, and nations bow down to thee: be lord over thy brethren, and let thy mother's sons bow down to thee: cursed be every one that curseth thee, and blessed be he that blesseth thee." **(6)** *Em* can represent blood relatives further removed than one's mother. In 1 Kin 15:10 the word means "grandmother": "And forty and one years reigned he in Jerusalem. And his [grand]mother's name was Maachah, the daughter of Abishalom." **(7)** This word can also mean "stepmother." When Joseph told his dream to his family, "his father rebuked him, and said unto him, What is this dream that thou hast dreamed? Shall I and thy [step]mother and thy brethren indeed come to bow down ourselves to thee to the earth?" (Gen 37:10; cf. 35:16ff., where we read that Rachel died). **(8)** The word can signify a mother-in-law, or the mother of one's wife: "And if a man take a wife and her mother, it is wickedness . . ." (Lev 20:14).

(9) The woman through whom a nation originated is called its "mother"; she is the first or tribal "mother," an ancestress: "Thus saith the LORD God unto Jerusalem; Thy birth and thy nativity is of the land of Canaan; thy father was an Amorite, and thy mother a Hittite" (Eze 16:3). Even further removed physically is Eve, "the mother of all living" (Gen 3:20). **(10)** *Em* can represent all one's female forebears: "Let the iniquity of his fathers be remembered with the LORD; and let not the sin of his mother be blotted out" (Ps 109:14). **(11)** A group of people, a people, or a city may be personified and called a "mother." Hosea calls the priests (probably) the "mother" of Israel: ". . . And the prophet also shall fall with thee in the night, and I will destroy thy mother" (Hos 4:5).

(12) The people of Israel, the northern kingdom, are the "mother" of Judah: "Where is the bill of your mother's divorcement, whom I have put away? or which of my creditors is it to whom I have sold you? Behold, for your iniquities have ye sold yourselves, and for your transgressions is your mother put away" (Is 50:1; cf. Hos 2:4, 7). **(13)** An important city may be called a "mother" of its citizens: ". . . Thou seekest to destroy a city and a mother in Israel . . ." (2 Sa 20:19). **(14)** The title "mother in Israel" was a title of respect in Deborah's day (Judg 5:7). **(15)** "The mother of a way" is the starting point for roads: "For the king of Babylon stood at the parting of the way, at the head of the two ways, to use divination . . ." (Eze 21:21). Syn.: 2545. See: TWOT—115a; BDB—51a, 51c.

518. אִם {43x} **ᵓîm**, *eem;* a prim. particle; used very widely as demonstr., *lo!;* interrog., *whether?;* or conditional, *if, although;* also *Oh that!, when;* hence, as a neg., *not:*—if, not, or, when, whether, surely, doubtless, while, neither, saving, verily = {43x}. See: TWOT—111; BDB—49c, 210b, 243d, 474c, 1090d, 1099a.

519. אָמָה {55x} **ᵓâmâh**, *aw-maw';* appar. a prim. word; a *maid-servant* or female slave:—handmaid {22x}, maidservant {19x}, maid {8x}, bondwoman {4x}, bondmaids {2x}. See: TWOT—112; BDB—51a, 1046c.

אֵמָה **ᵓêmâh**. See 367.

520. אַמָּה {245x} **ᵓammâh**, *am-maw';* prol. from 517; prop. a *mother* (i.e. *unit* of measure, or the *fore-arm* (below the elbow), i.e. a *cubit;* also a door-*base* (as a *bond* of the entrance):—cubit {242x}, measure {1x}, post {1x}, not translated {1x}.

Ammah (520) means "cubit." **(1)** It appears about 245 times in biblical Hebrew and in all periods, but especially in Ex 25—27; 37–38 (specifications of the tabernacle); 1 Kin 6—7 (the specifications of Solomon's temple and palace); and Eze 40—43 (the specifications of Ezekiel's temple). **(2)** In one passage, *ammah* means "pivot": "And the posts [literally, "sockets"] of the door moved at the voice of him that cried . . ." (Is 6:4). **(3)** In almost every other occurrence, the word means "cubit," the primary unit of linear measurement in the Old Testament. **(4)** A "cubit" ordinarily was the distance from one's elbow to the tip of the middle finger. Since this distance varied from individual to individual, the "cubit" was a rather imprecise measurement. Yet the first appearance of *ammah* (Gen 6:15) refers to the measurement of Noah's ark, which implies that the word must refer to a more precise length than the ordinary "cubit." Syn.: 3967, 4060. See: TWOT—115c; BDB—51a, 52a, 52c, 1081a.

521. אַמָּה {4x} **ᵓammâh** (Aram.), *am-maw';* corresp. to 520:—cubit {4x}. See: TWOT—2582; BDB—51a, 1081a.

522. אַמָּה {1x} **ᵓAmmâh**, *am-maw';* the same as 520; *Ammah*, a hill in Pal.:—*Ammah* {1x}. See: BDB—51a, 52a, 52c.

523. אֻמָּה {3x} **ᵓummâh**, *oom-maw';* from the same as 517; a *collection*, i.e. community of persons:—people {2x}, nation {1x}. See: TWOT—115e; BDB—52c, 1081a.

524. אֻמָּה {8x} **ᵓummâh** (Aram.), *oom-maw';* corresp. to 523:—nation {8x}. See: TWOT—2583; BDB—1081a.

525. אָמוֹן {1x} **ᵓâmôwn**, *aw-mone';* from 539, prob. in the sense of *training; skilled*, i.e. an architect [like 542]:—one brought up {1x}. See: TWOT—116L; BDB—54c.

526. אָמוֹן {17x} **ᵓÂmôwn**, *aw-mone';* the same as 525; *Amon*, the name of three Isr.:—Amon {17x}. See: BDB—51b, 54c.

527. אָמוֹן {3x} **ᵓâmôwn**, *aw-mone';* a var. for 1995; a *throng* of people:—multitude {2x}, populous {1x}. See: TWOT—116L; BDB—54c.

528. אָמוֹן {2x} ʾ**Âmôwn**, *aw-mone';* of Eg. der.; *Amon* (i.e. Ammon or Amn), a deity of Egypt (used only as an adjunct of 4996):—not translated {2x}. See: BDB—51b.

529. אֵמוּן {5x} ʾ**êmûwn**, *ay-moon';* from 539; *established,* i.e. (fig.) *trusty;* also (abstr.) *trustworthiness:*—faithful {3x}, truth {1x}, faith {1x}. See: TWOT—116d; BDB—53c.

530. אֱמוּנָה {49x} ʾ**ĕmûwnâh**, *em-oo-naw';* or (short.)

אֱמֻנָה ʾ**ĕmûnâh**, *em-oo-naw';* fem, of 529; lit. *firmness;* fig. *security;* mor. *fidelity:*—faithfulness {18x}, truth {13x}, faithfully {5x}, office {5x}, faithful {3x}, faith {1x}, stability {1x}, steady {1x}, truly {1x}, verily {1x}.

Emunah (530) means "firmness; faithfulness; truth; honesty; official obligation." **(1)** In Ex 17:12 (the first biblical occurrence), the word means "to remain in one place": "And his [Moses'] hands were steady until the going down of the sun." **(2)** Closely related to this use is that in Is 33:6: "And wisdom and knowledge shall be the stability of thy times. . . ." **(3)** In passages such as 1 Chr 9:22, *emunah* appears to function as a technical term meaning "a fixed position" or "enduring office": "All these which were chosen to be porters in the gates were two hundred and twelve. These were reckoned by their genealogy in their villages, whom David and Samuel the seer did ordain in their set [i.e., established] office." **(4)** The most frequent sense of *emunah* is "faithfulness," as illustrated by 1 Sa 26:23: "The LORD render to every man his righteousness and his faithfulness. . . ." The LORD repays the one who demonstrates that he does what God demands.

(5) Quite often, this word means "truthfulness," as when it is contrasted to false swearing, lying, and so on: "Run ye to and fro through the streets of Jerusalem, and see now, and know, and seek in the broad places thereof, if ye can find a man, if there be any that executeth judgment, that seeketh the truth [i.e., honesty]" (Jer 5:1; cf. Jer 5:2). Here *emunah* signifies the condition of being faithful to God's covenant, practicing truth, or doing righteousness. **(6)** On the other hand, the word can represent the abstract idea of "truth": "This is a nation that obeyeth not the voice of the Lord their God, nor receiveth correction: truth [*emunah*] is perished, and is cut off from their mouth" (Jer 7:28). These quotations demonstrate the two senses in which *emunah* means "true"—the personal sense, which identifies a subject as honest, trustworthy, faithful, truthful (Prov 12:22); and the factual sense, which identifies a subject as being factually true (cf. Prov 12:27), as opposed to that which is false.

(7) The essential meaning of *emunah* is "established" or "lasting," "continuing," "certain." **(7a)** So God says, "And in mercy shall the throne be established: and he shall sit upon it in truth in the tabernacle of David, judging, and seeking judgment, and hasting righteousness" (cf. 2 Sa 7:16; Is 16:5). **(7b)** Thus, the phrase frequently rendered "with lovingkindness and truth" should be rendered "with perpetual (faithful) lovingkindness" (cf. Josh 2:14). He who sows righteousness earns a "true" or "lasting" reward (Prov 11:18), a reward on which he can rely.

(8) In other contexts, *emunah* embraces other aspects of the concept of truth: "[The Lord] hath remembered his mercy and his truth toward the house of Israel . . ." (Ps 98:3). Here the word does not describe the endurance of God but His "truthfulness"; that which He once said He has maintained. The emphasis here is on truth as a subjective quality, defined personally. **(9)** In a similar sense, one can both practice (Gen 47:29) and speak the "truth" (2 Sa 7:28). In such cases, it is not a person's dependability (i.e., others can act on the basis of it) but his reliability (conformity to what is true) that is considered. The first emphasis is subjective and the second objective. It is not always possible to discern which emphasis is intended by a given passage. See: TWOT—116e; BDB—53c.

531. אָמוֹץ {13x} ʾ**Âmôwts**, *aw-mohts';* from 553; *strong, Amots,* an Isr.:—Amoz {13x}. See: BDB—55b.

532. אָמִי {1x} ʾ**Âmîy**, *aw-mee';* an abbrev. for 526; *Ami,* an Isr.:—Ami {1x}. See: BDB—51b, 54c.

אֲמִינוֹן ʾ**Ămîynôwn**. See 550.

533. אַמִּיץ {6x} ʾ**ammîyts**, *am-meets';* or (short.)

אַמִּץ ʾ**ammîts**, *am-meets';* from 553; *strong* or (abstr.) *strength:*—strong {4x}, mighty {1x}, courageous {1x}. See: TWOT—117d; BDB—55c.

534. אָמִיר {2x} ʾ**âmîyr**, *aw-meer';* appar. from 559 (in the sense of *self-exaltation*); a *summit* (of a tree or mountain:—bough {1x}, branch {1x}. See: TWOT—118d; BDB—57b, 1051c.

535. אָמַל {16x} ʾ**âmal**, *aw-mal';* a prim. root; to *droop;* by impl. to *be sick,* to *mourn:*—languish {14x}, feeble {1x}, weak {1x}. See: TWOT—114; BDB—51b.

536. אֻמְלַל {1x} ʾ**umlal**, *oom-lal';* from 535; *sick:*—weak {1x}. See: TWOT—114b; BDB—51c.

537. אֲמֵלָל {1x} ʾ**ămêlâl**, *am ay-lawl';* from 535; *languid:*—feeble {1x}. See: TWOT—114a; BDB—51c.

538. אֲמָם {1x} ʾ**Ămâm**, *am-awm';* from 517; *gathering*-spot; *Amam,* a place in Pal.:—*Amam* {1x}. See: BDB—52c.

539. אָמַן {108x} ʾ**âman**, *aw-man';* a prim. root; prop. to *build up* or *support;* to *foster* as a parent or nurse; fig. to *render* (or *be*) *firm* or faithful, to *trust* or believe, to *be permanent* or quiet; mor. to *be true* or certain; once (Is 30:21; interch. for 541) to *go to the right hand:*—believe {44x}, assurance {1x}, faithful {20x}, sure {11x}, established {7x}, trust {5x}, verified {3x}, steadfast {2x}, continuance {2x}, father {2x}, bring up {4x}, nurse {2x}, be nursed {1x}, surely be {1x}, stand fast {1x}, fail {1x}, trusty {1x}.

Aman means "to be firm, endure, be faithful, be true, stand fast, trust, have belief, believe." **(1)** It appears in all periods of biblical Hebrew (about 96 times) and only in the causative and passive stems. **(2)** In the passive stem, *aman* has several emphases: **(2a)** it indicates that a subject is "lasting" or "enduring," which is its meaning in Deut 28:59: "Then the LORD will make thy plagues wonderful, and the plagues of thy seed, even great plagues, and of long continuance, and sore sicknesses, and of long continuance." It also signifies the element of being "firm" or "trustworthy." **(2b)** In Is 22:23, *aman* refers to a "firm" place, a place into which a peg will be driven so that it will be immovable. The peg will remain firmly anchored, even though it is pushed so hard that it breaks off at the point of entry (Is 22:25). **(3)** The Bible also speaks of "faithful" people who fulfill their obligations (cf. 1 Sa 22:14; Prov 25:13). **(4)** The nuance meaning "trustworthy" also occurs: "He that is of a faithful spirit concealeth the matter" (Prov 11:13; cf. Is 8:2).

(5) An officebearer may be conceived as an "entrusted one": "He removeth away the speech of the trusty [entrusted ones], and taketh away the understanding of the aged" (Job 12:20). In this passage, *aman* is synonymously parallel (therefore equivalent in meaning) to "elders" or "officebearers." Thus, it should be rendered "entrusted ones" or "those who have been given a certain responsibility (trust)." Before receiving the trust, they are men "worthy of trust" or "trustworthy" (cf. 1 Sa 2:35; Neh 13:13). **(6)** In Gen 42:20 (the first biblical appearance of this word in this stem), Joseph requests that his brothers bring Benjamin to him; "so shall your words be verified," or "be shown to be true" (cf. 1 Kin 8:26; Hos 5:9). **(7)** In Hos 11:12, *aman* contrasts Judah's actions ("faithful") with those of Ephraim and Israel ("deceit"). So here *aman* represents both "truthfulness" and "faithfulness" (cf. Ps 78:37; Jer 15:18). **(8)** The word may be rendered "true" in several passages (1 Kin 8:26; 2 Chr 1:9; 6:17).

(9) A different nuance of *aman* is seen in Deut 7:9: ". . . the faithful God, which keepeth covenant and mercy. . . ." There is a good reason here to understand the word *aman* as referring to what God has done ("faithfulness"), rather than what He will do ("trustworthy"), because He has already proved Himself faithful by keeping the covenant. Therefore, the translation would become, ". . . faithful God who has kept His covenant and faithfulness, those who love Him kept . . ." (cf. Is 47:7). **(10)** In the causative stem, *aman* means "to stand fast," or "be fixed in one spot," which is demonstrated by Job 39:24: "He [a war horse] swalloweth the ground with fierceness and rage: neither believeth he that it is the sound of the trumpet." **(11)** Even more often, this stem connotes a psychological or mental certainty, as in Job 29:24: "If I laughed on them, they believed it not."

(12) Considering something to be trustworthy is an act of full trusting or believing. This is the emphasis in the first biblical occurrence of *aman:* "And [Abram] believed in the LORD; and he counted it to him for righteousness" (Gen 15:6). The meaning here is that Abram was full of trust and confidence in God, and that he did not fear Him (v. 1). It was not primarily in God's words that he believed, but in God Himself. Nor does the text tell us that Abram believed God so as to accept what He said as "true" and "trustworthy" (cf. Gen 45:26), but simply that he believed in God. In other words, Abram came to experience a personal relationship to God rather than an impersonal relationship with His promises. **(13)** Thus, in Ex 4:9 the meaning is, "if they do not believe **in** view of the two signs," rather than, "if they do not believe these two signs." The focus is on the act of believing, not on the trustworthiness of the signs. **(14)** A more precise sense of *aman* does appear sometimes: "That they may believe that the LORD . . . hath appeared unto thee" (Ex 4:5; cf. 1 Kin 10:7). **(15)** In other instances, *aman* has a cultic use, by which the worshiping community affirms its identity with what the worship leader says (1 Chr 16:32). The "God of the amen" (2 Chr 20:20; Is 65:16) is the God who always accomplishes what He says; He is a "God who is faithful." Syn.: 529, 530, 982. See: TWOT—116; BDB—52d, 1081a.

540. אֲמַן {3x} ʾ**ăman** (Aram.), *am-an';* corresp. to 539:—believe {1x}, sure {1x}, faithful {1x}. See: TWOT—2584; BDB—1081a.

541. אָמַן {1x} ʼâman, *aw-man'*; denom. from 3225; to take the *right hand* road:—turn to the right {1x}. Syn.: See 539. See: TWOT—872; BDB—54d, 411c, 412b.

542. אָמָן {1x} ʼâmân, *aw-mawn'*; from 539 (in the sense of *training*); an *expert:*—cunning workman {1x}. See: TWOT—116c; BDB—53b.

543. אָמֵן {30x} **ʼâmên**, *aw-mane'*; from 539; *sure;* abstr. *faithfulness;* adv. *truly:*—*amen* {27x}; truly {2x}, so be it {1x}.

Amen (543), an adverb, means "truly; genuinely; *amen;* so be it." **(1)** This Hebrew word usually appears as a response to a curse that has been pronounced upon someone, as the one accursed accepts the curse upon himself. By so doing, he binds himself to fulfill certain conditions or else be subject to the terms of the curse (cf. Deut 29:15–26). **(2)** Although signifying a voluntary acceptance of the conditions of a covenant, the *amen* was sometimes pronounced with coercion. Even in these circumstances, the one who did not pronounce it received the punishment embodied in the curse. **(3)** So the *amen* was an affirmation of a covenant, which is the significance of the word in Num 5:22, its first biblical occurrence. **(4)** Later generations or individuals might reaffirm the covenant by voicing their *amen* (Neh 5:1–13; Jer 18:6). **(5)** In 1 Kin 1:36, *amen* is noncovenantal. It functions as an assertion of a person's agreement with the intent of a speech just delivered: "And Benaiah the son of Jehoiada answered the king, and said, *Amen:* the LORD God of my lord the king say so too." However, the context shows that Benaiah meant to give more than just verbal assent; his *amen* committed him to carry out the wishes of King David. It was a statement whereby he obligated himself to do what David had indirectly requested of him (cf. Neh 8:6). Syn.: 539. See: TWOT—116b; BDB—53b.

544. אֹמֶן {1x} ʼômen, *oh-men'*; from 539; *verity:*—truth {1x}. See: TWOT—116a; BDB—53b.

545. אָמְנָה {1x} ʼomnâh, *om-naw'*; fem. of 544 (in the spec. sense of *training*); *tutelage:*—brought up {1x}. See: TWOT—116f; BDB—53d.

546. אָמְנָה {2x} ʼomnâh, *om-naw'*; fem. of 544 (in its usual sense); adv. *surely:*—indeed {2x}. See: TWOT—116g; BDB—53d.

547. אֹמְנָה {1x} ʼômᵉnâh, *om-me-naw'*; fem. act. part. of 544 (in the orig. sense of *supporting*); a *column:*—pillar {1x}. See: TWOT—116; BDB—52d.

548. אֲמָנָה {2x} ʼămânâh, *am-aw-naw'*; fem. of 543; something *fixed*, i.e. a *covenant*, an *allowance:*—sure {1x}, portion {1x}. See: TWOT—116h; BDB—53d.

549. אֲמָנָה {2x} ʼĂmânâh, *am-aw-naw'*; the same as 548; *Amanah*, a mountain near Damascus:—Amana {1x}, variant for Abana {1x}. See: BDB—53d.

550. אַמְנוֹן {28x} ʼAmnôwn, *am-nohn'*; or

אֲמִינוֹן ʼĂmîynôwn, *am-ee-nohn'*; from 539; *faithful; Amnon* (or Aminon), a son of David:—Amnon {28x}. See: BDB—54c.

551. אָמְנָם {9x} ʼomnâm, *om-nawm'*; adv. from 544; *verily:*—truth {3x}, indeed {2x}, true {1x}, no doubt {1x}, surely {1x}, indeed {1x}. Syn.: 571. See: TWOT—116j; BDB—53d.

552. אֻמְנָם {5x} ʼumnâm, *oom-nawm'*; an orth. var. of 551: —indeed {3x}, very deed {1x}, surety {1x}. See: TWOT—116i; BDB—53d.

553. אָמַץ {41x} **ʼâmats**, *aw-mats'*; a prim. root; to *be alert*, phys. (on foot) or ment. (in courage):—strengthen {12x}, courage {9x}, strong {5x}, courageous {2x}, harden {2x}, speed {2x}, stronger {2x}, confirm {1x}, established {1x}, fortify {1x}, increaseth {1x}, steadfastly minded {1x}, obstinate {1x}, prevailed {1x}. Syn.: 1369, 2388, 2392, 2428, 4581, 5797. Ref. TWOT—117; BDB—54d.

554. אָמֹץ {2x} ʼâmôts, *aw-mohts'*; prob. from 553; of a *strong* color, i.e. *red* (others *fleet*):—bay {2x}. See: TWOT—117c; BDB—55b.

555. אֹמֶץ {1x} ʼômets, *o'-mets;* from 553; *strength:*—stronger {1x}. See: TWOT—117a; BDB—55b.

אַמִּץ ʼammîts. See 533.

556. אַמְצָה {1x} ʼamtsâh, *am-tsaw'*; from 553; *force:*—strength {1x}. See: TWOT—117b; BDB—55b.

557. אַמְצִי {2x} ʼAmtsîy, *am-tsee'*; from 553; *strong; Amtsi*, an Isr.:—Amzi {2x}. See: BDB—55c.

558. אֲמַצְיָה {40x} ʼĂmatsyâh, *am-ats-yaw'*; or

אֲמַצְיָהוּ ʼĂmatsyâhûw, *am-ats-yaw'-hoo;* from 553 and 3050; *strength of Jah; Amatsjah*, the name of four Isr.:—Amaziah {40x}. See: BDB—55c.

559. אָמַר {5308x} **ʼâmar**, *aw-mar'*; a prim. root; to *say* (used with great latitude):—said {4874x}, speak {179x}, answer {99x}, command {30x}, tell {29x}, call {7x}, promised {6x}, misc. {84x} = appoint, avouch, bid, boast self, certify, challenge, charge, commandment, commune, consider, declare, demand, × desire, determine, × expressly, × indeed, × intend, name, × plainly, publish, report, require, × still, × suppose, talk, term, × that is, × think, use [speech], utter, × verily, × yet.

Amar means "to say, speak, tell, command, answer." **(1)** *Amar* refers to the simple act of communicating with the spoken word. Usually the word is used of direct speech ("say"), although it may be used of indirect speech as well ("speak"). **(2)** The usual subject of this verb is some self-conscious personality—man (Gen 2:23) or God (Gen 1:3—the first occurrence of the word). **(3)** Infrequently animals (Gen 3:1) or, in figures of speech such as personification, inanimate objects "say" something (Judg 9:8ff.). **(4)** This verb bears many connotations and in some passages is better translated accordingly. The KJV renders this verb "answer" 98 times ("say as a response").

(5) God speaks in Gen 9:8; 22:2; Ex 8:27. The force of God's speaking is more than merely making a statement: It is authoritative. **(6)** In addition to these frequently occurring connotations, *amar* is rendered with many words representing various aspects of spoken communication, such as **(6a)** "appoint" or "assign" (1 Kin 11:18), **(6b)** "mention" or "name" (Gen 43:27), **(6c)** "call" (Is 5:20), and **(6d)** "promise" (2 Kin 8:19). **(7)** Although not always so translated, this word can imply the act of thinking within oneself (Gen 44:28) and the intention to do something (Ex 2:14). **(8)** When used of divine speaking, this verb may refer to simple communication (Gen 1:26). **(9)** Often, however, there is a much fuller sense where God's saying effects the thing spoken (cf. Gen 1). **(10)** The phrase "thus says the Lord," so frequent in the prophets, has been analyzed as a message-formula. The Bible recognizes that behind the divine speaking is divine authority and power. Syn.: 1696, 5002. See: TWOT—118; BDB—59c, 1081a.

560. אֲמַר {71x} **ʼămar** (Aram.), *am-ar'*; corresp. to 559:—say {45x}, commanded {12x}, speak {4x}, tell {9x}, declare {1x}. Syn.: 1697, 4405. See 559. See: TWOT—2585; BDB—1081a.

561. אֵמֶר {49x} ʼêmer, *ay'-mer;* from 559; something *said:*—words {43x}, speeches {2x}, sayings {2x}, appointed {1x}, answer {1x}.

This noun appears 48 times. *ʼEmer* refers to "words" in Prov 2:1: "My son, if thou wilt receive my words, and hide my commandments with thee." Syn: Several other nouns are related to the verb *ʼamar. ʼImrah* (565) also means "word, speech," and it occurs 37 times. One occurrence of *ʼimrah* is in 2 Sa 22:31 (cf. Ps 18:30). The noun *ʼomer* (562) is found 6 times and means "word, speech, promise" (Ps 68:11; Hab 3:9). *Maʼamar* (3982) and *meʼmar* (3983) mean "word, command." *Maʼamar* occurs 3 times (Est 1:15; 2:22; 9:32), and *meʼmar* occurs twice (Ezra 6:9; Dan 4:17). *ʼEmer* simply refers to "words." Syn.: 373, 4405. See: TWOT—118a; BDB—57a.

562. אֹמֶר {6x} ʼômer, *o'-mer;* the same as 561:—word {2x}, speech {2x}, thing {1x}, promise {1x}. See: TWOT—118a; BDB—56d, 1051c.

563. אִמַּר {3x} ʼimmar (Aram.), *im-mar';* perh. from 560 (in the sense of *bringing forth*); a *lamb:*—lamb {3x}. See: TWOT—2585; BDB—1081b.

564. אִמֵּר {10x} ʼImmêr, *im-mare';* from 559; *talkative; Immer*, the name of five Isr.:—*Immer* {10x}. See: BDB—57b.

565. אִמְרָה {37x} ʼimrâh, *im-raw';* or

אֶמְרָה ʼemrâh, *em-raw';* fem. of 561, and mean. the same:—word {29x}, speech {7x}, commandment {1x}. Syn.: 561, 1697, 4405. See: TWOT—118b; BDB—57a, 57b.

566. אִמְרִי {2x} ʼImrîy, *im-ree';* from 564; *wordy; Imri*, the name of two Isr.:—Imri {2x}. See: BDB—57c.

567. אֱמֹרִי {87x} ʼĔmôrîy, *em-o-ree';* prob. a patron. from an unused name derived from 559 in the sense of *publicity*, i.e. prominence; thus, a *mountaineer;* an *Emorite*, one of the Canaanitish tribes:—Amorite {87x}. See: TWOT—119; BDB—57b.

568. אֲמַרְיָה {16x} ʼĂmaryâh, *am-ar-yaw';* or prol.

אֲמַרְיָהוּ ʼĂmaryâhûw, *am-ar-yaw'-hoo;* from 559 and 3050; *Jah has said* (i.e. promised); *Amarjah*, the name of nine Isr.:—Amariah {16x}. See: BDB—57c.

569. אַמְרָפֶל {2x} ʼAmrâphel, *am-raw-fel';* of uncert. (perh. for.) der.; *Amraphel*, a king of Shinar:—Amraphel {2x}. See: BDB—57d.

570. אֶמֶשׁ {5x} ʼemesh, *eh'-mesh;* time *past*, i.e. *yesterday* or *last night:*—yesternight {3x}, former time {1x}, yesterday {1x}. See: TWOT—120; BDB—57d.

571. אֱמֶת {127x} **ʼemeth**, *eh'-meth;* contr. from 539; *stability;* fig. *certainty, truth, trustworthiness:*—truth {92x}, true {18x}, truly {7x}, right {3x}, faithfully {2x}, assured {1x}, assuredly {1x}, establishment {1x}, faithful {1x}, sure {1x}, verity {1x}.

Emeth means "truth; right; faithful." **(1)** In Zec 8:3, Jerusalem is called "a city of truth." **(2)** Elsewhere, *emeth* is rendered as the word "right": "Howbeit thou art just in all that is brought upon us; for thou hast done right, but we have done wickedly . . ." (Neh 9:33). **(3)** Only infrequently (16 times) is *emeth* translated "faithful" as when Nehemiah is described as "a faithful man, and feared God above many" (Neh 7:2). Syn.: See: TWOT—116k; BDB—54a, 57d.

572. אַמְתַּחַת {15x} **ʾamtêchath**, *am-taykh'-ath;* from 4060; prop. something *expansive,* i.e. a flexible container for grain; a *bag:*—sack {15x}. See: TWOT—1265a; BDB—57d, 607c.

573. אֲמִתַּי {2x} **ʾĂmittay**, *am-it-tah'ee;* from 571; *veracious; Amittai,* an Isr.:—Amittai {2x}. See: BDB—54c, 57d.

574. אֵמְתָנִי {1x} **ʾemtânîy** (Aram.), *em-taw-nee';* from a root corresp. to that of 4975; well-*loined* (i.e. burly) or *mighty:*—terrible {1x}. See: TWOT—2571; BDB—1080a.

575. אָן {8x} **ʾân**, *awn;* or

אָנָה **ʾânâh**, *aw-naw';* contr. from 370; *where?;* hence, *whither?, when?;* also *hither* and *thither:*—whither, how, where, whithersoever, hither = {8x}. See: TWOT—75g; BDB—33a, 57d.

576. אֲנָא {16x} **ʾănâʾ** (Aram.), *an-aw';* or

אֲנָה **ʾănâh** (Aram.), *an-aw';* corresp. to 589; *I:*—I {14x}, me, {2x}. See: TWOT—2586; BDB—1081b.

577. אָנָּא {13x} **ʾânnâʾ**, *awn-naw';* or

אָנָּה **ʾânnâh**, *awn-naw';* appar. contr. from 160 and 4994; *oh now!:*—I beseech thee {8x}, I pray thee {2x}, Oh {x1}, O {2x}. See: TWOT—122; BDB—58a, 58c.

אֲנָה **ʾănâh**. See 576.

אָנָה **ʾânâh**. See 575.

578. אָנָה {2x} **ʾânâh**, *aw-naw';* a prim. root; to *groan:*—lament {1x}, mourn {1x}. See: TWOT—124; BDB—58b.

579. אָנָה {4x} **ʾânâh**, *aw-naw';* a prim. root [perh. rather ident. with 578 through the idea of *contraction* in anguish]; to *approach;* hence, to *meet* in various senses:—deliver {1x}, befall {1x}, happen {1x}, seeketh a quarrel {1x}. See: TWOT—126; BDB—58c, 1099c.

אָנָּה **ʾânnâh**. See 577.

580. אֲנוּ {1x} **ʾănûw**, *an-oo';* contr. for 587; *we:*—we {1x}. See: TWOT—128; BDB—58c, 59a.

אֹנוֹ **ʾÔnôw**. See 207.

581. אִנּוּן {4x} **ʾinnûwn** (Aram.), *in-noon';* or (fem.)

אִנִּין **ʾinnîyn** (Aram.), *in-neen';* corresp. to 1992; *they:*—are {2x}, these {1x}, them {1x}. See: TWOT—2587; BDB—1081c.

582. אֱנוֹשׁ {564x} **ʾĕnôwsh**, *en-oshe';* from 605; prop. a *mortal* (and thus differing from the more dignified 120); hence, a *man* in Gen (singly or collect.). It is often unexpressed in the English Version, espec. when used in apposition with another word.:—man {520x}, certain {10x}, husbands {3x}, some {3x}, merchantmen {2x}, persons {2x}, misc.: another, chap [-man], people, person, servant, some (× of them), + stranger, those - {24x}.

Enowsh means "man." **(1)** It occurs 25 times in biblical Aramaic and 42 times in biblical Hebrew. **(2)** Hebrew uses enosh exclusively in poetical passages. The only apparent exception is 2 Chr 14:11, but this is a prayer and, therefore uses poetical words. **(3)** *Enowsh* never appears with the definite article and at all times except once (Ps 144:3) sets forth a collective idea, "man." **(4)** In most cases where the word occurs in Job and the Psalms it suggests the frailty, vulnerability, and finitude of "man" as contrasted to God: "As for man, his days are as grass: as a flower of the field, so he flourisheth" (Ps 103:15). As such "man" cannot be righteous or holy before God: "Shall mortal man be more just than God? Shall a man be more pure than his Maker?" (Job 4:17). **(5)** In the Psalms this word is used to indicate the enemy: "Arise, O LORD; let not man prevail: let the heathen be judged in thy sight" (Ps 9:19). Here the parallelism shows that enosh is synonymous with "nations," or the enemy. They are, therefore, presented as weak, vulnerable, and finite: "Put them in fear, O LORD: that the nations may know themselves to be but men" (Ps 9:20).

(6) *Enowsh* may connote "men" as weak but not necessarily morally weak: "Blessed is the man that doeth this, and the son of man that layeth hold of it" (Is 56:2). In this passage the *enowsh* is blessed because he has been morally strong. **(7)** In a few places the word bears no moral overtones and represents "man" in a sense parallel to Hebrew adam. **(8)** He is finite as contrasted to the infinite God: "I said, I would scatter them into corners, I would make the remembrance of them to cease from among men" (Deut. 32:26—the first biblical occurrence). Syn.: Adam (120) connotes man as the creature created in God's image, the crown of all creation. Iysh (376) is used for man as the counterpart of woman and/or as distinguished in his maleness. Geber (1397) denotes a male as an antonym of a woman, many times suggesting strength, strong man. *ʾĔnôwsh* (582) sets forth a collective idea man suggesting the insignificance, frailty, vulnerability, and finitude of man as contrasted to God. Bachur (970) signifies the fully developed, vigorous, unmarried man is in his prime. See also: 376, 1167, 1397, 1400, 4962. See: TWOT—136a; BDB—60d, 1081d.

583. אֱנוֹשׁ {7x} **ʾĔnôwsh**, *en-ohsh';* the same as 582; *Enosh,* a son of Seth:—Enos {6x}, Enosh {1x}. See: BDB—60d.

584. אָנַח {12x} **ʾânach**, *aw-nakh';* a prim. root; to *sigh:*—sigh {10x}, groan {1x}, mourn {1x}. See: TWOT—127; BDB—58d.

585. אֲנָחָה {11x} **ʾănâchâh**, *an-aw-khaw';* from 584, *sighing:*—sighing {5x}, groanings {4x}, sighs {1x}, mourning {1x}. See: TWOT—127a; BDB—58d.

586. אֲנַחְנָא {4x} **ʾănachnâʾ** (Aram.), *an-akh'-naw;* or

אֲנַחְנָה **ʾănachnâh** (Aram.), *an-akh-naw';* corresp. to 587; *we:*—we {4x}. See: TWOT—2588; BDB—1081c.

587. אֲנַחְנוּ {6x} **ʾănachnûw**, *an-akh'-noo;* appar. from 595; *we:*—ourselves, us, we = {6x}. See: TWOT—128; BDB—58d, 59c.

588. אֲנָחֲרָת {1x} **ʾĂnâchărâth**, *an-aw-kha-rawth';* prob. from the same root as 5170; a *gorge* or narrow pass; *Anacharath,* a place in Pal.:—Anaharath. See: BDB—58d.

589. אֲנִי {13x} **ʾănîy**, *an-ee';* contr. from 595; *I:*—I, me, which, for I, mine = {13x}. See: TWOT—129; BDB—58d, 219a, 1081b.

590. אֳנִי {7x} **ʾŏnîy**, *on-ee';* prob. from 579 (in the sense of *conveyance*); a *ship* or (collect.) a *fleet:*—navy {5x}, navy of ships {1x}, galley {1x}. See: TWOT—125a,b; BDB—58b.

591. אֳנִיָּה {32x} **ʾŏnîyâh**, *on-ee-yaw';* fem. of 590; a *ship:*—ship {31x}, shipman + 582 {1x}. See: TWOT—125b; BDB—58b.

592. אֲנִיָּה {2x} **ʾănîyâh**, *an-ee-yaw';* from 578; *groaning:*—lamentation {1x}, sorrow {1x}. See: TWOT—124a; BDB—58b.

אִנִּין **ʾinnîyn**. See 581.

593. אֲנִיעָם {1x} **ʾĂnîyʿâm**, *an-ee-awm';* from 578 and 5971; *groaning of* (the) *people; Aniam,* an Isr.:—Aniam {1x}. See: BDB—58b.

594. אֲנָךְ {4x} **ʾănâk**, *an-awk';* prob. from an unused root mean. to *be narrow;* according to most a plumb-*line,* and to others a *hook:*—plumb-line {1x}. See: TWOT—129.1; BDB—59d.

595. אָנֹכִי {3x} **ʾânôkîy**, *aw-no-kee'* (sometimes *aw-no'-kee*); a prim. pron.; *I:*—I {1x}, me {1x}, which {1x}. See: TWOT—130; BDB—59a, 59d.

596. אָנַן {2x} **ʾânan**, *aw-nan';* a prim. root; to *mourn,* i.e. *complain:*—complain {2x}. See: TWOT—131; BDB—59d.

597. אָנַס {1x} **ʾânaç**, *aw-nas';* to *insist:*—compel {1x}. See: TWOT—132; BDB—60a.

598. אֲנַס {1x} **ʾănaç** (Aram.), *an-as';* corresp. to 597; fig. to *distress:*—troubleth {1x}. See: TWOT—2589; BDB—1081c.

599. אָנַף {14x} **ʾânaph**, *aw-naf';* a prim. root; to *breathe* hard, i.e. *be enraged:*—angry {13x}, displeased {1x}. The verb appears in Is 12:1and means angry: "O LORD, I will praise thee: though thou wast angry with me. . . ." Syn.: 639, 2734. See: TWOT—133; BDB—60a.

600. אֲנַף {2x} **ʾănaph** (Aram.), *an-af';* corresp. to 639 (only in the plur. as a sing.); the *face:*—face {1x}, visage {1x}. See: TWOT—2590; BDB—1081c.

601. אֲנָפָה {2x} **ʾănâphâh**, *an-aw-faw';* from 599; an unclean bird, perh. the *parrot* (from its *irascibility*):—heron {2x}. See: TWOT—133a; BDB—60b.

602. אָנַק {4x} **ʾânaq**, *aw-nak';* a prim. root; to *shriek:*—cry {3x}, groan {1x}. See: TWOT—134; BDB—60b.

603. אֲנָקָה {4x} **ʾănâqâh**, *an-aw-kaw';* from 602; *shrieking:*—sighing {2x}, crying out {1x}, groaning {1x}. See: TWOT—134a; BDB—60c.

604. אֲנָקָה {1x} **ʾănâqâh**, *an-aw-kaw';* the same as 603; some kind of lizard, prob. the *gecko* (from its *wail*):—ferret {1x}. See: TWOT—134b; BDB—60c.

605. אָנַשׁ {9x} **ʾânash**, *aw-nash';* a prim. root; to *be frail, feeble,* or (fig.) *melancholy:*—incurable {5x}, desperate {1x}, desperately wicked {1x}, woeful {1x}, sick {1x}. See: TWOT—135; BDB—60c.

606. אֱנָשׁ {25x} ʾĕnâsh (Aram.), *en-awsh';* or

אֱנַשׁ ʾĕnash (Aram.), *en-ash';* corresp. to 582; a *man:*—man {23x}, whosoever + 3606 {2x}. See: TWOT—2591; BDB—1081d.

אַנְתְּ ʾant. See 859.

607. אַנְתָּה {14x} ʾantâh (Aram.), *an-taw';* corresp. to 859; *thou:*—thou {13x}, thee {1x}. See: TWOT—2592; BDB—1082a.

608. אַנְתּוּן {1x} ʾantûwn (Aram.), *an-toon';* plur. of 607; *ye:*—ye {1x}. See: TWOT—2593; BDB—1082a.

609. אָסָא {58x} ʾÂçâʾ, *aw-saw';* of uncert. der.; *Asa,* the name of a king and of a Levite:—Asa {58x}. See: BDB—61d.

610. אָסוּךְ {1x} ʾâçûwk, *aw-sook';* from 5480; *anointed,* i.e. an oil-*flask:*—pot {1x}. See: TWOT—1474a; BDB—62a, 692a.

611. אָסוֹן {5x} ʾâçôwn, *aw-sone';* of uncert. der.; *hurt:*—mischief {3x}, mischief fellow {2x}. See: TWOT—138a; BDB—62a.

612. אֵסוּר {3x} ʾêçûwr, *ay-soor';* from 631; a *bond* (espec. *manacles* of a prisoner):—band {2x}, prison {1x}. See: TWOT—141a; BDB—64a, 1082a.

613. אֱסוּר {3x} ʾĕçûwr (Aram.), *es-oor';* corresp. to 612:—band {2x}, imprisonment {1x}. See: TWOT—2595a; BDB—1082b.

614. אָסִיף {2} ʾâçîyph, *aw-seef';* or

אָסִף ʾâçîph, *aw-seef';* from 622; *gathered,* i.e. (abstr.) a *gathering* in of crops:—ingathering {2x}. See: TWOT—140b; BDB—63b.

615. אָסִיר {12x} ʾâçîyr, *aw-sere';* from 631; *bound,* i.e. a *captive:*—prisoner {10x}, bound {2x}. See: TWOT—141b; BDB—64a.

616. אַסִּיר {3x} ʾaççîyr, *as-sere';* for 615:—prisoner {3x}. See: TWOT—141c; BDB—64b.

617. אַסִּיר {5x} ʾAççîyr, *as-sere';* the same as 616; *prisoner; Assir,* the name of two Isr.:—Assir {5x}. See: BDB—64b.

618. אָסָם {2x} ʾâçâm, *aw-sawm';* from an unused root mean. to *heap* together; a *storehouse* (only in the plur.):—barn {1x}, storehouse {1x}. See: TWOT—139a; BDB—62a.

619. אַסְנָה {1x} ʾAçnâh, *as-naw';* of uncert. der.; *Asnah,* one of the Nethinim:—Asnah {1x}. See: BDB—62a.

620. אָסְנַפַּר {1x} ʾOçnappar (Aram.), *os-nap-par';* of for. der.; *Osnappar,* an Ass. king:—Asnapper {1x}. See: BDB—1082a.

621. אָסְנַת {3x} ʾÂçᵉnath, *aw-se-nath';* of Eg. der.; *Asenath,* the wife of Joseph:—Asenath {3x}. See: BDB—62a.

622. אָסַף {200x} ʾâçaph, *aw-saf';* a prim. root; to *gather* for any purpose; hence, to *receive, take away,* i.e. remove (destroy, leave behind, put up, restore, etc.):—together {51x}, gather {86x}, assemble {15x}, rereward {5x}, misc. {51x}.

Acaph means "to gather, gather in, take away." **(1)** Basically, *acaph* refers to "bringing objects to a common point." This may mean to "gather" or "collect" something such as food. The first occurrence is when God told Noah to "gather" food to himself (Gen 6:21). Eventually, the food was to go into the ark. **(2)** This verb can also refer to "gathering" food at harvest time, or "harvesting": "And six years thou shalt sow thy land, and shalt gather in the fruits thereof" (Ex 23:10). **(3)** Second Kings 22:4 refers not to a process of going out and getting something together, but to standing still as someone brings money to one. **(4)** Also notice Gen 29:22: "And Laban gathered together all the men of the place, and made a feast"; this verse similarly focuses on the end product of gathering. But here the "gatherer" does not physically handle what is "gathered." He is simply the impetus or active cause for a congregating of all those men. **(5)** God may "gather" a man to his fathers—i.e., cause him to die (2 Kin 22:20). Here the emphasis is on the end product, and God as the agent who "gathers."

(6) *Acaph* may represent not only the process of bringing things to a common location; the word may also represent "bringing" things to oneself. After the harvest is brought ("gathered") in from the threshing floor and wine vat, the Feast of Booths is to be celebrated (Deut 16:13). **(7)** In Deut 22:2, a man is to "gather" into his home (bring home and care for) a lost animal whose owner cannot be found. **(8)** In this manner, God "gathers" to Himself those abandoned by their family (Ps 27:10). **(9)** A special application of this nuance is to "receive hospitality": ". . . When he went in he sat him down in a street of the city: for there was no man that took them into his house to lodging" (Judg 19:15). **(10)** "To gather in" also may mean "to be consumed by"—God promises that His people "shall be no more consumed with hunger" (Eze 34:29). **(11)** It is used in this way the verb can mean "to bring into," as when Jacob "gathered up his feet into the bed" (Gen 49:33).

(12) *Acaph* can emphasize "withdrawal" or "removal" of something; the action is viewed from the perspective of one who loses something because someone has taken it ("gathered it in"). In Ps 85:3, the "gathering" represents this sort of "withdrawal away from" the speaker. Thus, anger "disappears": "Thou hast taken away all thy wrath." Compare also Rachel's statement at the birth of Joseph: "God hath taken away my reproach" (Gen 30:23). In this case, Rachel speaks of the "destruction" of her reproach. **(13)** "To gather one's soul" is "to lose" one's life (Judg 18:25). **(14)** God can also be the agent who "gathers" or "takes away" a soul: "Gather not my soul with sinners . . ." (Ps 26:9). **(15)** In this sense, *acaph* can mean "being cured" of a disease; "Would God my lord were with the prophet that is in Samaria! for he would recover him of his leprosy" (2 Kin 5:3). Syn.: *ʾÂçaph* is a near synonym to qabats (6908 – {136x}), differing by having a more extensive range of meanings. *ʾÂçaph,* duplicates all the meanings of qabats. See: TWOT—140; BDB—62a.

623. אָסָף {46x} ʾÂçâph, *aw-sawf';* from 622; *collector; Asaph,* the name of three Isr., and of the family of the first:—Asaph {1x}. See: BDB—63a.

אָסִף ʾâçîph. See 614

624. אָסֻף {3x} ʾâçûph, *aw-soof';* pass. part. of 622; *collected* (only in the plur.), i.e. a *collection* (of offerings):—threshold {1x}, Asuppim {2x}. See: TWOT—140c; BDB—62b, 62c.

625. אֹסֶף {3x} ʾôçeph, *o'-sef;* from 622; a *collection* (of fruits):—the gathering {2x}, gather {1x}. See: TWOT—140a; BDB—63a.

626. אֲסֵפָה {1x} ʾăçêphâh, *as-ay-faw';* from 622; a *collection* of people (only adv.):—together {1x}. See: TWOT—140d; BDB—63b.

627. אֲסֻפָּה {1x} ʾăçuppâh, *as-up-paw';* fem. of 624.; a *collection* of (learned) men (only in the plur.):—assemblies {1x}. See: TWOT—140e; BDB—63b.

628. אֲסַפְסֻף {1x} ʾaçpᵉçûph, *as-pes-oof';* by redupl. from 624; *gathered up together,* i.e. a promiscuous *assemblage* (of people):—mixed multitude {1x}. See: TWOT—140f; BDB—63c.

629. אָסְפַּרְנָא {7x} ʾoçparnâʾ (Aram.), *os-par-naw';* of Pers. der.; *diligently:*—speedily {4x}, speed {1x}, fast {1x}, forthwith {1x}. See: TWOT—2594; BDB—1082a.

630. אַסְפָּתָא {1x} ʾAçpâthâʾ, *as-paw-thaw';* of Pers. der.; *Aspatha,* a son of Haman:—Aspatha {1x}. See: BDB—63c.

631. אָסַר {72x} ʾâçar, *aw-sar';* a prim. root; to *yoke* or *hitch;* by anal. to *fasten* in any sense, to *join* battle:—bind {47x}, prison {4x}, (-er {2x}), tie {4x}, misc.: fast, gird, harness, hold, keep, make ready, order, prepare, put in bonds, set in array – {15x}.

Acar means"to bind, imprison, tie, gird, to harness." **(1)** The first use of *acar* in the Hebrew text is in Gen 39:20, which tells how Joseph was "imprisoned" after being wrongfully accused by Potiphar's wife. **(2)** The common word for "tying up" for security and safety, *acar* is often used to indicate the tying up of horses and donkeys (2 Kin 7:10). **(3)** Similarly, oxen are "harnessed" to carts (1 Sa 6:7, 10). **(4)** Frequently, *acar* is used to describe the "binding" of prisoners with cords and various fetters (Gen 42:24; Judg 15:10, 12–13). **(5)** Samson misled Delilah as she probed for the secret of his strength, telling her to "bind" him with bowstrings (Judg 16:7) and new ropes (Judg 16:11), none of which could hold him. **(6)** Used in an abstract sense, *acar* refers **(6a)** to those who are spiritually "bound" (Ps 146:7; Is 49:9; 61:1) or **(6b)** a man who is emotionally "captivated" by a woman's hair (Song 7:5). **(7)** Strangely, the figurative use of the term in the sense of obligation or "binding" to a vow or an oath is found only in Num 30, but it is used there a number of times (vv. 3, 5–6, 8–9, 11–12). See: TWOT—141; BDB—63c, 1082a.

632. אֱסָר {11x} ʾĕçâr, *es-sawr';* or

אִסָּר ʾiççâr, *is-sawr';* from 631; an *obligation* or *vow* (of abstinence):—binding {1x}, bond {10x}. See: TWOT—141d; BDB—64b, 1082b.

633. אֱסָר {7x} ʾĕçâr (Aram.), *es-sawr';* corresp. to 632 in a legal sense; an *interdict:*—decree {7x}. See: TWOT—2595b; BDB—1082b.

634. אֵסַר־חַדּוֹן {3x} ʾÊçar-Chaddôwn, *ay-sar' chad-dohn';* of for. der.; *Esarchaddon,* an Assy. king:—Esar-haddon {3x}. See: BDB—64d.

635. אֶסְתֵּר {55x} ʾEçtêr, *es-tare';* of Pers. der.; *Ester,* the Jewish heroine:—Esther {55x}. See: BDB—64d.

636. אָע {5x} ʾâʿ (Aram.), *aw;* corresp. to 6086; a *tree* or *wood:*—timber {3x}, wood {2x}. See: TWOT—2596; BDB—1082b.

637. אַף {17x} ʾaph, *af;* a prim. particle; mean. *accession* (used as an adv. or conjunc.); *also* or *yea;* adversatively *though:*—also, even, yet, moreover, yea, with, low, therefore, much = {17x}. This is a conjunction denoting addition, especially of something greater. See: TWOT—142; BDB—64d, 210b, 1082b.

638. אַף {4x} ʾ**aph** (Aram.), *af;* corresp. to 637:—also {4x}. See: TWOT—2597; BDB—1082b.

639. אַף {276} ʾ**aph**, *af;* from 599; prop. the *nose* or *nostril;* hence, the *face,* and occasionally a *person;* also (from the rapid breathing in passion) *ire:*—anger {172x}, wrath {42x}, face {22x}, nostrils {13x}, nose {12x}, angry {4x}, longsuffering + 750 {4x}, before {2x}, countenance {1x}, forbearing {1x}, forehead {1x}, snout {1x}, worthy {1x}.

Aph (639) means "nose; nostrils; face; wrath; anger." **(1)** The fundamental meaning of the word is "nose," as a literal part of the body. *Aph* bears this meaning in the singular, while the dual refers to the "nostrils" through which air passes in and out: "And the LORD God formed man of the dust of the ground, and breathed into his nostrils the breath of life" (Gen 2:7—the first biblical occurrence). **(2)** In other contexts *aph* in the dual represents the "entire face." God cursed Adam saying: "In the sweat of thy face shalt thou eat bread, till thou return unto the ground . . ." (Gen 3:19). **(3)** This emphasis appears often with the phrase "to bow one's face to the ground": ". . . And Joseph's brethren came, and bowed down themselves before him with their faces to the earth" (Gen 42:6). **(4)** The words "length of face or nostrils" constitute an idiom meaning "longsuffering" or "slow to anger." **(4a)** It is used both of God and of man: "The LORD, The LORD God, merciful and gracious, long-suffering, and abundant in goodness and truth" (Ex 34:6). **(4b)** The contrasting idiom, meaning "quick to anger," might literally mean "short of face/nostrils." It implies a changeable countenance, a capricious disposition.

(5) Prov 14:17 uses this idiom with a little stronger emphasis: "He that is soon angry dealeth foolishly: and a man of wicked devices is hated." The accuracy of this translation is supported by the parallelism of the phrase and "a man of evil devices." **(6)** Clearly *aph* must mean something evil in God's sight. **(7)** Finally, the dual form can mean "wrath" (only in 4 passages): "Surely the churning of milk bringeth forth butter, and the wringing of the nose bringeth forth blood: so the forcing of wrath bringeth forth strife" (Prov 30:33; cf. Ex 15:8). **(8)** The singular form means "nose" about 25 times. In Num 11:19–20 the word represents a human nose: "You [Israel] shall . . . eat [the meat God will supply] . . . a whole month, until it comes out of your nostrils and becomes loathsome to you." **(9)** Is 2:22 makes it clear that the word represents the place where the breath is: "Cease ye from man, whose breath of life is in his nostrils. **(10)** *Aph* is applied also to the "nose" of animals. In Job 40:24, God speaks of a large water animal: "He taketh it with his eyes: his nose pierceth through snares."

(11) The word can be used anthropomorphically of God. Certainly passages such as Deut 4:15–19 make it clear that God is a Spirit (cf. Jn 4:24) and has not a body like men. Yet, speaking figuratively, it may be said: "They shall teach Jacob thy judgments, and Israel thy law: they shall put incense before thee [literally, "in thy nostrils"], and whole burnt sacrifice upon thine altar" (Deut 33:10; cf. Ps 18:8, 15). **(12)** The idiom "high of nose" means "haughty" (cf. the English idiom "to have one's nose in the air"): "The wicked, through the pride of his countenance, will not seek after God . . ." (Ps 10:4). **(13)** The singular form often means "anger" or "wrath." This meaning first appears in Gen 30:2: "And Jacob's anger was kindled against Rachel. . . ." **(14)** This meaning is applied to God as a figure of speech (anthropopathism) whereby He is attributed human emotions. Since God is infinite, eternal, and unchangeable and since anger is an emotion representing a change in one's reaction (cf. Num 25:4), God does not really become angry, He only appears to do so in the eyes of men (cf. Prov 29:8). **(15)** The Spirit of God can seize a man and move him to a holy "anger" (Judg 14:19; 1 Sa 11:6). Syn.: 3707. See: TWOT—133a; BDB—60a, 64d, 1081d.

640. אָפַד {2x} ʾ**âphad**, *aw-fad';* a prim. root [rather a denom. from 646]; to *gird* on (the ephod):—bind {1x}, gird {1x}. See: TWOT—142.1; BDB—65d.

אֵפֹד ʾ**êphôd**. See 646.

641. אֵפֹד {1x} ʾ**Êphôd**, *ay-fode';* the same as 646 short.; *Ephod,* an Isr.:—*Ephod* {1x}. See: BDB—65d.

642. אֵפֻדָּה {3x} ʾ**ephuddâh**, *ay-food-daw';* fem. of 646; a *girding* on (of the ephod); hence, Gen a *plating* (of metal):—ephod {2x}, ornament {1x}.

Ephuddah means "ephod; covering." This word is a feminine form of epod (or ephod). The word occurs 3 times, first in Ex 28:8: "And the curious girdle of the ephod, which is upon it, shall be of . . . gold, of blue, and purple, and scarlet, and fine twined linen." See: 142.1b; BDB—65d.

643. אַפֶּדֶן {1x} ʾ**appeden**, *ap-peh'-den;* appar. of for. der.; a *pavilion* or palace-tent:—palace {1x}. See: TWOT—142.2; BDB—66a.

644. אָפָה {25x} ʾ**âphâh**, *aw-faw';* a prim. root; to *cook,* espec. to *bake:*—bake {13x}, baker {11x}, bakemeats + 4639 {1x}. See: TWOT—143; BDB—66a.

אֵפָה ʾ**êphâh**. See 374.

645. אֵפוֹ {15x} ʾ**êphôw**, *ay-fo';* or

אֵפוֹא ʾ**êphôw**ʾ, *ay-fo';* from 6311; strictly a demonstr. particle, *here;* but used of time, *now* or *then:*—now {10x}, where {4x}, here {1x}. See: TWOT—144; BDB—66b.

646. אֵפוֹד {49x} ʾ**êphôwd**, *ay-fode';* rarely

אֵפֹד ʾ**êphôd**, *ay-fode';* prob. of for. der.; a *girdle;* spec. the *ephod* or high-priest's shoulder-piece; also Gen an *image:*—*ephod* {49x}.

Ephod is transliterated as "*ephod.*" **(1)** This word represents a close-fitting outer garment associated with worship. **(1a)** It was a kind of long vest, generally reaching to the thighs. **(1b)** The "*ephod*" of the high priest was fastened with a beautifully woven girdle (Ex 28:27–28) and had shoulder straps set in onyx stones, on which were engraved the names of the twelve tribes. **(1c)** Over the chest of the high priest was the breastplate, also containing twelve stones engraved with the tribal names. **(1d)** Rings attached it to the "*ephod.*" **(1e)** The Urim and Thummin were also linked to the breastplate. **(2)** Apparently, this "*ephod*" and attachments were prominently displayed in the sanctuary. David consulted the "*ephod*" to learn whether the people of Keilah would betray him to Saul (1 Sa 23:9–12); no doubt the Urim and Thummim were used. **(3)** The first biblical occurrence of the word refers to this high priestly *ephod:* "Onyx stones, and stones to be set in the *ephod,* and in the breastplate" (Ex 25:7). **(4)** So venerated was this "*ephod*" that replicas were sometimes made (Judg 8:27; 17:1–5) and even worshiped. **(5)** Lesser priests (1 Sa 2:28) and priestly trainees wore less elaborate "*ephods*" made of linen whenever they appeared before the altar. See: TWOT—142.1a; BDB—65b.

647. אֲפִיחַ {1x} ʾ**Ăphîyach**, *af-ee'-akh;* perh. from 6315; *breeze; Aphiach,* an Isr.:—Aphiah {1x}. See: BDB—66c.

648. אָפִיל {1x} ʾ**âphîyl**, *aw-feel';* from the same as 651 (in the sense of *weakness*); *unripe:*—grown up {1x}. See: TWOT—145d; BDB—66d.

649. אַפַּיִם {2x} ʾ**Appayim**, *ap-pah'-yim;* dual of 639; *two nostrils; Appajim,* an Isr.:—Appaim {2x}. See: BDB—60b.

650. אָפִיק {19x} ʾ**âphîyq**, *aw-feek';* from 622; prop. *containing,* i.e. a *tube;* also a *bed* or *valley* of a stream; also a *strong* thing or a *hero:*—river {10x}, channel {3x}, stream {2x}, brooks {1x}, mighty {1x}, scales {1x}, strong {1x}. See: TWOT—149a; BDB—67d.

651. אָפֵל {1x} ʾ**âphêl**, *aw-fale';* from an unused root mean. to *set* as the sun; *dusky:*—very dark {1x}. See: TWOT—145b; BDB—66c.

652. אֹפֶל {9x} ʾ**ôphel**, *o'fel;* from the same as 651; *dusk:*—darkness {7x}, privily {1x}, obscurity {1x}. See: TWOT—145a; BDB—66c.

653. אֲפֵלָה {10x} ʾ**ăphêlâh**, *af-ay-law';* fem. of 651; *duskiness,* fig. *misfortune;* concr. *concealment:*—darkness {6x}, gloominess {2x}, dark {1x}, thick {1x}. See: TWOT—145c, BDB—66c.

654. אֶפְלָל {2x} ʾ**Ephlâl**, *ef-lawl';* from 6419; *judge; Ephlal,* an Isr.:—*Ephlal* {2x}. See: BDB—66d, 813d.

655. אֹפֶן {1x} ʾ**ôphen**, *o'-fen;* from an unused root mean. to *revolve;* a *turn,* i.e. a *season:*—fitly {1x}. See: TWOT—146b; BDB—67a.

אֹפָן ʾ**ôphân**. See 212.

656. אָפֵס {5x} ʾ**âphêç**, *aw-face';* a prim. root; to *disappear,* i.e. *cease:*—fail {2x}, gone {1x}, end {1x}, brought to nought {1x}. See: TWOT—147; BDB—67a.

657. אֶפֶס {43x} ʾ**epheç**, *eh'-fes;* from 656; *cessation,* i.e. an *end* (espec. of the earth); often used adv. *no further;* also (like 6466) the *ankle* (in the dual), as being the extremity of the leg or foot:—ends {13x}, no {4x}, none {3x}, not {3x}, nothing {2x}, without {2x}, else {2x}, beside {1x}, but {1x}, cause {1x}, howbeit {1x}, misc. {10x}.

Ephec means "end; not; nothing; only." **(1)** Basically, the noun indicates that a thing "comes to an end" and "is no more." **(2)** The idea of the "far reaches" of a thing is seen in passages such as Prov 30:4: "Who hath gathered the wind in his fists? Who hath bound the waters in a garment? Who hath established all the ends [boundaries] of the earth?" (cf. Ps 72:8). **(3)** In other contexts, *ephec* means the "territory" of the nations other than Israel: ". . . With them he shall push the people together to the ends of the earth . . ." (Deut 33:17). **(4)** More often, this word represents the peoples who live outside the territory of Israel: "Ask of me, and I shall give thee the heathen for thine inheritance, and the [very ends] of the earth for thy possession" (Ps 2:8). **(5)** In Ps 22:27, the phrase, "the ends of the world," is synonymously parallel to "all the [families] of the nations." Therefore, "the ends of the earth" in such contexts represents all the peoples of the earth besides Israel.

(6) *Ephec* is used to express "non-existence" primarily in poetry, where it appears chiefly as a synonym of ayin ("none, nothing"). **(7)** In one instance, *ephec* is used expressing the "non-existence" of a person or thing and is translated "not" or "no": "Is there not yet any of the house of Saul, that I may show the kindness of God unto him?" (2 Sa 9:3). **(8)** In Is 45:6, the word means "none" or "no one": "That they may know from the rising of the sun, and from the west, that there is none beside me" (cf. v. 9). **(10)** In a few passages, *ephec* used as a particle of negation means "at an end" or "nothing": "And all her princes shall be nothing," or "unimportant" and "not exalted" to kingship (Is 34:12). **(11)** The force of this word in Is 41:12 is on the "non-existence" of those so described: ". . . They that war against thee shall be as nothing, and as a thing of nought."

(12) This word can also mean "nothing" in the sense of "powerlessness" and "worthlessness": "All nations before him are as nothing; and they are counted to him less than nothing, and [meaningless]" (Is 40:17). **(13)** In Num 22:35 *ephec* means "nothing other than" or "only": "Go with the men: but only the word that I shall speak unto thee, that thou shalt speak" (cf. Num 23:13). In such passages, *ephec* (with the Hebrew particle ki) qualifies the preceding phrase. **(14)** In 2 Sa 12:14, a special nuance of the word is represented by the English "howbeit." **(15)** In Is 52:4 *ephec* preceded by the preposition be ("by; because of") means "without cause": ". . . And the Assyrian oppressed them without cause." Syn.: 319, 3615, 7093, 7097, 7098. See: TWOT—147a; BDB—67a, 67b.

658. אֶפֶס דַּמִּים {1x} **ʾEpheç Dammîym**, *eh'-fes dam-meem';* from 657 and the plur. of 1818; *boundary of blood-*drops; *Ephes-Dammim,* a place in Pal.:—Ephes-dammim {1x}. See: BDB—67c, 819d.

659. אֶפַע {1x} **ʾêphaʿ**, *eh'-fah;* from an unused root prob. mean. to *breathe;* prop. a *breath,* i.e. *nothing:*—of nought {1x}. See: TWOT—1791a; BDB—67c.

660. אֶפְעֶה {3x} **ʾephʿeh**, *ef-eh';* from 659 (in the sense of *hissing*); an *asp* or other venomous serpent:—viper {3x}. See: TWOT—1791b; BDB—67c, 821a.

661. אָפַף {5x} **ʾâphaph**, *aw-faf';* a prim. root; to *surround:*—compass {5x}. See: TWOT—148; BDB—67c.

662. אָפַק {7x} **ʾâphaq**, *aw-fak';* a prim. root; to *contain,* i.e. (reflex.) *abstain:*—refrain {5x}, forced {1x}, restrained {1x}. See: TWOT—149; BDB—67c.

663. אֲפֵק {9x} **ʾĂphêq**, *af-ake';* or

אֲפִיק **ʾĂphîyq**, *af-eek';* from 662 (in the sense of *strength*); *fortress; Aphek* (or *Aphik*), the name of three places in Pal.:—Aphek {8x}, Aphik {1x}. See: BDB—67d.

664. אֲפֵקָה {1x} **ʾĂphêqâh**, *af-ay-kaw';* fem. of 663; *fortress; Aphekah,* a place in Pal.:—Aphekah {1x}. See: BDB—68a.

665. אֵפֶר {22x} **ʾêpher**, *ay'-fer;* from an unused root mean. to *bestrew; ashes:*—ashes {22x}. Ref.: TWOT—150a; BDB—68a.

666. אֲפֵר {2x} **ʾăphêr**, *af-ayr';* from the same as 665 (in the sense of *covering*); a *turban:*—ashes {2x}. See: TWOT—151a; BDB—68b.

667. אֶפְרֹחַ {2x} **ʾephrôach**, *ef-ro'-akh;* from 6524 (in the sense of *bursting* the shell); the *brood* of a bird:—young one {2x}, young {2x}. See: TWOT—1813c; BDB—68b, 827b.

668. אַפִּרְיוֹן {1x} **ʾappiryôwn**, *ap-pir-yone';* prob. of Eg. der.; a *palanquin:*—chariot {1x}. See: TWOT—151b; BDB—68b.

669. אֶפְרַיִם {180x} **ʾEphrayim**, *ef-rah'-yim;* dual of a masc. form of 672; *double fruit; Ephrajim,* a son of Joseph; also the tribe descended from him, and its territory:—Ephraim {176x}, Ephraimites {4x}. See: BDB—68b.

670. אֲפָרְסַי {1x} **ʾĂphârçay** (Aram.), *af-aw-re-sah'ee;* of for. or. (only in the plur.); an *Apharesite* or inhab. of an unknown region of Assyria:—Apharsite {1x}. See: BDB—1082b.

671. אֲפַרְסְכַי {2x} **ʾĂpharçekay** (Aram.), *af-ar-sek-ah'ee;* or

אֲפַרְסַתְכַי **ʾĂpharçathkay** (Aram.), *af-ar-sath-kah'ee;* of for. or. (only in the plur.); an *Apharsekite* or *Apharsathkite,* an unknown Ass. tribe:—Apharsachites {2x}, Apharsathchites {1x}. See: BDB—1082b, 1082c.

672. אֶפְרָת {10x} **ʾEphrâth**, *ef-rawth';* or

אֶפְרָתָה **ʾEphrâthâh**, *ef-raw'-thaw;* from 6509; *fruitfulness; Ephrath,* another name for Bethlehem; once (Ps 132:6) perh. for *Ephraim;* also of an Isr. woman:—Ephrath {5x}, Ephratah {5x}. See: BDB—68c, 68d.

673. אֶפְרָתִי {5x} **ʾEphrâthîy**, *ef-rawth-ee';* patrial from 672; an *Ephrathite* or an *Ephraimite:*—Ephraimite {1x}, Ephrathite {4x}. See: BDB—68d.

674. אַפְּתֹם {1x} **ʾappethôm** (Aram.), *ap-pe-thome';* of Pers. or.; *revenue;* others *at the last:*—revenue {1x}. See: TWOT—2601; BDB—1082c.

675. אֶצְבּוֹן {2x} **ʾEtsbôwn**, *ets-bone';* or

אֶצְבֹּן **ʾEtsbôn**, *ets-bone';* of uncert. der.; *Etsbon,* the name of two Isr.:—Ezbon. {2x}. See: BDB—69a.

676. אֶצְבַּע {32x} **ʾetsbaʿ**, *ets-bah';* from the same as 6648 (in the sense of *rasping*); something to *seize* with, i.e. a *finger;* by anal. a *toe:*—finger {32x}. See: TWOT—1873a; BDB—69a, 840c, 1109c.

677. אֶצְבַּע {3x} **ʾetsbaʿ** (Aram.), *ets-bah';* corresp. to 676:—finger {1x}, toe {2x}. See: TWOT—2602; BDB—1082c, 1109c.

678. אָצִיל {2x} **ʾâtsîyl**, *aw-tseel';* from 680 (in its second. sense of *separation*); an *extremity* (Is 41:9), also a *noble:*—nobles {1x}, chief men {1x}. See: TWOT—153b; BDB—69c.

679. אַצִּיל {3x} **ʾatstsîyl**, *ats-tseel';* from 680 (in its primary sense of *uniting*); a *joint* of the hand (i.e. *knuckle*); also (according to some) a *party-wall* (Eze 41:8):—armhole + 3027 {2x}, great {1x}. See: TWOT—153c; BDB—69c.

680. אָצַל {5x} **ʾâtsal**, *aw-tsal';* a prim. root; prop. to *join;* used only as a denom. from 681; to *separate;* hence, to *select, refuse, contract:*—take {2x}, reserved {1x}, kept {1x}, straitened {1x}. See: TWOT—153; BDB—69b.

681. אֵצֶל {58x} **ʾêtsel**, *ay'-tsel;* from 680 (in the sense of *joining*); a *side;* (as a prep.) *near:*—by {21x}, beside {12x}, by . . . {10x}, near {3x}, at {2x}, with . . . {2x}, from . . . {1x}, against {1x}, close {1x}, to {1x}, toward {1x}, unto {1x}, with {1x}. Syn.: 905, 5921. See: TWOT—153a; BDB—69a.

682. אָצֵל {7x} **ʾÂtsêl**, *aw-tsale';* from 680; *noble; Atsel,* the name of an Isr., and of a place in Pal.:—Azal {1x}, Azel {6x}. See: BDB—69b, 69c.

683. אֲצַלְיָהוּ {2x} **ʾĂtsalyâhûw**, *ats-al-yaw'-hoo;* from 680 and 3050 prol.; *Jah has reserved; Atsaljah,* an Isr.:—Azaliah {2x}. See: BDB—69c.

684. אֹצֶם {2x} **ʾÔtsem**, *o'-tsem;* from an unused root prob. mean. to *be strong; strength* (i.e. *strong*); *Otsem,* the name of two Isr.:—Ozem {2x}. See: BDB—69d.

685. אֶצְעָדָה {2x} **ʾetsʿâdâh**, *ets-aw-daw';* a var. from 6807; prop. a *step-chain;* by anal. a *bracelet:*—bracelet {1x}, chain {1x}. See: TWOT—1943e; BDB—69d, 858a.

686. אָצַר {5x} **ʾâtsar**, *aw-tsar';* a prim. root; to *store* up:—lay up in store {2x}, store up {1x}, make treasurer {1x}, treasured {1x}. See: TWOT—154; BDB—69d.

687. אֶצֶר {5x} **ʾEtser**, *ay'-tser;* from 686; *treasure; Etser,* an Idumæan:—Ezer {5x}. See: BDB—69d.

688. אֶקְדָּח {1x} **ʾeqdâch**, *ek-dawkh';* from 6916; *burning,* i.e. a *carbuncle* or other fiery gem:—carbuncle {1x}. See: TWOT—1987b; BDB—70a, 869b.

689. אַקּוֹ {1x} **ʾaqqôw**, *ak-ko';* prob. from 602; *slender,* i.e. the *ibex:*—wild goat {1x}. See: TWOT—155; BDB—70a.

690. אֲרָא {1x} **ʾĂrâ**, *ar-aw';* prob. for 738; *lion; Ara,* an Isr.:—Ara {1x}. See: BDB—70b.

691. אֶרְאֵל {1x} **ʾerʾêl**, *er-ale';* prob. for 739; a *hero* (collect.):—valiant one {1x}. See: TWOT—159a; BDB—70b, 72a.

692. אַרְאֵלִי {3x} **ʾArʾêlîy**, *ar-ay-lee';* from 691; *heroic; Areli* (or an *Arelite,* collect.), an Isr. and his desc.:—Areli {2x}, Arelites {1x}. See: BDB—70b, 72a.

693. אָרַב {42x} **ʾârab**, *aw-rab';* a prim. root; to *lurk:*—lay in wait {26x}, liers in wait {8x}, ambush {8x}. See: TWOT—156; BDB—70b, 936d.

694. אֲרָב {1x} **ʾĂrâb**, *ar-awb';* from 693; *ambush; Arab,* a place in Pal.:—*Arab* {1x}. See: BDB—70c.

695. אֶרֶב {2x} **ʾereb**, *eh'-reb;* from 693; *ambuscade:*—den {1x}, lie in wait {1x}. See: TWOT—156a; BDB—70c.

696. אֹרֶב {1x} **ʾôreb**, *o'-reb;* the same as 695:—wait {1x}. See: TWOT—156b; BDB—70c.

אַרְבֵּאל **ʾArbêl**. See 1009.

697. אַרְבֶּה {24x} **ʾarbeh**, *ar-beh';* from 7235; a *locust* (from its rapid *increase*):—grasshopper {4x}, locust {20x}.

This noun, which occurs 24 times, refers to a kind of swarming "locust": "Stretch out thine hand over the land of Egypt for the locusts, that they may come up upon the land of Egypt, and eat every herb of the land . . ." (Ex 10:12). Syn.: 1462, 2284, 5556. See: TWOT—2103a; BDB—70d, 916a.

698. אָרֳבָה {1x} **ʾorŏbâh**, *or-ob-aw';* fem. of 696 (only in the plur.); *ambuscades:*—spoils {1x}. See: TWOT—156c; BDB—70c.

699. אֲרֻבָּה {9x} **ʾărubbâh**, *ar-oob-baw'*; fem. part. pass. of 693 (as if for *lurking*); a *lattice;* (by impl.) a *window, dove-cot* (because of the pigeon-holes), *chimney* (with its apertures for smoke), *sluice* (with openings for water):—chimney {1x}, windows {1x}. Syn.: 2474. See: TWOT—156d; BDB—70c.

700. אֲרֻבּוֹת {1x} **ʾĂrubbôwth**, *ar-oob-both'*; plur. of 699; *Arubboth*, a place in Pal.:—Aruboth {1x}. See: BDB—70d.

701. אַרְבִּי {1x} **ʾArbîy**, *ar-bee'*; patrial from 694; an *Arbite* or native of Arab:—Arbite {1x}. See: BDB—70c.

702. אַרְבַּע {316x} **ʾarbaʿ**, *ar-bah'*; masc.

אַרְבָּעָה **ʾarbâʿâh**, *ar-baw-aw'*; from 7251; *four:*—four {265x}, fourteen + 6240 {19x}, fourteenth + 6240 {23x}, fourth {5x}, forty {2x}, three score and fourteen + 7657 {2x}. See: TWOT—2106a; BDB—70d, 916d, 112c.

703. אַרְבַּע {8x} **ʾarbaʿ** (Aram.), *ar-bah'*; corresp. to 702:—four {8x}. See: TWOT—2986a; BDB—1082c, 1112c.

704. אַרְבַּע {2x} **ʾArbaʿ**, *ar-bah'*; the same as 702; *Arba,* one of the Anakim:—*Arba* {2x}. See: BDB—70d, 917b.

אַרְבָּעָה **ʾarbâʿâh**. See 702.

705. אַרְבָּעִים {136x} **ʾarbâʿîym**, *ar-baw-eem'*; multiple of 702; *forty:*—forty {132x}, fortieth {4x}. See: TWOT—2106b; BDB—70d, 917b.

706. אַרְבַּעְתַּיִם {1x} **ʾarbaʿtayim**, *ar-bah-tah'-yim;* dual of 702; *fourfold:*—fourfold {1x}. See: TWOT—2106a; BDB—916d.

707. אָרַג {13x} **ʾârag**, *aw-rag';* a prim. root; to *plait* or *weave:*—weave {4x}, weaver {6x}, woven {3x}. See: TWOT—157; BDB—70d.

708. אֶרֶג {2x} **ʾereg**, *eh'-reg;* from 707; a *weaving;* a *braid;* also a *shuttle:*—beam {1x}, weaver's shuttle {1x}. See: TWOT—157a; BDB—71a.

709. אַרְגֹּב {5x} **ʾArgôb**, *ar-gobe';* from the same as 7263; *stony; Argob,* a district of Pal.:—Argob {1x}. See: BDB—71a, 918d.

710. אַרְגְּוָן {1x} **ʾargᵉvân**, *arg-ev-awn';* a var. for 713; *purple:*—purple {1x}. See: TWOT—157b; BDB—71a, 1082c.

711. אַרְגְּוָן {3x} **ʾargᵉvân** (Aram.), *arg-ev-awn';* corresp. to 710:—scarlet {3x}. *Argevan* is possibly a deep reddish-purple. See: TWOT—2603; BDB—1082c.

712. אַרְגָּז {3x} **ʾargâz**, *ar-gawz';* perh. from 7264 (in the sense of being *suspended*); a *box* (as a pannier):—coffer {3x}. See: TWOT—2112d; BDB—71a, 919c.

713. אַרְגָּמָן {38x} **ʾargâmân**, *ar-gaw-mawn';* of for. or.; *purple* (the color or the dyed stuff):—purple {38x}. See: TWOT—157b; BDB—71a, 1082c.

714. אַרְדְּ {2x} **ʾArd**, *ard;* from an unused root prob. mean. to *wander; fugitive; Ard,* the name of two Isr.:—*Ard* {2x}. See: BDB—71b.

715. אַרְדּוֹן {1x} **ʾArdôwn**, *ar-dohn';* from the same as 714; *roaming; Ardon,* an Isr.:—Ardon {1x}. See: BDB—71b.

716. אַרְדִּי {1x} **ʾArdîy**, *ar-dee;* patron. from 714; an *Ardite* (collect.) or desc. of Ard:—Ardites {1x}. See: BDB—71b.

717. אָרָה {2x} **ʾârâh**, *aw-raw';* a prim. root; to *pluck:*—gather {1x}, pluck {1x}. See: TWOT—158; BDB—71c, 1082c.

718. אֲרוּ {5x} **ʾărûw** (Aram.), *ar-oo';* prob. akin to 431; *lo!:*—behold {4x}, lo {1x}. See: TWOT—2604; BDB—1080d, 1082c.

719. אַרְוַד {2x} **ʾArvad**, *ar-vad';* prob. from 7300; a refuge for the *roving; Arvad,* an island-city of Pal.:—*Arvad* {2x}. See: BDB—71c.

720. אֲרוֹד {1x} **ʾĂrôwd**, *ar-ode';* an orth. var. of 719; *fugitive; Arod,* an Isr.:—Arod {1x}. See: BDB—71b.

721. אַרְוָדִי {2x} **ʾArvâdîy**, *ar-vaw-dee';* patrial from 719; an *Arvadite* or citizen of Arvad:—Arvadite {2x}. See: BDB—71c.

722. אֲרוֹדִי {2x} **ʾĂrôwdîy**, *ar-o-dee';* patron. from 721; an *Arodite* or desc. of Arod:—Arodi {1x}, Arodites {1x}. See: BDB—71b.

723. אֻרְוָה {3x} **ʾurvâh**, *oor-vaw';* or

אֲרָיָה **ʾărâyâh**, *ar-aw-yah';* from 717 (in the sense of *feeding*); a *herding-place* for an animal:—stall {3x}. See: TWOT—158b; BDB—71d.

724. אֲרוּכָה {6x} **ʾărûwkâh**, *ar-oo-kaw';* or

אֲרֻכָה **ʾărûkâh**, *ar-oo-kaw';* fem. pass. part. of 748 (in the sense of *restoring* to soundness); *wholeness* (lit. or fig.):—health {4x}, perfected {1x}, made up {1x}. See: TWOT—162d; BDB—74a.

725. אֲרוּמָה {1x} **ʾĂrûwmâh**, *ar-oo-maw';* a var. of 7316; *height; Arumah,* a place in Pal.:—Arumah {1x}. See: BDB—72b.

726. אֲרוֹמִי {1x} **ʾĂrôwmîy**, *ar-o-mee';* a clerical err. for 130; an *Edomite* (as in the marg.):—Syrian {1x}. See: BDB—10c.

727. אָרוֹן {202x} **ʾârôwn**, *aw-rone';* or

אָרֹן **ʾârôn**, *aw-rone';* from 717 (in the sense of *gathering*); a *box:*—ark {195x}, chest {6x}, coffin {1x}.

Aron (727)means "ark; coffin; chest; box." **(1)** In Gen 50:26, this word represents a coffin or sarcophagus. "So Joseph died, being a hundred and ten years old: and they embalmed him, and he was put in a coffin in Egypt." This coffin was probably quite elaborate and similar to those found in ancient Egyptian tombs. **(2)** During the reign of Joash (or Jehoash), when the temple was repaired, money for the work was deposited in a "chest" with a hole in its lid. The high priest Jehoida prepared this chest and put it at the threshold to the temple (2 Kin 12:9). **(3)** In most occurrences, *aron* refers to the "ark of the covenant." **(3a)** This piece of furniture functioned primarily as a container. **(3b)** As such the word is often modified by divine names or attributes. **(3b1)** The divine name first modifies *aron* in 1 Sa 3:3: "And ere the lamp of God went out in the temple of the LORD, where the ark of God was, and Samuel was laid down to sleep. . . ." **(3b2)** *Aron* is first modified by God's covenant name, Yahweh, in Josh 4:5. **(3b3)** Judg 20:27 is the first appearance of the "ark" as the ark of the covenant of Elohim. **(3b4)** First Samuel 5:11 uses the phrase "the ark of the God [elohim] of Israel," and 1 Chr 15:12 employs "the ark of the LORD [Yahweh] God [elohim] of Israel."

(4) Sometimes divine attributes replace the divine name: "Arise, O LORD, into thy rest; thou, and the ark of thy strength" (Ps 132:8). **(5)** Another group of modifiers focuses on divine redemption (cf. Heb. 8:5). Thus *aron* is often described as the "ark of the covenant" (Josh 3:6) or "the ark of the covenant of the LORD" (Num 10:33). **(6)** As such, the ark contained the memorials of God's great redemptive acts—the tablets upon which were inscribed the Ten Commandments, an omer or two quarts of manna, and Aaron's rod. **(7)** By Solomon's day, only the stone tablets remained in the ark (1 Kin 8:9). This chest was also called "the ark of the testimony" (Ex 25:22), which indicates that the two tablets were evidence of divine redemption. **(8)** Ex 25:10–22 tells us that this ark was made of acacia wood and measured 3¾ feet by 2¼ feet by 2¼ feet. It was gold-plated inside and outside, with a molding of gold. Each of its four feet had a golden ring at its top, through which passed unremovable golden carrying poles. The golden cover or mercy seat (place of propitiatory atonement) had the same dimensions as the top of the ark. Two golden cherubim sat on this cover facing each other, representing the heavenly majesty (Eze 1:10) that surrounds the living God.

(9) In addition to containing memorials of divine redemption, the ark represented the presence of God. To be before it was to be in God's presence (Num 10:35), although His presence was not limited to the ark (cf. 1 Sa 4:3–11; 7:2, 6). The ark ceased to have this sacramental function when Israel began to regard it as a magical box with sacred power (a palladium). **(10)** God promised to meet Moses at the ark (Ex 25:22). Thus, the ark functioned as a place where divine revelation was received (Lev 1:1; 16:2; Num 7:89). **(11)** The ark served as an instrument through which God guided and defended Israel during the wilderness wandering (Num 10:11). **(12)** Finally, it was upon this ark that the highest of Israel's sacraments, the blood of atonement, was presented and received (Lev 16:2ff.). See: TWOT—166a; BDB—75b.

728. אֲרַוְנָה {9x} **ʾĂravnâh**, *ar-av-naw';* or (by transp.)

אוֹרְנָה **ʾÔwrnâh**, *ore-naw';* or

אַרְנִיָּה **ʾArnîyah**, *ar-nee-yaw';* all by orth. var. for 771; *Aravnah* (or *Arnijah* or *Ornah*), a Jebusite:—Araunah {9x}. See: BDB—22d, 72b, 75d.

729. אָרַז {1x} **ʾâraz**, *aw-raz';* a prim. root; to *be firm;* used only in the pass. part. as a denom. from 730; of *cedar:*—made of cedar {1x}. See: TWOT—160c; BDB—72c, 72d.

730. אֶרֶז {73x} **ʾerez**, *eh-rez';* from 729; a *cedar* tree (from the tenacity of its roots):—cedar {67x}, cedar tree {6x}. See: TWOT—160a; BDB—72c.

731. אַרְזָה {1x} **ʾarzâh**, *ar-zaw';* fem. of 730; *cedar paneling:*—cedar work {1x}. See: TWOT—160b; BDB—72d.

732. אָרַח {5x} **ʾârach**, *aw-rakh';* a prim. root; to *travel:*—wayfaring man {4x}, goeth {1x}. See: TWOT—161; BDB—72d.

733. אָרַח {4x} **ʾÂrach**, *aw-rakh';* from 732; *wayfaring; Arach,* the name of three Isr.:—Arah {4x}. See: BDB—73b.

734. אֹרַח {58x} **ʾôrach**, *o'-rakh;* from 732; a well-trodden *road* (lit. or fig.); also a *caravan:*—way {26x}, path {25x}, highway {1x}, wayfaring man + 5674 08802 {1x}, manner {1x}, race {1x}, ranks {1x}, traveller {1x}, troops {1x}.

Orach means "way; path; course; conduct; manner." In meaning this word parallels Hebrew derek (1870), which it often synonymously parallels. **(1)** *Orach* means "path" or "way" conceived as a marked-out, well-traveled course: "Dan shall be a serpent by the way, an adder in the path, that biteth the horse heels . . ." (Gen 49:17). **(2)** In Judg 5:6 the word means "highway": "In the days of Shamgar . . . the highways were unoccupied, and the travelers walked through byways." **(3)** When the sun is likened to a "strong man" who rejoices "to run a race" (Ps 19:5), *orach* represents a race course rather than a highway or a primitive, snake-laden path.

(4) The man who makes his path straight goes directly on his journey, not turning aside for the beckoning harlot (Prov 9:15). So here the word represents the "course" one follows between his departure and arrival conceived in terms of small units, almost step by step. **(5)** In Ps. 8:8 the word represents the ocean currents: ". . . The fowl of the air and the fish of the sea, and whatsoever passeth through the paths of the seas." **(6)** *Orach* signifies the ground itself as the path upon which one treads: "He pursued them, and passed safely; even by the way that he had not gone with his feet" (Is 41:3). **(7)** In Job 30:12 the word seems to represent an obstruction or dam: ". . . They push away my feet, and they raise up against me the ways of their destruction."

(8) The word can refer to a recurring life event typical of an individual or a group. **(8a)** In its first biblical occurrence (Gen 18:11) it is used of "the manner of women" (menstruation). **(8b)** Job 16:22 mentions the "way whence I shall not return," or death, **(8c)** while other passages speak of life actions (Job 34:11; literally, "conduct") or life-style (Prov. 15:10: "Correction is grievous unto him that forsaketh the way . . ."—prescribed life-style; Prov. 5:6: "Lest thou shouldest ponder the path [which is typified by] life . . ."). **(8d)** Thus, *orach* sometimes figures a proper course of action or proceeding within a given realm—"the path of judgment" (Is 40:14). **(9)** The noun orchah, which occurs 3 times, represents a "wandering company" or a "caravan" (Gen 37:25). Syn.: 1870, 5410. See: TWOT—161a; BDB—73a.

735. אֹרַח {2x} **ʾôrach** (Aram.), *o'-rakh;* corresp. to 734; a *road:*—way {2x}. See: TWOT—2605; BDB—1082d.

736. אֹרְחָה {2x} **ʾôrᵉchâh**, *o-rekh-aw';* fem. act. part. of 732; a *caravan:*—(travelling) company {2x}. See: TWOT—161c; BDB—73c.

737. אֲרֻחָה {6x} **ʾărûchâh**, *ar-oo-khaw';* fem. pass. part. of 732 (in the sense of *appointing*); a *ration* of food:—allowance {2x}, diet {2x}, dinner {1x}, victuals {1x}. See: TWOT—161b; BDB—73c.

738. אֲרִי {80x} **ʾărîy**, *ar-ee';* or (prol.)

אַרְיֵה **ʾaryêh**, *ar-yay';* from 717 (in the sense of *violence*); a *lion:*—lion {79x}, untranslated variant {1x}. "lion." **(1)** The word represents a "full-grown lion." **(2)** This word should be compared to: **(2a)** *gur* (1482- Gen 49:9), a suckling lion; **(2b)** *shachal* (7826- Hos 5:14), a young lion which no longer is a suckling; and **(2c)** *kepir* (3715- Judg 14:5), a young lion which no longer is a suckling and which hunts for its food independently. **(3)** The "lion" was a much-feared beast (Amos 3:12) found mostly in the Trans-jordan (Jer 49:19) and in the mountainous areas (Song 4:8). **(4)** The various characteristics of the "lion" make it a frequent figure **(4a)** of strength and power (Judg 14:18), **(4b)** of plundering (Gen 49:9), and **(4c)** of malicious scheming (Ps 10:9). Syn.: 738, 744, 3715, 3833, 3918. See: TWOT—158a; BDB—71c, 1082c.

739. אֲרִיאֵל {2x} **ʾărîyʾêl**, *ar-ee-ale';* or

אֲרִאֵל **ʾărîʾêl**, *ar-ee-ale';* from 738 and 410; *lion of God,* i.e. *heroic:*—lionlike men {2x}. See: TWOT—159a; BDB—72a.

740. אֲרִאֵל {6x} **ʾĂrîʾêl**, *ar-ee-ale';* the same as 739; *Ariel,* a symb. name for Jerusalem, also the name of an Isr.:—*Ariel* {6x}. See: BDB—72a, 73c.

741. אֲרִאֵיל {3x} **ʾărîʾêyl**, *ar-ee-ale';* either by transp. for 739 or, more prob. an orth. var. for 2025; the *altar* of the Temple:—altar {3x}. See: TWOT—159a; BDB—72a, 72b, 73c.

742. אֲרִידַי {1x} **ʾĂrîyday**, *ar-ee-dah'-ee;* of Pers. or.; *Aridai,* a son of Haman:—Aridai {1x}. See: BDB—71c.

743. אֲרִידָתָא {1x} **ʾĂrîydâthâʾ**, *ar-ee-daw-thaw';* of Pers. or.; *Aridatha,* a son of Haman:—Aridatha {1x}. See: BDB—71c.

744. אַרְיֵה {10x} **ʾaryêh** (Aram.), *ar-yay';* corresp. to 738:—lion {10x}. See: TWOT—2606; BDB—71d, 1082c, 1082d.

745. אַרְיֵה {1x} **ʾAryêh**, *ar-yay';* the same as 738; *lion; Arjeh,* an Isr.:—Arieh {1x}. See: BDB—72a.

אֲרָיָה **ʾărâyâh**. See 723.

746. אֲרְיוֹךְ {7x} **ʾĂryôwk**, *ar-yoke';* of for. or.; *Arjok,* the name of two Babylonians:—Arioch {7x}. See: BDB—73c.

747. אֲרִיסַי {1x} **ʾĂriyçay**, *ar-ee-sah'-ee;* of Pers. or.; *Arisai,* a son of Haman:—Arisai {1x}. See: BDB—1121a.

748. אָרַךְ {34x} **ʾârak**, *aw-rak';* a prim. root; to *be* (caus. *make*) *long* (lit. or fig.):—prolong {18x}, long {5x}, lengthen {3x}, draw out {3x}, defer {2x}, tarried {1x}, . . . lived + 3117 0310 {2x}. See: TWOT—162; BDB—73c, 1082d.

749. אֲרַךְ {1x} **ʾărak** (Aram.), *ar-ak';* prop. corresp. to 748, but used only in the sense of *reaching* to a given point; to *suit:*—be meet {1x}. See: TWOT—2607; BDB—1082d.

750. אָרֵךְ {15x} **ʾârêk**, *aw-rake';* from 748; *long:*—slow {9x}, longsuffering + 639 {4x}, longwinged + 83 {1x}, patient {1x}. See: TWOT—162b; BDB—74a, 1082d.

751. אֶרֶךְ {1x} **ʾErek**, *eh'-rek;* from 748; *length; Erek,* a place in Bab.:—Erech {1x}. See: BDB—74b, 1083a.

752. אָרֹךְ {3x} **ʾârôk**, *aw-roke';* from 748; *long:*—long {2x}, longer {1x}. See: TWOT—162c; BDB—74a.

753. אֹרֶךְ {95x} **ʾôrek**, *o'rek';* from 748; *length:*—length {70x}, long {21x}, ever {2x}, as long as {1x}, high {1x}. *Orek* refers to length without limits. See: TWOT—162a; BDB—73d.

754. אַרְכָּא {1x} **ʾarkâʾ** (Aram.), *ar-kaw';* or

אַרְכָּה **ʾarkâh** (Aram.), *ar-kaw';* from 749; *length:*—prolonged {1x}. See: TWOT—2609; BDB—1082d.

755. אַרְכֻבָה {1x} **ʾarkûbâh** (Aram.), *ar-koo-baw';* from an unused root corresp. to 7392 (in the sense of *bending* the knee); the *knee:*—knees {1x}. See: TWOT—2608; BDB—1083a, 1085c.

אֲרֻכָה **ʾărûkâh**. See 724.

756. אַרְכְּוָי {1x} **ʾArkᵉvay** (Aram.), *ar-kev-ah'ee;* patrial from 751; an *Arkevite* (collect.) or native of Erek:—Archevites {1x}. See: BDB—1083a.

757. אַרְכִּי {6x} **ʾArkîy**, *ar-kee';* patrial from another place (in Pal.) of similar name with 751; an *Arkite* or native of Erek:—Archi {1x}, Archite {5x}. See: BDB—74b.

758. אֲרָם {132x} **ʾArâm**, *arawm';* from the same as 759; the *highland; Aram* or Syria, and its inhab.; also the name of a son of Shem, a grandson of Nahor, and of an Isr.:—Syria {67x}, Syrians {56x}, *Aram* {7x}, Syriadamascus + 4601 {1x}, Syriamaachah + 4601 {1x}. See: TWOT—163; BDB—74b, 591a.

759. אַרְמוֹן {32x} **ʾarmôwn**, *ar-mone';* from an unused root (mean. to *be elevated*); a *citadel* (from its *height*):—castle {1x}, palace {31x}. Syn.: 1002, 1003, 2038, 2918. See: TWOT—164a; BDB—74d.

760. אֲרַם צוֹבָה {1x} **ʾĂram Tsôwbâh**, *ar-am' tso-baw';* from 758 and 6678; *Aram of Tsoba* (or Cœle-Syria):—Aram-zobah {1x}. See: BDB—74b.

761. אֲרַמִּי {1x} **ʾĂrammîy**, *ar-am-mee';* patrial from 758; an *Aramite* or Aramæan:—Syrian {10x}, Aramitess {1x}. See: BDB—74c, 248c, 942b.

762. אֲרָמִית {5x} **ʾĂrâmîyth**, *ar-aw-meeth';* fem. of 761; (only adv.) *in Aramæan:*—Syrian language {2x}, Syrian tongue {2x}, Syriack {1x}. See: BDB—74c.

763. אֲרַם נַהֲרַיִם {6x} **ʾĂram Nahărayim**, *ar-am' nah-har-ah'-yim;* from 758 and the dual of 5104; *Aram of* (the) *two rivers* (Euphrates and Tigris) or Mesopotamia:—Aham-naharaim {1x}, Mesopotamia {6x}. See: BDB—74b, 74c.

764. אַרְמֹנִי {1x} **ʾArmônîy**, *ar-mo-nee';* from 759; *palatial; Armoni,* an Isr.:—Armoni {1x}. See: BDB—74d.

765. אֲרָן {2x} **ʾĂrân**, *ar-awn';* from 7442; *stridulous; Aran,* an Edomite:—*Aran* {2x}. See: BDB—75a.

766. אֹרֶן {1x} **ʾoren**, *o'-ren;* from the same as 765 (in the sense of *strength*); the *ash* tree (from its toughness):—ash {1x}. See: TWOT—165a; BDB—75a.

767. אֹרֶן {1x} **ʾÔren**, *o'-ren;* the same as 766; *Oren,* an Isr.:—*Oren* {1x}. See: BDB—75a.

אָרֹן **ʾârôn**. See 727.

768. אַרְנֶבֶת {2x} **ʾarnebeth**, *ar-neh'-beth;* of uncert. der.; the *hare:*—hare {2x}. See: TWOT—123a; BDB—58a, 75c.

769. אַרְנוֹן {25x} **ʾArnôwn**, *ar-nohn';* or

אַרְנֹן **ʾArnôn**, *ar-nohn';* from 7442; a *brawling* stream; the *Arnon,* a river east of the Jordan; also its territory:—*Arnon* {25x}. See: BDB—75a.

770. אַרְנָן {1x} **ʾArnân**, *ar-nawn';* prob. from the same as 769; *noisy; Arnan,* an Isr.:—*Arnan* {1x}. See: BDB—75a.

771. אָרְנָן {12x} **ʾOrnân**, *or-nawn';* prob. from 766; *strong; Ornan,* a Jebusite:—*Ornan* {12x}. Syn.: See 728. See: BDB—75a.

772. אֲרַע {21x} **ʾăraʿ** (Aram.), *ar-ah';* corresp. to 776; the *earth;* by impl. (fig.) *low:*—earth {20x}, interior {1x}. See: TWOT—2610; BDB—1083a.

773. אַרְעִית {1x} **ʾarʿîyth** (Aram.), *arh-eeth'*; fem. of 772; the *bottom:*—bottom {1x}. See: TWOT—2611; BDB—1083a.

774. אַרְפָּד {6x} **ʾArpâd**, *ar-pawd'*; from 7502; *spread* out; *Arpad*, a place in Syria:—*Arpad* {4x}, Arphad {2x}. See: BDB—75d, 951c.

775. אַרְפַּכְשַׁד {9x} **ʾArpakshad**, *ar-pak-shad'*; prob. of for. or.; *Arpakshad*, a son of Noah; also the region settled by him:—Arphaxad {9x}. See: BDB—75d.

776. אֶרֶץ {2504x} **ʾerets**, *eh'-rets;* from an unused root prob. mean. to *be firm;* the *earth* (at large, or partitively a *land*):—land {1543x}, earth {712x}, country {140x}, ground {98x}, world {4x}, way {3x}, common {1x}, field {1x}, nations {1x}, wilderness + 4057 {1x}.

Erets (776) means "earth; land." **(1)** *Erets* may be translated "earth," the temporal scene of human activity, experience, and history. **(2)** The material world had a beginning when God "made the earth by His power," "formed it," and "spread it out" (Is 40:28; 42:5; 45:12, 18; Jer 27:5; 51:15). **(2a)** Because He did so, it follows that "the earth is the LORD's" (Ps 24:1; Deut 10:1; Ex 9:29; Neh 9:6). **(2b)** No part of it is independent of Him, for "the very ends of the earth are His possession," including "the mountains," "the seas," "the dry land," "the depths of the earth" (Ps 2:8; 95:4–5; Amos 4:13; Jonah 1:9). **(2c)** God formed the earth to be inhabited (Is 45:18). **(2d)** Having "authority over the earth" by virtue of being its Maker, He decreed to "let the earth sprout vegetation: of every kind" (Job 34:13; Gen 1:11). **(2e)** It was never to stop its productivity, for "while the earth stands, seedtime and harvest, and cold and heat, and summer and winter, and day and night shall not cease" (Gen 8:22). "The earth is full of God's riches" and mankind can "multiply and fill the earth and subdue it" (Ps 104:24; Gen 1:28; 9:1). **(2f)** Let no one think that the earth is an independent, self-contained mechanism, for "the LORD reigns" as He "sits on the vault of the earth" from where "He sends rain on the earth" (Ps 97:1; Is 40:22; 1 Kin 17:14; Ps 104:4).

(3) As "the eyes of the LORD run to and fro throughout the earth," He sees that "there is not a just man on earth" (Eccl 7:20). At an early stage, God endeavored to "blot out man . . . from the face of the earth" (Gen 6:5–7). **(3a)** Though He relented and promised to "destroy never again all flesh on the earth," we can be sure that "He is coming to judge the earth" (Gen 7:16f.; Ps 96:13). **(3b)** At that time, "the earth shall be completely laid waste" so that "the exalted people of the earth fade away" (Jer 10:10; Joel 2:10; Is 33:3–6; Ps 75:8). **(3c)** But He also provides a way of escape for all who heed His promise: "Turn to me and be saved, all the ends of the earth" (Is 45:22). **(4)** What the Creator formed "in the beginning" is also to have an end, for He will "create a new heaven and a new earth" (Is 65:17; 66:22). **(5)** The Hebrew word *erets* also occurs frequently in the phrase "heaven and earth" or "earth and heaven." **(5a)** In other words, the Scriptures teach that our terrestrial planet is a part of an all-embracing cosmological framework which we call the universe. **(5b)** Not the result of accident or innate forces, the unfathomed reaches of space and its uncounted components owe their origin to the LORD "who made heaven and earth" (Ps 121:2; 124:8; 134:3).

(6) Because God is "the possessor of heaven and earth," the whole universe is to reverberate in the praise of His glory, which is "above heaven and earth" (Gen 14:19, 22; Ps 148:13). "Shout, O heavens and rejoice, O earth": "let the heavens be glad and let the earth rejoice" (Ps 49:13; 96:11). Such adoration is always appropriate, for "whatever the LORD pleases, He does in heaven and in earth, in the seas and in all deeps" (Ps 135:6). **(7)** *Erets* does not only denote the entire terrestrial planet, but is also used of some of the earth's component parts. English words like land, country, ground, and soil transfer its meaning into our language. **(7a)** Quite frequently, it refers to an area occupied by a nation or tribe. So we read of "the land of Egypt," "the land of the Philistines," "the land of Israel," "the land of Benjamin," and so on (Gen 47:13; Zec 2:5; 2 Kin 5:2, 4; Judg 21:21). **(7b)** Israel is said to live "in the land of the LORD" (Lev 25:33f.; Hos 9:13). When the people arrived at its border, Moses reminded them that it would be theirs only because the LORD drove out the other nations to "give you their land for an inheritance" (Deut 4:38). **(7c)** Moses promised that God would make its soil productive, for "He will give rain for your land" so that it would be "a fruitful land," "a land flowing with milk and honey, a land of wheat and barley" (Deut 11:13–15; 8:7–9; Jer 2:7). **(8)** The Hebrew noun may also be translated "the ground" (Job 2:13; Amos 3:5; Gen 24:52; Eze 43:14). Syn.: 127, 1471. See: TWOT—167; BDB—75d, 1083a.

777. אַרְצָא {1x} **ʾartsâʾ**, *ar-tsaw';* from 776; *earthiness; Artsa*, an Isr.:—Arza {1x}. See: BDB—76c.

778. אֲרַק {1x} **ʾăraq** (Aram.), *ar-ak';* by transm. for 772; the *earth:*—earth {1x}. See: TWOT—2612; BDB—1083a.

779. אָרַר {63x} **ʾârar**, *aw-rar';* a prim. root; to *execrate:*—curse {62x}, bitterly {1x}.

Arar (779) means "to curse." **(1)** The first occurrence is in Gen 3:14: "Thou [the serpent] art cursed above all cattle," and Gen 3:17: "Cursed is the ground for thy [Adam's] sake." **(2)** This form accounts for more than half of the occurrences. It is a pronouncement of judgment on those who break covenant, as: "Cursed is the man who . . ." (twelve times in Deut 27:15–26). **(3)** "Curse" is usually parallel with "bless." The two "curses" in Gen 3 are in bold contrast to the two blessings ("And God blessed them . . .") in Gen 1. **(4)** The covenant with Abraham includes: "I will bless them that bless thee, and curse [different root] him that curseth thee . . ." (Gen 12:3). **(5)** Compare Jeremiah's "Cursed be the man that trusteth in man" and "Blessed is the man that trusteth in the LORD" (17:5, 7). **(6)** Pagans used the power of "cursing" to deal with their enemies, as when Balak sent for Balaam: "Come . . . , curse me this people" (Num 22:6). Israel had the ceremonial "water that causeth the curse" (Num 5:18ff.).

(7) God alone truly "curses." It is a revelation of His justice, in support of His claim to absolute obedience. Men may claim God's "curses" by committing their grievances to God and trusting in His righteous judgment (cf. Ps 109:26–31). **(8)** "Curse" in the Old Testament is summed up in the statement: "Cursed be the man that obeyeth not the words of this covenant . . ." (Jer 11:3). **(9)** The New Testament responds: "Christ hath redeemed us from the curse of the law, being made a curse for us: for it is written, Cursed is every one that hangeth on a tree . . ." (Gal 3:13). Syn.: 423, 6895, 7045. See: TWOT—168; BDB—76c.

780. אֲרָרָט {4x} **ʾĂrârat**, *ar-aw-rat';* of for. or.; *Ararat* (or rather Armenia):—*Ararat* {2x}, Armenia {2x}. See: BDB—76d.

781. אָרַשׂ {11x} **ʾâras**, *aw-ras';* a prim. root; to *engage* for matrimony:—betroth {10x}, espouse {1x}. See: TWOT—170; BDB—76d.

782. אֲרֶשֶׁת {1x} **ʾăresheth**, *ar-eh'-sheth;* from 781 (in the sense of *desiring* to possess); a *longing* for:—request {1x}. See: TWOT—171a; BDB—77a.

783. אַרְתַּחְשַׁשְׂתָּא {15x} **ʾArtachshastâʾ** (Aram.), *ar-takh-shas-taw';* or

אַרְתַּחְשַׁשְׁתְּא **ʾArtachshastʾ** (Aram.), *ar-takh-shast';* or by perm.

אַרְתַּחְשַׁסְתְּא **ʾArtachshaçtʾ** (Aram.), *ar-takh-shast';* of for. or.; *Artachshasta* (or Artaxerxes), a title (rather than name) of several Pers. kings:—Artaxerxes {15x}. See: BDB—77a, 1083a.

784. אֵשׁ {379x} **ʾêsh**, *aysh;* a prim. word; *fire* (lit. or fig.):—fire {373x}, burning {1x}, fiery {1x}, untranslated variant {1x}, fire + 800 {1x}, flaming {1x}, hot {1x}.

Esh (784) means "fire." **(1)** In its first biblical appearance this word, *esh* represents God's presence as "a torch of fire": "And it came to pass, that, when the sun went down, and it was dark, behold a smoking furnace, and a [flaming torch] . . ." (Gen 15:17). **(2)** "Fire" was the instrument by which an offering was transformed into smoke, whose ascending heavenward symbolized God's reception of the offering (Lev 9:24). **(3)** God also consumed people with the "fire of judgment" (Num 11:1; Ps 89:46). **(4)** Various things were to be burnt as a sign of total destruction and divine judgment (Ex 32:20). **(5)** "Fire" often attended God's presence in theophanies (Ex 3:2). **(6)** Thus He is sometimes called a "consuming fire" (Ex 24:17). See: TWOT—172; BDB—77b, 1083b.

785. אֵשׁ {1x} **ʾêsh** (Aram.), *aysh;* corresp. to 784:—flame {1x}. See: TWOT—2614; BDB—1083b.

786. אִשׁ {2x} **ʾîsh**, *eesh;* ident. (in or. and formation) with 784; *entity;* used only adv., there *is* or *are:*—can {1x}, there {1x}. See: TWOT—173; BDB—78a.

787. אֹשׁ {3x} **ʾôsh** (Aram.), *ohsh;* corresp. (by transp. and abb.) to 803; a *foundation:*—foundation {3x}. See: TWOT—2613; BDB—1083b.

788. אַשְׁבֵּל {3x} **ʾAshbêl**, *ash-bale';* prob. from the same as 7640; *flowing; Ashbel*, an Isr.:—*Ashbel* {3x}. See: BDB—78a.

789. אַשְׁבֵּלִי {1x} **ʾAshbêlîy**, *ash-bay-lee';* patron. from 788; an *Ashbelite* (collect.) or desc. of Ashbel:—Ashbelites {1x}. See: BDB—78a.

790. אֶשְׁבָּן {1x} **ʾEshbân**, *esh-bawn';* prob. from the same as 7644; *vigorous; Eshban*, an Idumæan:—*Eshban* {1x}. See: BDB—78b.

791. אַשְׁבֵּעַ {1x} **ʾAshbêaʿ**, *ash-bay'-ah;* from 7650; *adjurer; Asbeä*, an Isr.:—*Ashbea* {1x}. See: BDB—78b.

792. אֶשְׁבַּעַל {2x} **ʾEshbaʿal**, *esh-bah'-al;* from 376 and 1168; *man of Baal; Eshbaal* (or Ishbosheth), a son of King Saul:—*Eshbaal* {2x}. See: BDB—36b, 78b.

793. אֶשֶׁד {1x} **ʾeshed**, *eh'-shed;* from an unused root mean. to *pour;* an *outpouring:*—stream {1x}. Syn.: 5104. See: TWOT—174a; BDB—78b.

794. אֲשֵׁדָה {6x} **ʾăshêdâh**, *ash-ay-daw';* fem. of 793; a *ravine:*—springs {3x}, variant {3x}. See: TWOT—174b; BDB—78b.

795. אַשְׁדּוֹד {17x} **ʾAshdôwd**, *ash-dode';* from 7703; *ravager; Ashdod,* a place in Pal.:—Ashdod {17x}. See: BDB—78b, 994c.

796. אַשְׁדּוֹדִי {5x} **ʾAshdôwdîy**, *ash-do-dee';* patrial from 795; an *Ashdodite* (often collect.) or inhab. of Ashdod:—Ashdodites {2x}, of Ashdod {3x}. See: BDB—78c.

797. אַשְׁדּוֹדִית {1x} **ʾAshdôwdîyth**, *ash-do-deeth';* fem. of 796; (only adv.) *in the language of Ashdod:*—in the speech of Ashdod {1x}. See: BDB—78c.

798. אַשְׁדּוֹת הַפִּסְגָּה {3x} **ʾAshdôwth hap-Piçgâh**, *ash-doth' hap-pis-gaw';* from the plur. of 794 and 6449 with the art. interposed; *ravines of the Pisgah; Ashdoth-Pisgah,* a place east of the Jordan:—Ashdoth-pisgah {3x}. See: BDB—820a.

799. אֶשְׁדָּת {1x} **ʾeshdâth**, *esh-dawth';* from 784 and 1881; a *fire-law:*—fiery {1x}. See: TWOT—174b; BDB—77d.

800. אֶשָּׁה {1x} **ʾeshshâh**, *esh-shaw';* fem. of 784; *fire:*—fire {1x}. See: TWOT—172; BDB—77d.

801. אִשֶּׁה {65x} **ʾishshâh**, *ish-shaw';* the same as 800, but used in a liturgical sense; prop. a *burnt-offering;* but occasionally of any *sacrifice:*—(offering, sacrifice), (made) by fire {65x}.

Ishshah means "fire offering." **(1)** Sixty-three of the 65 appearances of this word occur in the sacramental prescriptions of Exodus-Deuteronomy. The other two occurrences (Josh 13:14; 1 Sa 2:28) bear the same meaning and sacramental context. **(2)** All legitimate sacrifices had to be presented before God at His altar, and all of them involved burning to some degree. Thus they may all be called fire offerings (Ex 29:18). **(3)** The word *ishshah* first occurs in Ex 29:18: "And thou shalt burn the whole ram upon the altar: it is a burnt offering unto the LORD: it is a sweet savor, an offering made by fire unto the LORD." Syn.: 817, 4503, 5927, 5930, 7133, 8641. See: TWOT—172a; BDB—77d.

802. אִשָּׁה {780x} **ʾishshâh**, *ish-shaw';* fem. of 376 or 582; irreg. plur.

נָשִׁים **nâshîym**, *naw-sheem';* a *woman* (used in the same wide sense as 582) [*Often unexpressed in English.*]:—wife {425x}, woman {324x}, one {10x}, married {5x}, female {2x}, misc.: [adulter]ess, each, every, × many, + none, + together = {14x}.

Ishshah (802) means "woman; wife; betrothed one; bride; each." **(1)** This noun connotes one who is a female human being regardless of her age or virginity. **(1a)** Therefore, it appears in correlation to "man" (376 - ish): ". . . She shall be called Woman, because she was taken out of Man" (Gen 2:23). **(1b)** This is its meaning in its first biblical usage: "And the rib, which the LORD God had taken from man [120 - adam], made he a woman, and brought her unto the man" (Gen 2:22). **(1c)** The stress here is on identification of womanhood rather than a family role. **(2)** The stress on the family role of a "wife" appears in passages such as Gen 8:16: "Go forth of the ark, thou, and thy wife, and thy sons, and thy sons' wives with thee."

(3) In one special nuance the word connotes "wife" in the sense of a woman who is under a man's authority and protection; the emphasis is on the family relationship considered as a legal and social entity: "And Abram took Sarai his wife and Lot his brother's son, and all their substance that they had gathered . . ." (Gen 12:5). **(4)** In Lam 2:20 *ishshah* is a synonym for "mother": "Shall the women eat their [offspring, the little ones who were born healthy]?" **(5)** In Gen 29:21 (cf. Deut 22:24) it appears to connote "bride" or "betrothed one": "And Jacob said unto Laban, Give me my wife, for my days are fulfilled, that I may go in unto her." **(6)** Eccl 7:26 uses the word generically of "woman" conceived in general, or womanhood: "And I find more bitter than death the woman, whose heart is snares and nets . . ." (cf. Gen 31:35).

(7) This word is used only infrequently of animals: "Of every clean beast thou shalt take to thee by sevens, the male and his female: and of beasts that are not clean by two, the male and his female" (Gen 7:2). **(8)** This word can also be used figuratively describing foreign warriors and/or heroes as "women," in other words as weak, unmanly, and cowardly: "In that day shall Egypt be like unto women: and it shall be afraid and fear because of the shaking of the hand of the LORD of hosts . . ." (Is 19:16). **(9)** In a few passages *ishshah* means "each" or "every": "But every woman shall borrow of her neighbor, and of her that sojourneth in her house . . ." (Ex 3:22; cf. Amos 4:3). **(10)** A special use of this nuance occurs in passages such as Jer 9:20, where in conjunction with *reuwth* (7468 -"neighbor") it means "one" (female): "Yet hear the word of the LORD, O ye women, and let your ear receive the word of his mouth, and teach your daughters wailing, and every one her neighbor lamentation." See: TWOT—137a; BDB—61a, 78c, 84b, 1081d.

803. אֲשׁוּיָה {1x} **ʾăshuwyâh**, *ash-oo-yah';* fem. pass. part. from an unused root mean. to *found; foundation:*—foundation {1x}. See: TWOT—175a; BDB—78c.

804. אַשּׁוּר {151x} **ʾAshshûwr**, *ash-shoor';* or

אַשֻּׁר **ʾAshshûr**, *ash-shoor';* appar. from 833 (in the sense of *successful*); *Ashshur,* the second son of Shem; also his desc. and the country occupied by them (i.e. Assyria), its region and its empire:—Assyria {118x}, Assyrian {19x}, Asshur {8x}, Assyrian + 1121 {5x}, Assur {1x}. Syn.: See 838. See: TWOT—176; BDB—78c.

805. אֲשׁוּרִי {1x} **ʾĂshûwrîy**, *ash-oo-ree';* or

אַשּׁוּרִי **ʾAshshûwrîy**, *ash-shoo-ree';* from a patrial word of the same form as 804; an *Ashurite* (collect.) or inhab. of Ashur, a district in Pal.:—Asshurim {1x}, Ashurites {1x}. See: BDB—78d, 79a.

806. אַשְׁחוּר {2x} **ʾAshchûwr**, *ash-khoor';* prob. from 7835; *black; Ashchur,* an Isr.:—Ashur {2x}. See: BDB—79a, 1007b.

807. אֲשִׁימָא {1x} **ʾĂshîymâʾ**, *ash-ee-maw';* of for. or.; *Ashima,* a deity of Hamath:—Ashima {1x}. See: BDB—79a, 92d.

אֲשֵׁירָה **ʾăshêyrâh**. See 842.

808. אָשִׁישׁ {1x} **ʾâshîysh**, *aw-sheesh';* from the same as 784 (in the sense of *pressing* down firmly; comp. 803); a (ruined) *foundation:*—foundation {1x}. See: TWOT—185a; BDB—84b.

809. אֲשִׁישָׁה {4x} **ʾăshîyshâh**, *ash-ee-shaw';* fem. of 808; something closely *pressed* together, i.e. a *cake* of raisins or other comfits:—flagon {1x}. See: TWOT—185a; BDB—84b.

810. אֶשֶׁךְ {1x} **ʾeshek**, *eh'-shek;* from an unused root (prob. mean. to *bunch* together); a *testicle* (as a *lump*):—stone {1x}. See: TWOT—177; BDB—79a.

811. אֶשְׁכּוֹל {9x} **ʾeshkôwl**, *esh-kole';* or

אֶשְׁכֹּל **ʾeshkôl**, *esh-kole';* prob. prol. from 810; a *bunch of grapes* or other fruit:—cluster {8x}, cluster of grapes {1x}. See: TWOT—178; BDB—79a.

812. אֶשְׁכֹּל {6x} **ʾEshkôl**, *esh-kole';* the same as 811; *Eshcol,* the name of an Amorite, also of a valley in Pal.:—Eshcol {6x}. See: BDB—79b.

813. אַשְׁכְּנַז {3x} **ʾAshkᵉnaz**, *ash-ken-az';* of for. or.; *Ashkenaz,* a Japhethite, also his desc.:—*Ashkenaz* {3x}. See: BDB—79b.

814. אֶשְׁכָּר {2x} **ʾeshkâr**, *esh-kawr';* for 7939; a *gratuity:*—gift {1x}, present {1x}. See: BDB—79b, 1016d.

815. אֵשֶׁל {3x} **ʾêshel**, *ay'-shel;* from a root of uncert. signif.; a *tamarisk* tree; by extens. a *grove* of any kind:—grove {1x}, tree {2x}. A bona fide grove in contrast to the pagan grove, asherah (842). See: TWOT—179a; BDB—79b.

816. אָשַׁם {35x} **ʾâsham**, *aw-sham';* or

אָשֵׁם **ʾâshêm**, *aw-shame';* a prim. root; to *be guilty;* by impl. to *be punished* or *perish:*—guilty {14x}, desolate {6x}, offend {6x}, trespass {4x}, certainly {1x}, destroy {1x}, faulty {1x}, greatly {1x}, offence {1x}. See: TWOT—180; BDB—79c.

817. אָשָׁם {46x} **ʾâshâm**, *aw-shawm';* from 816; *guilt;* by impl. a *fault;* also a *sin-offering:*—trespass offering {34x}, trespass {8x}, offering for sin {1x}, sin {2x}, guiltiness {1x}.

Asham means "guilt offering; offense; guilt; gift of restitution; gift of atonement." **(1)** The noun *asham* occurs 46 times in biblical Hebrew; 33 of its occurrences are in the Pentateuch. **(2)** The most frequent meaning of the word is "guilt offering": "And he shall bring his trespass [guilt] offering unto the LORD for his sin which he hath sinned . . ." (Lev 5:6). **(3)** This specialized kind of sin offering (Lev 5:7) was to be offered when someone had been denied what was due to him. **(4)** The valued amount defrauded was to be repaid plus 20 percent (Lev 5:16; 6:5). **(5)** Ritual infractions and periods of leprosy and defilement took from God a commodity or service rightfully belonging to Him and required repayment plus restitution. **(6)** Every violation of property rights required paying full reparation and the restitution price (20 percent) to the one violated as well as presenting the guilt offering to God as the LORD of all (i.e., as a feudal lord over all). **(7)** If the offended party was dead, reparation and restitution were made to God (i.e. given to the priests; Num 5:5–10).

(8) Usually the "guilt offering" consisted of a ram (Lev 5:15) or a male lamb. **(8a)** The offerer presented the victim, laying his hands on it. **(8b)** The priest sprinkled its blood around the altar, burned the choice parts on the altar, and received the rest as food (Lev 7:2–7). **(8c)** When a cleansed leper made this offering, blood from the sacrifice was applied to the man's right ear, right thumb, and right big toe (Lev 14:14). **(9)** In some passages, *asham* is used of an offense against God and the guilt incurred by it: "And Abimelech said, What is this thou hast done unto us? One of the people might lightly have lain with thy wife, and thou shouldest have brought guiltiness upon us" (Gen 26:10—the first occurrence). There is an added sense here that the party offended would punish the perpetrator of the crime. **(10)** In two verses (Num 5:7–8), *asham* represents the repayment made to one who has been wronged: "Then they shall confess their sin which they have done: and he shall recompense his trespass with the principal thereof, and add unto it the fifth part thereof, and give it unto him against whom he hath trespassed." **(10a)** In the Hebrew the word is the value of the initial thing taken from the injured party, which value is to be returned to him, i.e., the reparation or restitution itself. **(10b)** This basic idea is extended so that the word comes to mean a gift made to God to remove guilt (1 Sa 6:3), or atone for sin (Is 53:10) other than the specified offerings to be presented at the altar.

(11) The noun implies the condition of guilt incurred through some wrongdoing (Gen 26:10); *Asham* refers **(12)** to the compensation given to satisfy an injured party [trespass offering or guilt offering] **(12a)** presented on the altar by the repentant offender **(12b)** after paying a compensation of six-fifths of the damage inflicted (Num 5:7–8). The trespass offering was **(12c)** the blood sacrifice of a ram (Lev 5:18; Lev 7:5, 7; 14:12–13). **(13)** The most significant theological statement containing *asham* is Is 53:10, which says that the servant of Yahweh was appointed as an *asham* for sinful mankind; suggesting that His death furnished a 120 percent compensation for the broken law of God. **(14)** It also is offense against God and the guilt incurred thereby (Gen 26:10). Syn. 801, 4503, 5927, 5030, 7133, 8641. See: TWOT—180b; BDB—79d.

818. **אָשֵׁם** {3x} **ʼâshêm**, *aw-shame';* from 816; *guilty;* hence, *presenting a sin-offering:*—guilty {2x}, faulty {1x}. See: TWOT—180a; BDB—79d.

819. **אַשְׁמָה** {19x} **ʼashmâh**, *ash-maw';* fem. of 817; *guiltiness, a fault,* the *presentation of a sin-offering:*—trespass {13x}, sin {4x}, offend {1x}, trespass offering {1x}. See: TWOT—180c; BDB—80a.

אַשְׁמוּרָה **ʼashmûwrâh**. See 821.

820. **אַשְׁמָן** {1x} **ʼashmân**, *ash-mawn';* prob. from 8081; a *fat* field:—desolate {1x}. See: TWOT—2410d; BDB—80b, 1032c.

821. **אַשְׁמֻרָה** {7x} **ʼashmûrâh**, *ash-moo-raw';* or **אַשְׁמוּרָה** **ʼashmûwrâh**, *ash-moo-raw';* or **אַשְׁמֹרֶת** **ʼashmôreth**, *ash-mo'-reth;* fem. from 8104; a night *watch:*—watch {5x}, night watch {2x}. Syn.: 4929, 4931, 6822, 8104, 8245. See: TWOT—2414e; BDB—80b, 1038a.

822. **אֶשְׁנָב** {2x} **ʼeshnâb**, *esh-nawb';* appar. from an unused root (prob. mean. to *leave small spaces between two things*); a latticed *window:*—casement {1x}, lattice {1x}. See: TWOT—2418a; BDB—80b, 1039d.

823. **אַשְׁנָה** **ʼAshnâh**, *ash-naw';* prob. a var. for 3466; *Ashnah,* the name of two places in Pal.:—*Ashnah* {2x}. See: BDB—80b.

824. **אֶשְׁעָן** {1x} **ʼEshʻân**, *esh-awn';* from 8172; *support; Eshan,* a place in Pal.:—Eshean {1x}. See: BDB—80b, 1043d.

825. **אַשָּׁף** {2x} **ʼashshâph**, *ash-shawf';* from an unused root (prob. mean. To *lisp,* i.e. *practice enchantment*); a *conjurer:*—astrologer {2x}.

Ashshaph means "enchanter." **(1)** The noun appears only twice in biblical Hebrew, and only in the Book of Daniel. **(2)** The vocation of ashipu is known from earliest times in the Akkadian (Old Babylonian) society. It is not clear whether the ashipu was an assistant to a particular order of Babylonian priests (mashmashu) or an order parallel in function to the mashmashu order. In either case, the ashipu offered incantations to deliver a person from evil magical forces (demons). The sick often underwent actual surgery while the incantations were spoken. **(3)** In the Bible, *ashshaph* first occurs in Dan 1:20: "And as for every matter of wisdom and understanding about which the king consulted them he found them ten times better than all the magicians and enchanters who were in his realm." See: TWOT—181; BDB—80b, 1083b.

826. **אַשָּׁף** {6x} **ʼashshâph** (Aram.), *ash-shawf';* corresp. to 825:—astrologer {6x}. The ungodly one who attempts to determine the future from the alignment of the stars. See: TWOT—2615; BDB—1083b.

827. **אַשְׁפָּה** {6x} **ʼashpâh**, *ash-paw';* perh. (fem.) from the same as 825 (in the sense of *covering*); a *quiver* or arrow-case:—quiver {6x}. See: TWOT—182a; BDB—80c, 251c, 1046a.

829. **אֶשְׁפָּר** {2x} **ʼeshpâr**, *esh-pawr';* of uncert. der.; a measured *portion:*—piece {1x}, flesh {1x}. See. TWOT—182.1; BDB—80c, 1051c.

830. **אַשְׁפֹּת** {7x} **ʼashpôth**, *ash-pohth';* or **אַשְׁפּוֹת** **ʼashpôwth**, *ash-pohth';* or (contr.) **שְׁפֹת** **shᵉphôth**, *shef-ohth';* plur. of a noun of the same form as 827, from 8192 (in the sense of *scraping*); a heap of *rubbish* or *filth:*—dung {4x}, dunghill {3x}. See: TWOT—2441b; BDB—80c, 1046b, 1052a.

831. **אַשְׁקְלוֹן** {12x} **ʼAshqᵉlôwn**, *ash-kel-one';* prob. from 8254 in the sense of *weighing*-place (i.e. *mart*); *Ashkelon,* a place in Pal.:—Ashkelon {9x}, Askalon {3x}. See: BDB—80c.

832. **אֶשְׁקְלוֹנִי** {1x} **ʼEshqᵉlôwnîy**, *esh-kel-o-nee';* patrial from 831; an *Ashkelonite* (collect.) or inhab. of Ashkelon:—Eshkalonites {1x}. See: BDB—80d.

833. **אָשַׁר** {16x} **ʼâshar**, *aw-shar';* or **אָשֵׁר** **ʼâshêr**, *aw-share';* a prim. root; to *be straight* (used in the widest sense, espec. to *be level, right, happy*); fig. to *go forward, be honest, prosper:*—blessed {7x}, lead {2x}, go {2x}, guide {1x}, happy {2x}, leaders {1x}, relieve {1x}. See: TWOT—183; BDB—80d.

834. **אֲשֶׁר** {111x} **ʼăsher**, *ash-er';* a prim. rel. pron. (of every gender and number); *who, which, what, that;* also (as adv. and conjunc.) *when, where, how, because, in order that,* etc.:—which, wherewith, because, when, soon, whilst, as if, as when, that, until, much, whosoever, whereas, wherein, whom, whose = {111x}. See: TWOT—184; BDB—81c, 84a, 455b, 606b, 758a, 774d, 775c, 979b, 979d, 980a, 1083d, 1087.

835. **אֶשֶׁר** {45x} **ʼesher**, *eh'-sher;* from 833; *happiness;* only in masc. plur. constr. as interj., how *happy!:*—blessed {27x}, happy {18x}.

Esher (835) means "blessed; happy." **(1)** All but 4 of the 44 biblical occurrences of this noun are in poetical passages, with 26 occurrences in the Psalms and 8 in Proverbs. **(2)** Basically, this word connotes the state of "prosperity" or "happiness" that comes when a superior bestows his favor (blessing) on one. **(2a)** In most passages, the one bestowing favor is God Himself: "Happy art thou, O Israel: who is like unto thee, O people saved by the LORD" (Deut 33:29). **(2b)** The state that the blessed one enjoys does not always appear to be "happy": "Behold, happy is the man whom God correcteth: therefore despise not thou the chastening of the Almighty: for he maketh sore, and bindeth up . . ." (Job 5:17–18). Eliphaz was not describing Job's condition as a happy one; it was "blessed," however, inasmuch as God was concerned about him. Because it was a blessed state and the outcome would be good, Job was expected to laugh at his adversity (Job 5:22).

(3) God is not always the one who makes one "blessed." At least, the Queen of Sheba flatteringly told Solomon that this was the case (1 Kin 10:8). **(4)** One's status before God (being "blessed") is not always expressed in terms of the individual or social conditions that bring what moderns normally consider to be "happiness." **(5)** So although it is appropriate to render *esher* as "blessed," the rendering of "happiness" does not always convey its emphasis to modern readers. Syn.: 833, 1288, 1293. See: TWOT—183a; BDB—80d.

836. **אָשֵׁר** {43x} **ʼÂshêr**, *aw-share';* from 833; *happy; Asher,* a son of Jacob, and the tribe descended from him, with its territory; also a place in Pal.:—*Asher* {43x}. See: BDB—81a.

837. **אֹשֶׁר** {1x} **ʼôsher**, *o'-sher;* from 833; *happiness:*—happy {1x}. See: TWOT—183b; BDB—81a.

838. **אָשׁוּר** {9x} **ʼâshshûwr**, *aw-shoor';* or **אַשֻּׁר** **ʼashshûr**, *ash-shoor';* from 833 in the sense of *going;* a *step:*—going {6x}, step {3x}. See: TWOT—183d; BDB—78c, 81a, 1083d.

839. **אֲשֻׁר** {1x} **ʼăshur**, *ash-oor';* contr. for 8391; the *cedar* tree or some other light elastic wood:—Ashurite {1x}. See: BDB—81b.

840. **אֲשַׂרְאֵל** {1x} **ʼĂsarʼêl**, *as-ar-ale';* by orth. var. from 833 and 410; *right of God; Asarel,* an Isr.:—Asareel {1x}. See: BDB—77b.

841. **אֲשַׂרְאֵלָה** {1x} **ʼĂsarʼêlâh**, *as-ar-ale'-aw;* from the same as 840; *right toward God; Asarelah,* an Isr.:—*Asarelah.* comp. 3480 {1x}. See: BDB—77b.

842. **אֲשֵׁרָה** {40x} **ʼăshêrâh**, *ash-ay-raw';* or **אֲשֵׁירָה** **ʼăshêyrâh**, *ash-ay-raw';* from 833; *happy; Asherah* (or Astarte) a Phœnician goddess; also an *image* of the same:—grove {40x}.

Asheyrah is transliterated "*Asherah,* Asherim (pl.)." **(1)** This noun first appears in the Bible in passages anticipating the settlement in Palestine. **(2)** The word's most frequent appearances, however, are usually in historical literature. Of its 40 appearances, 4 are in Israel's law code, 4 in Judges, 4 in prophetic books, and the rest are in 1 Kings and 2 Chronicles. **(3)** *Asheyrah* refers to a cultic object representing the presence of the Canaanite goddess *Asherah.* **(3a)** When the people of Israel entered Palestine, they were to have nothing to do with the idolatrous religions of its inhabitants. **(3b)** Rather, God said, "But ye shall destroy their altars, break their images, and cut down their groves [asherim] . . ." (Ex 34:13). **(4)** This cult object was manufactured from wood (Judg 6:26; 1 Kin 14:15) and it could be burned (Deut 12:3). Some scholars conclude that it was a sacred pole set up near an altar to Baal. Since there was only one goddess with this name, the plural (asherim) probably represents her several "poles."

(5) *Asherah* signifies the name of the goddess herself: "Now therefore send, and gather to me all Israel unto mount Carmel, and the prophets of Baal four hundred and fifty, and the prophets of the groves [*asherah*] four hundred, which eat at Jezebel's table" (1 Kin 18:19). **(6)** The Canaanites believed that *Asherah* ruled the sea, was the mother of all the gods including Baal, and sometimes was his deadly enemy. Apparently, the mythology of Canaan maintained that *Asherah* was the consort of Baal, who had displaced El as their highest god. Thus her sacred objects (poles) were immediately beside altars to Baal, and she was worshiped along with him. Syn.: comp. 6253. See: TWOT—183h; BDB—81b.

843. אָשֵׁרִי {1x} **ʾÂshêrîy**, *aw-shay-ree';* patron. from 836; an *Asherite* (collect.) or desc. of Asher:—Asherites {1x}. See: BDB—81b.

844. אַשְׂרִיאֵל {3x} **ʾAsrîyʾêl**, *as-ree-ale';* an orth. var. for 840; *Asriel*, the name of two Isr.:—Ashriel {2x}, Asriel {1x}. See: BDB—77b.

845. אַשְׂרִאֵלִי {1x} **ʾAsriʾêlîy**, *as-ree-ale-ee';* patron. from 844; an *Asrielite* (collect.) or desc. of Asriel:—Asrielites {1x}. See: BDB—77b.

846. אֻשַּׁרְנָא {2x} **ʾushsharnâʾ** (Aram.), *oosh-ar-naw';* from a root corresp. to 833; a *wall* (from its uprightness):—wall 2. See: TWOT—2616; BDB—1083b.

847. אֶשְׁתָּאֹל {7x} **ʾEshtâʾôl**, *esh-taw-ole';* or

אֶשְׁתָּאוֹל **ʾEshtâʾôwl**, *esh-taw-ole';* prob. from 7592; *intreaty; Eshtaol*, a place in Pal.:—Eshtaol {1x}. See: BDB—84b.

848. אֶשְׁתָּאֻלִי {1x} **ʾEshtâʾûlîy**, *esh-taw-oo-lee';* patrial from 847; an *Eshtaolite* (collect.) or inhab. of Eshtaol:—Eshtaulites {1x}. See: BDB—84b.

849. אֶשְׁתַּדּוּר {2x} **ʾeshtaddûwr** (Aram.), *esh-tad-dure';* from 7712 (in a bad sense); *rebellion:*—sedition {2x}. See: TWOT—3021a; BDB—1083b, 1114c.

850. אֶשְׁתּוֹן {2x} **ʾEshtôwn**, *esh-tone';* prob. from the same as 7764; *restful; Eshton*, an Isr.:—Eshton {2x}. See: BDB—84c.

851. אֶשְׁתְּמֹעַ {6x} **ʾEshtᵉmôaʿ**, *esh-tem-o'-ah;* or

אֶשְׁתְּמוֹעַ **ʾEshtᵉmôwaʿ**, *esh-tem-o'-ah;* or

אֶשְׁתְּמֹה **ʾEshtᵉmôh**, *esh-tem-o';* from 8085 (in the sense of *obedience*); *Eshtemoa* or *Eshtemoh*, a place in Pal.:—*Eshtemoa* {5x}, *Eshtemoh* {1x}. See: BDB—84c, 1035d.

852. אָת {3x} **ʾâth** (Aram.), *awth;* corresp. to 226; a *portent:*—sign {3x}. See: TWOT—2617; BDB—1079a, 1083c.

853. אֵת {22x} **ʾêth**, *ayth;* appar. contr. from 226 in the demonstr. sense of *entity;* prop. *self* (but Gen used to point out more def. the obj. of a verb or prep., *even* or *namely*):—not translated {22x}. See: TWOT—186; BDB—84c, 1096b.

854. אֵת {24x} **ʾêth**, *ayth;* prob. from 579; prop. *nearness* (used only as a prep. or an adv.), *near;* hence, Gen *with, by, at, among*, etc. [*Often with another prep. prefixed.*]:—against, among, before, by, for, from, in (-to), (out) of, with = {24x}. See: TWOT—187; BDB—85c.

855. אֵת {5x} **ʾêth**, *ayth;* of uncert. der.; a *hoe* or other digging implement:—coulter {2x}, plowshare {3x}. See: TWOT—192a; BDB—87b, 88a.

אַתְּ **ʾattâ**. See 859.

אָתָא **ʾâthâʾ**. See 857.

856. אֶתְבַּעַל {1x} **ʾEthbaʿal**, *eth-bah'-al;* from 854 and 1168; *with Baal; Ethbaal*, a Phœnician king:—*Ethbaal* {1x}. See: BDB—87a.

857. אָתָה {21x} **ʾâthâh**, *aw-thaw';* or

אָתָא **ʾâthâʾ**, *aw-thaw';* a prim. root [collat. to 225 contr.]; to *arrive:*—come {20x}, brought {1x}. See: TWOT—188; BDB—87b, 1083c.

858. אָתָה {16x} **ʾâthâh** (Aram.), *aw-thaw';* or

אָתָא **ʾâthâʾ** (Aram.), *aw-thaw';* corresp. to 857:—come {7x}, bring {9x}. See: TWOT—2618; BDB—1083c.

859. אַתָּה {1000's x} **ʾattâh**, *at-taw';* or (short.);

אַתָּ **ʾattâ**, *at-taw';* or

אַתְּ **ʾath**, *ath;* fem. (irreg.) sometimes

אַתִּי **ʾattîy**, *at-tee';* plur. masc.

אַתֶּם **ʾattem**, *at-tem';* fem.

אַתֶּן **ʾatten**, *at-ten';* or

אַתֵּנָה **ʾattênâh**, *at-tay'-naw;* or

אַתֵּנָּה **ʾattênnâh**, *at-tane'-naw;* a prim. pron. of the second pers.; *thou* and *thee*, or (plur.) *ye* and *you:*—thee, thou, ye, you = {1000's x}. See: TWOT—189; BDB—61c, 61d, 87b, 87c, 87d, 1082a.

860. אָתוֹן {34x} **ʾâthôwn**, *aw-thone';* prob. from the same as 386 (in the sense of *patience*); a female *ass* (from its docility):—(she) ass {34x}. See: TWOT—190a; BDB—87c.

861. אַתּוּן {10x} **ʾattûwn** (Aram.), *at-toon';* prob. from the corresp. to 784; prob. a *fire-place*, i.e. *furnace:*—furnace {10x}. See: TWOT—2619; BDB—1083c.

862. אַתּוּק {5x} **ʾattûwq**, *at-tooke';* or

אַתִּיק **ʾattîyq**, *at-teek';* from 5423 in the sense of *decreasing;* a *ledge* or offset in a building:—gallery {5x}. TWOT—191a; BDB—87d.

863. אִתַּי {9x} **ʾIttay**, *it-tah'ee;* or

אִיתַי **ʾIythay**, *ee-thah'ee;* from 854; *near; Ittai* or *Ithai*, the name of a Gittite and of an Isr.:—Ithai {1x}, Ittai {8x}. See: BDB—87a.

864. אֵתָם {4x} **ʾÊthâm**, *ay-thawm';* of Eg. der.; *Etham*, a place in the Desert:—*Etham* {4x}. See: BDB—87c.

אַתֶּן **ʾattem**. See 859.

865. אֶתְמוֹל {8x} **ʾethmôwl**, *eth-mole';* or

אִתְמוֹל **ʾithmôwl**, *ith-mole';* or

אֶתְמוּל **ʾethmûwl**, *eth-mool';* prob. from 853 or 854 and 4136; *heretofore;* def. *yesterday:*—time past + 8032 {2x}, herefore + 832 {1x}, beforetime + 8032 {1x}, yesterday {1x}, old {1x}, late {1x}, before {1x}. See: TWOT—2521; BDB—87c, 1069d.

866. אֶתְנָה {6x} **ʾethnâh**, *eth-naw';* from 8566; a *present* (as the price of harlotry):—reward {6x}. See: TWOT—2524a; BDB—1071d, 1072c.

אַתֵּנָה **ʾattênâh** or

אַתֵּנָּה **ʾattênnâh**. See 859.

867. אֶתְנִי {1x} **ʾEthnîy**, *eth-nee';* perh. from 866; *munificence; Ethni*, an Isr.:—Ethni {1x}. See: BDB—87d.

868. אֶתְנַן {11x} **ʾethnan**, *eth-nan';* the same as 866; a *gift* (as the price of harlotry or idolatry):—hire {8x}, reward {3x}. TWOT—2529a; BDB—87d, 1071d, 1072c.

869. אֶתְנַן {1x} **ʾEthnan**, *eth-nan';* the same as 868 in the sense of 867; *Ethnan*, an Isr.:—*Ethnan* {1x}. See: BDB—1071d, 1072c.

870. אֲתַר {8x} **ʾăthar** (Aram.), *ath-ar';* from a root corresp. to that of 871; a *place;* (adv.) *after:*—after {3x}, place {5x}. TWOT—2620; BDB—1079d, 1083c, 1084a, 1085d.

871. אֲתָרִים {1x} **ʾĂthârîym**, *ath-aw-reem';* plur. from an unused root (prob. mean. to *step*); *places; Atharim*, a place near Pal.:—spies {1x}. See: BDB—87d.

ב

872. בְּאָה {1x} **bᵉʾâh**, *bè-aw';* from 935; an *entrance* to a building:—entry {1x}. See: TWOT—212a, 99d.

873. בִּאוּשׁ {1x} **biʾûwsh** (Aram.), *be-oosh';* from 888; *wicked:*—bad {1x}. See: TWOT—2622a; BDB—1084a.

874. בָּאַר {3x} **bâʾar**, *baw-ar';* a prim. root; to *dig;* by anal. to *engrave;* fig. to *explain:*—plain {1x}, plainly {1x}, declare {1x}. See: TWOT—194; BDB—91b.

875. בְּאֵר {37x} **bᵉʾêr**, *bè-ayr';* from 874; a *pit;* espec. a *well:*—well {32x}, pit {3x}, slimepits {1x}, not translated {1x}.

Be'er means "pit; well." **(1)** This word appears 37 times in the Bible with no occurrences in the Old Testament prophetic books. **(2)** *Be'er* means a "well" in which there may be water. **(2a)** By itself the word does not always infer the presence of water. **(2b)** The word refers to the "pit" itself whether dug or natural: "And Abraham reproved Abimelech because of a well of water, which Abimelech's servants had violently taken away" (Gen 21:25). **(2c)** Such a "well" may have a narrow enough mouth that it can be blocked with a stone which a single strong man could move (Gen 29:2, 10). **(2d)** In the desert country of the ancient Near East a "well" was an important place and its water the source of deep satisfaction for the thirsty. This concept pictures the role of a wife for a faithful husband (Prov 5:15). **(3)** A "pit" may contain something other than water. In its first biblical appearance *be'er* is used of tar pits: "And the vale of Siddim was full of slimepits . . ." (Gen 14:10). **(4)** A "pit" may contain nothing as does the "pit" which becomes one's grave (Ps 55:23, "pit of the grave"). **(5)** In some passages the word was to represent more than a depository for the body but a place where one exists after death (Ps 69:15). See: TWOT—194a; BDB—91c.

876. בְּאֵר {2x} **Bᵉʾêr**, *bè-ayr';* the same as 875; *Beër*, a place in the Desert, also one in Pal.:—*Beer* {1x}. See: BDB—91d.

877. בֹּאר {2x} **bôʾr**, *bore;* from 874; a *cistern:*—cistern {2x}. Syn.: 953, 5869. See: TWOT—194d; BDB—92b.

878. בְּאֵרָא {1x} **Beʾêrâʾ**, *bè-ay-raw';* from 875; a *well; Beëra,* an Isr.:—*Beera* {1x}. See: BDB—92a.

879. בְּאֵר אֵלִים {1x} **Beʾêr ʾÊlîym**, *bè-ayr' ay-leem';* from 875 and the plur. of 410; *well of heroes; Beër-Elim,* a place in the Desert:—Beer-elim {1x}. See: BDB—91d.

880. בְּאֵרָה {1x} **Beʾêrâh**, *bè-ay-raw';* the same as 878; *Beërah,* an Isr.:—*Beerah* {1x}. See: BDB—92a.

881. בְּאֵרוֹת {5x} **Beʾêrôwth**, *bè-ay-rohth';* fem. plur. of 875; *wells; Beëroth,* a place in Pal.:—Beeroth {1x}. See: BDB—92a.

882. בְּאֵרִי {2x} **Beʾêrîy**, *bè-ay-ree';* from 875; *fountained; Beëri,* the name of a Hittite and of an Isr.:—Beeri {2x}. See: BDB—92b.

883. בְּאֵר לַחַי רֹאִי {3x} **Beʾêr la-Chay Rôʾîy**, *bè-ayr' lakh-ah'ee ro-ee';* from 875 and 2416 (with pref.) and 7203; *well of a living* (One) *my seer; Beër-Lachai-Rô,* a place in the Desert:—the well Lahairoi {2x}, Beerlahairoi {1x}. See: BDB—91d.

884. בְּאֵר שֶׁבַע {34x} **Beʾêr Shebaʿ**, *be-ayr' sheh'-bah;* from 875 and 7651 (in the sense of 7650); *well of an oath, Beër Sheba,* a place in Pal.:—Beer-shebah {34x}. See: BDB—92a, 989d.

885. בְּאֵרֹת בְּנֵי־יַעֲקָן {1x} **Beʾêrôth Benêy-Yaʿaqan**, *bè-ay-roth' be-nay' yah-a-kan';* from the fem. plur. of 875, and the plur. contr. of 1121, and 3292; *wells of* (the) *sons of Jaakan; Beëroth-Bene-Jaakan,* a place in the Desert:—Beeroth of the children of Jaakan {1x}. See: BDB—92b, 785c.

886. בְּאֵרֹתִי {5x} **Beʾêrôthîy**, *bè-ay-ro-thee';* patrial from 881; a *Beërothite* or inhab. of Beëroth:—Beerothite {1x}. See: BDB—92a.

887. בָּאַשׁ {17x} **bâʾash**, *baw-ash';* a prim. root; to *smell* bad; fig. to *be offensive* mor.:—stink {10x}, abhor {3x}, abomination {1x}, loathsome {1x}, stinking savour {1x}, utterly {1x} (inf. for emphasis). Syn.: 889, 8581. See: TWOT—195; BDB—1084a.

888. בְּאֵשׁ {1x} **beʾêsh** (Aram.), *bè-aysh';* corresp. to 887:—displease {1x}. See: TWOT—2622; BDB—1084a, 1094a.

889. בְּאֹשׁ {3x} **beʾôsh**, *bè-oshe';* from 877; a *stench:*—stink {3x}. See: TWOT—195a; BDB—93b.

890. בָּאְשָׁה {1x} **boʾshâh**, *bosh-aw';* fem. of 889; *stink-weed* or any other noxious or useless plant:—cockle {1x}. See: TWOT—195b; BDB—93b.

891. בְּאֻשִׁים {2x} **beʾûshîym**, *bè-oo-sheem';* plur. of 889; *poison-berries:*—wild grapes {2x}. See: TWOT—195c; BDB—93b.

892. בָּבָה {1x} **bâbâh**, *baw-baw';* fem. act. part. of an unused root mean. to *hollow* out; something *hollowed* (as a *gate*), i.e. the *pupil* of the eye:—apple [of the eye] {1x}. See: TWOT—196; BDB—93b.

893. בֵּבַי {6x} **Bêbay**, *bay-bah'ee;* prob. of for. or.; *Bebai,* an Isr.:—Bebai {1x}. See: BDB—93c.

894. בָּבֶל {262x} **Bâbel**, *baw-bel';* from 1101; *confusion; Babel* (i.e. Babylon), incl. Babylonia and the Bab. empire:—Babylon {257x}, Babylonian + 1121 {3x}, Babel {2x}. See: BDB—93c, 1084a.

895. בָּבֶל {25x} **Bâbel** (Aram.), *baw-bel';* corresp. to 894:—Babylon {25x}. See: BDB—1084a.

896. בַּבְלִי {1x} **Bablîy** (Aram.), *bab-lee';* patrial from 895; a *Babylonian:*—Babylonia {1x}. See: BDB—1084a.

897. בַּג {1x} **bag**, *bag;* a Pers. word; *food:*—spoil {1x}. See: TWOT—225a; BDB—93c, 103a.

898. בָּגַד {49x} **bâgad**, *baw-gad';* a prim. root; to *cover* (with a garment); fig. to *act covertly;* by impl. to *pillage:*—treacherously {23x}, transgressor {10x}, transgress {3x}, deceitfully {2x}, treacherous dealer {3x}, treacherous {2x}, very {2x} (inf. for emphasis), unfaithful man {1x}, treacherous men {1x}, offend {1x}, unfaithfully {1x}. Syn.: 6586. See: TWOT—198; BDB—93c.

899. בֶּגֶד {217x} **beged**, *behg'-ed;* from 898; a *covering,* i.e. clothing; also *treachery* or *pillage:*—garment {107x}, clothes {69x}, cloth {13x}, raiment {12x}, apparel {4x}, robe {4x}, wardrobe {2x}, very {2x}, clothing {1x}, lap {1x}, rags {1x}, vestures {1x}.

Beged means "garment; covering; cloth; blanket; saddlecloth." **(1)** The word signifies any kind of "garment" or "covering," usually for human wear. **(2)** *Beged* first appears in Gen 24:53: "And the servant brought forth jewels of silver, and jewels of gold, and raiment, and gave them to Rebekah. . . ." **(2a)** Here the word represents "garments made of precious materials." **(2b)** The "garments" of widows, on the other hand, must have been quite common and valueless (Gen 38:14). **(2c)** Certainly mourners' "garments" must have been very plain, if not torn (2 Sa 14:2). **(3)** *Beged* sometimes refers to "outer garments." **(3a)** Thus in 2 Kin 7:15, the Syrian soldiers who fled from Jerusalem left behind their "clothes" and equipment; they left behind everything that would hinder their escape. **(3b)** Surely this did not include their essential "clothing." **(4)** In Judg 14:12, however, the word is distinguished from linen wrappings ("outer garments")—Samson promised the Philistines that if they would solve his riddle, he would give them "thirty linen sheets and thirty change of garments" (cf. Judg 17:10).

(5) The "holy garments" Moses was commanded to make for Aaron included everything he was to wear while officiating before the Lord: ". . . A breastplate, and an ephod, and a robe, and an embroidered coat, a mitre, and a sash; and they shall make holy garments for Aaron . . ." (Ex 28:4). **(6)** In passages such as Num 4:6, *beged* means "covering," in the sense of a large flat piece of cloth material to be laid over something: "And [they] shall put thereon the covering of badgers' skins, and shall spread over it a cloth wholly of blue. . . ." **(7)** When put over people, such clothes were probably "blankets": "Now king David was old and stricken in years; and they covered him with clothes, but he gat no heat" (1 Kin 1:1). **(8)** When put over beasts, such coverings were "saddlecloths" (Eze 27:20). Syn.: 3801, 3847, 4403, 8008, 8071. See: TWOT—198a; BDB—93d.

900. בֹּגְדוֹת {1x} **bôgedôwth**, *bohg-ed-ōhth';* fem. plur. act. part. of 898; *treacheries:*—treacherous {1x}. TWOT—198b; BDB—93d.

901. בָּגוֹד {2x} **bâgôwd**, *baw-gode';* from 898; *treacherous:*—treacherous {2x}. See: TWOT—198c; BDB—93d.

902. בִּגְוַי {1x} **Bigvay**, *big-vah'ee;* prob. of for. or.; *Bigvai,* an Isr.:—Bigvai {1x}. See: BDB—94a.

903. בִּגְתָא {1x} **Bigthâʾ**, *big-thaw';* of Pers. der.; *Bigtha,* a eunuch of Xerxes:—*Bigtha* {1x}. See: BDB—94a.

904. בִּגְתָן {2x} **Bigthân**, *big-thawn';* or

בִּגְתָנָא **Bigthânâʾ**, *big-thaw'naw;* of similar der. to 903; *Bigthan* or *Bigthana,* a eunuch of Xerxes:—*Bigthan* {1x}, *Bigthana* {1x}. See: BDB—94b.

905. בַּד {56x} **bad**, *bad;* from 909; prop. *separation;* by impl. a *part* of the body, *branch* of a tree, *bar* for carrying; fig. *chief* of a city; espec. (with prep. pref.) as adv., *apart, only, besides:*—staves {37x}, beside {3x}, branches {3x}, alone {2x}, only {2x}, strength {2x}, apart {1x}, bars {1x}, each {1x}, except {1x}, beside him {1x}, like {1x}, themselves {1x}.

Bad (905) means "part; portion; limbs; piece of cloth; pole; shoot; alone; by themselves; only; apart from; besides; aside from." **(1)** First, *bad* means a "part or portion" of something. **(1a)** In Ex 30:34 it refers to the portion or amount of spices mixed together to make incense for the worship of God. **(1b)** In Job 18:13 the word represents the members or parts of the wicked (cf. Job 41:12—"limbs" of a crocodile). **(2)** Second, the word means a piece of cloth: **(2a)** "And thou shalt make them linen breeches to cover their nakedness . . ." (Ex 28:42—first occurrence of this nuance). **(2b)** This word is always used of a priestly garment or at least of a garment worn by one who appears before God or His altar. **(3)** Third, *bad* can mean a long piece of wood or woody material. **(3a)** The ark, altars, and table of the Bread of the Presence were carried by staves passed through rings attached to these articles: "And thou shalt put the staves into the rings by the sides of the ark, that the ark may be borne with them" (Ex 25:14—first occurrence of this nuance). **(3b)** In Eze 19:14 *bad* is used of the "shoots" or limbs of a vine; "And fire is gone out of a rod of her branches . . ." (cf. Eze 17:6). **(3c)** The gates of a city are badim (Job 17:16).

(4) Fourth, in most of its appearances (152x) this word is preceded by the preposition *le.* **(4a)** This use means "alone" (89x): "And the Lord God said, It is not good that the man should be alone; I will make him a help meet for him" (Gen 2:18—first occurrence of the word). **(4b)** In a second nuance the phrase identifies a unit by itself, a single unit: "And thou shalt couple five curtains by themselves, and six curtains by themselves . . ." (Ex 26:9). **(4c)** Twice the word is used as an adverb of limitation meaning "only": "Lo, this only have I found, that God hath made man upright; but they have sought out many inventions" (Eccl 7:29). **(4d)** When followed by the preposition *min* (or al) the word functions as an adverb meaning "apart from" or "besides": "And the children of Israel journeyed from Rameses to Succoth, about six hundred thousand on foot that were men, beside children" (Ex 12:37). **(4e)** In Num 29:39 the translation "besides" is appropriate: "These things ye shall do unto the Lord in your set feasts, beside your vows, and your freewill offerings. . . ." **(4f)** In 33 passages the word is preceded by the preposition *min* but still means "besides." See: TWOT—201a; BDB—94b, 94c, 571c.

906. בַּד {23x} **bad**, *bad;* perh. from 909 (in the sense of *divided* fibres); flaxen *thread* or yarn; hence, a *linen* garment:—linen {23x}. Syn.: 948, 6593, 8336. See: TWOT—199; BDB—94b.

907. בַּד {6x} **bad**, *bad;* from 908; a *brag* or *lie;* also a *liar:*—lie {3x}, liar {2x}, parts {1x}. Syn.: 3576. See: TWOT—202a; BDB—94b, 95a.

908. בָּדָא {2x} **bâdâʼ**, *baw-daw';* a prim. root; (fig.) to *invent:*—devise {1x}, feign {1x}. See: TWOT—200; BDB—94b.

909. בָּדַד {3x} **bâdad**, *baw-dad';* a prim. root; to *divide,* i.e. (reflex.) *be solitary:*—alone {3x}.

Badad means "to be isolated, be alone." One of its 3 appearances is in Ps 102:7: "I watch, and am as a sparrow alone upon the housetop." Syn.: 905. See: TWOT—201; BDB—94b.

910. בָּדָד {11x} **bâdâd**, *baw-dawd';* from 909; *separate;* adv. *separately:*—alone {7x}, solitary {2x}, only {1x}, desolate {1x}. See: TWOT—201b; BDB—94d.

911. בְּדַד {2x} **Bᵉdad**, *bed-ad';* from 909 {2x}. See: BDB—95a.

912. בֵּדְיָה {1x} **Bêdᵉyâh**, *bay-dè-yaw';* prob. short. form 5662; *servant of Jehovah; Bedejah,* an Isr.:—Bedeiah {1x}. See: BDB—95a.

913. בְּדִיל {6x} **bᵉdîyl**, *bed-eel';* from 914; *alloy* (because *removed* by smelting); by anal. *tin:*—tin {5x}, plummet + 68 {1x}. Syn. 4949. See: TWOT—203c; BDB—95d.

914. בָּדַל {42x} **bâdal**, *baw-dal';* a prim. root; to *divide* (in var. senses lit. or fig., *separate, distinguish, differ, select,* etc.):—separate {25x}, divide {8x}, difference {4x}, asunder {2x}, severed {2x}, sever out {1x}, separation {1x}, utterly {1x} (inf. for emphasis). Syn.: 2673, 5144, 6504. See: TWOT—203; BDB—95a.

915. בָּדָל {1x} **bâdâl**, *baw-dawl';* from 914; a *part:*—piece {1x}. See: TWOT—203a; BDB—95c.

916. בְּדֹלַח {2x} **bᵉdôlach**, *bed-o'-lakh;* prob. from 914; something in *pieces,* i.e. *bdellium,* a (fragrant) gum (perh. *amber*); others a *pearl:*—bdellium {2x}. See: TWOT—203d; BDB—95d.

917. בְּדָן {2x} **Bᵉdân**, *bed-awn';* prob. short. for 5658; *servile; Bedan,* the name of two Isr.:—*Bedan* {2x}. See: BDB—96a.

918. בָּדַק {1x} **bâdaq**, *baw-dak';* a prim. root; to *gap* open; used only as a denom. from 919; to *mend* a breach:—repair {1x}. See: TWOT—204; BDB—96a.

919. בֶּדֶק {10x} **bedeq**, *beh'-dek;* from 918; a *gap* or *leak* (in a building or a ship):—breach {8x}, calker + 2388 {2x}. See: TWOT—204a; BDB—96a.

920. בִּדְקַר {1x} **Bidqar**, *bid-car';* prob. from 1856 with prep. pref.; *by stabbing,* i.e. *assassin; Bidkar,* an Isr.:—Bidkar {1x}. See: BDB—96a.

921. בְּדַר {1x} **bᵉdar** (Aram.), *bed-ar';* corresp. (by transp.) to 6504; to *scatter:*—scatter {1x}. Syn.: 2219, 6340, 6566. See: TWOT—2623; BDB—1084a

922. בֹּהוּ {3x} **bôhûw**, *bo'-hoo;* from an unused root (mean. to *be empty*); a *vacuity,* i.e. (superficially) an undistinguishable *ruin:*—emptiness {1x}, void {2x}. See: TWOT—205a; BDB—96a.

923. בַּהַט {1x} **bahat**, *bah'-hat;* from an unused root (prob. mean. to *glisten*); white *marble* or perh. *alabaster:*—red [marble] {1x}. See: TWOT—206; BDB—96b.

924. בְּהִילוּ {1x} **bᵉhîylûw** (Aram.), *bè-hee-loo';* from 927; a *hurry;* only adv. *hastily:*—in haste {1x}. See: TWOT—2624a; BDB—1084b.

925. בָּהִיר {1x} **bâhîyr**, *baw-here';* from an unused root (mean. to *be bright*); *shining:*—bright {1x}. See: TWOT—211b; BDB—97c.

926. בָּהַל {39x} **bâhal**, *baw-hal';* a prim. root; to *tremble* inwardly (or *palpitate*), i.e. (fig.) *be* (caus. *make*) (suddenly) *alarmed* or *agitated;* by impl. to *hasten* anxiously:—trouble {17x}, haste {4x}, afraid {3x}, vexed {3x}, amazed {2x}, hasty {2x}, affrighted {1x}, dismayed {1x}, hastily {1x}, thrust him out {1x}, rash {1x}, speedily {1x}, speedy {1x}, vex {1x}. Syn.: 6862, 6869. See: TWOT—207; BDB—96b, 1084b.

927. בְּהַל {11x} **bᵉhal** (Aram.), *bè-hal';* corresp. to 926; to *terrify, hasten:*—in haste {3x}, trouble {8x}. See: TWOT—2624; BDB—1084a.

928. בֶּהָלָה {4x} **behâlâh**, *beh-haw-law';* from 926; *panic, destruction:*—terror {2x}, trouble {2x}. See: TWOT—207a; BDB—96d.

929. בְּהֵמָה {189x} **bᵉhêmâh**, *bè-hay-maw';* from an unused root (prob. mean. to *be mute*); prop. a *dumb* beast; espec. any large quadruped or *animal* (often collect.):—beast {136x}, cattle {53x}.

Behemah means "beast; animal; domesticated animal; cattle; riding beast; wild beast." **(1)** In Ex 9:25, this word clearly embraces even the larger "animals," all the animals in Egypt: "And the hail smote throughout all the land of Egypt all that was in the field, both man and beast. . . ." **(1a)** This meaning is especially clear in Gen 6:7: "I will destroy man whom I have created from the face of the earth; both man, and beast, and the creeping thing, and the fowls of the air. . . ." **(1b)** In 1Kin 4:33, this word seems to exclude birds, fish, and reptiles: "He [Solomon] spake also of beasts, and of fowl, and of creeping things, and of fishes."

(2) The word *behemah* can be used of all the domesticated beasts or animals other than man: "And God said, Let the earth bring forth the living creature after his kind, cattle, and creeping thing, and [wild] beast of the earth after his kind . . ." (Gen 1:24, first occurrence). **(2a)** Ps 8:7 uses *behemah* in synonymous parallelism with "oxen" and "sheep," as though it includes both: "All sheep and oxen, yea, and the beasts of the field." **(2b)** The word can, however, be used of cattle only: "Shall not their cattle and their substance and every animals of theirs be ours?" (Gen 34:23). **(3)** In a rare use of the word, it signifies a "riding animal," such as a horse or mule: "And I arose in the night, I and some few men with me; neither told I any man what my God had put in my heart to do at Jerusalem: neither was there any beast with me, save the beast that I rode upon" (Neh 2:12). **(4)** Infrequently, *behemah* represents any wild, four-footed, undomesticated beast: "And thy carcase shall be meat unto all fowls of the air, and unto the beasts of the earth, and no man shall [frighten] them away" (Deut 28:26). Syn.: 1165, 2416, 4735, 6629, 6728. See: TWOT—208a; BDB—96d.

930. בְּהֵמוֹת {1x} **bᵉhêmôwth**, *bè-hay-mōhth';* in form a plur. of 929, but really a sing. of Eg. der.; a *water-ox,* i.e. the *hippopotamus* or Nile-horse:—Behemoth {1x}. Could possibly be an extinct dinosaur. See: TWOT—208b; BDB—97a.

931. בֹּהֶן {16x} **bôhen**, *bo'-hen;* from an unused root appar. mean. to *be thick;* the *thumb* of the hand or *great toe* of the foot:—thumb {9x}, great toe {7x}. See: TWOT—209a; BDB—97b.

932. בֹּהַן {2x} **Bôhan**, *bo'han;* an orth. var. of 931; *thumb, Bohan,* an Isr.:—*Bohan* {2x}. See: BDB—97b.

933. בֹּהַק {1x} **bôhaq**, *bo'-hak;* from an unused root mean. to *be pale;* white *scurf:*—freckled spot {1x}. *Bohaq* is a harmless eruption of the skin; a pimple. See: TWOT—210a; BDB—97b.

934. בֹּהֶרֶת {13x} **bôhereth**, *bo-heh'-reth;* fem. act. part. of the same as 925; a *whitish* spot on the skin:—bright spot {13x}. See: TWOT—211a; BDB—97b.

935. בּוֹא {2577x} **bôwʼ**, *bo;* a prim. root; to *go* or *come* (in a wide variety of applications):—come {1435x}, bring {487x}, . . . in {233x}, enter {125x}, go {123x}, carry {17x}, . . . down {23x}, pass {13x}, . . . out {12x}, misc. {109x}.

Bow' (935) means "to go in, enter, come, go." **(1)** First, this verb connotes movement in space from one place toward another. **(1a)** The meaning "go in" or "enter" appears in Gen 7:7, where it is said that Noah and his family "entered" the ark. **(1b)** In the causative stem, this verb can signify "cause to enter" or "bring into" (Gen 6:19) or "bring unto" (its meaning in its first biblical occurrence, Gen 2:19). **(1c)** In Gen 10:19, the verb is used more absolutely in the phrase "as thou goest unto Sodom." **(1d)** Interestingly, this verb can also mean "to come" and "to return." Abram and his family "came" to the land of Canaan (Gen 12:5), **(1e)** while in Deut 28:6 God blessed the godly who "go forth" (to work in the morning) and "return" (home in the evening). **(2)** Sometimes *bow'* refers to the "going down" or "setting" of the sun (Gen 15:12). **(3)** It can connote dying, in the sense of "going to one's fathers" (Gen 15:15). **(4)** Another special use is the "going into one's wife" or "cohabitation" (Gen 6:4). *Bow'* can also be used of movement in time. For example, the prophets speak of the "coming" day of judgment (1 Sa 2:31). **(5)** Finally, the verb can be used of the "coming" of an event such as the sign predicted by a false prophet (Deut 13:2).

(6) There are three senses in which God is said "to come." **(6a)** God "comes" through an angel (Judg 6:11) or other incarnated being (cf. Gen 18:14). **(6a1)** He "appears" and speaks to men in dreams (Gen 20:3) and **(6a2)** in other actual manifestations (Ex 20:20). **(6a3)** For example, during the Exodus, God "appeared" in the cloud and fire that went before the people (Ex 19:9). **(6b)** Secondly, God promises to "come" to the faithful wherever and whenever they properly worship Him (Ex 20:24). **(6b1)** The Philistines felt that God had "come" into the Israelite camp when the ark of the covenant arrived (1 Sa 4:7). **(6b2)** This usage associated with formal worship may appear in Ps 24:7, where the gates of Zion are said to open as the King of glory "enters" Jerusalem. **(6b3)** Also, the Lord is "to return" ("come back") to the new temple described in Eze 43:2. **(6c)** Finally, there is a group of prophetic pictures of divine "comings." **(6c1)** This theme may have originated in the hymns sung of God's "coming" to aid His people in war (cf. Deut 33:2). **(6c2)** In the Psalms (e.g., 50:3) and prophets (e.g., Is 30:27), the Lord "comes" in judgment and blessing—a poetic figure of speech borrowed from ancient Near Eastern mythology (cf. Eze 1:4).

(7) *Bow'* also is used to refer to the "coming" of the Messiah. **(7a)** In Zec 9:9, the messianic king is pictured as "coming" on a foal of a donkey. **(7b)** Some of the passages pose especially difficult problems, such as Gen 49:10, which prophesies that the scepter will remain in Judah "until Shiloh come." **(7c)** Another difficult passage is Eze 21:27: "until he come whose right it is." **(8)** A very well-known prophecy using the verb *bow'* is that concerning the "coming" of the Son of Man (Dan 7:13). **(9)** Finally, there is the "coming" of the last day (Amos 8:2) and the Day of the Lord (Is 13:6). See: TWOT—212; BDB—97c.

936. בּוּז {12x} **bûwz**, *booz;* a prim. root; to *disrespect:*—despise {10x}, contemned {1x}, utterly (inf. for emphasis) {1x}. Syn.: 959, 3988. See: TWOT—213; BDB—100b.

937. בּוּז {11x} **bûwz**, *booz;* from 936; *disrespect:*—contempt {7x}, despised {2x}, contemptuously {1x}, shamed {1x}. See: TWOT—213a; BDB—100b.

938. בּוּז {3x} **Bûwz**, *booz;* the same as 937; *Buz,* the name of a son of Nahor, and of an Isr.:—Buz {3x}. See: BDB—100c.

939. בּוּזָה {1x} **bûwzâh**, *boo-zaw';* fem. pass. part. of 936; something *scorned;* an obj. of *contempt:*—despised {1x}. See: TWOT—213b; BDB—100c.

940. בּוּזִי {2x} **Bûwzîy**, *boo-zee';* patron. from 938; a *Buzite* or desc. of Buz:—Buzite {2x}. See: BDB—100c.

941. בּוּזִי {1x} **Bûwzîy**, *boo-zee';* the same as 940; *Buzi,* an Isr.:—Buzi {1x}. See: BDB—100c.

942. בַּוַּי {1x} **Bavvay**, *bav-vah'ee;* prob. of Pers. or.; *Bavvai,* an Isr.:—Bavai {1x}. See: BDB—100c.

943. בּוּךְ {3x} **bûwk**, *book;* a prim. root; to *involve* (lit. or fig.):—perplexed {2x}, entangled {1x}. See: TWOT—214; BDB—100c.

944. בּוּל {2x} **bûwl**, *bool;* for 2981; *produce* (of the earth, etc.):—food {1x}, stock {1x}. See: TWOT—835d; BDB—100d, 385b.

945. בּוּל {1x} **Bûwl**, *bool;* the same as 944 (in the sense of *rain*); *Bul,* the eighth Heb. month:—Bul {1x}. See: TWOT—215; BDB—100d.

946. בּוּנָה {1x} **Bûwnâh**, *boo-naw';* from 995; *discretion; Bunah,* an Isr.:—Bunah {1x}. See: BDB—100d, 107b.

בּוּנִי **Bûwnîy**. See 1138.

947. בּוּס {12x} **bûwç**, *boos;* a prim. root; to *trample* (lit. or fig.):—tread . . . {9x}, polluted {2x}, loath {1x}. See: TWOT—216; BDB—100d.

948. בּוּץ {8x} **bûwts**, *boots;* from an unused root (of the same form) mean. to *bleach,* i.e. (intr.) *be white;* prob. *cotton* (of some sort):—fine linen {7x}, white linen {1x}. See: TWOT—219; BDB—101b.

949. בּוֹצֵץ {1x} **Bôwtsêts**, *bo-tsates';* from the same as 948; *shining; Botsets,* a rock near Michmash:—Bozez {1x}. See: BDB—130d.

950. בּוּקָה {1x} **bûwqâh**, *boo-kaw';* fem. pass. part. of an unused root (mean. to *be hollow*); *emptiness* (as adj.):—empty {1x}. See: TWOT—220a; BDB—101c.

951. בּוֹקֵר {1x} **bôwkêr**, *bo-kare';* prop. act. part. from 1239 as denom. from 1241; a *cattle-tender:*—herdsman {1x}. See: TWOT—274b; BDB—133c.

952. בּוּר {1x} **bûwr**, *boor;* a prim. root; to *bore,* i.e. (fig.) *examine:*—declare {1x}. See: TWOT—221; BDB—101c.

953. בּוֹר {69x} **bôwr**, *bore;* from 952 (in the sense of 877); a pit *hole* (espec. one used as a *cistern* or a *prison*):—pit {42x}, cistern {4x}, dungeon {11x}, well {9x}, dungeon + 1004 {2x}, fountain {1x}. Syn.: 875. See: TWOT—194e; BDB—92b, 92d, 101c, 694c, 710a.

954. בּוֹשׁ {109x} **bûwsh**, *boosh;* a prim. root; prop. to *pale,* i.e. by impl. to *be ashamed;* also (by impl.) to *be disappointed,* or *delayed:*—ashamed {72x}, confounded {21x}, shame {9x}, all {2x} (inf. for emphasis), confusion {1x}, delayed {1x}, dry {1x}, long {1x}, shamed {1x}.

Buwsh means "to be ashamed, feel ashamed." **(1)** The word has overtones of being or feeling worthless. **(1)** *Buwsh* means "to be ashamed" in Is 1:29: "For they shall be ashamed of the oaks which ye have desired, and ye shall be confounded for the gardens that ye have chosen." Syn.: 1322, 2659, 3639, 7036. See: TWOT—222; BDB—101c.

955. בּוּשָׁה {4x} **bûwshâh**, *boo-shaw';* fem. part. pass. of 954; *shame:*—shame {4x}. See: TWOT—222a; BDB—102a.

956. בּוּת {1x} **bûwth** (Aram.), *booth;* appar. denom. from 1005; to *lodge* over night:—pass the night {1x}. See: TWOT—2629; BDB—1084c.

957. בַּז {25x} **baz**, *baz;* from 962; *plunder:*—prey {18x}, spoil {4x}, spoiled {2x}, booty {1x}. Syn.: 961, 962, 1497, 7998, 8154. See: TWOT—225a; BDB—102b, 103a.

958. בָּזָא {2x} **bâzâ'**, *baw-zaw';* a prim. root; prob. to *cleave:*—spoiled {2x}. Syn.: See 957. See: TWOT—223; BDB—102b.

959. בָּזָה {43x} **bazah**, *baw-zaw';* a prim. root; to *disesteem:*—despise {36x}, contemptible {3x}, contemned {1x}, disdained {1x}, vile person {1x}, scorn {1x}. Syn.: 936, 937, 3988. See: TWOT—224; BDB—102b.

960. בָּזֹה {1x} **bâzôh**, *baw-zo';* from 959; *scorned:*—despise {1x}. See: TWOT—224b; BDB—102b.

961. בִּזָּה {10x} **bizzâh**, *biz-zaw';* fem. of 957; *booty:*—prey {4x}, spoil {6x}. See: TWOT—225, 225b; BDB—102c, 103a.

962. בָּזַז {43x} **bâzaz**, *baw-zaz';* a prim. root; to *plunder:*—spoil {9x}, prey {9x}, spoiled {6x}, rob {6x}, take {6x}, take away {2x}, caught {1x}, gathering {1x}, robbers {1x}, took {1x}, utterly {1x}. Syn.: See 957. See: TWOT—225; BDB—102d.

963. בִּזָּיוֹן {1x} **bizzâyôwn**, *biz-zaw-yone';* from 959; *disesteem:*—contempt {1x}. See: TWOT—224a; BDB—102c.

964. בִּזְיוֹתְיָה {1x} **bizyôwthᵉyâh**, *biz-yo-thè-yaw';* from 959 and 3050; *contempts of Jah; Bizjothjah,* a place in Pal.:—Bizjothjah {1x}. See: BDB—103a.

965. בָּזָק {1x} **bâzâq**, *baw-zawk';* from an unused root mean. to *lighten;* a *flash* of lightning:—flash of lightning {1x}. See: TWOT—226a; BDB—103b.

966. בֶּזֶק {3x} **Bezeq**, *beh'-zek;* from 965; *lightning; Bezek,* a place in Pal.:—Bezek {3x}. See: BDB—103b.

967. בָּזַר {2x} **bâzar**, *baw-zar';* a prim. root; to *disperse:*—scatter {2x}. See: TWOT—227; BDB—103b, 1084a.

968. בִּזְתָא {1x} **Bizthâ'**, *biz-thaw';* of Pers. or.; *Biztha,* a eunuch of Xerxes:—*Biztha* {1x}. See: BDB—103b.

969. בָּחוֹן {1x} **bâchôwn**, *baw-khone';* from 974; an *assayer* of metals:—tower {1x}. See: TWOT—230d; BDB—103d.

970. בָּחוּר {45x} **bâchûwr**, *baw-khoor';* or

בָּחֻר **bâchûr**, *baw-khoor';* pass. part. of 977; prop. *selected,* i.e. a *youth* (often collect.):—young man {42x}, the chosen {1x}, young {1x}, not translated {1x}. Syn.: 972, 977, 4005, 7206.

Bachur means "young man." **(1)** This word signifies the fully developed, vigorous, unmarried man. **(2)** In its first occurrence *bachur* is contrasted to betulah (1330), "virgin": "The sword without, and terror within, shall destroy both the young man and the virgin, the suckling also with the man of gray hairs" (Deut 32:25). **(3)** The strength of the "young man" is contrasted with the gray hair (crown of honor) of old men (Prov 20:29). **(4)** The period during which a "young man" is in his prime (could this be the period during which he is eligible for the draft—i.e., age 20-50?) is represented by the two nouns, bechurim (979) and bechurot (970). Syn.: 'Adam (120) connotes man as the creature created in God's image, the crown of all creation. Iysh (376) is used for man as the counterpart of woman and/or as distinguished in his maleness. Geber (1397) denotes a male as an antonym of a woman, many times suggesting strength, strong man. Enowsh (582) sets forth a collective idea man suggesting the frailty, vulnerability, and finitude of man as contrasted to God. *Bâchûr* (970) signifies the fully developed, vigorous, unmarried man is in his prime. See also: 376, 582, 1167, 1397, 1400, 4962. See: TWOT—231a; BDB—104c.

בְּחוּרוֹת **bᵉchûwrôwth**. See 979.

בַּחוּרִים **Bachûwrîym**. See 980.

971. בַּחִין {1x} **bachîyn**, *bakh-een';* another form of 975; a watch-*tower* of besiegers:—tower {1x}. See: TWOT—230c; BDB—103d.

972. בָּחִיר {13x} **bâchîyr**, *baw-kheer';* from 977; *select:*—chosen {8x}, elect {4x}, chose {1x}.

Bachiyr means "chosen ones." It is used always of the Lord's "chosen ones": "Saul, whom the Lord did choose" (2 Sa 21:6); "ye children of Jacob, his chosen ones" (1 Chr 16:13). Syn.: See 970. See: TWOT—231c; BDB—104c.

973. בָּחַל {2x} **bâchal**, *baw-khal';* a prim. root; to *loathe:*—abhor {1x}, gotten hastily {1x}. See: TWOT—229; BDB—103b, 103c.

974. בָּחַן {29x} **bâchan**, *baw-khan';* a prim. root; to *test* (espec. metals); Gen and

fig. to *investigate:*—try {19x}, prove {7x}, examine {1x}, tempt {1x}, trial {1x}. Syn.: 5254. See: TWOT—230; BDB—103c.

975. בַּחַן {1x} **bachan**, *bakh'-an;* from 974 (in the sense of keeping a *look-out*); a watch-*tower:*—tower {1x}. See: TWOT—230b; BDB—103d.

976. בֹּחַן {1x} **bôchan**, *bo'-khan;* from 974; *trial:*—tried {1x}. See: TWOT—230a; BDB—103d.

977. בָּחַר {172x} **bâchar**, *baw-khar';* a prim. root; prop. to *try,* i.e. (by impl.) *select:*—choose {77x}, chosen {77x}, choice {6x}, choose . . . out {5x}, acceptable {1x}, appoint {1x}, excellent {1x}, chosen men {1x}, rather {1x}, require {1x}, not translated {1x}.

Bachar (977) means "to choose." **(1)** *Bachar* first occurs in the Bible in Gen 6:2: ". . . They took them wives of all which they chose." **(2)** It is often used with a man as the subject: "Lot chose [for himself] all the plain of Jordan . . ." (Gen 13:11). **(3)** In more than half of the occurrences, God is the subject of *bachar,* as in Num 16:5: ". . . The Lord will show who are his, and who is holy; . . . even him whom he hath chosen will he cause to come near unto him." **(4)** Neh 9:7–8 describes God's "choosing" (election) of persons as far back as Abram: "Thou *art* the Lord the God, who didst choose Abram, and broughtest him forth out of Ur of the Chaldees, and gavest him the name of Abraham. **(5)** *Bachar* is used 30 times in Deuteronomy, all but twice referring to God's "choice" of Israel or something in Israel's life. "Because he loved thy fathers, therefore he chose their seed after them . . ." (Deut 4:37). **(6)** Being "chosen" by God brings people into an intimate relationship with Him: ". . . The children of the Lord your God: . . . the Lord hath chosen thee to be a peculiar people unto himself, above all the nations that are upon the earth" (Deut 14:1–2).

(7) God's "choices" shaped the history of Israel; **(7a)** His "choice" led to their redemption from Egypt (Deut 7:7–8), **(7b)** sent Moses and Aaron to work miracles in Egypt (Ps 105:26–27), and **(7c)** gave them the Levites "to bless in the name of the Lord" (Deut 21:5). **(7d)** He "chose" their inheritance (Ps 47:4), including Jerusalem, where He dwelt among them (Deut 12:5; 2 Chr 6:5, 21). **(7e)** But "they have chosen their own ways, and . . . I also will choose their delusions, and will bring their fears upon them . . ." (Is 66:3–4). **(8)** The covenant called men to respond to God's election: ". . . I have set before you life and death . . . : therefore choose life . . ." (Deut 30:19; cf. Josh 24:22). Syn.: 970, 972, 4005. See: TWOT—231; BDB—103d.

978. בַּחֲרוּמִי {1x} **Bachărûwmîy**, *bakh-ar-oo-mee';* patrial from 980 (by transp.); a *Bacharumite* or inhab. of Bachurim:—Baharumite {1x}. See: BDB—104d, 138c.

979. בְּחֻרוֹת {3x} **b**^e**chûrôwth**, *bekh-oo-rothe';* or

בְּחוּרוֹת **b**^e**chûwrôwth**, *bekh-oo-roth';* fem. plur. of 970; also (masc. plur.)

בְּחֻרִים **b**^e**chûrîym**, *bekh-oo-reem'; youth* (collect. and abstr.):—young men {1x}, youth {2x}. See: TWOT—231b; BDB—104c.

980. בַּחֻרִים {5x} **Bachûrîym**, *bakh-oo-reem';* or

בַּחוּרִים **Bachûwrîym**, *bakh-oo-reem';* masc. plur. of 970; *young men; Bachurim,* a place in Pal.:—Bahurim {5x}. See: BDB—104c.

981. בָּטָא {4x} **bâṭâ'**, *baw-taw';* or

בָּטָה **bâṭâh**, *baw-taw';* a prim. root; to *babble;* hence, to *vociferate* angrily:—pronounce {2x}, speak {1x}, speak unadvisely {1x}. See: TWOT—232; BDB—104d.

982. בָּטַח {120x} **bâṭach**, *baw-takh';* a prim. root; prop. to *hie* for refuge [but not so *precipitately* as 2620]; fig. to *trust, be confident* or *sure:*—trust {103x}, confidence {4x}, secure {4x}, confident {2x}, bold {1x}, careless {1x}, hope {1x}, hoped {1x}, ones {1x}, sure {1x}, women {1x}.

(1) Betach is a noun meaning "security, trust." One occurrence is in Isa. 32:17: ". . . And the effect of righteousness quietness and assurance [betach] for ever." **(2)** *Batach* as a verb means "to be reliant, trust, be unsuspecting." The word means "to trust" in Deut 28:52: "And he shall besiege thee in all thy gates, until thy high and fenced walls come down, wherein thou trustedst, throughout all thy land. . . ." **(3)** Betah as an adjective means "secure." In two passages this word suggests trust and security: "And Gideon went up . . . and smote the host: for the host was secure [unsuspecting]" (Judg. 8:11; cf. Is 32:17). Syn.: 2620. See: TWOT—233; BDB—105a.

983. בֶּטַח {42x} **beṭach**, *beh'takh;* from 982; prop. a place of *refuge;* abstr. *safety,* both the fact (*security*) and the feeling (*trust*); often (adv. with or without prep.) *safely:*—safely {17x}, safety {9x}, carelessly {3x}, careless {2x}, safe {2x}, securely {2x}, assurance {1x}, boldly {1x}, care {1x}, confidence {1x}, hope {1x}, secure {1x}, surely {1x}.

(1) *Betach* as an adverb means "securely." **(2)** In its first occurrence *betach* emphasizes the status of a city which was certain of not being attacked: ". . . Two of the sons . . . took each man his sword, and came upon the city boldly, and slew all the males" (Gen 34:25). Thus the city was unsuspecting regarding the impending attack. **(3)** In passages such as Prov 10:9 (cf. Prov 1:33) *betach* emphasizes a confidence and the absence of impending doom: "He that walketh uprightly walketh surely: but he that perverteth his ways shall be known [faces certain judgment]." **(4)** Israel dwells in security **(4a)** apart from any possible doom or danger because God keeps her completely safe (Deut 33:12, 28; cf. 12:10). **(4b)** This condition is contingent on their faithfulness to God (Lev 25:18–19). **(5)** In the eschaton, however, such absence of danger is guaranteed by the Messiah's presence (Jer 23:5–6). See: TWOT—233a; BDB—105b.

984. בֶּטַח {1x} **Beṭach**, beh'-takh; the same as 983; *Betach,* a place in Syria:—Betah {1x}. See: BDB—105c.

985. בִּטְחָה {1x} **biṭchâh**, *bit-khaw';* fem. of 984; *trust:*—confidence {1x}. See: TWOT—233b; BDB—105c.

986. בִּטָּחוֹן {3x} **biṭṭâchôwn**, *bit-taw-khone';* from 982; *trust:*—confidence {2x}, hope {1x}. See: TWOT—233c; BDB—105c.

987. בַּטֻּחוֹת {1x} **baṭṭûchôwth**, *bat-too-khōth';* fem. plur. from 982; security:—secure {1x}. See: TWOT—233c; BDB—105c.

988. בָּטֵל {1x} **bâṭêl**, *baw-tale';* a prim. root; to *desist* from labor:—cease {1x}. See: TWOT—235; BDB—105d, 1084b.

989. בְּטֵל {6x} **b**^e**ṭêl** (Aram.), *bet-ale';* corresp. to 988; to *stop:*—(cause, make to), cease {5x}, hinder {1x}. See: TWOT—2625; BDB—1084b.

990. בֶּטֶן {72x} **beṭen**, *beh'-ten;* from an unused root prob. mean. to *be hollow;* the *belly,* espec. the *womb;* also the *bosom* or *body* of anything:—belly {30x}, womb {31x}, body {8x}, within {2x}, born {1x}. Syn.: 7358. See: TWOT—236a; BDB—105d.

991. בֶּטֶן {1x} **Beṭen**, *beh'-ten;* the same as 990; *Beten,* a place in Pal.:—*Beten* {1x}. See: BDB—106b.

992. בֹּטֶן {1x} **bôṭen**, *bo'-ten;* from 990; (only in plur.) a *pistachio*-nut (from its form):—nuts {1x}. See: TWOT—237a; BDB—106b.

993. בְּטֹנִים {1x} **B**^e**ṭônîym**, *bet-o-neem';* prob. plur. from 992; *hollows: Betonim,* a place in Pal.:—Betonim {1x}. See: BDB—106b.

994. בִּי {12x} **bîy**, *bee;* perh. from 1158 (in the sense of *asking*); prop. a *request;* used only adv. (always with "my Lord"); *Oh that!; with leave,* or *if it please:*—O {7x}, Oh {4x}, alas {1x}. See: TWOT—238a; BDB—106c.

995. בִּין {170x} **bîyn**, *bene;* a prim. root; to *separate* mentally (or *distinguish*), i.e. (Gen) *understand:*—understand {62x}, understanding {32x}, consider {22x}, prudent {8x}, perceive {7x}, regard {6x}, discern {3x}, instruct {3x}, misc. {27x}.

Bîyn basically means to understand, be able, deal wisely, consider, pay attention to, regard, notice, discern, perceive, inquire. **(1)** *Biyn* appears in Jer 9:12 with the meaning "to understand": "Who is the wise man, that may understand this?" **(2)** In Job 6:30 the word means "to discern," and in **(3)** Deut 32:7 it means "to consider." Syn.: 998, 7919. See: TWOT—239; BDB—106c.

996. בֵּין {32x} **bêyn**, *bane* (sometimes in the plur. masc. or fem.); prop. the constr. contr. form of an otherwise unused noun from 995; a *distinction;* but used only as a prep. *between* (repeated before each noun, often with other particles); also as a conj., *either . . . or:*—between, betwixt, asunder, within, between, out of, from = {32x}.

Beyn means "between; in the midst of; among; within; in the interval of." **(1)** This word nearly always (except in 1 Sa 17:4, 23) is a preposition meaning "in the interval of" or "between." **(2)** The word may represent "the area between" in general: "And it shall be for a sign unto thee upon thine hand, and for a memorial between thine eyes . . ." (Ex 13:9). **(3)** Sometimes the word means "within," in the sense of a person's or a thing's "being in the area of": "The slothful man saith, There is a lion in the way; a lion is in the streets" (Prov 26:13). **(4)** In other places, *beyn* means "among": "Shall the companions make a banquet of him [Leviathan]? Shall they part him among [give each a part] the merchants?" (Job 41:6). **(5)** In Job 34:37, the word means "in the midst of," in the sense of "one among a group": "For he addeth rebellion unto his sin, he clappeth his hands among us. . . ."

(6) The area separating two particular objects is indicated in several ways. **(6a)** First, by repeating *beyn* before each object: "And God divided the light from the darkness" [literally, "between the light and between the darkness"] (Gen 1:4); that is, He put an interval or space between them. **(6b)** In other places (more rarely), this concept is represented by putting *beyn* before one object and the preposition le before the second object: "Let there be a firmament in the midst [beyn] of the waters, and let it divide the waters from [le] the waters" (Gen 1:6). **(6c)** In still other instances, this idea is represented **(6c1)** by placing *beyn* before the first object plus the phrase meaning "with reference to" before the second (Joel 2:17), or **(6c2)** by *beyn* before the first object and the phrase "with reference to the interval of" before the second (Is 59:2). **(7)** *Beyn* is used in the sense of "distinguishing between" in many passages: "Let there be lights in the firmament of the heaven to divide the day from [ben] the night" (Gen 1:14).

(8) Sometimes *beyn* signifies a metaphorical relationship. For example, "This is the token of the covenant which I make between [beyn] me and you and every living creature . . ." (Gen 9:12). The covenant is a contractual relationship. **(9)** Similarly, the Bible speaks of an oath (Gen 26:28) and of goodwill (Prov 14:9) filling the metaphorical "space" between two parties. **(10)** This word is used to signify an "interval of days," or "a period of time": "Now that which was prepared for me was . . . once in ten days [literally, "at ten-day intervals"] store of all sorts of wine . . ." (Neh 5:18). **(11)** In the dual form, *beyn* represents "the space between two armies": "And there went out a champion [literally, "a man between the two armies"] out of the camp of the Philistines, named Goliath . . ." (1 Sa 17:4). In ancient warfare, a battle or even an entire war could be decided by a contest between two champions. See: TWOT—239a; BDB—107b, 108a, 120a, 1084b.

997. בֵּין {2x} **bêyn** (Aram.), *bane;* corresp. to 996:—among {1x}, between {1x}. See: TWOT—2626; BDB—1084b.

998. בִּינָה {38x} **bîynâh**, *bee-naw';* from 995; *understanding:*—understanding {32x}, wisdom {2x}, knowledge {1x}, meaning {1x}, perfectly {1x}, understand {1x}.

Biynah means "understanding." **(1)** *Biynah* appears 37 times and in all periods of biblical Hebrew even though it belongs primarily to the sphere of wisdom and wisdom literature. **(2)** This noun represents the "act of understanding": "And in all matters of wisdom and understanding, that the king inquired of them, he found them ten times better than all the magicians . . ." (Dan 1:20). **(3)** Elsewhere *biynah* signifies the faculty "understanding": ". . . The spirit of my understanding causeth me to answer" (Job 20:3). **(4)** In other passages the object of knowledge, in the sense of what one desires to know, is indicated by *biynah:* "Keep therefore and do them [God's laws]: for this is your wisdom and your understanding in the sight of the nations, which shall hear all these statutes . . ." (Deut 4:6; cf. 1 Chr 22:12). **(5)** God's law, therefore, is wisdom and "understanding"—what one should know. **(6)** This word is sometimes personified: "Yea, if thou criest after knowledge, and liftest up thy voice for understanding; if thou seekest her as silver, and searchest for her as for hid treasures . . ." (Prov 2:3–4). See also: 4905, 8394. See: TWOT—239b; BDB—108a, 1084b.

999. בִּינָה {1x} **bîynâh** (Aram.), *bee-naw';* corresp. to 998:—understanding {1x}. See: TWOT—2627; BDB—1084b.

1000. בֵּיצָה {1x} **bêytsâh**, *bay-tsaw';* from the same as 948; an *egg* (from its whiteness):—egg {1x}. See: TWOT—218a; BDB—101b.

1001. בִּירָא {1x} **bîyrâᵓ** (Aram.), *bee-raw';* corresp. to 1002; a *palace:*—palace {1x}. See: TWOT—2628; BDB—1084c.

1002. בִּירָה {16x} **bîyrâh**, *bee-raw';* of for. or.; a *castle* or *palace:*—palace {16x}. Syn.: 1964. See: TWOT—240; BDB—108b, 1084c.

1003. בִּירָנִית {2x} **bîyrânîyth**, *bee-raw-neeth';* from 1002; a *fortress:*—castle {2x}. See: TWOT—240; BDB—108c.

1004. בַּיִת {2055X} **bayith**, *bah'-yith;* prob. from 1129 abb.; a *house* (in the greatest var. of applications, espec. *family,* etc.):—house {1881x}, household {54x}, home {25x}, within {22x}, temple {11x}, prison {16x}, place {16x}, family {3x}, families + 1 {2x}, dungeon {2x}, misc. {23x}.

Bayith means "house or building; home; household; land." **(1)** First, this noun denotes a fixed, established structure made from some kind of material. **(1a)** As a "permanent dwelling place" it is usually distinguished from a tent (2 Sa 16:21, cf. v. 22). **(1c)** This word can even be applied to a one-room dwelling: "And he [Lot] said [to the two angels], Behold now, my lords, turn in, I pray you, into your servant's house . . ." (Gen 19:2). **(1d)** *Bayith* is also distinguished from temporary booths or huts: "And Jacob journeyed to Succoth, and built him a house, and made booths for his cattle . . ." (Gen 33:17). **(1e)** In Ps 132:3 the word means "dwelling-living-place" and is used in direct conjunction with "tent" (literally, "tent of my house"): "Surely I will not come into the tabernacle of my house, nor go up into my bed." **(1f)** A similar usage appears in 1 Chr 9:23 (literally, "the tent house"): "So they and their children had the oversight of the gates of the house of the Lord, namely, the house of the tabernacle, by wards."

(2) Second, in many passages (especially when the word is joined to the word God) *bayith* represents a place of worship or "sanctuary": "The first of the first fruits of thy land thou shalt bring into the house of the Lord thy God" (Ex 23:19). **(2a)** Elsewhere this noun signifies God's temple in Jerusalem: "And against the wall of the house he built chambers round about, against the walls of the house round about, both of the temple and of the oracle . . ." (1 Kin 6:5). **(2b)** Sometimes the word has this meaning although it is not further defined (cf. Eze 41:7). **(3)** Third, *bayith* can signify rooms and/or wings of a house: "And let the king appoint officers in all the provinces of his kingdom, that they may gather together all the fair young virgins unto Shushan the palace, to the [harem] (literally, to the house of the women; Est 2:3). . . ." **(3a)** In this connection *bayith* can also represent the inside of a building or some other structure as opposed to the outside: "Make thee an ark of gopher wood; rooms shalt thou make in the ark, and shalt pitch it within and without with pitch" (Gen 6:14—the first biblical occurrence).

(4) Fourth, *bayith* sometimes refers to the place where something or someone dwells or rests. So the underworld (Sheol) is termed a "home": "If I wait, the grave is mine house: I have made my bed in the darkness" (Job 17:13). **(4b)** An "eternal home" is one's grave: ". . . Man goeth to his long home, and the mourners go about the streets" (Eccl 12:5). **(4c)** "House" can also mean "place" when used with "grave," as in Neh 2:3: "Let the king live for ever: why should not my countenance be sad, when the city, the place of my fathers' sepulchers. . . ." **(4d)** *Bayith* means a receptacle in Is 3:20. **(4e)** In 1 Kin 18:32 the "house of two seeds" is a container for seed: "And with the stones he built an altar in the name of the Lord: and he made a trench about the altar, as great as would contain [literally, "a house of"] two measures of seed." **(4f)** Houses for bars are supports: "And thou shalt overlay the boards with gold, and make their rings of gold for places [literally, "houses"] for the bars" (Ex 26:29). **(4g)** Similarly, see "the places [house] of the two paths," a crossing of two paths, in Prov 8:2. **(4h)** The steppe is termed the "house of beasts": ". . . whose house I have made the wilderness, and the barren land his dwellings [house of beasts]" (Job 39:6).

(5) Fifth, *bayith* is often used of those who live in a house, i.e., a "household": "Come thou and all thy house into the ark . . ." (Gen 7:1). **(5a)** In passages such as Josh 7:14 this word means "family": ". . . And it shall be, that the tribe which the Lord taketh shall come according to the families thereof; and the family which the Lord shall take shall come by households [literally, by house or by those who live in a single dwelling]. . . ." **(5b)** In a similar nuance this noun means "descendants": "And there went a man of the house of Levi, and took to wife a daughter of Levi" (Ex 2:1). **(5c)** This word can be used of one's extended family and even of everyone who lives in a given area: "And the men of Judah came, and there they anointed David king over the house of Judah" (2 Sa 2:4). **(5d)** Gen 50:4, however, uses *bayith* in the sense of "a royal court" or all the people in a king's court: "And when the days of his mourning were past, Joseph spake unto the house of Pharaoh. . . ." **(5e)** The ideas "royal court" and "descendant" are joined in 1 Sa 20:16: "So Jonathan made a covenant with the house of David. . . ." **(5f)** In a few passages *bayith* means "territory" or "country": "Set the trumpet to thy mouth. He shall come as an eagle against the house of the Lord . . ." (Hos 8:1, 9:15, Jer 12:7, Zec 9:8). See: TWOT—241; BDB—108c, 111b, 143d, 476c, 1084c.

1005. בַּיִת {44x} **bayith** (Aram.), *bah-yith;* corresp. to 1004:—house {44x}. See: TWOT—2629a; BDB—1084c.

1006. בַּיִת {1x} **Bayith**, *bah'-yith;* the same as 1004; *Bajith,* a place in Pal.:—Bajith {1x}. See: BDB—110c.

1007. בֵּית אָוֶן {1x} **Bêyth ᵓÂven**, *bayth aw'-ven;* from 1004 and 205; *house of vanity; Beth-Aven,* a place in Pal.:—Beth-aven {1x}. See: BDB—110c.

1008. בֵּית־אֵל {70x} **Bêyth-ᵓÊl**, *bayth-ale';* from 1004 and 410; *house of God; Beth-El,* a place in Pal.:—Beth-el {70x}. See: TWOT—241a; BDB—110d.

1009. בֵּית אַרְבֵּאל {1x} **Bêyth ᵓArbêᵓl**, *bayth ar-bale';* from 1004 and 695 and 410; *house of God's ambush; Beth-Arbel,* a place in Pal.:—Beth-Arbel {1x}. See: BDB—70d, 111a.

1010. בֵּית בַּעַל מְעוֹן {2x} **Bêyth Baᶜal Mᵉᶜôwn**, *bayth bah'-al mè-own';* from 1004 and 1168 and 4583; *house of Baal* of (the) *habitation of* [appar. by transp.]; or (short.)

בֵּית מְעוֹן **Bêyth Mᵉᶜôwn**, *bayth mè-own'; house of habitation of* (Baal); *Beth-Baal-Meön,* a place in Pal.:—Beth-baal-meon {1x}, Bethmeon {1x}. Syn.: 1186 and 1194. See: BDB—111a, 112a.

1011. בֵּית בִּרְאִי {1x} **Bêyth Birᵓîy**, *bayth biree';* from 1004 and 1254; *house of a creative* one; *Beth-Biri,* a place in Pal.:—Beth-birei {1x}. See: BDB—111a, 111d, 135d, 740a.

1012. בֵּית בָּרָה {2x} **Bêyth Bârâh**, *bayth baw-raw'*; prob. from 1004 and 5679; *house of* (the) *ford; Beth-Barah*, a place in Pal.:—Beth-barah {2x}. See: BDB—111a.

1013. בֵּית־גָּדֵר {1x} **Bêyth-Gâdêr**, *bayth-gaw-dare'*; from 1004 and 1447; *house of* (the) *wall; Beth-Gader*, a place in Pal.:—Beth-gader {1x}. See: BDB—111b.

1014. בֵּית גָּמוּל {1x} **Bêyth Gâmûwl**, *bayth gaw-mool'*; from 1004 and the pass. part. of 1576; *house of* (the) *weaned; Beth-Gamul*, a place E. of the Jordan:—Beth-gamul {1x}. See: BDB—111b.

1015. בֵּית דִּבְלָתַיִם {1x} **Bêyth Diblâthayim**, *bayth dib-law-thah'-yim*; from 1004 and the dual of 1690; *house of* (the) *two figcakes; Beth-Diblathajim*, a place E. of the Jordan:—Beth-diblathaim {1x}. See: BDB—111b, 179c.

1016. בֵּית־דָּגוֹן {2x} **Bêyth-Dâgôwn**, *bayth-daw-gohn'*; from 1004 and 1712; *house of Dagon; Beth-Dagon*, the name of two places in Pal.:—Beth-dagon {2x}. See: BDB—111b.

1017. בֵּית הָאֱלִי {1x} **Bêyth hâ-ʼĔlîy**, *bayth haw-el-ee'*; patrial from 1008 with the art. interposed; a *Beth-elite*, or inhab. of Bethel:—Bethelite {1x}. See: BDB—111a.

1018. בֵּית הָאֵצֶל {1x} **Bêyth hâ-ʼÊtsel**, *bayth haw-ay'-tsel*; from 1004 and 681 with the art. interposed; *house of the side; Beth-ha-Etsel*, a place in Pal.:—Beth-ezel {1x}. See: BDB—111a.

1019. בֵּית הַגִּלְגָּל {1x} **Bêyth hag-Gilgâl**, *bayth hag-gil gawl'*; from 1004 and 1537 with the article interposed; *house of Gilgal* (or *rolling*); *Beth-hag-Gilgal*, a place in Pal.:—Beth-gilgal {1x}. See: BDB—111b.

1020. בֵּית הַיְשִׁימוֹת {4x} **Bêyth ha-Yᵉshîy-môwth**, *bayth hah-yesh-ee-mōth'*; from 1004 and the plur. of 3451 with the art. interposed; *house of the deserts; Beth-ha-Jeshimoth*, a town E. of the Jordan:—Beth-jeshimoth {4x}. See: BDB—111d.

1021. בֵּית הַכֶּרֶם {2x} **Bêyth hak-Kerem**, *bayth hak-keh'-rem*; from 1004 and 3754 with the art. interposed; *house of the vineyard; Beth-hak-Kerem*, a place in Pal.:—Beth-haccerem {2x}. See: BDB—111d.

1022. בֵּית הַלַּחְמִי {4x} **Bêyth hal-Lachmîy**, *bayth hal-lakh-mee'*; patrial from 1035 with the art. ins.; a *Beth-lechemite*, or native of Bethlechem:—Bethlehemite {1x}. See: BDB—112a.

1023. בֵּית הַמֶּרְחָק {1x} **Bêyth ham-Merchâq**, *bayth ham-mer-khawk'*; from 1004 and 4801 with the art. interposed; *house of the breadth; Beth-ham-Merchak*, a place in Pal.:—place that was far off {1x}. See: BDB—112a, 935d.

1024. בֵּית הַמַּרְכָּבוֹת {2x} **Bêyth ham-Markâ-bôwth**, *bayth ham-mar-kaw-both'*; or (short.)

בֵּית מַרְכָּבֹת **Bêyth Markâbôwth**, *bayth mar-kaw-both'*; from 1004 and the plur. of 4818 (with or without the art. interposed); *place of* (the) *chariots; Beth-ham-Markaboth* or *Beth-Markaboth*, a place in Pal.:—Beth-marcaboth {2x}. See: BDB—1121b.

1025. בֵּית הָעֵמֶק {1x} **Bêyth hâ-ʻÊmeq**, *bayth haw-ay'-mek*; from 1004 and 6010 with the art. interposed; *house of the valley; Beth-ha-Emek*, a place in Pal.:—Beth-emek {1x}. See: BDB—112b.

1026. בֵּית הָעֲרָבָה {3x} **Bêyth hâ-ʻĂrâbâh**, *bayth haw-ar-aw-baw'*; from 1004 and 6160 with the art. interposed; *house of the Desert; Beth-ha-Arabah*, a place in Pal.:—Beth-arabah {3x}. See: BDB—112c.

1027. בֵּית הָרָם {1x} **Bêyth hâ-Râm**, *bayth haw-rawm'*; from 1004 and 7311 with the art. interposed; *house of the height; Beth-ha-Ram*, a place E. of the Jordan:—Beth-aram {1x}. See: BDB—111b, 248b.

1028. בֵּית הָרָן {1x} **Bêyth hâ-Rân**, *bayth haw-rawn'*; prob. for 1027; *Beth-ha-Ran*, a place E. of the Jordan:—Beth-haran {1x}. See: BDB—111c.

1029. בֵּית הַשִּׁטָּה {1x} **Bêyth hash-Shiṭṭâh**, *bayth hash-shit-taw'*; from 1004 and 7848 with the art. interposed; *house of the acacia; Beth-hash-Shittah*, a place in Pal.:—Beth-shittah {1x}. See: BDB—112d.

1030. בֵּית הַשִּׁמְשִׁי {2x} **Bêyth hash-Shimshîy**, *bayth hash-shim-shee'*; patrial from 1053 with the art. ins.; a *Beth-shimshite*, or inhab. of Bethshemesh:—Bethshemite {2x}. See: BDB—113a.

1031. בֵּית חָגְלָה {3x} **Bêyth Choglâh**, *bayth chog-law'*; from 1004 and the same as 2295; *house of a partridge; Beth-Choglah*, a place in Pal.:—Beth-hoglah {2x}, Bethhogla {1x}. See: BDB—111c.

1032. בֵּית חוֹרוֹן {14x} **Bêyth Chôwrôwn**, *bayth kho-rone'*; from 1004 and 2356; *house of hollowness; Beth-Choron*, the name of two adjoining places in Pal.:—Beth-horon {14x}. See: BDB—111c, 357b, 751c.

בֵּית חָנָן **Bêyth Chânân**. See 358.

1033. בֵּית כַּר {1x} **Bêyth Kar**, *bayth kar*; from 1004 and 3733; *house of pasture; Beth-Car*, a place in Pal.:—Beth-car {1x}. See: BDB—111d.

1034. בֵּית לְבָאוֹת {1x} **Bêyth Lᵉbâʼôwth**, *bayth leb-aw-ōth'*; from 1004 and the plural of 3833; *house of lionesses; Beth-Lebaoth*, a place in Pal.:—Beth-lebaoth {1x}. Syn.: 3822. See: BDB—111d.

1035. בֵּית לֶחֶם {411x} **Bêyth Lechem**, *bayth leh'-khem*; from 1004 and 3899; *house of bread; Beth-Lechem*, a place in Pal.:—Beth-lehem {31x}, Bethlemjudah + 3063 {10x}. See: BDB—111d.

1036. בֵּית לְעַפְרָה {1x} **Bêyth lᵉ-ʻAphrâh**, *bayth lè-af-raw'*; from 1004 and the fem. of 6083 (with prep. interposed); *house to* (i.e. *of*) *dust; Beth-le-Aphrah*, a place in Pal.:—house of Aphrah {1x}. See: BDB—112a, 780b.

1037. בֵּית מִלּוֹא {4x} **Bêyth Millôwʼ**, *bayth mil-lo'*; or

בֵּית מִלֹּא **Bêyth Millôʼ**, *bayth mil-lo'*; from 1004 and 4407; *house of* (the) *rampart; Beth-Millo*, the name of two citadels:—house of Millo {4x} [or left untranslated]. See: BDB—112a, 571c.

1038. בֵּית מַעֲכָה {2x} **Bêyth Maʻâkâh**, *bayth mah-ak-aw'*; from 1004 and 4601; *house of Maakah; Beth-Maakah*, a place in Pal.:—Beth-maachah {2x}. See: BDB—112a, 591.

1039. בֵּית נִמְרָה {2x} **Bêyth Nimrâh**, *bayth nim-raw'*; from 1004 and the fem. of 5246; *house of* (the) *leopard; Beth-Nimrah*, a place east of the Jordan:—Beth-nimrah {2x}. Syn.: 5247. See: BDB—112b.

1040. בֵּית עֵדֶן {1x} **Bêyth ʻÊden**, *bayth ay'-den*; from 1004 and 5730; *house of pleasure; Beth-Eden*, a place in Syria:—Beth-eden {1x}. See: BDB—112b, 727a.

1041. בֵּית עַזְמָוֶת {1x} **Bêyth ʻAzmâveth**, *bayth az-maw'-veth*; from 1004 and 5820; *house of Azmaveth*, a place in Pal.:—Beth-az-maveth {1x}. Syn.: 5820. See: BDB—112b.

1042. בֵּית עֲנוֹת {1x} **Bêyth ʻĂnôwth**, *bayth an-ōth'*; from 1004 and a plur. from 6030; *house of replies; Beth-Anoth*, a place in Pal.:—Beth-anoth {1x}. See: BDB—112b, 779a.

1043. בֵּית עֲנָת {3x} **Bêyth ʻĂnâth**, *bayth an-awth'*; an orth. var. for 1042; *Beth-Anath*, a place in Pal.:—Beth-anath {3x}. See: BDB—112c, 779a.

1044. בֵּית עֵקֶד {2x} **Bêyth ʻÊqed**, *bayth ay'-ked*; from 1004 and a der. of 6123; *house of* (the) *binding* (for sheep-shearing); *Beth-Eked*, a place in Pal.:—shearing house {1x}, not translated {1x}. See: BDB—112c, 785b.

1045. בֵּית עַשְׁתָּרוֹת {1x} **Bêyth ʻAshtârôwth**, *bayth ash-taw-rōth'*; from 1004 and 6252; *house of Ashtoreths; Beth-Ashtaroth*, a place in Pal.:—house of Ashtaroth {1x}. Syn.: 1203, 6252. See: BDB—800a, 800b.

1046. בֵּית פֶּלֶט {2x} **Bêyth Pelet**, *bayth peh'-let*; from 1004 and 6412; *house of escape; Beth-Palet*, a place in Pal.:—Bethphelet {1x}, Bethpalet {1x}. See: BDB—112c.

1047. בֵּית פְּעוֹר {4x} **Bêyth Pᵉʻôwr**, *bayth pè-ore'*; from 1004 and 6465; *house of Peor; Beth-Peor*, a place E. of the Jordan:—Beth-peor {4x}. See: BDB—112c.

1048. בֵּית פַּצֵּץ {1x} **Bêyth Patstsêts**, *bayth pats-tsates'*; from 1004 and a der. from 6327; *house of dispersion; Beth-Patstsets*, a place in Pal.:—Beth-pazzez {1x}. See: BDB—112d, 823a.

1049. בֵּית צוּר {4x} **Bêyth Tsûwr**, *bayth tsoor'*; from 1004 and 6697; *house of* (the) *rock; Beth-Tsur*, a place in Pal.:—Beth-zur {4x}. See: BDB—112d.

1050. בֵּית רְחוֹב {2x} **Bêyth Rᵉchôwb**, *bayth rè-khobe'*; from 1004 and 7339; *house of* (the) *street; Beth-Rechob*, a place in Pal.:—Beth-rehob {1x}. See: BDB—112d.

1051. בֵּית רָפָא {1x} **Bêyth Râphâʼ**, *bayth raw-faw'*; from 1004 and 7497; *house of* (the) *giant; Beth-Rapha*, an Isr.:—Beth-rapha {1x}. See: BDB—112d, 951a.

1052. בֵּית שְׁאָן {9x} **Bêyth Shᵉʼân**, *bayth shè-awn'*; or

בֵּית שָׁן **Bêyth Shân**, *bayth shawn'*; from 1004 and 7599; *house of ease; Beth-Shean* or *Beth-Shan*, a place in Pal.:—Beth-shean {6x}, Beth-Shan {3x}. See: BDB—112d, 983b, 1039c.

1053. בֵּית שֶׁמֶשׁ {21x} **Bêyth Shemesh**, *bayth sheh'-mesh*; from 1004 and 8121; *house of* (the) *sun; Beth-Shemesh*, a place in Pal.:—Beth-shemesh {21x}. See: BDB—112d, 746d.

1054. בֵּית תַּפּוּחַ {1x} **Bêyth Tappûwach**, *bayth tap-poo'-akh*; from 1004 and 8598; *house of* (the) *apple; Beth-Tappuach*, a place in Pal.:—Beth-tappuah {1x}. See: BDB—113a.

1055. בִּיתָן {3x} **bîythân**, *bee-thawn';* prob. from 1004; a *palace* (i.e. *large house*):—palace {3x}. See: TWOT—241c; BDB—113a.

1056. בָּכָא {1x} **Bâkâ'**, *baw-kaw';* from 1058, *weeping; Baca,* a valley in Pal.:—Baca {1x}. See: BDB—113a.

1057. בָּכָא {4x} **bâkâ'**, *baw-kaw';* the same as 1056; the *weeping* tree (some gum-distilling tree, perh. the *balsam*):—mulberry tree {4x}. *Baka'* is a shrub which drips sap when cut. See: TWOT—242; BDB—113a.

1058. בָּכָה {114x} **bâkâh**, *baw-kaw';* a prim. root; to *weep;* Gen to *bemoan:*—weep {98x}, bewail {5x}, sore {3x} (inf. for emphasis) mourned {2x}, all {1x} (inf), complain {1x}, lamentation {1x}, more {1x} (inf.), weep over {1x}, tears {1x}. See: TWOT—243; BDB—113b.

1059. בֶּכֶה {1x} **bekeh**, *beh'-keh;* from 1058; a *weeping:*—× sore {1x}. See: TWOT—243a; BDB—113d.

1060. בְּכוֹר {117x} **bekôwr**, *bek-ore';* from 1069; *firstborn;* hence, *chief:*—firstborn {101x}, firstling {10x}, eldest {4x}, firstborn + 1121 {1x}, eldest son {1x}.

Bekowr means "firstborn." **(1)** The word represents the "firstborn" individual in a family (Gen 25:13); **(2)** the word can also represent the "firstborn" of a nation, collectively (Num 3:46). **(3)** The plural form of the word appears occasionally (Neh 10:36); in this passage, the word is applied to animals. **(4)** In other passages, the singular form of *bekowr* signifies a single "firstling" animal (Lev 27:26) or collectively the "firstborn" of a herd (Ex 11:5). **(5)** The "oldest" or "firstborn" son (Ex 6:14) had special privileges within the family. **(5a)** He received the special family blessing, which meant spiritual and social leadership and a double portion of the father's possessions—or twice what all the other sons received (Deut 21:17). **(5b)** He could lose this blessing through misdeeds (Gen 35:22) or by selling it (Gen 25:29–34).

(6) God claimed all Israel and all their possessions as His own. **(6a)** As a token of this claim, Israel was to give Him all its "firstborn" (Ex 13:1–16). **(6b)** The animals were to be sacrificed, redeemed, or killed, while the male children were redeemed either by being replaced with Levites or by the payment of a redemption price (Num 3:40ff.). **(7)** Israel was God's "firstborn"; it enjoyed a privileged position and blessings over all other nations (Ex 4:22; Jer 31:9). **(8)** The "first-born of death" is an idiom meaning a deadly disease (Job 18:13); **(9)** the "first-born of the poor" is the poorest class of people (Is 14:30). See: TWOT—244a; BDB—114a.

1061. בִּכּוּר {18x} **bikkûwr**, *bik-koor';* from 1069; the *first-fruits* of the crop:—firstfruit {14x}, firstripe {2x}, firstripe figs {1x}, hasty fruit {1x}.

Bikkuwr (1061) means "first fruits." **(1)** The "first grain and fruit" harvested was to be offered to God (Num 28:26) in recognition of God's ownership of the land and His sovereignty over nature. **(2)** Bread of the "first fruits" was bread made of the first harvest grain, presented to God at Pentecost (Lev 23:20). **(3)** The "day of the first fruits" was Pentecost (Num 28:26). See: TWOT 244e; BDB—114c.

1062. בְּכוֹרָה {15x} **bekôwrâh**, *bek-o-raw';* or (short.)

בְּכֹרָה **bekôrâh**, *bek-o-raw';* fem. of 1060; the *firstling* of man or beast; abstr. *primogeniture:*—birthright {9x}, firstling {5x}, firstborn {1x}. See: TWOT—244c; BDB—114c.

1063. בִּכּוּרָה {2x} **bikkûwrâh**, *bik-koo-raw';* fem. of 1061; the *early* fig:—firstripe {1x}, firstripe fruit {1x}. See: TWOT—244f; BDB—114c.

1064. בְּכוֹרַת {1x} **Bekôwrath**, *bek-o-rath';* fem. of 1062; *primogeniture; Bekorath,* an Isr.:—Bechorath {1x}. See: BDB—114c.

1065. בְּכִי {30x} **bekîy**, *bek-ee';* from 1058; a *weeping;* by anal. a *dripping:*—weep {24x}, overflowing {1x}, sore {1x}, wept + 1058 08799 {3x}, wept + 6963 {1x}. Syn.: 1058, 7857. See: TWOT—243b; BDB—113d.

1066. בֹּכִים {2x} **Bôkîym**, *bo-keem';* plur. act. part. of 1058; (with the art.) the *weepers; Bo-kim,* a place in Pal.:—Bochim {2x}. See: BDB—114a.

1067. בְּכִירָה {6x} **bekîyrâh**, *bek-ee-raw';* fem. from 1069; the *eldest* daughter:—firstborn {6x}. See: TWOT—244d; BDB—114c.

1068. בְּכִית {1x} **bekîyth**, *bek-eeth';* from 1058; a *weeping:*—mourning {1x}. See: TWOT—243d; BDB—114a.

1069. בָּכַר {4x} **bâkar**, *baw-kar';* a prim. root; prop. to *burst* the womb, i.e. (caus.) *bear* or *make early fruit* (of woman or tree); also (as denom. from 1061) to *give the birthright:*—firstborn {1x}, new fruit {1x}, firstling {1x}, first child {1x}. See: TWOT—244; BDB—114a.

1070. בֶּכֶר {1x} **beker**, *beh'-ker;* from 1069 (in the sense of *youth*); a young *camel:*—dromedary {1x}. See: TWOT—244b; BDB—114c.

1071. בֶּכֶר {5x} **Beker**, *beh'-ker;* the same as 1070; *Beker,* the name of two Isr.:—Becher {5x}. See: BDB—114b.

1072. בִּכְרָה {1x} **bikrâh**, *bik-raw';* fem. of 1070; a young *she-camel:*—dromedary {1x}. See: TWOT—244b; BDB—114c.

בְּכֹרָה **bekôrâh**. See 1062.

1073. בַּכֻּרָה {1x} **bakkûrâh**, *bak-koo-raw';* by orth. var. for 1063; a *first-ripe* fig:—firstripe {1x}. See: TWOT—244f; BDB—114c.

1074. בֹּכְרוּ {2x} **Bôkerûw**, *bo-ker-oo';* from 1069; *first-born; Bokeru,* an Isr.:—Bocheru {2x}. See: BDB—114b.

1075. בִּכְרִי {8x} **Bikrîy**, *bik-ree';* from 1069; *youth-ful; Bikri,* an Isr.:—Bichri {8x}. See: BDB—114b.

1076. בַּכְרִי {1x} **Bakrîy**, *bak-ree';* patron. from 1071; a *Bakrite* (collect.) or desc. of Beker:—Bachrites {1x}. See: BDB—114b.

1077. בַּל {9x} **bal**, *bal;* from 1086; prop. a *failure;* by impl. *nothing;* usually (adv.) *not* at all; also *lest:*—none, not, nor, lest, nothing, not, neither, no = {9x}. See: TWOT—246d; BDB—114d, 115b.

1078. בֵּל {3x} **Bêl**, *bale;* by contr. for 1168; *Bel,* the Baal of the Babylonians:—*Bel* {3x}. See: BDB—114d, 128c.

1079. בָּל {1x} **bâl** (Aram.), *bawl;* from 1080; prop. *anxiety,* i.e. (by impl.) the *heart* (as its seat):—heart {1x}. See: TWOT—2630; BDB—1084b, 1084c.

1080. בְּלָא {1x} **belâ'** (Aram.), *bel-aw';* corresp. to 1086 (but used only in a ment. sense); to *afflict:*—wear out {1x}. See: TWOT—2631; BDB—1094c.

1081. בַּלְאֲדָן {2x} **Bal'ădân**, *bal-ad-awn';* from 1078 and 113 (contr.); *Bel* (is his) *lord; Baladan,* the name of a Bab. prince:—*Baladan* {1x}. See: BDB—114d, 597d.

1082. בָּלַג {4x} **bâlag**, *baw-lag';* a prim. root; to *break off* or *loose* (in a favorable or unfavorable sense), i.e. *desist* (from grief) or *invade* (with destruction):—comfort {2x}, strength {1x}, strengthen {1x}. See: TWOT—245; BDB—114d.

1083. בִּלְגָּה {3x} **Bilgâh**, *bil-gaw';* from 1082; *desistance; Bilgah,* the name of two Isr.:—*Bilgah* {3x}. See: BDB—114d.

1084. בִּלְגַּי {1x} **Bilgay**, *bil-gah'-ee;* from 1082; *desistant; Bilgai,* an Isr.:—Bilgai {1x}. See: BDB—114d.

1085. בִּלְדַּד {5x} **Bildad**, *bil-dad';* of uncert. der.; *Bildad,* one of Job's friends:—*Bildad* {5x}. See: BDB—115a.

1086. בָּלָה {16x} **bâlâh**, *baw-law';* a prim. root; to *fail;* by impl. to *wear out, decay* (caus. *consume, spend*):—wax old {9x}, become old {2x}, consume {2x}, waste {1x}, enjoy {1x}, non translated variant {1x}. Syn.: 398, 3615. See: TWOT—246; BDB—115a, 1084c.

1087. בָּלֶה {5x} **bâleh**, *baw-leh';* from 1086; *worn out:*—old {5x}. See: TWOT—246a; BDB—115b.

1088. בָּלָה {1x} **Bâlâh**, *baw-law';* fem. of 1087; *failure; Balah,* a place in Pal.:—*Balah* {1x}. See: BDB—115a.

1089. בָּלַהּ {1x} **bâlahh**, *baw-lah';* a prim. root [rather by transp. for 926]; to *palpitate;* hence, (caus.) to *terrify:*—trouble {1x}. See: TWOT—247; BDB—117a.

1090. בִּלְהָה {11x} **Bilhâh**, *bil-haw';* from 1089; *timid; Bilhah,* the name of one of Jacob's concubines; also of a place in Pal.:—*Bilhah* {11x}. See: BDB—117b.

1091. בַּלָּהָה {10x} **ballâhâh**, *bal-law-haw';* from 1089; *alarm;* hence, *destruction:*—terror {10x}. Syn.: 928. See: TWOT—247a; BDB—117a.

1092. בִּלְהָן {4x} **Bilhân**, *bil-hawn';* from 1089; *timid; Bilhan,* the name of an Edomite and of an Isr.:—*Bilhan* {4x}. See: BDB—117b.

1093. בְּלוֹ {3x} **belôw** (Aram.), *bel-o';* from a root corresp. to 1086; *excise* (on articles consumed):—tribute {3x}. See: TWOT—2632; BDB—1084c.

1094. בְּלוֹא {3x} **belôw'**, *bel-o';* or (fully)

בְּלוֹי **belôwy**, *bel-o'-ee;* from 1086; (only in plur. constr.) *rags:*—old {3x}. See: TWOT—246b; BDB—115b.

1095. בֵּלְטְשַׁאצַּר {2x} **Bêltesha'tstsar**, *bale-tesh-ats-tsar';* of for. der.; *Belteshatstsar,* the Bab. name of Daniel:—Belteshazzar {2x}. See: BDB—117b, 1084d.

1096. בֵּלְטְשַׁאצַּר {8x} **Bêltesha'tstsar** (Aram.), *bale-tesh-ats-tsar';* corresp. to 1095:—Belteshazzar {8x}. See: BDB—1084d.

1097. בְּלִי {14x} **belîy**, *bel-ee';* from 1086; prop. *failure,* i.e. *nothing* or *destruction;* usually (with prep.) *without, not yet, because not, as long as,* etc.:—not, without, un . . . , lack of, so that no, corruption = {14x}. See: TWOT—246e; BDB—115c, 116a.

1098. בְּלִיל {3x} **bᵉlîyl**, *bel-eel';* from 1101; *mixed,* i.e. (spec.) *feed* (for cattle):—fodder {1x}, corn {1x}, provender {1x}. See: TWOT—248a; BDB—117d.

1099. בְּלִימָה {1x} **bᵉlîymâh**, *bel-ee-mah';* from 1097 and 4100; (as indef.) *nothing whatever:*—nothing {1x}. See: TWOT—246f; BDB—116a.

1100. בְּלִיַּעַל {27x} **bᵉlîyaʻal**, *bel-e-yah'-al;* from 1097 and 3276; *without profit, worthlessness;* by extens. *destruction, wickedness* (often in connection with 376, 802, 1121, etc.):—Belial {16x}, wicked {5x}, ungodly {3x}, evil {1x}, naughty {1x}, ungodly men {1x}.

Beliya'al means wickedness; wicked; destruction. **(1)** The basic meaning of this word appears in a passage such as Judg 20:13, where the sons of *beliya'al* are perpetrators of wickedness (they raped and murdered a man's concubine): "Now therefore deliver us the men, the children of Belial which are in Gibeah, that we may put them to death, and put away evil from Israel." **(2)** In its first appearance the word represents men who lead others into idolatry: "Certain men, the children of Belial, are gone out from among you, and have [seduced] the inhabitants of their city . . ." (Deut 13:13). **(3)** In Deut 15:9 the word modifies Hebrew dabar, "word" or "matter." Israel is warned to avoid "wicked" words (thoughts) in their hearts. **(4)** *Beliya'al* is a synonym for rasha' (7563 - "wicked rebellious one") in Job 34:18. **(5)** In Nah 1:11 the wicked counselor plots evil against God. **(6)** The psalmist uses *beliya'al* as a synonym of death: "The cords of death encompassed me, and the floods of ungodly men terrified me" (Ps 18:4). Syn.: 7451, 7455, 7489. See: TWOT—246g; BDB—116a.

1101. בָּלַל {44x} **bâlal**, *baw-lal';* a prim. root; to *overflow* (spec. with oil); by impl. to *mix;* also (denom. from 1098) to *fodder:*—mingled {37x}, confound {2x}, anointed {1x}, mixed {1x}, give provender {1x}, tempered {1x}, non translated variant {1x}. Syn.: 4537, 6148. See: TWOT—248; BDB—117b, 117d.

1102. בָּלַם {1x} **bâlam**, *baw-lam';* a prim. root; to *muzzle:*—held {1x}. See: TWOT—249; BDB—117d.

1103. בָּלַס {1x} **bâlaç**, *baw-las';* a prim. root; to *pinch* sycamore figs (a process necessary to ripen them):—gatherer {1x}. See: TWOT—250; BDB—118a.

1104. בָּלַע {49x} **bâlaʻ**, *baw-lah';* a prim. root; to *make away with* (spec. by *swallowing*); Gen to *destroy:*—swallow . . . {34x}, destroy {9x}, devour {3x}, covered {1x}, at . . . end {1x}.

Bala' means "to swallow, engulf." **(1)** *Balaʻ* is first used in Gen 41:7 in Pharaoh's dream of seven lean ears of grain "swallowing up" the seven plump ears. **(2)** While it is used of the normal physical swallowing of something quite frequently, such as Jonah's "being swallowed" by the great fish (Jonah 1:17), the word is used more often in the figurative sense, often implying destruction. **(2a)** Thus, the violent "overwhelm" the innocent (Prov 1:11–12); **(2b)** an enemy "swallows" those he conquers "like a dragon" (Jer 51:34); and **(2c)** the false prophet and priest "are swallowed up of wine" (Is 28:7). Syn.: 1572, 1866, 5693. See: TWOT—251; BDB—118a.

1105. בֶּלַע {2x} **belaʻ**, *beh'-lah;* from 1104; a *gulp;* fig. *destruction:*—devouring {1x}, swallowed {1x}. See: TWOT—251a; BDB—118c.

1106. בֶּלַע {14x} **Belaʻ**, *beh'-lah;* the same as 1105; *Bela,* the name of a place, also of an Edomite and of two Isr.:—*Bela* {13x}, Belah {1x}. See: BDB—118c, 118d, 858d.

1107. בִּלְעֲדֵי {17x} **bilʻădêy**, *bil-ad-ay';* or

בַּלְעֲדֵי **balʻădêy**, *bal-ad-ay';* constr. plur. from 1077 and 5703, *not till,* i.e. (as prep. or adv.) *except, without, besides:*—beside {7x}, save {4x}, without {4x}, not in me {1x}, not {1x}. See: TWOT—246h; BDB—116b, 118d.

1108. בַּלְעִי {1x} **Balʻîy**, *bal-ee';* patron. from 1106: a *Belaite* (collect.) or desc. of Bela:—Belaites {1x}. See: BDB—118c.

1109. בִּלְעָם {61x} **Bilʻâm**, *bil-awm';* prob. from 1077 and 5971; *not* (of the) *people,* i.e. *foreigner; Bilam,* a Mesopotamian prophet; also a place in Pal.:—Balaam {60x}, Bileam {1x}. See: TWOT—251b; BDB—118d.

1110. בָּלַק {2x} **bâlaq**, *baw-lak';* a prim. root; to *annihilate:*—(make) waste {2x}. TWOT—252; BDB—118d, 550b.

1111. בָּלָק {43x} **Bâlâq**, *baw-lawk';* from 1110; *waster; Balak,* a Moabitish king:—Balak {43x}. See: BDB—118d.

1112. בֵּלְשַׁאצַּר {1x} **Bêlshaʼtstsar**, *bale-shats-tsar';* or

בֵּלְאשַׁצַּר **Bêlʼshatstsar**, *bale-shats-tsar';* of for. or. (comp. 1095); *Belshatstsar,* a Bab. king:—Belshazzar {1x}. See: BDB—128d, 1084d.

1113. בֵּלְשַׁאצַּר {7x} **Bêlshaʼtstsar** (Aram.), *bale-shats-tsar';* corresp. to 1112:—Belshazzar {7x}. See: BDB—1084d.

1114. בִּלְשָׁן {2x} **Bilshân**, *bil-shawn';* of uncert. der.; *Bilshan,* an Isr.:—*Bilshan* {1x}. See: BDB—119a.

1115. בִּלְתִּי {30x} **biltîy**, *bil-tee';* constr. fem. of 1086 (equiv. to 1097); prop. a *failure of,* i.e. (used only as a neg. particle, usually with prep. pref.) *not, except, without, unless, besides, because not, until,* etc.:—but, except, save, nothing, lest, no, from, inasmuch, and not = {30x}. See: TWOT—246i; BDB—116c.

1116. בָּמָה {102x} **bâmâh**, *baw-maw';* from an unused root (mean. to *be high*); an *elevation:*—high place {100x}, heights {1x}, waves {1x}.

Bamah (1116) means "high place." **(1)** Bamah is used 102 times in biblical Hebrew, and the first occurrence is in Lev 26:30: "And I will destroy your high places, and cut down your images, and cast your carcases upon the carcases of your idols, and my soul shall abhor you." **(2)** Most of the uses are in the Books of Kings and Chronicles, with the sense of "cultic high place." The word is rarely used in the Pentateuch or in the poetic or prophetic literature. **(3)** *Bamah* refers to **(3a)** the heights of the clouds: "I will ascend above the heights [*bamah*] of the clouds; I will be like the most High" (Is 14:14), and **(3b)** the waves of the sea "[He] alone spreadeth out the heavens, and treadeth upon the waves [literally, "high places"] of the sea" (Job 9:8); **(3c)** *Bamah* can be understood idiomatically for authority: Ps. 18:33 (cf. 2 Sa 22:34; Hab 3:19): "He maketh my feet like hinds' feet, and setteth me upon my high places." **(4)** The word is used metaphorically to portray the Lord as providing for His people: "He made him ride on the high places of the earth, that he might eat the increase of the fields; and he made him to suck honey out of the rock, and oil out of the flinty rock" (Deut 32:13; cf. Is 58:14).

(5) The idiom, "to ride upon the high places of the earth," is a Hebraic way of expressing God's protection of His people. It expresses the exalted nature of Israel, whose God is the Lord. **(6)** Not every literal *bamah* was a cultic high place; the word may simply refer to a geographical unit; cf. "Therefore shall Zion for your sake be plowed as a field, and Jerusalem shall become heaps, and the mountain of the [temple] as the high places of the forest" (cf. Amos 4:13; Mic 3:12). **(7)** The Canaanites served their gods on these hills, where pagan priests presented the sacrifices to the gods: Israel imitated this practice (1 Kin 3:2), even when they sacrificed to the Lord. **(8)** The surrounding nations had high places dedicated to Chemosh (1 Kin 11:7), Baal (Jer 19:5), and other deities. **(9)** On the "high place," a temple was built and dedicated to a god: **(9a)** "[Jeroboam] made a house of high places, and **(9b)** made priests of the lowest of the people, which were not of the sons of Levi" (1 Kin 12:31). **(9c)** Cultic symbols were added as decoration; thus, the sacred pillars (842 - asherah) and sacred trees or poles (4676 - *matstsebah*) were associated with a temple: "For they also built them high places, and [sacred stones], and groves, on every high hill [1389 - *gib'ah*], and under every green tree" (1 Kin 14:23; cf. 2 Kin 16:4).

(10) Before the temple was built, Solomon worshiped the Lord at the great *bamah* of Gideon (1 Kin 3:4). **(10a)** This was permissible until the temple was constructed; however, **(10b)** history demonstrates that Israel soon adopted these "high places" for pagan customs. **(11)** The *bamah* was found in the cities of **(11a)** Samaria (2 Kin 23:19), and **(11b)** Judah (2 Chr 21:11), and even **(11c)** in Jerusalem (2 Kin 23:13). **(12)** The *bamah* was a place of cult prostitution: "[They] pant after the dust of the earth on the head of the poor, and turn aside the way of the meek: and a man and his father will go in unto the same maid, to profane my holy name: And they lay themselves down upon clothes laid to pledge by every altar, and they drink the wine of the condemned in the house of their god" (Amos 2:7–8). Syn.: 7413. See: TWOT—253; BDB—119a.

1117. בָּמָה {1x} **Bâmâh**, *baw-maw';* the same as 1116; *Bamah,* a place in Pal.:—*Bamah* {1x}. Syn.: 1120. See: BDB—119d.

1118. בִּמְהָל {1x} **Bimhâl**, *bim-hawl';* prob. from 4107 with prep. pref.; *with pruning; Bimhal,* an Isr.:—*Bimhal* {1x}. See: BDB—119d.

1119. בְּמוֹ {10x} **bᵉmôw**, *bem-o';* prol. for prep. pref.; *in, with, by,* etc.:—with {3x}, in {2x}, into {1x}, through {1x}, for {1x}, at {1x}, non translated variant {1x}. Syn.: See: TWOT—193; prep (poetic form); BDB—91b, 119d.

1120. בָּמוֹת {4x} **Bâmôwth**, *baw-mōth';* plur. of 1116; *heights;* or (fully)

בָּמוֹת בַּעַל **Bâmôwth Baʻal**, *baw-mōth' bah'-al;* from the same and 1168; *heights of Baal; Bamoth* or *Bamoth-Baal,* a place E. of the Jordan:—Bamoth {2x}, Baal {1x}, Bamothbaal {1x}. See: BDB—119d.

1121. בֵּן {4906x} **bên**, *bane;* from 1129; a *son* (as a *builder* of the family name), in the widest sense (of lit. and fig. relationship, incl. *grandson, subject, nation, quality* or *condition,* etc., [like 1, 251, etc.]):—son {2978x}, children {1568x}, old {135x}, first {51x}, man {20x}, young

{18x}, young + 1241 {17x}, child {10x}, stranger {10x}, people {5x}, misc. {92x}.

Ben means "son," *bat* (1323) means "daughter." **(1)** These nouns are derived from the verb banah. They are actually different forms of the same noun. **(1a)** Basically, this noun represents one's immediate physical male or female offspring. For example, Adam "begat sons and daughters" (Gen 5:4). **(1b)** The special emphasis here is on the physical tie binding a man to his offspring. **(2)** The noun can also be used of an animal's offspring: "Binding his foal unto the vine, and his ass's colt unto the choice vine . . ." (Gen 49:11). **(3)** Sometimes the word *ben,* which usually means "son," can mean "children" (both male and female). God told Eve that "in sorrow thou shalt bring forth children" (Gen 3:16—the first occurrence of this noun). **(4)** The words *ben* and *bat* can signify "descendants" in general—daughters, sons, granddaughters, and grandsons. Laban complained to Jacob that he had not allowed him "to kiss my sons and my daughters" (Gen 31:28; cf. v. 43).

(5) The phrase, "my son," may be used by a superior to a subordinate as a term of familiar address. Joshua said to Achan, "My son, give, I pray thee, glory to the Lord God of Israel . . ." (Josh 7:19). **(6)** On the lips of the subordinate, "son" signifies conscious submission. Ben-hadad's servant Hazael took gifts to Elisha, saying, "Thy son Benhadad king of Syria hath sent me to thee" (2 Kin 8:9). **(7)** *Ben* can also be used in a formula expressing a unique and unbreakable relationship: "Thou art my Son; this day have I begotten thee" (Ps 2:7). **(8)** *Ben* often is used in this sense of a king's relationship to God (i.e., he is God's adopted son). **(9)** Sometimes the same word expresses Israel's relationship to God: "When Israel was a child, then I loved him, and called my son out of Egypt" (Hos 11:1). **(10)** The Bible also refers to the heavenly court as the "sons of God" (Job 1:6). **(10a)** God called the elders of Israel the "children" of the Most High" (Ps 82:6). **(10b)** In Gen 6:2, the phrase "sons of God" is variously understood as **(10b1)** members of the heavenly court, **(10b2)** the spiritual disciples of God (the sons of Seth), and **(10b3)** the boastful among mankind.

(11) *Ben* may signify "young men" in general, regardless of any physical relationship to the speaker: "And [I] beheld among the simple ones, I discerned among the youths, a young man void of understanding" (Prov 7:7). **(12)** A city may be termed a "mother" and its inhabitants its "sons": "For he hath strengthened the bars of thy gates; he hath blessed thy children within thee" (Ps 147:13). **(13)** *Ben* is sometimes used to mean a single individual; thus Abraham ran to his flock and picked out a "son of a cow" (Gen 18:7). **(14)** The phrase "son of man" is used in this sense—God is asked to save the poor individuals, not the children of the poor (Ps 72:4). **(15)** *Ben* may also denote a member of a group. An example is a prophet who followed Elijah (1 Kin 20:35; cf. Amos 7:14). **(16)** This noun may also indicate someone worthy of a certain fate—e.g., "a stubborn and rebellious son" (Deut 21:18). **(17)** Used figuratively, "son of" can mean "something belonging to"—e.g., "the arrow [literally, "the son of a bow"] cannot make him flee" (Job 41:28). Syn.: 1247, 1248, 2860. See: TWOT—254; BDB—119d, 122b, 1085b.

1122. בֵּן {1x} **Bên,** *bane;* the same as 1121; *Ben,* an Isr.:—*Ben* {1x}. See: BDB—122a.

1123. בֵּן {11x} **bên** (Aram.), *bane;* corresp. to 1121:—children {6x}, son {3x}, young, of the captives + 1547 {1x}. See: TWOT—2639; BDB—1085b.

1124. בְּנָא {22x} **bᵉnâʾ** (Aram.), *ben-aw';* or

בְּנָה **bᵉnâh** (Aram.), *ben-aw';* corresp. to 1129; *to build:*—build {17x}, building {3x}, builded + 1934 {1x}, make {1x}. Syn.: 1129. See: TWOT—2633; BDB—1084d.

1125. בֶּן־אֲבִינָדָב {1x} **Ben-ʾÂbîynâdâb,** *ben-ab-ee"-naw-dawb';* from 1121 and 40; (the) *son of Abinadab; Ben-Abinadab,* an Isr.:—the son of Abinadab {1x}. See: BDB—122a.

1126. בֶּן־אוֹנִי {1x} **Ben-ʾÔwnîy,** *ben-o-nee';* from 1121 and 205; *son of my sorrow; Ben-Oni,* the orig. name of Benjamin:—Ben-oni {1x}. See: BDB—122b.

1127. בֶּן־גֶּבֶר {1x} **Ben-Geber,** *ben-gheh'-ber;* from 1121 and 1397; *son of* (the) *hero; Ben-Geber,* an Isr.:—the son of Geber {1x}. See: BDB—122b.

1128. בֶּן־דֶּקֶר {1x} **Ben-Deqer,** *ben-deh'-ker;* from 1121 and a der. of 1856; *son of piercing* (or *of a lance*); *Ben-Deker,* an Isr.:—the son of Dekar {1x}. See: BDB—122b.

1129. בָּנָה {376x} **bânâh,** *baw-naw';* a prim. root; *to build* (lit. and fig.):—build {340x}, build up {14x}, builder {10x}, made {3x}, built again + 8735 {2x}, repair {2x}, set up {2x}, have children + 8735 {1x}, obtain children + 8735 {1x}, surely {1x} (inf. for emphasis).

Banah means to build, establish, construct, rebuild. **(1)** In its basic meaning, *banah* appears in Gen 8:20, where Noah is said to have "constructed" an ark. **(2)** In Gen 4:17, *banah* means not only that Enoch built a city, but that he "founded" or "established" it. **(3)** This verb can also mean "to manufacture," or adding to an existing material to fashion a new object: **(3a)** as in Eze 27:5: "They have made all thy ship boards of fir trees. . . ." **(3b)** Somewhat in the same sense, we read that God "made" or "fashioned" Eve out of Adam's rib (Gen 2:22—the first biblical occurrence). **(3c)** In like manner, Asa began with the cities of Geba and Mizpah and "fortified" them (1 Kin 15:22). **(4)** *Banah* can also refer to "rebuilding" something that is destroyed. Joshua cursed anyone who would rise up and rebuild Jericho, the city that God had utterly destroyed (Josh 6:26). **(5)** Metaphorically or figuratively, the verb *banah* is used to mean "building one's house"—i.e., having children. Sarai said to Abram, "I pray thee, go in unto my maid; it may be that I may obtain children by her" (Gen 16:2). **(5a)** It was the duty of the nearest male relative to conceive a child with the wife of a man who had died childless (Deut 25:9); he thus helped "to build up the house" of his deceased relative. **(5b)** Used figuratively, "to build a house" may also mean "to found a dynasty" (2 Sa 7:27). Syn.: 1124. See: TWOT—255; BDB—124a, 1084d.

1130. בֶּן־הֲדַד {25x} **Ben-Hădad,** *ben-had-ad';* from 1121 and 1908; *son of Hadad; Ben-Hadad,* the name of several Syrian kings:—*Ben-hadad* {25x}. See: BDB—122b.

1131. בִּנּוּי {7x} **Binnûwy,** *bin-noo'-ee;* from 1129; *built* up; *Binnui,* an Isr.:—Binnui {7x}. See: BDB—125a.

1132. בֶּן־זוֹחֵת {1x} **Ben-Zôwchêth,** *ben-zo-khayth';* from 1121 and 2105; *son of Zocheth; Ben-Zocheth,* an Isr.:—Ben-zoketh {1x}. See: BDB—122b.

1133. בֶּן־חוּר {1x} **Ben-Chûwr,** *ben-khoor';* from 1121 and 2354; *son of Chur; Ben-Chur,* an Isr.:—the son of Hur {1x}. See: BDB—122b, 301b.

1134. בֶּן־חַיִל {1x} **Ben-Chayil,** *ben-khah'-yil;* from 1121 and 2428; *son of might; Ben-Chail,* an Isr.:—Ben-hail {1x}. See: BDB—122c.

1135. בֶּן־חָנָן {1x} **Ben-Chânân,** *ben-khaw-nawn';* from 1121 and 2605; *son of Chanan; Ben-Chanan,* an Isr.:—Ben-hanan {1x}. See: BDB—122c.

1136. בֶּן־חֶסֶד {1x} **Ben-Cheçed,** *ben-kheh'-sed;* from 1121 and 2617; *son of kindness; Ben-Chesed,* an Isr.:—the son of Hesed {1x}. See: BDB—122c.

1137. בָּנִי {15x} **Bânîy,** *baw-nee';* from 1129; *built; Bani,* the name of five Isr.:—Bani {15x}. See: BDB—125b.

1138. בֻּנִּי {3x} **Bunnîy,** *boon-nee';* or (fuller)

בּוּנִי **Bûwnîy,** *boo-nee';* from 1129; *built; Bunni* or *Buni,* an Isr.:—Bunni {3x}. See: BDB—100d, 1'25a, 125b.

1139. בְּנֵי־בְרַק {1x} **Bᵉnêy-Bᵉraq,** *ben-ay'-ber-ak';* from the plur. constr. of 1121 and 1300; *sons of lightning, Bene-berak,* a place in Pal.:—Bene-barak {1x}. See: BDB—122c, 140c.

1140. בִּנְיָה {1x} **binyâh,** *bin-yaw';* fem. from 1129; *a structure:*—building {1x}. See: TWOT—255; BDB—125b.

1141. בְּנָיָה {42x} **Bᵉnâyâh,** *ben-aw-yaw';* or (prol.)

בְּנָיָהוּ **Bᵉnâyâhûw,** *ben-aw-yaw'-hoo;* from 1129 and 3050; *Jah has built; Benajah,* the name of twelve Isr.:—Benaiah {42x}. See: BDB—125c.

1142. בְּנֵי יַעֲקָן {2x} **Bᵉnêy Yaʿăqân,** *ben-ay' yah-ak-awn';* from the plur. of 1121 and 3292; *sons of Yaakan; Bene-Jaakan,* a place in the Desert:—Bene-jaakan {2x}. See: BDB—122c, 785c.

1143. בֵּנַיִם {2x} **bênayim,** *bay-nah'-yim;* dual of 996; a *double interval,* i.e. the space between two armies:—champion {2x}.

Benayim literally means [a man] in the space between two armies; an army's representative, its champion. See: BDB—108a.

1144. בִּנְיָמִין {161x} **Binyâmîyn,** *bin-yaw-mene';* from 1121 and 3225; *son of* (the) *right hand; Binjamin,* youngest son of Jacob; also the tribe descended from him, and its territory:—Benjamin {161x}. See: TWOT—254a; BDB—122c.

1145. בֶּן־יְמִינִי {18x} **Ben-yᵉmîynîy,** *ben-yem-ee-nee';* sometimes (with the art. ins.)

בֶּן־הַיְמִינִי **Ben-ha-yᵉmînîy,** *ben-hah-yem-ee-nee';* with 376 ins. (1 Sa 9:1)

בֶּן־אִישׁ יְמִינִי **Ben-ʾÎysh Yᵉmîynîy,** *ben-eesh' yem-ee-nee'; son of a man of Jemini;* or short. (1 Sa 9:4; Est 2:5)

אִישׁ יְמִינִי **ʾÎysh Yᵉmîynîy,** *eesh yem-ee-nee'; a man of Jemini,* or (1 Sa 20:1) simply

יְמִינִי **Yᵉmînîy,** *yem-ee-nee'; a Jeminite;* (plur.

בְּנֵי יְמִינִי **Bᵉnîy Yᵉmîynîy,** *ben-ay' yem-ee-nee';* patron. from 1144; a *Benjaminite,* or descendent of Benjamin:—Benjamite {16x}, of Benjamin {1x}, Benjamite + 1121 {1x}. See: BDB—122d, 412b.

1146. בִּנְיָן {7x} **binyân**, *bin-yawn';* from 1129; an *edifice:*—building {7x}. Syn.: 1129. See: TWOT—255a; BDB—125c.

1147. בִּנְיָן {1x} **binyân** (Aram.), *bin-yawn';* corresp. to 1146:—building {1x}. See: TWOT—2633a; BDB—1084d.

1148. בְּנִינוּ {1x} **Beᵉnîynûw**, *ben-ee-noo';* prob. from 1121 with pron. suff.; *our son; Beninu,* an Isr.:—Beninu {1x}. See: BDB—123a.

1149. בְּנַס {1x} **bᵉnaç** (Aram.), *ben-as';* of uncert. affin.; to *be enraged:*—be angry {1x}. See: TWOT—2634. See: BDB—1084d.

1150. בִּנְעָא {2x} **Binᶜâʾ**, *bin-aw';* or

בִּנְעָה **Binᶜâh**, *bin-aw';* of uncert. der.; *Bina* or *Binah,* an Isr.:—Binea {2x}. See: BDB—126a.

1151. בֶּן־עַמִּי {1x} **Ben-ᶜAmmîy**, *ben-am-mee';* from 1121 and 5971 with pron. suff.; *son of my people; Ben-Ammi,* a son of Lot:—Ben-ammi {1x}. See: BDB—122c.

1152. בְּסוֹדְיָה {1x} **Bᵉçôwdᵉyâh**, *bes-o-deh-yaw';* from 5475 and 3050 with prep. pref.; *in* (the) *counsel of Jehovah; Besodejah,* an Isr.:—Besodeiah {1x}. See: BDB—126a, 691d.

1153. בְּסַי {2x} **Bᵉçay**, *bes-ah'-ee;* from 947; *domineering; Besai,* one of the Nethinim:—Besai {1x}. See: BDB—126a.

1154. בֶּסֶר {1x} **beçer**, *beh'-ser;* from an unused root mean. to *be sour;* an *immature* grape:—unripe grape {1x}. See: TWOT—257; BDB—126a.

1155. בֹּסֶר {4x} **bôçer**, *bo'ser;* from the same as 1154:—sour grape {4x}. See: TWOT—257a; BDB—126a.

1156. בְּעָא {12x} **bᵉᶜâʾ** (Aram.), *beh-aw';* or

בְּעָה **bᵉᶜâh** (Aram.), *beh-aw';* corresp. to 1158; to *seek* or *ask:*—seek {3x}, ask {3x}, desire {3x}, pray {3x}, request {3x}, make (petition) {1x}. See: TWOT—2635; BDB—1085a.

1157. בְּעַד {19x} **bᵉᶜad**, *beh-ad';* from 5704 with prep. pref.; *in up to* or *over against;* gen. *at, beside, among, behind, for,* etc.:—at, for, by, over, upon, about, up, through = {19x}. See: TWOT—258a; BDB—126b.

1158. בָּעָה {5x} **bâᶜâh**, *baw-aw';* a prim. root; to *gush* over, i.e. to *swell;* (fig.) to *desire* earnestly; by impl. to *ask:*—enquire {2x}, boil {1x}, sought up {1x}, swelling out {1x}.

Ba'ah basically means to conciliate the face of a person, and hence to pray with some prospect of success. Syn.: 1875, 7592. See: TWOT—259; BDB—126d, 1085a.

1159. בָּעוּ {1x} **bâᶜûw** (Aram.), *baw-oo';* from 1156; a *request:*—petition {1x}. See: TWOT—2635a; BDB—1085a.

1160. בְּעוֹר {10x} **Bᵉᶜôwr**, *beh-ore';* from 1197 (in the sense of *burning*); a *lamp; Beör,* the name of the father of an Edomitish king; also of that of Balaam:—Beor {10x}. See: BDB—129d.

1161. בִּעוּתִים {2x} **bîᶜûwthîym**, *be-oo-theme';* masc. plur. from 1204; *alarms:*—terrors {2x}. See: TWOT—265b; BDB—130a.

1162. בֹּעַז {24x} **Bôᶜaz**, *bo'-az;* from an unused root of uncert. mean.; *Boaz,* the ancestor of David; also the name of a pillar in front of the temple:—*Boaz* {24x}. See: BDB—126d.

1163. בָּעַט {2x} **bâᶜaṭ**, *baw-at';* a prim. root; to *trample* down, i.e. (fig.) *despise:*—kick {2x}. See: TWOT—261; BDB—127a.

1164. בְּעִי {1x} **bᵉᶜîy**, *beh-ee';* from 1158; a *prayer:*—grave {1x}. See: TWOT—1577d; BDB—127a, 730d.

1165. בְּעִיר {6x} **bᵉᶜîyr**, *beh-ere';* from 1197 (in the sense of *eating*); cattle:—beast {4x}, cattle {2x}. TWOT—264a; BDB—129c.

1166. בָּעַל {16x} **bâᶜal**, *baw-al';* a prim. root; to *be master;* hence, (as denom. from 1167) to *marry:*—marry {8x}, husband {3x}, dominion {2x}, wife {1x}, married wife {1x}, Beulah {1x}. *Ba'al* basically means to exercise dominion over. See: TWOT—262; BDB—127a.

1167. בַּעַל {82x} **baᶜal**, *bah'-al;* from 1166; a *master;* hence, a *husband,* or (fig.) *owner* (often used with another noun in modifications of this latter sense):—man {25x}, owner {14x}, husband {11x}, have {7x}, master {5x}, man given {2x}, adversary {1x}, archers {1x}, babbler + 3956 {1x}, bird + 3671 {1x}, captain {1x}, confederate + 1285 {1x}, misc. {12x}.

Ba'al means "master; *baal.*" **(1)** The word *ba'al* occurs 84 times in the Hebrew Old Testament, 15 times with the meaning of "husband" and 50 times as a reference to a deity. **(1)** The first occurrence of the noun *ba'al* is in Gen 14:13: "And there came one that had escaped, and told Abram the Hebrew; for he dwelt in the plain of Mamre the Amorite, brother of Eshcol, and brother of Aner: and these were confederate with [literally, "*ba'al's* of a covenant with"] Abram." **(2)** The primary meaning of *ba'al* is "possessor." Isaiah's use of *ba'al* in parallel with qanah (7069) clarifies this basic significance of *ba'al:* "The ox knoweth his owner [7069 - qanah], and the ass his master's [*ba'al*] crib: but Israel doth not know, my people doth not consider" (Is 1:3). **(3)** Man may be the owner [*ba'al*] of an animal (Ex 22:10), a house (Ex 22:7), a cistern (Ex 21:34), or even a wife (Ex 21:3). **(4)** A secondary meaning, "husband," is clearly indicated by the phrase *ba'al* ha-ishshah (literally, "owner of the woman"). For example: "If men strive, and hurt a woman with child, so that her fruit depart from her, and yet no mischief follow: he shall be surely punished, according as the woman's husband [*ba'al* ha-ishshah] will lay upon him; and he shall pay as the judges determine" (Ex 21:22).

(5) The meaning of *ba'al* is closely related to ish (376 - "man"), as is seen in the usage of these two words in one verse: "When the wife of Uriah heard that Uriah her husband [ish] was dead, she mourned for her husband [*ba'al*]" (2 Sa 11:26). **(6)** The word *ba'al* with another noun may signify a peculiar characteristic or quality: "And they said one to another, Behold, this master of dreams cometh" (Gen 37:19). **(7)** The word *ba'al* may denote any deity other than the God of Israel. **(7a)** *Baal* was a common name given to the god of fertility in Canaan. In the Canaanite city of Ugarit, *Baal* was especially recognized as the god of fertility. **(7b)** The Old Testament records that *Baal* was "the god" of the Canaanites. **(7c)** The Israelites worshiped *Baal* during **(7c1)** the time of the judges (Judg 6:25–32) and **(7c2)** of King Ahab. **(7c3)** Elijah stood as the opponent of the *Baal* priests at Mount Carmel (1 Kin 18:21ff.).

(8) Many cities made *Baal* a local god and honored him with special acts of worship: *Baal*-peor (Num 25:5), *Baal*-berith at Shechem (Judg 8:33), *Baal*-zebub (2 Kin 1:2–16) at Ekron, *Baal*-zephon (Num 33:7), and *Baal*-hermon (Judg 3:3). **(9)** Among the prophets, Jeremiah and Hosea mention *Baal* most frequently. **(9a)** Hosea pictured Israel as turning to the baals and only returning to the Lord after a time of despair (Hos 2:13, 17). **(9b)** He says that the name of *Baal* will no longer be used, not even with the meaning of "Lord" or "master," as the association was contaminated by the idolatrous practices: "And it shall be at that day, saith the Lord, that thou shalt call me Ishi; and shalt call me no more Ba-a-li [*ba'al*]. For I will take away the names of Ba-a-lim out of her mouth, and they shall no more be remembered by their name" (Hos 2:16–17). **(9c)** In Hosea's and Jeremiah's time, the *ba'al* idols were still worshiped, as the peoples sacrificed, built high places, and made images of the ba'alim (plural). Syn.: 113. See: TWOT—262a; BDB -127b, 127d, 1085a.

1168. בַּעַל {80x} **Baᶜal**, *bah'-al,* the same as 1167; *Baal,* a Phœnician deity:—*Baal* {62x}, Baalim {18x}. See: TWOT—262a; BDB—127c.

1169. בְּעֵל {3x} **bᵉᶜêl** (Aram.), *beh-ale';* corresp. to 1167:—chancellor + 2942 {3x}. See: TWOT—2636; BDB—1085a.

1170. בַּעַל בְּרִית {2x} **Baᶜal Bᵉrîyth**, *bah'-al ber-eeth';* from 1168 and 1285; *Baal of* (the) *covenant; Baal-Berith,* a special deity of the Shechemites:—Baal-berith {2x}. See: BDB—127d.

1171. בַּעַל גָּד {3x} **Baᶜal Gâd**, *bah'-al gawd;* from 1168 and 1409; *Baal of Fortune; Baal-Gad,* a place in Syria:—*Baal-gad* {1x}. See: BDB—128a.

1172. בַּעֲלָה {2x} **baᶜălâh**, *bah-al-aw';* fem. of 1167; a *mistress:*—mistress {2x}, hath (a familiar spirit) {2x}. See: TWOT—262b; BDB—128b.

1173. בַּעֲלָה {5x} **Baᶜălâh**, *bah-al-aw';* the same as 1172; *Baalah,* the name of three places in Pal.:—*Baalah* {5x}. See: BDB—128b.

1174. בַּעַל הָמוֹן {1x} **Baᶜal Hâmôwn**, *bah'-al haw-mone';* from 1167 and 1995; *possessor of a multitude; Baal-Hamon,* a place in Pal.:—Baal-hamon {1x}. See: BDB—128a.

1175. בְּעָלוֹת {2x} **Bᵉᶜâlôwth**, *beh-aw-lōth';* plur. of 1172; *mistresses; Beäloth,* a place in Pal.:—Bealoth {1x}, in Aloth {1x}. See: BDB—128c.

1176. בַּעַל זְבוּב {4x} **Baᶜal Zᵉbûwb**, *bah'-al zeb-oob';* from 1168 and 2070; *Baal of* (the) *Fly; Baal-Zebub,* a special deity of the Ekronites:—Baal-zebub {4x}. See: BDB—127d.

1177. בַּעַל חָנָן {5x} **Baᶜal Chânân**, *bah'-al khaw-nawn';* from 1167 and 2603; *possessor of grace; Baal-Chanan,* the name of an Edomite, also of an Isr.:—Baal-hanan {5x}. See: BDB—128a.

1178. בַּעַל חָצוֹר {1x} **Baᶜal Châtsôwr**, *bah'-al khaw-tsore';* from 1167 and a modif. of 2691; *possessor of a village; Baal-Chatsor,* a place in Pal.:—Baal-hazor {1x}. See: BDB—128a.

1179. בַּעַל חֶרְמוֹן {2x} **Baᶜal Chermôwn**, *bah'-al kher-mone';* from 1167 and 2768; *possessor of Hermon; Baal-Chermon,* a place in Pal.:—Baal-hermon {2x}. See: BDB—128a.

1180. בַּעֲלִי {1x} **Baᶜălîy**, *bah-al-ee';* from 1167 with pron. suff.; *my master; Baali,* a symb. name for Jehovah:—Baali {1x}. See: BDB—127b.

1181. בַּעֲלֵי בָּמוֹת {1x} **Baʿălêy Bâmôwth**, *bah-al-ay' baw-mōth'*; from the plur. of 1168 and the plur. of 1116; *Baals of* (the) *heights; Baale-Bamoth*, a place E. of the Jordan:—lords of the high places {1x}. See: BDB—127b.

1182. בְּעֶלְיָדָע {1x} **Beʿelyâdâʿ**, *beh-el-yaw-daw'*; from 1168 and 3045; *Baal has known; Beëljada*, an Isr.:—Beeliada {1x}. See: BDB—128c.

1183. בְּעַלְיָה {1x} **Beʿalyâh**, *beh-al-yaw'*; from 1167 and 3050; *Jah* (is) *master; Bealjah*, an Isr.:—Bealiah {1x}. See: BDB—128c.

1184. בַּעֲלֵי יְהוּדָה {1x} **Baʿălêy Yehûwdâh**, *bah-al-ay' yeh-hoo-daw'*; from the plural of 1167 and 3063; *masters of Judah; Baale-Jehudah*, a place in Pal.:—Baale of Judah {1x}. See: BDB—128b.

1185. בַּעֲלִיס {1x} **Baʿălîç**, *bah-al-ece'*; prob. from a der. of 5965 with prep. pref.; *in exultation; Baalis*, an Ammonitish king:—Baalis {1x}. See: BDB—128d.

1186. בַּעַל מְעוֹן {3x} **Baʿal Meʿôwn**, *bah-al meh-one'*; from 1168 and 4583; *Baal of* (the) *habitation* (of) [comp. 1010]; *Baal-Meön*, a place E. of the Jordan:—Baal-meon {3x}. See: BDB—128b.

1187. בַּעַל פְּעוֹר {6x} **Baʿal Peʿôwr**, *bah'-al peh-ore'*; from 1168 and 6465; *Baal of Peor; Baal-Peör*, a Moabitish deity:—Baal-peor {6x}. See: BDB—128b.

1188. בַּעַל פְּרָצִים {4x} **Baʿal Perâtsîym**, *bah'-al per-aw-tseem'*; from 1167 and the plur. of 6556; *possessor of breaches; Baal-Peratsim*, a place in Pal.:—Baal-perazim {4x}. See: BDB—128b.

1189. בַּעַל צְפוֹן {3x} **Baʿal Tsephôwn**, *bah'-al tsef-one'*; from 1168 and 6828 (in the sense of *cold*) [according to others an Eg. form of *Typhon*, the destroyer]; *Baal of winter; Baal-Tsephon*, a place in Egypt:—Baal-zephon {3x}. See: BDB—128b, 859d, 861b.

1190. בַּעַל שָׁלִשָׁה {1x} **Baʿal Shâlîshâh**, *bah'-al shaw-lee-shaw'*; from 1168 and 8031; *Baal of Shalishah, Baal-Shalishah*, a place in Pal.:—Baal-shalisha {1x}. See: BDB—128b.

1191. בַּעֲלָת {3x} **Baʿălâth**, *bah-al-awth'*; a modif. of 1172; *mistress-ship; Baalath*, a place in Pal.:—*Baalath* {3x}. See: BDB—128c.

1192. בַּעֲלַת בְּאֵר {1x} **Baʿălath Beʾêr**, *bah-al-ath' beh-ayr'*; from 1172 and 875; *mistress of a well; Baalath-Beër*, a place in Pal.:—*Baalath-beer* {1x}. See: BDB—127d, 128c, 928b.

1193. בַּעַל תָּמָר {1x} **Baʿal Tâmâr**, *bah'-al taw-mawr'*; from 1167 and 8558; *possessor of* (the) *palm-tree; Baal-Tamar*, a place in Pal.:—*Baal-tamar* {1x}. See: BDB—128b, 1071c.

1194. בְּעֹן {1x} **Beʿôn**, *beh-ohn'*; prob. a contr. of 1010; *Beön*, a place E. of the Jordan:—*Beon* {1x}. See: BDB—111a, 128d.

1195. בַּעֲנָא {3x} **Baʿănâʾ**, *bah-an-aw'*; the same as 1196; *Baana*, the name of four Isr.:—*Baana* {2x}, Baanah {1x}. See: BDB—128d.

1196. בַּעֲנָה {9x} **Baʿănâh**, *bah-an-aw'*; from a der. of 6031 with prep. pref.; *in affliction; Baanah*, the name of four Isr.:—*Baanah* {9x}. See: BDB—128d.

1197. בָּעַר {94x} **bâʿar**, *baw-ar'*; a prim. root; to *kindle*, i.e. *consume* (by fire or by eating); also (as denom. from 1198) to *be* (*-come*) *brutish*:—burn {41x}, . . . away {21x}, kindle {13x}, brutish {7x}, eaten {2x}, set {2x}, burn up {2x}, eat up {2x}, feed {1x}, heated {1x}, took {1x}, wasted {1x}. Syn.: 2787, 3341, 6999. 8313. See: TWOT—263; BDB—128d, 129c.

1198. בַּעַר {5x} **baʿar**, *bah'-ar*; from 1197; prop. *food* (as *consumed*); i.e. (by exten.) of cattle *brutishness*; (concr.) *stupid*:—brutish {4x}, foolish {1x}. See: TWOT—264b; BDB—129d.

1199. בָּעֲרָא {1x} **Bâʿărâʾ**, *bah-ar-aw'*; from 1198; *brutish: Baara*, an Isr. woman:—*Baara* {1x}. See: BDB—129d.

1200. בְּעֵרָה {1x} **beʿêrâh**, *bè-ay-raw'*; from 1197; a *burning*:—fire {1x}. Syn.: 784, 3857. See: TWOT 263a; BDB—129c.

1201. בַּעְשָׁא {28x} **Baʿshâʾ**, *bah-shaw'*; from an unused root mean. to *stink; offensiveness; Basha*, a king of Israel:—Baasha {28x}. See: BDB—129d.

1202. בַּעֲשֵׂיָה {1x} **Baʿăsêyâh**, *bah-as-ay-yaw'*; from 6213 and 3050 with a prep. pref.; *in* (the) *work of Jah; Baasejah*, an Isr.:—Baaseiah {1x}. See: BDB—129d.

1203. בְּעֶשְׁתְּרָה {1x} **Beʿeshterâh**, *beh-esh-ter-aw'*; from 6251 (as sing. of 6252) with prep. pref.; *with Ashtoreth; Beështerah*, a place E. of the Jordan:—*Beeshterah* {1x}. See: BDB—129d.

1204. בָּעַת {16x} **bâʿath**, *baw-ath'*; a prim. root; to *fear*:—afraid {10x}, terrify {3x}, affrighted {1x}, trouble {2x}. Syn.: 2729, 3372, 6342. See: TWOT—265; BDB—129d.

1205. בְּעָתָה {2x} **beʿâthâh**, *beh-aw-thaw'*, from 1204; *fear*:—trouble {2x}. See: TWOT—265a; BDB—130a.

1206. בֹּץ {1x} **bôts**, *botse*; prob. the same as 948; *mud* (as *whitish* clay):—mire {1x}. Syn.: 2916. See: TWOT—268a; BDB—130a, 130c.

1207. בִּצָּה {3x} **bitstsâh**, *bits-tsaw'*; intens. from 1206; a *swamp*:—mire {1x}, fens {1x}, miry place {1x}. See: TWOT—268b; BDB—130c.

1208. בָּצוֹר {1x} **bâtsôwr**, *baw-tsore'*; from 1219; *inaccessible*, i.e. *lofty*:—vintage {1x}. Syn.: 1210. See: TWOT—270f; BDB—131b.

1209. בֵּצַי {3x} **Bêtsay**, *bay-tsah'-ee*; perh. the same as 1153; *Betsai*, the name of two Isr.:—Bezai {3x}. See: BDB—130a.

1210. בָּצִיר {7x} **bâtsîyr**, *baw-tseer'*; from 1219; *clipped*, i.e. the *grape crop*:—vintage {1x}. See: TWOT—270f; BDB—131b.

1211. בֶּצֶל {1x} **betsel**, *beh'-tsel*; from an unused root appar. mean. to *peel*; an *onion*:—onion {1x}. See: TWOT—266a; BDB—130a.

1212. בְּצַלְאֵל {9x} **Betsalʾêl**, *bets-al-ale'*; prob. from 6738 and 410 with prep. pref.; *in* (the) *shadow* (i.e. protection) *of God; Betsalel*, the name of two Isr.:—Bezaleel {9x}. See: BDB—130b.

1213. בַּצְלוּת {2x} **Batslûwth**, *bats-looth'*; or בַּצְלִית **Batslîyth**, *bats-leeth'*; from the same as 1211; a *peeling; Batsluth* or *Batslith*, an Isr.:—Bazluth {2x}. See: BDB—130b.

1214. בָּצַע {16x} **bâtsaʿ**, *baw-tsah'*; a prim. root to *break* off, i.e. (usually) *plunder*; fig. to *finish*, or (intr.) *stop*:—cut me off {2x}, gained {2x}, given {2x}, greedy {2x}, coveteth {1x}, covetous {1x}, cut {1x}, finish {1x}, fulfilled {1x}, get {1x}, performed {1x}, wounded {1x}. See: TWOT—267; BDB—130b.

1215. בֶּצַע {23x} **betsaʿ**, *beh'-tsah*; from 1214; *plunder*; by extens. *gain* (usually unjust):—covetousness {10x}, gain {9x}, profit {3x}, lucre {1x}. See: TWOT—267a; BDB—130c.

1216. בָּצֵק {2x} **bâtsêq**, *baw-tsake'*; a prim. root; perh. to *swell* up, i.e. *blister*:—swell {2x}. See: TWOT—269; BDB—130d.

1217. בָּצֵק {5x} **bâtsêq**, *baw-tsake'*; from 1216; *dough* (as *swelling* by fermentation):—dough {4x}, flour {1x}. Syn.: 5560, 7058. See: TWOT—269a; BDB—130d.

1218. בָּצְקַת {2x} **Botsqath**, *bots-cath'*; from 1216; a *swell* of ground; *Botscath*, a place in Pal.:—Bozcath {1x}, Boskath {1x}. See: BDB—130d.

1219. בָּצַר {38x} **bâtsar**, *baw-tsar'*; a prim. root; to *clip* off; spec. (as denom. from 1210) to *gather* grapes; also to *be isolated* (i.e. *inaccessible* by height or fortification):—fenced {15x}, defenced {5x}, gather {4x}, grapegatherers {3x}, fortify {2x}, cut off {1x}, restrained {1x}, strong {1x}, mighty things {1x}, walled up {1x}, fenced up {1x}, walled {1x}, withholden {1x}, non translated variant {1x}. Syn.: 4013. See: TWOT—270; BDB—130d.

1220. בֶּצֶר {2x} **betser**, *beh'-tser*; from 1219; strictly a *clipping*, i.e. *gold* (as *dug* out):—gold {1x}, defence {1x}. See: TWOT—270a; BDB—131a.

1221. בֶּצֶר {5x} **Betser**, *beh'-tser*; the same as 1220, an *inaccessible* spot, *Betser*, a place in Pal.; also an Isr.:—Bezer {5x}. See: BDB—131a.

1222. בְּצַר {1x} **betsar**, *bets-ar'*; another form for 1220; *gold*:—gold {1x}. See: TWOT—270a; BDB—131a.

1223. בָּצְרָה {1x} **botsrâh**, *bots-raw'*; fem. from 1219; an *enclosure*, i.e. *sheep-fold*:—Bozrah {1x}. See: TWOT—270b; BDB—131a.

1224. בָּצְרָה {9x} **Botsrâh**, *bots-raw'*; the same as 1223; *Botsrah*, a place in Edom:—Bozrah {8x}, non translated variant {1x}. See: BDB—131b.

1225. בִּצָּרוֹן {1x} **bitstsârôwn**, *bits-tsaw-rone'*; masc. intens. from 1219; a *fortress*:—stronghold {1x}. See: TWOT—270c; BDB—131b.

1226. בַּצֹּרֶת {2x} **batstsôreth**, *bats-tso'-reth*; fem. intens. from 1219; *restraint* (of rain), i.e. *drought*:—dearth {1x}, drought {1x}. See: TWOT—270d; BDB—131b.

1227. בַּקְבּוּק {2x} **Baqbûwq**, *bak-book'*; the same as 1228; *Bakbuk*, one of the *Nethinim*:—Bakbuk {2x}. See: BDB—131c, 132d.

1228. בַּקְבֻּק {3x} **baqbûk**, *bak-book'*; from 1238; a *bottle* (from the gurgling in *emptying*):—bottle {2x}, cruse {1x}. See: TWOT—273a; BDB—131c, 132d.

1229. בַּקְבֻּקְיָה {3x} **Baqbuqyâh**, *bak-book-yaw'*; from 1228 and 3050; *emptying* (i.e. *wasting*) *of Jah; Bakbukjah*, an Isr.:—Bakbukiah {3x}. See: BDB—131c, 132d.

1230. בַּקְבַּקַּר {1x} **Baqbaqqar**, *bak-bak-kar'*; redupl. from 1239; *searcher; Bakbakkar*, an Isr.:—Bakbakkar {1x}. See: BDB—131c.

1231. בֻּקִּי {5x} **Buqqîy**, *book-kee';* from 1238; *wasteful; Bukki,* the name of two Isr.:—Bukki {5x}. See: BDB—131c.

1232. בֻּקִּיָּה {2x} **Buqqîyâh**, *book-kee-yaw';* from 1238 and 3050; *wasting of Jah; Bukkijah,* an Isr.:—Bukkiah {2x}. See: BDB—131c.

1233. בְּקִיעַ {2x} **bᵉqîyaʿ**, *bek-ee'-ah;* from 1234; a *fissure:*—breach {1x}, cleft {1x}. See: TWOT—271c; BDB—132c.

1234. בָּקַע **bâqaʿ**, *baw-kah';* a prim. root; to *cleave;* gen. to *rend, break, rip* or *open:*—cleave {10x}, . . .up {9x}, divide {5x}, rent {4x}, . . . out {3x}, break through {3x}, rend {3x}, breach {2x}, asunder {2x}, hatch {2x}, brake {1x}, burst {1x}, cleft {1x}, break forth {1x}, pieces {1x}, tare {1x}, tear {1x}, win {1x}.

Baqa (1234) means "to cleave, split, break open, break through." It is the origin of the name of the famous Beqa Valley (which means "valley" or "cleft") in Lebanon. **(1)** In its verbal forms, *baqa'* is found some 50 times in the Hebrew Old Testament. **(2)** The word is first used there in Gen 7:11, which states that the "fountains of the great deep [were] broken up," resulting in the Flood. **(3)** The everyday use of the verb is seen in references **(3a)** to "splitting" wood (Eccl 10:9) and **(3b)** the ground "splitting" asunder (Num 16:31). **(3c)** Serpents' eggs "split open" or "hatch out" their young (Is 59:5). **(4)** City walls are "breached" or "broken into" in order to take them captive (Jer 52:7). **(5)** One of the horrors of war was the "ripping open" of pregnant women by the enemy (2 Kin 8:12; 15:16). **(6)** Three times God is said "to split open" rocks or the ground in order to provide water for His people (Judg 15:19; Ps 74:15; Is 48:21).

(7) In the figurative sense, it is said that the light of truth will "break forth as the morning" (Is 58:8). **(8)** Using hyperbole or exaggeration, the historian who recorded the celebration for Solomon's coronation said that it was so loud "that the earth rent with the sound of them" (1 Kin 1:40). **(9)** As here, the KJV often renders *baqa'* by "rent." In other contexts, it may be translated "burst; clave (cleave); tear; divide; break." Syn.: 1692, 2673, 6536. See: TWOT—271; BDB—131c.

1235. בֶּקַע {2x} **beqaʿ**, *beh'-kah;* from 1234; a *section* (half) of a shekel, i.e. a *beka* (a weight and a coin):—bekah {1x}, half a shekel {1x}. See: TWOT—271a; BDB—132b.

1236. בִּקְעָא {1x} **biqʿâ'** (Aram.), *bik-aw';* corresp. to 1237:—plain {1x}. See: TWOT—2637; BDB—1085a.

1237. בִּקְעָה {20x} **biqʿâh**, *bik-aw';* from 1234; prop. a *split,* i.e. a wide level *valley* between mountains:—plain {7x}, valley {13x}. See: TWOT—271b; BDB—132c, 1085a.

1238. בָּקַק {9x} **bâqaq**, *baw-kak';* a prim. root; to *pour* out, i.e. to *empty,* fig. to *depopulate;* by anal. to *spread* out (as a fruitful vine):—empty {5x}, make void {1x}, emptiers {1x}, fail {1x}, utterly (inf for emphasis). See: TWOT—273; BDB—132c.

1239. בָּקַר {7x} **bâqar**, *baw-kar;* a prim. root; prop. to *plow,* or (gen.) *break* forth, i.e. (fig.) to *inspect, admire, care for, consider:*—enquire {3x}, seek {3x}, search {1x}.

(1) *Baqar* means "to attend, bestow care on, seek with pleasure." **(2)** Although this verb is found only 7 times in biblical Hebrew, it occurs in early, middle, and late periods and in both prose and poetry. **(3)** In Lev 13:36 *baqar* means "to attend to": ". . . If the scall be spread in the skin, the priest shall not seek for yellow hair. . . ." **(4)** The word implies "to seek with pleasure or delight" in Ps 27:4: ". . . to behold the beauty of the Lord, and *to inquire* in his temple." Syn.: 1875, 2664. See: TWOT—274; BDB—133a, 1085b.

1240. בְּקַר {5x} **bᵉqar** (Aram.), *bek-ar';* corresp. to 1239:—inquire {1x}, make search {4x}. See: TWOT—2638; BDB—1085a.

1241. בָּקָר {182x} **bâqâr**, *baw-kawr';* from 1239; a *beeve* or animal of the ox kind of either gender (as used for *plowing*); collect. a *herd:*—ox {78x}, herd {44x}, beeves {7x}, young {18x}, young + 1121 {17x}, bullock {6x}, bullock + 1121 {2x}, calf + 1121 {2x}, heifer {2x}, kine {2x}, bulls {1x}, cattle {1x}, cow's {1x}, great {1x}.

Baqar (1241) means "herd; cattle." **(1)** One meaning of the word is "cattle." **(1a)** Such beasts were slaughtered for food, and their hides were presented as offerings to God (Num 15:8). **(1b)** This meaning of *baqar* is in Gen 12:16 (the first biblical occurrence): "And he [Pharaoh] entreated Abram well for her [Sarah's] sake: and he had sheep, and oxen, and he asses. . . ." **(1c)** These were grazing beasts (1 Chr 27:29) and were eaten (1 Kin 4:23). **(1d)** These animals pulled carts (2 Sa 6:6) and plows (Job 1:14), and carried burdens on their backs (1 Chr 12:40). **(2)** *Baqar* often refers to a group of cattle or "herd" (both sexes), as it does in Gen 13:5: "And Lot also, which went with Abram, had flocks, and herds [in the Hebrew, this word appears in a singular form] and tents." **(3)** The word can represent a "small group of cattle" (not a herd; cf. Gen 47:17; Ex 22:1) or even a pair of oxen (Num 7:17). **(4)** A single ox is indicated either by some other Hebrew word or called an offspring of oxen (Gen 18:7). **(5)** *Baqar* also refers to statues of oxen: "It [the altar of burnt offerings] stood upon twelve oxen, three looking toward the north, and three looking toward the west, and three looking toward the south, and three looking toward the east . . ." (1 Kin 7:25). Syn.: 6499, 7794. See: TWOT—274a; BDB—133a.

1242. בֹּקֶר {204x} **bôqer**, *bo'-ker;* from 1239; prop. *dawn* (as the *break* of day); gen. *morning:*—morning {190x}, morrow {7x}, day {3x}, days + 6153 {1x}, early {3x}.

Boqer (1242) means "morning." **(1)** This word means "morning," **(1a)** though not the period of time before noon. **(1b)** Rather it indicates the point of time at which night is changing to day or that time at the end of night: "And Moses stretched forth his rod over the land of Egypt, and the Lord brought an east wind upon the land all that day, and all that night; and when it was morning, the east wind brought the locusts" (Ex 10:13). **(2)** *Boqer* can represent the time just before the rising of the sun. In Judg 19:25 we read that the men of Gibeah raped and abused the Levite's concubine "all the night until the morning: and when the day began to spring, they let her go" (cf. Ruth 3:13). **(3)** In the ancient Near East the night was divided into three watches. **(3a)** The last period of the night was called the morning watch (Ex 14:24). **(3b)** It lasted from 2:00 A.M. until sunrise, and in such a context the word indicates this period of time.

(4) *Boqer* can mean "daybreak" or "dawn." In Ex 14:27 it is reported that the water of the Red Sea "returned to his [normal state] when the morning appeared [literally, "at the turning of the morning"]." **(5)** *Boqer* is used as a synonym of "dawn" in Job 38:12: "Hast thou commanded the morning since thy days; and caused the dayspring to know his place . . . ?" **(6)** Sometimes *boqer* appears to mean "early morning," or shortly after daybreak: **(6a)** "And Joseph came in unto them in the morning, and looked upon them and, behold, they were sad" (Gen 40:6). **(6b)** Thus, Moses "rose up early in the morning" and went up to Mount Sinai; he arose before daybreak so he could appear before God in the "morning" as God had commanded (Ex 34:2, 4). **(6c)** In the "morning" Jacob saw that his bride was Leah rather than Rachel (Gen 29:25; cf. 1 Sa 29:10). **(7)** As the opposite of night the word represents the entire period of daylight. The psalmist prays that it is good "to show forth thy loving-kindness in the morning, and thy faithfulness every night" (Ps 92:2), in other words, to always be praising God (cf. Amos 5:8).

(8) In Ps 65:8 *boqer* represents a place, specifically, the place where the sun rises: "They also that dwell in the uttermost parts are afraid at thy tokens: thou makest the outgoings of the morning and evening to rejoice." **(9)** At least once the word appears to represent the resurrection: "Like sheep they [the ungodly] are laid in the grave; death shall feed on them; and the upright shall have dominion over them in the morning . . ." (Ps 49:14). **(10)** *Boqer* can mean "morrow" or "next day." This meaning first appears in Ex 12:10, where God tells Israel not to leave any of the Passover "until the morning; and that which remaineth of it until the morning ye shall burn with fire" (cf. Lev 22:30). Syn.: 5399, 7837. See: TWOT—274c; BDB—133c.

1243. בַּקָּרָה {1x} **baqqârâh**, *bak-kaw-raw';* intens. from 1239; a *looking after:*—seek out {1x}. See: TWOT—274d; BDB—134c.

1244. בִּקֹּרֶת {1x} **biqqôreth**, *bik-ko'-reth;* from 1239; prop. *examination,* i.e. (by impl.) *punishment:*—scourged {1x}. See: TWOT—274e; BDB—134c.

1245. בָּקַשׁ {225x} **bâqash**, *baw-kash';* a prim. root; to *search* out (by any method, spec. in worship or prayer); by impl. to *strive after:*—seek {189x}, require {14x}, request {4,x} seek out {4x}, enquired {3x}, besought {2x}, ask {2x}, sought for {2x}, begging {1x}, desire {1x}, get {1x}, inquisition {1x}, procureth {1x}.

Baqash means "to seek, search, consult." **(1)** Basically *baqash* means "to seek" to find something that is lost or missing, or, at least, whose location is unknown. **(1a)** In Gen 37:15 a man asks Joseph: "What seekest thou?" **(1b)** A special nuance of this sense is "to seek out of a group; to choose, select" something or someone yet undesignated, as in 1 Sa 13:14: ". . . The Lord hath sought him a man after his own heart. . . ." **(1c)** To seek one's face is "to seek" to come before him, or to have a favorable audience with him; all the world "was seeking" the presence of Solomon (1 Kin 10:24). **(1d)** In a similar sense one may "seek" God's face by standing before Him in the temple praying (2 Sa 21:1).

(2) The sense "seek to secure" emphasizes the pursuit of a wish or the accomplishing of a plan. **(2a)** Moses asked the Levites who rebelled against the unique position of Aaron and his sons: ". . . Seek ye the priesthood also?" (Num 16:10). **(2b)** This usage may have an emotional coloring, such as, "to aim at, devote oneself to, and be concerned about." So God asks the sons of men (mankind): ". . . How long will ye turn my glory into shame? How long will ye love vanity, and seek after [sin]?" (Ps 4:2). **(2c)** Cultically one may "seek" to secure God's favor or help: "And Judah gathered themselves together, to ask help of the Lord . . ." (2 Chr 20:4). **(2d)** In such usages the intellectual element usually is in the background; there is no seeking after information. **(2e)** An exception to this is Judg 6:29: "And when they inquired [1875 - darash] and asked [1245 - baqash], they said, Gideon the son of Joash hath done this thing."

(3) Infrequently this verb is used of seeking information from God (Ex 33:7). **(3a)** In a similar sense one may "seek" God's face (2 Sa 21:1). Here *baqash* is clearly used of searching for information (a cognitive pursuit). **(3b)** Also, compare the pursuit of wisdom (Prov. 2:4). **(4)** This sense of "seeking to secure" may also be used of seeking one's life (5315 - nepesh). **(4a)** God told Moses to "go, return into Egypt: for all the men are dead which sought thy life" (Ex 4:19). **(4b)** *Baqash* may be used with this same nuance but without *nepesh*—so Pharaoh "sought to slay Moses" (Ex 2:15). **(5)** Only twice is this nuance applied to seeking to procure one's good as in Ps 122:9: "Because of the house of the LORD our God I will seek thy good" [usually *darash* (1875) is used of seeking one's good].

(6) About 20 times *baqash* means to hold someone responsible for something because the speaker has a (real or supposed) legal right to it. In Gen 31:39 (the first biblical occurrence of the verb) Jacob points out to Laban that regarding animals lost to wild beasts, "of my hand didst thou require it." **(7)** Only infrequently is *baqash* used of seeking out a place, or as a verb of movement toward a place. So Joseph "sought [a place] to weep; and he entered into his chamber, and wept there" (Gen 43:30). **(8)** Theologically, this verb can be used not only "to seek" a location before the Lord (to stand before Him in the temple and seek to secure His blessing), but it may also be used of a state of mind: "But if from thence thou shalt seek the LORD thy God, thou shalt find him, if thou seek him [darash] with all thy heart and with all thy soul" (Deut 4:29). In instances such as this where the verb is used in synonymous parallelism with *darash*, the two verbs have the same meaning. Syn.: 1875, 7836. See: TWOT—276; BDB—134c.

1246. בַּקָּשָׁה {8x} **baqqâshâh**, *bak-kaw-shaw'*; from 1245; a *petition:*—request {8x}. See: TWOT—276a; BDB—135a.

1247. בַּר {8x} **bar** (Aram.), *bar;* corresp. to 1121; a *son, grandson,* etc.:—× old {1x}, son {7x}. See: TWOT—276a; BDB—1085b.

1248. בַּר {4x} **bar**, *bar;* borrowed (as a title) from 1247; the *heir* (apparent to the throne):—son {4x}. Syn.: 1121. See: TWOT—277; BDB—135a, 1085b.

1249. בַּר **bar**, *bar;* from 1305 (in its various senses); *beloved;* also *pure, empty:*—clean {3x}, pur {2x}, choice {1x}, clear {1x}. See: TWOT—288a; BDB—135a, 141a.

1250. בָּר {14x} **bâr**, *bawr;* or

בַּר **bar**, *bar;* from 1305 (in the sense of *winnowing*); *grain* of any kind (even while standing in the field); by extens. the open *country:*—corn {9x}, wheat {5x}. See: BDB—135a, 141b, 1085c.

1251. בַּר {8x} **bar** (Aram.), *bar;* corresp. to 1250; a *field:*—field {8x}. See: TWOT—2640; BDB—1085b, 1085c.

1252. בֹּר {6x} **bôr**, *bore;* from 1305; *purity:*—cleanness {4x}, pureness {1x}, never {1x}. See: TWOT—288d; BDB—101c, 141b.

1253. בֹּר {2x} **bôr**, *bore;* the same as 1252; vegetable *lye* (from its *cleansing*); used as a *soap* for washing, or a *flux* for metals:—purely {1x}, non translated variant {1x}. See: TWOT—288c; BDB—141b.

1254. בָּרָא {54x} **bârâʾ**, *baw-raw';* a prim. root; (absolutely) to *create;* (qualified) to *cut* down (a wood), *select, feed* (as formative processes):—create {42x}, creator {3x}, choose {2x}, make {2x}, cut down {2x}, dispatch {1x}, done {1x}, make fat {1x}.

Bara' means "to create, make." **(1)** This verb is of profound theological significance, since it has only God as its subject. **(1a)** Only God can "create" in the sense implied by *bara'*. **(1b)** The verb expresses creation out of nothing, an idea seen clearly in passages having to do with creation on a cosmic scale: "In the beginning God created the heaven and the earth" (Gen 1:1; cf. Gen 2:3; Is 40:26; 42:5). **(1c)** All other verbs for "creating" allow a much broader range of meaning; they have both divine and human subjects, and are used in contexts where bringing something or someone into existence is not the issue. **(2)** Objects of the verb include **(2a)** the heavens and earth (Gen 1:1; Is 40:26; 42:5; 45:18; 65:17), **(2b)** man (Gen 1:27; 5:2; 6:7; Deut 4:32; Ps 89:47; Is 43:7; 45:12); **(2c)** Israel (Is 43:1; Mal 2:10); **(2d)** a new thing (Jer 31:22); **(2e)** cloud and smoke (Is 4:5); **(2f)** north and south (Ps 89:12); **(2g)** salvation and righteousness (Is 45:8); **(2h)** speech (Is 57:19); **(2i)** darkness (Is 45:7); **(2j)** wind (Amos 4:13); and **(2k)** a new heart (Ps. 51:10).

(3) A careful study of the passages where *bara'* occurs shows that in the few non-poetic uses (primarily in Genesis), the writer uses scientifically precise language to demonstrate that God brought the object or concept into being from previously nonexistent material. **(4)** Especially striking is the use of *bara'* in Isaiah 40—65. **(4a)** Out of 49 occurrences of the verb in the Old Testament, 20 are in these chapters. **(4b)** Because Isaiah writes prophetically to the Jews in Exile, he speaks words of comfort based upon God's past benefits and blessings to His people. Isaiah especially wants to show that, since Yahweh is the Creator, He is able to deliver His people from captivity. The God of Israel has created all things: "I have made [6213 - 'asah] the earth, and created [*bara'*] man upon it: I, even my hands, have stretched out the heavens, and all their host have I commanded" (Is 45:12). **(4c)** The gods of Babylon are impotent nonentities (Is 44:12–20; 46:1–7), and so **(4d)** Israel can expect God to triumph by effecting a new creation (43:16–21; 65:17–25).

(5) Though a precisely correct technical term to suggest cosmic, material creation from nothing, *bara'* is a rich theological vehicle for communicating the sovereign power of God, who originates and regulates all things to His glory. Syn.: "For thus saith the LORD that created [*bara*] the heavens; God himself that formed [yatsar 3335] the earth and made [asah - 6213] it; he hath established [kun - 3559] it, he created [*bara*] it not in vain, he formed [yatsar - 3335] it to be inhabited: I am the LORD; and there is none else." (Is 45:18). The technical meaning of *bara* (to create out of nothing) may not hold in these passages; perhaps the verb was popularized in these instances for the sake of providing a poetic synonym. See: TWOT—278; BDB—135a, 135d.

1255. בְּרֹאדַךְ בַּלְאֲדָן {1x} **Beʳrôʾdak Balʾădân**, *ber-o-dak' bal-ad-awn';* a var. of 4757; *Berodak-Baladan,* a Bab. king:—Berodach-baladan {1x}. See: BDB—135d, 597d.

בִּרְאִי **Birʾîy**. See 1011.

1256. בְּרָאיָה {1x} **Beʳrâʾyâh**, *ber-aw-yaw';* from 1254 and 3050; *Jah has created; Berajah,* an Isr.:—Beraiah {1x}. See: BDB—135c.

1257. בַּרְבֻּר {1x} **barbûr**, *bar-boor';* by redupl. from 1250; a *fowl* (as fattened on *grain*):—fowl {1x}. See: TWOT—288g; BDB—135d, 141b.

1258. בָּרַד {1x} **bârad**, *baw-rad';* a prim. root, to *hail:*—hail {1x}. See: TWOT—280; BDB—136a.

1259. בָּרָד {29x} **bârâd**, *baw-rawd';* from 1258; *hail:*—hail {27x}, hailstones +68 {2x}. See: TWOT—280a; BDB—135d.

1260. בֶּרֶד {1x} **Bered**, *beh'red;* from 1258; *hail; Bered,* the name of a place south of Pal., also of an Isr.:—*Bered* {1x}. See: BDB—136a.

1261. בָּרֹד {4x} **bârôd**, *baw-rode';* from 1258; *spotted* (as if with *hail*):—grisled {4x}. See: TWOT—280b; BDB—136a.

1262. בָּרָה {7x} **bârâh**, *baw-raw';* a prim. root; to *select;* also (as denom. from 1250) to *feed;* also (as equiv. to 1305) to *render clear* (Eccl 3:18):—eat {4x}, choose {1x}, give {1x}, cause to eat {1x}. See: TWOT—281; BDB—136a.

1263. בָּרוּךְ {26x} **Bârûwk**, *baw-rook';* pass. part. from 1288; *blessed; Baruk,* the name of three Isr.:—Baruch {26x}. See: BDB—138c, 140a.

1264. בְּרוֹם {1x} **beʳrôwm**, *ber-ome';* prob. of for. or.; *damask* (stuff of variegated thread):—rich apparel {1x}. See: TWOT—286a; BDB—140b.

1265. בְּרוֹשׁ {20x} **beʳrôwsh**, *ber-ōsh';* of uncert. der.; a *cypress* (?) tree; hence, a *lance* or a *musical* instrument (as made of that wood):—fir tree {13x}, fir {7x}. See: TWOT—289a; BDB—137b, 141b.

1266. בְּרוֹת {1x} **beʳrôwth**, *ber-ōth';* a var. of 1265; the *cypress* (or some elastic tree):—fir {1x}. See: TWOT—289a; BDB—137b, 141c.

1267. בָּרוּת {1x} **bârûwth**, *baw-rooth';* from 1262; *food:*—meat {1x}. See: TWOT—281b; BDB—136a, 137b.

1268. בֵּרוֹתָה {2x} **Bêrôwthâh**, *bay-ro-thaw';* or

בֵּרֹתַי **Bêrôthay**, *bay-ro-tha'-ee;* prob. from 1266; *cypress* or *cypresslike; Berothah* or *Berothai,* a place north of Pal.:—Berothah {1x}, Berothai {1x}. See: BDB—92d, 137b, 467b.

1269. בִּרְזוֹת {1x} **Birzôwth**, *beer-zoth';* prob. fem. plur. from an unused root (appar. mean. to *pierce*); *holes; Birzoth,* an Isr.:—Birzavith {1x}. See. BDB—137b.

1270. בַּרְזֶל {76x} **barzel**, *bar-zel';* perh. from the root of 1269; *iron* (as *cutting*); by extens. an iron *implement:*—iron {73x}, (axe) head {2x}, smith + 2796 {1x}. See: TWOT—283a; BDB—137b, 1108d.

1271. בַּרְזִלַּי {12x} **Barzillay**, *bar-zil-lah'-ee;* from 1270; *iron*-hearted; *Barzillai,* the name of three Isr.:—Barzillai {12x}. See: BDB—137d.

1272. בָּרַח {65x} **bârach**, *baw-rakh';* a prim. root; to *bolt,* i.e. fig. to *flee* suddenly:—flee {52x}, . . .away {7x}, chased {1x}, fain {1x} (inf. for emphasis), flight {1x}, make haste {1x}, reach {1x}, shoot {1x}.

Barach means "to flee, pass through." **(1)** The word first appears in Gen 16:6, where it is said that Hagar "fled from her [Sarah's] face" as a result of Sarah's harsh treatment. **(2)** Men may "flee" from many things or situations. David "fled" from Naioth in Ramah in order to come to Jonathan (1 Sa 20:1). **(3)** Sometimes it is necessary to "flee" from weapons (Job 20:24). **(4)** In describing flight from a person, the Hebrew idiom "from the presence of" (literally, "from the face of") is often used (Gen 16:6, 8; 31:27; 35:1, 7). **(5)** In its figurative use, the word describes days "fleeing" away (Job 9:25) or frail man "fleeing" like a shadow (Job 14:2). **(6)** A rather paradoxical use is found in Song 8:14, in which "flee" must mean "come quickly": "Make haste [literally, "flee"], my beloved, and be thou like to a gazelle. . . ." Syn.: 5127. See: TWOT—284; BDB—137d.

1273. בַּרְחֻמִי {1x} **Barchûmîy**, *bar-khoo-mee';* by transp. for 978; a *Barchumite,* or native of *Bachurim:*—Barhumite {1x}. See: BDB—104d, 138c.

1274. בְּרִי {1x} **b^erîy**, *ber-ee';* from 1262; *fat:*—fat {1x}. See: TWOT—279a; BDB—135d, 138c.

1275. בֵּרִי {1x} **Bêrîy**, *bay-ree';* prob. by contr. from 882; *Beri,* an Isr.:—Beri {1x}. See: BDB—92d, 138c.

1276. בֵּרִי {1x} **Bêrîy**, *bay-ree';* of uncert. der.; (only in the plur. and with the art.) the *Berites,* a place in Pal.:—Berites {1x}. See: BDB—138c.

1277. בָּרִיא {13x} **bârîyʾ**, *baw-ree';* from 1254 (in the sense of 1262); *fatted* or *plump:*—fat {5x}, rank {2x}, fatfleshed + 1320 {2x}, firm {1x}, fatter {1x}, fed {1x}, plenteous {1x}. Syn.: 1878, 2459. See: TWOT—279a; BDB—135d.

1278. בְּרִיאָה {1x} **b^erîyʾâh**, *ber-ee-aw';* fem. from 1254; a *creation,* i.e. a *novelty:*—new thing {1x}. See: TWOT—278a; BDB—135c.

1279. בִּרְיָה {3x} **biryâh**, *beer-yaw';* fem. from 1262; *food:*—meat {1x}. See: BDB—135d, 136a, 138c.

1280. בְּרִיחַ {41x} **b^erîyach**, *ber-ee'-akh;* from 1272; a *bolt:*—bar {40x}, fugitive {1x}. See: TWOT—284b; BDB—138a.

1281. בָּרִיחַ {3x} **bârîyach**, *baw-ree'-akh;* or (short.)

בָּרִחַ **bârîach**, *baw-ree'-akh;* from 1272; a *fugitive,* i.e. the *serpent* (as *fleeing*), and the constellation by that name:—crooked {1x}, nobles {1x}, piercing {1x}. See: TWOT—284a; BDB—138a.

1282. בָּרִיחַ {1x} **Bârîyach**, *baw-ree'-akh;* the same as 1281; *Bariach,* an Isr.:—Bariah {1x}. See: BDB—138a.

1283. בְּרִיעָה {11x} **B^erîyʿâh**, *ber-ee'-aw;* appar. from the fem. of 7451 with prep. pref.; *in trouble; Beriah,* the name of four Isr.:—Beriah {11x}. See: BDB—140b.

1284. בְּרִיעִי {1x} **B^erîyʿîy**, *ber-ee-ee';* patron. from 1283; a *Beriite* (collect.) or desc. of Beriah:—Beerites {1x}. See: BDB—140b.

1285. בְּרִית {284x} **b^erîyth**, *ber-eeth';* from 1262 (in the sense of *cutting* [like 1254]); a *compact* (because made by passing between *pieces* of flesh):—covenant {264x}, league {17x}, confederacy {1x}, confederate {1x}, confederate + 1167 {1x}.

Beriyth means "covenant; league; confederacy." **(1)** The first occurrence of the word is in Gen 6:18: "But with thee [Noah] will I establish my covenant." **(2)** It is translated fifteen times as "league": ". . . Now therefore make ye a league with us" (Josh 9:6). **(2a)** These are all cases of political agreement within Israel (2 Sa 3:12–13, 21; 5:3) or **(2b)** between nations (1 Kin 15:19). **(2c)** In Judg 2:2: "And ye shall make no league with the inhabitants of this land. . . ." **(2d)** The command had been also given in Ex 23:32; 34:12–16; and Deut 7:2–6 ["covenant"]. **(3)** The word is used of "agreements between men," as **(3a)** Abraham and Abimelech (Gen 21:32): "Thus they made a covenant at Beer-sheba. . . ." **(3b)** David and Jonathan made a "covenant" of mutual protection that would be binding on David's descendants forever (1 Sa 18:3; 20:8, 16–18, 42). **(3c)** In these cases, there was "mutual agreement confirmed by oath in the name of the Lord." **(3d)** Sometimes there were also material pledges (Gen 21:28–31).

(4) Ahab defeated the Syrians: "So he made a covenant with [Ben-hadad], and sent him away" (1 Kin 20:34). **(5)** The king of Babylon "took of the king's seed [Zedekiah], and made a covenant with him, and hath taken an oath of him . . ." (Eze 17:13). In such "covenants," the terms were imposed by the superior military power; they were not mutual agreements. **(6)** In Israel, the kingship was based on "covenant": ". . . David made a league with them [the elders of Israel] in Hebron before the LORD . . ." (2 Sa 5:3). **(6a)** The "covenant" was based on their knowledge that God had appointed him (2 Sa 5:2); **(6b)** thus they became David's subjects (cf. 2 Kin 11:4, 17).

(7) The great majority of occurrences of *beriyth* are of God's "covenants" with men, as in Gen 6:18 above. **(7a)** The verbs used are important: "I will establish my covenant" (Gen 6:18)—literally, "cause to stand" or "confirm." **(7b)** "I will make my covenant" (Gen 17:2). **(7c)** "He declared to you his covenant" (Deut 4:13). **(7d)** "My covenant which I commanded them . . ." (Josh 7:11). **(7e)** "I have remembered my covenant. Wherefore . . . I will bring you out from under the burdens of the Egyptians" (Ex 6:5–6). **(7f)** God will not reject Israel for their disobedience so as "to destroy them utterly, and to break my covenant with them . . ." (Lev 26:44). **(7g)** "He will not . . . forget the covenant . . . which he sware unto them" (Deut 4:31). **(7h)** The most common verb is "to cut [karat] a covenant," which is always translated as in Gen 15:18: "The LORD made a covenant with Abram." This use apparently comes from the ceremony described in Gen 15:9–17 (cf. Jer 34:18), in which God appeared as "a smoking furnace, and a burning lamp [flaming torch] that passed between those pieces" (Gen 15:17). **(7i)** These verbs make it plain that God takes the sole initiative in covenant making and fulfillment.

(8) The words of the "covenant" were written in a book (Ex 24:4, 7; Deut 31:24–26) and on stone tablets (Ex 34:28). **(9)** Men "enter into" (Deut 29:12) or "join" (Jer 50:5) God's "covenant." **(10)** They are to obey (Gen 12:4) and "observe carefully" all the commandments of the "covenant" (Deut 4:6). **(11)** But above all, the "covenant" calls Israel to "love the LORD thy God with all thine heart, and with all thy soul, and with all thy might" (Deut 6:5). **(12)** God's "covenant" is a relationship of love and loyalty between the Lord and His chosen people: **(12a)** ". . . If ye will obey my voice indeed, and keep my covenant, then ye shall be a peculiar treasure unto me above all people . . . and ye shall be unto me a kingdom of priests, and a holy nation" (Ex 19:5–6). **(12b)** "All the commandments . . . shall ye observe to do, that ye may live, and multiply, and go in and possess the land which the LORD sware unto your fathers" (Deut 8:1). **(13)** In the "covenant," man's response contributes to covenant fulfillment; yet man's action is not causative. God's grace always goes before and produces man's response.

(14) Occasionally, Israel "made a covenant before the LORD, to walk after the LORD, and to keep his commandments . . . , to perform the words of this covenant that were written in this book" (2 Kin 23:3). **(14a)** This is like their original promise: "All that the LORD hath spoken we will do" (Ex 19:8; 24:7). **(14b)** Israel did not propose terms or a basis of union with God. They responded to God's "covenant." **(15)** The use of "Old Testament" and "New Testament" as the names for the two sections of the Bible indicates that God's "covenant" is central to the entire book. **(16)** The Bible relates God's "covenant" purpose, that man be joined to Him in loving service and know eternal fellowship with Him through the redemption that is in Jesus Christ. Syn: "Covenant" is parallel or equivalent to the Hebrew words **(A)** dabar (1697 - "word"), **(B)** hoq (2706 - "statute"), **(C)** piqqud (6490 - "precepts"—Ps 119:94), **(D)** ʿedah (5715 - "testimony"—Ps 25:10), **(E)** torah (8451 - "law"—Ps 78:10), and **(F)** checed (2617 - "lovingkindness"—Ps 17:7). These words emphasize the authority and grace of God in making and keeping the "covenant," and the specific responsibility of man under the covenant. See: TWOT—282a; BDB—136b, 138c.

1286. בְּרִית {1x} **B^erîyth**, *ber-eeth';* the same as 1285; *Berith,* a Shechemitish deity:—Berith {1x}. See: BDB—42c, 136c.

1287. בֹּרִית {1x} **bôrîyth**, *bo-reeth';* fem. of 1253; vegetable *alkali:*—soap {1x}. See: TWOT—288e; BDB—138c, 141b.

1288. בָּרַךְ {330x} **bârak**, *baw-rak';* a prim. root; to *kneel;* by impl. to *bless* God (as an act of adoration), and (vice-versa) man (as a benefit); also (by euphem.) to *curse* (God or the king, as treason):—bless {302x}, salute {5x}, curse {4x}, blaspheme {2x}, blessing {2x}, praised {2x}, kneel down {2x}, congratulate {1x}, kneel {1x}, make to kneel {1x}, misc. {8x}.

Barak means "to kneel, bless, be blessed, curse." **(1)** *Barak* occurs first in Gen 1:22: "And God blessed them, saying, Be fruitful and multiply, . . ." **(2)** God's first word to man is introduced in the same way: "And God blessed them, and God said unto them, Be fruitful, and multiply . . ." (v. 28). Thus the whole creation is shown to depend upon God for its continued existence and function (cf. Ps 104:27–30). **(3)** *Barak* is used again of man in Gen 5:2, at the beginning of the history of believing men, and again after the Flood in Gen 9:1: "And God blessed Noah and his sons. . . ."

(4) The central element of God's covenant with Abram is: "I will bless thee . . . and thou shalt be a blessing: And I will bless them that bless thee . . . and in thee shall all families of the earth be blessed" (Gen 12:2–3). **(4a)** This "blessing" on the nations is repeated in Gen 18:18; 22:18; and 28:14 (cf. Gen 26:4; Jer 4:2). **(4b)** In all of these instances, God's blessing goes out to the nations through Abraham or his seed. **(4c)** The covenant promise called the nations to seek the "blessing" (cf. Is 2:2–4), but made it plain that the initiative in blessing rests with God, and that Abraham and his seed were the instruments of it. **(5)** God, either directly or through His representatives, is the subject of this verb over 100 times. **(6)** The Levitical benediction is based on this order: "On this wise ye shall bless the children of Israel . . . the Lord bless thee . . . and they shall put my name upon the children of Israel; and I will bless them" (Num 6:23–27).

(7) The passive form of *barak* is used in pronouncing God's "blessing on men," as through Melchizedek: "Blessed be Abram of the most high God . . ." (Gen 14:19). **(8)** "Blessed be the LORD God of Shem . . ." (Gen 9:26) is an expression of praise. **(9)** "Blessed be the most high God, which hath delivered thine enemies into thy hand" (Gen 14:20) is mingled praise and thanksgiving. **(10)** A common form of greeting was, "Blessed be thou of the LORD" (1 Sa 15:13; cf. Ruth 2:4); "Saul went out to meet [Samuel], that he might salute him" (1 Sa 13:10). **(11)** The simple form of the verb is used in 2 Chr 6:13: "He . . . kneeled down. . . ." **(12)** Six times the verb is used to denote profanity, as in Job 1:5: "It may be that my sons have sinned, and cursed God in their hearts." See: TWOT—285; BDB—138c, 1085b.

1289. בְּרַךְ {5x} **bᵉrak** (Aram.), *ber-ak';* corresp. to 1288:—bless {4x}, kneel {1x}. See: TWOT—2641; BDB—1085b.

1290. בֶּרֶךְ {25x} **berek**, *beh'-rek;* from 1288; a *knee:*—knee {1x}. See: TWOT—285a; BDB—139c.

1291. בֶּרֶךְ {1x} **berek** (Aram.), *beh'-rek;* corresp. to 1290:—knee {1x}. See: TWOT—2641a; BDB—1085c.

1292. בָּרַכְאֵל {2x} **Bârakʼêl**, *baw-rak-ale';* from 1288 and 410, *God has blessed; Barakel,* the father of one of Job's friends:—Barachel {1x}. See: BDB—140a.

1293. בְּרָכָה {69x} **bᵉrâkâh**, *ber-aw-kaw';* from 1288; *benediction;* by impl. *prosperity:*—blessing {61x}, blessed {3x}, present {3x}, liberal {1x}, pools {1x}.

Berakah means "blessing." **(1)** It is used in conjunction with the verb barak ("to bless") 71 times in the Old Testament. **(2)** The word appears most frequently in Genesis and Deuteronomy. **(3)** The first occurrence is God's blessing of Abram: "I will make of thee a great nation, and I will bless thee, and make thy name great; and thou shalt be a blessing [*berakah*]" (Gen 12:2). **(4)** When expressed by men, a "blessing" was a wish or prayer for a blessing that is to come in the future: "And [God] give thee the blessing of Abraham, to thee, and to thy seed with thee; that thou mayest inherit the land wherein thou art a stranger, which God gave unto Abraham" (Gen 28:4). **(4a)** This refers to a "blessing" that the patriarchs customarily extended upon their children before they died. **(4b)** Jacob's "blessings" on the tribes (Gen 49) and **(4c)** Moses' "blessing" (Deut 33:1ff.) are other familiar examples of this.

(5) Blessing was the opposite of a cursing (*qelalah*): "My father peradventure will feel me, and I shall seem to him as a deceiver; and I shall bring a curse upon me, and not a blessing" (Gen 27:12). **(6)** The blessing might also be presented more concretely in the form of a gift. For example, "Take, I pray thee, my blessing that is brought to thee; because God hath dealt graciously with me, and because I have enough. And he urged him, and he took it" (Gen 33:11). **(7)** When a "blessing" was directed to God, it was a word of praise and thanksgiving, as in: "Stand up and bless the LORD your God for ever and ever: and blessed be thy glorious name, which is exalted above all blessing and praise" (Neh 9:5). **(8)** The LORD's "blessing" rests on those who are faithful to Him: "A blessing, if ye obey the commandments of the LORD your God, which I command you this day . . ." (Deut 11:27). His blessing brings **(8a)** righteousness (Ps 24:5), **(8b)** life (Ps. 133:3), **(8c)** prosperity (2 Sa 7:29), and **(8d)** salvation (Ps 3:8).

(9) The "blessing" is portrayed as a rain or dew: "I will make them and the places round about my hill a blessing; and I will cause the shower to come down in his season; there shall be showers of blessing" (Eze 34:26; cf. Ps 84:6). **(10)** In the fellowship of the saints, the LORD commands His "blessing": "[It is] as the dew of Hermon, and as the dew that descended upon the mountains of Zion: for there the LORD commanded the blessing, even life for evermore" (Ps 133:3). **(11)** In a few cases, the LORD made people to be a "blessing" to others. Abraham is a blessing to the nations (Gen 12:2). **(12)** His descendants are expected to become a blessing to the nations (Is 19:24; Zec 8:13). See: TWOT—285b; BDB—139c.

1294. בְּרָכָה {3x} **Bᵉrâkâh**, *ber-aw-kaw';* the same as 1293; *Berakah,* the name of an Isr., and also of a valley in Pal.:—Berachah {3x}. See: BDB—139d.

1295. בְּרֵכָה {17x} **bᵉrêkâh**, *ber-ay-kaw';* from 1288; a *reservoir* (at which camels *kneel* as a resting-place):—fishpools {1x}, pool {16x}. See: TWOT—285c; BDB—140a.

1296. בֶּרֶכְיָה {11x} **Berekyâh**, *beh-rek-yaw';* or בֶּרֶכְיָהוּ **Berekyâhûw**, *beh-rek-yaw'-hoo;* from 1290 and 3050; *knee* (i.e. *blessing*) of Jah; *Berekjah,* the name of six Isr.:—Berachiah {1x}, Berechiah {10x}. See: BDB—140a.

1297. בְּרַם {5x} **bᵉram** (Aram.), *ber-am';* perh. from 7313 with prep. pref.; prop. *highly,* i.e. *surely;* but used adversatively, *however:*—but {2x}, yet {2x}, nevertheless {1x}. See: TWOT—2642; BDB—1085c.

1298. בֶּרַע {1x} **Beraʻ**, *beh'-rah;* of uncert. der.; *Bera,* a Sodomitish king:—*Bera* {1x}. See: BDB—140b.

1299. בָּרַק {1x} **bâraq**, *baw-rak';* a prim. root; to *lighten* (lightning):—cast forth {1x}. See: TWOT—287; BDB—140b.

1300. בָּרָק {21x} **bârâq**, *baw-rawk';* from 1299; *lightning;* by anal. a *gleam;* concr. a *flashing* sword:—lightning {14x}, glittering {4x}, bright {1x}, glitter {1x}, glittering sword {1x}. See: TWOT—287a; BDB—140c.

1301. בָּרָק {13x} **Bârâq**, *baw-rawk';* the same as 1300; *Barak,* an Isr.:—Barak {13x}. See: BDB—140c.

1302. בַּרְקוֹס {2x} **Barqôwç**, *bar-kose';* of uncert. der.; *Barkos,* one of the Nethimim:—Barkos {2x}. See: BDB—140d.

1303. בַּרְקָן {2x} **barqân**, *bar-kwan';* from 1300; a *thorn* (perh. as burning *brightly*):—briers {2x}. See: TWOT—287e; BDB—140d.

1304. בָּרֶקֶת {3x} **bârᵉqath**, *baw-reh'-keth;* or בָּרְכַת **bârᵉkath**, *baw-rek-ath';* from 1300; a gem (as *flashing*), perh. the *emerald:*—carbuncle {3x}. See: TWOT—287d; BDB—140c, 140d.

1305. בָּרַר {18x} **bârar**, *baw-rar';* a prim. root; to *clarify* (i.e. *brighten*), *examine, select:*—pure {5x}, choice {2x}, chosen {2x}, clean {2x}, clearly {1x}, manifest {1x}, bright {1x}, purge out {1x}, polished {1x}, purge {1x}, purified {1x}. Syn.: 2134, 2141. See: TWOT—288; BDB—140d, 1085c.

1306. בִּרְשַׁע {1x} **Birshaʻ**, *beer-shah';* prob. from 7562 with a prep. pref.; *with wickedness; Birsha,* a king of Gomorrah:—*Birsha* {1x}. See: BDB—141d.

1307. בֵּרֹתִי {1x} **Bêrôthîy**, *bay-ro-thee';* patrial from 1268; a *Berothite,* or inhab. of Berothai:—Berothite {1x}. See: BDB—92d, 141d.

1308. בְּשׂוֹר {3x} **Bᵉsôwr**, *bes-ore';* from 1319; *cheerful; Besor,* a stream of Pal.:—Besor {1x}. See: BDB—143a.

1309. בְּשׂוֹרָה {6x} **bᵉsôwrâh**, *bes-o-raw';* or (short.) בְּשֹׂרָה **bᵉsôrâh**, *bes-o-raw';* fem. from 1319; glad *tidings;* by impl. *reward for good news:*—tidings {6x}. See: TWOT—291b; BDB—142d.

1310. בָּשַׁל {28x} **bâshal**, *baw-shal';* a prim. root; prop. to *boil* up; hence, to *be done* in cooking; fig. to *ripen:*—seethe {10x}, boil {6x}, sod {6x}, bake {2x}, ripe {2x}, roast {2x}. Syn.: 7570. See: TWOT—292; BDB—143a.

1311. בָּשֵׁל {2x} **bâshêl**, *baw-shale';* from 1310; *boiled:*—sodden {1x}, at all {1x} (inf. for emphasis). See: TWOT—292a; BDB—143b.

1312. בִּשְׁלָם {1x} **Bishlâm**, *bish-lawm';* of for. der.; *Bishlam,* a Pers.:—*Bishlam* {1x}. See: BDB—143b.

1313. בָּשָׂם {1x} **bâsâm**, *baw-sawm';* from an unused root mean. to *be fragrant;* [comp. 5561] the *balsam* plant:—spice {1x}. See: TWOT—290a; BDB—141d.

1314. בֶּשֶׂם {29x} **besem**, *beh'-sem;* or בֹּשֶׂם **bôsem**, *bo'-sem;* from the same as 1313; *fragrance;* by impl. *spicery;* also the *balsam* plant:—spice {24x}, sweet odours {2x}, sweet {2x}, sweet smell {1x}. TWOT—290a; BDB—141d.

1315. בָּשְׂמַת {7x} **Bosmath**, *bos-math';* fem. of 1314 (the second form); *fragrance; Bosmath,* the name of a wife of Esau, and of a daughter of Solomon:—Bashemath {6x}, Basmath {1x}. See: BDB—142a.

1316. בָּשָׁן {60x} **Bâshân**, *baw shawn';* of uncert. der.; *Bashan* (often with the art.), a region E. of the Jordan:—*Bashan* {59x}, Bashanhavothjair + 2334 {1x}. See: BDB—143b.

1317. בָּשְׁנָה {1x} **boshnâh**, *bosh-naw';* fem. from 954; *shamefulness:*—shame {1x}. See: TWOT—222b; BDB—102a, 143c.

1318. בָּשַׁס {1x} **bâshaç**, *baw-shas';* a prim. root; to *trample* down:—treading {1x}. See: TWOT—294; BDB—143c.

1319. בָּשַׂר **bâsar**, *baw-sar';* a prim. root; prop. to *be fresh,* i.e. *full* (*rosy,* (fig.) *cheerful*); to *announce* (glad news):—tidings {16x}, show forth {3x}, publish {3x}, messenger {1x}, preached {1x}. Syn.: 5046. See: TWOT—291; BDB—142a.

1320. בָּשָׂר {269x} **bâsâr**, *baw-sawr';* from 1319; *flesh* (from its *freshness*); by extens. *body, person;* also (by euphem.) the *pudenda* of a man:—flesh {256x}, body {2x}, fatfleshed + 1277 {2x}, leanfleshed + 1851 {2x}, kin {2x}, leanfleshed + 7534 {1x}, mankind + 376 {1x}, myself {1x}, nakedness {1x}, skin {1x}.

Basar means "flesh; meat." **(1)** The word means the "meaty part plus the skin" of men: "And the LORD God caused a deep sleep to fall upon Adam, and he slept: and he took one of his ribs, and closed up the flesh instead thereof"

(Gen 2:21—the first occurrence). **(2)** This word can also be applied to the "meaty part" of animals (Deut 14:8). **(2a)** Gen 41:2 speaks of seven cows, sleek and "fat of flesh." **(2b)** In Num 11:33, *basar* means the meat or "flesh" of the quail that Israel was still chewing. Thus the word means "flesh," whether living or dead. **(3)** *Basar* often means the "edible part" of animals. **(3a)** Eli's sons did not know God's law concerning the priests' portion, so "when any man offered sacrifice, the priest's [Eli's] servant came, while the flesh was [boiling], with a [three-pronged fork] in his hand" (1 Sa 2:13). **(3b)** However, they insisted that "before they burnt the fat . . . , Give flesh to roast for the priest; for he will not have [boiled] flesh of thee, but raw" (literally, "living"—1 Sa 2:15). **(3c)** *Basar,* then, represents edible animal "flesh" or "meat," whether cooked (Dan 10:3) or uncooked. **(3d)** The word sometimes refers to "meat" that one is forbidden to eat (cf. Ex 21:28).

(4) This word may represent a part of the body. **(4a)** At some points, the body is viewed as consisting of two components, "flesh" and bones: "This is now bone of my bones, and flesh of my flesh: she shall be called Woman, because she was taken out of Man" (Gen 2:23). **(4b)** That part of the "fleshly" element known as the foreskin was to be removed by circumcision (Gen 17:11). **(4c)** In other passages, the elements of the body are the "flesh," the skin, and the bones (Lam 3:4). **(4d)** Num. 19:5 mentions the "flesh," hide, blood, and refuse of a heifer. **(4e)** In Job 10:11, we read: "Thou hast clothed me with skin and flesh, and hast [knit] me with bones and sinews." **(5)** Flesh sometimes means "blood relative": "And Laban said to him [Jacob], Surely thou art my bone and my flesh" (Gen 29:14). **(5a)** The phrase "your flesh" or "our flesh" standing alone may bear the same meaning: "Come, and let us sell him to the Ishmaelites, and let not our hand be upon him; for he is our brother and our flesh" (Gen 37:27). **(5b)** The phrase she'er *basar* is rendered "near of kin" (Lev 18:6).

(6) About 50 times, "flesh" represents the "physical aspect" of man or animals as contrasted with the spirit, soul, or heart (the nonphysical aspect). **(6a)** In the case of men, this usage appears in Num 16:22: "O God, the God of the spirits of all flesh, shall one man sin, and wilt thou be wroth with all the congregation?" **(6b)** In such passages, then, *basar* emphasizes the "visible and structural part" of man or animal. **(7)** In a few passages, the word appears to mean "skin," or the part of the body that is seen: "By reason of the voice of my groaning my bones cleave to my skin" (Ps 102:5; 119:120). **(8)** In passages such as Lev. 13:2, the ideas "flesh" and "skin" are clearly distinguished. **(9)** The term "all flesh" has several meanings. **(9a)** It means "all mankind" in Deut 5:26: "For who is there of all flesh, that hath heard the voice of the living God . . . ?" **(9b)** In another place, this phrase refers to "all living creatures within the cosmos," or all men and animals (Gen 6:17). See: TWOT—291a; BDB—142b, 925b, 1085c.

1321. בְּשַׂר {3x} **bᵉsar** (Aram.), *bes-ar';* corresp. to 1320:—flesh {3x}. See: TWOT—2643; BDB—1085c.

בְּשֹׂרָה **bᵉsôrâh**. See 1309.

1322. בֹּשֶׁת {30x} **bôsheth**, *bo'-sheth;* from 954; *shame* (the feeling and the condition, as well as its cause); by impl. (spec.) an *idol:* —shame {20x}, confusion {7x}, ashamed {1x}, greatly {1x}, shameful thing {1x}.

Bosheth means "shame; shameful thing." **(1)** The 30 appearances of this noun are mostly in poetic materials—only 5 appearances are in historical literature. **(2)** This word means a "shameful thing" as a substitute for the name Baal: "For shame hath devoured the labor of our fathers from our youth . . ." (Jer 3:24; cf. Jer 11:13; Hos 9:10). **(3)** This substitution also occurs in proper names: Ish-*bosheth* (2 Sa 2:8), the "man of shame," was originally Esh-baal (cf. 1 Chr 8:33), the "man of Baal." **(4)** This word represents both "shame and worthlessness": "Thou son of the perverse rebellious woman, do not I know that thou hast chosen the son of Jesse . . . unto the confusion of thy mother's nakedness" (1 Sa 20:30). **(5)** The "shame of one's face" (2 Chr 32:21) may well mean being red-faced or embarrassed. See: TWOT—222b; BDB—102a, 143c, 574c.

1323. בַּת **bath**, *bath;* from 1129 (as fem. of 1121); a *daughter* (used in the same wide sense as other terms of relationship, lit. and fig.):—daughter {526x}, town {32x}, village {1x}2, owl + 3284 {8x}, first {3x}, apple {1x}, branches {1x}, children {1x}, company {1x}, daughter + 8676 {1x}, eye {1x}, old {1x}. For a discussion, see 1129. See: TWOT—254b; BDB—123a, 143c.

1324. בַּת {13x} **bath**, *bath;* prob. from the same as 1327; a *bath* or Heb. measure (as a means of *division*) of liquids:—*bath* {13x}. See: TWOT—298a; BDB—143d, 144c, 1085d.

1325. בַּת {2x} **bath** (Aram.), *bath;* corresp. to 1324:—*bath* {2x}. See: TWOT—2644; BDB—1085d.

1326. בָּתָה {1x} **bâthâh**, *baw-thaw';* prob. an orth. var. for 1327; *desolation:*—waste {1x}. See: TWOT—298c; BDB—144d.

1327. בַּתָּה {1x} **battâh**, *bat-taw';* fem. from an unused root (mean. to *break* in pieces); *desolation:*—desolate {1x}. See: TWOT—298b; BDB—144c.

1328. בְּתוּאֵל {10x} **Bᵉthûwʾêl**, *beth-oo-ale';* appar. from the same as 1326 and 410; *destroyed of God; Bethuel,* the name of a nephew of Abraham, and of a place in Pal.:—Bethuel {1x}. Syn.: comp. 1329. See: BDB—143d.

1329. בְּתוּל {1x} **Bᵉthûwl**, *beth-ool';* for 1328; *Bethul* (i.e. *Bethuel*), a place in Pal.:—Bethuel {1x}. See: BDB—143d.

1330. בְּתוּלָה {50x} **bᵉthûwlâh**, *beth-oo-law';* fem. pass. part. of an unused root mean. to *separate;* a *virgin* (from her *privacy*); sometimes (by continuation) a *bride;* also (fig.) a *city* or *state:*—virgin {38x}, maid {7x}, maiden {5x}.

Bethuwlah (1330) means "maiden, virgin." **(1)** This word can mean "virgin," as is clear in Deut 22:17, where if a man has charged that "I found not thy daughter a maid," the father is to say, "And yet these are the tokens of my daughter's virginity [betulim]. The text continues: "And they shall spread the cloth before the elders of the city." The husband was to be chastised and fined (which was given to the girl's father), "because he hath brought up an evil name upon a virgin of Israel" (Deut 22:19). If she was found not to be a "virgin," she was to be stoned to death "because she hath wrought folly in Israel, to play the whore in her father's house" (Deut 22:21). **(2)** In several passages this word merely means a grown-up girl or a "maiden"; it identifies her age and marital status. The prophets who denounce Israel for playing the harlot also called her the *bethuwlah* of Yahweh, or the *bethuwlah* (daughter) of Israel (Jer 31:4, 21). **(3)** The other nations are also called betuloth: Is 23:12—Zidon; Is 47:1—Babylon; Jer 46:11—Egypt. **(3a)** These nations are hardly being commended for their purity! **(3b)** In Ugaritic literature the word is used frequently of the goddess Anat, the sister of Baal and hardly a virgin. **(3c)** What was true of her and figuratively of these nations (including Israel) was that she was a vigorous young woman at the height of her powers and not married. **(3d)** Thus *bethuwlah* is often used in parallelism with the Hebrew bachur, which signifies a young man, regardless of his virginity, who is at the height of his powers (Deut 32:25). **(3e)** In such contexts virility and not virginity is in view. **(3f)** Because of this ambiguity Moses described Rebekah as a young girl (5291 - *na'arah*) who was "very fair to look upon, a virgin [betulah], neither had any man known her" (Gen 24:16—the first occurrence of the word). **(4)** It is safe to say that all virgins are maidens, but not all maidens are virgins. Syn.: 5659. See: TWOT—295a; BDB—143d.

1331. בְּתוּלִים {10x} **bᵉthûwlîym**, *beth-oo-leem';* masc. plur. of the same as 1330; (collect. and abstr.) *virginity;* by impl. and concr. the *tokens* of it:—virginity {8x}, maid {2x}. See: TWOT—295b; BDB—144a.

1332. בִּתְיָה {1x} **Bithyâh**, *bith-yaw';* from 1323 and 3050; *daughter* (i.e. worshipper) *of Jah; Bithjah,* an Eg. woman:—Bithiah {1x}. See: BDB—124a, 143d.

1333. בָּתַק {1x} **bâthaq**, *baw-thak';* a prim. root; to *cut* in pieces:—thrust through {1x}. See: TWOT—296; BDB—144a.

1334. בָּתַר {2x} **bâthar**, *baw-thar';* a prim. root, to *chop* up:—divide {2x}. See: TWOT—297; BDB—144a.

1335. בֶּתֶר {3x} **bether**, *beh'-ther;* from 1334; a *section:*—part {2x}, piece {1x}. See: TWOT—297a; BDB—144a.

1336. בֶּתֶר {1x} **Bether**, *beh'-ther;* the same as 1335; *Bether,* a (craggy) place in Pal.:—*Bether* {1x}. See: BDB—144b.

1337. בַּת רַבִּים {1x} **Bath Rabbîym**, *bath rabbeem';* from 1323 and a masc. plur. from 7227; the *daughter* (i.e. *city*) *of Rabbah:*—Bath-rabbim {1x}. See: BDB—123d.

1338. בִּתְרוֹן {1x} **Bithrôwn**, *bith-rone';* from 1334; (with the art.) the *craggy* spot; *Bithron,* a place E. of the Jordan:—Bithron {1x}. See: BDB—144c.

1339. בַּת־שֶׁבַע {11x} **Bath-Shebaʿ**, *bath-sheh'-bah;* from 1323 and 7651 (in the sense of 7650); *daughter of an oath; Bath-Sheba,* the mother of Solomon:—*Bath-sheba* {11x}. See: BDB—124a.

1340. בַּת־שׁוּעַ {2x} **Bath-Shûwaʿ**, *bath-shoo'-ah;* from 1323 and 7771; *daughter of wealth; Bath-shuä,* the same as 1339:—Bath-shua {2x}. See: BDB—124a.

ג

1341. גֵּא {1x} **gêʾ**, *gay';* for 1343; *haughty:*—proud {1x}. See: TWOT—299a; BDB—144b.

1342. גָּאָה {7x} **gâʾâh**, *gaw-aw';* a prim. root; to *mount* up; hence, in gen. to *rise,* (fig.) be *majestic:*—triumph {2x}, gloriously {2x}, risen {1x}, grow up {1x}, increase {1x}.

Ga'ah means "to be proud, be exalted." The word appears in Ex 15:1 in the sense of "to be exalted": "I will sing to the LORD, for He hath triumphed"; the horse and his rider hath He thrown into the sea." See: TWOT—299; BDB—144b, 1085d.

1343. גֵּאֶה {9x} **gêʾeh**, *gay-eh';* from 1342; *lofty;* fig. *arrogant:*—proud {9x}.

Ge'eh also means "proud" in its 9 occurrences, once in Is 2:12: "For the day of the LORD of hosts shall be upon every one that is proud and lofty. . . ." See: TWOT—299b; BDB—144b.

1344. גֵּאָה {1x} **gêʾâh**, *gay-aw';* fem. from 1342; *arrogance:*—pride {1x}. *Ge'ah* occurs once to mean "pride" (Prov 8:13). See: TWOT—299c; BDB—144d, 1085d.

1345. גְּאוּאֵל {1x} **Geʾûwʾêl**, *gheh-oo-ale';* from 1342 and 410; *majesty of God; Geel,* an Isr.:—Geuel {1x}. See: BDB—145b.

1346. גַּאֲוָה {19x} **gaʾăvâh**, *gah-av-aw';* from 1342; *arrogance* or *majesty;* by impl. (concr.) *ornament:*—pride {9x}, excellency {3x}, haughtiness {2x}, arrogancy {1x}, highness {1x}, proud {1x}, proudly {1x}, swelling {1x}.

The noun *ga'avah* which is found 19 times, also means "pride": "And all the people shall know, even Ephraim and the inhabitant of Samaria, that say in the pride and stoutness of heart . . ." (Is 9:9). See: TWOT—299d; BDB—144d.

1347. גָּאוֹן {49x} **gâʾôwn**, *gaw-ohn';* from 1342; the same as 1346:—pride {20x}, excellency {10x}, majesty {7x}, pomp {5x}, swelling {3x}, arrogancy {2x}, excellent {1x}, proud {1x}.

Ga'own means "pride." **(1)** This noun is a poetic word, which is found only in poetic books, the prophets (12 times in Isaiah), Moses' song (Ex 15:7), and Lev (26:19). **(2)** In a positive sense *ga'won,* like the verb, signifies "excellence" or "majesty." **(2a)** God's "majesty" was expressed in Israel's deliverance through the Red Sea (Ex 15:7). **(2b)** Israel as the redeemed people, then, is considered to be an expression of God's "majesty": "He shall choose our inheritance for us, the excellency of Jacob whom he loved" (Ps 47:4). **(3)** The meaning of *ga'won* is here close to that of kabod (3519), "glory." **(4)** Related to "majesty" is the word *ga'won* attributed to nature as something mighty, luxuriant, rich, and thick. The poets use the word to refer to the proud waves (Job 38:11) or the thick shrubbery by the Jordan; cf. "If thou hast run with the footmen, and they have wearied thee, then how canst thou contend with horses? And if in the land of peace, wherein thou trustedst, they wearied thee, then how wilt thou do in the swelling [literally, "majesty"] of Jordan?" (Jer 12:5; cf. 49:19; 50:44).

(5) The majority of the uses of *ga'won* are negative in that they connote human "pride" as an antonym for humility (Prov 16:18). **(5a)** Proverbs puts *ga'won* together with arrogance, evil behavior, and perverse speech. **(5b)** In her independence from the LORD, Israel as a majestic nation, having been set apart by a majestic God, had turned aside and claimed its excellence as a prerogative earned by herself. **(5c)** The new attitude of insolence was not tolerated by God: "The Lord God hath sworn by himself, saith the LORD the God of hosts, I abhor the excellency of Jacob, and hate his palaces: therefore will I deliver up the city with all that is therein" (Amos 6:8). See: TWOT—299e; BDB—144d.

1348. גֵּאוּת {8x} **gêʾûwth**, *gay-ooth';* from 1342; the same as 1346:—pride {2x}, majesty {2x}, proudly {1x}, raging {1x}, lifting up {1x}, excellent things {1x}.

Ge'uwth appears 8 times and refers to "majesty": "Let favor be showed to the wicked, yet will he not learn righteousness: in the land of uprightness will he deal unjustly, and will not behold the majesty of the LORD" (Is 26:10). See: TWOT—299f; BDB—145a.

1349. גַּאֲיוֹן {1x} **gaʾăyôwn**, *gah-ăh-yone';* from 1342: *haughty:*—proud {1x}. *Ga'ayown,* which means "pride," appears once in biblical Hebrew (Ps 123:4). See: TWOT—299g; BDB—145b.

1350. גָּאַל {104x} **gâʾal**, *gaw-al';* a prim. root, to *redeem* (according to the Oriental law of kinship), i.e. to *be the next of kin* (and as such to *buy back* a relative's property, *marry* his widow, etc.):—redeem {50x}, redeemer {18x}, kinsman {13x}, revenger {7x}, avenger {6x}, ransom {2x}, at all {2x}, deliver {1x}, kinsfolks {1x}, kinsman's part {1x}, purchase {1x}, stain {1x}, wise {1x}.

Ga'al means "to redeem, deliver, avenge, act as a kinsman." **(1)** The first occurrence of *ga'al* is in Gen 48:16: "The angel which redeemed me [Jacob] from all evil . . ." **(2)** Its basic use had to do with the deliverance of persons or property that had been sold for debt, as **(2a)** in Lev 25:25: "If thy brother be waxen poor, and hath sold away some of his possession, and if any of his kin come to redeem it, then shall he redeem that which his brother sold." **(2b)** If he prospers, the man himself may "redeem" it (Lev 25:26). **(2c)** A poor man may sell himself to a fellow Israelite (Lev 25:39) or to an alien living in Israel (Lev 25:47). **(3)** The responsibility "to redeem" belonged to the nearest relative—brother, uncle, uncle's son, or a blood relative from his family (Lev 25:25, 48–49). **(4)** The person who "redeemed" the one in financial difficulties was known as a **(4a)** kinsman in Ruth 2:20. **(4b)** In Deut 19:6 the redeemer is called the "avenger of blood" whose duty it was to execute the murderer of his relative. **(4b1)** The verb occurs in this sense 12 times and is translated "revenger" (Num 35:19, 21, 24, 27) or **(4b2)** "avenger" (Num 35:12).

(5) The Book of Ruth is a beautiful account of the kinsman-redeemer. **(5a)** His responsibility is summed up in Ruth 4:5: "What day thou buyest the field of the hand of Naomi, thou must buy it also of Ruth the Moabitess, the wife of the dead, to raise up the name of the dead upon his inheritance." **(5b)** Thus the kinsman-redeemer was responsible for preserving the integrity, life, property, and family name of his close relative or for executing justice upon his murderer. **(6)** The greater usage of this word group is of God who promised: ". . . I am the LORD . . . I will redeem you with a stretched out arm and with great judgments" (Ex 6:6; cf. Ps 77:15). **(6a)** Israel confessed: "Thou in thy mercy hast led forth the people which thou hast redeemed . . ." (Ex 15:13). **(6b)** "And they remembered that God was their rock, and the high God their redeemer" (Ps 78:35).

(7) The Book of Isaiah evidences the word "Redeemer" used of God 13 times, all in chapters 41–63, and *ga'al* is used 9 times of God, **(7a)** first in 43:1: "Fear not; for I have redeemed thee, I have called thee by thy name; thou art mine." **(7b)** *Ga'al* is used of deliverance from Egypt (51:10; 63:9) and **(7c)** from captivity in Babylon (48:20; 52:3, 9; 62:12). **(7d)** Israel's "Redeemer" is **(7d1)** "the Holy One of Israel" (41:14), **(7d2)** "the creator of Israel, your King" (43:14–15), **(7d3)** "the LORD of hosts" (44:6), and **(7d4)** "the mighty One of Jacob" (49:26). **(7e)** Those who share His salvation are "the redeemed" (35:9). **(8)** The Book of Psalms often places spiritual redemption in parallel with physical redemption. **(8a)** For example: "Draw nigh unto my soul, and redeem it: // deliver me because of mine enemies" (Ps 69:18). **(8b)** "Bless the Lord, O my soul, and forget not all his benefits: . . . who redeemeth thy life from destruction; who crowneth thee with loving-kindness and tender mercies" (Ps 103:2, 4). Syn.: 6299. See: TWOT—300; BDB—145b.

1351. גָּאַל {11x} **gâʾal**, *gaw-al';* a prim. root, [rather ident. with 1350, through the idea of *freeing,* i.e. *repudiating*]; to *soil* or (fig.) *desecrate:*—pollute {7x}, defile {3x}, stain {1x}. See: TWOT—301; BDB—146a.

1352. גֹּאֶל {1x} **gôʾel**, *go'-el;* from 1351; *profanation:*—defile {1x}. See: TWOT—301a; BDB—146a.

1353. גְּאֻלָּה {14x} **geʾullâh**, *gheh-ool-law';* fem. pass. part. of 1350; *redemption* (incl. the right and the object); by impl. *relationship:*—redeem {5x}, redemption {5x}, again {1x}, kindred {1x}, redeem + 4672 {1x}, right {1x}.

Ge'ullah means "(right of) redemption." **(1)** This word is used in regard to deliverance of persons or property that had been sold for debt. **(1a)** The law required that the "right of redemption" of land and of persons be protected (Lev 25:24, 48). **(1b)** The redemption price was determined by the number of years remaining until the release of debts in the year of jubilee (Lev 25:27–28). **(2)** The word *ge'ullah* also occurs in Jer 32:7: "Behold, Hanameel the son of Shallum thine uncle shall come unto thee, saying, Buy thee my field that is in Anathoth: for the right of redemption is thine to buy it." See: TWOT—300b; BDB—145d.

1354. גַּב {13x} **gab**, *gab;* from an unused root mean. to *hollow* or *curve;* the *back* (as *rounded* [comp. 1460 and 1479]; by anal. the *top* or *rim,* a *boss,* a *vault, arch* of eye, *bulwarks,* etc.:—eminent place {3x}, rings {2x}, bodies {2x}, back {1x}, backs {1x}, bosses {1x}, eyebrows {1x}, naves {1x}, higher place {1x}. See: TWOT—303a; BDB—146a, 146b, 1085d.

1355. גַּב {1x} **gab** (Aram.), *gab;* corresp. to 1354:—back {1x}. See: TWOT—2645; BDB—1085d.

1356. גֵּב {3x} **gêb**, *gabe;* from 1461; a *log* (as *cut* out); also *well* or *cistern* (as *dug*):—beam {1x}, ditch {1x}, pit {1x}. See: TWOT—323a,b; BDB—146b, 155d.

1357. גֵּב {1x} **gêb**, *gabe;* prob. from 1461 [comp. 1462]; a *locust* (from its *cutting*):—locust {1x}. See: TWOT—304a; BDB—146a, 146d.

1358. גֹּב {10x} **gôb** (Aram.), *gobe;* from a root corresp. to 1461; a *pit* (for wild animals) (as *cut* out):—den {10x}. See: BDB—1085d.

1359. גֹּב {2x} **Gôb**, *gobe;* or (fully)

גּוֹב **Gôwb**, *gobe;* from 1461; *pit; Gob,* a place in Pal.:—Gob {2x}. See: BDB—146b, 146c, 1085d.

1360. גֶּבֶא {3x} **gebeʾ**, *geh'-beh;* from an unused root mean. prob. to *collect;* a *reservoir;* by anal. a *marsh:*—marish {1x}, pit {2x}. See: TWOT—302a; BDB—146b.

1361. גָּבַהּ {42x} **gâbahh**, *gaw-bah';* a prim. root; to *soar,* i.e. *be lofty;* fig. to *be haughty:*—exalt {9x}, . . . up {9x}, haughty {5x}, higher {4x}, high {3x}, above {1x}, height {1x}, proud {1x}, upward {1x}. See: TWOT—305; BDB—146d.

1362. גָּבָהּ {4x} **gâbâhh**, *gaw-bawh';* from 1361; *lofty* (lit. or fig.):—high {2x}, proud {2x}.

Gabahh, as an adjective, means "to be high, exalted, lofty." **(1)** It may mean "to be high, lofty." **(1a)** In this sense, it is used of trees (Eze 19:11), **(1b)** the heavens (Job 35:5), and **(1c)** a man (1 Sa 10:23). **(2)** It may mean "to be exalted" in dignity and honor (Job 36:7). **(3)** Or it may simply mean "to be lofty," **(3a)** used in the positive sense of "being encouraged" (2 Chr. 17:6) or in **(3b)** the negative sense of "being haughty or proud" (2 Chr 26:16). Syn.: 1343, 2086. See: TWOT—305a; BDB—147a.

1363. גֹּבַהּ {17x} **gôbahh**, *go'-bah;* from 1361; *elation, grandeur, arrogance:*—height {9x}, high {3x}, pride {2x}, excellency {1x}, haughty {1x}, loftiness {1x}.

Gobahh, as a noun, means "height; exaltation; grandeur; haughtiness; pride." **(1)** This noun, which occurs 17 times in biblical Hebrew, refers to the "height" **(1a)** of things (2 Chr 3:4) and **(1b)** of men (1 Sa 17:4). **(2)** It may also refer **(2a)** to "exaltation" or "grandeur" (Job 40:10), and **(2b)** to "haughtiness" or "pride" (2 Chr 32:26). Syn.: 4791, 6967. See: TWOT—305b; BDB—147b.

1364. גָּבֹהַּ {37x} **gâbôahh**, *gaw-bo'-ah;* or (fully) גָּבוֹהַּ **gâbôwahh**, *gaw-bo'-ah;* from 1361; *elevated* (or *elated*), *powerful, arrogant:*—high {24x}, higher {5x}, lofty {2x}, exceeding {1x}, haughty {1x}, height {1x}, highest {1x}, proud {1x}, proudly {1x}.

Gabowahh, as an adjective means "high; exalted." **(1)** This word means "high, lofty, tall in dimension": "And the waters [of the flood] prevailed exceedingly upon the earth; and all the high hills, that were under the whole heaven, were covered" (Gen 7:19—the first occurrence). **(2)** When used of a man, *gaboahh* means "tall": Saul was "higher than any of the people" (1 Sa 9:2; cf. 16:7). **(3)** In Dan 8:2, *gabowahh* describes the length of a ram's horns: ". . . And the two horns were high; but one was higher than the other, and the higher came up last." **(4)** The word means "high or exalted in station": **(4a)** "Thus saith the Lord God; Remove the diadem, and take off the crown: this shall not be the same: exalt him that is low, and abase him that is high" (Eze 21:26). **(4b)** In Eccl 5:8, this connotation of "one of high rank" may be expressed in the translation "higher/highest." **(5)** *Gabowahh* may be used of a psychological state, such as "haughtiness": "Talk no more so exceeding proudly [this double appearance of the word emphasizes it]; let not arrogancy come out of your mouth . . ." (1 Sa 2:3). Syn.: 1116, 4791, 6967. See: TWOT—305a; BDB—147a.

1365. גַּבְהוּת {2x} **gabhûwth**, *gab-hooth';* from 1361; *pride:*—loftiness {1x}, lofty {1x}. See: TWOT—305c; BDB—147b.

1366. גְּבוּל {241x} **g**[e]**bûwl**, *gheb-ool';* or (short.) גְּבֻל **g**[e]**bûl**, *gheb-ool';* from 1379; prop. a *cord* (as *twisted*), i.e. (by impl.) a *boundary;* by extens. the *territory* inclosed:—border {158x}, coast {69x}, bound {5x}, landmark {4x}, space {2x}, limit {1x}, quarters {1x}, non translated variant {1x}.

Gebul (1366)means "boundary; limit; territory; closed area." **(1)** *Gebul* literally means "boundary" or "border." **(1a)** This meaning appears in Num 20:23, where it signifies the border or boundary of the entire land of Edom. **(1b)** Sometimes such an imaginary line was marked by a physical barrier: ". . . Arnon is the border of Moab, between Moab and the Amorites" (Num 21:13). **(1c)** Sometimes *gebul* denoted ethnic boundaries, such as the borders of the tribes of Israel: "And unto the Reubenites and unto the Gadites I gave from Gilead even unto the river Arnon half the valley, and the border even unto the river Jabbok, which is the border of the children of Ammon . . ." (Deut 3:16). **(1d)** In Gen 23:17, *gebul* represents the "border" of an individual's field or piece of ground: "And the field of Ephron, which was in Machpelah, which was before Mamre, the field, and the cave which was therein, and all the trees that were in the field, that were in all the borders round about, were made sure." **(1e)** Fields were delineated by "boundary marks," whose removal was forbidden by law (Deut 19:14; cf. Deut 27:17).

(2) *Gebul* can suggest the farthest extremity of a thing: "Thou hast set a bound that they may not pass over; that they turn not again to cover the earth" (Ps 104:9). **(3)** This word sometimes represents the concrete object marking the border of a thing or area (cf. Eze 40:12). **(3a)** The "border" of Ezekiel's altar is signified by *gebul* (Eze 43:13) and **(3b)** Jerusalem's "surrounding wall" is represented by this word (Is 54:12). **(4)** *Gebul* represents the territory within certain boundaries: "And the border of the Canaanites was from Sidon, as thou comest to Gerar, unto Gaza; as thou goest, unto Sodom, and Gomorrah, and Admah, and Zeboim, even unto Lasha" (Gen 10:19). **(5)** In Ex 34:24, Num 21:22, 1 Chr 21:12, and Ps 105:31–32, *gebul* is paralleled to the "territory" surrounding and belonging to a city. See: TWOT—307a; BDB—147c, 147d.

1367. גְּבוּלָה {10x} **g**[e]**bûwlâh**, *gheb-oo-law';* or (short.) גְּבֻלָה **g**[e]**bûlâh**, *gheb-oo-law';* fem. of 1366; a *boundary, region:*—coast {5x}, bounds {2x}, place {1x}, border {1x}, landmark {1x}.

Gebulah, the feminine form of gebul, occurs 9 times and means "boundary" in such passages as Is 10:13, and "territory" or "area" in other passages, such as Num 34:2. See: TWOT—307b; BDB—148b.

1368. גִּבּוֹר {158x} **gibbôwr**, *ghib-bore';* or (short.) גִּבֹּר **gibbôr**, *ghib-bore';* intens. from the same as 1397; *powerful;* by impl. *warrior, tyrant:*—mighty {63x}, mighty man {68x}, strong {4x}, valiant {3x}, . . . ones {4x}, mighties {2x}, man {2x}, valiant men {2x}, strong man {1x}, upright man {1x}, champion {1x}, chief {1x}, excel {1x}, giant {1x}, men's {1x}, mightiest {1x}, strongest {1x}.

Gibbor means "strong/mighty man" **(1)** The first occurrence of *gibbor* is in Gen 6:4: "There were giants in the earth in those days; and also after that, when the sons of God came in unto the daughters of men, and they bare children to them, the same became mighty men which were of old, men of renown." **(2)** In the context of battle, the word is better understood to refer to the category of warriors. **(2a)** The *gibbor* is the proven warrior; especially is this true when *gibbor* is used in combination with chayil (2428 - "strength"). **(2b)** The KJV gives a literal translation, "mighty men [*gibbor*] of valor [chayil]." **(3)** David, who had proven himself as a warrior, **(3a)** attracted "mighty men" to his band while he was being pursued by Saul (2 Sa 23). **(3b)** When David was enthroned as king, these men became a part of the elite military corps.

(4) The phrase *gibbor* chayil may also refer to a man of a high social class, the landed man who had military responsibilities. Saul came from such a family (1 Sa 9:1); so also Jeroboam (1 Kin 11:28). **(5)** The king symbolized the strength of his kingdom. **(5a)** He had to lead his troops in battle, and as commander he was expected to be a "mighty man." **(5b)** Early in David's life, he was recognized as a "mighty man" (1 Sa 18:7). **(5c)** The king is described as "mighty": "Gird thy sword upon thy thigh, O most Mighty, with thy glory and thy majesty" (Ps 45:3). **(6)** The messianic expectation included the hope that the Messiah would be "mighty": "For unto us a child is born, unto us a son is given: and the government shall be upon his shoulder; and his name shall be called Wonderful, Counselor, The mighty God, The everlasting Father, The Prince of Peace" (Is 9:6).

(7) Israel's God was a mighty God (Is 10:21). **(7a)** He had the power to deliver: "The Lord thy God in the midst of thee is mighty; he will save, he will rejoice over thee with joy; he will rest in his love, he will joy over thee with singing" (Zeph 3:17). **(7b)** Jeremiah's moving confession (32:17ff.) bears out the might of God in creation (v. 17) and in redemption (vv. 18ff.). **(7c)** The answer to the emphatic question, "Who is this King of glory?" in Ps 24 is: "The Lord strong and mighty, the Lord mighty in battle" (v. 8). **(8)** *Gibbor* may be translated by the adjective "strong" in the following contexts: **(8a)** a "strong" man (1 Sa 14:52), **(8b)** a "strong" lion (Prov 30:30), **(8c)** a mighty hunter (Gen 10:9), and **(8d)** the mighty ones (Gen 6:1–4). See: TWOT—310b; BDB—150a.

1369. גְּבוּרָה {61x} **g**[e]**bûwrâh**, *gheb-oo-raw';* fem. pass. part. from the same as 1368; *force* (lit. or fig.); by impl. *valor, victory:*—might {27x}, strength {17x}, power {9x}, mighty acts {4x}, mighty {2x}, force {1x}, mastery {1x}.

The primary meaning of *gebuwrah* is power or strength. **(1)** Certain animals are known for their strength, such as **(1a)** horses (Ps 147:10) and **(1b)** crocodiles (Job 41:4). **(2)** Man demonstrates might **(2a)** in heroic acts (Judg 8:21) and **(2b)** in war (Is 3:25). **(3)** David's powerful regime is a kingship of *gebuwrah* (1 Chr 29:30). **(4)** Both physical strength and wisdom were necessary for leadership, these two qualities are joined together **(4a)** in Wisdom (Prov 8:14), and **(4b)** in the Spirit-filled Micah (Mic 3:8). **(5)** The Messiah's special role will be a demonstration of might and counsel (Is 11:2). **(6)** God's might is lauded **(6a)** in psalms of praise (Ps 65:6), or **(6b)** in the context of prayer (Ps 54:1); and **(6c)** is a manifestation of His wisdom (Job 12:13). In the plural *gebuwrah* denotes God's mighty deeds of the past (Deut 3:24). See: TWOT—310c; BDB—150b.

1370. גְּבוּרָה {2x} **g**[e]**bûwrâh** (Aram.), *gheb-oo-raw';* corresp. to 1369; *power:*—might {2x}. See: TWOT—2647b; BDB—1086a.

1371. גִּבֵּחַ {1x} **gibbêach**, *ghib-bay'-akh;* from an unused root mean. to *be high* (in the forehead); *bald* in the forehead:—forehead bald {1x}. See: TWOT—306a; BDB—147c.

1372. גַּבַּחַת {4x} **gabbachath**, *gab-bakh'-ath;* from the same as 1371; *baldness* in the forehead; by anal. a *bare spot* on the right side of cloth:—bald forehead {3x}, × without {1x}. See: TWOT—306b; BDB—147c.

1373. גַּבַּי {1x} **Gabbay**, *gab-bah'-ee;* from the same as 1354; *collective; Gabbai,* an Isr.: Gabbai {1x}. See: BDB—146c, 147c.

1374. גֵּבִים {1x} **Gêbîym**, *gay-beem'*; plur. of 1356; *cisterns; Gebim*, a place in Pal.:—Gebim {1x}. See: BDB—147c, 155d.

1375. גְּבִיעַ {14x} **gᵉbîyaʿ**, *gheb-ee'-ah*; from an unused root (mean. to *be convex*); a *goblet;* by anal. the *calyx* of a flower:—bowl {8x}, cup {5x}, pot {1x}. See: TWOT—309b; BDB—149b.

1376. גְּבִיר {2x} **gᵉbîyr**, *gheb-eer'*; from 1396; a *master:*—lord {2x}. See: TWOT—310d; BDB—150c.

1377. גְּבִירָה {6x} **gᵉbîyrâh**, *gheb-ee-raw'*; fem. of 1376; a *mistress:*—queen {1x}. See: TWOT—310d; BDB—150c.

1378. גָּבִישׁ {1x} **gâbîysh**, *gaw-beesh'*; from an unused root (prob. mean. to *freeze*); *crystal* (from its resemblance to *ice*):—pearl {1x}. See: TWOT—311a; BDB—150d.

1379. גָּבַל **gâbal**, *gaw-bal'*; a prim. root; prop. to *twist* as a rope; only (as a denom. from 1366) to *bound* (as by a line):—border {2x}; set bounds {2x}, set {1x}. See: TWOT—307; BDB—148b.

1380. גְּבַל {1x} **Gᵉbal**, *gheb-al'*; from 1379 (in the sense of a *chain* of hills); a *mountain; Gebal*, a place in Phœnicia:—*Gebal* {1x}. See: BDB—148b.

1381. גְּבָל {1x} **Gᵉbâl**, *gheb-awl'*; the same as 1380; *Gebal*, a region in Idumæa:—*Gebal* {1x}. See: BDB—148c.

1382. גִּבְלִי {1x} **Giblîy**, *ghib-lee'*; patrial from 1380; a *Gebalite*, or inhab. of Gebal:—Giblites, stone-squarer {1x}. See: BDB—148c.

1383. גַּבְלֻת {2x} **gablûth**, *gab-looth'*; from 1379; a twisted *chain* or *lace:*—the ends {2x}. See: TWOT—307c; BDB—148b.

1384. גִּבֵּן {1x} **gibbên**, *gib-bane'*; from an unused root mean. to *be arched* or *contracted; hunch-backed:*—crookbackt {1x}. See: TWOT—308a; BDB—148c.

1385. גְּבִינָה {1x} **gᵉbînah**, *gheb-ee-naw'*; fem. from the same as 1384; *curdled* milk:—cheese {1x}. See: TWOT—308b; BDB—148c.

1386. גַּבְנֹן {2x} **gabnôn**, *gab-nohn'*; from the same as 1384; a *hump* or *peak* of hills:—high {2x}. See: TWOT—308c; BDB—148d.

1387. גֶּבַע {19x} **Gebaʿ**, *gheh'-bah*; from the same as 1375, a *hillock; Geba*, a place in Pal.:—*Geba* {13x}, Gibeah {4x}, Gaba {2x}. See: BDB—148d.

1388. גִּבְעָא {1x} **Gibʿâʾ**, *ghib-aw'*, by perm. for 1389; a *hill; Giba*, a place in Pal.:—Gibeah {1x}. See: BDB—148d.

1389. גִּבְעָה {69x} **gibʿâh**, *ghib-aw'*; fem. from the same as 1387; a *hillock:*—hill {69x}. See: TWOT—309a; BDB—148d.

1390. גִּבְעָה {44x} **Gibʿâh**, *ghib-aw'*; the same as 1389; *Gibah;* the name of three places in Pal.:—Gibeah {1x}. See: BDB—149b.

1391. גִּבְעוֹן {37x} **Gibʿôwn**, *ghib-ohn'*; from the same as 1387; *hilly; Gibon*, a place in Pal.:—Gibeon {37x}. See: BDB—149c.

1392. גִּבְעֹל {1x} **gibʿôl**, *ghib-ole'*; prol. from 1375; the *calyx* of a flower:—bolled {1x}. See: TWOT—309d; BDB—149c.

1393. גִּבְעֹנִי {8x} **Gibʿônîy**, *ghib-o-nee'*; patrial from 1391; a *Gibonite*, or inhab. of Gibon:—Gibeonite {8x}. See: BDB—149c.

1394. גִּבְעַת {1x} **Gibʿath**, *ghib-ath'*; from the same as 1375; *hilliness; Gibath:*—Gibeath {1x}. See: BDB—149b.

1395. גִּבְעָתִי {1x} **Gibʿâthîy**, *ghib-aw-thee'*; patrial from 1390; a *Gibathite*, or inhab. of Gibath:—Gibeathite {1x}. See: BDB—149b.

1396. גָּבַר **gâbar**, *gaw-bar'*; a prim. root; to *be strong;* by impl. to *prevail, act insolently:*—prevail {14x}, strengthen {3x}, great {2x}, confirm {1x}, exceeded {1x}, mighty {1x}, put {1x}, stronger {1x}, valiant {1x}.

Gabar means "to be strong." The root meaning "to be strong" appears in all Semitic languages as a verb or a noun, but the verb occurs only 25 times in the Old Testament. Job 21:7 contains an occurrence of *gabar:* "Wherefore do the wicked live, become old, yea, are mighty in power?" Syn.: 2388, 8630. See: TWOT—310; BDB—149c, 1085d.

1397. גֶּבֶר {68x} **geber**, *gheh'-ber*; from 1396; prop. a *valiant* man or *warrior;* gen. a *person* simply:—man {64x}, mighty {2x}, man child {1x}, every one {1x}. *Geber* means "man," **(1)** probably referring to a man strong enough to fulfill an assigned responsibility: 1 Chr 23:3: "Now the Levites were numbered from the age of thirty years and upward: and their number by their polls, man by man, was thirty and eight thousand." **(2)** This word occurs 68 times in the Hebrew Old Testament, and its frequency of usage is higher (32 times, nearly half of all the occurrences) in the poetical books. **(3)** The word occurs first in Ex 10:11: "Not so: go now ye that are men, and serve the Lord; for that ye did desire." **(4)** The root meaning "to be strong" is no longer obvious in the usage of *geber*, since it is a synonym of ish: "Thus saith the Lord, Write ye this man [ish] childless, a man [*geber*] that shall not prosper in his days: for no man of his seed shall prosper, sitting upon the throne of David . . ." (Jer 22:30).

(5) A *geber* denotes a "male," as an antonym of a "woman"; cf. "The woman [ishshah] shall not wear that which pertaineth unto a man, neither shall a man [*geber*] put on a woman's [ishshah] garment: for all that do so are abomination unto the Lord thy God" (Deut 22:5). **(6)** In standardized expressions of curse and blessing *geber* also functions as a synonym for ish, "man." The expression may begin with "Cursed be the man" (*geber;* Jer 17:5) or "Blessed is the man" (*geber;* Ps 34:8), but these same expressions also occur with ish (Ps 1:1; Deut 27:15). Syn: Other synonyms are zakar (2145 - "male" - Jer 30:6); enos (582 - "man" - Job 4:17); and adam (120 - "man" - Job 14:10). When compared to the weakness found in enosh, one can readily see that man is a marvelous combination of strength (*geber*) and weakness (enosh). Syn.: 120, 376, 582, 2145. See: TWOT—310a; BDB—149d.

1398. גֶּבֶר {1x} **Geber**, *gheh'-ber*; the same as 1397; *Geber*, the name of two Isr.:—*Geber* {1x}. See: BDB—150a.

1399. גְּבַר {1x} **gᵉbar**, *gheb-ar'*; from 1396; the same as 1397; a person:—man {1x}. See: TWOT—310a; BDB—149d, 989d, 1086a.

1400. גְּבַר {21x} **gᵉbar** (Aram.), *gheb-ar'*; corresp. to 1399:—certain {2x}, man {19x}. See: TWOT—2647a; BDB—1086a.

1401. גִּבָּר {1x} **gibbâr** (Aram.), *ghib-bawr'*; intens. of 1400; *valiant*, or *warrior:*—mighty {1x}. See: TWOT—2647b; BDB—1086a.

1402. גִּבָּר {1x} **Gibbâr**, *ghib-bawr'*; intens. of 1399; *Gibbar*, an Isr.:—*Gibbar* {1x}. See: BDB—150a.

גְּבֻרָה **gᵉbûrâh**. See 1369.

1403. גַּבְרִיאֵל **Gabrîyʾêl**, *gab-ree-ale'*; from 1397 and 410; *man of God; Gabriel*, an archangel:—Gabriel {1x}. See: BDB—150c.

1404. גְּבֶרֶת {9x} **gᵉbereth**, *gheb-eh'-reth*; fem. of 1376; *mistress:*—lady {2x}, mistress {9x}. See: TWOT—310e; BDB—150c.

1405. גִּבְּתוֹן {6x} **Gibbᵉthôwn**, *ghib-beth-one'*; intens. from 1389; a *hilly* spot; *Gibbethon*, a place in Pal.:—Gibbethon {6x}. See: BDB—146d, 150d.

1406. גָּג {30x} **gâg**, *gawg;* prob. by redupl. from 1342; a *roof;* by anal. the *top* of an altar:—roof {12x}, housetop {8x}, top {6x}, . . . house {4x}. See: TWOT—312; BDB—150d.

1407. גַּד {2x} **gad**, *gad;* from 1413 (in the sense of *cutting*); *coriander* seed (from its furrows):—coriander {2x}. See: TWOT—313c; BDB—151a, 151b.

1408. גַּד {2x} **Gad**, *gad;* a var. of 1409; *Fortune*, a Bab. deity:—that troop {2x}. See: TWOT—313e; BDB—151c.

1409. גָּד {2x} **gâd**, *gawd;* from 1464 (in the sense of *distributing*); *fortune:*—troop {2x}. See: TWOT—313d; BDB—151c.

1410. גָּד {70x} **Gâd**, *gawd;* from 1464; *Gad*, a son of Jacob, incl. his tribe and its territory; also a prophet:—*Gad* {1x}. See: BDB—151a, 151c.

1411. גְּדָבָר {2x} **gᵉdâbâr** (Aram.), *ghed-aw-bawr'*; corresp. to 1489; a *treasurer:*—treasurer {2x}. See: TWOT—2653; BDB—1086a, 1086b, 1089d.

1412. גֻּדְגֹּדָה {2x} **Gudgôdâh**, *gud-go'-daw;* by redupl. from 1413 (in the sense of *cutting*) *cleft; Gudgodah*, a place in the Desert:—Gudgodah {2x}. See: TWOT—2653; BDB—151a, 151d, 211c.

1413. גָּדַד {8x} **gâdad**, *gaw-dad'*; a prim. root [comp. 1464]; to *crowd;* also to *gash* (as if by *pressing* into):—cut {5x}, gather together {1x}, assemble by troop {1x}, gather {1x}.

The verb *gadad* means **(1)** to gather together against (Ps 94:21), **(2)** to make incisions into oneself as a religious act (Deut 14:1), **(3)** to roam about (Jer 30:23), or **(4)** to muster troops (Mic 5:1). See: TWOT—313; BDB—151a, 1086a.

1414. גְּדַד {2x} **gᵉdad** (Aram.), *ghed-ad'*; corresp. to 1413; to *cut down:*—hew down {2x}. See: TWOT—2649; BDB—1086a.

גְּדוּדָה **gᵉdûdâh**. See 1417.

1415. גָּדָה {4x} **gâdâh**, *gaw-daw'*; from an unused root (mean. to *cut* off); a *border* of a river (as *cut* into by the stream):—bank {1x}. See: TWOT—314a; BDB—152a.

גַּדָּה **Gaddâh**. See 2693.

1416. גְּדוּד {34x} **gᵉdûwd**, *ghed-ood'*; from 1413; a *crowd* (espec. of soldiers):—band {13x}, troop {11x}, army {5x}, company {4x}, men {1x}.

Geduwd (1416) means "band (of raiders); marauding band; raiding party; army; units (of an army); troops; bandits; raid." **(1)** Basically, this word represents individuals or a band of individuals who raid and plunder an enemy. **(1a)** The units that perform such raids may be a group of outlaws ("bandits"), **(1b)** a special unit of any army, or **(1c)** an entire army. **(2)** Ancient peoples frequently suffered raids from their neighbors. **(2a1)** When the Amalekites "raided" Ziklag, looting and burning it while taking captive the wives and families of the men who followed David, he inquired of God, "Shall I pursue after this troop? shall I overtake them?" (1 Sa 30:8). **(2a2)** In this case, the "raiding band" consisted of the entire army of Amalek. **(2b)** This meaning of *geduwd* occurs for the first time in Gen 49:19: ". . . A troop shall overcome him." Here the word is a collective noun referring to all the "band of raiders" to come. **(3)** When Job described the glory of days gone by, he said he "dwelt as a king in the army" (Job 29:25).

(4) When David and his followers were called a *geduwd,* they were being branded outlaws—men who lived by fighting and raiding (1 Kin 11:24). **(5)** In some passages, *geduwd* signifies a smaller detachment of troops or a military unit or division: **(5a)** "And Saul's son had two men that were captains of bands" (2 Sa 4:2). **(5b)** God sent against Jehoiakim "units" from the Babylonian army—"bands of the Chaldees, and bands of the Syrians, and bands of the Moabites, and bands of the children of Ammon . . ." (2 Kin 24:2). **(6)** The word can also represent individuals who are members of such raiding or military bands. **(6a)** The individuals in the household of Izrahiah, the descendant of Issachar, formed a military unit, "and with them by their generations, after the house of their fathers, were bands of soldiers for war, six and thirty thousand men . . ." (1 Chr 7:4). **(6b)** Bildad asks the rhetorical question concerning God, "Is there any number [numbering] of his armies?" (Job 25:3). See: TWOT—313a; BDB—151b.

1417. גְּדוּד {2x} **g^edûwd**, *ghed-ood';* or (fem.)

גְּדֻדָה **g^edûdâh**, *ghed-oo-daw';* from 1413; a *furrow* (as *cut*):—furrow {1x}, cutting {1x}. See: TWOT—313b; BDB—151b.

1418. גְּדוּדָה {1x} **g^edûwdâh**, *ghed-oo-daw';* fem. pass. part. of 1413; an *incision:*—cutting {1x}. See: TWOT—313b; BDB—151b.

1419. גָּדוֹל {529x} **gâdôwl**, *gaw-dole';* or (short.)

גָּדֹל **gâdôl**, *gaw-dole';* from 1431; *great* (in any sense); hence, *older;* also *insolent:*—great {397x}, high {22x}, greater {9x}, loud {9x}, greatest {9x}, elder {8x}, great man {8x}, mighty {7x}, eldest {6x}, misc. {44x}.

Gadol means "great." **(1)** The adjective *gadol* is the most frequently appearing word related to the verb gadal (1431). **(2)** Gadol is used **(2a)** of extended dimension (Gen 1:21), **(2b)** of number (Gen 12:2), **(2c)** of power (Deut 4:37), **(2d)** of punishment (Gen 4:13), and **(2e)** of value or importance (Gen 39:9). **(3)** The verb gadal (1431) and the related adjective *gadol* may each be used to make distinctive statements. **(3a)** In Hebrew one may say "he is great" both by using the verb alone and by using the pronoun and the adjective *gadol.* **(3a1)** The first sets forth a standing and existing condition—so Mal 1:5 could be rendered: "The Lord is magnified beyond the borders of Israel." **(3a2)** The second construction announces newly experienced information to the recipient, as in Is 12:6: ". . . Great is the Holy One of Israel in the midst of thee." This information was known previously, but recent divine acts have made it to be experienced anew. The emphasis is on the freshness of the experience. See: TWOT—315d; BDB—152d.

1420. גְּדוּלָה {12x} **g^edûwlâh**, *ghed-oo-law';* or (short.)

גְּדֻלָּה **g^edullâh**, *ghed-ool-law';* or (less accurately)

גְּדוּלָּה **g^edûwllâh**, *ghed-ool-law';* fem. of 1419; *greatness;* (concr.) *mighty acts:*—greatness {7x}, great things {3x}, majesty {1x}, dignity {1x}.

Geduwllah means "greatness; great dignity; great things." **(1)** This noun means "greatness" in Ps 71:21: "Thou shalt increase my greatness, and comfort me on every side." **(2)** *Geduwllah* may refer also to "great dignity" (Est 6:3) and **(3)** to "great things" (2 Sa 7:21). See: TWOT—315e; BDB—153c.

1421. גִּדּוּף {3x} **giddûwph**, *ghid-doof';* or (short.)

גִּדֻּף **giddûph**, *ghid-doof';* and (fem.)

גִּדּוּפָה **giddûwphâh**, *ghid-doo-faw';* or

גִּדֻּפָה **giddûphâh**, *ghid-doo-faw';* from 1422; *vilification:*—revilings {2x}, reproaches {1x}. See: TWOT—317b; BDB—154d.

1422. גְּדוּפָה {1x} **g^edûwphâh**, *ghed-oo-faw';* fem. pass. part. of 1442; a *revilement:*—taunt {1x}. See: TWOT—317g; BDB—154d.

גְּדוֹר **G^edôwr**. See 1446.

1423. גְּדִי {16x} **g^edîy**, *ghed-ee';* from the same as 1415; a young *goat* (from *browsing*):—kid {16x}. See: TWOT—314b; BDB—152a.

1424. גָּדִי {2x} **Gâdîy**, *gaw-dee';* from 1409; *fortunate; Gadi,* an Isr.:—Gadi {1x}. See: BDB—151d.

1425. גָּדִי {16x} **Gâdîy**, *gaw-dee';* patron. from 1410; a *Gadite* (collect.) or desc. of Gad:—Gadites {16x}. See: BDB—151d.

1426. גַּדִּי {1x} **Gaddîy**, *gad-dee';* intens. for 1424; *Gaddi,* an Isr.:—Gaddi {1x}. See: BDB—151d.

1427. גַּדִּיאֵל {1x} **Gaddîy'êl**, *gad-dee-ale';* from 1409 and 410; *fortune of God; Gaddiel,* an Isr.:—Gaddiel {1x}. See: BDB—151d.

1428. גִּדְיָה {1x} **gidyâh**, *ghid-yaw';* or

גַּדְיָה **gadyâh**, *gad-yaw';* the same as 1415; a river *brink:*—bank {1x}. See: TWOT—314a; BDB—152a.

1429. גְּדִיָּה {1x} **g^edîyâh**, *ghed-ee-yaw';* fem. of 1423; a young female *goat:*—kid {1x}. See: TWOT—314c; BDB—152a.

1430. גָּדִישׁ {3x} **gâdîysh**, *gaw-deesh';* from an unused root (mean. to *heap* up); a *stack* of sheaves; by anal. a *tomb:*—shock {2x}, stack {1x}, tomb {1x}. See: TWOT—319a, 320a; BDB—155c.

1431. גָּדַל **gâdal**, *gaw-dal';* a prim. root; prop. to *twist* [comp. 1434], i.e. to *be* (caus. *make*) *large* (in various senses, as in body, mind, estate or honor, also in pride):—magnify {32x}, great {26x}, grow {14x}, nourish up {7x}, grow up {6x}, greater {5x}, misc. {25x}.

Gadal means "to become strong, grow up, be great or wealthy, evidence oneself as great (magnified), be powerful, significant, or valuable." **(1)** This verb can signify the increasing of size and age as with the maturing process of human life: "And the child grew, and was weaned . . ." (Gen 21:8). **(2)** The word also depicts the "growing up" **(2a)** of animals (2 Sa 12:3) and **(2b)** plants (Is 44:14) and **(2c)** the maturing of animal horns (Dan 8:9) and **(2d)** other growing things. **(3)** In the intensive stem *gadal* indicates that this rearing has occurred: ". . . I have nourished and brought up children . . ." (Is 1:2). **(4)** This stem may also imply permission: ". . . [He] shall let the locks of the hair of his head grow" (Num 6:5). **(5)** *Gadal* can represent the status of "being great or wealthy." Abraham's servant reported: "And the Lord hath blessed my master greatly; and he is become great . . ." (Gen 24:35)—here the word represents the conclusion of a process.

(6) In the intensive stem the verb sets forth a fact, as when God said: "And I will make of thee a great nation, and I will bless thee, and make thy name great . . ." (Gen 12:2—the first biblical occurrence of the verb). **(7)** This word is sometimes used with the meaning "to be great, to evidence oneself as great": **(7a)** "And now, I beseech thee, let the power of my Lord be great, according as thou hast spoken . . ." (Num 14:17). **(7b)** Moses is praying that God will demonstrate that He is truly great, even as He has said, and do so not by destroying His people. **(7c)** Such an act (destroying Israel) would make onlookers conclude that God was not able to accomplish what He had promised. **(7d)** If, however, He would bring Israel into Palestine, this would exhibit His greatness before the nations. **(7e)** This same sense appears in 2 Sa 7:22, except with the added overtone of "magnified," "praised as great": "Wherefore thou art great, O Lord God: for there is none like thee, neither is there any God besides thee, according to all that we have heard with our ears."

(8) Another emphasis of *gadal* is "to be great, powerful, important, or valuable." This nuance arises when the word is applied to kings. Pharaoh said to Joseph: "Thou shalt be over my house, and according unto thy word shall all my people be ruled: only in the throne will I be greater [more powerful and honored] than thou" (Gen 41:40). **(9)** The Messiah "shall stand and feed in the strength of the Lord, in the majesty of the name of the Lord his God; and they shall abide: for now shall he be great unto the ends of the earth" (Mic 5:4); He will be powerful to the ends of the earth. **(10)** The nuance "to be valuable" appears in 1 Sa 26:24 when David said to Saul: "And, behold, as thy life was much set by this day in mine eyes, so let my life be much set by in the eyes of the Lord, and let him deliver me out of all tribulation." **(10a)** In this statement the second use of the verb is in the intensive stem. **(10b)** Perhaps the force of this could be expressed if one were to translate: "So may my life be very highly valued. . . ."

(11) In the reflexive stem *gadal* may signify "to magnify oneself." **(11a)** God says: "Thus will I magnify myself, and sanctify myself; and I will be known in the eyes of many nations . . ." (Eze 38:23). **(11b)** The context shows that He will bring judgment. **(11c)** In this way He "magnifies Himself," or shows Himself to be great and powerful. **(12)** On the other hand, a false statement of greatness and power is an empty boast. So *gadal* can mean "to boast": "Shall the axe boast itself against him that heweth therewith? or shall the saw magnify itself against him that shaketh it?" (Is 10:15). **(13)** In the causative stem the verb may signify "to assume great airs": "If indeed ye will magnify yourselves against me, and plead against me my reproach . . ." (Job 19:5). **(14)** A nuance appears in Job 7:17, where *gadal* is in the intensive stem, suggesting an estimation of greatness: "What is man, that thou shouldest magnify him? and that thou shouldest set thine heart upon him?" (Ps 8:4). When man is so insignificant, why then does God esteem him so important? See: TWOT—315; BDB—152a.

1432. גָּדֵל {4x} **gâdêl**, *gaw-dale'*; from 1431; *large* (lit. or fig.):—great {2x}, grew {2x}.

Another adjective *gadel* means "becoming great; growing up." This verbal adjective occurs 4 times, once in Gen 26:13: "And the man waxed great (1431), and went forward, and grew (1432) until he became very great (1431)." See: TWOT—315a; BDB—152c.

1433. גֹּדֶל {13x} **gôdel**, *go'-del*; from 1431; *magnitude* (lit. or fig.):—greatness {11x}, stout {1x}, stoutness {1x}.

Godel means "greatness" in terms **(1)** of size (Eze 31:7), **(2)** of divine power (Ps 79:11), **(3)** of divine dignity (Deut 32:3), **(4)** of divine majesty (Deut 3:24), **(5)** of divine mercy (Num 14:19), or **(6)** of the false greatness of one's heart (insolence; Is 9:9). See: TWOT—315b; BDB—152d.

1434. גְּדִל **g**e**dil**, *ghed-eel'*; from 1431 (in the sense of *twisting*); *thread*, i.e. a *tassel* or *festoon*:—fringe {1x}, wreath {1x}. See: TWOT—315c; BDB—152d.

1435. גִּדֵּל {4x} **Giddêl**, *ghid-dale'*; from 1431; *stout; Giddel*, the name of one of the Nethinim, also of one of "Solomon's servants":—*Giddel* {1x}. See: BDB—153c.

גָּדֹל **gâdôl**. See 1419.

גְּדֻלָּה **g**e**dullâh**. See 1420.

1436. גְּדַלְיָה {32x} **G**e**dalyâh**, *ghed-al-yaw'*; or (prol.)

גְּדַלְיָהוּ **G**e**dalyâhûw**, *ghed-al-yaw'-hoo*; from 1431 and 3050; *Jah has become great; Gedaljah*, the name of five Isr.:—Gedaliah {32x}. See: BDB—153c, 153d.

1437. גִּדַּלְתִּי {2x} **Giddaltîy**, *ghid-dal'-tee*; from 1431; *I have made great; Giddalti*, an Isr.:—Giddalti {2x}. See: BDB—153d.

1438. גָּדַע **gâdaʻ**, *gaw-dah'*; a prim. root; to *fell* a tree; gen. to *destroy* anything:—cut . . . down {11x}, cut off {7x}, cut asunder {3x}, cut in sunder {2x}. See: TWOT—316; BDB—154b.

1439. גִּדְעוֹן {39x} **Gidʻôwn**, *ghid-ohn'*; from 1438; *feller* (i.e. *warrior*); *Gidon*, an Isr.:—Gideon {39x}. See: TWOT—316a; BDB—154c.

1440. גִּדְעֹם {1x} **Gidʻôm**, *ghid-ohm'*; from 1438; a *cutting* (i.e. *desolation*); *Gidom*, a place in Pal.:—*Gidom* {1x}. See: BDB—154c.

1441. גִּדְעֹנִי {5x} **Gidʻônîy**, *ghid-o-nee'*; from 1438; *warlike* [comp. 1439]; *Gidoni*, an Isr.:—Gideoni {5x}. See: BDB—154c.

1442. גָּדַף {7x} **gâdaph**, *gaw-daf'*; a prim. root; to *hack* (with words), i.e. *revile*:—blaspheme {6x}, reproach {1x}. See: TWOT—317; BDB—154c.

גִּדּוּף **giddûph**, and

גִּדּוּפָה **giddûphâh**. See 1421.

1443. גָּדַר {10x} **gâdar**, *gaw-dar'*; a prim. root; to *wall* in or around:—make {3x}, mason {2x}, repairer {1x}, close up {1x}, fenced up {1x}, hedged {1x}, inclosed {1x}. See: TWOT—318; BDB—154d.

1444. גֶּדֶר {4x} **geder**, *gheh'-der*; from 1443; a *circumvallation*:—wall {1x}. See: TWOT—318a; BDB—154d.

1445. גֶּדֶר {1x} **Geder**, *gheh'-der*; the same as 1444; *Geder*, a place in Pal.:—*Geder* {1x}. See: BDB—155a.

1446. גְּדֹר {7x} **G**e**dôr**, *ghed-ore'*; or (fully)

גְּדוֹר **G**e**dôwr**, *ghed-ore'*; from 1443; *inclosure; Gedor*, a place in Pal.; also the name of three Isr.:—Gedor {7x}. See: BDB—155b.

1447. גָּדֵר {12x} **gâdêr**, *gaw-dare'*; from 1443; a *circumvallation*; by impl. an *inclosure*:—wall {7x}, hedge {4x}, fence {1x}. See: TWOT—318a; BDB—154d.

1448. גְּדֵרָה {10x} **g**e**dêrâh**, *ghed-ay-raw'*; fem. of 1447, *inclosure* (espec. for flocks):—hedge {4x}, fold {3x}, wall {1x}, sheepfold {1x}, sheepcote {1x}. See: TWOT—318b; BDB—155a.

1449. גְּדֵרָה **G**e**dêrâh**, *ghed-ay-raw'*; the same as 1448; (with the art.). *Gederah*, a place in Pal.:—*Gederah* {1x}. See: TWOT—318b; BDB—155b.

1450. גְּדֵרוֹת {2x} **G**e**dêrôwth**, *ghed-ay-rohth'*; plur. of 1448; *walls; Gederoth*, a place in Pal.:—Gederoth {2x}. See: BDB—155b.

1451. גְּדֵרִי {1x} **G**e**dêrîy**, *ghed-ay-ree'*; patrial from 1445; a *Gederite*, or inhab. of Geder:—Gederite {1x}. See: BDB—155b.

1452. גְּדֵרָתִי {1x} **G**e**dêrâthîy**, *ghed-ay-raw-thee'*; patrial from 1449; a *Gederathite*, or inhab. of Gederah:—Gederathite {1x}. See: BDB—155b.

1453. גְּדֵרֹתַיִם {1x} **G**e**dêrôthayim**, *ghed-ay-ro-thah'-yim*; dual of 1448; *double wall; Gederothajim*, a place in Pal.:—Gederothaim {1x}. See: BDB—155b.

1454. גֵּה {1x} **gêh**, *gay*; prob. a clerical err. for 2088; *this*:—this {1x}. See: TWOT—528; BDB—155c.

1455. גָּהָה {1x} **gâhâh**, *gaw-haw'*; a prim. root; to *remove* (a bandage from a wound, i.e. *heal* it):—cure {1x}. See: TWOT—321; BDB—155c.

1456. גֵּהָה {1x} **gêhâh**, *gay-haw'*; from 1455; a *cure*:—medicine {1x}. See: TWOT—321a; BDB—155c.

1457. גָּהַר {3x} **gâhar**, *gaw-har'*; a prim. root; to *prostrate* oneself:—stretch {2x}, cast himself down {1x}. See: TWOT—322; BDB—155c.

1458. גַּו {3x} **gav**, *gav*; another form for 1460; the *back*:—back {3x}. See: TWOT—326a; BDB—155c, 156a.

1459. גַּו {13x} **gav** (Aram.), *gav*; corresp. to 1460; the *middle*:—midst {10x}, within the same {1x}, wherein {1x}, therein {1x}. See: TWOT—2650; BDB—1086a.

1460. גֵּו {7x} **gêv**, *gave*; from 1342 [corresp. to 1354], the *back*; by anal. the *middle*:—back {5x}, among {1x}, body {1x}. See: TWOT—326b; BDB—156a, 156b, 1086a.

1461. גּוּב {1x} **gûwb**, *goob*; a prim. root; to *dig*:—husbandman {1x}. See: TWOT—323; BDB—146a, 155c.

1462. גּוֹב {2x} **gôwb**, *gobe*; from 1461; the *locust* (from its *grubbing* as a larvae):—grasshopper {2x}. See: TWOT—304b; BDB—146d, 147c, 155c.

1463. גּוֹג {10x} **Gôwg**, *gohg*; of uncert. der.; *Gog*, the name of an Isr., also of some northern nation:—Gog {10x}. See: TWOT—324; BDB—155d.

1464. גּוּד {3x} **gûwd**, *goode*; a prim. root [akin to 1413]; to *crowd* upon, i.e. *attack*:—invade {1x}, overcome {2x}. See: TWOT—325; BDB—156a.

1465. גֵּוָה {1x} **gêvâh**, *gay-vaw'*; fem. of 1460; the *back*, i.e. (by extens.) the *person*:—body {1x}. See: TWOT—326c; BDB—156b.

1466. גֵּוָה {3x} **gêvâh**, *gay-vaw'*; the same as 1465; *exaltation*; (fig.) *arrogance*:—lifting up {1x}, pride {2x}. See: TWOT—299h; BDB—145b, 156a.

1467. גֵּוָה {1x} **gêvâh** (Aram.), *gay-vaw'*; corresp to 1466:—pride {1x}. See: TWOT—2651; BDB—1085d, 1086b.

1468. גּוּז {2x} **gûwz**, *gooz*; a prim. root [comp. 1494]; prop. to *shear* off; but used only in the (fig.) sense of *passing* rapidly:—bring {1x}, cut off {1x}. See: TWOT—327; BDB—156d.

1469. גּוֹזָל {2x} **gôwzâl**, *go-zawl'*; or (short.)

גֹּזָל **gôzâl**, *go-zawl'*; from 1497; a *nestling* (as being comp. *nude* of feathers):—young {1x}, young pigeon {1x}. See: TWOT—337c; BDB—160a.

1470. גּוֹזָן {5x} **Gôwzân**, *go-zawn'*; prob. from 1468; a *quarry* (as a place of *cutting* stones); *Gozan*, a province of Assyria:—Gozan {1x}. See: BDB—157a.

1471. גּוֹי {558x} **gôwy**, *go'-ee*; rarely (short.)

גֹּי **gôy**, *go'-ee*; appar. from the same root as 1465 (in the sense of *massing*); a foreign *nation*; hence, a *Gentile*; also (fig.) a *troop* of animals, or a *flight* of locusts:—nation {374x}, heathen {143x}, Gentiles {30x}, people {11x}.

Goy means "nation; people; heathen." **(1)** *Goy* refers to a "people or nation," usually with overtones of territorial or governmental unity/identity. **(1a)** This emphasis is in the promise formulas where God promised to make someone a great, powerful, numerous "nation" (Gen 12:2). **(1b)** Certainly these adjectives described the future characteristics of the individual's descendants as compared to other peoples (cf. Num 14:12). **(1c)** So *goy* represents a group of individuals who are considered as a unit with respect to origin, language, land, jurisprudence, and government. **(1d)** This emphasis is in Gen 10:5 (the first occurrence): "By these were the isles of the Gentiles divided in their lands; every one after his tongue, after their families, in their nations." **(1e)** Deut 4:6 deals not with political and national identity but with religious unity, its wisdom, insight, righteous jurisprudence, and especially its nearness to God: "Keep therefore and do them; for this is your wisdom and your understanding in the sight of the nations, which shall hear all these statutes, and say, Surely this great nation is a wise and understanding people." **(1f)** Certainly all this is viewed as the result of divine election (Deut 4:32ff.). **(1g)** Israel's greatness is due to the greatness of her God and the great acts He has accomplished in and for her.

(2) *Goy* is sometimes almost a derogatory name for non-Israelite groups, or the "heathen": "And I will scatter you among the heathen, and will draw out a sword . . ." (Lev 26:33). **(2a)** This negative connotation is not always present, however, when the word is used of the heathen: "For from the top of the rocks I see him, and from the hills I behold him: lo, the people shall dwell alone, and shall not be reckoned among the nations" (Num 23:9). **(3)** Certainly in contexts dealing with worship the goyim are the non-Israelites: "They feared the Lord, and served their own gods, after the manner of the nations whom they carried away from thence" (2 Kin 17:33). **(4)** In passages such as Deut 4:38 goyim specifically describes the early inhabitants of Canaan prior to the Israelite conquest. **(4a)** Israel was to keep herself apart from and distinct from the "heathen" (Deut 7:1) and **(4b)** was to be an example of true godliness before them (Deut 4:6).

(5) On the other hand, Israel was to be the means by which salvation was declared to the nations (heathen) as a blessing to all the nations (Gen 12:2) and **(5a)** as a holy "nation" and kingdom of priests (Ex 19:6), and **(5b)** the nations came to recognize God's sovereignty (Is 60). **(6)** So the Messiah is the light of the nations (Is 49:6). Syn: **(A)** The word 'am (5971), "people, nation," suggests subjective personal interrelationships based on common familial ancestry and/or a covenantal union, while *goy* suggests a political entity with a land of its own: "Now therefore, I pray thee, if I have found grace in thy sight, show me thy way, that I may know thee, that I may find grace in thy sight: and consider that this nation is thy people" (Ex 33:13). **(B)** *Goy* may be used of a people, however, apart from its territorial identity: "And ye shall be unto me a kingdom of priests, and a holy nation" (Ex 19:6). Syn.: 5971. See: TWOT—326e; BDB—156c, 157a, 361d.

1472. גְּוִיָּה {13x} **gᵉvîyâh**, *ghev-ee-yaw';* prol. for 1465; a *body,* whether alive or dead:—body {9x}, corpse {2x}, carcase {2x}. See: TWOT—326d; BDB—156b, 157a.

1473. גּוֹלָה {42x} **gôwlâh**, *go-law';* or (short.)

גֹּלָה **gôlâh**, *go-law';* act. part. fem. of 1540; *exile;* concr. and collect. *exiles:*—captivity {26x}, carry away {7x}, captive {5x}, removing {2x}, remove {1x}, captivity + 3627 {1x}.

Golah means "exile; people exiled." **(1)** Ezra 2:1 uses the word of "people returning from the exile." **(2)** In other references, the word means "people in exile" (2 Kin 24:15). **(3)** In 1 Chr 5:22, *golah* refers to the era of the "exile." See: TWOT—350a; BDB—163c, 1086c.

1474. גּוֹלָן {4x} **Gôwlân**, *go-lawn';* from 1473; *captive; Golan,* a place E. of the Jordan:—Golan {4x}. See: BDB—157a.

1475. גּוּמָּץ {1x} **gûwmmâts**, *goom-mawts';* of uncert. der.; a *pit:*—pit {1x}. See: TWOT—362a; BDB—170a.

1476. גּוּנִי {4x} **Gûwnîy**, *goo-nee';* prob. from 1598; *protected; Guni,* the name of two Isr.:—Guni {1x}. See: BDB—157b.

1477. גּוּנִי {1x} **Gûwnîy**, *goo-nee';* patron. from 1476; a *Gunite* (collect. with art. pref.) or desc. of Guni:—Gunites {1x}. See: BDB—157b.

1478. גָּוַע {25x} **gâvaᶜ**, *gaw-vah';* a prim. root; to *breathe* out, i.e. (by impl.) *expire:*—die {12x}, give up the ghost {9x}, dead {1x}, perish {2x}, dead {1x}. See: TWOT—328; BDB—157b.

1479. גּוּף {1x} **gûwph**, *goof;* a prim. root; prop. to *hollow* or *arch,* i.e. (fig.) *close;* to *shut:*—shut {1x}. See: TWOT—329; BDB—157c.

1480. גּוּפָה {2x} **gûwphâh**, *goo-faw';* from 1479; a *corpse* (as *closed* to sense):—body {2x}. See: TWOT—329a; BDB—157c.

1481. גּוּר {98x} **gûwr**, *goor;* a prim. root; prop. to *turn* aside from the road (for a lodging or any other purpose), i.e. *sojourn* (as a guest); also to *shrink, fear* (as in a *strange* place); also to *gather* for hostility (as *afraid*):—sojourn {58x}, dwell {12x}, afraid {6x}, stranger {6x}, gather together {4x}, fear {3x}, abide {2x}, assemble {1x}, stand in awe {1x}, gathered {1x}, inhabitant {1x}, remain {1x}, sojourners {1x}, surely {1x}.

This verb means "to dwell or sojourn in a land as a client." The first occurrence of the word is in Gen 12:10, where it is reported that Abram journeyed to Egypt and dwelt there as a client. In Gen 21:23, Abraham makes a covenant with Abimelech, saying, ". . . According to the kindness that I have done unto thee, thou shalt do unto me, and to the land wherein thou hast sojourned." Syn.: 3427, 7931, 8453. See: TWOT—330, 332; BDB—157c, 158c, 158d.

1482. גּוּר {7x} **gûwr**, *goor;* or (short.)

גֻּר **gûr**, *goor;* perh. from 1481; a *cub* (as still *abiding* in the lair), espec. of the lion:—whelp {6x}, young one {1x}. See: TWOT—331b; BDB—158d.

1483. גּוּר {1x} **Gûwr**, *goor;* the same as 1482; *Gur,* a place in Pal.:—Gur {1x}. See: BDB—158a, 751c.

1484. גּוֹר {2x} **gôwr**, *gore;* or (fem.)

גֹּרָה **gôrâh**, *go-raw';* a var. of 1482:—whelp {1x}. See: TWOT—331a; BDB—158d, 177c.

1485. גּוּר־בַּעַל {1x} **Gûwr-Baᶜal**, *goor-bah'-al;* from 1481 and 1168; *dwelling of Baal; Gur-Baal,* a place in Arabia:—Gur-baal {1x}. See: BDB—158a.

1486. גּוֹרָל {77x} **gôwrâl**, *go-rawl';* or (short.)

גֹּרָל **gôrâl**, *go-ral';* from an unused root mean. to *be rough* (as stone); prop. a *pebble,* i.e. a *lot* (small stones being used for that purpose); fig. a *portion* or *destiny* (as if determined by lot):—lot {1x}.

Goral means "lot." **(1)** *Goral* represents the "lot" which was cast to discover the will of God in a given situation: "And Aaron shall cast lots upon the two goats; one lot for the Lord, and the other lot for the scapegoat" (Lev 16:8—the first occurrence). **(2)** Exactly what casting the "lot" involved is not known. **(3)** Since the land of Palestine was allocated among the tribes by the casting of the "lot," these allotments came to be known as their lots: "This then was the lot of the tribe of the children of Judah by their families; even to the border of Edom . . ." (Josh 15:1). **(4)** In an extended use the word *goral* represents the idea "fate" or "destiny": "And behold at eveningtide trouble; and before the morning he is not. This is the portion of them that spoil us, and the lot of them that rob us" (Is 17:14). **(5)** Since God is viewed as controlling all things absolutely, the result of the casting of the "lot" is divinely controlled: "The lot is cast into the lap; but the whole disposing thereof is of the Lord" (Prov 16:33). **(6)** Thus, providence (divine control of history) is frequently figured as one's "lot." See: TWOT—381a; BDB—174a.

1487. גּוּשׁ {1x} **gûwsh**, *goosh;* or rather (by perm.)

גִּישׁ **gîysh**, *gheesh;* of uncert. der.; a *mass* of earth:—clod {1x}. See: TWOT—333a; BDB—159a, 162c.

1488. גֵּז {4x} **gêz**, *gaze;* from 1494; a *fleece* (as *shorn*); also mown *grass:*—fleece {2x}, mowings {1x}, mown grass {1x}. See: TWOT—336a; BDB—159a, 159c.

1489. גִּזְבָּר {1x} **gizbâr**, *ghiz-bawr';* of for. der.; *treasurer:*—treasurer {1x}. See: TWOT—334; BDB—159b, 1086b.

1490. גִּזְבָּר {1x} **gizbâr** (Aram.), *ghiz-bawr';* corresp. to 1489:—treasurer {1x}. See: TWOT—2653; BDB—1086b.

1491. גָּזָה {1x} **gâzâh**, *gaw-zaw';* a prim. root [akin to 1468]; to *cut* off, i.e. *portion* out:—take {1x}. See: TWOT—335; BDB—159b.

1492. גָּזָּה {7x} **gazzâh**, *gaz-zaw';* fem. from 1494; a *fleece:*—fleece {7x}. See: TWOT—336b; BDB—159b, 159c.

1493. גִּזוֹנִי {1x} **Gizôwnîy**, *ghee-zo-nee';* patrial from the unused name of a place appar. in Pal.; a *Gizonite* or inhab. of Gizoh:—Gizonite {1x}. See: BDB—159b.

1494. גָּזַז {15x} **gâzaz**, *gaw-zaz';* a prim. root [akin to 1468]; to *cut* off; spec. to *shear* a flock or *shave* the hair; fig. to *destroy* an enemy:—shear {5x}, sheepshearer {3x}, shearers {3x}, cut off {1x}, poll {1x}, shave {1x}, cut down {1x}. Syn.: 5349. See: TWOT—336; BDB—159c.

1495. גָּזֵז {2x} **Gâzêz**, *gaw-zaze';* from 1494; *shearer; Gazez,* the name of two Isr.:—*Gazez* {1x}. See: BDB—159c.

1496. גָּזִית {11x} **gâzîyth**, *gaw-zeeth';* from 1491; something *cut,* i.e. *dressed* stone:—hewed, hewn stone {10x}, wrought {1x}. See: TWOT—335a; BDB—159b, 159d.

1497. גָּזַל {30x} **gâzal**, *gaw-zal';* a prim. root; to *pluck* off; spec. to *flay, strip* or *rob:*—spoil {8x}, take away {8x}, rob {4x}, pluck {3x}, caught {1x}, consume {1x}, exercised {1x}, force {1x}, pluck off {1x}, torn {1x}, violence {1x}. See: TWOT—337; BDB—159d.

1498. גָּזֵל {4x} **gâzêl**, *gaw-zale';* from 1497; *robbery,* or (concr.) *plunder:*—robbery {3x}, thing taken away by violence {1x}. See: TWOT—337a; BDB—160a.

1499. גֵּזֶל {2x} **gêzel**, *ghe'-zel;* from 1497; *plunder,* i.e. *violence:*—violence {1x}, violent perverting {1x}. See: BDB—160a.

גּוֹזָל **gôzâl**. See 1469.

1500. גְּזֵלָה {5x} **gᵉzêlâh**, *ghez-ay-law';* fem. of 1498 and mean. the same:—violence {3x}, robbed {1x}, that {1x}. See: TWOT—337b; BDB—160a.

1501. גָּזָם {3x} **gâzâm**, *gaw-zawm';* from an unused root mean. to *devour;* a kind of *locust:*—palmer-worm {3x}. See: TWOT—338a; BDB—160b.

1502. גַּזָּם {2x} **Gazzâm**, *gaz-zawm';* from the same as 1501; *devourer; Gazzam,* one of the Nethinim:—*Gazzam* {2x}. See: BDB—160b.

1503. גֶּזַע {3x} **gezaᶜ**, *geh'-zah;* from an unused root mean. to *cut* down (trees); the *trunk* or *stump* of a tree (as felled or as planted):—stem {1x}, stock {2x}. See: TWOT—339a; BDB—160b.

1504. גָּזַר {13x} **gâzar**, *gaw-zar';* a prim. root; to *cut* down or off; (fig.) to *destroy, divide, exclude,* or *decide:*—cut off {6x}, divide {3x}, decree {2x}, cut down {1x}, snatch {1x}. See: TWOT—340; BDB—160b, 1086b.

1505. גְּזַר {6x} **gᵉzar** (Aram.), *ghez-ar';* corresp. to 1504; to *quarry; determine:*—cut out {2x}, soothsayer {4x}.

The Chaldean soothsayer (Dan 2:27; 4:7; 5:7, 11) was no doubt an astrologer, who pretended to do what astrologers in many countries and in various eras have professed to do, namely, to calculate the destinies of man by interpreting the movements and conjunctions of the heavenly bodies. Their name comes from this verb which is literally to cut. Whether their name was applied to them from their marking out the heavens into certain divisions for purposes of observation, or whether they derived it from the fact that they cut off or decided the fate of those who came to them for advice, is a matter which perhaps cannot now be determined. See: TWOT—2654; BDB—1086b.

1506. גֶּזֶר {2x} **gezer**, *gheh'-zer;* from 1504; something *cut* off; a *portion:*—part {1x}, piece {1x}. See: TWOT—340a; BDB—160c.

1507. גֶּזֶר {15x} **Gezer**, *gheh'-zer;* the same as 1506; *Gezer*, a place in Pal.:—Gazer {2x}, *Gezer* {13x}. See: BDB—160c.

1508. גִּזְרָה {8x} **gizrâh**, *ghiz-raw';* fem. of 1506; the *figure* or person (as if *cut* out); also an *inclosure* (as *separated*):—polishing {1x}, separate place {7x}. See: TWOT—340c; BDB—160d.

1509. גְּזֵרָה {1x} **g**e**zêrâh**, *ghez-ay-raw';* from 1504; a *desert* (as *separated*):—not inhabited {1x}. See: TWOT—340b; BDB—160c.

1510. גְּזֵרָה {2x} **g**e**zêrâh** (Aram.), *ghez-ay-raw';* from 1505 (as 1504); a *decree:*—decree {1x}. See: TWOT—2654a; BDB—1086b.

1511. גִּזְרִי {1x} **Gizrîy** (in the marg.), *ghiz-ree';* patrial from 1507; a *Gezerite* (collect.) or inhab. of Gezer; but better (as in the text) by transp.

גִּרְזִי **Girzîy**, *gher-zee';* patrial of 1630; a *Girzite* (collect.) or member of a native tribe in Pal.:—Gezrites {1x}. See: BDB—160c, 173d.

1512. גָּחוֹן {2x} **gâchôwn**, *gaw-khone';* prob. from 1518; the external *abdomen, belly* (as the *source* of the fetus [comp. 1521]):—belly {1x}. See: TWOT—342a; BDB—161a.

גֵּחֲזִי **Gêchăzîy**. See 1522.

גָּחֹל **gâchol**. See 1513.

1513. גֶּחֶל {18x} **gechel**, *geh'-khel;* or (fem.)

גַּחֶלֶת **gacheleth**, *gah-kheh'-leth;* from an unused root mean. to *glow* or *kindle;* an *ember:*—coals {17x}, coals of fire {1x}. See: TWOT—341a; BDB—160d.

1514. גַּחַם {1x} **Gacham**, *gah'-kham;* from an unused root mean. to *burn; flame; Gacham*, a son of Nahor:—Gaham {1x}. See: BDB—161a.

1515. גַּחַר {1x} **Gachar**, *gah'-khar;* from an unused root mean. to *hide; lurker; Gachar,* one of the Nethinim:—Gahar {2x}. See: BDB—161a.

גּוֹי **gôy**. See 1471.

1516. גַּיְא {60x} **gay'**, *gah'-ee;* or (short.)

גַּי **gay**, *gah'-ee;* prob. (by transm.) from the same root as 1466 (abb.); a *gorge* (from its *lofty* sides; hence, narrow, but not a gully or winter-torrent):—valley {60x}. Syn.: 1237, 5158, 6010. See: TWOT—343; BDB—161a, 360d, 361d.

1517. גִּיד {7x} **gîyd**, *gheed;* prob. from 1464; a *thong* (as *compressing*); by anal. a *tendon:*—sinew {7x}. See: TWOT—344a; BDB—161c.

1518. גִּיחַ {6x} **gîyach**, *ghee'-akh;* or (short.)

גֹּחַ **gôach**, *go'-akh;* a prim. root; to *gush* forth (as water), gen. to *issue:*—come forth {3x}, take {1x}, bring forth {1x}, draw up {1x}. See: TWOT—345; BDB—157a, 160d, 161c.

1519. גִּיחַ {1x} **gîyach** (Aram.), *ghee'-akh;* or (short.)

גּוּחַ **gûwach** (Aram.), *goo'-akh;* corresp. to 1518; to *rush* forth:—strive {1x}. See: TWOT—345; BDB—1086b.

1520. גִּיחַ {1x} **Gîyach**, *ghee'-akh;* from 1518; a *fountain; Giach*, a place in Pal.:—Giah {1x}. See: BDB—161d.

1521. גִּיחוֹן {6x} **Gîychôwn**, *ghee-khone';* or (short.)

גִּחֹן **Gîchôwn**, *ghee-khone';* from 1518; *stream; Gichon*, a river of Paradise; also a valley (or pool) near Jerusalem:—Gihon {1x}. See: TWOT—345a; BDB—161d.

1522. גֵּיחֲזִי {12x} **Gêychăzîy**, *gay-khah-zee';* or

גֵּחֲזִי **Gêchăzîy**, *gay-khah-zee';* appar. from 1516 and 2372; *valley of a visionary; Gechazi*, the servant of Elisha:—Gehazi {12x}. See: BDB—160d, 161c, 162a.

1523. גִּיל {44x} **gîyl**, *gheel;* or (by perm.)

גּוּל **gûwl**, *gool;* a prim. root; prop. to *spin* round (under the influence of any violent emotion), i.e. usually *rejoice*, or (as *cringing*) *fear:*—rejoice {27x}, glad {10x}, joyful {4x}, joy {2x}, delight {1x}. See: TWOT—346; BDB—157a, 162a.

1524. גִּיל {10x} **gîyl**, *gheel;* from 1523; a *revolution* (of time, i.e. an *age*); also *joy:*—rejoice {3x}, joy {3x}, gladness {2x}, exceedingly {1x}, of your sort {1x}. Syn.: 5937, 7442, 8055. See: TWOT—346a,b; BDB—162b.

1525. גִּילָה {2x} **gîylâh**, *ghee-law';* or

גִּילַת **gîylath**, *ghee-lath';* fem. of 1524; *joy:*—joy {1x}, rejoicing {1x}. See: TWOT—346c; BDB—162b.

גִּילֹה **Gîylôh**. See 1542.

1526. גִּילֹנִי {2x} **Gîylônîy**, *ghee-lo-nee';* patrial from 1542; a *Gilonite* or inhab. of Giloh:—Gilonite {2x}. See: BDB—162b.

1527. גִּינַת {2x} **Gîynath**, *ghee-nath';* of uncert. der.; *Ginath*, an Isr.:—Ginath {2x}. See: BDB—162b. 171b.

1528. גִּיר {1x} **gîyr** (Aram.), *gheer;* corresp. to 1615; *lime:*—plaster {1x}. See: TWOT—2655; BDB—1086b.

1529. גֵּישָׁן {1x} **Gêyshân**, *gay-shawn';* from the same as 1487; *lumpish; Geshan*, an Isr.:—Geshan {1x}. See: BDB—162c.

1530. גַּל **gal**, *gal;* from 1556; something *rolled*, i.e. a *heap* of stone or dung (plural *ruins*), by anal. a *spring* of water (plur. *waves*):—heap {18x}, wave {4x}, spring {1x}, billow {1x}, of {1x}. See: TWOT—353a; BDB—162c, 164c.

1531. גֹּל {1x} **gôl**, *gole;* from 1556; a *cup* for oil (as *round*):—bowl {1x}. See: TWOT—353c; BDB—165a.

גְּלָא **g**e**lâ'**. See 1541.

1532. גַּלָּב {1x} **gallâb**, *gal-lawb';* from an unused root mean. to *shave;* a *barber:*—barber {1x}. See: TWOT—348; BDB—162c.

1533. גִּלְבֹּעַ {8x} **Gilbô'a**, *ghil-bo'-ah;* from 1530 and 1158; *fountain of ebullition; Gilboa*, a mountain of Pal.:—*Gilboa* {8x}. See: BDB—162c.

1534. גַּלְגַּל {11x} **galgal**, *gal-gal';* by redupl. from 1556; a *wheel;* by anal. a *whirlwind;* also *dust* (as *whirled*):—heaven {1x}, rolling thing {1x}, wheel {8x}, whirlwind {1x}. See: TWOT—353i; BDB—162c, 165d.

1535. גַּלְגַּל {1x} **galgal** (Aram.), *gal-gal';* corresp. to 1534; a *wheel:*—wheel {1x}. See: TWOT—2657a; BDB—1086b, 1086c.

1536. גִּלְגָּל {1x} **gilgâl**, *ghil-gawl';* a var. of 1534:—wheel {1x}. See: TWOT—353j; BDB—162c, 166a.

1537. גִּלְגָּל {41x} **Gilgâl**, *ghil-gawl';* the same as 1536 (with the art. as a prop. noun); *Gilgal*, the name of three places in Pal.:—*Gilgal* {41x}. See: BDB—166a. See also 1019.

1538. גֻּלְגֹּלֶת {12x} **gulgôleth**, *gul-go'-leth;* by redupl. from 1556; a *skull* (as *round*); by impl. a *head* (in enumeration of persons):—poll {7x}, scull {2x}, every man {2x}, head {1x}. See: TWOT—353l; BDB—162c, 166b.

1539. גֶּלֶד {1x} **geled**, *ghe'-led;* from an unused root prob. mean. to *polish;* the (human) *skin* (as *smooth*):—skin {1x}. See: TWOT—349; BDB—162d.

1540. גָּלָה {188x} **gâlâh**, *gaw-law';* a prim. root; to *denude* (espec. in a disgraceful sense); by impl. to *exile* (captives being usually *stripped*); fig. to *reveal:*—uncover {34x}, discover {20x}, captive {28x}, carry away {22x}, reveal {16x}, open {12x}, captivity {11x}, shew {9x}, remove {6x}, appear {3x}, misc. {18x} = + advertise, bewray, bring, depart, disclose, exile, be gone, × plainly, publish, × shamelessly, × surely, tell.

Galah means "to leave, depart, uncover, reveal." **(1)** *Intransitively, galah* signifies "depart" or "leave." **(1a)** This meaning is seen clearly in 1 Sa 4:21: "And she named the child Ichabod, saying, The glory is departed from Israel. . . ." **(1b)** Thus Isaiah 24:11: "The mirth of the land is gone." **(1c)** One special use of this sense of the verb is "to go into exile." The first biblical occurrence of *galah* carries this nuance: "And the children of Dan set up the graven image: and Jonathan . . . and his sons were priests to the tribe of Dan until the day of the captivity of the land" (Judg 18:30), or until they lost control of the land and were forced to serve other gods. **(1d)** The best-known Old Testament captivity was the one brought by God through the kings of Assyria and Babylon (1 Chr 5:26; cf. Jer 29:1).

(1e) Although *galah* is not used in this sense in the law of Moses, the idea is clearly present. If Israel does not "observe to do all the words of this law that are written in this book, that thou mayest fear this glorious and fearful name, The Lord Thy God; . . . ye shall be plucked from off the land whither thou goest to possess it. And the Lord shall scatter thee among all people . . ." (Deut 28:58, 63–64; cf. Lev 26:27, 33). **(1f)** This verb can also be used of the "exile of individuals," such as David (2 Sa 15:19). **(1g)** This word may signify "making oneself naked." Noah "drank of the wine, and was drunken; and he was uncovered within his tent" (Gen 9:21).

(2) The *transitive form* occurs less frequently, but has a greater variety of meanings. **(2a)** "To uncover" another person may mean "to have sexual relations with" him or her: "None of you shall approach to any [blood relative of his] to uncover their nakedness: I am the Lord" (Lev 18:6). **(2b)** Uncovering one's nakedness does not always, however, refer to sexual relations (cf. Ex

20:26). **(2c)** Another phrase, "to uncover someone's skirts," means to have sexual relations with a person (Deut 22:30). **(2d)** In Is 16:3, *galah* (in the intensive stem) signifies "betray": ". . . Hide the outcasts [do not betray the fugitive]. . . ." **(2e)** This verb may also be used of "discovering" things, of "laying them bare" so that they become visible: ". . . The foundations of the world were discovered at the rebuking of the Lord . . ." (2 Sa 22:16). **(2f)** In a related sense Eze 23:18 speaks of "uncovering" harlotries, of "exposing" them constantly or leading a life of harlotry. **(2g)** God's "uncovering" of Himself means that He "revealed" Himself (Gen 35:7).

(2h) "To uncover someone's ears" is to tell him something: **(2h1)** "Now the LORD had told Samuel in his ear [literally, "had uncovered the ear"] a day before Saul came, saying, to Samuel . . ." (1 Sa 9:15). **(2h2)** In this case, the verb means not simply "to tell," but "to tell someone something that was not known." **(2h3)** Used in this sense, *galah* is applied to the "revealing" of secrets (Prov 11:13) and of one's innermost feelings. **(2h4)** Hence, Jer 11:20 should be translated: "For unto thee have I revealed my case." **(2i)** Thus *galah* can be used of "making something" openly known, or of "publicizing" it: "The copy of the writing for a commandment to be given in every province was published unto all people, that they should be ready against that day" (Est 3:14). **(2j)** Another nuance appears in Jer 32:11, where *galah,* in connection with a deed of purchase, means "not sealed or closed up." See: TWOT—350; BDB—162d, 1086c.

1541. גְּלָה {9x} **gᵉlâh** (Aram.), *ghel-aw';* or

גְּלָא **gᵉlâʾ** (Aram.), *ghel-aw';* corresp. to 1540:—brought over {1x}, carry away {1x}, reveal {7x}. See: TWOT—2656; BDB—1086c.

גֹּלָה **gôlâh.** See 1473.

1542. גִּלֹה {2x} **Gilôh,** *ghee-lo';* or (fully)

גִּילֹה **Gîylôh,** *ghee-lo';* from 1540; *open; Giloh,* a place in Pal.:—Giloh {2x}. See: BDB—162b, 163d.

1543. גֻּלָּה {14x} **gullâh,** *gool-law';* fem. from 1556; a *fountain, bowl* or *globe* (all as *round*):—bowl {5x}, pommel {3x}, spring {6x}. See: TWOT—353c; BDB—163d, 165a.

1544. גִּלּוּל {48x} **gillûwl,** *ghil-lool';* or (short.)

גִּלֻּל **gillûl,** *ghil-lool';* from 1556; prop. a *log* (as *round*); by impl. an *idol:*—idol {47x}, image {1x}. See: TWOT—353h; BDB—165c.

1545. גְּלוֹם **gᵉlôwm,** *ghel-ome';* from 1563; *clothing* (as *wrapped*):—clothes {1x}. See: TWOT—354a; BDB—166b.

1546. גָּלוּת {1x} **gâlûwth,** *gaw-looth';* fem. from 1540; *captivity;* concr. *exiles* (collect.):—

גְּלוֹם {1x} **gᵉlôwm,** *ghel-ome';* from 1563; *clothing* (as *wrapped*):—captivity {10x}, captive captives {3x}, them that are carried away captive {2x}. See: clothes {1x}. See: TWOT—354a; BDB—166b. TWOT—350b; BDB—163c.

1547. גָּלוּת {4x} **gâlûwth** (Aram.), *gaw-looth';* corresp. to 1546:—captivity {3x}, captive {1x}. Syn.: 1473, 7617. See: TWOT—2656a; BDB—1086c.

1548. גָּלַח {23x} **gâlach,** *gaw-lakh';* a prim. root; prop. to *be bald,* i.e. (caus.) to *shave;* fig. to *lay waste:*—poll {2x}, shave {17x}, shave off {4x}. See: TWOT—351; BDB—164a.

1549. גִּלָּיוֹן {2x} **gillâyôwn,** *ghil-law-yone';* or

גִּלְיוֹן **gilyôwn,** *ghil-yone';* from 1540; a *tablet* for writing (as *bare*); by anal. a *mirror* (as a *plate*):—glass {1x}, roll {1x}. See: TWOT—350c; BDB—163d.

1550. גָּלִיל {4x} **gâlîyl,** *gaw-leel';* from 1556; a *valve* of a folding door (as *turning*); also a *ring* (as *round*):—folding {2x}, ring {2x}. See: TWOT—353f; BDB—165b.

1551. גָּלִיל {6x} **Gâlîyl,** *gaw-leel';* or (prol.)

גָּלִילָה **Gâlîylâh,** *gaw-lee-law';* the same as 1550; a *circle* (with the art.); *Galil* (as a special *circuit*) in the North of Pal.:—Galilee {6x}. See: BDB—165b.

1552. גְּלִילָה {5x} **gᵉlîylâh,** *ghel-ee-law';* fem. of 1550; a *circuit* or *region:*—border {3x}, coast {1x}, country {1x}. See: TWOT—353g; BDB—165b.

1553. גְּלִילוֹת {1x} **Gᵉlîylôwth,** *ghel-ee-lowth';* plur. of 1552; *circles; Geliloth,* a place in Pal.:—Geliloth {1x}. See: TWOT—353g; BDB—165c.

1554. גַּלִּים {2x} **Gallîym,** *gal-leem';* plur. of 1530; *springs; Gallim,* a place in Pal.:—Gallim {2x}. See: BDB—164d.

1555. גָּלְיַת {6x} **Golyath,** *gol-yath';* perh. from 1540; *exile; Goljath,* a Philistine:—Goliath {1x}. See: BDB—163d.

1556. גָּלַל {18x} **gâlal,** *gaw-lal';* a prim. root; to *roll* (lit. or fig.):—roll {9x}, roll . . . {3x}, seek occasion {1x}, wallow {1x}, trust {1x}, commit {1x}, remove {1x}, run down {1x}. See: TWOT—353; BDB—94a, 164b, 1086c.

1557. גָּלָל {1x} **gâlâl,** *gaw-lawl';* from 1556; *dung* (as in *balls*):—dung {1x}. See: TWOT—353d; BDB—165b.

1558. גָּלָל {10x} **gâlâl,** *gaw-lawl';* from 1556; a *circumstance* (as *rolled* around); only used adv., on *account* of:—because {4x}, . . . sake {4x}, because of thee {1x}, for {1x}. See: TWOT—352; BDB—164b.

1559. גָּלָל {3x} **Gâlâl,** *gaw-lawl';* from 1556, in the sense of 1560; *great; Galal,* the name of two Isr.:—*Galal* {3x}. See: BDB—165b.

1560. גְּלָל {2x} **gᵉlâl** (Aram.), *ghel-awl';* from a root corresp. to 1556; *weight* or *size* (as if *rolled*):—great {2x}. See: TWOT—2657; BDB—1086c.

1561. גֵּלֶל {4x} **gêlel,** *gay'-lel;* a var. of 1557; *dung* (plur. *balls* of dung):—dung {4x}. See: TWOT—353d; BDB—165a.

1562. גִּלֲלַי {1x} **Gîlălay,** *ghe-lal-ah'-ee;* from 1561; *dungy; Gilalai,* an Isr.:—Gilalai {1x}. See: BDB—165b.

1563. גָּלַם {1x} **gâlam,** *gaw-lam';* a prim. root; to *fold:*—wrap together {1x}. See: BDB—166b.

1564. גֹּלֶם {1x} **gôlem,** *go'-lem;* from 1563; a *wrapped* (and unformed *mass,* i.e. as the *embryo*):—substance yet being unperfect {1x}. See: TWOT—354b; BDB—166b.

1565. גַּלְמוּד {4x} **galmûwd,** *gal-mood';* prob. by prol. from 1563; *sterile* (as *wrapped* up too hard); fig. *desolate:*—desolate {2x}, solitary {2x}. See: TWOT—354c; BDB—166c.

1566. גָּלַע {3x} **gâlaʿ,** *gaw-lah';* a prim. root; to *be obstinate:*—intermeddle {1x}, meddle {2x}. See: TWOT—355; BDB—166c.

1567. גַּלְעֵד {2x} **Galʿêd,** *gal-ade';* from 1530 and 5707; *heap of testimony; Galed,* a memorial cairn E. of the Jordan:—Galeed {2x}. See: BDB—165a, 166d.

1568. גִּלְעָד {134x} **Gilʿâd,** *ghil-awd';* prob. from 1567; *Gilad,* a region E. of the Jordan; also the name of three Isr.:—Gilead {101x}, Ramothgilead + 7433 {18x}, Jabeshgilead + 3003 {12x}, Gileadites {2x}. See: TWOT—356; BDB—166d, 928c.

1569. גִּלְעָדִי {11x} **Gilʿâdîy,** *ghil-aw-dee';* patron. from 1568; a *Giladite* or desc. of Gilad:—Gileadite {11x}. See: TWOT—356a; BDB—167c.

1570. גָּלַשׁ {2x} **gâlash,** *gaw-lash';* a prim. root; prob. to *caper* (as a goat):—appear {2x}. See: TWOT—357; BDB—167c.

1571. גַּם {34x} **gam,** *gam;* by contr. from an unused root mean. to *gather;* prop. *assemblage;* used only adv. *also, even, yea, though;* often repeated as correl. *both . . . and:*—also {5x}, as {3x}, even {2x}, again {1x}, and {1x}, misc. {22x}. See: TWOT—361a; BDB—167c, 168d, 210b.

1572. גָּמָא {2x} **gâmâʾ,** *gaw-maw';* a prim. root (lit. or fig.) to *absorb:*—swallow {1x}, drink {1x}. See: TWOT—358; BDB—167c.

1573. גֹּמֶא {4x} **gômeʾ,** *go'-meh;* from 1572; prop. an *absorbent,* i.e. the *bulrush* (from its *porosity*); spec. the *papyrus:*—bulrush {2x}, rush {2x}. See: TWOT—358a; BDB—167d.

1574. גֹּמֶד {1x} **gômed,** *go'-med;* from an unused root appar. mean. to *grasp;* prop. a *span:*—cubit {1x}. See: TWOT—359a; BDB—167d.

1575. גַּמָּד {1x} **Gammâd,** *gam-mawd';* from the same as 1574; a *warrior* (as *grasping* weapons):—Gammadims {1x}. See: BDB—167d.

1576. גְּמוּל {19x} **gᵉmûwl,** *ghem-ool';* from 1580; *treatment,* i.e. an *act* (of good or ill); by impl. *service* or *requital:*—recompense {10x}, reward {3x}, benefit {2x}, given {1x}, serve + 1580 {1x}, deserve {1x}. See: TWOT—360a; BDB—168b.

1577. גָּמוּל {1x} **Gâmûwl,** *gaw-mool';* pass. part. of 1580; *rewarded; Gamul,* an Isr.:—Gamul {1x}. See also 1014.

1578. גְּמוּלָה {3x} **gᵉmûwlâh,** *ghem-oo-law';* fem. of 1576; mean. the same:—deed {1x}, recompense {1x}, such a reward {1x}. See: TWOT—360b; BDB—168c.

1579. גִּמְזוֹ {1x} **Gimzôw,** *ghim-zo';* of uncert. der.; Gimzo, a place in Pal.:—Gimzo {1x}. See: BDB—168a.

1580. גָּמַל {37x} **gâmal,** *gaw-mal';* a prim. root; to *treat* a person (well or ill), i.e. *benefit* or *requite;* by impl. (of *toil*), to *ripen,* i.e. (spec.) to *wean:*—wean {10x}, reward {8x}, dealt bountifully {4x}, do {4x}, bestowed {2x}, recompense {2x}, weaned child {2x}, do good {1x}, requite {1x}, ripening {1x}, served {1x}, yielded {1x}.

Gamal means "to deal out, deal with, wean, ripen." **(1)** While the basic meaning of the word is "to deal out, with," the wide range of meaning can be seen in its first occurrence in the biblical text: "And the child grew, and was weaned . . ." (Gen 21:8). **(2)** *Gamal* is used most frequently in the sense of "to deal out to," such as in Prov 31:12: "She will do him good and not evil. . . ." **(3)** The word is used twice in 1 Sa 24:17: ". . . Thou hast rewarded me good, whereas I have rewarded thee evil." **(4)** The psalmist rejoices and sings to the Lord "because he hath dealt bountifully with me" (Ps 13:6). **(5)** This word can express ripening of grapes (Is 18:5) or **(6)** bearing ripe almonds (Num 17:8). See: TWOT—360; BDB—168a.

1581. גָּמָל {54x} **gâmâl**, *gaw-mawl';* appar. from 1580 (in the sense of *labor* or *burden-bearing*); a *camel:*—camel {54x}. See: TWOT—360d; BDB—168c.

1582. גְּמַלִּי {1x} **Gemalliy**, *ghem-al-lee';* prob. from 1581; *camel-driver; Gemalli,* an Isr.:—Gemalli {1x}. See: BDB—168d.

1583. גַּמְלִיאֵל {5x} **Gamliyʼêl**, *gam-lee-ale';* from 1580 and 410; *reward of God; Gamliel,* an Isr.:—Gamaliel {5x}. See: BDB—168c.

1584. גָּמַר {5x} **gâmar**, *gaw-mar';* a prim. root; to *end* (in the sense of *completion* or *failure*):—cease {1x}, fail {1x}, come to an end {1x}, perfect {1x}, perform {1x}. See: TWOT—363; BDB—170a, 1086c.

1585. גְּמַר {1x} **gemar** (Aram.), *ghem-ar';* corresp. to 1584:—perfect {1x}. See: TWOT—2658; BDB—1086c.

1586. גֹּמֶר {6x} **Gômer**, *go'-mer;* from 1584; *completion; Gomer,* the name of a son of Japheth and of his desc.; also of a Hebrewess:—*Gomer* {6x}. See: BDB—170a.

1587. גְּמַרְיָה {5x} **Gemaryâh**, *ghem-ar-yaw';* or גְּמַרְיָהוּ **Gemaryâhûw**, *ghem-ar-yaw'-hoo;* from 1584 and 3050; *Jah has perfected; Gemarjah,* the name of two Isr.:—Gemariah {1x}. See: BDB—170b.

1588. גַּן {42x} **gan**, *gan;* from 1598; a *garden* (as *fenced*):—garden {42x}. Syn.: 1593. See: TWOT—367a; BDB—111b, 170b, 171a.

1589. גָּנַב {39x} **gânab**, *gaw-nab';* a prim. root; to *thieve* (lit. or fig.); by impl. to *deceive:*—steal {30x}, steal away {7x}, carry away {1x}, brought {1x}. See: TWOT—364; BDB—170b.

1590. גַּנָּב {17x} **gannâb**, *gaw-nab';* from 1589; a *stealer:*—thief {1x}. See: TWOT—364b; BDB—170c.

1591. גְּנֵבָה {2x} **genêbâh**, *ghen-ay-baw';* from 1589; *stealing,* i.e. (concr.) something *stolen:*—theft {2x}. See: TWOT—364a; BDB—170c.

1592. גְּנֻבַת {2x} **Genûbath**, *ghen-oo-bath';* from 1589; *theft; Genubath,* an Edomitish prince:—*Genubath* {2x}. See: BDB—170c.

1593. גַּנָּה {12x} **gannâh**, *gan-naw';* fem. of 1588; a *garden:*—garden {12x}. Syn.: 1594. See: TWOT—367b; BDB—171a.

1594. גִּנָּה {4x} **ginnâh**, *ghin-naw';* another form for 1593:—garden {4x}. See: TWOT—367b; BDB—171a.

1595. גֶּנֶז {3x} **genez**, *gheh'-nez;* from an unused root mean. to *store; treasure;* by impl. a *coffer:*—chest {1x}, treasury {3x}. See: TWOT—365a; BDB—170d, 1086c.

1596. גְּנַז {3x} **genaz** (Aram.), *ghen-az';* corresp. to 1595; *treasure:*—treasure {3x}. See: TWOT—2659; BDB—1086c.

1597. גִּנְזַךְ {1x} **ginzak**, *ghin-zak';* prol. from 1595; a *treasury:*—treasury {1x}. See: TWOT—366; BDB—170d.

1598. גָּנַן {8x} **gânan**, *gaw-nan';* a prim. root; to *hedge* about, i.e. (gen.) *protect:*—defend {8x}. See: TWOT—367; BDB—170d.

1599. גִּנְּתוֹן {3x} **Ginnethôwn**, *ghin-neth-ône';* or גִּנְּתוֹי **Ginnethôw**, *ghin-neth-o';* from 1598; *gardener; Ginnethon* or *Ginnetho,* an Isr.:—Ginnetho {1x}, Ginnethon {2x}. See: BDB—171b.

1600. גָּעָה {2x} **gâʻâh**, *gaw-aw';* a prim. root; to *bellow* (as cattle):—low {2x}. See: TWOT—368; BDB—171d.

1601. גֹּעָה {1x} **Gôʻâh**, *go-aw';* fem. act. part. of 1600; *lowing; Goah,* a place near Jerusalem:—Goath {1x}. See: BDB—171d.

1602. גָּעַל {10x} **gâʻal**, *gaw-al';* a prim. root; to *detest;* by impl. to *reject:*—abhor {5x}, lothe {3}, cast away {1x}, fail {1x}. See: TWOT—369; BDB—171d.

1603. גַּעַל {9x} **Gaʻal**, *gah'-al;* from 1602; *loathing; Gaal,* an Isr.:—*Gaal* {9x}. See: BDB—172a.

1604. גֹּעַל {1x} **gôʻal**, *go'-al;* from 1602; *abhorrence:*—loathing {1x}. See: TWOT—369a; BDB—172a.

1605. גָּעַר {14x} **gâʻar**, *gaw-ar';* a prim. root; to *chide:*—rebuke {12x}, corrupt {1x}, reprove {1x}. See: TWOT—370; BDB—172a.

1606. גְּעָרָה **geʻârâh**, *gheh-aw-raw';* from 1605; a *chiding:*—rebuke {13x}, reproof {2x}. Syn.: 3198. See: TWOT—370a; BDB—172a.

1607. גָּעַשׁ {10x} **gâʻash**, *gaw-ash';* a prim. root to *agitate* violently:—shake {5x}, move {3x}, trouble {1x}, toss themselves {1x}. See: TWOT—371; BDB—172b.

1608. גַּעַשׁ {4x} **Gaʻash**, *ga'-ash;* from 1607; a *quaking; Gaash,* a hill in Pal.:—*Gaash* {4x}. See: BDB—172b.

1609. גַּעְתָּם {3x} **Gaʻtâm**, *gah-tawm';* of uncert. der.; *Gatam,* an Edomite:—*Gatam* {3x}. See: BDB—172b.

1610. גַּף {4x} **gaph**, *gaf;* from an unused root mean. to *arch;* the *back;* by extens. the *body* or self:—highest places {1x}, himself {1x}. See: TWOT—373a; BDB—172b, 172c.

1611. גַּף {3x} **gaph** (Aram.), *gaf;* corresp. to 1610; a *wing:*—wing {3x}. See: TWOT—2660; BDB—1086d.

1612. גֶּפֶן {55x} **gephen**, *gheh'-fen;* from an unused root mean. to *bend;* a *vine* (as *twining*), espec. the grape:—vine {54x}, tree {1x}. See: TWOT—372a; BDB—172b.

1613. גֹּפֶר {1x} **gôpher**, *go'-fer;* from an unused root, prob. mean. to *house in;* a kind of tree or wood (as used for *building*), appar. the *cypress:*—*gopher* {1x}. See: TWOT—374; BDB—172d.

1614. גָּפְרִית {7x} **gophrîyth**, *gof-reeth';* prob. fem. of 1613; prop. cypress-*resin;* by anal. *sulphur* (as equally inflammable):—brimstone {7x}. See: TWOT—375; BDB—172d.

1615. גִּר {1x} **gîr**, *gheer;* perh. from 3564; *lime* (from being *burned* in a kiln):—chalkstone {1x}. See: TWOT—347a; BDB—162c, 173a, 1086b.

1616. גֵּר {92x} **gêr**, *gare;* or (fully) גֵּיר **gêyr**, *gare;* from 1481; prop. a *guest;* by impl. a *foreigner:*—stranger {87x}, alien {1x}, sojourner {1x}, stranger + 376 {1x}, stranger + 4480 {1x}, strangers + 582 {1x}.

Geyr means "client; stranger." **(1)** A "client" was not simply a foreigner (5237 - nakri) or a stranger (2114 - zar). **(1a)** He was a permanent resident, once a citizen of another land, who had moved into his new residence. **(1b)** Frequently he left his homeland under some distress, as when Moses fled to Midian (Ex 2:22). **(1c)** Whether the reason for his journey was to escape some difficulty or merely to seek a new place to dwell, he was one who sought acceptance and refuge. **(1d)** Consequently he might also call himself a toshab (8453), a settler. **(1e)** Neither the settler nor the "client" could possess land. **(1e1)** In the land of Canaan the possession of land was limited to members or descendants of the original tribal members. **(1e2)** Only they were full citizens who enjoyed all the rights of citizenry, which meant sharing fully in the inheritance of the gods and forefathers—the feudal privileges and responsibilities (cf. Eze 47:22).

(2) In Israel a *geyr,* like a priest, **(2a)** could possess no land and enjoyed the special privileges of the third tithe. **(2b)** Every third year the tithe of the harvest was to be deposited at the city gate with the elders and distributed among "the Levite, (because he hath no part nor inheritance with thee,) and the stranger, and the fatherless, and the widow, which are within thy gates . . ." (Deut 14:29). **(3)** In the eschaton such "clients" were to be treated as full citizens: "And it shall come to pass, that ye shall divide it [the land] by lot for an inheritance unto you, and to the strangers that sojourn among you, which shall beget children among you: and they shall be unto you as born in the country among the children of Israel; they shall have inheritance with you among the tribes of Israel" (Eze 47:22). **(4)** Under the Mosaic law aliens were not slaves but were usually in the service of some Israelite whose protection they enjoyed (Deut 24:14). **(4a)** This, however, was not always the case. **(4b)** Sometimes a "client" was rich and an Israelite would be in his service (Lev 25:47).

(5) The *ger* was to be treated (except for feudal privileges and responsibilities) as an Israelite, being responsible to and protected by the law: **(5a)** "Hear the causes between your brethren, and judge righteously between every man and his brother, and the stranger that is with him" (Deut 1:16); **(5b)** "ye shall therefore keep my statutes and my judgments, and shall not commit any of these abominations; neither any of your own nation, nor any stranger that sojourneth among you" (Lev 18:26); **(5c)** "ye shall have one manner of law, as well for the stranger, as for one of your own country: for I am the Lord your God" (Lev 24:22). **(6)** The *geyr* also enjoyed the Sabbath rest (Lev 25:6) and divine protection (Deut 10:18). **(7)** God commanded Israel to love the "client" as himself (Lev 19:34).

(8) The *geyr* could also be **(8a)** circumcised (Ex 12:48) and **(8b)** enjoy all the privileges of the true religion: **(8b1)** the Passover (Ex 12:48–49), **(8b2)** the Atonement feast (Lev 16:29), **(8b3)** presenting offerings (Lev 17:8), and **(8b4)** all the feasts (Deut 16:11). **(8c)** He was also obligated to keep the purity laws (Lev 17:15). **(9)** Israel is told that God is the true owner of all the land and its people are but "clients" owing Him feudal obedience (Lev 19:34; Deut 10:19). **(10)** They are admonished to treat the client with justice, righteousness, and love because like Abraham (Gen 23:4) they were "clients" in Egypt (Ex 22:21). **(11)** In legal cases the "client" could appeal directly to God the great feudal Lord (Lev 24:22).

Syn: Two other nouns related to *geyr* are megurim (4033) and gerut (1628). Megurim refers to the "status or condition of being a client" (Gen 17:8) and to a "dwelling where one is a client" (Job 18:19). Gerut refers to a "place where clients dwell" (Jer 41:17). See: TWOT—330a; BDB—158a, 162c, 173a.

1617. גֵּרָא {9x} **Gêrâʾ**, *gay-raw';* perh. from 1626; a *grain; Gera,* the name of six Isr.:—*Gera* {9x}. See: BDB—173a.

1618. גָּרָב {3x} **gârâb**, *gaw-rawb';* from an unused root mean. to *scratch; scurf* (from *itching*):—scab {1x}, scurvy {2x}. See: TWOT—376a; BDB—173a.

1619. גָּרֵב {3x} **Gârêb**, *gaw-rabe';* from the same as 1618; *scabby; Gareb,* the name of an Isr., also of a hill near Jerusalem:—*Gareb* {3x}. See: BDB—173a.

1620. גַּרְגַּר {1x} **gargar**, *gar-gar';* by redupl. from 1641; a *berry* (as if a pellet of *rumination*):—berry {1x}. See: TWOT—386c; BDB—173a, 176b.

1621. גַּרְגְּרוֹת {4x} **gargᵉrôwth**, *gar-gher-owth';* fem. plur. from 1641; the *throat* (as used in *rumination*):—neck {1x}. See: TWOT—386d; BDB—173a, 176b.

1622. גִּרְגָּשִׁי {7x} **Girgâshîy**, *ghir-gaw-shee';* patrial from an unused name [of uncert. der.]; a *Girgashite,* one of the native tribes of Canaan:—Girgashite {6x}, Girgasite {1x}. BDB—See: 173a.

1623. גָּרַד {1x} **gârad**, *gaw-rad';* a prim. root; to *abrade:*—scrape {1x}. See: TWOT—377; BDB—173b.

1624. גָּרָה {14x} **gârâh**, *gaw-raw';* a prim. root; prop. to *grate,* i.e. (fig.) to *anger:*—stir up {6x}, meddle {4x}, contend {3x}, strive {1x}. See: TWOT—378; BDB—173b.

1625. גֵּרָה {11x} **gêrâh**, *gay-raw';* from 1641; the *cud* (as *scraping* the throat):—cud {11x}. See: TWOT—386a; BDB—173d, 176a.

1626. גֵּרָה {5x} **gêrâh**, *gay-raw';* from 1641 (as in 1625); prop. (like 1620) a *kernel* (round as if *scraped*), i.e. a *gerah* or small weight (and coin):—*gerah* {5x}.

A *gerah,* was a weight, a 20th part of a shekel, equal to the weight of 16 barley grains or 4 to 5 carob beans. See: TWOT—386b; BDB—173d, 176a.

גֹּרָה **gôrâh**. See 1484.

1627. גָּרוֹן {8x} **gârôwn**, *gaw-rone';* or (short.)

גָּרֹן **gârôn**, *gaw-rone';* from 1641; the *throat* [comp. 1621] (as *roughened* by swallowing):—throat {4x}, neck {2x}, mouth {1x}, aloud {1x}. See: TWOT—378a; BDB—159a, 173c, 175c.

1628. גֵּרוּת {1x} **gêrûwth**, *gay-rooth';* from 1481; a (temporary) *residence:*—habitation {1x}. See: TWOT—330b; BDB—158c, 173d.

1629. גָּרַז {1x} **gâraz**, *gaw-raz';* a prim. root; to *cut* off:—cut off {1x}. See: TWOT—379; BDB—173d.

1630. גְּרִזִים {4x} **Gᵉrîzîym**, *gher-ee-zeem';* plur. of an unused noun from 1629 [comp. 1511], *cut* up (i.e. *rocky*); *Gerizim,* a mountain of Pal.:—Gerizim {4x}. See: BDB—173d.

1631. גַּרְזֶן {4x} **garzen**, *gar-zen';* from 1629; an *axe:*—ax {4x}. See: TWOT—379a; BDB—173d.

1632. גָּרֹל {1x} **gârôl**, *gaw-role';* from the same as 1486; *harsh:*—man of great {1x}. See: TWOT—381a; BDB—175a.

גֹּרָל **gôrâl**. See 1486.

1633. גָּרַם {3x} **gâram**, *gaw-ram';* a prim. root; to *be spare* or *skeleton-like;* used only as a denom. from 1634; (caus.) to *bone,* i.e. *denude* (by extens. *crunch*) the bones:—gnaw the bones {1x}, break {2x}. See: TWOT—382b; BDB—175.

1634. גֶּרֶם {5x} **gerem**, *gheh'-rem;* from 1633; a *bone* (as the *skeleton* of the body); hence, *self,* i.e. (fig.) *very:*—bone {3x}, strong {1x}, top {1x}. See: TWOT—382a; BDB—175a, 1086d.

1635. גְּרַם {1x} **gerem** (Aram.), *gheh'-rem;* corresp. to 1634; a *bone:*—bone {1x}. See: TWOT—382a; BDB—1086d.

1636. גַּרְמִי {1x} **Garmîy**, *gar-mee';* from 1634; *bony,* i.e. *strong:*—Garmite {1x}. See: BDB—175a.

1637. גֹּרֶן {36x} **gôren**, *go'-ren;* from an unused root mean. to *smooth;* a threshing-*floor* (as made *even*); by anal. any open *area:*—. threshingfloor {18x}, floor {11x}, place {2x}, barn {1x}, barnfloor {1x}, corn {1x}, cornfloor + 1715 {1x}, threshingplace {1x}. See: TWOT—383a; BDB—175b, 188d.

גָּרֹן **gârôn**. See 1627.

1638. גָּרַס {2x} **gâraç**, *gaw-ras';* a prim. root; to *crush;* also (intr. and fig.) to *dissolve:*—break {1x}. See: TWOT—387; BDB—175c, 176b.

1639. גָּרַע {21x} **gâraʿ**, *gaw-rah';* a prim. root; to *scrape* off; by impl. to *shave, remove, lessen,* or *withhold:*—diminish {8x}, take {3x}, . . .away {2x}, restrain {2x}, abated {1x}, keep back {1x}, clipped {1x}, minish {1x}, small {1x}, withdraweth {1x}. See: TWOT—384; BDB—175c.

1640. גָּרַף {1x} **gâraph**, *gaw-raf';* a prim. root; to *bear* off violently:—sweep away {1x}. See: TWOT—385; BDB—175d.

1641. גָּרַר {5x} **gârar**, *gaw-rar';* a prim. root; to *drag* off roughly; by impl. to *bring up* the cud (i.e. *ruminate*); by anal. to *saw:*—catch {1x}, destroy {1x}, chew {1x}, saw {1x}, continuing {1x}. See: TWOT—386; BDB—176a.

1642. גְּרָר {10x} **Gᵉrâr**, *gher-awr';* prob. from 1641; a *rolling* country; *Gerar,* a Philistine city:—*Gerar* {1x}. See: BDB—176b.

1643. גֶּרֶשׂ {2x} **geres**, *gheh'-res;* from an unused root mean. to *husk;* a *kernel* (collect.), i.e. *grain:*—beaten corn {2x}. See: TWOT—387a; BDB—176c.

1644. גָּרַשׁ {47x} **gârash**, *gaw-rash';* a prim. root; to *drive* out from a possession; espec. to *expatriate* or *divorce:*—drive out {20x}, cast out {8x}, thrust out {6x}, drive away {2x}, put away {2x}, divorced {2x}, driven {1x}, expel {1x}, drive forth {1x}, surely {1x}, troubled {1x}, cast up {1x}, divorced woman {1x}.

Garash means "to drive out, cast out." **(1)** An early occurrence in the Old Testament is in Ex 34:11: ". . . Behold, I drive out before thee the Amorite, and the Canaanite. . . ." **(2)** The word may be used of a divorced woman as in Lev 21:7—a woman that is "put away from her husband." See: TWOT—388; BDB—176c.

1645. גֶּרֶשׁ {1x} **geresh**, *gheh'-resh;* from 1644; *produce* (as if *expelled*):—put forth {1x}. See: TWOT—388a; BDB—177a.

1646. גְּרֻשָׁה {1x} **gᵉrûshâh**, *gher-oo-shaw';* fem. pass. part. of 1644; (abstr.) *dispossession:*—exaction {1x}. See: TWOT—388b; BDB—177a.

1647. גֵּרְשֹׁם {14x} **Gêrᵉshôm**, *gay-resh-ome';* for 1648; *Gereshom,* the name of four Isr.:—Gershom {14x}. See: BDB—177a.

1648. גֵּרְשׁוֹן {17x} **Gêrᵉshôwn**, *gay-resh-one';* or

גֵּרְשׁוֹם **Gêrᵉshôwm**, *gay-resh-ome';* from 1644; a *refugee; Gereshon* or *Gereshom,* an Isr.:—Gershon {17x}. See: TWOT—388b; BDB—177a.

1649. גֵּרְשֻׁנִּי {13x} **Gerᵉshunnîy**, *gay-resh-oon-nee';* patron. from 1648; a *Gereshonite* or desc. of Gereshon:—Gershonite, sons of Gershon {13x}. See: BDB—177b.

1650. גְּשׁוּר {9x} **Gᵉshûwr**, *ghesh-oor';* from an unused root (mean. to *join*); *bridge; Geshur,* a district of Syria:—Geshur {8x}, Geshurite {1x}. See: BDB—178a.

1651. גְּשׁוּרִי {6x} **Gᵉshûwrîy**, *ghe-shoo-ree';* patrial from 1650; a *Geshurite* (also collect.) or inhab. of Geshur:—Geshuri {2x}, Geshurites {4x}. See: BDB—178c.

1652. גָּשַׁם {1x} **gâsham**, *gaw-sham';* a prim. root; to *shower* violently:—(cause to) rain {1x}. See: TWOT—389; BDB—177d.

1653. גֶּשֶׁם {35x} **geshem**, *gheh'-shem;* from 1652; a *shower:*—rain {31x}, shower {4x}. See: TWOT—389a; BDB—177c, 1086d.

1654. גֶּשֶׁם {4x} **Geshem**, *gheh'-shem;* or (prol.)

גַּשְׁמוּ **Gashmûw**, *gash-moo';* the same as 1653; *Geshem* or *Gashmu,* an Arabian:—Geshem {3x}, Gashmu {1x}. See: BDB—177c, 177d.

1655. גֶּשֶׁם {5x} **geshem** (Aram.), *gheh'-shem;* appar. the same as 1653; used in a peculiar sense, the *body* (prob. for the [fig.] idea of a *hard* rain):—body {5x}. See: TWOT—2662; BDB—1086d.

1656. גֹּשֶׁם {1x} **gôshem**, *go'-shem;* from 1652; equiv. to 1653:—rained upon {1x}. See: TWOT—389; BDB—177d.

גַּשְׁמוּ **Gashmûw**. See 1654.

1657. גֹּשֶׁן {15x} **Gôshen**, *go'-shen;* prob. of Eg. or.; *Goshen,* the residence of the Isr. in Egypt; also a place in Pal.:—*Goshen* {15x}. See: TWOT—390; BDB—177d.

1658. גִּשְׁפָּא {1x} **Gishpâʾ**, *ghish-paw';* of uncert. der.; *Gishpa,* an Isr.:—Gispa {1x}. See: BDB—177d.

1659. גָּשַׁשׁ {2x} **gâshash**, *gaw-shash';* a prim. root; appar. to *feel* about:—grope {2x}. See: TWOT—391; BDB—178c.

1660. גַּת {5x} **gath**, *gath;* prob. from 5059 (in the sense of *treading* out grapes); a wine-*press* (or vat for holding the grapes in pressing them):—winepress {3x}, press {1x}, winefat {1x}. See: TWOT—841a; BDB—178c, 387c.

1661. גַּת {33x} **Gath**, *gath;* the same as 1660; *Gath,* a Philistine city:—*Gath* {33x}. See: BDB—178c, 387d, 440c.

1662. גַּת־הַחֵפֶר **Gath-ha-Chêpher**, *gath-hah-khay'-fer;* or (abridged)

גִּתָּה־חֵפֶר **Gittâh-Chêpher**, *ghit-taw-khay'-fer;* from 1660 and 2658 with the art. ins.; *wine-press of* (the) *well; Gath-Chepher,* a place in Pal.:—Gath-kephr {1x}, Gittah-kephr {1x}. See: BDB—387d.

1663. גִּתִּי {10x} **Gittîy**, *ghit-tee';* patrial from 1661; a *Gittite* or inhab. of Gath:—Gittite {10x}. See: BDB—178c, 388a.

1664. גִּתַּיִם {2x} **Gittayim**, *ghit-tah'-yim;* dual of 1660; *double wine-press; Gittajim,* a place in Pal.:—Gittaim {2x}. See: BDB—178c, 388a.

1665. גִּתִּית {3x} **Gittîyth**, *ghit-teeth';* fem. of 1663; a *Gittite* harp:—Gittith {3x}. See: BDB—178c, 388a.

1666. גֶּתֶר {2x} **Gether**, *gheh'-ther;* of uncert. der.; *Gether,* a son of Aram, and the region settled by him:—*Gether* {2x}. See: BDB—178c.

1667. גַּת־רִמּוֹן {4x} **Gath-Rimmôwn**, *gath-rim-mone';* from 1660 and 7416; *wine-press of* **(the)** *pomegranate; Gath-Rimmon,* a place in Pal.:—Gath-rimmon {4x}. See: BDB—387d.

ד

1668. דָּא {6x} **dâ'** (Aram.), *daw;* corresp. to 2088; *this:*—one {2x}, another {2x}, this {1x}. See: TWOT—2663; BDB—1086d.

1669. דָּאַב {3x} **dâ'ab**, *daw-ab';* a prim. root; to *pine:*—mourn {1x}, sorrow {1x}, sorrowful {1x}. See: TWOT—392; BDB—178a.

1670. דְּאָבָה {1x} **de'âbâh**, *dèh-aw-baw';* from 1669; prop. *pining;* by anal. *fear:*—sorrow {1x}. See: TWOT—392a; BDB—178b.

1671. דְּאָבוֹן {1x} **de'âbôwn**, *dèh-aw-bone';* from 1669; *pining:*—sorrow {1x}. See: TWOT—392b; BDB—178b.

1672. דָּאַג {7x} **dâ'ag**, *daw-ag';* a prim. root; *be anxious:*—afraid {3x}, sorrow {1x}, sorry {1x}, careful {1x}, take thought {1x}. See: TWOT—393; BDB—178b.

1673. דֹּאֵג {6x} **Dô'êg**, *do-ayg';* or (fully)

דּוֹאֵג **Dôw'êg**, *do-ayg';* act. part. of 1672; *anxious; Doëg,* an Edomite:—*Doeg* {6x}. See: BDB—178c.

1674. דְּאָגָה {6x} **de'âgâh**, *dèh-aw-gaw';* from 1672; *anxiety:*—carefulness {2x}, fear {1x}, heaviness {1x}, sorrow {1x}, with care {1x}. See: TWOT—393a; BDB—178c.

1675. דָּאָה {4x} **dâ'âh**, *daw-aw';* a prim. root; to *dart,* i.e. *fly* rapidly:—fly {4x}. See: TWOT—394; BDB—178d.

1676. דָּאָה {1x} **dâ'âh**, *daw-aw';* from 1675; the *kite* (from its rapid *flight*):—vulture {1x}. See 7201. See: TWOT—394a; BDB—178d, 906b.

1677. דֹּב {12x} **dôb**, *dobe;* or (fully)

דּוֹב **dôwb**, *dobe;* from 1680; the *bear* (as slow):—bear {12x}. See: TWOT—396a; BDB—179a, 187b, 1087a.

1678. דֹּב {1x} **dôb** (Aram.), *dobe;* corresp. to 1677:—bear {1x}. See: TWOT—2664; BDB—1087a.

1679. דֹּבֶא {1x} **dôbe'**, *do'-beh;* from an unused root (comp. 1680) (prob. mean. to *be sluggish,* i.e. *restful*); *quiet:*—strength {1x}. See: TWOT—395a; BDB—179a.

1680. דָּבַב {1x} **dâbab**, *daw-bab';* a prim. root (comp. 1679); to *move* slowly, i.e. *glide:*—cause to speak {1x}. See: TWOT—396; BDB—179a.

1681. דִּבָּה {9x} **dibbâh**, *dib-baw';* from 1680 (in the sense of *furtive* motion); *slander:* — evil report {3x}, slander {3x}, infamy {2x}, slander {1x}. See: TWOT—396b; BDB—179a.

1682. דְּבוֹרָה {4x} **debôwrâh**, *deb-o-raw';* or (short.)

דְּבֹרָה **debôrâh**, *deb-o-raw';* from 1696 (in the sense of *orderly* motion); the *bee* (from its *systematic* instincts):—bee {1x}. See: TWOT—399f; BDB—184b.

1683. דְּבוֹרָה {10x} **Debôwrâh**, *deb-o-raw';* or (short.)

דְּבֹרָה **Debôrâh**, *deb-o-raw';* the same as 1682; *Deborah,* the name of two Hebrewesses:—*Deborah* {1x}. See: BDB—184b.

1684. דְּבַח {1x} **debach** (Aram.), *deb-akh';* corresp. to 2076; to *sacrifice* (an animal):—offer sacrifice {1x}. See: TWOT—2665; BDB—1087a.

1685. דְּבַח {1x} **debach** (Aram.), *deb-akh';* from 1684; a *sacrifice:*—sacrifice {1x}. See: TWOT—2665a; BDB—1087a.

1686. דִּבְיוֹן {1x} **dibyôwn**, *dib-yone';* in the marg. for the textual reading

חֶרְיוֹן **cheryôwn**, *kher-yone';* both (in the plur. only and) of uncert. der.; prob. some cheap vegetable, perh. a bulbous root:—dove's dung {1x}. See: BDB—179b.

1687. דְּבִיר {16x} **debîyr**, *deb-eer';* or (short.)

דְּבִר **debîr**, *deb-eer';* from 1696 (appar. in the sense of *oracle*); the *shrine* or innermost part of the sanctuary:—oracle {1x}. The place from which deity speaks. See: TWOT—399g; BDB—184b.

1688. דְּבִיר {14x} **Debîyr**, *deb-eer';* or (short.)

דְּבִר **Debîr** (Josh 13:26 [but see 3810]), *deb-eer';* the same as 1687; *Debir,* the name of an Amoritish king and of two places in Pal.:—*Debir* {14x}. See: BDB—184c, 529a.

1689. דִּבְלָה {1x} **Diblâh**, *dib-law';* prob. an orth. err. for 7247; *Diblah,* a place in Syria:—Diblath {1x}. See: BDB—179c.

1690. דְּבֵלָה {5x} **debêlâh**, *deb-ay-law';* from an unused root (akin to 2082) prob. mean. to *press* together; a *cake* of pressed figs:—cake of figs {3x}, lump {2x}. See: TWOT—397a; BDB—179b.

1691. דִּבְלַיִם {1x} **Diblayim**, *dib-lah'-yim;* dual from the masc. of 1690; *two cakes; Diblajim,* a symb. name:—Diblaim {1x}. See: BDB—179c.

דִּבְלָתַיִם **Diblâthayim**. See 1015.

1692. דָּבַק {54x} **dâbaq**, *daw-bak';* a prim. root; prop. to *impinge,* i.e. *cling* or *adhere;* fig. to *catch* by pursuit:—cleave {32x}, follow hard {5x}, overtake {3x}, stick {3x}, keep fast {2x}, . . . together {2x}, abide {1x}, close {1x}, joined {1x}, pursued {1x}, take {1x}. *Dabaq* means "to cling, cleave, keep close." **(1)** *Dabaq* yields the noun form for "glue" and also the more abstract ideas of "loyalty, devotion." **(2)** In Gen 2:24: "Therefore shall a man leave his father and his mother, and shall cleave unto his wife: and they shall be one flesh." This usage reflects the basic meaning of one object's (person's) being joined to another. **(3)** In this sense, Eleazar's hand "cleaved" to the sword as he struck down the Philistines (2 Sa 23:10). **(4)** Jeremiah's linen waistcloth "clung" to his loins, symbolic of Israel's "clinging" to God (Jer 13:11). **(5)** In time of war and siege, the resulting thirst and famine caused the tongue "to cleave" to the roof of the mouth of those who had been so afflicted. **(6)** The figurative use of *dabaq* in the sense of "loyalty" and "affection" is based on the physical closeness of the persons involved, such as **(6a)** a husband's closeness to his wife (Gen 2:24), **(6b)** Shechem's affection for Dinah (Gen 34:3), or **(6c)** Ruth's staying with Naomi (Ruth 1:14). **(7)** "Cleaving" to God is equivalent to "loving" God (Deut 30:20). See: TWOT—398; BDB—179c, 1087a.

1693. דְּבַק {1x} **debaq** (Aram.), *deb-ak';* corresp. to 1692; to *stick* to:—cleave {1x}. See: TWOT—2666; BDB—1087a.

1694. דֶּבֶק {3x} **debeq**, *deh'-bek;* from 1692; a *joint;* by impl. *solder:*—joint {2x}, solder {1x}. See: TWOT—398a; BDB—180a.

1695. דָּבֵק {3x} **dâbêq**, *daw-bake';* from 1692; *adhering:*—cleave {1x}, joining {1x}, stick closer {1x}. See: TWOT—398?; BDB—180a.

1696. דָּבַר {1143x} **dâbar**, *daw-bar';* a prim. root; perh. prop. to *arrange;* but used fig. (of words), to *speak;* rarely (in a destructive sense) to *subdue:*—speak {840x}, say {118x}, talk {46x}, promise {31x}, tell {25x}, commune {20x}, pronounce {14x}, utter {7x}, command {4x} misc. {38x} = answer, appoint, bid, declare, destroy, give, name, rehearse, be spokesman, subdue, teach, think, use [entreaties], × well, × work. *Dabar* means "to speak, say." **(1)** This verb focuses not only on the content of spoken verbal communication but also and especially on the time and circumstances of what is said. **(2)** Unlike 'amar (559), "to say," *dabar* often appears without any specification of what was communicated. **(2a)** Those who "speak" are primarily persons (God or men) or organs of speech. **(2a1)** In Gen 8:15 (the first occurrence of this verb) God "spoke" to Noah, **(2a2)** while in Gen 18:5 one of the three men "spoke" to Abraham. **(3)** Exceptions to this generalization occur, for example **(3a)** in Job 32:7, where Elihu personifies "days" (a person's age) as that which has the right "to speak" first. **(3b)** In 2 Sa 23:2 David says that the Spirit of the Lord "spoke" to him; contrary to many (especially liberal) scholars, this is probably a reference to the Holy Spirit.

(4) Among the special meanings of this verb are **(4a)** "to say" (Dan 9:21), **(4b)** "to command" (2 Kin 1:9), **(4c)** "to promise" (Deut 6:3), **(4d)** "to commission" (Ex 1:17), **(4e)** "to announce" (Jer 36:31), **(4f)** "to order or command" (Deut 1:14), and **(4g)** "to utter a song" (Judg 5:12). **(4h)** Such secondary meanings are, however, quite infrequent. Syn.: Amar (559) usually focuses on the mode of revelation, whereas *dabar* focuses on the content. See: TWOT—399; BDB—180b.

1697. דָּבָר {1439x} **dâbâr**, *daw-baw';* from 1696; a *word;* by impl. a *matter* (as *spoken* of) or *thing;* adv. a *cause:*—word {807x}, thing {231x}, matter {63x}, acts {51x}, chronicles {38x}, saying {25x}, commandment {20x}, misc. {204x} = advice, affair, answer, × any such (thing), + because of, book, business, care, case, cause, certain rate, × commune (-ication), + concern [-ing], + confer, counsel, + dearth, decree, deed,

× disease, due, duty, effect, + eloquent, errand, [evil favoured-] ness, + glory, + harm, hurt, + iniquity, + judgment, language, + lying, manner, message, [no] thing, oracle, × ought, × parts, + pertaining, + please, portion, + power, promise, provision, purpose, question, rate, reason, report, request, × (as hast) said, sake, sentence, + sign, + so, some [uncleanness], somewhat to say, + song, speech, × spoken, talk, task, + that, × there done, thought, + thus, tidings, what [-soever], + wherewith, which, work.

Dabar means "word, matter; something." **(1)** The noun *dabar* refers, first, to what is said, to the actual "word" itself; whereas 'emer (561) is essentially oral communication (the act of speaking). **(2)** Before the dispersion from the tower of Babel all men spoke the same "words" or language (Gen 11:1). **(3)** This noun can also be used of the content of speaking. When God "did according to the word of Moses" (Ex 8:13), He granted his request. **(4)** The noun can connote "matter" or "affair," as in Gen 12:17, where it is reported that God struck Pharaoh's household with plagues because of Sarai." **(5)** A rather specialized occurrence of this sense appears in references to **(5a)** records of the "events of a period" (1 Kin 14:19) or **(5b)** the activities of a particular person (1 Kin 11:41; cf. Gen 15:1).

(6) *Dabar* can be used as a more general term in the sense of **(6a)** "something"—so in Gen 24:66 the "all things" is literally "all of something(s)"; **(6b)** it is an indefinite generalized concept rather than a reference to everything in particular. **(7)** This noun also appears to have had almost a technical status in Israel's law procedures. Anyone who had a "matter" before Moses had a law case (Ex 18:16). **(8)** As a biblical phrase "the word of the Lord" is quite important; it occurs about 242 times. **(8a)** Against the background just presented it is important to note that "word" here may focus on the content (meaning) of what was said, **(8b)** but it also carries overtones of the actual "words" themselves. **(8c)** It was the "word of the Lord" that came to Abram in a vision after his victory over the kings who had captured Lot (Gen 15:1). **(8d)** In most cases this is a technical phrase referring expressly to prophetic revelation (about 225 times). **(8e)** It has been suggested that this phrase has judicial overtones although there are only 7 passages where this is certain (cf. Num 15:31).

(9) This noun is used twice of God's "affairs" in the sense of the care of the temple (1 Chr 26:32). **(10)** The "word" of God indicates God's thoughts and will. **(10a)** This should be contrasted with His name, which indicates His person and presence. **(10b)** Therefore, God's "word" is called "holy" only once (cf. Ps 105:42), while His name is frequently called "holy." Syn: Several other nouns related to the verb *dabar* occur infrequently. **(A)** Dibrah (1700), which occurs 5 times, means "cause, manner" (Job 5:8). **(B)** Dabberet (1703) means "word" once (Deut 33:3). **(C)** Deborah (1682) appears 5 times and refers to "honey bee" (Deut 1:44; Ps 118:12). **(D)** Midbar (4057) refers to "speaking" once (Song 4:3). **(E)** *Dabar* refers to what is said, the actual word itself; whereas emer (561) is essentially oral communication (the act of speaking). See: TWOT—399a; BDB—182a.

1698. דֶּבֶר {49x} **deber**, *deh'-ber;* from 1696 (in the sense of *destroying*); a *pestilence:*—pestilence {47x}, plagues {1x}, murrain {1x}.

Deber means "pestilence." **(1)** The meaning of *deber* is best denoted by the English word "pestilence" or "plague." **(1a)** A country might be quickly reduced in population by the "plague" (cf. 2 Sa 24:13ff.). **(1b)** The nature of the "plague" (bubonic or other) is often difficult to determine from the contexts, as the details of medical interest are not given or are scanty. **(2)** In the prophetical writings, the "plague" occurs with other disasters: famine, flood, and the sword: "When they fast, I will not hear their cry; and when they offer burnt offering and an oblation, I will not accept them: but I will consume them by the sword, and by the famine, and by the pestilence" (Jer 14:12). See: TWOT—399b; BDB—184a.

1699. דֹּבֶר {2x} **dôber**, *do'-ber;* from 1696 (in its original sense); a *pasture* (from its *arrangement* of the flock):—fold {1x}, manner {1x}. See: TWOT—399c; BDB—184a.

דְּבִר **debîr** or

דְּבִר **Debîr**. See 1687, 1688.

1699′. דִּבֵּר {1x} **dibbêr**, *dib-bare';* for 1697:—word {1x}. See: BDB—184c.

1700. דִּבְרָה {5x} **dibrâh**, *dib-raw';* fem. of 1697; a *reason, suit* or *style:*—cause {1x}, end {1x}, estate {1x}, order {1x}, regard {1x}. See: TWOT—399e; BDB—184a, 1087a.

1701. דִּבְרָה {1x} **dibrâh** (Aram.), *dib-raw';* corresp. to 1700:—intent {1x}, sake {1x}. See: TWOT—2667; BDB—1087a.

דְּבֹרָה **debôrâh** or

דְּבֹרָה **Debôrâh**. See 1682, 1683.

1702. דֹּבְרָה {1x} **dôberâh**, *do-ber-aw';* fem. act. part. of 1696 in the sense of *driving* [comp. 1699]; a *raft:*—float {1x}. See: TWOT—399d; BDB—184a.

1703. דַּבָּרָה {1x} **dabbârâh**, *dab-baw-raw';* intens. from 1696; a *word:*—word {1x}. See: TWOT—399j; BDB—184c.

1704. דִּבְרִי {1x} **Dibrîy**, *dib-ree';* from 1697; *wordy; Dibri,* an Isr.:—Dibri {1x}. See: BDB—184c.

1705. דָּבְרַת {3x} **Dâberath**, *daw-ber-ath';* from 1697 (perh. in the sense of 1699); *Daberath,* a place in Pal.:—Dabareh {1x}, *Daberath* {1x}. See: BDB—184b.

1706. דְּבַשׁ {54x} **debash**, *deb-ash';* from an unused root mean. to *be gummy; honey* (from its *stickiness*); by anal. *syrup:*—honey {52x}, honeycomb + 3295 {1x}, honeycomb + 6688 {1x}. See: TWOT—400a; BDB—185a.

1707. דַּבֶּשֶׁת {1x} **dabbesheth**, *dab-beh'-sheth;* intens. from the same as 1706; a sticky *mass,* i.e. the *hump* of a camel:—hunch of a camel {1x}. See: TWOT—400b; BDB—185c.

1708. דַּבֶּשֶׁת {1x} **Dabbesheth**, *dab-beh'-sheth;* the same as 1707; *Dabbesheth,* a place in Pal.:—*Dabbesheth* {1x}. See: BDB—185c.

1709. דָּג {20x} **dâg**, *dawg;* or (fully)

דָּאג **dâ'g** (Neh. 13:16), *dawg;* from 1711; a *fish* (as *prolific*); or perh. rather from 1672 (as *timid*); but still better from 1672 (in the sense of *squirming,* i.e. moving by the vibratory action of the tail); a *fish* (often used collect.):—fish {20x}. See: TWOT—401a; BDB—178d, 185c.

1710. דָּגָה {15x} **dâgâh**, *daw-gaw';* fem. of 1709, and mean. the same:—fish {1x}. See: TWOT—401b; BDB—185d.

1711. דָּגָה {1x} **dâgâh**, *daw-gaw';* a prim. root; to *move rapidly;* used only as a denom. from 1709; to *spawn,* i.e. *become numerous:*—grow {1x}. See: TWOT—401; BDB—185c.

1712. דָּגוֹן {13x} **Dâgôwn**, *daw-gohn';* from 1709; the *fish-god; Dagon,* a Philistine deity:—Dagon {13x}.

1713. דָּגַל {4x} **dâgal**, *daw-gal';* a prim. root; to *flaunt,* i.e. *raise a flag;* fig. to *be conspicuous:*—set up banner {3x}, chiefest {1x}. See: TWOT—402b; BDB—186a, 186b.

1714. דֶּגֶל {14x} **degel**, *deh'-gel;* from 1713; a *flag:*—banner {1x}, standard {13x}. See: TWOT—402a; BDB—186b.

1715. דָּגָן {40x} **dâgân**, *daw-gawn';* from 1711; prop. *increase,* i.e. *grain:*—corn {37x}, wheat {2x}, cornfloor + 1637 {1x}. See: TWOT—403a; 186b.

1716. דָּגַר {2x} **dâgar**, *daw-gar';* a prim. root, to *brood* over eggs or young:—gather {1x}, sit {1x}. See: TWOT—404; BDB—186c.

1717. דַּד {4x} **dad**, *dad;* appar. from the same as 1730; the *breast* (as the seat of *love,* or from its shape):—breast {2x}, teat {2x}. See: TWOT—405; BDB—186d.

1718. דָּדָה {2x} **dâdâh**, *daw-daw';* a doubtful root; to *walk gently:*—went {1x}, go softly {1x}. See: TWOT—406; BDB—186d.

1719. דְּדָן {11x} **Dedân**, *ded-awn';* or (prol.)

דְּדָנֶה **Dedâneh** (Eze 25:13), *deh-daw'-neh;* of uncert. der.; *Dedan,* the name of two Cushites and of their territory:—Dedan {11x}. See: BDB—186d, 187a, 922b.

1720. דְּדָנִים {1x} **Dedânîym**, *ded-aw-neem';* plur. of 1719 (as patrial); *Dedanites,* the desc. or inhab. of Dedan:—Dedanim {1x}. See: BDB—187a.

1721. דֹּדָנִים {2x} **Dôdânîym**, *do-daw-neem';* or (by orth. err.)

רֹדָנִים **Rôdânîym** (1 Chr 1:7), *ro-daw-neem';* a plur. of uncert. der.; *Dodanites,* or desc. of a son of Javan:—Dodanim {1x}. See: BDB—187a, 922b, 922c.

1722. דְּהַב {23x} **dehab** (Aram.), *deh-hab';* corresp. to 2091; *gold:*—gold {14x} golden {9x}. See: TWOT—2668; BDB—1087a.

1723. דַּהֲוָא {1x} **Dahăvâ'** (Aram.), *dah-hav-aw';* of uncert. der.; *Dahava,* a people colonized in Samaria:—Dehavites {1x}. See: BDB—1087a.

1724. דָּהַם {1x} **dâham**, *daw-ham';* a prim. root (comp. 1740); to *be dumb,* i.e. (fig.) *dumb-founded:*—be astonied {1x}. See: TWOT—407; BDB—187a.

1725. דָּהַר {1x} **dâhar**, *daw-har';* a prim. root; to *curvet* or move irregularly:—pransing {1x}. See: TWOT—408; BDB—187b.

1726. דַּהֲהַר {2x} **dahăhar**, *dah-hah-har';* by redupl. from 1725; a *gallop:*—pransings {2x}. See: TWOT—408a; BDB—187b.

דּוֹאֵג **Dôw'êg**. See 1673.

1727. דּוּב {1x} **dûwb**, *doob;* a prim. root; to *mope,* i.e. (fig.) *pine:*—cast sorrow {1x}. See: TWOT—409; BDB—187b.

דּוֹב **dôwb**. See 1677.

1728. דַּוָּג {2x} **davvâg**, *dav-vawg';* an orth. var. of 1709 as a denom. 1771]; a *fisher-*

man:—fisher {2x}. See: TWOT—401d; BDB—186a, 187b.

1729. דּוּגָה {1x} **dûwgâh**, *doo-gaw';* fem. from the same as 1728; prop. *fishery,* i.e. a *hook* for fishing:—fishhook + 5518 {1x}. See: TWOT—401e; BDB—186a, 187b.

1730. דּוֹד **dôwd**, *dode;* or (short.)

דֹּד {61x} **dôd**, *dode;* from an unused root mean. prop. to *boil,* i.e. (fig.) to *love;* by impl. a *love-token, lover, friend;* spec. an *uncle:*—See: TWOT—410a; BDB—186d, 187c.

1731. דּוּד {7x} **dûwd**, *dood;* from the same as 1730; a *pot* (for *boiling*); also (by resemblance of shape) a *basket:*—basket {3x}, caldron {1x}, kettle {1x}, seething pot {2x}. See: TWOT—410e; BDB—188b.

1732. דָּוִד {1076x} **Dâvîd**, *daw-veed';* rarely (fully)

דָּוִיד **Dâvîyd**, *daw-veed';* from the same as 1730; *loving; David,* the youngest son of Jesse:—David {1076x}. See: TWOT—410c; BDB—187d.

1733. דּוֹדָה {3x} **dôwdâh**, *do-daw';* fem. of 1730; an *aunt:*—aunt {1x}, father's sister {1x}, uncle's wife {1x}. See: TWOT—410b; BDB—186d, 187d.

1734. דּוֹדוֹ {5x} **Dôwdôw**, *do-do';* from 1730; *loving; Dodo,* the name of three Isr.:—Dodo {5x}. See: BDB—186d, 187d.

1735. דּוֹדָוָהוּ {1x} **Dôwdâvâhûw**, *do-daw-vaw'-hoo;* from 1730 and 3050; *love of Jah; Dodavah,* an Isr.:—Dodavah {1x}. See: BDB—187d.

1736. דּוּדַי {7x} **dûwday**, *doo-dah'-ee;* from 1731; a *boiler* or *basket;* also the *mandrake* (as *aphrodisiac*):—basket {1x}, mandrake {7x}. See: TWOT—410d; BDB—188b.

1737. דּוֹדַי {1x} **Dôwday**, *do-dah'-ee;* formed like 1736; *amatory; Dodai,* an Isr.:—Dodai {1x}. See: BDB—187d.

1738. דָּוָה {1x} **dâvâh**, *daw-vaw';* a prim. root; to *be sick* (as if in menstruation):—infirmity {1x}. See: TWOT—411; BDB—188c.

1739. דָּוֶה {5x} **dâveh**, *daw-veh';* from 1738; *sick* (espec. in menstruation):—faint {2x}, menstruous cloth {1x}, she that is sick {1x}, having sickness {1x}. See: TWOT—411b; BDB—188c.

1740. דּוּחַ {4x} **dûwach**, *doo'-akh;* a prim. root; to *thrust* away; fig. to *cleanse:*—cast out {1x}, purge {1x}, wash {1x}. See: TWOT—412; BDB—188d.

1741. דְּוַי {2x} **d^evay**, *dev-ah'-ee;* from 1739; *sickness;* fig. *loathing:*—languishing {1x}, sorrowful {1x}. See: TWOT—411a; BDB—188c.

1742. דַּוָּי {3x} **davvây**, *dav-voy';* from 1739; *sick;* fig. *troubled:*—faint {3x}. See: TWOT—411d; BDB—188d.

דָּוִיד **Dâvîyd**. See 1732.

1743. דּוּךְ {1x} **dûwk**, *dook;* a prim. root; to *bruise* in a mortar:—beat {1x}. See: TWOT—413; BDB—188d.

1744. דּוּכִיפַת {2x} **dûwkîyphath**, *doo-kee-fath';* of uncert. der.; the *hoopoe* or else the *grouse:*—lapwing {2x}. See: TWOT—414; BDB—189a.

1745. דּוּמָה {2x} **dûwmâh**, *doo-maw';* from an unused root mean. to *be dumb* (comp. 1820); *silence;* fig. *death:*—silence {2x}. See: TWOT—415a; BDB—189a.

1746. דּוּמָה {4x} **Dûwmâh**, *doo-maw';* the same as 1745; *Dumah,* a tribe and region of Arabia:—Dumah {4x}. See: BDB—189a.

1747. דּוּמִיָּה {4x} **dûwmîyâh**, *doo-me-yaw';* from 1820; *stillness;* adv. *silently;* abstr. *quiet, trust:*—silence {1x}, silent {1x}, waiteth {2x}. See: TWOT—415b; BDB—189b.

1748. דּוּמָם {3x} **dûwmâm**, *doo-mawm';* from 1826; *still;* adv. *silently:*—dumb {1x}, silent {1x}, quietly wait {1x}. See: TWOT—415c; BDB—189b.

1749. דּוֹנַג {4x} **dôwnag**, *do-nag';* of uncert. der.; *wax:*—wax {4x}. See: TWOT—444a; BDB—200a.

1750. דּוּץ {1x} **dûwts**, *doots;* a prim. root; to *leap:*—turn into joy {1x}. See: TWOT—416; BDB—189b.

1751. דּוּק {1x} **dûwq** (Aram.), *dook;* corresp. to 1854; to *crumble:*—break into pieces {1x}. See: TWOT—2681; BDB—1089a.

1752. דּוּר {1x} **dûwr**, *dure;* a prim. root; prop. to *gyrate* (or move in a circle), i.e. to *remain:*—dwell {1x}. See: TWOT—418; BDB—189c, 1087b.

1753. דּוּר {7x} **dûwr** (Aram.), *dure;* corresp. to 1752; to *reside:*—dwell {5x}, inhabitant {2x}. See: TWOT—2669; BDB—1087b.

1754. דּוּר {3x} **dûwr**, *dure;* from 1752; a *circle, ball* or *pile:*—ball {1x}, burn {1x}, round about {1x}. See: TWOT—418a; BDB—189c, 462a.

1755. דּוֹר **dôwr**, *dore;* or (short.)

דֹּר {167x} **dôr**, *dore;* from 1752; prop. a *revolution* of time, i.e. an *age* or generation; also a *dwelling:*—generation {133x}, all {18x}, many {6x}, age {2x}, ever {5x}, × evermore {1x}, never {1x}, posterity {1x}.

Dor means "generation." **(1)** In the Old Testament, the word *dor* occurs about 167 times; as many as 74 of these are in the repetition "*dor* plus *dor,*" meaning "alway." **(2)** The first occurrence of the word is in Gen 6:9: "These are the generations of Noah [the account of Noah]: Noah was a just man and perfect in his generations, and Noah walked with God." **(3)** First the concrete meaning of "generation" is the "period during which people live": "And the Lord said unto Noah, Come thou and all thy house into the ark; for thee have I seen righteous before me in this generation" (Gen 7:1). **(4)** A "generation" may be described as **(4a)** "perverse" (Deut 32:5) or **(4b)** "righteous" (Ps 14:5).

(5) Close to this meaning is the temporal element of *dor:* A *dor* is roughly the period of time from one's birth to one's maturity, which in the Old Testament corresponds to a period of about 40 years (Num 14:33). **(6)** Abraham received the promise that four "generations" of his descendants were to be in Egypt before the Promised Land would be inherited. **(7)** Israel was warned to be faithful to the Lord, **(7a)** as the punishment for disobedience would extend to the fourth "generation" (Ex 20:5); **(7b)** but the Lord's love extends to a thousand "generations" of those who love Him (Deut 7:9). **(8)** The lasting element of God's covenantal faithfulness is variously expressed with the word *dor:* "Thy faithfulness is unto all generations: thou hast established the earth, and it abideth" (Ps 119:90)

(9) The use of *dor* in Isaiah 51 teaches the twofold perspective of "generation," with reference to the future as well as to the past. **(9a)** Isaiah spoke about the Lord's lasting righteousness and said that His deliverance is everlasting (literally, "generation of generations"—v. 8); **(9b)** but in view of Israel's situation, Isaiah petitioned the Lord to manifest His loving strength on behalf of Israel as in the past (literally, "generations forever"—v. 9). **(9c)** Thus, depending on the context, *dor* may refer to the past, the present, or the future. The psalmist recognized the obligation of one "generation" to the "generations" to come: "One generation shall praise thy works to another, and shall declare thy mighty acts" (Ps 145:4). **(10)** Even the grey-haired man has the opportunity to instruct the youth (Ps 71:17–18). See: TWOT—418b; BDB—189c, 201b, 1087b.

1756. דּוֹר {7x} **Dôwr**, *dore* or (by perm.)

דֹּאר **Dô'r** (Josh. 17:11; 1 Kings 4:11), *dore;* from 1755; *dwelling; Dor,* a place in Pal.:—*Dor* {1x}. See: BDB—178d, 190b.

1757. דּוּרָא {1x} **Dûwrâ'** (Aram.), *doo-raw';* prob. from 1753; *circle* or *dwelling; Dura,* a place in Bab.:—Dura {1x}. See: BDB—1087b.

1758. דּוּשׁ {14x} **dûwsh**, *doosh;* or

דּוֹשׁ **dôwsh**, *dōsh;* or

דִּישׁ **dîysh**, *deesh;* a prim. root; to *trample* or *thresh:*—thresh {9x}, tread out {3x}, break {1x}, tear {1x}, vr grass {1x}. See: TWOT—419; BDB—190b.

1759. דּוּשׁ {1x} **dûwsh** (Aram.), *doosh;* corresp. to 1758; to *trample:*—tread down {1x}. See: TWOT—2670; BDB—1087c.

1760. דָּחָה {11x} **dâchâh**, *daw-khaw';* or

דָּחַח **dâchach** (Jer 23:12), *daw-khakh';* a prim. root; to *push* down:—outcast {3x}, thrust {1x}, sore {1x}, overthrow {1x}, chase {1x}, tottering {1x}, driven away {1x}, driven on {1x}, cast down {1x}. See: TWOT—420; BDB—190d, 191a, 1087c.

1761. דַּחֲוָה {1x} **dachăvâh** (Aram.), *dakh-av-aw';* from the equiv. of 1760; prob. a musical *instrument* (as being *struck*):—instrument of music {1x}. See: TWOT—2671; BDB—1087c.

1762. דְּחִי {2x} **d^echîy**, *deh-khee';* from 1760; a *push,* i.e. (by impl.) a *fall:*—falling {2x}. See: TWOT—420a; BDB—191a.

1763. דְּחַל {6x} **d^echal** (Aram.), *deh-khal';* corresp. to 2119; to *slink,* i.e. (by impl.) to *fear,* or (caus.) *be formidable:*—make afraid {1x}, dreadful {2x}, fear {2x}, terrible {1x}. See: TWOT—2672; BDB—1087c.

1764. דֹּחַן {1x} **dôchan**, *do'-khan;* of uncert. der.; *millet:*—millet {1x}. See: TWOT—422a; BDB—191a.

1765. דָּחַף {4x} **dâchaph**, *daw-khaf';* a prim. root; to *urge,* i.e. *hasten:*—hasten {3x}, press {1x}. See: TWOT—423; BDB—191b.

1766. דָּחַק {2x} **dâchaq**, *daw-khak';* a prim. root; to *press,* i.e. *oppress:*—thrust {1x}, vex {1x}. See: TWOT—424; 191b.

1767. דַּי {38x} **day**, *dahee;* of uncert. der.; *enough* (as noun or adv.), used chiefly with prep. in phrases:—enough {6x}, sufficient {5x}, from {5x}, when {3x}, since {3x}, able {3x}, misc. {13x}: according to, after ability, among, as oft as, more than enough, in, much as is sufficient, sufficiently, too much, very.

Day means "sufficiency; the required enough." **(1)** The word is translated variously according to the needs of a given passage. **(1a)** The meaning "sufficiency" is clearly manifested in Ex 36:7: "For the stuff they had was sufficient for all the work to make it, and too much." **(1b)** A different translation is warranted in Jer 49:9: "If thieves [come] by night, they will destroy till they have enough" (cf. Obad 5). **(1c)** In Prov 25:16 the word means only what one's digestive system can handle: "Hast thou found honey? Eat so much as is sufficient for thee, lest thou be filled therewith, and vomit it." **(1d)** Other passages use this word of money (Deut 15:8). **(1e)** In Jer 51:58 day preceded by the preposition be means "only for": ". . . The people shall labor in vain [only for nothing], and the folk in the fire [only for fire], and they shall be weary." **(2)** The phrase "as long as there is need" signifies until there is no more required (Mal 3:10 - "that there shall not be room enough to receive it"). **(3)** The word first appears in Ex 36:5 and is preceded by the preposition min: "The people bring much more than enough for the service of the work, which the Lord commanded to make."

(4) There are many special uses of *day* where the basic meaning is in the background and the context dictates a different nuance. **(4a)** When preceded by the preposition ke, "as," the word usually means "according to": ". . . The judge shall cause him to lie down, and to be beaten before his face, according to his fault, by a certain number" (Deut 25:2). **(4b)** Preceded by min, "from," the word sometimes means "regarding the need." This illuminates passages such as 1 Sa 7:16: "And he [Samuel] went from year to year [according to the need of each year; "annually"] in circuit to Beth-el . . ." (cf. Is 66:23). **(4c)** In other places this phrase (*day* preceded by min) signifies "as often as": "Then the princes of the Philistines went forth: and it came to pass, after they went forth, that David behaved himself more wisely than all the servants of Saul . . ." (1 Sa 18:30). See: TWOT—425; BDB—95a, 191b, 461d, 552a.

1768. דִּי {19x} **dîy** (Aram.), *dee;* appar. for 1668; *that,* used as rel., conjunc., and espec. (with prep.) in adv. phrases; also as prep. *of:*—as {1x}, but {1x}, for {1x}, forasmuch {1x}, now {1x}, of {2x}, seeing {1x}, than {1x}, that {2x}, therefore {1x}, until {1x}, what soever {1x}, when {2x}, which {1x}, whom {1x}, whose {1x}. See: TWOT—2673; BDB—1087c, 1096c, 1096d.

1769. דִּיבוֹן {1x} **Dîybôwn**, *dee-bome';* or (short.)

דִּיבֹן **Dîybôn**, *dee-bone';* from 1727; *pining; Dibon,* the name of three places in Pal.:—Dibon {1x}. See: BDB—192a. [*Also, with* 1410 *added,* Dibon-gad.]

1770. דִּיג {1x} **dîyg**, *deeg;* denom. from 1709; to *fish:*—fish {1x}. See: TWOT—401c; BDB—185d, 192a.

1771. דַּיָּג {2x} **dayâg**, *dah-yawg';* from 1770; a *fisherman:*—fisher {2x}, See: TWOT—401d; BDB—186a, 192a.

1772. דַּיָּה {12x} **dayâh**, *dah-yaw';* intens. from 1675; a *falcon* (from its *rapid* flight):—vulture {1x}. See: TWOT—394b; BDB—178d, 192a.

1773. דְּיוֹ {1x} **d^e^yôw**, *deh-yo';* of uncert. der.; *ink:*—ink {1x}. See: TWOT—411e; BDB—188d, 192a.

1774. דִּי זָהָב {1x} **Dîy zâhâb**, *dee zaw-hawb';* as if from 1768 and 2091; *of gold; Dizahab,* a place in the Desert:—Dizahab {1x}. See: BDB—191d.

1775. דִּימוֹן {2x} **Dîymôwn**, *dee-mone';* perh. for 1769; *Dimon,* a place in Pal.:—Dimon {1x}. See: BDB—192a.

1776. דִּימוֹנָה {1x} **Dîymôwnâh**, *dee-mo-naw';* fem. of 1775; *Dimonah,* a place in Pal.:—Dimonah {1x}. See: BDB—192a.

1777. דִּין {24x} **dîyn**, *deen;* or (Gen 6:3)

דּוּן **dûwn**, *doon;* a prim. root [comp. 113]; to *rule;* by impl. to *judge* (as umpire); also to *strive* (as at law):—contend {1x}, execute (judgment) {1x}, judge {18x}, minister judgment {1x}, plead (the cause) {1x}, at strife {1x}, strive {1x}.

Diyn implies a settlement of what is right where there is a charge upon a person. *Diyn* is a judicial word marking the act whereby men's position and destiny are decided. Shaphath (8199) is an administrative word pointing to the mode in which men are to be governed and their affairs administered. See: TWOT—426; BDB—189b, 192a, 1088b.

1778. דִּין {2x} **dîyn** (Aram.), *deen;* corresp. to 1777; to *judge:*—judge {1x}, tread out {1x}. See: TWOT—2674; BDB—1088b.

1779. דִּין {20x} **dîyn**, *deen;* or (Job 19:29)

דּוּן **dûwn**, *doon;* from 1777; *judgement* (the suit, justice, sentence or tribunal); by impl. also *strife:*—cause {8x}, judgement {9x}, plea {2x}, strife {1x}. See: TWOT—426a; BDB—189b, 192c, 995a.

1780. דִּין {5x} **dîyn** (Aram.), *deen;* corresp. to 1779:—judgement {5x}. See: TWOT—2674?; BDB—1088b.

1781. דַּיָּן {2x} **dayân**, *dah-yawn';* from 1777; a *judge* or *advocate:*—judge {2x}. See: TWOT—426b; BDB—193a.

1782. דַּיָּן {1x} **dayân** (Aram.), *dah-yawn';* corresp. to 1781:—judge {1x}. See: TWOT—2674a; BDB—1088c.

1783. דִּינָה {8x} **Dîynâh**, *dee-naw';* fem. of 1779; *justice; Dinah,* the daughter of Jacob:—Dinah {8x}. See: BDB—192d.

1784. דִּינָי {1x} **Dîynay** (Aram.), *dee-nah'-ee;* patrial from an uncert. prim.; a *Dinaite* or inhab. of some unknown Ass. province:—Dinaite {1x}. See: BDB—1088c.

דִּיפַת **Dîyphath**. See 7384.

1785. דָּיֵק {6x} **dâyêq**, *daw-yake';* from a root corresp. to 1751; a *battering*-tower:—fort {6x}. See: TWOT—417a; BDB—189b, 193d.

1786. דַּיִשׁ {1x} **dayîsh**, *dah-yish';* from 1758; *threshing*-time:—threshing {1x}. See: TWOT—419a; BDB—190c, 193d.

1787. דִּישׁוֹן {7x} **Dîyshôwn**,

דִּישֹׁן **Dîyshôn**,

דִּשׁוֹן **Dîshôwn**, or

דִּשֹׁן **Dîshôn**, *dee-shone';* the same as 1788; *Dishon,* the name of two Edomites:—*Dishon* {7x}. See: BDB—190d, 193d.

1788. דִּישֹׁן {1x} **dîyshôn**, *dee-shone';* from 1758; the *leaper,* i.e. an *antelope:*—pygarg {1x}. See: TWOT—419c; BDB—190d, 193d.

1789. דִּישָׁן {5x} **Dîyshân**, *dee-shawn';* another form of 1787; *Dishan,* an Edomite:—Dishan {5x}. See: BDB—190d. 193d.

1790. דַּךְ {4x} **dak**, *dak;* from an unused root (comp. 1794); *crushed,* i.e. (fig.) *injured:*—afflicted {1x}, oppressed {3x}. See: TWOT—429a; BDB—194c.

1791. דֵּךְ {13x} **dêk** (Aram.), *dake;* or

דָּךְ **dâk** (Aram.), *dawk;* prol. from 1668; *this:*—the same {1x}, this {12x}. See: TWOT—2675; BDB—1080d, 1088c.

1792. דָּכָא {18x} **dâkâ'**, *daw-kaw';* a prim. root (comp. 1794); to *crumble;* tran. to *bruise* (lit. or fig.):—break {3x}, break in pieces {3x}, crush {3x}, bruise {2x}, destroy {2x}, contrite {1x}, smite {1x}, oppress {1x}, beat to pieces {1x}, humble {1x}. Syn.: 1854, 5310, 7489, 7533. See: TWOT—427; BDB—193d.

1793. דַּכָּא {3x} **dakkâ'**, *dak-kaw';* from 1792; *crushed* (lit. *powder,* or fig. *contrite*):—contrite {2x}, destruction {1x}. This word means to dash into pieces or crush. See: TWOT—427a, b; BDB—194b.

1794. דָּכָה {3x} **dâkâh**, *daw-kaw';* a prim. root (comp. 1790, 1792); to *collapse* (phys. or ment.):—break (sore) {3x}, contrite {1x}, crouch {1x}. See: TWOT—428; BDB—194d.

1795. דַּכָּה {1x} **dakkâh**, *dak-kaw';* from 1794 like 1793; *mutilated:*—+ wounded {1x}. See: TWOT—429b; BDB—194c.

1796. דֳּכִי {1x} **dŏkîy**, *dok-ee';* from 1794; a *dashing* of surf:—wave {1x}. See: TWOT—428a; BDB—194b.

1797. דִּכֵּן {1x} **dikkên** (Aram.), *dik-kane';* prol. from 1791; *this:*—same {1x}, that {1x}, this {1x}. See: TWOT—2676; BDB—1088c.

1798. דְּכַר {13} **d^e^kar** (Aram.), *dek-ar';* corresp. to 2145; prop. a *male,* i.e. of sheep:—ram {3x}. See: TWOT—2677a; BDB—1088d.

1799. דִּכְרוֹן {3x} **dikrôwn** (Aram.), *dik-rone';* or

דָּכְרָן **dokrân**, *dok-rawn'* (Aram.); corresp. to 2146; a *register:*—record {1x}. See: TWOT—2677b; BDB—1088d.

1800. דַּל {48x} **dal**, *dal;* from 1809; prop. *dangling,* i.e. (by impl.) *weak* or *thin:*—lean {1x}, needy {2x}, poor (man) {43x}, weaker {2x}.

Dal is "one who is low, poor, reduced, helpless, weak." **(1)** The dallim constituted the middle class of Israel—those who were physically deprived (in the ancient world the majority of people were poor). For example, the dallim may be viewed as the opposite of the rich (Ex 30:15; cf. Ruth 3:10; Prov 10:15). **(2)** In addition, the word may connote social poverty or lowliness. As such, *dal* describes those who are the counterparts of the great: "Ye shall do no unrighteousness in judgment: thou shalt not respect the person of the poor, nor honor the person of the mighty: but in righteousness shalt thou judge thy neighbor" (Lev 19:15; cf. Amos 2:7). **(3)** When Gideon challenged the Lord's summoning him to deliver Israel, he emphasized that his clan was too weak to do the job: "And he said unto him, Oh my Lord, wherewith shall I save Israel? behold, my family is poor in Manasseh . . ." (Judg 6:15; cf. 2 Sa 3:1). **(4)** God commands that society protect the poor, the lowly, and the weak: "Thou shalt not follow a multitude to do evil; neither shalt thou speak in a cause to decline after many to wrest judgment: neither shalt thou countenance a poor man in his cause" (Ex 23:2–3; cf. Lev 14:21; Is 10:2).

(5) He also warns that if men fail to provide justice, He will do so (Is 11:4). **(6)** In Gen 41:19 (the first biblical appearance of the word) *dal* is contrasted to "healthy" or "fat": "And behold, seven other kine came up after them, poor and very ill-favored and leanfleshed. . . ." **(6a)** Thus, *dal* indicates a physical condition and appearance of sickliness. **(6b)** It is used in this sense to describe Amnon's appearance as he longed for Tamar (2 Sa 13:4). **(7)** *Dal* is used (very infrequently) of spiritual poverty (in such cases it is sometimes paralleled to 'ebyon (34): "Therefore I said, Surely these are poor; they are foolish: for they know not the way of the Lord, nor the judgment of their God" (Jer 5:4). [Some scholars argue that here the word means "ignorance," and as the context shows, this is ignorance in the knowledge of God's word.] Syn: *Dal* is related to, but differs from, 'ani (6041 - which suggests affliction of some kind), 'ebyon (34 - which emphasizes need), and rash (7326 - which suggests destitution). See: TWOT—433a; BDB—194c, 195d.

1801. דָּלַג {5x} **dâlag**, *daw-lag';* a prim. root; to *spring:*—leap {5x}. See: TWOT—430; BDB—194c.

1802. דָּלָה {5x} **dâlâh**, *daw-law';* a prim. root (comp. 1809); prop. to *dangle,* i.e. to *let down* a bucket (for *drawing* out water); fig. to *deliver:*—draw out {3x}, enough {1x}, lift up {1x}. See: TWOT—431; BDB—194c.

1803. דַּלָּה {8x} **dallâh**, *dal-law';* from 1802, prop. something *dangling,* i.e. a loose *thread* or *hair;* fig. *indigent:*—poor {5x}, poorest sort {1x}, pinning sickness {1x}, hair {1x}.

Dallah, related to dal (1800) means "poverty; dishevelled hair." **(1)** The word appears in 2 Kin 24:14: ". . . none remained, save the poorest sort of the people of the land," where *dallah* emphasizes the social lowliness and "poverty" of those people whom it describes. **(2)** In Song 7:5 the word refers to "dishevelled hair" in the sense of something that hangs down. See: TWOT—433c; BDB—195d.

1804. דָּלַח {3x} **dâlach**, *daw-lakh';* a prim. root; to *roil* water:—trouble {3x}. See: TWOT—432; BDB—195c.

1805. דְּלִי {2x} **dᵉlîy**, *del-ee';* or

דֳּלִי **dŏlîy**, *dol-ee';* from 1802; a *pail* or *jar* (for *drawing* water):—bucket {2x}. See: TWOT—431c; BDB—194d.

1806. דְּלָיָה {7x} **Dᵉlâyâh**, *del-aw-yaw';* or (prol.)

דְּלָיָהוּ **Dᵉlâyâhûw**, *del-aw-yaw'-hoo;* from 1802 and 3050; *Jah has delivered; Delajah,* the name of five Isr.:—Dalaiah {1x}, Delaiah {6x}. See: BDB—195b.

1807. דְּלִילָה {6x} **Dᵉlîylâh**, *del-ee-law';* from 1809; *languishing; Delilah,* a Philistine woman:—Delilah {6x}. See: BDB—196a.

1808. דָּלִיָּה {8x} **dâlîyâh**, *daw-lee-yaw';* from 1802; something *dangling,* i.e. a *bough:*—branch {8x}. See: TWOT—431d; BDB—194d.

1809. דָּלַל {9x} **dâlal**, *daw-lal';* a prim. root (comp. 1802); to *slacken* or *be feeble;* fig. to *be oppressed:*—brought low {3x}, dried up {1x}, not equal {1x}, emptied {1x}, fail {1x}, impoverished {1x}, made thin {1x}.

Dalal means "to be low, hang down." **(1)** This verb appears always in poetical passages. **(2)** The word appears in Ps 79:8: "O remember not against us former iniquities: let thy tender mercies speedily prevent us; for we are brought very low." See: TWOT—433; BDB—195c.

1810. דִּלְעָן {1x} **Dilᶜân**, *dil-awn';* of uncert. der.; *Dilan,* a place in Pal.:—Dilean {1x}. See: 196a.

1811. דָּלַף {3x} **dâlaph**, *daw-laf';* a prim. root; to *drip;* by impl. to *weep:*—drop through {1x}, melt {1x}, pour out {1x}. See: TWOT—434; BDB—196a.

1812. דֶּלֶף {2x} **deleph**, *deh'-lef;* from 1811; a *dripping:* dropping {2x}. See: TWOT—434a; BDB—196a.

1813. דַּלְפוֹן {1x} **Dalphôwn**, *dal-fone';* from 1811; *dripping; Dalphon,* a son of Haman:—Dalphon {1x}. See: BDB—196a.

1814. דָּלַק {9x} **dâlaq**, *daw-lak';* a prim. root; to *flame* (lit. or fig.):—pursue {2x}, kindle {2x}, chase {1x}, persecute {1x}, persecutors {1x}, burning {1x}, inflame {1x}. See: TWOT—435; BDB—196a, 1088d.

1815. דְּלַק {1x} **dᵉlaq** (Aram.), *del-ak';* corresp. to 1814:—burn {1x}. See: TWOT—2678; BDB—1088d.

1816. דַּלֶּקֶת {1x} **dalleqeth**, *dal-lek'-keth;* from 1814; a *burning* fever:—inflammation {1x}. See: TWOT—435a; BDB—196b.

1817. דֶּלֶת {88x} **deleth**, *deh'-leth;* from 1802; something *swinging,* i.e. the *valve* of a door:—doors {69x}, gates {14x}, leaves {1x}, lid {1x}. See: TWOT—431a,e; BDB—194c, 194d, 195a, 196b. [In Ps 141:3, *dâl,* irreg.].

1818. דָּם {361x} **dâm**, *dawm;* from 1826 (comp. 119); *blood* (as that which when shed causes *death*) of man or an animal; by anal. the *juice* of the grape; fig. (espec. in the plur.) *bloodshed* (i.e. *drops* of blood):—blood {342x}, bloody {15x}, person + 5315 {1x}, bloodguiltiness {1x}, bloodthirsty + 582 {1x}, var. blood {1x}.

Dam means "blood." **(1)** *Dam* is used to denote the "blood" of animals, birds, and men (never of fish). **(2)** In Gen 9:4, "blood" is synonymous with "life": "But flesh with the life thereof, which is the blood thereof, shall ye not eat." **(3)** The high value of life as a gift of God led to the prohibition against eating "blood": "It shall be a perpetual statute for your generations throughout all your dwellings, that ye eat neither fat nor blood" (Lev 3:17). **(4)** Only infrequently does this word mean "blood-red," a color: "And they rose up early in the morning, and the sun shone upon the water, and the Moabites saw the water on the other side as red as blood" (2 Kin 3:22). **(5)** In two passages, *dam* represents "wine": "He washed his garments in wine, and his clothes in the blood of grapes" (Gen 49:11; cf. Deut 32:14).

(6) *Dam* bears several nuances. **(6a)** It can mean "blood shed by violence": "So ye shall not pollute the land wherein ye are: for blood it defileth the land: and the land cannot be cleansed of the blood that is shed therein . . ." (Num 35:33). **(6b)** Thus it can mean "death": "So will I send upon you famine and evil beasts, and they shall bereave thee; and pestilence and blood shall pass through thee; and I will bring the sword upon thee" (Eze 5:17). **(7)** Next, *dam* may connote an act by which a human life is taken, or blood is shed: "If there arise a matter too hard for thee in judgment, between blood and blood [one kind of homicide or another] . . ." (Deut 17:8).

(8) To "shed blood" is to commit murder: "Whoso sheddeth man's blood, by man shall his blood be shed . . ." (Gen 9:6). **(8a)** The second occurrence here means that the murderer shall suffer capital punishment. **(8b)** In other places, the phrase "to shed blood" refers to a nonritualistic slaughter of an animal: "What man soever there be of the house of Israel, that killeth an ox, or lamb . . . in the camp, or that killeth it out of the camp, and bringeth it not unto the door of the tabernacle of the congregation, to offer an offering unto the Lord before the tabernacle of the Lord; blood [guiltiness] shall be imputed unto that man" (Lev 17:3–4). **(9)** In judicial language, "to stand against one's blood" means to stand before a court and against the accused as a plaintiff, witness, or judge: "Thou shalt not go up and down as a talebearer among thy people: neither shalt thou stand against the blood [i.e., act against the life] of thy neighbor . . ." (Lev 19:16).

(10) The phrase, "his blood be on his head," signifies that the guilt and punishment for a violent act shall be on the perpetrator: "For everyone that curseth his father or his mother shall be surely put to death: he hath cursed his father or his mother; his blood [guiltiness] shall be upon him" (Lev 20:9). **(10a)** This phrase bears the added overtone that those who execute the punishment by killing the guilty party are not guilty of murder. **(10b)** So here "blood" means responsibility for one's dead: "And it shall be, that whosoever shall go out of the doors of thy house into the street, his blood shall be upon his head, and we will be guiltless: and whosoever shall be with thee in the house, his blood shall be on our head, if any hand be upon him" (Josh 2:19).

(11) Animal blood could take the place of a sinner's blood in atoning (covering) for sin: "For it is the blood that maketh an atonement for the soul" (Lev 17:11). **(11a)** Adam's sin merited death and brought death on all his posterity (cf. Rom 5:12); **(11b)** so the offering of an animal in substitution not only typified the payment of that penalty, but it symbolized that the perfect offering would bring life for Adam and all others represented by the sacrifice (cf. Heb. 10:4). **(11c)** The animal sacrifice prefigured and typologically represented the blood of Christ, who made the great and only effective substitutionary atonement, and whose offering was the only offering that gained life for those whom He represented. **(12c)** The shedding of His "blood" seals the covenant of life between God and man (cf. Matt. 26:28). See: TWOT—436; BDB—196b.

1819. דָּמָה {29x} **dâmâh**, *daw-maw';* a prim. root; to *compare;* by impl. to *resemble, liken, consider:*—like {14x}, liken {5x}, thought {6x}, compared {1x}, devised {1x}, meaneth {1x}, similitudes {1x}. *Damah* (1819) means "to be like, resemble, be or act like, liken or compare, devise, balance or ponder." **(1)** *Damah* means "to be like" in Ps 102:6: "I am like a pelican of the wilderness: I am like an owl of the desert." See: TWOT—437; BDB—197d, 1088d.

1820. דָּמָה {16x} **dâmâh**, *daw-maw';* a prim. root; to *be dumb* or *silent;* hence, to *fail* or *perish;* trans. to *destroy:*—cut off {3,x} cease {2x}, perish {2x}, bring to silence {2x}, liken {2x}, destroy {2x}, undone {1x}, utterly {1x}, cut down {1x}. See: TWOT—438; BDB—198c.

1821. דְּמָה {2x} **dᵉmâh** (Aram.), *dem-aw';* corresp. to 1819; to *resemble:*—be like {1x}. See: TWOT—2679; BDB—1088d.

1822. דֻּמָּה {1x} **dummâh**, *doom-maw';* from 1820; *desolation;* concr. *desolate:*—like the destroyed {1x}. See: TWOT—439b; BDB—199a.

1823. דְּמוּת {25x} **dᵉmûwth**, *dem-ooth'*; from 1819; *resemblance;* concr. *model, shape;* adv. *like:*—likeness {19x}, similitude {2x}, like {2x}, manner {1x}, fashion {1x}.

Demuwth means "likeness; shape; figure; form; pattern." **(1)** All but 5 of the 25 appearances of this word are in poetical or prophetical books of the Bible. **(2)** The word means "pattern," in the sense of the specifications from which an actual item is made: "Now King Ahaz went to Damascus . . . and saw an altar that *was* at Damascus: and king Ahaz sent to Urijah the priest the fashion of the altar, and the pattern of it, according to all the workmanship thereof" (2 Kin 16:10). **(3)** *Demuwth* means "shape" or "form," the thing(s) made after a given pattern. **(3a)** In 2 Chr 4:3 the word represents the "shape" of a bronze statue: "And under it was the similitude of oxen, which did compass it round about: ten in a cubit, compassing the sea round about."

(3b) In such passages *demuwth* means more than just "shape" in general; it indicates the "shape" in particular. **(3c)** In Eze 1:10, for example, the word represents the "form" or "likeness" of the faces of the living creatures Ezekiel describes. **(3d)** In Eze 1:26 the word refers to what something seemed to be rather than what it was: "And above the firmament that was over their heads was the likeness of a throne. . . ." **(4)** *Demuwth* signifies the original after which a thing is patterned: **(4a)** "To whom then will ye liken God? or what likeness will ye compare unto him?" (Is 40:18). **(4b)** This significance is in its first biblical appearance: "And God said, Let us make man in our image, after our likeness . . ." (Gen 1:26). **(5)** In Ps 58:4 the word appears to function merely to extend the form but not the meaning of the preposition ke: "Their poison is like the poison of a serpent. . . ." See: TWOT—437a; BDB—198b.

1824. דְּמִי {4x} **dᵉmîy**, *dem-ee'*; or

דֳּמִי **dŏmîy**, *dom-ee'*; from 1820; *quiet:*—cutting off {1x}, rest {1x}, silence {2x}. See: TWOT—438a; BDB—198c.

1825. דִּמְיוֹן **dimyôwn**, *dim-yone'*; from 1819; *resemblance:*—× like {1x}. See: TWOT—437b; BDB—198b.

1826. דָּמַם {30x} **dâmam**, *daw-mam'*; a prim. root [comp. 1724, 1820]; to *be dumb;* by impl. to *be astonished,* to *stop;* also to *perish:*—silence {6x}, still {6x}, silent {x}4, cut off {3x}, cut down {2x}, rest {2x}, cease {2x}, forbear 1, peace {1x}, quieted {1x}, tarry {1x}, wait {1x}. See: TWOT—439; BDB—198d, 199b.

1827. דְּמָמָה {3x} **dᵉmâmâh**, *dem-aw-maw'*; fem. from 1826; *quiet:*—calm {1x}, silence {1x}, still {1x}. See: TWOT—439a; BDB—199a.

1828. דֹּמֶן {6x} **dômen**, *do'-men;* of uncert. der.; *manure:*—dung {6x}. Syn.: 830, 1557, 2755, 6569, 6832. See: TWOT—441a; BDB—199b.

1829. דִּמְנָה {1x} **Dimnâh**, *dim-naw'*; fem. from the same as 1828; a *dung-heap; Dimnah,* a place in Pal.:—*Dimnah* {1x}. See: BDB—199b.

1830. דָּמַע {2x} **dâmaᶜ**, *daw-mah'*; a prim. root; to *weep:*—× sore {1x}, weep {1x}. See: BDB—199c.

1831. דֶּמַע {1x} **demaᶜ**, *dah'-mah;* from 1830; a *tear;* fig. *juice:*—liquor {1x}. Syn.: 4197, 4952. See: TWOT—442a; BDB—199c.

1832. דִּמְעָה {23x} **dimᶜâh**, *dim-aw'*; fem. of 1831; *weeping:*—tears {23x}. See: TWOT—442b; BDB—199c.

1833. דְּמֶשֶׁק {1x} **dᵉmesheq**, *dem-eh'-shek;* by orth. var. from 1834; *damask* (as a fabric of Damascus):—in Damascus {1x}. See: TWOT—433?; BDB—200a.

1834. דַּמֶּשֶׂק {45x} **Dammeseq**, *dam-meh'-sek;* or

דּוּמֶּשֶׂק **Dûwmeseq**, *doo-meh'-sek;* or

דַּרְמֶשֶׂק **Darmeseq**, *dar-meh'-sek;* of for. or.; *Damascus,* a city of Syria:—Damascus {44x}, Syriadamascus {1x}. See: BDB—199d, 204b, 217a.

1835. דָּן {71x} **Dân**, *dawn;* from 1777; *judge; Dan,* one of the sons of Jacob; also the tribe descended from him, and its territory; likewise a place in Pal. colonized by them:—*Dan* {71x}. See: BDB—75a, 192d, 200a.

1836. דֵּן {57x} **dên** (Aram.), *dane;* an orth. var. of 1791; *this:*—this {38x}, these {3x}, thus {2x}, hereafter {1x}, that {1x}, misc. {12x} = aforetime, + after this manner, one . . . another, such, therefore, wherefore, which. See: TWOT—2680; BDB—1080d, 1088d, 1096c.

דָּנִאֵל **Dânîʾêl**. See 1841.

1837. דַּנָּה {1x} **Dannâh**, *dan-naw'*; of uncert. der.; *Dannah,* a place in Pal.:—*Dannah* {1x}. See: BDB—200a.

1838. דִּנְהָבָה {1x} **Dinhâbâh**, *din-haw-baw'*; of uncert. der.; *Dinhabah,* an Edomitish town:—*Dinhabah* {2x}. See: BDB—200b.

1839. דָּנִי {5x} **Dânîy**, *daw-nee';* patron. from 1835; a *Danite* (often collect.) or desc. (or inhab.) of Dan:—Danites {4x}, of Dan {1x}. See: BDB—193a.

1840. דָּנִיֵּאל {29x} **Dânîyêʾl**, *daw-nee-yale';* in Eze.

דָּנִאֵל **Dânîʾêl**, *daw-nee-ale';* from 1835 and 410; *judge of God; Daniel* or *Danijel,* the name of two Isr.:—*Daniel* {29x}. See: BDB—193a, 200a, 200b.

1841. דָּנִיֵּאל {42x} **Dânîyêʾl** (Aram.), *daw-nee-yale';* corresp. to 1840; *Danijel,* the Heb. prophet:—Daniel {42x}. See: BDB—1088c.

1842. דָּן יַעַן {1x} **Dân Yaᶜan**, *dawn yah'-an;* from 1835 and (appar.) 3282; *judge of purpose; Dan-Jaan,* a place in Pal.:—Dan-jaan {1x}. See: BDB—193a, 419a.

1843. דֵּעַ **dêaᶜ**, *day'-ah;* from 3045; *knowledge:*—knowledge {2x}, opinion {3x}. Syn.: 1844, 1847. See: TWOT—848; BDB—200b, 395b.

1844. דֵּעָה {1x} **dêᶜâh**, *day-aw';* fem. of 1843; *knowledge:*—knowledge {6x}. Syn.: 1847. See: TWOT—848b; BDB—200b, 395c.

1845. דְּעוּאֵל {4x} **Dᵉᶜûwʾêl**, *deh-oo-ale';* from 3045 and 410; *known of God; Deel,* an Isr.:—Deuel {1x}. See: BDB—200b, 396a.

1846. דָּעַךְ {9x} **dâᶜak**, *daw-ak';* a prim. root; to *be extinguished;* fig. to *expire* or *be dried up:*—be extinct {1x}, consumed {1x}, put out {6x}, quenched {1x}. Syn.: 2193, 3518. See: TWOT—445; BDB—200b.

1847. דַּעַת {93x} **daᶜath**, *dah'-ath;* from 3045; *knowledge:*—knowledge {82x}, know {6x}, cunning {1x}, unwittingly 2 + 1097 {2x}, ignorantly + 1097 {1x}, unawares + 1097 {1x}.

Da'ath means "knowledge." **(1)** Several nouns are formed from yada' (3045) and the most frequently occurring is *da'ath* which appears 93 times in the Old Testament. **(2)** One appearance is in Gen 2:9: ". . . and the tree of knowledge of good and evil." **(2)** The word also appears in Ex 31:3. Syn.: 1843, 1844. See: TWOT—848c; BDB—200b, 395c.

1848. דֹּפִי {1x} **dôphîy**, *dof'-ee;* from an unused root (mean. to *push* over); a *stumbling*-block:—slanderest {1x}. Syn.: 1681, 3960, 7270. See: TWOT—446a; BDB—200c.

1849. דָּפַק {3x} **dâphaq**, *daw-fak';* a prim. root; to *knock;* by anal. to *press* severely:—beat {1x}, knock {1x}, overdrive {1x}. See: TWOT—447; BDB—200c.

1850. דָּפְקָה {2x} **Dophqâh**, *dof-kaw';* from 1849; a *knock; Dophkah,* a place in the Desert:—Dophkah {2x}. See: BDB—200c.

1851. דַּק {41x} **daq**, *dak;* from 1854; *crushed,* i.e. (by impl.) *small* or *thin:*—thin {5x}, small {5x}, leanfleshed + 1320 {2x}, dwarf {1x}, little thing {1x}. See: TWOT—448a; BDB—200c, 201a.

1852. דֹּק {1x} **dôq**, *doke;* from 1854; something *crumbling,* i.e. *fine* (as a *thin* cloth):—curtain {1x}. See: TWOT—448b; BDB—200c, 201a.

1853. דִּקְלָה {2x} **Diqlâh**, *dik-law';* of for. or.; *Diklah,* a region of Arabia:—Diklah {1x}. See: BDB—200c.

1854. דָּקַק {13x} **dâqaq**, *daw-kak';* a prim. root [comp. 1915]; to *crush* (or intr.) *crumble:*—beat small {2x}, powder {2x}, stamp {2x}, stamp small {2x}, bruise {2x}, small {1x}, made dust {1x}, beat in pieces {1x}. See: TWOT—448; BDB—200d, 1089c.

1855. דְּקַק {10x} **dᵉqaq** (Aram.), *dek-ak';* corresp. to 1854; to *crumble* or (trans.) *crush:*—break to pieces {1x}. See: TWOT—2681; BDB—1089a.

1856. דָּקַר **dâqar**, *daw-kar';* a prim. root; to *stab;* by anal. to *starve;* fig. to *revile:*—thrust through {8x}, pierced {1x}, wounded {1x}, stricken through {1x}. See: TWOT—449; BDB—201a.

1857. דֶּקֶר {1x} **Deqer**, *deh'-ker;* from 1856; a *stab; Deker,* an Isr.:—Dekar {1x}. See: BDB—201b.

1858. דַּר {1x} **dar**, *dar;* appar. from the same as 1865; prop. a *pearl* (from its sheen as rapidly *turned*); by anal. *pearl-stone,* i.e. mother-of-pearl or alabaster:—white {1x} Syn.: 3835, 3836, 6713. See: TWOT—454a; BDB—201b, 204d.

1859. דָּר {4x} **dâr** (Aram.), *dawr;* corresp. to 1755; an *age:*—generation {1x}. See: TWOT—2669a; BDB—1087b, 1089a.

דֹּר **dôr**. See 1755.

1860. דְּרָאוֹן **dᵉrâʾôwn**, *der-aw-one';* or

דֵּרָאוֹן {2x} **dêraʾôwn**, *day-raw-one';* from an unused root (mean. to *repulse*); an obj. of *aversion:*—abhorring {1x}, contempt {1x}. See: TWOT—450a; BDB—201b.

1861. דָּרְבוֹן {1x} **dorbôwn**, *dor-bone'* [also *dorbawn'*]; of uncert. der.; a *goad:*—goad {2x}. See: TWOT—451a,b; BDB—201c.

1862. דַּרְדַּע {1x} **Dardaᶜ**, *dar-dah';* appar. from 1858 and 1843; *pearl of knowledge; Darda,* an Isr.:—*Darda* {1x}. See: BDB—201c.

1863. דַּרְדַּר {2x} **dardar**, *dar-dar';* of uncert. der.; a *thorn:*—thistle {1x}. See: TWOT—454e; BDB—201d 205a.

1864. דָּרוֹם {17x} **dârôwm**, *daw-rome';* of uncert. der.; the *south;* poet. the *south wind:*—south {1x}. See: TWOT—454d; BDB—201d, 204.

1865. דְּרוֹר {8x} **dᵉrôwr**, *der-ore';* from an unused root (mean. to *move rapidly*); *freedom;* hence, *spontaneity* of outflow, and so *clear:*—liberty {7x}, pure {1x}. See: TWOT—454b; BDB—204d.

1866. דְּרוֹר {2x} **dᵉrôwr**, *der-ore';* the same as 1865, applied to a bird; the *swift,* a kind of swallow:—swallow {2x}. See: TWOT—454c; BDB—204d.

1867. דָּרְיָוֶשׁ {10x} **Dârᵉyâvêsh**, *daw-reh-yaw-vaysh';* of Pers. or.; *Darejavesh,* a title (rather than name) of several Pers. kings:—Darius {1x}. See: BDB—201d, 1089a.

1868. דָּרְיָוֶשׁ {15x} **Dârᵉyâvêsh** (Aram.), *daw-reh-yaw-vaysh';* corresp. to 1867:—Darius {15x}. See: BDB—1089a.

1869. דָּרַךְ {62x} **dârak**, *daw-rak';* a prim. root; to *tread;* by impl. to *walk;* also to *string* a bow (by treading on it in bending):—tread {23x}, bend {8x}, bent {7x}, lead {4x}, archer {2x}, tread down {2x}, come {1x}, go {2x}, treader {2x}, tread upon {2x}, walk {2x}, drew {1x}, lead forth {1x}, guide {1x}, tread out {1x}, go over {1x}, shoot {1x}, thresh {1x}. See: TWOT—453; BDB—201d.

1870. דֶּרֶךְ {705x} **derek**, *deh'-rek;* from 1869; a *road* (as *trodden*); fig. a *course* of life or *mode* of action, often adv.:—way {590x}, toward {31x}, journey {23x}, manner {8x}, misc. {53x} = along, away, because of, + by, conversation, custom, eastward, passenger, through, highway, pathway, wayside, whither, whithersoever.

Derek means "way (path, road, highway); distance; journey; manner, conduct; condition; destiny." **(1)** First, this word refers to a path, a road, or a highway. In Gen 3:24 (the first occurrence of the word) it means "path" or "route": ". . . And he placed at the east of the garden of Eden cherubim, and a flaming sword which turned every [direction], to [guard] the way of the tree of life." **(2)** Sometimes, as in Gen 16:7, the word represents a pathway, road, or route: "And the angel of the Lord found her by a fountain of water in the wilderness, by the fountain in the way to Shur." **(3)** The actual road itself is represented in Gen 38:21: "Where is the [temple prostitute], that was openly by the wayside?" **(4)** In Num 20:17 the word means "highway," a well-known and well-traveled road: ". . . We will go by the king's highway, we will not turn to the right hand nor to the left, until we have passed thy borders."

(5) This noun represents a "distance" (how far or how long) between two points: "And he set three days' journey [a distance of three days] betwixt himself and Jacob . . ." (Gen 30:36). **(6)** In other passages *derek* refers to the action or process of "taking a journey": "And to his father he sent after this manner; ten asses laden with the good things of Egypt, and ten she asses laden with corn and bread and meat for his father by the way [on the journey]" (Gen 45:23). **(7)** In an extended nuance *derek* means "undertaking": "If thou turn away thy foot from the sabbath, from doing thy pleasure on my holy day; and call the sabbath a delight, the holy of the Lord, honorable; and shalt honor him, not doing thine own ways, nor finding thine own pleasure . . ." (Is 58:13). Cf. Gen 24:21: "And the man wondering at her held his peace, to wit whether the Lord had made his journey prosperous or not" (cf. Deut 28:29).

(8) In another emphasis this word connotes how and what one does, a "manner, custom, behavior, mode of life": "Our father is old, and there is not a man in the earth to come in unto us after the manner of all the earth" (Gen 19:31). **(9)** In 1 Kin 2:4 *derek* is applied to an activity that controls one, one's life-style: "If thy children take heed to their way, to walk before me in truth with all their heart and with all their soul, there shall not fail thee . . . a man on the throne of Israel." **(10)** In 1 Kin 16:26 *derek* is used of Jeroboam's attitude: "For he walked in all the way of Jeroboam the son of Nebat, and in his sin wherewith he made Israel to sin. . . ." **(11)** Deeds, or specific acts, may be connoted by this noun: "Lo, these are parts of his ways; but how little a portion is heard of him? But the thunder of his power who can understand?" (Job 26:14).

(12) Derek refers to a "condition" in the sense of what has happened to someone. This is clear by the parallelism of Is 40:27: "Why sayest thou, O Jacob, and speakest, O Israel, My way is hid from the Lord, and [the justice due to me is passed away] from my God?" **(13)** In one passage *derek* signifies the overall course and fixed path of one's life, or his "destiny": "O Lord, I know that the way of man is not in himself: it is not in man that walketh to direct his steps" (Jer 10:23). **(14)** This word sometimes seems to bear the meaning of "power" or "rulership": "Only acknowledge thine iniquity, that thou hast transgressed against the Lord thy God, and hast scattered thy ways to the strangers under every green tree . . ." (Jer 3:13; cf. Job 26:14; 36:23; 40:19; Ps 67:2; 110:7; 119:37; 138:5; Prov 8:22; 19:16; 31:3; Hos 10:13; Amos 8:14). Some scholars, however, contest this explanation of these passages. Syn.: 734, 5410. See: TWOT—453a; BDB—202c, 1008b.

1871. דַּרְכְּמוֹן {4x} **darkᵉmôwn**, *dar-kem-one';* of Pers. or.; a "*drachma*," or coin:—dram {1x}. Syn.: 150. See: TWOT—453c; BDB—204b.

1872. דְּרָע {1x} **dᵉrâʿ** (Aram.), *der-aw';* corresp. to 2220; an *arm:*—arm {1x}. See: TWOT—2682a; BDB—1089a.

1873. דָּרַע {1x} **Dâraʿ**, *daw-rah';* prob. contr. from 1862; *Dara,* an Isr.:—*Dara* {1x}. See: BDB—201d, 204c.

1874. דַּרְקוֹן {2x} **Darqôwn**, *dar-kone';* of uncert. der.; *Darkon,* one of "Solomon's servants":—Darkon {1x}. See: BDB—204c.

1875. דָּרַשׁ {164x} **dârash**, *daw-rash';* a prim. root; prop. to *tread* or *frequent;* usually to *follow* (for pursuit or search); by impl. to *seek* or *ask;* spec. to *worship:*—seek {84x}, enquire {43x}, require {12x}, search {7x}, misc. {18x}: ask, × at all, care for, × diligently, make inquisition, [necro-] mancer, question, seek for, seek out, × surely.

Darash means "to seek, inquire, consult, ask, require, frequent." **(1)** Occurring more than 160 times in the Old Testament, *darash* is first used in Gen 9:5: "And surely your blood of your lives will I require . . ." It often has the idea of avenging an offense against God or the shedding of blood (see Eze 33:6). **(2)** One of the most frequent uses of this word is in the expression "to inquire of God," which sometimes **(2a)** indicates a private seeking of God in prayer for direction (Gen 25:22), and often **(2b)** it refers to the contacting of a prophet who would be the instrument of God's revelation (1 Sa 9:9; 1 Kin 22:8). **(3)** At other times this expression is found in connection with the use of the Urim and Thummim by the high priest as **(3a)** he sought to discover the will of God by the throwing of these sacred stones (Num 27:21). **(3b)** Just what was involved is not clear, but it may be presumed that only yes-or-no questions could be answered by the manner in which these stones fell.

(4) Pagan people and sometimes even apostate Israelites "inquired of" heathen gods. **(4a)** Thus, Ahaziah instructed messengers: "Go, inquire of Baal-zebub the god of Ekron whether I shall recover of this disease" (2 Kin 1:2). **(4b)** In gross violation of the Mosaic law (Deut 18:10–11), Saul went to the witch of Endor "to inquire of" her, which in this instance meant that she was to call up the spirit of the dead prophet Samuel. Saul went to the witch of Endor as a last resort, saying, "Seek me a woman that hath a familiar spirit, that I may go to her, and enquire of her. (1 Sa 28:7). **(5)** This word is often used to describe the "seeking of" the Lord in the sense of entering into covenantal relationship with Him. **(6)** The prophets often used *darash* as they called on the people to make an about-face in living and instead "seek ye the Lord while he may be found . . ." (Is 55:6). See: TWOT—455; BDB—201d, 205a.

1876. דָּשָׁא {2x} **dâshâʾ**, *daw-shaw';* a prim. root; to *sprout:*—bring forth {1x}, spring {1x}. See: TWOT—456; BDB—205d.

1877. דֶּשֶׁא {15x} **desheʾ**, *deh'-sheh;* from 1876; a *sprout;* by anal. *grass:*—(tender) grass {8x}, green {1x}, (tender) herb {6x}. See: TWOT—456a; BDB—206a, 1089b.

1878. דָּשֵׁן {11x} **dâshên**, *daw-shane';* a prim. root; to *be fat;* tran. to *fatten* (or regard as fat); spec. to *anoint;* fig. to *satisfy;* denom. (from 1880) to *remove* (fat) *ashes* (of sacrifices):—accept {1x}, anoint {1x}, take away the ashes {1x}, receive his ashes from {1x}, made fat {6x}, wax fat {1x}. See: TWOT—457; BDB—206a.

1879. דָּשֵׁן {3x} **dâshên**, *daw-shane';* from 1878; *fat;* fig. *rich, fertile:*—fat {3x}. See: TWOT—457b; BDB—206c.

1880. דֶּשֶׁן {15x} **deshen**, *deh'-shen;* from 1878; the *fat;* abstr. *fatness,* i.e. (fig.) *abundance;* spec. the (fatty) *ashes* of sacrifices:—ashes {8x}, fatness {7x}. See: TWOT—457a; BDB—206b.

1881. דָּת {22x} **dâth**, *dawth;* of uncert. (perh. for.) der.: a royal *edict* or statute:—law {9x}, decree {9x}, commandment {2x}, manner {1x}, commission {1x}. Syn.: 1882, 4941, 8451. See: TWOT—458; BDB—206c, 1089b.

1882. דָּת {14x} **dâth** (Aram.), *dawth;* corresp. to 1881:—decree {3x}, law {11x}. See: TWOT—2683; BDB—1089b.

1883. דֶּתֶא {2x} **detheʾ** (Aram.), *deh'-thay;* corresp. to 1877:—tender grass {2x}. See: TWOT—2684; BDB—1089b.

1884. דְּתָבָר {2x} **dᵉthâbâr** (Aram.), *deth-aw-bawr';* of Pers. or.; mean. one *skilled in law;* a *judge:*—counselor {2x}. See: TWOT—2685; BDB—1089b.

1885. דָּתָן {10x} **Dâthân**, *daw-thawn';* of uncert. der.; *Dathan,* an Isr.:—Dathan {10x}. See: BDB—206d.

1886. דֹּתָן {3x} **Dôthân**, *do'-thawn;* or (Chaldaizing dual)

דֹּתַיִן **Dôthayin** (Gen 37:17), *do-thah'-yin;* of uncert. der.; *Dothan,* a place in Pal.:—Dothan {3x}. See: BDB—206d.

ה

1887. הֵא {2x} **hê'**, *hay;* a prim. particle; *lo!:*—behold {1x}, lo {1x}. See: TWOT—461; BDB—210c, 1089c.

1888. הֵא {2x} **hê'** (Aram.), *hay;* or

הָא **hâ'** (Aram.), *haw;* corresp. to 1887:—even {1x}, lo {1x}. See: TWOT—02687, 02688; BDB—1089c.

1889. הֶאָח {13x} **he'âch**, *heh-awkh';* from 1887 and 253; *aha!:*—ah, aha, ha {13x}. See: TWOT—462; BDB—210c.

הָאֲרָרִי **Hâ'rârîy**. See 2043.

1890. הַבְהָב {1x} **habhâb**, *hab-hawb';* by redupl. from 3051; *gift* (in sacrifice), i.e. *holocaust:*—offering {1x}. See: TWOT—849b; BDB—210c, 396d.

1891. הָבַל {5x} **hâbal**, *haw-bal';* a prim. root; to *be vain* in act, word, or expectation; spec. to *lead astray:*—become vain {4x}, make vain {1x}. See: TWOT—463; BDB—211a.

1892. הֶבֶל {73x} **hebel**, *heh'-bel;* or (rarely in the abs.)

הֲבֵל **hăbêl**, *hab-ale';* from 1891; *emptiness* or *vanity;* fig. Something *transitory* and *unsatisfactory;* often used as an adv.:—vanity {61x}, vain {11x}, altogether {1x}.

Hebel means "breath; vanity; idol." **(1)** All but 4 of its 73 occurrences are in poetry (37 in Ecclesiastes). **(2)** The word represents human "breath" as a transitory thing: "I loathe it; I would not live always: let me alone; for my days are vanity [literally, but a breath]" (Job 7:16). **(3)** *Hebel* means something meaningless and purposeless: "Vanity of vanities, saith the Preacher, vanity of vanities; all is vanity" (Eccl 1:2). Cotton candy is an excellent example; it appears to offer a lot, when in reality it disappears when sampled. **(4)** This word signifies an "idol," which is unsubstantial, worthless, and vain: "They have moved me to jealousy with that which is not God; they have provoked me to anger with their vanities . . ." (Deut 32:21—the first occurrence). See: TWOT—463a; BDB—210c.

1893. הֶבֶל {8x} **Hebel**, *heh'-bel;* the same as 1892; *Hebel,* the son of Adam:—Abel {8x}. See: BDB—211a.

1894. הֹבֶן {1x} **hôben**, *ho'-ben;* only in plur., from an unused root mean. to *be hard; ebony:*—ebony {1x}. See: TWOT—464; BDB—211b.

1895. הָבַר {1x} **hâbar**, *haw-bar';* a prim. root of uncert. (perh. for.) der.; to *be a horoscopist:*—astrologer {1x}. Syn.: 825, 826. See: TWOT—465; BDB—211b.

1896. הֵגֵא {4x} **Hêgê'**, *hay-gay';* or (by perm.)

הֵגַי **Hêgay**, *hay-gah'-ee;* prob. of Pers. or.; *Hege* or *Hegai,* a eunuch of Xerxes:—Hegai {13}, Hege {1x}. See: BDB—211b, 212b.

1897. הָגָה {25x} **hâgâh**, *haw-gaw';* a prim. root [comp. 1901]; to *murmur* (in pleasure or anger); by impl. to *ponder:*—imagine {2x}, meditate {6x}, mourn {4x}, mutter {2x}, roar {1x}, × sore {1x}, speak {4x}, study {2x}, talk {1x}, utter {2x}.

Hagah means "to meditate, moan, growl, utter, speak." **(1)** Found only 25 times in the Hebrew Old Testament, **(1a)** it seems to be an onomatopoetic term, reflecting the sighing and low sounds one may make while musing, at least as the ancients practiced it. **(1b)** This meaning is seen in its first occurrence in the text: "This book of the law shall not depart out of thy mouth; but thou shalt meditate therein day and night . . ." (Josh 1:8). **(2)** Perhaps the most famous reference "to meditating" on the law day and night is Ps 1:2.

(3) *Hagah* also expresses the "growl" of lions (Is 31:4) and the "mourning" of doves (Is 38:14). **(4)** When the word is used in the sense of "to mourn," it apparently emphasizes the sorrowful sounds of mourning, as seen in this parallelism: "Therefore will I howl for Moab, and I will cry out for all Moab; mine heart shall mourn for the men of Kir-heres" (Jer 48:31). **(5)** The idea that mental exercise, planning, often is accompanied by low talking seems to be reflected by Prov 24:1–2: "Be not thou envious against evil men, . . . for their heart studieth destruction, and their lips talk of mischief." Syn.: 2803, 7878. See: TWOT—467; BDB—211c.

1898. הָגָה {3x} **hâgâh**, *haw-gaw';* a prim. root; to *remove:*—stay {1x}, take away {2x}. See: TWOT—468; BDB—212a.

1899. הֶגֶה {3x} **hegeh**, *heh'-geh;* from 1897; a *muttering* (in sighing, thought, or as thunder):—mourning {1x}, sound {1x}, tale {1x}. See: TWOT—467a; BDB—211d.

1900. הָגוּת {1x} **hâgûwth**, *haw-gooth';* from 1897; *musing:*—meditation {1x}. See: TWOT—467b; BDB—212a.

1901. הָגִיג {2x} **hâgîyg**, *haw-gheeg';* from an unused root akin to 1897; prop. a *murmur,* i.e. *complaint:*—meditation {1x}, musing {1x}. See: TWOT—466a; BDB—211c.

1902. הִגָּיוֹן {4x} **higgâyôwn**, *hig-gaw-yone';* intens. from 1897; a *murmuring* sound, i.e. a musical notation (prob. similar to the modern *affettuoso* to indicate solemnity of movement); by impl. a *machination:*—device {1x}, Higgaion {1x}, meditation {1x}, solemn sound {1x}. See: TWOT—467c; BDB—212a.

1903. הָגִין {1x} **hâgîyn**, *haw-gheen';* of uncert. der.; perh. *suitable* or *turning:*—directly {1x}. See: TWOT—469a; BDB—212b.

1904. הָגָר {12x} **Hâgâr**, *haw-gawr';* of uncert. (perhaps for.) der.; *Hagar,* the mother of Ishmael:—Hagar {12x}. See: BDB—212b.

1905. הַגְרִי {3x} **Hagrîy**, *hag-ree';* or (prol.)

הַגְרִיא **Hagrîy'**, *hag-ree';* perh. patron. from 1904; a *Hagrite* or member of a certain Arabian clan:—Hagarene {1x}, Hagarite {1x}, Haggeri {1x}. See: BDB—212b, 212c.

1906. הֵד {1x} **hêd**, *hade;* for 1959; a *shout:*—sounding again {1x}. See: TWOT—471b; BDB—212c, 212d.

1907. הַדָּבָר {4x} **haddâbâr** (Aram.), *had-dawbawr';* prob. of for. origin; a *vizier:*—counselor {4x}. See: TWOT—2689; BDB—1089c.

1908. הֲדַד {12x} **Hădad**, *had-ad';* prob. of for. or. [comp. 111]; *Hadad,* the name of an idol, and of several kings of Edom:—Hadad {12x}. See: TWOT—471c; BDB—212d.

1909. הֲדַדְעֶזֶר {9x} **Hădad'ezer**, *had-ad-eh'-zer;* from 1908 and 5828; *Hadad* (is his) *help; Hadadezer,* a Syrian king:—Hadadezer {9x}. Syn.: comp. 1928. See: BDB—212d.

1910. הֲדַדְרִמּוֹן {1x} **Hădadrimmôwn**, *had-ad-rim-mone';* from 1908 and 7417; *Hadad-Rimmon,* a place in Pal.:—Hadad-rimmon {1x}. 213a. See: BDB—213a.

1911. הָדָה {1x} **hâdâh**, *haw-daw';* a prim. root [comp. 3034]; to *stretch forth* the hand:—put. {1x}. See: TWOT—472; BDB—213a.

1912. הֹדוּ {2x} **Hôdûw**, *ho'-doo;* of for. or.; *Hodu* (i.e. Hindû-stan):—India {2x}. See: BDB—213a.

1913. הֲדוֹרָם {4x} **Hădôwrâm**, *had-o-rawm';* or

הֲדֹרָם **Hădôrâm**, *had-o-rawm';* prob. of for. der.; *Hadoram,* a son of Joktan, and the tribe descended from him:—Hadoram {4x}. See: BDB—213a, 214c.

1914. הִדַּי {1x} **Hidday**, *hid-dah'ee;* of uncert. der.; *Hiddai,* an Isr.:—Hiddai {1x}. See: BDB—213b, 301b.

1915. הָדַךְ {1x} **hâdak**, *haw-dak';* a prim. root [comp. 1854]; to *crush* with the foot:—tread down {1x}. See: TWOT—473; BDB—213b. Syn.: 947, 1758, 1869, 7429.

1916. הֲדֹם {6x} **hădôm**, *had-ome';* from an unused root mean. to *stamp* upon; a foot-*stool:*—footstool + 7272 {6x}. Syn.: 3534. See: TWOT—474; BDB—213b.

1917. הַדָּם {2x} **haddâm** (Aram.), *had-dawm';* from a root corresp. to that of 1916; something *stamped* to pieces, i.e. a *bit:*—pieces {1x}. See: TWOT—2690; BDB—1089d.

1918. הֲדַס {6x} **hădaç**, *had-as';* of uncert. der.; the *myrtle:*—myrtle {2x}, myrtle tree {4x}. See: TWOT—475; BDB—213c.

1919. הֲדַסָּה {1x} **Hădaççâh**, *had-as-saw';* fem. of 1918; *Hadassah* (or Esther):—Hadassah {1x}. See: BDB—213c.

1920. הָדַף {1x} **hâdaph**, *haw-daf';* a prim root; to *push* away or down:—thrust {3x}, drive {3x}, cast out {2x}, expel {1x}, thrust away {1x}, cast away {1x}. Syn.: 1644, 5974, 5090. See: TWOT—476; BDB—213c.

1921. הָדַר {7x} **hâdar**, *haw-dar';* a prim. root; to *swell* up (lit. or fig., act. or pass.); by impl. to *favor* or *honour, be high* or *proud:*—honour {3x}, countenance {1x}, crooked places {1x}, glorious {1x}, put forth {1x}.

Hadar means "to honor, prefer, exalt oneself, behave arrogantly." **(1)** This verb, which appears 7 times in biblical Hebrew means "to honor" or "to prefer" in Ex 23:3: "Neither shalt thou countenance a poor man in his cause." **(2)** In Prov 25:6 *hadar* means "to exalt oneself" or "to behave arrogantly." See: TWOT—477; BDB—213d, 1089d.

1922. הֲדַר {3x} **hădar** (Aram.), *had-ar';* corresp. to 1921; to *magnify* (fig.):—glorify {1x}, honour {2x}. See: TWOT—2691; BDB—1089d.

1923. הֲדַר {3x} **hădar** (Aram.), *had-ar';* from 1922; *magnificence:*—honour {2x}, majesty {1x}. See: TWOT—2691a; BDB—1089d.

1924. הֲדַר {1x} **Hădar**, *had-ar';* the same as 1926; *Hadar,* an Edomite:—Hadar {1x}. See: BDB—214c.

1925. הֶדֶר {1x} **heder**, *heh'-der;* from 1921; *honour;* used (fig.) for the *capital* city (Jerusalem):—glory {1x}. See: BDB—214a.

1926. הָדָר {30x} **hâdâr**, *haw-dawr';* from 1921; *magnificence*, i.e. ornament or splendor:—glory {7x}, majesty {7x}, honour {5x}, beauty {4x}, comeliness {3x}, excellency {2x}, glorious {1x}, goodly {1x}.

Hadar means "honor; splendor." **(1)** Its 30 appearances in the Bible are exclusively in poetic passages and in all periods. **(2)** *Hadar* refers to "splendor" in nature: "And ye shall take you on the first day the boughs of goodly trees [literally, trees of splendor or beauty] . . ." (Lev 23:40—the first occurrence). **(3)** This word is a counterpart to Hebrew words for "glory" and "dignity." **(3a)** Thus *hadar* means not so much overwhelming beauty as a combination of physical attractiveness and social position. **(3b)** The Messiah is said to have "no form nor [majesty]; and when we shall see him, there is no beauty that we should desire him" (Is 53:2). **(4)** Mankind is crowned with "glory and honor" in the sense of superior desirability (for God) and rank (Ps 8:5). **(5)** In Prov 20:29 *hadar* focuses on the same idea—an aged man's mark of rank and privilege is his gray hair. This reflects the theme present throughout the Bible that long life is a mark of divine blessing and results (often) when one is faithful to God, whereas premature death is a result of divine judgment.

(6) The ideas of glorious brilliance, preeminence, and lordship are included in *hadar* when it is applied to God: "Glory and honor are in his presence; strength and gladness are in his place" (1 Chr 16:27). **(6a)** Not only are these characteristics of His sanctuary (Ps 96:6) **(6b)** but He is clothed with them (Ps 104:1). **(7)** God gave David all good things: a crown of gold on his head, long life, and glory or "splendor" and majesty (Ps 21:3–5). **(8)** In the case of earthly kings their beauty or brilliance usually arises from their surroundings. So God says of Tyre: "They of Persia and of Lud and of Phut were in thine army, thy men of war: they hanged the shield and helmet in thee; they set forth thy comeliness [honor]. The men of Arvad with thine army were upon thy walls round about, and the Gammadim were in thy towers: they hanged their shields upon thy walls round about; they have made thy beauty perfect" (Eze 27:10–11). **(9)** God, however, manifests the characteristic of "honor or splendor" in Himself. Syn.: 3519. See: TWOT—477b; BDB—214a.

1927. הֲדָרָה {5x} **hădârâh**, *had-aw-raw';* fem. of 1926; *decoration:*—beauty {4x}, honour {1x}.

The noun *hadarah* means "majesty; splendor; exaltation; adornment." **(1)** This noun appears 5 times in the Bible. **(2)** The word implies "majesty or exaltation" in Prov 14:28: in the multitude of people *is* the king's honour: but in the want of people *is* the destruction of the prince. **(3)** *Hadarah* refers to "adornment" in Ps 29:2. See: TWOT—477c; BDB—214c.

1928. הֲדַרְעֶזֶר {12x} **Hădarʿezer**, *had-ar-eh'-zer;* from 1924 and 5828; *Hadar* (i.e. *Hadad,* 1908) is his *help; Hadarezer* (i.e. Hadadezer, 1909), a Syrian king:—Hadarezer {12x}. See: BDB—214c.

1929. הָהּ {1x} **hâhh**, *haw;* a short. form of 162; *ah!* expressing grief:—woe worth {1x}. See: BDB—214c.

1930. הוֹ **hôw**, *ho;* by perm. from 1929; *oh!:*—alas {1x}. See: TWOT—479; BDB—214c.

1931. הוּא {38x} **hûwʾ**, *hoo;* of which the fem. (beyond the Pentateuch) is

הִיא **hîyʾ**, *he;* a prim. word, the third pers. pron. sing., *he* (*she* or *it*); only expressed when emphat. or without a verb; also (intens.) *self,* or (espec. with the art.) the *same;* sometimes (as demonstr.) *this* or *that;* occasionally (instead of copula) *as* or *are:*—he, as for her, him (-self), it, the same, she (herself), such, that (. . . it), these, they, this, those, which (is), who. {38x}. See: TWOT—480; BDB—214d, 223d, 1090a.

1932. הוּא {7x} **hûwʾ** (Aram.), *hoo;* or (fem.)

הִיא **hîyʾ** (Aram.), *he;* corresp. to 1931:—to be {2x}, it {2x}, this {2x}, one {1x}. See: TWOT—2693; BDB—1081c, 1090a.

1933. הָוָא {6x} **hâvâʾ**, *haw-vaw';* or

הָוָה **hâvâh**, *haw-vaw';* a prim. root [comp. 183, 1961] supposed to mean prop. to *breathe; to be* (in the sense of existence):—be thou {2x}, be {1x}, shall be {1x}, may be {1x}, hath {1x}. See: TWOT—484, 491; BDB—216d, 217c.

1934. הֲוָא {69x} **hăvâʾ** (Aram.), *hav-aw';* or

הֲוָה **hăvâh** (Aram.), *hav-aw';* corresp. to 1933; to *exist;* used in a great variety of applications (espec. in connection with other words):—be {16x}, misc.: {52}: become, + behold, + came (to pass), + cease, + cleave, + consider, + do, + give, + have, + judge, + keep, + labour, + mingle (self), + put, + see, + seek, + set, + slay, + take heed, tremble, + walk, + would. See: TWOT—2692; BDB—1089d.

1935. הוֹד {24x} **hôwd**, *hode;* from an unused root; *grandeur* (i.e. an imposing form and appearance):—glory {9x}, honour {6x}, majesty {4x}, beauty {1x}, comeliness {1x}, glorious {1x}, goodly {1x}, honourable {1x}.

Howd means "splendor; majesty; authority." **(1)** All but 4 of its 24 biblical appearances occur in poetry. **(2)** The basic significance of "splendor and majesty" with overtones of superior power and position is attested in the application of this word to kings: **(2a)** "Therefore thus saith the LORD concerning Jehoiakim the son of Josiah king of Judah; They shall not lament for him, saying, Ah my brother! or, Ah sister! they shall not lament for him, saying, Ah lord! or, Ah his glory!" (Jer 22:18). **(2b)** This concept is equally prominent when the word is used of God: "Fair weather cometh out of the north: with God is terrible majesty" (Job 37:22).

(3) In many cases *howd* focuses on "dignity and splendor" with overtones of superior power and position but not to the degree seen in oriental kings: "And thou shalt put some of thine honor upon him, that all the congregation of the children of Israel may be obedient" (Num 27:20—the first occurrence of the word). **(4)** When used of the olive tree (Hos 14:6), *howd* focuses on its "splendor and dignity" as the most desired and desirable of the trees (cf. Judg 9:9–15). **(5)** The proud carriage of a war horse and seeming bravery in the face of battle lead God to say "The glory of his nostrils is terrible" (Job 39:20). **(6)** In every use of the word the one so described evokes a sense of amazement and satisfaction in the mind of the beholder. Syn.: 142, 3519, 6643. See: TWOT—482a; BDB—213a, 217a.

1936. הוֹד {1x} **Hôwd**, *hode;* the same as 1935; *Hod,* an Isr.:—Hod {1x}. See: BDB—217b.

1937. הוֹדְוָה {1x} **Hôwdᵉvâh**, *ho-dev-aw';* a form of 1938; *Hodevah* (or Hodevjah), an Isr.:—Hodevah {1x}. See: BDB—217b, 217c.

1938. הוֹדַוְיָה {3x} **Hôwdavyâh**, *ho-dav-yaw';* from 1935 and 3050; *majesty of Jah; Hodavjah,* the name of three Isr.:—Hodaviah {3x}. See: BDB—217b, 217c.

1939. הוֹדַיְוָהוּ {1x} **Howdayᵉvâhûw**, *ho-dah-yeh-vaw'-hoo;* a form of 1938; *Hodajvah,* an Isr.:—Hodaiah {1x}. See: BDB—217c.

1940. הוֹדִיָּה {1x} **Hôwdîyâh**, *ho-dee-yaw';* a form for the fem. of 3064; a *Jewess:*—Hodiah {1x}. See: BDB—217c.

1941. הוֹדִיָּה {5x} **Hôwdîyâh**, *ho-dee-yaw';* a form of 1938; *Hodijah,* the name of three Isr.:—Hodijah {5x}. See: BDB—217c.

הָוָה **hâvâh**. See 1933.

הֲוָה **hăvâh**. See 1934.

1942. הַוָּה {16x} **havvâh**, *hav-vaw';* from 1933 (in the sense of eagerly *coveting* and *rushing* upon; by impl. of *falling*); *desire;* also *ruin:*—calamity {4x}, wickedness {3x}, perverse thing {1x}, mischief {1x}, noisome {1x}, iniquity {1x}, substance {1x}, naughtiness {1x}, naughty {1x}, mischievous {1x}. See: TWOT—483a; BDB—217c.

1943. הֹוָה {3x} **hôvâh**, *ho-vaw';* another form for 1942; *ruin:*—mischief {3x}. See: TWOT—483c; BDB—217d.

1944. הוֹהָם {1x} **Hôwhâm**, *ho-hawm';* of uncert. der.; *Hoham,* a Canaanitish king:—Hoham. {1x}. See: BDB—222d.

1945. הוֹי {52x} **hôwy**, *hoh'-ee;* a prol. form of 1930 [akin to 188]; *oh!:*—woe {36x}, Ah {7x}, Ho {4x}, O {3x}, Alas {2x}. See: TWOT—485; BDB—222d.

1946. הוּךְ {4x} **hûwk** (Aram.), *hook;* corresp. to 1981; to *go;* caus. to *bring:*—go up {1x}, came {1x}, brought again {1x}, go {1x}. See: TWOT—2695; BDB—1090b.

1947. הוֹלֵלָה {4x} **hôwlêlâh**, *ho-lay-law';* fem. act. part. of 1984; *folly:*—madness {4x}. See: TWOT—501a; BDB—239c.

1948. הוֹלֵלוּת {1x} **hôwlêlûwth**, *ho-lay-looth';* from act. part. of 1984; *folly:*—madness {1x}. See: TWOT—501b; BDB—239c.

1949. הוּם {6x} **hûwm**, *hoom;* a prim. root [comp. 2000]; to *make an uproar,* or *agitate* greatly:—rang again {2x}, make a noise {2x}, moved {1x}, destroy {1x}. See: TWOT—486; BDB—223a, 228d.

1950. הוֹמָם {1x} **Hôwmâm**, *ho-mawm';* from 2000; *raging; Homam,* an Edomitish chieftain:—Homam {1x}. comp. 1967. See: BDB—223b, 243a.

1951. הוּן {1x} **hûwn**, *hoon;* a prim. root; prop. to *be naught,* i.e. (fig.) to *be* (caus. *act*) *light:*—be ready {1x}. See: TWOT—487; BDB—223b.

1952. הוֹן {26x} **hôwn**, *hone;* from the same as 1951 in the sense of 202; *wealth;* by impl. *enough:*—riches {11x}, substance {7x}, wealth {5x}, enough {2x}, nought {1x}.

Hown (1952) means "wealth; substance; riches; possessions; enough." **(1)** The 26 occurrences of this word are almost wholly in wisdom literature, with 17 of them in the Book of Proverbs. **(2)** This word appears only in the singular form.

(3) *Hown* usually refers to movable goods considered as "wealth": "But if he [the thief] be found, he shall restore seven-fold; he shall give all the substance of his house" (Prov 6:31; cf. Eze 27:12). **(4)** "Wealth" can be good and a sign of blessing: "Wealth and riches shall be in his [the righteous man's] house: and his righteousness endureth for ever" (Ps 112:3). **(5)** The creation is God's wealth: "I have rejoiced in the way of thy testimonies, as much as in all riches" (Ps 119:14). **(6)** In the Proverbs "wealth" is usually an indication of ungodliness: "The rich man's wealth is his strong city: the destruction of the poor is their poverty" (Prov 10:15). **(7)** This word can also represent any kind of concrete "wealth": ". . . If a man would give all the substance of his house for love, it would utterly be contemned" (Song 8:7). This is the significance of the word in its first occurrence: "Thou sellest thy people for nought and dost not increase thy wealth by their price" (Ps 44:12). **(9)** "Wealth" in general is meant in Prov 12:27: "The slothful man roasteth not that which he took in hunting: but the substance of a diligent man is precious." **(10)** Finally, *hown* means "enough" (only in Prov 30:15–16): "The horseleech hath two daughters, crying, Give, Give. There are three things that are never satisfied, yea, four things say not, It is enough: the grave; and the barren womb; the earth that is not filled with water; and the fire that saith not, It is enough." Syn.: 2428, 2633, 3502, 6239. See: TWOT—487a; BDB—223c.

1953. **הוֹשָׁמָע** {1x} **Hôwshâmâʿ**, *ho-shaw-maw';* from 3068 and 8085; *Jehovah has heard; Hoshama,* an Isr.:—Hoshama {1x}. See: BDB—221d, 223c.

1954. **הוֹשֵׁעַ** {17x} **Hôwshêaʿ**, *ho-shay'-ah;* from 3467; *deliverer; Hosheä,* the name of five Isr.:—Hosea {3x}, Hoshea {3x}, Oshea {3x}. See: BDB—223c, 448a.

1955. **הוֹשַׁעְיָה** {3x} **Hôwshaʿyâh**, *ho-shah-yaw';* from 3467 and 3050; *Jah has saved; Hoshajah,* the name of two Isr.:—Hoshaiah {3x}. See: BDB—448a.

1956. **הוֹתִיר** {2x} **Hôwthîyr**, *ho-theer';* from 3498; *he has caused to remain; Hothir,* an Isr.:—Hothir {2x}. See: BDB—223d, 452d.

1957. **הָזָה** {1x} **hâzâh**, *haw-zaw';* a prim. root [comp. 2372]; to *dream:*—sleep {1x}. See: TWOT—489; BDB—223d.

1958. **הִי** {1x} **hîy**, *he;* for 5092; *lamentation:*—woe {1x}. Syn.: 188, 190, 337, 480, 1929, 1945. See: TWOT—490; BDB—223d.

הִיא **hîyʾ**. See 1931, 1932.

1959. **הֵידָד** {7x} **hêydâd**, *hay-dawd';* from an unused root (mean. to *shout*); *acclamation:*—shouting {1x}. See: TWOT—471a; BDB—212c, 223d.

1960. **הֻיְּדָה** {1x} **huyᵉdâh**, *hoo-yed-aw';* from the same as 1959; prop. an *acclaim,* i.e. a *choir* of singers:—thanksgiving {1x}. Syn.: 8426. See: TWOT—847a; BDB—224a, 392d.

1961. **הָיָה** {75x} **hâyâh**, *haw-yaw;* a prim. root [comp. 1933]; to *exist,* i.e. *be* or *become, come to pass* (always emphat., and not a mere copula or auxiliary):—{75x} = beacon, × altogether, be (-come), accomplished, committed, like), break, cause, come (to pass), do, faint, fall, + follow, happen, × have, last, pertain, quit (one-) self, require, × use.

Hayah means "to become, occur, come to pass, be." **(1)** Often this verb indicates more than simple existence or identity (this may be indicated by omitting the verb altogether). **(1a)** Rather, the verb makes a strong statement about the being or presence of a person or thing. **(1b)** Yet the simple meaning "become" or "come to pass" appears often in the English versions. **(2)** The verb can be used to emphasize **(2a)** the presence of a person (e.g., God's Spirit—Judg 3:10), **(2c)** an emotion (e.g., fear—Gen 9:2), or **(2d)** a state of being (e.g., evil—Amos 3:6). **(2e)** In such cases, the verb indicates that their presence (or absence) is noticeable—it makes a real difference to what is happening. **(3)** On the other hand, in some instances *hayah* does simply mean "happen, occur." **(3a)** Here the focus is on the simple occurrence of the events—as seen, for example, in the statement following the first day of creation: "And so it happened" (Gen 1:7). **(3b)** In this sense, *hayah* is frequently translated "it came to pass."

(4) The use of this verb with various particles colors its emphasis accordingly. **(4a)** In passages setting forth blessing or cursing, for example, this verb not only is used to specify the object of the action but also the dynamic forces behind and within the action. **(4b)** Gen 12:2, for example, records that God told Abram: ". . . I will bless thee, and make thy name great; and thou shalt be [*hayah*] a blessing." **(4c)** Abram was already blessed, so God's pronouncement conferred upon him a future blessedness. **(4d)** The use of *hayah* in such passages declares the actual release of power, so that the accomplishment is assured—Abram will be blessed because God has ordained it. **(5)** In another set of passages, *hayah* constitutes intent rather than accomplishment. Hence, the blessing becomes a promise and the curse a threat (cf. Gen 15:5).

(6) Finally, in a still weaker use of *hayah,* the blessing or curse constitutes a wish or desire (cf. Ps 129:6). **(6a)** Even here the verb is somewhat dynamic, since the statement recognizes God's presence, man's faithfulness (or rebellion), and God's intent to accomplish the result pronounced. **(7)** In miracle accounts, *hayah* often appears at the climax of the story to confirm the occurrence of the event itself. **(7a)** Lot's wife looked back and "became" a pillar of salt (Gen 19:26); **(7b)** the use of *hayah* emphasizes that the event really occurred. **(7c)** This is also the force of the verb in Gen 1:3, in which God said, "Let there be light." He accomplished His word so that there was light. **(8)** The prophets use *hayah* to project God's intervention in the future. By using this verb, they emphasize not so much the occurrence of predicted events and circumstances as the underlying divine force that will effect them (cf. Is 2:2).

(9) Legal passages use *hayah* in describing God's relationship to His covenant people, to set forth what is desired and intended (cf. Ex 12:16). **(10)** When covenants were made between two partners, the formulas usually included *hayah* (Deut 26:17–18; Jer 7:23). **(11)** One of the most debated uses of *hayah* occurs in Ex 3:14, where God tells Moses His name. He says: "I am [*hayah*] that I am [*hayah*]." **(11a)** Since the divine name Jehovah or Yahweh was well-known long before (cf. Gen 4:1), this revelation seems to emphasize that the God who made the covenant was the God who kept the covenant. **(11b)** So Ex 3:14 is more than a simple statement of identity: "I am that I am"; **(11c)** it is a declaration of divine control of all things (cf. Hos 1:9). See: TWOT—491; BDB—218b, 224a, 1089d.

1962. **הַיָּה** {2x} **hayâh**, *hah-yaw';* another form for 1943; *ruin:*—calamity {2x}. See: TWOT—483b; BDB—217d, 228a.

1963. **הֵיךְ** {2x} **hêyk**, *hake;* another form for 349; *how?:*—how {1x}. See: TWOT—492; BDB—228a, 1089c.

1964. **הֵיכָל** {80x} **hêykâl**, *hay-kawl';* prob. from 3201 (in the sense of *capacity*); a large public building, such as a *palace* or *temple:*—palace {10x}, temple {70x}.

Heykal (1964) means "palace; temple." **(1)** The word occurs 78 times from First Samuel to Malachi, most frequently in Ezekiel. **(2)** The first usage pertains to the tabernacle at Shiloh (1 Sa 1:9). **(3)** The word "palace" in English versions may have one of three Hebrew words behind it: *heykal, bayit* (1004), or *'armon* (759). **(4)** The *heykal* with its 15 usages as "palace" refers to the palaces **(4a)** of Ahab (1 Kin 21:1), **(4b)** of the king of Babylon (2 Kin 20:18), and **(4c)** of Nineveh (Nah 2:6). **(5)** The "palace" was luxuriously decorated and the residents enjoyed the fulfillment of their pleasures; cf.: **(5a)** "And the wild beasts of the islands shall cry in their desolate houses, and dragons in their pleasant palaces: and her time is near to come, and her days shall not be prolonged" (Is 13:22). **(5b)** The psalmist compared beautiful girls to fine pillars in an ornate "palace": ". . . That our sons may be as plants grown up in their youth; that our daughters may be as corner stones, polished after the similitude of a palace" (Ps 144:12).

(6) Amos prophesied that the "songs of the temple" were to turn to wailing at the destruction of the northern kingdom (Amos 8:3). **(7)** *Heykal* with the meaning "temple" is generally clarified in the context by two markers that follow. **(7a)** The first marker is the addition "of the LORD": "And when the builders laid the foundation of the temple of the LORD, they set the priests in their apparel with trumpets, and the Levites the sons of Asaph with cymbals, to praise the LORD, after the ordinance of David king of Israel" (Ezra 3:10). **(7b)** The second marker is a form of the word *qodesh* (6944), "holy": "O God, the heathen are come into thine inheritance; thy holy temple have they defiled; they have laid Jerusalem on heaps" (Ps 79:1). **(8)** Sometimes the definite article suffices to identify the "temple in Jerusalem": "In the year that King Uzziah died I saw also the Lord sitting upon a throne, high and lifted up, and his train filled the temple" (Is 6:1), especially in a section dealing with the "temple" (Eze 41).

(9) The Old Testament also speaks about the heavenly *heykal,* the *heykal* of God. **(9a)** It is difficult to decide on a translation, whether "palace" or "temple." **(9b)** Most versions opt in favor of the "temple" idea: **(9b1)** "Hear, all ye people; hearken, O earth, and all that therein is: and let the Lord GOD be witness against you, the LORD from his holy temple" (Mic 1:2; cf. Ps 5:7; 11:4; Hab 2:20). **(9b2)** "In my distress I called upon the LORD, and cried to my God: and he did hear my voice out of his temple, and my cry did enter into his ears" (2 Sa 22:7). **(10)** However, since Scripture portrays the presence of the royal judgment throne in heaven, it is not altogether impossible that the original authors had a royal "palace" in mind. **(11)** The imagery of the throne, the "palace," and judgment seems to lie behind Ps 11:4–5. "The LORD is in his holy temple, the LORD's throne is in heaven: his eyes behold, his eyelids try, the children of men. The LORD trieth the righteous: but the wicked and him that loveth violence his soul hateth." See: TWOT—493; BDB—228a, 1090b.

1965. הֵיכַל {13x} **hêykal** (Aram.), *hay-kal';* corresp. to 1964:—palace {5x}, temple {8x}. See: TWOT—2694; BDB—1090b.

1966. הֵילֵל {1x} **hêylêl**, *hay-lale';* from 1984 (in the sense of *brightness*); the *morning-star:*—Lucifer {1x}. See: TWOT—499a; BDB—228d, 237d.

1967. הֵימָם {1x} **Hêymâm**, *hay-mawm';* another form for 1950; *Hemam,* an Idumæan:—Hemam {1x}. See: BDB—228d, 243a.

1968. הֵימָן {17x} **Hêymân**, *hay-mawn';* prob. from 539; *faithful; Heman,* the name of at least two Isr.:—Heman {17x}. See: BDB—54c, 228d.

1969. הִין {22x} **hîyn**, *heen;* prob. of Eg. or.; a *hin* or liquid measure:—hin {22x}. See: TWOT—494; BDB—228d.

1970. הָכַר {1x} **hâkar**, *haw-kar';* a prim. root; appar. to *injure:*—make self strange {1x}. See: TWOT—495; BDB—229a.

1971. הַכָּרָה {1x} **hakkârâh**, *hak-kaw-raw';* from 5234; *respect,* i.e. partiality:—shew {1x}. See: TWOT—1368e; BDB—229b, 648b.

הַל **hal**. See 1973.

1972. הָלָא {1x} **hâlâ'**, *haw-law';* prob. denom. from 1973; to *remove* or be *remote:*—cast far off {1x}. See: TWOT—496; BDB—229b, 229c.

1973. הָלְאָה {16x} **hâl'âh**, *haw-leh-aw';* from the prim. form of the art. [**hal**]; *to the distance,* i.e. *far away;* also (of time) *thus far:*—beyond {5x}, forward {5x}, hitherto {2x}, back {1x}; thenceforth {1x}, henceforth {1x}, yonder {1x}. See: See: TWOT—496a; BDB—210b, 229b.

1974. הִלּוּל {2x} **hillûwl**, *hil-lool';* from 1984 (in the sense of *rejoicing*); a *celebration* of thanksgiving for harvest:—merry {1x}, praise {1x}.

Hilluwlim [plural], which occurs twice, means "praise" in Lev 19:24: "But in the fourth year all the fruit thereof shall be holy to praise the LORD *withal.* See: TWOT—500a; BDB—239b.

1975. הַלָּז {1x} **hallâz**, *hal-lawz';* from 1976; *this* or *that:*—this {4x}, that {2x}, other side + 5676 {1x}. See: TWOT—497; BDB—229c, 534c.

1976. הַלָּזֶה {2x} **hallâzeh**, *hal-law-zeh';* from the art. [see 1973] and 2088; *this very:*—this {1x}. See: TWOT—497; BDB—229d, 534c.

1977. הַלֵּזוּ {1x} **hallêzûw**, *hal-lay-zoo';* another form of 1976; *that:*—this {1x}. See: TWOT—497; BDB—229d, 534c.

1978. הָלִיךְ {1x} **hâlîyk**, *haw-leek';* from 1980; a *walk,* i.e. (by impl.) a *step:*—step {1x}. *Haliyk* appears once with the meaning "steps" (Job 29:6). See: TWOT—498b; BDB—237b.

1979. הֲלִיכָה {7x} **hălîykâh**, *hal-ee-kaw';* fem. of 1978; a *walking;* by impl. a *procession* or *march,* a *caravan:*—ways {2x}, goings {2x}, companies {1x}, walk {1x}, way {1x}.

Haliykah means "course; doings; traveling company; caravan; procession." **(1)** This noun occurs 6 times in the Old Testament. **(2)** This word conveys several nuances. **(2a)** In Nah 2:5 *haliykah* refers to a "course": "He shall recount his worthies: they shall stumble in their walk. . . ." **(2b)** The word means "doings" in Prov 31:27. **(2c)** It may also mean "traveling-company" or "caravan" as in Job 6:19 or a "procession" as in Ps 68:24. See: TWOT—498c; BDB—237b.

1980. הָלַךְ {500x} **hâlak**, *haw-lak';* akin to 3212; a prim. root; to *walk* (in a great variety of applications, lit. and fig.):—go {217x}, walk {156x}, come {16x}, . . . away {7x}, . . . along {6x}, misc. {98x} = (all) along, apace, behave (self), come, (on) continually, be conversant, depart, + be eased, enter, exercise (self), + follow, forth, forward, get, go (about, abroad, along, away, forward, on, out, up and down), + greater, grow, be wont to haunt, lead, march, × more and more, move (self), needs, on, pass (away), be at the point, quite, run (along), + send, speedily, spread, still, surely, + talebearer, + travel (-ler), walk (abroad, on, to and fro, up and down, to places), wander, wax, [way-] faring man, × be weak, whirl.

Halak means "to go, walk, behave." **(1)** Essentially, this root refers to movement without any suggestion of direction in the sense of going, whether of **(1a)** man (Gen 9:23), **(1b)** beasts (Gen 3:14), or **(1c)** inanimate objects (Gen 2:14—the first occurrence of the word). **(2)** In cases other than men (where it means "to walk") *halak* may be translated "to go." **(2a)** It is used sometimes with a special emphasis on the end or goal of the action in mind; men are but flesh, "a wind that passeth [goes] away, and cometh not again" (Ps 78:39). **(2b)** Applied to human existence the word suggests "going to one's death," as in Gen 15:2, when Abraham says: "O Lord GOD, what wilt thou give me, seeing I go [am going to my death] childless . . , ?" **(3)** This verb can also be used of one's behavior, or the way one "walks in life." **(3a)** So he who "walks" uprightly shall be blessed of God (Is 33:15) **(3b)** This does not refer to walking upright on one's feet but to living a righteous life.

(4) This root is used in various other special ways. **(4a)** It may be used to emphasize that a certain thing occurred; **(4a1)** Jacob went and got the kid his mother requested, in other words, he actually did the action (Gen 27:14). **(4a2)** In Gen 8:3 the waters of the flood steadily receded from the surface of the earth. **(5)** Sometimes this verb implies movement away from, as in Gen 18:33, when the Lord "departed" from Abraham. **(6)** God is said to "walk" or "go in three senses. **(6a)** First, there are certain cases where He assumed some kind of physical form. **(6a1)** For example, Adam and Eve heard the sound of God "walking" to and fro in the garden of Eden (Gen 3:8). **(6a2)** He "walks" on the clouds (Ps 104:3) or in the heavens (Job 22:14); these are probably anthropomorphisms (God is spoken of as if He had bodily parts). **(6b)** Even more often God is said to accompany His people (Ex 33:14), **(6b1)** to go to redeem (deliver) them from Egypt (2 Sa 7:23), and **(6b2)** to come to save them (Ps 80:2). **(6c)** The idea of God's "going" ("walking") before His people in the pillars of fire and cloud (Ex 13:21) leads to the idea that His people must "walk" behind Him (Deut 13:5).

(7) Quite often the people are said to have "walked" or to be warned against "walking behind" foreign gods (Deut 4:3). **(8)** Thus, the rather concrete idea of following God through the wilderness moves to "walking behind" Him spiritually. **(9)** Some scholars suggest that "walking behind" pagan gods (or even the true God) arose from the pagan worship where the god was carried before the people as they entered the sanctuary. **(10)** Men may also "walk . . . after the imagination of their evil heart," or act stubbornly (Jer 3:17). **(11)** The pious followed or practiced God's commands; they "walked" **(11a)** in righteousness (Is 33:15), **(11b)** in humility (Mic 6:8), and **(11c)** in integrity (Ps 15:2). **(12)** They also "walk with God" (Gen 5:22), and **(13)** they live in His presence, and "walk before" Him (Gen 17:1), in the sense of living responsibly before Him. See: TWOT—498; BDB—229d, 539d, 540b.

1981. הֲלַךְ {3x} **hălak** (Aram.), *hal-ak';* corresp. to 1980 [comp. 1946]; to *walk:*—walk {1x}. See: TWOT—2695; BDB—1090b.

1982. הֵלֶךְ {2x} **hêlek**, *hay'-lek;* from 1980; prop. a *journey,* i.e. (by impl.) a *wayfarer;* also a *flowing:*—× dropped {1x}, traveler {1x}. *Helek* occurs twice and means a "visitor" (2 Sa 12:4). See: TWOT—498a; BDB—237a.

1983. הֲלָךְ {3x} **hălâk** (Aram.), *hal-awk';* from 1981; prop. a *journey,* i.e. (by impl.) *toll* on goods at a road:—custom {3x}. See: TWOT—2695a; BDB—1090b.

1984. הָלַל {165x} **hâlal**, *haw-lal';* a prim. root; to *be clear* (orig. of sound, but usually of color); to *shine;* hence, to *make a show,* to *boast;* and thus to *be* (clamorously) *foolish;* to *rave;* caus. to *celebrate;* also to *stultify:*—praise {117x}, glory {14x}, boast {10x}, be mad {8x}, shine {3x}, foolish {3x}, be fools {2x}, commended {2x}, rage {2x}, celebrate {1x}, give {1x}, give in marriage {1x}, renowned {1x}.

Halal means "to praise, celebrate, glory, sing (praise), boast." **(1)** The meaning "to praise" is actually the meaning of the intensive form of the Hebrew verb *halal,* which in its simple active form means "to boast." **(2)** Found more than 160 times in the Old Testament, *halal* is used for the first time in Gen 12:15, where it is noted that because of Sarah's great beauty, the princes of Pharaoh "commended" her to Pharaoh. **(3)** While *halal* is often used simply to indicate "praise" of people, including the king (2 Chr 23:12) or the beauty of Absalom (2 Sa 14:25), the word is usually used in reference to the "praise" of God. **(4)** Indeed, not only all living things but all created things, including the sun and moon, are called upon **(4a)** "to praise" God (Ps 148:2–5, 13; 150:1). **(4b)** Typically, such "praise" is called for and expressed in the sanctuary, especially in times of special festivals (Is 62:9).

(5) The Hebrew name for the Book of Psalms is simply the equivalent for the word "praises" and is a bit more appropriate than "Psalms," which comes from the Greek and has to do with the accompaniment of singing with a stringed instrument of some sort. **(5a)** It is little wonder that the Book of Psalms contains more than half the occurrences of *halal* in its various forms. **(5b)** Psalms 113—118 are traditionally referred to as the "Hallel Psalms," because they have to do with praise to God for deliverance from Egyptian bondage under Moses. **(5b1)** Because of this, they are an important part of the traditional Passover service. **(5b2)** There is no reason to doubt that these were the hymns sung by Jesus and His disciples on Maundy Thursday when He instituted the Lord's Supper (Mt 26:30).

(6) The word *halal* is the source of "Hallelujah," a Hebrew expression of "praise" to God **(6a)** which has been taken over into virtually every language of mankind. **(6b)** The Hebrew "Hallelujah" is generally translated "Praise the LORD!" **(6c)** The Hebrew term is more technically translated "Let us praise Yah," **(6c1)** the term "Yah" being a shortened form of "Yahweh," the unique Israelite name for God. **(6c2)** The term "Yah" is found in the KJV rendering of Ps 68:4, reflecting the Hebrew text. **(7)** Most versions follow the traditional translation "Lord," a practice begun in Judaism before New Testament times when the Hebrew term for "Lord" was substituted for "Yahweh," although it probably means something like "He who causes to be."

(8) The Greek approximation of "Hallelujah" is found 4 times in the New Testament in the form "Alleluia" (Rev 19:1, 3–4, 6). **(9)** Christian hymnody certainly would be greatly impoverished if the term "Hallelujah" were suddenly removed from our language of praise. Syn.: See: 1288, 3034. TWOT - 499, 500; BDB—237c, 237d, 239c.

1985. הִלֵּל {2x} **Hillêl**, *hil-layl';* from 1984; *praising* (namely God); *Hillel,* an Isr.:—Hillel {2x}. See: BDB—239b.

1986. הָלַם {9x} **hâlam**, *haw-lam';* a prim. root; to *strike* down; by impl. to *hammer, stamp, conquer, disband:*—smite {3x}, break down {2x}, break {1x}, beat down {1x}, beat {1x}, overcome {1x}. Syn.: 3807, 5060, 5062, 5221. See: TWOT—502; BDB—240c.

1987. הֶלֶם {1x} **Helem**, *heh'-lem;* from 1986; *smiter; Helem,* the name of two Isr.:—Helem {1x}. See: BDB—240c.

1988. הֲלֹם {11x} **hălôm**, *hal-ome';* from the art. [see 1973]; *hither:*—hither {6x}, hitherto {2x}, here {2x}, thither {1x}. See: TWOT—503; BDB—240d.

1989. הַלְמוּת {1x} **halmûwth**, *hal-mooth';* from 1986; a *hammer* (or *mallet*):—hammer {1x}. See: TWOT—502a; BDB—240d.

1990. חָם {1x} **Hâm**, *hawm;* of uncert. der.; *Ham,* a region of Pal.:—Ham {1x}. See: BDB—241a.

1991. הֵם {1x} **hêm**, *haym;* from 1993; *abundance,* i.e. *wealth:*—any of theirs {1x}. See: TWOT—505; BDB—241a.

1992. הֵם {44x} **hêm**, *haym;* or (prol.)

הֵמָּה **hêmmâh**, *haym'-maw;* masc. plur. from 1931; *they* (only used when emphat.):—it, like, × (how, so) many (soever, more as) they (be), (the) same, × so, × such, their, them, these, they, those, which, who, whom, withal, ye = {44x}. See: TWOT—504; BDB—216d, 241a, 1090b.

1993. הָמָה {34x} **hâmâh**, *haw-maw';* a prim. root [comp. 1949]; to *make a loud sound* (like the English "hum"); by impl. to *be in great commotion* or *tumult,* to *rage, war, moan, clamor:*—roar {8x}, noise {6x}, disquieted {4x}, sound {3x}, troubled {2x}, aloud {1x}, loud {1x}, clamorous {1x}, concourse {1x}, mourning {1x}, moved {1x}, raged {1x}, raging {1x}, tumult {1x}, tumultuous {1x}, uproar {1x}.

Hamah basically means "to make a noise, be tumultuous, roar, groan, bark, sound, moan." This verb occurs 34 times in biblical Hebrew. Psalm 83:2 contains one appearance: "For, lo, thine enemies make a tumult: and they that hate thee have lifted up the head." See: TWOT—505; BDB—242a.

1994. הִמּוֹ {11x} **himmôw** (Aram.), *him-mo';* or (prol.)

הִמּוֹן **himmôwn** (Aram.), *him-mone';* corresp. to 1992; *they:*—them {7x}, set + 3488 {1x}, are {1x}, those {1x}, men + 1400 {1x}. See: TWOT—2696; BDB—1090b.

1995. הָמוֹן {83x} **hâmôwn**, *haw-mone';* or

הָמֹן **hâmôn** (Eze 5:7), *haw-mone';* from 1993; a *noise, tumult, crowd;* also *disquietude, wealth:*—multitude {62x}, noise {4x}, tumult {4x}, abundance {3x}, many {3x}, store {2x}, company {1x}, multiplied {1x}, riches {1x}, rumbling {1x}, sounding {1x}.

Hamon means "multitude; lively commotion; agitation; tumult; uproar; commotion; turmoil; noise; crowd; abundance." **(1)** The word represents a "lively commotion or agitation": "Look down from heaven, and behold from the habitation of thy holiness and of thy glory: where is thy zeal and thy strength, the sounding of thy bowels and of thy mercies toward me?" (Is 63:15). **(2)** *Hamon* represents the stirring or agitation of a crowd of people: "When Joab sent the king's servant, and me thy servant, I saw a great tumult, but I knew not what it was" (2 Sa 18:29). **(3)** In Is 17:12 the word is synonymously parallel to *sha'on* (7588) "rushing": "Woe to the multitude of many people, which make a noise like the noise of the seas; and to the rushing of nations, that make a rushing like the rushing of mighty waters!" **(4)** Sometimes *hamon* represents the noise raised by an agitated crowd of people (a "tumult"): "And when Eli heard the noise of the crying, he said, "What meaneth the noise of this tumult [raised by the report that the battle was lost]?" (1 Sa 4:14).

(5) In Is 13:4 the word represents the mighty sound of a gathering army rather than the confused outcry of a mourning city: "The noise of a multitude in the mountains, like as of a great people; a tumultuous noise of the kingdoms of nations gathered together: the LORD of hosts mustereth the host of the battle." **(6)** A young lion eating his prey is not disturbed by the noise of a band of shepherds trying to scare him off (Is 31:4). **(7)** There are exceptions to the rule that the word represents the sound of a large number of people. **(7a)** In 1 Kin 18:41 *hamon* signifies the roar of a heavy downpour of rain (cf. Jer 10:13), and **(7b)** in Jer 47:3 it represents the tumult of chariots. **(8)** *Hamon* sometimes means a "multitude or crowd" from which a tumult may arise. **(9)** Frequently the word represents a large army: "And I will draw unto thee, to the river Kishon, Sisera, the captain of Jabin's army, with his chariots and his multitude . . ." (Judg 4:7; cf. 1 Sa 14:16).

(10) Elsewhere *hamon* represents a whole people: "And he dealt among all the people, even among the whole multitude of Israel . . ." (2 Sa 6:19). **(11)** Finally, any great throng, or a great number of people (Gen 17:4—the first occurrence) may be represented by this word. **(12)** A great number of things can be indicated by *hamon* "O LORD our God, all this store that we have prepared to build thee a house for thine holy name . . ." (1 Chr 29:16). **(13)** Abundance of possessions or wealth is indicated by *hamon,* as in: "A little that a righteous man hath is better than the riches of many wicked" (Ps 37:16; cf. Eccl 5:10—parallel to "silver" [money]; Is 60:5). **(14)** Finally, *hamon* refers to a group of people organized around a king, specifically, his courtiers: **(14a)** "Son of man, speak unto Pharaoh king of Egypt, and to his multitude [his train or royal retinue]; Whom art thou like in thy greatness?" (Eze 31:2). **(14b)** Thus in Ps 42:4 the word can represent a festival procession, a kind of train. Syn.: 527, 6951. See: TWOT—505a; BDB—242b.

הַמֹּלֶכֶת **ham-môleketh**. See 4447.

1996. הֲמוֹן גּוֹג {2x} **Hămôwn Gôwg**, *ham-one' gohg;* from 1995 and 1463; the *multitude of Gog;* the fanciful name of an emblematic place in Pal.:—Hamon-gog {2x}. See: BDB—155d, 242b.

1997. הֲמוֹנָה {1x} **Hămôwnâh**, *ham-o-naw';* fem. of 1995; *multitude; Hamonah,* the same as 1996:—Hamonah {1x}. See: BDB—242d.

הֲמוּנֵךְ **hămûwnêk**. See 2002.

1998. הֶמְיָה {1x} **hemyâh**, *hem-yaw';* from 1993; *sound:*—noise {1x}. Syn.: 7452. See: TWOT—505b; BDB—242d.

1999. הֲמֻלָּה {2x} **hămullâh**, *ham-ool-law';* or (too fully)

הֲמוּלָּה **hămûwllâh** (Jer 11:16), *ham-ool-law';* fem. pass. part. of an unused root mean. to *rush* (as rain with a windy roar); a *sound:*—speech {1x}, tumult {1x}. See: TWOT—506a; BDB—242d.

2000. הָמַם {13x} **hâmam**, *haw-mam';* a prim. root [comp. 1949, 1993]; prop. to *put in commotion;* by impl. to *disturb, drive, destroy:*—discomfit {5x}, destroy {3x}, vex {1x}, crush {1x}, break {1x}, consume {1x} trouble {1x}. See: TWOT—507; BDB—243a.

הָמָן **hâmôn**. See 1995.

2001. הָמָן {54x} **Hâmân**, *haw-mawn';* of for. der.; *Haman,* a Pers. vizier:—Haman {54x}. See: BDB—243b.

2002. הַמְנִיךְ {3x} **hamnîyk** (Aram.), *ham-neek';* but the text is

הֲמוּנֵךְ **hămûwnêk**, *ham-oo-nayk';* of for. or.; a *necklace:*—chain {3x}. See: TWOT—2697; BDB—1090c.

2003. הָמָס {1x} **hâmâç**, *haw-mawce';* from an unused root appar. mean. to *crackle;* a dry *twig* or *brushwood:*—melting {1x}. See: TWOT—508a; BDB—243b.

2004. הֵן {16x} **hên**, *hane;* fem. plur. from 1931; *they* (only used when emphat.):—therein {4x}, withal {3x}, which {2x}, they {2x}, for {1x}, like {1x}, them {1x}, thereby {1x}, wherein {1x}. See: TWOT—504; BDB—241d, 243b, 530a.

2005. הֵן {7x} **hên**, *hane;* a prim. particle; *lo!;* also (as expressing surprise) *if:*—behold, if, lo, though = {7x}. See: TWOT—510; BDB—243b, 530a, 1090c.

2006. הֵן {16x} **hên** (Aram.), *hane;* corresp. to 2005: *lo!* also *there* [-fore], [un-] *less, whether, but, if:*—if {2x}, or {2x}, whether {2x}. See: TWOT—2698; BDB—243d, 1090c, 1099a.

2007. הֵנָּה {26x} **hênnâh**, *hane'-naw;* prol. for 2004; *themselves* (often used emphat. for the copula, also in indirect relation):—× in, × such (and such things), their, (into) them, thence, therein, these, they (had), on this side, those, wherein = {26x}. See: TWOT—504; BDB—216d, 241b, 244d.

2008. הֵנָּה {14x} **hênnâh**, *hane'-naw;* from 2004; *hither* or *thither* (but used both of place and time):—here, hither [-to], now, on this (that) side, + since, this (that) way, thitherward, + thus far, to . . . fro, + yet = {14x}. See: TWOT—510b; BDB—244c.

2009. הִנֵּה {17x} **hinnêh**, *hin-nay';* prol. for 2005; *lo!:*—Behold, see, lo, here . . . I, and lo = {17x}. See: TWOT—510a; BDB—243d, 774b.

2010. הֲנָחָה {1x} **hănâchâh**, *han-aw-khaw';* from 5117; *permission* of rest, i.e. *quiet:*—release {1x}. See: TWOT—1323d; BDB—244d, 629c.

2011. הִנֹּם {13x} **Hinnôm**, *hin-nome';* prob. of for. or.; *Hinnom,* appar. a Jebusite:—Hinnom {13x}. See: BDB—244d.

2012. הֵנַע {3x} **Hênaʿ**, *hay-nah';* prob. of for. der.; *Hena,* a place appar. in Mesopotamia:—Hena {3x}. See: BDB—245a.

2013. הָסָה {8x} **hâçâh**, *haw-saw';* a prim. root; to *hush:*—keep silence {3x}, hold your peace {2x}, hold your tongue {1x}, still {1x}, (keep) silence {1x}. See: TWOT—511; BDB—245a, 245b.

2014. הֲפֻגָה {1x} **hăphûgâh**, *haf-oo-gaw';* from 6313; *relaxation:*—intermission {1x}. See: TWOT—1740b; BDB—245b, 806b.

2015. הָפַךְ **hâphak**, *haw-fak';* a prim. root; to *turn* about or over; by impl. to *change, overturn, return, pervert:*—turn {57x}, overthrow {13x}, overturn {5x}, change {3x}, turn . . . {6x}, become {1x}, came {1x}, converted {1x}, gave {1x}, make {1x}, perverse {1x}, perverted {1x}, retired {1x}, tumbled {1x}.

Haphak means "to turn, overturn, change, transform, turn back." **(1)** Used for the first time in the biblical text in Gen 3:24, the Hebrew verb form there indicates reflexive action: ". . . A flaming sword which turned every way [NAB, "revolving"; NEB, "whirling"] . . ." **(2)** In its simplest meaning, *hapak* expresses the turning from one side to another, such as **(2a)** "turning" one's back (Josh 7:8), or **(2b)** "as a man wipeth a dish, wiping it, and turning it upside down" (2 Kin 21:13). **(2c)** Similarly, Hosea refers to Israel as being "a cake not turned" (Hos 7:8). **(3)** The meaning of "transformation" or "change" is vividly illustrated in the story of Saul's encounter with the Spirit of God. **(3a)** Samuel promised that Saul "shalt be turned into another man" (1 Sa 10:6), and **(3b)** when the Spirit came on him, "God gave him another heart" (1 Sa 10:9).

(3c) Other examples of change are the "changing" of Pharaoh's mind (Ex 14:5; literally, "the heart of Pharaoh . . . was turned"); **(3d)** the "turning" of Aaron's rod into a serpent (Ex 7:15); **(3e)** dancing "turned" to mourning (Lam 5:14); **(3f)** water "turned" into blood (Ex 7:17); **(3g)** and the sun "turned" to darkness and the moon to blood (Joel 2:31). **(4)** Ps 41:3 "the LORD will strengthen him upon the bed of languishing: thou wilt make all his bed in his sickness." In view of the poetic parallelism involved, restoration of health must be meant. **(5)** The KJV rendering of Is 60:5 sounds strange to our modern ears: "The abundance of the sea shall be converted unto thee . . . " simply means the riches of the seas will be given back to thee. See: TWOT—512; BDB—245b.

2016. הֶפֶךְ {2x} **hephek**, *heh'-fek;* or

הֵפֶךְ **hêphek**, *hay'-fek;* from 2015; a *turn*, i.e. the *reverse:*—contrary {2x}. See: TWOT—512a; BDB—246a.

2017. הֹפֶךְ {1x} **hôphek**, *ho'-fek;* from 2015; an *upset*, i.e. (abstr.) *perversity:*—turning of things upside down {1x}. See: TWOT—512; BDB—246a.

2018. הֲפֵכָה {1x} **hăphêkâh**, *haf-ay-kaw';* fem. of 2016; *destruction:*—overthrow {1x}. See: TWOT—512b; BDB—246b.

2019. הֲפַכְפַּךְ {1x} **hăphakpak**, *haf-ak-pak';* by redupl. from 2015; *very perverse:*—froward {1x}. See: TWOT—512c; BDB—246b.

2020. הַצָּלָה {1x} **hatstsâlâh**, *hats-tsaw-law';* from 5337; *rescue:*—deliverance {1x}. See: TWOT—1404a; BDB—246c, 665a.

2021. הֹצֶן {1x} **hôtsen**, *ho'-tsen;* from an unused root mean. appar. to *be sharp* or *strong;* a *weapon* of war:—chariot {1x}. See: TWOT—513; BDB—246c.

2022. הַר {546x} **har**, *har;* a short. form of 2042; a *mountain* or *range* of hills (sometimes used fig.):—mountain {261x}, mount {224x}, hill {59x}, hill country {1x}, promotion {1x}.

Har means "mountain range; mountainous region; mount." **(1)** In its first biblical appearance *har* refers to the "mountain range" upon which Noah's ark came to rest (Gen 8:4). **(2)** In the singular form the word can mean a "mountain range" or the "mountains" of a given area: **(2a)** ". . . And [he] set his face toward the mount Gilead" (Gen 31:21). **(2)** Jacob was fleeing from Laban toward the "mountains" where he thought to find protection. **(2c)** A further extension of this meaning applies this word to an area which is primarily mountainous; the word focuses on the territory in general rather than on the mountains in particular: "And they gave them the city of Arba the father of Anak, which city is Hebron, in the hill country of Judah, with the suburbs thereof round about it" (Josh 21:11).

(3) The word can be used of particular "mountains": ". . . And he led the flock to the backside of the desert, and came to the mountain of God, even to Horeb" (Ex 3:1). **(3a)** In this particular instance "the mountain of God" refers to Horeb. **(3b)** Elsewhere it is Jerusalem: "Why leap ye, ye high hills? This is the hill which God desireth to dwell in; yea, the LORD will dwell in it for ever" (Ps 68:16). **(4)** *Har* signifies inhabitable sites situated on hills and/or mountainsides: **(4a)** "And at that time came Joshua, and cut off the Anakim from the mountains, from Hebron, from Debir, from Anab, and from all the mountains of Judah, and from all the mountains of Israel: Joshua destroyed them utterly with their cities" (Josh 11:21) **(4b)** In this regard, compare Deut 2:37: "Only unto the land of the children of Ammon thou camest not, nor unto any place of the river Jabbok, nor unto the cities in the mountains, nor unto whatsoever the LORD our God forbade us." **(4c)** A comparison of Judg 1:35 and Josh 19:41 shows that Mount Heres is the same as the city of Heres.

(5) In the poetical literature of the Old Testament, the view of the world held by men of that era finds its reflection. **(5a)** One can speak of the foundations of the mountains as rooted in the underworld (Deut 32:22), serving to support the earth as the "bars" of the earth (Jonah 2:6). **(5b)** Mountain peaks may be said to reach into the heavens where God dwells (Is 24:21; in Gen 11:4, the men who built the tower at Babel erroneously thought they were going to reach God's dwelling place). **(5c)** Although it would be wrong to conclude that God is setting forth this understanding of creation, yet He used it in explaining His word to men just as He used other contemporaneous ideas.

(6) Since "mountains" were associated with deity (Is 14:13), God chose to make great revelations on "mountains," concretely impressing the recipients with the solemnity and authority of the message (Deut 27; Josh 8:30–35). **(7)** At the same time such locations provided for better audibility and visibility (Judg 9:7; 2 Chr 13:4). **(8)** "Mountains" often serve as a symbol of strength (Zec 4:7) inasmuch as they carried mythological significance since many people thought of them as sacred areas (Jer 3:22–23), and they were the locations of strong fortresses (Josh 10:6). **(9)** Even the "mountains" tremble before the Lord; He is mightier than they are (Job 14:18). Syn.: 1389, 2042. See: TWOT—517a; BDB—219b, 223c, 246d, 249a, 251a.

2023. הֹר {1x} **Hôr**, *hore;* another form of 2022; *mountain; Hor,* the name of a peak in Idumæa and of one in Syria:—*Hor* {1x}. See: BDB—246d.

2024. הָרָא {1x} **Hârâ'**, *haw-raw';* perh. from 2022; *mountainousness; Hara,* a region of Media:—Hara {1x}. See: BDB—246d.

2025. הַרְאֵל {1x} **har'êl**, *har-ale';* from 2022 and 410; *mount of God;* fig. the *altar* of burnt-offering:—altar {1x}. Syn.: comp. 739. See: TWOT—159a; BDB—72b, 246d.

2026. הָרַג {167x} **hârag**, *haw-rag';* a prim. root; to *smite* with deadly intent:—slay {100x}, kill {24x}, kill . . . {3x}, murder {2x}, destroyed {1x}, murder {1x}, out of hand {1x}, made {1x}, put {1x}, slain {31x}, slayer {1x}, surely {1x}.

Harag means "to kill, slay, destroy." **(1)** The fact that it is found in the Old Testament some 167 times reflects how commonly this verb was used to indicate the taking of life, whether animal or human. **(2)** *Harag* is found for the first time in the Old Testament in the Cain and Abel story (Gen 4:8; also vv. 14–15). **(2)** Rarely suggesting premeditated killing or murder, this term generally is used for the "killing" of animals, including sacrificially, and for ruthless personal violence of man against man. **(3)** *Harag* is not the term used in the sixth commandment (Ex 20:13; Deut 5:17). The word there is *rashach* (7523), and since it implies premeditated killing, the commandment is better translated: "Do not murder," as most modern versions have it. **(4)** The word *harag* often means wholesale slaughter, both in battle and after battle (Num 31:7–8; Josh 8:24; 2 Sa 10:18). **(5)** The word is only infrequently used of men's killing at the command of God. In such instances, the causative form of the common Hebrew verb for "to die" is commonly found. **(6)** In general, *harag* refers to violent "killing" and destruction, sometimes even referring to the "killing" of vines by hail (Ps 78:47). Syn.: 7523, 7819. See: TWOT—514; BDB—246d.

2027. הֶרֶג {1x} **hereg**, *heh'-reg;* from 2026; *slaughter:*—be slain {1x}, slaughter {4x}. See: TWOT—514a; BDB—247c.

2028. הֲרֵגָה {5x} **hărêgâh**, *har-ay-gaw';* fem. of 2027; *slaughter:*—slaughter {5x}. See: TWOT—514b; 247c.

2029. הָרָה {43x} **hârâh**, *haw-raw';* a prim. root; to *be* (or *become*) *pregnant, conceive* (lit. or fig.):—conceive {38x}, woman with child {2x}, with child {2x}, again {1x}, bare {1x}, progenitors {1x}. See: TWOT—515; BDB—247c.

2030. הָרֶה {16x} **hâreh**, *haw-reh';* or

הָרִי **hârîy** (Hos 14:1), *haw-ree';* from 2029; *pregnant:*— . . . with child {13x}, conceive {3x}. See: TWOT—515a; BDB—248a.

2031. הַרְהֹר {1x} **harhôr** (Aram.), *har-hor';* from a root corresp. to 2029; a mental *conception:*—thought {1x}. See: TWOT—2700; BDB—1090d.

2032. הֵרוֹן {3x} **hêrôwn**, *hay-rone';* or

הֵרָיוֹן **hêrâyôwn**, *hay-raw-yone';* from 2029; *pregnancy:*—conception {3x}. See: TWOT—515c; BDB—248a.

2033. הֲרוֹרִי {1x} **Hărôwrîy**, *har-o-ree';* another form for 2043; a *Harorite* or mountaineer:—Harorite {1x}. See: BDB—248b, 353d.

2034. הֲרִיסָה {1x} **hărîyçâh**, *har-ee-saw';* from 2040; something *demolished:*—ruin {1x}. See: TWOT—516b; BDB—249a.

2035. הֲרִיסוּת {1x} **hărîyçûwth**, *har-ee-sooth';* from 2040; *demolition:*—destruction {1x}. See: TWOT—516c; BDB—249a.

2036. הֹרָם {1x} **Hôrâm**, *ho-rawm';* from an unused root (mean. to *tower* up); *high;*

Horam, a Canaanitish king:—Horam {1x}. See: BDB—248b.

2037. הָרֻם {1x} **Hârûm**, *haw-room'*; pass. part. of the same as 2036; *high; Harum*, an Isr.:—Harum {1x}. See: BDB—248b.

2038. הַרְמוֹן {1x} **harmôwn**, *har-mone'*; from the same as 2036; a *castle* (from its height):—palace {1x}. Syn.: 1002, 1964. See: BDB—248b.

2039. הָרָן {7x} **Hârân**, *haw-rawn'*; perh. from 2022; *mountaineer; Haran*, the name of two men:—Haran {7x}. See: BDB—248c.

2040. הָרַס {43x} **hâraç**, *haw-ras'*; a prim. root; to *pull* down or in pieces, *break, destroy*:—throw down {13x}, break down {9x}, overthrow {5x}, destroy {4x}, pull down {3x}, break through {2x}, ruined {2x}, beat down {1x}, pluck down {1x}, break {1x}, destroyers {1x}, utterly {1x}. Syn.: 5422. See: TWOT—516; BDB—248c.

2041. הֶרֶס {1x} **hereç**, *heh'-res*; from 2040; *demolition*:—destruction {1x}. See: TWOT—516a; BDB—249a, 256d.

2042. הָרָר {13x} **hârâr**, *haw-rawr'*; from an unused root mean. to *loom* up; a *mountain*:—hill {2x}, mountain {10x}, mount {1x}. See: TWOT—517; BDB—249a.

2043. הֲרָרִי {5x} **Hărârîy**, *hah-raw-ree'*; or הָרָרִי **Hârârîy** (2 Sa 23:11), *haw-raw-ree'*; or הָאֲרָרִי **Hâʾrârîy** (2 Sa 23:34, last clause), *haw-raw-ree'*; appar. from 2042; a *mountaineer*:—Hararite {5x}. See: BDB—76d, 210c, 251a.

2044. הָשֵׁם {1x} **Hâshêm**, *haw-shame'*; perh. from the same as 2828; *wealthy; Hashem*, an Isr.:—Hashem {1x}. See: BDB—251c.

2045. הַשְׁמָעוּת {1x} **hâshmâᶜûwth**, *hashmaw-ooth'*; from 8085; *announcement*:—to cause to hear {1x}. See: TWOT—2412e; 251c, 1036a.

2046. הִתּוּךְ {1x} **hittûwk**, *hit-took'*; from 5413; a *melting*:—is melted {1x}. See: TWOT—1442a; BDB—251c, 678a.

2047. הֲתָךְ {4x} **Hăthâk**, *hath-awk'*; prob. of for. or.; *Hathak*, a Pers. eunuch:—Hatach {4x}. See: BDB—251c.

2048. הָתַל {10x} **hâthal**, *haw-thal'*; a prim. root; to *deride*; by impl. to *cheat*:—mock {6x}, deceive {3x}, deal deceitfully {1x}. Syn.: 3931. See: TWOT—518; BDB—251c, 1068c.

2049. הָתֹל {1x} **hâthôl**, *haw-thole'*; from 2048 (only in plur. collect.); a *derision*:—mocker {1x}. See: TWOT—518a; BDB—251c, 1068c.

2050. הָתַת {1x} **hâthath**, *haw-thath'*; a prim. root; prop. to *break* in upon, i.e. to *assail*:—imagine mischief {1x}. See: TWOT—488; BDB—223c, 251d.

ו

2051. וְדָן {1x} **Vᵉdân**, *ved-awn'*; perh. for 5730; *Vedan* (or Aden), a place in Arabia:—Dan also {1x}. See: BDB—246c.

2052. וָהֵב {1x} **Vâhêb**, *vaw-habe'*; of uncert. der.; *Vaheb*, a place in Moab:—what he did {1x}. See: BDB—255a.

2053. וָו {13x} **vâv**, *vaw*; prob. a *hook* (the name of the sixth Heb. letter):—hook {13x}. See: TWOT—520; BDB—255b.

2054. וָזָר {1x} **vâzâr**, *vaw-zawr'*; presumed to be from an unused root mean. to *bear guilt; crime*:—× strange {1x}. See: TWOT—521; BDB—255c.

2055. וַיְזָתָא {1x} **Vayᵉzâthâʾ**, *vah-yez-aw'-thaw*; of for. or.; *Vajezatha*, a son of Haman:—Vajezatha {1x}. See: BDB—255c.

2056. וָלָד {2x} **vâlâd**, *vaw-lawd'*; for 3206; a *boy*:—child {2x}. See: BDB—255c, 409b.

2057. וַנְיָה {1x} **Vanyâh**, *van-yaw'*; perh. for 6043; *Vanjah*, an Isr.:—Vaniah {1x}. See: BDB—255c.

2058. וָפְסִי {1x} **Vophçîy**, *vof-see'*; prob. from 3254; *additional; Vophsi*, an Isr.:—Vophsi {1x}. See: BDB—255c.

2059. וַשְׁנִי {1x} **Vashnîy**, *vash-nee'*; prob. from 3461; *weak; Vashni*, an Isr.:—Vashni {1x}. See: BDB—255c.

2060. וַשְׁתִּי {10x} **Vashtîy**, *vash-tee'*; of Pers. or.; *Vashti*, the queen of Xerxes:—Vashti {10x}. See: BDB—255d.

ז

2061. זְאֵב {7x} **zᵉʾêb**, *zeh-abe'*; from an unused root mean. to *be yellow*; a *wolf*:—wolf {7x}. See: TWOT—522; BDB—255b.

2062. זְאֵב {6x} **Zᵉʾêb**, *zeh-abe'*; the same as 2061; *Zeëb*, a Midianitish prince:—Zeeb {6x}. See: BDB—255d.

2063. זֹאת {41x} **zôʾth**, *zothe'*; irreg. fem. of 2089; *this* (often used adv.):—hereby (-in, -with), it, likewise, the one (other, same), she, so (much), such (deed), that, therefore, these, this (thing), thus = {41x}. See: TWOT—528; BDB—256a, 260a.

2064. זָבַד {1x} **zâbad**, *zaw-bad'*; a prim. root; to *confer*:—endue {1x}. See: TWOT—524; BDB—256a.

2065. זֶבֶד {1x} **zebed**, *zeh'-bed*; from 2064; a *gift*:—dowry {1x}. Syn.: 4119. See: TWOT—524a; BDB—256b.

2066. זָבָד {8x} **Zâbâd**, *zaw-bawd'*; from 2064; *giver; Zabad*, the name of seven Isr.:—Zabad {8x}. See: BDB—256b.

2067. זַבְדִּי {61x} **Zabdîy**, *zab-dee'*; from 2065; *giving; Zabdi*, the name of four Isr.:—Zabdi {1x}. See: BDB—256c.

2068. זַבְדִּיאֵל {2x} **Zabdîyʾêl**, *zab-dee-ale'*; from 2065 and 410; *gift of God; Zabdiel*, the name of two Isr.:—Zabdiel {2x}. See: BDB—256c.

2069. זְבַדְיָה {9x} **Zᵉbadyâh**, *zeb-ad-yaw'*; or זְבַדְיָהוּ **Zᵉbadyâhûw**, *zeb-ad-yaw'-hoo*; from 2064 and 3050; *Jah has given; Zebadjah*, the name of nine Isr.:—Zebadiah {1x}. See: BDB—256c.

2070. זְבוּב {2x} **zᵉbûwb**, *zeb-oob'*; from an unused root (mean. to *flit*); a *fly* (espec. one of a stinging nature):—fly {2x}. See: TWOT—523a; BDB—256a.

2071. זָבוּד {1x} **Zâbûwd**, *zaw-bood'*; from 2064; *given; Zabud*, an Isr.:—Zabud {1x}. See: BDB—256b.

2072. זַבּוּד {1x} **Zabbûwd**, *zab-bood'*; a form of 2071; *given; Zabbud*, an Isr.:—Zabbud {1x}. See: BDB—256b.

2073. זְבוּל {5x} **zᵉbûwl**, *ze-bool'*; or זְבֻל **zᵉbûl**, *zeb-ool'*; from 2082; a *residence*:—dwell in {1x}, dwelling {1x}, habitation {3x}. See: TWOT—526a; BDB—259c.

2074. זְבוּלוּן {45x} **Zᵉbûwlûwn**, *zeb-oo-loon'*; or זְבֻלוּן **Zᵉbûlûwn**, *zeb-oo-loon'*; or זְבוּלֻן **Zᵉbûwlûn**, *zeb-oo-loon'*; from 2082; *habitation; Zebulon*, a son of Jacob; also his territory and tribe:—Zebulun {45x}. See: TWOT—526b; BDB—259d.

2075. זְבוּלֹנִי {3x} **Zᵉbûwlônîy**, *zeb-oo-lo-nee'*; patron. from 2074; a *Zebulonite* or desc. of Zebulun:—Zebulonite {1x}, Zebulunite {1x}. See: BDB—259d.

2076. זָבַח {134x} **zâbach**, *zaw-bakh'*; a prim. root; to *slaughter* an animal (usually in sacrifice):—sacrifice {85x}, offer {39x}, kill {5x}, slay {5x}.

Zabach means "to slaughter, sacrifice." **(1)** This word is a common Semitic term for sacrifice in general, although there are a number of other terms used in the Old Testament for specific sacrificial rituals. **(2)** There is no question that this is one of the most important terms in the Old Testament; *zabach* is found more than 130 times in its verbal forms and its noun forms occur over 500 times. **(3)** The first time the verb occurs is in **(3a)** Gen 31:54, where "Jacob offered sacrifice upon the mount." **(3b)** In Ex 20:24 the word is used in relation to the kinds of sacrifices to be made. **(4)** While there were grain and incense offerings prescribed as part of the Mosaic laws dealing with sacrifice (see Lev 2), the primary kind of sacrifice was the blood offering which required the slaughter of an animal (cf. Deut 17:1; 1 Chr 15:26).

(4a) This blood was poured around the altar, for the blood contained the life, as stated in Lev 17:11 "For the life of the flesh *is* in the blood: and I have given it to you upon the altar to make an atonement for your souls: for it *is* the blood *that* maketh an atonement for the soul." **(4b)** Since the blood was the vehicle of life, it belonged to God alone. **(4c)** Because the blood is the life, and because it is given to God in the process of pouring it about the altar, it becomes the means of expiating sin, as an offering for sin and not because it becomes a substitute for the sinner. **(5)** *Zabach* is also used as a term for "slaughter for eating." **(5a)** This usage is closely linked with "slaughter for sacrifice" since all eating of flesh was sacrificial among ancient Hebrews. **(5b)** The word carries this meaning in 1 Kin 19:21: "And he returned back from him, and took a yoke of oxen, and slew them, and boiled their flesh . . . and gave unto the people, and they did eat." See: TWOT—525; BDB—256d, 1087a.

2077. זֶבַח {162x} **zebach**, *zeh'-bakh*; from 2076; prop. a *slaughter*, i.e. the *flesh* of an animal; by impl. a *sacrifice* (the victim or the act):—sacrifice {155x}, offerings {6x}, offer {1x}.

Zebach properly means **(1)** to slay an animal for food, and accordingly rendered kill or slay. **(2)** The idea of a sacrifice is mistakenly thought to be performed solely by a priest. **(3)** A lay offerer, the head of the family, could also present and slay an animal before God's sanctuary (Deut 12:15, 21; 1 Sa 28:24; 2 Chr 18:2; Eze 34:3). **(3a)** The family or nation, following the priest's directions, offered the sacrifice through their representatives and **(3b)** partook of the flesh of the victims, entering thereby into communion with God. **(4)** The various ceremonies connected with the *zebach* are described in Lev 17:5–7. **(4a)** A man brought an unblemished animal to the door of the sacred tent, **(4b)** pressed his hands on its head, and **(4c)** slew it. **(4d)** The priest, **(4d1)** acting on God's behalf, **(4d2)** took the blood, which represented the life of the animal (and therefore the life of the offerer), and **(4d3)** poured it forth on the altar as an atonement (Lev 3:2). **(4d4)** He also burned the fat - to represent the fact that the richness or goodness of animal life proceeded from God, and was due to Him (Lev 3:4–5).

(4d5) The sacrifice demonstrated that without the shedding of blood there is no remission of sins (Lev 17:1; cf. Heb 9:22). **(4e)** A certain fixed portion of the flesh was **(4e1)** then given to the priest, to be eaten by himself and his family (Ex 29:28; Lev 7:31–35; Deut 18:3), and **(4e2)** the rest was eaten by the offerer and his household. **(4e3)** Because the people shared in the eating, the *zebach* was a communal meal in which the Lord hosted His people (Zeph 1:7). **(5)** Whether the feast was public or private, and whether the animal was offered by the elders of the nation or by the head of a family, these ceremonies were to symbolize the union between God and man, who were thus made partakers of the same food. **(6)** If it was impossible to perform the full rites connected with the sacrifice through distance from the tabernacle of the congregation, or from the place that God should subsequently choose to put His name, i.e., the temple, one point at any rate was to be observed: the blood of the slain animal was to be poured on the earth and covered with dust (Lev 7:13).

(7) The rites connected with the *zebach* were designed to produce a moral effect on the children of Israel. They were **(7a)** reminded of God's merciful disposition toward them, **(7b)** stimulated to live in conformity with His law, and **(7c)** were to deal mercifully with their poorer brethren. **(8)** The pious Israelite would be impressed **(8a)** that sin brought death into the world, and that **(8b)** he himself had sinned. His conscience would be stimulated through participating in **(8b1)** the death of the animal, **(8b2)** by the sprinkling of the blood, and **(8b3)** the burning of the fat. **(9)** He would thus have "a broken spirit" (Ps 51:17). **(10)** Through his sacrifice would be **(10a)** a strong call to righteousness (Ps 4:5), **(10b)** to obedience (1Sa 15:22), **(10c)** to joy (Ps 27:6), and **(10d)** to mercy (Hos 6:6). **(11)** Where the sacrifice had not this spirit, it lost all its value and significance. **(12)** *Zebach* was connected to covenant making, the sharing in food being a symbol of the oneness of the eaters (Gen 31:54; Ps 50:5).

(13) The prophets looked with condemnation on apostate Israel's sacrifices (Is 1:11). **(14)** Sacrifices, however, had their place **(15)** behind Israel's love for God (Hos 6:6), **(16)** less desired by God than obedience (1 Sa 15:22), and **(17)** a broken spirit and a contrite heart (Ps 51:16–17). **(18)** The Passover and the peace-offering were special kinds of *zebach*. **(19)** The "sacrifice" which was part of a covenant ritual involved the sprinkling of the blood on the people and upon the altar, which presumably symbolized God as the covenant partner (see Ex 24:6–8). **(20)** Another special "sacrifice" was "the sacrifice of the feast of the passover" (Ex 34:25). **(20a)** In this case the sacrificial lamb provided the main food for the passover meal, and **(20b)** its blood was sprinkled on the doorposts of the Israelite homes as a sign to the death angel. **(21)** The "sacrifice" of animals was in no way unique to Israelite religion, for sacrificial rituals generally are part of all ancient religious cults. **(21a)** Indeed, the mechanics of the ritual were quite similar, especially between Israelite and Canaanite religions. **(21b)** However, the differences are very clear in the meanings which the rituals had as they were performed either to capricious Canaanite gods or for the one true God who kept His covenant with Israel.

(22) The noun *zebach* is used of "sacrifices" to the one true God in Gen 46:1: "And Israel took his journey with all that he had . . . and offered sacrifices unto the God of his father Isaac" (cf. Ex 10:25; Neh 12:43). **(23)** The noun refers to "sacrifices" to other deities in Ex 34:15: "Lest thou make a covenant with the inhabitants of the land, and they go a whoring after their gods, and do sacrifice unto their gods, and one call thee, and thou eat of his sacrifice" (cf. Num 25:2; 2 Kin 10:19). **(24)** The idea of "sacrifice" certainly is taken over into the New Testament, for **(25)** Christ became "the Lamb of God, who takes away the sin of the world" (cf. Jn 1:29). **(26)** The writer of Hebrews makes much of the fact that with the "sacrifice" of Christ, no more sacrifices are necessary (cf. Heb 9). Syn.: The *zebach* (2077) or sacrifice was utterly distinct from the *'olath* (5930) or ascending-offering, which was wholly burned or turned into smoke, and from the sin-offering (2403), which was partly burned and partly eaten by the priest. comp. 801, 2282, 4503, 7133, 8426. See: TWOT—525a; BDB—257b.

2078. זֶבַח {12x} **Zebach**, *zeh'-bakh;* the same as 2077; *sacrifice; Zebach,* a Midianitish prince:—Zebah {12x}. See: BDB—258a.

2079. זַבַּי {1x} **Zabbay**, *zab-bah'-ee;* prob. by orth. err. for 2140; *Zabbai* (or Zaccai), an Isr.:—Zabbai {1x}. See: BDB—256a, 259b.

2080. זְבִידָה {1x} **Zᵉbîydâh**, *zeb-ee-daw';* fem. from 2064; *giving; Zebidah,* an Israelitess:—Zebudah {1x}. See: BDB—256b.

2081. זְבִינָא {1x} **Zᵉbîynâʼ**, *zeb-ee-naw';* from an unused root (mean. to *purchase*); *gainfulness; Zebina,* an Isr.:—Zebina {1x}. See: BDB—259b.

2082. זָבַל {1x} **zâbal**, *zaw-bal';* a prim. root; appar. prop. to *inclose,* i.e. to *reside:*—dwell with me {1x}. See: TWOT—526; BDB—259c.

2083. זְבֻל {6x} **Zᵉbûl**, *zeb-ool';* the same as 2073; *dwelling; Zebul,* an Isr.:—Zebul {1x}. See: BDB - 259d, 560d. Syn.: comp. 2073.

זְבֻלוּן **Zᵉbûlûwn**, See 2074

2084. זְבַן {1x} **zᵉban** (Aram.), *zeb-an';* corresp. to the root of 2081; to *acquire* by purchase:—gain {1x}. See: TWOT—2702; BDB—1091a.

2085. זָג {1x} **zâg**, *zawg;* from an unused root prob. mean. to *inclose;* the *skin* of a grape:—husk {1x}. See: TWOT—527a; BDB—260a.

2086. זֵד **zêd**, *zade';* from 2102; *arrogant:*—presumptuous {1x}, proud {13x}. See: TWOT—547a; BDB—260a, 267d.

2087. זָדוֹן {11x} **zâdôwn**, *zaw-done';* from 2102; *arrogance:*—presumptuously {2x}, pride {6x}, proud (man) {3x}. See: TWOT—547a; BDB—260a, 268a.

2088. זֶה **zeh**, *zeh;* a prim. word; the masc. demonstr. pron., *this* or *that:*—he, × hence, × here, it (-self), × now, × of him, the one . . . the other, × than the other, (× out of) the (self) same, such (an one) that, these, this (hath, man), on this side . . . on that side, × thus, very, which = {38x}. Syn.: 2063, 2090, 2097, 2098. See: TWOT—528; BDB—260a, 774b, 1086d, 1087c.

2089. זֶה {1x} **zeh** (1 Sa 17:34), *zeh;* by perm. for 7716; a *sheep:*—lamb {1x}. See: BDB—962a.

2090. זֹה {13x} **zôh**, *zo;* for 2088; *this* or *that:*—this {7x}, thus {3x}, that {1x}, what {1x}, another {1x}. See: BDB—262b, 1086d.

2091. זָהָב **zâhâb**, *zaw-hawb';* from an unused root mean. to *shimmer; gold,* fig. something *gold-colored* (i.e. *yellow*), as *oil,* a *clear sky:*—gold {348x}, golden {40x}, fair weather {1x}.

Zahab means "gold." **(1)** *Zahab* can refer to "gold ore," or "gold in its raw state." This is its meaning in its first biblical appearance: "The name of the first is Pison: that is it which compasseth the whole land of Havilah, where there is gold" (Gen 2:11). **(2)** The word can also be used of "gold" which has already been refined: "But he knoweth the way that I take: when he hath tried me, I shall come forth as gold" (Job 23:10). **(3)** "Gold" could be beaten (1 Kin 10:16) and **(4)** purified (Ex 25:11). **(5)** One can also speak of the best "gold" (2 Chr 3:5). **(6)** *Zahab* can be conceived of as an "object of wealth": "And Abram was very rich in cattle, in silver, and in gold" (Gen 13:2). **(6a)** As such, the emphasis is on "gold" as a valuable or precious commodity. **(6b)** Consequently, the word is used in comparisons: "The gold and the crystal cannot equal it: and the exchange of it shall not be for jewels of fine gold" (Job 28:17). **(7)** "Gold" was often one of the spoils of war: "But all the silver, and gold, and vessels of brass and iron, are consecrated unto the LORD: they shall come into the treasury of the LORD" (Josh 6:19). **(8)** "Gold" was bought and sold as an object of merchandise: "The merchants of Sheba and Raamah, they were thy merchants: they [paid for your wares] with chief of all spices, and with all precious stones, and gold" (Eze 27:22). **(9)** *Zahab* was used as a costly gift: "And Balaam answered and said unto the servants of Balak, If Balak would give me his house full of silver and gold, I [could not do anything] . . ." (Num 22:18). **(10)** This metal was used as a material to make jewelry and other valuable items: "And it came to pass, as the camels had done drinking, that the man took a golden earring of half a shekel weight, and two bracelets for her hands of ten shekels weight of gold . . ." (Gen 24:22). **(11)** Solomon's temple was adorned with "gold" (1 Kin 6:20–28). **(12)** Gold was used as money, being exchanged in various weights and values (according to its weight): "And he made three hundred shields of beaten gold; three pound of gold went to one shield . . ." (1 Kin 10:17; cf. 2 Sa 12:30). **(13)** "Gold" even existed in the form of "coins" (Ezra 2:69). **(14)** *Zahab* is used for the color "gold": "What be these two olive branches which through the two golden pipes empty the golden oil out of themselves?" (Zec 4:12). See: TWOT—529a; BDB—262c, 1087a.

2092. זָהַם {1x} **zâham**, *zaw-ham';* a prim. root; to *be rancid,* i.e. (tran.) to *loathe:*—abhor {1x}. See: TWOT—530; BDB—263d.

2093. זַהַם {1x} **Zaham**, *zah'-ham;* from 2092; *loathing; Zaham,* an Isr.:—Zaham {1x}. See: BDB—263d.

2094. זָהַר **zâhar**, *zaw-har';* a prim. root; to *gleam;* fig. to *enlighten* (by caution):—warn {18x}, admonish {2x}, teach {1x}, shine {1x}. See: TWOT—531, 532; BDB—263d, 264a, 1091a.

2095. זְהַר {1x} **zᵉhar** (Aram.), *zeh-har';* corresp. to 2094; (pass.) *be admonished:*—take heed {1x}. See: TWOT—2703; BDB—1091a.

2096. זֹהַר {2x} **zôhar**, *zo'-har;* from 2094; *brilliancy:*—brightness {2x}. See: TWOT—531a; BDB—264a.

2097. זוֹ {2x} **zôw**, *zo;* for 2088; *this* or *that:*—that {1x}, this {1x}. See: TWOT—528; BDB—262b, 264c.

2098. זוּ {15x} **zûw**, *zoo;* for 2088; *this* or *that:*—which {5x}, this {4x}, that {3x}, wherein {2x}, whom {1x}. See: TWOT—528; BDB—262b, 264c.

2099. זִו {2x} **Zîv**, *zeev';* prob. from an unused root mean. to *be prominent;* prop. *brightness* [comp. 2122], i.e. (fig.) the month of *flowers; Ziv* (corresp. to Ijar or May):—Zif {2x}. See: TWOT—533; BDB—264c.

2100. זוּב {42x} **zûwb**, *zoob;* a prim. root; to *flow* freely (as water), i.e. (spec.) to *have a* (sexual) *flux;* fig. to *waste* away; also to *overflow:*—flow {21x}, have an issue {14x}, gush out {3x}, pine away {1x}, hath {1x}, have {1x}, run {1x}. See: TWOT—534; BDB—264c.

2101. זוֹב {13x} **zôwb**, *zobe;* from 2100; a seminal or menstrual *flux:*—issue {13x}. See: TWOT—534a; BDB—264d.

2102. זוּד {10x} **zûwd**, *zood;* or (by perm.)

זִיד **zîyd**, *zeed;* a prim. root; to *seethe;* fig. to *be insolent:*—deal proudly {4x}, presumptuously {3x}, presume {1x}, be proud {1x}, sod {1x}. See: TWOT—547; BDB—264d, 267c, 1091a.

2103. זוּד {1x} **zûwd** (Aram.), *zood;* corresp. to 2102; to *be proud:*—in pride {1x}. See: TWOT—2704; BDB—1091a.

2104. זוּזִים {1x} **Zûwzîym**, *zoo-zeem';* plur. prob. from the same as 2123; *prominent; Zuzites,* an aboriginal tribe of Pal.:—Zuzims {1x}. See: BDB—265c.

2105. זוֹחֵת **Zôwchêth**, *zo-khayth';* of uncert. or.; *Zocheth,* an Isr.:—Zoheth {1x}. See: BDB—265d.

2106. זָוִית {2x} **zâvîyth**, *zaw-veeth';* appar. from the same root as 2099 (in the sense of *prominence*); an *angle* (as *projecting*), i.e. (by impl.) a *corner-column* (or *anta*):—corner {1x}, cornerstone {1x}. See: TWOT—2704; BDB—265a, 265d.

2107. זוּל {2x} **zûwl**, *zool;* a prim. root [comp. 2151]; prob. to *shake* out, i.e. (by impl.) to *scatter* profusely; fig. to *treat lightly:*—lavish {1x}, despise {1x}. See: TWOT—538; BDB—266a.

2108. זוּלָה {16x} **zûwlâh**, *zoo-law';* from 2107; prob. *scattering,* i.e. *removal;* used adv. *except:*—beside . . . {7x}, save {5x}, only {2x}, but me {1x}, but {1x}. See: TWOT—537a; BDB—265d.

2109. זוּן {1x} **zûwn**, *zoon;* a prim. root; perh. prop. to *be plump,* i.e. (tran.) to *nourish:*—feed {1x}. See: BDB—266a, 402c, 1091b.

2110. זוּן {1x} **zûwn** (Aram.), *zoon;* corresp. to 2109:—feed {1x}. See: BDB—1091b.

2111. זוּעַ {3x} **zûwâᶜ**, *zoo'-ah;* a prim. root; prop. to *shake* off, i.e. (fig.) to *agitate* (as with fear):—move {1x}, tremble {1x}, vex {1x}. See: TWOT—540; BDB—266a, 1091b.

2112. זוּעַ {2x} **zûwaᶜ** (Aram.), *zoo'-ah;* corresp. to 2111; to *shake* (with fear):—tremble {2x}. See: TWOT—2706; BDB—1091b.

2113. זְוָעָה {6x} **zᵉvâᶜâh**, *zev-aw-aw';* from 2111; *agitation, fear:*—be removed {1x}, trouble {4x}, vexation {1x}. See: TWOT—540a; BDB—266b. Syn.: comp. 2189.

2114. זוּר {77x} **zûwr**, *zoor;* a prim. root; to *turn* aside (espec. for lodging); hence, to *be a foreign, strange, profane;* spec. (act. part.) to *commit adultery:*—stranger {45x}, strange {18x}, estranged {4x}, stranger + 376 {3x}, another {2x}, strange woman {2x}, gone away {1x}, fanners {1x}, another place {1x}. Syn.: 1616, 5236. See: TWOT—541; BDB—266b, 266d, 268b.

2115. זוּר {3x} **zûwr**, *zoor;* a prim. root [comp. 6695]; to *press* together, *tighten:*—close {1x}, crush {1x}, thrust together {1x}. See: TWOT—543; BDB—266d.

2116. זוּרֶה {1x} **zûwreh**, *zoo-reh';* from 2115; *trodden* on:—that which is crushed {1x}. See: TWOT—543; BDB—266d.

2117. זָזָא {1x} **Zâzâᵓ**, *zaw-zaw';* prob. from the root of 2123; *prominent; Zaza,* an Isr.:—Zaza {1x}. See: BDB—265b, 267a.

2118. זָחַח {2x} **zâchach**, *zaw-khakh';* a prim. root; to *shove* or *displace:*—loose {2x}. See: TWOT—544; BDB—267b.

2119. זָחַל {3x} **zâchal**, *zaw-khal';* a prim. root; to *crawl;* by impl. to *fear:*—be afraid {1x}, serpent {1x}, worm {1x}. See: TWOT—545; BDB—267b, 267c, 1087c.

2120. זֹחֶלֶת {1x} **Zôcheleth**, *zo-keh'-leth;* fem. act. part. of 2119; *crawling* (i.e. *serpent*); *Zocheleth,* a boundary stone in Pal.:—Zoheleth {1x}. See: BDB—267b.

2121. זֵידוֹן {1x} **zêydôwn**, *zay-dohn';* from 2102; *boiling* of water, i.e. *wave:*—proud {1x}. See: TWOT—547c; BDB—268a.

2122. זִיו {6x} **zîyv** (Aram.), *zeev;* corresp. to 2099; (fig.) *cheerfulness:*—brightness {4x}, countenance {2x}. See: TWOT—2707; BDB—1091b.

2123. זִיז {3x} **zîyz**, *zeez;* from an unused root appar. mean. to *be conspicuous; fulness* of the breast; also a moving *creature:*—abundance {1x}, wild beast {2x}. See: TWOT—535a, 536a; BDB—265a, 265c, 268d.

2124. זִיזָא {2x} **Zîyzâᵓ**, *zee-zaw';* appar. from the same as 2123; *prominence; Ziza,* the name of two Isr.:—Ziza {1x}. See: BDB—265b, 268b.

2125. זִיזָה {1x} **Zîyzâh**, *zee-zaw';* another form for 2124; *Zizah,* an Isr.:—Zizah. See: BDB—265b, 268b.

2126. זִינָא {1x} **Zîynâᵓ**, *zee-naw';* from 2109; well-*fed;* or perh. an orth. err. for 2124; *Zina,* an Isr.:—Zina {1x}. See: BDB—265b, 286b.

2127. זִיעַ {1x} **Zîyaᶜ**, *zee'-ah;* from 2111; *agitation; Zia,* an Isr.:—Zia {1x}. See: BDB—266b, 268b.

2128. זִיף {10x} **Zîyph**, *zeef;* from the same as 2203; *flowing; Ziph,* the name of a place in Pal.; also of an Isr.:—Ziph {1x}. See: BDB—268b.

2129. זִיפָה {1x} **Zîyphâh**, *zee-faw';* fem. of 2128; a *flowing; Ziphah,* an Isr.:—Ziphah {1x}. See: BDB—268b.

2130. זִיפִי {3x} **Zîyphîy**, *zee-fee';* patrial from 2128; a *Ziphite* or inhab. of Ziph:—Ziphim {1x}, Ziphite {2x}. See: BDB—268b.

2131. זִיקָה {7x} **zîyqâh** (Isa. 50:11), *zee-kaw'* (fem.); and

זִק **zîq**, *zeek;* or

זֵק **zêq**, *zake;* from 2187; prop. what *leaps* forth, i.e. *flash* of fire, or a burning *arrow;* also (from the orig. sense of the root) a *bond:*—chain {3x}, spark {2x}, firebrand {1x}, fetter {1x}. See: TWOT—573; BDB—268b, 278a, 279b.

2132. זַיִת {38x} **zayith**, *zay'-yith;* prob. from an unused root [akin to 2099]; an *olive* (as yielding *illuminating* oil), the tree, the branch or the berry:—olive {17x}, olive tree {14x}, oliveyard {6x}, Olivet {1x}. See: TWOT—548; BDB—268b.

2133. זֵיתָן {1x} **Zêythân**, *zay-thawn';* from 2132; *olive* grove; *Zethan,* an Isr.:—Zethan {1x}. See: BDB—268d.

2134. זַךְ {11x} **zak**, *zak;* from 2141; *clear:*—clean {2x}, pure {9x}. See: TWOT—550a; BDB—269a, 269b.

2135. זָכָה {8x} **zâkâh**, *zaw-kaw';* a prim. root [comp. 2141]; to *be translucent;* fig. to *be innocent:*—be (make) clean {6x}, be clear {1x}, count pure {1x}. Syn.: See 2212, 2141, 2135. There are three roots closely connected together that all represent purity cleanness, or freedom from pollution, namely (1) *zaqaq* (2212 - Ps 12:6; Mal 3:3) (2) *zakak* (2141 - Job 8:6; 11:4), and (3) *zakah* (2135 - Job 15:14; Prov 20:9). These passages refer to moral purity and transparency of heart. They point to a character free from taint or sully as the object that man aims at, but which he fails to obtain by his own devices; and even at the best, that which seems perfectly pure in his sight is proved vile when seen in the light of God. See: TWOT—549; BDB—269a, 1091b.

2136. זָכוּ {1x} **zâkûw** (Aram.), *zaw-koo';* from a root corresp. to 2135; *purity:*—innocency {1x}. See: TWOT—2708; BDB—1091b.

2137. זְכוּכִית {1x} **zᵉkûwkîyth**, *zek-oo-keeth;* from 2135; prop. *transparency,* i.e. *glass:*—crystal {1x}. See: TWOT—550b; BDB—269a, 269b.

2138. זָכוּר {4x} **zâkûwr**, *zaw-koor';* prop. pass. part. of 2142, but used for 2145; a *male* (of man or animals):—males {3x}, menchildren {1x}. Syn.: 376, 2145. See: TWOT—551f; BDB—271d.

2139. זַכּוּר {10x} **Zakkûwr**, *zaw-koor';* from 2142; *mindful; Zakkur,* the name of seven Isr.:—Zaccur {8x}, Zacchur {1x}, var. trans. {1x}. See: TWOT—551f; BDB—271d.

2140. זַכַּי {3x} **Zakkay**, *zak-kah'-ee;* from 2141; *pure; Zakkai,* an Isr.:—Zaccai {3x}. See: BDB—269b.

2141. זָכַךְ {4x} **zâkak**, *zaw-kak';* a prim. root [comp. 2135]; to *be transparent* or *clean* (phys. or mor.):—be clean {2x}, make clean {1x}, be pure {1x}. Syn.: See 2135. See: TWOT—550; BDB—269a.

2142. זָכַר {233x} **zâkar**, *zaw-kar';* a prim. root; prop. to *mark* (so as to be recognized), i.e. to *remember;* by impl. to *mention;* also (as denom. from 2145) to *be male:*—remember {172x}, mention {21x}, remembrance {10x}, recorder {9x}, mindful {6x}, think {3x}, bring to remembrance {2x}, record {2x}, × burn {1x}, to burn incense {1x}, × earnestly {1x}, be male {2x}, recount {1x}, × still {1x}, × well {1x}.

Zakar means "to remember, think of, mention." **(1)** The group of words (the verb and the three nouns derived from it) is found throughout the Old Testament. **(2)** The first occurrence of *zakar* is in Gen 8:1 with God as the subject: **(2a)** "God remembered Noah . . . : and God made a wind to pass over the earth, and the waters assuaged." **(2b)** In Gen 9:15 God said to Noah: "And I will remember my covenant . . . ; and the waters shall no more become a flood to destroy all flesh." **(2c)** As in these two cases (cf. Gen 6:18), "remember" is used of God in respect to His covenant promises and is followed by an action to fulfill His covenant. **(2d)** God delivered Lot from Sodom because of His covenant with Abraham to bless all the nations through him (Gen 18:17–33): "God remembered Abraham, and sent Lot out of the midst of the overthrow" (Gen 19:29).

(3) This marks the history of Israel at every major point: "And I have also heard the groaning of the children of Israel, . . . and I have remembered my covenant. . . . and I will bring you out from under the burdens of the Egyptians . . ." (Ex 6:5–6). **(3a)** The promise "to remember" was repeated in the covenant at Sinai (Lev 26:40–45), **(3b)** God's remembrance was sung in the Psalms (98:3; 105:8, 42; 106:45), **(3c)** and the promise was repeated by the prophets in regard to restoration from captivity (Eze 16:60). **(3d)** The new covenant promise is: ". . . I will forgive their iniquity, and I will remember their sin no more" (Jer 31:34). **(4)** Because of this God's people pray, **(4a)** as Moses: "Turn from thy fierce wrath. . . . Remember Abraham, Isaac, and Israel, thy servants, to whom thou swarest . . ." (Ex 32:12–13); or **(4b)** Nehemiah: "Remember . . . the word that thou commandedst thy servant Moses . . ." (Neh 1:8, quoting Lev 26:33); or **(4c)** the psalmist: "Remember not the sins of my youth, nor my transgressions: according to thy mercy remember thou me . . ." (Ps 25:7); or **(4d)** Jeremiah: ". . . Remember, break not thy covenant with us" (Jer 14:21).

(5) Men also "remember." Joseph said to Pharaoh's butler: "But think on me . . . , and make mention of me unto Pharaoh . . ." (Gen 40:14). **(5a)** Again, "to remember" means more than "to recall"; **(5b)** it means "to retain in thought" so as to tell someone who can take action (cf. Ps 20:7). **(6)** *Zakar* may have more specific connotations in certain circumstances: "Hear ye this, O house of Jacob, . . . which swear by the name of the Lord, . . . and make mention of the God of Israel . . ." (Is 48:1), **(6a)** pointing to the mention of God's name in worship. **(6b)** David appointed "Levites as ministers before the ark of the LORD, to invoke . . . the LORD . . ." (1 Chr 16:4). **(7)** The covenant commanded Israel to **(7a)** "remember this day, in which ye came out from Egypt . . ." (Ex 13:3); **(7b)** to "remember the sabbath day . . ." (Ex 20:8); **(7c)** to "remember that thou wast a servant in the land of Egypt, and that the LORD thy God brought thee out thence through a mighty hand . . ." (Deut 5:15 and often); and **(7d)** to "remember his marvelous works . . ." (Ps 105:5; cf. 1 Chr 16:15). **(8)** But "the children of Israel remembered not the LORD their God, who had delivered them out of the hands of all their enemies . . ." (Judg 8:34; cf. Ps 78:42). See: TWOT—551; BDB—269c, 272c, 561b.

2143. זֵכֶר {23x} **zêker**, *zay'-ker;* or
זֶכֶר **zeker**, *zeh'-ker;* from 2142; a *memento*, abstr. *recollection* (rarely if ever); by impl. *commemoration:*—remembrance {11x}, memorial {5x}, memory {5x}, remembered {1x}, scent {1x}.

Zeker means "remembrance; memorial." **(1)** Of His covenant name, YHWH ("LORD"), God said: ". . . This is my memorial unto all generations" (Ex 3:15; cf. Ps 30:4; 135:13). **(1a)** The name would recall His acts of covenant fulfillment. **(1b)** Moses was told to write an account of the war with Amalek "for a memorial [2146 - *zikkaron*] in a book, and rehearse it in the ears of Joshua: for I will utterly put out the remembrance [*zeker*] of Amalek from under heaven" (Ex 17:14). **(2)** The name would recall His acts of covenant fulfillment (Ex 17:14). See: TWOT—551a; BDB—271a, 271b.

2144. זֶכֶר {1x} **Zeker**, *zeh'-ker;* the same as 2143; *Zeker*, an Isr.:—Zeker {1x}. See: BDB—271a.

2145. זָכָר {1x} **zâkâr**, *zaw-kawr';* from 2142; prop. *remembered*, i.e. a *male* (of man or animals, as being the most noteworthy sex):—male {67x}, man {7x}, child {4x}, mankind {2x}, him {1x}.

(1) *Zakar,* as a noun, means "male." **(1a)** It occurs 82 times and usually in early prose (Genesis through Deuteronomy), only 5 times in the biblical prophets, and never in biblical wisdom or poetical literature. **(1b)** *Zakar* emphasizes "maleness" as over against "femaleness"; this word focuses on the sex of the one so named. Thus, "God created man in his own image, in the image of God created he him; male and female created he them" (Gen 1:27). **(1c)** The word can be used not only of an "adult male" but also of a "male child" (Lev 12:7). **(1d)** *Zakar* is used collectively in many passages—in singular form, with a plural reference (Judg 21:11). **(1e)** In some contexts the word represents a "male animal": "And of every living thing of all flesh, two of every sort shalt thou bring into the ark, to keep them alive with thee; they shall be male and female" (Gen 6:19). **(2)** *Zakar,* the adjective, means "male." **(2a)** "Number all the firstborn of the males of the children of Israel from a month old and upward . . ." (Num 3:40). **(2b)** The word appears in Jer 20:15: "A man child is born unto thee; making him very glad." See: TWOT—551e; BDB—271b, 1088d.

2146. זִכָּרוֹן {24x} **zikrôwn**, *zik-rone';* from 2142; a *memento* (or memorable thing, day or writing):—memorial {17x}, remembrance {6x}, records {1x}.

Zikrown means "memorial." **(1)** God gave the bronze plates covering the altar (Num 16:40) and the heap of stones at the Jordan (Josh 4:7, 20–24) as perpetual "memorials" for the sons of Israel. **(2)** The names of the twelve tribes of Israel were engraved on two stones that were attached to the ephod as "stones of memorial unto the children of Israel: and Aaron shall bear their names before the LORD . . ." (Ex 28:12; cf. v. 29). **(3)** When Israel went into battle, and when they offered sacrifice, they were to blow trumpets "that they may be to you for a memorial before your God" (Num 10:9–10). See: TWOT—551b; BDB—272a, 1088d.

2147. זִכְרִי {12x} **Zikrîy**, *zik-ree';* from 2142; *memorable; Zicri,* the name of twelve Isr.:—Zichri {12x}. See: BDB—271d.

2148. זְכַרְיָה {3x} **Zᵉkaryâh**, *zek-ar-yaw';* or
זְכַרְיָהוּ **Zᵉkaryâhûw**, *zek-ar-yaw'-hoo;* from 2142 and 3050; *Jah has remembered; Zecarjah,* the name of twenty-nine Isr.:—Zachariah or Zechariah {43x}. See: BDB—272a, 1091c.

2149. זֻלּוּת {11x} **zullûwth**, *zool-looth';* from 2151; prop. a *shaking,* i.e. perh. a *tempest:*—vilest {1x}. See: TWOT—554a; BDB—273a.

2150. זַלְזַל {1x} **zalzal**, *zal-zal';* by redupl. from 2151; *tremulous,* i.e. a *twig:*—sprig {1x}. See: TWOT—553a; BDB—272d.

2151. זָלַל {8x} **zâlal**, *zaw-lal';* a prim. root [comp. 2107]; to *shake* (as in the wind), i.e. to *quake;* fig. to *be loose* morally, *worthless* or *prodigal:*—flow down {2x}, vile {2x}, glutton {2x}, riotous eaters {1x}, riotous {1x}. See: TWOT—553, BDB—272d.

2152. זַלְעָפָה {3x} **zalʿâphâh**, *zal-aw-faw';* or
זִלְעָפָף **zilʿâphâph**, *zil-aw-faw';* from 2196; a *glow* (of wind or anger); also a *famine* (as *consuming*):—horrible {1x}, horror {1x}, terrible {1x}. See: TWOT—555a; BDB—273a.

2153. זִלְפָּה {7x} **Zilpâh**, *zil-paw;* from an unused root appar. mean. to *trickle,* as myrrh; fragrant *dropping; Zilpah,* Leah's maid:—Zilpah {7x}. See: BDB—273a.

2154. זִמָּה {29x} **zimmâh**, *zim-maw';* or
זַמָּה **zammâh**, *zam-maw';* from 2161; a *plan,* espec. a bad one:—lewdness {14x}, wickedness {4x}, mischief {3x}, lewd {2x}, heinous crime {1x}, wicked devices {1x}, lewdly {1x}, wicked mind {1x}, purposes {1x}, thought {1x}.

Zimmah means "loose conduct; lewdness." **(1)** The 29 occurrences of this noun are all in legal and poetical books of the Bible, except for a single occurrence in Judges.

(2) This noun signifies "loose or infamous conduct" and is used most often with regard to illicit sexual conduct: "Thou shalt not uncover the nakedness of a woman and her daughter, . . . or her daughter's daughter, to uncover her nakedness; for they are her near kinswomen: it is wickedness" (Lev 18:17—the first occurrence). **(3)** Rejection of God's law or spiritual adultery may be represented by *zimmah* (Ps 119:150; cf. Eze 16:12–28). **(4)** A plan or scheme identified by the word is, therefore, a "harlotrous" plan (Ps 26:10). Syn: 2161, 4209. See: TWOT—556b; BDB—273b.

2155. זִמָּה {3x} **Zimmâh**, *zim-maw';* the same as 2154; *Zimmah,* the name of two Isr.:—Zimmah {3x}. See: BDB—273c.

2156. זְמוֹרָה {5x} **zᵉmôwrâh**, *zem-o-raw';* or
זְמֹרָה **zᵉmôrâh**, *zem-o-raw'* (fem.); and
זְמֹר **zᵉmôr**, *zem-ore'* (masc.); from 2168; a *twig* (as *pruned*):—branch {3x}, branches {1x}, slip {1x}. See: TWOT—559b; BDB—274d.

2157. זַמְזֹם {1x} **Zamzôm**, *zam-zome';* from 2161; *intriguing;* a *Zamzumite,* or native tribe of Pal.:—Zamzummim {1x}. See: BDB—273d.

2158. זָמִיר {6x} **zâmîyr**, *zaw-meer';* or
זָמִר **zâmîr**, *zaw-meer';* and (fem.)
זְמִרָה **zᵉmîrâh**, *zem-ee-raw';* from 2167; a *song* to be accompanied with instrumental music:—psalmist {2x}, singing {1x}, song {3x}. See: TWOT—558b; BDB—274b.

2159. זָמִיר {1x} **zâmîyr**, *zaw-meer';* from 2168; a *twig* (as *pruned*):—branch {1x}. See: BDB—254d.

2160. זְמִירָה {1x} **Zᵉmîyrâh**, *zem-ee-raw';* fem. of 2158; *song; Zemirah,* an Isr.:—Zemira {1x}. See: BDB—275b.

2161. זָמַם {13x} **zâmam**, *zaw-mam';* a prim. root; to *plan,* usually in a bad sense:—thought {5x}, devise {3x}, consider {1x}, purpose {1x}, imagine {1x}, plot {1x}.

Zamam, the verb, means "to ponder, to cogitate." In Zec 8:14–15 the word appears to carry the sense of "to ponder": "For thus saith the LORD of hosts; As I thought (*zamam*) to punish you, when your fathers provoked me to wrath . . . and I repented not: So again have I thought (*zamam*) in these days to do well unto Jerusalem and to the house of Judah: fear ye not." Syn: 2154, 2803, 4209. See: TWOT—556; BDB—273a.

2162. זָמָם {1x} **zâmâm**, *zaw-mawm';* from 2161; a *plot:*—wicked device {1x}. See: TWOT—556a; BDB—273b.

2163. זָמַן {3x} **zâman**, *zaw-man';* a prim. root; to *fix* (a time):—appoint {3x}. See: TWOT—557; BDB—273d.

2164. זְמַן {1x} **zᵉman** (Aram.), *zem-an';* corresp. to 2163; to *agree* (on a time and place):—prepare {1x}. See: TWOT—2709; BDB—1091c.

2165. זְמָן {4x} **zᵉmân**, *zem-awn';* from 2163; an *appointed* occasion:—season {1x}, time {3x}. Syn.: 6256, 6471. See: TWOT—557a; BDB—273d, 1091c.

2166. זְמָן {11x} **zᵉmân** (Aram.), *zem-awn';* from 2165; the same as 2165:—season {2x}, time {9x}. See: TWOT—2709a; BDB—1091c.

2167. זָמַר {45x} **zâmar**, *zaw-mar';* a prim. root [perh. ident. with 2168 through the idea of *striking* with the fingers]; prop. to *touch* the strings or parts of a musical instrument, i.e. *play* upon it; to make *music,* accompanied by the voice; hence, to *celebrate* in song and music:—praise {26x}, sing {16x}, sing psalms {2x}, sing forth {1x}. Syn.: 1984, 3034, 7891. See: TWOT—558; BDB—274a, 1091c.

2168. זָמַר {3x} **zâmar**, *zaw-mar';* a prim. root [comp. 2167, 5568, 6785]; to *trim* (a vine):—prune {3x}. See: TWOT—559; BDB—274d.

2169. זֶמֶר {1x} **zemer**, *zeh'-mer;* appar. from 2167 or 2168; a *gazelle* (from its lightly *touching* the ground):—chamois {1x}. See: TWOT—560b; BDB—275a.

2170. זְמָר {4x} **zᵉmâr** (Aram.), *zem-awr';* from a root corresp. to 2167; instrumental *music:*—musick {1x}. See: TWOT—2710a; BDB—1091c.

זָמִר **zâmîr**. See 2158.

זְמֹר **zᵉmôr**. See 2156.

2171. זַמָּר {1x} **zammâr** (Aram.), *zam-mawr';* from the same as 2170; an instrumental *musician:*—singer {1x}. See: TWOT—2710b; BDB—1091c.

2172. זִמְרָה {4x} **zimrâh**, *zim-raw';* from 2167; a *musical* piece or *song* to be accompanied by an instrument:—melody {2x}, psalm {2x}. Syn.: 4210. See: TWOT—558a; BDB—274b.

2173. זִמְרָה {1x} **zimrâh**, *zim-raw';* from 2168; *pruned* (i.e. *choice*) fruit:—best fruit {1x}. Syn.: 6529. See: TWOT—560a; BDB—275a.

זְמִרָה **zᵉmîrâh**. See 2158.

זְמֹרָה **zᵉmôrâh**. See 2156.

2174. זִמְרִי {15x} **Zimrîy**, *zim-ree';* from 2167; *musical; Zimri,* the name of five Isr., and of an Arabian tribe:—Zimri {15x}. See: BDB—275b.

2175. זִמְרָן {2x} **Zimrân**, *zim-rawn';* from 2167; *musical; Zimran,* a son of Abraham by Keturah:—*Zimran* {2x}. See: BDB—275b.

2176. זִמְרָת {3x} **zimrâth**, *zim-rawth';* from 2167; instrumental *music;* by impl. *praise:*—song {3x}. Syn.: 7892. See: TWOT—558a; BDB—274b.

2177. זַן {3x} **zan**, *zan;* from 2109; prop. *nourished* (or fully *developed*), i.e. a *form* or *sort:*—divers kinds {2x}, × all manner of store {1x}. See: TWOT—561; BDB—275b, 1091c.

2178. זַן {1x} **zan** (Aram.), *zan;* corresp. to 2177; *sort:*—kind {1x}. See: TWOT—2711; BDB—1091c.

2179. זָנַב {2x} **zânab**, *zaw-nab';* a prim. root mean. to *wag;* used only as a denom. from 2180; to *curtail,* i.e. *cut* off the rear:—smite the hindmost {2x}. See: TWOT—562; BDB—275c.

2180. זָנָב {11x} **zânâb**, *zaw-nawb';* from 2179 (in the orig. sense of *flapping*); the *tail* (lit. or fig.):—tail {11x}. See: TWOT—562a; BDB—275b.

2181. זָנָה {93x} **zânâh**, *zaw-naw';* a prim. root [highly-*fed* and therefore *wanton*]; to *commit adultery* (usually of the female, and less often of simple fornication, rarely of involuntary ravishment); fig. to *commit idolatry* (the Jewish people being regarded as the spouse of Jehovah):—harlot {36x}, go a whoring {19x}, . . . whoredom {15x}, whore {11x}, commit fornication {3x}, whorish {3x}, harlot + 802 {2x}, commit {1x}, continually {1x}, great {1x}, whore's + 802 {1x}.

Zanah means "to go a whoring, commit fornication, be a harlot, serve other gods." **(1)** This is the regular term denoting prostitution throughout the history of Hebrew, with special nuances coming out of the religious experience of ancient Israel. **(2)** It is used for the first time in the text at the conclusion of the story of the rape of Dinah by Shechem, as her brothers excuse their revenge by asking: "Should he deal with our sister as with a harlot?" (Gen 34:31). **(3)** While the term means "to commit fornication," whether by male or by female, **(3a)** it is to be noted that it is almost never used to describe sexual misconduct on the part of a male in the Old Testament. **(3b)** Part of the reason lies in the differing attitude in ancient Israel concerning sexual activity by men and women. **(3b)** The main reason, however, is the fact that this term is used most frequently to describe "spiritual prostitution" **(3b1)** in which Israel turned from God to strange gods.

(3b2) Deut 31:16 illustrates this meaning: "And the LORD said unto Moses, Behold, thou shalt sleep with thy fathers; and this people will rise up, and go a whoring after the gods of the strangers of the land, whither they go to be among them, and will forsake me, and break my covenant which I have made with them." **(4)** *Zanah* became, then, the common term for spiritual backsliding. **(4a)** The act of harloting after strange gods was more than changing gods, however. This was especially true when Israel went after the Canaanite gods, for the worship of these pagan deities involved actual prostitution with cult prostitutes connected with the Canaanite shrines. **(4b)** In the Old Testament sometimes the use of the phrase "go a whoring after" gods **(4b1)** implies an individual's involvement with cult prostitutes.

(4b2) An example might be in Ex 34:15–16: "Lest thou make a covenant with the inhabitants of the land, and they go a whoring after their gods, and do sacrifice unto their gods. . . . And thou take of their daughters unto thy sons, and their daughters go a whoring after their gods, and make thy sons go a whoring after their gods." **(5)** The religious theory behind such activity at the Canaanite shrine was that such **(5a)** sexual activity with cult prostitutes, both male and female, **(5b)** who represented the gods and goddesses of the Canaanite fertility cult, **(5c)** would stimulate fertility in their crops and flocks. **(5d)** Such cult prostitutes were not designated as prostitutes but rather "holy ones" or "set-apart ones," **(5d1)** since the Semitic term for "holy" means, first of all, to be set apart for a special use. **(5d2)** This is illustrated in Deut 23:17: "There shall be a whore of the daughters of Israel, neither shall there be a "sodomite of the sons of Israel."

(5e) This theme of religious harlotry looms large in the prophets who denounce this backsliding in no uncertain terms. **(5e1)** Ezekiel minces no words as he openly calls both Judah and Israel "harlots" and vividly describes their backsliding in sexual terms (Eze 16:6–63; 23). **(5e2)** The Book of Hosea, in which Hosea's wife Gomer became unfaithful and most likely was involved in such cult prostitution, again illustrates not only Hosea's heartbreak but also God's own heartbreak because of the unfaithfulness of his wife, Israel. Israel's unfaithfulness appears in Hos 9:1: "Rejoice not, O Israel, for joy, as other people: for thou hast gone a whoring from thy God, thou hast loved a reward upon every cornfloor." See: TWOT—563; BDB—266a, 275c.

2182. זָנוֹחַ {5x} **Zânôwach**, *zaw-no'-akh;* from 2186; *rejected; Zanoach,* the name of two places in Pal.:—Zanoah {5x}. See: BDB—276c.

2183. זְנוּן {12x} **zânûwn**, *zaw-noon';* from 2181; *adultery;* fig. *idolatry:*—whoredom {12x}. Syn.: 8457. See: TWOT—563a; BDB—276.

2184. זְנוּת {9x} **zᵉnûwth**, *zen-ooth';* from 2181; *adultery,* i.e. (fig.) *infidelity, idolatry:*—whoredom {9x}. Syn.: 8457. See: TWOT—563b; BDB—276a.

2185. זֹנוֹת {1x} **zônôwth**, *zo-noth';* regarded by some as if from 2109 or an unused root, and applied to military *equipments;* but evidently the fem. plur. act. part. of 2181; *harlots:*—armour {1x}. See: BDB—275d.

2186. זָנַח {20x} **zânach**, *zaw-nakh';* a prim. root mean. to *push* aside, i.e. *reject, forsake, fail:*—cast . . . off {17x}, cast away {1x}, turn . . . away {1x}, removed . . . far off {1x}. Syn.: 1644, 2904. See: TWOT—564; BDB—276b, 276c.

2187. זָנַק {1x} **zânaq**, *zaw-nak';* a prim. root; prop. to *draw together* the feet (as an animal about to dart upon its prey), i.e. to *spring* forward:—leap {1x}. See: TWOT—566; BDB—276c.

2188. זֵעָה {1x} **zêʿâh**, *zay-aw';* from 2111 (in the sense of 3154); *perspiration:*—sweat {1x}. See: TWOT—857b; BDB—276c, 402c.

2189. זַעֲוָה {7x} **zaʿăvâh**, *zah-av-aw';* by transp. for 2113; *agitation, maltreatment:* —× removed {6x}, trouble {1x}. See: TWOT—540a; BDB—266b, 276c.

2190. זַעֲוָן {2x} **Zaʿăvân**, *zah-av-awn';* from 2111; *disquiet; Zaavan,* an Idumæan:—*Zaavan* {2x}. See: BDB—266b, 276c.

2191. זְעֵיר {5x} **zᵉʿêyr**, *zeh-ayr';* from an unused root [akin (by perm.) to 6819], mean. to *dwindle; small:*—little {5x}. See: TWOT—571a; BDB—277d, 1091d.

2192. זְעֵיר {1x} **zᵉʿêyr** (Aram.), *zeh-ayr'*; corresp. to 2191:—little {1x}. See: TWOT—2712; BDB—1091d.

2193. זָעַךְ {1x} **zâʿak**, *zaw-ak'*; a prim. root; to *extinguish:*—be extinct {1x}. See: TWOT—567; BDB—276c.

2194. זָעַם {12x} **zâʿam**, *zaw-am'*; a prim. root; prop. to *foam* at the mouth, i.e. to *be enraged:*—indignation {4x}, defy {3x}, abhor {2x}, angry {2x}, abominable {1x}. Syn.: 7110. See: TWOT—568; BDB—276d.

2195. זַעַם **zaʿam**, *zah'-am*; from 2194; strictly *froth* at the mouth, i.e. (fig.) *fury* (espec. of God's displeasure with sin):—angry {1x}, indignation {20x}, rage {1x}. See: TWOT—568a; BDB—276d.

2196. זָעַף {5x} **zâʿaph**, *zaw-af'*; a prim. root; prop. to *boil* up, i.e. (fig.) to *be peevish* or *angry:*—fret {1x}, sad {1x}, worse liking {1x}, be wroth {2x}. See: TWOT—569; BDB—277a.

2197. זַעַף {6x} **zaʿaph**, *zah'-af*; from 2196; *anger:*—indignation {1x}, rage {2x}, raging {1x}, wrath {1x}. See: TWOT—569a; BDB—277a.

2198. זָעֵף {2x} **zâʿêph**, *zaw-afe'*; from 2196; *angry:*—displeased {2x}. See: TWOT—569b; BDB—277a.

2199. זָעַק {73x} **zâʿaq**, *zaw-ak'*; a prim. root; to *shriek* (from anguish or danger); by anal. (as a herald) to *announce* or *convene* publicly:—cry {50x}, cry out {11x}, assemble {3x}, called {3x}, gathered together {2x}, gathered {2x}, company {1x}, proclaimed {1x}.

Zaʿaq means "to cry, cry out, call." **(1)** Its first occurrence is in the record of the suffering of the Israelite bondage in Egypt: ". . . And the children of Israel sighed by reason of the bondage, and they cried [for help] . . ." (Ex 2:23). **(2)** *Zaʿaq* is perhaps most frequently used to indicate the "crying out" for aid in time of emergency, **(2a)** especially "crying out" for divine aid. **(2b)** God often heard this "cry" for help in the time of the judges, as Israel found itself in trouble because of its backsliding (Judg 3:9, 15; 6:7; 10:10). **(3)** The word is used also in appeals to pagan gods (Judg 10:14; Jer 11:12; Jonah 1:5). **(4)** That *zaʿaq* means more than a normal speaking volume is indicated in appeals to the king (2 Sa 19:28). **(5)** The word may imply **(5a)** a "crying out" in distress (1 Sa 4:13), **(5b)** a "cry" of horror (1 Sa 5:10), or **(5c)** a "cry" of sorrow (2 Sa 13:19). **(6)** Used figuratively, it is said that "the stone shall cry out of the wall" (Hab 2:11) of a house that is built by means of evil gain. Syn.: 6817, 7121, 7440, 77070. See: TWOT—570; BDB—277a, 1091c.

2200. זְעִק {1x} **zᵉʿîq** (Aram.), *zeh-eek'*; corresp. to 2199; to *make an outcry:*—cry {1x}. See: TWOT—2712; BDB—1091c.

2201. זַעַק {18x} **zaʿaq**, *zah'-ak*; and (fem.)

זְעָקָה **zᵉʿâqâh**, *zeh-aw-kaw'*; from 2199; a *shriek* or *outcry:*—cry {17x}, crying {1x}. See: TWOT—570a; BDB—277c.

2202. זִפְרֹן {1x} **Ziphrôn**, *zi-frone'*; from an unused root (mean. to *be fragrant*); *Ziphron*, a place in Pal.:—*Ziphron* {1x}. See: BDB—277d.

2203. זֶפֶת {3x} **zepheth**, *zeh'-feth*; from an unused root (mean. to *liquify*); *asphalt* (from its tendency to *soften* in the sun):—pitch {3x}. See: TWOT—572; BDB—278a.

זִק **zîq** or

זֵק **zêq**. See 2131.

2204. זָקֵן {27x} **zâqên**, *zaw-kane'*; a prim. root; to *be old:*—aged man {1x}, old {26x}.

Zaqen means "old man; old woman; elder; old." **(1)** The first occurrence is in Gen 18:11: "Now Abraham and Sarah were old and well stricken in age; and it ceased to be with Sarah after the manner of women." **(2)** In Gen 19:4, the word "old" is used as an antonym of "young": **(2a)** "But before they lay down, the men of the city, even the men of Sodom, compassed the house round, both old and young [5288 - *na'ar*, "young man"], all the people from every quarter" (cf. Josh 6:21). **(2b)** A similar usage of *zaqen* and "young" appears in other Bible references: "But [Rehoboam] forsook the counsel of the old men, which they had given him, and consulted with the young men [3206 - *yeled*, "boy; child"] that were grown up with him . . ." (1 Kin 12:8). **(2c)** "Then shall the virgin rejoice in the dance, both young men [970 - *bachur*] and old together: for I will turn their mourning into joy, and will comfort them, and make them rejoice from their sorrow" (Jer 31:13).

(3) The "old man" is described as **(3a)** being advanced in days (Gen 18:11), **(3b)** as being satisfied with life or full of years. **(4)** A feminine form of *zaqen* refers to an "old woman" (2205 - *zeqenah*). **(5)** The word *zaqen* has a more specialized use with the sense of "elder" (more than 100 times). **(5a)** The "elder" was recognized by the people for his gifts of leadership, wisdom, and justice. He was set apart to administer justice, settle disputes, and guide the people of his charge. **(5b)** Elders are also known as officers (7860 - *shotrim*), heads of the tribes, and judges; notice the parallel usage: "Joshua called for all Israel, and for their elders and for their heads, and for their judges, and for their officers, and said unto them; I am old and stricken in age . . ." (Josh 23:2).

(6) The "elders" were consulted by the king, but the king could determine his own course of action (1 Kin 12:8). **(7)** In a given city, the governing council was made up of the "elders," who were charged with the well-being of the town: "And Samuel did that which the LORD spake, and came to Bethlehem. And the elders of the town trembled at his coming, and said, Comest thou peaceably?" (1 Sa 16:4). **(8)** The elders met in session **(8a)** by the city gate (Eze 8:1). **(8b)** The place of meeting became known as the "seat" or "assembly") of the elders (Ps 107:32). **(9)** The KJV gives various translations of *zaqen:* "old; elder; old man; ancient." **(9a)** Note that the KJV distinguishes between "elder" and "ancient"; **(9b)** whenever the word *zaqen* does not apply to age or to rule, the KJV uses the word "ancient." See: TWOT—574; BDB—278b.

2205. זָקֵן {178x} **zâqên**, *zaw-kane'*; from 2204; *old:*—elders {115x}, old {23x}, old man {19x}, ancient {14x}, aged {3x}, eldest {1x}, ancient man {1x}, senators {1x}, old women {1x}.

(1) The word *zaqen* has a specialized use as elder **(1a)** recognized by the people for his gifts of leadership, wisdom, and justice; **(1b)** set apart to administer justice, settle disputes, and guide the people of his charge; **(1c)** known as officers (*shotrim* -7860), heads of the tribes, and judges (Josh 23:2); **(1d)** consulted by the king, but the king could determine his own course of action (1 Kin 12:8). **(2)** In a given city, the governing council was made up of the elders who **(2a)** were charged with the well-being of the town (1 Sa 16:4) and **(2b)** met in session by the city gate (Eze 8:1), with the place of meeting known as the seat/council/assembly of the elders (Ps 107:32). Whenever the word *zaqen* does not apply to age or to rule, the KJV uses the word ancient. See: TWOT—574b; BDB—278C.

2206. זָקָן {19x} **zâqân**, *zaw-kawn'*; from 2204; the *beard* (as indicating *age*):—beard.

Zaqan means "beard." **(1)** The word *zaqan* refers to a "beard" in Ps 133:2: "It is like the precious ointment upon the head, that ran down upon the beard, even Aaron's beard: that went down to the skirts of his garments. . . ." **(2)** The association of "old age" with a "beard" can be made, but should not be stressed. See: TWOT—574a; BDB—278a.

2207. זֹקֶן {1x} **zôqen**, *zo'-ken*; from 2204; old *age:*—age {1x}. See: TWOT—574c; BDB—279a.

2208. זָקֻן {4x} **zâqûn**, *zaw-koon'*; prop. pass. part. of 2204 (used only in the plur. as a noun); *old* age:—old age {4x}. See: TWOT—574e; BDB—279a.

2209. זִקְנָה {6x} **ziqnâh**, *zik-naw'*; fem. of 2205; old *age:*—old {3x}, old age {3x}. See: TWOT—574d; BDB—279a.

2210. זָקַף {2x} **zâqaph**, *zaw-kaf'*; a prim. root; to *lift*, i.e. (fig.) *comfort:*—raise (up) {2x}. See: TWOT—575; BDB—279a, 1091d.

2211. זְקַף {1x} **zᵉqaph** (Aram.), *zek-af'*; corresp. to 2210; to *hang*, i.e. *impale:*—set up {1x}. See: TWOT—2714; BDB—1091d.

2212. זָקַק {7x} **zâqaq**, *zaw-kak'*; a prim. root; to *strain*, (fig.) *extract, clarify:*—fine {1x}, pour down {1x}, purge {1x}, purify {1x}, refine {3x}. Syn.: See 2135. See: TWOT—576; 279b; BDB—279b.

2213. זֵר {10x} **zêr**, *zare*; from 2237 (in the sense of *scattering*); a *chaplet* (as *spread* around the top), i.e. (spec.) a border *moulding:*—crown {10x}. See: TWOT—543a; BDB—267a, 279c.

2214. זָרָא {1x} **zârâʾ**, *zaw-raw'*; from 2114 (in the sense of *estrangement*) [comp. 2219]; *disgust:*—loathsome {1x}. See: TWOT—542a; BDB—266d, 279c.

2215. זָרַב {1x} **zârab**, *zaw-rab'*; a prim. root; to *flow* away:—wax warm {1x}. See: TWOT—578; BDB—279c.

2216. זְרֻבָּבֶל {21x} **Zᵉrubbâbel**, *zer-oob-baw-bel'*; from 2215 and 894; *descended of* (i.e. from) *Babylon*, i.e. born there; *Zerubbabel*, an Isr.:—Zerubbabel {21x}. See: TWOT—578a; BDB—279c, 1091d.

2217. זְרֻבָּבֶל {1x} **Zᵉrubbâbel** (Aram.), *zer-oob-baw-bel'*; corresp. to 2216:—Zerubbabel {1x}. See: BDB—1091d.

2218. זֶרֶד {4x} **Zered**, *zeh'-red*; from an unused root mean. to *be exuberant* in growth; lined with *shrubbery*; *Zered*, a brook E. of the Dead Sea:—Zared {1x}, Zered {3x}. See: BDB—279c.

2219. זָרָה {39x} **zârâh**, *zaw-raw'*; a prim. root [comp. 2114]; to *toss* about; by impl. to *diffuse, winnow:*—scatter {19x}, disperse {8x}, fan {4x}, spread {2x}, winnowed {2x}, cast away {1x}, scatter away {1x}, compass {1x}, strawed {1x}. Syn.: 967, 2236, 6340, 6566. See: TWOT—579; BDB—279d, 561d.

2220. זְרוֹעַ {91x} **zᵉrôwaᶜ**, *zer-o'-ah;* or (short.)

זְרֹעַ **zᵉrôaᶜ**, *zer-o'-ah;* and (fem.)

זְרוֹעָה **zᵉrôwᶜâh**, *zer-o-aw';* or

זְרֹעָה **zᵉrôᶜâh**, *zer-o-aw';* from 2232; the *arm* (as *stretched* out), or (of animals) the *foreleg;* fig. *force:*—arm {83x}, power {3x}, shoulder {2x}, holpen {1x}, mighty {1x}, strength {1x}.

Zeroa' means "arm; power; strength; help." **(1)** *Zeroa'* means "arm," a part of the body: **(1a)** "Blessed be he that enlargeth Gad: he dwelleth as a lion, and teareth the arm with the crown of the head" (Deut 33:20). **(1b)** The word refers to arms in Gen 49:24 (the first occurrence): "But his bow abode in strength, and the arms of his hands were made strong. . . ." The strength of his arms enabled him to draw the bow. **(2)** In some passages, *zeroa'* refers especially to the forearm: "It shall be as when the harvestman gathereth the corn, and reapeth the ears with his arm. . . ." (Is 17:5). **(3)** Elsewhere, the word represents the shoulder: "And Jehu drew a bow with his full strength, and smote Jehoram between his arms . . ." (2 Kin 9:24). **(4)** *Zeroa'* connotes the "seat of strength": **(4a)** "He teacheth my hands to war, so that a bow of steel is broken by mine arms" (Ps 18:34). **(4b)** In Job 26:2, the poor are described as the arm that hath no strength. **(5)** God's strength is figured by anthropomorphisms (attributing to His human bodily parts), such as His "stretched out arm" (Deut 4:34) or His "strong arm" (Jer 21:5).

(6) In Is 30:30, the word seems to represent lightning bolts: "And the Lord shall cause his glorious voice to be heard, and shall show the lighting down of his arm, with the indignation of his anger, and with the flame of a devouring fire, with scattering, and tempest, and hailstones" (cf. Job 40:9). **(7)** The arm is frequently a symbol of strength, both of man (1 Sa 2:31) and of God (Ps 71:18): "Now also when I am old and grayheaded, O God, forsake me not; until I have showed thy strength unto this generation, and thy power to every one that is to come." **(8)** In Eze 22:6 *zeroa'* may be translated "power": "Behold, the princes of Israel, every one were in thee to their power to shed blood." **(9)** *Zeroa'* is also translated "help": "Assur also is joined with them: they have helped the children of Lot" (Ps 83:8). **(10)** The word can represent political or military forces: "And the arms of the south shall not withstand, neither his chosen people, neither shall there be any strength to withstand" (Dan 11:15; cf. Eze 17:9). **(11)** In Num 6:19 *zeroa'* is used of an animal's shoulder: "And the priest shall take the sodden shoulder of the ram . . ." (cf. Deut 18:3). See: TWOT—583a; BDB—283d, 1089a.

2221. זֵרוּעַ {2x} **zêrûwaᶜ**, *zay-roo'-ah;* from 2232; something *sown,* i.e. a *plant:*—sowing {1x}, thing that is sown {1x}. See: TWOT—582b; BDB—283b.

2222. זַרְזִיף {1x} **zarzîyph**, *zar-zeef';* by redupl. from an unused root mean. to *flow;* a *pouring rain:*—water {1x}. Syn.: 4325. See: TWOT—584a; BDB—280a, 284b.

זְרוֹעָה **zᵉrôwᶜâh**. See 2220.

2223. זַרְזִיר {1x} **zarzîyr**, *zar-zeer';* by redupl. from 2115; prop. tightly *girt,* i.e. prob. a *racer,* or some fleet animal (as being *slender* in the waist):—+ greyhound {1x}. See: TWOT—543b; BDB—267a, 280a.

2224. זָרַח **zârach**, *zaw-rakh';* a prim. root; prop. to *irradiate* (or shoot forth beams), i.e. to *rise* (as the sun); spec. to *appear* (as a symptom of leprosy):—arise {8x}, rise {6x}, rise up {2}, shine {1x}, up {1x}. See: TWOT—580; BDB—280b.

2225. זֶרַח {1x} **zerach**, *zeh'-rakh;* from 2224; a *rising* of light:—rising {1x}. See: TWOT—580a; BDB—280b.

2226. זֶרַח {21x} **Zerach**, *zeh'-rakh;* the same as 2225; *Zerach,* the name of three Isr., also of an Idumæan and an Ethiopian prince:—Zarah {20x}, Zerah {1x}. See: BDB—280b.

2227. זַרְחִי {6x} **Zarchîy**, *zar-khee';* patron. from 2226; a *Zarchite* or desc. of Zerach:—Zarchite {6x}. See: BDB—280c.

2228. זְרַחְיָה {5x} **Zᵉrachyâh**, *zer-akh-yaw';* from 2225 and 3050; *Jah has risen; Zerachjah,* the name of two Isr.:—Zerahiah {1x}. See: BDB—280c.

2229. זָרַם {2x} **zâram**, *zaw-ram';* a prim. root; to *gush* (as water):—carry away as with a flood {1x}, pour out {1x}. See: TWOT—581; BDB—281a.

2230. זֶרֶם {9x} **zerem**, *zeh'-rem;* from 2229; a *gush* of water:—flood {1x}, overflowing {1x}, shower {1x}, storm {3x}, tempest {3x}. See: TWOT—581a; BDB—281b.

2231. זִרְמָה {2x} **zirmâh**, *zir-maw';* fem. of 2230; a *gushing* of fluid (semen):—issue {2x}. See: TWOT—581b; BDB—281b.

2232. זָרַע {56x} **zâraᶜ**, *zaw-rah';* a prim. root; to *sow;* fig. to *disseminate, plant, fructify:*—sow {47x}, yielding {3x}, sower {2x}, bearing {1x}, conceive {1x}, seed {1x}, set {1x}.

Zara' means "to sow, scatter seed, make pregnant." **(1)** It occurs first in Gen 1:29 in the summary of the blessings of creation which God has given to mankind: ". . . In the which is the fruit of a tree yielding seed. . . ." **(2)** In an agricultural society such as ancient Israel, *zara'* would be most important and very commonly used, especially to describe the annual sowing of crops (Judg 6:3; Gen 26:12). **(3)** Used in the figurative sense, it is said that Yahweh "will sow" Israel in the land (Hos 2:23); in the latter days, Yahweh promises: ". . . I will sow the house of Israel and the house of Judah with the seed of man, and with the seed of beast" (Jer 31:27). **(4)** Of great continuing comfort are the words, "They that sow in tears shall reap in joy" (Ps 126:5). The universal law of the harvest, sowing and reaping, applies to all areas of life and experience.

(5) In Num 5, which describes the law of trial by ordeal in the case of a wife accused of infidelity. **(5a)** If she was found innocent, it was declared: ". . . She shall be free, and shall conceive [*zara'*] seed [*zera'*]" (Num 5:28). **(5b)** This phrase is literally: "She shall be acquitted and shall be seeded seed," or "She shall be made pregnant with seed." **(6)** An Old Testament name, Jezreel, has been connected with this root. Jezreel ("God sows") refers both to a city and valley near Mt. Gilboa (Josh 17:16; 2 Sa 2:9) and to the symbolically named son of Hosea (Hos 1:4). See: TWOT—582; BDB—281b, 1091d.

2233. זֶרַע {229x} **zeraᶜ**, *zeh'-rah;* from 2232; *seed;* fig. *fruit, plant, sowing-time, posterity:*—seed {221x}, child {2x}, carnally + 7902 {2x}, carnally {1x}, fruitful {1x}, seedtime {1x}, sowing time {1x}.

Zera' means "seed; sowing; seedtime; harvest; offspring; descendant(s); posterity." **(1)** *Zera'* refers to the process of scattering seed, or "sowing." **(1a)** This is the emphasis in Gen 47:24: "And it shall come to pass in the increase, that ye shall give the fifth part unto Pharaoh, and four parts shall be your own, for seed of the field, and for your food. . . ." **(1b)** Num. 20:5: ". . . it *is* no place of seed, or of figs, or of vines, or of pomegranates; neither *is* there any water to drink.: "." **(1c)** Eze 17:5 "He took also of the seed of the land, and planted it in a fruitful field;" **(1d)** A closely related emphasis occurs in passages such as Gen 8:22, where the word represents "sowing" as a regularly recurring activity: "While the earth remaineth, seedtime and harvest, and cold and heat . . . shall not cease."

(2) *Zera'* frequently means "seed." There are several nuances under this emphasis, **(2a)** the first being what is sown to raise crops for food. The Egyptians told Joseph: "Buy us and our land for bread, and we and our land will be servants unto Pharaoh: and give us seed, that we may live, and not die, that the land be not desolate" (Gen 47:19).

(2b) The word represents the product of a plant: "Let the earth bring forth grass, the herb yielding seed [food], and the fruit tree yielding fruit after his kind, whose seed is in itself . . ." (Gen 1:11-the first biblical appearance). **(2c)** In this and other contexts *zera'* specifically refers to "grain seed," or "edible seed" (cf. Lev 27:30). **(2d)** This may be the meaning of the word in 1 Sa 8:15: "And he will take the tenth of your seed, and of your vineyards. . . ." **(3)** In other contexts the word represents an entire "crop or harvest": "For the seed [harvest] shall be prosperous; the vine shall give her fruit, and the ground shall give her increase, and the heavens shall give their dew . . ." (Zec 8:12). **(4)** In Is 23:3 *zera'* and the usual Hebrew word for "harvest" (7105 - *qatsir*) are in synonymous parallelism. **(5)** *Zera'* sometimes means **(5a)** "semen," or a man's "seed": "And if any man's seed of copulation go out from him [if he has a seminal emission] . . ." (Lev 15:16). **(5b)** A beast's "semen" can also be indicated by this word (Jer 31:27).

(6) *Zera'* often means "offspring." **(6a)** "And I will put enmity between thee [the devil] and the woman [Eve], and between thy seed and her seed . . ." (Gen 3:15). **(6b)** This verse uses the word in several senses. **(6b1)** The first appearance means both the descendants of the snake and those of the spiritual being who used the snake (evil men). **(6b2)** The second appearance of the word refers to all the descendants of the woman and ultimately to a particular descendant (Christ). **(7)** In Gen 4:25 *zera'* appears not as a collective noun but refers to a particular and immediate "offspring"; upon the birth of Seth, Eve said: "God . . . hath appointed me another seed [offspring]. . . ." **(7a)** Gen 46:6 uses the word (in the singular) of one's entire family including children and grandchildren (cf. Gen 17:12). **(7b)** One's larger family, including all immediate relatives, is included in the word in passages such as 1 Kin 11:14. **(8)** The word is used of an entire nation of people in Est 10:3.

(9) *Zera'* is used of groups and individuals marked by a common moral quality. **(9a)** This usage was already seen in Gen 3:15. **(9b)** Is 65:23 mentions the "seed" of the blessed of God. The Messiah or Suffering Servant will see His "offspring," or those who believe in and follow Him (Is 53:10). **(10)** We also read about **(10a)** the followers of the righteous (Prov 11:21), **(10b)** the faithful "seed" (Jer 2:21), and **(10c)** godly "offspring." **(10d)** In each case this word represents those who are united by being typified by the modifier of *zera'*. **(11)** Several other passages exhibit the same nuance except that *zera'* is modified by an undesirable quality. See: TWOT—582a; BDB—282a, 1091d.

2234. זְרַע {1x} **zᵉraʿ** (Aram.), *zer-ah';* corresp. to 2233; *posterity:*—seed {1x}. See: TWOT—2715; BDB—1091d.

זְרֹעַ **zᵉrôaʿ**. See 2220.

זֵרֹעַ {2x} **zêrôaʿ**, *zay-ro'-ah;* or

2235. זֵרָעֹן **zêrâʿôn**, *zay-raw-ohn';* from 2232; something *sown* (only in the plur.), i.e. a *vegetable* (as food):—pulse {1x}. See: TWOT—582c; BDB—283b.

זְרֹעָה **zᵉrôʿâh**. See 2220.

2236. זָרַק **zâraq**, *zaw-rak';* a prim. root; to *sprinkle* (fluid or solid particles):—sprinkle {31x}, scatter {2x}, here and there {1x}, strowed {1x}. Syn.: 967, 5137.

Zaraq means "to throw; sprinkle; strew; toss; scatter abundantly." **(1)** Used 35 times in the text of the Hebrew Old Testament, **(1a)** in 26 of those times it expresses the "throwing" or "sprinkling" of blood against the sacrificial altar or on the people. **(1b)** Thus, it appears very often in Leviticus (1:5, 11; 3:2, 8, 13 et al.). **(2)** Ezekiel's version of "the New Covenant" includes the "sprinkling" of the water of purification (Eze 36:25). **(3)** In the first use of *zaraq* in the Old Testament, it describes the "throwing" of handsful of dust into the air which would settle down on the Egyptians and cause boils (Ex 9:8, 10). **(4)** In his reform, Josiah ground up the Canaanite idol images and "scattered, strewed," the dust over the graves of idol worshipers (2 Chr 34:4). **(5)** In Ezekiel's vision of the departure of God's glory from the temple, the man in linen takes burning coals and "scatters" them over Jerusalem (Eze 10:2). See: TWOT—585, BDB—284c.

2237. זָרַר {1x} **zârar**, *zaw-rar';* a prim. root [comp. 2114]; perh. to *diffuse*, i.e. (spec.) to *sneeze:*—sneeze {1x}. See: TWOT—586; BDB—284b.

2238. זֶרֶשׁ {4x} **Zeresh**, *zeh'-resh;* of Pers. or.; *Zeresh,* Haman's wife:—Zeresh {4x}. See: BDB—284d.

2239. זֶרֶת {7x} **zereth**, *zeh'-reth;* from 2219; the *spread* of the fingers, i.e. a *span:*—span {1x}. See: TWOT—587; BDB—284d.

2240. זַתּוּא {4} **Zattûwʾ**, *zat-too';* of uncert. der.; *Zattu,* an Isr.:—Zattu {1x}. See: BDB—285c.

2241. זֵתָם {2} **Zêthâm**, *zay-thawm';* appar. a var. for 2133; *Zetham,* an Isr.:—Zetham {2}. See: BDB—268d, 285c.

2242. זֵתַר {1x} **Zêthar**, *zay-thar';* of Pers. or.; *Zethar,* a eunuch of Xerxes:—Zethar {1x}. See: BDB—285c.

ח

2243. חֹב {1x} **chôb**, *khobe;* by contr. from 2245; prop. a *cherisher*, i.e. the *bosom:*—bosom {1x}. Syn.: 2436, 2683. See: TWOT—589a; BDB—285a, 285c.

2244. חָבָא {33x} **châbâʾ**, *khaw-baw';* a prim. root [comp. 2245]; to *secrete:*—× held {1x}, hide (self) {31x}, do secretly {1x}. Syn.: 2247, 2931, 5641, 5956. See: TWOT—588; BDB—285a.

2245. חָבַב {1x} **châbab**, *khaw-bab';* a prim. root [comp. 2244, 2247]; prop. to *hide* (as in the bosom), i.e. to *cherish* (with affection):—love {1x}. Syn.: 157, 160. See: TWOT—589; BDB—285c.

2246. חֹבָב {2x} **Chôbâb**, *kho-bawb';* from 2245; *cherished; Chobab,* father-in-law of Moses:—Hobab {2x}. See: BDB—285d.

2247. חָבָה {5x} **châbah**, *khaw-bah';* a prim. root [comp. 2245]; to *secrete:*—hide (self) {5x}. Syn.: 2244, 2931, 5641, 5956. See: TWOT—590; BDB—285d.

2248. חֲבוּלָה {1x} **chăbûwlâh** (Aram.), *khab-oo-law';* from 2255; prop. *overthrown,* i.e. (morally) *crime:*—hurt {1x}. See: TWOT—2716b; BDB—1092a.

2249. חָבוֹר {1x} **Châbôwr**, *khaw-bore';* from 2266; *united; Chabor,* a river of Assyria:—Habor {3x}. See: BDB—289c.

2250. חַבּוּרָה {7x} **chabbûwrâh**, *khab-boo-raw';* or

חַבֻּרָה **chabbûrâh**, *khab-boo-raw';* or

חֲבֻרָה **chăbûrâh**, *khab-oo-raw';* from 2266; prop. *bound* (with stripes), i.e. a *weal* (or black-and-blue mark itself):—stripe {3x}, hurt {1x}, wounds {1x}, blueness {1x}, bruise {1x}. Syn.: 2257. See: TWOT—598g; BDB—289a, 289c.

2251. חָבַט **châbat**, *khaw-bat';* a prim. root; to *knock* out or off:—beat out {2x}, beat off {1x}, beat down {1x}, threshed {1x}. Syn.: 1758. See: TWOT—591; BDB—286a.

2252. חֲבַיָּה {2x} **Chăbayâh**, *khab-ah-yaw';* or

חֲבָיָה **Chăbâyâh**, *khab-aw-yaw';* from 2247 and 3050; *Jah has hidden; Chabajah,* an Isr.:—Habaiah {2x}. See: BDB—285d, 286a.

2253. חֶבְיוֹן {1x} **chebyôwn**, *kheb-yone';* from 2247, a *concealment:*—hiding {1x}. Syn.: 2934. See: BDB—285d, 286a.

2254. חָבַל {29x} **châbal**, *khaw-bal';* a prim. root; to *wind* tightly (as a rope), i.e. to *bind;* spec. by a *pledge;* fig. to *pervert, destroy;* also to *writhe* in pain (espec. of parturition):—destroy {7x}, take a pledge {5x} pledge {5x}, bands {2x}, brought forth {2x}, at all {1x}, corrupt {1x}, corruptly {1x}, offend {1x}, spoil {1x}, travaileth {1x}, very {1x}, withholden {1x}. Syn.: 6, 343, 1104, 1820, 2040, 2475, 2717, 3615, 3772, 4135, 5395, 7665. See: TWOT—592, 593, 594, 595; BDB—286b, 287b, 1091d.

2255. חֲבַל {6x} **chăbal** (Aram.), *khab-al';* corresp. to 2254; to *ruin:*—destroy {5x}, hurt {1x}. See: TWOT—2716; BDB—1091d.

2256. חֶבֶל {60x} **chebel**, *kheh'-bel;* or

חֵבֶל **chêbel**, *khay'-bel;* from 2254; a *rope* (as *twisted*), espec. a measuring *line;* by impl. a *district* or *inheritance* (as *measured*); or a *noose* (as of *cords*); fig. a *company* (as if *tied* together); also a *throe* (espec. of parturition); also *ruin:*—sorrows {10x}, cord {16x}, line {7x}, coast {4x}, portion {4x}, region {3x}, lot {3x}, ropes {3x}, company {2x}, pangs {2x}, bands {1x}, country {1x}, destruction {1x}, pain {1x}, snare {1x}, tacklings {1x}.

Chebel means "cord; rope; tackle; measuring line; measurement; allotment; portion; region." **(1)** *Chebel* primarily means "cord" or "rope." "Then she let them down by a cord through the window: for her house *was* upon the town wall, and she dwelt upon the wall" (Josh 2:15). **(2)** The word is used of "tent ropes" in Is 33:20: ". . . A tabernacle that shall not be taken down . . . neither shall any of the cords thereof be broken." **(3)** A ship's "tackle" is the meaning of *chebel* in Is 33:23. **(4)** Used figuratively, *chebel* emphasizes "being bound." In 1 Kin 20:31, we read that the Syrians who fled into Aphek proposed to put sackcloth on their heads as a sign of repentance for attacking Israel, and to put "ropes" about their necks as a sign of submission to Israel's authority. **(5)** Snares used "cords" or "ropes," forming a web or a noose into which the prey stepped and was caught. In this manner, the wicked would be caught by God (Job 18:10).

(6) In many passages, death is pictured as a hunter whose trap has been sprung and whose quarry is captured by the "cords" of the trap: "the sorrows of hell compassed me about; the snares of death prevented me;" (2 Sa 22:6). **(7)** In other cases, the thing that "binds" is good: "I drew them with cords of a man, with bands of love . . ." (Hos 11:4). **(8)** Eccl 12:6 pictures human life as being held together by a silver "cord." **(9)** A "cord" could be used as a "measuring line": "And he smote Moab, and measured them with a line, casting them down to the ground; even with two lines measured he to put to death, and with one full line to keep alive" (2 Sa 8:2). **(9a)** This meaning of *chebel* also occurs in Ps 78:55: ". . . And [He] divided them an inheritance by line." **(9b)** Compare Mic 2:5: "Therefore thou shalt have none that shall cast a cord by lot in the congregation of the Lord." **(10)** The act referred to by Micah appears in Ps 16:6 as an image of one's life in general: "The lines are fallen unto me in pleasant places; yea, I have a goodly heritage."

(11) *Chebel* also means "the thing measured or allotted": **(11a)** "For the LORD's portion is his people; Jacob is the lot of his inheritance" (Deut 32:9). Here the use is clearly figurative, **(11b)** but in 1 Chr 16:18 the "portion" of Israel's inheritance is a concrete "measured thing"; **(11c)** this nuance first appears in Josh 17:5. **(12)** In passages such as Deut 3:4, the word is used of a "region" or "a measured area": ". . . Threescore cities, all the region of Argob, the kingdom of Og in Bashan." **(12)** The word may refer to a group of people, describing them as that which is tied together—"a band": ". . . Thou shalt meet a company of prophets coming down from the high place . . ." (1 Sa 10:5). See: TWOT—592b, 595a; BDB—286c, 286d, 287a, 287c.

2257. חֲבַל {3x} **chăbal** (Aram.), *khab-al';* from 2255; *harm* (personal or pecuniary):—damage {1x}, hurt {2x}. See: BDB—1092a.

2258. חֲבֹל {4x} **chăbôl**, *khab-ole';* or (fem.)

חֲבֹלָה **chăbôlâh**, *khab-o-law';* from 2254; a *pawn* (as security for debt):—pledge {4x}. Syn.: 5567, 6162. See: TWOT—593a; BDB—287a.

2259. חֹבֵל **chôbêl**, *kho-bale';* act. part. from 2254 (in the sense of handling *ropes*); a *sailor:*—pilot {4x}, shipmaster + 7227 {1x}. See: TWOT—592c; BDB—287a.

2260. חִבֵּל {1x} **chibbêl**, *khib-bale';* from 2254 (in the sense of furnished with *ropes*); a *mast:*—mast {1x}. See: TWOT—592d; BDB—287a.

2261. חֲבַצֶּלֶת {2x} **chăbatstseleth**, *khab-ats-tseh'-leth;* of uncert. der.; prob. *meadow-saffron:*—rose {2x}. See: TWOT—596.1; BDB—287c.

2262. חֲבַצִּנְיָה {1x} **Chăbatstsanyâh**, *khab-ats-tsan-yaw';* of uncert. der.; *Chabatstsanjah,* a Rechabite:—Habazaniah {1x}. See: BDB—287c.

2263. חָבַק {13x} **châbaq**, *khaw-bak';* a prim. root; to *clasp* (the hands or in embrace):—embrace {12x}, fold {1x}. See: TWOT—597; BDB—287d.

2264. חִבֻּק {2x} **chibbûq**, *khib-book';* from 2263; a *clasping* of the hands (in idleness):—fold {2x}. See: TWOT—597a; BDB—287d.

2265. חֲבַקּוּק {2x} **Chăbaqqûwq**, *khab-ak-kook';* by redupl. from 2263; *embrace; Chabakkuk,* the prophet:—Habakkuk {2x}. See: BDB—287d.

2266. חָבַר {29x} **châbar**, *khaw-bar';* a prim. root; to *join* (lit. or fig.); spec. (by means of spells) to *fascinate:*—couple {8x}, join {8x}, couple together {4x}, join together {3x}, compact {1x}, charmer + 2267 {1x}, charming + 2267 {1x}, have fellowship {1x}, league {1x}, heap up {1x}. See: TWOT—598; BDB—251c, 287d, 1092a.

2267. חֶבֶר {7x} **cheber**, *kheh'-ber;* from 2266; a *society;* also a *spell:*—wide {2x}, enchantment {2x}, company {1x}, charmer + 2266 {1x}, charming + 2266 {1x}. *Cheber* means binding, fascination and is rendered "enchantment" (Is 47:9, 12) and "[serpent] charmer" (Ps 58:5). Syn.: 328, 825, 826, 1505, 3858, 3907, 3909, 5172, 6049, See: TWOT—598a; BDB—288c.

2268. חֶבֶר {11x} **Cheber**, *kheh'-ber;* the same as 2267; *community; Cheber,* the name of a Kenite and of three Isr.:—Heber {1x}. See: BDB—288c.

2269. חֲבַר {3x} **chăbar** (Aram.), *khab-ar';* from a root corresp. to 2266; an *associate:*—companion {1x}, fellow {2x}. See: TWOT—2717, 2717a; BDB—1092a.

2270. חָבֵר {12x} **châbêr**, *khaw-bare';* from 2266; an *associate:*—companion {7x}, fellow {4x}, knit together {1x}. Syn.: 2271, 4828, 7453, 7462. See: TWOT—598c; BDB—288d.

2271. חַבָּר {1x} **chabbâr**, *khab-bawr';* from 2266; a *partner:*—companion {1x}. See: TWOT—598f; BDB—289a.

2272. חֲבַרְבֻּרָה {1x} **chăbarbûrâh**, *khab-ar-boo-raw';* by redupl. from 2266; a *streak* (like a *line*), as on the tiger:—spot {1x}. See: TWOT—598h; BDB—289a.

2273. חַבְרָה {1x} **chabrâh** (Aram.), *khab-raw';* fem. of 2269; an *associate:*—other {1x}. See: TWOT—2717b; BDB—1092a.

2274. חֶבְרָה {1x} **chebrâh**, *kheb-raw';* fem. of 2267; *association:*—company {1x}. Syn.: 2256. See: TWOT—598b; BDB—288d.

2275. חֶבְרוֹן {71x} **Chebrôwn**, *kheb-rone';* from 2267; seat of *association; Chebron,* a place in Pal., also the name of two Isr.:—Hebron {71x}. See: TWOT—598i; BDB—289b, 900c.

2276. חֶבְרוֹנִי {6x} **Chebrôwnîy**, *kheb-ro-nee';* or

חֶבְרֹנִי **Chebrônîy**, *kheb-ro-nee';* patron. from 2275; *Chebronite* (collect.), an inhab. of Chebron:—Hebronites {6x}. See: BDB—289c.

2277. חֶבְרִי {1x} **Chebrîy**, *kheb-ree';* patron. from 2268; a *Chebrite* (collect.) or desc. of Cheber:—Heberites {1x}. See: BDB—288d.

2278. חֲבֶרֶת {1x} **chăbereth**, *khab-eh'-reth;* fem. of 2270; a *consort:*—companion {1x}. See: TWOT—598d; BDB—289a.

2279. חֹבֶרֶת {4x} **chôbereth**, *kho-beh'-reth;* fem. act. part. of 2266; a *joint:*—which coupleth {2x}, coupling {2x}. See: TWOT—598e; BDB—289a.

2280. חָבַשׁ {33x} **châbash**, *khaw-bash';* a prim. root; to *wrap* firmly (espec. a turban, compress, or *saddle*); fig. to *stop,* to *rule:*—saddle {13x}, bind up {9x}, bind {5x}, put {2x}, about {1x}, girded {1x}, govern {1x}, healer {1x}. See: TWOT—599; BDB—289c.

2281. חָבֵת {1x} **châbêth**, *khaw-bayth';* from an unused root prob. mean. to *cook* [comp. 4227]; something *fried,* prob. a griddle-*cake:*—pan {1x}. See: TWOT—600a; BDB—290a.

2282. חַג {62x} **chag**, *khag;* or

חָג **châg**, *khawg;* from 2287; a *festival,* or a *victim* therefore:—feast {56x}, sacrifice {3x}, feast days {2x}, solemnity {1x}.

Chag means "feast; festal sacrifice." **(1)** Biblical Hebrew attests it about 62 times and in all periods, except in the wisdom literature. **(2)** This word refers especially to a "feast observed by a pilgrimage." That is its meaning in its first biblical occurrence, when Moses said to Pharaoh: "We will go with our young and with our old, with our sons and with our daughters, with our flocks and with our herds will we go; for we must hold a feast unto the LORD" (Ex 10:9). **(3)** *Chag* usually represents Israel's three annual "pilgrimage feasts," **(3a)** which were celebrated with processions and dances. **(3b)** These special feasts are distinguished from the sacred seasons ("festal assemblies"—Eze 45:17), the new moon festivals, and the Sabbaths (Hos 2:11). **(4)** There are two unique uses of *chag.* **(4a)** First, Aaron proclaimed a "feast to the LORD" at the foot of Mt. Sinai. This "feast" involved no pilgrimage but was celebrated with burnt offerings, communal meals, singing, and dancing. The whole matter was displeasing to God (Ex 32:5–7). **(4b)** In two passages, *chag* represents the "victim sacrificed to God" (perhaps during one of the three annual sacrifices): ". . . Bind the [festal] sacrifice with cords, even unto the horns of the altar" (Ps 118:27; cf. Ex 23:18). Syn.: 2077. See: TWOT—602a; BDB—290b, 290d.

2283. חָגָא {1x} **châgâ'**, *khaw-gaw';* from an unused root mean. to *revolve* [comp. 2287]; prop. *vertigo,* i.e. (fig.) *fear:*—terror {1x}. Syn.: 2847, 2851. See: TWOT—602b; BDB—290b, 291b.

2284. חָגָב {5x} **châgâb**, *khaw-gawb';* of uncert. der.; a *locust:*—locusts {1x}, grasshopper {2x}, grasshoppers {2x}. See: TWOT—601a; BDB—290b.

2285. חָגָב {1x} **Châgâb**, *khaw-gawb';* the same as 2284; *locust; Chagab,* one of the Nethinim:—Hagab {1x}. See: BDB—290c.

2286. חֲגָבָא {2x} **Chăgâbâ'**, *khag-aw-baw';* or

חֲגָבָה **Chăgâbâh**, *khag-aw-baw';* fem. of 2285; *locust; Chagaba* or *Chagabah,* one of the Nethinim:—Hagaba {1x}, Hagabah {1x}. See: BDB—290c.

2287. חָגַג {16x} **châgag**, *khaw-gag';* a prim. root [comp. 2283, 2328]; prop. to move in a *circle,* i.e. (spec.) to *march* in a sacred procession, to *observe* a festival; by impl. to *be giddy:*—keep {8x}, . . . feast {3x}, celebrate {1x}, keep a solemn feast {1x}, dancing {1x}, holy day {1x}, reel to and fro {1x}. See: TWOT—602; BDB—290c.

2288. חֲגָו {3x} **chăgâv**, *khag-awv';* from an unused root mean. to *take refuge;* a *rift* in rocks:—cleft {3x}. Syn.: 1233, 5366. See: TWOT—603a; BDB—291c.

2289. חָגוֹר {3x} **châgôwr**, *khaw-gore';* from 2296; *belted:*—girded with {1x}, girdle {2x}, girdles {1x}. Syn.: 73, 232, 247, 2280, 2296. See: TWOT—604b; BDB—292a.

2290. חֲגוֹר {6x} **chăgôwr**, *khag-ore';* or

חֲגֹר **chăgôr**, *khag-ore';* and (fem.)

חֲגוֹרָה **chăgôwrâh**, *khag-o-raw';* or

חֲגֹרָה **chăgôrâh**, *khag-o-raw';* from 2296; a *belt* (for the waist):—girdle {3x}, apron {1x}, armour {1x}, gird {1x}. See: TWOT—604a, 604c; BDB—292a.

2291. חַגִּי {3x} **Chaggîy**, *khag-ghee';* from 2287; *festive, Chaggi,* an Isr.; also (patron.) a *Chaggite,* or desc. of the same:—Haggi {2x}, Haggites {1x}. See: BDB—291b.

2292. חַגַּי {11x} **Chaggay**, *khag-gah'-ee;* from 2282; *festive; Chaggai,* a Heb. prophet:—Haggai {11x}. See: BDB—291b, 1092a.

2293. חַגִּיָּה {1x} **Chaggîyâh**, *khag-ghee-yaw';* from 2282 and 3050; *festival of Jah; Chaggijah,* an Isr.:—Haggiah {1x}. See: BDB—291b.

2294. חַגִּית {5x} **Chaggîyîth**, *khag-gheeth';* fem. of 2291; *festive; Chaggith,* a wife of David:—Haggith {5x}. See: BDB—291b.

2295. חָגְלָה {4x} **Choglâh**, *khog-law';* of uncert. der.; prob. a *partridge; Choglah,* an Israelitess:—Hoglah {4x}. Syn.: See also 1031. See: BDB—291c.

2296. חָגַר {43x} **châgar**, *khaw-gar';* a prim. root; to *gird* on (as a belt, armor, etc.):—gird {31x}, appointed {3x}, gird on {3x}, gird up {2x}, be afraid {1x}, put {1x}, restrain {1x}, on every side {1x}. See: TWOT—604; BDB—291c.

2297. חַד {1x} **chad**, *khad;* abridged from 259; *one:*—one {1x}. See: TWOT—61; BDB—26a, 292b.

2298. חַד {14x} **chad** (Aram.), *khad;* corresp. to 2297; as card. *one;* as art. *single;* as an ord. *first;* adv. *at once:*—one {5x}, first {4x}, a {4x}, together {1x}. See: TWOT—2718; BDB—1079c, 1092a, 1096c.

2299. חַד {4x} **chad**, *khad;* from 2300; *sharp:*—sharp {1x}. See: TWOT—605a; BDB—292b.

2300. חָדַד {6x} **châdad**, *khaw-dad';* a prim. root; to *be* (caus. *make*) *sharp* or (fig.) *severe:*—be fierce {1x}, sharpen {5x}. See: TWOT—605; BDB—292b, 292c.

2301. חֲדַד {1x} **Chădad**, *khad-ad';* from 2300; *fierce; Chadad,* an Ishmaelite:—Hadad {1x}. See: BDB—292c.

2302. חָדָה {3x} **châdâh**, *khaw-daw';* a prim. root; to *rejoice:*—make glad {1x}, be joined {1x}, rejoice {1x}. See: TWOT—607; BDB—292d.

2303. חַדּוּד {1x} **chaddûwd**, *khad-dood';* from 2300; a *point:*—sharp {1x}. See: TWOT—605b; BDB—292c.

2304. חֶדְוָה {2x} **chedvâh**, *khed-vaw';* from 2302; *rejoicing:*—gladness {1x}, joy {1x}. See: TWOT—607a; BDB—292d, 1092a.

2305. חֶדְוָה {1x} **chedvâh** (Aram.), *khed-vaw';* corresp. to 2304:—joy {1x}. See: TWOT—2719; BDB—1092a.

2306. חֲדִי {1x} **chădîy** (Aram.), *khad-ee';* corresp. to 2373; a *breast:*—breast {1x}. See: TWOT—2720; BDB—1092a.

2307. חֲדִיד {3x} **Châdîyd**, *khaw-deed'*; from 2300; a *peak; Chadid,* a place in Pal.:—Hadid {3x}. See: BDB—292c.

2308. חָדַל {59x} **châdal**, *khaw-dal'*; a prim. root; prop. to *be flabby,* i.e. (by impl.) *desist;* (fig.) *be lacking* or *idle:*—cease {20x}, forbear {16x}, leave {5x}, left off {5x}, let . . . alone {2x}, forbare {3x}, endeth {1x}, failed {1x}, forborn {1x}, forsake {1x}, rest {1x}, unoccupied {1x}, wanteth {1x}, nontranslated variant {1x}.

Chadal means "to cease, come to an end, desist, forbear, lack." **(1)** The first occurrence of *chadal* is in Gen 11:8 where, after man's language was confused, "and they left off to build the city." **(2)** The basic meaning of *chadal* is "coming to an end." Thus, Sarah's capacity for childbearing had long since "ceased" before an angel informed her that she was to have a son (Gen 18:11). **(3)** The Mosaic law made provision for the poor, since they would "never cease out of the land" (Deut 15:11; cf. Mt 26:11). **(4)** In Ex 14:12 this verb is better translated "let us alone" for the literal "cease from us." Syn.: 988, 1826, 3615, 7606, 7673, 7676. See: TWOT—609; BDB—292d.

2309. חֶדֶל {1x} **chedel**, *kheh'-del;* from 2308; *rest,* i.e. the state of the *dead:*—world {1x}. The place of rest, cessation, forbearance (Is 38:11). Syn.: 7465, 8398. See: TWOT—609a; BDB—293b.

2310. חָדֵל {3x} **châdêl**, *khaw-dale';* from 2308; *vacant,* i.e. *ceasing* or *destitute:*—he that forbeareth {1x}, frail {1x}, rejected {1x}. See: TWOT—609b; BDB—293b.

2311. חַדְלַי {1x} **Chadlay**, *khad-lah'-ee;* from 2309; *idle; Chadlai,* an Isr.:—Hadlai {1x}. See: BDB—293b.

2312. חֵדֶק {2x} **chêdeq**, *khay'-dek;* from an unused root mean. to *sting;* a *prickly* plant:—brier {1x}, thorn {1x}. Syn.: 329, 1303, 2336, 5285, 5544, 5636, 6975, 7898, 8068. See: TWOT—611a; BDB—293b.

2313. חִדֶּקֶל {2x} **Chiddeqel**, *khid-deh'-kel;* prob. of for. or.; the *Chiddekel* (or Tigris) river:—Hiddekel {2x}. See: BDB—293c.

2314. חָדַר {1x} **châdar**, *khaw-dar';* a prim. root; prop. to *inclose* (as a room), i.e. (by anal.) to *beset* (as in a siege):—enter a privy chamber {1x}. See: TWOT—612; BDB—293c.

2315. חֶדֶר **cheder**, *kheh'-der;* from 2314; an *apartment* (usually lit.):—chamber {21x}, inner {4x}, bedchamber + 4296 {3x}, bedchamber + 4904 {3x}, inward parts {2x}, innermost parts {2x}, parlours {1x}, south {1x}, within {1x}. See: TWOT—612a; BDB—293c.

2316. חֲדַר {1x} **Chădar**, *khad-ar';* another form for 2315; *chamber; Chadar,* an Ishmaelite:—Hadar {1x}. See: BDB—293c.

2317. חַדְרָךְ {1x} **Chadrâk**, *khad-rawk';* of uncert. der.; *Chadrak,* a Syrian deity:—Hadrach {1x}. See: BDB—293d.

2318. חָדַשׁ {10x} **châdash**, *khaw-dash';* a prim. root; to *be new;* caus. to *rebuild:*—renew {7x}, repair {3x}. *Chadash* means "to renew." **(1)** This verb occurs in post-Mosaic literature (with the exception of Job 10:17). **(2)** The first appearance of *chadash* in the Bible is in 1 Sa 11:14: "Then said Samuel to the people, Come, and let us go to Gilgal, and renew the kingdom there." Syn: 2319, 2320.See: TWOT—613; BDB—293d.

2319. חָדָשׁ {53x} **châdâsh**, *khaw-dawsh';* from 2318; *new:*—fresh {1x}, new {48x}, new thing {4x}. *Chadash,* the adjective, means "new; renewed." **(1)** *Chadash* means "new" both in the sense of recent or fresh and in the sense of something not previously existing (a new king - Ex 1:8). **(1a)** The first nuance appears in Lev 23:16: "Even unto the morrow after the seventh sabbath shall ye number fifty days; and ye shall offer a new meat offering unto the LORD." **(1b)** The first biblical occurrence of *chadash* (Ex 1:8) demonstrates the second meaning: "Now there arose up a new king over Egypt, which knew not Joseph." **(1b1)** This second nuance occurs in Isaiah's discussion of the future salvation. **(1b2)** For example, in Is 42:10 a new saving act of God will bring forth a new song of praise to Him: "Sing unto the LORD a new song, and his praise from the end of the earth. . . . " **(1b3)** The Psalter uses the phrase "a new song" in this sense; a new saving act of God has occurred and a song responding to that act celebrates it. **(1b4)** The "new" is often contrasted to the former: "Behold, the former things are come to pass, and new things do I declare: before they spring forth I tell you of them" (Is 42:9). **(1b5)** Jer 31:31–34 employs this same nuance speaking of the new covenant (cf. Eze 11:19; 18:31).

(2) A unique meaning appears in Lam 3:23, where *chadash* appears to mean "renewed"; just as God's creation is renewed and refreshed, so is His compassion and loving kindness: "They are new every morning: great is thy faithfulness." This nuance is more closely related to the verb from which this word is derived. Syn: 2318, 2320. See: TWOT—613a; BDB—294a, 1092a.

2320. חֹדֶשׁ {276x} **chôdesh**, *kho'-desh;* from 2318; the *new* moon; by impl. a *month:*—month {254x}, new moon {20x}, monthly {1x}, another {1x}.

Chodesh means "new moon; month." **(1)** The word refers to the day on which the crescent reappears: "So David hid himself in the field: and when the new moon was come, the king sat him down to eat meat" (1 Sa 20:24). **(2)** Is 1:14 uses this word of the feast which occurred on that day: "Your new moons [festivals] and your appointed feasts my soul hateth . . ." (cf. Num 28:14; 29:6). **(3)** *Chodesh* can refer to a "month," or the period from one new moon to another. The sense of a measure of time during which something happens occurs in Gen 38:24: "And it came to pass about three months after, that it was told Judah. . . . " **(4)** In a related nuance the word refers not so much to a measure of time as to a period of time, or a calendar month. These "months" are sometimes named (Ex 13:4) and sometimes numbered (Gen 7:11). Syn: 2318, 2319. See: TWOT—613b; BDB—294b.

2321. חֹדֶשׁ {1x} **Chôdesh**, *kho'-desh;* the same as 2320; *Chodesh,* an Israelitess:—Hodesh {1x}. See: BDB—295a.

2322. חֲדָשָׁה {1x} **Chădâshâh**, *khad-aw-shaw';* fem. of 2319; *new; Chadashah,* a place in Pal.:—Hadashah {1x}. See: BDB—295a.

2323. חֲדָת {1x} **chădath** (Aram.), *khad-ath';* corresp. to 2319; *new:*—new {1x}. See: TWOT—2721; BDB—1092a.

2324. חֲוָא {14x} **chăvâʾ** (Aram.), *khav-aw';* corresp. to 2331; to *show:*—shew {14x}. See: BDB—1092b.

2325. חוּב {1x} **chûwb**, *khoob;* also

חָיַב **châyab**, *khaw-yab';* a prim. root; prop. perh. to *tie,* i.e. (fig. and refl.) to *owe,* or (by impl.) to *forfeit:*—make endanger {1x}. See: TWOT—614; BDB—295a.

2326. חוֹב {1x} **chôwb**, *khobe;* from 2325; *debt:*—debtor {1x}. See: TWOT—614a; BDB—295a.

2327. חוֹבָה {1x} **chôwbâh**, *kho-baw';* fem. act. part. of 2247; *hiding* place; *Chobah,* a place in Syria:—Hobah {1x}. See: BDB—295b.

2328. חוּג {1x} **chûwg**, *khoog;* a prim. root [comp. 2287]; to describe a *circle.*—compass {1x}. See: TWOT—615; BDB—295b.

2329. חוּג {3x} **chûwg**, *khoog;* from 2328; a *circle:*—circle {1x}, circuit {1x}, compass {1x}. See: TWOT—615a; BDB—295b.

2330. חוּד {4x} **chûwd**, *khood;* a prim. root; prop. to *tie* a knot, i.e. (fig.) to *propound* a riddle:—put forth {4x}. See: TWOT—616; BDB—295c.

2331. חָוָה {6x} **châvâh**, *khaw-vah';* a prim. root; [comp. 2324, 2421]; prop. to *live;* by impl. (intens.) to *declare* or *show:*—shew {6x}. See: TWOT—618; BDB—296a, 1092b.

2332. חַוָּה {2x} **Chavvâh**, *khav-vaw';* caus. from 2331; *life-giver; Chavvah* (or Eve), the first woman:—Eve {2x}. See: BDB—295c.

2333. חַוָּה {4x} **chavvâh**, *khav-vaw';* prop. the same as 2332 (*life-giving,* i.e. *living-place*); by impl. an encampment or *village:*—(small) town {4x}. See: TWOT—617a; BDB—295d.

2334. חַוּוֹת יָעִיר {3x} **Chavvôwth Yâʿîyr**, *khav-vothe' yaw-eer';* from the plural of 2333 and a modif. of 3265; *hamlets of Jair,* a region of Pal.:—Bashanhavoth-jair {1x}, Havoth-jair {2x}. See: BDB—295d.

2335. חוֹזַי {1x} **Chôwzay**, *kho-zah'-ee;* from 2374; *visionary; Chozai,* an Isr.:—the seers {1x}. See: BDB—296a, 302c, 302d.

2336. חוֹחַ {11x} **chôwach**, *kho'-akh;* from an unused root appar. mean. to *pierce;* a *thorn;* by anal. a *ring* for the nose:—brambles {1x}, thistle(s) {5x}, thorn(s) {5x}. Syn.: 329, 1303, 2312, 5285, 5544, 5636, 6975, 7898, 8068. See: TWOT—620a, 620b; BDB—296a.

2337. חָוָח {1x} **châvâch**, *khaw-vawkh';* perh. the same as 2336; a *dell* or *crevice* (as if *pierced* in the earth):—thicket {1x}. See: TWOT—620a; BDB—296a.

2338. חוּט {1x} **chûwt** (Aram.), *khoot;* corresp. to the root of 2339, perhaps as a denom.; to *string* together, i.e. (fig.) to *repair:*—join {1x}. See: TWOT—2723; BDB—1092b.

2339. חוּט {7x} **chûwt**, *khoot;* from an unused root prob. mean. to *sew;* a *string;* by impl. a measuring *tape:*—cord {1x}, fillet {1x}, line {1x}, thread {4x}. See: TWOT—621a; BDB—296c, 1092b.

2340. חִוִּי {25x} **Chivvîy**, *khiv-vee';* perh. from 2333; a *villager;* a *Chivvite,* one of the aboriginal tribes of Pal.:—Hivite {25x}. See: BDB—295d, 296c.

2341. חֲוִילָה {7x} **Chăvîylâh**, *khav-ee-law';* prob. from 2342; *circular; Chavilah,* the name of two or three eastern regions; also perh. of two men:—Havilah {7x}. See: TWOT—622; BDB—296c.

2342. חוּל {62x} **chûwl**, *khool;* or

חִיל **chîyl**, *kheel;* a prim. root; prop. to *twist* or *whirl* (in a circular or spiral manner), i.e. (spec.) to *dance*, to *writhe* in pain (espec. of parturition) or fear; fig. to *wait*, to *pervert:*—pain {6x}, formed {5x}, bring forth {4x}, pained {4x}, tremble {4x}, travail {4x}, dance {2x}, calve {2x}, grieved {2x}, grievous {2x}, wounded {2x}, shake {2x}, misc. {23x} = bear, drive away, fear, great, hope, look, make, rest, shapen, (be) sorrow (-ful), stay, tarry, trust, wait carefully (patiently), See: TWOT—623; BDB—296d, 298c, 313d.

2343. חוּל {2x} **Chûwl**, *khool;* from 2342; a *circle; Chul,* a son of Aram; also the region settled by him:—Hul {2x}. See: BDB—299a.

2344. חוֹל {23x} **chôwl**, *khole;* from 2342; *sand* (as *round* or whirling particles):—sand {23x}. See: TWOT—623a; BDB—297c.

2345. חוּם {4x} **chûwm**, *khoom;* from an unused root mean. to *be warm,* i.e. (by impl.) *sunburnt* or *swarthy* (blackish):—brown {4x}. See: TWOT—625a; BDB—299b.

2346. חוֹמָה {133x} **chôwmâh**, *kho-maw';* fem. act. part. of an unused root appar. mean. to *join;* a *wall* of protection:—wall {131x}, walled {2x}.

Chowmah means "wall." **(1)** Its first occurrence is in Ex 14:22: "And the children of Israel went into the midst of the sea upon the dry ground: and the waters were a wall unto them on their right hand, and on their left." **(2)** It is rare in the Pentateuch, in the historical books, and in the poetical books. The most frequent use is in Nehemiah, where Nehemiah is in charge of the rebuilding of the "wall" of Jerusalem. **(3)** The primary meaning of *chowmah* is a "wall" around a city, since in ancient Israel people had to protect themselves by constructing such a well-fortified "wall" (cf. Lev 25:29–30). **(3a)** Stones were used in the construction of the "wall": "Now Tobiah the Ammonite was by him, and he said, Even that which they build, if a fox go up, he shall even break down their stone wall" (Neh 4:3). **(3b)** The "wall" was also strengthened by thickness and other devices.

(3c) From Solomonic times double walls (casemate) served a strategic purpose in that they were easy to construct and could be filled in with rocks and dirt in the case of a siege. **(3d)** There was also another possibility during a siege: "And the city was broken up, and all the men of war fled by night by the way of the gate between two walls, which is by the king's garden: (now the Chaldees were against the city round about:) . . ." (2 Kin 25:4). **(4)** In the case of war the enemy besieged a city and made efforts to breach the "wall" with a battering ram. **(4a)** The goal was to force a breach wide enough for the troops to enter into the city; "And Jehoash king of Israel took Amaziah king of Judah, the son of Jehoash the son of Ahaziah, at Beth-shemesh, and came to Jerusalem, and brake down the wall of Jerusalem from the gate of Ephraim unto the corner gate, four hundred cubits [about six hundred feet]" (2 Kin 14:13).

(4b) At the time of Nebuchadnezzar's invasion and victory over Jerusalem, he had the "walls" of the city demolished: "And they burnt the house of God, and brake down the wall of Jerusalem, and burnt all the palaces thereof with fire, and destroyed all the goodly vessels thereof" (2 Chr 36:19). **(4c)** For this reason Nehemiah had to help his unsuccessful compatriots to rebuild the "wall" about 135 years later: "Then said I unto them, Ye see the distress that we are in, how Jerusalem lieth waste, and the gates thereof are burned with fire: come, and let us build up the wall of Jerusalem, that we be no more a reproach" (Neh 2:17). **(5)** *Chowmah* also referred to any "wall," whether around buildings or parts of the city such as the temple precincts: "And behold a wall on the outside of the house round about, and in the man's hand a measuring reed of six cubits long by the cubit and a handbreadth: so he measured the breadth of the building, one reed; and the height, one reed" (Eze 40:5). See: TWOT—674c; BDB—299b, 327b.

2347. חוּס {24x} **chûwç**, *khoos;* a prim. root; prop. to *cover,* i.e. (fig.) to *compassionate:*—pity {7x}, regard {1x}, spare {16x}. See: TWOT—626; BDB—299b.

2348. חוֹף {7x} **chôwph**, *khofe;* from an unused root mean. to *cover;* a *cove* (as a *sheltered* bay):—haven {2x}, shore {2x}, coast {2x}, side {1x}. See: TWOT—710a; BDB—299c, 342b.

2349. חוּפָם {1x} **Chûwphâm**, *khoo-fawm';* from the same as 2348; *protection: Chupham,* an Isr.:—Hupham {1x}. See: BDB—299c.

2350. חוּפָמִי {1x} **Chûwphâmîy**, *khoo-faw-mee';* patron. from 2349; a *Chuphamite* or desc. of Chupham:—Huphamites {1x}. See: BDB—299c.

2351. חוּץ {164x} **chûwts**, *khoots;* or (short.)

חֻץ **chûts**, *khoots;* (both forms fem. in the plur.) from an unused root mean. to *sever;* prop. *separate* by a wall, i.e. *outside, outdoors:*—without {70x}, street {44x}, abroad {21x}, out {17x}, outside {2x}, fields {2x}, forth {2x}, highways {1x}, Kirjathhuzoth + 7155 {1x}, more {1x}, out of {1x}, outward {1x}, utter {1x}.

(1) *Chuts,* as a noun, means "street." **(1a)** A particular use of *chuts* denotes the place outside the houses in a city, or the "street." **(1a1)** The "street" was the place for setting up bazaars: "The cities, which my father took from thy father, I will restore; and thou shalt make streets for thee in Damascus, as my father made in Samaria" (1 Kin 20:34). **(1a2)** Craftsmen plied their trade on certain "streets" named after the guild—for example, the Bakers' Street: "Then Zedekiah the king commanded that they should commit Jeremiah into the court of the prison, and that they should give him daily a piece of bread out of the bakers' street, until all the bread in the city were spent" (Jer 37:21). **(1a3)** The absence of justice in the marketplace was an indication of the wickedness of the whole population of Jerusalem. Jeremiah was called to check in the "streets" to find an honest man: "Run ye to and fro through the streets of Jerusalem, and see now, and know, and seek in the broad places thereof, if ye can find a man, if there be any that executeth judgment, that seeketh the truth; and I will pardon it" (Jer 5:1). **(1b)** Other descriptions of the "streets" are given by the prophets. **(1b1)** Several mention that the "streets" were muddy: ". . . And to tread them down like the mire of the streets" (Is 10:6; cf. Mic 7:10; Zec 10:5). **(1b2)** Others make reference to the blood (Eze 28:23), **(1b3)** the famished (Lam 2:19), and **(1b4)** the dead (Nah 3:10) which filled the "streets" in times of war. **(1c)** The area outside a city was also known as the *chuts.* In this case it is better translated as "open country" or "field"; cf. "That our garners may be full, affording all manner of store, that sheep may bring forth thousands and ten thousands in our streets" (Ps 144:13; cf. Job 5:10; Prov 8:26). **(2)** *Chuts,* as an adverb, means "outside." **(2a)** The first occurrence of this word is in Gen 6:14: "Make thee an ark of gopher wood; rooms shalt thou make in the ark, and shalt pitch it within and without [*chuts*] with pitch." **(2b)** By *chuts* the general idea of "the outside" is intimated. **(2b1)** "Thou shalt have a place also without the camp, whither thou shalt go forth abroad" (Deut 23:12). **(2b2)** The area could be "outside" a home, tent, city, or camp—hence the adverbial usage of "outside." **(2c)** The word is also connected with a preposition with the sense of "in, to, on, toward the outside": "If he rise again, and walk abroad upon his staff, then shall he that smote him be quit: only he shall pay for the loss of his time, and shall cause him to be thoroughly healed" (Ex 21:19). See: TWOT—627a; BDB—299c.

חוֹק **chôwq**. See 2436.

חוּקֹק **Chûwqôq**. See 2712.

2352. חוּר {2x} **chûwr**, *khoor;* or (short.)

חֻר **chûr**, *khoor;* from an unused root prob. mean. to *bore;* the *crevice* of a serpent; the *cell* of a prison:—hole {2x}. See: TWOT—758b; BDB—301b, 351a, 359d.

2353. חוּר {2x} **chûwr**, *khoor;* from 2357; *white* linen:—white {2x}. See: TWOT—630a; BDB—301a.

2354. חוּר {15x} **Chûwr**, *khoor;* the same as 2353 or 2352; *Chur,* the name of four Isr. and one Midianite:—Hur {15x}. See: BDB—301a.

2355. חוֹר {1x} **chôwr**, *khore;* the same as 2353; *white* linen:—network {1x}. Syn.: comp. 2715. See: TWOT—630a; BDB—301a.

2356. חוֹר {7x} **chôwr**, *khore;* or (short.)

חֹר **chôr**, *khore;* the same as 2352; a *cavity, socket, den:*—cave {1x}, hole {6x}. See: TWOT—758a; BDB—351a, 359d.

2357. חָוַר {1x} **châvar**, *khaw-var';* a prim. root; to *blanch* (as with shame):—wax pale {1x}. See: TWOT—630; BDB—301a, 1092c.

2358. חִוָּר {1x} **chivvâr** (Aram.), *khiv-vawr';* from a root corresp. to 2357; *white:*—white {1x}. See: TWOT—2724; BDB—1092c.

חוֹרוֹן **Chôwrôwn**. See 1032.

חוֹרִי **chôwrîy**. See 2753.

2359. חוּרִי {1x} **Chûwrîy**, *khoo-ree';* prob. from 2353; *linen*-worker; *Churi,* an Isr.:—Huri {1x}. See: BDB—301b.

2360. חוּרַי {1x} **Chûwray**, *khoo-rah'ee;* prob. an orth. var. for 2359; *Churai,* an Isr.:—Hurai {1x}. See: BDB—213b. 301b.

2361. חוּרָם {13x} **Chûwrâm**, *khoo-rawm';* prob. from 2353; *whiteness,* i.e. noble; *Churam,* the name of an Isr. and two Syrians:—Huram {13x}. Syn.: comp. 2438. See: BDB—27c, 301b.

2362. חַוְרָן {2x} **Chavrân**, *khav-rawn';* appar. from 2357 (in the sense of 2352); *cavernous; Chavran,* a region E. of the Jordan:—Hauran {1x}. See: BDB—301c.

2363. חוּשׁ {20x} **chûwsh**, *koosh;* a prim. root; to *hurry;* fig. to *be eager* with excitement or enjoyment:—make haste {19x}, ready {1x}. Syn.: 926, 4116. See: TWOT—631; BDB—301c, 301d.

2364. חוּשָׁה {1x} **Chûwshâh**, *khoo-shaw';* from 2363; *haste; Chushah,* an Isr.:—Hushah {1x}. See: BDB—302a.

2365. חוּשַׁי {14x} **Chûwshay**, *khoo-shah'-ee;* from 2363; *hasty; Chushai,* an Isr.:—Hushai {14x}. See: BDB—302a.

2366. חוּשִׁים {4x} **Chûwshîym**, *khoo-sheem'*; or חֻשִׁים **Chûshîym**, *khoo-sheem'*; or חֻשִׁם **Chûshîm**, *khoo-shim'*; plur. from 2363; *hasters; Chushim*, the name of three Isr.:—Hushim {4x}. See: BDB—302a, 364d.

2367. חוּשָׁם {4x} **Chûwshâm**, *khoo-shawm'*; or חֻשָׁם **Chûshâm**, *khoo-shawm'*; from 2363; *hastily; Chusham*, an Idumæan:—Husham {4x}. See: BDB—302a, 364d.

2368. חוֹתָם {14x} **chôwthâm**, *kho-thawm'*; or חֹתָם **chôthâm**, *kho-thawm'*; from 2856; a *signature*-ring:—seal {5x}, signet {9x}. See: TWOT—780a; BDB—302a, 368a.

2369. חוֹתָם {2x} **Chôwthâm**, *kho-thawm'*; the same as 2368; *seal; Chotham*, the name of two Isr.:—Hotham {1x}, Hothan {1x}. See: BDB—302a, 368b.

2370. חֲזָא {31x} **chăzâ'** (Aram.), *khaz-aw'*; or חֲזָה **chăzâh** (Aram.), *khaz-aw'*; corresp. to 2372; to *gaze* upon; ment. to *dream, be usual* (i.e. *seem*):—see {17x}, saw + 1934 {6x}, beheld + 1934 {5x}, had {1x}, wont {1x}, beheld {1x}. See: TWOT—2725; BDB—1092c.

2371. חֲזָאֵל {23x} **Chăzâ'êl**, *khaz-aw-ale'*; or חֲזָהאֵל **Chăzâh'êl**, *khaz-aw-ale'*; from 2372 and 410; *God has seen; Chazaël*, a king of Syria:—Hazael {28x}. See: BDB—302a, 303c.

2372. חָזָה {51x} **châzâh**, *khaw-zaw'*; a prim. root; to *gaze* at; ment. to *perceive, contemplate* (with pleasure); spec. to *have a vision of*:—see {38x}, behold {7x}, look {3x}, prophesy {2x}, provide {1x}.

Chazah, as a verb, means "to see, behold, select for oneself." It means **(1)** "to see or behold" in general (Prov 22:29), **(2)** "to see" in a prophetic vision (Num 24:4), and **(3)** "to select for oneself" (Ex 18:21—the first occurrence of the word). **(4)** In Lam 2:14 the word means "to see" in relation to prophets' visions: "Thy prophets have seen vain and foolish things for thee: and they have not discovered thine iniquity. . . ." Syn: 2377, 2384. See: TWOT—633; BDB—302a, 1092d.

2373. חָזֶה {13x} **châzeh**, *khaw-zeh'*; from 2372; the *breast* (as most *seen* in front):—breast {13x}. Syn.: 1717, 2306, 7699. See: TWOT—634a; BDB—303d, 1092a.

2374. חֹזֶה {19x} **chôzeh**, *kho-zeh'*; act. part. of 2372; a *beholder* in vision; also a *compact* (as *looked upon* with approval):—agreement {1x}, prophet {1x}, see that {3x}, seer {16x}, stargazer {1x}.

One who sees a vision, not with the eye of sense but with the spiritual and intellectual faculties. Usually found in passages that refer to visions vouchsafed by God. Syn.: 5030. See: TWOT—633; BDB—302c.

חֲזָהאֵל **Chăzâh'êl**. See 2371.

2375. חֲזוֹ {1x} **Chăzow**, *khaz-o'*; from 2372; *seer; Chazo*, a nephew of Abraham:—Hazo {1x}. See: BDB—303d.

2376. חֵזֵו {13x} **chêzev** (Aram.), *khay'-zev*; from 2370; a *sight*:—look {1x}, vision {12x}. See: BDB—1092c.

2377. חָזוֹן {35x} **châzôwn**, *khaw-zone'*; from 2372; a *sight* (ment.), i.e. a *dream, revelation*, or *oracle*:—vision {35x}.

Chazown means "vision." **(1)** None of the 35 appearances of this word appear before First Samuel, and most of them are in the prophetic books. **(2)** *Chazown* almost always signifies a means of divine revelation. **(2a)** First, it refers to the means itself, to a prophetic "vision" by which divine messages are communicated: "The days are prolonged, and every vision faileth" (Eze 12:22). **(2b)** Second, this word represents the message received by prophetic "vision": "Where there is no vision, the people perish: but he that keepeth the law, happy is he" (Prov 29:18). **(2c)** Finally, *chazown* can represent the entirety of a prophetic or prophet's message as it is written down: "The vision of Isaiah the son of Amoz . . ." (Is 1:1). **(2d)** Thus the word inseparably related to the content of a divine communication focuses on the means by which that message is received: "And the word of the LORD was precious in those days; there was no open vision" (1 Sa 3:1—the first occurrence of the word). **(3)** In Is 29:7 this word signifies a non-prophetic dream. Syn: 2372, 2384. See: TWOT—633a; BDB—302d.

2378. חָזוֹת {1x} **châzôwth**, *khaw-zooth'*; from 2372; a *revelation*:—vision {1x}. See: TWOT—633c; BDB—303a.

2379. חֲזוֹת {2x} **chăzôwth** (Aram.), *khaz-oth'*; from 2370; a *view*:—sight {2x}. See: TWOT—2725b; 1092d; BDB—1092d.

2380. חָזוּת {4x} **châzûwth**, *khaw-zooth'*; from 2372; a *look*; hence, (fig.) striking *appearance, revelation*, or (by impl.) *compact*:—agreement {1x}, notable one {1x}, vision {2x}. See: TWOT—633d; BDB—303a.

2381. חֲזִיאֵל {1x} **Chăzîy'êl**, *khaz-ee-ale'*; from 2372 and 410; *seen of God; Chaziel*, a Levite:—Haziel {1x}. See: BDB—303c.

2382. חֲזָיָה {1x} **Chazayah**, *khaz-aw-yaw'*; from 2372 and 3050; *Jah has seen; Chazajah*, an Isr.:—Hazaiah {1x}. See: BDB—303c.

2383. חֶזְיוֹן {1x} **Chezyôwn**, *khez-yone'*; from 2372; *vision; Chezjon*, a Syrian:—Hezion {1x}. See: BDB—303c.

2384. חִזָּיוֹן {9x} **chizzâyôwn**, *khiz-zaw-yone'*; from 2372; a *revelation*, espec. by *dream*:—vision {9x}.

Chizzayown means "vision." This noun, which occurs 9 times, refers **(1)** to a prophetic "vision" in Joel 2:28: "And it shall come to pass afterward, that I will pour out my spirit upon all flesh; and your sons and your daughters shall prophesy, your old men shall dream dreams, your young men shall see visions." *Chizzayown* refers **(2)** to divine communication in 2 Sa 7:17 (the first biblical occurrence) and **(3)** to an ordinary dream in Job 4:13. Syn: 2372, 2377. See: TWOT—633e; BDB—303b.

2385. חֲזִיז {3x} **chăzîyz**, *khaw-zeez'*; from an unused root mean. to *glare*; a *flash* of lightning:—bright cloud {1x}, lightning {2x}. See: TWOT—635a; BDB—304a.

2386. חֲזִיר {7x} **chăzîyr**, *khaz-eer'*; from an unused root prob. mean. to *inclose*; a *hog* (perh. as *penned*):—boar {1x}, swine {1x}. See: TWOT—637a; BDB—306b.

2387. חֵזִיר {2x} **Chêzîyr**, *khay-zeer'*; from the same as 2386; perh. *protected; Chezir*, the name of two Isr.:—Hezir {2x}. See: BDB—306c.

2388. חָזַק {290x} **châzaq**, *khaw-zak'*; a prim. root; to *fasten* upon; hence, to *seize, be strong* (fig. *courageous*, caus. *strengthen, cure, help, repair, fortify*), *obstinate*; to *bind, restrain, conquer*:—strong {48x}, repair {47x}, hold {37x}, strengthened {28x}, strengthen {14x}, harden {13x}, prevail {10x}, encourage {9x}, take {9x}, courage {8x}, caught {5x}, stronger {5x}, hold {5x}, misc. {52x} = aid, amend, × calker, catch, cleave, confirm, be constant, constrain, continue, be established, fasten, force, fortify, help, lean, maintain, play the man, mend, become (wax) mighty, be recovered, retain, seize, be (wax) sore, be stout, be sure, be urgent, behave self valiantly, withstand.

Chazaq, as a verb, means "to be strong, strengthen, harden, take hold of." **(1)** The word first occurs in Gen 41:56: ". . . And the famine waxed sore in the land of Egypt." **(2)** In reference to Pharaoh, it means to brace up and strengthen and points to the hardihood with which he set himself to act in defiance against God and closed all the avenues to his heart to those signs and wonders which Moses wrought. **(2a)** Pharoah was responsible for his hard heart. Four times we read: "Pharaoh's heart was hardened" (Ex 7:13, 22; 8:19; 9:35). **(2b)** He hardened it. In Ex 9:34 Pharaoh's responsibility is made clear by the statement "he sinned yet more, and hardened his heart. . . . " **(2c)** God hardened it. The strong form of the verb is used in Ex 4:21: ". . . I will harden his [Pharaoh's] heart. . . ." This statement is found 8 times.

(3) In the sense of personal strength *chazaq* is first used in Deut 11:8 in the context of the covenant: **(3a)** "Therefore shall ye keep all the commandments which I command you this day, that ye may be strong, and go in and possess the land. . . . " **(3b)** Moses was commanded to "charge Joshua, and encourage him" (Deut 3:28). **(3c)** The covenant promise accompanies the injunction to "be strong and of a good courage": ". . . For the LORD thy God, he it is that doth go with thee; he will not fail thee, nor forsake thee" (Deut 31:6). **(3d)** The same encouragement was given to the returned captives as they renewed the work of rebuilding the temple (Zec 8:9; 13; cf. Hag 2:4). **(4)** If in the above examples there is moral strength combined with physical, the latter is the sense of Judg 1:28: **(4a)** "And it came to pass, when Israel was strong, that they put the Canaanites to [forced labor]. . . ." **(4b)** Israel sinned and the Lord "strengthened Eglon the king of Moab against Israel" (Judg 3:12).

(5) The word is used in reference **(5a)** to a building: ". . . The priests had not repaired the breaches of the house" (2 Kin 12:6), or **(5b)** to a city: "Moreover Uzziah built towers in Jerusalem . . . and fortified them" (2 Chr 26:9). **(6)** In battle *chazaq* means: "So David prevailed over the Philistine . . ." (1 Sa 17:50). **(7)** As the prophet said, "For the eyes of the LORD run to and fro throughout the whole earth to show himself strong in the behalf of them whose heart is perfect toward him" (2 Chr 16:9). **(8)** To His Servant, the Messiah, **(8a)** God said: "I . . . will hold thine hand . . ." (Is 42:6); and to **(8b)** Cyrus He said: ". . . Whose right hand I have holden . . ." (Is 45:1). **(9)** Other noteworthy uses of the word are: **(9a)** ". . . Thou shalt relieve him [a poor Israelite] . . ." (Lev 25:35); and **(9b)** ". . . [Saul] laid hold upon the skirt of his mantle, and it rent" (1 Sa 15:27). **(10)** In summary, **(10a)** this word group describes the physical and moral strength of man and society. **(10b)** God communicates strength to men, even to the enemies of His people as chastisement for His own. **(10c)** Men may turn their strength into stubbornness against God. See: TWOT—636; BDB—304a.

2389. חָזָק {56x} **châzâq**, *khaw-zawk'*; from 2388; *strong* (usually in a bad sense, *hard,* *bold, violent*):—strong {26x}, mighty {20x}, sore {3x}, stronger {2x}, harder {1x}, hottest {1x}, impudent {1x}, loud {1x}, stiffhearted {1x}.

Chazaq, as an adjective, means "strong; mighty; heavy; severe; firm; hard." **(1)** First, the word means "firm" or "hard" in the sense that something is impenetrable. **(1a)** In Eze 3:8–9 the prophet's face is compared to rock; **(1b)** God has made him determined to his task just as Israel is determined not to listen to him: "Behold, I have made thy face [hard] against their faces, and thy forehead [hard] against their foreheads. As an adamant harder than flint have I made thy forehead. . . ." **(1c)** Job 37:18 uses *chazaq* of molten solidified metal. **(2)** Second, this word means "strong." In its basic meaning it refers to physical strength. God's hand (an anthropomorphism; cf. Deut 4:15, 19) as a symbol of His effecting His will among men is "strong": "And I am sure that the king of Egypt will not let you go, no, not by a mighty hand" (Ex 3:19—the first biblical occurrence). **(2a)** This word modifies a noun, specifying that it is the opposite of weak, or unable to effect anything (Num 13:18). **(2b)** Isaiah speaks of God's "sore and great and strong sword" (27:1). **(2c)** When Ezekiel wrote of "fat and strong" animals, he probably meant that they were well fed and healthy (34:16). **(3)** Third, *chazaq* means "heavy." **(3a)** When applied to a battle or war, it describes the event(s) as severe (1 Sa 14:52). **(3b)** The word is also used to indicate **(3b1)** a severe sickness (1 Kin 17:17) and **(3b2)** famine (1 Kin 18:2). See: TWOT—636a; BDB—305c.

2390. חָזֵק {3x} **châzêq**, *khaw-zake'*; from 2388; *powerful:*—× wax louder {1x}, stronger {2x}. See: TWOT—636a; BDB—304a, 395d.

2391. חֵזֶק {1x} **chêzeq**, *khay'-zek*; from 2388; *help:*—strength {1x}. Syn.: 2392, 2482, 3581, 5797. See: TWOT—636b; BDB—305d.

2392. חֹזֶק {5x} **chôzeq**, *kho'-zek*; from 2388; *power:*—strength {5x}. See: TWOT—636c; BDB—305d.

2393. חֶזְקָה {5x} **chezqâh**, *khez-kaw'*; fem. of 2391; prevailing *power:*—strengthen self {1x}, strength {2x}, (was) strong {2x}. See: TWOT—636b; BDB—395d.

2394. חָזְקָה {6x} **chozqâh**, *khoz-kaw'*; fem. of 2392; *vehemence* (usually in a bad sense):—force {2x}, mightily {2x}, repair {1x}, sharply {1x}. See: TWOT—636d; BDB—306a.

2395. חִזְקִי {1x} **Chizqîy**, *khiz-kee'*; from 2388; *strong; Chizki*, an Isr.:—Hezeki {1x}. See: BDB—306a.

2396. חִזְקִיָּה {87x} **Chizqîyâh**, *khiz-kee-yaw'*; or

חִזְקִיָּהוּ **Chizqîyâhûw**, *khiz-kee-yaw'-hoo;* also

יְחִזְקִיָּה **Yᵉchizqîyâh**, *yekh-iz-kee-yaw'*; or

יְחִזְקִיָּהוּ **Yᵉchizqîyâhûw**, *yekh-iz-kee-yaw'-hoo;* from 2388 and 3050; *strengthened of Jah; Chizkijah*, a king of Judah, also the name of two other Isr.:—Hezekiah {85x}, Hizkiah {1x}, Hizkijah {1x}. Syn.: comp. 3169. See: BDB—306a.

2397. חָח {8x} **châch**, *khawkh;* once (Eze 29:4)

חָחִי **chăchîy**, *khakh-ee'*; from the same as 2336; a *ring* for the nose (or lips):—bracelet {1x}, chain {2x}, hook {5x}. See: TWOT—620b; BDB—296b, 306c.

חָחִי **châchîy**. See 2397.

2398. חָטָא {238x} **châṭâ'**, *khaw-taw'*; a prim. root; prop. to *miss;* hence, (fig. and gen.) to *sin;* by infer. to *forfeit, lack, expiate, repent,* (caus.) *lead astray, condemn:*—sin {188x}, purify {11x}, cleanse {8x}, sinner {8x}, committed {6x}, offended {4x}, blame {2x}, done {2x}, fault {1x}, harm {1x}, loss {1x}, miss {1x}, offender {1x}, purge {1x}, reconciliation {1x}, sinful {1x}, trespass {1x}.

Chata' means sin; sin-guilt; sin purification; sin offering. *Chata'*, as a verb, means "to miss, sin, be guilty, forfeit, purify." **(1)** The basic nuance of *chata'* is sin conceived as missing the road or mark; illustrated in Judg 20:16: **(1a)** "There were 700 left-handed Benjamite soldiers who "could sling stones at a hair breadth, and not miss." **(1b)** The meaning is extended in Prov 19:2: "He who makes haste with his feet sinneth." **(1c)** The intensive form is used in Gen 31:39: "That which was torn of beasts I brought not unto thee; I bare the loss of it. . . . " **(2)** From this basic meaning comes the word's chief usage to indicate moral failure toward both God and men, and certain results of such wrongs. **(2a)** The first occurrence of the verb is in Gen 20:6, God's word to Abimelech after he had taken Sarah: "Yea, I know that thou didst this in the integrity of thy heart; for I also withheld thee from sinning against me: therefore suffered I thee not to touch her. (cf. Gen 39:9). **(2b)** Sin against God is defined in Josh 7:11: "Israel hath sinned, and they have also transgressed my covenant which I commanded them. . . . " **(2c)** Also note Lev 4:27: "And if any one of the common people sin through ignorance, while he doeth somewhat against any of the commandments of the Lord concerning things which ought not to be done, and be guilty."

(3) The verb may also refer to the result of wrongdoing, as in Gen 43:9: ". . . Then let me bear the blame for ever." **(4)** Deut 24:1–4, after forbidding adulterous marriage practices, concludes: ". . . For that is abomination before the LORD: and thou shalt not cause the land to sin . . ." **(5)** Similarly, those who pervert justice are described as "those who by a word make a man out to be guilty" (Is 29:21). **(6)** This leads to the meaning in Lev 9:15: **(6a)** "And he . . . took the goat . . . and slew it, and offered it for sin. . . ." **(6b)** The effect of the offerings for sin is described in Ps 51:7: "Purge me with hyssop, and I shall be clean . . ." (cf. Num 19:1–13). **(7)** Another effect is seen in the word of the prophet to evil Babylon: "You have sinned against your life" (Hab. 2:10). **(8)** The word is used concerning acts committed against men, as in **(8a)** Gen 42:22: "Spake I not unto you, saying, Do not sin against the child . . . ?" and **(8b)** 1 Sa 19:4: "Do not let the king sin against his servant David, since he has not sinned against you . . ."

(9) Men are **(9a)** to turn from sin - a path/life-style, or act deviating from God's direction (1 Kin 8:35), **(9b)** to depart from sin (2 Kin 10:31), **(9c)** be concerned about it (Ps 38:18), and **(9d)** confess it (Num 5:7). **(10)** It also connotes the guilt or condition of sin (Gen 18:20), **(11)** means purification from sin (Num 8:7; 9:9), **(12)** the sin offering (Lev 4:1—5:13; 6:24–30) for **(12a)** some specific sin **(12b)** committed unwittingly, **(12c)** without intending to do it and **(12d)** perhaps even without knowing it at the time (Lev. 4:2; 5:15). Syn.: 205, 817, 599, 2403, 5674, 5771, 6588, 7451, 7563. See: TWOT—638; BDB—306c.

2399. חֵטְא {33x} **chêṭ'**, *khate;* from 2398; a *crime* or its *penalty:*—faults {1x}, × grievously {1x}, offences {1x}, (punishment of) sin {30x}.

(1) This word means "sin" in the sense of missing the mark or the path. **(1a)** This may be sin against either a man (Gen 41:9—the first occurrence of the word) or **(1b)** God (Deut 9:18). **(2)** Second, it connotes the "guilt" of such an act (Num 27:3). The psalmist confessed that his mother was in the condition of sin and guilt (cf. Rom 5:12) when he was conceived (Ps 51:5). See: TWOT—638a; BDB—307d, 1092d.

2400. חַטָּא {18x} **chaṭṭâ'**, *khat-taw'*; intens. from 2398; a *criminal*, or one accounted *guilty:*—offender {1x}, sinful {1x}, sinner {16x}.

(1) The noun *chatta'*, with the form reserved for those who are typified with the characteristic represented by the root, is used both as an adjective (emphatic) and as a noun. **(2)** The word occurs 18 times. **(3)** Men are described as "sinners" (1 Sa 15:18) and as those who are liable to the penalty of an offense (1 Kin 1:21). **(4)** The first occurrence of the word is in Gen 13:13: "But the men of Sodom were wicked and sinners before the Lord exceedingly." See: TWOT—638b; 308b.

2401. חֲטָאָה {8x} **chăṭâ'âh**, *khat-aw-aw'*; fem. of 2399; an *offence*, or a *sacrifice* for it:—sin offering {1x}, sin {7x}. See: TWOT—638d; BDB—308b.

2402. חַטָּאָה {1x} **chaṭṭâ'âh** (Aram.), *khat-taw-aw'*; corresp. to 2401; an *offence*, and the *penalty* or *sacrifice* for it:—sin (offering) {1x}. See: TWOT—2726b; BDB—308b.

2403. חַטָּאָה {296x} **chaṭṭâ'âh**, *khat-taw-aw'*; or

חַטָּאת **chaṭṭâ'th**, *khat-tawth'*; from 2398; an *offence* (sometimes habitual *sinfulness*), and its penalty, occasion, sacrifice, or expiation; also (concr.) an *offender:*—sin {182x}, sin offering {116x}, punishment {3x}, purification for sin {2x}, purifying {1x}, sinful {1x}, sinner {1x}.

Chatta'th, as a noun, means "sin; sin-guilt; sin purification; sin offering." **(1)** The basic nuance of this word is "sin" conceived as missing the road or mark (155 times). **(2)** *Chatta'th* can refer to an offense against a man: "And Jacob was wroth, and chode with Laban: and Jacob answered and said to Laban, What is my trespass [6588 - *pesha'*]? what is my sin, that thou hast so hotly pursued after me?" (Gen 31:36). **(2a)** It is such passages which prove that *chatta'th* is not simply a general word for "sin"; **(2b)** since Jacob used two different words, he probably intended two different nuances. **(3)** For the most part this word represents a sin against God (Lev 4:14). **(3a)** Men are to return from "sin," which is a path, a life-style, or act deviating from that which God has marked out (1 Kin 8:35). **(3b)** They should depart from "sin" (2 Kin 10:31), **(3c)** be concerned about it (Ps 38:18), and **(3d)** confess it (Num 5:7).

(4) The noun first appears in Gen 4:7, where Cain is warned that "sin lieth at the door." **(4a)** This citation may introduce a second nuance of the word—"sin" in general. **(4b)** Certainly such an emphasis appears in Ps 25:7, where the noun represents rebellious sin (usually indicated by *pêsha'* - 6588): "Remember not the sins of my youth, nor my transgressions. . . ." **(5)** In a few passages the term connotes the guilt or condition of sin: ". . . The cry of Sodom and Gomorrah is great, and . . . their sin is very grievous" (Gen 18:20). **(6)** The word means "purification from sin" in two passages: "And thus shalt thou do unto them, to cleanse them: Sprinkle water of purifying upon them . . ." (Num 8:7; cf. 19:9). **(7)** *Chatta'th* means "sin offering" (135 times). **(7a)** The law of the "sin offering" is recorded in Lev 4-5:13; 6:24–30. **(7b)** This was an offering for some specific "sin" committed unwittingly, without intending to do it and perhaps even without knowing it at the time (Lev 4:2; 5:15). **(7c)** Finally, several passages use this word for the idea of "punishment for sin" (Lev 20:20). Syn.: 801, 817, 2077, 4503, 5071, 5258, 5930, 6452, 7133, 8002, 8573. See: TWOT—638e; BDB—303b, 310d, 1092d.

2404. חָטַב {9x} **châṭab**, *khaw-tab'*; a prim. root; to *chop* or *carve* wood:—cut down {1x}, hew {1x}, hewer {1x}, hewers {5x}, polished {1x}. See: TWOT—639; BDB—310a.

2405. חֲטֻבָה {1x} **chăṭûbâh**, *khat-oo-baw'*; fem. pass. part. of 2404; prop. a *carving;* hence, a *tapestry* (as figured):—carved {1x}. See: TWOT—640a; 310b; BDB—310b.

2406. חִטָּה {30x} **chiṭṭâh**, *khit-taw'*; of uncert. der.; *wheat,* whether the grain or the plant:—wheat {29x}, wheaten {1x}. See: TWOT—691b; BDB—310b, 334d, 1093b.

2407. חַטּוּשׁ {5x} **Chaṭṭûwsh**, *khat-toosh'*; from an unused root of uncert. signif.; *Chattush,* the name of four or five Isr.:—Hattush {5x}. See: BDB—310d.

2408. חֲטִי {1x} **chăṭîy** (Aram.), *khat-ee'*; from a root corresp. to 2398; an *offence:*—sin {1x}. See: TWOT—2726a; BDB—1092d.

2409. חַטָּיָא {1x} **chaṭṭâyâʼ** (Aram.), *khat-taw-yaw'*; from the same as 2408; an *expiation:*—sin offering {1x}. See: TWOT—2726b; BDB—1092d.

2410. חֲטִיטָא {2x} **Chăṭîyṭaʼ**, *khat-ee-taw'*; from an unused root appar. mean. to *dig* out; *explorer; Chatita,* a temple porter:—Hatita {2x}. See: BDB—310b.

2411. חַטִּיל {2x} **Chaṭṭîyl**, *khat-teel'*; from an unused root appar. mean. to *wave; fluctuating; Chattil,* one of "Solomon's servants":—Hattil {2x}. See: BDB—310b.

2412. חֲטִיפָא {2x} **Chăṭîyphâʼ**, *khat-ee-faw'*; from 2414; *robber; Chatipha,* one of the Nethinim:—Hatipha {1x}. See: BDB—310c.

2413. חָטַם {1x} **châṭam**, *khaw-tam'*; a prim. root; to *stop:*—refrain {1x}. Syn.: 2820. See: TWOT—641; BDB—310c.

2414. חָטַף {3x} **châṭaph**, *khaw-taf'*; a prim. root; to *clutch;* hence, to *seize* as a prisoner:—catch {3x}. Syn.: 3920. See: TWOT—642; BDB—310c.

2415. חֹטֶר {2x} **chôṭer**, *kho'-ter*; from an unused root of uncert. signif.; a *twig:*—rod {2x}. Syn.: 4294, 4731, 7626. See: TWOT—643a; BDB—310d.

2416. חַי {501x} **chay**, *khah'-ee*; from 2421; *alive;* hence, *raw* (flesh); *fresh* (plant, water, year), *strong;* also (as noun, espec. in the fem. sing. and masc. plur.) *life* (or living thing), whether lit. or fig.:—live {197x}, life {144x}, beast {76x}, alive {31x}, creature {15x}, running {7x}, living thing {6x}, raw {6x}, misc. {19x} = + age, appetite, company, congregation, maintenance, + merry, multitude, + (be) old, quick, springing, troop.

Chay, in its **(1) masculine noun form,** means "living thing; life." **(1a)** The use of this word occurs only in the oath formula "as X lives," literally, "by the life of X": "And he said, They were my brethren, even the sons of my mother: as the LORD liveth, if ye had saved them alive, I would not slay you" (Judg 8:19). **(1b)** This formula summons the power of a superior to sanction the statement asserted. **(1b1)** In Judg 8:19 God is the witness to Gideon's pledge to kill his enemies and this statement that they brought the penalty on themselves. **(1b2)** A similar use appears in Gen 42:15 except that the power summoned is Pharaoh's: "Hereby ye shall be proved: By the life of Pharaoh ye shall not go forth hence, except your youngest brother come hither." **(1bc)** In 1 Sa 1:26 Hannah employs a similar phrase summoning Eli himself to attest the truthfulness of her statement: "And she said, Oh my lord, as thy soul liveth, my lord, I am the woman that stood by thee here, praying unto the LORD." **(1c)** Only God swears by His own power: "And the Lord said, I have pardoned according to thy word: But as truly as I live, all the earth shall be filled with the glory of the Lord" (Num 14:20–21).

(2) The **feminine form of the word,** *chayyah,* means "living being" and is especially used of animals. **(2a)** When so used, it usually distinguishes wild and undomesticated from domesticated animals; the word connotes that the animals described are untamed: **(2a1)** "And God remembered Noah, and every living thing, and all the cattle that was with him in the ark . . ." (Gen 8:1). **(2a2)** Job 37:8 uses *chayyah* of rapacious beasts: "Then the beasts go into dens, and remain in their places." **(2a3)** This same word may also connote "evil beast": "Come now therefore, and let us slay him, and cast him into some pit, and we will say, Some evil beast hath devoured him . . ." (Gen 37:20). **(2b)** In another nuance the word describes land animals as distinct from birds and fish: "Be fruitful, and multiply, and replenish the earth, and subdue it: and have dominion over the fish of the sea, and over the fowl of the air, and over every living thing that moveth upon the earth" (Gen 1:28). **(2c)** Infrequently *chayyah* represents a domesticated animal: "And the cities shall they have to dwell in; and the suburbs of them shall be for their cattle, and for their goods, and for all their beasts" (Num 35:3). **(2d)** Sometimes this word is used of "living beings" in general: "Also out of the midst thereof came the likeness of four living creatures: (Eze 1:5). In such passages the word is synonymous with the Hebrew word *nepesh* (5315).

(3) The **masculine plural of the noun** *chay, chayyim,* is a general word for the state of living as opposed to that of death. **(3a)** This meaning is in Deut 30:15: **(3a1)** "See, I have set before thee this day life and good, and death and evil." **(3a2)** Notice also Gen 27:46: "And Rebekah said to Isaac, I am weary of my life because of the daughters of Heth. . . . " **(3b)** In a second nuance the plural signifies "lifetime," or the days of one's life: ". . . And dust shalt thou eat all the days of thy life" (Gen 3:14). **(3c)** The phrase "the years of one's life" represents the same idea: "And Sarah was a hundred and seven and twenty years old: these were the years of the life of Sarah" (Gen 23:1). **(3d)** The "breath of life" in Gen 2:7 is the breath that brings "life": "And the LORD God formed man of the dust of the ground, and breathed into his nostrils the breath of life; and man became a living soul" (cf. Gen 6:17). **(3e)** The "tree of life" is the tree which gives one eternal, everlasting "life." Therefore, it is the tree whose fruit brings "life": "And out of the ground made the LORD God to grow every tree that is pleasant to the sight, and good for food; the tree of life also in the midst of the garden . . ." (Gen 2:9).

(3f) In another nuance this word suggests a special quality of "life," life as a special gift from God (a gift of salvation): "I call heaven and earth to record this day against you, that I have set before you life and death, blessing and cursing: therefore choose life, that both thou and thy seed may live" (Deut 30:19). **(3g)** The plural of the word can represent "persons who are alive," or living persons: "And he stood between the dead and the living; and the plague was stayed" (Num 16:48). **(4)** *Chay,* as **a masculine adjective,** means "alive; living." **(4a)** Used adjectivally it modifies men, animals, and God, but never plants. **(4a1)** In Gen 2:7 the word used with the noun *nepesh* (5315 - "soul, person, being") means a "living" person: "And the Lord God formed man of the dust of the ground, and breathed into his nostrils the breath of life; and man became a living soul." **(4a2)** The same two words are used in Gen 1:21 but with a slightly different meaning: "And God created . . . every living creature that moveth, which the waters brought forth abundantly, after their kind. . . ." Here a living *nepesh* ("creature") is an animal.

(4b) Deut 5:26 refers to God as the "living" God, distinguishing Him from the lifeless gods/idols of the heathen. **(4c)** In a related nuance *chay* describes flesh (animal meat or human flesh) under the skin, or "raw flesh." **(4c1)** In Lev 13:10 one reads that leprosy involved seeing quick (alive), raw (*chay*) flesh: "And the priest shall see him: and, behold, if the rising be white in the skin, and it have turned the hair white, and there be quick raw flesh in the rising. . . ." **(4c2)** The same words (*bashar chay*) are applied to dead, raw (skinned) animal flesh: "Give flesh to roast for the priest; for he will not have [boiled] flesh of thee, but raw" (1 Sa 2:15). **(4d)** Applied to liquids, *chay* means "running"; it is used metaphorically describing something that moves: "And Isaac's servants digged in the valley, and found there a well of springing water" (Gen 26:19). **(4e)** The Song of Solomon uses the word in a figure of speech describing one's wife; she is "a well of living waters" (4:15). The emphasis is not on the fact that the water flows but on its freshness; it is not stagnant, and therefore is refreshing and pleasant when consumed.

Chay, as an **masculine adjective,** means alive/living and modifies **(1)** man **(1a)** as man (Gen 2:7), or **(1b)** his flesh (Lev 13:10); **(2)** God (Deut 5:26); or **(3)** animals (1 Sa 2:15). **(4)** Applied to liquids, *chay* means running, being used metaphorically to describe something that moves: **(4a)** a well of springing water (Gen 26:19); **(4b)** living, life-giving waters (Jer 2:13; 17:3; Zec 14:8); **(4c)** one's wife; "a well of living waters" (Song 4:15). The emphasis is not on the fact that the water flows but on its freshness; it is not stagnant, and therefore is refreshing and pleasant when consumed. The **feminine** form, *chayyah,* means "living being" and is especially used of animals. **(1)** wild, untamed, undomesticated (Gen 8:1); **(1a)** rapacious beasts (Job 37:8); **(1b)** evil beasts (Gen 37:20); **(1c)** land animals as distinct from birds and fish (Gen 1:28). Infrequently *chayyah* represents

(2) a domesticated animal (Num 35:3). **(3)** Sometimes this word is used of living beings in general (Eze 1:5). The **masculine plural** of *chay, chayyim,* is a general word for **(1)** the state of living as opposed to that of death (Deut 30:15; Gen 27:46) and **(2)** signifies lifetime, or the days of one's life or the years of one's life (Gen 3:14; 23:1). **(3)** The "breath of life" (Gen 2:7; 6:17) is the breath that brings life. **(4)** The "tree of life" is the tree that gives one eternal, everlasting life (Gen 2:9). **(5)** This word also suggests a special quality of life, life as a special gift from God (a gift of salvation - Deut 30:19). **(6)** The plural can represent alive or living persons (Num 16:48). See: TWOT—644a; BDB—310d, 311d, 312c, 312d, 313a, 1092d.

2417. חַי {7x} **chay** (Aram.), *khah'-ee;* from 2418; *alive;* also (as noun in plur.) *life:*—life {2x}, that liveth {1x}, living {4x}. See: TWOT—2727a; BDB—1092d.

2418. חֲיָא {6x} **chăyâʾ** (Aram.), *khah-yaw';* or

חֲיָה **chăyâh** (Aram.), *khah-yaw';* corresp. to 2421; to *live:*—live {5x}, keep alive {1x}. See: TWOT—2727; BDB—1092d.

2419. חִיאֵל {1x} **Chîyʾêl**, *khee-ale';* from 2416 and 410; *living of God; Chiel,* an Isr.:—Hiel {1x}. See: BDB—27d, 310d, 313c.

חָיַב **châyab**. See 2325.

2420. חִידָה {17x} **chîydâh**, *khee-daw';* from 2330; a *puzzle,* hence, a *trick, conundrum,* sententious *maxim:*—riddle {9x}, dark sayings {3x}, hard question {2x}, dark sentence {1x}, proverb {1x}, dark speech {1x}. See: TWOT—616a; BDB—295b, 310d.

2421. חָיָה {262x} **châyâh**, *khaw-yaw';* a prim. root [comp. 2331, 2421]; to *live,* whether lit. or fig.; caus. to *revive:*—keep (leave, make) alive, × certainly, give (promise) life, (let, suffer to) live, nourish up, preserve (alive), quicken, recover, repair, restore (to life), revive, (× God) save (alive, life, lives), × surely, be whole.

Chayah means "to live." **(1)** In the ground stem this verb connotes "having life": **(1a)** "And Adam lived a hundred and thirty years . . ." (Gen 5:3). **(1b)** A similar meaning appears in Num 14:38 and Josh 9:21. **(2)** The intensive form of *chayah* means "to preserve alive": ". . . Two of every sort shalt thou bring into the ark, to keep them alive with thee . . ." (Gen 6:19). **(3)** This word may also mean "to bring to life" or "to cause to live": ". . . I dwell . . . with him also that is of a contrite and humble spirit, to revive the spirit of the humble, and to revive the heart of the contrite ones" (Is 57:15). **(4)** "To live" is more than physical existence. **(4a)** According to Deut 8:3, "man doth not live by bread only, but by every word that proceedeth out of the mouth of the LORD doth man live." **(4a)** Moses said to Israel: ". . . Love the LORD thy God . . . that thou mayest live and multiply" (Deut 30:16). See: TWOT—644; BDB—295c, 310d, 1092d.

2422. חָיֶה {1x} **châyeh**, *khaw-yeh';* from 2421; *vigorous:*—lively {1x}. See: TWOT—644e; BDB—313a.

2423. חֵיוָא {20x} **chêyvâʾ** (Aram.), *khay-vaw';* from 2418; an *animal:*—beast {20x}. See: TWOT—2727b; BDB—1092d.

2424. חַיּוּת {1x} **chayûwth**, *khah-yooth';* from 2421; *life:*—× living {1x}. See: TWOT—644g; BDB—313c.

2425. חָיַי {23x} **châyay**, *khaw-yah'-ee;* a prim. root [comp. 2421]; to *live;* caus. to *revive:*—live {21x}, save life {2x}. See: TWOT—644; BDB—310d.

2426. חֵיל {10x} **chêyl**, *khale;* or (short.)

חֵל **chêl**, *khale;* a collat. form of 2428; an *army;* also (by anal.) an *intrenchment:*—wall {2x}, rampart {2x}, host {2x}, trench {1x}, poor {1x}, bulwark {1x}, army {1x}. See: TWOT—623d; BDB—298a, 313d, 315d.

חִיל **chîyl**. See 2342.

2427. חִיל {6x} **chîyl**, *kheel;* and (fem.)

חִילָה **chîylâh**, *khee-law';* from 2342; a *throe* (espec. of childbirth):—pain {3x}, pang {2x}, sorrow {1x}. Syn.: 2342, 2479. See: TWOT—623b; 297d, 313d.

2428. חַיִל {243x} **chayil**, *khah'-yil;* from 2342; prob. a *force,* whether of men, means or other resources; an *army, wealth, virtue, valor, strength:*—army {56x}, man of valour {37x}, host {29x}, forces {14x}, valiant {13x}, strength {12x}, riches {11x}, wealth {10x}, power {9x}, substance {8x}, might {6x}, strong {5x}, misc. {33x} = able, activity, band of men (soldiers), company, goods, train, virtuous (-ly), war, worthy (-ily).

Chayil means strength; power; wealth; property; capable; valiant; army; troops; influential; upper-class people (courtiers). **(1)** First, this word signifies a faculty or "power," the ability to effect or produce something. **(1a)** The word is used of physical "strength" in the sense of power that can be exerted: "If the iron be blunt, and he do not whet the edge, then must he put to more strength . . ." (Eccl 10:10). **(1b)** Quite often this word appears in a military context. Here it is the physical strength, power, and ability to perform in battle that is in view. This idea is used of men in 1 Sa 2:4: "The bows of the mighty men are broken, and they that stumbled are girded with strength" (cf. Ps 18:32, 39). **(1c)** Ps 33:17 applies the word to a war horse. **(1d)** An interesting use of *chayil* appears in Num 24:17–18, where Balaam prophesied the destruction of Moab and Edom at the hands of Israel: "And Edom shall be a possession, Seir also shall be a possession for his enemies; and lsrael shall do valiantly" (v. 18). The idea here is dynamic; something is happening. **(1e)** One might also render this phrase: "Israel performs mightily." This translation of the word is somewhat inexact; a noun is translated as an adverb.

(2) Second, *chayil* means "wealth, property." **(2a)** This nuance of the word focuses on that which demonstrates one's ability, his wealth or goods; Levi, Simeon, and their cohorts attacked the Shechemites: "And all their wealth, and all their little ones, and their wives took they captive, and spoiled even all that was in the home" (Gen 34:29—the first biblical occurrence of the word). **(2b)** In Num 31:9 *chayil* includes all the possessions of the Midianites except the women, children, cattle, and flocks. Thus it seems to be a little narrower in meaning. **(2c)** When this nuance is used with the Hebrew word "to do or make," the resulting phrase means "to become wealthy or make wealth" (cf. Deut 8:18; Ruth 4:11). **(2d)** This is in marked contrast to the emphasis of the same construction in Num. 24:18. Joel 2:22 uses *chayil* in the sense of "wealth" or products of the ability of a tree to produce fruit.

(3) Third, several passages use the word in the sense of "able." **(3a)** In Gen 47:6 the ability to do a job well is in view. Pharaoh told Joseph: "The land of Egypt is before thee; in the best of the land make thy father and brethren to dwell; in the land of Goshen let them dwell: and if thou knowest any men of activity [capable men] among them, then make them rulers over my cattle." **(3b)** This word can also represent the domestic skills of a woman—Ruth is described as a woman of ability and, therefore, either potentially or actually a good wife (Ruth 3:11; Prov 12:4). **(3c)** When applied to men, *chayil* sometimes focuses on their ability to conduct themselves well in battle as well as being loyal to their commanders (1 Sa 14:52; 1 Kin 1:42). When used in such contexts, the word may be translated "valiant": "And there was sore war against the Philistines all the days of Saul: and when Saul saw any strong man, or any valiant man, he took him unto him" (1 Sa 14:52; cf. Num 24:18; 1 Sa 14:48).

(4) Fourth, this word sometimes means "army"; "And I will harden Pharaoh's heart, that he shall follow after them; and I will be honored upon Pharaoh, and upon all his host [army] . . ." (Ex 14:4). **(4a)** The word can also refer to the army as troops in the sense of a combination of a lot of individuals. **(4b)** Under such an idea the word can represent the members of an army distributed to perform certain functions. Jehoshaphat "placed forces in all the fenced cities of Judah, and set garrisons in the land of Judah . . ." (2 Chr 17:2). **(4c)** This is also the emphasis in 1 Kin 15:20: "Ben-hadad . . . sent the captains of the hosts which he had against the cities of Israel. . . ." **(5)** Fifth, *chayil* sometimes represents the "upper class," who, as in all feudal systems, were at once soldiers, wealthy, and influential; **(5a)** Sanballat "spake before his brethren and the army of Samaria," i.e., in the royal court (Neh 4:2). **(5b)** The Queen of Sheba was accompanied by a large escort of upperclass people from her homeland: "And she came to Jerusalem with a very great train . . ." (1 Kin 10:2). Syn.: 2426. See: TWOT—624a; BDB—298c, 313d, 1093a.

2429. חַיִל {7x} **chayil** (Aram.), *khah'-yil;* corresp. to 2428; an *army,* or *strength:*—aloud {3x}, army {2x}, power {1x}, most {1x}. See: TWOT—2728; BDB—1093a.

2430. חֵילָה {1x} **chêylâh**, *khay-law';* fem. of 2428; an *intrenchment:*—bulwark {1x}. See: TWOT—623e; BDB—298a.

2431. חֵילָם {2x} **Chêylâm**, *khay-lawm';* or

חֵלָאם **Chêlâʾm**, *khay-lawm';* from 2428; *fortress; Chelam,* a place E. of Pal.:—Helam {2x}. See: BDB—298a, 313d, 316a.

2432. חִילֵן {1x} **Chîylên**, *khee-lane';* from 2428; *fortress; Chilen,* a place in Pal.:—Hilen {1x}. See: BDB—298b.

2433. חִין {1x} **chîyn**, *kheen;* another form for 2580; *beauty:*—comely {1x}. See: TWOT—694c; BDB—313d, 336d.

2434. חַיִץ {1x} **chayits**, *khah'-yits;* another form for 2351; a *wall:*—wall {1x}. Syn.: 1444, 1447, 2346, 3796, 7791. See: TWOT—628a; BDB—300c, 313d.

2435. חִיצוֹן {25x} **chîytsôwn**, *khee-tsone';* from 2434; prop. the (outer) *wall side;* hence, *exterior;* fig. *secular* (as opposed to sacred):—utter {12x}, outward {7x}, without {5x}, outer {1x}. See: TWOT—627b; BDB—300b, 313d.

2436. חֵיק {39x} **chêyq**, *khake;* or

חֵק **chêq**, *khake;* and

חוֹק **chôwq**, *khoke;* from an unused root, appar. mean. to *inclose;* the *bosom* (lit. or fig.):—bosom {32x}, bottom {3x}, lap {1x}, midst {1x}, within {1x}, variant {1x}.

Cheq means "bosom; lap; base." **(1)** The word represents the "outer front of one's body" where beloved ones, infants, and animals are pressed closely: "Have I conceived all this people? have I begotten them, that thou shouldest say unto me, Carry them in thy bosom, as a nursing father beareth the sucking child . . ." (Num 11:12). **(2)** In its first biblical appearance, *cheq* is used of a man's "bosom": "And Sarai said unto Abram, My wrong be upon thee: I have given my maid into thy bosom; and when she saw that she had conceived, I was despised in her eyes . . ." (Gen 16:5). **(3)** The "husband of one's bosom" is **(3a)** a husband who is "held close to one's heart" or "cherished" (Deut 28:56). **(3b)** This figurative inward sense appears again in Ps 35:13: ". . . My prayer returned into mine own bosom" (cf. Job 19:27). **(3c)** In 1 Kin 22:35, the word means the "inside" or "heart" of a war chariot.

(4) *Cheq* represents a fold of one's garment above the belt where things are hidden: "And the Lord said furthermore unto him [Moses], Put now thine hand into thy bosom" (Ex 4:6). **(5)** This word is rendered as "lap": **(5a)** "The lot is cast into the lap; but the whole disposing thereof is of the LORD" (Prov 16:33). **(5b)** Yet "bosom" may be used, even where "lap" is clearly intended: "But the poor man had nothing, save one little ewe lamb, which he had bought and nourished up: and it grew up together with him, and with his children; it did eat of his own meat, and drank of his own cup, and lay in his bosom . . ." (2 Sa 12:3). **(6)** Finally, *cheq* means the "base of the altar," as described in Eze 43:13 (cf. Eze 43:17). Syn.: 2243, 2683, 6747. See: TWOT—629a; BDB—300c, 313d, 348d.

2437. חִירָה {2x} **Chîyrâh**, *khee-raw';* from 2357 in the sense of *splendor; Chirah,* an Adullamite:—Hirah {2x}. See: BDB—301b, 313d.

2438. חִירָם {24x} **Chîyrâm**, *khee-rawm';* or חִירֹם **Chîyrôm**, *khee-rome';* another form of 2361; *Chiram* or *Chirom,* the name of two Tyrians:—Hiram {23x}, Huram {1x}. See: BDB—27c, 313d.

2439. חִישׁ {1x} **chîysh**, *kheesh;* another form of 2363; to *hurry:*—make haste {1x}. Syn.: 926, 2363, 2648, 4116. See: TWOT—631; BDB—301c.

2440. חִישׁ {1x} **chîysh**, *kheesh;* from 2439; prop. a *hurry;* hence, (adv.) *quickly:*—soon {1x}. Syn.: 4116. See: TWOT—631a; BDB—301d.

2441. חֵךְ {15x} **chêk**, *khake;* prob. from 2596 in the sense of *tasting;* prop. the *palate* or inside of the mouth; hence, the *mouth* itself (as the organ of speech, taste and kissing):—roof of the mouth {5x}, mouth {9x}, taste {1x}. See: TWOT—692a, BDB—313d, 335a.

2442. חָכָה {14x} **châkâh**, *khaw-kaw';* a prim. root [appar. akin to 2707 through the idea of *piercing*]; prop. to *adhere* to; hence, to *await:*—long {1x}, tarry {2x}, wait {11x}. See: TWOT—645; BDB—314a.

2443. חַכָּה {3x} **chakkâh**, *khak-kaw';* prob. from 2442; a *hook* (as *adhering*):—angle {2x}, hook {1x}. Syn.: 2053, 8240. See: TWOT—693c; BDB—341a, 335c.

2444. חֲכִילָה {3x} **Chakîylâh**, *khak-ee-law';* from the same as 2447; *dark; Chakilah,* a hill in Pal.:—Hachilah {3x}. See: BDB—314b.

2445. חַכִּים {14x} **chakkîym** (Aram.), *khak-keem';* from a root corresp. to 2449; *wise,* i.e. a *Magian:*—wise {14x}. See: TWOT—2729a; BDB—1093a.

2446. חֲכַלְיָה {2x} **Chăkalyâh**, *khak-al-yaw';* from the base of 2447 and 3050; *darkness* (of) *Jah; Chakaljah,* an Isr.:—Hachaliah {2x}. See: BDB—314b.

2447. חַכְלִיל {1x} **chaklîyl**, *khak-leel';* by redupl. from an unused root appar. mean. to *be dark;* darkly *flashing* (only of the eyes); in a good sense, *brilliant* (as stimulated by wine):—red {1x}. Syn.: 119, 122, 132, 2448. See: TWOT—646a; BDB—314b.

2448. חַכְלִלוּת {1x} **chaklîlûwth**, *khak-lee-looth';* from 2447; *flash* (of the eyes); in a bad sense, *blearedness:*—redness {1x}. See: TWOT—646b; BDB—314b.

2449. חָכַם {27x} **châkam**, *khaw-kam';* a prim. root, to *be wise* (in mind, word or act):—wise {19x}, wiser {4x}, wisely {2x}, teach wisdom {1x}, exceeding {1x}.

Chakam means "to be wise, act wisely, make wise, show oneself wise." **(1)** The word means "to be wise" in Prov 23:15: "My son, if thine heart be wise, my heart shall rejoice, even mine." **(2)** In Ps 119:98 *chakam* means "to make wise": "Thou through thy commandments hast made me wiser than mine enemies: for they are ever with me." **(3)** This word represents the discernment of good and evil, prudence in secular matters, skill in arts, and experience in Divine things. **(4)** It is moral rather than intellectual; it is the adaptation of what we know to what we have (and ought) to do. Syn.: 995, 2450, 2454, 7919. See: TWOT—647; BDB—314b.

2450. חָכָם {137x} **châkâm**, *khaw-kawm';* from 2449; *wise,* (i.e. intelligent, skillful or artful):—wise {109x}, wise man {13x}, cunning {6x}, cunning men {4x}, subtil {1x}, unwise {2x}, wiser {2x}.

Chakam, the adjective, means "wise; skillful; practical." **(1)** This word plus the noun *chakemah* and the verb "to be wise" signify an important element of the Old Testament religious point of view. **(1a)** Religious experience was not a routine, a ritual, or faith experience. **(1b)** It was viewed as a mastery of the art of living in accordance with God's expectations. **(1c)** In their definition, the words "mastery" and "art" signify that wisdom was a process of attainment and not an accomplishment. **(2)** *Chakam* appears 132 times in the Hebrew Old Testament and occurs most frequently in Job, Proverbs, and Ecclesiastes, for which reason these books are known as "wisdom literature." **(3)** The first occurrence of *chakam* is in Gen 41:8: "And it came to pass in the morning that his spirit was troubled; and he sent and called for all the magicians of Egypt, and all the wise men thereof: and Pharaoh told them his dream; but there was none that could interpret them unto Pharaoh."

(4) The *chakam* in secular usage signified a man who was a "skillful" craftsman. **(4a)** The manufacturers of the objects belonging to the tabernacle were known to be wise, or experienced in their crafts (Ex 36:4). **(4b)** Even the man who was skillful in making idols was recognized as a craftsman (Is 40:20; cf. Jer 10:9). **(4c)** The reason for this is to be found in the man's skill, craftsmanship, and not in the object which was being manufactured. **(4d)** Those who were experienced in life were known as "wise," but their wisdom is not to be confused with the religious usage. **(4e)** Cleverness and shrewdness characterized this type of wisdom. **(4e1)** Amnon consulted Jonadab, who was known as a shrewd man (2 Sa 13:3), and followed his plan of seducing his sister Tamar. **(4e2)** Joab hired a "wise" woman to make David change his mind about Absalom (2 Sa 14:2).

(5) Based on the characterization of wisdom as a skill, a class of counselors known as "wise men" arose. **(5a)** They were to be found in Egypt (Gen 41:8), in Babylon (Jer 50:35), in Tyre (Eze 27:9), in Edom (Obad 8), and in Israel. **(5b)** In pagan cultures the "wise" man practiced magic and divination: **(5b1)** "Then Pharaoh also called the wise men and the sorcerers: now the magicians of Egypt, they also did in like manner with their enchantments" (Ex 7:11); and **(5b2)** ". . . that frustrateth the tokens of the liars, and maketh diviners mad; that turneth wise men backward, and maketh their knowledge foolish" (Is 44:25). **(6)** The religious sense of *chakam* excludes delusion, craftiness, shrewdness, and magic. **(6a)** God is the source of wisdom, as He is "wise": "Yet he also is wise, and will bring evil, and will not call back his words: but will arise against the house of the evildoers, and against the help of them that work iniquity" (Is 31:2).

(6b) The man or woman who, fearing God, lives in accordance with what God expects and what is expected of him in a God-fearing society is viewed as an integrated person. **(6c)** He is "wise" in that his manner of life projects the fear of God and the blessing of God rests upon him. **(6d)** Even as the craftsman is said to be skillful in his trade, the Old Testament *chakam* was learning and applying wisdom to every situation in life, and the degree in which he succeeded was a barometer of his progress on the road of wisdom. **(7)** The opposite of the *chakam* is the "fool" or wicked person, who stubbornly refuses counsel and depends on his own understanding: "For the turning away of the simple shall slay them, and the prosperity of fools shall destroy them" (Prov 1:32; cf. Deut 32:5–6; Prov 3:35). See: TWOT—647b; BDB—314c, 1093a.

2451. חָכְמָה {149x} **chokmâh**, *khok-maw';* from 2449; *wisdom* (in a good sense):—wisdom {145x}, wisely {2x}, skilful man {1x}, wits {1x}.

Chokmah, the noun, means "wisdom; experience; shrewdness." **(1)** Like *chakam,* most occurrences of this word are in Job, Proverbs, and Ecclesiastes. **(1a)** The *chakam* seeks after *chokmah,* "wisdom." **(1b)** Like *chakam,* the word *chokmah* can refer to technical skills or special abilities in fashioning something. **(1c)** The first occurrence of *chokmah* is in Ex 28:3: "And thou shalt speak unto all that are wisehearted, whom I have filled with the spirit of wisdom, that they may make Aaron's garments to consecrate him, that he may minister unto me in the priest's office." **(1c1)** This first occurrence of the word in the Hebrew Bible bears this out as well as the description of the workers on the tabernacle. **(1c2)** The artisan was considered to be endowed with special abilities given to him by God: "And he hath filled him with the spirit of God, in wisdom, in understanding, and in knowledge, and in all manner of workmanship" (Ex 35:31).

(2) *Chokmah* is the knowledge and the ability to make the right choices at the opportune time. **(2a)** The consistency of making the right choice is an indication of maturity and development. **(2b)** The prerequisite for "wisdom" is the fear of the Lord: "The fear of the Lord is the beginning of knowledge: but fools despise wisdom and instruction" (Prov 1:7). **(2c)** "Wisdom" is viewed as crying out for disciples who will do everything to pursue her (Prov 1:20). **(2d)** The person who seeks *chokmah* diligently **(2d1)** will receive understanding: "For the LORD giveth wisdom: out of his mouth cometh knowledge and understanding" (Prov 2:6); **(2d2)** he will benefit in his life by walking with God: "That thou mayest walk in the way of good men, and keep the paths of the righteous" (Prov 2:20). **(3)** The advantages of "wisdom" are many: "For length of days, and long life, and peace, shall they add to thee. Let not mercy and truth forsake thee: bind them about thy neck; write them upon the table of thine heart: so shalt thou find favor and good understanding in the sight of God and man" (Prov 3:2–4).

(4) The prerequisite is a desire to follow and imitate God as He has revealed Himself in Jesus Christ, without self-reliance and especially not in a spirit of pride: "A wise man will hear, and will increase learning; and a man of understanding shall attain unto wise counsels: to understand a proverb, and the interpretation; the words of the wise, and their dark sayings. The fear of the Lord is the beginning of knowledge: but fools despise wisdom and instruction" (Prov 1:5–7). **(5)** The fruits of *chokmah* are many, and the Book of Proverbs describes the characters of the *chakam* and *chokmah.* **(6)** In New Testament terms the fruits of "wisdom" are the same as the fruits of the Holy Spirit; cf. **(6a)** "But the fruit of the Spirit is love, joy, peace, long-suffering, gentleness, goodness, faith, meekness, temperance: against such there is no law" (Gal. 5:22–23); **(6b)** "But the wisdom that is from above is first pure, then peaceable, gentle, and easy to be entreated, full of mercy and good fruits, without partiality, and without hypocrisy. And the fruit of righteousness is sown in peace of them that make peace" (Jas 3:17–18).

(7) The importance of "wisdom" explains **(7a)** why books were written about it. **(7b)** Songs were composed in celebration of"wisdom" (Job 28). **(7c)** Even "wisdom" is personified in Proverbs. **(7c1)** *Chokmah* as a person stands for that divine perfection of "wisdom" which is manifest in God's creative acts. **(7c2)** As a divine perfection it is visible in God's creative acts: "Doth not wisdom cry: and understanding put forth her voice? . . . I wisdom dwell with prudence, and find out knowledge of witty inventions. . . . The LORD possessed me in the beginning of his way, before his works of old. . . . Then I was by him, as one brought up with him: and I was daily his delight, rejoicing always before him. . . . Now therefore hearken unto me, O ye children: for blessed are they that keep my ways" (Prov 8:1, 12, 22, 30, 32). See: TWOT—647a; BDB—315b.

2452. חָכְמָה {8x} **chokmâh** (Aram.), *khok-maw';* corresp. to 2451; *wisdom:*—wisdom {8x}. See: TWOT—2729b; BDB—1093a.

2453. חַכְמוֹנִי {2x} **Chakmôwnîy**, *khak-mo-nee';* from 2449; *skilful; Chakmoni,* an Isr.:—Hachmoni {1x}, Hachmonite {1x}. See: BDB—315d.

2454. חָכְמוֹת {5x} **chokmôwth**, *khok-mōth';* or

חַכְמוֹת **chakmôwth**, *khak-mōth';* collat. forms of 2451; *wisdom:*—wisdom {4x}, every wise [woman] {1x}. See: TWOT—647a; BDB—315b.

חֵל **chêl**. See 2426.

2455. חֹל {7x} **chôl**, *khole;* from 2490; prop. *exposed;* hence, *profane:*—common {2x}, profane {2x}, profane place {2x}, unholy {1x}.

Chol is that which is devoted to ordinary use in contrast to a sanctified, holy use. See: TWOT—623a, 661a; BDB—315d, 320d.

2456. חָלָא {1x} **châlâ'**, *khaw-law';* a prim. root [comp. 2470]; to *be sick:*—be diseased {1x}. See: TWOT—648; BDB—316a.

2457. חֶלְאָה {5x} **chel'âh**, *khel-aw';* from 2456; prop. *disease;* hence, *rust:*—scum {5x}. See: TWOT—649a; BDB—316a.

2458. חֶלְאָה {2x} **Chel'âh**, *khel-aw';* the same as 2457; *Chelah,* an Israelitess:—Helah {2x}. See: BDB—316a.

2459. חֶלֶב {92x} **cheleb**, *kheh'-leb;* or

חֵלֶב **chêleb**, *khay'-leb;* from an unused root mean. to *be fat; fat,* whether lit. or fig.; hence, the *richest* or *choice* part:—fat {79x}, fatness {4x}, best {5x}, finest {2x}, grease {1x}, marrow {1x}. See: TWOT—651a; BDB—316d.

2460. חֵלֶב {1x} **Chêleb**, *khay'-leb;* the same as 2459; *fatness; Cheleb,* an Isr.:—Heleb {1x}. See: BDB—317a.

2461. חָלָב {44x} **châlâb**, *khaw-lawb';* from the same as 2459; *milk* (as the *richness* of kine):—+ cheese {1x}, milk {42x}, sucking {1x}. See: TWOT—650a; BDB—316b.

2462. חֶלְבָּה {1x} **Chelbâh**, *khel-baw';* fem. of 2459; *fertility: Chelbah,* a place in Pal.:—Helbah {1x}. See: BDB—317a.

2463. חֶלְבּוֹן {1x} **Chelbôwn**, *khel-bone';* from 2459; *fruitful; Chelbon,* a place in Syria:—Helbon {1x}. See: BDB—317a.

2464. חֶלְבְּנָה {1x} **chelbᵉnâh**, *khel-ben-aw';* from 2459; *galbanam,* an odorous gum (as if *fatty*):—galbanum {1x}. See: TWOT—652; BDB—317b.

2465. חֶלֶד {5x} **cheled**, *kheh'-led;* from an unused root appar. mean. to *glide* swiftly; *life* (as a *fleeting* portion of time); hence, the *world* (as *transient*):—age {2x}, short time {1x}, world {2x}. This word stresses the transitory nature of things in this world which pass away. See: TWOT—653a; BDB—317b.

2466. חֵלֶד {1x} **Chêled**, *khay'-led;* the same as 2465; *Cheled,* an Isr.:—Heled {1x}. See: BDB—317c.

2467. חֹלֶד {1x} **chôled**, *kho'-led;* from the same as 2465; a *weasel* (from its *gliding* motion):—weasel {1x}. See: TWOT—654a; BDB—317c.

2468. חֻלְדָּה {2x} **Chuldâh**, *khool-daw';* fem. of 2467; *Chuldah,* an Israelitess:—Huldah {2x}. See: BDB—317c.

2469. חֶלְדַּי {2x} **Chelday**, *khel-dah'-ee;* from 2466; *worldliness; Cheldai,* the name of two Isr.:—Heldai {2x}. See: BDB—317c.

2470. חָלָה {75x} **châlâh**, *khaw-law';* a prim. root [comp. 2342, 2470, 2490]; prop. to *be rubbed* or *worn;* hence, (fig.) to *be weak, sick, afflicted;* or (caus.) to *grieve, make sick;* also to *stroke* (in flattering), *entreat:*—sick {34x}, beseech {6x}, be weak {4x}, grievous {4x}, be diseased {3x}, wounded {3x}, pray {3x}, intreat {3x}, grief {2x}, grieved {2x}, sore {2x}, pain {1x}, infirmity {1x}, intreated {1x}, laid {1x}, prayer {1x}, sorry {1x}, make suit {1x}, supplication {1x}, travail {1x}.

Chalah, as a verb, means "to be sick, weak." **(1)** It is found the first time near the end of the Book of Genesis when Joseph is told: "Behold, thy father is sick . . ." (Gen 48:1). **(2)** A survey of the uses of *chalah* shows that there was a certain lack of precision in many of its uses, and that the context would be the deciding factor in its meaning. **(2a)** When Samson told Delilah that if he were tied up with bowstrings he would "be weak, and be as another man" (Judg 16:7), the verb obviously did not mean "become sick," unless being sick implied being less than normal for Samson. **(2b)** When Joram is described as being sick because of wounds suffered in battle (2 Kin 8:29), perhaps it would be better to say that he was weak. **(2c)** Sacrificial animals that are described as being lame or "sick" (Mal 1:8) are actually imperfect or not acceptable for sacrifice. **(3)** This word is sometimes used in the figurative sense of overexerting oneself, thus becoming "weak." **(3a)** This is seen in Jer 12:13: "They have put themselves to pain . . ." **(3b)** Song 2:5, "sick of/with love," probably means "weak with passion." See: TWOT—655; BDB—317c, 318c.

2471. חַלָּה {14x} **challâh**, *khal-law';* from 2490; a *cake* (as usually *punctured*):—cake {14x}. Syn.: 4580, 5692, 6742. See: TWOT—660b; BDB—319c.

2472. חֲלוֹם {65x} **chălôwm**, *khal-ome';* or (short.)

חֲלֹם **chălôm**, *khal-ome';* from 2492; a *dream:*—dream {64x}, dreamer + 1167 {1x}.

Chalom, as a noun, means "dream." **(1)** The word means "dream." It is used of the ordinary dreams of sleep: "Then thou scarest me with dreams, and terrifiest me through visions . . ." (Job 7:14). **(2)** The most significant use of this word, however, is with reference to prophetic "dreams" and/or "visions." **(2a)** Both true and false prophets claimed to communicate with God by these dreams and visions. **(2b)** Perhaps the classical passage using the word in this sense is Deut 13:1ff.: "If there arise among you a prophet, or a dreamer of dreams, and giveth thee a sign or a wonder, and the sign or the wonder come to pass. . . . " **(2c)** This sense, that a dream is a means of revelation, appears in the first biblical occurrence of *chalom:* "But God came to Abimelech in a dream by night . . ." (Gen 20:3). Syn.: 2492. See: TWOT—663a; BDB—321c, 1093a.

2473. חֹלוֹן {3x} **Chôlôwn**, *kho-lone';* or (short.)

חֹלֹן **Chôlôn**, *kho-lone';* prob. from 2344; *sandy; Cholon,* the name of two places in Pal.:—Holon {3x}. See: BDB—298b, 322a.

2474. חַלּוֹן {31x} **challôwn**, *khal-lone';* a *window* (as *perforated*):—window {31x}. Syn.: 699, 6672. See: TWOT—660c; BDB—319d.

2475. חֲלוֹף {1x} **chălôwph**, *khal-ofe';* from 2498; prop. *surviving;* by impl. (collect.) *orphans:*—destruction {1x}. Syn.: 343, 816, 1104, 1820, 1949, 2254, 2717, 3772, 4288, 5255, 6979, 7665. See: TWOT—666b; BDB—322b.

2476. חֲלוּשָׁה {1x} **chălûwshâh**, *khal-oo-shaw';* fem. pass. part. of 2522; *defeat:*—being overcome {1x}. See: TWOT—671b; BDB—325d.

2477. חֲלַח {3x} **Chălach**, *khal-akh';* prob. of for. or.; *Chalach,* a region of Assyria:—Halah {3x}. See: BDB—318d.

2478. חַלְחוּל {1x} **Chalchûwl**, *khal-khool';* by redupl. from 2342; *contorted; Chalchul,* a place in Pal.:—Halhul {1x}. See: BDB—319a.

2479. חַלְחָלָה {4x} **chalchâlâh**, *khal-khaw-law';* fem. from the same as 2478; *writhing* (in childbirth); by impl. *terror:*—(great, much) pain {4x}. Syn.: 2342. See: TWOT—623f; BDB—298b, 319a.

2480. חָלַט {1x} **châlat**, *khaw-lat';* a prim. root; to *snatch* at:—catch {1x}. Syn.: 2414, 3920. See: TWOT—658; BDB—319a.

2481. חֲלִי {2x} **chălîy**, *khal-ee';* from 2470; a *trinket* (as *polished*):—jewel {1x}, ornament {1x}. See: TWOT—657a; BDB—316a, 318d.

2482. חָלִי {1x} **Chălîy**, *khal-ee';* the same as 2481; *Chali,* a place in Pal.:—Hali {1x}. See: BDB—318d.

2483. חֳלִי {24x} **chŏlîy**, *khol-ee';* from 2470; *malady, anxiety, calamity:*—sickness {12x}, disease {7x}, grief {4x}, sick {1x}.

Choliy means "sickness." **(1)** The use of this word in the description of the Suffering Servant in Is 53:3–4 is rendered "grief." **(2)** The meaning of "sickness" occurs in Deut 7:15: **(2a)** "And the Lord will take away from thee all sickness, and will put none of the evil diseases [4064 - *madweh*] of Egypt. . . . " **(2b)** *Choliy* is used metaphorically as a distress of the land in Hos 5:13. Syn.: 4245, 8463. See: TWOT—655a; BDB—318b.

2484. חֶלְיָה {1x} **chelyâh**, *khel-yaw';* fem. of 2481; a *trinket:*—jewel {1x}. See: TWOT—657b; BDB—318d.

2485. חָלִיל {4x} **châlîyl**, *khaw-leel';* from 2490; a *flute* (as *perforated*):—pipe {4x}. See: TWOT—660d; BDB—319d.

2486. חָלִילָה {21x} **châlîylâh**, *khaw-lee'-law;* or

חָלִלָה **châlîlâh**, *khaw-lee'-law;* a directive from 2490; lit. *for a profaned* thing; used (interj.) *far be it!:*—God forbid {9x}, far be it {4x}, be . . . far {4x}, Lord forbid {3x}, misc. {1x}. See: TWOT—661c; BDB—321a.

2487. חֲלִיפָה {12x} **chălîyphâh**, *khal-ee-faw';* from 2498; *alternation:*—change {11x}, course {1x}. See: TWOT—666c; BDB—322b.

2488. חֲלִיצָה {2x} **chălîytsâh**, *khal-ee-tsaw';* from 2502; *spoil:*—armour {1x}, spoil {1x}. Syn.: 957, 961, 7998. See: TWOT—667a, 668a; BDB—322d.

2489. חֶלְכָּא {4x} **chelᵉkâʾ**, *khay-lek-aw';* or

חֵלְכָה **chêlᵉkâh**, *khay-lek-aw';* appar. from an unused root prob. mean. to *be dark* or (fig.) *unhappy;* a *wretch,* i.e. *unfortunate:*—poor {2x}, variant {2x}. Syn.: 34, 1800, 1803, 4134, 4270, 4542, 6035. See: TWOT—659a; BDB—319a, 456c.

2490. חָלַל {141x} **châlal**, *khaw-lal';* a prim. root [comp. 2470]; prop. to *bore,* i.e. (by impl.) to *wound,* to *dissolve;* fig. to *profane* (a person, place or thing), to *break* (one's word), to *begin* (as if by an "opening wedge"); denom. (from 2485) to *play* (the flute):—begin {52x}, profane {36x}, pollute {23x}, defile {9x}, break {4x}, wounded {3x}, eat {2x}, slay {2x}, first {1x}, gather grapes {1x}, inheritance {1x}, men began {1x}, piped {1x}, players {1x}, prostitute {1x}, sorrow {1x}, stain {1x}, eat as common things {1x}.

Chalal (2490), means "to pollute, defile, profane, begin." **(1)** The most frequent use of this Hebrew root is in the sense of "to pollute, defile." **(1a)** This may be a ritual defilement, such as that resulting from contact with a dead body (Lev 21:4), or **(1b)** the ceremonial profaning of the sacred altar by the use of tools in order to shape the stones (Ex 20:25). **(1c)** Holy places may be profaned (Eze 7:24); **(1d)** the name of God (Eze 20:9) and **(1e)** even God Himself (Eze 22:26) may be profaned. **(1f)** The word is often used to describe the defilement which results from illicit sexual acts, such as harlotry (Lev 21:9) or violation of one's father's bed (Gen 49:4—the first occurrence). **(2)** In more than 50 instances, this root is used in the sense of "to begin." **(2a)** Perhaps the most important of such uses is found in Gen 4:26.

(2a1) There it is stated that after the birth of Seth, who was born to Adam and Eve after the murder of Abel by Cain, "then began men to call upon the name of the Lord." **(2a2)** One must ask whether the writer meant to say that it was not until the birth of Enosh, the son of Seth, that people "began" to call on the name of the Lord altogether, or whether he meant that this was the first time the name Yahweh was used. **(2a3)** In view of the accounts in Gen 1—3, neither of these seems likely. **(2a4)** Perhaps the writer is simply saying that in contrast to the apparent non-God-fearing attitude expressed by Cain, the generation beginning with Seth and his son Enosh was known for its God-fearing way of life. **(2a5)** Perhaps, in view of the passive intensive verb form used here, the meaning is something like this: "Then it was begun again to call on the name of the Lord." See: TWOT—660, 661; BDB—319b, 320a.

2491. חָלָל {94x} **châlâl**, *khaw-lawl';* from 2490; *pierced* (espec. to death); fig. *polluted:*—slay {78x}, wounded {10x}, profane {3x}, kill {2x}, slain man {1x}. See: TWOT—660a; BDB—319c, 321a.

חָלִלָה **châlîlâh**. See 2486.

2492. חָלַם {29x} **châlam**, *khaw-lam';* a prim. root; prop. to *bind* firmly, i.e. (by impl.) to *be* (caus. to *make*) *plump;* also (through the fig. sense of *dumbness*) to *dream:*—dreamed {20x}, dreamer {4x}, dream {1x}, dreameth {2x}, be in good liking {1x}, recover {1x}.

Chalam, as a verb, means "to become healthy or strong; to dream." **(1)** The meaning, "to become healthy," applies only to animals though "to dream" is used of human dreams. **(2)** Gen 28:12, the first occurrence, tells how Jacob "dreamed" that he beheld a ladder to heaven. See: TWOT—662, 663; BDB—321b.

2493. חֵלֶם {22x} **chêlem** (Aram.), *khay'-lem;* from a root corresp. to 2492; a *dream:*—dream {22x}. See: TWOT—2730; BDB—1093a.

2494. חֵלֶם {1x} **Chêlem**, *khay'lem;* from 2492; a *dream; Chelem,* an Isr.:—Helem {1x}. comp. 2469. See: BDB—321b.

2495. חַלָּמוּת {1x} **challâmûwth**, *khal-law-mooth';* from 2492 (in the sense of *insipidity*); prob. *purslain:*—egg {1x}. Syn.: 1000. See: TWOT—664; BDB—321d.

2496. חַלָּמִישׁ {5x} **challâmîysh**, *khal-law-meesh';* prob. from 2492 (in the sense of *hardness*); *flint:*—flint {3x}, flinty {1x}, rock {1x}. Syn.: 6864. See: TWOT—665; BDB—321d.

2497. חֵלֹן {5x} **Chêlôn**, *khay-lone';* from 2428; *strong; Chelon,* an Isr.:—Helon {5x}. See: BDB—298b, 322a.

2498. חָלַף **châlaph**, *khaw-laf';* a prim. root; prop. to *slide* by, i.e. (by impl.) to *hasten* away, *pass on, spring* up, *pierce* or *change:*—change {10x}, pass {3x}, renew {3x}, strike through {2x}, grow up {2x}, abolish {1x}, sprout again {1x}, alter {1x}, pass away {1x}, cut off {1x}, go on {1x}, pass on {1x}, over {1x}.

Chalaph means "to pass on, pass away, change, overstep, transgress." **(1)** When used in the simple active form, *chalaph* occurs only in poetry (except for 1 Sa 10:3), and it has the meaning of "to pass on, through." **(2)** The word is typically used in narrative or prose **(2a)** with the meaning of "to change." **(2b)** With this meaning *chalaph* first occurs in the Old Testament in Gen 31:7: ". . . Your father hath deceived me, and changed my wages ten times . . ." (cf. Gen 31:41). **(3b)** *Chalaph* expresses the "sweeping on" **(3b1)** of a flood (Is 8:8), **(3b2)** of a whirlwind (Is 21:1), and **(3b3)** of God Himself (Job 9:11). **(4)** The word has the meaning of "to pass away or to vanish," with reference **(4a)** to days (Job 9:26), **(4b)** the rain (Song 2:11), and **(4c)** idols (Is 2:18). **(5)** Not only wages, but garments are "changed" (Gen 35:2; Ps 102:26). **(6)** "To change" is "to renew" strength (Is 40:31; 41:1); **(7)** a tree appears "to be renewed" when it sprouts again (Job 14:7). See: TWOT—666; BDB—322a, 1025c, 1093a.

2499. חֲלַף {4x} **chălaph** (Aram.), *khal-af';* corresp. to 2498; to *pass* on (of time):—pass {4x}. See: TWOT—2731; BDB—1093a.

2500. חֵלֶף {2x} **chêleph**, *khay'-lef;* from 2498; prop. *exchange;* hence, (as prep.) *instead* of:—× for {2x}. See: TWOT—666a; BDB—322b.

2501. חֶלֶף {1x} **Cheleph**, *kheh'-lef;* the same as 2500; *change; Cheleph,* a place in Pal.:—Heleph {1x}. See: BDB—322b.

2502. חָלַץ {44x} **châlats**, *khaw-lats';* a prim. root; to *pull* off; hence, (intens.) to *strip,* (reflex.) to *depart;* by impl. to *deliver, equip* (for fight); *present, strengthen:*—deliver {15x}, arm {14x}, loose {2x}, armed men {2x}, prepared {2x}, take {2x}, army {1x}, make fat {1x}, put off {1x}, delivered out {1x}, draw out {1x}, armed soldiers {1x} withdrawn {1x}. See: TWOT—667, 668; BDB—322c, 323a.

2503. חֶלֶץ {5x} **Chelets**, *kheh'-lets;* or

חֵלֶץ **Chêlets**, *khay'-lets;* from 2502; perh. *strength; Chelets,* the name of two Isr.:—Helez {5x}. See: BDB—323b.

2504. חָלָץ **châlâts**, *khaw-lawts';* from 2502 (in the sense of *strength*); only in the dual; the *loins* (as the seat of vigor):—loins {9x}, reins {1x}. Syn.: 3629, 4975. See: TWOT—668 (668b); BDB—323b, 1093d.

2505. חָלַק {65x} **châlaq**, *khaw-lak';* a prim. root; to *be smooth* (fig.); by impl. (as smooth stones were used for *lots*) to *apportion* or *separate:*—divide {40x}, flatter {6x}, part {5x}, distribute {4x}, dealt {2x}, smoother {2x}, given {1x}, imparted {1x}, partner {1x}, portion {1x}, received {1x}, separate {1x}.

Chalaq, means "to divide, share, plunder, assign, distribute." **(1)** It appears for the first time in Gen 14:15, **(1a)** where it is said that Abram "divided himself against them" as he rescued his nephew Lot from the enemy. **(1b)** Apparently, Abram was "assigning" different responsibilities to his troops as part of his strategy. **(2)** The sense of "dividing" or "allotting" is found in Deut 4:19, **(2a)** where the sun, moon, and stars are said to have been "allotted" to all peoples by God. **(2b)** A similar use is seen in Deut 29:26, where God is said not to have "allotted" false gods to His people. **(3)** *Chalaq* is used in the legal sense of "sharing" an inheritance in Prov 17:2. **(4)** The word is used three times in reference to "sharing" the spoils of war in 1 Sa 30:24. **(5)** This verb describes the "division" of the people of Israel, as one half followed Tibni and the other half followed Omri (1 Kin 16:21). **(6)** The word *chalaq* is also important in the description of the "dividing" of the land of Canaan among the various tribes and clans (Num 26:52–55). Syn.: 2506, 2511, 2513. See: TWOT—669; BDB—323c, 325a, 1093b.

2506. חֵלֶק {66x} **chêleq**, *khay'-lek;* from 2505; prop. *smoothness* (of the tongue);

also an *allotment:*—portion {40x}, part {22x}, flattering {1x}, flattery {1x}, inheritance {1x}, partaker {1x}.

Cheleq, as a noun, means "portion; territory." It has a variety of meanings, such as **(1)** "booty" of war (Gen 14:24), **(2)** a "portion" of food (Lev 6:17), **(3)** a "tract" of land (Josh 18:5), **(4)** a spiritual "possession" or blessing (Ps 73:26), and **(5)** a chosen "pattern" or "life-style" (Ps 50:18). Syn.: 2511, 2513. See: TWOT—669a; BDB—324a, 325b.

2507. חֵלֶק {2x} **Chêleq**, *khay'-lek;* the same as 2506; *portion; Chelek,* an Isr.:—Helek {2x}. See: BDB—324c.

2508. חֲלָק {3x} **chălâq** (Aram.), *khal-awk';* from a root corresp. to 2505; a *part:*—portion {3x}. See: TWOT—2732a; BDB—1093b.

2509. חָלָק {4x} **châlâq**, *khaw-lawk';* from 2505; *smooth* (espec. of tongue):—flattering {2x}, smooth {1x}, smoother {1x}. Syn.: 2506, 2511, 2513. See: TWOT—670b; BDB—325b.

2510. חָלָק {2x} **Châlâq**, *khaw-lawk';* the same as 2509; *bare; Chalak,* a mountain of Idumæa:—Halak {2x}. See: BDB—325b.

2511. חַלָּק {1x} **challâq**, *khal-lawk';* from 2505; *smooth:*—smooth {1x}. Syn.: 2506, 2513. See: TWOT—670d; BDB—325b.

2512. חַלֻּק {1x} **challûq**, *khal-look';* from 2505; *smooth:*—smooth {1x}. See: TWOT—670d; BDB—325c.

2513. חֶלְקָה {29x} **chelqâh**, *khel-kaw';* fem. of 2506; prop. *smoothness;* fig. *flattery;* also an *allotment:*—portion {6x}, parcel {5x}, piece {5x}, field {3x}, flattering {2x}, plat {2x}, part {1x}, flattery {1x}, ground {1x}, places {1x}, smooth {1x}, smooth things {1x}. See: TWOT—670c; BDB—324c, 325c.

2514. חֲלַקָּה {1x} **chălaqqâh**, *khal-ak-kaw';* fem. from 2505; *flattery:*—flatteries {1x}. See: TWOT—670e; BDB—325c.

2515. חֲלֻקָּה {1x} **chăluqqâh**, *khal-ook-kaw';* fem. of 2512; a *distribution:*—division {1x}. See: TWOT—669c; BDB—324c.

2516. חֶלְקִי {1x} **Chelqîy**, *khel-kee';* patron. from 2507; a *Chelkite* or desc. of Chelek:—Helkites {1x}. See: BDB—324c.

2517. חֶלְקַי {1x} **Chelqay**, *khel-kah'ee;* from 2505; *apportioned; Chelkai,* an Isr.:—Helkai {1x}. See: BDB—324d.

2518. חִלְקִיָּה {34x} **Chilqîyâh**, *khil-kee-yaw';* or

חִלְקִיָּהוּ **Chilqîyâhûw**, *khil-kee-yaw'-hoo;* from 2506 and 3050; *portion* (of) *Jah; Chilhijah,* the name of eight Isr.:—Hilkiah {34x}. See: BDB—324d.

2519. חֲלַקְלַקָּה {4x} **chălaqlaqqâh**, *khal-ak-lak-kaw';* by redupl. from 2505; prop. something *very smooth;* i.e. a *treacherous* spot; fig. *blandishment:*—flatteries {2x}, slippery {2x}. See: TWOT—670f; BDB—325c.

2520. חֶלְקַת {2x} **Chelqath**, *khel-kath';* a form of 2513; *smoothness; Chelkath,* a place in Pal.:—Helkath {2x}. See: BDB—324d.

2521. חֶלְקַת הַצֻּרִים {1x} **Chelqath hats-Tsûrîym**, *khel-kath' hats-tsoo-reem';* from 2520 and the plur. of 6697, with the art. ins.; *smoothness of the rocks; Chelkath Hats-tsurim,* a place in Pal.:—Helkath-hazzurim {1x}. See: BDB—324d.

2522. חָלַשׁ {3x} **châlash**, *khaw-lash';* a prim. root; to *prostrate;* by impl. to *overthrow, decay:*—discomfit {1x}, waste away {1x}, weaken {1x}. See: TWOT—671; BDB—325d.

2523. חַלָּשׁ {1x} **challâsh**, *khal-lawsh';* from 2522; *frail:*—weak {1x}. Syn.: 535, 2470, 7390. See: TWOT—671a; BDB—325d.

2524. חָם {4x} **châm**, *khawm;* from the same as 2346; a *father-in-law* (as in *affinity*):—father in law {4x}. See: TWOT—674a; BDB—326a, 327a, 328d.

2525. חָם {2x} **châm**, *khawm;* from 2552; *hot:*—hot {1x}, warm {1x}. See: TWOT—677b; BDB—326a, 328d.

2526. חָם {16x} **Châm**, *khawm;* the same as 2525; *hot* (from the tropical habitat); *Cham,* a son of Noah; also (as a patron.) his desc. or their country:—Ham {16x}. See: BDB—325d, 328d.

2527. חֹם {14x} **chôm**, *khome;* from 2552; *heat:*—heat {9x}, to be hot {4x}, warm {1x}. Syn.: 2534, 2552. See: TWOT—677a; BDB—326a, 328b.

2528. חֶמָא {2x} **chĕmâʾ** (Aram.), *khem-aw';* or

חֲמָה **chămâh** (Aram.), *kham-aw';* corresp. to 2534; *anger:*—fury {1x}. See: TWOT—2733; BDB—1093b 1095c.

חֵמָא **chêmâʾ**. See 2534.

2529. חֶמְאָה {10x} **chemʾâh**, *khem-aw';* or (short.)

חֵמָה **chêmâh**, *khay-maw';* from the same root as 2346; curdled *milk* or *cheese:*—butter {1x}. See: TWOT—672a; BDB—326a, 328a.

2530. חָמַד {21x} **châmad**, *khaw-mad';* a prim. root; to *delight* in:—desire {11x}, covet {4x}, delight {2x}, pleasant {1x}, beauty {1x}, lust {1x}, delectable things {1x}. See: TWOT—673; BDB—326b, 326d.

2531. חֶמֶד {6x} **chemed**, *kheh'-med;* from 2530; *delight:*—desirable {3x}, pleasant {3x}. See: TWOT—673a; BDB—326c.

2532. חֶמְדָּה {25x} **chemdâh**, *khem-daw';* fem. of 2531; *delight:*—pleasant {12x}, desire {4x}, beloved {3x}, goodly {2x}, precious {4x}. See: TWOT—673b; BDB—326c.

2533. חֶמְדָּן {1x} **Chemdân**, *khem-dawn';* from 2531; *pleasant; Chemdan,* an Idumæan:—Hemdan {1x}. See: BDB—326d.

2534. חֵמָה {124x} **chêmâh**, *khay-maw';* or (Dan. 11:44)

חֵמָא **chêmâʾ**, *khay-maw';* from 3179; *heat;* fig. *anger, poison* (from its *fever*): fury {67x}, wrath {34x}, poison {6x}, furious {4x}, displeasure {3x}, rage {2x}, anger {1x}, bottles {1x}, furious + 1167 {1x}, furiously {1x}, heat {1x}, indignation {1x}, wrathful {1x}, wroth {1x}.

Chemah means "wrath; heat; rage; anger." **(1)** The noun, as well as the verb *yacham* (3179), denotes a strong emotional state. **(1a)** The noun is used 124 times, predominantly in the poetic and prophetic literature, especially Ezekiel. **(1b)** The first usage of *chemah* takes place in the story of Esau and Jacob. Jacob is advised to go to Haran with the hope that Esau's "anger" will dissipate: "And tarry with him a few days, until thy brother's fury turn away" (Gen 27:44). **(2)** The word indicates a state of anger. **(2a)** Most of the usage involves God's "anger." His "wrath" is expressed against Israel's sin in the wilderness: "For I was afraid of the anger and hot displeasure, wherewith the Lord was wroth against you to destroy you" (Deut 9:19). **(2b)** The psalmist prayed for God's mercy in the hour of God's "anger": "O LORD, rebuke me not in thine anger, neither chasten me in thy hot displeasure" (Ps 6:1).

(2c) God's "anger" against Israel was ultimately expressed in the exile of the Judeans to Babylon: "The Lord hath accomplished his fury; he hath poured out his fierce anger, and hath kindled a fire in Zion, and it hath devoured the foundations thereof" (Lam 4:11). **(2d)** The metaphor "cup" denotes the judgment of God upon His people. **(2d1)** His "wrath" is poured out: "Therefore he hath poured upon him the fury of his anger, and the strength of battle: and it hath set him on fire round about, yet he knew not; and it burned him, yet he laid it not to heart" (Is 42:25); **(2d2)** and the "cup of wrath" is drunk: "Awake, awake, stand up, O Jerusalem, which hast drunk at the hand of the LORD the cup of his fury; thou hast drunken the dregs of the cup of trembling . . ." (Is 51:17). **(3)** Thus, God as the Almighty Potentate is angered by the sins and the pride of His people, as they are an insult to His holiness. **(3a)** In a derived sense, the rulers on earth are also described as those who are angered, but their "anger" is aroused from circumstances over which they have no control.

(3a1) Naaman was angry with Elisha's advice (2 Kin 5:11–12); **(3a2)** Ahasuerus became enraged with Vashti's refusal to display her beauty before the men (Est 1:12).

(4) *Chemah* also denotes man's reaction to everyday circumstances. **(4a)** Man's "rage" is a dangerous expression of his emotional state, as it inflames everybody who comes close to the person in rage. **(4a1)** "Wrath" may arise for many reasons. Proverbs speaks strongly against *chemah,* as jealousy (6:34); cf. "Wrath is cruel, and anger is outrageous; but who is able to stand before envy?" (Prov 27:4; cf. Eze 16:38). **(4a2)** The man in rage may be culpable of crime and be condemned: "Be ye afraid of the sword: for wrath bringeth the punishments of the sword, that ye may know there is a judgment" (Job 19:29). **(4a3)** The wise response to "rage" is a soft answer: "A soft answer turneth away wrath: but grievous words stir up anger" (Prov 15:1).

(5) There are two special meanings of *chemah:* **(5a)** One is "heat," as in "the Spirit lifted me up, and took me away, and I went in bitterness, in the heat of my spirit; but the hand of the LORD was strong upon me" (Eze 3:14). **(5b)** The other is "poison," or "venom," as in Deut 32:33: "Their wine is the poison of dragons, and the cruel venom of asps." Syn: *Chemah* is associated with **(A)** *qin'ah* (7068), "jealousy," and also with **(B)** *naqam* (5358), "vengeance," as the angered person intends to save his name or avenge himself on the person who provoked him. In God's dealing with Israel He was jealous of His Holy name, for which reason He had to deal justly with idolatrous Israel by avenging Himself: "That it might cause fury to come up to take vengeance; I have set her blood upon the top of a rock, that it should not be covered" (Eze 24:8); but He also avenges His people against their enemies: "God is jealous, and the LORD revengeth; the LORD revengeth, and is furious; the LORD will take vengeance on his adversaries and he reserveth wrath for his enemies" (Nah 1:2). Other synonyms of *chemah* are **(C)** *'ap* (639) "anger," (Deut 29:27); and **(D)** *qetseph,* "wrath (7110)," (Jer 21:5). comp. 2529. See: TWOT—860a; BDB—326b, 328a, 404b, 1095c.

2535. חַמָּה {5x} **chammâh**, *kham-maw';* from 2525; *heat;* by impl. the *sun:*—heat {1x}, sun {5x}. See: TWOT—677c; BDB—328d.

2536. חַמּוּאֵל {1x} **Chammûwʾêl**, *kham-moo-ale';* from 2535 and 410; *anger* of God; Chammuel, an Isr.:—Hamuel {1x}. See: BDB—328a, 329b.

2537. חֲמוּטַל {3x} **Chămûwṭal**, *kham-oo-tal';* or חֲמִיטַל **Chămîyṭal**, *kham-ee-tal';* from 2524 and 2919; *father-in-law of dew; Chamutal* or *Chamital*, an Israelitess:—Hamutal {3x}. See: BDB—327d, 328a.

2538. חָמוּל {3x} **Châmûwl**, *khaw-mool';* from 2550; *pitied; Chamul*, an Isr.:—Hamul {3x}. See: BDB—328b.

2539. חָמוּלִי {1x} **Châmûwlîy**, *khaw-moo-lee';* patron. from 2538: a *Chamulite* (collect.) or desc. of Chamul:—Hamulites {1x}. See: BDB—328b.

2540. חַמּוֹן {2x} **Chammôwn**, *kham-mone';* from 2552; *warm* spring; *Chammon*, the name of two places in Pal.:—Hammon {2x}. See: BDB—329a.

2541. חָמוֹץ {1x} **châmôwts**, *khaw-motse';* from 2556; prop. *violent;* by impl. a *robber:*—oppressed {1x}. See: TWOT—681a; BDB—330b.

2542. חַמּוּק {1x} **chammûwq**, *kham-mook';* from 2559; a *wrapping*, i.e. *drawers:*—joints {1x}. See: TWOT—682a; BDB—330b.

2543. חֲמוֹר {96x} **chămôwr**, *kham-ore';* or (short.) חֲמֹר **chămôr**, *kham-ore';* from 2560; a male *ass* (from its dun *red*):—(he) ass {96x}. See: TWOT—685a; BDB—331a.

2544. חֲמוֹר {13x} **Chămôwr**, *kham-ore';* the same as 2543; *ass; Chamor*, a Canaanite:—Hamor {13x}. See: BDB—331c.

2545. חֲמוֹת {11x} **chămôwth**, *kham-ōth';* or (short.) חֲמֹת **chămôth**, *kham-ōth';* fem. of 2524; a *mother-in-law:*—mother in law {11x}. See: TWOT—674b; BDB—327b, 328a.

2546. חֹמֶט {1x} **chômeṭ**, *kho'-met;* from an unused root prob. mean. to *lie low;* a *lizard* (as *creeping*):—{1x} snail. See: TWOT—675a; BDB—328a.

2547. חֻמְטָה {1x} **Chumṭâh**, *khoom-taw';* fem. of 2546; *low; Chumtah*, a place in Pal.:—Humtah {1x}. See: BDB—328a.

2548. חָמִיץ {1x} **châmîyts**, *khaw-meets';* from 2556; *seasoned*, i.e. *salt* provender:—clean {1x}. See: TWOT—679c; BDB—330a.

2549. חֲמִישִׁי {45x} **chămîyshîy**, *kham-ee-shee';* or חֲמִשִּׁי **chamishshîy**, *kham-ish-shee';* ord. from 2568; *fifth;* also a *fifth:*—fifth {42x}, fifth part {3x}. Syn.: 2567, 2569. See: TWOT—686d; BDB—332c.

2550. חָמַל {41x} **châmal**, *khaw-mal';* a prim. root; to *commiserate;* by impl. to *spare:*—pity {18x}, spare {18x}, have compassion {5x}. See: TWOT—676; BDB—328a, 328b.

2551. חֶמְלָה {2x} **chemlâh**, *khem-law';* from 2550; *commiseration:*—merciful {1x}, pity {1x}. See: TWOT—676a; BDB—328b.

2552. חָמַם {13x} **châmam**, *khaw-mam';* a prim. root; to *be hot* (lit. or fig.):—warm {7x}, hot {3x}, heat {2x}, enflaming {1x}. See: TWOT—677; BDB—328a, 328c.

2553. חַמָּן {8x} **chammân**, *kham-mawn';* from 2535; a *sun*-pillar:—idol {1x}, image {8x}. Syn.: 4676. See: TWOT—677d; BDB—329a.

2554. חָמַס {8x} **châmaç**, *khaw-mas';* a prim. root; to *be violent;* by impl. to *maltreat:*—violence {2x}, violated {1x}, shake off {1x}, wrongfully imagine {1x}, violently taken away {1x}, wronged {1x}, made bare {1x}.

Chamac, as a verb, means "to treat violently." **(1)** This verb appears in Jer. 22:3 with the meaning of "to do no violence": ". . . And do no wrong, do no violence to the stranger, the fatherless, nor the widow, neither shed innocent blood in this place." See: TWOT—678; BDB—329b.

2555. חָמָס {60x} **châmâç**, *khaw-mawce';* from 2554; *violence;* by impl. *wrong;* by meton. unjust *gain:*—violence {39x}, violent {7x}, cruelty {4x}, wrong {3x}, false {2x}, cruel {1x}, damage {1x}, injustice {1x}, oppressor + 376 {1x}, unrighteous {1x}.

Chamac, as a noun, means "violence; wrong; maliciousness." **(1)** Basically *chamac* connotes the disruption of the divinely established order of things. **(2)** It has a wide range of nuances within this legal sphere. **(2a)** The expression "a witness in the case of violent wrongdoing" means someone who bears witness in a case having to do with such an offense (cf. Deut 19:16). **(2a1)** In this context the truthfulness of the witness is not established except upon further investigation (Deut 19:18). **(2a2)** Once he was established as a false witness, the penalty for the crime concerning which he bore false witness was to be executed against the liar (cf. Deut 19:19). **(2b)** In Ex 23:1 Israel is admonished: ". . . Put not thine hand with the wicked to be an unrighteous witness," i.e., a witness who in accusing someone of a violent crime intends to see the accused punished severely.

(3) *Chamac* perhaps connotes a "violent wrongdoing" which has not been righted, the guilt of which lies on an entire area (its inhabitants) disrupting their relationship with God and thereby interfering with His blessings. **(3a)** It is this latter sense which appears in the phrase "the earth was full of violent wrongdoing": "The earth also was corrupt before God, and the earth was filled with violence" (Gen 6:11—the first occurrence of the word). **(3b)** Thus, in Gen 16:5 Sarai summons God to judge between Abram and herself because he has not acted properly toward her keeping Hagar in submission: "My wrong [done me] be upon thee: I have given my maid into thy bosom; and when she saw that she had conceived, I was despised in her eyes: the LORD judge between me and thee." **(3c)** Abram as God's judge (in God's stead) accepts the correctness of her case and commits Hagar to Sarai's care to be dealt with properly. See: TWOT—678a; BDB—329c.

2556. חָמֵץ {8x} **châmêts**, *khaw-mates';* a prim. root; to *be pungent;* i.e. in taste (*sour*, i.e. lit. *fermented*, or fig. *harsh*), in color (*dazzling*):—leavened {5x}, cruel {1x}, dyed {1x}, grieved {1x}. See: TWOT—679, 680, 681; BDB—329d, 330a.

2557. חָמֵץ {11x} **châmêts**, *khaw-mates';* from 2556; *ferment*, (fig.) *extortion:*—leaven {5x}, leavened {1x}, leavened bread {5x}. See: TWOT—679a; BDB—329d, 330a.

2558. חֹמֶץ {6x} **chômets**, *kho'-mets;* from 2556; *vinegar:*—vinegar {6x}. See: TWOT—679b; BDB—330a.

2559. חָמַק {2x} **châmaq**, *khaw-mak';* a prim. root; prop. to *enwrap;* hence, to *depart* (i.e. turn about):—go about {1x}, withdraw self {1x}. See: TWOT—682; BDB—330b.

2560. חָמַר {6x} **châmar**, *khaw-mar';* a prim. root; prop. to *boil up;* hence, to *ferment* (with scum); to *glow* (with redness); as denom. (from 2564) to *smear* with pitch:—troubled {3x}, red {1x}, daub {1x}, foul {1x}. See: TWOT—683, 683d, 685; BDB—330b, 330d, 331a.

2561. חֶמֶר {2x} **chemer**, *kheh'-mer;* from 2560; *wine* (as *fermenting*):—× pure {1x}, red wine {1x}. See: TWOT—683a; BDB—330c, 1093b.

2562. חֲמַר {6x} **chămar** (Aram.), *kham-ar';* corresp. to 2561; *wine:*—wine {6x}. See: TWOT—2734; BDB—1093b.

חֲמֹר **chămôr**. See 2543.

2563. חֹמֶר {30x} **chômer**, *kho'mer;* from 2560; prop. a *bubbling* up, i.e. of water, a *wave;* of earth, *mire* or *clay* (cement); also a *heap;* hence, a *chomer* or dry measure:—clay {11x}, homer {11x}, mortar {4x}, mire {2x}, heap {2x}. Syn.: 2916. See: TWOT—683c; BDB—330c, 330d.

2564. חֵמָר {3x} **chêmâr**, *khay-mawr';* from 2560; *bitumen* (as *rising* to the surface):—slime {2x}, slimepit + 875 {1x}. See: TWOT—683b; BDB—330c.

2565. חֲמֹרָה {1x} **chămôrâh**, *kham-o-raw';* from 2560 [comp. 2563]; a *heap:*—heap {1x}. See: TWOT—684c; BDB—331a.

2566. חַמְרָן {1x} **Chamrân**, *kham-rawn';* from 2560; *red; Chamran*, an Idumæan:—Amran {1x}. See: BDB—331c.

2567. חָמַשׁ {1x} **châmash**, *khaw-mash';* a denom. from 2568; to *tax a fifth:*—take up the fifth part {1x}. Syn.: 2549, 2569. See: TWOT—686; BDB—332b.

2568. חָמֵשׁ {343x} **châmêsh**, *khaw-maysh';* masc. חֲמִשָּׁה **chămishshâh**, *kham-ish-shaw';* a prim. numeral; *five:*—five {300x}, fifteenth + 6240 {16x}, fifteen + 6240 {15x}, fifth {6x}, fifteen + 7657 {3x}, variant {1x}. See: TWOT—686a; BDB—331c.

2569. חֹמֶשׁ {1x} **chômesh**, *kho'-mesh;* from 2567; a *fifth* tax:—fifth part {1x}. Syn.: 2549. See: TWOT—686b; BDB—332b.

2570. חֹמֶשׁ {4x} **chômesh**, *kho'-mesh;* from an unused root prob. mean. to *be stout;* the *abdomen* (as *obese*):—fifth rib {4x}. See: TWOT—687a; BDB—332d.

2571. חָמֻשׁ {4x} **châmûsh**, *khaw-moosh';* pass. part. of the same as 2570; *staunch*, i.e. able-bodied *soldiers:*—armed {2x}, armed men {1x}, harnessed {1x}. See: TWOT—688a; BDB—332d.

חֲמִשָּׁה **chămishshâh**. See 2568.

חֲמִשִּׁי **chămishshîy**. See 2549.

2572. חֲמִשִּׁים {162x} **chămishshîym**, *kham-ish-sheem';* multiple of 2568; *fifty:*—fifty {151x}, fifties {6x}, fiftieth {4x}, fifty + 376 {1x}. See: TWOT—686c; BDB—332b.

2573. חֵמֶת {1x} **chêmeth**, *khay'-meth;* from the same as 2346; a skin *bottle* (as *tied* up):—bottle {1x}. Syn.: 1228, 4997, 5035. See: TWOT—689a; BDB—332d.

2574. חֲמָת {37x} **Chămâth**, *kham-awth';* from the same as 2346; *walled; Chamath*, a place in Syria:—Hamath {34x}, Hemath {3x}. See: TWOT—689a; BDB—333a.

חַמֹּת **chămôth**. See 2545.

2575. חַמַּת {1x} **Chammath**, *kham-math';* a var. for the first part of 2576; *hot* springs; *Chammath*, a place in Pal.:—Hammath {1x}. See: BDB—329a, 333b.

2576. חַמֹּת דֹּאר {1x} **Chammôth Dôʼr**, *kham-moth' dore;* from the plur. of 2535 and 1756; *hot* springs *of Dor; Chammath-Dor,* a place in Pal.:—Hamath-Dor {1x}. See: BDB—329a, 329b.

2577. חֲמָתִי {2x} **Chămâthîy**, *kham-aw-thee';* patrial from 2574; a *Chamathite* or native of *Chamath:*—Hamathite {2x}. See: BDB—333b.

2578. חֲמַת צוֹבָה {1x} **Chămath Tsôwbâh**, *kham-ath' tso-baw';* from 2574 and 6678; *Chamath of Tsobah; Chamath-Tsobah;* prob. the same as 2574:—Hamath-Zobah {1x}. See: BDB—333a, 844b, 844c.

2579. חֲמַת רַבָּה {1x} **Chămath Rabbâh**, *kham-ath' rab-baw';* from 2574 and 7237; *Chamath of Rabbah; Chamath-Rabbah,* prob. the same as 2574:—Hamath the great {1x}. See: BDB—333a.

2580. חֵן {69x} **chên**, *khane;* from 2603; *graciousness,* i.e. subj. (*kindness, favor*) or obj. (*beauty*):—grace {38x}, favour {26x}, gracious {2x}, pleasant {1x}, precious {1x}, well-favoured + 2896 {1x}.

Chen, as a noun, means "favor; grace." **(1)** The Hebrew noun *chen* occurs 69 times, **(1a)** mainly in the Pentateuch and in the historical books through Samuel. **(1b)** The word's frequency increases in the poetic books, but it is rare in the prophetic books. **(1c)** The first occurrence is in Gen 6:8: "But Noah found grace in the eyes of the LORD." **(2)** The basic meaning of *chen* is "favor." **(2a)** Whatever is "pleasant and agreeable" can be described by this word. When a woman is said to have *chen,* she is a "gracious" woman (Prov 11:16); **(2b)** or the word may have the negative association of being "beautiful without sense" (Prov 31:30). **(2c)** A person's speech may be characterized by "graciousness": "He that loveth pureness of heart, for the grace of his lips the king shall be his friend" (Prov 22:11; cf. Ps 45:2). **(3)** *Chen* also denotes the response to whatever is "agreeable." **(4)** The verbs used with "favor" are: **(4a)** "give favor" (Gen 39:21), **(4b)** "obtain favor" (Ex 3:21), and **(4c)** "find favor" (Gen 6:8). **(5)** The idioms are equivalent to the English verbs "to like" or "to love": "[She] said to him, Why have I found favor in your eyes, that you should take notice of me, when I am a foreigner?" (Ruth 2:10). See: TWOT—694a; BDB—333b, 336b.

2581. חֵן {1x} **Chên**, *khane;* the same as 2580; *grace; Chen,* a fig. name for an Isr.:—Hen {1x}. See: BDB—333b, 336d.

2582. חֵנָדָד {4x} **Chênâdâd**, *khay-naw-dawd';* prob. from 2580 and 1908; *favor of Hadad; Chenadad,* an Isr.:—Henadad {4x}. See: BDB—333b, 337b.

2583. חָנָה {143x} **chânâh**, *khaw-naw';* a prim. root [comp. 2603]; prop. to *incline;* by impl. to *decline* (of the slanting rays of evening); spec. to *pitch* a tent; gen. to *encamp* (for abode or siege):—pitch {78x}, encamp {47x}, camp {4x}, pitch . . . tent {4x}, abide {3x}, dwelt {2x}, lie {2x}, rested {2x}, grows to an end {1x}. See: TWOT—690; BDB—333b.

2584. חַנָּה {13x} **Channâh**, *khan-naw';* from 2603; *favored; Channah,* an Israelitess:—Hannah {13x}. See: BDB—333b, 336d.

2585. חֲנוֹךְ {16x} **Chănôwk**, *khan-oke';* from 2596; *initiated; Chanok,* an antediluvian patriarch:—Enoch {9x}, Hanoch {5x}, Henoch {2x}. See: BDB—335c.

2586. חָנוּן {11x} **Chânûwn**, *khaw-noon';* from 2603; *favored; Chanun,* the name of an Ammonite and of two Isr.:—Hanun {11x}. See: BDB—337a.

2587. חַנּוּן {13x} **channûwn**, *khan-noon';* from 2603; *gracious:*—gracious {13x}.

Channuwn, as an adjective, means "gracious." **(1)** One of the word's 13 occurrences is in Ex 34:6: "And the LORD passed by before him [Moses], and proclaimed, The LORD, The LORD God, merciful and gracious, long-suffering, and abundant in goodness and truth. . . . " **(2)** This adjective is used only of God and denotes the action that springs from His free and unmerited love to His creatures. See: TWOT—694d; BDB—337a.

2588. חָנוּת {1x} **chânûwth**, *khaw-nooth';* from 2583; prop. a *vault* or *cell* (with an arch); by impl. a *prison:*—cabins {1x}. See: TWOT—690a; BDB—333d.

2589. חַנּוֹת {2x} **channôwth**, *khan-nōth';* from 2603 (in the sense of *prayer*); *supplication:*—be gracious {1x}, intreated {1x}. See: TWOT—694; BDB—335d.

2590. חָנַט {5x} **chânaṭ**, *khaw-nat';* a prim. root; to *spice;* by impl. to *embalm;* also to *ripen:*—embalm {4x}, put forth {1x}. See: TWOT—691; 334c, 334d.

2591. חִנְטָא {2x} **chinṭâʼ** (Aram.), *khint-taw';* corresp. to 2406; *wheat:*—wheat {2x}. See: TWOT—2735; BDB—1093b.

2592. חַנִּיאֵל {2x} **Channîyʼêl**, *khan-nee-ale';* from 2603 and 410; *favor of God; Channiel,* the name of two Isr.:—Hanniel {1x}, Haniel {1x}. See: BDB—335a, 337a.

2593. חָנִיךְ {1x} **chânîyk**, *kaw-neek';* from 2596; *initiated;* i.e. *practiced:*—trained {1x}. See: TWOT—693a; BDB—335c.

2594. חֲנִינָה {1x} **chănîynâh**, *khan-ee-naw';* from 2603; *graciousness:*—favour {1x}. See: TWOT—694e; BDB—337a.

2595. חֲנִית {47x} **chănîyth**, *khan-eeth';* from 2583; a *lance* (for *thrusting,* like *pitching* a tent):—javelin {6x}, spear {41x}. Syn.: 3591, 7013, 7420. See: TWOT—690b; BDB—333d, 335a.

2596. חָנַךְ {5x} **chânak**, *khaw-nak';* a prim. root; prop. to *narrow* (comp. 2614); fig. to *initiate* or *discipline:*—dedicate {4x}, train up {1x}.

Chanak basically means "to initiate/ inaugurate/dedicate": **(1)** the altar (Num 7:10, 11), **(2)** the house of the Lord (2 Chr 7:5, 9), **(3)** the rebuilt temple (Ezr 6:16), **(4)** Jerusalem's wall (Neh 12:27), **(5)** Nebuchadnezzar's image (Dan 3:2). See: TWOT—693; BDB—335b.

2597. חֲנֻכָּא {4x} **chănukkâʼ** (Aram.), *chan-ook-kaw';* corresp. to 2598; *consecration:*—dedication {4x}. See: TWOT—2736; BDB—1093b.

2598. חֲנֻכָּה {8x} **chănukkâh**, *khan-ook-kaw';* from 2596; *initiation,* i.e. *consecration:*—dedicating {2x}, dedication {6x}. See: TWOT—693b; BDB—335c, 1093b.

2599. חֲנֹכִי {1x} **Chănôkîy**, *khan-o-kee';* patron. from 2585; a *Chanokite* (collect.) or desc. of Chanok:—Hanochites {1x}. See: BDB—335c.

2600. חִנָּם {32x} **chinnâm**, *khin-nawm';* from 2580; *gratis,* i.e. devoid of cost, reason or advantage:—without cause {15x}, for nought {6x}, causeless {2x}, in vain {2x}, free {1x}, without cost {1x}, freely {1x}, innocent {1x}, cost me nothing {1x}, for nothing {1x}, without wages {1x}.

Chinnam basically means "for nothing; for no purpose; useless; without a cause; for no reason." **(1)** This substantive is used chiefly as an adverb. It means "for nought": "And Laban said unto Jacob, Because thou art my brother, shouldest thou therefore serve me for nought? tell me, what shall thy wages be?" (Gen 29:15—the first occurrence). **(2)** The word means "in vain," or "for no purpose": "Surely in vain the net is spread in the sight of any bird" (Prov 1:17). **(3)** Finally, it means "for no cause": ". . . Wherefore then wilt thou sin against innocent blood, to slay David without a cause?" (1Sa 19:5). See: TWOT—694b; BDB—335d, 336c.

2601. חֲנַמְאֵל {4x} **Chănamʼêl**, *khan-am-ale';* prob. by orth. var. for 2606; *Chanamel,* an Isr.:—Hanameel {4x}. See: BDB—335d.

2602. חֲנָמָל {1x} **chănâmâl**, *khan-aw-mawl';* of uncert. der.; perh. the *aphis* or plant-louse:—frost {1x}. See: TWOT—693.1; BDB—335d.

2603. חָנַן {78x} **chânan**, *khaw-nan';* a prim. root [comp. 2583]; prop. to *bend* or *stoop* in kindness to an inferior; to *favor, bestow;* caus. to *implore* (i.e. move to favor by petition):—mercy {16x}, gracious {13x}, merciful {12x}, supplication {10x}, favour {7x}, besought {4x}, pity {4x}, fair {1x}, favourable {1x}, favoured {1x}, misc. {9x} = intreat, have pity upon, pray, × very.

Chanan, as a verb, means "to be gracious, considerate; to show favor." **(1)** The first time in Gen 33:5: "The children which God hath graciously given thy servant." **(2)** Generally, this word implies the extending of "favor," often when it is neither expected nor deserved. **(2a)** *Chanan* may express "generosity," a gift from the heart (Ps 37:21). **(2b)** God especially is the source of undeserved "favor" (Gen 33:11), and He is asked repeatedly for such "gracious" acts as only He can do (Num 6:25; Gen 43:29). The psalmist prays: ". . . Grant me thy law graciously" (Ps 119:29). **(3)** God's "favor" is especially seen in His deliverance from one's enemies or surrounding evils (Ps 77:9; Amos 5:15). **(4)** However, God extends His "graciousness" in His own sovereign way and will, to whomever He chooses (Ex 33:19). See: TWOT—694, 695; 335d, 337d, 1093b.

2604. חֲנַן {2x} **chănan** (Aram.), *khan-an';* corresp. to 2603; to *favor* or (caus.) to *entreat:*—shew mercy {1x}, make supplication {1x}. See: TWOT—2737; BDB—1093b.

2605. חָנָן {12x} **Chânân**, *khaw-nawn';* from 2603; *favor; Chanan,* the name of seven Isr.:—Canan {12x}. See: BDB—336d.

2606. חֲנַנְאֵל {4x} **Chănanʼêl**, *khan-an-ale';* from 2603 and 410; *God has favored; Chananel,* prob. an Isr., from whom a tower of Jerusalem was named:—Hananeel {4x}. See: BDB—337a.

2607. חֲנָנִי {11x} **Chănânîy**, *khan-aw-nee';* from 2603; *gracious; Chanani,* the name of six Isr.:—Hanani {11x}. See: BDB—337b.

2608. חֲנַנְיָה {29x} **Chănanyâh**, *khan-an-yaw';* or

חֲנַנְיָהוּ **Chănanyâhûw**, *khan-an-yaw'-hoo;* from 2603 and 3050; *Jah has favored; Chananjah,* the name of thirteen Isr.:—Hananiah {29x}. See: BDB—337b, 1093b.

2609. חָנֵס {1x} **Chânêç**, *khaw-nace'*; of Eg. der.; *Chanes*, a place in Egypt:—Hanes {1x}. See: BDB—337d.

2610. חָנֵף {11x} **chânêph**, *khaw-nafe'*; a prim. root; to *soil*, espec. in a mor. sense:—pollute {4x}, defile {4x}, greatly {1x}, corrupt {1x}, profane {1x}. See: TWOT—696; BDB—337d.

2611. חָנֵף {13x} **chânêph**, *khaw-nafe'*; from 2610; *soiled* (i.e. with sin), *impious:*—hypocrite {11x}, hypocritical {1x}. See: TWOT—696b; BDB—338a.

2612. חֹנֶף {1x} **chôneph**, *kho'-nef;* from 2610; moral *filth*, i.e. *wickedness:*—hypocrisy {1x}. See: TWOT—696a; BDB—338a.

2613. חֲנֻפָּה {1x} **chănûphâh**, *khan-oo-faw'*; fem. from 2610; *impiety:*—profaneness {1x}. See: TWOT—696c; BDB—338b.

2614. חָנַק {2x} **chânaq**, *khaw-nak'*; a prim. root [comp. 2596]; to *be narrow;* by impl. to *throttle*, or (reflex.) to *choke* oneself to death (by a rope):—hang self {1x}, strangle {1x}. See: TWOT—697; BDB—338b.

2615. חַנָּתֹן {1x} **Channâthôn**, *khan-naw-thone'*; prob. from 2603; *favored; Channathon*, a place in Pal.:—Hannathon {1x}. See: BDB—337b, 338b.

2616. חָסַד {3x} **châçad**, *khaw-sad'*; a prim. root; prop. perh. to *bow* (the neck only [comp. 2603] in courtesy to an equal), i.e. to *be kind;* also (by euphem. [comp. 1288], but rarely) to *reprove:*—shew self merciful {2x}, put to shame {1x}.

Chacad is a practical exhibition of loving-kindness toward our fellowman, whose only claim may be misfortune and whom it is in our power to help, though perhaps at the expense of time, money, convenience, and even religious or national prejudice. See: TWOT—698, 699; 338b, 340a. BDB—338b, 340a.

2617. חֶסֶד {248x} **cheçed**, *kheh'-sed;* from 2616; *kindness;* by impl. (toward God) *piety;* rarely (by opposition) *reproof*, or (subj.) *beauty:*—mercy {149x}, kindness {40x}, loving-kindness {30x}, goodness {12x}, kindly {5x}, merciful {4x}, favour {3x}, good {1x}, goodliness {1x}, pity {1x}, reproach {1x}, wicked thing {1x}.

Checed, as a noun, means "loving-kindness; steadfast love; grace; mercy; faithfulness; goodness; devotion." **(1)** This word is used 240 times in the Old Testament, and **(1a)** is especially frequent in the Psalter. **(1b)** The term is one of the most important in the vocabulary of Old Testament theology and ethics. **(2)** In general, one may identify three basic meanings of the word, which always interact: "strength," "steadfastness," and "love." Any understanding of the word that fails to suggest all three inevitably loses some of its richness. "Love" by itself easily becomes sentimentalized or universalized apart from the covenant. Yet "strength" or "steadfastness" suggests only the fulfillment of a legal or other obligation.

(3) The word refers primarily to mutual and reciprocal rights and obligations between the parties of a relationship (especially Yahweh and Israel). **(3a)** But *checed* is not only a matter of obligation; **(3b)** it is also of generosity. **(3c)** It is not only a matter of loyalty, but also of mercy. **(3d)** The weaker party seeks the protection and blessing of the patron and protector, but he may not lay absolute claim to it. **(3e)** The stronger party remains committed to his promise, but retains his freedom, especially with regard to the manner in which he will implement those promises. **(4)** *Checed* implies personal involvement and commitment in a relationship beyond the rule of law. **(5)** Marital love is often related to *checed.* **(5a)** Marriage certainly is a legal matter, and there are legal sanctions for infractions. **(5b)** Yet the relationship, if sound, far transcends mere legalities. **(5c)** The prophet Hosea applies the analogy to Yahweh's *checed* to Israel within the covenant (e.g., 2:21). **(6)** Hence, "devotion" is sometimes the single English word best capable of capturing the nuance of the original. **(7)** Hebrew writers often underscored the element of steadfastness (or strength) by pairing *checed* with *'emet* (571 - "truth, reliability") and *'emunah* (530 - "faithfulness").

(8) Biblical usage frequently speaks of someone "doing," "showing," or "keeping" *checed.* **(9)** The concrete content of the word is especially evident when it is used in the plural. **(9a)** God's "mercies," "kindnesses," or "faithfulnesses" are His specific, concrete acts of redemption in fulfillment of His promise. **(9b)** An example appears in Is 55:3: ". . . And I will make an everlasting covenant with you, even the sure mercies of David." **(10)** *Checed* has both God and man as its subject. **(10a)** When man is the subject of *checed*, the word usually describes the person's kindness or loyalty to another; cf. 2 Sa 9:7: "And David said . . . I will surely show thee [Mephibosheth] kindness for Jonathan thy father's sake. . . ." **(10b)** Only rarely is the term applied explicitly to man's affection or fidelity toward God; **(10c)** the clearest example is probably Jer 2:2: "Go and cry in the ears of Jerusalem, saying, thus saith the LORD; I remember thee, the kindness of thy youth, the love of thine espousals, when thou wentest after me in the wilderness. . . ." **(10d)** Man exercises *checed* toward various units within the community—toward family and relatives, but also to friends, guests, masters, and servants. **(10e)** *Checed* toward the lowly and needy is often specified.

(11) The Bible prominently uses the term *checed* to summarize and characterize a life of sanctification within, and in response to, the covenant. **(11a)** Thus, Hos 6:6 states that God desires "mercy and not sacrifice" (i.e., faithful living in addition to worship). **(11b)** Similarly, Mic 6:8 features *checed* in the prophets' summary of biblical ethics: ". . . and what doth the LORD require of thee, but . . . to love mercy . . . ?" **(12)** Behind all these uses with man as subject, however, stand the repeated references to God's *checed.* **(12a)** It is one of His most central characteristics. **(12b)** God's loving-kindness is offered to His people, who need redemption from sin, enemies, and troubles. **(12c)** A recurrent refrain describing God's nature is "abounding/plenteous in *checed*" (Ex 34:6; Neh 9:17; Ps 103:8; Jonah 4:2). **(12d)** The entire history of Yahweh's covenantal relationship with Israel can be summarized in terms of *checed.* **(12e)** It is the one permanent element in the flux of covenantal history. **(12f)** Even the Creation is the result of God's *checed* (Ps 136:5–9). **(12g)** His love lasts for a "thousand generations" (Deut 7:9; cf. Deut 5:10 and Ex 20:6), indeed "forever" (especially in the refrains of certain psalms, such as Ps 136).

(13) Words used in synonymous parallelism with *checed* help to define and explain it. **(13a)** The word most commonly associated with *checed* is *'emet* (571 - "fidelity; reliability"): ". . . Let thy loving-kindness [*checed*] and thy truth [*'emet*] continually preserve me." **(13b)** *'Emunah* (530) with a similar meaning is also common: "He hath remembered his mercy [*checed*] and his truth [*'emunah*] toward the house of Israel. . . ." **(14)** This emphasis is especially appropriate when God is the subject, because His *checed* is stronger and more enduring than man's. **(14a)** Etymological investigation suggests that *checed's* primitive significance may have been "strength" or "permanence." **(14b)** If so, a puzzling use of *checed* in Is 40:6 would be explained: "All flesh is grass, and all the goodliness thereof is as the flower of the field."

(15) The association of *checed* with "covenant" **(15a)** keeps it from being misunderstood as mere providence or love for all creatures; **(15b)** it applies primarily to God's particular love for His chosen and covenanted people. **(15c)** "Covenant" also stresses the reciprocity of the relationship; **(15d)** but since God's *checed* is ultimately beyond the covenant, it will not ultimately be abandoned, even when the human partner is unfaithful and must be disciplined (Is 54:8, 10). **(16)** Since its final triumph and implementation is eschatological, *checed* can imply the goal and end of all salvation-history (Ps 85:7, 10; 130:7; Mic 7:20). See: TWOT—698a, 699a; BDB—338c, 340a.

2618. חֶסֶד {1x} **Cheçed**, *kheh'-sed;* the same as 2617: *favor; Chesed*, an Isr.:—Hesed {1x}. See: BDB—122c.

2619. חֲסַדְיָה {1x} **Chăçadyâh**, *khas-ad-yaw'*; from 2617 and 3050; *Jah has favored; Chasadjah*, an Isr.:—Hasadiah {1x}. The proper noun *Chacadyah* (1Chr 3:20) is related to *checed* (2617). The name of Zerubbabel's son means "Yahweh is faithful/gracious," a fitting summary of the prophet's message. See: BDB—339d.

2620. חָסָה {37x} **châçâh**, *khaw-saw'*; a prim. root; to *flee* for protection [comp. 982]; fig. to *confide* in:—to trust {35x}, to make a refuge {1x}, have hope {1x}. It is often used where God is compared to a rock or a shield or one with protective wings. See: TWOT—700; BDB—340a.

2621. חֹסָה {5x} **Chôçâh**, *kho-saw'*; from 2620; *hopeful; Chosah*, an Isr.; also a place in Pal.:—Hosah {5x}. See: BDB—340b.

2622. חָסוּת {1x} **châçûwth**, *khaw-sooth'*; from 2620; *confidence:*—trust {1x}. See: TWOT—700a; BDB—340b.

2623. חָסִיד {32x} **châçîyd**, *khaw-seed'*; from 2616; prop. *kind*, i.e. (relig.) *pious* (a saint):—saints {19x}, holy {3x}, merciful {3x}, godly {2x}, good {1x}, godly man {1x}, Holy One {1x}, holy one {1x}, ungodly + 3808 {1x}.

Chaciyd, as an adjective, means "pious; devout; faithful; godly." **(1)** The adjective is often used to describe the faithful Israelite. **(1a)** God's *checed* provides the pattern, model, and strength by which the life of the *chaciyd* is to be directed. **(1b)** One reference to the "godly" man appears in Ps 12:1: "Help, LORD; for the godly man ceaseth; for the faithful fail from among the children of men." **(1c)** Usually a suffix or possessive pronoun referring to God is attached to the word, indicating His special attachment to those who pattern their lives after His: "O love the LORD, all ye his saints [literally, "His pious ones"]: for the LORD preserveth the faithful, and plentifully rewardeth the proud doer" (Ps 31:23). **(2)** Following the Greek *hosios* and Latin *sanctus*, the KJV often renders the word "saint"—which must be understood in the sense of sanctification [dependent upon grace], not moralistically [of native goodness]. See: TWOT—698b; BDB—339c.

2624. חֲסִידָה {6x} **chăçîydâh**, *khas-ee-daw';* fem. of 2623; the *kind* (maternal) bird, i.e. a *stork:*—× feathers {1x}, stork {5x}. See: TWOT—698c; BDB—339d.

2625. חָסִיל {6x} **chaçîyl**, *khaw-seel';* from 2628; the *ravager,* i.e. a *locust:*—caterpillar {6x}. See: TWOT—701a; BDB—340c.

2626. חָסִין {1x} **chăçîyn**, *khas-een';* from 2630; prop. *firm,* i.e. (by impl.) *mighty:*—strong {1x}. See: TWOT—703c; BDB—340d.

2627. חַסִּיר {1x} **chaççîyr** (Aram.), *khas-seer';* from a root corresp. to 2637; *deficient:*—wanting {1x}. Syn.: 47, 410, 533, 553, 1368, 2388, 2428, 2642, 5794. See: BDB—1093c.

2628. חָסַל {1x} **châçal**, *khaw-sal';* a prim. root; to *eat* off:—consume {1x}. Syn.: 3615. See: TWOT—701; BDB—340c.

2629. חָסַם {2x} **châçam**, *khaw-sam';* a prim. root; to *muzzle;* by anal. to *stop* the nose:—muzzle {1x}, stop {1x}. See: TWOT—702; BDB—340c.

2630. חָסַן {1x} **châçan**, *khaw-san';* a prim. root; prop. to *(be) compact;* by impl. to *hoard:*—lay up {1x}. See: TWOT—703; BDB—340d, 1093c.

2631. חֲסַן {2x} **chăçan** (Aram.), *khas-an';* corresp. to 2630; to *hold* in occupancy:—possess {2x}. See: TWOT—2738; BDB—1093c.

2632. חֱסֵן {2x} **chêçen** (Aram.), *khay'-sen;* from 2631; *strength:*—power {2x}. Syn.: 410, 2428, 3027, 3581, 5797. See: TWOT—2738a; BDB—1093c.

2633. חֹסֶן {5x} **chôçen**, *kho'-sen;* from 2630; *wealth:*—riches {1x}, strength {2x}, treasure {2x}. See: TWOT—703a; BDB—340d.

2634. חָסֹן {2x} **châçôn**, *khaw-sone';* from 2630; *powerful:*—strong {2x}. Syn.: 47, 533, 553, 1368, 2388, 2389, 5794, 5797. See: TWOT—703b; BDB—340d.

2635. חֲסַף {9x} **chăçaph** (Aram.), *khas-af';* from a root corresp. to that of 2636; a *clod:*—clay {9x}. Syn.: 2563, 2916, 4423. See: TWOT—2739; BDB—1093c.

2636. חַסְפַּס {1x} **chaçpaç**, *khas-pas';* redupl. from an unused root mean. appar. to *peel;* a *shred* or *scale:*—round thing {1x}. See: TWOT—704; BDB—341a, 1093c.

2637. חָסֵר {21x} **châçêr**, *khaw-sare';* a prim. root; to *lack;* by impl. to *fail, want, lessen:*—want {7x}, lack {6x}, fail {3x}, decreased {1x}, abated {1x}, have need {1x}, made lower {1x}, bereave {1x}. See: TWOT—705; BDB—341a, 1093c.

2638. חָסֵר {19x} **châçêr**, *khaw-sare';* from 2637; *lacking;* hence, *without:*—void {6x}, want {5x}, lack {4x}, fail {2x}, destitute {1x}, need {1x}. See: TWOT—705c; BDB—341c.

2639. חֶסֶר {2x} **cheçer**, *keh'-ler;* from 2637; *lack;* hence, *destitution:*—poverty {1x}, want {1x}. See: TWOT—705a; BDB—341c.

2640. חֹסֶר {3x} **chôçer**, *kho'-ser;* from 2637; *poverty:*—in want of {3x}. See: TWOT—705b; BDB—341c.

2641. חַסְרָה {1x} **Chaçrâh**, *khas-raw';* from 2637; *want; Chasrah,* an Isr.:—Hasrah {1x}. See: BDB—341c.

2642. חֶסְרוֹן {1x} **cheçrôwn**, *khes-rone';* from 2637; *deficiency:*—that which is wanting {1x}. See: TWOT—705d; 341c.

2643. חַף {1x} **chaph**, *khaf;* from 2653 (in the mor. sense of *covered* from soil); *pure:*—innocent {1x}. Syn.: 5355. See: TWOT—711a; BDB—341d, 342c.

2644. חָפָא {1x} **châphâ'**, *khaw-faw';* an orth. var. of 2645; prop. to *cover,* i.e. (in a sinister sense) to *act covertly:*—do secretly {1x}. See: TWOT—706; BDB—341d.

2645. חָפָה {12x} **châphâh**, *khaw-faw';* a prim. root (comp. 2644, 2653); to *cover;* by impl. to *veil,* to *incase, protect:*—ceiled {x}, covered {7x}, overlaid {4x}. See: TWOT—707; BDB—341d.

2646. חֻפָּה {3x} **chuppâh**, *khoop-paw';* from 2645; a *canopy:*—chamber {1x}, closet {1x}, defence {1x}. See: TWOT—710b; BDB—342a, 342c,

2647. חֻפָּה {1x} **Chuppâh**, *khoop-paw';* the same as 2646; *Chuppah,* an Isr.:—Huppah {1x}. See: BDB—342a, 342c.

2648. חָפַז {9x} **châphaz**, *khaw-faz';* a prim. root; prop. to *start* up suddenly, i.e. (by impl.) to *hasten* away, to *fear:*—haste {3x}, to haste {3x}, make haste {2x}, tremble {1x}. See: TWOT—708; BDB—342a.

2649. חִפָּזוֹן {3x} **chippâzôwn**, *khip-paw-zone';* from 2648; *hasty flight:*—haste {3x}. See: TWOT—708a; BDB—342a.

2650. חֻפִּים {3x} **Chuppîym**, *khoop-peem';* plur. of 2646 [comp. 2349]; *Chuppim,* an Isr.:—Huppim {3x}. See: BDB—342a, 342c.

2651. חֹפֶן {6x} **chôphen**, *kho'-fen;* from an unused root of uncert. signif.; a *fist* (only in the dual):—hand {4x}, fist {1x}, handful + 4393 {1x}. See: TWOT—709a; BDB—342b.

2652. חָפְנִי {5x} **Chophnîy**, *khof-nee';* from 2651; perh. *pugilist; Chophni,* an Isr.:—Hophni {5x}. See: BDB—342b.

2653. חָפַף {1x} **chôphaph**, *khaw-faf';* a prim. root (comp. 2645, 3182); to *cover* (in protection):—cover {1x}. See: TWOT—710; BDB—342b.

2654. חָפֵץ {75x} **châphêts**, *khaw-fates';* a prim. root; prop. to *incline* to; by impl. (lit. but rarely) to *bend;* fig. to *be pleased* with, *desire:*—delight {39x}, please {14x}, desire {9x}, will {3x}, pleasure {3x}, favour {2x}, like {2x}, moveth {1x}, would {1x}, at all {1x}.

Chaphets (2654), as a verb, means "to take pleasure in, take care of, desire, delight in, have delight in." **(1)** *Chaphets* means "to delight in" in 2 Sa 15:26: "But if he thus say, I have no delight in thee; behold, here am I, let him do to me as seemeth good unto him." **(2)** There is no reference to what we call favoritism, **(2a)** i.e., the overlooking of the claims of some so as to gratify the wishes of special friends; **(2b)** it is simply recorded that pleasure was found in certain persons, whatever the ground of it might be. **(3)** It is not so much an intense pleasurable emotion as a favorable disposition, or the prompting of the heart to take a certain course of action from a sense of fitness. See: TWOT—712, 713; BDB—342c, 33c.

2655. חָפֵץ {11x} **châphêts**, *khaw-fates';* from 2654; *pleased* with:—desire {3x}, have pleasure {2x}, whosoever would {1x}, if it please {1x}, willing {1x}, favour {1x}, wish {1x}, delight {1x}.

Chaphets means delighting in, having pleasure in (Ps 35:27): "Let the Lord be magnified, which hath pleasure in the prosperity of his servant." See: TWOT—712a; BDB—343a.

2656. חֵפֶץ **chêphets**, *khay'-fets;* from 2654; *pleasure;* hence, (abstr.) *desire;* concr. a *valuable* thing; hence, (by extens.) a *matter* (as something in mind):—pleasure {16x}, desire {12x}, delight {3x}, purpose {3x}, acceptable {1x}, delightsome {1x}, matter {1x}, pleasant {1x}, willingly {1x}.

Chephets, as a noun, means "pleasure; delight; desire; request; affair; thing." **(1)** This word often means "pleasure" or "delight": **(1a)** "Hath the LORD as great delight in burnt offerings and sacrifices, as in obeying the voice of the LORD?" (1 Sa 15:22—the first occurrence). **(1b)** Thus "the preacher [writer of Ecclesiastes] sought to find out acceptable [*chephets*] words: and that which was written was upright, even words of truth" (Eccl 12:10), words that were both true and aesthetically pleasing. **(2)** A good wife works with "hands of delight," or hands which delight in her work because of her love for her family; "she seeketh wool, and flax, and worketh willingly [in delight] with her hands" (Prov 31:13). **(2)** *Chephets* can mean not simply what one takes pleasure in or what gives someone delight but one's wish or desire: "Although my house be not so with God; yet he hath made with me an everlasting covenant, ordered in all things, and sure: for this is all my salvation, and all my desire, although he make it not to grow" (2 Sa 23:5).

(3) "To do one's desire" is to grant a request (1 Kin 5:8). **(4)** "Stones of desire" are precious stones (Is 54:12). **(5)** *Chephets* sometimes represents one's affairs as that in which one takes delight: **(5a)** ". . . There is . . . a time to every purpose [literally, delight] under the heaven" (Eccl 3:1). **(5b)** In Is 58:13 the first occurrence of this word means "pleasure" or "delight," while the last occurrence indicates an affair or matter in which one delights: "If thou turn away thy foot from the sabbath, from doing thy pleasure on my holy day; and call the sabbath a delight, the holy of the LORD, honorable; and shalt honor him, not doing thine own ways, nor finding thine own pleasure, nor speaking thine own words." **(6)** Finally, in one passage this word means "affair" in the sense of a "thing" or "situation": "If thou seest the oppression of the poor, and violent perverting of judgment and justice in a province, marvel not at the matter . . ." (Eccl 5:8). See: TWOT—712b; BDB—343a.

2657. חֶפְצִי־בָהּ {2x} **Chephtsîy bâhh**, *khef-tsee'-baw;* from 2656 with suffixes; *my delight* (is) *in her; Cheptsi-bah,* a fanciful name for Pal.:—Hephzi-bah {2x}. See: BDB—343b.

2658. חָפַר {22x} **châphar**, *khaw-far';* a prim. root; prop. to *pry* into; by impl. to *delve,* to *explore:*—dig {17x}, search out {3x}, paweth {1x}, seeketh {1x}. See: TWOT—714; BDB—343c.

2659. חָפֵר {17x} **châphêr**, *khaw-fare';* a prim. root [perhaps rath. the same as 2658 through the idea of *detection*]: to *blush;* fig. to *be ashamed, disappointed;* caus. to *shame, reproach:*—be ashamed {4x}, be confounded {6x}, be brought to confusion {2x}, be brought unto shame {4x}, bring reproach {1x}. See: TWOT—715; BDB—344a.

2660. חֵפֶר {9x} **Chêpher**, *khay'-fer;* from 2658 or 2659; a *pit* or *shame; Chepher,* a place in Pal.; also the name of three Isr.:—Hepher {9x}. See: BDB—343d.

2661. חָפֹר {1x} **chăphôr**, *khaf-ore';* from 2658; a *hole;* only in connection with 6512, which ought rather to be joined as one word, thus

חֲפַרְפֵּרָה **chăpharpêrâh**, *khaf-ar-pay-raw';* by redupl. from 2658; a *burrower,* i.e. prob. a *rat:*—+ mole {1x}. See: TWOT—714a; BDB—344a, 344b, 826c.

2662. חֶפְרִי {1x} **Chephrîy**, *khef-ree';* patron. from 2660; a *Chephrite* (collect.) or desc. of *Chepher:*—Hepherites {1x}. See: BDB—343d.

2663. חֲפָרַיִם {1x} **Chăphârayîm**, *khaf-aw-rah'-yim;* dual of 2660; *double pit; Chapharajim,* a place in Pal.:—Haphraim {1x}. See: BDB—343d.

חֲפַרְפֵּרָה **chăpharpêrâh**. See 2661.

2664. חָפַשׂ {23x} **châphas**, *khaw-fas';* a prim. root; to *seek;* caus. to *conceal* oneself (i.e. let be sought), or *mask:*—search {11x}, disguise {7x}, search out {2x}, changed {1x}, diligent {1x}, hidden {1x}. See: TWOT—716; BDB—344b.

2665. חֵפֶשׂ {1x} **chêphes**, *khay'-fes;* from 2664; something *covert,* i.e. a *trick:*—search {1x}. See: TWOT—716a; BDB—344c.

2666. חָפַשׁ {1x} **châphash**, *khaw-fash';* a prim. root; to *spread* loose; fig. to *manumit:*—be free {1x}. See: TWOT—717; BDB—344d.

2667. חֹפֶשׁ {1x} **chôphesh**, *kho'-fesh;* from 2666; something *spread* loosely, i.e. a *carpet:*—precious {1x}. See: TWOT—717a; BDB—344d.

2668. חֻפְשָׁה {1x} **chuphshâh**, *khoof-shaw';* from 2666; *liberty* (from slavery):—freedom {1x}. See: TWOT—717b; BDB—344d.

2669. חָפְשׁוּת {3x} **chôphshûwth**, *khof-shooth';* and

חָפְשִׁית **chophshîyth**, *khof-sheeth';* from 2666; *prostration* by sickness (with 1004, a *hospital*):—several {3x}. See: TWOT—717d; BDB—345a.

2670. חָפְשִׁי {17x} **chophshîy**, *khof-shee';* from 2666; *exempt* (from bondage, tax or care):—free {16x}, liberty {1x}.

2671. חֵץ {53x} **chêts**, *khayts;* from 2686; prop. a *piercer,* i.e. an *arrow;* by impl. a *wound;* fig. (of God) thunder-*bolt;* (by interchange for 6086) the *shaft* of a spear:—arrow {48x}, archers + 1167 {1x}, dart {1x}, shaft {1x}, wound {1x}, variant {1x}. See: TWOT—721b; BDB—345a, 346b.

חֻץ **chûts**. See 2351.

2672. חָצַב {25x} **châtsab**, *khaw-tsab',* or

חָצֵב **châtsêb**, *khaw-tsabe';* a prim. root; to *cut* or *carve* (wood, stone or other material); by impl. to *hew, split, square, quarry, engrave:*—dig {5x}, hew {4x}, hewers {4x}, hew out {4x}, mason {3x}, cut {1x}, divideth {1x}, graven {1x}, hewn {1x}, made {1x}.See: TWOT—718; BDB—345a.

2673. חָצָה {15x} **châtsâh**, *khaw-tsaw';* a prim. root [comp. 2686]); to *cut* or *split* in two; to *halve:*—divide {11x}, part {2x}, live out half {1x}, midst {1x}.

Chatsah, as a verb, means "to divide, reach unto." The word most commonly means "to divide," as in Ex 21:35: ". . . Then they shall sell the live ox, and divide the money of it. . . . " See: TWOT—719; BDB—345b.

2674. חָצוֹר {19x} **Châtsôwr**, *khaw-tsore';* a collect. form of 2691; *village; Chatsor,* the name (thus simply) of two places in Pal. and of one in Arabia:—Hazor {19x}. See: BDB—347d.

2675. חָצוֹר חֲדַתָּה {1x} **Châtsôwr Chădattâh**, *khaw-tsore' khad-at-taw';* from 2674 and a Chaldaizing form of the fem. of 2319 [comp. 2323]; *new Chatsor,* a place in Pal.:—Hazor, Hadattah [*as if two places*] {1x}. See: BDB—347d.

2676. חָצוֹת {3x} **châtsôwth**, *khaw-tsoth';* from 2673; the *middle* (of the night):—midnight {3x}. See: TWOT—719a; BDB—345c, 346a.

2677. חֵצִי {125x} **chêtsîy**, *khay-tsee';* from 2673; the *half* or *middle:*—half {108x}, midst {8x}, part {4x}, midnight + 3915, middle {1x}.

Chetsiy, as a noun, means "half; halfway; middle." **(1)** First, the word is used to indicate "half" of anything. This meaning first occurs in Ex 24:6: "And Moses took half of the blood, and put it in basins; and half of the blood he sprinkled on the altar." **(2)** Second, *chetsiy* can mean "middle," as it does in its first biblical appearance: "And it came to pass, that at midnight [literally, "the middle of the night"] the LORD smote all the first-born in the land of Egypt . . ." (Ex 12:29). **(3)** In Ex 27:5, the word means "halfway": "And thou shalt put it under the compass of the altar beneath, that the net may be even to the midst [i.e., up to the middle] of the altar." See: TWOT—719b; BDB—345c, 346a.

2678. חִצִּי {5x} **chitstsîy**, *khits-tsee';* or

חֵצִי **chêtsîy**, *khay-tsee';* prol. from 2671; an *arrow:*—arrow {5x}. Syn.: 2671. See: TWOT—719c, 721b; BDB—345d.

2679. חֲצִי הַמְּנֻחוֹת {1x} **Chătsîy ham-Mᵉnûchôwth**, *chat-tsee' ham-men-oo-khoth';* from 2677 and the plur. of 4496, with the art. interposed; *midst of the resting-places; Chatsi-ham-Menuchoth,* an Isr.:—half of the Manahethites {1x}. See: BDB—345d, 630a.

2680. חֲצִי הַמְּנַחְתִּי {1x} **Chătsîy ham-Mᵉnachtîy**, *khat-see' ham-men-akh-tee';* patron. from 2679; a *Chatsi-ham-Menachtite* or desc. of Chatsi-ham-Menuchoth:—half of the Manahethites {1x}. See: BDB—345d, 630a.

2681. חָצִיר {1x} **châtsîyr**, *khaw-tseer';* a collat. form of 2691; a *court* or *abode:*—court {1x}. See: TWOT—723b; BDB—347d.

2682. חָצִיר {21x} **châtsîyr**, *khaw-tseer';* perh. orig. the same as 2681, from the *greenness* of a courtyard; *grass;* also a *leek* (collect.):—grass {17x}, hay {2x}, herb {1x}, leek {1x}. See: TWOT—724a, 725a; BDB—348b.

2683. חֵצֶן {1x} **chêtsen**, *khay'-tsen;* from an unused root mean. to hold *firmly;* the *bosom* (as *comprised* between the arms):—bosom {1x}. Syn.: 2243, 2436, 6747. See: TWOT—720a; BDB—346a.

2684. חֹצֶן {2x} **chôtsen**, *kho'tsen;* a collat. form of 2683, and mean. the same:—arm {1x}, lap {1x}. See: TWOT—720b; BDB—346a.

2685. חֲצַף {2x} **chătsaph** (Aram.), *khats-af';* a prim. root; prop. to *shear* or cut close; fig. to *be severe:*—hasty {1x}, be urgent {1x}. See: TWOT—2740; BDB—1093c.

2686. חָצַץ {3x} **châtsats**, *khaw-tsats';* a prim. root [comp. 2673]; prop. to *chop* into, pierce or sever; hence, to *curtail,* to *distribute* (into ranks); as denom. from 2671, to *shoot* an arrow:—archer {1x}, × bands {1x}, cut off in the midst {1x}. See: TWOT—721, 721c; BDB—346a, 346d.

2687. חָצָץ {3x} **châtsâts**, *khaw-tsawts';* from 2687; prop. something *cutting;* hence, *gravel* (as *grit*); also (like 2671) an *arrow:*—arrow {1x}, gravel {1x}, stone {1x}. See: TWOT—721a; BDB—346b.

2688. חַצְצוֹן תָּמָר {1x} **Chatsᵉtsôwn Tâmâr**, *khats-ets-one' taw-mawr';* or

חַצֲצֹן תָּמָר **Chatsătsôn Tâmâr**, *khats-ats-one' taw-mawr';* from 2686 and 8558; *division* [i.e. perh. *row*] *of* (the) *palm-tree; Chatsetson-tamar,* a place in Pal.:—Hazezon-tamar {1x}. See: BDB—346c.

2689. חֲצֹצְרָה {29x} **chătsôtsᵉrâh**, *khats-o-tser-aw';* by redupl. from 2690; a *trumpet* (from its *sundered* or quavering note):—trumpet {1x}, trumpets {24x}, trumpeter {4x}. See: TWOT—726a; BDB—346d, 348c.

2690. חָצַר {11x} **châtsar**, *khaw-tsar';* a prim. root; prop. to *surround* with a stockade, and thus *separate* from the open country; but used only in the redupl. form

חֲצֹצֵר **chătsôtsêr**, *khast-o-tsare';* or (2 Chr 5:12)

חֲצֹרֵר **chătsôrêr**, *khats-o-rare';* as denom. from 2689; to *trumpet,* i.e. blow on that instrument:—sounded {2x}, blow {1x}, sound {1x}, trumpeters {1x}, sounded {1x}, variant {5x}. See: TWOT—726b; BDB—348b.

2691. חָצֵר {189x} **châtsêr**, *khaw-tsare'* (masc. and fem.); from 2690 in its orig. sense; a *yard* (as *enclosed* by a fence); also a *hamlet* (as similarly *surrounded* with walls):—court {141x}, villages {47x}, towns {1x}.

Chatser means "court; enclosure." **(1)** This word is related to a common Semitic verb that has two meanings: **(1a)** "to be present," in the sense of living at a certain place (encampment, residence, court), and **(1b)** "to enclose, surround, press together." **(1c)** In some Hebrew dictionaries, the usage of *chatser* as "settled abode," "settlement," or "village" is separated from the meaning "court." But most modern dictionaries identify only one root with two related meanings. **(2)** The first biblical occurrence of *chatser* is in Gen 25:16: "These are the sons of Ishmael, and these are their names, by their towns, and by their castles; twelve princes according to their nations." **(2a)** Here *chatser* is related to the first meaning of the root, this occurs less frequently than the usage meaning "court." **(3)** The *chatser* ("settlement") was a place where people lived without an enclosure to protect them. The word is explained in Lev 25:31: "But the houses of the villages which have no wall round about them shall be counted as the fields of the country: they may be redeemed, and they shall go out in the jubilee."

(3a) *Chatser* signifies the "settlements" of semi-nomadic peoples: the Ishmaelites (Gen 25:16), the Avim (Deut 2:23), and Kedar (Is 42:11). **(3b)** *Chatser* also denotes a "settlement" of people outside the city wall. The cities of Canaan were relatively small and could not contain the whole population. In times of peace, residents of the city might build homes and workshops for themselves outside the wall and establish a separate quarter. If the population grew, the king or governor often decided to enclose the new quarter by surrounding it with a wall and incorporating the section into the existing city, in order to protect the population from bandits and warriors. **(3c)** Jerusalem gradually extended its size westward; at the time of Hezekiah, it had grown into a large city. Huldah the prophetess lived in such a development, known in Hebrew as the *mishneh* (4932): "... she dwelt in Jerusalem in the college" (2 Kin 22:14).

(4) The Book of Joshua includes Israel's victories in Canaan's major cities as well as the suburbs: "Ain, Remmon, and Ether, and Ashan; four cities and their villages . . ." (19:7; cf. 15:45, 47; 21:12). **(5)** The predominant usage of *chatser* is "court," whether of a house, a palace, or the temple. **(5a)** Each house generally had a courtyard surrounded by a wall or else one adjoined several homes: "Nevertheless a lad saw them, and told Absalom: but they went both of them away quickly, and came to a man's house in Bahurim, which had a well in his court; whither they went down" (2 Sa 17:18). **(5b)** Solomon's palace had several "courts"—an outer "court," an "enclosed space" around the palace, and a "court" around which the palace was built. **(5c)** Similarly, the temple had various courts. The psalmist expressed his joy in being in the "courts" of the temple, where the birds built their nests (Ps 84:3); "For a day in thy courts is better than a thousand. I had rather be a doorkeeper in the house of my God, than to dwell in the tents of wickedness" (Ps 84:10). **(5d)** God's people looked forward to the thronging together of all the people in God's "courts": ". . . In the courts of the LORD's house, in the midst of thee, O Jerusalem" (Ps 116:19). See: TWOT—722a, 723a; BDB—346d, 347b.

2692. חֲצַר אַדָּר {1x} **Chătsar ʼAddâr**, *khats-ar' addawr';* from 2691 and 146; (the) *village of Addar; Chatsar-Addar,* a place in Pal.:—Hazar-addar {1x}. See: BDB—347b.

2693. חֲצַר גַּדָּה {1x} **Chătsar Gaddâh**, *khats-ar' gad-daw';* from 2691 and a fem. of 1408; (the) *village of* (female) *Fortune; Chatsar-Gaddah,* a place in Pal.:—Hazar-gaddah {1x}. See: BDB—151d, 347c.

2694. חֲצַר הַתִּיכוֹן {1x} **Chătsar hat-Tîykôwn**, *khats-ar' hat-tee-kone';* from 2691 and 8484 with the art. interposed; *village of the middle; Chatsar-hat-Tikon,* a place in Pal.:—Hazar-hatticon {1x}. See: BDB—347c, 1064a.

2695. חֶצְרוֹ {1x} **Chetsrôw**, *khets-ro';* by an orth. var. for 2696; *inclosure; Chetsro,* an Isr.:—Hezro {1x}, Hezrai {1x}. See: BDB—347d.

2696. חֶצְרוֹן {18x} **Chetsrôwn**, *khets-rone';* from 2691; *court-yard; Chetsron,* the name of a place in Pal.; also of two Isr.:—Hezron {18x}. See: BDB—348a.

2697. חֶצְרוֹנִי {2x} **Chetsrôwnîy**, *khets-ro-nee';* patron. from 2696; a *Chetsronite* or (collect.) desc. of Chetsron:—Hezronites {2x}. See: BDB—348a.

2698. חֲצֵרוֹת {6x} **Chătsêrowth**, *khats-ay-roth';* fem. plur. of 2691; *yards; Chatseroth,* a place in Pal.:—Hazeroth {6x}. See: BDB—348a.

2699. חֲצֵרִים {1x} **Chătsêrîym**, *khats-ay-reem';* plur. masc. of 2691; *yards; Chatserim,* a place in Pal.:—Hazerim {1x}. See: BDB—346d, 347b.

2700. חֲצַרְמָוֶת {2x} **Chătsarmâveth**, *khats-ar-maw'-veth;* from 2691 and 4194; *village of death; Chatsarmaveth,* a place in Arabia:—Hazarmaveth {1x}. See: BDB—348a.

2701. חֲצַר סוּסָה {1x} **Chătsar Çûwçâh**, *khats-ar' soo-saw';* from 2691 and 5484; *village of cavalry; Chatsar-Susah,* a place in Pal.:—Hazar-susah {1x}. See: BDB—347c.

2702. חֲצַר סוּסִים {1x} **Chătsar Çûwçîym**, *khats-ar' soo-seem';* from 2691 and the plur. of 5483; *village of horses; Chatsar-Susim,* a place in Pal.:—Hazar-susim {1x}. See: BDB—347c.

2703. חֲצַר עֵינוֹן {1x} **Chătsar ʻÊynôwn**, *khats-ar' ay-nōne';* from 2691 and a der. of 5869; *village of springs; Chatsar-Enon,* a place in Pal.:—Hazar-enon {1x}. See: BDB—347c, 745d.

2704. חֲצַר עֵינָן {3x} **Chătsar ʻÊynân**, *khats-ar' ay-nawn';* from 2691 and the same as 5881; *village of springs; Chatsar-Enan,* a place in Pal.:—Hazar-enan {3x}. See: BDB—347c, 745d.

2705. חֲצַר שׁוּעָל {4x} **Chătsar Shûwʻâl**, *khats-ar' shoo-awl';* from 2691 and 7776; *village of* (the) *fox; Chatsar-Shual,* a place in Pal.:—Hazar-shual {4x}. See: BDB—347c.

חֵק **chêq**. See 2436.

2706. חֹק {127x} **chôq**, *khoke;* from 2710; an *enactment;* hence, an *appointment* (of time, space, quantity, labor or usage):—statute {87x}, ordinance {9x}, decree {7x}, due {4x}, law {4x}, portion {3x}, bounds {2x}, custom {2x}, appointed {1x}, commandments {1x}, misc. {7x}: convenient, measure, × necessary, ordinary, set time, task.

Choq, as a noun, means "statute; prescription; rule; law; regulation." **(1)** This noun is derived from the verb *haqaq,* "to cut in, determine, decree." **(2)** The first usage of *choq* is in Gen 47:22: "Only the land of the priests bought he not; for the priests had a portion [*choq*] assigned them of Pharaoh. . . . " **(2a)** The meaning of *choq* in the first occurrence (Gen 47:22) differs from the basic meaning of "statute." **(2b)** It has the sense of something allotted or apportioned. **(2c)** A proverb speaks about "food convenient for me" (literally, "food of my prescription or portion"). **(2d)** Job recognized in his suffering that God does what is appointed for him: "For he performeth the thing that is appointed for me [literally, 'he will perform my Law'] . . ." (23:14). **(2e)** The "portion" may be something that is due to a person as an allowance or payment. The Egyptian priests received their income from Pharaoh (Gen 47:22), even as God permitted a part of the sacrifice to be enjoyed by the priests: "And it shall be Aaron's and his sons' [as their portion] for ever from the children of Israel: for it is a heave offering . . ." (Ex 29:28).

(3) The word *choq* also signifies "law," or "statute." **(3a)** In a general sense it refers to the "laws" of nature like rain: "When he made a decree for the rain, and a way for the lightning of the thunder" (Job 28:26; cf. Jer 5:22); **(3b)** and the celestial bodies: "He hath also stablished them for ever and ever: he hath made a decree which shall not pass" (Ps 148:6) **(3c)** "Thus saith the LORD, which giveth the sun for a light by day, and the ordinances of the moon and of the stars for a light by night, which divideth the sea when the waves thereof roar; The LORD of hosts is his name: If those ordinances depart from before me, saith the LORD, then the seed of Israel also shall cease from being a nation before me for ever" (Jer 31:35–36). **(4)** Moreover, the word *choq* denotes a "law" promulgated in a country: "And Joseph made it a law over the land of Egypt unto this day, that Pharaoh should have the fifth part; except the land of the priests only, which became not Pharaoh's" (Gen 47:26). **(5)** Finally, and most important, the "law" given by God is also referred to as a *choq:* "When they have a matter, they come unto me; and I judge between one and another, and I do make them know the statutes [*choq*] of God, and his laws [8451 - torah]" (Exod. 18:16). Syn: The word's synonyms are **(A)** mitswah (4687) "commandment"; **(B)** mishpat (4941) "judgment"; **(C)** berit (1285) "covenant"; **(D)** torah (8451)"law"; and **(E)** ʻedut (5713)"testimony." **(D)** It is not easy to distinguish between these synonyms, as they are often found in conjunction with each other: "Ye shall diligently keep the commandments [mitswah] of the LORD your God, and his testimonies [ʻedah], and his statutes [*choq*], which he hath commanded thee" (Deut 6:17). See: TWOT—728a; BDB—348d, 349b, 350c.

2707. חָקָה {4x} **châqah**, *khaw-kaw';* a prim. root; to *carve;* by impl. to *delineate;* also to *intrench:*—portrayed {2x}, carved work {1x}, set a print {1x}. See: TWOT—727; BDB—348d.

2708. חֻקָּה {104x} **chuqqâh**, *khook-kaw';* fem. of 2706, and mean. substantially the same:—statute {77x}, ordinance {22x}, custom {2x}, appointed {1x}, manners {1x}, rites {1x}.

Chuqqah (2708), as a noun means, "statute; regulation; prescription; term." **(1)** *Chuqqah* is found for the first time in God's words of commendation about Abraham to Isaac: "Because that Abraham obeyed my voice, and kept my charge [4931 – mishmeret], my commandments [4687 - mitswah], my statutes [*chuqqah*], and my laws [8451 - *torah*]" (Gen 26:5). **(1a)** The primary use of *chuqqah* is in the Pentateuch, especially in Leviticus and Numbers. **(1b)** It is extemely rare in the poetical books and in the prophetic writings (except for Jeremiah and Ezekiel). **(2)** The meaning of "fixed" is similar to the usage of *choq,* in the sense of the laws of nature: **(2a)** "Thus saith the LORD; If my covenant be not with day and night, and if I have not appointed the ordinances of heaven and earth" (Jer 33:25; cf. Job 38:33). **(2b)** Even as the Israelites had a period of rainfall from October to April, there was a fixed period of harvest (from April to June): "Neither say they in their heart, Let us now fear the LORD our God, that giveth rain, both the former and the latter, in his season: he reserveth unto us the appointed weeks of the harvest" (Jer 5:24). **(3)** In addition to regularity of nature, the word *chuqqah* signifies regular payment to the priests: "Which the LORD commanded to be given them of the children of Israel, in the day that he anointed them, by a statute for ever throughout their generations" (Lev 7:36).

(4) In non-religious usage, the word *chuqqah* refers to the customs of the nations: **(4a)** "After the doings of the land of Egypt, wherein ye dwelt, shall ye not do: and after the doings of the land of Canaan, whither I bring you, shall ye not do: neither shall ye walk in their ordinances" (Lev 18:3; cf. 20:23). **(4b)** The reason for the requirement to abstain from the pagan practices is that they were considered to be degenerate (Lev 18:30). **(5)** The most significant usage of *chuqqah* is God's "law." It is more specific in meaning than *choq* (2706). **(5a)** Whereas *choq* is a general word for "law," *chuqqah* denotes the "law" of a particular festival or ritual. **(5b)** There is the "law" of the Passover (Ex 12:14), Unleavened Bread (Ex 12:17), Feast of

Tabernacles (Lev 23:41), the Day of Atonement (Lev 16:29ff.), the priesthood (Ex 29:9), and the blood and fat (Lev 3:17). or **(6)** The "statutes" of people are to be understood as the practices contrary to God's expectations: "For the statutes of Omri are kept, and all the works of the home of Ahab, and ye walk in their counsels, that I should make thee a desolation, and the inhabitants thereof a hissing: therefore ye shall bear the reproach of my people" (Mic 6:16).

(7) The prophet Ezekiel condemned Judah for rejecting God's holy "statutes": **(7a)** "And she hath changed my judgments into wickedness more than the nations, and my statutes [*chuqqah*] more than the countries that are round about her: for they have refused my judgments and my statutes [*chuqqah*], they have not walked in them" (Eze 5:6). **(7b)** He also challenged God's people to repent and return to God's "statutes" that they might live: "If the wicked restore the pledge, give again that he had robbed, walk in the statutes of life, without committing iniquity; he shall surely live, he shall not die" (Eze 33:15). Syn: The word *chuqqah* has many synonyms. At times it forms a part of a series of three: "Beware that thou forget not the Lord thy God, in not keeping his **(1)** commandments [4687 - *mitswah*], and his **(2)** judgments [4941 - *mishpat*], and his statutes [*chuqqah*], which I command thee this day" (Deut 8:11), and at other times of a series of four: "Therefore thou shalt love the LORD thy God, and keep his charge **(3)** [4931 - *mishmeret*], and his statutes [*chuqqah*] and his judgments [4941 - *mishpat*], and his commandments [4687 - *mitswah*], always" (Deut 11:1; cf. Gen 26:5 with *torah* [8451] instead of *mishpat* [4941]). See: TWOT—728b; BDB—349a, 349d.

2709. חֲקוּפָא {2x} **Chăqûwphâʾ**, *khak-oo-faw';* from an unused root prob. mean. to *bend; crooked; Chakupha,* one of the Nethinim:—Hakupha {2x}. See: BDB—349a.

2710. חָקַק {19x} **châqaq**, *khaw-kak';* a prim. root; prop. to *hack,* i.e. *engrave* (Judg. 5:14, to *be a scribe* simply); by impl. to *enact* (laws being *cut* in stone or metal tablets in primitive times) or (gen.) *prescribe:*—lawgiver {6x}, governor {2x}, decree {2x}, to grave {2x}, portray {2x}, law {1x}, printed {1x}, set {1x}, note {1x}, appoint {1x}.

Chaqaq, as a verb, means "to cut in, determine, decree." **(1)** *Chaqaq* is used in Is 22:16 with the meaning "to cut in": ". . . That graveth a habitation for himself in a rock." **(2)** In Is 10:1 the verb is used of "enacting a decree": "Woe unto them that decree unrighteous decrees, and that write grievousness which they have prescribed." See: TWOT—728; BDB—349a.

2711. חֵקֶק {2x} **chêqeq**, *khay'-kek;* from 2710; an *enactment,* a *resolution:*—decree {1x}, thought {1x}. See: TWOT—728a; BDB—349b.

2712. חֻקֹּק {2x} **Chuqqôq**, *Khook-koke';* or (fully)

חוּקֹק **Chûwqôq**, *khoo-koke';* from 2710; *appointed; Chukkok* or *Chukok,* a place in Pal.:—Hukkok {1x}, Hukok {1x}. See: BDB—301a, 350c.

2713. חָקַר {27x} **châqar**, *khaw-kar';* a prim. root; prop. to *penetrate;* hence, to *examine* intimately:—search {12x}, search out {9x}, found out {2x}, seek out {1x}, seek {1x}, sounded {1x}, try {1x}. See: TWOT—729; BDB—350c.

2714. חֵקֶר {12x} **chêqer**, *khay'-ker;* from 2713; *examination, enumeration, deliberation:*—search {6x}, unsearchable {2x}, unsearchable + 369 {1x}, finding out {1x}, without number {1x} search out {1x}. See: TWOT—729a; BDB—350d.

2715. חֹר {13x} **chôr**, *khore;* or (fully)

חוֹר **chôwr**, *khore;* from 2787; prop. *white* or *pure* (from the *cleansing* or *shining* power of fire [comp. 2751]; hence, (fig.) *noble* (in rank):—noble {13x}. See: TWOT—757a; BDB—301c, 351a, 359d.

חֻר **chûr.** See 2352.

2716. חֶרֶא {1x} **chereʾ**, *kheh'-reh;* from an unused (and vulgar) root prob. mean. to *evacuate* the bowels: *excrement:*—dung {1x}. See: TWOT—730a; BDB—351a, 844b. Also

חֲרִי **chărîy**, *khar-ee'.*

2717. חָרַב {40x} **chârab**, *khaw-rab';* or

חָרֵב **chârêb**, *khaw-rabe';* a prim. root; to *parch* (through drought) i.e. (by anal.) to *desolate, destroy, kill:*—waste {16x}, dry {7x}, dry up {7x}, desolate {3x}, slay {2x}, decayeth {1x}, destroyed {1x}, destroyer {1x}, surely {1x}, utterly {1x}. See: TWOT—731, 732; BDB—351a, 351c, 352b, 1093d.

2718. חֲרַב {1x} **chărab** (Aram.), *khar-ab';* a root corresp. to 2717; to *demolish:*—destroy {1x}.

Charab means "to smite down, slaughter." The word appears in 2 Kin 3:23. "This is blood: the kings are surely slain. . . . " See: TWOT—2741; BDB—1093d.

2719. חֶרֶב {413x} **chereb**, *kheh'-reb;* from 2717; *drought;* also a *cutting* instrument (from its *destructive* effect), as a *knife, sword,* or other sharp implement:—sword {401x}, knife {5x}, dagger {3x}, axes {1x}, mattocks {1x}, tool {1x}, sword + 3027 {1x}.

Chereb, as a noun, means "sword; dagger; flint knife; chisel." **(1)** Usually *chereb* represents an implement that can be or is being used in war, such as a "sword." **(1a)** The exact shape of that implement, however, is not specified by this word. **(1b)** Present day archaeology has unearthed various sickle swords and daggers from the earliest periods. **(1b1)** Sickle swords are so named because they are shaped somewhat like a sickle with the outer edge of the arc being the cutting edge. **(1b2)** These were long one-edged "swords." This is what *chereb* refers to when one reads of someone's being slain with the edge of the "sword": "And they slew Hamor and Shechem his son with the edge of the sword, and took Dinah out of Shechem's house . . ." (Gen 34:26). **(1c)** The first biblical occurrence of the word (Gen 3:24) probably also represents such an implement: ". . . And he placed at the east of the garden of Eden cherubim, and a flaming sword which turned every way. . . . "

(2) The precise meaning of *chereb* is confused, however, by its application to what we know as a "dagger," a short two-edged sword: "But Ehud made him a dagger which had two edges, of a cubit [eighteen to twenty-four inches] length . . ." (Judg 3:16). **(3)** The sickle sword was probably the implement used up to and during the conquest of Palestine. About the same time the Sea Peoples (among whom were the Philistines) were invading the ancient Near East. They brought with them a new weapon—the long two-edged "sword." **(3a)** The first clear mention of such a "sword" in the biblical record appears in 1 Sa 17:51: "Therefore David ran, and stood upon the Philistine [Goliath], and took his sword, and drew it out of the sheath thereof, and slew him. . . ." **(3b)** Perhaps Saul also used the highly superior Philistine armor and "sword" (1 Sa 17:39), but this is not clear. **(3c)** It is also possible that the angel who confronted Balaam with a drawn "sword" wielded a long two-edged "sword" (Num 22:23). Certainly this would have made him (humanly speaking) a much more formidable sight. **(3d)** By the time of David, with his expertise and concern for warfare, the large two-edged "sword" was much more prominent if not the primary kind of "sword" used by Israel's heavy infantry.

(4) This two-edged "sword" can be compared **(4a)** to a tongue: ". . . Even the sons of men, whose teeth are spears and arrows, and their tongue a sharp sword" (Ps 57:4). This usage tells us not only about the shape of the "sword" but that such a tongue is a violent, merciless, attacking weapon. **(4b)** In Gen 27:40 "sword" is symbolic of violence: "And by thy sword shalt thou live. . . ." **(4c)** Prov 5:4 uses *chereb* (of a long twoedged "sword") to depict the grievous result of dealing with an adulteress; it is certain death: "But her end is bitter as wormwood, sharp as a two-edged sword." **(5)** The "sword" is frequently depicted as an agent of God. **(5a)** It is not only used to safeguard the garden of Eden, **(5b)** but figures the judgment of God executed upon His enemies: "For my sword shall be bathed in heaven: behold, it shall come down upon Idumea . . ." (Is 34:5; cf. Deut 28:22).

(6) *Chereb* may be used of various other cutting implements. **(6a)** In Josh 5:2 it means "knife": "Make thee sharp knives, and circumcise again the children of Israel the second time." **(6b)** Eze 5:1 uses *chereb* of a barber's "razor": "And thou, son of man, take thee a sharp knife, take thee a barber's razor, and cause it to pass upon thine head and upon thy beard. . . . " The exact size and shape of this tool cannot be determined, but it is clear that it was used as a razor. **(7)** This word can also be used of tools ("chisels") for hewing stone: "And if thou wilt make me an altar of stone, thou shalt not build it of hewn stone: for if thou lift up thy tool upon it, thou hast polluted it" (Ex 20:25). The fact that a "sword," an implement of death, would be used to cut the stone for an altar, the instrument of life, explains why this action would profane the altar. See: TWOT—732a; BDB—352b.

2720. חָרֵב {10x} **chârêb**, *khaw-rabe';* from 2717; *parched* or *ruined:*—desolate {2x}, dry {2x}, waste {6x}. See: TWOT—731a; BDB—351b, 351d.

2721. חֹרֶב {16x} **chôreb**, *kho'-reb;* a collat. form of 2719; *drought* or *desolation:*—heat {6x}, dry {3x}, drought {3x}, waste {2x}, desolation {1x}, utterly {1x}. See: TWOT—731b; BDB—351b, 351c.

2722. חֹרֵב {17x} **Chôrêb**, *kho-rabe';* from 2717; *desolate; Choreb,* a (gen.) name for the Sinaitic mountains:—Horeb {17x}. See: TWOT—731c; BDB—352a.

2723. חׇרְבָּה {42x} **chorbâh**, *khor-baw';* fem. of 2721; prop. *drought,* i.e. (by impl.) a *desolation:*—waste {18x}, desolation {8x}, desolate places {4x}, waste places {4x}, desert {3x}, desolate {3x}, decayed places {1x}, destructions {1x}. See: TWOT—731d; BDB—352a.

2724. חָרָבָה {8x} **chârâbâh**, *khaw-raw-baw';* fem. of 2720; a *desert:*—dry {1x}, dry ground {3x}, dry land {4x}. See: TWOT—731e; BDB—351c.

2725. חֲרָבוֹן {1x} **chărâbôwn**, *khar-aw-bone';* from 2717; parching *heat:*—drought {1x}. See: TWOT—731f; BDB—351c.

2726. חַרְבוֹנָא {2x} **Charbôwnâ'**, *khar-bo-naw';* or

חַרְבוֹנָה **Charbôwnâh**, *khar-bo-naw';* of Pers. or.; *Charbona* or *Charbonah,* a eunuch of Xerxes:—Harbona {1x}, Harbonah {1x}. See: BDB—353a.

2727. חָרַג {1x} **chârag**, *khaw-rag';* a prim. root; prop. to *leap* suddenly, i.e. (by impl.) to *be dismayed:*—be afraid {1x}. See: TWOT—733; BDB—353a.

2728. חָרְגֹּל {1x} **chargôl**, *khar-gole';* from 2727; the *leaping* insect, i.e. a *locust:*—beetle {1x}. See: TWOT—734a; BDB—353b.

2729. חָרַד {29x} **chârad**, *khaw-rad';* a prim. root; to *shudder* with terror; hence, to *fear;* also to *hasten* (with anxiety):—afraid {20x}, tremble {13x}, fray away {2x}, careful {1x}, discomfited {1x}, fray {1x}, quaked {1x}. See: TWOT—735; BDB—353b.

2730. חָרֵד {6x} **chârêd**, *khaw-rade';* from 2729; *fearful;* also *reverential:*—afraid {1x}, trembling {5x}. See: TWOT—735a; BDB—353d.

2731. חֲרָדָה {9x} **chărâdâh**, *khar-aw-daw';* fem. of 2730; *fear, anxiety:*—trembling {4x}, fear {2x}, exceedingly {1x}, care {1x}, quaking {1x}. See: TWOT—735b; BDB—353d.

2732. חֲרָדָה {2x} **Chărâdâh**, *khar-aw-daw';* the same as 2731; *Charadah,* a place in the Desert:—Haradah {2x}. See: BDB—354a.

2733. חֲרֹדִי {2x} **Chărôdîy**, *khar-o-dee';* patrial from a der. of 2729 [comp. 5878]; a *Charodite,* or inhab. of *Charod:*—Harodite {2x}. See: BDB—248b, 353d.

2734. חָרָה {90x} **chârâh**, *khaw-raw';* a prim. root [comp. 2787]; to *glow* or grow warm; fig. (usually) to *blaze* up, of anger, zeal, jealousy:—kindled {44x}, wroth {13x}, hot {10x}, angry {9x}, displease {4x}, fret {4x}, incensed {2x}, burn {1x}, earnestly {1x}, grieved {1x}, very {1x}.

Charah means "to get angry, be angry." **(1)** In the basic stem, the word refers to the "burning of anger" as in Jonah 4:1. **(2)** In the causative stem, it means "to become heated with work" or "with zeal for work" (Neh 3:20). Syn.: See 8474. See: TWOT—736; BDB—354a.

2735. חֹר הַגִּדְגָּד {2x} **Chôr hag-Gidgâd**, *khore hag-ghid-gawd';* from 2356 and a collat. (masc.) form of 1412, with the art. interposed; *hole of the cleft; Chor-hag-Gidgad,* a place in the Desert:—Hor-hagidgad {2x}. See: BDB—151d, 301b, 351a.

2736. חַרְהֲיָה {1x} **Charhăyâh**, *khar-hah-yaw';* from 2734 and 3050; *fearing Jah; Charhajah,* an Isr.:—Harhaiah {1x}. See: BDB—354c, 354d.

2737. חָרוּז {1x} **chârûwz**, *khaw-rooz';* from an unused root mean. to *perforate;* prop. *pierced,* i.e. a *bead* of pearl, gems or jewels (as strung):—chain {1x}. See: TWOT—737a; BDB—354d.

2738. חָרוּל {3x} **chârûwl**, *khaw-rool';* or (short.)

חָרֻל **chârûl**, *khaw-rool';* appar. a pass. part. of an unused root prob. mean. to *be prickly;* prop. *pointed,* i.e. a *bramble* or other thorny weed:—nettle {3x}. See: TWOT—743a; BDB—355b.

חֹרוֹן **chôrôwn**. See 1032, 2772.

2739. חֲרוּמַף {1x} **Chărûwmaph**, *khar-oo-maf';* from pass. part. of 2763 and 639; *snub-nosed; Charumaph,* an Isr.:—Harumaph {1x}. See: BDB—354d.

2740. חָרוֹן {41x} **chârôwn**, *khaw-rone';* or (short.)

חָרֹן **chârôn**, *khaw-rone';* from 2734; a *burning* of anger:—fierce {23x}, fierceness {9x}, wrath {6x}, fury {1x}, wrathful {1x}, displeasure {1x}.

Charon means "burning anger." This word refers exclusively to divine anger as that which is "burning." It first appears in Ex 32:12: "Turn from thy fierce wrath [*charon*], and repent of this evil against thy people." See: TWOT—736a; BDB—354c.

2741. חֲרוּפִי {1x} **Chărûwphîy**, *khar-oo-fee';* a patrial from (prob.) a collat. form of 2756; a *Charuphite* or inhab. of Charuph (or Chariph):—Haruphite {1x}. See: BDB—358b.

2742. חָרוּץ {18x} **chârûwts**, *khaw-roots';* or

חָרֻץ **chârûts**, *khaw-roots';* pass. part. of 2782; prop. *incised* or (act.) *incisive;* hence, (as noun masc. or fem.) a *trench* (as dug), *gold* (as mined), a *threshing-sledge* (having sharp teeth); (fig.) *determination;* also *eager:*—gold {6x}, diligent {5x}, decision {2x}, threshing instrument {2x}, sharp {1x}, sharp things {1x}, wall {1x}. See: TWOT—752a,b, 753a; BDB—358c, 358d, 359a.

2743. חָרוּץ {1x} **Chârûwts**, *khaw-roots';* the same as 2742; *earnest; Charuts,* an Isr.:—Haruz {1x}. See: BDB—358d.

2744. חַרְחוּר {2x} **Charchûwr**, *khar-khoor';* a fuller form of 2746; *inflammation; Charchur,* one of the Nethinim:—Harhur {2x}. See: BDB—354d, 359c.

2745. חַרְחַס {1x} **Charchaç**, *khar-khas';* from the same as 2775; perh. *shining; Charchas,* an Isr.:—Harhas {1x}. See: BDB—354d.

2746. חַרְחֻר {1x} **charchûr**, *khar-khoor';* from 2787; *fever* (as *hot*):—extreme burning {1x}. See: TWOT—756b; BDB—354d, 359c.

2747. חֶרֶט {2x} **cheret**, *kheh'-ret;* from a prim. root mean. to *engrave;* a *chisel* or *graver;* also a *style* for writing:—graving tool {1x}, pen {1x}. See: TWOT—738a; BDB—354d.

חָרִט **chârit**. See 2754.

2748. חַרְטֹם {11x} **chartôm**, *khar-tome';* from the same as 2747; a *horoscopist* (as *drawing* magical lines or circles):—magician {11x}. See: TWOT—738b; BDB—355a, 1093d.

2749. חַרְטֹם {5x} **chartôm** (Aram.), *khar-tome';* the same as 2748:—magician {5x}. See: TWOT—2742; BDB—1093d.

2750. חֳרִי {6x} **chôrîy**, *khor-ee';* from 2734; a *burning* (i.e. intense) anger:—fierce {3x}, great {2x}, heat {1x}. See: TWOT—736b; BDB—354c.

חֲרִי **chărîy**. See 2716.

2751. חֹרִי {1x} **chôrîy**, *kho-ree';* from the same as 2353; *white* bread:—white {1x}. Syn.: 3835, 3836, 7836. See: TWOT—740; BDB—301a, 355a.

2752. חֹרִי {6x} **Chôrîy**, *kho-ree';* from 2356; *cave-dweller* or troglodyte; a *Chorite* or aboriginal Idumæan:—Horims {2x}, Horites {4x}. See: BDB—355b, 360a.

2753. חֹרִי {4x} **Chôrîy**, *kho-ree';* or

חוֹרִי **Chôwrîy**, *kho-ree';* the same as 2752; *Chori,* the name of two men:—Hori {4x}. See: BDB—355b, 360a.

2754. חָרִיט {2x} **chârîyt**, *khaw-reet';* or

חָרִט **chârit**, *khaw-reet';* from the same as 2747; prop. *cut* out (or *hollow*), i.e. (by impl.) a *pocket:*—bag {1x}, crisping pin {1x}. See: TWOT—739a; BDB—355a.

2755. חֲרֵי־יוֹנִים {2x} **chărêy-yôwnîym**, *khar-ay'-yo-neem';* from the plur. of 2716 and the plur. of 3123; *excrements of doves* [or perh. rather the plur. of a single word].

חֲרָאיוֹן **chârâ'yôwn**, *khar-aw-yone';* of similar or uncert. der.], prob. a kind of vegetable:—doves' dung {2x}. See: TWOT—730a; BDB—351a, 355b.

2756. חָרִיף {2x} **Chârîyph**, *khaw-reef';* from 2778; *autumnal; Chariph,* the name of two Isr.:—Hariph {2x}. See: BDB—358b.

2757. חָרִיץ {2x} **chârîyts**, *khaw-reets';* or

חָרִץ **chârîts**, *khaw-reets';* from 2782; prop. *incisure* or (pass.) *incised* [comp. 2742]; hence, a *threshing-sledge* (with *sharp* teeth): also a *slice* (as cut):—+ cheese {1x}, harrow {1x}. See: TWOT—752c; BDB—358d.

2758. חָרִישׁ {3x} **chârîysh**, *khaw-reesh';* from 2790; *plowing* or its season:—earing (time) {2x}, ground {1x}. See: TWOT—760c; BDB—361a.

2759. חֲרִישִׁי {1x} **chărîyshîy**, *khar-ee-shee';* from 2790 in the sense of *silence; quiet,* i.e. *sultry* (as fem. noun, the *sirocco* or hot east wind):—vehement {1x}. See: TWOT—760e; BDB—362a.

2760. חָרַךְ {1x} **chârak**, *khaw-rak';* a prim. root; to *braid* (i.e. to *entangle* or snare) or *catch* (game) in a net:—roast {1x}. See: TWOT—741, 742; BDB—355b.

2761. חֲרַךְ {1x} **chărak** (Aram.), *khar-ak';* a root prob. allied to the equiv. of 2787; to *scorch:*—singe {1x}. See: TWOT—2743; BDB—1093d.

2762. חֶרֶךְ {1x} **cherek**, *kheh'-rek;* from 2760; prop. a *net,* i.e. (by anal.) *lattice:*—lattice {1x}. See: TWOT—742a; BDB—355b.

חָרֻל **chârûl**. See 2738.

2763. חָרַם {52x} **charam**, *khaw-ram';* a prim. root; to *seclude;* spec. (by a ban) to *devote* to relig. uses (espec. destruction); phys. and refl. to *be blunt* as to the nose:—destroy {34x}, utterly {10x}, devote {2x}, accursed {1x}, consecrate {1x}, forfeited {1x}, flat nose {1x}, utterly to make away {1x}, slay {1x}.

Charam is a religious word of great importance representing the devotion of some object to destruction or to a sacred use, not for the gratification of any selfish purpose. It is rendered **(1)** devote or dedicate **(1a)** a field (Lev 27:21), **(1b)** man (Lev 27:28), **(1c)** beast (Lev 27:28), and **(1d)** land (Lev 27:28–29) which rendered it priestly property (Num 18:14; Eze 44:29). **(2)** This word applied to the destruction of nations, **(2a)** because they were regarded as under the Divine doom, and **(2b)** because the destroyed nations' substance was dedicated to the LORD (Mic 4:13). **(3)** The word is used of the *accursed* (i.e., devoted) **(3a)** city and substance of Jericho (Josh 6:18), and **(3b)** Achan's conduct (Josh 22:20). Things which are cursed are **(3c)** the gold and silver from idols (Deut 7:26), **(3d)** the Edomites

(Is 34:5), **(3e)** Jacob (Is 43:28). *Charam* is rendered **(4)** destroy with reference to **(4a)** the Canaanites by Israel, **(4b)** the nations by Nebuchadnezzar (2 Kin 19:11), **(4c)** Egypt by the Lord (Is 11:15), and

(4d) Judah by Babylon (Jer 25:9). With regard to exterminating the Canaanites, note: **First,** it was not to accomplish personal revenge, for Israel had no grudge against Canaan; the people had to be almost goaded into the land. **Second,** it was not for plunder for all plunder was devoted to God; hence, *Charam,* accursed. **Third,** it was not to gratify thirst for military glory for the Hebrews, the smallest of nations, and were told beforehand their success would be in God's strength, not theirs. **Fourth,** it was not as a reward for merit; they were a rebellious and stiffnecked people, and would have perished in the wilderness had not God remembered His holy covenant. **Fifth,** the extermination of the Canaanites was to be a security against idolatry and demoralization on the part of Israel. **Last,** these nations had filled up the measure of their iniquity and the Israelites in destroying them were acting magisterially as God's agents. See: TWOT—744, 745; BDB—355c, 356d.

2764. חֵרֶם {38x} **chêrem**, *khay'-rem;* or (Zec 14:11)

חֶרֶם **cherem**, *kheh'-rem;* from 2763; phys. (as *shutting in*) a *net* (either lit. or fig.); usually a *doomed* object; abstr. *extermination:*—net {9x}, accursed thing {9x}, accursed {4x}, curse {4x}, cursed thing {3x}, devoted {3x}, destruction {2x}, devoted thing {2x}, dedicated thing {1x}, destroyed {1x}. See: TWOT—744a, 745a; BDB—356a, 357a.

2765. חֳרֵם {1x} **Chŏrêm**, *khor-ame';* from 2763; *devoted; Chorem,* a place in Pal.:—Horem {1x}. See: BDB—356c.

2766. חָרִם {11x} **Chârîm**, *khaw-reem';* from 2763; *snub-nosed; Charim,* an Isr.:—Harim {11x}. See: BDB—356c.

2767. חָרְמָה {9x} **Chormâh**, *khor-maw';* from 2763; *devoted; Chormah,* a place in Pal.:—Hormah {9x}. See: BDB—356c.

2768. חֶרְמוֹן {13x} **Chermôwn**, *kher-mone';* from 2763; *abrupt; Chermon,* a mount of Pal.:—Hermon {13x}. See: TWOT—744b; BDB—356d.

2769. חֶרְמוֹנִים {1x} **Chermôwnîym**, *kher-mo-neem';* plur. of 2768; *Hermons,* i.e. its peaks:—the Hermonites {1x}. See: BDB—356d.

2770. חֶרְמֵשׁ {2x} **chermêsh**, *kher-mashe';* from 2763; a *sickle* (as *cutting*):—sickle {2x}. See: TWOT—746; BDB—357a.

2771. חָרָן {12x} **Chârân**, *kaw-rawn';* from 2787; *parched; Charan,* the name of a man and also of a place:—Haran {12x}. See: TWOT—747; BDB—357a, 357b.

חָרֹן **chârôn**. See 2740.

2772. חֹרֹנִי {3x} **Chôrônîy**, *kho-ro-nee';* patrial from 2773; a *Choronite* or inhab. of Choronaim:—Horonite {3x}. See: BDB—357b.

2773. חֹרֹנַיִם {4x} **Chôrônayim**, *kho-ro-nah'-yim;* dual of a der. from 2356; *double cave-town; Choronajim,* a place in Moab:—Horonaim {4x}. See: BDB—357b.

2774. חַרְנֶפֶר {1x} **Charnepher**, *khar-neh'fer;* of uncert. der.; *Charnepher,* an Isr.:—Harnepher {1x}. See: BDB—357b.

2775. חֶרֶס {4x} **chereç**, *kheh'-res;* or (with a directive enclitic)

חַרְסָה **charçâh**, *khar'-saw;* from an unused root mean. to *scrape;* the *itch;* also [perh. from the mediating idea of 2777] the *sun:*—itch {1x}, sun {3x}. See: TWOT—759b, 748a; BDB—357b, 357c, 360b.

2776. חֶרֶס {1x} **Chereç**, *kheh'-res;* the same as 2775; *shining; Cheres,* a mountain in Pal.:—Heres {1x}. See: BDB—357c, 751c.

2777. חַרְסוּת {1x} **charçûwth**, *khar-sooth';* from 2775 (appar. in the sense of a red *tile* used for scraping); a *potsherd,* i.e. (by impl.) a *pottery;* the name of a gate at Jerusalem:—east {1x}. Syn.: 4217, 6921, 6924, 6926. See: TWOT—759c; BDB—357c, 360b.

2778. חָרַף {41x} **châraph**, *khaw-raf';* a prim. root; to *pull* off, i.e. (by impl.) to *expose* (as by *stripping*); spec. to *betroth* (as if a surrender); fig. to carp at, i.e. *defame;* denom. (from 2779) to spend the *winter:*—reproach {27x}, defy {8x}, betrothed {1x}, blasphemed {1x}, jeoparded {1x}, rail {1x}, upbraid {1x}, winter {1x}.

Charaph means "to say sharp things, reproach." **(1)** In Hebrew the verb refers to a manner of speech, i.e., to reproach someone. **(2)** Ps 42:10: "As with a sword in my bones, mine enemies reproach me; while they say daily unto me, Where is thy God?" See: TWOT—749, 750, 751; BDB—357c, 358b.

2779. חֹרֶף {7x} **chôreph**, *kho'-ref;* from 2778; prop. the *crop* gathered, i.e. (by impl.) the *autumn* (and winter) season; fig. *ripeness* of age:—winter {4x}, youth {1x}, cold {1x}, winterhouse + 1004 {1x}. See: TWOT—750a; BDB—358a.

2780. חָרֵף {1x} **Chârêph**, *khaw-rafe';* from 2778; *reproachful; Chareph,* an Isr.:—Hareph {1x}. See: BDB—358b.

2781. חֶרְפָּה {73x} **cherpâh**, *kher-paw';* from 2778; *contumely, disgrace,* the *pudenda:*—reproach {67x}, shame {3x}, rebuke {2x}, reproachfully {1x}.

Cherpah means "reproach." **(1)** It is rare in the Pentateuch and in the historical books. **(1a)** The noun appears most frequently in the Book of Psalms, in the major prophets, and in Daniel. **(1b)** The first occurrence is in Gen 30:23: "And she conceived, and bare a son; and said, God hath taken away my reproach." **(2)** "Reproach" denotes the state in which one finds himself. **(2a)** The unmarried woman (Is 4:1) or the woman without children (Gen 30:23) carried a sense of disgrace in a society where marriage and fertility were highly spoken of. **(2b)** The destruction of Jerusalem and the Exile brought Judah to the state of "reproach": "O Lord, according to all thy righteousness, I beseech thee, let thine anger and thy fury be turned away from thy city Jerusalem, thy holy mountain: because for our sins, and for the iniquities of our fathers, Jerusalem and thy people are become a reproach to all that are about us" (Dan 9:16). **(3)** The disgrace found in a person or a nation became the occasion for taunting the oppressed. **(3a)** The disgraced received abuse by the words spoken against them and by the rumors which were spread about them.

(3b) Whatever the occasion of the disgrace was whether defeat in battle, exile, or enmity, the psalmist prayed for deliverance from the "reproach": "Remove from me reproach and contempt; for I have kept thy testimonies" (Ps 119:22—see context; cf. Ps 109:25). **(3c)** The verbal abuse that could be heaped upon the unfortunate is best evidenced by the synonyms found with *cherpah* (2781) in Jer 24:9: "And I will deliver them to be removed into all the kingdoms of the earth for their hurt, to be a reproach and a proverb, a taunt and a curse, in all places whither I shall drive them." **(3d)** Several prophets predicted that Israel's judgment was partly to be experienced by the humiliating "reproach" of the nations: "And I will persecute them with the sword, with the famine, and with the pestilence, and will deliver them to be removed to all the kingdoms of the earth, to be a curse, and an astonishment, and a hissing, and a reproach among all the nations whither I have driven them" (Jer 29:18; cf. Eze 5:14). **(4)** However, the Lord graciously promised to remove the "reproach" at the accomplishment of His purpose: "He will swallow up death in victory; and the Lord GOD will wipe away tears from off all faces; and the rebuke of his people shall he take away from off all the earth . . ." (Is 25:8). See: TWOT—749a; BDB—357d.

2782. חָרַץ {12x} **chârats**, *khaw-rats';* a prim. root; prop. to *point* sharply, i.e. (lit.) to *wound;* fig. to *be alert,* to *decide:*—determined {6x}, move {2x}, decide {1x}, bestir {1x}, maim {1x}, decreed {1x}. See: TWOT—752; 358c.

2783. חֲרַץ {1x} **chărats** (Aram.), *khar-ats';* from a root corresp. to 2782 in the sense of *vigor;* the *loin* (as the seat of strength):—loin {1x}. See: TWOT—2744; BDB—1093d.

חָרֻץ **chârûts**. See 2742.

2784. חַרְצֻבָּה {2x} **chartsubbâh**, *khar-tsoob-baw';* of uncert. der.; a *fetter;* fig. a *pain:*—band {2x}. See: TWOT—754a; BDB—359a.

חָרִיץ **chârîts**. See 2757.

2785. חַרְצַן {1x} **chartsan**, *khar-tsan';* from 2782; a *sour* grape (as *sharp* in taste):—kernel {1x}. See: TWOT—752d; BDB—359a, 359b.

2786. חָרַק {5x} **châraq**, *khaw-rak';* a prim. root; to *grate* the teeth:—gnash {5x}. See: TWOT—755; BDB—359b.

2787. חָרַר {11x} **chârar**, *khaw-rar';* a prim. root; to *glow,* i.e. lit. (to *melt, burn, dry* up) or fig. (to *show* or *incite passion*):—burn {8x}, dried {1x}, angry {1x}, kindle {1x}. See: TWOT—756; BDB—359b.

2788. חָרֵר {1x} **chârêr**, *khaw-rare';* from 2787; *arid:*—parched place {1x}. See: TWOT—756a; BDB—359c.

2789. חֶרֶשׂ {17x} **cheres**, *kheh'-res;* a collat. form mediating between 2775 and 2791; a piece of *pottery:*—earthen {8x}, potsherd {5x}, sherd {2x}, stone {1x}, earth {1x}. See: TWOT—759a; BDB—360a.

2790. חָרַשׁ {73x} **chârash**, *khaw-rash';* a prim. root; to *scratch,* i.e. (by impl.) to *engrave, plow;* hence, (from the use of tools) to *fabricate* (of any material); fig. to *devise* (in a bad sense); hence, (from the idea of secrecy) to *be silent,* to *let alone;* hence, (by impl.) to *be deaf* (as an accompaniment of dumbness):—peace {26x}, plow {13x}, devise {5x}, keep . . . silence {5x}, hold . . . tongue {4x}, altogether {3x}, plowman {2x}, cease {1x}, conceal {1x}, deaf {1x}, to ear {1x}, graven {1x}, imagine {1x}, leave off speaking {1x}, hold peace {1x}, be quiet {1x}, rest {1x}, practise secretly {1x}, be silent {1x}, speak not a word {1x}, be still {1x}, worker {1x}.

Charash, as a verb, means "to plow, engrave, work in metals." **(1)** A fitting word for the agricultural nature of Israelite culture, *charash* is frequently used of "plowing" a field, usually with animals such as oxen (1 Kin 19:19). **(2)** The imagery of cutting up or tearing up a field with a plow easily lent itself to the figurative use of the word to mean mistreatment by others: "The plowers plowed upon my back: they made long their furrows" (Ps 129:3). **(3)** The word is used to express the plotting of evil against a friend in Prov 3:29: "Devise not evil against thy neighbor, seeing he dwelleth securely by thee [literally, "do not plow evil"]."

(4) The use of *charash* in the sense of "working or engraving" metals is not used in the Old Testament as much as it might have been if Israel had been as given to such craftsmanship as her neighbors, or perhaps because of the commandment against images (Ex 20:4). **(4a)** The word is used in 1 Kin 7:14: ". . . His father was a man of Tyre, a worker in brass [literally, 'a man who works in brass']. . . . " **(4b)** The first occurrence of *charash* is in Gen 4:22 where it is used of the "artificer in brass and iron." **(5)** The figurative use of "engraving" is vividly seen in the expression describing the extent of Israel's sin: "The sin of Judah is written with a pen of iron, and with the point of a diamond: it is graven upon the table of their heart . . ." (Jer 17:1). See: TWOT—760, 761; BDB—360b, 361a.

2791. חֶרֶשׁ {4x} **cheresh**, *kheh'-resh;* from 2790; magical *craft;* also *silence:*—craftsmen {2x}, artificer {1x}, secretly {1x}. See: TWOT—761b, 763a; BDB—361c, 361d.

2792. חֶרֶשׁ {1x} **Cheresh**, *kheh'-resh;* the same as 2791; *Cheresh,* a Levite:—Heresh {1x}. See: BDB—361d.

2793. חֹרֶשׁ {7x} **chôresh**, *kho'-resh;* from 2790; a *forest* (perh. as furnishing the material for fabric):—wood {4x}, forest {1x}, bough {1x}, shroud {1x}. See: TWOT—762a; BDB—361c.

2794. חֹרֵשׁ {1x} **chôrêsh**, *kho-rashe';* act. part. of 2790; a *fabricator* or mechanic:—artificer {1x}. See: TWOT—763a; BDB—360c.

2795. חֵרֵשׁ {9x} **chêrêsh**, *khay-rashe';* from 2790; *deaf* (whether lit. or spir.):—deaf {9x}. See: TWOT—761a; BDB—361b.

2796. חָרָשׁ {33x} **chârâsh**, *khaw-rawsh';* from 2790; a *fabricator* or any material:—carpenter {11x}, workman {6x}, craftsman {4x}, engraver {3x}, artificers {2x}, smith {2x}, makers {1x}, skilful {1x}, smith + 1270 {1x}, workers {1x}, wrought {1x}.

Charash, as a noun, means "engraver; artificer." **(1)** The prophets denounced the craftsmanship of these workers in metals when they made images (Is 40:20; Hos 8:6). **(2)** A more positive approach to the word is conveyed in 1 Chr 29:5: "The gold for things of gold . . . and for all manner of work to be made by the hands of artificers. And who then is willing to consecrate his service this day unto the Lord?" See: TWOT—760a; BDB—360d, 361d.

2797. חַרְשָׁא {2x} **Charshâ'**, *khar-shaw';* from 2792; *magician; Charsha,* one of the Nethinim:—Harsha {2x}. See: BDB—361d.

2798. חֲרָשִׁים {2x} **Chărâshîym**, *khar-aw-sheem';* plur. of 2796; *mechanics,* the name of a valley in Jerusalem:—Charashim {1x}, craftsmen {1x}. See: BDB—161b, 360d.

2799. חֲרֹשֶׁת {4x} **chărôsheth**, *khar-o'-sheth;* from 2790; mechanical *work:*—carving {2x}, cutting {2x}. See: TWOT—760b; BDB—360d.

2800. חֲרֹשֶׁת {3x} **Chărôsheth**, *khar-o'-sheth;* the same as 2799; *Charosheth,* a place in Pal.:—Harosheth {3x}. See: BDB—360d, 361d.

2801. חָרַת {1x} **chârath**, *khaw-rath';* a prim. root; to *engrave:*—graven {1x}. See: TWOT—764; BDB—362a.

2802. חֶרֶת {1x} **Chereth**, *kheh'-reth;* from 2801 [but equiv. to 2793]; *forest; Chereth,* a thicket in Pal.:—Hereth {1x}. See: BDB—362a.

2803. חָשַׁב {124x} **châshab**, *khaw-shab';* a prim. root; prop. to *plait* or interpenetrate, i.e. (lit.) to *weave* or (gen.) to *fabricate;* fig. to *plot* or contrive (usually in a malicious sense); hence, (from the ment. effort) to *think, regard, value, compute:*—count {23x}, devise {22x}, think {18x}, imagine {9x}, cunning {8x}, reckon {7x}, purpose {6x}, esteem {6x}, account {5x}, impute {4x}, forecast {2x}, regard {2x}, workman {2x}, conceived {1x}, misc. {9x} = consider, find out, hold, invent, be like, mean.

(1) Generally, this root signifies a mental process whereby some course is planned or conceived. It means "to think, account, reckon, devise, plan." **(2)** The first time it is found is in Gen 15:6 "And he believed in the LORD; and he counted it to him for righteousness." Here the term has the meaning of "to be imputed." **(3)** Frequently used in the ordinary sense of "thinking," or the normal thought processes (Is 10:7; 53:4; Mal 3:16), it **(4)** also is used in the sense of "devising evil plans" (Gen 50:20; Jer 48:2). **(5)** The word refers to craftsmen "inventing" instruments of music, artistic objects, and weapons of war (Ex 31:4; 2 Chr 26:15; Amos 6:5). See: TWOT—767; BDB—362d, 1093d.

2804. חֲשַׁב {1x} **chăshab** (Aram.), *khash-ab';* corresp. to 2803; to *regard:*—repute {1x}. See: TWOT—2745; BDB—1093d.

2805. חֵשֶׁב {8x} **chêsheb**, *khay'-sheb;* from 2803; a *belt* or strap (as being interlaced):—curious girdle {8x}. See: TWOT—2745; BDB—363d.

2806. חַשְׁבַּדָּנָה {1x} **Chashbaddânâh**, *khash-bad-daw'-naw;* from 2803 and 1777; *considerate judge; Chasbaddanah,* an Isr.:—Hasbadana {1x}. See: TWOT—2745; BDB—364c.

2807. חֲשֻׁבָה {1x} **Chăshûbâh**, *khash-oo-baw';* from 2803; *estimation; Cashubah,* an Isr.:—Hashubah {1x}. See: BDB—363d.

2808. חֶשְׁבּוֹן {3x} **cheshbôwn**, *khesh-bone';* from 2803; prop. *contrivance;* by impl. *intelligence:*—account {1x}, device {1x}, reason {1x}. See: TWOT—767b; BDB—363d.

2809. חֶשְׁבּוֹן {38x} **Cheshbôwn**, *khesh-bone';* the same as 2808; *Cheshbon,* a place E. of the Jordan:—Heshbon {38x}. See: BDB—363d.

2810. חִשָּׁבוֹן {2x} **chishshâbôwn**, *khish-shaw-bone';* from 2803; a *contrivance,* i.e. actual (a warlike *machine*) or ment. (a *machination*):—engine {1x}, invention {1x}. See: TWOT—767c; BDB—364a.

2811. חֲשַׁבְיָה {15x} **Chăshabyâh**, *khash-ab-yaw';* or

חֲשַׁבְיָהוּ **Chăshabyâhûw**, *khash-ab-yaw'-hoo;* from 2803 and 3050; *Jah has regarded; Chashabjah,* the name of nine Isr.:—Hashabiah {15x}. See: BDB—364a.

2812. חֲשַׁבְנָה {1x} **Chăshabnâh**, *khash-ab-naw';* fem. of 2808; *inventiveness; Chashnah,* an Isr.:—Hashabnah {1x}. See: BDB—364b.

2813. חֲשַׁבְנְיָה {2x} **Chăshabnᵉyâh**, *khash-ab-neh-yaw';* from 2808 and 3050; *thought of Jah; Chashabnejah,* the name of two Isr.:—Hashabniah {2x}. See: BDB—364b.

2814. חָשָׁה {16x} **châshâh**, *khaw-shaw';* a prim. root; to *hush* or keep quiet:—hold . . . peace {9x}, still {4x}, silence {2x}, silent {1x}. See: TWOT—768; BDB—364c.

2815. חַשּׁוּב {5x} **Chashshûwb**, *khash-shoob';* from 2803; *intelligent; Chashshub,* the name of two or three Isr.:—Hashub {4x}, Hasshub {1x}. See: BDB—363d.

2816. חֲשׁוֹךְ {1x} **chăshôwk** (Aram.), *khash-oke';* from a root corresp. to 2821; the *dark:*—darkness {1x}. See: TWOT—2747; BDB—1094a.

2817. חֲשׂוּפָא {2x} **Chăsûwphâ'**, *khas-oo-faw';* or

חֲשֻׂפָא **Chăsûphâ'**, *khas-oo-faw';* from 2834; *nakedness; Chasupha,* one of the Nethinim:—Hashupha {1x}, Hasupha {1x}. See: BDB—362d.

חָשׁוּק **châshûwq**. See 2838.

2818. חֲשַׁח {2x} **chăshach** (Aram.), *khash-akh';* a collat. root to one corresp. to 2363 in the sense of *readiness;* to *be necessary* (from the idea of *convenience*) or (tran.) to *need:*—careful {1x}, have need of {1x}. See: TWOT—2746; BDB—1093d.

2819. חַשְׁחוּת {1x} **chashchûwth** (Aram.), *khash-khooth';* from a root corresp. to 2818; *necessity:*—be needful {1x}. See: TWOT—2746b; BDB—1093d.

חֲשֵׁיכָה **chăshêykâh**. See 2825.

חֻשִׁים **Chûshîym**. See 2366.

2820. חָשַׂךְ {26x} **châsak**, *khaw-sak';* a prim. root; to *restrain* or (reflex.) *refrain;* by impl. to *refuse, spare, preserve;* also (by interch. with 2821) to *observe:*—spare {8x}, keep back {3x}, withhold {3x}, refrain {3x}, asswage {1x}, reserved {2x}, hold back {1x}, variant {1x}, forbear {1x}, hindereth {1x}, kept {1x}, punished {1x}, withholdeth {1x}. See: TWOT—765; BDB—362a.

2821. חָשַׁךְ {19x} **châshak**, *khaw-shak';* a prim. root; to *be dark* (as *withholding* light); tran. to *darken:*—darken {9x}, dark {5x}, blacker {1x}, darkness {1x}, dim {1x}, hideth {1x}, variant {1x}. See: TWOT—769; BDB—364d.

2822. חֹשֶׁךְ {80x} **chôshek**, *kho-shek';* from 2821; the *dark;* hence, (lit.) *darkness;* fig. *misery, destruction, death, ignorance, sorrow, wickedness:*—darkness {70x}, dark {7x}, obscurity {2x}, night {1x}. See: TWOT—769a; BDB—365a, 1094a.

2823. חָשֹׁךְ {1x} **châshôk**, *khaw-shoke';* from 2821; *dark* (fig. i.e. *obscure*):—mean {1x}. See: TWOT—769b; BDB—365b.

2824. חֶשְׁכָה {1x} **cheshkâh**, *khesh-kaw';* from 2821; *darkness:*—dark {1x}. See: BDB—365b.

2825. חֲשֵׁכָה {5x} **chăshêkâh**, *khash-ay-kaw';* or

חֲשֵׁיכָה **chăshêykâh**, *khash-ay-kaw';* from 2821; *darkness;* fig. *misery:*—darkness {1x}. See: TWOT—769c; BDB—365b.

2826. חָשַׁל {1x} **châshal**, *khaw-shal';* a prim. root; to *make* (intrans. *be*) *unsteady,* i.e. *weak:*—feeble {1x}. See: TWOT—770; BDB—365b.

2827. חֲשַׁל {1x} **chăshal** (Aram.), *khash-al';* a root corresp. to 2826; to *weaken,* i.e. *crush:*—subdue {1x}. See: TWOT—2748; BDB—1094a.

2828. חָשֻׁם {5x} **Châshûm**, *khaw-shoom';* from the same as 2831; *enriched; Chashum,* the name of two or three Isr.:—Hashum {5x}. See: BDB—365c.

חֻשָׁם **Chûshâm**. See 2367.

חֻשִׁים **Chûshîm**. See 2366.

2829. חֶשְׁמוֹן {1x} **Cheshmôwn**, *khesh-mone';* the same as 2831; *opulent; Cheshmon,* a place in Pal.:—Heshmon {1x}. See: BDB—365c.

2830. חַשְׁמַל {3x} **chashmal**, *khash-mal';* of uncert. der.; prob. *bronze* or polished spectrum metal:—amber {3x}. See: TWOT—770.1; BDB—365c.

2831. חַשְׁמַן {1x} **chashmân**, *khash-man';* from an unused root (prob. mean. *firm* or *capacious* in resources); appar. *wealthy:*—princes {1x}. See: TWOT—771; BDB—365c.

2832. חַשְׁמֹנָה {2x} **Chashmônâh**, *khash-mo-naw';* fem. of 2831; *fertile; Chasmonah,* a place in the Desert:—Hashmonah {2x}. See: BDB—365c.

2833. חֹשֶׁן {25x} **chôshen**, *kho'-shen;* from an unused root prob. mean. to *contain* or *sparkle;* perh. a *pocket* (as holding the Urim and Thummim), or *rich* (as containing gems), used only of the *gorget* of the high priest:—breastplate {25x}. See: TWOT—772a; BDB—365d.

2834. חָשַׂף {1x} **châsaph**, *khaw-saf';* a prim. root; to *strip* off, i.e. gen. to *make naked* (for exertion or in disgrace), to *drain* away or *bail* up (a liquid):—make bare {4x}, discover {2x}, uncover {2x}, take {1x}, clean {1x}, draw out {1x}. See: TWOT—766; BDB—362c, 362d.

2835. חָשִׂף {1x} **châsîph**, *khaw-seef';* from 2834; prop. *drawn off,* i.e. separated; hence, a small *company* (as divided from the rest):—little flocks {1x}. See: TWOT—766a; BDB—362c.

2836. חָשַׁק {11x} **châshaq**, *khaw-shak';* a prim. root; to *cling,* i.e. *join,* (fig.) to *love, delight* in; ellip. (or by interch. for 2820) to *deliver:*—desire {3x}, set his love {2x}, filleted {3x}, log {1x}, delight {1x}, in love {1x}. See: TWOT—773; BDB—365d, 366b.

2837. חֵשֶׁק {4x} **chêsheq**, *khay'-shek;* from 2836; *delight:*—desire {1x}, that {1x}, pleasure {1x}, desire + 2836 {1x}. See: TWOT—773a; BDB—366a.

2838. חָשֻׁק {8x} **châshûq**, *khaw-shook';* or

חָשׁוּק **châshûwq**, *khaw-shook';* pass. part. of 2836; *attached,* i.e. a fence-*rail* or rod connecting the posts or pillars:—fillet {8x}. See: TWOT—773b; BDB—366a.

2839. חִשֻּׁק {1x} **chishshûq**, *khish-shook';* from 2836; *conjoined,* i.e. a wheel-*spoke* or rod connecting the hub with the rim:—felloes {1x}. See: TWOT—773d; BDB—366b.

2840. חִשֻּׁר {1x} **chishshûr**, *khish-shoor';* from an unused root mean. to *bind* together; *combined,* i.e. the *nave* or hub of a wheel (as holding the spokes together):—spoke {1x}. See: TWOT—774b; BDB—366b.

2841. חַשְׁרָה {1x} **chashrâh**, *khash-raw';* from the same as 2840; prop. a *combination* or gathering, i.e. of watery *clouds:*—dark {1x}. See: TWOT—774a; BDB—366b.

חֲשֻׂפָא **Chăsûphâʼ**. See 2817.

2842. חָשַׁשׁ {2x} **châshash**, *khaw-shash';* by var. for 7179; dry *grass:*—chaff {2x}. See: TWOT—775a; BDB—366b.

2843. חֻשָׁתִי {5x} **Chûshâthîy**, *khoo-shaw-thee';* patron. from 2364; a *Chushathite* or desc. of Chushah:—Hushathite {5x}. See: TWOT—775a; 302a, 366c.

2844. חַת {4x} **chath**, *khath;* from 2865; concr. *crushed;* also *afraid;* abstr. *terror:*—broken {1x}, dismayed {1x}, dread {1x}, fear {1x}. See: TWOT—784a; BDB—366c, 369c.

2845. חֵת {14x} **Chêth**, *khayth;* from 2865; *terror; Cheth,* an aboriginal Canaanite:—Heth {14x}. See: TWOT—776; BDB—366c, 370c.

2846. חָתָה {4x} **châthâh**, *khaw-thaw';* a prim. root; to lay *hold* of; espec. to *pick* up fire:—heap {1x}, take {1x}, take away {1x}. See: TWOT—777; BDB—367a.

2847. חִתָּה {1x} **chittâh**, *khit-taw';* from 2865; *fear:*—terror {1x}. See: TWOT—784d; BDB—366c, 367b, 369d.

2848. חִתּוּל {1x} **chittûwl**, *khit-tool';* from 2853; *swathed,* i.e. a *bandage:*—roller {1x}. See: TWOT—779b; BDB—367c.

2849. חַתְחַת {1x} **chathchath**, *khath-khath';* from 2844; *terror:*—fear {1x}. See: TWOT—784e; BDB—369d.

2850. חִתִּי {48x} **Chittîy**, *khit-tee';* patron. from 2845; a *Chittite,* or desc. of Cheth:—Hittite {26x}, Hittites {22x}. See: TWOT—776a; BDB—366c, 370c.

2851. חִתִּית {8x} **chittîyth**, *khit-teeth';* from 2865; *fear:*—terror {8x}. See: TWOT—784f; BDB—369d.

2852. חָתַךְ {1x} **châthak**, *khaw-thak';* a prim. root, prop. to *cut* off, i.e. (fig.) to *decree:*—determine {1x}. See: TWOT—778; BDB—367b.

2853. חָתַל {2x} **châthal**, *khaw-thal';* a prim. root; to *swathe:*—× at all {1x}, swaddle {1x}. See: TWOT—779; BDB—367c.

2854. חֲתֻלָּה {1x} **chăthullâh**, *khath-ool-law';* from 2853; a *swathing* cloth (fig.):—swaddling band {1x}. See: TWOT—779a; BDB—367c.

2855. חֶתְלֹן {2x} **Chethlôn**, *kheth-lone';* from 2853; *enswathed; Chethlon,* a place in Pal.:—Hethlon {2x}. See: BDB—367c.

2856. חָתַם {27x} **châtham**, *khaw-tham';* a prim. root; to *close* up; espec. to *seal:*—seal {18x}, seal up {6x}, marked {1x}, stopped {1x}, variant {1x}. See: TWOT—780; BDB—367c, 1094a.

2857. חֲתַם {1x} **chătham** (Aram.), *khath-am';* a root corresp. to 2856; to *seal.*—seal {1x}. See: TWOT—2749; BDB—1094a.

חֹתָם **chôthâm**. See 2368.

2858. חֹתֶמֶת {1x} **chôthemeth**, *kho-the-meth;* fem. act. part. of 2856; a *seal:*—signet {1x}. See: TWOT—780b; BDB—368b.

2859. חָתַן {33x} **châthan**, *khaw-than';* a prim. root; to *give* (a daughter) *away* in marriage; hence, (gen.) to *contract affinity* by marriage:—join in affinity {3x}, father-in-law {21x}, make marriages {3x}, mother-in-law {1x}, son in law {5x}. See: TWOT—781b; BDB—368c, 368d.

2860. חָתָן {20x} **châthân**, *khaw-thawn';* from 2859; a *relative* by marriage (espec. through the bride); fig. a *circumcised* child (as a species of relig. espousal):—son-in-law {10x}, bridegroom {8x}, husband {2x}. See: TWOT—781c; BDB—368c.

2861. חֲתֻנָּה {1x} **chăthunnâh**, *khath-oon-naw';* from 2859; a *wedding:*—espousal {1x}. See: TWOT—781d; BDB—368d.

2862. חָתַף {1x} **châthaph**, *khaw-thaf';* a prim. root; to *clutch:*—take away {1x}. See: TWOT—782; BDB—368d.

2863. חֶתֶף {1x} **chetheph**, *kheh'-thef;* from 2862; prop. *rapine;* fig. *robbery:*—prey {1x}. See: TWOT—782a; BDB—369a.

2864. חָתַר **châthar**, *khaw-thar';* a prim. root; to *force* a passage, as by burglary; fig. with oars:—dig {7x}, row {1x}. See: TWOT—783; BDB—369a.

2865. חָתַת {54x} **châthath**, *khaw-thath';* a prim. root; prop. to *prostrate;* hence, to *break* down, either (lit.) by violence, or (fig.) by confusion and fear:—dismayed {27x}, afraid {6x}, break in pieces {6x}, broken {3x}, break down {2x}, abolished {1x}, affrighted {1x}, amazed {1x}, chapt {1x}, confound {1x}, discouraged {1x}, go down {1x}, beaten down {1x}, scarest {1x}, terrify {1x}.

Chathath means "to be dismayed, shattered, broken, terrified." **(1)** It occurs for the first time in Deut. 1:21 as Moses challenged Israel: "Do not fear or be discouraged." **(1a)** As here, *chathath* is often used in parallelism with the Hebrew term for "fear" (cf. Deut 31:8; Josh 8:1; 1Sa 17:11). **(1b)** Similarly, *chathath* is frequently used in parallelism with "to be ashamed" (Is 20:5; Jer 8:9). **(2)** An interesting figurative use of the word is found in Jer 14:4, where the ground "is chapt", for there was no rain." **(3)** The meaning "to be shattered" is usually employed in a figurative sense, **(3a)** as with reference to the nations coming under God's judgment (Is 7:8; 30:31). **(3b)** The coming Messiah is to "shatter" or "break" the power of all His enemies (Is 9:4). See: TWOT—784; BDB—369a.

2866. חֲתַת {1x} **chăthath**, *khath-ath';* from 2865; *dismay:*—casting down {1x}. See: TWOT—784c; 369c.

2867. חֲתַת {1x} **Chăthath**, *khath-ath';* the same as 2866; *Chathath,* an Isr.:—Hathath {1x}. See: BDB—369d.

ט

2868. טְאֵב {1x} **tᵉʼêb** (Aram.), *teh-abe';* a prim. root; to *rejoice:*—be glad {1x}. See: TWOT—2750; BDB—1094a.

2869. טָב {2x} **ṭâb** (Aram.), *tawb;* from 2868; the same as 2896; *good:*—fine {1x}, good {1x}. See: TWOT—2750a; BDB—1094b.

2870. טָבְאֵל {2x} **Ṭâbᵉʼêl**, *taw-beh-ale';* from 2895 and 410; *pleasing* (to) *God; Tabeël,* the name of a Syrian and of a Persian:—Tabeal {1x}, Tabeel {1x}. See: TWOT—2750a; BDB—370b.

2871. טָבוּל {1x} **ṭâbûwl**, *taw-bool';* pass. part. of 2881; prop. *dyed,* i.e. a *turban* (prob. as of *colored* stuff):—dyed attire {1x}. See: TWOT—788a; BDB—371b.

2872. טַבּוּר {2x} **ṭabbûwr**, *tab-boor';* from an unused root mean. to *pile* up; prop. *accumulated;* i.e. (by impl.) a *summit:*—middle {1x}, midst {1x}. Syn.: 2677, 3820, 7130, 8432, 8484. See: TWOT—790a; BDB—371d.

2873. טָבַח {11x} **ṭâbach**, *taw-bakh';* a prim. root; to *slaughter* (animals or men):—kill {1x}, killed {3x}, make slaughter {1x}, slaughter {3x}, slain {1x}, slay {2x}. Syn.: 2026, 2076, 2491, 4191, 5221, 7819. See: TWOT—786; BDB—370b.

2874. טֶבַח {12x} **ṭebach**, *teh'-bakh;* from 2873; prop. something *slaughtered;* hence, a *beast* (or *meat,* as butchered); abstr. *butchery* (or concr. a place of slaughter):—slaughter {9x}, slay {1x}, sore {1x}, beast {1x}. See: TWOT—786a; BDB—370d.

2875. טֶבַח {1x} **Ṭebach**, *teh'-bakh;* the same as 2874; *massacre; Tebach,* the name of a Mesopotamian and of an Isr.:—Tebah {1x}. See: BDB—370d.

2876. טַבָּח {32x} **ṭabbâch**, *tab-bawkh';* from 2873; prop. a *butcher;* hence, a *lifeguardsman* (because acting as an executioner); also a *cook* (as usually slaughtering the animal for food):—cook {30x}, guard {2x}. See: TWOT—786c; BDB—371a, 1094b.

2877. טַבָּח {1x} **ṭabbâch** (Aram.), *tab-bawkh';* the same as 2876; a *lifeguardsman:*—guard {1x}. See: TWOT—2751; BDB—1094b.

2878. טִבְחָה {3x} **ṭibhâh**, *tib-khaw';* fem. of 2874 and mean. the same:—flesh {1x}, slaughter {2x}. See: TWOT—786b; BDB—370d.

2879. טַבָּחָה {1x} **ṭabbâchâh**, *tab-baw-khaw';* fem. of 2876; a female *cook:*—cook {1x}. See: TWOT—786d; BDB—367b, 371a.

2880. טִבְחַת {1x} **Ṭibchath**, *tib-khath';* from 2878; *slaughter; Tibchath,* a place in Syria:—Tibhath {1x}. See: BDB—371a.

2881. טָבַל {16x} **ṭâbal**, *taw-bal';* a prim. root; to *dip:*—dip {15x}, plunge {1x}. This word means "dipped": **(1)** Joseph's coat (Gen 37:31), **(2)** the priest's finger (Lev 4:6), **(3)** Ruth's morsel (Ruth 2:14), and **(4)** Hazael's cloth (2 Kin 8:15). See: TWOT—787, 788; BDB—371a.

2882. טְבַלְיָהוּ {1x} **Ṭᵉbalyâhûw**, *teb-al-yaw'-hoo;* from 2881 and 3050; *Jah has dipped; Tebaljah,* an Isr.:—Tebaliah {1x}. See: BDB—371b.

2883. טָבַע {10x} **ṭâbaʿ**, *taw-bah';* a prim. root; to *sink:*—sink {7x}, drown {1x}, settle {1x}, fasten {1x}. See: TWOT—789; BDB—371c.

2884. טַבָּעוֹת {2x} **Ṭabbâʿôwth**, *tab-baw-othe';* plur. of 2885; *rings; Tabbaoth,* one of the Nethinim:—Tabbaoth {2x}. See: BDB—371d.

2885. טַבַּעַת {49x} **ṭabbaʿath**, *tab-bah'-ath;* from 2883; prop. a *seal* (as *sunk* into the wax), i.e. *signet* (for sealing); hence, (gen.) a *ring* of any kind:—ring {49x}. See: TWOT—789a; BDB—371c.

2886. טַבְרִמּוֹן {1x} **Ṭabrimmôwn**, *tab-rim-mone';* from 2895 and 7417; *pleasing* (to) *Rimmon; Tabrimmon,* a Syrian:—Tabrimmon {1x}. See: BDB—372a.

2887. טֵבֵת {1x} **Ṭêbeth**, *tay'-beth;* prob. of for. der.; *Tebeth,* the tenth Heb. month:—*Tebeth* {1x}. See: BDB—372a.

2888. טַבַּת {1x} **Ṭabbath**, *tab-bath';* of uncert. der.; *Tabbath,* a place E. of the Jordan:—*Tabbath* {1x}. See: BDB—372a.

2889. טָהוֹר {94x} **ṭâhôwr**, *taw-hore';* or

טָהֹר **ṭâhôr**, *taw-hore';* from 2891; *pure* (in a physical, chemical, ceremonial or moral sense):—clean {50x}, pure {40x}, fair {2x}, purer {1x}, variant {1x}.

Tahor, as an adjective, means "clean; pure." **(1)** The word denotes the absence of impurity, filthiness, defilement, or imperfection. **(2)** It is applied concretely to substances that are genuine or unadulterated as well as describing an unstained condition of a spiritual or ceremonial nature. **(3)** Gold is a material frequently said to be free of baser ingredients. **(3a)** Thus the ark of the covenant, the incense altar, and the porch of the temple were "overlaid with pure gold" (Ex 25:11; 37:11, 26; 2 Chr 3:4). **(3b)** Some of the furnishings and utensils in the temple—such as the mercy seat, the lampstand, the dishes, pans, bowls, jars, snuffers, trays—were of "pure gold" (Ex 37:6, 16–24). **(3c)** The high priest's vestment included "two chains of pure gold" and "a plate of pure gold" (Ex 28:14, 22, 36).

(4) God demands that His people have spiritual and moral purity, unsullied by sin. **(4a)** Anyone not clean of sin is subject to divine rejection and punishment. **(4b)** This contamination is never outgrown or overcome. **(4c)** Because sin pollutes one generation after another, Job asks: "Who can bring a clean thing out of an unclean?" (Job 14:4). **(4d)** All outward appearances to the contrary, it cannot be said that there is "one event . . . to the clean, and to the unclean" (Eccl 9:2). **(5)** Hope is available even to the chief of sinners, because any man can entreat the mercy of God and say: "Create in me a clean heart, O God; and renew a right spirit within me" (Ps 51:10). **(6)** In sharp contrast with mankind's polluted nature and actions, "the words of the LORD are pure words . . ." (Ps 12:6). The Lord is "of purer eyes than to behold evil" (Hab 1:13). **(7)** "Clean" most frequently describes the purity maintained by avoiding contact with other human beings, abstaining from eating animals, and using things that are declared ceremonially clean. **(8)** Conversely, cleansing results if ritual procedures symbolizing the removal of contamination are observed.

(9) The people of the old covenant were told that "he that toucheth the dead body of any man shall be unclean seven days" (Num 19:11). **(9a)** A priest was not to defile himself "for the dead among his people" except "for his kin, that is near unto him" (Lev 21:1–2). **(9b)** This relaxation of the rule was even denied the high priest and a Nazarite during "all the days that he separateth himself unto the LORD" (Num 6:6ff.). **(10)** Cleansing rituals emphasized the fact that the people were conceived and born in sin. **(10a)** Though conception and birth were not branded immoral (just as dying itself was not sinful), a woman who had borne a child remained unclean until she submitted to the proper purification rites (Lev 12). **(10b)** Chapter 15 of Leviticus prescribes ceremonial cleansing for a woman having her menstrual flow, for a man having seminal emissions, and for "the woman also with whom man shall lie with seed of copulation" (Lev 15:18). **(11)** To be ceremonially "clean," **(11a)** the Israelite also had to abstain from eating certain animals and even from touching them (Lev 11; Deut 14:3–21). **(11b)** After the Israelites settled in the Promised Land, some modifications were made in the regulations (Deut 12:15, 22; 15:22).

(12) Purification rites frequently involved the use of water. **(12a)** The person to be cleansed was required to wash himself and his clothes (Lev 15:27). **(12b)** Water was sprinkled on the individual, on his tent, and on all its furnishings: "And a clean person shall take hyssop, and dip it in the water, and sprinkle it upon the tent, and upon all the vessels, and upon the persons that were there, and upon him that touched a bone, or the slain, or one dead, or a grave" (Num 19:18). **(13)** Sometimes the person being cleansed also had to change garments (Lev 6:11). **(14)** However, the rites were not meritorious deeds, **(14a)** earning God's favor and forgiveness. **(14b)** Nor did the ceremonies serve their intended purpose if performed mechanically. **(14c)** Unless the rites expressed a person's contrite and sincere desire to be cleansed from the defilement of sin, they were an abomination to God and only aggravated a person's guilt. **(15)** Anyone who appeared before Him in ritual and ceremony with "hands . . . full of blood" (Is 1:15) and did not plead for cleansing of his crimes was judged to be as wicked as the people of Sodom and Gomorrah. **(16)** Zion's hope lay in this cleansing by means of an offering: "And they shall bring all your brethren for an offering unto the LORD out of all nations upon horses . . . as the children of Israel bring an offering in a clean vessel into the house of the LORD" (Is 66:20). See: TWOT—792d; BDB—373a.

2890. טְהוֹר {2x} **tᵉhôwr**, *teh-hore';* from 2891; *purity:*—pureness {2x}. See: TWOT—792b; BDB—373a, 779c.

2891. טָהֵר {94x} **ṭâhêr**, *taw-hare';* a prim. root; prop. to *be bright;* i.e. (by impl.) to *be pure* (phys. *sound, clear, unadulterated;* Levit. *uncontaminated;* mor. *innocent* or *holy*):—clean {80x}, purify {6x}, purge {5x}, pure {2x}, purifier {1x}.

Taher, means "to be clean, pure." **(1)** Since the fall of Adam and Eve, none of their offspring is clean in the sight of the holy God: **(1a)** "Who can say, I have made my heart clean, I am pure from my sin?" (Prov 20:9). **(1b)** Reminding Job that protestations of innocence are of no avail, Eliphaz asked: "Shall mortal man be more just than God? Shall a man be more pure than his Maker?" (Job 4:17). **(2)** There is hope, however, because God promised penitent Israel: **(2a)** "And I will cleanse them from all their iniquity, whereby they have sinned against me . . ." (Jer 33:8). **(2b)** He said: ". . . I will save them out of all their dwelling places, wherein they have sinned, and will cleanse them: so they shall be my people, and I will be their God" (Eze 37:23).

(3) The baleful effect of sin was recognized when a person contracted the dread disease of leprosy. After the priest diagnosed the disease, he could declare a person "clean" only after cleansing ceremonies had been performed: ". . . And he shall wash his clothes, also he shall wash his flesh in water, and he shall be clean" (Lev 14:9). **(4)** God required that His people observe purification rites when they came into His presence for worship. **(4a)** On the Day of Atonement, for example, prescribed ceremonies were performed to "cleanse" the altar from "the uncleanness of the children of Israel" and to "hallow it" (Lev 16:17–19; cf. Ex 29:36ff.). **(4b)** The priests were to be purified before they performed their sacred tasks. Moses was directed to "take the Levites . . . and cleanse them" (Num 8:6; cf. Lev 8:5–13).

(5) After they had been held captive in the unclean land of Babylon, ". . . the priests and the Levites purified themselves, and purified the people, and the gates, and the wall [of the rebuilt city of Jerusalem]" (Neh 12:30). **(6)** Cleansing might be achieved by physically removing the objects of defilement. During the reform of King Hezekiah, "the priests went into the inner part of the house of the LORD, to cleanse it, and brought out all the uncleanness that they found in the temple of the LORD . . ." (2 Chr 29:16). **(7)** Some rites required blood as the purifying agent: "And he shall sprinkle of the blood upon it [the altar] with his finger seven times, and cleanse it, and hallow it from the uncleanness of the children of Israel" (Lev 16:19). **(8)** Sacrifices were offered to make atonement for a mother after childbirth: ". . . she shall bring . . . the one for the burnt offering, and the other for a sin offering: and the priest shall make an atonement for her, and she shall be clean" (Lev 12:8). See: TWOT—792; BDB—372a.

2892. טֹהַר {4x} **ṭôhar**, *to'-har;* from 2891; lit. *brightness;* ceremonial *purification:*—clearness {1x}, glory {1x}, purifying {2x}. See: TWOT—792a; BDB—372d.

2893. טָהֳרָה {13x} **ṭohŏrâh**, *toh-or-aw';* fem. of 2892; ceremonial *purification;* moral *purity:*—× is cleansed {1x}, cleansing {7x}, purification {2x}, purifying {3x}. See: TWOT—792c; BDB—372d.

2894. טוּא {1x} **ṭûwʼ**, *too;* a prim. root; to *sweep away:*—sweep {1x}. See: TWOT—785; BDB—370a.

2895. טוֹב {33x} **ṭowb**, *tobe;* a prim. root, to *be* (tran. *do* or *make*) *good* (or *well*) in the widest sense:—well {10x}, good {9x}, please {6x}, goodly {2x}, better {2x}, cheer {1x}, comely {1x}, do {1x}, pleased + 5869 {1x}.

Towb means "to be joyful, glad, pleasant, lovely, appropriate, becoming, good, precious." Job 13:9 is one example of the word's meaning, "to be good": "Is it good that he should search you out?" See: TWOT—793; BDB—373b, 405c, 1094a.

2896. טוֹב {559x} **ṭôwb**, *tobe;* from 2895; *good* (as an adj.) in the widest sense; used likewise as a noun, both in the masc. and the fem., the sing. and the plur. (*good*, a *good* or *good* thing, a *good* man or woman; the *good*, *goods* or *good* things, *good* men or women), also as an adv. (*well*):—good {361x}, better {72x}, well {20x}, goodness {16x}, goodly {9x}, best {8x}, merry {7x}, fair {7x}, prosperity {6x}, precious {4x}, fine {3x}, wealth {3x}, beautiful {2x}, fairer {2x}, favour {2x}, glad {2x}, misc. {35x} = bountiful, cheerful, at ease, graciously, joyful, kindly, kindness, liketh (best), loving, × most, pleasant, + pleaseth, pleasure, ready, sweet, welfare.

Towb (2896), means "good; favorable; festive; pleasing; pleasant; well; better; right; best." **(1)** This adjective denotes "good" in every sense of that word. **(1a)** For example, *towb* is used in the sense "pleasant" or "delightful": "And he saw that [a resting place] was good, and the land that it was pleasant; and bowed his shoulder to bear [burdens] . . ." (Gen 49:15). **(1b)** An extension of this sense appears in Gen 40:16, where *towb* means "favorable" or "in one's favor": "When the chief baker saw that the interpretation was good, he said unto Joseph. . . ." **(1c)** In 1 Sa 25:8, the emphasis is on the nuance "delightful" or "festal": ". . . Let the young men find favor in thine eyes: for we come in a good day. . . ." **(2)** God is described as One who is "good," or One who gives "delight" and "pleasure": "But it is good for me to draw near to God: I have put my trust in the Lord GOD, that I may declare all thy works" (Ps 73:28).

(3) In 1 Sa 29:6, this word describes human activities: ". . . As the LORD liveth, thou hast been upright, and thy going out and thy coming in with me in the [army] is good in my sight. . . ." **(4)** *Towb* can be applied to scenic beauty, as in 2 Kin 2:19: "Behold, I pray thee, the situation of this city is pleasant, as my lord seeth: but the water is naught, and the ground barren." **(5)** Second Chr 12:12 employs a related nuance when it applies the word to the conditions in Judah under King Rehoboam, after he humbled himself before God: ". . . Things went well." **(6)** *Towb* often qualifies a common object or activity. **(6a)** When the word is used in this sense, no ethical overtones are intended. **(6b)** In 1 Sa 19:4, *towb* describes the way Jonathan spoke about David: "And Jonathan spake good of David unto Saul his father, and said unto him, Let not the king sin against his servant, against David; because he hath not sinned against thee, and because his works have been [toward thee] very good."

(7) First Sa 25:15 characterizes a people as "friendly" or "useful": "But the men were very good unto us, and we were not hurt, neither missed we any thing, as long as we were conversant with them, when we were in the fields. . . ." **(8)** Often this word bears an even stronger emphasis, as in 1 Kin 12:7, where the "good word" is not only friendly but eases the life of one's servants. God's "good word" promises life in the face of oppression and uncertainty: ". . . There hath not failed one word of all his good promise, which he promised by the hand of Moses his servant" (1 Kin 8:56). **(9)** *Towb* often characterizes a statement as an important assertion for salvation and prosperity (real or imagined): "Is not this the word that we did tell thee in Egypt, saying, Let us alone, that we may serve the Egyptians? For it had been better for us to serve the Egyptians, than that we should die in the wilderness" (Ex 14:12). **(10)** God judged that man's circumstance without a wife or helpmeet was not "good" (Gen 2:18).

(11) Elsewhere *towb* is applied to an evaluation of one's well-being or of the well-being of a situation or thing. "And God saw the light, that it was good: and God divided the light from the darkness" (Gen 1:4—the first occurrence). **(12)** *Towb* is used to describe land and agriculture: "And I am come down to deliver them out of the [power] of the Egyptians, and to bring them up out of that land unto a good [fertile] land and a large, unto a land flowing with milk and honey . . ." (Ex 3:8). **(12a)** This suggests its potential of supporting life (Deut 11:17). **(12b)** Thus the expression "the good land" is a comment about not only its existing, but its potential, productivity. **(12c)** In such contexts the land is viewed as one aspect of the blessings of salvation promised by God; thus the Lord did not permit Moses to cross the Jordan and enter the land which His people were to inherit (Deut 3:26–28). **(12d)** This aspect of the "good land" includes overtones of its fruitfulness and "pleasantness": "And he will take your fields, and your vineyards, and your oliveyards, even the best of them . . ." (1 Sa 8:14).

(13) *Towb* is used to describe men or women. **(13a)** Sometimes it is used of an "elite corps" of people: "And he will take your menservants, and your maidservants, and your goodliest young men, and your asses . . ." (1 Sa 8:16). **(13b)** In 2 Sa 18:27, Ahimaaz is described as a "good" man because he comes with "good" military news. **(14)** In 1 Sa 15:28, the word has ethical overtones: "The LORD hath rent the kingdom of Israel from thee this day, and hath given it to a neighbor of thine, that is better than thou" (cf. 1 Kin 2:32). **(15)** In other passages, *towb* describes physical appearance: "And the damsel was very fair to look upon [literally, "good of appearance"] . . ." (Gen 24:16). **(16)** When applied to one's heart, the word describes "well-being" rather than ethical status. Therefore, the parallel idea is "joyous and happy": ". . . And they . . . went unto their tents joyful and glad of heart for all the goodness that the LORD had done for David . . ." (1 Kin 8:66). **(17)** Dying "at a good old age" describes "advanced age," rather than moral accomplishment, but a time when due to divine blessings one is fulfilled and satisfied (Gen 15:15).

(18) *Towb* indicates that a given word, act, or circumstance contributes positively to the condition of a situation. **(18a)** Often this judgment does not mean that the thing is actually "good," only that it is so evaluated: "When the chief baker saw that the interpretation was good . . ." (Gen 40:16). **(18b)** The judgment may be ethical: "It is not good that ye do: ought ye not to walk in the fear of our God because of the reproach of the heathen . . .?" (Neh 5:9). **(19)** The word may also represent "agreement" or "concurrence": "The thing proceedeth from the LORD: we cannot speak unto thee bad or good" (Gen 24:50). **(20)** *Towb* is often used in conjunction with the Hebrew word *ra'ah* (7451 - "bad; evil"). **(20a)** Sometimes this is intended as a contrast; **(20b)** but in other contexts it may mean "everything from good [friendly] to bad [unfriendly]," which is a way of saying "nothing at all." **(20c)** In other contexts, more contrast is suggested: "And what the land is that they dwell in, whether it be good or bad . . ." (Num 13:19). In this case, the evaluation would determine whether the land could support the people well or not.

(21) In Gen 2:9, *towb* contrasted with evil has moral overtones: ". . . the tree of life also in the midst of the garden, and the tree of knowledge of good and evil." The fruit of this tree, if consumed, would reveal the difference between moral evil and moral "good." This reference also suggests that, by eating this fruit, man attempted to determine for himself what "good" and evil are. *Towb*, as an adjective, means "good." **(22)** And God saw the light, that *it was* good: and God divided the light from the darkness. **(22a)** God appraises each day's creative work as being "good," climaxing it with a "very good" on the sixth day: "And God saw every thing that he had made, and, behold, *it was* very good" (Gen 1:31). **(23)** As a positive term, the word is used to express many nuances of that which is "good," such as **(23a)** a "glad" heart: "And the priest's heart was glad, and he took the ephod, and the teraphim, and the graven image, and went in the midst of the people" (Judg 18:20), **(23b)** "pleasing" words: "And their words pleased Hamor, and Shechem Hamor's son" (Gen 34:18), and **(23c)** a "cheerful" face: "A merry heart maketh a cheerful countenance: but by sorrow of the heart the spirit is broken" (Prov 15:13). See: TWOT—793a; BDB—373c, 375a, 375c, 1094b.

2897. טוֹב {2x} **Ṭôwb**, *tobe;* the same as 2896; *good; Tob,* a region appar. E. of the Jordan:—Tob {2x}. See: BDB—376a.

2898. טוּב {32x} **ṭûwb**, *toob;* from 2895; *good* (as a noun), in the widest sense, espec. *goodness* (superl. concr. the *best*), *beauty, gladness, welfare:*—goodness {14x}, good {9x}, goods {3x}, good thing {2x}, fair {1x}, gladness {1x}, joy {1x}, well {1x}. See: TWOT—793b; BDB—375c.

2899. טוֹב אֲדֹנִיָּהוּ {1x} **Ṭôwb Ădônîyâhûw**, *tobe ado-nee-yah'-hoo;* from 2896 and 138; *pleasing* (to) *Adonijah; Tob-Adonijah,* an Isr.:—Tob-adonijah {1x}. See: BDB—375b.

2900. טוֹבִיָּה {18x} **Ṭôwbîyâh**, *to-bee-yaw';* or

טוֹבִיָּהוּ **Ṭôwbîyâhûw**, *to-bee-yaw'-hoo;* from 2896 and 3050; *goodness of*

Jehovah; Tobijah, the name of three Isr. and of one Samaritan:—Tobiah {15x}, Tobijah {1x}. See: BDB—375d.

2901. טָוָה {2x} **ṭâvâh**, *taw-vaw';* a prim. root; to *spin:*—spin {2x}. See: TWOT—794; BDB—376a.

2902. טוּחַ {12x} **ṭûwach**, *too'-akh;* a prim. root; to *smear,* espec. with lime:—daub {7x}, plaister {3x}, shut {1x}, overlay {1x}. Syn.: 2915, 7814. See: TWOT—795; BDB—376b, 377c.

2903. טוֹפָפָה {3x} **ṭôwphâphâh**, *to-faw-faw';* from an unused root mean. to *go around* or *bind;* a *fillet* for the forehead:—frontlet {3x}. See: TWOT—804a; BDB—376c, 377d.

2904. טוּל **ṭûwl**, *tool;* a prim. root; to *pitch* over or *reel;* hence, (tran.) to *cast* down or out:—*cast* {12x}, carry away {1x}, send out {1x}. See: TWOT—797; BDB—376c.

2905. טוּר {26x} **ṭûwr**, *toor;* from an unused root mean. to *range* in a reg. manner; a *row;* hence, a *wall:*—row {26x}. See: TWOT—798a; BDB—377a.

2906. טוּר {2x} **ṭûwr** (Aram.), *toor;* corresp. to 6697; a *rock* or hill:—mountain {2x}. See: TWOT—2752; BDB—1094b.

2907. טוּשׂ {1x} **ṭûws**, *toos;* a prim. root; to *pounce* as a bird of prey:—haste {1x}. See: TWOT—799; BDB—377b.

2908. טְוָת {1x} **ṭᵉvâth** (Aram.), *tev-awth';* from a root corresp. to 2901; *hunger* (as *twisting*):—fasting {1x}. See: TWOT—2753; BDB—1094b.

2909. טָחָה {1x} **ṭâchâh**, *taw-khaw';* a prim. root; to *stretch* a bow, as an *archer:*—bowshot + 7198 {1x}. See: TWOT—800; BDB—377b.

2910. טֻחָה {2x} **ṭûwchâh**, *too-khaw';* from 2909 (or 2902) in the sense of *overlaying;* (in the plur. only) the *kidneys* (as being *covered*); hence, (fig.) the inmost *thought:*—inward parts {2x}. See: TWOT—795b; BDB—376b.

2911. טְחוֹן {1x} **ṭᵉchôwn**, *tekh-one';* from 2912; a hand *mill;* hence, a *millstone:*—to grind {1x}. See: TWOT—802a; BDB—377c.

2912. טָחַן **ṭâchan**, *taw-khan';* a prim. root; to *grind* meal; hence, to *be a concubine* (that being their employment):—grind {7x}, grinder {1x}. See: TWOT—802; BDB—377c.

2913. טַחֲנָה {1x} **ṭachănâh**, *takh-an-aw';* from 2912; a hand *mill;* hence, (fig.) *chewing:*—grinding {1x}. See: TWOT—802b; BDB—377d.

2914. טְחֹר {8x} **ṭᵉchôr**, *tekh-ore';* from an unused root mean. to *burn;* a *boil* or ulcer (from the inflammation), espec. a tumor in the anus or pudenda (the piles):—emerod {8x}. See: TWOT—803a; BDB—377d.

2915. טִיחַ {1x} **ṭîyach**, *tee'akh;* from (the equiv. of) 2902; mortar or *plaster:*—daubing {1x}. See: TWOT—795a; BDB—376b, 378a.

2916. טִיט {13x} **ṭîyṭ**, *teet;* from an unused root mean. appar. to *be sticky* [rather perh. a denom. from 2894, through the idea of dirt to *be swept* away]; *mud* or *clay;* fig. *calamity:*—clay {3x}, dirt {2x}, mire {8x}. Syn.: 2563, 4423, 4568. See: TWOT—796a; BDB—376c, 378a.

2917. טִין {2x} **ṭîyn** (Aram.), *teen;* perh. by interchange, for a word corresp. to 2916; *clay:*—miry {2x}. See: TWOT—2754; BDB—1094b.

2918. טִירָה {7x} **ṭîyrâh**, *tee-raw';* fem. of (an equiv. to) 2905; a *wall;* hence, a *fortress* or a *hamlet:*—(goodly) castle {3x}, habitation {1x}, palace {2x}, row {1x}. See: TWOT—798b; BDB—377a, 378a.

2919. טַל {31x} **ṭal**, *tal;* from 2926; *dew* (as *covering* vegetation):—dew {31x}. See: TWOT—807a; BDB—378a, 378b, 1094b.

2920. טַל {5x} **ṭal** (Aram.), *tal;* the same as 2919:—dew {5x}. See: TWOT—2755; BDB—1094b.

2921. טָלָא {8x} **ṭâlâʾ**, *taw-law';* a prim. root; prop. to *cover* with pieces; i.e. (by impl.) to *spot* or *variegate* (as tapestry):—clouted {1x}, with divers colours {1x}, spotted {6x}. Syn.: 7553. See: TWOT—805; BDB—378a.

2922. טְלָא {1x} **ṭᵉlâʾ**, *tel-aw';* appar. from 2921 in the (orig.) sense of *covering* (for protection); a *lamb* [comp. 2924]:—lamb {1x}. Syn.: 3532, 3775. See: TWOT—806a; BDB—378b.

2923. טְלָאִים {1x} **Ṭᵉlâʾîym**, *tel-aw-eem';* from the plur. of 2922; *lambs; Telaim,* a place in Pal.:—Telaim {1x}. See: BDB—378a, 378b.

2924. טָלֶה {2x} **ṭâleh**, *taw-leh';* by var. for 2922; a *lamb:*—lamb {2x}. See: TWOT—806a; BDB—378b.

2925. טַלְטֵלָה {1x} **ṭalṭêlâh**, *tal-tay-law';* from 2904; *overthrow* or *rejection:*—captivity {1x}. See: TWOT—797a; BDB—376d.

2926. טָלַל {1x} **ṭâlal**, *taw-lal';* a prim. root; prop. to *strew* over, i.e. (by impl.) to *cover* in or *plate* (with beams):—cover {1x}. Syn.: 3680, 5526, 560, 6823. See: TWOT—808; BDB—378d, 1094b.

2927. טְלַל {1x} **ṭᵉlal** (Aram.), *tel-al';* corresp. to 2926; to *cover* with shade:—have a shadow {1x}. See: TWOT—2756; BDB—1094b.

2928. טֶלֶם {2x} **Ṭelem**, *teh'-lem;* from an unused root mean. to *break* up or treat violently; *oppression; Telem,* the name of a place in Idumæa, also of a temple doorkeeper:—*Telem* {2x}. See: BDB—378d.

2929. טַלְמוֹן {5x} **Ṭalmôwn**, *tal-mone';* from the same as 2728; *oppressive; Talmon,* a temple doorkeeper:—Talmon {5x}. See: BDB—379a.

2930. טָמֵא {161x} **ṭâmêʾ**, *taw-may';* a prim. root; to *be foul,* espec. in a cerem. or mor. sense (*contaminated*):—unclean {74x}, defile {71x}, pollute {14x}, uncleanness {1x}, utterly {1x}.

Tame', as a verb, means "to be unclean." **(1)** The verb occurs mainly in Leviticus, as in Lev 11:26: "The carcases of every beast which divideth the hoof, and is not clovenfooted, nor cheweth the cud, are unclean unto you: every one that toucheth them shall be unclean." **(2)** *Tame'* is the opposite of *taher* (2891), "to be pure." See: TWOT—809; BDB—379a, 380a.

2931. טָמֵא {87x} **ṭâmêʾ**, *taw-may';* from 2930; *foul* in a relig. sense:—unclean {79x}, defiled {5x}, infamous {1x}, polluted {1x}, pollution {1x}.

Tame', as an adjective, means "unclean." **(1)** The frequency of the word is high in Leviticus. **(2)** Its first occurrence is also in Leviticus: "Or if a soul touch any unclean thing, whether it be a carcase of an unclean beast, or a carcase of unclean cattle, or the carcase of unclean creeping things, and if it be hidden from him; he also shall be unclean, and guilty" (5:2). **(3)** The usage of *tame'* in the Old Testament resembles that of *tahor* (2889), "pure." **(3a)** First, uncleanness is a state of being. The leper was compelled to announce his uncleanness wherever he went (Lev 13:45); however, even here there is a religious overtone, in that his uncleanness was ritual. Hence, it is more appropriate to recognize that the second usage is most basic. **(3b)** *Tame'* in the religio-cultic sense is a technical term denoting a state of being ceremonially unfit. **(3b1)** Animals, carcases, unclean people, and objects conveyed the impurity to those who touched them: "And whatsoever the unclean person toucheth shall be unclean; and the soul that toucheth it shall lie unclean until even" (Num 19:22). **(3b2)** The impurity could also be brought about by a seminal issue (Lev 15:2) or a menstrual period (Lev 15:25), and whatever the unclean touched was also rendered "unclean." Syn.: 2490, 2610, 2933. See: TWOT—809a; BDB—379d.

2932. טֻמְאָה {37x} **ṭumʾâh**, *toom-aw';* from 2930; relig. *impurity:*—uncleanness {26x}, filthiness {7x}, unclean {4x}, unclean (-ness).

Tum'ah, as a noun, means "uncleanness." **(1)** The word occurs in Num 5:19: "And the priest shall charge her by an oath, and say unto the woman, If no man have lain with thee, and if thou hast not gone aside to uncleanliness with another instead of thine husband, be thou free from this bitter water that causeth the curse." Here the word refers to sexual "uncleanness." **(2)** *Tum'ah* occurs twice in Lev 16:16 and refers to ethical and religious "uncleanness." See: TWOT—809b; BDB—380a.

2933. טָמָה {2x} **ṭâmâh**, *taw-maw';* a collat. form of 2930; to *be impure* in a relig. sense:—be defiled {1x}, be reputed vile {1x}. See: TWOT—810; BDB—380b.

2934. טָמַן {32x} **ṭâman**, *taw-man';* a prim. root; to *hide* (by *covering* over):—hide {26x}, laid {2x}, lay privily {2x}, in secret {1x}. Syn.: 2244, 2447, 3582, 5641, 6845. See: TWOT—811; BDB—380b.

2935. טֶנֶא {4x} **ṭeneʾ**, *teh'-neh;* from an unused root prob. mean. to *weave;* a *basket* (of interlaced osiers):—basket {4x}. Syn.: 1731, 3619, 5536. See: TWOT—812a; BDB—380d.

2936. טָנַף {1x} **ṭânaph**, *taw-naf';* a prim. root; to *soil:*—defile {1x}. Syn.: 1351, 2490, 2930. See: TWOT—813; BDB—380d.

2937. טָעָה {1x} **ṭâʿâh**, *taw-aw';* a prim. root; to *wander;* caus. to *lead astray:*—seduce {1x}. See: TWOT—814; BDB—380d.

2938. טָעַם {11x} **ṭâʿam**, *taw-am';* a prim. root; to *taste;* fig. to *perceive:*—but taste {2x}, perceiveth {1x}, taste {5x}, tasted {2x}, tasteth {1x}. See: TWOT—815; BDB—380d, 1094b.

2939. טְעֵם {3x} **ṭᵉʿam** (Aram.), *teh-am';* corresp. to 2938; to *taste;* caus. to *feed:*—make to eat {1x}, feed {2x}. See: TWOT—2757; BDB—1094b.

2940. טַעַם {13x} **ṭaʿam**, *tah'-am;* from 2938; prop. a *taste,* i.e. (fig.) *perception;* by impl. *intelligence;* tran. a *mandate:*—advice {1x}, behaviour {2x}, decree {1x}, discretion {1x}, judgment {1x}, reason {1x}, taste {5x}, understanding {1x}. See: TWOT—815a; BDB—381a, 1094c.

2941. טַעַם {5x} taʿam (Aram.), *tah'-am;* from 2939; prop. a *taste,* i.e. (as in 2940) a judicial *sentence:*—account {1x}, to be commanded {1x}, commandment {2x}, matter {1x}. See: TWOT—2757a; 1094c.

2942. טְעֵם {25x} tᵉʿêm (Aram.), *teh-ame';* from 2939, and equiv. to 2941; prop. *flavor;* fig. *judgment* (both subj. and obj.); hence, *account* (both subj. and obj.):—decree {13x}, chancellor + 1169 {3x}, commanded + 7761 {3x}, regarded {1x}, commandment {2x}, regard + 7761 {1x}, tasted {1x}, wisdom {1x}. See: TWOT—2757a; BDB—1094c, 1096a.

2943. טָעַן {1x} ṭâʿan, *taw-an';* a prim. root; to *load* a beast:—lade {1x}. Syn.: 6006. See: TWOT—816; BDB—381b.

2944. טָעַן {1x} ṭâʿan, *taw-an';* a prim. root; to *stab:*—thrust through {1x}. Syn.: 1856. See: TWOT—817; BDB—381b.

2945. טַף {42x} ṭaph, *taf;* from 2952 (perh. referring to the *tripping* gait of children); a *family* (mostly used collect. in the sing.):—little ones {49x}, children {12x}, families {1x}.

Taph means "weaker one; child; little one." **(1)** Basically this word signifies those members of a nomadic tribe who are not able to march or who can only march to a limited extent. **(1a)** The word implies the "weaker ones." Thus we read of the men and the *taphim,* or the men and those who were unable to move quickly over long stretches: "And Judah said unto Israel, his father, Send the lad with me, and we will arise and go; that we may live, and not die, both we, and thou, and also our little ones" (Gen 43:8). **(1b)** This nuance is clearer in Gen 50:7–8: "And Joseph went up to bury his father; and with him went up all the servants of Pharaoh, the elders of his house, and all the elders of the land of Egypt, and all the house of Joseph, and his brethren and his father's house: only their little ones, and their flocks, and their herds, they left in the land of Goshen." They left the women and the aged to take care of the beasts and babies. These verses certainly make it clear that only men went along. **(2)** In several passages *taph* represents only the children and old ones: "And all their wealth, and all their little ones, and their wives took they captive, and spoiled even all that was in the house" (Gen 34:29, first occurrence). All the able-bodied men of Shechem were killed (Gen 34:26). **(3)** Sometimes the word means "children": "But all the women children, that have not known a man by lying with him, keep alive for yourselves" (Num 31:18; cf. v. 17). See: TWOT—821a; BDB—381b, 381d.

2946. טָפַח {2x} ṭâphach, *taw-fakh';* a prim. root; to *flatten* out or *extend* (as a tent); fig. to *nurse* a child (as *promotive* of growth); or perh. a denom. from 2947, from *dandling* on the palms:—span {1x} swaddle {1x}. See: TWOT—821; BDB—381b.

2947. טֵפַח {4x} ṭêphach, *tay'-fakh;* from 2946; a *spread* of the hand, i.e. a *palm-breadth* (not "span" of the fingers); arch. a *corbel* (as a supporting palm):—coping {1x}, hand-breadth {3x}. See: TWOT—818b; BDB—381c.

2948. טֹפַח {5x} ṭôphach, *to'-fakh;* from 2946 (the same as 2947):—hand-breadth {4x}, handbroad {1x}. See: TWOT—818c; BDB—381c.

182949. טִפֻּח {1x} ṭippûch, *tip-pookh';* from 2946; *nursing:*—span long {1x}. See: TWOT—818a; BDB—381c.

2950. טָפַל {3x} ṭâphal, *taw-fal';* a prim. root; prop. to *stick* on as a patch; fig. to *impute* falsely:—forge {1x}, forger {1x}, sew up {1x}. See: TWOT—819; BDB—381c.

2951. טִפְסַר {2x} ṭiphçar, *tif-sar';* of for. der.; a military *governor:*—captain {2x}. Syn.: 5057, 6346, 7218, 8269. See: TWOT—820; BDB—381d.

2952. טָפַף {1x} ṭâphaph, *taw-faf';* a prim. root; appar. to *trip* (with short steps) coquettishly:—mince {1x}. See: TWOT—821, BDB—381d.

2953. טְפַר {2x} tᵉphar (Aram.), *tef-ar';* from a root corresp. to 6852, and mean. the same as 6856; a finger-*nail;* also a *hoof* or *claw:*—nail {2x}. See: TWOT—2758; BDB—1094c.

2954. טָפַשׁ {1x} ṭâphash, *taw-fash';* a prim. root; prop. appar. to *be thick;* fig. to *be stupid:*—be fat {1x}. Syn.: 1277, 1878, 2459. See: TWOT—822; BDB—382a, 936a.

2955. טָפַת {1x} Ṭâphath, *taw-fath';* prob. from 5197; a *dropping* (of ointment); *Taphath,* an Israelitess:—Taphath {1x}. See: BDB—382a.

2956. טָרַד {2x} ṭârad, *taw-rad';* a prim. root; to *drive* on; fig. to *follow* close:—continual {2x}. See: TWOT—823; BDB—382a, 1094c.

2957. טְרַד {4x} tᵉrad (Aram.), *ter-ad';* corresp. to 2956; to *expel:*—drive {4x}. See: TWOT—2759; BDB—1094c.

2958. טְרוֹם {1x} tᵉrôwm, *ter-ome';* a var. of 2962; *not yet:*—before {1x}. See: TWOT—826; BDB—382c.

2959. טָרַח {1x} ṭârach, *taw-rakh';* a prim. root; to *overburden:*—weary {1x}. See: TWOT—825; BDB—382b.

2960. טֹרַח {2x} ṭôrach, *to'-rakh;* from 2959; a *burden:*—cumbrance {1x}, trouble {1x}. See: TWOT—825a; BDB—382b.

2961. טָרִי {2x} ṭârîy, *taw-ree';* from an unused root appar. mean. to *be moist;* prop. *dripping;* hence, *fresh* (i.e. recently made such):—new {1x}, putrefying {1x}. See: TWOT—824a; BDB—382b.

2962. טֶרֶם {9x} ṭerem, *teh'-rem;* from an unused root appar. mean. to *interrupt* or *suspend;* prop. *non-occurrence;* used adv. *not yet* or *before:*—before {5x}, ere {1x}, not yet {2x}, yet {1x}. See: TWOT—826; BDB—382c.

2963. טָרַף {25x} ṭâraph, *taw-raf';* a prim. root; to *pluck off* or *pull* to pieces; caus. to *supply* with food (as in morsels):—tear {6x}, tear in pieces {6x}, ravening {3x}, catch {2x}, doubt {1x}, feed {1x}, rent in pieces {1x}, prey {1x}, ravin {1x}, surely {1x}, not translated {1x}, torn {1x}. See: TWOT—827; BDB—382d.

2964. טֶרֶף {23x} ṭereph, *teh'-ref;* from 2963; something *torn,* i.e. a fragment, e.g. a *fresh* leaf, *prey, food:*—leaves {1x}, meat {3x}, prey {18x}, spoil {1x}. See: TWOT—827b; BDB—383a.

2965. טָרָף {1x} ṭârâph, *taw-rawf';* from 2963; recently *torn* off, i.e. *fresh:*—pluckt off {1x}. See: TWOT—827a; BDB—383a.

2966. טְרֵפָה {9x} tᵉrêphâh, *ter-ay-faw';* fem. (collect.) of 2964; *prey,* i.e. flocks devoured by animals:—ravin {1x}, (that which was) torn (of beasts, in pieces) {8x}. See: TWOT—827c; BDB—383c.

2967. טַרְפְּלָי {1x} Ṭarpᵉlay (Aram.), *tar-pel-ah'-ee;* from a name of for. der.; a *Tarpelite* (collect.) or inhab. of Tarpel, a place in Assyria:—Tarpelites {1x}. See: BDB—1094c.

י

2968. יָאַב {1x} yâʾab, *yaw-ab';* a prim. root; to *desire:*—long {1x}. See: TWOT—828; BDB—383b.

2969. יָאָה {1x} yâʾâh, *yaw-aw';* a prim. root; to *be suitable:*—appertain {1x}. See: TWOT—829; BDB—383b.

יְאוֹר yᵉʾôwr. See 2975.

2970. יַאֲזַנְיָה {4x} Yaʾăzanyâh, *yah-az-an-yaw';* or

יַאֲזַנְיָהוּ Yaʾăzanyâhûw, *yah-az-an-yaw'-hoo;* from 238 and 3050; *heard of Jah; Jaazanjah,* the name of four Isr.:—Jaazaniah {4x}. Syn.: comp. 3153. See: BDB—24d, 383b.

2971. יָאִיר {9x} Yâʾîyr, *yaw-ere';* from 215; *enlightener; Jaïr,* the name of four Isr.:—Jair {9x}. See: BDB—22c, 383b.

2972. יָאִרִי {1x} Yâʾîrîy, *yaw-ee-ree';* patron. from 2971; a *Jaïrite* or desc. of Jair:—Jairite {1x}. See: BDB—22c, 383b.

2973. יָאַל {4x} yâʾal, *yaw-al';* a prim. root; prop. to *be slack,* i.e. (fig.) to *be foolish:*—dote {1x}, be foolish {1x}, become foolish {1x}, do foolishly {1x}. See: TWOT—830, BDB—383b. Syn.: 191, 3684, 5034.

2974. יָאַל {19x} yâʾal, *yaw-al';* a prim. root [prob. rather the same as 2973 through the idea of mental *weakness*]; prop. to *yield,* espec. *assent;* hence, (pos.) to *undertake* as an act of volition:—content {7x}, please {4x}, would {3x}, taken upon me {2x}, began {1x}, assayed {1x}, willingly {1x}.

This word represents the volitional element in an act rather than the feelings, dispositions, or motives that have prompted it. See: TWOT—831; BDB—383d.

2975. יְאֹר {64x} yᵉʾôr, *yeh-ore';* of Eg. or.; a *channel,* e.g. a fosse, canal, shaft; spec. the *Nile,* as the one river of Egypt, incl. its collat. trenches; also the *Tigris,* as the main river of Assyria: brooks {5x}, flood {5x}, river {53x}, streams {1x}. Syn.: 5104. See: TWOT—832; BDB—383b, 384b, 456c.

2976. יָאַשׁ {6x} yâʾash, *yaw-ash';* a prim. root; to *desist,* i.e. (fig.) to *despond:*—(cause to) despair {2x}, one that is desperate {1x}, be no hope {3x}. See: TWOT—833; BDB—384c.

2977. יֹאשִׁיָּה {53x} Yôʾshîyâh, *yo-shee-yaw';* or

יֹאשִׁיָּהוּ Yôʾshîyâhûw, *yo-she-yaw'-hoo;* from the same root as 803 and 3050; *founded of Jah; Joshijah,* the name of two Isr.:—Josiah {53x}. See: BDB—78c, 384c.

2978. יְאִתוֹן {1x} yᵉʾîthôwn, *yeh-ee-thone';* from 857; an *entry:*—entrance {1x}. Syn.: 3996, 6607. See: TWOT—188a; BDB—36b, 87c.

2979. יְאָתְרַי {1x} Yᵉʾâthᵉray, *yeh-aw-ther-ah'ee;* from the same as 871; *stepping; Jeätherai,* an Isr.:—Jeaterai {1x}. See: BDB—384d.

2980. יָבַב {1x} yâbab, *yaw-bab';* a prim. root; to *bawl:*—cry out {1x}. Syn.: 2199, 6817, 7121. See: TWOT—834; BDB—384d.

2981. יְבוּל {13x} yᵉbûwl, *yeb-ool';* from 2986; *produce,* i.e. a *crop* or (fig.) *wealth:*—fruit {1x}, increase {10x}. Syn.: 6521, 7235. See: TWOT—835c; BDB—385b.

2982. יְבוּס {4x} **Yebûwç**, *yeb-oos'*; from 947; *trodden*, i.e. threshing-place; *Jebus*, the aboriginal name of Jerusalem:—Jebus {4x}. See: BDB—101a, 384d.

2983. יְבוּסִי {41x} **Yebûwçiy**, *yeb-oo-see'*; patrial from 2982; a *Jebusite* or inhab. of Jebus:—Jebusite (-s) {41x}. See: BDB—101a, 384d.

2984. יִבְחָר {3x} **Yibchar**, *yib-khar'*; from 977; *choice; Jibchar*, an Isr.:—Ibhar {3x}. See: BDB—104c, 384d.

2985. יָבִין {8x} **Yâbîyn**, *yaw-bene'*; from 995; *intelligent; Jabin*, the name of two Canaanitish kings:—Jabin {8x}. See: BDB—108a, 384d.

יָבֵישׁ **Yâbêysh**. See 3003.

2986. יָבַל {18x} **yâbal**, *yaw-bal'*; a prim. root; prop. to *flow;* caus. to *bring* (espec. with pomp):—bring {11x}, carry {4x}, bring forth {1x}, lead forth {1x}, lead {1x}. See: TWOT—835; BDB—384d, 1094d.

2987. יְבַל {3x} **yebal** (Aram.), *yeb-al'*; corresp. to 2986; to *bring:*—brought {2x}, carry {1x}. See: TWOT—2760; BDB—1094d.

יֹבֵל **yôbêl**. See 3104.

2988. יָבָל {2x} **yâbâl**, *yaw-bawl'*; from 2986; a *stream:*—[water-] course {1x}, stream {1x}. See: TWOT—835a; BDB—385a.

2989. יָבָל {1x} **Yâbâl**, *yaw-bawl'*; the same as 2988; *Jabal*, an antediluvian:—Jabal {1x}. See: BDB—385b.

יֹבֵל **yôbêl**. See 3104.

2990. יַבֶּל {1x} **yabbêl**, *yab-bale'*; from 2986; having *running* sores:—wen {1x}. See: TWOT—835f; BDB—385c, 386a.

2991. יִבְלְעָם {3x} **Yibleʽâm**, *yib-leh-awm'*; from 1104 and 5971; *devouring people; Jibleäm*, a place in Pal.:—Ibleam {3x}. See: BDB—385d.

2992. יָבַם {3x} **yâbam**, *yaw-bam'*; a prim. root of doubtful mean.; used only as a denom. from 2993; to *marry* a (deceased) brother's widow:—perform the duty of a husband's brother {2x}, marry {1x}. See: TWOT—836; BDB—386a.

2993. יָבָם {2x} **yâbâm**, *yaw-bawm'*; from (the orig. of) 2992; a *brother-in-law:*—husband's brother {2x}. See: TWOT—836a; BDB—386a.

2994. יְבֵמֶת {5x} **yebêmeth**, *yeb-ay'-meth*; fem. part. of 2992; a *sister-in-law:*—brother's wife {3x}, sister-in-law {2x}. See: TWOT—836b; BDB—386a.

2995. יַבְנְאֵל {2x} **Yabneʼêl**, *yab-neh-ale'*; from 1129 and 410; *built of God; Jabneël*, the name of two places in Pal.:—Jabneel {2x}. See: BDB—125c, 386b.

2996. יַבְנֶה {1x} **Yabneh**, *yab-neh'*; from 1129; a *building; Jabneh*, a place in Pal.:—Jabneh {1x}. See: BDB—125c, 386b.

2997. יִבְנְיָה {1x} **Yibneyâh**, *yib-neh-yaw'*; from 1129 and 3050; *built of Jah; Jibnejah*, an Isr.:—Ibneiah {1x}. See: BDB—125c, 386b.

2998. יִבְנִיָּה {1x} **Yibnîyâh**, *yib-nee-yaw'*; from 1129 and 3050; *building of Jah; Jibnijah*, an Isr.:—Ibnijah {1x}. See: BDB—125d, 386b.

2999. יַבֹּק {7x} **Yabbôq**, *yab-boke'*; prob. from 1238; *pouring* forth; *Jabbok*, a river E. of the Jordan:—Jabbok {1x}. See: BDB—132d, 391d.

3000. יְבֶרֶכְיָהוּ {1x} **Yeberekyâhûw**, *yeb-eh-rek-yaw'-hoo*; from 1288 and 3050: *blessed of Jah; Jeberekjah*, an Isr.:—Jeberechiah {1x}. See: BDB—140a, 386b.

3001. יָבֵשׁ {78x} **yâbêsh**, *yaw-bashe'*; a prim. root; to *be ashamed, confused* or *disappointed;* also (as failing) to *dry* up (as water) or *wither* (as herbage):—dry up {27x}, withered {22x}, confounded {9x}, ashamed {7x}, dry {7x}, wither away {2x}, clean {1x}, shamed {1x}, shamefully {1x}, utterly {1x}.

Yabesh means "to be dry, be dried up, be withered." **(1)** In its verbal form *yabesh* is found for the first time in Gen 8:7, when after the Flood, "the waters were dried up from the earth." However, the noun derivative, yabbashah, which means "dry ground," already occurs in Gen 1:9. **(2)** Physical "drying up" can involve **(2a)** bread (Josh 9:5), **(2b)** the ground in time of drought (Jer 23:10; Amos 4:7), **(2c)** brooks and streams (1 Kin 17:7), and **(2c)** crops (Is 42:15). **(3)** The shortness of man's life is compared to the "drying up" of grass (Ps 90:6; 102:11; Is 40:7). **(4)** Because of affliction, the heart too "withers" like the grass (Ps 102:4). **(5)** In his parable of the vine, Ezekiel likens God's judgment on Judah to the "withering" of a vine that is pulled up (Eze 17:9–10). **(6)** Because of his disobedience, Jeroboam's hand "is dried up" as judgment from God (1 Kin 13:4). **(7)** Psychosomatic awareness is clearly demonstrated in Prov 17:22: "A broken spirit drieth the bones." Syn.: 5034, 6784, 7060. See: TWOT—837; BDB—386b.

3002. יָבֵשׁ {9x} **yâbêsh**, *yaw-bashe'*; from 3001; *dry:*—dried {1x}, dried away {1x}, dry {7x}. See: TWOT—837a; BDB—386d.

3003. יָבֵשׁ {24x} **Yâbêsh**, *yaw-bashe'*; the same as 3002 (also

יָבֵישׁ **Yâbêysh**, *yaw-bashe'*; often with the addition of 1568, i.e. *Jabesh of Gilad*); *Jabesh*, the name of an Isr. and of a place in Pal.:—Jabesh {12x}, Jabeshgilead {12x}. See: BDB—386d.

3004. יַבָּשָׁה {14x} **yabbâshâh**, *yab-baw-shaw'*; from 3001; *dry* ground:—dry {10x}, dry land {2x}, dry ground {1x}, land {1x}. See: TWOT—837b; BDB—387a.

3005. יִבְשָׂם {1x} **Yibsâm**, *yib-sawm'*; from the same as 1314; *fragrant; Jibsam*, an Isr.:—Jibsam {1x}. See: BDB—142a.

3006. יַבֶּשֶׁת {2x} **yabbesheth**, *yab-beh'-sheth*; a var. of 3004; *dry* ground:—dry land {2x}. See: TWOT—837c; BDB—387a, 1094d.

3007. יַבֶּשֶׁת {1x} **yabbesheth** (Aram.), *yab-beh'-sheth*; corresp. to 3006; *dry* land:—earth {1x}. See: TWOT—2761; BDB—1094d.

3008. יִגְאָל {3x} **Yigʼâl**, *yig-awl'*; from 1350; *avenger; Jigal*, the name of three Isr.:—Igal {2x}, Igeal {1x}. See: BDB—145d, 387a.

3009. יָגַב {2x} **yâgab**, *yaw-gab'*; a prim. root; to *dig* or plow:—husbandman {2x}. See: TWOT—838; BDB—387a.

3010. יָגֵב {1x} **yâgêb**, *yaw-gabe'*; from 3009; a plowed *field:*—field {1x}. Syn.: 7704, 7709. See: TWOT—838a; BDB—387a.

3011. יָגְבְּהָה {2x} **Yogbehâh**, *yog-beh-haw'*; fem. from 1361; *hillock; Jogbehah*, a place E. of the Jordan:—Jogbehah {2x}. See: BDB—147b, 387a.

3012. יִגְדַּלְיָהוּ {1x} **Yigdalyâhûw**, *yig-dal-yaw'-hoo*; from 1431 and 3050; *magnified of Jah; Jigdaljah*, an Isr.:—Igdaliah {1x}. See: BDB—153d, 387a.

3013. יָגָה {8x} **yâgâh**, *yaw-gaw'*; a prim. root; to *grieve:*—afflict {4x}, cause grief {1x}, grieve {1x}, sorrowful {1x}, vex {1x}. Syn.: 3015, 6031. See: TWOT—839; BDB—387a.

3014. יָגָה {1x} **yâgâh**, *yaw-gaw'*; a prim. root [prob. rather the same as 3013 through the common idea of *dissatisfaction*]; to *push* away:—be removed {1x}. See: TWOT—840; BDB—387c.

3015. יָגוֹן {14x} **yâgôwn**, *yaw-gohn'*; from 3013; *affliction:*—grief {2x}, sorrow {12x}. See: TWOT—839a; BDB—387b.

3016. יָגוֹר {2x} **yâgôwr**, *yaw-gore'*; from 3025; *fearful:*—afraid {1x}, fearest {1x}. See: TWOT—843a; BDB—388d.

3017. יָגוּר {1x} **Yâgûwr**, *yaw-goor'*; prob. from 1481; a *lodging; Jagur*, a place in Pal.:—Jagur {1x}. See: BDB—158c, 387c.

3018. יְגִיעַ {16x} **yegîyaʽ**, *yeg-ee'-ah*; from 3021; *toil;* hence, a *work, produce, property* (as the result of labor):—labour {15x}, work {1x}. Syn.: 3021, 5639, 6467. See: TWOT—842e; BDB—388c.

3019. יָגִיעַ {1x} **yâgîyaʽ**, *yaw-ghee'-ah*; from 3021; *tired:*—weary {1x}. See: TWOT—842d; BDB—388c.

3020. יָגְלִי {1x} **Yoglîy**, *yog-lee'*; from 1540; *exiled; Jogli*, an Isr.:—Jogli {1x}. See: BDB—163d, 387c.

3021. יָגַע {26x} **yâgaʽ**, *yaw-gah'*; a prim. root; prop. to *gasp;* hence, to *be exhausted*, to *tire*, to *toil:*—faint {1x}, (make to) labour {12x}, (be) weary {13x}. Syn.: 3023. See: TWOT—842; 388a.

3022. יָגָע {1x} **yâgâʽ**, *yaw-gaw'*; from 3021; *earnings* (as the product of toil):—that which he laboured {1x} for. See: TWOT—842a; BDB—388b.

3023. יָגֵעַ {3x} **yâgêaʽ**, *yaw-gay'-ah*; from 3021; *tired;* hence, (tran.) *tiresome:*—full of labour {1x}, weary {2x}. See: TWOT—842b; 388b.

3024. יְגִעָה {1x} **yegîʽâh**, *yeg-ee-aw'*; fem. of 3019; *fatigue:*—weariness {1x}. See: TWOT—842c; BDB—388b.

3025. יָגֹר {5x} **yâgôr**, *yaw-gore'*; a prim. root; to *fear:*—be afraid {4x}, fear {1x}. Syn.: 3372, 6342. See: TWOT—843; BDB—388c.

3026. יְגַר שָׂהֲדוּתָא {1x} **Yegar Sahadûwthâʼ** (Aram.), *yegar' sah-had-oo-thaw'*; from a word derived from an unused root (mean. to *gather*) and a der. of a root corresp. to 7717; *heap of the testimony; Jegar-Sahadutha*, a cairn E. of the Jordan:—Jegar-Sahadutha {1x}. See: BDB—1094d.

3027. יָד {1614x} **yâd**, *yawd*; a prim. word; a *hand* (the *open* one [indicating *power, means, direction*, etc.], in distinction from 3709, the *closed* one); used (as noun, adv., etc.) in a great variety of applications, both lit. and fig., both prox. and remote [as follows]:—hand {1359x}, by {44x}, consecrate + 4390 {14x}, him {14x}, power {12x}, them {11x}, places {8x}, tenons {6x}, thee {6x}, coast {6x}, side {5x}, misc. {129x} = (+ be) able, × about, + armholes, at, axletree, because of, beside, border, × bounty, + broad, [broken-] handed, charge, + creditor, custody, debt, dominion, × enough, + fellowship, force,

× from, hand [-staves, -y work], × he, × in, labour, + large, ledge, [left-] handed, means, × mine, ministry, near, × of, × order, ordinance, × our, parts, pain, × presumptuously, service, sore, state, stay, draw with strength, stroke, + swear, terror, × thine own, × thou, through, × throwing, + thumb, times, × to, × under, × us, × wait on, [way-] side, where, + wide, × with (him, me, you), work, + yield, × yourselves.

Yad means "hand; side; border; alongside; hand-measure; portion; arm (rest); monument; manhood (male sex organ); power; rule." **(1)** The primary sense of this word is "hand": "And the Lord God said, Behold, the man is become as one of us, to know good and evil: and now, lest he put forth his hand, and take also of the tree of life . . ." (Gen 3:22—the first biblical occurrence). **(1a)** Sometimes the word is used in conjunction with an object that can be grasped by the "hand": "And if he smite him with throwing a stone [literally, "hand stone"] . . ." (Num 35:17). **(1b)** In a similar usage the word means "human": "He shall also stand up against the Prince of princes; but he shall be broken without hand [i.e., human agency]" (Dan 8:25; cf. Job 34:20). **(1c)** In Is 49:2, "hand" is used of God; God tells Moses that He will put His "hand" over the mouth of the cave and protect him. **(1c1)** This is a figure of speech, an anthropomorphism, by which God promises His protection. **(1c2)** God's "hand" is another term for God's "power" (cf. Jer 16:21). **(2)** *Yad* is employed in several other noteworthy phrases. **(2a)** The "lifting of the hand" may be involved in "taking an oath" (Gen 14:22). **(2b)** "Shaking" [literally, "giving one's hand"] is another oath-taking gesture (cf. Prov 11:21). **(2c)** For "one's hands to be on another" (Gen 37:27) or "laid upon another" (Ex 7:4) is to do harm to someone. **(2d)** "Placing one's hands with" signifies "making common cause with someone" (Ex 23:1). **(2e)** If one's hand does not "reach" something, he is "unable to pay" for it (Lev 5:7). **(2f)** When one's countryman is "unable to stretch out his hand to you," he is not able to support himself (Lev 25:35). **(2g)** "Putting one's hand on one's mouth" is a gesture of silence (Prov 30:32). **(2h)** "Placing one's hands under someone" means submitting to him (1 Chr 29:24). **(2i)** "Giving something into one's hand" is entrusting it to him (Gen 42:37). **(3)** A major group of passages uses *yad* to represent the location and uses of the hand. **(3a)** First, the word can mean "side," where the hand is located: "And Absalom rose up early, and stood beside the way of the gate . . ." (2 Sa 15:2). **(3b)** In 2 Chr 21:16, the word means "border": "Moreover the Lord stirred up against Jehoram the spirit of the Philistines, and of the Arabians, that were near [literally, "by the hand of"] the Ethiopians." **(3c)** A similar use in Ex 25 applies this word to the "banks" of the Nile River: "And the daughter of Pharaoh came down to wash herself at the river, and her maidens walked along by the [Nile]. . . ." In this sense, *yad* can represent "length and breadth." **(3d)** In Gen 34:21 we read that the land was (literally) "broad of hands": "These men are peaceable with us; therefore let them dwell in the land, and trade therein; for the land, behold, it is large enough for them. . . ."

(4) Since the hand can receive only a part or fraction of something, the word can signify a "part" or "fraction": "And he took and sent [portions] unto them from before him: but Benjamin's [portion] was five times so much as any of theirs" (Gen 43:34). **(5)** *Yad* comes to mean that which upholds something, a "support" (1 Kin 7:35ff.) or an "arm rest" (1 Kin 10:19). **(6)** Since a hand may be held up as a "sign," *yad* can signify a "monument" or "stele": ". . . Saul came to Carmel, and, behold, he set him up a place [monument], and is gone about, and passed on, and gone down to Gilgal" (1 Sa 15:12). **(7)** *Yad* sometimes represents the "male sex organ": ". . . And art gone up; thou hast enlarged thy bed, and made thee a covenant with them; thou lovedst their bed where thou sawest it [you have looked on their manhood]" (Is 57:8; cf. v. 10; 6:2; 7:20). **(8)** In several passages, *yad* is used in the sense of "power" or "rule": **(8a)** "And David smote Hadarezer king of Zobah unto Hamath, as he went to stablish his dominion by the river Euphrates" (1 Chr 18:3). **(8b)** "To be delivered into one's hands" means to be "given into one's power": "God hath delivered him into mine hand; for he is shut in, by entering into a town that hath gates and bars" (1 Sa 23:7; cf. Prov 18:21). **(8c)** "To fill someone's hand" may be a technical term for "installing him" in office: "And thou shalt put them upon Aaron thy brother, and his sons with him; and shalt anoint them, and consecrate them [literally, "fill their hands"], and sanctify them, that they may minister unto me in the priest's office" (Ex 28:41). **(9)** *Yad* is frequently joined to the preposition be and other prepositions as an extension; there is no change in meaning, only a longer form: "For what have I done? or what evil is in mine hand?" (1 Sa 26:18). See: TWOT—844; BDB—388d, 406d, 1094d.

3028. יַד {17x} **yad** (Aram.), *yad;* corresp. to 3027:—hand {16x}, power {1x}. See: TWOT—2763; BDB—1094d.

3029. יְדָא {2x} **yᵉdâʾ** (Aram.), *yed-aw';* corresp. to 3034; to *praise:*—thank {1x}, give thanks {1x}. See: TWOT—2764; BDB—1095a.

3030. יִדְאֲלָה {1x} **Yidʾălâh**, *yid-al-aw';* of uncert. der.; *Jidalah,* a place in Pal.:—Idalah {1x}. See: BDB—391d.

3031. יִדְבָּשׁ {1x} **Yidbâsh**, *yid-bawsh';* from the same as 1706; perh. *honeyed; Jidbash,* an Isr.:—Idbash {1x}. See: BDB—185c, 391d.

3032. יָדַד {3x} **yâdad**, *yaw-dad';* a prim. root; prop. to *handle* [comp. 3034], i.e. to *throw,* e.g. lots:—cast {3x}. See: TWOT—845, 846; BDB—391d.

3033. יְדִדוּת {1x} **yᵉdîdûwth**, *yed-ee-dooth';* from 3039; prop. *affection;* concr. a *darling* object:—dearly beloved {1x}. See: TWOT—846c; BDB—392a.

3034. יָדָה {114x} **yâdâh**, *yaw-daw';* a prim. root; used only as denom. from 3027; lit. to *use* (i.e. hold out) *the hand;* phys. to *throw* (a stone, an arrow) at or away; espec. to *revere* or *worship* (with extended hands); intens. to *bemoan* (by wringing the hands):—praise {53x}, give thanks {32x}, confess {16x}, thank {5x}, make confession {2x}, thanksgiving {2x}, cast {1x}, cast out {1x}, shoot {1x}, thankful {1x}.

Yadah means "to give thanks, laud, praise." **(1)** A common Hebrew word in all its periods, this verb is an important word in the language of worship. **(2)** *Yadah* is found 114 times in the Hebrew Bible, the first time being in the story of the birth of Judah, Jacob's son who was born to Leah: "And she conceived again, and bare a son: and she said, Now will I praise the LORD: therefore she called his name Judah; and left bearing (Gen 29:35). **(3)** The root, translated "confess" or "confession" about twenty times in the KJV, is also frequently rendered "praise" or "give thanks." **(3a)** At first glance, the meanings may appear unrelated. But upon closer inspection, it becomes evident that each sense profoundly illumines and interprets the other. **(3)** As is to be expected, this word is found most frequently in the Book of Psalms (some 70 times). **(3a)** *Yadah* overlaps in meaning with a number of other Hebrew words implying "praise," such as halal (1984 - whence hallelu-yah). **(3b)** As an expression of thanks or praise, it is a natural part of ritual or public worship as well as personal praise to God (Ps 30:9, 12; 35:18).

(3c) Man is occasionally the object of *yadah;* but far more commonly, God is the object. **(3d)** The usual context seems to be public worship, where the worshipers affirm and renew their relationship with God. **(3e)** The subject is not primarily the isolated individual, but the congregation. **(3f)** Especially in the hymns and thanksgivings of the Psalter, it is evident that *yadah* is a recital of, and thanksgiving for, Yahweh's mighty acts of salvation. **(3g)** An affirmation or confession of God's undeserved kindness throws man's unworthiness into sharp relief. **(3h)** Hence, a confession of sin may be articulated in the same breath as a confession of faith or praise and thanksgiving. **(3i)** The confession is not a moralistic, autobiographical catalogue of sins—individual infractions of a legal code—but a confession of the underlying sinfulness that engulfs all mankind and separates us from the holy God. **(4)** God is even to be praised for His judgments, by which He awakens repentance (e.g., Ps 51:4). **(4a)** So one is not surprised to find praises in penitential contexts, and vice versa (1 Kin 8:33ff.; Neh 9:2ff.; Dan 9:4ff.). **(4b)** If praise inevitably entails confession of sin, the reverse is also true: The sure word of forgiveness elicits praise and thanksgiving on the confessor's part. **(4c)** This wells up almost automatically from the new being of the repentant person.

(5) The vista of *yadah* expands both vertically and horizontally—vertically to include all creation, and horizontally stretching forward to that day when praise and thanksgiving shall be eternal (e.g., Ps 29; 95:10; 96:7–9; 103:19–22). **(6)** Thanks often are directed to the name of the Lord (Ps 106:47; 122:4). **(7)** An affirmation or confession of God's undeserved kindness throws man's unworthiness into sharp relief. **(8)** Hence, a confession of sin may be articulated in the same breath as a confession of faith or praise and thanksgiving. **(9)** The confession is not a moralistic, autobiographical catalogue of sins—individual infractions of a legal code—**(10)** but a confession of the underlying sinfulness that engulfs all mankind and separates us from the holy God. **(11)** God is even to be praised for His judgments, by which He awakens repentance (Ps 51:4). **(12)** So it is not surprising to find praises in penitential contexts, and vice versa (1 Kin 8:33; Neh 9:2; Dan 9:4).

(13) If praise inevitably entails confession of sin, the sure word of forgiveness elicits praise and thanksgiving on the confessor's part. This wells up almost automatically from the new being of the repentant person. **(14)** Often the direct object of *yadah* is the "name" of Yahweh (Ps 105:1; Is 12:4; 1 Chr 16:8). **(15)** This idiom is synonymous with praising Yahweh. **(16)** It introduces the entire dimension evoked by the "name" in biblical usage and reminds us that the holy God cannot be directly approached by fallen man, but only through His "name"—i.e., His Word and reputation, an anticipation of the incarnation. God reveals Himself only in His "name," especially in the sanctuary where He "causes His name to dwell." **(17)** *Yadah* expands vertically to include all creation, and horizontally stretching forward to that day when praise and thanksgiving shall be eternal (Ps 29; 95:10; 96:7–9; 103:19–22). See: TWOT—847; BDB—392a, 1095a.

3035. יִדּוֹ {2x} **Yiddôw**, *yid-do';* from 3034; *praised; Jiddo,* an Isr.:—Iddo {1x}, Jadua {1x}. See: BDB—392a.

3036. יָדוֹן {1x} **Yâdôwn**, *yaw-done';* from 3034; *thankful; Jadon,* an Isr.:—Jadon {1x}. See: BDB—193d.

3037. יַדּוּעַ {3x} **Yaddûwaʿ**, *yad-doo'-ah;* from 3045; *knowing; Jadduä,* the name of two Isr.:—Jaddua {3x}. See: BDB—396a.

3038. יְדוּתוּן {17x} **Yᵉdûwthûwn**, *yed-oo-thoon';* or

יְדֻתוּן **Yᵉdûthûwn**, *yed-oo-thoon';* or

יְדִיתוּן **Yᵉdîythûwn**, *yed-ee-thoon';* prob. from 3034; *laudatory; Jeduthun,* an Isr.:—Jeduthun {17x}. See: BDB—393a, 393b.

3039. יְדִיד {9x} **yᵉdîyd**, *yed-eed';* from the same as 1730; *loved:*—amiable {1x}, wellbeloved {1x}, beloved {5x}, loves {1x}. See: TWOT—846a; BDB—391d.

3040. יְדִידָה {1x} **Yᵉdîydâh**, *yed-ee-daw';* fem. of 3039; *beloved; Jedidah,* an Israelitess:—Jedidah {1x}. See: BDB—392a.

3041. יְדִידְיָה {1x} **Yᵉdîydᵉyâh**, *yed-ee-deh-yaw';* from 3039 and 3050; *beloved of Jah; Jedidejah,* a name of Solomon:—Jedidiah {1x}. See: BDB—392a, 393a.

3042. יְדָיָה {2x} **Yᵉdâyâh**, *yed-aw-yaw';* from 3034 and 3050; *praised of Jah; Jedajah,* the name of two Isr.:—Jedaiah {2x}. See: BDB—393a.

3043. יְדִיעֲאֵל {6x} **Yᵉdîyʿăʾêl**, *yed-ee-ah-ale';* from 3045 and 410; *knowing God; Jediaël,* the name of three Isr.:—Jediael {6x}. See: BDB—393a, 396a.

3044. יִדְלָף {1x} **Yidlâph**, *yid-lawf';* from 1811; *tearful; Jidlaph,* a Mesopotamian:—Jidlaph {1x}. See: BDB—393b.

3045. יָדַע {947x} **yâdaʿ**, *yaw-dah';* a prim. root; to *know* (prop. to ascertain by *seeing*); used in a great variety of senses, fig., lit., euphem. and infer. (incl. *observation, care, recognition;* and caus. *instruction, designation, punishment,* etc.) [as follow]:—know {645x}, known {105x}, knowledge {19x}, perceive {18x}, shew {17x}, tell {8x}, wist {7x}, understand {7x}, certainly {7x}, acknowledge {6x}, acquaintance {6x}, consider {6x}, declare {6x}, teach {5x}, misc. {85x} = advise, answer, appoint, assuredly, be aware, [un-] awares, can [-not], for a certainty, comprehend, × could they, cunning, be diligent, (can, cause to) discern, discover, endued with, familiar friend, famous, feel, can have, be [ig-] norant, instruct, kinsfolk, kinsman, + be learned, + lie by man, mark, privy to, × prognosticator, regard, have respect, skillful, can (man of) skill, be sure, of a surety, have [understanding], × will be, wit, wot.

Yada' means "to know." **(1)** Essentially *yada'* means: **(1a)** to know by observing and reflecting (thinking), and **(1b)** to know by experiencing. **(2)** The first sense appears in Gen 8:11, where Noah "knew" the waters had abated as a result of seeing the freshly picked olive leaf in the dove's mouth; he "knew" it after observing and thinking about what he had seen. **(2a)** He did not actually see or experience the abatement himself. In contrast to this knowing through reflection is the knowing which comes through experience with the senses, by investigation and proving, by reflection and consideration (firsthand knowing). **(2b)** Consequently *yada* is used in synonymous parallelism with **(2b1)** "hear" (Ex 3:7), **(2b2)** "see" (Gen 18:21), and **(2b3)** "perceive, see" (Job 28:7). **(2c)** Joseph told his brothers that were they to leave one of their number with him in Egypt then he would "know," by experience, that they were honest men (Gen 42:33). **(2d)** In the Garden of Eden, Adam and Eve were forbidden to eat of the tree whose fruit if eaten would give them the experience of evil and, therefore, the knowledge of both good and evil. **(2e)** Somewhat characteristically the heart plays an important role in knowing. Because they experienced the sustaining presence of God during the wilderness wandering, the Israelites "knew" in their hearts that God was disciplining or caring for them as a father cares for a son (Deut 8:5). Such knowing can be hindered by a wrongly disposed heart (Ps 95:10).

(3) Thirdly, this verb can represent that kind of knowing which one learns and can give back. **(3a)** So Cain said that he did not "know" he was Abel's keeper (Gen 4:9), and **(3b)** Abram told Sarai that he "knew" she was a beautiful woman (Gen 12:11). **(3c)** One can also "know" by being told—in Lev 5:1 a witness either sees or otherwise "knows" (by being told) pertinent information. **(3d)** In this sense "know" is paralleled **(3d1)** by "acknowledge" (Deut 33:9) and **(3d2)** "learn" (Deut 31:12–13). **(3e)** Thus, little children not yet able to speak do not "know" good and evil (Deut 1:39); **(3e1)** they have not learned it so as to tell another what it is. **(3e2)** In other words, their knowledge is not such that they can distinguish between good and evil.

(4) In addition to the essentially cognitive knowing already presented, this verb has a purely experiential side. **(4a)** The "knower" has actual involvement with or in the object of the knowing. **(4a1)** So Potiphar was unconcerned about (literally, "did not know about") what was in his house (Gen 39:6)—he had no actual contact with it. **(4a2)** In Gen 4:1 Adam's knowing Eve also refers to direct contact with her—in a sexual relationship. **(4b)** In Gen 18:19 God says He "knows" Abraham; He cared for him in the sense that He chose him from among other men and saw to it that certain things happened to him. The emphasis is on the fact that God "knew" him intimately and personally. **(4b1)** In fact, it is parallel in concept to "sanctified" (cf. Jer 1:5). **(4b2)** A similar use of this word relates to God's relationship to Israel as a chosen or elect nation (Amos 3:2).

(5) *Yada* in the intensive and causative stems is used to express a particular concept of revelation. **(5a)** God did not make Himself known by His name Jehovah to Abraham, Isaac, and Jacob. **(5b)** He did reveal that name to them, that He was the God of the covenant. **(5c)** Nevertheless, the covenant was not fulfilled (they did not possess the Promised Land) until the time of Moses. **(5d)** The statement in Ex 6:3 implies that now God was going to make Himself known "by His name"; He was going to lead them to possess the land. **(5e)** God makes Himself known through revelatory acts such as bringing judgment on the wicked (Ps 9:16) and deliverance to His people (Is 66:14). **(5f)** He also reveals Himself through the spoken word—for example, by the commands given through Moses (Eze 20:11), by promises like those given to David (2 Sa 7:21). **(5g)** Thus, God reveals Himself in law and promise. **(6)** "To know" God is to have an intimate experiential knowledge of Him. **(6a)** So Pharaoh denies that he knows Jehovah (Ex 5:2) or that he recognizes His authority over him. **(6b)** Positively "to know" God is paralleled to fear Him (1 Kin 8:43), to serve (1 Chr 28:9), and to trust (Is 43:10). Syn: *Yada'* is related to **(7)** da'at (1847) which means "knowledge": Gen 2:9: ". . . and the tree of knowledge of good and evil." The word also appears in Ex 31:3. It is related **(7a)** to the particle, madduá (4069) which is translated "why": Ex 1:18: ". . . Why have ye done this thing, and have saved the men children alive?" See also: 5234. See: TWOT—848; BDB—393b, 1095a.

3046. יְדַע {47x} **yᵉdaʿ** (Aram.), *yed-ah';* corresp. to 3045:—certify {4x}, know {18x}, make known {24x}, teach {1x}. See: TWOT—2765; BDB—1095a.

3047. יָדָע {2x} **Yâdâʿ**, *yaw-daw';* from 3045; *knowing; Jada,* an Isr.:—Jada {2x}. See: BDB—395b.

3048. יְדַעְיָה {11x} **Yᵉdaʿyâh**, *yed-ah-yaw';* from 3045 and 3050; *Jah has known; Jedajah,* the name of two Isr.:—Jedaiah {11x}. See: BDB—396a.

3049. יִדְּעֹנִי {11x} **yiddᵉʿônîy**, *yid-deh-o-nee';* from 3045; prop. a *knowing* one; spec. a *conjurer;* (by impl.) a *ghost:*—wizard {11x}.

These "knowing ones" are always ranked with those who deal in ʻowb (186 – necromancer) and are to be regarded with equal abhorrence. They were no doubt wise in their generation, prudent like the diviners, and skilled in the art of preying on the follies and superstitions of those who came in contact with them (Lev 19:31; 20:6; Deut 18:11; 1 Sa 28:8). See: TWOT—848d; BDB—396b.

3050. יָהּ {49x} **Yâhh**, *yaw;* contr. for 3068, and mean. the same; *Jah,* the sacred name:—JAH {1x}, the LORD {48x}, most vehement. comp. names in "-iah," "-jah." See: TWOT—484b; BDB—219c, 238a, 238b, 239c, 396c.

3051. יָהַב {34x} **yâhab**, *yaw-hab';* a prim. root; to *give* (whether lit. or fig.); gen. to *put;* imper. (refl.) *come:*—ascribe {1x}, bring {2x}, come on {1x}, give {23x}, go to {4x}, give out {1x}, set {1x}, take {1x}. See: TWOT—849; BDB—210c, 396c, 1095b.

3052. יְהַב {28x} **yᵉhab** (Aram.), *yeh-hab';* corresp. to 3051:—give {21x}, given + 1934 {2x}, delivered {1x}, laid {1x}, paid {1x}, prolonged {1x}, yielded {1x}. See: TWOT—2766; BDB—1095b.

3053. יְהָב {1x} **yᵉhâb**, *ye-hawb';* from 3051; prop. what is *given* (by Providence), i.e. a *lot:*—burden {1x}. Syn.: 4853, 5448. See: TWOT—849a; BDB—396d.

3054. יָהַד {1x} **yâhad**, *yaw-had';* denom. from a form corresp. to 3061; to *Judaize,* i.e. become Jewish:—become Jews {1x}. See: TWOT—850; BDB—397a, 397c.

3055. יְהֻד {1x} **Yᵉhûd**, *yeh-hood';* a briefer form of one corresp. to 3061; *Jehud,* a place in Pal.:—Jehud {1x}. See: BDB—397a.

3056. יֶהְדַּי {1x} **Yehday**, *yeh-dah'-ee;* perh. from a form corresp. to 3061; *Judaistic; Jehdai,* an Isr.:—Jehdai {1x}. See: BDB—213a, 397a.

3057. יְהוּדִיָּה {1x} **Yᵉhûdîyâh**, *yeh-hoo-dee-yaw';* fem. of 3064; *Jehudijah,* a Jewess:—Jehudijah {1x}. See: BDB—397c.

3058. יֵהוּא {58x} **Yêhûwʾ**, *yay-hoo';* from 3068 and 1931; *Jehovah (is) He; Jehu,* the name of five Isr.:—Jehu {58x}. See: BDB—219c, 397a.

3059. יְהוֹאָחָז {10x} **Yᵉhôwʼâchâz**, *yeh-ho-aw-khawz';* from 3068 and 270; *Jehovah-seized; Jehoächaz,* the name of three Isr.:—Jehoahaz {10x}. comp. 3099. See: BDB—219d.

3060. יְהוֹאָשׁ {17x} **Yᵉhôwʼâsh**, *yeh-ho-awsh';* from 3068 and (perh.) 784; *Jehovah-fired; Jehoäsh,* the name of two Isr. kings:—Jehoash {17x}. comp. 3101. See: BDB—219d.

3061. יְהוּד {7x} **Yᵉhûwd** (Aram.), *yeh-hood';* contr. from a form corresp. to 3063; prop. *Judah,* hence, *Judæa:*—Jewry {1x}, Judah {5x}, Judea {1x}. See: BDB—1095c.

3062. יְהוּדָאִי {10x} **Yᵉhûwdâʼîy** (Aram.), *yeh-hoo-daw-ee';* patrial from 3061; a *Jehudâte* (or Judaite), i.e. Jew:—Jew {10x}. See: BDB—1095c.

3063. יְהוּדָה {818x} **Yᵉhûwdâh**, *yeh-hoo-daw';* from 3034; *celebrated; Jehudah* (or Judah), the name of five Isr.; also of the tribe descended from the first, and of its territory:—Judah {808x}, Bethlehem-judah + 1035 {10x}. See: TWOT—850c; BDB—397a, 1095c.

3064. יְהוּדִי {76x} **Yᵉhûwdîy**, *yeh-hoo-dee';* patron. from 3063; a *Jehudite* (i.e. Judaite or Jew), or desc. of Jehudah (i.e. Judah):—Jew {74x}, Jew + 376 {1x}, Judah {1x}. See: TWOT—850a; BDB—397c, 1095c.

3065. יְהוּדִי {4x} **Yᵉhûwdîy**, *yeh-hoo-dee';* the same as 3064; *Jehudi,* an Isr.:—Jehudi {4x}. See: BDB—397c.

3066. יְהוּדִית {6x} **Yᵉhûwdîyth**, *yeh-hoo-deeth';* fem. of 3064; the *Jewish* (used adv.) language:—in the Jews' language {5x}, Jews' speech {1x}. See: BDB—397c.

3067. יְהוּדִית {1x} **Yᵉhûwdîyth**, *yeh-hoo-deeth';* the same as 3066; *Jewess; Jehudith,* a Canaanitess:—Judith {1x}. See: BDB—397c.

3068. יְהוָֹה {6519x} **Yᵉhôvâh**, *yeh-ho-vaw';* from 1961; (the) self-*Existent* or Eternal; *Jehovah,* Jewish national name of God:—LORD {6510x}, GOD {4x}, JEHOVAH {4x}, variant {1x}. Yehwah (3068), "Lord."

(1) The Tetragrammaton YHWH appears without its own vowels, and its exact pronunciation is debated (Jehovah, *Yehovah,* Jahweh, Yahweh). **(2)** The Hebrew text does insert the vowels for adonay (136), and Jewish students and scholars read adonay whenever they see the Tetragrammaton. **(3)** The divine name YHWH appears only in the Bible. **(4)** Its precise meaning is much debated. God chose it as His personal name by which He related specifically to His chosen or covenant people. Its first appearance in the biblical record is Gen 2:4: "These are the generations of the heavens and of the earth when they were created, in the day that the Lord God made the earth and the heavens." Apparently Adam knew Him by this personal or covenantal name from the beginning, since Seth both called his son Enosh (i.e., man as a weak and dependent creature) and began (along with all other pious persons) to call upon (formally worship) the name of YHWH, "the Lord" (Gen 4:26). The covenant found a fuller expression and application when God revealed Himself to Abraham (Gen 12:8), promising redemption in the form of national existence.

This promise became reality through Moses, to whom God explained that He was not only the "God who exists" but the "God who effects His will": "Thus shalt thou say unto the children of Israel, The Lord [YHWH] God of your fathers, the God of Abraham, the God of Isaac, and the God of Jacob, hath sent me unto you: this is my name for ever, and this is my memorial unto all generations. Go, and gather the elders of Israel together, and say unto them, The Lord [YHWH] God of your fathers, the God of Abraham, of Isaac, and of Jacob, appeared unto me, saying, I have surely visited you, and seen that which is done to you in Egypt: And I have said, I will bring you up out of the affliction of Egypt unto the land of the Canaanites . . ." (Ex 3:15–17). So God explained the meaning of "I am who I am" (Ex 3:14). He spoke to the fathers as YHWH, but the promised deliverance and, therefore, the fuller significance or experienced meaning of His name were unknown to them (Ex 6:2–8). Syn.: 113, 3050, 3069. See: TWOT—484a; BDB—217d, 397a, 397d, 398a.

3069. יְהוִֹה {305x} **Yᵉhôvîh**, *yeh-ho-vee';* a var. of 3068 [used after 136, and pronounced by Jews as 430, in order to prevent the repetition of the same sound, since they elsewhere pronounce 3068 as 136]:—God {304x}, LORD {1x}. See: BDB—217d, 397d.

3070. יְהוָֹה יִרְאֶה {1x} **Yᵉhôvâh Yirʼeh**, *yeh-ho-vaw' yir-eh';* from 3068 and 7200; *Jehovah will see* (to it); *Jehovah-Jireh,* a symb. name for Mt. Moriah:—Jehovah-jireh {1x}. See: BDB—907d.

3071. יְהוָֹה נִסִּי {1x} **Yᵉhôvâh Niççîy**, *yeh-ho-vaw' nis-see';* from 3068 and 5251 with the pron. suff.; *Jehovah* (is) *my banner; Jehovah-Nissi,* a symb. name of an altar in the Desert:—Jehovah nissi {1x}. See: BDB—651d.

3072. יְהוָֹה צִדְקֵנוּ {2x} **Yᵉhôvâh Tsidqênûw**, *ye-ho-vaw' tsid-kay'-noo;* from 3068 and 6664 with pron. suff.; *Jehovah* (is) *our right; Jehovah-Tsidkenu,* a symb. epithet of the Messiah and of Jerusalem:—the LORD our righteousness {2x}. See: BDB—842a.

3073. יְהוָֹה שָׁלוֹם {1x} **Yᵉhôvâh Shâlôwm**, *yeh-ho-vaw' shaw-lome';* from 3068 and 7965; *Jehovah* (is) *peace; Jehovah-Shalom,* a symb. name of an altar in Pal.:—Jehovah-shalom {1x}. See: BDB—1023a.

3074. יְהוָֹה שָׁמָּה {1x} **Yᵉhôvâh Shâmmâh**, *yeh-ho-vaw' shawm'-maw;* from 3068 and 8033 with directive enclitic; *Jehovah* (is) *thither; Jehovah-Shammah,* a symbol. title of Jerusalem:—Jehovah-shammah {1x}. See: BDB—1027c.

3075. יְהוֹזָבָד {4x} **Yᵉhôwzâbâd**, *yeh-ho-zaw-bawd';* from 3068 and 2064; *Jehovah-endowed; Jehozabad,* the name of three Isr.:—Jehozabad {4x}. Syn.: comp. 3107. See: BDB—220a.

3076. יְהוֹחָנָן {7x} **Yᵉhôwchânân**, *yeh-ho-khaw-nawn';* from 3068 and 2603; *Jehovah-favored; Jehochanan,* the name of eight Isr.:—Jehohanan {6x}, Johanan {1x}. See: BDB—220b. Syn.: comp. 3110.

3077. יְהוֹיָדָע {51x} **Yᵉhôwyâdâʻ**, *yeh-ho-yaw-daw';* from 3068 and 3045; *Jehovah-known; Jehojada,* the name of three Isr.:—Jehoiada {51x}. See: BDB—220b. Syn.: comp. 3111.

3078. יְהוֹיָכִין {10x} **Yᵉhôwyâkîyn**, *yeh-ho-yaw-keen';* from 3068 and 3559; *Jehovah will establish; Jehojakin,* a Jewish king:—Jehoiachin {10x}. See: BDB—220c, 408a, 487c. comp. 3112.

3079. יְהוֹיָקִים {37x} **Yᵉhôwyâqîym**, *yeh-ho-yaw-keem';* from 3068 abb. and 6965; *Jehovah will raise; Jehojakim,* a Jewish king:—Jehoiakim {37x}. See: BDB—220c. comp. 3113.

3080. יְהוֹיָרִיב {2x} **Yᵉhôwyârîyb**, *yeh-ho-yaw-reeb';* from 3068 and 7378; *Jehovah will contend; Jehojarib,* the name of two Isr.:—Jehoiarib {2x}. See: BDB—220d. comp. 3114.

3081. יְהוּכַל {1x} **Yᵉhûwkal**, *yeh-hoo-kal';* from 3201; *potent; Jehukal,* an Isr.:—Jehucal {1x}. See: BDB—220d, 397d, 408a. comp. 3116.

3082. יְהוֹנָדָב {8x} **Yᵉhôwnâdâb**, *yeh-ho-naw-dawb';* from 3068 and 5068; *Jehovah-largessed; Jehonadab,* the name of an Isr. and of an Arab:—Jehonadab {3x}, Jonadab {5x}. See: BDB—220d. comp. 3122.

3083. יְהוֹנָתָן {82x} **Yᵉhôwnâthân**, *yeh-ho-naw-thawn';* from 3068 and 5414; *Jehovah-given; Jehonathan,* the name of four Isr.:—Jonathan or Jehonathan {82x}. See: BDB—220d. comp. 3129.

3084. יְהוֹסֵף {1x} **Yᵉhôwçêph**, *yeh-ho-safe';* a fuller form of 3130; *Jehoseph* (i.e. Joseph), a son of Jacob:—Joseph {1x}. See: BDB—415c.

3085. יְהוֹעַדָּה {2x} **Yᵉhôwʻaddâh**, *yeh-ho-ad-daw';* from 3068 and 5710; *Jehovah-adorned; Jehoäddah,* an Isr.:—Jehoada {2x}. See: BDB—221a.

3086. יְהוֹעַדִּין {2x} **Yᵉhôwʻaddîyn**, *yeh-ho-ad-deen';* or

יְהוֹעַדָּן **Yᵉhôwʻaddân**, *yeh-ho-ad-dawn';* from 3068 and 5727; *Jehovah-pleased; Jehoäddin* or *Jehoäddan,* an Israelitess:—Jehoaddan {2x}. See: BDB—221a.

3087. יְהוֹצָדָק {8x} **Yᵉhôwtsâdâq**, *yeh-ho-tsaw-dawk';* from 3068 and 6663; *Jehovah-righted; Jehotsadak,* an Isr.:—Jehozadek {3x}, Josedech {6x}. See: BDB—221b. comp. 3136.

3088. יְהוֹרָם {29x} **Yᵉhôwrâm**, *yeh-ho-rawm';* from 3068 and 7311; *Jehovah-raised; Jehoram,* the name of a Syrian and of three Isr.:—Jehoram {23x}, Joram {6x}. See: BDB—221b. comp. 3141.

3089. יְהוֹשֶׁבַע {1x} **Yᵉhôwshebaʻ**, *yeh-ho-sheh'-bah;* from 3068 and 7650; *Jehovah-sworn; Jehosheba,* an Israelitess:—Jehosheba {1x}. See: BDB—221b, 989d. comp. 3090.

3090. יְהוֹשַׁבְעַת {2x} **Yᵉhôwshabʻath**, *yeh-ho-shab-ath';* a form of 3089; *Jehoshabath,* an Israelitess:—Jehoshabeath {2x}. See: BDB—221b, 221c.

3091. יְהוֹשׁוּעַ {218x} **Yᵉhôwshûwʻa**, *yeh-ho-shoo'-ah;* or

יְהוֹשֻׁעַ **Yᵉhôwshûʻa**, *yeh-ho-shoo'-ah;* from 3068 and 3467; *Jehovah-saved; Jehoshuä* (i.e. Joshua), the Jewish leader:—Jehoshua or Jehoshuah or Joshua {218x}. See: BDB—221c, 448a. comp. 1954, 3442.

3092. יְהוֹשָׁפָט {84x} **Yᵉhôwshâphâṭ**, *yeh-ho-shaw-fawt';* from 3068 and 8199; *Jehovah-judged; Jehoshaphat,* the name of six Isr.; also of a valley near Jerusalem:—Jehoshaphat {84x}. See: BDB—221d. comp. 3146.

3093. יָהִיר {2x} **yâhîyr**, *yaw-here';* prob. from the same as 2022; *elated;* hence, *arrogant:*—haughty {1x}, proud {1x}. See: TWOT—851a; BDB—397d.

3094. יְהַלֶּלְאֵל {2x} **Yᵉhallelᵓêl**, *yeh-hal-lel-ale';* from 1984 and 410; *praising God; Jehallelel,* the name of two Isr.:—Jehaleleel {1x}, Jehalelel {1x}. See: BDB—239c, 397d.

3095. יַהֲלֹם {3x} **yahălôm**, *yah-hal-ome';* from 1986 (in the sense of *hardness*); a precious stone, prob. *onyx:*—diamond {3x}. See: TWOT—502b; BDB—240d, 397d.

3096. יַהַץ {9x} **Yahats**, *yah'-hats;* or

יַהְצָה **Yahtsâh**, *yah'-tsaw;* or (fem.)

יַהְצָה **Yahtsâh**, *yah-tsaw';* from an unused root mean. to *stamp;* perh. *threshing*-floor; *Jahats* or *Jahtsah,* a place E. of the Jordan:—Jahaz {4x}, Jahazah {4x}, Jahzah {1x}. See: BDB—397d.

3097. יוֹאָב {145x} **Yôwᵓâb**, *yo-awb';* from 3068 and 1; *Jehovah-fathered; Joäb,* the name of three Isr.:—Joab {145x}. See: BDB—222a, 398a.

3098. יוֹאָח {11x} **Yôwᵓâch**, *yo-awkh';* from 3068 and 251; *Jehovah-brothered; Joach,* the name of four Isr.:—Joah {11x}. See: BDB—222a.

3099. יוֹאָחָז {4x} **Yôwᵓâchâz**, *yo-aw-khawz';* a form of 3059; *Joächaz,* the name of two Isr.:—Jehoahaz {3x}, Joahaz {1x}. See: BDB—219d, 222a.

3100. יוֹאֵל {19x} **Yôwᵓêl**, *yo-ale';* from 3068 and 410; *Jehovah* (is his) *God; Joël,* the name of twelve Isr.:—Joel {19x}. See: BDB—222a.

3101. יוֹאָשׁ {10x} **Yôwᵓâsh**, *yo-awsh';* or

יֹאָשׁ **Yôᵓâsh** (2 Chron. 24:1), *yo-awsh';* a form of 3060; *Joäsh,* the name of six Isr.:—Joash {47x}. See: BDB—219d, 222b.

3102. יוֹב {1x} **Yôwb**, *yobe;* perh. a form of 3103, but more prob. by err. transc. for 3437; *Job,* an Isr.:—Job {1x}. See: BDB—398a.

3103. יוֹבָב {9x} **Yôwbâb**, *yo-bawb';* from 2980; *howler; Jobab,* the name of two Isr. and of three foreigners:—Jobab {9x}. See: BDB—384d, 398a.

3104. יוֹבֵל {27x} **yôwbêl**, *yo-bale';* or

יֹבֵל **yôbêl**, *yob-ale';* appar. from 2986; the *blast* of a horn (from its *continuous* sound); spec. the *signal* of the silver trumpets; hence, the instrument itself and the festival thus introduced:—jubile {21x}, ram's horn {5x}, trumpet {1x}.

Yobel means "ram; ram's horn; jubilee year." **(1)** *Yobel* means ram's horn blown to assemble the people: "When the ram's horn [v, "trumpet"] sounds a long blast, they shall come up to the mountain" (Ex 19:13). **(2)** This word also signifies jubilee year (Lev 25:8–15; 27:16–25). **(2a)** In the fiftieth year on the Day of Atonement jubilee was to be declared. **(2b)** All land was returned to the individual or family to whom it had originally belonged by inheritance, even if he (or she) were in bondservice. **(2c)** When land was valued in anticipation of selling it or devoting it to God, it was to be valued in terms of anticipated productivity prior to the year of jubilee. **(2d)** Between jubilees land might be redeemed for its productivity value. **(2e)** City property, however, must be redeemed within a year of its sale or loss. **(2f)** Levitical property was not subject to these rules. **(2g)** Israelites who fell into bondage were to be released in the jubilee year, or redeemed in the interim period. See: TWOT—835e; BDB—385c, 398a.

3105. יוּבַל {1x} **yûwbal**, *yoo-bal';* from 2986; a *stream:*—river {1x}. Syn.: 180, 650, 2975. See: TWOT—835b; 385b, 398a.

3106. יוּבָל {1x} **Yûwbâl**, *yoo-bawl';* from 2986; *stream; Jubal,* an antediluvian:—Jubal {1x}. See: BDB—385b.

3107. יוֹזָבָד {10x} **Yôwzâbâd**, *yo-zaw-bawd';* a form of 3075; *Jozabad,* the name of ten Isr.:—Josabad {1x}, Jozabad {9x}. See: BDB—220a, 222b.

3108. יוֹזָכָר {1x} **Yôwzâkâr**, *yo-zaw-kawr';* from 3068 and 2142; *Jehovah-remembered; Jozacar,* an Isr.:—Jozachar {1x}. See: BDB—222b.

3109. יוֹחָא {2x} **Yôwchâᵓ**, *yo-khaw';* prob. from 3068 and a var. of 2421; *Jehovah-revived; Jocha,* the name of two Isr.:—Joha {2x}. See: BDB—398a.

3110. יוֹחָנָן {24x} **Yôwchânân**, *yo-khaw-nawn';* a form of 3076; *Jochanan,* the name of nine Isr.:—Johanan {24x}. See: BDB—220b, 222b.

יוּטָּה **Yûwṭâh**. See 3194.

3111. יוֹיָדָע {5x} **Yôwyâdâʻ**, *yo-yaw-daw';* a form of 3077; *Jojada,* the name of two Isr.:—Jehoiada {1x}, Joiada {4x}. See: BDB—220, 222b.

3112. יוֹיָכִין {1x} **Yôwyâkîyn**, *yo-yaw-keen';* a form of 3078; *Jojakin,* an Isr. king:—Jehoiachin {1x}. See: BDB—220c, 222c.

3113. יוֹיָקִים {4x} **Yôwyâqîym**, *yo-yaw-keem';* a form of 3079; *Jojakim,* an Isr.:—Joiakim {4x}. See: BDB—220c, 222c. comp. 3137.

3114. יוֹיָרִיב {5x} **Yôwyârîyb**, *yo-yaw-reeb';* a form of 3080; *Jojarib,* the name of four Isr.:—Joiarib {5x}. See: BDB—220d, 222c.

3115. יוֹכֶבֶד {2x} **Yôwkebed**, *yo-keh'-bed;* from 3068 contr. and 3513; *Jehovah-gloried; Jokebed,* the mother of Moses:—Jochebed {2x}. See: BDB—222c.

3116. יוּכַל {1x} **Yûwkal**, *yoo-kal';* a form of 3081; *Jukal,* an Isr.:—Jucal {1x}. See: BDB—220d, 222c, 398.

3117. יוֹם {2274x} **yôwm**, *yome;* from an unused root mean. to *be hot;* a *day* (as the *warm* hours), whether lit. (from sunrise to sunset, or from one sunset to the next), or fig. (a space of time defined by an associated term), [often used adv.]:—day {2008x}, time {64x}, chronicles + 1697 {37x}, daily {32x}, ever {17x}, year {14x}, continually {10x}, when {10x}, as {10x}, while {8x}, full {8x} always {4x}, whole {4x}, alway {4x}, misc. {44x} = age, + elder, × end, + evening, life, as (so) long as (. . . live), (even) now, + old, + outlived, + perpetually, presently, + remaineth, × required, season, × since, space, then, + in trouble, weather, + younger.

Yowm (3117) means "daylight; day; time; moment; year." **(1)** *Yowm* has several meanings. **(1a)** The word represents the period of "daylight" as contrasted with nighttime: "While the earth remaineth, seedtime and harvest, and cold and heat, and summer and winter, and day and night shall not cease" (Gen 8:22). **(1b)** The word denotes a period of twenty-four hours: "And it came to pass, as she spake to Joseph day by day . . ." (Gen 39:10). **(2)** *Yowm* can also signify a period of time of unspecified duration: "And God blessed the seventh day, and sanctified it: because that in it he had rested from all his work which God created and made" (Gen 2:3). **(2a)** In this verse, "day" refers to the entire period of God's resting from creating this universe. **(2b)** This "day" began after He completed the creative acts of the seventh day and extends at least to the return of Christ. **(2c)** Compare Gen 2:4: "These are the generations of the heavens and of the earth when they were created, in the day [beyom] that the Lord God made the earth and the heavens. . . ." **(2d)** Here "day" refers to the entire period envisioned in the first six days of creation. **(3)** Another nuance appears in Gen 2:17, where the word represents a "point of time" or "a moment": "But of the tree of the knowledge of good and evil, thou shalt not eat of it: for in the day [beyom] that thou eatest thereof thou shalt surely die."

(4) When used in the plural, the word may represent "year": "Thou shalt therefore keep this ordinance in his season from year to year [yamim]" (Ex 13:10). **(5)** There are several other special nuances of *yowm* when it is used with various prepositions. **(5a)** First, when used with ke ("as," "like"), it can connote **(5a1)** "first": "And Jacob said, Sell me this day [first] thy birthright" (Gen 25:31). **(5a2)** It may also mean "one day," or "about this day": "And it came to pass about this time, that Joseph went into the house to do his business . . ." (Gen 39:11). **(5a3)** On Joseph's lips, the phrase connotes "this present result" (literally, "as it is this day"): "But as for you, ye thought evil against me; but God meant it unto good, to bring to pass, as it is this day, to save much people alive" (Gen 50:20). **(5a4)** Adonijah used this same phrase to represent "today": "Let king Solomon swear unto me today that he will not slay his servant . . ." (1 Kin 1:51). **(5a5)** Yet another nuance appears in 1 Sa 9:13: "Now therefore get you up; for about this time ye shall find him." **(5b)** When used with the definite article ha, the noun may mean **(5b1)** "today" (as it does in Gen 4:14) or refer **(5b2)** to some particular "day" (1 Sa 1:4) and the "daytime" (Neh 4:16).

(6) The first biblical occurrence of *yowm* is found in Gen 1:5: "And God called the light Day, and the darkness he called Night. And the evening and the morning were the first day." **(7)** The second use introduces one of the most debated occurrences of the word, which is the duration of the days of creation. **(7a)** Perhaps the most frequently heard explanations are that these "days" are **(7a1)** 24 hours long, **(7a2)** indefinitely long (i.e., eras of time), or **(7a3)** logical rather than temporal categories (i.e., they depict theological categories rather than periods of time). **(7b)** However, we know that these were literal 24 hour days. God based the Sabbath day's rest on His 7 days of creation. God did not work "7 long periods of time." Ex 20:9–11 "Six days shalt thou labour, and do all thy work: But the seventh day *is* the sabbath of the LORD thy God: *in it* thou shalt not do any work, thou, nor thy son, nor thy daughter, thy manservant, nor thy maidservant, nor thy cattle, nor thy stranger that *is* within thy gates: For *in* six days the LORD made heaven and earth, the sea, and all that in them *is,* and rested the seventh day: wherefore the LORD blessed the sabbath day, and hallowed it."

(8) The "day of the Lord" is used to denote **(8a)** both the end of the age (eschatologically) or some occurrence during the present age (non-eschatologically). **(8b)** It may be a day of either judgment or blessing, or both (cf. Is 2). **(9)** It is noteworthy that Hebrew people did not divide the period of daylight into regular hourly periods, whereas nighttime was divided into three watches (Ex 14:24; Judg 7:19). **(10)** The beginning of a "day" is sometimes **(10)** said to be dusk

(Est 4:16) and sometimes **(11)** dawn (Deut 28:66–67). See: TWOT—852; BDB—398a, 1095c.

3118. יוֹם {16x} **yôwm** (Aram.), *yome;* corresp. to 3117; a *day:*—day {14x}, time {2x}. See: TWOT—2767; BDB—1095c.

3119. יוֹמָם {52x} **yôwmâm**, *yo-mawm';* from 3117; *daily:*—daily {2x}, (by, in the) day {41x}, daytime {7x}, time {1x}. See: TWOT—852a; BDB—401b.

3120. יָוָן {11x} **Yâvân**, *yaw-vawn';* prob. from the same as 3196; *effervescing* (i.e. hot and active); *Javan,* the name of a son of Joktan, and of the race (*Ionians,* i.e. Greeks) descended from him, with their territory; also of a place in Arabia:—Javan {7x}, Grecia {3x}, Greece {1x}. See: TWOT—855; BDB—75a, 42a.

3121. יָוֵן {1x} **yâvên**, *yaw-ven';* from the same as 3196; prop. *dregs* (as *effervescing*); hence, *mud:*—mire {1x}, miry {1x}. See: TWOT—853a; BDB—401c.

3122. יוֹנָדָב {7x} **Yôwnâdâb**, *yo-naw-dawb';* a form of 3082; *Jonadab,* the name of an Isr. and of a Rechabite:—Jonadab {7x}. See: BDB—220d, 222c.

3123. יוֹנָה {32x} **yôwnâh**, *yo-naw';* prob. from the same as 3196; a *dove* (appar. from the *warmth* of their mating):—dove {21x}, pigeon {10x}, variant + 1686 {1x}. See: TWOT—854a; BDB—351a, 401d.

3124. יוֹנָה {19x} **Yôwnâh**, *yo-naw';* the same as 3123; *Jonah,* an Isr.:—Jonah {19x}. See: BDB—402a.

3125. יְוָנִי {1x} **Yᵉvânîy**, *yev-aw-nee';* patron. from 3121; a *Jevanite,* or desc. of Javan:—Grecian {1x}. See: BDB—402b.

3126. יוֹנֵק {1x} **yôwnêq**, *yo-nake';* act. part. of 3243; a *sucker;* hence, a *twig* (of a tree felled and sprouting):—tender plant {1x}. See: TWOT—874a; BDB—413c.

3127. יוֹנֶקֶת {6x} **yôwneqeth**, *yo-neh'-keth;* fem. of 3126; a *sprout:*—tender branch {1x}, branch {4x}, young twigs {1x}. See: TWOT—874b; BDB—413c.

3128. יוֹנַת אֵלֶם רְחֹקִים {1x} **Yôwnath ʾêlem rᵉchôqîym**, *yo-nath' ay'-lem rekh-o-keem';* from 3123 and 482 and the plur. of 7350; *dove of* (the) *silence* (i.e. *dumb* Israel) *of* (i.e. *among*) *distances* (i.e. *strangers*); the title of a ditty (used for a name of its melody):—Jonath-elem-rechokim {1x}. See: BDB—401d.

3129. יוֹנָתָן {42x} **Yôwnâthân**, *yo-naw-thawn';* a form of 3083; *Jonathan,* the name of ten Isr.:—Jonathan {42x}. See: BDB—220d, 222c.

3130. יוֹסֵף {213x} **Yôwçêph**, *yo-safe';* future of 3254; *let him add* (or perh. simply act. part. *adding*); *Joseph,* the name of seven Isr.:—Joseph {213x}. See: BDB—402, 415c. comp. 3084.

3131. יוֹסִפְיָה {1x} **Yôwçiphyâh**, *yo-sif-yaw';* from act. part. of 3254 and 3050; *Jah* (is) *adding; Josiphjah,* an Isr.:—Josiphiah {1x}. See: BDB—402b, 415d.

3132. יוֹעֵאלָה {1x} **Yôwʿêʾlâh**, *yo-ay-law';* perh. fem. act. part. of 3276; *furthermore; Joelah,* an Isr.:—Joelah {1x}. See: BDB—402b, 418d.

3133. יוֹעֵד {1x} **Yôwʿêd**, *yo-ade';* appar. the act. part. of 3259; *appointer; Joed,* an Isr.:—Joed {1x}. See: BDB—222c.

3134. יוֹעֶזֶר {1x} **Yôwʿezer**, *yo-eh'-zer;* from 3068 and 5828; *Jehovah* (is his) *help; Joezer,* an Isr.:—Joezer {1x}. See: BDB—222c.

3135. יוֹעָשׁ {2x} **Yôwʿâsh**, *yo-awsh';* from 3068 and 5789; *Jehovah-hastened; Joash,* the name of two Isr.:—Joash {2x}. See: BDB—222c.

3136. יוֹצָדָק {5x} **Yôwtsâdâq**, *yo-tsaw-dawk';* a form of 3087; *Jotsadak,* an Isr.:—Jozadak {5x}. See: BDB—221b, 222c, 1095c.

3137. יוֹקִים {1x} **Yôwqîym**, *yo-keem';* a form of 3113; *Jokim,* an Isr.:—Jokim {1x}. See: BDB—220c, 222d.

3138. יוֹרֶה {2x} **yôwreh**, *yo-reh';* act. part. of 3384; *sprinkling;* hence, a *sprinkling* (or autumnal showers):—first rain {1x}, former [rain]{1x}. See: TWOT—910a; BDB—435c.

3139. יוֹרָה {1x} **Yôwrâh**, *yo-raw';* from 3384; *rainy; Jorah,* an Isr.:—Jorah {1x}. See: BDB—402b, 435c.

3140. יוֹרַי {1x} **Yôwray**, *yo-rah'-ee;* from 3384; *rainy; Jorai,* an Isr.:—Jorai {1x}. See: BDB—436c.

3141. יוֹרָם {20x} **Yôwrâm**, *yo-rawm';* a form of 3088; *Joram,* the name of three Isr. and one Syrian:—Joram {20x}. See: BDB—221b, 222d.

3142. יוּשַׁב חֶסֶד {1x} **Yûwshab Cheçed**, *yoo-shab' kheh'-sed;* from 7725 and 2617; *kindness will be returned; Jushab-Chesed,* an Isr.:—Jushab-hesed {1x}. See: BDB—402b, 1000b.

3143. יוֹשִׁבְיָה {1x} **Yôwshîbyâh**, *yo-shib-yaw';* from 3427 and 3050; *Jehovah will cause to dwell; Josibjah,* an Isr.:—Josibiah {1x}. See: BDB—444a.

3144. יוֹשָׁה {1x} **Yôwshâh**, *yo-shaw';* prob. a form of 3145; *Joshah,* an Isr.:—Joshah {1x}. See: BDB—402b, 444b.

3145. יוֹשַׁוְיָה {1x} **Yôwshavyâh**, *yo-shav-yaw';* from 3068 and 7737; *Jehovah-set; Joshavjah,* an Isr.:—Joshaviah {1x}. See: BDB—402b, 444b. comp. 3144.

3146. יוֹשָׁפָט **Yôwshâphâṭ**, *yo-shaw-fawt';* a form of 3092; *Joshaphat,* an Isr.:—Jehoshaphat {1x}, Joshaphat {1x}. See: BDB—221d, 222d.

3147. יוֹתָם {24x} **Yôwthâm**, *yo-thawm';* from 3068 and 8535; *Jehovah* (is) *perfect; Jotham,* the name of three Isr.:—Jotham {24x}. See: BDB—222d.

3148. יוֹתֵר **yôwthêr**, *yo-thare';* act. part. of 3498; prop. *redundant;* hence, *over and above,* as adj., noun, adv. or conjunc. [as follows]:—better {1x}, more {3x}, moreover {1x}, over {1x}, profit {1x}, further {1x}. See: TWOT—936d; BDB—452c.

3149. יְזַוְאֵל {1x} **Yᵉzavʾêl**, *yez-av-ale';* from an unused root (mean. to *sprinkle*) and 410; *sprinkled of God; Jezavel,* an Isr.:—Jeziel {1x}. See: BDB—402b.

3150. יִזִּיָּה {1x} **Yizzîyâh**, *yiz-zee-yaw';* from the same as the first part of 3149 and 3050; *sprinkled of Jah; Jizzijah,* an Isr.:—Jeziah {1x}. See: BDB—402c, 633c.

3151. יָזִיז {1x} **Yâzîyz**, *yaw-zeez';* from the same as 2123; *he will make prominent; Jaziz,* an Isr.:—Jaziz {1x}. See: BDB—265c, 402c.

3152. יִזְלִיאָה {1x} **Yizlîyʾah**, *yiz-lee-aw';* perh. from an unused root (mean. to *draw up*); *he will draw out; Jizliah,* an Isr.:—Jezliah {1x}. See: BDB—272c, 402c.

3153. יְזַנְיָה {2x} **Yᵉzanyâh**, *yez-an-yaw';* or יְזַנְיָהוּ **Yᵉzanyâhûw**, *yez-an-yaw'-hoo;* prob. for 2970; *Jezanjah,* an Isr.:—Jezaniah {2x}. See: BDB—24d, 402c.

3154. יֶזַע {1x} **yezaʿ**, *yeh'-zah;* from an unused root mean to *ooze; sweat,* i.e. (by impl.) a *sweating* dress:—any thing that causeth sweat {1x}. See: TWOT—857a; BDB—402c.

3155. יִזְרָח {1x} **Yizrâch**, *yiz-rawkh';* a var. for 250; a *Jizrach* (i.e. Ezrachite or Zarchite) or desc. of Zerach:—Izrahite {1x}. See: BDB—280d, 402c.

3156. יִזְרַחְיָה {3x} **Yizrachyâh**, *yiz-rakh-yaw';* from 2224 and 3050; *Jah will shine; Jizrachjah,* the name of two Isr.:—Izrahiah {1x}, Jezrahiah {1x}. See: BDB—280d, 402c.

3157. יִזְרְעֶאל {36x} **Yizrᵉʿêʾl**, *yiz-reh-ale';* from 2232 and 410; *God will sow; Jizreël,* the name of two places in Pal. and of two Isr.:—Jezreel {36x}. See: BDB—283b, 402c.

3158. יִזְרְעֵאלִי {8x} **Yizrᵉʿêʾlîy**, *yiz-reh-ay-lee';* patron. from 3157; a *Jizreëlite* or native of Jizreel:—Jezreelite {8x}. See: BDB—283c.

3159. יִזְרְעֵאלִית {5x} **Yizrᵉʿêʾlîyth**, *yiz-reh-ay-leeth';* fem. of 3158; a *Jezreëlitess:*—Jezreelitess {15x}. See: BDB—283c.

3160. יְחֻבָּה {1x} **Yᵉchubbâh**, *yekh-oob-baw';* from 2247; *hidden; Jechubbah,* an Isr.:—Jehubbah {1x}. See: BDB—285d, 286a, 402c.

3161. יָחַד {3x} **yâchad**, *yaw-khad';* a prim. root; to *be* (or *become*) *one:*—join {1x}, unite {2x}.

Yachad means "to be united, meet." Gen 49:6: "O my soul, come not thou into their secret; unto their assembly, mine honor, be not thou united. . . ." See: BDB—402d.

3162. יַחַד {142x} **yachad**, *yakh'-ad;* from 3161; prop. a *unit,* i.e. (adv.) *unitedly:*—together {120x}, altogether {5x}, alike {5x}, likewise {2x} withal {2x}, misc. {8x} = at all (once), both, only.

I. The adverbial form *yachad* means "together; alike; all at once; all together." **(1)** Used as an adverb, the word emphasizes a plurality in unity. **(2)** In some contexts the connotation is on community in action. Goliath challenged the Israelites, saying: "I defy the armies of Israel this day; give me a man, that we may fight together" (1 Sa 17:10). **(3)** Sometimes the emphasis is on commonality of place: ". . . And it came to pass, that they which remained were scattered, so that two of them were not left together" (1 Sa 11:11). **(4)** The word can be used of being in the same place at the same time: "And he delivered them into the hands of the Gibeonites, and they hanged them in the hill before the Lord: and they fell all seven together . . ." (2 Sa 21:9). **(5)** In other passages *yachad* means "at the same time": "O that my grief were thoroughly weighed, and my calamity laid in the balances together!" (Job 6:2). **(6)** In many poetic contexts *yachad* is a near synonym of kullam (3617), "altogether." **(6a)** *Yachad,* however, is more emphatic, meaning "all at once, all together." **(6b)** In Deut 33:5 (the first biblical occurrence) the word is used emphatically, meaning "all together," or "all of them together": "And he was king in Jeshurun, when the heads of the people and the tribes of Israel were gathered together."

(6c) Cf.: "Surely men of low degree are vanity, and men of high degree are a lie: to be laid in the balance, they are altogether lighter than vanity" (Ps 62:9). **(6d)** In such contexts *yachad* emphasizes the totality of a given group (cf. Ps 33:15). **(7)** *Yachad* also sometimes emphasizes that things are "alike" or that the same thing will happen to all of them: "likewise the fool and brutish person perish" (Ps 49:10). **II. The form yachdaw,** as an adverb, means "all alike; equally; all at once; all together." **(1)** It speaks of community **(1a)** in action (Deut 25:11), **(1b)** in place (Gen 13:6—the first biblical appearance of this form), and **(1c)** in time (Ps 4:8). **(2)** In other places it is synonymous with kullam (3617), "altogether." **(3)** In Is 10:8 yachdaw means "all alike," or "equally": "Are not my princes altogether kings?" **(4)** In Ex 19:8 this word implies "all at once" as well as "all together": "And all the people answered together, and said. . . ." **(5)** The sense "alike" appears in Deut 12:22: "Even as the roebuck and the hart is eaten, so thou shalt eat them: the unclean and the clean shall eat of them alike." See: TWOT—858b; BDB—403a, 403b.

3163. יַחְדּוֹ {1x} **Yachdôw**, *yakh-doe';* from 3162 with pron. suff.; *his unity,* i.e. (adv.) *together; Jachdo,* an Isr.:—Jahdo {1x}. See: BDB—403c.

3164. יַחְדִּיאֵל {1x} **Yachdîyʾêl**, *yakh-dee-ale';* from 3162 and 410; *unity of God; Jachdiël,* an Isr.:—Jahdiel {1x}. See: BDB—292d, 403d.

3165. יֶחְדִּיָּהוּ {2x} **Yechdîyâhûw**, *yekh-dee-yaw'-hoo;* from 3162 and 3050; *unity of Jah; Jechdijah,* the name of two Isr.:—Jehdeiah {2x}. See: BDB—292d.

יְחַוְאֵל **Yechavʾêl**. See 3171.

3166. יַחֲזִיאֵל {6x} **Yachăzîyʾêl**, *yakh-az-ee-ale';* from 2372 and 410; *beheld of God; Jachaziël,* the name of five Isr.:—Jahaziel {6x}. See: BDB—303c, 403d.

3167. יַחְזְיָה {1x} **Yachzeyâh**, *yakh-zeh-yaw';* from 2372 and 3050; *Jah will behold; Jachzejah,* an Isr.:—Jahaziah {1x}. See: BDB—303c, 403d.

3168. יְחֶזְקֵאל {3x} **Yechezqêʾl**, *yekh-ez-kale';* from 2388 and 410; *God will strengthen; Jechezkel,* the name of two Isr.:—Ezekiel {2x}, Jehezekel {1x}. See: BDB—306b, 403d.

3169. יְחִזְקִיָּה {44x} **Yechizqîyâh**, *yekh-iz-kee-yaw';* or

יְחִזְקִיָּהוּ **Yechizqîyâhûw**, *yekh-iz-kee-yaw'-hoo;* from 3388 and 3050; *strengthened of Jah; Jechizkijah,* the name of five Isr.:—Hezekiah {43x}, Jehizkiah {1x}. See: BDB—306a, 306b, 403d. comp. 2396.

3170. יַחְזֵרָה {1x} **Yachzêrâh**, *yakh-zay-raw';* from the same as 2386; perh. *protection; Jachzerah,* an Isr.:—Jahzerah {1x}. See: BDB—306c, 403d.

3171. יְחִיאֵל {14x} **Yechîyʾêl**, *yekh-ee-ale';* or (2 Chr 29:14)

יְחַוְאֵל **Yechavʾêl**, *yekh-av-ale';* from 2421 and 410; *God will live; Jechiël* (or *Jechavel*), the name of eight Isr.:—Jehiel {1x}. See: BDB—295d, 313c, 403d.

3172. יְחִיאֵלִי {2x} **Yechîyʾêlîy**, *yekh-ee-ay-lee';* patron. from 3171; a *Jechiëlite* or desc. of Jechiel:—Jehieli {2x}. See: BDB—313d, 403d.

3173. יָחִיד {12x} **yâchîyd**, *yaw-kheed';* from 3161; prop. *united,* i.e. *sole;* by impl. *beloved;* also *lonely;* (fem.) the *life* (as not to be replaced):—only {6x}, darling {2x}, only child {1x}, only son {1x}, desolate {1x}, solitary {1x}.

Yachiyd means "very self, only; solitary; lonely." **(1)** The word can be used meaning "self, my soul": "Deliver my soul from the sword, my darling from the power of the dog" (Ps 22:20; cf. Ps 35:17). **(2)** Sometimes this word means "only": "Take now thy son, thine only son Isaac, whom thou lovest . . ." (Gen 22:2—the first biblical occurrence of the word). **(3)** In two passages this word means "solitary" or "lonely": "Turn thee unto me, and have mercy upon me; for I am desolate and afflicted" (Ps 25:16; cf. Ps 68:6). **(4)** The noun yachad occurs only once to mean "unitedness." David said to the Benjaminites: "If ye be come peaceably unto me to help me, mine heart shall be knit unto you [I am ready to become one (or united) with you] . . ." (1 Chr 12:17). This usage of the word as a substantive is unusual. See: TWOT—858a; BDB—402d.

3174. יְחִיָּה {1x} **Yechîyâh**, *yekh-ee-yaw';* from 2421 and 3050; *Jah will live; Jechijah,* an Isr.:—Jehiah {1x}. See: BDB—313d, 403d.

3175. יָחִיל {1x} **yâchîyl**, *yaw-kheel';* from 3176; *expectant:*—should hope {1x}. This word signifies a long patient waiting. See: TWOT—859a; BDB—404a.

3176. יָחַל {42x} **yâchal**, *yaw-chal';* a prim. root; to *wait;* by impl. to *be patient, hope:*—(cause to, have, make to) hope {22x}, wait {12x}, tarry {3x}, trust {2x}, variant {2x}, stayed {1x}. See: TWOT—859; BDB—403d.

3177. יַחְלְאֵל {2x} **Yachleʾêl**, *yakh-leh-ale';* from 3176 and 410; *expectant of God; Jachleël,* an Isr.:—Jahleel {2x}. See: BDB—404b.

3178. יַחְלְאֵלִי {1x} **Yachleʾêlîy**, *yakh-leh-ay-lee';* patron. from 3177; a *Jachleëlite* or desc. of Jachleel:—Jahleelites {1x}. See: BDB—404b.

3179. יָחַם {10x} **yâcham**, *yaw-kham';* a prim. root; prob. to *be hot;* fig. to *conceive:*—get heat {1x}, be hot {2x}, conceive {6x}, be warm {1x}.

Yacham means "to be fiery, be hot." In Deut 19:6 *yacham* means "to be hot": "Lest the avenger of the blood pursue the slayer while his heart is hot, and overtake him. . . ." Syn.: 2029, 2030. See: TWOT—860; BDB—404b, 1095c.

3180. יַחְמוּר {2x} **yachmûwr**, *yakh-moor';* from 2560; a kind of *deer* (from the color; comp. 2543):—fallow deer {1x}. See: TWOT—685b; BDB—331c, 405a.

3181. יַחְמַי {1x} **Yachmay**, *yakh-mah'-ee;* prob. from 3179; *hot; Jachmai,* an Isr.:—Jahmai {1x}. See: BDB—327d, 405a.

3182. יָחֵף {5x} **yâchêph**, *yaw-khafe';* from an unused root mean. to *take off the shoes; unsandalled:*—barefoot {4x}, being unshod {1x}. See: TWOT—861a; BDB—405a.

3183. יַחְצְאֵל {2x} **Yachtseʾêl**, *yakh-tseh-ale';* from 2673 and 410; *God will allot; Jachtseël,* an Isr.:—Jahzeel {2x}. See: BDB—345d, 405a. comp. 3185.

3184. יַחְצְאֵלִי {1x} **Yachtseʾêlîy**, *yakh-tseh-ay-lee';* patron. from 3183; a *Jachtseëlite* (collect.) or desc. of Jachtseel:—Jahzeelites {1x}. See: BDB—345d, 405a.

3185. יַחְצִיאֵל {1x} **Yachtsîyʾêl**, *yakh-tsee-ale';* from 2673 and 410; *allotted of God; Jachtsiël,* an Isr.:—Jahziel {1x}. See: BDB—345d, 405a. Syn.: comp. 3183.

3186. יָחַר {1x} **yâchar**, *yaw-khar';* a prim. root; to *delay:*—tarry longer {1x}. See: TWOT—68; BDB—405b.

3187. יָחַשׂ **yâchas**, *yaw-khas';* a prim. root; to *sprout;* used only as denom. from 3188; to *enroll* by pedigree:—{12x}, genealogy {6x}, number . . . genealogy {2x}.

Yachas means "to reckon (according to race or family)." **(1)** In 1 Chr 5:17 *yachas* means "reckoned by genealogies": "All these were reckoned by genealogies in the days of Jothan King of Judah . . ." (cf. 1 Chr 7:5). **(2)** A similar use is found in Ezr 2:62: "These sought their register among those that were reckoned by genealogy, but they were not found . . ." See: TWOT—862; BDB—405b.

3188. יַחַשׂ {20x} **yachas**, *yakh'-as;* from 3187; a *pedigree* or family list (as *growing* spontaneously):—reckoned by genealogy {12x}, genealogy {6x}, number . . . genealogy {2x}.

Yachas means "genealogy." **(1)** This word appears in the infinitive form as a noun to indicate a register or table of genealogy: "And the number throughout the genealogy of them that were apt to the war, and to battle was twenty and six thousand men" (1 Chr 7:40; cf. 2 Chr 31:18). **(2)** Another rendering concerning the acts of Rehoboam, recorded in the histories of Shemaiah (2 Chr 12:15), meant that the particulars were related in a genealogical table. See: TWOT—862; BDB—405b.

3189. יַחַת {8x} **Yachath**, *yakh'-ath;* from 3161; *unity; Jachath,* the name of four Isr.:—Jahath {8x}. See: BDB—367a, 405c.

3190. יָטַב {107x} **yâṭab**, *yaw-tab';* a prim. root; to *be* (caus.) *make well,* lit. (*sound, beautiful*) or fig. (*happy, successful, right*):—well {35x}, good {21x}, please {14x}, merry {5x}, amend {4x}, better {4x}, accepted {2x}, diligently {2x}, misc. {20x} = use aright, benefit, seem best, make cheerful, be comely, + be content, dress, earnestly, find favour, give, be glad, shew more [kindness], skilfully, × very small, surely, make sweet, thoroughly, tire, trim, very.

(1) *Yatab* does not mean amend nor improve your ways but to make one's course line up with that which is pleasing to God and that which is well-pleasing in His sight. **(2)** *Yatab,* as a verb, means "to be good, do well, be glad, please, do good to go well, be pleasing, be delighted, be happy." **(3)** The meaning of the word, as expressed in Neh 2:6, is "pleased." **(4)** This verbal form is found first in the story of Cain and Abel, where it is used twice in one verse: "if thou doest well, shalt thou not be accepted? and if thou doest not well, sin lieth at the door. And unto thee *shall be* his desire, and thou shalt rule over him" (Gen 4:7). **(5)** Among other nuances of the verb are **(5a)** "to deal well": "therefore God dealt well with the midwives: and the people multiplied, and waxed very mighty" (Ex 1:20); **(5b)** "to play [a musical instrument] well": "and Saul said unto his servants, Provide me now a man that can play well, and bring *him* to me" (1 Sa 16:17), **(5c)** "to adorn, make beautiful": "And when Jehu was come to Jezreel, Jezebel heard *of it;* and she painted [*yatab*] her face, and tired her head, and looked out at a window" (2 Kin 9:30), and **(5d)** "to inquire diligently": "and it be told thee, and thou hast heard *of it,* and enquired diligently, and, behold, *it be* true, *and* the thing certain, *that* such abomination is wrought in Israel" (Deut 17:4). See: TWOT—863; BDB—405c.

3191. יְטַב {1x} **yᵉtab** (Aram.), *yet-ab'*; corresp. to 3190:—seem good {1x}. See: TWOT—2768; BDB—1095d.

3192. יָטְבָה {1x} **Yoṭbâh**, *yot-baw'*; from 3190; *pleasantness; Jotbah*, a place in Pal.:—Jotbah {1x}. See: BDB—406a.

3193. יָטְבָתָה {2x} **Yoṭbâthâh**, *yot-baw'-thaw;* from 3192; *Jotbathah*, a place in the Desert:—Jotbath {1x}, Jotbathah {2x}. See: BDB—406a.

3194. יֻטָּה {2x} **Yuṭṭâh**, *yoo-taw'*; or

יוּטָה **Yûwṭâh**, *yoo-taw'*; from 5186; *extended; Juttah* (or *Jutah*), a place in Pal.:—Juttah {2x}. See: BDB—398a, 406b, 641a.

3195. יְטוּר {3x} **Yᵉṭûwr**, *yet-oor'*; prob. from the same as 2905; *encircled* (i.e. *inclosed*); *Jetur*, a son of Ishmael:—Jetur {3x}. See: BDB—377b, 406b, 452d.

3196. יַיִן {140x} **yayin**, *yah'-yin;* from an unused root mean. to *effervesce; wine* (as fermented); by impl. *intoxication:*—banqueting {1x}, wine {138x}, winebibbers + 5433 {1x}.

Yayin means "wine." **(1)** This is the usual Hebrew word for fermented grape. **(2)** It is usually rendered "wine." Such "wine" was commonly drunk for refreshment: "And Melchizedek king of Salem brought forth bread and wine . . ." (Gen 14:18; cf. 27:25). **(3)** Passages such as Eze 27:18 inform us that "wine" was an article of commerce: "Damascus was thy merchant in the multitude of the wares of thy making, for the multitude of all riches; in the wine of Helbon, and white wool." **(4)** Strongholds were supplied with "wine" in case of siege: "and he fortified the strongholds, and put captains in them, and store of victual, and of oil and wine" (2 Chr 11:11). **(5)** Proverbs recommends that kings avoid "wine" and strong drink but that it be given to those troubled with problems that they might drink and forget their problems (Prov 31:4–7). **(6)** "Wine" was used to make merry, to make one feel good without being intoxicated: "Now Absalom had commanded his servants, saying, Mark ye now when Amnon's heart is merry with wine, and when I say unto you, Smite Amnon; then kill him, fear not: have not I commanded you? be courageous, and be valiant" (2 Sa 13:28).

(7) It was used in rejoicing before the Lord. **(7a)** Once a year all Israel is to gather in Jerusalem. **(7b)** The money realized from the sale of a tithe of all their harvest was to be spent "for whatsoever thy soul lusteth after, for oxen, or for sheep, or for wine, or for strong drink, or for whatsoever thy soul desireth: and thou shalt eat there before the Lord thy God, and thou shalt rejoice . . ." (Deut 14:26). **(8)** "Wine" was offered to God at His command as part of the prescribed ritual: "And with the one lamb a tenth deal of flour mingled with the fourth part of an hin of beaten oil; and the fourth part of an hin of wine *for* a drink offering" (Ex 29:40). **(9)** Thus it was part of the temple supplies available for purchase by pilgrims so that they could offer it to God: "*Some* of them also *were* appointed to oversee the vessels, and all the instruments of the sanctuary, and the fine flour, and the wine, and the oil, and the frankincense, and the spices" (1 Chr 9:29). **(10)** Pagans used "wine" in their worship, but "their wine is the poison of dragons, and the cruel venom of asps" (Deut 32:33).

(11) *Yayin* clearly represents an intoxicating beverage. **(11a)** This is evident in its first biblical appearance: "And Noah began to be a husbandman, and he planted a vineyard: and he drank of the wine, and was drunken . . ." (Gen 9:20–21). **(11b)** In Gen 9:24 *yayin* means drunkenness: "And Noah awoke from his wine. . . ." **(12)** People in special states of holiness were forbidden to drink "wine," such as **(12a)** the Nazarites: "He shall separate *himself* from wine and strong drink, and shall drink no vinegar of wine, or vinegar of strong drink, neither shall he drink any liquor of grapes, nor eat moist grapes, or dried" (Num 6:3), **(12b)** Samson's mother: "Now therefore beware, I pray thee, and drink not wine nor strong drink, and eat not any unclean *thing*" (Judg 13:4), and **(12c)** priests approaching God: "Do not drink wine nor strong drink, thou, nor thy sons with thee, when ye go into the tabernacle of the congregation, lest ye die: *it shall be* a statute for ever throughout your generations" (Lev 10:9). Syn:

(13) The word is used as a synonym of tirosh (8492), "new wine," in Hos 4:11, where it is evident that both can be intoxicating: "Whoredom and wine and new wine (tirosh) take away the heart." **(13a)** Tirosh is distinguished from *yayin* by referring only to new wine not fully fermented; *yayin* includes "wine" at any stage. **(13b)** In Gen 27:28 (the first biblical occurrence of the word) Jacob's blessing includes the divine bestowal of an abundance of new wine: "Therefore God give thee of the dew of heaven, and the fatness of the earth, and plenty of corn and wine." **(13c)** In 1 Sa 1:15 *yayin* parallels shekar (7941), "strong drink." **(13c1)** Shekar in early times included wine: "And the drink offering thereof *shall be* the fourth *part* of an hin for the one lamb: in the holy *place* shalt thou cause the strong wine to be poured unto the LORD *for* a drink offering" (Num 28:7); **(13c2)** but meant strong drink made from any fruit or grain: "He shall separate *himself* from wine and strong drink, and shall drink no vinegar of wine, or vinegar of strong drink, neither shall he drink any liquor of grapes, nor eat moist grapes, or dried" (Num 6:3). See: TWOT—864; BDB—406b.

3197. יַךְ {1x} **yak**, *yak;* by err. transc. for 3027; a *hand* or *side:*—[way-] side {1x}. See: TWOT—844; BDB—406d.

יָכוֹל **yâkôwl**. See 3201.

יְכוֹנְיָה **Yᵉkôwnᵉyâh**. See 3204.

3198. יָכַח {59x} **yâkach**, *yaw-kahh';* a prim. root; to *be right* (i.e. *correct*); recip. to *argue;* caus. to *decide, justify* or *convict:*—reprove {23x}, rebuke {12x}, correct {3x}, plead {3x}, reason {2x}, chasten {2x}, reprover + 376 {2x}, appointed {1x}, arguing {1x}, misc. {9x} = convince, daysman, dispute, judge, maintain, surely, in any wise.

Yakach (3198) means, "to decide, prove, convince, judge." **(1)** The first occurrence of the word is in Gen 20:16: "And unto Sarah he said, Behold, I have given thy brother a thousand *pieces* of silver: behold, he *is* to thee a covering of the eyes, unto all that *are* with thee, and with all *other:* thus she was reproved." Re-prove in English means to "prove over again"; hence, Sarah was proven chaste, untouched by another man. **(2)** It is evident in most of the uses of *yakach* that there is a value judgment involved, as in Ps 50:21: ". . . I will reprove thee, and [lay the charge before thee]." **(3)** Negative judgments may lead to reproof, especially by God (Job 5:17). **(3a)** Such divine reproof may be physical: ". . . I will chasten him with the rod of men . . ." (2 Sa 7:14). **(3b)** But it is the conviction of the wise man that "For whom the LORD loveth he correcteth; even as a father the son *in whom* he delighteth" (Prov 3:12). See: TWOT—865; BDB—406d.

יְכִילְיָה **Yᵉkîylᵉyâh**. See 3203.

3199. יָכִין {8x} **Yâkîyn**, *yaw-keen';* from 3559; *he* (or *it*) *will establish; Jakin*, the name of three Isr. and of a temple pillar:—Jachin {8x}. See: BDB—467c, 937b.

3200. יָכִינִי {1x} **Yâkîynîy**, *yaw-kee-nee';* patron. from 3199; a *Jakinite* (collect.) or desc. of Jakin:—Jachinites {1x}. See: BDB—467c.

3201. יָכֹל {195x} **yâkôl**, *yaw-kole';* or (fuller)

יָכוֹל **yâkôwl**, *yaw-kole';* a prim. root; to *be able*, lit. (*can, could*) or mor. (*may, might*):—could {46x}, able {43x}, cannot {34x}, prevail {22x}, may {16x}, can {12x}, canst {5x}, endure {2x}, might {2x}, misc. {13x} = any at all (ways), attain, overcome, have power, still, suffer.

Yakowl means "can, may, to be able, prevail, endure." **(1)** As in English, the Hebrew word usually requires another verb to make the meaning complete. **(2)** *Yakowl* first occurs in Gen 13:6: "And the land was not able to bear them, that they might dwell together. . . ." **(3)** God promised Abraham: "And I will make thy seed as the dust of the earth: so that if a man can number the dust of the earth, *then* shall thy seed also be numbered" (Gen 13:16; cf. Gen 15:5). **(4)** The most frequent use of this verb is in the sense of "can" or "to be able." **(4a)** The word may refer specifically to "physical ability," as in 1 Sa 17:33: "And Saul said to David, Thou art not able to go against this Philistine to fight with him: for thou *art but* a youth, and he a man of war from his youth." **(4b)** *Yakowl* may express "moral inability," **(4b1)** as in Josh 7:13: ". . . Thou canst not stand before thine enemies, until ye take away the accursed thing from among you." **(4b2)** For a similar sense, see Jer 6:10: "Behold, their ear is uncircumcised, and they cannot hearken. . . ."

(5) In the negative sense, it may be used to express "prohibition": "Thou mayest not eat within thy gates the tithe of thy corn, or of thy wine, or of thy oil, or the firstlings of thy herds or of thy flock, nor any of thy vows which thou vowest, nor thy freewill offerings, or heave offering of thine hand" (Deut 12:17). **(6)** Or the verb may indicate a "social barrier," as in Gen 43:32: ". . . The Egyptians might not eat bread with the Hebrews; for that is an abomination unto the Egyptians." **(7)** *Yakowl* is also used of God, as when Moses pleaded with God not to destroy Israel lest the nations say, "Because the LORD was not able to bring this people into the land which he sware unto them, therefore he hath slain them in the wilderness" (Num 14:16). **(8)** The word may indicate a positive sense: "If it be so, our God whom we serve is able to deliver us . . ." (Dan 3:17). **(9)** The word *yakowl* appears when God limits His patience with the insincere: "So that the LORD could no longer bear, because of the evil of your doings, *and* because of the abominations which ye have committed; therefore is your land a desolation, and an astonishment, and a curse, without an inhabitant, as at this day" (Jer 44:22).

(10) When *yakowl* is used without another verb, the sense is "to prevail" or "to overcome," as in the words of the angel to Jacob: "And he said, Thy name shall be called no more Jacob, but Israel: for as a prince hast thou power with God and with men, and hast prevailed" (Gen 32:28). **(11)** With the word *yakowl,* God rebukes Israel's insincerity: **(11a)** "Bring no more vain oblations; incense is an abomination unto me;

the new moons and sabbaths, the calling of assemblies, I cannot away with; *it is* iniquity, even the solemn meeting" (Is 1:13). **(11b)** "Thy calf, O Samaria, hath cast *thee* off; mine anger is kindled against them: how long *will it be* ere they attain to innocency?" (Hos 8:5). **(12)** There is no distinction in Hebrew between "can" and "may," **(12a)** since *yakowl* expresses both "ability" and "permission," or prohibition with the negative. **(12b)** Both God and man can act. **(12c)** There is no limit to God's ability apart from His own freely determined limits of patience with continued disobedience and insincerity (Is 59:1–2) and will (Dan 3:17–18). See: TWOT—866; BDB—407b, 1095d.

3202. יְכֵל {12x} **yᵉkêl** (Aram.), *yek-ale';* or יְכִיל **yᵉkîyl** (Aram.), *yek-eel';* corresp. to 3201:—be able {4x}, can {6x}, couldest {1x}, prevail {1x}. See: TWOT—2769; BDB—1095d. 1096d.

3203. יְכָלְיָה {2x} **Yᵉkolyâh**, *yek-ol-yaw';* and יְכָלְיָהוּ **Yᵉkolyâhûw**, *yek-ol-yaw'-hoo;* or (2 Chr 26:3) יְכִילְיָה **Yᵉkîylᵉyâh**, *yek-ee-leh-yaw';* from 3201 and 3050; *Jah will enable; Jekoljah* or *Jekiljah*, an Israelitess:—Jecholiah {1x}, Jecoliah {1x}. See: BDB—408a.

3204. יְכָנְיָה {7x} **Yᵉkonyâh**, *yek-on-yaw';* and יְכָנְיָהוּ **Yᵉkonyâhûw**, *yek-on-yaw'-hoo;* or (Jer 27:20) יְכוֹנְיָה **Yᵉkôwnᵉyâh**, *yek-o-neh-yaw';* from 3559 and 3050; *Jah will establish; Jekonjah*, a Jewish king:—Jeconiah {7x}. See: BDB—220c, 408a, 467c, 487c. comp. 3659.

3205. יָלַד {498x} **yâlad**, *yaw-lad';* a prim. root; to *bear* young; caus. to *beget;* medically, to *act as midwife;* spec. to *show lineage:*—beget {201x}, bare {110x}, born {79x}, bring forth {25x}, bear {23x}, travail {16x}, midwife {10x}, child {8x}, delivered {5x}, borne {3x}, birth {2x}, labour {2x}, brought up {2x}, misc. {12x} = calve, come, time of delivery, gender, hatch, declare pedigrees, be the son of.

Yalad means "to bear, bring forth, beget, be delivered." **(1)** Essentially, the word refers to the action of "giving birth" and its result, "bearing children." **(1a)** God cursed woman by multiplying her pain in "bringing forth" children (cf. Gen 3:16, the first occurrence of *yalad*). **(1b)** The second meaning is exemplified by Gen 4:18, which reports that Irad "begat" ("became the father of") Mehujael. **(1c)** This verb can also be used in reference to animals; in Gen 30:39, the strong among Laban's flocks "birthed" striped, speckled, and spotted offspring. **(2)** One recurring theme in biblical history is typified by Abram and Sarah. **(2a)** They had no heirs, but God made them a promise and gave them a son (Gen 16:1, 16). **(2a)** This demonstrates that God controls the opening of the womb (Gen 20:17–18) and bestows children as an indication of His blessing. **(3)** The prophets use the image of childbirth to illustrate the terror to overcome men in the day of the Lord: "And they shall be afraid: pangs and sorrows shall take hold of them; they shall be in pain as a woman that travaileth: they shall be amazed one at another; their faces *shall be as* flames" (Is 13:8).

(4) Hosea uses the image of marriage and childbearing to describe God's relationship to Israel (1:3, 6, 8). **(5)** Is 7:14, uses this verb to predict the "birth" of Immanuel: "Therefore the Lord himself shall give you a sign; Behold, a virgin shall conceive, and bear a son, and shall call his name Immanuel." **(6)** Finally, the prophets sometimes mourn the day of their "birth" (Jer 15:10). **(7)** *Yalad* describes the relationship between God and Israel at other places in the Bible as well. **(7a)** This relationship is especially relevant to the king who typifies the Messiah, the Son whom God "begot": "I will declare the decree: the LORD hath said unto me, Thou *art* my Son; this day have I begotten thee" (Ps 2:7). **(7b)** God also says He "begot" the nation of Israel as a whole: "Of the Rock *that* begat thee thou art unmindful, and hast forgotten God that formed thee" (Deut 32:18). **(7c)** This statement is in noticeable contrast to Moses' disclaimer that he did not "birth" them (Num 11:12) and, therefore, does not want to be responsible for them any longer.

(8) The motif that God "gave birth" to Israel is picked up by Jeremiah. In Jer 31:20, God states that His heart yearns for Ephraim His son (yeled). **(9)** Ezekiel develops this motif in the form of an allegory, giving the names Aholah and Aholibah to Samaria and Jerusalem respectively, to those whom He "bore" (Eze 23:4, 37). See: TWOT—867; BDB—408a, 529a.

3206. יֶלֶד {89x} **yeled**, *yeh'-led;* from 3205; something *born*, i.e. a *lad* or *offspring:*—child {72x}, young man {7x}, young ones {3x}, sons {3x}, boy {2x}, fruit {1x}, variant {1x}.

Yeled, as a noun, means "boy; child." **(1)** The noun *yeled* differs from ben (1121 - "son"), which more exactly specifies the parental relationship. **(2)** For example, the child that Naomi nursed was a "boy" (Ruth 4:16). Syn: *Yeled*, which appears 89 times in the Bible, has nouns built on it: **(2a)** yaldah (3207 - "girl"; 3 times), **(2b)** yalid (3211 - "son" or "slave"; 3 times), **(2c)** yillod (3209 - "newborn"; 5 times), **(2d)** walad (2056 - "child"; once), **(2e)** ledah (3205 - "bringing forth" or "birth"; 4 times), **(2f)** moledet (4138 - "offspring, kindred, parentage"; 22 times), and **(2g)** toledot (8435 - "descendants, contemporaries, generation, genealogy, record of the family"; 39 times), **(2h)** yaldoth (3208 - childhood, youth). See: TWOT—867b; BDB—409b.

3207. יַלְדָּה {3x} **yaldâh**, *yal-daw';* fem. of 3206; a *lass:*—damsel {1x}, girl {2x}. See: TWOT—867b; BDB—409c.

3208. יַלְדוּת {3x} **yaldûwth**, *yal-dooth';* abstr. from 3206; *boyhood* (or *girlhood*):—childhood {1x}, youth {2x}. See: TWOT—867c; BDB—409c.

3209. יִלּוֹד {5x} **yillôwd**, *yil-lode';* pass. from 3205; *born:*—born {5x}. See: TWOT—867d; BDB—409c.

3210. יָלוֹן {1x} **Yâlôwn**, *yaw-lone';* from 3885; *lodging; Jalon*, an Isr.:—Jalon {1x}. See: BDB—1124c.

3211. יָלִיד {13x} **yâlîyd**, *yaw-leed';* from 3205; *born:*—born {6x}, children {4x}, sons {2x}, homeborn + 1004 {1x}. See: TWOT—867e; BDB—409c.

3212. יָלַךְ {1043x} **yâlak**, *yaw-lak';* a prim. root [comp. 1980]; to *walk* (lit. or fig.); caus. to *carry* (in various senses):—go {628x}, walk {122x}, come {77x}, depart {66x}, . . . away {20x}, follow {20x}, get {14x}, lead {17x}, brought {8x}, carry {5x}, bring {4x}, misc. {62x} = × again, bear, flow, grow, let down, march, prosper, + pursue, cause to run, spread, take away ([-journey]), vanish, wax, × be weak. See: TWOT—498; BDB—229d.

3213. יָלַל {31x} **yâlal**, *yaw-lal';* a prim. root; to *howl* (with a wailing tone) or *yell* (with a boisterous one):—(make to) howl {29x}, be howling {2x}. See: TWOT—868; BDB—410a.

3214. יְלֵל {1x} **yᵉlêl**, *yel-ale';* from 3213; a *howl:*—howling {1x}. See: TWOT—868a; BDB—410b.

3215. יְלָלָה {5x} **yᵉlâlâh**, *yel-aw-law';* fem. of 3214; a *howling:*—howling {5x}. See: TWOT—868b; BDB—410b.

3216. יָלַע {1x} **yâlaʽ**, *yaw-lah';* a prim. root; to *blurt* or utter inconsiderately:—devour {1x}. See: TWOT—1098; BDB—410c, 534b.

3217. יַלֶּפֶת {2x} **yallepheth**, *yal-leh'-feth;* from an unused root appar. mean. to *stick* or *scrape; scurf* or *tetter:*—scabbed {2x}. See: TWOT—869a; BDB—410c.

3218. יֶלֶק {9x} **yekeq**, *yeh'-lek;* from an unused root mean. to *lick* up; a *devourer;* spec. the young *locust:*—cankerworm {6x}, caterpillar {3x}. See: TWOT—870a; BDB—410c.

3219. יַלְקוּט {1x} **yalqûwt**, *yal-koot';* from 3950; a travelling *pouch* (as if for gleanings):—scrip {1x}. See: TWOT—1125b; BDB—410c, 545a.

3220. יָם {396x} **yâm**, *yawm;* from an unused root mean. to *roar;* a *sea* (as breaking in *noisy* surf) or large body of water; spec. (with the art.), the *Mediterranean;* sometimes a large *river*, or an artificial *basin;* locally, the *west*, or (rarely) the *south:*—sea {321x}, west {47x}, westward {21x}, west side {4x}, seafaring men {1x}, south {1x}, western {1x}.

Yam means "sea; ocean." **(1)** This word refers to the body of water as distinct from the land bodies (continents and islands) and the sky (heavens): "For in six days the Lord made heaven and earth, the sea and all that in them is . . ." (Ex 20:11). **(1a)** Used in this sense *yam* means "ocean." **(1b)** This is its meaning in Gen 1:10, its first biblical appearance; unlike the use in the singular, where the word is a collective noun, it appears here in the plural: "And God called the dry land Earth; and the gathering together of the waters called he Seas. . . ." **(2)** *Yam* may be used of "seas," whether they are salty or fresh. **(2a)** The Great Sea is the Mediterranean: "From the wilderness and this Lebanon even unto the great river, the river Euphrates, all the land of the Hittites, and unto the Great Sea toward the going down of the sun, shall be your coast" (Josh 1:4). **(2b)** This sea is also called the sea of the Philistines (Ex 23:31) and **(2c)** the hinter or western sea (Deut 11:24 "uttermost sea"). **(3)** The Dead Sea is called **(3a)** the Salt Sea (Gen 14:3), **(3b)** the Arabah (Deut 3:17; "plain"), and **(3c)** the east sea (Eze 47:18).

(4) Thus, *yam* can be used of **(4a)** an inland salty "sea." **(4b)** It can also be used of a fresh water "sea" such as the Sea of Galilee: ". . . And the border shall descend, and shall reach unto the side of the Sea of Chinnereth eastward" (Num 34:11). **(5)** The word is sometimes used of the direction west or westward, in the sense of toward the (Great) Sea: "Lift up now thine eyes, and look from the place where thou art northward, and southward, and eastward, and westward" (Gen 13:14). **(5a)** In Gen 12:8 *yam* means "on the west side": "And he removed from thence unto a mountain on the east of Beth-el, and pitched his tent, having Beth-el on the west, and Hai on the east. . . ." **(5b)** This word can also refer to a side of something and not just a direction, but it is the side that faces westward: "He turned about to the west side . . ." (Eze 42:19). **(6)** Ex 10:19 uses *yam* as an adjective modifying "wind": "And the Lord turned a mighty strong west wind, which took away the locusts. . . ."

(7) *Yam* is used of the great basin immediately in front of the Holy Place: "And the pillars of brass that were in the house of the Lord, and the bases, and the brazen sea that was in the house of the Lord, did the Chaldees break in pieces, and carried the brass of them to Babylon" (2 Kin 25:13). This is also called **(7a)** the "molten sea" (of cast metal – 1 Kin 7:23) or simply **(7b)** the "sea" (Jer. 27:19). **(8)** *Yam* is used of mighty rivers such as the Nile: "And the waters shall fail from the sea, and the river shall be wasted and dried up" (Is 19:5). **(8a)** This statement occurs in the middle of a prophecy against Egypt. Therefore, "the river" is the Nile. **(8b)** But since the term "river" is in synonymous parallelism to "the sea," this latter term also refers to the Nile. **(8c)** Eze 32:2 uses *yam* of the branches of the Nile: ". . . And thou art as a whale in the seas: and thou camest forth with thy rivers, and troubledst the waters with thy feet, and fouledst their rivers."

(9) This word can also be used of the Euphrates River (Jer 51:36). **(10)** Some scholars believe that in some instances the word *yam* may represent the Canaanite god Yamm, "which alone spreadeth out the heavens, and treadeth upon the waves of the sea" (Job 9:8). **(10a)** If understood as a statement about Yamm, this passage would read: "and tramples upon the back of Yamm." **(10b)** The parallelism between "heavens" and "seas," however, would lead us to conclude that the reference here is to the literal "sea." **(10c)** Ps. 89:9–10 is a more likely place to see a mention of Yamm, for there the word is identified as one of God's enemies in immediate proximity to the goddess Rahab: "Thou rulest the raging of the sea [Yamm]: when the waves thereof arise, thou stillest them. Thou hast broken Rahab in pieces, as one that is slain; thou hast scattered thine enemies with thy strong arm." **(11)** Especially note Job 7:12: "Am I a sea [Yamm], or a whale, that thou settest a watch over me?" (cf. Job 26:12; Ps 74:13). See: TWOT—871a; BDB—410d, 1095d.

3221. יָם {2x} **yâm** (Aram.), *yawm;* corresp. to 3220:—sea {2x}. See: TWOT—2770; BDB—1095d.

3222. יֵם {1x} **yêm**, *yame;* from the same as 3117; a *warm* spring:—mule {1x}. Syn.: 6505. See: TWOT—871b; BDB—411b.

3223. יְמוּאֵל {2x} **Yᵉmûwʾêl**, *yem-oo-ale';* from 3117 and 410; *day of God; Jemuel,* an Isr.:—Jemuel {2x}. See: BDB—410c.

3224. יְמִימָה {1x} **Yᵉmîymâh**, *yem-ee-maw';* perh. from the same as 3117; prop. *warm,* i.e. *affectionate;* hence, *dove* [comp. 3123]; *Jemimah,* one of Job's daughters:—Jemimah {1x}. See: BDB—410d.

3225. יָמִין {139x} **yâmîyn**, *yaw-meen';* from 3231; the *right* hand or side (leg, eye) of a person or other object (as the *stronger* and more dexterous); locally, the *south:*—hand {105x}, right {24x}, side {5x}, south {3x}, left-handed + 334 {2x}.

Yamiyn means "right hand." **(1)** First, the word represents the bodily part called the "right hand": **(1a)** "And Joseph took them both, Ephraim in his right hand toward Israel's left hand, and Manasseh in his left hand toward Israel's right hand . . ." (Gen 48:13). **(1b)** Ehud was "bound as to his right hand"; he was lefthanded: "But when the children of Israel cried unto the Lord, the Lord raised them *up a deliverer, Ehud the son of Gera, a Benjamite, a man lefthanded . . .*" (Judg 3:15). **(2)** *Yamiyn* may be used in a figurative sense. God's taking one's "right hand" means that He strengthens him: "For I the Lord thy God will hold thy right hand, saying unto thee, Fear not: I will help thee" (Is 41:13). **(3)** The Bible speaks anthropomorphically, attributing to God human parts and, in particular, a "right hand" (Ex 15:6). **(3a)** The Bible teaches that God is a spirit and has no body or bodily parts (cf. Ex 20:4; Deut 4:15–19). **(3b)** This figure is used of God's effecting His will among men and of His working in their behalf (showing His favor): "And I said, This is my infirmity: but I will remember the years of the right hand of the Most High" (Ps 77:10).

(4) *Yamiyn* represents the direction, to the "right." In this use the word can specify the location of someone or something: "But the children of Israel walked upon dry land in the midst of the sea; and the waters were a wall unto them on their right hand, and on their left" (Ex 14:29). **(5)** In other contexts *yamiyn* signifies "direction toward": "Is not the whole land before thee? Separate thyself, I pray thee, from me: if thou wilt take the left hand, then I will go to the right; or if thou depart to the right hand, then I will go to the left" (Gen 13:9—the first biblical appearance). **(6)** *Yamiyn* can be used of bodily parts other than the right hand. In Judg 3:16 the word is used of one's thigh (literally, "thigh of the right hand"): "But Ehud made him a dagger which had two edges, of a cubit length; and he did gird it under his raiment upon his right thigh." **(6a)** The word is used in 1 Sa 11:2 in conjunction with one's eye and in **(6b)** Ex 29:22 with a thigh. **(7)** This word is used to mean "south," since the south is on one's "right" when he faces eastward: "Then came up the Ziphites to Saul to Gibeah, saying, Doth not David hide himself with us in strongholds in the wood, in the hill of Hachilah, which is on the south of Jeshimon?" (1 Sa 23:19). See: TWOT—872a; BDB—411c.

3226. יָמִין {6x} **Yâmîyn**, *yaw-meen';* the same as 3225; *Jamin,* the name of three Isr.:—Jamin {6x}. See: BDB—412c. See also: 1144.

3227. יְמִינִי {2x} **yᵉmîynîy**, *yem-ee-nee';* for 3225; *right:*—(on the) right (hand) {2x}. See: BDB—412a.

3228. יְמִינִי {1x} **Yᵉmîynîy**, *yem-ee-nee';* patron. from 3226; a *Jeminite* (collect.) or desc. of Jamin:—Jaminites {1x}. See: BDB—412b, 412c. See also 1145.

3229. יִמְלָא {4x} **Yimlâʾ**, *yeem-law';* or

יִמְלָה **Yimlâh**, *yim-law';* from 4390; *full; Jimla* or *Jimlah,* an Isr.:—Imla {2x}, Imlah {2x}. See: BDB—410d, 571c.

3230. יַמְלֵךְ {1x} **Yamlêk**, *yam-lake';* from 4427; *he will make king; Jamlek,* an Isr.:—Jamlech {1x}. See: BDB—576a.

3231. יָמַן {4x} **yâman**, *yaw-man';* a prim. root; to *be* (phys.) *right* (i.e. firm); but used only as denom. from 3225 and tran. to *be right-handed* or *take the right-hand* side:—go (turn) to (on, use) the right hand {4x}. See: TWOT—872c; BDB—412b.

3232. יִמְנָה {5x} **Yimnâh**, *yim-naw';* from 3231; *prosperity* (as betokened by the *right* hand); *Jimnah,* the name of two Isr.; also (with the art.) of the posterity of one of them:—Imna {1x}, Imnah {1x}, Jimnah {2x}, Jimnites {1x}. See: BDB—412c.

3233. יְמָנִי {33x} **yᵉmânîy**, *yem-aw-nee';* from 3231; *right* (i.e. at the right hand):—(on the) right (hand) {33x}.

Yemaniy, as a noun, means "right hand; on the right side; the right side (of one's body); southern." **(1)** *Yemaniy* means "right hand" in Ex 29:20: "Then shalt thou kill the ram, and take of his blood, and put *it* upon the tip of the right ear of Aaron, and upon the tip of the right ear of his sons, and upon the thumb of their right hand, and upon the great toe of their right foot, and sprinkle the blood upon the altar round about" (the first biblical occurrence). **(2)** In 1 Kin 7:21 the word refers to the "right side" in regard to a location. "And he set up the pillars in the porch of the temple: and he set up the right pillar, and called the name thereof Jachin: and he set up the left pillar, and called the name thereof Boaz." **(3)** *Yemaniy* appears in Eze 4:6 with the meaning of the "right side" of the body: "And when thou hast accomplished them, lie again on thy right side, and thou shalt bear the iniquity of the house of Judah forty days: I have appointed thee each day for a year." **(4)** The word implies "southern" in 1 Kin 6:8: "The door for the middle chamber was in the right side [southern side] of the house. . . ." See: TWOT—872d; BDB—412b. Syn.: 8486.

3234. יִמְנָע {1x} **Yimnâʿ**, *yim-naw';* from 4513; *he will restrain; Jimna,* an Isr.:—Imna {1x}. See: BDB—413a, 586b.

3235. יָמַר {2x} **yâmar**, *yaw-mar';* a prim. root; to *exchange;* by impl. to *change places:*—boast selves {1x}, change {1x}. See: TWOT—118; BDB—413a.

3236. יִמְרָה {1x} **Yimrâh**, *yim-raw';* prob. from 3235; *interchange; Jimrah,* an Isr.:—Imrah {1x}. See: BDB—413a, 598c.

3237. יָמַשׁ {1x} **yâmash**, *yaw-mash';* a prim. root; to *touch:*—feel {1x}. See: BDB—413a.

3238. יָנָה {21x} **yânâh**, *yaw-naw';* a prim. root; to *rage* or *be violent;* by impl. to *suppress,* to *maltreat:*—oppress {11x}, vex {4x}, destroy {1x}, oppressor {1x}, proud {1x}, do wrong {1x}, oppression {1x}, thrust out {1x}. See: TWOT—873; BDB—402a, 413a.

3239. יָנוֹחַ {3x} **Yânôwach**, *yaw-no'-akh;* or (with enclitic)

יָנוֹחָה **Yânôwchâh**, *yaw-no'-khaw;* from 3240; *quiet; Janoäch* or *Janochah,* a place in Pal.:—Janoah {1x}, Janohah {2x}. See: BDB—413b, 629c.

יָנוּם **Yânûm**. See 3241.

3240. יָנַח {75x} **yânach**, *yaw-nakh';* a prim. root; to *deposit;* by impl. to *allow to stay:*—leave {24x}, up {10x}, lay {8x}, suffer {5x}, place {4x}, put {4x}, set {4x}, . . . down {4x}, let alone {4x}, . . . him {2x}, bestowed {1x}, leave off {1x}, pacifieth {1x}, still {1x}, withdraw {1x}, withhold {1x}. (The Hiphil forms with the *dagesh* are here referred to, in accordance with the older grammarians; but if any distinction of the kind is to be made, these should rather be referred to 5117, and the others here.) See: TWOT—1323; BDB—628d.

3241. יָנִים {1x} **Yânîym**, *yaw-neem';* from 5123; *asleep; Janim,* a place in Pal.:—Janum {1x}. See: BDB—413b, 630b.

3242. יְנִיקָה {1x} **yᵉnîqâh**, *yen-ee-kaw';* from 3243; a *sucker* or sapling:—young twigs {1x}. See: TWOT—874c; BDB—413c.

3243. יָנַק {32x} **yânaq**, *yaw-nak';* a prim. root; to *suck;* caus. to *give milk:*—suck {14x}, nurse {7x}, suckling {6x}, sucking child {3x}, milch {1x}, nursing mothers {1x}. See: TWOT—874; BDB—413b, 568c, 586b.

3244. יַנְשׁוּף {3x} **yanshûwph**, *yan-shoof';* or

יַנְשׁוֹף **yanshôwph**, *yan-shofe';* appar. from 5398; an unclean (aquatic) bird; prob. the *heron* (perh. from its *blowing* cry, or because the *night*-heron is meant [comp. 5399]):—great owl {2x}, owl {1x}. See: TWOT—1434b; BDB—413d, 676a.

3245. יָסַד {42x} **yâçad**, *yaw-sad';* a prim. root; to *set* (lit. or fig.); intens. to *found;* refl. to *sit* down together, i.e. *settle, consult:*—foundation {15x}, lay {8x}, founded {8x}, ordain {2x}, counsel {2x}, established {2x}, foundation + 3117 {1x}, appointed {1x}, instructed {1x}, set {1x}, sure {1x}. See: TWOT—875; BDB—413d.

3246. יְסֻד {1x} **yᵉçûd**, *yes-ood';* from 3245; a *foundation* (fig. i.e. *beginning*):—× began {1x}. See: TWOT—875a; BDB—414b.

3247. יְסוֹד {20x} **yᵉçôwd**, *yes-ode';* from 3245; a *foundation* (lit. or fig.):—bottom {9x}, foundation {10x}, repairing {1x}. See: TWOT—875b; BDB—414b.

3248. יְסוּדָה {1x} **yᵉçûwdâh**, *yes-oo-daw';* fem. of 3246; a *foundation:*—foundation {1x}. See: TWOT—875c; BDB—414b.

3249. יָסוּר {1x} **yâçûwr**, *yaw-soor';* from 5493; *departing:*—they that depart {1x}. See: TWOT—1480; BDB—693c.

3250. יִסּוֹר {1x} **yiççôwr**, *yis-sore';* from 3256; a *reprover:*—instruct {1x}. See: TWOT—877a; BDB—416b.

3251. יָסַךְ {1x} **yâçak**, *yaw-sak';* a prim. root; to *pour* (intr.):—be poured {1x}. See: TWOT—1474; BDB—414c.

3252. יִסְכָּה {1x} **Yiçkâh**, *yis-kaw';* from an unused root mean. to *watch; observant; Jiskah,* sister of Lot:—Iscah {1x}. See: BDB—414c.

3253. יִסְמַכְיָהוּ {1x} **Yiçmakyâhûw**, *yis-mak-yaw-hoo';* from 5564 and 3050; *Jah will sustain; Jismakjah,* an Isr.:—Ismachiah {1x}. See: BDB—414d, 702b.

3254. יָסַף {213x} **yâçaph**, *yaw-saf';* a prim. root; to *add* or *augment* (often adv. to *continue* to do a thing):—more {70}, again {54x}, add {28x}, increase {16x}, also {6x}, exceed {4x}, put {4x}, further {4x}, henceforth {4x}, can {2x}, continued {2x}, give {2x}, misc. {17x} = × cease, + conceive again, × gather together, join, × longer (bring, do, make, much, put), proceed (further), prolong, be [strong-] er, × yet, yield.

Yacaph means "to add, continue, do again, increase, surpass." **(1)** Basically, *yacaph* signifies increasing the number of something. **(2)** It may also be used to indicate adding one thing to another, e.g., "And if a man eat of the holy thing unwittingly, then he shall put the fifth part thereof unto it, and shall give it unto the priest . . ." (Lev 22:14). **(3)** This verb may be used to signify the repetition of an act stipulated by another verb. For example, the dove that Noah sent out "returned not again" (Gen 8:12). **(4)** Usually the repeated action is indicated by an infinitive absolute, preceded by the preposition le—"And he did not have relations with her again." Literally, this reads "And he did not add again [5750 - 'od] to knowing her [intimately]" (Gen 38:26). **(5)** In some contexts *yacaph* means "to heighten," but with no suggestion of numerical increase. **(5a)** God says, "The meek also shall increase [*yacaph*] their joy in the Lord . . ." (Is 29:19).

(5b) This same emphasis appears in Ps 71:14: ". . . and will yet praise thee more and more [*yacaph*]' or literally, "And I will add to all Thy praises." **(5c)** In such cases, more than an additional quantity of joy or praise is meant. The author is referring to a new quality of joy or praise—i.e., a heightening of them. **(6)** Another meaning of *yacaph* is "to surpass." The Queen of Sheba told Solomon, "Thy wisdom and prosperity exceedeth the fame which I heard," or literally, "You add [with respect to] wisdom and prosperity to the report which I heard" (1 Kin 10:7). **(7)** This verb may also be used in covenantal formulas, e.g., Ruth summoned God's curse upon herself by saying, "The Lord do so to me, and more also [*yacaph*], if ought but death part thee and me," or literally, "Thus may the Lord do to me, and thus may he add, if . . ." (Ruth 1:17; cf. Lev 26; Deut 27—28). See: TWOT—876; BDB—414d, 1095d.

3255. יְסַף {1x} **yᵉçaph** (Aram.), *yes-af';* corresp. to 3254:—add {1x}. See: TWOT—2771; BDB—1095d.

3256. יָסַר {43x} **yâçar**, *yaw-sar';* a prim. root; to *chastise,* lit. (with blows) or fig. (with words); hence, to *instruct:*—chastise {21x}, instruct {8x}, correct {7x}, taught {2x}, bound {1x}, punish {1x}, reformed {1x}, reproveth {1x}, sore {1x}.

Yacar means "to discipline." The verb appears 43 times in the Old Testament; cf. Prov 19:18: "Chasten thy son while there is hope, and let not thy soul spare for his crying." See: TWOT—877; BDB—415d, 978d, 979a.

3257. יָע {9x} **yâᶜ**, *yaw;* from 3261; a *shovel:*—shovel {9x}. See: TWOT—879a; BDB—416d, 418b.

3258. יַעְבֵּץ {4x} **Yaᶜbêts**, *yah-bates';* from an unused root prob. mean. to *grieve; sorrowful; Jabets,* the name of an Isr., and also of a place in Pal.:—Jabez {4x}. See: BDB—416d, 716d.

3259. יָעַד {29x} **yâᶜad**, *yaw-ad';* a prim. root; to *fix* upon (by agreement or appointment); by impl. to *meet* (at a stated time), to *summon* (to trial), to *direct* (in a certain quarter or position), to *engage* (for marriage):—meet {7x}, together {5x}, assemble {4x}, appointed {3x}, set {3x}, time {2x}, betrothed {2x}, agreed {1x}, appointment {1x}, gather {1x}. See: TWOT—878; BDB—416d.

יֶעְדּוֹ **Yᵉᶜdôw**. See 3260.

3260. יֶעְדִּי {1x} **Yᵉᶜdîy**, *yed-ee';* from 3259; *appointed; Jedi,* an Isr.:—Iddo {1x}. See: BDB—418a, 723b. Syn.: 3035.

3261. יָעָה {1x} **yâᶜâh**, *yaw-aw';* a prim. root; appar. to *brush* aside:—sweep away {1x}. See: TWOT—879; BDB—418a.

3262. יְעוּאֵל {1x} **Yᵉᶜûwʼêl**, *yeh-oo-ale';* from 3261 and 410; *carried away of God; Jeel,* the name of four Isr.:—Jeuel {1x}. See: BDB—418b. comp. 3273.

3263. יְעוּץ {1x} **Yᵉᶜûwts**, *yeh-oots';* from 5779; *counsellor; Jets,* an Isr.:—Jeuz {1x}. See: BDB—418b, 734b.

3264. יָעוֹר {1x} **yâᶜôwr**, *yaw-ore';* a var. of 3293; a *forest:*—wood {1x}. Syn.: 2793. See: TWOT—888a; BDB—418b, 420c.

3265. יָעוּר {1x} **Yâᶜûwr**, *yaw-oor';* appar. pass. part. of the same as 3293; *wooded; Jar,* an Isr.:—Jair {1x}. See: BDB—418b, 418c, 753d.

3266. יְעוּשׁ {6x} **Yᵉᶜûwsh**, *yeh-oosh';* from 5789; *hasty; Jesh,* the name of an Edomite and of four Isr.:—Jehush {1x}, Jeush {5x}. See: BDB—418b, 736b. comp. 3274.

3267. יָעַז {1x} **yâᶜaz**, *yaw-az';* a prim. root; to *be bold* or *obstinate:*—fierce {1x}. See: TWOT—880; BDB—418b.

3268. יַעֲזִיאֵל {1x} **Yaᶜăzîyʼêl**, *yah-az-ee-ale';* from 3267 and 410; *emboldened of God; Jaaziël,* an Isr.:—Jaaziel {1x}. See: BDB—418c, 739c, 739d.

3269. יַעֲזִיָּהוּ {2x} **Yaᶜăzîyâhûw**, *yah-az-ee-yaw'-hoo;* from 3267 and 3050; *emboldened of Jah; Jaazijah,* an Isr.:—Jaaziah {2x}. See: BDB—418c, 739d.

3270. יַעֲזֵיר {13x} **Yaᶜăzêyr**, *yah-az-ayr';* or

יַעְזֵר **Yaᶜzêr**, *yah-zare';* from 5826; *helpful; Jaazer* or *Jazer,* a place E. of the Jordan:—Jaazer {2x}, Jazer {11x}. See: BDB—418c, 741b.

3271. יָעַט {1x} **yâᶜaṭ**, *yaw-at';* a prim. root; to *clothe:*—cover {1x}. See: TWOT—881; BDB—418c.

3272. יְעַט {3x} **yᵉᶜaṭ** (Aram.), *yeh-at';* corresp. to 3289; to *counsel;* refl. to *consult:*—counsellor {2x}, consult together {1x}. See: TWOT—2772; BDB—1095d, 1096a.

3273. יְעִיאֵל {13x} **Yᵉᶜîyʼêl**, *yeh-ee-ale';* from 3261 and 410; *carried away of God; Jêel,* the name of six Isr.:—Jeiel {11x}, Jehiel {2x}. See: TWOT—2772; BDB—418b. comp. 3262.

יָעִיר **Yâᶜîyr**. See 3265.

3274. יְעִישׁ {3x} **Yᵉᶜîysh**, *yeh-eesh';* from 5789; *hasty; Jêsh,* the name of an Edomite and of an Isr.:—Jeush {3x}. See: BDB—418c, 736b. comp. 3266.

3275. יַעְכָּן {1x} **Yaᶜkân**, *yah-kawn';* from the same as 5912; *troublesome; Jakan,* an Isr.:—Jachan {1x}. See: BDB—418c, 747c.

3276. יָעַל {23x} **yâᶜal**, *yaw-al';* a prim. root; prop. to *ascend;* fig. to *be valuable* (obj. *useful,* subj. *benefited*):—profit {19x}, at all {1x}, set forward {1x}, good {1x}, profitable {1x}. See: TWOT—882; BDB—418c.

3277. יָעֵל {3x} **yâᶜêl**, *yaw-ale';* from 3276; an *ibex* (as *climbing*):—wild goat {3x}. See: TWOT—883a; BDB—418d.

3278. יָעֵל {6x} **Yâᶜêl**, *yaw-ale';* the same as 3277; *Jaël,* a Canaanite:—Jael {6x}. See: BDB—418d.

3279. יַעֲלָא {2x} **Yaᶜălâʼ**, *yah-al-aw';* or

יַעֲלָה **Yaᶜălâh**, *yah-al-aw';* the same as 3280 or direct from 3276; *Jaala* or *Jaalah,* one of the Nethinim:—Jaala {1x}, Jaalah {1x}. See: BDB—419a.

3280. יַעֲלָה {1x} **yaᶜălâh**, *yah-al-aw';* fem. of 3277:—roe {1x}. See: TWOT—883b; BDB—418d.

3281. יַעְלָם {4x} **Yaᶜlâm**, *yah-lawm';* from 5956; *occult; Jalam,* an Edomite:—Jalam {4x}. See: BDB—419a, 761c.

3282. יַעַן {17x} **yaᶜan**, *yah'-an;* from an unused root mean. to *pay attention;* prop. *heed;* by impl. *purpose* (sake or account); used adv. to indicate the *reason* or cause:—because {7x}, because that {2x}, forasmuch {1x}, forasmuch as {4x}, seeing then that {1x}, whereas {1x}, + why {1x}. See: TWOT—1650e; BDB—419a, 774c.

3283. יָעֵן {1x} **yâᶜên**, *yaw-ane';* from the same as 3282; the *ostrich* (prob. from its *answering* cry:—ostrich {1x}. See: TWOT—884a; BDB—419a, 943d.

3284. יַעֲנָה {8x} **yaʿănâh**, *yah-an-aw';* fem. of 3283, and mean. the same:—+ owl {8x}. See: TWOT—884b; BDB—419a.

3285. יַעֲנַי {1x} **Yaʿănay**, *yah-an-ah'ee;* from the same as 3283; *responsive; Jaanai,* an Isr.:—Jaanai {1x}. See: BDB—419b.

3286. יָעַף {9x} **yâʿaph**, *yaw-af';* a prim. root; to *tire* (as if from wearisome *flight*):—faint {4x}, cause to fly {1x}, (be) weary (self) {4x}. See: TWOT—885; BDB—419b.

3287. יָעֵף {4x} **yâʿêph**, *yaw-afe';* from 3286; *fatigued;* fig. *exhausted:*—faint {2x}, wear {2x}. See: TWOT—885a; BDB—419b.

3288. יְעָף {1x} **yᵉʿâph**, *yeh-awf';* from 3286; *fatigue* (adv. utterly *exhausted*):—swiftly {1x}. See: TWOT—885b; BDB—419b.

3289. יָעַץ {80x} **yâʿats**, *yaw-ats';* a prim. root; to *advise;* refl. to *deliberate* or *resolve:*—counsel {25x}, counsellor {22x}, consult {9x}, give {7x}, purposed {5x}, advice {2x}, determined {2x}, advise {2x}, deviseth {2x}, taken {2x}, advertise {1x}, guide {1x}.

Ya'ats means to advise, counsel, or consult. **I.** *Ya'ats,* **as a verb,** means "to advise, counsel, consult." **(1)** *Ya'ats* is found first in Ex 18:19, where Jethro says to his son-in-law Moses: "I will give thee counsel, and God shall be with thee." **(2)** The word is found only one other time in the Hexateuch, and that is in Num 24:14: "And now, behold, I go unto my people: come *therefore, and* I will advertise thee what this people shall do to thy people in the latter days." **(3)** While *ya'ats* most often describes the "giving of good advice," the opposite is sometimes true. A tragic example was the case of King Ahaziah of Judah, whose mother "was his counselor to do wickedly" (2 Chr 22:3). **(4)** The idea of "decision" is expressed in Is 23:9: "The Lord of hosts hath purposed it."

II. Yo'es, **as a noun, means** "counselor." Perhaps the most familiar use of this root is the noun form found in the messianic passage, Is 9:6. On the basis of the syntax involved, it is probably best to translate: "Wonderful, Counselor." **III.** Ya'as, **as a participal,** refers to "those who give counsel, especially in connection with political and military leaders: **(1)** "And Absalom sent for Ahithophel the Gilonite, David's counsellor, from his city, *even* from Giloh, while he offered sacrifices. And the conspiracy was strong; for the people increased continually with Absalom" (2 Sa 15:12); **(2)** "And David consulted with the captains of thousands and hundreds, *and* with every leader" (1 Chr 13:1). See: TWOT—887; BDB—419c, 1095d.

3290. יַעֲקֹב {349x} **Yaʿăqôb**, *yah-ak-obe';* from 6117; *heel*-catcher (i.e. supplanter); *Jaakob,* the Isr. patriarch:—Jacob {349x}. See: BDB—420b, 784d.

3291. יַעֲקֹבָה {1x} **Yaʿăqôbâh**, *yah-ak-o'-baw;* from 3290; *Jaakobah,* an Isr.:—Jaakobah {1x}. See: BDB—420b, 785b.

3292. יַעֲקָן {1x} **Yaʿăqân**, *yah-ak-awn';* from the same as 6130; *Jaakan,* an Idumæan:—Jaakan {1x}. See: BDB—420c, 785c. comp. 1142.

3293. יַעַר {58x} **yaʿar**, *yah'-ar* from an unused root prob. mean. to *thicken* with verdure; a *copse* of bushes; hence, a *forest;* hence, *honey* in the *comb* (as hived in trees):—[honey-] comb {1x}, forest {37x}, forests {1x}, wood {19x}. See: TWOT—888, 889; BDB—420c, 421a.

3294. יַעְרָה {2x} **Yaʿrâh**, *yah-raw';* a form of 3295; *Jarah,* an Isr.:—Jarah {2x}. See: BDB—421a.

3295. יַעֲרָה {2x} **yaʿărâh**, *yah-ar-aw';* fem. of 3293, and mean. the same:—honeycomb + 1706 {1x}, forest {2x}. See: TWOT—889b; BDB—421a.

3296. יַעֲרֵי אֹרְגִים {1x} **Yaʿărêy ʾOrᵉgîym**, *yah-ar-ay' o-reg-eem';* from the plural of 3293 and the masc. plur. act. part. of 707; *woods of weavers; Jaare-Oregim,* an Isr.:—Jaare-oregim {1x}. See: BDB—421a.

3297. יְעָרִים {1x} **Yᵉʿârîym**, *yeh-aw-reem';* plur. of 3293; *forests; Jeärim,* a place in Pal.:—Jearim {1x}. See: BDB—421b. comp. 7157.

3298. יַעֲרֶשְׁיָה {1x} **Yaʿăreshyâh**, *yah-ar-esh-yaw';* from an unused root of uncert. signif. and 3050; *Jaareshjah,* an Isr.:—Jaresiah {1x}. See: BDB—421b, 793b.

3299. יַעֲשׂוּ {1x} **Yaʿăsûw**, *yah-as-oo';* from 6213; *they will do; Jaasu,* an Isr.:—Jaasau {1x}. See: BDB—421b, 795c.

3300. יַעֲשִׂיאֵל {2x} **Yaʿăsîyʾêl**, *yah-as-ee-ale';* from 6213 and 410; *made of God; Jaasiel,* an Isr.:—Jaasiel {1x}, Jasiel {1x}. See: BDB—421b, 795c.

3301. יִפְדְיָה {1x} **Yiphdᵉyâh**, *yif-deh-yaw';* from 6299 and 3050; *Jah will liberate; Jiphdejah,* an Isr.: Iphedeiah {1x}. See: BDB—421b.

3302. יָפָה {8x} **yâphâh**, *yaw-faw';* a prim. root; prop. to *be bright,* i.e. (by impl.) *beautiful:*—be beautiful {2x}, fair {3x}, make fair {1x}, fairer {1x}, deck {1x}. See: TWOT—890; BDB—421b.

3303. יָפֶה {41x} **yâpheh**, *yaw-feh';* from 3302; *beautiful* (lit. or fig.):—fair {21x}, beautiful {5x}, well {5x}, fairest {3x}, fair one {2x}, beauty {1x}, beautiful + 8389 {2x}, beauty {1x}, comely {1x}, pleasant {1x}. See: TWOT—890a; 421c.

3304. יְפֵה־פִיָּה {1x} **yᵉphêh-phîyâh**, *yef-eh' fee-yaw';* from 3302 by redupl.; *very beautiful:*—very fair {1x}. See: TWOT—890b; BDB—421d.

3305. יָפוֹ {4x} **Yâphôw**, *yaw-fo';* or
יָפוֹא **Yâphôwʾ** (Ezra 3:7), *yaw-fo';* from 3302; *beautiful; Japho,* a place in Pal.:—Japha {1x}, Joppa {3x}. See: BDB—421d.

3306. יָפַח {1x} **yâphach**, *yaw-fakh';* a prim. root; prop. to *breathe* hard, i.e. (by impl.) to *sigh:*—bewail {1x} self. See: TWOT—891; BDB—422a.

3307. יָפֵחַ {1x} **yâphêach**, *yaw-fay'-akh;* from 3306; prop. *puffing,* i.e. (fig.) *meditating:*—such as breathe out {1x}. See: TWOT—891a; BDB—422a.

3308. יֳפִי {19x} **yŏphîy**, *yof-ee';* from 3302; *beauty:*—beauty {19x}. See: TWOT—890c; BDB—421d.

3309. יָפִיעַ {5x} **Yâphîyaʿ**, *yaw-fee'-ah;* from 3313; *bright; Japhia,* the name of a Canaanite, an Isr., and a place in Pal.:—Japhia {5x}. See: BDB—422b.

3310. יַפְלֵט {1x} **Yaphlêṭ**, *yaf-late';* from 6403; *he will deliver; Japhlet,* an Isr.:—Japhlet {1x}. See: BDB—422a, 812d.

3311. יַפְלֵטִי {1x} **Yaphlêṭîy**, *yaf-lay-tee';* patron. from 3310; a *Japhletite* or desc. of Japhlet:—Japhleti {1x}. See: BDB—812d.

3312. יְפֻנֶּה {16x} **Yᵉphunneh**, *yef-oon-neh';* from 6437; *he will be prepared; Jephunneh,* the name of two Isr.:—Jephunneh {16x}. See: BDB—422a, 819c.

3313. יָפַע {8x} **yâphaʿ**, *yaw-fah';* a prim. root; to *shine:*—be light {1x}, shew self {1x}, shine {4x}, shine forth {2x}. See: TWOT—892; BDB—422a.

3314. יִפְעָה {1x} **yiphʿâh**, *yif-aw';* from 3313; *splendor* or (fig.) *beauty:*—brightness {1x}. See: TWOT—892a; BDB—422b.

3315. יֶפֶת {11x} **Yepheth**, *yeh'-feth;* from 6601; *expansion; Jepheth,* a son of Noah; also his posterity:—Japheth {11x}. See: BDB—422b, 834d.

3316. יִפְתָּח {30x} **Yiphtâch**, *yif-tawkh';* from 6605; *he will open; Jiphtach,* an Isr.; also a place in Pal.:—Jephthah {29x}, Jiphtah {1x}. See: BDB—422b, 836b.

3317. יִפְתַּח־אֵל {2x} **Yiphtach-ʾêl**, *yif-tach-ale';* from 6605 and 410; *God will open; Jiphtach-el,* a place in Pal.:—Jiphthah-el {2x}. See: BDB—422b, 836b.

3318. יָצָא { {1069x} **yâtsâʾ**, *yaw-tsaw';* a prim. root; to *go* (caus. *bring*) *out,* in a great variety of applications, lit. and fig., direct and proxim.:— . . . .out {518x}, ...forth {411x}, bring {24x}, come {24x}, proceed {16x}, go {13x}, depart {10x}, misc. {53x} = × after, appear, × assuredly, × begotten, + be condemned, in the end, escape, exact, fail, get away (hence,), grow, put away, be risen, × scarce, send with commandment, spread, × still, × surely, at any time, × to [and fro], utter.

Yatsa (3318), "to come forth, go out, proceed, go forth, bring out, come out." **(1)** Basically, this word means "movement away" from some point, even as bo' (935 - "come") means movement toward some point. **(2)** *Yatsa'* is the word used of "coming forth"—the observer is outside the point of departure but also speaks from the perspective of that departing point. **(2a)** For example, Gen 2:10 (the first occurrence of the word) reports that a river "came forth" or "flowed out" from the garden of Eden. **(2b)** In comparison to this continuing "going out," there is the one-time (punctiliar) "coming forth," as seen when all the animals "came out" of the ark (Gen 9:10). **(2c)** Thus, Goliath the champion of the Philistines "went forward" from the camp to challenge the Israelites to a duel: "And there went out a champion out of the camp of the Philistines, named Goliath, of Gath, whose height *was* six cubits and a span" (1 Sa 17:4). In the art of ancient warfare, a battle was sometimes decided on the basis of two duelers.

(3) This verb may be used with "come" (935 – bo') **(3a)** as an expression for "constant activity." **(3b)** The raven Noah sent out "went forth to and fro" (literally, "in and out") until the water had abated (Gen 8:7). **(4)** Various aspects of a man's personality may "go forth," indicating that they "leave" him. **(4a)** When one's soul "departs" the body, the person dies: "And it came to pass, as her soul was in departing, (for she died) that she called his name Benoni: but his father called him Benjamin" (Gen 35:18). **(4b)** When one's heart "departs," he loses all inner strength and confidence: "And he said unto his brethren, My money is restored; and, lo, *it is* even in my sack: and their heart failed *them,* and they were afraid, saying one to another, What *is* this *that* God hath done unto us?" (Gen 42:28).

(5) *Yatsa'* has a number of special uses. **(5a)** It can be used of "giving birth": If men strive, and hurt a woman with child, so that her fruit depart *from her,"* (Ex 21:22) or **(5b)** of "begetting" descendants: "And I will make thee exceeding fruitful, and I will make nations of thee, and kings shall come out of thee" (Gen 17:6). **(5c)** The "going forth" of a year is its close, as in the harvest season (Ex 23:16). **(5d)** Another special use of this verb has to do with "moving out" a camp for either a military campaign (1 Sa 8:20) or some other purpose (Deut 23:10). **(5e)** "Going and coming" may also be used of "fighting" in wars. **(5f)** Toward the end of his life Moses said he was unable to "come and go" (Deut 31:2; cf. Josh 14:11). He probably meant that he could not engage in war (Deut 31:3). **(5g)** On the other hand, this phrase can refer to the normal activities of life (1 Kin 3:7). **(6)** *Yatsa'* also has a cultic [religious] use, describing the "movement" of the priest in the tabernacle; bells were attached to the hem of the priest's robe so the people could follow his actions (Ex 28:35).

(7) When applied to God, the action of "going out" only infrequently refers to His "abandoning" a certain location. **(7a)** In Eze 10:18, the glory of the Lord "left" the "threshhold of the [temple], and stood over the cherubim," and eventually departed the temple altogether (Eze 10:19). **(7b)** Often this verb pictures the Lord as "going forth" to aid His people, especially in texts suggesting or depicting His appearances among men (theophanies; cf. Judg 5:4). **(7c)** In Egypt, the Lord "went out" into the midst of the Egyptians to smite their first born (Ex 11:4). **(7d)** The Lord's departure point in such cases is variously represented as Seir (Judg 5:4) and His heavenly dwelling place (Mic 1:3), although it is often unexpressed. **(8)** The messenger of God also "goes forth" to accomplish specific tasks (Num 22:32). **(9)** God's providential work in history is described by Laban and Bethuel as "the thing proceedeth from the Lord" (Gen 24:50). **(10)** Also, "going out" from the Lord are His hand (Ruth 1:13), His Word (Is 55:11), His salvation (Is 51:5), His justice (Is 45:23), and His wisdom (Is 51:4).

(11) *Yatsa'* is not used of God's initial creative act, but only of His using what already exists to accomplish His purposes, such as His causing water to "come out" of the rock (Deut 8:15). **(12)** Because *yatsa'* can mean "to bring forth," it is often used of "divine deliverance," as the One who "bringeth me forth from mine enemies" (2 Sa 22:49) "into a large place" (2 Sa 22:20). **(13)** One of the most important formulas in the Old Testament uses the verb *yatsa'*: "the Lord [who] brought [Israel] out of [Egypt]"; He brought them from slavery into freedom (Ex 13:3). Syn: 4161, 8444. See: TWOT—893; BDB—422b, 1115a.

3319. יְצָא {1x} **yᵉtsâʾ** (Aram.), *yets-aw';* corresp. to 3318:—finish {1x}. See: TWOT—3028; BDB—1096a, 1115a.

3320. יָצַב {48x} **yâtsab**, *yaw-tsab';* a prim. root; to *place* (anything so as to stay); refl. to *station, offer, continue:*—stand {24x}, present {9x}, set {6x}, stand still {2x}, stand up {2x}, withstand {1x}, stand fast {1x}, stand forth {1x}, remaining {1x}, resorted {1x}. See: TWOT—894; BDB—426a.

3321. יְצֵב {1x} **yᵉtsêb** (Aram.), *yets-abe';* corresp. to 3320; to *be firm;* hence, to *speak surely:*—truth {1x}. See: TWOT—2773; BDB—1096a.

3322. יָצַג {16x} **yâtsag**, *yaw-tsag';* a prim. root; to *place* permanently:—establish {1x}, leave {1x}, made {2x}, present {1x}, put {2x}, set {8x}, stay {1x}. See: TWOT—895; BDB—426c.

3323. יִצְהָר {23x} **yitshâr**, *yits-hawr';* from 6671; *oil* (as producing *light*); fig. *anointing:*—oil {22x}, oil {1x}. Syn.: 8081. See: TWOT—1883c; BDB—426d, 844a.

3324. יִצְהָר {9x} **Yitshâr**, *yits-hawr';* the same as 3323; *Jitshar,* an Isr.:—Izhar {8x}, Izehar {1x}. See: BDB—844b.

3325. יִצְהָרִי {4x} **Yitshârîy**, *yits-haw-ree';* patron. from 3324; a *Jitsharite* or desc. of Jitshar:—Izeharites {1x}, Izharites {3x}. See: BDB—844b.

3326. יָצוּעַ {11x} **yâtsûwaʿ**, *yaw-tsoo'-ah;* pass. part. of 3331; *spread,* i.e. a *bed;* (arch.) an *extension,* i.e. *wing* or *lean-to* (a single story or collect.):—bed {4x}, chamber {6x}, couch {1x}. See: TWOT—896a; BDB—426d, 427a.

3327. יִצְחָק {108x} **Yitschâq**, *yits-khawk';* from 6711; *laughter* (i.e. *mockery*); *Jitschak* (or Isaac), son of Abraham:—Isaac {108x}. See: TWOT—1905b; BDB—426d, 850c. Syn.: comp. 3446.

3328. יִצְחַר {1x} **Yitschar**, *yits-khar';* from the same as 6713; *he will shine; Jitschar,* an Isr.:—and Zehoar {1x}. See: BDB—426d, 850d.

3329. יָצִיא {1x} **yâtsîyʾ**, *yaw-tsee';* from 3318; *issue,* i.e. offspring:—those that came forth {1x}. See: TWOT—893a; BDB—425c.

3330. יַצִּיב {5x} **yatstsîyb** (Aram.), *yats-tseeb';* from 3321; *fixed, sure;* concr. *certainty:*—certain {1x}, certainty {1x}, true {2x}, truth {1x}. See: TWOT—2773a; BDB—1096a.

יָצִיעַ **yâtsîyaʿ**. See 3326.

3331. יָצַע {4x} **yâtsaʿ**, *yaw-tsah';* a prim. root; to *strew* as a surface:—make [one's] bed {1x}, × lie {1x}, spread {2x}. See: TWOT—896; BDB—426d.

3332. יָצַק {53x} **yâtsaq**, *yaw-tsak';* a prim. root; prop. to *pour* out (tran. or intr.); by impl. to *melt* or *cast* as metal; by extens. to *place* firmly, to *stiffen* or grow hard:—pour {21x}, cast {11x}, . . . out {7x}, molten {6x}, firm {2x}, set down {1x}, fast {1x}, groweth {1x}, hard {1x}, overflown {1x}, stedfast {1x}.

Yatsaq means "to pour, pour out, cast, flow." **(1)** The word is used first in **(1a)** Gen 28:18, where it is said that after Jacob had slept at Bethel with his head resting on a stone, he "poured oil upon the top of it." **(1b)** He again "poured" oil on a stone pillar at Bethel while on his return trip home twenty years later (Gen 35:14). **(1c)** The idea expressed in these two instances and others (Lev 8:12; 21:10) is that of anointing with oil; **(1c1)** it is not the ordinary term for "to anoint." **(1c2)** The regular term for "to anoint" is mashach (4886), which gives us the word "messiah." **(2)** Many things may "be poured out," such as **(2a)** oil in sacrifice: "And when any will offer a meat offering unto the LORD, his offering shall be *of* fine flour; and he shall pour oil upon it, and put frankincense thereon" (Lev 2:1), **(2b)** water for washing purposes: "But Jehoshaphat said, *Is there* not here a prophet of the LORD, that we may enquire of the LORD by him? And one of the king of Israel's servants answered and said, Here *is* Elisha the son of Shaphat, which poured water on the hands of Elijah" (2 Kin 3:11), and **(2c)** pottage for eating: "But he said, Then bring meal. And he cast *it* into the pot; and he said, Pour out for the people, that they may eat. And there was no harm in the pot" (2 Kin 4:41). **(3)** This verb is used to express the idea of "pouring out" or "casting" molten metals (Ex 25:12; 26:37; 1 Kin 7:46). **(4)** The idea of "pouring upon or infusing" someone is found in Ps 41:8: "An evil disease, *say they,* cleaveth fast unto him: and *now* that he lieth he shall rise up no more." The context seems to imply the infusion of a sickness. Syn.: 8210. See: TWOT—897; BDB—427a.

3333. יְצֻקָה {1x} **yᵉtsûqâh**, *yets-oo-kaw';* pass. part. fem. of 3332; *poured* out, i.e. *run* into a mould:—when it was cast {1x}. See: TWOT—897a; BDB—427c.

3334. יָצַר {9x} **yâtsar**, *yaw-tsar';* a prim. root; to *press* (intr.), i.e. *be narrow;* fig. *be in distress:*—be distressed {4x}, be narrow {1x}, be straitened (in straits) {2x}, be vexed {1x}. See: TWOT—1973; BDB—864c.

3335. יָצַר {62x} **yâtsar**, *yaw-tsar';* prob. ident. with 3334 (through the *squeezing* into shape); ([comp. 3331]); to *mould* into a form; espec. as a *potter;* fig. to *determine* (i.e. form a resolution):—form {26x}, potter {17x}, fashion {5x}, maker {4x}, frame {3x}, make {3x}, former {2x}, earthen {1x}, purposed {1x}.

Yatsar means "to form, mold, fashion." **(1)** The first occurrence in the Old Testament is in Gen 2:7: ". . . God formed man of the dust of the ground," reflecting the basic meaning of "molding" something to a desired shape. **(2)** *Yatsar* is a technical potter's word, and it is often used in connection with the potter at work (Is 29:16; Jer 18:4, 6). **(3)** The word is sometimes used as a general term of "craftsmanship or handiwork," whether molding, carving, or casting (Is 44:9–10, 12). **(3)** The word may be used to express the "Shall the throne of iniquity have fellowship with thee, which frameth mischief by a law?" (Ps 94:20). **(4)** *Yatsar* is frequently used to describe God's creative activity, whether literally or figuratively. **(4a)** Thus, God "formed" not only man (Gen 2:7–8) but **(4b)** the animals (Gen 2:19). **(4c)** God also "formed" the nation of Israel (Is 27:11; 45:9, 11); **(4d)** Israel was "formed" as God's special servant even from the womb (Is 44:2, 24; 49:5). **(4e)** While yet in the womb, Jeremiah was "formed" to be a prophet: "Before I formed thee in the belly I knew thee; and before thou camest forth out of the womb I sanctified thee, *and* I ordained thee a prophet unto the nations" (Jer 1:5).

(5) God "formed" **(5a)** locusts as a special visual lesson for Amos (Amos 7:1); **(5b)** the great sea monster, Leviathan, was "formed" to play in the seas (Ps 104:26). **(6)** The concreteness of ancient Hebrew thinking is vividly seen in a statement such as this: "I form the light, and create darkness . . ." (Is 45:7). **(7)** Similarly, the psalmist confessed to God: ". . . Thou hast made summer and winter" (Ps 74:17). **(8)** God "formed" **(8a)** the spirit of man (Zec 12:1), as well as **(8b)** the heart or mind of man (Ps 33:15). **(9)** *Yatsar* is used to express God's "planning" or "preordaining" according to His divine purpose (Is 22:11; 46:11). **(10)** Almost one half of the uses of this word in the Old Testament are found in the Book of Isaiah, with God as the subject of most of them. See: TWOT—898; BDB—427c, 849b.

3336. יֵצֶר {9x} **yêtser**, *yay'-tser;* from 3335; a *form;* fig. *conception* (i.e. *purpose*):—frame {1x}, thing framed {1x}, imagination {5x}, mind {1x}, work {1x}. See: TWOT—898a; BDB—428a.

3337. יֵצֶר {3x} **Yêtser**, *yay-tser;* the same as 3336; *Jetser,* an Isr.:—Jezer {3x}. See: BDB—428a.

3338. יָצֻר {1x} **yâtsûr**, *yaw-tsoor';* pass. part. of 3335; *structure,* i.e. limb or part:—member {1x}. See: TWOT—898b; BDB—428b.

3339. יִצְרִי {1x} **Yitsrîy**, *yits-ree';* from 3335; *formative; Jitsri,* an Isr.:—Isri {1x}. See: BDB—428b.

3340. יִצְרִי {1x} **Yitsrîy**, *yits-ree',* patron. from 3337; a *Jitsrite* (collect.) or desc. of Jetser:—Jezerites {1x}. See: BDB—428a.

3341. יָצַת {29x} **yâtsath**, *yaw-tsath';* a prim. root; to *burn* or *set on fire;* fig. to *desolate:*—burned {7x}, burn up {2x}, be desolate {1x}, set on fire {7x}, kindle {12x}. See: TWOT—899; BDB—428b, 850a.

3342. יֶקֶב {16x} **yeqeb**, *yeh'-keb;* from an unused root mean. to *excavate;* a *trough* (as dug out); spec. a wine-*vat* (whether the lower one, into which the juice drains; or the upper, in which the grapes are crushed):—winepresses {10x}, press {2x}, fats {2x}, pressfat {1x}, wine {1x}. See: TWOT—900a; BDB—428c.

3343. יְקַבְצְאֵל {1x} **Yᵉqabtsᵉʼêl**, *yek-ab-tseh-ale';* from 6908 and 410; *God will gather; Jekabtseël,* a place in Pal.:—Jekabzeel {1x}. See: BDB—428c, 868b. comp. 6909.

3344. יָקַד {9x} **yâqad**, *yaw-kad';* a prim. root; to *burn:*—(be) burn (-ing) {7x}, × from the hearth {1x}, kindle {1x}. See: TWOT—901; BDB—428d, 1096a.

3345. יְקַד {8x} **yᵉqad** (Aram.), *yek-ad';* corresp. to 3344:—burning {8x}. See: TWOT—2774; BDB—1096a.

3346. יְקֵדָא {1x} **yᵉqêdâʼ** (Aram.), *yek-ay-daw';* from 3345; a *conflagration:*—burning {1x}. See: TWOT—2774a; BDB—1096a.

3347. יָקְדְעָם {1x} **Yoqdᵉʻâm**, *yok-deh-awm';* from 3344 and 5971; *burning of* (the) *people; Jokdeäm,* a place in Pal.:—Jokdeam {1x}. See: BDB—429a.

3348. יָקֶה {1x} **Yâqeh**, *yaw-keh';* from an unused root prob. mean. to *obey; obedient; Jakeh,* a symb. name (for Solomon):—Jakeh {1x}. See: BDB—429a.

3349. יִקָּהָה {2x} **yiqqâhâh**, *yik-kaw-haw';* from the same as 3348; *obedience:*—gathering {1x}, to obey {1x}. Syn.: 8085. See: TWOT—902a; BDB—429b.

3350. יְקוֹד {1x} **yᵉqôwd**, *yek-ode';* from 3344; a *burning:*—burning {1x}. See: TWOT—901a; BDB—428d.

3351. יְקוּם {3x} **yᵉqûwm**, *yek-oom';* from 6965; prop. *standing* (extant), i.e. by impl. a *living thing:*—living substance {2x}, substance {1x}. See: TWOT—1999f; BDB—429b, 879c.

3352. יָקוֹשׁ {1x} **yâqôwsh**, *yaw-koshe';* from 3369; prop. *entangling;* hence, a *snarer:*—fowler {1x}. See: TWOT—906a; BDB—430c.

3353. יָקוּשׁ {3x} **yâqûwsh**, *yaw-koosh';* pass. part. of 3369; prop. *entangled,* i.e. by impl. (intr.) a *snare,* or (tran.) a *snarer:*—fowler {2x}, snare {1x}. See: TWOT—906b; BDB—430c.

3354. יְקוּתִיאֵל {1x} **Yᵉqûwthîyʼêl**, *yek-ooth-ee'-ale;* from the same as 3348 and 410; *obedience of God; Jekuthiël,* an Isr.:—Jekuthiel {1x}. See: BDB—429a, 429b.

3355. יָקְטָן {6x} **Yoqtân**, *yok-tawn';* from 6994; *he will be made little; Joktan,* an Arabian patriarch:—Joktan {6x}. See: BDB—429b.

3356. יָקִים {2x} **Yâqîym**, *yaw-keem';* from 6965; *he will raise; Jakim,* the name of two Isr.:—Jakim {2x}. See: BDB—879c. Syn.: comp. 3079.

3357. יַקִּיר {1x} **yaqqîyr**, *yak-keer';* from 3365; *precious:*—dear {1x}. See: TWOT—905c; BDB—430b.

3358. יַקִּיר {2x} **yaqqîyr** (Aram.), *yak-keer';* corresp. to 3357:—noble {1x}, rare {1x}. See: TWOT—2775a; BDB—1096a.

3359. יְקַמְיָה {3x} **Yᵉqamyâh**, *yek-am-yaw';* from 6965 and 3050; *Jah will rise; Jekamjah,* the name of two Isr.:—Jekamiah {2x}, Jecamiah {1x}. See: BDB—429b, 880c. comp. 3079.

3360. יְקַמְעָם {2x} **Yᵉqamʻâm**, *yek-am'-awm;* from 6965 and 5971; (the) *people will rise; Jekamam,* an Isr.:—Jekameam {2x}. See: BDB—429b, 880c. comp. 3079, 3361.

3361. יָקְמְעָם {2x} **Yoqmᵉʻâm**, *yok-meh-awm';* from 6965 and 5971; (the) *people will be raised; Jokmeäm,* a place in Pal.:—Jokmeam {2x}. See: BDB—429b, 880c. comp. 3360, 3362.

3362. יָקְנְעָם {3x} **Yoqnᵉʻâm**, *yok-neh-awm';* from 6969 and 5971; (the) *people will be lamented; Jokneäm,* a place in Pal.:—Jokneam {3x}. See: BDB—429b.

3363. יָקַע {8x} **yâqaʻ**, *yaw-kah';* a prim. root; prop. to *sever* oneself, i.e. (by impl.) to *be dislocated;* fig. to *abandon;* caus. to *impale* (and thus allow to drop to pieces by *rotting*):—be alienated {2x}, depart {1x}, hang (up) {4x}, be out of joint {1x}. See: TWOT—903; BDB—429b.

3364. יָקַץ {11x} **yâqats**, *yaw-kats';* a prim. root; to *awake* (intr.):—(be) awake (-d) {11x}. See: TWOT—904; BDB—429c.

יָקַף **yâqaph**. See 5362.

3365. יָקַר {11x} **yâqar**, *yaw-kar';* a prim. root; prop. appar. to *be heavy,* i.e. (fig.) *valuable;* caus. to *make rare* (fig. to *inhibit*):—be (make) precious {8x}, be prized {1x}, be set by {1x}, withdraw {1x}.

Yaqar, as a verb, means "to be difficult, be valued from, be valued or honored, be precious." The word means "to be precious" in 1 Sa 26:21: "Then said Saul, I have sinned: return, my son David: for I will no more do thee harm, because my soul was precious in thine eyes this day. . . ." See: TWOT—905; BDB—429, 429c.

3366. יְקָר {17x} **yᵉqâr**, *yek-awr';* from 3365; *value,* i.e. (concr.) *wealth;* abstr. *costliness, dignity:*—honour {12x}, precious {1x}, precious things {3x}, price {1x}.

Yeqar means precious thing; value; price; splendor; honor. *Yeqar,* as a noun, means "precious thing; value; price; splendor; honor." **(1)** The word signifies **(1a)** "value or price": "And the LORD said unto me, Cast it unto the potter: a goodly price that I was prised at of them. And I took the thirty *pieces* of silver, and cast them to the potter in the house of the LORD" (Zec 11:13), **(1b)** "splendor": "When he shewed the riches of his glorious kingdom and the honour of his excellent majesty many days, *even* an hundred and fourscore days" (Est 1:4), and **(1c)** "honor": "The Jews had light, and gladness, and joy, and honour" (Est 8:16). **(2)** In Jer 20:5 the word refers to "precious things": "Moreover I will deliver all the strength of this city, and all the labors thereof, and all the precious things thereof. . . ." See: TWOT—905b; BDB—430b, 1096a.

3367. יְקָר {7x} **yᵉqâr** (Aram.), *yek-awr';* corresp. to 3366:—glory {5x}, honour {2x}. See: TWOT—2775a; BDB—1096a.

3368. יָקָר {36x} **yâqâr**, *yaw-kawr';* from 3365; *valuable* (obj. or subj.):—precious {25x}, costly {4x} excellent {2x}, brightness {1x}, clear {1x}, fat {1x}, reputation {1x}, honourable women {1x}.

Yaqar, as an adjective means "precious; rare; excellent; weighty; noble." **(1)** First, *yaqar* means "precious" in the sense of being rare and valuable: "And he took their king's crown from off his head, the weight whereof was a talent of gold with the precious stones: and it was set on David's head" (2 Sa 12:30). **(2)** The emphasis is on the nuance "rare" in 1 Sa 3:1: "And the word of the Lord was precious in those days; there was no open vision." **(3)** The word can focus on the value of a thing: "How excellent is thy lovingkindness, O God!" (Ps 36:7). **(4)** This word means "weighty" or "noble": "Dead flies cause the ointment of the apothecary to send forth a stinking savour: *so doth* a little folly him that is in reputation for wisdom *and* honour" (Eccl 10:1); like dead flies which make perfume stink, so a little foolishness spoils wisdom and honor—it is worth more in a negative sense (cf. Lam 4:2). See: TWOT—905a; BDB—429d, 891b, 903b.

3369. יָקֹשׁ {8x} **yâqôsh**, *yaw-koshe';* a prim. root; to *ensnare* (lit. or fig.):—snare {5x}, lay a snare {1x}, laid {1x}, fowlers {1x}. See: TWOT—906; BDB—430b.

3370. יָקְשָׁן {4x} **Yoqshân**, *yok-shawn';* from 3369; *insidious; Jokshan,* an Arabian patriarch:—Jokshan {4x}. See: BDB—430d.

3371. יָקְתְאֵל {2x} **Yoqthᵉʼêl**, *yok-theh-ale';* prob. from the same as 3348 and 410; *veneration of God* [comp. 3354]; *Joktheël,* the name of a place in Pal., and of one in Idumæa:—Joktheel {2x}. See: BDB—430d.

יָרָא **yârâʼ**. See 3384.

3372. יָרֵא {341x} **yârêʼ**, *yaw-ray';* a prim. root; to *fear;* mor. to *revere;* caus. to *frighten:*—fear {188x}, afraid {78x}, terrible {23x}, terrible thing {6x}, dreadful {5x}, reverence {3x}, fearful {2x}, terrible acts {1x}, misc. {8x}.

Yare' means "to be afraid, stand in awe, fear." **(1)** Basically, this verb connotes the psychological reaction of "fear." **(1a)** *Yare'* may indicate being afraid of something or someone. **(1b)** Jacob prayed: "Deliver me, I pray thee, from the hand of my brother, from the hand of Esau: for I fear him, lest he will come and smite me, and the mother with the children" (Gen 32:11). **(2)** Used of a person in an exalted position, *yare'* connotes "standing in awe." **(2a)** This is not simple fear, but reverence, whereby an individual recognizes the power and position of the individual revered and renders him proper respect. **(2b)** In this sense, the word may imply submission to a proper ethical relationship to God; **(2c)** the angel of the Lord told Abraham: ". . . I know that thou fearest God, seeing thou hast not withheld thy son, thine only son from me" (Gen 22:12). **(3)** The verb can be used absolutely to refer to the heavenly and holy attributes of something or someone. So Jacob said of Bethel: "How [awesome] is this place! this is none other but the house of God, and this is the gate of heaven" (Gen 28:17).

(4) The people who were delivered from Egypt saw God's great power, "feared the Lord, and believed the Lord, and his servant Moses" (Ex 14:31). **(5)** There is more involved here than mere psychological fear. **(5a)** The people also showed proper "honor" ("reverence") for God and "stood in awe of" Him and of His servant, as their song demonstrates (Ex 15). **(5b)** After experiencing the thunder, lightning flashes, sound of the trumpet, and smoking mountain, they were "afraid" and drew back; but Moses told them not to be afraid, "for God is come to prove you, and that his fear may be before your faces, that ye sin not" (Ex 20:20). **(5c)** In this passage, the word represents "fear" or "dread" of the Lord. **(5d)** This sense is also found when God says, "fear not" (Gen 15:1).

(6) *Yare'* can be used absolutely (with no direct object), meaning "to be afraid." Adam told God: ". . . I was afraid, because I was naked; and I hid myself" (Gen 3:10—the first occurrence). **(7)** One may be "afraid" to do something, as when Lot "feared to dwell in Zoar" (Gen 19:30). See: TWOT—907, 908; BDB—431a, 1108c.

3373. יָרֵא {64x} **yârê'**, *yaw-ray';* from 3372; *fearing;* mor. *reverent:*—afraid {3x}, fear {59x}, fearful {2x}. See: TWOT—907a; BDB—431a, 531d.

3374. יִרְאָה {45x} **yir'âh**, *yir-aw';* fem. of 3373; *fear* (also used as infin.); mor. *reverence:*—fear {41x}, exceedingly + 1419 {2x}, dreadful {1x}, fearfulness {1x}.

Yir'ah means "fear; reverence." **(1)** It may mean "fear" of men: "This day will I begin to put the dread of thee and the fear of thee upon the nations *that are* under the whole heaven, who shall hear report of thee, and shall tremble, and be in anguish because of thee" (Deut 2:25), **(2)** of things: "And *on* all hills that shall be digged with the mattock, there shall not come thither the fear of briers and thorns: but it shall be for the sending forth of oxen, and for the treading of lesser cattle" (Is 7:25), **(3)** of situations: "Then were the men exceedingly afraid, and said unto him, Why hast thou done this? For the men knew that he fled from the presence of the LORD, because he had told them" (Jonah 1:10), and **(4)** of God: "And he said unto them, Take me up, and cast me forth into the sea; so shall the sea be calm unto you: for I know that for my sake this great tempest *is* upon you" (Jonah 1:12); **(5)** it may also mean "reverence" of God: "And Abraham said, Because I thought, Surely the fear of God *is* not in this place; and they will slay me for my wife's sake" (Gen 20:11). See: TWOT—907b; BDB—432a.

3375. יִרְאוֹן {1x} **Yir'ôwn**, *yir-ohn';* from 3372; *fearfulness; Jiron,* a place in Pal:—Iron {1x}. See: BDB—432a.

3376. יִרְאִיָּיה {2x} **Yir'îyâyh**, *yir-ee-yaw';* from 3373 and 3050; *fearful of Jah; Jirijah,* an Isr.:—Irijah {2x}. See: BDB—432c, 909d.

3377. יָרֵב {1x} **Yârêb**, *yaw-rabe';* from 7378; *he will contend; Jareb,* a symb. name for Assyria:—Jareb {1x} See: BDB—432c, 937a. comp. 3402.

3378. יְרֻבַּעַל {14x} **Y'rubba'al**, *yer-oob-bah'-al;* from 7378 and 1168; *Baal will contend; Jerubbaal,* a symbol. name of Gideon:—Jerubbaal {14x}. See: BDB—432c, 937c.

3379. יָרָבְעָם {104x} **Yârob'âm**, *yaw-rob-awm';* from 7378 and 5971; (the) *people will contend; Jarobam,* the name of two Isr. kings:—Jeroboam {104x}. See: BDB—432c, 914c, 937c.

3380. יְרֻבֶּשֶׁת {1x} **Y'rubbesheth**, *yer-oob-beh'-sheth;* from 7378 and 1322; *shame* (i.e. the idol) *will contend; Jerubbesheth,* a symbol. name for Gideon:—Jerubbesheth {1x}. See: BDB—432c, 937c.

3381. יָרַד {380x} **yârad**, *yaw-rad';* a prim. root; to *descend* (lit. to *go downwards;* or conventionally to a lower region, as the shore, a boundary, the enemy, etc.; or fig. to *fall*); caus. to *bring down* (in all the above applications):—(come, go, etc) down {340x}, descend {18x}, variant {2x}, fell {2x}, let {1x}, abundantly {1x}, down by {1x}, indeed {1x}, put off {1x}, light off {1x}, out {1x}, sank {1x}, subdued {1x}, take {1x}.

Yarad means "to descend, go down, come down." **(1)** Basically, this verb connotes "movement" from a higher to a lower location. **(1a)** In Gen 28:12, Jacob saw a "ladder set up on the earth, and the top of it reached to heaven: and behold the angels of God ascending and descending on it." **(1b)** In such a use, the speaker or observer speaks from the point of destination, and the movement is "downward" toward him. **(1c)** Thus one may "go down" below or under the ground's surface: "And the damsel *was* very fair to look upon, a virgin, neither had any man known her: and she went down to the well, and filled her pitcher, and came up" (Gen 24:16). **(1d)** The speaker may also speak as though he stands at the point of departure and the movement is away from him and "downward."

(1d1) Interestingly, one may "go down" to a lower spot in order to reach a city's gates (Judg 5:11) or **(1d2)** to get to a city located on a lower level than the access road (1 Sa 10:8)—**(1d3)** usually one goes up to a city and "goes down" to leave a city (1 Sa 9:27). **(1d4)** The journey from Palestine to Egypt is referred to as "going down" (Gen 12:10). This reference is not to a movement in space from a higher to a lower spot; it is a more technical use of the verb.

(2) *Yarad* is used frequently of "dying." **(2a)** One "goes down" to his grave. Here the idea of spatial movement is present, but in the background. **(2b)** This "going down" is much more of a removal from the world of conscious existence: For the grave cannot praise thee, death cannot celebrate thee: they that go down into the pit cannot hope for thy truth. The living, the living, he shall praise thee . . ." (Is 38:18–19). **(2c)** On the other hand, "going down to the dust" implies a return to the soil—i.e., a return of the body to the soil from which it came (Gen 3:19). "All they that go down to the dust shall bow before him . . ." (Ps 22:29). **(2d)** There is also the idea of the "descent" of the human soul into the realm of the dead. When Jacob mourned over Joseph whom he thought to be dead, he said: "For I will go down into the grave unto my son mourning" (Gen 37:35). **(2e)** Since one can "descend" into Sheol alive as a form of punishment (Num 16:30), this phrase means more than the end of human life. **(2f)** This meaning is further established because Enoch was rewarded by being taken off the earth: "And Enoch walked with God: and he was not; for God took him" (Gen 5:24); he was rewarded by not having "to descend" into Sheol.

(3) *Yarad* may also be used of "coming down," when the emphasis is on "moving downward" toward the speaker: "And the Lord came down to see the city and the tower" of Babel (Gen 11:5—the first biblical occurrence). **(4)** This verb may also be used to express coming down from the top of a mountain, as Moses did when he "descended" from Sinai (Ex 19:14). **(5)** The word may be used of "dismounting" from a donkey: "And when Abigail saw David, she hasted, and lighted off the ass . . ." (1 Sa 25:23). Abigail's entire body was not necessarily lower than before, so movement from a higher to a lower location is not indicated. However, she was no longer on the animal's back. So the verb here indicates "getting off" rather than getting down or descending. **(6)** In a somewhat related nuance, one may "get out" of bed. Elijah told Ahaziah: "Thou shalt not come down from that bed on which thou art gone up . . ." (2 Kin 1:4). Again, the idea is not of descending from something. When one comes down from a bed, he stands up; he is higher than he was while yet in the bed. Therefore, the meaning here is "get out of" rather than "descend."

(7) This verb is used also to describe what a beard does—it "hangs down" (Ps 133:2). **(8)** *Yarad* is used to indicate "coming away from" the altar: "And Aaron lifted up his hand toward the people, and blessed them, and came down from offering of the sin offering . . ." (Lev 9:22). This special use is best seen as the opposite of "ascending to" the altar, which is not just a physical movement from a lower to a higher plane but a spiritual ascent to a higher realm of reality. **(9)** For example, to "ascend" before a king is to go into the presence of someone who is on a higher social level. **(9a)** "To ascend" before God (represented by the altar) is to go before Someone on a higher spiritual plane. **(9b)** To stand before God is to stand in His presence before His throne, on a higher spiritual plane. **(10)** *Yarad* may thus be used of the humbled approach before God. God tells Moses that all the Egyptians shall "come down" to Him and bow themselves before Him (Ex 11:8). **(11)** Equally interesting is the occasional use of the verb to represent "descending" to a known sanctuary (cf. 2 Kings 2:2).

(12) Figuratively, the verb has many uses. **(12a)** The "going down" of a city is its destruction (Deut 20:20). **(12b)** When a day "descends," it comes to an end (Judg 19:11). **(12c)** The "descent" of a shadow is its lengthening (2 Kin 20:11). **(12d)** Tears "flow down" the cheeks when one weeps bitterly (Jer 13:17). **(13)** *Yarad* is also used figuratively of a "descent in social position": "The stranger that is within thee shall get up above thee very high; and thou shalt come down very low" (Deut 28:43). **(14)** At least once the word means "to go up." Jephthah's daughter said: "Let me alone two months, that I may go up and down upon the mountains, and bewail my virginity . . ." (Judg 11:37). See: TWOT—909; BDB—432c.

3382. יֶרֶד {7x} **Yered**, *yeh'-red;* from 3381; a *descent; Jered,* the name of an antediluvian, and of an Isr.:—Jared {2x}, Jarad {5x}. See: BDB—434b.

3383. יַרְדֵּן {182x} **Yardên**, *yar-dane';* from 3381; a *descender; Jarden,* the principal river of Pal.:—Jordan {182x}. See: BDB—434c.

3384. יָרָה {84x} **yârâh**, *yaw-raw';* or (2 Chron. 26:15)

יָרָא {84x} **yârâ'**, *yaw-raw';* a prim. root; prop. to *flow* as water (i.e. to *rain*); tran. to *lay* or *throw* (espec. an arrow, i.e. to *shoot*); fig. to *point* out (as if by *aiming* the finger), to *teach:*—teach {42x}, shoot {18x}, archers {5x}, cast {5x}, teacher {4x}, rain {2x}, laid {1x}, direct {1x}, inform {1x}, instructed {1x}, shewed {1x}, shooters {1x}, through {1x}, watered {1x}.

Yarah means to throw, cast (Gen 31:51), direct, teach (1 Sa 12:23), instruct, point out. *Yara'* means to cast, throw, teach, shoot, point out. **(1)** The basic meaning to cast is **(1a)** expressed in casting lots (Josh 18:6), by **(1b)** Pharaoh's army being cast into the sea (Ex 15:4), and **(1c)** a pillar cast: "And Laban said to Jacob, Behold this heap, and behold this pillar, which I have cast betwixt me and thee" (Gen 31:51). **(2)** The idea of "to throw" is easily extended to mean **(2a)** the shooting of arrows (1 Sa 20:36– 37); and **(2b)** "to throw" seems to be further extended to mean "to point," by which fingers are thrown in a certain direction (Gen 46:28; Prov. 6:13). **(3)** From this it is easy to see the concept of teaching as the "pointing out" of fact and truth. **(3a)** Thus, Bezaleel was inspired by God "to teach" others his craftsmanship: "And he hath put in his heart that he may teach, *both* he, and Aholiab, the son of Ahisamach, of the tribe of Dan" (Ex 35:34); **(3b)** the false prophets "teach" lies: "The ancient and honourable, he *is* the head; and the prophet that teacheth lies, he *is* the tail" (Is 9:15); and **(3c)** the father "taught" his son (Prov 4:4). **(4)** *Yarah* means "to teach" in 1 Sa 12:23: ". . . but I will teach you the good and the right way." **(5)** It was the responsibility of the priests to interpret and "to teach" those things that had to do with ceremonial requirements and God's judgments: "They shall teach Jacob thy judgments, and Israel thy law . . ." (Deut 33:10; cf. Deut 17:10-11). Interestingly, priests at a later time were said "to teach" for hire, presumably "to teach" what was wanted rather than true interpretation of God's word (Mic 3:11). **(6)** The noun torah (8451) is derived from this root. Syn: 8451. See: TWOT—910; BDB—432b, 434d.

3385. יְרוּאֵל {1x} **Yᵉrûwʾêl**, *yer-oo-ale';* from 3384 and 410; *founded of God; Jeruel,* a place in Pal.:—Jeruel {1x}. See: BDB—436c.

3386. יָרוֹחַ {1x} **Yârôwach**, *yaw-ro'-akh;* perh. denom. from 3394; (born at the) new *moon; Jaroäch,* an Isr.:—Jaroah {1x}. See: BDB—437b.

3387. יָרוֹק {1x} **yârôwq**, *yaw-roke';* from 3417; *green,* i.e. an herb:—green thing {1x}. See: TWOT—918c; BDB—438d.

3388. יְרוּשָׁא {2x} **Yᵉrûwshâʾ**, *yer-oo-shaw';* or

יְרוּשָׁה **Yᵉrûwshâh**, *yer-oo-shaw';* fem. pass. part. of 3423; *possessed; Jerusha* or *Jerushah,* an Israelitess:—Jerusha {1x}, Jerushah {1x}. See: BDB—440b.

3389. יְרוּשָׁלַםִ {643x} **Yᵉrûwshâlaim**, *yer-oo-shaw-lah'-im;* rarely

יְרוּשָׁלַיִם **Yᵉrûwshâlayim**, *yer-oo-shaw-lah'-yim;* a dual (in allusion to its two main hills [the true pointing, at least of the former reading, seems to be that of 3390]); prob. from (the pass. part. of) 3384 and 7999; *founded peaceful; Jerushalâm* or *Jerushalem,* the capital city of Pal.:—Jerusalem {643x}. See: BDB—436c, 1096b.

3390. יְרוּשָׁלֵם {26x} **Yᵉrûwshâlêm** (Aram.), *yer-oo-shaw-lame';* corresp. to 3389:—Jerusalem {26x}. See: BDB—1096b.

3391. יֶרַח {13x} **yerach**, *yeh'-rakh;* from an unused root of uncert. signif.; a *lunation,* i.e. *month:*—month {11x}, moon {2x}. See: TWOT—913b; BDB—437b, 1096b.

3392. יֶרַח {2x} **Yerach**, *yeh'-rakh;* the same as 3391; *Jerach,* an Arabian patriarch:—Jerah {2x}. See: BDB—437b.

3393. יְרַח {1x} **yᵉrach** (Aram.), *yeh-rakh';* corresp. to 3391; a *month:*—month {1x}. See: BDB—1096b.

3394. יָרֵחַ {26x} **yârêach**, *yaw-ray'-akh;* from the same as 3391; the *moon:*—moon {26x}. See: TWOT—913a; BDB—437a.

יְרֵחוֹ **Yᵉrêchôw**. See 3405.

3395. יְרֹחָם {10x} **Yᵉrôchâm**, *yer-o-khawm';* from 7355; *compassionate; Jerocham,* the name of seven or eight Isr.:—Jeroham {10x}. See: BDB—437b, 934a.

3396. יְרַחְמְאֵל {8x} **Yᵉrachmᵉʾêl**, *yer-akh-meh-ale';* from 7355 and 410; *God will compassionate; Jerachmeël,* the name of three Isr.:—Jerahmeel {8x}. See: BDB—437b, 934a.

3397. יְרַחְמְאֵלִי {2x} **Yᵉrachmᵉʾêlîy**, *yer-akh-meh-ay-lee';* patron. from 3396; a *Jerachmeëlite* or desc. of Jerachmeel:—Jerahmeelites {2x}. See: BDB—934a.

3398. יַרְחָע {2x} **Yarchâʿ**, *yar-khaw';* prob. of Eg. or.; *Jarcha,* an Eg.:—Jarha {2x}. See: BDB—437c.

3399. יָרַט {2x} **yârat**, *yaw-rat';* a prim. root; to *precipitate* or *hurl* (*rush*) headlong; (intr.) to *be rash:*—be perverse {1x}, turn over {1x}. See: TWOT—914; BDB—437c, 936a.

3400. יְרִיאֵל {1x} **Yᵉrîyʾêl**, *yer-ee-ale';* from 3384 and 410; *thrown of God; Jeriël,* an Isr.:—Jeriel {1x}. See: BDB—436c. comp. 3385.

3401. יָרִיב {3x} **yârîyb**, *yaw-rebe';* from 7378; lit. *he will contend;* prop. adj. *contentious;* used as noun, an *adversary:*—that content (-eth) {2x}, that strive {1x}. See: TWOT—2159b; BDB—937a.

3402. יָרִיב {3x} **Yârîyb**, *yaw-rebe';* the same as 3401; *Jarib,* the name of three Isr.:—Jarib {3x}. See: BDB—937b.

3403. יְרִיבַי {1x} **Yᵉrîybay**, *yer-eeb-ah'ee;* from 3401; *contentious; Jeribai,* an Isr.:—Jeribai {1x}. See: BDB—937a, 937b.

3404. יְרִיָּה {3x} **Yᵉrîyâh**, *yer-ee-yaw';* or

יְרִיָּהוּ **Yᵉrîyâhûw**, *yer-ee-yaw'-hoo;* from 3384 and 3050; *Jah will throw; Jerijah,* an Isr.:—Jeriah {1x}, Jerijah {2x}. See: BDB—436c.

3405. יְרִיחוֹ {57x} **Yᵉrîychôw**, *yer-ee-kho';* or

יְרֵחוֹ **Yᵉrêchôw**, *yer-ay-kho';* or var. (1 Kin 16:34)

יְרִיחֹה **Yᵉrîychôh**, *yer-ee-kho';* perh. from 3394; *its month;* or else from 7306; *fragrant; Jericho* or *Jerecho,* a place in Pal.:—Jericho {57x}. See: BDB—437b, 437c, 746d.

3406. יְרִימוֹת {13x} **Yᵉrîymôwth**, *yer-ee-mohth';* or

יְרֵימוֹת **Yᵉrêymôwth**, *yer-ay-mohth';* or

יְרֵמוֹת **Yᵉrêmôwth**, *yer-ay-mohth';* fem. plur. from 7311; *elevations; Jerimoth* or *Jeremoth,* the name of twelve Isr.:—Jeremoth {5x}, Jerimoth {8x}. See: BDB—438b, 928c.

3407. יְרִיעָה {1x} **yᵉrîyʿâh**, *yer-ee-aw';* from 3415; a *hanging* (as *tremulous*):—curtain {1x}. See: TWOT—917a; BDB—438c.

3408. יְרִיעוֹת {1x} **Yᵉrîyʿôwth**, *yer-ee-ohth';* plur. of 3407; *curtains; Jerioth,* an Israelitess:—Jerioth {1x}. See: BDB—438c.

3409. יָרֵךְ {34x} **yârêk**, *yaw-rake';* from an unused root mean. to *be soft;* the *thigh* (from its fleshy *softness*); by euphem. the *generative parts;* fig. a *shank, flank, side:*—× body {1x}, loins {2x}, shaft {3x}, side {7x}, thigh {21x}. See: TWOT—916a; BDB—437d, 1096b.

3410. יַרְכָא {1x} **yarkâʾ** (Aram.), *yar-kaw';* corresp. to 3411; a *thigh:*—thigh {1x}. See: TWOT—2777; BDB—1096b.

3411. יְרֵכָה {28x} **yᵉrêkâh**, *yer-ay-kaw';* fem. of 3409; prop. the *flank;* but used only fig., the *rear* or *recess:*—border {1x}, coasts {3x}, parts {2x}, quarter {1x}, side {21x}. See: TWOT—916b; BDB—438a.

3412. יַרְמוּת {7x} **Yarmûwth**, *yar-mooth';* from 7311; *elevation; Jarmuth,* the name of two places in Pal.:—Jarmuth {1x}. See: BDB—438b.

יְרֵמוֹת **Yᵉrêmôwth**. See 3406.

3413. יְרֵמַי {1x} **Yᵉrêmay**, *yer-ay-mah'-ee* from 7311; *elevated; Jeremai,* an Isr.:—Jeremai {1x}. See: BDB—438b.

3414. יִרְמְיָה {147x} **Yirmᵉyâh**, *yir-meh-yaw';* or

יִרְמְיָהוּ **Yirmᵉyâhûw**, *yir-meh-yaw'-hoo;* from 7311 and 3050; *Jah will rise; Jirmejah,* the name of eight or nine Isr.:—Jeremiah {147x}. See: BDB—438c, 941c.

3415. יָרַע {22x} **yâraʿ**, *yaw-rah';* a prim. root; prop. to *be broken* up (with any violent action) i.e. (fig.) to *fear:*—displease {9x}, grieved {4x}, grievous {3x}, evil {2x}, ill {2x}, harm {1x}, sad {1x}. See: TWOT—917; BDB—438c.

3416. יִרְפְּאֵל {1x} **Yirpᵉʾêl**, *yir-peh-ale';* from 7495 and 410; *God will heal; Jirpeël,* a place in Pal.:—Irpeel {1x}. See: BDB—438c, 951c.

3417. יָרַק {3x} **yâraq**, *yaw-rak';* a prim. root; to *spit:*—× but {1x}, spit {2x}. See: TWOT—918, 919; BDB—439a, 956d.

3418. יֶרֶק {6x} **yereq**, *yeh'-rek;* from 3417 (in the sense of *vacuity* of color); prop. *pallor,* i.e. hence, the yellowish *green* of young and sickly vegetation; concr. *verdure,* i.e. grass or vegetation:—grass {1x}, green {3x}, green thing {2x}. See: TWOT—918a; BDB—438d. Syn.: 1877, 2682, 3419, 6212.

3419. יָרָק {5x} **yârâq**, *yaw-rawk';* from the same as 3418; prop. *green;* concr. a *vegetable:*—green {2x}, herbs {3x}. See: TWOT—918b; BDB—438d.

יַרְקוֹן **Yarqôwn**. See 4313.

3420. יֵרָקוֹן {6x} **yêrâqôwn**, *yay-raw-kone';* from 3418; *paleness,* whether of persons (from fright), or of plants (from drought):—mildew {5x}, paleness {1x}. See: TWOT—918d; BDB—439a.

3421. יָרְקְעָם {1x} **Yorqᵉʿâm**, *yor-keh-awm';* from 7324 and 5971; *people will be poured forth; Jorkeäm,* a place in Pal.:—Jorkeam {1x}. See: BDB—439a.

3422. יְרַקְרַק {3x} **yᵉraqraq**, *yer-ak-rak';* from the same as 3418; *yellowishness:*—greenish {2x}, yellow {1x}. See: TWOT—918e; BDB—439a.

3423. יָרַשׁ {232x} **yârash**, *yaw-rash';* or

יָרֵשׁ **yârêsh**, *yaw-raysh';* a prim. root; to *occupy* (by *driving* out previous tenants, and *possessing* in their place); by impl. to *seize,* to *rob,* to *inherit;* also to *expel,* to *impoverish,* to *ruin:*—possess {116x}, . . . out {46x}, inherit {21x}, heir {10x}, possession {6x}, succeed {5x}, dispossess {4x}, poverty {3x}, drive {2x}, enjoy {2x}, poor {2x}, expelled {2x}, utterly {2x}, misc. {11x} = consume, destroy, disinherit, drive (-ing) out, × without fail, seize upon.

Yarash, as a verb, means "to inherit, subdue, take possession, dispossess, impoverish." **(1)** Basically *yarash* means "to inherit." The verb can connote the state of being designated as an heir. Abram said to God: "Behold, to me thou hast given no [offspring]: and, lo, one born in my house is mine heir [literally, "is the one who is inheriting me"]" (Gen 15:3—the first biblical occurrence of the word). **(1a)** Whatever Abram had to be passed on to his legal descendants was destined to be given to his servant. **(1b)** Hence his servant was his legally designated heir. **(2)** This root can also represent the status of having something as one's permanent possession, as a possession which may be passed on to one's legal descendants. God told Abram: "I am the Lord that brought thee out of Ur of the Chaldees, to give thee this land to inherit it" (Gen 15:7). **(3)** *Yarash* can mean "to take over as a permanent possession": "And if his father have no brethren, then ye shall give his inheritance unto his kinsman that is next to him of his family, and he shall possess it . . ." (Num 27:11).

(4) The verb sometimes means to take something over (in the case of the Promised Land) by conquest as a permanent possession: "The Lord shall make the pestilence cleave unto thee, until he have consumed thee from off the land, whither thou goest to possess it" (Deut 28:21). **(5)** When people are the object, *yarash* sometimes means "to dispossess" in the sense of taking away their inheritable goods and putting them in such a social position that they cannot hold possessions or inherit permanent possessions: "The Horim also dwelt in Seir beforetime; but the children of Esau succeeded them, when they had destroyed them from before them, and dwelt in their stead . . ." (Deut 2:12). **(6)** To cause someone to be dispossessed is "to impoverish" him: "The Lord maketh poor, and maketh rich . . ." (1 Sa 2:7), the Lord makes one to be without permanent inheritable possessions. See: TWOT—920; BDB—439a.

3424. יְרֵשָׁה {2x} **y^e^rêshâh**, *yer-ay-shaw';* from 3423; *occupancy:*—possession {2x}.

Yereshah, which appears twice, means "something given as a permanent possession; to be taken over by conquest": "And Edom shall be a possession, Seir also shall be a possession for his enemies; and Israel shall do valiantly" (Num 24:18). See: TWOT—920a; BDB—440b.

3425. יְרֻשָּׁה {14x} **y^e^rushshâh**, *yer-oosh-shaw';* from 3423; something *occupied;* a *conquest;* also a *patrimony:*—heritage {1x}, inheritance {1x}, possession {12x}.

Yerushshah occurs 14 times; it means **(1)** "to have as a possession": "Meddle not with them; for I will not give you of their land, no, not so much as a foot breadth; because I have given mount Seir unto Esau *for* a possession" (Deut 2:5), **(2)** "to be designated as a possession, to receive as a possession": "And the LORD said unto me, Distress not the Moabites, neither contend with them in battle: for I will not give thee of their land *for* a possession; because I have given Ar unto the children of Lot *for* a possession" (Deut 2:9). See: TWOT—920b; BDB—440b.

3426. יֵשׁ {133x} **yêsh**, *yaysh;* perh. from an unused root mean. to *stand* out, or *exist; entity;* used adv. or as a copula for the substantive verb (1961); there *is* or *are* (or any other form of the verb to *be,* as may suit the connection):—is {54x}, be {28x}, have {22x}, there {13x}, misc. {16x} = thou do, had, hast, (which) hath, substance, it was, ye will, thou wilt, wouldest.

Yesh means there is; substance; he/she/ it is/ are. **(1)** This particle is used substantively only in Prov 8:21: ". . . That I may cause those that love me to inherit substance; and I will fill their treasures." **(2)** In all other appearances the word asserts existence with emphasis. **(2a)** Sometimes *yesh* appears with a predicate following, **(2b)** as it does in Gen 28:16: "And Jacob awaked out of his sleep, and he said, Surely the Lord is in this place; and I knew it not." **(3)** In a few passages the word is used as a response to an inquiry: "Is the seer here? And they [the young maidens] answered them, and said, He is; behold, he is before you . . ." (1 Sa 9:11–12). **(4)** Used absolutely the word can mean "there is/are/was/ were," as it does in Gen 18:24 (the first biblical appearance): "Peradventure there be fifty righteous within the city . . ." **(5)** In many contexts *yesh* used in framing questions or protestations suggests doubt that the matter queried exists or is to be found: **(5a)** "As the Lord thy God liveth, there is no nation or kingdom, whither my lord hath not sent to seek thee: and when they said, He is not there; he took an oath of the kingdom and nation, that they found thee not" (1 Kin 18:10).

(5b) This is especially clear in Jer 5:1, where God commands the prophet to go and seek "if ye can find a man, if there be any that executeth judgment, that seeketh the truth. . . ." **(6)** There are several other special uses of *yesh.* **(6a)** Used with the particle *im* (518) and a participle, it emphasizes abiding intention: "And I came this day unto the well, and said, O Lord God of my master Abraham, if now thou do prosper my way which I go [literally, if there surely is a prospering of my way; or if it surely is that you intend to prosper] . . ." (Gen 24:42). **(6b)** Possession is sometimes indicated by *yesh* plus the preposition le: "And Esau said, I have enough, my brother . . ." (Gen 33:9). **(6c)** Used with the infinitive and the preposition le, *yesh* signifies possibility—Elisha told the Shunammite woman: "Behold, thou hast been careful for us with all this care; what is to be done for thee? wouldest thou be spoken for to the king, or to the captain of the host [is it possible that you want me to speak a word in your behalf to]?" (2 Kin 4:13). See: TWOT—921; BDB—441b, 930d, 1080a.

3427. יָשַׁב {1088x} **yâshab**, *yaw-shab';* a prim. root; prop. to *sit* down (spec. as judgement in ambush, in quiet); by impl. to *dwell,* to *remain;* caus. to *settle,* to *marry:*—dwell {437x}, inhabitant {221x}, sit {172x}, abide {70x}, inhabit {39x}, down {26x}, remain {23x}, in {22x}, tarry {19x}, set {14x}, continue {5x}, place {7x}, still {5x}, taken {5x}, misc. {23x} = ease self, endure, establish, × fail, habitation, haunt, make to keep [house], lurking, × marry (-ing), return, seat.

I. *Yashab,* **as a verb,** means "to dwell, sit, abide, inhabit, remain." **(1)** *Yashab* is first used in Gen 4:16, in its most common connotation of **(1a)** "to dwell": "Cain went out . . . and dwelt in the land of Nod. . . ." **(1b)** The word appears again in Gen 18:1: "He [Abraham] sat in the tent door." **(1c)** In Gen 22:5, *yashab* is translated: "Abide ye here with the ass; and I and the lad will go yonder and worship. . . ." **(1d)** The word has the sense of "to remain": **(1d1)** "Remain a widow at thy father's house . . ." (Gen 38:11), and **(1d2)** it is used of God in a similar sense: "Thou, O Lord, remainest for ever; thy throne from generation to generation . . ." (Lam 5:19). **(1e)** The promise of restoration from captivity was: "And they shall build houses and inhabit them . . ." (Is 65:21). **(2)** *Yashab* is sometimes combined with other words to form expressions in common usage. **(2a)** For example, "When he sitteth upon the throne of his kingdom" (Deut 17:18; cf. 1 Kin 1:13, 17, 24) carries the meaning "begins to reign." **(2b)** "To sit in the gate" means "to hold court" or "to decide a case," as in Ruth 4:1–2 and 1 Kin 22:10. **(2c)** "Sit thou at my right hand" (Ps 110:1) means to assume a ruling position as deputy. **(2d)** "There will I sit to judge all the heathen" (Joel 3:12) was a promise of eschatological judgment. **(2e)** "To sit in the dust" or "to sit on the ground" (Is 47:1) was a sign of humiliation and grief.

(3) *Yashab* is often used figuratively of God. The sentences, "I saw the Lord sitting on his throne" (1 Kin 22:19); "He that sitteth in the heavens shall laugh" (Ps 2:4); and "God sitteth upon the throne of his holiness" (Ps 47:8) all describe God as the exalted Ruler over the universe. **(4)** The idea that God also "dwells" among men is expressed by this verb: "Shalt thou [David] build me a house for me to dwell in?" (2 Sa 7:5; cf. Ps 132:14). **(5)** The usage of *yashab* in such verses as 1 Sa 4:4: ". . . The Lord of hosts, which dwelleth between the cherubim," describes His presence at the ark of the covenant in the tabernacle and the temple. **(6)** The word is also used to describe man's being in God's presence: **(6a)** "One thing have I desired of the Lord, . . . that I may dwell in the house of the Lord all the days of my life . . ." (Ps 27:4; cf. Ps 23:6). **(6b)** "Thou shalt bring them in, and plant them in the mountain of thine inheritance, in the place, O Lord, which thou hast made for thee to dwell in . . ." (Ex 15:17). **II.** *Yashab,* **as a participle,** means "remaining; inhabitant." **(1)** This participle is sometimes used as a simple adjective: "Jacob was a plain man, dwelling in tents" (Gen 25:27). **(2)** But the word is more often used as in Gen 19:25: ". . . All the inhabitants of the cities." Syn: 4908, 7931. See: TWOT—922; BDB—442a, 1096b.

3428. יֶשֶׁבְאָב {1x} **Yesheb'âb**, *yeh-sheb-awb';* from 3427 and 1; *seat of* (his) *father; Jeshebab,* an Isr.:—Jeshebeab {1x}. See: BDB—444a.

3429. יֹשֵׁב בַּשֶּׁבֶת {1x} **Yôshêb bash-Shebeth**, *yo-shabe' bash-sheh'-beth;* from the act. part. of 3427 and 7674, with a prep. and the art. interposed; *sitting in the seat; Josheb-bash-Shebeth,* an Isr.:—that sat in the seat {1x}. See: BDB—444a.

3430. יִשְׁבּוֹ בְּנֹב {1x} **Yishbôw b^e^-Nôb**, *yish-bo' beh-nobe';* from 3427 and 5011, with a pron. suff. and a prep. interposed; *his dwelling* (is) *in Nob; Jishbo-be-Nob,* a Philistine:—Ishbi-benob {1x}. See: BDB—444a.

3431. יִשְׁבַּח {1x} **Yishbach**, *yish-bakh';* from 7623; *he will praise; Jishbach,* an Isr.:—Ishbah {1x}. See: BDB—444c, 986d.

3432. יָשֻׁבִי {1x} **Yâshûbîy**, *yaw-shoo-bee';* patron. from 3437; a *Jashubite,* or desc. of Jashub:—Jashubites {1x}. See: BDB—444c, 1000b.

3433. יָשֻׁבִי לֶחֶם {1x} **Yâshûbîy Lechem**, *yaw-shoo-bee' leh'-khem;* from 7725 and 3899; *returner of bread; Jashubi-Lechem,* an Isr.:—Jashubi-lehem {1x}. See: BDB—1000b. or

יֹשְׁבֵי לֶחֶם **Yôsh^e^bêy Lechem**, *yo-sheh-bay' leh'-khem,* and rendered "(they were) inhab. of Lechem," i.e. of Bethlehem (by contr.). comp. 3902.

3434. יָשָׁבְעָם {3x} **Yâshobᶜâm**, *yaw-shob-awm';* from 7725 and 5971; *people will return; Jashobam,* the name of two or three Isr.:—Jashobeam {3x}. See: BDB—444c, 1000b.

3435. יִשְׁבָּק {2x} **Yishbâq**, *yish-bawk';* from an unused root corresp. to 7662; *he will leave; Jishbak,* a son of Abraham:—Ishbak {2x}. See: BDB—444c, 990b.

3436. יָשְׁבְּקָשָׁה {2x} **Yoshbᵉqâshâh**, *yosh-bek-aw-shaw';* from 3427 and 7186; a *hard seat; Joshbekashah,* an Isr.:—Joshbekashah {2x}. See: BDB—444a.

3437. יָשׁוּב {3x} **Yâshûwb**, *yaw-shoob';* or

יָשִׁיב **Yâshîyb**, *yaw-sheeb';* from 7725; *he will return; Jashub,* the name of two Isr.:—Jashub {3x}. See: BDB—445a, 445b, 1000a.

3438. יִשְׁוָה {2x} **Yishvâh**, *yish-vaw';* from 7737; *he will level; Jishvah,* an Isr.:—Ishvah {1x}, Isvah {1x}. See: BDB—445a, 1001a.

3439. יְשׁוֹחָיָה {1x} **Yᵉshôwchâyâh**, *yesh-o-khaw-yaw';* from the same as 3445 and 3050; *Jah will empty; Jeshochajah,* an Isr.:—Jeshoaiah {1x}. See: BDB—445a, 1001d, 1006a.

3440. יִשְׁוִי {4x} **Yishvîy**, *yish-vee';* from 7737; *level; Jishvi,* the name of two Isr.:—Ishuai {1x}, Ishvi {1x}, Isui {1x}, Jesui {1x}. See: BDB—445a, 1001a.

3441. יִשְׁוִי {1x} **Yishvîy**, *yish-vee';* patron. from 3440; a *Jishvite* (collect.) or desc. of Jishvi:—Jesuites {1x}. See: BDB—445a, 1001a.

3442. יֵשׁוּעַ {29x} **Yêshûwaᶜ**, *yay-shoo'-ah;* for 3091; *he will save; Jeshua,* the name of ten Isr., also of a place in Pal.:—Jeshua {29x}. See: BDB—221c, 222d, 445a, 448a, 1096b.

3443. יֵשׁוּעַ {1x} **Yêshûwaᶜ** (Aram.), *yay-shoo'-ah;* corresp. to 3442:—Jeshua {1x}. See: BDB—1096b.

3444. יְשׁוּעָה {78x} **yᵉshûwᶜâh**, *yesh-oo'-aw;* fem. pass. part. of 3467; something *saved,* i.e. (abstr.) *deliverance;* hence, *aid, victory, prosperity:*—salvation {65x}, help {4x}, deliverance {3x}, health {3x}, save {1x}, saving {1x}, welfare {1x}.

Yeshuw'ah, as a noun, means "deliverance." **(1)** This noun appears 78 times in the Old Testament, predominantly in the Book of Psalms (45 times) and Isaiah (19 times). **(2)** The first occurrence is in Jacob's last words: "I have waited for thy salvation, O Lord" (Gen 49:18). **(3)** "Salvation" in the Old Testament is not understood as a salvation from sin, since the word denotes broadly anything from which "deliverance" must be sought: distress, war, servitude, or enemies. **(3a)** There are both human and divine deliverers, but the word *yeshuw'ah* rarely refers to human "deliverance." **(3b)** A couple of exceptions are when Jonathan brought respite to the Israelites from the Philistine pressure (1 Sa 14:45), and when Joab and his men were to help one another in battle (2 Sa 10:11). **(4)** "Deliverance" is generally used with God as the subject. **(4a)** He is known as the salvation of His people: "But Jeshurun waxed fat, and kicked: thou art waxen fat, thou art grown thick, thou art covered with fatness; then he forsook God which made him, and lightly esteemed the Rock of his salvation" (Deut 32:15; cf. Is 12:2).

(4b) He worked many wonders in behalf of His people: "O sing unto the Lord a new song; for he hath done marvelous things: his right hand, and his holy arm, hath [worked salvation for him]" (Ps 98:1). **(5)** *Yeshuw'ah* occurs either in the context of rejoicing (Ps 9:14) or in the context of a prayer for "deliverance": "But I am poor and sorrowful: let thy salvation, O God, set me up on high" (Ps 69:29). **(6)** Habakkuk portrays the Lord's riding on chariots of salvation (3:8) to deliver His people from their oppressors: "Was the LORD displeased against the rivers? *was* thine anger against the rivers? *was* thy wrath against the sea, that thou didst ride upon thine horses *and* thy chariots of salvation?" **(7)** The worst reproach that could be made against a person was that God did not come to his rescue: "Many there be which say of my soul, there is no help for him in God [literally, "he has no deliverance in God"]" (Ps 3:2). **(9)** Many personal names contain a form of the root, such as Joshua ("the Lord is help"), Isaiah ("the Lord is help"), and Jesus (a Greek form of yeshu'ah). Syn: 3467, 5414, 8668. See: TWOT—929b; BDB—447b.

3445. יֶשַׁח {1x} **yeshach**, *yeh'-shakh;* from an unused root mean. to *gape* (as the empty stomach); *hunger:*—casting down {1x}. See: TWOT—924; BDB—445a.

3446. יִשְׂחָק {4x} **Yischâq**, *yis-khawk';* from 7831; *he will laugh; Jischak,* the heir of Abraham:—Isaac {4x}. See: TWOT—1905b; BDB—850c, 966a. comp. 3327.

3447. יָשַׁט {3x} **yâshat**, *yaw-shat';* a prim. root; to *extend:*—hold out {3x}. See: TWOT—925; BDB—445a.

3448. יִשַׁי {42x} **Yîshay**, *yee-shah'-ee;* by Aram.

אִישַׁי **ʾIyshay**, *ee-shah'-ee;* from the same as 3426; *extant; Jishai,* David's father:—Jesse {42x}. See: TWOT—926; BDB—36b, 445a.

יָשִׁיב **Yâshîyb**. See 3437.

3449. יִשִּׁיָּה {7x} **Yishshîyâh**, *yish-shee-yaw';* or

יִשִּׁיָּהוּ **Yishshîyâhûw**, *yish-shee-yaw'-hoo;* from 5383 and 3050; *Jah will lend; Jishshijah,* the name of five Isr.:—Ishiah {1x}, Isshiah {3x}, Ishijah {1x}, Jesiah {2x}. See: BDB—445b, 674d.

3450. יְשִׂימָאֵל {1x} **Yᵉsîymâʾêl**, *yes-eem-aw-ale';* from 7760 and 410; *God will place; Jesimaël,* an Isr.:—Jesimael {1x}. See: BDB—964d.

3451. יְשִׁימָה {1x} **yᵉshîymâh**, *yesh-ee-maw';* from 3456; *desolation:*—let death seize {1x}. See: TWOT—927a; BDB—445b.

3452. יְשִׁימוֹן {13x} **yᵉshîymôwn**, *yesh-ee-mone';* from 3456; a *desolation:*—desert {4x}, Jeshimon {6x}, solitary {1x}, wilderness {2x}. See: TWOT—927b; BDB—445b.

יְשִׁימוֹת **yᵉshîymôwth**. See 1020, 3451.

3453. יָשִׁישׁ {4x} **yâshîysh**, *yaw-sheesh';* from 3486; an *old* man:—aged {1x}, aged men {1x}, ancient {1x}, very old {1x}. Syn.: 2204, 2205, 2208, 2209, 3465, 5769, 7872. See: TWOT—931b; BDB—450a.

3454. יְשִׁישַׁי {1x} **Yᵉshîyshay**, *yesh-ee-shah'-ee;* from 3453; *aged; Jeshishai,* an Isr.:—Jeshishai {1x}. See: BDB—450b.

3455. יָשַׂם {2x} **yâsam**, *yaw-sam';* a prim. root; to *place;* intr. to *be placed:*—be put {1x}, set {1x}. See: TWOT—2243; BDB—441a.

3456. יָשַׁם {4x} **yâsham**, *yaw-sham';* a prim. root; to *lie waste:*—be desolate {4x}. Syn.: 1327, 2717, 2723, 8007. See: TWOT—927; BDB—445b.

3457. יִשְׁמָא {1x} **Yishmâʾ**, *yish-maw';* from 3456; *desolate; Jishma,* an Isr.:—Ishma {1x}. See: BDB—445c.

3458. יִשְׁמָעֵאל {48x} **Yishmâᶜêʾl**, *yish-maw-ale';* from 8085 and 410; *God will hear; Jishmaël,* the name of Abraham's oldest son, and of five Isr.:—Ishmael {48x}. See: BDB—445c, 1035d.

3459. יִשְׁמְעֵאלִי {8x} **Yishmâᶜêʾlîy**, *yish-maw-ay-lee';* patron. from 3458; a *Jishmaëlite* or desc. of Jishmael:—Ishmaelite {2x}, Ishmeelite {6x}. See: BDB—1035d.

3460. יִשְׁמַעְיָה {2x} **Yishmaᶜyâh**, *yish-mah-yaw';* or

יִשְׁמַעְיָהוּ **Yishmaᶜyâhûw**, *yish-mah-yaw'-hoo;* from 8085 and 3050; *Jah will hear; Jishmajah,* the name of two Isr.:—Ishmaiah {1x}, Ismaiah {1x}. See: BDB—1036a.

3461. יִשְׁמְרַי {1x} **Yishmᵉray**, *yish-mer-ah'-ee;* from 8104; *preservative; Jishmerai,* an Isr.:—Ishmerai {1x}. See: BDB—445c, 1038b.

3462. יָשֵׁן {19x} **yâshên**, *yaw-shane';* a prim. root; prop. to *be slack* or *languid,* i.e. (by impl.) *sleep* (fig. to *die*); also to *grow old, stale* or *inveterate:*—old {1x}, old store {1x}, remain long {1x}, (make to) sleep {16x}. See: TWOT—928; BDB—445c, 1096b.

3463. יָשֵׁן {9x} **yâshên**, *yaw-shane';* from 3462; *sleepy:*—asleep {2x}, sleep {3x}, sleepeth {2x}, sleeping {1x}, slept {1x}. See: TWOT 928a; BDB—445d.

3464. יָשֵׁן {1x} **Yâshên**, *yaw-shane';* the same as 3463; *Jashen,* an Isr.:—Jashen {1x}. See: BDB—445d

3465. יָשָׁן {7x} **yâshân**, *yaw-shawn';* from 3462; *old:*—old {7x}. See: TWOT—928b; BDB—445d.

3466. יְשָׁנָה {1x} **Yᵉshânâh**, *yesh-aw-naw';* fem. of 3465; *Jeshanah,* a place in Pal.:—Jeshanah {1x}. See: BDB—446a.

3467. יָשַׁע {205x} **yâshaᶜ**, *yaw-shah';* a prim. root; prop. to *be open, wide* or *free,* i.e. (by impl.) to *be safe;* caus. to *free* or *succor:*—save {149x}, saviour {15x}, deliver {13x}, help {12x}, preserved {5x}, salvation {3x}, avenging {2x}, at all {1x}, avenged {1x}, defend {1x}, rescue {1x}, safe {1x}, victory {1x}.

Yasha', means "to deliver, help." For example; "For thus saith the Lord God, the Holy One of Israel; In returning and rest shall ye be saved; in quietness and in confidence shall be your strength: and ye would not" (Is 30:15). See: TWOT—929; BDB—223c, 446b.

3468. יֶשַׁע {36x} **yeshaᶜ**, *yeh'-shah;* or

יֵשַׁע **yêshaᶜ**, *yay'-shah;* from 3467; *liberty, deliverance, prosperity:*—safety {1x}, salvation {32x}, saving {3x}.

Yesha', means "deliverance." This noun appears 36 times in the Old Testament. One appearance is in Ps 50:23: "Whoso offereth praise glorifieth me: and to him that ordereth his conversation aright will I show the salvation of God." See: TWOT—929a; BDB—447a.

3469. יִשְׁעִי {5x} **Yishᶜîy**, *yish-ee';* from 3467; *saving; Jishi,* the name of four Isr.:—Ishi {5x}. See: BDB—447d.

3470. יְשַׁעְיָה {39x} **Yᵉshaᶜyâh**, *yesh-ah-yaw';* or

יְשַׁעְיָהוּ **Yᵉshaᶜyâhûw**, *yesh-ah-yaw'-hoo;* from 3467 and 3050; *Jah has saved; Jeshajah,* the name of seven Isr.:—Isaiah

{32x}, Jesaiah {2x}, Jeshaiah {5x}. See: BDB—447d.

3471. יָשְׁפֵה {3x} **yâsh^ephêh**, *yaw-shef-ay';* from an unused root mean. to *polish;* a gem supposed to be *jasper* (from the resemblance in name):—jasper {3x}. See: TWOT—929.1; BDB—448C.

3472. יִשְׁפָּה {1x} **Yishpâh**, *yish-paw';* perh. from 8192; *he will scratch; Jishpah,* an Isr.:—Ispah {1x}. See: BDB—448c, 1046a.

3473. יִשְׁפָּן {1x} **Yishpân**, *yish-pawn';* prob. from the same as 8227; *he will hide; Jishpan,* an Isr.:—Ishpan {1x}. See: BDB—448c, 1051a.

3474. יָשַׁר {27x} **yâshar**, *yaw-shar';* a prim. root; to *be straight* or *even;* fig. to *be* (caus. to *make*) *right, pleasant, prosperous:*—please {6x}, straight {5x}, direct {4x}, right {3x}, well {2x}, fitted {1x}, good {1x}, make straight {1x}, meet {1x}, upright {1x}, uprightly {1x}.

Yashar, as a verb, means "to be straight, be smooth, be right." **(1)** This verb, which occurs rarely, has many derivatives in the Bible. **(2)** One occurrence of the verb is in 1 Chr 13:4: "And all the congregation said that they would do so: for the thing was right in the eyes of all the people." In this usage *yashar* has the sense of being pleasing or agreeable. **(3)** In Hab. 2:4 the word implies an ethical uprightness: "Behold, his soul *which* is lifted up is not upright in him: but the just shall live by his faith." See: TWOT—930; BDB—448c.

3475. יֵשֶׁר {1x} **Yêsher**, *yay'-sher;* from 3474; the *right; Jesher,* an Isr.:—Jesher {1x}. See: BDB—448c, 449c.

3476. יֹשֶׁר {14x} **yôsher**, *yo'-sher;* from 3474; the *right:*—equity {1x}, meet {1x}, right {2x}, upright {1x}, uprightness {9x}.

Yosher, as a noun, means "straightness." This noun occurs 14 times. One occurrence is in Prov 2:13: "Who leave the paths of uprightness, to walk in the ways of darkness." See: TWOT—930b; BDB—448c, 449c.

3477. יָשָׁר {119x} **yâshâr**, *yaw-shawr';* from 3474; *straight* (lit. or fig.):—right {53x}, upright {42x}, righteous {9x}, straight {3x}, convenient {2x}, Jasher {2x}, equity {1x}, just {1x}, meet {1x}, meetest {1x}, upright ones {1x}, uprightly {1x}, uprightness {1x}, well {1x}.

Yashar, as an adjective, means "upright; right; righteous; just." **(1)** This adjective occurs first in Exodus in the idiom "right in his eyes": "[He] said, If thou wilt diligently hearken to the voice of the Lord thy God, and wilt do that which is right in his sight, and wilt give ear to his commandments, and keep all his statutes, I will put none of these diseases upon thee, which I have brought upon the Egyptians: for I am the Lord that healeth thee" (Ex 15:26). **(2)** Its usage is infrequent in the Pentateuch and in the prophetical writings. Predominantly a poetic term, *yashar* also occurs idiomatically ("to do what is right") in the historical books; cf. 1 Kin 15:5: "Because David did that which was right in the eyes of the Lord, and turned not aside from any thing that he commanded him all the days of his life, save only in the matter of Uriah the Hittite." **(3)** The basic meaning is the root meaning "to be straight" in the sense of "to be level." **(3a)** The legs of the creatures in Ezekiel's vision were straight (Eze 1:7).

(3b) The Israelites designated an easy road for traveling as a "level road." It had few inclines and declines compared to the mountain roads (cf. Jer 31:9: "They shall come with weeping, and with supplications will I lead them: I will cause them to walk by the rivers of water in a straight way, wherein they shall not stumble: for I am a father to Israel, and Ephraim is my firstborn"). **(4)** *Yashar* with the meaning "right" pertains to things and to abstracts. **(4a)** Samuel promised himself to instruct God's people in "the good and the right way" (1 Sa 12:23). **(4b)** Nehemiah thanked God for having given just ordinances: "Thou camest down also upon mount Sinai, and spakest with them from heaven, and gavest them right judgments, and true laws, good statutes and commandments" (Neh 9:13). **(5)** Based on His revelation God expected His people to please Him in being obedient to Him: "And thou shalt do that which is right and good in the sight of the Lord: that it may be well with thee, and that thou mayest go in and possess the good land which the Lord sware unto thy fathers" (Deut 6:18).

(6) When *yashar* pertains to people, it is best translated "just" or "upright." God is the standard of uprightness for His people: "Good and upright is the Lord: therefore will he teach sinners in the way" (Ps 25:8): His word (Ps 33:4), His judgments (Ps 19:9), and His ways (Hos 14:9). He will reveal His uprightness as a blessing to His people. **(7)** The believer follows Him in being "upright" in heart: "Be glad in the Lord, and rejoice, ye righteous; and shout for joy, all ye that are upright in heart" (Ps 32:11; cf. 7:10; 11:2). **(7a)** In their daily walk they manifest that they are walking on the narrow road: "The wicked have drawn out the sword, and have bent their bow, to cast down the poor and needy, and to slay such as be of upright conversation" (Ps 37:14). **(7b)** The "just" are promised God's blessing upon their lives (Prov 11:10–11). **(8)** *Yashar* is also the abstract "rightness," especially when the Hebrew word has the definite article (hayyashar, "the right"): "Hear this, I pray you, ye heads of the house of Jacob, and princes of the house of Israel, that abhor judgment, and pervert all equity [all that is right]" (Mic 3:9). See: TWOT—930a; BDB—449a.

3478. יִשְׂרָאֵל {2505x} **Yisrâ'êl**, *yis-raw-ale';* from 8280 and 410; *he will rule* (as) *God; Jisraël,* a symb. name of Jacob; also (typ.) of his posterity:—Israel{2489x}, Israelites {16x}. See: BDB—441a, 975b, 1096b.

3479. יִשְׂרָאֵל {8x} **Yisrâ'êl** (Aram.), *yis-raw-ale';* corresp. to 3478:—Israel {8x}. See: BDB—1096.

3480. יְשַׂרְאֵלָה {1x} **Y^esar'êlâh**, *yes-ar-ale'-aw;* by var. from 3477 and 410 with directive enclitic; *right towards God; Jesarelah,* an Isr.:—Jesharelah {1x}. See: BDB—441a. Syn.: comp. 841.

3481. יִשְׂרְאֵלִי {1x} **Yisr^e'êlîy**, *yis-reh-ay-lee';* patron. from 3478; a *Jisreëlite* or desc. of Jisrael:—Israel + 3478 {1x}, Israelite {1x}. See: BDB—976a.

3482. יִשְׂרְאֵלִית {3x} **Yisr^e'êlîyth**, *yis-reh-ay-leeth';* fem. of 3481; a *Jisreëlitess* or female desc. of Jisrael:—Israelitiss {3x}. See: BDB—976a.

3483. יִשְׁרָה {1x} **yishrâh**, *yish-raw';* fem. or 3477; *rectitude:*—uprightness {1x}.

Yishrah means "uprightness" and occurs once: "And Solomon said, Thou hast shewed unto thy servant David my father great mercy, according as he walked before thee in truth, and in righteousness, and in uprightness of heart with thee; and thou hast kept for him this great kindness, that thou hast given him a son to sit on his throne, as *it is* this day" (1Kin 3:6). See: TWOT—930c; BDB—449c.

3484. יְשֻׁרוּן {4x} **Y^eshûrûwn**, *yesh-oo-roon';* from 3474; *upright; Jeshurun,* a symbol. name for Israel:—Jeshurun {3x}, Jesurun {1x}.

The noun *Yeshuruwn* is an honorific title for Israel: "But Jeshurun waxed fat, and kicked: thou art waxen fat, thou art grown thick, thou art covered *with fatness;* then he forsook God *which* made him, and lightly esteemed the Rock of his salvation" (Deut 32:15; 33:5). See: BDB—449c.

3485. יִשָּׂשכָר {43x} **Yissâ^skâr**, *yis-saw-kawr';* (strictly *yis-saws-kawr'*); from 5375 and 7939; *he will bring a reward; Jissaskar,* a son of Jacob:—Issachar {43x}. See: BDB—441a, 969b.

3486. יָשֵׁשׁ {1x} **yâshêsh**, *yaw-shaysh';* from an unused root mean. to *blanch; gray-haired,* i.e. an *aged* man:—stoop for age {1x}. See: TWOT—931a; BDB—450a.

3487. יַת {1x} **yath** (Aram.), *yath;* corresp. to 853; a sign of the object of a verb:—+ whom {1x}. See: TWOT—2779; BDB—1096b.

3488. יְתִב {5x} **y^ethîb** (Aram.), *yeth-eeb';* corresp. to 3427; to *sit* or *dwell:*—dwell {1x}, (be) set {2x}, sit {2x}. See: TWOT—2780; BDB—1096b.

3489. יָתֵד {24x} **yâthêd**, *yaw-thade';* from an unused root mean. to *pin* through or fast; a *peg:*—nail {8x}, paddle {1x}, pin {13x}, stake {2x}. See: TWOT—932a; BDB—450b.

3490. יָתוֹם {42x} **yâthôwm**, *yaw-thome';* from an unused root mean. to *be lonely;* a *bereaved* person:—fatherles {38x}, fatherless child {3x}, orphan {1x}. See: TWOT—934a; BDB—450c.

3491. יָתוּר {1x} **yâthûwr**, *yaw-thoor';* pass. part. of 3498; prop. what is *left,* i.e. (by impl.) a *gleaning:*—range {1x}. See: TWOT—936; BDB—1064b, 1064d.

3492. יַתִּיר {4x} **Yattîyr**, *yat-teer';* from 3498; *redundant; Jattir,* a place in Pal.:—Jattir {4x}. See: BDB—452d.

3493. יַתִּיר {8x} **yattîyr** (Aram.), *yat-teer';* corresp. to 3492; *preeminent;* adv. *very:*—exceeding {2x}, exceedingly {1x}, excellent {5x}. See: TWOT—2781; BDB—1096c.

3494. יִתְלָה {1x} **Yithlâh**, *yith-law';* prob. from 8518; it *will hang,* i.e. *be high; Jithlah,* a place in Pal.:—Jethlah {1x}. See: BDB—450c, 1068b.

3495. יִתְמָה {1x} **Yithmâh**, *yith-maw';* from the same as 3490; *orphanage; Jithmah,* an Isr.:—Ithmah {1x}. See: BDB—450d.

3496. יַתְנִיאֵל {1x} **Yathnîy'êl**, *yath-nee-ale';* from an unused root mean. to *endure,* and 410; *continued of God; Jathniël,* an Isr.:—Jathniel {1x}. See: BDB—451a, 1072a.

3497. יִתְנָן {1x} **Yithnân**, *yith-nawn';* from the same as 8577; *extensive; Jithnan,* a place in Pal.:—Ithnan {1x}. See: BDB—451a.

3498. יָתַר {107x} **yâthar**, *yaw-thar';* a prim. root; to *jut* over or *exceed;* by impl. to *excel;* (intr.) to *remain* or *be left;* caus. to *leave, cause to abound, preserve:*—leave {52x}, remain {23x}, rest {12x}, remainder {4x}, remnant {4x}, reserved {3x}, residue {3x}, plenteous {2x}, behind {1x}, excel {1x}, much {1x}, preserve {1x}.

Yathar, as a verb, means "to be left; remain over; excel; show excess." **(1)** *Yathar* occurs for the first time in the biblical text in Gen 30:36, **(1a)** where it is stated that "Jacob fed the rest of Laban's flocks." **(1b)** This statement reflects the word's frequent use to show separation from a primary group. **(1c)** Thus, Jacob "was left alone" (Gen 32:24) when his family and flocks went on beyond the brook Jabbok. **(2)** Sometimes the word indicates survivors, as in 2 Sa 9:1: "Is there yet any that is left of the house of Saul . . ." **(3)** The remnant idea is reflected in Eze 6:8: "Yet will I leave a remnant, that ye may have some that shall escape the sword. . . ." See: TWOT—936; 451a, 1096c.

3499. יֶתֶר {101x} **yether**, *yeh'-ther;* from 3498; prop. an *overhanging,* i.e. (by impl.) an *excess, superiority, remainder;* also a small *rope* (as hanging free):—rest {63x}, remnant {14x}, residue {8x}, leave {4x}, excellency {3x}, withs {3x}, cord {1x}, exceeding {1x}, excellent {1x}, more {1x}, plentifully {1x}, string {1x}.

Yether, as a noun, means "remainder; excess." **(1)** As "remainder, excess," it is used especially in the sense of a lesser number or quality as compared to something of primary importance. **(1a)** So, *yether* is used to refer to "the residue of the vessels that remain in this city" left in Jerusalem by Nebuchadnezzar (Jer 27:19–20), and **(1b)** the men who were left after Joab had assigned his picked men in the battle lines: "And the rest of the people he delivered into the hand of Abishai his brother, that he might put *them* in array against the children of Ammon" (2 Sa 10:10). **(2)** Occasionally *yether* is used to indicate "excess" in a negative way, so the literal "lip of excess" has the meaning of "lying lips": "Excellent speech becometh not a fool: much less do lying lips a prince" (Prov. 17:7). This is stressing that many times lying is adding to, instead of taking away from the truth. **(3)** A few times this noun implies "superiority" or "preeminence," as in Gen 49:3, where Jacob describes his son Reuben as being "Reuben, thou *art* my firstborn, my might, and the beginning of my strength, the excellency of dignity, and the excellency of power." **(4)** The name of Jethro (3503), Moses' father-in-law, is derived from this word. See: TWOT—936a; BDB—451d, 452a.

3500. יֶתֶר {9x} **Yether**, *yeh'-ther;* the same as 3499; *Jether,* the name of five or six Isr. and of one Midianite:—Jether {8x}, Jethro {1x}. See: BDB—452b. comp. 3503.

3501. יִתְרָא {1x} **Yithrâʾ**, *yith-raw';* by var. for 3502; *Jithra,* an Isr. (or Ishmaelite):—Ithra {1x}. See: BDB—452b.

3502. יִתְרָה {2x} **yithrâh**, *yith-raw';* fem. of 3499; prop. *excellence,* i.e. (by impl.) *wealth:*—abundance {1x}, riches {1x}. See: TWOT—936c; BDB—452b.

3503. יִתְרוֹ {9x} **Yithrôw**, *yith-ro';* from 3499 with pron. suff.; *his excellence; Jethro,* Moses' father-in-law:—Jethro {9x}. See: BDB—452b. comp. 3500.

3504. יִתְרוֹן {10x} **yithrôwn**, *yith-rone';* from 3498; *preeminence, gain:*—better {1x}, excellency {1x}, excelleth {2x}, profit {5x}, profitable {1x}. See: TWOT—936f; BDB—452c.

3505. יִתְרִי {1x} **Yithrîy**, *yith-ree';* patron. from 3500; a *Jithrite* or desc. of Jether:—Ithrite {1x}. See: BDB—452b.

3506. יִתְרָן {3x} **Yithrân**, *yith-rawn';* from 3498; *excellent; Jithran,* the name of an Edomite and of an Isr.:—Ithran {3x}. See: BDB—452d.

3507. יִתְרְעָם {2x} **Yithrᵉʿâm**, *yith-reh-awm';* from 3499 and 5971; *excellence of people; Jithreäm,* a son of David:—Ithream {2x}. See: BDB—453c.

3508. יֹתֶרֶת {11x} **yôthereth**, *yo-theh'-reth;* fem. act. part. of 3498; the *lobe* or *flap* of the liver (as if redundant or outhanging):—caul {11x}. See: TWOT—936e; BDB—452c.

3509. יְתֵת {2x} **Yᵉthêyth**, *yeh-thayth';* of uncert. der.; *Jetheth,* an Edomite:—Jetheth {1x}. See: BDB—453c.

ך

3510. כָּאַב {22x} **kâʾab**, *kaw-ab';* a prim. root; prop. to feel *pain;* by impl. to *grieve;* fig. to *spoil:*— . . . end {11x}, altogether {3x}, consume {3x}, consumption {2x}, consummation {1x}, determined {1x}, riddance {1x}. See: TWOT—982a; BDB—456a.

3511. כְּאֵב {6x} **kᵉʾêb**, *keh-abe';* from 3510; *suffering* (phys. or ment.), *adversity:*—sorrow {3x}, grief {2x}, pain {1x}. See: TWOT—940a; BDB—456b.

3512. כָּאָה {3x} **kâʾâh**, *kaw-aw';* a prim. root; to *despond;* caus. to *deject:*—broken {1x}, be grieved {1x}, make sad {1x}. See: TWOT—941; BDB—456c.

3513. כָּבַד {116x} **kâbad**, *kaw-bad';* or

כָּבֵד **kâbêd**, *kaw-bade';* a prim. root; to *be heavy,* i.e. in a bad sense (*burdensome, severe, dull*) or in a good sense (*numerous, rich, honorable*); caus. to *make weighty* (in the same two senses):—honour {34x}, glorify {14x}, honourable {14x}, heavy {13x}, harden {7x}, glorious {5x}, sore {3x}, made heavy {3x}, chargeable {2x}, great {2x}, many {2x}, heavier {2x}, promote {2x}, misc. {10x} = abounding with, more grievously afflict, boast, × be dim, be grievous, lade, × more be laid, nobles, prevail, be rich, stop.

Kabed means "to honor." **(1)** One occurrence of *kabed* is in Deut 5:16: "Honor thy father and thy mother, as the Lord thy God hath commanded thee. . . ." Syn.: 2388, 7185, 7188, 8631. See: TWOT—943; BDB—457a.

3514. כֹּבֶד {4x} **kôbed**, *ko'-bed;* from 3513; *weight, multitude, vehemence:*—grievousness {1x}, heavy {2x}, great number {1x}. See: TWOT—943c; BDB—458c.

3515. כָּבֵד {38x} **kâbêd**, *kaw-bade';* from 3513; *heavy,* fig. in a good sense (*numerous*) or in a bad sense (*severe, difficult, stupid*):—great {8x}, grievous {8x}, heavy {8x}, sore {4x}, hard {2x}, much {2x}, slow {2x}, hardened {1x}, heavier {1x}, laden {1x}, thick {1x}.

Kabed means "heavy; numerous, severe; rich." **(1)** Basically this adjective connotes "heavy." In Ex 17:12 the word is used of physical weight: "But Moses' hands were heavy; and they took a stone, and put it under him, and he sat thereon; and Aaron and Hur stayed up his hands. . . ." **(2)** This adjective bears the connotation of heaviness as an enduring, ever-present quality, a lasting thing. **(3)** Used in a negative but extended sense, the word depicts sin as a yoke ever pressing down upon one: "For mine iniquities are gone over mine head: as a heavy burden they are too heavy for me" (Ps 38:4). **(4)** A task can be described as "heavy" (Ex 18:18). **(4a)** Moses argued his inability to lead God's people out of Egypt because he was "slow of speech, and of a slow tongue"; **(4b)** his speech or tongue was not smooth-flowing but halting (heavy; Ex 4:10). **(4c)** This use of *kabed* appears with an explanation in Eze 3:6, where God is describing the people to whom Ezekiel is to minister: ". . . not to many people of a strange speech and of a hard language, whose words thou canst not understand."

(5) Another nuance of this word appears in Ex 7:14, where it is applied to Pharaoh's heart: "Pharaoh's heart is hardened, he refuseth to let the people go." **(6)** In all such contexts *kabed* depicts a burden which weighs down one's body (or some part of it) so that one is either disabled or unable to function successfully. **(7)** A second series of passages uses this word of something that falls upon or overcomes one. **(7a)** So God sent upon Egypt a "heavy" hail (Ex 9:18), a "great" swarm of insects (8:24), "numerous" locusts, and a "severe" pestilence (9:3). **(7b)** The first appearance of the word belongs to this category: ". . . The famine was [severe] in the land" of Egypt (Gen 12:10). **(8)** Used with a positive connotation, *kabed* can describe the amount of "riches" one has: "And Abram was very rich in cattle, in silver, and in gold" (Gen 13:2). **(8a)** This usage vividly illustrates the basic implications of the word. **(8b)** Whenever *kabed* is used, it reflects the idea of "weightiness," or that which is added to something else. Thus, to be "very rich" means that Abram was heavily "weighted down" with wealth. **(8c)** This idea also explains how the word can be used to indicate the state of "being honored" or "glorious," for honor and glory are additional qualities that are added to a person or thing.

(9) In Gen 50:9 the word is used to modify a group of people, **(9a)** "a very great company." **(9b)** The next verse uses *kabed* in the sense of "imposing" or "ponderous": "They mourned with a great and very sore lamentation. . . ." **(10)** This adjective is never used of God. **(11)** "To be heavy" includes negative as well as positive aspects. **(11a)** Thus, calamity is "heavier than the sand of the sea" (Job 6:3), and the hand of God is "very heavy" in punishing the Philistines (1 Sa 5:11). **(11b)** Bondage and heavy work are "heavy" on the people (Ex 5:9; Neh 5:18). **(11c)** Eyes (Gen 48:10) and ears (Is 59:1) that have become insensitive, or "dull," have had debilitating conditions added to them, whether through age or other causes. **(11d)** The heart of a man may become excessively "weighted" with stubbornness and thus become "hardened" (Ex 9:7).

(12) "To honor" or "glorify" anything is to add something which it does not have in itself, or that which others can give. **(12a)** Children are commanded to "honor" their parents (Ex 20:12; Deut 5:16); **(12b)** Balak promised "honor" to Balaam (Num 22:17); **(12c)** Jerusalem (Lam 1:8) and the Sabbath (Is 58:13) are "honored" or "made glorious." **(12d)** Above all, "honor" and "glory" are due to God, as repeatedly commanded in the biblical text: **(12d1)** "Honor the Lord with thy substance" (Prov 3:9); **(12d2)** "Let the Lord be glorified" (Is 66:5); **(12d3)** "Glorify ye the Lord" (Isa. 24:15). **(13)** *Kabed* is also the Hebrew word for "liver," apparently reflecting the sense that the liver is the heaviest of the organs of the body. See: TWOT—943a; BDB—458a, 1096b.

3516. כָּבֵד {1x} **kâbêd**, *kaw-bade';* the same as 3515; the *liver* (as the *heaviest* of the viscera):—liver {1x}. See: TWOT—943b; BDB—458b.

כָּבֹד **kâbôd**. See 3519.

3517. כְּבֵדֻת {1x} **kᵉbêdûth**, *keb-ay-dooth'*; fem. of 3515; *difficulty:*—× heavily {1x}. See: TWOT—943g; BDB—459c.

3518. כָּבָה {24x} **kâbâh**, *kaw-baw'*; a prim. root; to *expire* or (caus.) to *extinguish* (fire, light, anger):—go (put) out {7x}, quench {8x}, quenched {9x}. See: TWOT—944; BDB—459c.

3519. כָּבוֹד {200x} **kâbôwd**, *kaw-bode'*; rarely

כָּבֹד **kâbôd**, *kaw-bode'*; from 3513; prop. *weight*, but only fig. in a good sense, *splendor* or *copiousness:*—glory {156x}, honour {32x}, glorious {10x}, gloriously {1x}, honourable {1x}.

Kabod means "honor; glory; great quantity; multitude; wealth; reputation [majesty]; splendor."**(1)** *Kabod* refers to the great physical weight or "quantity" of a thing. **(2)** In Nah 2:9 one should read: "For there is no limit to the treasure—a great quantity of every kind of desirable object." **(3)** Is 22:24 likens Eliakim to a peg firmly anchored in a wall upon which is hung "all the [weighty things] of his father's house." **(4)** This meaning is required in Hos 9:11, where *kabod* represents a great crowd of people or "multitude": "As for Ephraim, their [multitude] shall fly away. . . ." **(5)** The word does not mean simply "heavy," but a heavy or imposing quantity of things. **(6)** *Kabod* often refers to both "wealth" and significant and positive "reputation" (in a concrete sense). **(6a)** Laban's sons complained that "Jacob hath taken away all that was our father's; and of that which was our father's hath he gotten all this [wealth]" (Gen 31:1—the first biblical occurrence). **(6b)** The second emphasis appears in Gen 45:13, where Joseph told his brothers to report to his "father . . . all my [majesty] in Egypt." Here this word includes a report of his position and the assurance that if the family came to Egypt, Joseph would be able to provide for them.

(7) Trees, forests, and wooded hills have an imposing quality, a richness or "splendor." God will punish the king of Assyria by destroying most of the trees in his forests, "and shall consume the glory of his forest, . . . and the rest of the trees of his forest shall be few, that a child may write them" (Is 10:18–19). **(8)** In Ps 85:9 the idea of richness or abundance predominates: **(8a)** "Surely his salvation is nigh them that fear him; that glory [or abundance] may dwell in our land." **(8b)** This idea is repeated in Ps 85:12: "Yea, the Lord shall give that which is good; and our land shall yield her increase."**(9)** *Kabod* can also have an abstract emphasis of "glory," imposing presence or position. Phinehas' wife named their son Ichabod, "saying, The glory is departed from Israel: because the ark of God was taken, and because of her father-in-law and her husband" (they, the high priests, had died; 1 Sa 4:21). **(10)** In Is 17:3 *kabod* represents the more concrete idea of a fullness of things including fortified cities, sovereignty (self-rule), and people.

(11) Among such qualities is "honor," or respect and position. In Is 5:13 this idea of "honor" is represented by *kabod:* ". . . And their [my people's] honorable men are famished, and their multitude dried up with thirst." **(12)** Thus the word *kabod* and its parallel (the multitude) represent all the people of Israel: the upper classes and the common people. **(13)** In many passages the word represents a future rather than a present reality: "In that day shall the branch of the Lord be beautiful and glorious . . ." (Is 4:2). **(14)** When used in the sense of "honor" or "importance" (cf. Gen 45:13) there are two nuances of the word. **(14a)** First, *kabod* can emphasize the position of an individual within the sphere in which he lives (Prov 11:16). **(14a1)** This "honor" can be lost through wrong actions or attitudes (Prov 26:1, 8) and evidenced in proper actions (Prov 20:3; 25:2). **(14a2)** This emphasis then is on a relationship between personalities. **(14b)** Second, there is a suggestion of nobility in many uses of the word, such as "honor" that belongs to a royal family (1 Kin 3:13). Thus, *kabod* can be used of the social distinction and position of respect enjoyed by nobility.

(15) When applied to God, the word represents a quality corresponding to Him and by which He is recognized. **(15a)** Joshua commanded Achan to give glory to God, to recognize His importance, worth, and significance (Josh 7:19). **(15b)** In this and similar instances "giving honor" refers to doing something; what Achan was to do was to tell the truth. **(16)** In other passages giving honor to God is a cultic recognition and confession of God as God (Ps 29:1). **(16a)** Some have suggested that such passages celebrate the sovereignty of God over nature wherein the celebrant sees His "glory" and confesses it in worship. **(16b)** In other places the word is said to point to God's sovereignty over history and specifically to a future manifestation of that "glory" (Is 40:5). **(16c)** Still other passages relate the manifestation of divine "glory" to past demonstrations of His sovereignty over history and peoples (Ex 16:7; 24:16). Syn.: 1926. See: TWOT—943d, 943e; BDB—458c.

3520. כְּבוּדָּה {3x} **kᵉbûwddâh**, *keb-ood-daw'*; irreg. fem. pass. part. of 3513; *weightiness*, i.e. *magnificence, wealth:*—carriage {1x}, all glorious {1x}, stately {1x}. See: TWOT—943f; BDB—458c, 459c.

3521. כָּבוּל {2x} **Kâbûwl**, *kaw-bool'*; from the same as 3525 in the sense of *limitation; sterile; Cabul*, the name of two places in Pal.:—Cabul {2x}. See: BDB—459d.

3522. כַּבּוֹן {1x} **Kabbôwn**, *kab-bone'*; from an unused root mean. to *heap* up; *hilly; Cabon*, a place in Pal.:—Cabbon {1x}. See: BDB—460a.

3523. כְּבִיר {2x} **kᵉbîyr**, *keb-eer*; from 3527 in the orig. sense of *plaiting;* a *matrass* (of intertwined materials):—pillow {2x}. Syn.: 3704, 4763. See: TWOT—948a; BDB—460d.

3524. כַּבִּיר {11x} **kabbîyr**, *kab-beer'*; from 3527; *vast*, whether in extent (fig. of power, *mighty;* of time, *aged*), or in number, *many:*—mighty {4x}, much {2x}, strong {1x}, most {1x}, mighty men {1x}, valiant + 47 {1x}, feeble + 3808 {1x}. See: TWOT—947a; BDB—460b.

3525. כֶּבֶל {2x} **kebel**, *keh'-bel;* from an unused root mean. to *twine* or braid together; a *fetter:*—fetter {2x}. See: TWOT—945a; BDB—459d.

3526. כָּבַס {51x} **kâbaç**, *kaw-bas'*; a prim. root; to *trample;* hence, to *wash* (prop. by stamping with the feet), whether lit. (incl. the *fulling* process) or fig.:—fuller {4x}, wash (-ing) {47x}.

Kabac means to wash [possibly by treading upon clothes in water?]. **(1)** A common term throughout the history of Hebrew for the "washing" of clothes, this word is found also in ancient Ugaritic and Akkadian, reflecting the treading aspect. **(2)** It is found for the first time in the Old Testament in Gen 49:11 as part of Jacob's blessing on Judah: ". . . He washed his garments in wine. . . ." **(3)** The word is used in the Old Testament primarily in the sense of "washing" clothes, both **(3a)** for ordinary cleansing: "And Mephibosheth the son of Saul came down to meet the king, and had neither dressed his feet, nor trimmed his beard, nor washed his clothes, from the day the king departed until the day he came *again* in peace" (2 Sa 19:24), and **(3b)** for ritual cleansing: "And the LORD said unto Moses, Go unto the people, and sanctify them to day and tomorrow, and let them wash their clothes" (Ex 19:10; cf. Lev 11:25).

(4) It is often used in parallelism with the expression "to wash oneself," as in Lev 14:8–9 "And he that is to be cleansed shall wash his clothes, and shave off all his hair, and wash himself in water, that he may be clean: and after that he shall come into the camp, and shall tarry abroad out of his tent seven days. But it shall be on the seventh day, that he shall shave all his hair off his head and his beard and his eyebrows, even all his hair he shall shave off: and he shall wash his clothes, also he shall wash his flesh in water, and he shall be clean." **(5)** *Kabac* is used in the sense of "washing" or "bathing" oneself only in the figurative sense and in poetic usage, as in Jer 4:14: "O Jerusalem, wash thine heart from wickedness, that thou mayest be saved." Syn.: 7364. See: TWOT—946; BDB—460a.

3527. כָּבַר {1x} **kâbar**, *kaw-bar'*; a prim. root; prop. to *plait* together, i.e. (fig.) to *augment* (espec. in number or quantity, to *accumulate*):—in abundance, multiply {1x}. See: TWOT—947; BDB—460b.

3528. כְּבָר {9x} **kᵉbâr**, *keb-awr'*; from 3527; prop. *extent* of time, i.e. a *great while;* hence, *long ago, formerly, hitherto:*—already {5x}, (seeing that which), now {4x}. See: TWOT—947c; BDB—460c.

3529. כְּבָר {8x} **Kᵉbâr**, *keb-awr'*; the same as 3528; *length; Kebar*, a river of Mesopotamia:—Chebar {8x}. See: TWOT—947d; BDB—460c. comp. 2249.

3530. כִּבְרָה {3x} **kibrâh**, *kib-raw'*; fem. of 3528; prop. *length*, i.e. a *measure* (of uncert. dimension):—× little {3x}. See: TWOT—947b; BDB—460c.

3531. כְּבָרָה {1x} **kᵉbârâh**, *keb-aw-raw'*; from 3527 in its orig. sense; a *sieve* (as netted):—sieve {1x}. See: TWOT—948b; BDB—460d.

3532. כֶּבֶשׂ {107x} **kebes**, *keh-bes';* from an unused root mean. to *dominate;* a *ram* (just old enough to *butt*):—lamb {105x}, sheep {2x}.

Kebes means "lamb (male); kid." **(1)** The *kebes* is a "young lamb" which is nearly always used for sacrificial purposes. **(2)** The first usage in Exodus pertains to the Passover: "Your lamb shall be without blemish, a male of the first year: ye shall take it out from the sheep, or from the goats" (Ex 12:5). **(3)** The word gedi (1423), "kid," is a synonym for *kebes:* "The wolf also shall dwell with the lamb [*kebes*], and the leopard shall lie down with the kid [gedi]; and the calf and the young lion and the fatling together; and a little child shall lead them" (Is 11:6). **(4)** The traditional translation "lamb" leaves the gender uncertain. In Hebrew the word *kebes* is masculine, whereas the kibshah (3535), "young ewe lamb," is feminine; cf. "And Abraham set seven ewe lambs of the flock by themselves" (Gen 21:28). Syn.: 1423, 2924, 3535, 3775, 7716. See: TWOT—949; BDB—461a.

3533. כָּבַשׁ {15x} **kâbash**, *kaw-bash'*; a prim. root; to *tread* down; hence, neg. to *disregard;* pos. to *conquer, subjugate, violate:*—

subdue {8x}, bring into subjection {3x}, bring into bondage {2x}, keep under {1x}, force {1x}. See: TWOT—951; BDB—461b.

3534. כֶּבֶשׁ {1x} **kebesh**, *keh'-besh;* from 3533; a *footstool* (as trodden upon):—footstool {1x}. See: TWOT—951a; BDB—461c.

3535. כִּבְשָׂה {8x} **kibsâh**, *kib-saw';* or כַּבְשָׂה **kabsâh**, *kab-saw';* fem. of 3532; a *ewe:*—ewe lamb {6x}, lamb {2x}. See: TWOT—950; BDB—461a.

3536. כִּבְשָׁן {4x} **kibshân**, *kib-shawn';* from 3533; a smelting *furnace* (as *reducing* metals):—furnace {4x}. See: TWOT—952; BDB—461c.

3537. כַּד {18x} **kad**, *kad;* from an unused root mean. to *deepen;* prop. a *pail;* but gen. of earthenware; a *jar* for domestic purposes:—barrel {4x}, pitcher {14x}. See: TWOT—953a; BDB—461c.

3538. כְּדַב {1x} **k^{e}dab** (Aram.), *ked-ab';* from a root corresp. to 3576; *false:*—lying {1x}. See: TWOT—2783; BDB—1096c.

3539. כַּדְכֹּד {2x} **kadkôd**, *kad-kode';* from the same as 3537 in the sense of *striking fire* from a metal forged; a *sparkling* gem, prob. the ruby:—agate {2x}. See: TWOT—953c; BDB—461d.

3540. כְּדָרְלָעֹמֶר {5x} **K^{e}dorlâ^{c}ômer**, *ked-or-law-o'-mer;* of for. or.; *Kedorlaomer,* an early Pers. king:—Chedorlaomer {5x}. See: BDB—462a.

3541. כֹּה {25x} **kôh**, *ko;* from the pref. *k* and 1931; prop. *like this,* i.e. by impl. (of manner) *thus* (or *so*); also (of place) *here* (or *hither*); or (of time) *now:*—{25x} = also, here, + hitherto, like, on the other side, so (and much), such, on that manner, (on) this (manner, side, way, way and that way), + mean while, yonder. See: TWOT—955; BDB—462a, 1096d.

3542. כָּה {1x} **kâh** (Aram.), *kaw;* corresp. to 3541:—hitherto {1x}. See: TWOT—2784; BDB—1096d.

3543. כָּהָה {8x} **kâhâh**, *kaw-haw';* a prim. root; *to be weak,* i.e. (fig.) to *despond* (caus. *rebuke*), or (of light, the eye) to *grow dull:*—darkened {1x}, be dim {3x}, fail {1x}, faint {1x}, restrained {1x}, × utterly {1x}. See: TWOT—957; BDB—462c, 462d.

3544. כֵּהֶה {9x} **kêheh**, *kay-heh';* from 3543; *feeble, obscure:*—somewhat dark {5x}, darkish {1x}, wax dim {1x}, heaviness {1x}, smoking {1x}. See: TWOT—957a; BDB—462d.

3545. כֵּהָה {1x} **kêhâh**, *kay-haw';* fem. of 3544; prop a *weakening;* fig. *alleviation,* i.e. cure:—healing {1x}. See: TWOT—957b; BDB—462d.

3546. כְּהַל {4x} **k^{e}hal** (Aram.), *keh-hal';* a root corresp. to 3201 and 3557; to *be able:*—be able {2x}, could {2x}. See: TWOT—2785; BDB—1096d.

3547. כָּהַן {23x} **kâhan**, *kaw-han';* a prim. root, appar. mean. to *mediate* in relig. services; but used only as denom. from 3548; to *officiate* as a priest; fig. to *put on regalia:*—priest's office {20x}, decketh {1x}, office of a priest {1x}, priest {1x}.

Kahan means "to act as a priest." **(1)** This verb, which appears 23 times in biblical Hebrew, is derived from the noun *kohen* (3548). **(2)** The verb appears only in the intensive stem. **(3)** One occurrence is in Ex 28:1: "And take thou unto thee Aaron thy brother, and his sons with him, from among the children of Israel, that he may minister unto me in the priest's office. . . ." See: TWOT—959; BDB—464c.

3548. כֹּהֵן {750x} **kôhên**, *ko-hane';* act. part. of 3547; lit. one *officiating,* a *priest;* also (by courtesy) an *acting priest* (although a layman):—priest {744x}, own {2x}, chief ruler {2x}, officer {1x}, princes {1x}.

Kohen means "priest." **(1)** This word is found 750 times in the Old Testament. **(1a)** More than one-third of the references to the "priests" are found in the Pentateuch. **(1b)** Leviticus, which has about 185 references, is called the "manual of the priests." **(2)** The term *kohen* was used to refer not only to the Hebrew priesthood but to Egyptian "priests" (Gen 41:50; 46:20; 47:26), the Philistine "priests" (1 Sa 6:2), the "priests" of Dagon (1 Sa 5:5), "priests" of Baal (2 Kin 10:19), "priests" of Chemosh (Jer 48:7), and "priests" of the Baalim and Asherim (2 Chr 34:5). **(2a)** Joseph married the daughter of the "priest" of On (Gen 41:45), and she bore him two sons, Ephraim and Manasseh (Gen 46:20). **(2b)** Joseph did not purchase the land of the "priests" of Egypt, because the Egyptian "priests" received regular allotments from Pharaoh (Gen 47:22). **(3)** A "priest" is an authorized minister of deity who officiates at the altar and in other cultic rites. A "priest" performs sacrificial, ritualistic, and mediatorial duties; he represents the people before God. By contrast, a "prophet" is an intermediary between God and the people.

(4) The Jewish priestly office was established by the Lord in the days of Moses. **(4a)** But prior to the institution of the high priesthood and the priestly office, we read of the priesthood of Melchizedek (Gen 14:18) and of Midianite "priests" (Ex 2:16; 3:1; 18:1). **(4b)** In Ex 19:24, other "priests" are mentioned: these may have been either Midianite "priests" or "priests" in Israel prior to the official establishment of the Levitical priesthood. **(4c)** No doubt priestly functions were performed in pre-Mosaic times by the head of the family, such as Noah, Abraham, and Job. **(4c1)** After the Flood, for example, Noah built an altar to the Lord (Gen 8:20–21). **(4c2)** At Bethel, Mamre, and Moriah, Abraham built altars. In Gen 22:12–13, we read that Abraham was willing to offer his son as a sacrifice. **(4c3)** Job offered up sacrifices for his sinning children (Job 1:5). **(5)** The priesthood constituted one of the central characteristics of Old Testament religion. A passage showing the importance of the priesthood is Num 16:5–7: "And he spake unto Korah and unto all his company, saying, Even tomorrow the Lord will show who are his, and who is holy; and will cause him to come near unto him: even him whom he hath chosen will he cause to come near unto him. This do; Take you censers, Korah, and all his company; And put fire therein, and put incense in them before the Lord . . . the man whom the Lord doth choose, he shall be holy. . . ."

(6) God established Moses, Aaron, and Aaron's sons Nadab, Abihu, Eleazar, and Ithamar as "priests" in Israel (Ex 28:1, 41; 29:9, 29–30). **(6a)** Because Nadab and Abihu were killed when they "offered strange fire before the Lord," **(6b)** the priesthood was limited to the lines of Eleazar and Ithamar (Lev 10:1–2; Num 3:4; 1 Chr 24:2). **(6c)** However, not all individuals born in the family of Aaron could serve as "priest." **(6c1)** Certain physical deformities excluded a man from that perfection of holiness which a "priest" should manifest before Yahweh (Lev 21:17–23). **(6c2)** A "priest" who was ceremonially unclean was not permitted to perform his priestly duties. **(6c3)** Lev 21:1–15 gives a list of ceremonial prohibitions that forbade a "priest" from carrying out his duties. **(7)** Ex 29:1–37 and Lev 8 describe the seven day consecration ceremony of Aaron and his sons. **(7a)** Both the high priest (*kohen* haggadol) and his sons were washed with water (Ex 29:4). **(7b)** Then Aaron the high priest dressed in holy garments with a breastplate over his heart, and there was placed on his head a holy crown—the mitre or turban (Ex 29:5–6). **(7c)** After that, Aaron was anointed with oil on his head (Ex 29:7; cf. Ps 133:2). **(7d)** Finally, the blood of a sacrificial offering was applied to Aaron and his sons (Ex 29:20–21). The consecrating bloodmark was placed upon the tip of the right ear, on the thumb of the right hand, and on the great toe of the right foot.

(8) The duties of the priesthood were very clearly defined by the Mosaic law. **(8a)** These duties were assumed on the eighth day of the service of consecration (Lev 9:1). **(8b)** The Lord told Aaron: "Therefore thou and thy sons with thee shall keep your priest's office for every thing of the altar, and within the veil; and ye shall serve . . ." (Num 18:7). **(9)** The "priests" were to act as teachers of the Law (Lev 10:10–11; Deut 33:10; 2 Chr 5:3; 17:7–9; Eze 44:23; Mal 2:6–9), a duty they did not always carry out (Mic 3:11; Mal 2:8). **(10)** In certain areas of health and jurisprudence, "priests" served as limited revelators of God's will. **(10a)** For example, it was the duty of the "priest" to discern the existence of leprosy and to perform the rites of cleansing (Lev 13—14). **(10b)** Priests determined punishments for murder and other civil matters (Deut 21:5; 2 Chr 19:8–11). See: TWOT—959a; BDB—463a, 1096d.

3549. כָּהֵן {8x} **kâhên** (Aram.), *kaw-hane';* corresp. to 3548:—priest {8x}. See: TWOT—2786; BDB—1096d.

3550. כְּהֻנָּה {4x} **k^{e}hunnâh**, *keh-hoon-naw';* from 3547; *priesthood:*—priesthood {9x}, priest's office {5x}. See: TWOT—959b; BDB—464d.

3551. כַּו {1x} **kav** (Aram.), *kav;* from a root corresp. to 3854 in the sense of *piercing;* a *window* (as a perforation):—window {1x}. Syn.: 699, 2474, 8261. See: BDB—1096d.

3552. כּוּב {1x} **Kûwb**, *koob;* of for. der.; *Kub,* a country near Egypt:—Chub {1x}. See: BDB—464d.

3553. כּוֹבַע {6x} **kôwba^{c}**, *ko'-bah;* from an unused root mean. to be *high* or *rounded;* a *helmet* (as *arched*):—helmet {6x}. See: TWOT—960; BDB—464d. comp. 6959.

3554. כָּוָה {2x} **kâvâh**, *kaw-vaw';* a prim. root; prop. to *prick* or *penetrate;* hence, to *blister* (as smarting or eating into):—burned {2x}. See: TWOT—961; BDB—464d.

כּוֹחַ **kôwach**. See 3581.

3555. כְּוִיָּה {1x} **k^{e}vîyâh**, *kev-ee-yaw';* from 3554; a *branding:*—burning {1x}. See: TWOT—961b; BDB—465a.

3556. כּוֹכָב {37x} **kôwkâb**, *ko-kawb';* prob. from the same as 3522 (in the sense of *rolling*) or 3554 (in the sense of *blazing*); a *star* (as *round* or as *shining*); fig. a *prince:*—star {36x}, stargazers + 3674 {1x}. See: TWOT—942a; BDB—456d, 465a.

3557. כּוּל {37x} **kûwl**, *kool;* a prim. root; prop. to *keep in;* hence, to *measure;* fig. to *maintain* (in various senses):—contain {6x}, feed

{6x}, sustain {4x}, abide {3x}, nourish {3x}, hold {2x}, receive {2x}, victual {2x}, bear {1x}, comprehended {1x}, misc. {7x} = forbearing, guide, be present, make provision, provide sustenance. See: TWOT—962; BDB—465a, 480d.

3558. כּוּמָז {2x} **kûwmâz**, *koo-mawz';* from an unused root mean. to *store* away; a *jewel* (prob. gold beads):—tablets {2x}. See: TWOT—990a; BDB—484d.

3559. כּוּן {219x} **kûwn**, *koon;* a prim. root; prop. to *be erect* (i.e. stand perpendicular); hence, (caus.) to *set up,* in a great variety of applications, whether lit. (*establish, fix, prepare, apply*), or fig. (*appoint, render sure, proper* or *prosperous*):—prepare {85x}, establish {58x}, ready {17x}, stablish {5x}, provide {5x}, right {5x}, fixed {4x}, set {4x}, direct {3x}, order {3x}, fashion {3x}, variant {2x}, certain {2x}, confirmed {2x}, firm {2x}, preparation {2x}, misc. {17x} = confirm, faithfulness, fasten, firm, be fitted, frame, be meet, ordain, perfect, (make) preparation, make provision, be stable, stand, tarry, × very deed.

Kuwn, as a verb, means "to be established, be readied, be prepared, be certain, be admissible." **(1)** This root used concretely connotes being firmly established, being firmly anchored and being firm. **(1a)** The first meaning is applied to a roof which is "firmly established" on pillars. So Samson said to the lad who was leading him: "Suffer me that I may feel the pillars whereupon the house standeth, that I may lean upon them" (Judg 16:26). **(1b)** In a similar sense the inhabited earth "is firmly established or anchored"; it is immovable: ". . . The world also is established, that it cannot be moved" (Ps 93:1). **(1c)** In Ps 75:3 the image shifts to the earth "firmly established" upon pillars. **(1d)** In Ps 65:6 the divine establishing of the mountains is synonymous with divine creating. **(2)** The verb also means "to be firm": "I have caused thee to multiply as the bud of the field, and thou hast increased and waxen great, and thou art come to excellent ornaments: *thy* breasts are fashioned [*kuwn*], and thine hair is grown, whereas thou *wast* naked and bare" (Eze 16:7).

(3) Used abstractly, *kuwn* can refer to a concept as "established," or "fixed" so as to be unchanging and unchangeable: "And for that the dream was doubled unto Pharaoh twice; it is because the thing is established by God, and God will shortly bring it to pass" (Gen 41:32—the first occurrence of the word). **(3a)** In somewhat the same sense one can speak of the light of day "being firmly established," or having fully arrived: "But the path of the just is as the shining light, that shineth more and more unto the perfect day" (Prov 4:18). **(3b)** *Kuwn* can be used of the "establishing" of one's descendants, of seeing them prosperous (Job 21:8). **(4)** Something can be "fixed" in the sense of "being prepared or completed": "Now all the work of Solomon was prepared unto the day of the foundation of the house of the Lord . . ." (2 Chr 8:16). **(5)** An "established" thing can be something that is enduring. **(5a)** In 1 Sa 20:31 Saul tells Jonathan: "For as long as the son of Jesse liveth upon the ground, thou shalt not be established, nor thy kingdom." **(5b)** Truthful lips (what they say) "shall be established," or will endure forever (Prov 12:19). **(5c)** One's plans "will endure" (be established) if he commits his works to the Lord (Prov 16:3).

(6) *Kuwn* can also mean "to be established" in the sense of "being ready." **(6a)** So Josiah told the people "to prepare" themselves for the Passover (2 Chr 35:4). **(6b)** This same sense appears in Ex 19:11 "And be ready against the third day: for the third day the Lord will come down in the sight of all the people upon mount Sinai." **(7)** A somewhat different nuance appears in Job 18:12; Bildad says that wherever godlessness breaks out, there is judgment: "Destruction shall be ready at his side." That is, calamity is "fixed or prepared" so that it exists potentially even before godlessness breaks out. **(8)** Something "fixed" or "established" can "be certain": "Then shalt thou inquire, and make search, and ask diligently; and, behold, if it be truth, and the thing certain . . ." (Deut 13:14). **(9)** In a somewhat different nuance the thing can be trustworthy or true. The psalmist says of the wicked that "there is no faithfulness in their mouth" (Ps 5:9). A further development of this emphasis is that a matter "may be admissible"—so Moses said to Pharaoh: "It is not meet so to do; for we shall sacrifice the abomination of the Egyptians to the Lord our God . . ." (Ex 8:26). **(10)** When one "fixes" an arrow on the bow, he takes aim or "prepares" to shoot his bow (cf. Ps 7:12). Syn.: 724, 3615, 3634. See: TWOT—964; BDB—465c.

3560. כּוּן {1x} **Kûwn**, *koon;* prob. from 3559; *established; Kun,* a place in Syria:—Chun {1x}. See: BDB—467b.

3561. כַּוָּן {2x} **kavvân**, *kav-vawn';* from 3559; something *prepared,* i.e. a sacrificial *wafer:*—cake {2x}. See: TWOT—964f; BDB—467d.

3562. כּוֹנַנְיָהוּ {3x} **Kôwnanyâhûw**, *ko-nan-yaw'-hoo;* from 3559 and 3050; *Jah has sustained; Conanjah,* the name of two Isr.:—Conaniah {1x}, Cononiah {2x}. See: BDB—467b, 487d. comp. 3663.

3563. כּוֹס {34x} **kôwç**, *koce;* from an unused root mean. to *hold* together; a *cup* (as a container), often fig. a *lot* (as if a potion); also some unclean bird, prob. an *owl* (perh. from the cup-like cavity of its eye):—cup {31x}, (small) owl {3x}. See: TWOT—965, 966; BDB—468a. comp. 3599.

3564. כּוּר {9x} **kûwr**, *koor;* from an unused root mean. prop. to *dig* through; a *pot* or *furnace* (as if excavated):—furnace {9x}. See: TWOT—967b, 968; BDB—468b. comp. 3600.

כֹּור **kôwr**. See 3733.

3565. כּוֹר עָשָׁן {1x} **Kôwr ʿÂshân**, *kore aw-shawn';* from 3564 and 6227; *furnace of smoke; Cor-Ashan,* a place in Pal.:—Chor-ashan {1x}. See: BDB—468b.

3566. כּוֹרֶשׁ {15x} **Kôwresh**, *ko'-resh;* or (Ezra 1:1 [last time], 2)

כֹּרֶשׁ **Kôresh**, *ko'-resh;* from the Pers.; *Koresh* (or Cyrus), the Pers. king:—Cyrus {15x}. See: BDB—468d, 503c, 1096d.

3567. כּוֹרֶשׁ {8x} **Kôwresh** (Aram.), *ko'-resh;* corresp. to 3566:—Cyrus {8x}. See: BDB—1096d.

3568. כּוּשׁ **Kûwsh**, *koosh;* prob. of for. or.; *Cush* (or Ethiopia), the name of a son of Ham, and of his territory; also of an Isr.:—Ethiopians {3x}, Cush {8x}, Ethiopia {19x}. See: TWOT—969; BDB—468d, 469a.

3569. כּוּשִׁי {23x} **Kûwshîy**, *koo-shee';* patron. from 3568; a *Cushite,* or desc. of Cush:—Cushi {8x}, Ethiopians {9x}, Ethiopia {6x}. See: TWOT—969a; BDB—469a.

3570. כּוּשִׁי {2x} **Kûwshîy**, *koo-shee';* the same as 3569; *Cushi,* the name of two Isr.:—Cushi {2x}. See: BDB—469b, 505b.

3571. כּוּשִׁית {2x} **Kûwshîyth**, *koo-sheeth';* fem. of 3569; a *Cushite woman:*—Ethiopian {2x}. See: BDB—469a.

3572. כּוּשָׁן {1x} **Kûwshân**, *koo-shawn';* perh. from 3568; *Cushan,* a region of Arabia:—Cushan {1x}. See: BDB—469b.

3573. כּוּשַׁן רִשְׁעָתַיִם {4x} **Kûwshan Rishʿâthâ-yim**, *koo-shan' rish-aw-thah'-yim;* appar. from 3572 and the dual of 7564; *Cushan of double wickedness; Cushan-Rishathajim,* a Mesopotamian king:—Chushan-rishathayim {4x}. See: BDB—469b, 958a.

3574. כּוֹשָׁרָה {1x} **kôwshârâh**, *ko-shaw-raw';* from 3787; *prosperity;* in plur. *freedom:*—× chain {1x}. See: TWOT—1052a; BDB—469b, 507a.

3575. כּוּת {2x} **Kûwth**, *kooth;* or (fem.)

כּוּתָה **Kûwthâh**, *koo-thaw';* of for. or.; *Cuth* or *Cuthah,* a province of Assyria:—Cuth {1x}, Cuthah {1x}. See: BDB—469b.

3576. כָּזַב {16x} **kâzab**, *kaw-zab';* a prim. root; to *lie* (i.e. *deceive*), lit. or fig.:—fail {1x}, liar {2x}, liars {1x}, lie {7x}, lying {1x}, lies {1x}, lied {2x}, be in vain {1x}. See: TWOT—970; BDB—469b, 1096c.

3577. כָּזָב {31x} **kâzâb**, *kaw-zawb';* from 3576; *falsehood;* lit. (*untruth*) or fig. (*idol*):—lie {23x}, lying {2x}, leasing {2x}, deceitful {1x}, false {1x}, liar {1x}, lies + 1697 {1x}. See: TWOT—970a; BDB—469c.

3578. כֹּזְבָא {1x} **Kôzᵉbâʾ**, *ko-zeb-aw';* from 3576; *fallacious; Cozeba,* a place in Pal.:—Choseba {1x}. See: BDB—469d.

3579. כָּזְבִּי {2x} **Kozbîy**, *koz-bee';* from 3576; *false; Cozbi,* a Midianitess:—Cozbi {2x}. See: BDB—469d.

3580. כְּזִיב {1x} **Kᵉzîyb**, *kez-eeb';* from 3576; *falsified; Kezib,* a place in Pal.:—Chezib {1x}. See: BDB—469d.

3581. כֹּחַ {126x} **kôach**, *ko'-akh;* or (Dan. 11:6)

כּוֹחַ **kôwach**, *ko'-akh;* from an unused root mean. to *be firm; vigor,* lit. (*force,* in a good or a bad sense) or fig. (*capacity, means, produce*); also (from its hardiness) a large *lizard:*—strength {58x}, power {47x}, might {7x}, force {3x}, ability {2x}, able {2x}, able + 6113 {1x}, chameleon {1x}, fruits {1x}, powerful {1x}, substance {1x}, wealth {1x}, weary + 3019 {1x}.

Kowach (3581)means "strength; power; force; ability." **(1)** *Kowach,* which occurs 126 times, is a poetic word as it is used most frequently in the poetic and prophetical literature. **(2)**

The basic meaning of *kowach* is an ability to do something. **(1a)** Samson's "strength" lay in his hair (Judg 16:5), and we must keep in mind that his "strength" had been demonstrated against the Philistines. **(1b)** Nations and kings exert their "powers" (Josh 17:17; Dan 8:24). **(1c)** It is even possible to say that a field has *kowach,* as it does or does not have vital "powers" to produce and harvest: "When thou tillest the ground, it shall not henceforth yield unto thee her strength [i.e., crops] . . ." (Gen 4:12—the first occurrence). **(2)** In the Old Testament it is recognized that by eating one gains "strength" (1 Sa 28:22), whereas one loses one's "abilities" in fasting (1Sa 28:20); "And he arose, and did eat and drink, and went in the strength of that meat forty days and forty nights unto Horeb the mount of God" (1 Kin 19:8). **(3)** The above definition of *kowach* fits well in the description of Daniel and his friends: **(3a)** "Children in whom was no blemish, but well-favored, and skillful in all wisdom, and cunning in knowledge, and understanding science, and such as had ability [*kowach*] in them to stand in the king's palace, and whom they might teach the learning and the tongue of the Chaldeans" (Dan 1:4).

(3b) The "ability" is here not physical but mental. **(3c)** They were talented in having the intellectual acumen of learning the skills of the Babylonians and thus training for being counselors to the king. **(4)** The internal fortitude was best demonstrated by the difficulties and frustrations of life. A strong man withstood hard times. The proverb bears out this important teaching: "If thou faint in the day of adversity, thy strength is small" (Prov 24:10). **(5)** A special sense of *kowach* is the meaning "property." **(5a)** The results of native "abilities," the development of special gifts, and the manifestation of one's "strength" led often to prosperity and riches. **(5b)** Those who returned from the Exile gave willingly out of their riches (*kowach*) to the building fund of the temple (Ezr 2:69). **(5c)** A proverb warns against adultery, because one's "strength," or one's wealth, may be taken by others: "Lest strangers be filled with thy wealth [*koach*]; and thy labors be in the house of a stranger" (Prov 5:10). **(6)** In the Old Testament, God had demonstrated His "strength" to Israel. **(6a)** The language of God's "strength" is highly metaphorical. **(6a1)** God's right hand gloriously manifests His "power" (Ex 15:6). **(6a2)** His voice is loud: "The voice of the Lord is powerful; the voice of the Lord is full of majesty" (Ps 29:4).

(6b) In His "power," He delivered Israel from Egypt (Ex 32:11) and brought them through the Red Sea (Ex 15:6; cf. Num 14:13). **(6c)** Even as He advances the rights of the poor and needy (Is 50:2), He brought the Israelites as a needy people into the Promised Land with His "power": "He hath showed his people the power of his works, that he may give them the heritage of the heathen" (Ps 111:6). **(7)** He delights in helping His people; however, the Lord does not tolerate self-sufficiency on man's part. **(7a)** Isaiah rebuked the king of Assyria for his arrogance in claiming to have been successful in his conquests (10:12–14), and he remarked that the axe (Assyria) should not boast over the one who chops (God) with it (v. 15). **(7b)** Likewise God had warned His people against pride in taking the land of Canaan: "And thou say in thine heart, My power [*kowach*] and the might of mine hand hath gotten me this wealth. But thou shalt remember the Lord thy God: for it is he that giveth thee power [*kowach*] to get wealth, that he may establish his covenant which he sware unto thy fathers, as it is this day" (Deut 8:17–18). **(8)** The believer must learn to depend upon God and trust in Him: "This is the word of the Lord unto Zerubbabel, saying, Not by might, nor by power, but by my spirit, saith the Lord of hosts" (Zec 4:6). See: TWOT—973.1; BDB—470a, 470b, 470c.

3582. כָּחַד {32x} **kâchad**, *kaw-khad'*; a prim. root; to *secrete*, by act or word; hence, (intens.) to *destroy:*—hide {16x}, cut off {10x}, conceal {4x}, desolate {1x}, cut down {1x}. See: TWOT—972; BDB—470b.

3583. כָּחַל {1x} **kâchal** *kaw-khal'*; a prim. root; to *paint* (with stibium):—paint {1x}. See: TWOT—974; BDB—471a, 806d.

3584. כָּחַשׁ {22x} **kâchash**, *kaw-khash'*; a prim. root; to *be untrue*, in word (to *lie, feign, disown*) or deed (to *disappoint, fail, cringe*):—lie {5x}, submit {3x}, deny {3x}, fail {3x}, denied {2x}, belied {1x}, deceive {1x}, dissembled {1x}, deal falsely {1x}, liars {1x}, submitted {1x}. Syn.: 3576, 8266. See: TWOT—975; BDB—471a.

3585. כַּחַשׁ {6x} **kachash**, *kakh'-ash;* from 3584; lit. a *failure* of flesh, i.e. *emaciation;* fig. *hypocrisy:*—leanness {1x}, lies {4x}, lying {1x}. See: TWOT—975a; BDB—471c.

3586. כֶּחָשׁ {1x} **kechâsh**, *kekh-awsh';* from 3584; *faithless:*—lying {1x}. See: TWOT—975b; BDB—471c.

3587. כִּי {1x} **kîy**, *kee;* from 3554; a *brand* or *scar:*—burning {1x}. See: TWOT—961a; BDB—465a, 475d.

3588. כִּי {46x} **kîy**, *kee;* a prim. particle [the full form of the prepositional prefix] indicating *causal* relations of all kinds, antecedent or consequent; (by impl.) very widely used as a rel. conjunc. or adv. [as below]; often largely modif. by other particles annexed:—{46x}= and, + (forasmuch, inasmuch, where-), as, assured [-ly], + but, certainly, doubtless, + else, even, + except, for, how, (because, in, so, than) that, + nevertheless, now, rightly, seeing, since, surely, then, therefore, + (al-) + though, + till, truly, + until, when, whether, while, whom, yea, yet. See: TWOT—976; BDB—210b, 465a, 471c, 474c, 475c, 758b, 774c, 774d, 1099a.

3589. כִּיד {1x} **kîyd**, *keed;* from a prim root mean. to *strike;* a *crushing;* fig. *calamity:*—destruction {1x}. Syn.: 3772, 5395, 7665. See: TWOT—977a; BDB—475d.

3590. כִּידוֹד {1x} **kîydôwd**, *kee-dode';* from the same as 3589 [comp. 3539]; prop. something *struck* off, i.e. a *spark* (as struck):—sparks {1x}. See: TWOT—953b; BDB—461d, 475d.

3591. כִּידוֹן {9x} **kîydôwn**, *kee-dohn';* from the same as 3589; prop. something to *strike* with, i.e. a *dart* (perh. smaller than 2595):—lance {1x}, shield {2x}, spear {5x}, target {1x}. See: TWOT—977b; BDB—475d.

3592. כִּידוֹן {1x} **Kîydôwn**, *kee-dohn';* the same as 3591; *Kidon*, a place in Pal.:—Chidon {1x}. See: BDB—475d, 647a.

3593. כִּידוֹר {1x} **kîydôwr**, *kee-dore';* of uncert. der.; perh. *tumult:*—battle {1x}. Syn.: 4421, 7128. See: TWOT—954a; BDB—461d, 475d.

3594. כִּיּוּן {1x} **Kîyûwn**, *kee-yoon';* from 3559; prop. a *statue*, i.e. idol; but used (by euphem.) for some heathen deity (perh. corresp. to Priapus or Baal-peor):—Chiun {1x}. See: BDB—475d.

3595. כִּיּוֹר {23x} **kîyôwr**, *kee-yore';* or

כִּיֹּר **kîyôr**, *kee-yore';* from the same as 3564; prop. something *round* (as *excavated* or *bored*), i.e. a chafing-*dish* for coals or a *caldron* for cooking; hence, (from similarity of form) a *washbowl;* also (for the same reason) a *pulpit* or platform:—hearth {1x}, laver {20x}, pan {1x}, scaffold {1x}. See: TWOT—967d; BDB—468c, 476a.

3596. כִּילַי {2x} **kîylay**, *kee-lah'-ee;* or

כֵּלַי **kêlay**, *kay-lah'-ee;* from 3557 in the sense of *withholding; niggardly:*—churl {2x}. See: TWOT—1366b; BDB—476a, 67d.

3597. כֵּילַף {1x} **kêylaph**, *kay-laf';* from an unused root mean. to *clap* or strike with noise; a *club* or sledge-hammer:—hammer {1x}. Syn.: 1989, 4717. See: TWOT—978.1; BDB—476a.

3598. כִּימָה {3x} **Kîymâh**, *kee-maw';* from the same as 3558; a *cluster* of stars, i.e. the *Pleiades:*—Pleiades {2x}, seven stars {1x}. See: BDB—465b, 476a.

3599. כִּיס {6x} **kîyç**, *keece;* a form for 3563; a *cup;* also a *bag* for money or weights:—bag {4x}, cup {1x}, purse {1x}. See: TWOT—979; BDB—476a.

3600. כִּיר {1x} **kîyr**, *keer;* a form for 3564 (only in the dual); a cooking *range* (consisting of two parallel stones, across which the boiler is set):—ranges for pots {1x}. See: TWOT—967c; BDB—468c, 476a.

כִּיֹּר **kîyôr**. See 3595.

3601. כִּישׁוֹר {1x} **kîyshôwr**, *kee-shore';* from 3787; lit. a *director*, i.e. the *spindle* or shank of a distaff (6418), by which it is twirled:—spindle {1x}. See: TWOT—1052c; BDB—476a, 507a.

3602. כָּכָה {9x} **kâkâh**, *kaw'-kaw;* from 3541; *just so,* referring to the previous or following context:—{9x}= after that (this) manner, this matter, (even) so, in such a case, thus. See: TWOT—956; BDB—462b, 476b.

3603. כִּכָּר {68x} **kikkâr**, *kik-kawr';* from 3769; a *circle*, i.e. (by impl.) a circumjacent *tract* or region, expec. the *Ghôr* or valley of the Jordan; also a (round) *loaf;* also a *talent* (or large [round] coin):—talent {48x}, plain {12x}, loaf {4x}, piece {2x}, country {1x}, morsel {1x}. See: TWOT 1046c; BDB—476b, 503a, 1098a.

3604. כִּכַּר {1x} **kikkêr** (C ald.), *kik-kare';* corresp. to 3603; a *talent:*—talent {1x}. See: TWOT—2804a; BDB—1096d, 1098a.

3605. כֹּל {25x} **kôl**, *kole;* or (Jer. 33:8)

כּוֹל **kôwl**, *kole;* from 3634; prop. the *whole;* hence, *all, any* or *every* (in the sing. only, but often in a plur. sense):—{25x} = (in) all (manner, [ye]), altogether, any (manner), enough, every (one, place, thing), howsoever, as many as, [no-] thing, ought, whatsoever, (the) whole, whoso (-ever).

Kowl, as a noun, means "all; the whole." **(1)** The word can be used alone, meaning "the entirety," "whole," or "all," as in: "And thou shalt put all [*kowl*] in the hands of Aaron, and in the hands of his sons . . ." (Ex 29:24). **(2)** *Kowl* can signify everything in a given unit whose members have been selected from others of their kind: "That the sons of God saw the daughters of men that they were fair; and they took them wives of all which they chose" (Gen 6:2). See: TWOT—985a; BDB—481a, 1097a.

3606. כֹּל {95x} **kôl** (Aram.), *kole;* corresp. to 3605:—all {51x}, any {8x}, whole {6x}, as {4x}, every {4x}, because + 6903 {4x}, as + 6903 {2x}, no {2x}, whosoever + 606 {2x}, misc. {12x} = + there (where) -fore, + though, (what, where) -soever.

Kol, as an adjective, means "all; whole; entirety; every; each." **(1)** When *kol* precedes a noun, it expresses a unit and signifies the whole: "These are the three sons of Noah: and of them was the whole (*kol*) earth overspread" (Gen 9:19). **(2)** *Kol* may also signify the entirety of a noun that does not necessarily represent a unit: "All the people, both small and great" entered into the covenant (2 Kin 23:2). The use of the word in such instances tends to unify what is not otherwise a unit. **(3)** *Kol* can precede a word that is only part of a larger unit or not part of a given unit at all. **(3a)** In this case, the prominent idea is that of "plurality," a heterogeneous unit: "And it came to pass from the time that he had made him overseer in his house, and over all that he had, that the Lord blessed the Egyptian's house for Joseph's sake; and the blessing of the Lord was upon all that he had in the house, and in the field" (Gen 39:5). **(3b)** Related to the preceding nuance is the use of *kol* to express comprehensiveness. **(3b1)** Not only does it indicate that the noun modified is a plurality, but also that the unit formed by the addition of *kol* includes everything in the category indicated by the noun: "All the cities were ten with their suburbs for the families of the children of Kohath that remained" (Josh 21:26).

(3b2) In Gen 1:21 (its first occurrence), the word precedes a collective noun and may be translated "every": "And God created great whales, and every living creature that moveth, . . ." **(4)** When used to refer to the individual members of a group, *kol* means "every": **(4a)** "His hand will be against every man, and every man's hand against him" (Gen 16:12). **(4b)** Another example: "Thy princes are rebellious, and companions of thieves: every one loveth gifts, and followeth after rewards" (Is 1:23). **(4c)** Related to this use is the meaning "none but." **(5)** In Deut 19:15, *kol* means "every kind of" or "any"; the word focuses on each and every member of a given unit: **(5a)** "One witness shall not rise up against a man for any iniquity, or for any sin, in any sin that he sinneth. . . ." **(5b)** A related nuance appears in Gen 24:10, but here the emphasis is upon "all sorts": "And the servant took ten camels of the camels of his master, and departed; for all [i.e., a variety of] the goods of his master were in his hand." See: TWOT—2789; BDB—1096d, 1097a.

3607. כָּלָא {18x} **kâlâ'**, *kaw-law'*; a prim. root; to *restrict*, by act (*hold* back or in) or word (*prohibit*):—shut up {4x}, stayed {3x}, refrained {2x}, restrained {2x}, withhold {2x}, keep back {1x}, finish {1x}, forbid {1x}, kept {1x}, retain {1x}. See: TWOT—980; BDB—476b, 478a.

3608. כֶּלֶא {10x} **kele'**, *keh'-leh;* from 3607; a *prison:*—prison {10x}. See: TWOT—980a; BDB—476c. comp. 3610, 3628.

3609. כִּלְאָב {1x} **Kil'âb**, *kil-awb';* appar. from 3607 and 1; *restraint of* (his) *father; Kilab,* an Isr.:—Chileab {1x}. See: BDB—476d.

3610. כִּלְאַיִם {4x} **kil'ayim**, *kil-ah'-yim;* dual of 3608 in the orig. sense of *separation; two heterogeneities:*—divers seeds {1x}, diverse kinds {1x}, mingled {1x}, mingled seed {1x}. See: TWOT—980d; BDB—476c.

3611. כֶּלֶב {32x} **keleb**, *keh'-leb;* from an unused root means. to *yelp,* or else to *attack;* a *dog;* hence, (by euphem.) a male *prostitute:*—dog {32x}. See: TWOT—981a; BDB—476d.

3612. כָּלֵב {35x} **Kâlêb**, *kaw-labe';* perh. a form of 3611, or else from the same root in the sense of *forcible; Caleb,* the name of three Isr.:—Caleb {35x}. See: BDB—477a.

3613. כָּלֵב אֶפְרָתָה {1x} **Kâlêb 'Ephrâthâh**, *kaw-labe' ef-raw'-thaw;* from 3612 and 672; *Caleb-Ephrathah,* a place in Egypt (if the text is correct):—Caleb-ephrathah {1x}. See: BDB—68d.

3614. כָּלִבּוֹ {1x} **Kâlibbôw**, *kaw-lib-bo';* prob. by err. transc. for

כָּלֵבִי **Kâlêbîy**, *kaw-lay-bee';* patron. from 3612; a *Calebite* or desc. of Caleb:—of the house of Caleb {1x}. See: BDB—477a.

3615. כָּלָה {206x} **kâlâh**, *kaw-law';* a prim. root; to *end,* whether intr. (to *cease, be finished, perish*) or tran. (to *complete, prepare, consume*):—consume {57x}, end {44x}, finish {20x}, fail {18x}, accomplish {12x}, done {9x}, spend {8x}, ended {7x}, determined {4x}, away {3x}, fulfil {3x}, fainteth {2x}, destroy {2x}, left {2x}, waste {2x}, misc. {13x} = cease, expire, × fully, × have, long, bring to pass, wholly reap, make clean riddance, quite take away.

Kalah (3615), as a noun, means "to cease, be finished, perish, be completed." **(1)** Basically, the word means "to cease or stop." **(1a)** *Kalah* may refer to the "end" of a process or action, such as the cessation of God's creating the universe: "And on the seventh day God ended his work which he had made . . ." (Gen 2:2—the first occurrence of the word). **(1b)** The word can also refer to the "disappearance" of something: "And the water was spent in the bottle . . ." (Gen 21:15). **(1c)** Finally, *kalah* can be used of "coming to an end" or "the process of ending": "The barrel of meal shall not waste" (1 Kin 17:14). **(2)** *Kalah* can have the more positive connotation of "successfully completing" something. **(2a)** First Kings 6:38 says that the house of the Lord was "finished throughout all the parts thereof, and according to all [its plans]." **(2b)** In this same sense, the word of the Lord "is fulfilled": "Now in the first year of Cyrus king of Persia, that the word of the Lord by the mouth of Jeremiah might be fulfilled, the Lord stirred up the spirit of Cyrus king of Persia, that he made a proclamation . . ." (Ezr 1:1). **(3)** *Kalah* sometimes means "making a firm decision." David tells Jonathan that if Saul is very angry, "be sure that evil is determined by him" (1 Sa 20:7). **(4)** Negatively, "to complete" something may mean "to make it vanish" or "go away." **(4a)** *Kalah* is used in this sense in Deut 32:23, when God says: "I will heap mischiefs upon them; I will spend mine arrows upon them." In other words, His arrows will "vanish" from His possession. **(4b)** This nuance is used especially of clouds: "As the cloud is consumed and vanisheth away . . ." (Job 7:9). **(4c)** Another negative nuance is to "destroy" something or someone: "the famine shall consume the land" (Gen 41:30). **(4d)** Along this same line is the use of *kalah* in Is 1:28: ". . . They that forsake the Lord shall be consumed"; here, however, the verb is a synonym for "dying" or "perishing." **(4e)** One's sight may also "vanish" and one may go blind: "But the eyes of the wicked shall fail, and they shall not escape . . ." (Job 11:20). **(5)** An altogether different emphasis appears when one's heart comes "to an end" or "stops within": "My soul longeth, yea, even fainteth for the courts of the Lord" (Ps 84:2); the psalmist probably meant that his desire for God's presence was so intense that nothing else had any meaning for him—he "died" to be there. **(6)** It can mean successfully completing something: "And in the eleventh year, in the month Bul, which *is* the eighth month, was the house finished throughout all the parts thereof, and according to all the fashion of it. So was he seven years in building it" (1 Kin 6:38). **(7)** The word of the Lord "is fulfilled" (Ezr 1:1). **(8)** It can mean making a firm decision: "If he say thus, *It is* well; thy servant shall have peace: but if he be very wroth, *then* be sure that evil is determined by him" (1 Sa 20:7). **(9)** Negatively, to complete something may mean "to make it vanish" or "go away" (Deut 32:23; clouds - Job 7:9). See: TWOT—982, 983, 984; BDB—477b.

3616. כָּלֶה {1x} **kâleh**, *kaw-leh';* from 3615; *pining:*—fail {1x}. See: TWOT—982b; BDB—479a.

3617. כָּלָה {22x} **kâlâh**, *kaw-law';* from 3615; a *completion;* adv. *completely;* also *destruction:*— . . . end {11x}, altogether {3x}, consume {3x}, consumption {2x}, consummation {1x}, determined {1x}, riddance {1x}.

Kalah, as a noun, means "consumption; complete annihilation." *Kalah* appears 22 times; one occurrence is Neh 9:31: "Nevertheless for thy great mercies' sake thou didst not utterly consume them, nor forsake them; . . . ." See: TWOT—982a; BDB—478d.

3618. כַּלָּה **kallâh**, *kal-law';* from 3634; a *bride* (as if *perfect*); hence, a *son's wife:*—bride {9x}, daughter-in-law {17x}, spouse {8x}. See: TWOT—986a; BDB—480c, 483c.

כְּלוּא **k^elûw'** See 3628.

3619. כְּלוּב {3x} **k^elûwb**, *kel-oob';* from the same as 3611; a bird-*trap* (as furnished with a *clap*-stick or treadle to spring it); hence, a *basket* (as resembling a wicker cage):—basket {1x}, cage {2x}. See: TWOT—981b; BDB—477b.

3620. כְּלוּב {2x} **K^elûwb**, *kel-oob';* the same as 3619; *Kelub,* the name of two Isr.:—Chelub {2x}. See: BDB—477b.

3621. כְּלוּבַי {1x} **K^elûwbay**, *kel-oo-bay'-ee;* a form of 3612; *Kelubai,* an Isr.:—Chelubai {1x}. See: BDB—477b.

3622. כְּלוּהַי {1x} **K^elûwhay**, *kel-oo-hah'-ee;* from 3615; *completed; Keluhai,* an Isr.:—Chelluh {1x}. See: BDB—479a.

3623. כְּלוּלָה {1x} **k^elûwlâh**, *kel-oo-law';* denom. pass. part. from 3618; *bridehood* (only in the plur.):—espousal {1x}. See: TWOT—986b; BDB—480c, 483c.

3624. כֶּלַח {2x} **kelach**, *keh'-lakh;* from an unused root mean. to *be complete; maturity:*—full age {1x}, old age {1x}. See: TWOT—984a; BDB—480c.

3625. כֶּלַח {2x} **Kelach**, *keh'-lakh;* the same as 3624; *Kelach,* a place in Assyria:—Calah {2x}. See: BDB—480d.

3626. כָּל־חֹזֶה {2x} **Kol-Chôzeh**, *kol-kho-zeh';* from 3605 and 2374; *every seer; Col-Chozeh,* an Isr.:—Col-hozeh {2x}. See: BDB—480d.

3627. כְּלִי {325x} **k^elîy**, *kel-ee';* from 3615; something *prepared,* i.e. any *apparatus* (as an implement, utensil, dress, vessel or weapon):—vessel {166x}, instrument {39x}, weapon {21x}, jewel {21x}, armourbearer + 5375 {18x}, stuff {14x}, thing {11x}, armour {10x}, furniture {7x}, carriage {3x}, bag {2x}, misc. {13x} = artillery, + furnish, that is made of, × one from another, that which pertaineth, pot, + psaltery, sack, tool, ware, + whatsoever.

Keliy means "vessel; receptacle; stuff clothing; utensil; tool; instrument; ornament or jewelry; armor or weapon." **(1)** This word is used of "receptacles" of various kinds used for storing and transporting. Thus Jacob said to Laban: "Whereas thou hast searched through all my stuff [literally, receptacles], what hast thou found of all thy household stuff [literally, from all the receptacles of thy house]?" (Gen 31:37). **(1a)** Such "receptacles" may be made of wood (Lev 11:32) or potsherd or clay (Lev 6:28). **(1b)** They may be used to hold documents (Jer 32:14), wine, oil, fruits (Jer 40:10), food (Eze 4:9), beverage (Ruth

2:9), or bread (1 Sa 9:7). **(1c)** Even a shepherd's bag is a *keliy* (1 Sa 17:40). **(1d)** In 1 Sa 17:22 the word is used of baggage, or "receptacles" (his shepherd's bag?) and what is in them: "And David left his carriage in the hand of the [baggage keeper]. . . ." **(1e)** The sailors on the ship in which Jonah sailed "cast forth the wares [cargo] . . . into the sea, to lighten it of them" (Jonah 1:5). **(2)** Ships are called "receptacles," presumably because they can hold people: "That sendeth ambassadors by the sea, even in vessels of bulrushes upon the waters . . ." (Is 18:2). **(3)** *Keliy* can mean "clothing": "The woman shall not wear that which pertaineth unto a man, neither shall a man put on a woman's garment: for all that do so are abomination unto the Lord thy God" (Deut 22:5).

(4) The word may be used of various "vessels and utensils": "And the four tables were of hewn stone for the burnt offering . . . : whereupon also they laid the instruments wherewith they slew the burnt offering and the sacrifice" (Eze 40:42). **(5)** In Gen 45:20 this word refers to movable but large possessions: Pharaoh told Joseph to tell his brothers to take wagons and bring their family to Egypt, and "regard not your stuff; for the good of all the land of Egypt is yours." **(6)** Thus in Ex 27:19 the word represents all the furniture and utensils of the tabernacle (cf. Num 3:8). **(7)** Samuel warned Israel that the king on whom they insisted would organize them into levees (work crews) "to [plow] his ground, and to reap his harvest, and to make his instruments of war, and instruments of his chariots" (1 Sa 8:12). **(8)** More narrowly, *keliy* may be used of oxen harnesses: ". . . Behold, here be oxen for burnt sacrifice, and threshing instruments and other instruments of the oxen for wood" (2 Sa 24:22). **(9)** This word may be used of various "implements or tools": "Simeon and Levi are brethren instruments of cruelty in their habitations" (Gen 49:5). **(10)** In Jer 22:7 the word represents "tools" with which trees may be cut down: "And I will prepare destroyers against thee, every one with his weapons: and they shall cut down thy choice cedars, and cast them into the fire."

(11) Isaac told Esau to take his gear, his quiver, and his bow, "and go out to the field, and take me some venison" (Gen 27:3). **(12)** Weapons for war are called "implements": "And they [the Israelites] went after them unto Jordan: and, lo, all the way was full of garments and vessels, which the Syrians had cast away in their haste" (2 Kin 7:15). **(12a)** A bearer of implements is an armor-bearer (Judg 9:54). **(12b)** A house of arms or an armory is referred to in 2 Kin 20:13. **(13)** In Amos 6:5 and such passages (2 Chr 5:13; 7:6; 23:13; cf. Ps 71:22) "musical instruments" are called kelim: "That chant to the sound of the viol, and invent to themselves instruments of music. . . ." **(14)** *Keliy* stands for various kinds of "precious ornaments": **(14a)** "And the servant brought forth jewels of silver, and jewels of gold, and raiment, and gave them to Rebekah . . ." (Gen 24:53—the first biblical appearance of the word). **(14b)** Such "precious ornaments" adorned the typical bride: "I will greatly rejoice in the Lord, my soul shall be joyful in my God; for he hath clothed me with the garments of salvation, he hath covered me with the robe of righteousness, as a bridegroom decketh himself with ornaments and as a bride adorneth herself with her jewels" (Is 61:10). See: TWOT—982g; BDB—479b, 480d.

3628. כְּלִיא {2x} **kᵉlîyʾ**, *kel-ee'*; or

כְּלוּא **kᵉlûwʾ**, *kel-oo'*; from 3607 [comp. 3608]; a *prison:*—prison = 1004 {2x}. See: TWOT—980b; BDB—476c.

3629. כִּלְיָה {31x} **kilyâh**, *kil-yaw'*; fem. of 3627 (only in the plur.); a *kidney* (as an essential *organ*); fig. the *mind* (as the interior self):—kidneys {18x}, reins {13x}. See: TWOT—983a; BDB—480b, 480d.

3630. כִּלְיוֹן {3x} **Kilyôwn**, *kil-yone'*; a form of 3631; *Kiljon*, an Isr.:—Chilion {3x}. See: BDB—479a.

3631. כִּלָּיוֹן {2x} **killâyôwn**, *kil-law-yone'*; from 3615; *pining, destruction:*—consumption {1x}, failing {1x}. See: TWOT—982c; BDB—479a, 480d.

3632. כָּלִיל {15x} **kâlîyl**, *kaw-leel'*; from 3634; *complete;* as noun, the *whole* (spec. a sacrifice *entirely consumed*); as adv. *fully:*—perfect {3x}, wholly {3x}, all {2x}, wholly burnt {1x}, flame {1x}, perfection {1x}, whole burnt sacrifice 1, utterly {1x}, every whit {1x}, whole {1x}.

Kaliyl means "the entire; whole, whole offering." **(1)** This word represents the "whole offering" from which the worshiper does not partake: "It is a statute for ever unto the Lord; it shall be wholly burnt" (Lev 6:22). **(2)** In Num 4:6, *kaliyl* refers to the "cloth wholly of blue." In other words, it indicates "the entire" cloth. Syn.: 5930. See: TWOT—985b; BDB—483a.

3633. כַּלְכֹּל {2x} **Kalkôl**, *kal-kole'*; from 3557; *sustenance; Calcol*, an Isr.:—Calcol {1x}, Chalcol {1x}. See: BDB—465b, 480d.

3634. כָּלַל {2x} **kâlal**, *kaw-lal'*; a prim. root; to *complete:*—made perfect {1x}, perfected {1x}.

Kalal, as a verb, means "to perfect." This common Semitic root appears in biblical Hebrew only 3 times. Eze 27:11 is a good example: ". . . They have made thy beauty perfect [*kalal*]." Syn.: 8003, 8549. See: TWOT—985, 986; BDB—480d, 1007a.

3635. כְּלַל {8x} **kᵉlal** (Aram.), *kel-al'*; corresp. to 3634; to *complete:*—finished {2x}, make up {2x}, set up {4x}. See: TWOT—2788; BDB—1097a, 115b.

3636. כְּלָל {1x} **Kᵉlâl**, *kel-awl'*; from 3634; *complete; Kelal*, an Isr.:—Chelal {1x}. See: BDB—483c.

3637. כָּלַם {38x} **kâlam**, *kaw-lawm'*; a prim. root; prop. to *wound;* but only fig., to *taunt* or *insult:*—ashamed {12x}, confounded {11x}, shame {7x}, blush {3x}, hurt {2x}, reproach {2x}, confusion {1x}. See: TWOT—987; BDB—483c.

3638. כִּלְמָד {1x} **Kilmâd**, *kil-mawd'*; of for. der.; *Kilmad*, a place appar. in the Ass. empire:—Chilmad {1x}. See: BDB—484b.

3639. כְּלִמָּה {30x} **kᵉlimmâh**, *kel-im-maw'*; from 3637; *disgrace:*—confusion {6x}, dishonour {3x}, reproach {1x}, shame {20x}. See: TWOT—987a; BDB—484a.

3640. כְּלִמּוּת {1x} **kᵉlimmu wth**, *kel-im-mooth'*; from 3639; *disgrace:*—shame {1x}. Syn.: 954, 1322, 2659, 7036. See: TWOT—987b; BDB—484b.

3641. כַּלְנֶה {3x} **Kalneh**, *kal-neh'*; or

כַּלְנֵה **Kalnêh**, *kal-nay'*; also

כַּלְנוֹ **Kalnôw**, *kal-no'*; of for. der.; *Calneh* or *Calno*, a place in the Ass. empire:—Calneh {2x}, Calno {1x}. See: BDB—484c. comp. 3656.

3642. כָּמַהּ {1x} **kâmahh**, *kaw-mah'*; a prim. root; to *pine* after:—long {1x}. Syn.: 183, 2968, 3700. See: TWOT—988; BDB—484c.

3643. כִּמְהָם {4x} **Kimhâm**, *kim-hawm'*; from 3642; *pining; Kimham*, an Isr.:—Chimham {4x}. See: BDB—158c, 484c, 484d.

3644. כְּמוֹ {20x} **kᵉmôw**, *kem-o'*; or

כָּמוֹ **kâmôw**, *kaw-mo'*; a form of the pref. *k*, but used separately [comp. 3651]; *as, thus, so:*—{20x} = according to, (such) as (it were, well as), in comp. of, like (as, to, unto), thus, when, worth. See: TWOT—938; BDB—455d, 484d.

3645. כְּמוֹשׁ {8x} **Kᵉmôwsh**, *kem-oshe'*; or (Jer. 48:7)

כְּמִישׁ **Kᵉmîysh**, *kem-eesh'*; from an unused root mean. to *subdue;* the *powerful; Kemosh*, the god of the Moabites:—Chemosh {8x}. See: BDB—484d.

3646. כַּמֹּן {3x} **kammôn**, *kam-mone'*; from an unused root mean. to *store* up or *preserve;* "*cummin*" (from its use as a *condiment*):—cummin {3x}. See: TWOT—991, 991b; BDB—485a.

3647. כָּמַס {1x} **kâmaç**, *kaw-mas'*; a prim. root; to *store* away, i.e. (fig.) in the memory:—laid up in store {1x}. See: TWOT—992; BDB—485a.

3648. כָּמַר {4x} **kâmar**, *kaw-mar'*; a prim. root; prop. to *intertwine* or *contract*, i.e. (by impl.) to *shrivel* (as with heat); fig. to *be* deeply *affected* with passion (love or pity):—be black {1x}, be kindled {1x}, yearn {2x}. See: TWOT—993, 994, 995; BDB—485a.

3649. כָּמָר {3x} **kâmâr**, *kaw-mawr'*; from 3648; prop. an *ascetic* (as if *shrunk* with self-maceration), i.e. an idolatrous *priest* (only in plur.):—Chemarims {1x}, (idolatrous) priests {2x}. Three out of the four places this word is used it refers to idolatrous priests (2 Kin 23:5; Hos 10:5; Zeph 1:4). See: TWOT—996; BDB—485c.

3650. כִּמְרִיר {1x} **kimrîyr**, *kim-reer'*; redupl. from 3648; *obscuration* (as if from *shrinkage* of light, i.e. an *eclipse* (only in plur.):—blackness {1x}. See: TWOT—994a; BDB—485b.

3651. כֵּן {42x} **kên**, *kane;* from 3559; prop. *set* upright; hence, (fig. as adj.) *just;* but usually (as adv. or conjunc.) *rightly* or *so* (in various applications to manner, time and relation; often with other particles):—so, thus, like manner, well, such thing, howbeit, state, after that, following, after this, therefore, wherefore, surely = {42x}.

Ken, as an adjective, means "right, veritable, honest." **(1)** The word implies "honest or righteous" in Gen 42:11: "We are all one man's sons; we are true men, thy servants are no spies." **(2)** The word means not "right" in 2 Kin 17:9: "And the children of Israel did secretly *those* things that *were* not right against the LORD their God, and they built them high places in all their cities, from the tower of the watchmen to the fenced city." See: TWOT—964a, 964b; BDB—467a, 467b, 475c, 485d, 487b, 540c, 1097b.

3652. כֵּן {8x} **kên** (Aram.), *kane;* corresp. to 3651; *so:*—thus {8x}. See: TWOT—2790; BDB—1097b.

3653. כֵּן {17x} **kên**, *kane;* the same as 3651, used as a noun; a *stand*, i.e. pedestal or station:—foot {8x}, estate {4x}, base {2x}, office {1x}, place {1x}, well {1x}. See: TWOT—998a; BDB—467b, 487b, 487c.

3654. כֵּן {7x} **kên**, *kane;* from 3661 in the sense of *fastening;* a *gnat* (from infixing its sting; used only in plur. [and irreg. in Exod. 8:17, 18; 13:14]):—lice {6x}, × manner {1x}. See: TWOT—999a; BDB—467b, 487b, 487c, 487d.

3655. כָּנָה {4x} **kânâh**, *kaw-naw';* a prim. root; to *address* by an additional name; hence, to *eulogize:*—give flattering titles {2x}, surname (himself) {2x}. See: TWOT—997; BDB—487b.

3656. כַּנֶּה {1x} **Kanneh**, *kan-neh';* for 3641; *Canneh,* a place in Assyria:—Canneh {1x}. See: BDB—487c.

3657. כַּנָּה {1x} **ka nâh**, *kaw-naw';* from 3661; a *plant* (as *set*):—× vineyard {1x}. Syn.: 3754. See: TWOT—999b; BDB—487c, 488a.

3658. כִּנּוֹר {42x} **kinnôwr**, *kin-nore';* from a unused root mean. to *twang;* a *harp:*—harp {42x}. See: TWOT—1004a; BDB—490a.

3659. כָּנְיָהוּ {3x} **Konyâhûw**, *kon-yaw'-hoo;* for 3204; *Conjah,* an Isr. king:—Coniah {3x}. See: BDB—220c.

3660. כְּנֵמָא {5x} **kᵉnêmâʼ** (Aram.), *ken-ay-maw';* corresp. to 3644; *so* or *thus:*—so {1x}, (in) this manner {1x}, sort {1x}, thus {2x}. See: TWOT—2791; BDB—1097b.

3661. כָּנַן {1x} **kânan**, *kaw-nan';* a prim. root; to *set* out, i.e. *plant:*—vineyard + 3657 {1x}. See: TWOT—999b; BDB—488a.

3662. כְּנָנִי {1x} **Kᵉnânîy**, *ken-aw-nee';* from 3661; *planted; Kenani,* an Isr.:—Chenani {1x}. See: BDB—487d.

3663. כְּנַנְיָה {3x} **Kᵉnanyâh**, *ken-an-yaw';* or כְּנַנְיָהוּ **Kᵉnanyâhûw**, *ken-an-yaw'-hoo;* from 3661 and 3050; *Jah has planted; Kenanjah,* an Isr.:—Chenaniah {3x}. See: BDB—487d.

3664. כָּנַס {11x} **kânaç**, *kaw-nas';* a prim. root; to *collect;* hence, to *enfold:*—gather {5x}, gather together {4x}, heap up {1x}, wrap {1x}.See: TWOT—1000; BDB—488a, 1097b.

3665. כָּנַע {36x} **kânaʻ**, *kaw-nah';* a prim. root; prop. to *bend* the knee; hence, to *humiliate, vanquish:*—humble {18x}, subdue {11x}, bring low {2x}, bring down {3x}, subjection {1x}, under {1x}.

Kana', means "to be humble, to humble, subdue." **(1)** The word can mean "to humble, to subdue," and it can have a passive or reflexive use, "to be humble" or "to humble oneself." **(1a)** While *kana'* occurs some 35 times in the Hebrew Old Testament, the word is not found until Deut 9:3: "The Lord thy God . . . shall destroy them, and he shall bring them down. . . ." **(1b)** *Kana'* is frequently used in this sense of "subduing, humbling," enemies: "And after this it came to pass, that David smote the Philistines, and subdued them: and David took Methegammah out of the hand of the Philistines" (2 Sa 8:1; cf. 1 Chr 17:10; Ps 81:14). **(1c)** "To humble oneself" before God in repentance is a common theme and need in the life of ancient Israel: "And *that* I also have walked contrary unto them, and have brought them into the land of their enemies; if then their uncircumcised hearts be humbled, and they then accept of the punishment of their iniquity" (Lev 26:41; cf. 2 Chr 7:14; 12:6–7, 12). Syn.: 8213. See: TWOT—1001; BDB—488b.

3666. כִּנְעָה {1x} **kinʻâh**, *kin-aw';* from 365 in the sense of *folding* [comp. 3664]; a *package:*—wares {1x}. See: TWOT—1001a; BDB—488c.

3667. כְּנַעַן {94x} **Kᵉnaʻan**, *ken-ah'-an;* from 3665; *humiliated; Kenaan,* a son of Ham; also the country inhabited by him:—Canaan {89x}, merchant {3x}, traffick {1x}, traffickers {1x}.

Kena'an means "Canaan" and *kena'ani* (3669) means "Canaanite; merchant." **(1)** "Canaan" is used 9 times as the name of a person and 80 times as a place name. **(1a)** "Canaanite" occurs 72 times of the descendants of "Canaan," the inhabitants of the land of Canaan. **(1c)** Most occurrences of these words are in Genesis through Judges, but they are scattered throughout the Old Testament. **(2)** "Canaan" is first used of a person in Gen 9:18: "and Ham is the father of Canaan" (cf. Gen 10:6). **(3)** After a listing of the nations descended from "Canaan," Gen 10:18–19 adds: "and afterward were the families of the Canaanites spread abroad. **(4)** And the border of the Canaanites was from Sidon, as thou comest to Gerar, unto Gaza; as thou goest, unto Sodom, and Gomorrah, ..." **(4a)** "Canaan" is the land west of the Jordan, as in Num 33:51: "When ye are passed over Jordan into the land of Canaan" (cf. Josh 22:9–11). **(4b)** At the call of God, Abram ". . . went forth to go into the land of Canaan; and into the land of Canaan they came. . . . And the Canaanite was then in the land" (Gen 12:5–6). **(4c)** Later God promised Abram: "Unto thy seed have I given this land, . . . [the land of] the Canaanites . . ." (Gen 15:18–20; cf. Ex 3:8, 17; Josh 3:10).

(5) "Canaanite" is a general term for all the descendants of "Canaan": **(5a)** "When the Lord thy God shall bring thee into the land whither thou goest to possess it, and hath cast out many nations before thee . . . the Canaanites . . ." (Deut 7:1). **(5b)** It is interchanged with Amorite in Gen 15:16: ". . . for the iniquity of the Amorites is not yet full" (cf. Josh 24:15, 18). **(6)** "Canaanite" is also used in the specific sense of one of the peoples of Canaan: **(6a)** ". . . and the Canaanites dwell by the sea, and by the coast of Jordan" (Num 13:29; cf. Josh 5:1; 2 Sa 24:7). **(6b)** As these peoples were traders, "Canaanite" is a symbol for "merchant" in Prov 31:24 and Job 41:6 and notably, in speaking of the sins of Israel, Hosea says, "He is a merchant, the balances of deceit are in his hand . . ." (Hos 7:12; cf. Zeph 1:11). **(7)** Gen 9:25–27 stamps a theological significance on "Canaan" from the beginning: "Cursed be Canaan; a servant of servants shall he be unto his brethren. . . . Blessed be the Lord God of Shem; and Canaan shall be his servant. And God shall enlarge Japheth . . . and Canaan shall be his servant."

(8) Noah prophetically placed this curse on "Canaan" because his father had stared at Noah's nakedness and reported it grossly to his brothers. **(8a)** Ham's sin, deeply rooted in his youngest son, is observable in the Canaanites in the succeeding history. **(8b)** Leviticus 18 gives a long list of sexual perversions that were forbidden to Israel prefaced by the statement: ". . . and after the doings of the land of Canaan, whither I bring you, shall ye not do . . ." (Lev 18:3). **(8c)** The list is followed by a warning: "Defile not ye yourselves in any of these things: for in all these the nations are defiled which I cast out before you" (Lev 18:24). **(9)** The command to destroy the "Canaanites" was very specific: **(9a)** "thou shalt smite them, and utterly destroy them. . . . ye shall destroy their altars, and break down their images. . . . For thou art a holy people unto the Lord thy God . . ." (Deut 7:2–6). **(9b)** But too often the house of David and Judah "built them high places, and images, and groves, on every high hill, and under every green tree. And there were also sodomites in the land: and they did according to all the abominations of the nations which the Lord cast out before the children of Israel" (1 Kin 14:23–24; cf. 2 Kin 16:3–4; 21:1–15).

(10) The nations were the "Canaanites"; thus "Canaanite" became synonymous with religious and moral perversions of every kind. **(11)** This fact is reflected in Zec 14:21: "and in that day there shall be no more the Canaanite in the house of the Lord of hosts." **(11a)** A "Canaanite" was not permitted to enter the tabernacle or temple; no longer would one of God's people who practiced the abominations of the "Canaanites" enter the house of the Lord. **(11b)** This prophecy speaks of the last days and will be fulfilled in the New Jerusalem, according to Rev 21:27: "And there shall in no wise enter into it any thing that defileth, neither whatsoever worketh abomination, or maketh a lie . . ." (cf. Rev 22:15). See: TWOT—1002, 1002b; BDB—488c, 488d.

3668. כְּנַעֲנָה {5x} **Kᵉnaʻănâh**, *ken-ah-an-aw';* fem. of 3667; *Kenaanah,* the name of two Isr.:—Chenaanah {5x}. See: BDB—489b.

3669. כְּנַעֲנִי {73x} **Kᵉnaʻănîy**, *ken-ah-an-ee';* patrial from 3667; a *Kenaanite* or inhab. of Kenaan; by impl. a *pedlar* (the Canaanites standing for their neighbors the Ishmaelites, who conducted mercantile caravans):—Canaanite {67x}, merchant {2x}, Canaan {1x}, Canaanitess {1x}, Canaanitish woman {2x}.

Kena'aniy means Canaanite, merchant, inhabitants of the land of Canaan (Gen 10:18–19). **(1)** Canaan is the land west of the Jordan (Gen 12:5–6; Num 33:51) **(2)** promised to Abraham (Gen 15:18–20; Ex 3:8). **(3)** Canaanite is a general term for all the descendants of Canaan (Deut 7:1) and interchanged with Amorite in Gen 15:16. **(4)** Canaanite is also used in the specific sense of one people of Canaan (Num 13:29; Josh 5:1; 2 Sa 24:7). **(5)** Gen 9:25–27 stamps a theological significance on Canaan from the beginning; they are cursed (Lev 18:1–24). The nations were the Canaanites; thus Canaanite became synonymous with religious and moral perversions of every kind. **(6)** Israel was to utterly destroy them (Deut 7:2–6), **(7)** failed to do so (1 Kin 14:23–24; 2 Kin 16:3–4; 21:1–15). **(8)** They will be destroyed (Zec 14:21). See: TWOT—1002a, 1002b; BDB—489a, 489b.

3670. כָּנַף {1x} **kânaph**, *kaw-naf';* a prim. root; prop. to *project* laterally, i.e. prob. (refl.) to *withdraw:*—be removed into a corner {1x}. See: TWOT—1003; BDB—489d.

3671. כָּנָף {108x} **kânâph**, *kaw-nawf';* from 3670; an *edge* or *extremity;* spec. (of a bird or army) a *wing,* (of a garment or bedclothing) a *flap,* (of the earth) a *quarter,* (of a building) a *pinnacle:*—wing {74x}, skirt {14x}, borders {2x}, corners {2x}, ends {2x}, feathered {2x}, sort {2x}, winged {2x}, misc. {8x} = + bird, × flying, + (one an-) other, overspreading, × quarters, uttermost part.

Kanaph means "wing." **(1)** In the Old Testament *kanaph* occurs first in the Creation account: "And God created great whales, and every living creature that moveth which the waters brought forth abundantly, after their kind, and every winged fowl after his kind: and God saw that it was good" (Gen 1:21; cf. Ps 78:27). **(2)** In the biblical usage the idiom "any winged fowl" denotes the class of birds; cf. "They, and every beast after his kind, and all the cattle after their kind, and every creeping thing that creepeth upon the earth after his kind, and every fowl after his kind, every bird of every sort" (Gen 7:14). **(3)** The word "wing" appears 109 times in the Hebrew Old Testament, **(3a)** with particular concentration in the description of the 2 cherubim of wood in Solomon's temple and in Ezekiel's vision of the "creatures," or cherubim. **(3b)** Elsewhere the Bible speaks of "wings" of the cherubim (Ex 25:20; 37:9) and of the seraphim (Is 6:2). **(4)** As an extension of the usage "wing," *kanaph* signifies "extremity." **(4a)** The seam or lower part of a garment was known as the *kanaph*. **(4b)** In the "skirt" (*kanaph*) of the garment one could carry things (Hag 2:12). **(4c)** Saul tore the skirt ("edge" - *kanaph*) of Samuel's robe (1 Sa 15:27).

(5) The extremity of a land on the world was also known by the word *kanaph* and is translated by "corner" in English: "And he shall set up an ensign for the nations, and shall assemble the outcasts of Israel, and gather together the dispersed of Judah from the four corners of the earth" (Is 11:12; cf. Job 37:3; 38:13; Eze 7:2). **(6)** In the metaphorical use God is said to protect His people as a bird protects her young with her "wings" (Deut 32:11). **(6a)** The psalmist expressed God's care and protection as a "shadow" of the "wings" (Ps 17:8; cf. 36:7; 57:1; 61:4; 63:7; 91:4). This may be a reference to the care afforded "under the wings of the cherubim over the mercy seat." **(6b)** In keeping with this usage Malachi looked forward to a new age, when "the Sun of righteousness [will] arise with healing in his wings, and ye shall go forth, and grow up as calves of the stall" (4:2). **(7)** When the nations are compared to birds, the association is that of terror and conquest. This is best expressed in Ezekiel's parable of the two eagles and the vine: "And say, Thus saith the Lord God; A great eagle with great wings, longwinged, full of feathers, which had divers colors, came unto Lebanon, and took the highest branch of the cedar: he cropped off the top of his young twigs, and carried it into a land of traffic; he set it in a city of merchants" (Eze 17:3–4). **(8)** The believer is enjoined to seek refuge with God when adversity strikes him or adversaries surround him: "He shall cover thee with his feathers, and under his wings shall thou trust: his truth shall be thy shield and buckler" (Ps 91:4). See: TWOT—1003a; BDB—489b.

3672. כִּנְּרוֹת {7x} **Kinnᵉrôwth**, *kin-ner-ōth'*; or

כִּנֶּרֶת **Kinnereth**, *kin-neh'-reth*; respectively plur. and sing. fem. from the same as 3658; perh. *harp*-shaped; *Kinneroth* or *Kinnereth*, a place in Pal.:—Chinnereth {1x}, Chinneroth {2x}, Cinneroth {1x}. See: BDB—490b.

3673. כְּנַשׁ {3x} **kânash** (Aram.), *kaw-nash'*; corresp. to 3664; to *assemble*:—gather together {3x}. See: TWOT—2792; BDB—1097b.

3674. כְּנָת {1x} **kᵉnâth**, *ken-awth'*; from 3655; a *colleague* (as having the same title):—companion {1x}. See: TWOT—1005; BDB—487c, 490c.

3675. כְּנָת {7x} **kᵉnâth** Aram.), *ken-awth'*; corresp. to 3674:—companion {7x}. See: TWOT—2793; BDB—1097c.

3676. כֵּס {1x} **kêç**, *kace*; appar. a contr. for 3678, but prob. by err. transc. for 5251:—sworn {1x}. See: TWOT—1007; BDB—490c, 490d.

3677. כֶּסֶא {2x} **keçeʾ**, *keh'-seh*; or

כֶּסֶה **keçeh**, *keh'-seh*; appar. from 3680; prop. *fulness* or the *full moon*, i.e. its festival:—(time) appointed {1x}. See: TWOT—1006; BDB—490c, 492c.

3678. כִּסֵּא {135x} **kiççêʾ**, *kis-say'*; or

כִּסֵּה **kiççêh**, *kis-say'*; from 3680; prop. *covered*, i.e. a *throne* (as *canopied*):—seat {1x}, stool {7x}, throne {127x}.

Kicce' means "throne; seat." **(1)** *Kicce'* occurs 130 times in the Hebrew Old Testament and, as is to be expected, the frequency is greater in the historical books and the prophetical works. It is rare in the Pentateuch. **(2)** The first usage of *kicce'* is in Gen 41:40: "Thou shalt be over my house, and according unto thy word shall all my people be ruled: only in the throne will I be greater than thou." **(3)** In the Old Testament the basic meaning of *kicce'* is "seat" or "chair." **(3a)** Visitors were seated on a chair (1 Kin 2:19), as well as guests (2 Kin 4:10) and older men (1 Sa 1:9). **(3b)** When the king or elders assembled to administer justice, they sat on the throne of justice (Prov 20:8; cf. Ps 9:4). **(3c)** In these contexts kicce' is associated with honor. **(3d)** However, in the case of the prostitute (Prov 9:14) and soldiers who set up their chairs (Jer 1:15—*kicce'* may mean "throne" here), *kicce'* signifies a place and nothing more. **(4)** The more frequent sense of *kicce'* is "throne" or "seat of honor," also known as the "royal seat": "And it shall be, when he sitteth upon the throne of his kingdom, that he shall write him a copy of this law in a book out of that which is before the priests the Levites" (Deut 17:18; cf. 1 Kin 1:46). **(5)** Since the Davidic dynasty received the blessing of God, the Old Testament has a number of references to "the throne of David" (2 Sa 3:10; Jer 22:2, 30; 36:30): "Of the increase of his government and peace there shall be no end, upon the throne of David, and upon his kingdom, to order it, and to establish it with judgment and with justice from henceforth even for ever" (Is 9:7). **(6)** The "throne of Israel" is a synonymous phrase for "throne of David" (1 Kin 2:4; cf. 8:20, 25; 9:5; 10:9; 2 Kin 10:30; 15:12, etc.). **(7)** The physical appearance of the "throne" manifested the glory of the king. Solomon's "throne" was an artistic product with ivory inlays, the wood covered with a layer of fine gold (1 Kin 10:18). **(8)** The word kicce' was also used to represent "kingship" and the succession to the throne. David had sworn that Solomon would sit on his "throne" (1 Kin 1:13; cf. 2 Kin 10:3). **(9)** Above all human kingship and "thrones" was the God of Israel: "God reigneth over the heathen: God sitteth upon the throne of his holiness" (Ps 47:8). **(10)** The Israelites viewed God as the ruler who was seated on a "throne." Micaiah said in the presence of Ahab and Jehoshaphat: "Hear thou therefore the word of the Lord: I saw the Lord sitting on his throne, and all the host of heaven standing by him on his right hand and on his left" (1 Kin 22:19). **(11)** Isaiah received a vision of God's glory revealed in the temple (Is 6:1). **(12)** The presence of the Lord in Jerusalem also gave rise to the conception that Jerusalem was the throne of God (Jer 3:17). See: TWOT—1007; BDB—490c, 492c, 1097c.

3679. כַּסְדַּי {1x} **Kaçday**, *kas-dah'-ee*; for 3778:—Chaldean {1x}. See: BDB—505a.

3680. כָּסָה {152x} **kâçâh**, *kaw-saw'*; a prim. root; prop. to *plump*, i.e. *fill up* hollows; by impl. to *cover* (for clothing or secrecy):—cover {135x}, hide {6x}, conceal {4x}, covering {2x}, overwhelmed {2x}, clad {1x}, closed {1x}, clothed {1x}. See: TWOT—1008; BDB—491b. comp. 3780.

כֶּסֶה **keçeh**. See 3677.

כִּסֵּה **kiççêh**. See 3678.

3681. כָּסוּי {2x} **kâçûwy**, *kaw-soo'-ee*; pass. part. of 3680; prop. *covered*, i.e. (as noun) a *covering*:—covering {2x}. See: TWOT—1008a; BDB—492b, 492d.

3682. כְּסוּת {8x} **kᵉçûwth**, *kes-ooth'*; from 3680; a *cover* (garment); fig. a *veiling*:—covering {6x}, raiment {1x}, vesture {1x}. See: TWOT—1008b; BDB—492b. 492d.

3683. כָּסַח {2x} **kâçach**, *kaw-sakh'*; a prim. root; to *cut off*:—cut down {1x}, cut up {1x}. See: TWOT—1010; BDB—492d.

3684. כְּסִיל {70x} **kᵉçîyl**, *kes-eel'*; from 3688; prop. *fat*, i.e. (fig.) stupid or *silly*:—fool {61x}, foolish {9x}.

Keciyl means "stupid fellow; dull person; fool." **(1)** This word occurs in the Old Testament 70 times with all of its occurrences being in wisdom literature except 3 in the Psalms. **(2)** The *keciyl* is "insolent" in religion and "stupid or dull" in wise living (living out a religion he professes). **(2a)** In Ps 92:6 the first emphasis is especially prominent: "A brutish man knoweth not; neither doth a fool understand this." **(2a1)** The psalmist is describing an enemy of God who knew God and His word but, seeing the wicked flourishing, reasoned that they have the right lifestyle: "When the wicked spring as the grass, and when all the workers of iniquity do flourish; *it is* that they shall be destroyed for ever" (Ps 92:7). **(2a2)** They have knowledge of God but do not properly evaluate or understand what they know. **(3)** The second emphasis is especially prominent in wisdom contexts: "How long, ye simple ones, will ye love simplicity? and the scorners delight in their scorning, and fools hate knowledge?" (Prov 1:22). **(3a)** In such contexts the person so described rejects the claims and teachings of wisdom. **(3b)** However, in the Bible wisdom is the practical outworking of one's religion. Therefore, even in these contexts there is a clear connotation of insolence in religion. Syn.: 191, 5036. See: TWOT—1011c; BDB—493a.

3685. כְּסִיל {4x} **Kᵉçîyl**, *kes-eel'*; the same as 3684; any notable *constellation*; spec. *Orion* (as if a *burly* one):—constellation {1x}, Orion{3}. See: TWOT—1011e; BDB—493a.

3686. כְּסִיל {1x} **Kᵉçîyl**, *kes-eel'*; the same as 3684; *Kesil*, a place in Pal.:—Chesil {1x}. See: BDB—493b.

3687. כְּסִילוּת {1} **kᵉçîylûwth**, *kes-eel-ooth'*; from 3684; *silliness*:—foolish {1x}. See: TWOT—1011d; BDB—493a.

3688. כָּסַל {1x} **kâçal**, *kaw-sal'*; a prim. root; prop. to *be fat*, i.e. (fig.) *silly*:—be foolish {1x}. See: TWOT—1011; BDB—492d.

3689. כֶּסֶל {13x} **keçel**, *keh'-sel*; from 3688; prop. *fatness*, i.e. by impl. (lit.) the *loin* (as the seat of the leaf *fat*) or (gen.) the *viscera*; also (fig.) *silliness* or (in a good sense) *trust*: flank {6x}, hope {3x}, folly {2x}, loins {1x}, confidence {1x}.

Kecel means "stupidity; imperturbability; confidence." **(1)** It means "stupidity": "I applied mine heart to know, and to search, and to seek out wisdom, and the reason *of things*, and to know the wickedness of folly, even of foolishness" (Eccl 7:25); and **(2)** "confidence": "For the LORD shall be thy confidence, and shall keep thy foot from being taken" (Prov 3:26). **(3)** The meaning of "confidence" also appears in Job 31:24: "If I have made gold my hope. . . ." See: TWOT—1011a; BDB—492d.

3690. כִּסְלָה {2x} **kiçlâh**, *kis-law'*; fem. of 3689; in a good sense, *trust*; in a bad one, *silliness:*—confidence {1x}, folly {1x}. See: TWOT—1011b; BDB—493a.

3691. כִּסְלֵו {2x} **Kîçlêv**, *kis-lave';* prob. of for. or.; *Kisleu,* the 9th Heb. month:—Chisleu {2x}. See: TWOT—1012; BDB—493b.

3692. כִּסְלוֹן {1x} **Kiçlôwn**, *kis-lone';* from 3688; *hopeful; Kislon,* an Isr.:—Chislon {1x}. See: BDB—493b.

3693. כְּסָלוֹן {1x} **Keçâlôwn**, *kes-aw-lone';* from 3688; *fertile; Kesalon,* a place in Pal.:—Chesalon {1x}. See: BDB—493b.

3694. כְּסֻלּוֹת {1x} **Keçullôwth**, *kes-ool-lōth';* fem. plur. of pass. part. of 3688; *fattened; Kesulloth,* a place in Pal.:—Chesulloth {1x}. See: BDB—493b, 1061d.

3695. כַּסְלֻחִים {2x} **Kaçlûchîym**, *kas-loo'-kheem;* a plur. prob. of for. der.; *Casluchim,* a people cognate to the Eg.:—Casluhim {2x}. See: BDB—493b.

3696. כִּסְלֹת תָּבֹר {1x} **Kiçlôth Tâbôr**, *kis-lōth' taw-bore';* from the fem. plur. of 3689 and 8396; *flanks of Tabor; Kisloth-Tabor,* a place in Pal.:—Chisloth-tabor {1x}. See: BDB—493b, 493c.

3697. כָּסַם {2x} **kâçam**, *kaw-sam';* a prim. root; to *shear:*—× only {1x}, poll {1x}. See: TWOT—1013; BDB—493c. comp. 3765.

3698. כֻּסֶּמֶת {3x} **kuççemeth**, *koos-seh'-meth;* from 3697; *spelt* (from its bristliness as if just *shorn*):—fitches {1x}, rie {2x}. See: TWOT—1013a; BDB—493c.

3699. כָּסַס {1x} **kâçaç**, *kaw-sas';* a prim. root; to *estimate:*—make your count {1x}. See: TWOT—1014; BDB—493c.

3700. כָּסַף {6x} **kâçaph**, *kaw-saf';* a prim. root; prop. to *become pale,* i.e. (by impl.) to *pine* after; also to *fear:*—[have] desire {2x}, be greedy {1x}, long {2x}, sore {1x}.

Kacaph means "to long for" in the sense of "to be pale by reason of longing": "And now, though thou wouldest needs be gone, because thou sore longedst after thy father's house, yet wherefore hast thou stolen my gods?" (Gen 31:30). See: TWOT—1015; BDB—493d.

3701. כֶּסֶף {403x} **keçeph**, *keh'-sef;* from 3700; *silver* (from its *pale* color); by impl. *money:*—silver {287x}, money {112x}, price {1x}, silverlings {1x}. money, price, silver (-ling).

Keceph means "silver; money; price; property." **(1)** This word represents the "metal ore silver": "Take away the dross from the silver, and there shall come forth a vessel for the finer" (Prov 25:4; cf. Job 28:1). **(2)** *Keceph* may signify the "metal silver," or what has been refined from silver ore: "And the servant brought forth jewels of silver, and jewels of gold . . ." (Gen 24:53). **(3)** As a precious metal, "silver" was not as valuable as gold—probably because it is not so rare: "And all king Solomon's drinking vessels were of gold, and all the vessels of the house of the forest of Lebanon were of pure gold; none were of silver: it was nothing accounted of in the days of Solomon" (1 Kin 10:21). **(4)** "Silver" was often a form of wealth. This is the meaning of *keceph* in Gen 13:2 (the first biblical occurrence): "And Abram was very rich in cattle, in silver, and in gold." **(5)** Silver pieces (not coins) were used as money: "Then Joseph commanded to fill their sacks with corn, and to restore every man's money into his sack . . ." (Gen 42:25).

(6) Frequently the word absolutely (by itself) and in the singular form means "pieces of silver": "Behold, I have given thy brother a thousand pieces of silver . . ." (Gen 20:16). **(7)** In Lev 25:50 the word is used in the general sense of "money, value, price": "And he shall reckon with him that bought him from the year that he was sold to him unto the year of jubilee: and the price of his sale shall be according unto the number of years. . . ." **(8)** Since it was a form of wealth, "silver" often was one of the spoils of war: "The kings came *and* fought, then fought the kings of Canaan in Taanach by the waters of Megiddo; they took no gain of money" (Judg 5:19). **(9)** This word may be used in the sense of "valuable property": "Notwithstanding, if he [the slave who has been beaten] continue a day or two, he shall not be punished: for he is his money" (Ex 21:21). **(10)** *Keceph* sometimes represents the color "silver": "Though ye have lain among the pots, yet shall ye be as the wings of a dove covered with silver, and her feathers with yellow gold" (Ps 68:13). See: TWOT—1015a; BDB—494a.

3702. כְּסַף {13x} **keçaph** (Aram.), *kes-af';* corresp. to 3701:—money {1x}, silver {12x}. See: TWOT—2794; BDB—1097c.

3703. כָּסִפְיָא {2x} **Kâçiphyâ'**, *kaw-sif-yaw';* perh. from 3701; *silvery; Casiphja,* a place in Bab.:—Casiphia {2x}. See: BDB—494d.

3704. כֶּסֶת {2x} **keçeth**, *keh'-seth;* from 3680; a *cushion* or pillow (as *covering* a seat or bed):—pillow {2x}. See: TWOT—1009a; BDB—492c, 492d.

3705. כְּעַן {13x} **ke'an** (Aram.), *keh-an';* prob. from 3652; *now:*—now {12x}, now therefore {1x}. See: TWOT—2795; BDB—1097c, 1107b.

3706. כְּעֶנֶת {4x} **ke'eneth** (Aram.), *keh-eh'-neth;* or

כְּעֶת **ke'eth** (Aram.), *keh-eth';* fem. of 3705; *thus* (only in the formula "and *so forth*"):—at such a time {4x}. See: TWOT—2796; BDB—1097c, 1107b, 1107c, 1108a.

3707. כָּעַס **kâ'aç**, *kaw-as';* a prim. root; to *trouble;* by impl. to *grieve, rage, be indignant:*—anger {43x}, provoke {3x}, angry {2x}, grieved {1x}, indignation {1x}, sorrow {1x}, vex {1x}, wrath {1x}, wroth {1x}.

Ka'ac means "to provoke, vex, make angry." **(1)** A word that is characteristic of the Book of Deuteronomy, it seems fitting that *ka'ac* is found for the first time in the Old Testament in that book: ". . . To provoke him to anger" (Deut 4:25). **(2)** The word is characteristic also of the books of Jeremiah and Kings. **(3)** A review of the uses of this verb shows that around 80 percent of them involve Yahweh's "being provoked to anger" by Israel's sin, especially its worship of other gods. One such example is in 2 Kin 23:19: "And all the houses also of the high places that were in the cities of Samaria, which the kings of Israel had made to provoke the Lord to anger, Josiah took away. . . ." See: TWOT—1016; BDB—494d.

3708. כַּעַס {25x} **ka'aç**, *kah'-as;* or (in Job)

כַּעַשׂ **ka'as**, *kah'-as;* from 3707; *vexation:*—grief {7x}, provocation {4x}, wrath {4x}, sorrow {3x}, anger {2x}, angry {1x}, indignation {1x}, provoking {1x}, sore {1x}, spite {1x}. See: TWOT—1016a; BDB—495b.

כְּעֶת **ke'eth**. See 3706.

3709. כַּף {191x} **kaph**, *kaf;* from 3721; the hollow *hand* or palm (so of the *paw* of an animal, of the *sole,* and even of the *bowl* of a dish or sling, the *handle* of a bolt, the *leaves* of a palm-tree); fig. *power:*—hand {127x}, spoon {24x}, sole {19x}, palm {5x}, hollow {3x}, handful {2x}, apiece {1x}, branches {1x}, breadth + 4096 {1x}, clouds {1x}, misc. {7x} = + foot, handle, [-led]), middle, paw, power.

Kaph means "palm (of hand)." **(1)** Basically, *kaph* represents the "palm," the hollow part of the hand as distinguished from its fingers, thumbs, and back. **(1a)** Thus we read that part of the ritual for cleansing a leper is that a "priest shall take some of the log of oil, and pour it into the palm of his own left hand" (Lev 14:15). **(1b)** The word represents the entire inside of the hand when it is cupped, or the "hollow of the hand." God told Moses: "While my glory passeth by, that I will put thee in a clift of the rock, and will cover thee with my hand while I pass by" (Ex 33:22; cf. Ps 139:5). **(2)** This word means fist, specifically the inside of a fist. The woman of Zarephath told Elijah: "I have not a cake, but a handful of meal in a barrel, and a little oil in a cruse . . ." (1 Kin 17:12). This was, indeed, a very small amount of flour—enough for only one little biscuit. **(3)** *Kaph* also refers to the flat of the hand, including the fingers and the thumb. These are what one claps together in joy and applause: "And he brought forth the king's son, and put the crown upon him, and gave him the testimony; and they made him king, and anointed him; and they clapped their hands, and said, God save the king" (2 Kin 11:12). **(4)** Clapping the hands may also be an expression of scorn and contempt (Num 24:10).

(5) The flat of the hands may be raised heavenward in prayer to symbolize one's longing to receive. Moses told Pharaoh: "As soon as I am gone out of the city, I will spread abroad my hands unto the Lord . . ." (Ex 9:29). **(6)** This word can suggest the inside part of a hand grasp as distinguished from the hand as a whole: "And the Lord said unto Moses, Put forth thine hand, and take it by the tail. And he put forth his hand, and caught it, and it became a rod in his hand" (Ex 4:4). **(7)** A mutual hand grasp may signify entrance into a pledge (Prov 6:1). **(8)** To take one's life (5315 - nepesh) into one's own hands is to put oneself into danger (Judg 12:3). **(9)** In many passages *kaph* is synonymous with the entire hand. Jacob tells Laban that "God hath seen . . . the labor of my hands . . ." (Gen 31:42). **(10)** Perhaps the same nuance occurs in passages such as Gen 20:5: "In the integrity of my heart and innocency of my hands have I done this." **(10)** The word may be used symbolically and figuratively meaning "power." **(10a)** Gideon complained to the Angel of the Lord that "now the Lord hath forsaken us, and delivered us into the hands [the power] of the Midianites" (Judg 6:13). **(10b)** Israel was not literally in the Midianites' hands but was dominated by them and under their control. **(11)** Once the word represents animal paws: "And whatsoever goeth upon his paws, among all manner of beasts that go on all four, those are unclean unto you . . ." (Lev 11:27).

(12) In many passages *kaph* signifies the sole of the foot, the hollow part. This meaning appears in Gen 8:9 (first biblical appearance): "But the dove found no rest for the sole of her foot . . ." (cf. Josh 3:13 where the word is used of the sole of a human foot). **(13)** Various hollow, bending, or beaten objects are represented by *kaph.* **(13a)** First, it is used of a thigh joint: "And when he [the Angel of the Lord] saw that he prevailed not against him [Jacob], he touched the hollow of his thigh; and the hollow of Jacob's thigh was out of joint, as he wrestled with him" (Gen 32:25). **(13b)** Second, a certain shaped pan or vessel is called a *kaph:* "And thou shalt make the dishes thereof, and spoons thereof, and covers thereof, and bowls thereof, to cover withal: of pure gold shalt thou make them" (Ex 25:29). **(13c)** Third, the word is used of the hollow of a sling: ". . . And the souls of thine enemies, them shall he sling out, as out of the middle of a sling" (1Sa 25:29). **(13d)** Next, the huge hand-shaped branches of palm trees are represented by the word: "And ye shall take you on the first day the boughs of goodly trees, branches of palm trees, and the boughs of thick trees . . ." (Lev 23:40). **(13e)** Finally, in Song 5:5 this word represents the bent piece of metal or wood which forms a door handle. See: TWOT—1022a; BDB—495b, 496a.

3710. כֵּף {2x} **kêph**, *kafe;* from 3721; a hollow *rock:*—rock {2x}. See: TWOT—1017; BDB—495b.

3711. כָּפָה {1x} **kâphâh**, *kaw-faw';* a p im. root; prop. to *bend,* i.e. (fig.) to *tame* or subdue:—pacify {1x}. See: TWOT—1018; BDB—495c.

3712. כִּפָּה {3x} **kippâh**, *k p-paw';* fem. of 3709; a *leaf* of a palm-tree:—branch {3x}. See: TWOT—1022b; BDB—495c, 497a.

3713. כְּפוֹר {9x} **k**^{e}**phôwr**, *kef-ore';* from 3722; prop. a *cover,* i.e. (by impl.) a *tankard* (or *covered* goblet); also white *frost* (as *covering* the ground):—bason {6x}, hoar (-y) frost {3x}. See: TWOT—1026a, 1026b; BDB—499b.

3714. כָּפִיס {1x} **kâphîyç**, *kaw-fece;* from an unused root mean. to *connect;* a *girder:*—beam {1x}. See: TWOT—1021a; BDB—496a.

3715. כְּפִיר {32x} **k**^{e}**phîyr**, *kef-eer';* from 3722; a *village* (as *covered* in by walls); also a young *lion* (perh. as *covered* with a mane):—young {1x}, lion {30x}, villages {1x}. See: TWOT—1025a, 1025d; BDB—498d. comp. 3723.

3716. כְּפִירָה {4x} **K**^{e}**phîyrâh**, *kef-ee-raw';* fem. of 3715; the *village* (always with the art.); *Kephirah,* a place in Pal.:—Chephirah {4x}. See: BDB—499a.

3717. כָּפַל {5x} **kâphal**, *kaw-fal';* a prim. root; to *fold* together; fig. to *repeat:*—double {5x}. See: TWOT—1019; BDB—495c.

3718. כֶּפֶל {3x} **kephel**, *keh'-fel;* from 3717; a *duplicate:*—double {3x}. See: TWOT—1019a; BDB—495c.

3719. כָּפַן {1x} **kâphan**, *kaw-fan';* a prim. root; to *bend:*—bend {1x}. See: TWOT—1020; BDB—495d.

3720. כָּפָן {2x} **kâphân**, *kaw-fawn';* from 3719; *hunger* (as making to *stoop* with emptiness and pain):—famine {2x}. See: TWOT—1020a; BDB—495d.

3721. כָּפַף {5x} **kâphaph**, *kaw-faf';* a prim. root; to *curve:*—bow down (self) {4x}, bow {1x}.

Kaphaph means "to bend, bow down." **(1)** This word appears 5 times in biblical poetry. **(2)** The verb occurs in Is 58:5: ". . . is it to bow down his head as a bulrush, and to spread sackcloth and ashes under him?" See: TWOT—1022; BDB—496a.

3722. כָּפַר {102x} **kâphar**, *kaw-far';* a prim. root; to *cover* (spec. with bitumen); fig. to *expiate* or *condone,* to *placate* or *cancel:*—atonement {71x}, purge {7x}, reconciliation {4x}, reconcile {3x}, forgive {3x}, purge away {2x}, pacify {2x}, atonement . . . made {2x}, merciful {2x}, cleansed {1x}, disannulled {1x}, appease {1x}, put off {1x}, pardon {1x}, pitch {1x}.

Kaphar means to cover over, propitiate, ransom, atone, expiate." **(1)** *Kaphar* has an initial secular and non-theological range quite parallel to padah (6299). **(1a)** In addition, however, *kaphar* became a technical term in Israel's sacrificial rituals. **(1b)** On its most basic level of meaning, *kaphar* denotes a material transaction or "ransom." **(2)** Sometimes man is the subject of *kaphar.* **(2a)** In 2 Sa 21:3, David asks the Gibeonites, ". . . And wherewith shall I make the atonement, that ye may bless the inheritance of the Lord?" He receives in answer the advice to hang seven of Saul's sons in compensation. **(2b)** In Ex 32:30, Moses ascends the mountain yet a third time in an effort to "make an atonement" for the people's sin (apparently merely by intercession, although this is not explicitly stated). **(2c)** Is 27:9 speaks of "purging" Israel's guilt by banishing idolatrous objects. **(2d)** In Num 25:13, Phinehas is said to have "made an atonement for the children of Israel" by spearing a couple during orgiastic worship of Baal.

(3) God is often the subject of *kaphar* in this general sense, too. **(3a)** In 2 Chr 30:18, Hezekiah prays for God to "pardon" those who were not ritually prepared for the Passover. **(3b)** At the conclusion of the Song of Moses, Yahweh is praised because He "will be merciful (3722) unto his land, *and* to his people. **(3c)** Similar general uses of the word appear in Ps 65:3; 78:38; and Dan 9:24. **(4)** Jeremiah once uses *kaphar* to pray bitterly that Yahweh not "forgive" the iniquity of those plotting to slay him (Jer 18:23). **(5)** In Ps 79:9 the word means "to purge" sin. **(6)** Most often *kaphar* is used in connection with specific rites, and the immediate subject is a priest. All types of ritual sacrifice are explained in terms of *kaphar.* **(6a)** We find the priests' smearing of blood on the altar during the "sin offering" (2403 - chatta't) described as "atonement" (Ex 29: 36–37; Lev 4:20, 31; 10:17; Num 28:22; 29:5; Neh 10:33).

(6b) The use of blood is not quite so prominent in sacrifices, but the relation to "atonement" still holds. It is clearly true of the "guilt offering" (Lev 5:16, 18; 6:7; 7:7; 14:21; 19:22; Num 5:8). **(6c)** The principle holds even when the poor cannot afford an animal or birds, and they sacrifice only a little flour—i.e., where obviously no blood is involved (Lev 5:11–13). **(7)** Making "atonement" (*kaphar*) is also part of the purpose of the "burnt offering" (Lev 1:4; Num 15:25). **(8)** The only major type of sacrifice not classified an "atonement" in Leviticus is the "cereal offering" (4503 - minchah) of chapter 2; but Eze 45:15, 17 does include it under that heading. **(9)** First Chr 6:49 applies the concept to the priestly ministry in general. **(10)** The connection of all of the rituals with *kaphar* peaks in the complex ceremony of the annual Day of Atonement (Yom Kippur), as described in detail in Lev 16. **(11)** All the sacrifices in the world would not satisfy God's righteousness (e.g., Mic 6:7; Ps 50:7–15). **(11a)** Hence God alone can provide an atonement for sin, by which His wrath is assuaged. **(11b)** The righteous God is neither implacable nor capricious, but provides Himself the "ransom" or substitute sacrifice that would satisfy Him. **(11c)** The priest at the altar represents God Himself, bringing the requisite offering before God; sacrifice is not essentially man's action, but God's own act of pardoning mercy. **(12)** *Kaphar* is first found in Gen 6:14, where it is used in its primary sense of "to cover over." Here God gives Noah instructions concerning the ark, including, "Pitch it within and without with pitch." **(13)** Most uses of the word, however, involve the theological meaning of "covering over," often with the blood of a sacrifice, in order to atone for some sin. This means that the "covering over" hides the sin from God's until the death of Christ takes away the sin of the world (cf. Jn 1:29; Heb 10:4).

(14) As might be expected, this word occurs more frequently in the Book of Leviticus than in any other book, since Leviticus deals with the ritual sacrifices that were made to atone for sin. **(14a)** For example, Lev 4:13–21 gives instructions for bringing a young bull to the tent of meeting for a sin offering. **(14b)** After the elders laid their hands on the bull (to transfer the people's sin to the bull), the bull was killed. **(14c)** The priest then brought some of the blood of the bull into the tent of meeting and sprinkled it seven times before the veil. **(14d)** Some of the blood was put on the horns of the altar and the rest of the blood was poured at the base of the altar of burnt offering. **(14e)** The fat of the bull was then burned on the altar. **(14f)** The bull itself was to be burned outside the camp. **(14g)** By means of this ritual, "the priest shall make an atonement [*kaphar*] for them, and it shall be forgiven them" (Lev 4:20).

(15) The term "atonement" is found at least 16 times in Lev 16, the great chapter concerning the Day of Atonement. **(15a)** Before anything else, the high priest had to "make atonement" for himself and his house by offering a bull as a sin offering. **(15b)** After lots were cast upon the two goats, one was sent away into the wilderness as an atonement (v. 10), while the other was sacrificed and its blood sprinkled on the mercy seat as an atonement for the people (vv. 15–20). **(15c)** The Day of Atonement was celebrated only once a year. **(15d)** Only on this day could the high priest enter the holy of holies of the tabernacle or temple on behalf of the people of Israel and make atonement for them. **(16)** Sometimes atonement for sin was made apart from or without blood offerings. **(16a)** During his vision-call experience, Isaiah's lips were touched with a coal of fire taken from the altar by one of the seraphim. With that, he was told, "Thy sin is purged [*kaphar*]" (Is 6:7). **(16b)** Isaiah's sin of unclean lips was purged (6:5); not sin purged unto salvation. See: TWOT—23, 1024, 1025, 1026; BDB—497b, 498b.

3723. כָּפָר {2x} **kâphâr**, *kaw-fawr';* from 3722; a *village* (as *protected* by walls):—village {2x}. See: TWOT—1025c; BDB—499a. comp. 3715.

3724. כֹּפֶר {17x} **kôpher**, *ko'-fer;* from 3722; prop. a *cover,* i.e. (lit.) a *village* (as *covered* in); (spec.) *bitumen* (as used for *coating*), and the *henna* plant (as used for *dyeing*); fig. a *redemption*-price:—ransom {8x}, satisfaction {2x}, bribe {2x}, camphire {2x}, pitch {1x}, sum of money {1x}, village {1x}. See: TWOT—1025b; BDB—497a, 498d, 499a.

3725. כִּפֻּר {8x} **kippûr**, *k p-poor';* from 3722; *expiation* (only in plur.):—atonement {8x}. See: TWOT—1023b; BDB—498c.

3726. כְּפַר הָעַמּוֹנִי {1x} **K**^{e}**phar hâ-ʿAmmôwnîy**, *kef-ar' haw-am-mo-nee';* from 3723 and 5984, with the art. interposed; *village of the Ammonite; Kefar-ha-Ammoni,* a place in Pal.:—Chefar-haamonai {1x}. See: BDB—499a.

3727. כַּפֹּרֶת {27x} **kappôreth**, *kap-po'-reth;* from 3722; a *lid* (used only of the *cover* of the sacred Ark):—mercy seat {26x}, mercy seatward {1x}.

Kapporeth, as a noun, means "mercy seat; throne of mercy." **(1)** It refers to a slab of gold that rested on top of the ark of the covenant.

(1a) Images of two cherubims stood on this slab, facing each other. **(1b)** This slab of gold represented the throne of God and symbolized His real presence in the worship shrine. **(1c)** On the Day of Atonement, the high priest sprinkled the blood of the sin offering on it, apparently symbolizing the blood's reception by God. **(1d)** Thus the *kapporeth* was the central point at which Israel, through its high priest, could come into the presence of God. **(2)** This is further seen in the fact that the temple proper was distinguished from its porches and other accompanying structures by the name "place of the mercy seat (*kapporeth*)" (1Chr 28:11). See: TWOT—1023c; BDB—498c.

3728. כָּפַשׁ {1x} **kâphash**, *kaw-fa h';* a prim. root; to *tread* down; fig. to *humiliate:*—cover {1x}. See: TWOT—1027; BDB—499b.

3729. כְּפַת {4x} **k^{e}phath** (Aram.), *kef-ath';* a root of uncert. correspondence; to *fetter:*—bind {4x}. See: TWOT—2798; BDB—1097c.

3730. כַּפְתֹּר {18x} **kaphtôr**, *kaf-tore';* or (Am. 9:1)

כַּפְתּוֹר **kaphtôwr**, *kaf-tore';* prob. from an unused root mean. to *encircle;* a *chaplet;* but used only in an architectonic sense, i.e. the *capital* of a column, or a wreath-like *button* or *disk* on the candelabrum:—knop {16x}, (upper) lintel {2x}. See: TWOT—1029; BDB—499b.

3731. כַּפְתֹּר {3x} **Kaphtôr**, *kaf-tore';* or (Am. 9:7)

כַּפְתּוֹר **Kaphtôwr**, *kaf-tore';* appar. the same as 3730; *Caphtor* (i.e. a *wreath*-shaped island), the orig. seat of the Philistines:—Caphtor {3x}. See: TWOT—1028; BDB—499c.

3732. כַּפְתֹּרִי {3x} **Kaphtôrîy**, *kaf-to-ree';* patrial from 3731; a *Caphtorite* (collect.) or native of Caphtor:—Caphthorim {1x}, Caphtorim (-s) {1x}. See: BDB—499c.

3733. כַּר {16x} **kar**, *kar;* from 3769 in the sense of *plumpness;* a *ram* (as *full-grown* and *fat*), incl. a *battering-ram* (as *butting*); hence, a *meadow* (as *for sheep*); also a *pad* or camel's saddle (as *puffed out*):—captain {1x}, furniture {1x}, lamb {10x}, (large) pasture {2x}, ram {2x}. Syn.: 352. See: TWOT—1046a; BDB—468b, 499c, 503a. See also 1033, 3746.

3734. כֹּר {9x} **kôr**, *kore;* from the same as 3564; prop. a deep round *vessel,* i.e. (spec.) a *cor* or measure for things dry:—cor {1x}, measure {8x}. See: TWOT—1031; BDB—499d, 1096d. Aram. the same.

3735. כְּרָא {1x} **kârâʾ** (Aram.), *kaw-raw';* prob. corresp. to 3738 in the sense of *piercing* (fig.); to *grieve:*—be grieved {1x}. See: TWOT—2799; BDB—1097d.

3736. כִּרְבֵּל {1x} **karbêl**, *kar-bale';* from the same as 3525; to *gird* or *clothe:*—clothed {1x}. See: TWOT—1032; BDB—499d, 1097d.

3737. כַּרְבְּלָא {1x} **karb^{e}lâʾ** (Aram.), *kar-bel-aw';* from a verb corresp. to that of 3736; a *mantle:*—hat {1x}. See: TWOT—2800; BDB—1097d.

3738. כָּרָה {16x} **kârâh**, *kaw-raw';* a prim. root; prop. to *dig;* fig. to *plot;* gen. to *bore* or *open:*—dig {12x}, make (a banquet) {2x}, pierce {1x}, open {1x}. See: TWOT—1033, 1034, 1035; BDB—456c, 468c, 500a.

3739. כָּרָה {4x} **kârâh**, *kaw-raw';* usually assigned as a prim. root, but prob. only a special application of 3738 (through the common idea of *planning* impl. in a bargain); to *purchase:*—buy {2x}, prepared {1x}, banquet {1x}. See: TWOT—1034; BDB—500b.

3740. כֵּרָה {1x} **kêrâh**, *kay-raw';* from 3739; a *purchase:*—provision {1x}. See: TWOT—1035a; BDB—500c.

3741. כָּרָה {1x} **kârâh**, *kaw-raw';* fem. of 3733; a *meadow:*—cottage {1x}. See: TWOT—1033a; BDB—500b, 504d.

3742. כְּרוּב {91x} **k^{e}rûwb**, *ker-oob';* of uncert. der.; a *cherub* or imaginary figure:—cherub {27x}, [*plur.*] cherubims {64x}. See: TWOT—1036; BDB—500c.

3743. כְּרוּב {2x} **K^{e}rûwb**, *ker-oob';* the same as 3742; *Kerub,* a place in Bab.:—Cherub {2x}. See: BDB—500c.

3744. כָּרוֹז {1x} **kârôwz** (Aram.), *kaw-roze';* from 3745; a *herald:*—herald {1x}. See: TWOT—2802; BDB—1097d.

3745. כְּרַז {1x} **k^{e}raz** (Aram.), *ker-az';* prob. of Gr. or. (κηρύσσω); to *proclaim:*—make a proclamation {1x}. See: TWOT—2801; BDB—1097d.

3746. כָּרִי {3x} **kârîy**, *kaw-ree';* perh. an abridged plur. of 3733 in the sense of *leader* (of the flock); a *life-guardsman:*—captains {2x}, Cherethites {1x}. See: BDB—501b.

3747. כְּרִית {2x} **K^{e}rîyth**, *ker-eeth';* from 3772; a *cut; Kerith,* a brook of Pal.:—Cherith {2x}. See: BDB—501b, 504d.

3748. כְּרִיתוּת {4x} **k^{e}rîythûwth**, *ker-ee-thooth';* from 3772; a *cutting* (of the matrimonial bond), i.e. *divorce:*—divorce {3x}, divorcement {1x}.

Keriythuwth, refers to a "bill of divorcement." **(1)** This word implies the cutting off of a marriage by means of a "bill of divorcement": "When a man hath taken a wife, and married her, and it come to pass that she find no favor in his eyes, because he hath found some uncleanness in her: then let him write her a bill of divorcement, and give it in her hand, and send her out of his house" (Deut 24:1). Syn.: 1644. See: TWOT—1048a; BDB—501b, 504d.

3749. כַּרְכֹּב {2x} **karkôb**, *kar-kobe';* expanded from the same as 3522; a *rim* or top margin:—compass {2x}. See: TWOT—1038a; BDB—501b.

3750. כַּרְכֹּם {1x} **ka kôm**, *kar-kome';* prob. of for. or.; the *crocus:*—saffron {1x}. See: TWOT—1039; BDB—501b.

3751. כַּרְכְּמִישׁ {3x} **Kark^{e}mîysh**, *kar-kem-eesh';* of for. der.; *Karkemish,* a place in Syria:—Carchemish {3x}. See: BDB—501c.

3752. כַּרְכַּס {1x} **Karkaç**, *kar-kas';* of Pers. or.; *Karkas,* a eunuch of Xerxes:—Carcas {1x}. See: BDB—501c.

3753. כִּרְכָּרָה {1x} **karkârâh**, *kar-kaw-raw';* from 3769; a *dromedary* (from its *rapid* motion as if dancing):—swift beast {1x}. See: TWOT—1046b; BDB—501c, 503a.

3754. כֶּרֶם {93x} **kerem**, *keh'-rem;* from an unused root of uncert. mean.; a *garden* or *vineyard:*—vines {3x}, (increase of the) vineyard (-s) {89x}, vintage {1x}.

Kerem means "vineyard." **(1)** The first occurrence is in Gen 9:20: "And Noah began *to be* an husbandman, and he planted a vineyard:" **(2)** Isaiah gives a vivid description of the work involved in the preparation, planting, and cultivation of a "vineyard" (Is 5:1–7). **(2a)** The "vineyard" was located on the slopes of a hill (Is 5:1). **(2b)** The soil was cleared of stones before the tender vines were planted (Is 5:2). **(2c)** A watchtower provided visibility over the "vineyard" (Is 5:2), and **(2d)** a winevat and place for crushing the grapes were hewn out of the rock (Is 5:2). **(2e)** When all the preparations were finished, the "vineyard" was ready and in a few years it was expected to produce crops. **(2f)** In the meantime the *kerem* required regular pruning (Lev 25:3–4). **(2g)** The time between planting and the first crop was of sufficient import as to free the owner from military duty: "And what man is he that hath planted a vineyard, and hath not yet eaten of it?" (Deut 20:6).

(3) The harvest time was a period of hard work and great rejoicing. **(3a)** The enjoyment of the "vineyard" was a blessing of God: "And they shall build houses, and inhabit them; and they shall plant vineyards, and eat the fruit of them" (Is 65:21). **(3b)** The failure of the "vineyard" to produce or the transfer of ownership of one's "vineyard" was viewed as God's judgment: "Forasmuch therefore as your treading is upon the poor, and ye take from him burdens of wheat: ye have built houses of hewn stone, but ye shall not dwell in them; ye have planted pleasant vineyards, but ye shall not drink wine of them" (Amos 5:11; cf. Deut 28:30). **(4)** The words "vineyard" and "olive grove' (2132 - zayit) are often found together in the biblical text. **(4a)** These furnished the two major permanent agricultural activities in ancient Israel, as both required much work and time before the crops came in. **(4b)** God promised that the ownership of the "vineyards" and orchards of the Canaanites was to go to His people as a blessing from Him (Deut 6:11–12).

(5) God's judgment to Israel extended to the "vineyards." **(5a)** The rejoicing in the "vineyard" would cease (Is 16:10) and **(5b)** the carefully cultivated "vineyard" would be turned into a thicket with thorns and briers (cf. Is 32:12–13). **(5c)** The "vineyard" would be reduced to a hiding place of wild animals and a grazing place for goats and wild donkeys (Is 32:14). **(6)** The postexilic hope lay in God's blessings on the agricultural activity of His people: "And I will bring again the captivity of my people of Israel, and they shall build the waste cities, and inhabit them; and they shall plant vineyards, and drink the wine thereof; they shall also make gardens, and eat the fruit of them" (Amos 9:14). **(7)** The "vineyards" were located mainly in the hill country and in the low-lying hill country. The Bible mentions the "vineyard" at Timnath (Judg 14:5), Jezreel (1 Kin 21:1), the hill country of Samaria (Jer 31:5), and even at Engedi (Song 1:14). **(8)** The metaphorical use of *kerem* **(8a)** allows the prophet Isaiah to draw an analogy between the "vineyard" and Israel: "For the vineyard of the Lord of hosts is the house of Israel . . ." (Is 5:7). See: TWOT—1040a; BDB—501c. See also 1021.

3755. כֹּרֵם {5x} **kôrêm**, *ko-rame';* act. part. of an imaginary denom. from 3754; a *vinedresser:*—vine dresser [*as one or two words*] {5x}. See: TWOT—1040; BDB—501d.

3756. כַּרְמִי {8x} **Karmîy**, *kar-mee';* from 3754; *gardener; Karmi,* the name of three Isr.:—Carmi {8x}. See: BDB—501d.

3757. כַּרְמִי {1x} **Karmîy**, *kar-mee';* patron. from 3756; a *Karmite* or desc. of *Karmi:*—Carmites {1x}. See: BDB—502a.

3758. כַּרְמִיל {3x} **karmîyl** *kar-mele';* prob. of for. or.; *carmine,* a deep red:—crimson {3x}. See: TWOT—1043; BDB—502b.

3759. כַּרְמֶל {13x} **karmel**, *kar-mel';* from 3754; a planted *field* (garden, orchard, vineyard or park); by impl. garden *produce:*—fruitful field {7x}, plentiful field {2x}, full ear {1x}, green ear {1x}, full ears of corn {1x}, plentiful {1x}. See: TWOT—1041; BDB—502a.

3760. כַּרְמֶל {26x} **Karmel**, *kar-mel';* the same as 3759; *Karmel,* the name of a hill and of a town in Pal.:—Carmel {26x}. See: TWOT—1042; BDB—502a.

3761. כַּרְמְלִי {5x} **Karmᵉlîy**, *kar-mel-ee';* patron. from 3760; a *Karmelite* or inhab. of Karmel (the town):—Carmelite {5x}. See: BDB—502b.

3762. כַּרְמְלִית {2x} **Karmᵉlîyth**, *kar-mel-eeth';* fem. of 3761; a *Karmelitess* or female inhab. of Karmel:—Carmelitess {2x}. See: BDB—502b.

3763. כְּרָן {2x} **Kᵉrân**, *ker-awn';* of uncert. der.; *Keran,* an aboriginal Idumæan:—Cheran {2x}. See: TWOT—1042; BDB—502b.

3764. כָּרְסֵא {1x} **korçêʾ** (Aram.), *kor-say';* corresp. to 3678; a *throne:*—throne {1x}. See: TWOT—2803; BDB—1097c, 1098a.

3765. כִּרְסֵם {1x} **kirçêm**, *kir-same';* from 3697; to *lay waste:*—waste {1x}. See: TWOT—1013b; BDB—493c, 502b.

3766. כָּרַע {36x} **kâraʿ**, *kaw-rah';* a prim. root; to *bend* the knee; by impl. to *sink,* to *prostrate:*—bow {14x}, . . . down {12x}, fell {2x}, subdued {2x}, brought low {1x}, couched {1x}, feeble {1x}, kneeling {1x}, very {1x}.

Kara' means "to bow, bow down, bend the knee." **(1)** *Kara'* appears for the first time in the deathbed blessing of Jacob as he describes Judah: ". . . He stooped down, he couched as a lion" (Gen 49:9). **(2)** The implication of *kara'* seems to be the bending of one's legs or knees, since a noun meaning "leg" is derived from it. **(3)** To "bow down" to drink was one of the tests for elimination from Gideon's army (Judg 7:5–6). **(4)** Kneeling" was a common attitude for the worship of God (1 Kin 8:54; Ezra 9:5; Is 45:23; cf. Phil. 2:10). **(5)** "Bowing down" before Haman was required by the Persian king's command (Est 3:2–5). **(6)** To "bow down upon" a woman was a euphemism for sexual intercourse (Job 31:10). **(7)** A woman in process of giving birth was said to "bow down": "And his daughter-in-law, Phinehas' wife, was with child, *near* to be delivered: and when she heard the tidings that the ark of God was taken, and that her father-in-law and her husband were dead, she bowed herself and travailed; for her pains came upon her" (1 Sa 4:19). **(8)** Tottering or feeble knees are those that "bend" from weakness or old age: "Thy words have upholden him that was falling, and thou hast strengthened the feeble knees" (Job 4:4). See: TWOT—1044; BDB—502c.

3767. כְּרָעַ {9x} **kârâʿ**, *kaw-raw';* from 3766; the *leg* (from the knee to the ankle) of men or locusts (only in the dual):—leg {9x}. See: TWOT—1044a; BDB—502d.

3768. כַּרְפַּס {1x} **karpaç** *kar-pas';* of for. or.; *byssus* or fine vegetable wool:—green {1x}. See: TWOT—1045; BDB—502d.

3769. כָּרַר {2x} **kârar**, *kaw-rar';* a prim. root; to *dance* (i.e. *whirl*):—dance (-ing) {2x}. Syn.: 2342, 4234. See: TWOT—1046; BDB—502d, 1098a.

3770. כְּרֵשׂ {1x} **kᵉrês**, *ker-ace';* by var. f om 7164; the *paunch* or belly (as *swelling* out):—belly {1x}. See: TWOT—1047a; BDB—503c.

כֹּרֶשׁ **Kôresh**. See 3567.

3771. כַּרְשְׁנָא {1x} **Karshᵉnâʾ**, *kar-shen-aw';* of for. or.; *Karshena,* a courtier of Xerxes:—Carshena {1x}. See: BDB—503c.

3772. כָּרַת {288x} **kârath**, *kaw-rath';* a prim. root; to *cut* (off, down or asunder); by impl. to *destroy* or *consume;* spec. to *covenant* (i.e. make an alliance or bargain, orig. by cutting flesh and passing between the pieces):—cut off {145x}, make {85x}, cut down {23x}, cut {9x}, fail {6x}, destroy {4x}, want {3x}, covenanted {2x}, hew {2x}, misc. {9x}= be chewed, feller, be freed, × lose, perish, × utterly.

Karath means "to cut off, cut down, fell, cut or make (a covenant or agreement)." **(1)** Basically *karath* means "to sever" something from something else by cutting it with a blade. **(1a)** The nuance depends upon the thing being cut off. **(1a1)** In the case of a branch, one "cuts it down" (Num 13:23), and one **(1a2)** "[swings] the axe to cut down the tree" (Deut 19:5). **(1b)** The word is also used of "chopping down" wooden idols (Ex 34:13). **(1c)** *Karath* can signify "chopping off" a man's head and feet (1 Sa 5:4). **(1d)** In Jer 34:18 this verb means "to cut into two pieces." **(1e)** "Cut off" may also imply cutting off in the sense of circumcision. In Ex 4:25 Zipporah took a flint knife and "cut off" her son's foreskin. **(1f)** In a related but different usage this word appears in Num. 11:33, where it means "to chew" meat. **(2)** "To cut off" can mean "to exterminate or destroy." God told Noah that "all flesh [shall never again] be cut off . . . by the waters of a flood . . ." (Gen 9:11–the first occurrence of the word). **(3)** *Karath* can be used of spiritual and social extermination. A person "cut off" in this manner is not necessarily killed but may be driven out of the family and removed from the blessings of the covenant. God told Abraham that "the uncircumcised man child whose flesh of his foreskin is not circumcised, that soul shall be cut off from his people; he hath broken my covenant" (Gen 17:14). **(4)** One of the best known uses of this verb is "to make" a covenant. **(4a)** The process by which God made a covenant with Abraham is called "cutting": "In the same day the Lord made a covenant with Abram . . ." (Gen 15:18). **(4b)** The word "covenant" appears nine times before this in Genesis, but it is not connected with *karath.* **(4c)** Furthermore, hereafter in Genesis and throughout the Bible *karath* is frequently associated with making a covenant. **(4d)** This verb, therefore, constitutes a rather technical term for making a covenant. **(4e)** In Genesis it often alludes to an act by which animals were cut in two and the party taking the oath passed between the pieces.

(5) Later, "cutting" a covenant did not necessarily include this act but seems to be an allusion to the Abrahamic covenantal process (cf. Jer 34:18). **(5a)** In such a covenant the one passing through the pieces pledged his faithfulness to the covenant. **(5b)** If that faithfulness was broken, he called death upon himself, or the same fate which befell the animals. **(6)** In some cases it is quite clear that no literal cutting took place and that *karath* is used in a technical sense of "making an agreement in writing": "And because of all this we make a sure *covenant,* and write *it;* and our princes, Levites, *and* priests, seal *unto it*" (Neh 9:38). See: TWOT—1048; BDB—503c.

3773. כָּרֻתָה {3x} **kârûthâh**, *kaw-rooth-aw';* pass. part. fem. of 3772; something *cut,* i.e. a hewn *timber:*—beam {3x}.

Karuthah means "beams." This noun, which occurs only 3 times, refers to "beams" in the sense of things "cut off" in 1 Kin 6:36: "And he built the inner court with three rows of hewed stone, and a row of cedar beams." See: TWOT—1048b; BDB—503c.

3774. כְּרֵתִי {10x} **Kᵉrêthîy**, *ker-ay-thee';* prob. from 3772 in the sense of *executioner,* a *Kerethite* or *life-guardsman* [comp. 2876] (only collect. in the sing. as plur.):—Cherethites {10x}. See: BDB—504d.

3775. כֶּשֶׂב {13x} **keseb**, *keh'-seb;* appar. by transp. for 3532; a young *sheep:*—lamb {4x}, sheep {9x}. See: TWOT—949; BDB—461a, 505a.

3776. כִּשְׂבָּה {1x} **kisbâh**, *kis-baw';* fem. of 3775; a young *ewe:*—lamb {1x}. See: TWOT—949; BDB—461b, 505a.

3777. כֶּשֶׂד {1x} **Kesed**, *keh'-sed;* from an unused root of uncert. mean.; *Kesed,* a relative of Abraham:—Chesed {1x}. See: BDB—505a.

3778. כַּשְׂדִּי {80x} **Kasdîy**, *kas-dee';* (occasionally with enclitic)

כַּשְׂדִּימָה **Kasdîymâh**, *kas-dee'-maw; toward* (the) *Kasdites* (into Chaldea), patron. from 3777 (only in the plur.); a *Kasdite,* or desc. of Kesed; by impl. a *Chaldæan* (as if so descended); also an *astrologer* (as if proverbial of that people:—Chaldeans {59x}, Chaldees {14x}, Chaldea {7x}. See: BDB—505a, 1098a.

3779. כַּשְׂדָּי {8x} **Kasday** (Aram.), *kas-dah'-ee;* corresp. to 3778; a *Chaldæan* or inhab. of Chaldæa; by impl. a *Magian* or professional astrologer:—Chaldean {8x}. See: BDB—1097c, 1098a.

3780. כָּשָׂה {1x} **kâsâh**, *kaw-saw';* a prim. root; to *grow fat* (i.e. *be covered* with flesh):—be covered {1x}. See: TWOT—1049; BDB—505b. comp. 3680.

3781. כַּשִּׁיל {1x} **kashshîyl** *kash-sheel';* from 3782; prop. a *feller,* i.e. an *axe:*—axes {1x}. See: TWOT—1050a; BDB—506a.

3782. כָּשַׁל {65x} **kâshal**, *kaw-shal';* a prim. root; to *totter* or *waver* (through weakness of the legs, espec. the ankle); by impl. to *falter, stumble,* faint or fall:—fall {27x}, stumble {19x}, cast down {4x}, feeble {4x}, overthrown {2x}, ruin {2x}, bereave + 7921 {1x}, decayed {1x}, faileth {1x}, utterly {1x}, weak {1x}, variant {2x}.

Kashal means "to stumble, stagger, totter, be thrown down." **(1)** It occurs the first time in Lev 26:37: "And they shall fall one upon another. . . ." **(1a)** This use illustrates the basic idea that one "stumbles" because of something or over something. **(1b)** Heavy physical burdens cause one "to stagger": ". . . The children fell under the [loads of] wood" (Lam 5:13). **(2)** This word is often used figuratively to describe the consequences of divine judgment on sin: "Behold, I will lay stumbling blocks before this people, and the fathers and the sons together shall fall upon them . . ." (Jer 6:21). **(3)** Babylon, too, will know God's judgment: "And the most proud shall stumble and fall . . ." (Jer 50:32). **(4)** When the psalmist says: "My knees totter from my fasting" (Ps 109:24, nab), he means: "My knees are weak." See: TWOT—1050; BDB—505b.

3783. כִּשָּׁלוֹן {1x} **kishshâlôwn**, *kish shaw-lone';* from 3782; prop. a *tottering,* i.e. *ruin:*—fall {1x}. See: TWOT—1050b; BDB—506a.

3784. כָּשַׁף {6x} **kâshaph**, *kaw-shaf';* a prim. root; prop. to *whisper* a spell, i.e. to *inchant* or practise magic:—sorcerer {3x}, witches {2x}, use witchcraft {1x}. See: TWOT—1051; BDB—506c.

3785. כֶּשֶׁף {6x} **kesheph**, *keh'-shef;* from 3784; *magic:*—sorcery {2x}, witchcraft {4x}. See: TWOT—1051a; BDB—506c.

3786. כַּשָּׁף {1x} **kashshâh**, *kash-shawf';* from 3784; a *magician:*—sorcerer {1x}. See: TWOT—1051b; BDB—506c.

3787. כָּשֵׁר {3x} **kâshêr**, *kaw-share';* a prim. root; prop. to *be straight* or *right;* by impl. to *be acceptable;* also to *succeed* or *prosper:*—direct {1x}, be right {1x}, prosper {1x}. See: TWOT—1052; BDB—506d.

3788. כִּשְׁרוֹן {3x} **kishrôwn**, *kish-rone';* from 3787; *success, advantage:*—equity {1x}, good {1x}, right {1x}. See: TWOT—1052b; BDB—507a.

3789. כָּתַב {223x} **kâthab**, *kaw-thab';* a prim. root; to *grave,* by impl. to *write* (describe, inscribe, prescribe, subscribe):—describe {7x}, recorded {1x}, prescribed {1x}, subscribe {4x}, write (-ing, -ten) {210x}.

Kathab means "to write, inscribe, describe, take dictation, engrave." **(1)** Basically, this verb represents writing down a message. **(2)** The judgment (ban) of God against the Amalekites was to be recorded in the book (scroll): "And the Lord said unto Moses, Write this for a memorial in a book, and rehearse it in the ears of Joshua: for I will utterly put out the remembrance of Amalek from under heaven" (Ex 17:14—the first biblical occurrence of the word). **(3)** One may "write" upon a stone or "write" a message upon it. Moses told Israel that after crossing the Jordan "thou shalt set thee up great stones, and plaster them with plaster: and thou shalt write upon them all the words of this law . . ." (Deut 27:2–3). **(3a)** This use of the word implies something more than keeping a record of something so that it will be remembered. **(3b)** This is obvious in the first passage because the memory of Amalek is "to be recorded" and also blotted out.

(3c) In such passages "to be recorded," therefore, refers to the unchangeableness and binding nature of the Word of God. **(3d)** God has said it, it is fixed, and it will occur. **(3e)** An extended implication in the case of divine commands is that man must obey what God "has recorded" (Deut 27:2–3). **(3f)** Thus, such uses of the word describe a fixed body of authoritative instruction, or a canon. **(3g)** These 2 passages also show that the word does not tell us anything specific about how the message was composed. **(3g1)** In the first instance Moses seems not to have merely "recorded" as a secretary but "to have written" creatively what he heard and saw. **(3g2)** Certainly in Ex 32:32 the word is used of creative writing by the author; God was not receiving dictation from anyone when He "inscribed" the Ten Commandments. **(3g3)** In Deut 27:2–3 the writers must reproduce exactly what was previously given (as mere secretaries).

(4) Sometimes *kathab* appears to mean "to inscribe" and "to cover with inscription." **(4a)** The 2 tablets of the testimony which were given to Moses by God were "tables of stone, written [fully inscribed] with the finger of God" (Ex 31:18). **(4b)** The verb means not only to write in a book but "to write a book," not just to record something in a few lines on a scroll but to complete the writing. **(4c)** Moses prays: "Yet now, if thou wilt forgive their sin—and if not, blot me, I pray thee, out of thy book which thou hast written" (Ex 32:32). **(4d)** Here "book" probably refers to a scroll rather than a book in the present-day sense. **(5)** Among the special uses of *kathab* is the meaning "to record a survey." **(5a)** At Shiloh, Joshua told Israel to choose three men from each tribe "and they shall arise, and go through the land, and describe it . . ." (Josh 18:4). **(6)** An extended nuance of *kathab* is "to receive dictation": "And Baruch wrote from the mouth of Jeremiah . . ." (Jer 36:4). **(7)** The word can also be used of signing one's signature: "And because of all this we make [are cutting] a sure covenant, and write it; and our princes, Levites, and priests, seal unto it" (Neh 9:38). **(7a)** Thus they "cut," or completed, the agreement by having the representatives sign it. **(7b)** The cutting was the signing. See: TWOT—1053; BDB—507a, 1098a.

3790. כְּתַב {8x} **k^{e}thab** (Aram.), *keth-ab';* corresp. to 3789:—write (-ten) {8x}. See: TWOT—2805; BDB—1098a.

3791. כְּתָב {17x} **kâthâb**, *kaw-thawb';* from 3789; something *written,* i.e. a *writing, record* or *book:*—register {2x}, scripture {1x}, writing {14x}.

Kathab means "something written; register; scripture." **(1)** In 1 Chr 28:19 *kathab* is used to mean "something written," such as an edict: "All this, said David, the Lord made me understand in writing by his hand upon me, even all the works of this pattern." **(2)** The word also refers to a "register": "These sought their register *among* those that were reckoned by genealogy, but they were not found: therefore were they, as polluted, put from the priesthood" (Ezr 2:62), and **(3)** to "scripture": "But I will shew thee that which is noted in the scripture of truth: and *there is* none that holdeth with me in these things, but Michael your prince" (Dan 10:21). See: TWOT—1053a; BDB—508b.

3792. כְּתָב {12x} **k^{e}thâb** (Aram.), *keth-awb';* corresp. to 3791:—prescribing {1x}, writing (-ten) {11x}. See: TWOT—2805a; 1098a.

3793. כְּתֹבֶת {1x} **k^{e}thôbeth**, *keth-o'-beth;* from 3789; a *letter* or other *mark* branded on the skin:—× any [mark]{1x}.

Kethobeth occurs once to mean something inscribed, specifically a "tatooing": "Ye shall not make any cuttings (*kethobeth*) in your flesh for the dead, nor print any marks upon you: I *am* the LORD" (Lev 19:28). See: TWOT—1053b; BDB—508b.

3794. כִּתִּי {8x} **Kittîy**, *kit-tee'* or

כִּתִּיִּי **Kittîyîy**, *kit-tee-ee';* patrial from an unused name denoting Cyprus (only in the plur.); a *Kittite* or Cypriote; hence, an *islander* in gen., i.e. the Greeks or Romans on the shores opposite Pal.:—Chittim {6x}, Kittim {2x}. See: BDB—508c.

3795. כָּתִית {5x} **kâthîyth**, *kaw-theeth';* from 3807; *beaten,* i.e. pure (oil):—beaten {1x}, pure {4x}. See: TWOT—1062a; BDB—508c, 510c.

3796. כֹּתֶל {1x} **kôthel**, *ko'-thel;* from an unused root mean. to *compact;* a *wall* (as *gathering* inmates):—wall {1x}. Syn.: 1444, 1447, 2346, 7023. See: TWOT—1054a; BDB—508c, 1098b.

3797. כְּתַל {2x} **k^{e}thal** (Aram.), *keth-al';* corresp. to 3796:—wall {2x}. See: TWOT—2806; BDB—1098b.

3798. כִּתְלִישׁ {1x} **Kithlîysh**, *kith-leesh';* from 3796 and 376; *wall of a man; Kithlish,* a place in Pal.:—Kithlish {1x}. See: BDB—508c.

3799. כָּתַם {1x} **kâtham**, *kaw-tham';* a prim. root; prop. to *carve* or *engrave,* i.e. (by impl.) to *inscribe* indelibly:—marked {1x}. See: TWOT—1055; BDB—508d.

3800. כֶּתֶם {9x} **kethem**, *keh'-them;* from 3799; prop. something *carved* out, i.e. *ore;* hence, *gold* (pure as orig. mined):—fine gold {4x}, gold {2x}, most {1x}, golden wedge {1x}, pure gold {1x}. Syn.: 1220, 2091, 2742, 6337. See: TWOT—1057; BDB—508d.

3801. כְּתֹנֶת {23x} **k^{e}thôneth**, *keth-o'-neth;* or

כֻּתֹּנֶת **kuttôneth**, *koot-to'-neth;* from an unused root mean. to *cover* [comp. 3802]; a *shirt:*—coat {23x}, garment {5x}, robe {1x}. See: TWOT—1058a; BDB—509a.

3802. כָּתֵף {67x} **kâthêph**, *kaw-thafe';* from an unused root mean. to *clothe;* the *shoulder* (proper, i.e. upper end of the arm; as being the spot where the garments hang); fig. *side-piece* or lateral projection of anything:—side {34x}, shoulders {22x}, shoulderpieces {4x}, undersetters {4x}, corner {2x}, arm {1x}. See: TWOT—1059; BDB—509b.

3803. כָּתַר {7x} **kâthar**, *kaw-thar';* a prim. root; to *enclose;* hence, (in a friendly sense) to *crown,* (in a hostile one) to *besiege;* also to *wait* (as restraining oneself):—compass (about) {3x}, inclosed {1x}, beset me round {1x}, suffer {1x}, crowned {1x}. See: TWOT—1060; BDB—509c.

3804. כֶּתֶר {1x} **kether**, *keh'-ther;* from 3803; prop. a *circlet,* i.e. a *diadem:*—crown {1x}. Syn.: 5850. See: TWOT—1060a; BDB—509d.

3805. כֹּתֶרֶת {1x} **kôthereth**, *ko-theh'-ret;* fem. act. part. of 3803; the *capital* of a column:—chapiter {1x}. See: TWOT—1060c; BDB—509d.

3806. כָּתַשׁ {1x} **kâthash** *kaw-thash';* a prim. root; to *butt* or *pound:*—bray {1x}. See: TWOT—1061; BDB—509d.

3807. כָּתַת {17x} **kâthath**, *kaw-thath';* a prim. root; to *bruise* or violently *strike:*—beat {4x}, destroyed {3x}, beat down {2x}, break in pieces {2x}, smite {2x}, beat in pieces {1x}, discomfited {1x}, crushed {1x}, stamped {1x}. See: TWOT—1062; BDB—510a.

ל

3808. לֹא **lô'**, *lo;* or

לוֹא **lôw'**, *lo;* or

לֹה {76x} **lôh** (Deut. 3:11), *lo;* a prim. particle; *not* (the simple or abs. negation); by impl. *no;* often used with other particles (as follows):—{76x} = not, no, none, nay, never, neither, ere, otherwise, before. See: TWOT—1064; BDB—210b, 518b, 529a, 530a, 1098c, 1099a.

3809. לָא {82x} **lâ'** (Aram.), *law;* or

לָה **lâh** (Aram.) (Dan. 4:32), *law;* corresp. to 3808:—not {49x}, no {9x}, nor {9x}, without {4x}, neither {3x}, none {3x}, cannot + 3202 {1x}, ever {1x}, never + 5957 {1x}, no + 3606 {1x}, nothing {1x}. See: TWOT—2808; BDB—1098c, 1098d, 1099a.

לֻא **lû'**. See 3863.

3810. לֹא דְבָר {3x} **Lô' Dᵉbar**, *lo deb-ar';* or
לוֹ דְבָר **Lôw Dᵉbar** (2 Sa 9:4, 5), *lo deb-ar';* or
לִדְבִר **Lidbîr** (Josh. 13:26), *lid-beer';* [prob. rather
לֹדְבַר **Lôdᵉbar**, *lo-deb-ar'*]; from 3808 and 1699; *pastureless; Lo-Debar,* a place in Pal.:—Lo-debar {3x}. See: BDB—520d, 529a, 530d.

3811. לָאָה {19x} **lâ'âh**, *law-aw';* a prim. root; to *tire;* (fig.) to *be* (or *make*) *disgusted:*—weary {15x}, grieve {2x}, faint {1x}, loath {1x}. See: TWOT—1066; BDB—521a.

3812. לֵאָה {34x} **Lê'âh**, *lay-aw';* from 3811; *weary; Leah,* a wife of Jacob:—Leah {34x}. See: BDB—521b.

לְאוֹם **lᵉôwm**. See 3816.

3813. לָאַט {1x} **lâ'at**, *law-at';* a prim. root; to *muffle:*—cover {1x}. See: TWOT—1067; BDB—521b.

3814. לָאט {1x} **lâ't**, *lawt;* from 3813 (or perh. for act part. of 3874); prop. *muffled,* i.e. *silently:*—softly {1x}. See: TWOT—1092a; BDB—521b, 532a.

3815. לָאֵל {1x} **Lâ'êl**, *law-ale';* from the prep. pref. and 410; (belonging) *to God; Laël,* an Isr.:—Lael {1x}. See: BDB—522b.

3816. לְאֹם {35x} **lᵉôm**, *leh-ome'* or
לְאוֹם **lᵉôwm**, *leh-ome';* from an unused root mean. to *gather;* a *community:*—nation {10x}, people {24x}, folk {1x}. This word usually speaks of a race of people (Gen 25:23). See: TWOT—1069a; BDB—522c.

3817. לְאֻמִּים {1x} **Lᵉummîym**, *leh-oom-meem';* plur. of 3816; *communities; Leümmim,* an Arabian:—Leummim {1x}. See: BDB—522c.

3818. לֹא עַמִּי {2x} **Lô' 'Ammîy**, *lo am-mee';* from 3808 and 5971 with pron. suff.; *not my people; Lo-Ammi,* the symbol. name of a son of Hosea:—Lo-ammi {2x}. See: BDB—520d.

3819. לֹא רֻחָמָה {2x} **Lô' Rûchâmâh**, *lo roo-khaw-maw';* from 3808 and 7355; *not pitied; Lo-Ruchamah,* the symbol. name of a son of Hosea:—Lo-ruhamah {1x}. See: BDB—520d, 933d.

3820. לֵב {592x} **lêb**, *labe;* a form of 3824; the *heart;* also used (fig.) very widely for the feelings, the will and even the intellect; likewise for the *center* of anything:—heart {508x}, mind {12x}, midst {11x}, understanding {10x}, hearted {7x}, wisdom {6x}, comfortably {4x}, well {4x}, considered {2x}, friendly {2x}, kindly {2x}, stouthearted + 47 {2x}, care + 7760 {2x}, misc. {20x} = consent, courage, courageous, × heed, × I, × regard, regarded, × themselves, × unawares, willingly.

I. *Leb* as a noun: Summary: The heart includes not only the motives, feelings, affections, and desires, but also the will, the aims, the principles, the thoughts, and the intellect of man. In fact, it embraces the whole inner man, the head never being regarded as the seat of intelligence. While it is the source of all action and the center of all thought and feeling the heart is also described as receptive to the influences both from the outer world and from God Himself. *Leb* means heart; mind; midst. It is used of God (Gen 6:6; Jer 32:41) and man. **(1)** Heart may refer to the organ of the body (Ex 28:29; 2 Sa 18:14). **(2)** *Leb* may also refer to the inner part or middle of a thing (Ex 15:8; Deut 4:11). **(3)** *Leb* is used of the man himself or his personality (Gen 17:17); or **(4)** his seat of desire, inclination, or will (Ex 7:14; 35:5). **(5)** Two people are in agreement when their hearts are right with each other (2 Kin 10:15).

(6) The heart is regarded as the seat of emotions (Deut 6:5; Ex 4:14); so there are **(6a)** merry hearts (Judg 16:25), **(6b)** fearful hearts (Is 35:4), and **(6c)** hearts that trembled (1 Sa 4:13). **(7)** The heart could be regarded as the seat of knowledge and wisdom and as a synonym of "mind" when "heart" appears with the verb "to know" (Deut 29:4; 1 Kin 3:9; cf. 4:29). **(8)** Memory is the activity of the heart (Job 22:22). **(10)** It may be the seat of conscience and moral character (Job 27:6; 2 Sa 24:10). **(11)** It is the fountain of man's deeds (Gen 20:5; 1 Kin 3:6; Is 38:3). **(12)** Rebellion and pride reside in the heart (Gen 8:21; Eze 28:2). **(13)** God controls the heart: He **(13a)** gives a new one (Eze 36:26); **(13b)** creates a clean one (Ps 51:10); **(13c)** unites the believer's heart to fear His name (Ps 86:11); and **(13d)** triest the heart (1 Chr 29:17). **(14)** Hence God's people seek His approval (Ps 26:2). **(15)** The heart stands for the inner being of man, the man himself, and is the fountain of all he does (Prov 4:4). All his thoughts, desires, words, and actions flow from deep within him. Yet a man cannot understand his own heart (Jer 17:9).

II. *Leb,* as an adverb, means "tenderly; friendly; comfortably." **(1)** *Leb* is used as an adverb in Gen 34:3: "And his soul clave unto Dinah . . . and he loved the damsel, and spake kindly (*leb*) unto the damsel." **(2)** In Ruth 4:13, the word means "friendly": ". . . thou hast spoken friendly unto thine handmaid. . . ." **(3)** The word means "comfortably" **(3a)** in 2 Chr 30:22: "And Hezekiah spake comfortably unto all the Levites that taught the good knowledge of the LORD: and they did eat throughout the feast seven days, offering peace offerings, and making confession to the LORD God of their fathers." and in **(3b)** Is 40:2 "Speak ye comfortably to Jerusalem, and cry unto her, that her warfare is accomplished, that her iniquity is pardoned: for she hath received of the LORD's hand double for all her sins."Syn.: 4578, 5315, 7023, 7130. See: TWOT—1071a; BDB—522, 523a, 524b, 525d, 925c, 1098d.

3821. לֵב {1x} **lêb** (Aram.), *labe;* corresp. to 3820:—heart {1x}. See: TWOT—2809a; BDB—1098d.

3822. לְבָאוֹת {1x} **Lᵉbâ'ôwth**, *leb-aw-ōth';* plur. of 3833; *lionesses; Lebaoth,* a place in Pal.:—Lebaoth {1x}. See: BDB—522d. See also 1034.

3823. לָבַב {5x} **lâbab**, *law-bab';* a prim. root; prop. *to be enclosed* (as if with *fat*); by impl. (as denom. from 3824) to *unheart,* i.e. (in a good sense) *transport* (with love), or (in a bad sense) *stultify;* also (as denom. from 3834) to *make cakes:*—ravished my heart {2x}, make {1x}, made cakes {1x}, be wise {1x}. See: TWOT—1071, 1071d; BDB—525d.

3824. לֵבָב {252x} **lêbâb**, *lay-bawb';* from 3823; the *heart* (as the most interior organ); used also like 3820:—heart {231x}, consider + 7760 {5x}, mind {4x}, understanding {3x}, misc. {9x} = + bethink themselves, breast, comfortably, courage, midst, × unawares.

Lebab, as a noun, means "heart; mind; midst." **(1)** "Heart" is used first of man in Gen 6:5: "And God saw that the wickedness of man was great in the earth, and that every imagination of the thoughts of his heart was only evil continually." **(2)** In Gen 6:6 it is used of God: "And it repented the Lord that he had made man on the earth, and it grieved him at his heart." **(3)** "Heart" may refer to the organ of the body: **(3a)** "And Aaron shall bear the names of the children of Israel in the breastplate of judgment upon his heart, when he goeth in unto the holy place . . ." (Ex 28:29); **(3b)** "[Joab] took three darts in his hand, and thrust them through the heart of Absalom . . ." (2 Sa 18:14); **(3c)** "My heart panteth . . ." (Ps 38:10). **(4)** *Lebab* may also refer to the inner part or middle of a thing: **(4a)** ". . . and the depths were congealed in the heart of the sea" (Ex 15:8); **(4b)** "and the mountain burned with fire in the midst [RSV, "to the heart"] of heaven . . ." (Deut 4:11); **(4c)** "Yea, thou shalt be as he that lieth down in the midst of the sea . . ." (Prov 23:34).

(5) *Lebab* can be used of the inner man, contrasted to the outer man, as **(5a)** in Deut 30:14: "But the word is very nigh unto thee, in thy mouth, and in thy heart, that thou mayest do it" (cf. Joel 2:13); **(5b)** "man looketh on the outward appearance, but the Lord looketh on the heart" (1 Sa 16:7). **(6)** *Lebab* is often compounded with "soul" for emphasis, as in 2 Chr 15:12; "And they entered into a covenant to seek the Lord God of their fathers with all their heart and with all their soul" (cf. 2 Chr 15:15). **(7)** Nepesh (5315 - "soul; life; self") is translated "heart" fifteen times in the KJV. **(7a)** Each time, it connotes the "inner man": **(7b)** "For as he thinketh in his heart [nepesh], so is he" (Prov 23:7). **(8)** *Lebab* can be used of the man himself or his personality: **(8a)** "Then Abraham fell upon his face and laughed, and said in his heart, . . ." (Gen 17:17); **(8b)** ". . . my heart had great experience . . ." (Eccl 1:16). **(8c)** *Lebab* is also used of God in this sense: "And I will give you pastors according to mine heart" (Jer 3:15).

(9) The seat of desire, inclination, or will can be indicated by "heart": **(9a)** "Pharaoh's heart is hardened . . ." (Ex 7:14); **(9b)** "whosoever is of a willing heart, let him bring it . . ." (Ex 35:5; cf. vv. 21, 29); **(9c)** "I will praise thee, O Lord my God, with all my heart . . ." (Ps. 86:12). **(9d)** *Lebab* is also used of God in this sense: ". . . and I will plant them in this land assuredly with my whole heart and with my whole soul" (Jer 32:41). **(10)** Two people are said to be in agreement when their "hearts" are right with each other: "Is thine heart right, as my heart is with thy heart?" (2 Kin 10:15). **(11)** In 2 Chr 24:4, "Joash was minded to repair the house of the Lord" (Heb. "had in his heart"). **(12)** The "heart" is regarded as the seat of emotions: **(12a)** "And thou shalt love the Lord thy God with all thine heart, . . ." (Deut 6:5); **(12b)** "and when he [Aaron] seeth thee, he will be glad in his heart" (Ex 4:14; cf. 1 Sa 2:1). **(12b)** So there are **(12b1)** "merry" hearts (Judg 16:25), **(12b2)** "fearful" hearts (Is 35:4), and **(12b3)** hearts that "trembled" (1 Sa 4:13).

(13) The "heart" could be regarded as the seat of knowledge and wisdom and as a synonym of "mind." **(13a)** This meaning often occurs when "heart" appears with the verb "to know": **(13a1)** "Thou shalt also consider [know] in your heart . . ." (Deut 8:5); and **(13a2)** "Yet the Lord hath not given you an heart to perceive [know] . . ." (Deut 29:4). **(13a3)** Solomon prayed, "Give therefore thy servant an understanding heart to judge thy people, that I may discern between good and bad . . ." (1 Kin 3:9; cf. 4:29). **(14)** Memory is the activity of the "heart," as in Job 22:22: ". . . lay up his [God's] words in thine heart." **(15)** The "heart" may be the seat of conscience and moral character. How does one respond to the revelation of God and of the world around him? **(15a)** Job answers: ". . . my heart shall not reproach me as long as I live" (27:6). **(15b)** On the contrary, "David's heart smote him . . ." (2 Sa 24:10). **(16)** The "heart" is the fountain of man's deeds: "in the integrity of my heart and innocency of my hands I have done this" (Gen 20:5; cf. v. 6). **(16a)** David walked "in uprightness of heart" (1 Kin 3:6) and **(16b)** Hezekiah walked "with a perfect heart" (Is 38:3) before God.

(17) Only the man with "clean hands, and a pure heart" (Ps 24:4) can stand in God's presence. **(18)** *Lebab* may refer to the seat of rebellion and pride. God said: ". . . for the imagination of man's heart is evil from his youth" (Gen 8:21). **(18a)** Tyre is like all men: "Because thine heart is lifted up, and thou hast said, I am a God" (Eze 28:2). **(18b)** They all become like Judah, whose "sin . . . is graven upon the table of their heart" (Jer 17:1). **(19)** God controls the "heart." **(19a)** Because of his natural "heart," man's only hope is in the promise of God: "A new heart also will I give you, . . . and I will take away the stony heart out of your flesh, and I will give you a heart of flesh" (Eze 36:26). **(19b)** So the sinner prays: "Create in me a clean heart, O God" (Ps 51:10); **(19c)** and "unite my heart [give me an undivided heart] to fear thy name" (Ps 86:11). **(19d)** Also, as David says, "I know also, my God, that thou triest the heart, and hast pleasure in uprightness" (1 Chr 29:17). **(19e)** Hence God's people seek His approval: ". . . try my reins and my heart" (Ps 26:2).

(20) The "heart" stands for the inner being of man, the man himself. As such, it is the fountain of all he does (Prov 4:4). **(20a)** All his thoughts, desires, words, and actions flow from deep within him. Yet a man cannot understand his own "heart" (Jer 17:9). **(20b)** As a man goes on in his own way, his "heart" becomes harder and harder. But God will circumcise (cut away the uncleanness of) the "heart" of His people, so that they will love and obey Him with their whole being (Deut 30:6). See: TWOT—1071a; BDB—523a, 925a, 1098d.

3825. לְבַב {1x} **lᵉbab** (Aram.), *leb-ab'*; corresp. to 3824:—heart {1x}. See: TWOT—2809b; BDB—1098d.

לְבִבָה **lᵉbîbâh**. See 3834.

3826. לִבָּה {1x} **libbâh**, *lib-baw'*; fem. of 3820; the *heart:*—heart {1x}. See: TWOT—1071b; BDB—525d.

3827. לַבָּה {1x} **labbâh**, *lab-baw'*; for 3852; *flame:*—flame {1x}. See: TWOT—1077b; BDB—529b.

3828. לְבוֹנָה {21x} **lᵉbôwnâh**, *leb-o-naw'*; or

לְבֹנָה **lᵉbonah**, *leb-o-naw'*; from 3836; *frankincense* (from its *whiteness* or perh. that of its smoke):—frankincense {15x}, incense {1x}. Syn.: 6999, 7004. See: TWOT—1074d; BDB—526c.

3829. לְבוֹנָה {1x} **Lᵉbôwnâh**, *leb-o- aw'*; the same as 3828; *Lebonah*, a place in Pal.:—Lebonah {1x}. See: TWOT—1074d; BDB—526d.

3830. לְבוּשׁ {32x} **lᵉbûwsh**, *leb-oosh'*; or

לְבֻשׁ **lᵉbûsh**, *leb-oosh'*; from 3847; a *garment* (lit. or fig.); by impl. (euphem.) a *wife:*—clothing {9x}, garment {9x}, apparel {8x}, vesture {2x}, clothed {1x}, put on {1x}, raiment {1x}, vestments {1x}. See: TWOT—1075a; BDB—528c, 1098d.

3831. לְבוּשׁ {1x} **lᵉbûwsh** (Aram.), *leb-oosh'*; corresp. to 3830:—garment {2x}. See: TWOT—2810a; BDB—1098d.

3832. לָבַט {3x} **lâbaṭ**, *l w-bat'*; a prim. root; to *overthrow;* intr. to *fall:*—fall {3x}. See: TWOT—1072; BDB—526a.

לֻבִּי **Lubbîy**. See 3864.

3833. לָבִיא {14x} **lâbîyʾ**, *law-bee'*; or (Eze 19:2)

לְבִיָּא **lᵉbîyâʾ**, *leb-ee-yaw'*; irreg. masc. plur.

לְבָאִים **lᵉbâʾîym**, *leb-aw-eem'*; irreg. fem. plur.

לְבָאוֹת **lᵉbâʾôwth**, *leb-aw-ōth'*; from an unused root mean. to *roar;* a *lion* (prop. a lion*ess* as the fiercer [although not a *roarer;* comp. 738]):—lion {5x}, great lion {3x}, old lion {2x}, stout lion {1x}, lioness {2x}, young {1x}. Syn.: 738, 3918, 7826. See: TWOT—1070b, 1070c; BDB—522d, 526a.

3834. לָבִיבָה {3x} **lâbîybâh**, *law-bee-baw'*; or rather

לְבִבָה **lᵉbîbâh**, *leb-ee-baw'*; from 3823 in its orig. sense of *fatness* (or perh. of *folding*); a *cake* (either as *fried* or *turned*):—cakes {3x}. See: TWOT—1071c; BDB—525d.

3835. לָבַן {8x} **lâban**, *law-ban'*; a prim. root; to *be* (or *become*) *white;* also (as denom. from 3843) to *make bricks:*—make white {3x}, make {2x}, make brick {1x}, be white {1x}, be whiter {1x}. See: TWOT—1074b, 1074h; BDB—526a, 527c.

3836. לָבָן {29x} **lâbân**, *law-bawn'*; or (Gen 49:12)

לָבֵן **lâbên**, *law-bane'*; from 3835; *white:*—white {29x}. See: TWOT—1074a; BDB—526b.

3837. לָבָן {55x} **Lâbân**, *law-bawn'*; the same as 3836; *Laban*, a Mesopotamian; also a place in the Desert:—Laban {55x}. See: BDB—526c.

לַבֵּן **Labbên**. See 4192.

3838. לְבָנָא {2x} **Lᵉbânâʾ**, *leb-aw-naw'*; or

לְבָנָה **Lᵉbânâh**, *leb-aw-naw'*; the same as 3842; *Lebana* or *Lebanah*, one of the Nethinim:—Lebana {1x}, Lebanah {1x}. See: BDB—526c.

3839. לִבְנֶה {2x} **libneh**, *lib-neh'*; from 38 5; some sort of *whitish* tree, perh. the *storax:*—poplar {2x}. See: TWOT—1074f; BDB—527b.

3840. לִבְנָה {1x} **libnâh**, *lib-naw'*; from 3 35; prop. *whiteness*, i.e. (by impl.) *transparency:*—paved {1x}. See: TWOT—1074g; BDB—527c.

3841. לִבְנָה {18x} **Libnâh**, *lib-naw'*; the sa e as 3839; *Libnah*, a place in the Desert and one in Pal.:—Libnah {18x}. See: TWOT—1074g; BDB—526c.

3842. לְבָנָה {3x} **lᵉbânâh**, *leb-aw-naw'*; from 3835; prop. (the) *white*, i.e. the *moon:*—moon {3x}. See: TWOT—1074c; BDB—526b. See also 3838.

3843. לְבֵנָה {11x} **lᵉbênâh**, *leb-ay-naw'*; from 3835; a *brick* (from the *whiteness* of the clay):—(altar of) brick {10x}, tile {1x}. See: TWOT—1074g; BDB—527b.

לְבֹנָה **lᵉbônâh**. See 3828.

3844. לְבָנוֹן {71x} **Lᵉbânôwn**, *leb-aw-nohn'*; from 3825; (the) *white* mountain (from its snow); *Lebanon*, a mountain range in Pal.:—Lebanon {71x}. See: TWOT—1074e; BDB—526d.

3845. לִבְנִי {5x} **Libnîy**, *lib-nee'*; from 3835; *white; Libni*, an Isr.:—Libni {5x}. See: TWOT—1074e; BDB—526d.

3846. לִבְנִי {2x} **Libnîy**, *lib-nee'*; patron. from 3845; a *Libnite* or desc. of Libni (collect.):—Libnites {2x}. See: TWOT—1074e; BDB—526d.

3847. לָבַשׁ {112x} **lâbash**, *law-bash'*; or

לָבֵשׁ **lâbêsh**, *law-bashe'*; a prim. root; prop. *wrap* around, i.e. (by impl.) to *put on* a garment or *clothe* (oneself, or another), lit. or fig.:—clothe {51x}, put on {22x}, put {18x}, array {6x}, wear {4x}, armed {3x}, came {3x}, apparel {1x}, apparelled {1x}, clothed them {1x}, came upon {1x}, variant {1x}.

Labesh means "to put on (a garment), clothe, wear, be clothed." **(1)** *Labash* is found very early in the Old Testament, **(1a)** in Gen 3:21: "Unto Adam also and to his wife did the Lord God make coats of skin, and clothed them." **(1b)** As always, God provided something much better for man than man could do for himself—in this instance, coats of skins to replace fig-leaf garments (Gen 3:7). **(2)** *Labash* is regularly used for the "putting on" of ordinary clothing (Gen 38:19; Ex 29:30; 1 Sa 28:8). **(3)** The word also describes the "putting on" of armor (Jer 46:4). **(4)** Many times it is used in a figurative sense, as **(4a)** in Job 7:5: "My flesh is clothed [covered] with worms. . . ." **(4b)** Jerusalem is spoken of as "putting on" the Jews as they return after the Exile (Is 49:18). **(4c)** Often the figurative garment is an abstract quality: "For he put on righteousness as a breastplate, . . . he put on garments of vengeance for clothing . . ." (Is 59:17).

(4d) God is spoken of as being "clothed with honor and majesty" (Ps 104:1). **(4e)** Job says, "I put on righteousness, and it clothed me . . ." (Job 29:14). **(5)** These abstract qualities are sometimes negative: **(5a)** "The prince shall be clothed with desolation" (Eze 7:27). **(5b)** "They that hate thee shall be clothed with shame" (Job 8:22). **(5c)** "Let mine adversaries be clothed with shame" (Ps 109:29). **(6)** A very important figurative use of *labash* is found in Judg 6:34, where the stative form of the verb may be translated, **(6a)** "The spirit of the Lord clothed itself [was clothed] with Gideon." **(6b)** The idea seems to be that the Spirit of the Lord incarnated Himself in Gideon and thus empowered him from within. **(6c)** The KJV renders it "came upon": "But the Spirit of the LORD came upon Gideon, and he blew a trumpet; and Abiezer was gathered after him." See: TWOT—1075; BDB—527d, 1098d.

3848. לְבַשׁ {3x} **lᵉbash** (Aram.), *leb-ash'*; corresp. to 3847:—clothe {3x}. See: TWOT—2810; BDB—1098d.

לְבֻשׁ **lᵉbûsh**. See 3830.

3849. לֹג {5x} **lôg**, *lohg;* from an unused root appar. mean. to *deepen* or *hollow* [like 3537]; a *log* or measure for liquids:—log [of oil] {5x}. See: TWOT—1076; BDB—528d.

3850. לֹד {4x} **Lôd**, *lode;* from an unused root of uncert. signif.; *Lod*, a place in Pal.:—Lod {4x}. See: BDB—528d.

לִדְבִר **Lidbîr**. See 3810.

3851. לַהַב {12x} **lahab**, *lah'-hab;* from an unused root mean. to *gleam;* a *flash;* fig. a sharply polished *blade* or *point* of a weapon:—blade {2x}, bright {1x}, flame {8x}, glittering {1x}. See: TWOT—1077, 1077a; BDB—529a.

3852. לֶהָבָה {19x} **lehâbâh**, *leh-aw-baw'*; or לַהֶבֶת **lahebeth**, *lah-eh'-beth;* fem. of 3851, and mean. the same:—flame {13x}, flaming {5x}, head [of a spear]{1x}. See: TWOT—1077b; BDB—529b.

3853. לְהָבִים {2x} **Lᵉhâbîym**, *leh-haw-beem';* plur. of 3851; *flames; Lehabim,* a son of Mizrain, and his desc.:—Lehabim {2x}. See: TWOT—1077b; BDB—529c.

3854. לַהַג {1x} **lahag**, *lah'-hag;* from an unused root mean. to *be eager;* intense mental *application:*—study {1x}. See: TWOT—1078a; BDB—529c.

3855. לַהַד {1x} **Lahad**, *lah'-had;* from an unused root mean. to *glow* [comp. 3851] or else to *be earnest* [comp. 3854]; *Lahad,* an Isr.:—Lahad {1x}. See: BDB—529c.

3856. לָהַהּ {2x} **lâhahh**, *law-hah';* a prim. root mean. prop. to *burn,* i.e. (by impl.) to *be rabid* (fig. *insane*); also (from the *exhaustion* of frenzy) to *languish:*—faint {1x}, mad {1x}. See: TWOT—1079; BDB—529c.

3857. לָהַט {11x} **lâhat**, *law-hat';* a prim. root; prop. to *lick,* i.e. (by impl.) to *blaze:*—set on fire {4x}, burn up {3x}, burn {2x}, kindle {1x}, flaming {1x}. See: TWOT—1081; BDB—529c.

3858. לַהַט {2x} **lahat**, *lah'-hat;* from 3857; a *blaze;* also (from the idea of *enwrapping*) *magic* (as *covert*):—flaming {1x}, enchantment {1x}. Those who practiced this did it in secrecy; compare "sleight of hand (Ex 7:11). See: TWOT—1081a; BDB—529d, 532a.

3859. לָהַם {2x} **lâham**, *law-ham'* a prim. root; prop. to *burn* in, i.e. (fig.) to *rankle:*—wound {1x}. See: TWOT—1082; BDB—529d.

3860. לָהֵן {2x} **lâhên**, *law-hane';* from the pref. prep. mean. *to* or *for* and 2005; prop. *for if;* hence, *therefore:*—for them {1x}. See: TWOT—1083; BDB—242a, 243b, 530a, 1099a.

3861. לָהֵן {10x} **lâhên** (Aram.), *law-hane';* corresp. to 3860; *therefore;* also *except:*—except {3x}, therefore {2x}, but {2x}, save {2x}, wherefore {1x}. See: TWOT—2811; BDB—242a, 539a, 1090d, 1099a.

3862. לַהֲקָה {1x} **lahăqâh**, *lah-hak-aw';* prob. from an unused root mean. to *gather;* an *assembly:*—company {1x}. Syn.: 5712, 6915. See: TWOT—1084; BDB—530a.

לוֹא **lôwʾ**. See 3808.

3863. לוּא {22x} **lûwʾ**, *loo;* or לֻא **lûʾ**, *loo;* or לוּ **lûw**, *loo;* a conditional particle; *if;* by impl. (interj. as a wish) *would that!:*—if {6x}, would God {4x}, O that {3x}, Oh {2x}, would it might be {1x}, if haply {1x}, peradventure {1x}, Oh that {1x}, pray thee {1x}, Though {1x}, would {1x}. See: TWOT—1085; BDB—520d, 530a.

3864. לוּבִי {4x} **Lûwbîy**, *loo-bee';* or לֻבִּי **Lubbiy** (Dan. 11:43) *loob-bee';* patrial from a name prob. derived from an unused root mean. to *thirst,* i.e. a *dry* region; appar. a *Libyan* or inhab. of interior Africa (only in plur.):—Lubim (-s) {3x}, Libyans {1x}. See: BDB—526a, 530c.

3865. לוּד {5x} **Lûwd**, *lood;* prob. of for. der.; *Lud,* the name of two nations:—Lud {4x}, Lydia {1x}. See: BDB—530d.

3866. לוּדִי {3x} **Lûwdîy**, *loo-dee';* or לוּדִיִּי **Lûwdîyîy**, *loo-dee-ee';* patrial from 3865; a *Ludite* or inhab. of Lud (only in plural):—Ludim {2x}, Lydians {1x}. See: BDB—530d.

3867. לָוָה {26x} **lâvâh**, *law-vaw';* a prim. root; prop. to *twine,* i.e. (by impl.) to *unite,* to *remain;* also to *borrow* (as a form of *obligation*) or (caus.) to *lend:*—join {10x}, lend {7x}, borrow {3x}, borrower {2x}, abide {1x}, cleave {1x}, lender {1x}, lender + 376 {1x}. See: TWOT—1087, 1088; BDB—530d, 531a.

3868. לוּז {6x} **lûwz**, *looz;* a prim. root; to *turn* aside [comp. 3867, 3874 and 3885], i.e. (lit.) to *depart,* (fig.) *be perverse:*—froward {2x}, depart {2x}, perverse {1x}, perverseness {1x}. See: TWOT—1090; BDB—531b.

3869. לוּז {1x} **lûwz**, *looz;* prob. of for. or.; some kind of *nut*-tree, perh. the *almond:*—hazel {1x}. See: TWOT—1090b; BDB—531c.

3870. לוּז {8x} **Lûwz**, *looz;* prob. from 3869 (as growing there); *Luz,* the name of two places in Pal.:—Luz {8x}. See: BDB—531c.

3871. לוּחַ {43x} **lûwach**, *loo'-akh;* or לֻחַ **lûach**, *loo' akh;* from a prim. root; prob. mean. to *glisten;* a *tablet* (as *polished*), of stone, wood or metal:—tables {38x}, boards {4x}, plates {1x}. See: TWOT—1091a; BDB—531d.

3872. לוּחִית {2x} **Lûwchîyth**, *loo-kheeth';* or לֻחוֹת **Lûchôwth** (Jer. 48:5), *loo-khoth';* from the same as 3871; *floored; Luchith,* a place E. of the Jordan:—Luhith {2x}. See: BDB—229d, 532a, 751c.

3873. לוֹחֵשׁ {2x} **Lôwchêsh**, *lo-khashe';* act. part. of 3907; (the) *enchanter; Lochesh,* an Isr.:—Hallohesh {1x}, Haloshesh [*includ. the art.*]{1x}. See: BDB—538a.

3874. לוּט {3x} **lûwt**, *loot;* a prim. root; to *wrap* up:—cast {1x}, wrapped {2x}. See: TWOT—1092; BDB—529d, 532a.

3875. לוֹט {1x} **lôwt**, *lote;* from 3874; a *veil:*—covering {1x}. Syn.: 3682, 4372, 4539. See: TWOT—1092b; BDB—532b.

3876. לוֹט {33x} **Lôwt**, *lote;* the same as 3875; *Lot,* Abraham's nephew:—Lot {33x}. See: BDB—532b.

3877. לוֹטָן {7x} **Lôwtân**, *lo-tawn';* from 3875; *covering; Lotan,* an Idumæan:—Lotan {7x}. See: BDB—532b.

3878. לֵוִי {64x} **Lêvîy**, *lay-vee';* from 3867; *attached; Levi,* a son of Jacob:—Levi {64x}. See: TWOT—1093; BDB—532b, 1099a. See also 3879, 3881.

3879. לֵוִי {4x} **Lêvîy** (Aram.), *lay-vee';* corresp. to 3880:—Levite {4x}. See: BDB—1099a.

3880. לִוְיָה {2x} **livyâh**, *liv-yaw';* from 3867; something *attached,* i.e. a *wreath:*—ornament {2x}. See: TWOT—1089a; BDB—531a.

3881. לֵוִיִּי {286x} **Lêvîyîy**, *lay-vee-ee';* or לֵוִי **Lêvîy**, *lay-vee';* patron. from 3878; a *Levite* or desc. of Levi:—Levite {286x}. See: BDB—532d.

3882. לִוְיָתָן {6x} **livyâthân**, *liv-yaw-thawn';* from 3867; a *wreathed* animal, i.e. a *serpent* (espec. the *crocodile* or some other large sea-monster); fig. the constellation of the *dragon;* also as a symbol of *Babylon:*—leviathan {5x}, mourning {1x}. See: TWOT—1089b; BDB—531b.

3883. לוּל {1x} **lûwl**, *lool;* from an unused root mean. to *fold* back; a *spiral* step:—winding stair {1x}. See: TWOT—1094; BDB—533b. comp. 3924.

3884. לוּלֵא {14x} **lûwlêʾ**, *loo-lay';* or לוּלֵי **lûwlêy**, *loo lay';* from 3863 and 3808; *if not:*—except {4x}, unless {4x}, if {3x}, had not {1x}, were it not {1x}, were it not that {1x}. See: TWOT—1085a; BDB—530b, 533b, 533c.

3885. לוּן {87x} **lûwn**, *loon;* or לִין **lîyn**, *leen;* a prim. root; to *stop* (usually over night); by impl. to *stay* permanently; hence, (in a bad sense) to *be obstinate* (espec. in words, to *complain*):—lodge {33x}, murmur {14x}, . . . the night {14x}, abide {7x}, remain {6x}, tarry {2x}, lodge in {2x}, continue {1x}, dwell {1x}, endure {1x}, grudge {1x}, left {1x}, lie {1x}, variant {3x}.

Luwn means "to remain, lodge, spend the night, abide." **(1)** Its first occurrence is in Gen 19:2, where it is used twice: "Behold now, my lords, turn in, I pray you, into your servant's house, and tarry all night (*luwn*). . . . And they said, Nay; but we will abide (*luwn*) in the street all night." **(2)** While it is usually used concerning human beings spending the night, *luwn* is sometimes used of animals, such as **(2a)** the unicorn (Job 39:9), **(2b)** the cormorant and the bittern (Zeph 2:14). **(3)** The word does not necessarily mean sleeping through the night, but may be used to indicate being located in one place for the night: "Thou shalt not . . . [let] the fat of my sacrifice remain until the morning [literally, "pass the night until morning"] (Ex 23:18). **(4)** In a similar way, the figurative use of the word often has the connotation of "abiding, remaining": **(4a)** ". . . Mine error remaineth with myself" (Job 19:4); **(4b)** ". . . Righteousness lodged in it . . ." (Is 1:21); **(4c)** "His soul shall dwell at ease . . ." (Ps 25:13); **(4d)** ". . . [He] shall abide satisfied . . ." (Prov 19:23). See: TWOT—1096, 1097; BDB—533c, 534a, 539b.

3886. לוּעַ {2x} **lûwaʿ**, *loo'-ah;* a prim. root; to *gulp;* fig. to *be rash:*—swallow down {1x}, swallowed up {1x}. See: TWOT—1098; BDB—534b, 541d, 542a.

3887. לוּץ {27x} **lûwts**, *loots;* a prim. root; prop. to *make mouths* at, i.e. to *scoff,* hence, (from the effort to pronounce a foreign language) to *interpret,* or (gen.) *intercede:*—scorner {14x}, scorn {4x}, interpreter {2x}, mocker {2x}, ambassadors {1x}, derision {1x}, mock {1x}, scornful {1x}, teachers {1x}. See: TWOT—1113; BDB—534c, 539b, 542c.

3888. לוּשׁ {5x} **lûwsh**, *loosh;* a prim. root; to *knead:*—knead {5x}. See: TWOT—1100; BDB—534c.

3889. לוּשׁ {1x} **Lûwsh**, *loosh;* from 3888; *kneading; Lush,* a place in Pal.:—Laish {1x}. See: BDB—534c, 539d. comp. 3919.

3890. לְוָת {1x} **lᵉvâth** (Aram.), *lev-awth';* from a root corresp. to 3867; prop. *adhe-*

sion, i.e. (as prep.) *with:*—× thee {1x}. See: TWOT—2813; BDB—1099a.

לֻחוֹת **Lûchôwth**. See 3872.

לָז **lâz** and

לָזֶה **lâzeh**. See 1975 and 1976.

3891. לְזוּת {1x} **l**e**zûwth**, *lez-ooth';* from 3868; *perverseness:*—perverse {1x}. See: TWOT—1090a; BDB—531c, 534c.

3892. לַח {6x} **lach**, *lakh;* from an unused root mean. to *be new; fresh,* i.e. unused or undried:—green {5x}, moist {1x}. See: TWOT—1102a; BDB—534c, 535a.

3893. לֵחַ {1x} **lêach**, *lay'-akh;* fr m the same as 3892; *freshness,* i.e. vigor:—natural force {1x}. See: TWOT—1102b; BDB—535a.

לֻחַ **lûach**. See 3871.

3894. לְחוּם {2x} **lâchûwm**, *law-khoom';* or

לְחֻם **lâchûm**, *law-khoom';* pass. part. of 3898; prop. *eaten,* i.e. *food;* also *flesh,* i.e. *body:*—while . . . is eating {1x}, flesh {1x}. See: TWOT—1104b; BDB—535d.

3895. לְחִי {21x} **l**e**chîy**, *lekh-ee';* from an unused root mean. to *be soft;* the *cheek* (from its *fleshiness*); hence, the *jaw*-bone:—cheek {10x}, bone {1x}, jaw {7x}, jawbone {3x}. See: TWOT—1101a; BDB—534c, 535a.

3896. לֶחִי {3x} **Lechîy**, *lekh'-ee;* a form of 3895; *Lechi,* a place in Pal.:—Lehi {3x}. See: BDB—534d, 535a. comp. also 7437.

3897. לָחַךְ {6x} **lâchak**, *law-khak';* a prim. root; to *lick:*—lick (up) {6x}. See: TWOT—1103; BDB—535a.

3898. לָחַם {177x} **lâcham**, *law-kham';* a prim. root; to *feed* on; fig. to *consume;* by impl. to *battle* (as *destruction*):—fight {149x}, to war {10x}, make war {8x}, eat {5x}, overcome {2x}, devoured {1x}, ever {1x}, prevail {1x}.

Lacham means "to fight, do battle, engage in combat." **(1)** *Lacham* appears first in Ex 1:10, where the Egyptian pharaoh expresses his fears that the Israelite slaves will multiply and join an enemy "to fight" against the Egyptians: "Come on, let us deal wisely with them; lest they multiply, and it come to pass, that, when there falleth out any war, they join also unto our enemies, and fight against us, and *so* get them up out of the land." **(2)** While the word is commonly used in the context **(2a)** of "armies engaged in pitched battle" against each other (Num 21:23; Josh 10:5; Judg 11:5), **(2b)** it is also used to describe "single, hand-to-hand combat": "And David said to Saul, Let no man's heart fail because of him; thy servant will go and fight with this Philistine. And Saul said to David, Thou art not able to go against this Philistine to fight with him: for thou *art but* a youth, and he a man of war from his youth" (1 Sa 17:32–33). **(3)** Frequently, God "fights" the battle for Israel (Deut 20:4). **(4)** Instead of swords, words spoken by a lying tongue are often used "to fight" against God's servants: "For the mouth of the wicked and the mouth of the deceitful are opened against me: they have spoken against me with a lying tongue" (Ps 109:2). See: TWOT—1104, 1105; BDB—535b, 536d.

3899. לֶחֶם {297x} **lechem**, *lekh'-em;* from 3898; *food* (for man or beast), espec. *bread,* or *grain* (for making it):—bread {237x}, food {21x}, meat {18x}, shewbread + 6440 {5x}, loaves {5x}, shewbread + 4635 {3x}, shewbread {2x}, victuals {2x}, eat {1x}, feast {1x}, fruit {1x}, provision {1x}.

Lechem means bread, meal, food, fruit. **(1)** This noun refers to "bread," as distinguished from meat. **(1a)** The diet of the early Hebrews ordinarily consisted of bread, meat, and liquids: "And he humbled thee, and suffered thee to hunger, and fed thee with manna, which thou knewest not, neither did thy fathers know; that he might make thee know that man doth not live by bread only, but by every word that proceedeth out of the mouth of the Lord . . ." (Deut 8:3). **(1b)** "Bread" was baked in loaves: "And it shall come to pass, that every one that is left in thine house shall come and crouch to him for a piece of silver and a morsel of bread . . ." (1 Sa 2:36). **(1c)** Even when used by itself, lechem can signify a "loaf of bread": **(1c1)** ". . . They will salute thee, and give thee two loaves of bread . . ." (1 Sa 10:4). **(1c2)** In this usage, the word is always preceded by a number. **(1d)** "Bread" was also baked in cakes (2 Sa 6:19).

(2) A "bit of bread" is a term for a modest meal. So Abraham said to his three guests, "Let a little water, I pray you, be fetched . . . and I will fetch a morsel of bread, and comfort ye your hearts . . ." (Gen 18:4–5). **(3)** In 1 Sa 20:27, *lechem* represents an entire meal: "Saul said unto Jonathan his son, Wherefore cometh not the son of Jesse to meat, neither yesterday, nor today?" **(4)** Thus, "to make bread" may actually mean "to prepare a meal": "A feast is made for laughter, and wine maketh merry . . ." (Eccl 10:19). **(5)** The "staff of bread" is the "support of life": "And when I have broken the staff of your bread, ten women shall bake your bread in one oven, and they shall deliver you your bread again by weight: and ye shall eat, and not be satisfied" (Lev 26:26). **(6)** The Bible refers to the "bread of the face" or "the bread of the Presence," which was the bread constantly set before God in the holy place of the tabernacle or temple: "And thou shalt set upon the table showbread before me always" (Ex 25:30).

(7) In several passages, *lechem* represents the grain from which "bread" is made: **(7a)** "And the seven years of dearth began to come, according as Joseph had said: and the dearth was in all the lands; but in all the land of Egypt there was bread" (Gen 41:54). **(7b)** The meaning "grain" is very clear in 2 Kin 18:32: "Until I come and take you away to a land like your own land, a land of corn and wine, a land of bread and vineyards. . . ." **(8)** *Lechem* can represent food in general. **(8a)** In Gen 3:19 (the first biblical occurrence), it signifies the entire diet: "In the sweat of thy face shalt thou eat bread. . . ." **(8b)** This nuance may include meat, as it does in Judg 13:15–16: "And Manoah said unto the angel of the Lord, I pray thee, let us detain thee, until we shall have made ready a kid for thee. And the angel of the Lord said unto Manoah, Though thou detain me, I will not eat of thy bread. . . ." **(8c)** In 1 Sa 14:24, 28, *lechem* includes honey, and in Prov 27:27 goat's milk.

(9) *Lechem* may also represent "food" for animals: "He giveth to the beast his food, and to the young ravens which cry" (Ps 147:9; cf. Prov 6:8). **(10)** Flesh and grain offered to God are called "the bread of God": "For the offerings of the Lord made by fire, and the bread of their God, they do offer . . ." (Lev 21:6; cf. 22:13). **(11)** There are several special or figurative uses of *lechem.* **(11a)** The "bread" of wickedness is "food" gained by wickedness: "For [evil men] eat the bread of wickedness, and drink the wine of violence" (Prov 4:17). **(11b)** Compare the "bread" or "food" gained by deceit (Prov 20:17) and lies (23:3). **(11c)** Thus, in Prov 31:27 the good wife "looketh well to the ways of her household, and eateth not the bread of idleness"—i.e., unearned food. **(11d)** The "bread of my portion" is the food that one earns (Prov 30:8). **(12)** Figuratively, men are the "food" or prey for their enemies: "Only rebel not ye against the Lord, neither fear ye the people of the land; for they are bread for us . . ." (Num 14:9).

(13) The Psalmist in his grief says his tears are his "food" (Ps 42:3). **(14)** Evil deeds are likened to food: "[The evil man's] meat in his bowels is turned, it is the gall of asps within him" (Job 20:14). **(15)** In Jer. 11:19, *lechem* represents "fruit from a tree" and is a figure of a man and his offspring: "And I knew not that they had devised devices against me, saying, Let us destroy the tree with the fruit thereof, and let us cut him off from the land of the living, that his name may be no more remembered." Syn.: 1036. See: TWOT—1105a; BDB—536d, 1099a.

3900. לְחֶם {1x} **l**e**chem** (Aram.), *lekh-em';* corresp. to 3899:—feast {1x}. See: TWOT—2814; BDB—1099a.

3901. לָחֶם {1x} **lâchem**, *law-khem';* from 3898, *battle:*—war {1x}. Syn.: 3898, 4421. See: TWOT—1104a; BDB—535d.

לָחֻם **lâchûm**. See 3894.

3902. לַחְמִי {1x} **Lachmîy**, *lakh-mee';* from 3899; *foodful; Lachmi,* a Philis.; or rather prob. a brief form (or perh. err. transc.) for 1022:—Lahmi {1x}. See: BDB—537c. See also 3433.

3903. לַחְמָס {1x} **Lachmâç**, *lakh-maws';* prob. by err. transc. for

לַחְמָם **Lachmâm**, *lakh-mawm';* from 3899; *food-like; Lachmam* or *Lachmas,* a place in Pal.:—Lahmam {1x}. See: BDB—537c.

3904. לְחֵנָה {3x} **l**e**chênâh** (Aram.), *lekh-ay-naw';* from an unused root of uncert. mean.; a *concubine:*—concubine {3x}. See: TWOT—2815; BDB—1099b.

3905. לָחַץ {19x} **lâchats**, *law-khats';* a prim. root; prop. to *press,* i.e. (fig.) to *distress:*—oppress {13x}, afflict {1x}, crushed {1x}, fast {1x}, forced {1x}, oppressors {1x}, thrust {1x}. See: TWOT—1106; BDB—537d.

3906. לַחַץ {12x} **lachats**, *lakh'-ats;* from 3905; *distress:*—affliction {5x}, oppression {7x}. See: TWOT—1106a; BDB—537d.

3907. לָחַשׁ {3x} **lâchash**, *law-khash';* a prim. root; to *whisper;* by impl. to *mumble* a spell (as a magician):—charmer {1x}, whisper (together) {2x}. The secret and sorrowful sighing of the oppressed (Is 26:16). Enchantment? (Ps. 58:5). See: TWOT—1107; BDB—538a.

3908. לַחַשׁ {5x} **lachash**, *lakh'-ash;* from 3907; prop. a *whisper,* i.e. by impl. (in a good sense) a private *prayer,* (in a bad one) an *incantation;* concr. an *amulet:*—charmed {1x}, earring {1x}, enchantment {1x}, orator {1x}, prayer {1x}. See: TWOT—1107a; BDB—538a.

3909. לָט {6x} **lât**, *lawt;* a form of 3814 or else part. from 3874; prop. *covered,* i.e. *secret;* by impl. *incantation;* also *secrecy* or (adv.) *covertly:*—enchantment {3x}, privily {1x}, secretly {1x}, softly {1x}. Syn.: 328, 825, 826, 2267, 3858, 3907, 5172, 6049. See: TWOT—1092a; BDB—532a, 538b.

3910. לֹט {2x} **lôt**, *lote;* prob. from 3874; a gum (from its *sticky* nature), prob. *ladanum:*—myrrh {2x}. See: TWOT—1108; BDB—538b.

3911. לְטָאָה {1x} **lᵉṭâʾâh**, *let-aw-aw';* from an unused root mean. to *hide;* a kind of *lizard* (from its *covert* habits):—lizard {1x}. See: TWOT—1109a; BDB—538b.

3912. לְטוּשִׁם {1x} **Lᵉṭûwshîm**, *let-oo-sheem';* masc. plur. of pass. part. of 3913; *hammered* (i.e. *oppressed*) ones; *Letushim,* an Arabian tribe:—Letushim {1x}. See: BDB—538c.

3913. לָטַשׁ {5x} **lâṭash**, *law-tash';* a prim. root; prop. to *hammer* out (an edge), i.e. to *sharpen:*—instructer {1x}, sharp {1x}, sharpen {2x}, whet {1x}. See: TWOT—1110, BDB—538b.

3914. לֹיָה {3x} **lôyâh**, *lo-yaw';* a form of 3880; a *wreath:*—addition {3x}. See: TWOT—1089a; BDB—531b, 538c.

3915. לַיִל {233x} **layil**, *lah'-yil;* or (Isa. 21:11)

לֵיל **lêyl**, *lale;* also

לַיְלָה **layᵉlâh**, *lah'-yel-aw;* from the same as 3883; prop. a *twist* (away of the light), i.e. *night;* fig. *adversity:*—night {205x}, nights {15x}, midnight + 2677 {4x}, season {3x}, midnight + 2676 {2x}, night + 1121 {2x}, midnight {1x}, midnight + 8432 {1x}.

Layelah means "night." **(1)** *Layelah* means "night," the period of time during which it is dark: "And God called the light Day, and the darkness he called Night" (Gen 1:5—the first biblical appearance). **(2)** In Ex 13:21 and similar passages the word means "by night," or "during the night": "And the Lord went before them by day in a pillar of cloud . . . and by night in a pillar of fire, to give them light; to go by day and night." **(3)** This word is used figuratively of protection: "Take counsel, execute judgment; make thy shadow as the night in the midst of the noonday; hide the outcasts; [betray] not him that wandereth" (Is 16:3). **(3)** *Layelah* also figures deep calamity without the comforting presence and guidance of God, and/or other kinds of distress: "Where is God my maker, who giveth songs in the night . . ." (Job 35:10). **(4)** During Old Testament times the "night" was divided into three watches: **(4a)** from sunset to 10 P.M., (Lam 2:19), **(4b)** from 10 P.M. to 2 A.M. (Judg 7:19), and **(4c)** from 2 A.M. to sunrise (Ex 14:24). See: TWOT—1111; BDB—538c, 1099b.

3916. לֵילְיָא {5x} **leylᵉyâʾ** (Aram.), *lay-leh-yaw';* corresp. to 3915:—night {5x}. See: TWOT—2816; BDB—1099b.

3917. לִילִית {1x} **lîylîyth**, *lee-leeth';* from 3915; a *night* spectre:—screech owl {1x}. Syn.: 3563. See: TWOT—1112; BDB—539b.

3918. לַיִשׁ {3x} **layish**, *lah'-yish;* from 3888 in the sense of *crushing;* a lion (from his destructive *blows*):—old lion {2x}, lion {1x}. See: TWOT—1114a; BDB—539d.

3919. לַיִשׁ {7x} **Layish**, *lah'-yish;* the same as 3918; *Laïsh,* the name of two places in Pal.:—Laish {7x}. See: BDB—534c, 539d. comp. 3889.

3920. לָכַד {121x} **lâkad**, *law-kad';* a prim. root; to *catch* (in a net, trap or pit); gen. to *capture* or occupy; also to *choose* (by lot); fig. to *cohere:*—take {112x}, catch {5x}, at all {1x}, frozen {1x}, holden {1x}, stick together {1x}.

Lakad (3920) means "to capture; seize; take captive." **(1)** It is found for the first time in the text in Num 21:32, where the Israelites are said to have taken the villages of the Amorites. **(2)** The act of "capturing, seizing" is usually connected with fighting wars or battles, so a variety of objects may be taken. **(2a)** Cities are often "captured" in war (Josh 8:21; 10:1; Judg 1:8, 12). **(2b)** Land or territory also is taken as booty of war (Josh 10:42; Dan 11:18). **(2c)** Strategic geographic areas such as watercourses "are captured" (Judg 3:28). **(2d)** Sometimes kings and princes "are seized" in battle (Judg 7:25; 8:12, 14), **(2e)** as well as fighting men and horses (2 Sa 8:4). **(2f)** Saul is spoken of as actually taking the kingdom, apparently by force of arms (1 Sa 14:47). **(3)** In establishing the source of Israel's defeat by Ai, lots were used "to take or separate" the guilty party, Achan and his family (Josh 7:14). **(4)** Occasionally *lakad* is used in the figurative sense, especially in terms of men "being caught" in the trap of divine judgment (Ps 9:15; Is 8:15; 24:18). Syn: 3948, 4455, 4457, 4727, 4728. See: TWOT—1115; BDB—539d.

3921. לֶכֶד {1x} **leked**, *leh'ked;* from 392; something to *capture* with, i.e. a *noose:*—being taken {1x}. See: TWOT—1115a; BDB—540b.

3922. לֵכָה {1x} **Lêkâh**, *lay-kaw';* from 3212; a *journey; Lekah,* a place in Pal.:—Lecah {1x}. See: BDB—540b.

3923. לָכִישׁ {24x} **Lâchîysh**, *law-keesh';* from an unused root of uncert. mean.; *Lakish,* a place in Pal.:—Lachish {24x}. See: BDB—540b.

3924. לֻלָאָה {13x} **lûlâʾâh**, *loo-law-aw';* from the same as 3883; a *loop:*—loop {13x}. See: TWOT—1095a; BDB—533b, 540c.

3925. לָמַד {86x} **lâmad**, *law-mad';* a prim. root; prop. to *goad,* i.e. (by impl.) to *teach* (the rod being an Oriental *incentive*):—teach {56x}, learn {22x}, instruct {3x}, diligently {1x}, expert {1x}, skilful {1x}, teachers {1x}, unaccustomed + 3808 {1x}.

Lamad means "to teach, learn, cause to learn." **(1)** In its simple, active form, this verb has the meaning "to learn," but it is also found in a form giving the causative sense, "to teach." **(2)** This word is first used in the Hebrew Old Testament in Deut 4:1: "Hearken, O Israel, unto the statutes and unto the judgments, which I teach you. . . ." **(3)** In Deut 5:1 *lamad* is used of learning God's laws: **(3a)** "Hear, O Israel, the statutes and judgments which I speak in your ears this day, that ye may learn them, and keep, and do them." **(3b)** A similar meaning occurs in Ps 119:7: "I will praise thee with uprightness of heart, when I shall have learned thy righteous judgments." **(4)** The word may be used of learning other things: works of the heathen (Ps 106:35); wisdom (Prov 30:3); and war (Mic 4:3).

(5) About half the occurrences of *lamad* are found in the books of Deuteronomy and Psalms, underlining the teaching emphasis found in these books. **(5a)** Judaism's traditional emphasis on teaching and thus preserving its faith clearly has its basis in the stress on teaching the faith found in the Old Testament, specifically Deut. 6:4–9, better known as the "Shema". **(5b)** Following the Shema', the "watchword of Judaism" that declares that Yahweh is One (Deut 6:4), is the "first great commandment" (Deut 6:5; Mark 12:28–29). **(5c)** When Moses delivered the Law to his people, he said, ". . . The Lord commanded me at that time to teach you statutes and judgments . . ." (Deut 4:14). **(6)** The later Jewish term Talmud [not a biblical word], "instruction," is derived from this verb. Syn.: 502, 995, 1696, 2094, 2449, 3256, 7919, 8150. See: TWOT—1116; BDB—540c.

לִמֻּד **limmûd**. See 3928.

3926. לְמוֹ {4x} **lᵉmôw**, *lem-o';* a prol. and separable form of the pref. prep.; *to* or *for:*—at {1x}, for {1x}, to {1x}, upon {1x}. See: TWOT—1063; BDB—518b, 530c, 541a.

3927. לְמוּאֵל {2x} **Lᵉmûwʾêl**, *lem-oo-ale';* or

לְמוֹאֵל **Lᵉmôwʾêl**, *lem-o-ale';* from 3926 and 410; (belonging) *to God; Lemuël* or *Lemoël,* a symbol. name of Solomon:—Lemuel {2x}. See: BDB—541a.

3928. לִמּוּד {6x} **limmûwd**, *lim-mood';* or

לִמֻּד **limmûd**, *lim-mood';* from 3925; *instructed:*—accustomed {1x}, disciple {1x}, learned {2x}, taught {1x}, used {1x}.

Limmud means "taught." **(1)** This adjective forms an exact equivalent to the New Testament idea of "disciple, one who is taught." **(2)** This is well expressed in Is 8:16: ". . . Seal the law among my disciples." **(3)** The word also occurs in Is 54:13: "And all thy children shall be taught of the Lord. . . ." See: TWOT—1116a; BDB—541a.

3929. לֶמֶךְ {11x} **Lemek**, *leh'-mek;* from an unused root of uncert. mean.; *Lemek,* the name of two antediluvian patriarchs:—Lamech {11x}. See: BDB—541a.

3930. לֹעַ {1x} **lôaʿ**, *lo'ah;* from 3886; the *gullet:*—throat {1x}. Syn.: 1627. See: TWOT—1098a; BDB—534b, 541b.

3931. לָעַב {1x} **lâʿab**, *law-ab';* a prim. root; to *deride:*—mock {1x}. See: TWOT—1117; BDB—541b.

3932. לָעַג {18x} **lâʿag**, *law-ag';* a prim. root; to *deride;* by impl. (as if imitating a foreigner) to *speak unintelligibly:*—mock {8x}, scorn {3x}, laugh {3x}, have in derision {2x}, laugh to scorn {1x}, stammering {1x}. See: TWOT—1118; BDB—541b.

3933. לַעַג {7x} **laʿag**, *lah'-ag;* from 3932; *derision, scoffing:*—derision {3x}, scorn (-ing) {4x}. See: TWOT—1118a; BDB—541c.

3934. לָעֵג {2x} **lâʿêg**, *law-ayg';* from 3932; a *buffoon;* also a *foreigner:*—mocker {1x}, stammering {1x}. See: TWOT—1118b; BDB—541d.

3935. לַעְדָּה {1x} **Laʿdâh**, *lah-daw';* from an unused root of uncert. mean.; *Ladah,* an Isr.:—Laadah {1x}. See: BDB—541d.

3936. לַעְדָּן {7x} **Laʿdân**, *lah-dawn';* from the same as 3935; *Ladan,* the name of two Isr.:—Laadan {7x}. See: BDB—541d.

3937. לָעַז {1x} **lâʿaz**, *law-az';* a p im. root; to *speak in a foreign tongue:*—strange language {1x}. See: TWOT—1119; BDB—541d.

3938. לָעַט {1x} **lâʿaṭ**, *la -at';* a prim. root; to *swallow* greedily; caus. to *feed:*—feed {1x}. See: TWOT—1120; BDB—542a.

3939. לַעֲנָה {8x} **laʿănâh**, *lah-an-aw';* from an unused root supposed to mean to *curse; wormwood* (regarded as *poisonous,* and therefore *accursed*):—hemlock {1x}, wormwood {7x}. See: TWOT—1121; BDB—542a.

3940. לַפִּיד {14x} **lappîyd**, *lap-peed';* or

לַפִּד **lappîd**, *lap-peed';* from an unused root prob. mean. to *shine;* a *flambeau, lamp* or *flame:*—lamp {7x}, firebrand {2x}, torch {2x}, brand {1x}, lightning {1x}, burning {1x}. See: TWOT—1122a; BDB—542a.

3941. לַפִּידוֹת {1x} **Lappîydôwth**, *lap-pee-dōth';* fem. plur. of 3940; *Lappidoth,* the husband of Deborah:—Lappidoth {1x}. See: BDB—542b.

3942. לִפְנֵי {1x} **liphnay**, *lif-nah'ee;* from the pref. prep. (*to* or *for*) and 6440; *anterior:*—before {1x}. See: TWOT—1782b; BDB—542b, 816d, 819b.

3943. לָפַת {3x} **lâphath**, *law-fath';* a prim. root; prop. to *bend*, i.e. (by impl.) to *clasp;* also (refl.) to *turn* around or aside:—take hold {1x}, turn {1x}, turn aside (self) {1x}. See: TWOT—1123; BDB—542b.

3944. לָצוֹן {3x} **lâtsôwn**, *law-tsone';* from 3887; *derision:*—scornful {2x}, scorning {1x}. See: TWOT—1113a; BDB—539c.

3945. לָצַץ {1x} **lâtsats**, *law-tsats';* a prim. root; to *deride:*—scorn {1x}. See: TWOT—1113; BDB—539b, 539c.

3946. לַקּוּם {1x} **Laqqûwm**, *lak-koom';* from an unused root thought to mean to *stop* up by a barricade; perh. *fortification; Lakkum*, a place in Pal.:—Lakum {1x}. See: BDB—542c.

3947. לָקַח {965x} **lâqach**, *law-kakh';* a prim. root; to *take* (in the widest variety of applications):—take {747x}, receive {61x}, take away {51x}, fetch {31x}, bring {25x}, get {6x}, take out {6x}, carry away {5x}, married {4x}, buy {3x}, misc. {26x} = accept, drawn, infold, × many, mingle, place, reserve, seize, send for, use, win.

Laqach means "to take, receive, take away." **(1)** Primarily this word means "to take, grasp, take hold of," as when Noah reached out and "took hold of" the dove to bring it back into the ark (Gen 8:9). **(2)** A secondary meaning is "to take away, remove, take to oneself," as when the invading kings "took away" and "took to themselves" all the movable goods of the cities of the plain (Gen 14:11). **(3)** Sometimes this verb implies "to receive something from someone." So Abraham asks Ephron the Hittite to "receive from" his hand payment for the field which contained the sepulchre (Gen 23:13). **(4)** With the particle "for" *laqach* means "to take someone or something," as when Joseph's brothers remarked that they were afraid he was scheming "to take" them to be slaves, mentioned in Gen 43:18. **(5)** Another secondary use of this word is "to transfer" a thing, concept, or emotion, such as **(5a)** "take vengeance" (Is 47:3), **(5b)** "receive reproach" (Eze 36:30), and **(5c)** "receive a [whisper]" (Job 4:12). **(6)** In other passages this verb is virtually a helping verb serving to prepare for an action stipulated in a subsequent verb; God "took" Adam and put him into the garden of Eden (Gen 2:15—the first occurrence of the verb).

(7) This word can be used elliptically, suggesting the phrase "take and bring," but only "taken" is written. Noah is told to "take" (and bring) clean animals by sevens into the ark (Gen 7:2). **(8)** This verb is used of God in several connections. **(8a)** Sometimes God is pictured as having bodily parts (anthropomorphically). **(8b)** This is the implication of Gen 2:15, where the Lord "took" Adam and put him into Eden. **(8b1)** God's taking sometimes connotes election, as when He "took" Abraham from his father's house (Gen 24:7). **(8b2)** He also "takes" in the sense of taking to Himself or accepting. Thus, He "accepts" offerings (Judg 13:23) and prayers (Ps 6:9). **(8c)** God "takes away" in judgment David's wives (2 Sa 12:11) and the kingdom (1 Kin 11:34). **(9)** Of special interest is the use of the verb in the absolute sense: God "took away" Enoch so that he was not found on earth (Gen 5:24). This meaning of receiving one into heaven to Himself seems to be the force of Ps 73:24 and perhaps of Ps 49:15. Syn: 3920, 4455, 4457, 4727, 4728. See: TWOT—1124; BDB—542c, 881c.

3948. לֶקַח **leqach**, *leh'-kakh;* from 3947; prop. something *received*, i.e. (ment.) *instruction* (whether on the part of the teacher or hearer); also (in an act. and sinister sense) *inveiglement:*—doctrine {4x}, learning {4x}, fair speech {1x}.

Leqach means teaching; instruction; persuasiveness; understanding, in the sense of something taken in. **(1)** The word is used in the sense of something taken in. **(2)** One occurrence is in Prov 1:5: "A wise man will hear, and will increase learning. . . ." **(3)** The word refers to "persuasiveness" in Prov 7:21. Syn: 3947, 4455, 4457, 4727, 4728. See: TWOT—1124a; BDB—544b.

3949. לִקְחִי {1x} **Liqchîy**, *lik-khee';* from 3947; *learned; Likchi*, an Isr.:—Likhi {1x}. See: BDB—544b.

3950. לָקַט {37x} **lâqaṭ**, *law-kat';* a prim. root; prop. to *pick* up, i.e. (gen.) to *gather;* spec. to *glean:*—gather {23x}, gather up {2x}, glean {12x}. See: TWOT—1125; BDB—544c.

3951. לֶקֶט {2x} **leqeṭ**, *leh'-ket;* from 3950; the *gleaning:*—gleaning {2x}. See: TWOT—1125a; BDB—545a.

3952. לָקַק {7x} **lâqaq**, *law-kak';* a prim. root; to *lick* or *lap:*—lap {4x}, lick {3x}. See: TWOT—1126; BDB—545a.

3953. לָקַשׁ {1x} **lâqash**, *l w-kash';* a prim. root; to *gather* the *after* crop:—gather {1x}. See: TWOT—1127c; BDB—545c.

3954. לֶקֶשׁ {2x} **leqesh**, *l h'-kesh;* from 3953; the *after crop:*—latter growth {2x}. See: TWOT—1127a; BDB—545b.

3955. לְשַׁד {2x} **lᵉshad**, *lesh-ad';* from an unused root of uncert. mean.; appar. *juice*, i.e. (fig.) *vigor;* also a sweet or fat *cake:*—fresh {1x}, moisture {1x}. See: TWOT—1128a; BDB—545c.

3956. לָשׁוֹן {117x} **lâshôwn**, *law-shone';* or
לָשֹׁן **lâshôn**, *law-shone';* also (in plur.) fem.
לְשֹׁנָה **lᵉshônâh**, *lesh-o-naw';* from 3960; the *tongue* (of man or animals), used lit. (as the instrument of licking, eating, or speech), and fig. (speech, an ingot, a fork of flame, a cove of water):—tongue {98x}, language {10x}, bay {3x}, wedge {2x}, babbler {1x}, flame {1x}, speaker + 376 {1x}, talkers {1x}.

Lashon means, "tongue; language; speech." **(1)** In the Hebrew Old Testament it appears 115 times, mainly in the poetic and, to a lesser extent, in the prophetical books. The first occurrence is in Gen 10:5: "By these were the isles of the Gentiles divided in their lands; every one after his tongue, after their families, in their nations." **(2)** The basic meaning of *lashon* is "tongue," which as an organ of the body refers **(2a)** to humans (Lam 4:4) and **(2b)** animals (Ex 11:7; Job 41:1). **(3)** The extended meaning of the word as an organ of speech occurs more frequently. **(3a)** A person may be "heavy" or "slow" of tongue (Ex 4:10); or **(3b)** he may be fluent and clear: "The heart also of the rash shall understand knowledge, and the tongue of the stammerers shall be ready to speak plainly" (Is 32:4). **(4)** And see the description of the "tongue" in Ps 45:1: "My heart is inditing a good matter: I speak of the things which I have made touching the King: my tongue is the pen of a ready writer."

(5) The word is often better translated as "speech," because of the negative and positive associations of *lashon.* **(5a)** Especially in the wisdom literature the manner of one's "speech" is considered to be the external expression of the character of the speaker. **(5b)** The fool's "speech" is unreliable (Ps 5:9), deceitful (Ps 109:2; 120:2–3; Prov 6:17), boastful (Ps 140:11), flattering (Prov 26:28), slanderous (Ps 15:3), and subversive (Prov 10:31). **(5c)** The "tongue" of the righteous man heals (Prov 15:4). **(5d)** While the "tongue" may be as sharp as a sword (Ps 57:4), it is a means of giving life to the righteous and death to the wicked: "Death and life are in the power of the tongue: and they that love it shall eat the fruit thereof" (Prov 18:21; cf. 21:23; 25:15). **(6)** The biblical authors speak of divine inspiration as the Lord's enabling them to speak: "The Spirit of the Lord spake by me, and his word was in my tongue" (2 Sa 23:2; cf. Prov 16:1).**(7)** "Tongue" with the meaning "speech" has as a synonym peh (6310), "mouth" (Ps 66:17), and more rarely sapah (8222), "lip" (Job 27:4).

(8) A further extension of meaning is "language." In Hebrew both *sapah* (8222) and *lashon* denote a foreign "language": "For with stammering lips and another tongue will he speak to this people" (Is 28:11). The foreigners to the "language" are well described in these words: "Thou shalt not see a fierce people, a people of a deeper speech than thou canst perceive; of stammering tongue, that thou canst not understand" (Is 33:19). **(9)** *Lashon* also refers to objects that are shaped in the form of a tongue. Most important is the "tongue of fire," which even takes the character of "eating" or "devouring": "Therefore as the [tongues of fire] devoureth the stubble, and the flame consumeth the chaff . . ." (Is 5:24). **(10)** The association in Isaiah of God's appearance in judgment with smoke and fire gave rise to a fine literary description of the Lord's anger: "Behold, the name of the Lord cometh from far, burning with his anger, and the burden thereof is heavy: his lips are full of indignation, and his tongue as a devouring fire" (Is 30:27). Notice the words "lips" and "tongue" here with the meaning of "flames of fire," even though the language evokes the representation of a tongue (as an organ of the body) together with a tongue (of fire). **(11)** Also a bar of gold (Josh 7:21) and a bay of the sea (Is 11:15) shaped in the form of a tongue were called *lashon.* Syn.: 6310, 8193. See: TWOT—1131a; BDB—546a, 1099b.

3957. לִשְׁכָּה {47x} **lishkâh**, *lish-kaw';* from an unused root of uncert. mean.; a *room* in a building (whether for storage, eating, or lodging):—chamber {46x}, parlour {1x}. See: TWOT—1129a; BDB—545c. comp. 5393.

3958. לֶשֶׁם {2x} **leshem**, *leh'-shem;* from an unused root of uncert. mean.; a *gem*, perh. the *jacinth:*—ligure {2x}. See: TWOT—1130; BDB—545d.

3959. לֶשֶׁם {2x} **Leshem**, *leh'-shem;* the same as 3958; *Leshem*, a place in Pal.:—Leshem {2x}. See: BDB—546a.

3960. לָשַׁן {3x} **lâshan**, *law-shan';* a prim. root; prop. to *lick;* but used only as a denom. from 3956; to *wag the tongue*, i.e. to *calumniate:*—accuse {1x}, slander {2x}. See: TWOT—1131; BDB—546d.

3961. לִשָּׁן {7x} **lishshân** (Aram.), *lish-shawn';* corresp. to 3956; *speech*, i.e. a *nation:*—language {7x}. See: TWOT—2817; BDB—1099b.

3962. לֶשַׁע {1x} **Leshaᶜ**, *leh'-shah;* from an unused root thought to mean to *break* through; a boiling *spring; Lesha,* a place prob. E. of the Jordan:—Lasha {1x}. See: BDB—546d.

3963. לֶתֶךְ {1x} **lethek**, *leh'-thek;* from an unused root of uncert. mean.; a *measure* for things dry:—half homer {1x}. See: TWOT—1133a; BDB—547c.

מ

מַ־ **ma-**, or

מָ־ **mâ-**. See 4100.

3964. מָא {1x} **mâ'** (Aram.), *maw;* corresp. to 4100; (as indef.) *that:*—+ what {1x}. See: TWOT—2822; BDB—1099b, 1099c.

3965. מַאֲבוּס {1x} **ma'ăbûwç**, *mah-ab-ooce';* from 75; a *granary:*—storehouse {1x}. Syn.: 618. See: TWOT—10b; BDB—7b, 547a.

3966. מְאֹד {299x} **m^e'ôd**, *meh-ode';* from the same as 181; prop. *vehemence,* i.e. (with or without prep.) *vehemently;* by impl. *wholly, speedily,* etc. (often with other words as an intens. or superl.; espec. when repeated):—very {137x}, greatly {49x}, sore {23x}, exceeding {18x}, great {12x}, exceedingly {11x}, much {10x}, exceeding + 3966 {6x}, exceedingly + 3966 {5x}, diligently {4x}, good {3x}, might {2x}, mightily {2x}, misc. {17x} = especially, far, fast, × louder and louder, quickly, utterly, well.

I. *Me'od*, as an adverb, means "exceedingly; very; greatly; highly." **(1)** *Me'od* functions adverbially, meaning "very." **(2)** The more superlative emphasis appears in Gen 7:18, where the word is applied to the "amount (quantity)" of a thing: "And the waters prevailed, and were increased greatly upon the earth. . . ." **(3)** In Ps 47:9, *me'od* is used of "magnifying" and "exaltation": ". . . For the shields of the earth belong unto God; he is greatly exalted." **(4)** The doubling of the word is a means of emphasizing its basic meaning, which is "very much": "And the waters prevailed exceedingly upon the earth . . ." (Gen 7:19). **II. *Me'od*, as a noun,** means "might." This word is used substantively in the sequence "heart . . . soul . . . might": "And thou shalt love the Lord thy God with all thine heart, and with all thy soul, and with all thy might" (Deut 6:5). See: TWOT—1134; BDB—547a.

3967. מֵאָה {581x} **mê'âh**, *may-aw';* or

מֵאיָה **mê'yâh**, *may-yaw';* prob. a prim. numeral; a *hundred;* also as a multiplicative and a fraction:—hundred {571x}, eleven hundred + 505 {3x}, hundredth {3x}, hundredfold {2x}, sixscore + 6242 {1x}, hundred times {1x}. See: TWOT—1135; BDB—547c, 549a, 1099b.

3968. מֵאָה {2x} **Mê'âh**, *may-aw';* the same as 3967; *Meäh,* a tower in Jerusalem:—Meah {2x}. See: BDB—548c.

3969. מְאָה {8x} **m^e'âh** (Aram.), *meh-aw';* corresp. to 3967:—hundred {8x}. See: TWOT—2818; BDB—1099b.

3970. מַאֲוַי {1x} **ma'ăvay**, *mah-av-ah'ee;* from 183; a *desire:*—desires {1x}. Syn.: 183, 2656. See: TWOT—40c; BDB—16c, 548c.

מוֹאל **môw'l**. See 4136.

3971. מאוּם {22x} **m'ûwm**, *moom;* usually

מוּם **mûwm**, *moom;* as if pass. part. from an unused root prob. mean. to *stain;* a *blemish* (phys. or mor.):—blemish {16x}, blot {3x}, spot {3x}. See: TWOT—1137a; BDB—548c, 558a.

3972. מְאוּמָה {32x} **m^e'ûwmâh**, *meh-oo'-maw;* appar. a form of 3971; prop. a *speck* or *point,* i.e. (by impl.) *something;* with neg. *nothing:*—anything {12x}, nothing {9x}, ought {5x}, any {2x}, fault {1x}, harm {1x}, nought {1x}, somewhat {1x}. See: TWOT—1136; BDB—548d.

3973. מָאוֹס {1x} **mâ'ôwç**, *maw-oce';* from 3988; *refuse:*—refuse {1x}. Syn.: 3985, 3988. See: TWOT—1139a; BDB—549d.

3974. מָאוֹר {19x} **mâ'ôwr**, *maw-ore';* or

מָאֹר **mâ'ôr**, *maw-ore';* also (in plur.) fem.

מְאוֹרָה **m^e'ôwrâh**, *meh-o-raw';* or

מְאֹרָה **m^e'ôrâh**, *meh-o-raw';* from 215; prop. a *luminous* body or *luminary,* i.e. (abstr.) *light* (as an element); fig. *brightness,* i.e. *cheerfulness;* spec. a *chandelier:*—bright {1x}, light {18x}. See: TWOT—52f; BDB—22c, 549a.

3975. מְאוּרָה {1x} **m^e'ûwrâh**, *meh-oo-raw';* fem. pass. part. of 215; something *lighted,* i.e. an *aperture;* by impl. a *crevice* or *hole* (of a serpent):—den {1x}. See: TWOT—52g; BDB—22d.

3976. מֹאזֵן {15x} **mô'zên**, *mo-zane';* from 239; (only in the dual) a pair of *scales:*—balances {15x}. See: TWOT—58a; BDB—24d, 549a, 1079b.

3977. מֹאזֵן {1x} **mô'zên** (Aram.), *mo-zane';* corresp. to 3976:—balances {1x}. See: TWOT—2819; BDB—1079b, 1099b.

מֵאיָה **me'yah**. See 3967.

3978. מַאֲכָל {30x} **ma'ăkâl**, *mah-ak-awl';* from 398; an *eatable* (includ. provender, flesh and fruit):—meat {22x}, food {5x}, fruit {1x}, manner {1x}, victual {1x}. See: TWOT—85d; BDB—38b, 549a.

3979. מַאֲכֶלֶת {4x} **ma'ăkeleth**, *mah-ak-eh'-leth;* from 398; something to *eat* with, i.e. a *knife:*—knife {4x}. See: TWOT—85e; BDB—38b, 549a.

3980. מַאֲכֹלֶת {2x} **ma'ăkôleth**, *mah-ak-o'-leth;* from 398; something *eaten* (by fire), i.e. *fuel:*—fuel {2x}. See: TWOT—85f; BDB—38c, 549a.

3981. מַאֲמָץ {1x} **ma'ămâts**, *mah-am-awts';* from 553; *strength,* i.e. (plur.) *resources:*—force {1x}. See: TWOT—117e; BDB—55c, 549a.

3982. מַאֲמַר {3x} **ma'ămar**, *mah-am-ar';* from 559; something (authoritatively) *said,* i.e. an *edict:*—commandment {2x}, decree {1x}. See: TWOT—118e; BDB—57d, 549a.

3983. מֵאמַר {2x} **mê'mar** (Aram.), *may-mar';* corresp. to 3982:—appointment {1x}, word {1x}. See: TWOT—2585a; BDB—1081b, 1099b.

3984. מָאן {7x} **mâ'n** (Aram.), *mawn;* prob. from a root corresp. to 579 in the sense of an *inclosure* by sides; a *utensil:*—vessel {7x}. See: TWOT—2820; BDB—1099c.

3985. מָאֵן {41x} **mâ'ên**, *maw-ane';* a prim. root; to *refuse:*—refuse {40x}, × utterly {1x}. See: TWOT—1138; BDB—549a.

3986. מָאֵן {4x} **mâ'ên**, *maw-ane';* from 3985; *unwilling:*—refuse {4x}. See: TWOT—1138a; BDB—549b.

3987. מֵאֵן {1x} **mê'ên**, *may-ane';* from 3985; *refractory:*—refuse {1x}. See: TWOT—1138b; BDB—549b.

3988. מָאַס {76x} **mâ'aç**, *maw-as';* a prim. root; to *spurn;* also (intr.) to *disappear:*—despise {25x}, refuse {9x}, reject {19x}, abhor {4x}, become loathsome {1x}, melt away {1x}, misc. {17x} = cast away (off), contemn, disdain, reprobate, × utterly, vile person.

Ma'ac means "to reject, refuse, despise." **(1)** It is found for the first time in Lev 26:15: "If ye shall despise my statutes. . . ." **(2)** God will not force man to do His will, so He sometimes must "reject" him: "Because thou hast rejected knowledge, I will also reject thee, that thou shalt be no priest to me . . ." (Hos 4:6). **(3)** Although God had chosen Saul to be king, Saul's response caused a change in God's plan for Saul: "Because thou hast rejected the word of the LORD, he hath also rejected thee from being king" (1 Sa 15:23). **(4)** As a creature of free choice, man may "reject" God: ". . . Ye have despised the LORD which is among you" (Num 11:20). **(5)** At the same time, man may "reject" evil (Is 7:15–16). When the things that God requires are done with the wrong motives or attitudes, God "despised" his actions: "I hate, I despise your feast days . . ." (Amos 5:21). **(6)** Purity of heart and attitude are more important to God than perfection and beauty of ritual. See: TWOT—1139, 1140; BDB—549b, 549d, 588a.

3989. מַאֲפֶה {1x} **ma'ăpheh**, *mah-af-eh';* from 644; something *baked,* i.e. a *batch:*—baken {1x}. See: TWOT—143a; BDB—66b, 549d.

3990. מַאֲפֵל {1x} **ma'ăphêl**, *mah-af-ale';* from the same as 651; something *opaque:*—darkness {1x}. See: TWOT—145e; BDB—66d, 549d.

3991. מַאֲפֵלְיָה {1x} **ma'ăphêl^eyâh**, *mah-af-ay-leh-yaw';* prol. fem. of 3990; *opaqueness:*—darkness {1x}. See: TWOT—145f; BDB—66d.

3992. מָאַר {4x} **mâ'ar**, *maw-ar';* a prim. root; to *be bitter* or (caus.) to *embitter,* i.e. *be painful:*—fretting {3x}, picking {1x}. See: TWOT—1141; BDB—549d.

מָאֹר **mâ'ôr**. See 3974.

3993. מַאֲרָב {5x} **ma'ărâb**, *mah-ar-awb';* from 693; an *ambuscade:*—ambushment {2x}, lurking place {1x}, lying in wait {2x}. See: TWOT—156e; BDB—70d, 550a.

3994. מְאֵרָה {5x} **m^e'êrâh**, *meh-ay-raw';* from 779; an *execration:*—curse {4x}, cursing {1x}. See: TWOT—168a; BDB—76d, 550a.

מְאֹרָה **m^e'ôrâh**. See 3974.

3995. מִבְדָּלָה {1x} **mibdâlâh**, *mib-daw-law';* from 914; a *separation,* i.e. (concr.) a *separate* place:—separate cities {1x}. See: TWOT—203b; BDB—95d, 550a.

3996. מָבוֹא {24x} **mâbôw'**, *maw-bo';* from 935; an *entrance* (the place or the act); spec. (with or without 8121) *sunset* or the *west;* also (adv. with prep.) *towards:*—going down {6x}, entry {5x}, come {3x}, entrance {3x}, enter {2x}, in {2x}, west {1x}, westward {2x}. See: TWOT—212b; BDB—99d, 550a.

3997. מְבוֹאָה {1x} **m^ebôw'âh**, *meb-o-aw';* fem. of 3996; a *haven:*—entry {1x}. See: TWOT—212b; BDB—99d.

3998. מְבוּכָה {2x} **m^ebûwkâh**, *meb-oo-kaw';* from 943; *perplexity:*—perplexity {2x}. See: TWOT—214a; BDB—100c, 550a.

3999. מַבּוּל {13x} **mabbûwl**, *mab-bool';* from 2986 in the sense of *flowing;* a *deluge:*—flood {13x}. See: TWOT—1142; BDB—550a.

4000. מָבוֹן {1x} **mâbôwn**, *maw-bone';* from 995; *instructing:*—taught {1x}. See: TWOT—239; BDB—107a, 108a, 550a.

4001. מְבוּסָה {3x} **m^ebûwçâh**, *meb-oo-saw';* from 947; a *trampling:*—treading (trodden) down (under foot) {3x}. See: TWOT—216b; BDB—101b, 550a.

4002. מַבּוּעַ {3x} **mabbûwaʿ**, *mab-boo'-ah;* from 5042; a *fountain:*—fountain {2x}, spring {1x}. See: TWOT—1287a; BDB—550a, 616a.

4003. מְבוּקָה {1x} **m^ebûwqâh**, *meb-oo-kah';* from the same as 950; *emptiness:*—void {1x}. See: TWOT—220b; BDB—101c.

4004. מִבְחוֹר {2x} **mibchôwr**, *mib-khore';* from 977; *select,* i.e. well fortified:—choice {2x}. See: TWOT—231e; BDB—104d, 550b.

4005. מִבְחָר {12x} **mibchâr**, *mib-khawr';* from 977; *select,* i.e. best:—choice {7x}, choicest {1x}, chosen {4x}. See: TWOT—231d; BDB—104d.

4006. מִבְחָר {1x} **Mibchâr**, *mib-khawr';* the same as 4005; *Mibchar,* an Isr.:—Mibhar {1x}. See: TWOT—231d; BDB—104d.

4007. מַבָּט {3x} **mabbâṭ**, *mab-bawt';* or

מֶבָּט **mebbâṭ**, *meb-bawt';* from 5027; something *expected,* i.e. (abstr.) *expectation:*—expectation {3x}. See: TWOT—1282a; BDB—550b, 613d.

4008. מִבְטָא {2x} **mibṭâʾ**, *mib-taw';* from 981; a rash *utterance* (hasty vow):—(that which . . .) uttered (out of) {2x}. See: TWOT—232a; BDB—105a, 550b.

4009. מִבְטָח {15x} **mibṭâch**, *mib-tawkh';* from 982; prop. a *refuge,* i.e. (obj.) *security,* or (subj.) *assurance:*—confidence {9x}, trust {4x}, sure {1x}, hope {1x}.

Mibtach means "the act of confiding; the object of confidence; the state of confidence or security." **(1)** The word refers to "the act of confiding" in Prov 21:22: "A wise man scaleth the city of the mighty, and casteth down the strength of the confidence thereof." **(2)** *Mibtach* means the "object of confidence" in Job 8:14 and **(3)** the "state of confidence or security" in Prov 14:26. See: TWOT—233e; BDB—105c, 550b.

4010. מַבְלִיגִית {1x} **mablîygîyth**, *mab-leeg-eeth';* from 1082; *desistance* (or rather *desolation*):—comfort self {1x}. See: TWOT—245a; BDB—114d, 550b.

4011. מִבְנֶה {1x} **mibneh**, *mib-neh';* from 1129; a *building:*—frame {1x}. See: TWOT—255c; BDB—125d, 550b.

4012. מְבֻנַּי {1x} **M^ebunnay**, *meb-oon-nah'-ee;* from 1129; *built* up; *Mebunnai,* an Isr.:—Mebunnai {1x}. See: BDB—125d, 550b.

4013. מִבְצָר {37x} **mibtsâr**, *mib-tsawr';* also (in plur.) fem. (Dan 11:15)

מִבְצָרָה **mibtsârâh**, *mib-tsaw-raw';* from 1219; a *fortification, castle,* or *fortified* city; fig. a *defender:*—hold {13x}, fenced {12x}, fortress {6x}, defenced {4x}, strong {2x}. See: TWOT—270g; BDB—131b, 550b.

4014. מִבְצָר {2x} **Mibtsâr**, *mib-tsawr';* the same as 4013; *Mibtsar,* an Idumæan:—Mibzar {2x}. See: BDB—550b.

מִבְצָרָה **mibtsârâh**. See 4013.

4015. מִבְרָח {1x} **mibrâch**, *mib-rawkh';* from 1272; a *refugee:*—fugitive {1x}. See: TWOT—284c; BDB—138b, 550b.

4016. מָבֻשׁ {1x} **mâbûsh**, *maw-boosh';* from 954; (plur.) the (male) *pudenda:*—secrets {1x}. See: TWOT—222d; BDB—102b, 550b.

4017. מִבְשָׂם {3x} **Mibsâm**, *mib-sawm';* from the same as 1314; *fragrant; Mibsam,* the name of an Ishmaelite and of an Isr.:—Mibsam {3x}. See: BDB—142a, 550b.

4018. מְבַשְּׁלָה {1x} **m^ebashsh^elâh**, *meb-ash-shel-aw';* from 1310; a cooking *hearth:*—boiling-place {1x}. See: TWOT—292b; BDB—143b, 550b.

מַג **Mâg**. See 7248, 7249.

4019. מַגְבִּישׁ {1x} **Magbîysh**, *mag-beesh';* from the same as 1378; *stiffening; Magbish,* an Isr., or a place in Pal.:—Magbish {1x}. See: BDB—150d, 550d.

4020. מִגְבָּלָה {1x} **migbâlâh**, *mig-baw-law';* from 1379; a *border:*—end {1x}. See: TWOT—307d; BDB—148b, 550b.

4021. מִגְבָּעָה {4x} **migbâʿâh**, *mig-baw-aw';* from the same as 1389; a *cap* (as *hemispherical*):—bonnet {4x}. See: TWOT—309c; BDB—149b, 550b.

4022. מֶגֶד {8x} **meged**, *meh'-ghed;* from an unused root prob. mean. to *be eminent;* prop. a *distinguished* thing; hence, something *valuable,* as a product or fruit:—pleasant {3x}, precious fruit {1x}, precious things {4x}. See: TWOT—1144a; BDB—550c.

4023. מְגִדּוֹן {12x} **M^egiddôwn** (Zec 12:11), *meg-id-dōne';* or

מְגִדּוֹ **M^egiddôw**, *meg-id-do';* from 1413; *rendezvous; Megiddon* or *Megiddo,* a place in Pal.:—Megiddo {11x}, Megiddon {1x}. See: BDB—151d, 550c.

4024. מִגְדּוֹל {7x} **Migdôwl**, *mig-dole';* or

מִגְדֹּל **Migdôl**, *mig-dole';* prob. of Eg. or.; *Migdol,* a place in Egypt:—Migdol {5x}, tower {2x}. See: BDB—154a.

4025. מַגְדִּיאֵל {2x} **Magdîyʾêl**, *mag-dee-ale';* from 4022 and 410; *preciousness of God; Magdiël,* an Idumæan:—Magdiel {2x}. See: BDB—550c.

4026. מִגְדָּל {50x} **migdâl**, *mig-dawl';* also (in plur.) fem.

מִגְדָּלָה **migdâlâh**, *mig-daw-law';* from 1431; a *tower* (from its size or height); by anal. a *rostrum;* fig. a (pyramidal) *bed* of flowers:—castles {1x}, flowers {1x}, tower {47x}, pulpit {1x}.

Migdal means "strong place; wooden podium." This noun usually refers **(1)** to a tower or a "strong place" (Gen 11:4–5), but **(2)** it also occurs once to refer to a "wooden podium": "And Ezra the scribe stood upon a pulpit of wood . . ." (Neh 8:4). See: BDB—153d, 550c, 955c. comp. the names following.

מִגְדֹּל **Migdôl**. See 4024.

מִגְדָּלָה **migdâlâh**. See 4026.

4027. מִגְדַּל־אֵל {1x} **Migdal-Êl**, *mig-dal-ale';* from 4026 and 410; *tower of God; Migdal-El,* a place in Pal.:—Migdal-el {1x}. See: BDB—154a.

4028. מִגְדַּל־גָּד {1x} **Migdal-Gâd**, *migdal-gawd';* from 4026 and 1408; *tower of Fortune; Migdal-Gad,* a place in Pal.:—Migdal-gad {1x}. See: BDB—154a.

4029. מִגְדַּל־עֵדֶר {1x} **Migdal-ʿÊder**, *mig-dal'-ay'-der;* from 4026 and 5739; *tower of a flock; Migdal-Eder,* a place in Pal.:—Migdal-eder, tower of the flock {1x}. See: BDB—154a.

4030. מִגְדָּנָה {4x} **migdânâh**, *mig-daw-naw';* from the same as 4022; *preciousness,* i.e. a *gem:*—precious things {3x}, presents {1x}. See: TWOT—1144b; BDB—550c.

4031. מָגוֹג {4x} **Mâgôwg**, *maw-gogue';* from 1463; *Magog,* a son of Japheth; also a barbarous northern region:—Magog {4x}. See: TWOT 324a; BDB—156a, 550c, 550d.

4032. מָגוֹר {8x} **mâgôwr**, *maw-gore';* or (Lam. 2:22)

מָגוּר **mâgûwr**, *maw-goor';* from 1481 in the sense of *fearing;* a *fright* (obj. or subj.):—fear {6x}, terror {2x}. See: TWOT—332a; BDB—159a, 550d. comp. 4036.

4033. מָגוּר {11x} **mâgûwr**, *maw-goor';* or

מָגֻר **mâgûr**, *maw-goor';* from 1481 in the sense of *lodging;* a temporary *abode;* by extens. a permanent *residence:*—dwellings {2x}, pilgrimage {4x}, where sojourn {1x}, be a stranger {4x}. See: TWOT—330c; BDB—158c. comp. 4032.

4034. מְגוֹרָה {1x} **m^egôwrâh**, *meg-o-raw';* fem. of 4032; *affright:*—fear {1x}. See: TWOT—332b; BDB—159a, 550d.

4035. מְגוּרָה {3x} **m^egûwrâh**, *meg-oo-raw';* fem. of 4032 or of 4033; a *fright;* also a *granary:*—barn {1x}, fear {2x}. See: TWOT—330d; BDB—158c, 550d.

4036. מָגוֹר מִסָּבִיב {1x} **Mâgôwr miç-Çâbîyb**, *maw-gore' mis-saw-beeb';* from 4032 and 5439 with the prep. ins.; *affright from around; Magor-mis-Sabib,* a symbol; name of Pashur:—Magor-missabib {1x}. See: BDB—159a, 687a.

4037. מַגְזֵרָה {1x} **magzêrâh**, *mag-zay-raw';* from 1504; a *cutting* implement, i.e. a *blade:*—axe {1x}. See: TWOT—340d; BDB—160d, 550d.

4038. מַגָּל {2x} **maggâl**, *mag-gawl';* from an unused root mean. to *reap;* a *sickle:*—sickle {2x}. See: TWOT—1292a; BDB—409d, 550d, 618c.

4039. מְגִלָּה {21x} **m^egillâh**, *meg-il-law';* from 1556; a *roll:*—roll {20x}, volume {1x}. See: TWOT—353m; BDB—166b, 550d, 1086c.

4040. מְגִלָּה {1x} **m^egillâh** (Aram.), *meg-il-law';* corresp. to 4039:—roll {1x}. See: TWOT—2657c; BDB—1086c, 1099c.

4041. מְגַמָּה {1x} **m^egammâh**, *meg-am-maw';* from the same as 1571; prop. *accumulation,* i.e. *impulse* or *direction:*—sup up {1x}. See: TWOT—361b; BDB—169d.

4042. מָגַן {3x} **mâgan**, *maw-gan';* a denom. from 4043; prop. to *shield; encompass* with; fig. to *rescue,* to *hand* safely *over* (i.e. *surrender*):—deliver {3x}. See: TWOT—367e; BDB—171c, 689b, 698c.

4043. מָגֵן {63x} **mâgên**, *maw-gane';* also (in plur.) fem.

מְגִנָּה **m^eginnâh**, *meg-in-naw';* from 1598; a *shield* (i.e. the small one or *buckler*); fig. a *protector;* also the scaly *hide* of the crocodile:—shield {48x}, buckler {9x}, armed {2x}, defence {2x}, rulers {1x}, scales + 650 {1x}. See: TWOT—367c; BDB—171b, 550d.

4044. מְגִנָּה {1x} **mᵉginnâh**, *meg-in-naw';* from 4042; a *covering* (in a bad sense), i.e. *blindness* or obduracy:—sorrow {1x}. See: TWOT—367d; BDB—171c, 550d. Syn.: 4043.

4045. מִגְעֶרֶת {1x} **migʿereth**, *mig-eh'-reth;* from 1605; *reproof* (i.e. curse):—rebuke {1x}. See: TWOT—370b; BDB—172a, 550d.

4046. מַגֵּפָה {26x} **maggêphâh**, *mag-gay-faw';* from 5062; a *pestilence;* by anal. *defeat:*—plague {21x}; slaughter {3x}, plagued {1x}, stroke {1x}. See: TWOT—1294b; BDB—550d, 620a.

4047. מַגְפִּיעָשׁ {1x} **Magpîyʿâsh**, *mag-pee-awsh';* appar. from 1479 or 5062 and 6211; *exterminator of* (the) *moth; Magpiash*, an Isr.:—Magpiash {1x}. See: BDB—550d.

4048. מָגַר {2x} **mâgar**, *maw-gar';* a prim. root; to *yield up;* intens. to *precipitate:*—cast down {1x}, terrors {1x}. See: TWOT—1145; BDB—550d, 1099c.

4049. מְגַר {1x} **mᵉgar** (Aram.), *meg-ar';* corresp. to 4048; to *overthrow:*—destroy {1x}. See: TWOT—2821; BDB—1099c.

4050. מְגֵרָה {4x} **mᵉgêrâh**, *meg-ay-raw';* from 1641; a *saw:*—axe {1x}, saw {3x}. See: TWOT—386e; BDB—176b, 551a.

4051. מִגְרוֹן {2x} **Migrôwn**, *mig-rone';* from 4048; *precipice; Migron*, a place in Pal.:—Migron {2x}. See: TWOT—386e; BDB—550d.

4052. מִגְרָעָה {1x} **migrâʿâh**, *mig-raw-aw';* from 1639; a *ledge* or offset:—narrowed rests {1x}. See: TWOT—384a; BDB—175d, 551a.

4053. מִגְרָפָה {1x} **migrâphâh**, *mig-raw-faw';* from 1640; something *thrown off* (by the spade), i.e. a *clod:*—clod {1x}. See: TWOT—385b; BDB—175d, 551a.

4054. מִגְרָשׁ {110x} **migrâsh**, *mig-rawsh';* also (in plur.) fem. (Eze 27:28).

מִגְרָשָׁה **migrâshâh**, *mig-raw-shaw';* from 1644; a *suburb* (i.e. open country whither flocks are *driven* for pasture); hence, the *area* around a building, or the *margin* of the sea:—cast out {1x}, suburb {109x}.

Migrash means "suburbs; pasture land; open land." **(1)** It denotes the untilled ground outside a city or the "pasture land" belonging to the cities: "For the children of Joseph were two tribes, Manasseh and Ephraim: therefore they gave no part unto the Levites in the land, save cities to dwell in, with their suburbs for their cattle and for their substance" (Josh 14:4). **(2)** Ezekiel describes a strip of land for the Levites around the city. Part of the land was to be used for houses and part to be left: "And the five thousand, that are left in the breadth over against the five and twenty thousand, shall be a profane place for the city, for dwelling, and for suburbs: and the city shall be in the midst thereof" (Eze 48:15). See: TWOT—388c; BDB—177b, 551a.

4055. מַד {12x} **mad**, *mad;* or

מֵד **mêd**, *made;* from 4058; prop. *extent*, i.e. *height;* also a *measure;* by impl. a *vesture* (as measured); also a *carpet:*—garment {4x}, armour {2x}, measure {2x}, raiment {1x}, judgement {1x}, variant {1x}, clothes {1x}, armour, clothes, garment, judgment, measure, raiment, stature. See: TWOT—1146a; BDB—551a, 551b.

4056. מַדְבַּח {1x} **madbach** (Aram.), *mad-bakh';* from 1684; a sacrificial *altar:*—altar {1x}. See: TWOT—2665b; BDB—1087a, 1099c.

4057. מִדְבָּר {271x} **midbâr**, *mid-bawr';* from 1696 in the sense of *driving;* a *pasture* (i.e. open field, whither cattle are driven); by impl. a *desert;* also *speech* (incl. its organs):—wilderness {255x}, desert {13x}, south {1x}, speech {1x}, wilderness + 776 {1x}. See: TWOT—399k, 399l; BDB—184c, 184d, 551a.

4058. מָדַד {51x} **mâdad**, *maw-dad';* a prim. root; prop. to *stretch;* by impl. to *measure* (as if by *stretching* a line); fig. to *be extended:*—measure {47x}, mete out {2x}, mete {1x}, stretched {1x}.

Madad, as a verb, means "to measure, measure off, extend." **(1)** This word has the nuance of "to survey." **(2)** The basic meaning of the verb is illustrated in its first occurrence in the Old Testament: ". . . they did mete it with an omer . . ." (Ex 16:18). **(3)** *Madad* is used not only of "measuring" volume but also of "measuring" distance (Deut 21:2) and length (Num 35:5). **(4)** A rather gruesome use is found in 2 Sa 8:2, where, after defeating the Moabites, David "measured them with a line, casting them down to the ground; even with two lines measured he to put to death, and with one full line to keep alive." **(5)** The greatness of the creator God is expressed in the question, "Who hath measured the waters in the hollow of his hand . . ." (Is 40:12). **(6)** Also, God "stood, and measured the earth" (Hab 3:6). **(7)** *Madad* can express the idea of extending, stretching: "And he stretched himself upon the child three times . . ." (1 Kin 17:21). See: TWOT—1146; BDB—551a.

4059. מִדַּד {1x} **middad**, *mid-dad';* from 5074; *flight:*—be gone {1x}. See: TWOT—1146; BDB—551a.

4060. מִדָּה {55x} **middâh**, *mid-daw';* fem. of 4055; prop. *extension*, i.e. height or breadth; also a *measure* (incl. its standard); hence, a *portion* (as measured) or a *vestment;* spec. *tribute* (as measured):—measure {37x}, piece {7x}, stature {4x}, size {3x}, meteyard {1x}, garments {1x}, tribute {1x}, wide {1x}.

Middah means "measure; measurement; extent; size; stature; section; area." **(1)** Of the 53 times this noun appears, 25 appearances are in Ezekiel. **(2)** This noun refers to the act of "measurement": "Ye shall do no unrighteousness in judgment, in meteyard, in weight, or in measure" (Lev 19:35). **(3)** In Eze 41:17 this word is used of length "measurement," and in Job 28:25 of liquid "measurement." **(4)** *Middah* means the thing measured, or the "size." Ex 26:2 (the first occurrence) specifies: ". . . Every one of the curtains shall have one measure [the same size]." **(5)** The word can also refer to the duration of one's life: "Lord, make me to know [realize] mine end, and the measure of my days [how short my life really is] . . ." (Ps 39:4). **(6)** A "man of measure" is one of great "stature or size": "And he [Benaiah] slew an Egyptian, a man of great stature, five cubits [about 7½ feet] high . . ." (1 Chr 11:23). **(7)** *Middah* sometimes represents a "measured portion" of a thing: "Malchijah the son of Harim, and Hashub the son of Pahath-moab, repaired the other piece, and the tower of the furnaces" (Neh 3:11). **(8)** In Eze 45:3 the word appears to represent a "measured area." See: TWOT—1146b; BDB—193c, 551c, 551d, 1101b.

4061. מִדָּה {4x} **middâh** (Aram.), *mid-daw'* or

מִנְדָּה **mindâh** (Aram.), *min-daw';* corresp. to 4060; *tribute* in money:—toll {3x}, tribute {1x}. See: TWOT—1147; BDB—1099c, 1101b.

4062. מַדְהֵבָה {1x} **madhêbâh**, *mad-hay-baw';* perh. from the equiv. of 1722; *gold-making*, i.e. *exactress:*—golden city {1x}. See: TWOT—2125d; BDB—551d, 923c.

4063. מֶדֶו {2x} **medev**, *meh'-dev;* from an unused root mean. to *stretch;* prop. *extent*, i.e. *measure;* by impl. a *dress* (as measured):—garment {2x}. See: TWOT—1148a; BDB—551d.

4064. מַדְוֶה {1x} **madveh**, *mad-veh';* from 1738; *sickness:*—diseases {2x}. See: TWOT—411c; BDB—188c, 551d.

4065. מַדּוּחַ {1x} **maddûwach**, *mad-doo'-akh;* from 5080; *seduction:*—causes of banishment {1x}. See: TWOT—1304a; BDB—551d, 623b.

4066. מָדוֹן {18x} **mâdôwn**, *maw-dohn';* from 1777; a *contest* or quarrel:—brawling {2x}, contention {3x}, contentions {2x}, contentious {3x}, discord {1x}, strife {7x}. See: TWOT—426c; BDB—193b, 551d, 552a. comp. 4079, 4090.

4067. מָדוֹן {1x} **mâdôwn**, *maw-dohn';* from the same as 4063; *extensiveness*, i.e. height:—stature {1x}. See: TWOT—1146d; BDB—193c, 551c, 551.

4068. מָדוֹן {1x} **Mâdôwn**, *maw-dohn';* the same as 4067; *Madon*, a place in Pal.:—Madon {1x}. See: BDB—193c.

4069. מַדּוּעַ {6x} **maddûwaʿ**, *mad-doo'-ah;* or

מַדֻּעַ **maddûaʿ**, *mad-doo'-ah;* from 4100 and the pass. part. of 3045; *what* (is) *known?;* i.e. (by impl.) (adv.) *why?:*—how {1x}, wherefore {2x}, why {3x}. This word is related to the verb *yadaʿ* (3045) and is found in Ex 1:18: ". . . Why have ye done this thing, and have saved the men children alive?" See: TWOT—848h; BDB—396c, 551d.

4070. מְדוֹר {4x} **mᵉdôwr** (Aram.), *med-ore';* or

מְדֹר **mᵉdôr** (Aram.), *med-ore';* or

מְדָר **mᵉdâr** (Aram.), *med-awr';* from 1753; a *dwelling:*—dwelling {4x}. See: TWOT—2669b; BDB—1087b, 1099c.

4071. מְדוּרָה {2x} **mᵉdûwrâh**, *med-oo-raw';* or

מְדֻרָה **mᵉdûrâh**, *med-oo-raw';* from 1752 in the sense of *accumulation;* a *pile* of fuel:—pile thereof {1x}, pile for fire {1x}. See: TWOT—418c; BDB—190b, 551d, 552b.

4072. מִדְחֶה {1x} **midcheh**, *mid-kheh';* from 1760; *overthrow:*—ruin {1x}. See: TWOT—420b; BDB—191a, 551d.

4073. מְדַחְפָה {1x} **mᵉdachphâh**, *med-akh-faw';* from 1765; a *push*, i.e. ruin:—overthrow {1x}. See: TWOT—423a; BDB—191b, 551d.

4074. מָדַי {16x} **Mâday**, *maw-dah'-ee;* of for. der.; *Madai*, a country of central Asia:—Madai {2x}, Medes {8x}, Media {6x}. See: BDB—552a, 1099c.

4075. מָדַי {1x} **Mâday**, *maw-dah'-ee;* patrial from 4074; a *Madian* or native of Madai:—Mede {1x}. See: BDB—552a, 1099c.

4076. מָדַי {5x} **Mâday** (Aram.), *maw-dah'-ee;* corresp. to 4074:—Medes {5x}. See: BDB—1099c.

4077. מָדַי {1x} **Mâday** (Aram.), *maw-dah'-ee;* corresp. to 4075:—Median {1x}. See: BDB—1099c.

4078. מַדַּי {1x} **madday**, *mad-dah'-ee;* from 4100 and 1767; *what* (is) *enough*, i.e.

sufficiently:—sufficiently {1x}. See: TWOT—425; BDB—552a, 553b.

4079. מִדְיָן {9x} **midyân**, *mid-yawn';* a var. for 4066:—brawling {2x}, contention {4x}, contentous {3x}. See: TWOT—426c; BDB—193b, 552a.

4080. מִדְיָן {59x} **Midyân**, *mid-yawn';* the same as 4079; *Midjan,* a son of Abraham; also his country and (collect.) his desc.:—Midian {39x}, Midianite {20x}. See: BDB—193c, 552a.

4081. מִדִּין {1x} **Middîyn**, *mid-deen';* a var. for 4080:—Middin {1x}. See: TWOT—426c; BDB—551d.

4082. מְדִינָה {44x} **m^{e}dîynâh**, *med-ee-naw';* from 1777; prop. a *judgeship,* i.e. *jurisdiction;* by impl. a *district* (as ruled by a judge); gen. a *region:*—(× every) province {44x}. See: TWOT—426d; BDB—193d, 552a, 1088c.

4083. מְדִינָה {11x} **m^{e}dîynâh** (Aram.), *med-ee-naw';* corresp. to 4082:—province {11x}. See: TWOT—2674c; BDB—1088c.

4084. מִדְיָנִי {7x} **Midyânîy**, *mid-yaw-nee';* patron. or patrial from 4080; a *Midjanite* or descend. (native) of Midjan:—Midianite {4x}, Midianitish woman {2x}, Midianitish {1x}. See: BDB—193c, 552a. comp. 4092.

4085. מְדֹכָה {1x} **m^{e}dôkâh**, *med-o-kaw';* from 1743; a *mortar:*—mortar {1x}. See: TWOT—413a; BDB—189a, 552a.

4086. מַדְמֵן {1x} **Madmên**, *mad-mane';* from the same as 1828; *dunghill; Madmen,* a place in Pal.:—Madmen {1x}. See: BDB—199b, 552a.

4087. מַדְמֵנָה {1x} **madmênâh**, *mad-may naw';* fem. from the same as 1828; a *dunghill:*—dunghill {1x}. See: TWOT—441b; BDB—199b, 552a.

4088. מַדְמֵנָה {1x} **Madmênâh**, *mad-may-naw';* the same as 4087; *Madmenah,* a place in Pal.:—Madmenah {1x}. See: BDB—199b, 552a.

4089. מַדְמַנָּה {2x} **Madmannâh**, *mad-man-naw';* a var. for 4087; *Madmannah,* a place in Pal.:—Madmannah {2x}. See: BDB—199b, 552a.

4090. מְדָן {3x} **m^{e}dân**, *med-awn';* a form of 4066:—discord {2x}, strifes {1x}. See: TWOT—426c; BDB—193b, 552a.

4091. מְדָן {2x} **M^{e}dân**, *med-awn;* the same as 4090; *Medan,* a son of Abraham:—Medan {2x}. See: TWOT—426c; BDB—193c, 552a.

4092. מְדָנִי {1x} **M^{e}dânîy**, *med-aw-nee';* a var. of 4084:—Midianite {1x}. See: BDB—193c.

4093. מַדָּע {6x} **maddâ^{c}**, *mad-daw';* or

מַדַּע **madda^{c}**, *mad-dah';* from 3045; *intelligence* or *consciousness:*—knowledge {4x}, science {1x}, thought {1x}. See: TWOT—848g; BDB—396b, 552a, 1095b.

מֹדָע **môdâ^{c}**. See 4129.

מַדּוּעַ **madûa^{c}**. See 4069.

4094. מַדְקָרָה {1x} **madqârâh**, *mad-kaw-raw';* from 1856; a *wound:*—piercing {1x}. See: TWOT—449a; BDB—201b, 552a.

מְדֹר **m^{e}dôr**. See 4070.

4095. מַדְרֵגָה {2x} **madrêgâh**, *mad-ray-gaw';* from an unused root mean. to *step;* prop. a *step;* by impl. a *steep* or inaccessible place:—stair {1x}, steep place {1x}. See: TWOT—452a; BDB—201c, 552b.

מְדֻרָה **m^{e}dûrâh**. See 4071.

4096. מִדְרָךְ {1x} **midrâk**, *mid-rawk';* from 1869; a *treading,* i.e. a place for stepping on:—[foot-] breadth {1x}. See: TWOT—453b; BDB—204a, 258a, 552b.

4097. מִדְרָשׁ {2x} **midrâsh**, *mid-rawsh';* from 1875; prop. an *investigation,* i.e. (by impl.) a *treatise* or elaborate compilation:—story {2x}.

Midrash can mean "study; commentary; story." This noun occurs a few times in late biblical Hebrew (2 Chr 13:22); it is commonly used in post-biblical Judaism to refer to the various traditional commentaries by the Jewish sages. One occurrence of the word is in 2 Chr 24:27: "Now concerning his sons, and the greatness of the burdens laid upon him . . . they are written in the story [commentary] of the Book of the Kings." See: TWOT—455a; BDB—205d, 552b.

4098. מְדֻשָׁה {1x} **m^{e}dushshâh**, *med-oosh-shaw';* from 1758; a *threshing,* i.e. (concr. and fig.) *down-trodden* people:—threshing {1x}. See: TWOT—419b; BDB—190c, 552b.

4099. מְדָתָא {5x} **M^{e}dâthâ**, *med-aw-thaw';* of Pers. or.; *Medatha,* the father of Haman:—Hammedatha {5x} [*incl. the art.*]. See: BDB—241a.

4100. מָה {27x} **mâh**, *maw;* or

מַה **mah**, *mah;* or

מָ־ **mâ**, *maw;* or

מַ־ **ma**, *mah;* also

מֶה **meh**, *meh;* a prim. particle; prop. interrog. *what?* (incl. *how? why? when?*); but also exclamation, *what!* (incl. *how!*), or indef. *what* (incl. *whatever,* and even rel. *that which*); often used with prefixes in various adv. or conjunc. senses:—what {8x}, how {3x}, why {3x}, whereby {1x}, wherein {1x}, how long {1x}, how oft {1x}, to what end {1x}; wherefore {3x}, wherewith {1x}, what good {1x}, howsoever {1x}, whereto {1x}, nothing {1x}. See: TWOT—1149; BDB—484d, 541a, 547a, 552a, 552b, 980a, 1099d.

4101. מָה {13x} **mâh** (Aram.), *maw;* corresp. to 4100:—how great {1x}, how mighty {1x}, that which {1x}, what {6x}, whatsoever {1x}, why {3x}. See: TWOT—2822; BDB—1099b, 1099c.

4102. מָהַהּ {9x} **mâhahh**, *maw-hah';* appar. a denom. from 4100; prop. to *question* or hesitate, i.e. (by impl.) to *be reluctant:*—delayed {1x}, linger {2x}, stay selves {1x}, tarry {5x}. See: TWOT—2822; BDB—554c.

4103. מְהוּמָה {12x} **m^{e}hûwmâh**, *meh-hoo-maw';* from 1949; *confusion* or uproar:—destruction {3x}, discomfiture {1x}, trouble {3x}, tumult {2x}, vexation {2x}, vexed {1x}. See: TWOT—486a; BDB—223b.

4104. מְהוּמָן {1x} **M^{e}hûwmân**, *meh-hoo-mawn';* of Pers. or.; *Mehuman,* a eunuch of Xerxes:—Mehuman {1x}. See: BDB—54d, 554c.

4105. מְהֵיטַבְאֵל {3x} **M^{e}hêytab^{e}êl**, *meh-hay-tab-ale';* from 3190 (augmented) and 410; *bettered of God; Mehetabel,* the name of an Edomitish man and woman:—Mehetabeel {1x}, Mehetabel {2x}. See: BDB—406b, 554c.

4106. מָהִיר {4x} **mâhîyr**, *maw-here';* or

מָהִר **mâhîr**, *maw-here';* from 4116; *quick;* hence, *skilful:*—diligent {1x}, hasty {1x}, ready {2x}. See: TWOT—1152c; BDB—554c, 555b.

4107. מָהַל {1x} **mâhal**, *maw-hal';* a prim. root; prop. to *cut down* or *reduce,* i.e. by impl. to *adulterate:*—mixed {1x}. See: TWOT—1151; BDB—554c.

4108. מַהְלֵךְ {1x} **mahlêk**, *mah-lake';* from 1980; a *walking* (plur. collect.), i.e. *access:*—place to walk {1x}. See: TWOT—498d; BDB—237b.

4109. מַהֲלָךְ {4x} **mahălâk**, *mah-hal-awk';* from 1980; a *walk,* i.e. a *passage* or a *distance:*—journey {3x}, walk {1x}. *Mahalak,* which appears 4 times, means "passage" (Eze 42:4) and "journey" (Neh 2:6). See: TWOT—498d; BDB—237b, 554c.

4110. מַהֲלָל {1x} **mahălâl**, *mah-hal-awl';* from 1984; *fame:*—praise {1x}. *Mahalal* occurs once (Prov 27:21) and denotes the degree of "praise" or its lack. See: TWOT—500b; BDB—239c, 554d.

4111. מַהֲלַלְאֵל {7x} **Mahălal^{e}êl**, *mah-hal-al-ale';* from 4110 and 410; *praise of God; Mahalalel,* the name of an antediluvian patriarch and of an Isr.:—Mahalaleel {7x}. See: BDB—239d, 554d.

4112. מַהֲלֻמָּה {2x} **mahălummâh**, *mah-hal-oom-maw';* from 1986; a *blow:*—stripes {1x}, strokes {1x}. See: TWOT—502c; BDB—240d, 554d.

4113. מַהֲמֹרָה {1x} **mahămôrâh**, *mah-ham-o-raw';* from an unused root of uncert. mean.; perh. an *abyss:*—deep pits {1x}. See: TWOT—509a; BDB—243b, 554d.

4114. מַהְפֵּכָה {6x} **mahpêkâh**, *mah-pay-kaw';* from 2015; a *destruction:*—when . . . overthrew {3x}, overthrow {2x}, overthrown {1x}. See: TWOT—512d; BDB—245c, 246b, 554d.

4115. מַהְפֶּכֶת {4x} **mahpeketh**, *mah-peh'-keth;* from 2015; a *wrench,* i.e. the *stocks:*—prison {2x}, stocks {2x}. See: TWOT—512e; BDB—246b, 554d.

4116. מָהַר {64x} **mâhar**, *maw-har';* a prim. root; prop. to *be liquid* or *flow* easily, i.e. (by impl.); to *hurry* (in a good or a bad sense); often used (with another verb) adv. *promptly:*—haste {42x}, swift {3x}, quickly {3x}, hastily {2x}, hasty {2x}, soon {2x}, speed {2x}, headlong {1x}, rash {1x}, fearful {1x}, ready {1x}, shortly {1x}, speedily {1x}, straightway {1x}, suddenly {1x}.

Mahar means "to hasten, make haste." This verb and various derivatives are common to both ancient and modern Hebrew. It occurs 64 times in the Hebrew Bible; it appears twice in the first verse in which it is found: "And Abraham hastened [*mahar*] into the tent unto Sarah, and said, Make ready quickly [*mahar*] three measures of fine meal . . ." (Gen 18:6). It often has an adverbial use when it appears with another verb, such as in Gen 18:7: ". . . hasted to dress it" (or "quickly prepared it"). See: TWOT—1152; BDB—554d, 555a.

4117. מָהַר {2x} **mâhar**, *maw-har';* a prim. root (perh. rather the same as 4116 through the idea of *readiness* in assent); to *bargain* (for a wife), i.e. to *wed:*—endow {1x}, × surely {1x}. See: TWOT—1153; BDB—555c.

4118. מַהֵר {18x} **mahêr**, *mah-hare'*; from 4116; prop. *hurrying;* hence, (adv.) *in a hurry:*—hasteth {1x}, hastily {2x}, at once {1x}, quickly {8x}, soon {1x}, speedily {4x}, suddenly {1x}. See: TWOT—1152a, 1152b; BDB—555a.

מָהִר **mâhîr**. See 4106.

4119. מֹהַר {3x} **môhar**, *mo'-har;* from 4117; a *price* (for a wife):—dowry {3x}. See: TWOT—1153a; BDB—555c.

4120. מְהֵרָה {20x} **m^ehêrâh**, *meh-hay-raw';* fem. of 4118; prop. a *hurry;* hence, (adv.) *promptly:*—quickly {10x}, speedily {4x}, make speed {1x}, soon {1x}, swiftly {1x}, hastily {1x}, with speed {1x}, shortly {1x}. See: TWOT—1152d; BDB—555b.

4121. מַהֲרַי {3x} **Mahăray**, *mah-har-ah'-ee;* from 4116; *hasty; Maharai*, an Isr.:—Maharai {3x}. See: BDB—555b.

4122. מַהֵר שָׁלָל חָשׁ בַּז {2x} **Mahêr Shâlâl Châsh Baz**, *mah-hare' shaw-lawl' khawsh baz;* from 4118 and 7998 and 2363 and 957; *hasting* (is he [the enemy] to the) *booty, swift* (to the) *prey; Maher-Shalal-Chash-Baz;* the symb. name of the son of Isaiah:—Maher-shalal-hash-baz {2x}. See: BDB—555b.

4123. מַהֲתַלָּה {1x} **mahăthallâh**, *mah-hath-al-law';* from 2048; a *delusion:*—deceit {1x}. See: TWOT—2514a; BDB—555c.

4124. מוֹאָב {181x} **Môw'âb**, *mo-awb;* from a prol. form of the prep. pref. *m-* and 1; *from* (her [the mother's]) *father; Moäb*, an incestuous son of Lot; also his territory and desc.:—Moab {166x}, Moabites {15x}. See: TWOT—1155; BDB—547a, 555d.

4125. מוֹאָבִי {16x} **Môw'âbîy**, *mo-aw-bee';* fem.

מוֹאָבִיָּה **Môw'âbîyâh**, *mo-aw-bee-yaw';* or

מוֹאָבִית **Môwâbîyth**, *mo-aw-beeth';* patron. from 4124; a *Moäbite* or *Moäbitess*, i.e. a desc. from Moab:—Moabite {7x}, Moabitess {6x}, Moab {2x}, Moabitish {1x}. See: TWOT—1155a; BDB—555d.

מוֹאל **môw'l**. See 4136.

4126. מוֹבָא {2x} **môwbâ'**, *mo-baw';* by transp. for 3996; an *entrance:*—coming {2x}. See: TWOT—212b; BDB—100a, 556a.

4127. מוּג {17x} **mûwg**, *moog;* a prim. root; to *melt*, i.e. lit. (to *soften, flow down, disappear*), or fig. (to *fear, faint*):—melt {5x}, dissolve {4x}, faint {3x}, melt away {2x}, consumed {1x}, fainthearted {1x}, soft {1x}. See: TWOT—1156; BDB—556a.

4128. מוּד {1x} **mûwd**, *mood;* a prim. root; to *shake:*—measure {1x}. See: TWOT—1157; BDB—551b, 556d.

4129. מוֹדַע {2x} **môwda'**, *mo-dah';* or rather

מֹדָע **môdâ'**, *mo-daw';* from 3045; an *acquaintance:*—kinswoman {1x}, kinsman {1x}. See: TWOT—848e; BDB—396b, 552a, 556d, 568a.

4130. מוֹדַעַת {1x} **môwda'ath**, *mo-dah'-ath;* from 3045; *acquaintance:*—kindred {1x}. See: TWOT—848f; BDB—396b, 552a.

4131. מוֹט {39x} **môwt**, *mote;* a prim. root; to *waver;* by impl. to *slip, shake, fall:*—moved {20x}, removed {5x}, slip {3x}, carried {1x}, cast {1x}, course {1x}, decay {1x}, falling down {1x}, exceedingly {1x}, fall {1x}, ready {1x}, shaketh {1x}, slide {1x}, variant {1x}. See: TWOT—1158; BDB—556d.

4132. מוֹט {6x} **môwt**, *mote;* from 4131; a *wavering*, i.e. *fall;* by impl. a *pole* (as shaking); hence, a *yoke* (as essentially a bent pole):—bar {3x}, be moved {1x}, staff {1x}, yoke {1x}. See: TWOT—1158a; BDB—557a.

4133. מוֹטָה {12x} **môwtâh**, *mo-taw';* fem. of 4132; a *pole;* by impl. an ox-*bow;* hence, a *yoke* (either lit. or fig.):—bands {2x}, heavy {1x}, staves {1x}, yoke {8x}. See: TWOT—1158b; BDB—557b.

4134. מוּךְ {5x} **mûwk**, *mook;* a prim. root; to *become thin*, i.e. (fig.) *be impoverished:*—be (waxen) poor {1x}, poorer {1x}. See: TWOT—1159; BDB—557b.

4135. מוּל {36x} **mûwl**, *mool;* a prim. root; to *cut* short, i.e. *curtail* (spec. the prepuce, i.e. to *circumcise*); by impl. to *blunt;* fig. to *destroy:*—circumcise {30x}, destroy {3x}, cut down {1x}, needs {1x}, cut in pieces {1x}.

Muwl (4135) means "to circumcise, cut off." **(1)** Most of the occurrences in the Old Testament take place in the Pentateuch (20 times) and Joshua (8 times). *Muwl* occurs most frequently in Genesis (17 times, 11 of them in Genesis 17 alone) and Joshua (8 times). **(2)** The physical act of circumcision was introduced by God as a sign of the Abrahamic covenant: **(2a)** "This *is* my covenant, which ye shall keep, between me and you and thy seed after thee; Every man child among you shall be circumcised. And ye shall circumcise the flesh of your foreskin; and it shall be a token of the covenant betwixt me and you" (Gen 17:10–11). **(2b)** It was a permanent "cutting off" of the foreskin of the male organ, and as such was a reminder of the perpetuity of the covenantal relationship. **(2c)** Israel was enjoined to be faithful in "circumcising" all males; each male baby was to be "circumcised" on the eighth day (Gen 17:12; Lev 12:3). **(2d)** Not only were the physical descendants of Abraham "circumcised," but also those who were servants, slaves, and foreigners in the covenant community (Gen 17:13–14).

(3) The special act of circumcision was a sign of God's gracious promise. With the promise and covenantal relations, God expected that His people would joyously and willingly live up to His expectations, and thus demonstrate His rule on earth. **(4)** To describe the "heart" attitude, several writers of Scripture use the verb "to circumcise." **(4a)** The "circumcision" of the flesh is a physical sign of commitment to God. **(4b)** Deuteronomy particularly is fond of the spiritual usage of the verb "to circumcise": "Circumcise therefore the foreskin of your heart, and be no more stiffnecked" (Deut 10:16; cf. 30:6). **(4c)** Jeremiah took over this usage: "Circumcise yourselves to the Lord, and take away the foreskins of your heart, ye men of Judah . . . , because of the evil of your doings" (Jer 4:4). **(5)** Few occurrences of the verb differ from the physical and the spiritual usage of "to circumcise." *Muwl* in the Book of Psalms has the meaning of "to cut off, destroy": "All nations compassed me about: but in the name of the LORD will I destroy them" (Ps 118:10; cf. vv. 11–12). See: TWOT—1161; BDB—557d.

4136. מוּל {36x} **mûwl**, *mool;* or

מוֹל **môwl** (Deut 1:1), *mole;* or

מוֹאל **môw'l** (Neh 12:38), *mole;* or

מֻל **mûl** (Num 22:5), *mool;* from 4135; prop. *abrupt*, i.e. a *precipice;* by impl. the *front;* used only adv. (with prep. pref.) *opposite:*—against {21x}, toward {3x}, forefront + 6440 {3x}, before {2x}, before it + 6440 {2x}, against + 6440 {1x}, forefront {1x}, from {1x}, Godward + 430 {1x}, with {1x}. See: TWOT—1160; BDB—541a, 556a, 557b.

4137. מוֹלָדָה {1x} **Môwlâdâh**, *mo-law-daw';* from 3205; *birth; Moladah*, a place in Pal.:—Moladah {1x}. See: BDB—409d, 558a.

4138. מוֹלֶדֶת {22x} **môwledeth**, *mo-leh'-deth;* from 3205; *nativity* (plur. *birth-place*); by impl. *lineage, native country;* also *offspring, family:*—kindred {11x}, nativity {6x}, born {2x}, begotten {1x}, issue {1x}, native {1x}. See: TWOT—867f; BDB—558a.

4139. מוּלָה {1x} **mûwlâh**, *moo-law';* from 4135; *circumcision:*—circumcision {1x}.

Muwlah is found in Ex 4:26: "So he let him go: then she said, A bloody husband *thou art*, because of the circumcision." See: TWOT—1161a; BDB—558a.

4140. מוֹלִיד {1x} **Môwlîyd**, *mo-leed';* from 3205; *genitor; Molid*, an Isr.:—Molid {1x}. See: BDB—410a, 558a.

מוּם **muwm**. See 3971.

מוּמְכָן **Môwmûkân**. See 4462.

4141. מוּסָב {1x} **mûwçâb**, *moo-sawb';* from 5437; a *turn*, i.e. *circuit* (of a building):—winding about {1x}.

Muwcab occurs once with the meaning of "circular passage": ". . . For the winding about of the house went still upward round about the house . . ." (Eze 41:7). See: TWOT—1456b; BDB—558a, 687c.

4142. מוּסַבָּה {5x} **mûwçabbâh**, *moo-sab-baw';* or

מֻסַבָּה **mûçabbâh**, *moo-sab-baw';* fem. of 4141; a *reversal*, i.e. the *backside* (of a gem), *fold* (of a double-leaved door), *transmutation* (of a name):—being changed {1x}, inclosed {2x}, be set {1x}, turning {1x}. See: TWOT—1456b; BDB—686d.

4143. מוּסָד {2x} **mûwçâd**, *moo-sawd';* from 3245; a *foundation:*—foundation {2x}. See: TWOT—875d; BDB—414b, 558a.

4144. מוֹסָד {3x} **môwçâd**, *mo-sawd';* from 3245; a *foundation:*—foundation {3x}. See: TWOT—875f; BDB—414c, 558a.

4145. מוּסָדָה {1x} **mûwçâdâh**, *moo-saw-daw';* fem. of 4143; a *foundation;* fig. an *appointment:*—grounded {1x}. See: TWOT—875e; BDB—414c, 558a. comp. 4328.

4146. מוֹסָדָה {10x} **môwçâdâh**, *mo-saw-daw';* or

מֹסָדָה **môçâdâh**, *mo-saw-daw';* fem. of 4144; a *foundation:*—foundation {10x}. See: TWOT—875f; BDB—414c.

4147. מוֹסֵר {11x} **môwçêr**, *mo-sare';* also (in plur.) fem.

מוֹסֵרָה **môwçêrâh**, *mo-say-raw';* or

מֹסְרָה **môç^erâh**, *mo-ser-aw';* from 3256; prop. *chastisement*, i.e. (by impl.) a *halter;* fig. *restraint:*—bands {6x}, bond {5x}. See: TWOT—141f; BDB—64c, 558a.

4148. מוּסָר {50x} **mûwçâr**, *moo-sawr';* from 3256; prop. *chastisement;* fig. *reproof, warning* or *instruction;* also *restraint:*—instruction {30x}, correction {8x}, chasten {4x}, chastisement {3x}, check {1x}, bond {1x}, discipline {1x}, doctrine {1x}, rebuker {1x}.

Muwcar means "instruction; chastisement; warning." **(1)** This noun occurs 50 times, mainly in Proverbs. **(2)** The first occurrence is in Deut 11:2: "... I speak not with your children which have not known, and which have not seen the chastisement of the LORD your God, his greatness, his mighty hand, and his stretched out arm." **(3)** One of the major purposes of the wisdom literature was to teach wisdom and *muwcar* (Prov 1:2). **(4)** *Muwcar* is discipline, but more. **(4a)** As "discipline" it teaches how to live correctly in the fear of the Lord, so that the wise man learns his lesson before temptation and testing: "Then I saw, and considered it well: I looked upon it, and received instruction" (Prov 24:32). **(4b)** This "discipline" is training for life; hence, paying attention to *muwcar* is important. **(4c)** Many verbs bear out the need for a correct response: "hear, obey, love, receive, obtain, take hold of, guard, keep." **(4d)** Moreover, the rejection is borne out by many verbs connected with *muwcar:* "reject, hate, ignore, not love, despise, forsake."

(5) When *muwcar* as "instruction" has been given, but was not observed, the *muwcar* as "chastisement" or "discipline" may be the next step: "Foolishness is bound in the heart of a child; but the rod of correction shall drive it far from him" (Prov 22:15). **(6)** Careful attention to "instruction" brings honor (Prov 1:9), life (Prov 4:13), and wisdom (Prov 8:33), and above all it pleases God: "For whoso findeth me findeth life, and shall obtain favor of the Lord" (Prov 8:35). **(7)** The lack of observance of "instruction" brings its own results: death (Prov 5:23), poverty, and shame (Prov 13:18), and is ultimately a sign that one has no regard for one's own life (Prov 15:32). **(8)** The receptivity for "instruction" from one's parents, teacher, the wise, or the king is directly corollary to one's subjugation to God's discipline. **(8a)** The prophets charged Israel with not receiving God's discipline: "O Lord, are not thine eyes upon the truth? thou hast stricken them, but they have not grieved; thou hast consumed them, but they have refused to receive correction: they have made their faces harder than a rock; they have refused to return" (Jer 5:3).

(8b) Jeremiah asked the men of Judah and the inhabitants in the besieged Jerusalem to pay attention to what was happening around them, that they still might subject themselves to "instruction" (35:13). **(9)** Isaiah predicted that God's chastisement on man was carried by the Suffering Servant, bringing peace to those who believe in Him: "But he was wounded for our transgressions, he was bruised for our iniquities: the chastisement of our peace was upon him; and with his stripes we are healed" (53:5). See: TWOT—877b; BDB—416b, 558a.

4149. מוֹסֵרָה {3x} **Môwçêrâh**, *mo-say-raw';* or (plur.)

מֹסֵרוֹת **Môçᵉrôwth**, *mo-ser-othe'* fem. of 4147; *correction* or *corrections; Moserah* or *Moseroth,* a place in the Desert:—Mosera {1x}, Moseroth {2x}. See: BDB—64c, 588b.

4150. מוֹעֵד {223x} **môwʿêd**, *mo-ade';* or

מֹעֵד **môʿêd**, *mo-ade';* or (fem.)

מוֹעָדָה **môwʿâdâh** (2 Chr 8:13), *mo-aw-daw';* from 3259; prop. an *appointment,* i.e. a fixed *time* or season; spec. a *festival;* conventionally a *year;* by impl. an *assembly* (as convened for a def. purpose); tech. the *congregation;* by extens. The *place of meeting;* also a *signal* (as appointed beforehand):—congregation {150x}, feast {23x}, season {13x}, appointed {12x}, time {12x}, assembly {4x}, solemnity {4x}, solemn {2x}, days {1x}, sign {1x}, synagogues {1x}.

Moʿed means "appointed place of meeting; meeting." **(1)** The noun *moʿed* appears in the Old Testament 223 times, of which 160 times are in the Pentateuch. **(2)** The word *moʿed* keeps its basic meaning of "appointed," **(2a)** but varies as to what is agreed upon or appointed according to the context: the time, the place, or the meeting itself. **(2b)** The usage of the verb in Amos 3:3 is illuminating: "Can two walk together, except they be agreed?" Whether they have agreed on a time or a place of meeting, or on the meeting itself, is ambiguous. **(3)** The meaning of *moʿed* is fixed within the context of Israel's religion. **(3a)** First, the festivals came to be known as the "appointed times" or the set feasts. These festivals were clearly prescribed in the Pentateuch.

(3b) The word refers to any "festival" or "pilgrimage festival," such as Passover (Lev 23:15ff.), the feast of first fruits (Lev 23:15ff.), the feast of tabernacles (Lev 23:33ff.), or the Day of Atonement (Lev 23:27). **(3b)** God condemned the people for observing the *moʿed* ritualistically: "Your new moons and your appointed feasts my soul hateth ..." (Is 1:14). **(4)** The word *moʿed* also signifies a "fixed place." **(4a)** This usage is not frequent: "For thou hast said in thine heart, I will ascend into heaven, I will exalt my throne above the stars of God: I will sit also upon the mount of the congregation [*moʿed*], in the sides of the north ..." (Is 14:13). **(4b)** "For I know that thou wilt bring me to death, and to the house appointed for all living" (Job 30:23). **(5)** In both meanings of *moʿed*—"fixed time" and "fixed place"—a common denominator is the "meeting" of two or more parties at a certain place and time—hence the usage of *moʿed* as "meeting." **(6)** The phrase, "tabernacle of the congregation," is a translation of the Hebrew *ʿohel moʿed* ("tent of meeting"). **(6a)** The phrase occurs 139 times—mainly in Exodus, Leviticus, and Numbers, rarely in Deuteronomy.

(6b) It signifies that the Lord has an "appointed place" by which His presence is represented and through which Israel was assured that their God was with them. **(6c)** The fact that the tent was called the "tent of meeting" signifies that Israel's God was among His people and that He was to be approached at a certain time and place that were "fixed" *(yaʿad)* in the Pentateuch. **(6d)** In the KJV, this phrase is translated as "tabernacle of the congregation" (Ex 28:43) because translators realized that the noun *ʿedah* ("congregation") is derived from the same root as *moʿed.* **(7)** Of the three meanings, the appointed "time" is most basic. The phrase "tent of meeting" lays stress on the "place of meeting." The "meeting" itself is generally associated with "time" or "place." Syn.: 5172. See: TWOT—878b; BDB—417b, 558a, 588d.

4151. מוֹעָד {1x} **môwʿâd**, *mo-awd';* from 3259; prop. an *assembly* [as in 4150]; fig. a *troop:*—appointed time {1x}. See: TWOT—878c; BDB—418a, 558a.

4152. מוּעָדָה {1x} **mûwʿâdâh**, *moo-aw-daw';* from 3259; an *appointed* place, i.e. *asylum:*—appointed {1x}. See: TWOT—878d; BDB—418a, 558a.

4153. מוֹעַדְיָה {1x} **Môwʿadyâh**, *mo-ad-yaw';* from 4151 and 3050; *assembly of Jah; Moädjah,* an Isr.:—Moadiah {1x}. See: BDB—558b, 588c. comp. 4573.

4154. מוּעֶדֶת {1x} **mûwʿedeth**, *moo-ay'-deth;* fem. pass. part. of 4571; prop. *made to slip,* i.e. *dislocated:*—out of joint {1x}. See: TWOT—1226; BDB—588c.

4155. מוּעָף {1x} **mûwʿâph**, *moo-awf';* from 5774; prop. *covered,* i.e. *dark;* abstr. *obscurity,* i.e. *distress:*—dimness {1x}. See: TWOT—1583a; BDB—558b, 734a.

4156. מוֹעֵצָה {7x} **môwʿêtsâh**, *mo-ay-tsaw';* from 3289; a *purpose:*—counsel {6x}, device {1x}. See: TWOT—887b; BDB—420b, 558b, 591d.

4157. מוּעָקָה {1x} **mûwʿâqâh**, *moo-aw-kaw';* from 5781; *pressure,* i.e. (fig.) *distress:*—affliction {1x}. See: TWOT—1585b; BDB—558b, 734c.

4158. מוֹפַעַת {4x} **Môwphaʿath** (Jer 48:21), *mo-fah'-ath;* or

מֵיפַעַת **Mêyphaʿath**, *may-fah'-ath;* or

מֵפַעַת **Mêphaʿath**, *may-fah'-ath;* from 3313; *illuminative; Mophaath* or *Mephaath,* a place in Pal.:—Mephaath {4x}. See: BDB—422b, 558b, 568c, 592b.

4159. מוֹפֵת {36x} **môwphêth**, *mo-faith';* or

מֹפֵת **môphêth**, *mo-faith';* from 3302 in the sense of *conspicuousness;* a *miracle;* by impl. a *token* or *omen:*—wonder {25x}, sign {8x}, miracle {2x}, wondered at {1x}.

Mowpheth means "wonder; sign; portent." **(1)** First, this word signifies a divine act or a special display of divine power: "When thou goest to return into Egypt, see that thou do all those wonders before Pharaoh, which I have put in thine hand ..." (Ex 4:21—the first biblical occurrence of the word). **(2)** Acts effecting the divine curses are called "wonders." Thus the word does not necessarily refer to a miraculous act, if "miracle" means something outside the realm of ordinary providence. **(3)** The word can represent a "sign" from God or a token of a future event: "This is the sign which the LORD hath spoken: Behold, the altar shall be rent, and the ashes that are upon it shall be poured out" (1 Kin 13:3). **(3a)** This sense sometimes has the nuance "symbol": "Hear now, O Joshua the high priest, thou, and thy fellows that sit before thee: for they *are* men wondered at *(mowpheth):* for, behold, I will bring forth my servant the BRANCH" (Zec 3:8; cf. Ps 71:7). See: TWOT—152a; BDB—68d, 558b.

4160. מוּץ {1x} **mûwts**, *moots;* a prim. root; to *press,* i.e. (fig.) to *oppress:* extortioner {1x}. See: TWOT—1162; BDB—568c, 592b.

4161. מוֹצָא {27x} **môwtsâʾ**, *mo-tsaw';* or

מֹצָא **môtsâʾ**, *mo-tsaw';* from 3318; a *going forth,* i.e. (the act) an *egress,* or (the place) an *exit;* hence, a *source* or *product;* spec. *dawn,* the *rising* of the sun (the *East*), *exportation, utterance,* a *gate,* a *fountain,* a *mine,* a *meadow* (as producing grass):—go out {7x}, go forth {5x}, spring {3x}, brought {2x}, watersprings + 4325 {2x}, bud {1x}, east {1x}, outgoings {1x}, proceeded {1x}, proceedeth {1x}, vein {1x}, come out {1x}, watercourse {1x}.

Motsaʾ means place of going forth; that which comes forth; going forth. **(1)** *Motsaʾ* is a word for "east" (cf. Ps 19:6), where the sun rises ("goes forth"): "His going forth *is* from the end of the heaven, and his circuit unto the ends of it: and there is nothing hid from the heat thereof." **(2)** The word also represents the "place of departure" or "exit" from the temple in Ezekiel's vision (Eze 42:11): "And the way before them *was* like the appearance of the chambers which *were* toward the north, as long as they, *and* as broad as they: and all their goings out *were* both according to their fashions, and according to their doors." **(3)** *Motsa'* also refers to the "starting point" of a journey (Num 33:2). **(4)** *Motsa'* may also refer to that which "comes forth," for example, **(4a)** an "utterance" (Num 30:13), and **(4b)** the "going forth" of the morning and evening, the dawn and dusk (Ps 65:8). **(5)** Finally, the word can represent the "actual going forth" itself. So Hosea says that the LORD's "going forth" to redeem His people is as certain as the sunrise (6:3). See: TWOT—893c; BDB—425c, 558b, 594b.

4162. מוֹצָא {5x} **Môwtsâʾ**, *mo-tsaw';* the same as 4161; *Motsa,* the name of two Isr.:—Moza {5x}. See: BDB—426a, 558b, 594b.

4163. מוֹצָאָה {2x} **môwtsâʾâh**, *mo-tsaw-aw';* fem. of 4161; a family *descent;* also a *sewer* [marg.; comp. 6675]:—draught house {1x}; goings forth {1x}. See: TWOT—893d; BDB—426a, 558b.

4164. מוּצַק {3x} **mûwtsaq**, *moo-tsak';* or

מוּצָק **mûwtsâq**, *moo-tsawk';* from 3332; *narrowness;* fig. *distress:*—anguish {1x}, is straitened {1x}, straitness {1x}. See: TWOT—1895c; BDB—558b, 848a.

4165. מוּצָק {2x} **mûwtsâq**, *moo-tsawk';* from 5694; prop. *fusion,* i.e. lit. a *casting* (of metal); fig. a *mass* (of clay):—casting {1x}, hardness {1x}. See: TWOT—897b; BDB—427c, 558b, 848a.

4166. מוּצָקָה {2x} **mûwtsâqâh**, *moo-tsaw-kaw';* or

מֻצָקָה **mûtsâqâh**, *moo-tsaw-kaw';* from 3332; prop. something *poured* out, i.e. a *casting* (of metal); by impl. a *tube* (as cast):—when it was cast {1x}, pipe {1x}. See: TWOT—897c; BDB—427c, 558b, 595b.

4167. מוּק {1x} **mûwq**, *mook;* a prim. root; to *jeer,* i.e. (intens.) *blaspheme:*—be corrupt {1x}. See: TWOT—1163; BDB—558b.

4168. מוֹקֵד {2x} **môwqêd**, *mo-kade';* from 3344; a *fire* or *fuel;* abstr. a *conflagration:*—burning {1x}, hearth {1x}. See: TWOT—901b; BDB—428d, 558c.

4169. מוֹקְדָה {1x} **môwqᵉdâh**, *mo-ked-aw';* fem. of 4168; *fuel:*—burning {1x}. See: TWOT—901c; BDB—429a, 558c.

4170. מוֹקֵשׁ {27x} **môwqêsh**, *mo-kashe';* or

מֹקֵשׁ **môqêsh**, *mo-kashe';* from 3369; a *noose* (for catching animals) (lit. or fig.); by impl. a *hook* (for the nose):—snare {20x}, gin {3x}, trap {2x}, ensnared {1x}, snared {1x}. See: TWOT—906c; BDB—430c, 558c.

4171. מוּר {14x} **mûwr**, *moor;* a prim. root; to *alter;* by impl. to *barter,* to *dispose of:*—change {10x}, at all {2x}, removed {1x}, exchange {1x}. See: TWOT—1164; BDB—558c.

4172. מוֹרָא {13x} **môwrâʾ**, *mo-raw';* or

מֹרָא **môrâʾ**, *mo-raw';* or

מוֹרָה **môrâh** (Ps 9:20), *mo-raw';* from 3372; *fear;* by impl. a *fearful* thing or deed:—fear {8x}, terror {3x}, dread {1x}, terribleness {1x}.

Morah means "fear." **(1)** The noun *morah,* which appears 13 times, is used exclusively of the fear of being before a superior kind of being. **(2)** Usually it is used to describe the reaction evoked in men by God's mighty works of destruction and sovereignty: **(2a)** "For the LORD thy God *is* a consuming fire, *even* a jealous God" (Deut 4:24). **(2b)** Hence, the word represents a very strong "fear" or "terror." **(3)** In the singular, this word emphasizes the divine acts themselves. *Morah* may suggest the reaction **(3a)** of animals to men: "And the fear of you and the dread of you shall be upon every beast of the earth, and upon every fowl of the air, upon all that moveth *upon* the earth, and upon all the fishes of the sea; into your hand are they delivered" (Gen 9:2); and **(3b)** of the nations to conquering Israel: "There shall no man be able to stand before you: *for* the LORD your God shall lay the fear of you and the dread of you upon all the land that ye shall tread upon, as he hath said unto you" (Deut 11:25). See: TWOT—907c, 907d; BDB—432a, 432b, 558d, 559a, 597b.

4173. מוֹרַג {3x} **môwrag**, *mo-rag';* or

מֹרַג **môrag**, *mo-rag';* from an unused root mean. to *triturate;* a threshing *sledge:*—threshing instrument {3x}. See: TWOT—1165; BDB—558d.

4174. מוֹרָד {5x} **môwrâd**, *mo-rawd';* from 3381; a *descent;* arch. an ornamental *appendage,* perh. a *festoon:*—going down {3x}, steep place {1x}, thin work {1x}. See: TWOT—909a; BDB—434b, 559a.

4175. מוֹרֶה {3x} **môwreh**, *mo-reh';* from 3384; an *archer;* also *teacher* or *teaching;* also the *early rain* [see 3138]:—former rain {2x}, rain {1x}. See: TWOT—910b, 910c; BDB—435a, 435c, 598c.

4176. מוֹרֶה {3x} **Môwreh**, *mo-reh';* or

מֹרֶה **Môreh**, *mo-reh';* the same as 4175; *Moreh,* a Canaanite; also a hill (perh. named from him):—Moreh {3x}. See: BDB—435d, 598c.

4177. מוֹרָה {3x} **môwrâh**, *mo-raw;* from 4171 in the sense of *shearing;* a *razor:*—razor {3x}. See: TWOT—1166; BDB—559a.

4178. מוֹרָט {5x} **môwrâṭ**, *mo-rawt';* from 3399; *obstinate,* i.e. independent:—peeled {2x}, furbished {2x}, bright {1x}. See: TWOT—1244; BDB—599a.

4179. מוֹרִיָּה {2x} **Môwrîyâh**, *mo-ree-yaw';* or

מֹרִיָּה **Môrîyâh**, *mo-ree-yaw';* from 7200 and 3050; *seen of Jah; Morijah,* a hill in Pal.:—Moriah {2x}. See: BDB—599a.

4180. מוֹרָשׁ {3x} **môwrâsh**, *mo-rawsh';* from 3423; a *possession;* fig. *delight:*—possession {2x}, thought {1x}.

The noun *mowrash* means "a place one has as a permanent possession": **(1)** "I will also make it a possession for the bittern . . ." (Is 14:23); and **(2)** "But upon mount Zion shall be deliverance, and there shall be holiness; and the house of Jacob shall possess their possessions" (Obad 17). See: TWOT—920d; BDB—440c, 559a.

4181. מוֹרָשָׁה {9x} **môwrâshâh**, *mo-raw-shaw';* fem. of 4180; a *possession:*—heritage {1x}, inheritance {2x}, possession {6x}.

Mowrashah, which occurs 9 times, can refer to **(1)** "a place one has as a permanent possession": "And I will bring you in unto the land, concerning the which I did swear to give it to Abraham, to Isaac, and to Jacob; and I will give it you for an heritage: I *am* the LORD" (Ex 6:8); **(2)** "a thing one has as a permanent possession": "Moses commanded us a law, *even* the inheritance of the congregation of Jacob" (Deut 33:4); and **(3)** "people to be dispossessed": "Behold, therefore I will deliver thee to the men of the east for a possession, and they shall set their palaces in thee, and make their dwellings in thee: they shall eat thy fruit, and they shall drink thy milk" (Eze 25:4). See: TWOT—920e; BDB—440c, 559a.

4182. מוֹרֶשֶׁת גַּת {1x} **Môwresheth Gath**, *moreh'-sheth gath;* from 3423 and 1661; *possession of Gath; Moresheth-Gath,* a place in Pal.:—Moresheth-gath {1x}. See: BDB—440c, 559a.

4183. מוֹרַשְׁתִּי {2x} **Mowrashtîy**, *mo-rash-tee';* patrial from 4182; a *Morashtite* or inhab. of Moresheth-Gath:—Morashthite {2x}. See: BDB—440d, 559a, 601c.

4184. מוּשׁ {3x} **mûwsh**, *moosh;* a prim. root; to *touch:*—feel {2x}, handle {1x}. See: TWOT—1168; BDB—559b.

4185. מוּשׁ {21x} **mûwsh**, *moosh;* a prim. root [perh. rather the same as 4184 through the idea of receding by *contact*]; to *withdraw* (both lit. and fig., whether intr. or tran.):—depart {12x}, remove {6x}, take away {1x}, gone back {1x}, cease {1x}. See: TWOT—1167; BDB—559a, 568c.

4186. מוֹשָׁב {44x} **môwshâb**, *mo-shawb';* or

מֹשָׁב **môshâb**, *mo-shawb';* from 3427; a *seat;* fig. a *site;* abstr. a *session;* by extens. an *abode* (the place or the time); by impl. *population:*—habitation {12x}, dwellings {8x}, seat {7x}, dwelling {4x}, dwellingplace {3x}, dwell {3x}, places {2x}, sitting {2x}, assembly {1x}, situation {1x}, sojourning {1x}. See: TWOT—922c; BDB—444b, 559b.

4187. מוּשִׁי {8x} **Mûwshîy**, *moo-shee';* or

מֻשִּׁי **Mushshîy**, *mush-shee';* from 4184; *sensitive; Mushi,* a Levite:—Mushi {8x}. See: BDB—559b, 603d.

4188. מוּשִׁי {2x} **Mûwshîy**, *moo-shee';* patron. from 4187; a *Mushite* (collect.) or desc. of Mushi:—Mushites {2x}. See: BDB—559b.

4189. מוֹשְׁכָה {1x} **môwshᵉkâh**, *mo-shek-aw';* act. part. fem. of 4900; something *drawing,* i.e. (fig.) a *cord:*—bands {1x}. See: TWOT—1257b; BDB—604d.

4190. מוֹשָׁעָה {1x} **môwshâʿâh**, *mo-shaw-aw';* from 3467; *deliverance:*—salvation {1x}. See: TWOT—929d; BDB—448a, 559b.

4191. מוּת {835x} **mûwth**, *mooth;* a prim. root; to *die* (lit. or fig.); caus. to *kill:*—die {424x}, dead {130x}, slay {100x}, death {83x}, surely {50x}, kill {31x}, dead man {3x}, dead body {2x}, in no wise {2x}, misc. {10x} = × at all, × crying, destroy (-er), necro [-mancer], × must needs, × very suddenly.

Muwth means "to die, kill." **(1)** Essentially, *muwth* means "to lose one's life." **(1a)** The word is used of physical "death," with reference to both man and beast. **(1a1)** Gen 5:5 records that Adam lived "nine hundred and thirty years: and he died." **(1a2)** Jacob explains to Esau that, were his livestock to be driven too hard (fast), the young among them would "die" (Gen 33:13). **(1b)** At one point, this verb is also used to refer to the stump of a plant (Job 14:8). **(1c)** Occasionally, *muwth* is used figuratively of land (Gen 47:19) or wisdom (Job 12:2). **(1d)** Then, too, there is the unique hyperbolic expression that Nabal's heart had "died" within him, indicating that he was overcome with great fear (1 Sa 25:37). **(2)** In an intensive stem, this root is used of the last act inflicted upon one who is already near death. Thus Abimelech, his head having been cracked by a millstone, asked his armor-bearer to "kill" him (Judg 9:54). **(3)** In the usual causative stem, this verb can mean "to cause to die" or "to kill"; God is the one who "puts to death" and gives life (Deut 32:39). **(4)** Usually, both the subject and object of this usage are personal, although there are exceptions—as when the Philistines personified the ark of the covenant, urging its removal so it would not "kill" them (1 Sa 5:11).

(5) Death in this sense may also be inflicted by animals (Ex 21:29). **(6)** This word describes "putting to death" in the broadest sense, including war and judicial sentences of execution (Josh 10:26). **(7)** God is clearly the ultimate Ruler of life and death (cf. Deut 32:39). **(7a)** This idea is especially clear in the Creation account, in which God tells man that he will surely die if he eats of the forbidden fruit (Gen 2:17—the first occurrence of the verb). **(7b)** Apparently there was no death before this time. When the serpent questioned Eve, she associated disobedience with death (Gen 3:3). The serpent repeated God's words, but negated them (Gen 3:4). **(7c)** When Adam and Eve ate of the fruit, both spiritual and physical death came upon Adam and Eve and their descendants (cf. Rom 5:12). **(7d)** They experienced spiritual death immediately, resulting in their shame and their attempt to cover their nakedness (Gen 3:7). **(7e)** Sin and/or the presence of spiritual death required a covering, but man's provision was inadequate; so God made a perfect covering in the form of a promised redeemer (Gen 3:15) and a typological covering of animal skins (Gen 3:21). See: TWOT—1169; BDB—559b, 607a, 1099d.

4192. מוּת {2x} **Mûwth** (Ps 48:14), *mooth;* or

מוּת לַבֵּן **Mûwth lab-bên**, *mooth lab-bane';* from 4191 and 1121 with the prep. and art. interposed; *"To die for the son"*, prob. the title of a popular song:—death {1x}, Muthlabben {1x}. See: BDB—527c, 761b, 761c, 763a.

4193. מוֹת {1x} **môwth** (Aram.), *mohth;* corresp. to 4194; *death:*—death {1x}. See: TWOT—2823; BDB—1099d.

4194. מָוֶת {160x} **mâveth**, *maw'-veth;* from 4191; *death* (nat. or violent); concr. the *dead,* their place or state (*hades*); fig. *pestilence, ruin:*—death {128x}, die {22x}, dead {8x}, deadly {1x}, slay {1x}.

Maveth means "death." **(1)** The word *maveth* occurs frequently as an antonym of *chayyim* (2416 - "life"): "I call heaven and earth to record this day against you, that I have set before you life and death, blessing and cursing: therefore choose life, that both thou and thy seed may live . . ." (Deut 30:19). **(2)** In the poetic language, *maveth* is used more often than in the historical books: Job-Proverbs (about 60 times), Joshua-Esther (about 40 times); but in the major prophets only about 25 times. **(3)** "Death" is the natural end of human life on this earth; it is an aspect of God's judgment on man: "But of the tree of the knowledge of good and evil, thou shalt not eat of it: for in the day that thou eatest thereof thou shalt surely die" (Gen 2:17). **(3a)** Hence all men die: "If these men die the common death of all men . . . then the LORD hath not sent me" (Num 16:29). **(3b)** The Old Testament uses "death" in phrases such as "the day of death" (Gen 27:2) and "the year of death" (Is 6:1), or to mark an event as occurring before (Gen 27:7, 10) or after (Gen 26:18) someone's passing away.

(4) "Death" may also come upon someone in a violent manner, as an execution of justice: "And if a man have committed a sin worthy of death and he be to be put to death, and thou hang him on a tree: his body shall not remain all night upon the tree . . ." (Deut 21:22–23). **(4a)** Saul declared David to be a "son of death" because he intended to have David killed (1 Sa 20:31; cf. Prov 16:14). **(4b)** In one of his experiences, David composed a psalm expressing how close an encounter he had had with death: "When the waves of death compassed me, the floods of ungodly men made me afraid; the sorrows of hell compassed me about; the snares of death prevented me" (2 Sa 22:5–6; cf. Ps 18:5–6). **(5)** Isaiah predicted the Suffering Servant was to die a violent death: "And he made his grave with the wicked, and with the rich in his death; because he had done no violence, neither was any deceit in his mouth" (Is 53:9).

(6) Associated with the meaning of "death" is the meaning of "death by a plague." **(6a)** In a besieged city with unsanitary conditions, pestilence would quickly reduce the weakened population. **(6b)** Jeremiah alludes to this type of death as God's judgment on Egypt (43:11); note that "death" refers here to "death of famine and pestilence." **(6c)** Lamentations describes the situation of Jerusalem before its fall: ". . . Abroad the sword bereaveth, at home there is as death" (Lam 1:20; cf. also Jer 21:8–9).

(7) The word *maveth* denotes the "realm of the dead" or *sheʾol.* This place of death has gates (Ps 9:13; 107:18) and chambers (Prov 7:27); the path of the wicked leads to this abode (Prov 5:5). **(8)** Isaiah expected "death" to be ended when the Lord's full kingship would be established: "He will swallow up death in victory; and the Lord GOD will wipe away tears from off all faces; and the rebuke of his people shall he take away from off all the earth: for the LORD hath spoken it" (Is 25:8). See: TWOT—1169a; BDB—560c.

מוּת לַבֵּן **Mûwth lab-bên.** See 4192.

4195. מוֹתָר {3x} **môwthâr**, *mo-thar';* from 3498; lit. *gain;* fig. *superiority:*—plenteousness {1x}, preeminence {1x}, profit {1x}. See: TWOT—936g; BDB—560d.

4196. מִזְבֵּחַ {402x} **mizbêach**, *miz-bay'-akh;* from 2076; an *altar:*—altar {402x}.

Mizbeach means "altar." **(1)** This frequent use is obviously another direct evidence of the centrality of the sacrificial system in Israel. **(2)** This word signifies a raised place where a sacrifice was made, as in Gen 8:20 (its first biblical appearance): "And Noah builded an altar unto the Lord; and took of every clean beast, and of every clean fowl, and offered burnt offerings on the altar." The first appearance of *mizbeach* is in Gen 8:20, where Noah built an "altar" after the Flood. **(3)** Countless "altars" are referred to as the story of Israel progresses on the pages of the Old Testament: that **(3a)** of Noah (Gen 8:20); **(3b)** of Abram at Sichem (Gen 12:7), **(3c)** at Beth-el (Gen 12:8), and **(3d)** at Moriah (Gen 22:9); **(3e)** of Isaac at Beersheba (Gen 26:25); **(3f)** of Jacob at Shechem (Gen 33:20); **(3g)** of Moses at Horeb (Ex 24:4), **(3h)** of Samuel at Ramah (1 Sa 7:17); **(3i)** of the temple in Jerusalem (1 Kin 6:20; 8:64); and **(3j)** of the two "altars" planned by Ezekiel for the restored temple (Eze 41:22; 43:13–17). **(4)** In later references, this word may refer to a table upon which incense was burned: "And thou shalt make an altar to burn incense upon: of shittim wood shalt thou make it" (Ex 30:1). **(5)** From the dawn of human history, offerings were made on a raised table of stone or ground (Gen 4:3).

(5) At first, Israel's altars were to be made of earth—i.e., they were fashioned of material that was strictly the work of God's hands. **(5a)** If the Jews were to hew stone for altars in the wilderness, they would have been compelled to use war weapons to do the work. (Notice that in Ex 20:25 the word for "tool" is *chereb,* "sword.") **(5b)** At Sinai, God directed Israel to fashion altars of valuable woods and metals. This taught them that true worship required man's best and that it was to conform exactly to God's directives; God, not man, initiated and controlled worship. **(6)** The altar that stood before the holy place (Ex 27:1–8) and the altar of incense within the holy place (Ex 30:1–10) had "horns." **(6a)** These horns had a vital function in some offerings (Lev 4:30; 16:18). **(6b)** For example, the sacrificial animal may have been bound to these horns in order to allow its blood to drain away completely (Ps 118:27). **(7)** *Mizbeach* is also used of pagan altars: "But ye shall destroy their altars, break their images, and cut down their groves" (Ex 34:13). **(8)** This noun is derived from the Hebrew verb *zabach* (2076), **(8a)** which literally means "to slaughter for food" or "to slaughter for sacrifice." **(8b)** Another Old Testament noun derived from *zabach* is *zebach* (162 times), which usually refers to a sacrifice that establishes communion between God and those who eat the thing offered. See: TWOT—525b; BDB—560d.

4197. מֶזֶג {1x} **mezeg**, *meh'-zeg;* from an unused root mean. to *mingle* (water with wine); *tempered* wine:—liquor {1x}. See: TWOT—1170a; BDB—561a.

4198. מָזֶה {1x} **mâzeh**, *maw-zeh';* from an unused root mean. to *suck* out; *exhausted:*—burnt {1x}. See: 1171a; BDB—561a.

4199. מִזָּה {3x} **Mizzâh**, *miz-zaw';* prob. from an unused root mean. to *faint* with fear; *terror; Mizzah,* an Edomite:—Mizzah {3x}. See: BDB—561a.

4200. מֶזֶו {1x} **mezev**, *meh'-zev;* prob. from an unused root mean. to *gather* in; a *granary:*—garner {1x}. See: TWOT—534b; BDB—265a, 561a.

4201. מְזוּזָה {1x} **m^e^zûwzâh**, *mez-oo-zaw';* or

מְזֻזָה **m^e^zûzâh**, *mez-oo-zaw';* from the same as 2123; a *door-post* (as *prominent*):—(door, side) post {19x}. See: TWOT—535b; BDB—265b, 561a.

4202. מָזוֹן {2x} **mâzôwn**, *maw-zone';* from 2109; *food:*—meat {1x}, victual {1x}. See: TWOT—539a; BDB—266a, 561a.

4203. מָזוֹן {2x} **mâzôwn** (Aram.), *maw-zone';* corresp. to 4202:—meat {2x}. See: TWOT—2705a; BDB—1091b, 1099d.

4204. מָזוֹר {1x} **mâzôwr**, *maw-zore';* from 2114 in the sense of *turning aside* from truth; *treachery,* i.e. a *plot:*—wound {1x}. See: TWOT—1175a; BDB—561a, 561c.

4205. מָזוֹר {3x} **mâzôwr**, *maw-zore';* or

מָזֹר **mâzôr**, *maw-zore';* from 2115 in the sense of *binding* up; a *bandage,* i.e. remedy; hence, a *sore* (as needing a compress):—bound up {1x}, wound {2x}. See: TWOT—543c; BDB—267a, 561a.

מְזֻזָה **m^e^zûzâh.** See 4201.

4206. מָזִיחַ {3x} **mâzîyach**, *maw-zee'-akh;* or

מֵזַח **mêzach**, *may-zakh';* from 2118; a *belt* (as movable):—girdle {1x}, strength {2x}. See: TWOT—1172a; BDB—561a, 561b.

4207. מַזְלֵג {7x} **mazlêg**, *maz-layg';* or (fem.)

מִזְלָגָה **mizlâgâh**, *miz-law-gaw';* from an unused root mean. to *draw* up; a *fork:*—fleshhook {7x}. See: TWOT—552a; BDB—272c, 561b.

4208. מַזָּלָה {1x} **mazzâlâh**, *maz-zaw-law';* appar. from 5140 in the sense of *raining;* a *constellation,* i.e. Zodiacal sign (perh. as affecting the weather):—planet {1x}. See: TWOT—1173; BDB—561b. comp. 4216.

4209. מְזִמָּה {19x} **mᵉzimmâh**, *mez-im-maw';* from 2161; a *plan,* usually evil (*machination*), sometimes good (*sagacity*):—discretion {4x}, wicked device {3x}, device {3x}, thought {3x}, intents {1x}, mischievous device {1x}, wickedly {1x}, witty inventions {1x}, lewdness {1x}, mischievous {1x}.

Mezimmah means "purpose; evil device; evil thoughts; discretion." **(1)** This noun occurs 19 times. **(2)** The word means "purpose" in Job 42:2 and is translated "thought": I know that thou canst do every *thing,* and *that* no thought can be withholden from thee." This stresses that what ever God thinks to be, is purposed and will happen. **(3)** *Mezimmah* refers to "evil device (lewdness)" in Jer 11:15: "What hath my beloved to do in mine house, seeing she hath wrought lewdness with many. . . ." **(4)** In Job 21:27 the word is used to mean "evil thoughts," and **(5)** in Prov 1:4 the word is used for "discretion." Syn: 2154, 2161. See: TWOT—556c; BDB—273c, 561b.

4210. מִזְמוֹר {57x} **mizmôwr**, *miz-more';* from 2167; prop. instrumental *music;* by impl. a *poem* set to notes:—psalm {57x}. See: TWOT—558c; BDB—274c, 561b.

4211. מַזְמֵרָה {4x} **mazmêrâh**, *maz-may-raw';* from 2168; a *pruning-knife:*—pruning-hooks {4x}. See: TWOT—559c; BDB—275a, 561c.

4212. מְזַמְּרָה {5x} **mᵉzammᵉrâh**, *mez-am-mer-aw';* from 2168; a *tweezer* (only in the plur.):—snuffers {5x}. See: TWOT—559d; BDB—275a, 561c.

4213. מִזְעָר {4x} **mizʿâr**, *miz-awr';* from the same as 2191; *fewness;* by impl. as superl. *diminutiveness:*—few {3x}, × very {1x}. See: TWOT—571b; BDB—277d, 561c.

מָזֹר **mâzôr**. See 4205.

4214. מִזְרֶה {2x} **mizreh**, *miz-reh';* from 2219; a winnowing *shovel* (as scattering the chaff):—fan {2x}. See: TWOT—570a; BDB—280a, 561d.

4215. מְזָרֶה {1x} **mᵉzâreh**, *mez-aw-reh';* appar. from 2219; prop. a *scatterer,* i.e. the north *wind* (as dispersing clouds; only in plur.):—out of the north {1x}. See: TWOT—579; BDB—280a.

4216. מַזָּרָה {1x} **Mazzârâh**, *maz-zaw-raw';* appar. from 5144 in the sense of *distinction;* some noted *constellation* (only in the plur.), perh. collect. the *zodiac:*—Mazzoroth {1x}. See: TWOT—1176; BDB—561d. comp. 4208.

4217. מִזְרָח {74x} **mizrâch**, *miz-rawkh';* from 2224; *sunrise,* i.e. the *east:*—east {30x}, eastward {20x}, sunrising + 8121 {9x}, rising {8x}, east side {5x}, east end {1x}, sunrising {1x}. See: TWOT—580c; BDB—280d, 561d.

4218. מִזְרָע {1x} **mizrâʿ**, *miz-raw';* from 2232; a planted *field:*—thing sown {1x}. See: TWOT—582f; BDB—283c, 561d.

4219. מִזְרָק {32x} **mîzrâq**, *miz-rawk';* from 2236; a *bowl* (as if for sprinkling):—basons {11x}, bowl {21x}. See: TWOT—585a; BDB—284c, 561d.

4220. מֵחַ {2x} **mêach**, *may'-akh;* from 4229 in the sense of *greasing; fat;* fig. *rich:*—fatling {1x}, fat one {1x}. See: TWOT—1181a; BDB—561d, 562d, 568a.

4221. מֹחַ {1x} **môach**, *mo'-akh;* from the same as 4220; *fat,* i.e. marrow:—marrow {1x}. See: TWOT—1181b; BDB—561d, 562d.

4222. מָחָא {3x} **mâchâ'**, *maw-khaw';* a prim. root; to *rub* or *strike* the hands together (in exultation):—clap {3x}. See: TWOT—1177; BDB—561d.

4223. מְחָא {4x} **mᵉchâ'** (Aram.), *mekh-aw';* corresp. to 4222; to *strike* in pieces; also to *arrest;* spec. to *impale:*—hanged {1x}, smote {3x}, stay {1x}. See: TWOT—2824; BDB—1099d.

4224. מַחֲבֵא {2x} **machăbê'**, *makh-ab-ay';* or

מַחֲבֹא **machăbô'**, *makh-ab-o';* from 2244; a *refuge:*—hiding place {1x}, lurking place {1x}. See: TWOT—588a, 589a; BDB—285c, 561d.

4225. מַחְבֶּרֶת {8x} **machbereth**, *makh-beh'-reth;* from 2266; a *junction,* i.e. seam or sewed piece:—coupling {8x}. See: TWOT—598j; BDB—289c, 561d.

4226. מְחַבְּרָה {2x} **mᵉchabbᵉrâh**, *mekh-ab-ber-aw';* from 2266; a *joiner,* i.e. brace or cramp:—coupling {1x}, joining {1x}. See: TWOT—598k; BDB—289c.

4227. מַחֲבַת {5x} **machăbath**, *makh-ab-ath';* from the same as 2281; a *pan* for baking in:—pan {5x}. See: TWOT—600b; BDB—290a, 561d.

4228. מַחֲגֹרֶת {1x} **machăgôreth**, *makh-ag-o'-reth;* from 2296; a *girdle:*—girding {1x}. See: TWOT—604d; BDB—292b, 561d.

4229. מָחָה {36x} **mâchâh**, *maw-khaw';* a prim. root; prop. to *stroke* or *rub;* by impl. to *erase;* also to *smooth* (as if with oil), i.e. *grease* or make fat; also to *touch,* i.e. reach to:—(blot, put, etc) . . . out {17x}, destroy {6x}, wipe {4x}, blot {3x}, wipe away {2x}, abolished {1x}, marrow {1x}, reach {1x}, utterly {1x}. See: TWOT—1178, 1179, 1181c; BDB—562a, 562b, 562c, 562d, 1099d.

4230. מְחוּגָה {1x} **mᵉchûwgâh**, *mekh-oo-gaw';* from 2328; an instrument for marking a circle, i.e. *compasses:*—compass {1x}. See: TWOT—615b; BDB—295b, 562c.

4231. מָחוֹז {1x} **mâchôwz**, *maw-khoze';* from an unused root mean. to *enclose;* a *harbor* (as *shut* in by the shore):—haven {1x}. See: TWOT—1180; BDB—562c.

4232. מְחוּיָאֵל {2x} **Mᵉchûwyâ'êl**, *mekh-oo-yaw-ale';* or

מְחִיָּיאֵל **Mᵉchîyyâ'êl**, *mekh-ee-yaw-ale';* from 4229 and 410; *smitten of God; Mechujael* or *Mechijael,* an antediluvian patriarch:—Mehujael {2x}. See: BDB—562c, 563a.

4233. מַחֲוִים {1x} **Machăvîym**, *makh-av-eem';* appar. a patrial, but from an unknown place (in the plur. only for a sing.); a *Machavite* or inhab. of some place named Machaveh:—Mahavite {1x}. See: BDB—296a, 562d.

4234. מָחוֹל {6x} **mâchôwl**, *maw-khole';* from 2342; a (round) *dance:*—dance {5x}, dancing {1x}. See: TWOT—623g; BDB—298b, 562d.

4235. מָחוֹל {1x} **Mâchôwl**, *maw-khole';* the same as 4234; *dancing; Machol,* an Isr.:—Mahol {1x}. See: BDB—562d.

מְחוֹלָה **mᵉchôwlâh**. See 65, 4246.

4236. מַחֲזֶה {4x} **machăzeh**, *makh-az-eh';* from 2372; a *vision:*—vision {4x}. See: TWOT—633f; BDB—303c, 562d.

4237. מֶחֱזָה {4x} **mechĕzâh**, *mekh-ez-aw';* from 2372; a *window:*—light {4x}. See: TWOT—633g; BDB—303d, 562d.

4238. מַחֲזִיאוֹת {2x} **Machăzîy'ôwth**, *makh-az-ee-oth';* fem. plur. from 2372; *visions; Machazioth,* an Isr.:—Mahazioth {2x}. See: BDB—303d, 562d.

4239. מְחִי {1x} **mᵉchîy**, *mekh-ee';* from 4229; a *stroke,* i.e. battering-*ram:*—engines {1x}. See: TWOT—1179a; BDB—562c, 562d.

4240. מְחִידָא {2x} **Mᵉchîydâ'**, *mekh-ee-daw';* from 2330; *junction; Mechida,* one of the Nethinim:—Mehida {2x}. See: BDB—563a.

4241. מִחְיָה {8x} **michyâh**, *mikh-yaw';* from 2421; *preservation of life;* hence, *sustenance;* also the live flesh, i.e. the *quick:*—reviving {2x}, quick {2x}, preserve life {1x}, sustenance {1x}, victuals {1x}, recover {1x}. See: TWOT—644h; BDB—313c, 563a.

מְחִיָּיאֵל **Mᵉchîyyâ'êl**. See 4232.

4242. מְחִיר {15x} **mᵉchîyr**, *mekh-eer';* from an unused root mean. to *buy; price, payment, wages:*—gain {1x}, hire {1x}, price {11x}, sold {1x}, worth {1x}. See: TWOT—1185c; BDB—564b.

4243. מְחִיר {1x} **Mᵉchîyr**, *mekh-eer';* the same as 4242; *price; Mechir,* an Isr.:—Mehir {1x}. See: BDB—564b.

4244. מַחְלָה {5x} **Machlâh**, *makh-law';* from 2470; *sickness; Machlah,* the name appar. of two Israelitesses:—Mahlah {4x}, Mahalah {1x}. See: BDB—563a.

4245. מַחֲלֶה {6x} **machăleh**, *makh-al-eh';* or (fem.)

מַחֲלָה **machălâh**, *makh-al-aw';* from 2470; *sickness:*—disease {2x}, infirmity {1x}, sickness {3x}. See: TWOT—655b, 655c; BDB—318b, 563a.

4246. מְחֹלָה {8x} **mᵉchôwlâh**, *mekh-o-law';* fem. of 4234; a *dance:*—company {1x}, dances {5x}, dancing {2x}. See: TWOT—623h; BDB—298b, 562d, 563a, 563b.

4247. מְחִלָּה {1x} **mᵉchillâ**, *mekh-il-law';* from 2490; a *cavern* (as if excavated):—cave {1x}. See: TWOT—660f; BDB—320a, 563a.

4248. מַחְלוֹן {4x} **Machlown**, *makh-lone';* from 2470; *sick; Machlon,* an Isr.:—Mahlon {4x}. See: TWOT—660f; BDB—563a.

4249. מַחְלִי {12x} **Machlîy**, *makh-lee';* from 2470; *sick; Machli,* the name of two Isr.:—Mahli {11x}, Mahali {1x}. See: BDB—563a.

4250. מַחְלִי {2x} **Machlîy**, *makh-lee';* patron. from 4249; a *Machlite* or (collect.) desc. of Machli:—Mahlites {2x}. See: BDB—563a.

4251. מַחֲלִי {1x} **machlûy**, *makh-loo'-ee;* from 2470; a *disease:*—disease {1x}. See: TWOT—655d; BDB—318c, 563a.

4252. מַחֲלָף {1x} **machălâph**, *makh-al-awf';* from 2498; a (sacrificial) *knife* (as *gliding* through the flesh):—knives {1x}. See: TWOT—666d; BDB—322c, 563b.

4253. מַחְלָפָה {2x} **machlâphâh**, *makh-law-faw';* from 2498; a *ringlet* of hair (as *gliding* over each other):—lock {2x}. See: TWOT—666e; BDB—322c, 563b.

4254. מַחֲלָצָה {2x} **machălâtsâh**, *makh-al-aw-tsaw';* from 2502; a *mantle* (as easily *drawn off*):—changeable suit of apparel {1x}, change of raiment {1x}. See: TWOT—667b; BDB—323a, 563b.

4255. מַחְלְקָה {1x} **machl**ᵉ**qâh** (Aram.), *makh-lek-aw';* corresp. to 4256; a *section* (of the Levites):—courses {1x}. See: TWOT—2732b; BDB—1093b, 1099d.

4256. מַחֲלֹקֶת {43x} **machălôqeth**, *makh-al-o'-keth;* from 2505; a *section* (of Levites, people or soldiers):—company {1x}, course {33x}, division {8x}, portion {1x}. See: TWOT—669d; BDB—324d, 563b, 1093b. See also 5555.

4257. מַחֲלַת {2x} **machălath**, *makh-al-ath';* from 2470; *sickness; Machalath,* prob. the title (initial word) of a popular song:—Mahalath {2x}. See: TWOT—623h or 655c; BDB—318d, 563b.

4258. מַחֲלַת {2x} **Machălath**, *makh-al-ath';* the same as 4257; *sickness; Machalath,* the name of an Ishmaelitess and of an Israelitess:—Mahalath {2x}. See: BDB—563b.

4259. מְחֹלָתִי {2x} **M**ᵉ**chôlâthîy**, *mekh-o-law-thee';* patrial from 65; a *Mecholathite* or inhab. of Abel-Mecholah:—Mecholathite {2x}. See: BDB—563b.

4260. מַחֲמָאָה {1x} **machămâ'âh**, *makh-am-aw-aw';* a denom. from 2529; something *buttery* (i.e. unctuous and pleasant), as (fig.) *flattery:*—× than butter {1x}. See: TWOT—1182; BDB—563b.

4261. מַחְמָד {13x} **machmâd**, *makh-mawd';* from 2530; *delightful;* hence, a *delight,* i.e. object of affection or desire:—beloved {1x}, desire {3x}, goodly {1x}, lovely {1x}, pleasant {4x}, pleasant thing {3x}. See: TWOT—673d, 673e; BDB—326d, 563b.

4262. מַחְמֻד {2x} **machmûd**, *makh-mood';* or

מַחְמוּד **machmûwd**, *makh-mood';* from 2530; *desired;* hence, a *valuable:*—pleasant thing {2x}. See: TWOT—673; BDB—327a, 563b.

4263. מַחְמָל {1x} **machmâl**, *makh-mawl';* from 2550; prop. *sympathy;* (by paronomasia with 4261) *delight:*—that which . . . pitieth {1x}. See: TWOT—676b; BDB—328c, 563c.

4264. מַחֲנֶה {216x} **machăneh**, *makh-an-eh';* from 2583; an *encampment* (of travellers or troops); hence, an *army,* whether lit. (of soldiers) or fig. (of dancers, angels, cattle, locusts, stars; or even the sacred courts):—camp {136x}, host {61x}, company {6x}, tents {5x}, armies {4x}, bands {2x}, battle {1x}, drove {1x}.

Machaneh means "camp; encampment; host." **(1)** Those who travel were called **(1a)** "campers," or a "company" as in Gen 32:8: Naaman stood before Elisha "with all his company" (2 Kin 5:15). **(1b)** Travelers, tradesmen, and soldiers spent much time on the road. They all set up "camp" for the night. Jacob "encamped" by the Jabbok with his retinue (Gen 32:10). **(2)** The name Mahanaim (Gen 32:2, "camps") owes its origin to Jacob's experience with the angels. **(2a)** He called the place Mahanaim in order to signify that it was God's "camp" (Gen 32:2), **(2b)** as he had spent the night "in the camp" (Gen 32:21) and wrestled with God (Gen 32:24). **(3)** Soldiers also established "camps" by the city to be conquered (Eze 4:2) **(4)** Usage of *machaneh* varies according to context. **(4a)** It signifies a nation set over against another (Ex 14:20). **(4b)** The word refers to a division concerning the Israelites; each of the tribes had a special "encampment" in relation to the tent of meeting (Num 1:52). **(4c)** The word "camp" is used to describe the whole people of Israel: "And it came to pass on the third day in the morning, that there were thunders and lightnings, and a thick cloud upon the mount, and the voice of the trumpet exceeding loud; so that all the people that was in the camp trembled" (Ex 19:16).

(5) God was present in the "camp" of Israel: "For the LORD thy God walketh in the midst of thy camp, to deliver thee, and to give up thine enemies before thee; therefore shall thy camp be holy: that he see no unclean thing in thee, and turn away from thee" (Deut 23:14). **(6)** As a result, sin could not be tolerated within the camp, and the sinner might have to be stoned outside the camp (Num 15:35). Syn.: 168, 4908. See: TWOT—690c; BDB—334a, 563c.

4265. מַחֲנֵה־דָן {1x} **Machănêh-Dân**, *makh-an-ay'-dawn;* from 4264 and 1835; *camp of Dan; Machaneh-Dan,* a place in Pal.:—Mahaneh-dan {1x}. See: BDB—334b, 563c.

4266. מַחֲנַיִם {3x} **Machănayim**, *makh-an-ah'-yim;* dual of 4264; *double camp; Machanajim,* a place in Pal.:—Mahanaim {13x}. See: BDB—334b, 563c.

4267. מַחֲנָק {1x} **machănaq**, *makh-an-ak';* from 2614; *choking:*—strangling {1x}. See: TWOT—697a; BDB—338b, 563c.

4268. מַחֲסֶה {20x} **machăçeh**, *makh-as-eh';* or

מַחְסֶה **machçeh**, *makh-seh';* from 2620; a *shelter* (lit. or fig.):—hope {2x}, (place of) refuge {15x}, shelter {2x}, trust {1x}. See: TWOT—700b; BDB—340b, 563c.

4269. מַחְסוֹם {1x} **machçôwm**, *makh-sohm';* from 2629; a *muzzle:*—bridle {1x}. See: TWOT—702a; BDB—340d, 563c.

4270. מַחְסוֹר {13x} **machçôwr**, *makh-sore';* or

מַחְסֹר **machçôr**, *makh-sore';* from 2637; *deficiency;* hence, *impoverishment:*—lack {1x}, need {1x}, penury {1x}, poor {1x}, poverty {1x}, want {8x}. See: TWOT—705e; BDB—341d, 563c.

4271. מַחְסֵיָה {2x} **Machçêyâh**, *makh-say-yaw';* from 4268 and 3050; *refuge of* (i.e. *in) Jah; Machsejah,* an Isr.:—Maaseiah {2x}. See: BDB—340c, 563c.

4272. מָחַץ {14x} **mâchats**, *maw-khats';* a prim. root; to *dash* asunder; by impl. to *crush, smash* or violently *plunge;* fig. to *subdue* or *destroy:*—dipped {1x}, pierce {2x}, pierce through {1x}, smite (through) {2x}, strike through {1x}, wound {7x}. See: TWOT—1183; BDB—563c.

4273. מַחַץ {1x} **machats**, *makh'-ats;* from 4272; a *contusion:*—stroke {1x}. See: TWOT—1183a; BDB—563d.

4274. מַחְצֵב {3x} **machtsêb**, *makh-tsabe';* from 2672; prop. a *hewing;* concr. a *quarry:*—hewed {1x}, hewn {1x}. See: TWOT—718a; BDB—345b, 563d.

4275. מֶחֱצָה {2x} **mechĕtsâh**, *mekh-ets-aw';* from 2673; a *halving:*—half {2x}. See: TWOT—719d; BDB—345d, 563d.

4276. מַחֲצִית {17x} **machătsîyth**, *makh-ats-eeth';* from 2673; a *halving* or the *middle:*—half {15x}, much {1x}, midday + 3117 {1x}. See: TWOT—719e; BDB—345d, 563d.

4277. מָחַק {1x} **mâchaq**, *maw-khak';* a prim. root; to *crush:*—smote off {1x}. See: TWOT—1184; BDB—563d.

4278. מֶחְקָר {1x} **mechqâr**, *mekh-kawr';* from 2713; prop. *scrutinized,* i.e. (by impl.) a *recess:*—deep places {1x}. See: TWOT—729b; BDB—350d, 563d.

4279. מָחָר {52x} **mâchar**, *maw-khar';* prob. from 309; prop. *deferred,* i.e. the *morrow;* usually (adv.) *tomorrow;* indef. *hereafter:*—time to come {8x}, tomorrow {44x}.

I. *Machar*, as a noun, means "tomorrow." **(1)** The word means the day following the present day: ". . . Tomorrow is the rest of the holy sabbath unto the LORD: bake that which ye will bake today . . ." (Ex 16:23). **(2)** *Machar* also occurs as a noun in Prov 27:1: "Boast not thyself of tomorrow; for thou knowest not what a day may bring forth." **II. *Machar*, as an adverb,** means "tomorrow." **(1)** The basic meaning of this word is clearly set forth in Ex 19:10: "And the LORD said unto Moses, Go unto the people, and sanctify them today and tomorrow, and let them wash their clothes." **(2)** In a few passages the phrase *yom machar* is used: "So shall my righteousness answer for me in time to come [later] . . ." (Gen 30:33). **(3)** In most passages *machar* by itself (used absolutely) means "tomorrow": "Behold, I go out from thee, and I will entreat the LORD that the swarms of flies may depart from Pharaoh, from his servants, and from his people, tomorrow . . ." (Ex 8:29). **(4)** Interestingly, in Ex 8:10 the phrase *lemachar* (which appears 5 times in the Bible) is used: "And he said, Tomorrow." **(5)** Used with the preposition *ke*, the word means "tomorrow about this time": "Behold, tomorrow about this time I will cause it to rain a very grievous hail . . ." (Ex 9:18). Syn.: 4283. See: TWOT—1185a; BDB—563d.

4280. מַחֲרָאָה {1x} **machărâ'âh**, *makh-ar-aw-aw';* from the same as 2716; a *sink:*—draught house {1x}. See: TWOT—730b; BDB—351a, 564c.

4281. מַחֲרֵשָׁה {1x} **machărêshâh**, *makh-ar-ay-shaw';* from 2790; prob. a *pickaxe:*—mattock {1x}. See: TWOT—760d; BDB—361a, 564c.

4282. מַחֲרֶשֶׁת {1x} **machăresheth**, *makh-ar-eh'-sheth;* from 2790; prob. a *hoe:*—share {1x}. See: TWOT—760d; BDB—361a, 564c.

4283. מָחֳרָת {32x} **machărâth**, *makh-ar-awth';* or

מָחֳרָתָם **machărâthâm** (1 Sa 30:17), *makh-ar-aw-thawm';* fem. from the same as 4279; the *morrow* or (adv.) *tomorrow:*—morrow {29x}, next day {2x}, next {1x}.

Macharath, as an adverb, means "the next day." **(1)** Closely related to the noun *machar* (4279) is this adverb, which occurs about 32 times and in all periods of biblical Hebrew. **(2)** About 28 times *macharat* is joined to the preposition *min* to mean "on the next day." This is its form and meaning in its first biblical appearance: "And it came to pass on the morrow . . ." (Gen 19:34). **(3)** In 3 passages this adverb is preceded by the preposition *le,* but the meaning is the same: "And David smote them from the twilight even unto the evening of the next day . . ." (1 Sa 30:17). **(4)** In Num 11:32 *macharath* appears after *yom,* "day," and is preceded by the definite article: "And the people stood up all that day, and all that night, and all the next day, and they gathered the quails. . . ." **(5)** First Chr 29:21 displays yet another construction, with the same meaning: ". . . On the morrow after that day. . . ." Syn.: 4279. See: TWOT—1185b; BDB—564a, 564c.

4284. מַחֲשָׁבָה {56x} **machăshâbâh**, *makh-ash-aw-baw';* or

מַחֲשֶׁבֶת **machăshebeth**, *makh-ash-eh'-beth;* from 2803; a *contrivance,* i.e. (concr.) a *texture, machine,* or (abstr.) *intention, plan* (whether bad, a *plot;* or good, *advice*):—thought {28x}, device {12x}, purpose {6x}, work {3x}, imaginations {3x}, cunning {1x}, devised {1x}, invented {1x}, means {1x}. See: TWOT—767d; BDB—364b, 564c.

4285. מַחְשָׁךְ {7x} **machshâk**, *makh-shawk';* from 2821; *darkness;* concr. a *dark place:*—darkness {4x}, dark places {2x}, dark {1x}. See: TWOT—769d; BDB—365b, 564c.

4286. מַחְשֹׂף {1x} **machsôph**, *makh-sofe';* from 2834; a *peeling:*—made appear {1x}. See: TWOT—766b; BDB—362d, 564c.

4287. מַחַת {3x} **Machath**, *makh'-ath;* prob. from 4229; *erasure; Machath,* the name of two Isr.:—Mahath {3x}. See: BDB—367b, 564c.

4288. מְחִתָּה {11x} **m^e^chittâh**, *mekh-it-taw';* from 2846; prop. a *dissolution;* concr. a *ruin,* or (abstr.) *consternation:*—destruction {7x}, terror {2x}, ruin {1x}, dismaying {1x}. Syn.: 3238, 3772, 4135. See: TWOT—784g; BDB—369d, 564c.

4289. מַחְתָּה {22x} **machtâh**, *makh-taw';* the same as 4288 in the sense of *removal;* a *pan* for live coals:—censer {15x}, firepans {2x}, snuffdishes {3x}. See: TWOT—777a; BDB—367b, 564c.

4290. מַחְתֶּרֶת {2x} **machtereth**, *makh-teh'-reth;* from 2864; a *burglary;* fig. *unexpected examination:*—breaking up {1x}, secret search {1x}. See: TWOT—783a; BDB—369a, 564c.

4291. מְטָא {8x} **m^e^ṭâʾ** (Aram.), *met-aw';* or

מְטָה **m^e^ṭâh** (Aram.) *met-aw';* appar. corresp. to 4672 in the intr. sense of being found *present;* to *arrive, extend* or *happen:*—come {5x}, reach {3x}. See: TWOT—783a; BDB—1100a.

4292. מַטְאֲטֵא {1x} **maṭʾăṭêʾ**, *mat-at-ay';* appar. a denom. from 2916; a *broom* (as removing *dirt* [comp. Engl. "to dust", i.e. remove dust]):—besom {1x}. See: TWOT—785a; BDB—370a, 564c,

4293. מַטְבֵּחַ {1x} **maṭbêach**, *mat-bay'-akh;* from 2873; *slaughter:*—slaughter {1x}. See: TWOT—786e; BDB—371a, 564c.

4294. מַטֶּה {251x} **maṭṭeh**, *mat-teh';* or (fem.)

מַטָּה **maṭṭâh**, *mat-taw';* from 5186; a *branch* (as *extending*); fig. a *tribe;* also a *rod,* whether for chastising (fig. *correction*), ruling (a *sceptre*), throwing (a *lance*), or walking (a *staff;* fig. a *support* of life, e.g. bread):—tribe {182x}, rod {52x}, staff {15x}, staves {1x}, tribe + 4294 {1x}.

Mattah means "rod; staff; tribe." **(1)** In Gen 38:18 the word refers to a shepherd's "staff": "And he said, What pledge shall I give thee? And she said, Thy signet, and thy bracelets, and thy staff that is in thine hand." **(2)** The word is used to refer to a number of kinds of "rods": **(2a)** A "rod" which symbolizes spiritual power, such as Moses' rod (Ex 4:2), **(2b)** Aaron's rod (Ex 7:9), **(2c)** the sorcerers' rods (Ex 7:12), and **(2d)** rods symbolizing authority (Num 17:7). **(3)** This noun is often used elliptically instead of "the rod of the tribe of"; the word signifies "tribe" (cf. Ex 31:2). **(4)** *Mattah* is also used in the phrase "the staff of bread,": "*And* when I have broken the staff of your bread, ten women shall bake your bread in one oven, and they shall deliver *you* your bread again by weight: and ye shall eat, and not be satisfied" (Lev 26:26). Syn.: 7626. See: TWOT—1352b; BDB—564c, 641c.

4295. מַטָּה {19x} **maṭṭâh**, *mat'-taw;* from 5786 with directive enclitic appended; *downward, below* or *beneath;* often adv. with or without prefixes:—beneath {7x}, downward {5x}, underneath {2x}, very {1x}, low {1x}, under {1x}, down {1x}, less {1x}.

Mattah, as an adverb, means "downwards; beneath." This word occurs 19 times. **(1)** It means "beneath": "And the LORD shall make thee the head, and not the tail; and thou shalt be above only, and thou shalt not be beneath; if that thou hearken unto the commandments of the LORD thy God, which I command thee this day, to observe and to do *them*" (Deut 28:13); **(2)** "downward": "And the remnant that is escaped of the house of Judah shall yet again take root downward, and bear fruit upward" (2 Kin 19:30); and **(3)** "underneath": "And two *other* rings of gold thou shalt make, and shalt put them on the two sides of the ephod underneath, toward the forepart thereof, over against the *other* coupling thereof, above the curious girdle of the ephod" (Ex 28:27). See: TWOT—1352a; BDB—564c, 641d.

4296. מִטָּה {29x} **miṭṭâh**, *mit-taw';* from 5186; a *bed* (as *extended*) for sleeping or eating; by anal. a *sofa, litter* or *bier:*—bed {26x}, bedchamber + 2315 {2x}, bier {1x}.

Mittah occurs about 29 times and means something which is stretched out. **(1)** *Mittah* is used of a couch: "Behold his bed, which *is* Solomon's; threescore valiant men *are* about it, of the valiant of Israel" (Song 3:7); **(2)** of a metal framework: "*Where were* white, green, and blue, *hangings,* fastened with cords of fine linen and purple to silver rings and pillars of marble: the beds (*mittah*) *were of* gold and silver, upon a pavement of red, and blue, and white, and black, marble" (Est 1:6); and of **(3)** a room, a bedchamber: "But Jehosheba, the daughter of king Joram, sister of Ahaziah, took Joash the son of Ahaziah, and stole him from among the king's sons *which were* slain; and they hid him, *even* him and his nurse, in the bedchamber from Athaliah, so that he was not slain" (2 Kin 11:2). See: TWOT—1352c; BDB—564c, 641d.

4297. מֻטֶּה {1x} **muṭṭeh**, *moot-teh';* from 5186; a *stretching,* i.e. *distortion* (fig. *iniquity*):—perverseness {1x}. See: TWOT—1352e; BDB—642a.

4298. מֻטָּה {1x} **muṭṭâh**, *moot-taw';* from 5186; *expansion:*—stretching out {1x}.

Muttot [plural] occurs once and refers to the "stretching out" of wings: "And he shall pass through Judah; he shall overflow and go over, he shall reach *even* to the neck; and the stretching out of his wings shall fill the breadth of thy land, O Immanuel"(Is 8:8). See: TWOT—1352d; BDB—564c, 642a.

4299. מַטְוֶה {1x} **maṭveh**, *mat-veh';* from 2901; something *spun:*—spun {1x}. See: TWOT—794a; BDB—376a, 564c.

4300. מְטִיל {1x} **m^e^ṭîyl**, *met-eel';* from 2904 in the sense of *hammering* out; an iron *bar* (as *forged*):—bar {1x}. See: TWOT—1186a; BDB—564c.

4301. מַטְמוֹן {5x} **maṭmôwn**, *mat-mone';* or

מַטְמֹן **maṭmôn**, *mat-mone';* or

מַטְמֻן **maṭmûn**, *mat-moon';* from 2934; a *secret* storehouse; hence, a *secreted* valuable (buried); gen. *money:*—hidden riches {1x}, (hid) treasure (-s) {5x}. See: TWOT—811a; BDB—380c, 564c.

4302. מַטָּע {6x} **maṭṭâ^c^**, *mat-taw';* from 5193; something *planted,* i.e. the place (a *garden* or vineyard), or the thing (a *plant,* fig. of men); by impl. the act, *planting:*—plant {2x}, plantation {1x}, planting {3x}. See: TWOT—1354c; BDB—564c, 642d.

4303. מַטְעַם {8x} **maṭ^c^am**, *mat-am';* or (fem.)

מַטְעַמָּה **maṭ^c^ammâh**, *mat-am-maw';* from 2938; a *delicacy:*—dainty (meat) {2x}, savoury meat {6x}. See: TWOT—815b; BDB—381b, 564d.

4304. מִטְפַּחַת {1x} **miṭpachath**, *mit-pakh'-ath;* from 2946; a wide *cloak* (for a woman):—vail {1x}, wimples {1x}. See: TWOT—818d; BDB—381c, 564d.

4305. מָטַר {17x} **mâṭar**, *maw-tar';* a prim. root; to *rain:*—(cause to) rain (upon) {17x}. See: TWOT—1187; BDB—565a.

4306. מָטָר {38x} **mâṭâr**, *maw-tawr';* from 4305; *rain:*—rain {36x}, great {1x}, small {1x}. See: TWOT—1187a; BDB—564d.

4307. מַטָּרָא {16x} **maṭṭârâʾ**, *mat-taw-raw';* or

מַטָּרָה **maṭṭârâh**, *mat-taw-raw';* from 5201; a *jail* (as a *guard*-house); also an *aim* (as being closely *watched*):—mark {3x}, prison {13x}. See: TWOT—1356a; BDB—565a, 643c.

4308. מַטְרֵד {2x} **Maṭrêd**, *mat-rade;* from 2956; *propulsive; Matred,* an Edomitess:—Matred {2x}. See: TWOT—1356a; BDB—382b.

4309. מַטְרִי {1x} **Maṭrîy**, *mat-ree';* from 4305; *rainy; Matri,* an Isr.:—Matri {1x}. See: TWOT—1356a; BDB—565a.

4310. מִי {12x} **mîy**, *me;* an interrog. pron. of persons, as 4100 is of things, *who?* (occasionally, by a peculiar idiom, of things); also (indef.) *whoever;* often used in oblique constr. with pref. or suff.:—any (man) {1x}, × he {1x}, for {1x}, + O that! {1x}, unto you {1x}, what {1x}, which {1x}, who {1x}, whom {1x}, whose {1x}, whosoever {1x}, + would to God {1x}. See: TWOT—1189; BDB—566a, 1100d.

4311. מֵידְבָא {5x} **Mêyd^e^bâʾ**, *may-deb-aw';* from 4325 and 1679; *water of quiet; Me-*

deba, a place in Pal.:—Medeba {5x}. See: BDB—567d.

4312. מֵידָד {1x} **Mêydâd,** *may-dawd';* from 3032 in the sense of *loving; affectionate; Medad,* an Isr.:—Medad {1x}. See: BDB—392a, 568a.

4313. מֵי הַיַּרְקוֹן {1x} **Mêy hay-Yarqôwn,** *may hah'-ee-yar-kone';* from 4325 and 3420 with the art. interposed; *water of the yellowness; Me-haj-Jarkon,* a place in Pal.:—Me-jarkon {1x}. See: BDB—438d.

4314. מֵי זָהָב {2x} **Mêy Zâhâb,** *may zaw-hawb';* from 4325 and 2091, *water of gold; Me-Zahab,* an Edomite:—Mezahab {2x}. See: BDB—566a.

4315. מֵיטָב {6x} **mêyṭâb,** *may-tawb';* from 3190; the *best* part:—best {6x}. See: TWOT—863a; BDB—406b, 568a.

4316. מִיכָא {5x} **Mîykâʾ,** *mee-kaw';* a var. for 4318; *Mica,* the name of two Isr.:—Micha {1x}, Micah {1x}. See: BDB—567d, 568a.

4317. מִיכָאֵל {13x} **Mîykâʾêl,** *me-kaw-ale';* from 4310 and (the pref. der. from) 3588 and 410; *who* (is) *like God?; Mikael,* the name of an archangel and of nine Isr.:—Michael {13x}. See: BDB—567c, 568a.

4318. מִיכָה {31x} **Mîykâh,** *mee-kaw';* an abbrev. of 4320; *Micah,* the name of seven Isr.:—Micah {26x}, Micaiah {1x}, Michah {4x}. See: BDB—567d, 568a.

4319. מִיכָהוּ {1x} **Mîykâhûw,** *me-kaw'-hoo;* a contr. for 4321; *Mikehu,* an Isr. prophet:—Micaiah {1x} (2 Chr 18:8). See: BDB—567c.

4320. מִיכָיָה {4x} **Mîykâyâh,** *me-kaw-yaw';* from 4310 and (the pref. der. from) 3588 and 3050; *who* (is) *like Jah?; Micajah,* the name of two Isr.:—Micah {1x}, Michaiah {3x}. See: BDB—567c, 568a. comp. 4318.

4321. מִיכָיְהוּ {20x} **Mîykâyᵉhûw,** *me-kaw-yeh-hoo';* or

מִכָיְהוּ **Mîkâyᵉhûw** (Jer 36:11), *me-kaw-yeh-hoo';* abbrev. for 4322; *Mikajah,* the name of three Isr.:—Michah {2x}, Micaiah {16x}, Michaiah {2x}. See: BDB—567c, 568a.

4322. מִיכָיָהוּ {2x} **Mîykâyâhûw,** *me-kaw-yaw'-hoo;* for 4320; *Mikajah,* the name of an Isr. and an Israelitess:—Michaiah {2x}. See: TWOT—863a; BDB—567c.

4323. מִיכָל {1x} **mîykâl,** *me-kawl'* from 3201; prop. a *container,* i.e. a *streamlet:*—brook {1x}. See: TWOT—1190; BDB—568a.

4324. מִיכַל {18x} **Mîykâl,** *me-kawl';* appar. the same as 4323; *rivulet; Mikal,* Saul's daughter:—Michal {18x}. See: BDB—568a.

4325. מַיִם {582x} **mayim,** *mah'-yim;* dual of a prim. noun (but used in a sing. sense); *water;* fig. *juice;* by euphem. *urine, semen:*—water {571x}, piss {2x}, waters + 6440 {2x}, watersprings {2x}, washing {1x}, watercourse + 4161 {1x}, waterflood {1x}, watering {1x}, variant {1x}.

Mayim means "water; flood." **(1)** First, "water" is one of the original basic substances. **(1a)** This is its significance in Gen 1:2 (the first occurrence of the word): "And the Spirit of God moved upon the face of the waters." **(1b)** In Gen 1:7 God separated the "waters" above and the "waters" below (cf. Ex 20:4) the expanse of the heavens. **(2)** Second, the word represents that which is in a well, "water" to be drunk (Gen 21:19). **(2a)** "Living water" is "water" that flows: "And Isaac's servants digged in the valley, and found there a well of springing [living] water . . ." (Gen 26:19). **(2b)** "Water" of oppression or affliction is so designated because it is drunk in prison: "Put this fellow in the prison, and feed him with bread of affliction and with water of affliction, until I come in peace" (1 Kin 22:27). **(2c)** Job 9:30 speaks of slush or snow water: "If I wash myself with snow water, and make my hands never so clean. . . ."

(3) Third, *mayim* can represent liquid in general: ". . . For the LORD our God hath put us to silence, and given us water of gall to drink, because we have sinned against the LORD" (Jer 8:14). **(3a)** The phrase, *me raglayim* ("water of one's feet") is urine: "Hath my master sent me to thy master, and to thee, to speak these words? hath he not sent me to the men which sit on the wall, that they may eat their own dung, and drink their own piss [water of their feet] with you?" (2 Kin 18:27; cf. Is 25:10). **(4)** Fourth, in Israel's cultus [rituals] "water" was poured or sprinkled (no one was ever immersed into water), symbolizing purification. **(4a)** So Aaron and his sons were to be washed with "water" as a part of the rite consecrating them to the priesthood: "And Aaron and his sons thou shalt bring unto the door of the tabernacle of the congregation, and shalt wash them with water" (Ex 29:4). **(4b)** Parts of the sacrificial animal were to be ritually cleansed with "water" during the sacrifice: "But his inwards and his legs shall he wash in water . . ." (Lev 1:9).

(4c) Israel's rites sometimes include consecrated "water": "And the priest shall take holy water in an earthen vessel; and of the dust that is in the floor of the tabernacle the priest shall take, and put it into the water" (Num 5:17). **(4d)** "Bitter water" was used in Israel's rituals, too: "And the priest shall set the woman before the LORD, and uncover the woman's head, and put the offering of memorial in her hands, which is the jealousy offering: and the priest shall have in his hand the bitter water that causeth the curse" (Num 5:18). **(4e)** It was "water" which when drunk brought a curse and caused bitterness (Num 5:24). **(5)** Fifth, in proper names this word is used of springs, streams, or seas and/or the area in the immediate vicinity of such bodies of water: "Say unto Aaron, Take thy rod, and stretch out thine hand upon the waters of Egypt, upon their streams, upon their rivers, and upon their ponds, and upon all their pools of water, that they may become blood . . ." (Ex 7:19).

(6) Sixth, this word is used figuratively in many senses. **(6a)** *Mayim* symbolizes danger or distress: "He sent from above, he took me; he drew me out of many waters" (2 Sa 22:17). **(6b)** Outbursting force is represented by *mayim* in 2 Sa 5:20: "The LORD hath broken forth upon mine enemies before me, as the [break-through] of waters." **(6c)** "Mighty waters" describes the onrush of the godless nations against God: "The nations shall rush like the rushing of many waters . . ." (Is 17:13). **(6d)** Thus the word is used to picture something impetuous, violent, and overwhelming: "Terrors take hold on him as waters, a tempest stealeth him away in the night" (Job 27:20). **(6e)** In other passages "water" is used to represent timidity: ". . . Wherefore the hearts of the people melted, and became as water" (Josh 7:5). **(6f)** Related to this nuance is the connotation "transitory": "Because thou shalt forget thy misery, and remember it as waters that pass away" (Job 11:16).

(6g) In Is 32:2 "water" represents that which is refreshing: "And a man shall be as a hiding place from the wind, and a covert from the tempest; as rivers of water in a dry place, as the shadow of a great rock in a weary land." **(6h)** Rest and peace are figured by waters of rest, or quiet waters: ". . . He leadeth me beside the still waters" (Ps 23:2). **(6i)** Similar ideas are involved when one's wife's charms are termed "water of life" or "water which enlivens": "Drink waters out of thine own cistern, and running waters out of thine own well" (Prov 5:15). **(6j)** Outpoured "water" represents bloodshed (Deut 12:16), wrath (Hos 5:10), judgment (Amos 5:24), and strong feelings (Job 3:24). See: TWOT—1188; BDB—555d, 565a, 568a.

4326. מִיָּמִן {4x} **Mîyâmîn,** *me-yaw-meem';* a form for 4509; *Mijamin,* the name of three Isr.:—Miamin {2x}, Mijamin {2x}. See: BDB—568a.

4327. מִין {31x} **mîyn,** *meen;* from an unused root mean. to *portion* out; a *sort,* i.e. *species:*—kind {31x}. See: TWOT—1191a; BDB—558a, 568b. comp. 4480.

4328. מְיֻסָּדָה {1x} **mᵉyuççâdâh,** *meh-yoos-saw-daw';* prop. fem. pass. part. of 3245; something *founded,* i.e. a *foundation:*—foundation {1x}. See: TWOT—875; BDB—414c.

4329. מֵיסָךְ {1x} **mêyçâk,** *may-sawk';* from 5526; a *portico* (as *covered*):—covert {1x}. See: TWOT—1492b; BDB—558a, 568c, 697b.

מֵיפַעַת **Mêyphaʿath.** See 4158.

4330. מִיץ {3x} **mîyts,** *meets;* from 4160; *pressure:*—churning {1x}, forcing {1x}, wringing {1x}. See: TWOT—1192b; BDB—568c.

4331. מֵישָׁא {1x} **Mêyshâʾ,** *may-shaw';* from 4185; *departure; Mesha,* a place in Arabia; also an Isr.:—Mesha {1x}. See: TWOT—1192b; BDB—568c.

4332. מִישָׁאֵל {7x} **Mîyshâʾêl,** *mee-shaw-ale';* from 4310 and 410 with the abbrev. insep. rel. [see 834] interposed; *who* (is) *what God* (is)*?; Mishaël,* the name of three Isr.:—Mishael {1x}. See: BDB—567d, 568c, 100a.

4333. מִישָׁאֵל {1x} **Mîyshâʾêl** (Aram.), *mee-shaw-ale';* corresp. to 4332; *Mishaël,* an Isr.:—Mishael {1x}. See: BDB—1100a.

4334. מִישׁוֹר {23x} **mîyshôwr,** *mee-shore';* or

מִישֹׁר **mîyshôr,** *mee-shore';* from 3474; a *level,* i.e. a *plain* (often used [with the art. pref.] as a prop. name of certain districts); fig. *concord;* also *straightness,* i.e. (fig.) *justice* (sometimes adv. *justly*):—plain {15x}, equity {2x}, straight {2x}, even place {1x}, right {1x}, righteously {1x}, uprightness {1x}.

Miyshor means "level place, uprightness." **(1)** In 1 Kin 20:23 *miyshor* refers to "level country": "And the servants of the king of Syria said unto him, Their gods *are* gods of the hills; therefore they were stronger than we; but let us fight against them in the plain, and surely we shall be stronger than they"; and **(2)** in Is 11:4 the word refers to "uprightness": ". . . And reprove with equity for the meek of the earth. . . ." See: TWOT—930f; BDB—449d.

4335. מֵישַׁךְ {1x} **Mêyshak,** *may-shak';* borrowed from 4336; *Meshak,* an Isr.:—Meshak {1x}. See: BDB—568d, 1100a.

4336. מֵישַׁךְ {14x} **Mêyshak** (Aram.), *may-shak';* of for. or. and doubtful signif.; *Me-*

shak, the Bab. name of 4333:—Meshak {14x}. See: BDB—1100a.

4337. מֵישַׁע {1x} **Mêyshâʿ**, *may-shah';* from 3467; *safety; Mesha,* an Isr.:—Mesha {1x}. See: BDB—448a, 568d.

4338. מֵישַׁע {1x} **Mêyshaʿ**, *may-shaw';* a var. for 4337; *safety; Mesha,* a Moabite:—Mesha {1x}. See: BDB—448a, 568d.

4339. מֵישָׁר {19x} **mêyshâr**, *may-shawr';* from 3474; *evenness,* i.e. (fig.) *prosperity* or *concord;* also *straightness,* i.e. (fig.) *rectitude* (only in plur. with sing. sense; often adv.):—equity {4x}, uprightly {3x}, uprightness {3x}, right things {2x}, agreement {1x}, aright {1x}, equal {1x}, right {1x}, righteously {1x}, sweetly {1x}, upright {1x}. See: TWOT—930e; BDB—449d, 606d.

4340. מֵיתָר {9x} **mêythâr**, *may-thar';* from 3498; a *cord* (of a tent) [comp. 3499] or the *string* (of a bow):—cord {8x}, string {1x}. See: TWOT—936h; BDB—452d, 568d.

4341. מַכְאֹב {16x} **makʾôb**, *mak-obe';* sometimes מַכְאוֹב **makʾôwb**, *mak-obe';* also (fem. Is 53:3) מַכְאֹבָה **makʾôbâh**, *mak-o-baw';* from 3510; *anguish* or (fig.) *affliction:*—grief {2x}, pain {2x}, sorrow {12x}. See: TWOT—940b; BDB—456b, 568d.

4342. מַכְבִּיר {1x} **makbîyr**, *mak-beer';* trans. part. of 3527; *plenty:*—abundance {1x}. See: TWOT—947; BDB—460b, 568d.

4343. מַכְבֵּנָא {1x} **Makbênâʾ**, *mak-bay-naw';* from the same as 3522; *knoll; Macbena,* a place in Pal. settled by him:—Machbenah {1x}. See: BDB—460a, 568d.

4344. מַכְבַּנַּי {1x} **Makbannay**, *mak-ban-nah'-ee;* patrial from 4343; a *Macbannite* or native of Macbena:—Machbanai {1x}. See: BDB—460a.

4345. מַכְבֵּר {6x} **makbêr**, *mak-bare';* from 3527 in the sense of *covering* [comp. 3531]; a *grate:*—grate {6x}. See: TWOT—948d; BDB—460d, 568d.

4346. מַכְבָּר {1x} **makbâr**, *mak-bawr';* from 3527 in the sense of *covering;* a cloth (as *netted* [comp. 4345]):—thick cloth {1x}. See: TWOT—948c; BDB—460d, 568d.

4347. מַכָּה {48x} **makkâh**, *mak-kaw';* or (masc.) מַכֶּה **makkeh**, *mak-keh';* (plur. only) from 5221; a *blow* (in 2 Chr 2:10, of the flail); by impl. a *wound;* fig. *carnage,* also *pestilence:*—wound {14x}, slaughter {14x}, plague {11x}, beaten {1x}, stripes {2x}, stroke {2x}, blow {1x}, smote {1x}, sores {1x}, wounded {1x}. See: TWOT—1364d; BDB—568d, 646d.

4348. מִכְוָה {5x} **mikvâh**, *mik-vaw';* from 3554; a *burn:*—that burneth {1x}, burning {4x}. See: TWOT—961c; BDB—465a, 568d.

4349. מָכוֹן {17x} **mâkôwn**, *maw-kone';* from 3559; prop. a *fixture,* i.e. a *basis;* gen. a *place,* espec. as an *abode:*—foundation {1x}, habitation {2x}, (dwelling-, settled) place {14x}.

Makown, which appears 17 times, means "an established place or site": "Thou shalt bring them in, and plant them in the mountain of thine inheritance, *in* the place, O LORD, *which* thou hast made for thee to dwell in, *in* the Sanctuary, O LORD, *which* thy hands have established" (Ex 15:17). See: TWOT—964c; BDB—467c, 467d, 568d.

4350. מְכוֹנָה {23x} **mᵉkôwnâh**, *mek-o-naw';* or מְכֹנָה **mᵉkônâh**, *mek-o-naw';* fem. of 4349; a *pedestal,* also a *spot:*—base {23x}.

Mekonah, as a noun, means "proper place; base." **(1)** This noun occurs 25 times; it means "proper place" in Ezra 3:3: "And they set the altar upon his bases. . . ." **(2)** The word refers to "bases" in 1 Kin 7:27: "And he made ten bases of brass; four cubits *was* the length of one base, and four cubits the breadth thereof, and three cubits the height of it." See: TWOT—964d; BDB—467d, 568d, 569a.

4351. מְכוּרָה {3x} **mᵉkûwrâh**, *mek-oo-raw';* or מְכֹרָה **mᵉkôrâh**, *mek-o-raw';* from the same as 3564 in the sense of *digging; origin* (as if a mine):—birth {1x}, habitation {1x}, nativity {1x}. See: TWOT—1033c; BDB—468d, 568d, 569d.

4352. מָכִי {1x} **Mâkîy**, *maw-kee';* prob. from 4134; *pining; Maki,* an Isr.:—Machi {1x}. See: BDB—568d.

4353. מָכִיר {22x} **Mâkîyr**, *maw-keer';* from 4376; *salesman; Makir,* an Isr.:—Machir {22x}. See: BDB—569c.

4354. מָכִירִי {1x} **Mâkîyrîy**, *maw-kee-re';* patron. from 4353; a *Makirite* or descend. of Makir:—of Machir {1x}. See: TWOT—1033c; BDB—569c.

4355. מָכַךְ {3x} **mâkak**, *maw-kak';* a prim. root; to *tumble* (in ruins); fig. to *perish:*—be brought low {2x}, decay {1x}. See: TWOT—1193; BDB—568d.

4356. מִכְלָאָה {3x} **miklâʾâh**, *mik-law-aw';* or מִכְלָה **miklâh**, *mik-law';* from 3607; a *pen* (for flocks):—fold {2x}, sheepfold + 6629 {1x}. comp. 4357. See: TWOT—980c; BDB—476c, 479a, 569a.

4357. מִכְלָה {1x} **miklâh**, *mik-law';* from 3615; *completion* (in plur. concr. adv. *wholly*):—perfect {1x}. See: TWOT—982d; BDB—476c, 479a, 569a. comp. 4356.

4358. מִכְלוֹל {2x} **miklôwl**, *mik-lole';* from 3634; *perfection* (i.e. concr. adv. *splendidly*):—most gorgeously {1x}, all sorts {1x}. See: TWOT—985c; BDB—483b, 569a.

4359. מִכְלָל {1x} **miklâl**, *mik-lawl';* from 3634; *perfection* (of beauty):—perfection {1x}. See: TWOT—985e; BDB—483b, 569a.

4360. מִכְלֻל {1x} **miklûl**, *mik-lool';* from 3634; something *perfect,* i.e. a splendid *garment:*—all sorts {1x}. See: TWOT—985d; BDB—483b, 569a.

4361. מַכֹּלֶת {1x} **makkôleth**, *mak-ko'-leth;* from 398; *nourishment:*—food {1x}. See: TWOT—85g, BDB—38c, 569a.

4362. מִכְמַן {1x} **mikman**, *mik-man';* from the same as 3646 in the sense of *hiding; treasure* (as *hidden*):—treasure {1x}. See: TWOT—991a; BDB—485a, 569a.

4363. מִכְמָס {11x} **Mikmâç** (Ezr 2:27; Neh. 7:31), *mik-maws';* or מִכְמָשׁ **Mikmâsh**, *mik-mawsh';* or מִכְמַשׁ **Mikmash** (Neh 11:31), *mik-mash';* from 3647; *hidden; Mikmas* or *Mikmash,* a place in Pal.:—Mikmas {2x}, Mikmash {9x}. See: BDB—485a, 569a.

4364. מַכְמָר {2x} **makmâr**, *mak-mawr';* or מִכְמֹר **mikmôr**, *mik-more';* from 3648 in the sense of *blackening* by heat; a (hunter's) *net* (as *dark* from concealment):—net {2x}. See: TWOT—995b; BDB—485b, 485c, 569a.

4365. מִכְמֶרֶת {3x} **mikmereth**, *mik-meh'-reth;* or מִכְמֹרֶת **mikmôreth**, *mik-mo'-reth;* fem. of 4364; a (fisher's) *net:*—drag {2x}, net {1x}. See: TWOT—995c; BDB—485c, 569a.

מִכְמָשׁ **Mikmâsh**. See 4363.

4366. מִכְמְתָת {2x} **Mikmᵉthâth**, *mik-meth-awth';* appar. from an unused root mean. to *hide; concealment; Mikmethath,* a place in Pal.:—Michmethath {2x}. See: BDB—485c, 569a.

4367. מַכְנַדְבַי {1x} **Maknadbay**, *mak-nad-bah'-ee;* from 4100 and 5068 with a particle interposed; *what* (is) *like* (a) *liberal* (man)?; *Maknadbai,* an Isr.:—Machnadebai {1x}. See: BDB—569a.

מְכֹנָה **mᵉkônâh**. See 4350.

4368. מְכֹנָה {1x} **Mᵉkônâh**, *mek-o-naw';* the same as 4350; a *base; Mekonah,* a place in Pal.:—Mekonah {1x}. See: BDB—569a.

4369. מְכֻנָה {1x} **mᵉkûnâh**, *mek-oo-naw';* the same as 4350; a *spot:*—base {1x}. See: TWOT—964d; BDB—467d.

4370. מִכְנָס {5x} **miknâç**, *mik-nawce';* from 3647 in the sense of *hiding;* (only in dual) *drawers* (from *concealing* the private parts):—breeches {5x}. See: TWOT—1000a; BDB—488b, 569a.

4371. מֶכֶס {6x} **mekeç**, *meh'-kes;* prob. from an unused root mean. to *enumerate;* an *assessment* (as based upon a *census*):—tribute {6x}. See: TWOT—1014a; BDB—493d, 569a.

4372. מִכְסֶה {16x} **mikçeh**, *mik-seh';* from 3680; a *covering,* i.e. weather-*boarding:*—covering {16x}. See: TWOT—1008c; BDB—492c, 569a.

4373. מִכְסָה {2x} **mikçâh**, *mik-saw';* fem. of 4371; an *enumeration;* by impl. a *valuation:*—according to the number {1x}, worth {1x}. See: TWOT—1014b; BDB—493d, 569a.

4374. מְכַסֶּה {4x} **mᵉkaççeh**, *mek-as-seh';* from 3680; a *covering,* i.e. *garment;* spec. a *coverlet* (for a bed), an *awning* (from the sun); also the *omentum* (as covering the intestines):—clothing {1x}, to cover {1x}, that which covereth {2x}. See: TWOT—1008d; BDB—492c, 569a.

4375. מַכְפֵּלָה {6x} **Makpêlâh**, *mak-pay-law';* from 3717; a *fold; Makpelah,* a place in Pal.:—Machpelah {6x}. See: TWOT—1019b; BDB—495d, 569a.

4376. מָכַר {80x} **mâkar**, *maw-kar';* a prim. root; to *sell,* lit. (as merchandise, a daughter in marriage, into slavery), or fig. (to *surrender*):—× at all {1x}, sell (away, self) {75x}, seller {4x}.

Makar means "to sell." **(1)** It is found for the first time in the Old Testament in Gen 25:31: "And Jacob said, Sell me this day thy birthright." **(2)** Anything tangible may be "sold," such as land (Gen 47:20), houses (Lev 25:29), animals (Ex 21:35), and human beings as slaves (Gen 37:27–28). **(3)** Daughters were usually "sold" for an agreed bride price (Ex 21:7). **(4)** *Makar* is often used in the figurative sense to express various actions. **(4a)** Nineveh is accused of "selling" or "betraying" other nations (Nah 3:4). **(4b)** Frequently it is said that God "sold" Israel into the power of her enemies, meaning that He gave them over entirely into their hands (Judg 2:14). **(4c)** Similarly, it was said that "the LORD shall sell Sisera into the hand of a woman" (Judg 4:9). **(5)** "To be sold" sometimes means to be given over to death (Est 7:4). See: TWOT—1194; BDB—569a.

4377. מֶכֶר {3x} **meker**, *meh'-ker;* from 4376; *merchandise;* also *value:*—pay for it {1x}, price {1x}, ware {1x}. See: TWOT—1194a; BDB—569c.

4378. מַכָּר {1x} **makkâr**, *mak-kawr';* from 5234; an *acquaintance:*—acquaintance {2x}. See: TWOT—1368f; BDB—569d, 648c.

4379. מִכְרֶה {1x} **mikreh**, *mik-reh';* from 3738; a *pit* (for salt):—saltpit + 4417 {1x}. See: TWOT—1033b; BDB—500b, 569d.

4380. מְכֵרָה {1x} **mᵉkêrâh**, *mek-ay-raw';* prob. from the same as 3564 in the sense of *stabbing;* a *sword:*—habitation {1x}. See: TWOT—1194d; BDB—468d, 569d.

מְכֹרָה **mᵉkôrâh**. See 4351.

4381. מִכְרִי {1x} **Mikrîy**, *mik-ree';* from 4376; *salesman; Mikri,* an Isr.:—Michri {1x}. See: BDB—569d.

4382. מְכֵרָתִי {1x} **Mᵉkêrâthîy**, *mek-ay-raw-thee';* patrial from an unused name (the same as 4380) of a place in Pal.; a *Mekerathite,* or inhab. of Mekerah:—Mecherathite {1x}. See: BDB—569d.

4383. מִכְשׁוֹל {14x} **mikshôwl**, *mik-shole';* or

מִכְשֹׁל **mikshôl**, *mik-shole';* masc. from 3782; a *stumbling-block,* lit. or fig. (*obstacle, enticement* [spec. an idol], *scruple*):—stumblingblock {8x}, offence {2x}, ruins {2x}, offend {1x}, fall {1x}. See: TWOT—1050c; BDB—506a, 569d.

4384. מַכְשֵׁלָה {2x} **makshêlâh**, *mak-shay-law';* fem. from 3782; a *stumbling-block,* but only fig. (*fall, enticement* [idol]):—ruin {1x}, stumbling-block {1x}. See: TWOT—1050d; BDB—506b, 569d.

4385. מִכְתָּב {9x} **miktâb**, *mik-tawb';* from 3789; a thing *written,* the *characters,* or a *document* (letter, copy, edict, poem):—writing {9x}.

Miktab means "something written, a writing": "And the tables *were* the work of God, and the writing *was* the writing of God, graven upon the tables" (Ex 32:16; cf. Is 38:9). See: TWOT—1053c; BDB—508b, 569d.

4386. מְכִתָּה {1x} **mᵉkittâh**, *mek-it-taw';* from 3807; a *fracture:*—bursting {1x}. See: TWOT—1062b; BDB—510c, 569d.

4387. מִכְתָּם {6x} **Miktâm**, *mik-tawm';* from 3799; an *engraving,* i.e. (techn.) a *poem:*—Michtam {6x}. See: TWOT—1056a; BDB—508d, 569d.

4388. מַכְתֵּשׁ {2x} **maktêsh**, *mak-taysh';* from 3806; a *mortar;* by anal. a *socket* (of a tooth):—hollow places {1x}, mortar {1x}. See: TWOT—1061a; BDB—509d, 569d.

4389. מַכְתֵּשׁ {1x} **Maktêsh**, *mak-taysh';* the same as 4388; *dell;* the *Maktesh,* a place in Jerusalem:—Maktesh {1x}. See: BDB—509d, 569d.

מַל **mûl**. See 4136.

4390. מָלֵא {249x} **mâlê'**, *maw-lay';* or

מָלָא **mâlâ'** (Est 7:5), *maw-law';* a prim. root, to *fill* or (intr.) *be full* of, in a wide application (lit. and fig.):—fill {107x}, full {48x}, fulfil {28x}, consecrate {15x}, accomplish {7x}, replenish {7x}, wholly {6x}, set {6x}, expired {3x}, fully {2x}, gather {2x}, overflow {2x}, satisfy {2x}, misc. {14x} = confirm, be at an end, be fenced, fulness, furnish, presume, space, take a [hand-] full.

I. *Male'*, as a verb, means "to fill, fulfill, overflow, ordain, endow." **(1)** Basically, *male'* means "to be full" in the sense of having something done to one. **(1a)** In 2 Kin 4:6, the word implies "to fill up": "And it came to pass, when the vessels were full, that she said. . . ." **(1b)** The verb is sometimes used figuratively as in Gen 6:13, when God noted that "the earth is filled with violence." **(2)** Used transitively, this verb means the act or state of "filling something." **(2a)** In Gen 1:22 (the first occurrence of the word), God told the sea creatures to "penetrate" the waters thoroughly but not exhaustively: "Be fruitful, and multiply and fill the waters in the seas." **(2b)** *Male'* can also mean "to fill up" in an exhaustive sense: ". . . And the glory of the Lord filled the tabernacle" (Ex 40:34). **(2c)** In this sense an appetite can be "filled up," "satiated," or "satisfied." **(3)** *Male'* is sometimes used in the sense "coming to an end" or "to be filled up," to the full extent of what is expected. **(3a)** For example, in 1 Kin 2:27 we read: "So Solomon thrust out Abiathar from being priest unto the Lord; that he might fulfill the word of the Lord, which he spake concerning the house of Eli in Shiloh." **(3b)** This constitutes a proof of the authority of the divine Word.

(4) In a different but related nuance, the verb signifies "to confirm" someone's word. Nathan told Bathsheba: "Behold, while thou yet talkest there with the king, I also will come in after thee, and confirm thy words" (1 Kin 1:14). **(5)** This verb is used to signify filling something to the full extent of what is necessary, in the sense of being "successfully completed": "When her days to be delivered were fulfilled . . ." (Gen 25:24). **(6)** This may also mean "to bring to an end"; so God tells Isaiah: "Speak ye comfortably to Jerusalem and cry unto her, that her warfare is accomplished . . ." (Is 40:2). **(7)** *Male'* is used of "filling to overflowing"—not just filling up to the limits of something, but filling so as to go beyond its limits: "For Jordan overfloweth all his banks all the time of harvest" (Josh 3:15). **(8)** A special nuance appears when the verb is used with "heart"; in such cases, it means "to presume." King Ahasuerus asked Esther: "Who is he, and where is he, that durst presume [literally, "fill his heart"] to do so?" (Est 7:5). **(9)** To call out "fully" is to cry aloud, as in Jer 4:5.

(10) The word often has a special meaning in conjunction with "hand." **(10a)** *Male'* can connote "endow" ("fill one's hand"), as in Ex 28:3: "And thou shalt speak unto all that are wisehearted, whom I have [endowed] with the spirit of wisdom. . . ." **(10b)** In Judg 17:5, "to fill one's hand" is "to consecrate" someone to priestly service. **(10c)** A similar idea appears in Eze 43:26, where no literal hand is filled with anything, but the phrase is a technical term for "consecration": "Seven days shall they [make atonement for] the altar and purify it; and they shall consecrate themselves." **(10c1)** This phrase is used not only of setting someone or something aside for special religious or cultic use, but of formally installing someone with the authority and responsibility to fulfill a cultic [religious] function (i.e., to be a priest). **(10c2)** So God commands concerning Aaron and his sons: "And thou . . . shalt anoint them, and consecrate them, and sanctify them, that they may minister unto me in the priest's office" (Ex 28:41).

(11) In military contexts, "to fill one's hand" is to prepare for battle. **(11a)** This phrase may be used of "becoming armed," as in Jer 51:11: "Make bright the arrows; gather the shields." **(11b)** In a fuller sense, the phrase may signify the step immediately before shooting arrows: "And Jehu drew [literally, "filled his hand with"] a bow with his full strength . . ." (2 Kin 9:24). **(11c)** It can also signify "being armed," or having weapons on one's person: "But the man that shall touch them must be [armed] with iron and the staff of a spear . . ." (2 Sa 23:7).

II. *Male'*, as an adjective, means "full." The basic meaning of the word is "full" or "full of": "I went out full, and the LORD hath brought me home again empty: why *then* call ye me Naomi, seeing the LORD hath testified against me, and the Almighty hath afflicted me?" (Ruth 1:21; cf. Deut 6:11). See: TWOT—1195; BDB—569d, 1100a.

4391. מְלָא {2x} **mᵉlâ'** (Aram.), *mel-aw';* corresp. to 4390; to *fill:*—fill {1x}, be full {1x}. See: TWOT—2826; BDB—1100a.

4392. מָלֵא {65x} **mâlê'**, *maw-lay';* from 4390; *full* (lit. or fig.) or *filling* (lit.); also (concr.) *fulness;* adv. *fully:*—full {57x}, fill {3x}, with child {1x}, fully {1x}, much {1x}, multitude {1x}, worth {1x}. See: TWOT—1195a; BDB—570d.

4393. מְלֹא {37x} **mᵉlô'**, *mel-o';* rarely

מְלוֹא **mᵉlôw'**, *mel-o';* or

מְלוֹ **mᵉlôw** (Eze 41:8), *mel-o';* from 4390; *fulness* (lit. or fig.):—full {12x}, fulness {8x}, all that is therein {7x}, all {2x}, fill {2x}, handful {2x}, multitude {2x}, handful + 7062 {1x}, handfuls + 2651 {1x}. See: TWOT—1195b; BDB—571a, 571d.

מִלֹּא **Millô'**. See 4407.

4394. מִלֻּא {15x} **millû'**, *mil-loo';* from 4390; a *fulfilling* (only in plur.), i.e. (lit.) a *setting* (of gems), or (tech.) *consecration* (also concr. a dedicatory *sacrifice*):—consecration {11x}, be set {4x}. See: TWOT—1195e; BDB—571b.

4395. מְלֵאָה {3x} **mᵉlê'âh**, *mel-ay-aw';* fem. of 4392; something *fulfilled,* i.e. *abundance* (of produce):—(first of ripe) fruit {1x}, fruit {1x}, fulness {1x}. See: TWOT—1195c; BDB—571b.

4396. מִלֻּאָה {3x} **millû'âh**, *mil-loo-aw';* fem. of 4394; a *filling,* i.e. *setting* (of gems):—inclosings {2x}, settings {1x}. See: TWOT—1195d; BDB—571b.

4397. מַלְאָךְ {214x} **mal'âk**, *mal-awk';* from an unused root mean. to *despatch* as a deputy; a *messenger;* spec. of God, i.e. an *angel* (also a prophet, priest or teacher):—angel {111x}, messenger {98x}, ambassadors {4x}, variant {1x}.

Mal'ak means "messenger; angel." **(1)** The noun *mal'ak* appears 213 times in the Hebrew Old Testament. **(1a)** Its frequency is especially great in the historical books, where it usually means "messenger": Judg (31 times), 2 Kin (20 times), 1 Sa (19 times), and 2 Sa (18 times). **(1b)** The prophetical works are very moderate in their usage of *mal'ak,* **(1c)** with the outstanding exception of the Book of Zechariah, where the angel of the Lord communicates God's message to Zechariah. **(1d)** For example: "Then I answered and said unto the angel that talked to me, 'What are these, my lord?' And the angel answered and said unto me, 'These are the four spirits [pl. of *malʾak*] of the heavens, which go forth from standing before the Lord of all the earth'" (Zec 6:4–5). **(2)** The word *malʾak* denotes someone sent over a great distance by an individual (Gen 32:3) or by a community (Num 21:21), in order to communicate a message. Often several messengers are sent together: "And Ahaziah fell down through a lattice in his upper chamber that was in Samaria, and was sick: and he sent messengers [pl. of *malʾak*] and said unto them, Go, inquire of Baal-zebub the god of Ekron whether I shall recover of this disease" (2 Kin 1:2).

(3) The introductory formula of the message borne by the *malʾak* often contains the phrase "Thus says . . . ," or "This is what . . . says," signifying the authority of the messenger in giving the message of his master: "Thus saith Jephthah, Israel took not away the land of Moab, nor the land of the children of Ammon" (Judg 11:15). **(4)** As a representative of a king, the *malʾak* might have performed the function of a diplomat. **(4a)** In 1 Kin 20:1ff., we read that Benhadad sent messengers with the terms of surrender: **(4b)** "He sent messengers to Ahab king of Israel into the city, and said unto him, Thus saith Benhadad . . ." (1 Kin 20:2). **(5)** These passages confirm the important place of the *malʾak*. **(5a)** Honor to the messenger signified honor to the sender, and the opposite was also true. **(5b)** David took personally the insult of Nabal (1 Sa 25:14ff.); and when Hanun, king of Ammon, humiliated David's servants (2 Sa 10:4ff.), David was quick to dispatch his forces against the Ammonites.

(6) God also sent messengers. **(6a)** First, there are the prophetic messengers: "And the LORD God of their fathers sent to them by his messengers, rising up betimes, and sending; because he had compassion on his people, and on his dwelling place: But they mocked the messengers of God, and despised his words, and misused his prophets, until the wrath of the LORD arose against his people, till there was no remedy" (2 Chr 36:15–16). **(6b)** Haggai called himself "the messenger of the LORD," *malʾak Yahweh*. **(7)** There were also angelic messengers. The English word angel is etymologically related to the Greek word *angelos,* whose translation is similar to the Hebrew: "messenger" or "angel." **(7a)** The angel is a supernatural messenger of the Lord sent with a particular message. **(7b)** Two angels came to Lot at Sodom: "And there came two angels to Sodom at even; and Lot sat in the gate of Sodom: and Lot seeing them rose up to meet them; and he bowed himself with his face toward the ground . . ." (Gen 19:1). **(7c)** The angels were also commissioned to protect God's people: "For he shall give his angels charge over thee, to keep thee in all thy ways" (Ps 91:11).

(8) Most significant, are the phrases *malʾak Yahweh,* "the angel of the LORD," and *malʾak ʿelohim,* "the angel of God." **(8a)** The phrase is always used in the singular. **(8b)** It denotes an angel who had mainly a saving and protective function: "For mine angel shall go before thee, and bring thee in unto the Amorites, and the Hittites, and the Perizzites, and the Canaanites, the Hivites, and the Jebusites: and I will cut them off" (Ex 23:23). **(8c)** He might also bring about destruction: "And David lifted up his eyes, and saw the angel of the LORD stand between the earth and the heaven, having a drawn sword in his hand stretched out over Jerusalem. Then David and the elders of Israel, who were clothed in sackcloth, fell upon their faces" (1 Chr 21:16). **(8d)** The relation between the Lord and the "angel of the LORD" is often so close that it is difficult to separate the two (Gen 16:7ff.; 21:17ff.; 22:11ff.; 31:11ff.; Ex 3:2ff.; Judg 6:11ff.; 13:21f.). **(8e)** This identification has led some interpreters to conclude that the "angel of the LORD" was the pre-incarnate Christ. See: TWOT—1068a; BDB—521c, 571c, 1098d.

4398. מַלְאַךְ {2x} **malʾak** (Aram.), *mal-ak';* corresp. to 4397; an *angel:*—angel {2x}. See: TWOT—2827; BDB—1098d, 1100a.

4399. מְלָאכָה {167x} **meˡlâʾkâh**, *mel-aw-kaw';* from the same as 4397; prop. *deputyship,* i.e. ministry; gen. *employment* (never servile) or work (abstr. or concr.); also *property* (as the result of *labor*):—work {129x}, business {12x}, workmen + 6213 {7x}, workmanship {5x}, goods {2x}, cattle {1x}, stuff {1x}, thing {1x}, misc. {9x} = + industrious, occupation, (+ -pied), + officer, use. See: TWOT—1068b; BDB—521d, 571c.

4400. מַלְאֲכוּת {1x} **malʾăkûwth**, *mal-ak-ooth';* from the same as 4397; a *message:*—message {1x}. See: TWOT—1068c; BDB—522b, 571c.

4401. מַלְאָכִי {1x} **Malʾâkîy**, *mal-aw-kee';* from the same as 4397; *ministrative; Malaki,* a prophet:—Malachi {1x}. See: BDB—522b, 571c.

4402. מִלֵּאת {1x} **millêʾth**, *mil-layth';* from 4390; *fulness,* i.e. (concr.) a *plump* socket (of the eye):—× fitly {1x}. See: TWOT—1195f; BDB—571c.

4403. מַלְבּוּשׁ {8x} **malbûwsh**, *mal-boosh';* or

מַלְבֻּשׁ **malbûsh**, *mal-boosh';* from 3847; a *garment,* or (collect.) *clothing:*—apparel {4x}, raiment {3x}, vestment {1x}. See: TWOT—1075b; BDB—528c, 571c.

4404. מַלְבֵּן {1x} **malbên**, *mal-bane';* from 3835 (denom.); a *brick-kiln:*—brickkiln {1x}. See: TWOT—1074i; BDB—527c, 571c, 576a.

4405. מִלָּה {38x} **millâh**, *mil-law';* from 4448 (plur. masc. as if from

מִלֶּה **milleh**, *mil-leh';* a *word;* collect. a *discourse;* fig. a *topic:*—word {23x}, speech {6x}, say {2x}, speaking {2x}, answer + 7725 {1x}, byword {1x}, matter {1x}, speak {1x}, talking {1x}. Syn.: 559, 1696. See: TWOT—1201a; BDB—571c, 576b.

4406. מִלָּה {24x} **millâh** (Aram.), *mil-law';* corresp. to 4405; a *word, command, discourse,* or *subject:*—commandment {1x}, matter {5x}, thing {11x}, word {7x}. See: TWOT—2831a; BDB—1100a, 1100c.

מְלוֹ **meˡlôw**. See 4393.

מְלוֹא **meˡlôwʾ**. See 4393.

4407. מִלּוֹא {10x} **millôwʾ**, *mil-lo';* or

מִלֹּא **millôʾ** (2 Kin 12:20) *mil-lo';* from 4390; a *rampart* (as *filled* in), i.e. the *citadel:*—Millo {10x}. See: BDB—571c. See also 1037.

4408. מַלּוּחַ {1x} **mallûwach**, *mal-loo'-akh;* from 4414; *sea-purslain* (from its *saltness*):—mallows {1x}. See: TWOT—1197c; BDB—572a.

4409. מַלּוּךְ {7x} **Mallûwk**, *mal-luke';* or

מַלּוּכִי **Mallûwkîy** (Neh 12:14) *mal-loo-kee';* from 4427; *regnant; Malluk,* the name of five Isr.:—Malluch {6x}, Melichu {1x}. See: BDB—576a.

4410. מְלוּכָה {24x} **meˡlûwkâh**, *mel-oo-kaw';* fem. pass. part. of 4427; something *ruled,* i.e. a *realm:*—kingdom {18x}, king's {2x}, × royal {4x}. See: TWOT—1199d; BDB—574c.

4411. מָלוֹן {8x} **mâlown**, *maw-lone';* from 3885; a *lodgment,* i.e. *caravanserai* or *encampment:*—inn {3x}, place where . . . lodged {1x}, lodgings {2x}, lodging place {2x}. See: TWOT—1096a; BDB—533d, 571d.

4412. מְלוּנָה {2x} **meˡlûwnâh**, *mel-oo-naw';* fem. from 3885; a *hut,* a *hammock:*—cottage {1x}, lodge {1x}. See: TWOT—1096b; BDB—534a, 571d.

4413. מַלּוֹתִי {2x} **Mallôwthîy**, *mal-lo'-thee;* appar. from 4448; *I have talked* (i.e. *loquacious*); *Mallothi,* an Isr.:—Mallothi {2x}. See: BDB—571d, 576c, 1100a.

4414. מָלַח {5x} **mâlach**, *maw-lakh';* a prim. root; prop. to *rub* to pieces or pulverize; intr. to *disappear* as dust; also (as denom. from 4417) to *salt* whether intern. (to *season* with salt) or extern. (to *rub* with salt):—× at all {1x}, salt {1x}, season {1x}, temper together {1x}, vanish away {1x}. See: TWOT—1196, 1197; BDB—571d, 572a, 1100b.

4415. מְלַח {1x} **meˡlach** (Aram.), *mel-akh';* corresp. to 4414; to *eat* salt, i.e. (gen.) *subsist:*—+ have maintenance {1x}. See: TWOT—2828; BDB—1090b, 1100b.

4416. מְלַח {3x} **meˡlach** (Aram.), *mel-akh',* from 4415; *salt:*—+ maintenance {1x}, salt {2x}. See: TWOT—2828a; BDB—1100a.

4417. מֶלַח {28x} **melach**, *meh'-lakh;* from 4414; prop. *powder,* i.e. (spec.) *salt* (as easily pulverized and dissolved:—salt {27x}, saltpits + 4379 {1x}. See: TWOT—1197a; BDB—571d, 1100a.

4418. מָלָח {2x} **mâlâch**, *maw-lawkh';* from 4414 in its orig. sense; a *rag* or old garment:—rotten rags {2x}. See: TWOT—1196a; BDB—571d.

4419. מַלָּח {4x} **mallâch**, *mal-lawkh';* from 4414 in its second. sense; a *sailor* (as following "the salt"):—mariner {4x}. See: TWOT—1197d; BDB—572a.

4420. מְלֵחָה {3x} **meˡlêchâh**, *mel-ay-khaw';* from 4414 (in its denom. sense); prop. *salted* (i.e. land [776 being understood]), i.e. a *desert:*—barren land {1x}, barreness {1x}, salt land {1x}. See: TWOT—1197b; BDB—572a.

4421. מִלְחָמָה {319x} **milchâmâh**, *mil-khaw-maw';* from 3898 (in the sense of *fighting*); a *battle* (i.e. the *engagement*); gen. *war* (i.e. *warfare*):—war {158x}, battle {151x}, fight {5x}, warriors + 6213 {2x}, fighting + 6213 {1x}, war + 376 {1x}, wars + 376 {1x}.

Milchamah means "battle; war." **(1)** This noun occurs more than 300 times in the Old Testament, indicating how large a part military experience and terminology played in the life of the ancient Israelites. **(2)** Gen 14:8 is an early occurrence of *milchamah:* "And there went out the king of Sodom, and the king of Gomorrah, . . . and they joined battle with them in the vale of Siddim." See: TWOT—1104c; BDB—536a, 572b.

4422. מָלַט {95x} **mâlat**, *maw-lat';* a prim. root; prop. to *be smooth,* i.e. (by impl.) to *escape* (as if by *slipperiness*); caus. to *release* or *rescue;* spec. to *bring forth* young, *emit* sparks:—escape {47x}, deliver {33x}, save {5x}, . . . out {4x}, alone {1x}, get away {1x}, lay {1x}, preserve {1x}, speedily {1x}, surely {1x}.

Malat means to escape, slip away, deliver, give birth. **(1)** The word appears twice in the first verse in which it is found: "And it came to pass, when they had brought them forth abroad, that he said, Escape for thy life; look not behind thee, neither stay thou in all the plain; escape to the mountain, lest thou be consumed" (Gen 19:17). **(2)** Sometimes *malat* is used in parallelism **(2a)** with *nuç* (5127) "to flee": And Saul sought to smite David even to the wall with the javelin; but he slipped away out of Saul's presence, and he smote the javelin into the wall: and David fled *(nuç),* and escaped *(malat)* that night" (1 Sa 19:10), or **(2b)** with *barach* (1272) "to flee": "So Michal let David down through a window: and he went, and fled *(barach),* and escaped *(nuç)*" (1 Sa 19:12). **(3)** The most common use of this word is to express the "escaping" from any kind of danger such as an enemy (Is 20:6), a trap (2 Kin 10:24), or a temptress (Eccl 7:26). **(4)** When Josiah's reform called for burning the bones of false prophets, a special directive was issued to spare the bones of a true prophet buried at the same place: ". . . So they let his bones alone . . ." (2 Kin 23:18; literally, "they let his bones escape"). **(5)** *Malat* is used once in the sense of "delivering a child" (Is 66:7). See: TWOT—1198; BDB—572b.

4423. מֶלֶט {1x} **melet**, *meh'-let;* from 4422, *cement* (from its plastic *smoothness*):—clay {1x}. See: TWOT—1198a; BDB—572d.

4424. מְלַטְיָה {1x} **Melatyâh**, *mel-at-yaw';* from 4423 and 3050; (whom) *Jah has delivered; Melatjah,* a Gibeonite:—Melatiah {1x}. See: TWOT—1198a; BDB—572d.

4425. מְלִילָה {1x} **meliylâh**, *mel-ee-law';* from 4449 (in the sense of *cropping* [comp. 4135]); a *head* of grain (as *cut* off):—ear {1x}. See: TWOT—1202a; BDB—576c.

4426. מְלִיצָה {2x} **melîytsâh**, *mel-ee-tsaw';* from 3887; an *aphorism;* also a *satire:*—interpretation {1x}, taunting {1x}. See: TWOT—1113b; BDB—539c, 572d.

4427. מָלַךְ {348x} **mâlak**, *maw-lak';* a prim. root; to *reign;* incept. to *ascend the throne;* caus. to *induct* into royalty; hence, (by impl.) to *take counsel:*—reign {289x}, king {46x}, made {4x}, queen {2x}, consulted {1x}, indeed {1x}, make {1x}, rule {1x}, set {1x}, surely {1x}, set up {1x}.

Malak means "to reign, be king (or queen)." **(1)** Basically the word means to fill the functions of ruler over someone. **(1a)** To hold such a position was to function as the commander-in-chief of the army, the chief executive of the group, and **(1b)** to be an important, if not central, religious figure. **(2)** The king was the head of his people and, therefore, in battle were the king to be killed, his army would disperse until a new king could be chosen. **(3)** The first appearance of *malak* is in Gen 36:31: "And these are the kings that reigned in the land of Edom, before there reigned any king over the children of Israel." **(4)** The king "reigned" as the earthly representative of the god (or God) who was recognized as the real king. **(4a)** Thus, he was considered to be god's (God's) son. **(4b)** This same idea recurs in Israel (Ps 2:6). In Israel, too, God was the King: "The Lord shall reign for ever and ever" (Ex 15:18). **(5)** That the word can also be used of what a queen does when she "reigns" proves that it refers to the function of anyone in the office of king: "And he was with her hid in the house of the Lord six years. And Athaliah did reign over the land" (2 Kin 11:3).

(6) *Malak* can also be used of the idea "to become king"—someone was made, or made himself, a king: "And Bela died, and Jobab the son of Zerah of Bozrah reigned in his stead" (Gen 36:33). **(7)** This verb can be used of the assumption of a kingly reign, or of "beginning to reign": "Saul reigned one year; and when he had reigned two years over Israel . . ." (1 Sa 13:1; cf. Prov 30:22). **(8)** Finally, the verb is used of receiving the title of queen (or king) whether or not one receives any political or military power. So it was said: "And let the maiden which pleaseth the king be queen instead of Vashti" (Est 2:4). See: TWOT—1199, 1200; BDB—573d, 576a, 1100b, 1100c.

4428. מֶלֶךְ {2523x} **melek**, *meh'-lek;* from 4427; a *king:*—king {2518x}, royal {2x}, Hammelech {1x}, Malcham {1x}, Moloch {1x}. See: TWOT—1199a; BDB—572d, 574c, 575d.

4429. מֶלֶךְ {3x} **Melek**, *meh'-lek;* the same as 4428; *king; Melek,* the name of two Isr.:—Melech {2x}, Hammelech {1x} [by includ. the art.]. See: BDB—573a, 574b, 1100b.

4430. מֶלֶךְ {180x} **melek** (Aram.), *meh'-lek;* corresp. to 4428; a *king:*—king {179x}, royal {1x}. See: TWOT—2829a; BDB—1100b.

4431. מְלַךְ {1x} **melak** (Aram.), *mel-ak';* from a root corresp. to 4427 in the sense of *consultation; advice:*—counsel {1x}. See: TWOT—2830a; BDB—1100c.

4432. מֹלֶךְ {8x} **Môlek**, *mo'-lek;* from 4427; *Molek* (i.e. king), the chief deity of the Ammonites:—Molech {8x}. See: TWOT—1199h; BDB—574c. comp. 4445.

4433. מַלְכָּא {2x} **malkâ'** (Aram.), *mal-kaw';* corresp. to 4436; a *queen:*—queen {2x}. See: TWOT—2829b; BDB—1100b.

4434. מַלְכֹּדֶת {1x} **malkôdeth**, *mal-ko'-deth;* from 3920; a *snare:*—trap {1x}. See: TWOT—1115b; BDB—540b, 576a.

4435. מִלְכָּה {11x} **Milkâh**, *mil-kaw';* a form of 4436; *queen; Milcah,* the name of a Hebrewess and of an Isr.:—Milcah {11x}. See: BDB—574c.

4436. מַלְכָּה {35x} **malkâh**, *mal-kaw';* fem. of 4428; a *queen:*—queen {35x}. See: TWOT—1199b; BDB—573c.

4437. מַלְכוּ {57x} **malkûw** (Aram.), *mal-koo';* corresp. to 4438; *dominion* (abstr. or concr.):—kingdom {49x}, kingly {1x}, realm {3x}, reign {4x}. See: TWOT—2829c; BDB—1100b.

4438. מַלְכוּת {91x} **malkûwth**, *mal-kooth';* or

מַלְכֻת **malkûth**, *mal-kooth';* or (in plur.)

מַלְכֻיָּה **malkûyâh**, *mal-koo-yâh';* from 4427; a *rule;* concr. a *dominion:*—kingdom {51x}, reign {21x}, royal {13x}, realm {4x}, empire {1x}, estate {1x}.

Malkuth means "kingdom; reign; rule." **(1)** The first occurrence is in Num 24:7: "He shall pour the water out of his buckets, and his seed shall be in many waters, and his king shall be higher than Agag, and his kingdom shall be exalted." **(2)** The word *malkuth* denotes: **(2a)** the territory of the kingdom: "When he showed the riches of his glorious kingdom and the honor of his excellent majesty many days, even a hundred and fourscore days" (Est 1:4); **(2b)** the accession to the throne: "For if thou altogether holdest thy peace at this time, then shall there enlargement and deliverance arise to the Jews from another place; but thou and thy father's house shall be destroyed: and who knoweth whether thou art come to the kingdom for such a time as this?" (Est 4:14); **(2c)** the year of rule: "So Esther was taken unto king Ahasuerus into his house royal in the tenth month, which is the month Tebeth, in the seventh year of his reign" (Est 2:16); and **(2d)** anything "royal" or "kingly": throne (Est 1:2), wine (Est 1:7), crown (Est 1:11), word (Est 1:19), garment (Est 6:8), palace (Est 1:9), scepter (Ps 45:6), and glory (Ps 145:11–12). See: TWOT—1199e; BDB—574d.

4439. מַלְכִּיאֵל {3x} **Malkîy'êl**, *mal-kee-ale';* from 4428 and 410; *king of* (i.e. appointed by) *God; Malkiël,* an Isr.:—Malchiel {3x}. See: BDB—575c.

4440. מַלְכִּיאֵלִי {1x} **Malkîy'êlîy**, *mal-kee-ay-lee';* patron. from 4439; a *Malkiëlite* or desc. of Malkiel:—Malchielite {1x}. See: BDB—575c.

4441. מַלְכִּיָּה {16x} **Malkîyâh**, *mal-kee-yaw';* or

מַלְכִּיָּהוּ **Malkîyâhûw** (Jer 38:6), *mal-kee-yaw'-hoo;* from 4428 and 3050; *king of* (i.e. appointed by) *Jah; Malkijah,* the name of ten Isr.:—Malchiah {10x}, Malchijah {6x}.

4442. מַלְכִּי־צֶדֶק {2x} **Malkîy-Tsedeq**, *mal-kee-tseh'-dek;* from 4428 and 6664; *king of right; Malki-Tsedek,* an early king in Pal.:—Melchizedek {2x}. See: TWOT—1199i; BDB—575d.

4443. מַלְכִּירָם {1x} **Malkîyrâm**, *mal-kee-rawm';* from 4428 and 7311; *king of a high one* (i.e. of exaltation); *Malkiram,* an Isr.:—Malchiram {1x}. See: BDB—575d.

4444. מַלְכִּישׁוּעַ {5x} **Malkîyshûwa'**, *mal-kee-shoo'-ah;* from 4428 and 7769; *king of wealth; Malkishua,* an Isr.:—Malchishua {5x}. See: BDB—575d.

4445. מַלְכָּם {4x} **Malkâm**, *mal-kawm';* or

מִלְכּוֹם **Milkôwm**, *mil-kome';* from 4428 for 4432; *Malcam* or *Milcom,* the national idol of the Ammonites:—Malcham {1x}, Milcom {3x}. See: BDB—575d.

4446. מְלֶכֶת {5x} **meleketh**, *mel-eh'-keth;* from 4427; a *queen:*—queen {5x}. See: TWOT—1199c; BDB—573d.

4447. מֹלֶכֶת {1x} **Môleketh**, *mo-leh'-keth;* fem. act. part. of 4427; *queen; Moleketh,* an Israelitess:—Hammoleketh {1x} [*incl. the art.*]. See: BDB—574c.

4448. מָלַל {5x} **mâlal**, *maw-lal';* a prim. root; to *speak* (mostly poet.) or *say:*—said {1x}, speak {2x}, utter {2x}. See: TWOT—1201; BDB—576a, 576c, 1100c.

4449. מְלַל {5x} **melal** (Aram.), *mel-al';* corresp. to 4448; to *speak:*—said {1x}, speak (-ing) {4x}. See: TWOT—2831; BDB—1100c.

4450. מִלֲלַי {1x} **Milâlay**, *mee-lal-ah'-ee;* from 4448; *talkative; Milalai,* an Isr.:—Milalai {1x}. See: BDB—576c.

4451. מַלְמָד {1x} **malmâd**, *mal-mawd';* from 3925; a *goad* for oxen:—goad {1x}. See: TWOT—1116b; BDB—541a, 576d.

4452. מָלַץ {1x} **mâlats**, *maw-lats;* a prim. root; to *be smooth,* i.e. (fig.) *pleasant:*—be sweet {1x}. See: TWOT—1205; BDB—576d.

4453. מֶלְצָר {2x} **Meltsâr**, *mel-tsawr';* of Pers. der.; the *butler* or other officer in the Bab. court:—Melzar {2x}. See: BDB—576d.

4454. מָלַק {2x} **mâlaq**, *maw-lak';* a prim. root; to *crack* a joint; by impl. to *wring* the neck of a fowl (without separating it):—wring off {2x}. See: TWOT—1207; BDB—577a.

4455. מַלְקוֹחַ {8x} **malqôwach**, *mal-ko'-akh;* from 3947; tran. (in dual) the *jaws* (as taking food); intr. *spoil* [and captives] (as taken):—booty {1x}, jaws {1x}, prey {6x}.

Malqowach refers **(1)** to "things taken in warfare,": "And the booty, *being* the rest of the prey which the men of war had caught, was six hundred thousand and seventy thousand and five thousand sheep" (Num 31:32). **(2)** *Malqowach* also means "jaws" once: "My strength is dried up like a potsherd; and my tongue cleaveth to my jaws; and thou hast brought me into the dust of death" (Ps 22:15). Syn: 3948, 4457, 4727, 4728. See: TWOT—1124b, 1124c; BDB—544b, 544c, 577a.

4456. מַלְקוֹשׁ {8x} **malqôwsh**, *mal-koshe';* from 3953; the spring *rain* (comp. 3954); fig. *eloquence:*—latter {2x}, latter rain {6x}. See: TWOT—1127b; BDB—545b, 577a.

4457. מֶלְקָח {6x} **melqâch**, *mel-kawkh';* or

מַלְקָח **malqâch**, *mal-kawkh';* from 3947; (only in dual) *tweezers:*—snuffers {1x}, tongs {5x}. *Melqachayim* [plural] refers to "snuffers" (Ex 37:23), and it is found 6 times. Syn: 3948, 4455, 4727, 4728. See: TWOT—1124d; BDB—544c, 577a.

4458. מֶלְתָּחָה {1x} **meltâchâh**, *mel-taw-khaw';* from an unused root mean. to *spread* out; a *wardrobe* (i.e. room where clothing is *spread*):—vestry {1x}. See: TWOT—1132a; BDB—547a, 577a.

4459. מַלְתָּעָה {1x} **maltâʿâh**, *mal-taw-aw';* transp. for 4973; a *grinder,* i.e. back *tooth:*—great tooth {1x}. See: TWOT—2516d; BDB—577a, 1069a.

4460. מַמְּגֻרָה {1x} **mammᵉgûrâh**, *mam-meg-oo-raw';* from 4048 (in the sense of *depositing*); a *granary:*—barn {1x}. See: TWOT—330e; BDB—158c, 577a.

4461. מֵמַד {1x} **mêmad**, *may-mad';* from 4058; a *measure:*—measures {1x}. See: TWOT—1146c; BDB—551d, 577a.

4462. מְמוּכָן {3x} **Mᵉmûwkân**, *mem-oo-kawn';* or (transp.)

מוֹמֻכָן **Môwmûkân** (Est 1:16), *mo-moo-kawn';* of Pers. der.; *Memucan* or *Momucan,* a Pers. satrap:—Memucan {3x}. See: BDB—558a, 577a.

4463. מָמוֹת {2x} **mâmôwth**, *maw-mothe';* from 4191; a mortal *disease;* concr. a *corpse:*—death {2x}. *Mamowth* refers to "death." *Mamoth* appears in Jer 16:4: "They shall die of grievous deaths . . ." (cf. Eze 28:8). See: TWOT—1169b; BDB—560d, 577a.

4464. מַמְזֵר {2x} **mamzêr**, *mam-zare';* from an unused root mean. to *alienate;* a *mongrel,* i.e. born of a Jewish father and a heathen mother:—bastard {2x}. See: TWOT—1174a; BDB—561c, 577a.

4465. מִמְכָּר {10x} **mimkâr**, *mim-kawr';* from 4376; *merchandise;* abstr. a *selling:*—that . . . sold {4x}, sale {2x}, that which cometh of the sale {1x}, ought {1x}, ware {1x}, sold {1x}. See: TWOT—1194b; BDB—569d, 577a.

4466. מִמְכֶּרֶת {1x} **mimkereth**, *mim-keh'-reth;* fem. of 4465; a *sale:*—+ sold as {1x}. See: TWOT—1194c; BDB—569d, 577a.

4467. מַמְלָכָה {117x} **mamlâkâh**, *mam-law-kaw';* from 4427; *dominion,* i.e. (abstr.) the estate (*rule*) or (concr.) the country (*realm*):—kingdom {110x}, royal {4x}, reign {2x}, king's {1x}.

Mamlakah means "kingdom; sovereignty; dominion; reign." **(1)** *Mamlakah* occurs first in Gen 10:10: "And the beginning of his kingdom was Babel, and Erech, and Accad, and Calneh, in the land of Shinar" in the sense of the "realm" of the kingdom. **(2)** The basic meaning of *mamlakah* is the area and people that constitute a "kingdom." **(2a)** The word refers to non-Israelite nations who are ruled by a *melek* (4428), "king": "And it shall come to pass after the end of seventy years, that the LORD will visit Tyre, and she shall turn to her hire, and shall commit fornication with all the kingdoms of the world upon the face of the earth" (Is 23:17). **(3)** *Mamlakah* is a synonym for *ʿam* (5971) "people," and *goy* (1471) "nation": ". . . they went from one nation to another, from one kingdom to another people" (Ps 105:13). **(4)** *Mamlakah* also denotes Israel as God's "kingdom": "And ye shall be unto me a kingdom of priests, and a holy nation" (Ex 19:6). **(5)** The Davidic king was the theocratic agent by whom God ruled over and blessed His people: "And thine house and thy kingdom shall be established for ever before thee: thy throne shall be established for ever" (2 Sa 7:16).

(6) Nevertheless, the one *mamlakah* after Solomon was divided into two kingdoms which Ezekiel predicted would be reunited: "And I will make them one nation in the land upon the mountains of Israel; and one king shall be king to them all: and they shall be no more two nations, neither shall they be divided into two kingdoms . . ." (Eze 37:22). **(7)** Close to the basic meaning is the usage of *mamlakah* to denote "king," **(7a)** as the king was considered to be the embodiment of the "kingdom." **(7b)** He was viewed as a symbol of the kingdom proper: "Thus saith the LORD God of Israel, I brought up Israel out of Egypt, and delivered you out of the hand of the Egyptians, and out of the hand of all kingdoms, and of them that oppressed you" (1 Sa 10:18); **(7c)** in Hebrew the noun "kingdoms" is feminine and the verb "oppress" has a masculine form, signifying that we must understand "kingdoms" as "kings". **(8)** The function and place of the king is important in the development of the concept "kingdom." **(8a)** "Kingdom" may signify the head of the kingdom.

(8b) The word further has the meaning of the royal "rule," the royal "sovereignty," and the "dominion." **(8b1)** The royal "sovereignty" was taken from Saul because of his disobedience (1 Sa 28:17). **(8b2)** "Royal sovereignty" is also the sense in Jer 27:1: "In the beginning of the reign of Jehoiakim. . . ." **(8c)** The Old Testament further defines as expressions of the royal "rule" all things associated with the king: **(8c1)** the throne: "And it shall be, when he sitteth upon the throne of his kingdom, that he shall write him a copy of this law in a book out of that which is before the priests the Levites" (Deut 17:18); **(8c2)** the pagan sanctuary supported by the throne: "But prophesy not again any more at Beth-el: for it is the king's chapel, and it is the king's court" (Amos 7:13); and **(8c3)** a royal city: "And David said unto Achish, If I have now found grace in thine eyes, let them give me a place in some town in the country, that I may dwell there: for why should thy servant dwell in the royal city with thee?" (1 Sa 27:5). **(9)** All human rule is under God's control. Consequently the Old Testament fully recognizes the kingship of God.

(9a) The Lord ruled as king over His people Israel (1 Chr 29:11). **(9b)** He graciously ruled over His people through David and his followers until the Exile (2 Chr 13:5). **(10)** In the New Testament usage all the above meanings are to be associated with the Greek word *basileia* ("kingdom"). **(10a)** This is the major translation of *mamlakah* in the Septuagint, and as such it is small wonder that the New Testament authors used this word to refer to God's "kingdom": the realm, the king, the sovereignty, and the relationship to God Himself as *melek* (4428), "king." See: TWOT—1199f; BDB—575a, 577a.

4468. מַמְלָכוּת {9x} **mamlâkûwth**, *mam-law-kooth';* a form of 4467 and equiv. to it:—kingdom {8x}, reign {1x}. See: TWOT—1199g; BDB—575c.

4469. מַמְסָךְ {2x} **mamçâk**, *mam-sawk';* from 4537; *mixture,* i.e. (spec.) wine *mixed* (with water or spices):—drink-offering {1x}, mixed wine {1x}. See: TWOT—1220b; BDB—577a, 587c.

4470. מֶמֶר {1x} **memer**, *meh'-mer;* from an unused root mean. to *grieve; sorrow:*—bitterness {1x}. See: TWOT—1248j; BDB—577a, 601b.

4471. מַמְרֵא {10x} **Mamrêʾ**, *mam-ray';* from 4754 (in the sense of *vigor*); *lusty; Mamre,* an Amorite:—Mamre {10x}. See: TWOT—1208; BDB—577b.

4472. מַמְרֹר {1x} **mamrôr**, *mam-ror';* from 4843; a *bitterness,* i.e. (fig.) calamity:—bitterness {1x}. See: TWOT—1248k; BDB—577a, 601b.

4473. מִמְשַׁח {1x} **mimshach**, *mim-shakh';* from 4886, in the sense of *expansion; outspread* (i.e. with outstretched wings):—anointed {1x}. See: TWOT—1255d; BDB—577b, 603d.

4474. מִמְשָׁל {3x} **mimshâl**, *mim-shawl';* from 4910; a *ruler* or (abstr.) *rule:*—dominion {2x}, that ruled {1x}. See: TWOT—1259b; BDB—577b, 606a.

4475. מֶמְשָׁלָה {17x} **memshâlâh**, *mem-shaw-law';* fem. of 4474; *rule;* also (concr. in plur.) a *realm* or a *ruler:*—dominion {10x}, rule {4x}, dominion + 3027 {1x}, government {1x}, power {1x}. See: TWOT—1259c; BDB—577b, 606a.

4476. מִמְשָׁק {1x} **mimshâq**, *mim-shawk';* from the same as 4943; a *possession:*—breeding {1x}. See: TWOT—1261b; BDB—577b, 606c.

4477. מַמְתָּק {2x} **mamtaq**, *mam-tak';* from 4985; something *sweet* (lit. or fig.):—(most) sweet {2x}. See: TWOT—1268d; BDB—577b, 609a.

4478. מָן {14x} **mân**, *mawn;* from 4100; lit. a *whatness* (so to speak), i.e. *manna* (so called from the question about it):—manna {14x}. See: TWOT—1208, 1209; BDB—577b, 577c.

4479. מַן {10x} **mân** (Aram.), *mawn;* from 4101; *who* or *what* (prop. interrog., hence, also indef. and rel.):—whomsoever {4x}, who {3x}, whoso {2x}, what {1x}. See: TWOT—2832; BDB—1100d.

4480. מִן {25x} **min**, *min;* or

מִנִּי **minnîy**, *min-nee';* or

מִנֵּי **minnêy** (constr. plur.) *min-nay';* (Is 30:11); for 4482; prop. a *part* of; hence, (prep.), *from* or *out of* in many senses (as follows):—{25x} = above, after, among, at, because of, by (reason of), from (among), in, × neither, × nor, (out) of, over, since, × then, through, × whether, with. See: TWOT—1212, 1213e; BDB—541b, 547a, 577a, 577c, 585d, 606b, 1100d.

4481. מִן {109x} **min** (Aram.), *min;* corresp. to 4480:—of {31x}, from {29x}, part {6x}, . . . I {4x}, . . . me {3x}, before {3x}, after {2x}, because {2x}, therefore {2x}, out {2x}, for {2x}, than {2x}, partly {2x}, misc. {19x} = according, by, × him, since, × these, to, upon, + when. See: TWOT—2833; BDB—1100d.

4482. מֵן {2x} **mên**, *mane;* from an unused root mean. to *apportion;* a *part;* hence, a musical *chord* (as parted into strings):—stringed instrument {1x}, whereby {1x}. See: TWOT—1211; BDB—577c, 585d.

4483. מְנָא {5x} **meᵉnâʾ** (Aram.), *men-aw';* or

מְנָה **meᵉnâh** (Aram.) *men-aw';* corresp. to 4487; to *count, appoint:*—number {1x}, ordain {1x}, set {3x}. See: TWOT—2835; BDB—1101b.

4484. מְנֵא {3x} **menêʾ** (Aram.), *men-ay';* pass. part. of 4483; *numbered:*—Mene {3x}. See: TWOT—2835a; BDB—1101b, 1108b, 1118c.

4485. מַנְגִּינָה {1x} **mangîynâh**, *man-ghee-naw';* from 5059; a *satire:*—music {1x}. See: TWOT—1291; BDB—584a, 618d.

מִנְדָּה **mindâh**. See 4061.

4486. מַנְדַּע {4x} **mandaʿ** (Aram.), *man-dah';* corresp. to 4093; *wisdom* or *intelligence:*—knowledge {2x}, reason {1x}, understanding {1x}. See: TWOT—2765a, 2834; BDB—1095b, 1101b.

מְנָה **meᵉnâh**. See 4483.

4487. מָנָה {28x} **mânâh**, *maw-naw';* a prim. root; prop. to *weigh* out; by impl. to *allot* or constitute officially; also to *enumerate* or enroll:—number {14x}, prepare {5x}, appointed {4x}, tell {3x}, count {1x}, set {1x}. See: TWOT—1213; BDB—584a, 1101b.

4488. מָנֶה {5x} **mâneh**, *maw-neh';* from 4487; prop. a fixed *weight* or measured amount, i.e. (techn.) a *maneh* or mina:—maneh {1x}, pound {4x}. See: TWOT—1213b; BDB—584b.

4489. מֹנֶה {2x} **môneh**, *mo-neh';* from 4487; prop. something *weighed* out, i.e. (fig.) a *portion* of time, i.e. an *instance:*—time {2x}. See: TWOT—1213c; BDB—584c.

4490. מָנָה {14x} **mânâh**, *maw-naw';* from 4487; prop. something *weighed* out, i.e. (gen.) a *division;* spec. (of food) a *ration;* also a *lot:*—such things as belonged {1x}, part {3x}, portion {10x}. See: TWOT—1213a; BDB—584b.

4491. מִנְהָג {2x} **minhâg**, *min-hawg';* from 5090; the *driving* (of a chariot):—driving {2x}. See: TWOT—1309a; BDB—584d, 624c.

4492. מִנְהָרָה {1x} **minhârâh**, *min-haw-raw';* from 5102; prop. a *channel* or fissure, i.e. (by impl.) a *cavern:*—den {1x}. See: TWOT—1316b; BDB—584d, 626a.

4493. מָנוֹד {1x} **mânôwd**, *maw-node';* from 5110 a *nodding* or *toss* (of the head in derision):—shaking {1x}. See: TWOT—1319c; BDB—584a, 627b.

4494. מָנוֹחַ {7x} **mânôwach**, *maw-no'-akh;* from 5117; *quiet,* i.e. (concr.) a *settled spot,* or (fig.) a *home:*—(place of) rest {7x}. See: TWOT—1323e; BDB—584d, 629c.

4495. מָנוֹחַ {18x} **Mânôwach**, *maw-no'-akh;* the same as 4494; *rest; Manoäch,* an Isr.:—Manoah {18x}. See: BDB—584d, 629d.

4496. מְנוּחָה {21x} **meᵉnûwchâh**, *men-oo-khaw';* or

מְנֻחָה **meᵉnûchâh**, *men-oo-khaw';* fem. of 4495; *repose* or (adv.) *peacefully;* fig. *consolation* (spec. *matrimony*); hence, (concr.) an *abode:*—rest {15x}, resting place {2x}, comfortable {1x}, ease {1x}, quiet {1x}, still {1x}. See: TWOT—1323f; BDB—584d, 629d.

4497. מָנוֹן {1x} **mânôwn** *maw-nohn';* from 5125; a *continuator,* i.e. *heir:*—son {1x}. See: TWOT—1213f; BDB—584d.

4498. מָנוֹס {8x} **mânôwç**, *maw-noce';* from 5127; a *retreat* (lit. or fig.); abstr. a *fleeing:*—× apace {1x}, escape {1x}, way to flee {1x}, flight {1x}, refuge {4x}. See: TWOT—1327a; BDB—651a.

4499. מְנוּסָה {2x} **meᵉnuwçâh**, *men-oo-saw';* or

מְנֻסָה **meᵉnûçâh**, *men-oo-saw';* fem. of 4498; *retreat:*—fleeing {1x}, flight {1x}. See: TWOT—1327b; BDB—586a, 631a.

4500. מָנוֹר {4x} **mânôwr**, *maw-nore';* from 5214; a *yoke* (prop. for *plowing*), i.e. the *frame* of a loom:—beam {4x}. See: TWOT—1361a; BDB—644d.

4501. מְנוֹרָה {40x} **meᵉnôwrâh**, *men-o-raw';* or

מְנֹרָה **meᵉnôrâh**, *men-o-raw';* fem. of 4500 (in the orig. sense of 5216); a *chandelier:*—candlestick {40x}. See: TWOT—1333c; BDB—586b, 633a.

4502. מִנְּזָר {1x} **minnᵉzâr**, *min-ez-awr';* from 5144; a *prince:*—crowned {1x}. See: TWOT—1340d; BDB—634d.

4503. מִנְחָה {211x} **minchâh**, *min-khaw';* from an unused root mean. to *apportion,* i.e. *bestow;* a *donation;* euphem. *tribute;* spec. a sacrificial *offering* (usually bloodless and voluntary):—offering {164x}, present {28x}, gift {7x}, oblation {6x}, sacrifice {5x}, meat {1x}.

Minchah means meat [cereal] offering; offering; tribute; present; gift; sacrifice; oblation. **(1)** The *minchah* must be regarded as a token of love, gratitude, and thanksgiving to God, who is Himself the Giver of all good gifts. **(1a)** It was an acknowledgement on the part of man that "the earth is the LORD's and the fullness thereof." **(1b)** Part of it was called the *memorial* and was burned with fire, and the rest was eaten by the priest and his family, not by the offerer. **(1c)** The KJV translates the word as meat offering, which is solid food in contrast to drink [liquids] and flesh [of animals]. The word "meat" in this KJV use really means "solid food/grain offering." **(2)** *Minchah* occurs for the first time in Gen 4:3: ". . . Cain brought of the fruit of the ground an offering unto the LORD." This use reflects the most common connotation of *minchah* as a "vegetable or cereal offering." **(3)** *Minchah* is used many times to designate a "gift" or "present" which is given by one person to another. **(3a)** For example, when Jacob was on his way back home after twenty years, his long-standing guilt and fear of Esau prompted him to send a rather large "present" (bribe) of goats, camels, and other animals (Gen 32:13–15).

(3b) Similarly, Jacob directed his sons to "carry down the man a present" (Gen 43:11) to appease the Egyptian ruler that later turned out to be his lost son Joseph. **(3c)** Those who came to hear Solomon's great wisdom all brought to him an appropriate "present" (1 Kin 10:25), doing so on a yearly basis. **(4)** Frequently *minchah* is used in the sense of "tribute" paid to a king or overlord. **(4a)** The delivering of the "tribute" of the people of Israel to the king of Moab by their judge-deliverer became the occasion for the deliverance of Israel from Moabite control as Ehud assassinated Eglon by a rather sly maneuver (Judg 3:15–23). **(4b)** Years later when David conquered the Moabites, they "became servants to David and brought gifts [tribute]" (2 Sa 8:2). **(4c)** Hosea proclaimed to Israel that its pagan bull-god would "be carried unto Assyria for a present [tribute]" (Hos 10:6). **(4d)** Other passages where *minchah* has the meaning of "tribute" are: Ps 72:10; 1 Kin 4:21; 2 Kin 17:3–4.

(5) *Minchah* is often used to refer to any "offering" or "gift" made to God, whether it was a "vegetable offering" or a "blood sacrifice." **(5a)** The story of Cain and Abel vividly illustrates this general usage: ". . . Cain brought of the fruit of the ground an offering unto the LORD. And Abel, he also brought of the firstlings of his flock and of the fat thereof. And the LORD had respect unto Abel and to his offering: But unto Cain and to his offering he had not respect" (Gen 4:3–5). **(5b)** The animal sacrifices which were misappropriated by the wicked sons of Eli were simply designated as "the offering of the LORD" (1 Sa 2:17). In each case "offering" is the translation of *minchah.* **(6)** A common use of *minchah,* especially in later Old Testament texts, is to designate "meat [grain/cereal] offerings." **(6a)** Sometimes it referred to the "meat [cereal] offering" of first fruits, "green ears of corn, dried by the fire. . . ." (Lev 2:14). **(6b)** Such offerings included oil and frankincense which were burned with the grain.

(6c) Similarly, the "meat [grain] offering" could be in the form of finely ground flour upon which oil and frankincense had been poured also. Sometimes the oil was mixed with the "meat [cereal] offering" (Lev 14:10, 21; 23:13; Num 7:13), again in the form of fine flour. The priest would take a handful of this fine flour, burn it as a memorial portion, and the remainder would belong to the priest (Lev 2:9–10). **(6d)** The "meat [cereal] offering" frequently was in the form of fine flour which was mixed with oil and then formed into cakes and baked, either in a pan or on a griddle (Lev 2:4–5). **(6e)** Other descriptions of this type of baked "meat [cereal] offering" are found in Num 6:15 and Lev 7:9. **(7e)** These baked "meat [cereal] offerings" were always to be made without leaven, but were to be mixed with salt and oil (Lev 2:11, 13). **(8)** The *minchah* was prescribed as a "meat offering" of flour kneaded with oil to be given along with the whole burnt offering. **(8a)** A libation of wine was to be given as well.

(9) This particular rule applied especially to the Feast of Weeks or Pentecost (Lev 23:18), to the daily "continual offering" (Ex 29:38–42), and to all the whole burnt offerings or general sacrifices (Num 15:1–16). **(9a)** The "meat [cereal] offering" was to be burned, **(9b)** while the wine seems to have been poured out at the foot of the altar like blood of the sacrificial animal. **(10)** The regular daily morning and evening sacrifices included the *minchah* and were specifically referred to **(10a)** as "the meat [cereal] offering of the morning" (Ex 29:41; cf. Num 28:8) and **(10b)** as "the evening meat [cereal] offering" (2 Kin 16:15; cf. Ezra 9:4–5 and Ps 141:2, "evening sacrifice"). **(11)** *Minchah* provides an interesting symbolism for the prophet when he refers to the restoration of the Jews: **(11a)** "And they shall bring all your brethren for an offering unto the LORD out of all nations upon horses, and in chariots . . . to my holy mountain Jerusalem, saith the LORD, as the children of Israel bring an offering in a clean vessel into the house of the LORD" (Is 66:20).

(11b) In his vision of the universal worship of God, even in Gentile lands, Malachi saw the *minchah* given as "a pure offering" to God by believers everywhere (Mal 1:11). Syn.: *ʾAsham* (817) means guilt offering, that which clears guilt away. *ʾIshsheh* (801) means those offerings made by fire. *ʾOlah* (5930) means whole burnt offering with nothing being shared or eaten. *Qorban* (7133) generally means offering, that which brings near to God. *Terumah* (8641) means that offering which was symbolically heaved/waved before God and then eaten by the priest and the one offering. See: TWOT—1214a; BDB—585a, 1101c.

4504. מִנְחָה {2x} **minchâh** (Aram.), *min-khaw';* corresp. to 4503; a sacrificial *offering:*—oblation {1x}, meat offering {1x}. See: TWOT—2836; BDB—1101c.

מְנֻחָה **mᵉnûchâh**. See 4496.

מְנֻחוֹת **Mᵉnûchôwth**. See 2679.

4505. מְנַחֵם {8x} **Mᵉnachêm**, *men-akh-ame';* from 5162; *comforter; Menachem,* an Isr.:—Menahem {8x}. See: BDB—637c.

4506. מָנַחַת {3x} **Mânachath**, *maw-nakh'-ath;* from 5117; *rest; Manachath,* the name of an Edomite and of a place in Moab:—Manahath {3x}. See: BDB—630a.

מְנַחְתִּי **Mᵉnachtîy**. See 2680.

4507. מְנִי {1x} **Mᵉnîy**, *men-ee';* from 4487; the *Apportioner,* i.e. Fate (as an idol):—number {1x}. See: BDB—584c.

מִנִּי **minnîy**. See 4480, 4482.

4508. מִנִּי {1x} **Minnîy**, *min-nee';* of for. der.; *Minni,* an Armenian province:—Minni {1x}. See: BDB—585d.

מְנָיוֹת **mᵉnâyôwth**. See 4521.

4509. מִנְיָמִין {3x} **Minyâmîyn**, *min-yaw-meen';* from 4480 and 3225; *from* (the) *right hand; Minjamin,* the name of two Isr.:—Miniamin {3x}. See: BDB—568a, 585d. comp. 4326.

4510. מִנְיָן {1x} **minyân** (Aram.), *min-yawn';* from 4483; *enumeration:*—number {1x}. See: TWOT—2835b; BDB—1101b, 1101c.

4511. מִנִּית {2x} **Minnîyth**, *min-neeth';* from the same as 4482; *enumeration; Minnith,* a place E. of the Jordan:—Minnith {2x}. See: TWOT—2835b; BDB—585d.

4512. מִנְלֶה {1x} **minleh**, *min-leh';* from 5239; *completion,* i.e. (in produce) *wealth:*—perfection {1x}. See: TWOT—1370a; BDB—585d, 649b.

מְנֻסָּה **mᵉnûçâh**. See 4499.

4513. מָנַע {29x} **mânaʿ**, *maw-nah';* a prim. root; to *debar* (neg. or pos.) from benefit or injury:—withhold {18x}, keep back {4x}, refrain {2x}, denied {1x}, deny {1x}, hinder {1x}, keep {1x}, restrained {1x}. See: TWOT—1216; BDB—586a.

4514. מַנְעוּל {6x} **manʿûwl**, *man-ool';* or

מַנְעֻל **manʿûl**, *man-ool';* from 5274; a *bolt:*—lock {6x}. See: TWOT—1383c; BDB—586b, 653b.

4515. מִנְעָל {1x} **minʿâl**, *min-awl';* from 5274; a *bolt:*—shoe {1x}. See: TWOT—1383d; BDB—586b, 653b.

4516. מַנְעַם {1x} **manʿam**, *man-am';* from 5276; a *delicacy:*—dainty {1x}. See: TWOT—1384d; BDB—586b, 654b.

4517. מְנַעְנַע {1x} **mᵉnaʿnaʿ**, *men-ah-ah';* from 5128; a *sistrum* (so called from its *rattling* sound):—cornet {1x}. See: TWOT—1328a; BDB—586b, 631c.

4518. מְנַקִּית {4x} **mᵉnaqqîyth**, *men-ak-keeth';* from 5352; a *sacrificial basin* (for holding blood):—bowl {3x}, cup {1x}. See: TWOT—1412d; BDB—586b, 667d.

מְנֹרָה **mᵉnôrâh**. See 4501.

4519. מְנַשֶּׁה {146x} **Mᵉnashsheh**, *men-ash-sheh';* from 5382; *causing to forget; Menashsheh,* a grandson of Jacob, also the tribe descended from him, and its territory:—Manasseh {146x}. See: TWOT—1217; BDB—586b.

4520. מְנַשִּׁי {4x} **Mᵉnashshîy**, *men-ash-shee';* from 4519; a *Menashshite* or desc. of Menashsheh:—of Manasseh {2x}, Manassites {2x}. See: BDB—586d.

4521. מְנָת {7x} **mᵉnâth**, *men-awth';* from 4487; an *allotment* (by courtesy, law or providence):—portion {7x}. See: TWOT—1213d; BDB—584a, 584c, 585d, 586d.

4522. מַס {23x} **maç**, *mas;* or

מִס **miç**, *mees;* from 4549; prop. a *burden* (as causing to *faint*), i.e. a *tax* in the form of forced *labor:*—tribute {12x}, tributary {5x}, levy {4x}, discomfited {1x}, taskmasters {1x}. See: TWOT—1218; BDB—586d.

4523. מָס {1x} **mâç**, *mawce;* from 4549; *fainting,* i.e. (fig.) *disconsolate:*—is afflicted {1x}. See: TWOT—1223a; BDB—587a, 588a.

4524. מֵסַב {5x} **mêçab**, *may-sab';* plur. masc.

מְסִבִּים **mᵉçibbîym**, *mes-ib-beem';* or fem.

מְסִבּוֹת **mᵉçibbôwth**, *mes-ib-bohth';* from 5437; a *divan* (as *enclosing* the room); abstr. (adv.) *around:*—round about {3x}, compass me about {1x}, at his table {1x}.

Meçab occurs 5 times, and it refers to "that which surrounds or is round." **(1)** *Mecab* refers to a "round table" (Song 1:12) and **(2)** to "places round about" Jerusalem: "And he put down the idolatrous priests, whom the kings of Judah had ordained to burn incense in the high places in the cities of Judah, and in the places round about Jerusalem; them also that burned incense unto Baal, to the sun, and to the moon, and to the planets, and to all the host of heaven" (2 Kin 23:5). See: TWOT—1456c; BDB—587a, 686d, 687b.

מֻסַבָּה **mûçabbâh**. See 4142.

4525. מַסְגֵּר {7x} **maçgêr**, *mas-gare';* from 5462; a *fastener,* i.e. (of a person) a *smith,* (of a thing) a *prison:*—prison {3x}, smith {4x}. See: TWOT—1462c; BDB—587a, 689d.

4526. מִסְגֶּרֶת {17x} **miçgereth**, *mis-gheh'-reth;* from 5462; something *enclosing,* i.e. a *margin* (of a region, of a panel); concr. a *stronghold:*—border {14x}, close place {2x}, hole {1x}. See: TWOT—1462d; BDB—587a, 689d.

4527. מַסַּד {1x} **maççad**, *mas-sad';* from 3245; a *foundation:*—foundation {1x}. See: TWOT—875g; BDB—414c, 587b.

מוֹסָדָה **môçâdâh**. See 4146.

4528. מִסְדְּרוֹן {1x} **miçdᵉrôwn**, *mis-der-ohn';* from the same as 5468; a *colonnade* or *internal portico* (from its *rows* of pillars):—porch {1x}. See: TWOT—1467c; BDB—587b, 690c.

4529. מָסָה {4x} **mâçâh**, *maw-saw';* a prim. root; to *dissolve:*—make to consume away {1x}, (make to) melt {2x}, water {1x}. See: TWOT—1219; BDB—587b.

4530. מִסָּה {1x} **miççâh**, *mis-saw';* from 4549 (in the sense of *flowing*); *abundance,* i.e. (adv.) *liberally:*—tribute {1x}. See: TWOT—1225; BDB—587b, 588b.

4531. מַסָּה {5x} **maççâh**, *mas-saw';* from 5254; a *testing,* of men (judicial) or of God (querulous):—temptation {4x}, trial {1x}. See: TWOT—1223b; BDB—587b, 588a, 650b.

4532. מַסָּה {4x} **Maççâh**, *mas-saw';* the same as 4531; *Massah,* a place in the desert:—Massah {4x}. See: BDB—587b, 650c.

4533. מַסְוֶה {3x} **maçveh**, *mas-veh';* appar. from an unused root mean. to *cover;* a *veil:*—vail {3x}. See: TWOT—1472b; BDB—587b, 691d.

4534. מְסוּכָה {1x} **mᵉçûwkah**, *mes-oo-kaw';* for 4881; a *hedge:*—thorn hedge {1x}. See: TWOT—1475a; BDB—587b, 692b.

4535. מַסָּח {1x} **maççâch**, *mas-sawkh';* from 5255 in the sense of *staving* off; a *cordon,* (adv.) or (as a) military *barrier:*—broken down {1x}. See: TWOT—1374a; BDB—587b, 650c.

4536. מִסְחָר {1x} **miçchâr**, *mis-khawr';* from 5503; *trade:*—traffic {1x}. See: TWOT—1486d; BDB—587b, 695c.

4537. מָסַךְ {5x} **mâçak**, *maw-sak';* a prim. root; to *mix,* espec. wine (with spices):—mingle {5x}. See: TWOT—1220; BDB—587c.

4538. מֶסֶךְ {1x} **meçek**, *meh'-sek;* from 4537; a *mixture,* i.e. of wine with spices:—mixture {1x}. See: TWOT—1220a; BDB—587c.

4539. מָסָךְ {25x} **mâçâk**, *maw-sawk';* from 5526; a *cover,* i.e. *veil:*—covering {7x}, curtain {1x}, hanging {17x}. See: TWOT—1492a; BDB—587c, 697a.

4540. מְסֻכָּה {1x} **mᵉçukkâh**, *mes-ook-kaw';* from 5526; a *covering,* i.e. garniture:—covering {1x}. See: TWOT—1492a; BDB—587c, 697b.

4541. מַסֵּכָה {28x} **maççêkâh**, *mas-say-kaw';* from 5258; prop. a *pouring* over, i.e. *fusion* of metal (espec. a *cast* image); by impl. a *libation,* i.e. league; concr. a *coverlet* (as if *poured* out):—covering {2x}, molten {7x}, image {18x}, vail {1x}. See: TWOT—1375c, 1376a; BDB—587c, 651a, 651b.

4542. מִסְכֵּן {4x} **miçkên**, *mis-kane';* from 5531; *indigent:*—poor {3x}, poor man {1x}. See: TWOT—1221; BDB—587c.

4543. מִסְכְּנָה {7x} **miçkᵉnâh**, *mis-ken-aw';* by transp. from 3664; a *magazine:*—

store {5x}, storehouse {1x}, treasure {1x}. See: TWOT—1494a; BDB—587b, 698b.

4544. מִסְכֵּנֻת {1x} **miçkênuth**, *mis-kay-nooth';* from 4542; *indigence:*—scarceness {1x}. See: TWOT—1222; BDB—587d, 698c.

4545. מַסֶּכֶת {2x} **maççeketh**, *mas-seh'-keth;* from 5259 in the sense of *spreading* out; something *expanded,* i.e. the *warp* in a loom (as *stretched* out to receive the woof):—web {2x}. See: TWOT—1376b; BDB—587c, 651c.

4546. מְסִלָּה {27x} **mᵉçillâh**, *mes-il-law';* from 5549; a *thoroughfare* (as *turnpiked*), lit. or fig.; spec. a *viaduct,* a *staircase:*—highway {19x}, causeway {2x}, path {2x}, way {2x}, courses {1x}, terraces {1x}. See: TWOT—1506d; BDB—587d, 700c.

4547. מַסְלוּל {1x} **maçlûwl**, *mas-lool';* from 5549; a *thoroughfare* (as turnpiked):—highway {1x}. See: TWOT—1506d; BDB—587d, 700c.

4548. מַסְמֵר {4x} **maçmêr**, *mas-mare';* or

מִסְמֵר **miçmêr**, *mis-mare';* also (fem.)

מַסְמְרָה **maçmᵉrâh**, *mas-mer-aw';* or

מִסְמְרָה **miçmᵉrâh**, *mis-mer-aw';* or even

מַשְׂמְרָה **masmᵉrâh** (Eccl 12:11), *mas-mer-aw';* from 5568; a *peg* (as *bristling* from the surface):—nail {4x}. See: TWOT—1518b; BDB—587d, 601d, 702c, 971b.

4549. מָסַס {21x} **mâçaç**, *maw-sas';* a prim. root; to *liquefy;* fig. to *waste* (with disease), to *faint* (with fatigue, fear or grief):—melt {13x}, faint {2x}, melt away {1x}, discouraged {1x}, loosed {1x}, molten {1x}, refuse {1x}, utterly {1x}. See: TWOT—1223; BDB—549d, 587d.

4550. מַסַּע {12x} **maççaᶜ**, *mas-sah';* from 5265; a *departure* (from *striking* the tents), i.e. march (not necessarily a single day's travel); by impl. a *station* (or point of *departure*):—journey {10x}, journeying {2x}. See: TWOT—1380a; BDB—588a, 652c.

4551. מַסָּע {2x} **maççâᶜ**, *mas-saw';* from 5265 in the sense of *projecting;* a *missile* (spear or arrow); also a *quarry* (whence stones are, as it were, *ejected*):—before it was brought {1x}, dart {1x}. See: TWOT—1380b, 1381a; BDB—588a, 652d.

4552. מִסְעָד {1x} **miçᶜâd**, *mis-awd'* from 5582; a *balustrade* (for stairs):—pillar {1x}. See: TWOT—1525a; BDB—588a, 703c.

4553. מִסְפֵּד {16x} **miçpêd**, *mis-pade';* from 5594; a *lamentation:*—lamentation {3x}, one mourneth {1x}, mourning {6x}, wailing {6x}. See: TWOT—1530a; BDB—588a, 704d.

4554. מִסְפּוֹא {5x} **miçpôwʾ**, *mis-po';* from an unused root mean. to *collect; fodder:*—provender {5x}. See: TWOT—1529a; BDB—588a, 704d.

4555. מִסְפָּחָה {2x} **miçpâchâh**, *mis-paw-khaw';* from 5596; a *veil* (as *spread* out):—kerchief {2x}. See: TWOT—1534c; BDB—588a, 705d.

4556. מִסְפַּחַת {3x} **miçpachath**, *mis-pakh'-ath;* from 5596; *scurf* (as *spreading* over the surface):—scab {3x}. See: TWOT—1534b; BDB—588a, 705c.

4557. מִסְפָּר {134x} **miçpâr**, *mis-pawr';* from 5608; a *number,* def. (arithmetical) or indef. (large, *innumerable;* small, a *few*); also (abstr.) *narration:*—number {110x}, few {6x}, all {3x}, innumerable {3x}, sum {2x}, time {2x}, account {1x}, abundance + 369 {1x}, infinite {1x}, innumerable + 369 {1x}, numbered {1x}, tale {1x}, telling {1x}, finite {1x}.

Miçpar (4557) means "measure; (a certain) number; account." **(1)** *Miçpar* can mean "measure" (quantity) as in Gen 41:49: "And Joseph gathered corn as the sand of the sea, very much, until he left numbering; for *it was* without number." **(2)** In Gen 34:30, the first biblical occurrence, the word refers to "a certain number" in the sense of the sum total of individuals that are counted: ". . . and I being few in number, they shall gather themselves together against me, and slay me. . . ." **(3)** The word means "account" (what is set forth in a detailed report) in Judg 7:15: "And it was *so,* when Gideon heard the telling of the dream, and the interpretation thereof, that he worshipped, and returned into the host of Israel, and said, Arise; for the LORD hath delivered into your hand the host of Midian." See: TWOT—1540e; BDB—588a, 708d.

4558. מִסְפָּר {1x} **Miçpâr**, *mis-pawr';* the same as 4457; *number; Mispar,* an Isr.:—Mizpar {1x}. See: BDB—588a, 709a. comp. 4559.

מֹסְרוֹת **Môçᵉrowth**. See 4149.

4559. מִסְפֶּרֶת {1x} **Miçpereth**, *mis-peh'-reth;* fem. of 4457; *enumeration; Mispereth,* an Isr.:—Mispereth {1x}. See: BDB—588a, 709a. comp. 4458.

4560. מָסַר {2x} **mâçar**, *maw-sar';* a prim. root; to *sunder,* i.e. (tran.) *set apart,* or (reflex.) *apostatize:*—commit {1x}, deliver {1x}. See: TWOT—1224; BDB—588a.

4561. מֹסָר {1x} **môçâr**, *mo-sawr';* from 3256; *admonition:*—instruction {1x}. See: TWOT—877b; BDB—416b, 416d, 558a, 588b.

4562. מָסֹרֶת {1x} **mâçôreth**, *maw-so'-reth;* from 631; a *band:*—bond {1x}. See: TWOT—141e; BDB—64b, 588b.

4563. מִסְתּוֹר {1x} **miçtôwr**, *mis-tore';* from 5641; a *refuge:*—covert {1x}. See: TWOT—1551c; BDB—588b, 712c.

4564. מַסְתֵּר {1x} **maçtêr**, *mas-tare';* from 5641; prop. a *hider,* i.e. (abstr.) a hiding, i.e. *aversion:*—hid {1x}. See: TWOT—1551e; BDB—588b, 712c.

4565. מִסְתָּר {10x} **miçtâr**, *mis-tawr';* from 5641; prop. a *concealer,* i.e. a *covert:*—secret {1x}, secretly {2x}, places {7x}. See: TWOT—1551d; BDB—588b, 712c.

מְעָא **mᵉᶜâʾ**. See 4577.

4566. מַעְבָּד {1x} **maᶜbâd**, *mah-bawd';* from 5647; an *act:*—work {1x}. See: TWOT—1553f; BDB—588b, 716a, 1105a.

4567. מַעְבָד {1x} **maᶜbâd** (Aram.), *mah-bawd';* corresp. to 4566; an *act:*—work {1x}. See: TWOT—2896c; BDB—1101c, 1105a.

4568. מַעֲבֶה {1x} **maᶜăbeh**, *mah-ab-eh';* from 5666; prop. *compact* (part of soil), i.e. *loam:*—clay {1x}. See: TWOT—1554b; BDB—588b, 716b.

4569. מַעֲבָר {11x} **maᶜăbâr**, *mah-ab-awr';* or fem.

מַעֲבָרָה **maᶜăbârâh**, *mah-ab-aw-raw';* from 5674; a *crossing*-place (of a river, a *ford;* of a mountain, a *pass*); abstr. a *transit,* i.e. (fig.) *overwhelming:*—ford {4x}, place where . . . pass {1x}, passage {6x}.

Maᶜabar, **the masculine form,** appears 3 times to mean: **(1)** "sweep" (of a staff): "And *in* every place where the grounded staff shall pass [*maᶜabar*], which the LORD shall lay upon him, *it* shall be with tabrets and harps: and in battles of shaking will he fight with it" (Is 30:32); **(2)** "ford" (Gen 32:22); and **(3)** "ravine" or "passage" (1 Sa 13:23). **(4)** *Maᶜbarah,* **the feminine form,** which appears 8 times, means **(4a)** "ford": "And the men pursued after them the way to Jordan unto the fords: and as soon as they which pursued after them were gone out, they shut the gate" (Josh 2:7); and **(4b)** "ravine" or "passage": "And between the passages [*maᶜbarah*], by which Jonathan sought to go over unto the Philistines' garrison, *there was* a sharp rock on the one side, and a sharp rock on the other side: and the name of the one *was* Bozez, and the name of the other Seneh" (1 Sa 14: 4). Syn.: 5674, 5676, 5680. See: TWOT—1556h; BDB—588c, 721b.

4570. מַעְגָּל {16x} **maᶜgâl**, *mah-gawl';* or fem.

מַעְגָּלָה **maᶜgâlâh**, *mah-gaw-law';* from the same as 5696; a *track* (lit. or fig.); also a *rampart* (as *circular*):—path {9x}, trench {3x}, goings {2x}, ways {1x}, wayside + 3027 {1x}. See: TWOT—1560f; BDB—588c, 722d.

4571. מָעַד {6x} **mâᶜad**, *maw-ad';* a prim. root; to *waver:*—make to shake {1x}, slide {2x}, slip {3x}. See: TWOT—1226; BDB—588c.

מֹעֵד **môᶜêd**. See 4150.

4572. מַעֲדַי {1x} **Maᶜăday**, *mah-ad-ah'-ee;* from 5710; *ornamental; Maadai,* an Isr.:—Maadai {1x}. See: BDB—588c.

4573. מַעַדְיָה {1x} **Maᶜadyâh**, *mah-ad-yaw';* from 5710 and 3050; *ornament of Jah; Maadjah,* an Isr.:—Maadiah {1x}. See: BDB—588b, 588c. comp. 4153.

4574. מַעֲדָן {4x} **maᶜădân**, *mah-ad-awn';* or (fem.)

מַעֲדַנָּה **maᶜădannâh**, *mah-ad-an-naw';* from 5727; a *delicacy* or (abstr.) *pleasure* (adv. *cheerfully*):—dainty {1x}, delicately {2x}, delight {1x}. See: TWOT—1567d; BDB—588d, 726d.

4575. מַעֲדַנָּה {1x} **maᶜădannâh**, *mah-ad-an-naw';* by tran. from 6029; a *bond,* i.e. *group:*—influence {1x}. See: TWOT—1649a; BDB—588d, 726d, 772c.

4576. מַעְדֵּר {1x} **maᶜdêr**, *mah-dare';* from 5737; a (weeding) *hoe:*—mattock {1x}. See: TWOT—1571a; BDB—588d, 727c.

4577. מְעָה {1x} **mᵉᶜâh** (Aram.), *meh-aw';* or

מְעָא **mᵉᶜâʾ** (Aram.), *meh-aw';* corresp. to 4578; only in plur. the *bowels:*—belly {1x}. See: TWOT—2837; BDB—1101c.

4578. מֵעֶה {32x} **mêᶜêh**, *may-eh';* from an unused root prob. mean. to *be soft;* used only in plur. the *intestines,* or (collect.) the *abdomen,* fig. *sympathy;* by impl. a *vest;* by extens. the *stomach,* the *uterus* (or of men, the seat of generation), the *heart* (fig.):—belly {3x}, bowels {27x}, × heart {1x}, womb {1x}. Syn.: 3820, 5315, 7023, 7130. See: TWOT—1227a; BDB—588d, 590c, 1101c.

4579. מֵעָה {1x} **mêᶜâh**, *may-aw';* fem. of 4578; the *belly,* i.e. (fig.) interior:—gravel {1x}. See: TWOT—1227b; BDB—589a.

4580. מָעוֹג {2x} **mâᶜôwg**, *maw-ogue';* from 5746; a *cake* of bread (with 3934 a *table-buffoon,* i.e. *parasite*):—cake {1x}, feast {1x}. See: TWOT—1575b; BDB—589b, 728b.

4581. מָעוֹז {37x} **mâʿôwz**, *maw-oze'* (also
מָעוּז **mâʿûwz**, *maw-ooz'*); or
מָעֹז **mâʿôz**, *maw-oze'* (also
מָעֻז **mâʿûz**, *maw-ooz'*); from 5810; a *fortified* place; fig. a *defence:*—strength {24x}, strong {4x}, fortress {3x}, hold {2x}, forces {1x}, fort {1x}, rock {1x}, strengthen {1x}. See: TWOT—1578a; BDB—589b, 731d.

4582. מָעוֹךְ {1x} **Mâʿôwk**, *maw-oke';* from 4600; *oppressed; Maok,* a Philistine:—Maoch {1x}. See: BDB—590d.

4583. מָעוֹן {19x} **mâʿôwn**, *maw-ohn';* or
מָעִין **mâʿîyn** (1 Chr 4:41), *maw-een';* from the same as 5772; an *abode,* of God (the Tabernacle or the Temple), men (their home) or animals (their lair); hence, a *retreat* (asylum):—habitation {10x}, dwelling {4x}, den {2x}, dwelling place {2x}, dwellingplace {1x}. See: TWOT—1581a; BDB—589b, 732d.

4584. מָעוֹן {8x} **Mâʿôwn**, *maw-ohn';* the same as 4583; a *residence; Maon,* the name of an Isr. and of a place in Pal.:—Maon {5x}, Maonites {3x}. See: BDB—589b, 733a. comp. 1010, 4586.

4585. מְעוֹנָה {9x} **meʿôwnâh**, *meh-o-naw';* or
מְעֹנָה **meʿônâh**, *meh-o-naw';* fem. of 4583, and mean. the same:—den {5x}, habitation {1x}, (dwelling) place {1x}, refuge {1x}. See: TWOT—1581b; BDB—589b, 591d, 733a.

4586. מְעוּנַי {3x} **Meʿûwnây**, *meh-oo-naw'-ee;* or
מְעִינִי **Meʿîyniy**, *meh-ee-nee';* prob. patrial from 4584; a *Meünite,* or inhab. of Maon (only in plur.):—Mehunim {1x}, Mehunims {1x}, Meunim {1x}. See: BDB—589b, 590c.

4587. מְעוֹנֹתַי {1x} **Meʿôwnôthay**, *meh-o-no-thah'-ee;* plur. of 4585; *habitative; Meonothai,* an Isr.:—Meonothai {1x}. See: BDB—589b, 733b.

4588. מָעוּף {1x} **mâʿûwph**, *maw-oof';* from 5774 in the sense of *covering* with shade [comp. 4155]; *darkness:*—dimness {1x}. See: TWOT—1583b; BDB—589b, 734a.

4589. מָעוֹר {1x} **mâʿôwr**, *maw-ore';* from 5783; *nakedness,* i.e. (in plur.) the *pudenda:*—nakedness {1x}. See: TWOT—1588a; BDB—589b, 735d.

מָעֹז **mâʿôz**. See 4581.

מָעֻז **mâʿûz**. See 4581.

4590. מַעַזְיָה {1x} **Maʿazyâh**, *mah-az-yaw';* or
מַעַזְיָהוּ **Maʿazyâhûw**, *mah-az-yaw'-hoo;* prob. from 5756 (in the sense of *protection*) and 3050; *rescue of Jah; Maazjah,* the name of two Isr.:—Maaziah {1x}. See: BDB—589b.

4591. מָעַט {22x} **mâʿaṭ**, *maw-at';* a prim. root; prop. to *pare* off, i.e. *lessen;* intr. to *be* (or caus. to *make*) *small* or *few* (or fig. *ineffective*):—diminish {5x}, few {4x}, less {4x}, little {3x}, fewness {1x}, least {1x}, minished {1x}, decrease {1x}, nothing {1x}, few in number {1x}. See: TWOT—1228; BDB—589b.

4592. מְעַט {102x} **meʿaṭ**, *meh-at';* or
מְעָט **meʿâṭ**, *meh-awt';* from 4591; a *little* or *few* (often adv. or compar.):—little {49x}, few {23x}, while {6x}, almost {5x}, small thing {4x}, small {3x}, some {2x}, matter {2x}, soon {2x}, fewer {1x}, fewest {1x}, lightly {1x}, very {1x}, little way {1x}, worth {1x}. See: TWOT—1228a; BDB—589d.

4593. מָעֹט {1x} **mâʿôṭ**, *maw-ote';* pass. adj. of 4591; *thinned* (as to the edge), i.e. *sharp:*—wrapped up {1x}. See: TWOT—1602; BDB—599a.

4594. מַעֲטֶה {1x} **maʿăṭeh**, *mah-at-eh';* from 5844; a *vestment:*—garment {1x}. See: TWOT—1601a; BDB—590c, 742a.

4595. מַעֲטָפָה {1x} **maʿăṭâphâh**, *mah-at-aw-faw',* from 5848; a *cloak:*—mantle {1x}. See: TWOT—1606a; BDB—590c, 742c.

4596. מְעִי {1x} **meʿîy**, *meh-ee';* from 5753; a *pile* of rubbish (as *contorted*), i.e. a *ruin* (comp. 5856):—heap {1x}. See: TWOT—1577e; BDB—590c, 730d.

4597. מָעַי {1x} **Mâʿay**, *maw-ah'-ee;* prob. from 4578; *sympathetic; Maai,* an Isr.:—Maai {1x}. See: BDB—590c.

4598. מְעִיל {28x} **meʿîyl**, *meh-eel';* from 4603 in the sense of *covering;* a *robe* (i.e. upper and outer *garment*):—cloke {1x}, coat {1x}, mantle {7x}, robe {19x}. See: TWOT—1230b; BDB—591c.

מֵעִים **mêʿîym**. See 4578.

מְעִין **meʿîyn** (Aram.). See 4577.

4599. מַעְיָן {23x} **maʿyân**, *mah-yawn';* or
מַעְיְנוֹ **maʿyenôw** (Ps 114:8) *mah-yen-o';* or (fem.)
מַעְיָנָה **maʿyânâh**, *mah-yaw-naw';* from 5869 (as a denom. in the sense of a *spring*); a *fountain* (also collect.), fig. a *source* (of satisfaction):—fountain {16x}, spring {2x}, well {5x}.

Maʿyan (4599) means "spring." **(1)** In Lev 11:36, *maʿyan* means "spring": "Nevertheless a fountain or pit, wherein there is plenty of water, shall be clean: but that which toucheth their carcase shall be unclean." **(2)** Another example is found in Gen 7:11: "In the six hundredth year of Noah's life, in the second month, . . . the same day were all the fountains of the great deep broken up, and the windows of heaven were opened." See: TWOT—1613a; BDB—590c, 745d.

מְעִינִי **Meʿîyniy**. See 4586.

4600. מָעַךְ {3x} **mâʿak**, *maw-ak';* a prim. root; to *press,* i.e. to *pierce, emasculate, handle:*—bruised {1x}, stuck {1x}, be pressed {1x}. See: TWOT—1229; BDB—590c.

4601. מַעֲכָה {23x} **Maʿăkâh**, *mah-ak-aw';* or
מַעֲכָת **Maʿăkâth** (Josh 13:13), *mah-ak-awth';* from 4600; *depression; Maakah* (or *Maakath*), the name of a place in Syria, also of a Mesopotamian, of three Isr., and of four Israelitesses and one Syrian woman:—Maachah {18x}, Maacah {3x}, Maachathites {1x}, Syriamaachah + 758 {1x}. See: BDB—590d, 591a. See also 1038.

4602. מַעֲכָתִי {8x} **Maʿăkâthîy**, *mah-ak-aw-thee';* patrial from 4601; a *Maakathite,* or inhab. of Maakah:—Maachathite {7x}, Maachathi. See: BDB—591a.

4603. מָעַל {35x} **mâʿal**, *maw-al';* a prim. root; prop. to *cover* up; used only fig. to *act covertly,* i.e. *treacherously:*—trespass {13x}, commit {11x}, transgress {10x}, done {1x}.

Maʿal means "to trespass, act unfaithfully." **(1)** Most of the time the noun *maʿal* will be combined with a verb into one phrase in which the verb takes the meaning of "to act" or "to commit"—e.g., Josh 7:1: "But the children of Israel committed [*maʿal*] a trespass [*maʿal*] in the accursed thing . . ." **(2)** The first occurrence of the verb (together with the noun) is found in Lev 5:15: "If a soul commit a trespass, and sin through ignorance. . . ." **(2a)** The sense of the verb is similar to the verb "to sin." **(2b)** In fact, in the next chapter the verb for "to sin" and *maʿal* are used together: "If a soul sin, and commit a trespass against the LORD, and lie unto his neighbor . . ." (Lev 6:2). **(2c)** The combining of these two usages in Leviticus is significant. **(2c1)** First, it shows that the verb may be a synonym for "to sin." *Maʿal* has basically this meaning in Lev 5:15, since the sin is here out of ignorance instead of a deliberate act of treachery. **(2c2)** Second, the meaning of *maʿal* is further expressed by a verb indicating the intent of being unfaithful to one's neighbor for personal profit ("commit a trespass against the LORD, and lie unto his neighbor . . .").

(3) The offense is against God, even when one acts unfaithfully against one's neighbor. **(3a)** In 2 Chr 29:6 we read: "For our fathers have trespassed, and done that which was evil in the eyes of the LORD our God, and have forsaken him . . ."; and **(3b)** Daniel prayed: ". . . Because of their trespass that they have trespassed against thee" (Dan 9:7). **(4)** When God spoke to Ezekiel: "Son of man, when the land sinneth against me by trespassing grievously, then will I stretch out mine hand upon it, and . . . cut off man and beast from it" (Eze 14:13), He communicated also His displeasure with Israel's rebellious, treacherous attitude. **(5)** The verb *maʿal* generally expresses man's unfaithfulness to God (Lev 26:40; Deut 32:51; 2 Chr 12:2; Ezra 10:2; Eze 14:13). **(6)** The word further signifies man's unfaithfulness to his fellow man; particularly it is illustrative of unfaithfulness in marriage: "If any man's wife go aside, and commit a trespass against him, And a man lie with her carnally . . ." (Num 5:12–13). See: TWOT—1230; BDB—591a.

4604. מַעַל {29x} **maʿal**, *mah'-al;* from 4603; *treachery,* i.e. sin:—trespass {17x}, transgression {6x}, trespassed {2x}, falsehood {1x}, grievously {1x}, sore {1x}, very {1x}.

Maʿal means "trespass; unfaithful, treacherous act." **(1)** In addition to the primary sense of "trespass," **(1a)** there may be an indication of the motivation through which the sin was committed. **(1b)** Most of the usages support the idea of "faithlessness, treachery." **(1c)** It is an act committed by a person who knows better but who, for selfish motives, acts in bad faith. **(1d)** The story of Achan bears out the attitude of treachery (Josh 7:1). **(1e)** Joshua challenged Israel not to follow the example of Achan: "Did not Achan the son of Zerah commit [*maʿal*] a trespass [*maʿal*] in the accursed thing, and wrath fell on all the congregation of Israel?" (Josh 22:20). **(2)** In 2 Chr 29:19 the "faithlessness" was committed against God: "Moreover all the vessels which king Ahaz in his reign did cast away in his transgression. . . ." **(3)** *Maʿal* also appears in Ezra 9:2: ". . . yea, the hand of the princes and rulers hath been chief in this trespass." See: TWOT—1230a; BDB—591b.

4605. מַעַל {138x} **maʿal**, *mah'-al;* from 5927; prop. the *upper* part, used only adv. with pref. *upward, above, overhead, from the top,* etc.:—upward {59x}, above {53x}, high {6x}, exceedingly {4x}, upon {4x}, very {2x}, forward {2x}, exceeding {2x}, over {2x}, above only {1x}, overturned + 2015 {1x}, above them {1x}, up + 935 {1x}. See: TWOT—1624k; BDB—591d, 751c.

מֵעַל **mêʿal**. See 5921.

4606. מֶעָל {1x} **mêʿal** (Aram.), *may-awl';* from 5954; (only in plur. as sing.) the *setting* (of the sun):—going down {1x}. See: TWOT—2911a; BDB—1101c, 1106d.

4607. מֹעַל {1x} **môʿal**, *mo'-al;* from 5927; a *raising* (of the hands):—lifting up {1x}. See: TWOT—1624i; BDB—591d, 751b.

4608. מַעֲלֶה {18x} **maʿăleh**, *mah-al-eh';* from 5927; an *elevation,* i.e. (concr.) *acclivity* or *platform;* abstr. (the relation or state) a *rise* or (fig.) *priority:*—up {11x}, ascent {2x}, before {1x}, chiefest {1x}, cliff {1x}, hill {1x}, stairs {1x}. See: TWOT—1624j; BDB—591d, 751b.

4609. מַעֲלָה {47x} **maʿălâh**, *mah-al-aw';* fem. of 4608; *elevation,* i.e. the act (lit. a *journey* to a higher place, fig. a *thought* arising), or (concr.) the condition (lit. a *step* or *grade*-mark, fig. a *superiority* of station); spec. a climactic *progression* (in certain Psalms):—degree {25x}, steps {11x}, stairs {5x}, dial {2x}, by {1x}, come {1x}, stories {1x}, go up {1x}.

Maʿalah means step; procession; pilgrimage. **(1)** It signifies a step or stair: "Neither shalt thou go up by steps unto mine altar, that thy nakedness be not discovered thereon" (Ex 20:26). **(2)** The word can mean procession: It is translated "degrees" in the titles of the Psalms sung by the men as they pilgrimed in procession to Jerusalem three times a year (Pss 120—134). See: TWOT—1624L, 1624m; BDB—591d, 752a.

4610. מַעֲלֵה עַקְרַבִּים {3x} **Maʿălêh ʿAqrabbîym**, *mah-al-ay' ak-rab-beem';* from 4608 and (the plur. of) 6137; *Steep of Scorpions,* a place in the Desert:—Maaleh-accrabim {2x}, the ascent (going up) of Akrabbim {1x}. See: BDB—751c, 785d.

4611. מַעֲלָל {41x} **maʿălâl**, *mah-al-awl';* from 5953; an *act* (good or bad):—doings {35x}, endeavours {1x}, inventions {2x}, works {3x}. See: TWOT—1627e; BDB—591d, 760b.

4612. מַעֲמָד {5x} **maʿămâd**, *mah-am-awd';* from 5975; (fig.) a *position:*—attendance {2x}, office {1x}, place {1x}, state {1x}.

Maʿamad, which occurs 5 times, refers **(1)** to "service or attendance upon": "And the meat of his table, and the sitting of his servants, and the attendance [*maʿamad*] of his ministers, and their apparel; his cupbearers also, and their apparel; and his ascent by which he went up into the house of the LORD; there was no more spirit in her" (2 Chr 9:4) and to **(2)** "office or function" (in someone's service): "Because their office [*maʿamad*] *was* to wait on the sons of Aaron for the service of the house of the LORD, in the courts, and in the chambers, and in the purifying of all holy things, and the work of the service of the house of God;" (1 Chr 23:28). Syn.: 4613, 5977, 5979, 5982. See: TWOT—1637d; BDB—591d, 765b.

4613. מָעֳמָד {1x} **mâʿŏmâd**, *maw-om-awd';* from 5975; lit. a *foothold:*—standing {1x}.

Maʿomad occurs once to mean "standing place" or "foothold": "I sink in deep mire, where *there is* no standing [maʿomad]: I am come into deep waters, where the floods overflow me" (Ps 69:2). Syn.: 4612, 5977, 5979, 5982. See: TWOT—1637e; BDB—591d, 765c.

4614. מַעֲמָסָה {1x} **maʿămâçâh**, *mah-am-aw-saw';* from 6006; *burdensomeness:*—burdensome {1x}. See: TWOT—1643a; BDB—591d, 770c.

4615. מַעֲמָק {5x} **maʿămâq**, *mah-am-awk';* from 6009; a *deep:*—deep {2x}, depths {3x}. See: TWOT—1644e; BDB—591d, 771b.

4616. מַעַן {10x} **maʿan**, *mah'-an;* from 6030; prop. *heed,* i.e. *purpose;* used only adv., *on account of* (as a motive or an aim), teleologically *in order that:*—{10x} = because of, to the end (intent) that, for (to, . . . 's sake), + lest, that, to. See: TWOT—1650g; BDB—541b, 591d, 775a.

4617. מַעֲנֶה {8x} **maʿăneh**, *mah-an-eh';* from 6030; a *reply* (favorable or contradictory):—answer {7x}, × himself {1x}. See: TWOT—1650f; BDB—591d, 775a, 775d.

4618. מַעֲנָה {2x} **maʿănâh**, *mah-an-aw';* from 6031, in the sense of *depression* or *tilling;* a *furrow:*—+ acre {1x}, furrows {1x}. See: TWOT—1651b; BDB—591d, 776a.

מְעֹנָה **meʿônâh**. See 4585.

4619. מַעַץ {1x} **Maʿats**, *mah'-ats; from 6095; closure; Maats,* an Isr.:—Maaz {1x}. See: BDB—591d.

4620. מַעֲצֵבָה {1x} **maʿătsêbâh**, *mah-ats-ay-baw';* from 6087; *anguish:*—sorrow {1x}. See: TWOT—1666f; BDB—591d, 781a.

4621. מַעֲצָד {2x} **maʿătsâd**, *mah-ats-awd';* from an unused root mean. to *hew;* an *axe:*—ax {1x}, tongs {1x}. See: TWOT—1668a; BDB—591d, 781b.

4622. מַעְצוֹר {1x} **maʿtsôwr**, *mah-tsore';* from 6113; obj. a *hindrance:*—restraint {1x}. See: TWOT—1675d; BDB—591d, 784a.

4623. מַעְצָר {1x} **maʿtsâr**, *mah-tsawr';* from 6113; subj. *control:*—rule {1x}. Prov 25:28 stresses self-restraint. See: TWOT—1675e; BDB—591d, 784a.

4624. מַעֲקֶה {1x} **maʿăqeh**, *mah-ak-eh';* from an unused root mean. to *repress;* a *parapet:*—battlement {1x}. See: TWOT—1679a; BDB—591d, 785b.

4625. מַעֲקָשׁ {1x} **maʿăqâsh**, *mah-ak-awsh';* from 6140; a *crook* (in a road):—crooked things {1x}. See: TWOT—1684c; BDB—591d, 786a.

4626. מַעַר {1x} **maʿar**, *mah'-ar;* from 6168; a *nude* place, i.e. (lit.) the *pudenda,* or (fig.) a vacant *space:*—nakedness {1x}, proportion {1x}. See: TWOT—1692d; BDB—591d, 789a.

4627. מַעֲרָב {9x} **maʿărâb**, *mah-ar-awb';* from 6148, in the sense of *trading; traffic;* by impl. mercantile *goods:*—market {4x}, merchandise {5x}. See: TWOT—1686c; BDB—591d.

4628. מַעֲרָב {14x} **maʿărâb**, *mah-ar-awb';* or (fem.)

מַעֲרָבָה **maʿărâbâh**, *mah-ar-aw-baw';* from 6150, in the sense of *shading;* the *west* (as a region of the *evening* sun):—west {10x}, westward {4x}. See: TWOT—1689b; BDB—591d, 788a.

4629. מַעֲרֶה {1x} **maʿăreh**, *mah-ar-eh';* from 6168; a *nude* place, i.e. a *common:*—meadows {1x}. See: TWOT—1692d; BDB—591d, 788b, 789a.

4630. מַעֲרָה {1x} **maʿărâh**, *mah-ar-aw';* fem. of 4629; an *open* spot:—armies {1x}. See: TWOT—1692d; BDB—592a, 790b.

4631. מְעָרָה {39x} **meʿârâh**, *meh-aw-raw';* from 5783; a *cavern* (as dark):—cave {36x}, den {2x}, hole {1x}. See: TWOT—1704a; BDB—592a, 792c.

4632. מְעָרָה {1x} **Meʿârâh**, *meh-aw-raw';* the same as 4631; *cave; Meärah,* a place in Pal.:—Mearah {1x}. See: BDB—792c.

4633. מַעֲרָךְ {1x} **maʿărâk**, *mah-ar-awk';* from 6186; an *arrangement,* i.e. (fig.) mental *disposition:*—preparation {1x}. See: TWOT—1694c; BDB—592a, 790a.

4634. מַעֲרָכָה {20x} **maʿărâkâh**, *mah-ar-aw-kaw';* fem. of 4633; an *arrangement;* concr. a *pile;* spec. a military *array:*—army {15x}, fight {1x}, be set in order {1x}, ordered place {1x}, rank {1x}, row {1x}. See: TWOT—1694d; BDB—592a, 790a.

4635. מַעֲרֶכֶת {9x} **maʿăreketh**, *mah-ar-eh'-keth;* from 6186; an *arrangement,* i.e. (concr.) a *pile* (of loaves):—shewbread + 3899 {5x}, shewbread {2x}, row {2x}. See: TWOT—1694e; BDB—592a, 790b.

4636. מַעֲרֹם {1x} **maʿărôm**, *mah-ar-ome';* from 6191, in the sense of *stripping; bare:*—naked {1x}. See: TWOT—1588d; BDB—592a, 736a, 791a.

4637. מַעֲרָצָה {1x} **maʿărâtsâh**, *mah-ar-aw-tsaw';* from 6206; *violence:*—terror {1x}. See: TWOT—1702c; BDB—592a, 792b.

4638. מַעֲרָת {1x} **Maʿărâth**, *mah-ar-awth';* a form of 4630; *waste; Maarath,* a place in Pal.:—Maarath {1x}. See: BDB—592a, 789b.

4639. מַעֲשֶׂה {235x} **maʿăseh**, *mah-as-eh';* from 6213; an *action* (good or bad); gen. a *transaction;* abstr. *activity;* by impl. a *product* (spec. a *poem*) or (gen.) *property:*—work {189x}, needlework + 7551 {5x}, acts {4x}, labour {4x}, doing {4x}, art {3x}, deed {3x}, misc. {23x} = + bakemeat, business, thing made, ware of making, occupation, thing offered, operation, possession, × well, wrought.

Maʿaseh means "work; deed; labor; behavior." **(1)** Lamech, Noah's father, in expressing his hope for a new world, used the noun for the first time in the Old Testament: "And he called his name Noah, saying, This same shall comfort us concerning our work and toil of our hands, because of the ground which the LORD hath cursed" (Gen 5:29). **(2)** The basic meaning of *maʿaseh* is "work." **(2a)** Lamech used the word to signify agricultural labor (Gen 5:29). **(2b)** The Israelites were commanded to celebrate the Festival of the Firstfruits, as it signified the blessing of God upon their "labors" (Ex 23:16). **(2c)** It is not to be limited to this. **(3)** As the word is the most general word for "work," it may be used to refer to the "work" of **(3a)** a skillful craftsman (Ex 26:1), **(3b)** a weaver (26:36), **(3c)** a jeweler (28:11), and **(3d)** a perfumer (30:25). **(4)** The finished product of the worker is also known as *maʿaseh:* **(4a)** "And in the uppermost basket there was of all manner of bakemeats [literally, "work of a baker"] for Pharaoh. . . ." (Gen 40:17); **(4b)** "And Moses and Eleazar the priest took the gold of them, even all wrought jewels" [literally, "articles of work"] (Num 31:51).

(5) The artisan plied his craft during the work week, known in Hebrew as "the days of work," and rested on the Sabbath: "Thus saith the Lord GOD; The gate of the inner court that looketh toward the east shall be shut the six working days; but on the sabbath it shall be opened, and in the day of the new moon it shall be opened" (Eze 46:1; cf. Ex 23:12). **(6)** The phrase "work of one's hands" signifies the worthlessness of the idols fashioned by human hands: "Asshur shall not save us; we will not ride upon horses: neither will we say any more to the work of our hands, Ye are our gods: for in thee the fatherless findeth mercy" (Hos 14:3). **(7)** However, the prayer of the psalmist includes the request that the "works" of God's people might be established: "And let the beauty of the LORD our God be upon us: and establish thou the work of our hands upon us; yea, the work of our hands establish thou it" (Ps 90:17). **(8)** Since the righteous work out God's work and are a cause of God's rejoicing, "the glory of the LORD shall endure for ever: the LORD shall rejoice in his works" (Ps 104:31).

(9) In addition to "work," *maʿaseh* also denotes "deed," "practice," or "behavior." Joseph asked his brothers, accused of having taken his cup of divination: "What deed is this that ye have done? wot ye not that such a man as I can certainly divine?" (Gen 44:15). **(10)** The Israelites were strongly commanded not to imitate the grossly immoral behavior of the Canaanites and the surrounding nations: "After the doings of the land of Egypt, wherein ye dwelt, shall ye not do: and after the doings of the land of Canaan, whither I bring you, shall ye not do: neither shall ye walk in their ordinances" (Lev 18:3; cf. Ex 23:24). **(11)** However, the Israelites did not listen to the warning, and they "were mingled among the heathen, and learned their works. . . . Thus were they defiled with their own works, and went a whoring with their own inventions" (Ps 106:35, 39). **(12)** Thus far, we have dealt with *maʿaseh* from man's perspective. **(12a)** The word may have a positive connotation ("work, deed") as **(12b)** well as a negative ("corrupt practice").

(13) The Old Testament also calls us to celebrate the "work" of God. The psalmist was overwhelmed with the majesty of the Lord, as he looked at God's "work" of creation: "When I consider thy heavens, the work of thy fingers, the moon and the stars, which thou hast ordained" (Ps 8:3; cf. 19:1; 102:25). **(14)** The God of Israel demonstrated His love by His mighty acts of deliverance on behalf of Israel: "And Israel served the LORD all the days of Joshua, and all the days of the elders that [out] lived Joshua, and which had known all the works of the LORD, that he had done for Israel" (Josh 24:31). **(15)** All of God's "works" are characterized by faithfulness to His promises and covenant: "For the word of the LORD is right; and all his works are done in truth" (Ps 33:4). See: TWOT—1708a; BDB—592a, 795c.

4640. מַעֲשַׁי {1x} **Maʿăsay**, *mah-as-ah'ee;* from 6213; *operative; Maasai*, an Isr.:—Maasiai {1x}. See: BDB—592a, 796b.

4641. מַעֲשֵׂיָה {23x} **Maʿăsêyâh**, *mah-as-ay-yaw';* or

מַעֲשֵׂיָהוּ **Maʿăsêyâhûw**, *mah-as-ay-yaw'-hoo;* from 4639 and 3050; *work of Jah; Maasejah*, the name of sixteen Isr.:—Maseiah {23x}. See: BDB—592a, 796b.

4642. מַעֲשַׁקָּה {2x} **maʿăshaqqâh**, *mah-ash-ak-kaw';* from 6231; *oppression:*—oppression {1x}, × oppressor {1x}. See: TWOT—1713e; BDB—592a, 799a.

4643. מַעֲשֵׂר {32x} **maʿăsêr**, *mah-as-ayr';* or

מַעֲשַׂר **maʿăsar**, *mah-as-ar';* and (in plur.) fem.

מַעַשְׂרָה **maʿasrâh**, *mah-as-raw';* from 6240; a *tenth;* espec. a *tithe:*—tithe {27x}, tenth part {2x}, tenth {2x}, tithing {1x}. See: TWOT—1711h; BDB—592a, 798b.

4644. מֹף {1x} **Môph**, *mofe;* of Eg. or.; *Moph*, the capital of Lower Egypt:—Memphis {1x}. See: BDB—592a. comp. 5297.

מְפִבֹשֶׁת **Mephîbôsheth**. See 4648.

4645. מִפְגָּע {1x} **miphgâʿ**, *mif-gaw';* from 6293; an *object of attack:*—mark {1x}. See: TWOT—1731b; BDB—592a, 803c.

4646. מַפָּח {1x} **mappâch**, *map-pawkh';* from 5301; a *breathing out* (of life), i.e. expiring:—giving up {1x}. See: BDB—592a, 656a.

4647. מַפֻּחַ {1x} **mappûach**, *map-poo'-akh;* from 5301; the *bellows* (i.e. *blower*) of a forge:—bellows {1x}. See: TWOT—1390b; BDB—592a, 656b.

4648. מְפִיבֹשֶׁת {15x} **Mephîybôsheth**, *mef-ee-bo'-sheth;* or

מְפִבֹשֶׁת **Mephîbôsheth**, *mef-ee-bo'-sheth;* prob. from 6284 and 1322; *dispeller of shame* (i.e. of Baal); *Mephibosheth*, the name of two Isr.:—Mephibosheth {15x}. See: BDB—592b, 937c.

4649. מֻפִּים {1x} **Muppîym**, *moop-peem';* a plur. appar. from 5130; *wavings, Muppim*, an Isr.:—Muppim {1x}. See: BDB—592b. comp. 8206.

4650. מֵפִיץ {1x} **mêphîyts**, *may-feets';* from 6327; a *breaker*, i.e. mallet:—maul {1x}. See: TWOT—1745a; BDB—592b, 807b.

4651. מַפָּל {1x} **mappâl**, *map-pawl';* from 5307; a *falling* off, i.e. chaff; also something *pendulous*, i.e. a flap:—flakes {1x}, refuse {1x}. See: TWOT—1392b; BDB—592b, 658c.

4652. מִפְלָאָה {1x} **miphlâʾâh**, *mif-law-aw';* from 6381; a *miracle:*—wondrous work {1x}. See: TWOT—1768c; BDB—592b, 811a.

4653. מִפְלַגָּה {1x} **miphlaggâh**, *mif-lag-gaw';* from 6385; a *classification:*—division {1x}. See: TWOT—1769d; BDB—592b, 811b.

4654. מַפָּלָה {3x} **mappâlâh**, *map-paw-law';* or

מַפֵּלָה **mappêlâh**, *map-pay-law';* from 5307; something *fallen*, i.e. a *ruin:*—ruin {1x}, ruinous {1x}. See: TWOT—1392d; BDB—592b, 658c.

4655. מִפְלָט {1x} **miphlâṭ**, *mif-lawt';* from 6403; an *escape:*—escape {1x}. See: TWOT—1774e; BDB—592b, 812d.

4656. מִפְלֶצֶת {4x} **miphletseth**, *mif-leh'-tseth;* from 6426; a *terror*, i.e. an idol:—idol {4x}. See: TWOT—1778b; BDB—592b, 814a.

4657. מִפְלָשׂ {1x} **miphlâs**, *mif-lawce';* from an unused root mean. to *balance;* a *poising:*—balancings {1x}. See: TWOT—1777b; BDB—592b, 814a.

4658. מַפֶּלֶת {8x} **mappeleth**, *map-peh'-leth;* from 5307; *fall*, i.e. *decadence;* concr. a *ruin;* spec. a *carcase:*—carcase {1x}, fall {5x}, ruin {2x}. See: TWOT—1392e; BDB—592b, 658c.

4659. מִפְעָל {3x} **miphʿâl**, *mif-awl';* or (fem.)

מִפְעָלָה **miphʿâlâh**, *mif-aw-law';* from 6466; a *performance:*—work {3x}. See: TWOT—1792c; BDB—592b. 821d.

4660. מַפָּץ {1x} **mappâts**, *map-pawts';* from 5310; a *smiting* to pieces:—slaughter {1x}. See: TWOT—1394b; BDB—592b, 658d.

4661. מַפֵּץ {1x} **mappêts**, *map-pates';* from 5310; a *smiter*, i.e. a war *club:*—battle ax {1x}. See: TWOT—1394c; BDB—592b, 659a.

4662. מִפְקָד {4x} **miphqâd**, *mif-kawd';* from 6485; an *appointment*, i.e. *mandate;* concr. a designated *spot;* spec. a *census:*—appointed place {1x}, commandment {1x}, number {2x}. See: TWOT—1802g; BDB—592b, 824c.

4663. מִפְקָד {1x} **Miphqâd**, *mif-kawd';* the same as 4662; *assignment; Miphkad*, the name of a gate in Jerusalem:—Miphkad {1x}. See: BDB—592b, 824c.

4664. מִפְרָץ {1x} **miphrâts**, *mif-rawts';* from 6555; a *break* (in the shore), i.e. a *haven:*—breaches {1x}. See: TWOT—1827a; BDB—592b, 830a.

4665. מִפְרֶקֶת {1x} **miphreketh**, *mif-reh'-keth;* from 6561; prop. a *fracture*, i.e. *joint* (*vertebra*) of the neck:—neck {1x}. See: TWOT—1828c; BDB—592b, 830b.

4666. מִפְרָשׂ {12x} **miphrâs**, *mif-rawce';* from 6566; an *expansion:*—that which . . . spreadest forth {1x}, spreadings {1x}. See: TWOT—1832a; BDB—592b, 831c.

4667. מִפְשָׂעָה {1x} **miphsâʿâh**, *mif-saw-aw';* from 6585; a *stride*, i.e. (by euphem.) the *crotch:*—buttocks {1x}. See: TWOT—1841b; BDB—592b, 832c.

מֹפֵת **môphêth**. See 4159.

4668. מַפְתֵּחַ {3x} **maphtêach**, *maf-tay'-akh;* from 6605; an *opener*, i.e. a *key:*—key {2x}, opening {1x}. See: TWOT—1854f; BDB—592b, 836b.

4669. מִפְתָּח {1x} **miphtâch**, *mif-tawkh';* from 6605; an *aperture*, i.e. (fig.) *utterance:*—opening {1x}. See: TWOT—1854e; BDB—592b, 836b.

4670. מִפְתָּן {8x} **miphtân**, *mif-tawn';* from the same as 6620; a *stretcher*, i.e. a *sill:*—threshold {8x}. See: TWOT—1858b; BDB—592, 837b.

4671. מֹץ {8x} **môts**, *motes;* or

מוֹץ **môwts** (Zeph 2:2), *motes;* from 4160; *chaff* (as *pressed* out, i.e. *winnowed* or [rather] threshed loose):—chaff {8x}. See: TWOT—1162a; BDB—558b, 592b.

4672. מָצָא {456x} **mâtsâʾ**, *maw tsaw';* a prim. root; prop. to *come* forth to, i.e. *appear* or *exist;* tran. to *attain*, i.e. *find* or *acquire;* fig. to *occur, meet* or *be present:*—find {359x}, present {20x}, find out {20x}, come {8x}, meet {5x}, befall {5x}, get {4x}, suffice {3x}, deliver {2x}, hit {2x}, left {2x}, hold {2x}, misc. {24x}= + be able, being, catch, × certainly, × have (here), be here, light (up-) on, × occasion serve, ready, speed.

Matsaʾ means "to find, meet, get." **(1)** *Matsaʾ* refers to "finding" someone or something that is lost or misplaced, or "finding" where it is. **(1a)** The thing may be found as the result of a purposeful search, as when the Sodomites were temporarily blinded by Lot's visitors and were not able to "find" the door to his house (Gen 19:11). **(1b)** In a very similar usage, the dove sent forth by Noah searched for a spot to land and was unable to "find" it (Gen 8:9). **(1c)** On other occasions, the location of something or someone may be found without an intentional search, as when Cain said: "[Whoever] findeth me shall slay me" (Gen 4:14). **(2)** *Matsa'* may connote not only "finding" a subject in a location, but "finding something" in an abstract sense. **(2a)** This idea is demonstrated clearly by Gen 6:8: "But Noah found grace in the eyes of the LORD." **(2b)** He found—"received"—something he did not seek.

(3) This sense also includes "finding" something one has sought in a spiritual or mental sense: **(3a)** "Mine hand had gotten much . . ." (Job 31:25). **(3b)** Laban tells Jacob: ". . . If I have found favor in thine eyes, [stay with me] . . ." (Gen 30:27). Laban is asking Jacob for a favor that he is seeking in an abstract sense. **(4)** *Matsa'* can also mean "to discover." **(4a)** God told Abraham: "If I find in Sodom fifty righteous within the city, then I will spare all the place for their sakes" (Gen 18:26). **(4b)** This same emphasis appears in the first biblical occurrence of the word: ". . . But for Adam there was not found a help meet for him" (Gen 2:20). **(5)** As noted earlier, there can be a connotation of the unintentional here, as when the Israelites "found" a man gathering wood on the Sabbath (Num 15:32). **(6)** Another special nuance is "to find out," in the sense of "gaining knowledge about." For example, Joseph's brothers said: "God hath found out the iniquity of thy servants . . ." (Gen 44:16).

(7) *Matsa'* sometimes suggests "being under the power" of something, in a concrete sense. David told Abishai: ". . . Take thou thy lord's servants, and pursue after him, lest he get him fenced cities, and escape us" (2 Sa 20:6). The idea is that Sheba would "find," enter, and defend himself in fortified cities. So to "find" them could be to "take them over." **(8)** This usage appears also in an abstract sense. Judah told Joseph: "For how shall I go up to my father, and the lad be not with me? lest peradventure I see the evil that shall come on my father" (Gen 44:34). **(9)** The word *matsa'*, therefore, can mean not only to "find" something, but to "obtain" it as one's own: "Then Isaac sowed in that land and received in the same year . . ." (Gen 26:12). **(10)** Infrequently, the word implies movement in a direction until one arrives at a destination. This sense is found in Job 11:7: "Canst thou by searching find out God?" (cf. 1 Sa 23:17). **(11)** In a somewhat different nuance, this meaning appears in Num 11:22: "Shall the flocks and the herds be slain for them, to suffice them?" See: TWOT—1231; BDB—592c.

מֹצָא **môtsâ'**. See 4161.

4673. מַצָּב {10x} **matstsâb**, *mats-tsawb';* from 5324; a fixed *spot;* fig. an *office,* a military *post:*—garrison {7x}, station {1x}, place where . . . stood {2x}. See: TWOT—1398c; BDB—594b, 662d.

4674. מֻצָּב {1x} **mutstsâb**, *moots-tsawb';* from 5324; a *station,* i.e. military *post:*—mount {1x}. See: TWOT—1398d; BDB—594b, 663a.

4675. מַצָּבָה {2x} **matstsâbâh**, *mats-tsaw-baw';* or

מִצָּבָה **mitstsâbâh**, *mits-tsaw-baw';* fem. of 4673; a military *guard:*—army {1x}, garrison {1x}. See: TWOT—1398f; BDB—594b, 663a.

4676. מַצֵּבָה {32x} **matstsêbâh**, *mats-tsay-baw';* fem. (caus.) part. of 5324; something *stationed,* i.e. a *column* or (memorial *stone*); by anal. an *idol:*—garrison {1x}, (standing) image {19x}, pillar {12x}.

Matstsebah means "pillar; monument; sacred stone." **(1)** This word refers to a "pillar" as a personal memorial in 2 Sa 18:18: "Now Absalom in his lifetime had taken and reared up for himself a pillar . . . and he called the pillar after his own name: and it is called unto this day, Absalom's place." **(2)** In Gen 28:18 the "monument" is a memorial of the Lord's appearance: "And Jacob rose up early in the morning, and took the stone that he had put *for* his pillows, and set it up *for* a pillar, and poured oil upon the top of it." **(3)** *Matstsebah* is used in connection with the altar built by Moses in Ex 24:4: "And Moses wrote all the words of the LORD, and rose up early in the morning, and builded an altar under the hill, and twelve pillars, according to the twelve tribes of Israel." Syn.: 352. See: TWOT—1398g; BDB—594b, 663a.

4677. מְצֹבָיָה {1x} **M**e**tsôbâyâh**, *mets-o-baw-yaw';* appar. from 4672 and 3050; *found of Jah; Metsobajah,* a place in Pal.:—Mesobaite {1x}. See: BDB—594b.

4678. מַצֶּבֶת {6x} **matstsebeth**, *mats-tseh'-beth;* from 5324; something *stationary,* i.e. a monumental *stone;* also the *stock* of a tree:—pillar {2x}, substance {4x}. See: TWOT—1398g; BDB—594b, 663a.

4679. מְצַד {11x} **m**e**tsad**, *mets-ad';* or

מְצָד **m**e**tsâd**, *mets-awd';* or (fem.)

מְצָדָה **m**e**tsâdâh**, *mets-aw-daw';* from 6679; a *fastness* (as a *covert* of ambush):—castle {1x}, fort {1x}, strongholds {5x}, holds {3x} munition {1x}. See: TWOT—1885c; BDB—594c, 844d, 845a.

מְצֻדָה **m**e**tsûdâh**. See 4686.

4680. מָצָה {7x} **mâtsâh**, *maw-tsaw';* a prim. root; to *suck* out; by impl. to *drain,* to *squeeze* out:—suck {1x}, wring (out) {6x}. See: TWOT—1232; BDB—594c.

4681. מֹצָה {1x} **Môtsâh**, *mo-tsaw';* act. part. fem. of 4680; *drained; Motsah,* a place in Pal.:—Mozah {1x}. See: BDB—594c.

4682. מַצָּה {53x} **matstsâh**, *mats-tsaw';* from 4711 in the sense of *greedily* devouring for sweetness; prop. *sweetness;* concr. *sweet* (i.e. not soured or bittered with yeast); spec. an *unfermented cake* or loaf, or (ellip.) the festival of *Passover* (because no leaven was then used):—unleavened bread {33x}, unleavened {14x}, cakes {5x}, without leaven {1x}.

Matstsah means "unleavened bread." **(1)** This noun occurs 53 times, **(1a)** all but 14 of them in the Pentateuch. **(1b)** The rest of the occurrences are in prose narratives or in Ezekiel's discussion of the new temple: "In the first *month,* in the fourteenth day of the month, ye shall have the passover, a feast of seven days; unleavened bread shall be eaten" (Eze 45:21). **(2)** In the ancient Orient, household bread was prepared **(2a)** by adding fermented dough to the kneading trough and working it through the fresh dough. **(2b)** Hastily made bread omitted the fermented (leavened) dough: Lot "made them a feast, and did bake unleavened bread, and they did eat" (Gen 19:3). In this case, the word represents bread hastily prepared for unexpected guests. **(3)** The feasts of Israel often involved the use of unleavened bread, perhaps because of the relationship between fermentation, rotting, and death (Lev 2:4ff.), or because unleavened bread reminded Jews of the hasty departure from Egypt and the rigors of the wilderness march. Syn.: 3899. See: TWOT—1105a; BDB—594c, 595a.

4683. מַצָּה {3x} **matstsâh**, *mats-tsaw';* from 5327; a *quarrel:*—contention {1x}, debate {1x}, strife {1x}. See: TWOT—1400a; BDB—594c, 663c.

4684. מַצְהָלָה {2x} **matshâlâh**, *mats-haw-law';* from 6670; a *whinnying* (through impatience for battle or lust):—neighing {1x}. See: TWOT—1881a; BDB—843d.

4685. מָצוֹד {6x} **mâtsôwd**, *maw-tsode';* or (fem.)

מְצוֹדָה **m**e**tsôwdâh**, *mets-o-daw';* or

מְצֹדָה **m**e**tsôdâh**, *mets-o-daw';* from 6679; a *net* (for *capturing* animals or fishes); also (by interch. for 4679) a *fastness* or (besieging) *tower:*—bulwark {1x}, hold {1x}, munition {1x}, net {2x}, snare {1x}. See: TWOT—1885d, 1885e; BDB—594c, 594d, 844d, 845a.

4686. מָצוּד {22x} **mâtsûwd**, *maw-tsood';* or (fem.)

מְצוּדָה **m**e**tsûwdâh**, *mets-oo-daw';* or

מְצֻדָה **m**e**tsûdâh**, *mets-oo-daw';* for 4685; a *net,* or (abstr.) *capture;* also a *fastness:*—fortress {6x}, hold {6x}, snare {2x}, strong hold {1x}, castle {1x}, net {1x}, strong place {1x}, hunted {1x}, strong hold {1x}, fort {1x}, defence {1x}. See: TWOT—1885g, 1885i; BDB—594c, 594d, 845a.

4687. מִצְוָה {181x} **mitsvâh**, *mits-vaw';* from 6680; a *command,* whether human or divine (collect. the *Law*):—commandments {177x}, precept {4x}, commanded {2x}, law {1x}, ordinances {1x}.

Mitsvah means "commandment." **(1)** Its first occurrence is in Gen 26:5, where *mitsvah* is synonymous with *choq* ("statute", 2706) and torah ("law", 8451): "Because that Abraham obeyed my voice, and kept my charge (4931 – *mishmeret*), my commandments (*mitsvah*), my statutes (2708 – *chuqqah* – plural), and my laws (8451 – *torah*). **(2)** In the Pentateuch, God is always the Giver of the *mitsvah.* "All the commandments which I command thee this day shall ye observe to do, that ye may live, and multiply, and go in and possess the land which the Lord sware unto your fathers. And thou shalt remember all the way which the LORD thy God led thee these forty years in the wilderness, to humble thee, and to prove thee, to know what was in thine heart, whether thou wouldest keep his commandments, or no" (Deut 8:1–2). **(3)** The "commandment" may be a prescription ("thou shalt do . . .") or a proscription ("thou shalt not do . . .").

(4) The commandments were **(4a)** given in the hearing of the Israelites (Ex 15:26; Deut 11:13), **(4b)** who were to "do" (Lev 4:2ff.) and "keep" (Deut 4:2; Ps 78:7) them. **(4c)** Any failure to do so signified a covenantal breach (Num 15:31), transgression (2 Chr 24:20), and apostasy (1 Kin 18:18). **(5)** The plural of *mitsvah* often denotes a "body of laws" given by divine revelation. **(5a)** They are God's "word": "Wherewithal shall a young man cleanse his way? By taking heed thereto according to thy word" (Ps 119:9). **(5b)** They are also known as "the commandments of God." **(6)** Outside the Pentateuch, "commandments" are given by kings (1 Kin 2:43), fathers (Jer 35:14), people (Is 29:13), and teachers of wisdom (Prov 6:20; cf. 5:13). Only about ten percent of all occurrences in the Old Testament fit this category. See: TWOT—1887b; BDB—594d, 846b.

4688. מְצוֹלָה {11x} **m^e^tsôwlâh**, *mets-o-law';* or מְצֹלָה **m^e^tsôlâh**, *mets-o-law';* also מְצוּלָה **m^e^tsûwlâh**, *mets-oo-law';* or מְצֻלָה **m^e^tsûlâh**, *mets-oo-law';* from the same as 6683; a *deep* place (of water or mud):—deep {5x}, deeps {3x}, depths {2x}, bottom {1x}. See: TWOT—1889b; BDB—594a, 595a, 846d.

4689. מָצוֹק {6x} **mâtsôwq**, *maw-tsoke';* from 6693; a *narrow* place, i.e. (abstr. and fig.) *confinement* or *disability:*—anguish {1x}, distress {1x}, straitness {4x}. See: TWOT—1895d; BDB—594d, 848a.

4690. מָצוּק {2x} **mâtsûwq**, *maw-tsook';* or מָצֻק **mâtsûq**, *maw-tsook';* from 6693; something *narrow,* i.e. a *column* or *hill*top:—pillar {1x}, situate {1x}. See: TWOT—1896a; BDB—594d, 595b, 848b.

4691. מְצוּקָה {7x} **m^e^tsûwqâh**, *mets-oo-kaw';* or מְצֻקָה **m^e^tsûqâh**, *mets-oo-kaw';* fem. of 4690; *narrowness,* i.e. (fig.) *trouble:*—anguish {1x}, distress {6x}. See: TWOT—1895e; BDB—594d, 595b, 848a.

4692. מָצוֹר {25x} **mâtsôwr**, *maw-tsore';* or מָצוּר **mâtsûwr**, *maw-tsoor';* from 6696; something *hemming* in, i.e. (obj.) a *mound* (of besiegers), (abstr.) a *siege,* (fig.) *distress,* or (subj.) a *fastness:*—siege {13x}, besieged {2x}, strong {2x}, besieged + 935 {2x}, bulwarks {1x}, defence {1x}, fenced {1x}, fortress {1x}, hold {1x}, tower {1x}. See: TWOT—1898a; BDB—594d, 848d.

4693. מָצוֹר {5x} **mâtsôwr**, *maw-tsore';* the same as 4692 in the sense of a *limit; Egypt* (as the *border* of Pal.):—besieged places {2x}, defence {1x}, fortress {1x}, fortified {1x}. See: TWOT—1898a; BDB—594d, 596a, 849a.

4694. מְצוּרָה {8x} **m^e^tsûwrâh**, *mets-oo-raw';* or מְצֻרָה **m^e^tsûrâh**, *mets-oo-raw';* fem. of 4692; a *hemming* in, i.e. (obj.) a *mound* (of siege), or (subj.) a *rampart* (of protection), (abstr.) *fortification:*—fenced (city) {5x}, fort {1x}, munition {1x}, strong hold {1x}. See: TWOT—1898b; BDB—596a, 849a.

4695. מַצּוּת {1x} **matstsûwth**, *mats-tsooth';* from 5327; a *quarrel:*—that contended {1x}. See: TWOT—1400b; BDB—594d, 596b, 663c.

4696. מֵצַח {11x} **mêtsach**, *may'-tsakh;* from an unused root mean. to *be clear,* i.e. *conspicuous;* the *forehead* (as *open* and *prominent*):—brow {1x}, forehead {11x}, + impudent {1x}. See: TWOT—1233a; BDB—594d.

4697. מִצְחָה {1x} **mitschâh**, *mits-khaw';* from the same as 4696; a *shin-piece* of armor (as *prominent*), only plur.:—greaves {1x}. See: TWOT—1233b; BDB—595a.

מְצִלָה **m^e^tsôlâh**. See 4688.

מְצֻלָה **m^e^tsûlâh**. See 4688.

4698. מְצִלָּה {1x} **m^e^tsillâh** *mets-il-law';* from 6750; a *tinkler,* i.e. a *bell:*—bell {1x}. See: TWOT—1919e; BDB—595a, 853a.

4699. מְצֻלָּה {1x} **m^e^tsullâh**, *mets-ool-law';* from 6751; *shade:*—bottom {1x}. See: TWOT—1889c; BDB—847a.

4700. מְצֵלֶת {13x} **m^e^tsêleth**, *mets-ay'-leth;* from 6750; (only dual) double *tinklers,* i.e. cymbals:—cymbals {13x}. See: TWOT—1919f; BDB—595a, 853a.

4701. מִצְנֶפֶת {12x} **mitsnepheth**, *mits-neh'-feth;* from 6801; a *tiara,* i.e. official *turban* (of a king or high priest):—diadem {1x}, mitre {11x}. See: TWOT—1940c; BDB—595a, 857b.

4702. מַצָּע {1x} **matstsâ^c^**, *mats-tsaw';* from 3331; a *couch:*—bed {1x}. See: TWOT—896c; BDB—427a, 595a.

4703. מִצְעָד {3x} **mits^c^âd**, *mits-awd';* from 6805; a *step;* fig. *companionship:*—goings {1x}, steps {2x}. See: TWOT—1943d; BDB—595a, 857d.

4704. מִצְּעִירָה {1x} **mitsts^ec^îyrâh**, *mits-tseh-ee-raw';* fem. of 4705; prop. *littleness;* concr. *diminutive:*—little {1x}. See: TWOT—1948c; BDB—859a.

4705. מִצְעָר {5x} **mits^c^âr**, *mits-awr';* from 6819; *petty* (in size or number); adv. a *short* (time):—little one {1x}, little while {1x}, small {2x}. See: TWOT—1948c; BDB—595a, 859b.

4706. מִצְעָר {1x} **Mits^c^âr**, *mits-awr';* the same as 4705; *Mitsar,* a peak of Lebanon:—Mizar {1x}. See: BDB—595a, 859b.

4707. מִצְפֶּה {2x} **mitspeh**, *mits-peh';* from 6822; an *observatory,* espec. for military purposes:—watch tower {2x}. See: TWOT—1950b; BDB—859d.

4708. מִצְפֶּה {15x} **Mitspeh**, *mits-peh';* the same as 4707; *Mitspeh,* the name of five places in Pal.:—Mizpeh {9x}, Mizpah {5x}, watch tower {1x}. See: BDB—595a, 859d. comp. 4709.

4709. מִצְפָּה {32x} **Mitspah**, *mits-paw';* fem. of 4708; *Mitspah,* the name of two places in Pal.:—Mitspah {18x}, Mitspeh {14x}. [This seems rather to be only an orth. var. of 4708 when "in pause".] See: BDB—595a, 859d.

4710. מִצְפֻּן {1x} **mitspûn**, *mits-poon';* from 6845; a *secret* (place or thing, perh. *treasure*):—hidden thing {1x}. See: TWOT—1953d; BDB—595a, 861b.

4711. מָצַץ {1x} **mâtsats**, *maw-tsats';* a prim. root; to *suck:*—milk {1x}. See: TWOT—1234; BDB—595a.

מְצָקָה **mûtsâqâh**. See 4166.

4712. מֵצַר {3x} **mêtsar**, *may-tsar';* from 6896; something *tight,* i.e. (fig.) *trouble:*—distress {1x}, pain {1x}, strait {1x}. See: TWOT—1973f; BDB—595b, 865c.

מָצֻק **mâtsûq**. See 4690.

מְצֻקָה **m^e^tsuqah**. See 4691.

מְצֻרָה **m^e^tsûrâh**. See 4694.

4713. מִצְרִי {30x} **Mitsrîy**, *mits-ree';* from 4714; a *Mitsrite,* or inhab. of Mitsrajim:—Egyptian {25x}, Egyptian + 376 {3x}, Egypt {1x}, Egyptian women {1x}. See: BDB—596a.

4714. מִצְרַיִם {681x} **Mitsrayim**, *mits-rah'-yim;* dual of 4693; *Mitsrajim,* i.e. Upper and Lower Egypt:—Egypt {586x}, Egyptian {90x}, Mizraim {4x}, Egyptians + 1121 {1x}. See: TWOT—1235; BDB—595c.

4715. מִצְרֵף {2x} **mitsrêph**, *mits-rafe';* from 6884; a *crucible:*—fining pot {2x}. See: TWOT—1972b; BDB—596b, 864c.

4716. מַק {2x} **maq**, *mak;* from 4743; prop. a *melting,* i.e. *putridity:*—rottenness {1x}, stink {1x}. See: TWOT—1237a; BDB—596b, 597a.

4717. מַקָּבָה {3x} **maqqâbâh**, *mak-kaw-baw';* from 5344; prop. a *perforatrix,* i.e. a *hammer* (as *piercing*):—hammer {3x}. See: TWOT—1409c; BDB—666a.

4718. מַקֶּבֶת {2x} **maqqebeth**, *mak-keh'-beth;* from 5344; prop. a *perforator,* i.e. a *hammer* (as *piercing*); also (intr.) a *perforation,* i.e. a *quarry:*—hammer {1x}, hole {1x}. See: TWOT—1409d; BDB—596b, 666c.

4719. מַקֵּדָה {9x} **Maqqêdâh**, *mak-kay-daw';* from the same as 5348 in the denom. sense of *herding* (comp. 5349); *fold; Makkedah,* a place in Pal.:—Makkedah {9x}. See: BDB—596b.

4720. מִקְדָּשׁ {74x} **miqdâsh**, *mik-dawsh';* or מִקְּדָשׁ **miqq^e^dâsh** (Ex 15:17), *mik-ked-awsh';* from 6942; a *consecrated* thing or place, espec. a *palace, sanctuary* (whether of Jehovah or of idols) or *asylum:*—sanctuary {69x}, holy place {3x}, chapel {1x}, hallowed part {1x}. See: TWOT—1990f; BDB—596b, 874a.

4721. מַקְהֵל {2x} **maqhêl**, *mak-hale';* or (fem.) מַקְהֵלָה **maqhêlâh**, *mak-hay-law';* from 6950; an *assembly:*—congregation {2x}. See: TWOT—1991d; BDB—596b, 875b.

4722. מַקְהֵלֹת {2x} **Maqhêlôth**, *mak-hay-loth';* plur. of 4721 (fem.); *assemblies; Makheloth,* a place in the Desert:—Makheloth {2x}. See: BDB—596b, 875b.

4723. מִקְוֶה {12x} **miqveh**, *mik-veh';* or מִקְוֵה **miqvêh** (1 Kin 10:28) *mik-vay';* or מִקְוֵא **miqvê^^** (2 Chr 1:16), *mik-vay';* from 6960; something *waited* for, i.e. *confidence* (obj. or subj.); also a *collection,* i.e. (of water) a *pond,* or (of men and horses) a *caravan* or *drove:*—abiding {1x}, gathering together {1x}, hope {4x}, linen yarn {4x}, plenty [of water] {1x}, pool {1x}. See: TWOT—1994c, 1995a; BDB—596b, 875c, 876a, 876c.

4724. מִקְוָה {1x} **miqvâh**, *mik-vaw';* fem. of 4723; a *collection,* i.e. (of water) a *reservoir:*—ditch {1x}. See: TWOT—1995a; BDB—596b, 876c.

4725. מָקוֹם {402x} **mâqôwm**, *maw-kome';* or מָקֹם **mâqôm**, *maw-kome';* also (fem.) מְקוֹמָה **m^e^qôwmâh**, *mek-o-mah';* or מְקֹמָה **m^e^qômâh**, *mek-o-mah';* from 6965; prop. a *standing,* i.e. a *spot;* but used widely of a *locality* (gen. or spec.); also (fig.) of a *condition* (of body or mind):—place {391x}, home {3x}, room {3x}, whithersoever {2x}, open {1x}, space {1x}, country {1x}.

Maqowm means "place; height; stature; standing." **(1)** It refers to the place where something **(1a)** stands: "And when they of Ashdod arose early on the morrow, behold, Dagon *was* fallen upon his face to the earth before the ark of the LORD. And they took Dagon, and set him in his place [*maqowm*] again" (1 Sa 5:3), **(1b)** sits: "The throne had six steps, and the top of the throne *was* round behind: and *there were* stays on either side on the place [*maqom*] of the seat, and two lions stood beside the stays."(1 Kin 10:19), **(1c)** dwells: "And I have set there a place [*maqom*] for the ark, wherein *is* the covenant of the LORD, which he made with our fathers, when he brought them out of the land of Egypt" (1 Kin 8:21), or **(1d)** is: "And God said, Let the waters under the heaven be gathered together unto one place [*maqom*], and let the dry *land* appear: and it was so" (Gen 1:9). **(2)** It may also refer to a larger location, such as a country (Ex 3:8) or to an undetermined "space between": "Then David went over to the other side and stood on the top of an hill afar off; a great space [*maqown*] *being* between them:" (1 Sa 26:13). **(3)** A "place" is sometimes a task or office: "If the spirit of the ruler rise up against thee, leave not thy place [*maqown*]; for yielding pacifieth great offences" (Eccl 10:4). **(4)** This noun is used to signify a sanctuary—i.e., a "place" of worship (Gen 22:3). See: TWOT—1999h; BDB—596b, 596c, 879d.

4726. מָקוֹר {18x} **mâqôwr**, *maw-kore'*; or

מָקֹר **mâqôr**, *maw-kore'*; from 6979; prop. something *dug*, i.e. a (gen.) *source* (of water, even when naturally flowing; also of tears, blood [by euphem. of the female *pudenda*]; fig. of happiness, wisdom, progeny):—fountain {11x}, issue {1x}, spring {3x}, wellspring {2x}, well {1x}. See: TWOT—2004a; BDB—596b, 881b.

4727. מִקָּח {1x} **miqqâch**, *mik-kawkh'*; from 3947; *reception:*—taking {1x}.

Miqqach occurs once to mean "taking": "Wherefore now let the fear of the LORD be upon you; take heed and do *it*: for *there is* no iniquity with the LORD our God, nor respect of persons, nor taking of gifts" (2 Chr 19:7). Syn: 3948, 4455, 4457, 4728. See: TWOT—1124e; BDB—544c.

4728. מַקָּחָה {1x} **maqqâchâh**, *mak-kaw-khaw'*; from 3947; something *received*, i.e. *merchandise* (purchased):—ware {1x}.

Maqqachot [plural] means "wares" once (Neh. 10:31). Syn: 3948, 4455, 4457, 4727. See: TWOT—1124f; BDB—544c.

4729. מִקְטָר {1x} **miqtâr**, *mik-tawr'*; from 6999; something to *fume* (incense) on, i.e. a *hearth* place:—to burn . . . upon {1x}.

Miqtar means a "place of sacrificial smoke; altar." The word appears once (Ex 30:1). Syn.: 4730, 6988, 6999, 7002, 7008. See: TWOT—2011d, 2011e; BDB—596b, 883b.

מְקַטְּרָה **mᵉqattᵉrâh**. See 6999.

4730. מִקְטֶרֶת {2x} **miqtereth**, *mik-teh'-reth*; fem. of 4729; something to *fume* (incense) in, i.e. a *coal-pan:*—censer {2x}.

Miqtereth means "censer; incense." **(1)** *Miqtereth* represents a "censer"—a utensil in which coals are carried—in 2 Chr 26:19. **(2)** The word refers to "incense" in Eze 8:11. Syn.: 6988, 6999, 7002, 7004, 7008. See: TWOT—2011f; BDB—596b, 883b.

4731. מַקֵּל {18x} **maqqêl**, *mak-kale*; or (fem.)

מַקְּלָה **maqqᵉlâh**, *mak-kel-aw'*; from an unused root mean. appar. to *germinate;* a *shoot*, i.e. *stick* (with leaves on, or for walking, striking, guiding, divining):—rod {8x}, staff {7x}, stave {2x}, handstave + 3027 {1x}. See: TWOT—1236; BDB—596b.

4732. מִקְלוֹת {4x} **Miqlôwth**, *mik-lohth'*; (or perh. *mik-kel-ohth'*); plur. of (fem.) 4731; *rods; Mikloth*, a place in the Desert:—Mikloth {4x}. See: BDB—596c.

4733. מִקְלָט {20x} **miqlât**, *mik-lawt'*; from 7038 in the sense of *taking* in; an *asylum* (as a *receptacle*):—refuge {20x}. See: TWOT—2026a; BDB—596c, 886a.

4734. מִקְלַעַת {4x} **miqlaʿath**, *mik-lah'-ath;* from 7049; a *sculpture* (prob. in bas-relief):—carved {1x}, carved figure {1x}, carving {1x}, graving {1x}. See: TWOT—2031a; BDB—596c, 887c.

מָקֹם **mâqôm**. See 4725.

מְקֹמָה **mᵉqômâh**. See 4725.

4735. מִקְנֶה {75x} **miqneh**, *mik-neh'*; from 7069; something *bought*, i.e. *property*, but only live *stock;* abstr. *acquisition:*—cattle {63x}, possession {5x}, flocks {3x}, substance {2x}, herds {1x}, purchase {1x}. See: TWOT—2039b; BDB—596d, 889b.

4736. מִקְנָה {15x} **miqnâh**, *mik-naw'*; fem. of 4735; prop. a *buying*, i.e. *acquisition;* concr. a piece of *property* (land or living); also the *sum* paid:—bought {7x}, purchase {5x}, price {2x}, possession {1x}. See: TWOT—2039c; BDB—596d, 889b.

4737. מִקְנֵיָהוּ {2x} **Miqnêyâhûw**, *mik-nay-yaw'-hoo;* from 4735 and 3050; *possession of Jah; Miknejah*, an Isr.:—Mikneiah {2x}. See: BDB—596d, 889c.

4738. מִקְסָם {2x} **miqçâm**, *mik-sawm'*; from 7080; an *augury:*—divination {2x}. See: TWOT—2044b; BDB—596d, 890d.

4739. מָקַץ {1x} **Mâqats**, *maw-kats'*; from 7112; *end; Makats*, a place in Pal.:—Makaz {1x}. See: BDB—596d.

4740. מַקְצוֹעַ {12x} **maqtsôwaʿ**, *mak-tso'-ah;* or

מַקְצֹעַ **maqtsôaʿ**, *mak-tso'-ah;* or (fem.)

מַקְצֹעָה **maqtsôʿâh**, *mak-tso-aw'*; from 7106 in the denom. sense of *bending;* an *angle* or recess:—corner {7x}, turning {12x}. See: TWOT—2057a; BDB—596d, 893a.

4741. מַקְצֻעָה {1x} **maqtsûʿâh**, *mak-tsoo-aw'*; from 7106; a *scraper*, i.e. a carving *chisel:*—plane {1x}. See: TWOT—2056b; BDB—596d, 893a.

4742. מְקֻצְעָה {2x} **mᵉqutsʿâh**, *mek-oots-aw'*; from 7106 in the denom. sense of *bending;* an *angle:*—corner {2x}. See: TWOT—2057a; BDB—596d, 893b.

4743. מָקַק {10x} **mâqaq**, *maw-kak'*; a prim. root; to *melt;* fig. to *flow, dwindle, vanish:*—consume away {4x}, be corrupt {1x}, dissolve {1x}, pine away {4x}. See: TWOT—1237; BDB—596d.

מָקֹר **mâqôr**. See 4726.

4744. מִקְרָא {23x} **miqrâʾ**, *mik-raw'*; from 7121; something *called* out, i.e. a public *meeting* (the act, the persons, or the place); also a *rehearsal:*—assemblies {2x}, calling {1x}, convocation {1x}, reading {1x}.

Miqraʾ means public worship service; convocation. **(1)** The word implies the product of an official summons to worship ("convocation") for the reading and exposition of the Law. The day was to be kept free from secular work and to be regarded as sacred by Divine command. **(2)** In Lev 23:2 it refers to Sabbaths as "convocation days": "Speak unto the children of Israel, and say unto them, *Concerning* the feasts of the LORD, which ye shall proclaim *to be* holy convocations, *even* these *are* my feasts." See: TWOT—2063d; BDB—597a, 896d.

4745. מִקְרֶה {10x} **miqreh**, *mik-reh'*; from 7136; something *met* with, i.e. an *accident* or *fortune:*—befall {4x}, event {3x}, hap {1x}, chance {1x}, happeneth {1x}. See: TWOT—2068c; BDB—597a, 899d.

4746. מְקָרֶה {1x} **mᵉqâreh**, *mek-aw-reh'*; from 7136; prop. something *meeting*, i.e. a *frame* (of timbers):—building {1x}. See: TWOT—2068f; BDB—597a, 900a.

4747. מְקֵרָה {2x} **mᵉqêrâh**, *mek-ay-raw'*; from the same as 7119; a *cooling* off:—× summer {2x}. See: TWOT—2077d; BDB—597a, 903b.

מֹקֵשׁ **môqêsh**. See 4170.

4748. מִקְשֶׁה {1x} **miqsheh**, *mik-sheh'*; from 7185 in the sense of *knotting* up round and hard; something *turned* (rounded), i.e. a *curl* (of tresses):—× well [set] hair {1x}. See: TWOT—2086a; BDB—597a, 904d.

4749. מִקְשָׁה {10x} **miqshâh**, *mik-shaw'*; fem. of 4748; *rounded* work, i.e. moulded by *hammering* (*repoussé*):—beaten work {6x}, beaten out of one piece {1x}, beaten {1x}, whole piece {1x}, upright {1x}. See: TWOT—2086b; BDB—597a, 904d.

4750. מִקְשָׁה {1x} **miqshâh**, *mik-shaw'*; denom. from 7180; lit. a *cucumbered* field, i.e. a *cucumber* patch:—garden of cucumbers {1x}. See: TWOT—2083b; BDB—597a, 903d, 904d.

4751. מַר {38x} **mar**, *mar;* or (fem.)

מָרָה **mârâh**, *maw-raw'*; from 4843; *bitter* (lit. or fig.); also (as noun) *bitterness*, or (adv.) *bitterly:*—bitter {20x}, bitterness {10x}, bitterly {3x}, chafed {1x}, angry {1x}, discontented {1x}, heavy {1x}, bitter thing {1x}. See: TWOT—1248a, 1248c; BDB—597a, 600c.

4752. מַר {1x} **mar**, *mar;* from 4843 in its orig. sense of *distillation;* a *drop:*—drop {1x}. See: TWOT—1249a; BDB—597a, 601c.

4753. מֹר {12x} **môr**, *more;* or

מוֹר **môwr**, *more;* from 4843; *myrrh* (as *distilling* in drops, and also as *bitter*):—myrrh {12x}. See: TWOT—1248b; BDB—558d, 597a, 600d.

4754. מָרָא {2x} **mârâʾ**, *maw-raw'*; a prim. root; to *rebel;* hence, (through the idea of *maltreating*) to *whip*, i.e. *lash* (self with wings, as the ostrich in running):—be filthy {1x}, lift up self {1x}. See: TWOT—1238; BDB—597a, 598a.

4755. מָרָא {1x} **Mârâʾ**, *maw-raw'*; for 4751 fem.; *bitter; Mara*, a symbol. name of Naomi:—Mara {1x}. See: BDB—597a, 600c.

4756. מָרֵא {4x} **mârêʾ** (Aram.), *maw-ray'*; from a root corresp. to 4754 in the sense of *domineering;* a *master:*—lord {2x}, Lord {2x}. See: TWOT—2839; BDB—1101c, 1101d.

מֹרָא **môrâʾ**. See 4172.

4757. מְרֹאדַךְ בַּלְאָדָן {1x} **Mᵉrôʾdak Balʾădân**, *mer-o-dak' bal-aw-dawn';* of for. der.; *Merodak-Baladan*, a Bab. king:—Merodach-baladan {1x}. See: BDB—596b, 597b, 597d. comp. 4781.

4758. מַרְאֶה {1x} **marʾeh**, *mar-eh'*; from 7200; a *view* (the act of seeing); also an *appearance* (the thing seen), whether (real) a *shape* (espec. if handsome, *comeliness;* often plur. the *looks*), or (mental) a *vision:*—appearance {35x}, sight {18x}, countenance {11x}, vision {11x}, favoured {7x}, look upon {4x}, fair + 2896 {2x}, misc. {15x} = × apparently, × as soon as beautiful (-ly), form, goodly, look [-eth], pattern, to see, seem, visage.

(1) *Marʾeh* and *toʾar* (8389) are descriptive of blessing in Gen 39:6: "And Joseph was *a* goodly [*toʾar*] *person*, and well favoured [*marʾeh*]." **(2)** *Marʾeh* refers more to external "appearance"

(Gen 2:9). **(3)** The word can also connote "sight" as in a range of vision (Lev 13:3) and **(4)** "sight" in the sense of a supernatural "sight" or manifestation (Ex 3:3). Syn.: 4759, 7207, 7209, 7210, 8389. See: TWOT—2095i; BDB—596b, 597b, 909c.

4759. מַרְאָה {12x} **marʾâh**, *mar-aw'*; fem. of 4758; a *vision;* also (caus.) a *mirror:*—looking glasses {1x}, vision {11x}.

Marʾah means "visionary appearance" or "(prophetic) vision" (Gen 46:2) and "looking glasses" (Ex 38:8). Syn.: 4758, 7207, 7209, 7210, 8389. See: TWOT—2095g, 2095h; BDB—597b, 909b, 909c.

4760. מֻרְאָה {1x} **murʾâh**, *moor-aw'*; appar. fem. pass. caus. part. of 7200; something *conspicuous,* i.e. the *craw* of a bird (from its *prominence*):—crop {1x}. See: TWOT—1239b; BDB—597b.

מְראוֹן **M[e]rʾôwn**. See 8112.

4761. מַרְאָשָׁה {1x} **marʾâshâh**, *mar-aw-shaw'*; denom. from 7218; prop. *headship,* i.e. (plur. for collect.) *dominion:*—principality {1x}. See: TWOT—2097f; BDB—912b.

4762. מַרְאֵשָׁה {8x} **Marʾêshâh**, *mar-ay-shaw'*; or

מָרֵשָׁה **Marêshâh**, *mar-ay-shaw'*; formed like 4761; *summit; Mareshah,* the name of two Isr. and of a place in Pal.:—Mareshah {8x}. See: BDB—597b, 601c, 912b.

4763. מְרַאֲשָׁה {8x} **m[e]raʾăshâh**, *mer-ah-ash-aw'*; formed like 4761; prop. a *headpiece,* i.e. (plur. for adv.) *at* (or *as*) the *head-rest* (or pillow):—bolster {5x}, head {1x}, pillow {2x}. See: TWOT—2097f; BDB—597b, 910c, 912a, 912b. comp. 4772.

4764. מֵרַב {3x} **Mêrâb**, *may-rawb'*; from 7231; *increase; Merab,* a daughter of Saul:—*Merab* {3x}. See: BDB—597b.

4765. מַרְבַד {1x} **marbad**, *mar-bad'*; from 7234; a *coverlet:*—covering of tapestry {1x}. See: TWOT—2102a; BDB—597b, 915a.

4766. מַרְבֶּה {2x} **marbeh**, *mar-beh'*; from 7235; prop. *increasing;* as noun, *greatness,* or (adv.) *greatly:*—great {1x}, increase {1x}. See: TWOT—2103b; BDB—597c, 916a.

4767. מִרְבָּה {1x} **mirbâh**, *meer-baw'*; from 7235; *abundance,* i.e. a great quantity:—much {1x}. See: TWOT—2103c; BDB—597c, 916b.

4768. מַרְבִּית {5x} **marbîyth**, *mar-beeth'*; from 7235; a *multitude;* also *offspring;* spec. *interest* (on capital):—greatest part {1x}, greatness {1x}, increase {2x}, multitude {1x}. See: TWOT—2103d; BDB—597c, 916b.

4769. מַרְבֵּץ {2x} **marbêts**, *mar-bates'*; from 7257; a *reclining* place, i.e. *fold* (for flocks):—couching place {1x}, place to lie down {1x}. See: TWOT—2109b; BDB—597c, 918c.

4770. מַרְבֵּק {4x} **marbêq**, *mar-bake'*; from an unused root mean. to *tie* up; a *stall* (for cattle):—× fat {1x}, fatted {1x}, stall {2x}. See: TWOT—2110a; BDB—597c, 918d.

מֹרַג **môrag**. See 4173.

4771. מַרְגּוֹעַ {1x} **margôwaʿ**, *mar-go'-ah*; from 7280; a *resting* place:—rest {1x}. See: TWOT—2117b; BDB—597c, 921b.

4772. מַרְגְּלָה {5x} **marg[e]lâh**, *mar-ghel-aw'*; denom. from 7272; (plur. for collect.) a *footpiece,* i.e. (adv.) *at the foot,* or (direct.) the *foot* itself:—feet {5x}. See: TWOT—2113c; BDB—597c, 920b. comp. 4763.

4773. מַרְגֵּמָה {1x} **margêmah**, *mar-gay-maw'*; from 7275; a *stone*-heap:—sling {1x}. See: TWOT—2114b; BDB—597c, 920c.

4774. מַרְגֵּעָה {1x} **margêʿâh**, *mar-gay-aw'*; from 7280; *rest:*—refreshing {1x}. See: TWOT—2117c; BDB—597c, 921c.

4775. מָרַד {25x} **mârad**, *maw-rad'*; a prim. root; to *rebel:*—rebel {23x}, rebels {1x}, rebellious {1x}. See: TWOT—1240, BDB—597c.

4776. מְרַד {1x} **m[e]rad** (Aram.), *mer-ad'*; from a root corresp. to 4775; *rebellion:*—rebellion {1x}. See: TWOT—2840a; BDB—597c, 1101c.

4777. מֶרֶד {1x} **mered**, *meh'-red*; from 4775; *rebellion:*—rebellion {1x}. See: TWOT—1240a; BDB—597c, 597d, 1101c.

4778. מֶרֶד {2x} **Mered**, *meh'-red;* the same as 4777; *Mered,* an Isr.:—*Mered* {2x}. See: BDB—597d.

4779. מָרָד {1x} **mârâd** (Aram.), *maw-rawd'*; from the same as 4776; *rebellious:*—rebellious {1x}. See: TWOT—2840b; BDB—1101c.

4780. מַרְדּוּת {1x} **mardûwth**, *mar-dooth'*; from 4775; *rebelliousness:*—× rebellious {1x}. See: TWOT—1240b; BDB—597d.

4781. מְרֹדָךְ {1x} **M[e]rôdâk**, *mer-o-dawk'*; of for. der.; *Merodak,* a Bab. idol:—Merodach {1x}. comp. 4757. See: TWOT—1241; BDB—597d.

4782. מָרְדְּכַי {60x} **Mord[e]kay**, *mor-dek-ah'-ee*; of for. der.; *Mordecai,* an Isr.:—Mordecai {60x}. See: BDB—598a.

4783. מֻרְדָּף {1x} **murdâph**, *moor-dawf'*; from 7291; *persecuted:*—persecuted {1x}. See: TWOT—2124a; BDB—598a, 022a, 923a.

4784. מָרָה {44x} **mârâh**, *maw-raw'*; a prim. root; to *be* (caus. *make*) *bitter* (or unpleasant); (fig.) to *rebel* (or resist; caus. to *provoke*):—rebel {19x}, rebellious {9x}, provoke {7x}, disobedient {2x}, against {1x}, bitter {1x}, changed {1x}, disobeyed {1x}, grievously {1x}, provocation {1x}, rebels {1x}.

Marah means "to rebel, be contentious." **(1)** *Marah* signifies an opposition to someone motivated by pride: **(1a)** "If a man have a stubborn [5637 - *carar*] and rebellious [*marah*] son, which will not obey the voice of his father . . ." (Deut 21:18). **(1b)** The sense comes out more clearly in Is 3:8: "For Jerusalem is ruined, and Judah is fallen: because their tongue and their doings *are* against the LORD, to provoke the eyes of his glory." **(2)** More particularly, the word generally connotes a rebellious attitude against God. Several prepositions are used to indicate the object of rebellion (*ʿim, et,* generally translated as "against"): **(2a)** ". . . Ye have been rebellious against [*ʿim*] the LORD" (Deut 9:7); **(2b)** ". . . She hath been rebellious against [*et*] me . . ." (Jer 4:17). **(3)** The primary meaning of *marah* is "to disobey." Several passages attest to this: **(3a)** ". . . Forasmuch as thou hast disobeyed the mouth of the LORD, and hast not kept the commandment which the LORD thy God commanded thee" (1 Kin 13:21); **(3b)** 1 Kin 13:26: "It is the man of God, who was disobedient unto the word of the LORD. . . ."

(4) The Old Testament sometimes specifically states that someone "rebelled" **(4a)** against the Lord; at other times it may refer to **(4b)** a rebelling against the word of the Lord (Ps 105:28; 107:11), or **(4c)** against the word of God (cf. Num 20:24; Deut 1:26, 43; 9:23; 1 Sa 12:14–15). **(4d)** The intent of the Hebrew is to signify the act of defying the command of God: "The LORD is righteous; for I have rebelled against his commandment . . ." (Lam 1:18). **(5)** The verb *marah* is at times strengthened by a form of the verb *carar* (5637 - "to be stubborn"): "[They] might not be as their fathers, a stubborn [*carar*] and rebellious [*marah*] generation; a generation that set not their heart aright . . ." (Ps 78:8; cf. Deut 21:18, 20; Jer 5:23). **(6)** An individual (Deut 21:18, 20), a nation (Num 20:24), and a city (Zeph 3:1) may be described as "being rebellious." **(7)** Zephaniah gave a vivid image of the nature of the rebellious spirit: "Woe to her that is filthy and polluted, to the oppressing city! She obeyed not the voice; she received not correction; she trusted not in the LORD; she drew not near to her God" (Zeph 3:1–2). See: TWOT—1242; BDB—597b, 598a, 598c.

4785. מָרָה {5x} **Mârâh**, *maw-raw';* the same as 4751 fem.; *bitter; Marah,* a place in the Desert:—*Marah* {5x}. See: BDB—598c, 600d.

מֹרֶה **Môreh**. See 4175.

4786. מֹרָה {1x} **môrâh**, *mo-raw'*; from 4843; *bitterness,* i.e. (fig.) *trouble:*—grief {1x}. See: TWOT—1248d; BDB—598c, 601a.

4787. מָרָּה {1x} **mârrâh**, *mawr-raw'*; a form of 4700, *trouble:*—bitterness {1x}. See: TWOT—1248c; BDB—598c, 601a.

4788. מָרוּד {3x} **mârûwd**, *maw-rood'*; from 7300 in the sense of *maltreatment,* an *outcast;* (abstr.) *destitution:*—cast out {1x}, misery {2x}. See: TWOT—2129a; BDB—598c, 924a.

4789. מֵרוֹז {1x} **Mêrôwz**, *may-roze'*; of uncert. der.; *Meroz,* a place in Pal.:—Meroz {1x}. See: BDB—72d, 598c.

4790. מְרוֹחַ {1x} **m[e]rôwach**, *mer-o-akh'*; from 4799; *bruised,* i.e. *emasculated:*—broken {1x}. See: BDB—598c.

4791. מָרוֹם {54x} **mârôwm**, *maw-rome'*; from 7311; *altitude,* i.e. concr. (an *elevated place*), abstr. (*elevation*), fig. (*elation*), or adv. (*aloft*):—high {29x}, height {10x}, above {5x}, high places {4x}, highest places {1x}, dignity {1x}, haughty {1x}, loftily {1x}, high ones {1x}, upward {1x}.

Marowm means "higher plane; height, high social position." **(1)** In its first biblical occurrence (Judg 5:18), *marowm* means "a higher plane on the surface of the earth." **(2)** Job 16:19 and Is 33:5 contain the word with the meaning of "the height" as the abode of God. **(3)** Job 5:11 uses the word to refer to "a high social position." **(4)** *Marowm* can also signify "self-exaltation" (2 Kin 19:22; Ps 73:8). See: TWOT—2133h; BDB—598c, 928d.

4792. מֵרוֹם {2x} **Mêrôwm**, *may-rome'*; formed like 4791; *height; Merom,* a lake in Pal.:—Merom {2x}. See: BDB—598c.

4793. מֵרוֹץ {1x} **mêrôwts**, *may-rotes'*; from 7323; a *run* (the trial of speed):—race {1x}. See: TWOT—2137a; BDB—598c, 930c.

4794. מְרוּצָה {4x} **m[e]rûwtsâh**, *mer-oo-tsaw'*; or

מְרֻצָה **m[e]rûtsâh**, *mer-oo-tsaw'*; fem. of 4793; a *race* (the act), whether the manner or the progress:—course {2x}, running {2x}. See: TWOT—2137a; BDB—598c, 599d, 930c, 954d. comp. 4835.

4795. מָרוּק {1x} **mârûwq**, *maw-rook'*; from 4838; prop. *rubbed;* but used abstr. a *rubbing* (with perfumery):—purification {1x}. See: TWOT—1246a; BDB—598c, 599d.

מְרוֹר **m^e^rôwr**. See 4844.

מְרוֹרָה **m^e^rôwrâh**. See 4846.

4796. מָרוֹת {1x} **Mârôwth**, *maw-rohth'*; plur. of 4751 fem.; *bitter* springs; *Maroth,* a place in Pal.:—Maroth {1x}. See: BDB—598c.

4797. מִרְזַח {1x} **mirzach**, *meer-zakh'*; from an unused root mean. to *scream;* a *cry,* i.e. (of joy), a *revel:*—banquet {1x}. See: TWOT—2140a; BDB—931a.

4798. מַרְזֵחַ {1x} **marzêach**, *mar-zay'-akh;* formed like 4797; a *cry,* i.e. (of grief) a *lamentation:*—mourning {1x}. See: TWOT—2140a; BDB—598d, 931a.

4799. מָרַח {1x} **mârach**, *maw-rakh'*; a prim. root; prop. to *soften* by rubbing or pressure; hence, (medicinally) to *apply* as an emollient:—lay for a plaister {1x}. See: TWOT—1243; BDB—598d.

4800. מֶרְחָב {6x} **merchâb**, *mer-khawb'*; from 7337; *enlargement,* either lit. (an *open space,* usually in a good sense), or fig. (*liberty*):—breadth {1x}, large place (room) {5x}. See: TWOT—2143c; BDB—598d, 932c.

4801. מֶרְחָק {18x} **merchâq**, *mer-khawk'*; from 7368; *remoteness,* i.e. (concr.) a *distant* place; often (adv.) *from afar:*—far {12x}, far off {4x}, afar off {1x}, far countries {1x}. See: TWOT—2151c; BDB—598d, 935d. See also 1023.

4802. מַרְחֶשֶׁת {2x} **marchesheth**, *mar-kheh'-sheth;* from 7370; a *stew*-pan:—frying pan {2x}. See: TWOT—2152a; BDB—598d, 935d.

4803. מָרַט {9x} **mâraṭ**, *maw-rat'*; a prim. root; to *polish;* by impl. to *make bald* (the head), to *gall* (the shoulder); also, to *sharpen:*—furbished {3x}, fallen {2x}, plucked off {2x}, peeled {1x}, plucked off their hair {1x}. See: TWOT—1244; BDB—590c, 598d, 1101d.

4804. מְרַט {1x} **m^e^raṭ** (Aram.), *mer-at'*; corresp. to 4803; to *pull* off:—be plucked {1x}. See: TWOT—2841; BDB—1101d.

4805. מְרִי {23x} **m^e^rîy**, *mer-ee'*; from 4784; *bitterness,* i.e. (fig.) *rebellion;* concr. *bitter,* or *rebellious:*—rebellious {17x}, rebellion {4x}, bitter {1x}, rebels {1x}.

I. *Meriy,* as a noun, means "rebellion." This word occurs infrequently: "For I know thy rebellion, and thy stiff neck . . ." (Deut 31:27; cf. Prov 17:11). **II. *Meriy,* as an adjective,** means "rebellious." **(1)** This word occurs 23 times, mainly in Ezekiel. **(2)** The word modifies "house" (referring to Israel) in Eze 2:8: ". . . Be not thou rebellious like that rebellious house. . . ." See: TWOT—1242a; BDB—598b, 599a.

4806. מְרִיא {8x} **m^e^rîy'**, *mer-ee'*; from 4754 in the sense of *grossness,* through the idea of *domineering* (comp. 4756); *stall-fed;* often (as noun) a *beeve:*—fatling {3x}, fat cattle {3x}, fed beast {1x}, fat beast {1x}. See: TWOT—1239a; BDB—597a.

4807. מְרִיב בַּעַל {3x} **M^e^rîyb Ba'al**, *mer-eeb' bah'-al;* from 7378 and 1168; *quarreller of Baal; Merib-Baal,* an epithet of Gideon:—Merib-baal {3x}. See: BDB—565a, 599a, 937c. comp. 4810.

4808. מְרִיבָה {7x} **m^e^rîybâh**, *mer-ee-baw'*; from 7378; *quarrel:*—strife {5x}, Meribahkadesh + 6946 {1x}, provocation {1x}. See: TWOT—2159c; BDB—599a, 937b.

4809. מְרִיבָה {9x} **M^e^rîybâh**, *mer-ee-baw'*; the same as 4808; *Meribah,* the name of two places in the Desert:—Meribah {6x}, strife {3x}. See: BDB—599a, 937b.

4810. מְרִי בַעַל {1x} **M^e^rîy Ba'al**, *mer-ee' bah'-al;* from 4805 and 1168; *rebellion of* (i.e. *against*) Baal; *Meri-Baal,* an epithet of Gideon:—Meri-baal {1x}. See: BDB—599a, 937c. comp. 4807.

4811. מְרָיָה {1x} **M^e^râyâh**, *mer-aw-yaw'*; from 4784; *rebellion; Merajah,* an Isr.:—Meraiah {1x}. See: BDB—599a. comp. 3236.

מֹרִיָּה **Môrîyâh**. See 4179.

4812. מְרָיוֹת {7x} **M^e^râyôwth**, *mer-aw-yohth'*; plur. of 4811; *rebellious; Merajoth,* the name of two Isr.:—Meraioth {7x}. See: BDB—599a.

4813. מִרְיָם {15x} **Miryâm**, *meer-yawm'*; from 4805; *rebelliously; Mirjam,* the name of two Israelitesses:—Miriam {15x}. See: BDB—599b.

4814. מְרִירוּת {1x} **m^e^rîyrûwth**, *mer-ee-rooth'*; from 4843; *bitterness,* i.e. (fig.) *grief:*—bitterness {1x}. See: TWOT—1248i; BDB—599b, 601b.

4815. מְרִירִי {1x} **m^e^rîyrîy**, *mer-ee-ree'*; from 4843; *bitter,* i.e. *poisonous:*—bitter {1x}. See: TWOT—1248h; BDB—599b, 601b.

4816. מֹרֶךְ {1x} **môrek**, *mo'-rek;* perh. from 7401; *softness,* i.e. (fig.) *fear:*—faintness {1x}. See: TWOT—2164c; BDB—599b, 940b.

4817. מֶרְכָּב {3x} **merkâb**, *mer-kawb';* from 7392; a *chariot;* also a *seat* (in a vehicle):—chariot {1x}, covering {1x}, saddle {1x}. See: TWOT—2163e; BDB—599b, 939c.

4818. מֶרְכָּבָה {44x} **merkâbâh**, *mer-kaw-baw'*; fem. of 4817; a *chariot:*—chariot {44x}.

Merkabah represents a war-chariot (Ex 14:25), which may have been used as a chariot of honor (Gen 41:43) and may also be translated traveling coach or cart (2 Kin 5:21). Syn.: 7393. See: TWOT—2163f; BDB—599b, 939c. See also 1024.

4819. מַרְכֹּלֶת {1x} **markôleth**, *mar-ko'-leth;* from 7402; a *mart:*—merchandise {1x}. See: TWOT—2165c; BDB—940c.

4820. מִרְמָה {39x} **mirmâh**, *meer-maw'*; from 7411 in the sense of *deceiving; fraud:*—deceit {20x}, deceitful {8x}, deceitfully {3x}, false {2x}, guile {2x}, feigned {1x}, craft {1x}, subtilty {1x}, treachery {1x}. See: TWOT—2169b; BDB—599b, 941b.

4821. מִרְמָה {1x} **Mirmâh**, *meer-maw'*; the same as 4820; *Mirmah,* an Isr.:—Mirma {1x}. See: BDB—599b, 941b.

4822. מְרֵמוֹת {6x} **M^e^rêmôwth**, *mer-ay-mohth'*; plur. from 7311; *heights; Meremoth,* the name of two Isr.:—Meremoth {6x}. See: BDB—599b.

4823. מִרְמָס {7x} **mirmâç**, *meer-mawce'*; from 7429; *abasement* (the act or the thing):—tread down {4x}, tread {2x}, trodden under foot {1x}. See: TWOT—2176a; BDB—599b, 942d.

4824. מֵרֹנֹתִי {2x} **Mêrônôthîy**, *may-ro-no-thee'*; patrial from an unused noun; a *Meronothite,* or inhab. of some (otherwise unknown) Meronoth.:—Meronothite {2x}. See: BDB—599c.

4825. מֶרֶס {1x} **Mereç**, *meh'-res;* of for. der.; *Meres,* a Pers.:—Meres {1x}. See: BDB—599c.

4826. מַרְסְנָא {1x} **Març^e^nâ'**, *mar-sen-aw'*; of for. der.; *Marsena,* a Pers.:—Marsena {1x}. See: BDB—599c.

4827. מֵרַע {1x} **mêra'**, *may-rah'*; from 7489; used as (abstr.) noun, *wickedness:*—do mischief {1x}. See: TWOT—2186f; BDB—949c, 949d.

4828. מֵרֵעַ {7x} **mêrêa'**, *may-ray'-ah;* from 7462 in the sense of *companionship;* a *friend:*—companion {4x}, friend {3x}. See: TWOT—2186f; BDB—599c, 946c.

4829. מִרְעֶה {13x} **mir'eh**, *meer-eh';* from 7462 in the sense of *feeding; pasture* (the place or the act); also the *haunt* of wild animals:—feeding place {1x}, pasture {12x}. See: TWOT—2185b; BDB—599c, 945c.

4830. מִרְעִית {10x} **mir'îyth**, *meer-eeth'*; from 7462 in the sense of *feeding; pasturage;* concr. a *flock:*—flock {1x}, pasture {9x}. See: TWOT—2185c; BDB—945c.

4831. מַרְעֲלָה {1x} **Mar'ălâh**, *mar-al-aw'*; from 7477; perh. *earthquake; Maralah,* a place in Pal.:—*Maralah* {1x}. See: BDB—599c, 947a.

4832. מַרְפֵּא {16x} **marpê'**, *mar-pay';* from 7495; prop. *curative,* i.e. lit. (concr.) a *medicine,* or (abstr.) a *cure;* fig. (concr.) *deliverance,* or (abstr.) *placidity:*—health {5x}, healing {3x}, remedy {3x}, incurable + 369 {1x}, cure {1x}, sound {1x}, wholesome {1x}, yielding {1x}. See: TWOT—2196c; BDB—599c, 951b.

4833. מִרְפָּשׂ {1x} **mirpâs**, *meer-paws';* from 7515; *muddled* water:—that which . . . have fouled {1x}. See: TWOT—2199a; BDB—590c, 952c.

4834. מָרַץ {4x} **mârats**, *maw-rats';* a prim. root; prop. to *press,* i.e. (fig.) to *be pungent* or vehement; to *irritate:*—embolden {1x}, be forcible {1x}, grievous {1x}, sore {1x}. See: TWOT—1245; BDB—599c.

4835. מְרֻצָה {1x} **m^e^rûtsâh**, *mer-oo-tsaw';* from 7533; *oppression:*—violence {1x}. See: TWOT—2212b; BDB—598c, 599d, 930d, 954d. See also 4794.

4836. מַרְצֵעַ {2x} **martsêa'**, *mar-tsay'-ah;* from 7527; an *awl:*—aul {2x}. See: TWOT—2209a; BDB—599d, 954b.

4837. מַרְצֶפֶת {1x} **martsepheth**, *mar-tseh'-feth;* from 7528; a *pavement:*—pavement {1x}. See: TWOT—2210b; BDB—599d, 954b.

4838. מָרַק {3x} **mâraq**, *maw-rak';* a prim. root; to *polish;* by impl. to *sharpen;* also to *rinse:*—bright {1x}, furbish {1x}, scour {1x}. See: TWOT—1246; BDB—599d.

4839. מָרָק {3x} **mârâq**, *maw-rawk';* from 4838; *soup* (as if a *rinsing*):—broth {3x}. See: TWOT—1247a; BDB—600a, 601d. See also 6564.

4840. מֶרְקָח {1x} **merqâch**, *mer-kawkh';* from 7543; a *spicy* herb:—× sweet {1x}. See: TWOT—2215f; BDB—600a, 955c.

4841. מֶרְקָחָה {2x} **merqâchâh**, *mer-kaw-khaw';* fem. of 4840; abstr. a *seasoning* (with spicery); concr. an *unguent-kettle* (for preparing spiced oil):—pot of ointment {1x}, × well {1x}. See: TWOT—2215g; BDB—600a, 955c.

4842. מִרְקַחַת {3x} **mirqachath**, *meer-kakh'-ath;* from 7543; an aromatic *unguent;* also an *unguent-pot:*—prepared by the apothecaries' art {1x}, compound {1x}, ointment {1x}. See: TWOT—2215h; BDB—600a, 955c.

4843. מָרַר {16x} **mârar**, *maw-rar';* a prim. root; prop. to *trickle* [see 4752]; but used only as a denom. from 4751; to *be* (caus. *make*) *bitter* (lit. or fig.):—bitterness {3x}, bitter {2x}, bitterly {2x}, choler {2x}, grieved {2x}, vexed {2x}, bitterness + 4751 {1x}, grieved him {1x}, provoke {1x}. See: TWOT—1248; BDB—600a.

4844. מְרֹר {3x} **m^erôr**, *mer-ore';* or

מְרוֹר **m^erôwr**, *mer-ore';* from 4843; a *bitter* herb:—bitter {2x}, bitterness {1x}. See: TWOT—1248e; BDB—601a.

4845. מְרֵרָה {1x} **m^erêrâh**, *mer-ay-raw';* from 4843; *bile* (from its bitterness):—gall {1x}. See: TWOT—1248g; BDB—601a.

4846. מְרֹרָה {4x} **m^erôrâh**, *mer-o-raw';* or

מְרוֹרָה **m^erôwrâh**, *mer-o-raw';* from 4843; prop. *bitterness;* concr. a *bitter thing;* spec. *bile;* also *venom* (of a serpent):—bitter {1x}, bitter thing {1x}, gall {2x}. See: TWOT—1248f; BDB—601a.

4847. מְרָרִי {39x} **M^erârîy**, *mer-aw-ree';* from 4843; *bitter; Merari,* an Isr.:—Merari {39x}. See: BDB—601b. See also 4848.

4848. מְרָרִי {1x} **M^erârîy**, *mer-aw-ree';* from 4847; a *Merarite* (collect.), or desc. of Merari:—Merarites {1x}. See: BDB—601b.

מָרֵשָׁה **Mârêshâh**. See 4762.

4849. מִרְשַׁעַת {1x} **mirshaʻath**, *meer-shah'-ath;* from 7561; a female *wicked doer:*—wicked woman {1x}. See: TWOT—2222d; BDB—601c, 958a.

4850. מְרָתַיִם {1x} **M^erâthayim**, *mer-aw-thah'-yim;* dual of 4751 fem.; *double bitterness; Merathajim,* an epithet of Bab.:—Merathaim {1x}.

The noun *merathayim* means "double rebellion." This reference to Babylon (Jer 50:21) is translated "Merathaim". See: BDB—601c.

4851. מַשׁ {1x} **Mash**, *mash;* of for. der.; *Mash,* a son of Aram, and the people desc. from him:—*Mash* {1x}. See: BDB—602a.

4852. מֵשָׁא {1x} **Mêshâ'**, *may-shaw';* of for. der.; *Mesha,* a place in Arabia:—*Mesha* {1x}. See: BDB—602a,.

4853. מַשָּׂא {66x} **massâ'**, *mas-saw';* from 5375; a *burden;* spec. *tribute,* or (abstr.) *porterage;* fig. an *utterance,* chiefly a *doom,* espec. *singing;* ment. *desire:*—burden {57x}, song {3x}, prophecy {2x}, set {1x}, exaction {1x}, carry away {1x}, tribute {1x}.

Massa' means "load; burden; tribute; delight." **(1)** The word means that which is borne by a man, an ass, a mule, or a camel: "If thou see the ass of him that hateth thee lying under his burden, and wouldest forbear to help him . . ." (Ex 23:5—the first occurrence). **(2)** A "load" may be hung on a peg (Is 22:25). **(3)** This word is used figuratively of spiritual "loads" one is carrying: "For mine iniquities are gone over mine head: as a heavy burden they are too heavy for me" (Ps 38:4). **(4)** *Massa'* means "burden" in the sense of something burdensome, a hardship. Moses asked God: ". . . Wherefore have I not found favor in thy sight, that thou layest the burden of all this people upon me?" (Num 11:11). **(5)** Once the word represents that which is borne to a lord, a "tribute": "Also some of the Philistines brought Jehoshaphat presents, and tribute silver . . ." (2 Chr 17:11). **(6)** In Eze 24:25 *massa'* bears a unique meaning: "Also, thou son of man, *shall it* not *be* in the day when I take from them their strength, the joy of their glory, the desire of their eyes, and that whereupon they set [*massa'*] their minds, their sons and their daughters."

(7) *Massa'* means "utterance" or "oracle," a "weighty message": "Then said Jehu to Bidkar his captain, Take up, *and* cast him in the portion of the field of Naboth the Jezreelite: for remember how that, when I and thou rode together after Ahab his father, the LORD laid this burden [*massa'*] upon him;" (2 Kin 9:25). **(8)** In Jer 23:33–38 the word appears to connote both a burden and an oracle. **(9)** By a burden we are to understand the message laid on the mind of the prophet, and by him pressed on the attention of the people. The message of the Lord ought not to have been regarded as a burden by the people; but it could not fail to be realized as such by the prophets, who at times felt heavily laden with the weight of their message (Jer 20:9; Nah 1:1, Hab 1:1). See: TWOT—1421d, 1421e; BDB—601d, 672c, 672d.

4854. מַשָּׂא {2x} **Massâ'**, *mas-saw';* the same as 4853; *burden; Massa,* a son of Ishmael:—*Massa* {2x}. See: BDB—601d, 672d.

4855. מַשָּׁא {2x} **mashshâ'**, *mash-shaw';* from 5383; a *loan;* by impl. *interest* on a debt:—exaction {1x}, usury {1x}. See: TWOT—1424a; BDB—600d, 601d, 602a, 673d.

4856. מַשֹּׂא {1x} **massô'**, *mas-so';* from 5375; *partiality* (as a *lifting* up):—respect {1x}. See: TWOT—1421f; BDB—601d, 673a.

4857. מַשְׁאָב {1x} **mash'âb**, *mash-awb';* from 7579; a *trough* for cattle to drink from:—place of drawing water {1x}. See: TWOT—2299.1a; BDB—602b, 980c.

מְשֹׁאָה **m^eshô'âh**. See 4875.

4858. מַשָּׂאָה {1x} **massâ'âh**, *mas-saw-aw';* from 5375; a *conflagration* (from the *rising* of smoke):—burden {1x}. See: TWOT—1421g; BDB—601d, 673a.

4859. מַשָּׁאָה {2x} **mashshâ'âh**, *mash-shaw-aw';* fem. of 4855; a *loan:*—anything {1x}, debt {1x}. See: TWOT—1424b; BDB—602a, 673d.

מַשֻּׁאָה **mashshû'âh**. See 4876.

4860. מַשָּׁאוֹן {1x} **mashshâ'ôwn**, *mash-shaw-ohn';* from 5377; *dissimulation:*—deceit {1x}. See: TWOT—1425a; BDB—602b, 674b.

4861. מִשְׁאָל {2x} **Mish'âl**, *mish-awl';* from 7592; *request; Mishal,* a place in Pal.:—*Mishal* {1x}, Misheal {1x}. See: TWOT—1425a; BDB—602b. comp. 4913.

4862. מִשְׁאָלָה {2x} **mish'âlâh**, *mish-aw-law';* from 7592; a *request:*—desire {1x}, petition {1x}. See: TWOT—2303b; BDB—602b, 982c.

4863. מִשְׁאֶרֶת {4x} **mish'ereth**, *mish-eh'-reth;* from 7604 in the orig. sense of *swelling;* a *kneading-trough* (in which the dough *rises*):—kneading trough {2x}, store {2x}. See: TWOT—1252; BDB—602b, 985a.

4864. מַשְׂאֵת {15x} **mas'êth**, *mas-ayth';* from 5375; prop. (abstr.) a *raising* (as of the hands in prayer), or *rising* (of flame); fig. an *utterance;* concr. a *beacon* (as *raised*); a *present* (as taken), *mess,* or *tribute;* fig. a *reproach* (as a burden):—burden {3x}, mess {3x}, collection {2x}, flame {2x}, gifts {1x}, oblations {1x}, reward {1x}, sign {1x}, lifting up {1x}. See: TWOT—1421h; BDB—601d, 673a.

מֹשָׁב **môshâb**. See 4186.

מְשֻׁבָה **m^eshûbâh**. See 4878.

4865. מִשְׁבְּצָה {9x} **mishb^etsâh**, *mish-bets-aw';* from 7660; a *brocade;* by anal. a (reticulated) *setting* of a gem:—ouches {8x}, wrought {1x}. See. TWOT—2320b; BDB—602b, 990b.

4866. מִשְׁבֵּר {3x} **mishbêr**, *mish-bare';* from 7665; the *orifice* of the womb (from which the fetus *breaks* forth):—birth {2x}, breaking forth {1x}. See: TWOT—2321c; BDB—602b, 991b.

4867. מִשְׁבָּר {5x} **mishbâr**, *mish-bawr';* from 7665; a *breaker* (of the sea):—billows {1x}, waves {4x}. See: TWOT—2321d; BDB—602b, 991c.

4868. מִשְׁבָּת {1x} **mishbâth**, *mish-bawth';* from 7673; *cessation,* i.e. destruction:—sabbaths {1x}. See: TWOT—2323e; BDB—602b, 992d.

4869. מִשְׂגָּב {16x} **misgâb**, *mis-gawb';* from 7682; prop. a *cliff* (or other *lofty* or *inaccessible* place); abstr. *altitude;* fig. a *refuge:*—defence {7x}, refuge {5x}, high tower {3x}, high fort {1x}, *Misgab* {1x}. See: TWOT—2234a; BDB—601d, 960d.

4869. מִשְׂגָּב {1x} **misgâb**, *mis-gawb'; Misgab,* a place in Moab:—*Misgab* {1x}.

4870. מִשְׁגֶּה {1x} **mishgeh**, *mish-gay';* from 7686; an *error:*—oversight {1x}. See: TWOT—2325b; BDB—602b, 993b.

4871. מָשָׁה {3x} **mâshâh**, *maw-shaw';* a prim. root; to *pull* out (lit. or fig.):—draw (out) {3x}. See: TWOT—1253; BDB—602b.

4872. מֹשֶׁה {766x} **Môsheh**, *mo-sheh';* from 4871; *drawing* out (of the water), i.e. *rescued; Mosheh,* the Isr. lawgiver:—Moses {766x}. See: TWOT—1254; BDB—602c, 1101d.

4873. מֹשֶׁה {1x} **Môsheh** (Aram.), *mo-sheh';* corresp. to 4872:—Moses {1x}. See: BDB—1101d.

4874. מַשֶּׁה {1x} **mashsheh**, *mash-sheh';* from 5383; a *debt:*—creditor + 1167 {1x}. See: TWOT—1427b; BDB—602d, 674c.

4875. מְשׁוֹאָה {3x} **m^eshôw'âh**, *mesh-o-aw';* or

מְשֹׁאָה **m^eshô'âh**, *mesh-o-aw';* from the same as 7722; (a) *ruin,* abstr. (the act) or concr. (the wreck):—desolation {1x}, waste {2x}. See: TWOT—2339b; BDB—602b, 602d, 674b, 996c.

4876. מַשּׁוּאָה {2x} **mashshûw'âh**, *mash-shoo-aw';* or

מַשֻּׁאָה **mashshû'âh**, *mash-shoo-aw';* for 4875; *ruin:*—desolation {1x}, destruction {1x}. See: TWOT—2339b; BDB—601d, 602b, 602f, 674b.

4877. מְשׁוֹבָב {1x} **M^eshôwbâb**, *mesh-o-bawb';* from 7725; *returned; Meshobab,* an Isr.:—Meshobab {1x}. See: BDB—1000c.

4878. מְשׁוּבָה {12x} **m^eshûwbâh**, *mesh-oo-baw';* or

מְשֻׁבָה **m^eshûbâh**, *mesh-oo-baw';* from 7725; *apostasy:*—backsliding {11x}, turning away {1x}.

Meshubah means "backturning; apostasy." This noun occurs 12 times, and it refers to "backsliding" in Hos 14:4: "I will heal their backsliding, I will love them freely: for mine anger is turned away from him." See: TWOT—2340c; BDB—602b, 602d, 1000b.

4879. מְשׁוּגָה {1x} **mᵉshûwgâh**, *mesh-oo-gaw';* from an unused root mean. to *stray; mistake:*—error {1x}. See: BDB—602d, 1000c.

4880. מָשׁוֹט {2x} **mâshôwt**, *maw-shote';* or

מִשְׁוֹט **mishshôwt**, *mish-shote';* from 7751; an *oar:*—oar {2x}. See: TWOT—2344e; BDB—602d, 1002b.

4881. מְשׂוּכָה {2x} **mᵉsûwkâh**, *mes-oo-kaw';* or

מְשֻׂכָה **mᵉsûkâh**, *mes-oo-kaw';* from 7753; a *hedge:*—hedge {2x}. See: TWOT—2241a; BDB—601d, 962b, 968a.

4882. מְשׁוּסָה {1x} **mᵉshûwçâh**, *mesh-oo-saw';* from an unused root mean. to *plunder; spoilation:*—spoil {1x}. See: TWOT—2426a; BDB—602d, 1042c, 1042d.

4883. מַשּׂוֹר {1x} **massôwr**, *mas-sore';* from an unused root mean. to *rasp;* a *saw:*—saw {1x}. See: TWOT—1423a; BDB—601d, 673d, 965a.

4884. מְשׂוּרָה {4x} **mᵉsûwrâh**, *mes-oo-raw';* from an unused root mean. appar. to *divide;* a *measure* (for liquids):—measure {4x}. See: TWOT—1250; BDB—601d.

4885. מָשׂוֹשׂ {17x} **mâsôws**, *maw-soce';* from 7797; *delight,* concr. (the cause or object) or abstr. (the feeling):—joy {12x}, mirth {3x}, rejoice {2x}. See: TWOT—2246b; BDB—601d, 965c.

4886. מָשַׁח {69x} **mâshach**, *maw-shakh';* a prim. root; to *rub* with oil, i.e. to *anoint;* by impl. to *consecrate;* also to *paint:*—anoint {68x}, painted {1x}.

Mashach means "to anoint, smear, consecrate." **(1)** The word is found for the first time in the Old Testament in Gen 31:13: ". . . where thou anointedst the pillar, and . . . vowedst a vow unto me . . ." **(1a)** This use illustrates the idea of anointing something or someone as an act of consecration. **(1b)** The basic meaning of the word, however, is simply to "smear" something on an object. **(1c)** Usually oil is involved, but it could be other substances, such as paint or dye (cf. Jer 22:14). **(2)** The expression "anoint the shield" in Is 21:5 probably has more to do with lubrication than consecration in that context. **(3)** When unleavened bread is "tempered with oil" in Ex 29:2, it is basically equivalent to our act of buttering bread. **(4)** The Old Testament most commonly uses *mashach* to indicate "anointing" in the sense of a special setting apart for an office or function. **(4a)** Thus, Elisha was "anointed" to be a prophet (1 Kin 19:16). **(4b)** More typically, kings were "anointed" for their office (1 Sa 16:12; 1 Kin 1:39). **(5)** Vessels used in the worship at the sacred shrine (both tabernacle and temple) were consecrated for use by "anointing" them (Ex 29:36; 30:26; 40:9–10). **(6)** In fact, the recipe for the formulation of this "holy anointing oil" is given in detail in Ex 30:22–25. See: TWOT—1255; BDB—602d, 1101d.

4887. מְשַׁח {2x} **mᵉshach** (Aram.), *mesh-akh';* from a root corresp. to 4886; *oil:*—oil {2x}. See: TWOT—2842; BDB—1101d.

4888. מִשְׁחָה {26x} **mishchâh**, *meesh-khaw';* or

מׇשְׁחָה **moshchâh**, *mosh-khaw';* from 4886; *unction* (the act); by impl. a consecratory *gift:*—anointing {24x}, anointed {1x}, ointment {1x}.

This noun occurs 26 times and only in Exodus, Leviticus, and Numbers. It always follows the Hebrew word for oil. The first occurrence is Ex 25:6: "Oil for the light, spices for anointing oil, and for sweet incense." See: TWOT—1255a, 1255b; BDB—603b, 603c.

4889. מַשְׁחִית {11x} **mashchîyth**, *mash-kheeth';* from 7843; *destructive,* i.e. (as noun) *destruction,* lit. (spec. a *snare*) or fig. (*corruption*):—destroy {4x}, corruption {2x}, destruction {2x}, set a trap {1x}, destroying {1x}, utterly {1x}. See: TWOT—2370a; BDB—603d, 1008c.

4890. מִשְׂחָק {1x} **mischâq** *mis-khawk';* from 7831; a *laughing-stock:*—scorn {1x}. See: TWOT—1905f; BDB—601d, 966a.

4891. מִשְׁחָר {1x} **mishchâr**, *mish-khawr';* from 7836 in the sense of day *breaking; dawn:*—morning {1x}. See: TWOT—2369b; BDB—603d, 1007d.

4892. מַשְׁחֵת {1x} **mashchêth**, *mash-khayth';* for 4889; *destruction:*—destroying {1x}. See: TWOT—2370b; BDB—603d, 1008c.

4893. מִשְׁחָת {2x} **mishchâth**, *mish-khawth';* or

מׇשְׁחָת **mâshchâth**, *mosh-khawth';* from 7843; *disfigurement:*—corruption {1x}, marred {1x}. See: TWOT—2370c; BDB—603d, 1008c.

4894. מִשְׁטוֹחַ {3x} **mishṭôwach**, *mish-to'-akh;* or

מִשְׁטַח **mishṭach**, *mish-takh';* from 7849; a *spreading*-place:—spread forth {1x}, spread upon {1x}, spreading {1x}. See: TWOT—2372b; BDB—603d, 1009a.

4895. מַשְׂטֵמָה {2x} **masṭêmâh**, *mas-tay-maw';* from the same as 7850; *enmity:*—hatred {2x}. See: TWOT—2251a; BDB—601d, 966b.

4896. מִשְׁטָר {1x} **mishṭâr**, *mish-tawr';* from 7860; *jurisdiction:*—dominion {1x}. See: TWOT—2374b; BDB—603d, 1009c.

4897. מֶשִׁי {2x} **meshîy**, *meh'-shee;* from 4871; *silk* (as *drawn* from the cocoon):—silk {2x}. See: TWOT—1256; BDB—603d.

מֻשִׁי **Mushîy**. See 4187.

4898. מְשֵׁיזַבְאֵל {3x} **Mᵉshêyzab'êl**, *mesh-ay-zab-ale';* from an equiv. to 7804 and 410; *delivered of God; Meshezabel,* an Isr.:—Meshezabeel {3x}. See: TWOT—1256; BDB—604a, 1115a.

4899. מָשִׁיחַ {39x} **mâshîyach**, *maw-shee'-akh;* from 4886; *anointed;* usually a *consecrated* person (as a king, priest, or saint); spec. the *Messiah:*—anointed {37x}, Messiah {2x}.

Mashiyach means "anointed one." **(1)** A word that is important both to Old Testament and New Testament understandings is the noun *mashiyach,* which gives us the term messiah. **(2)** As is true of the verb, *mashiyach* implies an anointing for a special office or function. **(2a)** Thus, David refused to harm Saul because Saul was "the Lord's anointed" (1 Sa 24:6). **(2b)** The Psalms often express the messianic ideals attached to the Davidic line by using the phrase "the Lord's anointed" (Ps 2:2; 18:50; 89:38, 51). **(3)** Interestingly enough, the only person named "messiah" in the Old Testament was Cyrus, the pagan king of Persia, **(3a)** who was commissioned by God to restore Judah to her homeland after the Exile (Is 45:1). **(3b)** The anointing in this instance was more figurative than literal, since Cyrus was not aware that he was being set apart for such a divine purpose. **(4)** The New Testament title of Christ is derived from the Greek *Christos* which is exactly equivalent to the Hebrew *mashiyach,* for it is also rooted in the idea of "to smear with oil." So the term Christ emphasizes the special anointing of Jesus of Nazareth for His role as God's chosen one. See: TWOT—1255c; BDB—603c.

4900. מָשַׁךְ {36x} **mâshak**, *maw-shak';* a prim. root; to *draw,* used in a great variety of applications (incl. to *sow,* to *sound,* to *prolong,* to *develop,* to *march,* to *remove,* to *delay,* to *be tall,* etc.):—draw {15x}, draw out {3x}, prolonged {3x}, scattered {2x}, draw along {1x}, draw away {1x}, continue {1x}, deferred {1x}, misc. {9x} = extend, forbear, × give, handle, make (sound) long, × sow, stretch out. See: TWOT—1257; BDB—604a.

4901. מֶשֶׁךְ {2x} **meshek**, *meh'shek;* from 4900; a *sowing;* also a *possession:*—precious {1x}, price {1x}. See: TWOT—1257a; BDB—604d.

4902. מֶשֶׁךְ {2x} **Meshek**, *meh'-shek;* the same in form as 4901, but prob. of for. der.; *Meshek,* a son of Japheth, and the people desc. from him:—Mesech {1x}, Meshech {1x}. See: BDB—604d.

4903. מִשְׁכַּב {6x} **mishkab** (Aram.), *mish-kab';* corresp. to 4904; a *bed:*—bed {6x}. See: TWOT—3029a; BDB—1101d, 1115b.

4904. מִשְׁכָּב {46x} **mishkâb**, *mish-kawb';* from 7901; a *bed* (fig. a *bier*); abstr. *sleep;* by euphem. carnal *intercourse:*—bed {34x}, bedchamber + 2315 {4x}, couch {1x}, misc. {7x} = lieth (lying) with.

Mishkab means a "place to lie; couch; bed; act of lying." **(1)** In Gen 49:4 *mishkab* is used to mean a "place to lie" or "bed": ". . . because thou wentest up to thy father's bed. . . ." **(2)** The word refers to the "act of lying" in Num 31:17: ". . . kill every woman that hath known man by lying with him." See: TWOT—2381c; BDB—605a, 1012d, 1115b.

מְשֻׂכָה **mᵉsûkâh**. See 4881.

4905. מַשְׂכִּיל {13x} **maskîyl**, *mas-keel';* from 7919; *instructive,* i.e. a *didactic* poem:—Maschil {13x}.

Maskiyl means a "didactic psalm(?)." **(1)** This noun form, derived from *sakal* (7919), is found in the title of 13 psalms and also in Ps 47:7. **(2)** Scholars are not agreed on the significance of this term, but on the basis of the general meaning of *sakal,* such psalms must have been considered didactic or teaching psalms. See: TWOT—2263b; BDB—601d, 968d.

מַשְׁכִּים **mashkîym**. See 7925.

4906. מַשְׂכִּית {6x} **maskîyth**, *mas-keeth';* from the same as 7906; a *figure* (carved on stone, the wall, or any object); fig. *imagination:*—conceit {1x}, image {1x}, imagery {1x}, picture {2x}, × wish {1x}. See: TWOT—2257c; BDB—601d, 967c.

4907. מִשְׁכַּן {1x} **mishkan** (Aram.), *mish-kan';* corresp. to 4908; *residence:*—habitation {1x}. See: TWOT—3031a; BDB—1101d.

4908. מִשְׁכָּן {139x} **mishkân**, *mish-kawn';* from 7931; a *residence* (incl. a shepherd's *hut,* the *lair* of animals, fig. the *grave;*

also the *Temple*); spec. the *Tabernacle* (prop. its wooden walls):—tabernacle {119x}, dwelling {9x}, habitation {5x}, dwellingplaces {3x}, place {1x}, dwelleth {1x}, tents {1x}.

Mishkan, "dwelling place; tent." **(1)** This word occurs nearly 140 times, and often refers to the wilderness "tabernacle" (Ex 25:9). **(2)** *Mishkan* was also used later to refer to the "temple" (4908). This usage probably prepared the way for the familiar term *shekinah,* which was widely used in later Judaism to refer to the "presence" of God. Syn: 3427, 7931. See: TWOT—2387c; BDB—605a, 1015c, 1115b.

4909. מַשְׂכֹּרֶת {4x} **maskôreth**, *mas-koh'-reth;* from 7936; *wages* or a *reward:*—reward {1x}, wages {3x}. See: TWOT—2264.1d; BDB—601d, 969b.

4910. מָשַׁל {81x} **mâshal**, *maw-shal';* a prim. root; to *rule:*—rule {38x}, ruler {19x}, reign {8x}, dominion {7x}, governor {4x}, ruled over {2x}, power {2x}, indeed {1x}.

Mashal means "to rule, reign, have dominion." **(1)** The word is used for the first time in the Old Testament in Gen 1:18, where the sun, moon, and stars are designated "to rule over the day and over the night. . . ." **(2)** *Mashal* is used most frequently in the text to express the "ruling or dominion" of one person over another (Gen 3:16; 24:2). **(2a)** Cain is advised "to rule over" or "master" sin (Gen 4:7). **(2b)** Joseph's brothers respond to his dreams with the angry question: "Shalt thou indeed reign over us?" (Gen 37:8; the Hebrew verb here is literally "ruling will you rule," the repetition of the same root giving the needed emphasis). **(3)** As Creator and Sovereign over His world, God "ruleth by his power for ever" (Ps 66:7). **(4)** When God allowed Israel to have a king, it was with the condition that God was still the ultimate King and that first loyalty belonged to Him (Deut 17:14–20). **(4a)** This theocratic ideal is perhaps best expressed by Gideon: "I will not rule over you, neither shall my son rule over you: the LORD shall rule over you" (Judg 8:23). **(4b)** With the possible exception of David, no king of Israel fully lived up to the theocratic ideal, and David himself had some problems with it. See: TWOT—1259; BDB—605c.

4911. מָשַׁל {16x} **mâshal**, *maw-shal';* denom. from 4912; to *liken,* i.e. (tran.) to use fig. language (an allegory, adage, song or the like); intr. to *resemble:*—like {5x}, proverb {4x}, speak {2x}, use {2x}, become {1x}, compare {1x}, utter {1x}. See: TWOT—1258, 1258b; BDB—605a, 605b.

4912. מָשָׁל {39x} **mâshâl**, *maw-shawl';* appar. from 4910 in some orig. sense of *superiority* in mental action; prop. a pithy *maxim,* usually of metaph. nature; hence, a *simile* (as an adage, poem, discourse):—proverb {19x}, parable {18x}, byword {1x}, like {1x}. See: TWOT—1258a; BDB—605a.

4913. מָשָׁל {1x} **Mâshâl**, *maw-shawl';* for 4861; *Mashal,* a place in Pal.:—Mashal {1x}. See: BDB—602b, 605a.

4914. מְשֹׁל {1x} **mᵉshôl**, *mesh-ol';* from 4911; a *satire:*—byword {1x}. See: TWOT—1258d; BDB—605c.

4915. מֹשֶׁל {3x} **môshel**, *mo'-shel;* (1) from 4910; *empire;* (2) from 4911; a *parallel:*—dominion {2x}, like {1x}. See: TWOT—1259a, 1258c; BDB—605c, 606a.

מִשְׁלוֹשׁ **mishlôwsh**. See 7969.

4916. מִשְׁלוֹחַ {10x} **mishlôwach**, *mish-lo'-akh;* or

מִשְׁלֹחַ **mishlôach**, *mish-lo'-akh;* also

מִשְׁלָח **mishlâch**, *mish-lawkh';* from 7971; a *sending* out, i.e. (abstr.) *presentation* (favorable), or *seizure* (unfavorable); also (concr.) a place of *dismissal,* or a *business* to be discharged:—to lay {1x}, to put {1x}, puttest {2x}, settest {3x}, sending {2x}, sending forth {1x}. See: TWOT—2394d, 2394e; BDB—606b, 1043c.

4917. מִשְׁלַחַת {2x} **mishlachath**, *mish-lakh'-ath;* fem. of 4916; a *mission,* i.e. (abstr.) and favorable) *release,* or (concr. and unfavorable) an *army:*—discharge {1x}, sending {1x}. See: TWOT—2394f; BDB—606b, 1020a.

4918. מְשֻׁלָּם {25x} **Mᵉshullâm**, *mesh-ool-lawm';* from 7999; *allied; Meshullam,* the name of seventeen Isr.:—*Meshullam* {25x}. See: BDB—606b, 1024b, 1024c.

4919. מְשִׁלֵּמוֹת {2x} **Mᵉshillêmôwth**, *mesh-il-lay-mohth';* plur. from 7999; *reconciliations; Meshillemoth,* an Isr.:—Meshillemoth {2x}. See: BDB—606b, 1024c. comp. 4921.

4920. מְשֶׁלֶמְיָה {4x} **Mᵉshelemyâh**, *mesh-eh-lem-yaw';* or

מְשֶׁלֶמְיָהוּ **Mᵉshelemyâhûw**, *mesh-eh-lem-yaw'-hoo;* from 7999 and 3050; *ally of Jah; Meshelemjah,* an Isr.:—Meshelemiah {4x}. See: BDB—606b, 1024b, 1024c.

4921. מְשִׁלֵּמִית {1x} **Mᵉshillêmîyth**, *mesh-il-lay-meeth';* from 7999; *reconciliation; Meshillemith,* an Isr.:—Meshillemith {1x}. See: BDB—606b, 1024c. comp. 4919.

4922. מְשֻׁלֶּמֶת {1x} **Mᵉshullemeth**, *mesh-ool-leh'-meth;* fem. of 4918; *Meshullemeth,* an Israelitess:—*Meshullemeth* {1x}. See: BDB—606b, 1024c.

4923. מְשַׁמָּה {7x} **mᵉshammâh**, *mesh-am-maw';* from 8074; a *waste* or *amazement:*—astonishment {1x}, desolate {6x}. See: TWOT—2409f; BDB—606b, 1031d.

4924. מַשְׁמָן {7x} **mashmân**, *mash-mawn';* from 8080; *fat,* i.e. (lit. and abstr.) *fatness;* but usually (fig. and concr.) a *rich* dish, a *fertile* field, a *robust* man:—fat {1x}, fat ones {1x}, fatness {4x}, fatest places {1x}. See: TWOT—2410e, 2410f; BDB—606b, 1032a, 1032c, 1032d, 1033b.

4925. מִשְׁמַנָּה {1x} **Mishmannâh**, *mish-man-naw';* from 8080; *fatness; Mashmannah,* an Isr.:—*Mishmannah* {1x}. See: BDB—606b, 1032d.

4926. מִשְׁמָע {1x} **mishmâᶜ**, *mish-maw';* from 8085; a *report:*—hearing {1x}. See: TWOT—2412f; BDB—606b, 1036a.

4927. מִשְׁמָע {4x} **Mishmâᶜ**, *mish-maw';* the same as 4926; *Mishma,* the name of a son of Ishmael, and of an Isr.:—*Mishma* {4x}. See: TWOT—2412f; BDB—606b, 1036a.

4928. מִשְׁמַעַת {4x} **mishmaᶜath**, *mish-mah'-ath;* fem. of 4926; *audience,* i.e. the royal *court;* also *obedience,* i.e. (concr.) a *subject:*—bidding {1x}, guard {2x}, obey {1x}. See: TWOT—2412g; BDB—606b, 1036a.

4929. מִשְׁמָר {22x} **mishmâr**, *mish-mawr';* from 8104; a *guard* (the man, the post, or the *prison*); fig. a *deposit;* also (as observed) a *usage* (abstr.), or an *example* (concr.):—ward {12x}, watch {4x}, guard {3x}, diligence {1x}, offices {1x}, prison {1x}.

Mishmar, as a noun, means "guard; guardpost." **(1)** In the first of its 22 occurrences *mishmar* means "guard": "And he put them in ward [*mishmar*] in the house of the captain of the guard, into the prison . . ." (Gen 40:3). **(2)** The word implies "guardpost" in Neh 7:3. **(3)** The word also refers to men on "guard" (Neh 4:23) and **(4)** to groups of attendants (Neh 12:24). Syn.: 5341, 8104. See: TWOT—2414f; BDB—606b, 1038b.

4930. מַסְמְרָה {1x} **masmᵉrâh**, *mas-mer-aw';* for 4548 fem.; a *peg:*—nail {1x}. See: TWOT—1518b; BDB—702d.

4931. מִשְׁמֶרֶת {78x} **mishmereth**, *mish-meh'-reth;* fem. of 4929; *watch,* i.e. the act (*custody*) or (concr.) the *sentry,* the *post;* obj. *preservation,* or (concr.) *safe;* fig. *observance,* i.e. (abstr.) *duty,* or (obj.) a *usage* or *party:*—charge {50x}, ward {9x}, watch {7x}, keep {7x}, ordinance {3x}, offices {1x}, safeguard {1x}.

Mishmereth means "those who guard; obligation." **(1)** The word refers to "those who guard" in 2 Kin 11:5: ". . . A third part of you that enter in on the sabbath shall even be keepers of the watch of the king's house." **(2)** In Gen 26:5 the word refers to an "obligation": "Because that Abraham obeyed my voice, and kept my charge, my commandments, my statutes, and my laws." See: TWOT—2414g; BDB—606b, 1038b.

4932. מִשְׁנֶה {35x} **mishneh**, *mish-neh';* from 8138; prop. a *repetition,* i.e. a *duplicate* (*copy* of a document), or a *double* (in amount); by impl. a *second* (in order, rank, age, quality or location):—second {11x}, double {8x}, next {7x}, college {2x}, copy {2x}, twice {2x}, fatlings {1x}, much {1x}, second order {1x}. See: TWOT—2421c; BDB—606b, 1032d, 1041c.

4933. מְשִׁסָּה {6x} **mᵉshiççâh**, *mesh-is-saw';* from 8155; *plunder:*—booty {2x}, spoil {4x}. See: TWOT—2426a; BDB—606b, 1042d.

4934. מִשְׁעוֹל {1x} **mishᶜôwl**, *mish-ole';* from the same as 8168; a *hollow,* i.e. a narrow passage:—path {1x}. See: TWOT—2432b; BDB—606c, 1043c.

4935. מִשְׁעִי {1x} **mishᶜîy**, *mish-ee';* prob. from 8159; *inspection:*—to supple {1x}. See: TWOT—1260a; BDB—606b.

4936. מִשְׁעָם {1x} **Mishᶜâm**, *mish-awm';* appar. from 8159; *inspection; Misham,* an Isr.:—Misham {1x}. See: BDB—606c.

4937. מִשְׁעֵן {5x} **mishᶜên**, *mish-ane';* or

מִשְׁעָן **mishᶜân**, *mish-awn';* from 8172; a *support* (concr.), i.e. (fig.) a *protector* or *sustenance:*—stay {5x}. See: TWOT—2434a, 2434b; BDB—606c, 1044a.

4938. מִשְׁעֵנָה {12x} **mishᶜênah**, *mish-ay-naw';* or

מִשְׁעֶנֶת **mishᶜeneth**, *mish-eh'-neth;* fem. of 4937; *support* (abstr.), i.e. (fig.) *sustenance* or (concr.) a *walking-stick:*—staff {11x}, stave {1x}. See: TWOT—2434c, 2434d; BDB—606c, 1044a.

4939. מִשְׂפָּח {1x} **mispâch**, *mis-pawkh';* from 5596; *slaughter:*—oppression {1x}. See: TWOT—1534d; BDB—705c, 974a.

4940. מִשְׁפָּחָה {300x} **mishpâchâh**, *mish-paw-khaw';* from 8192 [comp. 8198]; a *family,* i.e. circle of relatives; fig. a *class* (of persons), a *species* (of animals) or *sort* (of things); by extens. a *tribe* or *people:*—families {289x}, kinds {1x}, kindred {9x}.

Mishpachah means "family; clan." **(1)** The word is first used in Gen 8:19: "Every beast, every creeping thing, and every fowl, and whatsoever creepeth upon the earth, after their kinds, went forth out of the ark." **(2)** The noun *mishpachah* is used predominantly in the Pentateuch (as many as 154 times in Numbers) and in the historical books, but rarely in the poetical literature (5 times) and the prophetical writings. **(3)** All members of a group who were related by blood and who still felt a sense of consanguinity belonged to the "clan" or "the extended family." **(3a)** Saul argued that since he belonged to the least of the "clans," he had no right to the kingship (1 Sa 9:21). **(3b)** This meaning determined the extent of Rahab's family that was spared from Jericho: ". . . And they brought out all her kindred, and left them without the camp of Israel" (Josh 6:23). **(3c)** So the "clan" was an important division within the "tribe." **(3d)** The Book of Numbers gives a census of the leaders and the numbers of the tribes according to the "families" (Num 1–4; 26). **(3e)** In capital cases, where revenge was desired, the entire clan might be taken: "And, behold, the whole family is risen against thine handmaid, and they said, Deliver him that smote his brother, that we may kill him, for the life of his brother whom he slew; and we will destroy the heir also: and so they shall quench my coal which is left, and shall not leave to my husband neither name nor remainder upon the earth" (2 Sa 14:7). **(4)** A further extension of the meaning "division" or "clan" is the idiomatic usage of "class" or "group," such as "the families" of the animals that left the ark (Gen 8:19) or the "families" of the nations (Ps 22:28; 96:7; cf. Gen 10:5). **(5)** Even God's promise to Abraham had reference to all the nations: "And I will bless them that bless thee, and curse him that curseth thee: and in thee shall all families of the earth be blessed" (Gen 12:3). **(6)** The narrow meaning of *mishpachah* is similar to our usage of "family" and similar to the meaning of the word in modern Hebrew. Abraham sent his servant to his relatives in Padanaram to seek a wife for Isaac (Gen 24:38). **(7)** The law of redemption applied to the "close relatives in a family": "After that he is sold he may be redeemed again; one of his brethren may redeem him: Either his uncle, or his uncle's son, may redeem him, or any that is nigh of kin unto him of his family may redeem him; or if he be able, he may redeem himself" (Lev 25:48–49). See: TWOT—2442b; BDB—606c, 1046.

4941. מִשְׁפָּט {421x} **mishpât**, *mish-pawt';* from 8199; prop. a *verdict* (favorable or unfavorable) pronounced judicially, espec. a *sentence* or formal decree (human or [participant's] divine *law,* indiv. or collect.), incl. the act, the place, the suit, the crime, and the penalty; abstr. *justice,* incl. a participant's *right* or *privilege* (statutory or customary), or even a *style:*—judgment {296x}, manner {38x}, right {18x}, cause {12x}, ordinance {11x}, lawful {7x}, order {5x}, worthy {3x}, fashion {3x}, custom {2x}, discretion {2x}, law {2x}, measure {2x}, sentence {2x}, misc. {18x} = + adversary, ceremony, charge, × crime, desert, determination, disposing, due, form, to be judged, just (-ice, -ly), usest, + wrong.

Mishpat means "judgment; rights." **(1)** This word has two main senses; the first deals with the act of sitting as a judge, hearing a case, and rendering a proper verdict. Eccl 12:14 is one such occurrence: "For God shall bring every work into judgment, with every secret thing, whether it be good, or whether it be evil." **(2)** *Mishpat* can also refer to the "rights" belonging to someone: "Thou shalt not wrest the judgment of thy poor in his cause" (Ex 23:6). This second sense carries several nuances: **(2a)** the sphere in which things are in proper relationship to one's claims: "For I know him, that he will command his children and his household after him, and they shall keep the way of the LORD, to do justice and judgment; that the LORD may bring upon Abraham that which he hath spoken of him" (Gen 18:19—the first occurrence); **(2b)** a judicial verdict: "And thou shalt come unto the priests the Levites, and unto the judge that shall be in those days, and enquire; and they shall shew thee the sentence of judgment" (Deut 17:9); **(2c)** the statement of the case for the accused: "And Moses brought their cause before the LORD" (Num 27:5); and an established ordinance: "Now these *are* the judgments which thou shalt set before them" (Ex 21:1). See: TWOT—2443c; BDB—606c, 1048b.

4942. מִשְׁפָּת {2x} **mishpâth**, *mish-pawth';* from 8192; a *stall* for cattle (only dual):—burden {1x}, sheepfold {1x}. See: TWOT—2441c; BDB—606c, 1046b, 1052a.

4943. מֶשֶׁק {1x} **mesheq**, *meh'-shek;* from an unused root mean. to *hold; possession:*—+ steward {1x}. See: TWOT—1261a; BDB—606c.

4944. מַשָּׁק {1x} **mashshâq**, *mash-shawk';* from 8264; a *traversing,* i.e. rapid *motion:*—running to and fro {1x}. See: TWOT—2460a; BDB—606d, 1055b.

4945. מַשְׁקֶה {7x} **mashqeh**, *mash-keh';* from 8248; prop. *causing to drink,* i.e. a *butler;* by impl. (intr.), *drink* (itself); fig. a *well-watered* region:—drink {2x}, drinking {2x}, watered {1x}, butlership {1x}, fat pastures {1x}. See: TWOT—2452c; BDB—606d, 1052d.

4946. מִשְׁקוֹל {1x} **mishqôwl**, *mish-kole';* from 8254; *weight:*—weight {1x}. See: TWOT—2454b; BDB—606d, 1054a.

4947. מַשְׁקוֹף {3x} **mashqôwph**, *mash-kofe';* from 8259 in its orig. sense of *overhanging;* a *lintel:*—lintel {2x}, upper door post {1x}. See: TWOT—2458c; BDB—606d, 1054d.

4948. מִשְׁקָל {49x} **mishqâl**, *mish-kawl';* from 8254; *weight* (numerically estimated); hence, *weighing* (the act):—(full) weight {47x}, weigh {2x}. See: TWOT—2454c; BDB—606d, 1054a.

4949. מִשְׁקֶלֶת {2x} **mishqeleth**, *mish-keh'-leth;* or

מִשְׁקֹלֶת **mishqôleth**, *mish-ko'-leth;* fem. of 4948 or 4947; a *weight,* i.e. a *plummet* (with line attached):—plummet {1x}. See: TWOT—2454d; BDB—606d, 1054a.

4950. מִשְׁקָע {1x} **mishqâ^c^**, *mish-kaw';* from 8257; a *settling* place (of water), i.e. a pond:—deep {1x}. See: TWOT—2456a; BDB—606d, 1054b.

4951. מִשְׂרָה {2x} **misrâh**, *mis-raw';* from 8280; *empire:*—government {1x}. See: TWOT—2288a; BDB—601d, 976a.

4952. מִשְׁרָה {1x} **mishrâh**, *mish-raw';* from 8281 in the sense of *loosening; maceration,* i.e. steeped *juice:*—liquor {1x}. See: TWOT—2464a; BDB—606d, 1056a.

4953. מַשְׁרוֹקִי {4x} **mashrôwqîy** (Aram.), *mash-ro-kee';* from a root corresp. to 8319; a (musical) *pipe* (from its *whistling* sound):—flute {4x}. See: TWOT—3049a; BDB—1101d, 1117b.

4954. מִשְׁרָעִי {1x} **Mishrâ^c^îy**, *mish-raw-ee';* patrial from an unused noun from an unused root; prob. mean. to *stretch* out; *extension;* a *Mishraite,* or inhab. (collect.) of Mishra:—Mishraites {1x}. See: BDB—606d.

4955. מִשְׂרָפָה {2x} **misrâphâh**, *mis-raw-faw';* from 8313; *combustion,* i.e. *cremation* (of a corpse), or *calcination* (of lime):—burnings {2x}. See: TWOT—2292d; BDB—602a, 977c.

4956. מִשְׂרְפוֹת מַיִם {2x} **Misr^e^phôwth Mayim**, *mis-ref-ohth' mah'-yim;* from the plur. of 4955 and 4325; *burnings of water; Misrephoth-Majim,* a place in Pal.:—Misrephoth-mayim {2x}. See: BDB—602a, 977c.

4957. מַשְׂרֵקָה {2x} **Masrêqâh**, *mas-ray-kaw';* a form for 7796 used denom.; *vineyard; Masrekah,* a place in Idumæa:—Masrekah {2x}. See: BDB—602a, 977d.

4958. מַשְׂרֵת {1x} **masrêth**, *mas-rayth';* appar. from an unused root mean. to *perforate,* i.e. hollow out; a *pan:*—pan {1x}. See: TWOT—1251; BDB—602a.

4959. מָשַׁשׁ {9x} **mâshash**, *maw-shash';* a prim. root; to *feel* of; by impl. to *grope:*—feel {3x}, grope {4x}, search {2x}. See: TWOT—1262; BDB—606d.

4960. מִשְׁתֶּה {46x} **mishteh**, *mish-teh';* from 8354; *drink,* by impl. *drinking* (the act); also (by impl.) a *banquet* or (gen.) feast:—banquet {10x}, drink {5x}, feast ([-ed], -ing {31x}). See: TWOT—2477c; BDB—607a, 1059c, 1117c.

4961. מִשְׁתֵּה {1x} **mishteh** (Aram.), *mish-teh';* corresp. to 4960; a *banquet:*—banquet {1x}. See: TWOT—3051a; BDB—1101d, 1117c.

4962. מַת {22x} **math**, *math;* from the same as 4970; prop. an *adult* (as of full length); by impl. a *man* (only in the plur.):—men {14x}, few {2x}, few + 4557 {1x}, friends {1x}, number {1x}, persons {1x}, small {1x}, with {1x}. See: TWOT—1263; BDB—607a, 607d, 608a, 1071b.

4963. מַתְבֵּן {1x} **mathbên**, *math-bane';* denom. from 8401; *straw* in the heap:—straw {1x}. See: TWOT—2493a; BDB—607b, 1062a.

4964. מֶתֶג {4x} **metheg**, *meh-theg;* from an unused root mean. to *curb;* a *bit:*—bit {1x}, bridle {3x}. See: TWOT—1264a; BDB—607c.

4965. מֶתֶג הָאַמָּה {1x} **Metheg hâ-'Ammâh**, *meh'-theg haw-am-maw';* from 4964 and 520 with the art. interposed; *bit of the metropolis; Metheg-ha-Ammah,* an epithet of Gath:—Metheg-ammah {1x}. See: BDB—52a, 607c.

4966. מָתוֹק {12x} **mâthôwq**, *maw-thoke';* or

מָתוּק **mâthûwq**, *maw-thook';* from 4985; *sweet:*—sweet {8x}, sweetner {2x}, sweetness {2x}. See: TWOT—1268c; BDB—608b.

4967. מְתוּשָׁאֵל {2x} **M^e^thûwshâ'êl**, *meth-oo-shaw-ale';* from 4962 and 410, with the rel. interposed; *man who* (is) *of God; Methushaël,* an antediluvian patriarch:—Methusael {2x}. See: BDB—607b, 607c.

4968. מְתוּשֶׁלַח {6x} **M^e^thûwshelach**, *meth-oo-sheh'-lakh;* from 4962 and 7973; *man of a dart; Methushelach,* an antediluvian patriarch:—Methuselah {6x}. See: BDB—607b, 607c.

4969. מָתַח {1x} **mâthach**, *maw-thakh';* a prim. root; to *stretch* out:—spreadest them out {1x}. See: TWOT—1265; BDB—607c.

4970. מָתַי {3x} **mâthay**, *maw-thah'ee;* from an unused root mean. to *extend;* prop. *extent* (of time); but used only adv. (espec. with other particles pref.), *when* (either rel. or interrog.):—long {1x}, when {2x}. See: TWOT—1266; BDB—607d.

מְתִים **m^ethîym**. See 4962.

4971. מַתְכֹּנֶת {5x} **mathkôneth**, *math-ko'-neth;* or

מַתְכֻּנֶת **mathkûneth**, *math-koo'-neth;* from 8505 in the transferred sense of *measuring; proportion* (in size, number or ingredients):—composition {2x}, measure {1x}, state {1x}, tale {1x}. See: TWOT—2511c; BDB—607d, 1067c.

4972. מַתְּלָאָה {1x} **matt^elâ'âh**, *mat-tel-aw-aw';* from 4100 and 8513; *what a trouble!:*—what a weariness {1x}. See: TWOT—1066a; BDB—608a, 1067d.

4973. מְתַלְּעָה {3x} **m^ethall^e'âh**, *meth-al-leh-aw';* contr. from 3216; prop. a *biter,* i.e. a *tooth:*—cheek (jaw) {1x}, tooth {1x}, jaw {1x}. See: TWOT—1066a; BDB—577a, 608a, 1069a.

4974. מְתֹם {4x} **m^ethôm**, *meth-ohm';* from 8552; *wholesomeness;* also (adv.) *completely:*—men [*by reading* 4962]{1x}, soundness {3x}. See: TWOT—2522e; BDB—607a, 608a, 1071b.

מֶתֶן **Methen**. See 4981.

4975. מֹתֶן {47x} **môthen**, *mo'-then;* from an unused root mean. to *be slender;* prop. the *waist* or small of the back; only in plur. the *loins:*—+ greyhound {1x}, loins {42x}, side {4x}. See: TWOT—1267a; BDB—608a.

4976. מַתָּן {5x} **mattân**, *mat-tawn';* from 5414; a *present:*—gift {4x}, gifts {1x}. See: TWOT—1443b; BDB—608c, 682b.

4977. מַתָּן {3x} **Mattân**, *mat-tawn';* the same as 4976; *Mattan,* the name of a priest of Baal, and of an Isr.:—*Mattan* {3x}. See: BDB—608c, 682b.

4978. מַתְּנָא {3x} **matt^enâ'** (Aram.), *mat-ten-aw';* corresp. to 4979:—gift {3x}. See: TWOT—2880a; BDB—1101d, 1103d.

4979. מַתָּנָה {17x} **mattânâh**, *mat-taw-naw';* fem. of 4976; a *present;* spec. (in a good sense), a sacrificial *offering,* (in a bad sense) a *bribe:*—gift {16x}, as he is able {1x}. See: TWOT—1443c; BDB—608c, 682b.

4980. מַתָּנָה {1x} **Mattânâh**, *mat-taw-naw';* the same as 4979; *Mattanah,* a place in the Desert:—*Mattanah* {1x}. See: BDB—608c, 682c.

4981. מִתְנִי {1x} **Mithnîy**, *mith-nee';* prob. patrial from an unused noun mean. *slenderness;* a *Mithnite,* or inhab. of Methen:—Mithnite {1x}. See: BDB—608c.

4982. מַתְּנַי {3x} **Matt^enay**, *mat-ten-ah'ee;* from 4976; *liberal; Mattenai,* the name of three Isr.:—Mattenai {3x}. See: BDB—608c, 682c, 682d.

4983. מַתַּנְיָה {16x} **Mattanyâh**, *mat-tan-yaw';* or

מַתַּנְיָהוּ **Mattanyâhûw**, *mat-tan-yaw'-hoo;* from 4976 and 3050; *gift of Jah; Mattanjah,* the name of ten Isr.:—Mattaniah {16x}. See: BDB—608c, 682c.

מָתְנַיִם **mâthnayim**. See 4975.

4984. מִתְנַשֵּׂא {2x} **mithnassê'**, *mith-nas-say';* from 5375; (used as abstr.) supreme *exaltation:*—exalted {2x}. See: TWOT—1421; BDB—669d.

4985. מָתַק {5x} **mâthaq**, *maw-thak';* a prim. root; to *suck,* by impl. to *relish,* or (intr.) *be sweet:*—be (made, × take) sweet {5x}. See: TWOT—1268; BDB—608c.

4986. מֶתֶק {2x} **metheq**, *meh'-thek;* from 4985; fig. *pleasantness* (of discourse):—sweetness {2x}. See: TWOT—1268a; BDB—608d.

4987. מֹתֶק {1x} **môtheq**, *mo'-thek;* from 4985; *sweetness:*—sweetness {1x}. See: TWOT—1268b; BDB—608d.

4988. מָתָק {1x} **mâthâq**, *maw-thawk';* from 4985; a *dainty,* i.e. (gen.) *food:*—feed sweetly {1x}. See: TWOT—1268c?; BDB—608c.

4989. מִתְקָה {1x} **Mithqâh**, *mith-kaw';* fem. of 4987; *sweetness; Mithkah,* a place in the Desert:—Mithcah {1x}. See: BDB—609a.

4990. מִתְרְדָת {2x} **Mithr^edâth**, *mith-red-awth';* of Pers. or.; *Mithredath,* the name of two Pers.:—*Mithredath* {2x}. See: BDB—609c.

4991. מַתָּת {6x} **mattâth**, *mat-tawth';* fem. of 4976 abb.; a *present:*—gift {3x}, give {2x}, reward {1x}. See: TWOT—1443d; BDB—609c, 682c.

4992. מַתַּתָּה {1x} **Mattattâh**, *mat-tat-taw';* for 4993; *gift of Jah; Mattattah,* an Isr.:—Mattathah {1x}. See: BDB—609c, 683a.

4993. מַתִּתְיָה {8x} **Mattithyâh**, *mat-tith-yaw';* or

מַתִּתְיָהוּ **Mattithyâhûw**, *mat-tith-yaw'-hoo;* from 4991 and 3050; *gift of Jah; Mattithjah,* the name of four Isr.:—Mattithiah {8x}. See: BDB—609c, 682d.

נ

4994. נָא {1x} **nâ'**, *naw;* a prim. particle of incitement and entreaty, which may usually be rendered *I pray, now* or *then;* added mostly to verbs (in the imperative or future), or to interj., occasionally to an adv. or conjunc.:—{9x} = I beseech (pray) thee (you), go to, now, oh. Syn.: 577, 2603, 6279, 6419, 6739, 7592. See: TWOT—1269; BDB—609a, 644b.

4995. נָא {1x} **nâ'**, *naw;* appar. from 5106 in the sense of *harshness* from refusal; prop. *tough,* i.e. *uncooked* (flesh):—raw {1x}. See: TWOT—1358a; BDB—609d, 644b.

4996. נֹא {5x} **Nô'**, *no;* of Eg. or.; *No* (i.e. *Thebes*), the capital of Upper Egypt:—No {5x}. comp. 528. See: BDB—609d.

4997. נֹאד {6x} **nô'd**, *node;* or

נֹאוד **nô'wd**, *node;* also (fem.)

נֹאדָה **nô'dâh**, *no-daw';* from an unused root of uncert. signif.; a (skin or leather) *bag* (for fluids):—bottle {6x}. See: TWOT—1270; BDB—609d.

נְאדָרִי **ne'dârîy**. See 142.

4998. נָאָה {3x} **nâ'âh**, *naw-aw';* a prim. root; prop. to *be at home,* i.e. (by impl.) to be *pleasant* (or *suitable*), i.e. *beautiful:*—be beautiful {1x}, become {1x}, be comely {1x}. See: TWOT—1271; BDB—610a.

4999. נָאָה {12x} **nâ'âh**, *naw-aw';* from 4998; a *home;* fig. a *pasture:*—habitations {5x}, houses {1x}, pastures {5x}, pleasant places {1x}. See: TWOT—1322a; BDB—627d.

5000. נָאוֶה {9x} **nâ'veh**, *naw-veh';* from 4998 or 5116; *suitable,* or *beautiful:*—becometh {1x}, comely {6x}, seemly {2x}. See: TWOT—1271a; BDB—610a.

5001. נָאַם {1x} **nâ'am**, *naw-am';* a prim. root; prop. to *whisper,* i.e. (by impl.) to *utter* as an oracle:—say {1x}.

Na'am occurs only once in the entire Old Testament: "Behold, I am against the prophets, saith [5002 - *ne'um*] the LORD, that use their tongues, and say [*na'am*], He saith [5002 - *ne'um*]" (Jer 23:31). See: TWOT—1272; BDB—610c.

5002. נְאֻם {376x} **n^e'ûm**, *neh-oom';* from 5001; an *oracle:*—saith {366x}, said {9x}, spake {1x}.

I. *Ne'um*, as a verb, means, "to say, utter an affirmation, speak." **(1)** The word is a verbal form of the verb *na'am,* which occurs only once in the entire Old Testament: "Behold, I am against the prophets, saith [*ne'um*] the LORD, that use their tongues, and say [5001 - *na'am*], He saith [*ne'um*]" (Jer 23:31). **(2)** The word *ne'um* appears as many as 361 times and, because of the frequency in the prophetical books, it is characteristic of prophetic speech. **(3)** *Ne'um* is an indicator which generally appears at the end of the quotation: "What mean ye that ye beat my people to pieces, and grind the faces of the poor? saith [*ne'um*] the Lord GOD of hosts" (Is 3:15). **(4)** The word may also be found in the middle of an argument: "And I raised up of your sons for prophets, and of your young men for Nazarites. Is it not even thus, O ye children of Israel? saith [*ne'um*] the LORD. But ye gave the Nazarites wine to drink; and commanded the prophets, saying, Prophesy not" (Amos 2:11–12). **II. *Ne'um*,** as a noun, means "utterance; saying." **(1)** The use of *ne'um* is rare at the beginning of a statement: "The LORD said unto my Lord [literally, 'a statement of Jehovah to my Lord']. Sit thou at my right hand, until I make thine enemies thy footstool" (Ps 110:1).

(2) With one exception (Prov 30:1) in the sayings of Agur, the usage throughout the Old Testament is virtually limited to a word from God. **(3)** In Numbers the utterances of Balaam are introduced with the formula "and he uttered his oracle": "And he took up his parable, and said, Balaam the son of Beor hath said, and the man whose eyes are open hath said" (Num 24:3; cf. v. 15). **(4)** David's concluding words begin with these words: "Now these *be* the last words of David. David the son of Jesse said, and the man *who was* raised up on high, the anointed of the God of Jacob, and the sweet psalmist of Israel, said" (2 Sa 23:1). **(5)** Apart from these instances there are a few more examples, but as a rule *ne'um* is a prophetic term, which even beyond the prophetical literature is associated with a word from God. See: TWOT—1272a; BDB—610b.

5003. נָאַף {13x} **nâ'aph**, *naw-af';* a prim. root; to *commit adultery;* fig. to *apostatize:*—adultery {17x}, adulterer {8x}, adulteress {4x}, adulterous {1x}, women that break wedlock {1x}. See: TWOT—1273; BDB—610c.

5004. נִאֻף {2x} **nîʾûph**, *nee-oof'*; from 5003; *adultery:*—adulteries {2x}. See: TWOT—1273a; BDB—610d.

5005. נַאֲפוּף {1x} **naʾăphûwph**, *nah-af-oof'*; from 5003; *adultery:*—adulteries {1x}. See: TWOT—1273b; BDB—610d.

5006. נָאַץ {25x} **nâʾats**, *naw-ats'*; a prim. root; to *scorn;* or (Eccl 12:5) by interchange for 5132, to *bloom:*—despise {8x}, provoke {5x}, abhor {4x}, blaspheme {4x}, contemn {2x}, flourish {1x}, great occasion to blaspheme {1x}. See: TWOT—1274; BDB—610d, 665b.

5007. נְאָצָה {5x} **nᵉʾâtsâh**, *neh-aw-tsaw'*; or

נֶאָצָה **neʾâtsâh**, *neh-aw-tsaw'*; from 5006; *scorn:*—blasphemy {3x}, provocation {2x}. See: TWOT—1274a, 1274b; BDB—611a.

5008. נָאַק {2x} **nâʾaq**, *naw-ak'*; a prim. root; to *groan:*—groan {2x}. See: TWOT—1275; BDB—611a.

5009. נְאָקָה {4x} **nᵉʾâqâh**, *neh-aw-kaw'*; from 5008; a *groan:*—groaning {4x}. See: TWOT—1275a; BDB—611a.

5010. נָאַר {2x} **nâʾar**, *naw-ar'*; a prim. root; to *reject:*—abhorred {1x}, make void {1x}. See: TWOT—1276; BDB—611b.

5011. נֹב {6x} **Nôb**, *nobe;* the same as 5108; *fruit; Nob,* a place in Pal.:—*Nob* {6x}. See: BDB—611b, 612c.

5012. נָבָא {115x} **nâbâʾ**, *naw-baw'*; a prim. root; to *prophesy,* i.e. speak (or sing) by inspiration (in prediction or simple discourse):—prophesy {111x}, prophesying {2x}, prophet {2x}.

Nabaʾ means "to prophesy." **(1)** Its first appearance is in 1 Sa 10:6, where Saul is told by Samuel that when he meets a certain band of ecstatic prophets, he too will "prophesy with them, and . . . be turned into another man." **(2)** Most frequently *nabaʾ* is used to describe the function of the true prophet as he speaks God's message to the people, under the influence of the divine spirit (1 Kin 22:8; Jer 29:27; Eze 37:10). **(2a)** "To prophesy" was a task that the prophet could not avoid: "The Lord GOD hath spoken, who can but prophesy?" (Amos 3:8; cf. Jer 20:7, where Jeremiah says that he was both attracted to and forced into being a prophet). **(2b)** While the formula "The word of the LORD came [to the prophet]" is used literally hundreds of times in the Old Testament, **(2b1)** there is no real indication as to the manner in which it came—whether it came through the thought-processes, through a vision, or in some other way. **(2b2)** Sometimes, especially in the earlier prophets, it seems that some kind of ecstatic experience may have been involved, as in 1 Sa 10:6, 11; 19:20. **(2b3)** Music is sometimes spoken of as a means of prophesying, as in 1 Chr 25:1–3.

(3) The false prophets, although not empowered by the divine spirit, are spoken of as prophesying also: ". . . I have not spoken to them, yet they prophesied" (Jer 23:21). **(3a)** The false prophet is roundly condemned because he speaks a non-authentic word: ". . . . Prophesy against the prophets of Israel that prophesy, and say thou unto them that prophesy out of their own hearts, Hear ye the word of the LORD; . . . Woe unto the foolish prophets, that follow their own spirit, and have seen nothing!" (Eze 13:2–3). **(3b)** The false prophet especially is subject to frenzied states of mind which give rise to his prophesying, although the content of such activity is not clearly spelled out (1 Kin 22:10). **(3c)** The point is that in the biblical context "to prophesy" can refer to anything from the frenzied ecstaticism of a false prophet to the cold sober proclamation of God's judgment by an Amos or an Isaiah. **(4)** "To prophesy" is much more than the prediction of future events. **(4a)** Indeed, the first concern of the prophet is to speak God's word to the people of his own time, calling them to covenant faithfulness.

(4b) The prophet's message is conditional, dependent upon the response of the people. Thus, by their response to this word, the people determine in large part what the future holds, as is well illustrated by the response of the Ninevites to Jonah's preaching. **(4c)** Of course, prediction does enter the picture at times, such as in Nahum's prediction of the fall of Nineveh (Nah 2:13) and in the various messianic passages (Is 9:1–6; 11:1–9; 52:13–53:12). See: TWOT—1277; BDB—612a, 1101d.

5013. נְבָא {1x} **nᵉbâʾ** (Aram.), *neb-aw'*; corresp. to 5012:—prophesy {1x}. See: TWOT—2843a; BDB—1101d.

5014. נָבַב {4x} **nâbab**, *naw-bab'*; a prim. root; to *pierce;* to *be hollow,* or (fig.) *foolish:*—hollow {3x}, vain {1x}. See: TWOT—1278; BDB—612c.

5015. נְבוֹ {13x} **Nᵉbôw**, *neb-o'*; prob. of for. der.; *Nebo,* the name of a Bab. deity, also of a mountain in Moab, and of a place in Pal.:—Nebo {13x}. See: BDB—612d.

5016. נְבוּאָה {3x} **nᵉbûwʾâh**, *neb-oo-aw'*; from 5012; a *prediction* (spoken or written):—prophecy {3x}. See: TWOT—1277b; BDB—612c.

5017. נְבוּאָה {1x} **nᵉbûwʾâh** (Aram.), *neb-oo-aw'*; corresp. to 5016; inspired *teaching:*—prophesying {1x}. TWOT—2843b; See: BDB—1102a.

5018. נְבוּזַרְאֲדָן {15x} **Nᵉbûwzarʾădân**, *neb-oo-zar-ad-awn'*; of for. or.; *Nebuzaradan,* a Bab. general:—Nebuzaradan {15x}. See: BDB—613a.

5019. נְבוּכַדְנֶאצַּר {60x} **Nᵉbûwkadneʾtstsar**, *neb-oo-kad-nets-tsar'*; or

נְבֻכַדְנֶאצַּר **Nᵉbûkadneʾtstsar** (2 Kin 24:1, 10), *neb-oo-kad-nets-tsar'*; or

נְבוּכַדְנֶצַּר **Nᵉbûwkadnetstsar** (Est 2:6; Dan. 1:18), *neb-oo-kad-nets-tsar'*; or

נְבוּכַדְרֶאצַּר **Nᵉbûwkadreʾtstsar**, *neb-oo-kad-rets-tsar'*; or

נְבוּכַדְרֶאצּוֹר **Nᵉbûwkadreʾtstsôwr** (Ezr 2:1; Jer 49:28), *neb-oo-kad-rets-tsore'*; or for. der.; *Nebukadnetstsar* (or *-retstsar,* or *-retstsor*), king of Bab.:—Nebuchadnezzar {31x}, Nebuchadrezzar {29x}. See: BDB—613a, 1102a.

5020. נְבוּכַדְנֶצַּר {31x} **Nᵉbûwkadnetstsar** (Aram.), *neb-oo-kad-nets-tsar'*; corresp. to 5019:—Nebuchadnezzar {31x}. See: BDB—1102a.

5021. נְבוּשַׁזְבָּן {1x} **Nᵉbûwshazbân**, *neb-oo-shaz-bawn'*; of for. der.; *Nebushazban,* Nebuchadnezzar's chief eunuch:—Nebushazban {1x}. See: BDB—613b.

5022. נָבוֹת {22x} **Nâbôwth**, *naw-both'*; fem. plur. from the same as 5011; *fruits; Naboth,* an Isr.:—Naboth {22x}. See: BDB—613b.

5023. נְבִזְבָּה {2x} **nᵉbizbâh** (Aram.), *neb-iz-baw'*; of uncert. der.; a *largess:*—reward {2x}. See: TWOT—2844; BDB—1102a.

5024. נָבַח {1x} **nâbach**, *naw-bakh'*; a prim. root; to *bark* (as a dog):—bark {1x}. See: TWOT—1281; BDB—613b.

5025. נֹבַח {3x} **Nôbach**, *no'-bach;* from 5024; a *bark; Nobach,* the name of an Isr., and of a place E. of the Jordan:—Nobah {3x}. See: BDB—613b.

5026. נִבְחַז {1x} **Nibchaz**, *nib-khaz'*; of for. or.; *Nibchaz,* a deity of the Avites:—Nibhaz {1x}. See: BDB—613b.

5027. נָבַט {69x} **nâbaṭ**, *naw-bat'*; a prim. root; to *scan,* i.e. look intently at; by impl. to *regard* with pleasure, favor or care:—look {36x}, behold {13x}, consider {5x}, regard {4x}, see {4x}, respect {3x}, look down {2x}, look about {1x}, look back {1x}.

Nabat means "to look, regard, behold." **(1)** The first use of this term is in Gen 15:5, where it is used in the sense of "take a good look," as God commands Abraham: "Look now toward heaven, and [number] the stars. . . ." **(2)** While *nabat* is commonly used of physical "looking" (Ex 3:6), the word is frequently used in a figurative sense to mean a spiritual and inner apprehension. Thus, Samuel is told by God: "Look not on his countenance . . ." (1 Sa 16:7) as he searched for a king among Jesse's sons. **(3)** The sense of "consider" (with insight) is expressed in Is 51:1–2: ". . . Look unto the rock whence ye are hewn. . . . Look unto Abraham your father. . . ." **(4)** "Pay attention to" seems to be the meaning in Is 5:12: ". . . they regard not the work of the Lord. . . ." See: TWOT—1282; BDB—613c.

5028. נְבָט {25x} **Nᵉbâṭ**, *neb-awt'*; from 5027; *regard; Nebat,* the father of Jeroboam I:—*Nebat* {25x}. See: BDB—614a.

5029. נְבִיא {4x} **nᵉbiyʾ** (Aram.), *neb-ee'*; corresp. to 5030; a *prophet:*—prophet {4x}. See: TWOT—2843a; BDB—1101d.

5030. נָבִיא {316x} **nâbiyʾ**, *naw-bee'*; from 5012; a *prophet* or (gen.) *inspired* man:—prophet {312x}, prophecy {1x}, them that prophesy {1x}, prophet + 376 {1x}, variant {1x}.

Nabiyʾ means "prophet." **(1)** *Nabiyʾ* represents "prophet," whether a true or false prophet (cf. Deut 13:1–5). **(2)** True prophets were mouthpieces of the true God. **(3)** In 1 Chr 29:29 three words are used for "prophet": "Now the acts of David the king, first and last, behold, they are written in the Book of Samuel the Seer [7203 - *roʾeh*] and in the Book of Nathan the Prophet [*nabiyʾ*], and in the Book of Gad the Seer [2374 - *chozeh*]." **(4)** The words translated "seer" emphasize the means by which the "prophet" communicated with God but do not identify the men as anything different from prophets (cf. 1 Sa 9:9). **(5)** The first occurrence of *nabiyʾ* does not help to clearly define it either: "Now therefore restore the man [Abraham] his wife; for he is a prophet, and he shall pray for thee, and thou shalt live . . ." (Gen 20:7). **(6)** The second occurrence of *nabiyʾ* establishes its meaning: "And the LORD said unto Moses, See, I have made thee a god to Pharaoh: and Aaron thy brother shall be thy prophet" (Ex 7:1). The background of this statement is Ex 4:10–16, where Moses argued his inability to speak clearly. God promised to appoint Aaron (Moses' brother) to be the speaker: "And he shall be thy spokesman unto the people: and he shall be, even he shall be to thee instead of a mouth, and thou shalt be to him instead of God" (Ex 4:16).

(7) Ex 7:1 expresses the same idea in different words. It is clear that the word "prophet" is equal to one who speaks for another, or his mouth. **(8)** This basic meaning of *nabiyʼ* is supported by other passages. In the classical passage Deut 18:14–22, God promised to raise up another "prophet" like Moses who would be God's spokesman (v. 18). They were held responsible for what he told them and were admonished to obey him (Deut 18:19). However, if what the "prophet" said proved to be wrong, he was to be killed (Deut 18:20). Immediately, this constitutes a promise and definition of the long succession of Israel's prophets. Ultimately, it is a promise of the Great Prophet, Jesus Christ (cf. Acts 3:22–23). **(9)** The "prophet" or dreamer of dreams might perform miracles to demonstrate that he was God's man, but the people were to look to the message rather than the miracle before they heeded his message (Deut 13:1–5).

(10) In the plural *nabiyʼ* is used of some who do not function as God's mouthpieces. **(10a)** In the time of Samuel there were men who followed him. They went about praising God (frequently with song) and trying to stir the people to return to God (1 Sa 10:5, 10; 19:20). **(10b)** Followers of Elijah and Elisha formed into groups to assist and/or to learn from these masters. They were called sons of the prophets (1 Kin 20:35). **(10c)** Used in this sense, the word *nabiyʼ* means a companion and/or follower of a prophet. **(11)** The word is also used of "heathen prophets": "Now therefore send, and gather to me all Israel unto mount Carmel, and the prophets of Baal four hundred and fifty, and the prophets of the groves four hundred, which eat at Jezebel's table" (1 Kin 18:19). Syn.: 2374, 4853. See: TWOT—1277a; BDB—611c, 1101d.

5031. נְבִיאָה {6x} **nᵉbîyʼâh**, *neb-ee-yaw'*; fem. of 5030; a *prophetess* or (gen.) *inspired* woman; by impl. a *poetess;* by association a *prophet's wife:*—prophetess {6x}.

(1) In Ex 15:20 Miriam is called a "prophetess." **(2)** Isaiah's wife, too, is called a "prophetess" (Is 8:3). This usage may be related to the meaning "a companion and/or follower of a prophet." See: TWOT—1277c; BDB—612c.

5032. נְבָיוֹת {5x} **Nᵉbâyôwth**, *neb-aw-yoth'*; or נְבָית **Nᵉbâyôth**, *neb-aw-yoth'*; fem. plur. from 5107; *fruitfulnesses; Nebajoth,* a son of Ismael, and the country settled by him:—Nebaioth {2x}, Nebajoth {3x}. See: BDB—614a.

5033. נֵבֶךְ {1x} **nêbek**, *nay'-bek;* from an unused root mean. to *burst* forth; a *fountain:*—spring {1x}. Syn.: 1543, 4002, 4599. See: TWOT—1283; See: BDB—614a.

5034. נָבֵל {25x} **nâbêl**, *naw-bale';* a prim. root; to *wilt;* gen. to *fall* away, *fail, faint;* fig. to *be foolish* or (mor.) *wicked;* caus. to *despise, disgrace:*—fade {8x}, fade away {3x}, wear away {2x}, wither {2x}, disgrace {1x}, surely {1x}, dishonoureth {1x}, fall down {1x}, esteemed {1x}, falling {1x}, foolishly {1x}, come to nought {1x}, fall off {1x}, surely {1x}, make vile {1x}. See: TWOT—1286; BDB—614c, 615b.

5035. נֶבֶל {3x} **nebel**, *neh'-bel;* or נֵבֶל **nêbel**, *nay'-bel;* from 5034; a skin-*bag* for liquids (from *collapsing* when empty); hence, a *vase* (as similar in shape when full); also a *lyre* (as having a body of like form):—psalteries {23}, bottle {8x}, viol {4x}, flagons {1x}, pitchers {1x}, vessel {1x}. See: TWOT—1284a, 1284b; BDB—614b.

5036. נָבָל {18x} **nâbâl**, *naw-bawl';* from 5034; *stupid; wicked* (espec. *impious*):—fool {9x}, foolish {5x}, vile person {2x}, foolish man {1x}, foolish women {1x}. Syn.: 191, 3684. See: TWOT—1285a; BDB—614d.

5037. נָבָל {22x} **Nâbâl**, *naw-bawl';* the same as 5036; *dolt; Nabal,* an Isr.:—Nabal {18x}, Nabhal {4x}. See: BDB—615a.

5038. נְבֵלָה {48x} **nᵉbêlâh**, *neb-ay-law';* from 5034; a *flabby* thing, i.e. a *carcase* or *carrion* (human or bestial, often collect.); fig. an *idol:*—carcase {36x}, dead body {5x}, dieth of itself {4x}, dead of itself {1x}, died {1x}, body {1x}. See: TWOT—1286a; BDB—615c.

5039. נְבָלָה {13x} **nᵉbâlâh**, *neb-aw-law';* fem. of 5036; *foolishness,* i.e. (mor.) *wickedness;* concr. a *crime;* by extens. *punishment:*—folly {10x}, vile {1x}, villany {2x}.

Nebalah means "foolishness; senselessness; impropriety; stupidity." **(1)** It signifies "disregarding God's will": "Let not my lord, I pray thee, regard this man of Belial, *even* Nabal: for as his name *is,* so *is* he; Nabal *is* his name, and folly *is* with him: but I thine handmaid saw not the young men of my lord, whom thou didst send" (1 Sa 25:25). **(2)** *Nebalah* is most often used as a word for a serious sin: "And the sons of Jacob came out of the field when they heard *it:* and the men were grieved, and they were very wroth, because he had wrought folly [*nebalah*] in Israel in lying with Jacob's daughter; which thing ought not to be done" (Gen 34:7—the first occurrence). Syn.: 200. See: TWOT—1285b; BDB—615a.

5040. נַבְלוּת {1x} **nablûwth**, *nab-looth';* from 5036; prop. *disgrace,* i.e. the (female) *pudenda:*—lewdness {1x}. See: TWOT—1285c; BDB—615b.

5041. נְבַלָּט {1x} **Nᵉballât**, *neb-al-lawt';* appar. from 5036 and 3909; *foolish secrecy; Neballat,* a place in Pal.:—*Neballat* {1x}. See: BDB—615d.

5042. נָבַע {11x} **nâbaʻ**, *naw-bah';* a prim. root; to *gush* forth; fig. to *utter* (good or bad words); spec. to *emit* (a foul odor):—belch out {1x}, flowing, {1x} pour out {3x}, send forth {1x}, utter (abundantly) {5x}. See: TWOT—1287; BDB—615d.

5043. נֶבְרְשָׁא {1x} **nebrᵉshâʼ** (Aram.), *neb-reh-shaw';* from an unused root mean. to *shine;* a *light;* plur. (collect.) a *chandelier:*—candlestick {1x}. Syn.: 4501. See: TWOT—2845; BDB—1102a.

5044. נִבְשָׁן {1x} **Nibshân**, *nib-shawn';* of uncert. der.; *Nibshan,* a place in Pal.:—*Nibshan* {1x}. See: BDB—143c, 616a.

5045. נֶגֶב {112x} **negeb**, *neh'-gheb;* from an unused root mean. to *be parched;* the *south* (from its drought), spec. the *Negeb* or southern district of Judah, occasionally, *Egypt* (as south to Pal.):—south {89x}, southward {16x}, south side {5x}, south country {2x}. See: TWOT—1288a; BDB—616a, 918b.

5046. נָגַד {370x} **nâgad**, *naw-gad';* a prim. root; prop. to *front,* i.e. stand boldly out opposite; by impl. (caus.), to *manifest;* fig. to *announce* (always by word of mouth to one present); spec. to *expose, predict, explain, praise:*—tell {222x}, declare {63x}, shew {59x}, utter {5x}, shew forth {3x}, expound {2x}, messenger {2x}, report {2x}, misc. {13x} = bewray, × certainly, certify, denounce, × fully, plainly, profess, rehearse, speak, × surely.

Nagad means "to tell, explain, inform." **(1)** The first emphasis of the word is "to tell." This especially means that A (frequently a messenger or some other person who has witnessed something) "tells" B (the one to whom the report is made) C (the report). In such instances B (the one told) is spatially separated from the original source of the information. So, in Gen 9:22, Ham (A) saw his father naked and went outside the tent and "told" his brothers (B) what he had seen (C). **(2)** In another group of passages *nagad* represents the reporting of a messenger about a matter of life-or-death importance for the recipient. **(2a)** So a fugitive "came . . . and told Abram" that Lot had been captured and led away captive (Gen 14:13). **(2b)** A note of this emotionally charged situation is seen in Jacob's message to Esau: ". . . I have sent to tell my lord, that I may find grace in thy sight" (Gen 32:5). **(2c)** Although not a report from a messenger from afar, Gen 12:18 uses the verb of a report that is of crucial importance to the one addressed. Pharaoh asked Abram: "Why didst thou not tell me that she was thy wife?" **(2d)** Gen 12:17 reports that because Pharaoh had taken Sarai into his harem to become his wife, God had smitten his household with great plagues.

(3) *Nagad* means "to explain or reveal" something one does not otherwise know. **(3a)** In Gen 3:11 (the first biblical occurrence of the word) God asked Adam: "Who told thee that thou wast naked?" This was information immediately before them but not previously grasped by them. **(3b)** This usage appears in Gen 41:24, where Pharaoh said of his dream: ". . . I told this unto the magicians; but there was none that could declare it to me." **(3c)** Similarly, David made certain there were no survivors from the Philistine cities he looted so no one would "tell" it to Achish (1 Sa 27:11). **(4)** This word sometimes has a more forceful significance—God told the prophet to "show my people their transgression" (Is 58:1). See: TWOT—1289; BDB—616c.

5047. נְגַד {1x} **nᵉgad** (Aram.), *neg-ad';* corresp. to 5046; to *flow* (through the idea of *clearing* the way):—issue {1x}. See: TWOT—2846; BDB—1102a.

5048. נֶגֶד {23x} **neged**, *neh'-ghed;* from 5046; a *front,* i.e. part opposite; spec. a *counterpart,* or mate; usually (adv., espec. with prep.) *over against* or *before:*—{23x} = about, (over) against, × aloof, × far (off), × from, over, presence, × other side, sight, × to view.

Neged means "before; in the presence of; in the sight of, in front of; in one's estimation; straight ahead." **(1)** Basically the word indicates that its object is immediately "before" something or someone. **(1a)** It is used in Gen 2:18, where God said He would make Adam "a help meet for him," or someone to correspond to him, just as the males and females of the animals corresponded to (matched) one another. **(1b)** To be immediately "before" the sun is to be fully in the sunlight (Num 25:4). **(2)** In Ex 10:10 Pharaoh told Moses that evil was immediately "before" his face, or was in his mind. **(3)** *Neged* signifies "in front of" (Ex 19:2), **(4)** "before" in the sense of "in one's estimation" (Is 40:17), and **(5)** "straight ahead (before)" (Josh 6:5). **(6)** In combination with other particles *neged* means "contrary to" (Num 22:32). **(7)** The word indicates that its object is immediately "before" something or someone. As an adverb it means opposite, over against: "And she went, and sat her down over against him a good way off. . . ." (Gen 21:16). See: TWOT—1289a; BDB—617a, 1102a.

5049. נֶגֶד {1x} **neged** (Aram.), *neh'-ghed;* corresp. to 5048; *opposite:*—toward {1x}. See: TWOT—2846a; BDB—1102a.

5050. נָגַהּ {6x} **nâgahh**, *naw-găh';* a prim. root; to *glitter;* caus. to *illuminate:*—(en-) lighten {2x}, (cause to) shine {4x}. See: TWOT—1290; BDB—618b.

5051. נֹגַהּ {19x} **nôgahh**, *no'-găh;* from 5050; *brilliancy* (lit. or fig.):—brightness {11x}, light {1x}, bright {1x}, (clear) shining {6x}. See: TWOT—1290a; BDB—618b, 1102a.

5052. נֹגַהּ {2x} **Nôgahh**, *no'-găh;* the same as 5051; *Nogah,* a son of David:—Nogah {2x}. See: BDB—618b.

5053. נֹגַהּ {1x} **nogahh** (Aram.), *no'-găh;* corresp. to 5051; *dawn:*—morning {1x}. See: TWOT—2847; BDB—1102a.

5054. נְגֹהָה {1x} **n**e**gôhâh**, *neg-o-haw';* fem. of 5051; *splendor:*—brightness {1x}. See: TWOT—1290b; BDB—618c.

5055. נָגַח {11x} **nâgach**, *naw-gakh';* a prim. root; to *but* with the horns; fig. to *war* against:—gore {3x}, push (down, -ing) {8x}. See: TWOT—1291; BDB—618c.

5056. נַגָּח {2x} **naggâch**, *nag-gawkh';* from 5055; *butting,* i.e. *vicious:*—used (wont) to push {2x}. See: TWOT—1291a; BDB—618c.

5057. נָגִיד {44x} **nâgîyd**, *naw-gheed';* or

נָגִד **nâgîd**, *naw-gheed';* from 5046; a *commander* (as occupying the *front*), civil, military or religious; gen. (abstr. plur.), *honorable* themes:—ruler {20x}, prince {9x}, captain {6x}, leader {4x}, governor {3x}, nobles {1x}, excellent things {1x}.

Nagiyd means "chief leader." **(1)** In 1 Sa 9:16 the word is used as a "chief leader" that is equivalent to a king: "Tomorrow about this time I will send thee a man out of the land of Benjamin, and thou shalt anoint him to be captain over my people Israel. . . ." **(2)** *Nagiyd* appears in 1 Chr 9:11 to refer to a "chief leader" (ruler) of a smaller region: "And Azariah the son of Hilkiah, the son of Meshullam, the son of Zadok, the son of Meraioth, the son of Ahitub, the ruler of the house of God." **(3)** The word may also be used of a head of a family: "And Phinehas the son of Eleazar was the ruler over them in time past, *and* the LORD *was* with him" (1Chr 9:20). See: TWOT—1289b; BDB—618d.

5058. נְגִינָה {14x} **n**e**gîynâh**, *neg-ee-naw';* or

נְגִינַת **n**e**gîynath** (Ps 61:title), *neg-ee-nath';* from 5059; prop. instrumental *music;* by impl. a stringed *instrument;* by extens. a *poem* set to music; spec. an *epigram:*—stringed instruments {1x}, music {1x}, Neginoth [*plur.*] {6x}, song {5x}, Neginah {1x}. See: TWOT—1292.1a; BDB—618d.

5059. נָגַן {15x} **nâgan**, *naw-gan';* a prim. root; prop. to *thrum,* i.e. *beat* a tune with the fingers; espec. to *play* on a stringed instrument; hence, (gen.), to *make music:*—play {8x}, instrument {3x}, minstrel {2x}, melody {1x}, player {1x}. See: TWOT—1292.1; BDB—618d.

5060. נָגַע {150x} **nâga**c, *naw-gah';* a prim. root; prop. to *touch,* i.e. *lay the hand upon* (for any purpose; euphem. to *lie with* a woman); by impl. to *reach* (fig. to *arrive, acquire*); violently, to *strike* (punish, defeat, destroy, etc.):—touch {92x}, came {18x}, reach {11x}, bring {4x}, near {4x}, smite {4x}, nigh {3x}, plagued {3x}, happeneth {2x}, strike {2x}, beaten {1x}, cast {1x}, reach up {1x}, brought down {1x}, join {1x}, laid {1x}, get up {1x}.

Naga' means "to touch, strike, reach, smite." **(1)** *Naga'* first occurs in Gen 3:3 in the Garden of Eden story, where the woman reminds the serpent that God had said: "Ye shall not eat of [the fruit of the tree which is in the midst of the garden], neither shall ye touch it. . . ." **(2)** This illustrates the common meaning of physical touch involving various kinds of objects: **(2a)** Jacob's thigh was "touched" by the man at Jabbok (Gen 32:25, 32); **(2b)** the Israelites were commanded not "to touch" Mount Horeb under pain of death (Ex 19:12); and **(2c)** unclean things were not "to be touched" (Lev 5:2–3). **(3)** Sometimes *naga'* is used figuratively in the sense of emotional involvement: "And Saul also went home to Gibeah; and there went with him a band of men, whose hearts God had touched" (1 Sa 10:26). **(4)** The word is used to refer to sexual contact with another person, such as in Gen 20:6, where God tells Abimelech that He did not allow him "to touch" Sarah, Abraham's wife (cf. Prov 6:29). **(5)** To refer to the touch of God's hand means that divine chastisement has been received: ". . . Have pity upon me, O ye my friends; for the hand of God hath touched me" (Job 19:21). **(6)** The word is commonly used also to describe "being stricken" with a disease: King Uzziah "was smitten" with leprosy (2 Chr 26:20). See: TWOT—1293; BDB—619a.

5061. נֶגַע {78x} **nega**c, *neh'-gah;* from 5060; a *blow* (fig. *infliction*); also (by impl.) a *spot* (concr. a *leprous* person or dress):—plague {65x}, sore {5x}, stroke {4x}, stripes {2x}, stricken {1x}, wound {1x}.

Nega' means "plague: stroke; wound." **(1)** The word refers to a "plague" most frequently: "And the LORD plagued Pharaoh and his house with great plagues because of Sarai Abram's wife" (Gen 12:17; cf. Ex 11:1). **(2)** *Nega'* can also mean "stroke": "If there arise a matter too hard for thee in judgment, between blood and blood, between plea and plea, and between stroke and stroke, *being* matters of controversy within thy gates: then shalt thou arise, and get thee up into the place which the LORD thy God shall choose" (Deut 17:8; cf. 21:5) or **(3)** "wound": "A wound and dishonour shall he get; and his reproach shall not be wiped away" (Prov 6:33). **(4)** Each meaning carries with it the sense of a person "being stricken or smitten in some way." See: TWOT—1293a; BDB—619c.

5062. נָגַף {49x} **nâgaph**, *naw-gaf';* a prim. root; to *push, gore, defeat, stub* (the toe), *inflict* (a disease):—smite {27x}, put to the worse {5x}, smitten down {3x}, plague {3x}, hurt {2x}, slain {2x}, struck {2x}, stumble {2x}, beaten {1x}, dash {1x}, surely {1x}. Syn.: 4046, 5061. See: TWOT—1294; BDB—619d.

5063. נֶגֶף {7x} **negeph**, *neh'-ghef;* from 5062; a *trip* (of the foot); fig. an *infliction* (of disease):—plague {6x}, stumbling {1x}. See: TWOT—1294a; BDB—620a.

5064. נָגַר {10x} **nâgar**, *naw-gar';* a prim. root; to *flow;* fig. to *stretch* out; caus. to *pour* out or down; fig. to *deliver* over:—fall {1x}, flow away {1x}, pour down {1x}, pour out {2x}, run {1x}, shed {1x}, spilt {1x}, trickle down {1x}. See: TWOT—1295; BDB—620b.

5065. נָגַשׂ {23x} **nâgas**, *naw-gas';* a prim. root; to *drive* (an animal, a workman, a debtor, an army); by impl. to *tax, harass, tyrannize:*—oppressor {7x}, taskmasters {5x}, exact {4x}, distressed {2x}, oppressed {2x}, driver {1x}, exactors {1x}, taxes {1x}. See: TWOT—1296; BDB—620b.

5066. נָגַשׁ {125x} **nâgash**, *naw-gash';* a prim. root; to *be* or *come* (caus. *bring*) *near* (for any purpose); euphem. to *lie with* a woman; as an enemy, to *attack;* relig. to *worship;* caus. to *present;* fig. to *adduce* an argument; by reversal, to *stand back:*—(come, draw, etc) . . . near {55x}, come {14x}, (come, draw, etc) . . . nigh {12x}, bring {13x}, . . . hither {7x}, offer {7x}, approach {5x}, forth {3x}, misc. {9x} = give place, go hard (up), overtake, present, put, stand.

Nagash means "to approach, draw near, bring." **(1)** *Nagash* is used for the first time in the biblical text in Gen 18:23, where Abraham is said to "draw near" to God to plead that Sodom be spared. **(2)** The word is often used to describe ordinary "contact" of one person with another: "And Jacob went near unto Isaac his father; and he felt him, and said, The voice *is* Jacob's voice, but the hands *are* the hands of Esau" (Gen 27:22; cf. 43:19). **(3)** Sometimes *nagash* describes "contact" for the purpose of sexual intercourse: "And he said unto the people, Be ready against the third day: come not at *your* wives" (Ex 19:15). **(4)** More frequently, it is used to speak of the priests "coming into the presence of" God (Eze 44:13) or of the priests' "approach" to the altar (Ex 30:20). **(5)** Opposing armies are said "to go up" to battle each other (Judg 20:23). **(6)** Inanimate objects, such as the close-fitting scales of the crocodile, are said to be so "near" to each other that no air can come between them (Job 41:16). **(7)** Sometimes the word is used to speak of "bringing" an offering to the altar (Mal 1:7). See: TWOT—1297; BDB—620c.

5067. נֵד {6x} **nêd**, *nade;* from 5110 in the sense of *piling* up; a *mound,* i.e. *wave:*—heap {6x}. See: TWOT—1301a; BDB—621b, 622d.

5068. נָדַב {1x} **nâdab**, *naw-dab';* a prim. root; to *impel;* hence, to *volunteer* (as a soldier), to *present* spontaneously:—offered willingly {6x}, willingly offered {5x}, willing {2x}, offered {1x}, willing {1x}, offered freely {1x}, give willingly {1x}. See: TWOT—1299; BDB—621c, 1102b.

5069. נְדַב {4x} **n**e**dab** (Aram.), *ned-ab';* corresp. to 5068; *be* (or *give*) *liberal* (*-ly*):—freely offered {1x}, freewill offering {1x}, offering willingly {1x}, minded of their own freewill {1x}. See: TWOT—2848; BDB—1102b.

5070. נָדָב {20x} **Nâdâb**, *naw-dawb';* from 5068; *liberal; Nadab,* the name of four Isr.:—*Nadab* {20x}. See: BDB—621c.

5071. נְדָבָה {26x} **n**e**dâbâh**, *ned-aw-baw';* from 5068; prop. (abstr.) *spontaneity,* or (adj.) *spontaneous;* also (concr.) a *spontaneous* or (by infer., in plur.) *abundant* gift:—freewill offering {15x}, offerings {9x}, free offering {2x}, freely {2x}, willing offering {1x}, voluntary offering {1x}, plentiful {1x}, voluntarily {1x}, voluntary {1x}, willing {1x}, willingly {1x}.

This offering is always given willingly, bountifully, liberally, or as a prince would offer. It refers not to the nature of the offering or the external mode in which it is offered, but to the motive and spirit of the offerer. See: TWOT—1299a; BDB—621d.

5072. נְדַבְיָה {1x} **N**e**dabyâh**, *ned-ab-yaw';* from 5068 and 3050; *largess of Jah; Nedabjah,* an Isr.:—Nedabiah {1x}. See: BDB—622a.

5073. נִדְבָּךְ {2x} **nidbâk** (Aram.), *nid-bawk';* from a root mean. to *stick;* a *layer* (of building materials):—row {2x}. Syn.: 2905. See: TWOT—2849; BDB—1102b.

5074. נָדַד {28x} **nâdad**, *naw-dad';* a prim. root; prop. to *wave* to and fro (rarely to flap up and down); fig. to *rove, flee,* or (caus.) to *drive* away:—flee {9x}, wander {6x}, . . . away {4x}, wandereth abroad {1x}, flee apace {1x}, chased {1x}, misc. {6x} = × could not, depart, (re-) move, thrust away. See: TWOT—1300; BDB—622b, 1102b.

5075. נְדַד {1x} **nᵉdad** (Aram.), *ned-ad';* corresp. to 5074; to *depart:*—go from {1x}. See: TWOT—2850; BDB—1102b, 1102c.

5076. נָדוּד {1x} **nâdûd**, *naw-dood';* pass. part. of 5074; prop. *tossed;* abstr. a *rolling* (on the bed):—tossing to and fro {1x}. See: TWOT—1300a; BDB—622c.

5077. נָדָה {3x} **nâdâh**, *naw-daw';* or

נָדָא **nâdâ'** (2 Kin 17:21), *naw-daw';* a prim. root; prop. to *toss;* fig. to *exclude,* i.e. *banish, postpone, prohibit:*—cast out {1x}, drive {1x}, put far away {1x}. See: TWOT—1302; BDB—621b, 622d.

5078. נֵדֶה {1x} **nêdeh**, *nay'-deh;* from 5077 in the sense of freely *flinging* money; a *bounty* (for prostitution):—gifts {1x}. See: TWOT—1303a; BDB—622d.

5079. נִדָּה {29x} **niddâh**, *nid-daw';* from 5074; prop. *rejection;* by impl. *impurity,* espec. Pers. (menstruation) or mor. (idolatry, incest):—separation {14x}, put apart {2x}, filthiness {2x}, flowers {2x}, far {1x}, set apart {1x}, menstruous {1x}, removed {1x}, unclean thing {1x}, unclean {1x}, uncleanness {1x}, menstruous woman {1x}, removed woman {1x}. See: TWOT—1302a; BDB—622c, 622d.

5080. נָדַח {52x} **nâdach**, *naw-dakh';* a prim. root; to *push* off; used in a great variety of applications, lit. and fig. (to expel, mislead, strike, inflict, etc.): drive {18x}, drive out {6x}, . . . away {6x}, outcasts {5x}, cast out {3x}, banished {2x}, bring {1x}, go astray {1x}, chased {1x}, compelled {1x}, down {1x}, expelled {1x}, misc. {6x}= fetch a stroke, force, thrust away (out), withdraw.

Nadach means "to drive out, banish, thrust, move." **(1)** *Nadach* occurs approximately 50 times in the Hebrew Old Testament, and **(1a)** its first use is in the passive form: "And lest thou . . . shouldest be driven to worship them . . ." (Deut 4:19). **(1b)** The implication seems to be that an inner "drivenness" or "drawing away," as well as an external force, was involved in Israel's potential turning toward idolatry. **(2)** *Nadach* expresses the idea of "being scattered" in exile, as in Jer 40:12: "Even all the Jews returned out of all places whither they were driven. . . ." **(3)** Job complained that any resource he once possessed no longer existed, for it "is . . . driven quite from me" (Job 6:13). **(4)** Evil "shepherds" or leaders did not lead but rather "drove away" and scattered Israel (Jer 23:2). **(5)** The enemies of a good man plot against him "They only consult to cast *him* down from his excellency: they delight in lies: they bless with their mouth, but they curse inwardly" (Ps 62:4). See: TWOT—1304; BDB—623a.

5081. נָדִיב {28x} **nâdîyb**, *naw-deeb';* from 5068; prop. *voluntary,* i.e. generous; hence, *magnanimous;* as noun, a *grandee* (sometimes a *tyrant*):—prince {15x}, nobles {4x}, willing {3x}, free {2x}, liberal {2x}, liberal things {2x}. See: TWOT—1299b; BDB—622a.

5082. נְדִיבָה {1x} **nᵉdîybâh**, *ned-ee-baw';* fem. of 5081; prop. *nobility,* i.e. reputation:—soul {1x}. See: TWOT—1299c; BDB—622a.

5083. נָדָן {1x} **nâdân**, *naw-dawn';* prob. from an unused root mean. to *give;* a *present* (for prostitution):—gift {1x}. Syn.: 5078. See: TWOT—1305; BDB—623c.

5084. נָדָן {1x} **nâdân**, *naw-dawn';* of uncert. der.; a *sheath* (of a sword):—sheath {1x}. See: TWOT—1306; BDB—623c, 1102b.

5085. נִדְנֶה {1x} **nidneh** (Aram.), *nid-neh';* from the same as 5084; a *sheath;* fig. the *body* (as the receptacle of the soul):—body {1x}. See: TWOT—2851; BDB—1086, 1102b.

5086. נָדַף {9x} **nâdaph**, *naw-daf';* a prim. root; to *shove* asunder, i.e. *disperse:*—drive away {4x}, drive {1x}, thrust him down {1x}, shaken {1x}, driven to and fro {1x}, tossed to and fro {1x}. See: TWOT—1307; BDB—623c.

5087. נָדַר {31x} **nâdar**, *naw-dar';* a prim. root; to *promise* (pos., to do or give something to God):—make a vow {1x}, vow {30x}.

Nadar, as a verb, means "to vow." **(1)** Both men and women could "vow" a vow. **(2)** Numbers 30 deals with the law concerning vows; cf. **(2a)** Num 30:2: "If a man vow a vow unto the LORD, or swear an oath to bind his soul with a bond . . ."; and **(2b)** Num. 30:3: "If a woman also vow a vow unto the LORD, and bind herself by a bond. . . ." Syn.: 5088. See: TWOT—1308; BDB—623d.

5088. נֶדֶר {60x} **neder**, *neh'-der;* or

נֵדֶר **nêder**, *nay'-der;* from 5087; a *promise* (to God); also (concr.) a thing *promised:*—vow {58x}, vowed {2x}.

Neder, as a noun, means "vow; votive offering." **(1)** This noun occurs 60 times in biblical Hebrew and is often used in conjunction with the verb (19 times): ". . . Any of thy vows which thou vowest . . ." (Deut 12:17). **(2)** The vow has two basic forms, the unconditional and the conditional. **(2a)** The unconditional is an "oath" where someone binds himself without expecting anything in return: "I will pay my vows unto the LORD now in the presence of all his people" (Ps 116:14). The obligation is binding upon the person who has made a "vow." The word spoken has the force of an oath which generally could not be broken: "If a man vow a vow unto the Lord, or swear an oath to bind his soul with a bond; he shall not break his word, he shall do [everything he said]" (Num 30:2). **(2b)** The conditional "vow" generally had a preceding clause before the oath giving the conditions which had to come to pass before the "vow" became valid: "And Jacob vowed a vow, saying, If God will be with me, and will [watch over me] . . . , so that I come again to my father's house in peace; then shall the LORD be my God . . . and of all that thou shalt give me I will surely give the tenth unto thee" (Gen 28:20–22).

(3) "Vows" usually occurred in serious situations. **(3a)** Jacob needed the assurance of God's presence before setting out for Padan-aram (Gen 28:20–22); **(3b)** Jephthah made a rash "vow" before battle (Judg 11:30; cf. Num 21:1–3); **(3c)** Hannah greatly desired a child (1 Sa 1:11), when she made a "vow." **(3d)** Though conditional "vows" were often made out of desperation, there is no question of the binding force of the "vow." **(4)** Ecclesiastes amplifies the Old Testament teaching on "vowing": "When thou vowest a vow unto God, defer not to pay it. . . . Better is it that thou shouldest not vow, than that thou shouldest vow and not pay. . . . Neither say thou before the angel, that it was an error" (5:4–6). **(4a)** First, "vow" is always made to God. Even non-Israelites made "vows" to Him (Jonah 1:16). **(4b)** Second, a "vow" is made voluntarily. It is never associated with a life of piety or given the status of religious requirement in the Old Testament. **(4c)** Third, a "vow" once made must be kept. One cannot annul the "vow." **(4c1)** However, the Old Testament allows for "redeeming" the "vow"; by payment of an equal amount in silver, a person, a field, or a house dedicated by "vow" to the Lord could be redeemed (Lev 27:1–25). **(4c2)** This practice, however, declined in Jesus' time, and therefore the Talmud frowns upon the practice of "vowing" and refers to those who vow as "sinners."

(5) *Neder* signifies a kind of offering: "And thither ye shall bring your burnt offerings, and your sacrifices, and your tithes, and [contributions] of your hand, and your vows, and your freewill offerings . . ." (Deut 12:6). **(5a)** In particular the word represents a kind of peace or "votive offering" (Ezr 7:16). **(5b)** It also is a kind of thank offering: "Behold upon the mountains the feet of him that bringeth good tidings, that publisheth peace! . . . Perform thy vows . . ." (Nah 1:15). **(5c)** Here even Gentiles expressed their thanks to God presumably with a gift promised upon condition of deliverance (cf. Num 21:1–3). **(5d)** Such offerings may also be expressions of zeal for God (Ps 22:25). **(5e)** One can give to God anything not abominable to Him (Lev 27:9ff.; Deut 23:18), including one's services (Lev 27:2). **(6)** Pagans were thought to feed and/or tend their gods, while God denied that "vows" paid to Him were to be so conceived (Ps 50:9–13). **(6a)** In paganism the god rewarded the devotee because of and in proportion to his offering. **(6b)** It was a contractual relationship whereby the god was obligated to pay a debt thus incurred. In Israel no such contractual relationship was in view.

(7) The Israelites' unique and concrete demonstrations of love for God show that under Moses love (Deut 6:4) was more than pure legalism; it was spiritual devotion. **(8)** God's Messiah was pledged to offer Himself as a sacrifice for sin (Ps 22:25; cf. Lev 27:2ff.). This was the only sacrifice absolutely and unconditionally acceptable to God. **(9)** Every man is obliged to pay the "vow" before God: "Praise waiteth for thee, O God in Zion: and unto thee shall the vow be performed. . . . Unto thee shall all flesh come" (Ps 65:1–2). See: TWOT—1308a; BDB—623d.

5089. נֹהַּ {1x} **nôahh**, *no'-ăh;* from an unused root mean. to *lament; lamentation:*—wailing {1x}. Syn.: 4533, 5091, 5204. See: TWOT—1320a; BDB—624a, 627b.

5090. נָהַג {31x} **nâhag**, *naw-hag';* a prim. root; to *drive* forth (a person, an animal or chariot), i.e. *lead, carry away;* refl. to *proceed* (i.e. impel or guide oneself); also (from the *panting* induced by effort), to *sigh:*—lead {10x}, (carry, lead) . . . away {7x}, drive {6x}, forth {2x}, guide {2x}, brought {2x}, acquainting {1x}, brought in {1x}. See: TWOT—1309, 1310; BDB—624a, 624c.

5091. נָהָה {3x} **nâhâh**, *naw-haw';* a prim. root; to *groan,* i.e. *bewail;* hence, (through the idea of *crying* aloud), to *assemble* (as if on proclamation):—lament {2x}, wail {1x}. Syn.: 4533, 5089, 5204. See: TWOT—1311; BDB—624c.

5092. נְהִי {7x} **nᵉhîy**, *neh-hee';* from 5091; an *elegy:*—lamentation {3x}, wailing {4x}. See: TWOT—1311a; BDB—624c.

5093. נִהְיָה {1x} **nihyâh**, *nih-yaw';* fem. of 5092; *lamentation:*—doleful {1x}. See: TWOT—1311b; BDB—624d.

5094. נְהִיר {3x} **nᵉhîyr** (Aram.), *neh-heere';* or
נְהִירוּ **nâhîyrûw** (Aram.), *nâh-hee-roo';* from the same as 5105; *illumination,* i.e. (fig.) wisdom:—light {3x}. See: TWOT—2853a, 2853b; BDB—1102c.

5095. נָהַל {10x} **nâhal**, *naw-hal';* a prim. root; prop. to run with a *sparkle,* i.e. *flow;* hence, (tran.), to *conduct,* and (by infer.) to *protect, sustain:*—carry {1x}, feed {1x}, guide {5x}, lead (gently, on) {3x}. See: TWOT—1312; BDB—624d.

5096. נַהֲלָל {3x} **Nahălâl**, *năh-hal-awl';* or
נַהֲלֹל **Nahălôl**, *năh-hal-ole';* the same as 5097; *Nahalal* or *Nahalol,* a place in Pal.:—Nahalal {1x}, Nahallal {1x}, *Nahalol* {1x}. See: TWOT—1312; BDB—625b.

5097. נַהֲלֹל {1x} **nahălôl**, *năh-hal-ole';* from 5095; *pasture:*—bushes {1x}. See: TWOT—1312a; BDB—625b.

5098. נָהַם {5x} **nâham**, *naw-ham';* a prim. root; to *growl:*—mourn {2x}, roar {2x}, roaring {1x}. See: TWOT—1313; BDB—625b.

5099. נַהַם {2x} **naham**, *năh'-ham;* from 5098; a *snarl:*—roaring {2x}. See: TWOT—1313a; BDB—625b.

5100. נְהָמָה {2x} **nᵉhâmâh**, *neh-haw-maw';* fem. of 5099; *snarling:*—disquietness {1x}, roaring {1x}. See: TWOT—1313b; BDB—625b.

5101. נָהַק {2x} **nâhaq**, *naw-hak';* a prim. root; to *bray* (as an ass), *scream* (from hunger):—bray {2x}. See: TWOT—1314; BDB—625c.

5102. נָהַר {6x} **nâhar**, *naw-har';* a prim. root; to *sparkle,* i.e. (fig.) *be cheerful;* hence, (from the *sheen* of a running stream) to *flow,* i.e. (fig.) *assemble:*—flow {2x}, flow together {3x}, be lightened {1x}.

Nahar means "to flow." This verb occurs in Is 2:2: "And it shall come to pass in the last days that the mountain of the LORD's house shall be established in the top of the mountains, and shall be exalted above the hills; and all nations shall flow unto it." See: TWOT—1316, 1315; BDB—625c, 626a, 1102c.

5103. נְהַר {15x} **nᵉhar** (Aram.), *neh-har';* from a root corresp. to 5102; a *river,* espec. the Euphrates:—river {14x}, stream {1x}. See: TWOT—2852; BDB—1102c.

5104. נָהָר {120x} **nâhâr**, *naw-hawr';* from 5102; a *stream* (incl. the *sea;* espec. the Nile, Euphrates, etc.); fig. *prosperity:*—river {98x}, flood {18x}, streams {2x}, Aramnaharaim + 763 {1x}, river side {1x}.

Nahar (5104) means "river; stream; canal; current." **(1)** First, this word usually refers to permanent natural watercourses. **(1a)** In its first biblical appearance *nahar* represents the primeval "rivers" of Eden: "And a river went out of Eden to water the garden; and from thence it was parted, and became into four heads" (Gen 2:10). **(2)** In some passages *nahar* may represent a "canal(s)": "Say unto Aaron, Take thy rod, and stretch out thine hand upon the waters of Egypt, upon their streams [the branches of the Nile], upon their rivers [canals], and upon their ponds . . ." (Ex 7:19; cf. Eze 1:1). **(3)** Third, this word is used of "ocean currents": "For thou hadst cast me into the deep, in the midst of the seas; and the floods compassed me about: all thy billows and thy waves passed over me" (Jonah 2:3). **(4)** Fourth, *nahar* is used of underground streams: "For he hath founded it [the earth] upon the seas, and established it upon the floods" (Ps 24:2). This passage appears to be a literary allusion to the pagan concept of the creation and structure of the world—the next verse is "Who shall ascend into the hill of the LORD?" (Ps 24:3).

(5) This word plays a prominent role in the figure of divine blessing set forth in Ps 46:4: "There is a river, the streams whereof shall make glad the city of God. . . ." This may be an allusion to the primeval "river" in Eden whose water gave life to the garden. **(6)** In Is 33:21 the same Jerusalem is depicted as having "rivers" of blessing: ". . . A place of broad rivers and streams; wherein shall go no galley with oars, neither shall gallant ship pass thereby" (cf. Is 48:18). **(7)** In other passages a "river" is a figure of trouble and difficulty: "When thou passest through the waters, I will be with thee; and through the rivers, they shall not overflow thee . . ." (Is 43:2). **(8)** This is in marked contrast to the use of the same idea in Is 66:12, where an "overflowing stream" depicts respectively the onrush of God's glory and divine peace. Syn.: 5158. See: TWOT—1315a; BDB—625c.

5105. נְהָרָה {1x} **nᵉhârâh**, *neh-haw-raw';* from 5102 in its orig. sense; *daylight:*—light {1x}. See: TWOT—1316a; BDB—626a.

5106. נוּא {9x} **nûwʾ**, *noo;* a prim. root; to *refuse, forbid, dissuade,* or *neutralize:*—disallow {1x}, disallowed {3x}, discourage {2x}, discouraged {1x}, make to no effect {1x}, break {1x}. See: TWOT—1317; BDB—626b.

5107. נוּב {4x} **nûwb**, *noob;* a prim. root; to *germinate,* i.e. (fig.) to (caus. *make*) *flourish;* also (of words), to *utter:*—bring forth (fruit) {2x}, make cheerful {1x}, increase {1x}. See: TWOT—1318; BDB—626b.

5108. נוֹב {2x} **nôwb**, *nobe;* or
נֵיב **nêyb**, *nabe;* from 5107; *produce,* lit. or fig.:—fruit {2x}. Syn.: 6529. See: TWOT—1318a, 1318b; BDB—626c, 644b.

5109. נוֹבַי {1x} **Nôwbay**, *no-bah'ee;* from 5108; *fruitful; Nobai,* an Isr.:—Nebai {1x}. See: BDB—626c, 644b.

5110. נוּד {24x} **nûwd**, *nood;* a prim. root; to *nod,* i.e. waver; fig. to *wander, flee, disappear;* also (from *shaking* the head in sympathy), to *console, deplore,* or (from *tossing* the head in scorn) *taunt:*—bemoan {7x}, remove {5x}, vagabond {2x}, flee {1x}, get {1x}, mourn {1x}, move {1x}, pity {1x}, shaken {1x}, skippedst {1x}, sorry {1x}, wag {1x}, wandering {1x}. See: TWOT—1319; BDB—626c, 1102c.

5111. נוּד {1x} **nûwd** (Aram.), *nood;* corresp. to 5116; to *flee:*—get away {1x}. See: TWOT—2854; BDB—1102c.

5112. נוֹד {1x} **nôwd**, *node* [only defect.
נֹד **nôd**, *node*]; from 5110; *exile:*—wandering {1x}. See: TWOT—1319a; BDB—621b, 627a.

5113. נוֹד {1x} **Nôwd**, *node;* the same as 5112; *vagrancy; Nod,* the land of Cain:—Nod {1x}. See: BDB—627a.

5114. נוֹדָב {1x} **Nôwdâb**, *no-dawb';* from 5068; *noble; Nodab,* an Arab tribe:—Nodab {1x}. See: BDB—622a.

5115. נָוָה {2x} **nâvâh**, *naw-vaw';* a prim. root; to *rest* (as at home); caus. (through the impl. idea of *beauty* [comp. 5116]), to *celebrate* (with praises):—keep at home {1x}, prepare an habitation {1x}. See: TWOT—1321, 1322; BDB—627b, 627d.

5116. נָוֶה {36x} **nâveh**, *naw-veh';* or (fem.)
נָוָה **nâvâh**, *naw-vaw';* from 5115; (adj.) *at home;* hence, (by impl. of satisfaction) *lovely;* also (noun) a *home,* of God (temple), men (residence), flocks (pasture), or wild animals (*den*):—habitation {22x}, fold {4x}, dwelling {3x}, sheepcote {2x}, comely {1x}, stable {1x}, dwelling place {1x}, pleasant place {1x}, tarried {1x}. See: TWOT—1322a, 1322b, 1322c; BDB—610a, 627c, 627d.

5117. נוּחַ {64x} **nûwach**, *noo'-akh;* a prim. root; to *rest,* i.e. *settle* down; used in a great variety of applications, lit. and fig., intr., tran. and caus. (to *dwell, stay, let fall, place, let alone, withdraw, give comfort,* etc.):—rest {55x}, ceased {1x}, confederate {1x}, let down {1x}, set down {1x}, lay {1x}, quiet {2x}, remain {1x}, set {1x}.

Nuwach means "to rest, remain, be quiet." **(1)** The first occurrence is in Gen 8:4: "And the ark [came to rest] . . . upon the mountains of Ararat." **(1a)** This illustrates the frequent use of this word to show a physical settling down of something at some particular place. **(1b)** Other examples are birds (2 Sa 21:10), insects (Ex 10:14), and soles of feet in the waters of the Jordan (Josh 3:13). **(2)** "To rest" sometimes indicates a complete envelopment and thus permeation, as **(2a)** in the spirit of Elijah "resting" on Elisha (2 Kin 2:15), **(2b)** the hand of God "resting" on the mountain (Is 25:10), and **(2c)** when Wisdom "resteth in the heart of him that hath understanding" (Prov 14:33). **(3)** Frequently *nuwach* means "to be quiet" or "to rest" **(3a)** after hard work (Ex 20:11), **(3b)** from onslaught of one's enemies (Est 9:16), **(3c)** from trouble (Job 3:26), and **(3d)** in death (Job 3:17).

(4) The word may mean "to set one's mind at rest," as when a child receives the discipline of his parent (Prov 29:17). **(5)** Sometimes *nuwach* means "to leave at rest" or "to allow to remain." Thus, God "allowed" the pagan nations "to remain" in Canaan during Joshua's lifetime (Judg 2:23). **(6)** God threatened to abandon the Israelites in the wilderness (Num 32:15). **(7)** It should be noted that while *nuwach* is used sometimes as a synonym for *shabath* (7673), "to cease, to rest" (Ex 20:11), *shabath* really is basically "to cease" from work which may imply rest, but not necessarily so. The writer of Gen 2:3 is not stressing rest from work but rather God's ceasing from His creative work since it was complete. Syn.: 7673. See: TWOT—1323; BDB—628a. comp. 3241.

5118. נוּחַ {4x} **nûwach**, *noo'-akh;* or
נוֹחַ **nôwach**, *no'-akh;* from 5117; *quiet:*—rest {1x}, rested {2x}, resting place {1x}. See: TWOT—1323?; BDB—628a, 629a, 629b.

5119. נוֹחָה {1x} **Nôwchâh**, *no-chaw';* fem. of 5118; *quietude; Nochah,* an Isr.:—Nohah {1x}. See: BDB—629a.

5120. נוּט {1x} **nûwt**, *noot;* to *quake:*—be moved {1x}. See: TWOT—1324; BDB—630a.

5121. נָוִית {6x} **Nâvîyth**, *naw-veeth';* from 5115; *residence; Navith,* a place in Pal.:—Naioth {6x}. See: BDB—627d, 630b, 644b.

5122. נְוָלוּ {3x} **nᵉvâlûw** (Aram.), *nev-aw-loo';* or
נְוָלִי **nᵉvâlîy** (Aram.), *nev-aw-lee';* from an unused root prob. mean. to *be foul;* a *sink:*—dunghill {3x}. See: TWOT—2855; BDB—1102c.

5123. נוּם {6x} **nûwm**, *noom;* a prim. root; to *slumber* (from drowsiness):—slept

{1x}, slumber {5x}. See: TWOT—1325; BDB—630b.

5124. נוּמָה {1x} **nûwmâh**, *noo-maw';* from 5123; *sleepiness:*—drowsiness {1x}. See: TWOT—1325a; BDB—630b.

5125. נוּן {2x} **nûwn**, *noon;* a prim. root; to *re-sprout,* i.e. propagate by shoots; fig. to *be perpetual:*—be continued {2x}. See: TWOT—1326; BDB—630c.

5126. נוּן {30x} **Nûwn**, *noon;* or

נוֹן **Nôwn** (1 Chron. 7:27), *nohn;* from 5125; *perpetuity, Nun* or *Non,* the father of Joshua:—Non {1x}, Nun {29x}. See: BDB—630c.

5127. נוּס {161x} **nûwç**, *noos;* a prim. root; to *flit,* i.e. *vanish* away (subside, escape; caus. chase, impel, deliver):—flee {142x}, flee away {12x}, abated {1x}, displayed {1x}, flight {1x}, hide {1x}, flee out {1x}, lift up a standard {1x}, variant {1x}.

Nuwc means to flee, escape, take flight, depart. **(1)** *Nuwc* occurs for the first time in Gen 14:10, where it is used twice to describe the "fleeing" of the kings of Sodom and Gomorrah. **(2)** *Nuwc* is the common word for "fleeing" from an enemy or danger (Gen 39:12; Num 16:34; Josh 10:6). **(3)** The word is also used to describe "escape,": "Let not the swift flee away, nor the mighty man escape; they shall stumble, and fall toward the north by the river Euphrates" (Jer 46:6; cf. Amos 9:1). **(4)** In a figurative use, the word describes **(4a)** the "disappearance" of physical strength: "And Moses *was* an hundred and twenty years old when he died: his eye was not dim, nor his natural force abated" (Deut 34:7), **(4b)** the "fleeing" of evening shadows: "Until the day break, and the shadows flee away, turn, my beloved, and be thou like a roe or a young hart upon the mountains of Bether" (Song 2:17), and **(4c)** the "fleeing away" of sorrow: "And the ransomed of the LORD shall return, and come to Zion with songs and everlasting joy upon their heads: they shall obtain joy and gladness, and sorrow and sighing shall flee away" (Is 35:10). Syn.: 1272. See: TWOT—1327; BDB—630c.

5128. נוּעַ {42x} **nûwaʿ**, *noo'-ah;* a prim. root; to *waver,* in a great variety of applications, lit. and fig. (as subjoined):—shake {6x}, wander {6x}, move {6x}, promoted {3x}, fugitive {2x}, sift {2x}, stagger {2x}, wag {2x}, misc. {13x} = continually, × make, to [go] up and down, be gone away, reel, remove, scatter, set, to and fro, be vagabond. See: TWOT—1328; BDB—631a.

5129. נוֹעַדְיָה {2x} **Nôwʿadyâh**, *no-ad-yaw';* from 3259 and 3050; *convened of Jah; Noadjah,* the name of an Isr., and a false prophetess:—Noadiah {2x}. See: BDB—418a, 631d.

5130. נוּף {37x} **nûwph**, *noof;* a prim. root; to *quiver* (i.e. *vibrate* up and down, or *rock* to and fro); used in a great variety of applications (incl. *sprinkling, beckoning, rubbing, bastinadoing, sawing, waving,* etc.):—wave {16x}, shake {7x}, offer {5x}, lift up {4x}, move {1x}, perfumed {1x}, send {1x}, sift {1x}, strike {1x}. See: TWOT—1329, 1330; BDB—245a, 631d.

5131. נוֹף {1x} **nôwph**, *nofe;* from 5130; *elevation:*—situation {1x}. See: TWOT—1331a; BDB—632c. comp. 5297.

5132. נוּץ {3x} **nûwts**, *noots;* a prim. root; prop. to *flash;* hence, to *blossom* (from the brilliancy of color); also, to *fly* away (from the quickness of motion):—flee away {1x}, bud {1x}, bud forth {1x}. See: TWOT—1399; BDB—663b, 665b.

5133. נוֹצָה {4x} **nôwtsâh**, *no-tsaw';* or

נֹצָה **nôtsâh**, *no-tsaw';* fem. act. part. of 5327 in the sense of *flying;* a *pinion* (or wing feather); often (collect.) *plumage:*—feathers {3x}, ostrich {1x}. Syn.: 3283. See: TWOT—1399a; BDB—632c, 663b, 663d.

5134. נוּק {1x} **nûwq**, *nook;* a prim. root; to *suckle:*—nurse {1x}. Syn.: 3243. See: TWOT—1332; BDB—632d.

5135. נוּר {17x} **nûwr** (Aram.), *noor;* from an unused root (corresp. to that of 5216) mean. to *shine; fire:*—fiery {10x}, fire {7x}. See: TWOT—2856; BDB—1102c.

5136. נוּשׁ {1x} **nûwsh**, *noosh;* a prim. root; to *be sick,* i.e. (fig.) *distressed:*—be full of heaviness {1x}. See: TWOT—1334; BDB—633b.

5137. נָזָה {24x} **nâzâh**, *naw-zaw';* a prim. root; to *spirt,* i.e. *besprinkle* (espec. in expiation):—sprinkle {24x}. See: TWOT—1335, 1336; BDB—633b, 633c.

5138. נָזִיד {6x} **nâzîyd**, *naw-zeed';* from 2102; something *boiled,* i.e. *soup:*—pottage {6x}. See: TWOT—547d; BDB—268a, 633c.

5139. נָזִיר {16x} **nâzîyr**, *naw-zeer';* or

נָזִר **nâzîr**, *naw-zeer';* from 5144; *separate,* i.e. *consecrated* (as *prince,* a *Nazirite*); hence, (fig. from the latter) an *unpruned* vine (like an unshorn Nazirite):—Nazarite {12x}, separate {1x}, separated {1x}, vine undressed {2x}.

Nazir means "one who is separated; Nazarite." **(1)** There are 16 occurrences of the word in the Old Testament. **(1a)** The earliest use of *nazir* is found in Gen 49:26: "The blessings of thy father . . . shall be on the head of Joseph . . . that was separate from his brethren" (cf. Deut 33:16). **(1b)** Joseph was separated from his brethren to become the savior of his father, his brethren, and their families. **(2)** Most frequently in Old Testament usage, *nazir* is an appellation for one who vowed to refrain from certain things for a period of time: "And this is the law of the Nazarite, when the days of his separation are fulfilled: he shall be brought unto the door of the tabernacle of the congregation" (Num 6:13). **(2a)** According to Num 6, a lay person of either sex could take a special vow of consecration to God's service for a certain period of time. **(2b)** A "Nazarite" usually made a vow voluntarily; however, in the case of Samson, (Judg 13:5, 7) his parents dedicated him for life. **(3)** Num 6:1–23 laid down regulatory laws pertaining to Nazaritism. **(4)** There were two kinds of "Nazarites": the temporary and the perpetual. **(4a)** The temporary was much more common than the perpetual/life-long. **(4b)** From the Bible we have knowledge only of Samson, Samuel, and John the Baptist as persons who were lifelong "Nazarites." **(5)** The Bible does not specify the length of a Nazarite's separation. **(5a)** According to the Mishna, the normal time for keeping a Nazarite vow was thirty days; but sometimes a double vow was taken, lasting sixty days. **(5b)** In fact, a vow was sometimes undertaken for a hundred days. **(6)** During the time of his vow, **(6a)** a "Nazarite" was required to abstain from wine and every kind of intoxicating drink. **(6b)** He was also forbidden to cut the hair of his head or to approach a dead body, even that of his nearest relative. **(6c)** If a "Nazarite" accidently defiled himself, he had to undergo certain rites of purification and then had to begin the full period of consecration over again. **(7)** There is but one reference in the prophetic literature to "Nazarites": The prophet Amos complained that the Lord had given the Israelites, Nazarites and prophets as spiritual leaders, but that the people "gave the Nazarites wine to drink; and commanded the prophets, saying, Prophesy not" (Amos 2:11–12). **(8)** The New Testament occasionally refers to what appear to have been Nazarite vows. For example, Acts 18:18 says that Paul sailed with Priscilla and Aquila, "having shorn his head . . . for he had a vow" (cf. Acts 21:23–24). Syn.: 6504. See: TWOT—1340b; BDB—634c.

5140. נָזַל {16x} **nâzal**, *naw-zal';* a prim. root; to *drip,* or *shed* by trickling:—flood {3x}, flow {3x}, stream {2x}, pour out {1x}, distil {1x}, melted {1x}, drop {1x}, running waters {1x}, flow out {1x}, pour down {1x}, gush out {1x}. See: TWOT—1337; BDB—633c.

5141. נֶזֶם {17x} **nezem**, *neh'-zem;* from an unused root of uncert. mean.; a nose-*ring:*—earring {14x}, jewel {3x}. See: TWOT—1338a; BDB—633d.

5142. נְזַק {4x} **nᵉzaq** (Aram.), *nez-ak';* corresp. to the root of 5143; to *suffer* (caus. *inflict*) *loss:*—have endamage {1x}, damage {1x}, hurt {1x}, hurtful {1x}. See: TWOT—2857; BDB—1102c.

5143. נֵזֶק {1x} **nêzeq**, *nay'zek;* from an unused root mean. to *injure; loss:*—damage {1x}. See: TWOT—1339; BDB—413b, 634a.

5144. נָזַר {10x} **nâzar**, *naw-zar';* a prim. root; to *hold aloof,* i.e. (intr.) *abstain* (from food and drink, from impurity, and even from divine worship [i.e. *apostatize*]); spec. to *set apart* (to sacred purposes), i.e. *devote:*—consecrate {1x}, separate (-ing, self) {9x}.

Nazar, "to separate, be separated." **(1)** "To separate" and "to consecrate" are not distinguished from one another in the early Old Testament books. **(1a)** For example, the earliest use of *nazar* in the Pentateuch is in Lev 15:31: "Thus shall ye separate the children of Israel from their uncleanness; that they die not in their uncleanness, when they defile my tabernacle that is among them." **(1b)** Here Moses uses the word in a cultic [religious] sense, meaning a kind of "consecration." **(2)** In the days of the prophet Zechariah, Jews asked the Lord whether certain fasts which they had voluntarily adopted were to be continued and observed. **(2a)** "When they had sent unto the home of God Sherezer and Regemmelech, and their men, to pray before the Lord, and to speak unto the priests which were in the house of the Lord of hosts, and to the prophets, saying, Should I weep in the fifth month, separating myself, as I have done these so many years?" (Zec 7:2–3) **(2b)** The Lord's response stated that it was no longer necessary and therefore needed not to be continued.

(3) In prophetic literature, the verb *nazar* indicates Israel's deliberate separation **(3a)** from Jehovah to dedication of foreign gods or idols. **(3b)** Hos 9:10: "I found Israel like grapes in the wilderness; I saw your fathers as the firstripe in the fig tree at her first time: *but* they went to Baalpeor, and separated themselves unto *that* shame; and *their* abominations were according as they loved." **(4)** The prophet Ezekiel employed *nazar:* "For every one of the house of Israel, or of the stranger that sojourneth in Israel, which separateth himself from me, and setteth up his idols in his heart, and putteth the stumbling block of his iniquity before his face, and cometh to a prophet to inquire of him concerning me; I the Lord will answer him by myself" (Eze 14:7). See: TWOT—1340; BDB—634a, 634c.

5145. נֶזֶר {25x} **nezer**, *neh'-zer;* or

נֵזֶר **nêzer**, *nay'-zer;* from 5144; prop. something *set apart*, i.e. (abstr.) *dedication* (of a priest or Nazirite); hence, (concr.) unshorn *locks;* also (by impl.) a *chaplet* (espec. of royalty):—consecration {2x}, crown {11x}, hair {1x}, separation {11x}. See: TWOT—1340a; BDB—634b.

5146. נֹחַ {46x} **Nôach**, *no'-akh;* the same as 5118; *rest; Noach*, the patriarch of the flood:—Noah {46x}. See: TWOT—1323b; BDB—629b, 634d.

5147. נַחְבִּי {1x} **Nachbîy**, *nakh-bee';* from 2247; *occult; Nachbi*, an Isr.:—Nakbi {1x}. See: BDB—286a, 634d.

5148. נָחָה {39x} **nâchâh**, *naw-khaw';* a prim. root; to *guide;* by impl. to *transport* (into exile, or as colonists):—lead {24x}, guide {6x}, bring {4x}, bestowed {1x}, lead forth {1x}, govern {1x}, put {1x}, straiteneth {1x}. See: TWOT—1341; BDB—634d.

5149. נְחוּם {1x} **Nᵉchûwm**, *neh-khoom';* from 5162; *comforted; Nechum*, an Isr.:—Nehum {1x}. See: BDB—637b.

5150. נִחוּם {3x} **nichûwm**, *nee-khoom';* or

נִחֻם **nichûm**, *nee-khoom';* from 5162; prop. *consoled;* abstr. *solace:*—comfort {1x}, comfortable {1x}, repentings {1x}. See: TWOT—1344b; BDB—637b.

5151. נַחוּם {1x} **Nachûwm**, *nakh-oom';* from 5162; *comfortable; Nachum*, an Isr. prophet:—Nahum {1x}. See: BDB—637b.

5152. נָחוֹר {18x} **Nâchôwr**, *naw-khore';* from the same as 5170; *snorer; Nachor*, the name of the grandfather and a brother of Abraham:—Nahor {8x}. See: BDB—637d.

5153. נָחוּשׁ {1x} **nâchûwsh**, *naw-khoosh';* appar. pass. part. of 5172 (perh. in the sense of *ringing*, i.e. bell-metal; or from the *red* color of the throat of a serpent 5175, as denom. when hissing); *coppery*, i.e. (fig.) hard:—of brass {1x}. See: TWOT—1349b; BDB—639a.

5154. נְחוּשָׁה {10x} **nᵉchûwshâh**, *nekh-oo-shaw';* or

נְחֻשָׁה **nᵉchûshâh**, *nekh-oo-shaw';* fem. of 5153; *copper:*—brass {7x}, steel {3x}. See: TWOT—1349b; BDB—639a, 1102d. comp. 5176.

5155. נְחִילָה {1x} **Nᵉchîylâh**, *nekh-ee-law';* prob. denom. from 2485; a *flute:*—*[plur.]* Nehiloth {1x}. See: TWOT—1342b; BDB—636a.

5156. נְחִיר {1x} **nᵉchîyr**, *nekh-eer';* from the same as 5170; a *nostril:*—*[dual]* nostrils {1x}. See: TWOT—1346c; BDB—638a.

5157. נָחַל {62x} **nâchal**, *naw-khal';* a prim. root; to *inherit* (as a [fig.] mode of descent), or (gen.) to *occupy;* caus. to *bequeath*, or (gen.) *distribute, instate:*—inherit {30x}, inheritance {20x}, possess {5x}, have {2x}, had {1x}, divide {1x}, heritage {1x}, possession {1x}, defiled {1x}.

Nachal means to inherit, get possession of, take as a possession. **(1)** The first time *nachal* is used in the Old Testament text is in Ex 23:30: "inherit the land." **(2)** To inherit **(2a)** does not always require a "last will and testament." **(2b)** The basic meaning of *nachal* is to receive with the ability to control, possess, and direct. **(3)** One of the few instances of "to inherit" by last will and testament is in Deut 21:16: ". . . when he maketh his sons to inherit that which he hath. . . ." This clause is more literally translated "in the day he causes his sons to inherit that which is his." **(4)** When Moses prayed: ". . . O Lord, . . . take us for thine inheritance" (Ex 34:9), he did not mean that God should "inherit" through a will, but that He should "take possession of" Israel. **(5)** The meaning "to get as a possession" is seen in its figurative use. Thus, **(5a)** "the wise shall inherit [possess as their due] glory" (Prov 3:35); **(5b)** "the upright shall have good things in possession" (Prov 28:10); **(5c)** "our fathers have inherited lies" (Jer 16:19); **(5d)** "he that troubleth his own house shall inherit the wind" (Prov 11:29). See: TWOT—1342; BDB—635c.

5158. נַחַל {141x} **nachal**, *nakh'-al;* or (fem.)

נַחְלָה **nachlâh** (Ps 124:4), *nakh'-law;* or

נַחֲלָה **nachălâh** (Eze 47:19; 48:28), *nakh-al-aw';* from 5157 in its orig. sense; a *stream*, espec. a winter *torrent;* (by impl.) a (narrow) *valley* (in which a brook runs); also a *shaft* (of a mine):—brook {46x}, flood {5x}, river {56x}, stream {11x}, valley {23x}.

Nachalah means "wadi (or wady); torrent valley; torrent; river; shaft." **(1)** This noun represents a dry valley in which water runs during the rainy season: "And Isaac departed thence, and pitched his tent in the valley of Gerar, and dwelt there" (Gen 26:17—the first biblical appearance). **(2)** The word can signify the "wady" when it is full of rushing water. Indeed, it appears to describe the rushing water itself: "And he took them, and sent them over the brook . . ." (Gen 32:23). **(3)** Sometimes *nachalah* means a permanent stream or "river": "These shall ye eat of all that are in the waters: whatsoever hath fins and scales in the waters, in the seas, and in the rivers, them shall ye eat" (Lev 11:9). **(4)** The Pentateuch consistently distinguishes between extra-Egyptian waterways; calling them *nachalah*, 13 times, and nahar (5104), 13 times, and inter-Egyptian waterways (calling them ye'or). This distinction demonstrates the kind of first-hand knowledge and historical concern expected from a mature eyewitness. **(5)** *Nachalah* is used figuratively of many things that emerge and disappear suddenly or that have extreme on-rushing power such as the pride of nations (Is 66:12), the strength of the invader (Jer 47:2), and the power of the foe (Ps 18:4). **(6)** Torrents of oil do not please God if the offerer's heart is wrongly disposed (Mic 6:7). **(7)** God overfloods the godly with torrents of His good pleasure (Ps 36:8). **(8)** The eschaton is typified by streams, or torrents, in the desert (Eze 47:5–19; cf. Ex 17:3ff.). See: TWOT—1343a, 1343b; BDB—636a, 636d.

5159. נַחֲלָה {222x} **nachălâh**, *nakh-al-aw';* from 5157 (in its usual sense); prop. something *inherited*, i.e. (abstr.) *occupancy*, or (concr.) an *heirloom;* gen. an *estate, patrimony* or *portion:*—heritage {27x}, to inherit {2x}, inheritance {192x}, possession {1x}.

Nachalah means "possession; property; inheritance." **(1)** The first occurrence of the word is in Gen 31:14: "And Rachel and Leah answered and said unto him, Is there yet any portion or inheritance for us in our father's house?" **(2)** The basic translation of *nachalah* is "inheritance": "And Naboth said to Ahab, The Lord forbid it me, that I should give the inheritance of my fathers unto thee" (1 Kin 21:3). **(3)** The word stresses a "possession" to which one has received the legal claim. **(3a)** Technically, the 12 tribes were inheriting the land given to Abraham, Isaac, and Jacob. **(3b)** The usage of *nachalah* in the Pentateuch and Joshua indicates that the word often denotes that "possession" which all of Israel or a tribe or a clan received as their share in the Promised Land. **(3c)** The share was determined by lot (Num 26:56) shortly before Moses' death, and it fell upon Joshua to execute the division of the "possession": "So Joshua took the whole land, according to all that the Lord said unto Moses; and Joshua gave it for an inheritance unto Israel according to their divisions by their tribes" (Josh 11:23).

(3d) After the Conquest the term "inheritance" is no longer used to refer to newly gained territory by warfare. **(3e)** Once "possession" had been taken of the land, the legal process came into operation by which the hereditary property was supposed to stay within the family. **(3f)** For this reason Naboth could not give his rights over to Ahab (1 Kin 21:3–4). **(4)** One could redeem the property, whenever it had come into other hands, as did Boaz, in order to maintain the name of the deceased: "Moreover Ruth the Moabitess, the wife of Mahlon, have I purchased to be my wife, to raise up the name of the dead upon his inheritance, that the name of the dead be not cut off from among his brethren, and from the gate of his place" (Ruth 4:10). **(5)** Metaphorically, Israel is said to be God's "possession": "But the Lord hath taken you, and brought you forth out of the iron furnace, even out of Egypt, to be unto him a people of inheritance, as ye are this day" (Deut 4:20).

(6) Within the special covenantal status Israel experienced the blessing that its children were a special gift from the Lord (Ps 127:3). **(6a)** However, the Lord abandoned Israel as His "possession" to the nations (cf. Is 47:6), and **(6b)** permitted a remnant of the "possession" to return: "Who is a God like unto thee, that pardoneth iniquity, and passeth by the transgression of the remnant of his heritage? he retaineth not his anger for ever, because he delighteth in mercy" (Mic 7:18). **(7)** On the other hand, it can even be said that the Lord is the "possession" of His people. The priests and the Levites, whose earthly "possessions" were limited, were assured that their "possession" is the Lord: "Wherefore Levi hath no part nor inheritance with his brethren; the Lord is his inheritance, according as the Lord thy God promised him" (Deut 10:9; cf. 12:22; Num 18:23). See: TWOT—1342a; BDB—635a. comp. 5158.

5160. נַחֲלִיאֵל {2x} **Nachălîyʼêl**, *nakh-al-ee-ale';* from 5158 and 410; *valley of God; Nachaliël*, a place in the Desert:—Nahaliel {2x}. See: BDB—636d.

5161. נֶחֱלָמִי {3x} **Nechĕlâmîy**, *nekh-el-aw-mee';* appar. a patron. from an unused name (appar. pass. part. of 2492); *dreamed;* a *Nechelamite*, or desc. of Nechlam:—Nehelamite {3x}. See: BDB—636d.

5162. נָחַם {108x} **nâcham**, *naw-kham';* a prim. root; prop. to *sigh*, i.e. *breathe* strongly; by impl. to *be sorry*, i.e. (in a favorable sense) to *pity, console* or (refl.) *rue;* or (unfavorably) to *avenge* (oneself):—comfort {57x}, repent {41x}, comforter {9x}, ease {1x}.

Nacham means "to repent, comfort." **(1)** *Nacham* is translated "to repent" 41 times and "to comfort" 57 times in the Old Testament. **(1a)** To repent means to make a strong turning to a new course of action. **(1a1)** The emphasis is on *turning to* a positive course of action, not **(1a2)** *turning from* a less desirable course. **(1a3)** Comfort is derived from "com" (with) and "fort" (strength). **(1b)** Hence, when one repents, he exerts strength to change, to re-grasp the situation, and exert effort for the situation to take a different course of purpose and action. **(1c)** The stress is not upon new information or new facts which cause the change as it is upon the visible action taken. **(2)** Most uses of the term in the Old Testament are connected with God's repentance: **(2a)** "... It repented the Lord that he had made man ..." (Gen 6:6); **(2b)** "And the Lord repented of the evil which he thought to do unto his people" (Ex 32:14). **(2c)** Sometimes the Lord "repented" of the discipline He had planned to carry out concerning His people: "If that nation, against whom I have pronounced, turn from their evil, I will repent of the evil that I thought to do unto them" (Jer 18:8); **(2d)** "If it do evil in my sight, that it obey not my voice, then I will repent of the good ..." (Jer 18:10); **(2e)** "And rend your heart, and not your garments, and turn unto the Lord your God: for he is gracious and merciful, slow to anger ... and repenteth him of evil" (Joel 2:13).

(3) In other instances, the Lord exhibited new actions when man changed to make the right choices, **(3a)** but He could not change His attitude toward evil when man continued on the wrong course. **(3b)** As God demonstrated His actions, He always remained faithful to His own righteousness. **(4)** In some situations, God was weary of "repenting" (Jer 15:6), **(4a)** suggesting that He has grown weary with Israel's constant insincere repentance. **(4b)** An instance of this action was in Samuel's word to Saul, that God took the kingdom from Israel's first king and intended to give it to another; Samuel declared, "And also the Strength of Israel will not lie nor repent: for he *is* not a man, that he should repent" (1 Sa 15:29). **(5)** God usually "repented" of His actions because of man's intercession and repentance of his evil deeds. **(5a)** Moses pleaded with God as the intercessor for Israel: "Turn from thy fierce wrath, and repent of this evil against thy people" (Ex 32:12).

(5b) The Lord did that when He "... repented of the evil which he thought to do unto his people" (Ex 32:14). **(5c)** As God's prophet preached to Nineveh, "... God saw their works, that they turned from their evil way; and God repented of the evil, that he had said that he would do unto them ..." (Jonah 3:10). **(5d)** In such instances, God "repented," to bring about a change of plan than previously proclaimed by the prophet. Again, however, God remained faithful to His absolutes of righteousness in His relation to and with man. **(6)** Other passages refer to a change (or lack of it) in man's attitude. When man did not "repent" of his wickedness, he chose rebellion (Jer 8:6). **(7)** In the eschatological sense, when Ephraim (as a representative of the northern branch of Israel) will "repent" (Jer 31:19), God then will have mercy (Jer 31:20). **(8)** Man also expressed repentance to other men. Benjamin suffered greatly from the crime of immorality (Judg 19—20): "And the children of Israel [eleven tribes] repented them from Benjamin their brother, and said, There is one tribe cut off from Israel this day" (Judg 21:6; cf. v. 15).

(9) *Nacham* may also mean "to comfort." **(9a)** The refugees in Babylon would be "comforted" when survivors arrived from Jerusalem (Eze 14:23); the connection between "comfort" and "repent" here resulted from the calamity God brought upon Jerusalem as a testimony to the truth of His Word. **(9b)** David "comforted" Bathsheba after the death of her child born in sin (2 Sa 12:24); this probably indicates his repentance of what had happened in their indiscretion. **(10)** On the other hand, the word was used in the human sense of "comfort." Job asked his three companions, "How then comfort ye me in vain seeing in your answers there remaineth falsehood?" (Job 21:34; he meant that their attitude seemed cruel and unfeeling). **(11)** The psalmist looked to God for "comfort": "Thou shalt increase my greatness, and comfort me on every side" (Ps 71:21). **(12)** In an eschatological sense God indicated that He would "comfort" Jerusalem with the restoration of Israel, as a mother comforts her offspring (Is 66:13). See: TWOT—1344; BDB—636d.

5163. **נַחַם** {1x} **Nacham**, *nakh'-am;* from 5162; *consolation; Nacham,* an Isr.:—Naham {1x}. See: BDB—637b.

5164. **נֹחַם** {1x} **nôcham**, *no'-kham;* from 5162; *ruefulness,* i.e. *desistance:*—repentance {1x}. See: TWOT—1344a; BDB—637b.

5165. **נֶחָמָה** {2x} **nechâmâh**, *nekh-aw-maw';* from 5162; *consolation:*—comfort {2x}. See: TWOT—1344c; BDB—637c.

5166. **נְחֶמְיָה** {8x} **Nᵉchemyâh**, *nekh-em-yaw';* from 5162 and 3050; *consolation of Jah; Nechemjah,* the name of three Isr.:—Nehemiah {8x}. See: BDB—637c.

5167. **נַחֲמָנִי** {1x} **Nachămânîy**, *nakh-am-aw-nee';* from 5162; *consolatory; Nachamani,* an Isr.:—Nahamani {1x}. See: BDB—637c.

5168. **נַחְנוּ** {6x} **nachnûw**, *nakh-noo';* for 587; *we:*—we {6x}. See: TWOT—128a; BDB—59d, 637d.

5169. **נָחַץ** {1x} **nâchats**, *naw-khats';* a prim. root; to *be urgent:*—require hasted {1x}. See: TWOT—1345; BDB—637d.

5170. **נַחַר** {2x} **nachar**, *nakh'-ar;* and (fem.)

נַחֲרָה **nachărâh**, *nakh-ar-aw';* from an unused root mean. to *snort* or *snore;* a *snorting:*—nostrils {1x}, snorting {1x}. See: TWOT—1346, 1346a, 1346b; BDB—637d.

5171. **נַחֲרַי** {2x} **Nachăray**, *nakh-ar-ah'-ee;* or

נַחְרַי **Nachray**, *nakh-rah'-ee; from* the same as 5170; *snorer; Nacharai* or *Nachrai,* an Isr.:—Naharai {1x}, Nahari {1x}. See: BDB—638a.

5172. **נָחַשׁ** {11x} **nâchash**, *naw-khash';* a prim. root; prop. to *hiss,* i.e. *whisper* a (magic) spell; gen. to *prognosticate:*—enchantment {4x}, divine {2x}, enchanter {1x}, indeed {1x}, certainly {1x}, learn by experience {1x}, diligently observe {1x}. See: TWOT—1348; BDB—638c.

5173. **נַחַשׁ** {2x} **nachash**, *nakh'-ash;* from 5172; an *incantation* or *augury:*—enchantment {2x}. See: TWOT—1348a; BDB—638d.

5174. **נְחָשׁ** {9x} **nᵉchâsh** (Aram.), *nekh-awsh';* corresp. to 5154; *copper:*—brass {9x}. See: TWOT—2858; BDB—1102d.

5175. **נָחָשׁ** {31x} **nâchâsh**, *naw-khawsh';* from 5172; a *snake* (from its *hiss*):—serpent {31x}. See: TWOT—1347a; BDB—638a.

5176. **נָחָשׁ** {9x} **Nâchâsh**, *naw-khawsh';* the same as 5175; *Nachash,* the name of two persons appar. non-Isr.:—Nahash {9x}. See: BDB—638b.

נְחֻשָׁה **nᵉchûshâh**. See 5154.

5177. **נַחְשׁוֹן** {10x} **Nachshôwn**, *nakh-shone';* from 5172; *enchanter; Nachshon,* an Isr.:—Naashon {1x}, Nahshon {9x}. See: BDB—638b.

5178. **נְחֹשֶׁת** {141x} **nᵉchôsheth**, *nekh-o'-sheth;* for 5154; *copper,* hence, something made of that metal, i.e. *coin,* a *fetter;* fig. *base* (as compared with gold or silver):—brass {103x}, brasen {28x}, fetters {4x}, chain {3x}, copper {1x}, filthiness {1x}, steel {1x}.

Nechosheth means "brass, bronze; bronze chains, copper." **(1)** This word refers to the metal ore usually translated brass: "A land wherein thou shalt eat bread without scarceness, thou shalt not lack any thing in it; a land whose stones are iron, and out of whose hills thou mayest dig brass" (Deut 8:9). **(1b)** The word can also represent the refined ore: "And Zillah, she also bare Tubal-cain, an instructor of every artificer in brass and iron" (Gen 4:22). **(1c)** Copper ore rarely occurs in the earth in its pure state, hence, copper is a mixture in the earth of other metals; usually zinc, which is why the translation "brass" [a combination of zinc and copper]. **(2)** Inasmuch as it was a semi-precious metal, *nechosheth* is sometimes listed as a spoil of war (2 Sa 8:8). **(2a)** In such passages, it is difficult to know whether the reference is to copper or to copper mixed with tin (i.e., bronze). **(2b)** Certainly, "bronze" is intended in 1 Sa 17:5, where *nechosheth* refers to the material from which armor is made. **(2c)** Bronze is the material from which utensils (Lev 6:21), altars (Ex 38:30), and other objects were fashioned. **(2d)** This material could be polished (1 Kin 7:45) or shined (Ezra 8:27). **(2e)** This metal was less valuable than gold and more valuable than wood (Is 60:17).

(3) Still another meaning of *nechosheth* appears in Judg 16:21: "But the Philistines took [Samson], and put out his eyes, and brought him down to Gaza, and bound him with fetters of [bronze]; and he did grind in the prison house." Usually, when the word has this meaning it appears in the dual form (in the singular form only in Lam 3:7). **(4)** Deut 28:23 uses *nechosheth* to symbolize the cessation of life-giving rain and sunshine: "And thy heaven that is over thy head shall be [bronze], and the earth that is under thee shall be iron." See: TWOT—1349a, 1350a; BDB—638b, 639b, 1102d.

5179. **נְחֻשְׁתָּא** {1x} **Nᵉchushtâʾ**, *nekh-oosh-taw';* from 5178; *copper; Nechushta,* an Israelitess:—Nehushta {1x}. See: BDB—639a.

5180. **נְחֻשְׁתָּן** {1x} **Nᵉchushtân**, *nekh-oosh-tawn';* from 5178; something made of *copper,* i.e. the copper *serpent* of the Desert:—Nehushtan {1x}. See: TWOT—1347b; BDB—639b.

5181. **נָחַת** {9x} **nâchath**, *naw-khath';* a prim. root; to *sink,* i.e. *descend;* caus., to *press* or *lead* down:—broken {2x}, come down {2x}, enter {1x}, stick fast {1x}, settle {1x}, press sore {1x}, go down {1x. See: TWOT—1351; BDB—639b, 1102d.

5182. **נְחַת** {6x} **nᵉchath** (Aram.), *nekh-ath';* corresp. to 5181; to *descend;* caus., to *bring away, deposit, depose:*—come down {2x}, carry {1x}, place {1x}, laid up {1x}, deposed {1x}. See: TWOT—2859; BDB—1102d.

5183. **נַחַת** {8x} **nachath**, *nakh'-ath;* from 5182; a *descent,* i.e. imposition, unfavorable (*punishment*) or favorable (*food*); also (intr.; perh. from 5117), *restfulness:*—lighting down {1x}, quiet {1x}, quietness {1x}, to rest {4x}, be set on {1x}. See: TWOT—1323a, 1351a; BDB—629b, 639c.

5184. **נַחַת** {5x} **Nachath**, *nakh'-ath;* the same as 5183; *quiet; Nachath,* the name of an Edomite and of two Isr.:—Nahath {5x}. See: BDB—629b, 639c.

5185. נָחֵת {1x} **nâchêth**, *naw-khayth';* from 5181; *descending:*—come down {1x}. See: TWOT—1351b; BDB—639c.

5186. נָטָה {215x} **nâṭâh**, *naw-taw';* a prim. root; to *stretch* or spread out; by impl. to *bend* away (incl. mor. deflection); used in a great variety of application (as follows):—stretch out {60x}, incline {28x}, turn {16x}, stretch forth {15x}, turn aside {13x}, bow {8x}, decline {8x}, pitched {8x}, bow down {5x}, turn away {5x}, spread {5x}, stretched out still {4x}, pervert {4x}, stretch {4x}, extend {3x}, wrest {3x}, outstretched {3x}, carried aside {2x}, misc. {20x} = + afternoon, apply, deliver, go down, be gone, intend, lay, let down, offer, overthrown, prolong, put away, shew, take (aside), cause to yield.

Natah means "to stretch forth, spread out, stretch down, turn aside." **(1)** *Natah* connotes "extending something outward and toward" something or someone. So God told Moses: ". . . I will redeem you with a stretched out arm, and with great judgments" (Ex 6:6). **(1a)** This is a figure of God's active, sovereign, and mighty involvement in the affairs of men. **(1b)** So this phrase means "to stretch out" something until it reaches a goal. **(2)** The verb can also mean "to stretch out toward" but not to touch or reach anything. **(2a)** God told Moses to tell Aaron to take his staff in hand (cf. Ex 9:23) and "stretch it out." **(2b)** This act was to be done as a sign. **(2c)** The pointed staff was a visible sign that God's power was directly related to God's messengers: ". . . Take thy rod, and stretch out thine hand upon the waters of Egypt, upon their streams, upon their rivers, and upon their ponds . . . ," over all the water in Egypt (Ex 7:19). **(3)** God "stretched out" (offered) 3 things to David (1 Chr 21:10); this is a related sense with the absence of anything physical being "stretched out."

(4) This verb may connote "stretch out" but not toward anything. When a shadow "stretches out," it lengthens. Hezekiah remarked: "It is a light thing for the shadow to go down ten degrees . . ." (2 Kin 20:10), to grow longer. **(5)** *Natah* may be used in this sense without an object and referring to a day. The Levite was asked to "comfort thine heart, I pray thee. And they tarried until afternoon [literally, the "stretching" (of the day, or of the shadows)] . . ." (Judg 19:8). **(6)** "To stretch out" one's limbs full length is to recline: "And they lay themselves down upon clothes laid to pledge by every altar . . ." (Amos 2:8). This is a figure of temple prostitution. **(7)** This verb may also mean "to extend" in every direction. **(7a)** It represents what one does in pitching a tent by unrolling the canvas (or skins sewn together) and "stretching it out." **(7b)** The end product is that the canvas is properly "spread out." Abram "pitched his tent, having Beth-el on the west, and Hai on the east . . ." (Gen 12:8—the first appearance of the word). **(8)** This act and its result is used as a figure of God's creating the heavens: ". . . Which alone spreadeth out the heavens . . ." (Job 9:8). **(9)** This verb also implies "stretching down toward" so as to reach something. Earlier in the Bible Rebekah was asked to "let down thy pitcher, . . . that I may drink" (Gen 24:14); she was asked to "stretch it down" into the water.

(10) This is the nuance when God is said to have "inclined [stretched down] unto me, and heard my cry" (Ps 40:1). **(11)** Issachar is described as a donkey which "bowed his shoulder to bear [burdens]" (Gen 49:15). **(12)** In somewhat the same sense the heavens are bowed; the heavens are made to come closer to the earth. **(12a)** This is a figure of the presence of thick clouds: "He bowed the heavens also, and came down: and darkness was under his feet" (Ps 18:9). **(12b)** The somewhat new element here is that the heavens do not touch the speaker but only "stretch downward" toward him. **(13)** This verb may mean "to turn aside" in the sense of "to visit": ". . . Judah went down from his brethren, and turned in to [visited] a certain Adullamite . . ." (Gen 38:1). **(14)** Another special nuance appears in Num 22:23, where it means "to go off the way": "And the ass saw the angel of the Lord standing in the way . . . , and the ass turned aside out of the way. . . ." **(15)** Applied to human relationships, this may connote seduction: "With her much fair speech she caused him to yield . . ." (Prov 7:21). See: TWOT—1352; BDB—639d. Syn.: 4294, 4295.

5187. נְטִיל {1x} **neṭîyl**, *net-eel';* from 5190; *laden:*—that bear {1x}. See: TWOT—1353b; BDB—642b.

5188. נְטִיפָה {2x} **neṭîyphâh**, *net-ee-faw';* from 5197; a *pendant* for the ears (espec. of pearls):—chain {1x}, collar {1x}. See: TWOT—1355c; BDB—643b.

5189. נְטִישָׁה {3x} **neṭîyshâh**, *net-ee-shaw';* from 5203; a *tendril* (as an offshoot):—battlements {1x}, branches {1x}, plant {1x}. See: TWOT—1357a; BDB—644a.

5190. נָטַל {4x} **nâṭal**, *naw-tal';* a prim. root; to *lift;* by impl. to *impose:*—bare {1x}, hath borne {1x}, offer {1x}, taketh up {1x}. See: TWOT—1353; BDB—642a, 1102d.

5191. נְטַל {2x} **neṭal** (Aram.), *net-al';* corresp. to 5190; to *raise:*—lifted up {2x}. See: TWOT—2860; BDB—1102d.

5192. נֵטֶל {1x} **nêṭel**, *nay'-tel;* from 5190; a *burden:*—weighty {1x}. See: TWOT—1353a; BDB—642b.

5193. נָטַע {58x} **nâṭaᶜ**, *naw-tah';* a prim. root; prop. to *strike* in, i.e. *fix;* spec. to *plant* (lit. or fig.):—fastened {1x}, plant {56x}, planters {1x}.

Nata' means "to plant." **(1)** The word is used for the first time in the text in Gen 2:8: "And the Lord God planted a garden eastward in Eden. . . ." **(2)** The regular word for planting trees and vineyards, *nata'* is used figuratively of planting people: "Yet I had planted thee [Judah] a noble vine . . ." (Jer 2:21). **(3)** This use is a close parallel to the famous "Song of the Vineyard" (Is 5:1-10) where Israel and Judah are called God's "pleasant plant" (Is 5:7). **(4)** *Nata'* is used in Is 17:10 in an unusual description of idolatry: ". . . Therefore shalt thou plant pleasant plants, and shalt set it with strange slips." **(5)** "To plant" sometimes has the meaning of "to establish." Thus, God promises in the latter days, "I will plant them upon their land" (Amos 9:15). See: TWOT—1354; BDB—642b, 785c.

5194. נֶטַע {4x} **neṭaᶜ**, *neh'-tah;* from 5193; a *plant;* collect. a *plantation;* abstr. a *planting:*—plant {4x}. See: TWOT—1354a; BDB—642c.

5195. נָטִיעַ {1x} **nâṭîyaᶜ**, *naw-tee'-ah;* from 5193; a *plant:*—plants {1x}. See: TWOT—1354b; BDB—642d.

5196. נְטָעִים {1x} **Neṭâᶜîym**, *net-aw-eem';* plur. of 5194; *Netaim,* a place in Pal.:—among plants {1x}. See: BDB—642d.

5197. נָטַף {18x} **nâṭaph**, *naw-taf';* a prim. root; to *ooze,* i.e. *distil* gradually; by impl. to *fall in drops;* fig. to *speak* by inspiration:—drop {12x}, down {1x}, prophesy {4x}, prophet {1x}. See: TWOT—1355; BDB—642d.

5198. נָטָף {2x} **nâṭâph**, *naw-tawf';* from 5197; a *drop;* spec., an aromatic *gum* (prob. *stacte*):—drops {1x}, stacte {1x}. See: TWOT—1355a, 1355b; BDB—643a, 643b.

5199. נְטֹפָה {2x} **Neṭôphâh**, *net-o-faw';* from 5197; *distillation; Netophah,* a place in Pal.:—Netophah {2x}. See: BDB—643b.

5200. נְטֹפָתִי {11x} **Neṭôphâthîy**, *net-o-faw-thee';* patron. from 5199; a *Netophathite,* or inhab. of Netophah:—Netophathite {10x}, Netophathi {1x}. See: BDB—643b.

5201. נָטַר {9x} **nâṭar**, *naw-tar';* a prim. root; to *guard;* fig., to *cherish* (anger):—bear grudge {1x}, keep {4x}, keeper {2x}, reserve {2x}. See: TWOT—1356; BDB—643b, 1102d.

5202. נְטַר {1x} **neṭar** (Aram.), *net-ar';* corresp. to 5201; to *retain:*—keep {1x}. See: TWOT—2861; BDB—1102d.

5203. נָטַשׁ {40x} **nâṭash**, *naw-tash';* a prim. root; prop. to *pound,* i.e. *smite;* by impl. (as if beating out, and thus expanding) to *disperse;* also, to *thrust* off, down, out or upon (incl. *reject, let alone, permit, remit,* etc.):—forsake {15x}, leave {12x}, spread {3x}, spread abroad {1x}, drawn {1x}, fall {1x}, joined {1x}, lie {1x}, loosed {1x}, cast off {1x}, misc. {3x} = stretch out, suffer. See: TWOT—1357; BDB—643c.

5204. נִי {1x} **nîy**, *nee;* doubtful word; appar. from 5091; *lamentation:*—wailing {1x}. See: TWOT—1311c; BDB—624d, 644b.

5205. נִיד {1x} **nîyd**, *need;* from 5110; *motion* (of the lips in speech):—moving {1x}. See: TWOT—1319b; BDB—627a, 644b.

5206. נִידָה {1x} **nîydâh**, *nee-daw';* fem. of 5205; *removal,* i.e. exile:—removed {1x}. See: TWOT—1302b; BDB—622c, 627b, 644b.

5207. נִיחוֹחַ {43x} **nîychôwach**, *nee-kho'-akh;* or

נִיחֹחַ **nîychôach**, *nee-kho'-akh;* from 5117; prop. *restful,* i.e. *pleasant;* abstr. *delight:*—sweet {42x}, sweet odours {1x}. See: TWOT—1323c; BDB—629b, 644b, 1102d.

5208. נִיחוֹחַ {2x} **nîychôwach** (Aram.), *nee-kho'-akh;* or (short.)

נִיחֹחַ **nîychôach** (Aram.), *nee-kho'-akh;* corresp. to 5207; *pleasure:*—sweet odours {1x}, sweet odours {1x}. See: TWOT—2862; BDB—1102d.

5209. נִין {3x} **nîyn**, *neen;* from 5125; *progeny:*—son {3x}. See: TWOT—1326a; BDB—630c, 644b.

5210. נִינְוֵה {17x} **Nîyneᵉvêh**, *nee-nev-ay';* of for. or.; *Nineveh,* the capital of Assyria:—Nineveh {17x}. See: BDB—644b.

5211. נִיס {1x} **nîyç**, *neece;* from 5127; *fugitive:*—that fleeth {1x}. See: TWOT—1327; BDB—630d.

5212. נִיסָן {2x} **Nîyçân**, *nee-sawn';* prob. of for. or.; *Nisan,* the first month of the Jewish sacred year:—Nisan {2x}. See: TWOT—1359; BDB—644c.

5213. נִיצוֹץ {1x} **nîytsôwts**, *nee-tsotes';* from 5340; a *spark:*—spark {1x}. See: TWOT—1405a; BDB—665b.

5214. נִיר {2x} **nîyr**, *neer;* a root prob. ident. with that of 5216, through the idea of the *gleam* of a fresh furrow; to *till* the soil:—break up {2x}. See: TWOT—1360; BDB—644c.

5215. נִיר {4x} **nîyr**, *neer;* or
נִר **nîr**, *neer;* from 5214; prop. *plowing,* i.e. (concr.) freshly *plowed* land:—fallow ground {2x}, ploughing {1x}, tillage {1x}. See: TWOT—1360a; BDB—644c, 669c.

5216. נִיר {48x} **nîyr**, *neer* or
נִר **nîr**, *neer;* also
נֵיר **nêyr**, *nare;* or
נֵר **nêr**, *nare;* or (fem.)
נֵרָה **nêrâh**, *nay-raw';* from a prim. root [see 5214; 5135] prop. mean. to *glisten;* a *lamp* (i.e. the burner) or *light* (lit. or fig.):—candle {9x}, lamp {35x}, light {4x}. See: TWOT—1333b; BDB—632d, 633a, 644c, 669c, 1102c.

5217. נָכָא {1x} **nâkâʼ**, *naw-kaw';* a prim. root; to *smite,* i.e. *drive* away:—be viler {1x}. See: TWOT—1362; BDB—644d.

5218. נָכֵא {4x} **nâkêʼ**, *naw-kay';* or
נָכָא **nâkâʼ**, *naw-kaw';* from 5217; *smitten,* i.e. (fig.) *afflicted:*—broken {2x}, stricken {1x}, wounded {1x}. See: TWOT—1362a, 1362b; BDB—644d.

5219. נְכֹאת {2x} **nᵉkôʼth**, *nek-ohth';* from 5218; prop. a *smiting,* i.e. (concr.) an aromatic *gum* [perh. *styrax*] (as *powdered*):—spicery {1x}, spices {1x}. See: TWOT—1362c; BDB—644d.

5220. נֶכֶד {3x} **neked**, *neh'-ked;* from an unused root mean. to *propagate; offspring:*—nephew {2x}, son's son {1x}. See: TWOT—1363a; BDB—645a.

5221. נָכָה {500x} **nâkâh**, *naw-kaw';* a prim. root; to *strike* (lightly or severely, lit. or fig.):—smite {348x}, slay {92x}, kill {20x}, beat {9x}, slaughter {5x}, stricken {3x}, given {3x}, wounded {3x}, strike {2x}, stripes {2x}, misc. {13x} = cast forth, clap, × go forward, × indeed, murderer, punish, × surely. See: TWOT—1364; BDB—645a.

5222. נֵכֶה {1x} **nêkeh**, *nay-keh';* from 5221; a *smiter,* i.e. (fig.) *traducer:*—abjects {1x}. See: TWOT—1364b; BDB—646d.

5223. נָכֶה {3x} **nâkeh**, *naw-keh'; smitten,* i.e. (lit.) *maimed,* or (fig.) *dejected:*—contrite {1x}, lame {2x}. See: TWOT—1364a; BDB—646d.

5224. נְכוֹ {3x} **Nᵉkôw**, *nek-o';* prob. of Eg. or.; *Neko,* an Eg. king:—Necho {3x}. See: BDB—647a. comp. 6549.

5225. נָכוֹן {1x} **Nâkôwn**, *naw-kone';* from 3559; *prepared; Nakon,* prob. an Isr.:—Nachon {1x}. See: BDB—467d, 647a.

5226. נֵכַח {2x} **nêkach**, *nay'-kakh;* from an unused root mean. to *be straightforward;* prop. the *fore* part; used adv., *opposite:*—before {1x}, over against {1x}. See: TWOT—1365a; BDB—647b.

5227. נֹכַח {23x} **nôkach**, *no'-kakh;* from the same as 5226; prop., the *front* part; used adv. (espec. with prep.), *opposite, in front of, forward, in behalf of:*—against {10x}, before {9x}, directly {1x}, for {1x}, on {1x}, over {1x}. See: TWOT—1365a; BDB—647b.

5228. נָכֹחַ {4x} **nâkôach**, *naw-ko'-akh;* from the same as 5226; *straightforward,* i.e. (fig.), *equitable, correct,* or (abstr.), *integrity:*—plain {1x}, right {2x}, uprightness {1x}. See: TWOT—1365a; BDB—647c.

5229. נְכֹחָה {4x} **nᵉkôchâh**, *nek-o-khaw';* fem. of 5228; prop. *straightforwardness,* i.e. (fig.) *integrity,* or (concr.) a *truth:*—equity {1x}, right {1x}, right things {1x}, uprightness {1x}. See: TWOT—1365a; BDB—647c.

5230. נָכַל {4x} **nâkal**, *naw-kal';* a prim. root; to *defraud,* i.e. *act treacherously:*—beguile {1x}, conspire {1x}, deceiver {1x}, deal subtilly {1x}. See: TWOT—1366; BDB—647c.

5231. נֵכֶל {1x} **nêkel**, *nay'-kel;* from 5230; *deceit:*—wiles {1x}. See: TWOT—1366a; BDB—647d.

5232. נְכַס {2x} **nᵉkaç** (Aram.), *nek-as';* corresp. to 5233:—goods {2x}. See: TWOT—2863; BDB—1103a.

5233. נֶכֶס {5x} **nekeç**, *neh'-kes;* from an unused root mean. to *accumulate; treasure:*—riches {1x}, wealth {4x}. See: TWOT—1367; BDB—647d, 1103a.

5234. נָכַר {50x} **nâkar**, *naw-kar';* a prim. root; prop. to *scrutinize,* i.e. look intently at; hence (with *recognition* impl.), to *acknowledge, be acquainted with, care for, respect, revere,* or (with *suspicion* impl.), to *disregard, ignore, be strange* toward, *reject, resign, dissimulate* (as if ignorant or disowning):—know {16x}, acknowledge {7x}, discern {6x}, respect {4x}, knowledge {2x}, known {2x}, feign to another {2x}, misc. {11x} = × could, deliver, dissemble, estrange, perceive, regard, behave (make) self strange (-ly).

Nakar means "to know, regard, recognize, pay attention to, be acquainted with." **(1)** The first time is in Gen 27:23: ". . . he discerned him not." **(2)** The basic meaning of the term is a physical apprehension, whether through sight, touch, or hearing. **(2a)** Darkness sometimes makes recognition impossible (Ruth 3:14). **(2b)** People are often "recognized" by their voices (Judg 18:3). **(3)** *Nakar* sometimes has the meaning "pay attention to," a special kind of recognition: "Blessed be the man who took knowledge of you" (Ruth 2:19). **(4)** This verb can mean "to be acquainted with," a kind of intellectual awareness: ". . . neither shall his place know him any more" (Job 7:10; cf. Ps 103:16). **(5)** The sense of "to distinguish" is seen in Ezra 3:13: ". . . The people could not discern the noise of the shout of joy from the noise of the weeping of the people. . . ." Syn: 1847, 3045, 4069. See: TWOT—1368; BDB—647d, 649a.

5235. נֶכֶר {2x} **neker**, *neh'-ker;* or
נֹכֶר **nôker**, *no'-ker;* from 5234; something *strange,* i.e. unexpected *calamity:*—strange {1x}, stranger {1x}. See: TWOT—1368a; BDB—648c.

5236. נֵכָר {35x} **nêkar**, *nay-kawr';* from 5234; *foreign,* or (concr.) a *foreigner,* or (abstr.) *heathendom:*—strange {17x}, stranger + 1121 {10x}, stranger {7x}, alien {1x}. See: TWOT—1368b; BDB—648c.

5237. נָכְרִי {45x} **nokrîy**, *nok-ree';* from 5235 (second form); *strange,* in a variety of degrees and applications (*foreign, non-relative, adulterous, different, wonderful*):—stranger {18x}, strange {17x}, alien {4x}, strange woman {3x}, foreigner {2x}, outlandish {1x}, stranger + 376 {1x}. See: TWOT—1368c; BDB—648d.

5238. נְכֹת {2x} **nᵉkôth**, *nek-ōth';* prob. for 5219; *spicery,* i.e. (gen.) *valuables:*—precious things {2x}. See: TWOT—1369; BDB—649b.

5239. נָלָה {1x} **nâlâh**, *naw-law';* appar. a prim. root; to *complete:*—make an end {1x}. See: TWOT—1370; BDB—649b.

5240. נְמִבְזֶה {1x} **nᵉmibzeh**, *nem-ib-zeh';* from 959, *despised:*—vile {1x}. See: TWOT—224; BDB—102c, 649c.

5241. נְמוּאֵל {3x} **Nᵉmûwʼêl**, *nem-oo-ale';* appar. for 3223; *Nemuel,* the name of two Isr.:—Nemuel {3x}. See: BDB—649c.

5242. נְמוּאֵלִי {1x} **Nᵉmûwʼêlîy**, *nem-oo-ay-lee';* from 5241; a *Nemuelite,* or desc. of Nemuel:—Nemuelite {1x}. See: BDB—649c, 974b.

5243. נָמַל {5x} **nâmal**, *naw-mal';* a prim. root; to *become clipped* or (spec.) *circumcised:*—(branch to) be cut down {1x}, cut off {2x}, circumcised {1x}. See: TWOT—1161; BDB—576c, 576d.

5244. נְמָלָה {2x} **nᵉmâlâh**, *nem-aw-law';* fem. from 5243; an *ant* (prob. from its almost *bisected* form):—ant {2x}. See: TWOT—1371a; BDB—649c.

5245. נְמַר {1x} **nᵉmar** (Aram.), *nem-ar';* corresp. to 5246:—leopard {1x}. See: TWOT—2864; BDB—1103a.

5246. נָמֵר {6x} **nâmêr**, *naw-mare';* from an unused root mean. prop. to *filtrate,* i.e. *be limpid* [comp 5247 and 5249]; and thus to *spot* or *stain* as if by dripping; a *leopard* (from its stripes):—leopard {6x}. See: TWOT—1372a; BDB—649d, 1103a.

נִמְרֹד **Nimrôd**. See 5248.

5247. נִמְרָה {1x} **Nimrâh**, *nim-raw';* from the same as 5246; *clear* water; *Nimrah,* a place E. of the Jordan:—*Nimrah* {1x}. See: BDB—649d. See also 1039, 5249.

5248. נִמְרוֹד {4x} **Nimrôwd**, *nim-rode';* or
נִמְרֹד **Nimrôd**, *nim-rode';* prob. of for. or.; *Nimrod,* a son of Cush:—*Nimrod* {4x}. See: BDB—650a.

5249. נִמְרִים {2x} **Nimrîym**, *nim-reem';* plur. of a masc. corresp. to 5247; *clear* waters; *Nimrim,* a place E. of the Jordan:—Nimrim {2x}. See: BDB—649d. comp. 1039.

5250. נִמְשִׁי {5x} **Nimshîy**, *nim-shee';* prob. from 4871; *extricated; Nimshi,* the (grand-) father of Jehu:—Nimshi {5x}. See: BDB—650a.

5251. נֵס {20x} **nêç**, *nace;* from 5264; a *flag;* also a *sail;* by impl. a *flagstaff;* gen. a *signal;* fig. a *token:*—banner {2x}, sign {1x}, pole {2x}, sail {2x}, ensign {6x}, standard {7x}. See: TWOT—1379a; BDB—650a, 651d.

5252. נְסִבָּה {1x} **nᵉçibbâh**, *nes-ib-baw';* fem. pass. part. of 5437, prop. an *environment,* i.e. *circumstance* or *turn* of affairs:—cause {1x}.

Necibbah is found in 2 Chr 10:15 and is translated "cause" and means "turn of events: "So the king hearkened not unto the people: for the cause [*necibbah*] was of God, that the LORD might perform his word, which he spake by the hand of Ahijah the Shilonite to Jeroboam the son of Nebat." See: TWOT—1456a; BDB—650a, 687c.

5253. נָסַג {9x} **nâçag**, *naw-sag';* a prim. root; to *retreat:*—departing away {1x}, remove {5x}, take {1x}, take hold {1x}, turn away {1x}. See: TWOT—1469; BDB—690d.

נְסָה **nᵉçâh**. See 5375.

5254. נָסָה {36x} **nâçâh**, *naw-saw';* a prim. root; to *test;* by impl. to *attempt:*—adventure {1x}, assay {2x}, prove {20x}, tempt {12x}, try {1x}. See: TWOT—1373; BDB—650a.

5255. נָסַח {4x} **nâçach**, *naw-sakh';* a prim. root; to *tear* away:—destroy {1x}, pluck {2x}, root {1x}. See: TWOT—1373; BDB—650c, 1103a.

5256. נְסַח {1x} **nᵉçach** (Aram.), *nes-akh';* corresp. to 5255:—pulled down {1x}. See: TWOT—2865; BDB—1103a.

5257. נְסִיךְ {6x} **nᵉçîyk**, *nes-eek';* from 5258; prop. something *poured* out, i.e. a *libation;* also a molten *image;* by impl. a *prince* (as *anointed*):—drink offering {1x}, duke {1x}, prince {3x}, principal {1x}. See: TWOT—1375b, 1377a; BDB—651a, 651c.

5258. נָסַךְ {25x} **nâçak**, *naw-sak';* a prim. root; to *pour* out, espec. a libation, or to *cast* (metal); by anal. to *anoint* a king:—cover {3x}, melteth {1x}, molten {1x}, offer {2x}, pour {4x}, cause to pour out {12x}, set {1x}, set up {1x}. See: TWOT—1375, 1377; BDB—650c, 651c, 1103a.

5259. נָסַךְ {1x} **nâçak**, *naw-sak';* a prim. root [prob. ident. with 5258 through the idea of fusion]; to *interweave,* i.e. (fig.) to *overspread:*—that is spread {1x}. See: TWOT—1376; BDB—651b.

5260. נְסַךְ {1x} **nᵉçak** (Aram.), *nes-ak';* corresp. to 5258; to *pour* out a libation:—offer {1x}. See: TWOT—2866; BDB—1103a.

5261. נְסַךְ {1x} **nᵉçak** (Aram.), *nes-ak';* corresp. to 5262; a *libation:*—drink offering {1x}. See: TWOT—2866a; BDB—1103a.

5262. נֶסֶךְ {64x} **neçek**, *neh'-sek;* or

נֵסֶךְ **nêçek**, *nay'-sek;* from 5258; a *libation;* also a *cast idol:*—cover {1x}, drink offering {59x}, molten image {4x}. See: TWOT—1375a; BDB—651a, 1103a.

נִסְמָן **niçmân**. See 5567.

5263. נָסַס {1x} **nâçaç**, *naw-sas';* a prim. root; to *wane,* i.e. *be sick:*—standardbearer {1x}. See: TWOT—1378; BDB—651c.

5264. נָסַס {1x} **nâçaç**, *naw-sas';* a prim. root; to *gleam* from afar, i.e. to *be conspicuous* as a signal; or rather perh. a denom. from 5251 [and ident. with 5263, through the idea of a flag as *fluttering* in the wind]; to *raise a beacon:*—lift up as an ensign {1x}. See: TWOT—1379; BDB—651c.

5265. נָסַע {146x} **nâçaʿ**, *naw-sah';* a prim. root; prop. to *pull* up, espec. the tent-pins, i.e. *start* on a journey:—journey {41x}, departed {30x}, remove {28x}, forward {18x}, went {8x}, go away {3x}, brought {3x}, set forth {2x}, go forth {3x}, get {1x}, set aside {1x}, misc. {8x} = cause to blow, march, × still, be on his (go their) way.

Naca' means to journey, depart, set out, march. **(1)** It is probably the most common term in the Old Testament referring to the movement of clans and tribes. Indeed, the word is used almost 90 times in the Book of Numbers alone, since this book records the "journeying" of the people of Israel from Sinai to Canaan. **(2)** It occurs for the first time in Gen 11:2, where *naca'* refers to the "migration" of people to the area of Babylon: "And it came to pass, as they journeyed from the east, that they found a plain in the land of Shinar; and they dwelt there." **(3)** This word has the basic meaning of "pulling up" tent pegs (Is 33:20) in preparation for "moving" one's tent and property to another place; thus it lends itself naturally to the general term of "traveling" or "journeying": "Look upon Zion, the city of our solemnities: thine eyes shall see Jerusalem a quiet habitation, a tabernacle *that* shall not be taken down; not one of the stakes thereof shall ever be removed, neither shall any of the cords thereof be broken."

(4) Samson is said to have "pulled up" **(4a)** the city gate and posts (Judg 16:3), as well as **(4b)** the pin on the weaver's loom: "And she fastened *it* with the pin, and said unto him, The Philistines *be* upon thee, Samson. And he awaked out of his sleep, and went away with the pin of the beam, and with the web" (Judg 16:14). **(4)** *Naca'* describes the movement of the angel of God and the pillar of cloud as they came between Israel and the pursuing Egyptians at the Red Sea (Ex 14:19). **(5)** *Naca'* lends itself to a wide range of renderings, depending upon the context. See: TWOT—1380; BDB—652a.

5266. נָסַק {1x} **nâçaq**, *naw-sak';* a prim. root; to *go* up:—ascend {1x}. See: TWOT—1511; BDB—652d, 701c.

5267. נְסַק {3x} **nᵉçaq** (Aram.), *nes-ak';* corresp. to 5266:—take up {3x}. See: TWOT—2889; BDB—1103a, 1104b.

5268. נִסְרֹךְ {2x} **Niçrôk**, *nis-roke';* of for. or.; *Nisrok,* a Bab. idol:—Nisroch {2x}. See: TWOT—1382; BDB—652d.

5269. נֵעָה {1x} **Nêʿâh**, *nay-aw';* from 5128; *motion; Neäh,* a place in Pal.:—*Neah* {1x}. See: TWOT—1382; BDB—631c, 652d.

5270. נֹעָה {4x} **Nôʿâh**, *no-aw';* from 5128; *movement; Noah,* an Israelitess:—*Noah* {4x}. See: TWOT—1382; BDB—631c, 652d.

5271. נָעוּר {47x} **nâʿûwr**, *naw-oor';* or

נָעֻר **nâʿûr**, *naw-oor';* and (fem.)

נְעֻרָה **nᵉʿûrâh**, *neh-oo-raw';* prop. pass. part. from 5288 as denom.; (only in plur. collect. or emphat.) *youth,* the state (*juvenility*) or the persons (*young* people):—childhood {1x}, youth {46x}. See: TWOT—1389d, 1389e; BDB—655b, 655c.

5272. נְעִיאֵל {1x} **Nᵉʿîyʾêl**, *neh-ee-ale';* from 5128 and 410; *moved of God; Neiel,* a place in Pal.:—Neiel {1x}. See: BDB—653a.

5273. נָעִים {13x} **nâʿîym**, *naw-eem';* from 5276; *delightful* (obj. or subj., lit. or fig.):—pleasant {8x}, pleasures {2x}, sweet {2x}, sweet thing {1x}. See: TWOT—1384b, 1385a; BDB—653d, 654b.

5274. נָעַל {8x} **nâʿal**, *naw-al';* a prim. root; prop. to *fasten* up, i.e. with a bar or cord; hence, (denom. from 5275), to *sandal,* i.e. furnish with slippers:—bolt {2x}, inclosed {1x}, lock {2x}, shoe {2x}, shut up {1x}. See: TWOT—1383, 1383b; BDB—653a, 653b.

5275. נַעַל {22x} **naʿal**, *nah'-al;* or (fem.)

נַעֲלָה **naʿălâh**, *nah-al-aw';* from 5274; prop. a sandal *tongue;* by extens. a *sandal* or slipper (sometimes as a symbol of occupancy, a refusal to marry, or of something valueless):—shoe {20x}, dryshod {1x}, shoelatchet + 8288 {1x}. See: TWOT—1383a; BDB—653a.

5276. נָעֵם {8x} **nâʿêm**, *naw-ame';* a prim. root; to *be agreeable* (lit. or fig.):—pass in beauty {1x}, be delight {1x}, be pleasant {5x}, be sweet {1x}. See: TWOT—1384; BDB—653c.

5277. נַעַם {1x} **Naʿam**, *nah'-am;* from 5276; *pleasure; Naam,* an Isr.:—*Naam* {1x}. See: BDB—653d.

5278. נֹעַם {7x} **noʿam**, *no'-am;* from 5276; *agreeableness,* i.e. *delight, suitableness, splendor* or *grace:*—beauty {4x}, pleasant {2x}, pleasantness {1x}. See: TWOT—1384a; BDB—653c.

5279. נַעֲמָה {5x} **Naʿămâh**, *nah-am-aw';* fem. of 5277; *pleasantness; Naamah,* the name of an antediluvian woman, of an Ammonitess, and of a place in Pal.:—*Naamah* {5x}. See: BDB—653d, 654a.

5280. נַעֲמִי {1x} **Naʿămîy**, *nah-am-ee';* patron. from 5283; a *Naamanite,* or desc. of Naaman (collect.):—Naamites {1x}. See: BDB—654a, 654b.

5281. נָעֳמִי {21x} **Noʿŏmîy**, *no-ŏm-ee';* from 5278; *pleasant; Noomi,* an Israelitess:—Naomi {21x}. See: BDB—654a.

5282. נַעֲמָן {1x} **naʿămân**, *nah-am-awn';* from 5276; *pleasantness* (plur. as concr.):—pleasant {1x}. See: TWOT—1384c; BDB—654a.

5283. נַעֲמָן {16x} **Naʿămân**, *nah-am-awn';* the same as 5282; *Naaman,* the name of an Isr. and of a Damascene:—*Naaman* {16x}. See: BDB—654a.

5284. נַעֲמָתִי {4x} **Naʿămâthîy**, *nah-am-aw-thee';* patrial from a place corresp. in name (but not ident.) with 5279; a *Naamathite,* or inhab. of Naamah:—Naamathite {4x}. See: BDB—654b.

5285. נַעֲצוּץ {2x} **naʿătsûwts**, *nah-ats-oots';* from an unused root mean. to *prick;* prob. a *brier;* by impl. a *thicket* of thorny bushes:—thorn {2x}. See: TWOT—1386a; BDB—654c.

5286. נָעַר {1x} **nâʿar**, *naw-ar';* a prim. root; to *growl:*—yell {1x}. See: TWOT—1387; BDB—654c.

5287. נָעַר {4x} **nâʿar**, *naw-ar';* a prim. root [prob. ident. with 5286, through the idea of the *rustling* of mane, which usually accompanies the lion's roar]; to *tumble* about:—shake {4x}, shake out {3x}, overthrow {2x}, toss to and fro {1x}, shake off {1x}. See: TWOT—1388; BDB—654c.

5288. נַעַר {238x} **naʿar**, *nah'-ar;* from 5287; (concr.) a *boy* (as act.), from the age of infancy to adolescence; by impl. a *servant;* also (by interch. of sex), a *girl* (of similar latitude in age):—young man {76x}, servant {54x}, child {44x}, lad {33x}, young {15x}, children {7x}, youth {6x}, babe {1x}, boys {1x}, young {1x}.

Na'ar means "youth; lad; young man." **(1)** The root with the meaning of "youth" occurs only as a noun and occurs in Hebrew in the feminine (5291 - na'arah, "young girl") as well as the masculine form (e.g., Gen 24:14). **(1a)** *Na'ar* occurs 235 times in the Hebrew Old Testament. **(1b)** The first occurrence is in Gen 14:23–24: ". . . I will not take any thing . . . save only that which the young men have eaten, and the portion of the men which went with me, Aner, Eshcol, and Mamre; let them take their portion." **(3)** The basic meaning of *na'ar* is "youth," over against an older man. **(3a)** At times it may signify a very young child: "For before the child shall know to refuse the evil, and choose the good, the land that thou abhorrest shall be forsaken of both her kings" (Is 7:16). **(4)** Generally *na'ar* denotes a "young man" who is of marriageable age but is still a bachelor. **(4a)** When Jeremiah said: "Ah, Lord God! behold, I cannot speak: for I am a child" (Jer 1:6), he was not referring to his chronological age, but his inexperience as a spokesman for God. **(4b)** Absalom was considered a *na'ar*, even though he was old enough to lead the troups in rebellion against David: "And the king commanded Joab and Abishai and Ittai, saying, Deal gently for my sake with the young man, even with Absalom" (2 Sa 18:5).

(4c) A derived meaning of *na'ar* is "servant." Jonathan used a "servant" as armorbearer: "Now it came to pass upon a day, that Jonathan the son of Saul said unto the young man that bare his armor, Come, and let us go over to the Philistines' garrison, that is on the other side" (1 Sa 14:1). **(4c)** The *na'ar* ("servant") addressed his employer as "master": "And when they were by Jebus, the day was far spent; and the servant said unto his master, Come, I pray thee, and let us turn into this city of the Jebusites, and lodge in it" (Judg 19:11). **(4d)** Kings and officials had "servants" who were referred to by the title *na'ar*. In this context the word is better translated as "attendant," as in the case of the attendants of King Ahasuerus, who gave counsel to the king: "Then said the king's servants that ministered unto him, Let there be fair young virgins sought for the king" (Est 2:2). **(4e)** When a *na'ar* is commissioned to carry messages, he is a "messenger." **(4f)** Thus, we see that the meaning of the word *naar* as "servant" does not denote a "slave" or a performer of low duties. **(4g)** He carried important documents, was trained in the art of warfare, and even gave counsel to the king. See: TWOT—1389a; BDB—654d.

5289. נַעַר {1x} **naʿar**, *nah'-ar;* from 5287 in its der. sense of *tossing* about; a *wanderer:*—young one {1x}. See: TWOT—1388a; BDB—654d.

5290. נֹעַר {4x} **nôʿar**, *no'-ar;* from 5287; (abstr.) *boyhood* [comp. 5288]:—child {2x}, youth {2x}.

Another noun *no'ar* means "youth." This noun appears only 4 times in the Bible, once in Ps 88:15: "I am afflicted and ready to die from my youth up: while I suffer thy terrors I am distracted" (cf. Job 36:14). See: TWOT—1389b; BDB—655a.

נְעֻר **nâʿûr**. See 5271.

5291. נַעֲרָה {62x} **naʿărâh**, *nah-ar-aw';* fem. of 5288; a *girl* (from infancy to adolescence):—damsel {34x}, maid {7x}, maiden {16x}, young {4x}, young woman {1x}. See: TWOT—1389c; BDB—655a.

5292. נַעֲרָה {4x} **Naʿărâh**, *nah-ar-aw';* the same as 5291; *Naarah*, the name of an Israelitess, and of a place in Pal.:—*Naarah* {3x}, Naarath {1x}. See: BDB—655c.

נְעֻרָה **nᵉʿûrâh**. See 5271.

5293. נַעֲרַי {1x} **Naʿăray**, *nah-ar-ah'-ee;* from 5288; *youthful; Naarai*, an Isr.:—Naarai {1x}. See: BDB—655c.

5294. נְעַרְיָה {3x} **Nᵉʿaryâh**, *neh-ar-yaw';* from 5288 and 3050; *servant of Jah; Nearjah*, the name of two Isr.:—Neariah {3x}. See: BDB—655d.

5295. נַעֲרָן {1x} **Naʿărân**, *nah-ar-awn';* from 5288; *juvenile; Naaran*, a place in Pal.:—*Naaran* {1x}. See: BDB—655d.

5296. נְעֹרֶת {2x} **nᵉʿôreth**, *neh-o'-reth;* from 5287; something *shaken* out, i.e. *tow* (as the refuse of flax):—tow {2x}. See: TWOT—1388b; BDB—654d.

נַעֲרָתָה **Naʿărâthâh**. See 5292.

5297. נֹף {7x} **Nôph**, *nofe;* a var. of 4644; *Noph*, the capital of Upper Egypt:—*Noph* {7x}. See: BDB—592a, 655d.

5298. נֶפֶג {4x} **Nepheg**, *neh'-feg;* from an unused root prob. mean. to *spring* forth; a *sprout; Nepheg*, the name of two Isr.:—*Nepheg* {4x}. See: BDB—655d.

5299. נָפָה {4x} **nâphâh**, *naw-faw';* from 5130 in the sense of *lifting;* a *height;* also a *sieve:*—border {1x}, coast {1x}, region {1x}, sieve {1x}. See: TWOT—1331b, 1330a; BDB—190b, 632b, 632c, 655d.

5300. נְפוּשְׁסִים {2x} **Nᵉphûwshᵉçîym**, *nef-oo-shes-eem';* for 5304; *Nephushesim*, a Temple-servant:—Nephisesim {1x}, Nephusim {1x}. See: BDB—655d, 656b, 656c.

5301. נָפַח {12x} **nâphach**, *naw-fakh';* a prim. root; to *puff*, in various applications (lit., to *inflate, blow* hard, *scatter, kindle, expire;* fig., to *disesteem*):—blow {4x}, blown {1x}, breathe {2x}, give up {1x}, cause to lose [life]{1x}, seething {2x}, snuff {1x}. See: TWOT—1390; BDB—655d.

5302. נֹפַח {1x} **Nôphach**, *no'-fakh;* from 5301; a *gust; Nophach*, a place in Moab:—Nophah {1x}. See: BDB—656a.

5303. נְפִיל {3x} **nᵉphîyl**, *nef-eel';* or

נְפִל **nᵉphîl**, *nef-eel';* from 5307; prop., a *feller*, i.e. a *bully* or *tyrant:*—giant {3x}. See: TWOT—1393a; BDB—658c.

5304. נְפִיסִים {2x} **Nᵉphîyçîym**, *nef-ee-seem';* plur. from an unused root mean. See 5300. to *scatter; expansions; Nephisim*, a Temple-servant:—Nephusim {2x}. See: BDB—656b.

5305. נָפִישׁ {3x} **Nâphîysh**, *naw-feesh';* from 5314; *refreshed; Naphish*, a son of Ishmael, and his posterity:—Naphish {3x}. See: BDB—661c.

5306. נֹפֶךְ {4x} **nôphek**, *no'-fek;* from an unused root mean. to *glisten; shining;* a gem, prob. the *garnet:*—emerald {4x}. See: TWOT—1391; BDB—656c.

5307. נָפַל {434x} **nâphal**, *naw-fal';* a prim. root; to *fall*, in a great variety of applications (intr. or caus., lit. or fig.):—fall {318x}, fall down {25x}, cast {18x}, cast down {9x}, fall away {5x}, divide {5x}, overthrow {5x}, present {5x}, lay {3x}, rot {3x}, accepted {2x}, lie down {2x}, inferior {2x}, lighted {2x}, lost {2x}, misc. {22x} = cease, die, (let) fail, fell (-ing), fugitive, have [inheritance], be judged, lying, overwhelm, perish, slay, smite out, × surely, throw down. See: TWOT—1392; BDB—656c, 1103a.

5308. נְפַל {11x} **nᵉphal** (Aram.), *nef-al';* corresp. to 5307:—fall down {7x}, fall {3x}, have occasion {1x}. See: TWOT—2867; BDB—1103a.

5309. נֶפֶל {3x} **nephel**, *neh'-fel;* or

נֵפֶל **nêphel**, *nay'-fel;* from 5307; something *fallen*, i.e. an *abortion:*—untimely birth {3x}. See: TWOT—1392a; BDB—658b.

נְפִל **nᵉphîl**. See 5303.

5310. נָפַץ {22x} **nâphats**, *naw-fats';* a prim. root; to *dash* to pieces, or *scatter:*—break in pieces {9x}, scatter {3x}, break {3x}, dash {2x}, discharged {1x}, dispersed {1x}, overspread {1x}, dash in pieces {1x}, sunder {1x}. See: TWOT—1394; BDB—658c, 659a.

5311. נֶפֶץ {1x} **nephets**, *neh'-fets;* from 5310; a *storm* (as dispersing):—scattering {1x}. See: TWOT—1394a; BDB—658d.

5312. נְפַק {11x} **nᵉphaq** (Aram.), *nef-ak';* a prim. root; to *issue;* caus. to *bring out:*—take out {4x}, come forth {4x}, go forth {2x}, take forth {1x}. See: TWOT—2868; BDB—1103b.

5313. נִפְקָא {2x} **niphqâʾ** (Aram.), *nif-kaw';* from 5312; an *outgo*, i.e. expense:—expense {2x}. See: TWOT—2868a; BDB—1103b.

5314. נָפַשׁ {3x} **nâphash**, *naw-fash';* a prim. root; to *breathe;* pass., to *be breathed* upon, i.e. (fig.) *refreshed* (as if by a current of air):—refreshed {2x}, refreshed themselves {1x}.

Napash means "to breathe; respire; be refreshed." This verb appears 3 times in the Old Testament (Ex 23:12; 31:17). The other appearance is in 2 Sa 16:14: "And the king, and all the people that were with him, came weary and refreshed themselves there." See: TWOT—1395; BDB—661c.

5315. נֶפֶשׁ {753x} **nephesh**, *neh'-fesh;* from 5314; prop. a *breathing* creature, i.e. *animal* of (abstr.) *vitality;* used very widely in a lit., accommodated or fig. sense (bodily or ment.):—soul {475x}, life {117x}, person {29x}, mind {15x}, heart {15x}, creature {9x}, body {8x}, himself {8x}, yourselves {6x}, dead {5x}, will {4x}, desire {4x}, man {3x}, themselves {3x}, any {3x}, appetite {2x}, misc. {47x} = beast, breath, × [dis-] contented, × fish, ghost, + greedy, he, lust, me, mortally, one, own, pleasure, + slay, + tablet, they, thing, × would have it.

Nephesh means soul; self; life; person; heart. **(1)** The basic meaning comes from its verbal form, naphash (5314), which refers to the essence of life, the act of breathing, taking breath (Gen 2:7). From this many abstract meanings were developed. **(1a)** In its primary sense the noun appears in its first occurrence in Gen 1:20: "the moving creature that hath life," and **(1b)** in its second occurrence in Gen 2:7: "living soul." **(1c)** The best Biblical definition is found in Ps 103:1 where *nephesh* is defined as "all that is within" a person: "Bless the LORD, O my soul: and all that is within me, *bless* his holy name." **(2)** It is translated "soul" which makes sense in most passages. All other English translations, in the particular context, are stressing some aspect of the soul. **(3)** The Hebrew system of thought does not include the opposition of the terms "body" and "soul," which are really Greek and Latin in origin. **(3a)** The Hebrew compares/contrasts "the inner self" and "the outer appearance" or, as viewed in a different context, "what one is to oneself" as opposed to "what one appears to be to one's observers."

(3b) The goal of the Scriptures is to make the inner and the outer consistent. **(3c)** The inner person is *nephesh*, while the outer person, or reputation, is shem (8034), most commonly translated "name." **(4)** In narrative or historical passages of the Old Testament, *nephesh* is translated as "soul." as **(4a)** in Lev 17:11: "For the life of the flesh *is* in the blood: and I have given it to you upon the altar to make an atonement for your souls: for it *is* the blood *that* maketh an atonement for the soul." **(4b)** The soul of man, that immaterial part, which moves into the after life [the body is buried and decomposes] needs atonement to enter into God's presence upon death. **(5)** Hebrew parallelism brings out the various aspects contained in one's soul. **(5a)** Soul parallels the whole individual "him": Many *there be* which say of my soul, *There is* no help for him in God" (Ps 3:2); **(5b)** The Lord has a soul [stressing His inward attributes which are demonstrated in action]: "The LORD trieth the righteous: but the wicked and him that loveth violence His soul hateth" (Ps 11:5); **(5c)** Soul is parallel to the whole person "I": "My soul *is* continually in my hand: yet do I not forget thy law" (Ps 119:109). See: TWOT—1395a; BDB—659b, 925a, 925b, 925c.

5316. נֶפֶת {1x} **nepheth**, *neh'-feth;* for 5299; a *height:*—country {1x}. See: TWOT—1331c; BDB—190b, 632c, 661d.

5317. נֹפֶת {5x} **nôpheth**, *no'-feth;* from 5130 in the sense of *shaking* to pieces; a *dripping,* i.e. of *honey* (from the comb):—honeycomb {5x}. See: TWOT—1396; BDB—661d.

5318. נֶפְתּוֹחַ {2x} **Nephtôwach**, *nef-to'-akh;* from 6605; *opened,* i.e. a *spring; Nephtoach,* a place in Pal.:—Neptoah {2x}. See: BDB—661d, 836b.

5319. נַפְתּוּל {1x} **naphtûwl**, *naf-tool';* from 6617; prop. *wrestled;* but used (in the plur.) tran., a *struggle:*—wrestling {1x}. See: TWOT—1857c; BDB—661d, 836d.

5320. נַפְתֻּחִים {2x} **Naphtûchîym**, *naf-too-kheem';* plur. of for. or., *Naphtuchim,* an Eg. tribe:—Naptuhim {2x}. See: BDB—661d.

5321. נַפְתָּלִי {50x} **Naphtâlîy**, *naf-taw-lee';* from 6617; *my wrestling; Naphtali,* a son of Jacob, with the tribe desc. from him, and its territory:—Naphtali {50x}. See: BDB—661d, 836d.

5322. נֵץ {4x} **nêts**, *nayts;* from 5340; a *flower* (from its *brilliancy*); also a *hawk* (from it *flashing* speed):—blossom {1x}, hawk {3x}. See: TWOT—1405b, 1406a; BDB—661d, 665b, 665c.

5323. נָצָא {1x} **nâtsâ'**, *naw-tsaw';* a prim. root; to *go away:*—flee {1x}. See: TWOT—1397; BDB—661d.

5324. נָצַב {75x} **nâtsab**, *naw-tsab';* a prim. root; to *station,* in various applications (lit. or fig.):—stand {34x}, set {12x}, officers {6x}, set up {7x}, upright {2x}, appointed {1x}, deputy {1x}, erected {1x}, establish {1x}, Huzzab 1, misc. {9x} = lay, pillar, present, rear up, settle, sharpen, stablish, best state.

Natsab means "to stand, station, set up, erect." **(1)** Its first occurrence in the Old Testament is in Gen 18:2: ". . . Three men stood by him. . . ." **(2)** There are various ways of standing. One may "stand" for a definite purpose at a particular spot: "Get thee unto Pharaoh in the morning; lo, he goeth out unto the water; and thou shalt stand by the river's brink against he come; and the rod which was turned to a serpent shalt thou take in thine hand" (Ex 7:15). **(3)** One often stands upright: **(3a)** ". . . And stood every man at his tent door . . ." (Ex 33:8); **(3b)** ". . . my sheaf arose, and also stood upright . . ." (Gen 37:7). **(4)** One who is "stationed" in a position is usually over someone else: "And Azariah the son of Nathan was over the officers [literally, "those standing over" . . ." (1 Kin 4:5). **(5)** "To stand" something may be "to erect" something: "And Jacob set up a pillar . . ." (Gen 35:14). **(6)** The waters of the Sea of Reeds were said to "stand as a heap" (Ps 78:13). **(7)** To fix a boundary is "to establish or erect" a boundary marker (Deut 32:8). Syn.: 5975. See: TWOT—1398; BDB—246c, 662a, 663b, 1103b.

נְצִב **n^etsîb**. See 5333.

5325. נִצָּב {1x} **nitstsâb**, *nits-tsawb';* pass. part. of 5324; *fixed,* i.e. a *handle:*—haft {1x}. See: TWOT—1398a; BDB—662c.

5326. נִצְבָּה {1x} **nitsbâh** (Aram.), *nits-baw';* from a root corresp. to 5324; *fixedness,* i.e. *firmness:*—strength {1x}. TWOT—2869; See: BDB—1103b.

5327. נָצָה {11x} **nâtsâh**, *naw-tsaw';* a prim. root; prop. to *go forth,* i.e. (by impl.) to *be expelled,* and (consequently) *desolate;* caus. to *lay waste;* also (spec.), to *quarrel:*—be laid waste {1x}, ruinous {2x}, strive {2x}, strove together {3x}, strove against {2x}, strove {1x}. See: TWOT—1399, 1400, 1401; BDB—663c, 663d.

נֹצָה **nôtsâh**. See 5133.

5328. נִצָּה {2x} **nitstsâh**, *nits-tsaw';* fem. of 5322; a *blossom:*—flower {2x}. See: TWOT—1405c; BDB—663d, 665b.

נְצוּרָה **n^etsûwrâh**. See 5341.

5329. נָצַח {65x} **nâtsach**, *naw-tsakh';* a prim. root; prop. to *glitter* from afar, i.e. to *be eminent* (as a superintendent, espec. of the Temple services and its music); also (as denom. from 5331), to *be permanent:*—Musician {55x}, set forward {3x}, overseers {3x}, excel {1x}, oversee {1x}, perpetual {1x}, chief singer {1x}.

I. *Natsach*, as a verb, means (5329) "to keep, oversee, have charge over." **(1)** The word appears as "to set forward" in the sense of "to oversee or to lead": "Then stood Jeshua with his sons and his brethren, Kadmiel and his sons, the sons of Judah, together, to set forward the workmen in the house of God. . . ." (Ezra 3:9; cf. 1 Chr 23:4; 2 Chr 34:12). **(2)** The word appears as "to oversee" in 2 Chr 2:2: "And Solomon told out threescore and ten thousand men to bear burdens . . . and three thousand and six hundred to oversee them." **II. Natstseach, as a masculine participle**, means "overseer; director." **(1)** While this word is used approximately 65 times in the Hebrew Old Testament, almost all of them (except for 5 or 6) are participles, used as verbal-nouns. **(1a)** The participial form has the meaning of "overseer, director," reflecting the idea that one who is pre-eminent or conspicuous is an "overseer."

(1b) Thus, natstseach is found in the Book of Psalms a total of 55 times in the titles of various psalms (Ps 5, 6, 9, et al.) with the meaning, "To the chief musician." **(1c)** Of the 55 psalms involved, 39 are connected with the name of David, 9 with Korah, and 5 with Asaph, leaving only two anonymous psalms. **(1d)** The Hebrew preposition, *le,* used with this participle is a lamed of authorship. **(1e)** This title refers to the One who can bring harmony to all, the Coming One, the Messiah, the Chief Musician unto Whom all tune their songs and instruments. **(2)** This title is found also at the end of Hab 3, showing that this psalm was in the theme: "the just One shall live by faith." **(3)** The word refers to "overseers" in 2 Chr 2:18: ". . . and three thousand and six hundred overseers to set the people a work." **(4)** The feminine participle *natsach* is used only in Jer 8:5 in the sense of "enduring": "Why *then* is this people of Jerusalem slidden back by a perpetual [*natsach*] backsliding? they hold fast deceit, they refuse to return." See: TWOT—1402; BDB—663d, 1103b.

5330. נְצַח {1x} **n^etsach** (Aram.), *nets-akh';* corresp. to 5329; to *become chief:*—be preferred {1x}. See: TWOT—2870; BDB—1103b.

5331. נֶצַח {43x} **netsach**, *neh'-tsakh;* or

נֵצַח **nêtsach**, *nay'-tsakh;* from 5329; prop. a *goal,* i.e. the bright object at a distance travelled toward; hence, (fig.) *splendor,* or (subj.) *truthfulness,* or (obj.) *confidence;* but usually (adv.), *continually* (i.e. to the most distant point of view):—ever {24x}, never {4x}, perpetual {3x}, always {2x}, end {2x}, victory {2x}, strength {2x}, alway {1x}, constantly {1x}, evermore {1x}, never + 3808 {1x}. See: TWOT—1402a; BDB—664b.

5332. נֵצַח {2x} **nêtsach**, *nay'-tsakh;* prob. ident. with 5331, through the idea of *brilliancy* of color; *juice* of the grape (as blood red):—blood {1x}, strength {1x}. See: TWOT—1403a; BDB—664c.

5333. נְצִיב {12x} **n^etsîyb**, *nets-eeb';* or

נְצִב **n^etsîb**, *nets-eeb';* from 5324; something *stationary,* i.e. a *prefect,* a military *post,* a *statue:*—garrison {9x}, officer {2x}, pillar {1x}. See: TWOT—1398b; BDB—662c.

5334. נְצִיב {1x} **N^etsîyb**, *nets-eeb';* the same as 5333; *station; Netsib,* a place in Pal.:—Nezib {1x}. See: BDB—662d.

5335. נְצִיחַ {2x} **N^etsîyach**, *nets-ee'-akh;* from 5329; *conspicuous; Netsiach,* a Temple-servant:—Neziah {2x}. See: BDB—664c.

5336. נָצִיר {1x} **nâtsîyr**, *naw-tsere';* from 5341; prop. *conservative;* but used pass., *delivered:*—preserved {1x}. See: TWOT—1407a; BDB—666a.

5337. נָצַל {213x} **nâtsal**, *naw-tsal';* a prim. root; to *snatch* away, whether in a good or a bad sense:—deliver {179x}, recover {5x}, rid {3x}, escape {2x}, rescue {2x}, spoil {2x}, at all {2x}, take out {2x}, misc. {16x} = defend, × without fail, part, pluck, preserve, save, strip, × surely. See: TWOT—1404; BDB—664c, 1103b.

5338. נְצַל {3x} **n^etsal** (Aram.), *nets-al';* corresp. to 5337; to *extricate:*—deliver {2x}, rescue {1x}. See: TWOT—2871; BDB—1103b.

5339. נִצָּן {1x} **nitstsân**, *nits-tsawn';* from 5322; a *blossom:*—flower {1x}. See: TWOT—1405d; BDB—665a, 665b.

5340. נָצַץ {1x} **nâtsats**, *naw-tsats';* a prim. root; to *glare,* i.e. *be bright*-colored:—sparkle {1x}. See: TWOT—1405; BDB—665a.

5341. נָצַר {63x} **nâtsar**, *naw-tsar';* a prim. root; to *guard,* in a good sense (to *protect, maintain, obey,* etc.) or a bad one (to *conceal,* etc.):—keep {38x}, preserve {13x}, watchmen {3x}, besieged {2x}, keeper {1x}, monuments {1x}, observe + 7521 {1x}, preserver {1x}, subtil {1x}, hidden things {1x}, watchers {1x}.

Natsar means "to watch, to guard, to keep." **(1)** *Natsar* is found for the first time in the biblical text in Ex 34:7 where it has the sense of **(1a)** "keeping with faithfulness": "Keeping [*natsar*] mercy for thousands, forgiving iniquity and transgression and sin, and that will by no means clear *the guilty;* visiting the iniquity of the fathers upon the children, and upon the children's children, unto the third and to the fourth *generation.*" **(1b)** This meaning is usually found when man is the subject: **(1b1)** "keeping" the covenant (Deut 33:9); **(1b2)** "keeping" the law (Ps 105:45 and 10 times in Ps 119); **(1b3)** "keeping" the rules of parents (Prov 6:20). **(2)** *Natsar* is frequently used to express the idea of "guarding" something, such as a vineyard (Is 27:3) or a fortification (Nah 2:1).

(3) "To watch" one's speech is a frequent concern, so advice is given **(3a)** "to watch" one's mouth (Prov 13:3), **(3b)** the tongue (Ps 34:13), and **(3c)** the lips (Ps. 141:3). **(4)** Many references are made to God as the one who "preserves" His people from dangers of all kinds: "He found him in a desert land, and in the waste howling wilderness; he led him about, he instructed him, he kept him as the apple of his eye" (Deut 32:10; cf. Ps 31:23). **(5)** Generally, *natsar* is a close synonym to the much more common verb, shamar (8104), "to keep, tend." **(6)** Sometimes "to keep" has the meaning of "to besiege," as in Is 1:8, ". . . as a besieged city." Syn: 8104, 8105, 8107, 8108. See: TWOT—1407; BDB—665c, 666a, 1102d.

5342. נֵצֶר {4x} **nêtser**, *nay'-tser;* from 5341 in the sense of *greenness* as a striking color; a *shoot;* fig. a *descendant:*—branch {4x}. See: TWOT—1408a; BDB—666a.

5343. נְקֵא {1x} **n**[e]**qê'** (Aram.), *nek-ay';* from a root corresp. to 5352; *clean:*—pure {1x}. See: TWOT—2872; BDB—1103c.

5344. נָקַב {25x} **nâqab**, *naw-kab';* a prim. root; to *puncture,* lit. (to *perforate,* with more or less violence) or fig. (to *specify, designate, libel*):—curse {6x}, expressed {6x}, blaspheme {3x}, bore {2x}, name {2x}, pierce {2x}, appoint {1x}, holes {1x}, pierce through {1x}, strike through {1x}. See: TWOT—1409; BDB—666a, 666d.

5345. נֶקֶב {1x} **neqeb**, *neh'keb;* a *bezel* (for a gem):—pipe {1x}. See: TWOT—1409a; BDB—666b.

5346. נֶקֶב {1x} **Neqeb**, *neh'-keb;* the same as 5345; *dell; Nekeb,* a place in Pal.:—Nekeb {1x}. See: BDB—10a, 666c.

5347. נְקֵבָה {22x} **n**[e]**qêbâh**, *nek-ay-baw';* from 5344; *female* (from the sexual form):—female {18x}, woman {3x}, maid {1x}. See: BDB—666c.

5348. נָקֹד {9x} **nâqôd**, *naw-kode';* from an unused root mean. to *mark* (by *puncturing* or *branding*); *spotted:*—speckled {9x}. See: TWOT—1410a; BDB—666d.

5349. נֹקֵד {2x} **nôqêd**, *no-kade';* act. part. from the same as 5348; a *spotter* (of sheep or cattle), i.e. the owner or tender (who thus marks them):—herdman {1x}, sheepmaster {1x}. See: TWOT—1411a; BDB—667a.

5350. נִקֻּד {3x} **niqqud**, *nik-kood';* from the same as 5348; a *crumb* (as *broken* to spots); also a *biscuit* (as *pricked*):—cracknels {1x}, mouldy {2x}. See: TWOT—1410b; BDB—666d.

5351. נְקֻדָּה {1x} **n**[e]**quddâh**, *nek-ood-daw';* fem. of 5348; a *boss:*—studs {1x}. See: TWOT—1410c; BDB—667a.

5352. נָקָה {44x} **nâqâh**, *naw-kaw';* a prim. root; to *be* (or *make*) *clean* (lit. or fig.); by impl. (in an adverse sense) to *be bare,* i.e. *extirpated:*—unpunished {11x}, guiltless {5x}, innocent {5x}, clear {4x}, cleanse {3x}, free {2x}, by no means {2x}, acquit {2x}, altogether {2x}, cut off {2x}, at all {1x}, blameless {1x}, desolate {1x}, quit {1x}, utterly {1x}, wholly {1x}.

Naqah, as a verb, means "to be pure, innocent." **(1)** Isaiah described the future of Jerusalem as an empty ("desolate") city: "And her gates shall lament and mourn; and she *being* desolate shall sit upon the ground" (Is 3:26). **(2)** On the more positive side, a land may also be "cleansed" of robbers: "Then said he unto me, This *is* the curse that goeth forth over the face of the whole earth: for every one that stealeth shall be cut off [*naqah*] *as* on this side according to it; and every one that sweareth shall be cut off [*naqah*] *as* on that side according to it" (Zec 5:3). **(3)** The verb is more often used to mean being "free" (with the preposition min). **(3a)** The first occurrence in the Old Testament is in Gen 24:8, and is illustrative of this usage. **(3b)** Abraham ordered his servant to find a wife for Isaac. The servant pledged that he would fulfill his commission; however, if he did not succeed—that is, in case the woman was unwilling to make the long journey with him—Abraham would free him: ". . . Then thou shalt be clear from this my oath. . . ."

(4) The freedom may be **(4a)** from wrongdoing: "Then shall the man be guiltless from iniquity, and this woman shall bear her iniquity" (Num 5:31), or **(4b)** from punishment: "If he rise again, and walk abroad upon his staff, then shall he that smote *him* be quit [*naqah*]: only he shall pay *for* the loss of his time, and shall cause *him* to be thoroughly healed" (Ex 21:19; cf. Num 5:28). **(5)** The verb *naqah* also appears with the legal connotation of "innocence." **(5a)** First, a person may be declared "innocent," or "acquitted." David prayed: "Keep back thy servant also from presumptuous *sins;* let them not have dominion over me: then shall I be upright, and I shall be innocent from the great transgression" (Ps 19:13). **(5b)** On the other hand, the sinner is not "acquitted" by God: "I am afraid of all my sorrows, I know that thou wilt not hold me innocent" (Job 9:28). **(5c)** The punishment of the person who is not "acquitted" is also expressed by a negation of the verb *naqah:* "Thou shalt not take the name of the LORD thy God in vain; for the LORD will not hold him guiltless that taketh his name in vain" (Ex 20:7).

(5d) "For I *am* with thee, saith the LORD, to save thee: though I make a full end of all nations whither I have scattered thee, yet will I not make a full end of thee: but I will correct thee in measure, and will not leave thee altogether unpunished" (Jer 30:11). **(5e)** The fate of the wicked is the judgment of God: ". . . the wicked shall not be unpunished: but the seed of the righteous shall be delivered" (Prov 11:21). See: TWOT—1412; BDB—667a, 1103c.

5353. נְקוֹדָא {4x} **N**[e]**qôwdâ'**, *nek-o-daw';* fem. of 5348 (in the fig. sense of *marked*); *distinction; Nekoda,* a Temple-servant:—Nekoda {4x}. See: BDB—667a.

5354. נָקַט {1x} **nâqaṭ**, *naw-kat';* a prim. root; to *loathe:*—weary {1x}. See: TWOT—1996; BDB—667d, 876c.

5355. נָקִי {44x} **nâqîy**, *naw-kee';* or

נָקִיא **nâqîy'** (Joel 4:19; Jonah 1:14), *naw-kee';* from 5352; *innocent:*—innocent {31x}, guiltless {4x}, quit {2x}, blameless {2x}, clean {1x}, clear {1x}, exempted {1x}, free {1x}, variant {1x}.

Naqiy, as an adjective, means "innocent." This adjective appears 43 times in the Old Testament. One occurrence is in Ps 15:5, which says of the righteous man, "*He that* putteth not out his money to usury, nor taketh reward against the innocent [*naqiy*]. He that doeth these *things* shall never be moved." See: TWOT—1412a, 1412b; BDB—667c, 667d.

5356. נִקָּיוֹן {5x} **niqqâyôwn**, *nik-kaw-yone';* or

נִקָּיֹן **niqqâyôn**, *nik-kaw-yone';* from 5352; *clearness* (lit. or fig.):—cleanness {1x}, innocency {4x}. See: TWOT—1412c; BDB—667d, 874c.

5357. נָקִיק {3x} **nâqîyq**, *naw-keek';* from an unused root mean. to *bore;* a *cleft:*—hole {3x}. See: TWOT—1417a; BDB—669b.

5358. נָקַם {35x} **nâqam**, *naw-kam';* a prim. root; to *grudge,* i.e. *avenge* or *punish:*—avenge {18x}, vengeance {4x}, revenge {4x}, take {4x}, avenger {2x}, punished {2x}, surely {1x}.

Naqam means "to avenge, take vengeance, punish." **(1)** Lamech's sword song is a scornful challenge to his fellows and a blatant attack on the justice of God: ". . . for I have slain a man to my wounding, and a young man to my hurt. If Cain shall be avenged sevenfold, truly Lamech seventy and sevenfold" (Gen 4:23–24). **(2)** The Lord reserves vengeance as the sphere of His own action: "To me belongeth vengeance, and recompense . . . for he will avenge the blood of his servants, and will render vengeance to his adversaries" (Deut 32:35, 43). **(3)** The law therefore forbade personal vengeance: "Thou shalt not avenge, nor bear any grudge against the children of thy people, but thou shalt love thy neighbor as thyself: I am the Lord" (Lev 19:18). **(4)** Hence the Lord's people commit their case to Him, as David: "The Lord judge between me and thee [Saul], and the Lord avenge me of thee: but mine hand shall not be upon thee" (1 Sa 24:12). **(5)** The Lord uses men to take vengeance, as He said to Moses: "Avenge the children of Israel of the Midianites. . . . And Moses spake unto the people, saying, Arm some of yourselves unto the war, and let them go against the Midianites, and avenge the Lord of Midian" (Num 31:2–3).

(6) Vengeance for Israel is the Lord's vengeance. **(7)** The law stated, "And if a man smite his servant, or his maid, with a rod, and he die under his hand; he shall be surely punished" (Ex 21:20). **(7a)** In Israel, this responsibility was given to the "avenger of blood" (Deut 19:6). **(7b)** He was responsible to preserve the life and personal integrity of his nearest relative. **(8)** When a man was attacked because he was God's servant, he could rightly call for vengeance on his enemies, as Samson prayed for strength, ". . . that I may be at once avenged of the Philistines for my two eyes" (Judg 16:28). **(9)** In the covenant, God warned that His vengeance may fall on His own people: "And I will bring a sword upon you, that shall avenge the quarrel of my covenant . . ." (Lev 26:25). **(10)** Isaiah thus says of Judah: "Therefore saith the Lord, the Lord of hosts . . . Ah, I will ease me of mine adversaries, and avenge me of my enemies" (1:24). See: TWOT—1413; BDB—667d.

5359. נָקָם {17x} **nâqâm**, *naw-kawm';* from 5358; *revenge:*—+ avenged {1x}, quarrel {1x}, vengeance {15x}.

Naqam means "vengeance." **(1)** The noun is first used in the Lord's promise to Cain: "Therefore whosoever slayeth Cain, vengeance shall be taken on him sevenfold" (Gen 4:15). **(2)** In some instances a man may call for "vengeance" on his enemies, such as when another man has committed adultery with his wife: "For jealousy is the rage of a man: therefore he will not spare in the day of vengeance" (Prov 6:34). **(3)** The prophets frequently speak of God's "vengeance" on His enemies: Is 59:17; Mic 5:15; Nah 1:2. **(4)** It will come at a set time: "For it is the day of the Lord's vengeance, and the year of recompenses for the controversy of Zion" (Is 34:8). **(5)** Isaiah brings God's "vengeance" and redemption together in the promise of messianic salvation: **(5a)** "The Spirit of the Lord God is upon me; . . . he hath sent me . . . to proclaim the acceptable year of the Lord, and the day of vengeance of our God . . ." (61:1–2). **(5b)** When Jesus announced that this was fulfilled in Himself, He stopped short of reading the last clause; but His sermon clearly anticipated that "vengeance" that would come on Israel for rejecting Him. Isaiah also said: "For the day of vengeance is in mine heart, and the year of my redeemed is come" (63:4). See: TWOT—1413a; BDB—668b.

5360. נְקָמָה {27x} **nᵉqâmâh**, *nek-aw-maw'*; fem. of 5359; *avengement*, whether the act or the passion:—vengeance {18x}, avenge + 5414 {3x}, revenge {3x}, avenge + 5358 {1x}, avenged {1x}, take vengeance for thee + 5358 {1x}. See: TWOT—1413b; BDB—668c.

5361. נָקַע {3x} **nâqaʿ**, *naw-kah'*; a prim. root; to *feel aversion:*—be alienated {3x}. See: TWOT—1414; BDB—668c.

5362. נָקַף {19x} **nâqaph**, *naw-kaf'*; a prim. root; to *strike* with more or less violence (*beat, fell, corrode*); by impl. (of attack) to *knock together,* i.e. *surround* or *circulate:*—compass {7x}, go round about {3x}, go about {2x}, compass about {2x}, destroy {1x}, down {1x}, inclosed {1x}, kill {1x}, round {1x}. See: TWOT—1415, 1416; BDB—596d, 668c, 668d, 880d.

5363. נֹקֶף {2x} **nôqeph**, *no'-kef;* from 5362; a *threshing* (of olives):—shaking {2x}. See: TWOT—1415a; BDB—668d.

5364. נִקְפָּה {1x} **niqpâh**, *nik-paw'*; from 5362; prob. a *rope* (as *encircling*):—rent {1x}. See: TWOT—1416a; BDB—669a.

5365. נָקַר {6x} **nâqar**, *naw-kar'*; a prim. root; to *bore* (*penetrate, quarry*):—dig {1x}, pick out {1x}, pierce {1x}, put thrust out {1x}, put out {2x}. See: TWOT—1418; BDB—669b.

5366. נְקָרָה {2x} **nᵉqârâh**, *nek-aw-raw'*; from 5365, a *fissure:*—cleft {1x}, clift {1x}. See: TWOT—1418a; BDB—669b.

5367. נָקַשׁ {5x} **nâqash**, *naw-kash'*; a prim. root; to *entrap* (with a noose), lit. or fig.:—catch {1x}, lay a snare {2x}, snare {2x}. See: TWOT—1419; BDB—669b, 1103c.

5368. נְקַשׁ {1x} **nᵉqash** (Aram.), *nek-ash'*; corresp. to 5367; but used in the sense of 5362; to *knock:*—smote {1x}. See: TWOT—2873; BDB—1103c.

נֵר **nêr,**

נִר **nîr.** See 5215, 5216.

5369. נֵר {16x} **Nêr**, *nare;* the same as 5216; *lamp; Ner,* an Isr.:—*Ner* {6x}. See: TWOT—1333a; BDB—633a.

5370. נֵרְגַּל {1x} **Nêrgal**, *nare-gal';* of for. or.; *Nergal,* a Cuthite deity:—*Nergal* {1x}. See: BDB—669c.

5371. נֵרְגַל שַׁרְאֶצֶר {3x} **Nêrgal Sharʾetser**, *nare-gal' shar-eh'-tser;* from 5370 and 8272; *Nergal-Sharetser,* the name of two Bab.:—Nergal-sharezer {3x}. See: BDB—669c.

5372. נִרְגָּן {4x} **nirgân**, *neer-gawn';* from an unused root mean. to *roll* to pieces; a *slanderer:*—talebearer {3x}, whisperer {1x}. See: TWOT—2115; BDB—669d, 920d.

5373. נֵרְדְּ {3x} **nêrd**, *nayrd;* of for. or.; *nard,* an aromatic:—spikenard {3x}. See: TWOT—1420; BDB—669d.

נֵרָה **nêrâh.** See 5216.

5374. נֵרִיָּה {10x} **Nêrîyâh**, *nay-ree-yaw';* or

נֵרִיָּהוּ **Nêrîyâhûw**, *nay-ree-yaw'-hoo;* from 5216 and 3050; *light of Jah; Nerijah,* an Isr.:—Neriah {10x}. See: BDB—633a, 669d.

5375. נָשָׂא {654x} **nâsâʾ**, *naw-saw';* or

נָסָה **nâçâh** (Ps 4:6 7]) *naw-saw';* a prim. root; to *lift,* in a great variety of applications, lit. and fig., absol. and rel. (as follows):—(bare, lift, etc . . .) up {219x}, bear {115x}, take {58x}, bare {34x}, carry {30x}, (take, carry) . . . away {22x}, borne {22x}, armourbearer {18x}, forgive {16x}, accept {12x}, exalt {8x}, regard {5x}, obtained {4x}, respect {3x}, misc. {74x} = advance, arise, bring (forth), burn, cast, contain, desire, ease, exact, extol, fetch, furnish, further, give, go on, help, high, hold up, honorable (+ man), lade, lay, lift (self) up, lofty, marry, magnify, × needs, pardon, receive, spare, stir up, + swear, × utterly, wear, yield.

Nacah is used of the undertaking of the responsibilities for sins of others by substitution or representation (Ex 28:12; Lev 16:22; Is 53:12; cf. 1 Pe 2:24). Nashsha' means "to lift up, carry." This verb appears 654 times in the Old Testament; once in Gen 44:1: "Fill the men's sacks with food, as much as they can carry. . . ." See: TWOT—1421; BDB—650a, 669d, 959a, 962b, 1103c.

5376. נְשָׂא {3x} **nᵉsâʾ** (Aram.), *nes-aw';* corresp. to 5375:—carry away, make insurrection, take {3x}. See: TWOT—2874; BDB—1103c.

5377. נָשָׁא {12x} **nâshâʾ**, *naw-shaw';* a prim. root; to *lead astray,* i.e. (ment.) to *delude,* or (mor.) to *seduce:*—deceive {12x}, greatly {1x}, beguiled me {1x}, seize {1x}, utterly {1x}. See: TWOT—1425; BDB—674a.

5378. נָשָׁא {4x} **nâshâʾ**, *naw-shaw';* a prim. root [perh. ident. with 5377, through the idea of *imposition*]; to *lend* on interest; by impl. to *dun* for debt:—× debt {1x}, exact {2x}, giver of usury {1x}. See: TWOT—1424; BDB—673d, 674b.

נָשִׂא **nâsîʾ.** See 5387.

נְשֻׂאָה **nᵉsûʾâh.** See 5385.

5379. נִשֵּׂאת {1x} **nissêʾth**, *nis-sayth';* pass. part. fem. of 5375; something *taken,* i.e. a *present:*—gift {1x}. See: TWOT—1421; BDB—671c, 672a.

5380. נָשַׁב {3x} **nâshab**, *naw-shab';* a prim. root; to *blow;* by impl. to *disperse:*—(cause to) blow {2x}, drive away {1x}. See: TWOT—1426; BDB—674b.

5381. נָשַׂג {50x} **nâsag**, *naw-sag';* a prim. root; to *reach* (lit. or fig.):—overtake {23x}, hold {5x}, get {3x}, get + 3027 {3x}, attain {2x}, obtain {2x}, reach {2x}, ability + 3027 {1x}, able {1x}, able + 1767 {1x}, bring {1x}, layeth {1x}, put {1x}, remove {1x}, wax rich {1x}, surely {1x}, take {1x}.

Nasag means "to reach, overtake, attain." **(1)** It is used in the text of the Hebrew Old Testament approximately 50 times, the first time being Gen 31:25: "Then Laban overtook Jacob."**(2)** Often it is used in connection with the verb, "to pursue, follow," as in Gen 44:4: ". . . follow after the men; and when thou dost overtake them. . . ." **(3)** *Nasag* is sometimes used in the figurative sense to describe "being overtaken" by something undesirable or unwanted, such as **(3a)** war (Hos 10:9), **(3b)** the sword (Jer 42:16), or **(3c)** curses (Deut 28:15, 45). **(4)** Fortunately, blessings may "overtake" those who are obedient (Deut 28:2). **(5)** *Nasag* may mean "to attain to" something, "to come into contact" with it: "The sword of him that layeth at him [Leviathan] . . ." (Job 41:26). **(6)** Used figuratively, "The ransomed of the Lord . . . shall obtain joy and gladness . . ." (Is 35:10). **(7)** Jacob complained: ". . . the days of the years of my pilgrimage . . . have not attained unto the days of the years of the life of my fathers . . ." (Gen 47:9). See: TWOT—1422; BDB—673b.

5382. נָשָׁה {6x} **nâshâh**, *naw-shaw';* a prim. root; to *forget;* fig. to *neglect;* caus. to *remit, remove:*—forget {4x}, deprive {1x}, exact {1x}. See: TWOT—1428; BDB—674b, 674c.

5383. נָשָׁה {13x} **nâshâh**, *naw-shaw';* a prim. root [rather ident. with 5382, in the sense of 5378]; to *lend* or (by reciprocity) *borrow* on security or interest:—See: exact {3x}, lend {3x}, lend on usury {2x}, creditor {2x}, extortioner {1x}, taker of usury {1x}, usurer {1x}. See: TWOT—1427; BDB—673d.

5384. נָשֶׁה {2x} **nâsheh**, *naw-sheh';* from 5382, in the sense of *failure; rheumatic* or *crippled* (from the incident to Jacob):—which shrank {2x}. See: TWOT—1429; BDB—674d.

5385. נְשׂוּאָה {1x} **nᵉsûwʾâh**, *nes-oo-aw';* or rather,

נְשֻׂאָה **nᵉsûʾâh**, *nes-oo-aw';* fem. pass. part. of 5375; something *borne,* i.e. a *load:*—carriage {1x}. See: TWOT—1421a; BDB—672b.

5386. נְשִׁי {1x} **nᵉshîy**, *nesh-ee';* from 5383; a *debt:*—debt {1x}. See: TWOT—1427a; BDB—674c.

5387. נָשִׂיא {132x} **nâsîyʾ**, *naw-see';* or

נָשִׂא **nâsîʾ**, *naw-see';* from 5375; prop. an *exalted* one, i.e. a *king* or *sheik;* also a rising *mist:*—prince {96x}, captain 12, chief {10x}, ruler {6x}, vapours {3x}, governor {1x}, chief + 5387 {1x}, clouds {1x}, part {1x}, prince + 5387 {1x}.

Nasi' means prince; chief; leader. **(1)** Literally translated, it means one who bears responsibility, or who holds aloft an ensign. **(1a)** An early occurrence of *nashi'* is in Gen 23:6: "Hear us, my lord: thou art a mighty prince among us. . . ." **(1b)** The books of Numbers and Ezekiel use the word most frequently; elsewhere it rarely occurs. **(2)** Though the origin and meaning of *nashi'* are controversial, it is clearly associated with leadership, both Israelite and non-Israelite. **(2a)** Ishmael was promised to give rise to twelve "princes" (Gen 17:20; cf. 25:16); **(2b)** the Midianites had "princes" (Num 25:18), **(2c)** as well as the Amorites (Josh 13:21), **(2d)** the peoples of the sea (Eze 26:16), **(2e)** Kedar (Eze 27:21), **(2f)** Egypt (Eze 30:13), and **(2g)** Edom (Eze 32:29).

(3) Also Israel had her "princes" ("rulers"): ". . . On the sixth day they gathered twice as much bread, two omers for one man: and all the rulers of the congregation came and told Moses" (Ex 16:22). **(3a)** The "princes" ("leaders") of Israel did not only participate in the civil leadership; **(3b)** they were also regarded as pillars in Israelite religious life, the upholders of the covenantal way of life: "And Moses called unto them; and Aaron and all the rulers of the congregation returned unto him: and Moses talked with them" (Ex 34:31; cf. Josh 22:30). **(3c)** Hence, Israel was to obey her "leaders": "Thou shalt not revile the gods, nor curse the ruler of thy people" (Ex 22:28). **(4)** The masculine plural noun, which is found 4 times, means "vapors, clouds": "Whoso boasteth himself of a false gift is like clouds and wind without rain" (Prov 25:14; cf. Ps 135:7; Jer 10:13; 51:16). See: TWOT—1421b, 1421c; BDB—672b, 672c.

5388. נְשִׁיָּה {1x} **nᵉshîyâh**, *nesh-ee-yaw'*; from 5382; *oblivion:*—forgetfulness {1x}. See: TWOT—1428a; BDB—674d.

נָשִׁים **nâshîym**. See 802.

5389. נָשִׁין {1x} **nâshîyn** (Aram.), *naw-sheen'*; irreg. plur. fem. of 606:—women {1x}. See: TWOT—2875; BDB—1081d, 1103c.

5390. נְשִׁיקָה {2x} **nᵉshîyqâh**, *nesh-ee-kaw'*; from 5401; a *kiss:*—kisses {2x}. See: TWOT—1435a; BDB—676c.

5391. נָשַׁךְ {14x} **nâshak**, *naw-shak'*; a prim. root; to *strike* with a sting (as a serpent); fig. to *oppress* with interest on a loan:—bite {12x}, lend upon usury {2x}. See: TWOT—1430, 1430b; BDB—675a, 675b.

5392. נֶשֶׁךְ {12x} **neshek**, *neh'-shek;* from 5391; *interest* on a debt:—usury {12x}. See: TWOT—1430a; BDB—675b.

5393. נִשְׁכָּה {3x} **nishkâh**, *nish-kaw'*; for 3957; a *cell:*—chamber {3x}. See: TWOT—1431; BDB—675b.

5394. נָשַׁל {7x} **nâshal**, *naw-shal'*; a prim. root; to *pluck* off, i.e. *divest, eject,* or *drop:*—cast {1x}, cast out {1x}, drive {1x}, loose {1x}, put off {1x}, put out {1x}, slip {1x}. See: TWOT—1432; BDB—675b.

5395. נָשַׁם {1x} **nâsham**, *naw-sham'*; a prim. root; prop. to *blow* away, i.e. *destroy:*—destroy {1x}. See: TWOT—1433; BDB—675c, 1103c.

5396. נִשְׁמָא {1x} **nishmâʾ** (Aram.), *nish-maw'*; corresp. to 5397; vital *breath:*—breath {1x}. See: TWOT—2876; BDB 1103c.

5397. נְשָׁמָה {24x} **nᵉshâmâh**, *nesh-aw-maw'*; from 5395; a *puff,* i.e. *wind,* angry or vital *breath,* divine *inspiration, intellect,* or (concr.) an *animal:*—breath {17x}, blast {3x}, spirit {2x}, inspiration {1x}, souls {1x}.

A *neshamah* is literally a "breathing being": "But of the cities of these people, which the LORD thy God doth give thee *for* an inheritance, thou shalt save alive nothing that breatheth:" (Deut 20:16). See: TWOT—1433a; BDB—675c, 1103c.

5398. נָשַׁף {2x} **nâshaph**, *naw-shaf'*; a prim. root; to *breeze,* i.e. *blow* up fresh (as the wind):—blow {2x}. See: TWOT—1434; BDB—676a.

5399. נֶשֶׁף {12x} **nesheph**, *neh'-shef;* from 5398; prop. a *breeze,* i.e. (by impl.) *dusk* (when the evening breeze prevails):—twilight {6x}, night {3x}, dark {1x}, dawning of the morning {1x}, dawning of the day {1x}. See: TWOT—1434a; BDB—676a.

5400. נָשַׂק {3x} **nâsaq**, *naw-sak'*; a prim. root; to *catch* fire:—burn {1x}, kindle {2x}. See: TWOT—2266; BDB—673d, 969c.

5401. נָשַׁק {35x} **nâshaq**, *naw-shak'*; a prim. root [ident. with 5400, through the idea of *fastening* up; comp. 2388, 2836]; to *kiss,* lit. or fig. (*touch*); also (as a mode of *attachment*), to *equip* with weapons:—armed {2x}, armed men {1x}, ruled {1x}, kiss {29x}, that touched {1x}.

Nashaq means to kiss, whether as **(1)** a mark of respect: "Kiss the Son, lest he be angry, and ye perish *from* the way, when his wrath is kindled but a little. Blessed *are* all they that put their trust in him" (Ps 2:12) or otherwise is rendered **(2)** "rule": "Thou shalt be over my house, and according unto thy word shall all my people be ruled: only in the throne will I be greater than thou" (Gen 41:40). **(3)** It is applied to armor because it fits closely and is folded together: "The children of Ephraim, *being* armed, *and* carrying bows, turned back in the day of battle" (Ps 78:9). It is also applied to the wings of the living creatures that touched one another (Eze 3:13). See: TWOT—1435, 1436; BDB—676b, 676c.

5402. נֶשֶׁק {10x} **nesheq**, *neh'-shek;* or

נֵשֶׁק **nêsheq**, *nay'-shek;* from 5401; military *equipment,* i.e. (collect.) *arms* (offensive or defensive), or (concr.) an *arsenal:*—armed men {1x}, armour {3x}, armoury {1x}, battle {1x}, harness {1x}, weapon {3x}. See: TWOT—1436a; BDB—676d.

5403. נְשַׁר {2x} **nᵉshar** (Aram.), *nesh-ar'*; corresp. to 5404; an *eagle:*—eagle {2x}. See: TWOT—2877; BDB—1103c.

5404. נֶשֶׁר {26x} **nesher**, *neh'-sher;* from an unused root mean. to *lacerate;* the *eagle* (or other large bird of prey):—eagle {26x}. See: TWOT—1437; BDB—676d, 1103c.

5405. נָשַׁת {3x} **nâshath**, *naw-shath'*; a prim. root; prop. to *eliminate,* i.e. (intr.) to *dry* up:—fail {3x}. See: TWOT—1438; BDB—677a.

נְתִבָה **nᵉthîbâh**. See 5410.

5406. נִשְׁתְּוָן {2x} **nishtᵉvân**, *nish-tev-awn'*; prob. of Pers. or.; an *epistle:*—letter {2x}. See: TWOT—1439; BDB—677a, 1103c.

5407. נִשְׁתְּוָן {3x} **nishtᵉvân** (Aram.), *nish-tev-awn';* corresp. to 5406:—letter {3x}. See: TWOT—2878; BDB—1103c.

נְתוּן **Nathûwn**. See 5411.

5408. נָתַח {9x} **nâthach**, *naw-thakh'*; a prim. root; to *dismember:*—cut {5x}, cut into pieces {2x}, divided {1x}, hewed them in pieces {1x}. See. TWOT—1441; BDB—677c.

5409. נֵתַח {13x} **nêthach**, *nay'-thakh;* from 5408; a *fragment:*—parts {1x}, pieces {12x}. See: TWOT—1441a; BDB—677c.

5410. נָתִיב {26x} **nâthîyb**, *naw-theeb'*; or (fem.)

נְתִיבָה **nᵉthîybâh**, *neth-ee-baw'*; or

נְתִבָה **nᵉthîbâh** (Jer. 6:16), *neth-ee-baw'*; from an unused root mean. to *tramp;* a (beaten) *track:*—path {22x}, way {2x}, pathway {1x}, byways + 6128 {1x}. See: TWOT—1440a, 1440b; BDB—677a, 677b.

5411. נָתִין {18x} **Nâthîyn**, *naw-theen'*; or

נָתוּן **Nâthûwn** (Ezra 8:17), *naw-thoon'* (the proper form, as pass. part.), from 5414; one *given,* i.e. (in the plur. only) the *Nethinim,* or Temple-servants (as *given* to that duty):—Nethinims {18x}. See: TWOT—1443a; BDB—682a, 1103c.

5412. נְתִין {1x} **Nᵉthîyn** (Aram.), *netheen';* corresp. to 5411:—Nethinims {1x}. See: TWOT—2879; BDB—1103c.

5413. נָתַךְ {21x} **nâthak**, *naw-thak'*; a prim. root; to *flow* forth (lit. or fig.); by impl. to *liquefy:*—pour out {7x}, melt {4x}, poured {3x}, poured forth {3x}, gathered {1x}, molten {1x}, dropped {1x}, gathered together {1x}. See: TWOT—1442; BDB—677c.

5414. נָתַן {2008x} **nâthan**, *naw-than'*; a prim. root; to *give,* used with greatest latitude of application (*put, make,* etc.):—give {1078x}, put {191x}, deliver {174x}, made {107x}, set {99x}, up {26x}, lay {22x}, grant {21x}, suffer {18x}, yield {15x}, bring {15x}, cause {13x}, utter {12x}, laid {11x}, send {11x}, recompense {11x}, appoint {10x}, shew {7x}, misc. {167x} = add, apply, ascribe, assign, × avenge, × be ([healed]), bestow, cast, charge, come, commit, consider, count, + cry, direct, distribute, do, × doubtless, × without fail, fasten, frame, × get, hang (up), × have, × indeed, (give) leave, lend, let (out), lift up, + O that, occupy, offer, ordain, pay, perform, place, pour, print, × pull, render, requite, restore, shoot forth (up), + sing, + slander, strike, [sub-] mit, × surely, × take, thrust, trade, turn, + weep, × willingly, + withdraw, + would (to) God.

Nathan means "to deliver, give, place, set up, lay, make, do." **(1)** First, *nathan* represents the action by which something is set going or actuated. Achsah asked her father Caleb to "give" her a blessing, such as a tract of land with abundant water, as her dowry; she wanted him to "transfer" it from his possession to hers: "Who answered, Give me a blessing; for thou hast given me a south land; give me also springs of water. And he gave her the upper springs, and the nether springs" (Josh 15:19). **(2)** There is a technical use of this verb without an object: Moses instructs Israel to "give" generously to the man in desperate need: "Thou shalt surely give him, and thine heart shall not be grieved when thou givest unto him: because that for this thing the LORD thy God shall bless thee in all thy works, and in all that thou puttest thine hand unto" (Deut 15:10). **(3)** In some instances, *nathan* can mean to "send forth," as in "sending forth" a fragrance: "While the king *sitteth* at his table, my spikenard sendeth forth the smell thereof" (Song 1:12). **(4)** When used of a liquid, the word means to "send forth" in the sense of "spilling," for example, to spill blood: "Be merciful, O LORD, unto thy people Israel, whom thou hast redeemed, and lay not innocent blood unto thy people of Israel's charge. And the blood shall be forgiven them" (Deut 21:8).

(5) *Nathan* also has a technical meaning in the area of jurisprudence, meaning to hand something over to someone—for example: **(5a1)** "to pay": "That he may give me the cave of Machpelah, which he hath, which *is* in the end of his field; for as much money as it is worth he shall give it me for a possession of a burying place amongst you" (Gen 23:9); or **(5a2)** "to loan": "Thou shalt surely give him, and thine heart shall not be grieved when thou givest unto him: because that for this thing the LORD thy God shall bless thee in all thy works, and in all that thou puttest thine hand unto" (Deut 15:10). **(5b)** A girl's parent or someone else in a responsible position may "give" her to a man to be his wife (Gen 16:3), as well as presenting a bride price (Gen 34:12) and dowry (1 Kin 9:16). **(5c)** The verb also is used of "giving" or "granting" a request (Gen 15:2). **(6)** Sometimes, *nathan* can be used to signify "putting" ("placing") someone into custody (2 Sa 14:7) or into prison (Jer 37:4), or even of "destroying" something (Judg 6:30). **(7)** This same basic sense may be applied to "dedicating" ("handing over") something or someone to God, such as the first-born son (Ex 22:29). Levites are those who have been "handed over" in this way (Num 3:9).

(8) This word is used of "bringing reprisal" upon someone or of "giving" him what he deserves; in some cases, the stress is on the act of reprisal (1 Kin 8:32), or bringing his punishment on his head. **(9)** *Nathan* can be used of "giving" or "ascribing" something to someone, such as "giving" glory and praise to God (Josh 7:19). Obviously, nothing is passed from men to God; nothing is added to God, since He is perfect.

This means, therefore, that a worshiper recognizes and confesses what is already His. **(10)** Another major emphasis of *nathan* is the action of "giving" or "effecting" a result. For example, the land will "give" ("yield") its fruit (Deut 25:19). **(11)** In some passages, this verb means "to procure" ("to set up"), as when God "gave" ("procured, set up") favor for Joseph (Gen 39:21). **(12)** The word can be used of sexual activity, too, emphasizing the act of intercourse or "one's lying down" with an animal (Lev 18:23). **(13)** God "placed" (literally, "gave") the heavenly lights into the expanse of the heavens (Gen 1:17—the first occurrence of the verb). **(14)** A garland is "placed" (literally, "given") upon one's head (Prov 4:9).

(15) The children of Israel are commanded not to "set up" idols in their land. **(16)** Another meaning of *nathan* is seen in Gen 17:5: ". . . For a father of many nations have I made [literally, "given"] thee." There are several instances where the verb bears this significance. **(17)** *Nathan* has a number of special implications when used with bodily parts—for example, **(17a)** "to give" or "turn" a stubborn shoulder (Neh 9:29). Similarly, compare expressions such as **(17b)** "turning [giving] one's face" (2 Chr 29:6). **(17c)** To "turn [give] one's back" is to flee (Ex 23:27). **(17d)** "Giving one's hand" may be no more than "putting it forth," as in the case of the unborn Zarah (Gen 38:28). **(18)** This word can also signify **(18a)** an act of friendship as when Jehonadab "gave his hand" (instead of a sword) to Jehu to help him into the chariot (2 Kin 10:15); **(18b)** an act of oath-taking, as when the priests "pledged" ("gave their hands") to put away their foreign wives (Ezra 10:19); and **(18c)** "making" or "renewing" a covenant, as when the leaders of Israel "pledged" themselves ("gave their hands") to follow Solomon (1 Chr 29:24).

(19) "To give something into someone's hand" is to "commit" it to his care. **(19a)** So after the Flood, God "gave" the earth into Noah's hand (Gen 9:2). **(19b)** This phrase is used to express the "transfer of political power," such as the divine right to rule (2 Sa 16:8). **(20)** *Nathan* is used especially in a military and judicial sense, meaning "to give over one's power or control," or to grant victory to someone; so Moses said God would "give" the kings of Canaan into Israel's hands (Deut 7:24). **(21)** "To give one's heart" to something or someone is "to be concerned about it"; Pharaoh was not "concerned" about ("did not set his heart to") Moses' message from God (Ex 7:23). **(22)** "To put [give] something into one's heart" is to give one ability and concern to do something; thus God "put" it in the heart of the Hebrew craftsmen to teach others (Ex 36:2). **(23)** "To give one's face to" is **(23a)** to focus one's attention on something, as when Jehoshaphat was afraid of the alliance of the Transjordanian kings and "set [his face] to seek the Lord" (2 Chr 20:3). **(23b)** This same phrase can merely mean "to be facing someone or something" (cf. Gen 30:40).

(24) "To give one's face against" is a hostile action (Lev 17:10). **(25)** Used with lipne (lamed + 6440 - literally, "before the face of"), this verb may mean **(25a)** "to place an object before" or **(25b)** to "set it down before" (Ex 30:6). **(25c)** It may also mean **(25c1)** "to put before" (Deut 11:26), **(25c2)** "to smite" (cf. Deut 2:33), or **(25c3)** "to give as one's possession" (Deut 1:8). Syn.: 3467. See: TWOT—1443; BDB—678a, 1103c.

5415. נְתַן {7x} **nᵉthan** (Aram.), *neth-an'*; corresp. to 5414; *give:*—bestow {2x}, give {4x}, pay {1x}. See: TWOT—2880; BDB—1103c.

5416. נָתָן {42x} **Nâthân**, *naw-thawn'*; from 5414; *given; Nathan*, the name of five Isr.:—Nathan {42x}. See: BDB—681d.

5417. נְתַנְאֵל {14x} **Nᵉthanʾêl**, *neth-an-ale'*; from 5414 and 410; *given of God; Nethanel*, the name of ten Isr.:—Nethaneel {14x}. See: BDB—682a.

5418. נְתַנְיָה {20x} **Nᵉthanyâh**, *neth-an-yaw'*; or

נְתַנְיָהוּ **Nᵉthanyâhûw**, *neth-an-yaw'-hoo;* from 5414 and 3050; *given of Jah; Nethanjah*, the name of four Isr.:—Nethaniah {20x}. See: BDB—682b.

5419. נְתַן־מֶלֶךְ {1x} **Nᵉthan-Melek**, *neth-an' meh'-lek;* from 5414 and 4428; *given of* (the) *king; Nethan-Melek*, an Isr.:—Nathan-melech {1x}. See: BDB—682a.

5420. נָתַס {1x} **nâthaç**, *naw-thas'*; a prim. root; to *tear* up:—mar {1x}. See: TWOT—1444; BDB—683a.

5421. נָתַע {1x} **nâthaʿ**, *naw-thah'*; for 5422; to *tear* out:—break {1x}. See: TWOT—1445; BDB—683a.

5422. נָתַץ {42x} **nâthats**, *naw-thats'*; a prim. root; to *tear* down:—break down {22x}, throw down {5x}, destroy {5x}, cast down {3x}, beat down {3x}, pull down {2x}, break out {1x}, overthrow {1x}. See: TWOT—1446; 683a.

5423. נָתַק {27x} **nâthaq**, *naw-thak'*; a prim. root; to *tear* off:—break {12x}, drawn away {2x}, lifted up {2x}, plucked away {1x}, draw {1x}, drawn {1x}, break off {1x}, pluck off {1x}, root out {1x}, pull out {1x}, pluck {1x}, burst in sunder {1x}, break in sunder {2x}. See: TWOT—1447; BDB—683c.

5424. נֶתֶק {14x} **netheq**, *neh'-thek;* from 5423; *scurf:*—(dry) scall {14x}. See: TWOT—1447a; BDB—683d.

5425. נָתַר {8x} **nâthar**, *naw-thar'*; a prim. root; to *jump*, i.e. *be* violently *agitated;* caus., to *terrify, shake* off, *untie:*—drive asunder {1x}, leap {1x}, let loose {2x}, loose {1x}, × make {1x}, move {1x}, undo {1x}. See: TWOT—1448, 1449; BDB—684a.

5426. נְתַר {1x} **nᵉthar** (Aram.), *neth-ar'*; corresp. to 5425:—shake off {1x}. See: TWOT—2881; BDB—1083d, 1103d.

5427. נֶתֶר {2x} **nether**, *neh'-ther;* from 5425; mineral *potash* (so called from *effervescing* with acid):—nitre {2x}. See: TWOT—1450a; BDB—684a.

5428. נָתַשׁ {21x} **nâthash**, *naw-thash'*; a prim. root; to *tear* away:—pluck up {10x}, pluck out {3x}, destroyed {1x}, forsaken {1x}, root out {1x}, rooted {1x}, roots {1x}, root up {1x}, pull up {1x}, utterly {1x}. See: TWOT—1451; BDB—684c.

ס

5429. סְאָה {9x} **çᵉʾâh**, *seh-aw'*; from an unused root mean. to *define;* a *seah*, or certain measure (as *determinative*) for grain:—measure {9x}. See: TWOT—1452; BDB—684b.

5430. סְאוֹן {1x} **çᵉʾôwn**, *seh-own'*; from 5431; perh. a military *boot* (as a protection from *mud:*—battle {1x}. See: TWOT—1453a; BDB—684b.

5431. סָאַן {1x} **çâʾan**, *saw-an'*; a prim. root; to *be miry;* used only as denom. from 5430; to *shoe*, i.e. (act. part.) a *soldier* shod:—warrior {1x}. See: TWOT—1453; BDB—684b.

5432. סַאסְּאָה {1x} **çaʾçᵉʾâh**, *sah-seh-aw'*; for 5429; *measurement*, i.e. *moderation:*—measure {1x}. See: TWOT—1452; BDB—684b, 684d.

5433. סָבָא {6x} **çâbâʾ**, *saw-baw'*; a prim. root; to *quaff* to satiety, i.e. *become tipsy:*—See: drunkard {2x}, winebibbers {1x}, fill {1x}, drunken {1x}, variant {1x}. See: TWOT—1455; BDB—684b, 685a.

5434. סְבָא {4x} **Çᵉbâʾ**, *seb-aw'*; of for. or.; *Seba*, a son of Cush, and the country settled by him:—Seba {4x}. See: BDB—685b.

5435. סֹבֶא {3x} **çôbeʾ**, *so'-beh;* from 5433; *potation*, concr. (*wine*), or abstr. (*carousal*):—drink {1x}, drunken {1x}, wine {1x}. See: TWOT—1455a; BDB—685a.

5436. סְבָאִי {2x} **Çᵉbâʾîy**, *seb-aw-ee'*; patrial from 5434; a *Sebaite*, or inhab. of Seba:—Sabean {2x}. See: BDB—685b.

5437. סָבַב {154x} **çâbab**, *saw-bab'*; a prim. root; to *revolve, surround*, or *border;* used in various applications, lit. and fig. (as follows):—(stood, turned, etc.) about {54x}, compass {41x}, turn {34x}, turn away {4x}, remove {3x}, returned {2x}, round {2x}, side {2x}, turn aside {2x}, turn back {2x}, beset {2x}, driven {2x}, compass in {2x}, misc. {8x}.

Cabab means "to turn, go around, turn around (change direction)." **(1)** Basically this verb represents a circular movement—"to take a turning." It refers to such movement in general. **(2)** The first occurrence of *cabab* having this emphasis is in **(2a)** Gen 42:24, where Joseph "turned himself about" from his brothers and wept. Here the verb does not tell the precise direction of his departure, only that he left their presence. **(2b)** Similarly, when Samuel was told that Saul went to Carmel and "is gone about, and passed on, and gone down to Gilgal" (1 Sa 15:12), we are not told that he reversed direction in order to get from his origin to Carmel and Gilgal. **(3)** God led Israel out of the way (by an out-of-the-way route) when He took them into the Promised Land. **(3a)** He wanted to avoid having them face war with the Philistines, an event that was unavoidable if they proceeded directly north from Egypt to Palestine. **(3b)** Therefore, He led them through the wilderness—a back route into the land: "But God led the people about, through the way of the wilderness of the Red Sea . . ." (Ex 13:18).

(4) Perhaps one of the passages where this meaning is clearest is Prov 26:14, which speaks of the "turning" of a door on its hinges. **(4a)** An extension of this meaning occurs in 1 Sa 5:8–9, "to remove, to take away": "And they answered, Let the ark of the God of Israel be carried about [taken away] unto Gath. And they carried the ark of the God of Israel about thither" (cf. 2 Kin 16:18). **(5)** *Cabab* is "to go around," in the sense of to proceed or be arranged in a circle. **(5a)** Joseph tells his family: ". . . Lo, my sheaf arose, and also stood upright; and, behold, your sheaves stood round about, and made obeisance to my sheaf" (Gen 37:7). They moved so as to surround his sheaf. **(5b)** This is the action pictured when Israel besieged Jericho, except with the further nuance of encircling in a processional and religious march: "And ye shall compass the city, all ye men of war, and go round about the city once" (Josh 6:3). **(6)** "To travel" and "to return" are used together to represent traveling a circuit. It is said of Samuel that he used to go annually "in circuit" (1 Sa 7:16).

(7) Another variation of this emphasis is "to go around" a territory in order to avoid crossing through it: "And they journeyed from mount Hor by the way of the Red Sea, to compass [go around] the land of Edom: and the soul of the people was much discouraged because of the way" (Num 21:4). **(8)** *Cabab* is also used of the completion of this movement, the state of literally or figuratively surrounding something or someone. **(8a)** The very first biblical occurrence of the word carries this force (according to many scholars): "The name of the first is Pison: that is it which compasseth [flows around] the whole land of Havilah . . ." (Gen 2:11). **(8b)** Judg 16:2, where the Gazites "compassed [Samson] in, and laid wait for him all night in the gate of the city," represents another occurrence of this nuance. **(9)** When David spoke of the cords (as a trap) of Sheol "surrounding" him (2 Sa 22:6), he meant that they actually touched him and held him fast.

(10) *Cabab* can be used of sitting down around a table. So Samuel told Jesse to fetch David, "for we will not sit down till he come hither" (1 Sa 16:11). **(10)** This verb can mean "to change direction." **(10a)** This can be a change of direction toward:"Neither shall the inheritance remove from one tribe to another tribe . . ." (Num 36:9); **(10b)** the usual direction of passing on an inheritance is down family lines, and God's commandment that the daughters of Zelophehad marry within their father's families would make certain that this movement of things not be interrupted. **(10c)** This emphasis appears more clearly in 1 Sa 18:11: "And David [escaped] out of his presence twice"; it is certain that David is putting as much space between himself and Saul as possible. He is "running away or turning away" (cf. 1 Sa 22:17). **(11)** *Cabab* may also refer to a change of direction, as in Num 34:4: "And your border shall turn. . . ."

(12) There are three special nuances under this emphasis. **(12a)** First, the verb may mean "to roam through" as a scout looking for water: ". . . And they fetched a compass [made a circuit] of seven days' journey: and there was no water for the host, and for the cattle that followed them" (2 Kin 3:9). Some scholars suggest that this is the idea expressed in Gen 2:11 that the Pison meandered through Havilah rather than flowed around it. **(12b)** Second, *cabab* may be used of "turning something over" to someone. So Adonijah said of Solomon: ". . . The kingdom was mine, . . . howbeit the kingdom is turned about, and is become my brother's . . ." (1 Kin 2:15). **(12c)** Third, *cabab* may be used of "changing or turning one thing into another": "And the land shall be turned as a plain from Geba to Rimmon south of Jerusalem . . ." (Zec 14:10). Syn.: 2015. See: TWOT—1456; BDB—685b, 687a, 687b, 687c.

5438. סִבָּה {1x} **çibbâh**, *sib-baw';* from 5437; a (providential) *turn* (of affairs):—cause {1x}.

Cibbah is found in 1 Kin 12:15 and is translated "cause" and means "turn of events." See: TWOT—1456a; BDB—686d.

5439. סָבִיב {308x} **çâbîyb**, *saw-beeb';* or (fem.)

סְבִיבָה **çᵉbîybâh**, *seb-ee-baw';* from 5437; (as noun) a *circle, neighbour,* or *environs;* but chiefly (as adv., with or without prep.) *around:*—round about {25x}2, on every side {26x}, about {24x} compass {2x}, about us {2x}, circuits {1x}, about them {1x}.

Cebiybah, as a noun, means "area round about; circuit." **(1)** The word can be used as a noun, but it usually occurs as an adverb or preposition. **(2)** In 1 Chr 11:8 it refers to the "parts round about": "And he built the city round about, even from Millo round about. . . ." **(3)** The word may also be used for "circuits": ". . . And the wind returneth again according to his circuits" (Eccl 1:6). **(4)** The first biblical appearance of the word is in Gen 23:17, and it refers to "within the circuit of": "And the field of Ephron, which *was* in Machpelah, which *was* before Mamre, the field, and the cave which *was* therein, and all the trees that *were* in the field, that *were* in all the borders round about, were made sure." See: TWOT—1456b; BDB—686d.

5440. סָבַךְ {2x} **çâbak**, *saw-bak';* a prim. root; to *entwine:*—fold together, wrap {2x}. See: TWOT—1457; BDB—687c.

5441. סְבֹךְ {1x} **çôbek**, *so'-bek;* from 5440; a *copse:*—thicket {1x}. See: TWOT—1457b; BDB—687c.

5442. סְבָךְ {4x} **çᵉbâk**, *seb-awk';* from 5440, a *copse:*—thick {1x}, thicket {3x}. See: TWOT—1457a; BDB—687c.

5443. סַבְּכָא {4x} **çabbᵉkâʼ** (Aram.), *sab-bek-aw';* or

שַׂבְּכָא **sabbᵉkâʼ** (Aram.), *sab-bek-aw';* from a root corresp. to 5440; a *lyre:*—sackbut {4x}. See: TWOT—3003; BDB—1103d, 1113c.

5444. סִבְּכַי {4x} **Çibbᵉkay**, *sib-bek-ah'-ee;* from 5440; *copse-like; Sibbecai,* an Isr.:—Sibbecai {2x}, Sibbechai {2x}. See: BDB—687c.

5445. סָבַל {9x} **çâbal**, *saw-bal';* a prim. root; to *carry* (lit. or fig.), or (refl.) *be burdensome;* spec. to *be gravid:*—bear {1x}, be a burden {1x}, carry {4x}, strong to labour {1x}. Syn.: 5375. See: TWOT—1458; BDB—687d, 1103d.

5446. סְבַל {1x} **çᵉbal** (Aram.), *seb-al';* corresp. to 5445; to *erect:*—strongly laid {1x}. See: TWOT—2882; BDB—1103d.

5447. סֵבֶל {3x} **çêbel**, *say'-bel;* from 5445; a *load* (lit. or fig.):—burden {2x}, charge {1x}. See: TWOT—1458a; BDB—687d.

5448. סֹבֶל {3x} **çôbel**, *so'-bel;* [only in the form

סֻבָּל **çubbâl**, *soob-bawl'*]; from 5445; a *load* (fig.):—burden {3x}. See: TWOT—1458a; BDB—687d.

5449. סַבָּל {5x} **çabbâl**, *sab-bawl';* from 5445; a *porter:*—bearer of burden {3x}, . . . bear burden {1x}, burden {1x}. See: TWOT—1458b; BDB—687d, 688a.

5450. סְבָלָה {6x} **çᵉbâlâh**, *seb-aw-law';* from 5447; *porterage:*—burden {6x}. See: TWOT—1458c; BDB—688a.

5451. סִבֹּלֶת {1x} **Çibbôleth**, *sib-bo'-leth;* for **7641; an ear of grain:**—Sibboleth {1x}. See: TWOT—1458d; BDB—688a.

5452. סְבַר {1x} **çᵉbar** (Aram.), *seb-ar';* a prim. root; to *bear in mind,* i.e. *hope:*—think {1x}. See: TWOT—2883; BDB—1104a.

5453. סִבְרַיִם {1x} **Çibrayim**, *sib-rah'-yim;* dual from a root corresp. to 5452; *double hope; Sibrajim,* a place in Syria:—Sibraim {1x}. See: BDB—688a.

5454. סַבְתָּא {2x} **Çabtâʼ**, *sab-taw';* or

סַבְתָּה **Çabtâh**, *sab-taw';* prob. of for. der.; *Sabta* or *Sabtah,* the name of a son of Cush, and the country occupied by his posterity:—Sabta {1x}, Sabtah {1x}. See: BDB—688b.

5455. סַבְתְּכָא {2x} **Çabtᵉkâʼ**, *sab-tek-aw';* prob. of for. der.; *Sabteca,* the name of a son of Cush, and the region settled by him:—Sabtecha {1x}, Sabtechah {1x}. See: BDB—688b.

5456. סָגַד {4x} **çâgad**, *saw-gad';* a prim. root; to *prostrate* oneself (in homage):—fall down {4x}. See: TWOT—1459; BDB—688b, 1104a.

5457. סְגִד {12x} **çᵉgîd** (Aram.), *seg-eed';* corresp. to 5456:—worship {2x}. See: TWOT—2884; BDB—1104a.

5458. סְגוֹר {2x} **çᵉgôwr**, *seg-ore';* from 5462; prop. *shut up,* i.e. the *breast* (as inclosing the heart); also *gold* (as gen. *shut* up safely):—caul {1x}, gold {1x}. See: TWOT—1462a; BDB—689c.

5459. סְגֻלָּה {8x} **çᵉgullâh**, *seg-ool-law';* fem. pass. part. of an unused root mean. to *shut* up; *wealth* (as closely *shut* up):—peculiar treasure {3x}, peculiar {2x}, special {1x}, jewel {1x}, particular treasure {1x}.

(1) *Cegullah* means "possession." **(2)** *Cegullah* signifies "property" in the special sense of a private possession one personally acquired and carefully preserves. Six times this word is used of Israel as God's personally acquired (elected, delivered from Egyptian bondage, and formed into what He wanted them to be), carefully preserved, and privately possessed people: "Now therefore, if ye will obey my voice indeed, and keep my covenant, then ye shall be a peculiar treasure unto me above all people: for all the earth is mine" (Ex 19:5—first occurrence). See: TWOT—1460a; BDB—688c.

5460. סְגַן {5x} **çᵉgan** (Aram.), *seg-an';* corresp. to 5461:—governor {5x}. See: TWOT—2885; BDB—1104a.

5461. סָגָן {17x} **çâgân**, *saw-gawn';* from an unused root mean. to *superintend;* a *præfect* of a province:—prince {1x}, ruler {16x}. See: TWOT—1461; BDB—688c, 1104a.

5462. סָגַר {91x} **çâgar**, *saw-gar';* a prim. root; to *shut* up; fig. to *surrender:*—shut {40x}, shut up {12x}, deliver {9x}, pure {8x}, deliver up {7x}, shut in {3x}, give up {2x}, gave over {2x}, inclosed {1x}, repaired {1x}, closed {1x}, shutting {1x}, stop {1x}, straitly {1x}, together {1x}, close up {1x}.

Cagar means "to shut, close, shut up or imprison." **(1)** *Cagar* is used for the first time in the Old Testament in the story of the creation of the woman from the rib of the man: "And the Lord God . . . closed up the flesh instead thereof" (Gen 2:21). **(2)** The obvious use of this verb is to express the "shutting" of doors and gates, and it is used in this way many times in the text (Gen 19:10; Josh 2:7). **(3)** More specialized uses are: fat closing over the blade of a sword (Judg 3:22) and closing up a breach in city walls (1 Kin 11:27). **(4)** Figuratively, men may "close their hearts to pity" (Ps 17:10; KJV, "They are inclosed in their own fat," with "fat" symbolizing an unresponsive heart). **(5)** In the books of Samuel, *cagar* is used in the special sense of "to deliver up," implying that all avenues of escape "are closed": "This day will the Lord deliver thee into mine hand . . ." (1 Sa 17:46; cf. 1 Sa 24:18; 26:8; 2 Sa 18:28). **(6)** In Lev 13—14, in which the priest functions as a medical inspector of contagious diseases, *cagar* is used a number of times in the sense of "to isolate, to shut up" a sick person away from other people (see Lev 13:5, 11, 21, 26). **(7)** The more extreme sense of "to imprison" is found in Job 11:10: "If he cut off, and shut up, or gather together, then who can hinder him?" See: TWOT—1462; BDB—688d, 689b, 698c, 1104a.

5463. סְגַר {1x} **çᵉgar** (Aram.), *seg-ar';* corresp. to 5462:—shut up {1x}. See: TWOT—2886; BDB—1104a.

5464. סַגְרִיד {1x} **çagrîyd**, *sag-reed';* prob. from 5462 in the sense of *sweeping* away; a pouring rain:—very rainy {1x}. See: TWOT—1463a; BDB—690a.

5465. סַד {2x} **çad**, *sad;* from an unused root mean. to *estop;* the *stocks:*—stocks {2x}. See: TWOT—1464; BDB—690a.

5466. סָדִין {4x} **çâdîyn**, *saw-deen';* from an unused root mean. to *envelop;* a *wrapper,* i.e. *shirt:*—fine linen {2x}, sheet {2x}. See: TWOT—1466; BDB—690b.

5467. סְדֹם {39x} **Çᵉdôm**, *sed-ome';* from an unused root mean. to *scorch; burnt* (i.e. *volcanic* or *bituminous*) district; *Sedom,* a place near the Dead Sea:—Sodom {39x}. See: TWOT—1465; BDB—690a.

5468. סֶדֶר {1x} **çeder**, *seh'-der;* from an unused root mean. to *arrange; order:*—order {1x}. See: TWOT—1467a; BDB—690b.

5469. סַהַר {1x} **çahar**, *sah'-har;* from an unused root mean. to *be round; roundness:*—round {1x}. See: TWOT—1468a; BDB—690c.

5470. סֹהַר {8x} **çôhar**, *so'-har;* from the same as 5469; a *dungeon* (as *surrounded* by walls):—prison {8x}. See: TWOT—1468b; BDB—690c.

5471. סוֹא {1x} **Çôwʾ**, *so;* of for. der.; *So,* an Eg. king:—So {1x}. See: BDB—690c.

5472. סוּג {14x} **çûwg**, *soog;* a prim. root; prop. to *flinch,* i.e. (by impl.) to *go back,* lit. (to *retreat*) or fig. (to *apostatize*):—turned {6x}, turn away {2x}, go back {2x}, turn back {2x}, backslider {1x}, driven {1x}. See: TWOT—1469; BDB—690d.

5473. סוּג {1x} **çûwg**, *soog;* a prim. root [prob. rather ident. with 5472 through the idea of *shrinking* from a hedge; comp. 7735]; to *hem* in, i.e. *bind:*—set about {1x}. See: TWOT—1470; BDB—691b, 960d.

סוּג **çûwg**. See 5509.

5474. סוּגַר {1x} **çûwgar**, *soo-gar';* from 5462; an *inclosure,* i.e. *cage* (for an animal):—ward {1x}. See: TWOT—1462b; BDB—689c.

5475. סוֹד {21x} **çôwd**, *sode;* from 3245; a *session,* i.e. *company* of persons (in close deliberation); by impl. *intimacy, consultation,* a *secret:*—assembly {5x}, counsel {6x}, inward, {1x} secret (counsel) {9x}.

Cowd means "secret or confidential plan(s); secret or confidential talk; secret; council; gathering; circle." **(1)** *Cowd* means, first, "confidential talk": "Hide me from the secret counsel of the wicked . . ." (Ps 64:2). **(2)** In Prov 15:22: "Without counsel [sel-made] purposes are disappointed: but in the multitude of counselors they are established." **(3)** Sometimes the word signifies simply a talk about something that should be kept confidential: "Debate thy cause with thy neighbor himself; and discover not a secret to another" (Prov 25:9). **(4)** The word represents a group of intimates with whom one shares confidential matters: "O my soul, come not thou into their [Simeon's and Levi's] secret; unto their assembly, mine honor, be not thou united . . ." (Gen 49:6—the first occurrence of the word). **(5)** Jer 6:11 speaks of the "assembly [informal but still sharing confidential matters] of young men together." **(6)** To "have sweet counsel" is to be in a group where everyone both shares and rejoices in what is being discussed and/or done (Ps 55:14). See: TWOT—1471a; BDB—691c.

5476. סוֹדִי {1x} **Çôwdîy**, *so-dee';* from 5475; a *confidant; Sodi,* an Isr.:—Sodi {1x}. See: BDB—691d.

5477. סוּחַ {1x} **Çûwach**, *soo'-akh;* from an unused root mean. to *wipe* away; *sweeping; Suach,* an Isr.:—Suah {1x}. See: BDB—691d.

5478. סוּחָה {1x} **çûwchâh**, *soo-khaw';* from the same as 5477; something *swept* away, i.e. *filth:*—torn {1x}. See: TWOT—1473a; BDB—492c.

סוּט **çûwt**. See 7750.

5479. סוֹטַי {2x} **Çôwṭay**, *so-tah'-ee;* from 7750; *roving; Sotai,* one of the Nethinim:—Sotai {2x}. See: BDB—691d.

5480. סוּךְ {9x} **çûwk**, *sook;* a prim. root; prop. to *smear* over (with oil), i.e. *anoint:*—anoint (self) {8x}, × at all {1x}. See: TWOT—1474; BDB—414c, 691d.

סוֹלְלָה **çôwlᵉlâh**. See 5550.

5481. סוּמְפּוֹנְיָה {4x} **çûwmpôwnᵉyâh** (Aram.), *soom-po-neh-yaw';* or

סוּמְפֹּנְיָה **çûwmpônᵉyâh** (Aram.), *soom-po-neh-yaw';* or

סִיפֹנְיָא **çîyphônᵉyâʾ** (Dan. 3:10) (Aram.), *see-fo-neh-yaw';* of Gr. or. (sumfwniva); a *bagpipe* (with a double pipe):—dulcimer {4x}. See: BDB—1104a, 1104b.

5482. סְוֵנֵה {2x} **Çᵉvênêh**, *sev-ay-nay'* [rather to be written

סְוֵנָה **Çᵉvênâh**, *sev-ay'-naw;* for

סְוֵן **Çᵉvên**, *sev-ane';* i.e. *to Seven*]; of Eg. der.; *Seven,* a place in Upper Egypt:—Syene {2x}. See: BDB—692b.

5483. סוּס {140x} **çûwç**, *soos;* or

סֻס **çûç**, *soos;* from an unused root mean. to *skip* (prop. for joy); a *horse* (as leaping); also a *swallow* (from its rapid *flight*):—horse {133x}, crane {2x}, horseback {2x}, horseback + 7392 {2x}, horsehoofs + 6119 {1x}.

Cuc means "horse." **(1)** The first biblical appearance of *cuc* is in Gen 47:17: "And they brought their cattle unto Joseph: and Joseph gave them bread in exchange for horses, and for the flocks, and for the cattle of the herds, and for the asses. . . ." **(2)** In the second quarter of the second millennium the chariot became a major military weapon and "horses" a very desirable commodity. This was the time of Joseph. It was not until the end of the second millennium that a rudimentary cavalry appeared on the battlefield. **(3)** In the period of the eighth-century prophets and following, **(3a)** "horses" became a sign of luxury and apostasy: "Their land also is full of silver and gold, neither *is there any* end of their treasures; their land is also full of horses, neither *is there any* end of their chariots:" (Is 2:7; cf. Amos 4:10) **(3b)** inasmuch as Israel's hope for freedom and security was to be the Lord: "But he [the king] shall not multiply horses to himself, nor cause the people to return to Egypt, to . . . multiply horses . . ." (Deut 17:16). **(4)** The "horses" of God are the storm clouds with which he treads upon the sea: "Thou didst walk through the sea with thine horses, *through* the heap of great waters" (Hab 3:15). See: TWOT—1476, 1477; BDB—692b. comp. 6571.

5484. סוּסָה {1x} **çûwçâh**, *soo-saw';* fem. of 5483; a *mare:*—company of horses {1x}. See: TWOT—1477; BDB—692d.

5485. סוּסִי {1x} **Çûwçîy**, *soo-see';* from 5483; *horse-like; Susi,* an Isr.:—Susi {1x}. See: BDB—692d.

5486. סוּף {8x} **çûwph**, *soof;* a prim. root; to *snatch* away, i.e. *terminate:*—consume {5x}, have an end {1x}, perish {1x}, × be utterly {1x}. See: TWOT—1478; BDB—692d, 1104b.

5487. סוּף {2x} **çûwph** (Aram.), *soof;* corresp. to 5486; to *come to an end:*—consume {1x}, fulfill {1x}. See: TWOT—2888; BDB—1104b.

5488. סוּף {28x} **çûwph**, *soof;* prob. of Eg. or.; a *reed,* espec. the *papyrus:*—flag {3x}, Red [sea] {23x}, weeds {1x}. comp. 5489. See: TWOT—1479; BDB—693a.

5489. סוּף {1x} **Çûwph**, *soof;* for 5488 (by ellip. of 3220); the *Reed* (*Sea*):—Red Sea {1x}. See: TWOT—1479; BDB—693b.

5490. סוֹף {5x} **çôwph**, *sofe;* from 5486; a *termination:*—conclusion {1x}, end {3x}, hinder part {1x}. See: TWOT—1478a; BDB—693a.

5491. סוֹף {5x} **çôwph** (Aram.), *sofe;* corresp. to 5490:—end {5x}. See: TWOT—2888a; BDB—1104b.

5492. סוּפָה {16x} **çûwphâh**, *soo-faw';* from 5486; a *hurricane:*—storm {3x}, tempest {1x}, whirlwind {11x}, Red sea {1x}. See: TWOT—1478b; BDB—693a, 693b.

5493. סוּר {301x} **çûwr**, *soor;* or

שׂוּר **sûwr** (Hosea 9:12), *soor;* a prim. root; to *turn* off (lit. or fig.):—(put, take, . . .) away {97x}, depart {76x}, remove {35x}, aside {29x}, take {14x}, turn {12x}, turn in {9x}, take off {6x}, go {3x}, put {3x}, eschewed {3x}, misc. {14x} = be [-head], bring, call back, decline, get [you], × grievous, leave undone, be past, rebel, revolt, × be sour, withdraw, be without. See: TWOT—1480; BDB—693b, 694c, 963a, 965a.

5494. סוּר {1x} **çûwr**, *soor;* prob. pass. part. of 5493; *turned* off, i.e. *deteriorated:*—degenerate {1x}. See: TWOT—1480; BDB—693b, 694c.

5495. סוּר {1x} **Çûwr**, *soor;* the same as 5494; *Sur,* a gate of the Temple:—Sur {1x}. See: BDB—694c.

5496. סוּת {18x} **çûwth**, *sooth;* perh. denom. from 7898; prop. to *prick,* i.e. (fig.) stimulate; by impl. to *seduce:*—entice {1x}, move {5x}, persuade {5x}, provoke {1x}, remove {1x}, set on {2x}, stir up {2x}, take away {1x}. See: TWOT—1481; BDB—694c.

5497. סוּת {1x} **çûwth**, *sooth;* prob. from the same root as 4533; *covering,* i.e. *clothing:*—clothes {1x}. See: TWOT—1472a; BDB—691d, 694d.

5498. סָחַב {5x} **çâchab**, *saw-khab';* a prim. root; to *trail* along:—draw {2x}, draw out {2x}, tear {1x}. See: TWOT—1482; BDB—694d.

5499. סְחָבָה {2x} **çᵉchâbâh**, *seh-khaw-baw';* from 5498; a *rag:*—cast clout {2x}. See: TWOT—1482a; BDB—695a.

5500. סָחָה {1x} **çâchâh**, *saw-khaw';* a prim. root; to *sweep* away:—scrape {1x}. See: TWOT—1483; BDB—691d, 695a.

5501. סְחִי {1x} çᵉchîy, seh-khee'; from 5500; *refuse* (as *swept* off):—offscouring {1x}. See: TWOT—1483a; BDB—695a.

סָחִישׁ çâchîysh. See 7823.

5502. סָחַף {2x} çâchaph, saw-khaf'; a prim. root; to *scrape* off:—sweep away {1x}, sweeping away {1x}. See: TWOT—1485; BDB—695a.

5503. סָחַר {20x} çâchar, saw-khar'; a prim. root; to *travel* round (spec. as a *pedlar*); intens. to *palpitate*:—merchant {14x}, trade {2x}, about {1x}, merchantmen + 582 {1x}, panteth {1x}, traffick {1x}. See: TWOT—1486; BDB—695b.

5504. סַחַר {4x} çachar, sakh'-ar; from 5503; *profit* (from trade):—merchandise {4x}. See: TWOT—1486a; BDB—695c.

5505. סָחַר {3x} çâchar, saw-khar'; from 5503; an *emporium*; abstr. *profit* (from trade):—mart {1x}, merchandise {2x}. See: TWOT—1486a; BDB—695c.

5506. סְחֹרָה {1x} çᵉc ôrâh, sekh-o-raw'; from 5503; *traffic*:—merchandise {1x}. See: TWOT—1486b; BDB—695c.

5507. סֹחֵרָה {1x} çôchêrâh, so-khay-raw'; prop. act. part. fem. of 5503; something *surrounding* the person, i.e. a *shield*:—buckler {1x}. See: TWOT—1486c; BDB—695c.

5508. סֹחֶרֶת {1x} çôchereth, so-kheh'-reth; similar to 5507; prob. a (black) *tile* (or *tessara*) for laying borders with:—black marble {1x}. See: TWOT—1486e; BDB—695c.

סֵט çêt. See 7750.

5509. סִיג {8x} çîyg, seeg; or

סוּג çûwg (Eze 22:18), soog; from 5472 in the sense of *refuse*; *scoria*:—dross {8x}. See: TWOT—1469a; BDB—688c, 691a.

5510. סִיוָן {1x} Çîyvân, see-vawn'; prob. of Pers. or.; *Sivan*, the third Heb. month:—Sivan {1x}. See: TWOT—1487; BDB—695d.

5511. סִיחוֹן {37x} Çîychôwn, see-khone'; or

סִיחֹן Çîychôn, see-khone'; from the same as 5477; *tempestuous*; *Sichon*, an Amoritish king:—Sihon {37x}. See: BDB—695d.

5512. סִין {6x} Çîyn, seen; of uncert. der.; *Sin*, the name of an Eg. town and (prob.) desert adjoining:—Sin {6x}. See: BDB—695d.

5513. סִינִי {2x} Çîynîy, see-nee'; from an otherwise unknown name of a man; a *Sinite*, or desc. of one of the sons of Canaan:—Sinite {2x}. See: BDB—696b.

5514. סִינַי {35x} Çîynay, see-nah'-ee; of uncert. der.; *Sinai*, a mountain of Arabia:—Sinai {35x}. See: BDB—696a.

5515. סִינִים {1x} Çîynîym, see-neem'; plur. of an otherwise unknown name; *Sinim*, a distant Oriental region:—Sinim {1x}. See: BDB—692b, 696b.

5516. סִיסְרָא {21x} Çîyçᵉrâ', see-ser-aw'; of uncert. der.; *Sisera*, the name of a Canaanitish king and of one of the Nethinim:—Sisera {21x}. See: BDB—696b.

5517. סִיעָא {2x} Çîyᶜâ', see-ah'; or

סִיעֲהָא Çîyᶜăhâ', see-ah-haw'; from an unused root mean. to *converse*; *congregation*; *Sia*, or *Siaha*, one of the Nethinim:—Sia {1x}, Siaha {1x}.

סִיפֹנְיָא çîyphônᵉyâ'. See 5481.

5518. סִיר {34x} çîyr, seer; or (fem.)

סִירָה çîyrâh, see-raw'; or

סִרָה çîrâh (Jer. 52:18), see-raw'; from a prim. root mean. to *boil* up; a *pot*; also a *thorn* (as springing up rapidly); by impl. a *hook*:—pot {21x}, caldron {5x}, thorns {4x}, washpot + 7366 {2x}, pans {1x}, fishhooks + 1729 {1x}. See: TWOT—1489, 1490; BDB—696c.

5519. סָךְ {1x} çâk, sawk; from 5526; prop. a *thicket* of men, i.e. a *crowd*:—multitude {1x}. See: TWOT—1492c; BDB—697c.

5520. סֹךְ {4x} çôk, soke; from 5526; a *hut* (as of *entwined* boughs); also a *lair*:—covert {1x}, den {1x}, pavilion {1x}, tabernacle {1x}. See: TWOT—1492d; BDB—697c.

5521. סֻכָּה {31x} çukkâh, sook-kaw'; fem. of 5520; a *hut* or *lair*:—booth {11x}, cottage {1x}, covert {1x}, pavilion {5x}, tabernacle {12x}, tent {1x}. Syn.: 168, 4908, 6898. See: TWOT—1492d; BDB—697c.

5522. סִכּוּת {1x} çikkûwth, sik-kooth'; fem. of 5519; an (idolatrous) *booth*:—tabernacle {1x}. See: TWOT—1491; BDB—696d.

5523. סֻכּוֹת {18x} Çukkôwth, sook-kohth'; or

סֻכֹּת Çukkôth, sook-kohth'; plur. of 5521; *booths*; *Succoth*, the name of a place in Egypt and of three in Pal.:—Succoth {18x}. See: TWOT—1492e; BDB—697d.

5524. סֻכּוֹת בְּנוֹת {1x} Çukkôwth Bᵉnôwth, sook-kohth' ben-ohth'; from 5523 and the (irreg.) plur. of 1323; *booths of* (the) *daughters*; *brothels*, i.e. idolatrous *tents* for impure purposes:—Succoth-benoth {1x}. See: BDB—696d.

5525. סֻכִּי {1x} Çukkîy, sook-kee'; patrial from an unknown name (perh. 5520); a *Sukkite*, or inhab. of some place near Egypt (i.e. *hut-dwellers*):—Sukkiims {1x}. See: BDB—696d.

5526. סָכַךְ {23x} çâkak, saw-kak'; or

שָׂכַךְ sâkak (Exod. 33:22), saw-kak'; a prim. root; prop. to *entwine* as a screen; by impl. to *fence* in, *cover* over, (fig.) *protect*:—cover {15x}, covering {2x}, defence {1x}, defendest {1x}, hedge in {1x}, join together {1x}, set {1x}, shut up {1x}. See: TWOT—1475, 1492, 2259, 2260; BDB—692a, 696d, 697b, 697d, 698c, 962b, 967d, 968a.

5527. סְכָכָה {1x} Çᵉkâkâh, sek-aw-kaw'; from 5526; *inclosure*; *Secacah*, a place in Pal.:—Secacah {1x}. See: BDB—698a.

5528. סָכַל {8x} çâkal, saw-kal'; for 3688; to *be silly*:—done foolishly {5x}, turn into foolishness {1x}, make foolish {1x}, play the fool {1x}. See: TWOT—1493; BDB—698a.

5529. סֶכֶל {1x} çekel, seh'-kel; from 5520; *silliness*; concr. and collect. *dolts*:—folly {1x}. See: TWOT—1493b; BDB—698a.

5530. סָכָל {7x} çâkâl, saw-kawl'; from 5528; *silly*:—fool {4x}, foolish {2x}, sottish {1x}. See: TWOT—1493a; BDB—698a.

5531. סִכְלוּת {7x} çiklûwth, sik-looth'; or

שִׂכְלוּת siklûwth (Eccl. 1:17) sik-looth'; from 5528; *silliness*:—folly {5x}, foolishness {2x}. Syn.: 191, 200, 3689, 5036, 5528. See: TWOT—1493c, 1493d; BDB—698a, 968d.

5532. סָכַן {12x} çâkan, saw-kan'; a prim. root; to *be familiar* with; by impl. to *minister* to, *be serviceable* to, *be customary*:—acquaint {2x}, profitable {2x}, cherish {2x}, advantage {1x}, ever {1x}, profiteth {1x}, treasurer {1x}, unprofitable {1x}, wont {1x}. See: TWOT—1494; BDB—698b.

5533. סָכַן {2x} çâkan, saw-kan'; prob. a denom. from 7915; prop. to *cut*, i.e. *damage*; also to *grow* (caus. *make*) *poor*:—endangered {1x}, impoverished {1x}. See: TWOT—1495, 1496; BDB—698b, 698c.

5534. סָכַר {4x} çâkar, saw-kar'; a prim. root; to *shut* up; by impl. to *surrender*:—stopped {2x}, give over {1x}, impoverished {1x}. See: TWOT—1497, 1498, BDB—698c. See also 5462, 7936.

5535. סָכַת {1x} çâkath, saw-kath'; a prim. root; to *be silent*; by impl. to *observe* quietly:—take heed {1x}. See: TWOT—1499; BDB—698d.

סֻכֹּת Çukkôth. See 5523.

5536. סַל {15x} çal, sal; from 5549; prop. a willow *twig* (as *pendulous*), i.e. an *osier*; but only as woven into a *basket*:—basket {15x}. See: TWOT—1507a; BDB—698d, 700d.

5537. סָלָא {1x} çâlâ', saw-law'; a prim. root; to *suspend* in a balance, i.e. *weigh*:—compare {1x}. See: TWOT—1500; BDB—698d.

5538. סִלָּא {1x} Çillâ', sil-law'; from 5549; an *embankment*; *Silla*, a place in Jerusalem:—Silla {1x}. See: BDB—698d.

5539. סָלַד {1x} çâlad, saw-lad'; a prim. root; prob. to *leap* (with joy), i.e. *exult*:—harden self {1x}. See: TWOT—1501; BDB—698d.

5540. סֶלֶד {2x} Çeled, seh'-led; from 5539; *exultation*; *Seled*, an Isr.:—Seled {2x}. See: BDB—699a.

5541. סָלָה {4x} çâlâh, saw-law'; a prim. root; to *hang* up, i.e. *weigh*, or (fig.) *contemn*:—trodden down {1x}, trodden down under foot {1x}, valued {2x}. See: TWOT—1502, 1503; BDB—699a.

5542. סֶלָה {74x} Çelâh, seh'-law; from 5541; *suspension* (of music), i.e. *pause*:—Selah {74x}. See: TWOT—1506a; BDB—699a, 699d.

5543. סַלּוּ {6x} Çallûw, sal-loo'; or

סַלּוּא Çallûw', sal-loo'; or

סָלוּא Çâlûw, sal-loo'; or

סַלָּי Çallay, sal-lah'-ee; from 5541; *weighed*; *Sallu* or *Sallai*, the name of two Isr.:—Sallai {2x}, Sallu {3x}, Salu {1x}. See: BDB—699a, 699b.

5544. סִלּוֹן {2x} çillôwn, sil-lone'; or

סַלּוֹן çallôwn, sal-lone'; from 5541; a *prickle* (as if *pendulous*):—brier {1x}, thorn {1x}. See: TWOT—1504; BDB—699b.

5545. סָלַח {46x} çâlach, saw-lakh'; a prim. root; to *forgive*:—forgive {19x}, forgiven {13x}, pardon {13x}, spare {1x}.

Calach is reserved especially to mark the pardon extended to the sinner by God. **(1)** It is never used to denote that inferior kind and measure of forgiveness that is exercised by one man toward another. **(2)** It is the Divine restoration of an offender into favor, whether through his own repentance or the intercession of another. **(3)** Though not identical with atonement, the two are closely related. In fact, the covering of the sin and the forgiveness of the sinner can only be understood as two aspects of one truth; for both found their fullness in God's provision of mercy through Christ (cf. Heb 9:22). **(4)** God is always the subject of forgiveness. **(5)** No other Old Testament verb means "to forgive," although several verbs include "forgiveness" in the range of meanings given a particular context [e.g., (maca' - 4229 in Ex 32:32; and kapar - 3722 in Eze 16:63]. **(6)** The first biblical occurrence is in Moses' prayer of intercession on behalf of the Israelites: ". . . It is a stiffnecked people; and [forgive] our iniquity and our sin, and take us for thine inheritance" (Ex 34:9).

(7) Most occurrences of *calach* are in the sacrificial laws of Leviticus and Numbers. **(8)** In the typology of the Old Testament, sacrifices foreshadowed the accomplished work of Jesus Christ, and the Old Testament believer was assured of "forgiveness" based on sacrifice: "And the priest shall make an atonement [for him in regard to his sin]" (Num 15:25, 28), **(8a)** "And it shall be forgiven him" (Lev 4:26; cf. vv. 20, 31, 35; 5:10, 13, 16, 18). **(8b)** The mediators of the atonement were the priests who offered the sacrifice. **(8c)** The sacrifice was ordained by God to promise ultimate "forgiveness" in God's sacrifice of His own Son. **(8d)** Moreover, sacrifice was appropriately connected to atonement, as there is no forgiveness without the shedding of blood (Lev 4:20; cf. Heb 9:22). **(9)** Out of His grace, God alone "forgives" sin. **(9a)** The Israelites experienced God's "forgiveness" in the wilderness and in the Promised Land. **(9b)** As long as the temple stood, sacrificial atonement continued and the Israelites were assured of God's "forgiveness."

(10) When the temple was destroyed and sacrifices ceased, God sent the prophetic word that He graciously would restore Israel out of exile and "forgive" its sins: "And they shall teach no more every man his neighbour, and every man his brother, saying, Know the LORD: for they shall all know me, from the least of them unto the greatest of them, saith the LORD: for I will forgive their iniquity, and I will remember their sin no more" (Jer 31:34). **(11)** The psalmist appealed to God's great name in his request for "forgiveness": "For thy name's sake, O Lord, pardon mine iniquity; for it is great" (Ps 25:11). **(12)** David praised God for the assurance of "forgiveness" of sins: "Bless the Lord, O my soul . . . , who forgiveth all thine iniquities . . ." (Ps 103:2–3). **(13)** The Old Testament saints, while involved in sacrificial rites, put their faith in God. It was their faith in God that saved, not the sacrifices. See: TWOT—1505; BDB—699b.

5546. סַלָּח {1x} **çallâch**, *saw-lawkh';* from 5545; *placable:*—ready to forgive {1x}. See: TWOT—1505a; BDB—699c.

סַלַּי **Çallay**. See 5543.

5547. סְלִיחָה {3x} **çᵉlîychâh**, *sel-ee-khaw';* from 5545; *pardon:*—forgiveness {2x}, pardon {1x}. See: TWOT—1505b; BDB—699c.

5548. סַלְכָה {4x} **Çalkâh**, *sal-kaw';* from an unused root. mean. to *walk; walking; Salcah,* a place E. of the Jordan:—Salcah {2x}, Salchah {2x}. See: TWOT—1505b; BDB—699c.

5549. סָלַל {12x} **çâlal**, *saw-lal';* a prim. root; to *mound* up (espec. a turnpike); fig. to *exalt;* refl. to *oppose* (as by a dam):—cast up {6x}, raise up {2x}, exalt {2x}, extol {1x}, made plain {1x}. See: TWOT—1506; BDB—699c.

5550. סֹלְלָה {11x} **çôlᵉlâh**, *so-lel-aw';* or

סוֹלְלָה **çôwlᵉlâh**, *so-lel-aw';* act. part. fem. of 5549, but used pass.; a military *mound,* i.e. *rampart* of besiegers:—bank {3x}, mount {8x}. See: TWOT—1506b; BDB—700c.

5551. סֻלָּם {1x} **çullâm**, *sool-lawm';* from 5549; a *stair-case:*—ladder {1x}. See: TWOT—1506c; BDB—700c.

5552. סַלְסִלָּה {1x} **çalçillâh**, *sal-sil-law';* from 5541; a *twig* (as *pendulous*):—baskets {1x}. See: TWOT—1507b; BDB—700d.

5553. סֶלַע {60x} **çelaᶜ**, *seh'-lah;* from an unused root mean. to be *lofty;* a craggy *rock,* lit. or fig. (a *fortress*):—rock {57x}, strong hold {1x}, stones {1x}, stony {11x}. See: TWOT—1508a; BDB—700d.

5554. סֶלַע {2x} **Çelaᶜ**, *seh'-lah;* the same as 5553; *Sela,* the rock-city of Idumaea:—Sela {1x}, Selah {1x}. See: BDB—701a.

5555. סֶלַע הַמַּחְלְקוֹת {1x} **Çelaᶜ ham-machlᵉqôwth**, *seh'-lah ham-makh-lek-ōth';* from 5553 and the plur. of 4256 with the art. interposed; *rock of the divisions; Sela-ham-Machlekoth,* a place in Pal.:—Sela-hammalekoth {1x}. See: BDB—325d, 563b.

5556. סָלְעָם {1x} **çolᶜâm**, *sol-awm';* appar. from the same as 5553 in the sense of *crushing* as with a rock, i.e. consuming; a kind of *locust* (from its *destructiveness*):—bald locust {1x}. See: TWOT—1509; BDB—701b.

5557. סָלַף {7x} **çâlaph**, *saw-laf';* a prim. root; prop. to *wrench,* i.e. (fig.) to *subvert:*—overthrow {4x}, pervert {3x}. See: TWOT—1510; BDB—701b.

5558. סֶלֶף {2x} **çeleph**, *seh'-lef;* from 5557; *distortion,* i.e. (fig.) *viciousness:*—perverseness {2x}. See: TWOT—1510a; BDB—701b.

5559. סְלִק {5x} **çᵉlîq** (Aram.), *sel-eek';* a prim. root; to *ascend:*—came up {4x}, came {1x}. See: TWOT—2889; BDB—1104b.

5560. סֹלֶת {53x} **çôleth**, *so'-leth;* from an unused root mean. to *strip; flour* (as *chipped* off):—fine {1x}, flour {52x}. See: TWOT—1512; BDB—701c.

5561. סַם {17x} **çam**, *sam;* from an unused root mean. to *smell* sweet; an *aroma:*—sweet {14x}, sweet spices {3x}. See: TWOT—1516a; BDB—701c, 702c.

5562. סַמְגַּר נְבוֹ {1x} **Çamgar Nᵉbôw**, *sam-gar' neb-o';* of for. or.; *Samgar-Nebo,* a Bab. general:—Samgar-nebo {1x}. See: BDB—701c.

5563. סְמָדַר {3x} **çᵉmâdar**, *sem-aw-dar';* of uncert. der.; a vine *blossom;* used also adv. *abloom:*—tender grape {3x}. Syn.: 1154, 6025. See: TWOT—1513; BDB—701d.

5564. סָמַךְ {48x} **çâmak**, *saw-mak';* a prim. root; to *prop* (lit. or fig.); refl. to *lean* upon or *take hold* of (in a favorable or unfavorable sense):—lay {18x}, uphold {9x}, put {5x}, lean {3x}, stay {3x}, sustained {3x}, holden up {1x}, borne up {1x}, established {1x}, stand fast {1x}, lieth hard {1x}, rested {1x}, set {1x}. See: TWOT—1514; BDB—701d.

5565. סְמַכְיָהוּ {1x} **Çᵉmakyâhûw**, *sem-ak-yaw'-hoo;* from 5564 and 3050; *supported of Jah; Semakjah,* an Isr.:—Semachiah {1x}. See: BDB—702b.

5566. סֶמֶל {5x} **çemel**, *seh'-mel;* or

סֵמֶל **çêmel**, *say'-mel;* from an unused root mean. to *resemble;* a *likeness:*—figure {1x}, idol {2x}, image {2x}.

Cemel means an image, figure, or likeness; to be construed as a standardized likeness of a false deity in which it is imagined by its worshipers. Syn.: 2796, 4906, 6459, 6736, 6754, 8544. See: TWOT—1515; BDB—702b.

5567. סָמַן {1x} **çâman**, *saw-man';* a prim. root; to *designate:*—appointed {1x}. See: TWOT—1517; BDB—651c, 702c.

5568. סָמַר {2x} **çâmar**, *saw-mar';* a prim. root; to *be erect,* i.e. *bristle* as hair:—stood up {1x}, tremble {1x}. See: TWOT—1518; BDB—702c.

5569. סָמָר {1x} **çâmâr**, *saw-mar';* from 5568; *bristling,* i.e. *shaggy:*—rough {1x}. See: TWOT—1518a; BDB—702c.

5570. סְנָאָה {3x} **Çᵉnâ'âh**, *sen-aw-aw';* from an unused root mean. to *prick; thorny; Senaah,* a place in Pal.:—Senaah {2x}, Hassenaah [*with the art.*]{1x}. See: BDB—702d, 703a.

סְנֻאָה **çᵉnû'âh**. See 5574.

5571. סַנְבַלַּט {10x} **Çanballaṭ**, *san-bal-lat';* of for. or.; *Sanballat,* a Pers. satrap of Samaria:—Sanballat {10x}. See: BDB—702d.

5572. סְנֶה {6x} **çᵉneh**, *sen-eh';* from an unused root mean. to *prick;* a *bramble:*—bush {6x}. See: TWOT—1520; BDB—702d.

5573. סֶנֶה {1x} **Çeneh**, *seh-neh';* the same as 5572; *thorn; Seneh,* a crag in Pal.:—Seneh {1x}. See: BDB—702d.

סַנָּה **Çannâh**. See 7158.

5574. סְנוּאָה {2x} **Çᵉnûw'âh**, *sen-oo-aw';* or

סְנֻאָה **Çᵉnû'âh**, *sen-oo-aw'* from the same as 5570; *pointed;* (used with the art. as a proper name) *Senuah,* the name of two Isr.:—Hasenuah [*incl. the art.*] {1x}, Senuah {1x}. See: BDB—703a.

5575. סַנְוֵר {3x} **çanvêr**, *san-vare';* of uncert. der.; (in plur.) *blindness:*—blindness {3x}. See: TWOT—1520; BDB—703a.

5576. סַנְחֵרִיב {13x} **Çanchêrîyb**, *san-khay-reeb';* of for. or.; *Sancherib,* an Ass. king:—Sennacherib {13x}. See: BDB—703a.

5577. סַנְסִן {1x} **çançîn**, *san-seen';* from an unused root mean. to *be pointed;* a *twig* (as *tapering*):—boughs {1x}. See: TWOT—1522; BDB—703b.

5578. סַנְסַנָּה {1x} **Çançannâh**, *san-san-naw';* fem. of a form of 5577; a *bough; Sansannah,* a place in Pal.:—Sansannah {1x}. See: BDB—703a.

5579. סְנַפִּיר {1x} **çᵉnappîyr**, *sen-ap-peer';* of uncert. der.; a *fin* (collect.):—fins {1x}. See: TWOT—1523; BDB—703b.

5580. סָס {1x} **çâç**, *sawce;* from the same as 5483; a *moth* (from the *agility* of the fly):—moth {1x}. See: TWOT—1524; BDB—703b.

סֻס **çûç**. See 5483.

5581. סִסְמַי {2x} **Çiçmay**, *sis-mah'-ee;* of uncert. der.; *Sismai,* an Isr.:—Sisamai {2x}. See: BDB—703b.

5582. סָעַד {12x} **çâᶜad**, *saw-ad';* a prim. root; to *support* (mostly fig.):—comfort {3x}, strengthen {3x}, hold me up {3x}, upholden {1x}, establish {1x}, refresh {1x}. See: TWOT—1525; BDB—703c, 1104a.

5583. סְעַד {1x} **çᵉᶜad** (Aram.), *seh-ad';* corresp. to 5582; to *aid:*—helping {1x}. See: TWOT—2890; BDB—1104b.

5584. סָעָה {1x} **çâ'âh**, *saw-aw';* a prim. root; to *rush:*—storm {1x}. See: TWOT—1526; BDB—703c.

5585. סְעִיף {6x} **çâʿîyph**, *saw-eef'*; from 5586; a *fissure* (of rocks); also a *bough* (as *subdivided*):—(outmost) branches {2x}, clifts, top {3x}. See: TWOT—1527a; BDB—703d.

5586. סָעַף {1x} **çâʿaph**, *saw-af'*; a prim. root; prop. to *divide* up; but used only as denom. from 5585, to *disbranch* (a tree):—top {1x}. See: TWOT—1527c; BDB—703d.

5587. סָעִף {3x} **çâʿiph**, *saw-eef'* or

שָׂעִף **sâʿîph**, *saw-eef'*; from 5586; *divided* (in mind), i.e. (abstr.) a *sentiment:*—opinion {1x}, thoughts {2x}. See: TWOT—1527f; BDB—704a, 972a.

5588. סֵעֵף {1x} **çêʿêph**, *say-afe'*; from 5586; *divided* (in mind), i.e. (concr.) a *skeptic:*—thoughts {1x}. See: TWOT—1527e; BDB—704a.

5589. סְעַפָּה {2x} **çᵉʿappâh**, *seh-ap-paw'*; fem. of 5585; a *twig:*—bough {1x}, branch {1x}. See: TWOT—1527b; BDB—703d. comp. 5634.

5590. סָעַר {7x} **çâʿar**, *saw-ar'*; a prim. root; to *rush* upon; by impl. to *toss* (tran. or intr., lit. or fig.):—whirlwind {3x}, tempestuous {2x}, troubled {1x}, tossed with tempest {1x}. See: TWOT—1528b; BDB—704a.

5591. סַעַר {24x} **çaʿar**, *sah'-ar*; or (fem.)

סְעָרָה **çᵉʿârâh**, *seh-aw-raw'*; from 5590; a *hurricane:*—whirlwind {12x}, tempest {6x}, stormy {4x}, storm {1x}, whirlwind + 7307 {1x}. Syn.: 5036, 5492, 8183. See: TWOT 1528; BDB—704b, 973b.

5592. סַף {32x} **çaph**, *saf*; from 5605, in its orig. sense of *containing;* a *vestibule* (as a *limit*); also a *dish* (for holding blood or wine):—door {12x}, threshold {8x}, bason {4x}, posts {3x}, bowls {2x}, gates {2x}, cup {1x}. See: TWOT—1528b; BDB—704c, 706b.

5593. סַף {1x} **Çaph**, *saf;* the same as 5592; *Saph*, a Philistine:—Saph {1x}. See: BDB—704c, 706c. comp. 5598.

5594. סָפַד {30x} **çâphad**, *saw-fad'*; a prim. root; prop. to *tear* the hair and *beat* the breasts (as Orientals do in grief); gen. to *lament;* by impl. to *wail:*—lament {13x}, mourn {15x}, mourners {1x}, wail {1x}. Syn.: 56, 6969. See: TWOT—1530; BDB—704c, 973c.

5595. סָפָה {20x} **çâphâh**, *saw-faw'*; a prim. root; prop. to *scrape* (lit. to *shave;* but usually fig.) together (i.e. to *accumulate* or *increase*) or away (i.e. to *scatter, remove*, or *ruin;* intr. to *perish*):—add {3x}, augment {1x}, consume {6x}, destroy {5x}, heap {1x}, join {1x}, perish {2x}, put {1x}. See: TWOT—1531; BDB—705a.

5596. סָפַח {6x} **çâphach**, *saw-fakh'*; or

שָׂפַח **sâphach** (Isa. 3:17) *saw-fakh'*; a prim. root; prop. to *scrape* out, but in certain peculiar senses (of *removal* or *association*):—put {2x}, abiding {1x}, gather together {1x}, cleave {1x}, smite with the scab {1x}. See: TWOT—1532, 1534; BDB—705b, 705c, 974a.

5597. סַפַּחַת {2x} **çappachath**, *sap-pakh'-ath;* from 5596; the *mange* (as making the hair fall off):—scab {2x}. See: TWOT—1534a; BDB—705c.

5598. סִפַּי {1x} **Çippay**, *sip-pah'-ee;* from 5592; *bason-like; Sippai*, a Philistine:—Sippai {1x}. See: BDB—705d, 706c. comp. 5593.

5599. סָפִיחַ {5x} **çâphîyach**, *saw-fee'-akh;* from 5596; something (spontaneously) *falling* off, i.e. a *self-sown* crop; fig. a *freshet:*—grow of itself {2x}, things which grow {2x}, that which groweth {1x}. See: TWOT—1533a, 1533b; BDB—705b, 705c.

5600. סְפִינָה {1x} **çᵉphîynâh**, *sef-ee-naw'*; from 5603; a (sea-going) *vessel* (as *ceiled* with a deck):—ship {1x}. Syn.: 591, 6716. See: TWOT—1537b; BDB—706b.

5601. סַפִּיר {11x} **çappîyr**, *sap-peer'*; from 5608; a *gem* (perh. as used for *scratching* other substances), prob. the *sapphire:*—sapphire {10x}, sapphire stone {1x}. See: TWOT—1535; BDB—705d.

5602. סֵפֶל {2x} **çêphel**, *say'-fel;* from an unused root mean. to *depress;* a *basin* (as *deepened* out):—bowl {1x}, dish {1x}. See: TWOT—1536; BDB—705d.

5603. סָפַן {6x} **çâphan**, *saw-fan'*; a prim. root; to *hide* by covering; spec. to *roof* (pass. part. as noun, a *roof*) or *paneling;* fig. to *reserve:*—cieled {2x}, covered {3x}, seated {1x}. See: TWOT—1537; BDB—706a, 974a.

5604. סִפֻּן {1x} **çippûn**, *sip-poon'*; from 5603; a *wainscot:*—cieling {1x}. See: TWOT—1537a; BDB—706a.

5605. סָפַף {1x} **çâphaph**, *saw-faf'*; a prim. root; prop. to *snatch* away, i.e. *terminate;* but used only as denom. from 5592 (in the sense of a *vestibule*), to *wait at* (the) *threshold:*—be a doorkeeper {1x}. See: TWOT—1538c; BDB—706c.

5606. סָפַק {10x} **çâphaq**, *saw-fak'*; or

שָׂפַק **sâphaq** (1 Kings 20:10; Job 27:23; Isa. 2:6), *saw-fak'*; a prim. root; to *clap* the hands (in token of compact, derision, grief, indignation, or punishment); by impl. of satisfaction, to *be enough;* by impl. of excess, to *vomit:*—clap {2x}, smite {1x}, striketh {1x}, suffice {1x}, wallow {1x}, smote {1x}, smote together {1x}, clappeth {1x}, please {1x}. See: TWOT—1539; BDB—706c, 974a.

5607. סֵפֶק {2x} **çêpheq**, *say'-fek;* or

שֶׂפֶק **sepheq** (Job 20:22; 36:18) *seh'-fek;* from 5606; *chastisement;* also *satiety:*—stroke {1x}, sufficiency {1x}. See: TWOT—1539a; BDB—706d, 974a, 974b.

5608. סָפַר {161x} **çâphar**, *saw-far'*; a prim. root; prop. to *score* with a mark as a tally or record, i.e. (by impl.) to *inscribe*, and also to *enumerate;* intens. to *recount*, i.e. *celebrate:*—scribe {50x}, tell {40x}, declare {24x}, number {23x}, count {6x}, shew forth {5x}, writer {4x}, speak {2x}, accounted {1x}, commune {1x}, told out {1x}, reckon {1x}, penknife + 8593 {1x}, shewing {1x}, talk {1x}.

Caphar means "to number, count, proclaim, declare." **(1)** In the basic verbal form this verb signifies "to number or count." **(1a)** This meaning is in its first biblical appearance, Gen 15:5: "Look now toward heaven, and tell the stars, if thou be able to number them. . . ." **(1b)** Here the counting is a process which has no completion in view. **(1c)** In Lev 15:13 the emphasis is on a completed task: "And when [the man with the discharge becomes cleansed]; then he shall number to himself seven days for his cleansing, and wash his clothes, and bathe his flesh. . . ." **(1d)** Another nuance of this usage is "to count up" or "to take a census": "And David's heart smote him after that he had numbered the people" (2 Sa 24:10). **(2)** The verb is also used of assigning persons to particular jobs: "And Solomon told out threescore and ten thousand men to bear burdens . . ." (2 Chr 2:2). **(3)** Another special use appears in Ezra 1:8, where *capar* means "to count out according to a list" as the recipient listens: "Even those [the temple furnishings] did Cyrus king of Persia bring forth by the hand of Mithredath the treasurer, and numbered them unto Sheshbazzar, the prince of Judah." **(4)** In Ps 56:8 the word signifies "taking account of," or being aware and concerned about each detail of: "Thou tellest my wanderings. . . ."

(5) This verb can also mean "to measure," in the sense of what one does with grain: "And Joseph gathered corn as the sand of the sea, very much, until he left numbering; for it was without number" (Gen 41:49). **(6)** The verb *capar* can represent recording something in writing, or enumerating. So, "the Lord shall count, when he writeth up the people, that this man was born there" (Ps 87:6). **(7)** In about 90 instances this verb appears in an intensive form. **(7a)** For the most part the verb in this form means "to recount," to orally list in detail. **(7b)** The one exception to this significance is Job 38:37: "Who can number the clouds in wisdom? Or who can stay the bottles of heaven . . . ?" **(7c)** In every other instance the verb signifies a vocal statement (listing or enumeration) of a series of given facts. **(7c1)** In Gen 24:66 Eliezer, Abraham's servant, "told Isaac all things that he had done"; he gave him a summarized but complete account of his activities. Thus Isaac knew who Rebekah was, and why she was there, so he took her to be his wife. **(7c2)** In a similar but somewhat different sense Jacob "told Laban" who he was, that he was from the same family (Gen 29:13). In this case the word represents something other than a report; it represents an account of Jacob's genealogy and perhaps of the events of his parents' lives.

(8) This emphasis on accurate recounting is especially prominent in Num 13:27, where the spies report back to Moses concerning what they saw in Palestine. **(9)** Even more emphatic is Ex 24:3, where one word represents a detailed repetition of what Moses heard from God: "And Moses came and told the people all the words of the Lord, and all the judgments. . . ." **(10)** Again, in Is 43:26 a detailed and accurate recounting is clearly in view. In this case the prophet has in mind the presentation of a law case: "Put me in remembrance: let us plead together: declare thou, that thou mayest be justified." **(11)** Because of the predominant meaning presented above, Ps 40:5 could be translated: "If I would declare and speak of them, they would be too numerous to recount" (instead of "to count"). **(12)** In at least one case the verb in the intensive stem means "to exhibit," "to recount or list in detail by being a living example." This meaning first appears in Ex 9:16, where God tells Moses to say to Pharaoh: "And in very deed for this cause have I raised thee up, for to show in thee my power; and that my name may be declared throughout all the earth." See: TWOT—1540, 1540c; BDB—707d, 708b, 1104c.

5609. סְפַר {5x} **çᵉphar** (Aram.), *sef-ar'*; from a root corresp. to 5608; a *book:*—book {4x}, roll {1x}. See: TWOT—2891a; BDB—1104c.

5610. סְפָר {1x} **çᵉphâr**, *sef-awr'*; from 5608; a *census:*—numbering {1x}.

Cephar means a "numbering or census": "And Solomon numbered all the strangers that *were* in the land of Israel, after the numbering wherewith David his father had numbered them; and they were found an hundred and fifty thousand and three thousand and six hundred" (2 Chr 2:17). Syn: 5608, 5612, 5615.See: TWOT—1540d; BDB—708c.

5611. סְפָר {1x} **Çᵉphâr**, *sef-awr';* the same as 5610; *Sephar,* a place in Arabia:—Sephar {1x}. See: BDB—708c.

5612. סֵפֶר {184x} **çêpher**, *say'-fer;* or (fem.)

סִפְרָה **çiphrâh** (Psa. 56:8 [9]), *sif-raw';* from 5608; prop. *writing* (the art or a document); by impl. a *book:*—book {138x}, letter {29x}, evidence {8x}, bill {4x}, learning {2x}, register {1x}, learned + 3045 {1x}, scroll {1x}.

Cepher means book; tablet. **(1)** Basically this word represents something one writes upon. **(1a)** So in Ex 17:14 "the Lord said unto Moses, Write this for a memorial in a book." **(1b)** In Is 30:8 *cepher* represents a tablet: "Now go, write it before them in a table (3871 - luwach), and note it in a book (*cepher*), that it may be for the time to come for ever and ever." **(2)** In Gen 5:1 (the first biblical occurrence of this word) it signifies something that has been written upon, or a written record: "This is the book of the generations of Adam." **(3)** Such a written document may be a summary of God's law (Ex 24:7). **(4)** During the monarchy *cepher* came to represent a letter (2 Sa 11:14). **(5)** Even later it means a king's written decree sent throughout his empire (Est 1:22). **(6)** Usually the word means "book": **(6a)** "Yet now, if thou wilt forgive their sin—; and if not, blot me, I pray thee, out of thy book which thou hast written" (Ex 32:32)—a complete record of whatever one wants to preserve accurately. **(6b)** "Thou tellest my wanderings: put thou my tears into thy bottle: *are they* not in thy book?" (Ps 56:8). **(7)** Often this word can signify the way a people writes, the written language or script (Is 29:11).

(8) A manuscript **(8a)** was written (Ex 32:32; Deut 17:18) and **(8b)** sealed (Is 29:11), and **(8c)** to be read by the addressee (2 Kin 22:16). **(9)** In Is 30:8 *cepher* represents a tablet. **(9a)** *Cepher,* in Jer 36:6, is similar to scroll (4309 - megillah) and **(9b)** book (5612 - cipra - Ps. 56:8). **(9c)** In Gen 5:1 it signifies something that has been written down, or a written record. **(10)** Many books are named: the book of **(10a)** remembrance (Mal 3:16), **(10b)** life (Ps 69:28), **(10c)** Jasher (Josh 10:13), **(10d)** the generations (Gen 5:1), **(10e)** the Lord, **(10f)** the chronicles of the kings of Israel and of Judah (2 Chr 24:27). **(11)** Usually the word means "book" (Ex 32:32)—a complete record of whatever one wants to preserve accurately. **(12)** *Cepher* can represent a letter (2 Sa 11:14), **(13)** a king's written decree (Est 1:22). **(14)** Prophets wrote books: Nah 1:1; Jer 36. **(15)** Symbolically, Ezekiel ate a book (Eze 2:8—3:1). **(16)** In divorcing his wife, a man gave her a legal document known as the *cepher* of divorce (Deut 24:1). Syn.: 5608, 5610, 5615. See: TWOT—1540a, 1540b; BDB—706d, 707c, 708d, 1104c.

5613. סָפֵר {6x} **çâphêr** (Aram.), *saw-fare';* from the same as 5609; a *scribe* (secular or sacred):—scribe {6x}.

Capher means "scribe." **(1)** In the early monarchy the chief "scribe" was the highest court official next to the king (2 Sa 8:17). **(1a)** His job was to receive and evaluate all royal correspondence—to answer the unimportant and give the rest to the proper officer or to the king himself. **(1b)** He also wrote and/or composed royal communications to those within the kingdom. **(1c)** There was probably an entire corps of lesser scribes under his direction. **(1d)** As a highly trusted official he was sometimes involved in counting and managing great influxes of royal revenue (2 Kin 12:10) and in certain diplomatic jobs (2 Kin 19:2). **(2)** Later coper represented the Jewish official in the Persian court who was responsible for Jewish belongings (Ezra 7:11). **(3)** In the post-exilic community this word came to mean someone who was learned in the Old Testament Scripture and especially the Mosaic Law (the Pentateuch; Ezra 7:6). **(4)** The word first occurs in Judg 5:14: "they that handle the pen of the writer"). Syn.: 5610, 5612, 5615. See: TWOT—2891b; BDB—1104c.

5614. סְפָרָד {1x} **Çᵉphârâd**, *sef-aw-rawd';* of for. der.; *Sepharad,* a region of Assyria:—Sepharad {1x}. See: BDB—709b.

סִפְרָה **çiphrâh**. See 5612.

5615. סְפֹרָה {1x} **çᵉp ôrâh**, *sef-o-raw';* from 5608; a *numeration:*—number {1x}.

Ceporah, means a "number or sum": "My mouth shall shew forth thy righteousness *and* thy salvation all the day; for I know not the numbers *thereof*" (Ps 71:15). Syn.: 5608, 5610, 5612.See: TWOT—1540e; BDB—707d, 708d.

5616. סְפַרְוִי {1x} **Çᵉpharvîy**, *sef-ar-vee';* patrial from 5617; a *Sepharvite* or inhab. of Sepharvain:—Sepharvite {1x}. See: BDB—709c.

5617. סְפַרְוַיִם {6x} **Çᵉpharvayim** (dual), *sef-ar-vah'-yim;* or

סְפָרִים **Çᵉphârîym** (plur.), *sef-aw-reem';* of for. der.; *Sepharvajim* or *Sepharim,* a place in Assyria:—Sepharvaim {6x}. See: BDB—709b.

5618. סֹפֶרֶת {2x} **Çôphereth**, *so-feh'-reth;* fem. act. part. of 5608; a *scribe* (prop. female); *Sophereth,* a temple servant:—Sophereth {2x}. See: BDB—709b.

5619. סָקַל {22x} **çâqal**, *saw-kal';* a prim. root; prop. to *be weighty;* but used only in the sense of *lapidation* or its contrary (as if a delapidation):—stone {15x}, surely {2x}, cast {1x}, gather out {1x}, gather out stones {1x}, stoning {1x}, threw {1x}. See: TWOT—1541; BDB—709c, 920c.

5620. סַר {3x} **çar**, *sar;* from 5637 contr.; *peevish:*—heavy {2x}, sad {1x}. See: TWOT—1549a; BDB—709d.

5621. סָרָב {1x} **çârâb**, *saw-rawb';* from an unused root mean. to *sting;* a thistle:—brier {1x}. See: TWOT—1542; BDB—709d.

5622. סַרְבַּל {2x} **çarbal** (Aram.), *sar-bal';* of uncert. der.; a *cloak:*—coat {2x}. See: TWOT—2892; BDB—1104c.

5623. סַרְגּוֹן {1x} **Çargôwn**, *sar-gōne';* of for. der.; *Sargon,* an Assy. king:—Sargon {1x}. See: BDB—709d.

5624. סֶרֶד {2x} **Çered**, *seh'-red;* from a prim. root mean. to *tremble; trembling; Sered,* an Isr.:—Sered {2x}. See: BDB—710a.

5625. סַרְדִּי {1x} **Çardîy**, *sar-dee';* patron. from 5624; a *Seredite* (collect.) or desc. of Sered:—Sardites {1x}. See: BDB—710a.

5626. סִרָה {1x} **Çîrâh**, *see-raw';* from 5493; *departure; Sirah,* a cistern so-called:—Sirah {1x}. See: BDB—92d, 694c, 710a. See also 5518.

5627. סָרָה {8x} **çârâh**, *saw-raw';* from 5493; *apostasy, crime;* fig. *remission:*—× continual, rebellion {2x}, revolt {3x}, turn away {1x}, wrong {1x}. See: TWOT—1480a; BDB—694c, 710a.

5628. סָרַח {7x} **çârach**, *saw-rakh';* a prim. root; to *extend* (even to *excess*):—exceeding {1x}, hang {2x}, spread {1x}, stretch self {2x}, banish {1x}. See: TWOT—1543; BDB—710a.

5629. סֶרַח {1x} **çerach**, *seh'-rakh;* from 5628; a *redundancy:*—remnant {1x}. See: TWOT—1543a; BDB—710b.

5630. סִרְיֹן {2x} **çiyrôn**, *sir-yone';* for 8302; a coat of *mail:*—brigandine {2x}. See: TWOT—1544; BDB—710b.

5631. סָרִיס {42x} **çârîyç**, *saw-reece';* or

סָרִס **çârîç**, *saw-reece';* from an unused root mean. to *castrate;* a *eunuch;* by impl. *valet* (espec. of the female apartments), and thus, a *minister* of state:—chamberlain {13x}, eunuch {17x}, officer {12x}. See: TWOT—1545; BDB—710b. comp. 7249.

5632. סָרֵךְ {5x} **çârêk** (Aram.), *saw-rake';* of for. or.; an *emir:*—president {5x}. See: TWOT—2893; BDB—1104c.

5633. סֶרֶן {22x} **çeren**, *seh'-ren;* from an unused root of uncert. mean.; an *axle;* fig. a *peer:*—lord {22x}, plate {1x}. See: TWOT—1546, 1547; BDB—710c, 710d.

5634. סַרְעַפָּה {1x} **çarᶜappâh**, *sar-ap-paw';* for 5589; a *twig:*—bough {1x}. See: TWOT—1527d; BDB—703d, 710d.

5635. סָרַף {1x} **çâraph**, *saw-raf';* a prim. root; to *cremate,* i.e. to *be* (near) *of kin* (such being privileged to kindle the pyre):—burn {1x}. See: TWOT—2292; BDB—710d, 977a.

5636. סַרְפָּד {1x} **çarpâd**, *sar-pawd';* from 5635; a *nettle* (as stinging like a *burn*):—brier {1x}. See: TWOT—1548; BDB—710d.

5637. סָרַר {17x} **çârar**, *saw-rar';* a prim. root; to *turn* away, i.e. (mor.) *be refractory:*—rebellious {6x}, stubborn {4x}, revolters {2x}, revolting {1x}, slide back {1x}, backslide {1x}, away {1x}, withdrew {1x}. See: TWOT—1549; BDB—693c, 710d.

5638. סְתָו {1x} **çᵉthâv**, *seth-awv';* from an unused root mean. to *hide; winter* (as the dark season):—winter {1x}. See: TWOT—1549.1; BDB—711a.

5639. סְתוּר {1x} **Çᵉthûwr**, *seth-oor';* from 5641; *hidden; Sethur,* an Isr.:—Sethur {1x}. See: BDB—712c.

5640. סָתַם {14x} **çâtham**, *saw-tham';* or

שָׂתַם **sâtham** (Num. 24:15), *saw-tham';* a prim. root; to *stop* up; by impl. to *repair;* fig. to *keep secret:*—stop {8x}, shut up {2x}, hidden {1x}, shut out {1x}, secret {1x}, close up {1x}. See: TWOT—1550; BDB—711a, 979c.

5641. סָתַר {82x} **çâthar**, *saw-thar';* a prim. root; to *hide* (by covering), lit. or fig.:—hide {72x}, secret {4x}, close {2x}, absent {1x}, conceal {1x}, surely {1x}, variant {1x}.

Cathar means "to conceal, hide, shelter." **(1)** The word is found for the first time in Gen 4:14 as Cain discovers that because of his sin, he will be "hidden" from the presence of God, which implies a separation: "Behold, thou hast driven me out this day from the face of the earth; and from thy face shall I be hid; and I shall be a fugitive and a vagabond in the earth; and it shall come to pass, *that* every one that findeth me shall slay me."**(2)** In the so-called Mizpah Benediction (which is really a warning), *cathar* again has the sense of "separation": "The Lord watch between me and thee, when we are absent one from another" (Gen 31:49). **(3)** To "hide oneself" is to take refuge: "Doth not David hide himself with us . . . ?" (1 Sa 23:19). **(4)** Similarly, to "hide" someone is to "shelter" him from his enemy: ". . . The Lord hid them" (Jer 36:26). **(5)** To pray, "Hide thy face from my sins" (Ps 51:9), is to ask God to ignore them. **(6)** But when the prophet says, "And I will wait upon the Lord, that hideth his face from the house of Jacob . . ." (Is 8:17), he means that God's favor has been withdrawn. **(7)** Similarly, Judah's sins have "hidden" God's face from her: "But your iniquities have separated between you and your God, and your sins have hid *his* face from you, that he will not hear" (Is 59:2). See: TWOT—1551; BDB—711b, 1104c.

5642. סְתַר {2x} **çᵉthar** (Aram.), *seth-ar'*; corresp. to 5641; to *conceal;* fig. to *demolish:*—destroy {1x}, secret thing {1x}. See: TWOT—2894; BDB—1104c, 1104d.

5643. סֵתֶר {36x} **çêther**, *say'-ther;* or (fem.)
סִתְרָה **çithrâh** (Deut 32:38), *sith-raw';* from 5641; a *cover* (in a good or a bad, a lit. or a fig. sense):—secret {12x}, secretly {9x}, covert {5x}, secret place {3x}, hiding place {2x}, backbiting {1x}, covering {1x}, disguiseth {1x}, privily {1x}, protection {1x}. See: TWOT—1551a, 1551b; BDB—712a, 712c.

5644. סִתְרִי {1x} **Çithrîy**, *sith-ree';* from 5643; *protective; Sithri,* an Isr.:—Zithri {1x}. See: BDB—712c.

ע

5645. עָב {32x} **ʿâb**, *awb* (masc. and fem.); from 5743; prop. an *envelope,* i.e. *darkness* (or *density,* 2 Chr 4:17); spec. a (scud) *cloud;* also a *copse:*—clay {1x}, (thick) cloud {20x}, × thick {1x}, thicket {1x}. See: TWOT—1574a; BDB—712b, 716a, 728a. comp. 5672.

5646. עָב {3x} **ʿâb**, *awb;* or
עֹב **ʿôb**, *obe;* from an unused root mean. to *cover;* prop. equiv. to 5645; but used only as an arch. term, an *architrave* (as *shading* the pillars):—thick beam {2x}, plank {1x}. See: TWOT—1552a; BDB—712b, 728a.

5647. עָבַד {290x} **ʿâbad**, *aw-bad';* a prim. root; to *work* (in any sense); by impl. to *serve, till,* (caus.) *enslave,* etc.:—serve {227x}, do {15x}, till {9x}, servant {5x}, work {5x}, worshippers {5x}, service {4x}, dress {2x}, labour {2x}, ear {2x}, misc. {14x} = × be, keep in bondage, be bondmen, bond-service, compel, execute, + husbandman, keep, be wrought.

ʿAbad, as a verb, means "to serve, cultivate, enslave, work." **(1)** The verb is first used in **(1a)** Gen 2:5: ". . . And there was not a man to till the ground." **(1b)** God gave to man the task "to dress [the ground]" (Gen 2:15; 3:23). **(2)** In Gen 14:4 "they served Chedorlaomer . . ." means that they were his vassals. **(3)** God told Abraham that his descendants would "serve" the people of a strange land 400 years: "And he said unto Abram, Know of a surety that thy seed shall be a stranger in a land *that is* not theirs, and shall serve them; and they shall afflict them four hundred years" (Gen 15:13). **(4)** *ʿAbad* is often used toward God: ". . . Ye shall serve God upon this mountain" (Ex 3:12), meaning "to worship." **(5)** The word is frequently used with another verb: **(5a)** "Thou shalt fear the Lord thy God, and serve him . . ." (Deut 6:13), or **(5b)** ". . . hearken diligently unto my commandments which I command you this day, to love the Lord your God, and to serve him . . ." (Deut 11:13). **(6)** All nations are commanded: **(6a)** "Serve the Lord with gladness . . ." (Ps 100:2). **(6b)** In the reign of Messiah, "all nations shall serve him" (Ps 72:11). **(7)** The verb and the noun may be used together as in Num 8:11 "And Aaron shall offer the Levites before the Lord . . . that they may execute the service of the Lord." Syn.: 5650, 5656, 8334. See: TWOT—1553; BDB—712b, 1104d.

5648. עֲבַד {28x} **ʿăbad** (Aram.), *ab-bad';* corresp. to 5647; to *do, make, prepare, keep,* etc.:—do {10x}, made {7x}, cut {2x}, do + 1934 {2x}, do + 5922 {1x}, worketh {1x}, executed + 1934 {1x}, goeth {1x}, kept {1x}, moved {1x}, wrought {1x}. See: TWOT—2896; BDB—1104d.

5649. עֲבַד {7x} **ʿăbad** (Aram.), *ab-bad';* from 5648; a *servant:*—servant {7x}. See: TWOT—2896a; BDB—1105a.

5650. עֶבֶד {800x} **ʿebed**, *eh'-bed;* from 5647; a *servant:*—servant {744x}, manservant {23x}, bondman {21x}, bondage {10x}, bondservant {1x}, on all sides {1x}.

ʿEbed means "servant." **(1)** *ʿEbed* first appears in Gen 9:25: "And he said, Cursed *be* Canaan; a servant of servants shall he be unto his brethren." **(2)** A "servant" may be bought with money (Ex 12:44) or hired (1 Kin 5:6). **(3)** The often repeated statement of God's redemption of Israel is: "I brought you out of the house of bondage" (Ex 13:3). **(4)** *ʿEbed* was used as a mark of humility and courtesy, as in Gen 18:3: "Pass not away, I pray thee, from thy servant" (cf. Gen 42:10). **(5)** Moses addressed God: "O my Lord, I am not eloquent, neither heretofore, nor since thou hast spoken unto thy servant . . ." (Ex 4:10). **(6)** It is the mark of those called by God, as in Ex 14:31: "[They] believed the Lord, and his servant Moses." **(6b)** God claimed: "For unto me the children of Israel are servants . . ." (Lev 25:55; cf. Is 49:3). **(6c)** "And the Lord spake by his servants the prophets . . ." (2 Kin 21:10). **(6d)** The psalmist said: "I am thy servant" (116:16 indicating the appropriateness of the title to all believers).

(7) Of prime significance is the use of "my servant" for the Messiah in Isaiah (42:1–7; 49:1–7; 50:4–10; 52:13–53:12). **(7a)** Israel was a blind and deaf "servant" (Is 42:18–22). **(7b)** So the Lord called "my righteous servant" (Is 53:11; cf. 42:6) **(7b1)** "[to bear] the sin of many" (Is 53:12), **(7b2)** "that thou mayest be my salvation unto the end of the earth" (Is 49:6). **(8)** The "servant" was not a free man. **(8a)** He was subject to the will and command of his master. **(8b)** But one might willingly and lovingly submit to his master (Ex 21:5), remaining in his service when he was not obliged to do so: "And if the servant shall plainly say, I love my master, my wife, and my children; I will not go out free:" **(8c)** Hence it is a very fitting description of the relationship of man to God. Syn.: 5647, 5656, 8334. See: TWOT—1553a; BDB—713d, 1105a.

5651. עֶבֶד {6x} **ʿEbed**, *eh'-bed;* the same as 5650; *Ebed,* the name of two Isr.:—Ebed {6x}. See: BDB—711c.

5652. עֲבָד {1x} **ʿăbâd**, *ab-awd';* from 5647; a *deed:*—work {1x}. See: TWOT—1553b; BDB—715a.

5653. עַבְדָּא {2x} **ʿAbdâʾ**, *ab-daw';* from 5647; *work; Abda,* the name of two Isr.:—Abda {2x}. See: BDB—715a.

5654. עֹבֵד אֱדוֹם {20x} **ʿObêd ʾĔdôwm**, *o-bade' ed-ome';* from the act. part. of 5647 and 123; *worker of Edom; Obed-Edom,* the name of five Isr.:—Obed-edom {20x}. See: BDB—714d.

5655. עַבְדְּאֵל {1x} **ʿAbdᵉʾêl**, *ab-deh-ale';* from 5647 and 410; *serving God; Abdeel,* an Isr.:—Abdeel {1x}. See: BDB—715a. comp. 5661.

5656. עֲבֹדָה {141x} **ʿăbôdâh**, *ab-o-daw';* or
עֲבוֹדָה **ʿăbôwdâh**, *ab-o-daw';* from 5647; *work* of any kind:—service {96x}, servile {12x}, work {10x}, bondage {8x}, act {2x}, serve {2x}, servitude {2x}, tillage {2x}, effect {1x}, labour {1x}, misc. {5x} = + bondservant, ministering (-try), office, use, × wrought.

ʿAbodah, as a noun, means "work; labors; service." **(1)** This noun appears 141 times in the Hebrew Old Testament, and **(1a)** the occurrences are concentrated in Numbers and Chronicles. **(1b)** *ʿAbodah* is first used in Gen 29:27: "We will give thee this also for the service which thou shalt serve with me. . . ." **(2)** The more general meaning of *ʿabodah* is close to our English word for "work.": **(2a)** "Labor" in the field: "And over them that did the work of the field for tillage of the ground *was* Ezri the son of Chelub:" (1 Chr 27:26), **(2b)** daily "work" from morning till evening: "Man goeth forth unto his work and to his labour until the evening" (Ps 104:23), and **(2c)** "work" in the linen industry: "The sons of Shelah the son of Judah *were,* Er the father of Lecah, and Laadah the father of Mareshah, and the families of the house of them that wrought fine linen, of the house of Ashbea" (1 Chr 4:21) indicate a use with which we are familiar.

(3) To this, it must be added that *ʿabodah* may also be "hard labor," **(3a)** such as that of a slave: "And if thy brother *that dwelleth* by thee be waxen poor, and be sold unto thee; thou shalt not compel him to serve as a bondservant:" (Lev 25:39) or **(3b)** of Israel while in Egypt: "Go ye, get you straw where ye can find it: yet not aught of your work shall be diminished" (Ex 5:11). **(4)** The more limited meaning of the word is "service." Israel was in the "service" of the Lord: "But that it may be a witness between us, and you, and our generations after us, that we might do the service of the Lord before him with our burnt offerings, and with our sacrifices, and with our peace offerings; that your children may not say to our children in time to come, Ye have no part in the Lord" (Josh 22:27). **(5)** Whenever God's people were not fully dependent on Him, they had to choose to serve the Lord God or human kings with their requirements of forced "labor" and tribute: "Nevertheless they shall be his servants; that they may know my service, and the service of the kingdoms of the countries" (2 Chr 12:8).

(6) Further specialization of the usage is in association with the tabernacle and the temple. **(6a)** The priests were chosen for the "service" of the Lord: "And they shall keep his charge, and the charge of the whole congregation before the tabernacle of the congregation, to do the service of the tabernacle" (Num 3:7) **(6b)** The Levites also had many important functions in and around the temple; they sang, played musical instruments, and were secretaries, scribes, and doorkeepers (2 Chr 34:13; cf. 8:14). **(7)** Thus anything, people and objects (1 Chr 28:13), associated with the temple was considered to be in the "service" of the Lord. **(8)** Our understanding of "worship," with all its components, comes close to the Hebrew meaning of *ʿabodah* as "service"; cf. "So all the service of the Lord was prepared the same day, to keep the passover, and to offer burnt offerings upon the altar of the Lord, according to the commandment of King Josiah" (2 Chr 35:16). Syn.: 5647, 5650, 8334. See: TWOT—1553c; BDB—715a, 1105a.

5657. עֲבֻדָּה {2x} ʻăbuddâh, *ab-ood-daw';* pass. part. of 5647; something *wrought,* i.e. (concr.) *service:*—household {1x}, store of servants {1x}. See: TWOT—1553d; BDB—715c.

5658. עַבְדּוֹן {8x} ʻAbdôwn, *ab-dohn';* from 5647; *servitude; Abdon,* the name of a place in Pal. and of four Isr.:—Abdon {8x}. See: BDB—715c, 716c, 720d. comp. 5683.

5659. עַבְדוּת {3x} ʻabdûwth, *ab-dooth';* from 5647; *servitude:*—bondage {3x}. See: TWOT—1553e; BDB—715c.

5660. עַבְדִּי {3x} ʻAbdîy, *ab-dee';* from 5647; *serviceable; Abdi,* the name of two Isr.:—Abdi {3x}. See: BDB—715d.

5661. עַבְדִּיאֵל {1x} ʻAbdîyʼêl, *ab-dee-ale';* from 5650 and 410; *servant of God; Abdiel,* an Isr.:—Abdiel {1x}. See: BDB—715d. comp. 5655.

5662. עֹבַדְיָה {20x} ʻÔbadyâh, *o-bad-yaw';* or

עֹבַדְיָהוּ ʻÔbadyâhûw, *o-bad-yaw'-hoo;* act. part. of 5647 and 3050; *serving Jah; Obadjah,* the name of thirteen Isr.:—Obadiah {20x}. See: BDB—715d.

5663. עֶבֶד מֶלֶךְ {6x} ʻEbed Melek, *eh'-bed meh'-lek;* from 5650 and 4428; *servant of a king; Ebed-Melek,* a eunuch of *Zezekiah:*—Ebed-melech {6x}. See: BDB—715a.

5664. עֲבֵד נְגוֹ {1x} ʻĂbêd Nᵉgôw, *ab-ade' neg-o';* the same as 5665; *Abed-Nego,* the Bab. name of one of Daniel's companions:—Abed-nego {1x}. See: BDB—715a, 1105a.

5665. עֲבֵד נְגוֹא {4x} ʻĂbêd Nᵉgôwʼ (Aram.), *ab-ade' neg-o';* of for. or.; *Abed-Nego,* the name of Azariah:—Abed-nego {4x}. See: BDB—1105a.

5666. עָבָה {3x} ʻâbâh, *aw-baw';* a prim. root; to *be dense:*—thicker {2x}, thick {1x}. See: TWOT—1554; BDB—716a.

5667. עֲבוֹט {4x} ʻăbôwṭ, *ab-ote';* or

עֲבֹט ʻăbôṭ, *ab-ote';* from 5670; a *pawn:*—pledge {4x}. See: TWOT—1555a; BDB—716b.

5668. עָבוּר {8x} ʻâbûwr, *aw-boor';* or

עָבֻר ʻâbûr, *aw-boor';* pass. part. of 5674; prop. *crossed,* i.e. (abstr.) *transit;* used only adv. on *account* of, in *order* that:—sake {1x}, that {1x}, because of {1x}, to {3x}, to the intent that {1x}. See: TWOT—1556g; BDB—721a.

5669. עָבוּר {2x} ʻâbûwr, *aw-boor';* the same as 5668; *passed,* i.e. *kept* over; used only of *stored* grain:—old corn {2x}. See: TWOT—1556f; BDB—721a.

5670. עָבַט {6x} ʻâbaṭ, *aw-bat';* a prim. root; to *pawn;* caus. to *lend* (on security); fig. to *entangle:*—lend {2x}, fetch {1x}, borrow {1x}, surely {1x}, break {1x}. See: TWOT—1555; BDB—716b.

5671. עַבְטִיט {1x} ʻabṭîyṭ, *ab-teet';* from 5670; something *pledged,* i.e. (collect.) *pawned* goods:—thick clay {1x}. See: TWOT—1555b; BDB—716b.

5672. עֲבִי {4x} ʻăbîy, *ab-ee';* or

עֳבִי ʻŏbîy, *ob-ee';* from 5666; *density,* i.e. *depth* or *width:*—thickness {2x}, thick {2x}. See: TWOT—1554a; BDB—716a, 728a. comp. 5645.

5673. עֲבִידָה {6x} ʻăbîydâh (Aram.), *ab-ee-daw';* from 5648; *labor* or *business:*—work {3x}, affairs {2x}, service {1x}. See: TWOT—2896b; BDB—1105a.

5674. עָבַר {559x} ʻâbar, *aw-bar';* a prim. root; to *cross* over; used very widely of any *transition* (lit. or fig.; tran., intr., intens., or caus.); spec. to *cover* (in copulation):—(pass, went, . . .) over {174x}, pass {108x}, (pass, etc . . .) through {58x}, pass by {27x}, go {26x}, (put, pass, etc . . .) away {24x}, pass on {19x}, misc. {123x} = alienate, alter, × at all, beyond, bring (over, through), carry over, (over-) come (on, over), conduct (over), convey over, current, deliver, enter, escape, fail, gender, get over, lay, meddle, overrun, make partition, (cause to, make) + proclaim (-amation), perish, provoke to anger, rage, + raiser of taxes, remove, send over, set apart, + shave, cause to (make) sound, × speedily, × sweet smelling, (make to) transgress (-or), translate, [way-] faring man, be wrath.

This word communicates the idea of transgression, or crossing over the boundary of right and entering the forbidden land of wrong. *'Abar,* **the masculine form,** means "to pass away, pass over." **(1)** The verb refers primarily to spatial movement, to "moving over, through, or away from." **(1a)** This basic meaning can be used of "going over or through" a particular location to get to the other side, as when Jacob "crossed over" the Euphrates to escape Laban (Gen 31:21). **(1b)** Another specific use of this general meaning is to pass through something; Ps. 8:8 speaks of whatever "passes through" the sea as being under Adam's control. **(1c)** *'Abar* can also merely mean "to go as far as"—Amos tells his audience not to "cross over" to Beer-sheba (Amos 5:5). **(2)** "To go as far as" an individual is to overtake him: "But howsoever, *said he,* let me run. And he said unto him, Run. Then Ahimaaz ran by the way of the plain, and overran [*'abar*] Cushi" (2 Sa 18:23). **(3)** Abram "passed through" Canaan as far as Mamre; he did not go out of the land (cf. Gen 12:6). **(4)** The word can also be used of "passing by" something; Abraham begged the three men not "to pass by" him but to stop and refresh themselves: "And said, My Lord, if now I have found favour in thy sight, pass not away, I pray thee, from thy servant" (Gen 18:3).

(5) *'Abar* is sometimes used of "passing over" a law, order, or covenant as if it were not binding. When the people decided to enter Palestine against the command of God, Moses said, "Wherefore now do ye transgress the commandment of the Lord?" (Num 14:41). **(6)** This verb first occurs in Gen 8:1 where it means "pass over on top of.": "And God remembered Noah, and every living thing, and all the cattle that *was* with him in the ark: and God made a wind to pass over the earth, and the waters asswaged;" God caused the wind "to pass over" the flood waters and to carry them away. **(7)** The word can also mean "to pass away," to cease to be, as in Gen 50:4 where the days of mourning over Jacob "were past." **(8)** A number of technical phrases where this root has a regular and specialized meaning appear. **(8a)** For example, one who "passes over" the sea is a seafarer or sailor (Is 23:2). **(8b)** *'Abar* is used in business affairs with silver or money in the sense of reckoning money according to the "going" (passing) rate (Gen 23:16ff.). **(9)** In Song 5:5 the verb is used to mean "flow" as what a liquid does ("flowing" or "liquid" myrrh): "I rose up to open to my beloved; and my hands dropped [*'abar*] *with* myrrh, and my fingers *with* sweet smelling myrrh, upon the handles of the lock."

(10) The phrase "pass over to be numbered" is a phrase meaning to move from one status to another (to move into the ranks of the militia) in Ex 30:13–14: "This they shall give, every one that passeth among them that are numbered, half a shekel after the shekel of the sanctuary: (a shekel *is* twenty gerahs:) an half shekel *shall be* the offering of the LORD. Every one that passeth among them that are numbered, from twenty years old and above, shall give an offering unto the LORD." **(11)** The intensive stem of *'abar* is used in two special senses: **(11a)** of "overlaying" with precious metals: "So Solomon overlaid the house within with pure gold: and he made a partition by the chains of gold before the oracle; and he overlaid it with gold" (1 Kin 6:21), and **(11b)** of the ox's act of making a cow pregnant: "Their bull gendereth [*'abar*], and faileth not; their cow calveth, and casteth not her calf" (Job 21:10).

(12) The verb also has special meanings in the causative stem: **(12a)** "to devote" the firstborn to the Lord: "That thou shalt set apart [*'abar*] unto the LORD all that openeth the matrix, and every firstling that cometh of a beast which thou hast; the males *shall be* the LORD'S" (Ex 13:12); **(12b)** "to offer" a child by burning him in fire: "There shall not be found among you *any one* that maketh his son or his daughter to pass through [*'abar*] the fire, *or* that useth divination, *or* an observer of times, or an enchanter, or a witch," (Deut 18:10); **(12c)** "to make" a sound "come forth": "Then shalt thou cause the trumpet of the jubile to sound [*'abar*] on the tenth *day* of the seventh month, in the day of atonement shall ye make the trumpet sound throughout all your land." (Lev 25:9); **(12c)** "to sovereignly transfer" a kingdom or cause it to pass over to another's leadership: "To translate [*'abar*] the kingdom from the house of Saul, and to set up the throne of David over Israel and over Judah, from Dan even to Beersheba" (2 Sa 3:10); **(12d)** "to put away or cause to cease": "And he took away [*'abar*] the sodomites out of the land, and removed all the idols that his fathers had made" (1 Kin 15:12); **(12e)** and "to turn" something "away": "Turn away [*'abar*] mine eyes from beholding vanity; *and* quicken thou me in thy way" (Ps 119:37).

(13) 'Abarah, **the feminine noun form** which occurs twice, means "crossing or ford": "And there went over a ferry boat to carry over ['abarah] the king's household, and to do what he thought good. And Shimei the son of Gera fell down before the king, as he was come over ['abarah] Jordan" (2 Sa 19:18). **(14)** *'Abar,* **as a verb,** occurs only when it refers to sin. **(15)** *'Abar* often carries the sense of "transgressing" a covenant or commandment—i.e., the offender "passes beyond" the limits set by God's law and falls into transgression and guilt. **(15a)** This meaning appears in Num 14:41: "And Moses said, wherefore now do ye transgress the commandment of the Lord? but it shall not prosper." **(15b)** Another example is in Judg 2:20: "And the anger of the Lord was hot against Israel; and he said, Because that this people hath transgressed my covenant which I commanded their fathers, and have not hearkened unto my voice" (cf. 1 Sa 15:24; Hos 8:1).

(16) Most frequently, *'abar* illustrates the motion of "crossing over" or "passing over." **(16a)** This word refers to crossing a stream or boundage ("pass through," Num 21:22), **(16b)** invading a country ("passed over," Judg 11:32), **(11c)** crossing a boundary against a hostile army ("go over," 1 Sa 14:4), **(16d)** marching over ("go over," Is 51:23), **(16e)** overflowing the banks of a river or other natural barriers ("pass through," Is 23:10), **(16f)** passing a razor over one's head ("come upon," Num 6:5), and **(16g)** the passing of time ("went over," 1 Chr 29:30). See: TWOT—1556; BDB—716d, 720d, 1105b.

5675. עֲבַר {14x} ʿăbar (Aram.), *ab-ar';* corresp. to 5676:—beyond {7x}, side {7x}. See: TWOT—2897; BDB—1105a.

5676. עֵבֶר {91x} ʿêber, *ay'-ber;* from 5674; prop. a region *across;* but used only adv. (with or without a prep.) on the *opposite* side (espec. of the Jordan; usually mean. the *east*):—side {58x}, beyond {21x}, straight {3x}, passage {2x}, by {1x}, from {1x}, other {1x}, against {1x}, over {1x}, quarter {1x}, Strong's synonym {1x}.

'Eber, which occurs 91 times, refers to the **(1)** "side": "Now it came to pass upon a day, that Jonathan the son of Saul said unto the young man that bare his armour, Come, and let us go over to the Philistines' garrison, that *is* on the other side. But he told not his father" (1 Sa 14:1) or **(2)** "edge" of something: "And thou shalt make two rings of gold, and thou shalt put them upon the two ends of the breastplate in the border thereof, which *is* in the side of the ephod inward" (Ex 28:26). **(3)** When speaking of rivers or seas, *'eber* means the "edge or side opposite the speaker" or "the other side": "For we have heard how the LORD dried up the water of the Red sea for you, when ye came out of Egypt; and what ye did unto the two kings of the Amorites, that *were* on the other side Jordan, Sihon and Og, whom ye utterly destroyed" (Josh 2:10). Syn.: 4569, 5676, 5680. See: TWOT—1556a; BDB—719b, 1105a.

5677. עֵבֶר {15x} ʿÊber, *ay'-ber;* the same as 5676; *Eber,* the name of two patriarchs and four Isr.:—*Eber* {13x}, Heber {2x}. See: BDB—720a

5678. עֶבְרָה {34x} ʿebrâh, *eb-raw';* fem. of 5676; an *outburst* of passion:—wrath {31x}, rage {2x}, anger {1x}. See: TWOT—1556d; BDB—720c.

5679. עֲבָרָה {3x} ʿăbârâh, *ab-aw-raw';* from 5674; a *crossing*-place:—ferry boat {1x}, variant {2x}. See: TWOT—1556c; BDB—720b.

5680. עִבְרִי {34x} ʿIbrîy, *ib-ree';* patron. from 5677; an *Eberite* (i.e. Hebrew) or desc. of Eber:—Hebrew {29x}, Hebrew woman {2x}, Hebrew + 376 {1x}, Hebrewess {1x}, Hebrew man {1x}.

'Ibriy means "Hebrew." **(1)** The origin and meaning of this word, which appears 34 times, is much debated. **(2)** The word is an early generic term for a variety of Semitic peoples and is somewhat akin to our word barbarian. **(3)** So Abram is identified as a "Hebrew" (Gen 14:13). **(4)** This ethnic term indicates family origin whereas the term "sons of Israel" is a political and religious term. **(5)** Unquestionably in the ancient Near East "Hebrew" was applied to a far larger group than the Israelites. **(6)** The word occurs in Ugaritic, Egyptian, and Babylonian writings describing a diverse mixture of nomadic wanderers or at least those who appear to have at one time been nomadic. **(7)** Sometimes the word seems to be a term of derision. Such usage recalls 1 Sa 29:3, where the Philistine leaders asked Achish, "What do these Hebrews here?" **(8)** There is considerable debate about identifying Hebrew with the well-known Habiru (Semitic warlords) who occupied Egypt in the first half of the second millennium B.C. Syn.: 4569, 5674, 5676. See: BDB—720a.

5681. עִבְרִי {1x} ʿIbrîy, *ib-ree';* the same as 5680; *Ibri,* an Isr.:—Ibri {1x}. See: BDB—720b.

5682. עֲבָרִים {4x} ʿĂbârîym, *ab-aw-reem';* plur. of 5676; regions *beyond; Abarim,* a place in Pal.:—Abarim {4x}. See: BDB—720d.

5683. עֶבְרֹן {1x} ʿEbrôn, *eb-rone';* from 5676; *transitional; Ebron,* a place in Pal.:—Hebron {1x}. See: BDB—715c, 720d.

5684. עֶבְרֹנָה {2x} ʿEbrônâh, *eb-raw-naw';* fem. of 5683; *Ebronah,* a place in the Desert:—*Ebronah* {2x}. See: BDB—720d.

5685. עָבַשׁ {1x} ʿâbash, *aw-bash';* a prim. root; to *dry* up:—rotten {1x}. See: TWOT—1557; BDB—721b.

5686. עָבַת {1x} ʿâbath, *aw-bath';* a prim. root; to *interlace,* i.e. (fig.) to *pervert:*—wrap it up {1x}. See: TWOT—1558; BDB—721c.

5687. עָבֹת {4x} ʿâbôth, *aw-both';* or

עָבוֹת ʿâbôwth, *aw-both';* from 5686; *intwined,* i.e. *dense:*—thick {4x}. See: TWOT—1558a; BDB—721c.

5688. עֲבֹת {25x} ʿăbôth, *ab-oth';* or

עֲבוֹת ʿăbôwth, *ab-oth';* or (fem.)

עֲבֹתָה ʿăbôthâh, *ab-oth-aw';* the same as 5687; something *intwined,* i.e. a *string, wreath* or *foliage:*—wreathen {7x}, cords {5x}, ban {4x}, boughs {3x}, rope {3x}, chains {2x}, branches {1x}. See: TWOT—1558b; BDB—716b, 721c.

5689. עָגַב {7x} ʿâgab, *aw-gab';* a prim. root; to *breathe* after, i.e. to *love* (sensually):—doted {6x}, lovers {1x}. This word is used of impure love. Syn.: 157, 1730, 2617, 2836, 3039, 7355. See: TWOT—1558b; BDB—721d.

5690. עֶגֶב {2x} ʿegeb, *eh'-gheb;* from 5689; *love* (concr.), i.e. *amative* words:—much love {1x}, very lovely {1x}. See: TWOT—1559a; BDB—721d.

5691. עֲגָבָה {1x} ʿăgâbâh, *ag-aw-baw';* from 5689; *love* (abstr.), i.e. *amorousness:*—inordinate love {1x}. See: TWOT—1559b; BDB—721d.

5692. עֻגָּה {7x} ʿuggâh, *oog-gaw';* from 5746; an *ash-cake* (as *round*):—cake (upon the hearth) {7x}. See: TWOT—1575a; BDB—722a, 728a.

עָגוֹל ʿâgôwl. See 5696.

5693. עָגוּר {2x} ʿâgûwr, *aw-goor';* pass. part. [but with act. sense] of an unused root mean. to *twitter;* prob. the *swallow:*—swallow {2x}. See: TWOT—1563a; BDB—723a.

5694. עָגִיל {2x} ʿâgîyl, *aw-gheel';* from the same as 5696; something *round,* i.e. a *ring* (for the ears):—earring {2x}. See: TWOT—1560e; BDB—722d.

5695. עֵגֶל {35x} ʿêgel, *ay-ghel;* from the same as 5696; a (male) *calf* (as *frisking* round), espec. one nearly grown (i.e. a *steer*):—bullock {2x}, calf {33x}. See: TWOT—1560a; BDB—722a.

5696. עָגֹל {6x} ʿâgôl, *aw-gole';* or

עָגוֹל ʿâgôwl, *aw-gole';* from an unused root mean. to *revolve, circular:*—round {6x}. See: TWOT—1560c; BDB—722c.

5697. עֶגְלָה {14x} ʿeglâh, *eg-law';* fem. of 5695; a (female) *calf,* espec. one nearly grown (i.e. a *heifer*):—calf {1x}, cow {1x}, heifer {12x}. See: TWOT—1560b; BDB—722b, 722c, 1026b.

5698. עֶגְלָה {2x} ʿEglâh, *eg-law';* the same as 5697; *Eglah,* a wife of David:—*Eglah* {2x}. See: BDB—722c.

5699. עֲגָלָה {25x} ʿăgâlâh, *ag-aw-law';* from the same as 5696; something *revolving,* i.e. a wheeled *vehicle:*—cart {15x}, chariot {1x}, wagon {9x}. See: TWOT—1560d; BDB—722c.

5700. עֶגְלוֹן {13x} ʿEglôwn, *eg-lawn';* from 5695; *vituline; Eglon,* the name of a place in Pal. and of a Moabitish king:—Eglon {13x}. See: BDB—722d.

5701. עָגַם {1x} ʿâgam, *aw-gam';* a prim. root; to *be sad:*—grieve {1x}. See: TWOT—1561; BDB—723a.

5702. עָגַן {1x} ʿâgan, *a -gan';* a prim. root; to *debar,* i.e. from marriage:—stay {1x}. See: TWOT—1562; BDB—723a.

5703. עַד {49x} ʿad, *ad;* from 5710; prop. a (peremptory) *terminus,* i.e. (by impl.) *duration,* in the sense of *advance* or *perpetuity* (substantially as a noun, either with or without a prep.):—ever {41x}, everlasting {2x}, end {1x}, eternity {1x}, ever + 5769 {1x}, evermore {1x}, old {1x}, perpetually {1x}. Syn.: 753, 1755, 5331, 6256, 6783, 6924. See: TWOT—1565a; BDB—723b, 723c.

5704. עַד {99x} ʿad, *ad;* prop. the same as 5703 (used as a prep., adv. or conjunc.; espec. with a prep.); *as far* (or *long,* or *much*) *as,* whether of space (*even unto*) or time (*during, while, until*) or degree (*equally with*):—{99x} = against, and, as, at, before, by (that), even (to), for (-asmuch as), [hither-] to, + how long, into, as long (much) as, (so) that, till, toward, until, when, while, (+ as) yet. See: TWOT—1565c; BDB—723b, 723d, 774b, 1105b.

5705. עַד {32x} ʿad (Aram.), *ad;* corresp. to 5704:—till {11x}, until {5x}, unto {4x}, ever {2x}, for {2x}, to {2x}, but at {1x}, even {1x}, hitherto + 3542 {1x}, mastery + 7981 {1x}, on {1x}, within {1x}. See: TWOT—2899; BDB—1105b.

5706. עַד {3x} ʿad, *ad;* the same as 5703 in the sense of the *aim* of an attack; *booty:*—prey {3x}. See: TWOT—1565b; BDB—723b, 723d.

5707. עֵד {69x} ʿêd, *ayd;* contr. from 5749; concr. a *witness;* abstr. *testimony;* spec. a *recorder,* i.e. *prince:*—witness {69x}.

'Ed means a "witness." **(1)** This word has to do with the legal or judicial sphere. **(1a)** First, in the area of civil affairs the word can mean someone who is present at a legal transaction and can confirm it if necessary. **(1b)** Such people worked as notaries, e.g., for an oral transfer of property: "Now this was the manner in former time in Israel concerning redeeming and concerning changing, for to confirrn all things. . . . And Boaz said unto the elders, and unto all the people, Ye are witnesses this day, that I have bought all that was Elimelech's, and all that was Chilion's and Mahlon's, of the hand of Naomi" (Ruth 4:7, 9). **(2)** At a later time the "witnesses" not only acted to attest the transaction and to confirm it orally, but they signed a document or deed of purchase. **(2a)** Thus "witness" takes on the new nuance of those able and willing to affirm the truth of a transaction by affixing their signatures: **(2b)** "And I gave the evidence of the purchase unto Baruch the son of Neriah . . . in the sight of Hanameel mine uncle's son, and in the presence of the witnesses that subscribed the book of the purchase . . ." (Jer 32:12).

(3) An object or animal(s) can signify the truthfulness of an act or agreement. **(3a)** Its very existence or the acceptance of it by both parties (in the case of the animals given to Abimelech in Gen 21:30) bears witness: "Now therefore come thou, let us make a covenant, I and thou; and let it be for a witness between me and thee [let it attest to our mutual relationship]" (Gen 31:44—the first biblical occurrence of the word). **(3b)** Jacob then set up a stone pillar or heap as a further "witness" (Gen 31:48) calling upon God to effect judgment if the covenant were broken. **(4)** In Mosaic criminal law the accused has the right to be faced by his/her accuser and to give evidence of his/her innocence. **(4a)** In the case of a newly married woman charged by her own husband, his testimony is sufficient to prove her guilty of adultery unless her parents have clear evidence proving her virginity before her marriage (Deut 22:14ff.). **(4b)** Usually the accused is faced with someone who either saw or heard of his guilt: "And if a soul sin, and hear the voice of swearing, and is a witness, whether he hath seen or known of it . . ." (Lev 5:1).

(5) Heavy penalties fell on anyone who lied to a court. **(5a)** The ninth commandment may well have immediate reference to such a concrete court situation (Ex 20:16). **(5b)** If so, it serves to sanction proper judicial procedure, to safeguard individuals from secret accusation and condemnation and giving them the right and privilege of self-defense. **(6)** In the exchange between Jacob and Laban mentioned above, Jacob also cites God as a "witness" (Gen 31:50) between them, the one who will see violations; God, however, is also the Judge: "If thou shalt afflict my daughters, or if thou shalt take *other* wives beside my daughters, no man *is* with us; see, God *is* witness betwixt me and thee." **(7)** Although human courts are (as a rule) to keep judge and "witness" separate, the "witnesses" do participate in executing the penalty upon the guilty party (Deut 17:7), even as God does: "The hands of the witnesses shall be first upon him to put him to death, and afterward the hands of all the people. So thou shalt put the evil away from among you." Syn.: 5749. See: TWOT—1576b; BDB—723b, 729c, 1113d.

5708. עֵד {1x} **ʿêd**, *ayd;* from an unused root mean. to *set* a period [comp. 5710, 5749]; the *menstrual* flux (as periodical); by impl. (in plur.) *soiling:*—filthy {1x}. See: TWOT—1564a; BDB—723b, 726b.

עֹד **ʿôd**. See 5750.

5709. עֲדָא {9x} **ʿădâʾ** (Aram.), *ad-aw';* or

עֲדָה **ʿădâh** (Aram.), *ad-aw';* corresp. to 5710:—take away {3x}, passed {1x}, departed {1x}, altereth {1x}, took {1x}, pass away {1x}, removeth {1x}. See: TWOT—2898; BDB—1105b.

עֹדֵד **ʿÔdêd**. See 5752.

5710. עָדָה {10x} **ʿâdâh**, *aw-daw';* a prim. root; to *advance,* i.e. *pass* on or *continue;* caus. to *remove;* spec. to *bedeck* (i.e. bring an ornament upon):—deck . . . {6x}, adorn {2x}, passed {1x}, take away {1x}. See: TWOT—1565; BDB—723c, 725c, 1105b.

5711. עָדָה {8x} **ʿÂdâh**, *aw-daw';* from 5710; *ornament; Adah,* the name of two women:—*Adah* {8x}. See: BDB—725b.

5712. עֵדָה {149x} **ʿêdâh**, *ay-daw';* fem. of 5707 in the orig. sense of *fixture;* a stated *assemblage* (spec. a *concourse,* or gen. a *family* or *crowd*):—congregation {124x}, company {13x}, assembly {9x}, multitude {1x}, people {1x}, swarm {1x}.

ʿEdah means "congregation." **(1)** In ordinary usage, *ʿedah* refers to a "group of people." **(1a)** It occurs 149 times in the Old Testament, most frequently in the Book of Numbers. **(1b)** The first occurrence is in Ex 12:3, where the word is a synonym for qahal (6951), "assembly": "Speak ye unto all the congregation of Israel, saying, In the tenth *day* of this month they shall take to them every man a lamb, according to the house of *their* fathers, a lamb for an house:" **(2)** The most general meaning of *ʿedah* is "group," whether of animals—such as a swarm of bees (Judg 14:8), a herd of bulls (Ps 68:30), and the flocking together of birds (Hos 7:12)—or of people, such as the righteous (Ps 1:5), the evildoers (Ps 22:16), and the nations (Ps 7:7). **(3)** The most frequent reference is to the "congregation of Israel" (9 times), "the congregation of the sons of Israel" (26 times), "the congregation" (24 times), or "all of the congregation" (30 times). **(4)** Elders (Lev 4:15), family heads (Num 31:26), and princes (Num 16:2; 31:13; 32:2) were placed in charge of the "congregation" in order to assist Moses in a just rule. Syn.: 4150, 6951. See: TWOT—878a; BDB—417a, 726b, 729d. comp. 5713.

5713. עֵדָה {22x} **ʿêdâh**, *ay-daw';* fem. of 5707 in its techn. sense; *testimony:*—testimonies {22x}, witness {4x}. See: TWOT—1576c, 1576e; BDB—726b, 729d, 730a. comp. 5712.

5714. עִדּוֹ {10x} **ʿIddôw**, *id-do';* or

עִדּוֹא **ʿIddôwʾ**, *id-do';* or

עִדִּיא **ʿIddîyʾ**, *id-dee';* from 5710; *timely; Iddo* (or *Iddi*), the name of five Isr.:—Iddo {10x}. See: BDB—418a, 723b, 726b. comp. 3035, 3260.

5715. עֵדוּת {59x} **ʿêdûwth**, *ay-dooth';* fem. of 5707; *testimony:*—testimony {55x}, witness {4x}.

ʿEduwth means "testimony; ordinance." **(1)** This word refers to the Ten Commandments as a solemn divine charge or duty. **(1a)** In particular, it represents those commandments as written on the tablets and existing as a reminder and "testimony" of Israel's relationship and responsibility to God: "And he gave unto Moses, when he had made an end of communing with him upon Mount Sinai, two tables of testimony, tables of stone, written with the finger of God" (Ex 31:18). **(1c)** Elsewhere these tablets are called simply "the testimony": "And thou shalt put into the ark the testimony which I shall give thee" (Ex 25:16). **(1d)** Since they were kept in the ark, it became known as the "ark of the testimony" (Ex 25:22) or simply "the testimony": "As the Lord commanded Moses, so Aaron laid it up before the Testimony, to be kept" (Ex 16:34—the first biblical occurrence of the word). **(1e)** The tabernacle as the housing for the ark containing these tablets was sometimes called the "tabernacle of testimony" (Ex 38:21) or the "tent of the testimony" (Num 9:15).

(2) The word sometimes refers to the entire law of God: "The law of the Lord is perfect, converting the soul: the testimony of the Lord is sure, making wise the simple" (Ps 19:7). Here ʿedut is synonymously parallel to "law," making it a synonym to that larger concept. **(3)** Special or particular laws are sometimes called "testimonies": "And keep the charge of the Lord thy God, to walk in his ways, to keep his statutes, and his commandments, and his judgments, and his testimonies, as it is written in the law of Moses, that thou mayest prosper in all that thou doest, and whithersoever thou turnest thyself:" (1 Kin 2:3). **(4)** In Ps 122:4 the annual pilgrimage feasts are called "the testimony of Israel": "Whither the tribes go up, the tribes of the LORD, unto the testimony of Israel, to give thanks unto the name of the LORD." See: TWOT—1576f; BDB—726b, 730b.

5716. עֲדִי {13x} **ʿădîy**, *ad-ee';* from 5710 in the sense of *trappings; finery;* gen. an *outfit;* spec. a *headstall:*—mouth {2x}, ornament {11x}. See: TWOT—1566a; BDB—725d, 726b.

5717. עֲדִיאֵל {3x} **ʿĂdîyʾêl**, *ad-ee-ale';* from 5716 and 410; *ornament of God; Adiel,* the name of three Isr.:—Adiel {3x}. See: BDB—726a, 726b.

5718. עֲדָיָה {9x} **ʿĂdâyâh**, *ad-aw-yaw';* or

עֲדָיָהוּ **ʿĂdâyâhûw**, *ad-aw-yaw'-hoo;* from 5710 and 3050; *Jah has adorned; Adajah,* the name of eight Isr.:—Adaiah {9x}. See: BDB—726a, 726b.

5719. עָדִין {1x} **ʿâdîyn**, *aw-deen';* from 5727; *voluptuous:*—given to pleasures {1x}. See: TWOT—1567c; BDB—726d, 783b.

5720. עָדִין {4x} **ʿÂdîyn**, *aw-deen';* the same as 5719; *Adin,* the name of two Isr.:—Adin {4x}. See: BDB—726d.

5721. עֲדִינָא {1x} **ʿĂdîynâʾ**, *ad-ee-naw';* from 5719; *effeminacy; Adina,* an Isr.:—Adina {1x}. See: BDB—726d.

5722. עֲדִינוֹ {1x} **ʿădîynôw**, *ad-ee-no';* prob. from 5719 in the orig. sense of *slender* (i.e. a *spear*); *his spear:*—Adino {1x}. See: BDB—726d.

5723. עֲדִיתַיִם {1x} **ʿĂdîythayim**, *ad-ee-thah'-yim;* dual of a fem. of 5706; *double prey; Adithajim,* a place in Pal.:—Adithaim {1x}. See: BDB—726b.

5724. עַדְלַי {1x} **ʿAdlay**, *ad-lah'-ee;* prob. from an unused root of uncert. mean.; *Adlai,* an Isr.:—Adlai {1x}. See: BDB—726b.

5725. עֲדֻלָּם {8x} **ʿĂdullâm**, *ad-ool-lawm';* prob. from the pass. part. of the same as 5724; *Adullam,* a place in Pal.:—*Adullam* {8x}. See: BDB—726b.

5726. עֲדֻלָּמִי {3x} **ʿĂdullâmîy**, *ad-ool-law-mee';* patrial from 5725; an *Adullamite* or native of Adullam:—Adullamite {3x}. See: BDB—726c.

5727. עָדַן {1x} **ʿâdan**, *aw-dan';* a prim. root; to *be soft* or *pleasant;* fig. and refl. to *live voluptuously:*—delighted themselves {1x}. See: TWOT—1567; BDB—726c.

5728. עֲדֶן {2x} **ʿăden**, *ad-en';* or

עֲדֶנָּה **ʿădennâh**, *ad-en'-naw;* from 5704 and 2004; *till now:*—yet {2x}. See: TWOT—1565c?; BDB—725c, 727a.

5729. עֶדֶן {3x} **ʿEden**, *eh'-den;* from 5727; *pleasure; Eden,* a place in Mesopotamia:—Eden {3x}. See: BDB—726c, 727a.

5730. עֵדֶן {4x} **ʿêden**, *ay'-den;* or (fem.)

עֶדְנָה **ʿednâh**, *ed-naw';* from 5727; *pleasure:*—delicates {1x}, delights {1x}, pleasure {2x}. See: TWOT—1567a; BDB—726c, 726d. See also 1040.

5731. עֵדֶן {17x} **ʿÊden**, *ay'-den;* the same as 5730 (masc.); *Eden,* the region of Adam's home:—Eden {17x}. See: TWOT—1568; BDB—727a.

5732. עִדָּן {13x} **ʿiddân** (Aram.), *id-dawn';* from a root corresp. to that of 5708; a set *time;* tech. a *year:*—time {13x}. See: TWOT—2900; BDB—1105c.

5733. עַדְנָא {2x} **ʿAdnâʾ**, *ad-naw'* from 5727; *pleasure; Adna,* the name of two Isr.:—*Adna* {2x}. See: BDB—726c, 726d.

5734. עַדְנָה {2x} ʽ**Adnâh**, *ad-naw';* from 5727; *pleasure; Adnah,* the name of two Isr.:—*Adnah* {2x}. See: BDB—726c, 726d, 727a.

5735. עֲדְעָדָה {1x} ʽ**Ădʽâdâh**, *ad-aw-daw';* from 5712; *festival; Adadah,* a place in Pal.:—*Adadah* {1x}. See: BDB—727a, 793a.

5736. עָדַף {9x} ʽ**âdaph**, *aw-daf';* a prim. root; to *be* (caus. *have*) *redundant:*—remains {4x}, overplus {1x}, more {1x}, odd number {1x}, over and above {1x}, over {1x}. See: TWOT—1569; BDB—727a.

5737. עָדַר {11x} ʽ**âdar**, *aw-dar';* a prim. root; to *arrange,* as a battle, a vineyard (to *hoe*); hence, to *muster* and so to *miss* (or find *wanting*):—dig {2x}, fail {4x}, keep {1x}, keep rank {1x}, lack {3x}. See: TWOT—1570, 1571, 1572; BDB—727b, 727c.

5738. עֶדֶר {1x} ʽ**Eder**, *eh'-der;* from 5737; an *arrangement* (i.e. drove); *Eder,* an Isr.:—Ader {1x}. See: BDB—727d.

5739. עֵדֶר {38x} ʽ**êder**, *ay'-der;* from 5737; an *arrangement,* i.e. *muster* (of animals):—drove {4x}, flock {32x}, herds {2x}. See: TWOT—1572a; BDB—727c.

5740. עֵדֶר {3x} ʽ**Êder**, *ay'-der;* the same as 5739; *Eder,* the name of an Isr. and of two places in Pal.:—*Eder* {3x}. See: BDB—727d.

5741. עַדְרִיאֵל {2x} ʽ**Adrîyʼêl**, *ad-ree-ale';* from 5739 and 410; *flock of God; Adriel,* an Isr.:—Adriel {2x}. See: BDB—727b.

5742. עָדָשׁ {4x} ʽ**âdâsh**, *aw-dawsh';* from an unused root of uncert. mean.; a *lentil:*—lentiles {4x}. See: TWOT—1573; BDB—727d.

עַוָּא ʽ**Avvâʼ**. See 5755.

5743. עוּב {1x} ʽ**ûwb**, *oob;* a prim. root; to *be dense* or *dark,* i.e. to *becloud:*—cover with a cloud {1x}. See: TWOT—1574; BDB—728a, 743b, 726b.

5744. עוֹבֵד {10x} ʽ**Ôwbêd**, *o-bade';* act. part. of 5647; *serving; Obed,* the name of five Isr.:—Obed {10x}. See: BDB—714d.

5745. עוֹבָל {1x} ʽ**Ôwbâl**, *o-bawl';* of for. der.; *Obal,* a son of Joktan:—Obal {1x}. See: BDB—716c.

5746. עוּג {1x} ʽ**ûwg**, *oog;* a prim. root; prop. to *gyrate;* but used only as a denom. from 5692, to *bake* (round cakes on the hearth):—bake {1x}. See: TWOT—1575; BDB—728b.

5747. עוֹג {22x} ʽ**Ôwg**, *ogue;* prob. from 5746; *round; Og,* a king of Bashan:—Og {22x}. See: BDB—721d, 728b.

5748. עוּגָב {4x} ʽ**ûwgâb**, *oo-gawb';* or

עֻגָּב ʽ**uggâb**, *oog-gawb';* from 5689 in the orig. sense of *breathing;* a *reed*-instrument of music:—organ {2x}, flute {1x}. pipe {1x}. See: TWOT—1559c; BDB—721d, 728b.

5749. עוּד ʽ**ûwd**, *ood;* a prim. root; to *duplicate* or *repeat;* by impl. to *protest, testify* (as by reiteration); intens. to *encompass, restore* (as a sort of redupl.):—testify {15x}, protest {6x}, witness {6x}, record {3x}, charge {2x}, solemnly {2x}, take {3x}, admonished {1x}, misc. {7x} = earnestly, lift up, relieve, rob, stand upright, give warning.

ʽ*Uwd* means "to take as witness, bear witness, repeat, admonish, warn, assure protection, relieve." **(1)** In 1 Kin 21:10 ʽ*uwd* means "to bear witness": "And set two men, sons of Belial, before him, to bear witness against him. . . ." **(2)** The word means "to warn" in Jer 6:10: "To whom shall I speak, and give warning, that they may hear?" **(3)** The Law of God is His testimony, because it is His own affirmation concerning His nature, attributes, and consequent demands. See: TWOT—1576, 1576d; BDB—728c, 729d.

5750. עוֹד {30x} ʽ**ôwd**, *ode;* or

עֹד ʽ**ôd**, *ode;* from 5749; prop. *iteration* or *continuance;* used only adv. (with or without prep.), *again, repeatedly, still, more:*—{30x} = again, × all life long, at all, besides, but, else, further (-more), henceforth, (any) longer, (any) more (-over), × once, since, (be) still, when, (good, the) while (having being), (as, because, whether, while) yet (within). See: TWOT—1576a; BDB—723b, 728c, 1105c.

5751. עוֹד {1x} ʽ**ôwd** (Aram.), *ode;* corresp. to 5750:—while {1x}. See: TWOT—2901; BDB—1105c.

5752. עוֹדֵד {3x} ʽ**Ôwdêd**, *o-dade';* or

עֹדֵד ʽ**Ôdêd**, *o-dade';* from 5749; *reiteration; Oded,* the name of two Isr.:—*Oded* {3x}. See: BDB—723b, 729c.

5753. עָוָה {17x} ʽ**âvâh**, *aw-vaw';* a prim. root; to *crook,* lit. or fig. (as follows):—iniquity {4x}, perverse {2x}, perversely {2x}, perverted {2x}, amiss {1x}, turn {1x}, crooked {1x}, bowed down {1x}, troubled {1x}, wickedly {1x}, wrong {1x}.

(1) The perversion or distortion of nature that is caused by evildoing is represented by this word. ʽ*Avah* means "to do iniquity." **(2)** ʽ*Avah* is often used as a synonym of chata' (2398), "to sin," as in Ps 106:6: "We have sinned [chata'] with our fathers, we have committed iniquity [ʽ*avah*], we have done wickedly [7561 – rasha']." See: TWOT—1577; BDB—730c, 731c, 1105c.

5754. עַוָּה {3x} ʽ**avvâh**, *av-vaw';* intens. from 5753 abb.; *overthrow:*—overturn {3x}. See: TWOT—1577b; BDB—730c, 731d.

5755. עִוָּה {4x} ʽ**Ivvâh**, *iv-vaw';* or

עַוָּא ʽ**Avvâʼ** (2 Kin 17:24) *av-vaw';* for 5754; *Ivvah* or *Avva,* a region of Assyria:—Ava {1x}, Ivah {3x}. See: BDB—727d, 731d.

עָוֹן ʽ**avôwn**. See 5771.

5756. עוּז {4x} ʽ**ûwz**, *ooz;* a prim. root; to *be strong;* caus. to *strengthen,* i.e. (fig.) to *save* (by flight):—gather . . . {2x}, gather {1x}, retire {1x}. See: TWOT—1578; BDB—731d.

5757. עַוִּי {1x} ʽ**Avvîy**, *av-vee';* patrial from 5755; an *Avvite* or native of Avvah (only plur.):—Avites {1x}. See: BDB—731d, 732a.

5758. עִוְיָא {1x} ʽ**ivyâʼ** (Aram.), *iv-yaw';* from a root corresp. to 5753; *perverseness:*—iniquities {1x}. See: TWOT—2902; BDB—1105c.

5759. עֲוִיל {2x} ʽ**ăvîyl**, *av-eel';* from 5764; a *babe:*—young children {1x}, little ones {1x}. See: TWOT—1579b; BDB—732a, 732b.

5760. עֲוִיל {1x} ʽ**ăvîyl**, *av-eel';* from 5765; *perverse* (morally):—ungodly {1x}. See: TWOT—1580d; BDB—732b, 732d.

5761. עַוִּים {3x} ʽ**Avvîym**, *av-veem';* plur. of 5757; *Avvim* (as inhabited by Avvites), a place in Pal. (with the art. pref.):—Avim {2x}, Avites {1x}. See: BDB—731d, 732a.

5762. עֲוִית {2x} ʽ**Ăvîyth**, *av-veeth';* or [perh.

עַיּוֹת ʽ**Ayôwth**, *ah-yōth',* as if plur. of 5857]

עַיּוּת ʽ**Ayûwth**, *ah-yōth';* from 5753; *ruin; Avvith* (or *Avvoth*), a place in Pal.:—Avith {2x}. See: BDB—732a, 743b.

5763. עוּל {5x} ʽ**ûwl**, *ool;* a prim. root; to *suckle,* i.e. *give milk:*—milch {2x}, young {1x}, ewes great with young {1x}, those that are young {1x}. See: TWOT—1579; BDB—732b.

5764. עוּל {2x} ʽ**ûwl**, *ool;* from 5763; a *babe:*—sucking child {1x}, infant {1x}. See: TWOT—1579a; BDB—732b.

5765. עָוַל {2x} ʽ**âval**, *aw-val';* a prim. root; to *distort* (morally):—deal unjustly {1x}, unrighteous {1x}.

This word is thought to designate the want of integrity and rectitude that is the accompaniment, if not the essential part, of wrongdoing. This word is taken in its original sense as a departure from that which equal and right. See: TWOT—1580; BDB—732c.

עוֹל ʽ**ôwl**. See 5923.

5766. עֶוֶל {55x} ʽ**evel**, *eh'-vel;* or

עָוֶל ʽ**âvel**, *aw'-vel;* and (fem.)

עַוְלָה ʽ**avlâh**, *av-law';* or

עוֹלָה ʽ**ôwlâh**, *o-law';* or

עֹלָה ʽ**ôlâh**, *o-law';* from 5765; (moral) *evil:*—iniquity {36x}, wickedness {7x}, unrighteousness {3x}, unjust {2x}, perverseness {1x}, unjustly {1x}, unrighteously {1x}, wicked {1x}, wickedly {1x}, variant {2x}. See: TWOT—1580a, 1580b; BDB—732b, 732c, 732d, 759b, 763c.

5767. עַוָּל {5x} ʽ**avvâl**, *av-vawl';* intens. from 5765; *evil* (morally):—wicked {3x}, unjust {1x}, unrighteous {1x}. See: TWOT—1580c; BDB—732d.

עוֹלָה ʽ**ôwlâh**. See 5930.

5768. עוֹלֵל {20x} ʽ**ôwlêl**, *o-lale';* or

עֹלָל ʽ**ôlâl**, *o-lawl';* from 5763; a *suckling:*—children {13x}, infant {3x}, babes {2x}, child {1x}, little ones {1x}. See: TWOT—1579c; BDB—732d, 760c.

5769. עוֹלָם {439x} ʽ**ôwlâm**, *o-lawm';* or

עֹלָם ʽ**ôlâm**, *o-lawm';* from 5956; prop. *concealed,* i.e. the *vanishing* point; gen. time *out of mind* (past or future), i.e. (practically) *eternity;* freq. adv. (espec. with prep. pref.) *always:*—ever {272x}, everlasting {63x}, old {22x}, perpetual {22x}, evermore {15x}, never {13x}, time {6x}, ancient {5x}, world {4x}, always {3x}, alway {2x}, long {2x}, more {2x}, never + 408 {2x}, misc. {6x}.

ʽ*Olam* means "eternity; remotest time; perpetuity." **(1)** First, in a few passages the word means "eternity" in the sense of not being limited to the present. Thus, in Eccl. 3:11 we read that God had bound man to time and given him the capacity to live "above time" (i.e., to remember yesterday, plan for tomorrow, and consider abstract principles); yet He has not given him divine knowledge: "He hath made every thing beautiful in his time: also he hath set the world in their heart, so that no man can find out the work that God maketh from the beginning to the end."

(2) Second, the word signifies "remotest time" or "remote time." **(2a)** In 1 Chr 16:36, God is described as blessed "for ever and ever," or from the most distant past time to the most distant future time: "Blessed *be* the LORD God of Israel for ever and ever. And all the people said, Amen, and praised the LORD." **(2b)** In passages where God is viewed as the One who existed before the creation was brought into existence, ʽ*olam* means: **(2b1)** "at the very beginning": "Remember the former things [the beginning things at the very beginning] of old: for I am God, and there is none else . . ." (Is 46:9); or **(2b2)** "from eternity, from the pre-creation, till now": "Remember, O Lord, thy tender mercies and thy lovingkindnesses; for they have been ever of old [from eternity]" (Ps 25:6). **(3)** In other passages, the word means "from (in) olden times": ". . . Mighty men which were of old, men of renown" (Gen 6:4).

(4) In Is 42:14, the word is used hyperbolically meaning "for a long time": "I have long time holden my peace; I have been still, and refrained myself. . . ." **(5)** This word may include all the time between the ancient beginning and the present: "The prophets that have been before me and before thee of old prophesied . . ." (Jer 28:8). **(6)** The word can mean "long ago" (from long ago): "For [long ago] I have broken thy yoke, and burst thy bands . . ." (Jer 2:20). **(7)** In Josh 24:2, the word means "formerly; in ancient times." **(8)** The word is used in Jer 5:15, where it means "ancient": "Lo, I will bring a nation upon you from far, O house of Israel, saith the Lord: it is a mighty nation, it is an ancient nation. . . ." **(9)** When used with the negative, *ʻolam* can mean "never": "We are thine: thou never barest rule [literally, "not ruled from the most distant past"] over them . . ." (Is 63:19). **(10)** Similar meanings emerge when the word is used without a preposition and in a genitive relationship to some other noun.

(11) With the preposition ʻad, the word can mean **(11a)** "into the indefinite future": "An Ammonite or Moabite shall not enter into the congregation of the Lord; even to their tenth generation shall they not enter into the congregation of the Lord for ever" (Deut 23:3). **(11b)** The same construction can signify "as long as one lives": "I will not go up until the child be weaned, and then I will bring him, that he may appear before the Lord, and there abide for ever" (1 Sa 1:22). **(11c)** This construction then sets forth an extension into the indefinite future, beginning from the time of the speaker. **(12)** In the largest number of its occurrences, *ʻolam* appears with the preposition le. **(12a)** This construction is weaker and less dynamic in emphasis than the previous phrase, insofar as it envisions a "simple duration." **(12b)** This difference emerges in 1 Kin 2:33, where both phrases occur: "Their blood shall therefore return upon the head of Joab, and upon the head of his seed for ever (le *ʻolam*): but upon David, and upon his seed, and upon his house, and upon his throne, shall there be peace for ever (ʻad *ʻolam*) from the LORD." **(12b1)** Le *ʻolam* is applied to the curse set upon the dead Joab and his descendants. The other more dynamic phrase (ʻad *ʻolam*), applied to David and his descendants, emphasizes the ever-continued, ever-acting presence of the blessing extended into the "indefinite future."

(13) In Ex 21:6 the phrase le *ʻolam* means "as long as one lives": ". . . And his master shall bore his ear through with an awl; and he shall serve him for ever." **(13a)** This phrase emphasizes "continuity," "definiteness," and "unchangeability." **(13b)** This is its emphasis in Gen 3:22, the first biblical occurrence of *ʻolam:* ". . . And now, lest he put forth his hand, and take also of the tree of life, and eat, and live for ever. . . ." **(14)** The same emphasis on "simple duration" pertains when *ʻolam* is used in passages such as **(14a)** Ps 61:8, where it appears by itself: "So will I sing praise unto thy name for ever, that I may daily perform my vows." **(14b)** The parallelism demonstrates that *ʻolam* means "day by day," or "continually." **(15)** In Gen 9:16, the word (used absolutely) means the "most distant future": "And the bow shall be in the cloud; and I will look upon it, that I may remember the everlasting covenant between God and every living creature. . . ." **(16)** In other places, the word means "without beginning, without end, and ever-continuing": "Trust ye in the Lord for ever: for in the Lord Jehovah is everlasting strength" (Is 26:4). **(17)** The plural of this word is an intensive form. Syn.: 5331, 5703. See: TWOT—1631a; BDB—732d, 761d, 1106d.

5770. עָוַן {1x} **ʻâvan**, *aw-van';* denom. from 5869; to *watch* (with jealousy):—eyed {1x}. See: TWOT—1612; BDB—745a.

5771. עָוֹן {230x} **ʻâvôn**, *aw-vone';* or

עָווֹן **ʻâvôwn** (2 Kin 7:9; Ps 51:5 [7]), *aw-vone';* from 5753; *perversity,* i.e. (moral) *evil:*—iniquity {220x}, punishment {5x}, fault {2x}, Iniquities + 1697 {1x}, mischief {1x}, sin {1x}.

Avown means "iniquity; guilt; punishment." **(1)** This word is derived from the root ʻavah (5753), which means "to be bent, bowed down, twisted, perverted" or "to twist, pervert." **(2)** *ʻAvown* portrays sin as **(2a)** a perversion of life (a twisting out of the right way), **(2b)** a perversion of truth (a twisting into error), or **(2c)** a perversion of intent (a bending of rectitude into willful disobedience). **(3)** The word "iniquity" is the best single-word equivalent. **(4)** The first use of *ʻavown* comes from Cain's lips, where the word takes the special meaning of "punishment": "And Cain said unto the Lord, My punishment is greater than I can bear" (Gen 4:13). **(2)** The word signifies **(2a)** an offense, intentional or not, against God's law. **(2b)** This meaning is also most basic to the word *chatta't* (2403), "sin," in the Old Testament, and for this reason the words *chatta't* and *ʻawon* are virtually synonymous; "Lo, this [the live coal] hath touched thy [Isaiah's] lips; and thine iniquity [*ʻawon*] is taken away, and thy sin [*chatta't*] purged" (Is 6:7). **(3)** "Iniquity" as an offense to God's holiness is punishable. The individual is warned that the Lord punishes man's transgression: "But every one shall die for his own iniquity: every man that eateth the sour grape, his teeth shall be set on edge" (Jer 31:30).

(4) There is also a collective sense in that the one is responsible for the many: "Thou shalt not bow down thyself to them, nor serve them: for I the Lord thy God am a jealous God, visiting the iniquity of the fathers upon the children unto the third and fourth generation of them that hate me" (Ex 20:5). **(5)** No generation, however, was to think that it bore God's judgment for the "iniquity" of another generation: "Yet say ye, Why? doth not the son bear the iniquity of the father? When the son hath done that which is lawful and right, and hath kept all my statutes, and hath done them, he shall surely live. The soul that sinneth, it shall die. The son shall not bear the iniquity of the father, neither shall the father bear the iniquity of the son: the righteousness of the righteous shall be upon him, and the wickedness of the wicked shall be upon him" (Eze 18:19–20). **(6)** Israel went into captivity for the sin of their fathers and for their own sins: "And the heathen shall know that the house of Israel went into captivity for their iniquity; because they trespassed against me, therefore hid I my face from them, and gave them into the hand of their enemies: so fell they all by the sword" (Eze 39:23).

(7) Serious as "iniquity" is in the covenantal relationship between the Lord and His people, the people are reminded that He is a living God who willingly forgives "iniquity": "Keeping mercy for thousands, forgiving iniquity and transgression and sin, and that will by no means clear the guilty; visiting the iniquity of the fathers upon the children, and upon the children's children, unto the third and to the fourth generation" (Ex 34:7). **(8)** God expects **(8a)** confession of sin: "I acknowledged my sin unto thee, and mine iniquity have I not hid. I said, I will confess my transgressions unto the Lord; and thou forgavest the iniquity of my sin" (Ps 32:5), and **(8b)** a trusting, believing heart which expresses the humble prayer: "Wash me thoroughly from mine iniquity, and cleanse me from my sin" (Ps 51:2). **(9)** Isaiah 53 teaches that God put upon Jesus Christ our "iniquities" (v. 6), that He having been bruised for our "iniquities" (v. 5) might justify those who believe on Him: "He shall see of the travail of his soul, and shall be satisfied: by his knowledge shall my righteous servant justify many; for he shall bear their iniquities" (Is 53:11).

(10) The usage of ʻawon includes the whole area of sin, judgment, and "punishment" for sin. The Old Testament teaches that God's forgiveness of "iniquity" extends to the actual sin, the guilt of sin, God's judgment upon that sin, and God's punishment of the sin. "Blessed is the man unto whom the Lord imputeth not iniquity, and in whose spirit there is no guile" (Ps 32:2). **(11a)** The penitent wrongdoer recognized his "iniquity" in Is 59:12: "For our transgressions are multiplied before thee, and our sins testify against us: for our transgressions are with us; and as for our iniquities, we know them" (cf. 1 Sa 3:13). **(11b)** "Iniquity" is something to be confessed: **(11b1)** "And Aaron shall lay both his hands upon the head of the live goat, and confess over him all the iniquities of the children of Israel . . ." (Lev 16:21). **(11b2)** "And the seed of Israel . . . confessed their sins, and the iniquities of their fathers" (Neh 9:2; cf. Ps 38:18). **(12)** The grace of God may **(12a)** remove or forgive "iniquity": "And unto him he said, Behold, I have caused thine iniquity to pass from thee . . ." (Zec 3:4; cf. 2 Sa 24:10). **(12b)** His atonement may cover over "iniquity": "By mercy and truth iniquity is purged; and by the fear of the Lord men depart from evil" (Prov 16:6; cf. Ps 78:38).

(13) *ʻAvown* may refer to "the guilt of iniquity," as in Eze 36:31: "Then shall ye remember your own evil ways . . . and shall loathe yourselves in your own sight for your iniquities and for your abominations" (cf. Eze 9:9). **(14)** The word may also refer to "punishment for iniquity": "And Saul sware to her by the Lord, saying, As the Lord liveth, there shall no punishment happen to thee for this thing" (1 Sa 28:10). **(15)** In Ex 28:38, *ʻavown* is used as the object of natsaʼ (5375 - "to bear, carry away, forgive"): "And it shall be upon Aaron's forehead, that Aaron may bear (natsaʼ) the iniquity (*ʻavown*) of the holy things, which the children of Israel shall hallow in all their holy gifts; and it shall be always upon his forehead, that they may be accepted before the LORD." **(15a)** to suggest bearing the punishment for the "iniquity" of others. **(15b)** In Is 53:11, we are told that the servant of Yahweh bears the consequences of the "iniquities" of sinful mankind, including Israel. Syn: ʻAwon occurs frequently throughout the Old Testament in parallelism with other words related to sin, such as **(A)** chatta't (2403 - "sin") and **(B)** peshaʼ (6588 - "transgression"). **(B1)** Some examples are 1 Sa 20:1: "And David . . . said before Jonathan, what have I done? what is mine iniquity [5771 – *ʻawon*]? and what is my sin [2403 – *chatta't*] before thy father, that he seeketh my life?" (cf. Is 43:24; Jer 5:25). **(B2)** Also note Job 14:17: "My transgression [6588 – peshaʼ] is sealed up in a bag, and thou sewest up mine iniquity [5771 - 'awon]" (cf. Ps 107:17; Is 50:1). See: TWOT—1577a; BDB—730d, 733b, 773b, 1105c.

5772. עוֹנָה {1x} ʿôwnâh, *o-naw';* from an unused root appar. mean. to *dwell* together; sexual (*cohabitation*):—duty of marriage {1x}. See: TWOT—1650a; BDB—733b, 773b.

5773. עַוְעֶה {1x} ʿavʿeh, *av-eh';* from 5753; *perversity:*—perverse {1x}. See: TWOT—1577c; BDB—730c, 733b.

5774. עוּף {32x} ʿûwph, *oof;* a prim. root; to *cover* (with wings or obscurity); hence, (as denom. from 5775) to *fly;* also (by impl. of dimness) to *faint* (from the darkness of swooning):—fly {17x}, (fly, flee . . .) away {6x}, faint {3x}, brandish {1x}, shine forth {1x}, set {1x}, weary {1x}, variant {2x}. See: TWOT—1582, 1583, 1583c; BDB—733b, 734a, 746a, 1074a, 1105c.

5775. עוֹף {71x} ʿôwph, *ofe;* from 5774; a *bird* (as *covered* with feathers, or rather as *covering* with wings), often collect.:—fowl {59x}, bird {9x}, flying {2x}, flieth {1x}. See: TWOT—1582a; BDB—733d.

5776. עוֹף {2x} ʿôwph (Aram.), *ofe;* corresp. to 5775:—fowl {2x}. See: TWOT—2903; BDB—1105c.

5777. עוֹפֶרֶת {9x} ʿôwphereth, *o-feh'-reth;* or

עֹפֶרֶת ʿôphereth, *o-feh'-reth;* fem. part. act. of 6080; *lead* (from its *dusty* color):—lead {9x}. See: TWOT—1665b; BDB—780b.

5778. עוֹפַי {1x} ʿÔwphay, *o-fah'-ee;* from 5775; *birdlike; Ephai,* an Isr.:—Ephai {1x}. See: BDB—734a, 746a.

5779. עוּץ {2x} ʿûwts, *oots;* a prim. root; to *consult:*—take advice {1x}, take . . . together {1x}. See: TWOT—1584; BDB—734a.

5780. עוּץ {8x} ʿÛwts, *oots;* appar. from 5779; *consultation; Uts,* a son of Aram, also a Seirite, and the regions settled by them.:—Uz {8x}. See: BDB—734b.

5781. עוּק {2x} ʿûwq, *ook;* a prim. root; to *pack:*—be pressed {2x}. See: TWOT—1585; BDB—734b.

5782. עוּר {81x} ʿûwr, *oor;* a prim. root [rather ident. with 5783 through the idea of *opening* the eyes]; to *wake* (lit. or fig.):—(stir, lift . . . .) up {40x}, awake {25x}, wake {6x}, raise {6x}, arise {1x}, master {1x}, raised out {1x}, variant {1x}.

'Uwr means "to awake, stir up, rouse oneself, rouse." **(1)** Its first use in the Old Testament has the sense **(1a)** of "rousing" someone to action: "Awake, awake, Deborah" (Judg 5:12). **(1b)** This same meaning is reflected in Ps 7:6, where it is used in parallelism with "arise": "Arise, O Lord, in thine anger, . . . awake for me to the judgment that thou hast commanded." **(2)** *'Uwr* commonly signifies awakening out of ordinary sleep: "And the angel that talked with me came again, and waked me, as a man that is wakened out of his sleep," (Zec 4:1) or **(3)** out of the sleep of death: "So man lieth down, and riseth not: till the heavens *be* no more, they shall not awake, nor be raised out of their sleep" (Job 14:12). **(4)** In Job 31:29, it expresses the idea of "being excited" or "stirred up": "If I . . . lifted up myself when evil found him. . . ." **(5)** This verb is found several times in the Song of Solomon, for instance, **(5a)** in contrast with sleep: "I sleep, but my heart waketh . . ." (5:2). **(5b)** It is found three times in an identical phrase: ". . . that you stir not up, nor awake my love, till he please" (Song 2:7; 3:5; 8:4). See: TWOT—1587; BDB—BDB—734d.

5783. עוּר {1x} ʿûwr, *oor;* a prim. root; to *(be) bare:*—naked {1x}. See: TWOT—1588; BDB—735d.

5784. עוּר {1x} ʿûwr (Aram.), *oor; chaff* (as the *naked* husk):—chaff {1x}. See: TWOT—2904; BDB—1105c.

5785. עוֹר {99x} ʿôwr, *ore;* from 5783; *skin* (as *naked*); by impl. *hide, leather:*—skin {96x}, hide {2x}, leather {1x}. See: TWOT—1589a; BDB—736a.

5786. עָוַר {5x} ʿâvar, *aw-var';* a prim. root [rather denom. from 5785 through the idea of a *film* over the eyes]; to *blind:*—put out {3x}, blind {2x}. See: TWOT—1586; BDB—734c. See also 5895.

5787. עִוֵּר {26x} ʿivvêr, *iv-vare';* intens. from 5786; *blind* (lit. or fig.):—blind {25x}, blind men {1x}. See: TWOT—1586a; BDB—734c.

עוֹרֵב ʿôwrêb. See 6159.

5788. עִוָּרוֹן {3x} ʿivvârôwn, *iv-vaw-rone';* and (fem.)

עַוֶּרֶת ʿavvereth, *av-veh'-reth;* from 5787; *blindness:*—blindness {2x}, blind {1x}. See: TWOT—1586b, 1586c; BDB—734d.

5789. עוּשׁ {1x} ʿûwsh, *oosh;* a prim. root; to *hasten:*—assemble yourselves {1x}. See: TWOT—1590; BDB—736b.

5790. עוּת {1x} ʿûwth, *ooth;* for 5789; to *hasten,* i.e. *succor:*—speak {1x}. See: TWOT—1592; BDB—736c.

5791. עָוַת {11x} ʿâvath, *aw-vath';* a prim. root; to *wrest:*—pervert {3x}, crooked {2x}, bow {1x}, bow down {1x}, falsifying {1x}, overthrown {1x}, perversely {1x}, subvert {1x}. See: TWOT—1591; BDB—736c.

5792. עַוָּתָה {1x} ʿavvâthâh, *av-vaw-thaw';* from 5791; *oppression:*—my wrong {1x}. See: TWOT—1591a; BDB—736c.

5793. עוּתַי {2x} ʿÛwthay, *oo-thah'-ee;* from 5790; *succoring; Uthai,* the name of two Isr.:—Uthai {2x}. See: BDB—736d, 800d.

5794. עַז {23x} ʿaz, *az;* from 5810; *strong, vehement, harsh:*—strong {12x}, fierce {4x}, mighty {3x}, power {1x}, greedy {1x}, roughly {1x}, stronger {1x}. See: TWOT—1596a; BDB—736d, 738c.

5795. עֵז {74x} ʿêz, *aze;* from 5810; a she-*goat* (as *strong*), but masc. in plur. (which also is used ellipt. for *goat's hair*):—goat {63x}, kid + 1423 {5x}, kid {4x}, he {1x}, kids + 1121 {1x}. See: TWOT—1654a; BDB—736d, 777c, 1107c.

5796. עֵז {1x} ʿêz (Aram.), *aze;* corresp. to 5795:—goats {1x}. See: TWOT—2920a; BDB—1105d, 1107c.

5797. עֹז {93x} ʿôz, *oze;* or (fully)

עוֹז ʿôwz, *oze;* from 5810; *strength* in various applications (*force, security, majesty, praise*):—strength {60x}, strong {17x}, power {11x}, might {2x}, boldness {1x}, loud {1x}, mighty {1x}. See: TWOT—1596b; BDB—731d, 736d, 738d.

5798. עֻזָּא {14x} ʿUzzâʾ, *ooz-zaw';* or

עֻזָּה ʿUzzâh, *ooz-zaw';* fem. of 5797; *strength; Uzza* or *Uzzah,* the name of five Isr.:—Uzza {10x}, *Uzzah* {4x}. See: BDB—736d, 738a, 739b, 739c.

5799. עֲזָאזֵל {4x} ʿăzâʾzêl, *az-aw-zale';* from 5795 and 235; *goat of departure;* the *scapegoat:*—scapegoat {4x}. See: TWOT—1593; BDB—736d.

5800. עָזַב {215x} ʿâzab, *aw-zab';* a prim. root; to *loosen,* i.e. *relinquish, permit,* etc.:—forsake {129x}, leave {72x}, leave off {4x}, faileth {2x}, fortify {2x}, help {2x}, committeth {1x}, destitute {1x}, refuseth {1x}, surely {1x}.

'Azab means "to leave, forsake, abandon, leave behind, be left over, let go." **(1)** Basically *'azab* means "to depart from something," or "to leave." **(1a)** This is the meaning of the word in its first biblical appearance: "[For this cause] shall a man leave his father and his mother, and shall cleave unto his wife . . ." (Gen 2:24). **(1b)** A special nuance of the word is "to leave in the lurch," or to leave someone who is depending upon one's services. So Moses said to Hobab the Midianite (Kenite): "Leave us not [in the lurch] I pray thee; forasmuch as thou knowest how we are to encamp in the wilderness, and thou mayest be to us instead of eyes" (Num 10:31). **(2)** The word also carries the meaning "forsake," or "leave entirely." Such passages convey a note of finality or completeness. So Isaiah is to preach that ". . . the land that thou abhorrest shall be forsaken of both her kings" (Is 7:16). **(3)** In other places, the abandonment is complete but not necessarily permanent. God says that Israel is "as a woman forsaken and grieved in spirit. . . . For a small moment have I forsaken thee; but with great mercies will I gather thee" (Is 54:6–7).

(4) This word carries a technical sense of "completely and permanently abandoned" or "divorced." Isaiah employs this sense in 62:4: "Thou shalt no more be termed Forsaken; . . . but thou shalt be called [My delight is in her], and thy land [Married]. . . ." **(5)** Another special use of the word is "to disregard advice": "But he forsook the counsel of the old men which they had given him . . ." (1 Kin 12:8).**(6)** A second emphasis of *'azab* is "to leave behind," meaning to allow something to remain while one leaves the scene. In Gen 39:12, Joseph "left" his garment in the hand of Potiphar's wife and fled. **(7)** The word may also refer to an intentional "turning over one's possessions to another's trust," or "leaving something in one's control." Potiphar "left all that he had in Joseph's hand" (Gen 39:6). **(8)** In a somewhat different nuance, the word means to "let someone or something alone with a problem": "If thou see the ass of him that hateth thee lying under his burden, and wouldest forbear to help him . . ." (Ex 23:5). **(9)** Used figuratively, *'azab* means to "put distance between" in a spiritual or intellectual sense: "Cease from anger, and forsake wrath . . ." (Ps 37:8).

(10) The emphasis of the word is "to be left over," or "to take most of something and leave the rest behind": "And thou shalt not glean thy vineyard, neither shalt thou gather every grape of thy vineyard; thou shalt leave them [over] for the poor and stranger: I am the Lord your God" (Lev 19:10). **(11)** Finally, *'azab* can mean "to let go" or "allow to leave." The "stupid and senseless men" are those who make no provision for the future; they die leaving ("allowing it to go") their wealth to others (Ps 49:10). **(12)** A different nuance occurs in Ruth 2:16, where the verb means "to let something lie" on the ground. **(13)** *'Azab* can also mean "to give up": "He that covereth his sins shall not prosper: but whoso confesseth and forsaketh them [gives them up] shall have mercy" (Prov 28:13), and **(14)** the word can mean "to set free," as in 2 Chr 28:14: "So the armed men left the captives and the spoil before the princes and all the congregation." **(15)** *'Azab* can signify "let go," or "make it leave." Concerning evil, Zophar remarks, ". . . [The wicked] forsake it not, but keep it still within his mouth" (Job 20:13).

(16) *'Azab* can mean to "allow someone to do something," as in 2 Chr 32:31, where "God left [Hezekiah], to try him, that he might know all that was in his heart"; God "let" Hezekiah do whatever he wanted. **(17)** "Letting an activity go" may also signify its discontinuance: "I pray you, let us leave off this usury" (Neh 5:10). **(18)** *'Azab* is sometimes used in a judicial technical sense of "being free," which is the opposite of being in bondage. The Lord will vindicate His people, and will have compassion on His servants "when he seeth that their power is gone, and there is none shut up, or left" (Deut 32:36). See: TWOT—1594, 1595; BDB—736d, 738a, 1115a.

5801. עִזָּבוֹן {7x} **ʿizzâbôwn**, *iz-zaw-bone'*; from 5800 in the sense of *letting go* (for a price, i.e. *selling*); *trade*, i.e. the place (*mart*) or the payment (*revenue*):—fair {6x}, wares {1x}. See: TWOT—1594b; BDB—738a.

5802. עַזְבּוּק {1x} **ʿAzbûwq**, *az-book'*; from 5794 and the root of 950; *stern depopulator; Azbuk*, an Isr.:—Azbuk {1x}. See: BDB—738a, 739d.

5803. עַזְגָּד {4x} **ʿAzgâd**, *az-gawd'*; from 5794 and 1409; *stern troop; Azgad*, an Isr.:—*Azgad* {4x}. See: BDB—738a, 739d.

5804. עַזָּה {2x} **ʿAzzâh**, *az-zaw'*; fem. of 5794; *strong; Azzah*, a place in Pal.:—*Azzah* {18x}, Gaza {3x}. See: BDB—738a.

5805. עֲזוּבָה {1x} **ʿăzûwbâh**, *az-oo-baw'*; fem. pass. part. of 5800; *desertion* (of inhabitants):—forsaking {1x}. See: BDB—737d.

5806. עֲזוּבָה {4x} **ʿĂzûwbâh**, *az-oo-baw'*; the same as 5805; *Azubah*, the name of two Israelitesses:—Azubah {4x}. See: BDB—738a.

5807. עֱזוּז {3x} **ʿĕzûwz**, *ez-ooz'*; from 5810; *forcibleness:*—might {2x}, strength {1x}. See: TWOT—1596c; BDB—739b.

5808. עִזּוּז {2x} **ʿizzûwz**, *iz-zooz'*; from 5810; *forcible;* collect. and concr. an *army:*—strong {1x}, power {1x}. See: TWOT—1596d; BDB—739b.

5809. עַזּוּר {3x} **ʿAzzûwr**, *az-zoor'*; or
עַזֻּר **ʿAzzûr**, *az-zoor'*; from 5826; *helpful; Azzur*, the name of three Isr.:—Azur {2x}, *Azzur* {1x}. See: BDB—741a.

5810. עָזַז {12x} **ʿâzaz**, *aw-zaz'*; a prim. root; to *be stout* (lit. or fig.):—strengthen {6x}, prevail {3x}, strong {1x}, impudent {1x}, hardeneth {1x}. See: TWOT—1596; BDB—738b.

5811. עָזָז {1x} **ʿÂzâz**, *aw-zawz'*; from 5810; *strong; Azaz*, an Isr.:—*Azaz* {1x}. See: BDB—739b.

5812. עֲזַזְיָהוּ {3x} **ʿĂzazyâhûw**, *az-az-yaw'-hoo*; from 5810 and 3050; *Jah has strengthened; Azazjah*, the name of three Isr.:—Azaziah {3x}. See: BDB—739c.

5813. עֻזִּי {11x} **ʿUzzîy**, *ooz-zee'*; from 5810; *forceful; Uzzi*, the name of six Isr.:—Uzzi {11x}. See: BDB—739d.

5814. עֻזִּיָּא {1x} **ʿUzzîyâ'**, *ooz-zee-yaw'*; perh. for 5818; *Uzzija*, an Isr.:—Uzzia {1x}. See: BDB—739d.

5815. עֲזִיאֵל {1x} **ʿĂzîy'êl**, *az-ee-ale'*; from 5756 and 410; *strengthened of God; Aziël*, an Isr.:—Aziel {1x}. See: BDB—739d. comp. 3268.

5816. עֻזִּיאֵל {16x} **ʿUzzîy'êl**, *ooz-zee-ale'*; from 5797 and 410; *strength of God; Uzziël*, the name of six Isr.:—Uzziel {16x}. See: BDB—739c.

5817. עָזִּיאֵלִי {2x} **ʿOzzîy'êlîy**, *oz-zee-ay-lee'*; patron. from 5816; an *Uzziëlite* (collect.) or desc. of Uzziel:—Uzzielites {2x}. See: BDB—739c.

5818. עֻזִּיָּה {27x} **ʿUzzîyâh**, *ooz-zee-yaw'*; or
עֻזִּיָּהוּ **ʿUzzîyâhûw**, *ooz-zee-yaw'-hoo*; from 5797 and 3050; *strength of Jah; Uzzijah*, the name of five Isr.:—Uzziah {27x}. See: BDB—739c.

5819. עֲזִיזָא {1x} **ʿĂzîyzâ'**, *az-ee-zaw'*; from 5756; *strengthfulness; Aziza*, an Isr.:—Aziza {1x}. See: BDB—739c.

5820. עַזְמָוֶת {8x} **ʿAzmâveth**, *az-maw'-veth*; from 5794 and 4194; *strong* (one) *of death; Azmaveth*, the name of three Isr. and of a place in Pal.:—*Azmaveth* {8x}. See: BDB—730a. See also 1041.

5821. עַזָּן {1x} **ʿAzzân**, *az-zawn'*; from 5794; *strong* one; *Azzan*, an Isr.:—*Azzan* {1x}. See: BDB—740a.

5822. עָזְנִיָּה {2x} **ʿozniyâh**, *oz-nee-yaw'*; prob. fem. of 5797; prob. the *sea-eagle* (from its *strength*):—osprey {2x}. See: TWOT—1596e; BDB—740a.

5823. עָזַק {1x} **ʿâzaq**, *aw-zak'*; a prim. root; to *grub* over:—fenced {1x}. See: TWOT—1597; BDB—740a, 1105d.

5824. עִזְקָא {2x} **ʿizqâ'** (Aram.), *iz-kaw'*; from a root corresp. to 5823; a *signet*-ring (as engraved):—signet {2x}. See: TWOT—2905; BDB—1105d.

5825. עֲזֵקָה {7x} **ʿĂzêqâh**, *az-ay-kaw'*; from 5823; *tilled; Azekah*, a place in Pal.:—Azekah {7x}. See: BDB—740a.

5826. עָזַר {82x} **ʿâzar**, *aw-zar'*; a prim. root; to *surround*, i.e. *protect* or *aid:*—help {64x}, helper {11x}, holpen {3x}, succour {3x}, variant {1x}.

'Azar means "to help, assist, aid." **(1)** *'Azar* is first found in the Old Testament in Jacob's deathbed blessing of Joseph: ". . . The God of thy father, who shall help thee . . ." (Gen 49:25). **(2)** Help or aid comes from a variety of sources: Thirty-two kings "helped" Ben-hadad (1 Kin 20:6); one city "helps" another (Josh 10:33); even false gods are believed to be of "help" (2 Chr. 28:23). **(3)** Of course, the greatest source of help is God Himself; **(3a)** He is "the helper of the fatherless" (Ps 10:14). **(3b)** God promises: "I will help thee" (Is 41:10); "and the Lord shall help them, and deliver them . . ." (Ps 37:40). See: TWOT—1598; BDB—740a.

5827. עֶזֶר {1x} **ʿEzer**, *eh'-zer*; from 5826; *help; Ezer*, the name of two Isr.:—*Ezer* {1x}. See: BDB—740d. comp. 5829.

5828. עֵזֶר {21x} **ʿêzer**, *ay'-zer*; from 5826; *aid:*—help {19x}, help meet {2x}. See: TWOT—1598a; BDB—740c.

5829. עֵזֶר {4x} **ʿÊzer**, *ay'-zer*; the same as 5828; *Ezer*, the name of four Isr.:—Ezer {4x}. See: BDB—740d. comp. 5827.

עַזֻּר **ʿAzzûr**. See 5809.

5830. עֶזְרָא {22x} **ʿEzrâ'**, *ez-raw'*; a var. of 5833; *Ezra*, an Isr.:—*Ezra* {22x}. See: BDB—740d, 1105d.

5831. עֶזְרָא {3x} **ʿEzrâ'** (Aram.), *ez-raw'*; corresp. to 5830; *Ezra*, an Isr.:—*Ezra* {3x}. See: BDB—1105d.

5832. עֲזַרְאֵל {6x} **ʿĂzar'êl**, *az-ar-ale'*; from 5826 and 410; *God has helped; Azarel*, the name of five Isr.:—Azareel {5x}, Azarael {1x}. See: BDB—741a.

5833. עֶזְרָה {26x} **ʿezrâh**, *ez-raw'*; or
עֶזְרָת **ʿezrâth** (Ps 60:11 [13]; 108:12 [13]), *ez-rawth'*; fem. of 5828; *aid:*—help {25x}, helpers {1x}. See: TWOT—1598b; BDB—740d.

5834. עֶזְרָה {1x} **ʿEzrâh**, *ez-raw'*; the same as 5833; *Ezrah*, an Isr.:—*Ezrah* {1x}. See: BDB—741a.

5835. עֲזָרָה {9x} **ʿăzârâh**, *az-aw-raw'*; from 5826 in its orig. mean. of *surrounding;* an *inclosure;* also a *border:*—settle {6x}, court {3x}. See: TWOT—1599a; BDB—741c.

5836. עֶזְרִי {1x} **ʿEzrîy**, *ez-ree'*; from 5828; *helpful; Ezri*, an Isr.:—Ezri {1x}. See: BDB—741b.

5837. עַזְרִיאֵל {3x} **ʿAzrîy'êl**, *az-ree-ale'*; from 5828 and 410; *help of God; Azriël*, the name of three Isr.:—Azriel {3x}. See: BDB—741a.

5838. עֲזַרְיָה {48x} **ʿĂzaryâh**, *az-ar-yaw'*; or
עֲזַרְיָהוּ **ʿĂzaryâhûw**, *az-ar-yaw'-hoo*; from 5826 and 3050; *Jah has helped; Azarjah*, the name of nineteen Isr.:—Azariah {48x}. See: BDB—741a, 1105d.

5839. עֲזַרְיָה {1x} **ʿĂzaryâh** (Aram.), *az-ar-yaw'*; corresp. to 5838; *Azarjah*, one of Daniel's companions:—Azariah {1x}. See: BDB—1105d.

5840. עַזְרִיקָם {6x} **ʿAzrîyqâm**, *az-ree-kawm'*; from 5828 and act. part. of 6965; *help of an enemy; Azrikam*, the name of four Isr.:—Azrikam {6x}. See: BDB—741b.

5841. עַזָּתִי {2x} **ʿAzzâthîy**, *az-zaw-thee'*; patrial from 5804; an *Azzathite* or inhab. of Azzah:—Gazites {1x}, Gazathites {1x}. See: BDB—738b, 741c.

5842. עֵט {4x} **ʿêṭ**, *ate*; from 5860 (contr.) in the sense of *swooping*, i.e. *side-long stroke;* a *stylus* or marking stick:—pen {4x}. See: TWOT—1600; BDB—741c.

5843. עֵטָא {1x} **ʿêṭâ'** (Aram.), *ay-taw'*; from 3272; *prudence:*—counsel {1x}. See: TWOT—2772b; BDB—1096a, 1105d.

5844. עָטָה {17x} **ʿâṭâh**, *aw-taw'*; a prim. root; to *wrap*, i.e. *cover, veil, clothe*, or *roll:*—cover {10x}, array {1x}, turn aside {1x}, clad {1x}, covering {1x}, filleth {1x}, put on {1x}, surely {1x}. See: TWOT—1601, 1602; BDB—741d, 742a.

5845. עֲטִין {1x} **ʿăṭîyn**, *at-een'*; from an unused root mean. appar. to *contain;* a *receptacle* (for milk, i.e. *pail;* fig. *breast*):—breasts {1x}. See: TWOT—1604a; BDB—742b.

5846. עֲטִישָׁה {1x} **ʿăṭîyshâh**, *at-ee-shaw'*; from an unused root mean. to *sneeze; sneezing:*—sneezings {1x}. See: TWOT—1609a; BDB—743a.

5847. עֲטַלֵּף {3x} **ʿăṭallêph**, *at-al-lafe'*; of uncert. der.; a *bat:*—bat {3x}. See: TWOT—1603; BDB—742a.

5848. עָטַף {16x} ʻâṭaph, *aw-taf';* a prim. root; to *shroud*, i.e. *clothe* (whether tran. or reflex.); hence, (from the idea of *darkness*) to *languish:*—overwhelmed {5x}, faint {3x}, swoon {2x}, covereth {1x}, fail {1x}, feeble {1x}, feebler {1x}, hideth {1x}, covered over {1x}. See: TWOT—1605, 1606, 1607; BDB—742b, 742c.

5849. עָטַר {7x} ʻâṭar, *aw-tar';* a prim. root; to *encircle* (for attack or protection); espec. to *crown* (lit. or fig.):—crown {4x}, compass {2x}, crowning {1x}. See: TWOT—1608, 1608b; BDB—742c, 742d.

5850. עֲטָרָה {23x} ʻăṭârâh, *at-aw-raw';* from 5849; a *crown:*—crown {23x}. See: TWOT—1608a; BDB—742d.

5851. עֲטָרָה {1x} ʻĂṭârâh, *at-aw-raw';* the same as 5850; *Atarah*, an Israelitess:—*Atarah* {1x}. See: BDB—742d.

5852. עֲטָרוֹת {5x} ʻĂṭârôwth, *at-aw-rōth';* or

עֲטָרֹת ʻĂṭârôth, *at-aw-rōth';* plur. of 5850; *Ataroth*, the name (thus simply) of two places in Pal.:—*Ataroth* {5x}. See: BDB—743a.

5853. עַטְרוֹת אַדָּר {2x} ʻAṭrôwth ʼAddâr, *at-rōth' ad-dawr';* from the same as 5852 and 146; *crowns of Addar; Atroth-Addar*, a place in Pal.:—Atarothadar {1x}, Atarothaddar {1x}. See: BDB—743a.

5854. עַטְרוֹת בֵּית יוֹאָב {1x} ʻAṭrôwth Bêyth Yôwʼâb, *at-rōth' bayth yo-awb';* from the same as 5852 and 1004 and 3097; *crowns of* (the) *house of Joäb; Atroth beth Joab*, a place in Pal.:—the house of Joab {1x}. See: BDB—743a.

5855. עַטְרוֹת שׁוֹפָן {1x} ʻAṭrôwth Shôwphân, *at-rōth' sho-fawn';* from the same as 5852 and a name otherwise unused [being from the same as 8226] mean. *hidden; crowns of Shophan; Atroth-Shophan*, a place in Pal.:—Atroth Shophan {1x}. See: BDB—743a, 1051a.

5856. עִי {4x} ʻîy, *ee;* from 5753; a *ruin* (as if overturned):—heap {4x}. See: TWOT—1577d; BDB—730c, 743b.

5857. עַי {41x} ʻAy, *ah'ee;* or (fem.)

עַיָּא ʻAyâʼ (Neh. 11:31), *ah-yaw';* or

עַיָּת ʻAyâth (Isa. 10:28), *ah-yawth';* for 5856; *Ai, Aja* or *Ajath*, a place in Pal.:—Ai {36x}, Hai {2x}, Aiath {1x}, city {1x}. See: BDB—743b, 747b.

5858. עֵיבָל {8x} ʻÊybâl, *ay-bawl';* perh. from an unused root prob. mean. to *be bald; bare; Ebal*, a mountain of Pal.:—Ebal {8x}. See: BDB—743b.

עַיָּה ʻAyâh. See 5857.

5859. עִיּוֹן {3x} ʻIyôwn, *ee-yone';* from 5856; *ruin; Ijon*, a place in Pal.:—Ijon {3x}. See: BDB—743b.

5860. עִיט {3x} ʻîyṭ, *eet;* a prim. root; to *swoop* down upon (lit. or fig.):—fly {2x}, rail {1x}. See: TWOT—1610, 1610b; BDB—743b, 743c.

5861. עַיִט {8x} ʻayiṭ, *ah'-yit;* from 5860; a *hawk* or other bird of prey:—fowl {4x}, bird {2x}, ravenous bird {2x}. See: TWOT—1610a; BDB—743c.

5862. עֵיטָם {5x} ʻÊyṭâm, *ay-tawm';* from 5861; *hawk-ground; Etam*, a place in Pal.:—Etam {5x}. See: BDB—743c.

5863. עִיֵּי הָעֲבָרִים {2x} ʻIyêy hâ-ʻĂbârîym, *ee-yay' haw-ab-aw-reem';* from the plur. of 5856 and the plur. of the act. part. of 5674 with the art. interposed; *ruins of the passers; Ije-ha-Abarim*, a place near Pal.:—Ijeabarim {2x}. See: BDB—743d.

5864. עִיִּים {2x} ʻIyîym, *ee-yeem';* plur. of 5856; *ruins; Ijim*, a place in the Desert:—Iim {2x}. See: BDB—743d.

5865. עֵילוֹם {1x} ʻêylôwm, *ay-lome';* for 5769:—for ever {1x}. See: TWOT—1631a; BDB—743d, 761d, 763a.

5866. עִילַי {1x} ʻÎylay, *ee-lah'-ee;* from 5927; *elevated; Ilai*, an Isr.:—Ilai {1x}. See: BDB—743d.

5867. עֵילָם {28x} ʻÊylâm, *ay-lawm';* or

עוֹלָם ʻÔwlâm (Ezra 10:2; Jer. 49:36), *o-lawm';* prob. from 5956; *hidden*, i.e. *distant; Elam*, a son of Shem, and his desc., with their country; also of six Isr.:—Elam {28x}. See: BDB—743d, 1106d.

5868. עֲיָם {1x} ʻăyâm, *ah-yawm';* of doubtful or. and authenticity; prob. mean. *strength:*—mighty {1x}. See: TWOT—1611; BDB—744a.

5869. עַיִן {887x} ʻayin, *ah'-yin;* prob. a prim. word; an *eye* (lit. or fig.); by anal. a *fountain* (as the *eye* of the landscape):—eye {495x}, sight {216x}, seem {19x}, colour {12x}, fountain {11x}, well {11x}, face {10x}, pleased + 3190 {10x}, presence {8x}, displeased + 3415 {8x}, before {8x}, pleased + 3474 {4x}, conceit {4x}, think {4x}, misc. {66x} = affliction, outward appearance, + think best, + be content, countenance, + favour, furrow, × him, + humble, knowledge, look, (+ well), × me, open (-ly), + regard, resemblance, × thee, × them, × us, × you (-rselves).

ʻAyin means "eye; well; surface; appearance; spring." **(1)** First, the word represents the bodily part, "eye." **(1a)** In Gen 13:10, *ʻayin* is used of the "human eye": "And Lot lifted up his eyes, and beheld all the plain of Jordan. . . ." **(1b)** It is also used of the "eyes" of animals (Gen 30:41), idols (Ps 115:5), and God (Deut 11:12—anthropomorphism). **(2)** The expression "between the eyes" means "on the forehead": "And it shall be for a sign unto thee upon thine hand, and for a memorial between thine eyes, that the Lord's law may be in thy mouth . . ." (Ex 13:9). **(3)** "Eyes" are used as typical of one's "weakness" or "hurt": "And it came to pass, that when Isaac was old, and his eyes were dim, so that he could not see, he called Esau his eldest son, and said . . ." (Gen 27:1). **(4)** The "apple of the eye" is the central component, the iris: "Keep me as the apple of the eye" (Ps 17:8). **(5)** "Eyes" might be a special feature of "beauty": "Now he was ruddy, and withal [fair of eyes], and goodly to look to" (1 Sa 16:12). **(6)** *ʻAyin* is often used in connection with expressions of "seeing": "And, behold, your eyes see, and the eyes of my brother Benjamin, that it is my mouth that speaketh unto you" (Gen 45:12). **(7)** The expression "to lift up one's eyes" is explained by a verb following it: one lifts up his eyes to do something—whatever the verb stipulates (cf. Gen 13:10).

(8) "Lifting up one's eyes" may also be an act expressing "desire," "longing," "devotion": "And it came to pass after these things, that his master's wife [looked with desire at] Joseph . . ." (Gen 39:7). **(9)** The "eyes" may be used in gaining or seeking a judgment, in the sense of "seeing intellectually," "making an evaluation," or "seeking an evaluation or proof of faithfulness": "And thou saidst unto thy servants, Bring him down unto me, that I may set mine eyes upon him" (Gen 44:21). **(10)** "Eyes" sometimes show mental qualities, such as regret: "Also regard not [literally, "do not let your eye look with regret upon"] your stuff; for the good of all the land of Egypt is yours" (Gen 45:20). **(11)** "Eyes" are used figuratively of mental and spiritual abilities, acts and states. So the "opening of the eyes" in Gen 3:5 (the first occurrence) means to become autonomous by setting standards of good and evil for oneself. **(12)** In passages such as Prov 4:25, "eye" represents a moral faculty: "Let thine eyes look right on, and let thine eyelids look straight before thee." **(13)** Prov 23:6 uses the word of a moral state (literally"evil eye"): "Eat thou not the bread of [a selfish man], neither desire thou his dainty meats."

(14) An individual may serve as a guide, or one's "eyes": "And he said, Leave us not, I pray thee; forasmuch as thou knowest how we are to encamp in the wilderness, and thou mayest be to us instead of eyes" (Num 10:31). **(15)** The phrase, "in the eye of," means "in one's view or opinion": "And he went in unto Hagar, and she conceived: and when she saw that she had conceived, her mistress was despised in her eyes" (Gen 16:4). **(16)** Another phrase, "from the eyes of," may signify that a thing or matter is "hidden" from one's knowledge: "And a man lie with her carnally, and it be hid from the eyes of her husband, and [she be undetected] . . ." (Num 5:13). **(17)** In Ex 10:5, the word represents the "visible surface of the earth": "And they shall cover the face of the earth, that one cannot be able to see the earth. . . ." **(18)** Lev 13:5 uses *ʻayin* to represent "one's appearance": "And the priest shall look on him the seventh day: and behold, if the plague in his sight be at a stay . . ." **(19)** A "gleam or sparkle" is described in the phrase, "to give its eyes," in passages such as Prov 23:31: "Look not thou upon the wine when it is red, when it giveth his color [gives its eyes] in the cup. . . ." **(20)** *ʻAyin* also represents a "spring" (literally, an "eye of the water"): "And the angel of the Lord found her by a fountain of water in the wilderness, by the fountain on the way to Shur" (Gen 16:7). See: TWOT—1612a, 1613; BDB—733b, 744a, 745a, 1044d, 1105d.

5870. עַיִן {5x} ʻayin (Aram.), *ah'-yin;* corresp. to 5869; an *eye:*—eye {5x}. See: TWOT—2906; BDB—1105d.

5871. עַיִן {5x} ʻAyin, *ah'-yin;* the same as 5869; *fountain; Ajin*, the name (thus simply) of two places in Pal.:—Ain {5x}. See: BDB—745a, 745b, 745c, 942a.

5872. עֵין גֶּדִי {6x} ʻÊyn Gedîy, *ane geh'-dee;* from 5869 and 1423; *fountain of a kid; En-Gedi*, a place in Pal.:—Engedi {6x}. See: BDB—745b.

5873. עֵין גַּנִּים {3x} ʻÊyn Gannîym, *ane gan-neem';* from 5869 and the plur. of 1588; *fountain of gardens; En-Gannim*, a place in Pal.:—Engannim {3x}. See: BDB—745c.

5874. עֵין־דֹּאר {3x} ʻÊyn-Dôʼr, *ane-dore';* or

עֵין דּוֹר ʻÊyn Dôwr, *ane dore;* or

עֵין־דֹּר ʻÊyn-Dôr, *ane-dore';* from 5869 and 1755; *fountain of dwelling; En-Dor*, a place in Pal.:—Endor {3x}. See: BDB—745c.

5875. עֵין הַקּוֹרֵא {1x} ʻÊyn haq-Qôwrêê, a place near Pal.:—Enhakkore {1x}. See: BDB—745b.

עֵינוֹן ʻÊynôwn. See 2703.

5876. עֵין חַדָּה {1x} ʿ**Êyn Chaddâh**, *ane khad-daw'*; from 5869 and the fem. of a der. from 2300; *fountain of sharpness; En-Chaddah*, a place in Pal.:—Enhaddah {1x}. See: BDB—292c, 745c.

5877. עֵין חָצוֹר {1x} ʿ**Êyn Châtsôwr**, *ane khaw-tsore'*; from 5869 and the same as 2674; *fountain of a village; En-Chatsor*, a place in Pal.:—Enhazor {1x}. See: BDB—745c.

5878. עֵין חֲרֹד {1x} ʿ**Êyn Chărôd**, *ane khar-ode'*; from 5869 and a der. of 2729; *fountain of trembling; En-Charod*, a place in Pal.:—well of Harod {1x}. See: BDB—353d, 745b, 745c.

5879. עֵינַיִם {1x} ʿ**Êynayim**, *ay-nah'-yim*; or

עֵינָם ʿ**Êynâm**, *ay-nawm'*; dual of 5869; *double fountain; Enajim* or *Enam*, a place in Pal.:—Enam {1x}. See: BDB—745d.

5880. עֵין מִשְׁפָּט {1x} ʿ**Êyn Mishpâṭ**, *ane mish-pawt'*; from 5869 and 4941; *fountain of judgment; En-Mishpat*, a place near Pal.:—En-mishpat {1x}. See: BDB—745c, 874a.

5881. עֵינָן {5x} ʿ**Êynân**, *ay-nawn'*; from 5869; *having eyes; Enan*, an Isr.:—Enan {5x}. See: BDB—745d. comp. 2704.

5882. עֵין עֶגְלַיִם {1x} ʿ**Êyn ʿEglayim**, *ane eg-lah'-yim*; from 5869 and the dual of 5695; *fountain of two calves; En-Eglajim*, a place in Pal.:—Eneglaim {1x}. See: BDB—722d, 745c.

5883. עֵין רֹגֵל {4x} ʿ**Êyn Rôgêl**, *ane ro-gale'*; from 5869 and the act. part. of 7270; *fountain of a traveller; En-Rogel*, a place near Jerusalem:—Enrogel {4x}. See: BDB—745b, 920b.

5884. עֵין רִמּוֹן {1x} ʿ**Êyn Rimmôwn**, *ane rim-mone'*; from 5869 and 7416; *fountain of a pomegranate; En-Rimmon*, a place in Pal.:—Enrimmon {1x}. See: BDB—745b, 745c, 942a.

5885. עֵין שֶׁמֶשׁ {2x} ʿ**Êyn Shemesh**, *ane sheh'-mesh*; from 5869 and 8121; *fountain of* (the) *sun; En-Shemesh*, a place in Pal.:—Enshemesh {2x}. See: BDB—745d.

5886. עֵין תַּנִּים {1x} ʿ**Êyn Tannîym**, *ane tan-neem'*; from 5869 and the plur. of 8565; *fountain of jackals; En-Tannim*, a pool near Jerusalem:—strong's synonym {1x}.

5887. עֵין תַּפּוּחַ {1x} ʿ**Êyn Tappûwach**, *ane tap-poo'-akh*; from 5869 and 8598; *fountain of an apple tree; En-Tappuäch*, a place in Pal.:—Entappuah {1x}. See: BDB—745d.

5888. עָיֵף {1x} ʿ**âyêph**, *aw-yafe'*; a prim. root; to *languish*:—wearied {1x}. See: TWOT—1614a; BDB—746a.

5889. עָיֵף {17x} ʿ**âyêph**, *aw-yafe'*; from 5888; *languid*:—weary {8x}, faint {6x}, thirsty {3x}. See: TWOT—1614a; BDB—746a.

5890. עֵיפָה {2x} ʿ**êyphâh**, *ay-faw'*; fem. from 5774; *obscurity* (as if from *covering*):—darkness {2x}. See: TWOT—1583d; BDB—734a, 746a, 780c.

5891. עֵיפָה {5x} ʿ**Êyphâh**, *ay-faw'*; the same as 5890; *Ephah*, the name of a son of Midian, and of the region settled by him; also of an Isr. and of an Israelitess:—Ephah {5x}. See: BDB—734a, 746a.

5892. עִיר {1089x} ʿ**îyr**, *eer*; or (in the plur.)

עָר ʿ**âr**, *awr*; or

עָיַר ʿ**âyar** (Judg 10:4), *aw-yar'*; from 5782 a *city* (a place guarded by *waking* or a watch) in the widest sense (even of a mere *encampment* or *post*):—city {1074x}, town {7x}, every one {2x}, variant {6x}.

ʿ*Iyr* means city; town; village; quarter [of a city]. **(1)** This word suggests a village, maybe with or without walls: "All these cities *were* fenced with high walls, gates, and bars; beside unwalled towns [ʿ*iyr*] a great many" (Deut 3:5); an unwalled village being Hebrew word chatser (2968). **(2)** ʿ*Iyr* can signify a village in a permanent place, even though the dwellings are tents: "And Saul came to a city [ʿ*iyr*] of Amalek, and laid wait in the valley" (1 Sa 15:5). **(3)** In Gen 4:17 ʿ*iyr* means a permanent dwelling center consisting of residences of stone and clay: "And Cain knew his wife; and she conceived, and bare Enoch: and he builded a city, and called the name of the city, after the name of his son, Enoch." **(4)** As a rule, there are usually no political overtones to the word; **(4a)** ʿ*iyr* simply represents the place where people dwell on a permanent basis. **(4b)** ʿ*Iyr*, however, can represent a political entity: "And to *them* which *were* in Rachal, and to *them* which *were* in the cities of the Jerahmeelites, and to *them* which *were* in the cities of the Kenites," (1 Sa 30:29). **(5)** This word can represent those who live in a given town: "And when he came, lo, Eli sat upon a seat by the wayside watching: for his heart trembled for the ark of God. And when the man came into the city, and told *it*, all the city cried out" (1 Sa 4:13). **(6)** ʿ*Iyr* can signify only a part of a city, such as a part that is surrounded by a wall: "Nevertheless David took the strong hold of Zion: the same *is* the city of David" (2 Sa 5:7). See: TWOT—1587a, 1615; BDB—735c, 746b, 746d.

5893. עִיר {1x} ʿ**Îyr**, *eer*; the same as 5892; *Ir*, an Isr.:—Ir {1x}. See: BDB—746d.

5894. עִיר {3x} ʿ**îyr** (Aram.), *eer*; from a root corresp. to 5782; a *watcher*, i.e. an *angel* (as guardian):—watcher {3x}. See: TWOT—2907; BDB—1105d.

5895. עַיִר {8x} ʿ**ayîr**, *ah'-yeer*; from 5782 in the sense of *raising* (i.e. *bearing* a burden); prop. a young *ass* (as just broken to a load); hence, an ass-*colt*:—colt {4x}, foal {2x}, young ass {2x}. See: TWOT—1616a; BDB—736b, 747a.

5896. עִירָא {6x} ʿ**Îyrâʾ**, *ee-raw'*; from 5782; *wakefulness; Ira*, the name of three Isr.:—Ira {6x}. See: BDB—747a.

5897. עִירָד {2x} ʿ**Îyrâd**, *ee-rawd'*; from the same as 6166; *fugitive; Irad*, an antediluvian:—Irad {2x}. See: BDB—747a.

5898. עִיר הַמֶּלַח {1x} ʿ**Îyr ham-Melach**, *eer ham-meh'-lakh*; from 5892 and 4417 with the art. of substance interp.; *city of* (the) *salt; Ir-ham-Melach*, a place near Pal.:—city of Salt {1x}. See: BDB—746d.

5899. עִיר הַתְּמָרִים {4x} ʿ**Îyr hat-Temârîym**, *eer hat-tem-aw-reem'*; from 5892 and the plur. of 8558 with the art. interpolated; *city of the palmtrees; Ir-hat-Temarim*, a place in Pal.:—variant {2x}, (city of palm) trees {2x}. See: BDB—746d.

5900. עִירוּ {1x} ʿ**Îyrûw**, *ee-roo'*; from 5892; a *citizen; Iru*, an Isr.:—Iru {1x}. See: BDB—747a.

5901. עִירִי {1x} ʿ**Îyrîy**, *ee-ree'*; from 5892; *urbane; Iri*, an Isr.:—Iri {1x}. See: BDB—747a.

5902. עִירָם {2x} ʿ**Îyrâm**, *ee-rawm'*; from 5892; *city-wise; Iram*, an Idumæan:—Iram {2x}. See: BDB—747a.

5903. עֵירֹם {10x} ʿ**êyrôm**, *ay-rome'*; or

עֵרֹם ʿ**êrôm**, *ay-rome'*; from 6181; *nudity*:—naked {9x}, nakedness {1x}. See: TWOT—1588b; BDB—735d, 747a, 790d.

5904. עִיר נָחָשׁ {1x} ʿ**Îyr Nâchâsh**, *eer naw-khawsh'*; from 5892 and 5175; *city of a serpent; Ir-Nachash*, a place in Pal.:—Irnahash {1x}. See: BDB—638b, 746d.

5905. עִיר שֶׁמֶשׁ {1x} ʿ**Îyr Shemesh**, *eer sheh'-mesh*; from 5892 and 8121; *city of* (the) *sun; Ir-Shemesh*, a place in Pal.:—Irshemesh {1x}. See: BDB—747b.

5906. עַיִשׁ {2x} ʿ**Ayish**, *ah'-yish*; or

עָשׁ ʿ**Âsh**, *awsh*; from 5789; the constellation of the Great *Bear* (perh. from its *migration* through the heavens):—Arcturus {2x}. See: TWOT—1617; BDB—747a, 798b.

עַיָּת ʿ**Ayâth**. See 5857.

5907. עַכְבּוֹר {7x} ʿ**Akbôwr**, *ak-bore'*; prob. for 5909; *Akbor*, the name of an Idumæan and two Isr.:—Achbor {7x}. See: BDB—747b.

5908. עַכָּבִישׁ {2x} ʿ**akkâbîysh**, *ak-kaw-beesh'*; prob. from an unused root in the lit. sense of *entangling*; a *spider* (as *weaving* a network):—spider {2x}. See: TWOT—1619; BDB—747B.

5909. עַכְבָּר {6x} ʿ**akbâr**, *ak-bawr'*; prob. from the same as 5908 in the second. sense of *attacking*; a *mouse* (as *nibbling*):—mouse {6x}. See: TWOT—1618; BDB—747b.

5910. עַכּוֹ {1x} ʿ**Akkôw**, *ak-ko'*; appar. from an unused root mean. to *hem* in; *Akko* (from its situation on a *bay*):—Accho {1x}. See: BDB—747b.

5911. עָכוֹר {5x} ʿ**Âkôwr**, *aw-kore'*; from 5916; *troubled; Akor*, the name of a place in Pal.:—Achor {5x}. See: TWOT—1621a; BDB—747d.

5912. עָכָן {6x} ʿ**Âkân**, *aw-kawn'*; from an unused root mean. to *trouble; troublesome; Akan*, an Isr.:—Achan {6x}. See: BDB—747c. comp. 5917.

5913. עָכַס {1x} ʿ**âkaç**, *aw-kas'*; a prim. root; prop. to *tie*, spec. with fetters; but used only as denom. from 5914; to *put on anklets*:—tinkling {1x}. See: TWOT—1620; BDB—747c.

5914. עֶכֶס {2x} ʿ**ekeç**, *eh'-kes*; from 5913; a *fetter*; hence, an *anklet*:—stocks {1x}, tinkling ornament {1x}. See: TWOT—1620a; BDB—747c.

5915. עַכְסָה {5x} ʿ**Akçâh**, *ak-saw'*; fem. of 5914; *anklet; Aksah*, an Israelitess:—Achsah {5x}. See: BDB—747c.

5916. עָכַר {14x} ʿ**âkar**, *aw-kar'*; a prim. root; prop. to *roil* water; fig. to *disturb* or *afflict*:—trouble {12x}, stirred {1x}, troubler {1x}. See: TWOT—1621; BDB—747c.

5917. עָכָר {1x} ʿ**Âkâr**, *aw-kawr'*; from 5916; *troublesome; Akar*, an Isr.:—Achar {1x}. See: BDB—747c, 747d. comp. 5912.

5918. עָכְרָן {5x} ʻ**Okrân**, *ok-rawn';* from 5916; *muddler; Okran,* an Isr.:—Ocran {5x}. See: BDB—747d.

5919. עַכְשׁוּב {1x} ʻ**akshûwb**, *ak-shoob';* prob. from an unused root mean. to *coil;* an *asp* (from lurking *coiled* up):—adder {1x}. See: TWOT—1622; BDB—747d.

5920. עַל {6x} ʻ**al**, *al;* from 5927; prop. the *top;* spec. the *Highest* (i.e. *God*); also (adv.) *aloft, to Jehovah:*—above {3x}, most High {2x}, on high {1x}. See: TWOT—1624p; BDB—748a, 752b.

5921. עַל {48x} ʻ**al**, *al;* prop. the same as 5920 used as a prep. (in the sing. or plur. often with pref., or as conjunc. with a particle following); *above, over, upon,* or *against* (yet always in this last relation with a downward aspect) in a great variety of applications (as follow):—{48x} = upon, in, on, over, by, for, both, beyond, through, throughout, against, beside, forth, off, from off. See: TWOT—1624p; BDB—475c, 591d, 748a, 752b, 752c, 759d, 761b, 763a, 1106a.

5922. עַל {99x} ʻ**al** (Aram.), *al;* corresp. to 5921:—upon {19x}, over {13x}, unto {9x}, against {7x}, concerning {6x}, in {6x}, for {4x}, unto me {4x}, about {3x}, in him {3x}, misc. 25. See: TWOT—2908; BDB—1105d, 1106a.

5923. עֹל {40x} ʻ**ôl**, *ole;* or

עוֹל ʻ**ôwl**, *ola;* from 5953; a *yoke* (as *imposed* on the neck), lit. or fig.:—yoke {40x}. See: TWOT—1628a; BDB—748a, 760d.

5924. עֵלָּא {1x} ʻ**êllâʼ** (Aram.), *ale-law';* from 5922; *above:*—over {1x}. See: TWOT—2909a; BDB—1105d, 1106a.

5925. עֻלָּא {1x} ʻ**Ullâʼ**, *ool-law';* fem. of 5923; *burden; Ulla,* an Isr.:—*Ulla* {1x}. See: BDB—748a.

5926. עִלֵּג {1x} ʻ**illêg**, *il-layg';* from an unused root mean. to *stutter; stuttering:*—stammerers {1x}. See: TWOT—1623a; BDB—748a.

5927. עָלָה {889x} ʻ**âlâh**, *aw-law';* a prim. root; to *ascend,* intr. (*be high*) or act. (*mount*); used in a great variety of senses, primary and second., lit. and fig. (as follow):—(come, etc . . .) up {676x}, offer {67x}, come {22x}, bring {18x}, ascend {15x}, go {12x}, chew {9x}, offering {8x}, light {6x}, increase {4x}, burn {3x}, depart {3x}, put {3x}, spring {2x}, raised {2x}, arose {2x}, break {2x}, exalted {2x}, misc. {33}.

ʻAlah means "to go up, ascend, offer up." **(1)** Basically, *ʻalah* suggests movement from a lower to a higher place. **(1a)** That is the emphasis in Gen 2:6 (the first occurrence of the word), which reports that Eden was watered by a mist or stream that "went up" over the ground. **(1b)** *ʻAlah* may also mean "to rise up" or "ascend." The king of Babylon [satan] said in his heart, "I will ascend into heaven" (Is 14:13). **(2)** This word may mean "to take a journey," as in traveling from Egypt (Gen 13:1) toward Palestine or other points northward. **(3)** The verb may be used in a special sense meaning "to extend, reach"—for example, the border of Benjamin "went up ["extended, reached"] through the mountains westward" (Josh 18:12). **(4)** The use of *ʻalah* to describe the journey from Egypt to Palestine is such a standard phrase that it often appears without the geographical reference points. Joseph told his brothers to "go up" to their father in peace (Gen 44:17). **(5)** Even the return from the Exile, which was a journey from north to south (Palestine), is described as a "going up" (Ezra 2:1). **(6)** Thus, the reference may be not so much to physically "going up," but to a figurative or spiritual "going up." This usage appears long before Ezra's time, when it is said that one "goes up" to the place where the sanctuary is located (cf. Deut 17:8).

(7) The verb became a technical term for "making a pilgrimage" (Ex 34:24) or "going up" before the Lord; in a secular context, compare Joseph's "going up" before Pharaoh (Gen 46:31). **(8)** In instances where an enemy located himself in a superior position (frequently a higher place), one "goes up" to battle (Josh 22:12). **(9)** The verb can also refer merely to "going out" to make war against someone, even though there is no movement from a lower to a higher plane. So Israel "went up" to make war against the Moabites, who heard of the Israelites' approach while still dwelling in their cities (2 Kin 3:21). **(10)** Even when *ʻalah* is used by itself, it can mean "to go to war"; the Lord told Phinehas, "Go up; for tomorrow I will deliver them into thine hand" (Judg 20:28). **(11)** On the other hand, if the enemy is recognized to be on a lower plane, one can "go down" (3381 - yarad) to fight (Judg 1:9). **(12)** The opposite of "going up" to war is not descending to battle, but "leaving off" (*ʻalah* me'al), literally, "going up from against." **(12)** Another special use of *ʻalah* is "to overpower" (literally, "to go up from"). For example, the Pharaoh feared the Israelites lest in a war they join the enemy, fight against Egypt, and "overpower" the land (Ex 1:10).

(13) "To go up" may also be used of "increasing in strength," as the lion that becomes strong from his prey: The lion "goes up from his prey" (Gen 49:9; cf. Deut 28:43). **(14)** Not only physical things can "go up." *ʻAlah* can be used also of the "increasing" of wrath (2 Sa 11:20), the "ascent" of an outcry before God (Ex 2:23), and the "continual" sound of battle (although "sound of" is omitted; cf. 1 Kin 22:35). **(15)** The word can also be used passively to denote mixing two kinds of garments together, causing one "to lie upon" or "be placed upon" the other (Lev 19:19). **(16)** Sometimes "go up" means "placed," even when the direction is downward, as when placing a yoke upon an ox (Num 19:2) or going to one's grave (Job 5:26). This may be an illustration of how Hebrew verbs can sometimes mean their opposite. **(17)** The verb is also used of "recording" a census (1 Chr 27:24). **(18)** The verb *ʻalah* is used in a causative stem to signify "presenting an offering" to God. In 63 cases, the word is associated with the presentation of the whole burnt offering (ʻolah). **(19)** *ʻAlah* is used of the general act of "presenting offerings" when the various offerings are mentioned in the same context (Lev 14:20), or when the purpose of the offering is not specifically in mind (Is 57:6). **(20)** Sometimes this verb means merely "to offer" (e.g., Num 23:2). See: TWOT—1624; BDB—748a, 1105d.

5928. עֲלָה {1x} ʻ**ălâh** (Aram.), *al-aw';* corresp. to 5930; a *holocaust:*—burnt offerings {1x}. See: TWOT—2909e; BDB—1106a, 1106d.

5929. עָלֶה {18x} ʻ**âleh**, *aw-leh';* from 5927; a *leaf* (as *coming up* on a tree); collect. *foliage:*—leaf {12x}, branch {5x}, branches + 6086 {1x}. See: TWOT—1624a; BDB—750a.

5930. עֹלָה {289x} ʻ**ôlâh**, *o-law';* or

עוֹלָה ʻ**ôwlâh**, *o-law';* fem. act. part. of 5927; a *step* or (collect. *stairs,* as *ascending*); usually a *holocaust* (as *going up* in smoke):—burnt offering {264x}, burnt sacrifice {21x}, ascent {1x}, go up {1x}.

ʻOlah means "whole burnt offering." **(1)** In its first biblical occurrence *olah* identifies a kind of "offering" presented to God: "And Noah builded an altar unto the Lord; and took of every clean beast, and of every clean fowl, and offered burnt offerings on the altar" (Gen 8:20). **(2)** Its second nuance appears in Lev 1:4, where it represents the "thing being offered":"And he shall put his hand upon the head of the burnt offering; and it shall be accepted for him to make atonement for him." **(3)** This kind of "offering" could be made **(3a)** with a bull (Lev 1:3–5), a sheep, a goat (Lev 1:10), or a bird (Lev 1:14). **(3b)** The offerer laid his hands on the sacrificial victim, symbolically transferring his sin and guilt to it. **(3c)** After he slew the animal (on the north side of the altar), the priest took its blood, which was presented before the Lord prior to being sprinkled around the altar. **(3d)** A bird was simply given to the priest, but he wrung its neck and allowed its blood to drain beside the altar (Lev 1:15). **(3e)** This sacrifice effected an atonement, a covering for sin necessary before the essence of the sacrifice could be presented to God. **(3f)** Next, the "offering" was divided into sections. They were carefully purified (except those parts which could not be purified) and arranged on the altar (Lev 1:6–9, 12–13). **(3g)** The entire sacrifice was then consumed by the fire and its essence sent up to God as a placating (pleasing) odor. **(3h)** The animal skin was given to the priest as his portion (Lev 7:8).

(4) The word *olah* was listed first in Old Testament administrative prescriptions and descriptions as the most frequent offering. **(4a)** Every day required the presentation of a male lamb morning and evening—the continual "whole burnt offering" (Ex 29:38–42). **(4b)** Each month was consecrated by a "whole burnt offering," of two young bulls, one ram, and seven male lambs (Num 28:11–14). **(4c)** The same sacrifice was mandated, for each day of the Passover-Unleavened Bread feast (Num 28:19–24), and the Feast of Weeks (Num 28:26–29). **(5)** Other stated feasts required "burnt offerings" as well. **(6)** The various purification rites mandated both "burnt" and sin "offerings." **(7)** The central significance of *owlah* as the "whole burnt offering" was the total surrender of the heart and life of the offerer to God. **(7a)** Sin offerings could accompany them when the offerer was especially concerned with a covering or expiation for sin (2 Chr 29:27). **(7b)** When peace offerings accompanied "burnt offerings," the offerer's concern focused on fellowship with God (2 Chr 29:31–35). **(7c)** Before the Mosaic legislation, it appears, the "whole burnt offering" served the full range of meanings expressed in all the various Mosaic sacrifices. Syn.: 2077. See: TWOT—1624c, 1624d; BDB—732d, 750b, 751a. See also 5766.

5931. עִלָּה {3x} ʻ**illâh** (Aram.), *il-law';* fem. from a root corresp. to 5927; a *pretext* (as *arising* artificially):—occasion {3x}. See: TWOT—2910; BDB—1105d, 1106c.

5932. עַלְוָה {1x} ʻ**alvâh**, *al-vaw';* for 5766; *moral perverseness:*—iniquity {1x}. See: TWOT—1580b; BDB—759b.

5933. עַלְוָה {2x} ʻ**Alvâh**, *al-vaw';* or

עַלְיָה ʻ**Alyâh**, *al-yaw';* the same as 5932; *Alvah* or *Aljah,* an Idumæan:—Aliah {1x}, Alvah {1x}. See: BDB—759b, 759d.

5934. עָלוּם {4x} ʻ**âlûwm**, *aw-loom';* pass. part. of 5956 in the denom. sense of 5958; (only in plur. as abstr.) *adolescence;* fig. *vigor:*—youth {4x}. See: TWOT—1630c; BDB—761c.

5935. עַלְוָן {2x} ʿ**Alvân**, *al-vawn';* or

עַלְיָן ʿ**Alyân**, *al-yawn';* from 5927; *lofty; Alvan* or *Aljan,* an Idumæan:—Alian {1x}, Alvan {1x}. See: BDB—759b, 759d.

5936. עֲלוּקָה {1x} ʿ**ălûwqâh**, *al-oo-kaw';* fem. pass. part. of an unused root mean. to *suck;* the *leech:*—horseleach {1x}. See: TWOT—1636a; BDB—763c.

5937. עָלַז {16x} ʿ**âlaz**, *aw-laz';* a prim. root; to *jump* for joy, i.e. *exult:*—rejoice {12x}, triumph {2x}, joyful {2x}. See: TWOT—1625; BDB—759c.

5938. עָלֵז {1x} ʿ**âlêz**, *aw-laze';* from 5937; *exultant:*—rejoice {1x}. See: TWOT—1625a; BDB—759c.

5939. עֲלָטָה {4x} ʿ**ălâṭâh**, *al-aw-taw';* fem. from an unused root mean. to *cover; dusk:*—twilight {3x}, dark {1x}. See: TWOT—1626; BDB—759c.

5940. עֱלִי {1x} ʿ**ĕlîy**, *el-ee';* from 5927; a *pestle* (as *lifted*):—pestle {1x}. See: TWOT—1624b; BDB—750a, 759c.

5941. עֵלִי {33x} ʿ**Êlîy**, *ay-lee';* from 5927; *lofty; Eli,* an Isr. high-priest:—Eli {33x}. See: BDB—750a, 759c.

5942. עִלִּי {2x} ʿ**illîy**, *il-lee';* from 5927; *high;* i.e. comparative:—upper {2x}. See: TWOT—1624e; BDB—751a, 759c.

5943. עִלַּי {10x} ʿ**illay** (Aram.), *il-lah'-ee;* corresp. to 5942; *supreme* (i.e. *God*):—the most High {5x}, most high {4x}, high {1x}. See: TWOT—2909d; BDB—1106a.

עַלְיָה ʿ**Alyâh**. See 5933.

5944. עֲלִיָּה {20x} ʿ**ălîyâh**, *al-ee-yaw';* fem. from 5927; something *lofty,* i.e. a *stairway;* also a *second-story* room (or even one on the roof); fig. the *sky:*—chamber {12x}, parlour {4x}, going up {2x}, ascent {1x}, loft {1x}. See: TWOT—1624f; BDB—751a, 759c, 1106a.

5945. עֶלְיוֹן {53x} ʿ**elyôwn**, *el-yone';* from 5927; an *elevation,* i.e. (adj.) *lofty* (comp.); as title, the *Supreme:*—High {18x}, most high {9x}, high {9x}, upper {8x}, higher {4x}, highest {2x}, above {1x}, Highest {1x}, uppermost {1x}.

ʿ*Elyown* means "the upper; the highest." **(1)** The use of ʿ*elyown* in Gen 40:17 means "the upper" as opposed to "the lower": "And in the uppermost basket *there was* of all manner of bakemeats for Pharaoh; and the birds did eat them out of the basket upon my head." **(2)** Where referring to or naming God, ʿ*elyown* means "the highest": "And Melchizedek king of Salem brought forth bread and wine: and he *was* the priest of the most high God" (Gen 14:18). See: TWOT—1624g; BDB—751b, 759c, 1106a.

5946. עֶלְיוֹן {4x} ʿ**elyôwn** (Aram.), *el-yone';* corresp. to 5945; the *Supreme:*—the most high {4x}. See: TWOT—2909c; BDB—1106a.

5947. עַלִּיז {7x} ʿ**allîyz**, *al-leez';* from 5937; *exultant:*—rejoice {4x}, joyous {3x}. See: TWOT—1625b; BDB—759c.

5948. עֲלִיל {1x} ʿ**ălîyl**, *al-eel';* from 5953 in the sense of *completing;* prob. a *crucible* (as *working* over the metal):—furnace {1x}. See: TWOT—1628b; BDB—760d.

5949. עֲלִילָה {24x} ʿ**ălîylâh**, *al-ee-law';* or

עֲלִלָה ʿ**ălîlâh**, *al-ee-law';* from 5953 in the sense of *effecting;* an *exploit* (of God), or a *performance* (of man, often in a bad sense); by impl. an *opportunity:*—doing {14x}, works {3x}, deeds {2x}, occasions {2x}, actions {1x}, acts {1x}, inventions {1x}. See: TWOT—1627c; BDB—760a.

5950. עֲלִילִיָּה {1x} ʿ**ălîylîyâh**, *al-ee-lee-yaw';* for 5949; (miraculous) *execution:*—work {1x}. See: TWOT—1627d; BDB—760b.

עַלְיָן ʿ**Alyân**. See 5935.

5951. עֲלִיצוּת {1x} ʿ**ălîytsûwth**, *al-ee-tsooth';* from 5970; *exultation:*—rejoicing {1x}. See: TWOT—1635a; BDB—763c.

5952. עַלִּית {1x} ʿ**allîyth** (Aram.), *al-leeth';* from 5927; a *second-story* room:—chamber {1x}. See: BDB—1106a. comp. 5944.

5953. עָלַל {20x} ʿ**âlal**, *aw-lal';* a prim. root; to *effect* thoroughly; spec. to *glean* (also fig.); by impl. (in a bad sense) to *overdo,* i.e. maltreat, be saucy to, pain, impose (also lit.):—glean {4x}, done {3x}, abuse {3x}, mock {2x}, affecteth {1x}, children {1x}, do {1x}, defiled {1x}, practise {1x}, throughly {1x}, wrought wonderfully {1x}, wrought {1x}. See: TWOT—1627, 1627b, 1628; BDB—759d, 760a, 760c, 1106c.

5954. עֲלַל {13x} ʿ**ălal** (Aram.), *al-al';* corresp. to 5953 (in the sense of *thrusting* oneself in), to *enter;* caus. to *introduce:*—bring in {6x}, come in {2x}, went in {2x}, bring {1x}, went {1x}, come {1x}. See: TWOT—2911; BDB—1106c.

עֹלָל ʿ**ôlâl**. See 5768.

עֲלִלָה ʿ**ălîlâh**. See 5949.

5955. עֹלֵלָה {6x} ʿ**ôlêlâh**, *o-lay-law';* fem. act. part. of 5953; only in plur. *gleanings;* by extens. *gleaning-time:*—gleaning grapes {3x}, grapegleanings {1x}, gleaning of the grape {1x}, grapes {1x}. See: TWOT—1627a; BDB—760a.

5956. עָלַם {28x} ʿ**âlam**, *aw-lam';* a prim. root; to *veil* from sight, i.e. *conceal* (lit. or fig.):—hide {22x}, blind {1x}, dissemblers {1x}, hidden {1x}, secret {1x}, secret thing {1x}, any ways {1x}. See: TWOT—1629; BDB—761a.

5957. עָלַם {20x} ʿ**âlam** (Aram.), *aw-lam';* corresp. to 5769; *remote* time, i.e. the *future* or *past* indefinitely; often adv. *forever:*—ever {12x}, everlasting {4x}, old {2x}, ever + 5705 {1x}, never {1x}. See: TWOT—2912; BDB—1106d.

5958. עֶלֶם {2x} ʿ**elem**, *eh'-lem;* from 5956; prop. something *kept out of sight* [comp. 5959], i.e. a *lad:*—young man {1x}, stripling {1x}.

The only 2 appearances of the masculine form (5958 - ʿ*elem*) are in First Samuel: "And the king said, Enquire thou whose son the stripling [ʿ*elem*] *is*" (17:56); and "But if I say thus unto the young man [ʿ*elem*], Behold, the arrows *are* beyond thee; go thy way: for the LORD hath sent thee away" (20:22). See: TWOT—1630a; BDB—761c.

עֹלָם ʿ**ôlâm**. See 5769.

5959. עַלְמָה {7x} ʿ**almâh**, *al-maw';* fem. of 5958; a *lass* (as *veiled* or private):—virgin {4x}, maid {2x}, damsels {1x}.

ʿ*Almah* means virgin; maiden. **(1)** That ʿ*almah* means virgin is quite clear in **(1a1)** Gen 24:43 the word describes Rebekah, "Behold, I stand by the well of water; and it shall come to pass, that when the virgin cometh forth to draw *water,* and I say to her, Give me, I pray thee, a little water of thy pitcher to drink;" **(1a2)** and that she was a "maiden" with whom no man had had relations: "And the damsel *was* very fair to look upon, a virgin, neither had any man known her: and she went down to the well, and filled her pitcher, and came up" (Gen 24:16). Then again in **(1b)** Song 6:8: "There are threescore queens, and fourscore concubines, and virgins without number." **(1b1)** Thus all the women in the court are described. **(1b2)** The word ʿ*almah* represents those who are eligible for marriage but are neither wives (queens) nor concubines. **(1b3)** These "virgins" all loved the king and longed to be chosen to be with him (to be his bride), **(1b4)** even as did the Shulamite who became his bride (1:3–4). **(2)** It is used more of the concept "virgin" than that of "maiden," **(3)** yet always of a woman who had not borne a child. **(4)** Solomon wrote that the process of wooing a woman was mysterious to him (Prov 30:19). **(4a)** Certainly in that day a man ordinarily wooed one whom he considered to be a "virgin." **(4b)** There are several contexts, therefore, in which a young girl's virginity is expressly in view.

(5) All virgins are maidens, but not all maidens are necessarily a virgin. **(6)** This makes it the ideal word to be used in Is 7:14, since the word betulah emphasizes virility more than virginity (although it is used with both emphases, too). **(6a)** The reader of Is 7:14 in the days preceding the birth of Jesus would read that a "virgin who is a maiden" would conceive a child. **(6b)** This was a possible, but irregular, use of the word since the word can refer merely to the unmarried status of the one so described. **(6c)** The child immediately in view was the son of the prophet and his wife (cf. Is 8:3) who served as a sign to Ahaz that his enemies would be defeated by God. **(6c)** On the other hand, the reader of that day must have been extremely uncomfortable with this use of the word, since its primary connotation is "virgin" rather than "maiden." **(6d)** Thus the clear translation of the Greek in Mt 1:23 whereby this word is rendered "virgin" satisfies its fullest implication. **(6e)** Therefore, there was no embarrassment to Isaiah when his wife conceived a son by him, since the word ʿ*almah* allowed for this. Neither is there any embarrassment in Matthew's understanding of the word. See: TWOT—1630b; BDB—761c.

5960. עַלְמוֹן {1x} ʿ**Almôwn**, *al-mone';* from 5956; *hidden; Almon,* a place in Pal.:—Almon {1x}. See: BDB—761b. See also 5963.

5961. עֲלָמוֹת {2x} ʿ**Ălâmôwth**, *al-aw-mōth';* plur. of 5959; prop. *girls,* i.e. the *soprano* or female voice, perh. *falsetto:*—Alamoth {2x}. See: BDB—761b, 761c, 763a.

עַלְמוּת ʿ**almûwth**. See 4192.

5962. עַלְמִי {1x} ʿ**Almîy** (Aram.), *al-mee';* patrial from a name corresp. to 5867 contr.; an *Elamite* or inhab. of Elam:—Elamites {1x}. See: BDB—1106d.

5963. עַלְמֹן דִּבְלָתָיְמָה {2x} ʿ**Almôn Diblâthâyᵉmâh**, *al-mone' dib-law-thaw'-yem-aw;* from the same as 5960 and the dual of 1690 [comp. 1015] with enclitic of direction; *Almon toward Diblathajim; Almon-Diblathajemah,* a place in Moab:—Almondiblathaim {2x}. See: BDB—761b.

5964. עָלֶמֶת {4x} ʿ**Âlemeth**, *aw-leh'-meth;* from 5956; a *covering; Alemeth,* the name of a place in Pal. and of two Isr.:—*Alemeth* {3x}, Alameth {1x}. See: BDB—761b.

5965. עָלַס {3x} ʿ**âlaç**, *aw-las';* a prim. root; to *leap* for joy, i.e. *exult, wave* joyously:—rejoice {1x}, peacock {1x}, solace {1x}. See: TWOT—1632; BDB—763a.

5966. עָלַע {1x} ʿ**âlaʿ**, *aw-lah';* a prim root; to *sip* up:—suck up {1x}. See: TWOT—1633; BDB—763a.

5967. עֲלַע {1x} ʿ**âlaʿ** (Aram.), *al-ah';* corresp. to 6763; a *rib:*—ribs {1x}. See: TWOT—2913; BDB—1106d.

5968. עָלַף {5x} ʿ**âlaph**, *aw-laf';* a prim. root; to *veil* or *cover;* fig. to *be languid:*—faint {3x}, overlaid {1x}, wrapped {1x}. TWOT—1634; BDB—763a.

5969. עֻלְפֶּה {1x} ʿ**ulpeh**, *ool-peh';* from 5968; an *envelope,* i.e. (fig.) *mourning:*—fainted {1x}. See: TWOT—1634; BDB—763b.

5970. עָלַץ {8x} ʿ**âlats**, *aw-lats';* a prim. root; to *jump* for joy, i.e. *exult:*—rejoice {6x}, joyful {1x}, triumph {1x}. See: TWOT—1635; BDB—763b.

5971. עַם {1861x} ʿ**am**, *am;* from 6004; a *people* (as a congregated *unit*); spec. a *tribe* (as those of Israel); hence, (collect.) *troops* or *attendants;* fig. a *flock:*—people {1836x}, nation {17x}, people + 1121 {4x}, folk {2x}.

Ammi {1x}, men {1x}. *ʿAm* means "people; relative." **(1)** The word bears subjective and personal overtones. **(1a)** *ʿAm* represents a familial relationship. **(1b)** In Ruth 3:11 the word means "male kinsmen" with special emphasis on the paternal relationship: **(1b1)** "And now, my daughter, fear not; I will do to thee all that thou requirest: for all the city of my people doth know that thou art a virtuous woman." **(1b2)** Here the word is a collective noun insofar as it occurs in the singular; indeed, it is almost an abstract noun. **(2)** In the plural the word refers to all the individuals who are related to a person through his father: "But he shall not defile himself, being a chief man among his people, to profane himself" (Lev 21:4). **(3)** The word is quite often combined with divine names and titles in people's names (theophoric names) where God is set forth as the God of a particular tribe, clan, or family—for example, **(3a)** Jekameam (God has raised up a clan or family, 1 Chr 23:19) and **(3b)** Jokneam (God has created a clan or family, Josh 12:22). **(4)** *ʿAm* may signify those relatives (including women and children) who are grouped together locally whether or not they permanently inhabit a given location: "Then Jacob was greatly afraid and distressed: and he divided the people that was with him, and the flocks, and herds, and the camels, into two bands" (Gen 32:7).

(5) This word may refer to the whole of a nation formed and united primarily by their descent from a common ancestor. Such a group has strong blood ties and social interrelationships and interactions. **(5a)** Often they live and work together in a society in a common location. **(5b)** This is the significance of the word in its first biblical appearance: "And the Lord said, Behold, the people is one, and they have all one language . . ." (Gen 11:6). **(5c)** Hence, in this usage *ʿam* refers not simply to male relatives but to men, women, and children. **(5d)** *ʿAm* may also include those who enter by religious adoption and marriage. **(6)** The people of Israel initially were the descendants of Jacob (Israel) and their families: "And he said unto his people [Egyptians], Behold, the people of the children of Israel are more and mightier than we" (Ex 1:9).

(7) Later the basic unity in a common covenant relationship with God becomes the unifying factor underlying *ʿam.* **(7a)** When they left Egypt, the people of Israel were joined by many others: "And a mixed multitude went up also with them; and flocks, and herds, even very much cattle" (Ex 12:38). **(7b)** Such individuals and their families were taken into Israel before they observed the Passover: "And when a stranger shall sojourn with thee, and will keep the passover to the Lord, let all his males be circumcised, and then let him come near and keep it; and he shall be as one that is born in the land . . ." (Ex 12:48). **(7c)** There is another mention of this group (perhaps) in Num 11:4: "And the mixed multitude that was among them fell a lusting: and the children of Israel also wept again, and said. . . ." **(7d)** After that, however, we read of them no more. By the time of the conquest we read only of the "people" (*ʿam*) of Israel entering the land of Canaan and inheriting it (Judg 5:11). **(7e)** Passages such as Deut 32:9 clearly focus on this covenantal relationship as the basis of unity: "For the Lord's portion is his people; Jacob is the lot of his inheritance." **(7f)** This sense certainly emerges in the concept "to be cut off from one's people": "And the uncircumcised man child whose flesh of his foreskin is not circumcised, that soul shall be cut off from his people; he hath broken my covenant" (Gen 17:14).

(8) *ʿAm* can mean all those physical ancestors who lived previously and are now dead. **(8a)** So Abraham was gathered to his people: "Then Abraham gave up the ghost, and died in a good old age, an old man, and full of years; and was gathered to his people" (Gen 25:8). **(8b)** There might be covenantal overtones here in the sense that Abraham was gathered to all those who were true believers. Jesus argued that such texts taught the reality of life after death (cf. Mt 22:32). **(9)** *ʿAm* can represent the individuals who together form a familial (and covenantal) group within a larger group: "Zebulun and Naphtali were a people that jeoparded their lives unto the death in the high places of the field [on the battlefield]" (Judg 5:18). **(9a)** Some scholars have suggested that the reference here is to a fighting unit with the idea of blood relationship in the background. **(9b)** One must never forget, however, that among nomadic and seminomadic tribes there is no distinction between the concepts "militia" and "kinsmen": "And the Lord said unto Joshua, Fear not, neither be thou dismayed: take all the people of war with thee, and arise . . ." (Josh 8:1). **(9c)** Compare Josh 8:5 where *ʿam* by itself means fighting unit: "And I, and all the people that are with me, will approach unto the city . . ." (cf. Gen 32:7).

(10) *ʿAm* may signify the inhabitants of a city regardless of their familial or covenantal relationship; it is a territorial or political term: "And Boaz said unto the elders, and unto all the people, Ye are witnesses . . ." (Ruth 4:9). **(11)** This noun can be used of those who are privileged. In the phrase "people of the land" *ʿam* may signify those who have feudal rights, or those who may own land and are especially protected under the law: "And Abraham stood up, and bowed himself to the people of the land, even to the children of Heth" (Gen 23:7).

(12) This sense of a full citizen appears when the phrase is used of Israel, too (cf. 2 Kin 11:14ff.). **(12a)** In some contexts this phrase excludes those of high office such as the king, his ministers, and priests; "For, behold, I have made thee this day a defenced city, and an iron pillar, and brazen walls against the whole land, against the kings of Judah, against the princes thereof, against the priests thereof, and against the people of the land" (Jer 1:18). **(12b)** In Lev 4:27 this same phrase signifies the entire worshiping community of Israel: "And if any one of the common people [people of the land] sin through ignorance. . . ." **(12c)** The sense of privileged people with a proper relationship to and unique knowledge of God appears in Job 12:2: "No doubt but ye are the people, and wisdom shall die with you." **(12d)** Could it be that in Is 42:5 all mankind are conceived to be the privileged recipients of divine revelation and blessing: "Thus saith God the Lord, he that created the heavens, and stretched them out; he that spread forth the earth, and that which cometh out of it; he that giveth breath unto the people upon it, and spirit to them that walk therein."

(13) Finally, sometimes *ʿam* used of an entire nation has political and territorial overtones. As such it may be paralleled to the Hebrew word with such overtones (1471 - goy): "For thou art a holy people unto the Lord thy God, and the Lord hath chosen thee to be a peculiar people unto himself, above all the nations that are upon the earth" (Deut 14:2; cf. Ex 19:5–6). Syn.: 523, 1471. See: TWOT—1640a, 1640e; BDB—763c, 766b, 769b, 770c, 1107a.

5972. עַם {15x} ʿ**am** (Aram.), *am;* corresp. to 5971:—people {15x}. See: TWOT—2914; BDB—1107a.

5973. עִם {26x} ʿ**im**, *eem;* from 6004; adv. or prep., *with* (i.e. in *conjunction* with), in varied applications; spec. *equally with;* often with prep. pref. (and then usually unrepresented in English):—{26x} = with, unto, by, as long, neither, from between, from among, to, unto. See: TWOT—1640b; BDB—763c, 765c, 767a, 769b, 1107a.

5974. עִם {20x} ʿ**im** (Aram.), *eem;* corresp. to 5973:—with {9x}, with . . . {3x}, to {2x}, from {2x}, toward {1x}, like {1x}, unto {1x}, by {1x}. See: TWOT—2915; BDB—1107a.

5975. עָמַד {521x} ʿ**âmad**, *aw-mad';* a prim. root; to *stand,* in various relations (lit. and fig., intr. and tran.):—stood {171x}, stand {137x}, (raise, stand . . .) up {42x}, set {32x}, stay {17x}, still {15x}, appointed {10x}, standing {10x}, endure {8x}, remain {8x}, present {7x}, continue {6x}, withstand {6x}, waited {5x}, establish {5x}, misc. {42x} = abide (behind), arise, cease, confirm, dwell, be employed, leave, make, ordain, be [over], place, raise up, repair, + serve, tarry.

ʿAmad means "to take one's stand; stand here or be there; stand still." **(1)** The basic meaning of this verb is "to stand upright." **(1a)** This is its meaning in Gen 18:8, its first biblical occurrence: "And he took butter, and milk, and the calf which he had dressed, and set *it* before them; and he stood by them under the tree, and they did eat." **(1b)** It is what a soldier does while on watch: "And the king said *unto him,* Turn aside, *and* stand here. And he turned aside, and stood still" (2 Sa 18:30). **(2)** From this basic meaning comes the meaning "to be established, immovable, and standing upright" on a single spot; **(2a)** the soles of the priests' feet "rested" (stood still, unmoving) in the waters of the Jordan (Josh 3:13). **(2b)** Also, the sun and the moon "stood still" at Joshua's command (Josh 10:13). **(3)** Idols "stand upright" in one spot, never moving. The suggestion here is that they never do anything that is expected of living things (Is 46:7).

(4) *ʿAmad* may be used of the existence of a particular experience. **(4a)** In 2 Sa 21:18 there "was" (1961 - hayah) war again, **(4b)** while in 1 Chr 20:4 war "existed" or "arose" (*ʿamad*) again. **(5)** Cultically (with reference to the formal worship activities) this verb is used of approaching the altar to make a sacrifice. **(5a)** It describes the last stage of this approaching, "to stand finally and officially" before the altar (before God; cf. Deut 4:11). **(5b)** Such standing is not just a standing still doing nothing but includes all that one does in ministering before God (Num 16:9). **(6)** In other contexts *'amad* is used as the opposite of verbs indicating various kinds of movement. **(6a)** The psalmist praises the man who does not walk (behave according to) in the counsel of the ungodly or "stand" (serve) in the path of the sinful (Ps 1:1). **(6b)** Laban told Abraham not "to stand" (remain stationary, not entering) outside his dwelling but to come in (Gen 24:31).

(7) The verb can suggest "immovable," or not being able to be moved. So the "house of the righteous shall stand" (Prov 12:7). **(8)** Yet another nuance appears in Ps 102:26, which teaches the indestructibility and/or eternity of God—the creation perishes but He "shalt endure [will ever stand]." **(8a)** This is not the changelessness of doing nothing or standing physically upright, **(8b)** but the changelessness of ever-existing being, a quality that only God has in Himself. **(8c)** All other existing depends upon Him; the creation and all creatures are perishable. **(9)** In a more limited sense the man who does not die as the result of a blow "stands," or remains alive (Ex 21:21). **(10)** In a military context "to stand" refers to gaining a victory: "Behold, two kings stood not before him: how then shall we stand?" (2 Kin 10:4; cf. Judg 2:14). **(11)** *'Amad* can be used of the ever unchanged content and/or existence of **(11a)** a document (Jer 32:14), **(11b)** a city (1 Kin 15:4), **(11c)** a people (Is 66:22), and **(11d)** a divine worship (Ps. 19:9).

(12) Using the causative aspect of the Hebrew verb, Jeroboam "ordained" (made to stand, to minister) priests in Bethel (1 Kin 12:32). **(13)** Certain prepositions sometimes give this verb special meanings. **(13a)** With "to" the verb can signify being in a certain place to accomplish a predesignated task—**(13a1)** so Moses said that certain tribes should "stand upon mount Gerizim to bless the people" (Deut 27:12). **(13a2)** With this same preposition this verb can be used **(13a2i)** judicially of the act of being in court, or standing before a judge (1 Kin 3:16), and **(13a2ii)** the position (whether literal or figurative) assumed by a judge when pronouncing the sentence (Eze 44:24) or **(13a2iii)** delivering judgment (Is 3:13; cf. Ex 17:6). **(13a3)** With the preposition "before" *'amad* is used to describe the service of a servant before a master—so Joshua "stood" before Moses (Deut 1:38). This is not inactivity but activity. **(14)** In Neh 8:5 the verb means "to stand up or rise up"; when Ezra opened the book, all the people "stood up" (cf. Dan 12:13). Syn.: 4612, 4613, 5977, 5979, 5982. See: TWOT—1637; BDB—763c.

5976. **עָמַד** {1x} **ʻâmad**, *aw-mad';* for 4571; to *shake:*—to be at a stand {1x}. See: TWOT—1637; BDB—588c.

5977. **עֹמֶד** {10x} **ʻômed**, *o'-med;* from 5975; a *spot* (as being *fixed*):—place {6x}, upright {2x}, where I stood {1x}, I stood {1x}.

'Omed occurs 10 times and refers to "standing places": "And they stood in their place after their manner, according to the law of Moses the man of God:" (2 Chr 30:16). Syn.: 4612, 4613, 5979, 5982. See: TWOT—1637a; BDB—765a.

5978. **עִמָּד** {12x} **ʻimmâd**, *im-mawd';* prol. for 5973; along *with:*—with me {1x}, within me {1x}, by me {1x}, upon me {1x}, mine {1x}, against me {1x}, unto me {1x}, me {1x}, from me {1x}, of me {1x}, that I take {1x}, in me {1x}. See: TWOT—1640b; BDB—767a.

עַמֻּד **ʻammûd**. See 5982.

5979. **עֶמְדָּה** {1x} **ʻemdâh**, *em-daw';* from 5975; a *station*, i.e. domicile:—standing {1x}.

'Emdah means "standing ground" once: "Pass ye away, thou inhabitant of Saphir, having thy shame naked: the inhabitant of Zaanan came not forth in the mourning of Bethezel; he shall receive of you his standing" (Mic 1:11). Syn.: 4612, 4613, 5977, 5982.See: TWOT—1637b; BDB—765a.

5980. **עֻמָּה** {32x} **ʻummâh**, *oom-maw';* from 6004; *conjunction*, i.e. *society;* mostly adv. or prep. (with prep. pref.), *near, beside, along with:*—against {26x}, beside {2x}, answerable {1x}, at {1x}, hard {1x}, points {1x}. See: TWOT—1640f; BDB—769c.

5981. **עֻמָּה** {1x} **ʻUmmâh**, *oom-maw';* the same as 5980; *association; Ummah*, a place in Pal.:—*Ummah* {1x}. See: BDB—769d.

5982. **עַמּוּד** {110x} **ʻammûwd**, *am-mood';* or **עַמֻּד** **ʻammûd**, *am-mood';* from 5975; a *column* (as *standing*); also a *stand*, i.e. platform:—pillar {109x}, apiece + 259 {1x}. *'Ammud* means "pillar; standing place." **(1)** The noun *'ammud* occurs 110 times and usually signifies something that stands upright like a "pillar": "And thou shalt hang it upon four pillars of shittim *wood* overlaid with gold: their hooks *shall be of* gold, upon the four sockets of silver" (Ex 26:32; cf. Judg 16:25). **(2)** It may occasionally refer to a "standing place": "And when she looked, behold, the king stood by a pillar, as the manner *was*, and the princes and the trumpeters by the king, and all the people of the land rejoiced," (2 Kin 11:14). Syn.: 4612, 4613, 5977, 5979. See: TWOT—1637c; BDB—765a.

5983. **עַמּוֹן** {105x} **ʻAmmôwn**, *am-mone';* from 5971; *tribal*, i.e. *inbred; Ammon*, a son of Lot; also his posterity and their country:—Ammon {90x}, Ammonites + 1121 {13x}, Ammonites {2x}. See: TWOT—1642; BDB—769d.

5984. **עַמּוֹנִי** {18x} **ʻAmmôwnîy**, *am-mo-nee';* patron. from 5983; an *Ammonite* or (adj.) *Ammonitish:*—Ammonite {17x}, Ammon {1x}. See: TWOT—1642a; BDB—770a.

5985. **עַמּוֹנִית** {4x} **ʻAmmôwnîyth**, *am-mo-neeth';* fem. of 5984; an *Ammonitess:*—Ammonitess {4x}. See: BDB—770a.

5986. **עָמוֹס** {7x} **ʻÂmôwç**, *aw-moce';* from 6006; *burdensome; Amos*, an Isr. prophet:—Amos {7x}. See: BDB—770c.

5987. **עָמוֹק** {2x} **ʻÂmôwq**, *aw-moke';* from 6009; *deep; Amok*, an Isr.:—Amok {2x}. See: BDB—771b.

5988. **עַמִּיאֵל** {6x} **ʻAmmîyʼêl**, *am-mee-ale';* from 5971 and 410; *people of God; Ammiël*, the name of three or four Isr.:—Ammiel {6x}. See: BDB—765c, 770a.

5989. **עַמִּיהוּד** {10x} **ʻAmmîyhûwd**, *am-mee-hood';* from 5971 and 1935; *people of splendor; Ammihud*, the name of three Isr.:—Ammihud {10x}. See: BDB—770a.

5990. **עַמִּיזָבָד** {1x} **ʻAmmîyzâbâd**, *am-mee-zaw-bawd';* from 5971 and 2064; *people of endowment; Ammizabad*, an Isr.:—Ammizabad {1x}. See: BDB—770b.

5991. **עַמִּיחוּר** {1x} **ʻAmmîychûwr**, *am-mee-khoor';* from 5971 and 2353; *people of nobility; Ammichur*, a Syrian prince:—Ammihud {1x}. See: BDB—770a, 770b.

5992. **עַמִּינָדָב** {13x} **ʻAmmîynâdâb**, *am-mee-naw-dawb';* from 5971 and 5068; *people of liberality; Amminadab*, the name of four Isr.:—Amminadab {13x}. See: BDB—770b.

5993. **עַמִּי נָדִיב** {1x} **ʻAmmîy Nâdîyb**, *am-mee' naw-deeb';* from 5971 and 5081; *my people* (is) *liberal; Ammi-Nadib*, prob. an Isr.:—Amminadib {1x}. See: BDB—766c.

5994. **עֲמִיק** {1x} **ʻămîyq** (Aram.), *am-eek';* corresp. to 6012; *profound*, i.e. unsearchable:—deep {1x}. See: TWOT—2916; BDB—1107a.

5995. **עָמִיר** {4x} **ʻâmîyr**, *aw-meer';* from 6014; a *bunch* of grain:—sheaf {3x}, handful {1x}. See: TWOT—1645c; BDB—771c.

5996. **עַמִּישַׁדַּי** {5x} **ʻAmmîyshadday**, *am-mee-shad-dah'ee;* from 5971 and 7706; *people of* (the) *Almighty; Ammishaddai*, an Isr.:—Ammishaddai {5x}. See: BDB—770b.

5997. **עָמִית** {12x} **ʻâmîyth**, *aw-meeth';* from a prim. root mean. to *associate; companionship;* hence, (concr.) a *comrade* or kindred man:—neighbour {9x}, another {2x}, fellow {1x}. See: TWOT—1638a; BDB—765c.

5998. **עָמַל** {11x} **ʻâmal**, *aw-mal';* a prim. root; to *toil*, i.e. *work severely* and with irksomeness:—labour {8x}, take {3x}.

'Amal means to labor: "Then I looked on all the works that my hands had wrought, and on the labour that I had laboured to do: and, behold, all *was* vanity and vexation of spirit, and *there was* no profit under the sun" (Eccl 2:11, cf. 11:19, 21; 5:16; Ps 127:1). See: TWOT—1639; BDB—765c, 766a.

5999. **עָמָל** {55x} **ʻâmâl**, *aw-mawl';* from 5998; *toil*, i.e. *wearing effort;* hence, *worry*, wheth. of body or mind:—labour {25x}, mischief {9x}, misery {3x}, travail {3x}, trouble {3x}, sorrow {2x}, grievance {1x}, grievousness {1x}, iniquity {1x}, miserable {1x}, pain {1x}, painful {1x}, perverseness {1x}, toil {1x}, wearisome {1x}, wickedness {1x}.

'Amal means labor; toil; anguish; troublesome work; trouble; misery, evil; trouble; misfortune; mischief; grievance; wickedness. **(1)** The Book of Ecclesiastes clearly represents this use: **(1a)** "Yea, I hated all my labor which I had taken under the sun . . ." (Eccl 2:18). **(1b)** "And also that every man should eat and drink, and enjoy the good of all his labor . . ." (Eccl 3:13). **(1c)** A related example appears in Ps 107:12: "Therefore he brought down their heart with labor; they fell down and there was none to help." **(2)** In general, *'amal* refers either to the trouble and suffering which sin causes the sinner or to the trouble that he inflicts upon others. **(2a)** Jer 20:18 depicts self-inflicted sorrow: "Wherefore came I forth out of the womb to see labor [*'amal*] and sorrow [3015 - yagon], that my days should be consumed with shame?" **(2b)** Another instance is found in Deut 26:7: "And when we cried unto the Lord God of our fathers, the Lord heard our voice, and looked on our affliction [6040 - *'oni*], and our labor [*'amal*], and our oppression [3906 - *lachats*]."

(3) Job 4:8 illustrates the sense of trouble as mischief inflicted on others: ". . . They that plow iniquity [205 - 'awen], and sow wickedness [*'amal*] reap the same." **(3a)** The word appears in Ps 140:9: "As for the head of those that compass me about, let the mischief of their own lips cover them." **(3b)** Hab 1:3 also refers to the trouble inficted on others: "Why dost thou show me iniquity [205 - *'awen*], and cause me to behold grievance [*'amal*]? For spoiling and violence are before me; and there are that raise up strife and contention." **(4)** The word means labor in the sense of toil or oppression, **(4a)** generally (Deut 26:7) or **(4b)** of Messiah (Is 53:11). **(5)** Something gained by toil or labor is *ʿamal* (Ps 105:44). **(6)** *ʿAmal* means troublesome work, emphasizing the difficulty involved in a task or work as troublesome and burdensome (Eccl 1:3). **(7)** It can ethically connote sin (Ps 7:14; cf. Job 4:8). See: TWOT—1639a; BDB—765d.

6000. עָמָל {1x} **ʿÂmâl**, *aw-mawl';* the same as 5999; *Amal,* an Isr.:—*Amal* {1x}. See: BDB—765d.

6001. עָמֵל {9x} **ʿâmêl**, *aw-male';* from 5998; *toiling;* concr. a *laborer;* fig. *sorrowful:*—labour {4x}, take {2x}, workman {1x}, misery {1x}, wicked {1x}. See: TWOT—1639b, 1639c; BDB—766a.

6002. עֲמָלֵק {39x} **ʿĂmâlêq**, *am-aw-lake';* prob. of for. or.; *Amalek,* a desc. of Esau; also his posterity and their country:—Amalek {24x}, Amalekites {15x}. See: BDB—766a.

6003. עֲמָלֵקִי {12x} **ʿĂmâlêqîy**, *am-aw-lay-kee';* patron. from 6002; an *Amalekite* (or collect. the *Amalekites*) or desc. of Amalek:—Amalekite {11x}, Amalekite + 376 {1x}. See: BDB—766a.

6004. עָמַם {3x} **ʿâmam**, *aw-mam';* a prim. root; to *associate;* by impl. to *overshadow* (by *huddling* together):—hide {2x}, dim {1x}. See: TWOT—1641; BDB—770b.

6005. עִמָּנוּאֵל {2x} **ʿImmânûwʾêl**, *im-maw-noo-ale';* from 5973 and 410 with a pron. suff. ins.; *with us* (is) *God; Immanuel,* a typical name of Isaiah's son:—Immanuel + 410 {2x}. See: TWOT—1640d; BDB—769b, 770c.

6006. עָמַס {9x} **ʿâmaç**, *aw-mas';* or

עָמַשׂ **ʿâmas**, *aw-mas';* a prim. root; to *load,* i.e. *impose* a burden (or fig. infliction):—lade {4x}, load {2x}, put {1x}, borne {1x}, burden {1x}. See: TWOT—1643; BDB—770c, 771d.

6007. עֲמַסְיָה {1x} **ʿĂmaçyâh**, *am-as-yaw';* from 6006 and 3050; *Jah has loaded; Amasjah,* an Isr.:—Amasiah {1x}. See: BDB—770c.

6008. עַמְעָד {1x} **ʿAmʿâd**, *am-awd';* from 5971 and 5703; *people of time; Amad,* a place in Pal.:—*Amad* {1x}. See: BDB—770c.

6009. עָמַק {9x} **ʿâmaq**, *aw-mak';* a prim. root; *to be* (caus. *make*) *deep* (lit. or fig.):—deep {5x}, deeply {2x}, depth {1x}, profound {1x}. See: TWOT—1644; BDB—770d.

6010. עֵמֶק {69x} **ʿêmeq**, *ay'-mek;* from 6009; a *vale* (i.e. broad *depression*):—valley {63x}, vale {4x}, dale {2x}. See: TWOT—1644a; BDB—770d. See also 1025.

6011. עֹמֶק {1x} **ʿômeq**, *o'-mek;* from 6009; *depth:*—depth {1x}. See: TWOT—1644b; BDB—771b.

6012. עָמֵק {4x} **ʿâmêq**, *aw-make';* from 6009; *deep* (lit. or fig.):—strange {2x}, depths {1x}, deeper {1x}. See: TWOT—1644c; BDB—771b, 1107a.

6013. עָמֹק {16x} **ʿâmôq**, *aw-moke';* from 6009; *deep* (lit. or fig.):—deeper {8x}, deep {7x}, deep things {1x}. See: TWOT—1644d; BDB—771b, 1008a.

6014. עָמַר {3x} **ʿâmar**, *aw-mar';* a prim. root; prop. appar. to *heap;* fig. to *chastise* (as if *piling* blows); spec. (as denom. from 6016) to *gather* grain:—merchandise {2x}, sheaves {1x}. See: TWOT—1645, 1646; BDB—771c.

6015. עֲמַר {1x} **ʿămar** (Aram.), *am-ar';* corresp. to 6785; *wool:*—wool {1x}. See: TWOT—2917; BDB—1107a.

6016. עֹמֶר {14x} **ʿômer**, *o'-mer;* from 6014; prop. a *heap,* i.e. a *sheaf;* also an *omer,* as a dry measure:—sheaf {8x}, *omer* {6x}. See: TWOT—1645b, 1645a; BDB—771b, 771c.

6017. עֲמֹרָה {16x} **ʿĂmôrâh**, *am-o-raw';* from 6014; a (ruined) *heap; Amorah,* a place in Pal.:—Gomorrah {16x}. See: BDB—771c.

6018. עָמְרִי {18x} **ʿOmrîy**, *om-ree';* from 6014; *heaping; Omri,* an Isr.:—Omri {18x}. See: BDB—771d.

6019. עַמְרָם {14x} **ʿAmrâm**, *am-rawm';* prob. from 5971 and 7311; *high people; Amram,* the name of two Isr.:—Amram {14x}. See: BDB—771d.

6020. עַמְרָמִי {2x} **ʿAmrâmîy**, *am-raw-mee';* patron. from 6019; an *Amramite* or desc. of Amram:—Amramites {2x}.See: BDB—771d.

עָמַשׂ **ʿâmas**. See 6006.

6021. עֲמָשָׂא {16x} **ʿĂmâsâʾ**, *am-aw-saw';* from 6006; *burden; Amasa,* the name of two Isr.:—Amasa {16x}. See: BDB—771d.

6022. עֲמָשַׂי {5x} **ʿĂmâsay**, *am-aw-sah'-ee;* from 6006; *burdensome; Amasai,* the name of three Isr.:—Amasai {5x}. See: BDB—772a.

6023. עֲמַשְׁסַי {1x} **ʿĂmashçay**, *am-ash-sah'-ee;* prob. from 6006; *burdensome; Amashsay,* an Isr.:—Amashai {1x}. See: BDB—772a.

6024. עֲנָב {2x} **ʿĂnâb**, *an-awb';* from the same as 6025; *fruit; Anab,* a place in Pal.:—*Anab* {2x}. See: BDB—772b.

6025. עֵנָב {19x} **ʿênâb**, *ay-nawb';* from an unused root prob. mean. to *bear* fruit; a *grape:*—grape {18x}, wine {1x}. See: TWOT—1647a; BDB—772a.

6026. עָנַג {10x} **ʿânag**, *aw-nag';* a prim. root; to *be soft* or *pliable,* i.e. (fig.) *effeminate* or luxurious:—delight {7x}, delicate {1x}, delicateness {1x}, sport {1x}. See: TWOT—1648; BDB—772b.

6027. עֹנֶג {2x} **ʿôneg**, *o'-neg;* from 6026; *luxury:*—pleasant {1x}, delight {1x}. See: TWOT—1648a; BDB—772b.

6028. עָנֹג {3x} **ʿânôg**, *aw-nogue';* from 6026; *luxurious:*—delicate {2x}, delicate woman {1x}. See: TWOT—1648b; BDB—772b.

6029. עָנַד {2x} **ʿânad**, *aw-nad';* a prim. root; to *lace* fast:—tie {1x}, bind {1x}. See: TWOT—1649; BDB—772c.

6030. עָנָה {329x} **ʿânâh**, *aw-naw';* a prim. root; prop. to *eye* or (gen.) to *heed,* i.e. *pay attention;* by impl. to *respond;* by extens. to *begin* to speak; spec. to *sing, shout, testify, announce:*—answer {242x}, hear {42x}, testify {12x}, speak {8x}, sing {4x}, bear {3x}, cry {2x}, witness {2x}, give {1x}, misc. {13x}.

ʿAnah means "to respond, answer, reply." **(1)** *ʿAnah* means "to respond," but not necessarily with a verbal response. **(1a)** For example, in Gen 35:3 Jacob tells his household, "And let us arise, and go up to Bethel; and I will make there an altar unto God, who answered [*ʿanah*] me in the day of my distress. . . ." **(1a1)** In Gen 28:10ff., where this "answering" is recorded, it is quite clear that God initiated the encounter and that, although He spoke with Jacob, **(1a2)** the emphasis is on the vision of the ladder and the relationship with God that it represented. **(1b)** This meaning is even clearer in Ex 19:18, where we read that God reacted to the situation at Sinai with a sound (of thunder). **(1c)** A nonverbal reaction is also indicated in Deut 20:11. God tells Israel that before they besiege a city they should demand its surrender. Its inhabitants are to live as Israel's slaves "if it [the city] make thee answer of peace [literally, "responds peaceably"], and open unto thee. . . ." **(1d)** In Job 30:20, Job says he cried out to God, who did not "respond" to him (i.e., did not pay any attention to him). **(1e)** In Is 49:8 the Lord tells the Messiah, "In an acceptable time have I heard thee, and in a day of salvation have I helped thee. . . ." Here responding ("hearing") is synonymously parallel to helping—i.e., it is an action (cf. Ps 69:17; Is 41:17).

(2) A second major meaning of *ʿanah* is "to respond with words," as when one engages in dialogue. **(2a)** In Gen 18:27 (the first occurrence of *ʿanah*), we read: "Abraham answered and said" to the Lord, who had just spoken. **(2a1)** In this formula, the two verbs represent one idea (i.e., they form an hendiadys). **(2a2)** A simpler translation might be "respond," since God had asked no question and required no reply. **(2b)** On the other hand, when the sons of Heth "answer and say" (Gen 23:5), they are responding verbally to the implied inquiry made by Abraham (v. 4). Therefore, they really do answer. **(3)** *ʿAnah* may mean "respond" in the special sense of verbally reacting to a truth discovered: **(3a)** "Then answered the five men that went to spy out the country of Laish, and said . . ." (Judg 18:14). Since no inquiry was addressed to them, this word implies that they gave a report; they responded to what they had discovered. **(3b)** In Deut 21:7, the children of Israel are told how to respond to the rite of the heifer—viz., "They shall answer and say, Our hands have not shed this blood, neither have our eyes seen it."

(4) *ʿAnah* can also be used in the legal sense of "testify": "Thou shalt not bear false witness against thy neighbor" (Ex 20:16). **(4a)** Or we read in Ex 23:2: "Thou shalt not follow a multitude to do evil. . . ." **(4b)** In a similar sense, Jacob proposed that Laban give him all the spotted and speckled sheep of the flock, so that "my righteousness [will] answer [i.e., testify] for me in time to come, when it shall come [to make an investigation] for my hire before thy face . . ." (Gen 30:33). See: TWOT—1650, 1653; BDB—732d, 772c, 777a, 1107a. See also 1042, 1043.

6031. עָנָה {84x} **ʿânâh**, *aw-naw';* a prim. root [possibly rather ident. with 6030 through the idea of *looking* down or *browbeating*]; to *depress* lit. or fig., tran. or intr. (in various applications, as follows):—afflict {50x}, humble {11x}, force {5x}, exercised {2x}, sing {2x}, Leannoth {1x}, troubled {1x}, weakened {1x}, misc. {11}.

ʿAnah, as a verb, means "to be afflicted, be bowed down, be humbled, be meek." **(1)** This word, common to both ancient and modern Hebrew, is the source of several important words in the history and experience of Judaism: "humble, meek, poor, and affliction." **(2)** It is found for the first time in Gen 15:13: ". . . they shall afflict them four hundred years." **(3)** *ʿAnah* often expresses harsh and painful treatment. **(3a)** Sarai "dealt hardly" with Hagar (Gen 16:6). **(3b)** When Joseph was sold as a slave, his feet were hurt with fetters (Ps 105:18). **(4)** Frequently the verb expresses the idea that God sends affliction for disciplinary purposes: ". . . the Lord thy God led thee these forty years in the wilderness, to humble thee, and to prove thee, to know what was in thine heart . . ." (Deut 8:2; see also 1 Kin

11:39; Ps 90:15). **(5)** To take a woman sexually by force may be "to humble" her (Gen 34:2). **(6)** In the Day of Atonement observance, "to humble oneself" is probably connected with the requirement for fasting on that day (Lev 23:28–29). **(7)** *ʿAnah* means "to be exercised": "And I gave my heart to seek and search out by wisdom concerning all *things* that are done under heaven: this sore travail hath God given to the sons of man to be exercised therewith" (Eccl 1:13). See: TWOT—1651, 1652; BDB—775d, 776a, 1107c.

6032. עֲנָה {30x} **ʿănâh** (Aram.), *an-aw';* corresp. to 6030:—answered {16x}, spake {14x}. See: TWOT—2918; BDB—1107a.

6033. עֲנָה {1x} **ʿănâh** (Aram.), *an-aw';* corresp. to 6031:—poor {1x}. See: TWOT—2919a; BDB—1107c.

6034. עֲנָה {12x} **ʿĂnâh**, *an-aw';* prob. from 6030; an *answer; Anah,* the name of two Edomites and one Edomitess:—*Anah* {12x}. See: BDB—777b.

6035. עָנָו {26x} **ʿânâv**, *aw-nawv';* or [by intermixture with 6041]

עָנָיו **ʿânâyv**, *aw-nawv';* from 6031; *depressed* (fig.), in mind (*gentle*) or circumstances (*needy,* espec. *saintly*):—meek {13x}, humble {5x}, poor {5x}, lowly {2x}, very meek {1x}.

ʿAnayv, as an adjective, means "humble; poor; meek." **(1)** This adjective, which appears about 21 times in biblical Hebrew, is closely related to ʿani (6041) and derived from the same verb. **(1a)** Sometimes this word is synonymous with ʿani. Perhaps this is due to the well-known waw-yodh interchange. **(1b)** *ʿAnayv* appears almost exclusively in poetical passages and describes the intended outcome of affliction from God, namely "humility." **(2)** In its first appearance the word depicts the objective condition as well as the subjective stance of Moses. He was entirely dependent on God and saw that he was: "Now the man Moses was very meek, above all the men which were upon the face of the earth" (Num 12:3). See: TWOT—1652a; BDB—776c, 1107c. comp. 6041.

6036. עָנוּב {1x} **ʿÂnûwb**, *aw-noob';* pass. part. from the same as 6025; *borne* (as fruit); *Anub,* an Isr.:—Anub {1x}. See: BDB—772b.

6037. עַנְוָה {2x} **ʿanvâh**, *an-vaw';* fem. of 6035; *mildness* (royal); also (concr.) *oppressed:*—gentleness {1x}, meekness {1x}.

This word occurs only 5 times, setting forth the two characteristics gained from affliction: "humility and gentleness." Applied to God, it represents His submission to His own nature: "And in thy majesty ride prosperously because of truth and meekness *and* righteousness; and thy right hand shall teach thee terrible things" (Ps 45:4). See: TWOT—1652b; BDB—776c.

6038. עֲנָוָה {5x} **ʿănâvâh**, *an-aw-vaw';* from 6035; *condescension,* human and subj. (*modesty*), or divine and obj. (*clemency*):—humility {3x}, gentleness {1x}, meekness {1x}. See: TWOT—1652b; BDB—776c.

6039. עֱנוּת {1x} **ʿênûwth**, *en-ooth';* from 6031; *affliction:*—affliction {1x}. See: TWOT—1652c; BDB—776d.

6040. עֳנִי {37x} **ʿŏnîy**, *on-ee';* from 6031; *depression,* i.e. misery:—affliction {32x}, trouble {3x}, afflicted + 1121 {1x}, variant {1x}.

The noun *ʿoniy,* means "affliction." **(1)** *ʿOniy* represents the state of pain and/or punishment resulting from affliction. **(2)** In Deut 16:3 the shewbread is termed the bread of "affliction" because it is a physical reminder of **(2a)** sin, the cause of "affliction": "Look upon mine affliction and my pain; and forgive all my sins" (Ps 25:18), **(2b)** the hardship involved in sin (especially the Egyptian bondage), and **(2c)** divine deliverance from sin: "This *is* my comfort in my affliction: for thy word hath quickened me" (Ps 119:50). See: TWOT—1652e; BDB—777a.

6041. עָנִי {80x} **ʿânîy**, *aw-nee';* from 6031; *depressed,* in mind or circumstances [practically the same as 6035, although the marg. constantly disputes this, making 6035 subj. and 6041 obj.]:—poor {58x}, afflicted {15x}, lowly {1x}, man {1x}, variant {3x}.

ʿAniy, as a noun, means "poor; weak; afflicted; humble." **(1)** This noun is frequently used in synonymous parallelism with ʿebyon (34 - "needy") and/or dal (1802 - "poor"). **(1a)** It differs from both in emphasizing some kind of disability or distress. **(1b)** A hired servant as one who is in a lower (oppressive) social and material condition is described both as an ʿebyon and *ʿaniy:* "Thou shalt not oppress a hired servant that is poor and needy, whether he be of thy brethren, or of thy strangers that are in thy land within thy gates: At his day thou shalt give him his hire, neither shall the sun go down upon it; for he is poor, and setteth his heart upon it: lest he cry against thee unto the Lord, and it be sin unto thee" (Deut 24:14–15). **(1c)** If wrongly oppressed, he can call on God for defense.

(2) Financially, the *ʿaniy* lives from day to day and is socially defenseless, being subject to oppression. **(2a)** In its first biblical occurrence the *ʿaniy* is guaranteed (if men obey God's law) his outer garment for warmth at night even though that garment might be held as collateral during the day: "If thou lend money to any of my people that is poor by thee, thou shall not be to him as a usurer, neither shalt thou lay upon him usury" (Ex 22:25). **(2b)** The godly protect and deliver the "afflicted" (Is 10:2; Eze 18:17), while the ungodly take advantage of them, increasing their oppressed condition: "*Is it* not to deal thy bread to the hungry, and that thou bring the poor that are cast out to thy house? when thou seest the naked, that thou cover him; and that thou hide not thyself from thine own flesh?" (Is 58:7). **(2c)** The king is especially charged to protect the *ʿaniy:* "Open thy mouth, judge righteously, and plead the cause of the poor and needy" (Prov 31:9.)

(3) *ʿAniy* can refer to one who is physically oppressed: "Therefore hear now this, thou afflicted, and drunken, but not with wine" (Is 51:21). **(4)** Physical oppression is sometimes related to spiritual oppression as in Ps 22:24: "For he hath not despised nor abhorred the affliction of the afflicted; neither hath he hid his face from him. . . ." Outward affliction frequently leads to inner spiritual affliction and results in an outcry to God: "Turn thee unto me, and have mercy upon me; for I am desolate and afflicted" (Ps 25:16). **(5)** Even apart from outward affliction, the pious are frequently described as the "afflicted" or "poor" for whom God provides: "Thy congregation hath dwelt therein: thou, O God, hast prepared of thy goodness for the poor" (Ps 68:10). In such cases spiritual poverty and want are clearly in view. **(6)** Sometimes the word means "humble" or "lowly," as it does in Zec 9:9, where it describes the Messiah: "Behold, thy King cometh unto thee: he is just, and having salvation; lowly, and riding upon an ass . . ." (cf. Ps 18:27; Prov 3:34; Is 66:2). See: TWOT—1652d; BDB—776c, 776d, 1107c.

6042. עֻנִּי {3x} **ʿUnnîy**, *oon-nee';* from 6031; *afflicted; Unni,* the name of two Isr.:—Unni {3x}. See: BDB—777b, 777d.

6043. עֲנָיָה {2x} **ʿĂnâyâh**, *an-aw-yaw';* from 6030; *Jah has answered; Anajah,* the name of two Isr.:—Anaiah {2x}. See: BDB—777d.

עָנָיו **ʿânâyv** See 6035.

6044. עָנִים {1x} **ʿÂnîym**, *aw-neem';* for plur. of 5869; *fountains; Anim,* a place in Pal.:—Anim {1x}. See: BDB—745d.

6045. עִנְיָן {8x} **ʿinyân**, *in-yawn';* from 6031; *ado,* i.e. (gen.) *employment* or (spec.) an *affair:*—travail {6x}, business {2x}. See: TWOT—1651a; BDB—775d.

6046. עָנֵם {1x} **ʿÂnêm**, *aw-name';* from the dual of 5869; *two fountains; Anem,* a place in Pal.:—*Anem* {1x}. See: BDB—745c.

6047. עֲנָמִים {2x} **ʿĂnâmîm**, *an-aw-meem';* as if plur. of some Eg. word; *Anamim,* a son of Mizraim and his desc., with their country:—*Anamim* {2x}. See: BDB—777d.

6048. עֲנַמֶּלֶךְ {1x} **ʿĂnammelek**, *an-am-meh'-lek;* of for. or.; *Anammelek,* an Ass. deity:—Anammelech {1x}. See: BDB—777d.

6049. עָנַן {11x} **ʿânan**, *aw-nan';* a prim. root; to *cover;* used only as a denom. from 6051, to *cloud* over; fig. to *act covertly,* i.e. practise magic:—observer of times {5x}, soothsayer {2x}, bring {1x}, sorceress {1x}, enchanter {1x}, Meonemin.

(1) A mode of attempting to obtain information was by the examination of the clouds. **(2)** These observers are ranked with all the other intruders into unlawful pursuits in Deut 18:10, under the title of soothsayers. **(3)** They are called "sons of the sorceress" (Is 57:3) and are classed with the vile, the impure, and the idolater. **(4)** They are called enchanters (Jer 27:9). **(5)** They are also called "observers of times," persons who by examining the clouds profess to be able to tell at what exact crisis any event is to be expected to take place, and when a good opportunity arrives for doing a certain work (Lev 1:26; 2 Kin 21:6; 2 Chr 33:6). Syn.: 825, 826, 1505, 2267, 3858, 3907, 5172. See: TWOT—1655, 1656; BDB—778a, 1107c.

6050. עֲנַן {1x} **ʿănan** (Aram.), *an-an';* corresp. to 6051:—cloud {1x}. See: TWOT—2921; BDB—1107c.

6051. עָנָן {81x} **ʿânân**, *aw-nawn';* from 6049; a *cloud* (as *covering* the sky), i.e. the *nimbus* or thunder-cloud:—cloud {81x}, cloudy {6x}.

ʿAnan, means "cloud; fog; storm cloud; smoke." **(1)** The word commonly means "cloud mass." **(1a)** *ʿAnan* is used especially of the "cloud mass" that evidenced the special presence of God: "And the Lord went before them by day in a pillar of a cloud, to lead them the way . . ."(Ex 13:21). **(1b)** In Ex 34:5, this presence is represented by *ʿanan* only: "And the Lord descended in the cloud, and stood with him [Moses] there, and proclaimed the name of the Lord." **(2)** When the ark of the covenant was brought into the holy place, "The cloud filled the house of the Lord, so that the priests could not stand to minister because of the cloud: for the glory of the Lord had filled the house of the Lord" (1 Kin 8:10–11). **(2a)** Thus the "cloud" evidenced the presence of God's glory. **(2b)** So the psalmist wrote that God was surrounded by "clouds and darkness" (Ps 97:2); hence, **(2b)** God appears as the controller and sovereign of nature. **(3)** The "cloud" is a sign and figure of "divine protection": "And the LORD will create upon every dwelling place of mount Zion, and upon her assemblies, a cloud and smoke by day, and the shining of a flaming fire by night: for upon all the glory *shall be* a defence" (Is 4:5), and

(4) serves as a barrier hiding the fullness of divine holiness and glory, as well as barring sinful man's approach to God: "Thou hast covered thyself with a cloud, that *our* prayer should not pass through" (Lam 3:44). Man's relationship to God, therefore, is God-initiated and God-sustained, not humanly initiated or humanly sustained. **(5)** In its first biblical occurrence, *ʿanan* is used in conjunction with God's sign that He would never again destroy the earth by a flood: "I do set my bow in the cloud, and it shall be for a token of a covenant between me and the earth" (Gen 9:13). **(6)** Elsewhere, the transitory quality of a cloud is used to symbolize **(6a)** the loyalty: "O Ephraim, what shall I do unto thee? O Judah, what shall I do unto thee? for your goodness *is* as a morning cloud, and as the early dew it goeth away" (Hos 6:4) and **(6b)** existence of Israel: "Therefore they shall be as the morning cloud, and as the early dew that passeth away, as the chaff *that* is driven with the whirlwind out of the floor, and as the smoke out of the chimney" (Hos 13:3).

(7) In Is 44:22, God says that after proper punishment He will wipe out, "as a thick cloud, thy transgressions, and, as a cloud, thy sins. . . ." **(8)** *ʿAnan* can mean "storm cloud" and is used **(8a)** to symbolize "an invading force": "Thou shalt ascend and come like a storm, thou shalt be like a cloud to cover the land, thou, and all thy bands, and many people with thee" (Eze 38:9; cf. Jer 4:13). **(8b)** In Job 26:8, the storm cloud is said to be God's: "He bindeth up the waters in his thick clouds; and the cloud is not rent under them." **(8c)** In several passages, the thick storm cloud and the darkness accompanying it are symbols of "gloom" (Eze 30:18) and/or "divine judgment" (Eze 30:3). **(9)** *ʿAnan* can represent the "smoke" arising from burning incense: "And he shall put the incense upon the fire before the Lord, that the cloud of the incense may cover the mercy seat that is upon the testimony, that he die not . . ." (Lev 16:13). **(9a)** This "cloud of smoke" may represent the covering between God's presence (above the mercy seat) and sinful man. **(9b)** If so, it probably also symbolizes the "divine glory." **(9c)** On the other hand, many scholars feel it represents the human prayers offered up to God. See: TWOT—1655a; BDB—777d, 1107c.

6052. עָנָן {1x} **ʿÂnân**, *aw-nawn';* the same as 6051; *cloud; Anan,* an Isr.:—*Anan* {1x}. See: BDB—778b.

6053. עֲנָנָה {1x} **ʿănânâh**, *an-aw-naw';* fem. of 6051; *cloudiness:*—cloud {1x}. See: TWOT—1655a; BDB—778a.

6054. עֲנָנִי {1x} **ʿĂnânîy**, *an-aw-nee';* from 6051; *cloudy; Anani,* an Isr.:—Anani {1x}. See: BDB—778b.

6055. עֲנַנְיָה {2x} **ʿĂnanyâh**, *an-an-yaw';* from 6049 and 3050; *Jah has covered; Ananjah,* the name of an Isr. and of a place in Pal.:—Ananiah {2x}. See: BDB—778b.

6056. עֲנַף {4x} **ʿănaph** (Aram.), *an-af';* or

עֶנֶף **ʿeneph** (Aram.), *eh'-nef;* corresp. to 6057:—branches {3x}, boughs {1x}. See: TWOT—2922; BDB—1107c.

6057. עָנָף {7x} **ʿânâph**, *aw-nawf';* from an unused root mean. to *cover;* a *twig* (as *covering* the limbs):—branch {4x}, boughs {3x}. See: TWOT—1657a; BDB—778c, 1107c.

6058. עָנֵף {1x} **ʿânêph**, *aw-nafe';* from the same as 6057; *branching:*—branches {1x}. See: TWOT—1657b; BDB—778c.

6059. עָנַק {3x} **ʿânaq**, *aw-nak';* a prim. root; prop. to *choke;* used only as denom. from 6060, to *collar,* i.e. adorn with a necklace; fig. to *fit out* with supplies:—compass {1x}, furnish {1x}, liberally {1x}. See: TWOT—1658c; BDB—778d.

6060. עָנָק {3x} **ʿânâq**, *aw-nawk';* from 6059; a *necklace* (as if *strangling*):—chain {3x}. See: TWOT—1658b, 1658a; BDB—778d.

6061. עֲנָק {9x} **ʿÂnâq**, *aw-nawk';* the same as 6060; *Anak,* a Canaanite:—Anak {9x}. See: BDB—778c.

6062. עֲנָקִי {9x} **ʿĂnâqîy**, *an-aw-kee';* patron. from 6061; an *Anakite* or desc. of Anak:—Anakim {9x}. See: BDB—778c.

6063. עָנֵר {3x} **ʿÂnêr**, *aw-nare';* prob. for 5288; *Aner,* a Amorite, also a place in Pal.:—*Aner* {3x}. See: BDB—778d.

6064. עָנַשׁ {9x} **ʿânash**, *aw-nash';* a prim. root; prop. to *urge;* by impl. to *inflict* a penalty, spec. to *fine:*—punish {5x}, condemned {2x}, amerce {1x}, surely {1x}. See: TWOT—1659; BDB—778d.

6065. עֲנַשׁ {1x} **ʿănash** (Aram.), *an-ash';* corresp. to 6066; a *mulct:*—confiscation {1x}. See: TWOT—2923; BDB—1107c.

6066. עֹנֶשׁ {2x} **ʿônesh**, *o'-nesh;* from 6064; a *fine:*—tribute {1x}, punishment {1x}. See: TWOT—1659a; BDB—778d, 1107c.

עֵנֶת **ʿeneth** See 3706.

6067. עֲנָת {2x} **ʿĂnâth**, *an-awth';* from 6030; *answer; Anath,* an Isr.:—*Anath* {2x}. See: BDB—779a.

6068. עֲנָתוֹת {15x} **ʿĂnâthôwth**, *an-aw-thōth';* plur. of 6067; *Anathoth,* the name of two Isr., also of a place in Pal:—Anathoth {15x}. See: BDB—779a.

6069. עַנְתֹתִי {5x} **ʿAnthôthîy**, *an-tho-thee';* or

עַנְּתוֹתִי **ʿAnnᵉthôwthîy**, *an-ne-tho-thee';* patrial from 6068; a *Antothite* or inhab. of Anathoth:—Anethothite {2x}, Antothite {2x}, Anathoth {1x}. See: BDB—779a.

6070. עַנְתֹתִיָּה {1x} **ʿAnthôthîyâh**, *an-tho-thee-yaw';* from the same as 6068 and 3050; *answers of Jah; Anthothijah,* an Isr.:—Antothijah {1x}. See: BDB—779a.

6071. עָסִיס {5x} **ʿâçîyç**, *aw-sees';* from 6072; *must* or fresh grape-juice (as just *trodden* out):—new wine {2x}, sweet wine {2x}, juice {1x}. See: TWOT—1660a; BDB—779b.

6072. עָסַס {1x} **ʿâçaç**, *aw-sas';* a prim. root; to *squeeze* out juice; fig. to *trample:*—tread down {1x}. See: TWOT—1660; BDB—779a.

6073. עֳפֶא {1x} **ʿŏpheʾ**, *of-eh';* from an unused root mean. to *cover;* a *bough* (as covering the tree):—branches {1x}. See: TWOT—1661; BDB—779b, 1107c.

6074. עֳפִי {3x} **ʿŏphîy** (Aram.), *of-ee';* corresp. to 6073; a *twig;* bough, i.e. (collect.) *foliage:*—leaves {3x}. See: TWOT—2924; BDB—1107c.

6075. עָפַל {2x} **ʿâphal**, *aw-fal';* a prim. root; to *swell;* fig. *be elated:*—lifted up {1x}, presume {1x}. See: TWOT—1662, 1663; BDB—779b, 779c.

6076. עֹפֶל {9x} **ʿôphel**, *o'-fel;* from 6075; a *tumor;* also a *mound,* i.e. *fortress:*—forts {1x}, strong hold {1x}, tower {1x}, variant for emerods {6x}. See: TWOT—1662a, 1662b; BDB—779b.

6077. עֹפֶל {5x} **ʿÔphel**, *o'-fel;* the same as 6076; *Ophel,* a ridge in Jerusalem:—*Ophel* {5x}. See: TWOT—1662a; BDB—779b.

6078. עָפְנִי {1x} **ʿOphnîy**, *of-nee';* from an unused noun [denoting a place in Pal.; from an unused root of uncert. mean.]; an *Ophnite* (collect.) or inhab. of Ophen:—Ophni {1x}. See: BDB—779c.

6079. עַפְעַף {10x} **ʿaphʿaph**, *af-af';* from 5774; an *eyelash* (as *fluttering*); fig. morning *ray:*—eyelid {9x}, dawning {1x}. See: TWOT—1582b; BDB—733d, 779c.

6080. עָפַר {1x} **ʿâphar**, *aw-far';* a prim. root: mean. either to *be gray* or perh. rather to *pulverize;* used only as denom. from 6083, to *be dust:*—cast {1x}. See: TWOT—1664; BDB—780a.

6081. עֵפֶר {4x} **ʿÊpher**, *ay'-fer;* prob. a var. of 6082; *gazelle; Epher,* the name of an Arabian and of two Isr.:—*Epher* {4x}. See: BDB—780b.

6082. עֹפֶר {5x} **ʿôpher**, *o'-fer;* from 6080; a *fawn* (from the *dusty* color):—young {5x}. See: TWOT—1665a; BDB—780a.

6083. עָפָר {110x} **ʿâphâr**, *aw-fawr';* from 6080; *dust* (as *powdered* or *gray*); hence, *clay, earth, mud:*—dust {93x}, earth {7x}, powder {3x}, rubbish {2x}, ashes {2x}, morter {2x}, ground {1x}.

ʿApar means "dust; clods; plaster; ashes." **(1)** This noun represents the "porous loose earth on the ground," or "dust." **(2)** In its first biblical occurrence, *ʿapar* appears to mean this porous loose earth: "And the Lord God formed man of the dust of the ground, and breathed into his nostrils the breath of life . . ." (Gen 2:7). **(3)** In Gen 13:16, the word means the "fine particles of the soil": "And I will make thy [descendants] as the dust of the earth. . . ." **(4)** In the plural, the noun can mean "dust masses" or "clods" of earth: ". . . While as yet he had not made the earth, nor the fields, nor the highest part of the dust of the world" (Prov 8:26). **(5)** *ʿApar* can signify "dry crumbled mortar or plaster": "And he shall cause the house to be scraped within round about, and they shall pour out the dust that they scrape off without the city into an unclean place . . ." (Lev 14:41). **(6)** In Lev 14:42, the word means "wet plaster": "And they shall take other stones, and put them in the place of those stones; and he shall take other mortar, and shall plaster the house."**(7)** *ʿApar* represents "finely ground material" in Deut 9:21: "And I took your sin, the calf which ye had made, and burnt it with fire, and stamped it, and ground it very small, even until it was as small as dust: and I cast the dust thereof into the brook that descended out of the mount."

(8) *ʿApar* can represent the "ashes" of something that has been burned: **(8a)** "And the king commanded Hilkiah the high priest, and the priests of the second order, and the keepers of the door, to bring forth out of the temple of the Lord all the vessels that were made for Baal, and for the grove, and for all the host of heaven: and he burned them [outside] Jerusalem . . . and carried the ashes of them unto Bethel" (2 Kin 23:4). **(8a)** In a similar use, the word represents the "ashes" of a burnt offering (Num 19:17). **(9)** The "rubble" of a destroyed city sometimes is called "dust": "And Ben-hadad sent unto him, and said, The gods do so unto me, and more also, if the dust of Samaria shall suffice for handfuls for all the people that follow me" (1 Kin 20:10). **(10)** In Gen 3:14 the serpent was cursed with "dust" as his perpetual food (cf. Is 65:25; Mic 7:17). **(11)** Another nuance arising from the characteristics of dust appears in Job 28:6, where the word parallels "stones." Here the word seems to represent "the ground": "The stones of it are the place of sapphires: and it hath dust of gold."

(12) *'Apar* may be used as a symbol of a "large mass" or "superabundance" of something. This use, already cited (Gen 13:16), appears again in its fulfillment in Num 23:10: "Who can count the dust of Jacob, and the number of the fourth part of Israel?" **(13)** "Complete destruction" is represented by *'apar* in 2 Sa 22:43: "Then did I beat them as small as the dust of the earth: I did stamp them as the mire of the street. . . ." **(14)** In Ps 7:5, the word is used of "valuelessness" and "futility": "Let the enemy persecute my soul, and take it; yea, let him tread down my life upon the earth, and lay mine honor in the dust." **(15)** To experience defeat is "to lick the dust" (Ps 72:9), and **(16)** to be restored from defeat is "to shake oneself from the dust" (Is 52:2). **(17)** To throw "dust" ("dirt") at someone is a sign of shame and humiliation (2 Sa 16:13), **(18)** while mourning is expressed by various acts of self-abasement, which may include throwing "dust" or "dirt" on one's own head (Josh 7:6). **(19)** Abraham says he is but "dust and ashes," not really important (Gen 18:27). **(20)** In Job 7:21 and similar passages, *'apar* represents "the earth" of the grave: "For now shall I sleep in the dust; and thou shalt seek me in the morning, but I shall not be." **(21)** This word is also used as a simile for a "widely scattered army": "For the king of Syria had destroyed them, and had made them like the dust by threshing" (2 Kin 13:7). See: TWOT—1664a; BDB—779c.

עֲפָרָה **ʽAphrâh**. See 1036.

6084. עָפְרָה {8x} **ʽOphrâh**, *of-raw'*; fem. of 6082; *female fawn; Ophrah,* the name of an Isr. and of two places in Pal.:—*Ophrah* {8x}. See: BDB—780b.

6085. עֶפְרוֹן {14x} **ʽEphrôwn**, *ef-rone'*; from the same as 6081; *fawn-like; Ephron,* the name of a Canaanite and of two places in Pal.:—Ephron {13x}, Ephrain {1x}. See: BDB—780b.

עֹפֶרֶת **ʽôphereth**. See 5777.

6086. עֵץ {328x} **ʽêts**, *ates;* from 6095; a *tree* (from its *firmness*); hence, *wood* (plur. *sticks*):—tree {162x}, wood {107x}, timber {23x}, stick {14x}, gallows {8x}, staff {4x}, stock {4x}, carpenter + 2796 {2x}, branches {1x}, helve {1x}, planks {1x}, stalks {1x}.

'Ets means "tree; wood; timber; stick; stalk." **(1)** In its first biblical appearance *'ets* is used as a collective noun representing all trees bearing fruit (Gen 1:11). **(2)** In Ex 9:25 the word means "tree" indiscriminately: ". . . And the hail smote every herb of the field, and brake every tree of the field." **(3)** God forbids Israel to destroy the orchards around besieged cities: "When thou shalt besiege a city a long time, in making war against it to take it, thou shalt not destroy the trees . . . : for thou mayest eat of them [literally, ". . . its tree or orchard . . . for you may eat from it . . ."] . . ." (Deut 20:19). **(4)** This word may signify a single "tree," as it does in Gen 2:9: "The tree of life also in the midst of the garden, and the tree of knowledge of good and evil." **(5)** This word may be used of the genus "tree." So Is 41:19 lists the olive "tree" and the box "tree" in the midst of a long list of various species of trees. **(6)** *'Ets* can mean "wood." Thus, Deut 16:21: "Thou shalt not plant thee a grove of any trees near unto the altar of the LORD thy God, which thou shalt make thee."

(7) This word can represent "wood" as a material from which things are constructed, as a raw material to be carved: "And in carving of timber, to work in all manner of workmanship" (Ex 31:5). **(7a)** Large unprocessed pieces of "wood or timber" are also signified by *'ets:* "Go up to the mountain, and bring wood [timber], and build the house . . ." (Hag 1:8). **(7b)** The end product of wood already processed and fashioned into something may be indicated by *'ets:* "And upon whatsoever any of them, when they are dead, doth fall, it shall be unclean; whether it be any vessel of wood . . ." (Lev 11:32). **(8)** This word means "stick" or "piece of wood" in Eze 37:16: ". . . Thou son of man, take thee one stick, and write upon it. . . ." **(9)** This may also refer to a "pole" or "gallows": ". . . Within three days shall Pharaoh lift up thy head from off thee, and shall hang thee on a tree [gallows or pole] . . ." (Gen 40:19).

(10) *'Ets* once means "stalk": "But she had brought them up to the roof of the house, and hid them with the stalks of flax, which she had laid in order upon the roof" (Josh 2:6). Syn.: **(A)** 'Ayil (352) means "large, mighty tree." This word occurs 4 times and only in poetical passages. This does not mean a particular genus or species of tree but merely a large, mighty tree: "For they shall be ashamed of the oaks which ye have desired . . ." (Is 1:29—the first biblical occurrence). **(B)** 'Elon (436) means "large tree." **(B1)** This noun is probably related to 'ayil (352), "large tree." 'Elon occurs 10 times and only in relation to places of worship. It may well be that these were all ancient cultic sites. **(B2)** The word does not represent a particular genus or species of tree but, like the noun to which it is related, simply a "big tree": "And Gaal spake again and said, See there come people down by the middle of the land, and another company come along by the plain of Meonenim" (Judg 9:37). **(B3)** Judg 9:6 speaks of the "plain ('elon) of the pillar" in Shechem where the men of Shechem and Beth-millo made Abimelech king." This is probably stressing a lone tree on a plain. See: TWOT—1670a; BDB—780c, 781c, 1082b.

6087. עָצַב {17x} **ʽâtsab**, *aw-tsab';* a prim. root; prop. to *carve,* i.e. *fabricate* or *fashion;* hence, (in a bad sense) to *worry, pain* or *anger:*—grieve {10x}, displeased {1x}, hurt {1x}, made {1x}, sorry {1x}, vexed {1x}, worship {1x}, wrest {1x}.

In Jer 44:19 this word signifies the fashioning of cakes as images of the "the queen of heaven." See: TWOT—1666, 1667; BDB—780c, 781a, 1107d.

6088. עֲצַב {1x} **ʽătsab** (Aram.), *ats-ab';* corresp. to 6087; to *afflict:*—lamentable {1x}. See: TWOT—2925; BDB—1107d.

6089. עֶצֶב {7x} **ʽetseb**, *eh'-tseb;* from 6087; an earthen *vessel;* usually (painful) *toil;* also a *pang* (whether of body or mind):—sorrow {3x}, labour {2x}, grievous {1x}, idol {1x}. See: TWOT—1666a, 1667a; BDB—780d, 781a.

6090. עֹצֶב {4x} **ʽôtseb**, *o'-tseb;* a var. of 6089; an *idol* (as fashioned); also *pain* (bodily or mental):—sorrow {2x}, wicked {1x}, idol {1x}. See: TWOT—1666b, 1667b; BDB—780d, 781b.

6091. עָצָב {17x} **ʽâtsâb**, *aw-tsawb';* from 6087; an (idolatrous) *image:*—idol {16x}, image {1x}.

The stress of this word is labor [see 6090, 6092]. Does this mean that worship is laborious? Scripture always teaches that true worship is not wearisome to the child of God whereas the worship of idols is hard labor without profit. Syn.: 205, 367, 457, 1534, 4656, 6089, 8251. See: TWOT—1667c; BDB—781b.

6092. עָצֵב {1x} **ʽâtsêb**, *aw-tsabe';* from 6087; a (hired) *workman:*—labours {1x}. See: TWOT—1666c; BDB—780d.

6093. עִצָּבוֹן {3x} **ʽitstsâbôwn**, *its-tsaw-bone';* from 6087; *worrisomeness,* i.e. *labor* or *pain:*—sorrow {2x}, toil {1x}. See: TWOT—1666e; BDB—781a.

6094. עַצֶּבֶת {5x} **ʽatstsebeth**, *ats-tseh'-beth;* from 6087; an *idol;* also a *pain* or *wound:*—sorrow {4x}, wounds {1x}. See: TWOT—1666d; BDB—781a.

6095. עָצָה {1x} **ʽâtsâh**, *aw-tsaw';* a prim. root; prop. to *fasten* (or *make firm*), i.e. to *close* (the eyes):—shut {1x}. See: TWOT—1669; BDB—781b, 783b.

6096. עָצֶה {1x} **ʽâtseh**, *aw-tseh';* from 6095; the *spine* (as giving *firmness* to the body):—backbone {1x}. See: TWOT—1671a; BDB—782b.

6097. עֵצָה {1x} **ʽêtsâh**, *ay-tsaw';* fem. of 6086; *timber:*—tree {1x}. See: TWOT—1670b; BDB—782a.

6098. עֵצָה {88x} **ʽêtsâh**, *ay-tsaw';* from 3289; *advice;* by impl. *plan;* also *prudence:*—counsel {79x}, counsels {2x}, purpose {2x}, advice {1x}, counsellors + 582 {1x}, advisement {1x}, counsel + 3289 + 8799 {1x}, counsellor + 376 {1x}. See: TWOT—887a; BDB—420a.

6099. עָצוּם {31x} **ʽâtsûwm**, *aw-tsoom';* or

עָצֻם **ʽâtsûm**, *aw-tsoom';* pass. part. of 6105; *powerful* (spec. a *paw*); by impl. *numerous:*—strong {13x}, mighty {8x}, mightier {7x}, feeble {1x}, great {1x}, much {1x}. See: TWOT—1673d; BDB—783a, 783b.

6100. עֶצְיוֹן גֶּבֶר {7x} **ʽEtsyôwn** (short.

עֶצְיֹן **ʽEtsyôn) Geber**, *ets-yone' gheh'ber;* from 6096 and 1397; *backbone-like of a man; Etsjon-Geber,* a place on the Red Sea:—Eziongeber {4x}, Eziongaber {3x}. See: BDB—782b.

6101. עָצַל {1x} **ʽâtsal**, *aw-tsal';* a prim. root; to *lean* idly, i.e. to *be indolent* or *slack:*—slothful {1x}. See: TWOT—1672; BDB—782b.

6102. עָצֵל {14x} **ʽâtsêl**, *aw-tsale';* from 6101; *indolent:*—slothful {8x}, sluggard {6x}. See: TWOT—1672a; BDB—782b.

6103. עַצְלָה {2x} **ʽatslâh**, *ats-law';* fem. of 6102; (as abstr.) *indolence:*—slothfulness {2x}. See: TWOT—1672b; BDB—782b.

6104. עַצְלוּת {1x} **ʽatslûwth**, *ats-looth';* from 6101; *indolence:*—idleness {1x}. See: TWOT—1672c; BDB—782c.

6105. עָצַם {20x} **ʽâtsam**, *aw-tsam';* a prim. root; to *bind* fast, i.e. *close* (the eyes); intr. to *be* (caus. *make*) *powerful* or *numerous;* denom. (from 6106) to *crunch* the bones:—increased {4x}, mighty {4x}, . . . strong {4x}, more {2x}, broken his bones {1x}, closed {1x}, great {1x}, mightier {1x}, shutteth {1x}, stronger {1x}. See: TWOT—1673, 1674; BDB—782c, 783b.

6106. עֶצֶם {126x} **ʽetsem**, *eh'tsem;* from 6105; a *bone* (as *strong*); by extens. the *body;* fig. the *substance,* i.e. (as pron.) *selfsame:*—

bone {104x}, selfsame {11x}, same {5x}, body {2x}, very {2x}, life {1x}, strength {1x}.

(1) This word commonly represents a human bone as one of the constitutent parts of the human body: "Thou hast clothed me with skin and flesh, and hast fenced me with bones and sinews" (Job 10:11). **(2)** *ʿEtsem* used with flesh (1320) can indicate a blood relationship: "And Laban said to him, Surely thou *art* my bone and my flesh. And he abode with him the space of a month" (Gen 29:14). **(3)** In Job 2:5, used with flesh (1320), *ʿetsem* represents one's body: "But put forth thine hand now, and touch his bone and his flesh, and he will curse thee to thy face." **(4)** The plural form represents **(4a)** the seat of vigor or sensation: "His bones are full *of the sin* of his youth, which shall lie down with him in the dust" (Job 20:11; cf. 4:14), or **(4b)** one's whole being: "Have mercy upon me, O LORD; for I *am* weak: O LORD, heal me; for my bones are vexed" (Ps 6:2). **(5)** This word is frequently used for the bones of the dead (Num 19:16) or **(6)** human remains, including a mummified corpse (Gen 50:25). **(7)** *ʿEtsem* sometimes represents animal bones (Ex 12:46). See: TWOT—1673c; BDB—782c.

6107. עֶצֶם {3x} **ʿEtsem**, *eh'-tsem;* the same as 6106; *bone; Etsem,* a place in Pal.:—Azem {2x}, Ezem {1x}. See: BDB—783a.

6108. עֹצֶם {3x} **ʿôtsem**, *o'-tsem;* from 6105; *power;* hence, *body:*—might {1x}, strong {1x}, substance {1x}. See: TWOT—1673a; BDB—782c.

עָצוּם **ʿâtsûm**. See 6099.

6109. עׇצְמָה {3x} **ʿotsmâh**, *ots-maw';* fem. of 6108; *powerfulness;* by extens. *numerousness:*—strength {2x}, abundance {1x}. See: TWOT—1673b; BDB—782c.

6110. עַצֻּמָה {1x} **ʿatstsûmâh**, *ats-tsoo-maw';* fem. of 6099; a *bulwark,* i.e. (fig.) *argument:*—strong {1x}. See: TWOT—1674b; BDB—783a, 783b.

6111. עַצְמוֹן {3x} **ʿAtsmôwn**, *ats-mone';* or

עַצְמֹן **ʿAtsmôn**, *ats-mone';* from 6107; *bone-like; Atsmon,* a place near Pal.:—Azmon {3x}. See: BDB—783b.

6112. עֵצֶן {1x} **ʿÊtsen**, *ay'-tsen;* from an unused root mean. to *be sharp* or *strong;* a *spear:*—Eznite {1x}. See: BDB—783b.

6113. עָצַר {46x} **ʿâtsar**, *aw-tsar';* a prim. root; to *inclose;* by anal. to *hold back;* also to *maintain, rule, assemble:*—shut up {15x}, stayed {7x}, retain {3x}, detain {3x}, able {2x}, withhold {2x}, keep {2x}, prevail {1x}, recover {1x}, refrained {1x}, reign {1x}, misc. {8x}. See: TWOT—1675; BDB—783c.

6114. עֶצֶר {1x} **ʿetser**, *eh'-tser;* from 6113; *restraint:*—magistrate {1x}. See: TWOT—1675a; BDB—783d.

6115. עֹצֶר {3x} **ʿôtser**, *o'-tser;* from 6113; *closure;* also *constraint:*—oppression {1x}, barren {1x}, prison {1x}. See: TWOT—1675b; BDB—783d.

6116. עֲצָרָה {11x} **ʿătsârâh**, *ats-aw-raw';* or

עֲצֶרֶת **ʿătsereth**, *ats-eh'-reth;* from 6113; an *assembly,* espec. on a *festival* or *holiday:*—solemn assembly {9x}, solemn meeting {1x}, assembly {1x}. See: TWOT—1675c; BDB—783d.

6117. עָקַב {5x} **ʿâqab**, *aw-kab';* a prim. root; prop. to *swell* out or up; used only as denom. from 6119, to *seize by the heel;* fig. to *circumvent* (as if *tripping* up the heels); also to *restrain* (as if holding by the heel):—supplant {2x}, take by the heel {1x}, stay {1x}, utterly {1x}. See: TWOT—1676; BDB—784b.

6118. עֵקֶב {15x} **ʿêqeb**, *ay'-keb;* from 6117 in the sense of 6119; a *heel,* i.e. (fig.) the *last* of anything (used adv. *for ever*); also *result,* i.e. *compensation;* and so (adv. with prep. or rel.) on *account* of:—× because {6x}, reward {3x}, end {2x}, because + 834 {1x}, by {1x}, for {1x}, if {1x}. See: TWOT—1676e; BDB—784c.

6119. עָקֵב {13x} **ʿâqêb**, *aw-kabe';* or (fem.)

עִקְּבָה **ʿiqqᵉbâh**, *ik-keb-aw';* from 6117; a *heel* (as *protuberant*); hence, a *track;* fig. the *rear* (of an army):—heel {6x}, footsteps {3x}, horsehoofs {1x}, at the last {1x}, steps {1x}, liers in wait {1x}. See: TWOT—1676a; BDB—784a.

6120. עָקֵב {1x} **ʿâqêb**, *aw-kabe';* from 6117 in its denom. sense; a *lier in wait:*—heels {1x}. See: TWOT—1676b; BDB—784c.

6121. עָקֹב {3x} **ʿâqôb**, *aw-kobe';* from 6117; in the orig. sense, a *knoll* (as *swelling* up); in the denom. sense (tran.) *fraudulent* or (intr.) *tracked:*—crooked {1x}, deceitful {1x}, polluted {1x}. See: TWOT—1676c; BDB—784c.

6122. עׇקְבָה {1x} **ʿoqbâh**, *ok-baw';* fem. of an unused form from 6117 mean. a *trick; trickery:*—subtilty {1x}. See: TWOT—1676d; BDB—784c.

6123. עָקַד {1x} **ʿâqad**, *aw-kad';* a prim. root; to *tie* with thongs:—bound {1x}. See: TWOT—1677; BDB—785b.

עֵקֶד **ʿÊqed**. See 1044.

6124. עָקֹד {7x} **ʿâqôd**, *aw-kode';* from 6123; *striped* (with *bands*):—ringstraked {7x}. See: TWOT—1678a; BDB—785b.

6125. עָקָה {1x} **ʿâqâh**, *aw-kaw';* from 5781; *constraint:*—oppression {1x}. See: TWOT—1585a; BDB—734b, 785b.

6126. עַקּוּב {8x} **ʿAqqûwb**, *ak-koob';* from 6117; *insidious; Akkub,* the name of five Isr.:—Akkub {8x}. See: BDB—784d.

6127. עָקַל {1x} **ʿâqal**, *aw-kal';* a prim. root; to *wrest:*—wrong {1x}. See: TWOT—1680; BDB—785b.

6128. עֲקַלְקַל {2x} **ʿăqalqal**, *ak-al-kal';* from 6127; *winding:*—byways + 5410 {1x}, crooked ways {1x}. See: TWOT—1680a; BDB—785c.

6129. עֲקַלָּתוֹן {1x} **ʿăqallâthôwn**, *ak-al-law-thone';* from 6127; *tortuous:*—crooked {1x}. See: TWOT—1680b; BDB—785c.

6130. עָקָן {1x} **ʿÂqân**, *aw-kawn';* from an unused root mean. to *twist; tortuous; Akan,* an Idumæan:—Akan {1x}. See: BDB—785c. comp. 3292.

6131. עָקַר {7x} **ʿâqar**, *aw-kar';* a prim. root; to *pluck* up (espec. by the roots); spec. to *hamstring;* fig. to *exterminate:*—hough {4x}, pluck up {1x}, rooted up {1x}, digged down {1x}. See: TWOT—1681, 1682; BDB—785c.

6132. עֲקַר {1x} **ʿăqar** (Aram.), *ak-ar';* corresp. to 6131:—plucked up by the roots {1x}. See: TWOT—2926; BDB—1107d.

6133. עֵקֶר {1x} **ʿêqer**, *ay'-ker;* from 6131; fig. a *transplanted* person, i.e. naturalized citizen:—stock {1x}. See: TWOT—1681a; BDB—785c.

6134. עֵקֶר {1x} **ʿÊqer**, *ay'-ker;* the same as 6133; *Eker,* an Isr.:—Eker {1x}. See: BDB—785d.

6135. עָקָר {12x} **ʿâqâr**, *aw-kawr';* from 6131; *sterile* (as if *extirpated* in the generative organs):—barren {12x}. See: TWOT—1682a; BDB—785d.

6136. עִקַּר {3x} **ʿiqqar** (Aram.), *ik-kar';* from 6132; a *stock:*—stump {3x}. See: TWOT—2926a; BDB—1107d.

6137. עַקְרָב {6x} **ʿaqrâb**, *ak-rawb';* of uncert. der.; a *scorpion;* fig. a *scourge* or knotted whip:—scorpion {6x}. See: TWOT—1683; BDB—785d.

6138. עֶקְרוֹן {22x} **ʿEqrôwn**, *ek-rone';* from 6131; *eradication; Ekron,* a place in Pal.:—Ekron {22x}. See: BDB—785d.

6139. עֶקְרוֹנִי {2x} **ʿEqrôwnîy**, *ek-ro-nee';* or

עֶקְרֹנִי **ʿEqrônîy**, *ek-ro-nee';* patrial from 6138; an *Ekronite* or inhab. of Ekron:—Ekronites {2x}. See: BDB—785d.

6140. עָקַשׁ {5x} **ʿâqash**, *aw-kash';* a prim. root; to *knot* or *distort;* fig. to *pervert* (act or declare perverse):—perverse {2x}, pervert {2x}, crooked {1x}. See: TWOT—1684; BDB—786a.

6141. עִקֵּשׁ {11x} **ʿiqqêsh**, *ik-kashe';* from 6140; *distorted;* hence, *false:*—froward {6x}, perverse {4x}, crooked {1x}. See: TWOT 1684a; BDB—786a.

6142. עִקֵּשׁ {3x} **ʿIqqêsh**, *ik-kashe';* the same as 6141; *perverse; Ikkesh,* an Isr.:—Ikkesh {2x}. See: BDB—786a.

6143. עִקְּשׁוּת {2x} **ʿiqqᵉshûwth**, *ik-kesh-ooth';* from 6141; *perversity:*—froward {2x}. See: TWOT—1684b; BDB—786A.

עָר **ʿâr**. See 5892.

6144. עָר {6x} **ʿÂr**, *awr;* the same as 5892; a *city; Ar,* a place in Moab:—*Ar* {6x}. See: BDB—786a.

6145. עָר {6x} **ʿâr**, *awr;* from 5782; a *foe* (as *watchful* for mischief):—city {3x}, enemy {2x}, Strong's synonym {1x}. See: TWOT—1684+; BDB—786b, 1108a.

6146. עָר {1x} **ʿâr** (Aram.), *awr;* corresp. to 6145:—enemies {1x}. See: TWOT—2930a; BDB—1107d, 1108a.

6147. עֵר {10x} **ʿÊr**, *ayr;* from 5782; *watchful; Er,* the name of two Isr.:—*Er* {10x}. See: BDB—735c, 786b.

6148. עָרַב {22x} **ʿârab**, *aw-rab';* a prim. root; to *braid,* i.e. *intermix;* tech. to *traffic* (as if by barter); also to *give* or *be security* (as a kind of exchange).—surety {9x}, meddle {2x}, mingled {2x}, pledges {2x}, becometh {1x}, engaged {1x}, intermeddle {1x}, mortgaged {1x}, occupiers {1x}, occupy {1x}, undertake {1x}. See: TWOT—1686; BDB—786c, 1107d.

6149. עָרֵב {8x} **ʿârêb**, *aw-rabe'* a prim. root [rather ident. with 6148 through the idea of close *association*]; to *be agreeable:*—sweet {5x}, pleasure {1x}, pleasing {1x}, pleasant {1x}. See: TWOT—1687a; BDB—787a, 1107d.

6150. עָרַב {3x} **ʿârab**, *aw-rab';* a prim. root [rather ident. with 6148 through the idea of *covering* with a texture]; to *grow dusky* at sundown:—evening {2x}, darkened {1x}. See: TWOT—1689; BDB—788a.

6151. עֲרַב {4x} ʿ**ărab** (Aram.), *ar-ab';* corresp. to 6148; to *commingle:*—mix {3x}, mingle {1x}. See: TWOT—2927; BDB—1107d.

6152. עֲרָב {5x} ʿ**Ărâb**, *ar-awb'* or

עֲרַב ʿ**Ărab**, *ar-ab';* from 6150 in the fig. sense of *sterility; Arab* (i.e. *Arabia*), a country E. of Pal.:—Arabia {5x}. See: TWOT—1688a, 1688c; BDB—787a, 787b.

6153. עֶרֶב {137x} ʿ**ereb**, *eh'-reb;* from 6150; *dusk:*—even {72x}, evening {47x}, night {4x}, mingled {2x}, people {2x}, eventide {2x}, eveningtide + 6256 {2x}, Arabia {1x}, days {1x}, even + 996 {1x}, evening + 3117 {1x}, evening + 6256 {1x}, eventide + 6256 {1x}.

ʿ*Ereb* means "evening, night." **(1)** This word represents the time of the day immediately preceding and following the setting of the sun. **(1a)** During this period, the dove returned to Noah's ark (Gen 8:11). **(1b)** Since it was cool, women went to the wells for water in the "evening" (Gen 24:11). **(1c)** It was at "evening" that David walked around on top of his roof to refresh himself and cool off, and observed Bathsheba taking a bath (2 Sa 11:2). In its first biblical appearance, ʿ*ereb* marks the "opening of a day": "And the evening and the morning were the first day" (Gen 1:5). **(1d)** The phrase "in the evening" [literally, "between the evenings"] means the period between sunset and darkness, "twilight" (Ex 12:6; KJV, "in the evening"). **(2)** Second, in poetical use, the word can mean "night": "When I lie down, I say, When shall I arise, and the night be gone? And I am full of tossings to and fro unto the dawning of the day" (Job 7:4). See: TWOT—1689a; BDB—787d.

6154. עֵרֶב {11x} ʿ**êreb**, *ay'-reb;* or

עֶרֶב ʿ**ereb** (1 Kin 10:15), (with the art. pref.), *eh'-reb;* from 6148; the *web* (or transverse threads of cloth); also a *mixture*, (or *mongrel* race):—woof {9x}, mixed multitude {2x}. See: TWOT—1685a, 1685b; BDB—786b, 786c.

6155. עָרָב {5x} ʿ**ârâb**, *aw-rawb';* from 6148; a *willow* (from the use of osiers as wattles):—willow {5x}. See: TWOT—1690b; BDB—788b.

6156. עָרֵב {2x} ʿ**ârêb**, *aw-rabe';* from 6149; *pleasant:*—sweet {2x}. See: TWOT—1687a; BDB—787a.

6157. עָרֹב {9x} ʿ**ârôb**, *aw-robe';* from 6148; a *mosquito* (from its *swarming*):—swarm {7x}, divers sorts of flies {2x}. See: TWOT—1685c; BDB—786c.

6158. עֹרֵב {10x} ʿ**ôrêb**, *o-rabe';* or

עוֹרֵב ʿ**ôwrêb**, *o-rabe';* from 6150; a *raven* (from its *dusky* hue):—raven {10x}. See: TWOT—1690a; BDB—788b.

6159. עֹרֵב {7x} ʿ**Ôrêb**, *o-rabe';* or

עוֹרֵב ʿ**Ôwrêb**, *o-rabe';* the same as 6158; *Oreb*, the name of a Midianite and of a cliff near the Jordan:—Oreb {7x}.

6160. עֲרָבָה {61x} ʿ**ărâbâh**, *ar-aw-baw';* from 6150 (in the sense of *sterility*); a *desert;* espec. (with the art. pref.) the (gen.) sterile valley of the Jordan and its continuation to the Red Sea:—plain {42x}, desert {9x}, wilderness {5x}, Arabah {2x}, champaign {1x}, evenings {1x}, heavens {1x}. See: TWOT—1688d; BDB—787b. See also 1026.

6161. עֲרֻבָּה {2x} ʿ**ărubbâh**, *ar-oob-baw';* fem. pass. part. of 6148 in the sense of a *bargain* or *exchange;* something given as *security*, i.e. (lit.) a *token* (of safety) or (metaph.) a *bondsman:*—pledge {1x}, surety {1x}. See: TWOT—1686a; BDB—786d.

6162. עֲרָבוֹן {3x} ʿ**ărâbôwn**, *ar-aw-bone';* from 6148 (in the sense of *exchange*); a *pawn* (given as security):—pledge {3x}. See: TWOT—1686b; BDB—786d.

6163. עֲרָבִי {9x} ʿ**Ărâbîy**, *ar-aw-bee';* or

עַרְבִי ʿ**Arbîy**, *ar-bee';* patrial from 6152; an *Arabian* or inhab. of Arab (i.e. Arabia):—Arabian {9x}. See: BDB—787b.

6164. עַרְבָתִי {2x} ʿ**Arbâthîy**, *ar-baw-thee';* patrial from 1026; an *Arbathite* or inhab. of (Beth-) Arabah:—Arbathite {2x}. See: BDB—112c, 787c.

6165. עָרַג {3x} ʿ**ârag**, *aw-rag';* a prim. root; to *long* for:—pant {2x}, cry {1x}. See: TWOT—1691; BDB—788b.

6166. עֲרָד {5x} ʿ**Ărâd**, *ar-awd';* from an unused root mean. to *sequester* itself; *fugitive; Arad*, the name of a place near Pal., also of a Canaanite and an Isr.:—*Arad* {5x}. See: BDB—788c.

6167. עֲרָד {1x} ʿ**ărâd** (Aram.), *ar-awd';* corresp. to 6171; an *onager:*—wild ass {1x}. See: TWOT—2928; BDB—1107d.

6168. עָרָה {15x} ʿ**ârâh**, *aw-raw';* a prim. root; to *be* (caus. *make*) *bare;* hence, to *empty, pour* out, *demolish:*—uncover {3x}, discover {3x}, emptied {2x}, rase {2x}, leave destitute {1x}, make naked {1x}, poured out {1x}, poured {1x}, spreading {1x}.

ʿ*Arah*, as a verb, means "to pour out, make bare, destroy, spread oneself out." **(1)** The word means "to pour out" in Is 32:15: " Until the spirit be poured upon us from on high. . . ." **(2)** The verb implies "to make bare" in Lev 20:19: "And thou shalt not uncover the nakedness of thy mother's sister, nor of thy father's sister: for he uncovereth his near kin: they shall bear their iniquity." **(3)** ʿ*Arah* is used in the sense of "to destroy" in Is 3:17: "Therefore the LORD will smite with a scab the crown of the head of the daughters of Zion, and the Lord will discover their secret parts." **(4)** In Ps 37:35 the word means "to spread oneself out": "I have seen the wicked in great power, and spreading himself like a green bay tree." See: TWOT—1692; BDB—788c, 1107d.

6169. עָרָה {1x} ʿ**ârâh**, *aw-raw';* fem. from 6168; a *naked* (i.e. level) plot:—paper reeds {1x}. See: TWOT—1692a; BDB—788d.

6170. עֲרוּגָה {4x} ʿ**ărûwgâh**, *ar-oo-gaw';* or

עֲרֻגָה ʿ**ărûgâh**, *ar-oo-gaw';* fem. pass. part. of 6165; something *piled* up (as if [fig.] *raised* by mental aspiration), i.e. a *parterre:*—bed {2x}, furrow {2x}. See: TWOT—1691a; BDB—788c.

6171. עָרוֹד {1x} ʿ**ârôwd**, *aw-rode';* from the same as 6166; an *onager* (from his *lonesome* habits):—wild ass {1x}. See: TWOT—1693; BDB—789b, 1107d.

6172. עֶרְוָה {54x} ʿ**ervâh**, *er-vaw';* from 6168; *nudity*, lit. (espec. the *pudenda*) or fig. (*disgrace, blemish*):—nakedness {50x}, nakedness + 1320 {1x}, shame {1x}, unclean {1x}, uncleanness {1x}.

ʿ*Ervah*, as a noun, means "nakedness; indecent thing." **(1)** Thirty-two of the 54 occurrences of this noun are in the social laws of Lev 18, 20. **(2)** This word represents the male sexual organ. In its first biblical appearance ʿerwah implies shameful exposure: "And Ham, the father of Canaan, saw the nakedness of his father. . . . And Shem and Japheth took a garment, and laid it upon both their shoulders, and went backward, and covered the nakedness of their father; and their faces were backward, and they saw not their father's nakedness" (Gen 9:22–23). **(3)** This word is often used of female nakedness (the uncovered sex organs) and **(3a)** is symbolical of shame. **(3b)** In Lam 1:8 plundered, devastated Jerusalem is pictured as a woman whose nakedness is exposed. **(4)** To uncover one's nakedness is a frequent euphemism for cohabitation: "None of you shall approach to any that is near of kin to him, to uncover their nakedness: I am the Lord" (Lev 18:6).

(5) The phrase "indecent thing" represents any uncleanness in a military camp or any violation of the laws of sexual abstinence—nocturnal emission not properly cleansed, sexual cohabitation and other laws of purity (for example, excrement buried in the camp): "For the Lord thy God walketh in the midst of thy camp, to deliver thee, and to give up thine enemies before thee; therefore shall thy camp be holy: that he see no unclean thing [literally, "a matter of an indecent thing"] in thee, and turn away from thee" (Deut 23:14). **(6)** In Deut 24:1 ʿ*ervah* appears to bear this emphasis on any violation of the laws of purity—if a groom is dissatisfied with his bride "because he hath found some uncleanness in her," he may divorce her. Obviously this evidence is not of previous cohabitation, since such a sin merits death (Deut 22:13ff.).

(7) The "undefended parts" or "nakedness" of a land is represented by ʿ*ervah* in Gen 42:9: "Ye are spies; to see the nakedness of the land ye are come." Syn.: Other nouns related to this word appear less often. **(A)** Ma'ar (4626), which refers to "sexual nakedness," appears in a figurative sense in Nah 3:5: "Behold, I *am* against thee, saith the LORD of hosts; and I will discover thy skirts upon thy face, and I will shew the nations thy nakedness, and the kingdoms thy shame." **(B)** ʿErom (6174) appears as a noun abstract in several instances. This word represents the more general idea of being without clothes, with no necessary suggestion of shamefulness; it means the "state of being unclothed." In Eze 16:7, 39 the word ʿerom appears as "naked," but it can literally be translated as "nakedness" or one being in his "nakedness." **(C)** Ta'ar (8593), which occurs 13 times, means "razor" (Num 6:5), a "knife" to sharpen scribal pens (Jer 36:23), or "sword sheath" (1 Sa 17:51). **(D)** Morah (4177) also means "razor"(1 Sa 1:11). See also: 4626, 5903. See: TWOT—1692b; BDB—788d.

6173. עַרְוָה {1x} ʿ**arvâh** (Aram.), *ar-vaw';* corresp. to 6172; *nakedness*, i.e. (fig.) *impoverishment:*—dishonour {1x}. See: TWOT—2929; BDB—1107d.

6174. עָרוֹם {16x} ʿ**ârôwm**, *aw-rome';* or

עָרֹם ʿ**ârôm**, *aw-rome';* from 6191 (in its orig. sense); *nude*, either partially or totally:—naked {16x}.

ʿ*Arowm*, as an adjective, means "naked." The first occurrence is in Gen 2:25: "And they were both naked, the man and his wife, and were not ashamed." Syn.: 5903. See: TWOT—1588c; BDB—736a, 790d.

6175. עָרוּם {11x} ʿ**ârûwm**, *aw-room';* pass. part. of 6191; *cunning* (usually in a bad sense):—prudent {8x}, crafty {2x}, subtil {1x}. See: TWOT—1698c; BDB—791a.

6176. עֲרוֹעֵר {1x} ʿărôwʿêr, *ar-o-ayr'*; or
עַרְעָר ʿarʿâr, *ar-awr'*; from 6209 redupl.; a *juniper* (from its *nudity* of situation):—heath {1x}. See: TWOT—1705b, 1705c; BDB—791b, 792d.

6177. עֲרוֹעֵר {16x} ʿĂrôwʿêr, *ar-o-ayr'*; or
עֲרֹעֵר ʿĂrôʿêr, *ar-o-ayr'*; or
עַרְעוֹר ʿArʿôwr, *ar-ore'*; the same as 6176; *nudity* of situation; *Aroër*, the name of three places in or near Pal.:—Aroer {16x}. See: BDB—791b, 792d.

6178. עָרוּץ {1x} ʿârûwts, *aw-roots'*; pass. part. of 6206; *feared*, i.e. (concr.) a *horrible* place or *chasm:*—cliff {1x}. See: TWOT—1702a; BDB—792a.

6179. עֵרִי {2x} ʿÊrîy, *ay-ree'*; from 5782; *watchful; Eri*, an Isr.:—Eri {2x}.See: BDB—735c.

6180. עֵרִי {1x} ʿÊrîy, *ay-ree'*; patron. of 6179; a *Erite* (collect.) or desc. of Eri:—Erites {1x}. See: BDB—735c.

6181. עֶרְיָה {6x} ʿeryâh, *er-yaw'*; for 6172; *nudity:*—bare {4x}, naked {1x}, quite {1x}.

Another adjective, found 6 times, is *ʿeryah*. One appearance is in Eze 16:22: ". . . When thou wast naked and bare. . . ." See: TWOT—1692c; BDB—789a.

6182. עֲרִיסָה {4x} ʿărîyçâh, *ar-ee-saw'*; from an unused root mean. to *comminute; meal:*—dough {4x}. See: TWOT—1699a; BDB—791b.

6183. עָרִיף {1x} ʿârîyph, *aw-reef'*; from 6201; the *sky* (as *drooping* at the horizon):—heavens {1x}. See: TWOT—1701a; BDB—791d.

6184. עָרִיץ {20x} ʿârîyts, *aw-reets'*; from 6206; *fearful*, i.e. *powerful* or *tyrannical:*—terrible {8x}, terrible one {5x}, oppressor {3x}, mighty {1x}, power {1x}, strong {1x}, violent {1x}. See: TWOT—1702b; BDB—792a.

6185. עֲרִירִי {4x} ʿărîyrîy, *ar-e-ree'*; from 6209; *bare*, i.e. destitute (of children):—childless {4x}. See: TWOT—1705a; BDB—792d.

6186. עָרַךְ {75x} ʿârak, *aw-rak'*; a prim. root; to set in a *row*, i.e. *arrange*, put in *order* (in a very wide variety of applications):—array {26x}, order {21x}, prepare {5x}, expert {3x}, value {3x}, compare {2x}, direct {2x}, equal {2x}, estimate {2x}, furnish {2x}, ordained {2x}, misc. {4x}.

ʿArak means "to arrange, set in order, compare." **(1)** The word is first found in the Old Testament in Gen 14:8: ". . . They joined battle [literally, "they arranged," referring to opposing battle lines]. . . ." It is used in this way many times in the record of the battles of Israel. **(2)** A common word in everyday life, *ʿarak* often refers to "arranging" a table: "Prepare the table, watch in the watchtower, eat, drink: arise, ye princes, and anoint the shield" (Is 21:5; cf. Eze 23:41). **(3)** The word is used several times in the Book of Job with reference to "arranging" or "setting" words "in order," **(3a)** as in an argument or rebuttal (Job 32:14; 33:5; 37:19). **(3b)** In Job 13:18, Job declares: "Behold now, I have ordered my cause [literally, "I have set my judgment in order"]. . . ." **(3c)** "To arrange in order" makes it possible "to compare" one thing with another. **(4)** So, to show the superiority of God over the idols, the prophet asks: "To whom then will ye liken God? or what likeness will ye compare unto him?" (Is 40:18). See: TWOT—1694; BDB—789b, 790a.

6187. עֵרֶךְ {33x} ʿêrek, *eh'rek*; from 6186; a *pile, equipment, estimate:*—estimation {24x}, set at {1x}, equal {1x}, set in order {1x}, price {1x}, proportion {1x}, set {1x}, suit {1x}, taxation {1x}, valuest {1x}. See: TWOT—1694a; BDB—789d.

6188. עָרֵל {2x} ʿârêl, *aw-rale'*; a prim. root; prop. to *strip;* but used only as denom. from 6189; to *expose* or *remove* the *prepuce*, whether lit. (to *go naked*) or fig. (to *refrain* from using):—count as uncircumcised {1x}, foreskin be uncovered {1x}. See: TWOT—1695; BDB—790c, 947a.

6189. עָרֵל {35x} ʿârêl, *aw-rale'*; from 6188; prop. *exposed*, i.e. projecting loose (as to the prepuce); used only tech. *uncircumcised* (i.e. still having the prepuce uncurtailed):—uncircumcised {34x}, uncircumcised person {1x}. See: TWOT—1695b; BDB—790c.

6190. עָרְלָה {16x} ʿorlâh, *or-law'*; fem. of 6189; the *prepuce:*—foreskin {13x}, uncircumcised {3x}. See: TWOT—1695a; BDB—790b.

6191. עָרַם {5x} ʿâram, *aw-ram'*; a prim. root; prop. to *be* (or *make*) *bare;* but used only in the der. sense (through the idea perh. of *smoothness*) to *be cunning* (usually in a bad sense):—subtilty {1x}, crafty {1x}, prudent {1x}, beware {1x}, very {1x}. TWOT—1698; BDB—791a.

6192. עָרַם {1x} ʿâram, *aw-ram'* a prim. root; to *pile* up:—gathered together {1x}. See: TWOT—1696; BDB—790d.

6193. עֹרֶם {1x} ʿôrem, *o'-rem;* from 6191; a *stratagem:*—craftiness {1x}. See: TWOT—1698a; BDB—791a.

עֵרֹם ʿÊrôm. See 5903.

עָרֹם ʿârôm. See 6174.

6194. עָרֵם {10x} ʿârêm (Jer 50:26), *aw-rame'*; or (fem.)
עֲרֵמָה ʿărêmâh, *ar-ay-maw'*; from 6192; a *heap;* spec. a *sheaf:*—heap {8x}, heap of corn {1x}, sheaves {1x}. See: TWOT—1696a; BDB 790d.

6195. עָרְמָה {5x} ʿormâh, *or-maw'*; fem. of 6193; *trickery;* or (in a good sense) *discretion:*—guile {1x}, wilily {1x}, subtilty {1x}, wisdom {1x}, prudence {1x}. See: TWOT—1698b; BDB—791a.

עֲרֵמָה ʿarêmâh. See 6194.

6196. עַרְמוֹן {2x} ʿarmôwn, *ar-mone'*; prob. from 6191; the *plane* tree (from its *smooth* and shed bark):—chestnut tree {2x}. See: TWOT—1697a; BDB—790d.

6197. עֵרָן {1x} ʿÊrân, *ay-rawn'*; prob. from 5782; *watchful; Eran*, an Isr.:—*Eran* {1x}. See: BDB—735d, 791b.

6198. עֵרָנִי {1x} ʿÊrâniy, *ay-raw-nee'*; patron. from 6197; an *Eranite* or desc. (collect.) of Eran:—Eranites {1x}. See: BDB—735d, 791b.

עַרְעוֹר ʿArʿôwr. See 6177.

6199. עַרְעָר {2x} ʿarʿâr, *ar-awr'*; from 6209; *naked*, i.e. (fig.) *poor:*—destitute {1x}, health {1x}. See: TWOT—1705b; BDB—791b, 792d. See also 6176.

עֲרֹעֵר ʿĂrôʿêr. See 6177.

6200. עֲרֹעֵרִי {1x} ʿĂrôʿêrîy, *ar-o-ay-ree'*; patron. from 6177; an *Aroërite* or inhab. of Aroër:—Aroerite {1x}. See: BDB—793a.

6201. עָרַף {2x} ʿâraph, *aw-raf'*; a prim. root; to *droop;* hence, to *drip:*—drop {1x}, drop down {1x}. See: TWOT—1701; BDB—791c.

6202. עָרַף {6x} ʿâraph, *aw-raf'*; a prim. root [rather ident. with 6201 through the idea of *sloping*]; prop. to *bend* downward; but used only as a denom. from 6203, to *break the neck;* hence, (fig) to *destroy:*—break neck {2x}, strike off {1x}, break down {1x}, cut off . . . neck {1x}, behead {1x}. See: TWOT—1700; BDB—791c.

6203. עֹרֶף {33x} ʿôreph, *o-ref'*; from 6202; the *nape* or back of the neck (as *declining*); hence, the *back* generally (whether lit. or fig.):—neck {17x}, back {7x}, stiffnecked + 7186 {4x}, stiffnecked {3x}, backs + 310 {1x}, stiffnecked + 7185 {1x}. See: TWOT—1700a; BDB—791b.

6204. עָרְפָּה {2x} ʿOrpâh, *or-paw'*; fem. of 6203; *mane; Orpah*, a Moabitess:—*Orpah* {2x}. See: BDB—791c.

6205. עֲרָפֶל {15x} ʿărâphel, *ar-aw-fel'*; prob. from 6201; *gloom* (as of a *lowering* sky):—thick darkness {8x}, darkness {3x}, gross darkness {2x}, dark cloud {1x}, dark {1x}. See: TWOT—1701b; BDB—791d.

6206. עָרַץ {15x} ʿârats, *aw-rats'*; a prim. root; to *awe* or (intr.) to *dread;* hence, to *harass:*—afraid {3x}, fear {3x}, dread {2x}, terribly {2x}, break {1x}, affrighted {1x}, oppress {1x}, prevail {1x}, terrified {1x}. See: TWOT—1702; BDB—592a, 791d.

6207. עָרַק {2x} ʿâraq, *aw-rak'*; a prim. root; to *gnaw*, i.e. (fig.) *eat* (by hyperbole); also (part.) a *pain:*—fleeing {1x}, sinew {1x}. See: TWOT—1703; BDB—792b.

6208. עַרְקִי {2x} ʿArqîy, *ar-kee'*; patrial from an unused name mean. a *tush;* an *Arkite* or inhab. of Erek:—Arkite {2x}. See: BDB—792b.

6209. עָרַר {4x} ʿârar, *aw-rar'*; a prim. root; to *bare;* fig. to *demolish:*—make bare {1x}, raise up {1x}, utterly {1x}, broken {1x}. See: TWOT—1705; BDB—792c.

6210. עֶרֶשׂ {10x} ʿeres, *eh'res;* from an unused root mean. perh. to *arch;* a *couch* (prop. with a *canopy*):—bed {5x}, couch {3x}, bedstead {2x}. See: TWOT—1706a; BDB—793a.

6211. עָשׁ {12x} ʿâsh, *awsh;* from 6244; a *moth:*—moth {7x}, grass {5x}. See: TWOT—1715a, 1617, 2931; BDB—747b, 798b, 799c. See also 5906.

6211'. עֲשַׂב {33x} ʿăsab (Aram.), *as-ab'*; 6212:—herb {17x}, grass {16x}. See: TWOT—1707a.

6212. עֶשֶׂב {33x} ʿeseb, *eh'seb;* from an unused root mean. to *glisten* (or *be green*); *grass* (or any tender shoot):—herb {17x}, grass {16x}. See: TWOT—1707a; BDB—793b, 1108a.

6213. עָשָׂה {2633x} ʿâsâh, *aw-saw'*; a prim. root; to *do* or *make*, in the broadest sense and widest application (as follows):—do {1333x}, make {653x}, wrought {52x}, deal {52x}, commit {49x}, offer {49x}, execute {48x}, keep {48x}, shew {43x}, prepare {37x}, work {29x}, do so {21x}, perform {18x}, get {14x}, dress {13x}, maker {13x}, maintain {7x}, misc. {154x} = accomplish, advance, appoint, apt, be at, become, bear, bestow, bring forth, bruise, be busy, × certainly, have the charge of, deck, + displease, exercise, fashion, + feast, [fight-]ing man, + finish, fit, fly, follow, fulfill, furnish, gather, go about, govern, grant, great, + hinder, hold ([a feast]), × indeed, + be industrious, + journey, labour, be meet, observe, be occupied, + officer, pare, bring (come) to pass, practise, procure, provide, put, requite, × sacrifice, serve, set, × sin, spend, × surely, take, × throughly, trim, × very, + vex, be [warr-] ior, yield, use.

ʿ*Asah* means "to create, do, make." I. CREATION: **(1)** This verb, which occurs over 2600 times in the Old Testament, is used as a synonym for "create" only about 60 times. **(1a)** There is nothing inherent in the word to indicate the nature of the creation involved; **(1b)** it is only when ʿ*asah* is parallel to *bara'* that we can be sure that it implies creation. **(1c)** Because ʿ*asah* describes the most common of human (and divine) activities, it is ill-suited to communicate theological meaning—except where it is used with bara' or other terms whose technical meanings are clearly established. **(1d)** The most instructive occurrences of ʿ*asah* are in the early chapters of Genesis. **(1d1)** Gen 1:1 uses the verb bara' to introduce the Creation account, and Gen 1:7 speaks of its detailed execution: "And God made [ʿ*asah*] the firmament. . . ." **(1d2)** Whether or not the firmament was made of existing material cannot be determined, since the passage uses only ʿ*asah*. **(1d3)** But it is clear that the verb expresses creation, since it is used in that context and follows the technical word bara'. The same can be said of other verses in Genesis: 1:16 (the lights of heaven); 1:25, 3:1 (the animals); 1:31; 2:2 (all his work); and 6:6 (man). **(1d4)** In Gen 1:26–27, however, ʿ*asah* must mean creation from nothing, since it is used as a synonym for bara'. The text reads, "Let us make [ʿ*asah*] man in our image, after our likeness. . . . So God created [bara'] man in his own image. . . ." **(1d5)** Similarly, Gen 2:4 states: "These are the generations of the heavens and of the earth when they were created [bara'], in the day that the Lord God made [ʿ*asah*] the earth and the heavens." **(1d6)** Finally, Gen 5:1 equates the two as follows: "In the day that God created [bara'] man, in the likeness of God made [ʿ*asah*] he him." **(1d7)** The unusual juxtaposition of bara' and ʿ*asah* in Gen 2:3 refers to the totality of creation, which God had "created" by "making." **(2)** It is unwarranted to overly refine the meaning of ʿ*asah* to suggest that it means creation from something, as opposed to creation from nothing. **(3)** Only context can determine its special nuance. It can mean either, depending upon the situation.

II. GENERAL: ʿAshah means "to make, do, create." **(1)** In its primary sense this verb represents the production of various objects. **(1a)** This includes making images and idols: "Thou shalt not make unto thee any graven image . . ." (Ex 20:4). **(1b)** The verb can mean to make something into something: "And the residue thereof he maketh a god, even his graven image . . ." (Is 44:17). **(2)** In an extended use this verb means to prepare a meal, a banquet, or even an offering: "And he [Abraham] took butter, and milk, and the calf which he had dressed, and set it before them [his three guests] . . ." (Gen 18:8). **(3)** In Gen 12:5 ʿashah means "to acquire" (as it often does): "And Abram took Sarai his wife, and Lot his brother's son, and all their substance that they had gathered, and the souls that they had gotten in Haran. . . ." The "souls that they had gotten" probably were slaves. **(4)** Used in association with "Sabbath" or the name of other holy days, this word signifies "keeping" or "celebrating": "All the congregation of Israel shall keep it [the Passover]" (Ex 12:47).

(5) In a related sense the word means "to spend" a day: "For who knoweth what is good for man in this life, all the days of his vain life which he spendeth as a shadow?" (Eccl 6:12). **(6)** Depending upon its object, ʿashah has several other nuances within the general concept of producing some product. **(6a)** For example, with the object "book" the verb means "to write": ". . . Of making many books there is no end . . ." (Eccl 12:12). **(6b)** The Bible also uses this word of the process of war: "These made war with Bera king of Sodom . . ." (Gen 14:2). **(6c)** Sometimes the word represents an action: "And Joshua made peace with them, and made a league with them . . ." (Josh 9:15). **(6d)** "To make a mourning" is to observe it: ". . . And he [Joseph] made a mourning for his father seven days" (Gen 50:10). **(6d)** With "name" the verb means "to gain prominence and fame": "Go to, let us build us a city and a tower, whose top may reach unto heaven; and let us make us a name . . ." (Gen 11:4). **(6e)** With the word "workmanship" the word signifies "to work": "And I have filled him with the spirit of God . . . , and in all manner of workmanship, . . . to work in gold, and in silver, and in brass" (Ex 31:3–4). **(7)** ʿAshah may represent the relationship of an individual to another in his action or behavior, in the sense of what one does. So Pharaoh asks Abram: "What is this that thou hast done unto me?" (Gen 12:18).

(8) Israel pledged: "All that the Lord hath said will we do, and be obedient" (Ex 24:7). **(9)** With the particle le the verb signifies inflicting upon another some act or behavior: "Then Abimelech called Abraham, and said unto him, What hast thou done unto us?" (Gen 20:9). **(10)** With the particle ʿim the word may mean "to show," or "to practice" something toward someone. The emphasis here is on an ongoing mutual relationship between two parties obligating them to a reciprocal act: "O Lord God of my master Abraham, I pray thee, send me good speed this day, and show kindness unto my master Abraham" (Gen 24:12). **(11)** In Gen 26:29 ʿashah appears twice in the sense "to practice toward": "That thou wilt do us no harm, as we have not touched thee, and as we have done unto thee nothing but good. . . ." **(12)** Used absolutely this verb sometimes means "to take action": "Let Pharaoh do this, and let him appoint officers over the land . . ." (Gen 41:34). **(12a)** In the Hebrew ʿashah has no object in this passage—it is used absolutely. **(12b)** Used in this manner it may also signify "to be active": "She seeketh wool, and flax, and worketh willingly with her hands" (Prov 31:13). **(13)** In 1 Chr 28:10 the verb (used absolutely) means "to go to work," to go about doing a task: "Take heed now; for the Lord hath chosen thee to build a house for the sanctuary: be strong, and do it."

(14) This verb used of plants signifies "bringing forth." In Gen 1:11 it means "to bear" fruit: ". . . And the fruit tree [bearing] fruit after his kind. . . ." **(15)** In another nuance this verb represents what a plant does in producing grain: ". . . It hath no stalk: the bud shall yield no meal . . ." (Hos 8:7). **(16)** The word signifies the production of branches, too: "It was planted in a good soil by great waters, that it might bring forth branches, and that it might bear fruit, that it might be a goodly vine" (Eze 17:8). **(17)** ʿAshah is used theologically of man's response to divine commands. **(17a)** God commanded Noah: "Make thee an ark of gopher wood . . ." (Gen 6:14). **(17b)** Similarly Israel was commanded "to construct" a sanctuary for God (Ex 25:8). **(18)** The manipulation of the blood of the sacrifice is what the priest is to do (Lev 4:20). **(19)** The entire cultic [religious] activity is described by ʿashah: "As he hath done this day, so the Lord hath commanded to do . . ." (Lev 8:34). **(20)** Thus in his acts a man demonstrates his inward commitment and, therefore, his relationship to God (Deut 4:13). **(21)** Doing God's commands brings life upon a man (Lev 18:5).

(22) This verb is also applied specifically to all aspects of divine acts and actions. **(22a)** In the general sense of His actions toward His people Israel, the word first occurs in Gen 12:2, where God promises "to make" Abram a great nation. **(22b)** ʿAshah is also the most general Old Testament expression for divine creating. Every aspect of this activity is described by this word: "For in six days the Lord made heaven and earth . . ." (Ex 20:11). This is its meaning in its first biblical occurrence: "And God made the firmament, and divided the waters which were under the firmament from the waters which were above the firmament . . ." (Gen 1:7). **(23)** This word is used of God's acts effecting the entire created world and individual men (Ex 20:6). **(24)** God's acts and words perfectly correspond, so that what He says He does, and what He does is what He has said (Gen 21:1; Ps 115:3). Syn.: 1254, 3335, 3559, 6466, 7069. See: TWOT—1708, 1709; BDB—793c, 796b.

6214. עֲשָׂהאֵל {18x} **ʿĂsâhʾêl**, *as-aw-ale'*; from 6213 and 410; *God has made; Asahel*, the name of four Isr.:—*Asahel* {18x}. See: BDB—795c.

6215. עֵשָׂו {97x} **ʿÊsâv**, *ay-sawv'*; appar. a form of the pass. part. of 6213 in the orig. sense of *handling; rough* (i.e. sensibly *felt*); *Esau*, a son of Isaac, incl. his posterity:—Esau {97x}. See: BDB—796c.

6216. עָשׁוֹק {1x} **ʿâshôwq**, *aw-shoke'*; from 6231; *oppressive* (as noun, a *tyrant*):—oppressor {1x}. See: TWOT—1713c; BDB—799a.

6217. עָשׁוּק {3x} **ʿâshûwq**, *aw-shook'*; or

עָשֻׁק **ʿâshûq**, *aw-shook'*; pass. part. of 6231; used in plur. masc. as abstr. *tyranny:*—oppression {2x}, oppressed {1x}. See: TWOT—1713d; BDB—799a.

6218. עָשׂוֹר {16x} **ʿâsôwr**, *aw-sore'*; or

עָשֹׂר **ʿâsôr**, *aw-sore'*; from 6235; *ten;* by abbrev. ten *strings,* and so a *decachord:*—tenth {12x}, instrument of ten strings {3x}, ten {1x}. See: TWOT—1711d; BDB—797c.

6219. עָשׁוֹת {1x} **ʿâshôwth**, *aw-shōth'*; from 6245; *shining,* i.e. *polished:*—bright {1x}. See: TWOT—1716b; BDB—799d.

6220. עַשְׁוָת {1x} **ʿAshvâth**, *ash-vawth'*; for 6219; *bright; Ashvath*, an Isr.:—*Ashvath* {1x}. See: BDB—798b.

6221. עֲשִׂיאֵל {1x} **ʿĂsîyʾêl**, *as-ee-ale'*; from 6213 and 410; *made of God; Asiël*, an Isr.:—Asiel {1x}. See: BDB—795c.

6222. עֲשָׂיָה {8x} **ʿĂsâyâh**, *aw-saw-yaw'*; from 6213 and 3050; *Jah has made; Asajah*, the name of three or four Isr.:—Asaiah {8x}. See: BDB—795c.

6223. עָשִׁיר {23x} **ʿâshîyr**, *aw-sheer'*; from 6238; *rich*, whether lit. or fig. (*noble*):—rich {20x}, rich man {3x}. See: TWOT—1714b; BDB—799b.

6224. עֲשִׂירִי {29x} **ʿăsîyrîy**, *as-ee-ree'*; from 6235; *tenth;* by abb. *tenth month* or (fem.)

part:—tenth {27x}, tenth part {2x}. See: TWOT—1711f; BDB—798a.

6225. עָשַׁן {6x} ʿ**âshan**, *aw-shan'*; a prim. root; to *smoke*, whether lit. or fig.:—smoke {5x}, angry {1x}. See: TWOT—1712; BDB—798c.

6226. עָשֵׁן {2x} ʿ**âshên**, *aw-shane'*; from 6225; *smoky:*—smoking {2x}. See: TWOT—1712b; BDB—798c.

6227. עָשָׁן {25x} ʿ**âshân**, *aw-shawn'*; from 6225; *smoke*, lit. or fig. (*vapor, dust, anger*):—smoke {24x}, smoking {1x}. See: TWOT—1712a; BDB—798c.

6228. עָשָׁן {4x} ʿ**Âshân**, *aw-shawn'*; the same as 6227; *Ashan*, a place in Pal.:—*Ashan* {4x}. See: BDB—92d, 798c.

6229. עָשַׂק {1x} ʿ**âsaq**, *aw-sak'*; a prim. root (ident. with 6231); to *press upon*, i.e. *quarrel:*—strove {1x}. See: TWOT—1710; BDB—796c.

6230. עֵשֶׂק {1x} ʿ**Êseq**, *ay'sek*; from 6229; *strife:*—Esek {1x}. See: BDB—796c.

6231. עָשַׁק {37x} ʿ**âshaq**, *aw-shak'*; a prim. root (comp. 6229); to *press* upon, i.e. *oppress, defraud, violate, overflow:*—oppress {23x}, oppressor {4x}, defraud {3x}, wrong {2x}, deceived {1x}, deceitfully gotten {1x}, oppression {1x}, drink up {1x}, violence {1x}. See: TWOT—1713; BDB—798d.

6232. עֵשֶׁק {1x} ʿ**Êsheq**, *ay-shek'*; from 6231; *oppression*, *Eshek*, an Isr.:—Eshek {1x}. See: BDB—799a.

6233. עֹשֶׁק {15x} ʿ**ôsheq**, *o'-shek*; from 6231; *injury, fraud*, (subj.) *distress*, (concr.) *unjust gain:*—oppression {11x}, cruelly {1x}, extortion {1x}, oppression + 6231 {1x}, thing {1x}. See: TWOT—1713a; BDB—799a.

עָשֻׁק ʿ**âshûq**. See 6217.

6234. עָשְׁקָה {1x} ʿ**oshqâh**, *osh-kaw'*; fem. of 6233; *anguish:*—oppressed {1x}. See: TWOT—1713b; BDB—799a.

6235. עֶשֶׂר {175x} ʿ**eser**, *eh'ser*; masc.

עֲשָׂרָה ʿ**ăsârâh**, *as-aw-raw'*; from 6237; *ten* (as an *accumulation* to the extent of the digits):—ten {172x}, fifteen + 2568 {1x}, seventeen + 7651 {1x}, ten times {1x}. See: TWOT—1711a; BDB—796c, 797d, 1108a.

6236. עֲשַׂר {6x} ʿ**ăsar** (Aram.), *as-ar'*; masc.

עַשְׂרָה ʿ**asrâh** (Aram.), *as-raw'*; corresp. to 6235; *ten:*—ten {4x}, twelve + 8648 {2x}. See: TWOT—2932; BDB—1108a.

6237. עָשַׂר {9x} ʿ**âsar**, *aw-sar'*; a prim. root (ident. with 6238); to *accumulate;* but used only as denom. from 6235; to *tithe*, i.e. *take* or *give a tenth:*—tithe {4x}, take . . . tenth {2x}, give tenth {1x}, surely {1x}, truly {1x}. See: TWOT—1711c, BDB—797c.

6238. עָשַׁר {17x} ʿ**âshar**, *aw-shar'*; a prim. root; prop. to *accumulate;* chiefly (spec.) to *grow* (caus. *make*) *rich:*—be (-come, make, make self, wax) rich {13x}, enrich {3x}, richer {1x}. See: TWOT—1714; BDB—799a. See 6240.

6239. עֹשֶׁר {37x} ʿ**ôsher**, *o'-sher*; from 6238; *wealth:*—× far [richer]{1x}, riches {36x}. See: TWOT—1714a; BDB—799b.

6240. עָשָׂר {335x} ʿ**âsâr**, *aw-sawr'*; for 6235; *ten* (only in combination), i.e. *teen;* also (ord.) *-teenth:*—eleven + 259 {9x}, eleven + 6249 {6x}, eleventh + 6249 {13x}, eleventh + 259 {4x}, twelve + 8147 {106x}, twelfth + 8147 {21x}, thirteen + 7969 {13x}, thirteenth + 7969 {11x} to nineteen {152x}. See: TWOT—1711b; BDB—797a.

עָשֹׂר ʿ**âsôr**. See 6218.

6241. עִשָּׂרוֹן {28x} ʿ**issârôwn**, *is-saw-rone'*; or

עִשָּׂרֹן ʿ**issârôn**, *is-saw-rone'*; from 6235; (fractional) a *tenth* part:—tenth {3x}, tenth deal {25x}. See: TWOT—1711h; BDB—798a.

6242. עֶשְׂרִים {315x} ʿ**esrîym**, *es-reem'*; from 6235; *twenty;* also (ord.) *twentieth:*—twenty {278x}, twentieth {36x}, sixscore + 3967 {1x}. See: TWOT—1711c; BDB—796d, 797d.

6243. עֶשְׂרִין {1x} ʿ**esrîyn** (Aram.), *es-reen'*; corresp. to 6242:—twenty {1x}. See: TWOT—2932a; BDB—1108a.

6244. עָשֵׁשׁ {3x} ʿ**âshêsh**, *aw-shaysh'*; a prim. root; prob. to *shrink*, i.e. *fail:*—be consumed {3x}. See: TWOT—1715; BDB—799c.

6245. עָשַׁת {2x} ʿ**âshath**, *aw-shath'*; a prim. root; prob. to *be sleek*, i.e. *glossy;* hence, (through the idea of *polishing*) to *excogitate* (as if *forming* in the mind):—shine {1x}, think {1x}. See: TWOT—1716, 1717; BDB—799c, 799d, 1108a.

6246. עֲשִׁת {1x} ʿ**âshîth** (Aram.), *ash-eeth'*; corresp. to 6245; to *purpose:*—think {1x}. See: TWOT—2933; BDB—1108a.

6247. עֶשֶׁת {1x} ʿ**esheth**, *eh'-sheth*; from 6245; a *fabric:*—bright {1x}. See: TWOT—1716a; BDB—799d.

6248. עַשְׁתּוּת {1x} ʿ**ashtûwth**, *ash-tooth'*; from 6245; *cogitation:*—thought {1x}. See: TWOT—1717a; BDB—799d.

6249. עַשְׁתֵּי {19x} ʿ**ashtêy**, *ash-tay'*; appar. masc. plur. constr. of 6247 in the sense of an *afterthought* (used only in connection with 6240 in lieu of 259) *eleven* or (ord.) *eleventh:*—eleven + 6240 {19x}. See: TWOT—1717c; BDB—799d.

6250. עֶשְׁתֹּנָה {1x} ʿ**eshtônâh**, *esh-to-naw'*; from 6245; *thinking:*—thought {1x}. See: TWOT—1717b; BDB—799d.

6251. עַשְׁתְּרָה {4x} ʿ**ashtᵉrâh**, *ash-ter-aw'*; prob. from 6238; *increase:*—flock {4x}. See: TWOT—1718a; BDB—800b.

6252. עַשְׁתָּרוֹת {12x} ʿ**Ashtârôwth**, *ash-taw-rōth'*; or

עַשְׁתָּרֹת ʿ**Ashtârôth**, *ash-taw-rōth'*; plur. of 6251; *Ashtaroth*, the name of a Sidonian deity, and of a place E. of the Jordan:—*Ashtaroth* {11x}, Astaroth {1x}. See: BDB—800b, 902b. See also 1045, 6253, 6255.

6253. עַשְׁתֹּרֶת {3x} ʿ**Ashtôreth**, *ash-to'reth*; prob. for 6251; *Ashtoreth*, the Phœnician goddess of love (and *increase*):—*Ashtoreth* {3x}. See: TWOT—1718; BDB—800a.

6254. עַשְׁתְּרָתִי {1x} ʿ**Ashtᵉrâthîy**, *ash-ter-aw-thee'*; patrial from 6252; an *Ashterathite* or inhab. of Ashtaroth:—Ashterathite {1x}. See: BDB—800c.

6255. עַשְׁתְּרֹת קַרְנַיִם {1x} ʿ**Ashtᵉrôth Qarnayim**, *ash-ter-ōth' kar-nah'-yim;* from 6252 and the dual of 7161; *Ashtaroth of* (the) *double horns* (a symbol of the deity); *Ashteroth-Karnâm*, a place E. of the Jordan:—Ashtoreth Karnaim {1x}. See: BDB—800b.

6256. עֵת {296x} ʿ**êth**, *ayth;* from 5703; *time*, espec. (adv. with prep.) *now, when*, etc.:—time {257x}, season {16x}, when {7x}, always {4x}, eveningtide + 6153 {2x}, misc. {10x} = + after, × certain, + continually, + evening, long, so [long] as.

ʿEth means "time; period of time; appointed time; proper time; season." **(1)** Basically this noun connotes "time" conceived as an opportunity or season. **(1a)** First, the word signifies an appointed, fixed, and set time or period. This is what astrologers claimed to discern: "Then the king said to the wise men, which knew the times . . ." (Est 1:13). **(1b)** God alone, however, knows and reveals such "appointed times": ". . . In the time of their visitation they shall be cast down, saith the Lord" (Jer 8:12). **(2)** This noun also is used of the concept "proper or appropriate time." This nuance is applied to the "time" God has appointed for one to die: "Be not over much wicked, neither be thou foolish: why shouldest thou die before thy time?" (Eccl 7:17). **(2a)** It is used of the "appropriate or suitable time" for a given activity in life: "He hath made every thing beautiful in his time . . ." (Eccl 3:11; cf. Ps 104:27). **(2b)** Finally, the "appropriate time" for divine judgment is represented by *ʿeth:* "It is time for thee, Lord, to work: for they have made void thy law" (Ps 119:126).

(3) A third use connotes "season," or a regular fixed period of time such as springtime: "And he said, I will certainly return unto thee according to the time of life; and, lo, Sarah thy wife shall have a son" (Gen 18:10). **(3a)** Similarly, the word is used of the rainy "season" (Ezra 10:13), **(3b)** the harvest "time" (Jer 50:16), **(3c)** the migratory "period" (Jer 8:7), and **(3d)** the mating "season" (Gen 31:10). **(4)** This noun also is applied to differing "extensions of time." In its first biblical appearance, for example, *ʿeth* represents the "time" (period of the day) when the sun is setting: "And the dove came in to him in the evening [literally, time of the evening] . . ." (Gen 8:11). **(5)** The word is used of special occasions such as the birth of a child: "Therefore will he give them up, until the time *that* she which travaileth hath brought forth: then the remnant of his brethren shall return unto the children of Israel" (Mic 5:3) and **(6)** of periods during which certain conditions persist: "And let them judge the people at all seasons: and it shall be, *that* every great matter they shall bring unto thee, but every small matter they shall judge: so shall it be easier for thyself, and they shall bear *the burden* with thee" (Ex 18:22; cf. Dan 12:11). See: TWOT—1650b; BDB—773b, 800c.

6257. עָתַד {2x} ʿ**âthad**, *aw-thad'*; a prim. root; to *prepare:*—make fit {1x}, be ready to become heaps {1x}. See: TWOT—1719; BDB—800c, 1108a.

עַתֻּד ʿ**attûd**. See 6260.

6258. עַתָּה {9x} ʿ**attâh**, *at-taw'*; from 6256; at *this time*, whether adv., conjunc. or expletive:—{9x} = henceforth, now, straightway, this time, whereas. See: TWOT—1650c; BDB—773d, 800d, 1107b.

6259. עָתוּד {2x} ʿ**âthûwd**, *aw-thood'*; pass. part. of 6257; *prepared:*—ready {1x}, treasures {1x}. See: TWOT—1719a; BDB—800c.

6260. עַתּוּד {29x} ʿ**attûwd**, *at-tood'*; or

עַתֻּד ʿ**attûd**, *at-tood'*; from 6257; *prepared*, i.e. *full grown;* spoken only (in plur.) of *he-goats*, or (fig.) *leaders* of the people:—chief one {1x}, (he) goat {2x}, ram {26x}. See: TWOT—1719b; BDB—800c.

6261. עִתִּי {1x} ʿ**ittîy**, *it-tee'*; from 6256; *timely:*—fit {1x}. See: TWOT—1650d; BDB—774c, 800d.

6262. עַתַּי {4x} ʽ**Attay**, *at-tah'ee;* for 6261; *Attai,* the name of three Isr.:—Attai {4x}. See: BDB—774c, 800d.

6263. עֲתִיד {1x} ʽ**ăthîyd** (Aram.), *ath-eed';* corresp. to 6264; *prepared:*—ready {1x}. See: TWOT—2934; BDB—1108a.

6264. עָתִיד {6x} ʽ**âthîyd**, *aw-theed';* from 6257; *prepared;* by impl. *skilful;* fem. plur. the *future;* also *treasure:*—things that shall come {1x}, ready {4x}, treasures {1x}. See: TWOT—1719a; BDB—800c, 1108a.

6265. עֲתָיָה {1x} ʽ**Âthâyâh**, *ath-aw-yaw';* from 5790 and 3050; *Jah has helped; Athajah,* an Isr.:—Athaiah {1x}. See: BDB—800d.

6266. עָתִיק {1x} ʽ**âthîyq**, *aw-theek';* from 6275; prop. *antique,* i.e. *venerable* or *splendid:*—durable {1x}. See: TWOT—1721c; BDB—801b.

6267. עַתִּיק {2x} ʽ**attîyq**, *at-teek';* from 6275; *removed,* i.e. *weaned;* also *antique:*—ancient {1x}, drawn {1x}. See: TWOT—1721d; BDB—801c, 1108a.

6268. עַתִּיק {3x} ʽ**attîyq** (Aram.), *at-teek';* corresp. to 6267; *venerable:*—ancient {3x}. See: TWOT—2935; BDB—810a, 1108a.

6269. עֲתָךְ {1x} ʽ**Âthâk**, *ath-awk';* from an unused root mean. to *sojourn; lodging; Athak,* a place in Pal.:—Athach {1x}. See: BDB—800d, 801d.

6270. עַתְלַי {1x} ʽ**Athlay**, *ath-lah'ee;* from an unused root mean. to *compress; constringent; Athlai,* an Isr.:—Athlai {1x}. See: BDB—800d.

6271. עֲתַלְיָה {17x} ʽ**Âthalyâh**, *ath-al-yaw';* or

עֲתַלְיָהוּ ʽ**Ăthalyâhûw**, *ath-al-yaw'-hoo;* from the same as 6270 and 3050; *Jah has constrained; Athaljah,* the name of an Israelitess and two Isr.:—Athaliah {17x}. See: BDB—800d.

6272. עָתַם {1x} ʽ**âtham**, *aw-tham';* a prim. root; prob. to *glow,* i.e. (fig.) *be desolated:*—be darkened {1x}. See: TWOT—1720; BDB—801a.

6273. עָתְנִי {1x} ʽ**Otnîy**, *oth-nee';* from an unused root mean. to *force; forcible; Othni,* an Isr.:—Othni {1x}. See: BDB—801a.

6274. עָתְנִיאֵל {7x} ʽ**Othnîyʼêl**, *oth-nee-ale';* from the same as 6273 and 410; *force of God; Othniël,* an Isr.:—Othniel {7x}. See: BDB—801a.

6275. עָתַק {9x} ʽ**âthaq**, *aw-thak';* a prim. Root; to *remove* (intr. or tran.) fig. to *grow old;* spec. to *transcribe:*—copy out {1x}, leave off {1x}, become old {1x}, wax old {1x}, removed {5x}. See: TWOT—1721; BDB—801a, 1108a.

6276. עָתֵק {1x} ʽ**athêq**, *aw-thake';* from 6275; *antique,* i.e. *valued:*—durable {1x}. See: TWOT—1721b; BDB—801b.

6277. עָתָק {4x} ʽ**âthâq**, *aw-thawk';* from 6275 in the sense of *license; impudent:*—arrogancy {1x}, grievous things {1x}, hard things {1x}, stiff {1x}. See: TWOT—1721a; BDB—801b.

6278. עֵת קָצִין {1x} ʽ**Êth Qâtsîyn**, *ayth kaw-tseen';* from 6256 and 7011; *time of a judge; Eth-Katsin,* a place in Pal.:—Ittah-kazin {1x}. See: BDB—773d.

6279. עָתַר {20x} ʽ**âthar**, *aw-thar';* a prim. root [rather denom. from 6281]; to burn *incense* in worship, i.e. *intercede* (recip. *listen* to prayer):—intreat {18x}, pray {1x}, prayer {1x}. See: TWOT—1722; BDB—801c.

6280. עָתַר {2x} ʽ**âthar**, *aw-thar';* a prim. root; to *be* (caus. *make*) *abundant:*—deceitful {1x}, multiply {1x}. See: TWOT—1723; BDB—801d.

6281. עֶתֶר {2x} ʽ**Ether**, *eh'ther;* from 6280; *abundance; Ether,* a place in Pal.:—*Ether* {2x}. See: BDB—800d, 801d.

6282. עָתָר {2x} ʽ**âthâr**, *aw-thawr';* from 6280; *incense* (as increasing to a *volume* of smoke); hence, (from 6279) a *worshipper:*—suppliant {1x}, thick {1x}. See: TWOT—1722a, 1724a; BDB—801c, 801d.

6283. עֲתֶרֶת {1x} ʽ**ăthereth**, *ath-eh'-reth;* from 6280; *copiousness:*—abundance {1x}. See: TWOT—1723a;BDB—801d.

פ

פֹּא **pôʼ**. See 6311.

6284. פָּאָה {1x} **pâʼâh**, *paw-aw';* a prim. root; to *puff,* i.e. *blow* away:—scatter into corners {1x}. See: TWOT—1725; BDB—802a.

6285. פֵּאָה {86x} **pêʼâh**, *pay-aw';* fem. of 6311; prop. *mouth* in a fig. sense, i.e. *direction, region, extremity:*—corner {16x}, end {1x}, part {1x}, quarter {4x}, side {64x}. See: TWOT—1725a; BDB—802a.

6286. פָּאַר {14x} **pâʼar**, *paw-ar';* a prim. root; to *gleam,* i.e. (caus.) *embellish;* fig. to *boast;* also to *explain* (i.e. make clear) oneself; denom. from 6288, to *shake* a tree:—beautify {3x}, boast self {1x}, go over the boughs {1x}, glorify self {7x}, glory {1x}, vaunt self {1x}.

Pa'ar means "to glorify." One appearance of this verb is in Is 60:9: ". . . And to the Holy One of Israel, because he hath gloried thee." See: TWOT—1726, 1727; BDB—802b, 802d.

6287. פְּאֵר {7x} **peʼêr**, *peh-ayr';* from 6286; an *embellishment,* i.e. fancy *head-dress:*—beauty {1x}, bonnets {2x}, goodly {1x}, ornament {1x}, tire of thine head {1x}, tires {1x}. See: TWOT—1726a; BDB—802c.

6288. פְּאֹרָה {7x} **peʼôrâh**, *peh-o-raw';* or

פֹּרָאה **pôrâʼh**, *po-raw';* or

פֻּארָה **pûʼrâh**, *poo-raw';* from 6286; prop. *ornamentation,* i.e. (plur.) *foliage* (incl. the limbs) as *bright* green:—bough {2x}, branch {4x}, sprig {1x}. See: TWOT—1727a; BDB—802d, 825b.

6289. פָּארוּר {2x} **pâʼrûwr**, *paw-roor';* from 6286; prop. *illuminated,* i.e. a *glow;* as noun, a *flush* (of anxiety):—blackness {2x}. See: TWOT—1727b; BDB—802d.

6290. פָּארָן {11x} **Pâʼrân**, *paw-rawn';* from 6286; *ornamental; Paran,* a desert of Arabia:—*Paran* {11x}. See: TWOT—1728; BDB—803a.

6291. פַּג {1x} **pag**, *pag;* from an unused root mean. to *be torpid,* i.e. *crude;* an *unripe* fig:—green figs {1x}. See: TWOT—1729a; BDB—803a.

6292. פִּגּוּל {4x} **piggûwl**, *pig-gool';* or

פִּגֻּל **piggûl**, *pig-gool';* from an unused root mean. to *stink;* prop. *fetid,* i.e. (fig.) *unclean* (ceremonially):—abominable {2x}, abominable things {1x}, abomination {1x}. See: TWOT—1730a; BDB—803b.

6293. פָּגַע {46x} **pâgaʽ**, *paw-gah';* a prim. root; to *impinge,* by accident or violence, or (fig.) by importunity:—fall {12x}, meet {11x}, reach {7x}, intercession {4x}, intreat {2x}, entreat {1x}, misc. {9x} = come (betwixt), lay, light [upon], pray, run. See: TWOT—1731; BDB—803b.

6294. פֶּגַע {2x} **pegaʽ**, *peh'-gah;* from 6293; *impact* (casual):—chance {1x}, occurrent {1x}. See: TWOT—1731a; BDB—803c.

6295. פַּגְעִיאֵל {5x} **Pagʽîyʼêl**, *pag-ee-ale';* from 6294 and 410; *accident of God; Pagiël,* an Isr.:—Pagiel {5x}. See: BDB—803c.

6296. פָּגַר {2x} **pâgar**, *paw-gar';* a prim. root; to *relax,* i.e. *become exhausted:*—be faint {2x}. See: TWOT—1732; BDB—803c.

6297. פֶּגֶר {22x} **peger**, *peh'gher;* from 6296; a *carcase* (as *limp*), whether of man or beast; fig. an idolatrous *image:*—carcase (carcass) {14x}, corpse {2x}, dead body {6x}. Syn.: 5038. See: TWOT—1732a; BDB—803d.

6298. פָּגַשׁ {14x} **pâgash**, *paw-gash';* a prim. root; to *come in contact with,* whether by accident or violence; fig. to *concur:*—meet (with, together) {14x}. See: TWOT—1732a; BDB—803d.

6299. פָּדָה {59x} **pâdâh**, *paw-daw';* a prim. root; to *sever,* i.e. *ransom;* gen. to *release, preserve:*—redeem {48x}, deliver {5x}, ransom {2x}, rescued {1x}, misc. {3x} = × at all, × by any means, × surely.

Padah means "to redeem, ransom." **(1)** *Padah* indicates that some intervening or substitutionary action effects a release from an undesirable condition. **(1a)** In more secular contexts, it implies a payment of some sort. **(1b)** But 1 Sa 14:45 indicates that money is not intrinsic in the word; Saul is determined to execute Jonathan for his involuntary transgression, but ". . . the people rescued Jonathan, that he died not." **(1c)** Slavery appears as a condition from which one may be "ransomed" (Ex 21:8; Lev 19:20). **(2)** The word is connected with the laws of the firstborn. As a reminder of slaying all the Egyptian firstborn but sparing the Israelites, God retained an eternal claim on the life of all Israelite firstborn males, both of men and of cattle. The latter were often sacrificed, "but all the firstborn of my children I redeem" (Ex 13:15). **(3)** God accepted the separation of the tribe of Levi for liturgical service in lieu of all Israelite firstborn (Num 3:40ff.). However, the Israelite males still had to be "redeemed" (*padah*) from this service by payment of specified "redemption money" (Num 3:44–51).

(4) When God is the subject of *padah,* the word emphasizes His complete, sovereign freedom to liberate human beings. **(5)** Sometimes God is said to "redeem" **(5a)** individuals (Abraham, Is 29:22; David, 1 Kin 1:29; Ps 26:11; 21:5; 71:23); **(5b)** but usually Israel, the elect people, is the beneficiary. **(5c)** Sometimes the redemption or deliverance is proclaimed absolutely (2 Sa 7:23; Ps 44:26; Hos 7:13); but the subject is said to be "ransomed" from a specific oppression. **(5d)** At other times, the reference is less explicit—e.g., from "troubles" (Ps 25:22) and from "wicked" men (Jer 15:21). **(6)** Only once is *padah* used to describe liberation from sin or iniquity: "And he shall redeem Israel from all his iniquity" (Ps 130:8). Syn.: 1350, 1353, 3722, 6304. Syn.: 1350, 3724. See: TWOT—1734; BDB—804a, 804b.

6300. פְּדַהְאֵל {1x} **Pedahʼêl**, *ped-ah-ale';* from 6299 and 410; *God has ransomed; Pedahel,* an Isr.:—*Pedahel* {1x}. See: BDB—804b.

6301. פְּדָהצוּר {5x} **Peʼdâhtsûwr**, *ped-aw-tsoor';* from 6299 and 6697; a *rock* (i.e.

God) *has ransomed; Pedahtsur,* an Isr.:—Pedahzur {5x}. See: BDB—804c.

6302. פָּדוּי {4x} **pâdûwy**, *paw-doo'-ee;* pass. part. of 6299; *ransomed* (and so occurring under 6299); as abstr. (in plur. masc.) a *ransom:*—(that are) to be (that were) redeemed {4x}. See: TWOT—1734a; BDB—804a, 804b.

6303. פָּדוֹן {2x} **Pâdôwn**, *paw-done';* from 6299; *ransom; Padon,* one of the Nethinim:—Padon {2x}. See: BDB—804b.

6304. פְּדוּת {4x} **pᵉdûwth**, *ped-ooth';* or

פְּדֻת **pᵉduth**, *ped-ooth';* from 6299; *distinction;* also *deliverance:*—division {1x}, redeem {1x}, redemption {2x}.

The noun related to padah (6299) is *peduth.* It occurs about 5 times and means "ransom or redemption": "He sent redemption unto his people: he hath commanded his covenant for ever . . ." (Ps 111:9). See: TWOT—1734b; BDB—804b.

6305. פְּדָיָה {8x} **Pᵉdâyâh**, *ped-aw-yaw';* or

פְּדָיָהוּ **Pᵉdâyâhûw**, *ped-aw-yaw'-hoo;* from 6299 and 3050; *Jah has ransomed; Pedajah,* the name of six Isr.:—Pedaiah {8x}. See: BDB—804c.

6306. פִּדְיוֹם {4x} **pidyôwm**, *pid-yome';* or

פִּדְיֹם **pidyôm**, *pid-yome';* also

פִּדְיוֹן **pidyôwn**, *pid-yone';* or

פִּדְיֹן **pidyôn**, *pid-yone';* from 6299; a *ransom:*—ransom {1x}, that were redeemed {1x}, redemption {2x}.

6307. פַּדָּן {11x} **Paddân**, *pad-dawn';* from an unused root mean. to *extend;* a *plateau;* or

פַּדַּן אֲרָם **Paddan ʼĂrâm**, *pad-dan' ar-awm';* from the same and 758; the *table-land of Aram; Paddan* or *Paddan-Aram,* a region of Syria:—Padan {1x}, Padan-aram {11x}. See: TWOT—1735; BDB—804c.

6308. פָּדַע {1x} **pâdaʻ**, *paw-dah';* a prim. root; to *retrieve:*—deliver {1x}. See: TWOT—1736; BDB—804c.

6309. פֶּדֶר {3x} **peder**, *peh'der;* from an unused root mean. to *be greasy; suet:*—fat {3x}. See: TWOT—1737; BDB—804d.

פְּדֻת **pᵉdûth**. See 6304.

6310. פֶּה {498x} **peh**, *peh;* from 6284; the *mouth* (as the means of *blowing*), whether lit. or fig. (particularly *speech*); spec. *edge, portion* or *side;* adv. (with prep.) *according to:*—mouth {340x}, commandment {37x}, edge {35x}, according {22x}, word {15x}, hole {6x}, end {3x}, appointment {2x}, portion {2x}, tenor {2x}, sentence {2x}, misc. {32x} = after, assent, collar, × eat, entry, + file, × in, mind, part, × (should) say (-ing), skirt, sound, speech, × spoken, talk, × to, + two-edged, wish.

Peh means mouth; edge; opening; entrance; collar; utterance; order; command; evidence. **(1)** The word means mouth of **(1a)** a human (Ex 4:16), **(1b)** an animal (Num 22:28), **(1c)** a bird's beak (Gen 8:11). **(2)** Figuratively, it speaks of the mouth of **(2a)** the ground (Gen 4:11), **(2b)** the grave (Ps 141:7), **(2c)** a well (Gen 29:2), **(2d)** brooks (Is 19:7), **(2e)** a sack (Gen 42:27), **(2f)** a cave (Josh 10:18), **(2g)** a city gate (Prov 8:3), **(2h)** a tunic's collar (Ex 28:32). **(3)** *Peh* represents the edge of a sword, perhaps in the sense of the part that consumes and/or bites (Gen 34:26). **(4)** Several noteworthy idioms employ *peh:* **(4a)** In Josh 9:2 "with one mouth" means "with one accord;" **(4b1)** "mouth to mouth" means person to person (Num 12:8; Jer 32:3, 4), or **(4b2)** "from end to end" (2 Kin 10:21); **(4c)** "with open mouth" emphasizes greedy consumption (Is 9:12); **(4d)** Placing one's hands on one's mouth is a gesture of silence (Job 29:9); **(4e)** "To ask someone's mouth" is to ask him personally (Gen 24:57); **(4f)** "The mouth of two witnesses" means their testimony (Num 35:30); **(4g)** In Jer. 36:4 "from the mouth of Jeremiah" means "by dictation."

(5) This word can also stand for utterance or order (Gen 41:40). **(6)** *Peh* used with various prepositions has special meanings. **(6a)** Used with ke, it means **(6a1)** "according to" (Num 7:5), or **(6a2)** "in proportion to" (Lev 25:52), or **(6a3)** "as much as" (Ex 16:21). **(7)** When the word is preceded by le, it means **(7a)** "in proportion to" (Lev 25:51), **(7b)** "according to" (Jer 29:10). **(8)** With ʻal the word also means "according to" or "in proportion to" (cf. Lev 27:18). **(9)** The phrase pi shenayim (literally, "two mouths") has two different meanings. **(9a)** In Deut 21:17 it means "double portion" (two parts); and **(9b)** in Zec 13:8 it means "two thirds." Syn.: 6680. See: TWOT—1738; BDB—804d, 809d, 810a, 1108c.

6311. פֹּה {8x} **pôh**, *po;* or

פֹּא **pôʼ** (Job 38:11), *po;* or

פּוֹ **pôw**, *po;* prob. from a prim. inseparable particle פְּ **p** (of demonstr. force) and 1931; *this place* (French *içi*), i.e. *here* or *hence:*—here {2x}, hither {1x}, hitherto {1x}, on this side {1x}, on that side {1x}, on the one side {1x}, on the other side {1x}. See: TWOT—1739, BDB—802a, 805d.

פּוֹא **pôwʼ**. See 375.

6312. פּוּאָה {4x} **Pûwʼâh**, *poo-aw'* or

פֻּוָּה **Puvvâh**, *poov-vaw';* from 6284; a *blast; Puäh* or *Puvvah,* the name of two Isr.:—Puah {2x}, Pua {1x}, Phuvah {1x}. See: BDB—806a, 806d.

6313. פּוּג {4x} **pûwg**, *poog;* a prim. root; to *be sluggish:*—cease {1x}, be feeble {1x}, faint {1x}, be slacked {1x}. See: TWOT—1740; BDB—806a.

6314. פּוּגָה {1x} **pûwgâh**, *poo-gaw';* from 6313; *intermission:*—rest {1x}. See: TWOT—1740b; BDB—806b.

פֻּוָּה **Puvvâh**. See 6312.

6315. פּוּחַ {14x} **pûwach**, *poo'akh;* a prim. root; to *puff,* i.e. blow with the breath or air; hence, to *fan* (as a breeze), to *utter,* to *kindle* (a fire), to *scoff:*—blow (upon) {2x}, break {2x}, puff {2x}, bring into a snare {1x}, speak {6x}, utter {1x}. See: TWOT—1741; BDB—806b.

6316. פּוּט {7x} **Pûwṭ**, *poot;* of for. or.; *Put,* a son of Ham, also the name of his desc. or their region, and of a Pers. tribe:—Put {2x}, Phut {2x}, Libyan {2x}, Libya {1x}. See: BDB—806c.

6317. פּוּטִיאֵל {1x} **Pûwṭîyʼêl**, *poo-tee-ale';* from an unused root (prob. mean. to *disparage*) and 410; *contempt of God; Putiël,* an Isr.:—Putiel {1x}. See: BDB—806c.

6318. פּוֹטִיפַר {2x} **Pôwṭîyphar**, *po-tee-far';* of Eg. der.; *Potiphar,* an Eg.:—Potiphar {2x}. See: BDB—806c.

6319. פּוֹטִי פֶרַע {3x} **Pôwṭîy Pheraʻ**, *po-tee feh'-rah;* of Eg. der.; *Poti-Phera,* an Eg.:—Poti-pherah {3x}. See: BDB—806c.

6320. פּוּךְ {4x} **pûwk**, *pook;* from an unused root mean. to *paint; dye* (spec. *stibium* for the eyes):—fair colours {1x}, glistering {1x}, painted {1x}, painting {1x}. See: TWOT—1742; BDB—806c.

6321. פּוֹל {2x} **pôwl**, *pole;* from an unused root mean. to *be thick;* a *bean* (as *plump*):—beans {2x}. See: TWOT—1743; BDB—806d.

6322. פּוּל {4x} **Pûwl**, *pool;* of for. or.; *Pul,* the name of an Ass. king and of an Ethiopian tribe:—Pul {4x}. See: BDB—806d.

6323. פּוּן {1x} **pûwn**, *poon;* a prim. root mean. to *turn,* i.e. *be perplexed:*—be distracted {1x}. See: TWOT—1744;BDB—67a, 806d.

6324. פּוּנִי {1x} **Pûwnîy**, *poo-nee';* patron. from an unused name mean. a *turn;* a *Punite* (collect.) or desc. of an unknown Pun:—Punites {1x}. See: BDB—806a, 806d.

6325. פּוּנֹן {2x} **Pûwnôn**, *poo-none';* from 6323; *perplexity; Punon,* a place in the Desert:—Punon {2x}. See: BDB—806d.

6326. פּוּעָה {1x} **Pûwʻâh**, *poo-aw';* from an unused root mean. to *glitter; brilliancy; Puäh,* an Israelitess:—Puah {1x}. See: BDB—806d.

6327. פּוּץ {..} **pûwts**, *poots;* a prim. root; to *dash* in pieces, lit. or fig. (espec. to *disperse*):—scatter {48x}, scatter abroad {6x}, disperse {3x}, spread abroad {2x}, cast abroad {2x}, drive {1x}, break to pieces {1x}, shake to pieces {1x}, dash to pieces {1x}, retired {1x}.

Puwts means "to scatter, disperse, be scattered." **(1)** The word is found for the first time in Gen 10:18: ". . . The families of the Canaanites spread abroad." **(2)** The word is used 3 times in the story of the tower of Babel (Gen 11:4, 8–9), apparently to emphasize how men and their languages "were spread" throughout the world. **(3)** *Puwts,* in the sense of "scattering," often has an almost violent connotation to it. **(3a)** Thus, when Saul defeated the Ammonites, "they which remained were scattered, so that two of them were not left together" (1 Sa 11:11) **(3b)** Such "scattering" of forces seems to have been a common thing after defeats in battle (1 Kin 22:17; 2 Kin 25:5). **(4)** Many references are made to Israel as a people and nation "being scattered" among the nations, especially in the imagery of a scattered flock of sheep (Eze 34:5–6; Zec 13:7). **(5)** Ezekiel also promises the gathering together of this scattered flock: ". . . I will even gather you from the people, . . . where ye have been scattered . . ." (Eze 11:17; 20:34, 41). **(6)** In a figurative sense, this word is used to refer to lightning as arrows which God "scatters" (2 Sa 22:15). **(7)** No harvest is possible unless first the seeds "are scattered" in rows (Is 28:25). See: TWOT—1745, 1746, 1800; BDB—806d, 807b, 822d.

6328. פּוּק {2x} **pûwq**, *pook;* a prim. root; to *waver:*—stumble {1x}, move {1x}. See: TWOT—1747; BDB—807b.

6329. פּוּק {7x} **pûwq**, *pook;* a prim. root [rather ident. with 6328 through the idea of *dropping* out; comp. 5312], to *issue,* i.e. *furnish;* caus. to *secure;* fig. to *succeed:*—afford {1x}, draw out {1x}, further {1x}, get {1x}, obtain {3x}. See: TWOT—1748; BDB—807c.

6330. פּוּקָה {1x} **pûwqâh**, *poo-kaw';* from 6328; a *stumbling-block:*—grief {1x}. See: TWOT—1747a; BDB—807c.

6331. פּוּר {3x} **pûwr**, *poor;* a prim. root; to *crush:*—break {1x}, bring to nought {1x}, × utterly take {1x}. See: TWOT—1750; BDB—830b, 830c.

6332. פּוּר {8x} **Pûwr**, *poor;* also (plur.)

פּוּרִים **Pûwrîym**, *poo-reem';* or

פֻּרִים **Pûrîym**, *poo-reem';* from 6331; a *lot* (as by means of a *broken* piece):—

Pur {3x}, Purim {5x}. See: TWOT—1749; BDB—807c.

6333. פּוּרָה {2x} **pûwrâh**, *poo-raw';* from 6331; a *wine-press* (as *crushing* the grapes):—winepress {1x}, press {1x}. See: TWOT—1750a; BDB—802d, 807d.

פּוּרִים **Pûwrîym**. See 6332.

6334. פּוֹרָתָא {1x} **Pôwrâthâ᾽**, *po-raw-thaw';* of Pers. or.; *Poratha,* a son of Haman:—Poratha {1x}. See: BDB—807d.

6335. פּוּשׁ {4x} **pûwsh**, *poosh;* a prim. root; to *spread;* fig. *act proudly:*—spread {1x}, grow up {1x}, grown fat {1x}, scattered {1x}. See: TWOT—1751, 1752; BDB—807d.

6336. פּוּתִי {1x} **Pûwthîy**, *poo-thee';* patron. from an unused name mean. a *hinge;* a *Puthite* (collect.) or desc. of an unknown Puth:—Puhites {1x}. See: BDB—807d.

6337. פָּז {9x} **pâz**, *pawz;* from 6338; *pure* (gold); hence, *gold* itself (as refined):—fine {8x},pure {1x}. See: TWOT—1753a; BDB—808a.

6338. פָּזַז {1x} **pâzaz**, *paw-zaz';* a prim. root; to *refine* (gold):—best {1x}. See: TWOT—1753; BDB—558b, 808a.

6339. פָּזַז {2x} **pâzaz**, *paw-zaz';* a prim. root [rather ident. with 6338]; to *solidify* (as if by *refining*); also to *spring* (as if *separating* the limbs):—made strong {1x}, leaping {1x}. See: TWOT—1754; BDB—808a.

6340. פָּזַר {10x} **pâzar**, *paw-zar';* a prim. root; to *scatter,* whether in enmity or bounty:—scattered {9x}, dispersed {1x}. See: TWOT—1755; BDB—808a.

6341. פַּח {27x} **pach**, *pakh;* from 6351; a (metallic) *sheet* (as *pounded* thin); also a spring *net* (as spread out like a *lamina*):—snare {22x}, gin {2x}, plate {2x}, snares + 3027 {1x}. See: TWOT—1759a, 1759b; BDB—808b, 809a.

6342. פָּחַד {25x} **pâchad**, *paw-khad';* a prim. root; to *be startled* (by a sudden alarm); hence, to *fear* in general:—fear {14x}, afraid {9x}, awe {1x}, shake {1x}. See: TWOT—1756; BDB—808b, 1108c.

6343. פַּחַד {49x} **pachad**, *pakh'-ad;* from 6342; a (sudden) *alarm* (prop. the object feared, by impl. the feeling):—fear {40x}, dread {3x}, great {2x}, terror {2x}, dreadful {1x}, greatly {1x}. See: TWOT—1756a; BDB—808b.

6344. פַּחַד {1x} **pachad**, *pakh'-ad;* the same as 6343; a *testicle* (as a cause of *shame* akin to fear):—stones {1x}. See: TWOT—1756c; BDB—808c.

6345. פַּחְדָּה {1x} **pachdâh**, *pakh-daw';* fem. of 6343; *alarm* (i.e. *awe*):—fear {1x}. See: TWOT—1756b; BDB—808c.

6346. פֶּחָה {28x} **pechâh**, *peh-khaw';* of for. or.; a *prefect* (of a city or small district):—governor {17x}, captain {9x}, deputies {2x}. Syn.: 1166, 3027, 4427, 4910, 5057, 5401, 7980, 7985, 8269. See: TWOT—1757; BDB—808d, 1108b.

6347. פֶּחָה {10x} **pechâh** (Aram.), *peh-khaw';* corresp. to 6346:—governor {6x}, captain {4x}. See: TWOT—2936; BDB—1108b.

6348. פָּחַז {2x} **pâchaz**, *paw-khaz';* a prim. root; to *bubble* up or *froth* (as boiling water), i.e. (fig.) to *be unimportant:*—light {2x}. See: TWOT—1758; BDB—808d.

6349. פַּחַז {1x} **pachaz**, *pakh'-az;* from 6348; *ebullition,* i.e. froth (fig. lust):—unstable {1x}. See: TWOT—1758a; BDB—808d.

6350. פַּחֲזוּת {1x} **pachăzûwth**, *pakh-az-ooth';* from 6348; *frivolity:*—lightness {1x}. See: TWOT—1758b; BDB—808d.

6351. פָּחַח {1x} **pâchach**, *paw-khakh';* a prim. root; to *batter* out; but used only as denom. from 6341, to *spread a net:*—snared {1x}. See: TWOT—1759; BDB—809a.

6352. פֶּחָם {3x} **pechâm**, *peh-khawm';* perh. from an unused root prob. mean. to *be black;* a *coal,* whether charred or live:—coals {3x}. See: TWOT—1760a; BDB—809a, 809b.

6353. פֶּחָר {1x} **pechâr** (Aram.), *peh-khawr';* from an unused root prob. mean. to *fashion;* a *potter:*—potter {1x}. See: TWOT—2937; BDB—1108b.

6354. פַּחַת {10x} **pachath**, *pakh'-ath;* prob. from an unused root appar. mean. to *dig;* a *pit,* espec. for catching animals:—pit {8x}, hole {1x}, snare {1x}. See: TWOT—1761a; BDB—809b.

6355. פַּחַת מוֹאָב {6x} **Pachath Môw᾽âb**, *pakh'-ath mo-awb';* from 6354 and 4124; *pit of Moäb; Pachath-Moäb,* an Isr.:—Pahathmoab {6x}. See: BDB—809b.

6356. פְּחֶתֶת {1x} **pᵉchetheth**, *pekh-eh'-theth;* from the same as 6354; a *hole* (by mildew in a garment):—fret inward {1x}. See: TWOT—1761b; BDB—809b.

6357. פִּטְדָה {4x} **pitdâh**, *pit-daw';* of for. der.; a *gem,* prob. the *topaz:*—topaz {4x}. See: TWOT—1762; BDB—809b.

6358. פָּטוּר {2x} **pâṭûwr**, *paw-toor';* pass. part. of 6362; *opened,* i.e. (as noun) a *bud:*—dismissed {1x}, shoot out {1x}. See: TWOT—1764; BDB—809c.

6359. פָּטִיר {1x} **pâṭîyr**, *paw-teer';* from 6362; *open,* i.e. *unoccupied:*—free {1x}. See: TWOT—1764; BDB—809c.

6360. פַּטִּישׁ {3x} **paṭṭîysh**, *pat-teesh';* intens. from an unused root mean. to *pound;* a *hammer:*—hammer {3x}. See: TWOT—1763; BDB—809c.

6361. פַּטִּישׁ {2x} **paṭṭîysh** (Aram.), *pat-teesh';* from a root corresp. to that of 6360; a *gown* (as if *hammered* out wide):—hosen {2x}. See: TWOT—2938; BDB—1108b.

6362. פָּטַר {7x} **pâṭar**, *paw-tar';* a prim. root; to *cleave* or burst through, i.e. (caus.) to *emit,* whether lit. or fig. (*gape*):—open {4x}, slip away {1x}, free {1x}, let out {1x}. See: TWOT—1764; BDB—809c, 809d.

6363. פֶּטֶר {12x} **peṭer**, *peh'-ter;* or

פִּטְרָה **pitrâh**, *pit-raw';* from 6362; a *fissure,* i.e. (concr.) *firstling* (as *opening* the matrix):—firstling {4x}, openeth {6x}, such as open {1x}. See: TWOT—1764a, 1764b; BDB—809d.

6364. פִּי־בֶסֶת {1x} **Pîy-Beçeth**, *pee beh'-seth;* of Eg. or.; *Pi-Beseth,* a place in Egypt:—Pi-beseth {1x}. See: BDB—809d.

6365. פִּיד {3x} **pîyd**, *peed;* from an unused root prob. mean. to *pierce;* (fig.) *misfortune:*—destruction {2x}, ruin {1x}. See: TWOT—1765a; BDB—810a.

6366. פֵּיָה {1x} **pêyâh**, *pay-aw';* or

פִּיָה **pîyâh**, *pee-yaw';* fem. of 6310; an *edge:*—two edged {1x}. See: TWOT—1738; BDB—804d.

6367. פִּי הַחִרֹת {4x} **Piy ha-Chîrôth**, *pee hah-khee-rōth';* from 6310 and the fem. plur. of a noun (from the same root as 2356), with the art. interpolated; *mouth of the gorges; Pi-ha-Chiroth,* a place in Egypt:—Pi-hahiroth {4x}. See: BDB—809d.

6368. פִּיחַ {2x} **pîyach**, *pee'-akh;* from 6315; a *powder* (as easily *puffed* away), i.e. *ashes* or *dust:*—ashes {2x}. See: TWOT—1741a; BDB—806b.

6369. פִּיכֹל {3x} **Pîykôl**, *pee-kole';* appar. from 6310 and 3605; *mouth of all; Picol,* a Philistine:—Phichol {3x}. See: BDB—810a.

6370. פִּילֶגֶשׁ {37x} **pîylegesh**, *pee-leh'-ghesh;* or

פִּלֶגֶשׁ **pîlegesh**, *pee-leh'-ghesh;* of uncert. der.; a *concubine;* also (masc.) a *paramour:*—concubine {35x}, concubine + 802 {1x}, paramour]. See: TWOT—1770; BDB—810a, 811b.

6371. פִּימָה {1x} **pîymâh**, *pee-maw';* prob. from an unused root mean. to *be plump; obesity:*—collops of fat {1x}. See: TWOT—1766a; BDB—802b, 810a.

6372. פִּינְחָס {25x} **Pîynᵉchâç**, *pee-nekh-aws';* appar. from 6310 and a var. of 5175; *mouth of a serpent; Pinechas,* the name of three Isr.:—Phinehas {25x}. See: BDB—810a, 819c.

6373. פִּינֹן {2x} **Pîynôn**, *pee-none';* prob. the same as 6325; *Pinon,* an Idumæan:—Pinon {2x}. See: BDB—810a.

6374. פִּיפִיָּה {2x} **pîyphîyâh**, *pee-fee-yaw';* for 6366; an *edge* or *tooth:*—teeth {1x}, × two-edged {1x}. See: TWOT—1738; BDB—804d, 810a.

6375. פִּיק {1x} **pîyq**, *peek;* from 6329; a *tottering:*—smite together {1x}. See: TWOT—1747b; BDB—807c, 810a, 823a.

6376. פִּישׁוֹן {1x} **Pîyshôwn**, *pee-shone';* from 6335; *dispersive; Pishon,* a river of Eden:—Pison {1x}. See: BDB—810b.

6377. פִּיתוֹן {2x} **Pîythôwn**, *pee-thone';* prob. from the same as 6596; *expansive; Pithon,* an Isr.:—Pithon {2x}. See: BDB—810b.

6378. פַּךְ {3x} **pak**, *pak;* from 6379; a *flask* (from which a liquid may *flow*):—box {2x}, vial {1x}. See: TWOT—1767a; BDB—810b.

6379. פָּכָה {1x} **pâkâh**, *paw-kaw';* a prim. root; to *pour:*—ran out {1x}. See: TWOT—1767b; BDB—810b.

6380. פֹּכֶרֶת צְבָיִים {2x} **Pôkereth Tsᵉbâyiym**, *po-keh'-reth tseb-aw-yeem';* from the act. part. (of the same form as the first word) fem. of an unused root (mean. to *entrap*) and plur. of 6643; *trap of gazelles; Pokereth-Tsebajim,* one of the "servants of Solomon":—Pochereth of Zebaim {2x}. See: BDB—810b.

6381. פָּלָא {71x} **pâlâ᾽**, *paw-law';* a prim. root; prop. perh. to *separate,* i.e. *distinguish* (lit. or fig.); by impl. to *be* (caus. *make*) *great, difficult, wonderful:*—(wondrous, marvellous . . .) work {18x}, wonders {9x}, marvellous {8x}, wonderful {8x}, . . . things {6x}, hard {5x}, wondrous {3x}, wondrously {2x}, marvellously {2x}, performing {2x}, misc. {8x} = accomplish, hidden, things too high, miracles, perform, separate, make singular.

Pala', as a verb, means "to be marvelous, be extraordinary, be beyond one's power to do, do wonderful acts." **(1)** As a denominative verb, it is based on the noun for "wonder, marvel," so it expresses the idea of doing or making a wondrous thing. **(2)** The verb is found for the first time in Gen 18:14: "Is any thing too hard for the Lord?" **(3)** *Pala'* is used primarily with God as its subject, expressing actions that are beyond the bounds of human powers or expectations. This idea is well expressed by the psalmist: "This is the Lord's doing; it is marvelous in our eyes" (Ps 118:23). **(4)** Deliverance from Egypt was the result of God's wondrous acts: "And I will stretch out my hand, and smite Egypt with all my wonders which I will do in [it] . . ." (Ex 3:20). **(5)** Praise is constantly due God for all His wonderful deeds (Ps 9:1). **(6)** At the same time, God does not require anything of His people that is too hard for them (Deut 30:11). **(7)** Although something may appear impossible to man, it still is within God's power: "If it be marvelous in the eyes of the remnant of this people in these days, should it also be marvelous in mine eyes? saith the Lord of hosts" (Zec 8:6). See: TWOT—1768; BDB—810c.

6382. פֶּלֶא {13x} **peleʼ**, *peh'-leh;* from 6381; a *miracle:*—marvellous thing {1x}, wonder {8x}, wonderful {3x}, wonderfully {1x}.

Pele', as a noun, means "wonder; marvel." **(1)** This noun frequently expresses the "wonder," the extraordinary aspects, of God's dealings with His people: "Who *is* like unto thee, O LORD, among the gods? who *is* like thee, glorious in holiness, fearful *in* praises, doing wonders?" (Ex 15:11; cf. Ps 77:11; Is 29:14). **(2)** The messianic title, "wonderful counselor" (Is 9:6) points toward God's Anointed continuing the marvelous acts of God. See: TWOT—1768a; BDB—810b.

6383. פִּלְאִי {4x} **pilʼîy**, *pil-ee';* or

פָּלִיא **pâlîyʼ**, *paw-lee';* from 6381; *remarkable:*—secret {1x}, wonderful {1x}, variant {2x}. See: TWOT—1768b; BDB—811a, 813a.

6384. פַּלֻּאִי {1x} **Palluʼîy**, *pal-loo-ee';* patron. from 6396; a *Palluïte* (collect.) or desc. of Pallu:—Palluites {1x}. See: BDB—811a.

פְּלָאיָה **Pᵉlâʼyâh**. See 6411.

פִּלְאֶסֶר **Pilʼeçer**. See 8407.

6385. פָּלַג {4x} **pâlag**, *paw-lag';* a prim. root; to *split* (lit. or fig.):—divide {4x}. See: TWOT—1769; BDB—811a, 1108b.

6386. פְּלַג {1x} **pᵉlag** (Aram.), *pel-ag';* corresp. to 6385:—divided {1x}. See: TWOT—2939; BDB—1108b.

6387. פְּלַג {1x} **pᵉlag** (Aram.), *pel-ag';* from 6386; a *half:*—dividing {1x}. See: TWOT—2939a; BDB—1108b.

6388. פֶּלֶג {10x} **peleg**, *peh'-leg;* from 6385; a *rill* (i.e. small *channel* of water, as in irrigation):—river {9x}, stream {1x}. See: TWOT—1769a; BDB—811b.

6389. פֶּלֶג {7x} **Peleg**, *peh'-leg;* the same as 6388; *earthquake; Peleg*, a son of Shem:—*Peleg* {7x}. See: BDB—811b.

6390. פְּלַגָּה {3x} **pᵉlaggâh**, *pel-ag-gaw';* from 6385; a *runlet*, i.e. *gully:*—division {2x}, river {1x}. See: TWOT—1769b; BDB—811b

6391. פְּלֻגָּה {1x} **pᵉluggâh**, *pel-oog-gaw';* from 6385; a *section:*—divisions {1x}. See: TWOT—1769c; BDB—811b.

6392. פְּלֻגָּה {1x} **pᵉluggâh** (Aram.), *pel-oog-gaw';* corresp. to 6391:—divisions {1x}. See: TWOT—2939b; BDB—1108c.

פִּלֶגֶשׁ **pîlegesh**. See 6370.

6393. פְּלָדָה {1x} **pᵉlâdâh**, *pel-aw-daw';* from an unused root mean. to *divide;* a *cleaver*, i.e. iron *armature* (of a chariot):—torches {1x}. See: TWOT—1771; BDB—811c.

6394. פִּלְדָּשׁ {1x} **Pildâsh**, *pil-dawsh';* of uncert. der.; *Pildash*, a relative of Abraham:—*Pildash* {1x}. See: BDB—811c.

6395. פָּלָה {7x} **pâlâh**, *paw-law';* a prim. root; to *distinguish* (lit. or fig.):—sever {2x}, separated {1x}, wonderfully {1x}, set apart {1x}, marvellous {1x}, put a difference {1x}. See: TWOT—1772; BDB—811c.

6396. פַּלּוּא {5x} **Pallûwʼ**, *pal-loo';* from 6395; *distinguished; Pallu*, an Isr.:—Pallu {4x}, Phallu {1x}. See: BDB—811a.

6397. פְּלוֹנִי {3x} **Pᵉlôwnîy**, *pel-o-nee';* patron. from an unused name (from 6395) mean. *separate;* a *Pelonite* or inhab. of an unknown Palon:—Pelonite {3x}. See: BDB—812a, 813d.

6398. פָּלַח {5x} **pâlach**, *paw-lakh';* a prim. root; to *slice*, i.e. *break* open or *pierce:*—cut {1x}, shred {1x}, cleave {1x}, bring forth {1x}, strike through {1x}. See: TWOT—1773; BDB—812a.

6399. פְּלַח {10x} **pᵉlach** (Aram.), *pel-akh';* corresp. to 6398; to *serve* or worship:—serve {9x}, ministers {1x}. See: TWOT—2940; BDB—1108c.

6400. פֶּלַח {6x} **pelach**, *peh'-lakh;* from 6398; a *slice:*—piece {6x}. See: TWOT—1773a; BDB—812a.

6401. פִּלְחָא {1x} **Pilchâʼ**, *pil-khaw';* from 6400; *slicing; Pilcha*, an Isr.:—*Pilcha* {1x}. See: BDB—812a.

6402. פָּלְחָן {1x} **polchân** (Aram.), *pol-khawn';* from 6399; *worship:*—service {1x}. See: TWOT—2940a; BDB—1108c.

6403. פָּלַט {25x} **pâlaṭ**, *paw-lat';* a prim. root; to *slip* out, i.e. *escape;* caus. to *deliver:*—deliver {16x}, deliverer {5x}, calveth {1x}, escape {2x}, safe {1x}. See: TWOT—1774; BDB—812b.

6404. פֶּלֶט {2x} **Peleṭ**, *peh'-let;* from 6403; *escape; Pelet*, the name of two Isr.:—*Pelet* {2x}. See: BDB—812b. See also 1046.

פָּלֵט **pâlêṭ**. See 6412.

6405. פַּלֵּט {5x} **pallêṭ**, *pal-late';* from 6403; *escape:*—deliverance {1x}, escape {4x}. See: TWOT—1774a; BDB—812c.

פְּלֵטָה **pᵉlêṭâh**. See 6413.

6406. פַּלְטִי {2x} **Palṭîy**, *pal-tee';* from 6403; *delivered; Palti*, the name of two Isr.:—Palti {1x}, Phalti {1x}. See: BDB—812d.

6407. פַּלְטִי {1x} **Palṭîy**, *pal-tee';* patron. from 6406; a *Paltite* or desc. of Palti:—Paltite {1x}. See: BDB—112c.

6408. פִּלְטַי {1x} **Pilṭay**, *pil-tah'-ee;* for 6407; *Piltai*, an Isr.:—Piltai {1x}. See: BDB—812d.

6409. פַּלְטִיאֵל {2x} **Palṭîyʼêl**, *pal-tee-ale';* from the same as 6404 and 410; *deliverance of God; Paltiël*, the name of two Isr.:—Paltiel {1x}, Phaltiel {1x}. See: BDB—812d.

6410. פְּלַטְיָה {5x} **Pᵉlaṭyâh**, *pel-at-yaw';* or

פְּלַטְיָהוּ **Pᵉlaṭyâhûw**, *pel-at-yaw'-hoo;* from 6403 and 3050; *Jah has delivered; Pelatjah*, the name of four Isr.:—Pelatiah {5x}. See: BDB—812d.

פָּלִיא **pâlîyʼ**. See 6383.

6411. פְּלָיָה {3x} **Pᵉlâyâh**, *pel-aw-yaw';* or

פְּלָאיָה **Pᵉlâʼyâh**, *pel-aw-yaw';* from 6381 and 3050; *Jah has distinguished; Pelajah*, the name of three Isr.:—Pelaiah {3x}. See: BDB—811a, 813a.

6412. פָּלִיט {21x} **pâlîyṭ**, *paw-leet';* or

פָּלֵיט **pâlêyṭ**, *paw-late';* or

פָּלֵט **pâlêṭ**, *paw-late';* from 6403; a *refugee:*—escape {20x}, fugitive {1x}. See: TWOT—1774b, 1774c; BDB—812c.

6413. פְּלֵיטָה {28x} **pᵉlêyṭâh**, *pel-ay-taw';* or

פְּלֵטָה **pᵉlêṭâh**, *pel-ay-taw';* fem. of 6412; *deliverance;* concr. an *escaped* portion:—deliverance {5x}, escape {22x}, remnant {1x}. See: TWOT—1774d; BDB—812c.

6414. פָּלִיל {3x} **pâlîyl**, *paw-leel';* from 6419; a *magistrate:*—judge {3x} See: TWOT—1776b; BDB—813c.

6415. פְּלִילָה {1x} **pᵉlîylâh**, *pel-ee-law';* fem. of 6414; *justice:*—judgment {1x}. See: TWOT—1776c; BDB—813d.

6416. פְּלִילִי {1x} **pᵉlîylîy**, *pel-ee-lee';* from 6414; *judicial:*—judge {1x}. See: TWOT—1776d; BDB—813d.

6417. פְּלִילִיָּה {1x} **pᵉlîylîyâh** *pel-ee-lee-yaw';* fem. of 6416; *judicature:*—judgment {1x}. See: TWOT—1776e; BDB—813d.

6418. פֶּלֶךְ {10x} **pelek**, *peh'-lek;* from an unused root mean. to *be round;* a *circuit* (i.e. *district*); also a *spindle* (as *whirled*); hence, a *crutch:*—distaff {1x}, staff {1x}, part {8x}. See: TWOT—1775a; BDB—813a.

6419. פָּלַל {84x} **pâlal**, *paw-lal';* a prim. root; to *judge* (officially or mentally); by extens. to *intercede, pray:*—pray {74x}, made {3x}, judge {2x}, intreat {1x}, judgment {1x}, prayer {1x}, supplication {1x}, thought {1x}.

Palal, as a verb, means "to pray, intervene, mediate, judge." **(1)** The word is used 4 times in the intensive verbal form; the remaining 80 times are found in the reflexive or reciprocal form, in which the action generally points back to the subject. **(1a)** In the intensive form *palal* expresses the idea of "to mediate, to come between two parties," always between human beings. **(1b)** Thus, "If one man sins against another, the judge shall judge him: but if a man sins against the LORD, who shall intreat for him?" (1 Sa 2:25). **(1c)** "To mediate" requires "making a judgment," as in Eze 16:52: "Thou also, which hast judged thy sisters. . . ." **(1d)** In the remaining 2 references in which the intensive form is used, *palal* expresses **(1d1)** "having thought" in Gen 48:11: "And Israel said unto Joseph, I had not thought [*palal*] to see thy face: and, lo, God hath shewed me also thy seed." and **(1d2)** "coming between/executing judgment for another" in Ps 106:30: "Then stood up Phinehas, and executed judgment [*palal*]: and *so* the plague was stayed."

(2) The reflexive/reciprocal form: The first occurrence of *palal* in the Old Testament is in Gen 20:7, where the reflexive or reciprocal form of the verb expresses the idea of "interceding for, prayer in behalf of": ". . . He shall pray for thee. . . ." Such intercessory praying is frequent in the Old Testament: **(2a)** Moses "prays" for the people's deliverance from the fiery serpents (Num 21:7); **(2b)** he "prays" for Aaron (Deut 9:20); and **(2c)** Samuel "intercedes" continually for Israel (1 Sa 12:23). **(3)** Prayer is directed not only toward Yahweh but toward pagan idols as well

(Is 44:17). **(4)** Sometimes prayer is made to Yahweh that He would act against an enemy: "That which thou hast prayed to me against Sennacherib king of Assyria I have heard" (2 Kin 19:20). **(5)** Just why this verb form is used to express the act of praying is not completely clear. **(5a)** Since this verb form points back to the subject, in a reflexive sense, perhaps it emphasizes the part which the person praying has in his prayers. **(5b)** Also, since the verb form can have a reciprocal meaning between subject and object, it may emphasize the fact that prayer is basically communication, which always has to be two-way in order to be real. **(6)** Prayer is directed also toward pagan idols (Is 44:17). Syn.: 1777, 6279, 6739, 7592, 8199, 8605. See: TWOT—1776; BDB—813a.

6420. **פָּלָל** {1x} **Pâlâl**, *paw-lawl';* from 6419; *judge; Palal*, an Isr.:—*Palal* {1x}. See: BDB—813c.

6421. **פְּלַלְיָה** {1x} **Pᵉlalyâh**, *pel-al-yaw';* from 6419 and 3050; *Jah has judged; Pelaljah*, an Isr.:—Pelaliah {1x}. See: BDB—813d.

6422. **פַּלְמוֹנִי** {1x} **palmôwnîy**, *pal-mo-nee';* prob. for 6423; a *certain* one, i.e. *so-and-so:*—certain {1x}. See: TWOT—1772a; BDB—812a, 813d.

פִּלְנְאֶסֶר **Pilnᵉeçer.** See 8407.

6423. **פְּלֹנִי** {3x} **pᵉlônîy**, *pel-o-nee';* from 6395; *such* a one, i.e. a specified *person:*—such {3x}. See: TWOT—1772a; BDB—811d.

פִּלְנֶסֶר **Pilneçer.** See 8407.

6424. **פָּלַס** **pâlaç**, *paw-las';* a prim. root; prop. to *roll* flat, i.e. *prepare* (a road); also to *revolve*, i.e. *weigh* (mentally):—made {1x}, ponder {3x}, weigh {2x}. See: TWOT—1777; BDB—814a, 814b.

6425. **פֶּלֶס** {2x} **peleç**, *peh'-les;* from 6424; a *balance:*—scales {1x}, weight {1x}. See: TWOT—1777a; BDB—813d.

פְּלֶסֶר **Pᵉleçer.** See 8407.

6426. **פָּלַץ** {1x} **pâlats**, *paw-lats';* a prim. root; prop. perh. to *rend*, i.e. (by impl.) to *quiver:*—tremble {1x}. See: TWOT—1778; BDB—814a.

6427. **פַּלָּצוּת** {4x} **pallâtsûwth**, *pal-law-tsooth';* from 6426; *affright:*—fearfulness {1x}, horror {2x}, trembling {1x}. See: TWOT—1778a; BDB—814a.

6428. **פָּלַשׁ** {5x} **pâlash**, *paw-lash';* a prim. root; to *roll* (in dust):—roll {2x}, wallow {3x}. See: TWOT—1779; BDB—814b.

6429. **פְּלֶשֶׁת** {8x} **Pᵉlesheth**, *pel-eh'-sheth;* from 6428; *rolling*, i.e. *migratory; Pelesheth*, a region of Syria:—Palestina {3x}, Palestine {1x}, Philistia {3x}, Philistines {1x}. See: BDB—814b.

6430. **פְּלִשְׁתִּי** {288x} **Pᵉlishtîy**, *pel-ish-tee';* patrial from 6429; a *Pelishtite* or inhab. of Pelesheth:—Philistine {287x}, Philistim {1x}. See: BDB—814b.

6431. **פֶּלֶת** {2x} **Peleth**, *peh'-leth;* from an unused root mean. to *flee; swiftness; Peleth*, the name of two Isr.:—*Peleth* {2x}. See: BDB—814c.

6432. **פְּלֵתִי** {7x} **Pᵉlêthîy**, *pel-ay-thee';* from the same form as 6431; a *courier* (collect.) or official *messenger:*—Pelethites {7x}. See: BDB—814c.

6433. **פֻּם** {6x} **pûm** (Aram.), *poom;* prob. for 6310; the *mouth* (lit. or fig.):—mouth {6x}. See: TWOT—2941; BDB—1108c.

6434. **פֵּן** {2x} **pên**, *pane;* from an unused root mean. to *turn;* an *angle* (of a street or wall):—corner {2x}. See: TWOT—1783a; BDB—819c.

6435. **פֵּן** {4x} **pên**, *pane;* from 6437; prop. *removal;* used only (in the constr.) adv. as conjunc. *lest:*—(lest) (peradventure), that . . . not {4x}. See: TWOT—1780; BDB—814c.

6436. **פַּנַּג** {1x} **Pannag**, *pan-nag';* of uncert. der.; prob. *pastry:*—Pannag {1x}. See: TWOT—1781;BDB—815a.

6437. **פָּנָה** {135x} **pânâh**, *paw-naw';* a prim. root; to *turn;* by impl. to *face*, i.e. *appear, look*, etc.:—turn {53x}, look {42x}, prepare {6x}, regard {4x}, respect {4x}, look back {4x}, turn away {2x}, turn back {2x}, misc. {16x} = appear, at [even-] tide, behold, cast out, come on, × corner, dawning, empty, go away, lie, mark, pass away, × right [early].

Panah, as a verb, means "to turn towards, turn back, turn around, attach to, pass away, make clear." **(1)** Most occurrences of this verb carry the sense "to turn in another direction"; this is a verb of either physical or mental motion. **(1a)** Used of physical motion, the word signifies turning so as to move in another direction: "Ye have compassed this mountain long enough: turn you northward" (Deut 2:3). **(1b)** *Panah* can also mean to turn so as to face or look at something or someone: "And it came to pass, as Aaron spake unto the whole congregation of the children of Israel, that they looked toward the wilderness . . ." (Ex 16:10). **(2)** "Turning toward" something may also signify looking at, or seeing it: "Remember thy servants, Abraham, Isaac, and Jacob; look not unto [do not see] the stubbornness of this people, nor to their wickedness, nor to their sin" (Deut 9:27). **(3)** A further extension in meaning is seen in Hag 1:9, where *panah* means "to look for," or to expect: "Ye looked for much, and, lo, it came to little. . . ."**(4)** Another focus of meaning is "to turn back" so as to see. This is found in Josh 8:20: "And when the men of Ai looked behind them, they saw, and, behold, the smoke of the city ascended up to heaven, and they had no power to flee this way or that way: and the people that fled to the wilderness turned back upon the pursuers."

(5) In other passages the verb means "to turn around," in the sense of to look in every direction. So Moses "looked this way and that way, and when he saw there was no man, he slew the Egyptian, and hid him in the sand" (Ex 2:12). **(6)** In the sense of "to turn around" *panah* is used of changing one's direction so as to leave the scene. So "the men turned their faces from thence, and went toward Sodom . . ." (Gen 18:22—the first biblical occurrence of the verb). **(7)** Used of intellectual and spiritual turning, this verb signifies attaching oneself to something. God commanded Israel: "Turn ye not unto idols, nor make to yourselves molten gods . . ." (Lev 19:4); they should not shift their attention to and attach themselves to idols. In an even stronger use this verb represents dependence on someone: ". . . Which bringeth their iniquity to remembrance, when they shall look after [depend on] them . . ." (Eze 29:16). **(8)** "To turn towards" sometimes means to pay attention to someone. Job tells his friends: "Now . . . look upon me; for it is evident unto you if I lie" (Job 6:28).

(9) In a still different emphasis the word connotes the "passing away" of something, such as the turning away of a day: "And Isaac went out to meditate in the field at the eventide . . ."—he went out "at the turning of the evening" (Gen 24:63). **(9a)** Similarly the Bible speaks of the dawn as the "turning of the morning" (Ex 14:27). **(9b)** The "turning of the day" is the end of the day (Jer 6:4). **(10)** Used in a military context, *panah* can signify giving up fighting or fleeing before one's enemies. Because of Achan's sin the Lord was not with Israel at the battle of Ai: "Therefore the children of Israel could not stand before their enemies, but turned their backs before their enemies, because they were accursed . . ." (Josh 7:12). **(11)** In the intensive stem the verb means "to remove," to take away: "The Lord hath taken away thy judgments, he hath cast out thine enemy . . ." (Zeph 3:15). **(12)** "To clear a house" (to set things in order) is often the means by which conditions are prepared for guests: "Come in, thou blessed of the Lord; wherefore standest thou without? for I have prepared the house . . ." (Gen 24:31). **(13)** Another nuance is "to prepare" a road for a victory march; Isaiah says: "Prepare ye the way of the Lord, make straight in the desert a highway for our God" (Is 40:3; cf. Mt 3:3). See: TWOT—1782; BDB—806d, 815a.

פָּנֶה **pâneh.** See 6440.

6438. **פִּנָּה** {28x} **pinnâh**, *pin-naw';* fem. of 6434; an *angle;* by impl. a *pinnacle;* fig. a *chieftain:*—bulwarks {1x}, chief {2x}, corner {22x}, stay {1x}, towers {2x}.

Pinnah, as a noun, means "corner." **(1)** The word refers to "corners" in Ex 27:2: "And thou shalt make the horns of it upon the four corners thereof . . ." **(2)** In 2 Kin 14:13 the word refers to a corner-tower, and **(3)** in Judg 20:2 *pinnah* is used figuratively of a "chief" as the "corner" or defense of the people. See: TWOT—1783a; BDB—806d, 819c.

6439. **פְּנוּאֵל** {9x} **Pᵉnûwʼêl**, *pen-oo-ale';* or (more prop.)

פְּנִיאֵל **Pᵉnîyʼêl**, *pen-ee-ale';* from 6437 and 410; *face of God; Penuël* or *Peniël*, a place E. of Jordan; also (as Penuel) the name of two Isr.:—Peniel {1x}, Penuel {8x}. See: BDB—819c.

פָּנִי **pânîy.** See 6443.

6440. **פָּנִים** {2109x} **pânîym**, *paw-neem';* plur. (but always as sing.) of an unused noun.

פָּנֶה **pâneh**, *paw-neh';* from 6437]; the *face* (as the part that *turns*); used in a great variety of applications (lit. and fig.); also (with prep. pref.) as a prep. (*before*, etc.):—before {1137x}, face {390x}, presence {76}, because {67x}, sight {40x}, countenance {30x}, from {27x}, person {21x}, upon {20x}, of {20x}, . . . me {18x}, against {17x}, . . . him {16x}, open {13x}, for {13x}, toward {9x}, misc. {195x} = + accept, a- fore (-time), anger, × as (long as), at, + battle, + beseech, edge, + employ, endure, + enquire, favour, fear of, forefront (-part), form (-er time, -ward), front, heaviness, + honourable, + impudent, + in, it, look [-eth] (-s), + meet, × more than, mouth, off, (of) old (time), × on, + out of, over against, the partial, + please, propect, was purposed, by reason, of, + regard, right forth, + serve, × shewbread, state, straight, + street, × thee, × them (-selves), through (+ -out), till, time (-s) past, unto, upside (+ down), with (-in, + -stand), × ye, × you.

Paniym means "face." **(1)** This noun appears in biblical Hebrew about 2,100 times and in all periods, except when it occurs with the names of persons and places, it always appears in the plural. **(2)** In its most basic meaning, this noun refers to the "face" of something. **(2a)** First, it refers to the "face" of a human being: "And Abram fell on his face: and God talked with him . . ." (Gen 17:3). **(2b)** In a more specific application, the word represents the look on one's face, or one's "countenance": "And Cain was very [angry], and his countenance fell" (Gen 4:5). **(3)** To pay something to someone's "face" is to pay it to him personally (Deut 7:10); in such contexts, the word connotes the person himself. **(4)** *Paniym* can also be used of the surface or visible side of a thing, as in Gen 1:2: "The Spirit of God moved upon the face of the waters." **(5)** In other contexts, the word represents the "front side" of something: "And thou shalt couple five curtains by themselves, and six curtains by themselves and shalt double the sixth curtain in the forefront of the tabernacle" (Ex 26:9).

(6) When applied to time, the word (preceded by the preposition le) means "formerly": "The Horim also dwelt in Seir [formerly] . . . (Deut 2:12). **(7)** This noun is sometimes used anthropomorphically of God; the Bible speaks of God as though He had a "face": ". . . For therefore I have seen thy face, as though I had seen the face of God" (Gen 33:10). **(7a)** The Bible clearly teaches that God is a spiritual being and ought not to be depicted by an image or any likeness whatever (Ex 20:4). **(7b)** Therefore, there was no image or likeness of God in the innermost sanctuary—only the ark of the covenant was there, and God spoke from above it (Ex 25:22). **(8)** The word *paniym,* then, is used to identify the bread that was kept in the holy place, "the shewbread" (Num 4:7). This bread was always kept in the presence of God. Syn.: 977, 5375, 7521. See: TWOT—1782a; BDB—542b, 815d, 819d, 819c.

6441. פְּנִימָה {14x} **pᵉnîymâh**, *pen-ee'-maw;* from 6440 with directive enclitic; *faceward,* i.e. *indoors:*—within {10x}, inward {2x}, in {1x}, inner part {1x}.

Peniymah, as an adverb, means "within." One appearance is in 1 Kin 6:18: "And the cedar of the house within was carved with knobs and open flowers. . . ." Here the word refers to the inside of the house. See: TWOT—1782c; BDB—542b, 819b.

6442. פְּנִימִי {32x} **pᵉnîymîy**, *pen-ee-mee';* from 6440; *interior:* inner {30x}, inward {1x}, within {1x}.

Peniymiy, as an adjective, means "inner." This adjective occurs 32 times, and it refers to a part of a building, usually a temple. One occurrence is in 1 Kin 6:27: "And he set the cherubim within the inner house. . . ." See: TWOT—1782d; BDB—819b.

6443. פָּנִין {6x} **pânîyn**, *paw-neen';* or

פָּנִי **pânîy**, *paw-nee';* from the same as 6434; prob. a *pearl* (as *round*):—rubies {6x}. See: TWOT—1783b; BDB—819c.

6444. פְּנִנָּה {3x} **Pᵉninnâh**, *pen-in-naw';* prob. fem. from 6443 contr.; *Peninnah,* an Israelitess:—*Peninnah* {3x}. See: BDB—819d.

6445. פָּנַק {1x} **pânaq**, *paw-nak';* a prim. root; to *enervate:*—delicately bring up {1x}. See: TWOT—1784; BDB—819d.

6446. פַּס {5x} **paç**, *pas;* from 6461; prop. the *palm* (of the hand) or *sole* (of the foot) [comp. 6447]; by impl. (plur.) a *long and sleeved* tunic (perh. simply a *wide* one; from the orig. sense of the root, i.e. of *many breadths*):—colours {5x}. See: TWOT—1789a; BDB—819d, 821a, 1108d.

6447. פַּס {2x} **paç** (Aram.), *pas;* from a root corresp. to 6461; the *palm* (of the hand, as being *spread* out):—part {2x}. See: TWOT—2942; BDB—1108c, 1108d.

6448. פָּסַג {1x} **pâçag**, *paw-sag';* a prim. root; to *cut up,* i.e. (fig.) *contemplate:*—consider {1x}. See: TWOT—1785; BDB—819d.

6449. פִּסְגָּה {5x} **Piçgâh**, *pis-gaw';* from 6448; a *cleft; Pisgah,* a mountain E. of Jordan:—Pisgah {5x}. See: BDB—820a.

6450. פַּס דַּמִּים {1x} **Paç Dammîym**, *pas dam-meem';* from 6446 and the plur. of 1818; *palm* (i.e. *dell*) *of bloodshed; Pas-Dammim,* a place in Pal.:—Pasdammim {1x}. See: BDB—67c. comp. 658.

6451. פִּסָּה {1x} **piççâh**, *pis-saw';* from 6461; *expansion,* i.e. *abundance:*—handful {1x}. See: TWOT—1789b; BDB—820a, 821a.

6452. פָּסַח {7x} **pâçach**, *paw-sakh';* a prim. root; to *hop,* i.e. (fig.) *skip* over (or *spare*); by impl. to *hesitate;* also (lit.) to *limp,* to *dance:*—pass over {4x}, halt {1x}, become lame {1x}, leap {1x}. See: TWOT—1786, 1787; BDB—820a, 820c.

6453. פֶּסַח {49x} **Peçach**, *peh'-sakh;* from 6452; a *pretermission,* i.e. *exemption;* used only tech. of the Jewish *Passover* (the festival or the victim):—Passover {46x}, passover offerings {3x}. See: TWOT—1786a; BDB—820a.

6454. פָּסֵחַ {4x} **Pâçêach**, *paw-say'-akh;* from 6452; *limping; Paseach,* the name of two Isr.:—Paseah {3x}, Phaseah {1x}. See: BDB—820c.

6455. פִּסֵּחַ {14x} **piççêach**, *pis-say'-akh;* from 6452; *lame:*—lame {14x}. See: TWOT—1787a; BDB—820c.

6456. פְּסִיל {23x} **pᵉçîyl**, *pes-eel';* from 6458; an *idol:*—graven images {18x}, carved images {3x}, quarries {2x}. See: TWOT—1788b; BDB—820d.

6457. פָּסַךְ {1x} **Pâçak**, *paw-sak';* from an unused root mean. to *divide; divider; Pasak,* an Isr.:—Pasach {1x}. See: BDB—820d.

6458. פָּסַל {6x} **pâçal**, *paw-sal';* a prim. root; to *carve,* whether wood or stone:—hew {5x}, graven {1x}. See: TWOT—1788; BDB—820d.

6459. פֶּסֶל {31x} **peçel**, *peh'-sel;* from 6458; an *idol:*—graven image {28x}, carved image {2x}, graven {1x}. Syn.: 2796, 4906, 5566, 6754. See: TWOT—1788a; BDB—820d.

6460. פְּסַנְטֵרִין {4x} **pᵉçantêrîyn** (Aram.), *pes-an-tay-reen';* or

פְּסַנְתֵּרִין **pᵉçantêrîyn**, *pes-an-tay-reen';* a transliteration of the Gr. **ψαλτήριον** *psaltērion, a lyre:*—psaltery {4x}. See: TWOT—2943; BDB—1108c.

6461. פָּסַס {1x} **paçaç**, *paw-sas';* a prim. root; prob. to *disperse,* i.e. (intr.) *disappear:*—fail {1x}. See: TWOT—1790; BDB—821a.

6462. פִּסְפָּה {1x} **Piçpâh**, *pis-paw';* perh. from 6461; *dispersion; Pispah,* an Isr.:—Pispah {1x}. See: BDB—821a.

6463. פָּעָה {1x} **pâʿâh**, *paw-aw';* a prim. root; to *scream:*—cry {1x}. See: TWOT—1791; BDB—821a.

6464. פָּעוּ {2x} **Pâʿûw**, *paw-oo';* or

פָּעִי **Pâʿîy**, *paw-ee';* from 6463; *screaming; Paü* or *Paï,* a place in Edom:—Pai {1x}, Pau {1x}. See: BDB—821b.

6465. פְּעוֹר {5x} **Pᵉʿôwr**, *peh-ore';* from 6473; a *gap; Peör,* a mountain E. of Jordan; also (for 1187) a deity worshipped there:—Peor {5x}. See: BDB—822b. See also 1047.

פָּעִי **Pâʿîy**. See 6464.

6466. פָּעַל {56x} **pâʿal**, *paw-al';* a prim. root; to *do* or *make* (systematically and habitually), espec. to *practise:*—work {19x}, workers {19x}, do {10x}, make {4x}, commit {1x}, doers {1x}, Maker {1x}, ordaineth {1x}.

Pa'al means "to do, work." **(1)** Found only 56 times in the Hebrew Old Testament, **(1a)** it is used primarily as a poetic synonym for the much more common verb 'ashah (6213), "to do, to make." **(1b)** Thus, almost half the occurrences of this verb are in the Book of Psalms. **(2)** *Pa'al* is used for the first time in the Old Testament in the Song of Moses: ". . . The place, O Lord, which thou hast made for thee to dwell in . . ." (Ex 15:17). **(3)** There is no distinction in the use of this verb, whether God or man is its subject. In Ps 15:2 man is the subject: "He that walketh uprightly and worketh righteousness, and speaketh the truth in his heart." Syn.: 6213. See: TWOT—1792; BDB—821b.

6467. פֹּעַל {38x} **pôʿal**, *po'-al;* from 6466; an *act* or *work* (concr.):—work {30x}, act {3x}, deeds {2x}, do {1x}, getting {1x}, maker {1x}. See: TWOT—1792a; BDB—821c.

6468. פְּעֻלָּה {14x} **pᵉʿullâh**, *peh-ool-law';* fem. pass. part. of 6466; (abstr.) *work:*—work {10x}, labour {2x}, reward {1x}, wages {1x}. See: TWOT—1792b; BDB—821c.

6469. פְּעֻלְּתַי {1x} **Pᵉullᵉthay**, *peh-ool-leh-thah'-ee;* from 6468; *laborious; Peülletha,* an Isr.:—Peulthai {1x}. See: BDB—821d.

6470. פָּעַם {5x} **pâʿam**, *paw-am';* a prim. root; to *tap,* i.e. *beat regularly;* hence, (gen.) to *impel* or *agitate:*—troubled {4x}, move {1x}. See: TWOT—1793; BDB—821d.

6471. פַּעַם {112x} **paʿam**, *pah'-am;* or (fem.)

פַּעֲמָה **paʿămâh**, *pah-am-aw';* from 6470; a *stroke,* lit. or fig. (in various applications, as follow):— . . . time {58x}, once {14x}, now {7x}, feet {6x}, twice {5x}, thrice + 7969 {4x}, steps {4x}, corners {3x}, ranks {2x}, oftentimes {2x}, misc. {7x}= hoofbeats, pedestal, stroke, anvil.

I. *Pa'am,* as a noun, means "step; foot; hoofbeats; pedestal; stroke; anvil." **(1)** The nuances of this word are related to the basic meaning "a human foot." The psalmist uses this meaning in Ps 58:10: "The righteous shall rejoice when he seeth the vengeance: he shall wash his feet in the blood of the wicked." **(2)** In Ex 25:12 the word is applied to the "pedestals or feet" of the ark of the covenant: "And thou shalt cast four rings of gold for it, and put them in the four [feet] thereof; and two rings shall be in the one side of it, and two rings in the other side of it." **(3)** Elsewhere the word signifies the "steps" one takes, or "footsteps": "Hold up my goings in thy paths, that my footsteps slip not" (Ps 17:5). **(4)** Judg 5:28 applies the word to the "steps" of a galloping horse, or its hoofbeats. **(5)** This focus on the falling of a foot once is extended to the "stroke" of a spear: "Then said Abishai to David, God hath delivered thine enemy into thine hand this day: now therefore let me smite him, I pray thee, with the spear even to the earth at once, and I will not *smite* him the second time" (1 Sa 26:8).

(6) Finally, *pa'am* represents a foot-shaped object, an "anvil" (Is 41:7). **II.** *Pa'am* **as an adverb,** means "once; now; anymore." **(1)** This word functions as an adverb with the focus on an occurrence or time. **(2)** In Ex 10:17 the word bears this emphasis: "Now therefore forgive, I pray thee, my sin only this once, and entreat the Lord your God. . . ." **(3)** The first biblical appearance of the word focuses on the finality, the absoluteness, of an event: "This is now bone of my bones . . ." (Gen 2:23). **(4)** The thrust of this meaning appears clearly in the translation of Gen 18:32—Abraham said to God: "Oh, let not the Lord be angry, and I will speak yet but this once [only one more time]. . . ." See: TWOT—1793a; BDB—821d.

6472. פַּעֲמֹן {7x} **paʿămôn**, *pah-am-one';* from 6471; a *bell* (as *struck*):—bell {7x}. See: TWOT—1793b; BDB—822b.

6473. פָּעַר {4x} **pâʿar**, *paw-ar';* a prim. root; to *yawn,* i.e. *open* wide (lit. or fig.):—open {3x}, gaped {1x}. See: TWOT—1794; BDB—822b.

6474. פַּעֲרַי {1x} **Paʿăray**, *pah-ar-ah'-ee;* from 6473; *yawning; Paarai,* an Isr.:—Paarai {1x}. See: BDB—822b

6475. פָּצָה {15x} **pâtsâh**, *paw-tsaw';* a prim. root; to *rend,* i.e. *open* (espec. the mouth):—open {10x}, rid {2x}, gaped {1x}, utter {1x}, deliver {1x}. See: TWOT—1795; BDB—822c.

6476. פָּצַח {8x} **pâtsach**, *paw-tsakh';* a prim. root; to *break* out (in joyful sound):—break forth {6x}, break {1x}, make a loud noise {1x}. See: TWOT—1796; BDB—822c.

6477. פְּצִירָה {1x} **pᵉtsîyrâh**, *pets-ee-raw';* from 6484; *bluntness:*—file {1x}. See: TWOT—1801a; BDB—823a.

6478. פָּצַל {2x} **pâtsal**, *paw-tsal';* a prim. root; to *peel:*—pilled {2x}. See: TWOT—1797; BDB—822d.

6479. פְּצָלָה {1x} **pᵉtsâlâh**, *pets-aw-law';* from 6478; a *peeling:*—strake {1x}. See: TWOT—1797a; BDB—822d.

6480. פָּצַם {1x} **pâtsam**, *paw-tsam';* a prim. root; to *rend* (by earthquake):—broken {1x}. See: TWOT—1798; BDB—822d.

6481. פָּצַע {3x} **pâtsaʿ**, *paw-tsah';* a prim. root; to *split,* i.e. *wound:*—wounded {3x}. See: TWOT—1799; BDB—822d.

6482. פֶּצַע {8x} **petsaʿ**, *peh'-tsah;* from 6481; a *wound:*—wound {7x}, wounding {1x}. See: TWOT—1799a; BDB—822d.

פַּצֵּץ **Patstsets.** See 1048.

6483. פִּצֵּץ {1x} **Pitstsêts**, *pits-tsates';* from an unused root mean. to *dissever; dispersive; Pitstsets,* a priest:—Aphses {1x}. See: BDB—823a.

6484. פָּצַר {7x} **pâtsar**, *paw-tsar';* a prim. root; to *peck* at, i.e. (fig.) *stun* or *dull:*—urge {4x}, press {2x}, stubbornness {1x}. See: TWOT—1801; BDB—823a.

6485. פָּקַד {305x} **pâqad**, *paw-kad';* a prim. root; to *visit* (with friendly or hostile intent); by anal. to *oversee, muster, charge, care for, miss, deposit,* etc.:—number {119x}, visit {59x}, punish {31x}, appoint {14x}, commit {6x}, miss {6x}, set {6x}, charge {5x}, governor {5x}, lack {4x}, oversight {4x}, officers {4x}, counted {3x}, empty {3x}, ruler {3x}, overseer {3x}, judgment {2x}, misc. {28x}. × at all, avenge, bestow, deliver to keep, enjoin, go see, hurt, do judgment, lay up, look, make, × by any means, reckon, (call to) remember (-brance), sum, × surely, want.

Paqad means to number, visit, be concerned with, look after, make a search for, punish. **(1)** The first occurrence is in Gen 21:1 **(1a)** ("The Lord visited Sarah") in the special sense of "to intervene on behalf of," so as to demonstrate the divine intervention in the normal course of events to bring about or fulfill a divine intent. **(1b)** Often this intervention is by miraculous means. **(2)** The verb is used in an expression which is unique to Hebrew and which shows great intensity of meaning. **(2a)** Such an occurrence appears in Ex 3:16ff. **(2b)** in which it is used twice in two different grammatical forms to portray the intensity of the action; the text reads (literally): "Looking after, I have surely visited". **(2c)** The usage refers to God's intervention in His saving the children of Israel from their bondage in Egypt.

(3) The same verb in a similar expression can also be used for divine intervention for punishment: "Shall I not visit them for these things?" (Jer 9:9), which means literally: "Shall I not punish them for these things?" **(4)** Hebrew usage also allows a use which applies to the speaker in a nearly passive sense. **(4a)** This is termed the reflexive, since it turns back upon the speaker. **(4b)** *Paqad* is used in such a sense meaning "be missed, be lacking," as in 1 Sa 25:7: ". . . Neither was there aught missing. . . ." **(5)** However, the most common usage of the verb in the whole of the Old Testament is in the sense of "drawing up, mustering, or numbering," as of troops for marching or battle (Ex 30:12 and very frequently in Num; less so in 1 and 2 Samuel). Syn.: 502, 7101, 7218, 7336. See: TWOT—1802; BDB—823a, 824b.

פִּקֻּד **piqqûd.** See 6490.

6486. פְּקֻדָּה {32x} **pᵉquddâh**, *pek-ood-daw';* fem. pass. part. of 6485; *visitation* (in many senses, chiefly official):—visitation {13x}, office {5x}, charge {2x}, oversight {2x}, officers {2x}, orderings {1x}, account {1x}, custody {1x}, numbers {1x}, misc. 4. See: TWOT—1802a; BDB—824a.

6487. פִּקָּדוֹן {3x} **piqqâdôwn**, *pik-kaw-done';* from 6485; a *deposit:*—that which was delivered {2x}, store {1x}. See: TWOT—1802f; BDB—824c.

6488. פְּקִדֻת {1x} **pᵉqîdûth**, *pek-ee-dooth';* from 6496; *supervision:*—ward {1x}. See: TWOT—1802d; BDB—824b.

6489. פְּקוֹד {2x} **Pᵉqôwd**, *pek-ode';* from 6485; *punishment; Pekod,* a symbol. name for Bab.:—Pekod {2x}. See: BDB—824c.

6490. פִּקּוּד {24x} **piqqûwd**, *pik-kood';* or

פִּקֻּד **piqqûd**, *pik-kood';* from 6485; prop. *appointed,* i.e. a *mandate* (of God; plur. only, collect. for the *Law*):—precept {21x}, commandment {2x}, statute {1x}. See: TWOT—1802e; BDB—824b.

6491. פָּקַח {20x} **pâqach**, *paw-kakh';* a prim. root; to *open* (the senses, espec. the eyes); fig. to *be observant:*—open {20x}. See: TWOT—1803; BDB—824c.

6492. פֶּקַח {11x} **Peqach**, *peh'-kakh;* from 6491; *watch; Pekach,* an Isr. king:—Pekah {11x}. See: BDB—842d.

6493. פִּקֵּחַ {2x} **piqqêach**, *pik-kay'-akh;* from 6491; *clear-sighted;* fig. *intelligent:*—seeing {1x}, wise {1x}. See: TWOT—1803a; BDB—824d.

6494. פְּקַחְיָה {3x} **Pᵉqachyâh**, *pek-akh-yaw';* from 6491 and 3050; *Jah has observed; Pekachjah,* an Isr. king:—Pekahiah {3x}. See: BDB—824d.

6495. פְּקַח־קוֹחַ {1x} **pᵉqach-qôwach**, *pek-akh-ko'-akh;* from 6491 redoubled; *opening* (of a dungeon), i.e. *jail-delivery* (fig. *salvation* from sin):—opening of the prison {1x}. See: TWOT—1803b; BDB—824d, 876c.

6496. פָּקִיד {13x} **pâqîyd**, *paw-keed';* from 6485; a *superintendent* (civil, military, or religious):—officer {6x}, overseer {5x}, governor {1x}, which had the charge {1x}.

Paqiyd, as a noun, means "one who looks after." **(1)** This noun, derived from paqad (6485) in the sense "to number, muster, draw up (troops)," possibly means "one who draws up troops," hence "officer" (2 Chr 24:11). **(2)** Another example of this meaning occurs in Jer 20:1: "Now Pashur the son of Immer the priest, who was also chief governor in the house of the Lord. . . ." See: TWOT—1802c; BDB—824b.

6497. פֶּקַע {3x} **peqaʿ**, *peh'-kah;* from an unused root mean. to *burst;* only used as an arch. term of an ornament similar to 6498, a *semi-globe:*—knops {3x}. See: TWOT—1804a; BDB—825a.

6498. פַּקֻּעָה {1x} **paqqûʿâh**, *pak-koo-aw';* from the same as 6497; the *wild cucumber* (from *splitting* open to shed its seeds):—gourd {1x}. See: TWOT—1804b; BDB—825a.

6499. פַּר {133x} **par**, *par;* or

פָּר **pâr**, *pawr;* from 6565; a *bullock* (appar. as *breaking* forth in wild strength, or perh. as *dividing* the hoof):—bullock {127x}, bulls {2x}, oxen {2x}, calves {1x}, young {1x}.

***Par,* the masculine noun,** means "bullock." **(1)** *Par* means "young bull," which is the significance in its first biblical appearance (Gen 32:15), which tells us that among the gifts Jacob sent to placate Esau were "ten bulls." **(2)** In Ps 22:12, the word is used to describe "fierce, strong enemies": "Many bulls have compassed me: strong bulls of Bashan have beset me round." **(3)** When God threatens the nations with judgment in Is 34:7, He describes their princes and warriors as "young bulls," which He will slaughter (cf. Jer 50:27; Eze 39:18). **(4) Parah, the feminine form of** *par,* is used disdainfully of women in Amos 4:1: "Hear this word, you kine of Bashan . . ." See: TWOT—1831a; BDB—825a, 830d.

6500. פָּרָא {1x} **pârâʾ**, *paw-raw';* a prim. root; to *bear fruit:*—fruitful {1x}. See: TWOT—1805; BDB—825a, 826b.

6501. פֶּרֶא {10x} **pereʾ**, *peh'-reh;* or

פֶּרֶה **pereh** (Jer. 2:24), *peh'-reh;* from 6500 in the second. sense of *running* wild; the *onager:*—wild ass {9x}, wild {1x}. See: TWOT—1805a; BDB—825b, 826c.

פֹּרָאה **pôrâʾh.** See 6288.

6502. פִּרְאָם {1x} **Pirʾâm**, *pir-awm';* from 6501; *wildly; Piram,* a Canaanite:—*Piram* {1x}. See: BDB—825b.

6503. פַּרְבָּר {3x} **Parbâr**, *par-bawr';* or

פַּרְוָר **Parvâr**, *par-vawr';* of for. or.; *Parbar* or *Parvar,* a quarter of Jerusalem:—Parbar {2x}, suburb {1x}. See: BDB—825b, 826c.

6504. פָּרַד {26x} **pârad**, *paw-rad';* a prim. root; to *break* through, i.e. *spread* or *separate* (oneself):—separate {12x}, part {4x}, divided {3x}, scattered abroad {1x}, dispersed {1x}, joint {1x}, scattered {1x}, severed {1x}, stretched {1x}, sundered {1x}.

Parad (6504) means "to divide, separate." **(1)** *Parad* occurs for the first time in the text in Gen 2:10: "And a river went out of Eden . . . and from thence it was parted, and became into four heads." The meaning here must be "dividing into four branches." **(2)** This word often expresses separation of people from each other, sometimes with hostility: "Separate thyself . . . from me . . ." (Gen 13:9). **(3)** A reciprocal separation seems to be implied in the birth of Jacob and Esau: "Two nations are in thy womb, and two manner of people shall be separated from thy bowels . . ." (Gen 25:23). **(4)** Sometimes economic status brings about separation: ". . . The poor is separated from his neighbor" (Prov 19:4). **(5)** Generally speaking, *parad* has more negative than positive connotations. Syn.: 5139, 5144. See: TWOT—1806; BDB—825b.

6505. פֶּרֶד {15x} **pered**, *peh'-red;* from 6504; a *mule* (perh. from his *lonely* habits):—mule {15x}. See: TWOT—1807a; BDB—825d.

6506. פִּרְדָּה {3x} **pirdâh**, *pir-daw';* fem. of 6505; a *she-mule:*—mule {3x}. See: TWOT—1807b; BDB—825d.

6507. פְּרֻדָה {1x} **perûdâh**, *per-oo-daw';* fem. pass. part. of 6504; something *separated,* i.e. a *kernel:*—seed {1x}. See: TWOT—1806a; BDB—825c.

6508. פַּרְדֵּס {3x} **pardêç**, *par-dace';* of for. or.; a *park:*—orchard {2x}, forest {1x}. See: TWOT—1808; BDB—825d.

6509. פָּרָה {29x} **pârâh**, *paw-raw';* a prim. root; to *bear fruit* (lit. or fig.):—fruitful {19x}, increased {3x}, grow {2x}, beareth {1x}, forth {1x}, bring fruit {1x}, make fruitful {1x}.

Parah, the verb, means "to be fruitful, bear fruit." Its first occurrence is in Gen 1:22: "And God blessed them, saying, Be fruitful, and multiply, . . ." See: TWOT—1809; BDB—825a, 826a, 832c.

6510. פָּרָה {26x} **pârâh**, *paw-raw';* fem. of 6499; a *heifer:*—kine {18x}, heifer {6x}, cow {2x}. See: TWOT—1831b; BDB—826c, 831a.

6511. פָּרָה {1x} **Pârâh**, *paw-raw';* the same as 6510; *Parah,* a place in Pal.:—*Parah* {1x}. See: BDB—826c, 831a.

פֶּרֶה **pereh**. See 6501.

6512. פֵּרָה {1x} **pêrâh**, *pay-raw';* from 6331; a *hole* (as *broken,* i.e. *dug*):—moles {1x}. See: TWOT—714a; BDB—344a, 826c. comp. 2661.

6513. פֻּרָה {2x} **Pûrâh**, *poo-raw';* for 6288; *foliage; Purah,* an Isr.:—Phurah {2x}. See: BDB—826c.

6514. פְּרוּדָא {2x} **Perûwdâʾ**, *per-oo-daw';* or

פְּרִידָא **Perîydâʾ**, *per-ee-daw';* from 6504; *dispersion; Peruda* or *Perida,* one of "Solomon's servants":—Peruda {1x}, Perida {1x}. See: BDB—825c.

פְּרוֹזִי **perôwzîy**. See 6521.

6515. פָּרוּחַ {1x} **Pârûwach**, *paw-roo'-akh;* pass. part. of 6524; *blossomed; Paruäch,* an Isr.:—Paruah {1x}. See: BDB—827c.

6516. פַּרְוַיִם {1x} **Parvayim**, *par-vah'-yim;* of for. or.; *Parvajim,* an Oriental region:—Parvaim {1x}. See: BDB—826c.

6517. פָּרוּר {3x} **pârûwr**, *paw-roor';* pass. part. of 6565 in the sense of *spreading* out [comp. 6524]; a *skillet* (as *flat* or *deep*):—pot {2x}, pan {1x}. See: TWOT—1750b, 1810; BDB—807d.

פַּרְוָר **Parvâr**. See 6503.

6518. פָּרָז {1x} **pârâz**, *paw-rawz';* from an unused root mean. to *separate,* i.e. *decide;* a *chieftain:*—villages {1x}. See: TWOT—1812?; BDB—826d.

6519. פְּרָזָה {3x} **perâzâh**, *per-aw-zaw';* from the same as 6518; an *open* country:—unwalled town {1x}, unwalled village {1x}, town without walls {1x}. See: TWOT—1812a; BDB—826d.

6520. פְּרָזוֹן {2x} **perâzôwn**, *per-aw-zone';* from the same as 6518; *magistracy,* i.e. *leadership* (also concr. *chieftains*):—village {2x}. See: TWOT—1812b; BDB—826d.

6521. פְּרָזִי {3x} **perâzîy**, *per-aw-zee';* or

פְּרוֹזִי **perôwzîy**, *per-o-zee';* from 6519; a *rustic:*—village {1x}, country {1x}, unwalled {1x}. See: TWOT—1812c; BDB—826d.

6522. פְּרִזִּי {23x} **Perizzîy**, *per-iz-zee';* for 6521; inhab. *of the open country;* a *Perizzite,* one of the Canaanitish tribes:—Perizzite {23x}. See: BDB—827a.

6523. פַּרְזֶל {20x} **parzel** (Aram.), *par-zel';* corresp. to 1270; *iron:*—iron {20x}. See: TWOT—2944; BDB—1108d.

6524. פָּרַח {36x} **pârach**, *paw-rakh';* a prim. root; to *break* forth as a bud, i.e. *bloom;* gen. to *spread;* spec. to *fly* (as extending the wings); fig. to *flourish:*—flourish {10x}, bud {5x}, blossom {4x}, grow {3x}, break {3x}, fly {2x}, spring {2x}, break forth {2x}, abroad {1x}, abundantly {1x}, break out {1x}, spreading {1x}, spring up {1x}. See: TWOT—1813, 1814, 1815; BDB—827a, 827b, 827c.

6525. פֶּרַח {17x} **perach**, *peh'-rakh;* from 6524; a *calyx* (nat. or artif.); gen. *bloom:*—flower {14x}, bud {2x}, blossom {1x}. See: TWOT—1813a; BDB—827b.

6526. פִּרְחַח {1x} **pirchach**, *pir-khakh';* from 6524; *progeny,* i.e. a *brood:*—youth {1x}. See: TWOT—1813b; BDB—827b, 1107b.

6527. פָּרַט {1x} **pâraṭ**, *paw-rat';* a prim. root; to *scatter* words, i.e. *prate* (or *hum*):—chant {1x}. See: TWOT—1816; BDB—827c.

6528. פֶּרֶט {1x} **pereṭ**, *peh'-ret;* from 6527; a *stray* or *single* berry:—grape {1x}. See: TWOT—1816a; BDB—827c, 1107b.

6529. פְּרִי {119x} **perîy**, *per-ee';* from 6509; *fruit* (lit. or fig.):—fruit {113x}, fruitful {2x}, boughs {1x}, firstfruits + 7225 {1x}, reward {1x}, fruit thereof {1x}.

Periy, as a noun, means "fruit; reward; price; earnings; product; result." **(1)** First, *periy* represents the mature edible product of a plant, which is its "fruit." **(1a)** This broad meaning is evident in Deut 7:13: "He will also bless the fruit of thy womb, and the fruit of thy land, thy corn, and thy wine, and thine oil, the increase of thy kine and the flocks of thy sheep. . . ." **(1b)** In its first biblical appearance, the word is used to signify both "trees" and the "fruit" of trees: "And God said, Let the earth bring forth grass, the herb yielding seed, and the fruit tree yielding fruit after his kind . . ." (Gen 1:11). **(1c)** In Ps 107:34, the word is used as a modifier of land. The resulting term is "a fruitful land" in the sense of a "land of fruit." **(2)** Second, *periy* means "offspring," or the "fruit of a womb." **(2a)** In Deut 7:13, the word represents "human offspring," but it can also be used **(2b)** of animal "offspring" (Gen 1:22).

(3) Third, the "product" or "result" of an action is, in poetry, sometimes called its "fruit": **(3a)** "A man shall say, Verily there is a reward [*periy*] for the righteous: verily he is a God that judgeth in the earth" (Ps 58:11). **(3b)** Is 27:9 speaks of "all the fruit to take away his sin"), i.e., the result of God's purifying acts toward Israel. **(3c)** The wise woman buys and plants a field with her earnings or the "fruit of her hands" (Prov 31:16). In other words, she is to be rewarded by receiving the "product" of her hands (Prov 31:31). **(3d)** The righteous will be rewarded "I the LORD search the heart, *I* try the reins, even to give every man according to his ways, *and* according to the fruit of his doings" (Jer 17:10; cf. 21:14). See: TWOT—1809a; BDB—826b.

פְּרִידָא **Perîydâʾ**. See 6514.

פֻּרִים **Pûrîym**. See 6332.

6530. פְּרִיץ {6x} **perîyts**, *per-eets';* from 6555; *violent,* i.e. a *tyrant:*—robber {4x}, destroyer {1x}, ravenous {1x}. See: TWOT—1826b; BDB—829b.

6531. פֶּרֶךְ {6x} **perek**, *peh'-rek;* from an unused root mean. to *break* apart; *fracture,* i.e. *severity:*—rigour {5x}, cruelty {1x}. See: TWOT—1817a; BDB—827d.

6532. פֹּרֶכֶת {25x} **pôreketh**, *po-reh'-keth;* fem. act. part. of the same as 6531; a *separatrix,* i.e. (the sacred) *screen:*—vail {25x}. See: TWOT—1817a; BDB—827d.

6533. פָּרַם {3x} **pâram**, *paw-ram';* a prim. root; to *tear:*—rend {3x}. See: TWOT—1819; BDB—827d.

6534. פַּרְמַשְׁתָּא {1x} **Parmashtâʾ**, *par-mash-taw';* of Pers. or.; *Parmashta,* a son of Haman:—*Parmashta* {1x}. See: BDB—828a.

6535. פַּרְנַךְ {1x} **Parnak**, *par-nak';* of uncert. der.; *Parnak,* an Isr.:—Parnach {1x}. See: BDB—828a.

6536. פָּרַס {14x} **pâraç**, *paw-ras';* a prim. root; to *break* in pieces, i.e. (usually without violence) to *split, distribute:*—divide {9x}, parteth {2x}, deal {1x}, hoofs {1x}, tear {1x}. See: TWOT—1821; BDB—828a, 1108d.

6537. פְּרַס {3x} **peraç** (Aram.), *per-as';* corresp. to 6536; to *split* up:—UPHARSIN {1x}, PERES {1x}, divided {1x}. See: TWOT—2945; BDB—1101b, 1108d.

6538. פֶּרֶס {2x} **pereç**, *peh'-res;* from 6536; a *claw;* also a kind of *eagle:*—ossifrage {2x}. See: TWOT—1821a; BDB—828b.

6539. פָּרַס {28x} **Pâraç**, *paw-ras';* of for. or.; *Paras* (i.e. *Persia*), an E. country, incl. its inhab.:—Persia {27x}, Persian {1x}. See: TWOT—1820; BDB—828a, 1108d.

6540. פָּרַס {6x} **Pâraç** (Aram.), *paw-ras';* corresp. to 6539:—Persians {4x}, Persia {2x}. See: BDB—1108d.

6541. פַּרְסָה {19x} **parçâh**, *par-saw';* fem. of 6538; a *claw* or split *hoof:*—hoof {17x}, claws {2x}. See: TWOT—1821b; BDB—828b.

6542. פַּרְסִי {1x} **Parçîy**, *par-see';* patrial from 6539; a *Parsite* (i.e. *Persian*), or inhab. of Peres:—Persian {1x}. See: BDB—828a.

6543. פַּרְסִי {1x} **Parçîy** (Aram.), *par-see';* corresp. to 6542:—Persian {1x}. See: BDB—1108d.

6544. פָּרַע {16x} **pâraʻ**, *paw-rah';* a prim. root; to *loosen;* by impl. to *expose, dismiss;* fig. *absolve, begin:*—refuse {3x}, uncover {3x}, naked {2x}, avenging {1x}, avoid {1x}, go back {1x}, bare {1x}, let {1x}, made naked {1x}, set at nought {1x}, perish {1x}. See: TWOT—1822, 1823, 1824; BDB—828c, 828d.

6545. פֶּרַע {2x} **peraʻ**, *peh'-rah;* from 6544; the *hair* (as *dishevelled*):—locks {2x}. See: TWOT—1823a, 1822a; BDB—828c, 828d.

6546. פַּרְעָה {2x} **parʻâh**, *par-aw';* fem. of 6545 (in the sense of *beginning*); *leadership* (plur. concr. *leaders*):—revenge {1x}, avenge {1x}. See: TWOT—1822a; BDB—828d.

6547. פַּרְעֹה {268x} **Parʻôh**, *par-o';* of Eg. der.; *Paroh,* a gen. title of Eg. kings:—Pharaoh {268x}. See: TWOT—1825; BDB—829a.

6548. פַּרְעֹה חָפְרַע {1x} **Parʻôh Chophraʻ**, *par-o' khof-rah';* of Eg. der.; *Paroh-Chophra,* an Eg. king:—Pharaohhophra {1x}. See: BDB—344b.

6549. פַּרְעֹה נְכֹה {5x} **Parʻôh Nᵉkôh**, *par-o' nek-o';* or

פַּרְעֹה נְכוֹ **Parʻôh Nᵉkôw**, *par-o' nek-o';* of Eg. der.; *Paroh-Nekoh* (or *-Neko*), an Eg. king:—Pharaoh-necho {5x}. See: BDB—647a.

6550. פַּרְעֹשׁ {2x} **parʻôsh**, *par-oshe';* prob. from 6544 and 6211; a *flea* (as the *isolated insect*):—flea {2x}. See: TWOT—1825.1; BDB—829a.

6551. פַּרְעֹשׁ {6x} **Parʻôsh**, *par-oshe';* the same as 6550; *Parosh,* the name of four Isr.:—*Parosh* {5x}, Pharosh {1x}. See: BDB—829b.

6552. פִּרְעָתוֹן {1x} **Pirʻâthôwn**, *pir-aw-thone';* from 6546; *chieftaincy; Pirathon,* a place in Pal.:—Pirathon {1x}. See: BDB—828c.

6553. פִּרְעָתוֹנִי {5x} **Pirʻâthôwnîy**, *pir-aw-tho-nee';* or

פִּרְעָתֹנִי **Pirʻâthônîy**, *pir-aw-tho-nee';* patrial from 6552; a *Pirathonite* or inhab. of Pirathon:—Pirathonite {5x}. See: BDB—828d.

6554. פַּרְפַּר {1x} **Parpar**, *par-par';* prob. from 6565 in the sense of *rushing; rapid; Parpar,* a river of Syria:—Pharpar {1x}. See: BDB—829b.

6555. פָּרַץ {49x} **pârats**, *paw-rats';* a prim. root; to *break* out (in many applications, dir. and indirect, lit. and fig.):—break down {11x}, break forth {5x}, increase {5x}, break {4x}, abroad {3x}, breach {2x}, break in {2x}, made {2x}, break out {2x}, pressed {2x}, break up {2x}, break away {1x}, breaker {1x}, compelled {1x}, misc. {6x}. See: TWOT—1826; BDB—829b.

6556. פֶּרֶץ {19x} **perets**, *peh'-rets;* from 6555; a *break* (lit. or fig.):—breach {14x}, gap {2x}, breaking {1x}, breaking forth {1x}, breaking in {1x}. See: TWOT—1826a; BDB—829c.

6557. פֶּרֶץ {15x} **Perets**, *peh'-rets;* the same as 6556; *Perets,* the name of two Isr.:—Pharez {12x}, Perez {3x}. See: BDB—829d.

6558. פַּרְצִי {1x} **Partsîy**, *par-tsee';* patron. from 6557; a *Partsite* (collect.) or desc. of Perets:—Pharzites {1x}. See: BDB—829d.

6559. פְּרָצִים {1x} **Pᵉrâtsîym**, *per-aw-tseem';* plur. of 6556; *breaks; Peratsim,* a mountain in Pal.:—Perazim {1x}. See: BDB—829c.

6560. פֶּרֶץ עֻזָּא {2x} **Perets ʻUzzâʼ**, *peh'-rets ooz-zaw';* from 6556 and 5798; *break of Uzza; Perets-Uzza,* a place in Pal.:—Perezuzza {2x}. See: BDB—829d.

6561. פָּרַק {10x} **pâraq**, *paw-rak';* a prim. root; to *break* off or *crunch;* fig. to *deliver:*—break off {3x}, break {2x}, rent {1x}, rend in pieces {1x}, redeem {1x}, deliver {1x}, tear in pieces {1x}. See: TWOT—1828; BDB—830a, 1108d.

6562. פְּרַק {1x} **pᵉraq** (Aram.), *per-ak';* corresp. to 6561; to *discontinue:*—break off {1x}. See: TWOT—2946; BDB—1108d.

6563. פֶּרֶק {2x} **pereq**, *peh'-rek;* from 6561; *rapine;* also a *fork* (in roads):—crossway {1x}, robbery {1x}. See: TWOT—1828a; BDB—830a.

6564. פָּרָק {1x} **pârâq**, *paw-rawk';* from 6561; *soup* (as full of *crumbed* meat):—broth {1x}. See also 4832.

6565. פָּרַר {50x} **pârar**, *paw-rar';* a prim. root; to *break* up (usually fig., i.e. to *violate, frustrate:*—break {25x}, make void {5x}, defeat {2x}, disannul {2x}, disappoint {2x}, frustrate {2x}, come to nought {2x}, break asunder {1x}, cause to cease {1x}, clean {1x}, dissolved {1x}, divide {1x}, misc. {5x}. See: TWOT—1829, 1830, 1831; BDB—830b, 830c.

6566. פָּרַשׂ {67x} **pâras**, *paw-ras';* a prim. root; to *break* apart, *disperse,* etc.:—spread {31x}, spread forth {12x}, spread out {6x}, spread abroad {5x}, stretch {3x}, stretch forth {2x}, stretch out {2x}, scattered {2x}, breaketh {1x}, lay open {1x}, chop in pieces {1x}, spread up {1x}.

Paras, as a verb, means "to spread out, scatter, display." **(1)** It is found for the first time in Ex 9:29: ". . . I will spread abroad my hands unto the Lord. . . ." Such stretching of the hands probably reflected the characteristic posture of prayer in the Bible (cf. Ps 143:6; Is 1:15). **(2)** *Paras* sometimes expresses the "spreading out" of a garment to its widest extent (Judg 8:25). **(3)** It is commonly used of wings' "being spread," opened fully (Deut 32:11; 1 Kin 6:27). **(4)** "To spread out" a net is to set a snare or trap (Hos 7:12). **(5)** Sometimes "to spread out" is "to display": ". . . A fool layeth open his folly" (Prov 13:16). **(6)** "To spread" may mean "to cover over" and thus to hide from vision: "And the woman took and spread a covering over the well's mouth, and spread ground corn thereon; and the thing was not known" (2 Sa 17:19). **(7)** In some instances, "to spread" may have a more violent meaning of "to scatter": ". . . They that remain shall be scattered toward all winds . . ." (Eze 17:21). See: TWOT—1832; BDB—831A.

6567. פָּרַשׁ {5x} **pârash**, *paw-rash';* a prim. root; to *separate,* lit. (to *disperse*) or fig. (to *specify*); also (by impl.) to *wound:*—shew {1x}, scatter {1x}, declare {1x}, distinctly {1x}, sting {1x}. See: TWOT—1833, 1834; BDB—831c, 831d, 1109a.

6568. פְּרַשׁ {1x} **pᵉrash** (Aram.), *per-ash';* corresp. to 6567; to *specify:*—plainly {1x}. See: TWOT—2947; BDB—1109a.

6569. פֶּרֶשׁ {7x} **peresh**, *peh'-resh;* from 6567; *excrement* (as *eliminated*):—dung {7x}. See: TWOT—1835a; BDB—831d.

6570. פֶּרֶשׁ {1x} **Peresh**, *peh'-resh;* the same as 6569; *Peresh,* an Isr.:—*Peresh* {1x}. See: BDB—831d.

6571. פָּרָשׁ {57x} **pârâsh**, *paw-rawsh';* from 6567; a *steed* (as *stretched* out to a vehicle, not single nor for mounting [comp. 5483]); also (by impl.) a *driver* (in a chariot), i.e. (collect.) cavalry:—horsemen {56x}, horsemen + 1167 {1x}. See: TWOT—1836a; BDB—832a.

6572. פַּרְשֶׁגֶן {4x} **parshegen**, *par-sheh'-ghen;* or

פַּתְשֶׁגֶן **pathshegen**, *path-sheh'-gen;* of for. or.; a *transcript:*—copy {4x}. See: TWOT—1837; BDB—832b, 837d, 1109a.

6573. פַּרְשֶׁגֶן {3x} **parshegen** (Aram.), *par-sheh'-ghen;* corresp. to 6572:—copy {3x}. See: TWOT—2948; BDB—1109a.

6574. פַּרְשְׁדֹן {1x} **parshᵉdôn**, *par-shed-one';* perh. by compounding 6567 and 6504 (in the sense of *straddling*) [comp. 6576]; the *crotch* (or *anus*):—dirt {1x}. See: TWOT—1838; BDB—832b.

6575. פָּרָשָׁה {2x} **pârâshâh**, *paw-raw-shaw';* from 6567; *exposition:*—sum {1x}, declaration {1x}. See: TWOT—1833a; BDB—831d.

6576. פַּרְשֵׁז {1x} **parshêz**, *par-shaze';* a root appar. formed by compounding 6567 and that of 6518 [comp. 6574]; to *expand:*—spread {1x}. See: TWOT—1832; BDB—831c, 832b.

6577. פַּרְשַׁנְדָּתָא {1x} **Parshandâthâʼ**, *par-shan-daw-thaw';* of Pers. or.; *Parshandatha,* a son of Haman:—*Parshandatha* {1x}. See: BDB—832b.

6578. פְּרָת {19x} **Pᵉrâth**, *per-awth';* from an unused root mean. to *break* forth; *rushing; Perath* (i.e. *Euphrates*), a river of the East:—Euphrates {19x}. See: BDB—832b.

פֹּרָת **pôrâth**. See 6509.

6579. פַּרְתְּמִים {3x} **partam**, *par-tam';* of Pers. or.; a *grandee:*—noble {2x}, prince {1x}. See: TWOT—1839; BDB—832c.

6580. פַּשׁ {1x} **pash**, *pash;* prob. from an unused root mean. to *disintegrate; stupidity* (as a result of *grossness* or of *degeneracy*):—extremity {1x}. See: TWOT—1843; BDB—832d.

6581. פָּשָׂה {22x} **pâsâh**, *paw-saw';* a prim. root; to *spread:*—spread {15x}, spread much {4x}, abroad {3x}. See: TWOT—1840; BDB—832c.

6582. פָּשַׁח {1x} **pâshach**, *paw-shakh';* a prim. root; to *tear* in pieces:—pulled in pieces {1x}. See: TWOT—1844; BDB—832d.

6583. פַּשְׁחוּר {14x} **Paschûwr**, *pash-khoor';* prob. from 6582; *liberation; Pashchur,* the name of four Isr.:—Pashur {14x}. See: BDB—832d.

6584. פָּשַׁט {43x} **pâshat**, *paw-shat';* a prim. root; to *spread* out (i.e. *deploy* in hostile array); by anal. to *strip* (i.e. *unclothe, plunder, flay,* etc.):—strip {13x}, put off {6x}, flay {4x}, invaded {4x}, spoil {3x}, strip off {2x}, fell {2x}, spread abroad {1x}, forward {1x}, invasion {1x}, pull off {1x}, made a road {1x}, rushed {1x}, set {1x}, spread {1x}, ran upon {1x}. See: TWOT—1845; BDB—832d.

6585. פָּשַׂע {1x} **pâsaʻ**, *paw-sah';* a prim. root; to *stride* (from *spreading* the legs), i.e. *rush* upon:—go {1x}. See: TWOT—1841; BDB—832c.

6586. פָּשַׁע {41x} **pâshaʻ**, *paw-shah';* a prim. root [rather ident. with 6585 through the idea of *expansion*]; to *break* away (from just authority), i.e. *trespass, apostatize, quarrel:*—transgress {17x}, transgressor {9x}, rebelled {6x}, revolt {6x}, offended {1x}, transgression {1x}, trespassed {1x}.

Pasha' means to transgress, rebel. **(1)** The basic sense of *pasha'* is to rebel with one of two rebellion's stages in focus: **(1a)** a goal of independence (2 Kin 1:1), and **(1b)** the state of independence itself (2 Kin 8:20). **(2)** A more radical meaning is the state of rebellion in which there is no end of the rebellion in view; it is no longer goal-oriented (1 Kin 12:19). **(3)** When the act is committed against the Lord it is usually translated "transgress" (Hos 7:13; Is 66:24) and is an expression of an apostate way of life (Is 59:13). See: TWOT—1846; BDB—833b.

6587. פֶּשַׂע {1x} **pesaʿ**, *peh'-sah;* from 6585; a *stride:*—step {1x}. See: TWOT—1841a; BDB—832c.

6588. פֶּשַׁע {93x} **peshaʿ**, *peh'-shah;* from 6586; a *revolt* (national, moral, or religious):—transgression {84x}, trespass {5x}, sin {3x}, rebellion {1x}.

Pesha', as a noun, means "transgression; guilt; punishment; offering." **(1)** Basically, this noun signifies willful deviation from, and therefore rebellion against, the path of godly living. **(2)** This emphasis is especially prominent in Amos 2:4: "For three transgressions of Judah, and for four, I will not turn away the punishment thereof; because they have despised the law of the Lord, and have not kept his commandments, and their lies caused them to err, after the which their fathers have walked." Such a willful rebellion from a prescribed or agreed-upon path may be perpetrated against another man: ". . . **(3)** Jacob answered and said to Laban, What is my trespass? what is my sin, that thou hast so hotly pursued after me?" (Gen 31:36—the first occurrence of the word). Jacob is asking what he has done by way of violating or not keeping his responsibility (contract) with Laban.

(4) A nation can sin in this sense against another nation: "For three transgressions of Damascus, and for four . . . because they have threshed Gilead with threshing instruments of iron" (Amos 1:3). **(5)** Usually, however, *pesha'* has immediate reference to one's relationship to God. **(6)** This word sometimes represents the guilt of such a transgression: "I am clean, without [guilt of] transgression, I am innocent; neither is there iniquity in me" (Job 33:9). **(7)** *Pesha'* can signify the punishment for transgression: **(7a)** "And a host was given him against the daily sacrifice by reason of transgression . . ." (Dan 8:12); **(7b)** "How long shall be the vision concerning the daily sacrifice, and [punishment for] the transgression of desolation, to give both the sanctuary and the host to be trodden under foot?" (Dan 8:13). **(8)** Finally, in Mic 6:7 *pesha'* signifies an offering for "transgression": "Shall I give my first-born for my transgression . . .?"

See: TWOT—1846a; BDB—833b. Syn.: 2398, 5771, 7686.

6589. פָּשַׂק {2x} **pâsaq**, *paw-sak';* a prim. root; to *dispart* (the feet or lips), i.e. *become licentious:*—open {1x}, open wide {1x}. See: TWOT—1842; BDB—832d.

6590. פְּשַׁר {2x} **pᵉshar** (Aram.), *pesh-ar';* corresp. to 6622; to *interpret:*—make {1x}, interpreting {1x}. See: TWOT—2949; BDB—1109a.

6591. פְּשַׁר {31x} **pᵉshar** (Aram.), *pesh-ar';* from 6590; an *interpretation:*—interpretation {31x}. See: TWOT—2949a; BDB—1109a.

6592. פֵּשֶׁר {1x} **pêsher**, *pay'-sher;* corresp. to 6591:—interpretation {1x}. See: TWOT—1847; BDB—833d, 1109a.

6593. פִּשְׁתֶּה {16x} **pishteh**, *pish-teh';* from the same as 6580 as in the sense of *comminuting; linen* (i.e. the thread, as *carded*):—linen {9x}, flax {7x}. See: TWOT—1848; BDB—833d.

6594. פִּשְׁתָּה {4x} **pishtâh**, *pish-taw';* fem. of 6593; *flax;* by impl. a *wick:*—flax {3x}, tow {1x}. See: TWOT—1849; BDB—834a.

6595. פַּת {15x} **path**, *path;* from 6626; a *bit:*—morsel {9x}, piece {5x}, meat {1x}. See: TWOT—1862a; BDB—834a, 837d.

6596. פֹּת {2x} **pôth**, *pohth;* or

פֹּתָה **pothâh** (Eze 13:19), *po-thaw';* from an unused root mean. to *open;* a *hole,* i.e. *hinge* or the female *pudenda:*—hinge {1x}, secret parts {1x}. See: TWOT—1850; BDB—834a.

פְּתָאִי **pᵉthâʾiy**. See 6612.

6597. פִּתְאוֹם {25x} **pithʾôwm**, *pith-ome';* or

פִּתְאֹם **pithʾôm**, *pith-ome';* from 6621; *instantly:*—suddenly {22x}, sudden {2x}, straightway {1x}. See: TWOT—1859a; BDB—834a, 837b.

6598. פַּתְבַּג {6x} **pathbag**, *pathbag';* of Pers. or.; a *dainty:*—portion of meat {4x}, meat {2x}. See: TWOT—1851; BDB—834a.

6599. פִּתְגָם {2x} **pithgâm**, *pith-gawm';* of Pers. or.; a (judicial) *sentence:*—decree {1x}, sentence {1x}. See: TWOT—1852; BDB—834a, 1109b.

6600. פִּתְגָם {6x} **pithgâm** (Aram.), *pith-gawm';* corresp. to 6599; a *word, answer, letter* or *decree:*—answer {2x}, matter {2x}, word {1x}, letter {1x}. See: TWOT—2950; BDB—1109b.

6601. פָּתָה **pâthâh**, *paw-thaw';* a prim. root; to *open,* i.e. *be* (caus. *make*) *roomy;* usually fig. (in a mental or moral sense) to *be* (caus. *make*) *simple* or (in a sinister way) *delude:*—entice {10x}, deceive {8x}, persuade {4x}, flatter {2x}, allure {1x}, enlarge {1x}, silly one {1x}, silly {1x}. See: TWOT—1853; BDB—834b, 834c, 1109b.

6602. פְּתוּאֵל {1x} **Pᵉthûwʾêl**, *peth-oo-ale';* from 6601 and 410; *enlarged of God; Pethuël,* an Isr.:—Pethuel {1x}. See: BDB—834b.

6603. פִּתּוּחַ {11x} **pittûwach**, *pit-too'-akh;* or

פִּתֻּחַ **pittûach**, *pit-too'-akh;* pass. part. of 6605; *sculpture* (in low or high relief or even intaglio):—engravings {5x}, graving {2x}, carved {1x}, grave + 6605 {1x}, graven {1x}, carved work {1x}. See: TWOT—1855a; BDB—836c.

6604. פְּתוֹר {2x} **Pᵉthôwr**, *peth-ore';* of for. or.; *Pethor,* a place in Mesopotamia:—Pethor {2x} See: BDB—834b.

6605. פָּתַח {144x} **pâthach**, *paw-thakh';* a prim. root; to *open* wide (lit. or fig.); spec. to *loosen, begin, plow, carve:*—open {107x}, loose {13x}, grave {7x}, wide {3x}, engrave {2x}, put off {2x}, out {2x}, appear {1x}, drawn {1x}, break forth {1x}, set forth {1x}, let go free {1x}, ungird {1x}, unstop {1x}, have vent {1x}.

Pathach, as a verb, means "to open." **(1)** The first occurrence is in Gen 7:11: "In the six hundredth year of Noah's life, in the second month, the seventeenth day of the month, the same day were all the fountains of the great deep broken up, and the windows of heaven were opened." **(2)** Although the basic meaning of *pathach* is "to open," the word is extended to mean "to cause to flow," "to offer for sale," "to conquer," "to surrender," "to draw a sword," "to solve [a riddle]," "to free." **(3)** In association with min, the word becomes "to deprive of." See: TWOT—1854, 1855; BDB—834d, 836b, 1109b.

6606. פְּתַח {2x} **pᵉthach** (Aram.), *peth-akh';* corresp. to 6605; to *open:*—open {2x}. See: TWOT—2951; BDB—1109b.

6607. פֶּתַח {163x} **pethach**, *peh'-thakh;* from 6605; an *opening* (lit.), i.e. *door* (*gate*) or *entrance* way:—door {126x}, entering {10x}, entry {8x}, gate {7x}, in {7x}, entrance {3x}, openings {1x}, place {1x}.

Pethach, as a noun, means "doorway; opening; entrance; gate." **(1)** *Pethach* basically represents the "opening through which one enters a building, tent, tower (fortress), or city." **(1a)** Abraham was sitting at the "doorway" of his tent in the heat of the day when his three heavenly visitors appeared (Gen 18:1). **(1b)** Lot met the men of Sodom at the "doorway" of his home, having shut the door behind him (Gen 19:6). **(2)** Larger buildings had larger entryways, so in Gen 43:19 *pethach* may be rendered by the more general word, "entrance." **(3)** In Gen 38:14, *pethach* may be translated "gateway": Tamar "sat in the open place." **(4)** Thus a *pethach* was both a place to sit (a location) and an opening for entry (a passageway): ". . . And the incense altar, and his staves, and the anointing oil, and the sweet incense, and the hanging for the door at the entering in of the tabernacle . . ." (Ex 35:15). **(5)** There are a few notable special uses of *pethach.* **(5a)** The word normally refers to a part of the intended construction plans of a dwelling, housing, or building; **(5a)** but in Eze 8:8 it represents an "entrance" not included in the original design of the building: ". . . When I had digged in the wall, behold a door." **(5b)** This is clearly not a doorway.

(6) This word may be used of a cave's "opening," as when Elijah heard the gentle blowing that signified the end of a violent natural phenomenon: ". . . He wrapped his face in his mantle, and went out, and stood in the entering in of the cave" (1 Kin 19:13). **(7)** In the plural form, *pethach* sometimes **(7a)** represents the "city gates" themselves: "And her [Zion's] gates shall lament and mourn . . ." (Is 3:26). **(7b)** This form of the word is used as a figure for one's lips; in Mic 7:5, for example, the prophet mourns the low morality of his people and advises his hearers to trust no one, telling them to guard their lips (literally, the "openings" of their mouths). **(8)** In its first biblical occurrence, *pethach* is used figuratively. The heart of men is depicted as a house or building with the Devil crouching at the "entrance," ready to subdue it utterly and destroy its occupant (Gen 4:7). See: TWOT—1854a; BDB—835d.

6608. פֵּתַח {1x} **pêthach**, *pay'-thakh;* from 6605; *opening* (fig.) i.e. *disclosure:*—entrance {1x}. See: TWOT—1854b; BDB—836a.

פְּתֻחַ **pâthûach**. See 6603.

6609. פְּתִחָה {1x} **pᵉthîchâh**, *peth-ee-khaw';* from 6605; something *opened,* i.e. a *drawn* sword:—drawn sword {1x}. See: TWOT—1854d; BDB—836a.

6610. פִּתְחוֹן {2x} **pithchôwn**, *pith-khone';* from 6605; *opening* (the act):—open {1x}, opening {1x}. See: TWOT—1854c; BDB—836a.

6611. פְּתַחְיָה {4x} **Pᵉthachyâh**, *peth-akh-yaw';* from 6605 and 3050; *Jah has opened; Pethachjah*, the name of four Isr.:—Pethakiah {4x}. See: BDB—836a.

6612. פְּתִי {19x} **pᵉthîy**, *peth-ee';* or

פֶּתִי **pethîy**, *peh'-thee;* or

פְּתָאִי **pᵉthâʾîy**, *peth-aw-ee';* from 6601; *silly* (i.e. *seducible*):—foolish {2x}, simple {15x}, simplicity {1x}, simple ones {1x}. See: TWOT—1853a; BDB—834a, 834b, 834c, 836a.

6613. פְּתַי {2x} **pᵉthay** (Aram.), *peth-ah'-ee;* from a root corresp. to 6601; *open*, i.e. (as noun) *width:*—breadth {2x}. See: TWOT—2952; BDB—1109b.

6614. פְּתִיגִיל {1x} **pᵉthîygîyl**, *peth-eeg-eel';* of uncert. der.; prob. a figured *mantle* for holidays:—stomacher {1x}. See: TWOT—1856; BDB—836c.

6615. פְּתַיּוּת {1x} **pᵉthayûwth**, *peth-ah-yooth';* from 6612; *silliness* (i.e. *seducibility*):—simple {1x}. See: TWOT—1853a; BDB—834c, 836b.

6616. פָּתִיל {11x} **pâthîyl**, *paw-theel';* from 6617; *twine:*—bound {1x}, bracelet {2x}, lace {4x}, line {1x}, ribband {1x}, thread {1x}, wire {1x}. See: TWOT—1857a; BDB—836d.

6617. פָּתַל {5x} **pâthal**, *paw-thal';* a prim. root; to *twine*, i.e. (lit.) to *struggle* or (fig.) *be* (morally) *tortuous:*—shew self froward {1x}, forward {2x}, shew self unsavoury {1x}, wrestle {1x}. See: TWOT—1857; BDB—836c.

6618. פְּתַלְתֹּל {1x} **pᵉthaltôl**, *peth-al-tole';* from 6617; *tortuous* (i.e. crafty):—crooked {1x}. See: TWOT—1857b; BDB—836d.

6619. פִּתֹם {1x} **Pîthôm**, *p e-thome';* of Eg. der.; *Pithom*, a place in Egypt:—Pithom {1x}. See: TWOT—1857b; BDB—837a.

6620. פֶּתֶן {6x} **pethen**, *peh'-then;* from an unused root mean. to *twist;* an *asp* (from its *contortions*):—adder {2x}, asp {4x}. See: TWOT—1858a; BDB—837a.

6621. פֶּתַע {7x} **pethaʿ**, *peh'-thah;* from an unused root mean. to *open* (the eyes); a *wink*, i.e. *moment* [comp. 6597] (used only [with or without prep.] adv. *quickly* or *unexpectedly*):—at an instant {1x}, suddenly {4x}, × very {1x}. See: TWOT—1859; BDB—837b.

6622. פָּתַר {9x} **pâthar**, *paw-thar';* a prim. root; to *open* up, i.e. (fig.) *interpret* (a dream):—interpret {4x}, interpreted {3x}, interpreter {1x}, interpretation {1x}. See: TWOT—1860; BDB—837a.

6623. פִּתְרוֹן {5x} **pithrôwn**, *pith-rone';* or

פִּתְרֹן **pithrôn**, *pith-rone';* from 6622; *interpretation* (of a dream):—interpretation {5x}. See: TWOT—1860a; BDB—837a.

6624. פַּתְרוֹס {5x} **Pathrôwç**, *path-roce';* of Eg. der.; *Pathros*, a part of Egypt:—Pathros {5x}. See: BDB—837d.

6625. פַּתְרֻסִי {2x} **Pathrûçîy**, *path-roo-see';* patrial from 6624; a *Pathrusite*, or inhab. of Pathros:—Pathrusim {2x}. See: BDB—837d.

פַּתְשֶׁגֶן **pathshegen**. See 6572.

6626. פָּתַת {1x} **pathath**, *paw-thath';* a prim. root; to *open*, i.e. *break:*—part {1x}. See: TWOT—1862; BDB—834b, 837d.

ץ

6627. צָאָה **tsâʾâh**, *tsaw-aw';* from 3318; *issue*, i.e. (human) *excrement:*—that which cometh from thee {1x}, that cometh out of; {2x}. See: TWOT—1884a; BDB—838a, 844b.

צֹאָה **tsôʾâh**. See 6675.

צְאוֹן **tsᵉʾôwn**. See 6629.

6628. צֶאֱל {2x} **tseʾel**, *tseh'-el;* from an unused root mean. to *be slender;* the *lotus* tree:—shady trees {2x}. See: TWOT—1863; BDB—838a.

6629. צֹאן {274x} **tsôʾn**, *tsone;* or

צְאוֹן **tsᵉʾôwn** (Psa. 144:13) *tseh-one';* from an unused root mean. to *migrate;* a collect. name for a *flock* (of sheep or goats); also fig. (of men):—flock {138x}, sheep {110x}, cattle {15x}, shepherd + 7462 {2x}, lamb + 1121 {2x}, lamb {1x}, sheep + 4480 {1x}, sheepcotes + 1448 {1x}, sheepfold + 1448 {1x}, sheepfold + 4356 {1x}, sheepshearers + 1494 {1x}, shepherd + 7462 {1x}.

Ts'own means flock; small cattle; sheep; goats. **(1)** The primary meaning of *ts'own* is small cattle, to be distinguished from baqar (1241 - herd). **(2)** The word may refer to **(2a)** sheep only (1 Sa 25:2), or **(2b)** to both sheep and goats (Gen 30:33). **(3)** The flock was important economically with the animals being **(3a)** eaten (1 Sa 14:32; Ps 44:11), **(3b)** shorn for their wool (Gen 31:19), **(3c)** milked (Deut 32:14), and offered as a sacrifice (Gen 4:4). **(4)** Metaphorically, it applies to people (Eze 36:38) with God viewed as the shepherd (Ps 100:3; Ps 23; 79:13; Mic 7:14). **(5)** God's people are considered as **(5a)** sheep for the slaughter (Ps 44:22); **(5b)** a flock without a shepherd (1 Kin 22:17; Zec 10:2; 13:7); **(5c)** guided astray by their shepherds, or leaders (Jer 50:6); **(5d)** individually going astray (Is 53:6); and **(5e)** prophetically promised to be regathered **(5e1)** under Messiah (Jer 23:3) **(5e2)** as Israel's Shepherd (Exe 34:23–24). See: 1864a; BDB—838a.

6630. צַאֲנָן {1x} **Tsaʾănân**, *tsah-an-awn';* from the same as 6629 used denom.; *sheep pasture; Zaanan*, a place in Pal.:—Zaanan {1x}. See: BDB—838c.

6631. צֶאֱצָא {11x} **tseʾĕtsâ**, *tseh-ets-aw';* from 3318; *issue*, i.e. *produce, children:*—that which cometh forth {1x}, which cometh out {1x}, offspring {1x}. See: TWOT—893b; BDB—425c, 838c.

6632. צָב {3x} **tsâb**, *tsawb;* from an unused root mean. to *establish;* a *palanquin* or *canopy* (as a *fixture*); also a species of *lizard* (prob. as clinging *fast*):—covered wagon {1x}, litter {1x}, tortoise {1x}. See: TWOT—1866a, 1867a; BDB—838c, 839d.

6633. צָבָא {13x} **tsâbâʾ**, *tsaw-baw';* a prim. root; to *mass* (an army or servants):—fight {4x}, assemble {3x}, mustered {2x}, warred {2x}, perform {1x}, wait {1x}.

Tsaba', as a verb, means "to wage war, to muster an army, to serve in worship." **(1)** *Tsaba'* means "to wage war" in Num 31:7: "And they warred against the Midianites, as the Lord commanded Moses. . . ." **(2)** The word is used in 2 Kin 25:19 to refer to "mustering an army." **(3)** Another sense of *tsaba'* appears in Num. 4:23 with the meaning of "serving in worship": ". . . all that enter in to perform the service, to do the work in the tabernacle of the congregation." See: TWOT—1865; BDB—838c, 1109b.

6634. צְבָא {10x} **tsᵉbâʾ** (Aram.), *tseb-aw';* corresp. to 6633 in the fig. sense of *summoning* one's wishes; to *please:*—will {9x}, his will {1x}. See: TWOT—2953; BDB—1109b.

6635. צָבָא {485x} **tsâbâʾ**, *tsaw-baw';* or (fem.)

צְבָאָה **tsᵉbâʾâh**, *tseb-aw-aw';* from 6633; a *mass* of persons (or fig. things), espec. reg. organized for war (an *army*); by impl. a *campaign*, lit. or fig. (spec. *hardship, worship*):—host {393x}, war {41x}, army {29x}, battle {5x}, service {5x}, appointed time {3x}, warfare {2x}, soldiers {1x}, company {1x}, misc. {5x}.

Tsaba', as a noun, means "host; military service; war; army; service; labor; forced labor; conflict." **(1)** This word involves several interrelated ideas: a group; impetus; difficulty; and force. **(1a)** These ideas undergird the general concept of "service" which one does for or under a superior rather than for himself. **(1b)** *Tsaba'* is usually applied to "military service" but is sometimes used of "work" in general (under or for a superior). **(1c)** In Num 1:2–3 the word means "military service": "Take ye the sum of all the congregation of the children of Israel . . . from twenty years old and upward, all that are able to go forth to war in Israel. . . ." **(1d)** The idea is more concrete in Josh 22:12, where the word represents serving in a military campaign: "And when the children of Israel heard of it, the whole congregation of the children of Israel gathered themselves together at Shiloh, to go to war against them." **(1e)** Num 31:14 uses *tsaba'* of the actual battling itself: "And Moses was wroth with the officers of the host [army], . . . which came from the battle."

(2) The word can also represent an "army host": **(2a)** "And Eleazer the priest said unto the men of war which went to the battle . . ." (Num 31:21). **(2b)** Even clearer is Num 31:48: "And the officers which were over thousands of the host, the captains of thousands, and captains of hundreds, came near unto Moses. **(2c)** "This meaning first appears in Gen 21:22, which mentions Phichol, the captain of Abimelech's "army." **(3)** At several points this is the meaning of the feminine plural: "And it shall be, when the officers have made an end of speaking unto the people, that they shall make captains of the armies to lead the people" (Deut 20:9). **(4)** In Num 1, 2, and 10, where *tsaba'* occurs with regard to a census of Israel, it is suggested that this was a military census by which God organized His "army" to march through the wilderness. **(4a)** Some scholars have noted that the plan of the march, or the positioning of the tribes, recalls the way ancient armies were positioned during military campaigns. **(4b)** On the other hand, groupings of people might be indicated regardless of military implications, as seems to be the case in passages such as Ex 6:26: "These are that Aaron and Moses, to whom the Lord said, Bring out the children of Israel from the land of Egypt according to their armies."

(5) That *tsaba'* can refer to a "nonmilitary host" is especially clear in Ps 68:11: "The Lord gave the word: great was the company of those that published it." **(6)** The phrase "hosts of heaven" signifies the stars as visual indications of the gods of the heathen: **(6a)** "And them that worship the host of heaven upon the housetops; and them that worship and that swear by the Lord, and that swear by Malcham . . ." (Zeph 1:5). **(6b)** This meaning first appears in Deut 4:19: "And lest thou lift up thine eyes unto heaven, and when thou seest the sun, and the moon, and the stars, *even* all the host of heaven, shouldest be driven to worship them, and serve them, which the LORD thy God hath divided unto all nations under the whole heaven."

(7) Sometimes this phrase refers to the "host of heaven," or the angels: "And [Micaiah] said, Hear thou therefore the word of the Lord: I saw the Lord sitting on his throne, and all the host of heaven [the angels] standing by him on his right hand and on his left" (1 Kin 22:19). **(7a)** God Himself is the commander of this "host" (Dan 8:10–11). **(7b)** In Josh 6:14 the commander of the "host" of God confronted Joshua. **(7c)** This heavenly "host" not only worships God but serves to do all His will: "Bless ye the Lord, all ye his hosts; ye ministers of his, that do his pleasure" (Ps 103:21). **(7d)** Another meaning of the phrase "the host(s) of heaven" is simply "the numberless stars": "As the host of heaven cannot be numbered, neither the sand of the sea measured: so will I multiply the seed of David my servant, and the Levites that minister unto me" (Jer 33:22). **(7e)** This phrase can include all the heavenly bodies, as it does in Ps 33:6: "By the word of the Lord were the heavens made; and all the host of them by the breath of his mouth." **(8)** In Gen 2:1 *tsaba'* includes the heavens, the earth, and everything in the creation: "Thus the heavens and the earth were finished, and all the host of them."

(9) The meaning "nonmilitary service in behalf of a superior" emerges in Num 4:2–3: "Take the sum of the sons of Kohath . . . from thirty years old and upward even until fifty years old, all that enter [the service], to do the work in the tabernacle of the congregation." **(10)** In Job 7:1 the word represents the burdensome everyday "toil" of mankind: "Is there not an appointed time to man upon earth? Are not his days also like the days of a hireling?" **(11)** In Job 14:14 *tsaba'* seems to represent "forced labor." **(12)** In Dan 10:1 the word is used for "conflict": "In the third year of Cyrus king of Persia a thing was revealed unto Daniel, whose name was called Belteshazzar; and the thing *was* true, but the time appointed *was* long: and he understood the thing, and had understanding of the vision." See: TWOT—1865a, 1865b; BDB—219b, 838d.

6636. צְבֹאִים {5x} **Tsᵉbôʾiym**, *tseb-o-eem'*; or (more correctly)

צְבִיִּים **Tsᵉbîyîym**, *tseb-ee-yeem'*; or

צְבִיִם **Tsᵉbîyîm**, *tseb-ee-yeem'*; plur. of 6643; *gazelles; Tseboïm* or *Tsebijim*, a place in Pal.:—Zeboim {3x}, Zeboiim {2x}. See: BDB—839c, 840d.

6637. צֹבֵבָה {1x} **Tsôbêbâh**, *tso-bay-baw'*; fem. act. part. of the same as 6632; the *canopier* (with the art.); *Tsobebah*, an Israelitess:—Zobebah {1x}. See: BDB—839d.

6638. צָבָה {3x} **tsâbâh**, *tsaw-baw'*; a prim. root; to *amass*, i.e. *grow turgid;* spec. to *array* an army against:—swell {2x}, fight {1x}. See: TWOT—1868; BDB—839d.

6639. צָבֶה {1x} **tsâbeh**, *tsaw-beh'*; from 6638; *turgid:*—swell {1x}. See: TWOT—1868a; BDB—839d.

צֹבָה **Tsôbâh**. See 6678.

6640. צְבוּ {1x} **tsᵉbûw** (Aram.), *tseb-oo'*; from 6634; prop. *will;* concr. an *affair* (as a matter of *determination*):—purpose {1x}. See: TWOT—2953a; BDB—1109c.

6641. צָבוּעַ {1x} **tsâbûwaᶜ**, *tsaw-boo'-ah;* pass. part. of the same as 6648; *dyed* (in stripes), i.e. the *hyena:*—speckled {1x}. See: TWOT—1872b; BDB—840c.

6642. צָבַט {1x} **tsâbaṭ**, *tsaw-bat'*; a prim. root; to *grasp*, i.e. *hand* out:—reached {1x}. See: TWOT—1871; BDB—840b.

6643. צְבִי {32x} **tsᵉbîy**, *tseb-ee'*; from 6638 in the sense of *prominence; splendor* (as *conspicuous*); also a *gazelle* (as *beautiful*):—roe {9x}, roebuck {5x}, glory {8x}, glorious {6x}, beautiful {1x}, beauty {1x}, goodly {1x}, pleasant {1x}. See: TWOT—1869a, 1870a; BDB—839c, 840a.

6644. צִבְיָא {1x} **Tsibyâʾ**, *tsib-yaw'*; for 6645; *Tsibja*, an Isr.:—Zibia {1x}. See: BDB—840b.

6645. צִבְיָה {2x} **Tsibyâh**, *tsib-yaw'*; for 6646; *Tsibjah*, an Israelitess:—Zibiah {2x}. See: BDB—840b.

6646. צְבִיָּה {2x} **tsᵉbîyâh**, *tseb-ee-yaw'*; fem. of 6643; a *female* gazelle:—roe {2x}. See: TWOT—1870b; BDB—840b.

צְבִיִּים **Tsᵉbîyîym**. See 6636.

צְבָיִם **Tsᵉbâyîm**. See 6380.

6647. צְבַע {5x} **tsᵉbaᶜ** (Aram.), *tseb-ah'*; a root corresp. to that of 6648; to *dip:*—wet {5x}. See: TWOT—2954; BDB—1109c.

6648. צֶבַע {3x} **tsebaᶜ**, *tseh'-bah;* from an unused root mean. to *dip* (into coloring fluid); a *dye:*—diverse colours {3x}. See: TWOT—1872a; BDB—840c, 1109c.

6649. צִבְעוֹן {8x} **Tsibᶜôwn**, *tsib-one'*; from the same as 6648; *variegated; Tsibon*, an Idumæan:—Zibeon {8x}. See: BDB—840d.

6650. צְבֹעִים {2x} **Tsᵉbôᶜîym**, *tseb-o-eem'*; plur. of 6641; *hyenas; Tseboïm*, a place in Pal.:—Zeboim {2x}. See: BDB—840d.

6651. צָבַר {7x} **tsâbar**, *tsaw-bar'*; a prim. root; to *aggregate:*—heap up {3x}, heap {1x}, gather {2x}, lay {1x}. See: TWOT—1874; BDB—840d.

6652. צִבֻּר {1x} **tsibbûr**, *tsib-boor'*; from 6551; a *pile:*—heap {1x}. See: TWOT—1874a; BDB—840d.

6653. צֶבֶת {1x} **tsebeth**, *tseh'-beth;* from an unused root appar. mean. to *grip;* a *lock* of stalks:—handful {1x}. See: TWOT—1875a; BDB—841a.

6654. צַד {33} **tsad**, *tsad;* contr. from an unused root mean. to *sidle* off; a *side;* fig. an *adversary:*—side {9x}beside {3x}, another {1x}. See: TWOT—1876a; BDB—841a, 1109c.

6655. צַד {2x} **tsad** (Aram.), *tsad;* corresp. to 6654; used adv. (with prep.) at or upon the *side* of:—concerning {1x}, against {1x}. See: TWOT—2955; BDB—1109c.

6656. צְדָא {1x} **tsᵉdâʾ** (Aram.), *tsed-aw'*; from an unused root corresp. to 6658 in the sense of *intentness;* a (sinister) *design:*—true {1x}. Syn.: 539, 543, 571, 3330. See: TWOT—2956; BDB—1109c.

6657. צְדָד {2x} **Tsᵉdâd**, *tsed-awd'*; from the same as 6654; a *siding; Tsedad*, a place near Pal.:—Zedad {2x}. See: BDB—841a.

6658. צָדָה {3x} **tsâdâh**, *tsaw-daw'*; a prim. root; to *chase;* by impl. to *desolate:*—wait {1x}, hunt {1x}, destroyed {1x}. Syn.: 5362, 5422, 5595. See: TWOT—1877, 1878; BDB—841b, 1109c.

צֵדָה **tsêdâh**. See 6720.

6659. צָדוֹק {53x} **Tsâdôwq**, *tsaw-doke'*; from 6663; *just; Tsadok*, the name of eight or nine Isr.:—Zadok {53x}. See: BDB—843b.

6660. צְדִיָּה {2x} **tsᵉdîyâh**, *tsed-ee-yaw'*; from 6658; *design* [comp. 6656]:—laying of wait {2x}. See: TWOT—1877a; BDB—841b, 1109c.

6661. צִדִּים {1x} **Tsiddîym**, *tsid-deem'*; plur. of 6654; *sides; Tsiddim* (with the art.), a place in Pal.:—Ziddim {1x}. See: BDB—841b.

6662. צַדִּיק {206x} **tsaddîyq**, *tsad-deek'*; from 6663; *just:*—righteous {162x}, just {42x}, righteous man {1x}, lawful {1x}.

Tsaddiyq, as an adjective, means "righteous; just." **(1)** The word is used of God in Ex 9:27: "I have sinned this time: the Lord is righteous, and I and my people are wicked." **(2)** *Tsaddiq* is used of a nation in Gen 20:4: ". . . And he said, Lord, wilt thou slay also a righteous nation?" See: TWOT—1879c; BDB—843a.

צִדֹנִי **Tsîdônîy**. See 6722.

6663. צָדַק {41x} **tsâdaq**, *tsaw-dak'*; a prim. root; to *be* (caus. *make*) *right* (in a moral or forensic sense):—justify {23x}, righteous {10x}, just {3x}, justice {2x}, cleansed {1x}, clear ourselves {1x}, righteousness {1x}.

The basic meaning of *tsadaq* is to be righteous, be in the right, be justified, be just. **(1)** Originally this word meant to be stiff or straight. **(1a)** This word is used of man as regarded as having obtained deliverance from condemnation, and as being thus entitled to a certain inheritance. **(1b)** Thus a man is accounted or dealt with as righteous. It is really the reception and exercise of *tsedeq* (6664). **(1c)** Nowhere is the issue of righteousness more appropriate than in the problem of the suffering of the righteous presented to us in Job, **(1c1)** where the verb occurs 17 times. **(1c2)** Apart from the Book of Job the frequency of *tsadaq* in the various books is small. **(1d)** The first occurrence of the verb is in Gen 38:26, where Judah admits that Tamar was just in her demands: "She hath been more righteous than I; because that I gave her not to Shelah my son."

(2) The basic meaning of *tsadaq* is "to be righteous." **(2a)** It is a legal term which involves the whole process of justice. **(2b)** God "is righteous" in all of His relations, and **(2c)** in comparison with Him man is not righteous: "Shall mortal man be more just [righteous] than God?" (Job 4:17). **(3)** In a derived sense, the case presented may be characterized as a just cause in that all facts indicate that the person is to be cleared of all charges. **(3a)** Isaiah called upon the nations to produce witnesses who might testify that their case was right: "Let them bring forth their witnesses that they may be justified: or let them hear, and say, It is truth" (43:9). **(3b)** Job was concerned about his case and defended it before his friends: ". . . Though I were righteous, yet would I not answer, but I would make supplication to my judge" (9:15). **(4)** *Tsadaq* may also be used to signify the outcome of the verdict, when a man is pronounced "just" and is judicially cleared of all charges. Job believed that the Lord would ultimately vindicate him against his opponents (Job 13:18).

(5) In its causative pattern, the meaning of the verb brings out more clearly the sense of a judicial pronouncement of innocence: "If there be a controversy between men, and they come unto judgment, that the judges may judge them; then they shall justify [*tsadaq*] the righteous [*tsaddiq*], and condemn the wicked" (Deut 25:1). **(6)** The Israelites were charged with upholding righteousness in all areas of life. **(6a)** When the court system failed because of corruption, the wicked were falsely "justified" and the poor were robbed of justice because of trumped-up charges. **(6b)** Absalom, thus, gained a large following by promising justice to the landowner (2 Sa 15:4). **(7)** God, however, assured Israel that justice would be done in the end: "Thou shalt not wrest the judgment of thy poor in his cause. Keep thee far from a false matter; and the innocent and righteous slay thou not: for I will not justify the wicked" (Ex 23:6–7). The righteous person followed God's example. **(8)** The psalmist exhorts his people to change their judicial system: "Defend the poor and fatherless: do justice to the afflicted and needy" (Ps 82:3). **(9)** Job's ultimate hope was in God's declaration of justification. The Old Testament is in agreement with this hope. When injustice prevails, God is the One who "justifies." See: TWOT—1879; BDB—842c, 1109d.

6664. צֶדֶק {116x} **tsedeq**, *tseh'-dek;* from 6663; the *right* (nat., mor. or legal); also (abstr.) *equity* or (fig.) *prosperity:*—righteousness {77x}, just {11x}, justice {10x}, righteous {8x}, righteously {3x}, right {3x}, righteous cause {1x}, unrighteousness {1x}, misc. {2x}.

Tsedeq, the masculine noun form, and tsedaqah (6666), the feminine form of the noun, **(1)** mean "righteousness." **(1a)** The feminine form of the word tsedaqah, which occurs 157 times, is found throughout the Old Testament (except for Ex, Lev, 2 Kin, Eccl, Lam, Hab, and Zeph). **(1b)** *Tsedeq,* which occurs 119 times, is found mainly in poetic literature. **(1b1)** The first usage of *tsedeq* is: "Ye shall do no unrighteousness in judgment: thou shalt not respect the person of the poor, nor honor the person of the mighty: but in righteousness shalt thou judge thy neighbor" (Lev 19:15); and **(1b2)** of *tsedaqah* is: "[Abram] believed in the Lord; and he counted it to him for righteousness" (Gen 15:6).

(2) Exegetes have spilled much ink in an attempt to understand contextually the words *tsedeq* and tsedaqah. **(2a)** The conclusions of the researchers indicate a two-fold significance: relational and legal. **(2a1)** On the one hand, the relationships among people and of a man to his God can be described as *tsedeq,* supposing the parties are faithful to each other's expectations. It is a **relational word. (2a2)** In Jacob's proposal to Laban, Jacob used the word *tsedaqah* to indicate the relationship. The KJV gives the following translation of tsedaqah: "So shall my righteousness answer for me in time to come, when it shall come for my hire before thy face . . ." (Gen 30:33). **(2b)** On the other hand "righteousness" as an abstract or as the **legal status** of a relationship is also present in the Old Testament. The *locus classicus* is Gen 15:6: ". . . And he [the Lord] counted it to him [Abraham] for righteousness." **(2c)** Regrettably, in a discussion of the dynamic versus the static sense of the word, one or the other wins out, though both elements are present. **(2c1)** The books of Psalms and of the prophets particularly use the sense of **"righteousness" as a state;** cf. "Hearken to me, ye that follow after righteousness, ye that seek the Lord: look unto the rock whence ye are hewn, and to the hole of the pit whence ye are digged" (Is 51:1); and **(2c2)** "My righteousness is near; my salvation is gone forth, and mine arms shall judge the people; the isles shall wait upon me, and on mine arm shall they trust" (Is 51:5). **(2d)** Thus, in the discussion of the two nouns below the meanings lie between the dynamic and the static.

(3) *Tsedeq* and *tsedaqah* are legal terms signifying justice in conformity **(3a)** with the legal corpus (the Law; Deut 16:20), **(3b)** the judicial process (Jer 22:3), **(3c)** the justice of the king as judge (1 Kin 10:9; Ps 119:121; Prov 8:15), and also **(3d)** the source of justice, God Himself: "Judge me, O Lord my God, according to thy righteousness; and let them not rejoice over me. . . . And my tongue shall speak of thy righteousness and of thy praise all the day long" (Ps 35:24, 28). **(4)** The word "righteousness" also embodies all that God expects of His people. **(4a)** The verbs associated with "righteousness" indicate the practicality of this concept. One judges, deals, sacrifices, and speaks righteously; and one learns, teaches, and pursues after righteousness. **(4b)** Based upon a special relationship with God, the Old Testament saint asked God to deal righteously with him: "Give the king thy judgments, O God, and thy righteousness unto the king's son" (Ps 72:1). See: TWOT—1879a; BDB—575d, 841c.

6665. צִדְקָה {1x} **tsidqâh** (Aram.), *tsid-kaw';* corresp. to 6666; *beneficence:*—righteousness {1x}. See: TWOT—2957; BDB—1109d.

6666. צְדָקָה {157x} **tsᵉdâqâh**, *tsed-aw-kaw';* from 6663; *rightness* (abstr.), subj. (*rectitude*), obj. (*justice*), mor. (*virtue*) or fig. (*prosperity*):—righteousness {128x}, justice {15x}, right {9x}, righteous acts {3x}, moderately {1x}, righteously {1x}. For a complete discussion, see 6664. See: TWOT—1879b; BDB—842a, 1109d.

6667. צִדְקִיָּה {63x} **Tsidqîyâh**, *tsid-kee-yaw';* or

צִדְקִיָּהוּ **Tsidqîyâhûw**, *tsid-kee-yaw'-hoo;* from 6664 and 3050; *right of Jah; Tsidkijah,* the name of six Isr.:—Zedekiah {62x}, Zidkijah {1x}. See: BDB—843b.

6668. צָהַב {1x} **tsâhab**, *tsaw-hab';* a prim. root; to *glitter,* i.e. *be golden* in color:—fine {1x}. See: TWOT—1880; BDB—843c.

6669. צָהֹב {3x} **tsâhôb**, *tsaw-obe';* from 6668; *golden* in color:—yellow {3x}. See: TWOT—1880a; BDB—843c.

6670. צָהַל {9x} **tsâhal**, *tsaw-hal';* a prim. root; to *gleam,* i.e. (fig.) *be cheerful;* by transf. to *sound* clear (of various animal or human expressions):—cry aloud {2x}, bellow {1x}, neighed {1x}, cry out {1x}, rejoiced {1x}, shine {1x}, shout {1x}, lift up {1x}. See: TWOT—1881, 1882; BDB—843c, 843d.

6671. צָהַר {1x} **tsâhar**, *tsaw-har';* a prim. root; to *glisten;* used only as denom. from 3323, to *press* out *oil:*—make oil {1x}. See: TWOT—1883d; BDB—844a.

6672. צֹהַר {24x} **tsôhar**, *tso'-har;* from 6671; a *light* (i.e. *window*): dual *double light,* i.e. *noon:*—noon {11x}, noonday {9x}, day {1x}, midday {1x}, noontide + 6256 {1x}, window {1x}. See: TWOT—1883a, 1883b; BDB—843d, 844a.

6673. צַו {9x} **tsav**, *tsav;* or

צָו **tsâv;**, *tsawv;* from 6680; an *injunction:*—precept {8x}, commandment {1x}. See: TWOT—1887c; BDB—844b, 846c.

6674. צוֹא {2x} **tsôwʼ**, *tso;* or

צֹא **tsôʼ**, *tso;* from an unused root mean. to *issue; soiled* (as if *excrementitious*):—filthy {2x}. See: TWOT—1884; BDB—838a, 844b.

6675. צוֹאָה {5x} **tsôwʼâh**, *tso-aw';* or

צֹאָה **tsôʼâh**, *tso-aw':* fem. of 6674; *excrement;* gen. *dirt;* fig. *pollution:*—dung {2x}, filthiness {2x}, filth {1x}. See: TWOT—1884b; BDB—838a, 844b. [*marg. for* 2716.]

6676. צַוַּאר {3x} **tsavvaʼr** (Aram.), *tsav-var';* corresp. to 6677:—neck {3x}. See: TWOT—2958; BDB—1109d.

6677. צַוָּאר {42x} **tsavvâʼr**, *tsav-vawr';* or

צַוָּר **tsavvâr** (Neh. 3:5), *tsav-vawr';* or

צַוָּרֹן **tsavvârôn** (Cant. 4:9), *tsav-vaw-rone';* or (fem.)

צַוָּארָה **tsavvâʼrâh** (Mic. 2:3) *tsav-vaw-raw';* intens. from 6696 in the sense of *binding;* the back of the *neck* (as that on which burdens are *bound*):—neck {42x}. See: TWOT—1897a; BDB—844b, 848b, 848c, 850a, 1109d.

6678. צוֹבָא {12x} **Tsôwbâʼ**, *tso-baw';* or

צוֹבָה **Tsôwbâh**, *tso-baw';* or

צֹבָה **Tsôbâh**, *tso-baw';* from an unused root mean. to *station;* a *station; Zoba* or *Zobah,* a region of Syria:—Zobah {10x}, Zoba {2x}. See: BDB—844b.

6679. צוּד {18x} **tsûwd**, *tsood;* a prim. root; to *lie* alongside (i.e. in wait); by impl. to *catch* an animal (fig. men); (denom. from 6718) to *victual* (for a journey):—hunt {13x}, take {2x}, chased {1x}, provision {1x}, sore {1x}. See: TWOT—1885; BDB—844c, 845b.

6680. צָוָה {494x} **tsâvâh**, *tsaw-vaw';* a prim. root; (intens.) to *constitute, enjoin:*—command {514x}, charge {39x}, commandment {9x}, appoint {5x}, bade {3x}, order {3x}, commander {1x}, misc. {4x}.

This word signifies to set up or appoint. *Tsavah,* as a verb, means "to command." **(1)** Essentially, this verb refers to verbal communication by which a superior "orders" or "commands" a subordinate. **(1a)** The word implies the content of what was said. **(1b)** Pharaoh "ordered" ("commanded") his men concerning Abraham, and they escorted Abraham and his party out of Egypt (Gen 12:20). **(1c)** This "order" defines an action relevant to a specific situation. **(2)** *Tsavah* can also connote "command" in the sense of the establishment of a rule by which a subordinate is to act in every recurring similar situation. **(2a)** In the Garden of Eden (the first appearance of this word in the Bible), God "commanded" ("set down the rule"): "Of every tree of the garden thou mayest freely eat: . . ." (Gen 2:16). **(2b)** In this case, the word does not contain the content of the action but focuses on the action itself. **(2c)** One of the recurring formulas in the Bible is "X did all that Y commanded him"—e.g., Ruth "did according to all that her mother-in-law bade her" (Ruth 3:6). This means that she carried out Naomi's "orders." **(2d)** A similar formula, "X did just as Y commanded," is first found in Num 32:25, where the sons of Reuben and Gad say to Moses that they "will do as my lord commandeth." **(2e)** These formulas indicate the accomplishment of, or the intention to accomplish, the "orders" of a superior.

(3) The verb *tsavah* can be used of a commission or charge, such as the act of "commanding," "telling," or "sending" someone to do a particular task. **(3a)** In Gen 32:4, Jacob "commissioned" his servants to deliver a particular message to his brother Esau. They acted as his emissaries. **(3b)** Jacob commissioned (literally, "commanded") his sons to bury him in the cave of Machpelah (Gen 49:30), and then he died. This "command" constituted a last will and testament—an obligation or duty. The verb again indicates, therefore, appointing someone to be one's emissary. **(4)** The most frequent subject of this verb is God. **(4a)** However, He is not to be questioned or "commanded" to explain the work of His hands (Is 45:11). **(4b)** He tells Israel that His "commands" are unique, requiring an inner commitment and not just external obedience, as the commands of men do (Gen 29:13). **(4c)** His "ordering" is given to Moses from above the mercy seat (Ex 25:22) and from His "commands" at Sinai (Lev 7:38; cf. 17:1ff.). **(4d)** At other times when He "commands," the thing simply occurs; His word is active and powerful (Ps 33:9). **(4e)** He also issues "orders" through and to the prophets (Jer 27:4) who explain, apply, and speak His "commands" (Jer 1:17). See: TWOT—1887; BDB—845b.

6681. **צָוַח** {1x} **tsâvach**, *tsaw-vakh';* a prim. root; to *screech* (exultingly):—shout {1x}. See: TWOT—1888; BDB—846d.

6682. **צְוָחָה** {4x} **tsᵉvâchâh**, *tsev-aw-khaw';* from 6681; a *screech* (of anguish):—cry {2x}, crying {1x}, complaining {1x}. See: TWOT—1888a; BDB—846d.

6683. **צוּלָה** {1x} **tsûwlâh**, *tsoo-law';* from an unused root mean. to *sink;* an *abyss* (of the sea):—deep {1x}. See: TWOT—1889a; BDB—846d.

6684. **צוּם** {21x} **tsûwm**, *tsoom;* a prim. root; to *cover* over (the mouth), i.e. to *fast:*—fast {20x}, at all {1x}. See: TWOT—1890; BDB—847a.

6685. **צוֹם** {26x} **tsôwm**, *tsome;* or

צֹם **tsôm**, *tsome;* from 6684; a *fast:*—fast {16x}, fasting {9x}, fasted + 6684 {1x}. See: TWOT—1890a; BDB—847b.

6686. **צוּעָר** {5x} **Tsûwʿâr**, *tsoo-awr';* from 6819; *small; Tsuär,* an Isr.:—Zuar {5x}. See: BDB—859b.

6687. **צוּף** {3x} **tsûwph**, *tsoof;* a prim. root; to *overflow:*—flow {1x}, overflow {1x}, swim {1x}. See: TWOT—1892; BDB—847b.

6688. **צוּף** {2x} **tsûwph**, *tsoof;* from 6687; *comb* of honey (from *dripping*):—honeycomb {2x}. See: TWOT—1892a; BDB—847b.

6689. **צוּף** {4x} **Tsûwph**, *tsoof;* or

צוֹפַי **Tsôwphay**, *tso-fah'-ee;* or

צִיף **Tsîyph**, *tseef;* from 6688; *honeycomb; Tsuph* or *Tsophai* or *Tsiph,* the name of an Isr. and of a place in Pal.:—Zuph {4x}. See: BDB—847c, 851c.

6690. **צוֹפַח** {2x} **Tsôwphach**, *tso-fakh';* from an unused root mean. to *expand, breadth; Tsophach,* an Isr.:—Zophah {2x}. See: BDB—860c.

צוֹפַי **Tsôwphay**. See 6689.

6691. **צוֹפַר** {4x} **Tsôwphar**, *tso-far';* from 6852; *departing; Tsophar,* a friend of Job:—Zophar {4x}. See: BDB—862b.

6692. **צוּץ** {9x} **tsûwts**, *tsoots;* a prim. root; to *twinkle,* i.e. *glance;* by anal. to *blossom* (fig. *flourish*):—flourish {5x}, blossom {2x}, bloomed {1x}, shewing {1x}. See: TWOT—1893, 1894; BDB—847c, 847d.

6693. **צוּק** {11x} **tsûwq**, *tsook;* a prim. root; to *compress,* i.e. (fig.) *oppress, distress:*—distress {5x}, oppressor {2x}, sore {1x}, press {1x}, straiten {1x}. See: TWOT—1895; BDB—847d.

6694. **צוּק** {3x} **tsûwq**, *tsook;* a prim. root [rather ident. with 6693 through the idea of *narrowness* (of orifice)]; to *pour* out, i.e. (fig.) *smelt, utter:*—pour {2x}, molten {1x}. See: TWOT—1896; BDB—848b, 862c.

6695. **צוֹק** {4x} **tsôwq**, *tsoke;* or (fem.)

צוּקָה **tsûwqâh**, *tsoo-kaw';* from 6693; a *strait,* i.e. (fig.) *distress:*—anguish {4x}. See: TWOT—1895a, 1895b; BDB—848a.

6696. **צוּר** {38x} **tsûwr**, *tsoor;* a prim. root; to *cramp,* i.e. *confine* (in many applications, lit. and fig., formative or hostile):—besiege {21x}, lay siege {3x}, distress {3x}, bind {2x}, adversaries {1x}, assault {1x}, bags {1x}, beset {1x}, cast {1x}, fashioned {1x}, fortify {1x}, inclose {1x}, bind up {1x}. See: TWOT—1898, 1899, 1900; BDB—848d, 849a, 849b, 1109d.

6697. **צוּר** {78x} **tsûwr**, *tsoor;* or

צֻר **tsûr**, *tsoor;* from 6696; prop. a *cliff* (or sharp rock, as *compressed*); gen. a *rock* or *boulder;* fig. a *refuge;* also an *edge* (as *precipitous*):—rock {64x}, strength {5x}, sharp {2x}, God {2x}, beauty {1x}, edge {1x}, stones {1x}, mighty One {1x}, strong {1x}.

(1) *Tsur* means rocky wall or cliff (Ex 17:6; 33:21–22). **(2)** It frequently means rocky hill or mountains (Is 2:10, 19). **(3)** Figuratively, **(3a)** the rock flowing with honey and oil pictures the abundant overflowing blessing of God (Deut 32:13); **(3b)** The rock (or mountain) serves as a figure of security (Ps 61:2), firmness (Job 14:18), and something that endures (Job 19:24). **(4)** *Tsur* can mean rocky ground or perhaps a large flat rock (2 Sa 21:10; Prov 30:19). **(5)** The word means boulder in the sense of a rock large enough to serve as an altar (Judg 6:21). **(6)** Rock frequently pictures God's support and defense of His people (Deut 32:15). **(7)** It can be a name **(7a)** of God (Deut 32:4), or **(7b)** of heathen gods (Deut 32:31). **(8)** Abraham is the source (rock) from which Israel was hewn (Is 51:1). See: TWOT—1901a; BDB—849c, 866a. See also 1049.

6698. **צוּר** {5x} **Tsûwr**, *tsoor;* the same as 6697; *rock; Tsur,* the name of a Midianite and of an Isr.:—Zur {5x}. See: BDB—849d.

צוֹר **Tsôwr**. See 6865.

צַוָּר **tsavvâr**. See 6677.

6699. **צוּרָה** {4x} **tsûwrâh**, *tsoo-raw';* fem. of 6697; a *rock* (Job 28:10); also a *form* (as if *pressed* out):—form {4x}. See: TWOT—1900a; BDB—849b, 849c, 849d.

צַוָּרֹן **tsavvârôn**. See 6677.

6700. **צוּרִיאֵל** {1x} **Tsûwrîyʾêl**, *tsoo-ree-ale';* from 6697 and 410; *rock of God; Tsuriël,* an Isr.:—Zuriel {1x}. See: BDB—849d.

6701. **צוּרִישַׁדַּי** {5x} **Tsûwrîyshadday**, *tsoo-ree-shad-dah'-ee;* from 6697 and 7706; *rock of* (the) *Almighty; Tsurishaddai,* an Isr.:—Zurishaddai {5x}. See: BDB—849d.

6702. **צוּת** {1x} **tsûwth**, *tsooth;* a prim. root; to *blaze:*—burn {1x}. See: TWOT—899; BDB—850a.

6703. **צַח** {4x} **tsach**, *tsakh;* from 6705; *dazzling,* i.e. *sunny, bright,* (fig.) *evident:*—white {1x}, clear {1x}, plainly {1x}, dry {1x}. See: TWOT—1903a; BDB—850a.

צִחָא **Tsîchâʾ**. See 6727.

6704. **צִחֶה** {1x} **tsîcheh**, *tsee-kheh';* from an unused root mean. to *glow; parched:*—dried up {1x}. See: TWOT—1902a; BDB—850a.

6705. **צָחַח** {1x} **tsâchach**, *tsaw-khakh';* a prim. root; to *glare,* i.e. *be dazzling* white:—whiter {1x}. See: TWOT—1903; BDB—850a.

6706. **צְחִיחַ** {5x} **tsᵉchîyach**, *tsekh-ee'-akh;* from 6705; *glaring,* i.e. *exposed* to the bright sun:—top {4x}, higher places {1x}. See: TWOT—1903b; BDB—850a.

6707. **צְחִיחָה** {1x} **tsᵉchîychâh**, *tsekh-ee-khaw';* fem. of 6706; a *parched* region, i.e. the *desert:*—dry land {1x}. See: TWOT—1903c; BDB—850b.

6708. **צְחִיחִי** {1x} **tsᵉchîychîy**, *tsekh-ee-khee';* from 6706; *bare* spot, i.e. in the *glaring* sun:—higher place {1x}. See: TWOT—1903b; BDB—850a.

6709. **צַחֲנָה** {1x} **tsachănâh**, *tsakh-an-aw';* from an unused root mean. to *putrefy; stench:*—ill savour {1x}. See: TWOT—1904a; BDB—850b.

6710. **צַחְצָחָה** {1x} **tsachtsâchâh**, *tsakh-tsaw-khaw';* from 6705; a *dry* place, i.e. *desert:*—drought {1x}. See: TWOT—1903d; BDB—850b.

6711. **צָחַק** {13x} **tsâchaq**, *tsaw-khak';* a prim. root; to *laugh* outright (in merriment or scorn); by impl. to *sport:*—laugh {6x}, mock {4x}, sport {2x}, play {1x}. See: TWOT—1905; BDB—850b.

6712. **צְחֹק** {2x} **tsᵉchôq**, *tsekh-oke';* from 6711; *laughter* (in pleasure or derision):—laugh {2x}. See: TWOT—1905a; BDB—850b.

6713. **צַחַר** {1x} **tsachar**, *tsakh'-ar;* from an unused root mean. to *dazzle; sheen,* i.e. *whiteness;*—white {1x}. See: TWOT—1906a; BDB—850c.

6714. **צֹחַר** {5x} **Tsôchar**, *tso'-khar;* from the same as 6713; *whiteness; Tsochar,* the name of a Hittite and of an Isr.:—Zoar {4x}, Jezoar {1x}. See: BDB—850c. comp. 3328.

6715. **צָחֹר** {1x} **tsâchôr**, *tsaw-khore';* from the same as 6713; *white:*—white {1x}. See: TWOT—1906b; BDB—850c.

6716. **צִי** {4x} **tsîy**, *tsee;* from 6680; a *ship* (as a *fixture*):—ship {4x}. See: TWOT—1907; BDB—850d, 851c.

6717. **צִיבָא** {16x} **Tsîybâʾ**, *tsee-baw';* from the same as 6678; *station; Tsiba,* an Isr.:—Ziba {16x}. See: BDB—850d.

6718. **צַיִד** {19x} **tsayid**, *tsah'-yid;* from a form of 6679 and mean. the same; the *chase;* also *game* (thus taken); (gen.) *lunch* (espec. for a journey):—venison {8x}, hunter {3x}, victuals {2x}, provision {2x}, hunting {1x}, catch {1x}, food {1x}, hunting {1x}. See: TWOT—1885a, 1886a; BDB—844d, 845b.

6719. **צַיָּד** {1x} **tsayâd**, *tsah'-yawd;* from the same as 6718; a *huntsman:*—hunter {1x}. See: TWOT—1885b; BDB—844d.

6720. **צֵידָה** {10x} **tsêydâh**, *tsay-daw';* or

צֵדָה **tsêdâh**, *tsay-daw';* fem. of 6718; *food:*—victuals {6x}, provision {2x}, meat {1x}, venison {1x}. See: TWOT—1886b; BDB—841b, 845b.

6721. **צִידוֹן** {22x} **Tsîydôwn**, *tsee-done';* or

צִידֹן **Tsîydôn**, *tsee-done';* from 6679 in the sense of *catching* fish; *fishery; Tsidon,* the name of a son of Canaan, and of a place in Pal.:—Zidon {20x}, Sidon {2x}. See: BDB—850d.

6722. **צִידֹנִי** {16x} **Tsîydônîy**, *tsee-do-nee';* patrial from 6721; a *Tsidonian* or inhab. of Tsidon:—Zidonians {10x}, Sidonians {5x}, them of Zidon {1x}. See: BDB—841b, 851a.

6723. **צִיָּה** {16x} **tsîyâh**, *tsee-yaw';* from an unused root mean. to *parch; aridity;*

concr. a *desert:*—dry {7x}, dry land {2x}, wilderness {2x}, drought {2x}, dry places {1x}, solitary place {1x}, barren {1x}. See: TWOT—1909a; BDB—851a.

6724. צִיוֹן {2x} **tsîyôwn**, *tsee-yone';* from the same as 6723; a *desert:*—dry place {2x}. See: TWOT—1909b; BDB—851b, 851c.

6725. צִיּוּן {3x} **tsîyûwn**, *tsee-yoon';* from the same as 6723 in the sense of *conspicuousness* [comp. 5329]; a monumental or guiding *pillar:*—title {1x}, waymark {1x}, sign {1x}. See: TWOT—1887a; BDB—846b, 851c.

6726. צִיּוֹן {154x} **Tsîyôwn**, *tsee-yone';* the same (reg.) as 6725; *Tsijon* (as a permanent *capital*), a mountain of Jerusalem:—Zion {153x}, Sion {1x}. See: TWOT—1910; BDB—851b.

6727. צִיחָא {3x} **Tsîychâʾ**, *tsee-khaw';* or

צִחָא **Tsîchâʾ**, *tsee-khaw';* as if fem. of 6704; *drought; Tsicha,* the name of two Nethinim:—Ziha {3x}. See: BDB—850a, 851c.

6728. צִיִּי {6x} **tsîyîy**, *tsee-ee';* from the same as 6723; a *desert-dweller,* i.e. *nomad* or wild *beast:*—desert {3x}, wilderness {3x}. See: TWOT—1908; BDB—850d, 851c.

6729. צִינֹק {1x} **tsîynôq**, *tsee-noke';* from an unused root mean. to *confine;* the *pillory:*—stocks {1x}. See: TWOT—1941a; BDB—851c, 857b.

6730. צִיעֹר {1x} **Tsîyᶜôr**, *tsee-ore';* from 6819; *small; Tsior,* a place in Pal.:—Zior {1x}. See: BDB—851c, 859b.

צִיף **Tsîyph**. See 6689.

6731. צִיץ {15x} **tsîyts**, *tseets;* or

צִץ **tsîts**, *tseets;* from 6692; prop. *glistening,* i.e. a burnished *plate;* also a *flower* (as *bright* colored); a *wing* (as *gleaming* in the air):—flower {10x}, plate {3x}, blossom {1x}, wings {1x}. See: TWOT—1911; BDB—751c, 847c, 847d, 851c, 862c.

6732. צִיץ {1x} **Tsîyts**, *tseets;* the same as 6731; *bloom; Tsits,* a place in Pal.:—Ziz {1x}. See: BDB—847d, 851d.

6733. צִיצָה {1x} **tsîytsâh**, *tsee-tsaw';* fem. of 6731; a *flower:*—flower {1x}. See: BDB—847d, 851c.

6734. צִיצִת {4x} **tsîytsîth**, *tsee-tseeth';* fem. of 6731; a *floral* or *wing*-like projection, i.e. a *fore-lock* of hair, a *tassel:*—fringe {3x}, lock {1x}. See: TWOT—1912; BDB—851d.

צִיקְלַג **Tsîyqᵉlag**. See 6860.

6735. צִיר {12x} **tsîyr**, *tseer;* from 6696; a *hinge* (as *pressed* in turning); also a *throe* (as a physical or mental *pressure*); also a *herald* or errand-doer (as *constrained* by the principal):—ambassador {4x}, pang {3x}, messenger {2x}, pains {1x}, hinge {1x}, sorrow {1x}. See: TWOT—1913a, 1914a, 1914b; BDB—851d, 852a. comp. 6736.

6736. צִיר {2x} **tsîyr**, *tseer;* the same as 6735; a *form* (of beauty; as if *pressed* out, i.e. *carved*); hence, an (idolatrous) *image:*—idol {1x}, variant {1x}. Syn.: 5566, 6754, 8544. See: TWOT—1900b; BDB—849c, 851d.

6737. צָיַר {1x} **tsâyar**, *tsaw-yar';* a denom. from 6735 in the sense of *ambassador;* to *make an errand,* i.e. *betake* oneself:—ambassador {1x}. See: BDB—851d.

6738. צֵל {49x} **tsêl**, *tsale;* from 6751; *shade,* whether lit. or fig.:—shadow {45x}, defence {3x}, shade {1x}. See: TWOT—1921a; BDB—852a, 853b, 853c.

6739. צְלָא {2x} **tsᵉlâʾ** (Aram.), *tsel-aw';* prob. corresp. to 6760 in the sense of *bowing; pray:*—pray {2x}. Syn.: 577, 1156, 4994, 6279, 6419, 7592. See: TWOT—2959; BDB—1109d.

6740. צָלָה {3x} **tsâlâh**, *tsaw-law';* a prim. root; to *roast:*—roast {3x}. See: TWOT—1915; BDB—852a.

6741. צִלָּה {3x} **Tsillâh**, *tsil-law';* fem. of 6738; *Tsillah,* an antediluvian woman:—Zillah {3x}. See: BDB—852a, 853c.

6742. צְלוּל {2x} **tsᵉlûwl**, *tsel-ool';* from 6749 in the sense of *rolling;* a (round or flattened) *cake:*—cake {1x}, variant {1x}. See: TWOT—1922a; BDB—853d.

6743. צָלַח {65x} **tsâlach**, *tsaw-lakh';* or

צָלֵחַ **tsâlêach**, *tsaw-lay'-akh;* a prim. root; to *push* forward, in various senses (lit. or fig., tran. or intr.):—prosper {44x}, come {6x}, prosperous {5x}, come mightily {2x}, effected {1x}, good {1x}, meet {1x}, break out {1x}, went over {1x}, misc. {3x}.

Tsaleach means "to succeed, prosper." **(1)** The word is first found in Gen 24:21: ". . . whether the Lord had made his journey prosperous [literally, "to prosper"] or not." **(2)** This word generally expresses the idea of a successful venture, as contrasted with failure. The source of such success is God: ". . . as long as he sought the Lord, God made him to prosper" (2 Chr 26:5). **(3)** In spite of that, the circumstances of life often raise the question, "Wherefore doth the way of the wicked prosper?" (Jer 12:1). **(4)** It is sometimes used in such a way as to indicate "victory": "In your majesty ride prosperously" (Ps 45:4). See: TWOT—1916, 1917; BDB—852a, 852b, 1109d.

6744. צְלַח {4x} **tsᵉlach** (Aram.), *tsel-akh';* corresp. to 6743; to *advance* (tran. or intr.):—prosper {3x}, promote {1x}. See: TWOT—2960; BDB—1109d.

6745. צֵלָחָה {1x} **tsêlâchâh**, *tsay-law-khaw';* from 6743; something *protracted* or flattened out, i.e. a *platter:*—pan {1x}. See: TWOT—1918a; BDB—852c.

6746. צְלֹחִית {1x} **tsᵉlôchîyth**, *tsel-o-kheeth';* from 6743; something *prolonged* or tall, i.e. a *vial* or salt-*cellar:*—cruse {1x}. See: TWOT—1918c; BDB—852d.

6747. צַלַּחַת {3x} **tsallachath**, *tsal-lakh'-ath;* from 6743; something *advanced* or deep, i.e. a *bowl;* fig. the *bosom:*—bosom {2x}, dish {1x}. See: TWOT—1918b; BDB—852c.

6748. צָלִי {3x} **tsâlîy**, *tsaw-lee';* pass. part. of 6740; *roasted:*—roast {3x}. See: TWOT—1915a; BDB—852a, 852d.

6749. צָלַל {1x} **tsâlal**, *tsaw-lal';* a prim. root; prop. to *tumble* down, i.e. *settle* by a waving motion:—sink {1x}. See: TWOT—1920; BDB—853a. comp. 6750, 6751.

6750. צָלַל {4x} **tsâlal**, *tsaw-lal';* a prim. root [rather ident. with 6749 through the idea of *vibration*]; to *tinkle,* i.e. *rattle* together (as the ears in *reddening* with shame, or the teeth in *chattering* with fear):—tingle {3x}, quiver {1x}. See: TWOT—1919; BDB—852d.

6751. צָלַל {2x} **tsâlal**, *tsaw-lal';* a prim. root [rather ident. with 6749 through the idea of *hovering* over (comp. 6754)]; to *shade,* as twilight or an opaque object:—begin to be dark {1x}, shadowing {1x}. See: TWOT—1921; BDB—853a, 1094b.

6752. צֵלֶל {4x} **tsêlel**, *tsay'-lel;* from 6751; *shade:*—shadow {4x}. See: TWOT—1921a; BDB—853b.

6753. צְלֶלְפּוֹנִי {1x} **Tsᵉlelpôwnîy**, *tsel-el-po-nee';* from 6752 and the act. part. of 6437; *shade-facing; Tselelponi,* an Israelitess:—Hazelelponi {1x}. See: BDB—853c.

6754. צֶלֶם {17x} **tselem**, *tseh'-lem;* from an unused root mean. to *shade;* a *phantom,* i.e. (fig.) *illusion, resemblance;* hence, a representative *figure,* espec. an *idol:*—image {16x}, vain shew {1x}.

(1) This word means statue (2 Kin 11:18; Num 33:52). **(2)** It signifies a replica (1 Sa 6:5). **(3)** In Eze 23:14 *tselem* represents a wall painting of some Chaldeans. **(4)** The word means image in the sense of essential nature: **(4a)** human nature in its internal and external characteristics rather than an exact duplicate: "And Adam lived an hundred and thirty years, and begat *a son* in his own likeness, after his image; and called his name Seth:" (Gen 5:3); or **(4b)** God made man in His own image, **(4b1)** reflecting some of His own perfections: perfect in knowledge, righteousness, and holiness, and with dominion over the creatures (Gen 1:26). **(4b2)** Being created in God's image meant being created male and female, in a loving unity of more than one person (Gen 1:27). **(5)** In Ps 39:6 *tselem* means shadow of a thing which represents the original very imprecisely, or it means merely a phantom, a thing which represents the original more closely but lacks its essential characteristic [reality]: "Surely every man walketh in a vain shew: surely they are disquieted in vain: he heapeth up *riches,* and knoweth not who shall gather them." **(6)** In Ps 73:20 the word represents a dream image: "As a dream when *one* awaketh; *so,* O Lord, when thou awakest, thou shalt despise their image." See: TWOT—1923a; BDB—853d, 1109d.

6755. צֶלֶם {17x} **tselem** (Aram.), *tseh'-lem;* or

צְלֵם **tsᵉlem** (Aram.), *tsel-em';* corresp. to 6754; an idolatrous *figure:*—form {16x}, image {1x}. See: TWOT—2961; BDB—1109d.

6756. צַלְמוֹן {3x} **Tsalmôwn**, *tsal-mone';* from 6754; *shady; Tsalmon,* the name of a place in Pal. and of an Isr.:—Zalmon {2x}, Salmon {1x}. See: BDB—854a.

6757. צַלְמָוֶת {18x} **tsalmâveth**, *tsal-maw'-veth;* from 6738 and 4194; *shade of death,* i.e. the *grave* (fig. *calamity*):—shadow of death {18x}. See: TWOT—1921b; BDB—853c, 854a.

6758. צַלְמֹנָה {2x} **Tsalmônâh**, *tsal-mo-naw';* fem. of 6757; *shadiness; Tsalmonah,* a place in the desert:—Zalmonah {2x}. See: BDB—854a.

6759. צַלְמֻנָּע {12x} **Tsalmunnâᶜ**, *tsal-moon-naw';* from 6738 and 4513; *shade has been denied; Tsalmunna,* a Midianite:—Zalmunna {12x}. See: BDB—854a.

6760. צָלַע {4x} **tsâlaᶜ**, *tsaw-lah';* a prim. root: prob. to *curve;* used only as denom. from 6763, to *limp* (as if *one-sided*):—halt {4x}. See: TWOT—1925; BDB—854b.

6761. צֶלַע {3x} **tselaᶜ**, *tseh'-lah;* from 6760; a *limping* or *full* (fig.):—halt {1x}, adversity {1x}, variant {1x}. See: TWOT—1925a; BDB—854c.

6762. צֶלַע {2x} **Tselaᶜ**, *tseh'-lah;* the same as 6761; *Tsela,* a place in Pal.:—Zelah {2x}. See: BDB—854b.

6763. צֵלָע {41x} **tsêlâᶜ**, *tsay-law'*; or (fem.)

צַלְעָה **tsalᶜâh**, *tsal-aw'*; from 6760; a *rib* (as *curved*), lit. (of the body) or fig. (of a door, i.e. *leaf*); hence, a *side*, lit. (of a person) or fig. (of an object or the sky, i.e. *quarter*); arch. a (espec. floor or ceiling) *timber* or *plank* (single or collect., i.e. a *flooring*):—side {19x}, chamber {11x}, boards {2x}, corners {2x}, rib {2x}, another {1x}, beams {1x}, halting {1x}, leaves {1x}, planks {1x}. See: TWOT—1924a; BDB—854b, 1106d.

6764. צָלָף {1x} **Tsâlâph**, *tsaw-lawf'*; from an unused root of unknown mean.; *Tsalaph*, an Isr.:—Zalaph {1x}. See: BDB—854c.

6765. צְלָפְחָד {11x} **Tsᵉlophchâd**, *tsel-of-chawd'*; from the same as 6764 and 259; *Tselophchad*, an Isr.:—Zelophehad {11x}. See: BDB—854c.

6766. צֶלְצַח {1x} **Tseltsach**, *tsel-tsakh'*; from 6738 and 6703; *clear shade; Tseltsach*, a place in Pal.:—Zelzah {1x}. See: BDB—854c.

6767. צְלָצַל {6x} **tsᵉlâtsal**, *tsel-aw-tsal'*; from 6750 redupl.; a *clatter*, i.e. (abstr.) *whirring* (of wings); (concr.) a *cricket;* also a *harpoon* (as *rattling*), a *cymbal* (as *clanging*):—cymbal {3x}, locust {1x}, spear {1x}, shadowing {1x}. See: TWOT—1919a, 1919b, 1919c; BDB—852d, 854c.

6768. צֶלֶק {2x} **Tseleq**, *tseh'-lek;* from an unused root mean. to *split; fissure; Tselek*, an Isr.:—Zelek {2x}. See: BDB—854c.

6769. צִלְּתַי {2x} **Tsillᵉthay**, *tsil-leth-ah'-ee;* from the fem. of 6738; *shady; Tsillethai*, the name of two Isr.:—Zilthai {2x}. See: BDB—853c, 854c.

צֹם **tsôm**. See 6685.

6770. צָמֵא {10x} **tsâmêʾ**, *tsaw-may';* a prim. root; to *thirst* (lit. or fig.):—thirst {5x}, athirst {2x}, thirsty {1x}, suffer thirst {1x}, suffer thirst {1x}. See: TWOT—1926; BDB—854c.

6771. צָמֵא {9x} **tsâmêʾ**, *tsaw-may';* from 6770; *thirsty* (lit. or fig.):—thirsty {7x}, thirst {2x}. See: TWOT—1926b; BDB—854d.

6772. צָמָא **tsâmâʾ**, *tsaw-maw';* from 6770; *thirst* (lit. or fig.):—thirst {16x}, thirsty {1x}. See: TWOT—1926a; BDB—854d.

6773. צִמְאָה {1x} **tsimʾâh**, *tsim-aw';* fem. of 6772; *thirst* (fig. of *libidinousnes*):—thirst {1x}. See: TWOT—1926c; BDB—854d.

6774. צִמָּאוֹן {3x} **tsimmâʾôwn**, *tsim-maw-one';* from 6771; a *thirsty* place, i.e. *desert:*—drought {1x}, dry ground {1x}, thirsty land {1x}. See: TWOT—1926d; BDB—855a.

6775. צָמַד {5x} **tsâmad**, *tsaw-mad';* a prim. root; to *link*, i.e. *gird;* fig. to *serve*, (mentally) *contrive:*—join {3x}, fasten {1x}, frame {1x}. See: TWOT—1927; BDB—855a.

6776. צֶמֶד {15x} **tsemed**, *tseh'-med;* a *yoke* or *team* (i.e. *pair*); hence, an *acre* (i.e. day's task for a yoke of cattle to plow):—yoke {7x}, couple {4x}, two {2x}, together {1x}, acres {1x}. See: TWOT—1927a; BDB—855a.

6777. צַמָּה {4x} **tsammâh**, *tsam-maw';* from an unused root mean. to *fasten* on; a *veil:*—locks {4x}. See: TWOT—1929a; BDB—855b, 855d.

6778. צִמּוּק {4x} **tsammûwq**, *tsam-mook';* from 6784; a cake of *dried* grapes:—cluster of raisins {2x}, bunch of raisins {2x}. See: TWOT—1930a; BDB—856a.

6779. צָמַח {33x} **tsâmach**, *tsaw-makh';* a prim. root; to *sprout* (tran. or intr., lit. or fig.):—grow {13x}, spring forth {6x}, spring up {4x}, grow up {2x}, bring forth {2x}, bud {2x}, spring out {2x}, beareth {1x}, bud forth {1x}. See: TWOT—1928; BDB—855b.

6780. צֶמַח {12x} **tsemach**, *tseh'-makh;* from 6779; a *sprout* (usually concr.), lit. or fig.:—Branch {4x}, bud {3x}, branch {1x}, that which grew {1x}, spring {1x}, springing {1x}, grew {1x}. See: TWOT—1928a; BDB—855c.

6781. צָמִיד {7x} **tsâmîyd**, *tsaw-meed';* or

צָמִד **tsâmîd**, *tsaw-meed';* from 6775; a *bracelet* or *arm-clasp;* gen. a *lid:*—bracelet {6x}, covering {1x}. See: TWOT—1927b, 1927c; BDB—855b.

6782. צַמִּים {2x} **tsammîym**, *tsam-meem';* from the same as 6777; a *noose* (as *fastening*); fig. *destruction:*—robber {2x}. See: TWOT—1929b; BDB—855d.

6783. צְמִיתֻת {2x} **tsᵉmîythûth**, *tsem-ee-thooth';* or

צְמִתֻת **tsᵉmîthûth**, *tsem-ee-thooth';* from 6789; *excision*, i.e. *destruction;* used only (adv.) with prep. pref. to *extinction*, i.e. *perpetually:*—for ever {2x}. Syn.: 753, 5331, 5703, 8548. See: TWOT—1932a; BDB—855d, 856c.

6784. צָמַק {1x} **tsâmaq**, *tsaw-mak';* a prim. root; to *dry* up:—dry {1x}. See: TWOT—1930; BDB—855d.

6785. צֶמֶר {16x} **tsemer**, *tseh'-mer;* from an unused root prob. mean. to *be shaggy; wool:*—woollen {5x}, wool {11x}. See: TWOT—1931a; BDB—856a, 1107a.

6786. צְמָרִי {2x} **Tsᵉmârîy**, *tsem-aw-ree';* patrial from an unused name of a place in Pal.; a *Tsemarite* or branch of the Canaanites:—Zemarite {2x}. See: BDB—856a.

6787. צְמָרַיִם {2x} **Tsᵉmârayim**, *tsem-aw-rah'-yim;* dual of 6785; *double fleece; Tsemarajim*, a place in Pal.:—Zemaraim {2x}. See: BDB—856b.

6788. צַמֶּרֶת {5x} **tsammereth**, *tsam-meh'-reth;* from the same as 6785; *fleeciness*, i.e. *foliage:*—top {3x}, highest branch {2x}. See: TWOT—1931b; BDB—856a.

6789. צָמַת {15x} **tsâmath**, *tsaw-math';* a prim. root; to *extirpate* (lit. or fig.):—cut off {8x}, destroy {5x}, vanish {1x}, consume {1x}. See: TWOT—1932; BDB—856b.

צְמִתֻת **tsᵉmîthûth**. See 6783.

6790. צִן {10x} **Tsîn**, *tseen;* from an unused root mean. to *prick;* a *crag; Tsin*, a part of the Desert:—Zin {10x}. See: BDB—851c, 856c.

6791. צֵן {2x} **tsên**, *tsane;* from an unused root mean. to *be prickly;* a *thorn;* hence, a cactus-*hedge:*—thorn {2x}. See: TWOT—1936a; BDB—856c, 856d.

6792. צֹנֵא {2x} **tsônêʾ**, *tso-nay';* or

צֹנֶה **tsôneh**, *tso-neh';* for 6629; a *flock:*—sheep {2x}. See: TWOT—1864a, 1933; BDB—856c.

6793. צִנָּה {22x} **tsinnâh**, *tsin-naw';* fem. of 6791; a *hook* (as *pointed*); also a (large) *shield* (as if guarding by *prickliness*); also *cold* (as *piercing*):—shield {10x}, buckler {5x}, target {5x}, hook {1x}, cold {1x}. See: TWOT—1936b, 1937a, 1938a; BDB—856c, 856d, 857a.

6794. צִנּוּר {2x} **tsinnûwr**, *tsin-noor';* from an unused root perh. mean. to *be hollow;* a *culvert:*—gutter {1x}, waterspout {1x}. See: TWOT—1942a; BDB—857c.

6795. צָנַח {3x} **tsânach**, *tsaw-nakh';* a prim. root; to *alight;* (tran.) to *cause to descend*, i.e. *drive* down:—lighted {2x}, fasten {1x}. See: TWOT—1934; BDB—856c.

6796. צָנִין {2x} **tsânîyn**, *tsaw-neen';* or

צָנִן **tsânîn**, *tsaw-neen';* from the same as 6791; a *thorn:*—thorn {2x}. See: TWOT—1936c; BDB—856d.

6797. צָנִיף {6x} **tsânîyph**, *tsaw-neef';* or

צָנוֹף **tsânôwph**, *tsaw-nofe';* or (fem.)

צָנִיפָה **tsânîyphâh**, *tsaw-nee-faw';* from 6801; a *head-dress* (i.e. piece of cloth *wrapped* around):—diadem {2x}, mitre {2x}, hood {1x}, variant {1x}. See: TWOT—1940a; BDB—857b.

6798. צָנַם {1x} **tsânam**, *tsaw-nam';* a prim. root; to *blast* or *shrink:*—withered {1x}. See: TWOT—1935; BDB—856d.

6799. צְנָן {1x} **Tsᵉnân**, *tsen-awn';* prob. for 6630; *Tsenan*, a place near Pal.:—Zenan {1x}. See: BDB—838c, 857a.

צָנִן **tsânîn**. See 6796.

6800. צָנַע {2x} **tsânaᶜ**, *tsaw-nah';* a prim. root; to *humiliate:*—lowly {1x}, humbly {1x}. See: TWOT—1939; BDB—857a.

6801. צָנַף {3x} **tsânaph**, *tsaw-naf';* a prim. root; to *wrap*, i.e. *roll* or *dress:* attired {1x}, violently turn {1x}, surely {1x}. See: TWOT—1940; BDB—857a.

6802. צְנֵפָה {1x} **tsᵉnêphâh**, *tsen-ay-faw';* from 6801; a *ball:*—toss {1x}. See: TWOT—1940b; BDB—857b.

6803. צִנְצֶנֶת {1x} **tsintseneth**, *tsin-tseh'-neth;* from the same as 6791; a *vase* (prob. a vial *tapering* at the top):—pot {1x}. See: TWOT—1938b; BDB—857a.

6804. צַנְתָּרָה {1x} **tsantârâh**, *tsan-taw-raw';* prob. from the same as 6794; a *tube:*—pipe {1x}. See: TWOT—1942b; BDB—857c.

6805. צָעַד {8x} **tsâᶜad**, *tsaw-ad';* a prim. root; to *pace*, i.e. *step* regularly; (upward) to *mount;* (along) to *march;* (down and caus.) to *hurl:*—go {3x}, march {3x}, run over {1x}, bring {1x}. See: TWOT—1943; BDB—857c.

6806. צַעַד {14x} **tsaᶜad**, *tsah'-ad;* from 6804; a *pace* or *regular step:*—step {11x}, pace {1x}, goings {1x}, go {1x}. See: TWOT—1943a; BDB—857d.

6807. צְעָדָה {3x} **tsᵉᶜâdâh**, *tseh-aw-daw';* fem. of 6806; a *march;* (concr.) an (ornamental) *ankle-chain:*—going {2x}, ornaments of the legs {1x}. See: TWOT—1943b, 1943c; BDB—857d.

6808. צָעָה {5x} **tsâᶜâh**, *tsaw-aw';* a prim. root; to *tip* over (for the purpose of *spilling* or *pouring* out), i.e. (fig.) *depopulate;* by impl. to *imprison* or *conquer;* (refl.) to *lie down* (for coitus, sexual intercourse):—wander {2x}, captive exile {1x}, travelling {1x}, wanderer {1x}. See: TWOT—1944; BDB—858a.

צָעוֹר **tsâᶜôwr**. See 6810.

6809. צָעִיף {3x} **tsâʿîyph**, *tsaw-eef';* from an unused root mean. to *wrap* over; a *veil:*—vail {3x}. See: TWOT—1946a; BDB—858b.

6810. צָעִיר {22x} **tsâʿîyr**, *tsaw-eer';* or

צָעוֹר **tsâʿôwr**, *tsaw-ore';* from 6819; *little;* (in number) *few;* (in age) *young,* (in value) *ignoble:*—younger {8x}, least {4x}, youngest {3x}, little {2x}, little ones {2x}, small one {1x}, small {1x}, young + 3117 {1x}. See: TWOT—1948a; BDB—859a.

6811. צָעִיר {1x} **Tsâʿîyr**, *tsaw-eer';* the same as 6810; *Tsaïr,* a place in Idumæa:—Zair {1x}. See: BDB—859a.

6812. צְעִירָה {1x} **tseʿîyrâh**, *tseh-ee-raw';* fem. of 6810; *smallness* (of age), i.e. *juvenility:*—youth {1x}. See: TWOT—1948b; BDB—859a.

6813. צָעַן {1x} **tsâʿan**, *tsaw-an';* a prim. root; to *load* up (beasts), i.e. to *migrate:*—taken down {1x}. See: TWOT—1945; BDB—858a.

6814. צֹעַן {7x} **Tsôʿan**, *tso'-an;* of Eg. der.; *Tsoän,* a place in Egypt:—Zoan {7x}. See: BDB—130c, 858a.

6815. צַעֲנַנִּים {2x} **Tsaʿănannîym**, *tsah-an-an-neem';* or (dual)

צַעֲנַיִם **Tsaʿănayim**, *tsah-an-ah'-yim;* plur. from 6813; *removals; Tsaanannim* or *Tsaanajim,* a place in Pal.:—Zaannannim {1x}, Zaanaim {1x}. See: BDB—858b.

6816. צַעְצֻעַ {1x} **tsaʿtsûaʿ**, *tsah-tsoo'-ah;* from an unused root mean. to *bestrew* with carvings; *sculpture:*—image {1x}. See: TWOT—1891a; BDB—847b, 858b.

6817. צָעַק {55x} **tsâʿaq**, *tsaw-ak';* a prim. root; to *shriek;* (by impl.) to *proclaim* (an assembly):—cry {44x}, gather together {4x}, cry out {3x}, at all {1x}, called {1x}, gathered {1x}, call together {1x}.

Tsa'aq means "to cry, cry out, call." **(1)** Its first occurrence is in the record of the suffering of the Israelite bondage in Egypt: ". . . And the children of Israel sighed by reason of the bondage, and they cried [for help] . . ." (Ex 2:23). **(2)** *Tsa'aq* is perhaps most frequently used to indicate the "crying out" for aid in time of emergency, **(2a)** especially "crying out" for divine aid. **(2b)** God often heard this "cry" for help in the time of the judges, as Israel found itself in trouble because of its backsliding (Judg 3:9, 15; 6:7; 10:10). **(3)** The word is used also in appeals to pagan gods (Judg 10:14; Jer 11:12; Jonah 1:5). **(4)** That *tsa'aq* means more than a normal speaking volume is indicated in appeals to the king: "For all *of* my father's house were but dead men before my lord the king: yet didst thou set thy servant among them that did eat at thine own table. What right therefore have I yet to cry any more unto the king?" (2 Sa 19:28). **(5)** The word may imply **(5a)** a "crying out" in distress (1 Sa 4:13), **(5b)** a "cry" of horror (1 Sa 5:10), or **(5c)** a "cry" of sorrow (2 Sa 13:19). **(6)** Used figuratively, it is said that "the stone shall cry out of the wall" (Hab 2:11) of a house that is built by means of evil gain. Syn.: 2199. See: TWOT—1947; BDB—858b.

6818. צְעָקָה {21x} **tsaʿăqâh**, *tsah-ak-aw';* from 6817; a *shriek:*—cry {19x}, crying {2x}. See: TWOT—1947a; BDB—858c.

6819. צָעַר {3x} **tsâʿar**, *tsaw-ar';* a prim. root; to *be small,* i.e. (fig.) *ignoble:*—brought low {1x}, shall be small {1x}, little ones {1x}. See: TWOT—1948; BDB—858d.

6820. צֹעַר {10x} **Tsôʿar**, *tso'ar;* from 6819; *little; Tsoär,* a place E. of the Jordan:—Zoar {10x}. See: BDB—118d, 858d.

6821. צָפַד {1x} **tsâphad**, *tsaw-fad';* a prim. root; to *adhere:*—cleaveth {1x}. See: TWOT—1949; BDB—859b.

6822. צָפָה {37x} **tsâphâh**, *tsaw-faw';* a prim. root; prop. to *lean* forward, i.e. to *peer* into the distance; by impl. to *observe, await:*—watchman {20x}, watch {8x}, behold {2x}, look {2x}, espy {1x}, look up {1x}, waited {1x}, look well {1x}, variant for Zophim {1x}.

I. *Tsapah,* as a verb, means "to overlay, spy, keep watch." **(1)** It occurs for the first time in the Old Testament in the so-called Mizpah Benediction: "The Lord watch between me and thee . . ." (Gen 31:49). **(1a)** The meaning in this context is "to watch" with a purpose, that of seeing that the covenant between Laban and Jacob was kept. **(1b)** Thus, the statement by Laban is more of a threat than a benediction. **(2)** Similarly, when God's "eyes behold the nations" (Ps 66:7), it is much more than a casual look. Perhaps in most uses, the connotation of "to spy" would be the most accurate. **II. As a participle,** *tsaphah* is often used as a noun, tsopeh, meaning "watchman," or one whose task it is "to keep close watch": "But Absalom fled. And the young man that kept the watch lifted up his eyes, and looked, and, behold, there came much people by the way of the hill side behind him" (2 Sa 13:34). See: TWOT—1950; BDB—859b.

6823. צָפָה {46x} **tsâphâh**, *tsaw-faw';* a prim. root [prob. rather ident. with 6822 through the idea of *expansion* in outlook, transferring to act]; to *sheet* over (espec. with metal):—overlay {40x}, covered {5x}, garnished {1x}. See: TWOT—1951; BDB—860a.

6824. צָפָה {1x} **tsâphâh**, *tsaw-faw';* from 6823; an *inundation* (as *covering*):—swim {1x}. See: TWOT—1892b; BDB—847c, 859b.

6825. צְפוֹ {3x} **Tsephôw**, *tsef-o';* or

צְפִי **Tsephîy**, *tsef-ee';* from 6822; *observant; Tsepho* or *Tsephi,* an Idumæan:—Zepho {2x}, Zephi {1x}. See: BDB—859d, 860c.

6826. צִפּוּי {5x} **tsippûwy**, *tsip-poo'-ee;* from 6823; *encasement* (with metal):—covering {3x}, overlay {2x}. See: TWOT—1951a; BDB—860b.

6827. צְפוֹן {1x} **Tsephôwn**, *tsef-one';* prob. for 6837; *Tsephon,* an Isr.:—Zephon {1x}. See: BDB—859d.

6828. צָפוֹן {153x} **tsâphôwn**, *tsaw-fone';* or

צָפֹן **tsâphôn**, *tsaw-fone';* from 6845; prop. *hidden,* i.e. *dark;* used only of the *north* as a quarter (*gloomy* and *unknown*):—north {116x}, northward {24x}, north side {11x}, northern {1x}, north wind {1x}. See: TWOT—1953b; BDB—859d, 860d, 861b.

6829. צָפוֹן {1x} **Tsâphôwn**, *tsaw-fone';* the same as 6828; *boreal; Tsaphon,* a place in Pal.:—Zaphon {1x}. See: BDB—861b.

6830. צְפוֹנִי {1x} **tsephôwnîy**, *tsef-o-nee';* from 6828; *northern:*—northern {1x}. See: TWOT—1953c; BDB—859d, 861a.

6831. צְפוֹנִי {1x} **Tsephôwnîy**, *tsef-o-nee';* patron. from 6827; a *Tsephonite,* or (collect.) desc. of Tsephon:—Zephonites {1x}. See: BDB—859d, 861b.

6832. צְפוּעַ {1x} **tsephûwaʿ**, *tsef-oo'-ah;* from the same as 6848; *excrement* (as *protruded*):—dung {1x}. See: TWOT—1955a; BDB—861c.

6833. צִפּוֹר {40x} **tsippôwr**, *tsip-pore';* or

צִפֹּר **tsippôr**, *tsip-pore';* from 6852; a little *bird* (as *hopping*):—bird {32x}, fowl {6x}, sparrow {2x}. See: TWOT—1959a; BDB—861d, 1110a.

6834. צִפּוֹר {7x} **Tsippôwr**, *tsip-pore';* the same as 6833; *Tsippor,* a Moabite:—Zippor {7x}. See: BDB—862a.

6835. צַפַּחַת {7x} **tsappachath**, *tsap-pakh'-ath;* from an unused root mean. to *expand;* a *saucer* (as *flat*):—cruse {7x}. See: TWOT—1952a; BDB—860b.

6836. צְפִיָּה {1x} **tsephîyâh**, *tsef-ee-yaw';* from 6822; *watchfulness:*—watching {1x}. See: TWOT—1950a; BDB—859d, 860c, 871a.

6837. צִפְיוֹן {1x} **Tsiphyôwn**, *tsif-yone';* from 6822; *watch*-tower; *Tsiphjon,* an Isr.:—Ziphion {1x}. See: BDB—859d, 860c. comp. 6827.

6838. צַפִּיחִת {1x} **tsappîychîth**, *tsap-pee-kheeth';* from the same as 6835; a flat thin *cake:*—wafers {1x}. See: TWOT—1952b; BDB—860c.

6839. צֹפִים {1x} **Tsôphîym**, *tso-feem';* plur. of act. part. of 6822; *watchers; Tsophim,* a place E. of the Jordan:—Zophim {1x}. See: BDB—859c.

6840. צָפִין {1x} **tsâphîyn**, *tsaw-feen';* from 6845; a *treasure* (as *hidden*):—thy hid (treasure) {1x}. See: TWOT—1953a; BDB—860d.

6841. צְפִיר {1x} **tsephîyr** (Aram.), *tsef-eer';* corresp. to 6842; a he-*goat:*—he {1x}. See: TWOT—2963; BDB—1110a.

6842. צָפִיר {6x} **tsâphîyr**, *tsaw-feer';* from 6852; a male *goat* (as *prancing*):—he {3x}, goat {2x}, he goat {1x}. See: TWOT—1962a; BDB—862b, 1110a.

6843. צְפִירָה {3x} **tsephîyrâh**, *tsef-ee-raw';* fem. formed like 6842; a *crown* (as *encircling* the head); also a *turn* of affairs (i.e. *mishap*):—morning {2x}, diadem {1x}. See: TWOT—1960a; BDB—862a.

6844. צָפִית {1x} **tsâphîyth**, *tsaw-feeth';* from 6822; a *sentry:*—watchtower {1x}. See: TWOT—1951b; BDB—860b, 860c.

6845. צָפַן {33x} **tsâphan**, *tsaw-fan';* a prim. root; to *hide* (by *covering* over); by impl. to *hoard* or *reserve;* fig. to *deny;* spec. (favorably) to *protect,* (unfavorably) to *lurk:*—hide {16x}, lay up {7x}, esteemed {1x}, lurk {1x}, hidden ones {1x}, privily {1x}, secret places {1x}, secret {1x}, misc. {4x}. See: TWOT—1953; BDB—860c, 860d.

צָפֹן **tsâphôn**. See 6828.

6846. צְפַנְיָה {10x} **Tsephanyâh**, *tsef-an-yaw';* or

צְפַנְיָהוּ **Tsephanyâhûw**, *tsef-an-yaw'-hoo;* from 6845 and 3050; *Jah has secreted; Tsephanjah,* the name of four Isr.:—Zephaniah {10x}. See: BDB—861b.

6847. צָפְנַת פַּעְנֵחַ {1x} **Tsophnath Paʿnêach**, *tsof-nath' pah-nay'-akh;* of Eg. der.; *Tsophnath-Paneäch,* Joseph's Eg. name:—Zaphnathpaaneah {1x}. See: BDB—861b.

6848. צֶפַע {5x} **tsephaʿ**, *tseh'-fah;* or

צִפְעֹנִי **tsiphʿônîy**, *tsif-o-nee';* from an unused root mean. to *extrude;* a *viper* (as *thrusting* out the tongue, i.e. *hissing*):—

cockatrice {4x}, adder {1x}. See: TWOT—1954a, 1954b; BDB—861c.

6849. צְפִעָה {1x} tsᵉphîʿâh, *tsef-ee-aw';* fem. from the same as 6848; an *outcast* thing:—issue {1x}. See: TWOT—1953a; BDB—861c.

צִפְעֹנִי tsiphʿônîy. See 6848.

6850. צָפַף {4x} tsâphaph, *tsaw-faf';* a prim. root; to *coo* or *chirp* (as a bird):—peep {2x}, chatter {1x}, whisper {1x}. See: TWOT—1957; BDB—861c.

6851. צַפְצָפָה {1x} tsaphtsâphâh, *tsaf tsaw faw';* from 6687; a *willow* (as growing in *overflowed* places):—willow tree {1x}. See: TWOT—1957a; BDB—861d.

6852. צָפַר {1x} tsâphar, *tsaw-far';* a prim. root; to *skip* about, i.e. *return:*—depart early {1x}. See: TWOT—1958; BDB—861d.

6853. צְפַר {4x} tsᵉphar (Aram.), *tsef-ar';* corresp. to 6833; a *bird:*—fowl {3x}, like birds {1x}. See: TWOT—2962; BDB—1110a.

צִפֹּר tsippôr. See 6833.

6854. צְפַרְדֵּעַ {13x} tsᵉphardêaʿ, *tsef-ar-day'-ah;* from 6852 and a word elsewhere unused mean. a *swamp;* a *marsh-leaper,* i.e. *frog:*—frog {13x}. See: TWOT—1963; BDB—862c.

6855. צִפֹּרָה {3x} Tsippôrâh, *tsip-po-raw';* fem. of 6833; *bird; Tsipporah,* Moses' wife:—Zipporah {3x}. See: BDB—862a.

6856. צִפֹּרֶן {2x} tsippôren, *tsip-po'-ren;* from 6852 (in the denom. sense [from 6833] of *scratching*); prop. a *claw,* i.e. (human) *nail;* also the *point* of a style (or pen, tipped with adamant):—nail {1x}, point {1x}. See: TWOT—1961a; BDB—862b, 1094c.

6057. צְפַת {1x} Tsᵉphath, *tsef-ath';* from 6822; *watch*-tower; *Tsephath,* a place in Pal.:—Zephath {1x}. See: BDB—862c.

6858. צֶפֶת {1x} tsepheth, *tseh'-feth;* from an unused root mean. to *encircle;* a *capital* of a column:—chapiter {1x}. See: TWOT—1951c; BDB—860b, 862c.

6859. צְפָתָה {1x} Tsᵉphâthâh, *tsef-aw'-thaw;* the same as 6857; *Tsephathah,* a place in Pal.:—Zephathah {1x}. See: BDB—862c.

צִץ tsits. See 6732.

6860. צִקְלַג {15x} Tsiqlâg, *tsik-lag';* or

צִיקְלַג Tsîyqᵉlag (1 Chron. 12:1, 20), *tsee-kel-ag';* of uncert. der.: *Tsiklag* or *Tsikelag,* a place in Pal.:—Ziklag {15x}. See: BDB—851d, 862c.

6861. צִקְלֹן {1x} tsiqlôn, *tsik-lone';* from an unused root mean. to *wind;* a *sack* (as *tied* at the mouth):—husk {1x}. See: TWOT—1964; BDB—862d.

6862. צַר {105x} tsar, *tsar;* or

צָר tsâr, *tsawr;* from 6887; *narrow;* (as a noun) a *tight* place (usually fig., i.e. *trouble*); also a *pebble* (as in 6864); (tran.) an *opponent* (as *crowding*):—enemy {37x}, adversary {26x}, trouble {17x}, distress {5x}, affliction {3x}, foes {2x}, narrow {2x}, strait {2x}, flint {1x}, sorrow {1x}, misc. {9x} = afflicted, anguish, close, small, tribulation.

Tsar, **as a noun,** means "adversary; enemy; foe; distress; affliction." **(1)** This word also occurs mostly in poetry. **(1a)** In Prov 24:10, *tsar* means "scarcity" or the "distress" caused by scarcity: "*If* thou faint in the day of adversity, thy strength *is* small." **(1b)** The emphasis of the noun is sometimes on the feeling of "dismay" arising from a distressful situation (Job 7:11). In this usage the word *tsar* represents a psychological or spiritual status. **(1c)** In Is 5:30, the word describes conditions that cause distress: ". . . If one look unto the land, behold darkness and sorrow . . ." (cf. Is 30:20). This nuance appears to be the most frequent use represented by *tsar.* **(1d)** The first use of the noun is in Gen 14:20: "And blessed be the most high God, which hath delivered thine enemies into thy hand." **(2)** *Tsar* is a general designation for "enemy." **(2a)** The "enemy" may be a nation (2 Sa 24:13) or, **(2b)** more rarely, the "opponent" of an individual (cf. Gen 14:20; Ps 3:1).

(3) The Lord may also be the "enemy" of His sinful people as His judgment comes upon them (cf. Deut 32:41–43). Hence, the Book of Lamentations describes God as an "adversary" of His people: "He hath bent his bow like an enemy [341 - oyeb]: he stood with his right hand as an adversary [*tsar*], and slew all that were pleasant to the eye in the tabernacle of the daughter of Zion: he poured out his fury like fire" (Lam 2:4). **(4)** *Tsar* means scarcity or the distress caused by scarcity with the emphasis on the psychological or spiritual feeling of dismay arising from that distressful situation (Job 7:11). **(5)** In Is 5:30, the word describes conditions that cause distress (cf. Is 30:20). This nuance appears to be the most frequent use represented by *tsar.* **(6)** *Tsar,* **as an adjective,** describes a space as narrow and easily blocked by a single person (Num 22:26). Syn: The word *tsar* has several synonyms: **(A)** *oyeb* (341), "enemy" (cf. Lam 2:5); **(B)** *sone* (8130), "hater" (Ps 44:7); **(C)** *rodep* (7291), "persecutor" (Ps 119:157); **(D)** *arits* (6184), "tyrant; oppressor" (Job 6:23). See: TWOT—1973a, 1973b, 1974a, 1975a; BDB—862d, 865a, 865d, 866a, 1108a.

6863. צֵר {1x} Tsêr, *tsare;* from 6887; *rock; Tser,* a place in Pal.:—Zer {1x}. See: BDB—862d.

6864. צֹר {2x} tsôr, *tsore;* from 6696; a *stone* (as if *pressed* hard or to a point); (by impl. of use) a *knife:*—sharp stone {1x}, flint {1x}. See: TWOT—1975b; BDB—862d, 863a, 866a.

6865. צֹר {42x} Tsôr, *tsore;* or

צוֹר Tsôwr, *tsore;* the same as 6864; a *rock; Tsor,* a place in Pal.:—Tyrus {22x}, Tyre {20x}. See: TWOT—1965; BDB—850a, 862d, 863c, 866a.

צֻר tsûr. See 6697.

6866. צָרַב {1x} tsârab, *tsaw-rab';* a prim. root; to *burn:*—burned {1x}. See: TWOT—1966; BDB—863a.

6867. צָרֶבֶת {3x} tsârebeth, *tsaw-reh'-beth;* from 6686; *conflagration* (of fire or disease):—burning {2x}, inflammation {1x}. See: TWOT—1966a, 1966b; BDB—863a.

6868. צְרֵדָה {2x} Tsᵉrêdâh, *tser-ay-daw';* or

צְרֵדָתָה Tsᵉrêdâthâh, *tser-ay-daw'-thaw;* appar. from an unused root mean. to *pierce; puncture; Tseredah,* a place in Pal.:—Zereda {1x}, Zeredathah {1x}. See: BDB—863a, 866c.

6869. צָרָה {73x} tsârâh, *tsaw-raw';* fem. of 6862; *tightness* (i.e. fig. *trouble*); tran. a female *rival:*—trouble {44x}, distress {8x}, affliction {7x}, adversity {5x}, anguish {5x}, tribulation {3x}, adversary {1x}.

Tsarah, as a noun, means "distress; straits." **(1)** The 73 appearances of *tsarah* occur in all periods of biblical literature, although most occurrences are in poetry (poetical, prophetical, and wisdom literature). **(2)** *Tsarah* means "straits" or "distress" in a psychological or spiritual sense, which is its meaning in Gen 42:21 (the first occurrence): "We are verily guilty concerning our brother, in that we saw the anguish of his soul, when he besought us, and we would not hear. . . ." See: TWOT—1973c, 1974b; BDB—863a, 865b, 865d.

6870. צְרוּיָה {26x} Tsᵉrûwyâh, *tser-oo-yaw';* fem. pass. part. from the same as 6875; *wounded; Tserujah,* an Israelitess:—Zeruiah {26x}. See: BDB—863b, 863c.

6871. צְרוּעָה {1x} Tsᵉrûwʿâh, *tser-oo-aw';* fem. pass. part. of 6879; *leprous; Tseruäh,* an Israelitess:—Zeruah {1x}. See: BDB—864a.

6872. צְרוֹר {11x} tsᵉrôwr, *tser-ore';* or (short.)

צְרֹר tsᵉrôr, *tser-ore';* from 6887; a *parcel* (as *packed* up); also a *kernel* or *particle* (as if a *package*):—bundle {4x}, bag {3x}, bindeth {1x}, grain {1x}, stone {1x}, Zeror {1x}. See: TWOT—1973e, 1975c; BDB—865c, 866a, 866c.

6873. צָרַח {2x} tsârach, *tsaw-rakh';* a prim. root; to *be clear* (in tone, i.e. *shrill*), i.e. to *whoop:*—cry {1x}, roar {1x}. See: TWOT—1968; BDB—863c.

6874. צְרִי {1x} Tsᵉrîy, *tser-ee';* the same as 6875; *Tseri,* an Isr.:—Zeri {1x}. See: BDB—863b. comp. 3340.

6875. צְרִי {6x} tsᵉrîy, *tser-ee';* or

צֳרִי tsŏrîy, *tsor-ee';* from an unused root mean. to *crack* [as by *pressure*], hence, to *leak; distillation,* i.e. *balsam:*—balm {6x}. See: TWOT—1967a; BDB—863b, 863c.

6876. צֹרִי {5x} Tsôrîy, *tso-ree';* patrial from 6865; a *Tsorite* or inhab. of Tsor (i.e. *Syrian*):— . . .of Tyre {5x}. See: BDB—863a.

6877. צְרִיחַ {4x} tsᵉrîyach, *tser-ee'-akh;* from 6873 in the sense of *clearness* of vision; a *citadel:*—hold {3x}, high places {1x}. See: TWOT—1969a; BDB—863c.

6878. צֹרֶךְ {1x} tsôrek, *tso'-rek;* from an unused root mean. to *need; need:*—need {1x}. See: TWOT—1970a; BDB—863d.

6879. צָרַע {20x} tsâraʿ, *tsaw-rah';* a prim. root; to *scourge,* i.e. (intr. and fig.) to *be stricken with leprosy:*—leper {14x}, leprous {6x}. See: TWOT—1971; BDB—863d.

6880. צִרְעָה {3x} tsirʿâh, *tsir-aw';* from 6879; a *wasp* (as *stinging*):—hornet {3x}. See: TWOT—1971b; BDB—864a.

6881. צָרְעָה {10x} Tsorʿâh, *tsor-aw';* appar. another form for 6880; *Tsorah,* a place in Pal.:—Zorah {8x}, Zoreah {1x}, Zareah {1x}. See: BDB—864a.

6882. צָרְעִי {3x} Tsorʿîy, *tsor-ee';* or

צָרְעָתִי Tsorʿâthîy, *tsor-aw-thee';* patrial from 6881; a *Tsorite* or *Tsorathite,* i.e. inhab. of Tsorah:—Zorites {1x}, Zorathites {1x}, Zareathites {1x}. See: BDB—864a.

6883. צָרַעַת {35x} tsâraʿath, *tsaw-rah'-ath;* from 6879; *leprosy:*—leprosy {35x}. See: TWOT—1971a; BDB—863d.

6884. צָרַף {33x} tsâraph, *tsaw-raf';* a prim. root; to *fuse* (metal), i.e. *refine* (lit. or fig.):—try {11x}, founder {5x}, goldsmith {5x}, refine {3x}, refiner {2x}, melt {2x}, pure {2x}, purge away {1x}, casteth {1x}, finer {1x}.

(1) *Tsaraph* means to refine, try, smelt, test. **(2)** It means to test, to find out who is qualified for battle: "And the LORD said unto Gideon, The people *are* yet *too* many; bring them down unto the water, and I will try them for thee there: and it shall be, *that* of whom I say unto thee, This shall go with thee, the same shall go with thee; and of whomsoever I say unto thee, This shall not go with thee, the same shall not go" (Judg 7:4). **(3)** The word is equivalent to the English "smith" (Jer 17:4 - a silversmith). **(3a)** Jeremiah describes the process of smelting, refining, and also its failures (Jer 6:29–30). **(3b)** Isaiah details the work of the smith as involving smelting, refining, and particularly the use of the refined metals in making the final product (Is 40:19; 41:7). **(4)** Metaphorically, it is used with the sense "to refine by means of suffering" (Ps 66:10–12). **(5)** God's judgment is also described as a process of refining: "And I will turn my hand upon thee, and purely purge away thy dross, and take away all thy tin:" (Is 1:25).

(6) Those purified call on the name of the Lord and receive the gracious benefits of the covenant: "And I will bring the third part through the fire, and will refine them as silver is refined, and will try them as gold is tried: they shall call on my name, and I will hear them: I will say, It *is* my people: and they shall say, The LORD *is* my God." (Zec 13:9). **(8)** The coming of the messenger of the covenant (Jesus Christ) is compared to the work of a smith: "But who may abide the day of his coming? and who shall stand when he appeareth? for he *is* like a refiner's fire, and like fullers' soap: And he shall sit *as* a refiner and purifier of silver: and he shall purify the sons of Levi, and purge them as gold and silver, that they may offer unto the LORD an offering in righteousness" (Mal 3:2–3). **(9)** The believer can take comfort in the Word of God which alone on earth is tried and purified and by which we can be purified (Ps 119:140; Ps 18:30; Prov 30:5). See: TWOT—1972; BDB—864a.

6885. צֹרְפִי {1x} **Tsôrᵉphîy**, *tso-ref-ee'*; from 6884; *refiner; Tsorephi* (with the art.), an Isr.:—goldsmith {1x}. See: TWOT—1972a; BDB—864c.

6886. צָרְפַת {3x} **Tsârᵉphath**, *tsaq-ref-ath'*; from 6884; *refinement; Tsarephath*, a place in Pal.:—Zarephath {3x}. See: BDB—864c.

6887. צָרַר {58x} **tsârar**, *tsaw-rar'*; a prim. root; to *cramp*, lit. or fig., tran. or intr. (as follows):—enemy {14x}, distress {7x}, bind up {6x}, vex {6x}, afflict {4x}, besiege {4x}, adversary {3x}, strait {3x}, trouble {2x}, bound {2x}, pangs {2x}, misc. {5x} = be in affliction, narrower, oppress, shut up.

Tsarar means to wrap, tie up, be narrow, be in pangs of birth, be distressed: "And Jephthah said unto the elders of Gilead, Did not ye hate me, and expel me out of my father's house? and why are ye come unto me now when ye are in distress?" (Judg 11:7). See: TWOT—1973, 1974; BDB—864c, 865b, 865c, 865d.

6888. צְרֵרָה {1x} **Tsᵉrêrâh**, *tser-ay-raw'*; appar. by err. transc. for 6868; *Tsererah* for *Tseredah:*—Zererath {1x}. See: BDB—866c.

6889. צֶרֶת {1x} **Tsereth**, *tseh'-reth;* perh. from 6671; *splendor; Tsereth*, an Isr.:—Zereth {1x}. See: BDB—866c.

6890. צֶרֶת הַשַּׁחַר {1x} **Tsereth hash-Shachar**, *tseh'-reth hash-shakh'-ar;* from the same as 6889 and 7837 with the art. interposed; *splendor of the dawn; Tsereth-hash-Shachar*, a place in Pal.:—Zarethshahar {1x}. See: BDB—866c.

6891. צָרְתָן {3x} **Tsârᵉthân**, *tsaw-reth-awn';* perh. for 6868; *Tsarethan*, a place in Pal.:—Zarthan {1x}, Zaretan {1x}, Zartanah {1x}. See: BDB—863a, 866c.

ק

6892. קֵא {1x} **qêʾ**, *kay;* or

קִיא **qîyʾ**, *kee;* from 6958; *vomit:*—vomit {1x}. See: TWOT—2013a, 2013b; BDB—866b, 883c.

6893. קָאַת {5x} **qâʾath**, *kaw-ath';* from 6958; prob. the *pelican* (from *vomiting*):—cormorant {3x}, pelican {2x}. See: TWOT—1976; BDB—866b.

6894. קַב {1x} **qab**, *kab;* from 6895; a *hollow*, i.e. vessel used as a (dry) *measure:*—cab {1x}. See: TWOT—1977a; BDB—866b.

6895. קָבַב {8x} **qâbab**, *kaw-bab';* a prim. root; to *scoop* out, i.e. (fig.) to *malign* or *execrate* (i.e. *stab* with words):—× at all {1x}, curse {7x}. See: TWOT—1978; BDB—866d.

6896. קֵבָה {1x} **qêbâh**, *kay-baw';* from 6895; the *paunch* (as a *cavity*) or first stomach of ruminants:—maw {1x}. See: TWOT—1979a; BDB—867a, 869a.

6897. קֹבָה {1x} **qôbâh**, *ko'-baw;* from 6895; the *abdomen* (as a cavity):—belly {1x}. See: TWOT—1979a; BDB—867a, 869a.

6898. קֻבָּה {1x} **qubbâh**, *koob-baw';* from 6895; a *pavilion* (as a domed *cavity*):—tent {1x}. Syn.: 168, 4264, 4908. 5521. See: TWOT—1977b; BDB—866d.

6899. קִבּוּץ {1x} **qibbûwts**, *kib-boots';* from 6908; a *throng:*—company {1x}. See: TWOT—1983a; BDB—868b.

6900. קְבוּרָה {14x} **qᵉbûwrâh**, *keb-oo-raw';* or

קְבֻרָה **qᵉbûrâh**, *keb-oo-raw';* fem. pass. part. of 6912; *sepulture;* (concr.) a *sepulchre:*—burial {4x}, burying place {1x}, grave {4x}, sepulchre {5x}. See: TWOT—1984b; BDB—869a.

6901. קָבַל {13x} **qâbal**, *kaw-bal';* a prim. root; to *admit*, i.e. *take* (lit. or fig.):—receive {6x}, took {3x}, choose {1x}, held {1x}, take hold {1x}, undertook {1x}. See: TWOT—1980; BDB—867a, 1110b.

6902. קְבַל {3x} **qᵉbal** (Aram.), *keb-al';* corresp. to 6901; to *acquire:*—receive {1x}, take {2x}. See: TWOT—2964; BDB—1110b.

6903. קְבֵל {29x} **qᵉbêl** (Aram.), *keb-ale';* or

קֳבֵל **qŏbêl** (Aram.), *kob-ale';* (corresp. to 6905; (adv.) *in front of;* usually (with other particles) *on account of, so as, since, hence:*—as + 3606 {5x}, because + 3606 {4x}, therefore + 3606 {3x}, before {3x}, as {2x}, wherefore + 3606 {2x}, according {1x}, against {1x}, misc. {8x} = + for this cause, + by this means, by reason of, + that, + though. See: TWOT—2965; BDB—1097b, 1110a.

6904. קֹבֶל {1x} **qôbel**, *ko'-bel;* from 6901 in the sense of *confronting* (as standing *opposite* in order to receive); a *battering*-ram:—war {1x}. See: TWOT—1980a; BDB—867b.

6905. קָבָל {1x} **qâbâl**, *kaw-bawl';* from 6901 in the sense of *opposite* [see 6904]; the *presence*, i.e. (adv.) *in front of:*—before {1x}. See: TWOT—1980a;BDB—867b.

6906. קָבַע {6x} **qâbaʿ**, *kaw-bah';* a prim. root; to *cover*, i.e. (fig.) *defraud:*—rob {4x}, spoil {2x}. See: TWOT—1981; BDB—867b.

6907. קֻבַּעַת {2x} **qubbaʿath**, *koob-bah'-ath;* from 6906; a *goblet* (as deep like a *cover*):—dregs {2x}. See: TWOT—1982; BDB—867c.

6908. קָבַץ {127x} **qâbats**, *kaw-bats';* a prim. root; to *grasp*, i.e. *collect:*—gather {70x}, gather together {42x}, assemble {6x}, gather up {3x}, heap {1x}, gather out {1x}, resort {1x}, surely {1x}, take up {2x}.

(1) *Qabats* means "to collect, gather, assemble." **(2)** *Qabats* means "to gather" things together into a single location. **(2a)** The word may focus on the process of "gathering," as in Gen 41:35 (the first occurrence): Joseph advised Pharaoh to appoint overseers to "gather all the food of those good years that come, and lay up corn under the hand of Pharaoh. . . ." **(2b)** The verb may also focus on the result of the process, as in Gen 41:48: "And he gathered up all the food of the seven years, which were in the land of Egypt. . . ." **(3)** Only in one passage does *qabats* mean "to harvest" (Is 62:9): "But they that have gathered [harvested] it [grain] shall eat it and praise the Lord;" **(4)** This verb is used metaphorically of things that can be "gathered" only in a figurative sense. So in Ps 41:6, the enemy's "heart gathereth iniquity to itself" —i.e., the enemy considers how he can use everything he hears and sees against his host.

(5) It is often used of "gathering" people or "assembling" them. This "gathering" is usually a response to a summons, but not always. In 1 Kin 11:24, David "gathered men unto him, and became captain over a [marauding] band." This action was not the result of a summons David issued, but resulted from reports that circulated about him. The entire story makes it quite clear that David was not seeking to set up a force rivaling Saul's. But when men came to him, he marshalled them. **(6)** Quite often this verb is used of "summoning" people to a central location. When Jacob blessed his sons, for example, he "summoned" them to him and then told them to gather around closer (Gen 49:2). **(7)** This same word is used of "summoning" the militia. All able-bodied men in Israel between the ages of 20 and 40 were members of the militia. In times of peace they were farmers and tradesmen; but when danger threatened, a leader would "assemble" them or "summon" them to a common location and organize them into an army (cf. Judg 12:4).

(8) All Israel could be "summoned" or "gathered" for battle (as a militia); thus ". . . Saul gathered all Israel together, and they pitched in Gilboa" (1 Sa 28:4). **(9)** This military use may also signify "marshalling" a standing army in the sense of "setting them up" for battle. The men of Gibeon said: "All the kings of the Amorites that dwell in the mountains are gathered together against us" (Josh 10:6). **(10)** In 1 Kin 20:1, *qabats* carries this sense in addition to overtones of "concentrating" an entire army against a particular point: "And Ben-hadad the king of Syria gathered all his host together: and there were thirty and two kings with him, and horses, and chariots: and he went up and besieged Samaria, and warred against it." **(11)** Ordered assemblies may include assemblies for covenant-making: "And Abner said unto David, I will arise and go, and will gather all Israel unto my lord the king, that they may make a league with thee . . ." (2 Sa 3:21). **(12)** In several instances, assemblies are "convened" for public worship activities: "Samuel said, Gather all Israel to Mizpeh. . . . And they gathered together to Mizpeh, and drew water, and poured it out before the Lord, and fasted on that day . . ." (1 Sa 7:5–6; cf. Joel 2:16).

(13) When *qabats* appears in the intensive stem, God is often the subject. This usage connotes that something will result that would not result if things were left to themselves. The verb is used in this sense to refer to "divine judgment": "As they gathered silver, and brass . . . into the midst of the furnace, to blow the fire upon it, to melt it; so will I gather you in mine anger and in my fury (Eze 22:20). **(14)** *Qabats* is also applied to "divine deliverance": ". . . The Lord thy God will turn thy captivity, and have compassion upon thee, and will return and gather thee from all the nations, whither the Lord thy God hath scattered thee" (Deut 30:3). **(15)** A special use of the verb *qabats* appears in Joel 2:6, namely "to glow" or "glow with excitement" or "become pale [white]": "Before their face the people shall be much pained: all faces shall gather blackness." Syn.: The verb 'acaph (622) is a near synonym to *qabats,* differing from it only by having a more extensive range of meanings and duplicating all the meanings of *qabats*. See: TWOT—1983; BDB—867c.

6909. קַבְצְאֵל {3x} **Qabtsᵉêl**, *kab-tseh-ale';* from 6908 and 410; *God has gathered; Kabtseël,* a place in Pal.:—Kabzeel {3x}. See: BDB—868b. comp. 3343.

6910. קְבֻצָה {1x} **qᵉbûtsâh**, *keb-oo-tsaw';* fem. pass. part. of 6908; a *hoard:*—× gather {1x}. See: BDB—868b.

6911. קִבְצַיִם {1x} **Qibtsayim**, *kib-tsah'-yim,* dual from 6908; a *double heap; Kibtsajim,* a place in Pal.:—Kibzaim {1x}. See: BDB—868b.

6912. קָבַר **qâbar**, *kaw-bar';* a prim. root; to *inter:*—bury {131x}, buriers {1x}, in any wise {1x}.

Qabar, as a verb, means "to bury." **(1)** This root is used almost exclusively of burying human beings, the act of placing a dead body into a grave or tomb. **(1a)** In its first biblical appearance, *qabar* bears this meaning. God told Abraham, "And thou shalt go to thy fathers in peace; thou shalt be buried in a good old age" (Gen 15:15). **(1b)** A proper burial was a sign of special kindness and divine blessing. As such, it was an obligation of the responsible survivors. Abraham bought the cave of Machpelah so that he might bury his dead. **(1c)** David thanked the men of Jabesh-gilead for their daring reclamation of the bodies of Saul and Jonathan (1 Sa 31:11–13), and for properly "burying" them. He said, "Blessed be ye of the Lord, that ye have showed this kindness unto your lord, even unto Saul, and have buried him" (2 Sa 2:5). **(1d)** Later, David took the bones of Saul and Jonathan and buried them in their family tomb (2 Sa. 21:14); here the verb means both "bury" and "rebury." **(1e)** A proper burial was not only a kindness; it was a necessity. If the land were to be clean before God, all bodies had to be "buried" before nightfall: "His body shall not remain all night upon the tree, but thou shalt in any wise bury him that day; (for he that is hanged is accursed of God;) that thy land be not defiled, which the Lord thy God giveth thee for an inheritance" (Deut 21:23). **(1f)** Thus, if a body was not buried, divine approval was withdrawn.

(2) Not to be "buried" was a sign of divine disapproval, both on the surviving kinsmen and on the nation. **(2a)** Ahijah the prophet told Jeroboam's wife, "And all Israel shall mourn for him [Jeroboam's son], and bury him: for he only of Jeroboam shall come to the grave" (1 Kin 14:13). **(2b)** As for the rest of his family, they would be eaten by dogs and birds of prey (v. 11; cf. Jer 8:2). Jeremiah prophesied that Jehoiakim would "be buried with the burial of an ass, drawn and cast forth beyond the gates of Jerusalem" (Jer 22:19). **(3)** Bodies may be "buried" in caves (Gen 25:9), sepulchers (Judg 8:32), and graves (Gen 50:5). **(4)** In a few places, *qabar* is used elliptically of the entire act of dying. So in Job 27:15 we read: "Those that remain of him [his survivors] shall be buried in death: and his widows shall not weep." Syn.: 6913. See: TWOT—1984; BDB—868b.

6913. קֶבֶר {67x} **qeber**, *keh'-ber;* or (fem.)

קִבְרָה **qibrâh**, *kib-raw';* from 6912; a *sepulchre:*—burying place {6x}, grave {35x}, sepulchre {25x}.

(1) The state that we call death, i.e., the condition cosequent on the act of dying, is to be viewed in three aspects: **(1a)** first, there is the tomb or sepulcher; the location of the physical frame called *qeber* (6913 – Gen 50:5); **(1b)** secondly, there is the corruption whereby the body itself is dissolved, which is represented by shachath (7843); and **(1c)** thirdly, there is sheowl (7585) which represents the locality or condition of the departed. **(2)** *Qeber* refers to a **(2a)** a tomb-grave/sepulcher (Gen 23:4), **(2b)** grave (Jer 5:16), and **(2c)** in Ps 88:11, it is used of a grave that is the equivalent of the underworld. **(3)** In Judg 8:32, the word signifies a family sepulcher. **(4)** Jer 26:23 uses the word for a burial place, an open pit. See: TWOT—1984a; BDB—868d.

קְבֻרָה **qᵉbûrâh**. See 6900.

6914. קִבְרוֹת הַתַּאֲוָה {5x} **Qibrôwth hat-Taʾăvâh**, *kib-roth' hat-tah-av-aw';* from the fem. plur. of 6913 and 8378 with the art. interposed; *graves of the longing; Kibroth-hat-Taavh,* a place in the Desert:—Kibroth-hattaavah {5x}. See: BDB—869a.

6915. קָדַד {15x} **qâdad**, *kaw-dad';* a prim. root; to *shrivel* up, i.e. *contract* or *bend* the body (or neck) in deference:—bow {2x}, bow down the head {11x}, stoop {2x}. See: TWOT—1985; BDB—869a.

6916. קִדָּה {2x} **qiddâh**, *kid-daw';* from 6915; *cassia* bark (as in *shrivelled* rolls):—cassia {2x}. See: TWOT—1986b; BDB—869b.

6917. קְדוּמִים {1x} **qâdûwm**, *kaw-doom';* pass. part. of 6923; a *pristine* hero:—ancient {1x}. See: TWOT—1988g; BDB—870c.

6918. קָדוֹשׁ {116x} **qâdôwsh**, *kaw-doshe';* or

קָדֹשׁ **qâdôsh**, *kaw-doshe';* from 6942; *sacred* (cerem. or mor.); (as noun) *God* (by eminence), an *angel,* a *saint,* a *sanctuary:*—holy {65x}, Holy One {39x}, saint {12x}. **(1)**

Qadosh, as an adjective, means "holy." **(1)** The word describes something or someone. **(1a)** In Hebrew the verb qadash and the word qadesh combine both elements: the descriptive and the static. **(1b)** The traditional understanding of "separated" is only a derived meaning, and not the primary. **(1c)** The first of its 116 occurrences is in Ex 19:16: "And ye shall be unto me a kingdom of priests, and a holy nation. These are the words which thou shalt speak unto the children of Israel." **(2)** In the Old Testament *qadosh* has a strongly religious connotation. **(2a)** In one sense the word describes an object or place or day to be "holy" with the meaning of "devoted" or "dedicated" to a particular purpose: "And the priest shall take holy water in an earthen vessel . . ." (Num 5:17). **(2b)** Particularly the sabbath day is "devoted" as a day of rest: "If thou turn away thy foot from the sabbath, from doing thy pleasure on my holy day; and call the sabbath a delight, the holy of the Lord, honorable; and shalt honor him, not doing thine own ways, nor finding thine own pleasure, nor speaking thine own words: Then shalt thou delight thyself in the Lord . . ." (Is 58:13–14). **(2c)** The prescription is based on Gen 2:3 where the Lord "sanctified," or "dedicated," the sabbath.

(3) God has dedicated Israel as His people. **(3a)** They are "holy" by their relationship to the "holy" God. **(3b)** All of the people are in a sense "holy," as members of the covenant community, irrespective of their faith and obedience: "And they gathered themselves together against Moses and against Aaron, and said unto them, Ye take too much upon you, seeing all the congregation are holy, every one of them, and the Lord is among them: wherefore then lift ye up yourselves above the congregation of the Lord?" (Num 16:3). **(4)** God's intent was to use this "holy" nation as a "holy," royal priesthood amongst the nations (Ex 19:6). **(5)** Based on the intimate nature of the relationship, God expected His people to live up to His "holy" expectations and, thus, to demonstrate that they were a "holy nation": "And ye shall be holy unto me: for I the Lord am holy, and have severed you from other people, that ye should be mine" (Lev 20:26).

(5) The priests were chosen to officiate at the Holy Place of the tabernacle/temple. Because of their function as intermediaries between God and Israel and because of their proximity to the temple, they were dedicated by God to the office of priest: "They shall be holy unto their God, and not profane the name of their God: for the offerings of the Lord made by fire, and the bread of their God, they do offer: therefore they shall be holy. They shall not take a wife that is a whore, or profane; neither shall they take a woman put away from her husband: for he is holy unto his God. Thou shalt sanctify him therefore; for he offereth the bread of thy God: he shall be holy unto thee: for I the Lord, which sanctify you, am holy" (Lev 21:6–8). **(6)** Aaron as the high priest was "They envied Moses also in the camp, *and* Aaron the saint of the LORD" (Ps 106:16).

(7) The Old Testament clearly and emphatically teaches that God is "holy." **(7a)** He is "the Holy One of Israel" (Is 1:4), the "holy God" (Is 5:16), and "the Holy One" (Is 40:25). **(7b)** His name is "Holy": "For thus saith the high and lofty One that inhabiteth eternity, whose name is Holy; I dwell in the high and holy place, with him also that is of a contrite and humble spirit, to revive the spirit of the humble, and to revive the heart of the contrite ones" (Is 57:15). **(7c)** The negative statement, "There is none holy as the Lord: for there is none besides thee: neither is there any rock like our God" (1 Sa 2:2), explains that He is most "holy" and that no one is as "holy" as He is. **(8)** Also the angels in the heavenly entourage are "holy": "And ye shall flee *to* the valley of the mountains; for the valley of the mountains shall reach unto Azal: yea, ye shall flee, like as ye fled from before the earthquake in the days of Uzziah king of Judah: and the LORD my God shall come, *and* all the saints with thee" (Zec 14:5). **(9)** The seraphim proclaimed to each other the holiness of God: "And one cried unto another, and said, "Holy, holy, holy, is the Lord of hosts: the whole earth is full of his glory" (Is 6:3). See: TWOT—1990b; BDB—872c, 1110d.

6919. קָדַח {5x} **qâdach**, *kaw-dakh';* a prim. root; to *inflame:*—burn {1x}, kindle {4x}. See: TWOT—1987; BDB—869b.

6920. קַדַּחַת {2x} **qaddachath**, *kad-dakh'-ath;* from 6919; *inflammation,* i.e. febrile disease:—burning ague {1x}, fever {1x}. See: TWOT—1987a; BDB—869b.

6921. קָדִים {69x} **qâdîym**, *kaw-deem';* or

קָדִם **qâdîm**, *kaw-deem';* from 6923; the *fore* or front part; hence, (by orientation) the *East* (often adv. *eastward,* for brevity the *east wind*):—east {50x}, east wind {10x}, eastward {7x}, eastward + 1870 {1x}, east side {1x}. See: TWOT—1988d; BDB—870b.

6922. קַדִּישׁ {13x} **qaddîysh** (Aram.), *kad-deesh';* corresp. to 6918:—holy {4x}, holy One {3x}, saint {6x}. See: TWOT—2967; BDB—872d.

6923. קָדַם {26x} **qâdam**, *kaw-dam';* a prim. root; to *project* (one self), i.e. *precede;* hence, to *anticipate, hasten, meet* (usually for help):—prevent {15x}, before {6x}, met {2x}, come {1x}, disappoint {1x}, go {1x}.

Most often, this verb is used in a martial context. Such confrontations may be peaceful, as in the meeting of allies: "For thou [dost meet] him with the blessings of goodness . . ." (Ps 21:3). They may also be hostile: "The sorrows of hell compassed me about; the snares of death confronted (KJV, "prevented") me" (2 Sa 22:6). See: TWOT—1988; BDB—869d, 870c.

6924. קֶדֶם {87x} **qedem**, *keh'-dem;* or

קֵדְמָה **qêdmâh**, *kayd'-maw;* from 6923; the *front,* of place (absolutely, the *fore part,* rel. the *East*) or time (*antiquity*); often used adv. (*before, anciently, eastward*):—east {32x}, old {17x}, eastward {11x}, ancient {6x}, east side {5x}, before {3x}, east part {2x}, ancient time {2x}, aforetime {1x}, eternal {1x}, misc. {7x} = × ever (-lasting), forward, past. See: TWOT—1988a; BDB—869c, 870a, 870b, 1110c. comp. 6783, 6926.

6925. קֳדָם {42x} **qŏdâm** (Aram.), *kod-awm';* or

קְדָם **qᵉdâm** (Aram.) (Dan. 7:13), *ked-awm';* corresp. to 6924; *before:*—before {29x}, before + 4481 {2x}, of + 4481 {2x}, him {2x}, misc. {7x} = × from, × I (thought), × me, + of, × it pleased, presence. See: TWOT—2966a; BDB—1110b.

קָדִם **qâdîm**. See 6921.

6926. קִדְמָה {4x} **qidmâh**, *kid-maw';* fem. of 6924; the *forward* part (or rel.) *East* (often adv. *on* (the) *east* or *in front*):—east {3x}, eastward {1x}. See: TWOT—1988a; BDB—870b.

6927. קַדְמָה {6x} **qadmâh**, *kad-maw';* from 6923; *priority* (in time); also used adv. (*before*):—former estate {3x}, old estate {1x}, afore {1x}, antiquity {1x}. See: TWOT—1988c; BDB—870b, 1110c.

6928. קַדְמָה {2x} **qadmâh** (Aram.), *kad-maw';* corresp. to 6927; *former* time:—ago {1x}, aforetime + 4481 + 1836 {1x}. See: TWOT—2966b; BDB—1110c.

קֵדְמָה **qêdmâh**. See 6924.

6929. קֵדְמָה {2x} **Qêdᵉmâh**, *kayd'-maw;* from 6923; *precedence; Kedemah,* a son of Ishmael:—Kedemah {2x}. See: BDB—870b.

6930. קַדְמוֹן {1x} **qadmôwn**, *kad-mone';* from 6923; *eastern:*—east {1x}. See: TWOT—1988e; BDB—870c.

6931. קַדְמוֹנִי {10x} **qadmôwnîy**, *kad-mo-nee';* or

קַדְמֹנִי **qadmônîy**, *kad-mo-nee';* from 6930; (of time) *anterior* or (of place) *oriental:*—east {4x}, former {2x}, ancients {1x}, that went before {1x}, things of old {1x}, old {1x}. See: TWOT—1988f; BDB—870c.

6932. קְדֵמוֹת {4x} **Qᵉdêmôwth**, *ked-ay-mothe';* from 6923; *beginnings; Kedemoth,* a place in eastern Pal.:—Kedemoth {4x}. See: BDB—870d.

6933. קַדְמַי {3x} **qadmay** (Aram.), *kad-mah'-ee;* from a root corresp. to 6923; *first:*—first {3x}. See: TWOT—2966c; BDB—1110c.

6934. קַדְמִיאֵל {8x} **Qadmîyʼêl**, *kad-mee-ale';* from 6924 and 410; *presence of God; Kadmiël,* the name of three Isr.:—Kadmiel {8x}. See: BDB—870d.

קַדְמֹנִי **qadmônîy**. See 6931.

6935. קַדְמֹנִי {1x} **Qadmônîy**, *kad-mo-nee';* the same as 6931; *ancient,* i.e. aboriginal; *Kadmonite* (collect.), the name of a tribe in Pal.:—Kadmonites {1x}. See: BDB—870d.

6936. קָדְקֹד {11x} **qodqôd**, *kod-kode';* from 6915; the *crown* of the head (as the part most *bowed*):—crown of the head {6x}, top of the head {2x}, crown {1x}, pate {1x}, scalp {1x}. See: TWOT—1986a; BDB—869a, 903a.

6937. קָדַר {17x} **qâdar**, *kaw-dar';* a prim. root; to *be ashy,* i.e. *dark*-colored; by impl. to *mourn* (in sackcloth or sordid garments):—mourn {6x}, black {4x}, dark {4x}, blackish {1x}, darkened {1x}, heavily {1x}. See: TWOT—1989; BDB—871a.

6938. קֵדָר {12x} **Qêdâr**, *kay-dawr';* from 6937; *dusky* (of the skin or the tent); *Kedar,* a son of Ishmael; also (collect.) *bedawin* (as his desc. or representatives):—Kedar {12x}. See: BDB—871a.

6939. קִדְרוֹן {11x} **Qidrôwn**, *kid-rone';* from 6937; *dusky* place; *Kidron,* a brook near Jerusalem:—Kidron {11x}. See: BDB—871b.

6940. קַדְרוּת {1x} **qadrûwth**, *kad-rooth';* from 6937; *duskiness:*—blackness {1x}. See: TWOT—1989a; BDB—871a.

6941. קְדֹרַנִּית {1x} **qᵉdôranniyth**, *ked-o-ran-neeth';* adv. from 6937; *blackish ones* (i.e. *in sackcloth*); used adv. in *mourning* weeds:—mournfully {1x}. See: TWOT—1989b; BDB—871a.

6942. קָדַשׁ {172x} **qâdâsh**, *kaw-dash';* a prim. root; to *be* (caus. *make, pronounce* or *observe* as) *clean* (cerem. or mor.):—sanctify {108x}, hallow {25x}, dedicate {10x}, holy {7x}, prepare {7x}, consecrate {5x}, appointed {1x}, bid {1x}, purified {1x}, misc. {7x} = defile, keep, proclaim, × wholly.

(1) This word is used in some form or another to represent being set apart for the work of God. Qadesh, or *qadash,* as verbs, mean "to be holy; to sanctify." This verb, which occurs 172 times, can mean **(2)** "to be holy": "Seven days thou shalt make an atonement for the altar, and sanctify it; and it shall be an altar most holy: whatsoever toucheth the altar shall be holy" (Ex 29:37; cf. Lev 6:18) or **(3)** "to sanctify": "Hear me, ye Levites, sanctify now yourselves, and sanctify the house of the Lord God of your fathers, and carry forth the filthiness out of the holy place" (2 Chr 29:5). See: TWOT—1990; BDB—872d.

6943. קֶדֶשׁ {12x} **Qedesh**, *keh'-desh;* from 6942; a *sanctum; Kedesh,* the name of four places in Pal.:—Kedesh {11x}, Kedeshnaphtali {1x}. See: TWOT—1990d; BDB—873d, 904d.

6944. קֹדֶשׁ {468x} **qôdesh**, *ko'-desh;* from 6942; a *sacred* place or thing; rarely abstr. *sanctity:*—holy {262x}, sanctuary {68x}, (holy, hallowed, . . .) things {52x}, most {44x}, holiness {30x}, dedicated {5x}, hallowed {3x}, consecrated {1x}, misc. {3x}.

Qodesh, as a noun, means "holiness; holy thing; sanctuary." This noun occurs 469 times with the meanings: **(1)** "holiness": "Who *is* like unto thee, O LORD, among the gods? who *is* like thee, glorious in holiness, fearful *in* praises, doing wonders?" (Ex 15:11); **(2)** "holy thing": "And when Aaron and his sons have made an end of covering the sanctuary, and all the vessels of the sanctuary, as the camp is to set forward; after that, the sons of Kohath shall come to bear *it:* but they shall not touch *any* holy thing, lest they die" (Num 4:15); and **(3)** "sanctuary": "And all the wise men, that wrought all the work of the sanctuary, came every man from his work which they made;" (Ex 36:4). See: TWOT—1990a; BDB—871c, 873d, 874a, 874b.

6945. קָדֵשׁ {6x} **qâdêsh**, *kaw-dashe';* from 6942; a (quasi) *sacred* person, i.e. (tech.) a (male) *devotee* (by prostitution) to licentious idolatry:—sodomite {5x}, unclean {1x}.

Another noun, *qadesh,* means "temple-prostitute" or "sodomite": "There shall be no whore of the daughters of Israel, nor a sodomite of the sons of Israel" (Deut 23:17). Syn.: 6948. See: TWOT—1990c; BDB—873c.

6946. קָדֵשׁ {18x} **Qâdêsh**, *kaw-dashe';* the same as 6945; *sanctuary; Kadesh,* a place in the desert:—Kadesh {17x}, Meribahkadesh + 4808 {1x}. See: TWOT—1990e; BDB—872c, 873d, 937b. comp. 6947.

קָדֹשׁ **qâdôsh**. See 6918.

6947. קָדֵשׁ בַּרְנֵעַ {10x} **Qâdêsh Barnêaʿ**, *kaw-dashe' bar-nay'-ah;* from the same as 6946 and an otherwise unused word (appar. compounded of a correspondent to 1251 and a der. of 5128) mean. *desert of a fugitive; Kadesh of* (the) *Wilderness of Wandering; Kadesh-Barneä,* a place in the desert:—Kadeshbarnea {10x}. See: BDB—140b, 745c, 873d, 874a.

6948. קְדֵשָׁה {5x} **qᵉdêshâh**, *ked-ay-shaw';* fem. of 6945; a female *devotee* (i.e. *prostitute*):—harlot {4x}, whore {1x}.

Qadesh, means temple-prostitute or sodomite (Deut 23:17). This word stresses the separation aspect of the word. These two individuals are totally separate to the extreme from God, instead of to Him alone. See: TWOT 1990c; BDB—873d.

6949. קָהָה {4x} **qâhâh**, *kaw-haw';* a prim. root; to *be dull:*—set on edge {3x}, blunt {1x}. See: TWOT—1990.1; BDB—874b.

6950. קָהַל {39x} **qâhal**, *kaw-hal';* a prim. root; to *convoke:*—(gather, assemble) together {14x}, gather {16x}, assembled {9x}.

Qahal means to gather for conflict or war, for religious purposes, and for judgment (1 Kin 8:1). See: TWOT—1991; BDB—874d.

6951. קָהָל {123x} **qâhâl**, *kaw-hawl';* from 6950; *assemblage* (usually concr.):—congregation {86x}, assembly {17x}, company {17x}, multitude {3x}.

(1) *Qahal* can mean an assembly gathered to plan or execute war (Gen 49:6; 1 Kin 12:3; Eze 17:17). **(2)** It can denote a gathering to judge or deliberate (Eze 23:45–47). **(3)** It may signify an assembly representing a larger group (1 Chr 13:1–2; 2 Chr 1:2; Lev 4:13). **(4)** Sometimes *qahal* represents all the males of Israel who were eligible to bring sacrifices to the Lord (Deut 23:1). **(5)** In Num 16:3 and 33, it is clear that the "assembly" was the worshiping, voting community (cf. 18:4). **(6)** The word *qahal* also signifies all the people of Israel (Ex 16:31; Gen 28:3). See: TWOT—1991a; BDB—874c.

6952. קְהִלָּה {2x} **qᵉhillâh**, *keh-hil-law';* from 6950; an *assemblage:*—congregation {1x}, assembly {1x}. See: TWOT—1991b; BDB—875a.

6953. קֹהֶלֶת {7x} **qôheleth**, *ko-heh'-leth;* fem. of act. part. from 6950; a (female) *assembler* (i.e. *lecturer*): abstr. *preaching* (used as a "nom de plume", *Koheleth*):—preacher {7x}. See: TWOT—1991c; BDB—875a.

6954. קְהֵלָתָה {2x} **Qᵉhêlâthâh**, *keh-hay-law'-thaw;* from 6950; *convocation; Kehelathah*, a place in the desert:—Kehelathah {2x}. See: BDB—875b.

6955. קְהָת {32x} **Qᵉhâth**, *keh-hawth';* from an unused root mean. to *ally* oneself; *allied; Kehath*, an Isr.:—Kohath {32x}. See: BDB—875b.

6956. קֳהָתִי {15x} **Qŏhâthîy**, *ko-haw-thee';* patron. from 6955; a *Kohathite* (collect.) or desc. of Kehath:—Kohathite {15x}. See: BDB—875c.

6957. קַו {21x} **qav**, *kav;* or

קָו **qâv**, *kawv;* from 6960 [comp. 6961]; a *cord* (as *connecting*), espec. for measuring; fig. a *rule;* also a *rim*, a musical *string* or *accord:*—line {20x}, rule {1x}. See: TWOT—1992, 1994a; BDB—875c, 876a, 876a. comp. 6978.

6958. קוֹא {8x} **qôwʾ**, *ko;* or

קָיָה **qâyâh** (Jer. 25:27), *kaw-yaw';* a prim. root; to *vomit:*—vomit {5x}, spue {3x}. See: TWOT—2014; BDB—883c, 883d.

6959. קוֹבַע {2x} **qôwbaʿ**, *ko'-bah or ko-bah';* a form collat. to 3553; a *helmet:*—helmet {2x}. See: TWOT—1993; BDB—875c.

6960. קָוָה {49x} **qâvâh**, *kaw-vaw';* a prim. root; to *bind* together (perh. by *twisting*), i.e. *collect;* (fig.) to *expect:*—wait {29x}, look {13x}, wait for {1x}, look for {1x}, gathered {1x}, misc. {4x}.

This word stresses the straining of the mind in a certain direction with an expectant attitude. . . . a forward look with assurance. See: TWOT—1994, 1995; BDB—875c, 876b.

6961. קָוֶה {3x} **qâveh**, *kaw-veh';* from 6960; a (measuring) *cord* (as if for *binding*):—line. See: TWOT—1994a; BDB—876a.

קוֹחַ **qôwach**. See 6495.

6962. קוּט {7x} **qûwt**, *koot;* a prim. root; prop. to *cut off*, i.e. (fig.) *detest:*—grieve {3x}, lothe {3x}, very {1x}. See: TWOT—1996; BDB—876c, 878c.

6963. קוֹל {506x} **qowl**, *kole;* or

קֹל **qôl**, *kole;* from an unused root mean. to *call* aloud; a *voice* or *sound:*—voice {383x}, noise {49x}, sound {39x}, thunder {10x}, proclamation + 5674 {4x}, send out + 5414 {2x}, thunderings {2x}, fame {1x}, misc. {16x} = + aloud, bleating, crackling, cry (+ out), fame, lightness, lowing, + hold peace, proclaim, + sing, + spark, + yell.

(1) It denotes a sound produced by vocal cords including **(1a)** the human voice (Josh 10:14), **(1b)** the vocal sounds produced by animals (1 Sa 15:14), and **(1c)** the voice of personified inanimate objects or things: "And he said, What hast thou done? the voice of thy brother's blood crieth unto me from the ground" (Gen 4:10). **(2)** This word also covers a great variety of noises and sounds, such as **(2a)** the noise or sound of battle (Ex 32:17), **(2b)** the sound of words (Deut 1:34), **(2c)** water (Eze 1:24), **(2d)** weeping (Is 65:19), and **(2e)** thunder (Ex 9:23). **(3)** The word can represent the thing that is spoken (Gen 3:17) even if written down (2 Kin 10:6). **(4)** There are several special phrases related to *qol:* **(4a)** "To lift up one's voice and weep" signifies **(4a1)** crying out for help (Gen 39:14), **(4a2)** mourning for present or anticipated tragedy (Gen 21:16), **(4a3)** the sound of disaster (Num 16:34), **(4a4)** or joy (Gen 29:11). **(4b)** "To hearken to one's voice" means **(4b1)** taking note of something and believing it (Gen 4:23), **(4b2)** following another's suggestions (Gen 3:17), **(4b3)** complying with another's request (Gen 21:12), **(4b4)** obeying another's command (Gen 22:18), and **(4b5)** answering a prayer (2 Sa 22:7).

(5) Theologically the word is crucial in prophecy. **(5a)** The prophet's voice is God's voice (Ex 3:18; 7:1; Deut 18:18–19). **(5b)** God's voice is sometimes **(5b1)** the roar of thunder, demonstrating His tremendous power which evokes fear and submission (Ex 9:23, 29); or **(5b2)** a "still small voice" (1 Kin 19:12). **(5c)** In covenantal contexts God stipulates that His voice, heard in both the roar of thunder and the prophetic message, is authoritative and when obeyed brings reward (Ex 19:5; 1 Sa 12:14–18). See: TWOT—1998a, 2028b; BDB—876d, 877b, 885c, 887a, 1110d.

6964. קוֹלָיָה {2x} **Qôwlâyâh**, *ko-law-yaw';* from 6963 and 3050; *voice of Jah; Kolajah*, the name of two Isr.:—Kolaiah {2x}. See: BDB—877b.

6965. קוּם {628x} **qûwm**, *koom;* a prim. root; to *rise* (in various applications, lit., fig., intens. and caus.):—(stood, rise, etc . . .) up {240x}, arise {211x}, raise {47x}, establish {27x}, stand {27x}, perform {25x}, confirm {9x}, again {5x}, set {5x}, stablish {3x}, surely {3x}, continue {3x}, sure {2x}, abide {1x}, accomplish {1x}, misc. {19x} = × be clearer, decree, × be dim, endure, × enemy, enjoin, make good, help, hold, make, × but newly, ordain, pitch, remain, strengthen, succeed.

Quwm means "to arise, stand up, come about." **(1)** It may denote any movement to an erect position, **(1a)** such as getting up out of a bed (Gen 19:33), or **(1b)** it can be used as the opposite of sitting or kneeling, as when Abraham "stood up from before his dead" (Gen 23:3). **(1c)** It can also refer to the result of arising, as when Joseph saw his sheaf arise and remain erect (Gen 37:7). **(2)** *Quwm* may be used by itself, with no direct object to refer to the origin of something, as when Isaiah says, "It shall not stand . . ." (Is 7:7). **(3)** Sometimes *quwm* is used in an intensive mood to signify empowering or strengthening: "Strengthen thou me according unto thy word" (Ps 119:28). **(4)** It is also used to denote the inevitable occurrence of something predicted or prearranged: "They have seen vanity and lying divination, saying, The LORD saith: and the LORD hath not sent them: and they have made *others* to hope that they would confirm [qum] the word" (Eze 13:6). **(5)** In a military context, *quwm* may mean "to engage in battle." In Ps 18:38, for instance, God says, "I have wounded them that were not able to rise . . ." (cf. 2 Sa 23:10).

(6) *Quwm* may also be used very much like ʿamad (5975) to indicate the continuation of something—e.g., "Thy kingdom shall not continue" (1 Sa 13:14). **(7)** Sometimes it indicates validity, as when a woman's vow shall not "stand" (be valid) if her father forbids it (Num 30:5). **(8)** Also see Deut 19:15, which states that a matter may be "confirmed" only by the testimony of two or more witnesses. **(9)** In some passages, *quwm* means "immovable"; so Eli's eyes were "set" (1 Sa 4:15). **(10)** Another special use of *quwm* is "rise up again," as when a childless widow complains to the elders, "My husband's brother refuseth to raise up unto his brother a name in Israel . . ." (Deut 25:7). In other words, the brother refuses to continue that name or "raise it up again." **(11)** When used with another verb, *quwm* may suggest simply the beginning of an action. When Scripture says that "[Jacob] rose up, and passed over the [Euphrates] river" (Gen 31:21), it does not mean that he literally stood up—merely that he began to cross the river.

(12) Sometimes *quwm* is part of a compound verb and carries no special meaning of its own. This is especially true in commands. Thus Gen 28:2 could simply be rendered, "Go to Padan-aram," rather than, "Arise, go . . ." (KJV). **(13)** Other special meanings emerge when *quwm* is used with certain particles. **(13a)** With ʿal, "against," it often means "to fight against or attack": "A man riseth against his neighbor, and slayeth him . . ." (Deut 22:26). This is its meaning in Gen 4:8, the first biblical occurrence. **(13b)** With the particle be ("against"), *quwm* means "make a formal charge against": "One witness shall not rise up against a man . . ." (Deut 19:15). **(13c)** With le ("for"), *quwm* means "to testify in behalf of": "Who will rise up for me against the evildoers?" (Ps 94:16). **(13c)** The same construction can mean "to deed over," as when Ephron's field was made sure"—Gen 23:17). Syn.: 4725. See: TWOT—1999; BDB—525d, 877c, 879d, 1110d.

6966. קוּם {35x} **qûwm** (Aram.), *koom;* corresp. to 6965:—set up {11x}, arise {5x}, stand {5x}, set {4x}, establish {3x}, rise up {3x}, appointeth {1x}, stood by {1x}, made {1x}, rise {1x}. See: TWOT—2968; BDB—1110d.

6967. קוֹמָה {45x} **qôwmâh**, *ko-maw';* from 6965; *height:*—height {30x}, stature {7x}, high {5x}, tall {2x}, along {1x}. See: TWOT—1999a; BDB—879b.

6968. קוֹמְמִיּוּת {1x} **qôwmᵉmîyûwth**, *ko-mem-ee-yooth';* from 6965; *elevation*, i.e. (adv.) *erectly* (fig.):—upright {1x}. See: TWOT—1999e; BDB—879c.

6969. קוּן {8x} **qûwn**, *koon;* a prim. root; to *strike* a musical note, i.e. *chant* or *wail* (at a funeral):—lament {7x}, mourning women {1x}. See: TWOT—2018; BDB—880c, 884b.

6970. קוֹעַ {1x} **Qôwaʿ**, *ko'-ah;* prob. from 6972 in the orig. sense of *cutting* off; *curtailment; Koä*, a region of Bab.:—Koa {1x}. See: BDB—880c.

6971. קוֹף {2x} **qôwph**, *kofe;* or

קֹף **qôph**, *kofe;* prob. of for. or.; a *monkey:*—apes {2x}. See: TWOT—2000; BDB—880d.

6972. קוּץ {1x} **qûwts**, *koots;* a prim. root; to *clip* off; used only as denom. from 7019; to *spend the harvest* season:—summer {1x}. See: BDB—884d.

6973. קוּץ {9x} **qûwts**, *koots;* a prim. root [rather ident. with 6972 through the idea of *severing* oneself from (comp. 6962)]; to *be* (caus. *make*) *disgusted* or *anxious:*—abhor {3x}, weary {2x}, loath {1x}, distressed {1x}, vex {1x}, grieved {1x}. See: TWOT—2002; BDB—880d.

6974. קוּץ {22x} **qûwts**, *koots;* a prim. root [rather ident. with 6972 through the idea of *abruptness* in starting up from sleep (comp. 3364)]; to *awake* (lit. or fig.):—awake {18x}, wake {2x}, arise {1x}, watch {1x}. See: TWOT—904a, 2019; BDB—884c.

6975. קוֹץ {12x} **qôwts**, *kotse;* or

קֹץ **qôts**, *kotse;* from 6972 (in the sense of *pricking*); a *thorn:*—thorn {12x}. See: TWOT—2003a; BDB—881a.

6976. קוֹץ {6x} **Qôwts**, *kotse;* the same as 6975; *Kots,* the name of two Isr.:—Koz {4x}, Coz {1x}, Hakkoz {1x}. See: BDB—881a.

6977. קְוֻצָּה {2x} **qᵉvutstsâh**, *kev-oots-tsaw';* fem. pass. part. of 6972 in its orig. sense; a *forelock* (as *shorn*):—lock {2x}. See: TWOT—2003b; BDB—881b.

6978. קַו־קַו {2x} **qav-qav**, *kav-kav';* from 6957 (in the sense of a *fastening*); *stalwart:*—meted out {2x}. See: TWOT—1994b; BDB—876a.

6979. קוּר {6x} **qûwr**, *koor;* a prim. root; to *trench;* by impl. to *throw forth;* also (denom. from 7023) to *wall up,* whether lit. (to *build* a wall) or fig. (to *estop*):—dig {2x}, cast out {2x}, destroy {1x}, break down {1x}. See: TWOT—2004, 2077; BDB—876a, 881b, 903b.

6980. קוּר {2x} **qûwr**, *koor;* from 6979; (only plur.) *trenches,* i.e. a *web* (as if so formed):—web {2x}. See: TWOT—2005a; BDB—881c.

6981. קוֹרֵא {3x} **Qôwrêʾ**, *ko-ray';* or, the name of two Isr.:—Kore {3x}. See: BDB—881c, 896c.

6982. קוֹרָה {5x} **qôwrâh**, *ko-raw';* or

קֹרָה **qôrâh**, *ko-raw';* from 6979; a *rafter* (forming *trenches* as it were); by impl. a *roof:*—beam {4x}, roof {1x}. See: TWOT—2068d; BDB—881c, 900a.

6983. קוֹשׁ {1x} **qôwsh**, *koshe;* a prim. root; to *bend;* used only as denom. for 3369, to *set a trap:*—snare {1x}. See: TWOT—2006; BDB—881c.

6984. קוּשָׁיָהוּ {1x} **Qûwshâyâhûw**, *koo-shaw-yaw'-hoo;* from the pass. part. of 6983 and 3050; *entrapped of Jah; Kushajah,* an Isr.:—Kushaiah {1x}. See: BDB—881c, 885c.

6985. קַט {1x} **qaṭ**, *kat;* from 6990 in the sense of *abbreviation;* a *little,* i.e. (adv.) *merely:*—very {1x}. See: TWOT—2006.1; BDB—876c, 881c.

6986. קֶטֶב {3x} **qeṭeb**, *keh'-teb;* from an unused root mean. to *cut* off; *ruin:*—destruction {2x}, destroying {1x}. See: TWOT—2007a; BDB—881c.

6987. קֹטֶב {1x} **qôṭeb**, *ko'-teb;* from the same as 6986; *extermination:*—destruction {1x}. See: TWOT—2007a; BDB—881c.

6988. קְטוֹרָה {1x} **qᵉṭôwrâh**, *ket-o-raw';* from 6999; *perfume:*—incense {1x}.

Qetowrah, means "incense." This word's only appearance is in Deut 33:10. Syn.: 4730, 6999, 7002, 7004, 7008. See: TWOT—2011a; BDB—882c.

6989. קְטוּרָה {4x} **Qᵉṭûwrâh**, *ket-oo-raw';* fem. pass. part. of 6999; *perfumed; Keturah,* a wife of Abraham:—Keturah {4x}. See: BDB—882c.

6990. קָטַט {1x} **qâṭaṭ**, *kaw-tat';* a prim. root; to *clip* off, i.e. (fig.) *destroy:*—shall be cut off {1x}. See: TWOT—1997; BDB—876c.

6991. קָטַל {3x} **qâṭal**, *kaw-tal';* a prim. root; prop. to *cut* off, i.e. (fig.) *put to death:*—slay {2x}, kill {1x}. See: TWOT—2008; BDB—881d, 1111a.

6992. קְטַל {7x} **qᵉṭal** (Aram.), *ket-al';* corresp. to 6991; to *kill:*—slay {7x}. See: TWOT—2969; BDB—1111a.

6993. קֶטֶל {1x} **qeṭel**, *keh'-tel;* from 6991; a violent *death:*—slaughter {1x}. See: TWOT—2008a; BDB—881d.

6994. קָטֹן {4x} **qâṭôn**, *kaw-tone';* a prim. root [rather denom. from 6996]; to *diminish,* i.e. *be* (caus. *make*) *diminutive* or (fig.) *of no account:*—was a small thing {2x}, make small {1x}, am not worthy {1x}.

Qaton (6994) and qatan (6996) are synonomous adjectives meaning small; youngest, insignificant: "I am not worthy of the least of all the mercies, and of all the truth, which thou hast shewed unto thy servant;" (Gen 32:10). **(1)** They bear the sense **(1a)** younger: "And Noah awoke from his wine, and knew what his younger son had done unto him" (Gen 9:24), **(1b)** smaller and less significant: "And God made two great lights; the greater light to rule the day, and the lesser light to rule the night:" (Gen 1:16), **(1c)** small, with reference to **(1c1)** the size of a set of weights (Deut 25:13), **(1c2)** the size of the smallest finger of one's hand (1 Kin 12:10), and **(1c3)** to the degree of seriousness of a given sin: "And Balaam answered and said unto the servants of Balak, If Balak would give me his house full of silver and gold, I cannot go beyond the word of the LORD my God, to do less or more" (Num 22:18).

(2) In the sense of young these words refer to the relative age of an individual: "And the Syrians had gone out by companies, and had brought away captive out of the land of Israel a little [*qaton*] maid; and she waited on Naaman's wife" (2 Kin 5:2, 14; Gen 42:15). **(3)** These adjectives can represent the idea of **(3a)** insignificant, small in importance or strength: (Deut 1:17); **(3b)** low in social standing: "And Samuel said, When thou *wast* little in thine own sight, *wast* thou not *made* the head of the tribes of Israel, and the LORD anointed thee king over Israel?" (1 Sa 15:17), or **(3c)** triviality: "And let them judge the people at all seasons: and it shall be, *that* every great matter they shall bring unto thee, but every small matter they shall judge:" (Ex 18:22). See: TWOT—2009; BDB—881d.

6995. קֹטֶן {2x} **qôṭen**, *ko'-ten;* from 6994; a *pettiness,* i.e. the *little finger:*—finger {2x}. See: TWOT—2009c; BDB—882b.

6996. קָטָן {101x} **qâṭân**, *kaw-tawn';* or

קָטֹן **qâṭôn**, *kaw-tone';* from 6962; *abbreviated,* i.e. *diminutive,* lit. (in quantity, size or number) or fig. (in age or importance):—small {33x}, little {19x}, youngest {15x}, younger {14x}, least {10x}, less {3x}, lesser {2x}, little one {2x}, smallest {1x}, small things {1x}, young {1x}. See 6994 for discussion. See: TWOT—2009a, 2009b; BDB—881d, 882b.

6997. קָטָן {1x} **Qâṭân**, *kaw-tawn';* the same as 6996; *small; Katan,* an Isr.:—Hakkatan {1x}. See: BDB—882a.

6998. קָטַף {5x} **qâṭaph**, *kaw-taf';* a prim. root; to *strip* off:—crop off {2x}, pluck {1x}, cut up {1x}, cut down {1x}. See: TWOT—2010; BDB—882b.

6999. קָטַר {117x} **qâṭar**, *kaw-tar';* a prim. root [rather ident. with 7000 through the idea of fumigation in a *close* place and perh. thus *driving* out the occupants]; to *smoke,* i.e. turn into fragrance by fire (espec. as an act of worship):—incense {59x}, burn {49x}, offer {3x}, kindle {1x}, offering {1x}, misc. {4x}.

This word stresses the turning of a substance into a vapor. **(1)** Technically this verb means offering true offerings every time it appears in the causative stem (Hos 4:13; 11:2), although it may refer only to the burning of incense (2 Chr 13:11). **(2)** Offerings are burned to change the offering into smoke (the ethereal essence of the offering), which would ascend to God as a pleasing savor. **(3)** The things sacrificed were mostly common foods, and in this way Israel offered up to God life itself, their labors, and the fruit of their labors. **(4)** Such offerings represent both the giving of the thing offered and a vicarious substitution of the offering for the offerer. **(5)** Because of man's sinfulness (Gen 8:21), he was unable to initiate a relationship with God. **(6)** Therefore, God Himself told man what was necessary in order to worship and serve Him. **(7)** God specified that only the choicest of one's possessions could be offered, and the best of the offering belonged to Him (Lev 4:10). **(8)** Only His priests were to offer sacrifices (2 Kin 16:13). **(9)** All offerings were to be made at the designated place; after the conquest, this was the central sanctuary (Lev 17:6).

(10) Some of Israel's kings tried to legitimatize their idolatrous offerings, although they were in open violation of God's directives. Thus the causative stem is used to describe, for example, Jeroboam's idolatrous worship: "So he offered upon the altar which he had made in Beth-el the fifteenth day of the eighth month, even in the month which he had devised of his own heart; and ordained a feast unto the children of Israel: and he offered upon the altar, and burnt incense" (1 Kin 12:33; cf. 2 Kin 16:13; 2 Chr 28:4). **(11)** The intensive stem (occurring only after the Pentateuch) always represents "false worship." **(11a)** This form of *qatar* may represent the "total act of ritual" (2 Chr. 25:14). **(11b)** Such an act was usually a conscious act of idolatry, imitative of Canaanite worship (Is 65:7). **(11c)** Such worship was blasphemous and shameful (Jer 11:17). **(11d)** Those who performed this "incense-burning" were guilty of forgetting God (Jer 19:4), **(11e)** while the practice itself held no hope for those who were involved in it (Jer 11:12). **(11f)** Amos ironically told Israelites to come to Gilgal and Bethel (idolatrous altars) and "offer" a thank offering. This irony is even clearer in the Hebrew, for Amos uses *qatar* in the intensive stem. Syn.: 5930. See: TWOT—2011, 2011e, 2011g; BDB—882b, 883b.

7000. קָטַר {1x} **qâṭar**, *kaw-tar';* a prim. root; to *inclose:*—joined {1x}. See: TWOT—2012; BDB—883b, 1111b.

7001. קְטַר {3x} **qᵉṭar** (Aram.), *ket-ar';* from a root corresp. to 7000; a *knot* (as *tied* up), i.e. (fig.) a *riddle;* also a *vertebra* (as if a knot):—doubts {2x}, joints {1x}. See: TWOT—2970; BDB—1111b.

7002. קִטֵּר {1x} **qiṭṭêr**, *kit-tare';* from 6999; *perfume:*—incense {1x}.

Qitter means "incense." This word appears once in Jer 44:21. Syn.: 4730, 6988, 6999, 7004, 7008. See: TWOT—2011c; BDB—883b.

7003. קִטְרוֹן {1x} **Qiṭrôwn**, *kit-rone';* from 6999; *fumigative; Kitron,* a place in Pal.:—Kitron {1x}. See: BDB—883c.

7004. קְטֹרֶת {60x} **qᵉṭôreth**, *ket-o'-reth;* from 6999; a *fumigation:*—incense {57x}, perfume {3x}.

Qetorel, as a noun, means "incense." **(1)** The first biblical occurrence of *qetoreth* is in Ex 25:6: "Oil for the light, spices for anointing oil, and for sweet incense." **(2)** The word represents "perfume" in Prov 27:9. Syn.: 4730. See: TWOT—2011a; BDB—882c.

7005. קַטָּת {1x} **Qattâth**, *kat-tawth';* from 6996; *littleness; Kattath,* a place in Pal.:—Kattath {1x}. See: BDB—883c.

7006. קָיָה {1x} **qâyâh**, *kaw-yaw';* a prim. root; to *vomit:*—spue {1x}. See: TWOT—2013, 2013b; BDB—883d.

7007. קַיִט {1x} **qâyiṭ** (Aram.), *kah'-yit;* corresp. to 7019; *harvest:*—summer {1x}. See: TWOT—2971; BDB—1111b.

7008. קִיטוֹר {4x} **qîyṭôwr**, *kee-tore';* or

קִיטֹר **qîyṭôr**, *kee-tore';* from 6999; a *fume,* i.e. *cloud:*—smoke {3x}, vapour {1x}.

Qiytowr refers to "smoke; vapor." This word does not refer to the smoke of an offering, but to other kinds of smoke or vapor. The reference in Ps 148:8 ("vapor") is one of its four biblical occurrences. Syn.: **(A)** Muqtar means "the kindling of incense." The word is used only once, and that is in Mal 1:11: ". . . And in every place incense shall be offered unto my name. . . ." **(B)** Meqatterah refers to "incense altar." The word occurs once (2 Chr 26:19). See also: 4730, 6988, 7002, 7004, 7008. See: TWOT—2011b; BDB—882c, 883d.

7009. קִים {1x} **qîym**, *keem;* from 6965; an *opponent* (as *rising* against one), i.e. (collect.) enemies:—substance {1x}. See: TWOT—1999c; BDB—879c, 883d.

7010. קְיָם {2x} **qᵉyâm** (Aram.), *keh-yawm';* from 6966; an *edict* (as *arising* in law):—decree {1x}, statute {1x}. See: TWOT—2968a; BDB—1111a, 1111b.

7011. קַיָּם {2x} **qayâm** (Aram.), *kah-yawm';* from 6966; *permanent* (as *rising* firmly):—sure {1x}, steadfast {1x}. See: TWOT—2968b; BDB—1111a, 1111b.

7012. קִימָה {1x} **qîymâh**, *kee-maw';* from 6965; an *arising:*—rising up {1x}. See: TWOT—1999d; BDB—879c, 883d.

קִימוֹשׁ **Qîymôwsh**. See 7057.

7013. קַיִן {1x} **qayin**, *kah'-yin;* from 6969 in the orig. sense of *fixity;* a *lance* (as *striking fast*):—spear {1x}. See: TWOT—2015a; BDB—883d.

7014. קַיִן {18x} **Qayin**, *kah'-yin;* the same as 7013 (with a play upon the affinity to 7069); *Kajin,* the name of the first child, also of a place in Pal., and of an Oriental tribe:—Cain {17x}, Kenite {1x}. See: TWOT—2017, 2016; BDB—883d, 884a.

7015. קִינָה {18x} **qîynâh**, *kee-naw';* from 6969; a *dirge* (as accompanied by *beating* the breasts or on instruments):—lamentation {18x}. See: TWOT—2018a; BDB—884b.

7016. קִינָה {1x} **Qîynâh**, *kee-naw';* the same as 7015; *Kinah,* a place in Pal.:—Kinah {1x}. See: BDB—884a.

7017. קֵינִי {13x} **Qêynîy**, *kay-nee';* or

קִינִי **Qîynîy** (1 Chron. 2:55) *kee-nee';* patron. from 7014; a *Kenite* or member of the tribe of Kajin:—Kenite {13x}. See: TWOT—2016; BDB—884a, 889d.

7018. קֵינָן {6x} **Qêynân**, *kay-nawn';* from the same as 7064; *fixed; Kenan,* an antediluvian:—Cainan {5x}, Kenan {1x}. See: BDB—884b.

7019. קַיִץ {20x} **qayits**, *kah'-yits;* from 6972; *harvest* (as the *crop*), whether the product (grain or fruit) or the (dry) season:—summer {11x}, summer fruit {9x}. See: TWOT—2020a; BDB—884d, 1111b.

7020. קִיצוֹן {4x} **qîytsôwn**, *kee-tsone';* from 6972; *terminal:*—uttermost {3x}, outmost {1x}. See: TWOT—2060b; BDB—884d, 894a.

7021. קִיקָיוֹן {5x} **qîyqâyôwn**, *kee-kaw-yone';* perh. from 7006; the *gourd* (as *nauseous*):—gourd {5x}. See: TWOT—2021; BDB—884d.

7022. קִיקָלוֹן {1x} **qîyqâlôwn**, *kee-kaw-lone';* from 7036; intense *disgrace:*—shameful spewing {1x}. See: TWOT—2028f; BDB—884d, 887b.

7023. קִיר {74x} **qîyr**, *keer;* or

קִר **qîr** (Isa. 22:5), *keer;* or (fem.)

קִירָה **qîyrâh**, *kee-raw';* from 6979; a *wall* (as built in a *trench*):—wall {66x}, side {4x}, masons {2x}, town {1x}, very {1x}. Syn.: 3820, 5315, 4578, 7130. See: TWOT—2022; BDB—885a, 885b, 894d.

7024. קִיר {5x} **Qîyr**, *keer;* the same as 7023; *fortress; Kir,* a place in Ass.; also one in Moab:—Kir {5x}. See: BDB—885b. comp. 7025.

7025. קִיר חֶרֶשׂ {5x} **Qîyr Cheres**, *keer kheh'-res;* or (fem. of the latter word)

קִיר חֲרֶשֶׂת **Qîyr Chăreseth**, *keer khareh'-seth;* from 7023 and 2789; *fortress of earthenware; Kir-Cheres* or *Kir-Chareseth,* a place in Moab:—Kirheres {2x}, Kirharaseth {1x}, Kirhareseth {1x}, Kirharesh {1x}. See: BDB—885b.

7026. קֵירֹס {2x} **Qêyrôç**, *kay-roce';* or

קֵרֹס **Qêrôç**, *kay-roce';* from the same as 7166; *ankled, Keros,* one of the Nethinim:—Keros {2x}. See: BDB—885b, 902b.

7027. קִישׁ {21x} **Qîysh**, *keesh;* from 6983; a *bow; Kish,* the name of five Isr.:—Kish {21x}. See: BDB—885c.

7028. קִישׁוֹן {6x} **Qîyshôwn**, *kee-shone';* from 6983; *winding; Kishon,* a river of Pal.:—Kishon {6x}. See: BDB—885c.

7029. קִישִׁי {1x} **Qîyshîy**, *kee-shee';* from 6983; *bowed; Kishi,* an Isr.:—Kishi {1x}. See: BDB—881c, 885c.

7030. קִיתָרֹס {8x} **qîythârôç** (Aram.), *kee-thaw-roce';* of Gr. or. (kivqari"); a *lyre:*—harp {4x}, variant spelling {4x}. See: TWOT—2972; BDB—1111b, 1112a.

7031. קַל {13x} **qal**, *kal;* contr. from 7043; *light;* (by impl.) *rapid* (also adv.):—swift {9x}, swiftly {2x}, swifter {1x}, light {1x}. See: TWOT—2028a; BDB—885c, 886d.

7032. קָל {7x} **qâl** (Aram.), *kawl;* corresp. to 6963:—sound {4x}, voice {3x}. See: TWOT—2973; BDB—1110b, 1111b.

קֹל **qôl**. See 6963.

7033. קָלָה {4x} **qâlâh**, *kaw-law';* a prim. root [rather ident. with 7034 through the idea of *shrinkage* by heat]; to *toast,* i.e. *scorch* partially or slowly:—roasted {1x}, dried {1x}, parched {1x}, loathsome {1x}. See: TWOT—2023; BDB—885c.

7034. קָלָה {6x} **qâlâh**, *kaw-law';* a prim. root; to *be light* (as impl. in *rapid* motion), but fig. only (*be* [caus. *hold*] *in contempt*):—seem vile {1x}, shall be condemned {1x}, lightly esteemed {1x}, despised {1x}, base {1x}, settest light {1x}. See: TWOT—2024; BDB—885d.

7035. קָלַהּ {1x} **qâlahh**, *kaw-lah';* for 6950; to *assemble:*—gather together {1x}. See: TWOT—1991; BDB—874d, 885c.

7036. קָלוֹן {17x} **qâlôwn**, *kaw-lone';* from 7034; *disgrace;* (by impl.) the *pudenda:*—shame {13x}, confusion {1x}, dishonour {1x}, ignominy {1x}, reproach {1x}. See: TWOT—2024a; BDB—885d.

7037. קַלַּחַת {2x} **qallachath**, *kal-lakh'-ath;* appar. but a form for 6747; a *kettle:*—caldron {2x}. See: TWOT—2025; BDB—886a.

7038. קָלַט {1x} **qâlaṭ**, *kaw-lat';* a prim. root; to *maim:*—lacking in his parts {1x}. See: TWOT—2027; BDB—886a.

7039. קָלִי {6x} **qâlîy**, *kaw-lee';* or

קָלִיא **qâlîyʾ**, *kaw-lee';* from 7033; *roasted* ears of grain:—parched corn {5x}, parched {1x}. See: TWOT—2023a; BDB—885d, 886b.

7040. קַלַּי {1x} **Qallay**, *kal-lah'-ee;* from 7043; *frivolous; Kallai,* an Isr.:—Kallai {1x}. See: BDB—886b, 887a.

7041. קֵלָיָה {1x} **Qêlâyâh**, *kay-law-yaw';* from 7034; *insignificance; Kelajah,* an Isr.:—Kelaiah {1x}. See: BDB—886b.

7042. קְלִיטָא {3x} **Qᵉlîyṭâʾ**, *kel-ee-taw';* from 7038; *maiming; Kelita,* the name of three Isr.:—Kelita {3x}. See: BDB—886b.

7043. קָלַל {82x} **qâlal**, *kaw-lal';* a prim. root; to *be* (caus. *make*) *light,* lit. (*swift, small, sharp,* etc.) or fig. (*easy, trifling, vile,* etc.):—curse {39x}, swifter {5x}, light thing {5x}, vile {4x}, lighter {4x}, despise {3x}, abated {2x}, ease {2x}, light {2x}, lighten {2x}, slightly {2x}, misc. {12x} = make bright, bring into contempt, accurse, eas (-y, -ier), × slight, be swift, revile, whet.

Qalal means "to be trifling, light, swift; to curse." **(1)** As will be seen, its various nuances grow out of the basic idea of being "trifling" or "light," with somewhat negative connotations involved. **(2)** *Qalal* is found for the first time in Gen 8:8: ". . . To see if the waters had abated;" indicating a lessening of what had existed. **(2)** The idea of "to be swift" is expressed in the Hebrew comparative form. So, Saul and Jonathan "were swifter than eagles" (2 Sa 1:23—literally, "more than eagles they were light"). **(3)** A similar idea is expressed in 1 Sa 18:23: "And David said, Seemeth it to you a light thing to a king's son-in-law . . . ?" **(4)** *Qalal* frequently includes the idea of "cursing" or "making little or contemptible": "And he that curseth [belittles] his father, or his mother, shall surely be put to death" (Ex 21:17). **(5)** "To curse" had the meaning of an "oath" when related to one's gods: "And the Philistine cursed David by his gods" (1 Sa 17:43). **(6)** The negative aspect of "non-blessing" was expressed by the passive form: ". . . The sinner being a hundred years old shall be accursed [by death]" (Is 65:20). Similar usage is reflected in: ". . . Their portion is cursed in the earth . . ." (Job 24:18). **(7)** The causative form of the verb sometimes expressed the idea of "lightening, lifting a weight": ". . . Peradventure he will lighten his hand from off you . . ." (1 Sa 6:5); ". . . so shall it be easier for thyself . . ." (Ex 18:22). Syn.: 423, 779. See: TWOT—2028; BDB—886b.

7044. קָלָל {2x} **qâlâl**, *kaw-lawl';* from 7043; *brightened* (as if *sharpened*):—burnished {1x}, polished {1x}. See: TWOT—2028c; BDB—887a.

7045. קְלָלָה {33x} **qᵉlâlâh**, *kel-aw-law';* from 7043; *vilification:*—curse {27x}, cursing {5x}, accursed {1x}. See: TWOT—2028d; BDB—887a.

7046. קָלַס {4x} **qâlaç**, *kaw-las';* a prim. root; to *disparage,* i.e. ridicule:—mock {2x}, scorn {1x}, scoff {1x}. See: TWOT—2029; BDB—887b.

7047. קֶלֶס {3x} **qeleç**, *keh'-les;* from 7046; a *laughing-stock:*—derision {3x}. See: TWOT—2029a; BDB—887b.

7048. קַלָּסָה {1x} **qallâçâh**, *kal-law-saw';* intens. from 7046; *ridicule:*—mocking {1x}. See: TWOT—2029b; BDB—887b.

7049. קָלַע {7x} **qâlaʿ**, *kaw-lah';* a prim. root: to *sling;* also to *carve* (as if a *circular* motion, or into *light* forms):—sling {4x}, carve {3x}. See: TWOT—2030, 2031; BDB—887b, 887c.

7050. קֶלַע {22x} **qelaʿ**, *keh'-lah;* from 7049; a *sling;* also a (door) *screen* (as if *slung* across), or the *valve* (of the door) itself:—hangings {15x}, sling {4x}, sling + 3709 {1x}, slingstones + 68 {1x}, leaves {1x}. See: TWOT—2030a, 2030c; BDB—887c.

7051. קַלָּע {1x} **qallâʿ**, *kal-law';* intens. from 7049; a *slinger:*—slinger {1x}. See: TWOT—2030b; BDB—887c.

7052. קְלֹקֵל {1x} **qᵉlôqêl**, *kel-o-kale';* from 7043; *insubstantial:*—light {1x}. See: TWOT—2028e; BDB—887b, 887d.

7053. קִלְּשׁוֹן {1x} **qillᵉshôwn**, *kil-lesh-one';* from an unused root mean. to *prick;* a *prong,* i.e. hay-fork:—fork {1x}. See: TWOT—2032; BDB—887d.

7054. קָמָה {10x} **qâmâh**, *kaw-maw';* fem. of act. part. of 6965; something that *rises,* i.e. a *stalk* of grain:—standing corn {5x}, corn {2x}, grown up {2x}, stalk {1x}. See: TWOT—1999b; BDB—879b, 887d.

7055. קְמוּאֵל {3x} **Qᵉmûwʾêl**, *kem-oo-ale';* from 6965 and 410; *raised of God; Kemuël,* the name of a rel. of Abraham, and of two Isr.:—Kemuel {3x}. See: BDB—887d.

7056. קָמוֹן {1x} **Qâmôwn**, *kaw-mone';* from 6965; an *elevation; Kamon,* a place E. of the Jordan:—Camon {1x}. See: BDB—879c, 887d.

7057. קִמּוֹשׁ {2x} **qimmôwsh**, *kim-moshe';* or

קִימוֹשׁ **qîymôwsh**, *kee-moshe';* from an unused root mean. to *sting;* a *prickly* plant:—nettles {2x}. See: TWOT—2037a; BDB—883d, 888b. comp. 7063.

7058. קֶמַח {14x} **qemach**, *keh'-makh;* from an unused root prob. mean. to *grind; flour:*—meal {10x}, flour {4x}. See: TWOT—2033a; BDB—887d.

7059. קָמַט {2x} **qâmat**, *kaw-mat';* a prim. root; to *pluck,* i.e. *destroy:*—cut down {1x}, filled me with wrinkles {1x}. See: TWOT—2034; BDB—888a.

7060. קָמַל {2x} **qâmal**, *kaw-mal';* a prim. root; to *wither:*—wither {1x}, hewn down {1x}. See: TWOT—2035; BDB—888a.

7061. קָמַץ {3x} **qâmats**, *kaw-mats';* a prim. root; to *grasp* with the hand:—take {2x}, take a handful {1x}. See: TWOT—2036; BDB—888a.

7062. קֹמֶץ {4x} **qômets**, *ko'mets;* from 7061; a *grasp,* i.e. *handful:*—handful {2x}, handful + 4393 {2x}. See: TWOT—2036a; BDB—888a.

7063. קִמָּשׁוֹן {1x} **qimmâshôwn**, *kim-maw-shone';* from the same as 7057; a *prickly* plant:—thorn {1x}. See: TWOT—2037a; BDB—888b.

7064. קֵן {13x} **qên**, *kane;* contr. from 7077; a *nest* (as *fixed*), sometimes incl. the *nestlings;* fig. a *chamber* or *dwelling:*—nest {12x}, room {1x}. See: TWOT—2042a; BDB—888b, 890a.

7065. קָנָא {33} **qânâʾ**, *kaw-naw';* a prim. root; to *be* (caus. *make*) *zealous,* i.e. (in a bad sense) *jealous* or *envious:*—jealous {10x}, envy {9x}, jealousy {5x}, envious {4x}, zealous {2x}, very {2x}, zeal {1x}.

Qana' means "to be jealous; to be zealous." **(1)** At the interhuman level *qana'* has a strongly competitive sense. **(1a)** In its most positive sense the word means "to be filled with righteous zeal or jealousy." **(1b)** The law provides that a husband who suspects his wife of adultery can bring her to a priest, who will administer a test of adultery. **(1c)** Whether his accusation turns out to be grounded or not, the suspicious man has a legitimate means of ascertaining the truth. **(1d)** In his case a spirit of jealousy has come over him, as he "is jealous" of his wife (Num 5:30). **(1e)** However, even in this context (Num 5:12–31), the jealousy has arisen out of a spirit of rivalry which cannot be tolerated in a marriage relationship. **(1f)** The jealousy must be cleared by a means ordained by the law and administered by the priests. **(1g)** *Qana'*, then, in its most basic sense is the act of advancing one's rights to the exclusion of the rights of others: **(1g1)** ". . . Ephraim shall not envy Judah, and Judah shall not vex Ephraim" (Is 11:13). **(1g2)** Saul sought to murder the Gibeonite enclave "in his zeal to the children of Israel and Judah" (2 Sa 21:2).

(2) Next, the word signifies the attitude of envy toward an opponent. **(2a)** Rachel in her barren state "envied her sister" (Gen 30:1) and in the state of envy approached Jacob: "Give me children, or else I die." **(2b)** The Philistines envied Isaac because of the multitude of his flocks and herds (Gen 26:14). **(3)** The Bible contains a strong warning against being envious of sinners, who might prosper and be powerful today, but will be no more tomorrow: "Envy thou not the oppressor, and choose none of his ways" (Prov 3:31; cf. Ps 37:1). **(4)** In man's relation to God, the act of zeal is more positively viewed as the act of the advancement of God and His glory over against substitutes. **(4a)** The tribe of Levi received the right to service because "he was zealous for his God" (Num 25:13). **(4b)** Elijah viewed himself as the only faithful servant left in Israel: "I have been very jealous for the Lord God of hosts: for the children of Israel have forsaken thy covenant . . . And I, even I only, am left . . ." (1 Kin 19:10).

(5) However, the sense of *qana'* is "to make jealous," that is, "to provoke to anger": "They provoked him to jealousy with strange gods, with abominations provoked they him to anger" (Deut 32:16). **(6)** God is not tainted with the negative connotation of the verb. **(6a)** His holiness does not tolerate competitors or those who sin against Him. **(6b)** In no single passage in the whole Old Testament is God described as envious. **(6c)** When God is the subject of the verb *qana'*, the meaning is "be zealous," and the preposition le ("to, for") is used before the object: His holy name (Eze 39:25); His land (Joel 2:18); and His inheritance (Zec 1:14). Cf. Zec 8:2: "Thus saith the LORD of hosts; I was jealous for Zion with great jealousy, and I was jealous for her with great fury." See: TWOT—2038; BDB—888c.

7066. קְנָא {1x} **qᵉnâʾ** (Aram.), *ken-aw';* corresp. to 7069; to *purchase:*—buy {1x}. See: TWOT—2974; BDB—1111b.

7067. קַנָּא {6x} **qannâʾ**, *kan-naw';* from 7065; *jealous:*—jealous {6x}.

Qanna', as an adjective, means "jealous." **(1)** The word refers directly to the attributes of God's justice and holiness, as He is the sole object of human worship and does not tolerate man's sin. **(2)** One appearance is in Ex 20:5: ". . . For I the Lord thy God am a jealous God, visiting the iniquity of the fathers upon the children unto the third and fourth generation of them that hate me." See: TWOT—2038b; BDB—888d. comp. 7072.

7068. קִנְאָה {43x} **qinʾâh**, *kin-aw';* from 7065; *jealousy* or *envy:*—jealousy {25x}, zeal {9x}, envy {8x}, for my sake {1x}.

Qin'ah means "ardor; zeal; jealousy." This noun occurs 43 times in biblical Hebrew. One occurrence is in Deut 29:20: "The Lord will not spare him, but then the anger of the Lord and his jealousy shall smoke against that man. . . ." See: TWOT—2038a; BDB—888b.

7069. קָנָה **qânâh**, *kaw-naw';* a prim. root; to *erect,* i.e. *create;* by extens. to *procure,* espec. by purchase (caus. *sell*); by impl. to *own:*—buy {46x}, get {15x}, purchased {5x}, buyer {3x}, possessor {3x}, possessed {2x}, owner {1x}, recover {1x}, redeemed {1x}, misc. {7x} = attain, teach to keep cattle, provoke to jealousy, × surely, × verily.

(1) In Gen 4:1 Eve says "I have gotten a man from the Lord" expressing God's creating or bringing into being; thus Eve said "I have created a man-child with the help of the Lord" (cf. Gen 14:19, 22). **(2)** In Deut 32:6, God is called the father who created Israel; a father begets or creates, rather than acquires children. **(3)** *Qanah* expresses one person making a purchase agreement with another; buying a slave (Ex 21:2) or land (Gen 47:20). **(4)** Some have related *qanah* to creation: *Qanah* means "to get, acquire, earn" and these basic meanings are dominant in the Old Testament, but certain poetic passages have long suggested that this verb means "create." **(4a)** In Gen 14:19, Melchizedek blessed Abram and said: "Blessed be Abram by God Most High, possessor of heaven and earth. **(4b)** Gen 14:22 repeats this divine epithet. **(4c)** Deut 32:6 makes this meaning certain in that *qanah* is parallel to (6213 - 'asah, "to make"): "is not he thy father *that* hath bought (7069 - *qanah*) thee? hath he not made (6213 - 'asah) thee, and established (3559 - kun) thee? **(4d)** Ps 78:54; 139:13; and Prov 8:22–23 also suggest the idea of creation. See: TWOT—2039; BDB—888d, 1111b.

7070. קָנֶה {62x} **qâneh**, *kaw-neh';* from 7069; a *reed* (as *erect*); by resemblance a *rod* (espec. for measuring), *shaft, tube, stem,* the *radius* (of the arm), *beam* (of a steelyard):—reed {28x}, branch {24x}, calamus {3x}, cane {2x}, stalk {2x}, balance {1x}, bone {1x}, spearmen {1x}. See: TWOT—2040a; BDB—889c.

7071. קָנָה {3x} **Qânâh**, *kaw-naw';* fem. of 7070; *reediness; Kanah,* the name of a stream and of a place in Pal.:—Kanah {3x}. See: BDB—889d.

7072. קַנּוֹא {2x} **qannôwʾ**, *kan-no';* for 7067; *jealous* or *angry:*—jealous {2x}.

The adjective *qannow'* means "jealous." **(1)** Josh 24:19 is one example: "And Joshua said unto the people, Ye cannot serve the Lord: for he is a holy God; he is a jealous God; he will not forgive your transgressions nor your sins." **(2)** Nah. 1:2

contains the other occurrence of *qannow'*: "God *is* jealous, and the LORD revengeth; the LORD revengeth, and *is* furious; the LORD will take vengeance on his adversaries, and he reserveth *wrath* for his enemies." See: TWOT—2038c; BDB—888d.

7073. קְנַז {11x} **Qᵉnaz**, *ken-az';* prob. from an unused root mean. to *hunt; hunter; Kenaz*, the name of an Edomite and of two Isr.:—Kenaz {11x}. See: BDB—889d.

7074. קְנִזִּי {4x} **Qᵉnizzîy**, *ken-iz-zee';* patron. from 7073; a *Kenizzite* or desc. of Kenaz:—Kenezite {3x}, Kenizzites {1x}. See: BDB—889d.

7075. קִנְיָן {10x} **qinyân**, *kin-yawn';* from 7069; *creation*, i.e. (concr.) *creatures;* also *acquisition, purchase, wealth:*—substance {4x}, of . . . getting {2x}, goods {2x}, riches {1x}, with {1x}. See: TWOT—2039a; BDB—889a.

7076. קִנָּמוֹן {3x} **qinnâmôwn**, *kin-naw-mone';* from an unused root (mean. to *erect*); *cinnamon* bark (as in *upright* rolls):—cinnamon {3x}. See: TWOT—2041; BDB—890a.

7077. קָנַן {5x} **qânan**, *kaw-nan';* a prim. root; to *erect;* but used only as denom. from 7064; to *nestle*, i.e. *build* or *occupy* as a nest:—make . . . nest {5x}. See: TWOT—2042; BDB—890a.

7078. קֶנֶץ {1x} **qênets**, *kay'-nets;* from an unused root prob. mean. to *wrench; perversion:*—end {1x}. See: TWOT—2043a; BDB—890b.

7079. קְנָת {2x} **Qᵉnâth**, *ken-awth';* from 7069; *possession; Kenath*, a place E. of the Jordan:—Kenath {2x}. See: BDB—890b.

7080. קָסַם {20x} **qâçam**, *kaw-sam';* a prim. root; prop. to *distribute*, i.e. *determine* by lot or magical scroll; by impl. to *divine:*—divine {7x}, diviners {7x}, use {3x}, divination {1x}, prudent {1x}, soothsayer {1x}.

(1) Divination was a pagan parallel to prophesying (Deut 18:10, 14–15). **(2)** *Qacam* is a seeking after the will of the gods, in an effort to learn their future action or divine blessing on some proposed future action (Josh 13:22). **(3)** It seems probable that the diviners conversed with demons (cf. 1 Cor 10:20). **(4)** The practice of divination might involve **(4a)** offering sacrifices to the deity on an altar (Num 23:1ff.), **(4b)** the use of a hole (?) in the ground, through which the diviner spoke to the spirits of the dead: "And Saul disguised himself, and put on other raiment, and he went, and two men with him, and they came to the woman by night: and he said, I pray thee, divine unto me by the familiar spirit, and bring me *him* up, whom I shall name unto thee" (1 Sa 28:8), **(4c)** the shaking of arrows, **(4d)** consulting with household idols, or **(4e)** studying the livers of dead animals (Eze 21:21). **(5)** Divination was one of man's attempts to know and control the world and the future, apart from the true God. **(6)** It was the opposite of true prophecy, the submission to God's sovereignty (Deut 18:14). See: TWOT—2044; BDB—890c.

7081. קֶסֶם {11x} **qeçem**, *keh'-sem;* from 7080; a *lot;* also *divination* (incl. its *fee*), *oracle:*—divination {9x}, witchcraft {1x}, divine sentence {1x}. See: TWOT—2044a; BDB—890c.

7082. קָסַס {1x} **qâçaç**, *kaw-sas';* a prim. root; to *lop* off:—cut off {1x}. See: TWOT—2045; BDB—890d.

7083. קֶסֶת {3x} **qeçeth**, *keh'-seth;* from the same as 3563 (or as 7185); prop. a *cup*, i.e. an *ink-stand:*—inkhorn {3x}. See: TWOT—2080b; BDB—890d, 1099c.

7084. קְעִילָה {18x} **Qᵉʻîylâh**, *keh-ee-law';* perh. from 7049 in the sense of *inclosing; citadel; Keïlah*, a place in Pal.:—Keilah {18x}. See: BDB—890d.

7085. קַעֲקַע {1x} **qaʻăqaʻ**, *kah-ak-ah';* from the same as 6970; an *incision* or gash:—mark {1x}. See: TWOT—2046a; BDB—891a.

7086. קְעָרָה {17x} **qᵉʻârâh**, *keh-aw-raw';* prob. from 7167; a *bowl* (as *cut* out hollow):—charger {14x}, dish {3x}. See: TWOT—2047a; BDB—891a.

קֹף **qôph**. See 6971.

7087. קָפָא {5x} **qâphâʼ**, *kaw-faw';* a prim. root; to *shrink*, i.e. *thicken* (as unracked wine, curdled milk, clouded sky, frozen water):—congeal {1x}, settled {1x}, curdle {1x}, variant {1x}, dark {1x}. See: TWOT—2048, 2048a; BDB—891a, 891b.

7088. קָפַד {1x} **qâphad**, *kaw-fad';* a prim. root; to *contract*, i.e. *roll together:*—cut off {1x}. See: TWOT—2049; BDB—891b.

7089. קְפָדָה {1x} **qᵉphâdâh**, *kef-aw-daw';* from 7088; *shrinking*, i.e. *terror:*—destruction {1x}. See: TWOT—2049b; BDB—891c.

7090. קִפּוֹד {3x} **qippôwd**, *kip-pode';* or

קִפֹּד **qippôd**, *kip-pode';* from 7088; a species of bird, perh. the *bittern* (from its *contracted* form):—bittern {3x}. See: TWOT—2049a; BDB—891b.

7091. קִפּוֹז {1x} **qippôwz**, *kip-poze';* from an unused root mean. to *contract*, i.e. *spring* forward; an *arrow-snake* (as *darting* on its prey):—great owl {1x}. See: TWOT—2050a; BDB—891c.

7092. קָפַץ {7x} **qâphats**, *kaw-fats';* a prim. root; to *draw together*, i.e. close; by impl. to *leap* (by *contracting* the limbs); spec. to *die* (from *gathering* up the feet):—shut {2x}, stop {2x}, shut up {1x}, take out of the way {1x}, skip {1x}. See: TWOT—2051; BDB—891c.

7093. קֵץ {67x} **qêts**, *kates;* contr. from 7112: an *extremity;* adv. (with prep. pref.) *after:*—end {52x}, after {10x}, border {3x}, infinite {1x}, process {1x}.

Qets means "end." **(1)** First, the word is used to denote the "end of a person" or "death": **(1a)** "And God said unto Noah, The end of all flesh is come before me . . ." (Gen 6:13). **(1b)** In Ps 39:4, *qets* speaks of the "farthest extremity of human life," in the sense of how short it is: "Lord, make me to know mine end, and the measure of my days, what it is; that I may know how frail I am." **(2)** Second, *qets* means "end" as the state of "being annihilated": "He setteth an end to darkness, and searcheth out all perfection . . ." (Job 28:3). **(3)** Third, related to the previous meaning but quite distinct, is the connotation "farthest extremity of," such as the "end of a given period of time": "And after certain years [literally, "at the end of years"] he went down to Ahab to Samaria . . ." (2 Chr 18:2; cf. Gen 4:3—the first biblical appearance). **(4)** A fourth nuance emphasizes a "designated goal," not simply the extremity but a conclusion toward which something proceeds: "For the vision is yet for an appointed time, but at the end it shall speak, and not lie . . ." (Hab 2:3). **(5)** In another emphasis, *qets* represents the "boundary" or "limit" of something: "I have seen an end of all perfection" (Ps 119:96). **(6)** In 2 Kin 19:23, the word (with the preposition le) means "farthest": ". . . And I will enter into the lodgings of his borders, and into the forest of his Carmel." See: TWOT—2060a; BDB—891d, 893d.

קֹץ **qôts**. See 6975.

7094. קָצַב {2x} **qâtsab**, *kaw-tsab';* a prim. root; to *clip*, or (gen.) *chop:*—cut down {1x}, shorn {1x}. See: TWOT—2052; BDB—891d.

7095. קֶצֶב {3x} **qetseb**, *keh'-tseb;* from 7094; *shape* (as if *cut* out); *base* (as if there *cut* off):—size {2x}, bottom {1x}. See: TWOT—2052a; BDB—891d.

7096. קָצָה {5x} **qâtsâh**, *kaw-tsaw';* a prim. root; to *cut* off; (fig.) to *destroy;* (partially) to *scrape* off:—cut off {2x}, cut short {1x}, scrape {1x}, scrape off {1x}. See: TWOT—2053; BDB—891d.

7097. קָצֶה {96x} **qâtseh**, *kaw-tseh';* or (neg. only)

קֵצֶה **qêtseh**, *kay'-tseh;* from 7096: an *extremity* (used in a great variety of applications and idioms; comp. 7093):—end {56x}, . . . part {7x}, edge {6x}, border {3x}, outside {3x}, utmost {3x}, uttermost {3x}, coast {2x}, quarter {2x}, misc. {11x} = × after, brim, brink, [in-] finite, frontier, shore, side, × some.

Qatseh means "end; border; extremity." **(1)** In Gen 23:9, *qatseh* means "end" in **(1a)** the sense of "extremity": "That he may give me the cave of Machpelah, which he hath, which is in the end of his field. . . ." **(1b)** The word means "[nearest] edge or border" in Ex 13:20: "And they took their journey from Succoth, and encamped in the Etham, in the edge of the wilderness." **(1c)** At other points, the word clearly indicates the "farthest extremity": "If any of thine be driven out unto the outmost parts of heaven, from thence will the Lord thy God gather thee, and from thence will he fetch thee" (Deut 30:4). **(2)** Second, *qatseh* can signify a "temporal end," such as the "end of a period of time"; that is the use in Gen 8:3, the first biblical occurrence of the word: ". . . After the end of the hundred and fifty days the waters were abated."

(3) One special use of *qatseh* occurs in Gen 47:2, where **(3a)** the word is used with the preposition min ("from"): "And from among his brothers he took five men and presented them to Pharaoh" (cf. Eze 33:2). **(3b)** In Gen 19:4, the same construction means "from every quarter (or "part") of a city": ". . . The men of the city, even the men of Sodom, compassed the house round, both old and young, all the people from every quarter." **(3c)** A similar usage occurs in Gen 47:21, except that the phrase is repeated twice and is rendered "from one end of the borders of Egypt to the other." **(3d)** In Jer 51:31, the phrase means "in every quarter" or completely." See: TWOT—2053a, 2053c; BDB—892a, 892c, 1111b.

7098. קָצָה {35x} **qâtsâh**, *kaw-tsaw';* fem. of 7097, a *termination* (used like 7097):—end {22x}, lowest {3x}, uttermost part {2x}, edges {2x}, selvedge {2x}, misc. {4x} = coast, corner.

Qatsah means "end; border; edge; extremity." This word refers primarily to concrete objects. In a few instances. however, *qatsah* is used of abstract objects; one example is of God's way (Job 26:14). See: TWOT—2053b; BDB—892b.

7099. קֶצֶו {7x} **qetsev**, *keh'-tsev;* and (fem.)

קִצְוָה **qitsvâh**, *kits-vaw';* from 7096; a *limit* (used like 7097, but with less variety):—end {4x}, uttermost {1x}, variant {2x}. See: TWOT—2053d; BDB—892c.

7100. קֶצַח {3x} **qetsach**, *keh'-tsakh;* from an unused root appar. mean. to *incise; fen-*

nel-flower (from its *pungency*):—fitches {3x}. See: TWOT—2055a; BDB—892d.

7101. קָצִין {12x} **qâtsîyn**, *kaw-tseen'*; from 7096 in the sense of *determining;* a *magistrate* (as *deciding*) or other *leader:*—ruler {4x}, prince {4x}, captain {3x}, guide {1x}. See: TWOT—2054a; BDB—892d. comp. 6278.

7102. קְצִיעָה {1x} **qᵉtsîyʿâh**, *kets-ee-aw'*; from 7106; *cassia* (as *peeled;* plur. the *bark*):—cassia {1x}. See: TWOT—2056a; BDB—893a, 893b.

7103. קְצִיעָה {1x} **Qᵉtsîyʿâh**, *kets-ee-aw'*; the same as 7102; *Ketsiah*, a daughter of Job:—Kezia {1x}. See: BDB—893a.

7104. קְצִיץ {1x} **Qᵉtsîyts**, *kets-eets'*; from 7112; *abrupt; Keziz*, a valley in Pal.:—Keziz {1x}. See: BDB—894a.

7105. קָצִיר {54x} **qâtsîyr**, *kaw-tseer'*; from 7114; *severed*, i.e. *harvest* (as *reaped*), the crop, the time, the reaper, or fig.; also a *limb* (of a tree, or simply *foliage*):—harvest {47x}, boughs {3x}, branch {2x}, harvestman {1x}, harvest time {1x}. See: TWOT—2062a, 2062b; BDB—894c, 894d.

7106. קָצַע {2x} **qâtsaʿ**, *kaw-tsah'*; a prim. root; to *strip* off, i.e. (partially) *scrape;* by impl. to *segregate* (as an angle):—cause to scrape {1x}, corner {1x}. See: TWOT—2056, 2057; BDB—892d.

7107. קָצַף {34x} **qâtsaph**, *kaw-tsaf'*; a prim. root; to *crack* off, i.e. (fig.) *burst* out in rage:—wroth {22x}, wrath {5x}, displeased {3x}, angry {2x}, angered {1x}, fret {1x}.

Qatsaph, as a verb, means "to be wroth, angry." **(1)** The general meaning of *qatsap* is a strong emotional outburst of anger, especially when man is the subject of the reaction. **(1a)** The first usage of the word brings this out: "And Pharaoh was wroth against two of his officers . . . and he put them in [custody] . . ." (Gen 40:2–3; cf. 41:10). **(1b)** Moses became bitterly angry with the disobedient Israelites (Ex 16:20). **(1c)** The leaders of the Philistines "were wroth" with Achish (1 Sa 29:4), and **(1d)** Naaman was strongly irritated by Elisha's lack of a sense of protocol (2 Kin 5:11). **(1e)** Elisha expressed his anger with Joash, king of Israel (2 Kin 13:19). **(1f)** King Ahasuerus deposed Vashti in his anger (Est 1:12). **(1g)** In these examples an exalted person (generally a king) demonstrated his royal anger in radical measures against his subjects. He was in a position "to be angered" by the response of his subjects. **(2)** It is rarer for a person "to become angry" with an equal. **(3)** It is even rarer for a subject "to be angry" with his superior: ". . . Two of the king's chamberlains . . . were wroth, and sought to lay hand on the king Ahasuerus" (Est 2:21).

(4) The verb *qatsap* is used 11 times to describe man's anger and 18 times to refer to God's anger. This fact, coupled with the observation that the verb generally is an expression of a superior against a subject, explains why the biblical text more frequently uses *qatsap* to describe God's anger. **(5)** The object of the anger is often indicated by the preposition 'al ("against"). "For I was afraid of the anger [639 - 'ap] and hot displeasure [2534 - chemah], wherewith the Lord was wroth [*qatsap*] against ['al] you to destroy you" (Deut 9:19). **(6)** The Lord's anger expresses itself against disobedience (Lev 10:6) and sin (Eccl 5:5ff.). **(6a)** However, people themselves can be the cause for God's anger (Ps 106:32). **(6b)** In the wilderness the Israelites provoked God to wrath by their disobedience and lack of faith: "Remember, and forget not, how thou provokedst the Lord thy God to wrath in the wilderness: from the day that thou didst depart out of the land of Egypt, until ye came unto this place, ye have been rebellious against the Lord" (Deut 9:7; cf. vv. 8, 22). **(6c)** Moses spoke about God's wrath against Israel's disobedience which would in time be the occasion for the Exile (Deut 29:27), and the prophets amplify Moses' warning of God's coming "wrath" (Jer 21:5). **(7)** After the Exile, God had compassion on Israel and turned His anger against Israel's enemies (Is 34:2). See: TWOT—2058; BDB—893b.

7108. קְצַף {1x} **qᵉtsaph** (Aram.), *kets-af'*; corresp. to 7107; to *become enraged:*—be furious {1x}. See: TWOT—2975; BDB—1111c.

7109. קְצַף {1x} **qᵉtsaph** (Aram.), *kets-af'*; from 7108; *rage:*—wrath {1x}. See: TWOT—2975a; BDB—1111c.

7110. קֶצֶף {29x} **qetseph**, *keh'-tsef;* from 7107; a *splinter* (as *chipped* off); fig. *rage* or *strife:*—wrath {23x}, indignation {3x}, sore {2x}, foam {1x}.

Qetseph (7110), as a noun, means "wrath." **(1)** This noun occurs 28 times in biblical Hebrew and **(1a)** generally with reference to God. **(1b)** One occurrence of God's "wrath" is in 2 Chr 29:8: "Wherefore the wrath of the Lord was upon Judah and Jerusalem. . . ." **(2)** An example of man's "wrath" appears in Est 1:18: "Likewise shall the ladies of Persia and Media say this day unto all the king's princes, which have heard of the deed of the queen. Thus shall there arise too much contempt and wrath" (cf. Eccl 5:17). See: TWOT—2058a, 2059b; BDB—893c.

7111. קְצָפָה {1x} **qᵉtsâphâh**, *kets-aw-faw'*; from 7107; a *fragment:*—barked {1x}. See: TWOT—2059a; BDB—893c.

7112. קָצַץ {14x} **qâtsats**, *kaw-tsats'*; a prim. root; to *chop* off (lit. or fig.):—cut off {6x}, utmost {3x}, cut in pieces {2x}, cut {1x}, cut asunder {1x}, cut in sunder {1x}. See: TWOT—2060; BDB—893c.

7113. קְצַץ {1x} **qᵉtsats** (Aram.), *kets-ats';* corresp. to 7112:—cut off {1x}. See: BDB—893c.

7114. קָצַר {49x} **qâtsar**, *kaw-tsar'*; a prim. root; to *dock* off, i.e. *curtail* (tran. or intr., lit. or fig.); espec. to *harvest* (grass or grain):—reap {22x}, reaper {8x}, shortened {5x}, shorter {2x}, discouraged {1x}, lothed {1x}, straitened {1x}, misc. {9x} = × at all, cut down, much, grieve, harvestman, mourn, trouble, vex. See: TWOT—2061, 2062; BDB—894a, 894b, 894d.

7115. קֹצֶר {1x} **qôtser**, *ko'-tser;* from 7114; *shortness* (of spirit), i.e. *impatience:*—anguish {1x}. See: TWOT—2061b; BDB—894b.

7116. קָצֵר {5x} **qâtsêr**, *kaw-tsare'*; from 7114; *short* (whether in size, number, life, strength or temper):—small {2x}, few {1x}, soon {1x}, hasty {1x}. See: TWOT—2061a; BDB—894b.

7117. קְצָת {5x} **qᵉtsâth**, *kets-awth'*; from 7096; a *termination* (lit. or fig.); also (by impl.) a *portion;* adv. (with prep. pref.) *after:*—end {3x}, part {1x}, some {1x}. See: TWOT—2053e; BDB—596d, 892c, 892d, 894d, 1111c.

7118. קְצָת {4x} **qᵉtsâth** (Aram.), *kets-awth';* corresp. to 7117:—end {2x}, partly {2x}. See: TWOT—2976; BDB—1111c.

7119. קַר {3x} **qar**, *kar;* contr. from an unused root mean. to *chill; cool;* fig. *quiet:*—cold {2x}, variant {1x}. See: TWOT—2077a; BDB—894d.

קִר **qîr**. See 7023.

7120. קֹר {1x} **qôr**, *kore;* from the same as 7119; *cold:*—cold {1x}. See: TWOT—2077b; BDB—894d, 903b.

7121. קָרָא {735x} **qârâ'**, *kaw-raw'*; a prim. root [rather ident. with 7122 through the idea of *accosting* a person met]; to *call* out to (i.e. prop. *address* by name, but used in a wide variety of applications):—call {528x}, cried {98x}, read {38x}, proclaim {36x}, named {7x}, guests {4x}, invited {3x}, gave {3x}, renowned {3x}, bidden {2x}, preach {2x}, misc. {11x} = bewray [self], (be) famous, mention, (make) proclamation, pronounce, publish, say.

Qara' means "to call, call out, recite." **(1)** *Qara'* may signify the "specification of a name." **(1a)** Naming a thing is frequently an assertion of sovereignty over it, which is the case in the first use of *qara'*: "And God called the light Day, and the darkness he called Night" (Gen 1:5). **(1b)** God's act of creating, "naming," and numbering includes the stars (Ps 147:4) and all other things (Is 40:26). **(2)** He allowed Adam to "name" the animals as a concrete demonstration of man's relative sovereignty over them (Gen 2:19). **(3)** Divine sovereignty and election are extended over all generations, for God "called" them all from the beginning (Is 41:4; cf. Amos 5:8). **(4)** "Calling" or "naming" an individual **(4a)** may specify the individual's primary characteristic: "And he said, Is not he rightly named Jacob? for he hath supplanted me these two times: he took away my birthright; and, behold, now he hath taken away my blessing" (Gen 27:36); **(4b)** it may consist of a confession or evaluation (Is 58:13; 60:14); and **(4c)** it may recognize an eternal truth: "Therefore the Lord himself shall give you a sign; Behold, a virgin shall conceive, and bear a son, and shall call his name Immanuel" (Is 7:14).

(5) This verb also is used to indicate "calling to a specific task." **(5a)** In Ex 2:7, Moses' sister Miriam asked Pharaoh's daughter if she should go and "call" (summon) a nurse. **(5b)** Israel was "called" (elected) by God to be His people (Is 65:12), as were the Gentiles in the messianic age (Is 55:5). **(6)** To "call" on God's name is to summon His aid. **(6a)** This emphasis appears in Gen 4:26, where men began to "call" on the name of the Lord. **(6b)** Such a "calling" on God's name occurs against the background of the Fall and the murder of Abel. **(6c)** The "calling" on God's name is clearly not the beginning of prayer, since communication between God and man existed since the Garden of Eden; nor is it an indication of the beginning of formal worship, since formal worship began at least as early as the offerings of Cain and Abel (Gen 4:7ff.). **(7)** The sense of "summoning" God to one's aid was surely in Abraham's mind when he "called upon" God's name (Gen 12:8). **(7a)** "Calling" in this sense constitutes a prayer prompted by recognized need and **(7b)** directed to One who is able and willing to respond (Ps 145:18; Is 55:6).

(8) Basically, *qara'* means "to call out loudly" in order to get someone's attention so that contact can be initiated. So Job is told: "Call now, if there be any that will answer thee; and to which of the saints wilt thou turn?" (Job 5:11). **(9)** Often this verb represents sustained communication, paralleling "to say" (559 - 'amar), as in Gen 3:9: "And the Lord God called unto Adam, and said unto him. . . ." **(10)** *Qara'* can also mean "to call out a warning," so that direct contact may be avoided: "And the leper in whom the plague is, his clothes shall be rent, and his head bare, and he shall put a covering upon his upper lip, and shall cry, Unclean, unclean" (Lev 13:45). **(11)** *Qara'* may mean "to shout" or "to call out loudly." **(11a)** Goliath "shouted" toward the ranks of Israel (1 Sa 17:8) and challenged them to individual combat (duel). **(11b)** Sometimes ancient peoples settled battles through such combatants. **(11c)** Before battling an enemy, Israel was directed to offer them peace: "When thou comest nigh unto a city to fight against it, then proclaim peace unto it [call out to it in terms of peace]" (Deut 20:10).

(12) *Qara'* may also mean "to proclaim" or "to announce," as when Israel proclaimed peace to the sons of Benjamin (Judg 21:13). **(12a)** This sense first occurs in Gen 41:43, where we are told that Joseph rode in the second chariot; "and they cried before him, Bow the knee." **(12b)** Haman recommended to King Ahasuerus that he adorn the one to be honored and "proclaim" ("announce") before him, "Thus shall it be done to the man whom the king delighteth to honor" (Est 6:9). This proclamation would tell everyone that the man so announced was honored by the king. **(13)** The two emphases, "proclamation" and "announce," occur in Ex 32:5: ". . . Aaron made proclamation, and said, Tomorrow is a feast to the Lord." This instance implies "summoning" an official assemblage of the people. **(14)** In prophetic literature, *qara'* is a technical term for "declaring" a prophetic message: "For the saying which he cried by the word of the Lord . . . shall surely come to pass" (1 Kin 13:32).

(15) Another major emphasis of *qara'* is "to summon." **(15a)** When Pharaoh discovered Abram's deceit concerning Sarai, he "summoned" ("called") Abram so that he might correct the situation (Gen 12:18). **(15b)** Often the summons is in the form of a friendly invitation, as when Reuel (or Jethro) told his daughters to "invite him [Moses] that he may eat bread," (Ex 2:20). **(16)** The participial form of *qara'* is used to denote "invited guests": "As soon as ye be come into the city, ye shall straightway find him, before he go up to the high place to eat: for the people will not eat until he come, because he doth bless the sacrifice; *and* afterwards they eat that be bidden. Now therefore get you up; for about this time ye shall find him" (1 Sa 9:13). **(17)** This verb is also used in judicial contexts, to mean being "summoned to court" if a man is accused of not fulfilling his levirate responsibility, "then the elders of his city shall call him, and speak unto him . . ." (Deut 25:8). **(18)** *Qara'* is used of "summoning" someone and/or "mustering" an army: "Why hast thou served us thus, that thou calledst us not, when thou wentest to fight with the Midianites?" (Judg 8:1).

(19) The meaning "to read" apparently arose from the meaning "to announce" and "to declare," inasmuch as reading was done out loud so that others could hear. This sense appears in Ex 24:7: "And he took the book of the covenant, and read in the audience of the people: and they said, All that the LORD hath said will we do, and be obedient." **(20)** *Qara'* means "to read to oneself" only in a few passages. **(21)** At least once, the verb *qara'* means "to dictate": "Then Baruch answered them, He [dictated] all these words unto me . . . and I wrote them with ink in the book" (Jer. 36:18). Syn.: 1319, 4744. See: TWOT—2063; BDB—894d, 1111c.

7122. קָרָא {16x} **qârâʼ**, *kaw-raw';* a prim. root: to *encounter,* whether accidentally or in a hostile manner:—befall {5x}, come {4x}, chance {2x}, happened {2x}, met {2x}, fall out {1x}.

(1) *Qara'* represents an intentional confrontation, whereby one person is immediately before another person. This may be **(1a)** friendly (Gen 14:17; Josh 9:11) or **(1b)** hostile (Josh 8:5; Amos 4:12). **(2)** Religiously, one meets God or is met by God (Ex 5:3). **(3)** This verb infrequently represents an accidental meeting, so it is translated "befall" (Gen 42:4). See: TWOT—2064; BDB—896d, 897a.

7123. קְרָא {11x} **qᵉrâʼ** (Aram.), *ker-aw';* corresp. to 7121:—read {7x}, cry {3x}, called {1x}. See: TWOT—2977; BDB—1111c.

7124. קֹרֵא {2x} **qôrêʼ**, *ko-ray';* prop. act. part. of 7121; a *caller,* i.e. *partridge* (from its *cry*):—partridge {2x}. See: TWOT—2063a; BDB—896c. See also 6981.

7125. קִרְאָה {121x} **qîrʼâh**, *keer-aw';* from 7122; an *encountering,* accidental, friendly or hostile (also adv. *opposite*):—meet {76x}, against {40x}, come {2x}, help {1x}, seek {1x}, way {1x}. See: TWOT—2064; BDB—896d, 897a.

7126. קָרַב {280x} **qârab**, *kaw-rab';* a prim. root; to *approach* (caus. *bring near*) for whatever purpose:—offer {95x}, (come, draw, . . .) near {58x}, bring {58x}, (come, draw, . . .) nigh {18x}, come {12x}, approach {10x}, at hand {4x}, presented {2x}, misc. {13x} = join, produce, make ready, stand, take.

(1) This word stresses to approach or draw near and is often used of man's entrance into the presence of the living God; a nearness of the closest and most intimate kind (Num 16:9; Ps 65:4). **(1a)** In general *qarab* signifies approach or coming near someone or something apart from any sense of intimacy. *Qarab* (7126), as a verb, means "to offer, come near, approach." **(1b)** In general *qarab* signifies "approach or coming near someone or something" apart from any sense of intimacy. **(1c)** In Gen 12:11 (the first biblical occurrence) the word is used of spatial proximity, of being spatially close to something: "And it came to pass, when he was come near to enter into Egypt, that he said unto Sarai his wife. . . ." **(1d)** Usually the word represents being so close to something (or someone) that the subject can see (Ex 32:19), speak to (Num 9:6), or even touch (Ex 36:2) the object or person in question. **(2)** This verb also is used of temporal nearness, in the sense that something is about to occur. **(2a)** *Qarab* can be used of the imminence of joyous occasions, such as religious feasts: "Beware that there be not a thought in thy wicked heart, saying, The seventh year, the year of release, is at hand . . ." (Deut 15:9). **(2b)** The word is also used of the imminence of foreboding events: ". . . Esau said in his heart, The days of mourning for my father are at hand [literally, "my father will soon die"] . . ." (Gen 27:41).

(3) *Qarab* is used in a number of technical senses. In all these instances personal involvement is suggested; the idea is not simply being close to something (someone) but being actively and personally involved with it (him). **(3a)** In military contexts the word signifies armed conflict. **(3a1)** In Deut 2:37 the Lord commended Israel because "unto the land of the children of Ammon thou camest not." **(3a2)** Yet in Deut. 2:19 He allowed them to "come nigh" that land: "And when thou comest nigh over against the children of Ammon, distress them not, nor meddle with them. . . ." **(3a3)** The later passage (Deut 2:37) uses the word technically, to close in battle. Therefore, Israel did not come close to the land of Ammon; they did not close in battle with them (cf. Josh 8:5). **(3b)** In some passages this martial coloring is not immediately obvious to the casual reader but is nonetheless present: "When the wicked . . . came upon me to eat up my flesh . . ." (Ps 27:2). Ps 27:3 ("though a host should encamp against me") substantiates that this use of the verb is "to close in battle" (cf. Ps 91:10; 119:150).

(4) *Qarab* is used technically of having sexual relations. In Gen 20:4 before Abimelech states his innocence with regard to Sarah we read he "had not come near her" (cf. Deut 22:14; Is 8:3). **(5)** In another technical use the word represents every step one performs in presenting his offering and worship to God. **(5a)** This idea first appears in Ex 3:5 where God tells Moses not to "draw near" before removing his sandals. **(5b)** Later Israel's meeting with God's representative was a drawing near to God (Ex 16:9). **(5c)** At Sinai they drew near to receive God's law (Deut 5:23, 27). **(6)** In the causative stem the verb often represents the sacrificial presentation of offerings (Lev 1:14) through the priests (Lev 1:5) to the Lord (Lev 1:13). **(7)** Israel also came near the Lord's representative in serious legal cases so that God the great King and Judge could render a decision (Josh 7:14). **(8)** In the eschaton all peoples are to gather before God; they are "to come near" Him to hear and receive His judgment (Is 41:1; 48:16). See: TWOT—2065; BDB—897b, 1111c.

7127. קְרֵב {9x} **qᵉrêb** (Aram.), *ker-abe';* corresp. to 7126:—come near {4x}, offer {2x}, come {1x}, bring near {1x}, offer {1x}. See: TWOT—2978; BDB—1111c.

7128. קְרָב {9x} **qᵉrâb**, *ker-awb';* from 7126; hostile *encounter:*—battle {5x}, war {4x}.

(1) The word *qerab,* means "war, battle," or the actual engaging in battle (Ps 55:18). **(2)** It is used of hand to hand combat. Syn.: 7131, 7132, 7138. See: TWOT—2065b; BDB—898b, 1111d.

7129. קְרָב {1x} **qᵉrâb** (Aram.), *ker-awb';* corresp. to 7128:—war {1x}. See: TWOT—2978a; BDB—1111d.

7130. קֶרֶב {227x} **qereb**, *keh'-reb;* from 7126; prop. the *nearest* part, i.e. the *center,* whether lit., fig. or adv. (espec. with prep.):—among {76x}, midst {73x}, within {24x}, inwards {22x}, in {6x}, misc. {26x} = × before, bowels, × unto charge, + eat (up), × heart, × him, + out of, purtenance, × therein, × through.

I. *Qereb* (7130), as a preposition, means "among." The first usage of this preposition is in Genesis: "Abram dwelled in the land of Canaan, and Lot dwelled in [among] the cities of the plain, and pitched his tent toward Sodom" (13:12). **II. *Qereb,* as a noun,** means "inward part; midst." **(1)** One idiomatic usage of *qereb* denotes an inward part of the body that is the seat of laughter (Gen 18:12) and of thoughts (Jer 4:14). **(2)** The Bible limits another idiomatic usage, meaning "inner parts," to animals: "Eat not of it raw, nor sodden at all with water, but roast with fire—his head with his legs, and with the purtenance thereof" (Ex 12:9). **(3)** The noun approximates the prepositional use with the meaning of "midst" or "in." **(3a)** Something may be "in the midst of" a place: "Peradventure there be fifty righteous within [*qereb*] the city: wilt thou also destroy and not spare the place for the fifty righteous that are therein?" (Gen 18:24). **(3b)** It may be in the midst of people: "Then Samuel took the horn of oil, and anointed him in the midst [*qereb*] of his brethren: and the Spirit of the Lord came upon David from that day forward" (1 Sa 16:13).

(4) God is said to be in the midst of the land (Ex 8:22), the city of God (Ps 46:4), and Israel (Num 11:20). **(4a)** Even when He is close to His people, God is nevertheless holy: **(4b)** "Cry out and shout, thou inhabitant of Zion: for great is the Holy One of Israel in the midst [*qereb*] of thee" (Is 12:6; cf. Hos 11:9). **(5)** The idiomatic use of *qereb* in Psalm 103:—"Bless the Lord, O my soul: and all that is within me, bless his holy name"—has the noun in the plural. **(5a)** It seems best to take "all that is within me" as a reference to the Psalmist's whole being, **(5b)** rather than to a distinct part of the body that is within him. See: TWOT—2066a; BDB—899a.

7131. קָרֵב {11x} **qârêb**, *kaw-rabe';* from 7126; *near:*—come nigh {4x}, come near {3x}, draw near {2x}, approach {1x}, came {1x}.

Qareb, which occurs 11 times, means "near"; it represents intimate proximity (usually in a cultic context referring to cultic activity). One appearance is in Eze 45:4: "The holy portion of the land shall be for the priests the ministers of the sanctuary, which shall come near to minister unto the Lord. . . ." Syn.: 7128, 7132, 7138. See: TWOT—2065a; BDB—898a.

קָרֹב **qârôb**. See 7138.

7132. קְרָבָה {2x} **qᵉrâbâh**, *ker-aw-baw';* from 7126; *approach:*—draw near {1x}, approach {1x}.

Qerabah occurs twice with the meaning of drawing near to worship God and offer sacrifice (Ps 73:28; Is 58:2). Syn.: 7128, 7131, 7138. See: TWOT—2065c; BDB—898b.

7133. קָרְבָּן {82x} **qorbân**, *kor-bawn';* or

קֻרְבָּן **qurbân**, *koor-bawn';* from 7126; something *brought near* the altar, i.e. a sacrificial *present:*—offering {68x}, oblation {12x}, offered {1x}, sacrifice {1x}.

Qorban means "offering; oblation; sacrifice." **(1)** While the root, "to come/bring near," is found literally hundreds of times in the Old Testament, the derived noun *qorban* occurs 82 times. All but two of the occurrences in the Old Testament are found in the books of Numbers and Leviticus. The two exceptions are in Ezekiel (20:28; 40:43), a book which has a great concern for ritual. The word occurs for the first time in Lev. 1:2. **(2)** *Qorban* may be translated as "that which one brings near to God or the altar." It is not surprising, then, that the word is used as a general term for all sacrifices, whether animal or vegetable. The very first reference to "sacrifice" in Leviticus is to the *qorban* as a burnt "offering": "If any man of you bring an offering unto the Lord, ye shall bring your offering of the cattle, even of the herd, and of the flock. If his offering be a burnt sacrifice . . ." (Lev 1:2–3; cf. Lev 1:10; 3:2, 6; 4:23). **(3)** The first reference to *qorban* as a "meat [cereal] offering" is in Lev. 2:1: "And when any will offer a meat offering unto the Lord, his offering shall be of fine flour. . . ."

(4) What is perhaps the best concentration of examples of the use of *qorban* is Numbers 7. In this one chapter, the word is used some 28 times, referring to all kinds of animal and meat [cereal] offerings, but with special attention to the various silver and gold vessels which were offered to the sanctuary. For example, Eliab's "offering was one silver charger, the weight whereof was a hundred and thirty shekels, one silver bowl of seventy shekels, . . . both of them full of fine flour mingled with oil for a meat offering; One golden spoon of ten shekels, full of incense; One young bullock, one ram, one lamb of the first year, for a burnt offering" (Num 7:25–27). **(5)** In the two uses found in Ezekiel, both are in the general sense of "offering." **(5a)** In Eze 20:28 the word refers to the pagan "provocation of their offering" which apostate Israel gave to other gods, while **(5b)** in Eze 40:43, *qorban* refers to regular animal sacrifices. **(6)** *Qurban* means "wood offering." *Qurban* is closely related to *qorban,* and it is found in Neh 10:34; 13:31. Here it refers to the "wood offering" which was to be provided for the burning of the sacrifices in the Second Temple. Lots were to be cast among the people, priests, and Levites to determine who would bring in the "wood offering" or fuel at the scheduled times throughout the year. Syn.: 801, 2077, 2282. See: TWOT—2065e; BDB—898d.

7134. קַרְדֹּם {5x} **qardôm**, *kar-dome';* perh. from 6923 in the sense of *striking* upon; an *axe:*—ax {5x}. See: TWOT—2067; BDB—899c.

7135. קָרָה {5x} **qârâh**, *kaw-raw';* fem. of 7119; *coolness:*—cold {5x}. See: TWOT—2067; BDB—899c, 903b.

7136. קָרָה {27x} **qârâh**, *kaw-raw';* a prim. root; to *light upon* (chiefly by accident); caus. to *bring about;* spec. to *impose* timbers (for roof or floor):—happen {7x}, meet {5x}, beams {4x}, befall {3x}, brought {1x}, misc. {7x} = appoint, come (to pass unto), floor, [hap] was, send good speed. See: TWOT—2068, 2068e; BDB—899c, 900a.

7137. קָרֶה {1x} **qâreh**, *kaw-reh';* from 7136; an (unfortunate) *occurrence,* i.e. some accidental (ceremonial) *disqualification:*—uncleanness that chanceth {1x}. See: TWOT—2068a; BDB—899d.

קֹרָה **qôrâh**. See 6982.

7138. קָרוֹב {78x} **qârôwb**, *kaw-robe';* or

קָרֹב **qârôb**, *kaw-robe';* from 7126; *near* (in place, kindred or time):—near {35x}, nigh {13x}, at hand {6x}, neighbour {5x}, next {5x}, kin {3x}, approach {2x}, short {2x}, kinsfolk {1x}, kinsmen {1x}, misc. {5x} = allied, approach, more ready, short (-ly).

This word stresses kinsman or near neighbor. *Qarob,* as an adjective, means "near." **(1)** *Qarob* can represent nearness in space: "Behold now, this city *is* near to flee unto, and it *is* a little one" (Gen 19:20—the first biblical occurrence) and **(2)** an epistemological nearness: "But the word *is* very nigh unto thee, in thy mouth, and in thy heart, that thou mayest do it" (Deut 30:14). **(3)** The adjective also appears in Eze 6:12: "He that is far off shall die of the pestilence; and he that is near shall fall by the sword. . . ." **(4)** It means neighbor in Ex 32:27. Syn.: 7128, 7131, 7132. See: TWOT—2065d; BDB—898b.

7139. קָרַח {5x} **qârach**, *kaw-rakh';* a prim. root; to *depilate:*—make bald {4x}, make {1x}. TWOT—2069; BDB—901a.

7140. קֶרַח {7x} **qerach**, *keh'-rakh;* or

קֹרַח **qôrach**, *ko'-rakh;* from 7139; *ice* (as if bald, i.e. *smooth*); hence, *hail;* by resemblance, rock *crystal:*—frost {3x}, ice {3x}, crystal {1x}. See: TWOT—2070a; BDB—901c.

7141. קֹרַח {37x} **Qôrach**, *ko'rakh;* from 7139; *ice; Korach,* the name of two Edomites and three Isr.:—Korah {37x}. See: BDB—901b.

7142. קֵרֵחַ {3x} **qêrêach**, *kay-ray'-akh;* from 7139; *bald* (on the back of the head):—bald {3x}. See: TWOT—2069a; BDB—901b.

7143. קָרֵחַ {14x} **Qârêach**, *kaw-ray'-akh;* from 7139; *bald; Kareäch,* an Isr.:—Kareah {13x}, Careah {1x}. See: BDB—901b.

7144. קָרְחָה {11x} **qorchâh**, *kor-khaw';* or

קָרְחָא **qorchâ'** (Eze 27:31), *kor-khaw';* from 7139; *baldness:*—baldness {9x}, bald {1x}, utterly {1x}. See: TWOT—2069b; BDB—901b.

7145. קָרְחִי {8x} **Qorchîy**, *kor-khee';* patron. from 7141; a *Korchite* (collect.) or desc. of Korach:—Korhites {4x}, Korahite {3x}, Kore {1x}. See: BDB—687c, 901c.

7146. קָרַחַת {4x} **qârachath**, *kaw-rakh'-ath;* from 7139; a *bald* spot (on the back of the head); fig. a *threadbare* spot (on the back side of the cloth):—bald head {3x}, bare within {1x}. See: TWOT—2069c; BDB—901b.

7147. קְרִי {7x} **qᵉrîy**, *ker-ee';* from 7136; hostile *encounter:*—contrary {7x}. See: TWOT—2068b; BDB—899d, 901c.

7148. קָרִיא {3x} **qârîy'**, *kaw-ree';* from 7121; *called,* i.e. *select:*—famous {2x}, variant {1x}. See: TWOT—2063b; BDB—896c.

7149. קִרְיָא {9x} **qiryâ'** (Aram.), *keer-yaw';* or

קִרְיָה **qiryâh** (Aram.), *keer-yaw';* corresp. to 7151:—city {9x}. See: TWOT—2979; BDB—1111d.

7150. קְרִיאָה {1x} **qᵉrîy'âh**, *ker-ee-aw';* from 7121; a *proclamation:*—preaching {1x}. See: TWOT—2063c; BDB—896d.

7151. קִרְיָה {31x} **qiryâh**, *kir-yaw';* from 7136 in the sense of *flooring,* i.e. *building;* a *city:*—city {31x}. See: TWOT—2068g; BDB—900a, 901c, 1111d.

7152. קְרִיּוֹת {4x} **Qᵉrîyôwth**, *ker-ee-yōth';* plur. of 7151; *buildings; Kerioth,* the name of two places in Pal.:—Kerioth {4x}. See: BDB—901a, 901c.

7153. קִרְיַת אַרְבַּע {9x} **Qiryath 'Arba'**, *keer-yath' ar-bah';* or (with the art. interposed)

קִרְיַת הָאַרְבַּע **Qiryath hâ-'Arba'** (Neh. 11:25), *keer-yath' haw-ar-bah';* from 7151 and 704 or 702; *city of Arba,* or *city of the four* (giants); *Kirjath-Arba* or *Kirjath-ha-Arba,* a place in Pal.:—Kirjatharba {6x}, city of Arba {1x}, synonym {2x}. See: BDB—900b, 917b.

7154. קִרְיַת בַּעַל {2x} **Qiryath Ba'al**, *keer-yath' bah'-al;* from 7151 and 1168; *city of Baal; Kirjath-Baal,* a place in Pal.:—Kirjathbaal {2x}. See: BDB—900c.

7155. קִרְיַת חֻצוֹת {1x} **Qiryath Chûtsôwth**, *keer-yath' khoo-tsōth';* from 7151 and the fem. plur. of 2351; *city of streets; Kirjath-Chutsoth,* a place in Moab:—Kirjathhuzoth {1x}. See: BDB—900c.

7156. קִרְיָתַיִם {6x} **Qiryâthayim**, *keer-yaw-thah'-yim;* dual of 7151; *double city; Kirjathaïm,* the name of two places in Pal.:—Kirjathaim {3x}, Kiriathaim {3x}. See: BDB—900b, 1001a.

7157. קִרְיַת יְעָרִים **Qiryath Yᵉ'ârîym**, *keer-yath' yeh-aw-reem';* or (Jer. 26:20) with the art. interposed; or (Josh. 18:28) simply the former part of the word; or

קִרְיַת עָרִים **Qiryath 'Ârîym**, *keer-yath' aw-reem';* from 7151 and the plur. of 3293 or 5892; *city of forests,* or *city of towns; Kirjath-Jeärim* or *Kirjath-Arim,* a place in Pal.:—Kirjathjearim {19x}, Kirjath {1x}. See: BDB—900b, 900c, 900d, 901c.

7158. קִרְיַת סַנָּה **Qiryath Çannâh**, *keer-yath' san-naw';* or

קִרְיַת סֵפֶר **Qiryath Çêpher**, *keer-yath' say-fer;* from 7151 and a simpler fem. from the same as 5577, or (for the latter name) 5612; *city of branches,* or *of a book; Kirjath-Sannah* or *Kirjath-Sepher,* a place in Pal.:—Kirjathsepher {4x}, Kirjathsannah {1x}. See: BDB—703a, 707c, 900d.

7159. קָרַם {2x} **qâram**, *kaw-ram';* a prim. root; to *cover:*—cover {2x}. See: TWOT—2071; BDB—901c.

7160. קָרַן {4x} **qâran**, *kaw-ran';* a prim. root; to *push* or gore; used only as denom. from 7161, to *shoot out horns; fig. rays:*—shine {3x}, has horns {1x}. See: TWOT—2072; BDB—902a.

7161. קֶרֶן {76x} **qeren**, *keh'-ren;* from 7160; a *horn* (as *projecting*); by impl. a *flask, cornet;* by resembl. an elephant's *tooth* (i.e. *ivory*), a *corner* (of the altar), a *peak* (of a mountain), a *ray* (of light); fig. *power:*—horn {75x}, hill {1x}. See: TWOT—2072a; BDB—901d, 902b, 1111d.

7162. קֶרֶן {14x} **qeren** (Aram.), *keh'-ren;* corresp. to 7161; a *horn* (lit. or for sound):—horn {10x}, cornet {4x}. See: TWOT—2980; BDB—1111d.

7163. קֶרֶן הַפּוּךְ {1x} **Qeren Hap-pûwk**, *keh'-ren hap-pook';* from 7161 and 6320; *horn of cosmetic; Keren-hap-Puk,* one of Job's daughters:—Keren-happuch {1x}. See: BDB—806c, 902a.

7164. קָרַס {2x} **qâraç**, *kaw-ras';* a prim. root; prop. to *protrude;* used only as denom. from 7165 (for alliteration with 7167), to *hunch,* i.e. be hump-backed:—stoop {2x}. See: TWOT—2073; BDB—902b.

7165. קֶרֶס {10x} **qereç**, *keh'-res;* from 7164; a *knob* or belaying pin (from its swelling form):—tache {10x}. See: TWOT—2073a; BDB—902b.

קֵרֹס **Qêrôç**. See 7026.

7166. קַרְסֹל {2x} **qarçôl**, *kar-sole';* from 7164; an *ankle* (as a *protuberance* or joint):—feet {2x}. See: TWOT—2073b; BDB—902b.

7167. קָרַע {62x} **qâra'**, *kaw-rah';* a prim. root; to *rend,* lit. or fig. (*revile, paint* the eyes, as if enlarging them):—rent {54x}, tear {4x}, rend away {2x}, cut {1x}, cut out {1x}, surely {1x}. "to rend, tear, tear away."

(1) It is found for the first time in Gen 37:29: ". . . He rent his clothes." **(2)** In the expression, "to tear one's clothes," *qara'* is used 39 times. Usually such "rending" of clothes is an expression of grief (Gen 37:34; 44:13; 2 Sa 13:19). **(3)** Sometimes the word is used in a symbolic act, such as Ahijah's "tearing" a new garment into twelve pieces and sending them to the twelve tribes as a symbol of coming division (1 Kin 11:30). **(4)** Samuel used *qara'* figuratively when he said to Saul: "The Lord hath rent the kingdom of Israel from thee this day . . ." (1 Sa 15:28). **(5)** Wild animals "rend" or "tear" their prey (Hos 13:8). See: TWOT—2074; BDB—902b.

7168. קֶרַע {4x} **qera'**, *keh'-rah;* from 7167; a *rag:*—piece {3x}, rags {1x}. See: TWOT—2074; BDB—902d.

7169. קָרַץ {5x} **qârats**, *kaw-rats';* a prim. root; to *pinch,* i.e. (partially) to *bite* the lips, *blink* the eyes (as a gesture of malice), or (fully) to *squeeze* off (a piece of clay in order to mould a vessel from it):—winketh {3x}, moving {1x}, formed {1x}. See: TWOT—2075; BDB—902d.

7170. קְרַץ {2x} **qᵉrats** (Aram.), *ker-ats';* corresp. to 7171 in the sense of a *bit* (to "eat the *morsels* of" any one, i.e. *chew* him up [fig.] by *slander*):—accused {2x}. See: TWOT—2981; BDB—1111d.

7171. קֶרֶץ {1x} **qerets**, *keh'-rets;* from 7169; *extirpation* (as if by *constriction*):—destruction {1x}. See: TWOT—2075a; BDB—903a, 1111d.

7172. קַרְקַע {8x} **qarqa'**, *kar-kah';* from 7167; *floor* (as if a pavement of pieces or *tesseræ*), of a building or the sea:—floor {6x}, other {1x}, bottom {1x}. See: TWOT—2076; BDB—903a.

7173. קַרְקַע {1x} **Qarqa'**, *kar-kah';* the same as 7172; *ground-floor; Karka* (with the art. pref.), a place in Pal.:—Karkaa {1x}. See: BDB—903a.

7174. קַרְקֹר {1x} **Qarqôr**, *kar-kore';* from 6979; *foundation; Karkor,* a place E. of the Jordan:—Karkor {1x}. See: BDB—903a.

7175. קֶרֶשׁ {51x} **qeresh**, *keh'-resh;* from an unused root mean. to *split* off; a *slab* or plank; by impl. a *deck* of a ship:—board {50x}, benches {1x}. See: TWOT—2079a; BDB—903c.

7176. קֶרֶת {5x} **qereth**, *keh'-reth;* from 7136 in the sense of building; a *city:*—city {5x}. See: TWOT—2068h; BDB—900d, 903c.

7177. קַרְתָּה {1x} **Qartâh**, *kar-taw';* from 7176; *city; Kartah,* a place in Pal.:—Kartah {1x}. See: BDB—900d.

7178. קַרְתָּן {1x} **Qartân**, *kar-tawn';* from 7176; *city-plot; Kartan,* a place in Pal.:—Kartan {1x}. See: BDB—900b, 900d.

7179. קַשׁ {16x} **qash**, *kash;* from 7197; *straw* (as *dry*):—stubble {16x}. See: TWOT—2091a; BDB—903b.

7180. קִשֻּׁא {1x} **qishshû'**, *kish-shoo';* from an unused root (mean. to *be hard*); a *cucumber* (from the difficulty of *digestion*):—cucumbers {1x}. See: TWOT—2083a; BDB—903d.

7181. קָשַׁב {46x} **qâshab**, *kaw-shab';* a prim. root; to *prick up* the ears, i.e. *hearken:*—hearken {27x}, attend {10x}, heed {3x}, hear {2x}, incline {1x}, marked {1x}, regarded {1x}, mark well {1x}. See: TWOT—2084; BDB—904a.

7182. קֶשֶׁב {4x} **qesheb**, *keh'-sheb;* from 7181; a *hearkening:*—record {1x}, hearing {1x}, diligently {1x}, heed {1x}. See: TWOT—2084a; BDB—904a.

7183. קַשָּׁב {5x} **qashshâb**, *kash-shawb';* or

קַשֻּׁב **qashshûb**, *kash-shoob';* from 7181; *hearkening:*—attentive {3x}, attent {2x}. See: TWOT—2084b, 2084c; BDB—903c, 904a, 904b.

7184. קָשָׂה {4x} **qâsâh**, *kaw-saw';* or

קַשְׂוָה **qasvâh**, *kas-vaw';* from an unused root mean. to *be round;* a *jug* (from its shape):—cover {3x}, cup {1x}. See: TWOT—2080, 2080a; BDB—903c.

7185. קָשָׁה {28x} **qâshâh**, *kaw-shaw';* a prim. root; prop. to *be dense,* i.e. *tough* or *severe* (in various applications):—harden {12x}, hard {4x}, stiffnecked + 6203 {2x}, grievous {2x}, misc. {8x} = be cruel, be fiercer, be sore, (be, make) stiff (-en).

This word marks the restlessness, impatience, petulance, and irritability with which Pharaoh's course of action was characterized while he was resisting the urgent appeals of both Moses and his own people. Syn.: 7188, 8631. See: TWOT—2085; BDB—904b.

7186. קָשֶׁה {36x} **qâsheh**, *kaw-sheh';* from 7185; *severe* (in various applications):—stiffnecked + 6203 {6x}, hard {5x}, roughly {5x}, cruel {3x}, grievous {3x}, sore {2x}, churlish {1x}, hardhearted {1x}, heavy {1x}, misc. {9x} = + impudent, obstinate, prevailed, sorrowful, stubborn, + in trouble. See: TWOT—2085a; BDB—904c.

7187. קְשׁוֹט {2x} **qᵉshôwṭ** (Aram.), *kesh-ote';* or

קְשֹׁט **qᵉshôṭ** (Aram.), *kesh-ote';* corresp. to 7189; *fidelity:*—truth {2x}. See: TWOT—2982; BDB—1112a.

7188. קָשַׁח {2x} **qâshach**, *kaw-shakh';* a prim. root; to *be* (caus. *make*) *unfeeling:*—harden {2x}. See: TWOT—2087; BDB—905a.

7189. קֹשֶׁט {2x} **qôsheṭ**, *ko'-shet;* or

קֹשְׁט **qôshṭ**, *kōsht;* from an unused root mean. to *balance; equity* (as evenly *weighed*), i.e. *reality:*—certainty {1x}, truth {1x}. See: TWOT—2088, 2089a; BDB—905a, 1112a.

קשׁט **qôshôṭ**. See 7187.

7190. קְשִׁי {1x} **qᵉshîy**, *kesh-ee';* from 7185; *obstinacy:*—stubbornness {1x}. See: TWOT—2085b; BDB—904d, 905a.

7191. קִשְׁיוֹן {2x} **Qishyôwn**, *kish-yone';* from 7190; *hard ground; Kishjon,* a place in Pal.:—Kishion {1x}, Kishon {1x}. See: BDB—904d, 905a.

7192. קְשִׂיטָה {3x} **qᵉsîyṭah**, *kes-ee-taw';* from an unused root (prob. mean. to *weigh* out); an *ingot* (as def. *estimated* and stamped for a coin):—piece of money {2x}, piece of silver {1x}. See: TWOT—2081a; BDB—903d.

7193. קַשְׂקֶשֶׂת {8x} **qasqeseth**, *kas-keh'-seth;* by redupl. from an unused root mean. to *shale* off as bark; a *scale* (of a fish); hence, a coat of *mail* (as composed of or covered with jointed *plates* of metal):—scale {7x}, mail {1x}. See: TWOT—2082a; BDB—903d.

7194. קָשַׁר {44x} **qâshar**, *kaw-shar';* a prim. root: to *tie,* phys. (*gird, confine, compact*) or ment. (in *love, league*):—conspired {18x}, bind {14x}, made {5x}, stronger {2x}, misc. {5x} = conspiracy, conspirator, join together, knit, work [treason]. See: TWOT—2090; BDB—905a.

7195. קֶשֶׁר {16x} **qesher**, *keh'-sher;* from 7194; an (unlawful) *alliance:*—conspiracy {9x}, treason {5x}, confederacy {2x}. See: TWOT—2090a; BDB—905c.

7196. קִשֻּׁר {2x} **qishshûr**, *kish-shoor';* from 7194; an (ornamental) *girdle* (for women):—headband {1x}, attire {1x}. See: TWOT—2090b; BDB—905c.

7197. קָשַׁשׁ {8x} **qâshash**, *kaw-shash';* a prim. root; to *become sapless* through drought; used only as denom. from 7179; to *forage* for straw, stubble or wood; fig. to *assemble:*—gather {6x}, gather together {2x}. See: TWOT—2091, 2092; BDB—905d.

7198. קֶשֶׁת {77x} **qesheth**, *keh'-sheth;* from 7185 in the orig. sense (of 6983) of *bending; a bow,* for *shooting* (hence, fig. *strength*) or the *iris:*—bow {68x}, archers + 3384 {3x}, archers {2x}, archers + 1869 {1x}, misc. {3x}. See: TWOT—2093; BDB—905d.

7199. קַשָּׁת {1x} **qashshâth**, *kash-shawth';* intens. (as denom.) from 7198; a *bowman:*—archer {1x}. See: TWOT—2094; BDB—906c.

ר

7200. רָאָה {1313x} **râ'âh**, *raw-aw';* a prim. root; to *see,* lit. or fig. (in numerous applications, dir. and impl., tran., intr. and caus.):—see {879x}, look {104x}, behold {83x}, shew {68x}, appear {66x}, consider {22x}, seer

{12x}, spy {6x}, respect {5x}, perceive {5x}, provide {4x}, regard {4x}, enjoy {4x}, lo {3x}, foreseeth {2x}, heed {2x}, misc. {74x} = advise self, approve, × certainly, discern, have experience, gaze, × indeed, × joyfully, mark, meet, × be near, present, seem, × sight of others, espy, stare, × surely, × think, view, visions.

Ra'ah is variously translated to see, observe, perceive, get acquainted with, gain understanding, examine, look after (see to), choose, discover. *Ra'ah,* as a verb, means "to see, observe, perceive, get acquainted with, gain understanding, examine, look after (see to), choose, discover." **(1)** Basically *ra'ah* connotes seeing with one's eyes: **(1a)** Isaac's "eyes were dim, so that he could not see" (Gen 27:1). **(1b)** This is its meaning in Gen 1:4, its first biblical appearance. **(1c)** The word can be used in the sense of seeing only what is obvious: ". . . For the Lord seeth not as man seeth . . ." (1 Sa 16:7). **(1d)** This verb can also mean "to observe": ". . . And there were upon the roof about three thousand men and women, that beheld while Samson made sport" (Judg 16:27). **(2)** The second primary meaning is "to perceive," or to be consciously aware of—so idols "neither see, nor hear" (Deut 4:28). **(3)** Third, *ra'ah* can represent perception in the sense of hearing something—God brought the animals before Adam "to see what he would call them" (Gen 2:19).

(4) In Is 44:16 the verb means "to enjoy": ". . . I am warm, I have seen the fire." **(5)** It can also mean "to realize" or "to get acquainted with": "When I applied mine heart to know wisdom, and to see the business that is done upon the earth . . ." (Eccl 8:16). **(6)** The rebellious men of Jerusalem tell God they will not "see sword nor famine"; they will not experience it (Jer 5:12). **(7)** This verb has several further extended meanings. For example, *ra'ah* can refer to "perceiving or ascertaining" something apart from seeing it with one's eyes, as when Hagar saw that she had conceived (Gen 16:4). **(8)** It can represent mentally recognizing that something is true: "We saw certainly that the Lord was with thee . . ." (Gen 26:28). **(9)** Seeing and hearing together can mean "to gain understanding": ". . . Kings shall shut their mouths at him: for that which had not been told them shall they see; and that which they had not heard shall they consider" (Is 52:15). **(10)** In Mal 3:18 the verb means "to distinguish": "Then shall ye return, and discern between the righteous and the wicked. . . ."

(11) The word can mean to consider the fact that Israel is God's people (Ex 33:13). **(12)** In addition to these uses of *ra'ah* referring to intellectual seeing, there is seeing used in the sense of living. **(12a)** "To see the light" is to live life (Job 3:16; cf. 33:28). **(12b)** It can mean "experience" in the sense of what one is aware of as he lives: "Even as I have seen, they that plow iniquity . . . reap the same" (Job 4:8). **(12c)** In 2 Kin 25:19 the verb is used in the unique sense of "having trusted concourse with" when it speaks of the five advisors of the king. **(13)** Another idea of seeing is "to examine": "And the Lord came down to see the city and the tower . . ." (Gen 11:5). **(13a)** This examining can have to do with more than looking something over; it can refer to looking after or supervising something (Gen 39:23). **(13b)** Used in this sense *ra'ah* can imply looking upon with joy or pain. Hagar asked that she not be allowed to look on the death of Ishmael (Gen 21:16).

(14) This verb may be used of attending to or visiting—so Jonadab said to Amnon: ". . . When thy father cometh to see thee, say unto him . . ." (2 Sa 13:5). **(15)** When Joseph advised Pharaoh "to look out a man discreet and wise," he was telling him to choose or select such a man (Gen 41:33). **(16)** "To examine" may also be "to observe" someone **(16a)** in order to imitate what he does (Judg 7:17), or **(16b)** "to discover" something (find it out; Judg 16:5). See: TWOT—2095; BDB—906b, 909b, 1112a.

7201. רָאָה {1x} **râʼâh,** *raw-aw';* from 7200; a *bird* of prey (prob. the *vulture,* from its sharp *sight*):—glede {1x}. See: TWOT—394a; BDB—906b. comp. 1676.

7202. רָאֶה {1x} **râʼeh,** *raw-eh';* from 7200; *seeing,* i.e. experiencing:—see {1x}. See: TWOT—2095a; BDB—909a.

7203. רֹאֶה {1x} **rôʼeh,** *ro-eh';* act. part. of 7200; a *seer* (as often rendered); but also (abstr.) a *vision:*—vision {1x}.

Ro'eh, as a noun, means "vision": "But they also have erred through wine, and through strong drink are out of the way; the priest and the prophet have erred through strong drink, they are swallowed up of wine, they are out of the way through strong drink; they err in vision, they stumble *in* judgment" (Is 28:7). See: TWOT—2095b, 2095c; BDB—906d, 909a, 909b.

7204. רֹאֵה {1x} **Rôʼêh,** *ro-ay';* for 7203; *prophet; Roëh,* an Isr.:—Haroeh {1x}. See: BDB—909b.

7205. רְאוּבֵן {72x} **Rᵉʼûwbên,** *reh-oo-bane';* from the imper. of 7200 and 1121; *see* ye a *son; Reben,* a son of Jacob:—Reuben {72x}. See: BDB—910a.

7206. רְאוּבֵנִי {18x} **Rᵉʼûwbênîy,** *reh-oob-aynee';* patron. from 7205; a *Rebenite* or desc. of Reüben:—Reubenite {17x}, Reuben {1x}. See: BDB—910a.

7207. רַאֲוָה {1x} **raʼăvâh,** *rah-av-aw';* from 7200; *sight,* i.e. *satisfaction:*—beholding + 7212 {1x}.

Re'ut [from *ra'avah*] occurs once, and it means "look" (Eccl 5:11). Syn.: 4758, 4759, 7209, 7210, 8389. See: TWOT—2095; BDB—906d, 908a, 909b.

7208. רְאוּמָה {1x} **Rᵉʼûwmâh,** *reh-oo-maw';* fem. pass. part. of 7213; *raised; Remah,* a Syrian woman:—Reumah {1x}. See: BDB—910b.

7209. רְאִי {1x} **rᵉʼîy,** *reh-ee';* from 7200; a *mirror* (as *seen*):—looking glass {1x}.

Re'iy appears once to mean "looking-glass" (Job 37:18). Syn.: 4758, 4759, 7207, 7210, 8389. See: TWOT—2095e; BDB—909b, 910b.

7210. רֳאִי {6x} **rôʼîy,** *ro-ee';* from 7200; *sight,* whether abstr. (*vision*) or concr. (a *spectacle*):—see {4x}, look {1x}, gazingstock {1x}.

Ro'iy, which occurs 6 times, means "looking, appearance": "Now he *was* ruddy, *and* withal of a beautiful countenance, and goodly to look to [*ro'iy*]" (1 Sa 16:12). Syn.: 4758, 4759, 7207, 7209, 8389. See: TWOT—2095f; BDB—909b, 910b.

7211. רְאָיָה {4x} **Rᵉʼâyâh,** *reh-aw-yaw';* from 7200 and 3050; *Jah has seen; Reäjah,* the name of three Isr.:—Reaiah {3x}, Reaia {1x}. See: BDB—909b, 909d, 910b.

7212. רְאִית {1x} **rᵉʼîyth,** *reh-eeth';* from 7200; *sight:*—beholding {1x}. See: TWOT—2095d; BDB—909b, 910b.

7213. רָאַם {1x} **râʼam,** *raw-am';* a prim. root; to *rise:*—lifted up {1x}. See: TWOT—2096; BDB—910b, 910c, 926c.

7214. רְאֵם {9x} **rᵉʼêm,** *reh-ame';* or
רְאֵים **rᵉʼêym,** *reh-ame';* or
רֵים **rêym,** *rame;* or
רֵם **rêm,** *rame;* from 7213; a wild *bull* (from its *conspicuousness*):—unicorn {9x}. See: TWOT—2096a; BDB—910b, 937c, 941a.

7215. רָאמָה {2x} **râʼmâh,** *raw-maw';* from 7213; something *high* in value, i.e. perh. *coral:*—coral {2x}. See: TWOT—2096b; BDB—910c.

7216. רָאמוֹת {4x} **Râʼmôwth,** *raw-mōth';* or
רָאמֹת **Râmôth,** *raw-mōth';* plur. of 7215; *heights; Ramoth,* the name of two places in Pal.:—*Ramoth* {4x}. See: BDB—910c.

7217. רֵאשׁ {14x} **rêʼsh** (Aram.), *raysh;* corresp. to 7218; the *head;* fig. the *sum:*—head {12x}, sum {1x}, chief {1x}. See: TWOT—2983; BDB—1112a.

7218. רֹאשׁ {598x} **rôʼsh,** *roshe;* from an unused root appar. mean. to *shake;* the *head* (as most easily *shaken*), whether lit. or fig. (in many applications, of place, time, rank, etc.):—head {349x}, chief {91x}, top {73x}, beginning {14x}, company {12x}, captain {10x}, sum {9x}, first {6x}, principal {5x}, chapiters {4x}, rulers {2x}, misc. {23x} = band, end, × every [man], excellent, forefront, height, (on) high (-est part, [priest]), × lead, × poor.

Ro'sh, means "head; top; first; sum." **(1)** This word often represents a "head," **(1a)** a bodily part (Gen 40:20). **(1b)** *Rosh* is also used of a decapitated "head" (2 Sa 4:8), **(1c)** an animal "head" (Gen 3:15), and **(1d)** a statue "head" (Dan 2:32). **(1e)** In Dan 7:9, where God is pictured in human form, His "head" is crowned with hair like pure wool (i.e., white).

(2) To "lift up one's own head" may be **(2a)** a sign of declaring one's innocence: "If I be wicked, woe unto me; and if I be righteous, yet will I not lift up my head. I am full of confusion; therefore see thou mine affliction" (Job 10:15). **(2b)** This same figure of speech may indicate an intention to begin a war, the most violent form of self-assertion: "For, lo, thine enemies make a tumult: and they that hate thee have lifted up the head" (Ps 83:2). **(2c)** With a negation, this phrase may symbolize submission to another power: "Thus was Midian subdued before the children of Israel, so that they lifted up their heads no more" (Judg 8:28). **(2d)** Used transitively (i.e., to lift up someone else's "head"), this word may connote restoring someone to a previous position: "Yet within three days shall Pharaoh lift up thine head, and restore thee unto thy place . . ." (Gen 40:13). **(2e)** It can also denote the release of someone from prison: ". . . Evil-Merodach king of Babylon in the year that he began to reign did lift up the head of Jehoiachin king of Judah out of prison" (2 Kin 25:27). **(3)** With the verb *rum* (7311 - "to raise"), **(3a)** *ro'sh* can signify the victory and power of an enthroned king—God will "lift up [His] head," or exert His rule (Ps 110:7). **(3b)** When God lifts up (rum) one's "head," He fills one with hope and confidence: "But thou, O Lord, art a shield for me; my glory, and the lifter up of mine head" (Ps 3:3).

(4) There are many secondary nuances of *ro'sh.* **(4a)** First, the word can represent the "hair on one's head": "But it shall be on the seventh day, that he shall shave all his hair off his head and his beard and his eyebrows, even all his hair he shall shave off:" (Lev 14:9). **(4b)** The word can connote unity, representing every individual in a given group: "Have they not sped? have they not divided the prey; to every man a damsel or two . . ." (Judg 5:30). **(4c)** This word may be used numerically, meaning the total number of persons or individuals in a group: "Take ye the sum (*ro'sh*) of all the congregation of the children of Israel, after their families, by the house of their fathers, with the number of their names, every male by their polls" (Num 1:2). **(4d)** *Ro'sh* can also emphasize the individual: "And there was a great famine in Samaria: and, behold, they besieged it, until an ass's head [i.e., an individual donkey] was sold for fourscore pieces of silver . . ." (2 Kin 6:25). **(4e)** It is upon the "head" (upon the person himself) that curses and blessings fall: "The blessings of thy father have prevailed above the blessings of my progenitors . . . : they shall be on the head of Joseph . . ." (Gen 49:26). **(4f)** *Ro'sh* sometimes means "leader," whether appointed, elected, or self-appointed. The word can be used of the tribal fathers, who are the leaders of a group of people: "And Moses chose able men out of all Israel, and made them heads over the people . . ." (Ex 18:25). **(4g)** Military leaders are also called "heads": "These be the names of the mighty men whom David had: The Tachmonite that sat in the seat, chief among the captains . . ." (2 Sa 23:8). **(4h)** In Num 1:16, the princes are called "heads" (cf. Judg 10:18). **(4i)** This word is used of those who represent or lead the people in worship (2 Kin 25:18—the chief priest).

(5) When used of things, *ro'sh* means "point" or "beginning." **(5a)** With a local emphasis, the word refers to the "top" or summit of a mountain or hill: ". . . Tomorrow I will stand on the top of the hill with the rod of God in mine hand" (Ex 17:9). **(5b)** Elsewhere the word represents the topmost end of a natural or constructed object: "Go to, let us build us a city and a tower, whose top may reach unto heaven . . ." (Gen 11:4). **(5c)** In Gen 47:31, the word denotes the "head" of a bed, or where one lays his "head." **(5d)** In 1 Kin 8:8, *ro'sh* refers to the ends of poles. **(5e)** The word may be used of the place where a journey begins: "Thou hast built thy high place at every head of the way . . ." (Eze 16:25; cf. Dan 7:1: "the sum of the matters. . . ."). **(5f)** This sense of the place of beginning appears in Gen 2:10 (the first occurrence): "And a river went out of Eden to water the garden; and from thence it was parted, and became [the source of four rivers]." **(5g)** This nuance identifies a thing as being placed spatially in front of a group; it stands in front or at the "head" (Deut 20:9; cf. 1 Kin 21:9). **(5h)** The "head" of the stars is a star located at the zenith of the sky (Job 22:12). **(5i)** The "head" cornerstone occupies a place of primary importance. It is the stone by which all the other stones are measured; it is the chief cornerstone (Ps 118:22).

(6) This word may have a temporal significance meaning "beginning" or "first." **(6a)** The second sense is seen in Ex 12:2: "This month shall be unto you the beginning of months. . . ." **(6b)** In 1 Chr 16:7 the word describes the "first" in a whole series of acts: "Then on that day David delivered first this psalm to thank the Lord into the hand of Asaph and his brethren." **(7)** *Ro'sh* may also have an estimative connotation: "Take thou also unto thee [the finest of] spices . . ." (Ex 30:23). Syn.: 7101, 7336. See: TWOT—2097; BDB—910c, 1112a.

7219. רֹאשׁ {12x} **rôʼsh**, *roshe;* or
רוֹשׁ **rôwsh** (Deut. 32:32), *roshe;* appar. the same as 7218; a poisonous *plant*, prob. the *poppy* (from its conspicuous *head*); gen. *poison* (even of serpents):—gall {9x}, venom {1x}, poison {1x}, hemlock {1x}. See: TWOT—2098; BDB—911b, 912c, 930d.

7220. רֹאשׁ {1x} **Rôʼsh**, *roshe;* prob. the same as 7218; *Rosh*, the name of an Isr. and of a for. nation:—*Rosh* {1x}. See: BDB—911b, 912c.

רֵאשׁ **rêʼsh**. See 7389.

7221. רִאשָׁה {1x} **riʼshâh**, *ree-shaw';* from the same as 7218; a *beginning:*—beginnings {1x}. See: TWOT—2097a; BDB—911c.

7222. רֹאשָׁה {1x} **rôʼshâh**, *ro-shaw';* fem. of 7218; the *head:*—headstone + 68 {1x}. See: TWOT—2097b; BDB—911c.

7223. רִאשׁוֹן {185x} **riʼshôwn**, *ree-shone';* or
רִאשֹׁן **riʼshôn**, *ree-shone';* from 7221; *first*, in place, time or rank (as adj. or noun):—first {129x}, former {26x}, former things {6x}, beginning {4x}, chief {3x}, before {3x}, old time {2x}, foremost {3x}, aforetime {1x}, misc. {8x} = ancestor, eldest, forefather, past.

Ri'shon (7223), as an adjective, means "first; foremost; preceding; former." **(1)** It denotes the "first" in a temporal sequence: "And it came to pass in the six hundredth and first year, in the first month, the first day of the month . . ." (Gen 8:13). **(2)** In Ezra 9:2, *ri'shon* is used both of precedence in time and of leadership: ". . . The holy seed have mingled themselves with the people of those lands: yea, the hand of the princes and rulers hath been chief (*ri'shon*) in this trespass." **(3)** Another meaning of this adjective is "preceding" or "former": ". . . Unto the place of the altar, which he had made there at the first . . ." (Gen 13:4). **(4)** Gen 33:2 uses this word locally: "And he put the handmaids and their children foremost (*ri'shon*), and Leah and her children after, and Rachel and Joseph hindermost." **(5)** The "former ones" are "ancestors": "But I will for their sakes remember the covenant of their ancestors, whom I brought forth out of the land of Egypt in the sight of the heathen . . ." (Lev 26:45). **(6)** But in most cases, this adjective has a temporal emphasis. See: TWOT—2097c; BDB—910b, 911c, 938c.

7224. רִאשֹׁנִי {1x} **riʼshônîy**, *ree-sho-nee';* from 7223; *first:*—first {1x}. See: TWOT—2097d; BDB—912a.

7225. רֵאשִׁית {51x} **rêʼshîyth**, *ray-sheeth';* from the same as 7218; the *first*, in place, time, order or rank (spec. a *firstfruit*):—beginning {18x}, firstfruits {11x}, first {9x}, chief {8x}, misc. {5x}.

Re'shiyth (7225), means "beginning; first; choicest." **(1)** The abstract word *re'shiyth* corresponds to the temporal and estimative sense of ro'sh (7218). **(1a)** *Re'shiyth* connotes the "beginning" of a fixed period of time: ". . . The eyes of the Lord thy God are always upon it, from the beginning of the year even unto the end of the year" (Deut 11:12). **(1b)** The "beginning" of one's period of life is intended in Job 42:12: "So the Lord blessed the latter end of Job more than his beginning. . . ." **(2)** This word can represent a point of departure, as it does in Gen 1:1 (the first occurrence): "In the beginning God created the heaven and the earth." **(3)** Estimatively, this word can mean the "first" or "choicest": "The first of the first fruits of thy land thou shalt bring into the house of the Lord thy God" (Ex 23:19). **(4)** This nuance of *re'shiyth* may appear in the comparative sense, meaning "choicest" or "best." Dan 11:41 exhibits the nuance of "some": ". . . But these shall escape out of his hand, even Edom, and Moab, and the chief of the children of Ammon" (Dan 11:41).

(5) Used substantively, the word can mean "first fruits": **(5a)** "As for the oblation of the first fruits, ye shall offer them unto the Lord: but they shall not be burnt on the altar for a sweet savor" (Lev 2:12). **(5b)** "The first fruits of them which they shall offer unto the Lord, them have I given thee" (Num 18:12). **(6)** Sometimes this word represents the "first part" of an offering: "Ye shall offer up a cake of the first of your dough for a heave offering . . ." (Num 15:20). See: TWOT—2097e; BDB—912a, 957a.

7226. רַאֲשֹׁת {1x} **raʼăshôth**, *rah-ash-ōth';* from 7218; a *pillow* (being for the *head*):—bolster {1x}. See: TWOT—2097f; BDB—910c, 912a.

7227. רַב {458x} **rab**, *rab;* by contr. from 7231; *abundant* (in quantity, size, age, number, rank, quality):—many {190x}, great {118x}, much {36x}, captain {24x}, more {12x}, long {10x}, enough {9x}, multitude {7x}, mighty {5x}, greater {4x}, greatly {3x}, misc. {40x} = (in) abound (-undance, -ant, -antly), elder, exceedingly, full, increase, manifold, things, a time), ([ship-]) master, multiply, officer, often [-times], plenteous, populous, prince, process [of time], suffice (-ient).

I. *Rab*, **as a noun,** means "chief." **(1)** The first appearance: "And it came to pass, that at midnight [literally, "the middle of the officers] of his house]. . . ." **(2)** *Rab*, designating chief, is **(2a)** an indication of military rank similar to our word general (Jer 39:3). **(2b)** One should especially note the titles in Jeremiah: "And all the princes [officials] of the king of Babylon came in, and sat in the middle gate, even Nergal-sharezer, Samgar-nebo, Sarsechim, Rab-saris, Nergal-sharezer, Rab-mag, with all the residue of the princes of the king of Babylon" (39:3). Verses 9, 10, 11, and 13 of Jeremiah 39 mention Nebuzaradan as the "captain" of the bodyguard. **II.** *Rab*, **as an adjective,** means "many; great; large; prestigious; powerful." **(1)** First, this word represents plurality in number or amount, whether applied to people or to things. **(1a)** *Rab* is applied to people in Gen 26:14: "For he [Isaac] had possession of flocks, and possession of herds, and great store of servants. . . ." **(1b)** In Gen 13:6, the word is applied to things: "And the land was not able to bear them, that they might dwell together: for their substance was great, so that they could not dwell together." This word is sometimes used of "large groups of people" (Ex 5:5).

(2) This basic idea of "numerical multiplicity" is also applied to amounts of liquids or masses of non-liquids: **(2a)** "And Moses lifted up his hand, and with his rod he smote the rock twice: and the water came out abundantly . . ." (Num 20:11); a "great" amount of water came forth. **(2b)** Rebekah told Abraham's servant that her father had "straw and provender enough, and room to lodge in" (Gen 24:25). **(3)** The phrase "many waters" is a fixed phrase meaning the "sea": **(3a)** ". . . Thou whom the merchants of Zidon, that pass over the sea, have replenished. And by great waters the seed of Sihor, the harvest of the river, is her revenue . . ." (Is 23:2–3). **(3b)** "And the channels of the sea appeared, the foundations of the world were discovered, at the rebuking of the Lord, at the blast of the breath of his nostrils. He sent from above, he took me; he drew me out of many waters . . ." (2 Sa 22:16–17). **(3c)** This imagery is used in several Old Testament poetical passages; it would be wrong to conclude that this view of the world was true or actual. **(3d)** On the other hand, Gen 7:11 uses a related phrase as a figure of the "sources of all water": ". . . The same day were all the fountains of the great deep broken up. . . ."

(4) Used in conjunction with "days" or "years," *rab* means "long," and the resulting phrase means "a long time": "And Abraham sojourned in the Philistines' land many days" (Gen 21:34). **(5)** The word can be used metaphorically, describing an abstract concept: "And God saw that the wickedness of man was great in the earth, and that every imagination of the thoughts of his heart was only evil continually" (Gen 6:5—the first biblical occurrence). **(5a)** This use of *rab* does not describe the relative value of the thing modified, but its numerical recurrence. **(5b)** The statement implies, however, that man's constant sinning was more reprehensible than the more occasional sinning previously committed. **(6)** When *rab* is applied to land areas, it means "large" (1 Sa 26:13). This usage is related to the usual meaning of the Semitic cognates, which represent "size" rather than numerical multiplicity (also cf. gadal - 1431): "And the Lord delivered them into the hand of Israel, who smote them, and chased them unto great Zidon . . ." (Josh 11:8).

(7) When God is called the "great King" (Ps 48:2), the adjective refers to His superior power and sovereignty over all kings (vv. 4ff.). **(7a)** This meaning emerges in Job 32:9: "The great may not be wise, nor may elders understand justice" (cf. Job 35:9). **(7b)** Uses such as these in Job emphasize "greatness in prestige," whereas passages such as 2 Chr 14:11 emphasize "strength and might": "And Asa cried unto the LORD his God, and said, LORD, *it is* nothing with thee to help, whether with many, or with them that have no power: help us, O LORD our God; for we rest on thee, and in thy name we go against this multitude. O LORD, thou *art* our God; let not man prevail against thee." See: TWOT—2099a, 2099b; BDB—912c, 912d, 913c, 914d, 918d, 1112a.

7228. רַב {2x} **rab**, *rab;* by contr. from 7232; an *archer* [or perh. the same as 7227]:—archer {2x}. See: TWOT—2100a; BDB—912c, 914d.

7229. רַב {15x} **rab** (Aram.), *rab;* corresp. to 7227:—great {9x}, master {2x}, stout {1x}, chief {1x}, captain {1x}, lord {1x}. See: TWOT—2984a; BDB—1112a, 1112c.

רִב **rîb**. See 7378.

7230. רֹב {155x} **rôb**, *robe;* from 7231; *abundance* (in any respect):—multitude {70x}, abundance {35x}, great {9x}, greatness {8x}, much {8x}, abundantly {4x}, plenty {3x}, many {3x}, long {2x}, excellent {1x}, misc. {12x} = all, × common [sort], greatly, huge, be increased, more in number, most, plentifully, × very [age].

Rob, as a noun, means "multitude; abundance." **(1)** The word basically means "multitude" or "abundance"; it has numerical implications apparent in its first biblical appearance: "I will multiply thy seed exceedingly, that it shall not be numbered for multitude" (Gen 16:10). **(2)** When applied to time or distance, *rob* indicates a "large amount" or "long": "And these bottles of wine, which we filled, were new; and, behold, they be rent: and these our garments and our shoes are become old by reason of the very long journey" (Josh 9:13). **(3)** In several passages, the word is applied to abstract ideas or qualities. In such cases, *rob* means "great" or "greatness": ". . . This that is glorious in his apparel, traveling in the greatness of his strength" (Is 63:1).

(4) The preposition le when prefixed to the noun *rob* sometimes forms an adverbial phrase **(4a)** meaning "abundantly": "For it was little which thou hadst before I came, and it is now increased unto a multitude . . ." (Gen 30:30). **(4b)** The same phrase bears a different sense in 1 Kin 10:10, where it seems to be almost a substantive: "There came no more such abundance of spices as these which the queen of Sheba gave to king Solomon." **(4c)** The phrase literally appears to mean "great" with respect to "multitude." **(4d)** This phrase is applied to Uzziah's building activities: ". . . And on the wall of Ophel he built much" (2 Chr 27:3), where it means "much." **(4e)** This phrase is extended by the addition of 'ad (5704). Thus we have 'ad lerob, meaning "exceeding much": "Since the people began to bring the offerings into the house of the Lord, we have had enough to eat, and have left plenty [literally, "the remainder is exceeding much"] . . ." (2 Chr 31:10). See: TWOT—2099c; BDB—912c, 913d, 923d.

7231. רָבַב {17x} **râbab**, *raw-bab';* a prim. root; prop. to *cast* together [comp. 7241], i.e. *increase,* espec. in number; also (as denom. from 7233) to *multiply by the myriad:*—are many {6x}, are multiplied {3x}, increased {3x}, are more {2x}, manifold {1x}, ten thousands {1x}, multiply {1x}.

Rabab, as a verb, means "to be numerous, great, large, powerful." **(1)** The first occurrence means "to be (or become) numerous": "And it came to pass, when men began to multiply on the face of the earth, and daughters were born unto them," (Gen 6:1). **(2)** *Rabab* can also mean "to be great" in size, prestige, or power: "And the LORD said, Because the cry of Sodom and Gomorrah is great, and because their sin is very grievous;" (Gen 18:20; cf. Job 33:12; Ps 49:16). **(3)** With a subject indicating time, this verb **(3a)** implies "lengthening": "And in process of time the daughter of Shuah Judah's wife died;" (Gen 38:12), and **(3b)** with special subjects the word may imply "extension of space": "And if the way be too long for thee, so that thou art not able to carry it; *or* if the place be too far from thee, which the LORD thy God shall choose to set his name there, when the LORD thy God hath blessed thee:" (Deut 14:24). Syn.: 3515. See: TWOT—2099; BDB—912c, 912d, 914b, 914c, 1112a.

7232. רָבַב {2x} **râbab**, *raw-bab';* a prim. root [rather ident. with 7231 through the idea of *projection*]; to *shoot* an arrow:—shot {1x}, shot out {1x}. See: TWOT—2100; BDB—914d.

7233. רְבָבָה {16x} **r^{e}bâbâh**, *reb-aw-baw';* from 7231; *abundance* (in number), i.e. (spec.) a *myriad* (whether def. or indef.):—ten thousand {13x}, million {1x}, many {1x}, multiply {1x}. See: TWOT—2099d; BDB—914b.

7234. רָבַד {1x} **râbad**, *raw-bad';* a prim. root; to *spread:*—deck {1x}. See: TWOT—2102; BDB—914d.

7235. רָבָה **râbâh**, *raw-baw';* a prim. root; to *increase* (in whatever respect):—multiply {74x}, increase {40x}, much {29x}, many {28x}, more {12x}, great {8x}, long {3x}, store {2x}, exceedingly {2x}, greater {2x}, abundance {2x}, misc. {24x} = [bring in] abundance (× -antly), + archer [*by mistake for* 7232], be in authority, bring up, × continue, enlarge, excel, exceeding (-ly), be full of, grow up, heap, nourish, plenty (-eous), × process [of time], sore, store, thoroughly, very.

Rabah, as a verb, means "to multiply, become numerous, become great." **(1)** Basically this word connotes numerical increase. **(1a)** It can refer to the process of increasing numerically: God told the sea and air creatures to "be fruitful, and multiply" (Gen 1:22—the first occurrence). **(1b)** In Gen 38:12 the word refers to the end result in the sense that a great many of something existed: "And in process of time the daughter of Shuah Judah's wife died [literally, "and the days became multiplied"]. . . ." **(1c)** When used with "days," the word may also signify "long life": ". . . I shall multiply my days as the sand" (Job 29:18: cf. Prov 4:10). **(2)** *Rabah* sometimes refers to increasing in wealth, although in such cases the material is clearly specified (cf. Deut 8:13: ". . . and thy silver and thy gold is multiplied"). **(3)** This verb can be used of being quantitatively large. In Gen 7:17 the waters are said to have "increased, and bare up the ark, and it was lifted up above the earth." **(3a)** So here the verb means "to increase in quantity." **(3b)** A similar use occurs in Gen 15:1, where God tells Abram: "I am . . . thy exceeding great reward." **(3c)** The first instance speaks of the process of increasing and the latter of the end product (something that is larger).

(4) In a special nuance this verb signifies the process of growing up: "Their young ones are in good liking, they grow up [in the open field]" (Job 39:4). **(5)** *Rabah* can also be used of the end product: "I have caused thee to multiply as the bud of the field, and thou hast increased and waxen great, and thou art come to excellent ornaments: thy breasts are fashioned, and thine hair is grown . . ." (Eze 16:7). **(6)** A somewhat different nuance occurs in Eze 19:2, where the verb speaks of a parent's care for an offspring: ". . . She nourished her whelps." **(7)** *Rabah* is sometimes used with another verb to signify its increase in occurrence or frequency. **(7a)** In some passages it signifies that a process is continuing: "The people bring much more than enough for the service of the work . . ." (Ex 36:5), literally, "the people continue to bring." **(7b)** It can also signify a great number of times with the sense of "repeatedly." **(8)** The sinner is urged to return to God, **(8a)** "for he will abundantly pardon" (Is 55:7). **(8b)** This sense appears clearly in Amos 4:4: "Come to Beth-eland transgress; at Gilgal multiply transgression. . . ." Syn.: 697, 4766, 4768, 8635, 8636. See: TWOT—2103, 2104; BDB—915a, 916c, 1112b.

7236. רְבָה {6x} **r^{e}bâh** (Aram.), *reb-aw';* corresp. to 7235:—grow {5x}, great {1x}. Syn.: 7101, 7218, 7336. See: TWOT—2985; BDB—1112b.

7237. רַבָּה {15x} **Rabbâh**, *rab-baw';* fem. of 7227; *great; Rabbah,* the name of two places in Pal., East and West:—*Rabbah*{13x}, Rabbath {2x}. See: BDB—851a, 913d, 916c.

7238. רְבוּ **r^{e}bûw** (Aram.), *reb-oo';* from a root corresp. to 7235; *increase* (of dignity):—majesty {4x}, greatness {1x}. See: TWOT—2985a; BDB—1112c.

7239. רִבּוֹ {11x} **ribbôw**, *rib-bo';* from 7231; or
רִבּוֹא **ribbôw'**, *rib-bo';* from 7231; a *myriad,* i.e. indef. *large number:*— . . . . thousand {4x}, forty, etc . . . (thousand) {4x}, ten thousand {2x}, variant {1x}. See: TWOT—2099e; BDB—914b, 916c, 1112a.

7240. רִבּוֹ {2x} **ribbôw** (Aram.), *rib-bo';* corresp. to 7239:—ten thousand {2x}. See: TWOT—2984b; BDB—1112b.

7241. רְבִיב {6x} **râbîyb**, *raw-beeb';* from 7231; a *rain* (as an *accumulation* of drops):—shower {6x}. See: TWOT—2099f; BDB—914c.

7242. רְבִיד {2x} **râbîyd**, *raw-beed';* from 7234; a *collar* (as *spread* around the neck):—chain {2x}. See: TWOT—2101a; BDB—914d.

7243. רְבִיעִי {56x} **rᵉbîyʿîy**, *reb-ee-ee'*; or

רְבִעִי **rᵉbîʿîy**, *reb-ee-ee'*; from 7251; *fourth;* also (fractionally) a *fourth:*—fourth {51x}, fourth part {4x}, foursquare {1x}. See: TWOT—2107c; BDB—917d, 1112c.

7244. רְבִיעַי {6x} **rᵉbîyʿay** (Aram.), *reb-ee-ah'-ee;* corresp. to 7243:—fourth {6x}. See: TWOT—2986b; BDB—1112c.

7245. רַבִּית {1x} **Rabbîyth**, *rab-beeth';* from 7231; *multitude; Rabbith,* a place in Pal.:—Rabbith {1x}. See: BDB—914c, 916c.

7246. רָבַךְ {3x} **râbak**, *raw-bak';* a prim. root; to *soak* (bread in oil):—fried {2x}, baken {1x}. See: TWOT—2105; BDB—916c.

7247. רִבְלָה {11x} **Riblâh**, *rib-law';* from an unused root mean. to *be fruitful; fertile; Riblah,* a place in Syria:—*Riblah* {11x}. See: BDB—916c.

7248. רַב־מָג {2x} **Rab-Mâg**, *rab-mawg';* from 7227 and a for. word for a Magian; *chief Magian; Rab-Mag,* a Bab. official:—*Rabmag* {2x}. See: TWOT—1143; BDB—550b, 913c, 916c.

7249. רַב־סָרִיס {3x} **Rab-Çârîyç**, *rab-saw-reece';* from 7227 and a for. word for a eunuch; *chief chamberlain; Rab-Saris,* a Bab. official:—Rabsaris {3x}. See: BDB—913c, 916c.

7250. רָבַע {3x} **râbaʿ**, *raw-bah';* a prim. root; to *squat* or *lie* out flat, i.e. (spec.) in copulation:—lie down {2x}, gender {1x}. See: TWOT—2108; BDB—918a.

7251. רָבַע {12x} **râbaʿ**, *raw-bah';* a prim. root [rather ident. with 7250 through the idea of *sprawling* "at all fours" (or possibly the reverse is the order of der.); comp. 702]; prop. to *be four* (sided); used only as denom. of 7253; to *be quadrate:*—foursquare {8x}, square {4x}. See: TWOT—2107; BDB—917c.

7252. רֶבַע {1x} **rebaʿ**, *reh'-bah;* from 7250; *prostration* (for sleep):—lying down {1x}. See: TWOT—2108; BDB—918a.

7253. רֶבַע {7x} **rebaʿ**, *reh'-bah;* from 7251; a *fourth* (part or side):—sides {3x}, fourth part {2x}, squares {2x}. See: TWOT—2107a; BDB—917d.

7254. רֶבַע {2x} **Rebaʿ**, *reh'-bah;* the same as 7253; *Reba,* a Midianite:—*Reba* {2x}. See: BDB—918b.

7255. רֹבַע {2x} **rôbaʿ**, *ro'-bah;* from 7251; a *quarter:*—fourth part {2x}. See: TWOT—2107b; BDB—917d.

7256. רִבֵּעַ {4x} **ribbêaʿ**, *rib-bay'-ah;* from 7251; a desc. of the *fourth* generation, i.e. *great great grandchild:*—fourth {4x}. See: TWOT—2107d; BDB—918a.

רְבִיעִי **rᵉbîyʿîy**. See 7243.

7257. רָבַץ {30x} **râbats**, *raw-bats';* a prim. root; to *crouch* (on all four legs folded, like a recumbent animal); by impl. to *recline, repose, brood, lurk, imbed:*—lay down {15x}, lay {9x}, couch beneath {1x}, couched {1x}, misc. {4x} = crouch (down), fall down, make a fold, lay, (cause to, make to) lie (down), make to rest, sit. See: TWOT—2109; BDB—918b.

7258. רֵבֶץ {4x} **rêbets**, *ray'-bets;* from 7257; a *couch* or place of repose:—resting place {2x}, where each lay {1x}, to lie down in {1x}. See: TWOT—2109a; BDB—918c.

7259. רִבְקָה {30x} **Ribqâh**, *rib-kaw';* from an unused root prob. mean. to *clog* by tying up the fetlock; *fettering* (by beauty); *Ribkah,* the wife of Isaac:—Rebekah {30x}. See: BDB—918d.

7260. רַבְרַב {8x} **rabrab** (Aram.), *rab-rab';* from 7229; *huge* (in size); *domineering* (in character):—great {6x}, great things {2x}. See: TWOT—2984a; BDB—1112b, 1112c.

7261. רַבְרְבָן {8x} **rabrᵉbân** (Aram.), *rab-reb-awn';* from 7260; a *magnate:*—lord {6x}, prince {2x}. See: TWOT—2984c; BDB—1112b, 1112c.

7262. רַבְשָׁקֵה {16x} **Rabshâqêh**, *rab-shaw-kay';* from 7227 and 8248; *chief butler; Rabshakeh,* a Bab. official:—Rabshakeh {15x}, Rabshakeh + 5631 + 7227 {1x}. See: BDB—913d, 918d.

7263. רֶגֶב {2x} **regeb**, *reh'-gheb;* from an unused root mean. to *pile* together; a *lump* of clay:—clod {2x}. See: TWOT—2111a; BDB—918d.

7264. רָגַז {41x} **râgaz**, *raw-gaz';* a prim. root; to *quiver* (with any violent emotion, espec. anger or fear):—tremble {12x}, move {7x}, rage {5x}, shake {3x}, disquiet {3x}, troubled {3x}, quake {2x}, afraid {1x}, misc. {5x} = stand in awe, fall out, fret, provoke, be wroth. See: TWOT—2112; BDB—919a, 1112c.

7265. רְגַז {1x} **rᵉgaz** (Aram.), *reg-az';* corresp. to 7264:—provoke unto wrath {1x}. See: TWOT—2987; BDB—1112c.

7266. רְגַז {1x} **rᵉgaz** (Aram.), *reg-az';* from 7265; violent *anger:*—rage {1x}. See: TWOT—2987a; BDB—1112c.

7267. רֹגֶז {7x} **rôgez**, *ro'-ghez;* from 7264; *commotion, restlessness* (of a horse), *crash* (of thunder), *disquiet, anger:*—trouble {2x}, troubling {1x}, noise {1x}, rage {1x}, fear {1x}, wrath {1x}. See: TWOT—2112a; BDB—919c.

7268. רַגָּז {1x} **raggâz**, *rag-gawz';* intens. from 7264; *timid:*—trembling {1x}. See: TWOT—2112c; BDB—919c.

7269. רׇגְזָה {1x} **rogzâh**, *rog-zaw';* fem. of 7267; *trepidation:*—trembling {1x}. See: TWOT—2112b; BDB—919c.

7270. רָגַל {25x} **râgal**, *raw-gal';* a prim. root; to *walk* along; but only in spec. applications, to *reconnoiter,* to *be a tale-bearer* (i.e. *slander*); also (as denom. from 7272) to *lead about:*—spy {12x}, spy out {8x}, view {2x}, backbiteth {1x}, espy out {1x}, slandered {1x}. See: TWOT—2113; BDB—920a, 1076a.

7271. רְגַל {7x} **rᵉgal** (Aram.), *reg-al';* corresp. to 7272:—feet {7x}. See: TWOT—2988; BDB 1112c.

7272. רֶגֶל {247x} **regel**, *reh'-gel;* from 7270; a *foot* (as used in *walking*); by impl. a *step;* by euphem. the *pudenda:*—feet {216x}, footstool + 1916 {6x}, after {4x}, times {4x}, follow {4x}, piss + 4325 {2x}, toes {2x}, journey {1x}, legs {1x}, misc. {7x} = × be able to endure, × according as, × coming, × follow, × haunt, + possession.

Regel, means "foot; leg." **(1)** Its first occurrence in Gen 8:9: "But the dove found no rest for the sole of her foot, and she returned unto him into the ark," **(2)** *Regel* may refer to the "foot" of a human (Gen 18:4), an animal (Eze 29:11), a bird (Gen 8:9), or even a table (a rare usage; Ex. 25:26). **(3)** The word's usage is also extended to signify the "leg": "And he had greaves of brass upon his legs, and a target of brass between his shoulders" (1 Sa 17:6). **(4)** *Regel* is used euphemistically for urine; the "water of the legs" (2 Kin 18:27). **(5)** The foot's low place gave rise to an idiom: "From the sole of the foot to the crown of the head" (cf. Deut 28:35), signifying the "total extent of the body." **(6)** "Foot" may be a metaphor of "arrogance": "Let not the foot of pride come against me, and let not the hand of the wicked remove me" (Ps 36:11). **(7)** It is used to represent Israel: "Neither will I make the feet of Israel move any more out of the land which I gave their fathers; only if they will observe to do according to all that I have commanded them, and according to all the law that my servant Moses commanded them" (2 Kin 21:8).

(8) In anthropomorphic expressions, God has "feet." **(8a)** Thus God revealed Himself with a pavement of sapphire as clear as the sky under His "feet" (Ex 24:10). **(8b)** The authors of Scripture portray God as having darkness (Ps 18:9) and clouds of dust beneath His "feet" (Nah 1:3), and sending a plague out from His "feet" (Hab 3:5). **(8c)** His "feet" are said to rest on the earth (Is 66:1); the temple is also the resting place of His "feet": ". . . And I will make the place of my feet glorious" (Is 60:13). **(9)** Similarly, **(9a)** the seraphim had "feet," which they covered with a pair of wings as they stood in the presence of God (Is 6:2); **(9b)** the cherubim had "feet" that Ezekiel described (Eze 1:7). See: TWOT—2113a; BDB—919c, 1112c.

7273. רַגְלִי {12x} **raglîy**, *rag-lee';* from 7272; a *footman* (soldier):—footman {7x}, footman + 376 {4x}, foot {1x}. See: TWOT—2113b; BDB—920b.

7274. רֹגְלִים {2x} **Rôgᵉlîym**, *ro-gel-eem';* plur. of act. part. of 7270; *fullers* (as *tramping* the cloth in washing); *Rogelim,* a place E. of the Jordan:—Rogelim {2x}. See: BDB—920c.

7275. רָגַם {16x} **râgam**, *raw-gam';* a prim. root [comp. 7263, 7321, 7551]; to *cast* together (stones), i.e. to *lapidate:*—stone {15x}, certainly {1x}. See: TWOT—2114; BDB—920c.

7276. רֶגֶם {1x} **Regem**, *reh'-gem;* from 7275; stone-*heap; Regem,* an Isr.:—*Regem* {1x}. See: BDB—920d.

7277. רִגְמָה {1x} **rigmâh**, *rig-maw';* fem. of the same as 7276; a *pile* (of stones), i.e. (fig.) a *throng:*—council {1x}. See: TWOT—2114a; BDB—920c.

7278. רֶגֶם מֶלֶךְ {1x} **Regem Melek**, *reh'-gem meh'-lek;* from 7276 and 4428; *king's heap; Regem-Melek,* an Isr.:—Regemmelech {1x}. See: BDB—920d.

7279. רָגַן {3x} **râgan**, *raw-gan';* a prim. root; to *grumble,* i.e. *rebel:*—murmur {3x}. See: TWOT—2115; BDB—920d.

7280. רָגַע {13x} **râgaʿ**, *raw-gah';* a prim. root; prop. to *toss* violently and suddenly (the sea with waves, the skin with boils); fig. (in a favorable manner) to *settle,* i.e. *quiet;* spec. to *wink* (from the motion of the eye-lids):—break {1x}, divide {2x}, find ease {1x}, be a moment {1x}, (cause, give, make to) rest {5x}, make suddenly {2x}. See: TWOT—2116, 2117, 2118; BDB—920d, 921b, 921c.

7281. רֶגַע {22x} **regaʿ**, *reh'-gah;* from 7280. a *wink* (of the eyes), i.e. a very *short space* of time:—instant {2x}, moment {18x}, space {1x}, suddenly {1x}. See: TWOT—2116a; BDB—921a.

7282. רָגֵעַ {1x} **râgêaʿ**, *raw-gay'-ah;* from 7280; *restful,* i.e. *peaceable:*—that are quiet {1x}. See: TWOT—2117a; BDB—921b.

7283. רָגַשׁ {1x} **râgash**, *raw-gash';* a prim. root; to *be tumultuous:*—rage {1x}. See: TWOT—2119; BDB—921c, 1112c.

7284. רְגַשׁ {3x} **rᵉgash** (Aram.), *reg-ash';* corresp. to 7283; to *gather* tumultuously:—assembled {2x}, assembled together {1x}. See: TWOT—2989; BDB—1112c.

7285. רֶגֶשׁ {2x} **regesh**, *reh'-ghesh;* or (fem.)

רִגְשָׁה **rigshâh**, *rig-shaw';* from 7283; a tumultuous *crowd:*—company {1x}, insurrection {1x}. See: TWOT—2119a, 2119b; BDB—920c, 921c.

7286. רָדַד {4x} **râdad**, *raw-dad';* a prim. root; to *tread* in pieces, i.e. (fig.) to *conquer,* or (spec.) to *overlay:*—spend {1x}, spread {1x}, subdue {2x}. See: TWOT—2120; BDB—921c.

7287. רָדָה {27x} **râdâh**, *raw-daw';* a prim. root; to *tread* down, i.e. *subjugate;* spec. to *crumble* off:—rule {13x}, dominion {1x}9, take {1x}2, prevaileth {1x}1, reign {1x}1, ruler {1x}. See: TWOT—2121, 2122; BDB—921d, 922a.

7288. רַדַּי {1x} **Radday**, *rad-dah'-ee;* intens. from 7287; *domineering; Raddai,* an Isr.:—Raddai {1x}. See: BDB—921d, 922b.

7289. רָדִיד {2x} **râdîyd**, *raw-deed';* from 7286 in the sense of *spreading;* a *veil* (as expanded):—vails {2x}, veil {1x}. See: TWOT—2120a; BDB—921d.

7290. רָדַם {7x} **râdam**, *raw-dam';* a prim. root; to *stun,* i.e. *stupefy* (with sleep or death):— . . . deep sleep {3x}, was fast asleep {2x}, sleep {1x}, sleeper {1x}. See: TWOT—2123; BDB—922b.

7291. רָדַף רָדַף **râdaph**, *raw-daf';* a prim. root; to *run after* (usually with hostile intent; fig. [of time] *gone by*):—pursue {74x}, persecute {20x}, follow {18x}, chase {13x}, persecutors {7x}, pursuer {6x}, follow after {1x}, flight {1x}, misc. {3x}.

Radaph, means "to pursue, follow after, pass away, persecute." **(1)** The basic meaning of this verb is "to pursue after" an enemy with the intent of overtaking and defeating him. **(1a)** In most of its occurrences *radaph* is a military term. **(1b)** It first occurs in Gen 14:14, where it is reported that Abram mustered his 318 men and "pursued them [men who took his nephew, Lot] unto Dan." **(1c)** A nuance of this verb is "to pursue" a defeated enemy with the intent of killing him: "And he divided himself against them, he and his servants, by night, and smote them, and pursued them unto Hobah, which is on the left hand of Damascus" (Gen 14:15). **(2)** The one pursued is not always a hostile force—so Laban "took his brethren [army] with him, and pursued after him [Jacob] seven days' journey; and they overtook him in the mount Gilead" (Gen 31:23).

(3) At times *radaph* signifies pursuing without having a specific location or direction in mind, as in hunting for someone. This meaning is in 1 Sa 26:20—David asked Saul why he was exerting so much effort on such an unimportant task (namely, pursuing him), "as when one doth hunt a partridge in the mountains." **(4)** The word occurs in Josh 2:5, where Rahab tells the soldiers of Jericho: ". . . Whither the men [Israelite spies] went I wot not: pursue after them quickly; for ye shall overtake them." **(4a)** This verse embodies the meaning first mentioned, but by **(4b)** Josh 2:22 the emphasis has shifted to hunting, not intentional pursuit after an enemy whose location is known but a searching for an enemy in order to kill him: "And they went, and came unto the mountain, and abode there three days, until the pursuers were returned: and the pursuers sought them throughout all the way, but found them not." **(5)** In another nuance *radaph* can signify "to put to flight" or "to confront and cause to flee." **(5a)** Moses reminded the Israelites that "the Amorites . . . came out against you, and chased you, as bees do, and destroyed you in Seir, even unto Hormah" (Deut 1:44). **(5b)** Bees do not pursue their victims, but they certainly do put them to flight, or cause them to flee. **(5c)** In Josh 23:10 Israel is reminded: "One man of you shall chase a thousand: for the Lord your God he it is that fighteth for you, as he hath promised you" (cf. Lev 26:8). **(6)** Used in another sense, *radaph* signifies the successful accomplishment of a pursuit; the pursuer overtakes the pursued but does not utterly destroy him (in the case of an army) and, therefore, continues the pursuit until the enemy is utterly destroyed. **(6a)** So Israel is warned of the penalty of disobedience to God: "The Lord shall smite thee with a consumption, and with a fever . . . ; and they shall pursue thee until thou perish" (Deut 28:22; cf. v. 45). **(6b)** This is the emphasis when God admonishes Israel: "That which is altogether just shalt thou follow, that thou mayest live, and inherit the land . . ." (Deut 16:20). **(7)** Israel is "to pursue" justice and only justice, as a goal always achieved but never perfected. **(7a)** They are to always have justice in their midst, and always "to pursue" it. This same sense appears in other figurative uses of the word: "Surely goodness and mercy shall follow me all the days of my life . . ." (Ps 23:6; cf. Is 1:23; 5:11; Hos 6:3). **(8)** In a related meaning *radaph* can signify "follow after." **(8a)** This is not with any intention to do harm to the one pursued but merely "to overtake" him. **(8b)** So Gehazi "pursued" (followed after) Naaman, overtook him, and asked him for a talent of silver and two changes of clothes (2 Kin 5:21–22). **(9)** The word also means "to follow after" in the sense of "practicing," or following a leader: "They also that render evil for good are mine adversaries; because I follow the thing that good is" (Ps 38:20; cf. 119:150; Prov 21:21). **(10)** Another meaning of *radaph,* "to persecute," represents the constant infliction of pain or trouble upon one's enemies. This meaning is seen in Deut 30:7: "And the Lord thy God will put all these curses upon thine enemies, and on them that hate thee, which persecuted thee" (cf. Job 19:22, 28). **(11)** A special use of *radaph* appears in Eccl 3:15: ". . . God requireth [holds men accountable for] that which is past." Men should serve God (literally, "fear him") because God controls all things. Men should be on His side, since He is totally sovereign. **(12)** The intensive stem sometimes means to pursue relentlessly and passionately as a harlot "pursues" her lovers (Prov 11:19). See: TWOT—2124; BDB—922c, 923b.

7292. רָהַב {4x} **râhab**, *raw-hab';* a prim. root; to *urge* severely, i.e. (fig.) *importune, embolden, capture, act insolently:*—overcome {1x}, behave self proudly {1x}, make sure {1x}, strengthen {1x}. See: TWOT—2125; BDB—923b.

7293. רַהַב {3x} **rahab**, *rah'-hab;* from 7292, *bluster (-er):*—proud {2x}, strength {1x}. See: TWOT—2125c; BDB—923c.

7294. רַהַב {3x} **Rahab**, *rah'-hab;* the same as 7293; *Rahab* (i.e. *boaster*), an epithet of Egypt:—*Rahab* {3x}. See: BDB—923c.

7295. רָהָב {1x} **râhâb**, *raw-hawb';* from 7292; *insolent:*—proud {1x}. See: TWOT—2125a; BDB—923b.

7296. רֹהַב {1x} **rôhab**, *ro'-hab;* from 7292; *pride:*—strength {1x}. See: TWOT—2125b; BDB—923b.

7297. רָהָה {1x} **râhâh**, *raw-haw';* a prim. root; to *fear:*—be afraid {1x}. See: TWOT—2126; BDB—436c, 923c.

7298. רַהַט {4x} **rahat**, *rah'-hat;* from an unused root appar. mean. to *hollow out;* a *channel* or watering-box; by resemblance a *ringlet* of hair (as forming parallel lines):—gallery {1x}, gutter {2x}, trough {1x}. See: TWOT—2127a, 2128a; BDB—923d.

7299. רֵו {2x} **rêv** (Aram.), *rave;* from a root corresp. to 7200; *aspect:*—form {2x}. See: TWOT—2990; BDB—1112a, 1112b.

רוּב **rûwb**. See 7378.

7300. רוּד {4x} **rûwd**, *rood;* a prim. root; to *tramp* about, i.e. *ramble* (free or disconsolate):—have the dominion {1x}, be lord {1x}, mourn {1x}, rule {1x}. See: TWOT—2129; BDB—923d.

7301. רָוָה {14x} **râvâh**, *raw-vaw';* a prim. root; to *slake* the thirst (occasionally of other appetites):—water {4x}, make drun {2x}, fill {2x}, satiate {2x}, bathed {1x}, satisfied {1x}, abundantly satisfy {1x}, soaked {1x}. See: TWOT—2130; BDB—924a.

7302. רָוֶה {3x} **râveh**, *raw-veh';* from 7301; *sated* (with drink):—drunkenness {1x}, watered {2x}. See: TWOT—2130b; BDB—924b.

7303. רוֹהֲגָה {1x} **Rôwhăgâh**, *ro-hag-aw';* from an unused root prob. mean. to *cry* out; *outcry; Rohagah,* an Isr.:—Rohgah {1x}. See: BDB—923c, 924b.

7304. רָוַח {3x} **râvach**, *raw-vakh';* a prim. root [rather ident. with 7306]; prop. to *breathe* freely, i.e. *revive;* by impl. to *have ample room:*—be refreshed {2x}, large {1x}. See: TWOT—2132; BDB—926b. This word connotes being refreshed (1 Sa 16:23; Job 32:20).

7305. רֶוַח {2x} **revach**, *reh'-vakh;* from 7304; *room,* lit. (an *interval*) or fig. (*deliverance*):—enlargement {1x}, space {1x}. See: TWOT—2132a; BDB—926c.

7306. רוּחַ {11x} **rûwach**, *roo'-akh;* a prim. root; prop. to *blow,* i.e. *breathe;* only (lit.) to *smell* or (by impl.) *perceive* (fig. to *anticipate, enjoy*):—accept {1x}, smell {8x}, × touch {1x}, make of quick understanding {1x}.

(1) This word means to smell; hence, to be keen or quick of understanding: "And shall make him of quick understanding (*ruwach*) in the fear of the LORD: and he shall not judge after the sight of his eyes, neither reprove after the hearing of his ears:" (Is 11:3). **(2)** *Ruwach* means to perceive, enjoy, smell: "And the Lord smelled a sweet savor. . . ." (Gen 8:21). See: TWOT—2131; BDB—926b.

7307. רוּחַ {378x} **rûwach**, *roo'-akh;* from 7306; *wind;* by resemblance *breath,* i.e. a sensible (or even violent) exhalation; fig. *life, anger, unsubstantiality;* by extens. a *region* of the sky; by resemblance *spirit,* but only of a rational being (incl. its expression and functions):—Spirit or spirit {232x}, wind {92x}, breath {27x}, side {6x}, mind {5x}, blast {4x}, vain {2x}, air {1x}, anger {1x}, cool {1x}, courage {1x}, misc. {6x} = × cool, × quarter, spiritual, tempest, whirlwind, windy.

Introduction: It is clear that the wind is regarded in Scripture as a fitting emblem of the mighty penetrating power of the invisible God. Moreover, the breath is suppose to symbolize not only the deep feelings that are generated within man, such as sorrow and anger; but also kindred feelings in the Divine nature. It is revealed that God and God alone has the faculty of communicating His Spirit or life to His creatures, who are thus enabled to feel, think, speak, and act in accordance with the Diving will. *Ruwach* (7307), means "breath; air; strength; wind; breeze; spirit; courage; temper; Spirit." **(1)** First, this word means "breath," air for breathing, air that is being breathed. **(1a)** This meaning is especially evident in Jer 14:6: "And the wild asses did stand in the high places, they snuffed up the wind like dragons. . . ." **(1b)** When one's "breath" returns, he is revived: ". . . When he [Samson] had drunk [the water], his spirit [literally, "breath"] came again, and he revived . . ." (Judg 15:19). **(1c)** Astonishment may take away one's "breath": "And when the queen of Sheba had seen all Solomon's wisdom, and the home that he had built, And the meat of his table, . . . there was no more spirit in her [she was overwhelmed and breathless]" (1 Kin 10:4–5). **(1d)** *Ruwach* may also represent speaking, or the breath of one's mouth: "By the word of the Lord were the heavens made; and all the host of them by the breath of his mouth"(Ps 33:6; cf. Ex 15:8; Job 4:9; 19:17). **(2)** Second, this word can be used with emphasis on the invisible, intangible, fleeting quality of "air": "O remember that my life is wind: mine eyes shall no more see good" (Job 7:7). **(2a)** There may be a suggestion of purposelessness, uselessness, or even vanity (emptiness) when *ruwach* is used with this significance: "And the prophets shall become wind, and the word is not in them . . ." (Jer 5:13). **(2b)** "Windy words" are really "empty words" (Job 16:3), just as "windy knowledge" is "empty knowledge" (Job 15:2; cf. Eccl 1:14, 17—"meaningless striving"). **(2c)** In Prov 11:29 *ruwach* means "nothing": "He that troubleth his own house shall inherit the wind. . . ." This nuance is especially prominent in Eccl 5:15–16: "And he came forth of his mother's womb, naked shall he return to go as he came, and shall take nothing of his labor, which he may carry away in his hand. And this also is a sore evil, that in all points as he came, so shall he go: and what profit hath he that hath labored for the wind?" **(3)** Third, *ruwach* can mean "wind." **(3a)** In Gen 3:8 it seems to mean the gentle, refreshing evening breeze so well known in the Near East: "And they heard the voice of the Lord God walking in the garden in the cool [literally, "breeze"] of the day. . . ." **(3b)** It can mean a strong, constant wind: ". . . And the Lord brought an east wind upon the land all that day, and all that night . . ." (Ex 10:13). **(3c)** It can also signify an extremely strong wind: "And the Lord turned a mighty strong west wind . . ." (Ex 10:19). **(3d)** In Jer 4:11 the word appears to represent a gale or tornado (cf. Hos 8:7). **(3e)** God is the Creator (Amos 4:13) and sovereign Controller of the winds (Gen 8:1; Num 11:31; Jer 10:13). **(4)** Fourth, the wind represents direction. **(4a)** In Jer 49:36 the four winds represent the four ends of the earth, which in turn represent every quarter: "And upon Elam will I bring the four winds [peoples from every quarter of the earth] from the four quarters of heaven, and will scatter them toward all those winds; and there shall be no nation whither the outcasts of Elam shall not come." **(5)** Fifth, *ruwach* frequently represents the element of life in a man, his natural "spirit": "And all flesh died that moved upon the earth, . . . All in whose nostrils was the breath of life . . ." (Gen 7:21–22). **(5a)** In these verses the animals have a "spirit" (cf Ps. 104:29). **(5b)** On the other hand, in Prov 16:2 the word appears to mean more than just the element of life; it seems to mean "soul": "All the ways of a man are clean in his own eyes; but the Lord weigheth the spirits." **(5c)** Thus, Isaiah can put nepesh (5315), "soul," and *ruwach* in synonymous parallelism: "With my soul have I desired thee in the night; yea, with my spirit within me will I seek thee early . . ." (26:9). **(5d)** It is the "spirit" of a man that returns to God (Eccl 12:7). **(6)** Sixth, *ruwach* is often used of a man's mind-set, disposition, or "temper": "Blessed is the man unto whom the Lord imputeth not iniquity, and in whose spirit there is no guile" (Ps 32:2). **(6a)** In Eze 13:3 the word is used of one's mind or thinking: "Woe unto the foolish prophets, that follow their own spirits, and have seen nothing" (cf. Prov 29:11). **(6b)** *Ruwach* can represent particular dispositions, as it does in Josh 2:11: "And as soon as we had heard these things, our hearts did melt, neither did there remain any more courage in any man, because of you . . ." (cf. Josh 5:1; Job 15:13). **(6c)** Another disposition represented by this word is "temper": "If the spirit [temper] of the ruler rise up against thee, leave not thy place . . ." (Eccl 10:4). **(6d)** David prayed that God would "restore unto me the joy of thy salvation; and uphold me with thy free Spirit" (Ps 51:12). In this verse "joy of salvation" and "free Spirit" are parallel and, therefore, synonymous terms. Therefore, "Spirit" refers to the One who restores that "joy." **(7)** Seventh, the Bible often speaks of God's "Spirit," the third person of the Trinity. **(7a)** This is the use of the word in its first biblical occurrence: "And the earth was without form, and void; and darkness was upon the face of the deep. And the Spirit of God moved upon the face of the waters" (Gen 1:2). **(7b)** Is 63:10–11 and Ps 51:12 specifically speak of the "holy or free Spirit." **(8)** Eighth, the non-material beings (angels) in heaven are sometimes called "spirits": "And there came forth a spirit, and stood before the Lord, and said, I will persuade him" (1 Kin 22:21; cf. 1 Sa 16:14). **(9)** Ninth, the "spirit" may also be used of that which enables a man to do a particular job or that which represents the essence of a quality of man: **(9a)** "And Joshua the son of Nun was full of the spirit of wisdom; for Moses had laid his hands upon him . . ." (Deut 34:9). **(9b)** Elisha asked Elijah for a double portion of his "spirit" (2 Kin 2:9) and received it. Syn.: 5397. See: TWOT—2131a; BDB—924c, 1112d.

7308. רוּחַ {11x} **rûwach** (Aram.), *roo'-akh;* corresp. to 7307:—mind {1x}, spirit {8x}, wind {2x}. See: TWOT—2991a; BDB—1112d.

7309. רְוָחָה {2x} **r^{e}vâchâh**, *rev-aw-khaw';* fem. of 7305; *relief:*—breathing {1x}, respite {1x}. See: TWOT—2132b; BDB—926c.

7310. רְוָיָה {2x} **r^{e}vâyâh**, *rev-aw-yaw';* from 7301; *satisfaction:*—runneth over {1x}, wealthy {1x}. See: TWOT—2130c; BDB—924b, 926c.

7311. רוּם {194x} **rûwm**, *room;* a prim. root; to *be high;* act. to *rise* or *raise* (in various applications, lit. or fig.):—(lift, hold, etc . . .) up {63x}, exalt {47x}, high {25x}, offer {13x}, give {5x}, heave {3x}, extol {3x}, lofty {3x}, take {3x}, tall {3x}, higher {2x}, misc. {24x} = haughty, levy, (X a-) loud, + presumptuously, (be) promote (-ion), proud, taller, breed worms.

Ruwm, means "to be high, exalted." **(1)** Basically, *ruwm* represents either the "state of being on a higher plane" or "movement in an upward direction." **(1a)** The former meaning appears in the first biblical occurrence of the word: "And the flood was forty days upon the earth; and the waters increased, and bare up the ark, and it was lifted [rose] up above the earth" (Gen 7:17). **(1b)** Used of men, this verb may refer to their "physical stature"; for example, the spies sent into Canaan reported that "the people is greater and taller than we; the cities are great and walled up to heaven . . ." (Deut 1:28). **(1c)** The other emphasis, representing what is done to the subject or what it does to itself, appears in Ps 12:8: "The wicked walk on every side, when the vilest men are exalted." **(1d)** The psalmist confesses that the Lord will "set me up upon a rock" so as to be out of all danger (Ps 27:5). **(1e)** A stormy wind (Ps 107:25) "lifts up" the waves of the sea. **(2)** *Ruwm* is used of the building of an edifice. Ezra confessed that God had renewed the people of Israel, allowing them "to set up the house of our God, and to repair the desolations thereof, and to give us a wall in Judah and Jerusalem" (Ezra 9:9; cf. Gen 31:45).

(3) In Eze 31:4, this verb is used of "making a plant grow larger": "The waters made him [the cedar in Lebanon] great, the deep set him up on high. . . ." **(4)** Since in Deut. 1:28 gadal (1419 - "larger") and *ruwm* ("taller") are used in close connection, Eze 31:4 could be translated: "The waters made it grow bigger, the deep made it grow taller." **(5)** Closely related to this nuance is the use of *ruwm* to represent the process of child-rearing. God says through Isaiah: ". . . I have nourished [1419 - gadal] and brought up children, and they have rebelled against me" (Is 1:2). **(6)** *Ruwm* sometimes means "to take up away from," as in Is 57:14: "Cast ye up, cast ye up, prepare the way, take up the stumbling block out of the way of my people." **(7)** When used in reference to offerings, the word **(7a)** signifies the "removal of a certain portion" (Lev 2:9). **(7b)** The presentation of the entire offering is also referred to as an "offering up" (Num 15:19).

(8) In extended applications, *ruwm* has both negative and positive uses. **(8a)** Positively, this word can signify "to bring to a position of honor." **(8a1)** So God says: "Behold, my servant shall deal prudently, he shall be exalted and extolled, and be very high" (Is 52:13). **(8a2)** This same meaning occurs in 1 Sa 2:7, where Hannah confessed: "The Lord maketh poor, and maketh rich: he bringeth low, and lifteth up." **(8b)** Used in a negative sense, *ruwm* means "to be haughty": "And the afflicted people thou wilt save: but thine eyes are upon the haughty, that thou mayest bring them down" (2 Sa 22:28). **(9)** *Ruwm* is often used with other words in special senses. **(9a)** For example, to lift one's voice is "to cry aloud." Potiphar's wife reported that when Joseph attacked her, she "raised" her voice screaming. These two words (rum and "voice") are used together to mean "with a loud voice" (Deut 27:14). **(10)** The raising of the hand **(10a)** serves as a symbol of power and strength and signifies being "mighty" or "triumphant": "Were it not that I feared the wrath of the enemy, lest their adversaries should behave themselves strangely, and lest they should say, Our hand is high [literally, "is raised"] . . ." (Deut 32:27). **(10b)** To raise one's hand against someone is to rebel against him. Thus, "Jeroboam . . . lifted up his hand against the king" (1 Kin 11:26).

(11) The raising of one's horn suggests the picture of a wild ox standing in all its strength. **(11a)** This is a picture of "triumph" over one's enemies: "My heart rejoiceth in the Lord, mine horn is exalted in the Lord; my mouth is enlarged over mine enemies . . ." (1 Sa 2:1). **(11b)** Moreover, horns symbolized the focus of one's power. Thus, when one's horn is "exalted," one's power is exalted. When one exalts another's horn, he gives him "strength": ". . . He [the Lord] shall give strength unto his king, and exalt the horn of his anointed" (1 Sa 2:10). **(12)** Raising one's head may be a public gesture of "triumph and supremacy," as in Ps 110:7, where it is said that after defeating all His enemies the Lord will "lift up the head." **(12a)** This nuance is sometimes used transitively, as when someone else lifts a person's head. Some scholars suggest that in such cases the verb signifies the action of a judge who has pronounced an accused person innocent by raising the accused's head. **(12b)** This phrase also came to signify "to mark with distinction," "to give honor to," or "to place in a position of strength": "But thou, O Lord, art a shield for me, my glory, and the lifter up of mine head" (Ps 3:3). **(13)** To raise one's eyes or heart is to be "proud" and "arrogant": "Then thine heart be lifted up, and thou forget the Lord thy God, which brought thee forth out of the land of Egypt" (Deut 8:14). See: TWOT—2133; BDB—575d, 910b, 926c, 941a, 942c, 1112d.

7312. רוּם {6x} **rûwm**, *room;* or

רֻם **rûm**, *room;* from 7311; (lit.) *elevation* or (fig.) *elation:*—haughtiness {3x}, height {1x}, × high {2x}.

Ruwm, as a noun, means "height; haughtiness." **(1)** This word occurs 6 times, and it means "height" in Prov 25:3. **(2)** *Rum* signifies "haughtiness" in Is 2:11. Syn.: 4791. See: TWOT—2133a; BDB—927d, 941a.

7313. רוּם {4x} **rûwm** (Aram.), *room;* corresp. to 7311; (fig. only):—extol {1x}, lift up (self) {2x}, set up {1x}. See: TWOT—2992; BDB—1112d.

7314. רוּם {5x} **rûwm** (Aram.), *room;* from 7313; (lit.) *altitude:*—height {5x}. See: TWOT—2992a; BDB—1112d.

7315. רוֹם {1x} **rôwm**, *rome;* from 7311; *elevation,* i.e. (adv.) *aloft:*—on high {1x}. See: TWOT—2133b; BDB—927d.

7316. רוּמָה {1x} **Rûwmâh**, *roo-maw';* from 7311; *height; Rumah,* a place in Pal.:—Rumah {1x}. See: BDB—928a.

7317. רוֹמָה {1x} **rôwmâh**, *ro-maw';* fem. of 7315; *elation,* i.e. (adv.) *proudly:*—haughtily {1x}. See: BDB—928a.

7318. רוֹמָם {1x} **rôwmâm**, *ro-mawm';* from 7426; *exaltation,* i.e. (fig. and spec.) *praise:*—be extolled {1x}. See: TWOT—2133f; BDB—928c.

7319. רוֹמְמָה {1x} **rôwmᵉmâh**, *ro-mem-aw';* fem. act. part. of 7426; *exaltation,* i.e. *praise:*—high {1x}. See: TWOT—2133f?;BDB—927a, 928c.

7320. רוֹמַמְתִּי עֶזֶר {2x} **Rôwmamtîy ᶜEzer** (or רֹמַמְתִּי **Rômamtîy**), *ro-mam'-tee eh'-zer;* from 7311 and 5828; *I have raised* up a *help; Romamti-Ezer,* an Isr.:—Romamti-ezer {2x}. See: BDB—928d, 942c.

7321. רוּעַ {46x} **rûwaᶜ**, *roo-ah';* a prim. root; to *mar* (espec. by breaking); fig. to *split* the ears (with sound), i.e. *shout* (for alarm or joy):—shout {23x}, noise {7x}, . . . alarm {4x}, cry {4x}, triumph {3x}, smart {1x}, misc. {4x} = destroy, smart, sound an alarm. See: TWOT—2135; BDB—929c, 937c.

7322. רוּף {1x} **rûwph**, *roof;* a prim. root; prop. to *triturate* (in a mortar), i.e. (fig.) to *agitate* (by concussion):—tremble {1x}. See: TWOT—2201; BDB—952c.

7323. רוּץ {104x} **rûwts**, *roots;* a prim. root; to *run* (for whatever reason, espec. to *rush*):—run {72x}, guard (14x}, post {8x}, run away {2x}, speedily {1x}, misc. {7x} = break down, footman, bring hastily, stretch out.

(1) *Ruwts* signifies moving very quickly or hastening rather than running (Gen 18:2, 7; 41:14; Ps 68:31). **(2)** It can mean to run (Josh 8:19). **(3)** In a military sense, the charging into battle, **(3a)** metaphorically describes the lifestyle of the wicked—they rush headlong at God (Job 15:26). **(3b)** This emphasis explains 2 Sa 22:30 which means to charge at the enemy. **(4)** *Ruwts* also means running away from something or someone (Judg 7:21). **(5)** *Ruwts* can signify running into somewhere not only in a hostile sense but in order to be united with or hidden by it: "The name of the LORD *is* a strong tower: the righteous runneth (7323) into it, and is safe" (Prov 18:10). **(6)** Runners **(6a)** preceded kings and pretenders to the throne (2 Sa 15:1) and **(6a)** served as official messengers (2 Sa 18:19). See: TWOT—2137; BDB—929c, 930a, 943b, 952d.

7324. רוּק {19x} **rûwq**, *rook;* a prim. root; to *pour* out (lit. or fig.), i.e. *empty:*—(pour, draw . . .) out {7x}, empty {7x}, draw {3x}, armed {1x}, pour forth {1x}. See: TWOT—2161; BDB—937d.

7325. רוּר {1x} **rûwr**, *roor;* a prim. root; to *slaver* (with spittle), i.e. (by anal.) to *emit* a fluid (ulcerous or natural):—run {1x}. See: TWOT—2162; BDB—938b.

7326. רוּשׁ {24x} **rûwsh**, *roosh;* a prim. root; to *be destitute:*—poor {19x}, poor man {3x}, lack {1x}, needy {1x}. See: TWOT—2138; BDB—910c, 930d, 957a.

רוֹשׁ **rôwsh**. See 7219.

7327. רוּת {12x} **Rûwth**, *rooth;* prob. for 7468; *friend; Ruth,* a Moabitess:—Ruth {12x}. See: BDB—930d, 946c.

7328. רָז {9x} **râz** (Aram.), *rawz;* from an unused root prob. mean. to *attenuate,* i.e. (fig.) *hide;* a *mystery:*—secret {9x}. See: TWOT—2993; BDB—1112d.

7329. רָזָה {2x} **râzâh**, *raw-zaw';* a prim. root; to *emaciate,* i.e. *make* (*become*) *thin* (lit. or fig.):—famish {1x}, wax lean {1x}. See: TWOT—2139; BDB—930d.

7330. רָזֶה {2x} **râzeh**, *raw-zeh';* from 7329; *thin:*—lean {2x}. See: TWOT—2139a; BDB—931a.

7331. רְזוֹן {1x} **Rᵉzôwn**, *rez-one';* from 7336; *prince; Rezon,* a Syrian:—Rezon {1x}. See: BDB—931b.

7332. רָזוֹן {3x} **râzôwn**, *raw-zone';* from 7329; *thinness:*—leanness {2x}, × scant {1x}. See: TWOT—2139c; BDB—931a, 931b.

7333. רָזוֹן {1x} **râzôwn**, *raw-zone';* from 7336; a *dignitary:*—prince {1x}. See: TWOT—2142a; BDB—931a, 931b.

7334. רָזִי {2x} **râzîy**, *raw-zee';* from 7329; *thinness:*—leanness {2x}. See: TWOT—2139b; BDB—931a.

7335. רָזַם {1x} **râzam**, *raw-zam';* a prim. root; to *twinkle* the eye (in mockery):—wink {1x}. See: TWOT—2141; BDB—931b.

7336. רָזַן {6x} **râzan**, *raw-zan';* a prim. root; prob. to *be heavy,* i.e. (fig.) *honorable:*—prince {5x}, ruler {1x}. See: TWOT—2142; BDB—931b.

7337. רָחַב {25x} **râchab**, *raw-khab';* a prim. root; to *broaden* (intr. or tran., lit. or fig.):—enlarge {18x}, wide {3x}, large {2x}, make room {2x}. See: TWOT—2143; BDB—931b.

7338. רַחַב {2x} **rachab**, *rakh'-ab;* from 7337; a *width:*—breadth {1x}, broad place {1x}. See: TWOT—2143a; BDB—931d.

7339. רְחֹב {43x} **rᵉchôb**, *rekh-obe';* or

רְחוֹב **rᵉchôwb**, *rekh-obe';* from 7337; a *width,* i.e. (concr.) *avenue* or *area:*—broad places {1x}, broad ways {2x}, street {40x}.

Rechowb represents the town square immediately near the gate(s) which often served for social functions such as assemblies, courts, and official proclamations (Gen 19:2). See: TWOT—2143d; BDB—932a. See also 1050.

7340. רְחֹב {10x} **Rᵉchôb**, *rekh-obe';* or

רְחוֹב **Rᵉchôwb**, *rekh-obe';* the same as 7339; *Rechob,* the name of a place in Syria, also of a Syrian and an Isr.:—Rehob {10x}. See: BDB—932b.

7341. רֹחַב {101x} **rôchab**, *ro'-khab;* from 7337; *width* (lit. or fig.):—breadth {74x}, broad {21x}, thickness {2x}, largeness {1x}, thick {1x}, as broad as + 3651 {1x}, wideness {1x}.

Rochab, means "breadth; width; expanse." **(1)** First, the word refers to how broad a flat expanse is. In Gen 13:17, we read: "Arise, walk through the land in the length of it and in the breadth of it; for I will give it unto thee." **(1a)** *Rochab* itself sometimes represents the concept of length, breadth, or the total territory: ". . . And the stretching out of his wings shall fill the breadth of thy land, O Immanuel" (Is 8:8; cf. Job 37:10). **(1b)** This idea is used figuratively in 1 Kin 4:29, describing the dimensions of Solomon's discernment: "And God gave Solomon wisdom and understanding exceeding much, and largeness [*rochab*] of heart, even as the sand that is on the seashore." **(2)** Second, *rochab* is used to indicate the "thickness" or "width" of an object. **(2a)** In its first biblical occurrence the word is used of Noah's ark: "The length of the ark shall be three hundred cubits, the breadth of it fifty cubits, and the height of it thirty cubits" (Gen 6:15). **(2b)** In Eze 42:10, the word represents the "thickness" of a building's wall in which there were chambers (cf. Eze 41:9). See: TWOT—2143b; BDB—931d.

7342. רָחָב {21x} **râchâb**, *raw-khawb';* from 7337; *roomy,* in any (or every) direction, lit. or fig.:—broad {5x}, broader {1x}, large {8x}, at liberty {1x}, proud {3x}, wide {3x}. See: TWOT—2143c; BDB—932a.

7343. רָחָב {5x} **Râchâb**, *raw-khawb';* the same as 7342; *proud; Rachab,* a Canaanitess:—Rahab {5x}. See: BDB—932a.

7344. רְחֹבוֹת {4x} **Rᵉchôbôwth**, *rekh-o-bōth';* or

רְחֹבֹת **Rᵉchôbôth**, *rekh-o-bōth';* plur. of 7339; *streets; Rechoboth,* a place in Assyria and one in Pal.:—Rehoboth {4x}. See: BDB—932c.

7345. רְחַבְיָה {5x} **Rᵉchabyâh**, *rekh-ab-yaw';* or

רְחַבְיָהוּ **Rᵉchabyâhûw**, *rek-ab-yaw'-hoo;* from 7337 and 3050; *Jah has enlarged; Rechabjah,* an Isr.:—Rehabiah {5x}. See: BDB—932c.

7346. רְחַבְעָם {50x} **Rᵉchabᶜâm**, *rekh-ab-awm';* from 7337 and 5971; a *people* *has enlarged; Rechabam,* an Isr. king:—Rehoboam {50x}. See: BDB—932c.

רְחֹבֹת **R^e^chôbôth**. See 7344.

7347. רֵחֶה {5x} **rêcheh**, *ray-kheh';* from an unused root mean. to *pulverize;* a *mill*-stone:—mill {2x}, millstone {2x}, nether {1x}. See: TWOT—2144a; BDB—932d.

רְחֹוב **R^e^chôwb**. See 7339, 7340.

7348. רְחוּם {8x} **R^e^chûwm**, *rekh-oom';* a form of 7349; *Rechum,* the name of a Pers. and of three Isr.:—Rehum {8x}. See: BDB—933d, 1113a.

7349. רַחוּם {13x} **rachûwm**, *rakh-oom';* from 7355; *compassionate:*—merciful {8x}, compassion {5x}.

The adjective is used in that important proclamation of God's name to Moses: "The Lord, The Lord God, merciful and gracious . . ." (Ex 34:6). See: TWOT—2146c; BDB—933d.

7350. רָחוֹק {84x} **râchôwq**, *raw-khoke';* or

רָחֹק **râchôq**, *raw-khoke';* from 7368; *remote,* lit. or fig., of place or time; spec. *precious;* often used adv. (with prep.):—(far, afar . . .) off {39x}, far {30x}, long ago {3x}, far from {3x}, come {2x}, afar {2x}, old {2x}, far abroad {1x}, long {1x}, space {1x}. See: TWOT—2151b; BDB—935b, 1113a.

7351. רְחִיט {2x} **r^e^chîyt**, *rekh-eet';* from the same as 7298; a *panel* (as resembling a *trough*):—rafter {1x}, variant {1x}. See: TWOT—2128b; BDB—923d, 932d.

7352. רַחִיק {1x} **rachîyq** (Aram.), *rakh-eek';* corresp. to 7350:—far {1x}. See: TWOT—2994; BDB—1113a.

7353. רָחֵל {4x} **râchêl**, *raw-kale';* from an unused root mean. to *journey;* a *ewe* [the *females* being the predominant element of a flock] (as a good *traveller*):—ewe {2x}, sheep {2x}. See: TWOT—2145a; BDB—932d.

7354. רָחֵל {47x} **Râchêl**, *raw-khale';* the same as 7353; *Rachel,* a wife of Jacob:—*Rachel* {46x}, Rahel {1x}. See: BDB—932d.

7355. רָחַם {47x} **râcham**, *raw-kham';* a prim. root; to *fondle;* by impl. to *love,* espec. to *compassionate:*— . . . mercy {32x}, . . . compassion {8x}, pity {3x}, love {1x}, merciful {1x}, Ruhamah {1x}, surely {1x}.

Racham, the verb, means "to have compassion, be merciful, pity." **(1)** The verb is translated "love" once: "I will love thee, O Lord . . ." (Ps 18:1). **(2)** *Racham* is also used in God's promise to declare His name to Moses: "I will make all my goodness pass before thee, and I will proclaim the name of the Lord before thee; and will be gracious to whom I will be gracious, and will show mercy on whom I will show mercy" (Ex 33:19). **(3)** So men pray: "Remember, O Lord, thy tender mercies and thy loving-kindnesses" (Ps 25:6); and **(4)** Isaiah prophesies messianic restoration: ". . . With great mercies will I gather thee. . . . But with everlasting kindness will I have mercy on thee, saith the Lord thy Redeemer" (Is 54:7–8). This is the heart of salvation by the suffering Servant-Messiah. See: TWOT—2146; BDB—933c.

7356. רַחַם {44x} **racham**, *rakh'-am;* from 7355; *compassion* (in the plur.); by extens. the *womb* (as *cherishing* the fetus); by impl. a *maiden:*—mercy {30x}, compassion {4x}, womb {4x}, bowels {2x}, pity {2x}, damsel {1x}, tender love {1x}.

(1) *Racham* expresses a deep and tender feeling of compassion, such as is aroused by the sight of weakness or suffering in those who are dear to us or need our help. Rachamim, as a plural noun, means "bowels; mercies; compassion." **(2)** This noun, always used in the plural intensive, occurs in Gen 43:14: "And God Almighty give you mercy." **(3)** In Gen 43:30, it is used of Joseph's feelings toward Benjamin: "His bowels did yearn upon his brother." **(4)** Rachamim is most often used of God, as by David in 2 Sa 24:14: "Let us fall now into the hand of the Lord; for his mercies are great. . . ." **(5)** We have the equivalent Aramaic word in Daniel's request to his friends: "That they would desire mercies of the God of heaven concerning this secret . . ." (Dan 2:18). Syn.: 2896. See: TWOT—2146a; BDB—933a, 933b, 1113a.

7357. רַחַם {1x} **Racham**, *rakh'-am;* the same as 7356; *pity; Racham,* an Isr.:—Raham {1x}. See: BDB—933d.

7358. רֶחֶם {26x} **rechem**, *rekh'-em;* from 7355; the *womb* [comp. 7356]:—womb {21x}, matrix {5x}.

Rechem, as a noun, means "bowels; womb; mercy." **(1)** The first use of *rechem* is in its primary meaning of "womb": "The Lord had fast closed up all the wombs of the house of Abimelech" (Gen 20:18). **(2)** The word is personified in Judg 5:30: "Have they not divided the prey; to every man a damsel or two . . . ?" **(3)** In another figurative sense, in 1 Kin 3:26: "Her bowels yearned upon her son." See: TWOT—2146a; BDB—933a.

7359. רְחֵם {1x} **r^e^chêm** (Aram.), *rekh-ame';* corresp. to 7356; (plur.) *pity:*—mercies {1x}. See: TWOT—2995; BDB—1113a.

7360. רָחָם {2x} **râchâm**, *raw-khawm';* or (fem.)

רָחָמָה **râchâmâh**, *raw-khaw-maw';* from 7355; a kind of *vulture* (supposed to be *tender* toward its young):—gier eagle. See: TWOT—2147a; BDB—934b.

7361. רַחֲמָה {1x} **rachămâh**, *rakh-am-aw';* fem. of 7356; a *maiden:*—two {1x}. See: TWOT—2146a; BDB—933a.

7362. רַחְמָנִי {1x} **rachmânîy**, *rakh-maw-nee';* from 7355; *compassionate:*—pitiful {1x}. See: TWOT—2146d; BDB—933d.

7363. רָחַף {3x} **râchaph**, *raw-khaf';* a prim. root; to *brood;* by impl. to *be relaxed:*—shake {1x}, move {1x}, flutter {1x}. See: TWOT—2148, 2149; BDB—934b.

7364. רָחַץ {72x} **râchats**, *raw-khats';* a prim. root; to *lave* (the whole or a part of a thing):—wash {53x}, bathe {18x}, wash away {1x}.

Rachats means "to wash, bathe." **(1)** The first occurrence of the word in the text illustrates one of its most common uses: "Let a little water . . . be fetched, and wash your feet . . ." (Gen 18:4). **(2)** When the word is used figuratively to express vengeance, the imagery is a bit more gruesome: ". . . He shall wash his feet in the blood of the wicked" (Ps 58:10). **(3)** Pilate's action in Mt 27:24 is reminiscent of the psalmist's statement "I will wash mine hands in innocency" (Ps 26:6). **(4)** The parts of a sacrificial animal usually "were washed" before they were burned on the altar (Ex 29:17). **(5)** *Rachats* is frequently used in the sense of "bathing" or "washing" oneself (Ex 2:5; 2 Sa 11:2). **(6)** Beautiful eyes are figuratively described as "washed with milk" (Song 5:12). Syn.: 1740, 3526, 7857. See: TWOT—2150; BDB—934b.

7365. רְחַץ {1x} **r^e^chats** (Aram.), *rekh-ats';* corresp. to 7364 [prob. through the accessory idea of *ministering* as a servant at the bath]; to *attend* upon:—trust {1x}. See: TWOT—2996; BDB—1113a.

7366. רַחַץ {2x} **rachats**, *rakh'-ats;* from 7364; a *bath:*—washpot {2x}. See: TWOT—2150a; BDB—934d.

7367. רַחְצָה {2x} **rachtsâh**, *rakh-tsaw';* fem. of 7366; a *bathing* place:—washing {2x}. See: TWOT—2150b; BDB—934d.

7368. רָחַק {58x} **râchaq**, *raw-khak';* a prim. root; to *widen* (in any direction), i.e. (intr.) *recede* or (tran.) *remove* (lit. or fig., of place or relation):— . . . far {36x}, . . . off {9x}, . . . away {7x}, remove {5x}, good way {1x}.

Rachaq, means "far." **(1)** The word is used about 55 times in the Hebrew Old Testament and it occurs for the first time in Gen 21:16: "And she went, and sat her down over against *him* a good way off (*rachaq*), as it were a bowshot:" **(2)** *Rachaq* is used to express "distance" of various types. It may be "distance" from a place (Deut. 12:21), as when Job felt that his friends kept themselves "aloof" from him (Job 30:10). **(3)** Sometimes the word expresses "absence" altogether: ". . . The comforter that should relieve my soul is far from me . . ." (Lam 1:16). **(4)** "To be distant" was also "to abstain": "Keep thee far from a false matter" (Ex 23:7). **(5)** Sometimes *rachaq* implies the idea of "exile": ". . . The Lord [removes] men far away" (Is 6:12). **(6)** "To make the ends of the land distant" is "to extend the boundaries": ". . . thou hast increased the [borders of the land]" (Is 26:15). See: TWOT—2151; BDB—934d, 1113a.

7369. רָחֵק {1x} **râchêq**, *raw-khake';* from 7368; *remote:*—far from thee {1x}. See: TWOT—2151a, 2151b; BDB—935b.

רָחֹק **râchôq**. See 7350.

7370. רָחַשׁ {1x} **râchash**, *raw-khash';* a prim. root; to *gush:*—inditing {1x}. See: TWOT—2152; BDB—935d.

7371. רַחַת {1x} **rachath**, *rakh'-ath;* from 7306; a *winnowing*-fork (as *blowing* the chaff away):—shovel {1x}. See: TWOT—2153; BDB—935d.

7372. רָטַב {1x} **râtab**, *raw-tab';* a prim. root; to *be moist:*—wet {1x}. See: TWOT—2154; BDB—936a.

7373. רָטֹב {1x} **râṭôb**, *raw-tobe';* from 7372; *moist* (with sap):—green {1x}. See: TWOT—2154a; BDB—936a.

7374. רֶטֶט {1x} **retet**, *reh'-tet;* from an unused root mean. to *tremble; terror:*—fear {1x}. See: TWOT—2156a; BDB—936a.

7375. רֻטֲפַשׁ {1x} **rûwṭăphash**, *roo-taf-ash';* a root compounded from 7373 and 2954; to *be rejuvenated:*—fresher {1x}. See: TWOT—2157; BDB—936a.

7376. רָטַשׁ {6x} **râtash**, *raw-tash';* a prim. root; to *dash* down:—dash . . . pieces {5x}, dash {1x}. See: TWOT—2158; BDB—936b.

7377. רִי {1x} **rîy**, *ree;* from 7301; *irrigation,* i.e. *a shower:*—watering {1x}. See: TWOT—2130a; BDB—138c, 924b, 936b.

7378. רִיב {67x} **rîyb**, *reeb;* or

רוּב **rûwb**, *roob;* a prim. root; prop. to *toss,* i.e. *grapple;* mostly fig. to *wrangle,* i.e. *hold a controversy;* (by impl.) to *defend:*—plead {27x}, strive {13x}, contend {12x}, chide {6x}, debate {2x}, misc. {7x} = adversary, complain, × ever, × lay wait, rebuke, × thoroughly.

Riyb, as a verb, means "to plead, strive, conduct a legal case, make a charge." **(1)** It appears in the text for the first time in Gen 26:20: "And the herdmen of Gerar did strive with Isaac's herdmen. . . ." **(2)** Such "striving" with words is found frequently in the biblical text (Gen 31:36; Ex 17:2). **(3)** Sometimes contentious words lead to bodily struggle and injury: "And if men strive together, and one smite another . . ." (Ex 21:18). **(4)** The prophets use *riyb* frequently to indicate that God has an indictment, a legal case, against Israel: "The Lord standeth up to plead (*riyb*), and standeth to judge the people" (Is 3:13). **(5)** In one of his visions, Amos noted: ". . . the Lord God called to contend by fire . . ." (Amos 7:4). **(6)** Micah 6 is a classic example of such a legal case against Judah, calling on the people "to plead" their case (6:1) and progressively showing how only God has a valid case (6:8). See: TWOT—2159; BDB—912c, 923d, 936b.

7379. רִיב {62x} **rîyb**, *reeb;* or

רִב **rîb**, *reeb;* from 7378; a *contest* (personal or legal):—cause {24x}, strife {16x}, controversy {13x}, contention {2x}, misc. {7x} = + adversary, chiding, contend, multitude, pleading, strive (-ing), suit.

Riyb, as a noun, means "strife; dispute." The word appears twice in Mic 6:2: "Hear ye, O mountains, the Lord's controversy, and ye strong foundations of the earth: for the Lord hath a controversy with his people, and he will plead with Israel." See: TWOT—2159a; BDB—936d.

7380. רִיבַי {2x} **Rîybay**, *ree-bah'-ee;* from 7378; *contentious; Ribai,* an Isr.:—Ribai {2x}. See: BDB—937a.

7381. רֵיחַ {58x} **rêyach**, *ray'-akh;* from 7306; *odor* (as if *blown*):—savour {45x}, smell {11x}, scent {2x}.

Reyach, as a noun, means "savor; smell; fragrance; aroma." **(1)** Of the 61 appearances of this word, 43 refer specifically to sacrifices made to God and appear in Genesis–Numbers and Ezekiel. **(2)** This word refers to the "scent or smell" of a person or thing: "And he [Jacob] came near, . . . and he [Isaac] smelled the smell of his raiment . . ." (Gen 27:27). **(3)** In Song 1:12 reach signifies the "fragrance" of perfume and in Song 2:3 the "fragrance" of a flower. **(4)** This word is used of a bad "smell" in Ex 5:21: ". . . Because ye have made our savor to be abhorred [have made us odious] in the eyes of Pharaoh. . . ." **(5)** Most frequently reach is used of the "odor" of a sacrifice being offered up to God. The sacrifice, or the essence of the thing it represents, ascends to God as a placating "odor": "And the Lord smelled a sweet savor . . ." (Gen 8:21—the first occurrence of the word). See: TWOT—2131b; BDB—926b, 937c, 1112d.

7382. רֵיחַ {1x} **rêyach** (Aram.), *ray'-akh;* corresp. to 7381:—smell {1x}. See: TWOT—2991b; BDB—1112d, 1113a.

רֵים **rêym**. See 7214.

רֵיעַ **rêyaʿ**. See 7453.

7383. רִיפָה {2x} **rîyphâh**, *ree-faw';* or

רִפָה **rîphâh**, *ree-faw';* from 7322; (only plur.), *grits* (as *pounded*):—ground corn {1x}, wheat {1x}. See: TWOT—2160a; BDB—937d, 952b.

7384. רִיפַת {2x} **Rîyphath**, *ree-fath';* or (prob. by orth. err.)

דִּיפַת **Dîyphath**, *dee-fath';* of for. or.; *Riphath,* a grandson of Japheth and his desc.:—Riphath {2x}. See: BDB—193d, 937d.

7385. רִיק {12x} **rîyq**, *reek;* from 7324; *emptiness;* fig. a *worthless* thing; adv. *in vain:*—vain {7x}, vanity {2x}, no purpose {1x}, empty {1x}, vain thing {1x}. See: TWOT—2161b; BDB—938a, 938b.

7386. רֵיק {14x} **rêyq**, *rake;* or (short.)

רֵק **rêq**, *rake;* from 7324; *empty;* fig. *worthless:*—empty {6x}, vain {5x}, emptied {1x}, vain men {1x}, vain fellows {1x}. See: TWOT—2161a; BDB—938a, 938b, 954d.

7387. רֵיקָם {16x} **rêyqâm**, *ray-kawm';* from 7386; *emptily;* fig. (obj.) *ineffectually,* (subj.) *undeservedly:*—empty {12x}, without cause {2x}, void {1x}, vain {1x}. See: TWOT—2161c; BDB—938b.

7388. רִיר {2x} **rîyr**, *reer;* from 7325; *saliva;* by resemblance *broth:*—spittle {1x}, white [of an egg] {1x}. See: TWOT—2162a; BDB—938c.

7389. רֵישׁ {7x} **rêysh**, *raysh;* or

רֵאשׁ **rêʾsh**, *raysh;* or

רִישׁ **rîysh**, *reesh;* from 7326; *poverty:*—poverty {7x}. See: TWOT—2138a, 2138b; BDB—910c, 930d, 938c.

7390. רַךְ {16x} **rak**, *rak;* from 7401; *tender* (lit. or fig.); by impl. *weak:*—tender {9x}, soft {3x}, fainthearted + 3824 {1x}, one {1x}, weak {1x}, tenderhearted + 3824 {1x}. See: TWOT—2164a; BDB—938c, 940a.

7391. רֹךְ {1x} **rôk**, *roke;* from 7401; *softness* (fig.):—tenderness {1x}. See: TWOT—2164b; BDB—938c, 940a.

7392. רָכַב {78x} **râkab**, *raw-kab';* a prim. root; to *ride* (on an animal or in a vehicle); caus. to *place upon* (for riding or gen.), to *despatch:*—ride {50x}, rider {12x}, horseback {3x}, put {3x}, set {2x}, carried {2x}, misc. {6x} = get [oneself] up, on horse.

Rakab means "to ride upon, drive, mount (an animal)." The first occurrence is in Gen 24:61: "And Rebekah arose, and her damsels, and they rode upon the camels. . . ." See: TWOT—2163; BDB—938c.

7393. רֶכֶב {120x} **rekeb**, *reh'-keb;* from 7392; a *vehicle;* by impl. a *team;* by extens. *cavalry;* by anal. a *rider,* i.e. the upper millstone:—chariot {115x}, millstone {3x}, wagons {1x}, variant {1x}.

Rekeb means "chariotry; chariot units; chariot horse; chariot; train; upper millstone." **(1)** The word is used collectively of an entire force of "military chariotry": "And he took six hundred chosen chariots, and all the chariots (Ex 14:7). **(1a)** This use of *rekeb* might well be rendered "chariot-units" (the chariot, a driver, an offensive and a defensive man). **(1b)** The immediately preceding verse uses *rekeb* of a single "war-chariot" (or perhaps "chariot unit"). **(1c)** The following translation distinguishes the separate units in Ex 14:6–7: "So he made his chariot ready and took his courtiers with him, and he took six hundred select chariot units, and all the chariotry of Egypt with defensive men." **(2)** In its first biblical appearance, *rekeb* means "chariotry": "And there went up with him both chariots and horsemen . . ." (Gen 50:9). **(3)** In 2 Sa 8:4, the word represents "chariot-horse": ". . . And David hocked all the chariot horses. . . ."

(4) *Rekeb* also is used of the "chariot" itself: ". . . And the king was stayed up in his chariot against the Syrians . . ." (1 Kin 22:35). **(5)** Next, *rekeb* refers to a "column" or "train of donkeys and camels": "And he saw a chariot with a couple of horsemen, a chariot of asses, and a chariot of camels . . ." (Is 21:7). **(6)** Finally, *rekeb* sometimes signifies an "upper millstone": "No man shall take the nether or the upper millstone to pledge . . ." (Deut 24:6; cf. Judg 9:53; 2 Sa 11:21). Syn.: 4818. See: TWOT—2163a; BDB—939a.

7394. רֵכָב {13x} **Rêkâb**, *ray-kawb';* from 7392; *rider; Rekab,* the name of two Arabs and of two Isr.:—Rechab {13x}. See: BDB—939c.

7395. רַכָּב {3x} **rakkâb**, *rak-kawb';* from 7392; a *charioteer:*—driver of his chariot {1x}, horseman {1x}, chariot man {1x}. See: TWOT—2163c; BDB—939b.

7396. רִכְבָּה {1x} **rikbâh**, *rik-baw';* fem. of 7393; a *chariot* (collect.):—chariot {1x}. See: TWOT—2163b; BDB—939b.

7397. רֵכָה {5x} **Rêkâh**, *ray-kaw';* prob. fem. from 7401; *softness; Rekah,* a place in Pal.:—Rechabites {4x}, Rechah {1x}. See: BDB—939d.

7398. רְכוּב {1x} **rᵉkûwb**, *rek-oob';* from pass. part. of 7392; a *vehicle* (as *ridden* on):—chariot {1x}. See: TWOT—2163d; BDB—939c.

7399. רְכוּשׁ {28x} **rᵉkûwsh**, *rek-oosh';* or

רְכֻשׁ **rᵉkûsh**, *rek-oosh';* from pass. part. of 7408; *property* (as *gathered*):—goods {12x}, substance {11x}, riches {5x}. See: TWOT—2167b; BDB—940d.

7400. רָכִיל {6x} **râkîyl**, *raw-keel';* from 7402 a *scandal-monger* (as *travelling* about):—slander {2x}, talebearer {2x}, talebearer + 1980 {1x}, carry tales {1x}. See: TWOT—2165b; BDB—940c.

7401. רָכַךְ {8x} **râkak**, *raw-kak';* a prim. root; to *soften* (intr. or tran.), used fig.:—tender {2x}, faint {2x}, fainthearted + 3824 {1x}, mollified {1x}, soft {1x}, softer {1x}. See: TWOT—2164; BDB—939d.

7402. רָכַל {17x} **râkal**, *raw-kal';* a prim. root; to *travel* for trading:—merchant {17x}. See: TWOT—2165; BDB—940b.

7403. רָכָל {1x} **Râkâl**, *raw-kawl';* from 7402; *merchant; Rakal,* a place in Pal.:—Rachal {1x}. See: BDB—940b.

7404. רְכֻלָּה {4x} **rᵉkullâh**, *rek-ool-law';* fem. pass. part. of 7402; *trade* (as *peddled*):—merchandise {2x}, traffick {2x}. See: TWOT—2165a; BDB—940b.

7405. רָכַס {2x} **râkaç**, *raw-kas';* a prim. root; to *tie:*—bind {2x}. See: TWOT—2166; BDB—940c.

7406. רֶכֶס {1x} **rekeç**, *reh'-kes;* from 7405; a mountain *ridge* (as of *tied* summits):—rough places {1x}. See: TWOT—2166a; BDB—940c.

7407. רֹכֶס {1x} **rôkeç**, *ro'-kes;* from 7405; a *snare* (as of *tied* meshes):—pride {1x}. See: TWOT—2166b; BDB—940c.

7408. רָכַשׁ {5x} **râkash**, *raw-kash';* a prim. root; to *lay up,* i.e. *collect:*—got {4x}, gather {1x}. See: TWOT—2167; BDB—940d.

7409. רֶכֶשׁ {4x} **rekesh**, *reh'-kesh;* from 7408; a *relay* of animals on a post-route (as *stored* up for that purpose); by impl. a *courser:*—

mule {2x}, dromedaries {1x}, swift beast {1x}. See: TWOT—2167a; BDB—940d.

רְכֻשׁ **rᵉkûsh**. See 7399.

רֵם **rêm**. See 7214.

7410. רָם {7x} **Râm**, *rawm;* act. part. of 7311; *high; Ram,* the name of an Arabian and of an Isr.:—*Ram* {7x}. See: BDB—928a. See also 1027.

רֻם **rûm**. See 7311.

7411. רָמָה {12x} **râmâh**, *raw-maw';* a prim. root; to *hurl;* spec. to *shoot;* fig. to *delude* or *betray* (as if causing to fall):—deceived {4x}, beguiled {2x}, thrown {2x}, betray {1x}, bowmen + 7198 {1x}, carrying {1x}, deceived so {1x}. See: TWOT—2168, 2169; BDB—941a, 1113a.

7412. רְמָה {12x} **rᵉmâh** (Aram.), *rem-aw';* corresp. to 7411; to *throw, set,* (fig.) *assess:*—cast {10x}, impose {1x}, cast down {1x}. See: TWOT—2997; BDB—1113a.

7413. רָמָה {4x} **râmâh**, *raw-maw';* fem. act. part. of 7311; a *height* (as a seat of idolatry):—high place {4x}. See: TWOT—2133d; BDB—928a, 941d.

7414. רָמָה {37x} **Râmâh**, *raw-maw';* the same as 7413; *Ramah,* the name of four places in Pal.:—*Ramah* {37x}. See: BDB—910b, 910c, 928a, 928c, 941d.

7415. רִמָּה {7x} **rimmâh**, *rim-maw';* from 7426 in the sense of *breeding* [comp. 7311]; a *maggot* (as rapidly *bred*), lit. or fig.:—worm {7x}. See: TWOT—2175a; BDB—941d, 942c.

7416. רִמּוֹן {32x} **rimmôwn**, *rim-mone';* or

רִמֹּן **rimmôn**, *rim-mone';* from 7426; a *pomegranate,* the tree (from its *upright* growth) or the fruit (also an artificial ornament):—pomegranate {31x}, pomegranate tree {1x}. See: TWOT—2170; BDB—745c, 941d.

7417. רִמּוֹן {16x} **Rimmôwn**, *rim-mone';* or (short.)

רִמֹּן **Rimmôn**, *rim-mone';* or

רִמּוֹנוֹ **Rimmôwnôw** (1 Chron. 6:62 [77]), *rim-mo-no';* the same as 7416; *Rimmon,* the name of a Syrian deity, also of five places in Pal.:—*Rimmon* {16x}. See: TWOT—2171; BDB—942a, 942b. The addition "-methoar" (Josh. 19:13) is

הַמְּתֹאָר **ham-mᵉthô'âr**, *ham-meth-o-awr';* pass. part. of 8388 with the art.; *the* (one) *marked off,* i.e. *which pertains;* mistaken for part of the name.

רָמוֹת **Râmôwth**. See 7418, 7433.

7418. רָמוֹת־נֶגֶב {1x} **Râmôwth-Negeb**, *raw-moth-neh'-gheb;* or

רָמַת נֶגֶב **Râmath Negeb**, *raw'-math neh'-gheb;* from the plur. or constr. form of 7413 and 5045; *heights* (or *height*) of (the) *South; Ramoth-Negeb* or *Ramath-Negeb,* a place in Pal.:—Ramoth {1x}. See: BDB—910c, 928b, 928c.

7419. רָמוּת {1x} **râmûwth**, *raw-mooth';* from 7311; a *heap* (of carcases):—height {1x}. See: TWOT—2133e; BDB—928c, 942b.

7420. רֹמַח {15x} **rômach**, *ro'-makh;* from an unused root mean. to *hurl;* a *lance* (as *thrown*); espec. the iron *point:*—spear {12x}, javelin {1x}, lancet {1x}, buckler {1x}. See: TWOT—2172; BDB—942b.

7421. רַמִּי {1x} **rammîy**, *ram-mee';* for 761; a *Ramite,* i.e. Aramæan:—Syrian {1x}. See: BDB—74c.

7422. רַמְיָה {1x} **Ramyâh**, *ram-yaw';* from 7311 and 3050; *Jah has raised; Ramjah,* an Isr.:—Ramiah {1x}. See: BDB—941d, 942b.

7423. רְמִיָּה {15x} **rᵉmîyâh**, *rem-ee-yaw';* from 7411; *remissness, treachery:*—deceitful {4x}, deceitfully {3x}, deceit {2x}, slothful {2x}, false {1x}, guile {1x}, idle {1x}, slack {1x}. See: TWOT—2169a; BDB—941a, 941c, 942b, 945a.

7424. רַמָּךְ {1x} **rammâk**, *ram-mawk';* of for. or.; a brood *mare:*—dromedaries {1x}. See: TWOT—2173; BDB—942b.

7425. רְמַלְיָהוּ {13x} **Rᵉmalyâhûw**, *rem-al-yaw'-hoo;* from an unused root and 3050 (perh. mean. to *deck*); *Jah has bedecked; Remaljah,* an Isr.:—Remaliah {13x}. See: BDB—942b.

7426. רָמַם {7x} **râmam**, *raw-mam';* a prim. root; to *rise* (lit. or fig.):—exalted {3x}, get [oneself] up {1x}, lifted up (self) {2x}, mount up {1x}. See: TWOT—2174; BDB—942c.

7427. רֹמֵמֻת {1x} **rômêmûth**, *ro-may-mooth';* from the act. part. of 7426; *exaltation:*—lifting up of self {1x}. See: TWOT—2133g; BDB—928c.

רִמֹּן **rimmôn**. See 7416.

7428. רִמֹּן פֶּרֶץ {2x} **Rimmôn Perets**, *rim-mone' peh'-rets;* from 7416 and 6556; *pomegranate of* (the) *breach; Rimmon Perets,* a place in the desert:—Rimmon-parez {2x}. See: BDB—829d, 942a.

7429. רָמַס {19x} **râmaç**, *raw-mas';* a prim. root; to *tread* upon (as a potter, in walking or abusively):—tread down {7x}, trea {5x}, stamped {2x}, trample . . . feet {1x}, oppressors {1x}, tread under foot {1x}, trample {1x}, trodden {1x}. See: TWOT—2176; BDB—942c.

7430. רָמַשׂ {17x} **râmas**, *raw-mas';* a prim. root; prop. to *glide* swiftly, i.e. to *crawl* or *move* with short steps; by anal. to *swarm:*—creep {11x}, move {6x}. See: TWOT—2177; BDB—942d.

7431. רֶמֶשׂ {17x} **remes**, *reh'-mes;* from 7430; a *reptile* or any other rapidly moving animal:—that creepeth {1x}, creeping thing {15x}, moving thing {1x}. See: TWOT—2177a; BDB—943a.

7432. רֶמֶת {1x} **Remeth**, *reh'-meth;* from 7411; *height; Remeth,* a place in Pal.:—*Remeth* {1x}. See: BDB—928c, 928d, 943a.

7433. רָמֹת גִּלְעָד {22x} (or רָמוֹת **Râmôwth**) **Râmôth Gilᶜâd** (2 Chron. 22:5), *raw-moth' gil-awd';* from the plur. of 7413 and 1568; *heights of Gilad; Ramoth-Gilad,* a place E. of the Jordan:—Ramoth-gilead + 1568 {19x}, Ramoth {3x}. See: BDB—928b. See also 7216.

7434. רָמַת הַמִּצְפֶּה {1x} **Râmath ham-Mitspeh**, *raw-math' ham-mits-peh';* from 7413 and 4707 with the art. interpolated; *height of the watch*-tower; *Ramath-ham-Mitspeh,* a place in Pal.:—Ramath-mizpeh {1x}. See: BDB—859d, 928b.

7435. רָמָתִי {1x} **Râmâthîy**, *raw-maw-thee';* patron. of 7414; a *Ramathite* or inhab. of Ramah:—Ramathite {1x}. See: BDB—928b, 943a.

7436. רָמָתַיִם צוֹפִים {1x} **Râmâthayim Tsôwphîym**, *raw-maw-thah'-yim tso-feem';* from the dual of 7413 and the plur. of the act. part. of 6822; *double height of watchers; Ramathajim-Tsophim,* a place in Pal.:—Ramathaim-zophim {1x}. See: BDB—847c, 928a, 928c, 943a.

7437. רָמַת לֶחִי {1x} **Râmath Lechîy**, *raw'-math lekh'-ee;* from 7413 and 3895; *height of* (a) *jaw-bone; Ramath-Lechi,* a place in Pal.:—Ramath-lehi {1x}. See: BDB—928b.

רָן **Rân**. See 1028.

7438. רֹן {1x} **rôn**, *rone;* from 7442; a *shout* (of deliverance):—song {1x}. See: TWOT—2179a; BDB—943a, 943c.

7439. רָנָה {1x} **rânâh**, *raw-naw';* a prim. root; to *whiz:*—rattle {1x}. See: TWOT—2178; BDB—943a.

7440. רִנָּה {33x} **rinnâh**, *rin-naw';* from 7442; prop. a *creaking* (or shrill sound), i.e. *shout* (of joy or grief):—cry {12x}, singing {9x}, rejoicing {3x}, joy {3x}, gladness {1x}, proclamation {1x}, shouting {1x}, sing {1x}, songs {1x}, triumph {1x}. See: TWOT—2179c; BDB—943a, 943c.

7441. רִנָּה {1x} **Rinnâh**, *rin-naw';* the same as 7440; *Rinnah,* an Isr.:—*Rinnah* {1x}. See: BDB—943a, 943d.

7442. רָנַן {52x} **rânan**, *raw-nan';* a prim. root; prop. to *creak* (or emit a stridulous sound), i.e. to *shout* (usually for joy):—sing {20x}, rejoice {11x}, sing aloud {4x}, shout {4x}, shout for joy {3x}, sing for joy {2x}, crieth {2x}, cry out {2x}, shout aloud {1x}, misc. {3x}.

Ranan, as a verb, means "to sing, shout, cry out." **(1)** It occurs approximately 50 times in the Hebrew Old Testament, with about half of these uses being in the Book of Psalms, where there is special emphasis on "singing" and "shouting" praises to God. **(2)** *Ranan* is found for the first time in Lev 9:24 at the conclusion of the consecration of Aaron and his sons to the priesthood. When the fire fell and consumed the sacrifice, the people "shouted, and fell on their faces." **(3)** *Ranan* is often used to express joy, exultation, which seems to demand loud singing, especially when it is praise to God: "Cry out and shout, thou inhabitant of Zion: for great is the Holy One of Israel in the midst of thee" (Is 12:6). **(4)** When Wisdom calls, she cries aloud to all who will hear (Prov 8:3). **(5)** To shout for joy (Ps 32:11) is to let joy ring out! Syn.: 7891. See: TWOT—2134, 2179; BDB—929c, 930c, 943b, 943c.

7443. רֶנֶן {1x} **renen**, *reh'-nen;* from 7442; an *ostrich* (from its *wail*):—× goodly {1x}. See: TWOT—2179d; BDB—943d.

7444. רַנֵּן {2x} **rannên**, *ran-nane';* intens. from 7442; *shouting* (for joy):—singing {1x}, joy {1x}. See: TWOT—2179; BDB—943b.

7445. רְנָנָה {4x} **rᵉnânâh**, *ren-aw-naw';* from 7442; a *shout* (for joy):—joyful {1x}, joyful voice {1x}, singing {1x}, triumphing {1x}. See: TWOT—2179b; BDB—943c.

7446. רִסָּה {2x} **Riççâh**, *ris-saw';* from 7450; a *ruin* (as *dripping* to pieces); *Rissah,* a place in the 1Desert:—Rissah {2x}. See: BDB—943d.

7447. רָסִיס {2x} **râçîyç**, *raw-sees';* from 7450; prop. *dripping* to pieces, i.e. a *ruin;* also a dew-*drop:*—breach {1x}, drop {1x}. See: TWOT—2181a, 2182a; BDB—944a.

7448. רֶסֶן {4x} **reçen**, *reh'-sen;* from an unused root mean. to *curb;* a *halter* (as *restraining*); by impl. the *jaw:*—bridle {4x}. See: TWOT—2180a; BDB—943d.

7449. רֶסֶן {1x} **Reçen**, *reh'-sen;* the same as 7448; *Resen*, a place in Ass.:—Resen {1x}. See: BDB—944a.

7450. רָסַס {1x} **râçaç**, *raw-sas';* a prim. root; to *comminute;* used only as denom. from 7447, to *moisten* (with drops):—temper {1x}. See: TWOT—2181; BDB—944a.

7451. רַע {663x} **raʿ**, *rah;* from 7489; *bad* or (as noun) *evil* (nat. or mor.):—evil {442x}, wickedness {59x}, wicked {25x}, mischief {21x}, hurt {20x}, bad {13x}, trouble {10x}, sore {9x}, affliction {6x}, ill {5x}, adversity {4x}, favoured {3x}, harm {3x}, naught {3x}, noisome {2x}, grievous {2x}, sad {2x}, misc. {34x} = calamity, + displease (-ure), distress, + exceedingly, × great, grief, heavy, hurtful, + mark, misery, + not please, sorrow, vex, worse (-st), wretchedness, wrong.

Introduction: This word combines together in one the wicked deed and its consequences. It generally indicates the rough exterior of wrongdoing as a breach of harmony, and as breaking up of what is good and desirable in man and in society. While the prominent characteristic of the godly is lovingkindness (2617), one of the most marked features of the ungodly man is that his course is an injury both to himself and to everyone around him. **(1)** *Ra'* refers to that which is "bad" or "evil," in a wide variety of applications. A greater number of the word's occurrences signify something morally evil or hurtful, often referring to man or men: **(1a)** "Then answered all the wicked men and men of Belial, of those that went with David . . ." (1 Sa 30:22). **(1b)** "And Esther said, the adversary and enemy is the wicked Haman" (Est 7:6). **(1c)** "There they cry, but none giveth answer, because of the pride of evil men" (Job 35:12; cf. Ps 10:15).

(2) *Ra'* is also used to denote **(2a)** evil words (Prov 15:26), **(2b)** evil thoughts (Gen 6:5), or **(2c)** evil actions (Deut 17:5, Neh 13:17). **(3)** Eze 6:11 depicts grim consequences for Israel as a result of its actions: "Thus saith the Lord God; smite with thine hand, and stamp with thy foot, and say, Alas for all the evil abominations of the house of Israel! For they shall fall by the sword, by the famine, and by the pestilence." **(4)** *Ra'* may mean "bad" or unpleasant in the sense of giving pain or calming unhappiness: **(4a)** "And Jacob said unto Pharaoh, . . . Few and evil have the days of the years of my life been . . ." (Gen 47:9). **(4b)** "And when the people heard these evil tidings, they mourned . . ." (Ex 33:4; cf. Gen 37:2). **(4c)** "Correction is grievous [*ra'*] unto him that forsaketh the way: and he that hateth reproof shall die" (Prov 15:10).

(5) *Ra'* may also connote a fierceness or wildness: **(5a)** "He cast upon them the fierceness of his anger, wrath, and indignation, and trouble, by sending evil [*ra'*] angels among them" (Ps 78:49). **(5b)** "Some evil beast hath devoured him . . ." (Gen 37:20; cf. Gen 37:33; Lev 26:6). **(6)** In less frequent uses, *ra'* implies **(6a)** severity: "For thus saith the Lord God; How much more when I send my four sore [*ra'*] judgments upon Israel . . ." (Eze 14:21; cf. Deut 6:22); **(6b)** unpleasantness: "And the Lord will take away from thee all sickness, and will put more of the evil diseases of Egypt . . . upon thee . . ." (Deut 7:15; cf. Deut 28:59); **(6c)** deadliness: "When I shall send upon them the evil arrows of famine, which shall be for their destruction . . ." (Eze 5:16; cf. "hurtful sword," Ps 144:10); **(6d)** or sadness: "Wherefore the king said unto me, why is thy countenance sad . . ." (Neh 2:2).

(7) The word may also refer to something of poor or inferior quality, such as **(7a)** "bad" land (Num 13:19), **(7b)** "naughty" figs (Jer 24:2), **(7c)** "ill-favored" cattle (Gen 41:3, 19), or **(7d)** a "bad" sacrificial animal (Lev 27:10, 12, 14). **(8)** In Is 45:7 Yahweh describes His actions by saying, ". . . I make peace, and create evil [*ra'*] . . ."; **(8a)** moral "evil" is not intended in this context, but rather the antithesis of shalom ("peace; welfare; well-being"). **(8b)** The whole verse affirms that as absolute Sovereign, the Lord creates a universe governed by a moral order. Calamity and misfortune will surely ensue from the wickedness of ungodly men. **(8c)** When He purposely withdraws His powerful hand, resorting to providence and sovereignty, and leaves the situation to ungodly men, He has created a situation wherein peace and wholesomeness will not stand. **(8d)** The ungodly men will wreck the peace and establish that which is poor, less than His reflection, and hurtful to all considered. Syn.: 205, 817, 2403, 5674, 5771, 5999. See: TWOT—2191a, 2191c; BDB—944a, 948a, 948c, 949a. [incl. Fem.

רָעָה **râʿâh**; *as adj. or noun.*]

7452. רֵעַ {3x} **rêaʿ**, *ray'-ah;* from 7321; a *crash* (of thunder), *noise* (of war), *shout* (of joy):—× aloud {1x}, noise {1x}, shouted {1x}. See: TWOT—2135a; BDB—929d, 944a, 946b.

7453. רֵעַ {188x} **rêaʿ**, *ray'-ah;* or

רֵיעַ **rêyaʿ**, *ray'-ah;* from 7462; an *associate* (more or less close):—neighbour {102x}, friend {42x}, another {23x}, fellow {10x}, companion {5x}, other {2x}, brother {1x}, husband {1x}, lovers {1x}, neighbour + 1121 {1x}.

Rea', as a noun, means "friend; companion." **(1)** The basic meaning of *rea'* is in the narrow usage of the word. A *rea'* is a "personal friend" with whom one shares confidences and to whom one feels very close: "And the Lord spake unto Moses face to face, as a man speaketh unto his friend" (Ex 33:11). **(1a)** The closeness of relationship is best expressed by those texts where the *rea'* is like a brother or son, a part of the family: "For my brethren and companions' sakes . . ." (Ps 122:8, cf. Deut 13:6). For this reason, when Zimri became king over Israel he killed not only all relatives of Baasha, but also his "friends" (1 Kin 16:11). **(1b)** In this sense, the word is a synonym of 'ah (251 - "brother") and of qarob (7138 - "kin"): ". . . Go in and out from gate to gate throughout the camp, and slay every man his brother ('ah), and every man his companion (*rea'*), and every man his neighbor (qarob)" (Ex 32:27). **(2)** Similar to the above is the sense of "marriage partner": "His mouth is most sweet: yea, he is altogether lovely. This is my beloved, and this is my friend, O daughters of Jerusalem" (Song 5:16).

(6) However, *rea'* may also signify "illegitimate partners": ". . . If a man put away his wife, and she go from him, and become another man's, shall he return unto her again? shall not that land be greatly polluted? but thou has played the harlot with many lovers (*rea'*); yet return again to me, saith the Lord" (Jer 3:1). **(7)** The wider usage of *rea'* resembles the English word neighbor, the person with whom one associates regularly or casually without establishing close relations. **(7a)** One may borrow from his "neighbor" (Ex 22:14), but not bear false witness (Ex 20:16) nor covet his neighbor's possessions (Ex 20:17–18). The laws regulate how one must not take advantage of one's "neighbors." **(7b)** The second greatest commandment, which Jesus reiterated—"Love thy neighbor as thyself" (Lev 19:18)—receives reinforcement in the laws of the Pentateuch. **(7c)** The prophets charged Israel with breaking the commandment: They oppressed each other (Is 3:5) and desired their neighbors' wives (Jer 5:8); they committed adultery with these women (Eze 18:6); they did not pay wages to the worker (Jer 22:13); and they improperly took advantage of their "neighbors" (Eze 22:12).

(8) According to Proverbs, not loving one's neighbor is a sign of foolishness: "He that is void of wisdom despiseth his neighbour: but a man of understanding holdeth his peace" (Prov 11:12). **(9)** The wider meaning comes to expression in the proverb of the rich man and his "friends": "Wealth maketh many friends; but the poor is separated from his neighbor" (Prov 19:4). Here the "friend" is a person whose association is not long-lasting, whose friendship is superficial. Syn.: 1730, 2617, 2836, 3039, 5689, 7463, 7464, 7468, 7474. See: TWOT—2186a; BDB—929d, 937c, 944a, 945d, 946c.

7454. רֵעַ {2x} **rêaʿ**, *ray'-ah;* from 7462; a *thought* (as *association* of ideas):—thought {2x}. See: TWOT—2187a;BDB—929d, 944a, 946b, 946d.

7455. רֹעַ {19x} **rôaʿ**, *ro'-ah;* from 7489; *badness* (as *marring*), phys. or mor.:—evil {11x}, wickedness {3x}, bad {1x}, badness {1x}, naughtiness {1x}, sorrow {1x}, sadness {1x}. See: TWOT—2191b; BDB—944a, 947d.

7456. רָעֵב {11x} **râʿêb**, *raw-abe';* a prim. root; to *hunger:*— . . . hunger {5x}, hungry {4x}, suffer famish {1x}, famished {1x}.

Ra'eb, as a verb, means to be hungry, suffer hunger: "And when all the land of Egypt was famished. . . ." (Gen 41:55). See: TWOT—2183; BDB—944a.

7457. רָעֵב {21x} **râʿêb**, *raw-abe';* from 7456; *hungry* (more or less intensely):—hunger bitten {1x}, hungry {20x}.

The first biblical occurrence is in 1 Sa 2:5: ". . . And they that were hungry ceased: . . ." See: TWOT—2183b; BDB—944c.

7458. רָעָב {101x} **râʿâb**, *raw-awb';* from 7456; *hunger* (more or less extensive):—dearth {5x}, famine {87x}, + famished {1x}, hunger {8x}.

Ra'ab, as a noun, means "famine; hunger." **(1)** *Ra'ab* means "hunger" as opposed to "thirst": "Therefore shalt thou serve thine enemies which the Lord shall send against thee, in hunger, and in thirst, and in nakedness, and in want of all things . . ." (Deut 28:48). **(2)** Another meaning of the word is "famine," or the lack of food in an entire geographical area: "And there was a famine in the land: and Abram went down into Egypt . . ." (Gen 12:10—the first occurrence). **(2a)** God used a "famine" as a means of judgment (Jer 5:12), **(2b)** of warning (1 Kin 17:1), **(2c)** of correction (2 Sa 21:1), or **(2d)** of punishment (Jer 14:12). **(2d)** The "famine" was always under divine control, being planned and used by Him. **(3)** *Ra'ab* was also used to picture the "lack of God's word" (Amos 8:11; cf. Deut 8:3). See: TWOT—2183a; BDB—944b.

7459. רְעָבוֹן {3x} **rᵉʿâbôwn**, *reh-aw-bone';* from 7456; *famine:*—famine {3x}. See: TWOT—2183c; BDB—944c.

7460. רָעַד {3x} **râʿad**, *raw-ad';* a prim. root: to *shudder* (more or less violently):—tremble {3x}. See: TWOT—2184; BDB—944c.

7461. רַעַד {6x} **raʿad**, *rah'-ad;* or (fem.)

רְעָדָה **rᵉʿâdâh**, *reh-aw-daw';* from 7460; a *shudder:*—trembling {4x}, fearful {1x}, fearfulness {1x}. See: TWOT—2184a, 2184b; BDB—944c, 944d.

7462. רָעָה {173x} **râʿâh**, *raw-aw';* a prim. root; to *tend* a flock; i.e. *pasture* it; intr. to *graze* (lit. or fig.); gen. to *rule;* by extens. to *associate* with (as a friend):—feed {75x}, shepherd {63x}, pastor {8x}, herdmen {7x}, keep {3x}, companion {2x}, broken {1x}, company {1x}, devour {1x}, eat {1x}, entreateth {1x}, misc. {10x} = use as a friend, make friendship with, + shearing house, wander, waste.

Ra'ah, as a verb, means "to associate with." This word appears in Prov 22:24: "Make no friendship with an angry man; and with a furious man thou shalt not go. . . ." See: TWOT—2185, 2186; BDB—944d, 945c, 946b, 950a, 1113b.

7463. רֵעֶה {3x} **rêʿeh**, *ray-eh';* from 7462; a (male) *companion:*—friend {3x}.

Re'eh also means "friend." This noun appears in 1 Kin 4:5: ". . . Zabud the son of Nathan was principal officer, and the king's friend. . . ." Syn.: 7453, 7464, 7468, 7474. See: TWOT—2186b; BDB—946b.

7464. רֵעָה {3x} **rêʿâh**, *ray'-aw;* fem. of 7453; a female *associate:*—companion {2x}, fellows {1x}.

Re'ah refers to a "female friend." See Judg 11:37 for this usage: "And she said unto her father . . . let me alone two months, that I may go up and down upon the mountains, and bewail my virginity, I and my fellows" (cf. Judg 11:38; Ps 45:14). Syn.: 7453, 7463, 7468, 7474. See: TWOT—2186c; BDB—946b.

7465. רֹעָה {1x} **rôʿâh**, *ro-aw';* for 7455; *breakage:*—broken {1x}. See: TWOT—2192; BDB—949d.

7466. רְעוּ {5x} **Rᵉʿûw**, *reh-oo';* for 7471 in the sense of 7453; *friend; Re,* a postdiluvian patriarch:—Reu {5x}. See: BDB—946c.

7467. רְעוּאֵל {11x} **Rᵉʿûwʾêl**, *reh-oo-ale';* from the same as 7466 and 410; *friend of God; Reüel,* the name of Moses' father-in-law, also of an Edomite and an Isr.:—Raguel {1x}, Reuel {10x}. See: BDB—946c.

7468. רְעוּת {6x} **rᵉʿûwth**, *reh-ooth';* from 7462 in the sense of 7453; a female *associate,* gen. an *additional* one:—neighbour {2x}, another {2x}, mate {2x}.

Re'uwth refers to a "fellow woman." This word is usually translated idiomatically in a reciprocal phrase of "one another," as in Zec 11:9: "Then said I, I will not feed you: that that dieth, let it die; and that that is to be cut off, let it be cut off; and let the rest eat every one the flesh of another (*re'uwth*)." Syn.: 7453, 7463, 7464, 7468, 7474. See: TWOT—2186e; BDB—946b.

7469. רְעוּת {7x} **rᵉʿûwth**, *reh-ooth';* prob. from 7462; a *feeding* upon, i.e. *grasping* after:—vexation {7x}. See: TWOT—2187b; BDB—946d.

7470. רְעוּת {2x} **rᵉʿûwth** (Aram.), *reh-ooth';* corresp. to 7469; *desire:*—pleasure {1x}, will {1x}. See: TWOT—2998a; BDB—1113b.

7471. רְעִי {1x} **rᵉʿîy**, *reh-ee';* from 7462; *pasture:*—pasture {1x}. See: TWOT—2185a; BDB—945c.

7472. רֵעִי {1x} **Rêʿîy**, *ray-ee';* from 7453; *social; Rê,* an Isr.:—Rei {1x}. See: BDB—946c.

7473. רֹעִי {2x} **rôʿîy**, *ro-ee';* from act. part. of 7462; *pastoral;* as noun, a *shepherd:*—shepherd {2x}. See: BDB—944d, 945a, 945c.

7474. רַעְיָה {10x} **raʿyâh**, *rah-yaw';* fem. of 7453; a female *associate:*—love {9x}, variant {1x}.

The noun *ra'yah* means "beloved companion; bride." *Ra'yah* occurs many times in the Song of Solomon: 1:9, 15; 2:2, 10, 13; 4:1, 7; 5:2; 6:4. Syn.: 7453, 7463, 7464, 7468. See: TWOT—2186d; BDB—946b.

7475. רַעְיוֹן {3x} **raʿyôwn**, *rah-yone';* from 7462 in the sense of 7469; *desire:*—vexation {3x}. See: TWOT—2187c; BDB—946d.

7476. רַעְיוֹן {6x} **raʿyôwn** (Aram.), *rah-yone';* corresp. to 7475; a *grasp,* i.e. (fig.) mental *conception:*—thought {5x}, cogitation {1x}. See: TWOT—2998b; BDB—1113b.

7477. רָעַל {1x} **râʿal**, *raw-al';* a prim. root; to *reel,* i.e. (fig.) to *brandish:*—terribly shaken {1x}. See: TWOT—2188; BDB—947a.

7478. רַעַל {1x} **raʿal**, *rah'-al;* from 7477; a *reeling* (from intoxication):—trembling {1x}. See: TWOT—2188a; BDB—947a.

7479. רְעָלָה {1x} **raʿălâh**, *rah-al-aw';* fem. of 7478; a long *veil* (as *fluttering*):—muffler {1x}. See: TWOT—2188b; BDB—947a.

7480. רְעֵלָיָה {1x} **Rᵉʿêlâyâh**, *reh-ay-law-yaw';* from 7477 and 3050; *made to tremble* (i.e. *fearful*) *of Jah; Reëlajah,* an Isr.:—Reeliah {1x}. See: BDB—947a, 947c.

7481. רָעַם {13x} **râʿam**, *raw-am';* a prim. root; to *tumble,* i.e. *be* violently *agitated;* spec. to *crush* (of thunder); fig. to *irritate* (with anger):—thunder {8x}, roar {3x}, trouble {1x}, fret {1x}. See: TWOT—2189; BDB—947b.

7482. רַעַם {6x} **raʿam**, *rah'am;* from 7481; a *peal* of thunder:—thunder {6x}. See: TWOT—2189a; BDB—947b.

7483. רַעְמָה {1x} **raʿmâh**, *rah-maw';* fem. of 7482; the *mane* of a horse (as *quivering* in the wind):—thunder {1x}. See: TWOT—2189b; BDB—947c.

7484. רַעְמָה {5x} **Raʿmâh**, *rah-maw';* the same as 7483; *Ramah,* the name of a grandson of Ham, and of a place (perh. founded by him):—Raamah {5x}. See: BDB—947c.

7485. רַעַמְיָה {1x} **Raʿamyâh**, *rah-am-yaw';* from 7481 and 3050; *Jah has shaken; Raamjah,* an Isr.:—Raamiah {1x}. See: BDB—947a, 947c.

7486. רַעְמְסֵס {5x} **Raʿmᵉçêç**, *rah-mes-ace';* or

רַעַמְסֵס **Raʿamçêç**, *rah-am-sace';* of Eg. or.; *Rameses* or *Raamses,* a place in Egypt:—Rameses {5x}, Raamses {1x}. See: BDB—947c.

7487. רַעֲנָן {1x} **raʿănan** (Aram.), *rah-aw-nan';* corresp. to 7488; *green,* i.e. (fig.) *prosperous:*—flourishing {1x}. See: TWOT—2999; BDB—1113b.

7488. רַעֲנָן {20x} **raʿănân**, *rah-an-awn';* from an unused root mean. to *be green; verdant;* by anal. *new;* fig. *prosperous:*—green {18x}, fresh {1x}, flourishing {1x}. See: TWOT—2190a; BDB—947d, 1113b.

7489. רָעַע {83x} **râʿaʿ**, *raw-ah';* a prim. root; prop. to *spoil* (lit. by *breaking* to pieces); fig. to *make* (or *be*) *good for nothing,* i.e. *bad* (physically, socially or morally):—evil {20x}, evildoer {10x}, hurt {7x}, wickedly {5x}, worse {5x}, afflict {5x}, wicked {4x}, break {3x}, doer {3x}, ill {3x}, harm {3x}, displease {2x}, misc. {13x} = associate selves, show self friendly, × indeed, do mischief, punish, still, vex. Syn.: 2398, 3256, 5358, 5771, 6064. See: TWOT—2191, 2192; BDB—945b, 948a, 949b, 949d, 1084a.

7490. רְעַע {2x} **rᵉʿaʿ** (Aram.), *reh-ah';* corresp. to 7489:—bruise {1x}, break {1x}. See: TWOT—3000; BDB—1113b.

7491. רָעַף {5x} **râʿaph**, *raw-af';* a prim. root; to *drip:*—drop {3x}, drop down {1x}, distil {1x}. See: TWOT—2193; BDB—950a.

7492. רָעַץ {2x} **râʿats**, *raw-ats';* a prim. root; to *break* in pieces; fig. *harass:*—dash in pieces {1x}, vex {1x}. See: TWOT—2194; BDB—950a.

7493. רָעַשׁ {30x} **râʿash**, *raw-ash;* a prim. root; to *undulate* (as the earth, the sky, etc.; also a field of grain), partic. through fear; spec. to *spring* (as a locust):—shake {16x}, tremble {9x}, moved {2x}, afraid {1x}, quake {1x}, remove {1x}. See: TWOT—2195; BDB—950a.

7494. רַעַשׁ {17x} **raʿash**, *rah'-ash;* from 7493; *vibration, bounding, uproar:*—earthquake {6x}, rushing {3x}, shake {3x}, fierceness {1x}, confused noise {1x}, commotion {1x}, rattling {1x}, quaking {1x}. See: TWOT—2195a; BDB—950b.

7495. רָפָא {67x} **râphâʾ**, *raw-faw';* or

רָפָה **râphâh**, *raw-faw';* a prim. root; prop. to *mend* (by stitching), i.e. (fig.) to *cure:*—heal {57x}, physician {5x}, cure {1x}, repaired {1x}, misc. {3x} = × thoroughly, make whole.

(1) *Rapah* means to heal, a restoring to normal, an act which God typically performs (Gen 20:17). **(2)** Thus, appeals to God for healing are common (Jer 17:14). **(3)** Not only are human diseases healed, but **(3a)** bad water is restored to normal or healed (2 Kin 2:22); **(3b)** salt water is healed or made fresh (Eze 47:8); even **(3c)** pottery is healed or restored (Jer 19:11). **(4)** Nations are healed—such healing not only involves God's grace and forgiveness, but also the nation's repentance. Divine discipline leads to repentance and healing (Hos 6:1; Jer 30:17). **(5)** Foreign cities and powers can know God's healing if they repent (Jer 51:8–9). **(6)** False prophets are condemned because they deal only with the symptoms and not with the deep spiritual hurts of the people: "They have healed also the hurt of the daughter of my people slightly, saying, Peace, peace; when there is no peace" (Jer 6:14; also 8:11). Syn.: 7503. See: TWOT—2196; BDB—950c.

7496. רָפָא {8x} **râphâʾ**, *raw-faw';* from 7495 in the sense of 7503; prop. *lax,* i.e. (fig.) a *ghost* (as *dead;* in plur. only):—dead {7x}, deceased {1x}. See: TWOT—2198c; BDB—951a, 952b.

7497. רָפָא {25x} **râphâʾ**, *raw-faw';* or

רָפָה **râphâh**, *raw-faw';* from 7495 in the sense of *invigorating;* a *giant:*—giant {17x}, Rephaim {8x}. Syn.: 1368, 5307. See: TWOT—2198d; BDB—951a, 952b. See also 1051.

7498. רָפָא {2x} **Râphâʾ**, *raw-faw';* or

רָפָה **Râphâh**, *raw-faw';* prob. the same as 7497; *giant; Rapha* or *Raphah,* the name of two Isr.:—*Rapha* {2x}. See: BDB—951a, 951b, 952a, 952b.

7499. רְפֻאָה {3x} **rᵉphûʾâh**, *ref-oo-aw';* fem. pass. part. of 7495; a *medicament:*—medicine {2x}, healed {1x}. See: TWOT—2196a; BDB—951b.

7500. רִפְאוּת {1x} **riphʼûwth**, *rif-ooth'*; from 7495; a *cure:*—health {1x}. See: TWOT—2196b; BDB—951b.

7501. רְפָאֵל {1x} **Rᵉphâʼêl**, *ref-aw-ale'*; from 7495 and 410; *God has cured; Rephaël,* an Isr.:—*Rephael* {1x}. See: BDB—951b.

7502. רָפַד {3x} **râphad**, *raw-fad'*; a prim. root; to *spread* (a bed); by impl. to *refresh:*—spread {1x}, made {1x}, comfort {1x}. See: TWOT—2197; BDB—951c.

7503. רָפָה {46x} **râphâh**, *raw-faw'*; a prim. root; to *slacken* (in many applications, lit. or fig.):—feeble {6x}, fail {4x}, weaken {4x}, go {4x}, alone {4x}, idle {3x}, stay {3x}, slack {3x}, faint {2x}, forsake {2x}, abated {1x}, cease {1x}, misc. {9x} = consume, draw [toward evening], leave, be still, be slothful. See: TWOT—2198; BDB—951c, 952a. See 7495.

7504. רָפֶה {4x} **râpheh**, *raw-feh'*; from 7503; *slack* (in body or mind):—weak {4x}. See: TWOT—2198a; BDB—952a.

רָפָה **râphâh, Râphâh.** See 7497, 7498.

רִפָה **riphâh.** See 7383.

7505. רָפוּא {1x} **Râphûwʼ**, *raw-foo'*; pass. part. of 7495; *cured; Raphu,* an Isr.:—Raphu {1x}. See: BDB—951b.

7506. רֶפַח {1x} **Rephach**, *reh'-fakh;* from an unused root appar. mean. to *sustain; support; Rephach,* an Isr.:—Rephah {1x}. See: BDB—952c.

7507. רְפִידָה {1x} **rᵉphîydâh**, *ref-ee-daw'*; from 7502; a *railing* (as *spread* along):—bottom {1x}. See: TWOT—2197a;BDB—951c.

7508. רְפִידִים {5x} **Rᵉphîydîym**, *ref-ee-deem'*; plur. of the masc. of the same as 7507; *ballusters; Rephidim,* a place in the Desert:—Rephidim {5x}. See: BDB—951c.

7509. רְפָיָה {5x} **Rᵉphâyâh**, *ref-aw-yaw'*; from 7495 and 3050; *Jah has cured; Rephajah,* the name of five Isr.:—Rephaiah {5x}. See: BDB—951b, 952c.

7510. רִפְיוֹן {1x} **riphyôwn**, *rif-yone'*; from 7503; *slackness:*—feebleness {1x}. See: TWOT—2198b; BDB—952a, 952c.

7511. רָפַס {2x} **râphaç**, *raw-fas'*; a prim. root; to *trample,* i.e. *prostrate:*—humble thyself {1x}, submit thyself {1x}. See: TWOT—2199; BDB—952c, 952d, 1113b.

7512. רְפַס {2x} **rᵉphaç** (Aram.), *ref-as'*; corresp. to 7511:—stamp {2x}. See: TWOT—3001; BDB—1113b.

7513. רַפְסֹדָה {1x} **raphçôdâh**, *raf-so-daw'*; from 7511; a *raft* (as *flat* on the water):—flote {1x}. See: TWOT—2200; BDB—952c.

7514. רָפַק {1x} **râphaq**, *raw-fak'*; a prim. root; to *recline:*—lean {1x}. See: TWOT—2202; BDB—952d.

7515. רָפַשׂ {3x} **râphas**, *raw-fas'*; a prim. root; to *trample,* i.e. *roil* water:—foul {2x}, trouble {1x}. See: TWOT—2199; BDB—952c, 952d.

7516. רֶפֶשׁ {1x} **rephesh**, *reh'-fesh;* from 7515; *mud* (as *roiled*):—mire {1x}. See: TWOT—2203a; BDB—952d.

7517. רֶפֶת {1x} **repheth**, *reh'-feth;* prob. from 7503; a *stall* for cattle (from their *resting* there):—stall {1x}. See: TWOT—2204; BDB—952d.

7518. רַץ {1x} **rats**, *rats;* contr. from 7533; a *fragment:*—piece {1x}. See: TWOT—2212a; BDB—952d, 954d.

7519. רָצָא {1x} **râtsâʼ**, *raw-tsaw'*; a prim. root; to *run;* also to *delight* in:—run {1x}. See: TWOT—2205; BDB—952d.

7520. רָצַד {1x} **râtsad**, *raw-tsad'*; a prim. root; prob. to *look askant,* i.e. (fig.) *be jealous:*—leap {1x}. See: TWOT—2206; BDB—952d.

7521. רָצָה {57x} **râtsâh**, *raw-tsaw'*; a prim. root; to *be pleased with;* spec. to *satisfy* a debt:—accept {22x}, please {6x}, pleasure {6x}, delight {5x}, enjoy {4x}, favourable {3x}, acceptable {1x}, accomplish {1x}, affection {1x}, approve {1x}, misc. {7x} = consent with, like, observe, pardon, reconcile self.

Ratsah, the verb, means to be pleased with or favorable to (Gen 33:10), be delighted with, be pleased to make friends with; be graciously received; make oneself favored. **(1)** It is evident that by the Divine acceptance is to be understood the pleasure with which God welcomes into personal contact with Himself those who approach Him in His own appointed way, and in a spirit cognate to His own. **(2)** An evildoer, as such, is not acceptable to God even though he offers sacrifices. He must be sheltered by atonement, and must have the germ at least of a Divine life working in him if he would be regarded by God with pleasure. **(3)** When God is pleased with someone, it is translated "to be delighted," which seems to reflect a sense of greater pleasure (Is 42:1). **(4)** When one must merit *ratsah,* it is translated with "to please" or "to accept" (Mic 6:7; Amos 5:22). **(4)** *Ratsah* can be used in the sense of "to pay for" or "to satisfy a debt," especially as it relates to land lying fallow in the sabbath years (Lev 26:34). Syn.: 977, 2656, 5375, 7613. See: TWOT—2207; BDB—952d, 953a.

7522. רָצוֹן {56x} **râtsôwn**, *raw-tsone'*; or

רָצֹן **râtsôn**, *raw-tsone'*; from 7521; *delight* (espec. as shown):—favour {15x}, will {14x}, acceptable {8x}, delight {5x}, pleasure {5x}, accepted {4x}, desire {3x}, acceptance {1x}, selfwill {1x}.

Ratson means "favor; goodwill; acceptance; will; desire; pleasure." **(1)** *Ratson* represents a concrete reaction of the superior to an inferior. **(1a)** When used of God, *ratson* may represent that which is shown in His blessings: "And for the precious things of the earth and fullness thereof, and for the good will of him that dwelt in the bush" (Deut 33:16). **(1b)** Thus Isaiah speaks of the day, year, or time of divine "favor"—in other words, the day of the Lord when all the blessings of the covenant shall be heaped upon God's people (Is 49:8; 58:5; 61:2). **(2)** In wisdom literature, this word is used in the sense of "what men can bestow": **(2a)** "He that diligently seeketh good procureth favor: but he that seeketh mischief, it shall come unto him" (Prov 11:27). **(2b)** In Prov 14:35, *ratson* refers to what a king can or will do for someone he likes. **(3)** This word represents the position one enjoys before a superior who is favorably disposed toward him. **(3a)** This nuance is used only of God and frequently in a cultic [religious worship] context: ". . . And it [the plate engraved with "holy to the Lord"] shall be always upon his [the high priest's] forehead, that they may be accepted before the Lord" (Ex 28:38). **(3b)** Being "accepted" means that God subjectively feels well disposed toward the petitioner.

(4) *Ratson* also signifies a voluntary or arbitrary decision. **(4a)** Ezra told the people of Israel to do the "will" of God, to repent and observe the law of Moses (Ezra 10:11). **(4b)** This law was dictated by God's own nature; His nature led Him to be concerned for the physical well-being of His people. **(4c)** Ultimately, His laws were highly personal; they were simply what God wanted His people to be and do. Thus the psalmist confessed his delight in doing God's "will," or His law (Ps 40:8). **(5)** When a man does according to his own "will," he does "what he desires": "I saw the ram pushing westward, and northward, and southward; so that no beasts might stand before him, neither was there any that could deliver out of his hand; but he did according to his will and became great" (Dan 8:4). **(6)** In Ps 145:16, the word *ratson* means "one's desire" or "what one wants" (cf. Est 1:8). **(7)** This emphasis is found in Gen 49:6 (the first occurrence): ". . . And in their self-will they [brought disaster upon themselves]." See: TWOT—2207a; BDB—953c.

7523. רָצַח {47x} **râtsach**, *raw-tsakh'*; a prim. root; prop. to *dash* in pieces, i.e. *kill* (a human being), espec. to *murder:*—slayer {16x}, murderer {14x}, kill {5x}, murder {3x}, slain {3x}, manslayer {2x}, killing {1x}, slayer + 310 {1x}, slayeth {1x}, death {1x}.

Ratsach means "to kill, murder, slay." **(1)** This verb occurs 47 times in the Old Testament, and its concentration is in the Pentateuch. **(2)** *Ratsach* occurs primarily in the legal material of the Old Testament. **(2a)** This is not a surprise, as God's law included regulations on life and provisions for dealing with the murderer. **(2b)** The Decalogue gives the general principle in a simple statement, which contains the first occurrence of the verb: "Thou shalt not kill [murder]" (Ex 20:13). **(3)** Another provision pertains to the penalty: "Whoso killeth any person, the murderer shall be put to death by the mouth of witnesses . . ." (Num 35:30). However, before a person is put to death, he is assured of a trial.

(4) The Old Testament recognizes the distinction between premeditated murder and unintentional killing. **(4a)** In order to assure the rights of the manslayer, who unintentionally killed someone, the law provided for three cities of refuge (Num 35; Deut 19; Josh 20; 21) on either side of the Jordan, to which a manslayer might flee and seek asylum: ". . . that the slayer may flee thither, which killeth any person at unawares" (Num 35:11). **(4b)** The provision gave the manslayer access to the court system, for he might be "killed" by the blood avenger if he stayed within his own community (Num 35:21). **(4c)** He is to be tried (Num 35:12), and **(4d)** if he is found to be guilty of unintentional manslaughter, he is required to stay in the city of refuge until the death of the high priest (Num 35:28). **(4e)** The severity of the act of murder is stressed in the requirement of exile even in the case of unintentional murder. **(4f)** The man guilty of manslaughter is to be turned over to the avenger of blood, who keeps the right of killing the manslayer if the manslayer goes outside the territory of the city of refuge before the death of the high priest. **(4g)** On the other hand, if the manslayer is chargeable with premeditated murder (examples of which are given in Num 35:16–21), the blood avenger may execute the murderer without a trial. **(4h)** In this way the Old Testament underscores the principles of the sanctity of life and of retribution; only in the cities of refuge is the principle of retribution suspended.

(5) The prophets use *ratsach* to describe the effect of injustice and lawlessness in Israel: ". . . because there is no truth, nor mercy, nor knowledge of God in the land. By swearing, and lying, and killing, and stealing, and committing adultery . . ." (Hos 4:1–2; cf. Is 1:21; Jer 7:9). **(6)** The psalmist, too, metaphorically expresses the deprivation of the rights of helpless murder victims: "They slay the widow and the stranger, and murder the fatherless" (Ps 94:6). **(7)** The KJV gives these senses: "kill; murder; be put to death; be slain." Syn.: 2026, 7819. See: TWOT—2208; BDB—953d.

7524. רֶצַח {2x} **retsach**, *reh-tsakh;* from 7523; a *crushing;* spec. a *murder*-cry:—slaughter {1x}, sword {1x}. See: TWOT—2208a; BDB—954a.

7525. רִצְיָא {1x} **Ritsyâʾ**, *rits-yaw';* from 7521; *delight; Ritsjah,* an Isr.:—Rezia {1x}. See: BDB—954a.

7526. רְצִין {11x} **R^{e}tsîyn**, *rets-een';* prob. for 7522; *Retsin,* the name of a Syrian and of an Isr.:—Rezin {11x}. See: BDB—954a.

7527. רָצַע {1x} **râtsaʿ**, *raw-tsah';* a prim. root; to *pierce:*—bore {1x}. See: TWOT—2209; BDB—954a.

7528. רָצַף {1x} **râtsaph**, *raw-tsaf';* a denom. from 7529; to *tessellate,* i.e. embroider (as if with bright stones):—pave {1x}. See: TWOT—2210; BDB—954b.

7529. רֶצֶף {1x} **retseph**, *reh'-tsef;* for 7565; a red-hot *stone* (for baking):—coals {1x}. See: TWOT—2232a; BDB—954b, 954c.

7530. רֶצֶף {2x} **Retseph**, *reh'-tsef;* the same as 7529; *Retseph,* a place in Ass.:—Rezeph {2x}. See: BDB—954b.

7531. רִצְפָּה {8x} **ritspâh**, *rits-paw';* fem. of 7529; a hot *stone;* also a tessellated *pavement:*—live coal {1x}, pavement {1x}. See: TWOT—2210a, 2211a; BDB—954b, 954c.

7532. רִצְפָּה {4x} **Ritspâh**, *rits-paw';* the same as 7531; *Ritspah,* an Israelitess:—Rizpah {4x}. See: BDB—954c.

7533. רָצַץ **râtsats**, *raw-tsats';* a prim. root; to *crack* in pieces, lit. or fig.:—oppressed {6x}, broken {4x}, break {3x}, bruised {2x}, crush {2x}, discouraged {1x}, struggle together {1x}. See: TWOT—2212; BDB—930d, 954c, 1113b.

7534. רַק {3x} **raq**, *rak;* from 7556 in its orig. sense; *emaciated* (as if *flattened* out):—lean {1x}, thin {1x}, leanfleshed + 1320 {1x}. See: TWOT—2218a; BDB—954d, 956b.

7535. רַק **raq**, *rak;* the same as 7534 as a noun; prop. *leanness,* i.e. (fig.) *limitation;* only adv. *merely,* or conjunc. *although:*—but {1x}, even {1x}, except {1x}, howbeit {1x}, howsoever {1x}, nevertheless {1x}, nothing but {1x}, notwithstanding {1x}, only {1x}, save {1x}, so {1x}, so that {1x}, surely {1x}, yet {1x}, yet so {1x}, in any wise {1x}. See: TWOT—2218a; BDB—954d, 956b.

7536. רֹק {3x} **rôq**, *roke;* from 7556; *spittle:*—spit {1x}, spitting {1x}, spittle {1x}. See: TWOT—2219a; BDB—954d, 956d.

7537. רָקַב {2x} **râqab**, *raw-kab';* a prim. root; to *decay* (as by worm-eating):—rot {2x}. See: TWOT—2213; BDB—955a.

7538. רָקָב {5x} **râqâb**, *raw-kawb';* from 7537; *decay* (by *caries*):—rottenness {4x}, rotten thing {1x}. See: TWOT—2213a; BDB—955a.

7539. רִקָּבוֹן {1x} **riqqâbôwn**, *rik-kaw-bone';* from 7538; *decay* (by *caries*):—rotten {1x}. See: TWOT—2213b; BDB—955a.

7540. רָקַד {9x} **râqad**, *raw-kad';* a prim. root; prop. to *stamp,* i.e. to *spring* about (wildly or for joy):—dance {4x}, skip {3x}, leap {1x}, jump {1x}. See: TWOT—2214; BDB—955a.

7541. רַקָּה {5x} **raqqâh**, *rak-kaw';* fem. of 7534; prop. *thinness,* i.e. the *side* of the head:—temple {5x}. See: TWOT—2218c; BDB—955b, 956d.

7542. רַקּוֹן {1x} **Raqqôwn**, *rak-kone';* from 7534; *thinness; Rakkon,* a place in Pal.:—Rakkon {1x}. See: BDB—955b, 956d.

7543. רָקַח {8x} **râqach**, *raw-kakh';* a prim. root; to *perfume:*—apothecary {4x}, compound {1x}, make ointment {1x}, prepare {1x}, spice {1x}. See: TWOT—2215; BDB—955b.

7544. רֶקַח {1x} **reqach**, *reh'-kakh;* from 7543; prop. *perfumery,* i.e. (by impl.) *spicery* (for flavor):—spiced {1x}. See: TWOT—2215a; BDB—955b.

7545. רֹקַח {2x} **rôqach**, *ro'-kakh;* from 7542; an *aromatic:*—confection {1x}, ointment {1x}. See: TWOT—2215b; BDB—955b.

7546. רַקָּח {1x} **raqqâch**, *rak-kawkh';* from 7543; a male *perfumer:*—apothecaries {1x}. See: TWOT—2215c; BDB—955c.

7547. רַקֻּחַ {1x} **raqqûach**, *rak-koo'-akh;* from 7543; a *scented* substance:—perfume {1x}. See: TWOT—2215e; BDB—955c.

7548. רַקָּחָה {1x} **raqqâchâh**, *rak-kaw-khaw';* fem. of 7547; a female *perfumer:*—confectionaries {1x}. See: TWOT—2215d; BDB—955c.

7549. רָקִיעַ {17x} **râqîyaʿ**, *raw-kee'-ah;* from 7554; prop. an *expanse,* i.e. the *firmament* or (appar.) visible arch of the sky:—firmament {17x}.

(1) *Raqiya* means that which is fixed and steadfast, rather than that which is solid. **(1a)** The application to the heavenly bodies is simple and beautiful: **(1b)** they are not fickle and uncertain in their movements, but are regulated by a law that they cannot pass over. **(2)** It comes from raqa (7554) which means spread out. The firmament, then is that which is spread or stretched out—hence an expanse. Thus it is extended and fixed, or fixed space. **(3)** The interplanetary spaces are measured out by God, and though the stars are ever moving, they generally preserve fixed relative positions; their movements are not erratic, not in straight lines, but in orbits, and thus, though ever changing, they are always the same. See: TWOT—2217a; BDB—956a.

7550. רָקִיק {8x} **râqîyq**, *raw-keek';* from 7556 in its orig. sense; a thin *cake:*—cake {1x}, wafer {7x}. See: TWOT—2218b; BDB—956d.

7551. רָקַם {9x} **râqam**, *raw-kam';* a prim. root; to *variegate* color, i.e. *embroider;* by impl. to *fabricate:*—needlework + 4639 {4x}, needlework {2x}, embroiderer {2x}, curiously wrought {1x}.

7552. רֶקֶם {6x} **Reqem**, *reh'-kem;* from 7551; *versi-color; Rekem,* the name of a place in Pal., also of a Midianite and an Isr.:—Rekem {6x}. See: BDB—955d.

7553. רִקְמָה {12x} **riqmâh**, *rik-maw';* from 7551; *variegation* of color; spec. *embroidery:*—broidered work {5x}, needlework {3x}, divers colours {2x}, broidered {2x}. See: TWOT—2216a; BDB—955d.

7554. רָקַע {11x} **râqaʿ**, *raw-kah';* a prim. root; to *pound* the earth (as a sign of passion); by anal. to *expand* (by hammering); by impl. to *overlay* (with thin sheets of metal):—spread . . . {6x}, stamp {2x}, stretch {1x}, beat {1x}, made broad {1x}. See: TWOT—2217; BDB—955d. See 7549 for discussion of the firmament.

7555. רִקֻּעַ {1x} **riqqûaʿ**, *rik-koo'-ah;* from 7554; *beaten* out, i.e. a (metallic) *plate:*—broad {1x}. See: TWOT—2217b; BDB—956b.

7556. רָקַק {1x} **râqaq**, *raw-kak';* a prim. root; to *spit:*—spit {1x}. See: TWOT—2219; BDB—956d.

7557. רַקַּת {1x} **Raqqath**, *rak-kath';* from 7556 in its orig. sense of *diffusing;* a *beach* (as *expanded* shingle); *Rakkath,* a place in Pal.:—Rakkath {1x}. See: BDB—957a.

7558. רִשְׁיוֹן {1x} **rîshyôwn**, *rish-yone';* from an unused root mean. to *have leave;* a *permit:*—grant {1x}. See: TWOT—2220a; BDB—957a.

7559. רָשַׁם {1x} **râsham**, *raw-sham';* a prim. root; to *record:*—note {1x}. See: TWOT—2221; BDB—957a, 1113b.

7560. רְשַׁם {7x} **r^{e}sham** (Aram.), *resh-am';* corresp. to 7559:—sign {5x}, write {2x}. See: TWOT—3002; BDB—1113b.

7561. רָשַׁע {34x} **râshaʿ**, *raw-shah';* a prim. root; to *be* (caus. *do* or *declare*) *wrong;* by impl. to *disturb, violate:*—condemn {15x}, wickedly {10x}, wicked {4x}, departed {2x}, trouble {1x}, vexed {1x}, wickedness {1x}.

(1) This verb appears in 2 Chr 6:37: "Yet if they bethink themselves in the land whither they are carried captive, and turn and pray unto thee in the land of their captivity, saying, We have sinned, we have done amiss, and have dealt wickedly." **(2)** This word means to deal with or account as wicked. Syn.: 8199. See: TWOT—2222; BDB—957d.

7562. רֶשַׁע {30x} **reshaʿ**, *reh'-shah;* from 7561; a *wrong* (espec. moral):—iniquity {1x}, wicked {4x}, wickedness {25x}.

Resha', found 30 times, usually means "wickedness": "Remember thy servants, Abraham, Isaac, and Jacob; look not unto the stubborness of this people, nor to their wickedness (*resha'*), nor to their sin" (Deut 9:27). See: TWOT—2222a; BDB—957c.

7563. רָשָׁע {263x} **râshâʿ**, *raw-shaw';* from 7561; morally *wrong;* concr. an (actively) *bad* person:—wicked {249x}, ungodly {8x}, wicked man {3x}, misc. {3x} = + condemned, guilty, that did wrong.

I. *Rasha'*, as a noun, means "wicked; ungodly; guilty." **(1)** The narrow meaning of *rasha'* lies in the concept of "wrongdoing" or "being in the wrong." **(1a)** It is a legal term. **(1b)** *Rasha'* means wicked; guilty enough to deserve punishment (Deut 25:2), and maybe even death (2 Sa 4:11; cf. Eze 3:18–19). **(1c)** *Rasha'* generally connotes a turbulence and restlessness (cf. Is 57:21) or something disjointed or ill-regulated; thus suggesting that it refers to the tossing and confusion in which the wicked live, and to the perpetual agitation they came to others. **(2)** In some instances, *rasha'* carries the sense of being "guilty of crime": **(2a)** "Thou shalt not raise a false report: put not thine hand with the wicked to be an unrighteous witness" (Ex 23:1). **(2b)** "Take away the wicked from before the king, and his throne shall be established in righteousness" (Prov 25:5). **(2c)** "An ungodly witness scorneth judgment: and the mouth of the wicked [plural form] devoureth iniquity"

(Prov 19:28; cf. Prov 20:26). **(3)** Justifying the "wicked" is classed as a heinous crime: "He that justifieth the wicked, and he that condemneth the just, even they both are abomination to the Lord" (Prov 17:15; cf. Ex 23:7).

(4) The *rasha'* is guilty of hostility to God and His people: **(4a)** "Arise, O Lord, disappoint him, cast him down: deliver my soul from the wicked, which is thy sword" (Ps 17:13); "**(4b)** Oh let the wickedness of the wicked [plural form] come to an end; but establish the just . . ." (Ps 7:9). **(5)** The word is applied to the people **(5a)** of Babylon in Is 13:11 and **(5b)** to the Chaldeans in Hab 1:13. **(6)** The *rasha'* is guilty of hostility to God and His people (Ex 9:27; Ps 17:13). **(7)** Its narrow meaning—a legal term asserting one has sinned against the law—lies in the concept of wrongdoing or being in the wrong (Prov 28:4). **(8)** When in Israel's history justice did not prevail, the guilty were acquitted (Prov 29:2; cf. 2 Chr 6:23). **(9)** Its more general meaning denotes the category of people who have done wrong, are still living in sin, and are intent on continuing with wrongdoing (Ps 10:4). **(9a)** He challenges God (Ps 10:13), **(9b)** loves violence (Ps 11:5), **(9c)** oppresses the righteous (Ps 17:9), **(9d)** does not repay his debts (Ps 37:21), and **(9e)** lays a snare to trap the righteous (Ps 119:110). **(9f)** Ps 37 gives a vivid description of the acts of the wicked and also of God's judgment upon them.

(10) Facing the terrible force of the wicked, the righteous prayed for God's deliverance and for His judgment upon them (Ps 1:6). **(10a)** The expectation of the righteous includes God's judgment on the wicked in this life that they might **(10a1)** be ashamed (Ps 31:17), **(10a2)** be overcome by sorrows (Ps 32:10), **(10a3)** fall by their devices (Ps 141:10), **(10a4)** die a premature death (Prov 10:27), and **(10a5)** that their remembrance will be no more (Prov 10:7). **(10b)** It is expected that at the time of their death there will be great shouting (Prov 11:10). **(11)** In the typical example of Deut 25:2, this word refers to a person "guilty of a crime": **(11a)** "And it shall be, if the wicked man be worthy to be beaten, that the judge shall cause him . . . to be beaten. . . ." **(11b)** A similar reference appears in Jer 5:26: "For among my people are found wicked [plural form] men: they lay wait, as he that setteth snares; they set a trap, they catch men." **(12)** *Rasha'* is used specifically of murderers in 2 Sa 4:11: **(12a)** "How much more, when wicked men have slain a righteous person in his own house upon his bed? . . ." **(12b)** The expression "guilty of death" (*rasha'* lamut) occurs in Num 35:31 and is applied to a murderer.

(13) Pharaoh and his people are portrayed as "wicked" people guilty of hostility to God and His people (Ex 9:27). **(14)** The person who has sinned against the law is guilty: "They that forsake the law praise the wicked: but such as keep the law contend with them" (Prov 28:4). **(15)** When in Israel's history justice did not prevail, the "guilty" were acquitted: ". . . When the wicked beareth rule, the people mourn" (Prov 29:2; cf. 2 Chr 6:23). **(16)** *Rasha'* also denotes the category of people who have done wrong, are still living in sin, and are intent on continuing with wrongdoing. This is the more general meaning of the word. **(17)** The first psalm exhorts the godly not to imitate the deeds and behavior of the ungodly, wicked people. **(18)** The "wicked" **(18a)** does not seek God (Ps 10:4); **(18)** he challenges God (Ps 10:13). **(18c)** In his way of life the "wicked" loves violence (Ps 11:5), **(18d)** oppresses the righteous (Ps 17:9), **(18e)** does not repay his debts (Ps 37:21), and **(18f)** lays a snare to trap the righteous (Ps 119:110). **(18g)** Ps. 37 gives a vivid description of the acts of the "wicked" and also of God's judgment upon them.

(19) Facing the terrible force of the "wicked," the righteous prayed for God's deliverance and for His judgment upon them. **(19a)** This theme of judgment has already been anticipated in Ps 1:6: "For the Lord knoweth the way of the righteous: but the way of the ungodly shall perish." **(19b)** The expectation of the righteous includes God's judgment on the "wicked" in this life that they might be ashamed (Ps 31:17), be overcome by sorrows (Ps 32:10), fall by their devices (Ps 141:10), die a premature death (Prov 10:27), and that their remembrance will be no more (Prov 10:7). **(19c)** It is expected that at the time of their death there will be great shouting: "When it goeth well with the righteous, the city rejoiceth: when the wicked perish, there is shouting" (Prov 11:10). **(20)** The judgment upon the "wicked" is particularly strong in Proverbs, where the author contrasts the advantages of wisdom and righteousness and the disadvantages of the "wicked" (cf. 2:22: "But the wicked shall be cut off from the earth, and the transgressors shall be rooted out of it"). **(21)** In Job another theme finds expression: why are the "wicked" not cut off? "Wherefore do the wicked live, become old, yea, are mighty in power?" (21:7). There is no clear answer to this question in the Old Testament. **(22)** Malachi predicts a new age in which the distinction of the righteous and the "wicked" will be clear and where the righteous will triumph: "Then shall ye return, and discern between the righteous and the wicked, between him that serveth God and him that seeth him not" (Mal 3:18).

II. *Rasha'*, as an adjective, means "wicked; guilty." **(1)** In some cases a person is so guilty that he deserves death: ". . . If the wicked man be worthy to be beaten, that the judge shall cause him to lie down, and to be beaten before his face . . . by a certain number" (Deut 25:2). **(2)** The characteristics of a "wicked" person qualify him as a godless, impious man: "How much more, when wicked men have slain a righteous person in his own house upon his bed? shall I not therefore now require his blood of your hand, and take you away from the earth?" (2 Sa 4:11; cf. Eze 3:18–19). Syn.: 7562, 7564. See: TWOT—2222b; BDB—957b.

7564. רִשְׁעָה {15x} **rish'âh**, *rish-aw';* fem. of 7562; *wrong* (espec. moral):—fault {1x}, wickedly {1x}, wickedness {13x}.

Rish'ah, which appears 15 times, refers to "wickedness" or "guilt": "For my righteousness the Lord hath brought me in to possess this land: but for the wickedness of these nations the Lord doth drive them out from before thee" (Deut 9:4). See: TWOT—2222c; BDB—957d, 958a.

7565. רֶשֶׁף {7x} **resheph**, *reh'-shef;* from 8313; a live *coal;* by anal. *lightning;* fig. an *arrow,* (as *flashing* through the air); spec. *fever:*—coals {2x}, burning coals {1x}, burning heat {1x}, spark {1x}, arrow {1x}, hot thunderbolt {1x}. See: TWOT—2223a; BDB—958b.

7566. רֶשֶׁף {1x} **Resheph**, *reh'-shef;* the same as 7565; *Resheph,* an Isr.:—*Resheph* {1x}. See: BDB—958b.

7567. רָשַׁשׁ {2x} **râshash**, *raw-shash';* a prim. root; to *demolish:*—impoverish {2x}. See: TWOT—2224; BDB—930d, 958b.

7568. רֶשֶׁת {20x} **resheth**, *reh'-sheth;* from 3423; a *net* (as *catching* animals):—net {20x}, network + 4639 {1x}. See: TWOT—920c; BDB—440b, 958b.

7569. רַתּוֹק {1x} **rattôwq**, *rat-toke';* from 7576; a *chain:*—chain {1x}. See: TWOT—2227b; BDB—958d.

7570. רָתַח {3x} **râthach**, *raw-thakh';* a prim. root; to *boil:*—boil {3x}. See: TWOT—2225; BDB—958b.

7571. רֶתַח {1x} **rethach**, *reh'-thakh;* from 7570; a *boiling:*—× [boil] well {1x}. See: TWOT—2225a; BDB—958c.

7572. רַתִּיקָה {2x} **rattîyqâh**, *rat-tee-kaw';* from 7576; a *chain:*—chain {2x}. See: TWOT—2227b; BDB—958d.

7573. רָתַם {1x} **râtham**, *raw-tham';* a prim. root; to *yoke* up (to the pole of a vehicle):—bind {1x}. See: TWOT—2226; BDB—958c.

7574. רֶתֶם {4x} **rethem**, *reh'-them;* or

רֹתֶם **rôthem**, *ro'-them;* from 7573; the Spanish *broom* (from its pole-like stems):—juniper {2x}, juniper tree {2x}. See: TWOT—2226a; BDB—958c.

7575. רִתְמָה {2x} **Rithmâh**, *rith-maw';* fem. of 7574; *Rithmah,* a place in the Desert:—*Rithmah* {2x}. See: BDB—958c.

7576. רָתַק {2x} **râthaq**, *raw-thak';* a prim. root; to *fasten:*—loose {1x}, bound {1x}. See: TWOT—2227; BDB—958d.

7577. רְתֻקָה {1x} **r'thûqâh**, *reth-oo-kaw';* fem. pass. part. of 7576; something *fastened,* i.e. a *chain:*—chain {1x}. See: TWOT—2227a; BDB—958d.

7578. רְתֵת {1x} **r'thêth**, *reth-ayth';* for 7374; *terror:*—trembling {1x}. See: TWOT—2228a; BDB—958d.

ש

7579. שָׁאַב {19x} **shâ'ab**, *sahw-ab';* a prim. root; to *bale* up water:—draw {15x}, drawer {4x}. See: TWOT—2299.1; BDB—980b.

7580. שָׁאַג {21x} **shâ'ag**, *shaw-ag';* a prim. root; to *rumble* or *moan:*—roar {20x}, mightily {1x}. See: TWOT—2300; BDB—980c.

7581. שְׁאָגָה {7x} **sh'âgâh**, *sheh-aw-gaw';* from 7580; a *rumbling* or *moan:*—roaring {7x}. See: TWOT—2300a; BDB—980d.

7582. שָׁאָה {6x} **shâ'âh**, *shaw-aw';* a prim. root; to *rush;* by impl. to *desolate:*—lay waste {2x}, rushing {2x}, waste {1x}, desolate {1x}. See: TWOT—2301; BDB—980d.

7583. שָׁאָה {1x} **shâ'âh**, *shaw-aw';* a prim. root [rather ident. with 7582 through the idea of *whirling* to giddiness]; to *stun,* i.e. (intr.) *be astonished:*—wondering + 8693 {1x}. See: TWOT—2302; BDB—981b.

7584. שַׁאֲוָה {1x} **sha'ăvâh**, *shah-av-aw';* from 7582; a *tempest* (as *rushing*):—desolation {1x}. See: TWOT—2301a; BDB—981a.

7585. שְׁאוֹל {65x} **sh'ôwl**, *sheh-ole';* or

שְׁאֹל **sh'ôl**, *sheh-ole';* from 7592; *hades* or the world of the dead (as if a subterranean *retreat*), incl. its accessories and inmates:—grave {31x}, hell {31x}, pit {3x}.

Sheol is the abode of the dead, a place of degradation, the locality or condition of those who have died or have been destroyed. It is implied that although, so far as the world is concerned, they have perished, yet they are still in a state of existence and are within God's cognizance. **(1)** *She'ol* is the place of the dead. It refers to the netherworld or the underground cavern to which all buried dead go. **(2)** It was not understood to be a place of punishment, but simply the ultimate resting place of all mankind (Gen 37:35). **(3)** Thus, it was thought to be the land of no return (Job 16:22; 17:14–16). **(4)** It was a place to be dreaded, not only because it meant the end of physical life on earth, but also because there was no praise of God there (Ps 6:5). **(5)** Deliverance from going there was a blessing (Ps 30:3). **(6)** Everything about *she'ol* was negative. **(6a)** First, there is the tomb or sepulcher; the local habitation of the physical frame called *qeber* (6913). **(6b)** Secondly, there is the corruption whereby the body itself is dissolved, which is represented by the word *shachath* (7843); and **(6b)** thirdly, there is *sheol,* the locality or condition of the departed.

(7) *Sheol* is the netherworld. **(8)** It is not used in one single passage for punishment after the resurrection. **(9)** It is contrasted, in regards to locality, with heaven, the one being regarded as down and the other up. **(10)** It is spoken of as an abode for those who have departed from the way of life and have chosen the path of evil. **(11)** It involves deprivation of the only kind of existence about which we have any definite knowledge, but some passages where it occurs imply a certain companionship. **(12)** Though man knows so little about it, *sheol* is naked and open before God. He can find men there; He can hide them there; He can redeem them thence. Syn.: 6, 2011 + 1510. See: TWOT—2303c; BDB—982c, 982d.

7586. שָׁאוּל {406x} **Shâ'ûwl,** *shaw-ool';* pass. part. of 7592; *asked; Shaül,* the name of an Edomite and two Isr.:—Saul {399x}, Shaul {7x}. See: BDB—982b.

7587. שָׁאוּלִי {1x} **Shâ'ûwlîy,** *shaw-oo-lee';* patron. from 7856, a *Shaülite* or desc. of Shaul:—Shaulites {1x}. See: BDB—982c.

7588. שָׁאוֹן {17x} **shâ'ôwn,** *shaw-one';* from 7582; *uproar* (as of *rushing*); by impl. *destruction:*—noise {8x}, tumult {3x}, tumultuous {2x}, rushing {2x}, horrible {1x}, pomp {1x}. See: TWOT—2301c; BDB—981a.

7589. שְׁאָט {3x} **sh**e**'âṭ,** *sheh-awt';* from an unused root mean. to *push* aside; *contempt:*—despiteful {2x}, despite {1x}. See: TWOT—2345a; BDB—981b, 1002b.

7590. שָׁאט {3x} **shâ't,** *shawt;* for act. part of 7750 [comp. 7589]; one *contemning:*—despise {3x}. See: TWOT—2345; BDB—1002b.

7591. שְׁאִיָּה {1x} **sh**e**'îyâh,** *sheh-ee-yaw';* from 7582; *desolation:*—destruction {1x}. See: TWOT—2301b; BDB—981a, 981b.

7592. שָׁאַל {173x} **shâ'al,** *shaw-al';* or

שָׁאֵל **shâ'êl,** *shaw-ale';* a prim. root; to *inquire;* by impl. to *request;* by extens. to *demand:*—ask {94x}, enquire {22x}, desire {9x}, require {7x}, borrow {6x}, salute {4x}, demand {4x}, lent {4x}, request {3x}, earnestly {2x}, beg {2x}, misc. {16x} = lay to charge, consult, + greet, obtain leave, pray, × straitly, × surely, wish.

Sha'el means to ask, inquire, consult **(1)** It is commonly used for simple requests (Judg 5:25). **(2)** *Sha'el* is sometimes used in the sense of praying for something (Ps 122:6). **(3)** "To ask another of his welfare" carries the sense of a greeting (Ex 18:7; Judg 18:15; 1 Sa 10:4). **(4)** Frequently, it is used to indicate someone's asking for God's direction or counsel (Josh 9:14; Is 30:2). **(5)** In Ps 109:10 it is used to indicate begging. Syn.: 577, 6279, 6419, 6739. See: TWOT—2303; BDB—981b, 1114a.

7593. שְׁאֵל {6x} **sh**e**'êl** (Aram.), *sheh-ale';* corresp. to 7592:—ask {3x}, require {2x}, demand {1x}. See: TWOT—3012; BDB—1114a.

7594. שְׁאָל {1x} **Sh**e**'âl,** *sheh-awl';* from 7592; *request; Sheäl,* an Isr.:—Sheal {1x}. See: BDB—982b.

שְׁאֹל **sh**e**'ôl.** See 7585.

7595. שְׁאֵלָא {1x} **sh**e**'êlâ'** (Aram.), *sheh-ay-law';* from 7593; prop. a *question* (at law), i.e. judicial *decision* or mandate:—demand {1x}. See: TWOT—3012a; BDB—1114a.

7596. שְׁאֵלָה {14x} **sh**e**'êlâh,** *sheh-ay-law';* or

שֵׁלָה **shêlâh** (1 Sa 1:17), *shay-law';* from 7592; a *petition;* by impl. a *loan:*—petition {10x}, request {3x}, loan {1x}. See: TWOT—2303a; BDB—982c, 1017c, 1115c.

7597. שְׁאַלְתִּיאֵל {9x} **Sh**e**'altîy'êl,** *sheh-al-tee-ale';* or

שַׁלְתִּיאֵל **Shaltîy'êl,** *shal-tee-ale';* from 7592 and 410; *I have asked God; Sheältiël,* an Isr.:—Shealtiel {8x}, Salathiel {1x}. See: BDB—982c, 1027a.

7598. שְׁאַלְתִּיאֵל {1x} **Sh**e**'altîy'êl** (Aram.), *sheh-al-tee-ale';* corresp. to 7597:—Shealtiel {1x}. See: BDB—982d.

7599. שָׁאַן {5x} **shâ'an,** *shaw-an';* a prim. root; to *loll,* i.e. *be peaceful:*—at ease {2x}, quiet {2x}, rest {1x}. See: TWOT—2304; BDB—983b. See also 1052.

7600. שַׁאֲנָן {10x} **sha'ănân,** *shah-an-awn';* from 7599; *secure;* in a bad sense, *haughty:*—ease {6x}, quiet {2x}, tumult {2x}. See: TWOT—2304a; BDB—983b. comp. 7946.

7601. שָׁאַס {1x} **shâ'aç,** *shaw-as';* a prim. root; to *plunder:*—spoil {1x}. See: TWOT—2426; BDB—983c.

7602. שָׁאַף {14x} **shâ'aph,** *shaw-af';* a prim. root; to *inhale* eagerly; fig. to *covet;* by impl. to *be angry;* also to *hasten:*—swallow up {6x}, snuff up {2x}, pant {2x}, earnestly desire {1x}, desire {1x}, devour {1x}, hast {1x}. See: TWOT—2305, 2306; BDB—983c.

7603. שְׂאֹר {5x} **s**e**'ôr,** *seh-ore';* from 7604; *barm* or yeast-cake (as *swelling* by fermentation):—leaven {5x}. See: TWOT—2229a; BDB—959a.

7604. שָׁאַר {133x} **shâ'ar,** *shaw-ar';* a prim. root; prop. to *swell* up, i.e. *be* (caus. *make*) *redundant:*—leave {75x}, remain {46x}, remnant {4x}, let {3x}, rest {2x}, misc. {3x} = (be) left, reserve.

(1) Noah and his family were a remnant delivered through the Flood (Gen 7:23). **(2)** Seven thousand remained true to God during the days of Elijah (1 Kin 19:18). **(3)** Remants were considered holy (Is 4:3). **(4)** The doctrine of the remnant was revealed early in Israel's history by Moses (Deut 4:27; 28:62). **(5)** Conditions for the remnant were not always ideal (Neh 1:2–3). See: TWOT—2307, 2308; BDB—983d.

7605. שְׁאָר {26x} **sh**e**'âr,** *sheh-awr';* from 7604; a *remainder:*—remnant {11x}, rest {10x}, residue {4x}, other {1x}.

(1) Isaiah characterizes the remnant of Israel (Is 10:20). **(2)** He also describes the twofold theme which emerges from most prophetic passages concerning the remnant: **(2a)** A remnant will survive when the people are subjected to punishment, and **(2b)** the fact that a remnant does survive and does remain contains a note of hope for the future (Is 10:20–21; 11:11). See: TWOT—2307a; BDB—984b, 1114b.

7606. שְׁאָר {12x} **sh**e**'âr** (Aram.), *sheh-awr';* corresp. to 7605:—rest {9x}, residue {2x}, rest {1x}. See: TWOT—3013; BDB—1114b.

7607. שְׁאֵר {16x} **sh**e**'êr,** *sheh-ayr';* from 7604; *flesh* (as *swelling* out), as living or for food; gen. *food* of any kind; fig. *kindred* by blood:—flesh {7x}, near kinswoman {2x}, food {1x}, near {1x}, nigh {1x}, near kin {1x}, kin {1x}, body {1x}, kinsman {1x}. See: TWOT—2308a; BDB—984d, 985a.

7608. שַׁאֲרָה {1x} **sha'ărâh,** *shah-ar-aw';* fem. of 7607; female *kindred* by blood:—near kinswomen {1x}. See: TWOT—2308a; BDB—985a.

7609. שֶׁאֱרָה {1x} **She'ĕrâh,** *sheh-er-aw';* the same as 7608; *Sheërah,* an Israelitess:—Sherah {1x}. See: BDB—985a.

7610. שְׁאָר יָשׁוּב {1x} **Sh**e**'âr Yâshûwb,** *sheh-awr' yaw-shoob';* from 7605 and 7725; a *remnant will return; Sheär-Jashub,* the symbol. name of one of Isaiah's sons:—Shear-jashub {1x}. See: BDB—984c, 1000b.

7611. שְׁאֵרִית **sh**e**'êrîyth,** *sheh-ay-reeth';* from 7604; a *remainder* or residual (surviving, final) portion:—remnant {44x}, residue {13x}, rest {3x}, remainder {2x}, escaped {1x}, misc. {3x} = that had escaped, be left, posterity.

(1) The idea of the remnant plays a prominent part in the divine economy of salvation throughout the Old Testament. **(1a)** The remnant concept is applied especially to the Israelites who survived such calamities as war, pestilence, and famine—**(1b)** people whom the Lord in His mercy spared to be His chosen people (2 Kin 19:31; cf. Ezra 9:14). **(2)** The Israelites repeatedly suffered major catastrophes **(2a)** that brought them to the brink of extinction. **(2b)** So they often prayed as in Jer 42:2. **(3)** Isaiah prayed for the remnant which would be left after the Assyrian invasions (Is 37:32). **(4)** Micah announced the regathering of the Jewish people after the Exile in Babylon (2:12; 4:7; 5:7–8). **(5)** Jeremiah discussed the plight of the Jews who fled to Egypt after Jerusalem's capture by Nebuchadnezzar (Jer 40:11, 15). **(6)** Zephaniah identified the remnant with the poor and humble (2:3, 7; 3:12–13). **(7)** Zechariah announced that a remnant would be present at the time of the coming of the Messiah's kingdom (12:10–13:1; 13:8–9). See: TWOT—2307b; BDB—984c, 1056c.

7612. שֵׁאת {1x} **shê'th,** *shayth;* from 7582: *devastation:*—desolation {1x}. See: TWOT—2301d; BDB—981b, 985a, 1059a.

7613. שְׂאֵת {14x} **s**e**'êth,** *seh-ayth';* from 5375; an *elevation* or leprous scab; fig. *elation* or cheerfulness; *exaltation* in rank or character:—rising {7x}, dignity {2x}, excellency {2x}, accepted {1x}, highness {1x}, raise up {1x}. See: TWOT—1421j; BDB—673b, 979c.

7614. שְׁבָא {23x} **Sh**e**bâ',** *sheb-aw';* of for. or.; *Sheba,* the name of three early progenitors of tribes and of an Ethiopian district:—*Sheba* {23x}. See: BDB—985a.

7615. שְׁבָאִי {1x} **Sh**e**bâ'îy,** *sheb-aw-ee';* patron. from 7614; a *Shebaïte* or desc. of Sheba:—Sabeans {1x}. See: BDB—985b.

7616. שָׁבָב {1x} **shâbâb,** *shaw-bawb';* from an unused root mean. to *break* up; a *fragment,* i.e. *ruin:*—broken in pieces {1x}. See: TWOT—2309a; BDB—985b.

7617. שָׁבָה {47x} **shâbâh,** *shaw-baw';* a prim. root; to *transport* into captivity:—(carry, take away, . . .) captive {37x}, (take, drive, . . .)

away {8x}, take {2x}. See: TWOT—2311; BDB—985c.

7618. שְׁבוֹ {2x} **sh^ebûw**, *sheb-oo';* from an unused root (prob. ident. with that of 7617 through the idea of *subdivision* into flashes or streamers [comp. 7632] mean. to *flame;* a *gem* (from its sparkle), prob. the *agate:*—agate {2x}. See: TWOT—2311e; BDB—986b.

7619. שְׁבוּאֵל {6x} **Sh^ebûw'êl**, *sheb-oo-ale';* or שׁוּבָאֵל **Shûwbâ'êl**, *shoo-baw-ale';* from 7617 (abbrev.) or 7725 and 410; *captive* (or *returned*) *of God; Shebuël* or *Shubaël,* the name of two Isr.:—Shebuel {3x}, Shubael {3x}. See: BDB—986c.

7620. שָׁבוּעַ {20x} **shâbûwa^c**, *shaw-boo'-ah;* or שָׁבֻעַ **shâbûa^c**, *shaw-boo'-ah;* also (fem.) שְׁבֻעָה **sh^ebû^câh**, *sheb-oo-aw';* prop. pass. part. of 7650 as a denom. of 7651; lit. *sevened,* i.e. a *week* (spec. of years):—week {19x}, seven {1x}.

(1) In Gen 29:27 it refers to an entire week of feasting. **(2)** Ex 34:22 speaks of a special feast in Israel's religious calendar. **(3)** In Lev 12:5 the word appears with the dual suffix and signifies a period of two weeks. See: TWOT—2318d; BDB—988d.

7621. שְׁבוּעָה {30x} **sh^ebûw^câh**, *sheb-oo-aw';* fem. pass. part. of 7650; prop. something *sworn,* i.e. an *oath:*—oath {28x}, sworn + 1167 {1x}, curse {1x}. See: TWOT—2319a; BDB—989d.

7622. שְׁבוּת {44x} **sh^ebûwth**, *sheb-ooth';* or שְׁבִית **sh^ebîyth**, *sheb-eeth';* from 7617; *exile,* concr. *prisoners;* fig. a *former state* of prosperity:—captivity {31x}, captives {1x}. See: TWOT—2311d; BDB—986a, 987b, 1000a.

7623. שָׁבַח {11x} **shâbach**, *shaw-bakh';* a prim. root; prop. to *address* in a loud tone, i.e. (spec.) *loud;* fig. to *pacify* (as if by words):—praise {5x}, still {2x}, keep it in {1x}, glory {1x}, triumph {1x}, commend {1x}. Syn.: 1288, 1984, 2167, 3034. See: TWOT—2312, 2313; BDB—986c, 1114b.

7624. שְׁבַח {5x} **sh^ebach** (Aram.), *sheb-akh';* corresp. to 7623; to *adulate,* i.e. *adore:*—praise {5x}. See: TWOT—3014; BDB—1114b.

7625. שְׁבַט {1x} **sh^ebaṭ** (Aram.), *sheb-at';* corresp. to 7626; a *clan:*—tribe {1x}. See: TWOT—3015; BDB—1114b.

7626. שֵׁבֶט {190x} **shêbet**, *shay'-bet;* from an unused root prob. mean. to *branch* off; a *scion,* i.e. (lit.) a *stick* (for punishing, writing, fighting, ruling, walking, etc.) or (fig.) a *clan:*—tribe {140x}, rod {34x}, scepter {10x}, staff {2x}, misc. {4x} = × correction, dart.

Shebet, means a "tribe; rod." **(1)** The "rod" as a tool is used by the shepherd (Lev 27:32) and the teacher (2 Sa 7:14). **(2)** It is a symbol of authority in the hands of a ruler, whether it is the scepter (Amos 1:5, 8) or an instrument of warfare and oppression: "Thou shalt break them with a rod of iron; thou shalt dash them in pieces like a potter's vessel" (Ps 2:9; cf. Zec 10:11). **(3)** The symbolic element comes to expression in a description of the messianic rule: "But with righteousness shall he judge the poor, and reprove with equity for the meek of the earth: and he shall smite the earth with the rod of his mouth . . ." (Is 11:4). **(4)** The word *shebet* is most frequently used (143 times) to denote a "tribe," a division in a nation. It is the preferred term for the twelve "tribes" of Israel (Gen 49:16; Ex 28:21). **(5)** Jeremiah referred to all of Israel as the "tribe": "The portion of Jacob is not like them; for he is the former of all things: and Israel is the rod of his inheritance: the Lord of hosts is his name" (51:19). Syn.: 2945, 4294, 4940. See: TWOT—2314a; BDB—986d, 1114b.

7627. שְׁבָט {1x} **Sh^ebâṭ**, *sheb-awt';* of for. or.; *Shebat,* a Jewish month:—Sebat {1x}. See: BDB—987b.

7628. שְׁבִי {49x} **sh^ebîy**, *sheb-ee';* from 7618; *exiled; captured;* as noun, *exile* (abstr. or concr. and collect.); by extens. *booty:*—captivity {35x}, captive {10x}, prisoners {2x}, taken away {1x}, taken {1x}. See: TWOT—2311a; BDB—985d, 987b.

7629. שֹׁבִי {1x} **Shôbîy**, *sho-bee';* from 7617; *captor; Shobi,* an Ammonite:—Shobi {1x}. See: BDB—986b.

7630. שֹׁבַי {2x} **Shôbay**, *sho-bah'-ee;* for 7629; *Shobai,* an Isr.:—Shobai {2x}. See: BDB—986b.

7631. שְׂבִיב {2x} **s^ebîyb** (Aram.), *seb-eeb';* corresp. to 7632:—flame {2x}. See: TWOT—3016; BDB—1114b.

7632. שָׁבִיב {1x} **shâbîyb**, *shaw-beeb';* from the same as 7616; *flame* (as *split* into tongues):—spark {1x}. See: TWOT—2310a; BDB—985b.

7633. שִׁבְיָה {9x} **shibyâh**, *shib-yaw';* fem. of 7628; *exile* (abstr. or concr. and collect.):—captive {8x}, captivity {1x}. See: TWOT—2311c; BDB—986a, 987b.

7634. שָׁבְיָה {1x} **Shobyâh**, *shob-yaw';* fem. of the same as 7629; *captivation; Shobjah,* an Isr.:—Shachia {1x}. See: BDB—967d.

7635. שָׁבִיל {3x} **shâbîyl**, *shaw-beel';* from the same as 7640; a *track* or passageway (as if *flowing* along):—path {3x}. See: TWOT—2316d; BDB—987c.

7636. שָׁבִיס {1x} **shâbîyç**, *shaw-beece';* from an unused root mean. to *interweave;* a *netting* for the hair:—caul {1x}. See: TWOT—2317a; BDB—987d.

7637. שְׁבִיעִי {98x} **sh^ebîy^cîy**, *sheb-ee-ee';* or שְׁבִעִי **sh^ebî^cîy**, *sheb-ee-ee';* ord. from 7657; *seventh:*—seventh {96x}, seventh time {1x}, seven {1x}. See: TWOT—2318b; BDB—988c.

שְׁבִית **sh^ebîyth**. See 7622.

7638. שָׂבָךְ {1x} **sâbâk**, *saw-bawk';* from an unused root mean. to *intwine;* a *netting* (ornament to the capital of a column):—net {1x}. See: TWOT—2230; BDB—959a, 959b.

שַׂבְּכָא **sabb^ekâ'**. See 5443.

7639. שְׂבָכָה {15x} **s^ebâkâh**, *seb-aw-kaw';* fem. of 7638; a *net-work,* i.e (in hunting) a *snare,* (in arch.) a *ballustrade;* also a *reticulated* ornament to a pillar:—network {7x}, wreath {3x}, wreathen work {2x}, checker {1x}, lattice {1x}, snare {1x}. See: TWOT—2230b; BDB—959a, 959b, 1113c.

7640. שֹׁבֶל {1x} **shôbel**, *show'-bel;* from an unused root mean. to *flow;* a lady's *train* (as *trailing* after her):—leg {1x}. See: TWOT—2316a; BDB—987c.

7641. שִׁבֹּל {19x} **shibbôl**, *shib-bole';* or (fem.) שִׁבֹּלֶת **shibbôleth**, *shib-bo'-leth;* from the same as 7640; a *stream* (as *flowing*); also an *ear* of grain (as *growing* out); by anal. a *branch:*—ears {11x}, ears of corn {3x}, branches {1x}, channel {1x}, floods {1x}, *Shibboleth* {1x}, waterflood + 4325 {1x}. comp. 5451. See: TWOT—2316b, 2316c; BDB—987c.

7642. שַׁבְלוּל {1x} **shablûwl**, *shab-lool';* from the same as 7640; a *snail* (as if *floating* in its own slime):—snail {1x}. See: TWOT—248c; BDB—117d, 987c.

שִׁבֹּלֶת **shibbôleth**. See 7641.

7643. שְׂבָם {6x} **S^ebâm**, *seb-awm';* or (fem.) שִׂבְמָה **Sibmâh**, *sib-maw';* prob. from 1313; *spice; Sebam* or *Sibmah,* a place in Moab:—Shebam {1x}, Shibmah {1x}, *Sibmah* {4x}. See: BDB—959b.

7644. שֶׁבְנָא {9x} **Shebnâ'**, *sheb-naw';* or שֶׁבְנָה **Shebnâh**, *sheb-naw';* from an unused root mean. to *grow; growth; Shebna* or *Shebnah,* an Isr.:—*Shebna* {9x}. See: BDB—987d.

7645. שְׁבַנְיָה {7x} **Sh^ebanyâh**, *sheb-an-yaw';* or שְׁבַנְיָהוּ **Sh^ebanyâhûw**, *sheb-an-yaw'-hoo;* from the same as 7644 and 3050; *Jah has grown* (i.e. *prospered*); *Shebanjah,* the name of three or four Isr.:—Shebaniah {7x}. See: BDB—987d.

7646. שָׂבַע {95x} **sâba^c**, *saw-bah';* or שָׂבֵעַ **sâbêa^c**, *saw-bay'-ah;* a prim. root; to *sate,* i.e. *fill* to satisfaction (lit. or fig.):—satisfy {47x}, fill {25x}, full {15x}, plenty {2x}, enough {2x}, satiate {1x}, sufficed {1x}, unsatiable {1x}, weary {1x}.

(1) *Sabea'* expresses the idea of being filled, sated (Ex 16:8). **(2)** Figuratively, Israel is compared to sated cattle or sheep (Jer 50:19). **(3)** The earth too can be sated, have its fill, of rain (Job 38:27). **(4)** *Sabea'* sometimes expresses over-indulgence (Prov 25:16). **(5)** God too can become surfeited, especially when men offer sacrifices with the wrong motives (Is 1:11). **(6)** The lazy man shall have poverty enough (Prov 28:19). **(7)** *Sabea'* often expresses God's satisfying, supplying, man with his material needs (Ps 103:5). See: TWOT—2231; BDB—959b.

7647. שָׂבָע {8x} **sâbâ^c**, *saw-baw';* from 7646; *copiousness:*—abundance {1x}, plenty {4x}, plenteous {3x}. See: TWOT—2231c; BDB—960a.

7648. שֹׂבַע {8x} **sôba^c**, *so'-bah;* from 7646; *satisfaction* (of food or [fig.] joy):—full {5x}, fulness {1x}, satisfying {1x}, sufficed {1x}. See: TWOT—2231a; BDB—959d.

7649. שָׂבֵעַ {10x} **sâbêa^c**, *saw-bay'-ah;* from 7646; *satiated* (in a pleasant or disagreeable sense):—full (of) {8x}, satisfied (with) {2x}. See: TWOT—2231d; BDB—960a.

7650. שָׁבַע **shâba^c**, *shaw-bah';* a prim. root; prop. to *be complete,* but used only as a denom. from 7651; to *seven* oneself, i.e. *swear* (as if by repeating a declaration seven times):—sware {167x}, charge {8x}, oath {7x}, adjure {3x}, straitly {2x}.

(1) Often to swear or to take an oath is to strongly affirm a promise (Gen 21:23–24; Josh 6:22; 1 Sa 20:17). **(2)** Allegiance to God is pledged by an oath (Is 19:18). **(3)** Zephaniah condemns the idolatrous priests that swear by the Lord and by Malcham [the Ammonite god] (Zeph 1:5). **(4)** In making and upholding His promises to men, God often swears by Himself. (Gen 22:16–17; cf. Isa 45:23; Jer 22:5). **(5)** God also swears by His holiness (Amos 4:2). **(5)** The root for "to swear" and the root for "seven" are the same in Hebrew, and since the number seven is the "perfect number," some have conjectured that "to swear" is to somehow "seven oneself," thus to bind oneself with seven things. Perhaps this is paralleled by the use of "seven" in Samson's allowing himself to be bound by seven fresh bowstrings (Judg 16:7) and weaving the seven locks of his head (Judg. 16:13). The relationship between "to swear" and "seven" is inconclusive. See: TWOT—2318; BDB—989a.

7651. שֶׁבַע {394x} **sheba'**, *sheh'-bah;* or (masc.) שִׁבְעָה **shib'âh**, *shib-aw';* from 7650; a prim. cardinal number; *seven* (as the sacred *full* one); also (adv.) *seven times;* by impl. a *week;* by extens. an *indefinite* number:—seven 355, seventh {13x}, seventeen + 6240 {8x}, seven times {6x}, seventeenth + 6240 {6x}, seventeenth {5x}, sevens + 7657 {2x}, seven men {1x}, sevenfold {1x}, seventeen + 6235 {1x}, seventeen + 7657 {1x}. See: TWOT—2318; BDB—987d, 988d, 1114b. comp. 7658.

7652. שֶׁבַע {10x} **Sheba'**, *sheh'-bah;* the same as 7651; *seven; Sheba,* the name of a place in Pal., and of two Isr.:—*Sheba* {10x}. See: BDB—989d.

שָׁבֻעַ **shâbûa'**. See 7620.

7653. שִׂבְעָה {1x} **sib'âh**, *sib-aw';* fem. of 7647; *satiety:*—fulness {1x}. See: TWOT—2231b; BDB—960a.

7654. שָׂבְעָה {6x} **sob'âh**, *sob-aw';* fem. of 7648; *satiety:*—satisfy {2x}, enough {2x}, full {1x}, sufficiently {1x}. See: TWOT—2231b; BDB—960a.

שִׁבְעָה **shib'âh**. See 7651.

7655. שִׁבְעָה {6x} **shib'âh** (Aram.), *shib-aw';* corresp. to 7651:—seven {5x}, seven times {1x}. See: TWOT—3017; BDB—1114b.

7656. שִׁבְעָה {1x} **Shib'âh**, *shib-aw';* masc. of 7651; *seven (-th); Shebah,* a well in Pal.:—Shebah {1x}. See: BDB—988b.

שְׁבֻעָה **sh'bû'âh**. See 7620.

שְׁבִיעִי **sh'bîy'îy**. See 7637.

7657. שִׁבְעִים {91x} **shib'îym**, *shib-eem';* multiple of 7651; *seventy:*—seventy {58x}, three score and (ten, twelve, etc . . .) {33x}. See: TWOT—2318b; BDB—988c.

7658. שִׁבְעָנָה {1x} **shib'ânâh**, *shib-aw-naw';* prol. for the masc. of 7651; *seven:*—seven {1x}. See: TWOT—2318; BDB—988d.

7659. שִׁבְעָתַיִם {7x} **shib'âthayim**, *shib-aw-thah'-yim;* dual (adv.) of 7651; *seven-times:*—sevenfold {6x}, seven times {1x}. See: TWOT—2318c; BDB—988d.

7660. שָׁבַץ {2x} **shâbats**, *shaw-bats';* a prim. root; to *interweave* (colored) threads in squares; by impl. (*of reticulation*) to *inchase* gems in gold:—embroider {1x}, set {1x}. See: TWOT—2320; BDB—990a.

7661. שָׁבָץ {1x} **shâbâts**, *shaw-bawts';* from 7660; *intanglement,* i.e. (fig.) *perplexity:*—anguish {1x}. See: TWOT—2320a; BDB—990b.

7662. שְׁבַק {5x} **sh'baq** (Aram.), *sheb-ak';* corresp. to the root of 7733; to *quit,* i.e. *allow to remain:*—leave {4x}, let alone {1x}. See: TWOT—3018; BDB—1114c.

7663. שָׂבַר {8x} **sâbar**, *saw-bar';* err. שָׁבַר **shâbar** (Neh. 2:13, 15), *shaw-bar';* a prim. root; to *scrutinize;* by impl. (of *watching*) to *expect* (with hope and patience):—hope {3x}, tarry {1x}, view {2x}, wait {2x}. See: TWOT—2232; BDB—960b, 1104a.

7664. שֵׂבֶר {2x} **sêber**, *say'-ber;* from 7663; *expectation:*—hope {2x}. See: TWOT—2232a; BDB—960b.

7665. שָׁבַר {148x} **shâbar**, *shaw-bar';* a prim. root; to *burst* (lit. or fig.):—break {115x}, destroy {9x}, break in pieces {8x}, break down {4x}, hurt {3x}, torn {2x}, give birth {1x}, crush {1x}, quench {1x}, misc. {6x} = broken ([-hearted]), × quite, view [*by mistake for* 7663].

(1) The common word for breaking things, *shabar* describes the breaking of **(1a)** earthen vessels (Judg 7:20; Jer 19:10), **(1b)** bows (Hos 1:5), **(1c)** doors (Gen 19:9), **(1d)** swords (Hos 2:18), **(1e)** bones (Ex 12:46), and **(1f)** yokes or bonds (Jer 28:10, 12–13). **(2)** Figuratively, it describes a shattered heart or emotion (Ps 69:20; Eze 6:9). **(3)** Intensively, *shabar* connotes shattering something, such as **(3a)** the tablets of the Law (Ex 32:19), **(3b)** idol images (2 Kin 11:18), or **(3c)** trees by hail (Ex 9:25). Syn.: 7591, 7703, 8074, 8154. See: TWOT—2321; BDB—990c, 991b, 1117c.

7666. שָׁבַר {21x} **shâbar**, *shaw-bar';* denom. from 7668; to *deal* in grain:—buy {15x}, sell {6x}. See: TWOT—2322; BDB—991c.

7667. שֶׁבֶר {44x} **sheber**, *sheh'-ber;* or שֵׁבֶר **shêber**, *shay'-ber;* from 7665; a *fracture,* fig. *ruin;* spec. a *solution* (of a dream):—destruction {21x}, breach {7x}, hurt {4x}, breaking {3x}, affliction {2x}, bruise {2x}, crashing {1x}, interpretation {1x}, vexation {1x}, broken footed {1x}, broken handed {1x}. See: TWOT—2321a; BDB—991a, 991c.

7668. שֶׁבֶר {9x} **sheber**, *sheh'-ber;* the same as 7667; *grain* (as if *broken* into kernels):—corn {8x}, victuals {1x}. See: TWOT—2322a; BDB—991c.

7669. שֶׁבֶר {1x} **Sheber**, *sheh'-ber;* the same as 7667; *Sheber,* an Isr.:—*Sheber* {1x}. See: BDB—991b.

7670. שִׁבְרוֹן {2x} **shibrôwn**, *shib-rone';* from 7665; *rupture,* i.e. a *pang;* fig. *ruin:*—breaking {1x}, destruction {1x}. See: TWOT—2321b; BDB—991b.

7671. שְׁבָרִים {1x} **Sh'bârîym**, *sheb-aw-reem';* plur. of 7667; *ruins; Shebarim,* a place in Pal.:—Shebarim {1x}. See: BDB—991b.

7672. שְׁבַשׁ {1x} **sh'bash** (Aram.), *sheb-ash';* corresp. to 7660; to *intangle,* i.e. *perplex:*—be astonied {1x}. See: TWOT—3019; BDB—1114c.

7673. שָׁבַת {71x} **shâbath**, *shaw-bath';* a prim. root; to *repose,* i.e. *desist* from exertion; used in many impl. relations (caus., fig. or spec.):—cease {47x}, rest {11x}, away {3x}, fail {2x}, celebrate {1x}, misc. {7x} = keep (sabbath), suffer to be lacking, leave, rid, still.

Shabath means "to rest, cease." **(1)** The verb first occurs in Gen 2:2–3: "And on the seventh day God ended his work which he had made; and he rested on the seventh day from all his work which he had made. And God blessed the seventh day, and sanctified it: because that in it he had rested from all his work which God created and made." **(2)** The basic and most frequent meaning of *shabath* is shown in Gen 8:22: "While the earth remaineth, seedtime and harvest, and cold and heat, and summer and winter, and day and night shall not cease." **(3)** This promise became a prophetic sign of God's faithfulness: "If those ordinances depart from before me, saith the Lord, then the seed of Israel also shall cease from being a nation before me for ever" (Jer 31:36). **(4)** We find a variety of senses: **(4a)** ". . . Even the first day ye shall put away (*shabath*) leaven out of your houses . . ." (Ex 12:15). **(4b)** "Neither shalt thou suffer the salt of the covenant of thy God to be lacking from thy meat offering" (Lev 2:13). **(4c)** Josiah "put down (*shabath*) the idolatrous priests . . ." (2 Kin 23:5). **(4d)** "I will also rid (*shabath*) beasts out of the land" (Lev 26:6). Syn: 2308, 7676. See: TWOT—2323, 2323c; BDB—991d, 992c.

7674. שֶׁבֶת {3x} **shebeth**, *sheh'-beth;* from 7673; *rest, interruption, cessation:*—cease {1x}, sit still {1x}, loss of time {1x}. See: TWOT—2323a; BDB—444a, 992a.

7675. שֶׁבֶת {4x} **shebeth**, *sheh'-beth;* infin. of 3427; prop. *session;* but used also concr. an *abode* or *locality:*—place {1x}, seat {3x}. See: TWOT—922a; BDB—443d. comp. 3429.

7676. שַׁבָּת {107x} **shabbâth**, *shab-bawth';* intens. from 7673; *intermission,* i.e (spec.) the *Sabbath:*—(+ every) sabbath {107x}, another {1x}.

Shabbath, as a noun, means "the sabbath." **(1)** The verb *sabat* (7673) is the root of *shabbat:* "Six days you are to do your work, but on the seventh day you shall rest . . ." (Ex 23:12). **(2)** In Ex 31:15, the seventh day is called the "sabbath rest." **(3)** A man's "rest" was to include his animals and servants (Ex 23:12): even "in earing time and in harvest thou shalt rest" (Ex 34:21). **(4)** "It is a sign between me and the children of Israel for ever: for in six days the Lord made heaven and earth, and on the seventh day he rested, and was refreshed" (Ex 31:17). **(5)** ". . . Then shall the land keep a sabbath unto the Lord" (Lev 25:2). Six years' crops will be sown and harvested, but the seventh year "shall be a sabbath of rest unto the land, a sabbath for the Lord . . ." (Lev 25:4). **(6)** The feast of trumpets, the Day of Atonement, and the first and eighth days of the Feast of Tabernacles are also called "a sabbath observance" or "a sabbath of complete rest" (Lev 23:24, 32, 39). **(7)** The "sabbath" was a "day of worship" (Lev 23:3) as well as a "day of rest and refreshment" for man (Ex 23:12). **(8)** God "rested and was refreshed" (Ex 31:17).

(9) The "sabbath" was the covenant sign of God's lordship over the creation. **(9a)** By observing the "sabbath," Israel confessed that they were God's redeemed people, subject to His lordship to obey the whole of His law. **(9b)** They were His stewards to show mercy with kindness and liberality to all (Ex 23:12; Lev 25). **(10)** By "resting," man witnessed his trust in God to give fruit to his labor; he entered into God's "rest." Thus "rest" and the "sabbath" were eschatological in perspective, looking to the accomplishment of God's ultimate purpose through the redemption of His people, to whom the "sabbath" was a covenant sign. **(11)** The prophets rebuked Israel for their neglect of the sabbath (Is 1:13; Jer 17:21–27; Eze 20:12–24; Amos 8:5). **(12)** They also proclaimed "sabbath" observance as a blessing in the messianic age and a sign of its fullness (Is 56:2–4; 58:13; 66:23; Eze 44:24; 45:17; 46:1, 3–4, 12). **(13)** The length of the Babylonian Captivity was determined by the extent of Israel's abuse of the sabbatical year (2 Chr 36:21; cf. Lev 26:34–35). Syn: 2308, 7673. See: TWOT—2323b; BDB—992a.

7677. שַׁבָּתוֹן {11x} **shabbâthôwn**, *shab-baw-thone'*; from 7676; a *sabbatism* or special holiday:—rest {8x}, sabbath {3x}. See: TWOT—2323d; BDB—992d.

7678. שַׁבְּתַי {3x} **Shabbᵉthay**, *shab-beth-ah'-ee*; from 7676; *restful; Shabbethai*, the name of three Isr.:—Shabbethai {3x}. See: BDB—992d.

7679. שָׂגָא {2x} **sâgâʼ**, *saw-gaw'*; a prim. root; to *grow*, i.e. (caus.) to *enlarge*, (fig.) *laud:*—increase {1x}, magnify {1x}. See: TWOT—2233; BDB—960b, 1113c.

7680. שְׂגָא {3x} **sᵉgâʼ** (Aram.), *seg-aw'*; corresp. to 7679; to *increase:*—grow {1x}, be multiplied {2x}. See: TWOT—3004; BDB—1113c.

7681. שָׁגֵא {1x} **age**, an Isr.:—Shage {1x}. See: BDB—992d, 993b.

7682. שָׂגַב **sâgab**, *saw-gab'*; a prim. root; to *be* (caus. *make*) *lofty*, espec. *inaccessible;* by impl. *safe, strong;* used lit. and fig.—high {6x}, exalted {6x}, defend {2x}, safe {2x}, excellent {1x}, misc. {3x} = lofty, be too strong. See: TWOT—2234; BDB—960c.

7683. שָׁגַג {5x} **shâgag**, *shaw-gag'*; a prim. root; to *stray*, i.e. (fig.) *sin* (with more or less apology):—× also for that {1x}, deceived {1x}, err {1x}, go astray {1x}, sin ignorantly {1x}. See: TWOT—2324; BDB—992d.

7684. שְׁגָגָה {19x} **shᵉgâgâh**, *sheg-aw-gaw'*; from 7683; a *mistake* or inadvertent *transgression:*—error {2x}, through ignorance {6x}, by ignorance {2x}, in ignorance {1x}, ignorance {3x}, at unawares {4x}, unwittingly {1x}. See: TWOT—2324a; BDB—993a.

7685. שָׂגָה {4x} **sâgâh**, *saw-gaw'*; a prim. root; to *enlarge* (espec. upward, also fig.):—grow (up) {2x}, increase {2x}. See: TWOT—2233b; BDB—960d.

7686. שָׁגָה {21x} **shâgâh**, *shaw-gaw'*; a prim. root; to *stray* (caus. *mislead*), usually (fig.) to *mistake*, espec. (mor.) to *transgress;* by extens. (through the idea of intoxication) to *reel*, (fig.) *be enraptured:*—err {11x}, ravished {2x}, wander {3x}, deceiver {1x}, cause to go astray {1x}, sin through ignorance {1x}, go astray {1x}, deceived {1x}. Syn.: 2398, 5771, 6588. See: TWOT—2325; BDB—993a.

7687. שְׂגוּב {3x} **Sᵉgûwb**, *seg-oob'*; from 7682; *aloft; Segub*, the name of two Isr.:—Segub {3x}. See: BDB—960d.

7688. שָׁגַח {3x} **shâgach**, *shaw-gakh'*; a prim. root; to *peep*, i.e. *glance* sharply at:—look (narrowly) {3x}. See: TWOT—2326; BDB—993b.

7689. שַׂגִּיא {2x} **saggîyʼ**, *sag-ghee'*; from 7679; (superl.) *mighty:*—excellent {1x}, great {1x}. See: TWOT—2233a; BDB—960c.

7690. שַׂגִּיא {13x} **saggîyʼ** (Aram.), *sag-ghee'*; corresp. to 7689; *large* (in size, quantity or number, also adv.):—exceeding {1x}, great {3x}, greatly {1x}; many {2x}, much {4x}, sore {1x}, very {1x}. See: TWOT—3004a; BDB—1113c.

7691. שְׁגִיאָה {1x} **shᵉgîyʼâh**, *sheg-ee-aw'*; from 7686; a moral *mistake:*—error {1x}. See: TWOT—2325a; BDB—993b.

7692. שִׁגָּיוֹן {2x} **Shiggâyôwn**, *shig-gaw-yone'*; or

שִׁגָּיֹנָה **Shiggâyônâh**, *shig-gaw-yo-naw'*; from 7686; prop. *aberration*, i.e. (tech.) a *dithyramb* or rambling poem:—Shiggaion {1x}, Shigionoth {1x}. See: BDB—993a, 993c.

7693. שָׁגַל {4x} **shâgal**, *shaw-gal'*; a prim. root; to *copulate* with:—lie with {1x}, ravish {3x}. See: TWOT—2327; BDB—993c.

7694. שֵׁגָל {2x} **shêgâl**, *shay-gawl'*; from 7693; a *queen* (from cohabitation):—queen {2x}. See: TWOT—2327a; BDB—993c, 1114c.

7695. שֵׁגַל {3x} **shêgâl** (Aram.), *shay-gawl'*; corresp. to 7694; a (legitimate) *queen:*—wife {3x}. See: TWOT—3020; BDB—1114c.

7696. שָׁגַע {7x} **shâgaʻ**, *shaw-gah'*; a prim. root; to *rave* through insanity:—mad {5x}, mad man {2x}. See: TWOT—2328; BDB—993c.

7697. שִׁגָּעוֹן {3x} **shiggâʻôwn**, *shig-gaw-yone'*; from 7696; *craziness:*—furiously {1x}, madness {2x}. See: TWOT—2328a; BDB—993d.

7698. שֶׁגֶר {5x} **sheger**, *sheh'-ger;* from an unused root prob. mean. to *eject;* the *fetus* (as finally *expelled*):—that cometh of {1x}, increase {4x}. See: TWOT—2329a; BDB—993d.

7699. שַׁד {24x} **shad**, *shad;* or

שֹׁד **shôd**, *shode;* prob. from 7736 (in its orig. sense) contr.; the *breast* of a woman or animal (as *bulging*):—breast {22x}, pap {1x}, teat {1x}. See: TWOT—2332a; BDB—993d, 994c, 994d.

7700. שֵׁד {2x} **shêd**, *shade;* from 7736; a *demon* (as *malignant*):—devil {2x}. Syn.: 7854, 8163. See: TWOT—2330; BDB—993d.

7701. שֹׁד {25x} **shôd**, *shode;* or

שׁוֹד **shôwd** (Job 5:21), *shode;* from 7736; *violence, ravage:*—spoil {10x}, destruction {7x}, desolation {2x}, robbery {2x}, wasting {2x}, oppression {1x}, spoiler {1x}. See: TWOT—2331a; BDB—994a, 994c, 1000c.

7702. שָׂדַד {3x} **sâdad**, *saw-dad';* a prim. root; to *abrade*, i.e. *harrow* a field:—break clods {2x}, harrow {1x}. See: TWOT—2235; BDB—961a.

7703. שָׁדַד {58x} **shâdad**, *shaw-dad';* a prim. root; prop. to *be burly*, i.e. (fig.) *powerful* (pass. *impregnable*); by impl. to *ravage:*—spoil {30x}, spoiler {11x}, waste {8x}, destroy {2x}, robbers {2x}, misc. {5x} = dead, destroyer, oppress, × utterly. Syn.: 5302, 7591, 7665, 7722, 8074. See: TWOT—2331; BDB—994a, 1000d.

7704. שָׂדֶה {333x} **sâdeh**, *saw-deh';* or

שָׂדַי **sâday**, *saw-dah'-ee;* from an unused root mean. to *spread* out; a *field* (as *flat*):—field {292x}, country {17x}, land {11x}, wild {8x}, ground {4x}, soil {1x}.

The form, *sadeh,* means "field; country; domain [of a town]." **(1)** This word often represents the "open field" where the animals roam wild. **(1a)** That is its meaning in its first biblical appearance: "And every plant of the field before it was in the earth, and every herb of the field before it grew: for the Lord God had not caused it to rain upon the earth . . ." (Gen 2:5). **(1b)** Thus, "Esau was a cunning hunter, a man of the field; and Jacob was a plain man, dwelling in tents" (Gen 25:27). **(1c)** A city in the "open field" was unfortified; David wisely asked Achish for such a city, showing that he did not intend to be hostile (1 Sa 27:5). Dwelling in an unfortified city meant exposure to attack. **(2)** *Sadeh* represents the "fields surrounding a town" (Josh 21:12; cf. Neh 11:25). **(3)** "Arable land," land that is either cultivated or to be cultivated, is also signified by *sadeh:* "If it be your mind that I should bury my dead out of my sight; hear me, and entreat for me to Ephron the son of Zohar, that he may give me the cave of Machpelah, which he hath, which is in the end of his field . . ." (Gen 23:8–9).

(4) The entirety of one's cultivated or pasture land is called his "field": "And the king [David] said unto him [Mephibosheth], Why speakest thou any more of thy matters? I have said, Thou and Ziba divide the land [previously owned by Saul]" (2 Sa 19:29). **(5)** Sometimes particular sections of land are identified by name: "And after this, Abraham buried Sarah his wife in the cave of the field of Machpelah before Mamre . . ." (Gen 23:19). **(6)** The form, *saday,* also means "open field." *Saday* occurs 12 times, only in poetical passages. Deut 32:13 is the first biblical appearance: "He made him ride on the high places of the earth, that he might eat the increase of the fields; . . ." Syn.: 127, 776. See: TWOT—2236a, 2236b; BDB—961a, 961b.

7705. שִׁדָּה {2x} **shiddâh**, *shid-dah';* from 7703; a *wife* (as *mistress* of the house):—× all sorts, musical instrument {2x}. See: TWOT—2332b; BDB—994d.

7706. שַׁדַּי {48x} **Shadday**, *shad-dah'-ee;* from 7703; the *Almighty:*—Almighty {48x}.

(1) The title *Shadday* really indicates the fullness and riches of God's grace, and would remind the Hebrew reader that from God comes every good and perfect gift—that He is never weary of pouring forth His mercies on His people, and that He is more ready to give than they are to receive. **(2)** Bountiful expresses the sense most exactly. **(3)** El (410) sets forth the might of God and the title *Shadday* points to the inexhaustible stores of His bounty. See: TWOT—2333; BDB—994c, 994d.

7707. שְׁדֵיאוּר {5x} **Shᵉdêyʼûwr**, *shed-ay-oor';* from the same as 7704 and 217; *spreader of light; Shedejur,* an Isr.:—Shedeur {5x}. See: BDB—994d.

7708. שִׂדִּים {3x} **Siddîym**, *sid-deem';* plur. from the same as 7704; *flats; Siddim,* a valley in Pal.:—Siddim {3x}. See: BDB—961a, 961d.

7709. שְׁדֵמָה {6x} **shᵉdêmâh**, *shed-ay-maw';* appar. from 7704; a cultivated *field:*—blasted {1x}, field {5x}. See: TWOT—2334a; BDB—995a, 1056c.

7710. שָׁדַף {3x} **shâdaph**, *shaw-daf';* a prim. root; to *scorch:*—blast {3x}. See: TWOT—2335; BDB—995b.

7711. שְׁדֵפָה {6x} **shᵉdêphâh**, *shed-ay-faw';* or

שִׁדָּפוֹן **shiddâphôwn**, *shid-daw-fone';* from 7710; *blight:*—blasted {1x}, blasting {5x}. See: TWOT—2335a, 2335b; BDB—995b

7712. שְׁדַר {1x} **shᵉdar** (Aram.), *shed-ar';* a prim. root; to *endeavor:*—laboured {1x}. See: TWOT—3021; BDB—1114c.

7713. שְׂדֵרָה {4x} **sᵉdêrâh**, *sed-ay-raw';* from an unused root mean. to *regulate;* a *row,* i.e. *rank* (of soldiers), *story* (of rooms):—board {1x}, range {3x}. See: TWOT—1467b; BDB—690b, 961d.

7714. שַׁדְרַךְ {1x} **Shadrak**, *shad-rak';* prob. of for. or.; *Shadrak,* the Bab. name of one of Daniel's companions:—Shadrach {1x}. See: BDB—995b, 1114c.

7715. שַׁדְרַךְ {14x} **Shadrak** (Aram.), *shad-rak';* the same as 7714:—Shadrach {14x}. See: BDB—1114c.

7716. שֶׂה {46x} **seh**, *seh;* or

שֵׂי **sêy**, *say;* prob. from 7582 through the idea of *pushing* out to graze; a member of a flock, i.e. a *sheep* or *goat:*—sheep {18x}, cattle {10x}, lamb {16x}, ewe {1x}, lamb + 3532 {1x}. See: TWOT—2237; BDB—961d, 966d. comp. 2089.

7717. שָׂהֵד {1x} **sâhêd**, *saw-hade';* from an unused root mean. to *testify;* a *witness:*—record {1x}. See: TWOT—2238; BDB—962a, 1113c.

7718. שֹׁהַם {11x} **shôham**, *sho'-ham;* from an unused root prob. mean to *blanch;* a gem, prob. the *beryl* (from its *pale* green color):—onyx {11x}. See: TWOT—2337; BDB—965d.

7719. שֹׁהַם {1x} **Shôham**, *sho'-ham;* the same as 7718; *Shoham*, an Isr.:—*Shoham* {1x}. See: BDB—996a.

7720. שַׂהֲרֹן {3x} **sahărôn**, *sah-har-one';* from the same as 5469; a round *pendant* for the neck:—ornament {2x}, round tires like the moon {1x}. See: TWOT—2239a; BDB—962a.

שַׁו **shav**. See 7723.

7721. שׂוֹא {1x} **sôw'**, *so;* from an unused root (akin to 5375 and 7722) mean. to *rise;* a *rising:*—arise {1x}. See: TWOT—1421; BDB—962b.

7722. שׁוֹא {13x} **shôw'**, *sho;* or (fem.)

שׁוֹאָה **shôw'âh**, *sho-aw';* or

שֹׁאָה **shô'âh**, *sho-aw';* from an unused root mean. to *rush* over; a *tempest;* by impl. *devastation:*—desolation {5x}, destruction {3x}, desolate {2x}, destroy {1x}, storm {1x}, wasteness {1x}. Syn.: 7591, 8074, 8154. See: TWOT—2339, 2339a; BDB—980b, 980d, 996b.

7723. שָׁוְא {53x} **shâv'**, *shawv;* or

שַׁו **shav**, *shav;* from the same as 7722 in the sense of *desolating; evil* (as *destructive*), lit. (*ruin*) or mor. (espec. *guile*); fig. *idolatry* (as false, subj.), *uselessness* (as deceptive, obj.; also adv. in *vain*):—vain {22x}, vanity {22x}, false {5x}, lying {2x}, falsely {1x}, lies {1x}.

Shav' means "deceit; deception; malice; falsity; vanity; emptiness." **(1)** The 53 occurrences of *shav'* are primarily in poetry. **(2)** The basic meaning of this word is "deceit" or "deception," "malice," and "falsehood." **(2a)** This meaning emerges when it is used in a legal context: "Put not thine hand with the wicked to be an unrighteous witness" (Ex 23:1). **(2b)** Used in cultic [religious worship] contexts, the word bears these same overtones but may be rendered variously. For example, in Ps 31:6 the word may be rendered "lying", in the sense of "deceitful" (cf. Eze 12:24). Eliphaz described the ungodly as those who trust in "emptiness" or "deception," though they gain nothing but emptiness as a reward for that trust (Job 15:31). See: TWOT—2338a; BDB—981a, 996a.

7724. שְׁוָא {1x} **Sh^evâ'**, *shev-aw';* from the same as 7723; *false; Sheva*, an Isr.:—*Sheva* {1x}. See: BDB—976a, 996a, 1009d.

7725. שׁוּב {1066x} **shûwb**, *shoob;* a prim. root; to *turn* back (hence, away) tran. or intr., lit. or fig. (not necessarily with the idea of *return* to the starting point); gen. to *retreat;* often adv. *again:*—return {391x}, . . . again {248x}, turn {123x}, . . . back {65x}, . . . away {56x}, restore {39x}, bring {34x}, render {19x}, answer {18x}, recompense {8x}, recover {6x}, deliver {5x}, put {5x}, withdraw {5x}, requite {4x}, misc. {40x} = × in any case (wise), × at all, averse, call [to mind], cease, × certainly, × consider, + continually, convert, + deny, × fro, [go] out, hinder, let, [see] more, × needs, be past, × pay, pervert, recall, refresh, relieve, rescue, retrieve, reverse, reward, + say nay, still, × surely.

Shuwb means "to return or go back, bring back." **(1)** The basic meaning of the verb is movement back to the point of departure (unless there is evidence to the contrary). **(1a)** In the first occurrence of this verb God told Adam that he and Eve would "eat bread, till thou return unto the ground;" (Gen 3:19). **(1b)** Used in this emphasis, *shuwb* can be applied specifically of returning along a path already traversed: "So Esau returned that day on his way unto Seir" (Gen 33:16). **(2)** The word can mean "turn away from," as **(2a)** in Ps 9:3: "When mine enemies are turned back . . . ," or **(2b)** "reverse a direction," as in 2 Kin 20:10: ". . . Let the shadow return backward ten degrees." **(3)** It can mean the opposite of going out, as when the raven Noah sent forth was constantly going "to and fro" (Gen 8:7)—this phrase, however, may also mean merely constant movement; the raven went about constantly "here and there." **(4)** In Gen 8:3 the word is used of the receding of the flood water: "And the waters returned (*shuwb*) from off the earth continually (1980 – halak): and after the end of the hundred and fifty days the waters were abated." **(5)** The verb can also mean "to follow after": "Behold, thy sister-in-law is gone back unto her people, and unto her gods: return thou after thy sister-in-law" (Ruth 1:15).

(6) *Shuwb* can imply the cessation of something. In this sense, the word can imply "to go away or disappear": "And tarry with him a few days, until thy brother's fury turn away" (Gen 27:44). **(7)** It can refer to the initiation of the cessation of something. In some cases violence is the means of bringing something to cease: "How then wilt thou turn away the face of one captain of the least of my master's servants . . ." (2 Kin 18:24). **(8)** In Is 47:10 the verb implies both turning away and destroying: "Thy wisdom and thy knowledge, it hath perverted thee. . . ." **(9)** In the case of spiritually returning (metaphorically) to the Lord, *shuwb* can mean **(9a)** "turning away from" following Him (Num 14:43), **(9b)** "turning from" pursuing evil (1 Kin 8:35), and **(9c)** "to return" to Him and obey Him (Deut 30:2). **(10)** The verb can also be used in close relation to another verb to indicate the repetition of an action presented by the other verb: ". . . I will again feed and keep thy flock" (Gen 30:31). **(11)** The process called conversion or turning to God is in reality a re-turning or a turning back again to Him from whom sin has separated us, but whose we are by virtue of creation, preservation and redemption. Syn.: 2105, 4878, 5162, 8666. See: TWOT—2340; BDB—996d, 1000a, 1117d.

שׁוּבָאֵל **Shûwbâ'êl**. See 7619.

7726. שׁוֹבָב {4x} **shôwbâb**, *sho-bawb';* from 7725; *apostate*, i.e. *idolatrous:*—backsliding {2x}, frowardly {1x}, turn away [*from marg.*] {1x}. See: TWOT—2340c; BDB—1000a.

7727. שׁוֹבָב {4x} **Shôwbâb**, *sho-bawb';* the same as 7726; *rebellious; Shobab*, the name of two Isr.:—Shobab {4x}. See: BDB—1000a.

7728. שׁוֹבֵב {2x} **shôwbêb**, *sho-babe';* from 7725; *apostate*, i.e. *heathenish* or (actually) *heathen:*—backsliding {2x}. See: TWOT—2340d; BDB—1000a.

7729. שׁוּבָה {1x} **shûwbâh**, *shoo-baw';* from 7725; a *return:*—returning {1x}. 7729 *Shuwbah* occurs once to mean "coming back" or "turning back": "For thus saith the Lord God, the Holy One of Israel; In returning (*shuwbah*) and rest shall ye be saved; in quietness and in confidence shall be your strength: and ye would not" (Is 30:15). See: TWOT—2340a; BDB—1000a.

7730. שׂוֹבֶךְ {1x} **sôwbek**, *so'-bek;* for 5441; a *thicket*, i.e. interlaced branches:—thick boughs {1x}. See: TWOT—2230a; BDB—959a.

7731. שׁוֹבָךְ {2x} **Shôwbâk**, *sho-bawk';* perh. for 7730; *Shobak*, a Syrian.—Shobach {2x}. See: BDB—1000c.

7732. שׁוֹבָל {9x} **Shôwbâl**, *sho-bawl';* from the same as 7640; *overflowing; Shobal*, the name of an Edomite and two Isr.:—Shobal {9x}. See: BDB—987c, 1000c.

7733. שׁוֹבֵק {1x} **Shôwbêq**, *sho-bake';* act. part. from a prim. root mean. to *leave* (comp. 7662); *forsaking; Shobek*, an Isr.:—Shobek {1x}. See: BDB—990b, 1000c, 1114c.

7734. שׂוּג {1x} **sûwg**, *soog;* a prim. root; to *retreat:*—turned back {1x}. See: TWOT—1469; BDB—690d.

7735. שׂוּג {1x} **sûwg**, *soog;* a prim. root; to *hedge* in:—make to grow {1x}. See: TWOT—1470; BDB—691b.

7736. שׁוּד {1x} **shûwd**, *shood;* a prim. root; prop. to *swell* up, i.e. fig. (by impl. of *insolence*) to *devastate:*—waste {1x}. See: TWOT—2331; BDB—994a, 1000d.

שׁוֹד **shôwd**. See 7699, 7701.

7737. שָׁוָה {21x} **shâvâh**, *shaw-vaw';* a prim. root; prop. to *level*, i.e. *equalize;* fig. to *resemble;* by impl. to *adjust* (i.e. *counterbalance, be suitable, compose, place, yield*, etc.):—laid {3x}, equal {3x}, like {2x}, compared {2x}, profit {2x}, set {1x}, misc. {8x} = avail, behave, bring forth, countervail, make plain, reckon. See: TWOT—2342, 2343; BDB—1000d, 1001a, 1114d.

7738. שָׁוָה {1x} **shâvâh**, *shaw-vaw';* a prim. root; to *destroy:*—× substance {1x} [*from the marg.*]. See: TWOT—2343; BDB—996c.

7739. שְׁוָה {2x} **sh^evâh** (Aram.), *shev-aw';* corresp. to 7737; to *resemble:*—made {2x}. See: TWOT—3023, 3024; BDB—1114d.

7740. שָׁוֵה {1x} **Shâvêh**, *shaw-vay';* from 7737; *plain; Shaveh*, a place in Pal.:—*Shaveh* {1x}. See: TWOT—2342a; BDB—1001a.

7741. שָׁוֵה קִרְיָתַיִם {1x} **Shâvêh Qiryâthayim**, *shaw-vay' kir-yaw-thah'-yim;* from the same as 7740 and the dual of 7151; *plain of a double city; Shaveh-Kirjathajim*, a place E. of the Jordan:—Shaveh Kiriathaim {1x}. See: BDB—1001a.

7742. שׂוּחַ {1x} **sûwach**, *soo'-akh;* a prim. root; to *muse* pensively:—meditate {1x}. See: TWOT—2255; BDB—962b, 1002a.

7743. שׁוּחַ {3x} **shûwach**, *shoo'-akh;* a prim. root; to *sink*, lit. or fig.:—bow down {1x}, incline {1x}, humble {1x}. See: TWOT—2343.1; BDB—1001b, 1008a, 1009d, 1060c.

7744. שׁוּחַ {2x} **Shûwach**, *shoo'-akh;* from 7743; *dell; Shûach*, a son of Abraham:—Shuah {2x}. See: BDB—1001d.

7745. שׁוּחָה {5x} **shûwchâh**, *shoo-khaw';* from 7743; a *chasm:*—ditch {4x}, pit {1x}. See: TWOT—2343.1a; BDB—1001c.

7746. שׁוּחָה {1x} **Shûwchâh**, *shoo-khaw';* the same as 7745; *Shuchah,* an Isr.:—Shuah {1x}. See: BDB—1001d.

7747. שׁוּחִי {5x} **Shuchîy**, *shoo-khee';* patron. from 7744; a *Shuchite* or desc. of Shuach:—Shuhite {5x}. See: BDB—1001d.

7748. שׁוּחָם {1x} **Shûwchâm**, *shoo-khawm';* from 7743; *humbly; Shucham,* an Isr.:—Shuham {1x}. See: BDB—1001d.

7749. שׁוּחָמִי {2x} **Shûwchâmîy**, *shoo-khaw-mee';* patron. from 7748; a *Shuchamite* (collect.):—Shuhamites {2x}. See: BDB—1001d.

7750. שׂוּט {2x} **sûwt**, *soot;* or (by perm.)

סוּט **çûwt**, *soot;* a prim. root; to *detrude,* i.e. (intr. and fig.) *become derelict* (wrongly practise; namely, idolatry):—turn aside to {2x}. See: TWOT—2240; BDB—962b.

7751. שׁוּט {13x} **shûwt**, *shoot;* a prim. root; prop. to *push* forth; (but used only fig.) to *lash,* i.e. (the sea with oars) to *row;* by impl. to *travel:*—run to and fro {6x}, go to and fro {2x}, go about {1x}, gone {1x}, mariners {1x}, rowers {1x}, go through {1x}. See: TWOT—2344, 2344d; BDB—967b, 1001d, 1002b.

7752. שׁוֹט {11x} **shôwt**, *shote;* from 7751; a *lash* (lit. or fig.):—scourge {5x}, whip {6x}. See: TWOT—2344a; BDB—1002a, 1002b.

7753. שׂוּךְ {3x} **sûwk**, *sook;* a prim. root; to *entwine,* i.e. *shut* in (for formation, protection or restraint):—fence {1x}, make an hedge {1x}, hedge up {1x}. See: TWOT—2241; BDB—962b, 968a.

7754. שׂוֹךְ {2x} **sôwk**, *soke;* or (fem.)

שׂוֹכָה **sôwkâh**, *so-kaw';* from 7753; a *branch* (as *interleaved*):—bough {2x}. See: TWOT—2242a, 2242b; BDB—962c.

7755. שׂוֹכֹה {8x} **Sôwkôh**, *so-ko';* or

שֹׂכֹה **Sôkôh**, *so-ko';* or

שׂוֹכוֹ **Sôwkôw**, *so-ko';* from 7753; *Sokoh* or *Soko,* the name of two places in Pal.:—Socoh {2x}, Shochoh {2x}, Sochoh {1x}, Shoco {1x}, Socho {1x}, Shocho {1x}. See: BDB—962c.

7756. שׂוּכָתִי {1x} **Sûwkâthîy**, *soo-kaw-thee';* prob. patron. from a name corresp. to 7754 (fem.); a *Sukathite* or desc. of an unknown Isr. named Sukah:—Suchathite {1x}. See: BDB—962c.

7757. שׁוּל {11x} **shûwl**, *shool;* from an unused root mean. to *hang* down; a *skirt;* by impl. a bottom *edge:*—hem {6x}, skirt {4x}, train {1x}. See: TWOT—2346a; BDB—1002c.

7758. שׁוֹלָל {4x} **shôwlâl**, *sho-lawl';* or

שֵׁילָל **shêylâl** (Mic. 1:8), *shay-lawl';* from 7997; *nude* (espec. bare-foot); by impl. *captive:*—spoiled {2x}, stripped {2x}. See: TWOT—2399a; BDB—1002c, 1010a, 1021d.

7759. שׁוּלַמִּית {2x} **Shûwlammîyth**, *shoo-lam-meeth';* from 7999; *peaceful* (with the art. always pref., making it a pet name); the *Shulammith,* an epithet of Solomon's queen:—Shulamite {2x}. See: BDB—1002c, 1025a.

7760. שׂוּם {586x} **sûwm**, *soom;* or

שִׂים **sîym**, *seem;* a prim. root; to *put* (used in a great variety of applications, lit., fig., infer. and ellip.):—put {155x}, make {123x}, set {119x}, lay {64x}, appoint {19x}, give {11x}, set up {10x}, consider {8x}, turn {5x}, brought {4x}, ordain {3x}, place {3x}, take {3x}, shew {2x}, regard {2x}, mark {2x}, disposed {2x}, care {2x}, misc. {49x} = × any wise, call [a name], cast in, change, charge, commit, convey, determine, + disguise, do, get, heap up, hold, impute, leave, look, + name, × on, order, + paint, preserve, purpose, rehearse, reward, + stedfastly, × tell, + tread down, × wholly, work.

Siym means **(1)** to put or place someone somewhere (Gen 2:8). **(2)** In Ex 40:8 it means to set up, putting something so that it is perpendicular or vertical. **(3)** Figuratively, **(3a)** a "wall" is erected before someone (Mic 5:1; 1 Kin 20:12; 1 Sa 15:2); or **(3b)** something is set or put before one's mind (Ps 54:3; cf. Eze 14:4). **(4)** *Siym* denotes to set over, impose on negatively (Ex 1:11). **(5)** A more positive use of the word is to appoint (1 Sa 8:5). **(6)** *Siym* also means to put down in the sense of literally setting something on the ground, on a chair, or a flat surface (Gen 22:9). **(7)** In a related sense one puts down a distance or space between himself and someone else (Gen 30:36). **(8)** In Job 4:18 the word means to charge someone with an error, or to put it down against him. **(9)** It means to impute, lay to one's charge (1 Sa 22:15) or **(10)** to bring guilt upon one's self (Deut 22:8). **(11)** This verb is used of putting clothing on, setting it down upon one's body (Ruth 3:3).

(12) One may obligate someone with a task, impose/set it upon him (Ex 5:8). **(13)** When used **(13a)** with hand, it signifies **(13a1)** putting (Ex 4:21) or **(13b1)** taking something (Judg 4:21) into one's grasp, or **(13b)** putting hands on to arrest (2 Kin 11:16). **(14)** This verb may be used in giving in behalf of (Job 17:3) as the Servant of the Lord would "make his soul an offering for sin" (Is 53:10). **(15)** In Dan 1:7 *siym* signifies to assign something to, or give to as new names. **(16)** To place or put something on one's heart means **(16a)** to consider it (Is 47:7) or **(16b)** to pay heed to it (1 Sa 21:12). **(17)** The meaning to fix, as to fix something in a particular place, appears in Gen 24:47. **(18)** The word signifies the creation of the thing [fixing its nature] and its use [its disposition] in Ex 4:11 (cf. Gen 13:16). **(19)** It means to state, to appoint, or to assign (Ex 21:13). **(20)** It can mean to assign to continue, or to preserve (Gen 45:7; Ex 8:12). Syn.: 2803, 8667. See: TWOT—2243; BDB—962c, 965a, 967c, 1113d.

7761. שׂוּם {26x} **sûwm** (Aram.), *soom;* corresp. to 7760:—made {15x}, commanded {3x}, give {2x}, laid {2x}, have {1x}, named {1x}, misc. {2x} = + regard, set. See: TWOT—3006; BDB—1113d.

7762. שׁוּם {1x} **shûwm**, *shoom;* from an unused root mean. to *exhale; garlic* (from its rank *odor*):—garlic {1x}. See: TWOT—2347; BDB—1002c.

7763. שׁוֹמֵר {2x} **Shôwmêr**, *sho-mare';* or

שֹׁמֵר **Shômêr**, *sho-mare';* act. part. of 8104; *keeper; Shomer,* the name of two Isr.:—*Shomer* {2x}. See: BDB—1037c.

7764. שׁוּנִי {2x} **Shûwnîy**, *shoo-nee';* from an unused root mean. to *rest; quiet; Shuni,* an Isr.:—Shuni {2x}. See: BDB—1002c.

7765. שׁוּנִי {1x} **Shûwnîy**, *shoo-nee';* patron. from 7764; a *Shunite* (collect.) or desc. of Shuni:—Shunites {1x}. See: BDB—1002c.

7766. שׁוּנֵם {3x} **Shûwnêm**, *shoo-name';* prob. from the same as 7764; *quietly; Shunem,* a place in Pal:—Shunem {3x}. See: BDB—1002d.

7767. שׁוּנַמִּית {8x} **Shûwnammîyth**, *shoo-nam-meeth';* patrial from 7766; a *Shunammitess,* or female inhab. of Shunem:—Shunamite {8x}. See: BDB—1002d.

7768. שָׁוַע {21x} **shâvaʿ**, *shaw-vah';* a prim. root; prop. to *be free;* but used only caus. and refl. to *halloo* (for help, i.e. *freedom* from some trouble):—cried {17x}, cry out {2x}, aloud {1x}, shout {1x}. See: TWOT—2348; BDB—1002d.

7769. שׁוּעַ {2x} **shûwaʿ**, *shoo'-ah;* from 7768; a *halloo:*—cry {1x}, riches {1x}. See: TWOT—2348a; BDB—447d, 575d, 1002d, 1003a.

7770. שׁוּעַ {2x} **Shûwaʿ**, *shoo'-ah;* the same as 7769; *Shuä,* a Canaanite:—Shuah {2x}. See: BDB—447c.

7771. שׁוֹעַ {3x} **shôwaʿ**, *sho'-ah;* from 7768 in the orig. sense of *freedom;* a *noble,* i.e. *liberal, opulent;* also (as noun in the der. sense) a *halloo:*—bountiful {1x}, crying {1x}, rich {1x}. See: TWOT—929c, 2348b; BDB—447c, 1003a.

7772. שׁוֹעַ {1x} **Shôwaʿ**, *sho'-ah;* the same as 7771; *rich; Shoä,* an Oriental people:—Shoa {1x}. See: BDB—447c, 1003a.

7773. שֶׁוַע {1x} **shevaʿ**, *sheh'-vah;* from 7768; a *halloo:*—cry {1x}. See: TWOT—2348a; BDB—1002d.

7774. שׁוּעָא {2x} **Shûwʿâʾ**, *shoo-aw';* from 7768; *wealth; Shuä,* an Israelitess:—Shua {2x}. See: BDB—447d, 1003a.

7775. שַׁוְעָה {11x} **shavʿâh**, *shav-aw';* fem. of 7773; a *hallooing:*—cry {11x}. See: TWOT—2348c; BDB—1003a.

7776. שׁוּעָל {7x} **shûwʿâl**, *shoo-awl';* or

שֻׁעָל **shûʿâl**, *shoo-awl';* from the same as 8168; a *jackal* (as a *burrower*):—fox {7x}. See: TWOT—2433a; BDB—1043c.

7777. שׁוּעָל {2x} **Shûwʿâl**, *shoo-awl';* the same as 7776; *Shuäl,* the name of an Isr. and of a place in Pal.:—Shual {2x}. See: BDB—1043c.

7778. שׁוֹעֵר {37x} **shôwʿêr**, *sho-are';* or

שֹׁעֵר **shôʿêr**, *sho-are';* act. part. of 8176 (as denom. from 8179); a *janitor:*—doorkeepers {2x}, porter {35x}. See: TWOT—2437b; BDB—1045b.

7779. שׁוּף {4x} **shûwph**, *shoof;* a prim. root; prop. to *gape,* i.e. *snap* at; fig. to *overwhelm:*—break {1x}, bruise {2x}, cover {1x}. See: TWOT—2349; BDB—1003a.

7780. שׁוֹפָךְ {2x} **Shôwphâk**, *sho-fawk';* from 8210; *poured; Shophak,* a Syrian:—Shophach {2x}. See: BDB—1000c, 1003a.

7781. שׁוּפָמִי {1x} **Shûwphâmîy**, *shoo-faw-mee';* patron. from 8197; a *Shuphamite* (collect.) or desc. of Shephupham:—Shuphamites {1x}. See: BDB—1003a, 1050d, 1051b.

שׁוֹפָן **Shôwphân**. See 5855.

7782. שׁוֹפָר {72x} **shôwphâr**, *sho-far';* or

שֹׁפָר **shôphâr**, *sho-far';* from 8231 in the orig. sense of *incising;* a *cornet* (as giving a *clear* sound) or curved horn:—trumpet {68x}, cornet {4x}. See: TWOT—2449c; BDB—1051c.

7783. שׁוּק {3x} **shûwq**, *shook;* a prim. root; to *run* after or over, i.e. *overflow:*—overflow {2x}, water {1x}. See: TWOT—2351; BDB—1003b.

7784. שׁוּק {4x} **shûwq**, *shook;* from 7783; a *street* (as *run* over):—street {4x}. See: TWOT—2350b; BDB—1003b.

7785. שׁוֹק {19x} **shôwq**, *shoke;* from 7783; the (lower) *leg* (as a *runner*):—shoulder {13x}, legs {4x}, hip {1x}, thigh {1x}. See: TWOT—2350a; BDB—1003b, 1114d.

7786. שׂוּר {3x} **sûwr**, *soor;* a prim. root; prop. to *vanquish;* by impl. to *rule* (caus. *crown*):—reign {1x}, have power {1x}, made prince {1x}. See: TWOT—2287; BDB—975b, 979a. See 5493.

7787. שׂוּר {1x} **sûwr**, *soor;* a prim. root [rather ident. with 7786 through the idea of *reducing* to pieces; comp. 4883]; to *saw:*—cut {1x}. See: TWOT—2245; BDB—963a, 965a, 975b.

7788. שׁוּר {2x} **shûwr**, *shoor;* a prim. root; prop. to *turn,* i.e. *travel* about (as a harlot or a merchant):—went {1x}, sing {1x}. See: TWOT—2353; BDB—1003c. See also 7891.

7789. שׁוּר {16x} **shûwr**, *shoor;* a prim. root [rather ident. with 7788 through the idea of *going round* for inspection]; to *spy* out, i.e. (gen.) *survey,* (for evil) *lurk for,* (for good) *care for:*—behold {5x}, see {4x}, look {2x}, observe {2x}, lay wait {1x}, regard {1x}, perceive {1x}. See: TWOT—2354; BDB—1003d.

7790. שׁוּר {1x} **shûwr**, *shoor;* from 7889; a *foe* (as *lying in wait*):—enemy {1x}. See: TWOT—2354a; BDB—1004a.

7791. שׁוּר {4x} **shûwr**, *shoor;* from 7788; a *wall* (as *going about*):—wall {4x}. See: TWOT—2355b; BDB—1004b, 1004c, 1114d.

7792. שׁוּר {3x} **shûwr** (Aram.), *shoor;* corresp. to 7791:—wall {3x}. See: TWOT—3025; BDB—1114d.

7793. שׁוּר {6x} **Shûwr**, *shoor;* the same as 7791; *Shur,* a region of the Desert:—Shur {6x}. See: BDB—1004b.

7794. שׁוֹר {78x} **shôwr**, *shore;* from 7788; a *bullock* (as a *traveller*):—ox {62x}, bullock {12x}, cow {2x}, bull {1x}, wall {1x}. See: TWOT—2355a; BDB—1004a, 1117d.

7795. שׂוֹרָה {1x} **sôwrâh**, *so-raw';* from 7786 in the prim. sense of 5493; prop. a *ring,* i.e. (by anal.) a *row* (adv.):—principal {1x}. See: TWOT—2245a; BDB—965a, 975b.

שׂוֹרֵק **sôwrêq**. See 8321.

7796. שׂוֹרֵק {1x} **Sôwrêq**, *so-rake';* the same as 8321; a *vine; Sorek,* a valley in Pal.:—Sorek {1x}. See: BDB—977d.

7797. שׂוּשׂ {27x} **sûws**, *soos;* or

שִׂישׂ **sîys**, *sece;* a prim. root; to *be bright,* i.e. *cheerful:*—rejoice {20x}, glad {4x}, greatly {1x}, joy {1x}, mirth {1x}. See: TWOT—2246; BDB—965a.

7798. שַׁוְשָׁא {1x} **Shavshâ'**, *shav-shaw';* from 7797; *joyful; Shavsha,* an Isr.:—Shavsha {1x}. See: BDB—1004c.

7799. שׁוּשַׁן {15x} **shûwshan**, *shoo-shan';* or

שׁוֹשָׁן **shôwshân**, *sho-shawn';* or

שֹׁשָׁן **shôshân**, *sho-shawn';* and (fem.)

שׁוֹשַׁנָּה **shôwshannâh**, *sho-shan-naw';* from 7797; a *lily* (from its *whiteness*), as a flower or arch. ornament; also a (straight) *trumpet* (from the *tubular* shape):—lily {13x}, Shoshannim {2x}. See: TWOT—2356; BDB—1004c.

7800. שׁוּשַׁן {21x} **Shûwshan**, *shoo-shan';* the same as 7799; *Shushan,* a place in Pers.:—Shushan {21x}. See: BDB—1004d.

7801. שׁוּשַׁנְכִי {1x} **Shûwshankîy** (Aram.), *shoo-shan-kee';* of for. or.; a *Shushankite* (collect.) or inhab. of some unknown place in Ass.:—Susanchites {1x}. See: BDB—1114d.

7802. שׁוּשַׁן עֵדוּת {2x} **Shûwshan ʽÊdûwth**, *shoo-shan' ay-dooth';* or (plur. of former)

שׁוֹשַׁנִּים עֵדוּת **Shôwshannîym ʽÊdûwth**, *sho-shan-neem' ay-dooth';* from 7799 and 5715; *lily* (or *trumpet*) *of assemblage; Shushan-Eduth* or *Shoshannim-Eduth,* the title of a popular song:—Shoshannimeduth {1x}, Shushaneduth {1x}. See: BDB—1004c.

שׁוּשַׁק **Shûwshaq**. See 7895.

7803. שׁוּתֶלַח {4x} **Shûwthelach**, *shoo-theh'-lakh;* prob. from 7582 and the same as 8520; *crash of breakage; Shuthelach,* the name of two Isr.:—Shuthelah {4x}. See: BDB—1004d.

7804. שְׁזַב {9x} **shᵉzab** (Aram.), *shez-ab';* corresp. to 5800; to *leave,* i.e. (caus.) *free:*—deliver {9x}. See: TWOT—3027; BDB—1095c, 1115a.

7805. שָׁזַף {3x} **shâzaph**, *shaw-zaf';* a prim. root; to *tan* (by sun-burning); fig. (as if by a piercing ray) to *scan:*—see {2x}, look {1x}. See: TWOT—2357; BDB—1004d.

7806. שָׁזַר {21x} **shâzar**, *shaw-zar';* a prim. root; to *twist* (a thread of straw):—twine {21x}. See: TWOT—2358; BDB—1004d.

7807. שַׁח {1x} **shach**, *shakh;* from 7817; *sunk,* i.e. *downcast:*—+ humble {1x}. See: TWOT—2361a; BDB—1005a, 1006a.

7808. שֵׂחַ {1x} **sêach**, *say'-akh;* for 7879; *communion,* i.e. (refl.) *meditation:*—thought {1x}. See: TWOT—2255c; BDB—965c, 967b.

7809. שָׁחַד {2x} **shâchad**, *shaw-khad';* a prim. root; to *donate,* i.e. *bribe:*—reward {1x}, hire {1x}. See: TWOT—2359; BDB—1005a, 1007c.

7810. שַׁחַד {23x} **shachad**, *shakh'-ad;* from 7809; a *donation* (venal or redemptive):—gift {10x}, reward {7x}, bribes {3x}, present {2x}, bribery {1x}. See: TWOT—2359a; BDB—1005a.

7811. שָׂחָה {3x} **sâchâh**, *saw-khaw';* a prim. root; to *swim;* caus. to *inundate:*—swim {3x}. See: TWOT—2247; BDB—965c.

7812. שָׁחָה {172x} **shâchâh**, *shaw-khaw';* a prim. root; to *depress,* i.e. *prostrate* (espec. refl. in homage to royalty or God):—worship {99x}, bow {31x}, bow down {18x}, obeisance {9x}, reverence {5x}, fall down {3x}, themselves {2x}, stoop {1x}, crouch {1x}, misc. {3x}.

Shachah portrays **(1)** the act of bowing down in homage by an inferior **(1a)** before a superior ruler (1 Sa 24:8), and **(1b)** before a social or economic superior to whom one bows (Ruth 2:10). **(2)** It is the common term for coming before God in worship (1 Sa 15:25; Jer 7:2). **(3)** Other gods and idols are also the object of such worship by one's prostrating oneself before them (Is 2:20; 44:15, 17). Syn.: 5457. See: TWOT—2360; BDB—1005b.

7813. שָׂחוּ {1x} **sâchûw**, *saw'-khoo;* from 7811; a *pond* (for *swimming*):—swim {1x}. See: TWOT—2247a; BDB—965c.

7814. שְׂחוֹק {15x} **sᵉchôwq**, *sekh-oke';* or

שְׂחֹק **sᵉchôq**, *sekh-oke';* from 7832; *laughter* (in merriment or defiance):—laughter {6x}, derision {5x}, laughing {1x}, mock {1x}, laugh to scorn {1x}, sport {1x}. See: TWOT—1905d; BDB—966a.

7815. שְׁחוֹר {1x} **shᵉchôwr**, *shekh-ore';* from 7835; *dinginess,* i.e. perh. *soot:*—coal {1x}. See: TWOT—2368a; BDB—1005d, 1007a.

שִׁחוֹר **shîchôwr**. See 7883.

שָׁחוֹר **shâchôwr**. See 7838.

7816. שְׁחוּת {1x} **shᵉchûwth**, *shekh-ooth';* from 7812; *pit:*—pit {1x}. See: TWOT—2360a; BDB—1005c.

7817. שָׁחַח {21x} **shâchach**, *shaw-khakh';* a prim. root; to *sink* or *depress* (refl. or caus.):—bow down {5x}, cast down {4x}, bring down {3x}, brought low {2x}, bow {2x}, bending {1x}, couch {1x}, humbleth {1x}, low {1x}, stoop {1x}. See: TWOT—2361; BDB—1001c, 1005d.

7818. שָׂחַט {1x} **sâchaṭ**, *saw-khat';* a prim. root; to *tread* out, i.e. *squeeze* (grapes):—press {1x}. See: TWOT—2248; BDB—965c.

7819. שָׁחַט {81x} **shâchaṭ**, *shaw-khat';* a prim. root; to *slaughter* (in sacrifice or massacre):—kill 42, slay 36, offer {1x}, shot out {1x}, slaughter {1x}.

Shachat means "to slaughter, kill." **(1)** It first appears in Gen 22:10: "And Abraham . . . took the knife to slay his son." **(2)** Expressing "slaying" for sacrifice is the most frequent use of *shachat* (51 times); and as might be expected, the word is found some 30 times in the Book of Leviticus alone. **(3)** *Shachat* sometimes implies the "slaughtering" of animals for food (1 Sa 14:32, 34; Is 22:13). **(4)** The word is used of the "killing" of people a number of times (Judg 12:6; 1 Kin 18:40; 2 Kin 10:7, 14). **(5)** Sometimes God is said "to slay" people (Num 14:16). **(6)** Backslidden Judah went so far as "to slaughter" children as sacrifices to false gods (Eze 16:21; 23:39; Is 57:5). Syn.: 2026, 7523. See: TWOT—2362; BDB—1006a, 1006b.

7820. שָׁחַט {5x} **shâchaṭ**, *shaw-khat';* a prim. root [rather ident. with 7819 through the idea of *striking*]; to *hammer* out:—beaten {5x}. See: TWOT—2362; BDB—1006a.

7821. שְׁחִיטָה {1x} **shᵉchîyṭâh**, *shekh-ee-taw';* from 7819; *slaughter:*—killing {1x}. See: TWOT—2362a; BDB—1006b.

7822. שְׁחִין {13x} **shᵉchîyn**, *shekh-een';* from an unused root prob. mean. to *burn; inflammation,* i.e. an *ulcer;*—boil {11x}, botch {2x}. See: TWOT—2364a; BDB—1006b, 1006c.

7823. שָׁחִיס {2x} **shâchîyç**, *shaw-khece';* or

סָחִישׁ **çâchîysh**, *saw-kheesh';* from an unused root appar. mean. to *sprout; after-growth:*—that which springeth of the same {2x}. See: TWOT—1484; BDB—695a, 1006b.

7824. שָׁחִיף {1x} **shâchîyph**, *shaw-kheef';* from the same as 7828; a *board* (as *chipped* thin):—cieled {1x}. See: TWOT—2249; BDB—965d, 1006b.

7825. שְׁחִית {2x} **shᵉchîyth**, *shekh-eeth';* from 7812; a *pit*-fall (lit. or fig.):—destruction {1x}, pit {1x}. See: TWOT—2360b; BDB—1005d.

7826. שַׁחַל {7x} **shachal**, *shakh'-al;* from an unused root prob. mean. to *roar;* a *lion* (from his characteristic *roar*):—lion {4x}, fierce lion {3x}. See: TWOT—2363a; BDB—1006c.

7827. שְׁחֵלֶת {1x} **shᵉchêleth**, *shekh-ay'-leth;* appar. from the same as 7826 through some obscure idea, perh. that of *peeling* off by concussion of sound; a *scale* or shell, i.e. the aromatic *mussel:*—onycha {1x}. See: TWOT—2363b; BDB—1006c.

7828. שָׁחַף {2x} **shachaph**, *shakh'-af;* from an unused root mean. to *peel,* i.e. *emaciate;* the *gull* (as *thin*):—cuckow {2x}. See: TWOT—2365a; BDB—1006d.

7829. שַׁחֶפֶת {2x} **shachepheth**, *shakh-eh'-feth;* from the same as 7828; *emaciation:*—consumption {2x}. See: TWOT—2365b; BDB—1006d.

7830. שַׁחַץ {2x} **shachats**, *shakh'-ats;* from an unused root appar. mean. to *strut; haughtiness* (as evinced by the attitude):—lion {1x}, pride {1x}. See: TWOT—2366a; BDB—1006d.

7831. שַׁחֲצוֹם {1x} **Shachatsôwm**, *shakh-ats-ome';* from the same as 7830; *proudly; Shachatsom,* a place in Pal.:—Shahazimah {1x}. See: BDB—1006d.

7832. שָׂחַק {36x} **sâchaq**, *saw-khak';* a prim. root; to *laugh* (in pleasure or detraction); by impl. to *play:*—play {10x}, laugh {10x}, rejoice {3x}, scorn {3x}, sport {3x}, merry {2x}, mock {2x}, deride {1x}, derision {1x}, mockers {1x}. See: TWOT—1905c; BDB—965d.

7833. שָׁחַק {4x} **shâchaq**, *shaw-khak';* a prim. root; to *comminate* (by trituration or attrition):—beat {3x}, wear {1x}. See: TWOT—2367; BDB—1006d.

7834. שַׁחַק {21x} **shachaq**, *shakh'-ak;* from 7833; a *powder* (as *beaten* small): by anal. a thin *vapor;* by extens. the *firmament:*—cloud {11x}, sky {7x}, heaven {2x}, small dust {1x}. Syn.: 1534, 6160, 8064. See: TWOT—2367a; BDB—1007a.

שְׂחֹק **s**ᵉ**chôq**. See 7814.

7835. שָׁחַר {1x} **shâchar**, *shaw-khar';* a prim. root [rather ident. with 7836 through the idea of the *duskiness* of early dawn]; to *be dim* or dark (in color):—black {1x}. See: TWOT—2368; BDB—1007a, 1009d.

7836. שָׁחַר {12x} **shâchar**, *shaw-khar';* a prim. root; prop. to *dawn,* i.e. (fig.) *be* (up) *early* at any task (with the impl. of earnestness); by extens. to *search* for (with painstaking):—seek early {4x}, seek {2x}, diligently seek {2x}, betimes {1x}, misc. {3x} = [do something] betimes, enquire early, rise (seek) betimes, seek (diligently) early, in the morning. See: TWOT—2369; BDB—1007c.

7837. שַׁחַר {24x} **shachar**, *shakh'-ar;* from 7836; *dawn* (lit., fig. or adv.):—morning {12x}, day {6x}, early {2x}, dayspring {1x}, light {1x}, riseth {1x}, Shahar {1x}. See: TWOT—2369a; BDB—1007b.

שִׁחֹר **Shîchôr**. See 7883.

7838. שָׁחֹר {6x} **shâchôr**, *shaw-khore';* or

שָׁחוֹר **shâchôwr**, *shaw-khore';* from 7835; prop. *dusky,* but also (absol.) *jetty:*—black {6x}. See: TWOT—2368b; BDB—1007b.

7839. שַׁחֲרוּת {1x} **shachărûwth**, *shakh-ar-ooth';* from 7836; a *dawning,* i.e. (fig.) *juvenescence:*—youth {1x}. See: TWOT—2368c; BDB—1007b, 1007d.

7840. שְׁחַרְחֹרֶת {1x} **sh**ᵉ**charchôreth**, *shekh-ar-kho'-reth;* from 7835; *swarthy:*—black {1x}. See: TWOT—2368d; BDB—1007b.

7841. שְׁחַרְיָה {1x} **Sh**ᵉ**charyâh**, *shekh-ar-yaw';* from 7836 and 3050; *Jah has sought; Shecharjah,* an Isr.:—Sheariah {1x}. See: BDB—1007d.

7842. שַׁחֲרַיִם {1x} **Shachărayim**, *shakh-ar-ah'-yim;* dual of 7837; *double dawn; Shacharajim,* an Isr.:—Shaharaim {1x}. See: BDB—1007d.

7843. שָׁחַת {147x} **shâchath**, *shaw-khath';* a prim. root; to *decay,* i.e. (caus.) *ruin* (lit. or fig.):—destroy {96x}, corrupt {22x}, mar {7x}, destroyer {3x}, corrupters {2x}, waster {2x}, spoilers {2x}, battered {1x}, corruptly {1x}, misc. {11x} = cast off, destruction, lose, perish, spill, × utterly, waste.

This word especially marks dissolution or corruption and also to the physical destruction of all that was living on the earth and of the earth itself. **(1)** Anything that is good can be corrupted or spoiled: **(1a)** all on the earth (Gen 6:11–12, 17); **(1b)** Jeremiah's loincloth (Jer 13:7), **(1c)** a vineyard (Jer 12:10), **(1d)** cities (Gen 13:10), and **(1e)** a temple (Lam 2:6). **(2)** *Shachath* has the meaning of to waste when words are inappropriately spoken (Prov 23:8). **(3)** In its participial form, it describes **(3a)** a destroying lion (Jer 2:30v) and **(3b)** the destroying angel (1 Chr 21:15). **(4)** The word symbolizes a trap in Jer 5:26. **(5)** *Shachath* is used frequently by the prophets in the sense of "to corrupt morally" (Is 1:4; Eze 23:11; Zeph 3:7). Syn.: 7585. See: TWOT—2370; BDB—1007d, 1115a.

7844. שְׁחַת {3x} **sh**ᵉ**chath** (Aram.), *shekh-ath';* corresp. to 7843:—fault {2x}, corrupt {1x}. See: TWOT—3026; BDB—1115a.

7845. שַׁחַת {23x} **shachath**, *shakh'-ath;* from 7743; a *pit* (espec. as a trap); fig. *destruction:*—corruption {4x}, pit {14x}, destruction {2x}, ditch {2x}, grave {1x}. See: TWOT—2343.1c, 2370d; BDB—1001c, 1008b, 1008d.

7846. שֵׂט {1x} **sêt**, *sayte;* or

סֵט **çêt**, *sayt;* from 7750; a *departure* from right, i.e. *sin:*—revolters {1x}. See: TWOT—2240a; BDB—962b, 966a.

7847. שָׂטָה {6x} **sâṭâh**, *saw-taw';* a prim. root; to *deviate* from duty:—go aside {4x}, turn {1x}, decline {1x}. See: TWOT—2250; BDB—966a.

7848. שִׁטָּה {28x} **shiṭṭâh**, *shit-taw';* fem. of a der. [only in the plur.

שִׁטִּים **shiṭṭîym**, *shit-teem';* mean. the *sticks* of wood] from the same as 7850; the *acacia* (from its *scourging* thorns):—shittim {27x}, shittah tree {1x}. See: TWOT—2371; BDB—1008d. See also 1029.

7849. שָׁטַח {6x} **shâṭach**, *shaw-takh';* a prim. root; to *expand:*—spread {3x}, enlarge {1x}, stretch out {1x}, all abroad {1x}. See: TWOT—2372; BDB—1008d.

7850. שֹׁטֵט {1x} **shôṭêṭ**, *sho-tate';* act. part. of an otherwise unused root mean. (prop. to *pierce;* but only as a denom. from 7752) to *flog;* a *goad:*—scourge {1x}. See: TWOT—2344b; BDB—1002b, 1009a.

7851. שִׁטִּים {5x} **Shiṭṭîym**, *shit-teem';* the same as the plur. of 7848; *acacia* trees; *Shittim,* a place E. of the Jordan:—Shittim {5x}. See: BDB—1008d.

7852. שָׂטַם {6x} **sâṭam**, *saw-tam';* a prim. root; prop. to *lurk* for, i.e. *persecute:*—hate {5x}, oppose {1x}. See: TWOT—2251; BDB—966b.

7853. שָׂטַן {6x} **sâṭan**, *saw-tan';* a prim. root; to *attack,* (fig.) *accuse:*—adversary {5x}, resist {1x}. See: TWOT—2252; BDB—966c.

7854. שָׂטָן {27x} **sâṭân**, *saw-tawn';* from 7853; an *opponent;* espec. (with the art. pref.) *Satan,* the arch-enemy of good:—*Satan* {19x}, adversary {7x}, withstand {1x}.

Satan is an adversary or plotter, one who devises means for opposition. *Satan* means "adversary; *Satan.*" **(1)** In Ps 38:20, David cried out because he was the target of attack by his "adversaries": "They also that render evil for good are mine adversaries; because I follow *the thing that* good *is.*" **(2)** In another psalm of distress by an individual, a godly man expressed his deep faith in the Lord. The writer prayed concerning those who were "adversaries" to his soul: "Let them be confounded and consumed that are adversaries to my soul; let them be covered with reproach and dishonor that seek my hurt" (Ps 71:13). He expressed the reality of the powers of darkness against an individual who sought to live for God.

(3) Imprecatory psalms call for judgment upon one's enemies. **(3a)** David's enemies became his "adversaries," but he continued to pray for them (Ps 109:4). **(3b)** Because those enemies repaid him evil for good and hatred for his love, the king prayed: "Set thou a wicked man over him: and let *Satan* stand at his right hand" (Ps 109:6). **(3c)** When they spoke evil against his soul, David called for the Lord's reward against his "adversaries" (Ps 109:20), and finally, **(3d)** because David's accusers had intended him so much harm, he asked that his accusers be clothed with shame and dishonor (Ps 109:29). **(3e)** In all of these passages, God worked indirectly by permitting individuals to act as "adversaries" of His people. **(4)** In another instance, David was merciful with members of Saul's family who cursed him and wished him harm when he fled from Absalom (2 Sa 16:5ff.). **(4a)** David restrained his army commanders from killing Saul's family who had repented of their misdeeds. **(4b)** The king did not want his officers to be his "adversaries" on the day of victory and joy (2 Sa 19:22).

(5) God can also be the "adversary." When Balaam went to curse the sons of Israel, God warned him not to do so. **(5a)** When the prophet persisted, God disciplined him: "And God's anger was kindled because he went: and the angel of the Lord stood in the way for an adversary against him" (Num 22:22). **(5b)** God stood as an "adversary" because no curse could undo the covenants and agreements already made with Israel. **(6)** God took up a controversy with Solomon. **(6a)** When Solomon added more and more pagan wives to his harem, God was greatly displeased (Deut 17:17). **(6b)** But when the king built pagan shrines for his wives, God raised up "adversaries" against him (1 Kin 11:14), a direct action which caused the Edomites and Syrians to revolt against Israel. **(7)** Another special instance of intervention was the occasion when ". . . *Satan* [literally, "an adversary"] stood up against Israel, and provoked David to number Israel" (1 Chr 21:1). (No definite article is here in Hebrew and, therefore, "an adversary" is in mind.)

(8) In a parallel passage the Lord moved David to number Israel and Judah (2 Sa 24:1). Even as the Lord stirred up an "adversary" against Solomon, so here God took a direct action to test David to help him learn a vital lesson. God tests believers to help them make the right choices and not depend upon their own human strength. **(9)** In the Book of Job, the word *Satan* always has the definite article preceding it (Job 1:6–12; 2:1–7), so the term emphasizes *Satan*'s role as "the adversary." **(9a)** God permitted *Satan* to test Job's faith, and the adversary inflicted the patriarch with many evils and sorrows. **(9b)** *Satan* was not all-powerful because he indicated that he could not get beyond God's protection of Job (Job 1:10).

(9c) He penetrated the "hedge" only with God's permission and only for specific instances that would demonstrate God's righteousness.

(10) Zechariah recorded a vision of "... Joshua the high priest standing before the angel of the Lord, and *Satan* standing at his right hand to resist him" (literally, "be his adversary"; Zec 3:1). **(10a)** The Lord rebuked "the adversary" (Zec 3:2). **(10b)** *Satan* was once again in conflict with God's purposes and the angels of God, but "the adversary" was not all-powerful and was subject to rebuke by God Himself **(11)** A general usage of *satan* ("adversary") appears in 1 Kin 5:4: "But now the Lord my God hath given me rest on every side, so that there is neither adversary or evil occurrent." **(12)** In another instance, David went over to the side of the Philistines; in attempting to fight with them against Israel, some of the Philistine leaders doubted David's sincerity and felt that he would be "an adversary" in any battle between the two armies (1 Sa 29:4). Syn.: 7700, 8163. See: TWOT—2252a; BDB—966b.

7855. שִׂטְנָה {1x} **sitnâh**, *sit-naw';* from 7853; *opposition* (by letter):—accusation {1x}. See: TWOT—2252b; BDB—966c.

7856. שִׂטְנָה {1x} **Sitnâh**, *sit-naw';* the same as 7855; *Sitnah*, the name of a well in Pal.:—*Sitnah* {1x}. See: BDB—966c.

7857. שָׁטַף {13x} **shâṭaph**, *shaw-taf';* a prim. root; to *gush;* by impl. to *inundate, cleanse;* by anal. to *gallop, conquer:*—overflow {20x}, rinsed {3x}, wash away {2x}, drown {1x}, flowing {1x}, misc. {4x} = overwhelm, run, rush. Syn.: 1740, 3526, 7364. See: TWOT—2373; BDB—1009a.

7858. שֶׁטֶף {6x} **sheṭeph**, *sheh'-tef;* or

שֵׁטֶף **shêṭeph**, *shay'-tef;* from 7857; a *deluge* (lit. or fig.):—flood {1x}, overflowing of waters {1x}, outrageous {1x}. See: TWOT—2373a; BDB—1009b.

7859. שְׁטַר {1x} **sᵉṭar** (Aram.), *set-ar';* of uncert. der.; a *side:*—one side {1x}. See: TWOT—3007; BDB—1113d.

7860. שֹׁטֵר {25x} **shôṭêr**, *sho-tare';* act. part. of an otherwise unused root prob. mean. to *write;* prop. a *scribe*, i.e. (by anal. or impl.) an official *superintendent* or *magistrate:*—officers {23x}, ruler {1x}, overseer {1x}. See: TWOT—2374a; BDB—1009c, 1104c.

7861. שִׁטְרַי {1x} **Shitray**, *shit-rah'-ee;* from the same as 7860; *magisterial; Shitrai*, an Isr.:—Shitrai {1x}. See: BDB—1009c, 1056c.

7862. שַׁי {3x} **shay**, *shah'-ee;* prob. from 7737; a *gift* (as *available*):—present {3x}. See: TWOT—2375; BDB—1009c.

7863. שִׂיא {1x} **sîyʾ**, *see;* from the same as 7721 by perm.; *elevation:*—excellency {1x}. See: TWOT—1421i; BDB—673b, 966c.

7864. שְׁיָא {1x} **Shᵉyâʾ**, *sheh-yaw';* for 7724; *Sheja*, an Isr.:—Sheva {1x}. See: BDB—1009d.

7865. שִׂיאֹן {1x} **Sîyʾôn**, *see-ohn';* from 7863; *peak; Sion*, the summit of Mt. Hermon:—Sion {1x}. See: BDB—673b, 966c.

7866. שִׁאיוֹן {1x} **Shîʾyôwn**, *shee-ohn';* from the same as 7722; *ruin; Shijon*, a place in Pal.:—Shion {1x}. See: BDB—1009d.

7867. שִׂיב {2x} **sîyb**, *seeb;* a prim. root; prop. to *become aged*, i.e. (by impl.) to *grow gray:*—grayheaded {2x}. See: TWOT—2253; BDB—959a, 966c.

7868. שִׂיב {5x} **sîyb** (Aram.), *seeb;* corresp. to 7867:—elder {5x}. See: TWOT—3008; BDB—1114a.

7869. שֵׂיב {1x} **sêyb**, *sabe;* from 7867; old *age:*—age {1x}. See: TWOT—2253a; BDB—966c, 1114a.

7870. שִׁיבָה {1x} **shîybâh**, *shee-baw';* by perm. from 7725; a *return* (of property):—captivity {1x}. See: TWOT—2340b; BDB—1000a, 1009d.

7871. שִׁיבָה {1x} **shîybâh**, *shee-baw';* from 3427; *residence:*—lay {1x}. See: TWOT—922b; BDB—444a, 1000a, 1009d.

7872. שֵׂיבָה {19x} **sêybâh**, *say-baw';* fem. of 7869; old *age:*—old age {6x}, gray hairs {6x}, hoar head {3x}, hoary head {2x}, grayheaded {1x}, hoary {1x}. See: TWOT—2253b; BDB—966c.

7873. שִׂיג {1x} **sîyg**, *seeg;* from 7734; a *withdrawal* (into a private place):—pursuing {1x}. See: TWOT—1469a; BDB—691a, 966d.

7874. שִׂיד {2x} **sîyd**, *seed;* a prim. root prob. mean. to *boil* up (comp. 7736); used only as denom. from 7875; to *plaster:*—plaister {2x}. See: TWOT—2254; BDB—966d.

7875. שִׂיד {4x} **sîyd**, *seed;* from 7874; *lime* (as *boiling* when slacked):—plaister {2x}, lime {2x}. See: TWOT—2254a; BDB—966d.

7876. שָׁיָה {1x} **shâyâh**, *shaw-yaw';* a prim. root; to *keep* in memory:—be unmindful {1x}. See: TWOT—1428; BDB—1009d. [Render Deut 32:18, "A Rock bore thee, *thou must recollect;* and (yet) thou hast forgotten," etc.]

7877. שִׁיזָא {1x} **Shîyzâʾ**, *shee-zaw';* of unknown der.; *Shiza*, an Isr.:—Shiza {1x}. See: BDB—1009d.

7878. שִׂיחַ {20x} **sîyach**, *see'-akh;* a prim. root; to *ponder*, i.e. (by impl.) *converse* (with oneself, and hence, aloud) or (tran.) *utter:*—talk {5x}, meditate {5x}, speak {4x}, complain {2x}, pray {1x}, commune {1x}, muse {1x}, declare {1x}. See: TWOT—2255; BDB—967a, 1002a.

7879. שִׂיחַ {14x} **sîyach**, *see'-akh;* from 7878; a *contemplation;* by impl. an *utterance:*—complaint {9x}, meditation {1x}, prayer {1x}, talking {1x}, communication {1x}, babbling {1x}. See: TWOT—2255a; BDB—967a.

7880. שִׂיחַ {4x} **sîyach**, *see'-akh;* from 7878; a *shoot* (as if *uttered* or put forth), i.e. (gen.) *shrubbery:*—bush {2x}, plant {1x}, shrub {1x}. See: TWOT—2256a; BDB—967b.

7881. שִׂיחָה {3x} **sîychâh**, *see-khaw';* fem. of 7879; *reflection;* by extens. *devotion:*—meditation {2x}, prayer {1x}. Syn.: 577, 4994, 6279, 6419, 6739, 7592. See: TWOT—2255b; BDB—967a.

7882. שִׁיחָה {3x} **shîychâh**, *shee-khaw';* for 7745; a *pit-*fall:—pit {3x}. See: TWOT—2343.1b; BDB—1001c, 1009d.

7883. שִׁיחוֹר {4x} **Shîychôwr**, *shee-khore';* or

שִׁחוֹר **Shîchôwr**, *shee-khore';* or

שִׁחֹר **Shîchôr**, *shee-khore';* prob. from 7835; *dark*, i.e. *turbid; Shichor*, a stream of Egypt:—Shihor {1x}, Sihor {3x}. See: BDB—1005d, 1007a, 1009d.

7884. שִׁיחוֹר לִבְנָת {1x} **Shîychôwr Libnâth**, *shee-khore' lib-nawth';* from the same as 7883 and 3835; *darkish whiteness; Shichor-Libnath*, a stream of Pal.:—Shihor-libnath {1x}. See: BDB—527d, 1009d.

7885. שַׁיִט {2x} **shayiṭ**, *shay'-yit;* from 7751; an *oar;* also (comp. 7752) a *scourge* (fig.):—oar {2x}. See: TWOT—2344c; BDB—1002a, 1002b, 1009d.

7886. שִׁילֹה {1x} **Shîylôh**, *shee-lo';* from 7951; *tranquil; Shiloh*, an epithet of the Messiah:—Shiloh {1x}. See: BDB—1010a.

7887. שִׁילֹה {32x} **Shîylôh**, *shee-lo';* or

שִׁלֹה **Shîlôh**, *shee-lo';* or

שִׁילוֹ **Shîylôw**, *shee-lo';* or

שִׁלוֹ **Shîlôw**, *shee-lo';* from the same as 7886; *Shiloh*, a place in Pal.:—Shiloh {32x}. See: BDB—1009d, 1017d.

7888. שִׁילוֹנִי {6x} **Shiylôwnîy**, *shee-lo-nee';* or

שִׁילֹנִי **Shîylônîy**, *shee-lo-nee';* or

שִׁלֹנִי **Shîlônîy**, *shee-lo-nee';* from 7887; a *Shilonite* or inhab. of Shiloh:—Shilonite {6x}. See: BDB—1009d, 1017c, 1018a, 1025b.

שֵׁילָל **shêylâl**. See 7758.

7889. שִׁימוֹן {1x} **Shîymôwn**, *shee-mone';* appar. for 3452; *desert; Shimon*, an Isr.:—Shimon {1x}. See: BDB—1010a.

7890. שַׁיִן {2x} **shayin**, *shah'-yin;* from an unused root mean. to *urinate; urine:*—piss {2x}. See: TWOT—2377a; BDB—1010a.

7891. שִׁיר {87x} **shîyr**, *sheer;* or (the orig. form)

שׁוּר **shûwr** (1 Sa 18:6), *shoor;* a prim. root [rather ident. with 7788 through the idea of *strolling* minstrelsy]; to *sing:*—sing {41x}, singer {37x}, singing men {4x}, singing women {4x}, behold {1x}.

I. ***Shiyr* (7891), as a verb,** means "to sing." **(1)** While it occurs 87 times in the Hebrew Old Testament, it is not used until Ex 15:1: "Then sang Moses and the children of Israel this song unto the Lord. . . ." One might wonder if it took the miracle of the Exodus from Egypt to give the Israelites something "to sing" about! **(2)** Over one quarter of the instances of *shiyr* are found in the Book of Psalms, often in the imperative form, calling the people to express their praise to God in singing. One such example is found in Ps 96:1: "O sing unto the Lord a new song: sing unto the Lord, all the earth." **(3)** Frequently *shiyr* is found in parallelism with *zamar* (2167), "to sing" (Ps 68:4, 32). **II. Shir, as a participle,** means "singers." **(1)** In the Books of Chronicles, *shiyr* is used in the participial form some 33 times to designate the Levitical "singers" (1 Chr 15:16). **(2)** "Female singers" are referred to occasionally (2 Sa 19:35; 2 Chr 35:25; Eccl 2:8). See: TWOT—2378; BDB—1010c.

7892. שִׁיר {90x} **shîyr**, *sheer;* or fem.

שִׁירָה **shîyrâh**, *shee-raw',* from 7891; a *song;* abstr. *singing:*—song {74x}, musick {7x}, singing {4x}, musical {2x}, sing {1x}, singers {1x}, song + 1697 {1x}.

Shiyr, as a noun, means "song." **(1)** This noun is found about 30 times in the titles of various psalms as well as elsewhere in the Old Testament. **(2)** *Shiyr* is used of a joyous "song" in Gen 31:27: ". . . And didst not tell me, that I might have sent thee away with mirth, and with songs, with tabret, and with harp?" **(3)** In Judg 5:12 the word refers to a triumphal "song," and **(4)** in Neh 12:46 the word is used of a religious "song" for worship. **(5)** The book that is commonly designated "The Song of Solomon" actually has the title "The Song of Songs" in Hebrew, a love "song," pure and simple, and that love has its rightful place in the divine plan for mature men and women. See: TWOT—2378a, 2378b; BDB—1010b, 1010c.

שִׂישׂ **sîys**. See 7797.

7893. שַׁיִשׁ {1x} **shayish**, *shah'-yish;* from an unused root mean. to *bleach,* i.e. *whiten; white,* i.e. *marble:*—marble {1x}. See: TWOT—2379; BDB—1010d. See 8336.

7894. שִׁישָׁא {1x} **Shîyshâ'**, *shee-shaw';* from the same as 7893; *whiteness; Shisha,* an Isr.:—Shisha {1x}. See: BDB—1010d.

7895. שִׁישַׁק {7x} **Shîyshaq**, *shee-shak';* or

שׁוּשַׁק **Shûwshaq**, *shoo-shak';* of Eg. der.; *Shishak,* an Eg. king:—Shishak {7x}. See: BDB—1004d, 1011a.

7896. שִׁית {85x} **shîyth**, *sheeth;* a prim. root; to *place* (in a very wide application):—set {23x}, made {19x}, lay {13x}, put {11x}, appoint {3x}, regard {2x}, misc. {14x} = apply, array, bring, consider, let alone, × look, mark, shew, be stayed, × take.

Shiyth, as a verb, means "to put, place, set, station, fix." **(1)** It occurs 85 times in the Hebrew Old Testament, for the first time in Gen 3:15: "And I will put enmity between thee and the woman. . . ." **(2)** Generally speaking, this word is a term of physical action, typically expressing movement from one place to another. **(3)** Often it expresses "putting" hands on someone or something: ". . . Joseph shall put his hand upon thine eyes [close your eyes]" (Gen 46:4). **(3a)** One may "put on" ornaments (Ex 33:4); **(3b)** Naomi laid her "grandchild" Obed in her bosom (Ruth 4:16); **(3c)** a fine may be "laid" on someone for injury (Ex 21:22). **(3d)** Sheep may be "set" or stationed, at a particular place (Gen 30:40). **(4)** "To set" one's heart to something is **(4a)** to give heed to, to pay attention (Ex 7:23). **(4b)** To set one's heart may also be to reflect: "Then I saw, and considered it [set my heart to it] . . ." (Prov 24:32).

(5) "To set" boundaries is "to set," or "fix," limits: "And I will set thy bounds from the Red Sea even unto the sea of the Philistines . . ." (Ex 23:31). **(6)** When Job cries: "Oh . . . that thou wouldest appoint me a set time, and remember me!" (Job 14:13), he wants limits "set" for him. **(7)** *Shiyth* is sometimes used to express the making of something: **(7a)** ". . . I will make him prince . . ." (1 Kin 11:34); **(7b)** "And I will lay it waste . . ." (Is 5:6); **(7c)** ". . . I will make thee a wilderness . . ." (Jer 22:6). See: TWOT—2380; BDB—1004d, 1011a, 1011d.

7897. שִׁית {1x} **shîyth**, *sheeth;* from 7896; a *dress* (as *put* on):—attire {1x}. See: TWOT—2380a; BDB—1011c.

7898. שַׁיִת {7x} **shayith**, *shah'-yith;* from 7896; *scrub* or *trash,* i.e. wild *growth* of weeds or briers (as if *put* on the field):—thorns {7x}. See: TWOT—2380c; BDB—1011d.

7899. שֵׂךְ {1x} **sêk**, *sake;* from 5526 in the sense of 7753; a *brier* (as of a hedge):—prick {1x}. See: TWOT—2262a; BDB—967c, 968a.

7900. שֹׂךְ {1x} **sôk**, *soke;* from 5526 in the sense of 7753; a *booth* (as *interlaced*):—tabernacle {1x}. Syn.: 168, 4264, 4908, 5521. See: TWOT—2260a; BDB—967c, 968a.

7901. שָׁכַב {212x} **shâkab**, *shaw-kab';* a prim. root; to *lie* down (for rest, sexual connection, decease or any other purpose):—lie {106x}, sleep {48x}, lie down {43x}, rest {3x}, lien {2x}, misc. {10x} = × at all, cast down, lodge, ravish, stay.

Shakab means "to lie down, lie, have sexual intercourse with." **(1)** Basically this verb signifies a person's lying down—**(1a)** though in Job 30:17 and Eccl 2:23 it refers to something other than a human being. **(1b)** *Shakab* is used of the state of reclining as opposed to sitting: "And every thing that she lieth upon in her [menstruation] shall be unclean: every thing also that she sitteth upon . . ." (Lev 15:20). **(2)** This general sense appears in several nuances. **(2a)** There is the meaning "to lie down to rest." **(2a1)** Elisha "came thither, and he turned into the chamber [which the Shunammite had prepared for his use], and lay there" (2 Kin 4:11). **(2a2)** Job remarks that his gnawing pains "take no rest" (Job 30:17; cf. Eccl 2:23). **(3)** *Shakab* can also be used of lying down on a bed, for example, when one is sick. Jonadab told Amnon: "Lay thee down on thy bed, and make thyself [pretend to be] sick . . ." (2 Sa 13:5). **(4)** The word can be used as an equivalent of the phrase "to go to bed": "But before they [Lot's visitors] lay down, the men of the city, even the men of Sodom, compassed the house round . . ." (Gen 19:4—the first occurrence of the verb).

(5) *Shakab* also signifies "lying down asleep." The Lord told Jacob: ". . . The land whereon thou liest, to thee will I give it, and to thy seed" (Gen 28:13). **(6)** In Ex 22:26–27 the verb denotes the act of sleeping more than the lying down: "If thou at all take thy neighbor's raiment to pledge, thou shalt deliver it unto him by that the sun goeth down . . . [In what else] shall he sleep?" **(7)** *Shakab* can also be used to mean "lodge" and thus refers to sleeping and eating. Israel's spies lodged with Rahab: "And they went, and came into a harlot's house, named Rahab, and lodged there" (Josh 2:1; cf. 2 Kin 4:11). **(8)** This verb can mean "to lie down" in a figurative sense of to be humbled or to be robbed of power. The trees of Lebanon are personified and say concerning the king of Babylon: "Since thou art laid down, no feller [tree cutter] is come up against us" (Is 14:8). **(9)** Used reflexively, *shakab* means "to humble oneself, to submit oneself": "We lie down in our shame . . ." (Jer 3:25). **(10)** Another special nuance is "to put something on its side": "Who can number the clouds in wisdom? Or who can [tip] the bottles of heaven, when the dust groweth into hardness, and the clods cleave fast together?" (Job 38:37–38).

(11) An emphasis of *shakab* is "to die," to lie down in death. Jacob instructed his sons as follows: "But I will lie with my fathers, and thou shalt carry me out of Egypt, and bury me in their burying place" (Gen 47:30). **(12)** This phrase ("lie down with one's fathers") does not necessarily refer to being buried or to dying an honorable death (cf. 1 Kin 22:40) but is a synonym for a human's dying. (It is never used of animals or inanimate things.) **(13)** The idea is that when one dies he no longer stands upright. Therefore, to "lie with one's fathers" parallels the concept of "lying down" in death. **(14)** *Shakab,* as 1 Kin 22:40 suggests, can refer to the state of being dead ("so Ahab slept with his fathers"), since v. 37 already reports that he had died and was buried in Samaria. **(15)** The verb used by itself may mean "to die," or "to lie dead"; cf. "At her feet he bowed, he fell, he lay [dead]: at her feet he bowed, he fell: where he bowed, there he fell down dead" (Judg 5:27). **(16)** Another major use of *shakab* is "to have sexual relations with." The first occurrence of this use is in Gen 19:32, where Lot's daughters say: "Come, let us make our father drink wine, and we will lie with him, that we may preserve seed of our father."

(17) Even when a physical "lying down" is not necessarily in view, the word is used of having sexual relations: "Whosoever lieth with a beast shall surely be put to death" (Ex 22:19). **(18)** The word is also used of homosexual activities (Lev 18:22). See: TWOT—2381; BDB—1011d, 1014d, 1115b.

7902. שְׁכָבָה {9x} **shᵉkâbâh**, *shek-aw-baw';* from 7901; a *lying* down (of dew, or for the sexual act):—copulation {3x}, lie {2x}, carnally {2x}, from him {1x}, not translated {1x}.

Shekabah means "layer of dew." In one of its 9 appearances, sekabah refers to a "layer of dew": ". . . and in the morning the dew lay round about the host" (Ex 16:13). See: TWOT—2381a; BDB—1012c.

7903. שְׁכֹבֶת {4x} **shᵉkôbeth**, *shek-o'-beth;* from 7901; a (sexual) *lying* with:—× lie {4x}.

Shekobeth refers to "copulation." This noun occurs rarely (4 times), as in Lev 18:20: "Moreover thou shalt not lie carnally with thy neighbor's wife, to defile thyself with her." See: TWOT—2381b; BDB—1012d.

7904. שָׁכָה {1x} **shâkâh**, *shaw-kaw';* a prim. root; to *roam* (through lust):—in the morning {1x}. See: TWOT—2382; BDB—1013a.

7905. שֻׂכָּה {1x} **sukkâh**, *sook-kaw';* fem. of 7900 in the sense of 7899; a *dart* (as pointed like a *thorn*):—barbed irons {1x}. See: TWOT—2262b; BDB—967c, 968a.

7906. שֵׂכוּ {1x} **Sêkûw**, *say'-koo;* from an unused root appar. mean. to *surmount;* an *observatory* (with the art.); *Seku,* a place in Pal.:—Sechu {1x}. See: BDB—967d.

7907. שֶׂכְוִי {1x} **sekvîy**, *sek-vee';* from the same as 7906; *observant,* i.e. (concr.) the *mind:*—heart {1x}. See: TWOT—2257a; BDB—967c.

7908. שְׁכוֹל {3x} **shᵉkôwl**, *shek-ole';* infin. of 7921; *bereavement:*—loss of children {2x}, spoiling {1x}. See: TWOT—2385a; BDB—1013d.

7909. שַׁכּוּל {6x} **shakkuwl**, *shak-kool';* or

שַׁכֻּל **shakkul**, *shak-kool';* from 7921; *bereaved:*—barren {2x}, robbed of whelps {2x}, bereaved of children {1x}, bereaved of whelps {1x}. See: TWOT—2385b, 2385c; BDB—1014a.

7910. שִׁכּוֹר {13x} **shikkôwr**, *shik-kore';* or

שִׁכֹּר **shikkôr**, *shik-kore';* from 7937; *intoxicated,* as a state or a habit:—drunken {5x}, drunkard {5x}, drunk {2x}, drunken man {1x}. See: TWOT—2388b; BDB—1016c.

7911. שָׁכַח {102x} **shâkach**, *shaw-kakh';* or

שָׁכֵחַ **shâkêach**, *shaw-kay'-akh;* a prim. root; to *mislay,* i.e. to *be oblivious of,* from want of memory or attention:—forget {61x}, forgotten {40x}, at all {1x}.

Shakeach, means "to forget." **(1)** *Shakeach* is found for the first time in the Old Testament in Gen 27:45, when Rebekah urges Jacob to flee his home until Esau "forget that which thou hast done to him." **(2)** As the people worshiped strange gods, Jeremiah reminded Judah that "all thy lovers have forgotten thee; they seek thee not" (Jer 30:14). **(3)** But God does not "forget" His people: "Can a woman forget her suckling child, that she should not have compassion on the son of her womb? yea, they may forget, yet will I not forget thee" (Is 49:15). **(4)** In spite of this, when destruction came, Judah complained: "Wherefore dost thou forget us for ever . . . ?" (Lam 5:20). **(5)** Israel would often "forget" God's law (Hos 4:6) and God's name (Jer 23:27). See: TWOT—2383; BDB—1013a.

7912. שְׁכַח {18x} **sh^ekach** (Aram.), *shek-akh';* corresp. to 7911 through the idea of disclosure of a *covered* or *forgotten* thing; to *discover* (lit. or fig.):—find {18x}. See: BDB—1115b.

7913. שָׁכֵחַ {2x} **shâkêach**, *shaw-kay'-akh;* from 7911; *oblivious:*—forget {2x}. See: TWOT—2383a; BDB—1013c.

7914. שְׂכִיָּה {1x} **s^ekîyâh**, *sek-ee-yaw';* fem. from the same as 7906; a *conspicuous* object:—picture {1x}. See: TWOT—2257b; BDB—967c.

7915. שַׂכִּין {1x} **sakkîyn**, *sak-keen';* intens. perh. from the same as 7906 in the sense of 7753; a *knife* (as *pointed* or edged):—knife {1x}. See: TWOT—2258; BDB—967d.

7916. שָׂכִיר {17x} **sâkîyr**, *saw-keer';* from 7936; a man *at wages* by the day or year:—hired servant {8x}, hireling {6x}, hired {2x}, hired man {1x}. See: TWOT—2264.1c; BDB—969b.

7917. שְׂכִירָה {1x} **s^ekîyrâh**, *sek-ee-raw';* fem. of 7916; a *hiring:*—hired {1x}. See: TWOT—2264.1c; BDB—969b.

7918. שָׁכַךְ {5x} **shâkak**, *shaw-kak';* a prim. root; to *weave* (i.e. *lay*) a trap; fig. (through the idea of *secreting*) to *allay* (passions; phys. *abate* a flood):—pacified {1x}, appeased {1x}, set {1x}, asswage {1x}, cease {1x}. See: TWOT—2384; BDB—968a, 1013c.

7919. שָׂכַל {63x} **sâkal**, *saw-kal';* a prim. root; to *be* (caus. *make* or *act*) *circumspect* and hence, *intelligent:*—understand {12x}, wise {12x}, prosper {8x}, wisely {6x}, understanding {5x}, consider {4x}, instruct {3x}, prudent {2x}, skill {2x}, teach {2x}, misc. {7x} = expert, prosper, have good success, wisdom, guide wittingly.

Sakal means "to be prudent, act wisely, give attention to, ponder, prosper." **(1)** Its first use in the text, in Gen 3:6, contributes to an interesting paradox, for while the forbidden fruit was "to be desired to make one wise," it was a very unwise thing to take it! **(2)** The basic meaning of *sakal* seems to be "to look at, to give attention to," as illustrated in this parallelism: "That they may see, and know, and consider, and understand . . ." (Is 41:20). **(3)** From this develops the connotation of insight, intellectual comprehension: "Let not the wise man glory in his wisdom . . . But let him that glorieth glory in this, that he understandeth and knoweth me . . ." (Jer 9:23–24). **(4)** As here, it is frequently used along with and in parallelism to the Hebrew yada (3045), "to know" (primarily experientially). **(5)** As is true of chakam (2450), "to be wise," *sakal* never concerns abstract prudence, but acting prudently: "Therefore the prudent shall keep silence . . ." (Amos 5:13); ". . . He hath left off to be wise . . ." (Ps 36:3). Syn.: 502, 995, 998, 2094, 2449, 3256, 4905, 8150, 8394. See: TWOT—2263, 2264; BDB—968a, 968d, 1114a.

7920. שְׂכַל {1x} **s^ekal** (Aram.), *sek-al';* corresp. to 7919:—consider {1x}. See: TWOT—3009; BDB—1114a.

7921. שָׁכֹל {25x} **shâkôl**, *shaw-kole';* a prim. root; prop. to *miscarry,* i.e. *suffer abortion;* by anal. to *bereave* (lit. or fig.):—bereave {10x}, barren {2x}, childless {2x}, cast young {2x}, cast a calf {1x}, lost children {1x}, rob of children {1x}, deprived {1x}, misc. {5x} = destroy, × expect, miscarry, spoil. See: TWOT—2385; BDB—1013c, 1014a.

7922. שֶׂכֶל {16x} **sekel**, *seh'-kel;* or

שֵׂכֶל **sêkel**, *say'-kel;* from 7919; *intelligence;* by impl. *success:*—understanding {7x}, wisdom {3x}, wise {1x}, prudence {1x}, knowledge {1x}, sense {1x}, discretion {1x}, policy {1x}. See: TWOT—2263a; BDB—968c.

שַׁכֻּל **shakkûl**. See 7909.

שִׂכְלוּת **siklûwth**. See 5531.

7923. שִׁכֻּלִים {1x} **shikkûlîym**, *shik-koo-leem';* plur. from 7921; *childlessness* (by continued bereavements):—have, after you have lost the other {1x}. See: TWOT—2385d; BDB—1014a.

7924. שָׂכְלְתָנוּ {3x} **sokl^ethânûw** (Aram.), *sok-leth-aw-noo';* from 7920; *intelligence:*—understanding {3x}. See: TWOT—3009a; BDB—1114a.

7925. שָׁכַם {65x} **shâkam**, *shaw-kam';* a prim. root; prop. to *incline* (the shoulder to a burden); but used only as denom. from 7926; lit. to *load up* (on the back of man or beast), i.e. to *start early* in the morning:—(rise up, get you, . . .) early {61x}, betimes {2x}, morning {2x}.

Shakam means "to rise early, start early." **(1)** It is found for the first time in Gen 19:2: ". . . And ye shall rise up early, and go on your ways." **(2)** As in this instance, many of the instances of the use of *shakam* are in connection with traveling. **(2a)** Thus, it may be used with verbs of going (as above) or **(2b)** encamping (Judg 7:1). **(3)** The word is used some 30 times in reference to rising early in the morning, as in 1 Sa 29:10, in which this phrase appears twice: "Wherefore now rise up early in the morning with thy master's servants that are come with thee: and as soon as ye be up early in the morning, and have light, depart." **(4)** A number of times in the Book of Jeremiah, "rising up early" is used with "speaking" (7:13; 25:3; 35:14), "sending" (7:25; 25:4; 29:19; 35:15; 44:4), "protesting" (11:7), or "teaching" (32:33). **(5)** Ps 127:2 gives some interesting advice while using this word: "It is vain for you to rise up early, to sit up late, to eat the bread of sorrows: for so he giveth his beloved sleep." See: TWOT—2386; BDB—1014c.

7926. שְׁכֶם {22x} **sh^ekem**, *shek-em';* from 7925; the *neck* (between the shoulders) as the place of burdens; fig. the *spur* of a hill:—shoulder {17x}, back {2x}, consent {2x}, portion {1x}. See: TWOT—2386a; BDB—1014a.

7927. שְׁכֶם {63x} **Sh^ekem**, *shek-em';* the same as 7926; *ridge; Shekem,* a place in Pal.:—Shechem {61x}, Sichem {1x}, consent {1x}. See: TWOT—2386b; BDB—1014b.

7928. שֶׁכֶם {3x} **Shekem**, *sheh'-kem;* for 7926; *Shekem,* the name of a Hivite and two Isr.:—Shechem {3x}. See: BDB—1014c.

7929. שִׁכְמָה {1x} **shikmâh**, *shik-maw';* fem. of 7926; the *shoulder*-bone:—shoulder blade {1x}. See: TWOT—2386a; BDB—1014a, 1014b.

7930. שִׁכְמִי {1x} **Shikmîy**, *shik-mee';* patron. from 7928; a *Shikmite* (collect.), or desc. of Shekem:—Shechemites {1x}. See: BDB—1014c.

7931. שָׁכַן {129x} **shâkan**, *shaw-kan';* a prim. root [appar. akin (by transm.) to 7901 through the idea of *lodging;* comp. 5531, 7925]; to *reside* or permanently stay (lit. or fig.):—dwell {92x}, abide {8x}, place {7x}, remain {5x}, inhabit {4x}, rest {3x}, set {2x}, continue {1x}, dwellers {1x}, dwelling {1x}, misc. {5x} = continue, have habitation, lay.

Shakan, means "to dwell, inhabit, settle down, abide." **(1)** *Shakan* is first used in the sense of "to dwell" in **(1a)** Gen 9:27: ". . . And he shall dwell in the tents of Shem." **(1b)** Moses was commanded: "And let them make me a sanctuary, that I may dwell among them" (Ex 25:8). **(2)** *Shakan* is a word from nomadic life, meaning "to live in a tent." Thus, Balaam "saw Israel abiding in his tents according to their tribes" (Num 24:2). **(2a)** In that verse, *shakan* refers to temporary "camping," **(2b)** but it can also refer to being permanently "settled": "But thou *art* the same, and thy years shall have no end" (Ps 102:28). **(3)** God promised to give Israel security, "that they may dwell in a place of their own, and move no more . . ." (2 Sa 7:10). Syn: 3427, 4908. See: TWOT—2387; BDB—1014d, 1015c, 1115b.

7932. שְׁכַן {2x} **sh^ekan** (Aram.), *shek-an';* corresp. to 7931:—habitation {1x}, dwell {1x}.

Shakan means "to dwell, inhabit." One occurrence of the verb is in Ps 37:27: "Depart from evil, and do good; and dwell for evermore." See: TWOT—3031; BDB—1115b.

7933. שֶׁכֶן {1x} **sheken**, *sheh'-ken;* from 7931; a *residence:*—habitation {1x}. See: TWOT—387a; BDB—1015c.

7934 שָׁכֵן {20x} **shâkên**, *shaw-kane';* from 7931; a *resident;* by extens. a fellow-*citizen:*—neighbour {17x}, inhabitant {2x}, nigh thereunto {1x}. See: TWOT—2387b; BDB—1015c.

7935. שְׁכַנְיָה {10x} **Sh^ekanyâh**, *shek-an-yaw';* or (prol.)

שְׁכַנְיָהוּ **Sh^ekanyâhûw**, *shek-an-yaw'-hoo;* from 7931 and 3050; *Jah has dwelt; Shekanjah,* the name of nine Isr.:—Shechaniah {8x}, Shecaniah {2x}. See: BDB—1016a.

7936. שָׂכַר {21x} **sâkar**, *saw-kar';* or (by perm.)

סָכַר **çâkar** (Ezra 4:5), *saw-kar';* a prim. root [appar. akin (by prosthesis) to 3739 through the idea of temporary *purchase;* comp. 7937]; to *hire:*—hire {15x}, rewardeth {2x}, wages {2x}, surely {1x}, hire out {1x}. See: TWOT—2264.1; BDB—698d, 968d.

7937. שָׁכַר {19x} **shâkar**, *shaw-kar';* a prim. root; to *become tipsy;* in a qualified sense, to *satiate* with a stimulating drink or (fig.) influence:—drunken {12x}, drunk {4x}, filled with drink {1x}, abundantly {1x}, were merry {1x}. See: TWOT—2388; BDB—1016a. [Superlative of 8248.]

7938. שֶׂכֶר {2x} **seker**, *seh'-ker;* from 7936; *wages:*—reward {1x}, sluices {1x}. See: TWOT—2264.1a; BDB—969a.

7939. שָׂכָר {28x} **sâkâr**, *saw-kawr';* from 7936; *payment* of contract; concr. *salary, fare, maintenance;* by impl. *compensation, benefit:*—hire {9x}, reward {9x}, wages {6x}, price {2x}, fare {1x}, worth {1x}. See: TWOT—2264.1b; BDB—969a.

7940. שָׂכָר {2x} **Sâkar**, *saw-kar';* the same as 7939; *recompense; Sakar,* the name of two Isr.:—Sacar {2x}. See: BDB—969b.

7941. שֵׁכָר {23x} **shêkâr**, *shay-kawr';* from 7937; an *intoxicant,* i.e. intensely alcoholic *liquor:*—strong drink {21x}, strong wine {1x}, drunkard {1x}. See: TWOT—2388a; BDB—1016b.

שִׁכֹּר **shikkôr**. See 7910.

7942. שִׁכְּרוֹן {1x} **Shikk^erôwn**, *shik-ker-one'*; for 7943; *drunkenness, Shikkeron,* a place in Pal.:—Shicron {1x}. See: BDB—1016c.

7943. שִׁכָּרוֹן {3x} **shikkârôwn**, *shik-kaw-rone'*; from 7937; *intoxication:*—drunkenness {2x}, drunken {1x}. See: TWOT—2388c; BDB—1016c.

7944. שַׁל {1x} **shal**, *shal;* from 7952 abbrev.; a *fault:*—error {1x}. See: TWOT—2389.1; BDB—1016d.

7945. שֶׁל {3x} **shel**, *shel;* for the rel. 834; used with prep. pref., and often followed by some pron. aff.; on *account* of, *what*soever, *which*soever:—though {1x}, for whose cause {1x}, for my sake {1x}. See: TWOT—184; BDB—979b, 980a, 1016d.

7946. שַׁלְאֲנָן {1x} **shal'ănân**, *shal-an-awn';* for 7600; *tranquil:*—ease {1x}. See: TWOT—2304a; BDB—1016d.

7947. שָׁלַב {2x} **shâlab**, *shaw-lab';* a prim. root; to *space* off; intens. (*evenly*) to *make equidistant:*—set in order {1x}, equally distant {1x}. See: TWOT—2390; BDB—1016d.

7948. שָׁלָב {3x} **shâlâb**, *shaw-lawb';* from 7947; a *spacer* or raised *interval,* i.e. the *stile* in a frame or panel:—ledge {3x}. See: TWOT—2390a; BDB—1016d.

7949. שָׁלַג {1x} **shâlag**, *shaw-lag';* a prim. root; prop. mean. to *be white;* used only as denom. from 7950; to *be snow-white* (with the linen clothing of the slain):—snow {1x}. See: TWOT—2391; BDB—1017a.

7950. שֶׁלֶג {20x} **sheleg**, *sheh'-leg;* from 7949; *snow* (prob. from its *whiteness*):—snow {19x}, snowy {1x}. See: TWOT—2391a; BDB—1017a, 1117d.

7951. שָׁלָה {5x} **shâlâh**, *shaw-law';* or

שָׁלַו **shâlav** (Job 3:26), *shaw-lav';* a prim. root; to *be tranquil,* i.e. *secure* or *successful:*—prosper {3x}, safety {1x}, happy {1x}. See: TWOT—2392; BDB—1017a, 1115c.

7952. שָׁלָה {2x} **shâlâh**, *shaw-law';* a prim. root [prob. rather ident. with 7953 through the idea of *educing*]; to *mislead:*—negligent {1x}, deceive {1x}. See: BDB—1017b, 1017d.

7953. שָׁלָה {1x} **shâlâh**, *shaw-law';* a prim. root [rather cognate (by contr.) to the base of 5394, 7997 and their congeners through the idea of *extracting*]; to *draw* out or off, i.e. *remove* (the soul by death):—take away {1x}. See: TWOT—2393; BDB—1017b, 1017d.

7954. שְׁלָה {1x} **sh^elâh** (Aram.), *shel-aw';* corresp. to 7951; to *be secure:*—at rest {1x}. See: TWOT—3032; BDB—1115c.

שִׁלֹה **Shilôh**. See 7887.

7955. שָׁלָה {1x} **shâlâh** (Aram.), *shaw-law';* from a root corresp. to 7952; a *wrong:*—anything amiss {1x}. See: BDB—1115c.

שֵׁלָה **shêlâh**. See 7596.

7956. שֵׁלָה {8x} **Shêlâh**, *shay-law';* the same as 7596 (short.); *request; Shelah,* the name of a postdiluvian patriarch and of an Isr.:—*Shelah* {8x}. See: BDB—982c, 1017c, 1018a.

7957. שַׁלְהֶבֶת {3x} **shalhebeth**, *shal-heh'-beth;* from the same as 3851 with sibilant pref.; a *flare* of fire:—(flaming) flame {3x}. See: TWOT—1077c; BDB—529b, 1018a.

שָׁלַו **shâlav**. See 7951.

7958. שְׂלָו {4x} **s^elâv**, *sel-awv';* or

שְׂלָיו **s^elâyv**, *sel-awv';* by orth. var. from 7951 through the idea of *sluggishness;* the *quail* collect. (as *slow* in flight from its weight):—quails {4x}. See: TWOT—2265; BDB—969b.

7959. שֶׁלֶו {1x} **shelev**, *sheh'-lev;* from 7951; *security:*—prosperity {1x}. See: TWOT—2392a; BDB—1017b, 1017d.

שִׁלוֹ **Shîlôw**. See 7887.

7960. שָׁלוּ {4x} **shâlûw** (Aram.), *shaw-loo';* or

שָׁלוּת **shâlûwth** (Aram.), *shaw-looth';* from the same as 7955; a *fault:*—error {1x}, × fail {2x}, thing amiss {1x}. See: BDB—1115c.

7961. שָׁלֵו {8x} **shâlêv**, *shaw-lave';* or

שָׁלֵיו **shâlêyv**, *shaw-lave';* fem.

שְׁלֵוָה **sh^elêvâh**, *shel-ay-vaw';* from 7951; *tranquil;* (in a bad sense) *careless;* abstr. *security:*—at ease {2x}, peaceable {1x}, quietness {1x}, prosperity {1x}, quiet {1x}, prosper {1x}, wealthy {1x}. See: TWOT—2392c; BDB—1017c.

7962. שַׁלְוָה {8x} **shalvâh**, *shal-vaw';* from 7951; *security* (genuine or false):—prosperity {3x}, peaceably {2x}, quietness {1x}, abundance {1x}, peace {1x}. See: TWOT—2392d; BDB—1017b, 1017c.

7963. שְׁלֵוָה {1x} **sh^elêvâh** (Aram.), *shel-ay-vaw';* corresp. to 7962; *safety:*—tranquillity {1x}. See: TWOT—3032b; BDB—1115c. See also 7961.

7964. שִׁלּוּחַ {3x} **shillûwach**, *shil-loo'-akh;* or

שִׁלֻּחַ **shillûach**, *shil-loo'-akh;* from 7971; (only in plur.) a *dismissal,* i.e. (of a wife) *divorce* (espec. the document); also (of a daughter) *dower:*—presents {2x}, have sent back {1x}.

Shilluachim [plural] occurs 3 times and means "presents" in the sense of something sent out to or with someone (1 Kin 9:16). Syn.: 7971, 7973, 7975, 7999, 8002, 8003. See: TWOT—2394b; BDB—1019d.

7965. שָׁלוֹם {236x} **shâlôwm**, *shaw-lome';* or

שָׁלֹם **shâlôm**, *shaw-lome';* from 7999; *safe,* i.e. (fig.) *well, happy, friendly;* also (abstr.) *welfare,* i.e. *health, prosperity, peace:*—peace {175x}, well {14x}, peaceably {9x}, welfare {5x}, salute + 7592 {4x}, prosperity {4x}, did {3x}, safe {3x}, health {2x}, peaceable {2x}, misc. {15x} = familiar, × fare, favour, + friend, × great, prosperous, rest, safety, × wholly.

Shalom, as a noun, means "peace; completeness; welfare; health." **(1)** The first two occurrences in Genesis already indicate the changes in meaning: **(1a)** "And thou shalt go to thy fathers in peace [*shalom* in the sense of "in tranquility," "at ease," "unconcerned"]; thou shalt be buried in a good old age" (Gen 15:15); and **(1b)** "that thou wilt do us no hurt, as we have not touched thee, and as we have done unto thee nothing but good, and have sent thee away in peace [*shalom* with the meaning of "unharmed" and "unhurt"] . . ." (Gen 26:29). **(1c)** Yet, both uses are essentially the same, as they express the root meaning of "to be whole." **(2)** The phrase *ish shelomi* ("friend of my peace") in Ps 41:9, "Yea, mine own familiar friend [literally, "friend of my peace"], in whom I trusted, which did eat of my bread, hath lifted up his heel against me" (cf. Jer 20:10), **(2a)** signifies a state in which one can feel at ease, comfortable with someone. **(2b)** The relationship is one of harmony and wholeness, which is the opposite of the state of strife and war: "I am for peace: but when I speak, they are for war" (Ps 120:7).

(3) *Shalom* as a harmonious state of the soul and mind encourages the development of the faculties and powers. **(3a)** The state of being at ease is experienced both externally and internally. **(3a)** In Hebrew it finds expression in the phrase beshalom ("in peace"): **(3b)** "I will both lay me down in peace [beshalom], and sleep: for thou, Lord, only makest me dwell in safety" (Ps 4:8). **(4)** Closely associated to the above is the meaning "welfare," specifically personal "welfare" or "health." **(4a)** This meaning is found in questions: "And Joab said to Amasa, Art thou in health, my brother? And Joab took Amasa by the beard with the right hand to kiss him" (2 Sa 20:9), or **(4b)** in the prepositional phrase leshalom with the verb "to ask": "And he asked them of their welfare, and said, Is your father well, the old man of whom ye spake? Is he yet alive?" (Gen 43:27).

(5) *Shalom* also signifies "peace," indicative of a prosperous relationship between two or more parties. **(5a)** *Shalom* in this sense finds expression in speech: "Their tongue is as an arrow shot out; it speaketh deceit: one speaketh peaceably [literally, "in peace"] to his neighbor with his mouth, but in heart he layeth his wait" (Jer 9:8); **(5b)** in diplomacy: "Howbeit Sisera fled away on his feet to the tent of Jael the wife of Heber the Kenite: for there was peace between Jabin the king of Hazor and the house of Heber the Kenite" (Judg 4:17); **(5c)** and in warfare: ". . . If it make thee answer of peace, and open unto thee, then it shall be, that all the people that is found therein shall be tributaries unto thee, and they shall serve thee" (Deut 20:11). **(6)** Isaiah prophesied concerning the "prince of peace" (Is 9:6), whose kingdom was to introduce a government of "peace" (Is 9:7).

(7) Ezekiel spoke about the new covenant as one of "peace": "Moreover I will make a covenant of peace with them; it shall be an everlasting covenant with them: and I will place them, and multiply them, and will set my sanctuary in the midst of them for evermore" (Eze 37:26). **(8)** Psalm 122 is one of those great psalms in celebration of and in prayer for the "peace of Jerusalem": "Pray for the peace of Jerusalem: they shall prosper that love thee" (Ps 122:6). **(9)** In benedictions God's peace was granted to His people: ". . . Peace shall be upon Israel" (Ps 125:5). Syn.: 7999, 8002, 8003. See: TWOT—2401a; BDB—1022d.

7966. שִׁלּוּם {3x} **shillûwm**, *shil-loom';* or

שִׁלֻּם **shillûm**, *shil-loom';* from 7999; a *requital,* i.e. (secure) *retribution,* (venal) a *fee:*—recompense {2x}, reward {1x}. See: TWOT—2401h; BDB—1024b.

7967. שַׁלּוּם {27x} **Shallûwm**, *shal-loom';* or (short.)

שַׁלֻּם **Shallûm**, *shal-loom';* the same as 7966; *Shallum,* the name of fourteen Isr.:—*Shallum* {27x}. See: BDB—1024b, 1024c, 1025a.

שְׁלוֹמִית **Sh^elôwmîyth**. See 8019.

7968. שַׁלּוּן {1x} **Shallûwn**, *shal-loon';* prob. for 7967; *Shallun,* an Isr.:—Shallum {1x}. See: BDB—1024c.

7969. שָׁלוֹשׁ {430x} **shâlôwsh**, *shaw-loshe'*; or
שָׁלֹשׁ **shâlôsh**, *shaw-loshe'*; masc.
שְׁלוֹשָׁה **shᵉlôwshâh**, *shel-o-shaw'*; or
שְׁלֹשָׁה **shᵉlôshâh**, *shel-o-shaw'*; a prim. number; *three;* occasionally (ord.) *third,* or (multipl.) *thrice:*—three {388x}, thirteen + 6240 {13x}, thirteenth + 6240 {11x}, third {9x}, thrice + 6471 {4x}, threescore and thirteen + 7657 {2x}, stories {1x}, forks + 7053 {1x}, oftentimes + 6471 {1x}. See: TWOT—2403a; BDB—606b, 1025c, 1118a. comp. 7991.

7970. שְׁלוֹשִׁים {175x} **shᵉlôwshîym**, *shel-o-sheem'*; or
שְׁלֹשִׁים **shᵉlôshîym**, *shel-o-sheem'*; multiple of 7969; *thirty;* or (ord.) *thirtieth:*—thirty {163x}, thirtieth {9x}, captains {1x}, variant {2x}. See: TWOT—2403d; BDB—1026c. comp. 7991.

שָׁלוּת **shâlûwth**. See 7960.

7971. שָׁלַח {847x} **shâlach**, *shaw-lakh'*; a prim. root; to *send* away, for, or out (in a great variety of applications):—send {566x}, go {73x}, (send, put, . . .) forth {54x}, send away {48x}, lay {14x}, send out {12x}, put {10x}, put away {7x}, cast out {7x}, stretch out {5x}, cast {5x}, set {5x}, put out {4x}, depart {4x}, soweth {3x}, loose {3x}, misc. {22x} = × any wise, appoint, bring (on the way), conduct, × earnestly, forsake, give (up), grow long, lay, leave, let depart (down, go), push away, reach forth, spread.

Shalach, as a verb, means "to send, stretch forth, get rid of." **(1)** Basically this verb means "to send," in the sense of **(1a)** to initiate and to see that such movement occurs: "Judah sent the kid by the hand of his friend . . . , he found her not"; it never reached its goal (Gen 38:20), or **(1b)** to successfully conclude such an action: ". . . these animals are a present sent unto my lord Esau." (Gen 32:18). **(1c)** In 1 Sa 15:20 Saul told Samuel about the "way which the lord sent" him; here, too, the emphasis is on the initiation of the action. **(2)** The most frequent use of *shalach* suggests the sending of someone or something as a messenger to a particular place: **(2a)** ". . . He shall send his angel before thee, and thou shalt take a wife unto my son from thence" (Gen 24:7); **(2b)** God's angel (messenger) will be sent to Nahor to prepare things for the successful accomplishment of the servant's task. **(2c)** One may also "send a word" by the hand of a messenger (fool), **(2c1)** one may send a message (Prov 26:6), **(2c2)** send a letter (2 Sa 11:14), and **(2c3)** send instructions (Gen 20:2). **(3)** *Shalach* can refer to shooting arrows by sending them to hit a particular target: "And he sent out arrows, and scattered them . . ." (2 Sa 22:15). **(4)** In Ex 9:14 God "sends" His plague into the midst of the Egyptians; He "sends" them forth and turns them loose among them. **(5)** Other special meanings of this verb include letting something go freely or without control: "Thou givest thy mouth to evil . . ." (Ps 50:19). **(6)** Quite often this verb means "to stretch out." God was concerned lest after the Fall Adam "put forth his hand, and take also of the tree of life" (Gen 3:22). **(7)** One may stretch forth a staff (1 Sa 14:27) or a sickle (Joel 3:13). **(8)** For the most part **the intensive stems** merely intensify the meanings already set forth, but the meaning "to send away" is especially frequent: ". . . And, behold, the servants of David and Joab came from *pursuing* a troop, and brought in a great spoil with them: but Abner *was* not with David in Hebron; for he had sent him away, and he was gone in peace. . . ." (2 Sa 3:22). **(9)** God sent man out of the garden of Eden; **(9a)** He made man leave (Gen 3:23—the first occurrence of the verb). **(9b)** Noah sent forth a raven (Gen 8:7). **(10)** *Shalach* can also mean to give someone a send off, or "to send" someone on his way in a friendly manner: ". . . And Abraham went with them to bring them on the way [send them off]" (Gen 18:16). **(11)** In Deut 22:19 the word is used of divorcing a wife, or sending her away. **(12)** This verb can signify "to get rid of" something: "They bow themselves, they bring forth their young ones, they cast out their [labor pains]" (Job 39:3). **(13)** It can also be used of setting a bondservant free: "And when thou sendest him out free from thee, thou shalt not let him go away empty" (Deut 15:13). **(14)** In a less technical sense *shalach* can mean to release someone held by force. The angel with whom Jacob wrestled said: "Let me go, for the day breaketh" (Gen 32:26). **(15)** Yet another nuance is "to hand someone over," as in Ps 81:12: "So I gave them up unto their own hearts' lust. . . ." **(16)** *Shalach* can also mean to set something afire, as in "set the city on fire" (Judg 1:8). **(17)** In the **passive sense** the verb has some additional special meanings; in Prov 29:15 it means "to be left to oneself": ". . . But a child left to himself [who gets his own way] bringeth his mother to shame." Syn.: 7964, 7973, 7975, 7999, 8002, 8003.See: TWOT—2394; BDB—1018a, 1115c.

7972. שְׁלַח {14x} **shᵉlach** (Aram.), *shel-akh'*; corresp. to 7971:—put {1x}, send {13x}. See: TWOT—3033; BDB—1115c.

7973. שֶׁלַח {8x} **shelach**, *sheh'-lakh;* from 7971, a *missile* of attack, i.e. *spear;* also (fig.) a *shoot* of growth; i.e. *branch:*—sword {3x}, weapon {2x}, dart {1x}, plant {1x}, put them off {1x}.

(1) *Shelach* means "something sent forth as a missile," and it can refer to a sword or a weapon. **(2)** *Shelach* occurs 8 times (2 Chr 32:5; Job 33:18; Neh 4:17). Syn.: 7964, 7971, 7975, 7999, 8002, 8003. See: TWOT—2394a; BDB—1019c.

7974. שֶׁלַח {9x} **Shelach**, *sheh'-lakh;* the same as 7973; *Shelach,* a postdiluvian patriarch:—Salah {6x}, Shelah {3x}. See: BDB—1019d. comp. 7975.

7975. שִׁלֹחַ {2x} **Shilôach**, *shee-lo'-akh;* or (in imitation of 7974)
שֶׁלַח **Shelach** (Neh. 3:15), *sheh'-lakh;* from 7971; *rill; Shiloäch,* a fountain of Jerusalem:—Siloah {2x}. Shiloah appears in Is 8:6 and refers to a channel through which water is sent forth. Syn.: 7964, 7971, 7973, 7999, 8002, 8003. See: BDB—1019d.

שִׁלֻּחַ **shillûach**. See 7964.

7976. שִׁלֻּחָה {1x} **shilluchâh**, *shil-loo-khaw'*; fem. of 7964; a *shoot:*—branch {1x}. See: TWOT—2394c; BDB—1020a.

7977. שִׁלְחִי {2x} **Shilchîy**, *shil-khee'*; from 7973; *missive,* i.e. *armed; Shilchi,* an Isr.:—Shilhi {2x}. See: BDB—1019d.

7978. שִׁלְחִים {1x} **Shilchîym**, *shil-kheem'*; plur. of 7973; *javelins* or *sprouts; Shilchim,* a place in Pal.:—Shilhim {1x}. See: BDB—1019d.

7979. שֻׁלְחָן {70x} **shulchân**, *shool-khawn'*; from 7971; a *table* (as *spread* out); by impl. a *meal:*—table {70x}. See: TWOT—2395a; BDB—1020b.

7980. שָׁלַט {8x} **shâlaṭ**, *shaw-lat'*; a prim. root; to *dominate,* i.e. *govern;* by impl. to *permit:*—(bear, have) rule {4x}, have dominion {1x}, give (have) power {3x}. Syn.: 4427, 4910, 7985. See: TWOT—2396; BDB—1020c, 1115c.

7981. שְׁלֵט {7x} **shᵉlêṭ** (Aram.), *shel-ate'*; corresp. to 7980:—have the mastery {1x}, have power {1x}, bear rule {1x}, be (make) ruler {4x}. See: TWOT—3034; BDB—1115c.

7982. שֶׁלֶט {7x} **sheleṭ**, *sheh'-let;* from 7980; prob. a *shield* (as *controlling,* i.e. protecting the person):—shield {7x}. See: TWOT—2397a; BDB—1020d.

7983. שִׁלְטוֹן {2x} **shilṭôwn**, *shil-tone'*; from 7980; a *potentate:*—power {2x}. See: TWOT—2396b; BDB—1020d.

7984. שִׁלְטוֹן {2x} **shilṭôwn** (Aram.), *shil-tone';* or
שִׁלְטֹן **shilṭôn**, *shil-tone'*; corresp. to 7983:—ruler {2x}. See: TWOT—3034c; BDB—[does not appear in BDB]

7985. שָׁלְטָן {14x} **sholṭân** (Aram.), *shol-tawn';* from 7981; *empire* (abstr. or concr.):—dominion {14x}. See: TWOT—3034a; BDB—1115d.

7986. שַׁלֶּטֶת {1x} **shalleṭeth**, *shal-leh'-teth;* fem. from 7980; a *vixen:*—imperious {1x}. See: TWOT—2396c; BDB—1020d.

7987. שְׁלִי {1x} **shᵉlîy**, *shel-ee';* from 7951; *privacy:*—+ quietly {1x}. See: TWOT—2392b; BDB—1017b.

7988. שִׁלְיָה {1x} **shilyâh**, *shil-yaw';* fem. from 7953; a *fetus* or *babe* (as *extruded* in birth):—young one {1x}. See: TWOT—2393a; BDB—1017d.

שְׁלָיו **sᵉlâyv**. See 7958.

שַׁלֵיו **shalêyv**. See 7961.

7989. שַׁלִּיט {4x} **shallîyṭ**, *shal-leet';* from 7980; *potent;* concr. a *prince* or *warrior:*—governor {1x}, mighty {1x}, that hath power {1x}, ruler {1x}. See: TWOT—2396a; BDB—1020c, 1020d.

7990. שַׁלִּיט {10x} **shallîyṭ** (Aram.), *shal-leet';* corresp. to 7989; *mighty;* abstr. *permission;* concr. a *premier:*—captain {1x}, be lawful {1x}, rule {6x}, ruler {2x}. See: TWOT—3034b; BDB—1115d.

7991. שָׁלִישׁ {20x} **shâlîysh**, *shaw-leesh';* or
שָׁלוֹשׁ **shâlôwsh** (1 Chr 11:11; 12:18), *shaw-loshe';* or
שָׁלֹשׁ **shâlôsh** (2 Sa 23:13), *shaw-loshe';* from 7969; a *triple,* i.e. (as a musical instrument) a *triangle* (or perh. rather *three*-stringed lute); also (as an indef. great quantity) a *three*-fold measure (perh. a *treble* ephah); also (as an officer) a general of the *third* rank (upward, i.e. the highest):—captain {11x}, lord {4x}, instrument of musick {1x}, great measure {1x}, excellent thing {1x}, measure {1x}, prince {1x}. See: TWOT—2403e, 2403f, 2403g; BDB—1026b, 1026c, 1026d.

7992. שְׁלִישִׁי {108x} **shᵉlîyshîy**, *shel-ee-shee';* ord. from 7969; *third;* fem. a *third* (part); by extens. a *third* (day, year or time); spec. a *third*-story cell):—third {84x}, third part {18x}, three years old {2x}, three {2x}, third rank {1x}, third time {1x}. See: TWOT—2403b; BDB—722c, 1026a.

7993. שָׁלַךְ {125x} **shâlak**, *shaw-lak;* a prim. root; to *throw* out, down or away (lit. or fig.):—cast {77x}, cast out {15x}, cast away {11x}, cast down {11x}, cast forth {4x}, cast off {2x}, adventured {1x}, hurl {1x}, misc. {3x} = cast out, pluck, throw.

Shalak means to throw, fling, cast, overthrow. **(1)** Its first use is in Gen 21:15, where Hagar cast the Ishmael under one of the shrubs. **(2)** It describe the throwing or casting of anything tangible: **(2a)** Moses threw a tree into water to sweeten it (Ex 15:25); **(2b)** Aaron claimed he threw gold into the fire and a golden calf walked out (Ex 32:24). **(2c)** Trees shed or cast off wilted blossoms (Job 15:33). **(3)** *Shalak* indicates rejection in Lam 2:1. **(4)** The word is used figuratively in Ps 55:22. See: TWOT—2398; BDB—1020d.

7994. שָׁלָךְ {2x} **shâlâk**, *shaw-lawk';* from 7993; *bird of prey,* usually thought to be the *pelican* (from *casting* itself into the sea):—cormorant {2x}. See: TWOT - 2398a; BDB—1021c.

7995. שַׁלֶּכֶת {1x} **shalleketh**, *shal-leh'-keth;* from 7993; a *felling* (of trees):—when cast {1x}. See: TWOT—2398b; BDB—1021c.

7996. שַׁלֶּכֶת {1x} **Shalleketh**, *shal-leh'-keth;* the same as 7995; *Shalleketh,* a gate in Jerusalem:—*Shalleketh* {1x}. See: BDB—1021c.

7997. שָׁלַל {16x} **shâlal**, *shaw-lal';* a prim. root; to *drop* or *strip;* by impl. to *plunder:*—spoil {8x}, take {5x}, fall {1x}, prey {1x}, purpose {1x}. See: TWOT—2399, 2400; BDB—1021c, 1021d.

7998. שָׁלָל {73x} **shâlâl**, *shaw-lawl';* from 7997; *booty:*—prey {10x}, spoil {63x}.

Shalal **(1)** literally means prey which an animal tracks down, kills, and eats (Gen 49:27). **(2)** The word may mean booty or spoil of war, which includes **(2a)** anything and everything a soldier or army captures from an enemy and carries off (Deut 20:14) up to **(2b)** an entire nation as plunder or a spoil of war (Jer 50:10). **(3)** To save one's own life as booty is to have one's life spared (cf. Jer 21:9). **(4)** *Shalal* is used private plunder (Is 10:1–2). **(5)** This word may also represent private gain (Prov 31:11). See: TWOT—2400a; BDB—1021d.

7999. שָׁלַם {116x} **shâlam**, *shaw-lam';* a prim. root; to *be safe* (in mind, body or estate); fig. to *be* (caus. *make*) *completed;* by impl. to *be friendly;* by extens. to *reciprocate* (in various applications):—pay {19x}, peace {11x}, recompense {11x}, reward {10x}, render {9x}, restore {8x}, repay {7x}, perform {7x}, good {6x}, end {4x}, requite {4x}, restitution {4x}, finished {3x}, again {3x}, amends {1x}, full {1x}, misc. {8x} = full, peaceable, that is perfect, (make) prosper (-ous), requite, × surely.

Shalam means to finish, complete, repay, reward. **(1)** The Hebrew root denotes perfection in the sense that a condition or action is complete. When sufficient building materials were at hand and workmen had enough time to apply them, the wall of Jerusalem was finished (Neh 6:15). **(2)** Perfection and completeness is primarily attributed to God. He is deficient in nothing; His attributes are not marred by any shortcomings; His power is not limited by weakness. God reminded Job of His uninhibited independence and absolute self-sufficiency (Job 41:11). **(3)** Israel's social law required one to meet his obligations in full; either by **(3a)** equal replacement (Ex 22:14; Lev 24:18), **(3b)** double (Ex 22:9), or **(3c)** fourfold (2 Sa 12:6). **(4)** Debts were not to be left unpaid (2 Kin 4:7; Ps 37:21). **(5)** National relationships were established on the basis of complete negotiations, making peace (Josh 10:1; 1 Kin 22:44). **(6)** Shalem as a verb, means "to be complete, be sound." **(6a)** The word signifies "to be complete" in 1 Kin 9:25: "So he finished the house." **(6b)** Another form of the verb, *shalam,* means "to make peace": "When a man's ways please the Lord, he maketh even his enemies to be at peace with him" (Prov 16:7). Syn.: 7964, 7971, 7973, 7975, 8002, 8003. See: TWOT—2401c; BDB—1022b, 1023d, 1115d.

8000. שְׁלַם {3x} **sheʻlam** (Aram.), *shel-am';* corresp. to 7999; to *complete,* to *restore:*—deliver {1x}, finish {2x}. See: TWOT—3035; BDB—1115d.

8001. שְׁלָם {4x} **sheʻlâm** (Aram.), *shel-awm';* corresp. to 7965; *prosperity:*—peace {4x}. See: TWOT—3035a; BDB—1116a.

8002. שֶׁלֶם {87x} **shelem**, *sheh'-lem;* from 7999; prop. *requital,* i.e. a (voluntary) sacrifice in *thanks:*—peace offering {81x}, peace {6x}.

(1) *Shelem* conveys the idea of completeness or perfection, and also of compensation, as well as that of peace. **(2)** It was a special kind of *zebach* (2077) or sacrificial feast, occasioned by some particular event in family life that called for a thankful acknowledgement of God's goodness, and a rendering to Him of what return was due and possible. **(3)** *Shelem,* means "peace offering": "And he sent young men of the children of Israel, which offered burnt offerings, and sacrificed peace offerings of oxen unto the Lord" (Ex 24:5). Syn.: 7964, 7971, 7973, 7975, 7999, 8003. See: TWOT—2401b; BDB—1023b.

8003. שָׁלֵם {27x} **shâlêm**, *shaw-lame';* from 7999; *complete* (lit. or fig.); espec. *friendly:*—perfect {16x}, whole {4x}, full {2x}, just {1x}, peaceable {1x}, misc. {3x} = made ready, quiet, *Shalem.*

Shalem, as an adjective, means "complete; perfect." **(1)** This word is found in Gen 15:16 with the meaning of not quite "complete": "But in the fourth generation they shall come hither again: for the iniquity of the Amorites is not yet full." **(2)** The word means "perfect" in Deut 25:15. **(3)** God demanded total obedience from His people: "Let [their] heart therefore be perfect with the Lord our God, to walk in his statutes, and to keep his commandments . . ." (1 Kin 8:61). **(4)** Solomon failed to meet this requirement because ". . . his heart was not perfect with the Lord his God" (1 Kin 11:4). **(5)** Hezekiah, on the other hand, protested: ". . . I have walked before thee in truth and with a perfect heart" (2 Kin 20:3). **(6)** In business transactions, the Israelites were required to ". . . have a perfect and just weight, a perfect and just measure . . ." (Deut 25:15). Syn.: 7964, 7971, 7973, 7975, 7999, 8002. See: TWOT—2401d; BDB—1023d.

8004. שָׁלֵם {3x} **Shâlêm**, *shaw-lame';* the same as 8003; *peaceful; Shalem,* an early name of Jerusalem:—Salem {2x}, Shalem {1x}. See: BDB—1024a.

שָׁלֹם **shâlôm**. See 7965.

8005. שִׁלֵּם {1x} **shillêm**, *shil-lame';* from 7999; *requital:*—recompense {1x}. See: TWOT—2401e; BDB—1024a.

8006. שִׁלֵּם {2x} **Shillêm**, *shil-lame';* the same as 8005; *Shillem,* an Isr.:—*Shillem* {2x}. See: BDB—1024a.

שִׁלֻּם **shillûm**. See 7966.

שַׁלֻּם **Shallûm**. See 7967.

8007. שַׂלְמָא {4x} **Salmâʼ**, *sal-maw';* prob. for 8008; *clothing; Salma,* the name of two Isr.:—*Salma* {4x}. See: BDB—969c.

8008. שַׂלְמָה {16x} **salmâh**, *sal-maw';* transp. for 8071; a *dress:*—clothes {3x}, garment {8x}, raiment {5x}. See: TWOT—2270b; BDB—969c, 971a, 1070b.

8009. שַׂלְמָה {1x} **Salmâh**, *sal-maw';* the same as 8008; *clothing; Salmah,* an Isr.:—Salmon {1x}. See: BDB—969c, 971b. comp. 8012.

8010. שְׁלֹמֹה {293x} **Sheʻlômôh**, *shel-o-mo';* from 7965; *peaceful; Shelomah,* David's successor:—Solomon {293x}. See: BDB—1024c.

8011. שִׁלֻּמָה {1x} **shillumâh**, *shil-loo-maw';* fem. of 7966; *retribution:*—reward {1x}. See: TWOT—2401h; BDB—1024b.

8012. שַׂלְמוֹן {1x} **Salmôwn**, *sal-mone';* from 8008; *investiture; Salmon,* an Isr.:—Salmon {1x}. See: BDB—969c. comp. 8009.

8013. שְׁלֹמוֹת {5x} **Sheʻlômôwth**, *shel-o-moth';* fem. plur. of 7965; *pacifications; Shelomoth,* the name of two Isr.:—Shelomith {3x}, Shelomoth {2x}. See: BDB—1024d. comp. 8019.

8014. שַׂלְמַי {1x} **Salmay**, *sal-mah'-ee;* from 8008; *clothed; Salmai,* an Isr.:—Shalmai {1x}. See: BDB—969c, 971b, 1030c.

8015. שְׁלֹמִי {1x} **Sheʻlômîy**, *shel-o-mee';* from 7965; *peaceable; Shelomi,* an Isr.:—Shelomi {1x}. See: BDB—1025a.

8016. שִׁלֵּמִי {1x} **Shillêmîy**, *shil-lay-mee';* patron. from 8006; a *Shilemite* (collect.) or desc. of Shillem:—Shillemites {1x}. See: BDB—1024b.

8017. שְׁלֻמִיאֵל {5x} **Sheʻlumîyʼêl**, *shel-oo-mee-ale';* from 7965 and 410; *peace of God; Shelumiel,* an Isr.:—Shelumiel {5x}. See: BDB—1025a.

8018. שֶׁלֶמְיָה {10x} **Shelemyâh**, *shel-em-yaw';* or

שֶׁלֶמְיָהוּ **Shelemyâhuw**, *shel-em-yaw'-hoo;* from 8002 and 3050; *thank-offering of Jah; Shelemjah,* the name of nine Isr.:—Shelemiah {10x}. See: BDB—1024b, 1024c, 1025a.

8019. שְׁלֹמִית {8x} **Sheʻlômîyth**, *shel-o-meeth';* or

שְׁלוֹמִית **Sheʻlôwmiyth** (Ezra 8:10), *shel-o-meeth';* from 7965; *peaceableness; Shelomith,* the name of five Isr. and three Israelitesses:—Shelomith {8x}. See: BDB—1024d, 1025a.

8020. שַׁלְמַן {1x} **Shalman**, *shal-man';* of for. der.; *Shalman,* a king appar. of Assyria:—*Shalman* {1x}. See: BDB—1025a. comp. 8022.

8021. שַׁלְמֹן {1x} **shalmôn**, *shal-mone';* from 7999; a *bribe:*—reward {1x}. See: TWOT—2401f; BDB—1024b.

8022. שַׁלְמַנְאֶסֶר {2x} **Shalmanʼeçer**, *shal-man-eh'-ser;* of for. der.; *Shalmaneser,* an Ass. king:—Shalmaneser {2x}. See: BDB—1025b. Comp 8020.

8023. שִׁלֹנִי {1x} **Shîlônîy**, *shee-lo-nee';* the same as 7888; *Shiloni,* an Isr.:—Shiloni {1x}. See: BDB—1017c, 1018a, 1025b.

8024. שֵׁלָנִי {1x} **Shêlânîy**, *shay-law-nee';* from 7956; a *Shelanite* (collect.), or desc. of Shelah:—Shelanites {1x}. See: BDB—1017c, 1025b.

8025. שָׁלַף {25x} **shâlaph**, *saw-laf';* a prim. root; to *pull* out, up or off:—draw {22x}, pluck off {2x}, grow up {1x}. See: TWOT—2402; BDB—1025b.

8026. שֶׁלֶף {2x} **Sheleph**, *sheh'-lef;* from 8025; *extract; Sheleph,* a son of Jokthan:—*Sheleph* {2x}. See: BDB—1025c.

8027. שָׁלַשׁ {9x} **shâlash**, *shaw-lash';* a prim. root perh. orig. to *intensify,* i.e. *treble;* but appar. used only as denom. from 7969, to *be* (caus. *make*) *triplicate* (by restoration, in portions, strands, days or years):—three years old {3x}, third time {2x}, threefold {1x}, three {1x}, three parts {1x}, three days {1x}. See: TWOT—2403; BDB—1026a.

8028. שֶׁלֶשׁ {1x} **Shelesh**, *sheh'-lesh;* from 8027; *triplet; Shelesh,* an Isr.:—*Shelesh* {1x}. See: BDB—1026d.

שָׁלֹשׁ **shâlôsh**. See 7969.

8029. שִׁלֵּשׁ {5x} **shillêsh**, *shil-laysh';* from 8027; a desc. of the *third* degree, i.e. *great grandchild:*—third {5x}. See: TWOT—2403h; BDB—1026d.

8030. שִׁלְשָׁה {1x} **Shilshâh**, *shil-shaw';* fem. from the same as 8028; *triplication; Shilshah,* an Isr.:—*Shilshah* {1x}. See: BDB—1027a.

8031. שָׁלִשָׁה {1x} **Shâlîshâh**, *shaw-lee-shaw';* fem. from 8027; *trebled* land; *Shalishah,* a place in Pal.:—Shalisha {1x}. See: BDB—1027a.

שְׁלֹשָׁה **shâlôshâh**. See 7969.

8032. שִׁלְשׁוֹם {25x} **shilshôwm**, *shil-shome';* or שִׁלְשֹׁם **shilshôm**, *shil-shome';* from the same as 8028; *trebly,* i.e. (in time) *day before yesterday:*—times past + 8543 {7x}, heretofore + 8543 {6x}, before {3x}, past + 8865 {2x}, beforetime + 8543 {2x}, beforetime + 865 {1x}, misc. {4x} = excellent things, three days. See: TWOT—2403c; BDB—1026b, 1026d, 1070a.

שְׁלֹשִׁים **sh**e**lôshîym**. See 7970.

שַׁלְתִּיאֵל **Shaltîy'êl**. See 7597.

8033. שָׁם {10x} **shâm**, *shawm;* a prim. particle [rather from the rel. 834]; *there* (transferring to time) *then;* often *thither,* or *thence:*—{10x} = there, therein, thither, whither, in it, thence, thereout. See: TWOT—2404; BDB—1027a, 1030b, 1031d, 1118b.

8034. שֵׁם {864x} **shêm**, *shame;* a prim. word [perh. rather from 7760 through the idea of def. and conspicuous *position;* comp. 8064]; an *appellation,* as a mark or memorial of individuality; by impl. *honor, authority, character:*—name {832x}, renown {7x}, fame {4x}, famous {3x}, named {3x}, named + 7121 {2x}, famous + 7121 {1x}, infamous + 2931 {1x}, report {1x}, misc. {10x} = + base, report.

Shem means name; reputation; memory; renown. **(1)** Names were not always indicative of the persons who bore them such as "dog" (Caleb) and "bee" (Deborah). **(2)** Perhaps some names indicated a single decisive characteristic of their bearer. **(3)** In other cases, a name recalls an event or mood which the parent(s) experienced at or shortly before the child's birth and/or naming. **(4)** Other names make a statement about an individual. **(5)** The sense of a name as an identification appears in Gen 2:19: "And out of the ground the LORD God formed every beast of the field, and every fowl of the air; and brought *them* unto Adam to see what he would call them: and whatsoever Adam called every living creature, that *was* the name thereof." **(6)** The names by which God revealed Himself do reflect something of His person and work.

(7) *Shem* can be a synonym for reputation or fame: "And they said, Go to, let us build us a city and a tower, whose top *may reach* unto heaven; and let us make us a name, lest we be scattered abroad upon the face of the whole earth." (Gen 11:4). **(8)** To "give a name for one" is to make him famous (2 Sa 7:23). **(9)** This word is sometimes a synonym for memory or reputation (2 Sa 14:7). In this respect name may include property, or an inheritance (Num 27:4). **(10)** *Shem* can connote **(10a)** renown (Num 16:2) and **(10b)** continuance (Ruth 4:5; Deut 9:14). See: TWOT—2405; BDB—1027d, 1116a.

8035. שֵׁם {17x} **Shêm**, *shame;* the same as 8034; *name; Shem,* a son of Noah (often includ. his posterity):—*Shem* {17x}. See: BDB—1028d.

8036. שֻׁם {12x} **shum** (Aram.), *shoom;* corresp. to 8034:—name {11x}, named + 7761 {1x}. See: TWOT—3036; BDB—1116a.

8037. שַׁמָּא {1x} **Shammâ'**, *sham-maw';* from 8074; *desolation; Shamma,* an Isr.:—*Shamma* {1x}. See: BDB—1031c.

8038. שֶׁמְאֵבֶר {1x} **Shem'êber**, *shem-ay'-ber;* appar. from 8034 and 83; *name of pinion,* i.e. *illustrious; Shemeber,* a king of Zeboim:—*Shemeber* {1x}. See: BDB—1028d.

8039. שִׁמְאָה {1x} **Shim'âh**, *shim-aw';* perh. for 8093; *Shimah,* an Isr.:—Shimeah {1x}. See: BDB—1029a. comp. 8043.

8040. שְׂמֹאול {54x} **s**e**môwl**, *sem-ole';* or שְׂמֹאל **s**e**mô'l**, *sem-ole';* a prim. word [rather perh. from the same as 8071 (by insertion of א) through the idea of *wrapping* up]; prop. *dark* (as *enveloped*), i.e. the *north;* hence (by orientation), the *left* hand:—left {36x}, left hand {17x}, left side {1x}. See: TWOT—2267a; BDB—541a, 965a, 969d.

8041. שָׂמַאל {5x} **sâma'l**, *saw-mal';* a prim. root [rather denom. from 8040]; to use the *left* hand or pass in that direction):—left {5x}. See: TWOT—2267; BDB—970a, 971b.

8042. שְׂמָאלִי {9x} **s**e**mâ'lîy**, *sem-aw-lee';* from 8040; situated on the *left* side:—left {7x}, left hand {2x}. See: TWOT—2267b; BDB—970a.

8043. שִׁמְאָם {1x} **Shim'âm**, *shim-awm';* for 8039 [comp. 38]; *Shimam,* an Isr.:—Shimeam {1x}. See: BDB—1029a.

8044. שַׁמְגַּר {2x} **Shamgar**, *sham-gar';* of uncert. der.; *Shamgar,* an Isr. judge:—*Shamgar* {2x}. See: BDB—1029a.

8045. שָׁמַד {90x} **shâmad**, *shaw-mad';* a prim. root; to *desolate:*—destroy {83x}, destruction {1x}, overthrown {1x}, perished {1x}, misc. {4x} = bring to nought, pluck down, × utterly.

Shamad means to destroy, annihilate, exterminate. **(1)** This word always expresses complete destruction or annihilation: **(1a)** of people (Deut 2:12; Judg 21:16), **(1b)** of the pagan high places (Hos 10:8), and **(1c)** of Baal and his images (2 Kin 10:28). **(2)** When God wants to completely destroy, He will sweep with the [broom] of destruction (Is 14:23). Syn.: 6, 343, 7665, 7843. See: TWOT—2406; BDB—1029a, 1116a.

8046. שְׁמַד {1x} **sh**e**mad** (Aram.), *shem-ad';* corresp. to 8045:—consume {1x}. TWOT—3037; BDB—1116a.

שָׁמֶה **shâmeh**. See 8064.

8047. שַׁמָּה {39x} **shammâh**, *sham-maw';* from 8074; *ruin;* by impl. *consternation:*—astonishment {13x}, desolation {12x}, desolate {10x}, waste {3x}, wonderful {1x}. See: TWOT—2409d; BDB—1030b, 1031c.

8048. שַׁמָּה {8x} **Shammâh**, *sham-maw';* the same as 8047; *Shammah,* the name of an Edomite and four Isr.:—*Shammah* {8x}. See: BDB—1030b, 1031c, 1035a.

8049. שַׁמְהוּת {1x} **Shamhûwth**, *sham-hooth';* for 8048; *desolation; Shamhuth,* an Isr.:—Shamhuth {1x}. See: BDB—1030b, 1031c.

8050. שְׁמוּאֵל {140x} **Sh**e**mûw'êl**, *sehm-oo-ale';* from the pass. part. of 8085 and 410; *heard of God; Shemuel,* the name of three Isr.:—Samuel {137x}, Shemuel {3x}. See: BDB—1028d, 1030b.

שְׁמוֹנֶה **sh**e**môwneh**. See 8083.

שְׁמוֹנָה **sh**e**môwnâh**. See 8083.

שְׁמוֹנִים **sh**e**môwnîym**. See 8084.

8051. שַׁמּוּעַ {5x} **Shammûwa'**, *sham-moo'-ah;* from 8074; *renowned; Shammua,* the name of four Isr.:—Shammua {5x}. See: BDB—1035a, 1035b.

8052. שְׁמוּעָה {27x} **sh**e**mûw'âh**, *sehm-oo-aw';* fem. pass. part. of 8074; something *heard,* i.e. an *announcement:*—rumour {9x}, tidings {8x}, report {4x}, fame {2x}, bruit {1x}, doctrine {1x}, mentioned {1x}, news {1x}. Syn.: *Shoma* (8089) means things heard by accident; hearsay (Josh 6:27). *Shema* (8088) is something heard by design; report (Gen 29:13). *Shemuw'ah* means revelation; something heard, doctrine (Is 28:9). See: TWOT—2412d; BDB—1035b.

8053. שָׁמוּר {1x} **Shâmûwr**, *shaw-moor';* pass. part. of 8103; *observed; Shamur,* an Isr.:—Shamir {1x}. See: BDB—1038d, 1039a.

8054. שַׁמּוֹת {1x} **Shammôwth**, *sham-mōth';* plur. of 8047; *ruins; Shammoth,* an Isr.:—Shammoth {1x}. See: BDB—1030b, 1031c.

8055. שָׂמַח {152x} **sâmach**, *saw-makh';* a prim. root; prob. to *brighten* up, i.e. (fig.) *be* (caus. *make*) *blithe* or *gleesome:*—rejoice {95x}, glad {45x}, joy {5x}, joyful {2x}, merry {2x}, misc. {3x} = cheer up, × very.

(1) *Samach* usually refers to a spontaneous emotion or extreme happiness which is expressed in some visible and/or external manner. **(1a)** It does not normally represent an abiding state of well-being or feeling. **(1b)** This emotion arises at festivals, circumcision feasts, wedding feasts, harvest feasts, the overthrow of one's enemies (1 Sa 11:9), and other such events. **(2)** The emotion expressed in the verb *samach* usually finds a visible expression. **(2a)** In Jer 50:11 the Babylonians are denounced as being glad and jubilant over the pillage of Israel. **(2b)** Their emotion is expressed externally by their skipping about like a threshing heifer and neighing like stallions. **(2c)** The emotion represented in the verb (and concretized in the noun *simchah*—43) is sometimes accompanied by dancing, singing, and playing musical (1 Sa 18:6). **(2d)** This emotion is usually described as the product of some external situation, circumstance, or experience (Ex 4:14). **(2d1)** This passage speaks of inner feeling which **(2d2)** is visibly expressed as Aaron was overcome with joy and kissed him (4:27).

(3) The verb *samach* suggests three elements: **(3a)** a spontaneous, unsustained feeling of jubilance, **(3b)** a feeling so strong that it finds expression in some external act, and **(3c)** a feeling prompted by some external and unsustained stimulus. **(4)** This verb intransitively signifies that the action is focused on the subject (1 Sa 11:9). **(4a)** God is sometimes the subject, the one who rejoices and is jubilant (Ps 104:31). **(4b)** The godly are to be glad in the Lord, rejoice, and shout for joy (Ps 32:11). **(5)** *Samach* can also mean to be joyful or glad (Deut 12:7) describing a state into which one places submits himself. **(6)** It describes all that one does in making a feast before God (Lev 23:40). **(7)** In a few cases the verb describes an on-going state (1 Kin 4:20). See: TWOT—2268; BDB—970a.

8056. שָׂמֵחַ {23x} **sâmêach**, *saw-may'-akh;* from 8055; *blithe* or *gleeful:*—rejoice {11x}, glad {4x}, joyful {3x}, merry {3x}, merrily {1x}, merryhearted {1x}.

The first biblical occurrence is in Deut 16:15: "Seven days shalt thou keep a solemn feast unto the Lord thy God in the place which the Lord shall choose: because the Lord thy God shall bless thee . . . therefore thou shalt surely rejoice." See: TWOT—2268a; BDB—970c.

8057. שִׂמְחָה {94x} **simchâh**, *sim-khaw';* from 8056; *blithesomeness* or *glee,* (relig. or festival):—joy {44x}, gladness {31x}, mirth {8x}, rejoice {3x}, rejoicing {2x}, misc. {6x} = × exceeding (-ly), joyfulness, pleasure.

This noun is both **(1)** a technical term for the external expression of "joy" (Gen 31:27—the first biblical occurrence; cf. 1 Sa 18:6; Jer 50:11) and **(2)** (usually) a representation of the abstract feeling or concept "joy" (Deut 28:47). **(3)** In another technical use this noun signifies the entire activity of making a feast before God: "And all the people went their way to eat, and to drink, and to send portions, and to make great mirth [literally, "to make a great rejoicing"] . . ." (Neh 8:12). **(4)** The noun catches the concrete coloring of the verb, as in Is 55:12: "For ye shall go out with joy . . . : the mountains and the hills shall break forth before you into singing, and all the trees of the field shall clap their hands." See: TWOT—2268b; BDB—965a, 970d.

8058. שָׁמַט {9x} **shâmaṭ**, *shaw-mat';* a prim. root; to *fling* down; incipiently to *jostle;* fig. to *let alone, desist, remit:*—release {2x}, throw down {2x}, shake {1x}, stumble {1x}, discontinue {1x}, overthrown {1x}, let rest {1x}. See: TWOT—2408; BDB—1030c.

8059. שְׁמִטָּה {5x} **sh**^e^**miṭṭâh**, *shem-it-taw';* from 8058; *remission* (of debt) or *suspension* of labor):—release {5x}. See: TWOT—2408a; BDB—1030d.

8060. שַׁמַּי {6x} **Shammay**, *sham-mah'-ee;* from 8073; *destructive; Shammai,* the name of three Isr.:—Shammai {6x}. See: BDB—1030c, 1031d.

8061. שְׁמִידָע {3x} **Sh**^e^**mîydâ**^c^, *shem-ee-daw';* appar. from 8034 and 3045; *name of knowing; Shemida,* an Isr.:—Shemida {3x}. See: BDB—1029a, 1030c.

8062. שְׁמִידָעִי {1x} **Sh**^e^**mîydâ**^c^**îy**, *shem-ee-daw-ee';* patron. from 8061; a *Shemidaite* (collect.) or desc. of Shemida:—Shemidaites {1x}. See: BDB—1029a, 1030c.

8063. שְׂמִיכָה {1x} **s**^e^**mîykâh**, *sem-ee-kaw';* from 5564; a *rug* (as *sustaining* the Oriental sitter):—mantle {1x}. See: TWOT—2269a; BDB—970d.

8064. שָׁמַיִם {420x} **shâmayim**, *shaw-mah'-yim;* dual of an unused sing.

שָׁמֶה **shâmeh**, *shaw-meh';* from an unused root mean. to *be lofty;* the *sky* (as *aloft;* the dual perh. alluding to the visible arch in which the clouds move, as well as to the higher ether where the celestial bodies revolve):—heaven {398x}, air {21x}, astrologers + 1895 {1x}.

Introduction: Sometimes it signifies the atmosphere immediately surrounding the earth, in which the fowls of the air fly. Sometimes it is used of the space in which the clouds are floating. In other places it refers to the vast expanse through which the stars are moving in their courses. It is opposed to *sheowl* (7585), the one being regarded as a place of exaltation, the other of degradation; the one being represented as the dwelling place of the Most High and the angels of God, the other as the abode of the dead. It includes all space that is not occupied by the terrestrial globe, and extends from the air we breathe and the winds we feel around us to the firmament or expanse that contains the innumerable stars. This it includes, and exceeds for where our intellect ceases to operate, and fails to find a limit to the extension of space, there faith comes in. And while before the eye of the body there is spread out an infinity of space, the possession of a super-material nature brings us into communion with a Being whose nature and condition cannot adequately be described by terms of locality or extension. The heavens and the heaven of heavens cannot contain Him. The countless stars are not only known and numbered by Him, but are called into existence and fixed in their courses by His will and wisdom. Where He is, there the true heaven is; and the glories of the firmament faintly shadow forth the ineffable bliss that those must realize who are brought into relationship with Him.

(1) *Shamayim* is the usual for the sky and the realm of the sky **(1a)** birds fly (Deut 4:17). **(1b)** This area, high above the ground but below the stars and heavenly bodies, is often the locus of visions (1 Chr 21:16). **(2)** This word represents an area farther removed from the earth's surface **(2a)** from which come such things as **(2a1)** frost (Job 38:29), **(2a2)** snow (Is 55:10), **(2a3)** fire (Gen 19:24), **(2a4)** dust (Deut 28:24), **(2a5)** hail (Josh 10:11), and **(2a6)** rain (Gen 8:2). **(2b)** This realm is God's storehouse; God is **(3a)** the dispenser of the stores and Lord of the realm (Deut 28:12). **(2c)** This meaning of *shamayim* occurs in Gen 1:7–8. **(3)** *Shamayim* also represents the realm in which the sun, moon, and stars are located (Gen 1:14). **(4)** The phrase "heaven and earth" may denote the entire creation (Gen 1:1). **(5)** Heaven is the dwelling place of God (Ps 2:4; Deut 4:39; 26:15). **(5a)** Another expression representing the dwelling place of God is "the highest heaven [literally, the heaven of heavens] (Deut 10:14). **(5b)** This does not indicate height, but an absolute—i.e., God's abode is a unique realm not to be identified with the physical creation. Syn.: 7834. See: TWOT—2407a; BDB—1029c, 1116a.

8065. שָׁמַיִן {38x} **shâmayin** (Aram.), *shaw-mah'-yin;* corresp. to 8064:—heaven {38x}. See: TWOT—3038; BDB—1116a.

8066. שְׁמִינִי {28x} **sh**^e^**mîynîy**, *shem-ee-nee';* from 8083; *eight:*—eight {28x}. See: TWOT—2411c; BDB—1033b.

8067. שְׁמִינִית {3x} **sh**^e^**mîynîyth**, *shem-ee-neeth';* fem. of 8066; prob. an *eight*-stringed lyre:—Sheminith {3x}. See: TWOT—2411c; BDB—1033b.

8068. שָׁמִיר {11x} **shâmîyr**, *shaw-meer';* from 8104 in the orig. sense of *pricking;* a *thorn;* also (from its *keenness* for scratching) a gem, prob. the *diamond:*—brier {8x}, adamant {1x}, adamant stone {1x}, diamond {1x}. See: TWOT—2416a; BDB—1038d, 1039a.

8069. שָׁמִיר {3x} **Shâmîyr**, *shaw-meer';* the same as 8068; *Shamir,* the name of two places in Pal.:—Shamir {3x}. See: BDB—1039a. comp. 8053.

8070. שְׁמִירָמוֹת {4x} **Sh**^e^**mîyrâmôwth**, *shem-ee-raw-mōth';* or

שְׁמָרִימוֹת **Sh**^e^**mârîymôwth**, *shem-aw-ree-mōth';* prob. from 8034 and plur. of 7413; *name of heights; Shemiramoth,* the name of two Isr.:—Shemiramoth {4x}. See: BDB—1029a, 1030d.

8071. שִׂמְלָה {29x} **simlâh**, *sim-law';* perh. by perm. for the fem. of 5566 (through the idea of a *cover* assuming the shape of the object beneath); a *dress,* espec. a *mantle:*—raiment {11x}, clothes {6x}, garment {6x}, apparel {2x}, cloth {2x}, clothing {2x}. See: TWOT—2270a; BDB—969c, 971a. comp. 8008.

8072. שַׂמְלָה {4x} **Samlâh**, *sam-law';* prob. for the same as 8071; *Samlah,* an Edomite:—*Samlah* {4x}. See: BDB—971a.

8073. שַׁמְלַי {1x} **Shamlay**, *sham-lah'-ee;* for 8014; *Shamlai,* one of the Nethinim:—Shalmai {1x}. See: BDB—969c, 1030c.

8074. שָׁמֵם {92x} **shâmêm**, *shaw-mame';* a prim. root; to *stun* (or intr. *grow numb*), i.e. *devastate* or (fig.) *stupefy* (both usually in a pass. sense):—desolate {49x}, astonished {20x}, desolation {7x}, waste {5x}, destroy {3x}, wondered {2x}, amazed {1x}, astonishment {1x}, misc. {4x} = be astonied, be destitute.

(1) *Shamem* means to be desolate (2 Sa 13:20), astonished (Job 21:5), appalled, devastated (Hos 2:12), ravaged. **(2)** What one sees sometimes is so horrible that it "horrifies" or "appalls": "Mark me, and be astonished, and lay your hand upon your mouth [i.e., be speechless]" (Job 21:5). Syn.: 7591, 7665, 7703, 7722. See: TWOT—2409; BDB—1030d, 1031c, 1116b.

8075. שְׁמַם {1x} **sh**^e^**mam** (Aram.), *shem-am';* corresp. to 8074:—be astonied {1x}. See: TWOT—3039; BDB—1116b.

8076. שָׁמֵם {2x} **shâmêm**, *shaw-mame';* from 8074; *ruined:*—desolate {2x}. See: TWOT—2409a; BDB—1031b.

8077. שְׁמָמָה {58x} **sh**^e^**mâmâh**, *shem-aw-maw';* or

שִׁמָמָה **shîmâmâh**, *shee-mam-aw';* fem. of 8076; *devastation;* fig. *astonishment:*—desolate {40x}, desolation {14x}, waste {1x}, misc. {3x} = (laid, × most) desolate (-ion), waste. See: TWOT—2409b, 2409c; BDB—1031b, 1031c.

8078. שִׁמָּמוֹן {2x} **shimmâmôwn**, *shim-maw-mone';* from 8074; *stupefaction:*—astonishment {2x}. See: TWOT—2409e; BDB—1031d.

8079. שְׂמָמִית {1x} **s**^e^**mâmîyth**, *sem-aw-meeth';* prob. from 8074 (in the sense of *poisoning*); a *lizard* (from the superstition of its *noxiousness*):—spider {1x}. See: TWOT—2271; BDB—971b, 1031d.

8080. שָׁמַן {5x} **shâman**, *shaw-man';* a prim. root; to *shine,* i.e. (by anal.) *be* (caus. *make*) *oily* or *gross:*—wax fat {3x}, make fat {1x}, became fat {1x}.

Shaman, the verb, means to grow or be fat (Neh 9:25; Jer 5:28). See: TWOT—2410; BDB—1031d.

8081. שֶׁמֶן {193x} **shemen**, *sheh'-men;* from 8080; *grease,* espec. liquid (as from the olive, often perfumed); fig. *richness:*—oil {165x}, ointment {14x}, olive {4x}, oiled {2x}, fat {2x}, things {2x}, misc. {4x} = anointing, × fruitful, + pine.

Shemen means **(1)** (olive) oil used to anoint **(1a)** a memorial (Gen 28:18), **(1b)** a future office bearer (Ex 25:6; 2 Kin 9:6); **(1c)** one's head as a sign of mourning (2 Sa 14:2); **(1d)** one's head as a sign of rejoicing (Ps 23:5); and **(1e)** one's ear lobe, thumb, and toe as signs of dedication: to hear only God [the ear], to do only God's will [right thumb = power], and to go only where He leads [right big toe] (Lev 14:17). **(2)** *Shemen* is used **(2a)** as a preservative on shield-leather (2 Sa 1:21); **(2b)** in baking (Ex 29:2); and **(2c)** as a medication (Eze 16:9). **(3)** This oil is burned for light (Ex 25:6). **(4)** Its many uses made olive oil a valuable trade item (Eze 27:17). **(5)** *Shemen* perhaps means the olive itself (Jer 40:10). **(6)** *Shemen* is a kind of perfume or mixed with certain odors to make a perfume (Song 1:3). **(7)** *Shemen* sometimes modifies wood (1 Kin 6:23). See: TWOT—2410c; BDB—1032a.

8082. שָׁמֵן {10x} **shâmên**, *shaw-mane'*; from 8080; *greasy*, i.e. *gross*; fig. *rich:*—fat {8x}, plenteous {1x}, lusty {1x}.

The adjective *shamen* means **(1)** fat (Eze 34:16); **(2)** rich in the sense of fattening (Gen 49:20); **(3)** fertile (Num 13:20); **(4)** robust or muscular (Judg 3:29); and **(5)** large (Hab 1:16). See: TWOT—2410a; BDB—1032a.

8083. שְׁמֹנֶה {109x} **shᵉmôneh**, *shem-o-neh'*; or

שְׁמוֹנֶה **shᵉmôwneh**, *shem-o-neh'*; fem.

שְׁמֹנָה **shᵉmônâh**, *shem-o-naw'*, or

שְׁמוֹנָה **shᵉmôwnâh**, *shem-o-naw'*; appar. from 8082 through the idea of *plumpness*, a cardinal number, *eight* (as if a *surplus* above the "perfect" seven); also (as ord.) *eighth:*—eight {74x}, eighteen + 6240 {18x}, eighteenth + 6240 {11x}, eighth {5x}, eighteen thousand + 7239 {1x}. See: TWOT—2411a; BDB—1032d.

8084. שְׁמֹנִים {38x} **shᵉmônîym**, *shem-o-neem'*; or

שְׁמוֹנִים **shᵉmôwnîym**, *shem-o-neem'*; mult. from 8083; *eighty*, also *eightieth:*—four fourscore {34x}, eighty {3x}, eightieth {1x}. See: TWOT—2411b; BDB—1033b.

8085. שָׁמַע {1159x} **shâmaᶜ**, *shaw-mah'*; a prim. root; to *hear* intelligently (often with impl. of attention, obedience, etc.; caus. to *tell*, etc.):—hear {785x}, hearken {196x}, obey {81x}, publish {17x}, understand {9x}, obedient {8x}, diligently {8x}, shew {6x}, sound {3x}, declare {3x}, discern {2x}, noise {2x}, perceive {2x}, tell {2x}, reported {2x}, misc. {33x} = × attentively, call (gather) together, × carefully, × certainly, consent, consider, be content, give ear, × indeed, listen, (make a) proclaim (-ation), regard, × surely, whosoever [heareth], witness.

(1) Basically, this verb means to hear something with one's ears, but there are several other nuances. **(1a)** In Gen 37:17, a man unintentionally overheard. **(1b)** *Shama* can also be used of eavesdropping, or intentionally listening in on a conversation (Gen 18:10). **(1c)** *Shama* means to give undivided attention (Gen 37:6; 1 Chr 28:2). **(2)** To hear something may imply to have knowledge (Gen 21:26). **(3)** *Shama* may also imply to gain or get knowledge (Jer 37:5). **(4)** It may mean to come into knowledge about something (Num 9:8). **(5)** The verb can represent the mere hearing of something (Gen 3:8). **(6)** To make someone hear something (without any specification of what was heard) suggests summoning the person (1 Kin 15:22). **(7)** Hearing can be both intellectual and spiritual. **(7a)** Spiritually, one may hear God's Word (Num 24:4). Gen 17:20). **(8)** To hear means not only to hear what is said, but to agree with its intention or petition (Gen 16:11; 17:20). **(9)** In the case of hearing and hearkening to a higher authority, *shama* can mean to obey (Gen 22:18). **(10)** To have a hearing heart is to have discernment or understanding (1 Kin 3:9). **(11)** Certainly when Moses told Israel's judges to "hear" cases, he meant more than listening with one's ear. He meant for them to examine the merits of a case, so as to render a just decision (Deut 1:16). See: TWOT—2412, 2412a; BDB—1033b, 1116b.

8086. שְׁמַע {9x} **shᵉmaᶜ** (Aram.), *shem-ah'*; corresp. to 8085:—hear {8x}, obey {1x}. See: TWOT—3040; BDB—1116b.

8087. שֶׁמַע {5x} **Shemaᶜ**, *sheh'-mah*; for the same as 8088; *Shema*, the name of a place in Pal. and of four Isr.:—*Shema* {5x}. See: BDB—1034d, 1035c.

8088. שֵׁמַע {18x} **shêmaᶜ**, *shay'-mah*; from 8085; something *heard*, i.e. a *sound*, *rumor*, *announcement*; abstr. *audience:*—fame {5x}, report {5x}, hear {3x}, tidings {2x}, bruit {1x}, loud {1x}, speech {1x}. Syn.:

(1) *Shema* is something heard by design; report (Gen 29:13). **(2)** *Shoma* (8089) means things heard by accident; hearsay (Josh 6:27). **(3)** *Shemuw'ah* (8052) means revelation; something heard, doctrine (Is 28:9). See: TWOT—2412b; BDB—1034d.

8089. שֹׁמַע {4x} **shômaᶜ**, *sho'-mah*; from 8085; a *report:*—fame {4x}. Syn.:

(A) *Shoma* means things heard by accident; hearsay (Josh 6:27). **(B)** *Shema* (8088) is something heard by design; report (Gen 29:13). **(C)** *Shemuw'ah* (8052) means revelation; something heard, doctrine (Is 28:9). See: TWOT—2412c; BDB—1035a.

8090. שְׁמָע {1x} **Shᵉmâᶜ**, *shem-aw'*; for 8087; *Shema*, a place in Pal.:—*Shema* {1x}. See: BDB—1035a.

8091. שָׁמָע {1x} **Shâmâᶜ**, *shaw-maw'*; from 8085; *obedient; Shama*, an Isr.:—*Shama* {1x}. See: BDB—1035a.

8092. שִׁמְעָא {6x} **Shimᶜâ'**, *shim-aw'*; for 8093; *Shima*, the name of four Isr.:—*Shimea* {6x}. See: BDB—1031c, 1035a, 1035b, 1035c.

8093. שִׁמְעָה {2x} **Shimᶜâh**, *shim-aw'*; fem. of 8088; *annunciation; Shimah*, an Isr.:—*Shimeah* {2x}. See: BDB—1031c, 1035a.

8094. שְׁמָעָה {1x} **Shᵉmâᶜâh**, *shem-aw-aw'*; for 8093; *Shemaah*, an Isr.:—*Shemaah* {1x}. See: BDB—1035a.

8095. שִׁמְעוֹן {44x} **Shimᶜôwn**, *shim-ōne'*; from 8085; *hearing; Shimon*, one of Jacob's sons, also the tribe desc. from him:—Simeon {43x}, Shimeon {1x}. See: BDB—1035b.

8096. שִׁמְעִי {43x} **Shimᶜiy**, *shim-ee'*; from 8088; *famous; Shimi*, the name of twenty Isr.:—Shimei {41x}, Shimhi {1x}, Shimi {1x}. See: BDB—1031c, 1034d, 1035c.

8097. שִׁמְעִי {2x} **Shimᶜiy**, *shim-ee'*; patron. from 8096; a *Shimite* (collect.) or desc. of Shimi:—Shimites {1x}, Shimei {1x}. See: BDB—1035c.

8098. שְׁמַעְיָה {41x} **Shᵉmaᶜyâh**, *shem-aw-yaw'*; or

שְׁמַעְיָהוּ **Shᵉmaᶜyâhûw**, *shem-aw-yaw'-hoo*; from 8085 and 3050; *Jah has heard; Shemajah*, the name of twenty-five Isr.:—Shemaiah {41x}. See: BDB—1035c.

8099. שִׁמְעֹנִי {4x} **Shimᶜôniy**, *shim-o-nee'*; patron. from 8095; a *Shimonite* (collect.) or desc. of Shimon:—Simeonite {3x}, Simeon {1x}. See: BDB—1035c.

8100. שִׁמְעָת {2x} **Shimᶜâth**, *shim-awth'*; fem. of 8088; *annunciation; Shimath*, an Ammonitess:—*Shimeath* {2x}. See: BDB—1035a.

8101. שִׁמְעָתִי {1x} **Shimᶜâthiy**, *shim-aw-thee'*; patron. from 8093; a *Shimathite* (collect.) or desc. of Shimah:—Shimeathites {1x}. See: BDB—1035a.

8102. שֶׁמֶץ {2x} **shemets**, *sheh'-mets*; from an unused root mean. to *emit* a sound; an *inkling:*—little {2x}. See: TWOT—2413a; BDB—1036b.

8103. שִׁמְצָה {1x} **shimtsâh**, *shim-tsaw'*; fem. of 8102; scornful *whispering* (of hostile spectators):—shame {1x}. See: TWOT—2413b; BDB—1036b.

8104. שָׁמַר {468x} **shâmar**, *shaw-mar'*; a prim. root; prop. to *hedge* about (as with thorns), i.e. *guard*; gen. to *protect*, *attend to*, etc.:—keep {283x}, observe {46x}, heed {35x}, keeper {28x}, preserve {21x}, beware {9x}, mark {8x}, watchman {8x}, wait {7x}, watch {7x}, regard {5x}, save {2x}, misc. {9x} = be circumspect, look narrowly, reserve, sure.

Shamar means "to keep, tend, watch over, retain." **(1)** *Shamar* means "to keep" in the sense of "tending" and taking care of. **(1a)** So God put Adam "into the garden of Eden to dress it and to keep it" (Gen 2:15—the first occurrence). **(1b)** In 2 Kin 22:14 Harhas is called "keeper of the wardrobe" (the priest's garments). **(1c)** Satan was directed "to keep," or "to tend" (so as not to allow it to be destroyed) Job's life: "Behold, he is in thine hand; but save his life" (Job 2:6). **(1d)** In this same sense God is described as the keeper of Israel (Ps 121:4). **(2)** The word also means "to keep" in the sense of "watching over" or giving attention to. David, ironically chiding Abner for not protecting Saul, says: "Art not thou a valiant man? and who is like to thee in Israel? wherefore then hast thou not kept thy lord the king?" (1 Sa 26:15). **(3)** In extended application this emphasis comes to mean "to watch, observe": "And it came to pass, as she continued praying before the Lord, that Eli [was watching] her mouth" (1 Sa 1:12). **(4)** Another extended use of the verb related to this emphasis appears in covenantal contexts. **(4a)** In such cases "keep" means "to watch over" in the sense of seeing that one observes the covenant, keeping one to a covenant. **(4b)** God says of Abraham: "For I know him, that he will command his children and his household after him, and they shall keep the way of the Lord, to do justice and judgment . . ." (Gen 18:19). **(4c)** As God had said earlier, "Thou shalt keep my covenant therefore, thou, and thy seed after thee in their generations" (Gen 17:9). **(5)** When used in close connection with another verb, *shamar* can signify carefully or watchfully doing that action: "And he answered and said, Must I not take heed to speak that which the Lord hath put in my mouth?" (Num 23:12). **(6)** Not only does *shamar* signify watching, but it signifies doing it as a watchman in the sense of fulfilling a responsibility: "And the spies saw a man come forth out of the city . . ." (Judg 1:24). **(7)** This verb means "to keep" in the sense of saving or "retaining." **(7a)** When Jacob told his family about his dream, "his brethren envied him; but his father observed the saying" (Gen 37:11); he "retained" it mentally. **(7b)** Joseph tells Pharaoh to appoint overseers to gather food: "And let them . . . lay up corn under the hand of Pharaoh, and let them keep food in the cities" (Gen 41:35); let them not give it out but see that it is "retained" in storage. **(8)** *Shamar* seems to mean, "to revere." So the psalmist says: "I have hated them that regard [revere] lying vanities: but I trust in the Lord" (Ps 31:6). Syn.: 821, 4929, 4931, 5341, 8105, 8107, 8108. See: TWOT—2414; BDB—1036b.

8105. שֶׁמֶר {5x} **shemer**, *sheh'-mer;* from 8104; something *preserved,* i.e. the *settlings* (plur. only) of wine:—lees {4x}, dregs {1x}.

Shemerim [plural] refers to "dregs of wine, lees." One of the 4 appearances of this word is in Is 25:6: ". . . shall the Lord of hosts make unto all people a feast of fat things, a feast of wines on the lees (shemarim), of fat things full of marrow, of wines on the lees (*shemarim*) well refined." See: TWOT—2415a; BDB—1038d.

8106. שֶׁמֶר {5x} **Shemer**, *sheh'-mer;* the same as 8105; *Shemer,* the name of three Isr.:—*Shemer* {2x}, Shamer {2x}, Shamed {1x}. See: BDB—1029c, 1037c, 1038d.

8107. שִׁמֻּר {2x} **shimmûr**, *shim-moor';* from 8104; an *observance:*—observed {2x}. *Shimmurim* [plural] means a "night vigil." In Ex 12:42 this word carries the meaning of "night vigil" in the sense of "night of watching": "It is a night to be much observed (shimmurim) unto the Lord for bringing them out from the land of Egypt: this is that night of the Lord to be observed (*shummurim*) of all the children of Israel in their generations." This noun occurs twice in this entry and in no other verse. Syn.: 821, 4929, 4931, 5341, 8108. See: TWOT—2414c; BDB—1037d.

שֹׁמֵר **Shômêr**. See 7763.

8108. שָׁמְרָה {1x} **shomrâh**, *shom-raw';* fem. of an unused noun from 8104 mean. a *guard; watchfulness:*—watch {1x}.

The noun *shomrah* means "guard, watch." The single appearance of this word is in Ps 141:3: "Set a watch (*shomrah*), O LORD, before my mouth; keep the door of my lips." Syn.: 821, 4929, 4931, 5341, 8107. See: TWOT—2414a; BDB—1037c.

8109. שְׁמֻרָה {1x} **shᵉmûrâh**, *shem-oo-raw';* fem. of pass. part. of 8104; something *guarded,* i.e. an *eye-lid:*—waking {1x}. See: TWOT—2414b; BDB—1037d.

8110. שִׁמְרוֹן {5x} **Shimrôwn**, *shim-rone';* from 8105 in its orig. sense; *guardianship; Shimron,* the name of an Isr. and of a place in Pal.:—Shimron {5x}. See: BDB—1038a.

8111. שֹׁמְרוֹן {109x} **Shômᵉrown**, *sho-mer-ōne';* from the act. part. of 8104; *watch-station; Shomeron,* a place in Pal.:—Samaria {109x}. See: TWOT—2414d; BDB—1037d, 1116b.

8112. שִׁמְרוֹן מְראוֹן {1x} **Shimrôwn Mᵉrʼôwn**, *shim-rone' mer-one';* from 8110 and a der. of 4754; *guard of lashing; Shimron-Meron,* a place in Pal.:—Shimronmeron {1x}. See: BDB—597b, 598c, 1038a.

8113. שִׁמְרִי {4x} **Shimriy**, *shim-ree';* from 8105 in its orig. sense; *watchful; Shimri,* the name of four Isr.:—Shimri {4x}. See: BDB—1037c.

8114. שְׁמַרְיָה {4x} **Shᵉmaryâh**, *shem-ar-yaw';* or שְׁמַרְיָהוּ **Shᵉmaryâhûw**, *shem-ar-yaw'-hoo;* from 8104 and 3050; *Jah has guarded; Shemarjah,* the name of four Isr.:—Shemariah {4x}. See: BDB—1037d.

שְׁמָרִימוֹת **Shᵉmârîymôwth**. See 8070.

8115. שָׁמְרַיִן {2x} **Shomrayin** (Aram.), *shom-rah'-yin;* corresp. to 8111; *Shomrain,* a place in Pal.:—Samaria {2x}. See: BDB—1116b.

8116. שִׁמְרִית {1x} **Shimrîyth**, *shim-reeth';* fem. of 8113; *female guard; Shimrith,* a Moabitess:—Shimrith {1x}. See: BDB—1037d.

8117. שִׁמְרֹנִי {1x} **Shimrônîy**, *shim-ro-nee';* patron. from 8110; a *Shimronite* (collect.) or desc. of Shimron:—Shimronites {1x}. See: BDB—1038a.

8118. שֹׁמְרֹנִי {1x} **Shômᵉrônîy**, *sho-mer-o-nee';* patrial from 8111; a *Shomeronite* (collect.) or inhab. of Shomeron:—Samaritans {1x}. See: BDB—1038a.

8119. שִׁמְרָת {1x} **Shimrâth**, *shim-rawth';* from 8104; *guardship; Shimrath,* an Isr.:—*Shimrath* {1x}. See: BDB—1037d.

8120. שְׁמַשׁ {1x} **shᵉmash** (Aram.), *shem-ash';* corresp. to the root of 8121 through the idea of *activity* impl. in day-light; to *serve:*—ministered {1x}. See: TWOT—3042; BDB—1116b.

8121. שֶׁמֶשׁ **shemesh**, *sheh'-mesh;* from an unused root mean. to *be brilliant;* the *sun;* by impl. the *east;* fig. a *ray,* i.e. (arch.) a notched *battlement:*—sun {119x}, sunrising + 4217 {9x}, east side + 4217 {2x}, windows {1x}, eastward + 4217 {1x}, west + 3996 {1x}, westward + 3996 {1x}.

(1) This word means sun (Gen 15:12). **(2)** The "wings of the sun" are probably its rays (Mal 4:2). **(3)** The sun's regularity **(3a)** is supported by divine sovereignty (Gen 8:22) and **(3b)** figures the security of God's allies (Judg 5:31). **(4)** God can **(4a)** make the sun stand still when He wishes (Josh 10:12–13) or **(4b)** darken **(4b1)** as an indication of His judgment upon His enemies and **(4b2)** salvation for His people (Joel 2:31–32). **(5)** The sun and all the heavenly bodies were created by God (Gen 1:16) and **(6)** are summoned to praise Him (Ps 148:3). **(7)** The Canaanites and other people worshipped the sun as a god, and this paganism appeared among Israelites in times of spiritual decline (Deut 4:19). **(8)** The east is "the rising of the sun" (Num 21:11). **(9)** The west is "the setting of the sun" (Deut 11:30). **(10)** To be "before the sun" or "before the eyes of the sun" is to be openly exposed (Num 25:4). **(11)** To "see the sun" is "to live" (Ps 58:8). **(12)** Something "under the sun" is life lived on the earth apart from God in contrast to life lived on earth with a proper relationship with God (Eccl 1:3). See: TWOT—2417a; BDB—1039a, 1116b. See also 1053.

8122. שֶׁמֶשׁ {1x} **shemesh** (Aram.), *sheh'-mesh;* corresp. to 8121; the *sun:*—sun {1x}. See: TWOT—3041; BDB—1116b.

8123. שִׁמְשׁוֹן {38x} **Shimshôwn**, *shim-shone';* from 8121; *sunlight; Shimshon,* an Isr.:—Samson {38x}. See: BDB—1039c.

שִׁמְשִׁי **Shimshîy**. See 1030.

8124. שִׁמְשַׁי {4x} **Shimshay** (Aram.), *shim-shah'-ee;* from 8122; *sunny; Shimshai,* a Samaritan:—Shimshai {4x}. See: BDB—1116c.

8125. שַׁמְשְׁרַי {1x} **Shamshᵉray**, *sham-sher-ah'-ee;* appar. from 8121; *sunlike; Shamsherai,* an Isr.:—Shamsherai {1x}. See: BDB—1039c.

8126. שֻׁמָתִי {1x} **Shûmâthîy**, *shoo-maw-thee';* patron. from an unused name from 7762 prob. mean. *garlic*-smell; a *Shumathite* (collect.) or desc. of Shumah:—Shumathites {1x}. See: BDB—1002c, 1029c, 1039c.

8127. שֵׁן {55x} **shên**, *shane;* from 8150; a *tooth* (as *sharp*); spec. (for 8143) *ivory;* fig. a *cliff:*—teeth {31x}, tooth {10x}, ivory {10x}, sharp {2x}, crag {1x}, forefront {1x}. See: TWOT—2422a; BDB—1039c, 1042a, 1116d.

8128. שֵׁן {3x} **shên** (Aram.), *shane;* corresp. to 8127; a *tooth:*—teeth {3x}. See: TWOT—3043; BDB—1116c, 1116d.

8129. שֵׁן {1x} **Shên**, *shane;* the same as 8127; *crag; Shen,* a place in Pal.:—*Shen* {1x}. See: BDB—1039c, 1042b.

8130. שָׂנֵא {146x} **sânêʼ**, *saw-nay';* a prim. root; to *hate* (personally):—hate {136x}, enemies {3x}, enemy {2x}, foes {1x}, hateful {1x}, misc. {3x} = hater, odious, × utterly.

(1) *Sane'* represents an emotion ranging from intense hatred to the much weaker set against and is used of persons and things (including ideas, words, inanimate objects). **(2)** The strong sense of the word typifies the emotion of jealousy (Gen 37:4; cf. v. 11). The word covers emotion ranging from bitter disdain to outright hatred (Gen 37:18ff). **(3)** This emphasis can be further heightened by a double use of the root [literally, "hating, you hated her"] (Judg 15:2). **(4)** One special use of *sane'* is ingressive, indicating the initiation of the emotion (2 Sa 13:15; Hos 9:15; Jer 12:8). **(5)** In a weaker sense, *sane'* signifies being set against something (Ex 18:21). **(6)** It means to be unloved (Deut 22:16; Eze 23:28). See: TWOT—2272; BDB—971b, 1114a.

8131. שְׂנֵא {1x} **sᵉnêʼ** (Aram.), *sen-ay';* corresp. to 8130:—them that hate thee {1x}. See: TWOT—3010; BDB—1114a.

8132. שָׁנָא {3x} **shânâʼ**, *shaw-naw';* a prim. root; to *alter:*—change {3x}. See: TWOT—2419; BDB—1039c, 1039d, 1040a.

8133. שְׁנָא {21x} **shᵉnâʼ** (Aram.), *shen-aw';* corresp. to 8132:—change {14x}, diverse {5x}, alter {2x}. See: BDB—1039d.

שֵׁנָא **shênâʼ**. See 8142.

8134. שִׁנְאָב {1x} **Shinʼâb**, *shin-awb';* prob. from 8132 and 1; a *father has turned; Shinab,* a Canaanite:—*Shinab* {1x}. See: BDB—1039c.

8135. שִׂנְאָה {16x} **sinʼâh**, *sin-aw';* from 8130; *hate:*—hatred {13x}, hated {2x}, hatefully {1x}. See: TWOT—2272b; BDB—971d.

8136. שִׁנְאָן {1x} **shinʼân**, *shin-awn';* from 8132; *change,* i.e. *repetition:*—angels {1x}. See: TWOT—2421d; BDB—1039c, 1041d.

8137. שֶׁנְאַצַּר {1x} **Shenʼatstsar**, *shen-ats-tsar';* appar. of Bab. or.; *Shenatstsar,* an Isr.:—Shenazar {1x}. See: BDB—1039c.

8138. שָׁנָה {22x} **shânâh**, *shaw-naw';* a prim. root; to *fold,* i.e. *duplicate* (lit. or fig.); by impl. to *transmute* (tran. or intr.):—change {7x}, second time {3x}, again {3x}, diverse {2x}, alter {1x}, disguise {1x}, doubled {1x}, pervert {1x}, preferred {1x}, repeateth {1x}, misc. {1x} = disguise, return. See: TWOT—2421; BDB—1039c, 1039d, 1040d.

8139. שְׁנָה {1x} **shᵉnâh** (Aram.), *shen-aw';* corresp. to 8142:—sleep {1x}. See: TWOT—2778a; BDB—1096b, 1116d.

8140. שְׁנָה {7x} **shᵉnâh** (Aram.), *shen-aw';* corresp. to 8141:—year {7x}. See: BDB—1096b, 1116d.

8141. שָׁנֶה {875x} **shâneh** (in plur. only), *shaw-neh'*; or (fem.)

שָׁנָה **shânâh**, *shaw-naw'*; from 8138; a *year* (as a *revolution* of time):—year {797x}, not translated {55x}, yearly {3x}, yearly + 8141 {2x}, year + 1121 {1x}, live + 2416 {1x}, old + 2416 + 3117 {1x}, misc. {4x}.

Shanah means year (Gen 1:14). **(1)** The year may be based on the relationship between the seasons and the sun, the solar year or agricultural year (Ex 23:16; Deut 16:9–12). **(2)** It can be based on a correlation of the seasons and the moon (lunar year) (Num 28.11–15). **(3)** These systems appear side by side at least from the time of Moses. An exact picture of the Old Testament year is difficult to obtain. See: TWOT—2419a; BDB—1040a.

8142. שֵׁנָה {23x} **shênâh**, *shay-naw'*; or

שֵׁנָא **shênâʾ** (Ps 127:2), *shay-naw'*; from 3462; *sleep:*—sleep {23x}. See: TWOT—928c; BDB—446a, 1039c, 1041d, 1042b, 1096b.

8143. שֶׁנְהַבִּים {2x} **shenhabbîym**, *shen-hab-beem'*; from 8127 and the plur. appar. of a for. word; prob. *tooth of elephants,* i.e. *ivory tusk:*—ivory {2x}. See: TWOT—2422c; BDB—1041d, 1042b.

8144. שָׁנִי {42x} **shânîy**, *shaw-nee'*; of uncert. der.; *crimson,* prop. the insect or its color, also stuff dyed with it:—scarlet {34x}, scarlet + 8438 {5x}, scarlet thread {2x}, crimson {1x}. See: TWOT—2420a; BDB—1040c.

8145. שֵׁנִי {156x} **shênîy**, *shay-nee'*; from 8138; prop. *double,* i.e. *second;* also adv. *again:*—second {87x}, other {37x}, time {13x}, again {7x}, another {7x}, more {3x}, either {1x}, second rank {1x}. See: TWOT—2421b; BDB—1041b, 1118b.

8146. שָׂנִיא {1x} **sânîyʾ**, *saw-nee'*; from 8130; *hated:*—hated {1x}. See: TWOT—2272a; BDB—971d.

8147. שְׁנַיִם {768x} **shenayim**, *shen-ah'-yim;* dual of 8145; fem.

שְׁתַּיִם **shettayim**, *shet-tah'-yim; two;* also (as ord.) *twofold:*—two {533x}, twelve + 6240 {105x}, both {69x}, twelfth + 6240 {21x}, second {10x}, twain {7x}, both of them {5x}, twice {5x}, double {5x}, misc. {8x} = couple, twain, + twenty (sixscore) thousand. See: TWOT—2421a; BDB—1040d, 1060a, 1118b.

8148. שְׁנִינָה {4x} **shenîynâh**, *shen-ee-naw'*; from 8150; something *pointed,* i.e. a *gibe:*—byword {3x}, taunt {1x}. See: TWOT—2422b; BDB—1042b.

8149. שְׁנִיר {4x} **Shenîyr**, *shen-eer'*; or

שְׂנִיר **Senîyr**, *sen-eer'*; from an unused root mean. to *be pointed; peak; Shenir* or *Senir,* a summit of Lebanon:—Senir {2x}, Shenir {2x}. See: BDB—972a.

8150. שָׁנַן {9x} **shânan**, *shaw-nan'*; a prim. root; to *point* (tran. or intr.); intens. to *pierce;* fig. to *inculcate:*—sharp {4x}, whet {2x}, sharpen {1x}, prick {1x}, teach diligently {1x}. Syn.: 502, 2094, 3384, 3925, 7919. See: TWOT—2422; BDB—1041d, 1116d.

8151. שָׁנַס {1x} **shânaç**, *shaw-nas'*; a prim. root; to *compress* (with a belt):—gird up {1x}. See: TWOT—2423; BDB—1042b.

8152. שִׁנְעָר {8x} **Shinʿâr**, *shin-awr'*; prob. of for. der.; *Shinar,* a plain in Bab.:—*Shinar* {7x}, Babylonish {1x}. See: TWOT—2424; BDB—1042b.

8153. שְׁנָת {1x} **shenâth**, *shen-awth'*; from 3462; *sleep:*—sleep {1x}. See: TWOT—928c; BDB—445c, 446a, 1042b, 1042c.

8154. שָׁסָה {12x} **shâçâh**, *shaw-saw'*; or

שָׁשָׂה **shâsâh** (Isa. 10:13), *shaw-saw';* a prim. root; to *plunder:*—destroyer {1x}, rob {2x}, spoil {7x}, spoiler {2x}. Syn.: 7591, 7665, 7722, 7703. See: TWOT—2425; BDB—983c, 1042c, 1042d, 1058b.

8155. שָׁסַס {5x} **shâçaç**, *shaw-sas'*; a prim. root; to *plunder:*—rifle {1x}, spoil {4x}. See: TWOT—2426; BDB—983c, 1042c.

8156. שָׁסַע {9x} **shâçaʿ**, *shaw-sah'*; a prim. root; to *split* or *tear;* fig. to *upbraid:*—clovenfooted {3x}, cleave {2x}, rent {2x}, cleft {1x}, stayed {1x}. See: TWOT—2427; BDB—1042d, 1043c.

8157. שֶׁסַע {4x} **sheçaʿ**, *sheh'-sah;* from 8156; a *fissure:*—clovenfooted + 8156 {3x}, cleave {1x}. See: TWOT—2427a; BDB—1043a.

8158. שָׁסַף {1x} **shâçaph**, *shaw-saf'*; a prim. root; to *cut* in pieces, i.e. *slaughter:*—hew in pieces {1x}. See: TWOT—2428; BDB—1043a.

8159. שָׁעָה {15x} **shâʿâh**, *shaw-aw'*; a prim. root; to *gaze* at or about (prop. for help); by impl. to *inspect, consider, compassionate, be nonplussed* (as looking around in amazement) or *bewildered:*—look {5x}, respect {3x}, dismay {2x}, turn {1x}, regard {1x}, spare {1x}, be dim {1x}, depart {1x}. See: TWOT—2429; BDB—1043a, 1044b.

8160. שָׁעָה {5x} **shâʿâh** (Aram.), *shaw-aw';* from a root corresp. to 8159; prop. a *look,* i.e. a *moment:*—hour {5x}. See: TWOT—3044; BDB—1116d.

שְׂעוֹר **seʿôwr**. See 8184.

שְׂעוֹרָה **seʿôwrâh**. See 8184.

8161. שַׁעֲטָה {1x} **shaʿățâh**, *shah'-at-aw;* fem. from an unused root mean. to *stamp;* a *clatter* (of hoofs):—stamping {1x}. See: TWOT—2430a; BDB—1043b.

8162. שַׁעַטְנֵז {2x} **shaʿaṭnêz**, *shah-at-naze';* prob. of for. der.; *linsey-woolsey,* i.e. cloth of linen and wool carded and spun together:—garment of divers sorts {1x}, linen and woollen {1x}. See: TWOT—2431; BDB—1043b.

8163. שָׂעִיר {59x} **sâʿîyr**, *saw-eer';* or

שָׂעִר **sâʿir**, *saw-eer';* from 8175; *shaggy;* as noun, a *he-goat;* by anal. a *faun:*—kid {28x}, goat {24x}, devil {2x}, satyr {2x}, hairy {2x}, rough {1x}.

Sa'ir is translated "devils" (Lev 17:7). This passage demonstrates that the word represents beings that were objects of pagan worship, appearing under Jeroboam I [929–909 B.C.] (2 Chr 11:15). Josiah's revival probably involved the breaking down of the high places of these devils (2 Kin 23:8). Some translate them as "goat-demons; goat-idols." Syn.: 7700, 7854. See: TWOT—2274c, 2274e; BDB—972c, 972d.

8164. שָׂעִיר {1x} **sâʿîyr**, *saw-eer';* formed the same as 8163; a *shower* (as *tempestuous*):—small rain {1x}. See: TWOT—2277a; BDB—973c.

8165. שֵׂעִיר {39x} **Sêʿîyr**, *say-eer';* formed like 8163; *rough; Seir,* a mountain of Idumaea and its aboriginal occupants, also one in Pal.:—Seir {39x}. See: TWOT—2274h, 2274g; BDB—973a, 1043b.

8166. שְׂעִירָה {2x} **seʿîyrâh**, *seh-ee-raw';* fem. of 8163; a *she-goat:*—kid {2x}. See: BDB—972c.

8167. שְׂעִירָה {1x} **Seʿîyrâh**, *seh-ee-raw';* formed as 8166; *roughness; Seirah,* a place in Pal.:—Seirath {1x}. See: BDB—972c.

8168. שֹׁעַל {3x} **shôʿal**, *sho'-al;* from an unused root mean. to *hollow* out; the *palm;* by extens. a *handful:*—handful {2x}, hollow of his hand {1x}. See: TWOT—2432a; BDB—1043b.

שֻׁעָל **shûʿâl**. See 7776.

8169. שַׁעַלְבִים {3x} **Shaʿalbîym**, *shah-al-beem';* or

שַׁעֲלַבִּין **Shaʿălabbîyn**, *shah al ab been';* plur. from 7776; *fox-holes; Shaalbim* or *Shaalabbin,* a place in Pal.:—Shaalbim {2x}, Shaalabbin {1x}. See: BDB—1043c.

8170. שַׁעַלְבֹנִי {2x} **Shaʿalbônîy**, *shah-al-bo-nee';* patrial from 8169; a *Shaalbonite* or inhab. of Shaalbin:—Shaalbonite {2x}. See: BDB—1043d.

8171. שַׁעֲלִים {1x} **Shaʿălîym**, *shah-al-eem';* plur. of 7776; *foxes; Shaalim,* a place in Pal.:—Shalim {1x}. See: BDB—1043d.

8172. שָׁעַן {22x} **shâʿan**, *shaw-an';* a prim. root; to *support* one's self:—lean {9x}, stay {5x}, rely {4x}, rest {3x}, lieth {1x}. See: TWOT—2434; BDB—1043d.

8173. שָׁעַע {9x} **shâʿaʿ**, *shaw-ah';* a prim. root; (in a good acceptation) to *look* upon (with complacency), i.e. *fondle, please* or *amuse* (self); (in a bad one) to *look* about (in dismay), i.e. *stare:*—delight {4x}, cry {1x}, cry out {1x}, play {1x}, dandle {1x}, shut {1x}. See: TWOT—2435, 2436; BDB—1043a, 1044a, 1044b.

שָׂעִף **sâʿiph**. See 5587.

8174. שַׁעַף {2x} **Shaʿaph**, *shah'-af;* from 5586; *fluctuation; Shaaph,* the name of two Isr.:—*Shaaph* {2x}. See: BDB—1044c.

8175. שָׂעַר {8x} **sâʿar**, *saw-ar';* a prim. root; to *storm;* by impl. to *shiver,* i.e. *fear:*—be (horrible) afraid {4x}, come like (to take away as with) a whirlwind {2x}, be tempestuous {1x}, hurl as a storm {1x}. See: TWOT—2274d, 2275, 2276; BDB—972b, 972c, 973b.

8176. שָׁעַר {1x} **shâʿar**, *shaw-ar';* a prim. root; to *split* or *open,* i.e. (lit., but only as denom. from 8179) to *act as gate-keeper* (see 7778): (fig.) to *estimate:*—think {1x}. See: TWOT—2438; BDB—1045c.

8177. שְׂעַר {3x} **seʿar** (Aram.), *seh-ar';* corresp. to 8181; *hair:*—hair {3x}. See: TWOT—3011; BDB—1114a.

8178. שַׂעַר {4x} **saʿar**, *sah'-ar;* from 8175; a *tempest;* also a *terror:*—storm {1x}, affrighted + 270 {1x}, sore {1x}, horribly {1x}. See: TWOT—2275a; BDB—972c, 973b. See 8181.

8179. שַׁעַר {371x} **shaʿar**, *shah'-ar;* from 8176 in its orig. sense; an *opening,* i.e. *door* or *gate:*—gate {364x}, city {3x}, door {2x}, port {1x}, porters {1x}.

(1) Basically, this word represents a structure closing and enclosing a large opening through a wall, or a barrier through which people and things pass to an enclosed area. **(2)** The gate of a city often was a fortified structure deeper than the wall. This is especially true of strong, well-fortified cities (Gen 19:1). **(3)** Within major cities there were usually strongly fortified citadels with gates (Neh 2:8). **(4)** Certain gates were only the thickness of a curtain (Ex 27:16). **(5)** The temple had large openings between its various courts (Jer 7:2). **(5)** Both the **(5a)** underworld (Job 38:17) and **(5b)** heaven, the domain of God (Gen 28:17), are pictured as cities with gates. **(6)** The gates of ancient cities sometimes enclosed city squares or were immediately in front of squares (2 Chr 32:6). **(6a)** The entry way (2 Chr 23:15) could be secured with heavy doors that were attached to firmly embedded pillars and reinforced by bars (Judg 16:3; cf. Ps 147:13; Neh 3:3). **(6b)** Palaces could be citadels with strongly fortified gates large enough to have rooms over them (2 Sa 18:33). **(6c)** Gates had rooms to house guards (Eze 40:7). **(6d)** The rooms bordering the gates could also be used to store siege supplies (Neh 12:25). **(7)** The gates were the place where local courts convened (Deut 25:7). **(7a)** The sentence sometimes was executed at the city gates (Jer 15:7). See: TWOT—2437a; BDB—745b, 1044c, 1118d.

8180. שַׁעַר {1x} **shaʿar**, *shah'-ar;* from 8176; a *measure* (as a *section*):—hundredfold + 3967 {1x}. See: TWOT—2438a; BDB—1045c.

שָׂעִר **sâʿîr**. See 8163.

8181. שֵׂעָר {28x} **sêʿâr**, *say-awr';* or

שַׂעַר **saʿar** (Is 7:20), *sah'-ar;* from 8175 in the sense of *dishevelling; hair* (as if *tossed* or *bristling*):—hair {24x}. hairy {3x}, × rough {1x} See: TWOT—2274a; BDB—972b, 1114a.

שֹׁעֵר **shôʿêr**. See 7778.

8182. שֹׁעָר {1x} **shôʿâr**, *sho-aw';* from 8176; *harsh* or *horrid,* i.e. *offensive:*—vile {1x}. See: TWOT—2439a; BDB—1045d.

8183. שְׂעָרָה {2x} **s^{e}ʿârâh**, *seh-aw-raw';* fem. of 8178; a *hurricane:*—storm {1x}, tempest {1x}. See: TWOT—2275b; BDB—973b.

8184. שְׂעֹרָה {34x} **s^{e}ʿôrâh**, *seh-o-raw';* or

שְׂעוֹרָה **s^{e}ʿôwrâh**, *seh-o-raw'* (fem. mean. the *plant*); and (masc. mean. the *grain*); also

שְׂעֹר **s^{e}ʿôr**, *seh-ore';* or

שְׂעוֹר **s^{e}ʿôwr**, *seh-ore';* from 8175 in the sense of *roughness; barley* (as *villose*):—barley {34x}. See: TWOT—2274f; BDB—972d.

8185. שַׂעֲרָה {1x} **saʿărâh**, *sah-ar-aw';* fem. of 8181; *hairiness:*—hair {1x}. See: TWOT—2274b; BDB—972b.

8186. שַׁעֲרוּרָה {4x} **shaʿărûwrâh**, *shah-ar-oo-raw';* or

שַׁעֲרִירִיָּה **shaʿărîyrîyâh**, *shah-ar-ee-ree-yaw';* or

שַׁעֲרֻרִת **shaʿărûrîth**, *shah-ar-oo-reeth';* fem. from 8176 in the sense of 8175; something *fearful:*—horrible thing {4x}. See: TWOT—2439b; BDB—1045d.

8187. שְׁעַרְיָה {2x} **Sh^{e}ʿaryâh**, *sheh-ar-yaw';* from 8176 and 3050; *Jah has stormed; Shearjah,* an Isr.:—Sheariah {2x}. See: BDB—1045c.

8188. שְׂעֹרִים {1x} **S^{e}ʿôrîym**, *seh-o-reem';* masc. plur. of 8184; *barley* grains; *Seorim,* an Isr.:—Seorim {1x}. See: BDB—972d.

8189. שַׁעֲרַיִם {3x} **Shaʿărayim**, *shah-ar-ah'-yim;* dual of 8179; *double gates; Shaarajim,* a place in Pal.:—Sharaim {1x}, Shaarim {2x}. See: BDB—1045c.

שַׁעֲרִירִיָּה **shaʿărîyrîyâh**. See 8186.

שַׁעֲרֻרִת **shaʿărûrîth**. See 8186.

8190. שַׁעַשְׁגַּז {1x} **Shaʿashgaz**, *shah-ash-gaz';* of Pers. der.; *Shaashgaz,* a eunuch of Xerxes:—Shaashgaz {1x}. See: BDB—1045d.

8191. שַׁעְשֻׁעַ {9x} **shaʿshûaʿ**, *shah-shoo'-ah;* from 8173; *enjoyment:*—delight {7x}, pleasure {2x}. See: TWOT—2436a; BDB—1044b.

8192. שָׁפָה {2x} **shâphâh**, *shaw-faw';* a prim. root; to *abrade,* i.e. *bare:*—high {1x}, stick out {1x}. See: TWOT—2440; BDB—1045d, 1046a.

8193. שָׂפָה {176x} **sâphâh**, *saw-faw';* or (in dual and plur.)

שֶׂפֶת **sepheth**, *sef-eth';* prob. from 5595 or 8192 through the idea of *termination* (comp. 5490); the *lip* (as a nat. boundary); by impl. *language;* by anal. a *margin* (of a vessel, water, cloth, etc.):—lip {112x}, bank {10x}, brim {8x}, edge {8x}, language {7x}, speech {6x}, shore {6x}, brink {5x}, border {3x}, side {3x}, prating {2x}, vain {2x}, misc. {4x} = band, binding, talk.

(1) Lip is a part of the body (Is 6:7). **(2)** With the lips, or human speech, **(2a)** one may flatter (Ps 12:3), **(2b)** lie (Ps 31:18), **(2c)** speak mischief (Ps 140:9), and **(2d)** speak perversity (Prov 4:24). **(3)** The lip (speech) of the people of God is described as **(3a)** not sinful (Job 2:10), **(3b)** rejoicing (Job 8:21), **(3c)** prayerful (Ps 17:1), **(3d)** speaking God's word (Ps 119:13), **(3e)** truthful (Prov 12:19), **(3f)** wise (Prov 14:7; 15:7), **(3g)** righteous (Prov 16:13), and **(3h)** excellent (Prov 17:7). **(4)** Metaphorically, *saphah* (edge) denotes **(4a1)** the shore of a sea (Gen 22:17), the edge **(4a2)** of a river (Gen 41:3), **(4b)** the edge of material (Ex 26:4), or **(4c)** the brim of a vessel (1 Kin 7:23). See: TWOT—2278a; BDB—973c.

8194. שָׁפָה {1x} **shâphâh**, *shaw-faw';* from 8192 in the sense of *clarifying;* a *cheese* (as *strained* from the whey):—cheese {1x}. See: TWOT—2440a; BDB—1045d.

8195. שְׁפוֹ {2x} **Sh^{e}phôw**, *shef-o';* or

שְׁפִי **Sh^{e}phîy**, *shef-ee';* from 8192; *baldness* [comp. 8205]; *Shepho* or *Shephi,* an Idumaean:—Shephi {1x}, Shepho {1x}. See: BDB—1046a.

8196. שְׁפוֹט {2x} **sh^{e}phôwṭ**, *shef-ote';* or

שְׁפוּט **sh^{e}phûwṭ**, *shef-oot';* from 8199; a judicial *sentence,* i.e. *punishment:*—judgment {2x}. See: TWOT—2443b; BDB—1048a.

8197. שְׁפוּפָם {2x} **Sh^{e}phûwphâm**, *shef-oo-fawm';* or

שְׁפוּפָן **Sh^{e}phûwphân**, *shef-oo-fawn';* from the same as 8207; *serpent-like; Shephupham* or *Shephuphan,* an Isr.:—Shupham {1x}, Shephuphan {1x}. See: BDB—1051b.

8198. שִׁפְחָה {63x} **shiphchâh**, *shif-khaw';* fem. from an unused root mean. to *spread* out (as a *family;* see 4940); a *female slave* (as a member of the *household*):—handmaid {29x}, maid {12x}, maidservant {8x}, bondwomen {3x}, maiden {3x}, womenservants {3x}, handmaidens {2x}, bondmaid {1x}, servant {1x}, wench {1x}. See: TWOT—2442a; BDB—1046c.

8199. שָׁפַט {203x} **shâphaṭ**, *shaw-fat';* a prim. root; to *judge,* i.e. pronounce *sentence* (for or against); by impl. to *vindicate* or *punish;* by extens. to *govern;* pass. to *litigate* (lit. or fig.):—judge (v) {119x}, judge (n) {60x}, plead {11x}, avenged {2x}, condemn {2x}, execute {2x}, judgment {2x}, defend {1x}, deliver {1x}, misc. {3x} = × needs, reason, rule.

Shaphat means "to judge, deliver, rule." **(1)** In many contexts this root has a judicial sense. **(1a)** *Shaphat* refers to the activity of a third party who sits over two parties at odds with one another. **(1b)** This third party hears their cases against one another and decides where the right is and what to do about it (he functions as both judge and jury). **(1c)** So Sarai said to Abram: "My wrong [outrage done me] be upon thee [in your lap]: I have given my maid into thy bosom; and when she saw that she had conceived, I was despised in her eyes: the Lord judge between me and thee" (Gen 16:5—the first occurrence of the word). **(1d)** Sarai had given Hagar to Abram in her stead. This act was in keeping with ancient Nuzu law, which Abram apparently knew and followed. The legal rights to the child would be Sarai's. This would mean that Hagar "did all the work" and received none of the privileges. Consequently she made things miserable for Sarai. As the tribal and family head Abram's responsibility was to keep things in order. This he did not do. Thus Sarai declares that she is innocent of wrongdoing; she has done nothing to earn Hagar's mistreatment, and Abram is at fault in not getting the household in order. Her appeal is: since Abram has not done his duty (normally he would be the judge of tribal matters), "the Lord decide" between us, that is, in a judicial sense, as to who is in the right. Abram granted the legitimacy of her case and handed Hagar over to her to be brought into line (Gen 16:6).

(2) *Shaphat* also speaks of the accomplishing of a sentence. Both this concept and those of hearing the case and rendering a decision are seen in **(2a)** Gen 18:25, where Abraham speaks of "the Judge [literally, "One who judges"] of all the earth." **(2b)** In 1 Sa 3:13 the emphasis is solely on "delivering" the sentence: "For I have told him that I will judge his house for ever for the iniquity which he knoweth. . . ." **(3)** In some cases "judging" really means delivering from injustice or oppression. David says to Saul: "The Lord therefore be judge and judge between me and thee, and see, and plead my cause, and deliver me out of thine hand" (1 Sa 24:15). **(4)** This sense (in addition to the judicial sense), "to deliver," is to be understood when one speaks of the judges of Israel (Judg 2:16): "Nevertheless the Lord raised up judges, which delivered them out of the hand of those that [plundered] them." **(5)** *Shaphat* can be used not only of an act of deliverance, but of a process whereby order and law are maintained within a group. This idea also is included in the concept of the judges of Israel: "And Deborah, a prophetess, the wife of Lapidoth, she judged Israel at that time" (Judg 4:4). The judge had two roles: to discern the will of God and then to lead an army to overthrow the oppressors. Deborah could discern the will of God, but she could not lead men into battle. Barak did that. (Judg 4:4–9).

(6) Certainly ruling is in mind in Num 25:5: "And Moses said unto the judges of Israel, 'Slay ye every one his men that were joined unto Baal-Peor'" (cf. 1 Sa 8:1). **(7)** The military deliverer was the head over a volunteer army summoned when danger threatened (militia). In the time of Samuel this procedure proved inadequate for Israel. They wanted a leader who would organize and lead a standing army. They asked Samuel, therefore, for a king such as the other nations had, one who was apt and trained in warfare, and whose successor (son) would be carefully trained, too. There would be more continuity in leadership as a result. Included in this idea of a king who would "judge" them like the other nations was the idea of a ruler; in order to sustain a permanent army and its training, the people had to be organized for taxation and conscription. This is what is in view in 1 Sa 8:6–18 as Samuel explains. These men were raised up from time to time to be rulers over the land, to defend the people from enemies, to save them from their oppressors, to teach them the truth, and to uphold them in the right course. Syn.: 1777, 2940, 3198, 6419, 7561. See: TWOT—2443; BDB—251c, 1047a, 1117a.

8200. שְׁפַט {1x} **shᵉphaṭ** (Aram.), *shef-at';* corresp. to 8199; to *judge:*—magistrates {1x}. See: TWOT—2045; BDB—1117a.

8201. שֶׁפֶט {16x} **shepheṭ**, *sheh'-fet;* from 8199; a *sentence*, i.e. *infliction:*—judgment {16x}.

The noun *shephet* [plural – *shepatim*] refers to "acts of judgment." One of the 16 occurrences is in Num 33:4: "For the Egyptians buried all their firstborn, which the Lord had smitten among them: upon their gods also the Lord executed judgments." See: TWOT—2443a; BDB—1048a.

8202. שָׁפָט {8x} **Shâphâṭ**, *shaw-fawt';* from 8199; *judge; Shaphat,* the name of four Isr.:—*Shaphat* {8x}. See: BDB—1048b.

8203. שְׁפַטְיָה {13x} **Shᵉphaṭyâh**, *shef-at-yaw';* or שְׁפַטְיָהוּ **Shᵉphaṭyâhûw**, *shef-at-yaw'-hoo;* from 8199 and 3050; *Jah has judged; Shephatjah,* the name of ten Isr.:—Shephatiah {13x}. See: BDB—1049b.

8204. שִׁפְטָן {1x} **Shiphṭân**, *shif-tawn';* from 8199; *judge-like; Shiphtan,* an Isr.:—*Shiphtan* {1x}. See: BDB—1049b.

8205. שְׁפִי {10x} **shᵉphîy**, *shef-ee';* from 8192; *bareness;* concr. a *bare* hill or plain:—high place {9x}, variant {1x}. See: TWOT—2440b, BDB—1045d, 1046a.

8206. שֻׁפִּים {3x} **Shuppîym**, *shoop-peem';* plur. of an unused noun from the same as 8207 and mean. the same; *serpents; Shuppim,* an Isr.:—Shuppim {3x}. See: BDB—1047a, 1049b, 1050d, 1051b.

8207. שְׁפִיפֹן {1x} **shᵉphîyphôn**, *shef-ee-fone';* from an unused root mean. the same as 7779; a kind of *serpent* (as *snapping*), prob. the *cerastes* or horned adder:—adder {1x}. See: TWOT—2448a; BDB—1051b.

8208. שָׁפִיר {1x} **Shâphîyr**, *shaf-eer';* from 8231; *beautiful; Shaphir,* a place in Pal.:—Saphir {1x}. See: BDB—1051c.

8209. שַׁפִּיר {2x} **shappîyr** (Aram.), *shap-peer';* intens. of a form corresp. to 8208; *beautiful:*—fair {2x}. See: TWOT—3046a; BDB—1117a.

8210. שָׁפַךְ {115x} **shâphak**, *shaw-fak';* a prim. root; to *spill* forth (blood, a libation, liquid metal; or even a solid, i.e. to *mound* up); also (fig.) to *expend* (life, soul, complaint, money, etc.); intens. to *sprawl* out:—pour out {46x}, shed {36x}, pour {20x}, cast {6x}, gush out {1x}, misc. {6x} = shedder, slip.

Shaphak means "to pour out, pour, shed." **(1)** In its first use in the Old Testament, the word is part of the general principle concerning the taking of human life: "Whoso sheddeth man's blood, by man shall his blood be shed . . ." (Gen 9:6). **(2)** While it is frequently used in this sense of "shedding" or "pouring out" blood, **(3)** the word is commonly used of the "pouring out" of the contents of a vessel, such as water (Ex 4:9; 1 Sa 7:6), plaster or dust (Lev 14:41), and drink offerings to false gods (Is 57:6). **(4)** In its figurative use, *shaphak* indicates the "pouring out" **(4a)** of God's wrath (Hos 5:10), **(4b)** of contempt (Job 12:21), **(4c)** of wickedness (Jer 14:16), and **(4d)** of the Spirit of God (Eze 39:29). **(5)** The psalmist describes his helpless condition in this picturesque phrase: "I am poured out like water" (Ps 22:14). See: TWOT—2444; BDB—706c, 1049b.

8211. שֶׁפֶךְ {2x} **shephek**, *sheh'-fek;* from 8210; an *emptying* place, e.g. an ash-*heap:*—poured out {2x}. See: TWOT—2444a; BDB—1050a.

8212. שָׁפְכָה {1x} **shophkâh**, *shof-kaw';* fem. of a der. from 8210; a *pipe* (for *pouring* forth, e.g. wine), i.e. the *penis:*—privy member {1x}. See: TWOT—2444b; BDB—1050a.

8213. שָׁפֵל {29x} **shâphêl**, *shaw-fale';* a prim. root; to *depress* or *sink* (expec. fig. to *humiliate,* intr. or tran.):— . . . low {10x}, . . . down {8x}, humble {7x}, abase {2x}, debase {1x}, put lower {1x}.

Shaphel means "to be low, become low; sink down; be humiliated; be abased." **(1)** *Shaphel* occurs about twenty-nine times in the Old Testament. It is a poetic term. **(2)** The verb, as can be expected in poetic usage, is generally used in a figurative sense. **(3)** *Shaphel* rarely denotes a literal lowness. Even in passages where the meaning may be taken literally, the prophet communicates a spiritual truth: ". . . The high [trees] of stature shall be hewn down, and the haughty shall be humbled" (Is 10:33), or "Every valley shall be exalted, and every mountain and hill shall be made low . . ." (Is 40:4).

(4) Isaiah particularly presented Judah's sin as one of rebellion, self-exaltation, and pride: "And the loftiness of man shall be bowed down, and the haughtiness of men shall be made low: and the LORD alone shall be exalted in that day. (2:17; cf. 3:16–17). **(4a)** In the second chapter he repeated God's indictment on human pride. When the Lord comes in judgment, He will not tolerate pride: ". . . The Lord alone shall be exalted in that day" (Is 2:11); then "the Lord of hosts shall be upon every one that is proud and lofty, and upon every one that is lifted up; and he shall be brought low" (Is 2:12). **(4b)** Isaiah applied to Judah the principle found in Proverbs: "A man's pride shall bring him low: but honor shall uphold the humble in spirit" (Prov 29:23). **(4c)** Pride and self-exaltation have no place in the life of the godly, as the Lord "brings low" a person, a city, and a nation: "The Lord maketh poor, and maketh rich: he bringeth low, and lifteth up" (1 Sa 2:7).

(5) The prophets called the people to repent and to demonstrate their return to God by lowliness. Their call was generally unheeded. Ultimately the Exile came, and the people were humbled by the Babylonians. Nevertheless, the promise came that, regardless of the obstacles, God would initiate the redemption of His people. Isaiah expressed the greatness of the redemption in this way: "Prepare ye the way of the Lord. . . . Every valley shall be exalted, and every mountain and hill shall be made low. . . . And the glory of the Lord shall be revealed. . . ." (Is 40:3–5). **(6)** It is translated as "to be low"; "to bring low"; "to be humble." See: TWOT—2445; BDB—1050a, 1117a.

8214. שְׁפַל {4x} **shᵉphal** (Aram.), *shef-al';* corresp. to 8213:—humble {1x}, abase {1x}, subdue {1x}, put down {1x}. See: BDB—1117a.

8215. שְׁפַל {1x} **shᵉphal** (Aram.), *shef-al';* from 8214; *low:*—basest {1x}. See: BDB—1117a.

8216. שֵׁפֶל {2x} **shêphel**, *shay'-fel;* from 8213; an *humble* rank:—low estate {1x}, low place {1x}. *Shephel,* as a noun, refers to a "low condition, low estate" and appears twice (Ps 136:23; Eccl 10:6). See: TWOT—2445a; BDB—1050c.

8217. שָׁפָל {19x} **shâphâl**, *shaw-fawl';* from 8213; *depressed,* lit. or fig.:—low {5x}, lower {4x}, base {4x}, humble {4x}, basest {1x}, lowly {1x}. *Shaphal* as an adjective means "low; humble." **(1)** This word means "low" in Eze 17:24: "And all the trees of the field shall know that I the Lord have brought down the high tree, have exalted the low tree. . . ." **(2)** In Is 57:15 *shaphal* refers to "humble": ". . . I dwell in the high and holy place, with him also that is of a contrite and humble spirit, to revive the spirit of the humble, and to revive the heart of the contrite ones." See. TWOT—2445c, BDB—1050c.

8218. שִׁפְלָה {1x} **shiphlâh**, *shif-law';* fem. of 8216; *depression:*—low place {1x}.

The noun *shiphlah* means a "humiliated state" and occurs once: "When it shall hail, coming down on the forest; and the city shall be low in a low place" (Is 32:19); the city is leveled completely. See: TWOT—2445b; BDB—1050c.

8219. שְׁפֵלָה {20x} **shᵉphêlâh**, *shef-ay-law';* from 8213; *Lowland,* i.e. (with the art.) the maritime slope of Pal.:—valley {8x}, vale {5x}, plain {3x}, low country {2x}, low plain {2x}.

Shephelah means "lowland" and is used most often as a technical designation for the low-lying hills of the Judean hill country (cf. Deut 1:7; Josh 9:1). See: TWOT—2445d; BDB—1050c.

8220. שִׁפְלוּת {1x} **shiphlûwth**, *shif-looth';* from 8213; *remissness:*—idleness {1x}.

Shiphluwth refers to a "sinking" and it's single appearance is in Eccl 10:18: "By much slothfulness the building decayeth; and through idleness [*shiphluwth*] of the hands the house droppeth through." The word implies a negligence or "sinking" of the hands. See: TWOT—2445e; BDB—1050d.

8221. שְׁפָם {2x} **Shᵉphâm**, *shef-awm';* prob. from 8192; *bare* spot; *Shepham,* a place in or near Pal.:—*Shepham* {2x}. See: BDB—1050d.

8222. שָׂפָם {5x} **sâphâm**, *saw-fawm';* from 8193; the *beard* (as a *lip-piece*):—lip {3x}, upper lip {1x}, beard {1x}. See: TWOT—2279; BDB—974a.

8223. שָׁפָם {1x} **Shâphâm**, *shaw-fawm';* formed like 8221; *baldly; Shapham,* an Isr.:—*Shapham* {1x}. See: BDB—1050d.

8224. שִׂפְמוֹת {1x} **Siphmôwth**, *sif-mōth';* fem. plur. of 8221; *Siphmoth,* a place in Pal.:—Siphmoth {1x}. See: BDB—974a, 1050d.

8225. שִׁפְמִי {1x} **Shiphmîy**, *shif-mee';* patrial from 8221; a *Shiphmite* or inhab. of Shepham:—Shiphmite {1x}. See: BDB—1050d.

8226. שָׂפַן {1x} **sâphan**, *saw-fan';* a prim. root; to *conceal* (as a valuable):—treasure {1x}. See: TWOT—1537; BDB—706a.

8227. שָׁפָן {34x} **shâphân**, *shaw-fawn';* from 8226; a species of *rock-rabbit* (from its *hiding*), i.e. prob. the *hyrax:*—*Shaphan* {30x}, coney {4x}. See: TWOT—2446a; BDB—1050d.

8228. שֶׁפַע {1x} **shephaᶜ**, *sheh'-fah;* from an unused root mean. to *abound; resources:*—abundance {1x}. See: TWOT—2447a; BDB—1051a.

8229. שִׁפְעָה {6x} **shiphᶜâh**, *shif-aw';* fem. of 8228; *copiousness:*—abundance {3x}, company {2x}, multitude {1x}. See: TWOT—2447b; BDB—1051a.

8230. שִׁפְעִי {1x} **Shiphᶜîy**, *shif-ee';* from 8228; *copious; Shiphi,* an Isr.:—Shiphi {1x}. See: BDB—1051b.

שָׂפַק **sâphaq**. See 5606.

8231. שָׁפַר {1x} **shâphar**, *shaw-far'*; a prim. root; to *glisten*, i.e. (fig.) *be* (caus. *make*) *fair:*—goodly {1x}. See: TWOT—2449; BDB—1051c.

8232. שְׁפַר {3x} **sh^ephar** (Aram.), *shef-ar'*; corresp. to 8231; to *be beautiful:*—think it good {1x}, please {1x}, acceptable {1x}. See: TWOT—3046; BDB—1117a.

8233. שֶׁפֶר {1x} **shepher**, *sheh'-fer;* from 8231; *beauty:*—goodly {1x}. See: TWOT—2449a; BDB—1051c.

8234. שֶׁפֶר {2x} **Shepher**, *sheh'-fer;* the same as 8233; *Shepher*, a place in the Desert:—Shapher {2x}. See: BDB—1051c.

שֹׁפָר **shôphâr**. See 7782.

8235. שִׁפְרָה {1x} **shiphrâh**, *shif-raw';* from 8231; *brightness:*—garnished {1x}. See: TWOT—2449b; BDB—1051c.

8236. שִׁפְרָה {1x} **Shiphrâh**, *shif-raw';* the same as 8235; *Shiphrah*, an Israelitess:—*Shiphrah* {1x}. See: BDB—1051c.

8237. שַׁפְרוּר {1x} **shaphrûwr**, *shaf-roor';* from 8231; *splendid*, i.e. a *tapestry* or *canopy:*—royal pavilion {1x}. See: TWOT—2449d; BDB—1051d.

8238. שְׁפַרְפַּר {1x} **sh^epharphar** (Aram.), *shef-ar-far';* from 8231; the *dawn* (as *brilliant* with aurora):—early in the morning. See: TWOT—3046b; BDB—1117a.

8239. שָׁפַת {5x} **shâphath**, *shaw-fath';* a prim. root; to *locate*, i.e. (gen.) *hang* on or (fig.) *establish, reduce:*—set on {3x}, brought {1x}, ordain {1x}. See: TWOT—2441a; BDB—1046a, 1052a.

8240. שָׁפָת {2x} **shâphâth**, *shaw-fawth';* from 8239; a (double) *stall* (for cattle); also a (two-pronged) *hook* (for flaying animals on):—pot {1x}, hook {1x}. See: TWOT—2450; BDB—1046b, 1052a.

8241. שֶׁצֶף {1x} **shetseph**, *sheh'-tsef;* from 7857 (for alliteration with 7110); an *outburst* (of anger):—little {1x}. See: TWOT—2373a; BDB—1009b, 1052a.

8242. שַׂק {48x} **saq**, *sak;* from 8264; prop. a *mesh* (as allowing a liquid to *run* through), i.e. coarse loose cloth or *sacking* (used in mourning and for bagging); hence, a *bag* (for grain, etc.):—sackcloth {41x}, sack {6x}, sackclothes {1x}. See: TWOT—2282a; BDB—974b.

8243. שָׁק {1x} **shâq** (Aram.), *shawk;* corresp. to 7785; the *leg:*—legs {1x}. See: TWOT—3047; BDB—1114d, 1117b.

8244. שָׂקַד {1x} **sâqad**, *saw-kad';* a prim. root; to *fasten:*—bound {1x}. See: TWOT—2281; BDB—974b.

8245. שָׁקַד {12x} **shâqad**, *shaw-kad';* a prim. root; to *be alert*, i.e. *sleepless;* hence, to *be on the lookout* (whether for good or ill):—watch {9x}, wake {1x}, remain {1x}, hasten {1x}. See: TWOT—2451; BDB—1052a.

8246. שָׁקַד {6x} **shâqad**, *shaw-kad';* a denom. from 8247; to *be* (intens. *make*) *almond-shaped:*—almonds {6x}. See: TWOT—2451b; BDB—1052b.

8247. שָׁקֵד {4x} **shâqêd**, *shaw-kade';* from 8245; the *almond* (tree or nut; as being the *earliest* in bloom):—almond {2x}, almond tree {2x}. See: TWOT—2451a; BDB—1052b.

8248. שָׁקָה {74x} **shâqâh**, *shaw-kaw';* a prim. root; to *quaff*, i.e. (caus.) to *irrigate* or *furnish a potion* to:—drink {43x}, water {17x}, butler {9x}, cupbearer {3x}, misc. {1x}.

Shaqah, as a verb, means "to give drink, water." **(1)** The word usually occurs in the causative sense, while its much more common counterpart, shatah (8354), is used primarily in the simple active form, "to drink." **(1a)** In its first occurrence in the biblical text, *shaqah* expresses the idea of "to water": **(1b)** "But there went up a mist from the earth, and watered the whole face of the ground" (Gen 2:6). **(2)** The dry climate of the Middle East makes *shaqah* a most important word, since it expresses the act of "irrigating" or "watering" crops ["waterest with thy foot" means directing the water into the irrigation canals with the foot serving as a deflector/director for the water] (Deut 11:10).

(3) God "waters" the earth and causes plants to grow (Ps 104:13–14). **(4)** Figuratively, He "irrigates" His vineyard, Israel (Is 27:3). **(5)** A frequent use of *shaqah* is to express the "giving of water to drink" to animals (Gen 24:14, 46; 29:2–3, 7–8, 10). **(6)** Men are given a variety of things to drink, such as water (Gen 24:43), wine (Gen 19:32; Amos 2:12), milk (Judg 4:19), and vinegar (Ps 69:21). **(7)** In a symbol of divine judgment, God is said to give "water of gall to drink" to Israel (Jer 8:14; 9:15; 23:15). **(8)** In this time of judgment and mourning, Israel was not to be given "the cup of consolation to drink" (Jer 16:7). **(9)** A healthy person is one whose bones "are moistened" with marrow (Job 21:24; literally, whose bones "are watered" or "irrigated" with marrow). See: TWOT—2452; BDB—913d, 1052b, 1054b. See 7937, 8354.

8249. שִׁקֻּו {1x} **shiqqûv**, *shik-koov';* from 8248; (plur. collect.) a *draught:*—drink {1x}. See: TWOT—2452a; BDB—1052d.

8250. שִׁקּוּי {2x} **shiqqûwy**, *shik-koo'-ee;* from 8248; a *beverage; moisture*, i.e. (fig.) *refreshment:*—marrow {1x}, drink {1x}. See: TWOT—2452a; BDB—1052c.

8251. שִׁקּוּץ {28x} **shiqqûwts**, *shik-koots';* or

שִׁקֻּץ **shiqqûts**, *shik-koots';* from 8262; *disgusting*, i.e. *filthy;* espec. *idolatrous* or (concr.) an *idol:*—abomination {20x}, detestable things {5x}, detestable {1x}, abominable filth {1x}, abominable idols {1x}.

This word is often used to testify to God's hatred of the whole system of idolatry. Syn.: 205, 367. See: TWOT—2459b; BDB—1055a.

8252. שָׁקַט {41x} **shâqat**, *shaw-kat';* a prim. root; to *repose* (usually fig.):—rest {16x}, quiet {16x}, quietness {4x}, still {2x}, appeaseth {1x}, idleness {1x}, settled {1x}. See: TWOT—2453; BDB—1052d.

8253. שֶׁקֶט {1x} **sheqet**, *sheh'-ket;* from 8252; *tranquillity:*—quietness {1x}. See: TWOT—2453a; BDB—1053b.

8254. שָׁקַל **shâqal**, *shaw-kal';* a prim. root; to *suspend* or *poise* (espec. in trade):—weigh {14x}, pay {4x}, throughly {1x}, receive {1x}, receiver {1x}, spend {1x}. See: TWOT—2454a; BDB—1053b, 1118c.

8255. שֶׁקֶל {88x} **sheqel**, *sheh'-kel;* from 8254; prob. a *weight;* used as a commercial standard:—shekel {88x}. See: TWOT—2454a; BDB—1053c, 1118c.

8256. שָׁקָם {7x} **shâqâm**, *shaw-kawm';* or (fem.)

שִׁקְמָה **shiqmâh**, *shik-maw';* of uncert. der.; a *sycamore* (usually the tree):—sycamore {1x}, sycamore fruit {1x}, sycamore tree {5x}. See: TWOT—2455; BDB—1054a.

8257. שָׁקַע {6x} **shâqa^c**, *shaw-kah';* (abb. Am. 8:8); a prim. root; to *subside;* by impl. to *be overflowed, cease;* caus. to *abate, subdue:*—make deep {1x}, let down {1x}, drown {2x}, quench {1x}, sink {1x}. See: TWOT—2456; BDB—1052c, 1054b.

8258. שְׁקַעֲרוּרָה {1x} **sh^eqa^crûwrâh**, *shek-ah-roo-raw';* from 8257; a *depression:*—hollow strakes {1x}. See: TWOT—2047b; BDB—891a, 1054c.

8259. שָׁקַף {22x} **shâqaph**, *shaw-kaf';* a prim. root; prop. to *lean out* (of a window), i.e. (by impl.) *peep* or *gaze* (pass. *be a spectacle*):—look {11x}, look down {6x}, look out {3x}, look forth {1x}, appear {1x}. See: TWOT—2457; BDB—1054c.

8260. שֶׁקֶף {1x} **sheqeph**, *sheh'-kef;* from 8259; a *loophole* (for *looking out*), to admit light and air:—window {1x}. See: TWOT—2458a; BDB—1054d.

8261. שָׁקֻף {2x} **shâqûph**, *shaw-koof';* pass. part. of 8259; an *embrasure* or opening [comp. 8260] with bevelled jam:—light {1x}, window {1x}. See: TWOT—2458b; BDB—1054d.

8262. שָׁקַץ {7x} **shâqats**, *shaw-kats';* a prim. root; to *be filthy*, i.e. (intens.) to *loathe, pollute:*—abhor {1x}, make abominable {2x}, have in abomination {2x}, detest {1x}, × utterly {1x}. See: TWOT—2459; BDB—1055a.

8263. שֶׁקֶץ {11x} **sheqets**, *sheh'-kets;* from 8262; *filth*, i.e. (fig. and spec.) an *idolatrous* object:—abominable {2x}, abomination {9x}. See: TWOT—2459a, 2459b; BDB—1054d.

שִׁקֻּץ **shiqqûts**. See 8251.

8264. שָׁקַק {6x} **shâqaq**, *shaw-kak';* a prim. root; to *course* (like a beast of prey); by impl. to *seek* greedily:—have appetite {1x}, justle one against another {1x}, long {1x}, range {1x}, run {1x}, run to and fro {1x}. See: TWOT—2460; BDB—1055b.

8265. שָׂקַר {1x} **sâqar**, *saw-kar';* a prim. root; to *ogle*, i.e. *blink* coquettishly:—wanton {1x}. See: TWOT—2283; BDB—974c.

8266. שָׁקַר {6x} **shâqar**, *shaw-kar';* a prim. root; to *cheat*, i.e. *be untrue* (usually in words):—fail {1x}, deal falsely {2x}, lie {3x}. See: TWOT—2461; BDB—1055d.

8267. שֶׁקֶר {113x} **sheqer**, *sheh'-ker;* from 8266; an *untruth;* by impl. a *sham* (often adv.):—lie {28x}, lying {21x}, false {20x}, falsehood {13x}, falsely {13x}, vain {5x}, wrongfully {4x}, deceitful {2x}, deceit {1x}, liar {1x}, misc. {5x} = without a cause, feignedly, vain thing.

Sheqer, as a noun, means "falsehood; lie." **(1)** It is rare in all but the poetic and prophetic books, and even in these books its usage is concentrated in Psalms (24 times) Proverbs (20 times), and Jeremiah (37 times). **(2)** The first occurrence is in Ex 5:9: "Let there more work be laid upon the men, that they may labor therein: and let them not regard vain words [lies]." **(3)** In about thirty-five passages, *sheqer* describes the nature of "deceptive speech": "to speak" (Is 59:3), "to teach" (Is 9:15), "to prophesy" (Jer 14:14), and "to lie" (Mic 2:11). **(4)** It may also indicate a "deceptive character," as expressed in one's acts: "to deal treacherously" (2 Sa 18:13) and "to deal falsely" (Hos 7:1).

(5) Thus *sheqer* defines a way of life that goes contrary to the law of God. **(5a)** The psalmist, desirous of following God, prayed: "Remove from me the way of lying: and grant me thy law graciously. I have chosen the way of truth: thy judgments have I laid before me" (Ps 119:29–30; cf. vv. 104, 118, 128). **(5b)** Here we see the opposites: "falsehood" and "faithfulness." **(5c)** As "faithfulness" is a relational term, "falsehood" denotes "one's inability to keep faith" with what one has said or to respond positively to the faithfulness of another being. **(6)** The Old Testament saint was instructed to avoid "deception" and the liar: "Keep thee far from a false matter; and the innocent and righteous slay thou not: for I will not justify the wicked" (Ex 23:7; cf. Prov 13:5). See: TWOT—2461a; BDB—1055b.

8268. שֹׁקֶת {2x} **shôqeth**, *sho'-keth;* from 8248; a *trough* (for *watering*):—trough {2x}. See: TWOT—2452b; BDB—1052d, 1055d.

8269. שַׂר {421x} **sar**, *sar;* from 8323; a *head* person (of any rank or class):—prince {208x}, captain {130x}, chief {33x}, ruler {33x}, governor {6x}, keeper {3x}, principal {2x}, general {1x}, lords {1x}, misc. {4x} = task master, master, steward.

Sar, means "official; leader; commander; captain; chief; prince; ruler." **(1)** The word is often applied to certain non-Israelite "officials or representatives of the king." **(1a)** This meaning appears in Gen 12:15, its first biblical appearance: "The princes also of Pharaoh saw her [Sarah], and commended her before Pharaoh. . . ." **(1b)** In other contexts *sar* represents "men who clearly have responsibility over others"; they are "rulers or chieftains." **(2)** *Sar* may mean simply a "leader" of a profession, a group, or a district, **(2a)** as Phichol was the "commander" of Abimelech's army (Gen 21:22) and **(2b)** Potiphar was "an officer of Pharaoh's and captain of the [body]guard" (Gen 37:36). **(2c)** In such usage, "chief" means "head official" (cf. Gen 40:2). **(2d)** *Sarim* (plural) were "honored men" (Is 23:8).

(3) *Sar* is used of certain "notable men" within Israel. **(3a)** When Abner was killed by Joab, David said to his servants (palace officials), "Know ye not that there is a prince and a great man fallen this day in Israel?" (2 Sa 3:38; cf. Num 21:18). **(3b)** Joab, Abishai, and Ittai were "commanders" in David's army (cf. 2 Sa 23:19). **(3c)** "Local leaders in Israel" are also called sarim: "And the princes of Succoth said . . ." (Judg 8:6). **(4)** In several passages, *sar* refers to the task of "ruling." **(4a)** Moses tried to break up a fight between two Hebrews and one of them asked him, "Who made thee a prince and a judge over us?" (Ex 2:14). **(4b)** In such a context, *sar* means "leader," "ruler," and "judge": "Moreover thou shalt provide out of all the people able men, such as fear God, men of truth, hating covetousness; and place such over them, to be rulers of thousands, and rulers of hundreds, rulers of fifties, and rulers of tens . . ." (Ex 18:21).

(5) The "commander" of Israel's army was called a *sar* (1 Sa 17:55). **(6)** In Judg 8:6, *sar* represents a "ruler" of a city. **(7)** Any government official might be called a *sar* (Neh 3:14). **(8)** "Religious officiants" who served in the temple of God were also called sarim (Jer 35:4). **(9)** The "leaders" or "chiefs" of the Levites (1 Chr 15:16) or priests (Ezra 8:24) are sarim. **(10)** In 1 Chr 24:5, the word appears to be a title: "Thus were they divided by lot, one sort with another; for the governors of the sanctuary [*sarim qodes*] and governors of the house of God [*sarim ha'elohim*], were of the sons of Eleazar and of the sons of Ithamar." **(11)** In the Book of Daniel, *sar* is used of "superhuman beings" or "patron angels." Thus, Michael is the "prince" of Judah (Dan 10:21; cf. Josh 5:14). Daniel 8:25 speaks of a king who will arise and "stand up against the Prince of princes" (i.e., the Messiah). See: TWOT—2295a; BDB—694a, 974c, 978a, 979.

8270. שֹׁר {2x} **shôr**, *shore;* from 8324; a *string* (as *twisted* [comp. 8306]), i.e. (spec.) the umbilical cord (also fig. as the centre of strength):—navel {2x}. See: TWOT—2469a; BDB—1055d, 1057a.

8271. שְׁרֵא {6x} **sh^{e}rê'** (Aram.), *sher-ay';* a root corresp. to that of 8293; to *free, separate;* fig. to *unravel, commence;* by impl. (of unloading beasts) to *reside:*—begin {1x}, dissolve {2x}, dwell {1x}, loose {2x}. See: TWOT—3048; BDB—1117b.

8272. שַׁרְאֶצֶר {3x} **Shar'etser**, *shar-eh'-tser;* of for. der.; *Sharetser*, the name of an Ass. and an Isr.:—Sharezer {2x}, Sherezer {1x}. See: TWOT—3048; BDB—974c, 1055d.

8273. שָׁרָב {2x} **shârâb**, *shaw-rawb';* from an unused root mean. to *glare;* quivering *glow* (of the air), expec. the *mirage:*—heat {1x}, parched ground {1x}. See: TWOT—2462a; BDB—1055d.

8274. שֵׁרֵבְיָה {8x} **Shêrêbyâh**, *shay-rayb-yaw';* from 8273 and 3050; *Jah has brought heat; Sherebjah*, the name of two Isr.:—Sherebiah {8x}. See: BDB—1055d.

8275. שַׁרְבִיט {4x} **sharbîyt**, *shar-beet';* for 7626; a *rod* of empire:—sceptre {4x}. See: TWOT—2314b; BDB—987b, 1056a.

8276. שָׂרַג {2x} **sârag**, *saw-rag';* a prim. root; to *intwine:*—wrap together {1x}, wreath {1x}. See: TWOT—2284; BDB—974d.

8277. שָׂרַד {1x} **sârad**, *saw-rad';* a prim. root; prop. to *puncture* [comp. 8279], i.e. (fig. through the idea of *slipping* out) to *escape* or survive:—remained {1x}. See: TWOT—2285; BDB—974d.

8278. שְׂרָד {4x} **s^{e}râd**, *ser-awd';* from 8277; *stitching* (as *pierced* with a needle):—service {4x}. See: TWOT—2286a; BDB—975a.

8279. שֶׂרֶד {1x} **sered**, *seh'-red;* from 8277; a (carpenter's) *scribing-awl* (for *pricking* or scratching measurements):—line {1x}. See: TWOT—2286b; BDB—975b.

8280. שָׂרָה {2x} **sârâh**, *saw-raw';* a prim. root; to *prevail:*—power {2x}. See: TWOT—2287; BDB—975b.

8281. שָׁרָה {2x} **shârâh**, *shaw-raw';* a prim. root; to *free:*—remnant {1x}, it {1x}. See: TWOT—2463; BDB—1056a, 1056c, 1117b.

8282. שָׂרָה {5x} **sârâh**, *saw-raw';* fem. of 8269; a *mistress*, i.e. *female noble:*—lady {2x}, princess {2x}, queen {1x}. See: TWOT—2295b; BDB—979a, 994d.

8283. שָׂרָה {38x} **Sârâh**, *saw-raw';* the same as 8282; *Sarah*, Abraham's wife:—*Sarah* {38x}. See: BDB—979a.

8284. שָׁרָה {1x} **shârâh**, *shaw-raw';* prob. fem. of 7791; a *fortification* (lit. or fig.):—wall {1x}. See: TWOT—2355b; BDB—1004b, 1056c.

8285. שֵׁרָה {1x} **shêrâh**, *shay-raw';* from 8324 in its orig. sense of *pressing;* a wrist*band* (as *compact* or *clasping*):—bracelet {1x}. See: TWOT—2469b; BDB—1056b, 1057b.

8286. שְׂרוּג {5x} **S^{e}rûwg**, *ser-oog';* from 8276; *tendril; Serug*, a postdiluvian patriarch:—Serug {5x}. See: BDB—974d.

8287. שָׁרוּחֶן {1x} **Shârûwchen**, *shaw-roo-khen';* prob. from 8281 (in the sense of *dwelling* [comp. 8271] and 2580; *abode of pleasure; Sharuchen*, a place in Pal.:—Sharuhen {1x}. See: BDB—1056b.

8288. שְׂרוֹךְ {2x} **s^{e}rôwk**, *ser-oke';* from 8308; a *thong* (as *laced* or *tied*):—latchet {1x}, shoelatchet + 5275 {1x}. See: TWOT—2290a; BDB—976c.

8289. שָׁרוֹן {7x} **Shârôwn**, *shaw-rone';* prob. abridged from 3474; *plain, Sharon*, the name of a place in Pal.:—Sharon {6x}, Lasharon {1x}. See: BDB—450a, 546d, 1056c.

8290. שָׁרוֹנִי {1x} **Shârôwnîy**, *shaw-ro-nee';* patrial from 8289; a *Sharonite* or inhab. of Sharon:—Sharonite {1x}. See: BDB—1056c.

8291. שָׂרוּק {1x} **sarûwq**, *sar-ook';* pass. part. from the same as 8321; a *grapevine:*—principal plant {1x}. See: TWOT—2294b; BDB—977d. See 8320, 8321.

8292. שְׁרוּקָה {3x} **sh^{e}rûwqâh**, *sher-oo-kaw';* or (by perm.)

שְׁרִיקָה **sh^{e}rîyqâh**, *sher-ee-kaw';* fem. pass. part. of 8319; a *whistling* (in scorn); by anal. a *piping:*—hissing {2x}, bleating {1x}. See: TWOT—2468b; BDB—1057a.

8293. שֵׁרוּת {1x} **shêrûwth**, *shay-rooth';* from 8281 abb.; *freedom:*—variant {1x}. See: TWOT—2463; BDB—1056a.

8294. שֶׂרַח {3x} **Serach**, *seh'-rakh;* by perm. for 5629; *superfluity; Serach*, an Israelitess:—Serah {2x}, Sarah {1x}. See: BDB—976a.

8295. שָׂרַט {3x} **sâraṭ**, *saw-rat';* a prim. root; to *gash:*—cut in pieces {1x}, in pieces {1x}, make {1x}. See: TWOT—2289; BDB—976b.

8296. שֶׂרֶט {2x} **sereṭ**, *seh'-ret;* and

שָׂרֶטֶת **sâreṭeth**, *saw-reh'-teth;* from 8295; an *incision:*—cuttings {2x}. See: TWOT—2289a; BDB—976b.

8297. שָׂרַי {17x} **Sâray**, *saw-rah'-ee;* from 8269; *dominative; Sarai*, the wife of Abraham:—Sarai {17x}. See: BDB—976b, 979c.

8298. שָׁרַי {1x} **Shâray**, *shaw-rah'-ee;* prob. from 8324; *hostile; Sharay*, an Isr.:—Sharai {1x}. See: BDB—1056c.

8299. שָׂרִיג {3x} **sârîyg**, *saw-reeg';* from 8276; a *tendril* (as *intwining*):—branch {3x}. See: TWOT—2284a; BDB—974d.

8300. שָׂרִיד {28x} **sârîyd**, *saw-reed';* from 8277; a *survivor:*—remain {12x}, remaining {9x}, left {3x}, remnant {2x}, alive {1x}, rest {1x}. See: TWOT—2285a; BDB—975a.

8301. שָׂרִיד {2x} **Sârîyd**, *saw-reed';* the same as 8300; *Sarid*, a place in Pal.:—Sarid {2x}. See: BDB—975a.

8302. שִׁרְיוֹן {9x} **shiryôwn**, *shir-yone';* or

שִׁרְיֹן **shiryôn**, *shir-yone';* and

שִׁרְיָן **shiryân**, *shir-yawn';* also (fem.)

שִׁרְיָה **shiryâh**, *shir-yaw';* and

שִׁרְיֹנָה **shiryônâh**, *shir-yo-naw';* from 8281 in the orig. sense of *turning;* a *corslet* (as if *twisted*):—habergeon {3x}, coat {2x}, harness {2x}, coat of mail {1x}, breastplate {1x}. See: TWOT—2466a, 2465a; BDB—1056b, 1056c. See 5630.

8303. שִׁרְיוֹן {2x} **Shiryôwn**, *shir-yone';* and

שִׂרְיֹן **Siryôn**, *sir-yone';* the same as 8304 (i.e. *sheeted* with snow); *Shirjon* or *Sirjon*, a peak of the Lebanon:—Sirion {2x}. See: BDB—976b.

8304. שְׂרָיָה {20x} **S^erâyâh**, *ser-aw-yaw';* or

שְׂרָיָהוּ **S^erâyâhûw**, *ser-aw-yaw'-hoo;* from 8280 and 3050; *Jah has prevailed; Serajah,* the name of nine Isr.:—Seraiah {20x}. See: BDB—976a, 976b, 996a.

8305. שְׂרִיקָה {1x} **s^erîyqâh**, *ser-ee-kaw';* from the same as 8321 in the orig. sense of *piercing; hetchelling* (or combing flax), i.e. (concr.) *tow* (by extens. *linen* cloth):—fine {1x}. See: TWOT—2293a; BDB—977c.

8306. שָׂרִיר {1x} **shârîyr**, *shaw-reer';* from 8324 in the orig. sense as in 8270 (comp. 8326); a *cord,* i.e. (by anal.) *sinew:*—navel {1x}. See: TWOT—2469c; BDB—1057b.

8307. שְׁרִירוּת {10x} **sh^erîyrûwth**, *sher-ee-rooth';* from 8324 in the sense of *twisted,* i.e. *firm; obstinacy:*—imagination {9x}, lust {1x}. See: TWOT—2469d; BDB—1057b.

8308. שָׂרַךְ {1x} **sârak**, *saw-rak';* a prim. root; to *interlace:*—traversing {1x}. See: TWOT—2290; BDB—976c.

8309. שְׁרֵמָה {1x} **sh^erêmâh**, *sher-ay-maw';* prob. by an orth. err. for 7709; a *common:*—field {1x}. See: TWOT—2334a; BDB—995a, 1056c.

8310. שַׂרְסְכִים {1x} **Sarç^ekîym**, *sar-seh-keem';* of for. der.; *Sarsekim,* a Bab. general:—Sarsechim {1x}. See: BDB—976c.

8311. שָׂרַע {3x} **sâra^c**, *saw-rah';* a prim. root; to *prolong,* i.e. (reflex.) *be deformed* by excess of members:—superfluous {2x}, stretch out {1x}. See: TWOT—2291; BDB—976c.

8312. שַׂרְעַף {2x} **sar^caph**, *sar-af';* for 5587; *cogitation:*—thought {2x}. See: TWOT—2273b; BDB—972a, 976d.

8313. שָׂרַף {117x} **sâraph**, *saw-raf';* a prim. root; to *be* (caus. *set*) *on fire:*—burn {112x}, burn up {2x}, kindled {1x}, made {1x}, utterly {1x}.

(1) Since burning is the main characteristic of fire, the term *saraph* is used to describe the destroying of objects of all kinds: **(1a)** the door of a city tower (Judg 9:52), **(1b)** various cities (Josh 6:24; 1 Sa 30:1), **(1c)** chariots (Josh 11:6, 9), **(1d)** idols (Ex 32:20; Deut 9:21), and **(1e)** the scroll that Jeremiah had dictated to Baruch (Jer 36:25, 27–28). **(2)** Some burnings were abominable: **(2a)** the Moabites' burning of the bones of the king of Edom (Amos 2:1) and **(2b)** burning of men's bodies on the sacred altar was a great act of desecration (1 Kin 13:2). **(3)** Ezekiel burned a third of his hair as a symbol that part of the people of Judah would be destroyed (Eze 5:4).

(4) The burning of a red heifer produced ashes for purification (Lev 19:5, 8). Syn.: It is important to notice that throughout the Levitical ritual two distinct words are used to represent burning. *Qatar* (6999) which properly means to turn into smoke or vapor, is used of the burning of the *Olah* (5930), of the memorial portion of the *minchah* (4503), and of the fat of the *zebach* (2077), all of which were intended as offerings for God's good pleasure and not for sin. This burning took palace of the altar at the door of the tabernacle. *Saraph* means to consume or burn up, and is used of the burning of the bodies of certain sin-offerings. Nothing is said of their smoke ascending as a sweet savor to God, because they represent "the body of sin, "an object that is by no means pleasing in His sight. This is the aspect of the matter presented by the sin-offering that the priest offered for himself, and still more emphatically by the offering of the goat for the sins for the people on the great Day of Atonement. Ordinary sin-offerings were eaten by the priest. See: TWOT—2292; BDB—976d.

8314. שָׂרָף {7x} **sârâph**, *saw-rawf';* from 8313; *burning,* i.e. (fig.) *poisonous* (serpent); spec. a *saraph* or symb. creature (from their copper color):—fiery serpent {3x}, fiery {2x}, seraphim {2x}.

(1) *Saraph,* in the singular, means burning one; fiery being (Num 21:6, 8; cf. Is 14:29; 30:6). **(2)** *Seraphim,* the plural form, means burning, noble. Seraphim refers to the ministering beings in Is 6:2, 6, and may imply either a serpentine form (albeit with wings, human hands, and voices) or beings that have a glowing quality about them. See: TWOT—2292a, 2292b; BDB—977b.

8315. שָׂרָף {1x} **Sâraph**, *saw-raf';* the same as 8314; *Saraph,* an Isr.:—*Saraph* {1x}. See: BDB—977b.

8316. שְׂרֵפָה {13x} **s^erêphâh**, *ser-ay-faw';* from 8313; *cremation:*—burning {9x}, burn {3x}, throughly {1x}. See: TWOT—2292c; BDB—977b.

8317. שָׁרַץ {14x} **shârats**, *shaw-rats';* a prim. root; to *wriggle,* i.e. (by impl.) *swarm* or *abound:*—creep {6x}, bring forth abundantly {5x}, move {1x}, breed abundantly {1x}, increase abundantly {1x}. See: TWOT—2467; BDB—1056c.

8318. שֶׁרֶץ {15x} **sherets**, *sheh'-rets;* from 8317; a *swarm,* i.e. active mass of minute animals:—creeping thing {11x}, creep {2x}, creature {1x}, move {1x}. See: TWOT—2467a; BDB—1056d.

8319. שָׁרַק {12x} **shâraq**, *shaw-rak';* a prim. root; prop. to *be shrill,* i.e. to whistle or *hiss* (as a call or in scorn):—hiss {12x}. See: TWOT—2468; BDB—1056d, 1117b.

8320. שָׂרֻק {1x} **sâruq**, *saw-rook';* from 8319; *bright red* (as *piercing* to the sight), i.e. *bay:*—speckled {1x}. See: TWOT—2294a; BDB—977d. See 8291.

8321. שֹׂרֵק {3x} **sôrêq**, *so-rake';* or

שׂוֹרֵק **sôwrêq**, *so-rake';* and (fem.)

שֹׂרֵקָה **sôrêqâh**, *so-ray-kaw';* from 8319 in the sense of *redness* (comp. 8320); a *vine* stock (prop. one yielding *purple* grapes, the richest variety):—choice wine {2x}, noble wine {1x}. See: TWOT—2294c; BDB—977d. comp. 8291.

8322. שְׁרֵקָה {7x} **sh^erêqâh**, *sher-ay-kaw';* from 8319; a *derision:*—hissing {7x}. See: TWOT—2468a; BDB—1056d.

8323. שָׂרַר {5x} **sârar**, *saw-rar';* a prim. root; to *have* (tran. *exercise;* refl. *get*) *dominion:*—rule {3x}, make prince {1x}, altogether {1x}. See: TWOT—2295; BDB—965a, 979a.

8324. שָׁרַר {5x} **shârar**, *shaw-rar';* a prim. root; to *be hostile* (only act. part. an *opponent*):—enemies {5x}. See: TWOT—2469; BDB—1004a.

8325. שָׁרָר {1x} **Shârâr**, *shaw-rawr';* from 8324; *hostile; Sharar,* an Isr.:—*Sharar* {1x}. See: BDB—1057a.

8326. שֹׁרֶר {1x} **shôrer**, *sho'-rer;* from 8324 in the sense of *twisting* (comp. 8270); the umbilical *cord,* i.e. (by extens.) a *bodice:*—navel {1x}. See: TWOT—2469a; BDB—1057a.

8327. שָׁרַשׁ {8x} **shârash**, *shaw-rash';* a prim. root; to *root,* i.e. strike into the soil, or (by impl.) to pluck from it:—. . . root {7x}, root out {1x}. See: TWOT—2471; BDB—1057d.

8328. שֶׁרֶשׁ {33x} **sheresh**, *sheh'-resh;* from 8327; a *root* (lit. or fig.):—root {30x}, bottom {1x}, deep {1x}, heels {1x}. See: TWOT—2471a; BDB—1057c, 1117b.

8329. שֶׁרֶשׁ {1x} **Sheresh**, *sheh'-resh;* the same as 8328; *Sheresh,* an Isr.:—*Sheresh* {1x}. See: BDB—1058a, 1058c.

8330. שֹׁרֶשׁ {3x} **shôresh** (Aram.), *sho'-resh;* corresp. to 8328:—root {3x}. See: TWOT—3050a; BDB—1117b.

8331. שַׁרְשָׁה {1x} **sharshâh**, *shar-shaw';* from 8327; a *chain* (as *rooted,* i.e. *linked*):—chain {1x}. See: TWOT—2470; BDB—1057b, 1058a. comp. 8333.

8332. שְׁרֹשׁוּ {1x} **sh^erôshûw** (Aram.), *sher-o-shoo';* from a root corresp. to 8327; *eradication,* i.e. (fig.) *exile:*—banishment {1x}. See: TWOT—3050b; BDB—1117b.

8333. שַׁרְשְׁרָה {7x} **sharsh^erâh**, *shar-sher-aw';* from 8327 [comp. 8331]; a *chain;* (arch.) prob. a *garland:*—chain {7x}. See: TWOT—2470; BDB—1057b, 1058a.

8334. שָׁרַת {97x} **shârath**, *shaw-rath';* a prim. root; to *attend* as a menial or worshipper; fig. to *contribute* to:—minister (v) {62x}, minister (n) {17x}, serve {8x}, servant {5x}, service {3x}, servitor {1x}, waited {1x}.

I. *Sharath,* as a noun, means "to serve, minister." **(1a)** This word occurs less than 100 times in the Old Testament. **(1b)** In the vast majority of instances, *sharath* appears in the form of an infinitive or participle. **(1c)** When the participle is translated as a verbal noun, such as "servant" or "minister," it loses the connotation of duration or repetition. [see below] **(1d)** Another grammatical feature of *sharath* is its usage exclusively in the intensive form. **(2)** *Sharath* often denotes "service" rendered in connection with Israel's worship; about 60 of its 97 occurrences have this meaning. **(2a)** When Samuel was still a boy, he ". . . did minister unto the Lord before Eli the priest" (1 Sa 2:11), and **(2b)** the Lord called to him while he ". . . ministered unto the Lord before Eli" (1 Sa 3:1). **(2c)** This kind of "service" was to honor only the Lord, for Israel was not to be "as the heathen, as the families of the countries; to serve wood and stone" (Eze 20:32).

(3) In the temple of Ezekiel's vision, those Levites who had ". . . ministered unto them [the people] before their idols . . ." were forbidden by the Lord to serve as priests (Eze 44:12). **(4)** Furthermore, ". . . the Lord separated the tribe of Levi . . . to minister unto him, and to bless in his name . . ." (Deut 10:8). **(5)** From the tribe of Levi, Moses was to anoint Aaron and his sons and consecrate them, that they may "minister" as priests (Ex 29:30). **(6)** Those not of the family of Aaron, though chosen "to minister unto him forever," acted as assistants to the priests, performing such physical tasks as keeping the gates, slaughtering the burnt offering, caring for the altars and the utensils of the sanctuary: "Then David said, None ought to carry the ark of God but the Levites: for them hath the LORD chosen to carry the ark of God, and to minister unto him for ever" (1 Chr 15:2; cf. Eze 44:11). **(7)** But Isaiah foresees the time when ". . . the sons of strangers . . . shall minister unto thee" (Is 60:10).

(8) In a number of situations, the word is used to denote "service" rendered to a fellow human being. **(8a)** Though the person "served" usually is of a higher rank or station in life, this word never describes a slave's servitude to his master. **(8b)** Moses was instructed: "Bring the tribe of Levi near, and present them before Aaron, the priest, that they may minister unto him" (Num 3:6; cf. 8:26). **(8c)** Elisha "ministered" to Elijah: "And he returned back from him, and took a yoke of oxen, and slew them, and boiled their flesh with the instruments of the oxen, and gave unto the people, and they did eat. Then he arose, and went after Elijah, and ministered unto him." (1 Kin 19:21). **(8d)** Abishag is said to have "ministered" unto David: "And Bathsheba went in unto the king into the chamber: and the king was very old; and Abishag the Shunammite ministered unto the king" (1 Kin 1:15). **(8e)** Various kinds of officials "ministered" to David: "And David assembled all the princes of Israel, the princes of the tribes, and the captains of the companies that ministered to the king by course, and the captains over the thousands, and captains over the hundreds, and the stewards over all the substance and possession of the king, and of his sons, with the officers, and with the mighty men, and with all the valiant men, unto Jerusalem" (1 Chr 28:1). **(8f)** David's son Amnon had a "servant that ministered unto him" (2 Sa 13:17). **(9)** There were seven eunuchs that "served in the presence of Ahasuerus the king . . ." (Est 1:10). He also had "servants that ministered unto him . . ." (Esth 2:2).

II. *Sharath,* as a participle, means "servant; minister." **(1)** This word is most regularly translated "minister." Josh 1:1 is one example: "Now after the death of Moses the servant ['ebed] of the Lord it came to pass, that the Lord spake unto Joshua, the son of Nun, Moses' minister [*sharath*]. . . ." **(2)** Eze 40:24 refers to a place in the temple complex which is reserved for ". . . the ministers of the house. . . .": "Then said he unto me, These *are* the places of them that boil, where the ministers of the house shall boil the sacrifice of the people." **(3)** The privilege of serving the Lord is not restricted to human beings: **(3a)** "Bless ye the Lord, all ye his hosts [angels]; ye ministers of his, that do his pleasure" (Ps 103:21). **(3b)** Fire and wind, conceived poetically as persons, are also God's "ministers": "Who layeth the beams of his chambers in the waters: who maketh the clouds his chariot: who walketh upon the wings of the wind: Who maketh his angels spirits; his ministers a flaming fire:" (Ps 104:3–4).

(4) Joshua was the "minister" of Moses (Ex 24:13), and **(5)** Elisha had a "servitor": "And his servitor said, What, should I set this before an hundred men? He said again, Give the people, that they may eat: for thus saith the LORD, They shall eat, and shall leave *thereof*" (2 Kin 4:43). Syn.: 5647, 5650, 5656. See: TWOT—2472; BDB—1058a.

8335. שָׁרֵת {2x} **shârêth**, *shaw-rayth';* infin. of 8334; *service* (in the Temple):—ministry {1x}, minister {1x}. See: TWOT—2472a; BDB—1058b.

8336. שֵׁשׁ {42x} **shêsh**, *shaysh;* or (for alliteration with 4897)

שְׁשִׁי **sh^eshiy**, *shesh-ee';* for 7893; *bleached* stuff, i.e. *white* linen or (by anal.) marble:—linen {20x}, fine linen {17x}, marble {3x}, silk {1x}, variant {1x}. See: TWOT—2473, 2379a; BDB—1010d, 1058b, 1058c.

8337. שֵׁשׁ {215x} **shêsh**, *shaysh;* masc.

שִׁשָּׁה **shishshâh**, *shish-shaw';* a prim. number; *six* (as an overplus [see 7797] beyond five or the fingers of the hand); as ord. *sixth:*—six {187x}, sixteen + 6240 {21x}, sixteenth + 6240 {3x}, sixth {2x}, sixteen + 7657 {1x}, threescore + 7239 {1x}. See: 995c, 1010d, 1058b, 1114d.

8338. שָׁשָׁו {1x} **shâwshâw**, *shaw-shaw';* a prim. root; appar. to *annihilate:*—leave the sixth part of thee {1x}. See: TWOT—2474; BDB—995d.

8339. שֵׁשְׁבַּצַּר {2x} **Shêshbatstsar**, *shaysh-bats-tsar';* of for. der.; *Sheshbatstsar,* Zerubbabel's Pers. name:—Sheshbazzar {2x}. See: BDB—1058c.

8340. שֵׁשְׁבַּצַּר {2x} **Shêshbatstsar** (Aram.), *shaysh-bats-tsar';* corresp. to 8339:—Sheshbazzar {2x}. See: BDB—1058c.

שָׂשָׂה **shâsâh**. See 8154.

8341. שָׁשָׁה {1x} **shâshâh**, *shaw-shaw';* a denom. from 8337; to *sixth* or divide into sixths:—sixth part {1x}. See: TWOT—2336d; BDB—995d.

8342. שָׂשׂוֹן {22x} **sâsôwn**, *saw-sone';* or

שָׂשֹׂן **sâsôn**, *saw-sone';* from 7797; *cheerfulness;* spec. *welcome:*—joy {15x}, gladness {3x}, mirth {3x}, rejoicing {1x}. See: TWOT—2246a; BDB—965b, 979c.

8343. שָׁשַׁי {1x} **Shâshay**, *shaw-shah'-ee;* perh. from 8336; *whitish; Shashai,* an Isr.:—Shashai {1x}. See: BDB—1058d.

8344. שֵׁשַׁי {3x} **Shêshay**, *shay-shah'-ee;* prob. for 8343; *Sheshai,* a Canaanite:—Sheshai {3x}. See: BDB—1058d.

8345. שִׁשִּׁי {28x} **shishshîy**, *shish-shee';* from 8337; *sixth,* ord. or (fem.) fractional:—sixth {25x}, sixth part {3x}. See: TWOT—2336b; BDB—995d, 1058d.

8346. שִׁשִּׁים {59x} **shishshîym**, *shish-sheem';* multiple of 8337; *sixty:*—threescore {47x}, sixty {12x}. See: TWOT—2336c; BDB—995d, 1058d.

8347. שֵׁשַׁךְ {2x} **Shêshak**, *shay-shak';* of for. der.; *Sheshak,* a symbol. name of Bab.:—Sheshach {2x}. See: TWOT—2475; BDB—525d, 1058d.

8348. שֵׁשָׁן {5x} **Shêshân**, *shay-shawn';* perh. for 7799; *lily; Sheshan,* an Isr.:—*Sheshan* {5x}. See: BDB—1058d.

שֹׁשָׁן **Shôshân**. See 7799.

8349. שָׁשַׁק {2x} **Shâshaq**, *shaw-shak';* prob. from the base of 7785; *pedestrian; Shashak,* an Isr.:—Shashak {2x}. See: BDB—1059a.

8350. שָׁשַׁר {2x} **shâshar**, *shaw-shar';* perh. from the base of 8324 in the sense of that of 8320; *red* ochre (from its *piercing* color):—vermilion {2x}. See: TWOT—2476; BDB—1059a.

8351. שֵׁת {1x} **shêth** (Num. 24:17), *shayth;* from 7582; *tumult:*—*Sheth* {1x}. TWOT—2301d, 2478a; BDB—981b, 1059a.

8352. שֵׁת {9x} **Shêth**, *shayth;* from 7896; *put,* i.e. *substituted; Sheth,* third son of Adam:—Seth {7x}, *Sheth* {2x}. See: BDB—1011c, 1059a.

8353. שֵׁת {2x} **shêth** (Aram.), *shayth;* or

שִׁת **shîth** (Aram.), *sheeth;* corresp. to 8337:—sixth {1x}, six {1x}. See: TWOT—3022a; BDB—1114d, 1117b.

8354. שָׁתָה {217x} **shâthâh**, *shaw-thaw';* a prim. root; to *imbibe* (lit. or fig.):—drink {208x}, drinkers {1x}, drunkards {1x}, banquet {1x}, misc. {6x} = × assuredly, × certainly, drinking, surely. See: TWOT—2477; BDB—1059a, 1117c. [*prop. intens. of* 8248.]

8355. שְׁתָה {5x} **sh^ethâh** (Aram.), *sheth-aw';* corresp. to 8354:—to drink {5x}.

(1) This verb primarily means to drink or to consume a liquid, and is used of inanimate subjects (land – Deut 11:1), as well as of persons (Gen 9:21), or animals (Gen 24:19). **(2)** "To drink a cup" is a metaphor for consuming all that a cup may contain (Is 51:17). **(3)** Not only liquids may be drunk (Job 15:16). **(4)** This word may be used of a communal activity (Judg 9:27). **(5)** The phrase "eat and drink" may mean **(5a)** to eat a meal (Gen 24:54); or **(5b)** to banquet, which included many activities in addition to just eating and drinking, or participating in a feast (1 Kin 1:25). **(6)** The phrase, "eating and drinking," may signify a religious meal—i.e., a communion meal with God (Ex 24:11), sacramentally uniting with God (cf. 1 Cor. 10:19). **(7)** The phrase, "eating and drinking," may also signify life in general (1 Kin 4:20; cf. Eccl 2:24; 5:18; Jer 22:15). See: TWOT—3051; BDB—1083b, 1117c.

8356. שָׁתָה {2x} **shâthâh**, *shaw-thaw';* from 7896; a *basis,* i.e. (fig.) political or moral *support:*—foundations {1x}, purposes {1x}. See: TWOT—2380b; BDB—1011d, 1059a, 1059d, 1060a.

8357. שֵׁתָה {2x} **shêthâh**, *shay-thaw';* from 7896; the *seat* (of the person):—buttocks {2x}. See: TWOT—2478a; BDB—1011d, 1059a, 1059d.

8358. שְׁתִי {1x} **sh^ethîy**, *sheth-ee';* from 8354; *intoxication:*—drunkenness {1x}. See: TWOT—2477a; BDB—1059c.

8359. שְׁתִי {9x} **sh^ethîy**, *sheth-ee';* from 7896; a *fixture,* i.e. the *warp* in weaving:—warp {9x}. See: TWOT—2479a; BDB—1059d.

8360. שְׁתִיָּה {1x} **sh^ethîyâh**, *sheth-ee-yaw';* fem. of 8358; *potation:*—drinking {1x}. See: TWOT—2477b; BDB—1059c.

שְׁתַּיִם **sh^ettayim**. See 8147.

8361. שִׁתִּין {4x} **shittîyn** (Aram.), *shit-teen';* corresp. to 8346 [comp. 8353]; *sixty:*—threescore {4x}. See: TWOT—3022b; BDB—1114d, 1117c.

8362. שָׁתַל {10x} **shâthal**, *shaw-thal';* a prim. root; to *transplant:*—plant {10x}. See: TWOT—2480; BDB—1060a.

8363. שְׁתִל {1x} **sh^ethîyl**, *sheth-eel';* from 8362; a *sprig* (as if *transplanted*), i.e. *sucker:*—plant {1x}. See: TWOT—2480a; BDB—1060a.

8364. שֻׁתַלְחִי {1x} **Shûthalchîy**, *shoo-thal-kee';* patron. from 7803; a *Shuthalchite* (collect.) or desc. of Shuthelach:—Shuthalhites {1x}. See: BDB—1004d.

שָׂתַם **sâtham**. See 5640.

8365. שָׁתַם {2x} **shâtham**, *shaw-tham';* a prim. root; to *unveil* (fig.):—open {2x}. See: TWOT—2481; BDB—1060c.

8366. שָׁתַן {6x} **shâthan**, *shaw-than';* a prim. root; (caus.) to *make water,* i.e. *urinate:*—pisseth {6x}. See: TWOT—2377; BDB—1010b, 1060c.

8367. שָׁתַק {4x} **shâthaq**, *shaw-thak';* a prim. root; to *subside:*—calm {2x}, quiet {1x}, cease {1x}. See: TWOT—2482; BDB—1060c.

8368. שָׂתַר {1x} **sâthar**, *saw-thar';* a prim. root; to *break* out (as an eruption):—secret parts {1x}. See: TWOT—2297; BDB—979c, 1104d.

8369. שֵׁתָר {1x} **Shêthâr**, *shay-thawr';* of for. der.; *Shethar,* a Pers. satrap:—*Shethar* {1x}. See: BDB—1060c.

8370. שְׁתַר בּוֹזְנַי {4x} **Shᵉthar Bôwzᵉnay**, *sheth-ar' bo-zen-ah'-ee;* of for. der.; *Shethar-Bozenai,* a Pers. officer:—Shetharboznai {4x}. See: BDB—1117c.

8371. שָׁתַת {2x} **shâthath**, *shaw-thath';* a prim. root; to *place,* i.e. *array;* reflex. to *lie:*—laid {1x}, set {1x}. See: TWOT—2483; BDB—1001c, 1060c.

ת

8372. תָּא {13x} **tâʼ**, *taw;* and (fem.)

תָּאָה **tâʼâh** (Eze 40:12), *taw-aw';* from (the base of) 8376; a *room* (as *circumscribed*):—little chamber {11x}, chamber {2x}. See: TWOT—2484; BDB—1060b.

8373. תָּאַב {2x} **tâʼab**, *taw-ab';* a prim. root; to *desire:*—long {2x}. See: TWOT—2485; BDB—1060b.

8374. תָּאַב {1x} **tâʼab**, *taw-ab';* a prim. root [prob. rather ident. with 8373 through the idea of *puffing* disdainfully at; comp. 340]; to *loathe* (mor.):—abhor {1x}. See: TWOT—2486; BDB—1060b.

8375. תַּאֲבָה {1x} **taʼăbâh**, *tah-ab-aw';* from 8374 [comp. 15]; *desire:*—longing {1x}. See: TWOT—2485a; BDB—1060b.

8376. תָּאָה {2x} **tâʼâh**, *taw-aw';* a prim. root; to *mark* off, i.e. (intens.) *designate:*—point out {2x}. See: TWOT—2487; BDB—1060d, 1061c, 1063b.

8377. תְּאוֹ {2x} **tᵉʼôw**, *teh-o';* and

תּוֹא **tôwʼ** (the orig. form), *toh;* from 8376; a species of *antelope* (prob. from the white *stripe* on the cheek):—wild ox {1x}, wild bull {1x}. See: TWOT—2488; BDB—1060d, 1063a.

8378. תַּאֲוָה {20x} **taʼăvâh**, *tah-av-aw';* from 183 (abb.); a *longing;* by impl. a *delight* (subj. *satisfaction,* obj. a *charm*):—desire {13x}, lust {1x}, greedily {1x}, pleasent {1x}, misc. {4x} = dainty, × exceedingly, lusting. See: TWOT—40d; BDB—16c. See also 6914.

8379. תַּאֲוָה {1x} **taʼăvâh**, *tah-av-aw';* from 8376; a *limit,* i.e. *full extent:*—utmost bound {1x}. See: TWOT—2496b; BDB—1060d, 1063b.

8380. תָּאוֹם {4x} **tâʼôwm**, *taw-ome';* or

תָּאֹם **tâʼôm**, *taw-ome';* from 8382; a *twin* (in plur. only), lit. or fig.:—twin {4x}. See: TWOT—2489a; BDB—1060d, 1063a, 1064a.

8381. תַּאֲלָה {1x} **taʼălâh**, *tah-al-aw';* from 422; an *imprecation:*—curse {1x}. See: TWOT—94b; BDB—46d, 1060d.

8382. תָּאַם {6x} **tâʼam**, *taw-am';* a prim. root; to *be complete;* but used only as denom. from 8380, to *be* (caus. *make*) *twinned,* i.e. (fig.) *duplicate* or (arch.) *jointed:*—coupled together {3x}, bear twins {2x}, coupled {1x}. See: TWOT—2489; BDB—1060d, 1069c, 1071a.

תָּאֹם **tâʼôm**. See 8380.

8383. תְּאֻן {1x} **tᵉʼun**, *teh-oon';* from 205; *naughtiness,* i.e. *toil:*—lies {1x}. See: TWOT—48b; BDB—20b, 1061b.

8384. תְּאֵן {39x} **tᵉʼên**, *teh-ane';* or (in the sing., fem.)

תְּאֵנָה **tᵉʼênâh**, *teh-ay-naw';* perh. of for. der.; the *fig* (tree or fruit):—fig tree {23x}, fig {16x}. See: TWOT—2490; BDB—1061a.

8385. תַּאֲנָה {2x} **taʼănâh**, *tah-an-aw';* or

תֹּאֲנָה **tôʼănâh**, *to-an-aw';* from 579; an *opportunity* or (subj.) *purpose:*—occasion {2x}. See: TWOT—126a, 126b; BDB—58c, 1061a.

8386. תַּאֲנִיָּה {2x} **taʼănîyâh**, *tah-an-ee-yaw';* from 578; *lamentation:*—heaviness {1x}, mourning {1x}. See: TWOT—124b; BDB—1061b.

8387. תַּאֲנַת שִׁלֹה {1x} **Taʼănath Shîlôh**, *tah-an-ath' shee-lo';* from 8385 and 7887; *approach of Shiloh; Taanath-Shiloh,* a place in Pal.:—Taanathshiloh {1x}. See: BDB—1061b.

8388. תָּאַר {7x} **tâʼar**, *taw-ar';* a prim. root; to *delineate;* reflex. to *extend:*—draw {5x}, mark out {2x}. See: TWOT—2491, 2491b; BDB—1060d, 1061b, 1061c.

8389. תֹּאַר {15x} **tôʼar**, *to'-ar;* from 8388; *outline,* i.e. *figure* or *appearance:*—form {3x}, goodly {2x}, beautiful + 3303 {2x}, favoured {2x}, comely {1x}, countenance {1x}, fair + 3303 {1x}, goodly + 2896 {1x}, resembled {1x}, visage {1x}.

The noun *to'ar* means **(1)** "form, shape" in 1 Sa 28:14 and **(2)** "stately appearance" in 1 Sa 25:3. Syn.: 4758, 4759, 7207, 7209, 7210.See: TWOT—2491a; BDB—1061b, 1064c.

8390. תַּאֲרֵעַ {1x} **Taʼărêaʻ**, *tah-ar-ay'-ah;* perh. from 772; *Taarea,* an Isr.:—Tarea {1x}. See: BDB—357c, 1061c. See 8475.

8391. תְּאַשּׁוּר {2x} **tᵉʼashshûwr**, *teh-ash-shoor';* from 833; a species of *cedar* (from its *erectness*):—box tree {1x}, box {1x}. See: TWOT—183g; BDB—81b, 1061c.

8392. תֵּבָה {28x} **têbâh**, *tay-baw';* perh. of for. der.; a *box:*—ark {28x}. See: TWOT—2492; BDB—1061c.

8393. תְּבוּאָה {42x} **tᵉbûwʼâh**, *teb-oo-aw';* from 935; *income,* i.e. *produce* (lit. or fig.):—increase {23x}, fruit {13x}, revenue {5x}, gain {1x}. See: TWOT—212c; BDB—100a, 1061d.

8394. תָּבוּן {43x} **tâbûwn**, *taw-boon';* and (fem.)

תְּבוּנָה **tᵉbûwnâh**, *teb-oo-naw';* or

תּוֹבֻנָה **tôwbûnâh**, *to-boo-naw';* from 995; *intelligence;* by impl. an *argument;* by extens. *caprice:*—understanding {38x}, discretion {1x}, reasons {1x}, misc. {3x} = skilfulness, wisdom.

Tobuwnah means "understanding." **(1)** This word is a wisdom term. **(2)** Like binah (995), it represents the act of wisdom: "He divideth the sea with his power, and by his understanding he smiteth through the proud" (Job 26:12), **(3)** the faculty of wisdom: "And I have filled him with the spirit of God, in wisdom, and in understanding, and in knowledge, and in all manner of workmanship," (Ex 31:3), **(4)** the object of wisdom: "Yea, if thou criest after knowledge, and liftest up thy voice for understanding;" (Prov 2:3), and **(5)** the personification of wisdom (Prov 8:1). Syn.: 995, 998, 4905, 7919, 8394. See: TWOT—239c; BDB—108a, 108b, 1061d, 1063b.

8395. תְּבוּסָה {1x} **tᵉbûwçâh**, *teb-oo-saw';* from 947; a *treading down,* i.e. *ruin:*—destruction {1x}. See: TWOT—216c; BDB—101b, 1061d.

8396. תָּבוֹר {10x} **Tâbôwr**, *taw-bore';* from a root corresp. to 8406; *broken region; Tabor,* a mountain in Pal., also a city adjacent:—Tabor {10x}. See: BDB—58b, 493b, 1061d.

8397. תֶּבֶל {2x} **tebel**, *teh'-bel;* appar. from 1101; *mixture,* i.e. *unnatural* bestiality:—confusion {2x}. See: TWOT—248d; BDB—117d, 1061d.

8398. תֵּבֵל {36x} **têbêl**, *tay-bale';* from 2986; the *earth* (as *moist* and therefore inhabited); by extens. the *globe;* by impl. its *inhabitants;* spec. a partic. *land,* as Babylonia, Pal.:—world {35x}, habitable part {1x}.

This word signified, first, the solid material on which man dwells, and that was formed, founded, established, and disposed by God; and secondly, the inhabitants thereof. See: TWOT—835h; BDB—385c, 1061d.

תֻּבַל **Tûbal**. See 8422.

8399. תַּבְלִית {1x} **tablîyth**, *tab-leeth';* from 1086; *consumption:*—destruction {1x}. See: TWOT—246c; BDB—115b, 1061d.

8400. תְּבַלֻּל {1x} **tᵉballûl**, *teb-al-lool';* from 1101 in the orig. sense of *flowing:*—a *cataract* (in the eye):—blemish {1x}. See: TWOT—248e; BDB—117d, 1061d.

8401. תֶּבֶן {17x} **teben**, *teh'-ben;* prob. from 1129; prop. *material,* i.e. (spec.) refuse *haum* or stalks of grain (as *chopped* in threshing and used for fodder):—straw {15x}, stubble {1x}, chaff {1x}. See: TWOT—2493; BDB—1061d.

8402. תִּבְנִי {3x} **Tibnîy**, *tib-nee';* from 8401; *strawy; Tibni,* an Isr.:—Tibni {3x}. See: BDB—1062a.

8403. תַּבְנִית {20x} **tabnîyth**, *tab-neeth';* from 1129; *structure;* by impl. a *model, resemblance:*—pattern {9x}, likeness {5x}, form {3x}, similitude {2x}, figure {1x}. See: TWOT—255d; BDB—125d, 1062a.

8404. תַּבְעֵרָה {2x} **Tabʻêrâh**, *tab-ay-raw';* from 1197; *burning; Taberah,* a place in the desert:—*Taberah* {2x}. See: BDB—1062a.

8405. תֵּבֵץ {3x} **Têbêts**, *tay-bates';* from the same as 948; *whiteness; Tebets,* a place in Pal.:—Thebez {3x}. See: BDB—1062a.

8406. תְּבַר {1x} **tᵉbar** (Aram.), *teb-ar';* corresp. to 7665; to *be fragile* (fig.):—break {1x}. See: TWOT—3052; BDB—1117c.

8407. תִּגְלַת פִּלְאֶסֶר {6x} **Tiglath Pilʼeçer**, *tig-lath' pil-eh'-ser;* or

תִּגְלַת פְּלֶסֶר **Tiglath Pᵉleçer**, *tig-lath pel-eh-ser;* or

תִּלְּגַת פִּלְנְאֶסֶר **Tilgath Pilnᵉʼeçer**, *til-gath' pil-neh-eh'-ser;* or

תִּלְּגַת פִּלְנֶסֶר **Tilgath Pilneçer**, *til-gath' pil-neh'-ser;* of for. der.; *Tiglath-Pileser* or *Tilgath-pilneser,* an Assy. king:—Tiglath-pileser {3x}, Tilgath-pilneser {3x}. See: BDB—129c, 1062a, 1067d.

8408. תַּגְמוּל {1x} **tagmûwl**, *tag-mool';* from 1580; a *bestowment:*—benefit {1x}. See: TWOT—360c; BDB—1062b.

8409. תִּגְרָה {1x} **tigrâh**, *tig-raw';* from 1624; *strife,* i.e. *infliction:*—blow {1x}. See: TWOT—378b; BDB—173d, 1062b.

תֹּגַרְמָה **Tôgarmâh**. See 8425.

8410. תִּדְהָר {2x} **tidhâr**, *tid-hawr';* appar. from 1725; *enduring;* a species of hardwood or *lasting* tree (perh. *oak*):—pine {1x}, pine tree {1x}. See: TWOT—408b; BDB—187b, 1062b.

8411. תְּדִירָא {2x} **tᵉdîyrâʼ** (Aram.), *ted-ee-raw';* from 1753 in the orig. sense of *enduring; permanence,* i.e. (adv.) *constantly:*—continually {2x}. See: TWOT—2669d; BDB—1087b, 1117c.

8412. תַּדְמֹר {2x} **Tadmôr**, *tad-more'*; or

תַּמֹּר **Tammôr** (1 Kings 9:18), *tam-more'*; appar. from 8558; *palm*-city; *Tadmor*, a place near Pal.:—Tadmor {2x}. See: BDB—1062b.

8413. תִּדְעָל {2x} **Tidʻâl**, *tid-awl'*; perh. from 1763; *fearfulness; Tidal*, a Canaanite:—*Tidal* {2x}. See: BDB—1062b.

8414. תֹּהוּ {20x} **tôhûw**, *to'-hoo*; from an unused root mean. to lie *waste*; a *desolation* (of surface), i.e. *desert*; fig. a *worthless* thing; adv. in *vain*:—vain {4x}, vanity {4x}, confusion {3x}, without form {2x}, wilderness {2x}, nought {2x}, nothing {1x}, empty place {1x}, waste {1x}. See: TWOT—2494a; BDB—1062c.

8415. תְּהוֹם {36x} **tᵉhôwm**, *teh-home'*; or

תְּהֹם **tᵉhôm**, *teh-home'*; (usually fem.) from 1949; an *abyss* (as a *surging* mass of water), espec. the *deep* (the *main* sea or the subterranean *water-supply*):—deep {20x}, depth {15x}, deep places {1x}.

Tehom means "deep water; ocean; water table; waters; flood of waters." **(1)** The word represents the "deep water" whose surface freezes when cold: "The waters are hid as with a stone, and the face of the deep is frozen" (Job 38:30). **(2)** In Ps 135:6 *tehom* is used of the "ocean" in contrast to the seas: "Whatsoever the Lord pleased, that did he in heaven, and in earth, in the seas, and all deep places [in the entire ocean]" (cf. Ps 148:7 et al.). **(3)** The word has special reference to the deep floods or sources of water. **(3a)** Sailors in the midst of a violent storm "mount up to the heaven, they go down again to the depths" (Ps 107:26). **(3b)** This is hyperbolic or exaggerated poetical talk, but it presents the "depths" as the opposite of the heavens or skies. **(3c)** This emphasis is especially prominent in the Song of Moses, where the word represents the ever-existing (but not eternal), ever-threatening, and perilous "deep," not simply an element of nature but a dangerous element: "The depths have covered them: they sank into the bottom as a stone" (Ex 15:5). **(3d)** On the other hand, in such contexts *tehom* may mean no more than "deep water" into which heavy objects quickly sink.

(4) *Tehom* can represent an inexhaustible source of water or, by way of poetic comparison, of blessing: ". . . With blessings of heaven above, blessings of the deep that lieth under . . ." (Gen 49:25). **(4a)** In such contexts the word represents the "water table" always available below the surface of the earth—what was tapped by digging wells, out of which flowed springs, and what was one with the waters beneath the surface of oceans, lakes, seas, and rivers. **(4b)** This was what God opened together with the waters above the expanse (Gen 7:11; cf. 1:7) and what later was closed to cause and terminate the great Flood (Gen 8:2; cf. Ps 33:6; 104:6; Eze 26:19). **(4c)** In such contexts the word represents a "flood of waters" (Ps 33:6). **(5)** In Gen 1:2 (the first occurrence of the word) *tehom* is used of "all waters" which initially covered the surface of the entire earth: ". . . And darkness was upon the face of the deep" (cf. Prov 3:20; 8:24, 27–28). Syn.: 4325. See: TWOT—2495a; BDB—1062d.

8416. תְּהִלָּה {57x} **tᵉhillâh**, *teh-hil-law'*; from 1984; *laudation*; spec. (concr.) a *hymn*:—praise {57x}.

Tehillah means "glory; praise; song of praise; praiseworthy deeds." **(1)** This word denotes a quality or attribute of some person or thing, "glory or praiseworthiness": "He is thy praise, and he is thy God, that hath done for thee these great and terrible things, which thine eyes have seen" (Deut 10:21). **(2)** Israel is God's "glory" when she exists in a divinely exalted and blessed state: "And give him no rest, till he establish, and till he make Jerusalem a praise in the earth" (Is 62:7; cf. Jer 13:11). **(3)** In some cases *tehillah* represents the words or song by which God is publicly lauded, or by which His "glory" is publicly declared: **(3a)** "My praise [the Messiah is speaking here] shall be of thee in the great congregation . . ." (Ps 22:25). **(3b)** Ps 22:22 is even clearer: "I will declare thy name unto my brethren: in the midst of the congregation will I praise thee."

(4) *Tehillah* is a technical-musical term for a song (7892 - shir) which exalts or praises God: "David's psalm of praise" (heading for Ps 145; v. 1 in the Hebrew). **(5)** Perhaps Neh 11:17 refers to a choirmaster or one who conducts such singing of "praises": "And Mattaniah . . . , the son of Asaph, was the principal to begin the thanksgiving in prayer [who at the beginning was the leader of praise at prayer]. . . ." **(6)** Finally, *tehillah* may represent deeds which are worthy of "praise," or deeds for which the doer deserves "praise and glory." This meaning is in the word's first biblical appearance: "Who is like unto thee, O Lord, among the gods? Who is like thee, glorious in holiness, fearful in praises [in praiseworthy deeds], doing wonders [miracles]?" (Ex 15:11). See: TWOT—500c; BDB—239d, 1062d.

8417. תָּהֳלָה {1x} **tohŏlâh**, *to-hol-aw'*; fem. of an unused noun (appar. from 1984) mean. *bluster; braggadocio*, i.e. (by impl.) *fatuity*:—folly {1x}. See: TWOT—2494b; BDB—1062d.

8418. תַּהֲלֻכָה {1x} **tahălûkâh**, *tah-hal-oo-kaw'*; from 1980; a *procession*:—× went {1x}.

Tahalukot [plural of *tahalukah*] occurs once to mean "procession," specifically a thanksgiving procession (Neh 12:31). See: TWOT—498e; BDB—237c, 1062d.

תְּהֹם **tᵉhôm**. See 8415.

8419. תַּהְפֻּכָה {10x} **tahpûkâh**, *tah-poo-kaw'*; from 2015; a *perversity* or *fraud*:—froward {4x}, frowardness {3x}, froward things {2x}, perverse things {1x}. See: TWOT—512f; BDB—246c, 1063a.

8420. תָּו {3x} **tâv**, *tawv*; from 8427; a *mark*; by impl. a *signature*:—desire {1x}, mark {2x}. See: TWOT—2496a; BDB—1063a, 1063b.

8421. תּוּב {8x} **tûwb** (Aram.), *toob*; corresp. to 7725, to *come back*; spec. (tran. and ellip.) to *reply*:—answer {2x}, restore {1x}, return {4x}, return an answer {1x}. See: TWOT—3053; BDB—1117d.

8422. תּוּבַל {8x} **Tûwbal**, *too-bal'*; or

תֻּבַל **Tûbal**, *too-bal'*; prob. of for. der.; *Tubal*, a postdiluvian patriarch and his posterity:—*Tubal* {8x}. See: BDB—1061d, 1063a.

8423. תּוּבַל קַיִן {2x} **Tûwbal Qayin**, *too-bal' kah'-yin*; appar. from 2986 (comp. 2981) and 7014; *offspring of Cain; Tubal-Kajin*, an antediluvian patriarch:—Tubal-cain {2x}. See: BDB—1063b.

תּוֹבֻנָה **tôwbûnâh**. See 8394.

8424. תּוּגָה {4x} **tûwgâh**, *too-gaw'*; from 3013; *depression* (of spirits); concr. a *grief*:—heaviness {3x}, sorrow {1x}. See: TWOT—839b; BDB—387b.

8425. תּוֹגַרְמָה {4x} **Tôwgarmâh**, *to-gar-maw'*; or

תֹּגַרְמָה **Tôgarmâh**, *to-gar-maw'*; prob. of for. der.; *Togarmah*, a son of Gomer and his posterity:—*Togarmah* {4x}. See: BDB—1062b.

8426. תּוֹדָה {32x} **tôwdâh**, *to-daw'*; from 3034; prop. an *extension* of the hand, i.e. (by impl.) *avowal*, or (usually) *adoration*; spec. a *choir* of worshipers:—thanksgiving {18x}, praise {6x}, thanks {3x}, thank offerings {3x}, confession {2x}.

(1) *Towdah* means "thanksgiving." **(2)** In the Hebrew text *towdah* is used to indicate "thanksgiving" in songs of worship (Ps 26:7; 42:4). **(3)** Sometimes the word is used to refer to the thanksgiving choir or procession (Neh 12:31, 38). **(4)** One of the peace offerings, or "sacrings," was designated the thanksgiving offering (Lev 7:12). Syn.: 1984, 2026, 2077, 3034, 4503, 5930, 7133, 8416. See: TWOT—847b; BDB—392d, 1063b.

8427. תָּוָה {2x} **tâvâh**, *taw-vaw'*; a prim. root; to *mark* out, i.e. (prim.) *scratch* or (def.) *imprint*:—scrabble {1x}, set [a mark] {1x}. See: TWOT—2496; BDB—1061c, 1063b.

8428. תָּוָה {1x} **tâvâh**, *taw-vaw'*; a prim. root [or perh. ident. with 8427 through a similar idea from *scraping* to pieces]; to *grieve*:—limit {1x}. See: TWOT—2497; BDB—1063b.

8429. תְּוַהּ {1x} **tᵉvahh** (Aram.), *tev-ah'*; corresp. to 8539 or perh. to 7582 through the idea of *sweeping* to ruin [comp. 8428]; to *amaze*, i.e. (reflex. by impl.) *take alarm*:—be astonied {1x}. See: TWOT—3054; BDB—1117d.

8430. תּוֹחַ {1x} **Tôwach**, *to'-akh*; from an unused root mean. to *depress; humble; Toach*, an Isr.:—Toah {1x}. See: BDB—1063c.

8431. תּוֹחֶלֶת {6x} **tôwcheleth**, *to-kheh'-leth*; from 3176; *expectation*:—hope {6x}. See: TWOT—859b; BDB—404b, 1063c, 1064a.

תּוֹךְ **tôwk**. See 8496.

8432. תָּוֶךְ {415x} **tâvek**, *taw'-vek*; from an unused root mean. to *sever*; a *bisection*, i.e. (by impl.) the *centre*:—midst {209x}, among {140x}, within {20x}, middle {7x}, in {6x}, between {3x}, therein {3x}, through {2x}, into {2x}, misc. {23x} = amongst, half, × wherein, mid [-night], × out (of).

(1) *Tavek* indicates the part of a space, place, number of people, things, or line which is not on the end or outside edge (Gen 9:21). **(2)** The word means among, not necessarily in the middle (Gen 40:20). **(3)** Ex 14:29 uses *tavek* as an extension of the word through. **(4)** This word also sometimes means simply "in" in the sense of "mixed into something" (Ex 39:3). **(5)** *Tavek* can mean middle when applied to an object or person between two others (Ex 39:25). **(6)** In Num 35:5 the word means "in the center." **(7)** This word signifies the hypothetical center line dividing something into two equal parts (Gen 15:10; Eze 15:4). **(8)** *Tavek* is used substantively, meaning the middle or the center part of a thing (Josh 12:2). See: TWOT—2498; BDB—1063c.

8433. תּוֹכֵחָה {28x} **tôwkêchâh**, *to-kay-khaw'*; and

תּוֹכַחַת **tôwkachath**, *to-kakh'-ath*; from 3198; *chastisement*; fig. (by words) *correction, refutation, proof* (even in defence):—reproof {14x}, rebuke {7x}, reproved {2x}, arguments {1x}, misc. {4x} = × chastened, correction, reasoning. See: TWOT—865a, 865b; BDB—407b, 1064a.

תּוּכִּיִּי **tûwkkîy**. See 8500.

8434. תּוֹלָד {1x} **Tôwlâd**, *to-lawd'*; from 3205; *posterity; Tolad*, a place in Pal.:—Tolad {1x}. See: BDB—410a, 1064a. comp. 513.

8435. תּוֹלְדָה {39x} **tôwlᵉdâh**, *to-led-aw';* or

תֹּלְדָה **tôlᵉdâh**, *to-led-aw';* from 3205; (plur. only) *descent,* i.e. *family;* (fig.) *history:*—generations {38x}, birth {1x}. See: TWOT—867g; BDB—410a, 1064a.

8436. תּוּלוֹן {1x} **Tûwlôn**, *too-lone';* from 8524; *suspension; Tulon,* an Isr.:—Tilon {1x}. See: BDB—1064a, 1066c, 1066d.

8437. תּוֹלָל {1x} **tôwlâl**, *to-lawl';* from 3213; *causing to howl,* i.e. an *oppressor:*—they that wasted us {1x}. See: TWOT—868c; BDB—1064a.

8438. תּוֹלָע {43x} **tôwlâ'**, *to-law';* and (fem.)

תּוֹלֵעָה **tôwlê'âh**, *to-lay-aw';* or

תּוֹלַעַת **tôwla'ath**, *to-lah'-ath;* or

תֹּלַעַת **tôla'ath**, *to-lah'-ath;* from 3216; a *maggot* (as *voracious*); spec. (often with ellip. of 8144) the crimson-*grub,* but used only (in this connection) of the color from it, and cloths dyed therewith:—scarlet {34x}, worm {8x}, crimson {1x}. See: TWOT—2516b; BDB—1068d, 1069a.

8439. תּוֹלָע {6x} **Tôwlâ'**, *to-law';* the same as 8438; *worm; Tola,* the name of two Isr.:—Tola {6x}. See: BDB—1064d, 1069a.

8440. תּוֹלָעִי {1x} **Tôwlâ'îy**, *to-law-ee';* patron. from 8439; a *Tolaite* (collect.) or desc. of Tola:—Tolaites {1x}. See: BDB—1046b, 1069a.

8441. תּוֹעֵבָה {117x} **tôw'êbâh**, *to-ay-baw';* or

תֹּעֵבָה **tô'êbâh**, *to-ay-baw';* fem. act. part. of 8581; prop. something *disgusting* (mor.), i.e. (as noun) an *abhorrence;* espec. *idolatry* or (concr.) an *idol:*—abomination {113x}, abominable thing {2x}, abominable {2x}.

To'ebah means abomination; loathsome, detestable thing. **(1)** *To'ebah* defines something or someone as essentially unique in the sense of being dangerous, sinister, and repulsive to another individual (Gen 43:32; 46:34; Prov 29:27). **(2)** When used with reference to God, this word describes people, things, acts, relationships, and characteristics that are detestable to Him because they are contrary to His nature; such as **(2a)** things related to death and idolatry (Deut 14:3); **(2b)** people with loathsome habits are themselves detestable to Him (Deut 22:5). **(3)** It is used in some contexts to describe pagan practices and objects (Deut 7:25–26). **(4)** It describes the repeated failures to observe divine regulations (Eze 5:7, 9). **(5)** *To'ebah* may represent **(5a)** the pagan cultic practices themselves (Deut 12:31), or **(5b)** the people who perpetrate such practices (Deut 18:12). **(6)** It is used in the sphere of jurisprudence and of family or tribal relationships; certain acts or characteristics are destructive of societal and familial harmony; both such things and the people who do them are described by *to'ebah* (Prov 6:16–19). See: TWOT—2530a; BDB—1072d.

8442. תּוֹעָה {2x} **tôw'âh**, *to-aw';* fem. act. part. of 8582; *mistake,* i.e. (mor.) *impiety,* or (political) *injury:*—hinder {1x}, error {1x}. See: TWOT—2531a; BDB—1064a, 1073c.

8443. תּוֹעָפָה {4x} **tôw'âphâh**, *to-aw-faw';* from 3286; (only in plur. collect.) *weariness,* i.e. (by impl.) *toil* (*treasure* so obtained) or *speed:*—strength {3x}, plenty {1x}. See: TWOT—886a; BDB—419b, 1064a.

8444. תּוֹצָאָה {23x} **tôwtsâ'âh**, *to-tsaw-aw';* or

תֹּצָאָה **tôtsâ'âh**, *to-tsaw-aw';* from 3318; (only in plur. collect.) *exit,* i.e. (geographical) *boundary,* or (fig.) *deliverance,* (act.) *source:*—goings out {11x}, outgoings {7x}, going forth {2x}, issues {2x}, borders {1x}.

Totsa'ah means "departure; place of departure." The word *totsa'ah* can connote both **(1)** the source of "departure": "Keep thy heart with all diligence; for out of it *are* the issues of life" (Prov 4:23) and **(2)** the actual "departure" itself: "*He that is* our God *is* the God of salvation; and unto GOD the Lord *belong* the issues from death" ("escape," Ps 68:20). **(3)** However, the word may also represent the extremity of a territory or its "border"—the place where one departs a given territory: "And the border went up toward Debir from the valley of Achor, . . .and the goings out thereof were at Enrogel:" (Josh 15:7). Syn.: 3318, 4161. See: TWOT—893e; BDB—426a, 1064a.

8445. תּוֹקְהַת {1x} **Tôwqahath**, *to-kah'-ath;* from the same as 3349; *obedience; Tokahath,* an Isr.:—Tikvath {1x}. See: BDB—876b, 1064b, 1075b.

8446. תּוּר {23x} **tûwr**, *toor;* a prim. root; to *meander* (caus. *guide*) about, espec. for trade or reconnoitring:—search {11x}, search out {3x}, spy out {2x}, seek {2x}, chapmen + 582 {1x}, descry {1x}, espied {1x}, excellent {1x}, merchantmen + 582 {1x}. See: TWOT—2500; BDB—451d, 1064b, 1064d.

8447. תּוֹר {4x} **tôwr**, *tore;* or

תֹּר **tôr**, *tore;* from 8446; a *succession,* i.e. a *string* or (abstr.) *order:*—turn {2x}, row {1x}, border {1x}. See: TWOT—2500a; BDB—1061b, 1064c, 1076a.

8448. תּוֹר {1x} **tôwr**, *tore;* prob. the same as 8447; a *manner* (as a sort of *turn*):—estate {1x}. See: TWOT—2500a; BDB—1061b, 1064c, 1076a.

8449. תּוֹר {14x} **tôwr**, *tore;* or

תֹּר **tôr**, *tore;* prob. the same as 8447; a *ring*-dove, often (fig.) as a term of endearment:—turtledove {9x}, turtle {5x}. See: TWOT—2500c; BDB—1064d, 1076a.

8450. תּוֹר {7x} **tôwr** (Aram.), *tore;* corresp. (by perm.) to 7794; a *bull:*—oxen {4x}, bullock {3x}. See: TWOT—3055; BDB—1117d.

8451. תּוֹרָה {219x} **tôwrâh**, *to-raw';* or

תֹּרָה **tôrâh**, *to-raw';* from 3384; a *precept* or *statute,* espec. the *Decalogue* or *Pentateuch:*—law {219x}.

Summary: *Torah* signifies primarily direction, teaching, instruction (Prov 13:14). It is derived from the verb, *yarah* "to project, point out" (3384) and hence to point out or teach. The law of God is that which points out or indicates His will to man. It is not an arbitrary rule, still less is it a subjective impulse; it is rather to be regarded as a course of guidance from above. Seen against the background of the verb *yarah,* it becomes clear that *torah* is much more than law or a set of rules. *Torah* is not restriction or hindrance, but instead the means whereby one can reach a goal or ideal. In the truest sense, *torah* was given to Israel to enable her to truly become and remain God's special people. One might say that in keeping *torah,* Israel was kept. Unfortunately, Israel fell into the trap of keeping *torah* as something imposed, and for itself, rather than as a means of becoming what God intended for her. The means became the end. Instead of seeing *torah* as a guideline, it became an external body of rules, and thus a weight rather than a freeing and guiding power. This burden, plus the legalism of Roman law, forms the background of the New Testament tradition of law, especially as Paul struggles with it in his letter to the church at Rome.

(1) In the wisdom literature, where the noun does not appear with a definite article, **(1a)** *torah* signifies primarily "direction, teaching, instruction": **(1a1)** "The law of the wise is a fountain of life, to depart from the snares of death" (Prov 13:14), and **(1a2)** "Receive, I pray thee, the law from his mouth, and lay up his words in thine heart" (Job 22:22). **(2)** The "instruction" of the sages of Israel, who were charged with the education of the young, was intended to cultivate in the young a fear of the Lord so that they might live in accordance with God's expectations. **(2a)** The sage was a father to his pupils: "Whoso keepeth the law is a wise son: but he that is a companion of riotous men shameth his father" (Prov 28:7; cf. 3:1; 4:2; 7:2). **(2b)** The natural father might also instruct his son in wise living, even as a God-fearing woman was an example of kind "instruction": "She openeth her mouth with wisdom; and in her tongue is the law of kindness" (Prov 31:26).

(3) The "instruction" given by God to Moses and the Israelites became **(3a)** known as "the law" or **(3b)** "the direction" (ha-*torah*), and quite frequently **(3c)** as "the Law of the Lord": "Blessed are the undefiled in the way, who walk in the law of the Lord" (Ps 119:1), or **(3d)** "the Law of God": "Also day by day, from the first day unto the last day, [Ezra] read in the book of the law of God" (Neh 8:18), and also **(3e)** as "the Law of [given through] Moses": "Remember ye the law of Moses my servant, which I commanded unto him in Horeb for all Israel . . ." (Mal 4:4). **(4)** The word can refer to **(4a)** the whole of the "law": "For he established a testimony in Jacob, and appointed a law in Israel, which he commanded our fathers, that they should make them known to their children" (Ps 78:5), or **(4b)** or particulars: "And this is the law which Moses set before the children of Israel . . ." (Deut 4:44). **(5)** God had communicated the "law" that Israel might observe and live: "And what nation is there so great, that hath statutes and judgments so righteous as all this law, which I set before you this day?" (Deut 4:8). **(6)** The king was instructed to have a copy of the "law" prepared for him at his coronation (Deut 17:18).

(7) The priests were charged with the study and teaching of, as well as the jurisprudence based upon, the "law" (Jer 18:18). **(7a)** Because of rampant apostasy the last days of Judah were times when there were no teaching priests (2 Chr 15:3); in fact, **(7b)** in Josiah's days the "law" (whether the whole *Torah,* or a book or a part) was recovered: "And Hilkiah . . . said to Shaphan the scribe, I have found the book of the law in the house of the Lord" (2 Chr 34:15). **(8)** The prophets called Israel to repent by returning to the *torah* ("instruction") of God (Is 1:10). **(8a)** Jeremiah prophesied concerning God's new dealing with His people in terms of the New Covenant, in which God's law is to be internalized, God's people would willingly obey Him: "But this shall be the covenant that I will make with the house of Israel; After those days, saith the Lord, I will put my law in their inward parts, and write it in their hearts; and will be their God, and they shall be my people" (Jer 31:33). **(8b)** The last prophet of the Old Testament reminded the priests of their obligations (Mal 2) and challenged God's people to remember the "law" of Moses in preparation for the coming Messiah (Mal 4:4). Syn.: 3384. See: TWOT—910d; BDB—435d, 1064c, 1064d.

8452. תּוֹרָה {1x} **tôwrâh**, *to-raw';* prob. fem. of 8448; a *custom:*—manner {1x}. See: TWOT—910d; BDB—435d, 1064c, 1064d.

8453. תּוֹשָׁב {14x} **tôwshâb**, *to-shawb';* or תֹּשָׁב **tôshâb** (1 Kings 17:1), *to-shawb';* from 3427; a *dweller* (but not outlandish [5237]); espec. (as distinguished from a native citizen [act. part. of 3427] and a temporary inmate [1616] or mere lodger [3885]) resident *alien:*—sojourner {9x}, stranger {3x}, foreigner {2x}. See: TWOT—922d; BDB—444c, 1064d, 1077b.

8454. תּוּשִׁיָּה {12x} **tuwshîyâh**, *too-shee-yaw';* or תֻּשִׁיָּה **tûshîyâh**, *too-shee-yaw';* from an unused root prob. mean. to *substantiate; support* or (by impl.) *ability,* i.e. (direct) *help,* (in purpose) an *undertaking,* (intellectual) *understanding:*—wisdom {7x}, enterprise {1x}, thing as it is {1x}, that which is {1x}, substance {1x}, working {1x}. Syn.: 995, 2450, 7919. See: TWOT—923a; BDB—444d, 1064d, 1077b.

8455. תּוֹתָח {1x} **tôwthâch**, *to-thawkh';* from an unused root mean. to *smite;* a *club:*—darts {1x}. Syn.: 2671. See: TWOT—933a; BDB—450c, 1064d.

8456. תָּזַז {1x} **tâzaz**, *taw-zaz';* a prim. root; to *lop* off:—cut down {1x}. See: TWOT—2501; BDB—1064d.

8457. תַּזְנוּת {20x} **taznûwth**, *taz-nooth';* or תַּזְנֻת **taznûth**, *taz-nooth';* from 2181; *harlotry,* i.e. (fig.) *idolatry:*—fornication {2x}, whoredom {18x}. See: TWOT—563c; BDB—276b, 1064d.

8458. תַּחְבֻּלָה {6x} **tachbûlâh**, *takh-boo-law';* or תַּחְבּוּלָה **tachbûwlâh**, *takh-boo-law';* from 2254 as denom. from 2256; (only in plur.) prop. *steerage* (as a management of *ropes*), i.e. (fig.) *guidance* or (by impl.) a *plan:*—good advice {1x}, (wise) counsels {5x}. See: TWOT—596a; BDB—287a, 1064d.

8459. תֹּחוּ {1x} **Tôchûw**, *to'-khoo;* from an unused root mean. to *depress; abasement; Tochu,* an Isr.:—Tohu {1x}. See: BDB—1063c, 1064d.

8460. תְּחוֹת {4x} **tᵉchôwth** (Aram.), *tekh-??th';* or תְּחֹת **tᵉchôth** (Aram.), *tekh-ōth';* corresp. to 8478; *beneath:*—under {4x}. Syn.: 8478. See: TWOT—3056; BDB—1117d.

8461. תַּחְכְּמֹנִי {1x} **Tachkᵉmônîy**, *takh-kem-o-nee';* prob. for 2453; *sagacious; Tachkemoni,* an Isr.:—Tachmonite {1x}. See: BDB—315d, 1064d.

8462. תְּחִלָּה {22x} **tᵉchillâh**, *tekh-il-law';* from 2490 in the sense of *opening;* a *commencement;* rel. *original* (adv. *-ly*):—beginning {14x}, first {5x}, first time {2x}, begin {1x}. See: TWOT—661d; BDB—321a, 1064d.

8463. תַּחֲלוּא {5x} **tachălûwʾ**, *takh-al-oo';* or תַּחֲלֻא **tachălûʾ**, *takh-al-oo';* from 2456; a *malady:*—disease {2x}, × grievous {1x}, (that are) sick {1x}, sickness {1x}. See: TWOT—648a; BDB—316a, 1066d.

8464. תַּחְמָס {2x} **tachmâç**, *takh-mawce';* from 2554; a species of unclean bird (from its *violence*), perh. an *owl:*—night hawk {2x}. See: TWOT—678b; BDB—329d, 1064d.

8465. תַּחַן {2x} **Tachan**, *takh'-an;* prob. from 2583; *station; Tachan,* the name of two Isr.:—Tahan {2x}. See: BDB—334c, 1064d.

8466. תַּחֲנָה {1x} **tachănâh**, *takh-an-aw';* from 2583; (only plur. collect.) an *encampment:*—camp {1x}. Syn.: 2583, 4264. See: TWOT—690d; BDB—334c, 1064d.

8467. תְּחִנָּה {25x} **tᵉchinnâh**, *tekh-in-naw';* from 2603; *graciousness;* caus. *entreaty:*—supplication {23x}, favour {1x}, grace {1x}. See: TWOT—694f; BDB—337c, 1064d.

8468. תְּחִנָּה {1x} **Tᵉchinnâh**, *tekh-in-naw';* the same as 8467; *Techinnah,* an Isr.:—Tehinnah {1x}. See: BDB—337c.

8469. תַּחֲנוּן {18x} **tachănûwn**, *takh-an-oon';* or (fem.) תַּחֲנוּנָה **tachănûwnâh**, *takh-an-oo-naw';* from 2603; earnest *prayer:*—supplications {17x}, intreaties {1x}. See: TWOT—694g; BDB—337c, 1064d.

8470. תַּחֲנִי {1x} **Tachănîy**, *takh-an-ee';* patron. from 8465; a *Tachanite* (collect.) or desc. of Tachan:—Tahanites {1x}. See: BDB—334c, 1064d, 1071d.

8471. תַּחְפַּנְחֵס {7x} **Tachpanchêç**, *takh-pan-khace';* or תְּחַפְנְחֵס **Tᵉchaphnᵉchêç** (Eze 30:18), *tekh-af-nekh-ace';* or תַּחְפְּנֵס **Tachpᵉnêç** (Jer 2:16), *takh-pen-ace';* of Eg. der.; *Tachpanches, Techaphneches* or *Tachpenes,* a place in Egypt:—Tahpanhes {5x}, Tahapanes {1x}, Tehaphnehes {1x}. See: BDB—1064d.

8472. תַּחְפְּנֵיס {3x} **Tachpᵉnêyç**, *takh-pen-ace';* of Eg. der.; *Tachpenes,* an Eg. woman:—Tahpenes {3x}. See: BDB—1065a.

8473. תַּחֲרָא {2x} **tachărâʾ**, *takh-ar-aw';* from 2734 in the orig. sense of 2352 or 2353; a linen *corslet* (as *white* or *hollow*):—habergeon {2x}. See: TWOT—2502; BDB—1065a.

8474. תַּחָרָה {2x} **tachârâh**, *takh-aw-raw';* a factitious root from 2734 through the idea of the *heat* of jealousy; to *vie* with a rival:—closest {1x}, contend {1x}. See: TWOT—736; BDB—354a.

8475. תַּחְרֵעַ {1x} **Tachrêaʿ**, *takh-ray'-ah;* for 8390; *Tachrea,* an Isr.:—Tahrea {1x}. See: BDB—357c, 1065a.

8476. תַּחַשׁ {14x} **tachash**, *takh'-ash;* prob. of for. der.; a (clean) animal with fur, prob. a species of *antelope:*—badger {14x}. See: TWOT—2503; BDB—1065a.

8477. תַּחַשׁ {1x} **Tachash**, *takh'-ash;* the same as 8476; *Tachash,* a rel. of Abraham:—Thahash {1x}. See: BDB—1065a.

8478. תַּחַת {24x} **tachath**, *takh'-ath;* from the same as 8430; the *bottom* (as *depressed*); only adv. *below* (often with prep. pref. *underneath*), in *lieu of,* etc.:—{24x} = instead, under, for, as, with, from, flat, in the same place. See: TWOT—2504; BDB—1065a, 1117d.

8479. תַּחַת {1x} **tachath** (Aram.), *takh'-ath;* corresp. to 8478:—under {1x}. See: TWOT—3056; BDB—1117d.

8480. תַּחַת {6x} **Tachath**, *takh'-ath;* the same as 8478; *Tachath,* the name of a place in the desert, also of three Isr.:—Tahath {6x}. See: BDB—1066c.

תְּחֹת **tᵉchôth**. See 8460.

8481. תַּחְתּוֹן {13x} **tachtôwn**, *takh-tone';* or תַּחְתֹּן **tachtôn**, *takh-tone';* from 8478; *bottommost:*—lower {5x}, lowest {2x}, nether {5x}, nethermost {1x}. See: TWOT—2504a; BDB—1066b.

8482. תַּחְתִּי {19x} **tachtîy**, *takh-tee';* from 8478; *lowermost;* as noun (fem. plur.) the *depths* (fig. a *pit,* the *womb*):—nether parts {5x}, nether {4x}, lowest {3x}, lower {2x}, lower parts {2x}, misc. {3x}. See: TWOT—2504b; BDB—1066d.

8483. תַּחְתִּים חָדְשִׁי {1x} **Tachtîym Chodshîy**, *takh-teem' khod-shee';* appar. from the plur. masc. of 8482 or 8478 and 2320; *lower* (ones) *monthly; Tachtim-Chodshi,* a place in Pal.:—Tahtim-hodshi {1x}. See: BDB—295a, 874a, 1066c.

8484. תִּיכוֹן {11x} **tîykôwn**, *tee-kone';* or תִּיכֹן **tîykôn**, *tee-kone';* from 8432; *central:*—middle {8x}, middlemost {2x}, midst {1x}. See: TWOT—2498a; BDB—1064a, 1066c.

8485. תֵּימָא {5x} **Têymâʾ**, *tay-maw';* or תֵּמָא **Têmâʾ**, *tay-maw';* prob. of for. der.; *Tema,* a son of Ishmael, and the region settled by him:—*Tema* {5x}. See: BDB—1066d, 1069b.

8486. תֵּימָן {23x} **têymân**, *tay-mawn';* or תֵּמָן **têmân**, *tay-mawn';* denom. from 3225; the *south* (as being on the *right* hand of a person facing the east):—south {11x}, southward {8x}, south side {2x}, south coast {1x}, south wind {1x}.

(1) *Teman* means "south; southern quarter; southwards." **(2)** In its first biblical occurrence (Ex 26:18), the word refers to the direction "southward." **(3)** *Teman* can mean "south" or "southern quarter" as in Josh 15:1: "This then was the lot of the tribe of the children of Judah by their families; *even* to the border of Edom the wilderness of Zin southward *was* the uttermost part of the south coast." Syn.: 3233. See: TWOT—872e; BDB—412c, 1066d, 1071b.

8487. תֵּימָן {11x} **Têymân**, *tay-mawn';* or תֵּמָן **Têmân**, *tay-mawn';* the same as 8486; *Teman,* the name of two Edomites, and of the region and desc. of one of them:—*Teman* {11x}. See: BDB—412d, 1064a, 1071b.

8488. תֵּימְנִי {1x} **Têymᵉnîy**, *tay-men-ee';* prob. for 8489; *Temeni,* an Isr.:—Temeni {1x}. See: BDB—412d, 1066d.

8489. תֵּימָנִי {8x} **Têymânîy**, *tay-maw-nee';* patron. from 8487; a *Temanite* or desc. of Teman:—Temani {1x}, Temanite {7x}. See: BDB—412d, 1066d, 1071b.

8490. תִּימָרָה {2x} **tîymârâh**, *tee-maw-raw';* or תִּמָרָה **tîmârâh**, *tee-maw-raw';* from the same as 8558; a *column,* i.e. *cloud:*—pillar {2x}. Syn.: 4676, 5982. See: TWOT—2523d; BDB—1066d.

8491. תִּיצִי {1x} **Tîytsîy**, *tee-tsee';* patrial or patron. from an unused noun of uncert. mean.; a *Titsite* or desc. or inhab. of an unknown Tits:—Tizite {1x}. See: BDB—1066d.

8492. תִּירוֹשׁ {38x} **tîyrôwsh**, *tee-roshe';* or תִּירֹשׁ **tîyrôsh**, *tee-roshe';* from 3423 in the sense of *expulsion; must* or fresh grape-juice (as just *squeezed* out); by impl. (rarely) fermented *wine:*—(new, sweet) wine {38x}. Syn.: 3196, 4469, 6071. See: TWOT—2505; BDB—440d, 1066d.

8493. תִּירְיָא {1x} **Tîyrᵉyâʼ**, *tee-reh-yaw'*; prob. from 3372; *fearful, Tirja*, an Isr.:—Tiria {1x}. See: BDB—432b, 1066d.

8494. תִּירָס {2x} **Tîyrâç**, *tee-rawce'*; prob. of for. der.; *Tiras*, a son of Japheth:—Tiras {2x}. See: BDB—1066d.

תִּירֹשׁ **tîyrôsh**. See 8492.

8495. תַּיִשׁ {4x} **tayish**, *tah'-yeesh*; from an unused root mean. to *butt*; a *buck* or he-goat (as given to *butting*):—he goat {4x}. Syn.: 5795, 6842, 8163. See: TWOT—2506; BDB—1066d.

8496. תֹּךְ {3x} **tôk**, *toke*; or

תּוֹךְ **tôwk** (Psa. 72:14), *toke*; from the same base as 8432 (in the sense of *cutting* to pieces); *oppression*:—deceit {2x}, fraud {1x}. See: TWOT—2509a; BDB—1063c, 1067a.

8497. תָּכָה {1x} **tâkâh**, *taw-kaw'*; a prim. root; to *strew*, i.e. *encamp*:—sat down {1x}. See: TWOT—2507; BDB—1067a.

8498. תְּכוּנָה {2x} **tᵉkûwnâh**, *tek-oo-naw'*; fem. pass. part. of 8505; *adjustment*, i.e. *structure*; by impl. *equipage*:—fashion {1x}, store {1x}.

Tekuwnah means "fixed matter" as in Eze 43:11: ". . . Show them the form of the house, and the fashion [*tekunah*] thereof . . ." See: 8499. See: TWOT—964e; BDB—467d, 1067a.

8499. תְּכוּנָה {1x} **tᵉkûwnâh**, *tek-oo-naw'*; from 3559; or prob. ident. with 8498; something *arranged* or *fixed*, i.e. a *place*:—seat {1x}.

Tekuwnah means "fixed place" as in Job 23:3: "Oh that I knew where I might find him! *that* I might come *even* to his seat!" See: TWOT—964e; BDB—467d, 1067a.

8500. תֻּכִּי {2x} **tukkîy**, *took-kee'*; or

תּוּכִּי **tûwkkîy**, *took-kee'*; prob. of for. der.; some imported creature, prob. a *peacock*:—peacock {2x}. See: TWOT—2508; BDB—1064a, 1067a.

8501. תָּכָךְ {1x} **tâkâk**, *taw-kawk'*; from an unused root mean. to *dissever*, i.e. *crush*:—deceitful {1x}. See: TWOT—2509?; BDB—1067a.

8502. תִּכְלָה {1x} **tiklâh**, *tik-law'*; from 3615; *completeness*:—perfection {1x}. See: TWOT—982e; BDB—479a, 1067a.

8503. תַּכְלִית {5x} **taklîyth**, *tak-leeth'*; from 3615; *completion*; by impl. an *extremity*:—end {2x}, perfect {1x}, perfection {2x}. See: TWOT—982f; BDB—479b, 1067a.

8504. תְּכֵלֶת {50x} **tᵉkêleth**, *tek-ay'-leth*; prob. for 7827; the cerulean *mussel*, i.e. the color (*violet*) obtained therefrom or stuff dyed therewith:—blue {50x}. See: TWOT—2510; BDB—1067a.

8505. תָּכַן {18x} **tâkan**, *taw-kan'*; a prim. root; to *balance*, i.e. *measure* out (by weight or dimension); fig. to *arrange, equalize*, through the idea of *levelling* (ment. *estimate, test*):—equal {7x}, weigh {3x}, pondereth {2x}, unequal {2x}, directed {1x}, misc. {3x} = bear up, mete, tell. See: TWOT—2511; BDB—1067b.

8506. תֹּכֶן {2x} **tôken**, *to'-ken*; from 8505; a fixed *quantity*:—measure {1x}, tale {1x}. See: TWOT—2511a; BDB—1067c.

8507. תֹּכֶן {1x} **Tôken**, *to'-ken*; the same as 8506; *Token*, a place in Pal.:—Tochen {1x}. See: BDB—1067c.

8508. תָּכְנִית {2x} **tokniyth**, *tok-neeth'*; from 8506; *admeasurement*, i.e. *consummation*:—pattern {1x}, sum {1x}. See: TWOT—2511b; BDB—1067c.

8509. תַּכְרִיךְ {1x} **takrîyk**, *tak-reek'*; appar. from an unused root mean. to *encompass*; a *wrapper* or robe:—garment {1x}. See: TWOT—1037a; BDB—501b, 1067c.

8510. תֵּל {5x} **têl**, *tale*; by contr. from 8524; a *mound*:—heap {4x}, × strength {1x}. See: TWOT—2513a; BDB—1067c, 1068b, 1068d.

8511. תָּלָא {3x} **tâlâʼ**, *taw-law'*; a prim. root; to *suspend*; fig. (through *hesitation*) to *be uncertain*; by impl. (of mental *dependence*) to *habituate*:—be bent {1x}, hang (in doubt) {2x}. See: BDB—1067d.

8512. תֵּל אָבִיב {1x} **Têl ʼÂbîyb**, *tale aw-beeb'*; from 8510 and 24; *mound* of *green* growth; *Tel-Abib*, a place in Chaldaea:—Tel-abib {1x}. See: BDB—1068b.

8513. תְּלָאָה {4x} **tᵉlâʼâh**, *tel-aw-aw'*; from 3811; *distress*:—travail {2x}, travel {1x}, trouble {1x}. See: TWOT—1066a; BDB—521b.

8514. תַּלְאוּבָה {1x} **talʼûwbâh**, *tal-oo-baw'*; from 3851; *desiccation*:—great drought {1x}. See: TWOT—1065a;BDB—520d, 1067d.

8515. תְּלַאשַּׂר {2x} **Tᵉlaʼssar**, *tel-as-sar'*; or

תְּלַשַּׂר **Tᵉlassar**, *tel-as-sar'*; of for. der.; *Telassar*, a region of Assyria:—*Telassar* {1x}, Thelasar {1x}. See: BDB—1067d.

8516. תַּלְבֹּשֶׁת {1x} **talbôsheth**, *tal-bo'-sheth*; from 3847; a *garment*:—clothing {1x}. Syn.: 3830. See: TWOT—1075c; BDB—528d, 1067d.

8517. תְּלַג {1x} **tᵉlag** (Aram.), *tel-ag'*; corresp. to 7950; *snow*:—snow {1x}. See: TWOT—3057; BDB—1117d.

תִּלְגַת **Tilgath**. See 8407.

תֹּלְדָה **tôlᵉdâh**. See 8435.

8518. תָּלָה {28x} **tâlâh**, *taw-law'*; a prim. root; to *suspend* (espec. to *gibbet*):—hang {25x}, hang up {3x}. See: TWOT—2512; BDB—1067d.

8519. תְּלוּנָּה {8x} **tᵉlûwnâh**, *tel-oo-naw'*; or

תְּלֻנָּה **tᵉlunnâh**, *tel-oon-naw'*; from 3885 in the sense of *obstinacy*; a *grumbling*:—murmuring {8x}. See: TWOT—1097a; BDB—534b, 1068d.

8520. תֶּלַח {1x} **Telach**, *teh'-lakh*; prob. from an unused root mean. to *dissever*; *breach*; *Telach*, an Isr.:—Telah {1x}. See: BDB—1068b.

8521. תֵּל חַרְשָׁא {2x} **Têl Charshâʼ**, *tale kharshaw'*; from 8510 and the fem. of 2798; *mound of workmanship*; *Tel-Charsha*, a place in Bab.:—Tel-haresha {1x}, Tel-harsa {1x}. See: BDB—1068b.

8522. תְּלִי {1x} **tᵉlîy**, *tel-ee'*; prob. from 8518; a *quiver* (as *slung*):—quiver {1x}. See: TWOT—2512a; BDB—1068a.

8523. תְּלִיתַי {2x} **tᵉlîythay** (Aram.), *tel-ee-thah'-ee*; or

תַּלְתִּי **taltîy** (Aram.), *tal-tee'*; ord. from 8532; *third*:—third {2x}. See: TWOT—3058c; BDB—1118a.

8524. תָּלַל {1x} **tâlal**, *taw-lal'*; a prim. root; to *pile* up, i.e. *elevate*:—eminent {1x}. See: TWOT—2513; BDB—1068c. comp. 2048.

8525. תֶּלֶם {5x} **telem**, *teh'-lem*; from an unused root mean. to *accumulate*; a *bank* or *terrace*:—furrow {4x}, ridge {1x}. See: TWOT—2515a; BDB—1068d.

8526. תַּלְמַי {6x} **Talmay**, *tal-mah'-ee*; from 8525; *ridged*; *Talmai*, the name of a Canaanite and a Syrian:—Talmai {6x}. See: BDB—1068d.

8527. תַּלְמִיד {1x} **talmîyd**, *tal-meed'*; from 3925; a *pupil*:—scholar {1x}. See: TWOT—1116c; BDB—541a, 1068d.

8528. תֵּל מֶלַח {2x} **Têl Melach**, *tale meh'-lakh*; from 8510 and 4417; *mound of salt*; *Tel-Melach*, a place in Bab.:—Tel-melah {2x}. See: BDB—1068b.

תְּלֻנָּה **tᵉlunnâh**. See 8519.

8529. תָּלַע {1x} **tâlaʻ**, *taw-law'*; a denom. from 8438; to *crimson*, i.e. dye that color:—scarlet {1x}. See: TWOT—2516c; BDB—1069a.

תֹּלַעַת **tôlaʻath**. See 8438.

8530. תַּלְפִּיָּה {1x} **talpîyâh**, *tal-pee-yaw'*; fem. from an unused root mean. to *tower*; something *tall*, i.e. (plur. collect.) *slenderness*:—armoury {1x}. See: TWOT—2517; BDB—1069b.

תְּלַשַּׂר **Tᵉlassar**. See 8515.

8531. תְּלַת {2x} **tᵉlath** (Aram.), *tel-ath'*; from 8532; a *tertiary* rank:—third {2x}. See: TWOT—3058b; BDB—1118a.

8532. תְּלָת {11x} **tᵉlâth** (Aram.), *tel-awth'*; masc.

תְּלָתָה **tᵉlâthâh** (Aram.), *tel-aw-thaw'*; or

תְּלָתָא **tᵉlâthâʼ** (Aram.), *tel-aw-thaw'*; corresp. to 7969; *three* or *third*:—three {10x}, third {1x}. See: TWOT—3058a; BDB—1118a.

תַּלְתִּי **taltiy**. See 8523.

8533. תְּלָתִין {2x} **tᵉlâthîyn** (Aram.), *tel-aw-theen'*; mult. of 8532; *ten times three*:—thirty {2x}. See: TWOT—3058d; BDB—1118a.

8534. תַּלְתַּל {1x} **taltal**, *tal-tal'*; by redupl. from 8524 through the idea of *vibration*; a trailing *bough* (as *pendulous*):—bushy {1x}. See: TWOT—2513c; BDB—1068c, 1069b.

8535. תָּם {13x} **tâm**, *tawm*; from 8552; *complete*; usually (mor.) *pious*; spec. *gentle, dear*:—perfect {9x}, undefiled {2x}, plain {1x}, upright {1x}.

Tam means perfect and stresses integrity (Job 1:1). See: TWOT—2522c; BDB—1069b, 1070d.

8536. תָּם {4x} **tâm** (Aram.), *tawm*; corresp. to 8033; *there*:—there {2x}, where {1x}, thence {1x}. See: TWOT—3059; BDB—1118a.

8537. תֹּם {23x} **tôm**, *tome*; from 8552; *completeness*; fig. *prosperity*; usually (mor.) *innocence*:—integrity {11x}, upright {2x}, uprightly {2x}, uprightness {2x},venture {2x}, full {1x}, perfect {1x}, perfection {1x}, simplicity {1x}.

Tom signifies completeness in the following senses: **(1)** fullness (Job 21:23), **(2)** innocency or simplicity (2 Sa 15:11), **(3)** integrity (Gen 20:5). See: TWOT—2522a; BDB—1069b, 1070d, 1071b. See 8550.

תֵּמָא **Têmâʼ**. See 8485.

8538. תֻּמָּה {5x} **tummâh**, *toom-maw'*; fem. of 8537; *innocence*:—integrity {5x}. See: TWOT—2522b; BDB—1069b, 1070d.

8539. תָּמַהּ {9x} **tâmahh**, *taw-mah';* a prim. root; to *be in consternation:*—marvel {3x}, wonder {2x}, marvellously {1x}, astonied {1x}, astonished {1x}, amazed {1x}. See: TWOT—2518; BDB—1069b.

8540. תְּמַהּ {3x} **tᵉmahh** (Aram.), *tem-ah';* from a root corresp. to 8539; a *miracle:*—wonder {3x}. See: TWOT—3060; BDB—1118b.

8541. תִּמָּהוֹן {2x} **timmâhôwn**, *tim-maw-hone';* from 8539; *consternation:*—astonishment {2x}. See: TWOT—2518a; BDB—1069b.

8542. תַּמּוּז {1x} **Tammûwz**, *tam-mooz';* of uncert. der.; *Tammuz,* a Phoenician deity:—Tammuz {1x}. See: TWOT—2519; BDB—1069c.

8543. תְּמוֹל {23x} **tᵉmôwl**, *tem-ole';* or

תְּמֹל **tᵉmôl**, *tem-ole';* prob. for 865; prop. *ago,* i.e. a (short or long) *time since;* espec. *yesterday,* or (with 8032) *day before* yesterday:—times past + 8032 {7x}, heretofore + 8032 {6x}, yesterday {4x}, as {3x}, beforetime + 8032 {2x}, about these days {1x}. See: TWOT—2521; BDB—1069d.

8544. תְּמוּנָה {10x} **tᵉmûwnâh**, *tem-oo-naw';* or

תְּמֻנָה **tᵉmûnâh**, *tem-oo-naw';* from 4327; *something portioned* (i.e. *fashioned*) out, as a *shape,* i.e. (indef.) *phantom,* or (spec.) *embodiment,* or (fig.) *manifestation* (of favor):—likeness {5x}, similitude {4x}, image {1x}.

This word does not refer to an idol; but to some form or outline that presented itself in vision; a likeness (see Ps 17:15). Syn.: 5566. See: TWOT—1191b; BDB—568b, 1069c.

8545. תְּמוּרָה {6x} **tᵉmûwrâh**, *tem-oo-raw';* from 4171; *barter, compensation:*—exchange {2x}, change {1x}, changing {1x}, recompense {1x}, restitution {1x}. See: TWOT—1164a; BDB—558c, 1069c.

8546. תְּמוּתָה {2x} **tᵉmûwthâh**, *tem-oo-thaw';* from 4191; *execution* (as a doom):—die {1x}, death {1x}.

Temuwthah means "death." One occurrence is in Ps 79:11: "Let the sighing of the prisoner come before thee; according to the greatness of thy power preserve thou those that are appointed to die [literally, sons of death]" (cf. Ps 102:20). See: TWOT—1169c; BDB—560d, 1069c.

8547. תֶּמַח {2x} **Temach**, *teh'-makh;* of uncert. der.; *Temach,* one of the Nethinim:—Thamah {1x}, Tamah {1x}. See: BDB—1069c.

8548. תָּמִיד {104x} **tâmîyd**, *taw-meed';* from an unused root mean. to *stretch;* prop. *continuance* (as indef. *extension*); but used only (attributively as adj.) *constant* (or adv. *constantly*); ellipt. the *regular* (daily) sacrifice:—continually {53x}, continual {26x}, daily {7x}, always {6x}, alway {4x}, ever {3x}, perpetual {2x}, continual employment {1x}, evermore {1x}, never {1x}.

Tamiyd means always; continually: regularly. **(1)** *Tamiyd* expresses continually, with continuity (Ex 25:30; Is 21:8; 2 Sa 9:7). **(2)** *Tamiyd* occurs most frequently of the daily rituals in the tabernacle and temple (Ex 29:38). **(2a)** Both ideas—regularity and continuousness—are present in the word. **(2b)** These rituals were to be performed regularly and without interruption for the duration of the old covenant. **(3)** The word is also used of God describing **(3a)** His visible presence at the tabernacle (Num 9:16), and **(3b)** His care for His people (Ps 40:11). **(4)** *Tamiyd* is also used of Jerusalem (Is 49:16). **(5)** The word describes man's response to God (Ps. 16:8; 34:1;119:44). **(6)** it is said of Zion eschatologically: "Therefore thy gates shall be open continually; they shall not be shut day nor night" (Is 60:11). **(7)** *Tamiyd,* the adjective, means continual (Ex 30:7–8; Num 28:6; Eze 46:15). Syn.: 753, 5331, 5703. See: TWOT—1157a; BDB—556b, 1069c.

8549. תָּמִים {91x} **tâmîym**, *taw-meem';* from 8552; *entire* (lit., fig. or mor.); also (as noun) *integrity, truth:*—without blemish {44x}, perfect {18x}, upright {8x}, without spot {6x}, uprightly {4x}, whole {4x}, sincerely {2x}, complete {1x}, full {1x}, sincerity {1x}, sound {1x}, undefiled {1x}.

Tamiym means perfect; blameless; sincerity; entire; whole; complete; full. **(1)** *Tamiym* means complete, in the sense of the entire or whole thing: **(1a)** the whole day (Josh 10:13), **(1b)** seven complete sabbaths (Lev 23:15), **(1c)** a full year (Lev 25:30). **(2)** This word may mean intact, not cut up into pieces (Eze 15:5). **(3)** *Tamiym* may mean incontestable or free from objection: **(3a)** God's work (Deut 32:4), **(3b)** an unblemished sacrifice (Lev 22:18–21). **(4)** When one is described by *tamiym,* there is nothing in his outward activities or internal disposition that is odious to God (Gen 6:9). This word describes his entire relationship to God. **(5)** Another adjective, tam, means **(5a)** complete or perfect (Song 5:2), **(5b)** sound or wholesome (Gen 25:27), and **(5c)** complete, morally innocent, having integrity (Job 1:8). See: TWOT—2522d; BDB—1070d.

8550. תֻּמִּים {5x} **Tummîym**, *toom-meem';* plur. of 8537; *perfections,* i.e. (tech.) one of the epithets of the objects in the high-priest's breastplate as an emblem of *complete* Truth:—Thummim {5x}. See: BDB—1070d.

8551. תָּמַךְ {21x} **tâmak**, *taw-mak';* a prim. root; to *sustain;* by impl. to *obtain, keep fast;* fig. to *help, follow close:*—hold {7x}, uphold {5x}, retain {4x}, hold up {2x}, misc. {3x} = maintain {1x}, stay {1x}, stay up {1x}. See: TWOT—2520; BDB—1064a, 1069c.

תְּמֹל **tᵉmôl**. See 8543.

8552. תָּמַם {64x} **tâmam**, *taw-mam';* a prim. root; to *complete,* in a good or a bad sense, lit. or fig., tran. or intr. (as follows):—consume {26x}, end {9x}, finished {4x}, clean {3x}, upright {3x}, spent {3x}, perfect {2x}, done {2x}, failed {2x}, accomplish {2x}, misc. {8x} = cease, come to the full, be all gone, × be all here, sum, be wasted, whole.

Tamam means to be complete, finished, perfect, spent, sound, used up, have integrity. **(1)** The basic meaning of this word is that of being complete or finished, with nothing else expected or intended. **(2)** The temple was finished or complete (1 Kin 6:22). **(3)** *Tamam* is sometimes used to express the fact that something is completed or finished with regard to its supply: **(3a)** money (Gen 47:15, 18); **(3b)** bread (Jer 37:21); and **(3c)** a people (Num 14:35). **(4)** *Tamam* expresses moral and ethical soundness (Ps 19:13). See: TWOT—2522; BDB—1064a, 1070b.

תֵּמָן **têmân**, **Têmân**. See 8486, 8487.

8553. תִּמְנָה {12x} **Timnâh**, *tim-naw';* from 4487; a *portion* assigned; *Timnah,* the name of two places in Pal.:—Timnath {8x}, *Timnah* {3x}, Thimnathah {1x}. See: BDB—584c, 1071b.

תְּמֻנָה **tᵉmûnâh**. See 8544.

8554. תִּמְנִי {1x} **Timnîy**, *tim-nee';* patrial from 8553; a *Timnite* or inhab. of Timnah:—Timnite {1x}. See: BDB—584d, 1071b.

8555. תִּמְנָע {6x} **Timnâʿ**, *tim-naw';* from 4513; *restraint; Timna,* the name of two Edomites:—*Timna* {4x}, Timnah {2x}. See: BDB—586b, 1071b.

8556. תִּמְנַת חֶרֶס {3x} **Timnath Chereç**, *tim-nath kheh'-res;* or

תִּמְנַת סֶרַח **Timnath Çerach**, *tim-nath seh'-rakh;* from 8553 and 2775; *portion of* (the) *sun; Timnath-Cheres,* a place in Pal.:—Timnathserah {2x}, Timnathheres {1x}. See: BDB—584b, 1071b.

8557. תֶּמֶס {1x} **temeç**, *teh'-mes;* from 4529; *liquefaction,* i.e. *disappearance:*—melt {1x}. See: TWOT—1223c; BDB—588a, 1071b.

8558. תָּמָר {12x} **tâmâr**, *taw-mawr';* from an unused root mean. to *be erect;* a *palm* tree:—palm tree {12x}. See: TWOT—2523; BDB—1071c.

8559. תָּמָר {24x} **Tâmâr**, *taw-mawr';* the same as 8558; *Tamar,* the name of three women and a place:—*Tamar* {24x}. See: BDB—1062b, 1071c.

8560. תֹּמֶר {2x} **tômer**, *to'-mer;* from the same root as 8558; a *palm* trunk:—palm tree {2x}. See: TWOT—2523a; BDB—1071c.

8561. תִּמֹּר {19x} **timmôr** (plur. only), *tim-more';* or (fem.)

תִּמֹּרָה **timmôrâh** (sing. and plur.), *tim-mo-raw';* from the same root as 8558; (arch.) a *palm*-like pilaster (i.e. *umbellate*):—palm tree {19x}. See: TWOT—2523c; BDB—1071c.

תַּמֹּר **Tammôr**. See 8412.

תִּמָרָה **timârâh**. See 8490.

8562. תַּמְרוּק {4x} **tamrûwq**, *tam-rook';* or

תַּמְרֻק **tamrûq**, *tam-rook';* or

תַּמְרִיק **tamrîyq**, *tam-reek';* from 4838; prop. a *scouring,* i.e. *soap* or *perfumery* for the bath; fig. a *detergent:*—things for purification {2x}, purifying {1x}, cleanse {1x}. See: TWOT—1246b; BDB—600a, 1071d.

8563. תַּמְרוּר {3x} **tamrûwr**, *tam-roor';* from 4843; *bitterness* (plur. as collect.):—bitter {2x}, bitterly {1x}. See: TWOT—1248L; BDB—601b, 1071d.

תַּמְרֻק **tamrûq** and

תַּמְרִיק **tamriyq**. See 8562.

8564. תַּמְרוּר {1x} **tamrûwr**, *tam-roor';* from the same root as 8558; an *erection,* i.e. *pillar* (prob. for a guide-board):—high heaps {1x}. See: TWOT—2523e; BDB—1071d.

8565. תַּן {1x} **tan**, *tan;* from an unused root prob. mean. to *elongate;* a *monster* (as preternaturally formed), i.e. a *sea-serpent* (or other huge marine animal); also a *jackal* (or other hideous land animal):—whale {1x}. See: TWOT—2528a; BDB—1071d, 1072b. comp. 8577.

8566. תָּנָה {2x} **tânâh**, *taw-naw';* a prim. root; to *present* (a mercenary inducement), i.e. *bargain* with (a harlot):—hired {2x}. See: TWOT—2524; BDB—1071d.

8567. תָּנָה {2x} **tânâh**, *taw-naw';* a prim. root [rather ident. with 8566 through the idea of *attributing* honor]; to *ascribe* (praise), i.e. *celebrate, commemorate:*—lament {1x}, rehearse {1x}. See: TWOT—2525; BDB—1072a.

8568. תַּנָּה {1x} **tannâh**, *tan-naw';* prob. fem. of 8565; a female *jackal:*—dragon {1x}. See: TWOT—2528b; BDB—1072b.

8569. תְּנוּאָה {2x} **tᵉnûwʾâh**, *ten-oo-aw';* from 5106; *alienation;* by impl. *en-*

mity:—occasion {1x}, breach of promise {1x}. See: TWOT—1317a; BDB—626b, 1072a.

8570. תְּנוּבָה {5x} **tᵉnûwbâh**, *ten-oo-baw';* from 5107; *produce:*—fruit {3x}, increase {2x}. See: TWOT—1318c; BDB—626c, 1072a.

8571. תְּנוּךְ {8x} **tᵉnûwk**, *ten-ook';* perh. from the same as 594 through the idea of *protraction;* a *pinnacle,* i.e. *extremity:*—tip {8x}. See: TWOT—2527a; BDB—1072a.

8572. תְּנוּמָה {5x} **tᵉnûwmâh**, *ten-oo-maw';* from 5123; *drowsiness,* i.e. *sleep:*—slumber {4x}, slumbering {1x}. See: TWOT—1325b; BDB—630b, 1072a.

8573. תְּנוּפָה {30x} **tᵉnûwphâh**, *ten-oo-faw';* from 5130; a *brandishing* (in threat); by impl. *tumult;* spec. the official *undulation* of sacrificial offerings:—wave offering {14x}, wave {8x}, offering {6x}, shaking {2x}. See: TWOT—1330b; BDB—632b, 1072a.

8574. תַּנּוּר {15x} **tannûwr**, *tan-noor';* from 5216; a *fire-pot:*—oven {11x}, furnace {4x}. See: TWOT—2526; BDB—1072a.

8575. תַּנְחוּם {5x} **tanchûwm**, *tan-khoom';* or

תַּנְחֻם **tanchûm**, *tan-khoom';* and (fem.)

תַּנְחוּמָה **tanchûwmâh**, *tan-khoo-maw';* from 5162; *compassion, solace:*—consolation {4x}, comfort {1x}. See: TWOT—1344d; BDB—637c, 1072b.

8576. תַּנְחֻמֶת {2x} **Tanchûmeth**, *tan-khoo'-meth;* for 8575 (fem.); *Tanchumeth,* an Isr.:—Tanhumeth {2x}. See: BDB—637c, 1072b.

8577. תַּנִּין {28x} **tannîyn**, *tan-neen';* or

תַּנִּים **tannîym** (Eze 29:3), *tan-neem';* intens. from the same as 8565; a marine or land *monster,* i.e. *sea-serpent* or *jackal:*—dragon {21x}, serpent {3x}, whale {3x}, sea monster {1x}. See: TWOT—2528b; BDB—1072c.

8578. תִּנְיָן {1x} **tinyân** (Aram.), *tin-yawn';* corresp. to 8147; *second:*—second {1x}. See: TWOT—3061a; BDB—1118b.

8579. תִּנְיָנוּת {1x} **tinyânûwth** (Aram.), *tin-yaw-nooth';* from 8578; a *second time:*—again {1x}. See: TWOT—3061b; BDB—1118b.

8580. תִּנְשֶׁמֶת {3x} **tanshemeth**, *tan-sheh'-meth;* from 5395; prop. a hard *breather,* i.e. the name of two unclean creatures, a lizard and a bird (both perh. from changing color through their *irascibility*), prob. the *tree-toad* and the *water-hen:*—swan {2x}, mole {1x}. See: TWOT—1433b; BDB—675d, 1072d.

8581. תָּעַב {22x} **tâᶜab**, *taw-ab';* a prim. root; to *loathe,* i.e. (mor.) *detest:*—abhor {14x}, abominable {6x}, abominably {1x}, utterly {1x}.

Ta'ab means to abhor, treat as abhorrent, cause to be an abomination, act abominably: Deut 7:26: "Neither shalt thou bring an abomination into thine house. . . ." See: TWOT—2530; BDB—1073a.

תּוֹעֵבָה **tôᶜêbâh**. See 8441.

8582. תָּעָה {50x} **tâᶜâh**, *taw-aw';* a prim. root; to *vacillate,* i.e. *reel* or *stray* (lit. or fig.); also caus. of both:—err {17x}, astray {12x}, wander {10x}, seduced {3x}, stagger {2x}, out of the way {2x}, away {1x}, deceived {1x}, dissemble {1x}, pant {1x}. See: TWOT—2531; BDB—1073b.

8583. תֹּעוּ {5x} **Tôᶜûw**, *to'-oo;* or

תֹּעִי **Tôᶜîy**, *to'-ee;* from 8582; *error, Tou* or *Toi,* a Syrian king:—Toi {3x}, Tou {2x}. See: BDB—1073d.

8584. תְּעוּדָה {3x} **tᵉᶜûwdâh**, *teh-oo-daw';* from 5749; *attestation,* i.e. a *precept, usage:*—testimony {3x}. See: TWOT—1576g; BDB—730c, 1073d.

8585. תְּעָלָה {11x} **tᵉᶜâlâh**, *teh-aw-law';* from 5927; a *channel* (into which water is *raised* for irrigation); also a *bandage* or *plaster* (as placed *upon* a wound):—conduit {4x}, trench {3x}, watercourse {1x}, healing {1x}, cured {1x}, little rivers {1x}. See: TWOT—1624n, 1624o; BDB—752b, 1073d.

8586. תַּעֲלוּל {2x} **taᶜălûwl**, *tah-al-ool';* from 5953; *caprice* (as a fit *coming on*), i.e. *vexation;* concr. a *tyrant:*—babe {1x}, delusion {1x}. See: TWOT—1627f; BDB—760c, 1073d.

8587. תַּעֲלֻמָּה {3x} **taᶜălummâh**, *tah-al-oom-maw';* from 5956; a *secret:*—secret {2x}, thing that is hid {1x}. See: TWOT—1629a; BDB—761b, 1073d.

8588. תַּעֲנוּג {5x} **taᶜănûwg**, *tah-an-oog';* or

תַּעֲנֻג **taᶜănûg**, *tah-an-oog';* and (fem.)

תַּעֲנֻגָה **taᶜănûgâh**, *tah-ah-oog-aw';* from 6026; *luxury:*—delight {3x}, delicate {1x}, pleasant {1x}. See: TWOT—1648c; BDB—772c, 1073b.

8589. תַּעֲנִית {1x} **taᶜănîyth**, *tah-an-eeth';* from 6031; *affliction* (of self), i.e. *fasting:*—heaviness {1x}. See: TWOT—1652f; BDB—777a, 1073d.

8590. תַּעְנָךְ {7x} **Taᶜănâk**, *tah-an-awk';* or

תַּעְנַךְ **Taᶜnâk**, *tah-nawk';* of uncert. der.; *Taanak* or *Tanak,* a place in Pal.:—Taanach {6x}, Tanach {1x}. See: BDB—1073d.

8591. תָּעַע {2x} **tâᶜaᶜ**, *taw-ah';* a prim. root; to *cheat;* by anal. to *maltreat:*—deceiver {1x}, misused {1x}. See: TWOT—2532; BDB—1073d.

8592. תַּעֲצֻמָה {1x} **taᶜătsûmâh**, *tah-ats-oo-maw';* from 6105; *might* (plur. collect.):—power {1x}. See: TWOT—1673e; BDB—783b, 1074a.

8593. תַּעַר {13x} **taᶜar**, *tah'-ar;* from 6168; a *knife* or *razor* (as *making* bare): also a *scabbard* (as *being bare,* i.e. *empty*):—sheath {6x}, razor {4x}, penknife {1x}, scabbard {1x}, shave {1x}.

Ta'ar means "razor" (Num 6:5), a "knife" to sharpen scribal pens (Jer 36:23), or "sword sheath" (1 Sa 17:51). Syn.: Morah (4177) also means "razor"(1 Sa 1:11). See: TWOT—1692e; BDB—789b, 1074a.

8594. תַּעֲרֻבָה {2x} **taᶜărûbâh**, *tah-ar-oo-baw';* from 6148; *suretyship,* i.e. (concr.) a *pledge:*—hostage {2x}. See: TWOT—1686d; BDB—787a, 1074a.

8595. תַּעְתֻּעַ {2x} **taᶜtûaᶜ**, *tah-too'-ah;* from 8591; a *fraud:*—error {2x}. See: TWOT—2532a; BDB—1074a.

8596. תֹּף {17x} **tôph**, *tofe;* from 8608 contr.; a *tambourine:*—timbrel {9x}, tabret {8x}. See: TWOT—2536a; BDB—1074a, 1074b.

8597. תִּפְאָרָה {51x} **tiphʼârâh**, *tif-aw-raw';* or

תִּפְאֶרֶת **tiphʼereth**, *tif-eh'-reth;* from 6286; *ornament* (abstr. or concr., lit. or fig.):—glory {22x}, beauty {10x}, beautiful {6x}, honour {4x}, fair {3x}, glorious {3x}, bravery {1x}, comely {1x}, excellent {1x}.

Tiph'ereth means "glory; beauty; ornament; distinction; pride." **(1)** The word represents "beauty," in the sense of the characteristic enhancing one's appearance: "And thou shalt make holy garments for Aaron thy brother for glory and for beauty" (Ex 28:2—the first occurrence). **(2)** In Is 4:2, the word identifies the fruit of the earth as the "beauty" or "adornment" of the survivors of Israel. **(3)** *Tip'ereth* (or the feminine form, *tip'arah*) means "glory" in several instances. **(3a)** The word is used of one's rank. A crown of "glory" is a crown which, by its richness, indicates high rank—Wisdom will "[present you with] a crown of glory" (Prov 4:9). **(3b)** "The hoary head is a crown of glory" (Prov 16:31), **(3c)** a reward for righteous living. **(3c)** In Is 62:3, the phrase "crown of glory" is paralleled by "royal diadem." **(4)** This word also modifies **(4a)** the greatness of a king (Est 1:4) and **(4b)** the greatness of the inhabitants of Jerusalem (Zec 12:7). **(4c)** In each of these instances, this word emphasizes the rank of the persons or things so modified. **(5)** The word is used of one's renown: ". . . And to make thee high above all nations which he hath made, in praise, and in name, and in honor [distinction]" (Deut 26:19). **(6)** In another related nuance, *tip'eret* (or *tip'arah*) is used of God, to emphasize His rank, renown, and inherent "beauty": "Thine, O Lord, is the greatness, and the power, and the glory, and the victory, and the majesty . . ." (1 Chr 29:11). **(7)** This word represents the "honor" of a nation, in the sense of its position before God: **(7a)** "[He has] cast down from heaven unto the earth the beauty [honor or pride] of Israel . . ." (Lam 2:1). **(7b)** This nuance is especially clear in passages such as Judg 4:9: "I will surely go with thee: notwithstanding the journey that thou takest shall not be for thine honor [i.e., distinction]; for the Lord shall sell Sisera into the hand of a woman." **(8)** In Is 10:12, *tip'eret* (or *tip'arah*) represents a raising of oneself to a high rank in one's own eyes: ". . . I will punish the fruit of the stout heart of the king of Assyria, and the glory of his high looks." Syn.: 6286. See: TWOT—1726b; BDB—802c, 1074a.

8598. תַּפּוּחַ {6x} **tappûwach**, *tap-poo'-akh;* from 5301; an *apple* (from its *fragrance*), i.e. the fruit or the tree (prob. includ. others of the *pome* order, as the quince, the orange, etc.):—apple tree {3x}, apple {3x}. See: TWOT—1390c; BDB—656b, 745d, 1074a. See also 1054.

8599. תַּפּוּחַ {6x} **Tappûwach**, *tap-poo'-akh;* the same as 8598; *Tappuach,* the name of two places in Pal., also of an Isr.:—Tappuah {6x}. See: BDB—656b, 1074a.

8600. תְּפוֹצָה {1x} **tᵉphôwtsâh**, *tef-o-tsaw';* from 6327; a *dispersal:*—dispersion {1x}. See: TWOT—1745b; BDB—807b, 1074a.

8601. תֻּפִין {1x} **tûphîyn**, *too-feen';* from 644; *cookery,* i.e. (concr.) a *cake:*—baken {1x}. See: TWOT—2533; BDB—1074a.

8602. תָּפֵל {7x} **tâphêl**, *taw-fale';* from an unused root mean. to *smear; plaster* (as *gummy*) or *slime;* (fig.) *frivolity:*—untempered {5x}, foolish {1x}, unsavoury {1x}. See: TWOT—2534a, 2535a; BDB—1074a, 1074b.

8603. תֹּפֶל {1x} **Tôphel**, *to'-fel;* from the same as 8602; *quagmire; Tophel,* a place near the desert:—*Tophel* {1x}. See: BDB—1074b.

8604. תִּפְלָה {3x} **tiphlâh**, *tif-law';* from the same as 8602; *frivolity:*—folly {2x}, foolishly {1x}. See: TWOT—2534b; BDB—1074a.

8605. תְּפִלָּה {77x} **tᵉphillâh**, *tef-il-law';* from 6419; *intercession, supplication;* by impl. a *hymn:*—prayer {77x}.

Tephillah means "prayer." **(1)** This word is the most general Hebrew word for "prayer." **(1a)** It first appears in 1 Kin 8:28: "Yet have thou respect unto the prayer of thy servant, and to his supplication. . . ." **(1b)** In the eschaton God's house will be a house of "prayer" for all peoples (Is 56:7); **(1c)** it will be to this house that all nations will come to worship God. **(2)** The word can mean both a non-liturgical, non-poetical "prayer" and a liturgical, poetical "prayer." **(2a)** In the latter special meaning *tephillah* is used as a psalm title in 5 psalms and as the title of Habakkuk's prayer (Hab 3:1). **(2c)** In these uses *tephillah* means a prayer set to music and sung in the formal worship service. **(3)** In Ps 72:20 the word describes all the psalms or "prayers" of Psalms 1—72, only one of which is specifically called a "prayer" (17:1). Syn.: 6419. See: TWOT—1776a; BDB—813c, 1074b.

8606. תִּפְלֶצֶת {1x} **tiphletseth**, *tif-leh'-tseth;* from 6426; *fearfulness:*—terribleness {1x}. See: TWOT—1778c; BDB—814a, 1074b.

8607. תִּפְסַח {2x} **Tiphçach**, *tif-sakh';* from 6452; *ford; Tiphsach,* a place in Mesopotamia:—Tiphsah {2x}. See: BDB—820b, 1074b.

8608. תָּפַף {2x} **tâphaph**, *taw-faf';* a prim. root; to *drum,* i.e. play (as) on the tambourine:—playing with timbrels {1x}, tabering {1x}. See: TWOT—2536; BDB—1074c.

8609. תָּפַר {4x} **tâphar**, *taw-far';* a prim. root; to *sew:*—sew {4x}. See: TWOT—2537; BDB—1074c.

8610. תָּפַשׂ {65x} **tâphas**, *taw-fas';* a prim. root; to *manipulate,* i.e. *seize,* chiefly to *capture, wield;* spec. to *overlay;* fig. to *use* unwarrantably:—take {27x}, taken {12x}, handle {8x}, hold {8x}, catch {4x}, surprised {2x}, misc. {4x} = stop, × surely.

Taphas means to catch, seize, lay hold of, grasp, play. **(1)** This verb expresses the idea of grasping something in one's hand in order to use it (Gen 4:21). **(2)** Other things that are seized with the hand are: **(2a)** swords (Eze 21:11), **(2b)** shields (Jer 46:9), **(2c)** bows (Amos 2:15), and **(2d)** sickles (Jer 50:16). **(3)** To seize someone may be to arrest him (Jer 37:14). **(4)** Frequently, *taphas* is used in the sense of to capture (Josh 8:23). Syn.: 270. See: TWOT—2538; BDB—1074c.

8611. תֹּפֶת {1x} **tôpheth**, *to'-feth;* from the base of 8608; a *smiting,* i.e. (fig.) *contempt:*—spit {1x}. See: TWOT—2499a; BDB—1064b, 1075a.

8612. תֹּפֶת {9x} **Tôpheth**, *to'-feth;* the same as 8611; *Topheth,* a place near Jerusalem:—Tophet {8x}, *Topheth* {1x}. See: TWOT—2539; BDB—1064b, 1075a, 1075b.

8613. תָּפְתֶּה {1x} **Tophteh**, *tof-teh';* prob. a form of 8612; *Tophteh,* a place of cremation:—Tophet {1x}. See: BDB—1075a.

8614. תִּפְתָּי {2x} **tiphtay** (Aram.), *tif-tah'-ee;* perh. from 8199; *judicial,* i.e. a *lawyer:*—sheriffs {2x}. See: TWOT—3062; BDB—1118b.

תֹּצָאָה **tôtsâ'âh**. See 8444.

8615. תִּקְוָה {34x} **tiqvâh**, *tik-vaw';* from 6960; lit. a *cord* (as an *attachment* [comp. 6961]); fig. *expectancy:*—hope {23x}, expectation {7x}, line {2x}, the thing that I long for {1x}, expected {1x}. See: TWOT—1994d, 1994e; BDB—876c, 1075b.

8616. תִּקְוָה {3x} **Tiqvâh**, *tik-vaw';* the same as 8615; *Tikvah,* the name of two Isr.:—Tikvah {2x}, Tikvath {1x}. See: BDB—876b, 1075b.

8617. תְּקוּמָה {1x} **tᵉqûwmâh**, *tek-oo-maw';* from 6965; *resistfulness:*—power to stand {1x}. See: TWOT—1999g; BDB—879c, 1075b.

8618. תְּקוֹמֵם {1x} **tᵉqôwmêm**, *tek-o-mame';* from 6965; an *opponent:*—that rise up against thee {1x}. See: TWOT—1999; BDB—878c, 879d, 1075b.

8619. תָּקוֹעַ {1x} **tâqôwaᶜ**, *taw-ko'-ah;* from 8628 (in the musical sense); a *trumpet:*—trumpet {1x}. See: TWOT—2541b; BDB—1075d.

8620. תְּקוֹעַ {7x} **Tᵉqôwaᶜ**, *tek-o'-ah;* a form of 8619; *Tekoa,* a place in Pal.:—Tekoa {6x}, Tekoah {1x}. See: BDB—1075d.

8621. תְּקוֹעִי {17x} **Tᵉqôwᶜîy**, *tek-o-ee';* or

תְּקֹעִי **Tᵉqôᶜîy**, *tek-o-ee';* patron. from 8620; a *Tekoite* or inhab. of Tekoah:—Tekoite {5x}, Tekoah {2x}. See: BDB—1075d.

8622. תְּקוּפָה {4x} **tᵉqûwphâh**, *tek-oo-faw';* or

תְּקֻפָה **tᵉqûphâh**, *tek-oo-faw';* from 5362; a *revolution,* i.e. (of the sun) *course,* (of time) *lapse:*—end {2x}, circuit {1x}, come about {1x}. See: TWOT—2001a; BDB—880d, 1075b.

8623. תַּקִּיף {1x} **taqqîyph**, *tak-keef';* from 8630; *powerful:*—mightier {1x}. See: TWOT—2542b; BDB—1076a.

8624. תַּקִּיף {5x} **taqqîyph** (Aram.), *tak-keef';* corresp. to 8623:—strong {3x}, mighty {2x}. See: TWOT—3065c; BDB—1118c.

8625. תְּקַל {3x} **tᵉqal** (Aram.), *tek-al';* corresp. to 8254; to *balance:*—Tekel {2x}, weighed {1x}. See: TWOT—3063, 3063a; BDB—1101b, 1118c.

8626. תָּקַן {3x} **tâqan**, *taw-kan';* a prim. root; to *equalize,* i.e. *straighten* (intr. or tran.); fig. to *compose:*—make straight {2x}, set in order {1x}. See: TWOT—2540; BDB—1075b, 1118c.

8627. תְּקַן {1x} **tᵉqan** (Aram.), *tek-an';* corresp. to 8626; to *straighten* up, i.e. *confirm:*—established {1x}. See: TWOT—3064; BDB—1118c.

8628. תָּקַע {69x} **tâqaᶜ**, *taw-kah';* a prim. root; to *clatter,* i.e. *slap* (the hands together), *clang* (an instrument); by anal. to *drive* (a nail or tent-pin, a dart, etc.); by impl. to *become bondsman* (by handclasping):—blow {46x}, fasten {5x}, strike {4x}, pitch {3x}, thrust {2x}, clap {2x}, sounded {2x}, cast {1x}, misc. {4x} = smite, × suretiship.

Taqa' means to strike, give a blast, clap, blow, drive. **(1)** Striking or driving a tent peg means **(1a)** pitching a tent (Gen 31:25); and **(1b)** was used of Jael's driving the peg into Sisera's temple (Judg 4:21). **(2)** *Taqa'* describes **(2a)** the strong west wind that drove the locusts into the Red Sea (Ex 10:19), **(2b)** striking one's hands in praise or triumph (Ps 47:1), or **(2c)** to shake hands was a surety or guarantor of the agreement. (Prov 6:1; 17:18; 22:26). **(3)** *Taqa'* expresses giving a blast on a trumpet (Josh 6:4, 8–9, 13, 16, 20). See: TWOT—2541; BDB—1075b.

8629. תֵּקַע {1x} **têqaᶜ**, *tay-kah';* from 8628; a *blast* of a trumpet:—sound {1x}. See: TWOT—2541a; BDB—1075d.

תְּקֹעִי **Tᵉqôᶜîy**. See 8621.

8630. תָּקַף {3x} **tâqaph**, *taw-kaf';* a prim. root; to *overpower:*—prevail {3x}. See: TWOT—2542; BDB—1075d, 1118c.

8631. תְּקֵף {5x} **tᵉqêph** (Aram.), *tek-afe';* corresp. to 8630; to *become* (caus. *make*) *mighty* or (fig.) *obstinate:*— . . . strong {3x}, harden {1x}, make firm {1x}. Syn.: 2388, 3513, 7188. See: TWOT—3065; BDB—1118c.

8632. תְּקֹף {2x} **tᵉqôph** (Aram.), *tek-ofe';* corresp. to 8633; *power:*—strength {1x}, might {1x}. See: TWOT—3065b; BDB—1118c.

8633. תֹּקֶף {3x} **tôqeph**, *to'-kef;* from 8630; *might* or (fig.) *positiveness:*—power {1x}, strength {1x}, authority {1x}. See: TWOT—2542a; BDB—1076a.

תְּקֻפָה **tᵉqûphâh**. See 8622.

תֹּר **tôr**. See 8447, 8449.

8634. תַּרְאֲלָה {1x} **Tar'ălâh**, *tar-al-aw';* prob. for 8653; a *reeling; Taralah,* a place in Pal.:—*Taralah* {1x}. See: BDB—1076a.

8635. תַּרְבּוּת {1x} **tarbûwth**, *tar-booth';* from 7235; *multiplication,* i.e. *progeny:*—increase {1x}.

Tarbuwth has a single appearance to mean "increase": "And, behold, ye are risen up in your fathers' stead, an increase (*tarbuwth*) of sinful men, to augment yet the fierce anger of the LORD toward Israel" (Num 32:14). See: TWOT—2103e; BDB—916b, 1076a.

8636. תַּרְבִּית {6x} **tarbîyth**, *tar-beeth';* from 7235; *multiplication,* i.e. *percentage* or *bonus* in addition to principal:—increase {5x}, unjust gain {1x}.

Tarbiyth can mean "interest, increment, usury": "Take thou no usury of him, or increase: but fear thy God; that thy brother may live with thee" (Lev 25:36). See: TWOT—2103f; BDB—916b.

8637. תִּרְגַּל {1x} **tirgal**, *teer-gal';* a denom. from 7270; to *cause to walk:*—to go {1x}. See: TWOT—2113; BDB—920b, 1076a.

8638. תִּרְגֵּם {1x} **tirgam**, *teer-gam';* a denom. from 7275 in the sense of *throwing* over; to *transfer,* i.e. *translate:*—interpreted {1x}. See: TWOT—2543; BDB—1076a.

תֹּרָה **tôrâh**. See 8451.

8639. תַּרְדֵּמָה {7x} **tardêmâh**, *tar-day-maw';* from 7290; a *lethargy* or (by impl.) *trance:*—deep sleep {7x}. See: TWOT—2123a; BDB—922b, 1076b.

8640. תִּרְהָקָה {2x} **Tirhâqâh**, *teer-haw'-kaw;* of for. der.; *Tirhakah,* a king of Kush:—Tirhakah {2x}. See: BDB—1076b.

8641. תְּרוּמָה {76x} **tᵉrûwmâh**, *ter-oo-maw';* or

תְּרֻמָה **tᵉrûmâh** (Deut 12:11), *ter-oo-maw';* from 7311; a *present* (as offered *up*), espec. in *sacrifice* or as *tribute:*—offering {51x}, oblation {19x}, heave {4x}, gifts {1x}, offered {1x}.

Terumah means "heave offering; offering; oblation." **(1)** *Terumah* is used for the first time in Ex 25:2: "Speak unto the children of Israel, that they bring me an offering: of every man that giveth it willingly with the heart ye shall take my offering." **(2)** In more than a third of its occurrences in the text, the KJV translates *terumah* as "heave offering," all of these instances being found in Exodus, Leviticus, Numbers (where the majority are found), and Deuteronomy. **(2a)** This translation apparently is derived from the fact that the word is based on the common Semitic root, "to be high, exalted." **(2b)** The inference seems to be that such "offerings" were raised high by the priest in some sort of motion as it was placed on the altar. **(2c)** This is clearly illustrated in Num 15:20: "Ye shall offer up a cake of the first of your dough for a heave offering: as ye do the heave offering of the threshing floor, so shall ye heave it." **(2d)** From texts like this, it appears that *terumah* was used in the early period to refer to "contributions" or "gifts" which consisted of the produce of the ground, reflecting the agricultural character of early Israel. See Deut 12:6, 11, 17 for other examples.

(3) *Terumah* often is used to designate those gifts or contributions to God, but which were set apart specifically for the priests: "And every offering of all the holy things of the children of Israel, which they bring unto the priest, shall be his" (Num 5:9). **(3a)** Such "offerings" were to go to the priests because of a special covenant God had made: "All the holy offerings which the people of Israel present to the Lord I give to you [Aaron], and to your sons and daughters with you, as a perpetual due; it is a covenant of salt for ever before the Lord for you and for your offspring with you" (Num 18:19). **(3b)** Such offerings, or contributions, sometimes were of grain or grain products: "Besides the cakes, he shall offer for his offering leavened bread with the sacrifice of thanksgiving of his peace offerings. And of it he shall offer one out of the whole oblation for a heave offering unto the Lord, and it shall be the priest's that sprinkleth the blood of the peace offerings" (Lev 7:13–14).

(4) Part of the animal sacrifices was also designated as a *terumah* for the priests: "And the right shoulder shall ye give unto the priest for a heave offering of the sacrifices of your peace offerings" (Lev 7:32; cf. Lev 10:14–15; Num 6:20). Such contributions to the priests obviously were given to provide the needed foodstuffs for the priests and their families since their tribe, Levi, was given no land on which to raise their own food. **(5)** While all the priests had to be from the tribe of Levi, inheriting their office through their fathers, not all Levites could function as priests. For one thing, there were too many of them. Also, some were needed to work in the tabernacle, and later the temple, as maintenance and cleanup people, something that is readily understandable when one thinks of all that was involved in the sacrificial system. The Levites actually lived in various parts of Israel, and they were the welfare responsibility of the Israelites among whom they lived. They, like the widow, the orphan, and the resident alien, were to be given the tithe of all farm produce every third year (Deut 14:28–29). The Levites, then, were to tithe the tithe they received, giving their own tithe from what they received from the people to the Lord. Part of that tithe was to be a *terumah* or "heave offering" to the priests, the descendants of Aaron (see Num 18:25–32).

(6) In order to provide for the materials necessary for the construction of the wilderness tabernacle, Moses was instructed to receive an "offering" or *terumah*. **(6a)** The "offering" was to consist of all kinds of precious metals and stones, as well as the usual building materials such as wood and skins (Ex 25:3–9). **(6b)** When Moses announced this to the people of Israel, he said: "Take ye from among you an offering unto the Lord; whosoever is of a willing heart, let him bring it, an offering of the Lord . . ." (Ex 35:5), following this with a list of the needed materials (Ex 35:6–8). **(6)** The implication here is twofold: the *terumah* is really the Lord's, and it is best given freely, willingly, from a generous heart. **(7)** In the Second Temple Period, following the Exile, the silver and gold and the vessels for the temple are called "the offering for the house of our God" (Ezra 8:25), also signifying a contribution.

(8) The *terumah* sometimes was an "offering" which had the meaning of a tax, an obligatory assessment which was made against every Israelite male who was twenty years old or older, to be paid for the support of the tabernacle and later, the temple (Ex 30:11–16). **(8a)** This tax was levied on all males without any allowance for their financial situation: "The rich shall not give more, and the poor shall not give less than half a shekel, when they give an offering unto the Lord, to make an atonement for your souls" (Ex 30:15). **(8c)** This tax actually had its basis in the census or count of the male population, the tax then being required as a ransom or atonement from the wrath of God because such a census was taken (2 Sa 24:1). **(8d)** The practical aspect of it was that it provided needed financial support for the sanctuary. **(9)** Another example of *terumah* in the sense of taxes may be seen in Prov 29:4: "The king by judgment establisheth the land; but he that receiveth gifts overthroweth it." Solomon's heavy taxation which led to the split of the kingdom may be a case in point (1 Kin 12).

(10) A very different use of *terumah* is found in Eze 45:1; 48:9, 29–21, where it refers to an "oblation" which was that portion of land on which the post-exilic temple was to be built, as well as accommodations for the priests and Levites. **(10a)** This tract of land is referred to as "the holy oblation" (Eze 48:20), **(10b)** since it belongs to God just as much as the *terumah* which was given to Him as a sacrifice. Syn.: 801, 817, 4503, 5930, 7133. See: TWOT—2133i; BDB—929a, 1076b.

8642. תְּרוּמִיָּה {1x} **tᵉrûwmîyâh**, *ter-oo-mee-yaw';* formed as 8641; a sacrificial *offering:*—oblation {1x}. See: TWOT—2133j; BDB—929b, 1076b.

8643. תְּרוּעָה {36x} **tᵉrûwʿâh**, *ter-oo-aw';* from 7321; *clamor,* i.e. *acclamation* of joy or a *battle-cry;* espec. *clangor* of trumpets, as an *alarum:*—shout {11x}, shouting {8x}, alarm {6x}, sound {3x}, blowing {2x}, joy {2x}, jubile {1x}, loud noise {1x}, rejoicing {1x}, sounding {1x}. See: TWOT—2135b; BDB—929d, 1076b.

8644. תְּרוּפָה {1x} **tᵉrûwphâh**, *ter-oo-faw';* from 7322 in the sense of its congener 7495; a *remedy:*—medicine {1x}. See: TWOT—2136a; BDB—930a, 1076b.

8645. תִּרְזָה {1x} **tirzâh**, *teer-zaw';* prob. from 7329; a species of tree (appar. from its *slenderness*), perh. the *cypress:*—cypress {1x}. See: TWOT—2543.1; BDB—1076b.

8646. תֶּרַח {13x} **Terach**, *teh'-rakh;* of uncert. der.; *Terach,* the father of Abraham; also a place in the desert:—Terah {11x}, Tarah {1x}, Tahath {1x}. See: BDB—1076b.

8647. תִּרְחֲנָה {1x} **Tirchănâh**, *teer-khan-aw';* of uncert. der.; *Tirchanah,* an Isr.:—Tirhanah {1x}. See: BDB—934b, 1076c.

8648. תְּרֵין {4x} **tᵉrêyn** (Aram.), *ter-ane';* fem. תַּרְתֵּין **tartêyn**, *tar-tane';* corresp. to 8147; *two:*—twelve + 6236 {2x}, two {1x}, second {1x}. See: TWOT—3061c; BDB—1118b, 1118d.

8649. תָּרְמָה {6x} **tormâh**, *tor-maw';* and תַּרְמוּת **tarmûwth**, *tar-mooth';* or תַּרְמִית **tarmîyth**, *tar-meeth';* from 7411; *fraud:*—deceit {4x}, deceitful {1x}, privily {1x}. See: TWOT—2169c; BDB—941b, 941c, 1076c.

תְּרֻמָה **tᵉrûmâh**. See 8641.

8650. תֹּרֶן {3x} **tôren**, *to'-ren;* prob. for 766; a *pole* (as a mast or flag-staff):—mast {2x}, beacon {1x}. See: TWOT—2544; BDB—1076c.

8651. תְּרַע {2x} **tᵉraʿ** (Aram.), *ter-ah';* corresp. to 8179; a *door;* by impl. a *palace:*—gate {1x}, mouth {1x}. See: TWOT—3066; BDB—1118d.

8652. תָּרָע {1x} **târâʿ** (Aram.), *taw-raw';* from 8651; a *doorkeeper:*—porters {1x}. See: TWOT—3067; BDB—1118d.

8653. תַּרְעֵלָה {3x} **tarʿêlâh**, *tar-ay-law';* from 7477; *reeling:*—trembling {2x}, astonishment {1x}. See: TWOT—2188c; BDB—947a, 1076c.

8654. תִּרְעָתִי {1x} **Tirʿâthîy**, *teer-aw-thee';* patrial from an unused name mean. *gate;* a *Tirathite* or inhab. of an unknown Tirah:—Tirathites {1x}. See: BDB—1076c.

8655. תְּרָפִים {15x} **tᵉrâphîym**, *ter-aw-feme';* plur. perh. from 7495; a *healer; Teraphim* (sing. or plur.) a family idol:—image {7x}, teraphim {6x}, idol {1x}, idolatry {1x}.

Teraphiym means "idol; household idol; divine symbol." **(1)** Its basic meaning is "spirit" or "demon." **(2)** *Teraphiym* first appears in Gen 31:19: "And Laban went to shear his sheep: and Rachel had stolen the [household gods] that were her father's." Hurrian law of this period recognized "household idols" as deeds to the family's succession and goods. This makes these *terapim* (possibly a plural of majesty as is *elohim* when used of false gods; cf. 1 Kin 11:5, 33) extremely important to Laban in every way. **(3)** In 1 Sa 19:13 we read that "Michal took the terapim [here a plural of "majesty"] and laid it on the bed, and put a quilt of goat's hair at its head, and covered it with blankets" (author's translation). In view of 1 Sa 19:11, where it is said that they were in David's private quarters, supposing that this terapim was a "household idol" is difficult, although not impossible. This was probably a statue instead of an idol.

(4) In Judg 17:5: ". . . Micah had a house of gods, and made an ephod, and terapim, and consecrated one of his sons, who became his priest." In Judg 18:14 terapim appears to be distinguished from idols: ". . . there is in these houses an ephod, and terapim, and a graven image, and a molten image?" The verses that follow suggest that the graven image and the molten image may have been the same thing: Judg 18:17 uses all four words in describing what the Danites stole; Judg 18:20 omits "molten image" from the list; and Judg 18:31 reports that only the graven image was set up for worship. We know that the ephod was a special priestly garment. Syn.: 457. See: TWOT—2545; BDB—1076c.

8656. תִּרְצָה {18x} **Tirtsâh**, *teer-tsaw';* from 7521; *delightsomeness; Tirtsah,* a place in Pal.; also an Israelitess:—Tirzah {18x}. See: BDB—953c, 1076d.

8657. תֶּ֫רֶשׁ {2x} **Teresh**, *teh'-resh;* of for. der.; *Teresh,* a eunuch of Xerxes:—*Teresh* {2x}. See: BDB—1076d.

8658. תַּרְשִׁישׁ {7x} **tarshîysh**, *tar-sheesh';* prob. of for. der. [comp. 8659]; a gem, perh. the *topaz:*—beryl {7x}. See: TWOT—2546; BDB—1076d.

8659. תַּרְשִׁישׁ {28x} **Tarshîysh**, *tar-sheesh';* prob. the same as 8658 (as the region of the stone, or the reverse); *Tarshish,* a place on the Mediterranean, hence, the epithet of a *merchant* vessel (as if for or from that port); also the name of a Pers. and of an Isr.:—Tarshish {24x}, Tharshish {4x}. See: TWOT—2547; BDB—1076d.

8660. תִּרְשָׁתָא {5x} **Tirshâthâʾ**, *teer-shaw-thaw';* of for. der.; the title of a Pers. deputy or *governor:*—Tirshatha {5x}. See: TWOT—2548; BDB—1077a.

תַּרְתֵּין **tartêyn**. See 8648.

8661. תַּרְתָּן {2x} **Tartân**, *tar-tawn';* of for. der.; *Tartan,* an Ass.:—*Tartan* {2x}. See: TWOT—2549; BDB—1077a.

8662. תַּרְתָּק {1x} **Tartâq**, *tar-tawk';* of for. der.; *Tartak,* a deity of the Avvites:—Tartak {1x}. See: BDB—1077b.

8663. תְּשֻׁאָה {4x} **t^eshuʾâh**, *tesh-oo-aw';* from 7722; a *crashing* or loud *clamor:*—noise {1x}, crying {1x}, stirs {1x}, shouting {1x}. See: TWOT—2339c; BDB—996c, 1077b.

תֹּשָׁב **tôshâb**. See 8453.

8664. תִּשְׁבִּי {6x} **Tishbîy**, *tish-bee';* patrial from an unused name mean. *recourse;* a *Tishbite* or inhab. of Tishbeh (in Gilead):—Tishbite {6x}. See: BDB—986c, 1077b.

8665. תַּשְׁבֵּץ {1x} **tashbêts**, *tash-bates';* from 7660; *checkered* stuff (as *reticulated*):—broidered {1x}. See: TWOT—2320c; BDB—990b, 1077b.

8666. תְּשׁוּבָה {8x} **t^eshûwbâh**, *tesh-oo-baw';* or

תְּשֻׁבָה **t^eshûbâh**, *tesh-oo-baw';* from 7725; a *recurrence* (of time or place); a *reply* (as *returned*):—return {3x}, expired {3x}, answers {2x}.

Teshubah may mean **(1)** "return" or "beginning": "And his return was to Ramah; for there was his house; and there he judged Israel; and there he built an altar unto the LORD" (1 Sa 7:17); and **(2)** "answer": "How then comfort ye me in vain, seeing in your answers (*teshubah*) there remaineth falsehood?" (Job 21:34). See: TWOT—2340f; BDB—1000c, 1077b.

8667. תְּשׂוּמֶת {1x} **t^esûwmeth**, *tes-oo-meth';* from 7760; a *deposit,* i.e. *pledging:*—fellowship {1x}. Syn.: 7760. See: TWOT—2243a; BDB—965a, 1077b.

8668. תְּשׁוּעָה {34x} **t^eshûwʿâh**, *tesh-oo-aw';* or

תְּשֻׁעָה **t^eshûʿâh**, *tesh-oo-aw';* from 7768 in the sense of 3467; *rescue* (lit. or fig., Pers., national or spir.):—salvation {17x}, deliverance {5x}, help {5x}, safety {4x}, victory {3x}.

Teshu'ah means "deliverance." One example is Is 45:17: "But Israel shall be saved in the Lord with an everlasting salvation: ye shall not be ashamed nor confounded world without end." Syn.: 3444, 3467, 3468, 5414. See: TWOT—929e; BDB—448b, 1077b.

8669. תְּשׁוּקָה {3x} **t^eshûwqâh**, *tesh-oo-kaw';* from 7783 in the orig. sense of *stretching* out after; a *longing:*—desire {3x}. See: TWOT—2352a; BDB—1003c, 1077b.

8670. תְּשׁוּרָה {1x} **t^eshûwrâh**, *tesh-oo-raw';* from 7788 in the sense of *arrival;* a *gift:*—present {1x}. See: TWOT—2353a; BDB—1003d, 1077b.

תַּשְׁחֵת **tashchêth**. See 516.

תֻּשִׁיָּה **tûshîyâh**. See 8454.

8671. תְּשִׁיעִי {18x} **t^eshîyʿîy**, *tesh-ee-ee';* ord. from 8672; *ninth:*—ninth {18x}. See: TWOT—2551; BDB—1077d.

תְּשֻׁעָה **t^eshûʿâh**. See 8668.

8672. תֵּשַׁע {58x} **têshaʿ**, *tay'-shah;* or (masc.)

תִּשְׁעָה **tishʿâh**, *tish-aw';* perh. from 8159 through the idea of a *turn* to the next or full number ten; *nine* or (ord.) *ninth:*—nine {45x}, ninth {6x}, nineteenth + 6240 {4x}, nineteen + 6240 {3x}. See: TWOT—2550; BDB—1077c.

8673. תִּשְׁעִים {20x} **tishʿîym**, *tish-eem';* multiple from 8672; *ninety:*—ninety {20x}. See: TWOT—2552; BDB—1077d.

8674. תַּתְּנַי {4x} **Tatt^enay**, *tat-ten-ah'-ee;* of for. der., *Tattenai,* a Pers.:—Tatnai {4x}. See: BDB—1118d.

The New Strong's®

Expanded Dictionary

of the Words in the

Greek New Testament

with their Renderings in the

King James Version

and with Additional Definitions

Adapted from W. E. Vine

and Cross-references to Other

Word Study Resources

Note regarding the Greek Dictionary: The numbering of Greek words skips *2717* and from *3202* to *3303*. This error in numbering is part of the original edition of the Dictionary. Because the original numbering system (with these errors) has been used by so many Bible students and other Bible reference works, it has been left unchanged to avoid the confusion that would result from having an old and a new Strong's numbering system. The only error is the skipping of *numbers, not* the omission of Greek words. No Greek words that Strong listed in the original are missing from this dictionary.

Read this first!

How to Use the Greek Dictionary

For many people Strong's unique system of numbers continues to be *the* bridge between the original languages of the Bible and the English of the *King James Version* (AV). *Strong's Greek Dictionary* is a fully integrated companion to the main concordance, and its entries contain a wealth of information about the words of the Bible in their original language. In order to enhance the strategic importance of the *Dictionary* for Bible students, significant features have been added in this new, expanded edition.

New Features

The *Dictionary* is designed to provide thorough information so that your word studies are enriching and satisfying. The most significant enhancement is the expanded definitions, which come from the best of standard word study resources such as *Vine's Complete Expository Dictionary of Old and New Testament Words* and *Thayer's Greek-English Lexicon of the New Testament*. The expanded definitions reveal the entire range of meanings so that the user can conduct more precise and accurate word studies. In addition, they help to convey the depth and richness of Greek words.

The second item that has been added is the frequency word counts, which appear in curly brackets {}. Frequency counts are provided for both the Greek and English words used in the King James Bible. For example, the Greek word *agathos* (entry *#18*) has {102x} following it. This means that this Greek word occurs 102 times in the Greek text. Then after the :— symbol, a list of English translations along with the number of times this English word is used in the AV is given. For example, the Greek word *agathos* is translated 77 times as "good," 14 times as "good thing," etc.

For those wanting to conduct more advanced word studies, a cross-reference to other lexicons is given at the end of the definition. These lexicons are *A Greek-English Lexicon of the New Testament and Other Christian Literature,* 2d ed., edited by Walter Bauer, William F. Arndt, F. Wilbur Gingrich, and Frederick Danker (University of Chicago, 1979); *Theological Dictionary of the New Testament,* edited by Gerhard Kittel and Gerhard Friedrich (Eerdmans, 1964–1974 [9-volume edition]; 1985 [1-volume edition]); and *Thayer's Greek-English Lexicon of the New Testament* (Baker, 1977). These first two lexicons are abbreviated as BAGD and TDNT. Thayer's lexicon is not abbreviated.

Using the Dictionary with the Main Concordance

To use this *Dictionary,* locate the number given to the biblical reference for any particular entry in the main concordance. For example, under "prepare" you find *Strong's* number *2090* next to the Bible reference Mk 14:12. Since this reference is in the New Testament, and since this numeral is set in italic type (not regular type), you know that it refers to the *Greek Dictionary.*

Using the Dictionary to Do Word Studies

Careful Bible students do word studies, and *The New Strong's® Expanded Exhaustive Concordance* with enhanced *Greek Dictionary* offers unique assistance. Consider the word "love" as found in the AV. By skimming the main concordance, you find these numbers for Greek words that the King James Bible translates with the English word "love": *25, 5368, 26, 2309, 5360, 5365, 5362, 5388, 5363, 5361.* Now for any one Bible reference in this entry there is only one Greek word cited and you may be interested only in establishing the precise meaning for just that word in that occurrence. If so, it will be very helpful for you to observe that same Greek word in *each* of its occurrences in the Bible. In that way, you develop an idea of its possible range of meanings, and you can help clarify what is most likely the precise meaning in the specific Bible reference you are studying.

But don't overlook exploring each Greek word translated as "love." You may wish to take notes as you look up each occurrence of the word that goes with *25,* and then each occurrence of the word that goes with *26,* and so forth. This method gives you an excellent basis for understanding all that the New Testament signifies with the AV's word "love."

Now see the *Dictionary* entry *25* itself, and notice that after the symbol :— all the words and word prefixes and suffixes are listed. These show you that this one Greek word, *agapoa,* is translated into several different but related words in the King James Bible: beloved, love, loved. This list tells you the range of uses of the one Greek word in the AV. This information can help you distinguish between the nuances of the meaning found where this and the other Greek words are translated by these same words and similar ones in the King James Bible.

These three ways of using the *Dictionary* in conjunction with the main concordance show you only a sampling of the many ways *The New Strong's® Expanded Exhaustive Concordance of the Bible* can enrich your study of the Bible. (See also *Getting the Most from Your New Strong's® Exhaustive Bible Concordance,* Nelson, 2000.) The examples given above also show why it is important that you take the time to become familiar with each feature in the *Dictionary* as illustrated on the following page.

Greek

An Example from the Greek New Testament Dictionary

Strong's number in *italics*, corresponding to the numbers at the ends of the context lines in the main concordance.

An unnumbered cross-reference entry.

The word as it appears in the original Greek spelling.

Where appropriate, important discussion of multiple uses and functions of the word.

The Greek word represented in English letters in **bold** type (the transliteration).

Strong's syllable-by-syllable pronunciation in *italics*, with the emphasized syllable marked by the accent.

When the Greek word relates to a Hebrew or Aramaic word from the Old Testament, the Strong's numbers is encased in square brackets [...].

Brief English definitions (shown by italics).

ἀπέπω **apĕpō**. See *550*.

728. ἀῤῥαβών **arrhabōn**, *ar-hrab-ohn´;* of Heb. or. [6162]; a *pledge*, i.e. part of the purchase-money or property given in advance as *security* for the rest:— earnest.

3360. μέχρι **mĕchri** *mekh´-ree;* or

μεχρίς **mĕchris** *mekh-ris´;* from *3372; as far as*, i.e. *up to* a certain point (as a prep. of extent [denoting the *terminus*, whereas *891* refers espec. to the *space* of time or place intervening] or a conjunc.):— till, (un-) to, until.

3361. μή **mē** *may;* a primary particle of qualified *negation* (whereas *3756* expresses an absolute denial); (adv.) *not*, (conjunc.) *lest;* also (as an interrog. implying a *neg*. answer [whereas *3756* expects an *affirmative* one]) *whether:*— any, but (that), × forbear, + God forbid, + lack, lest, neither, never, no (× wise in), none, nor, [can-] not, nothing, that not, un [-taken], without. Often used in compounds in substantially the same relations. See also *3362, 3363, 3364, 3372, 3373, 3375, 3378*.

See "Special Symbols."

Italic Strong's numbers refer to related Greek words in this Dictionary.

After the long dash (—), there is a complete, alphabetical listing of all ways this Greek word is translated in the KJV. (See also "Special Symbols").

Improved, consistent abbreviations. All abbreviations occur with their full spelling in the list of abbreviations.

Note that Greek spelling variations are conveniently indented for easy comparison.

Plan of the Greek Dictionary

1. All the original words are presented in their alphabetical order (according to Greek). They are numbered for easy matching between this Dictionary and the main part of the Concordance. Many reference books also use these same numbers which were originally created by Dr. Strong.

2. Immediately after each word, the exact equivalent of each sound (phoneme) is given in English characters, according to the transliteration system given below.

3. Next follows the precise pronunciation with the proper stress mark.

4. Then comes the etymology, root meaning, and common uses of the word, along with any other important related details.

5. In the case of proper names, the normal English spelling is given, accompanied by a few words of explanation.

6. Finally, after the colon and the dash (:—), all the different ways that the word appears in the Authorized Version (KJV) are listed in alphabetical order. When the Greek word appears in English as a phrase, the main word of the phrase is used to alphabetize it.

By looking up these words in the main concordance and by noting the passages which display the same number in the right-hand column, the reader also possesses a complete *Greek New Testament Concordance*, expressed in the words of the Authorized Version.

Transliteration and Pronunciation of the Greek

The following shows how the Greek words are transliterated into English in this Dictionary.

1. The *Alphabet* is as follows:

No.	Form upper	Form lower	Name	Transliteration and Pronunciation
1.	**Α**	α	Alpha (*al´-fah*)	**a**, as in *Arm* or *mAn* [1]
2.	**Β**	β	Bēta (*bay´-tah*)	**b**
3.	**Γ**	γ	Gamma (*gam´-mah*)	**g**, as in *Guard* [2]
4.	**Δ**	δ	Dĕlta (*del´-tah*)	**d**
5.	**Ε**	ϵ	Ĕpsilŏn (*ep´-see-lon*)	**ĕ**, as in *mEt*
6.	**Ζ**	ζ	Zēta (*dzay´-tah*)	**z**, as in *aDZe* [3]
7.	**Η**	η	Ēta (*ay´-tah*)	**ē**, as in *thEy*
8.	**Θ**	θ	Thēta (*thay´-tah*)	**th**, as in *THin* [4]
9.	**Ι**	ι	Iota (*ee-o´-tah*)	**i**, as in *machIne* [5]
10.	**Κ**	κ	Kappa (*kap´-pah*)	**k**
11.	**Λ**	λ	Lambda (*lamb´-dah*)	**l**
12.	**Μ**	μ	Mu (*moo*)	**m**
13.	**Ν**	ν	Nu (*noo*)	**n**
14.	**Ξ**	ξ	Xi (*ksee*)	**x** = *ks*
15.	**Ο**	ο	Omikrŏn (*om´-e-cron*)	**ŏ**, as in *not*
16.	**Π**	π	Pi (*pee or pai*)	**p**
17.	**Ρ**	ρ	Rhō (*hro*)	**r**
18.	**Σ**	σ, final ς	Sigma (*sig´-mah*)	**s** sharp
19.	**Τ**	τ	Tau (*tŏw*)	**t**, as in *Tree* [6]
20.	**Υ**	υ	Upsilŏn (*u´-pse-lon*)	**u**, as in *fUll*
21.	**Φ**	φ	Phi (*fee or fai*)	**ph** = *f*
22.	**Χ**	χ	Chi (*khee or khai*)	German **ch** [7]
23.	**Ψ**	ψ	Psi (*psee or psai*)	**ps**
24.	**Ω**	ω	Omĕga (*o´-meg-ah*)	**ō**, as in *no*

[1] α, when *final*, or before a final ρ or followed by any *other* consonant, is sounded like *a* in *Arm*; elsewhere like *a* in *mAn*.

[2] γ, when followed by γ, **k**, **c**, or ξ is sounded like *ng* in *kiNG*.

[3] ζ is always sounded like *dz*.

[4] θ never has the guttural sound, like *th* in *THis*.

[5] ι has the sound of *ee* when it *ends* an *accented* syllable; in other situations a more obscure sound, like *i* in *amIable* or *Imbecile*.

[6] τ never has an s-sound, like *t* in *naTion*.

[7] From the difficulty of producing the true sound of χ, it is generally sounded like *k*.

2. The mark ʽ, placed over the *initial* vowel of a word, is called the *Rough Breathing*, and is equivalent to the English *h*, by which we have accordingly represented it. Its *absence* over an initial vowel is indicated by the mark ʼ, called the *Smooth Breathing*, which is silent, and is therefore not represented in our method of transliteration.[8]

3. The following are the Greek *diphthongs*, properly so called:[9]

Form	Transliteration and Pronunciation
αι	**ai** (*ah´ee*) [ă + ē]
ει	**ei**, as in *hEIght*
οι	**oi**, as in *OIl*
υι	**we**, as in *sWEet*
αυ	**ow**, as in *nOW*
ευ	**eu**, as in *fEUd*
ου	**ou**, as in *thrOUgh*

4. The *accent* (stress of voice) falls on the syllable where it is written.[10] It occurs in three forms: the *acute* (ʹ), which is the only true accent; the *grave* (`) which is its substitute; and the *circumflex* (˜), which is the union of the two. The acute may stand on any one of the last *three* syllables, and in case it occurs on the final syllable, before another word in the same sentence, it is written as a grave. The grave is understood (but never written as such) on every other syllable. The circumflex is written on any syllable (necessarily the last syllable or next to the last syllable of a word) formed by the contraction of two syllables, of which the *first* would properly have the acute accent.

5. The following *punctuation* marks are used: the comma (,), the semicolon (·), the colon or period (.), the question mark (;), and by some editors, also the exclamation mark, parentheses, and quotation marks.

Special Symbols

+ (*addition*) denotes a rendering in the A.V. of one or more Greek words in connection with the one under consideration. For example, in Rev. 17:17, No. 1106, γνώμη (**gnōmē**) is translated as a verb ("to agree"), when it is actually a noun and part of a Greek idiom that is literally translated "to do one mind."

× (*multiplication*) denotes a rendering in the A.V. that results from an idiom peculiar to the Greek. For example, in Heb. 12:21, the whole Greek phrase in which ἔντρομος, **ĕntrŏmŏs** (1790) appears is a way of expressing great anxiety. The same idiom is used about Moses in Acts 7:32.

( ) (*parentheses*), in the renderings from the A.V., denote a word or syllable which is sometimes given in connection with the principal word to which it is attached. In Mark 15:39 there are two Greek prepositions (1537 and 1727) which are used together ("over against"). One English preposition, "opposite," communicates the same idea.

[ ] (*brackets*), in the rendering from the A.V., denote the inclusion of an additional word in the Greek. For example, No. 2596 κατά (**kata**) is translated "daily" in Luke 19:47, along with No. 2250 ἡμέρα (**hēmĕra**). So, two Greek words were translated by one English word.

Italics, at the end of a rendering from the A.V., denote an explanation of the variations from the usual form.

Note

Because of some changes in the numbering system (while the original work was in progress) no Greek words are cited for 2717 or 3203-3302. These numbers were dropped altogether. This will not cause any problems in *Strong's* numbering system. **No Greek words have been left out.** Because so many other reference works use this numbering system, it has **not** been revised. If it were revised, much confusion would certainly result.

---

[8] These signs are placed over the *second* vowel of a *diphthong*. The same is true of the accents.

The *Rough* Breathing always belongs to an initial υ.

The *Rough* Breathing is always used with ρ, when it begins a word. If this letter is doubled in the middle of a word, the first ρ takes the Smooth Breathing mark and the second ρ takes the Rough Breathing mark.

Since these signs cannot conveniently be written above the first letter of a word, when it is a *capital*, they are placed *before* it in such cases. This observation applies also to the *accents*. The aspiration *always* begins the syllable.

Occasionally, in consequence of a contraction (*crasis*), the Smooth Breathing is made to stand in the middle of a word, and is then called *Coro´nis*.

[9] The above are combinations of two *short* vowels, and are pronounced like their respective elements, but in more rapid succession than otherwise. Thus, αι is midway between *i* in *hIgh*, and *ay* in *sAY*.

Besides these, there are what are called *improper* diphthongs, in which the former is a *long* vowel. In these,

ᾳ sounds like α
ῃ " η
ῳ " ω
ηυ " η + υ
ωυ " ω + υ

the second vowel, when it is ι, is written *under* the first vowel (unless it is a capital), and is *silent*; when it is υ, it is sounded separately. When the initial vowel is a capital, the ι is placed after it, but it does not take a breathing mark or any accent.

The sign ¨ is called *diær;esis*. It is placed over the *second* of two vowels, indicating that they do *not* form a diphthong.

[10] Every word (except a few monosyllables, called *Aton´ics*) must have one accent; several small words (called *Enclit´ics*) put their accent (always as an acute) on the last syllable of the preceding word (in addition to its own accent, which still has the principal stress), where this is possible.

Abbreviations

abb. = abbreviated
abbreviation
abstr. = abstract
abstractly
act. = active (voice)
actively
acc. = accusative (case) [1]
adj. = adjective
adjectivally
adv. = adverb
adverbial
adverbially
aff. = affix [2]
affixed
affin. = affinity
alt. = alternate
alternately
anal. = analogy
appar. = apparent
apparently
arch. = architecture
architectural
architecturally
art. = article [3]
artif. = artificial
artificially
Ass. = Assyrian
A.V. = Authorized Version
(King James Version)
Bab. = Babylon
Babylonia
Babylonian
caus. = causative [4]
causatively
cerem. = ceremony
ceremonial
ceremonially
Chald. = Chaldee (Aramaic)
Chaldaism
(Aramaism)
Chr. = Christian
collat. = collateral
collaterally
collect. = collective
collectively
comp. = compare [5]
comparison
comparative
comparatively
concr. = concrete
concretely
conjec. = conjecture
conjectural
conjecturally
conjug. = conjugation [6]
conjugational
conjugationally
conjunc. = conjunction
conjunctional
conjunctionally
constr. = construct [7]
construction
constructive
constructively
contr. = contracted [8]
contraction
correl. = correlated
correlation
correlative
correlatively
corresp. = corresponding
correspondingly
dat. = dative (case) [9]
def. = definite [10]
definitely
demonstr. = demonstrative[11]
denom. = denominative [12]
denominatively
der. = derived
derivation
derivative
derivatively
desc. = descended
descendant
descendants
dimin. = diminutive [13]
dir. = direct
directly
E. = East
Eastern
eccl. = ecclesiastical
ecclesiastically
e.g. = for example
Eg. = Egypt
Egyptian
Egyptians
ellip. = ellipsis [14]
elliptical
elliptically
emphat. = emphatic
emphatically
equiv. = equivalent
equivalently
err. = error
erroneous
erroneously
espec. = especially
etym. = etymology [15]
etymological
etymologically
euphem. = euphemism [16]
euphemistic
euphemistically
euphon. = euphonious [17]
euphonically
extens. = extension [18]
extensive
extern. = external
externally
fem. = feminine (gender)
fig. = figurative
figuratively
for. = foreign
foreigner
freq. = frequentative
frequentatively
fut. = future
gen. = general
generally
generic
generical
generically
Gr. = Greek
Graecism
gut. = guttural [19]
Heb. = Hebrew
Hebraism
i.e. = that is
ident. = identical
identically
immed. = immediate
immediately
imper. = imperative [20]
imperatively
imperf. = imperfect [21]
impers. = impersonal
impersonally
impl. = implied
impliedly
implication
incept. = inceptive [22]
inceptively
incl. = including
inclusive
inclusively
indef. = indefinite
indefinitely
ind. = indicative [23]
indicatively
indiv. = individual
individually
infer. = inference
inferential
inferentially
infin. = infinitive
inhab. = inhabitant
inhabitants
ins. = inserted
intens. = intensive
intensively
interch. = interchangeable
intern. = internal
internally
interj. = interjection [24]
interjectional
interjectionally
interrog. = interrogative [25]
interrogatively
intr. = intransitive [26]
intransitively
invol. = involuntary
involuntarily
irreg. = irregular
irregularly
Isr. = Israelite
Israelites
Israelitish
Lat. = Latin
Levit. = Levitical
Levitically
lit. = literal
literally
marg. = margin
marginal reading
masc. = masculine (gender)
mean. = meaning
ment. = mental
mentally
metaph. = metaphorical
metaphorically
mid. = middle (voice) [27]
modif. = modified
modification
mor. = moral
morally
mult. = multiplicative [28]
nat. = natural
naturally
neg. = negative
negatively
neut. = neuter (gender)
obj. = object
objective
objectively
obs. = obsolete
ord. = ordinal [29]
or. = origin
orig. = original
originally
orth. = orthography [30]
orthographical
orthographically
Pal. = Palestine
part. = participle
pass. = passive (voice)
passively
patron. = patronymic [31]
patronymical
patronymically
perh. = perhaps
perm. = permutation [32] (of
adjacent letters)
pers. = person
personal
personally
Pers. = Persia
Persian
Persians
phys. = physical
physically
plur. = plural
poet. = poetry
poetical
poetically
pos. = positive
positively
pref. = prefix
prefixed
prep. = preposition
prepositional
prepositionally
prim. = primitive
prob. = probable
probably
prol. = prolonged [33]
prolongation
pron. = pronoun
pronominal
pronominally
prop. = properly
prox. = proximate
proximately
recip. = reciprocal
reciprocally
redupl. = reduplicated [34]
reduplication
refl. = reflexive [35]
reflexively
reg. = regular
rel. = relative
relatively
relig. = religion
religious
religiously
Rom. = Roman
second. = secondary
secondarily
signif. = signification
signifying
short. = shorter
shortened
sing. = singular
spec. = specific
specifically
streng. = strengthening
subdiv. = subdivision
subdivisional
subdivisionally
subj. = subjectively
subjective
subject
substit. = substituted
suff. = suffix
superl. = superlative [36]
superlatively
symb. = symbolic
symbolical
symbolically
tech. = technical
technically
term. = termination
tran. = transitive [37]
transitively
transc. = transcription
transm. = transmutation [38]
transp. = transposed [39]
transposition
typ. = typical
typically
uncert. = uncertain
uncertainly
var. = various
variation
voc. = vocative (case) [40]
vol. = voluntary
voluntarily

---

1 often indicating the direct object of an action verb

2 part of a word which, when attached to the beginning of the word is called a prefix; if attaching within a word, an infix; and if at the end, a suffix

3 "the" is the definite article; "a" and "an" are indefinite articles

4 expressing or denoting causation

5 the comparative of an adjective or adverb expresses a greater degree of an attribute, e.g. "higher"; "more slowly"

6 a systematic array of various verbal forms

7 the condition in Hebrew and Aramaic when two adjacent nouns are combined semantically as follows, e.g."sword" + "king" = "(the) sword of (the) king" or "(the) king's sword". These languages tend to throw the stress of the entire noun phrase toward the end of the whole expression.

8 a shortened form of a word. It is made by omitting or combining some elements or by reducing vowels or syllables, e.g. "is not" becomes "isn't".

9 often the indirect object of an action verb

10 the definite article ("the")

11 demonstrative pronouns which point (show), e.g. "this," "that"

12 derived from a noun

13 a grammatical form which expresses smallness and/or endearment

14 a construction which leaves out understood words

15 the historical origin of a word

16 the use of a pleasant, polite, or harmless-sounding word or phrase to hide harsh, rude, or infamous truths, e.g. "to pass away" = "to die"

17 a linguistic mechanism to make pronunciation easier, e.g. "an" before "hour" instead of "a"

18 when a general term can denote an entire class of things

19 speech sounds which are produced deep in the throat

20 the mood which expresses a command

21 used of a tense which expresses a continuous but unfinished action or state

22 used of a verbal aspect which denotes the beginning of an action

23 used of the mood which expresses a verbal action as actually occurring (not hypothetical)

24 an exclamation which expresses emotion

25 indicating a question

26 referring to verbs which do not govern direct objects

27 reflexive

28 capable of multiplying or tending to multiply

29 This shows the position or the order within a series, e.g. "second"; the corresponding cardinal number is "two".

30 the written system of spelling in a given language

31 a name derived from that of a paternal ancestor, often created by an affix in various languages

32 a rearrangement

33 lengthening a pronunciation

34 the repetition of a letter or syllable to form a new, inflected word

35 denoting an action by the subject upon itself

36 expressing the highest degree of comparison of the quality indicated by an adjective or an adverb, e.g. "highest"; "most timely"

37 expressing an action directed toward a person or a thing (the direct object)

38 the change of one grammatical element to another

39 switching word order

40 an inflection which is used when one is addressing a person or a thing directly, e.g. "John, come here!"

GREEK DICTIONARY OF THE NEW TESTAMENT.

A

1. Α {4x} **A**, *al'-fah;* of Heb. or.; the first letter of the alphabet; fig. only (from its use as a numeral) the *first.* Often used (usually ἄν **an**, before a vowel) also in composition (as a contr. from *427*) in the sense of *privation;* so in many words beginning with this letter; occasionally in the sense of *union* (as a contr. of *260*).:—Alpha {4x}. See: TDNT—1:1,*; BAGD—1a; THAYER—1a.

2. **Ἀαρών** {5x} **Aarōn**, *ah-ar-ohn';* of Heb. or. [175]; *Aaron,* the brother of Moses:—*Aaron* {5x}. See: TDNT—1:3, 1; BAGD—1a; THAYER—1b.

3. **ʼαβαδδών** {1x} **Abaddōn**, *ab-ad-dohn';* of Heb. or. [11]; a destroying *angel:*—*Abaddon* {1x}. See: TDNT—1:4, 1; BAGD—1a; THAYER—1b.

4. **ἀβαρής** {1x} **abarēs**, *ab-ar-ace';* from *1* (as a neg. particle) and *922; weightless,* i.e. (fig.) *not burdensome:*—from being burdensome {1x}.

Abares means without weight "without weight" lit. "I kept myself burdensomeless." (2 Cor 11:9). See: BAGD—1b, THAYER—1c.

5. **Ἀββᾶ** {3x} **Abba**, *ab-bah';* of Chald. or. *father* (as a voc.):—*Abba* {3x}.

Father, customary title used of God in prayer. *Abba,* approximating a personal name, framed by the lips of infants betokens unreasoning trust. Father expresses an intelligent apprehension of the relationship by the child. The two together express the love and intelligent confidence of the child (Mk 14:36; Rom 8:15; Gal 4:6). See: TDNT—1:5, 1; BAGD—1b; THAYER—1c.

6. **Ἄβελ** {4x} **Abĕl**, *ab'-el;* of Heb. or. [1893]; *Abel,* "vanity/transitory," the second son of Adam:—*Abel* {4x}. See: TDNT—*, 2; BAGD—1c; THAYER—1d.

7. **Ἀβιά** {3x} **Abia**, *ab-ee-ah';* of Heb. or. [29]; *Abijah,* "my father is Jehovah," the name of two Isr.:—*Abia* {3x}. See: BAGD—1c; THAYER—1d.

8. **Ἀβιάθαρ** {1x} **Abiathar**, *ab-ee-ath'-ar;* of Heb. or. [54]; *Abiathar,* "father of abundance," an Isr.:—*Abiathar* {1x}. See: BAGD—1c; THAYER—1d.

9. **Ἀβιληνή** {1x} **Abilēnē**, *ab-ee-lay-nay';* of for. or. [comp. 58]; *Abilene,* "grassy meadow," a region of Syria:—*Abilene* {1x}. See: BAGD—1d; THAYER—2a.

10. **Ἀβιούδ** {2x} **Abiŏud**, *ab-ee-ood';* of Heb. or. [31]; *Abihud,* "my father is majesty," an Isr.:—Abiud {2x}. See: BAGD—1d; THAYER—2a.

11. **Ἀβραάμ** {73x} **Abraam**, *ab-rah-am';* of Heb. or. [85]; *Abraham,* "father of a multitude," the Heb. patriarch:—Abraham {73x}. See: TDNT—1:8, 2; BAGD—1d; THAYER—2a.

12. **ἄβυσσος** {9x} **abussŏs**, *ab'-us-sos;* from *1* (as a neg. particle) and a var. of *1037; depthless,* i.e. (spec.) (infernal) *"abyss":*—deep {2x}, bottomless {2x}, bottomless pit {5x}.

Abussos means bottomless. It describes an immeasurable depth, the underworld, the lower regions, the abyss of Sheol, the lower region, the abode of demons (Rev 11:7; 17:8). See: TDNT—1:9, 2; BAGD—2a; THAYER—2a.

13. **Ἄγαβος** {2x} **Agabŏs**, *Ag'-ab-os;* of Heb. or. [comp. 2285]; *Agabus,* "locust," an Isr.:—Agabus {2x}. See: BAGD—2b; THAYER—2b.

14. **ἀγαθοεργέω** {1x} **agathŏĕrgĕō**, *ag-ath-o-er-gheh'-o;* from *18* and *2041;* to *work good:*—do good {1x}.

In 1 Ti 6:18 the rich are enjoined to do good: "That they do good, that they be rich in good works, ready to distribute, willing to communicate." Syn.: 14, 18, 19, 2095, 2109, 2140, 2570, 2573, 5544. See: TDNT—1:17, 3; BAGD—2b; THAYER—2b.

15. **ἀγαθοποιέω** {11x} **agathŏpŏiĕō**, *ag-ath-op-oy-eh'-o;* from *17; to be a well-doer* (as a favor or a duty):—do good {7x}, well doing {2x}, do well {2x}.

This word is used **(1)** in a general way, "to do well": "For so is the will of God, that with well doing ye may put to silence the ignorance of foolish men:" (1 Pet 2:15; cf, vs. 20; 3:6, 17; 3 Jn 11); and **(2)** with pointed reference "to the benefit of another": "Then said Jesus unto them, I will ask you one thing; Is it lawful on the sabbath days to do good, or to do evil? to save life, or to destroy *it?*" (Lk 6:9; cf. 33, 35). Syn.: 16, 17, 2569. See: TDNT—1:17, 3; BAGD—2c; THAYER—2b.

16. **ἀγαθοποιΐα** {1x} **agathŏpŏiïa**, *ag-ath-op-oy-ee'-ah;* from *17; well-doing,* i.e. *virtue:*—well-doing {1x}.

This word occurs in occurs in 1 Pt 4:19 – "Wherefore let them that suffer according to the will of God commit the keeping of their souls *to him* in well doing, as unto a faithful Creator." Syn.: 15, 17, 2569. See: TDNT—1:17, 3; BAGD—2c; THAYER—2b.

17. **ἀγαθοποιός** {1x} **agathŏpŏiŏs**, *ag-ath-op-oy-os';* from *18* and *4160;* a *well-doer,* i.e. *virtuous:*—them that do well {1x}.

This word means "doing good, beneficent," and is translated "them that do well" in 1 Pt 2:14 [lit., "well-doing (ones)."]. See: TDNT—1:17, 3; BAGD—2c.; THAYER—2c.

18. **ἀγαθός** {102x} **agathŏs**, *ag-ath-os';* a prim. word; *"good"* (in any sense, often as noun):—good 77, good thing {14x}, that which is good + 3588 {8x}, the thing which is good + 3588 {1x}, well {1x}, benefit {1x}.

Agathos, as an adjective, describes that which, being "good" in its character or constitution, is beneficial in its effect. **(1)** It is used **(1a)** of things physical, **(1a1)** e.g., a tree: "Even so every good tree bringeth forth good fruit; but a corrupt tree bringeth forth evil fruit." (Mt 7:17); **(1a2)** ground: "And other fell on good ground, and sprang up, and bare fruit an hundredfold." (Lk 8:8); **(1b)** in a moral sense, frequently of persons and things. **(1b1)** God is essentially, absolutely and consummately "good": "And he said unto him, Why callest thou me good? *there is* none good but one, *that is,* God:" (Mt 19:17; cf. Mk 10:18; Lk 18:19). **(1b2)** To certain persons the word is applied: "Is it not lawful for me to do what I will with mine own? Is thine eye evil, because I am good?" (Mt 20:15; cf. 25:21, 23; Lk 19:17; 23:50; Jn 7:12; Acts 11:24; Titus 2:5); and **(1c)** in a general application: "That ye may be the children of your Father which is in heaven: for He maketh His sun to rise on the evil and on the good, and sendeth rain on the just and on the unjust." (Mt 5:45; cf. 12:35; Lk 6:45; Rom 5:7; 1 Pet 2:18).

(2) The neuter of the adjective with the definite article signifies that which is "good," lit., "the good," as being morally honorable, pleasing to God, and therefore beneficial. **(2a)** Christians are to prove it (Rom 12:2); **(2b)** to cleave to it (Rom 12:9); **(2c)** to do it (Rom 13:3; cf. Gal 6:10); **(2d)** to work it (Rom 2:10; Eph 4:28; 6:8); **(2e)** to follow after it (1 Th 5:15); **(2f)** to be zealous of it (1 Pt 3:13); **(2g)** to imitate it (3 Jn 11); **(2h)** to overcome evil with it (Rom 12:21). **(3)** Governmental authorities are ministers of "good," i.e., that which is salutary, suited to the course of human affairs: "For he is the minister of God to thee for good. But if thou do that which is evil, be afraid;" (Rom 13:4). **(4)** The neuter plural is also used of material "goods," riches, etc.: "He hath filled the hungry with good things; and the rich he hath sent empty away." (Lk 1:53; cf. 12:18, 19; 16:25; Gal 6:6 (of temporal supplies).

(5) In Rom 10:15, the "good" things are the benefits provided through the sacrifice of Christ, in regard both to those conferred through the gospel and to those of the coming messianic kingdom: "And how shall they preach, except they be sent? as it is written, How beautiful are the feet of them that preach the gospel of peace, and bring glad tidings of good things!" (cf. Heb 9:11; 10:1). Syn.: **(A)** Kalos (2570) and *agathos* occur together in Lk 8:15: "But that on the good (kalos) ground are they, which in an honest (kalos) and good (*agathos*) heart, having heard the word, keep *it,* and bring forth fruit with patience." An "honest" (kalos) heart is the attitude which is right towards God and a "good" (*agathos*) heart is one that, instead of working ill to a neighbor, acts beneficially towards him. **(B)** In Rom 7:18, "in me . . . dwelleth no good thing" (*agathos*) signifies that in him is nothing capable of doing "good," and hence he lacks the power "to do that which is good" (kalos). **(C)** In 1 Th 5:15, "follow after that which is good" (*agathos*), the "good" is that which is beneficial; in v. 21, "hold fast that which is good (kalos)," the "good" describes the intrinsic value of the teaching. See also: 2108, 2110, 2570, 5543, 5485. See: TDNT—1:10, 3; BAGD—2d; THAYER—2c.

19. **ἀγαθωσύνη** {4x} **agathōsunē**, *ag-ath-o-soo'-nay;* from *18; goodness,* i.e. *virtue* or *beneficence:*—goodness {4x}.

(1) *Agathosune,* as a noun, means "goodness," and **(1a)** signifies that moral quality which is described by the adjective agathos (18): being "good" in its character or constitution, is beneficial in its effect. **(1b)** This word means a zeal for goodness and truth. **(2)** It is used, in the NT, of regenerate persons (Rom 15:14; Gal 5:22; Eph 5:9; 2 Th 1:11). Syn.: **(A)** Chrestotes (5544) describes the kindlier aspects of "goodness," a kindly disposition towards others. Christ illustrates this quality in His dealings with the penitent woman (Lk 7:37–50). **(B)** *Agathosune* includes the sterner qualities by which doing "good" to others is not necessarily by gentle means; yet the sterner element in the ideal character which acts in a manner for the benefit of others. Christ illustrates this quality in cleansing the temple (Mt 21:12, 13) and in denouncing the scribes and Pharisees (Mt 23:13–29). Syn.: 5544. See: TDNT—1:18, 3; BAGD—3d; THAYER—3b.

20. **ἀγαλλίασις** {5x} **agalliasis**, *ag-al-lee'-as-is;* from *21; exultation;* spec. *welcome:*—gladness {3x}, exceeding joy {1x}, joy {1x}.

This word means "exultation, exuberant joy" is translated **(1)** "gladness": "And thou [Elisabeth] shalt have joy and gladness; and many shall rejoice at his birth." (Lk 1:14; cf. Acts 2:6; Heb 1:9); **(2)** "joy": "For, lo, as soon as the voice of thy salutation sounded in mine ears, the babe leaped in my womb for joy." (Lk 1:44); and **(3)** "exceeding joy": "Now unto him that is able to keep you from falling, and to present *you* faultless before the presence of his glory with exceeding joy," (Jude 24). Syn.: It indicates a more exultant "joy" than chara (5479). See: TDNT—1:19, 4; BAGD—3d; THAYER—3b.

21. **ἀγαλλιάω** {11x} **agalliaō**, *ag-al-lee-ah'-o;* from ἄγαν **agan** (*much*) and *242;* prop. to *jump for joy,* i.e. *exult:*—rejoice {7x}, be exceeding glad {1x}, be glad {1x}, greatly rejoice {1x}, with exceeding joy {1x}.

Agalliao, as a verb, means "to exult, rejoice greatly," is chiefly used in the middle voice. It conveys the idea of jubilant exultation, spiritual "gladness": **(1)** "Rejoice, and be exceeding glad: for great *is* your reward in heaven: for so persecuted they the prophets which were before you." (Mt 5:12 - the Lord's command to His disciples); **(2)** Lk 1:47 - in Mary's song; **(3)** Lk 10:21 - of Christ's exultation ("rejoiced"); **(4)** Jn 8:56 - of Abraham; **(5)** Acts 16:34 - of the Philippian jailor; **(6)** 1 Pt 1:6, 8; 4:13 - "with exceeding joy", of believers in general. Syn.: 2165, 5463. See: TDNT—1:19, *; BAGD—3d; THAYER—3c.

22. **ἄγαμος** {4x} **agamŏs**, *ag'-am-os;* from *1* (as a neg. particle) and *1062; unmarried:*—unmarried {4x}.

This word is translated "unmarried" and occurs in 1 Cor 7:8, 11, 32, 34. See: BAGD—4b; THAYER—3c.

23. **ἀγανακτέω** {7x} **aganaktĕō**, *ag-an-ak-teh'-o;* from ἄγαν **agan** (*much*) and ἄχθος **achthŏs** (*grief;* akin to the base of *43*); to *be greatly afflicted,* i.e. (fig.) *indignant:*—have indignation {2x}, be much displeased {2x}, with indignation {2x}, be sore displeased {1x}.

Aganakteo means to be indignant, feel a violent irritation, to be moved with indignation and is translated **(1)** "were moved with indignation" of the ten disciples against James and John (Mt 20:24); **(2)** "they were sore displeased" of the chief priests and scribes against Christ and the children (Mt 21:15); **(3)** "they had indignation" of the disciples against the woman who anointed Christ's feet (Mt 26:8); **(4)** "he was much displeased" of Christ against the disciples for rebuking the children (Mk 10:14); and **(5)** "(answered) with indignation of the ruler of the synagogue against Christ for healing on the Sabbath (Lk 13:14). Syn.: 2371, 4360. See: BAGD—4b; THAYER—3d.

24. **ἀγανάκτησις** {1x} **aganaktēsis**, *ag-an-ak'-tay-sis;* from *23; indignation:*—indignation {1x}. See: BAGD—4b; THAYER—3d.

25. **ἀγαπάω** {142x} **agapaō**, *ag-ap-ah'-o;* perh. from ἄγαν **agan** (*much*) [or comp. 5689]; to *love* (in a social or moral sense):—love {135x), beloved {7x}.

Agapao, **in its perfect participle passive form,** is translated "beloved" in Rom 9:25; Eph 1:6; Col 3:12; 1 Th 1:4; 2 Th 2:13. Syn.: 5368. See: TDNT—1:21, 5; BAGD—4d; THAYER—3d. comp. *5368.*

26. **ἀγάπη** {116x} **agapē**, *ag-ah'-pay;* from *25; love,* i.e. *affection* or *benevolence;* spec. (plur.) a *love-feast:*—love {86x}, charity {27}, dear {1x}, charitably+2596 {1x}, feast of charity {1x}.

(1) The attitude of God toward His Son (Jn 17:26), the human race (Jn 3:16; Rom 5:8); and to believers on the Lord Jesus Christ particularly (Jn 14:2). **(2)** It is His will to His children concerning their attitude **(2a)** one toward another (Jn 13:34), and **(2b)** toward all men (1 Th 3:12; 1 Cor 16:14; 2 Pet 1:7). **(3)** He desires for them to express His essential nature (1 Jn 4:8). **(4)** Love can be known only from the actions it prompts as God's love is seen in the gift of His Son (1 Jn 4:9, 10). **(5)** This is not the love drawn out by any excellency in its objects (Rom 5:8). **(6)** It was an exercise of the divine will in deliberate choice, made without assignable cause save that which lies in the nature of God Himself (cf. Deut 7:7, 8). **(7)** Love had its perfect expression among men in the Lord Jesus Christ (2 Cor 5:14; Eph 2:4; 3:19; 5:2). **(8)** Christian love is the fruit of His Spirit in the Christian (Gal 5:22).

(9) Christian love has God for its primary object, and expresses itself first of all in implicit obedience to His commandments (Jn 14:15, 21, 23; 15:10; 1 Jn 2:5; 5:3; 2 Jn 6). **(10)** Self-will, that is, self-pleasing, is the negation of love to God. **(11)** Christian love, whether exercised toward the brethren, or toward men generally, is not an impulse from the feelings, it does not always run with the natural inclinations, nor does it spend itself only upon those for whom some affinity is discovered. **(10a)** Love seeks the welfare of all (Rom 15:2), and **(10b)** works no ill to any (Rom 13:8–10); **(10c)** seeks opportunity to do good to 'all men, and especially toward them that are of the household of the faith,' (Gal 6:10). **(11)** See further 1 Cor 13 and Col 3:11–14. **(12)** In respect of *agapao* as used of God, **(12a)** it expresses the deep and constant love and interest of a perfect Being towards entirely unworthy objects, **(12b)** producing and fostering a reverential love in them towards the Giver, **(12c)** a practical love towards those who are partakers of the same, and **(12d)** a desire to help others to seek the Giver.

(13) *Agape* is used in the plural in Jude 12, signifying "feasts of charity." Syn.: *Agape* expresses a more reasoning attachment, of choice and selection, from a seeing in the object upon whom it is bestowed that which is worthy of regard; or else from a sense that such is due toward the person so regarded, as being a benefactor or the like. Phileo (5368), without being necessarily an unreasoning attachment, does yet give less account of itself to itself; is more instinctive, is more of the feelings or natural affections, implies more passion. In the NT agapao is purged of all coldness, and is deeper than phileo. . . . phileo implies an instinctive, affectionate attachment; but agapao of a sentiment based on judgment and adulation, which selects its object for a reason. See also: 1062, 1173, 1403, 1859. See: TDNT—1:21, 5; BAGD—5b; THAYER—4b.

27. **ἀγαπητός** {62x} **agapētŏs**, *ag-ap-ay-tos';* from *25; beloved:*—beloved {47x}, dearly beloved {9x}, well beloved {3x}, dear {3x}.

Agapetos, as an adjective, from agapao (25), means "loved," is used of **(1)** Christ as loved by God: "And lo a voice from heaven, saying, This is my beloved Son, in whom I am well pleased." (Mt 3:17); **(2)** of believers: "To all that be in Rome, beloved of God, called *to be* saints:" (Rom 1:7); **(3)** of believers, one of another: "I write not these things to shame you, but as my beloved sons I warn *you.*" (1 Cor 4:14); **(4)** often, as a form of address: "Wherefore, my dearly beloved, flee from idolatry." (e.g. 1 Cor 10:14). See: TDNT—1:21, 5; BAGD—6b; THAYER—4d.

28. **Ἄγαρ** {2x} **Agar**, *ag'-ar;* of Heb. or. [1904]; *Hagar,* the concubine of Abraham:—Hagar {2x}. See: TDNT—1:55, 10; BAGD—6d; THAYER—5a.

29. **ἀγγαρεύω** {3x} **aggarĕuō**, *ang-ar-yew'-o;* of for. or. [comp. 104]; prop. to *be a courier,* i.e. (by impl.) to *press* into public service:—compel (to go) {3x}.

Aggareuo means to impress into service and is used of compelling a person to go a mile (Mt 5:41) or impressing of Simon to bear Christ's cross (Mt 27:32; Mk 15:21). Syn.: 315. See: BAGD—6d; THAYER—5b.

30. **ἀγγεῖον** {2x} **aggĕiŏn**, *ang-eye'-on;* from ἄγγος **aggŏs** (a *pail,* perh. as *bent;* comp. the base of *43*); a *receptacle:*—vessel {2x}. See: BAGD—6d; THAYER—5b.

31. **ἀγγελία** {1x} **aggĕlia**, *ang-el-ee'-ah;* from *32;* an *announcement,* i.e. (by impl.) *precept:*—message {1x}.

Aggelia means to bring a message, to proclaim, denoting a message, a proclamation, news (1 Jn 1:5). Syn.: 189, 2782. See: TDNT—1:56, 10; BAGD—7a; THAYER—5c.

32. **ἄγγελος** {186x} **aggĕlŏs**, *ang'-el-os;* from ἀγγέλλω **aggĕllō** [prob. der. from *71;* comp. *34*] (to *bring tidings*); a *messenger;* esp. an "*angel*"; by impl. a *pastor:*—angel {179x}, messenger {7x}.

(1) *Angelos* is a messenger sent by God or by man or by satan. **(2)** It is also used of a guardian or representative in Rev 1:20. **(3)** The word most frequently refers to an order of created beings **(3a)** superior to man (Heb 2:7; Ps 8:5), **(3b)** belonging to Heaven (Mt 24:36), **(3c)** belonging to God (Lk 12:8), and **(3d)** engaged in His service (Ps 103:20). **(4)** Angels are **(4a)** spirits, **(4b)** not having material bodies as men (Heb 1:14), **(4c1)** are either human in form, or **(4c2)** can assume the human form when necessary (cf. Lk 24:4 with v. 23, Acts 10:3 with v. 30), and **(4d)** they are called holy (Mk 8:38) and elect (1 Ti 5:21). See: TDNT—1:74, 12; BAGD—7; THAYER—5c.

33. **ἄγε** {2x} **agĕ**, *ag'-eh;* imper. of *71;* prop. *lead,* i.e. *come* on:—go to {2x}. See: BAGD—8b; THAYER—6a.

34. **ἀγέλη** {8x} **agĕlē**, *ag-el'-ay;* from *71* [comp. *32*]; a *drove:*—herd {8x}.

It is used in the NT only of swine (Mt 8:30–32; Mk 5:11, 13; Lk 8:32, 33). See: BAGD—8b; THAYER—6a.

35. **ἀγενεαλόγητος** {1x} **agĕnĕalŏgētŏs**, *ag-en-eh-al-og'-ay-tos;* from *1* (as neg. particle) and *1075; unregistered* as to birth:—without descent {1x}.

This word is rendered "without genealogy" in Heb 7:3. See: TDNT—1:665, 114; BAGD—8c; THAYER—6a.

36. **ἀγενής** {1x} **agĕnēs**, *ag-en-ace';* from *1* (as neg. particle) and *1085;* prop. *without kin,* i.e. (of unknown descent, and by impl.) *ignoble:*—base things {1x}.

Agenes means of low birth; hence, denoting that which is of no reputation, of no account. It is translated "the base things of the world," i.e., those which are of no account or fame in the world's esteem and being in the neuter plural of the adjective bears reference to persons (1 Cor 1:28; note esp. vs. 26). Syn.: 60, 5011. See: BAGD—8c; THAYER—6b.

37. **ἁγιάζω** {29x} **hagiazō**, *hag-ee-ad'-zo;* from *40;* to *make holy,* i.e. (cer.) *purify* or *consecrate;* (mentally) to *venerate:*—sanctify {26x}, hallow {2x}, be holy {1x}.

(1) *Hagiazo* means to make holy and signifies to set apart for God, to sanctify, to make a person or thing the opposite of koinos (2839–common). **(2)** It is translated "Hallowed," with reference to the name of God, the Father, in the Lord's Prayer (Mt 6:9; Lk 11:2). **(3)** In the passive voice, it means "to be made holy, be sanctified," and **(3a)** is translated "let him be made holy" (Rev 22:11), **(3b)** the tense expressing the definiteness and completeness of the divine act; **(3c)** elsewhere it is rendered by the verb "to sanctify." See: TDNT—1:111, 14; BAGD—8c; THAYER—6b.

38. **ἁγιασμός** {10x} **hagiasmŏs**, *hag-ee-as-mos';* from *37;* prop. *purification,* i.e. (the state) *purity;* concr. (by Heb.) a *purifier:*—holiness {5x}, sanctification {5x}.

Hagiasmos signifies **(1)** separation to God (1 Cor 1:30; 2 Th 2:13; 1 Pet 1:2) and **(2)** the resultant state, the conduct befitting those so separated (1 Th 4:3, 4, 7). **(3)** It is translated "holiness" in Rom 6:19, 22; 1 Th 4:7; 1 Ti 2:15; Heb 12:14. **(4)** Sanctification is thus the state predetermined by God for believers, into which in grace He calls them, and in which they begin their Christian course and so pursue it. **(5)** Hence they are called "saints" (40 - hagioi). Syn.: 40, 41, 42, 3741, 3743. See: TDNT—1:113, 14; BAGD—9a; THAYER—6d.

39. **ἅγιον** {11x} **hagiŏn**, *hag'-ee-on;* neut. of *40;* a *sacred* thing (i.e. spot):—sanctuary {4x}, holy place {3x}, holiest of all {3x}, holiness {1x}.

Hagion, the neuter of the adjective hagios (40), means holy and is used **(1)** of those structures which are set apart to God: **(1a)** of the tabernacle in the wilderness (Heb 9:1), and **(1b)** in 9:2 the outer part is called the Holy place (KJV, "the sanctuary"). **(2)** It is used of heaven itself, i.e., the immediate presence of God and His throne (Heb 8:2, "the sanctuary). Syn.: 3485. See: BAGD—9b; THAYER—6d.

40. **ἅγιος** {229x} **hagiŏs**, *hag'-ee-os;* from ἅγος **hagŏs** (an *awful* thing) [comp. *53, 2282*]; *sacred* (phys. *pure,* mor. *blameless* or *religious,* cer. *consecrated*):—holy {161x}, saints {61x}, Holy One {4x}, misc. {3x} = holy one, holy thing.

Hagios fundamentally signifies separated, and hence, in Scripture in its moral and spiritual significance, separated from sin and therefore consecrated to God, sacred. **(1)** It is predicated of God (as the absolutely "Holy" One, in His purity, majesty and glory): **(1a)** of the Father (Lk 1:49; Jn 17:11; 1 Pet 1:15), **(1b)** of the Son (Lk 1:35; Acts 3:14; 4:27), and **(1c)** of the Spirit (Mt 1:18; 2 Ti 1:14). **(2)** It is used of men and things in so far as they are devoted to God. **(2a)** Indeed the quality, as attributed to God, is often presented in a way which involves divine demands upon the conduct of believers who are called hagioi, "saints," "sanctified," or "holy" ones. **(3)** This sainthood is not an attainment, **(3a)** it is a state into which God in grace calls men; yet **(3b)** believers are called to sanctify themselves **(3b1)** consistently with their calling (2 Ti 1:9), **(3b2)** cleansing themselves from all defilement, **(3b3)** forsaking sin, **(3b4)** living a holy manner of life (1 Pet 1:15; 2 Pet 3:11), and **(3b5)** experiencing fellowship with God in His holiness.

(4) The saints are thus figuratively spoken of as a holy temple **(4a)** (1 Cor 3:17—a local church); **(4b)** (Eph 2:21—the whole Church). **(5)** *Hagios* expresses something more and higher than sacred, outwardly associated with God; something more than worthy, honorable; something more than pure, free from defilement. *Hagios* is more comprehensive. It is characteristically godlikeness. **(6)** The **adjective** is used **(6a)** of the outer part of the tabernacle (Heb 9:2 "sanctuary" = "the holy place"); **(6b)** of the inner sanctuary (Heb 9:3 "holiest of all" = "the Holy of Holies"; **(6c)** of the city of Jerusalem (Rev 11:2); **(6d)** its temple (Acts 6:13); **(6e)** of the faith (Jude 20); **(6f)** of the greetings of saints (1 Cor 16:20); **(6g)** of angels (Mk 8:38); **(6h)** of apostles and prophets (Eph 3:5); **(6i)** of the future heavenly Jerusalem (Rev 21:2, 10; 22:19). Syn.: 38, 41, 42, 3741, 3742, 3743. See: TDNT—1:88, 14; BAGD—9b; THAYER—6d.

41. **ἁγιότης** {1x} **hagiŏtēs**, *hag-ee-ot'-ace;* from *40; sanctity* (i.e. prop. the state):—holiness {1x}.

Hagiotes means sanctity, the abstract quality of holiness, and is used of God: "For they verily for a few days chastened *us* after their own pleasure; but he for *our* profit, that *we* might be partakers of his holiness" (Heb 12:10). Syn.: 38, 40, 42, 3741, 3742, 3743. See: TDNT—1:114, 14; BAGD—10b; THAYER—7c.

42. **ἁγιωσύνη** {3x} **hagiōsunē**, *hag-ee-o-soo'-nay;* from *40; sacredness* (i.e. prop. the quality):—holiness {3x}.

Hagiosune denotes the manifestation of the quality of holiness in personal conduct and is used **(1)** in Rom 1:4 of the absolute holiness of Christ in the days of His flesh, **(1a)** which distinguished Him from all merely human beings; this (which is indicated in the phrase "the spirit of holiness") and **(1b)** (in vindication of it) His resurrection from the dead, marked Him out as (He was "declared to be") the Son of God;

(2) believers are to be "perfecting holiness in the fear of God," (2 Cor 7:1, **(2a)** i.e., bringing "holiness" to its predestined end), whereby **(2b)** they may be found "unblameable in holiness" in the Parousia of Christ (1 Th 3:13). **(2c)** In each place character is in view, **(2c1)** perfect in the case of the Lord Jesus, and **(2c2)** growing toward perfection in the case of the Christian. **(2d)** Here the exercise of love is declared to be the means God uses to develop likeness to Christ in His children. **(2e)** The sentence may be paraphrased thus:—The Lord enable you more and more to spend your lives in the interests of others, in order that He may so establish you in Christian character now, that you may be vindicated from every charge that might possibly be brought against you at the Judgment-seat of Christ (cf. 1 Jn 4:16, 17). Syn.: 38, 40, 41, 3741, 3743. See: TDNT—1:114, 14; BAGD—10b; THAYER—7c.

43. **ἀγκάλη** {1x} **agkalē**, *ang-kal'-ay;* from ἄγκος **agkŏs** (a *bend,* "ache"); an *arm* (as *curved*):—arm {1x}.

Ankale, used in the plural, in Lk 2:28, originally denoted the curve, or the inner angle, of the arm. Syn.: Brachion (1023), "the shorter part of the arm, from the shoulder to the elbow," is used metaphorically to denote strength, power, and always in the NT of the power of God (Lk 1:51; Jn 12:38; Acts 13:17). Syn.: 1023. See: BAGD—10c; THAYER—7c.

44. **ἄγκιστρον** {1x} **agkistrŏn**, *ang'-kis-tron;* from the same as *43;* a *hook* (as *bent*):—hook {1x}.

Agkistron is a fish-hook" and is used in Mt 17:27. See: BAGD—10c; THAYER—7d.

45. **ἄγκυρα** {4x} **agkura**, *ang'-koo-rah;* from the same as *43;* an *"anchor"* (as *crooked*):—anchor {4x}.

Agkura was so called because of its curved form [ankos, "a curve"] (Acts 27:29–30, 40; Heb 6:19). See: BAGD—10c; THAYER—7d.

46. **ἄγναφος** {2x} **agnaphŏs**, *ag'-naf-os;* from *1* (as a neg. particle) and the same as *1102;* prop. *unfulled,* i.e. (by impl.) *new* (cloth):—new {2x}.

Agnaphos literally means "uncarded" (*a,* negative, *knapto,* "to card wool"), is rendered "undressed/new," of cloth, in Mt 9:16 and Mk 2:21. See: BAGD—10d; THAYER—7d.

47. **ἁγνεία** {2x} **hagnĕia**, *hag-ni'-ah;* from *53; cleanliness* (the quality), i.e. (spec.) *chastity:*—purity {2x}.

Hagneia occurs in 1 Ti 4:12; 5:2, where it denotes the chastity which excludes all impurity of spirit, manner, or act. Syn.: 54. See: TDNT—1:123, 19; BAGD—10d; THAYER—7d

48. **ἁγνίζω** {7x} **hagnizō**, *hag-nid'-zo;* from *53;* to *make clean,* i.e. (fig.) *sanctify* (cer. or mor.):—purify {5x}, purify self {2x}.

Hagnizo is used of purifying **(1)** ceremonially (Jn 11:55; Acts 21:24, 26), **(2a)** morally, the heart (Jas 4:8), **(2b)** the soul (1 Pet 1:22), or **(2c)** oneself (1 Jn 3:3). Syn.: 2511. See: TDNT—1:123, 19; BAGD—11a; THAYER—7d.

49. **ἁγνισμός** {1x} **hagnismŏs**, *hag-nis-mos';* from *48;* a *cleansing* (the act), i.e. (cer.) *lustration:*—purification {1x}.

Hagnismos denotes a ceremonial purification (Acts 21:26; cf. Num. 6:9–13). Syn.: 2512, 2514. See: TDNT—1:124, 19; BAGD—11a; THAYER—ba.

50. **ἀγνοέω** {22x} **agnŏĕō**, *ag-no-eh'-o;* from *1* (as a neg. particle) and *3539; not to know* (through lack of information or intelligence); by impl. to *ignore* (through disinclination):—be ignorant {7x}, ignorant {4x}, know not {4x}, understand not {3x}, ignorantly {2x}, unknown {2x}.

Agnoeo, as a verb, signifies **(1)** "to be ignorant, not to know," either **(1a)** intransitively **(1a1)** 1 Cor 14:38: "But if any man be ignorant, let him be ignorant," **(1a2)** 1 Ti 1:13: "Who was before a blasphemer, and a persecutor, and injurious: but I obtained mercy, because I did *it* ignorantly in unbelief." [lit., "being ignorant (I did it)"]; or **(1a3)** Heb 5:2: "Who can have compassion on the ignorant, and on them that are out of the way; for that he himself also is compassed with infirmity"; or **(2)** transitively, **(2a)** 2 Pet 2:12: "But these, as natural brute beasts, made to be taken and destroyed, speak evil of the things that they understand not [*agnoeo*]; and shall utterly perish in their own corruption;" **(2a2)** Acts 13:27: "For they that dwell at Jerusalem, and their rulers, because they knew him not [*agnoeo*]," **(2a3)** Acts 17:23: "For as I passed by, and beheld your devotions, I found an altar with this inscription, TO THE UNKNOWN GOD. Whom therefore ye ignorantly [*agnoeo*] worship, him declare I unto you." [lit., "what not knowing ye worship").

(3) This word is also rendered by the verb **(3a)** "to be ignorant that," or "to be ignorant of" (Rom 1:13; 10:3; 11:25; 1 Cor 10:1; 12:1; 2 Cor 1:8; 2:11; 1 Th 4:13); **(3b)** to know not (Rom 2:4; 6:3; 7:1); **(3c)** to be unknown [passive voice] (2 Cor 6:9; Gal 1:22); **(3c)** "not to understand" (Mk 9:32; Lk 9:45). Syn.: 51, 52, 56, 2399, 2990. See: TDNT—1:115, 18; BAGD—11b; THAYER—8a. Syn.: 2990.

51. **ἀγνόημα** {1x} **agnŏēma**, *ag-no'-ay-mah;* from *50;* a thing *ignored*, i.e. *shortcoming:*—error {1x}.

Agnoema, as a noun, means **(1)** "a sin of ignorance" and **(2)** occurs in Heb 9:7: "But into the second *went* the high priest alone once every year, not without blood, which he offered for himself, and *for* the errors of the people." **(3)** What is especially in view in these passages is unwitting error. **(3a)** For Israel a sacrifice was appointed, greater in proportion to the culpability of the guilty, greater, for instance, for a priest or ruler than for a private person. **(3b)** Sins of "ignorance," being sins, must be expiated. **(3c)** A believer guilty of a sin of "ignorance" needs the efficacy of the expiatory sacrifice of Christ, and finds "grace to help." **(3d)** Yet, as the conscience of the believer receives enlightenment, what formerly may have been done in "ignorance" becomes a sin against the light and demands a special confession, to receive forgiveness (1 Jn 1:8, 9). **(4)** It is a sin that resulted from a weakness of the flesh—not a highhanded sin—from an imperfect insight into God's law, and from a lack of due circumspection that afterwards was viewed with shame and regret. Syn.: 50, 52, 56, 2399, 2990. See: TDNT—1:115, 18; BAGD—11c; THAYER—8b.

52. **ἄγνοια** {4x} **agnŏia**, *ag'-noy-ah;* from *50; ignorance* (prop. the quality):—ignorance {4x}.

Agnoia, as a noun, literally means "want of knowledge or perception" and denotes "ignorance" **(1)** on the part of the Jews regarding Christ (Acts 3:17); **(2)** of Gentiles in regard to God (Acts 17:30; cf. Eph 4:18 which includes the idea of willful blindness: see Rom 1:28, not the "ignorance" which mitigates guilt); **(3)** of the former unregenerate condition of those who became believers (1 Pet 1:14). Syn.: 50, 51, 56, 2399, 2990. See: TDNT—1:116, 18; BAGD—11d; THAYER—8b.

53. **ἁγνός** {8x} **hagnŏs**, *hag-nos';* from the same as *40;* prop. *clean*, i.e. (fig.) *innocent, modest, perfect:*—chaste {3x}, clean {1x}, pure {4x}.

Hagnos signifies **(1)** pure from every fault, immaculate, clear (2 Cor 7:11; Phil 4:8; 1 Ti 5:22); or **(2)** pure from carnality, modest (2 Cor 11:2; Titus 2:5). Syn.: **(A)** Hagios (40), holy, as being free from admixture of evil; **(B)** hosios (3741), holy, as being free from defilement; **(C)** *eilikrines* (1506), pure, as being tested, lit., judged by the sunlight, and **(D)** *katharos* (2513), pure, as being cleansed. See: TDNT—1:122, 19; BAGD—11d; THAYER—8b.

54. **ἁγνότης** {1x} **hagnŏtēs**, *hag-not'-ace;* from *53; cleanness* (the state), i.e. (fig.) *blamelessness:*—pureness {1x}.

Hagnotes occurs in 2 Cor 6:6 and means "pureness." Syn.: 47. See: TDNT—1:124, 19; BAGD—12a; THAYER—8b.

55. **ἁγνῶς** {1x} **hagnōs**, *hag-noce';* adv. from *53; purely*, i.e. *honestly:*—sincerely {1x}.

Hagnos denotes "with pure motives" and is rendered "sincerely" in Phil 1:16: "The one preach Christ of contention, not sincerely, supposing to add affliction to my bonds:" See: BAGD—12a; THAYER—8b.

56. **ἀγνωσία** {2x} **agnōsia**, *ag-no-see'-ah;* from *1* (as neg. particle) and *1108; ignorance* (prop. the state):—ignorance {1x}, not the knowledge {1x}.

Agnosia as a noun, denotes **(1)** "ignorance" as directly opposed to gnosis [1108 - which signifies "knowledge" as a result of observation and experience (a, negative, ginosko, "to know"; cf. Eng., "agnostic")]. **(2)** It is used in 1 Cor 15:34 ("no knowledge"), and 1 Pet 2:15. **(3)** In both these passages reprehensible "ignorance" is suggested. Syn.: 50, 51, 52, 2399, 2990. See: TDNT—1:116, 18; BAGD—12b; THAYER—8b.

57. **ἄγνωστος** {1x} **agnōstŏs**, *ag'-noce-tos';* from *1* (as neg. particle) and *1110; unknown:*—unknown {1x}.

This word is found only in Acts 17:23: For as I passed by, and beheld your devotions, I found an altar with this inscription, "TO THE UNKNOWN GOD." See: TDNT—1:119, 18; BAGD—12b; THAYER—8c.

58. **ἀγορά** {11x} **agŏra**, *ag-or-ah';* from ἀγείρω **agĕirō** (to *gather;* prob. akin to *1453*); prop. the *town-square* (as a place of public resort); by impl. a *market* or *thoroughfare:*—market {6x}, marketplace {4x}, street {1x}.

Agora denotes a place of assembly, a public place or forum, a marketplace. **(1)** A variety of events occurred there: **(1a)** business dealings such as the hiring of laborers (Mt 20:3); **(1b)** the buying and selling of goods (Mk 7:4); **(1c)** the games of children (Mt 11:16; Lk 7:32); **(1d)** exchange of greetings (Mt 23:7; Mk 12:38; Lk 11:43; 20:46); **(1e)** the holding of trials (Acts 16:19); or **(1f)** public discussions (Acts 17:17). **(2)** Mk 6:56 records the bringing of the sick there. **(7)** The word always carries with it the idea of publicity, in contrast to private circumstances. See: BAGD—12c; THAYER—8c.

59. **ἀγοράζω** {31x} **agŏrazō**, *ag-or-ad'-zo;* from *58;* prop. to *go to market*, i.e. (by impl.) to *purchase;* spec. to *redeem:*—buy {28x}, redeem {3x}.

Agorazo, means primarily, "to frequent the market-place," the agora; hence to do business there, to buy or sell. **(1)** It is used literally in Mt 14:15: "And when it was evening, his disciples came to him, saying, This is a desert place, and the time is now past; send the multitude away, that they may go into the villages, and buy themselves victuals." **(2)** Figuratively, Christ is spoken of as having bought His redeemed, making them His property at the price of His blood (1 Cor 6:20; 7:23; 2 Pet 2:1; Rev 5:9; 14:3–4). Syn.: 5608. See: TDNT—1:124, 19; BAGD—12d; THAYER—8c.

60. **ἀγοραῖος** {2x} **agŏraiŏs**, *ag-or-ah'-yos;* from *58; relating to the market-place*, i.e. *forensic* (times); by impl. *vulgar:*—baser sort {1x}, low {1x}.

Agoraios, literally signifies relating to the market place; hence, **(1)** frequenting markets, and so sauntering about idly. **(2)** It is also used of affairs usually transacted in the market-place such as judicial assemblies (Acts 19:38 - law). Syn.: 36, 5011. See: BAGD—13a; THAYER—8d.

61. **ἄγρα** {2x} **agra**, *ag'-rah;* from *71;* (abstr.) a *catching* (of fish); also (concr.) a *haul* (of fish):—draught {2x}.

(1) *Agra* means to go hunting or catching and is used only **(2)** in connection with fishing. **(2a)** In Lk 5:4 it signifies the act of catching fish and **(2b)** in Lk 5:9 it stands for the catch itself. Syn.: 856. See: BAGD—13a; THAYER—8d.

62. **ἀγράμματος** {1x} **agrammatŏs**, *ag-ram-mat-os;* from *1* (as neg. particle) and *1121; unlettered*, i.e. *illiterate:*—unlearned {1x}.

In its only occurrence, Acts 4:13, the disciples are accused of being unversed in the learning of the Jewish schools. Syn.: 261, 521, 2399. See: BAGD—13b; THAYER—8d.

63. **ἀγραυλέω** {1x} **agraulĕō**, *ag-row-leh'-o;* from *68* and *832* (in the sense of *833*); to *camp out:*—abide in the field {1x}.

Agrauleo means to lodge in a fold in a field (Lk 2:8). Syn.: 390, 835, 1304, 1961, 2476, 2650, 3306, 3887, 4160, 4357, 5278. See: BAGD—13b; THAYER—8d.

64. **ἀγρεύω** {1x} **agrĕuō**, *ag-rew'-o;* from *61;* to *hunt*, i.e. (fig.) to *entrap:*—catch {1x}. See: BAGD—13b; THAYER—9a.

65. **ἀγριέλαιος** {2x} **agriĕlaiŏs**, *ag-ree-el'-ah-yos;* from *66* and *1636;* an *oleaster:*—wild olive tree {1x}, olive tree which is wild {1x}.

Agrielaios is an adjective used as a noun in Rom 11:17, 24 —a wild olive tree. Syn.: 1636, 1638, 2565. See: BAGD—13b; THAYER—9a.

66. **ἄγριος** {3x} **agriŏs**, *ag'-ree-os;* from *68; wild* (as pertaining to the *country*), lit. (*natural*) or fig. (*fierce*):—wild {2x}, raging {1x}.

Agrios denotes **(1)** of or in fields; hence, not domestic, said of honey (Mt 3:4; Mk 1:6); or **(2)** savage, fierce, used metaphorically in Jude 13, raging waves. See: BAGD—13c; THAYER—9a.

67. **Ἀγρίππας** {12x} **Agrippas**, *ag-rip'-pas;* appar. from *66* and *2462; wild-horse* tamer; *Agrippas*, one of the Herods:—Agrippa {12x}. See: BAGD—13d; THAYER—9b.

68. **ἀγρός** {36x} **agrŏs**, *ag-ros';* from *71;* a *field* (as a *drive* for cattle); gen. the *country;* spec. a *farm*, i.e. *hamlet:*—field {22x}, country {8x}, land {4x}, farm {1x}, piece of ground {1x}.

Agros denotes a field, especially a cultivated field; hence, the country in contrast to the town (Mk 5:14; 6:36; 15:21; 16:12; Lk 8:34; 9:12). Syn.: 3313, 3968, 4066, 5561. See: BAGD—13d; THAYER—9b.

69. **ἀγρυπνέω** {4x} **agrupnĕō**, *ag-roop-neh'-o;* ultimately from *1* (as neg. particle) and *5258;* to *be sleepless*, i.e. *keep awake:*—watch {4x}.

Agrupneo means **(1)** to be sleepless and is used metaphorically to be watchful (Mk 13:33; Lk 21:36; Eph 6:18; Heb 13:17). The word expresses not mere wakefulness, but the watchfulness of those who are intent upon a thing. Syn.: 1127, 3525, 3906. See: TDNT—2:338, 195; BAGD—14a; THAYER—9b.

70. **ἀγρυπνία** {2x} **agrupnia**, *ag-roop-nee'-ah;* from *69; sleeplessness*, i.e. a *keeping awake:*—watching {2x}.

Agrupnia means sleeplessness and is rendered watchings (2 Cor 6:5; 11:27). Syn.: 2892, 5438. See: BAGD—14a; THAYER—9c.

71. **ἄγω** {72x} **agō**, *ag'-o;* a prim. verb; prop. to *lead;* by impl. to *bring, drive,* (refl.) *go,* (spec.) *pass* (time), or (fig.) *induce:*—bring {45x}, lead {12x}, go {7x}, bring forth {2x}, bring {1x}, misc. {5x} = be, carry, keep, be open.

Ago means to lead, to lead along, to bring, and connotes to bring: "For if we believe that Jesus died and rose again, even so them also which sleep in Jesus will God bring (*ago*) with Him" (1 Th 4:14; cf. 2 Ti 4:11; Heb 2:10). Syn.: 321, 520, 1521, 3919, 4254, 4311, 5342. See: BAGD—14b; THAYER—9c.

72. **ἀγωγή** {1x} **agōgē**, *ag-o-gay';* redupl. from *71;* a *bringing* up, i.e. *mode of living:*—manner of life {1x}.

Agoge properly denotes **(1)** a teaching; figuratively, **(2)** a training, discipline, and so, **(1)** the life led, a way or course of life, conduct (2 Ti 3:10 – manner of life). See: TDNT—1:128, 20; BAGD—14d; THAYER—10a.

73. **ἀγών** {6x} **agōn**, *ag-one';* from *71;* prop. a place of *assembly* (as if *led*), i.e. (by impl.) a *contest* (held there); fig. an *effort* or *anxiety:*—conflict {2x}, fight {2x}, contention {1x}, race {1x}.

Agon means to lead and signifies **(1)** a place of assembly especially the place where the Greeks assembled for the Olympic and Pythian games; **(2)** a contest of athletes, metaphorically, and translated **(2a1)** "fight" (1 Ti 6:12; 2 Ti 4:7), or **(2a2)** "race" (Heb 12:1). Hence, **(3)** the inward conflict of the soul is often the result, or the accompaniment, of outward conflict (Phil 1:30; 1 Th 2:2). It implies a contest against spiritual foes, as well as human adversaries (Col 2:1—conflict). Syn.: 119. See: TDNT—1:135, 20; BAGD—15a; THAYER—10a.

74. **ἀγωνία** {1x} **agōnia**, *ag-o-nee'-ah;* from *73;* a *struggle* (prop. the state), i.e. (fig.) *anguish:*—agony {1x}.

Agonia [cf. Eng., "agony"] was used among the Greeks **(1)** as an alternative to *agon* (73), "a place of assembly"; **(2)** then for the contests or games which took place there, and then **(3)** to denote intense emotion. **(3a)** It was more frequently used eventually in this last respect, to denote severe emotional strain and anguish. **(3b)** So in Lk 22:44, of the Lord's "agony" in Gethsemane (Lk 22:44). See: TDNT—1:140, 20; BAGD—15a; THAYER—10b.

75. **ἀγωνίζομαι** {7x} **agōnizŏmai**, *ag-o-nid'-zom-ahee;* from *73;* to *struggle,* lit. (to *compete* for a prize), fig. (to *contend* with an adversary), or gen. (to *endeavor* to accomplish something):—strive {3x}, fight {3x}, labour fervently {1x}.

Agonizomai denotes **(1)** to contend in the public games (1 Cor 9:25); **(2)** to fight, engage in conflict: "Jesus answered, My kingdom is not of this world: if my kingdom were of this world, then would my servants fight, that I should not be delivered to the Jews: but now is my kingdom not from hence." (Jn 18:36); **(3)** metaphorically, **(3a)** to contend perseveringly against opposition and temptation: "Fight [*aganizomai*] the good fight [73 – agon] of faith, lay hold on eternal life, whereunto thou art also called, and hast professed a good profession before many witnesses." (1 Ti 6:12; cf. 2 Ti 4:7); **(3b)** to strive as in a contest for a prize, straining every nerve to attain to the object: "Strive [*aganizomai*] to enter in at the strait gate: for many, I say unto you, will seek to enter in, and shall not be able." (Lk 13:24); **(3c)** to put forth every effort, involving toil (Col 1:29; 1 Ti 4:10); **(3d)** to wrestle earnestly in prayer: "Epaphras, who is *one* of you, a servant of Christ, saluteth you, always labouring fervently [*aganizomai*] for you in prayers, that ye may stand perfect and complete in all the will of God." (Col 4:12). Syn.: 2341, 3164, 4438. See: TDNT—1:135, 20; BAGD—15b; THAYER—10b.

76. **Ἀδάμ** {9x} **Adam**, *ad-am';* of Heb. or. [121]; *Adam,* the first man; typ. (of Jesus) *man* (as his representative):—Adam {9x}. See: TDNT—1:141, 21; BAGD—15c; THAYER—10c.

77. **ἀδάπανος** {1x} **adapanŏs**, *ad-ap'-an-os;* from *1* (as neg. particle); and *1160; costless,* i.e. *gratuitous:*—without charge {1x}.

Adapanos, literally means "without expense" and is used in 1 Cor 9:18 as without charge of service in the gospel. See: BAGD—15d; THAYER—10c.

78. **Ἀδδί** {1x} **Addi**, *ad-dee';* prob. of Heb. or. [comp. 5716]; *Addi,* an Isr.:—*Addi* {1x}. See: BAGD—15d; THAYER—10c.

79. **ἀδελφή** {24x} **adĕlphē**, *ad-el-fay';* fem of *80;* a *sister* (nat. or eccl.):—sister {24x}.

Adelphe is used **(1)** natural relationship (e.g., Mt 19:29; of the "sisters" of Christ, the children of Joseph and Mary after the virgin birth of Christ (cf. Mt 13:56); **(2)** of "spiritual kinship" with Christ, an affinity marked by the fulfillment of the will of the Father: "For whosoever shall do the will of my Father which is in heaven, the same is my brother, and sister, and mother." (Mt 12:50; Mk 3:35); **(3)** of spiritual relationship based upon faith in Christ: "I commend unto you Phebe our sister, which is a servant of the church which is at Cenchrea:"(Rom 16:1; cf. 1 Cor 7:15; 9:5). See: TDNT—1:144, 22; BAGD—15d; THAYER—10c.

80. **ἀδελφός** {346x} **adĕlphŏs**, *ad-el-fos';* from *1* (as a connective particle) and δελφύς **dĕlphus** (the *womb*); a *brother* (lit. or fig.) near or remote [much like 1]:—brother {346x}.

Adelphos denotes a brother, or near kinsman; in the plural, a community based on identity of origin or life. It is used of: **(1)** male children of the same parents: "Abraham begat Isaac; and Isaac begat Jacob; and Jacob begat Judas and his brethren;" (Mt 1:2; cf. 14:3); **(2)** male descendants of the same parents: "And when he was full forty years old, it came into his heart to visit his brethren the children of Israel." (Acts 7:23; cf. 7:26; Heb 7:5); **(3)** male children of the same mother: "Is not this the carpenter's son? is not his mother called Mary? and his brethren, James, and Joses, and Simon, and Judas?" (Mt 13:55; cf. 1 Cor 9:5; Gal 1:19); **(4)** people of the same nationality: "And now, brethren, I wot that through ignorance ye did *it,* as *did* also your rulers." (Acts 3:17; cf. 3:22; Rom 9:3); **(5)** any man, a neighbor: "But I say unto you, That whosoever is angry with his brother (*adelphos*) without a cause shall be in danger of the judgment: and whosoever shall say to his brother (*adelphos*), Raca, shall be in danger of the council: but whosoever shall say, Thou fool, shall be in danger of hell fire." (Mt 5:22; cf. 7:3);

(6) persons united by a common interest: "And if ye salute your brethren only, what do ye more *than others?* do not even the publicans so?" (Mt 5:47); **(7)** persons united by a common calling: "Then saith he unto me, See *thou do it* not: for I am thy fellowservant, and of thy brethren the prophets, and of them which keep the sayings of this book: worship God." (Rev 22:9); **(8)** mankind: "Wherefore in all things it behoved him to be made like unto *his* brethren, that he might be a merciful and faithful high priest in things *pertaining* to God, to make reconciliation for the sins of the people." (Heb 2:17); **(9)** the disciples, and so, by implication, all believers: "Then said Jesus unto them, Be not afraid: go tell my brethren that they go into Galilee, and there shall they see me." (Mt 28:10; cf. Jn 20:17); **(10)** believers, apart from sex (Mt 23:8; Acts 1:15; Rom 1:13; 1 Th 1:4; Rev 19:10 [the word "sisters" is used of believers, only in 1 Ti 5:2). Syn.: **A.** adelphotes (81), primarily, a brotherly relation; the community possessed of this relation, a brotherhood (1 Pet 2:17); **B.** philadelphos (5361), fond of one's brethren (1 Pet 3:8); **C.** philadelphia (5359), brotherly love (Rom 12:10; 1 Th 4:9); **D.** pseudadelphos (5569) false brethren (2 Cor 11:26; Gal 2:4). See: TDNT—1:144, 22; BAGD—15d; THAYER—10d.

81. **ἀδελφότης** {2x} **adĕlphŏtēs**, *ad-el-fot'-ace;* from *80; brotherhood* (prop. the feeling of *brotherliness*), i.e. the (Chr.) *fraternity:*—brotherhood {1x}, brethren {1x}. See: TDNT—1:144, 22; BAGD—16c; THAYER—11b.

82. **ἄδηλος** {2x} **adēlŏs**, *ad'-ay-los;* from *1* (as a neg. particle) and *1212; hidden,* fig. *indistinct:*—appear not {1x}, uncertain {1x}.

Adelos denotes **(1)** unseen; with the article, translated "which appear not": "Woe unto you, scribes and Pharisees, hypocrites! for ye are as graves which appear not (*adelos*), and the men that walk over *them* are not aware *of them.*" (Lk 11:44); and **(2)** uncertain, indistinct: "For if the trumpet give an uncertain sound, who shall prepare himself to the battle?" (1 Cor 14:8). See: BAGD—16d; THAYER—11b.

83. **ἀδηλότης** {1x} **adēlŏtēs**, *ad-ay-lot'-ace;* from *82; uncertainty:*—uncertain {1x}. *Adelotes* means uncertainty [of riches] and occurs in 1 Tim 6:17. See: BAGD—16d; THAYER—11b.

84. **ἀδήλως** {1x} **adēlōs**, *ad-ay'-loce;* adv. from *82; uncertainly:*—uncertainly {1x}.

Adelos is translated as "uncertainly" in 1 Cor 9:26: "I therefore so run, not as uncertainly; so fight I, not as one that beateth the air." See: BAGD—16d; THAYER—11b.

85. **ἀδημονέω** {3x} **adēmŏnĕō**, *ad-ay-mon-eh'-o;* from a der. of ἀδέω **adeo** (to be *sated* to loathing); to *be in distress* (of mind):—be very heavy {2x}, be full of heaviness {1x}.

Ademoneo means to be troubled, much distressed and is used of **(1)** the Lord's sorrow in Gethsemane: "And he took with him Peter and the two sons of Zebedee, and began to be sorrowful and very heavy (*ademoneo*)" (Mt 26:37; cf. Mk 14:33); and **(2)** of Epaphroditus: "For he longed after you all, and was full of heaviness, because that ye had heard that he had been sick." (Phil 2:26). Syn.: 916, 3076. See: BAGD—16d; THAYER—11b.

86. **ᾅδης** {11x} **haidēs**, *hah'-dace;* from *1* (as neg. particle) and *1492;* prop. *unseen,* i.e. "*Hades*" or the place (state) of departed souls:—hell {10x}, grave {1x}.

Hades is **(1)** the region of departed spirits of the lost (but including the blessed dead in periods preceding the ascension of Christ). **(2)** It corresponds to Sheol in the OT. **(3)** For the condition of the inhabitants see Lk 16:23–31. **(3)** The word is used always by the Lord (Mt 11:23; 16:18; Lk 10:15; 16:23). **(4)** It is used with reference to the soul of Christ (Acts 2:27, 31). **(5)** Christ declares that He has the keys of it (Rev 1:18). **(6)** In Rev 6:8 it is personified, **(6a)** with the signification of the temporary destiny of the doomed; **(6b)** it is to give up those who are therein (Rev 20:13), and **(6c)** it is to be cast into the lake of fire (Rev 20:14). See: TDNT—1:146, 22; BAGD—16d; THAYER—11c.

87. **ἀδιάκριτος** {1x} **adiakritŏs**, *ad-ee-ak'-ree-tos;* from *1* (as a neg. particle) and a der. of *1252;* prop. *undistinguished,* i.e. (act.) *impartial:*—without partiality {1x}.

Adiakritos primarily signifies not to be parted; hence, without uncertainty, or indecision, without partiality: "But the wisdom that is from above is first pure, then peaceable, gentle, *and* easy to be intreated, full of mercy and good fruits, without partiality (*adiakritos*), and without hypocrisy." (Jas 3:17). See: TDNT—3:950, 469; BAGD—17a; THAYER—11d.

88. **ἀδιάλειπτος** {2x} **adialĕiptŏs**, *ad-ee-al'-ipe-tos;* from *1* (as a neg. particle) and a der. of a compound of *1223* and *3007; unintermitted,* i.e. *permanent:*—continual {1x}, without ceasing {1x}.

Adialeiptos means unceasing and is used **(1)** of incessant, continual heart pain: KJV Romans 9:2 "That I have great heaviness and continual sorrow in my heart." (Rom 9:2); and **(2)** in 2 Ti 1:3 of remembrance in prayer: "I thank God, whom I serve from *my* forefathers with pure conscience, that without ceasing I have remembrance of thee in my prayers night and day." **(3)** The meaning in each place is not that of unbroken continuity, but without the omission of any occasion. See: BAGD—17b; THAYER—11d.

89. **ἀδιαλείπτως** {4x} **adialĕiptōs**, *ad-ee-al-ipe'-toce;* adv. from *88; uninteruptedly,* i.e. *without omission* (on an appropriate occasion):—without ceasing {4x}.

Adialeiptos means unceasingly, without ceasing and is used with the same significance as the adjective (88); not of what is not interrupted, but of that which is constantly recurring: **(1)** prayer: "For God is my witness, whom I serve with my spirit in the gospel of his Son, that without ceasing I make mention of you always in my prayers;" (Rom 1:9; cf. 1 Th 5:17); **(2)** in 1 Th 1:3 of the remembrance of the work, labor and patience of saints: "Remembering without ceasing your work of faith, and labour of love, and patience of hope in our Lord Jesus Christ, in the sight of God and our Father;" and **(3)** in 1 Th 2:13 of thanksgiving: "For this cause also thank we God without ceasing." See: BAGD—17b; THAYER—11d.

90. **ἀδιαφθορία** {1x} **adiaphthŏria**, *ad-ee-af-thor-ee'-ah;* from a der. of a compound of *1* (as a neg. particle) and a der. of *1311; incorruptibleness,* i.e. (fig.) *purity* (of doctrine):—uncorruptness {1x}. See: BAGD—17b; THAYER—11d.

91. **ἀδικέω** {28x} **adikĕō**, *ad-ee-keh'-o;* from *94;* to *be unjust,* i.e. (act.) *do wrong* (mor., socially or phys.):—hurt {10x}, do wrong {8x}, wrong {2x}, suffer wrong {2x}, be unjust {2x}, take wrong {1x}, injure {1x}, be an offender {1x}, hope {1x}.

Adikeo signifies, **(1)** intransitively, to do wrong, do hurt, act unjustly: "For their power is in their mouth, and in their tails: for their tails *were* like unto serpents, and had heads, and with them they do hurt." (Rev 9:19); and **(2)** transitively to wrong, hurt or injure a person: "Behold, I give unto you power to tread on serpents and scorpions, and over all the power of the enemy: and nothing shall by any means hurt you." (Lk 10:19; cf. Rev 6:6; 7:2). Syn.: 984, 2559. See: TDNT—1:157, 22; BAGD—17c; THAYER—11d.

92. **ἀδίκημα** {3x} **adikēma**, *ad-eek'-ay-mah;* from *91;* a *wrong* done:—matter of wrong {1x}, evil doing {1x}, iniquity {1x}.

Adikema denotes a wrong, injury, misdeed and is translated **(1)** a matter of wrong: "And when Paul was now about to open *his* mouth, Gallio said unto the Jews, If it were a matter of wrong or wicked lewdness, O *ye* Jews, reason would that I should bear with you:" (Acts 18:14); **(2)** evildoing: "Or else let these same *here* say, if they have found any evil doing in me, while I stood before the council," (Acts 24:20); **(3)** iniquities: "For her sins have reached unto heaven, and God hath remembered her iniquities." (Rev 18:5). Syn.: 93, 458, 3892, 4189. See: TDNT—1:161, 22; BAGD—17d; THAYER—12a.

93. **ἀδικία** {25x} **adikia**, *ad-ee-kee'-ah;* from *94;* (legal) *injustice* (prop. the quality, by impl. the act); mor. *wrongfulness* (of character, life or act):—unrighteousness {16x}, iniquity {6x}, unjust {2x}, wrong {1x}.

Adikia denotes **(1)** unrighteousness, literally, unrightness, a condition of not being right, whether with God, according to the standard of His holiness and righteousness, or with man, according to the standard of what man knows to be right by his conscience. **(2)** The word is usually translated "unrighteousness," but is rendered "iniquity" in Lk 13:27; Acts 1:18; 8:23; 1 Cor 13:6. **(3)** In Lk 16:8 and 18:6, the phrases lit. are, "the steward of unrighteousness" and "the judge of injustice," the subjective genitive describing their character; in 18:6 the meaning is "injustice" and so perhaps in Rom 9:14. Syn.: 92, 458, 3892, 4189. See: TDNT—1:153, 22; BAGD—17d; THAYER—12a.

94. **ἄδικος** {12x} **adikŏs**, *ad'-ee-kos;* from *1* (as a neg. particle) and *1349; unjust;* by extens. *wicked;* by impl. *treacherous;* spec. *heathen:*—unjust {8x}, unrighteous {4x}.

Adikos means "not in conformity with *dike* (1349 - 'right,')" and is rendered "unjust": "That ye may be the children of your Father which is in heaven: for he maketh his sun to rise on the evil and on the good, and sendeth rain on the just and on the unjust." (Mt 5:45; cf. Lk 18:11; Acts 24:15). See: TDNT—1:149, 22; BAGD—18b; THAYER—12b.

95. **ἀδίκως** {1x} **adikōs**, *ad-ee'-koce;* adv. from *94; unjustly:*—wrongfully {1x}.

This word occurs only in 1 Pet 2:19: "For this *is* thankworthy, if a man for conscience toward God endure grief, suffering wrongfully." See: BAGD—18b; THAYER—12c.

96. **ἀδόκιμος** {8x} **adŏkimŏs**, *ad-ok'-ee-mos;* from *1* (as a neg. particle) and *1384; unapproved,* i.e. *rejected;* by impl. *worthless* (lit. or mor.):—reprobate {6x}, castaway {1x}, rejected {1x}.

Adokimos signifies not standing the test, rejected. It is said of things **(1)** the land as rejected (Heb 6:8); and **(2)** of persons as **(2a)** reprobate in mind (Rom 1:28); **(2b)** reprobate concerning the faith (Titus 1:16); and **(2b)** castaway (1 Cor 9:27). See: TDNT—2:255, 181; BAGD—18c; THAYER—12c.

97. **ἄδολος** {1x} **adŏlŏs**, *ad'-ol-os;* from *1* (as a neg. particle) and *1388; undeceitful,* i.e. (fig.) *unadulterated:*—sincere {1x}.

Adolos, as a noun, means "without guile," "pure, unadulterated," and is used metaphorically of the teaching of the Word of God: "As newborn babes, desire the sincere milk of the word, that ye may grow thereby" (1 Pet 2:2). Syn.: As the akakos (172) has no harmfulness in him, and the *adolos* (97) no guile, so the akeraios (185) no foreign mixture, and the haplous (573) no folds or wrinkles. See also: 185. See: BAGD—18d; THAYER—12c.

98. **᾿Αδραμυττηνός** {1x} **Adramuttēnŏs**, *ad-ram-oot-tay-nos';* from ᾿Αδραμύττειον **Adramuttĕiŏn** (a place in Asia Minor); *Adramyttene* or belonging to Adramyttium:—Adramyttium {1x}. See: BAGD—18d; THAYER—12c.

99. **᾿Αδρίας** {1x} **Adrias**, *ad-ree'-as;* from ᾿Αδρία **Adria** (a place near its shore); the *Adriatic* sea (incl. the Ionian):—Adria {1x}. See: BAGD—18d; THAYER—12d.

100. **ἁδρότης** {1x} **hadrŏtēs**, *had-rot'-ace;* from ἁδρός **hadrŏs** (stout); *plumpness,* i.e. (fig.) *liberality:*—abundance {1x}.

Hadrotes means thick, fat, full-grown, rich; so regarding the offering in 2 Cor 8:20 the thought is that of bountiful giving, a fat offering, not mere abundance. Syn.: 4050. See: BAGD—18d; THAYER—12d.

101. **ἀδυνατέω** {2x} **adunatĕō**, *ad-oo-nat-eh'-o;* from *102;* to *be unable,* i.e. (pass.) *impossible:*—be impossible {2x}.

Adunateo signifies to be impossible, unable, and in the NT it is used only of things: **(1)** nothing to a believer: "And Jesus said unto them, Because of your unbelief: for verily I say unto you, If ye have faith as a grain of mustard seed, ye shall say unto this mountain, Remove hence to yonder place; and it shall remove; and nothing shall be impossible unto you." (Mt 17:20); **(2)** nothing with God: "For with God nothing shall be impossible" (Lk 1:37). See: TDNT—2:284, 186; BAGD—19a; THAYER—12d.

102. **ἀδύνατος** {10x} **adunatŏs**, *ad-oo'-nat-os;* from *1* (as a neg. particle) and *1415; unable,* i.e. *weak* (lit. or fig.); pass. *impossible:*—impossible {6x}, impotent {1x}, could not do {1x}, weak {1x}, not possible {1x}. See: TDNT—2:284, 186; BAGD—19a; THAYER—12d.

103. **ᾄδω** {5x} **a̧dō**, *ad'-o'* a prim. verb; to *sing:*—sing {5x}.

Ado is used always of "praise to God," **(1)** intransitively: "Speaking to yourselves in psalms and hymns and spiritual songs, singing and making melody in your heart to the Lord;" (Eph 5:19; cf. Col 3:16); **(2)** transitively: "And they sung a new song, saying, Thou art worthy to take the book, and to open the seals thereof" (Rev 5:9; cf. 14:3; 15:3). Syn.: 5214, 5567. See: TDNT—1:163, 24; BAGD—19b; THAYER—13a.

104. **ἀεί** {8x} **aĕi**, *ah-eye';* from an obs. prim. noun (appar. mean. continued *duration*); "*ever,*" by qualification *regularly;* by impl. *earnestly:*—always {4x}, always {3x}, ever {1x}.

Aei has two meanings: **(1)** "perpetually, incessantly": "Ye stiffnecked and uncircumcised in heart and ears, ye do always (*aei*) resist the Holy Ghost: as your fathers *did,* so *do* ye." (Acts 7:51; cf. 2 Cor 4:11; 6:10; Titus 1:12; Heb 3:10; **(2)** "invariably, at any and every time," of successive occurrences, when some thing is to be repeated, according to the circumstances: "But sanctify the Lord God in your hearts: and *be* ready always to *give* an answer to every man that asketh you a reason of the hope that is in you with meekness and fear:" (1 Pet 3:15; cf. 2 Pet 1:12). See: BAGD—19c; THAYER—13a.

105. **ἀετός** {4x} **aĕtŏs**, *ah-et-os';* from the same as *109;* an *eagle* (from its *wind*-like flight):—eagle {4x}. See: BAGD—19d; THAYER—13a.

106. **ἄζυμος** {9x} **azumŏs**, *ad'-zoo-mos;* from *1* (as a neg. particle) and *2219; unleavened,* i.e. (fig.) *uncorrupted;* (in the neut. plur.) spec. (by impl.) the *Passover* week:—unleavened bread {8x}, unleavened {1x}.

Azumos denotes "unleavened bread," i.e., without any process of fermentation; hence, **(1)** metaphorically, **(1a)** "of a holy, spiritual condition": "Purge out therefore the old leaven (*azumos*), that ye may be a new lump, as ye are unleavened. For even Christ our passover is sacrificed for us:" (1 Cor 5:7), and **(1b)** of "sincerity and truth": "Therefore let us keep the feast, not with old leaven (*azumos*), neither with the leaven of malice and wickedness; but with the unleavened *bread* of sincerity and truth." (1 Cor 5: 8). **(2)** With the article it signifies the feast of unleavened bread: "Now the first *day* of the *feast of* unleavened bread the disciples came to Jesus, saying unto him, Where wilt thou that we prepare for thee to eat the passover?" (Mt 26:17; cf. Mk 14:1, 12; Lk 22:1, 7; Acts 12:3; 20:6). See: TDNT—2:902, 302; BAGD—19d; THAYER—13b.

107. **Ἀζώρ** {2x} **Azōr**, *ad-zore';* of Heb. or. [comp. 5809]; *Azor,* an Isr.:—*Azor* {2x}. See: BAGD—20a; THAYER—13b.

108. **Ἄζωτος** {1x} **Azōtŏs**, *ad'-zo-tos;* of Heb. or. [795]; *Azotus* (i.e. Ashdod), a place in Pal.:—Azotus {1x}. See: BAGD—20a; THAYER—13b.

109. **ἀήρ** {7x} **aēr**, *ah-ayr';* from ἄημι **aēmi** (to *breathe* unconsciously, i.e. *respire;* by anal. to *blow*); *"air"* (as naturally *circumambient*):—air {7x}.

This word signifies "the atmosphere" **(1)** certainly in five of the seven occurrences (Acts 22:23; 1 Cor 9:26; 14:9; Rev 9:2; 16:11), and **(2)** almost certainly in the other two (Eph 2:2 and 1 Th 4:17). See: TDNT—1:165, 25; BAGD—20b; THAYER—13c. Syn.: 3772, 5594.

ἀθά **atha**. See *3134*.

110. **ἀθανασία** {3x} **athanasia**, *ath-an-as-ee'-ah;* from a compound of *1* (as a neg. particle) and *2288; deathlessness:*—immortality {3x}.

Athanasia literally means deathlessness and is rendered **(1)** "immortality" **(1a)** of the glorified body of the believer (1 Cor 15:53, 54); and **(1b)** of the nature of God (1 Ti 6:16). **(2)** In the NT *athanasia* expresses more than deathlessness, it suggests the quality of the life enjoyed because for the believer what is mortal is to be "swallowed up of life": "For we that are in *this* tabernacle do groan, being burdened: not for that we would be unclothed, but clothed upon, that mortality might be swallowed up of life." (2 Cor 5:4). See: TDNT—3:22, 312; BAGD—20c; THAYER—13c.

111. **ἀθέμιτος** {2x} **athĕmitŏs**, *ath-em'-ee-tos;* from *1* (as a neg. particle) and a der. of θέμις **thĕmis** (*statute;* from the base of *5087*); *illegal;* by impl. *flagitious:*—unlawful thing {1x}, abominable {1x}.

Athemitos occurs in Acts 10:28, "unlawful," and 1 Pet 4:3, "abominable." Syn.: 947. See: TDNT—1:166, 25; BAGD—20d; THAYER—13d.

112. **ἄθεος** {1x} **athĕŏs**, *ath'-eh-os;* from *1* (as a neg. particle) and *2316; godless:*—without God {1x}.

Atheos (112), means "atheist," primarily signifying godless, destitute of God. In Eph 2:12 the phrase indicates, not only that the Gentiles were void of any true recognition of God, and hence became morally godless (Rom 1:19–32); but, being given up by God, they were excluded from communion with God and from the privileges granted to Israel (cf. Gal 4:8). See: TDNT—3:120, 322; BAGD—20d; THAYER—13d.

113. **ἄθεσμος** {2x} **athĕsmŏs**, *ath'-es-mos;* from *1* (as a neg. particle) and a der. of *5087* (in the sense of *enacting*); *lawless,* i.e. (by impl.) *criminal:*—wicked {2x}.

Athesmos means lawless, wicked: "And delivered just Lot, vexed with the filthy conversation of the wicked:" (2 Pet 2:7; cf. 3:17). Syn.: 4190. See: TDNT—1:167, 25; BAGD—21a; THAYER—13d.

114. **ἀθετέω** {16x} **athĕtĕō**, *ath-et-eh'-o;* from a compound of *1* (as a neg. particle) and a der. of *5087; to set aside,* i.e. (by impl.) to *disesteem, neutralize* or *violate:*—despise {8x}, reject {4x}, bring to nothing {1x}, frustrate {1x}, disannul {1x}, cast off {1x}.

Atheteo signifies to put as of no value; hence, **(1)** to act towards anything as though it were annulled; to deprive a law of its force by opinions or acts contrary to it: "Brethren, I speak after the manner of men; Though *it be* but a man's covenant, yet *if it be* confirmed, no man disannulleth (*atheteo*), or addeth thereto." (Gal 3:15); or **(2)** to thwart the efficacy of anything, to nullify, to frustrate it, reject it: "But the Pharisees and lawyers rejected (*atheteo*) the counsel of God against themselves, being not baptized of him" (Lk 7:30); **(2a)** "will I reject": "For it is written, I will destroy the wisdom of the wise, and will bring to nothing (*atheteo*) the understanding of the prudent." (1 Cor 1:19), **(2c)** make void/frustrate: "I do not frustrate (*atheteo*) the grace of God: for if righteousness *come* by the law, then Christ is dead in vain." (Gal 2:21); **(2d)** set at nought/despise: "Likewise also these *filthy* dreamers defile the flesh, despise dominion, and speak evil of dignities." (Jude 8). Syn.: 208. See: TDNT—8:158, 1176; BAGD—21a; THAYER—13d.

115. **ἀθέτησις** {2x} **athĕtēsis**, *ath-et'-ay-sis;* from *114; cancellation* (lit. or fig.):—disannulling {1x}, to put away + 1519 {1x}.

Athetesis means a setting aside, abolition, and is translated **(1)** disannulling (Heb 7:18) with reference to a commandment; and **(2)** to put away (lit. "for a putting away") with reference to sin (Heb 9:26). See: TDNT—8:158, 1176; BAGD—21b; THAYER—14a.

116. **Ἀθῆναι** {6x} **Athēnai**, *ath-ay-nahee;* plur. of Ἀθήνη **Athēnē** (the goddess of wisdom, who was reputed to have founded the city); *Athenæ,* the capitol of Greece:—Athens {6x}. See: BAGD—21b; THAYER—14a.

117. **Ἀθηναῖος** {2x} **Athēnaiŏs**, *ath-ay-nah'-yos;* from *116;* an *Athenæan* or inhab. of Athenæ:—Athenians {1x}, of Athens {1x}. See: BAGD—21b; THAYER—14b.

118. **ἀθλέω** {2x} **athlĕō**, *ath-leh'-o;* from ἄθλος **athlŏs** (a *contest* in the public lists); to *contend* in the competitive games:—strive {2x}.

Athleo means to engage in a contest (cf. Eng., "athlete"), to contend in public games, is used both times in 2 Tim 2:5: "And if a man also strive for masteries (*athleo*), *yet* is he not crowned, except he strive (*athleo*) lawfully." Syn.: 1252, 1864. See: TDNT—1:167, 25; BAGD—21b; THAYER—14b

119. **ἄθλησις** {1x} **athlēsis**, *ath'-lay-sis;* from *118;* a *struggle* (fig.):—fight {1x}.

Athlesis denotes a combat, contest of athletes; hence, a struggle, fight, affliction: "But call to remembrance the former days, in which, after ye were illuminated, ye endured a great fight of afflictions;" (Heb 10:32). Syn.: 73. See: TDNT—1:167, 25; BAGD—21c; THAYER—14b.

120. **ἀθυμέω** {1x} **athumĕō**, *ath-oo-meh'-o;* from a comp. of *1* (as a neg. particle) and *2372;* to *be spiritless,* i.e. *disheartened:*—be discouraged {1x}.

Athumeo means "to be disheartened, dispirited, discouraged" (*a,* negative, *thumos,* "spirit, courage," from the root *thu,* found in *thuo,* "to rush," denoting "feeling, passion"; hence Eng., "fume"), and is found in Col 3:21: "Fathers, provoke not your children *to anger,* lest they be discouraged (*athumeo*)." See: BAGD—21c; THAYER—14b.

121. **ἄθῳος** {2x} **athōŏs**, *ath'-o-os;* from *1* (as a neg. particle) and prob. a der. of *5087* (mean. a *penalty*); *not guilty:*—innocent {2x}.

Athoos primarily denotes "unpunished" (*a,* negative, *thoe,* "a penalty"); then, "innocent": **(1)** "[Judas] Saying, I have sinned in that I have betrayed the innocent blood. And they said, What *is that* to us? see thou *to that.*" (Mt 27:4), **(1a)** "innocent blood," i.e., the blood of an "innocent" person, the word "blood" being used both by synecdoche (a part standing for the whole), and **(1b)** by metonymy (one thing standing for another), i.e., for death by execution; **(2)** In Mt 27: 24 Pilate speaks of himself as "innocent": **(2a)** "When Pilate saw that he could prevail nothing, but *that* rather a tumult was made, he took water, and washed *his* hands before the multitude, saying, I am innocent of the blood of this just person: see ye *to it.*" **(2b)** Pilate is declaring his innocence, and hence, he asserts he should go unpunished for his part in the crucifixion. Syn.: 172. See: BAGD—21d; THAYER—14b.

122. **αἴγειος** {1x} **aigĕiŏs**, *ah'-ee-ghi-os;* from αἴξ **aix** (a *goat*); belonging to a *goat:*—goatskin + 1192 {1x}. See: BAGD—21d; THAYER—14c.

123. **αἰγιαλός** {6x} **aigialŏs**, *ahee-ghee-al-os';* from ἀΐσσω **aïssō** (to *rush*) and *251* (in the sense of the *sea,* a *beach* (on which the *waves dash*):—shore {6x}. See: BAGD—21d; THAYER—14c.

124. **Αἰγύπτιος** {5x} **Aiguptiŏs**, *ahee-goop'-tee-os;* from *125;* an *gyptian* or inhab. of Aegyptus:—Egyptian {3x}, Egyptians {2x}. See: BAGD—21d; THAYER—14c.

125. **Αἴγυπτος** {24x} **Aiguptŏs**, *ah'-ee-goop-tos;* of uncert. der.; *gyptus,* the land of the Nile:—Egypt {24x}. See: BAGD—22a; THAYER—14c.

126. **ἀΐδιος** {2x} **aïdiŏs**, *ah-id'-ee-os;* from *104; everduring* (forward and backward, or forward only):—eternal {1x}, everlasting {1x}.

Aidios denotes "everlasting" (from *aei,* "ever"): "And the angels which kept not their first estate, but left their own habitation, he hath reserved in everlasting chains under darkness unto the judgment of the great day." (Jude 6). Syn.: Aionios (166) should always be translated "eternal" and *aidios,* "everlasting." Aionios **stresses time** and negates the end either of a space of time or of unmeasured time, and is used chiefly where something future is spoken of, *aidios* **stresses quality,** excluding interruption and lays stress upon permanence and unchangeableness. See: TDNT—1:168, 25; BAGD—22a; THAYER—14d.

127. **αἰδώς** {2x} **aidōs**, *ahee-doce';* perh. from *1* (as a neg. particle) and *1492* (through the idea of *downcast* eyes); *bashfulness,* i.e. (toward men), *modesty* or (toward God) *awe:*—shamefacedness {1x}, reverence {1x}.

(1) This word stresses an innate moral response to the performing of dishonorable acts. **(2)** It is self-motivated and implies a reverence for the good as good, not merely as that to which honor and reputation are attached. **(3)** *Aidos* is a sense of shame, modesty" and is used regarding the demeanor of women in the church: "In like manner also, that women adorn themselves in modest apparel, with shamefacedness (*aidos*) and sobriety; not with braided hair, or gold, or pearls, or costly array; (1 Ti 2:9). **(3a)** Shamefacedness is that which is fast or rooted [shamefastness - 1611 KJV] in the character . . . **(3b)** which is reflected in the face. **(4)** It is translated "reverence" in Heb 12:28 "Wherefore we receiving a kingdom which cannot be moved, let us have grace, whereby we may serve God acceptably with reverence and godly fear:" Syn.: As to *aidos* and aischune (152), *aidos* is more objective, having regard to others; it is the stronger word. *Aidos* would always restrain a good man from an unworthy act, *aischune* would sometimes restrain a bad one. Syn.: 152, 1791, 4997. See: TDNT—1:169, 26; BAGD—22b; THAYER—14d.

128. **Αἰθίοψ** {2x} **Aithiŏps**, *ahee-thee'-ops;* from αἴθω **aithō** (to *scorch*) and ὤψ **ōps** (the *face,* from *3700; an thiopian* (as a *blackamoor*):—Ethiopian {2x}. See: BAGD—22b; THAYER—14d.

129. **αἷμα** {99x} **haima**, *hah'-ee-mah;* of uncert. der.; *blood,* lit. (of men or animals), fig. (the *juice* of grapes) or spec. (the atoning *blood* of Christ); by impl. *bloodshed,* also *kindred:*—blood {99x}.

'*Aima,* (Eng., prefix haem—), besides its natural meaning of blood, stands **(1)** in conjunction with *sarx* (4651 flesh) as "flesh and blood," and signifies man, human beings: "And Jesus answered and said unto him, Blessed art thou, Simon Barjona: for flesh and blood hath not revealed *it* unto thee, but my Father which is in heaven." (Mt 16:17; cf. 1 Cor 15:50); **(2)** for human generation: "Which were born, not of blood, nor of the will of the flesh, nor of the will of man, but of God." (Jn 1:13); **(3)** for blood shed by violence: "That upon you may come all the righteous blood shed upon the earth, from the blood of righteous Abel unto the blood of Zacharias son of Barachias, whom ye slew between the temple and the altar." (Mt 23:35; cf. Rev 17:6); **(4)** for the blood of sacrificial victims (Heb 9:7); **(5)** for the blood of Christ, which betokens **(5a)** His death by the shedding of His blood in propiatory sacrifice; and **(5b)** to drink His blood is to appropriate the saving effects of His propiatory death: "Then Jesus said unto them, Verily, verily, I say unto you, Except ye eat the flesh of the Son of man, and drink his blood, ye have no life in you" (Jn 6:53). Syn.: 130. See: TDNT—1:172, 26; BAGD—22c; THAYER—15a.

130. **αἱματεκχυσία** {1x} **haimatĕkchusia**, *hahee-mat-ek-khoo-see'-ah;* from *129* and a der. of *1632;* an *effusion of blood:*—shedding of blood {1x}.

Haimatekchusia denotes "shedding of blood": KJV Hebrews 9:22 "And almost all things are by the law purged with blood; and without shedding of blood is no remission." (Heb 9:22). Syn.: 129. See: TDNT—1:176, 26; BAGD—23b; THAYER—15d.

131. **αἱμοῤῥέω** {1x} **haimŏrrhĕō**, *hahee-mor-hreh'-o;* from *129* and *4482;* to *flow blood,* i.e. *have a hemorrhage:*—diseased with an issue of blood {1x}.

Haimorrhoeo means to flow (Eng., hemorrhage), and signifies to suffer from a flow of blood: "And, behold, a woman, which was diseased with an issue of blood twelve years, came behind *him,* and touched the hem of his garment:" (Mt 9:20). See: BAGD—23c; THAYER—15d.

132. **Αἰνέας** {2x} **Ainĕas**, *ahee-neh'-as;* of uncert. der.; *Æneas,* an Isr.:—Aeneas {2x}. See: BAGD—23c; THAYER—16a.

133. **αἴνεσις** {1x} **ainĕsis**, *ah'-ee-nes-is;* from *134;* a *praising* (the act), i.e. (spec.) a *thank* (-offering):—praise {1x}.

Ainesis means praise and is found in Heb 13:15 where it is metaphorically represented as a sacrificial offering: "By him therefore let us offer the sacrifice of praise to God continually, that is, the fruit of *our* lips giving thanks to His name." Syn.: 136, 1868. See: BAGD—23c; THAYER—16a.

134. **αἰνέω** {9x} **ainĕō**, *ahee-neh'-o;* from *136;* to *praise* (God):—praise {9x}.

Aineo means to speak in praise of, to praise and is always used of praise to God: **(1)** by angels: "And it came to pass, as the angels were gone away from them into heaven, the shepherds said one to another, Let us now go even unto Bethlehem, and see this thing which is come to pass, which the Lord hath made known unto us." (Lk 2:13); **(2)** by men: "And when he was come nigh, even now at the descent of the mount of Olives, the whole multitude of the disciples began to rejoice and praise God with a loud voice for all the mighty works that they had seen;" (Lk 19:37; cf. 24:53; Acts 2:20; Rom 15:11). Syn.: 1843, 1867, 5214, 5567. See: TDNT—1:177, 27; BAGD—23c; THAYER—16a.

135. **αἴνιγμα** {1x} **ainigma**, *ah'-ee-nig-ma;* from a der. of *136* (in its prim. sense); an *obscure* saying ("enigma"), i.e. (abstr.) *obscureness:*—darkly + 1722 {1x}. See: TDNT—1:178, 27; BAGD—23c; THAYER—16a.

136. **αἶ-νος** {2x} **ainŏs**, *ah'-ee-nos;* appar. a prim. word; prop. a *story,* but used in the sense of *1868; praise* (of God):—praise {2x}.

Ainos primarily means a tale, narration, and came to denote detailed praise in the NT only of praise to God (Mt 21:16; Lk 18:43). Syn.: 133, 1868. See: TDNT—1:177, 27; BAGD—23d; THAYER—16b.

137. **Αἰνών** {1x} **Ainōn**, *ahee-nohn';* of Heb. or. [a der. of 5869, *place of springs*]; *Ænon,* a place in Pal.:—Aenon {1x}. See: BAGD—23d; THAYER—16b.

138. **αἱρέομαι** {3x} **hairĕŏmai**, *hahee-reh'-om-ahee;* prob. akin to *142;* to *take for oneself,* i.e. to *prefer:*—choose {3x}.

Haireomai means to take, and is used in the middle voice only, in the sense of taking for oneself, choosing **(1)** by God: "But we are bound to give thanks alway to God for you, brethren beloved of the Lord, because God hath from the beginning chosen you to salvation through sanctification of the Spirit and belief of the truth:" (2 Th 2:13); or **(2)** by man: "But if I live in the flesh, this *is* the fruit of my labour: yet what I shall choose I wot not." (Phil 1:22; cf. Heb 11:25). **(3)** Its special significance is to select rather by the act of taking, than by showing preference or favor. Syn.: 140, 1586, 1951, 4401, 5500. See: TDNT—1:180, 27; BAGD—24a; THAYER—16c.

139. **αἵρεσις** {9x} **hairĕsis**, *hah'-ee-res-is;* from *138;* prop. a *choice,* i.e. (spec.) a *party* or (abstr.) *disunion:*—sect {5x}, heresy {4x}.

Hairesis denotes **(1)** a choosing, choice; then **(2)** that which is chosen, and hence, **(3)** an opinion, **(3a)** especially a self-willed opinion, **(3b)** which is substituted for submission to the power of truth, and **(3c)** leads to division and the formation of sects: "Idolatry, witchcraft, hatred, variance, emulations, wrath, strife, seditions, heresies," (Gal 5:20). **(4)** Such erroneous opinions are **(4a)** frequently the outcome of personal preference or the prospect of advantage: "But there were false prophets also among the people, even as there shall be false teachers among you, who privily shall bring in damnable heresies, even denying the Lord that bought them, and bring upon themselves swift destruction." (2 Pet 2:1—damnable signifies leading to ruin) and create **(4b1)** sects: "Then the high priest rose up, and all they that were with him, (which is the sect [*hairesis*] of the Sadducees,) and were filled with indignation," (Acts 5:17; cf. 15:5; 24:5, 14) and **(4b2)** "heresies": "For there must be also heresies among you, that they which are approved may be made manifest among you." (1 Cor 11:19). See: TDNT—1:180, 27; BAGD—23d; THAYER—16b.

140. **αἱρετίζω** {1x} **hairĕtizō**, *hahee-ret-id'-zo;* from a der. of *138;* to *make a choice:*—choose {1x}.

Hairetizo means that which may be taken and signifies to take. It implies that what is taken is eligible or suitable; hence, to choose by reason of suitability: "Behold my servant, whom I have chosen; my beloved, in whom my soul is well pleased: I will put my spirit upon him, and He shall shew judgment to the Gentiles." (Mt 12:18—of God's delight in Christ as His chosen). Syn.: 138, 1586, 1951, 4401, 5500. See: TDNT—1:184, 27; BAGD—24a; THAYER—16c.

141. **αἱρετικός** {1x} **hairĕtikŏs**, *hahee-ret-ee-kos';* from the same as *140;* a *schismatic:*—that is a heretick {1x}.

This word primarily denotes capable of choosing; hence, causing division by a party spirit, factious: "A man that is an heretick after the first and second admonition reject;" (Titus 3:10). [Heretick is now spelled heretic.] See: TDNT—1:184, 27; BAGD—24a; THAYER—16c.

142. **αἴρω** {102x} **airō**, *ah'-ee-ro;* a prim. verb; to *lift;* by impl. to *take up* or *away;* fig. to *raise* (the voice), *keep in suspense* (the mind), spec. to *sail* away (i.e. *weigh anchor*); by Heb. [comp. 5375] to *expiate* sin:—take up {32x}, take away {25x}, take {25x}, away with {5x}, lift up {4x}, bear {3x}, misc. {8x} = carry, loose, make to doubt, put away, remove.

Airo signifies **(1)** to raise up to lift, to take upon oneself and carry what has been raised, physically: "Every branch in me that beareth not fruit He [God] taketh away: and every *branch* that beareth fruit, he purgeth it, that it may bring forth more fruit." (Jn 15:2) [*Airo* here indicates those branches which are on the ground, hence unable to bear fruit, God raises up so the branch can be fruitful.], or **(2)** as applied to the mind, to suspend, to keep in suspense: "Then came the Jews round about him, and said unto him, How long dost thou make us to doubt? If thou be the Christ, tell us plainly." (Jn 10:24, lit., "How long doth thou suspend our souls?"); **(3)** to take away what is attached to anything, to remove, as of Christ, in taking away the sin of the world (Jn 1:29); **(4)** Christ was manifested to take away sins: "And ye know that He was manifested to take away our sins; and in Him is no sin." (1 Jn 3:5), where, not the nature of the Atonement is in view, but its effect in the believer's life. Syn.: 399, 430, 941, 1627, 3114, 3356, 4064, 4160, 4722, 5159, 5297, 5342, 5409. See: TDNT—1:185, 28; BAGD—24b; THAYER—16c.

143. **αἰσθάνομαι** {1x} **aisthanŏmai**, *ahee-sthan'-om-ahee;* of uncert. der.; to *apprehend* (prop. by the senses):—perceive {1x}.

Aisthenomai means "to perceive, to notice, understand," and is used in Lk 9:45: "But they understood not this saying, and it was hid from them, that they perceived it not: and they feared to ask him of that saying." See: TDNT—1:187, 29; BAGD—24d; THAYER—17b.

144. **αἴσθησις** {1x} **aisthēsis**, *ah'-ee-sthay-sis;* from *143; perception,* i.e. (fig.) *discernment:*—judgment {1x}. See: TDNT—1:187, 29; BAGD—25a; THAYER—17b.

145. **αἰσθητήριον** {1x} **aisthētēriŏn**, *ahee-sthay-tay'-ree-on;* from a der. of *143;* prop. an *organ of perception,* i.e. (fig.) *judgment:*—senses {1x}.

Aistheterion is the faculty of perception, the organ of sense, the senses, the capacities for spiritual apprehension: "But strong meat belongeth to them that are of full age, *even* those who by reason of use have their senses (*aistheterion*) exercised to discern both good and evil." (Heb 5:14). See: TDNT—1:187, 29; BAGD—25a; THAYER—17b.

146. **αἰσχροκερδής** {3x} **aischrŏkĕrdēs**, *ahee-skhrok-er-dace';* from *150* and κέρδος **kerdos** (*gain*); *sordid:*—greedy of filthy lucre {2x}, given to filthy lucre {1x}.

This word means "greedy of base gain" and is used in 1 Ti 3:3, 8 and Titus 1:7: "greedy of filthy lucre." Syn.: 150, 1508. See: BAGD—25a; THAYER—17b.

147. **αἰσχροκερδῶς** {1x} **aischrŏkĕrdōs**, *ahee-skhrok-er-doce';* adv. from *146; sordidly:*—for filthy lucre {1x}.

Aischrokerdos means an "eagerness for base gain": "Feed the flock of God which is among you, taking the oversight *thereof,* not by constraint, but willingly; not for filthy lucre, but of a ready mind;" (1 Pet 5:2). See: BAGD—25b; THAYER—17b.

148. **αἰσχρολογία** {1x} **aischrŏlŏgia**, *ahee-skhrol-og-ee'-ah;* from *150* and *3056; vile conversation:*—filthy communication {1x}.

This word indicates every kind of foul-mouthed abusiveness, not just the most obvious and offensive kind; an outbreak of a loveless spirit toward our neighbor: "But now ye also put off all these; anger, wrath, malice, blasphemy, filthy communication out of your mouth." (Col 3:8). Syn.: Morologia (3473) refers to foolishness, *aischrologia* to foulness, and eutrapelia (2160) to false refinement, to discourse that is not reasoned with the salt of grace. All three of these are sins of speech are noted and condemned. See: BAGD—25b; THAYER—17b.

149. **αἰσχρόν** {3x} **aischrŏn**, *ahee-skhron';* neut. of *150;* a *shameful* thing, i.e. *indecorum:*—shame {3x}. See: BAGD—25b; THAYER—17c.

150. **αἰσχρός** {1x} **aischrŏs**, *ahee-skhros';* from the same as *153; shameful,* i.e. *base* (spec. *venal*):—filthy {1x}.

Aischros means "a shameful thing": "For if the woman be not covered, let her also be shorn: but if it be a shame for a woman to be shorn or shaven, let her be covered. "(1 Cor 11:6; cf. 14:35; Eph 5:12). Syn.: 150, 152, 422, 808, 818, 819, 1788, 1791, 2617. See: TDNT—1:189, 29; BAGD—25b; THAYER—17c.

151. **αἰσχρότης** {1x} **aischrŏtēs**, *ahee-skhrot'-ace;* from *150; shamefulness,* i.e. *obscenity:*—filthiness {1x}.

This word represents all that is contrary to purity (Eph 5:4). Syn.: 766, 3436, 4507. See: TDNT—1:189, 29; BAGD—25b; THAYER—17c.

152. **αἰσχύνη** {6x} **aischunē**, *ahee-skhoo'-nay;* from *153; shame* or *disgrace* (abstr. or concr.):—shame {5x}, dishonesty {1x}.

This word refers to the feeling that leads to shun what is unworthy out of anticipation of dishonor; a fear of anticipated ill-repute. *Aischune* means shame and signifies **(1)** subjectively, **(1a)** the confusion of one who is ashamed of anything, a sense of shame (Lk 14:9); **(1b)** those things which shame conceals (2 Cor 4:2); and **(2)** objectively, **(2a)** ignominy, that which is visited on a person by the wicked (Heb 12:2); and **(2b)** that which should arise from guilt (Phil 3:19); **(3)** concretely, a thing to be ashamed of (Rev 3:18; Jude 13). Syn.: 127, 1791. See: TDNT—1:189, 29; BAGD—25b; THAYER—17c.

153. **αἰσχύνομαι** {5x} **aischunŏmai**, *ahee-skhoo'-nom-ahee;* from αἶσχος **aischŏs** (*disfigurement,* i.e. *disgrace*); to *feel shame* (for oneself):—be ashamed {5x}.

Aischuno means shame and always being in the passive voice, signifies **(1)** to have a feeling of fear or shame which prevents a person from doing a thing (Lk 16:3); and **(2)** the feeling of shame arising from something that has been done (2 Cor 10:8; Phil 1:20), or **(3)** of the possibility of being ashamed before the Lord Jesus His Parousia with His saints (1 Jn 2:28); and **(4)** in 1 Pet 4:16 of being ashamed of suffering as a Christian. Syn.: 1788, 1870, 2617. See: TDNT—1:189, 29; BAGD—25c; THAYER—17c.

154. **αἰτέω** {71x} **aitĕō**, *ahee-teh'-o;* of uncert. der.; to *ask* (in gen.):—ask {48x}, desire {17x}, beg {2x}, require {2x}, crave {1x}, call for {1x}.

Aiteo, as a verb, means "to ask." **(1)** *Aiteo* more frequently suggests the attitude of a suppliant, the petition of one who is lesser in position than he to whom the petition is made. **(1a)** in the case of men in asking something from God: "Ask (*aiteo*), and it shall be given you; seek, and ye shall find; knock, and it shall be opened unto you:" (Mt 7:7); **(1b)** a child from a parent (Mt 7:9–10); **(1c)** a subject from a king: (Acts 12:20); **(1d)** priests and people from Pilate: "And they were instant with loud voices, requiring (*aiteo*) that he might be crucified." (Lk 23:23); **(1e)** a beggar from a passer by: (Acts 3:2). **(2)** With reference to petitioning God, this verb is found in Paul's epistles in Eph 3:20 and Col 1:9; in Jas four times, 1:5–6; 4:1–3; in 1 Jn, five times, 3:22; 5:14, 15 (twice), 16. Syn.: *Aiteo* is the more submissive and suppliant term; erotao (2065) implies an equality between the one who asks and the one who is asked—a king of another king (Lk 14:32); or if not equality, then a familiarity that lends authority to the request. See also: 155, 350, 1833, 1905, 2065, 3004, 4441. See: TDNT—1:191, 30; BAGD—25d; THAYER—17d.

155. **αἴτημα** {3x} **aitēma**, *ah'-ee-tay-mah;* from *154;* a *thing asked* or (abstr.) an *asking:*—require {1x}, request {1x}, petition {1x}.

Aitema means lit., "that which has been asked for" is used of: **(1)** "as what is required": "And Pilate gave sentence that it should be as they required." (Lk 23:24); **(2)** "requests": "Be careful for nothing; but in every thing by prayer and supplication with thanksgiving let your requests be made known unto God." (Phil 4:6); and **(3)** "petitions": "And if we know that he hear us, whatsoever we ask, we know that we have the petitions that we desired of him." (1 Jn 5:15). Syn.: Several aitemata (155) make up one proseuche (4335). See also: 154, 155, 1833, 1905, 2065, 3004, 4441. See: TDNT—1:193, 30; BAGD—26b; THAYER—18a.

156. **αἰτία** {20x} **aitia**, *ahee-tee'-a;* from the same as *154;* a *cause* (as if *asked* for), i.e. (logical) *reason* (motive, matter), (legal) *crime* (alleged or proved):—cause {9x}, wherefore + 1223 & 3739 {3x}, accusation {3x}, fault {3x}, case {1x}, crime {1x}.

(1) *Aitia,* as a noun, has the primary meaning of "a cause, especially an occasion of something evil, hence a charge, an accusation." **(2)** It is used in a forensic sense, of **(2a)** an accusation: "Against whom when the accusers stood up, they brought none accusation of such things as I supposed:" (Acts 25:18); or **(2b)** a crime: "And set up over his head his accusation written, THIS IS JESUS THE KING OF THE JEWS" (Mk 15:26; cf. Jn 18:38; 19:4, 6; Acts 13:28; 23:28; 28:18). Syn.: *Aitia* refers to an accusation that may be true or false. It is a term that was used in an accusation made against the Lord (Mt 27:37). *Elenchos* (1650) refers to an accusation that is true, and often implies an inward or outward acknowledgment of that truthfulness on the part of the accused. See also: 157, 1225, 1458, 1462, 1908, 2723, 2724, 4811. See: BAGD—26b; THAYER—18b.

157. **αἰτίαμα** {1x} **aitiama**, *ahee-tee'-am-ah;* from a der. of *156;* a *thing charged:*—complaint {1x}.

Aitioma, as a noun, means "an accusation," expressing aitia (156) more concretely, and is found in Acts 25:7: "And when he was come, the Jews which came down from Jerusalem stood round about, and laid many and grievous complaints (aitioma) against Paul, which they could not prove." Syn.: 156, 1225, 1458, 1462, 1908, 2723, 2724, 4811. See: BAGD—26c; THAYER—18b, 18c.

158. **αἴτιον** {4x} **aitiŏn**, *ah'-ee-tee-on;* neut. of *159;* a *reason* or *crime* [like *156*]:—fault {2x}, cause {2x}.

Aition means a fault, synonymous with *156* but more limited in scope, and is translated **(1)** "cause (of death)" in Lk 23:22; **(2)** "cause" (of a riot) in Acts 19:40; and **(3)** "fault" in Luke 23:4, 14. Syn.: 156, 3056. See: BAGD—26d; THAYER—18b.

159. **αἴτιος** {1x} **aitiŏs**, *ah'-ee-tee-os;* from the same as *154; causative,* i.e. (concr.) a *causer:*—author {1x}.

Aitios, as an adjective (cf. 156 - aitia, a cause), denotes "that which causes something;" literally, one who causes an event to happen. **(1)** This and archegos (747) are both translated "author" in Hebrews. **(2)** *Aitios,* in Heb 5:9, describes Christ as the "Author of eternal salvation unto all them that obey Him," **(2a)** signifying that Christ, exalted and glorified as our High Priest, on the ground of His finished work on earth, has become the personal mediating cause of eternal salvation. **(2b)** Christ is not the merely formal cause of our salvation. He is the concrete and active cause of it. **(2c)** He has not merely caused or effected it, He is, as His name, "Jesus," implies, our salvation itself (Lk 2:30; 3:6). Syn.: 747. See: BAGD—26d; THAYER—18b.

160. **αἰφνίδιος** {2x} **aiphnidiŏs**, *aheef-nid'-ee-os;* from a comp. of *1* (as a neg. particle) and *5316* [comp. *1810*] (mean.

non-apparent); *unexpected,* i.e. (adv.) *suddenly:*—unawares {1x}, sudden {1x}.

Aiphnidios, as an adjective, means **(1)** "sudden": "For when they shall say, Peace and safety; then sudden (*aiphnidios*) destruction cometh upon them, as travail upon a woman with child; and they shall not escape" (1 Th 5:3); or **(2)** "unawares": "And take heed to yourselves, lest at any time your hearts be overcharged with surfeiting, and drunkenness, and cares of this life, and *so* that day come upon you unawares (*aiphnidios*). Syn.: 869, 1810, 1819. See: BAGD—26d; THAYER—18c.

161. **αἰχμαλωσία** {3x} **aichmalōsia**, *aheekh-mal-o-see'-ah;* from *164; captivity:*—captivity {3x}.

Aichmalosia, as a noun, means **(1)** "captivity," is found in Rev 13:10: "He that leadeth into captivity shall go into captivity: he that killeth with the sword must be killed with the sword." **(2)** Eph 4:8 reads "He led captivity captive" **(2a)** which seems to be an allusion to the triumphal procession by which a victory was celebrated, the "captives" taken forming part of the procession. **(2b)** The quotation is from Ps 68:18, and probably is a forceful expression for Christ's victory, through His death, and that at His ascension Christ transferred the redeemed Old Testament saints from Sheol to His own presence in glory. Syn.: 162, 163, 164, 2221. See: TDNT—1:195, 31; BAGD—26d; THAYER—18c.

162. **αἰχμαλωτεύω** {2x} **aichmalōtĕuō**, *aheekh-mal-o-tew'-o;* from *164;* to *capture* [like *163*]:—lead captive {2x}.

Aichmaloteuo, as a verb, signifies "to make a prisoner of war": "Wherefore he saith, When he ascended up on high, he led captivity captive, and gave gifts unto men" (Eph 4:8). Syn.: 161, 163, 164, 2221. See: TDNT—1:195, 31; BAGD—26d; THAYER—18c.

163. **αἰχμαλωτίζω** {3x} **aichmalōtizō**, *aheekh-mal-o-tid'-zo;* from *164;* to *make captive:*—bring into captivity {2x}, lead away captive {1x}.

Aichmalotizo, practically synonymous with aichmaloteuo (162), denotes **(1)** "to lead away captive": "And they shall fall by the edge of the sword, and shall be led away captive into all nations:" (Lk 21:24), or **(2)** "to subjugate, to bring under control": "But I see another law in my members, warring against the law of my mind, and bringing me into captivity to the law of sin which is in my members" [said of the effect of the Law in one's members in bringing the person into captivity under the law of sin] (Rom 7:23); or **(3)** of subjugating the thoughts to the obedience of Christ: "Casting down imaginations, and every high thing that exalteth itself against the knowledge of God, and bringing into captivity every thought to the obedience of Christ;" (2 Cor 10:5); or **(4)** of those who took captive "silly women laden with sins" (2 Ti 3:6). Syn.: 161, 162, 164, 2221. See: TDNT—1:195, 31; BAGD—27a; THAYER—18c.

164. **αἰχμαλωτός** {1x} **aichmalōtŏs**, *aheekh-mal-o-tos';* from αἰχμή **aichmē** (a *spear*) and a der. of the same as *259;* prop. a *prisoner of war,* i.e. (gen.) a *captive:*—captive {1x}.

Aichmalotos, as a noun, literally means "one taken by the spear" (from aichme, "a spear," and halotos, a verbal adjective, from *halonai,* "to be captured"); hence denotes "a captive": "The Spirit of the Lord *is* upon me, because he hath anointed me to preach the gospel to the poor; he hath sent me to heal the brokenhearted, to preach deliverance to the captives, and recovering of sight to the blind, to set at liberty them that are bruised." Syn.: 161, 162, 163, 2221. See: TDNT—1:195, 31; BAGD—27a; THAYER—18d.

165. **αἰών** {128x} **aiōn**, *ahee-ohn';* from the same as *104;* prop. an *age;* by extens. *perpetuity* (also past); by impl. the *world;* spec. (Jewish) a Messianic period (present or future):—ever {71x}, world {38x}, never + 3364 + 1519 + 3588 {6x}, evermore {4x}, age {2x}, eternal {2x}, misc. {5x} = course, forever.

The primary stress of this word is time in its unbroken duration. *Aion,* as a noun, means **(1)** "an age, era" and **(1a)** signifies a period of indefinite duration, or **(1b)** time viewed in relation to what takes place in the period. **(1c)** The force attaching to the word is not so much that of the actual length of a period, but that of a period marked by spiritual or moral characteristics. **(1d)** This is illustrated in the use of the adjective in the phrase "life eternal," in Jn 17:3, in respect of the increasing knowledge of God. **(1e)** Eternal life stresses the quality of life; everlasting life stresses its length. **(2)** The phrases containing this word should not be rendered literally, but consistently with its sense of indefinite duration. **(2a)** Thus *"eis ton aiona"* does not mean "unto the age" but "for ever": "As he saith also in another *place,* Thou *art* a priest for ever after the order of Melchisedec" (Heb 5:6). **(2b)** The Greeks contrasted that which came to an end with that which was expressed by this phrase, which shows that they conceived of it as expressing interminable duration. **(3)** The word occurs most frequently in the Gospel of John, the Hebrews and Revelation. Syn.: 166, 1074, 2244, 2250, 5046, 5230. See: TDNT—1:197, 31; BAGD—27b; THAYER—18d. comp. *5550.*

166. **αἰώνιος** {71x} **aiōniŏs**, *ahee-o'-nee-os;* from *165; perpetual* (also used of past time, or past and future as well):—eternal {42x}, everlasting {25x}, the world began + 5550 {2x}, since the world began + 5550 {1x}, for ever {1x}.

Aionios, the adjective, describes **(1)** duration, **(1a)** either undefined but not endless: "Now to him that is of power to stablish you according to my gospel, and the preaching of Jesus Christ, according to the revelation of the mystery, which was kept secret since the world began (*aionios*)" (Rom 16:25; cf. 2 Ti 1:9; Titus 1:2); or **(1b)** undefined because endless: "But now is made manifest, and by the scriptures of the prophets, according to the commandment of the everlasting (*aionios*) God, made known to all nations for the obedience of faith" (Rom 16:26). **(1c)** *Aionios,* denoting "eternal," is set in contrast with proskairos (4340), lit., "for a season": "While we look not at the things which are seen, but at the things which are not seen: for the things which are seen *are* temporal (proskairos); but the things which are not seen *are* eternal (*aionios*)" (2 Cor 4:18).

(2) It is used of that which in nature is endless, as, e.g., **(2a)** of God (Rom 16:26), **(2b)** His power (1 Ti 6:16), **(2c)** His glory (1 Pet 5:10), **(2d)** the Holy Spirit (Heb 9:14), **(2e)** redemption (Heb 9:12), **(2f)** salvation (Heb 5:9), **(2g)** life in Christ (Jn 3:16), **(2h)** the resurrection body (2 Cor 5:1), **(2i)** the future rule of Christ (2 Pet 1:11), which is declared to be without end (Lk 1:33), **(2j)** of sin that never has forgiveness (Mk 3:29), **(2k)** the judgment of God (Heb 6:2), and **(2l)** of fire, one of judgment's instruments (Mt 18:8; 25:41; Jude 7). **(2m)** the punishment referred to in 2 Th 1:9, is not temporary, but final, and, accordingly, the phraseology shows that its purpose is not remedial but retributive. Syn.: 126, 165, 1074, 2244, 2250, 5046, 5230. See: TDNT—1:208, 31; BAGD—28b; THAYER—20c.

167. **ἀκαθαρσία** {10x} **akatharsia**, *ak-ath-ar-see'-ah;* from *169; impurity* (the quality), phys. or mor.:—uncleanness {10x}.

Akatharsia, as a noun, denotes "uncleanness": **(1)** physical: "Woe unto you, scribes and Pharisees, hypocrites! for ye are like unto whited sepulchres, which indeed appear beautiful outward, but are within full of dead *men's* bones, and of all uncleanness" (Mt 23:27; **(2)** moral: "Wherefore God also gave them up to uncleanness through the lusts of their own hearts, to dishonour their own bodies between themselves:" (Rom 1:24; cf. 6:19; 2 Cor 12:21; Gal 5:19; Eph 4:19; 5:3; Col 3:5; 1 Th 2:3 -suggestive of the fact that sensuality and evil doctrine are frequently associated; 4:7). Syn.: 169, 2839, 2840, 3394. See: TDNT—3:427, 381; BAGD—28d; THAYER—21a.

168. **ἀκαθάρτης** {1x} **akathartēs**, *ak-ath-ar'-tace;* from *169; impurity* (the state), mor.:—filthiness {1x}. See: BAGD—29a; THAYER—21a.

169. **ἀκάθαρτος** {30x} **akathartŏs**, *ak-ath'-ar-tos;* from *1* (as a neg. particle) and a presumed der. of *2508* (mean. *cleansed*); *impure* (cer., mor. [*lewd*] or spec. [*demonic*]):—unclean {28x}, foul {2x}.

Akathartos, as an adjective, means "unclean, impure" [*a,* negative, *kathairo* (2508), "to purify"], and is used **(1)** of "unclean" spirits: "There came also a multitude *out* of the cities round about unto Jerusalem, bringing sick folks, and them which were vexed with unclean spirits: and they were healed every one" (Acts 5:16); **(1a)** frequently in the Synoptists, **(1b)** not in John's gospel; **(2)** ceremonially unclean: "But Peter said, Not so, Lord; for I have never eaten any thing that is common or unclean" (Acts 10:14, cf. 10:28; 11:8; 1 Cor 7:14);

(3) morally unclean: "Wherefore come out from among them, and be ye separate, saith the Lord, and touch not the unclean *thing;* and I will receive you" (2 Cor 6:17), including **(3a)** an "unclean person": "For this ye know, that no whoremonger, nor unclean person, nor covetous man, who is an idolater, hath any inheritance in the kingdom of Christ and of God" (Eph 5:5); **(3b)** "the filthiness/unclean things": "And the woman was arrayed in purple and scarlet colour, and decked with gold and precious stones and pearls, having a golden cup in her hand full of abominations and filthiness (168/169) of her fornication": (Rev 17:4); **(3c)** always, in the Gospels, of unclean spirits; **(3d)** it is translated "foul": "When Jesus saw that the people came running together, he rebuked the foul spirit, saying unto him, *Thou* dumb and deaf spirit, I charge thee, come out of him, and enter no more into him" (Mk 9:25; c. Rev 18:2). **(3e)** Since the word primarily had a ceremonial significance, the moral significance is less prominent as applied to a spirit, than when *poneros* (4190), "wicked," is so applied. Syn.: 167, 2839, 2840, 3394. See: TDNT—3:427, 381; BAGD—29a; THAYER—21b.

170. **ἀκαιρέομαι** {1x} **akairĕŏmai**, *ak-ahee-reh'-om-ahee;* from a comp. of *1* (as a neg. particle) and *2540* (mean. *unseasonable*); to *be inopportune* (for one-self), i.e. to *fail of a proper occasion:*—lack of opportunity {1x}.

Akaireomai, as a verb, means "to have no opportunity": "But I rejoiced in the Lord greatly, that now at the last your care of me hath flourished again; wherein ye were also careful, but ye lacked opportunity" (Phil 4:10) [a, negative, and kairos (2540), "season"]. Syn.: 2119, 2120,

2540, 5117. See: TDNT—3:462,*; BAGD—29b; THAYER—21b.

171. **ἀκαίρως** {1x} **akairōs**, *ak-ah'-ee-roce;* adv. from the same as *170; inopportunely:*—out of season {1x}.

Akairos, as an adverb, denotes "out of season, unseasonably": "Preach the word; be instant in season, out of season (*akairos*); reprove, rebuke, exhort with all longsuffering and doctrine" (2 Tim 4:2). Syn.: 2111, 2122, 2540, 3641, 4340, 5550, 5610. See: TDNT—3:462, 389; BAGD—29b; THAYER—21b.

172. **ἄκακος** {2x} **akakŏs**, *ak'-ak-os;* from *1* (as a neg. particle) and *2556; not bad,* i.e. (obj.) *innocent* or (subj.) *unsuspecting:*—simple {1x}, harmless {1x}.

(1) *Akakos* lit. means without evil, free from evil and signifies simple, guileless, unsuspecting, innocent, free from admixture of evil: **(1a)** of believers: "For they that are such serve not our Lord Jesus Christ, but their own belly; and by good words and fair speeches deceive the hearts of the simple (*akakos*)" (Rom 16:18); **(1b)** of the character of Christ: "For such an high priest became us, *who is* holy, harmless, undefiled, separate from sinners, and made higher than the heavens" (Heb. 7:26). **(2)** The absence of all evil implies the presence of all good. Syn.: *Akakos* contains no harmfulness, so the adolos (97) has no guile, the *akeraios* (185) contains no foreign mixture, and the *haplous* (573) has no folds or wrinkles. See also: 185. See: TDNT—3:482, 391, BAGD—29b; THAYER—21b.

173. **ἄκανθα** {14x} **akantha**, *ak'-an-thah;* prob. from the same as *188;* a *thorn:*—thorns {14x}.

Akantha, as a noun, means **(1)** "a brier, a thorn" is always used in the plural in the NT (Mt 7:16; Lk 6:44; Mt 13:7 (twice); Mt 13:22); **(2)** in Mt 27:29 and Jn 19:2, of the crown of "thorns" placed on Christ's head in mock imitation of the garlands worn by emperors. Syn.: 174, 4647. See: BAGD—29c; THAYER—21c.

174. **ἀκάνθινος** {2x} **akanthinŏs**, *ak-an'-thee-nos;* from *173; thorny:*—of thorns {2x}.

Akanthinos, as an adjective, means "of thorns": "And they clothed him with purple, and platted a crown of thorns, and put it about his *head*" (Mk 15:17; cf. Jn 19:5). Syn.: 173, 4647. See: BAGD—29c; THAYER—21c.

175. **ἄκαρπος** {7x} **akarpŏs**, *ak'-ar-pos;* from *1* (as a neg. particle) and *2590; barren* (lit. or fig.):—unfruitful {6x}, without fruit {1x}.

Akarpos, as an adjective, means "unfruitful" and is used figuratively **(1)** of "the word of the Kingdom," rendered "unfruitful" in the case of those influenced by the cares of the world and the deceitfulness of riches (Mt 13:22; Mk 4:19); **(2)** of the understanding of one praying with a "tongue," which effected no profit to the church without an interpretation of it (1 Cor 14:14); **(3)** of the works of darkness (Eph 5:11); **(4)** of believers who fail "to maintain good works," indicating the earning of one's living so as to do good works to others (Titus 3:14); **(5)** of the effects of failing to supply in one's faith the qualities of virtue, knowledge, temperance, patience, godliness, love of the brethren, and love (2 Pet 1:8). **(6)** In Jude 12 it is rendered "without fruit," of ungodly men, who oppose the gospel while pretending to uphold it, depicted as "autumn trees." Syn.: 2590, 2592, 2593, 3703, 5352. See: TDNT—3:616, 416; BAGD—29d; THAYER—21c.

176. **ἀκατάγνωστος** {1x} **akatagnōstŏs**, *ak-at-ag'-noce-tos;* from *1* (as a neg. particle) and a der. of *2607; unblamable:*—that cannot be condemned {1x}.

Akatagnostos, as an adjective, means, with negative prefix, *a,* "not to be condemned" and is said of sound speech: "Sound speech, that cannot be condemned; that he that is of the contrary part may be ashamed, having no evil thing to say of you" (Titus 2:8). Syn.: 843, 2607, 2613, 2631, 2632, 2633, 2917, 2919, 2920. See: TDNT—1:714, 119; BAGD—29d; THAYER—21c.

177. **ἀκατακάλυπτος** {2x} **akatakaluptŏs**, *ak-at-ak-al'-oop-tos;* from *1* (as a neg. particle) and a der. of a comp. of *2596* and *2572; unveiled:*—uncovered {2x}.

Akatakaluptos means "uncovered" and is used in 1 Cor 11:5 with reference to the injunction forbidding women to be "unveiled" in a church gathering: "But every woman that prayeth or prophesieth with *her* head uncovered dishonoureth her head: for that is even all one as if she were shaven" (cf. 1 Cor 11:13). See: BAGD—29d; THAYER—21d.

178. **ἀκατάκριτος** {2x} **akatakritŏs**, *ak-at-ak'-ree-tos;* from *1* (as a neg. particle) and a der. of *2632; without* (legal) *trial:*—uncondemned {2x}.

Akatakritos is rendered "uncondemned" in Acts 16:37 and properly means "without trial, not yet tried": "But Paul said unto them, They have beaten us openly uncondemned (*akatakritos*), being Romans, and have cast *us* into prison; and now do they thrust us out privily? nay verily; but let them come themselves and fetch us out" (cf. Acts 22:25). See: TDNT—3:952, 469; BAGD—29d; THAYER—21d.

179. **ἀκατάλυτος** {2x} **akatalutŏs**, *ak-at-al'-oo-tos;* from *1* (as a neg. particle) and a der. of *2647; indissoluble,* i.e. (fig.) *permanent:*—endless {2x}.

Akatalutos denotes indissoluble, Heb 7:16, "endless": "Who is made, not after the law of a carnal commandment, but after the power of an endless life"i.e., a life which makes its possessor the holder of His priestly office for evermore. Syn.: 562. See: TDNT—3:952, 469; BAGD—30a; THAYER—21d.

180. **ἀκατάπαυστος** {1x} **akatapaustŏs**, *ak-at-ap'-ow-stos;* from *1* (as a neg. particle) and a der. of *2664; unrefraining:*—that cannot cease {1x}. See: BAGD—30a; THAYER—21d.

181. **ἀκαταστασία** {5x} **akatastasia**, *ak-at-as-tah-see'-ah;* from *182; instability,* i.e. *disorder:*—commotion {1x}, confusion {2x}, tumult {2x}.

Akatastasia, as a noun, means "instability" and denotes **(1)** "a state of disorder, disturbance, confusion, tumult": "For God is not *the author* of confusion, but of peace, as in all churches of the saints" (1 Cor 14:33); **(2)** "revolution or anarchy": "For where envying and strife *is,* there *is* confusion (akatasia) and every evil work" (Jas 3:16); **(3)** "commotions": "But when ye shall hear of wars and commotions, be not terrified: for these things must first come to pass; but the end *is* not by and by" (Lk 21:9); **(4)** "tumults" 2Cor 6:5; 12:20). Syn.: 2617, 4797, 4799. See: TDNT—3:446, 387; BAGD—30a; THAYER—21d.

182. **ἀκατάστατος** {1x} **akatastatŏs**, *ak-at-as'-tat-os;* from *1* (as a neg. particle) and a der. of *2525; inconstant:*—unstable {1x}.

Akatastatos means "unsettled, unstable, disorderly" is translated "unstable" in Jas. 1:8. See: TDNT—3:447, 387; BAGD—30b; THAYER—22a.

183. **ἀκατάσχετος** {1x} **akataschĕtŏs**, *ak-at-as'-khet-os;* from *1* (as a neg. particle) and a der. of *2722; unrestrainable:*—unruly {1x}.

Akataschetos is translated "unruly" in Jas 3:8. See: BAGD—30b.; THAYER—22a.

184. **Ἀκελδαμά** {1x} **Akeldama**, *ak-el-dam-ah';* of Chald. or. [mean. *field of blood;* corresp. to 2506 and 1818]; *Akeldama,* a place near Jerusalem:—Aceldama {1x}. See: BAGD—30b; THAYER—22a.

185. **ἀκέραιος** {3x} **akĕraiŏs**, *ak-er'-ah-yos;* from *1* (as a neg. particle) and a presumed der. of *2767; unmixed,* i.e. (fig.) *innocent:*—harmless {2x}, simple {1x}.

Akeraios, literally means "unmixed, with absence of foreign mixture, pure" and is used **(1)** metaphorically of what is guileless, sincere, harmless: "Behold, I send you forth as sheep in the midst of wolves: be ye therefore wise as serpents, and harmless as doves" (Mt 10:16), i.e., with the simplicity of a single eye, discerning what is evil, and choosing only what glorifies God (cf. Phil 2:15); **(2)** "simple": "For your obedience is come abroad unto all *men.* I am glad therefore on your behalf: but yet I would have you wise unto that which is good, and simple concerning evil" (Rom 16:19). Syn.: As the *akakos* (172) has no harmfulness in him, and the *adolos* (97) no guile, so the *akeraios* no foreign mixture, and the haplous (573) no folds. See: TDNT—1:209, 33; BAGD—30b; THAYER—22a.

186. **ἀκλινής** {1x} **aklinēs**, *ak-lee-nace';* from *1* (as a neg. particle) and *2827; not leaning,* i.e. (fig.) *firm:*—without wavering {1x}.

Aklines means "without bending/without wavering" and occurs in Heb 10:23: "Let us hold fast the profession of *our* faith without wavering; (for he *is* faithful that promised)." See: BAGD—30c; THAYER—22a.

187. **ἀκμάζω** {1x} **akmazō**, *ak-mad'-zo;* from the same as *188;* to *make a point,* i.e. (fig.) *mature:*—be fully ripe {1x}.

Akmazo, means "to be at the prime, to be ripe" and is translated "are fully ripe": "And another angel came out from the altar, which had power over fire; and cried with a loud cry to him that had the sharp sickle, saying, Thrust in thy sharp sickle, and gather the clusters of the vine of the earth; for her grapes are fully ripe" (Rev 14:18). Syn.: 3583, 3860. See: BAGD—30d; THAYER—22a.

188. **ἀκμήν** {1x} **akmēn**, *ak-mane';* acc. of a noun ("*acme*") akin to ἀκή **akē** (a *point*) and mean. the same; adv. *just* now, i.e. *still:*—yet {1x}. See: BAGD—30d; THAYER—22a.

189. **ἀκοή** {24x} **akŏē**, *ak-o-ay';* from *191; hearing* (the act, the sense or the thing heard):—hearing {10x}, ears {4x}, fame {3x}, rumour {2x}, report {2x}, audience {1x}, which ye heard {1x}, preached {1x}.

Akoe means "hearing" denotes **(1)** the sense of "hearing" (1 Cor 12:17; 2 Pet 2:8); **(2)** that which is "heard," a report (Mt 4:24); **(3)** the physical organ (Mk 7:35), standing for the sense of "hearing"; **(4)** so in Lk 7:1 for "audience"; **(5)** Acts 17:20; 2 Tim 4:3–4 - "being tickled as to the ears"); **(5)** a message or teaching (Jn 12:38; Rom 10:16–17; Gal 3:2, 5; 1 Th 2:13; Heb 4:2 - "(the word) preached." **(6)** A combination of verb and noun is used in phrases which have been termed Hebraic as they express somewhat literally an OT phraseology **(6a)** "by hearing ye shall hear" (Mt 13:14; Acts 28:26 a mode of expression conveying emphasis); **(6b)** "the receiving of a message" Rom 10:17, something more than the mere sense of "hearing"; an interaction with the Word and a decision is always made [compare a courtroom hearing]. Syn.: 191, 1251, 1522, 1873, 1874, 3775, 3878, 4257, 5621. See: TDNT—1:221, 34; BAGD—30d; THAYER—22b.

190. **ἀκολουθέω** {92x} **akŏlŏuthĕō**, *ak-ol-oo-theh'-o;* from *1* (as a particle of union) and κέλευθος **kĕlĕuthŏs** (a *road*); prop. to *be in the same way with,* i.e. to *accompany* (spec. as a disciple):—follow {91x}, reach {1x}.

Akoloutheo, as a verb, gives rise to be an akolouthos, "a follower," or "companion" (from the prefix a, here expressing "union, likeness," and keleuthos, "a way"; hence, "one going in the same way") and is used **(1)** frequently in the literal sense (Mt 4:25); **(2)** metaphorically, of "discipleship" (Mk 8:34; 9:38; 10:21). **(3)** It is used 77 times in the Gospels, of "following" Christ, and only once otherwise: "And he sendeth forth two of his disciples, and saith unto them, Go ye into the city, and there shall meet you a man bearing a pitcher of water: follow him" (Mk 14:13). Syn.: 1096, 1377, 1811, 1872, 2614, 2628, 3877, 4870. See: TDNT—1:210, 33; BAGD—31a; THAYER—22b.

191. **ἀκούω** {437x} **akŏuō**, *ak-oo'-o;* a prim. verb; to *hear* (in various senses):—hear {418x}, hearken {6x}, give audience {3x}, hearer {2x}, misc. {8x} = come (to the ears), be noised, be reported, understand.

Akouo, as a verb, is the usual word denoting "to hear" is used **(1)** intransitively: "He that hath ears to hear, let him hear" (Mt 11:15; cf. Mk 4:23); **(2)** transitively when the object is expressed, sometimes in the accusative case, sometimes in the genitive. **(2a)** Thus in Acts 9:7, "hearing the voice," the noun "voice" is in the partitive genitive case [i.e., hearing (something) of], whereas in 22:9, "they heard not the voice," the construction is with the accusative. **(2b)** This removes the idea of any contradiction. The former indicates a "hearing" of the sound, the latter indicates the meaning or message of the voice (this they did not hear). **(2c)** The former denotes the sensational perception, the latter (the accusative case) the thing perceived. **(3)** In Jn 5:25, 28, **(3a)** the genitive case is used, indicating a "sensational perception" that the Lord's voice is sounding; **(3b)** in 3:8, of "hearing" the wind, the accusative is used, stressing "the thing perceived."

(4) That God "hears" prayer signifies that He answers prayer (Jn 9:31; 1 Jn 5:14, 15). **(5)** Sometimes the verb is used with para ("from beside"), **(5a)** e.g., Jn 1:40, "one of the two which heard John speak," lit., "heard from beside John," suggesting that he stood beside him; **(5b)** in Jn 8:26, 40, indicating the intimate fellowship of the Son with the Father; **(5c)** the same construction is used in Acts 10:22 and 2 Ti 2:2, in the latter case, of the intimacy between Paul and Timothy. Syn.: 189, 1251, 1522, 1873, 1874, 3878, 4257. See: TDNT—1:216, 34; BAGD—31d; THAYER—22c.

192. **ἀκρασία** {2x} **akrasia**, *ak-ras-ee'-a;* from *193; want of self-restraint:*—excess {1x}, incontinency {1x}.

Akrasia literally denotes "want of strength," hence, "want of self-control, incontinence, excess": **(1)** "Woe unto you, scribes and Pharisees, hypocrites! for ye make clean the outside of the cup and of the platter, but within they are full of extortion and excess (*akrasia*)" (Mt 23:25); **(2)** "Defraud ye not one the other, except *it be* with consent for a time, that ye may give yourselves to fasting and prayer; and come together again, that Satan tempt you not for your incontinency" (1 Cor 7:5). Syn.: 193, 401. See: TDNT—2:339, 196; BAGD—33a; THAYER—23d.

193. **ἀκράτης** {1x} **akratēs**, *ak-rat'-ace;* from *1* (as a neg. particle) and *2904; powerless,* i.e. *without self-control:*—incontinent {1x}.

Akrates, "powerless, incontinent": "Without natural affection, truce breakers, false accusers, incontinent, fierce, despisers of those that are good" (2 Ti 3:3 - "without self-control"). Syn.: 192, 401. See: TDNT—2:339, 196; BAGD—33a; THAYER—23d.

194. **ἄκρατος** {1x} **akratŏs**, *ak'-rat-os;* from *1* (as a neg. particle) and a presumed der. of *2767; undiluted:*—without mixture {1x}. See: BAGD—33a; THAYER—23d.

195. **ἀκρίβεια** {1x} **akribĕia**, *ak-ree'-bi-ah;* from the same as *196; exactness:*—perfect manner {1x}.

Akribeia, as a noun, means "exactness, precision": "I am verily a man *which am* a Jew, born in Tarsus, *a city* in Cilicia, yet brought up in this city at the feet of Gamaliel, *and* taught according to the perfect manner of the law of the fathers, and was zealous toward God, as ye all are this day" (Acts 22:3). Syn.: 1485, 2239, 3634, 3668, 3697, 3779, 4169, 4187, 4217, 4459, 5158, 5159, 5179, 5615. See: BAGD—33a; THAYER—23d.

196. **ἀκριβέστατος** {1x} **akribĕstatŏs**, *ak-ree-bes'-ta-tos;* superlative of ἀκρίβης **akribēs** (a der. of the same as *206*); *most exact:*—most straitest {1x}.

This word means "accurate, exact" and occurs in Acts 26:5 "the most straitest (sect)." See: BAGD—33b; THAYER—23d.

197. **ἀκριβέστερον** {4x} **akribĕstĕrŏn**, *ak-ree-bes'-ter-on;* neut. of the comparative of the same as *196;* (adv.) *more exactly:*—more perfectly {3x}, more perfect {1x}.

This word means "accurately, carefully" is translated **(1)** "more perfectly" (Acts 18:26; 23:15); **(2)** "more perfect" (Acts 23: 20; 24:22, lit., "knowing more exactly"). See: BAGD—33b; THAYER—23d.

198. **ἀκριβόω** {2x} **akribŏō**, *ak-ree-bŏ'-o;* from the same as *196; to be exact,* i.e. *ascertain:*—enquire diligently {2x}.

Akriboo, as a verb, means "to learn carefully" is translated "diligently enquired" (Mt 2:7, 16). Syn.: 1097, 3129, 3453. See: BAGD—33b; THAYER—24a.

199. **ἀκριβῶς** {5x} **akribōs**, *ak-ree-boce';* adv. from the same as *196; exactly:*—diligently {2x}, perfect {1x}, perfectly {1x}, circumspectly {1x}.

The word expresses that "accuracy" which is the outcome of carefulness. *Akribos* is translated **(1)** "having had perfect understanding" (Lk 1:3 "having traced the course of all things accurately"). **(2)** It is used in Mt 2:8 of Herod's command to the wise men as to searching for the young Child "diligently"; **(3)** in Acts 18:25 of Apollos' teaching of "the things concerning Jesus" ("carefully/diligently"); **(4)** in Eph 5:15 of the way in which believers are to walk ("circumspectly"); **(5)** in 1 Th 5:2 of the knowledge gained by the saints through the apostle's teaching concerning the Day of the Lord ("perfectly"). See: BAGD—33b; THAYER—24a.

200. **ἀκρίς** {4x} **akris**, *ak-rece';* appar. from the same as *206;* a *locust* (as *pointed,* or as *lightning* on the *top* of vegetation):—locust {4x}.

Akris occurs **(1)** in Mt 3:4 and Mk 1:6 **(1a)** of the insects themselves, **(1b)** as forming part of the diet of John the Baptist; **(1c)** they are used as food; **(1d)** the Arabs stew them with butter, after removing the head, legs and wings. **(2)** In Rev 9:3, 7, they appear as monsters representing satanic agencies, let loose by divine judgments inflicted upon men for five months, the time of the natural life of the "locust." See: BAGD—33c; THAYER—24a.

201. **ἀκροατήριον** {1x} **akrŏatēriŏn**, *ak-rŏ-at-ay'-ree-on;* from *202;* an *audience-room:*—place of hearing {1x}.

Akroaterion, as a noun, denotes "a place of audience" [cf. akroaomai - 202 "to listen"], "a place of hearing": "And on the morrow, when Agrippa was come, and Bernice, with great pomp, and was entered into the place of hearing (*akroaterion*), with the chief captains, and principal men of the city, at Festus' commandment Paul was brought forth" (Acts 25:23). Syn.: 402, 1096, 1502, 3837, 4042, 5117, 5247, 5564, 5602. See: BAGD—33c; THAYER—24b.

202. **ἀκροατής** {4x} **akrŏatēs**, *ak-rŏ-at-ace';* from ἀκροάομαι **akrŏaŏmai** (to *listen;* appar. an intens. of *191*); a *hearer* (merely):—hearer {4x}.

This word means "to listen" and is used of being a hearer **(1)** "of the Law": "For not the hearers of the law *are* just before God, but the doers of the law shall be justified" (Rom 2:13); **(2)** "of the word" (Jas 1:22, 23); and **(3)** in Jas 1: 25 one should not be "a [forgetful] hearer [of the word]." See: BAGD—33c; THAYER—24b.

203. **ἀκροβυστία** {20x} **akrŏbustia**, *ak-rob-oos-tee'-ah;* from *206* and prob. a modified form of πόσθη **pŏsthē** (the *penis* or male sexual organ); the *prepuce;* by impl. an *uncircumcised* (i.e. *gentile,* fig. *unregenerate*) state or person:—uncircumcision {16x}, being circumcised {2x}, uncircumcised + 2192 {1x}, though not circumcised {1x}.

Akrobustia, as a noun, means "uncircumcision" and is used **(1)** of the physical state, in contrast to the act of "circumcision": **(1a)** "having uncircumcision (Acts 11:3); **(1b)** "though they be in uncircumcision" (Rom 2:25–26; 4:10–11, 12; 1 Cor 7:18–19; Gal 5:6; 6:15; Col 3:11); **(2)** by metonymy, for Gentiles (e.g., Rom 2:26–27; 3:30; 4:9; Gal 2:7; Eph 2:11); **(3)** in a metaphorical or transferred sense, of the moral condition in which the corrupt desires of the flesh still operate (Col 2:13). Syn.: 564, 1986, 4059, 4061. See: TDNT—1:225, 36; BAGD—33d; THAYER—24b.

204. **ἀκρογωνιαῖος** {2x} **akrŏgōniaiŏs**, *ak-rog-o-nee-ah'-yos;* from *206* and *1137;* belonging to the extreme *corner:*—chief corner {2x}.

This words denotes "a chief corner-stone" [from *akros,* "highest, extreme," *gonia,* "a corner, angle"] (Eph 2:20; 1 Pet 2:6). See: TDNT—1:792, 137; BAGD—33d; THAYER—24c.

205. **ἀκροθίνιον** {1x} **akrŏthiniŏn**, *ak-roth-in'-ee-on;* from *206* and θίς **this** (a *heap*); prop. (in the plur.) the *top of the heap,* i.e. (by impl.) *best of the booty:*—spoils {1x}.

Akrothinion, primarily means the top of a heap; hence firstfruit offerings, and in war the choicest spoils: "Now consider how great this man *was,* unto whom even the patriarch Abraham gave the tenth of the spoils" (Heb 7:4). Syn.: 724, 4661. See: BAGD—33d; THAYER—24c.

206. **ἄκρον** {6x} **akrŏn**, *ak'-ron;* neut. of an adj. prob. akin to the base of *188;* the *extremity:*—uttermost part {2x}, one end {1x}, other + 846 {1x}, tip {1x}, top {1x}.

This word means "the top, an extremity," is translated "tip" in Luke 16:24. See: BAGD—34a; THAYER—24d.

207. **'Ακύλας** {6x} **Akulas**, *ak-oo'-las;* prob. for Lat. *aquila* (an *eagle*); *Akulas*, an Isr.:—Aquila {6x}. See: BAGD—34b; THAYER—24d.

208. **ἀκυρόω** {3x} **akurŏō**, *ak-oo-rŏ'-o;* from *1* (as a neg. particle) and *2964;* to *invalidate:*—make of none effect {2x}, disannul {1x}.

This word means **(1)** "to deprive of authority"; hence, "to make of none effect": "And honour not his father or his mother, *he shall be free.* Thus have ye made the commandment of God of none effect by your tradition" (Mt 15:6; cf. Mk 7:13, with reference to the commandment or word of God); and **(2)** "to disannul": "And this I say, *that* the covenant, that was confirmed before of God in Christ, the law, which was four hundred and thirty years after, cannot disannul, that it should make the promise of none effect" (Gal 3:17 of the inability of the Law to deprive of force God's covenant with Abraham). **(3)** This verb stresses the effect of the act, while atheteo (114) stresses the attitude of the rejector. Syn.: 114, 115. See: TDNT—3:1099, 494; BAGD—34b; THAYER—24d.

209. **ἀκωλύτως** {1x} **akōlutōs**, *ak-o-loo'-toce;* adv. from a compound of *1* (as a neg. particle) and a der. of *2967;* in *an unhindered manner*, i.e. *freely:*—no man forbidding him {1x}.

This word means "without hindrance" and is translated "none forbidding him" (Acts 28:31). It is interesting to read the triumphant note on which the word brings the Acts to a close. See: BAGD—34b; THAYER—24d.

210. **ἄκων** {1x} **akōn**, *ak'-ohn;* from *1* (as a neg. particle) and *1635; unwilling:*—against (one's) will {1x}.

This word means "unwillingly," occurs in 1 Cor 9:17, and is translated "against my will." Syn.: 1635. See: TDNT—2:469, 221; BAGD—34b; THAYER—24d.

211. **ἀλάβαστρον** {4x} **alabastrŏn**, *al-ab'-as-tron;* neut. of ἀλάβαστρος **alabastrŏs** (of uncert. der.), the name of a stone; prop. an "*alabaster*" box, i.e. (by extens.) a perfume *vase* (of any material):—alabaster box {3x}, box {1x}.

This word means "an alabaster vessel" and is translated "box" (Mt 26:7; Mk 14:3; Lk 7:37). The breaking refers to the seal, not to the box or cruse. See: BAGD—34c; THAYER—24d.

212. **ἀλαζονεία** {2x} **alazŏnĕia**, *al-ad-zon-i'-a;* from *213; braggadocio*, i.e. (by impl.) *self-confidence:*—boasting {1x}, pride {1x}.

Alazoneia is **(1)** the practice of an *alazon* (213) and denotes **(2)** quackery; hence, arrogant display, or boastings: "But now ye rejoice in your boastings: all such rejoicing is evil" (Jas 4:16); and **(2)** pride: "For all that *is* in the world, the lust of the flesh, and the lust of the eyes, and the pride of life, is not of the Father, but is of the world" (1 Jn 2:16). Syn.: 2744, 3166. See: TDNT—1:226, 36; BAGD—34c; THAYER—25a.

213. **ἀλαζών** {2x} **alazōn**, *al-ad-zone';* from ἄλη **alē** (*vagrancy*); *braggart:*—boaster {2x}.

Alazon means a boaster and primarily signifies "a wanderer about the country, a vagabond; hence, an impostor; one who is full of empty and boastful professions and only while in the company of others": "For men shall be lovers of their own selves, covetous, boasters, proud, blasphemers, disobedient to parents, unthankful, unholy" (2 Ti 3:2; Rom 1:30). Syn.: *Alazon,* hyperephanos (5244) and hybristes (5197) portray an ascending scale of guilt, respectively designating those who are boastful in words (213), those who are proud and overbearing in thoughts (5244), and those who are insolent and injurious in deeds (5197). See also: 2744, 3166, 5197, 5244. See: TDNT—1:226, 36; BAGD—34d; THAYER—25a.

214. **ἀλαλάζω** {2x} **alalazō**, *al-al-ad'-zo;* from ἀλαλή **alalē** (a *shout, "halloo"*); to *vociferate*, i.e. (by impl.) to *wail;* fig. to *clang:*—wail {1x}, tinkle {1x}.

This word is derived from the battle-cry, *alala*, is used of "raising the shout of battle" (cf. Josh 6:20); hence, **(1)** "to make a loud cry or shout": "And He cometh to the house of the ruler of the synagogue, and seeth the tumult, and them that wept and wailed (*alalazo*) greatly" (cf. Ps 47:1; Jer 29:2; of wailing mourners); and **(2)** in 1 Cor 13:1 of the "tinkling" of cymbals. See: TDNT—1:227, 36; BAGD—34d; THAYER—25b.

215. **ἀλάλητος** {1x} **alalētŏs**, *al-al'-ay-tos;* from *1* (as a neg. particle) and a der. of *2980; unspeakable:*—which cannot be uttered {1x}. See: BAGD—34d; THAYER—25b.

216. **ἄλαλος** {3x} **alalŏs**, *al'-al-os;* from *1* (as a neg. particle) and *2980; mute:*—dumb {3x}.

Alolos, as an adjective, literally means "speechless" (a, negative, and laleo, "to speak"), and is found in Mk 7:37: "And were beyond measure astonished, saying, He hath done all things well: He maketh both the deaf to hear, and the dumb to speak" (cf. 9:17, 25). Syn.: *Aphonos* (880), lit., "voiceless, or soundless" has reference to voice, while *alalos* (216) has reference to words. See also: 880, 2974, 4623. See: BAGD—34d; THAYER—25b.

217. **ἅλας** {8x} **halas**, *hal'-as;* from *251; salt;* fig. *prudence:*—salt {8x}. See: TDNT—1:228, 36; BAGD—35a; THAYER—25b.

218. **ἀλείφω** {9x} **alĕiphō**, *al-i'-fo;* from *1* (as particle of union) and the base of *3045;* to *oil* (with perfume):—anoint {9x}.

Aleipho, as a verb, is a general term used for "an anointing" of any kind, whether **(1)** of physical refreshment after washing: "But thou, when thou fastest, anoint thine head, and wash thy face" (Mt 6:17; cf. Lk 7:38, 46; Jn 11:2; 12:3); or **(2)** of the sick: "And they cast out many devils, and anointed with oil many that were sick, and healed *them*" (Mk 6:13; cf. Jas 5:14); or **(3)** a dead body: "And when the sabbath was past, Mary Magdalene, and Mary the *mother* of James, and Salome, had bought sweet spices, that they might come and anoint Him"(Mk 16:1).

(4) The material used was either oil, or ointment: "And stood at His feet behind *him* weeping, and began to wash His feet with tears, and did wipe *them* with the hairs of her head, and kissed His feet, and anointed *them* with the ointment" (Lk 7:38; cf. vs 46). Syn.: Aleiphein and chriein (5548) are clearly distinguished. Chriein is absolutely restricted to the Father's anointing of the Son with the Holy Spirit for the accomplishment of the Son's greater office. Chriein has no profane or common uses. Aleiphein is used as the mundane and profane term, and is used indiscriminately of all actual anointings whether with oil or with ointment. See also: 1472, 1637, 2025, 3462, 3464, 5545, 5548. See: TDNT—1:229, 37; BAGD—35b; THAYER—25d.

219. **ἀλεκτοροφωνία** {1x} **alektŏrŏphōnia**, *al-ek-tor-of-o-nee'-ah;* from *220* and *5456; cock-crow*, i.e. the third night-watch:—cockcrowing {1x}.

This word denotes "cock-crowing." **(1)** There were two "cock-crowings," one after midnight, the other before dawn. **(2)** In these watches the Jews followed the Roman method of dividing the night. **(2a)** The first "cock-crowing" was at the third watch of the night. **(2b)** That is the one mentioned in Mk 13:35. **(2c)** Mark mentions both; see 14:30. **(3)** The latter, the second, is that referred to in the other Gospels and is mentioned especially as "the cock-crowing." See: BAGD—35b; THAYER—25d.

220. **ἀλέκτωρ** {12x} **alĕktōr**, *al-ek'-tore;* from ἀλέκω **(to *ward* off)**; a *cock* or male fowl:—cock {12x}. See: BAGD—35c; THAYER—26a.

221. **'Αλεξανδρεύς** {2x} **Alĕxandrĕus**, *al-ex-and-reuce';* from 'Αλεξάνδρεια (the city so called); an *Alexandreian* or inhab. of Alexandria:—Alexandrian {1x}, born at Alexander + 1085 {1x}. See: BAGD—35c; THAYER—26a.

222. **'Αλεξανδρίνος** {2x} **Alĕxandrinŏs**, *al-ex-an-dree'-nos;* from the same as *221; Alexandrine*, or belonging to Alexandria:—of Alexandria {2x}. See: BAGD—35c; THAYER—26a.

223. **'Αλέξανδρος** {6x} **Alĕxandrŏs**, *al-ex'-an-dros;* from the same as (the first part of) *220* and *435; man-defender; Alexander*, the name of three Isr. and one other man:—Alexander {6x}. See: BAGD—35c; THAYER—26a.

224. **ἄλευρον** {2x} **alĕurŏn**, *al'-yoo-ron;* from ἀλέω **alĕō** (to *grind*); *flour:*—meal {2x}.

This verb for this word means "to grind," and therefore, literally, "what is ground": "Another parable spake he unto them; The kingdom of heaven is like unto leaven, which a woman took, and hid in three measures of meal, till the whole was leavened" (Mt. 13:33; cf. Lk 13:21). See: BAGD—35d; THAYER—26a.

225. **ἀλήθεια** {110x} **alēthĕia**, *al-ay'-thi-a;* from *227; truth:*—truth {107x}, truly + 1909 {1x}, true {1x}, verity {1x}.

Aletheia, as a noun, means "truth" and is used **(1)** objectively, **(1a)** signifying the reality lying at the basis of an appearance; the manifested, veritable essence of a matter: "I say the truth in Christ, I lie not, my conscience also bearing me witness in the Holy Ghost" (Rom 9:1; cf. 2 Cor 11:10); **(1b)** especially of Christian doctrine: "To whom we gave place by subjection, no, not for an hour; that the truth of the gospel might continue with you" (Gal 2:5, where "the truth of the Gospel" denotes the "true" teaching of the Gospel, in contrast to perversions of it); **(1c)** Rom 1:25 where "the truth of God" may be "the truth concerning God" or "God whose existence is a verity"; **(1d)** but in Rom 15:8 **(1d1)** "the truth of God" is indicative of His faithfulness in the fulfillment of His promises as exhibited in Christ; **(1d2)** the word has an absolute force in Jn 14:6; 17:17; 18:37, 38; **(1d3)** in Eph 4:21 "as the truth is in Jesus", the meaning is not merely ethical "truth," but "truth" in all its fullness and scope, as embodied in Him; **(1e)** He was the perfect expression of the truth; this is virtually equivalent to His statement in Jn 14:6;

(2) subjectively, **(2a)** "truthfulness/truth," not merely verbal, but sincerity and integrity of character: "Ye are of *your* father the devil, and the lusts of your father ye will do. He was a murderer from the beginning, and abode not in the truth, because there is no truth in him" (Jn 8:44; cf. 3 John 3). Syn.: 226, 227, 228, 230, 1103, 1104. See: TDNT—1:232, 37; BAGD—35d; THAYER—26a.

226. **ἀληθεύω** {2x} **alēthĕuō**, *al-ayth-yoo'-o;* from *227; to be true* (in doctrine and profession):—tell the truth {1x}, speak the truth {1x}.

Aletheuo, as a verb, signifies "to deal faithfully or truly with anyone." **(1)** "speaking the truth": "But speaking the truth in love, may grow up into him in all things, which is the head, *even* Christ" (Eph 4:15); **(2)** "I tell [you] the truth": "Am I therefore become your enemy, because I tell you the truth?" (Gal 4:16 - where probably the apostle is referring to the contents of his epistle). Syn.: 225, 227, 228, 230, 1103, 1104. See: TDNT—1:251, 37; BAGD—36c; THAYER—26d.

227. **ἀληθής** {25x} **alēthēs**, *al-ay-thace';* from *1* (as a neg. particle) and *2990; true* (as *not concealing*):—true {23x}, truly {1x}, truth {1x}.

Alethes, as an adjective, means primarily "unconcealed, manifest"; hence, actual, "true to fact" and is used **(1)** of "truthful" persons: "And they sent out unto him their disciples with the Herodians, saying, Master, we know that thou art true, and teachest the way of God in truth, neither carest thou for any *man:* for thou regardest not the person of men"(Mt 22:16; cf. Mk 12:14; Jn 3:33; 7:18; 8:26; Rom 3:4; 2 Cor 6:8); **(2)** of "true" things, conforming to reality" "For thou hast had five husbands; and he whom thou now hast is not thy husband: in that saidst thou truly" (Jn 4:18; cf. 10:41; 19:35; 21:24; Acts 12:9; Phil 4:8; Titus 1:13; 1 Pet 5:12; 2 Pet 2:22; 1 Jn 2:8, 27; 3 Jn 2). Syn.: Alethinos (228) is related to *alethes* as form to contents or substances; *alethes* denotes the reality of the thing, alethinos defines the relation of the conception to the thing to which it corresponds = genuine." Syn.: 225, 226, 228, 230, 1103, 1104. See: TDNT—1:247, 37; BAGD—36d; THAYER—27a.

228. **ἀληθινός** {27x} **alēthinŏs**, *al-ay-thee-nos';* from *227; truthful:*—true {27x}.

Alethinos, as an adjective, denotes "true" in the sense of real, ideal, genuine. It is used **(1)** of God: "Then cried Jesus in the temple as he taught, saying, Ye both know me, and ye know whence I am: and I am not come of myself, but He that sent me is true, whom ye know not" (Jn 7:28; cf. 17:3; 1 Th 1:9; Rev 6:10). These declare that God fulfills the meaning of His Name; He is "very God," in distinction from all other gods, false gods; it signifies that He is veracious, "true" to His utterances, He cannot lie; **(2)** of Christ: "And we know that the Son of God is come, and hath given us an understanding, that we may know him that is true, and we are in him that is true, *even* in his Son Jesus Christ. This is the true God, and eternal life" (1 Jn 5:20; cf. Rev 3:7, 14; 19:11); **(3)** Christ's judgment: "And yet if I judge, my judgment is true: for I am not alone, but I and the Father that sent me" (Jn 8:16);

(4) God's words: "And herein is that saying true, One soweth, and another reapeth" (Jn 4:37; cf. Rev 19:9, 21:5; 22:6); **(5)** His ways: "And they sing the song of Moses the servant of God, and the song of the Lamb, saying, Great and marvellous *are* thy works, Lord God Almighty; just and true *are* thy ways, thou King of saints" (Rev 15:3); **(6)** His judgments: "And I heard another out of the altar say, Even so, Lord God Almighty, true and righteous *are* thy judgments" (Rev 16:7; cf. 19:2); **(7)** His worshipers: "But the hour cometh, and now is, when the true worshippers shall worship the Father in spirit and in truth: for the Father seeketh such to worship Him" (Jn 4:23); **(8)** believers' hearts: "Let us draw near with a true heart in full assurance of faith, having our hearts sprinkled from an evil conscience, and our bodies washed with pure water" (Heb 10:22);

(9) the witness of the apostle John: "And he that saw *it* bare record, and his record is true: and he knoweth that he saith true, that ye might believe" (Jn 19:35); **(10)** the spiritual, antitypical tabernacle: "A minister of the sanctuary, and of the true tabernacle, which the Lord pitched, and not man" (Heb 8:2; cf. 9:24, not that the wilderness tabernacle was false, but that it was a weak and earthly copy of the heavenly). Syn.: *Alethinos* is related to *alethes* (227) as form to contents or substances; alethes denotes the reality of the thing, *alethinos* defines the relation of the conception to the thing to which it corresponds = genuine." See also: 225, 226, 227, 230, 1103, 1104. See: TDNT—1:249, 37; BAGD—37a; THAYER—27a.

229. **ἀλήθω** {2x} **alēthō**, *al-ay'-tho;* from the same as *224; to grind at the mill:*—grinding {2x}.

Aletho, as a verb, signifies "to grind at the mill" (Mt 24:41; Lk 17:35). See: BAGD—37b; THAYER—27b.

230. **ἀληθῶς** {21x} **alēthōs**, *al-ay-thoce';* adv. from *227; truly:*—of a truth {6x}, indeed {6x}, surely {3x}, truly {2x}, very {1x}, misc. {3x} = of a surety, verily.

Alethos, as an adverb, means "truly, surely" and is rendered **(1)** "of a truth": "Then they that were in the ship came and worshipped him, saying, Of a truth thou art the Son of God" (Mt 14:33; cf. 26:73); **(2)** "surely": "And he denied it again. And a little after, they that stood by said again to Peter, Surely thou art *one* of them: for thou art a Galilaean, and thy speech agreeth *thereto*" (Mk 14:70; cf. Lk 9:27; 12:44; 21:3; Jn 6:14; 7:40; 17:8; **(3)** "of a surety": "And when Peter was come to himself, he said, Now I know of a surety, that the Lord hath sent his angel, and hath delivered me out of the hand of Herod, and *from* all the expectation of the people of the Jews" (Acts 12:11); **(4)** "in truth": "For this cause also thank we God without ceasing, because, when ye received the word of God which ye heard of us, ye received *it* not *as* the word of men, but as it is in truth, the word of God, which effectually worketh also in you that believe" (1 Th 2:13); **(5)** "truly": "Now when the centurion, and they that were with him, watching Jesus, saw the earthquake, and those things that were done, they feared greatly, saying, Truly this was the Son of God" (Mt 27:54; cf. Mk 15:39). Syn.: 225, 226, 227, 228, 1103, 1104. Syn.: 1104. See: BAGD—37b; THAYER—27b.

231. **ἁλιεύς** {5x} **haliĕus**, *hal-ee-yoos';* from *251; a sailor* (as engaged on the *salt* water), i.e. (by impl.) a *fisher:*—fishers {4x}, fishermen {1x}.

This word means "a fisherman, fisher" and occurs in Mt 4:18, 19; Mk 1:16, 17; Lk 5:2). See: BAGD—37c; THAYER—27c.

232. **ἁλιεύω** {1x} **haliĕuō**, *hal-ee-yoo'-o;* from *231; to be a fisher,* i.e. (by impl.) to *fish:*—a fishing {1x}.

Halieuo means "to fish" and occurs in Jn 2:3. See: BAGD—37d; THAYER—27c.

233. **ἁλίζω** {3x} **halizō**, *hal-id'-zo;* from *251;* to *salt:*—to salt {3x}.

Halizo, as a verb, signifies "to sprinkle" or "to season with salt" (Mt 5:13; Mk 9:49). Syn.: 251, 252, 358. See: BAGD—37d; THAYER—27c.

234. **ἀλίσγεμα** {1x} **alisgĕma**, *al-is'-ghem-ah;* from ἀλισγέω **alisgĕō** (to *soil*); (cer.) *defilement:*—pollution {1x}.

This word denotes a pollution, contamination (Acts 15:20—"pollutions of idols," i.e., all the contaminating associations connected with idolatry including meats from sacrifices offered to idols. See: BAGD—37d; THAYER—27d.

235. **ἀλλά** {637x} **alla**, *al-lah';* neut. plur. of *243;* prop. *other* things, i.e. (adv.) *contrariwise* (in many relations):—but {573x}, yea {15x}, yet {11x}, nevertheless {10x}, howbeit {9x}, nay {4x}, therefore {3x}, save {2x}, not tr {2x}, misc. {8x} = and, indeed, no, notwithstanding. Syn.: 3304, 3756, 3780. See: BAGD—38a; THAYER—27d.

236. **ἀλλάσσω** {6x} **allassō**, *al-las'-so;* from *243;* to *make different:*—change {6x}.

Allasso means **(1)** to make other than it is, to transform, change, and is used **(1a)** of the effect of the gospel upon the precepts of the Law (Acts 6:14); **(1b)** of the effect, on the body of a believer, of Christ's return (1 Cor 15:51–52); **(1c)** of the final renewal of the material creation (Heb 1:12); **(1d)** of a change in the apostle's mode of speaking or dealing (Gal 4:20). **(2)** In Rom 1:23 it means to exchange. Syn.: 3328, 3337, 3346. See: TDNT—1:251, 40; BAGD—39a; THAYER—28c.

237. **ἀλλαχόθεν** {1x} **allachŏthĕn**, *al-lakh-oth'-en;* from *243; from elsewhere:*—some other way {1x}. See: BAGD—39b; THAYER—28d.

238. **ἀλληγορέω** {1x} **allēgŏrĕō**, *al-lay-gor-eh'-o;* from *243* and ἀγορέω **agŏrĕō** (to *harangue* [comp. *58*]); to *allegorize:*—be an allegory {1x}.

Allegoreo is translated in Gal 4:24 "are an allegory" and came to signify to speak, not according to the primary sense of the word, but so that the facts stated are applied to illustrate principles. Using a text in an allegorical way does not do away with the literal historical narrative from which the allegory is taken. See: TDNT—1:260, 42; BAGD—39b; THAYER—28d.

239. **ἀλληλουϊα** {4x} **allēlŏuïa**, *al-lay-loo'-ee-ah;* of Heb. or. [imper. of 1984 and 3050]; *praise ye Jah!,* an adoring exclamation:—alleluia {4x}. See: TDNT—1:264, 43; BAGD—39c; THAYER—28d.

240. **ἀλλήλων** {100x} **allēlōn**, *al-lay'-lone;* a reciprocal pronoun; gen. plur. from *243* redupl.; *one another:*—one another {76x}, themselves {12x}, yourselves {3x}, misc. {9x} = each other, mutual, the other. [*sometimes with 3326 or 4314*]. See: BAGD—39c; THAYER—28d.

241. **ἀλλογενής** {1x} **allŏgĕnēs**, *al-log-en-ace';* from *243* and *1085; foreign,* i.e. not a Jew:—stranger {1x}.

Allogenes (241) (allos, "another," genos, "a race") occurs in Lk 17:18 of a Samaritan. Syn.: 245, 3580, 3581. See: TDNT—1:266, 43; BAGD—39c; THAYER—28d.

242. **ἅλλομαι** {3x} **hallŏmai**, *hal'-lom-ahee;* mid. voice of appar. a prim. verb; to *jump;* fig. to *gush:*—leap {2x}, spring up {1x}.

Hallomai means to leap **(1)** metaphorically, of the springing up of water (Jn 4:14); **(2)** literally, of the leaping of healed cripples (Acts 3:8; 14:10). Syn.: 1814, 2177, 4640. See: BAGD—39d; THAYER—28d.

Greek

243. **ἄλλος** {160x} **allŏs**, *al'-los;* a prim. word; "*else*," i.e. *different* (in many applications):—other(s) {81x}, another {62x}, some {11x}, one {4x}, misc. {2x} = more, one.

Allos (243) and heteros (2087) **(1)** have a difference in meaning, which despite a tendency to be lost, is to be observed in numerous passages. **(1a1)** *Allos* expresses a numerical difference and denotes "another of the same sort"; **(1a2)** heteros expresses a qualitative difference and denotes "another of a different sort." **(3)** Examples are: **(3a)** Christ promised to send "another Comforter" (*allos,* "another like Himself," not heteros), John 14:16. **(3b)** Paul says "I see another law," heteros, a law different from that of the spirit of life (not *allos,* "a law of the same sort"), Rom. 7:23. **(3b)** After Joseph's death "another king arose," heteros, one of quite a different character, Acts 7:18. **(3c)** Paul speaks of "a different gospel (heteros), which is not another" (*allos,* another like the one he preached), Gal. 1:6–7. **(4)** They are not interchangeable. See: TDNT—1:264, 43; BAGD—39d; THAYER—29a.

244. **ἀλλοτριεπίσκοπος** {1x} **allotriĕpiskŏpŏs**, *al-lot-ree-ep-is'-kop-os;* from *245* and *1985; overseeing others'* affairs, i.e. a *meddler* (spec. in Gentile customs):—a busybody in other men's matters {1x}.

Allotrioepiskopos, [from allotrios, "belonging to another person," and episkopos, "an overseer,"] is translated "busybody" (1 Pet 4:15). It was a legal term for a charge brought against Christians as being hostile to civilized society, their purpose being to make Gentiles conform to Christian standards. Syn.: 4020, 4021. See: TDNT—2:620, 244; BAGD—40c; THAYER—29a.

245. **ἀλλότριος** {14x} **allŏtriŏs**, *al-lot'-ree-os;* from *243; another's,* i.e. not one's own family/country; by extens. *foreign, not akin, hostile:*—stranger {4x}, another man's {4x}, strange {2x}, other men's {2x}, other {1x}, alien {1x}. See: TDNT—1:265, 43; BAGD—40c; THAYER—29b.

246. **ἀλλόφυλος** {1x} **allŏphulŏs**, *al-lof'-oo-los;* from *243* and *5443; for.,* i.e. (spec.) *Gentile:*—one of another nation {1x}. Syn.: 1085, 1484. See: TDNT—1:267, 43; BAGD—41a; THAYER—29b.

247. **ἄλλως** {1x} **allōs**, *al'-loce;* adv. from *243; differently:*—otherwise {1x}. Syn.: 243, 1893, 2088. See: BAGD—41a; THAYER—29b.

248. **ἀλοάω** {3x} **alŏaō**, *al-o-ah'-o;* from the same as *257;* to *tread* out grain:—tread out the corn {2x}, thresh {1x}. See: BAGD—41a; THAYER—29b.

249. **ἄλογος** {3x} **alŏgŏs**, *al'-og-os;* from *1* (as a neg. particle) and *3056; irrational:*—brute {2x}, unreasonable {1x}.

The stress in this word is on being without the possession of reason. See. TDNT—4.141, 505; BAGD—41a; THAYER—29b.

250. **ἀλοή** {1x} **alŏē**, *al-o-ay';* of for. or. [comp. 174]; *aloes* (the gum):—aloes {1x}. See: BAGD—41b; THAYER—29c.

251. **ἅλς** {1x} **hals**, *halce;* a prim. word; "*salt*":—salt {1x}.

Halas, as a noun, is used **(1)** literally (Mt 5:13; Mk 9:50; Lk 14:34; **(2)** metaphorically, **(2a)** of "believers" (Mt 5:13); **(2b)** of their "character and condition": "Salt *is* good: but if the salt have lost his saltness, wherewith will ye season it? Have salt in yourselves, and have peace one with another" (Mk 9:50); **(2c)** of "wisdom" exhibited in their speech (Col 4:6).

(3) Being possessed of purifying, perpetuating and antiseptic qualities, "salt" became emblematic of fidelity and friendship. **(3a)** In Scripture, it is an emblem of the covenant between God and His people (cf. Num 18:19; 2 Chr 13:5); **(3b)** so again when the Lord says "Have salt in yourselves, and be at peace one with another" (Mk 9:50). **(3c)** In the Lord's teaching it is also symbolic of that spiritual health and vigor essential to Christian virtue and counteractive of the corruption that is in the world (e.g. Mt 5:13, see (2a) above. **(3d)** Food is seasoned with "salt." **(3e)** Every meal offering was to contain it, and it was to be offered with all offerings presented by Israelites, as emblematic of the holiness of Christ, and as betokening the reconciliation provided for man by God on the ground of the death of Christ (cf. Lev 2:13). **(3f)** To refuse God's provision in Christ and the efficacy of His expiatory sacrifice is to expose oneself to the doom of being "salted with fire" (Mk 9:49). Syn.: 233, 252, 358. See: BAGD—41b; THAYER—29c.

252. **ἁλυκός** {1x} **halukŏs**, *hal-oo-kos';* from *251; briny:*—salt {1x}.

Halukos occurs in Jas 3:12 and means "salt (water)." Syn.: 233, 251, 358. See: BAGD—41c; THAYER—29c.

253. **ἀλυπότερος** {1x} **alupŏtĕrŏs**, *al-oo-pot'-er-os;* comparative of a comp. of *1* (as a neg. particle) and *3077; more without grief:*—less sorrowful {1x}.

Alupos, as an adjective, denotes "free from grief, less sorrowful": "I sent him therefore the more carefully, that, when ye see him again, ye may rejoice, and that I may be the less sorrowful" (Phil 2:28, their joy would mean the removal of a burden from his heart). Syn.: 3076, 3077, 3600, 3601, 3997, 4036, 5604. See: TDNT—4:323,*; BAGD—41c; THAYER—29c.

254. **ἅλυσις** {11x} **halusis**, *hal'-oo-sis;* of uncert. der.; a *fetter* or *manacle:*—chain {10x}, bonds {1x}.

Halusis, as a noun, denotes "bonds/chains": "For which I am an ambassador in bonds: that therein I may speak boldly, as I ought to speak" (Eph 6:20). Syn.: 1198, 1199, 4886. See: BAGD—41c; THAYER—29c.

255. **ἀλυσιτελής** {1x} **alusitĕlēs**, *al-oo-sit-el-ace';* from *1* (as a neg. particle) and the base of *3081; gainless,* i.e. (by impl.) *pernicious:*—unprofitable {1x}.

Alusiteles, as an adjective, means "not advantageous, not making good the expense involved": "Obey them that have the rule over you, and submit yourselves: for they watch for your souls, as they that must give account, that they may do it with joy, and not with grief: for that *is* unprofitable (*alusiteles*) for you" (Heb 13:17). Syn.: 512, 888, 889, 890. See: BAGD—41c; THAYER—29d.

256. **Ἀλφαῖος** {5x} **Alphaiŏs**, *al-fah'-yos;* of Heb. or. [comp. 2501]; *Alphæus,* an Isr.:—Alphaeus (father of James) {4x}, Alphaeus (father of Levi) {1x}. See: BAGD—41c; THAYER—29d.

257. **ἅλων** {2x} **halōn**, *hal'-ohn;* prob. from the base of *1507;* a threshing-*floor* (as *rolled* hard), i.e. (fig.) the *grain* (and chaff, as just threshed):—floor {2x}.

Halon is "a threshing floor," is so translated "floor" in Mt 3:12, and Lk 3:17, perhaps by metonymy for the grain. See: BAGD—41d; THAYER—29d.

258. **ἀλώπηξ** {3x} **alōpēx**, *al-o'-pakes;* of uncert. der.; a *fox,* i.e. (fig.) a *cunning* person:—fox {3x}.

Alopex is **(1)** literal in Mt 8:20; Lk 9:58; and **(2)** metaphorically, of Herod, in Lk 13:32. See: BAGD—41d; THAYER—29d.

259. **ἅλωσις** {1x} **halōsis**, *hal'-o-sis;* from a collat. form of *138; capture:*—to be taken + 1519 {1x}. See: BAGD—42a; THAYER—30a.

260. **ἅμα** {10x} **hama**, *ham'-ah;* a prim. particle; prop. *at the "same" time,* but freely used as a prep. or adv. denoting close association:—together {3x}, withal {3x}, with {1x}, and {1x}, also {2x}.

Hama (260), "at once," is translated "together" and stresses the temporal "together at the same time": "Then we which are alive *and* remain shall be caught up together with them in the clouds, to meet the Lord in the air: and so shall we ever be with the Lord" (1 Th 4:17; cf. 1 Th 5:10; Rom 3:12). Syn.: Homou (3674) stresses together at the same place. See: BAGD—42a; THAYER—30a.

261. **ἀμαθής** {1x} **amathēs**, *am-ath-ace';* from *1* (as a neg. particle) and *3129; ignorant:*—unlearned {1x}.

Amathes, as an adjective, means "unlearned" (3129 - *manthano,* "to learn"), is translated "unlearned": "As also in all *his* epistles, speaking in them of these things; in which are some things hard to be understood, which they that are unlearned and unstable wrest, as *they do* also the other scriptures, unto their own destruction" (2 Pet 3:16). Syn.: 62, 521. See: BAGD—42b; THAYER—30a.

262. **ἀμαράντινος** {1x} **amarantinŏs**, *am-ar-an'-tee-nos;* from *263;* "*amaranthine*", i.e. (by impl.) *fadeless:*—that fadeth not away {1x}.

Amarantinos, as an adjective, primarily signifies "composed of amaranth"; hence, "unfading," 1 Pet 5:4, of the crown of glory promised to faithful elders. Syn.: This word stresses that the inheritance is intrinsically strong; whereas amarantos (263) focuses on forces which can attempt to affect its worth. See also: 862, 3133. See: BAGD—42b; THAYER—30a.

263. **ἀμάραντος** {1x} **amarantŏs**, *am-ar'-an-tos;* from *1* (as a neg. particle) and a presumed der. of *3133; unfading,* i.e. (by impl.) *perpetual:*—that fadeth not away {1x}.

Amarantos, as an adjective, means "unfading." whence the "amaranth," an unfading flower, a symbol of perpetuity is used in 1 Pet 1:4 of the believer's inheritance, "that fadeth not away." Syn.: 262, 3133.

Our inheritance is without corruption from within itself (862), without defilement from outside itself (283), and will not wither or fade away (263). See also: 262, 862, 3133. See: BAGD—42b; THAYER—30b.

264. **ἁμαρτάνω** {43x} **hamartanō**, *ham-ar-tan'-o;* perh. from *1* (as a neg. particle) and the base of *3313;* prop. to *miss* the mark (and so *not share* in the prize), i.e. (fig.) to *err,* esp. (mor.) to *sin:*—sin {38x}, trespass {3x}, offend {1x}, for your faults {1x}.

Hamartano, as a verb, means literally "to miss the mark" and is used **(1)** of "sinning" against God **(1a)** by angels (2 Pet 2:4); **(1b)** by man (Mt 27:4; Lk 15:18, 21 [heaven standing, by metonymy, for God]; Jn 5:14; 8:11; 9:2, 3; Rom 2:12 [twice]; 3:23; 5:12, 14, 16; 6:15; 1 Cor 7:28 [twice], 36; 15:34; Eph 4:26; 1 Ti 5:20; Titus 3:11; Heb 3:17; 10:26; 1 Jn 1:10; in 2:1 [twice]), the aorist tense in each place, referring to an act of "sin"; on the contrary, in 3:6 [twice], 8, 9, the present tense indicates, not the committal of an act, but the continuous practice of "sin"; in 5:16 [twice] the present tense indicates the condition resulting from an act, "unto death" signifying "tending towards death"; **(2)** against Christ (1 Cor 8:12); **(3)** against man, **(3a)** a brother (Mt 18:15 - "trespass"; v. 21; Lk 17:3, 4 - "trespass"; 1 Cor 8:12; **(3b)** in Lk 15:18, 21, against the father by the Prodigal Son, "in thy sight" being suggestive of befitting reverence; **(3c)** against Jewish law, the Temple, and Caesar (Acts 25:8, - "offended"); **(4)** against one's own body, by fornication (1 Cor 6:18); **(5)** against earthly masters by servants (1 Pet 2:20 - "(when ye be buffeted) for your faults," lit., "having sinned"). Syn.: 265, 266, 361, 4258. See: TDNT—1:267, 44; BAGD—42b; THAYER—30b.

265. **ἁμάρτημα** {4x} **hamartēma**, *ham-ar'-tay-mah;* from *264;* a *sin* (prop. concr.):—sin {4x}.

Hamartema, as a noun, denotes "an act of disobedience to divine law" (plural in Mk 3:28; Rom 3:25; 1 Cor 6:18). Syn.: 264, 266, 361, 4258. See: TDNT—1:267, 44; BAGD—42c; THAYER—30c.

266. **ἁμαρτία** {174x} **hamartia**, *ham-ar-tee'-ah;* from *264; sin* (prop. abstr.):—sin {172x}, sinful {1x}, offense {1x}.

Hamartia, as a verb, is literally **(1)** "a missing of the mark" but this etymological meaning is largely lost sight of in the NT. **(1a)** It is the most comprehensive term for moral deviations. **(1b)** It is used of "sin" as **(1b1)** a principle or source of action, or an inward element producing acts: "What then? are we better *than they?* No, in no wise: for we have before proved both Jews and Gentiles, that they are all under sin" (Rom 3:9; cf. 5:12, 13, 20; 6:1, 2; 7:7 [abstract for concrete]; 7:8 [twice], 9, 11, 13, "sin, that it might be shown to be sin," i.e., "sin became death to me, that it might be exposed in its heinous character": in the last clause, "sin might become exceeding sinful," i.e., through the holiness of the Law, the true nature of sin was designed to be manifested to the conscience; **(1b2)** a governing principle or power: "Knowing this, that our old man is crucified with *him,* that the body of sin might be destroyed, that henceforth we should not serve sin" (Rom 6:6, "[the body] of sin," here "sin" is spoken of as an organized power, acting through the members of the body, though the seat of "sin" is in the will [the body is the organic instrument]; in the next clause, and in other passages, as follows, this governing principle is personified (e.g., Rom 5:21; 6:12, 14, 17; 7:11, 14, 17, 20, 23, 25; 8:2; 1 Cor 15:56; Heb 3:13; 11:25; 12:4; Jas 1:15).

(2) This word is also **(2a)** a generic term [distinct from specific terms such as *hamartema* (265) yet sometimes inclusive of concrete wrong doing (e.g., Jn 8:21, 34, 46; 9:41; 15:22, 24; 19:11)]; **(2b)** in Rom 8:3, "God, sending His own Son in the likeness of sinful flesh," **(2b1)** means Christ had a human nature, but He did not have a sinful human nature (2 Cor 5:21; 1 Jn 3:5; Jn 14:30; Jn 8:46; Heb 4:15; 1 Pet 2:22). **(2b2)** Christ, preexistently the Son of God, assumed human flesh; **(2b3)** the reality of incarnation was His, without taint of sin (3667 - *homoioma,* "likeness"], and **(2b4)** as an offering for sin," i.e., "a sin offering" (Heb 9:28; cf. Lev 4:32; 5:6, 7, 8, 9), **(2b5)** "condemned sin in the flesh," i.e., Christ, having taken human nature, "sin" apart (Heb 4:15), and having lived a sinless life, died under the condemnation and judgment due to our "sin." **(2b6)** In 2 Cor 5:21, "Him . . . He made to be sin" indicates that God dealt with Him as He must deal with "sin," and that Christ fulfilled what was typified in the guilt offering. Syn.: 264, 265, 361, 4258. See: TDNT—1:267, 44; BAGD—43a; THAYER—30d.

267. **ἀμάρτυρος** {1x} **amarturŏs**, *am-ar'-too-ros;* from *1* (as a neg. particle) and a form of *3144; unattested:*—without witness {1x}.

Amarturos, as an adjective, denotes "without witness": "Nevertheless He left not himself without witness, in that He did good, and gave us rain from heaven, and fruitful seasons, filling our hearts with food and gladness" (Acts 14:17). Syn.: 2649, 3140, 3141, 3142, 3143, 3144, 4828, 4901, 5571, 5576, 5577. See: BAGD—44a; THAYER—31c.

268. **ἁμαρτωλός** {47x} **hamartōlŏs**, *ham-ar-to-los';* from *264; sinful,* i.e. a *sinner:*—sinner {43x}, sinful {4x}.

Hamartolos is used as an adjective "sinful": "Whosoever therefore shall be ashamed of me and of my words in this adulterous and sinful generation; of him also shall the Son of man be ashamed, when He cometh in the glory of His Father with the holy angels" (Mk 8:38; cf. Lk 5:8; 19:7 [lit., "a sinful man"]; 24:7; Jn 9:16, and 24 [lit., "a man sinful"]; Rom 7:13). See: TDNT—1:317, 51; BAGD—44a; THAYER—31c.

269. **ἄμαχος** {2x} **amachŏs**, *am'-akh-os;* from *1* (as a neg. particle) and *3163; peaceable:*—not a brawler {1x}, no brawler {1x}.

Amachos (*a,* negative, *mache,* a fight), an adjective, literally means "not fighting" and came to denote, metaphorically, "not contentious, not a brawler" (1 Ti 3:3; Titus 3:2). Syn.: 3943. See: TDNT—4:527, 573; BAGD—44c; THAYER—31d.

270. **ἀμάω** {1x} **amaō**, *am-ah'-o;* from *260;* prop. to *collect,* i.e. (by impl.) *reap:*—reap down {1x}.

Amao is translated "have reaped down " (Jas 5:4) with the sense that cutting down is primary and that of gathering-in secondary. See: BAGD—44c; THAYER—31d.

271. **ἀμέθυστος** {1x} **amĕthustŏs**, *am-eth'-oos-tos;* from *1* (as a neg. particle) and a der. of *3184;* the *"amethyst"* (supposed to *prevent intoxication*):—amethyst {1x}.

Some feel this jewel gets its name from its reddish purple, almost wine, color. See: BAGD—44d; THAYER—31d.

272. **ἀμελέω** {5x} **amĕlĕō**, *am-el-eh'-o;* from *1* (as a neg. particle) and *3199;* to *be careless* of; not to care:—neglect {2x}, make light of {1x}, regard not {1x}, be negligent {1x}.

Ameleo denotes "to be careless, not to care" (Mt 22:5 - "they made light of (it)," lit. "making light of it);" an aorist participle, indicating the definiteness of their decision. See: BAGD—44d; THAYER—31d.

273. **ἄμεμπτος** {5x} **amĕmptŏs**, *am'-emp-tos;* from *1* (as a neg. particle) and a der. of *3201; irreproachable:*—blameless {3x}, unblameable {1x}, faultless {1x}.

Amemptos, as an adjective, related to memphomai (3201), is translated **(1)** "unblameable" (1 Th 3:13); **(2)** "blameless" (Lk 1:6; Phil 2:15; 3:6); and **(3)** "faultless" (Heb 8:7). Syn.: If *amomos* (299) is the "unblemished," *amemptos* (273) is the "unblamed." Christ was *amomos* in that there was in Him no spot or blemish, and He could say, "Which of you convinceth Me of sin? (Jn 8:46);" but in strictness of speech He was not *amemptos* (unblamed), nor is this epithet ever given to Him in the NT, seeing that He endured the contradiction of sinners against Himself, who slandered His footsteps and laid to His charge 'things that He knew not' (i.e., of which He was guiltless). Syn.: 274, 298, 299, 338, 410, 423, 2607, 3201, 3469. See: TDNT—4:571, 580; BAGD—45a; THAYER—31d.

274. **ἀμέμπτως** {2x} **amĕmptōs**, *am-emp'-toce;* adv. from *273; faultlessly:*—unblameably {1x}, blameless {1x}.

Amemptos, as an adverb, is translated **(1)** "unblameably": "Ye *are* witnesses, and God *also,* how holily and justly and unblameably we behaved ourselves among you that believe" (1 Th 2:10); **(2)** "blameless": "And the very God of peace sanctify you wholly; and *I pray God* your whole spirit and soul and body be preserved blameless unto the coming of our Lord Jesus Christ" (1 Th 5:23) which is said of believers at the judgment-seat of Christ in His Parousia [His presence after His coming], as the outcome of present witness and steadfastness. Syn.: 273, 298, 299, 338, 410, 423, 2607, 3201, 3469. See: BAGD—45a; THAYER—32a.

275. **ἀμέριμνος** {2x} **amĕrimnŏs**, *am-er'-im-nos;* from *1* (as a neg. particle) and *3308; not anxious:*—secure + 4060 {1x}, without carefulness {1x}. See: TDNT—4:593, 584; BAGD—45b; THAYER—32a.

276. **ἀμετάθετος** {2x} **amĕtathĕtŏs**, *am-et-ath'-et-os;* from *1* (as a neg. particle) and a der. of *3346; unchangeable,* or (neut. as abstr.) *unchangeability:*—immutability {1x}, immutable {1x}.

Ametathetos is an adjective signifying "immutable" (*a,* negative, *metatithemi,* "to change") and is used in Heb 6:18, where the "two immutable things" are the promise and the oath. In v. 17 the word is used in the neuter with the article, as a noun, denoting "the immutability," with reference to God's counsel. See: BAGD—45b; THAYER—32a.

277. **ἀμετακίνητος** {1x} **amĕtakinētŏs**, *am-et-ak-in'-ay-tos;* from *1* (as a neg. particle) and a der. of *3334; firm, immoveable:*—unmoveable {1x}.

Ametakinetos, as an adjective, means "firm, immoveable": "Therefore, my beloved brethren, be ye stedfast, unmoveable, always abounding in the work of the Lord, forasmuch as ye know that your labour is not in vain in the Lord" (1 Cor 15:58). Syn.: 383, 761, 2795, 2796, 3334, 4525, 4531, 4579, 4787, 5342. See: BAGD—45c; THAYER—32a.

278. **ἀμεταμέλητος** {2x} **amĕtamĕlētŏs**, *am-et-am-el'-ay-tos;* from *1* (as a neg. particle) and a presumed der. of *3338; irrevocable:*—without repentance {1x}, not to be repented of {1x}.

Ametameletos, as an adjective, means "not repented of" and is translated **(1)** "not to be repented of": "For godly sorrow worketh repentance to salvation not to be repented of: but the sorrow of the world worketh death" (2 Cor 7:10); and **(2)** "without repentance": "For the gifts and calling of God *are* without repentance" (Rom 11:29). Syn.: 3338. See: TDNT—4:626, 589; BAGD—45c; THAYER—32a.

279. **ἀμετανόητος** {1x} **amĕtanŏētŏs**, *am-et-an-o'-ay-tos;* from *1* (as a neg. particle) and a presumed der. of *3340; unrepentant:*—impenitent {1x}. See: TDNT—4:1009, 636; BAGD—45c; THAYER—32a.

280. **ἄμετρος** {2x} **amĕtrŏs**, *am'-et-ros;* from *1* (as a neg. particle) and *3358; immoderate:*—things without measure {2x}.

Ametros, as an adjective, means **(1)** "without measure" and **(2)** is used in the neuter plural in an adverbial phrase in 2 Cor. 10:13, 15, *eis ta ametra,* "(we will not boast) of things without measure," [lit., "unto the (things) without measure"] **(3)** referring to the sphere divinely appointed for the apostle as to his gospel ministry; **(4)** this had reached to Corinth, and by the increase of the faith of the church there, would extend to regions beyond. **(5)** His opponents had no scruples about intruding into the spheres of other men's work. Syn.: 488, 943, 2884, 3313, 3354, 3358, 4057, 4568, 5234, 5249, 5518. See: TDNT—4:632, 590; BAGD—45d; THAYER—32b.

281. **ἀμήν** {152x} **amēn**, *am-ane'*; of Heb. or. [543]; prop. *firm,* i.e. (fig.) *trustworthy;* adv. *surely* (often as interj. *so be it*):—verily {101x}, amen {51x}.

Amen is **(1)** transliterated from Hebrew into both Greek and English. **(2)** Its meanings may be seen in such passages as **(2a)** Deut 7:9, 'the faithful (the *Amen*) God' **(2b)** Is 49:7, 'Jehovah that is faithful.' **(2c)** Is 65:16, 'the God of truth,' **(2d)** And if God is faithful His testimonies and precepts are "sure *(amen)*," Ps 19:7; 111:7, as **(2e)** are also His warnings, Hos 5:9, and **(2f)** promises, Is 33:16; 55:3. **(3)** *'Amen'* is used of men also, e.g., Prov 25:13. **(4)** There are cases where the people used it to express their assent to a law and their willingness to submit to the penalty attached to the breach of it, Deut 27:15, cf. Neh 5:13. **(5)** It is also used to express acquiescence in another's prayer, 1 Kin 1:36, where it is defined as "(let) God say so too," or **(6)** in another's thanksgiving, 1 Chr 16:36, whether **(6a)** by an individual, Jer 11:5, or by **(6b)** the congregation, Ps 106:48. **(7)** Thus *"Amen"* said by God "it is and shall be so," and by men, "so let it be." **(8)** Once in the NT *'Amen'* is a title of Christ, Rev 3:14, because through Him the purposes of God are established, 2 Cor 1:20. **(9)** The early Christian churches followed the example of Israel in associating themselves audibly with the prayers and thanksgivings offered on their behalf, 1 Cor 14:16, where the article 'the' points to a common practice. **(10)** Moreover this custom conforms to the pattern of things in the Heavens, see Rev 5:14. **(11)** The individual also said *"Amen"* to express his "let it be so" in response to the Divine "thus it shall be,'" Rev 22:20. **(12)** Frequently the speaker adds *"Amen"* to his own prayers and doxologies, as is the case at Eph 3:21. **(13)** The Lord Jesus often used *"Amen,"* translated "verily," to introduce new revelations of the mind of God. **(14)** In John's Gospel it is always repeated, *"Amen, Amen,"* but not elsewhere. Luke does not use it at all, but where Matthew, 16:28, and Mark, 9:1, have *"Amen,"* Luke has "of a truth"; thus by varying the translation of what the Lord said, Luke throws light on His meaning. See: TDNT—1:335, 53; BAGD—45d; THAYER—32b.

282. **ἀμήτωρ** {1x} **amētōr**, *am-ay'-tore; from 1* (as a neg. particle) and *3384; motherless,* i.e. *of unknown maternity:*—without mother {1x}.

Ametor, "without a mother" is used in Heb 7:3, of the Genesis record of Melchizedek, certain details concerning him being purposely omitted, in order to conform the description to facts about Christ as the Son of God. Syn.: 3384, 3389. See: BAGD—46a; THAYER—32b.

283. **ἀμίαντος** {4x} **amiantŏs**, *am-ee'-an-tos;* from *1* (as a neg. particle) and a der. of *3392; unsoiled,* i.e. (fig.) *pure; free from contamination:*—undefiled {4x}.

Amiantos means "undefiled, free from contamination" and is used **(1)** of Christ: "For such an high priest became us, *who is* holy, harmless, undefiled, separate from sinners, and made higher than the heavens" (Heb 7:26); **(2)** of pure religion (Jas 1:27); **(3)** of the eternal inheritance of believers (1 Pet 1:4); and **(4)** of the marriage bed as requiring to be free from unlawful sexual intercourse (Heb 13:4). See: TDNT—4:647, 593; BAGD—46b; THAYER—32c.

284. **Ἀμιναδάβ** {3x} **Aminadab**, *am-ee-nad-ab';* of Heb. or. [5992]; *Aminadab,* an Isr.:—*Aminadab* {3x}. See: BAGD—46b; THAYER—32c.

285. **ἄμμος** {5x} **ammŏs**, *am'-mos;* perh. from *260; sand* (as *heaped* on the beach):—sand {5x}.

Ammos means "sand" or "sandy ground" and describes **(1)** an insecure foundation (Mt 7:26); **(2)** numberlessness, vastness: "Esaias also crieth concerning Israel, Though the number of the children of Israel be as the sand of the sea, a remnant shall be saved" (Rom 9:27; cf. Heb 11:12; Rev 20:8); and **(3)** symbolically in Rev 13:1: "And I stood upon the sand of the sea, and saw a beast rise up out of the sea, having seven heads and ten horns, and upon his horns ten crowns, and upon his heads the name of blasphemy" the position taken up by John, to view the rising of the Beast out of the sea (emblematic of the restless condition of nations). See: BAGD—46b; THAYER—32c.

286. **ἀμνός** {4x} **amnŏs**, *am-nos';* appar a prim. word; a *lamb:*—lamb {4x}. Syn.: 704, 721.

Amnos, "a lamb," is used figuratively of Christ: **(1)** Jn 1:29, 36, with the article, pointing Him out as the expected One, the One to be well known as the personal fulfillment and embodiment of all that had been indicated in the OT, the One by whose sacrifice deliverance from divine judgment was to be obtained; **(2)** in Acts 8:32 and 1 Pet 1:19, the absence of the article stresses the nature and character of His sacrifice as set forth in the symbolism. **(3)** The reference in each case is to the lamb of God's providing, Gen 22:8, and the Paschal lamb of God's appointment for sacrifice in Israel (e.g. cf. Ex 12:5, 14, 27; and cf. 1 Cor 5:7). Syn.: See discussion under 721. See: TDNT—1:338, 54; BAGD—46c; THAYER—32d.

287. **ἀμοιβή** {1x} **amŏibē**, *am-oy-bay';* from ἀμείβω **amĕibō** (to *exchange*); *requital:*—requite + 591 {1x}.

Amoibe means "a requital, recompence," is used with the verb *apodidomi* (591 - "to render") in 1 Ti 5:4, and is translated "to requite": "But if any widow have children or nephews, let them learn first to shew piety at home, and to requite their parents: for that is good and acceptable before God." See: BAGD—46c; THAYER—32d.

288. **ἄμπελος** {8x} **ampĕlŏs**, *am'-pel-os;* prob. from the base of *297* and that of *257;* a *vine* (as *coiling about* a support):—vine {8x}.

This word is used **(1)** of a literal vine (Mt 26:29; Jas 3:12); **(2)** figuratively, **(2a)** of Christ (Jn 15:1, 4, 5); **(2b)** of His enemies (Rev 14:18, 19 - "the vine of the earth"). TDNT—1:342, 54; BAGD—46d; THAYER—32d.

289. **ἀμπελουργός** {1x} **ampĕlŏurgŏs**, *am-pel-oor-gos';* from *288* and *2041;* a *vine-worker,* i.e. *pruner:*—dresser of vineyard {1x}.

This word means "a worker in a vineyard" and is rendered "vinedresser" in Lk 13:7. See: BAGD—47a; THAYER—32d.

290. **ἀμπελών** {23x} **ampĕlōn**, *am-pel-ohn';* from *288;* a *vineyard:*—vineyard {23x}.

Ampelon is used 22 times in the Synoptic Gospels; elsewhere in 1 Cor 9:7: ". . . who planteth a vineyard, and eateth not of the fruit thereof?" See: BAGD—47a; THAYER—32d.

291. **Ἀμπλίας** {1x} **Amplias**, *am-plee'-as;* contr. for Lat. *ampliatus* [*enlarged*]; *Amplias,* a Rom. Chr.:—Amplias {1x}. See: BAGD—47a; THAYER—32d.

292. **ἀμύνομαι** {1x} **amunŏmai**, *am-oo'-nom-ahee;* mid. voice of a prim. verb; to *ward off* (for oneself), i.e. *protect:*—defend {1x}.

Amunomai means "to ward off," is used in the middle voice in Acts 7:24, of the assistance given by Moses to his fellow Israelite against an Egyptian (translated, "defended"). The middle voice indicates the special personal interest Moses had in the act. See: BAGD—47a; THAYER—33a.

293. **ἀμφίβληστρον** {2x} **amphiblēstrŏn**, *am-feeb'-lace-tron;* from a comp. of the base of *297* and *906;* a (fishing) *net* (as *thrown about* the fish):—net {2x}.

Amphiblestron literally means "something thrown around" and denotes a casting net, a somewhat small net, cast over the shoulder, spreading out in a circle and made to sink by weights (Mt 4:18). Syn.: *Diktyon* (1350) is the more general term for nets, including the hunting net and the fishing nets. *Amphiblestron* (293) and sagene (4522) are types of fishing nets. See also: 1350, 4522. See: BAGD—47b; THAYER—33b.

294. **ἀμφιέννυμι** {4x} **amphiĕnnumi**, *am-fee-en'-noo-mee;* from the base of *297* and ἕννυμι **hĕnnumi** (to *invest*); to *enrobe:*—clothes {4x}.

Amphiennumi, as a verb, means "to put clothes round" signifies, in the middle voice, to put clothing on oneself (Mt 6:30; 11:8; Lk 7:25; 12:28). Syn.: 1463, 1737, 1746, 1902, 2439, 4016. See: BAGD—47c; THAYER—33a.

295. **Ἀμφίπολις** {1x} **Amphipŏlis**, *am-fip'-ol-is;* from the base of *297* and *4172;* a *city surrounded* by a river; *Amphipolis,* a place in Macedonia:—*Amphipolis* {1x}. See: BAGD—47c; THAYER—33b.

296. **ἄμφοδον** {1x} **amphŏdŏn**, *am'-fod-on;* from the base of *297* and *3598;* a *fork* in the road:—place where two ways meet {1x}.

Amphodon, as a noun, properly means "a way around, where two ways meet": "And they went their way, and found the colt tied by the door without in a place where two ways met; and they loose him" (Mk 11:4). Syn.: 4113, 4505. See: BAGD—47c; THAYER—33b.

297. **ἀμφότερος** {14x} **amphŏtĕrŏs**, *am-fot'-er-os;* comp. of ἀμφί **amphi** (*around*); (in plur.) *both:*—both {14x}. See: BAGD—47c; THAYER—33b.

298. **ἀμώμητος** {2x} **amōmētŏs**, *am-o'-may-tos;* from *1* (as a neg. particle) and a der. of *3469; unblameable:*—without rebuke {1x}, blameless {1x}.

Amometos, as an adjective, is translated **(1)** "without rebuke": "That ye may be blameless and harmless, the sons of God, without rebuke (*amometos*), in the midst of a crooked and perverse nation, among whom ye shine as lights in the world" (Phil 2:15), and is rendered "blameless": "Wherefore, beloved, seeing that ye look for such things, be diligent that ye may be found of him in peace, without spot, and blameless" (2 Pet 3:14). Syn.: 273, 274, 299, 338, 410, 423, 2607, 3201, 3469. See: TDNT—4:831, 619; BAGD—47d; THAYER—33c.

299. **ἄμωμος** {7x} **amōmŏs**, *am'-o-mos;* from *1* (as a neg. particle) and *3470; unblemished* (lit. or fig.):—without rebuke {2x}, without blame {1x}, unblameable {1x}, without spot {1x}, faultless {1x}, without fault {1x}.

Amomos, as an adjective, means "without blame": "According as He hath chosen us in Him before the foundation of the world, that we should be holy and without blame before Him in love" (Eph 1:4). Syn.: If *amomos* (299) is the "unblemished," amemptos (273) is the "unblamed." Christ was *amomos* in that there was in Him no spot or blemish, and He could say, "Which of you convinceth Me of sin? (Jn 8:46);" but in strictness of speech He was not amemptos (unblamed), nor is this epithet ever given to Him in the NT, seeing that He endured the contradiction of sinners against Himself, who slandered His footsteps and laid to His charge 'things that He knew not' (i.e., of which He was guiltless). Syn.: 273, 274, 298, 338, 410, 423, 2607, 3201, 3469. See: TDNT—4:830, 619; BAGD—47d; THAYER—33c.

300. **'Αμών** {2x} **Amōn**, *am-one';* of Heb. or. [526]; *Amon,* an Isr.:—*Amon* {2x}. See: BAGD—48a; THAYER—33c.

301. **'Αμώς** {1x} **Amōs**, *am-oce';* of Heb. or. [531]; *Amos,* an Isr.:—*Amos* {1x}. See: BAGD—48a; THAYER—33c.

302. **ἄν** {191x} **an**, *an;* a prim. particle, denoting a *supposition, wish, possibility* or *uncertainty:*—whosoever {35x}, whatsoever {7x}, whomsoever {5x}, whereinsoever {1x}, what things soever {1x}, whatsoever + 3745 {7x}, an many as + 3745 {4x}, whosoever + 3745 {2x}, what things so ever + 3745 {1x}, wherewith soever + 3745 {1x}, whithersoever + 3699 {4x}, wheresoever + 3699 {2x}, whatsoever + 3748 {5x}, whosoever + 3748 {3x}, whose soever + 5100 {2x}, not tr {111x}. See: BAGD—48a; THAYER—33c. Also contr. for *1437.*

303. **ἀνά** {15x} **ana**, *an-ah';* a prim. prep. and adv.; prop. *up;* but (by extens.) used (distributively) *severally,* or (locally) *at* (etc.):—by {3x}, apiece {2x}, every man {2x}, each {1x}, several {1x}, two and two + 1417 {1x}, among {1x}, through {1x}, between {1x}, by {1x}, in {1x}. In compounds (as a prefix) it often means (by impl.) *repetition, intensity, reversal,* etc.

Ana is used with numerals or measures of quantity with a distributive force, is translated **(1)** "apiece" **(1a)** in Lk 9:3, "two coats apiece"; **(1b)** in Jn 2:6, "two or three firkins apiece." **(2)** In Mt 20:9–10, "every man a penny," is a free rendering for "a penny apiece"; **(3)** in Lk 10:1, *ana duo* is "two by two"; and **(4)** Rev 4:8, "each."

304. **ἀναβαθμός** {2x} **anabathmŏs**, *an-ab-ath-mos';* from *305* [comp. *898*]; a *stairway:*—stairs {2x}.

Anabathmos is "an ascent" and denotes "a flight of stairs" (Acts 21:35, 40). These were probably the steps leading down from the castle of Antonia to the Temple. See: BAGD—50a; THAYER—35a.

305. **ἀναβαίνω** {82x} **anabainō**, *an-ab-ah'-ee-no;* from *303* and the base of *939;* to *go up* (lit. or fig.):—go up {37x}, come up {10x}, ascend {10x}, ascend up {8x}, climb up {2x}, spring up {2x}, grow up {2x}, come {2x}, enter {2x}, arise {2x}, rise up {2x}, misc. {2x}, vr ascend {1x}. Syn.: 450, 1096, 1326, 1453, 1525, 1817, 4911.

Anabaino, as a verb, means "to go up, to ascend," is rendered **(1)** "arise"- of thoughts/reasonings: "And He said unto them, Why are ye troubled? and why do thoughts arise in your hearts?" (Lk 24:38); **(2)** "rise up" - of the beast: "And I stood upon the sand of the sea, and saw a beast rise up out of the sea" (Rev 13:1); **(3)** "ascend" - of the beast: "The beast that thou sawest was, and is not; and shall ascend out of the bottomless pit" (Rev 17:8); **(4)** "rose up" - of the smoke of burning Babylon: "And again they said, Alleluia. And her smoke rose up for ever and ever" (Rev 19:3). Syn.: 393, 450, 1096, 1326, 1453, 1525, 1817, 4911. See: TDNT—1:519, 90; BAGD—50a; THAYER—35a.

306. **ἀναβάλλομαι** {1x} **anaballŏmai**, *an-ab-al'-lom-ahee;* mid. voice from *303* and *906;* to *put off* (for oneself); to postpone:—defer {1x}.

This word literally means "to throw up"; hence; "to postpone," and is used in the middle voice in Acts 24:22, in the forensic sense of "deferring" the hearing of a case. See: BAGD—50c; THAYER—35c.

307. **ἀναβιβάζω** {1x} **anabibazō**, *an-ab-ee-bad'-zo;* from *303* and a der. of the base of *939;* to *cause to go up,* i.e. *haul* (a net):—draw {1x}.

Anabibazo, as a verb, a causal form of anabaino (305 - "to go up") denotes, lit., "to make go up, cause to ascend"; hence, "to draw a boat up on land" (Mt 13:48). Syn.: 385, 392, 501, 502, 645, 868, 1096, 1670, 1448, 1828, 2020, 2464, 4317, 4334, 4358, 4685, 4951, 5288, 5289. See: BAGD—50d; THAYER—35c.

308. **ἀναβλέπω** {26x} **anablĕpō**, *an-ab-lep'-o;* from *303* and *991;* to *look up;* by impl. to *recover sight:*—receive sight {15x}, look up {9x}, look {1x}, see {1x}.

Anablepo, as a verb, denotes **(1)** "looking up": "And He commanded the multitude to sit down on the grass, and took the five loaves, and the two fishes, and looking up to heaven, he blessed" (Mt 14:19; Mk 8:24, 25; **(2)** "to recover sight": "The blind receive their sight, and the lame walk" (Mt 11:5; 20:34; Jn 9:11). Syn.: 352, 578, 816, 872, 991, 1689, 1896, 1914, 1980, 1983, 2300, 2334, 3706, 3708, 3879, 4017, 4648. See: BAGD—50d; THAYER—35c.

309. **ἀνάβλεψις** {1x} **anablĕpsis**, *an-ab'-lep-sis;* from *308; restoration of sight:*—recovering of sight {1x}.

Anablepsis, as a verb, denotes "recovering of sight": "The Spirit of the Lord *is* upon Me, because He hath anointed me to preach the gospel . . . and recovering of sight to the blind . . ." (Lk 4:18). See: BAGD—51a; THAYER—35d.

310. **ἀναβοάω** {3x} **anabŏaō**, *an-ab-o-ah'-o;* from *303* and *994;* to *halloo:*—cry 1, cry aloud {1x}, cry out {1x}.

Anaboao, as a verb, [ana makes it intesive] means "to lift up the voice, cry out" and is said **(1)** of Christ at the moment of His death, a testimony to His supernatural power in giving up His life: "And about the ninth hour Jesus cried with a loud voice, saying, Eli, Eli, lama sabachthani? that is to say, My God, my God, why hast thou forsaken me?" (Mt 27:46); **(2)** of the multitude: "And the multitude crying aloud began to desire *him to do* as he [Pilate] had ever done unto them" (Mk 15:8); **(3)** of a man out of a company (Lk 9:38). Syn.: 349, 994, 995, 1916, 2019, 2896, 2905, 2906, 5455. See: BAGD—51a; THAYER—35d.

311. **ἀναβολή** {1x} **anabŏlē**, *an-ab-ol-ay';* from *306;* a *putting off:*—delay + 4160 {1x}.

Anabole, as a noun, literally signifies "that which is thrown up"; hence "a delay": "Therefore, when they were come hither, without any delay on the morrow I sat on the judgment seat, and commanded the man to be brought forth" (Acts 25:17). Syn.: 3635, 5549. Syn.: 3635, 5549. See: BAGD—51a; THAYER—35d.

312. **ἀναγγέλλω** {18x} **anaggĕllō**, *an-ang-el'-lo;* from *303* and the base of *32;* to *announce* (in detail):—tell {6x}, show {6x}, declare {3x}, rehearse {1x}, speak {1x}, report {1x}.

Anaggello, as a verb, means "to declare, announce," is used especially of heavenly messages, and is translated **(1)** "reported" in 1 Pet 1:12: "Unto whom it was revealed, that not unto themselves, but unto us they did minister the things, which are now reported unto you . . .", or **(2)** "declare": "This then is the message which we have heard of Him, and declare unto you . . ." (1 Jn 1:5). See: TDNT—1:61, 10; BAGD—51b; THAYER—36a.

313. **ἀναγεννάω** {2x} **anagĕnnaō**, *an-ag-en-nah'-o;* from *303* and *1080;* to *beget* or (by extens.) *bear* (again):—begat again {1x}, be born again {1x}.

Anagennao, as a verb, means "begotten": "Blessed *be* the God and Father of our Lord Jesus Christ, which according to His abundant mercy hath begotten us again . . ." (1 Pet 1:3; cf. 1:23). Syn.: 616, 738, 1080, 1084, 1085, 1626, 5088. Syn.: 1080. See: TDNT—1:673, 114; BAGD—51c; THAYER—36a.

314. **ἀναγινώσκω** {33x} **anaginōskō**, *an-ag-in-oce'-ko;* from *303* and *1097;* to *know again,* i.e. (by extens.) to *read:*—read {33x}.

Anaginosko, as a verb, means primarily "to know certainly, to know again, recognize" and is used of **(1)** "reading" written characters: "But He said unto them, Have ye not read what David did, when he was an hungered, and they that were with him" (Mt 12:3; cf. 12:5; 21:16; 24:15); **(1a)** of the private "reading" of Scripture (Acts 8:28, 30, 32); **(1b)** of the public "reading" of Scripture (Lk 4:16; Acts 13:27; 15:21; 2 Cor 3:15; Col 4:16 [thrice]; 1 Th 5:27; Rev 1:3). **(2)** In 2 Cor 1:13 there is a purposive play upon words; firstly, "we write none other things unto you, than what ye read (*anaginosko*)" signifies that there is no hidden or mysterious meaning in his epistles; whatever doubts may have arisen and been expressed in this respect, he means what he says; then follows the similar verb *epiginosko* (1921), "to acknowledge," "or even acknowledge, and I hope ye will acknowledge unto the end." **(3)** Similarly, in 2 Cor 3:2 the verb *ginosko* (1097), "to know," and *anaginosko,* "to read," are put in that order, and metaphorically applied to the church at Corinth as being an epistle, a message to the world, written by the apostle and his fellow missionaries, through their ministry of the gospel and the consequent change in the lives of the converts, an epistle "known and read of all men." Syn.: 320. See: TDNT—1:343, 55; BAGD—51c; THAYER—36b.

315. **ἀναγκάζω** {9x} **anagkazō**, *an-ang-kad'-zo;* from *318;* to *necessitate:*—compel {5x}, constrain {4x}.

Anankazo denotes "to put constraint upon, to constrain, to compel, whether by threat, entreaty, force or persuasion." **(1)** Christ "constrained" the disciples to get into a boat (Mt 14:22; Mk 6:45); **(2)** the servants of the man who made a great supper were to compel people to come in (Lk 14:23); **(3)** Saul of Tarsus "compelled" saints to blaspheme (Acts 26:11); **(4)** Titus, though a Greek, was not "compelled" to be circumcised (Gal 2:3), as Galatian converts were "constrained" (6:12); **(5)** Peter was "compelling"

Gentiles to live as Jews (Gal 2:14); **(6)** Paul was "constrained" to appeal to Caesar (Acts 28:19), and **(7)** was "compelled" by the church at Corinth to become foolish in speaking of himself (2 Cor 12:11). Syn.: 29. See: TDNT—1:344, 55; BAGD—52a; THAYER—36b.

316. **ἀναγκαῖος** {8x} **anagkaiŏs**, *an-ang-kah'-yos;* from *318; necessary;* by impl. *close* (of kin):—necessary {5x}, near {1x}, more needful {1x}, of necessity {1x}.

Anankaios, as an adjective means "necessary" and is used in a secondary sense of persons connected by bonds of nature or friendship, with the meaning "intimate": "And the morrow after they entered into Caesarea. And Cornelius waited for them, and had called together his kinsmen and near (*anankaios*) friends" (Acts 10:24 "(his) near friends)." Syn.: 1448, 1451, 1452, 4139, 4317, 4334. See: TDNT—1:344, 55; BAGD—52b; THAYER—36b.

317. **ἀναγκαστῶς** {1x} **anagkastōs**, *an-ang-kas-toce';* adv. from a der. of *315; by force, unwillingly, compulsorily:*—by constraint {1x}.

Anankastos, as an adverb, means "by force, unwillingly, by constraint": "Feed the flock of God which is among you, taking the oversight *thereof,* not by constraint, but willingly; not for filthy lucre, but of a ready mind" (1 Pet 5:2). Syn.: 315, 3849, 4912. See: BAGD—52b; THAYER—36c.

318. **ἀναγκή** {18x} **anagkē**, *an-ang-kay';* from *303* and the base of *43; constraint* (lit. or fig.); by impl. *distress:*—necessity {7x}, must needs {3x}, distress {3x}, must of necessity {2x}, need + 2192 {1x}, necessary {1x}, needful {1x}.

Anagke denotes **(1)** a necessity imposed whether **(1a)** by external circumstances: "For of necessity (ananke) he [Pilate] must release one unto them at the feast" (Lk 23:17) or **(1b)** inward pressure: "For though I preach the gospel, I have nothing to glory of: for necessity (*anagke*) is laid upon me; yea, woe is unto me, if I preach not the gospel!" (1 Cor 9:16); **(2)** straits, distress: "But woe unto them that are with child, and to them that give suck, in those days! for there shall be great distress (ananke) in the land, and wrath upon this people" (Lk 21:23; cf. 1 Cor 7:26; 1 Th 3:7). Syn.: 928, 2347, 2669, 4660, 4729, 4730, 4928. See: TDNT—1:344, 55; BAGD—52b; THAYER—36c.

319. **ἀναγνωρίζομαι** {1x} **anagnōrizŏmai**, *an-ag-no-rid'-zom-ahee;* mid. voice from *303* and *1107;* to *make* (oneself) *known:*—be made known {1x}. See: BAGD—52d; THAYER—36c.

320. **ἀνάγνωσις** {3x} **anagnōsis**, *an-ag'-no-sis;* from *314;* (the act of) *reading:*—reading {3x}.

Anagnosis, as a noun, means "reading"; the public "reading" of Scripture: "And after the reading of the law and the prophets the rulers of the synagogue sent unto them . . ." (Acts 13:15; cf. 2 Cor 3:14; 1 Ti 4:13 where the context makes clear that the reference is to the care required in reading the Scriptures to a company, a duty ever requiring the exhortation "take heed"). Syn.: 314. See: TDNT—1:343, 55; BAGD—52d; THAYER—36d.

321. **ἀνάγω** {24x} **anagō**, *an-ag'-o;* from *303* and *71; to lead up;* by extens. to *bring out;* spec. to *sail* away:—bring {3x}, loose {3x}, sail {3x}, launch {3x}, depart {3x}, misc. {9x} = lead (up), loose, offer, set forth, take up.

Anago, as a verb, means **(1)** "to lead or bring up to": "And when the days of her purification according to the law of Moses were accomplished, they brought Him to (*anago*) Jerusalem, to present *him* to the Lord" (Lk 2:22; cf. Acts 9:39); **(2)** "to bring forth": "And when he [Herod] had apprehended him [Peter], he put *him* in prison, and delivered *him* to four quaternions of soldiers to keep him; intending after Easter to bring him forth (*anago*) to the people" (Acts 12:4); **(3)** "to bring again": "Now the God of peace, that brought again (*anago*) from the dead our Lord Jesus, that great shepherd of the sheep, through the blood of the everlasting covenant" (Heb 13:20); **(4)** "to bring up again": "Or, Who shall descend into the deep? (that is, to bring up Christ again (*anago*) from the dead)" (Rom 10:7). See: BAGD—53a; THAYER—36d.

322. **ἀναδείκνυμι** {2x} **anadĕiknumi**, *an-ad-ike'-noo-mee;* from *303* and *1166; to exhibit,* i.e. (by impl.) to *indicate, appoint:*—appoint {1x}, show {1x}.

Anadeiknumi, as a verb, means literally "to show up, to show clearly" and signifies "to appoint to a position or a service." It is used in this sense of the 70 disciples: "After these things the Lord appointed other seventy also, and sent them two and two before His face into every city and place, whither He himself would come" (Lk 10:1). Syn.: 1299, 1303, 2476, 2525, 4929, 5021, 5087. See: TDNT—2:30, 141; BAGD—53b; THAYER—36d.

323. **ἀνάδειξις** {1x} **anadĕixis**, *an-ad'-ike-sis;* from *322;* (the act of) *exhibition:*—showing {1x}.

Anadeixis means "a shewing forth" [*ana,* "up or forth," and *deiknumi* "to show") and is translated "showing" in Lk 1:80: "And the child grew, and waxed strong in spirit, and was in the deserts till the day of His shewing unto Israel." See: TDNT—2:31, 141; BAGD—53c; THAYER—37a.

324. **ἀναδέχομαι** {2x} **anadĕchŏmai**, *an-ad-ekh'-om-ahee;* from *303* and *1209;* to *entertain* (as a guest); to receive gladly:—receive {2x}.

Anadechomai, as a verb, means "to receive gladly" is used **(1)** in Acts 28:7 of the reception by Publius of the shipwrecked company in Melita; **(2)** in Heb 11:17, of Abraham's reception of God's promises, "gladly received": **(3)** This means that Abraham was taking the responsibility of something, becoming security for, undertaking. **(3a)** The predominance of this meaning suggests its application in Heb 11:17. **(3b)** The statement that Abraham had 'undertaken,' 'assumed the responsibility of,' the promises, means that the responsibility would surely be that of his faith in "receiving" the promises. **(3c)** It is a little difficult to attach any other sense to the circumstances, save perhaps that Abraham's faith undertook to exercise the assurance of the fulfillment of the promises. Syn.: 353, 354, 568, 588, 618, 1209, 1523, 1926, 2210, 2865, 2975, 2983, 3028, 3335, 3336, 3858, 3880, 3970, 4327, 4355, 4356, 4380, 4381, 4382, 5562, 5264, 5274. See: BAGD—53c; THAYER—37a.

325. **ἀναδίδωμι** {1x} **anadidōmi**, *an-ad-eed'-om-ee;* from *303* and *1325;* to *hand over:*—deliver {1x}.

Anadidomi, as a verb, means "to deliver over, give up" and is used of "delivering" the letter mentioned in Acts 23:33: "Who, when they came to Caesarea, and delivered the epistle to the governor, presented Paul also before him." Syn.: 525, 629, 591, 859, 1325, 1560, 1659, 1807, 1929, 3086, 3860, 4506, 5483. See: BAGD—53c; THAYER—37a.

326. **ἀναζάω** {5x} **anazaō**, *an-ad-zah'-o* from *303* and *2198;* to *recover life* (lit. or fig.):—be alive again {2x}, revive {2x}, live again {1x}.

Anazao, as a verb, denotes "to live again, to revive": "For this my son was dead, and is alive again; he was lost, and is found. And they began to be merry" (Lk 15:24); and "to manifest activity again": "For I was alive without the law once: but when the commandment came, sin revived, and I died" (Rom 7:9). Syn.: 390, 980, 1236, 2198, 2225, 4176, 4800, 5225. See: TDNT—2:872, 290; BAGD—53d; THAYER—37a.

327. **ἀναζητέω** {2x} **anazētĕō**, *an-ad-zay-teh'-o;* from *303* and *2212;* to *search* out:—seek {2x}.

Anazeteo, as a verb, means "to seek carefully" (ana, "up," used intensively), and is used of searching for human beings, difficulty in the effort being implied: "But they, supposing Him to have been in the company, went a day's journey; and they sought Him among *their* kinsfolk and acquaintance"(Lk 2:44; Acts 11:25). Syn.: 1567, 1934, 2206, 2212, 3713. Syn.: 1567, 1934, 2212, 3713. See: BAGD—53d; THAYER—37b.

328. **ἀναζώννυμι** {1x} **anazōnnumi**, *an-ad-zone'-noo-mee;* from *303* and *2224;* to *gird afresh:*—gird up {1x}.

Anazonnumi, as a verb, means "to gird up" and is used **(1)** metaphorically of the loins of the mind: "Wherefore gird up (*anazunnomi*) the loins of your mind, be sober, and hope to the end for the grace that is to be brought unto you at the revelation of Jesus Christ" (1 Pet 1:13; cf. Lk 12:35). **(2)** The figure is taken from the circumstances of the Israelites as they ate the Passover in readiness for their journey (cf. Ex 12:11); **(3)** the Christian is to have his mental powers alert in expectation of Christ's coming. **(4)** The verb is in the middle voice, indicating the special interest the believer is to take in so doing. Syn.: 1241, 2224, 4024. Syn.: 1241, 2224, 4024. See: BAGD—53d; THAYER—37b.

329. **ἀναζωπυρέω** {1x} **anazōpurĕō**, *an-ad-zo-poor-eh'-o;* from *303* and a comp. of the base of *2226* and *4442;* to *re-enkindle:*—stir up {1x}.

Anazopureo, as a verb, denotes "to kindle afresh" or "keep in full flame" [ana, "up," or "again," zoos, "alive," pur, "fire"], and is used metaphorically: "Wherefore I put thee in remembrance that thou stir up the gift of God, which is in thee by the putting on of my hands" (2 Ti 1:6, where "the gift of God" is regarded as a fire capable of dying out through neglect). Syn.: 383, 387, 1326, 1892, 2042, 3947, 3951, 4531, 4579, 4787, 4797, 5017. See: BAGD—54a; THAYER 37b.

330. **ἀναθάλλω** {1x} **anathallō**, *an-ath-al'-lo;* from *303* and θάλλω **thallō** (to *flourish*); to *revive:*—flourish {1x}.

Anathallo means "to flourish anew" [*ana,* "again, anew," *thallo,* "to flourish or blossom"], hence, "to revive," is used metaphorically in Phil 4:10: "But I rejoiced in the Lord greatly, that now at the last your care of me hath flourished again; wherein ye were also careful, but ye lacked opportunity." See: BAGD—54a; THAYER—37c.

331. **ἀνάθεμα** {6x} **anathĕma**, *an-ath'-em-ah;* from *394;* a (religious) *ban* or (concr.) *excommunicated* (thing or person):—accursed {4x}, anathema {1x}, bind under a great curse + 332 {1x}.

Anathema, as a noun, is transliterated from the Greek, is **(1)** "a thing devoted to God," whether **(1a)** for His service, as the sacrifices (cf. Lev 27:28), or **(1b)** for its destruction, as **(1b1)** an idol (cf. Deut 7:26), or **(1b2)** a city (Josh 6:17). **(1c)** Later it acquired the more general meaning of "the disfavor of Jehovah" (e.g., Zech 14:11). **(2)** This is the meaning in the NT. It is used **(2a)** of the sentence pronounced: "And they came to the chief priests and elders, and said, We have bound ourselves under a great curse that we will eat nothing until we have slain Paul." [lit., "cursed themselves with a curse"; see *anathematizo* – 332]. **(2b)** of the object on which the "curse" is laid, "accursed": "For I could wish that myself were accursed from Christ for my brethren, my kinsmen according to the flesh:"(Rom 9:3; cf. 1 Cor 12:3; 16:22; Gal 1:8–9, all of which the kjv renders by "accursed" except 1 Cor 16:22, where it has "*Anathema*").

(3) In Gal 1:8–9, the apostle declares in the strongest manner that the gospel he preached was the one and only way of salvation, and that to preach another was to nullify the death of Christ: "But though we, or an angel from heaven, preach any other gospel unto you than that which we have preached unto you, let him be accursed. As we said before, so say I now again, If any *man* preach any other gospel unto you than that ye have received, let him be accursed." **(4)** This word stresses that which is dedicated to God's honor but to its own destruction. Syn.: 332, 334, 685, 1944, 2552, 2652, 2653, 2671, 2672. See: TDNT—1:354, 57; BAGD—54b; THAYER—37c.

332. **ἀναθεματίζω** {4x} **anathĕmatizō,** *an-ath-em-at-id'-zo;* from *331;* to *declare* or *vow* under penalty of execration:—curse {1x}, bind under a curse {1x}, bind with an oath {1x}, bind under a great curse + 331 {1x}.

Anathematizo, as a verb, signifies **(1)** "to declare anathema," i.e., "devoted to destruction, accursed, to curse": "But he began to curse and to swear, *saying,* I know not this man of whom ye speak." (Mk 14:71, or **(2)** "to bind by a curse": "And when it was day, certain of the Jews banded together, and bound themselves under a curse, saying that they would neither eat nor drink till they had killed Paul." (Acts 23:12; cf. vss. 14, 21). Syn.: 331, 685, 1944, 2551, 2652, 2653, 2671, 2672. See: TDNT—1:355, 57; BAGD—54a; THAYER—37d.

333. **ἀναθεωρέω** {2x} **anathĕōrĕō,** *an-ath-eh-o-reh'-o;* from *303* and *2334;* to *look again* (i.e. *attentively*) at (lit. or fig.):—behold {1x}, consider {1x}.

Anatheoreo, [ana, "up" (intensive)], as a verb, means "to view with interest, consider contemplatively," is translated **(1)** "beheld": "For as I passed by, and beheld (*anatheoreo*) your devotions, I found an altar with this inscription, TO THE UNKNOWN GOD. Whom therefore ye ignorantly worship, him declare I unto you" (Acts 17:23); **(2)** "considering": "Remember them which have the rule over you, who have spoken unto you the word of God: whose faith follow, considering (anathereo) the end of *their* conversation" (Heb 13:7). Syn.: 816, 991, 1689, 1896, 2029, 2300, 2334, 2657, 2734, 3708. See: BAGD—54c; THAYER—38a.

334. **ἀνάθημα** {1x} **anathēma,** *an-ath'-ay-mah;* from *394* [like *331,* but in a good sense]; a *votive* offering:—gift {1x}.

Anathema denotes a gift set up in a temple, a votive offering (Lk 21:5). Syn.: 331, 3646, 4376, 4689. This word stresses that which was dedicated to God for its own honor as well as for God's glory. See: TDNT—1:354, 57; BAGD—54c; THAYER—38a.

335. **ἀναίδεια** {1x} **anaidĕia,** *an-ah'-ee-die-ah';* from a comp. of *1* (as a neg. particle [comp. *427*]) and *127; impudence,* i.e. (by impl.) *importunity:*—importunity {1x}.

Anaideia denotes shamelessness, importunity and is used in the Lord's illustration concerning the need of earnestness and perseverance in prayer (Lk 11:8). If shameless persistence can obtain a boon from a neighbor, then certainly earnest prayer will receive our Father's answer. See: BAGD—54c; THAYER—38a.

336. **ἀναίρεσις** {2x} **anairĕsis,** *an-ah'-ee-res-is;* from *337;* (the act of) *killing:*—death {2x}.

Anairesis, another word for "death" literally signifies "a taking up or off" as of the taking of a life, or "putting to death." It is found in Acts 8:1, of the murder of Stephen (cf. Acts 22:20). Syn.: 520, 615, 1935, 2288, 2289, 5054. See: BAGD—54d; THAYER—38b.

337. **ἀναιρέω** {23x} **anairĕō,** *an-ahee-reh'-o;* from *303* and (the act. of) *138;* to *take up,* i.e. *adopt;* by impl. to *take away* (violently), i.e. *abolish, murder:*—kill {10x}, slay {8x}, put to death {2x}, take up {1x}, do {1x}, take away {1x}.

Anaireo literally means to take or lift up or away; hence, **(1)** to put to death and is usually translated "to kill, slay, put to death" (Lk 23:32; Acts 26:10). It is used 17 times, with this meaning, in Acts. Syn.: 520, 615, 1935, 2288, 2289, 5054. See: BAGD—54d; THAYER—38b.

338. **ἀναίτιος** {2x} **anaitiŏs,** *an-ah'-ee-tee-os;* from *1* (as a neg. particle) and *159* (in the sense of *156*); *innocent:*—blameless {1x}, guiltless {1x}.

Anaitios, as an adjective, means "guiltless" and is translated **(1)** "blameless": "Or have ye not read in the law, how that on the sabbath days the priests in the temple profane the sabbath, and are blameless?" (Mt 12:5) and **(2)** "guiltless": "But if ye had known what *this* meaneth, I will have mercy, and not sacrifice, ye would not have condemned the guiltless" (Mt 12:7). Syn.: 273, 274, 298, 299, 410, 423, 2607, 3201, 3469. See: BAGD—55b; THAYER—38b.

339. **ἀνακαθίζω** {2x} **anakathizō,** *an-ak-ath-id'-zo;* from *303* and *2523;* prop. to *set up,* i.e. (refl.) to *sit up:*—sit up {2x}.

Anakathizo, as a verb, means "to set up" and is used intransitively, "to sit up," of two who were raised from the dead: "And he that was dead sat up, and began to speak. And He delivered him to his mother" (Lk 7:15; and Acts 9:40). Syn.: 345, 347, 377, 1910, 2516, 2521, 2621, 2523, 2625, 4775, 4776, 4873. See: BAGD—55b; THAYER—38b.

340. **ἀνακαινίζω** {1x} **anakainizō,** *an-ak-ahee-nid'-zo;* from *303* and a der. of *2537;* to *restore:*—renew {1x}. See: TDNT—3:451, 388; BAGD—55b; THAYER—38c.

341. **ἀνακαινόω** {2x} **anakainŏō,** *an-ak-ahee-nŏ'-o;* from *303* and a der. of *2537;* to *renovate:*—renew {2x}.

Anakainoo means to make new, not recent but different, to renew and is **(1)** used in the passive voice in 2 Cor 4:16 of the daily renewal of the inward man (in contrast to the physical frame), i.e., of the renewal of spiritual power; and **(2)** in Col 3:10, of the new man (in contrast to the old unregenerate nature), which is being renewed unto the true knowledge in Christ, as opposed to heretical teachings. Syn.: *Anakainoo* means substantially different but not recently new; whereas, *anaeoo* (365) means recently new but not substantially different. See: TDNT—3:452, 388; BAGD—55c; THAYER—38c.

342. **ἀνακαίνωσις** {2x} **anakainōsis,** *an-ak-ah'-ee-no-sis;* from *341; renovation:*—renewing {2x}.

Anakainosis means "a renewal" and is used **(1)** in Rom 12:2 "the renewing (of your mind)," i.e., the adjustment of the moral and spiritual vision and thinking to the mind of God, which is designed to have a transforming effect upon the life; and **(1b)** stresses the willing response on the part of the believer. **(2)** In Titus 3:5, "the renewing of the Holy Spirit" is **(2a)** not a fresh bestowment of the Spirit, but **(2b)** a revival of His power, **(2a1)** developing the Christian life, **(2a2)** stressing the continual operation of the indwelling Spirit of God. Syn.: 3824. Palingenesis (3824) stresses the new birth; whereas, anakainosis stresses the process of sanctification. See: TDNT—3:453, 388; BAGD—55c; THAYER—38c.

343. **ἀνακαλύπτω** {2x} **anakaluptō,** *an-ak-al-oop'-to;* from *303* (in the sense of *reversal*) and *2572;* to *unveil:*—untaken away + 3361 {1x}, open {1x}.

Anakalupto means "to uncover, unveil," and is used in **(1)** 2 Cor 3:14 with the negative *me,* "not," is rendered "untaken away. "The best rendering seems to be, "the veil remains unlifted (for it is in Christ that it is done away)." Judaism does not recognize the vanishing of the glory of the Law as a means of life, under God's grace in Christ. **(2)** In 2 Cor 3:18 "open" continues the metaphor of the veil (vv. 13–17), referring to hindrances to the perception of spiritual realities, hindrances removed in the unveiling. See: TDNT—3:560, 405; BAGD—55c; THAYER—38c.

344. **ἀνακάμπτω** {4x} **anakamptō,** *an-ak-amp'-to;* from *303* and *2578;* to *turn back:*—return {3x}, turn again {1x}.

Anakampto, as a verb, means "to turn or bend back": "And being warned of God in a dream that they [the magi] should not return to Herod, they departed into their own country another way" (Mt 2:12; cf. Lk 10:6; Acts 18:21; Heb 11:15). Syn.: 360, 390, 1880, 1877, 1994, 5290. See: BAGD—55c; THAYER—38d.

345. **ἀνακεῖμαι** {14x} **anakĕimai,** *an-ak-i'-mahee;* from *303* and *2749;* to *recline* (as a corpse or at a meal):—sit at meat {5x}, guests {2x}, sit {2x}, sit down {1x}, be set down {1x}, lie {1x}, lean {1x}, at the table {1x}.

Anakeimai, as a verb, means "to recline at table" and is rendered **(1)** "to sit at meat" (Mt 9:10; 26:7); **(2)** Mt 26:20"He sat down" (cf. Mk 16:14; Lk 7:37; 22:27 [twice]); **(3)** in Mk 14:18, "sat"; **(4)** in Jn 6:11 "were set down." Syn.: 339, 347, 377, 1910, 2516, 2521, 2621, 2523, 2625, 4775, 4776, 4873. See: TDNT—3:654, 425; BAGD—55d; THAYER—38d.

346. **ἀνακεφαλαίομαι** {2x} **anakĕphalaiŏmai,** *an-ak-ef-al-ah'-ee-om-ahee;* from *303* and *2775* (in its or. sense); to *sum up:*—briefly comprehend {1x}, gather together in one {1x}.

Anakephalaioo means to sum up, gather up, to present as a whole and is used **(1)** in the passive voice in Rom 13:9: "For this, Thou shalt not commit adultery, Thou shalt not kill, Thou shalt not steal, Thou shalt not bear false witness, Thou shalt not covet; and if *there be* any other commandment, it is briefly comprehended (*anakephalaiomai*) in this saying, namely, Thou shalt love thy neighbour as thyself"; i.e., the one commandment expresses all that the Law enjoins, and to obey this one is to fulfil the Law (cf. Gal 5:14); and **(2)** in the middle voice in Eph 1:10: "That in the dispensation of the fulness of times He might gather together (anakephalaioo) in one all things in Christ, both which are in heaven, and which are on earth; *even* in Him", of God's purpose to "sum up" all things in the heavens and on the earth in Christ, a consummation extending beyond the limits of the church, though the latter is to be a factor in its realization. See: TDNT—3:681, 429; BAGD—55d; THAYER—38d.

347. **ἀνακλίνω** {8x} **anaklinō**, *an-ak-lee'-no;* from *303* and *2827;* to *lean back:*—sit down {3x}, make sit down {2x}, sit down to meat {1x}, make sit down to meat {1x}, lay {1x}.

Anaklino, as a verb, means "to cause to recline, make to sit down," and is used **(1)** in the active voice: "Blessed *are* those servants, whom the lord when he cometh shall find watching: verily I say unto you, that he shall gird himself, and make them to sit down (*anaklino*) to meat, and will come forth and serve them" (Lk 12:37; cf. Lk 2:7 of "laying" the infant Christ in the manger); and **(2)** in the passive: "And I say unto you, That many shall come from the east and west, and shall sit down with Abraham, and Isaac, and Jacob, in the kingdom of heaven" (Mt 8:11; 14:19; Mk 6:39; Lk 7:36; 9:15; 13:29). Syn.: 339, 345, 377, 1910, 2516, 2521, 2621, 2523, 2625, 4775, 4776, 4873. See: BAGD—56a; THAYER—39a.

348. **ἀνακόπτω** {1x} **anakŏptō**, *an-ak-op'-to;* from *303* and *2875;* to *beat back,* i.e. *check:*—hinder {1x}. See: BAGD—56b; THAYER—39a.

349. **ἀνακράζω** {5x} **anakrazō**, *an-ak-rad'-zo;* from *303* and *2896;* to *scream up* (aloud):—cry out {5x}.

Anakrazo, as a verb, [ana, "up," intensive], signifies "to cry out loudly": "And there was in their synagogue a man with an unclean spirit; and he cried out" (Mk 1:23; 6:49; Lk 4:33; 8:28; 23:18). Syn.: 310, 994, 995, 1916, 2019, 2896, 2905, 2906, 5455. See: TDNT—3:898, 465; BAGD—56b; THAYER—39a.

350. **ἀνακρίνω** {16x} **anakrinō**, *an-ak-ree'-no;* from *303* and *2919;* prop. to *scrutinize,* i.e. (by impl.) *investigate, interrogate, determine:*—examine {6x}, judge {6x}, ask question {2x}, search {1x}, discern {1x}.

Anakrino, as a verb, means "to judge," and sometimes has the meaning to ask a question: "Whatsoever is sold in the shambles, *that* eat, asking no question for conscience sake:" (1 Cor 10:25; cf. 10:27). Syn.: 154, 155, 1833, 1905, 2065, 3004, 4441. See: TDNT—3:943, 469; BAGD—56b; THAYER—39b.

351. **ἀνάκρισις** {1x} **anakrisis**, *an-ak'-ree-sis;* from *350;* a (judicial) *investigation:*—examination {1x}.

This word means to distinguish and was a legal term denoting the preliminary investigation for gathering evidence for the information of the judges: "Of whom I have no certain thing to write unto my lord. Wherefore I have brought him forth before you, and specially before thee, O king Agrippa, that, after examination (*anakrisis*) had, I might have somewhat to write" (Acts 25:26). See: TDNT—3:943, 469; BAGD—56c; THAYER—39b.

352. **ἀνακύπτω** {4x} **anakuptō**, *an-ak-oop'-to;* from *303* (in the sense of *reversal*) and *2955;* to *unbend,* i.e. *rise;* fig. *be elated:*—lift up (one's) self {3x}, look up {1x}.

Anakupto, as a verb, means "to lift oneself up" and is translated "look up": "And when these things begin to come to pass, then look up (*anakupto*), and lift up your heads; for your redemption draweth nigh" (Lk 21:28 of being elated in joyous expectation). Syn.: 308, 578, 816, 872, 991, 1689, 1896, 1914, 1980, 1983, 2300, 2334, 3706, 3708, 3879, 4017, 4648. See: BAGD—56c; THAYER—39c.

353. **ἀναλαμβάνω** {13x} **analambanō**, *an-al-am-ban'-o;* from *303* and *2983;* to *take up:*—take up {4x}, receive up {3x}, take {3x}, take in {2x}, take into {1x}.

Analambano, as a verb, means "to take up, to take to oneself, receive" and is rendered "to receive": "So then after the Lord had spoken unto them, He was received up into heaven, and sat on the right hand of God" (Mk 16:19; cf. Acts 1:2, 11, 22; 10:16; 1 Ti 3:16). Syn.: 324, 354, 568, 588, 618, 1209, 1523, 1926, 2210, 2865, 2975, 2983, 3028, 3335, 3336, 3858, 3880, 3970, 4327, 4355, 4356, 4380, 4381, 4382, 5562, 5264, 5274. See: TDNT—4:7, 495; BAGD—56d; THAYER—39c.

354. **ἀνάληψις** {1x} **analēpsis**, *an-al'-aip-sis;* from *353; ascension:*—receive up {1x}.

Analepsis, as a noun, means "a taking up" and is used in Lk 9:51 with reference to Christ's ascension; "that He should be received up" is, lit., "of the receiving up (of Him): "And it came to pass, when the time was come that He should be received up (*analepsis*), He stedfastly set His face to go to Jerusalem." Syn.: 324, 353, 568, 588, 618, 1209, 1523, 1926, 2210, 2865, 2975, 2983, 3028, 3335, 3336, 3858, 3880, 3970, 4327, 4355, 4356, 4380, 4381, 4382, 5562, 5264, 5274. See: TDNT—4:7, 495; BAGD—57a; THAYER—39c.

355. **ἀναλίσκω** {3x} **analiskō**, *an-al-is'-ko;* from *303* and a form of the alt. of *138;* prop. to *use up,* i.e. *destroy:*—consume {3x}.

Analisko means to use up, spend up, especially in a bad sense, to destroy and is said of the destruction of persons **(1)** literally: "And when His disciples James and John saw *this,* they said, Lord, wilt thou that we command fire to come down from heaven, and consume them, even as Elias did?" (Lk 9:54); and **(2)** metaphorically: "But if ye bite and devour one another, take heed that ye be not consumed one of another" (Gal 5:15; 2 Th 2:8). Syn: 2654, 853. See: BAGD—57a; THAYER—39c.

356. **ἀναλογία** {1x} **analŏgia**, *an-al-og-ee'-ah;* from a comp. of *303* and *3056; proportion:*—proportion {1x}.

Analogia [cf. Eng., "analogy"] signified the right relation, the coincidence or agreement existing or demanded according to the standard of the several relations, not agreement as equality. **(1)** It is used in Rom 12:6: "Having then gifts differing according to the grace that is given to us, whether prophecy, *let us prophesy* according to the proportion (*analogia*) of faith" where "let us prophesy according to the proportion of faith." **(2)** It recalls 12: 3: "For I say, through the grace given unto me, to every man that is among you, not to think *of himself* more highly than he ought to think; but to think soberly, according as God hath dealt to every man the measure of faith." **(3)** It is a warning against going beyond what God has given and faith receives. **(4)** "Proportion" here represents its true meaning. **(5)** The fact that there is a definite article before "faith" in the original does not necessarily afford an intimation that the faith, the body of Christian doctrine, is here in view. **(5a)** The presence of the definite article is due to the fact that faith is an abstract noun. **(5b)** The meaning "the faith" is not relevant to the context. See: TDNT—1:347, 56; BAGD—57b; THAYER—39d.

357. **ἀναλογίζομαι** {1x} **analŏgizŏmai**, *an-al-og-id'-zom-ahee;* mid. voice from *356;* to *estimate,* i.e. (fig.) *contemplate:*—consider {1x}.

Analogizomai means "to consider": "For consider Him that endured such contradiction of sinners against Himself, lest ye be wearied and faint in your minds" (Heb 12:3). See: BAGD—57b; THAYER—39d.

358. **ἄναλος** {1x} **analŏs**, *an'-al-os;* from *1* (as a neg. particle) and *251; saltless,* i.e. *insipid:*—lose saltness + 1096 {1x}.

Analos denotes "saltless, insipid, have lost its saltness" lit., "have become (ginomai) saltless (*analos*)" (Mk 9:50). Salt looses its saltness when it clumps together and becomes useless. Syn.: 233, 251, 252. See: BAGD—57b; THAYER—39d.

359. **ἀνάλυσις** {1x} **analusis**, *an-al'-oo-sis;* from *360; departure:*—departure {1x}.

Analusis, as a noun, means "an unloosing" [as of things woven], "a dissolving into separate parts" [Eng., "analysis"], and is once used of "departure from life": "For I am now ready to be offered, and the time of my departure is at hand" (2 Ti 4:6), where the metaphor is either nautical, from loosing from moorings [thus used in Greek poetry], or military, from breaking up an encampment. Syn.: 867, 1841. See: TDNT—4:337, 543; BAGD—57b; THAYER—39d.

360. **ἀναλύω** {2x} **analuō**, *an-al-oo'-o;* from *303* and *3089;* to *break up,* i.e. *depart* (lit. or fig.):—return {1x}, depart {1x}.

(1) *Analuo* literally means to unloose, undo, and signifies to depart in the sense of departing from life; a metaphor drawn from loosing moorings preparatory to setting sail. **(2)** *Analuo,* as a verb, means "to depart [die]" in Phil 1:23: "For I am in a strait betwixt two, having a desire to depart, and to be with Christ; which is far better" and **(3)** signifies "to return" in Lk 12:36, used in a simile of the "return" of a lord for his servants after a marriage feast. Syn.: 344, 390, 630, 868, 1880, 1877, 1994, 3327, 3332, 5290. See: TDNT—4:337, 543; BAGD—57c; THAYER—40a.

361. **ἀναμάρτητος** {1x} **anamartētŏs**, *an-am-ar'-tay-tos;* from *1* (as a neg. particle) and a presumed der. of *264; sinless:*—without sin {1x}.

Anamartetos, as an adjective, means "without sin": "So when they continued asking Him, He lifted up himself, and said unto them, He that is without sin among you, let him first cast a stone at her" (Jn 8:7). Syn.: 264, 265, 266, 4258. See: TDNT—1:333, 51; BAGD—57c; THAYER—40a.

362. **ἀναμένω** {1x} **anamĕnō**, *an-am-en'-o;* from *303* and *3306;* to *await:*—wait for {1x}.

Anameno, as a verb, means "to wait for" [*ana,* "up," used intensively, and *meno,* "to abide"], and is used in 1 Th 1:10 of "waiting" for the Son of God from heaven: "And to wait for His Son from heaven, whom He raised from the dead, *even* Jesus, which delivered us from the wrath to come." The word carries with it the suggestion of "waiting" with patience and confident expectancy. See: BAGD—57d; THAYER—40a.

363. **ἀναμιμνήσκω** {6x} **anamimnēskō**, *an-am-im-nace'-ko;* from *303* and *3403;* to *remind;* (refl.) to *recollect:*—call to remembrance {2x}, call to mind {1x}, bring to

remembrance {1x}, remember {1x}, put to remembrance {1x}.

Anamimnesko, as a verb, means "to remind, call to remembrance" [*ana,* "up," *mimnesko,* "to remind", and is translated "called to mind": "And the second time the cock crew. And Peter called to mind the word that Jesus said unto him, Before the cock crow twice, thou shalt deny me thrice. And when he thought thereon, he wept" in Mk 14:72 (passive voice). See: BAGD—57d; THAYER—40b.

364. **ἀνάμνησις** {4x} **anamnēsis**, *an-am'-nay-sis;* from *363; recollection:*—remembrance {3x}, remembrance again {1x}.

Anamnesis means a remembrance and is used **(1)** in Christ's command in the institution of the Lord's Supper: "And He took bread, and gave thanks, and brake *it,* and gave unto them, saying, This is My body which is given for you: this do in remembrance of Me" (Lk 22:19; cf. 1 Cor 11:24, 25); not in memory of as in remembering a deceased loved one, but in an affectionate calling of the Person Himself to mind; **(2)** of the remembrance of sins: ""But in those *sacrifices there is* a remembrance again *made* of sins every year" (Heb 10:3). This is not just an external bringing to remembrance but an awakening of mind; a heart-felt conviction. Syn.: 3403, 3420, 3421, 5279, 5280. See: TDNT—1:348, 56; BAGD—58a; THAYER—40b.

365. **ἀνανεόω** {1x} **ananĕŏō**, *an-an-neh-o'-o;* from *303* and a der. of *3501;* to *renovate,* i.e. *reform:*—renew {1x}.

Ananeoo means to renew, make young and is used in Eph 4:23 "be renewed (in the spirit of your mind)." The renewal here mentioned is not that of the mind itself in its natural powers of memory, judgment and perception, but "the spirit of the mind"; which, under the controlling power of the indwelling Holy Spirit, directs its bent and energies God-ward in the enjoyment of fellowship with the Father and with His Son, Jesus Christ, and of the fulfillment of the will of God. Syn.: 340, 341, 342. See: TDNT—4:899, 628; BAGD—58a; THAYER—40b.

366. **ἀνανήφω** {1x} **ananēphō**, *an-an-ay'-fo;* from *303* and *3525;* to become *sober again,* i.e. (fig.) *regain* (one's) *senses:*—recover (one's) self {1x}.

Ananepho means to return to soberness as from a state of delirium or drunkenness and is used in 2 Ti 2:26: "And *that* they may recover themselves out of the snare of the devil, who are taken captive by him at his will"; said of those who, opposing the truth through accepting perversions of it, fall into the snare of the devil, become intoxicated with error. Syn.: 4982. See: BAGD—58b; THAYER—40c.

367. **Ἀνανίας** {11x} **Ananias**, *an-an-ee'-as;* of Heb. or. [2608]; *Ananias,* the name of three Isr.:—*Ananias* (of Damascus) {6x}, *Ananias* (of Jerusalem) {3x}, *Ananias* (high priest) {2x}. See: BAGD—58b; THAYER—40c.

368. **ἀναντίῤῥητος** {1x} **anantirrhētŏs**, *an-an-tir'-hray-tos;* from *1* (as a neg. particle) and a presumed der. of a comp. of *473* and *4483; indisputable:*—cannot be spoken against + 5607 {1x}.

Anantirrhetos literally means "not to be spoken against" [*a,* negative, *n,* euphonic, *anti,* "against," *rhetos,* "spoken"], and is rendered "cannot be gainsaid, spoken against": "Seeing then that these things cannot be spoken against, ye ought to be quiet, and to do nothing rashly" (Acts 19:36). Syn.: 369, 483, 485. See: BAGD—58c; THAYER—40c.

369. **ἀναντιῤῥήτως** {1x} **anantirrhētōs**, *an-an-tir-hray'-toce;* adv. from *368; promptly:*—without gainsaying {1x}.

Anantirrhetos, corresponds to 368 and is translated "without gainsaying": "Therefore came I *unto you* without gainsaying, as soon as I was sent for: I ask therefore for what intent ye have sent for me?" (Acts 10:29 it might be rendered "unquestioningly"). See: BAGD—58c; THAYER—40c.

370. **ἀνάξιος** {1x} **anaxiŏs**, *an-ax'-ee-os;* from *1* (as a neg. particle) and *514; unfit:*—unworthy {1x}.

Anaxios [*a,* negative, *n,* euphonic, *axios,* "worthy"] means "unworthy" and is used in 1 Cor 6:2: "Do ye not know that the saints shall judge the world? and if the world shall be judged by you, are ye unworthy to judge the smallest matters?" See: TDNT—1:379, 63; BAGD—58c; THAYER—40d.

371. **ἀναξίως** {2x} **anaxiōs**, *an-ax-ee'-oce;* adv. from *370; irreverently:*—unworthily {2x}.

Anaxios is used in 1 Cor 11:27 of partaking of the Lord's Supper "unworthily," i.e., treating it as a common meal, the bread and cup as common things, not apprehending their solemn symbolic import: "Wherefore whosoever shall eat this bread, and drink *this* cup of the Lord, unworthily, shall be guilty of the body and blood of the Lord (cf. 11:19)." Syn.: 370. See: BAGD—58d; THAYER—40d.

372. **ἀνάπαυσις** {5x} **anapausis**, *an-ap'-ŏw-sis;* from *373; intermission;* by impl. *recreation:*—rest {4x}, rest + 2192 {1x}.

Anapausis means cessation, refreshment, rest, and is used in Mt 11:29: "Take My yoke upon you, and learn of Me; for I am meek and lowly in heart: and ye shall find rest unto your souls"; where the contrast is with the burdens imposed by the Pharisees. Christ's rest is not a rest from work, but in work; not the rest of inactivity but of the harmonious working of all the faculties and affections—of will, heart, imagination, conscience—because each has found in God the ideal sphere for its satisfaction and development. Syn.: 373, 425, 1879, 1981, 2270, 2663, 2664, 2681, 2838, 4520. See: TDNT—1:350, 56; BAGD—58d; THAYER—40d.

373. **ἀναπαύω** {12x} **anapauō**, *an-ap-ow'-o;* from *303* and *3973;* (refl.) to *repose* (lit. or fig. [*be exempt*], *remain*); by impl. to *refresh:*—rest {4x}, refresh {4x}, take rest {2x}, give rest {1x}, take ease {1x}.

(1) *Anapauo* signifies to give intermission from labor, to give rest, to refresh so to recover strength. **(2)** It signifies "to cause or permit one to cease from any labor or movement" so as to recover strength. **(2a)** It implies previous toil and care. **(2b)** Its chief significance is that of taking, or causing to take, rest. **(2c)** It is used in the middle voice in Lk 12:19: "And I will say to my soul, Soul, thou hast much goods laid up for many years; take thine ease, eat, drink, *and* be merry," **(3)** "take (thine) ease" is indicative of unnecessary, self-indulgent relaxation. (cf. Mt 11:28; Lk 12:19; 1 Cor 16:18). Syn.: 372, 425, 1879, 1981, 2270, 2663, 2664, 2681, 2838, 4520. See: TDNT—1:350, 56; BAGD—58d; THAYER—40d.

374. **ἀναπείθω** {1x} **anapĕithō**, *an-ap-i'-tho;* from *303* and *3982;* to *incite:*—persuade {1x}.

Anapeitho means "to persuade, induce," in an evil sense and is used in Acts 18:13: "Saying, This *fellow* persuadeth men to worship God contrary to the law." See: BAGD—59b; THAYER—41a.

375. **ἀναπέμπω** {4x} **anapĕmpō**, *an-ap-em'-po;* from *303* and *3992;* to *send up* or *back:*—send {2x}, send again {2x}.

Anapempo denotes **(1)** to send up to a higher authority: "And as soon as he [Pilate] knew that He belonged unto Herod's jurisdiction, he sent Him to Herod, who himself also was at Jerusalem at that time" (Lk 23:7; cf; 23:15; Acts 25:21); and **(2)** to send back: "And Herod with his men of war set Him at nought, and mocked *Him,* and arrayed Him in a gorgeous robe, and sent Him again to Pilate" (Lk 23:11; cf. Philem 12). Syn.: 649, 1599, 1821, 3343, 3992, 4842, 4882. See: BAGD—59b; THAYER—41a.

376. **ἀνάπηρος** {2x} **anapērŏs**, *an-ap'-ay-ros*); from *303* (in the sense of *intensity*) and πῆρος **pērŏs** (*maimed*); *crippled:*—maimed {2x}.

Anaperos means "crippled, maimed" [from *ana,* "up," and *peros,* "disabled in a limb"], and is found in Lk 14:13: "But when thou makest a feast, call the poor, the maimed (*anaperos*), the lame, the blind" (cf. Lk 14: 21). Syn.: 2948. See: BAGD—59c; THAYER—41b.

377. **ἀναπίπτω** {11x} **anapiptō**, *an-ap-ip'-to;* from *303* and *4098;* to *fall back,* i.e. *lie down, lean back:*—sit down {7x}, sit down to meat {2x}, be set down {1x}, lean {1x}.

Anapipto, as a verb, means literally "to fall back" [*ana,* "back," *pipto,* "to fall"], and is used of reclining at a repast and translated **(1)** "leaning back, [as he was, on Jesus' breast]": "He [the apostle John] then lying on Jesus' breast saith unto Him, Lord, who is it?" (Jn 13:25); **(2)** "leaned back": "Then Peter, turning about, seeth the disciple whom Jesus loved following; which also leaned on His breast at supper, and said, Lord, which is he that betrayeth thee?" (Jn 21:20 the apostle's reminder of the same event in his experience). **(3)** *Anapipto* also means "to fall back" and denotes "to recline for a repast [meal]": "And He commanded the multitude to sit down (*anapipto*) on the ground" (Mt 15:35; cf. Mk 6:40; 8:6; Lk 11:37; 14:10; 17:7; 22:14; Jn 6:10 [twice]; 13:12). Syn.: 339, 345, 347, 1910, 2516, 2521, 2621, 2523, 2625, 4775, 4776, 4873. See: BAGD—59c; THAYER—41b.

378. **ἀναπληρόω** {6x} **anaplērŏō**, *an-ap-lay-rŏ'-o;* from *303* and *4137;* to *complete;* by impl. to *occupy, supply;* fig. to *accomplish* (by coincidence or obedience):—fulfil {2x}, supply {2x}, occupy {1x}, fill up {1x}.

Anapleroo means "to fill up adequately, completely" and is translated **(1)** by the verb "occupieth": "Else when thou shalt bless with the spirit, how shall he that occupieth (*anapleroo*) the room of the unlearned say Amen at thy giving of thanks, seeing he understandeth not what thou sayest?" (1 Cor 14:16 of a believer as a member of an assembly, who "fills" the position or condition [not one who "fills" it by assuming it] of being unable to understand the language of him who had the gift of tongues; and **(2)** "to fill up their sins" of the Jews who persisted in their course of antagonism and unbelief: "Forbidding us to speak to the Gentiles that they might be saved, to fill up their sins alway: for the wrath is come upon them to the uttermost" (1 Th 2:16). Syn.: 466, 1072, 1705, 2880, 3325, 4130, 4137, 4845. See: TDNT—6:305, 867; BAGD—59d; THAYER—41b.

379. **ἀναπολόγητος** {2x} **anapŏlŏgētŏs**, *an-ap-ol-og'-ay-tos;* from *1* (as a neg. particle) and a presumed der. of *626;*

indefensible:—without excuse {1x}, inexcuseable {1x}.

Anapologetos means **(1)** "without excuse, inexcusable": "For the invisible things of Him from the creation of the world are clearly seen, being understood by the things that are made, *even* His eternal power and Godhead; so that they are without excuse", (Rom 1:20 "without excuse," of those who reject the revelation of God in creation); or **(1)** "inexcusable": "Therefore thou art inexcusable, O man, whosoever thou art that judgest: for wherein thou judgest another, thou condemnest thyself, for thou that judgest doest the same things" (Rom 2:1 of the Jew who judges the Gentile). See: BAGD—60a; THAYER—41c.

380. **ἀναπτύσσω** {1x} **anaptussō**, *an-ap-toos'-so;* from *303* (in the sense of *reversal*) and *4428;* to *unroll* (a scroll or volume):—open {1x}.

Anaptusso literally means "to unroll" [*ana,* "back," *ptusso,* "to roll"], and is found in Lk 4:17 (of the roll of Isaiah): "And there was delivered unto Him the book of the prophet Esaias. And when He had opened (*anaptusso*) the book, He found the place where it was written . . ." See: BAGD—60a; THAYER—41c.

381. **ἀνάπτω** {3x} **anaptō**, *an-ap'-to;* from *303* and *681;* to *enkindle:*—kindle {3x}.

Anapto means "to light up" and is used **(1)** literally, translated "kindleth" in Jas 3:5: "Even so the tongue is a little member, and boasteth great things. Behold, how great a matter a little fire kindleth!" (cf. Acts 28:2). **(2)** Metaphorically, in the passive voice, in Luke 12:49, of the "kindling" of the fire of hostility: "I am come to send fire on the earth; and what will I, if it be already kindled?" Syn.: 681, 4012. See: BAGD—60a; THAYER—41d.

382. **ἀναρίθμητος** {1x} **anarithmētŏs**, *an-ar-ith' may tos;* from *1* (as a neg. particle) and a der. of *705; unnumbered,* i.e. *without number:*—innumerable {1x}.

Anarithmetos, as a verb, [*a,* negative, *n,* euphonic, *arithmeo* "to number"] means a number too large to count: "Therefore sprang there even of one, and him [Abraham] as good as dead, *so many* as the stars of the sky in multitude, and as the sand which is by the sea shore innumerable" (Heb 11:12). Syn.: 3461. See: BAGD—60a; THAYER—41d.

383. **ἀνασείω** {2x} **anasĕiō**, *an-as-i'-o;* from *303* and *4579;* fig. to *excite:*—move {1x}, stir up {1x}.

Anaseio, as a verb, primarily denotes "to shake back or out, move to and fro"; then, "to stir up," used metaphorically **(1)** in Mk 15:11: "But the chief priests moved the people, that he [Pilate] should rather release Barabbas unto them" (cf. Lk 23:5). Syn.: 329, 387, 1326, 1892, 2042, 3947, 3951, 4531, 4579, 4787, 4797, 5017. See: BAGD—60a; THAYER—41d.

384. **ἀνασκευάζω** {1x} **anaskĕuazō**, *an-ask-yoo-ad'-zo;* from *303* (in the sense of *reversal*) and a der. of *4632;* prop. to *pack up* (baggage), i.e. (by impl. and fig.) to *upset:*—subvert {1x}.

Anaskeuazo primarily means "to pack up baggage"; hence, from a military point of view, to dismantle a town, to plunder and is used metaphorically in Acts 15:24, of unsettling or subverting the souls of believers: "Forasmuch as we have heard, that certain which went out from us have troubled you with words, subverting (*anaskeuazo*) your souls, saying, *Ye must* be circumcised, and keep the law: to whom we gave no *such* commandment." See: BAGD—60b; THAYER—41d.

385. **ἀνασπάω** {2x} **anaspaō**, *an-as-pah'-o;* from *303* and *4685;* to *take up* or *extricate:*—pull out {1x}, draw out {1x}.

Anaspao, as a verb, means "to draw up" and is used **(1)** of "drawing up, pulling out" an animal out of a pit: "And answered them, saying, Which of you shall have an ass or an ox fallen into a pit, and will not straightway pull him out on the sabbath day?" (Lk 14:5), and **(2)** of the "drawing" up of the sheet into heaven, in the vision in Acts 11:10: "And this was done three times: and all were drawn up again into heaven." Syn.: 307, 392, 501, 502, 645, 868, 1096, 1670, 1448, 1828, 2020, 2464, 4317, 4334, 4358, 4685, 4951, 5288, 5289. See: BAGD—60b; THAYER—41d.

386. **ἀνάστασις** {42x} **anastasis**, *an-as'-tas-is;* from *450;* a *standing up* again, i.e. (lit.) a *resurrection* from death (individual, gen. or by impl. [its author]), or (fig.) a (moral) *recovery* (of spiritual truth):—resurrection {39x}, rising again {1x}, that should rise {1x}, raised to life again + 1537 {1x}.

Anastasis denotes **(1)** a raising up, or rising; literally, "to cause to stand up on one's feet again": "And Simeon blessed them, and said unto Mary his mother, Behold, this *child* is set for the fall and rising again of many in Israel; and for a sign which shall be spoken against" (Lk 2:34—the Child would be like a stone over which many in Israel would stumble; while many others would find in its strength and firmness a means of their salvation and spiritual life. They would be caused to rise up and once again to lean upon the Creator they had been rejecting. Jesus, the stone, the corner stone would be the One against Whom they would return and lean against (cf. Mt 21:24; Acts 4:11; 26:26; Eph 2:20; 1 Pet 2:6–7);

(2) of resurrection from the dead, **(2a)** of Christ: "Beginning from the baptism of John, unto that same day that He was taken up from us, must one be ordained to be a witness with us of His resurrection" (Acts 1:22; cf. 2:31; 4:33; Rom 1:4; 6:5; Phil 3:10); **(2b)** of those who are Christ's at His Parousia: "And thou shalt be blessed; for they cannot recompense thee: for thou shalt be recompensed at the resurrection of the just" (Lk 14:14); **(2c)** of the rest of the dead, after the Millennium: "But the rest of the dead lived not again until the thousand years were finished. This *is* the first resurrection" (Rev 20:5); **(2d)** of those who were raised in more immediate connection with Christ's resurrection: "That Christ should suffer, *and* that He should be the first that should rise from the dead, and should shew light unto the people, and to the Gentiles" (Acts 26:23); **(2e)** of the resurrection spoken of in general terms: "The same day came to Him the Sadducees, which say that there is no resurrection, and asked Him" (Mt 22:23; Mk 12:18); **(2f)** of those who were raised in OT times, to die again: "Women received their dead raised to life again: and others were tortured, not accepting deliverance; that they might obtain a better resurrection" (Heb 11:35). Syn.: *Anastasis* stresses the final state of the one raised [upon his own feet]; whereas, exanastasis (1815) stresses the state from which the one was raised; and *egersis* (1454) stresses the invigoration which raises the one up. See: TDNT—1:371, 60; BAGD—60b; THAYER—41d.

387. **ἀναστατόω** {3x} **anastatŏō**, *an-as-tat-ŏ'-o;* from a der. of *450* (in the sense of *removal*); prop. to *drive out* of home, i.e. (by impl.) to *disturb* (lit. or fig.):—turn upside down {1x}, make an uproar {1x}, trouble {1x}.

Anastatoo, as a verb, means "to excite, unsettle" and is used **(1)** of "stirring up, turned upside down" to sedition, and tumult: "And when they found them not, they drew Jason and certain brethren unto the rulers of the city, crying, These that have turned the world upside down are come hither also" (Acts 17:6; cf. 21:38); **(2)** "to upset, trouble" by false teaching: "I would they were even cut off which trouble you" (Gal 5:12). Syn.: 329, 383, 1326, 1892, 2042, 3947, 3951, 4531, 4579, 4787, 4797, 5017. See: BAGD—61a; THAYER—42b.

388. **ἀνασταυρόω** {1x} **anastaurŏō**, *an-as-tŏw-rŏ'-o;* from *303* and *4717;* to *recrucify* (fig.):—crucify afresh {1x}.

Anastauroo is used in Heb 6:6 of Hebrew apostates, who as merely nominal Christians, in turning back to Judaism, were thereby virtually guilty of "crucifying" Christ again: "If they shall fall away, to renew them again unto repentance; seeing they crucify to themselves the Son of God afresh, and put *Him* to an open shame" See: TDNT—7:583, 1071; BAGD—61a; THAYER—42b.

389. **ἀναστενάζω** {1x} **anastĕnazō**, *an-as-ten-ad'-zo;* from *303* and *4727;* to *sigh deeply:*—sigh deeply {1x}.

Anastenazo means "to sigh deeply" [*ana,* "up," suggesting "deep drawn," and *stenazo* (4727), "to groan,"], and occurs in Mk 8:12: "And He sighed deeply in His spirit, and saith, Why doth this generation seek after a sign? verily I say unto you, There shall no sign be given unto this generation" See: BAGD—61b; THAYER—42b.

390. **ἀναστρέφω** {11x} **anastrĕphō**, *an-as-tref'-o;* from *303* and *4762;* to *overturn;* also to *return;* by impl. to *busy* oneself, i.e. *remain, live:*—return {2x}, have conversation {2x}, live {2x}, abide {1x}, overthrow {1x}, behave (one's) self {1x}, be used {1x}, pass {1x}.

Anastrepho, as a verb, used metaphorically, in the middle voice, "to conduct oneself, behave, live," is translated "to live": **(1)** "honestly: "Pray for us: for we trust we have a good conscience, in all things willing to live honestly" (Heb 13:18); and **(2)** "in error": "For when they speak great swelling *words* of vanity, they allure through the lusts of the flesh, *through much* wantonness, those that were clean escaped from them who live in error" (2 Pet 2:18). Syn.: 326, 980, 1236, 2198, 2225, 4176, 4800, 5225. See: TDNT—7:715, 1093; BAGD—61b; THAYER—42b.

391. **ἀναστροφή** {13x} **anastrŏphē**, *an-as-trof-ay';* from *390; behavior:*—conversation {13x}.

Anastropha, as a noun, means literally "a turning back" and is translated "manner of life, living, conversation": "For ye have heard of my conversation in time past in the Jews' religion, how that beyond measure I persecuted the church of God, and wasted it" (Gal 1:13; Eph 4:22; 1 Ti 4:12; Heb 13:7; Jas 3:13; 1 Pet 1:15, 18; 2:1 "behavior"; 3:1, 2, 16; 2 Pet 2:7; 3:11). "Conversation" in English primarily means "give and take, back and forth" and pictures a life style of going and coming in every day events. Syn.: 2688. See: TDNT—7:715, 1093; BAGD—61c; THAYER—42c.

392. **ἀνατάσσομαι** {1x} **anatassŏmai**, *an-at-as'-som-ahee;* from *303* and the mid. voice of *5021;* to *arrange:*—set forth in order {1x}.

Anatassomai, as a verb, means "to arrange in order": "Forasmuch as many have taken in hand to set forth in order (*anatassomai*) a declaration of those things which are most surely believed among us" (Lk 1:1 - some interpret the word to mean to "bring together" from memory assisted by the Holy Spirit). Syn.: 307, 385, 501, 502, 645, 868, 1096, 1670, 1448, 1828, 2020,

2464, 4317, 4334, 4358, 4685, 4951, 5288, 5289. See: TDNT—8:32,*; BAGD—61d; THAYER—42d.

393. **ἀνατέλλω** {9x} **anatĕllō**, *an-at-el'-lo;* from *303* and the base of *5056;* to (*cause* to) *arise:*—be up {2x}, rise {2x}, spring up {1x}, make rise {1x}, at the rising of {1x}, spring {1x}, arise {1x}.

Anatello, as a verb, means "to arise" and is used especially of things in the natural creation: **(1)** metaphorically, of light: "The people which sat in darkness saw great light; and to them which sat in the region and shadow of death light is sprung up" (Mt 4:16); **(2)** of the sun: "That ye may be the children of your Father which is in heaven: for He maketh His sun to rise on the evil and on the good" (Mt 5:45; Mk 4:6; Jas 1:11); **(3)** of a cloud: "And He said also to the people, When ye see a cloud rise out of the west, straightway ye say, There cometh a shower; and so it is" (Lk 12:54); **(4)** of the day-star: "We have also a more sure word of prophecy; whereunto ye do well that ye take heed, as unto a light that shineth in a dark place, until the day dawn, and the day star arise in your hearts" (2 Pet 1:19); **(5)** metaphorically, of the Incarnation of Christ: "Our Lord hath sprung out of Judah" (Heb 7:14 - more lit., "Our Lord hath arisen out of Judah," as of the rising of the light of the sun). Syn.: 305, 450, 1096, 1326, 1453, 1525, 1817, 4911. See: TDNT—1:351, 57; BAGD—62a; THAYER—42d.

394. **ἀνατίθεμαι** {2x} **anatithĕmai**, *an-at-ith'-em-ahee;* from *303* and the mid. voice of *5087;* to *set forth* (for oneself), i.e. *propound:*—declare {1x}, communicate {1x}.

Anatithemai means to put up or before and is used of laying a case, declaring/detailing its parts, before an authority: "And when they had been there many days, Festus declared (*anathemai*) Paul's cause unto the king, saying, There is a certain man left in bonds by Felix" (Acts 25:14; cf. Gal 2:2). See: TDNT—1:353, 57; BAGD—62a; THAYER—42d.

395. **ἀνατολή** {10x} **anatŏlē**, *an-at-ol-ay';* from *393;* a *rising* of light, i.e. *dawn* (fig.); by impl. the *east* (also in plur.):—east {9x}, dayspring {1x}.

Anatole literally means "a rising up" and is used of the rising of the sun; **(1)** it chiefly means the east: "Now when Jesus was born in Bethlehem of Judaea in the days of Herod the king, behold, there came wise men from the east to Jerusalem" (Mt 2:1; cf. 2:2, 9; 8:11; 24:27; Lk 13:29; Rev 7:2; 16:12; 21:13); and it is also rendered **(2)** "dayspring": "Through the tender mercy of our God; whereby the dayspring from on high hath visited us" (Lk 1:78). See: TDNT—1:352, 57; BAGD—62b; THAYER—43a.

396. **ἀνατρέπω** {2x} **anatrĕpō**, *an-at-rep'-o;* from *303* and the base of *5157;* to *overturn* (fig.):—overthrow {1x}, subvert {1x}.

Anatrepo literally means "to turn up or over" [*ana,* "up," *trepo,* "to turn"] "to upset, overthrow" and is used metaphorically **(1)** in 2 Ti 2:18: "Who concerning the truth have erred, saying that the resurrection is past already; and overthrow the faith of some"; and **(2)** "subvert" in Titus 1:11: "Whose mouths must be stopped, who subvert whole houses, teaching things which they ought not, for filthy lucre's sake." See: BAGD—62c; THAYER—43a.

397. **ἀνατρέφω** {3x} **anatrĕphō**, *an-at-ref'-o;* from *303* and *5142;* to *rear* (phys. or ment.):—nourish {1x}, nourish up {1x}, bring up {1x}.

Anatrepho, as a verb, means **(1)** "to nourish": "In which time Moses was born, and was exceeding fair, and nourished up (*anatrepho*) in his father's house three months" (Acts 7:20; cf. 7:21); **(2)** "brought up": "I am verily a man *which am* a Jew, born in Tarsus, *a city* in Cilicia, yet brought up (*anatrepho*) in this city at the feet of Gamaliel" (Acts 22:3). See: BAGD—62d; THAYER—43a.

398. **ἀναφαίνω** {2x} **anaphainō**, *an-af-ah'-ee-no;* from *303* and *5316;* to *show,* i.e. (refl.) *appear,* or (pass.) to *have pointed* out:—appear {1x}, discover {1x}.

This word means to bring to light, hold up to view, to show, to appear, be made apparent. *Anaphaino* means "forth, or up," perhaps originally a nautical term, "to come up into view," hence, in general, "to appear suddenly," and is used **(1)** in the passive voice, in Lk 19:11, of the Kingdom of God: "And as they heard these things, He added and spake a parable, because He was nigh to Jerusalem, and because they thought that the kingdom of God should immediately appear (*anaphaino*)"; **(2)** active voice, in Acts 21:3 "to come in sight of": "Now when we had discovered (*anaphaino*) Cyprus, we left it on the left hand, and sailed into Syria, and landed at Tyre: for there the ship was to unlade her burden." See: BAGD—63a; THAYER—43b.

399. **ἀναφέρω** {10x} **anaphĕrō**, *an-af-er'-o;* from *303* and *5342;* to *take up* (lit. or fig.):—offer up {3x}, bear {2x}, offer {2x}, bring up {1x}, lead up {1x}, carry up {1x}.

Anaphero means up and is used of leading persons up to a higher place: **(1)** of the Lord's ascension: "And it came to pass, while He blessed them, He was parted from them, and carried up (*anaphero*) into heaven" (Lk 24:51); or **(2)** of the Lord's propitiatory sacrifice, in His bearing sins on the cross: "So Christ was once offered to bear the sins of many; and unto them that look for him shall he appear the second time without sin unto salvation" (Heb 9:28; cf. 1 Pet 2:24). **(3)** *Anaphero* also denotes "to bring up": "And after six days Jesus taketh Peter, James, and John his brother, and bringeth them up (*anaphero*) into an high mountain apart" (Mt 17:1). Syn.: 941, 5342. See: TDNT—9:60, 1252; BAGD—63a; THAYER—43b.

400. **ἀναφωνέω** {1x} **anaphōnĕō**, *an-af-o-neh'-o;* from *303* and *5455;* to *exclaim:*—speak out {1x}.

In Lk 1:42 *anaphoneo* means "to lift up one's voice," and is rendered "spake out": "And she spake out with a loud voice, and said, Blessed *art* thou among women, and blessed *is* the fruit of thy womb." See: BAGD—63b; THAYER—43c.

401. **ἀνάχυσις** {1x} **anachusis**, *an-akh'-oo-sis;* from a comp. of *303* and χέω **chĕō** (to *pour*); prop. *effusion,* i.e. (fig.) *license:*—excess {1x}.

Anachusis, literally means "a pouring out, overflowing" and is used metaphorically in 1 Pet 4:4: "Wherein they think it strange that ye run not with *them* to the same excess of riot, speaking evil of *you*" said of the riotous conduct described in vs 3. Syn.: 192, 193. See: BAGD—63c; THAYER—43c.

402. **ἀναχωρέω** {14x} **anachōrĕō**, *an-akh-o-reh'-o;* from *303* and *5562;* to *retire:*—depart {8x}, withdraw (one's) self {2x}, go aside {2x}, turn aside {1x}, give place {1x}.

Anachoreo, as a verb, means "to withdraw, to go back, recede, retire" [*ana,* "back or up," *choreo,* "to make room for, betake oneself," *choros,* "a place"], and is translated **(1)** "departed": "When Jesus therefore perceived that they would come and take Him by force, to make Him a king, He departed again into a mountain Himself alone" (Jn 6:15; cf. Mt 2:12–14; 4:12; 14:13; 15:21; 27:5); and **(2)** "turned aside": "But when he [Joseph] heard that Archelaus did reign in Judaea in the room of his father Herod, he was afraid to go thither: notwithstanding, being warned of God in a dream, he turned aside into the parts of Galilee" (Mt 2:22); and **(3)** "give place": "He said unto them, Give place: for the maid is not dead, but sleepeth. And they laughed him to scorn" (Mt 9:24). Syn.: 201, 1096, 1502, 3837, 4042, 5117, 5247, 5564, 5602. See: BAGD—63c; THAYER—43c.

403. **ἀνάψυξις** {1x} **anapsuxis**, *an-aps'-ook-sis;* from *404;* prop. a *recovery of breath,* i.e. (fig.) *revival:*—refeshing {1x}.

Anapsuxis means "a refreshing" and occurs in Acts 3:19: "Repent ye therefore, and be converted, that your sins may be blotted out, when the times of refreshing shall come from the presence of the Lord." See: TDNT—9:664, 1342; BAGD—63c; THAYER—43c.

404. **ἀναψύχω** {1x} **anapsuchō**, *an-aps-oo'-kho;* from *303* and *5594;* prop. to *cool off,* i.e. (fig.) *relieve:*—refresh {1x}.

This word means to cool again, to cool off, recover from the effects of heat; to refresh one's spirit [*ana,* "back," *psucho,* "to cool"] and is used in 2 Ti 1:16: "The Lord give mercy unto the house of Onesiphorus; for he oft refreshed me, and was not ashamed of my chain." See: TDNT—9:663, 1342; BAGD—63d; THAYER—43d.

405. **ἀνδραποδιστής** {1x} **andrapŏdistēs**, *an-drap-od-is-tace';* from a der. of a comp. of *435* and *4228;* an *enslaver* (as bringing *men* to his *feet*):—menstealer {1x}.

This word means "a slave dealer, kidnapper," from *andrapodon,* "a slave captured in war" a word found in the plural in the papyri, e.g., in a catalogue of property and in combination with *tetrapoda,* "four-footed things" (*andrapodon, aner,* "a man," *pous,* "a foot"); *andrapodon* "was never an ordinary word for slave; it was too brutally obvious a reminder of the principle which made quadruped and human chattels differ only in the number of their legs. The verb *andrapodizo* supplied the noun "with the like odious meaning": "For whoremongers, for them that defile themselves with mankind, for menstealers, for liars, for perjured persons, and if there be any other thing that is contrary to sound doctrine" (1Ti 1:10). See: BAGD—63d; THAYER—43d.

406. **Ἀνδρέας** {13x} **Andrĕas**, *an-dreh'-as;* from *435; manly; Andreas,* an Isr.:—Andrew {13x}. See: BAGD—63d; THAYER—43d.

407. **ἀνδρίζομαι** {1x} **andrizŏmai**, *an-drid'-zom-ahee;* mid. voice from *435;* to *act manly:*—quit you like men {1x}.

This word means to quit something that will free you to be a man; thus "quit you like men" means "stop present activities which frees you to be the man God calls you to be;" to make a man of or make brave; to show one's self a man: "Watch ye, stand fast in the faith, quit you like men, be strong." See: TDNT—1:360, 59; BAGD - 64a; THAYER—43d.

408. **Ἀνδρόνικος** {1x} **Andrŏnikŏs**, *an-dron'-ee-kos;* from *435* and *3534; man of victory; Andronicos,* an Isr.:—Adronicus {1x}. See: BAGD—64a; THAYER—43d.

409. **ἀνδροφόνος** {1x} **andrŏphŏnŏs**, *an-drof-on'-os;* from *435* and *5408;* a *murderer:*—manslayer {1x}.

This word comes from *aner,* "a man," and *phoneus,* "a murderer," and occurs in the plural in 1 Tim 1:9: "Knowing this, that the law is not made for a righteous man, but for the lawless and disobedient, for the ungodly and for sinners, for unholy and profane, for murderers of fathers and murderers of mothers, for manslayers (*androphonos*)." See: BAGD—64a; THAYER—44a.

410. **ἀνέγκλητος** {5x} **anĕgklētŏs**, *an-eng'-klay-tos;* from *1* (as a neg. particle) and a der. of *1458; unaccused,* i.e. (by impl.) *irreproachable:*—blameless {4x}, unreproveable {1x}.

Anenkletos, as an adjective, signifies "that which cannot be called to account" [from *a,* negative, *n,* euphonic, and *enkaleo,* "to call in"], i.e., with nothing laid to one's charge, as the result of public investigation, and is translated **(1)** "blameless": "Who shall also confirm you unto the end, *that ye may be* blameless in the day of our Lord Jesus Christ" (1 Cor 1:8; cf. 1 Ti 3:10; Titus 1:6–7); and **(2)** "unreproveable": "In the body of His flesh through death, to present you holy and unblameable and unreproveable in His sight" (Col 1:22). **(3)** It implies not merely acquittal, but the absence of even a charge or accusation against a person. This is to be the case with elders: "And let these also first be proved; then let them use the office of a deacon, being *found* blameless" (1 Ti 3:10; cf. Titus 1:6–7). Syn.: 273, 274, 298, 299, 338, 423, 2607, 3201, 3469. See: TDNT—1:356, 58; BAGD—64b; THAYER—44a.

411. **ἀνεκδιήγητος** {1x} **anĕkdiēgētŏs**, *an-ek-dee-ay'-gay-tos;* from *1* (as a neg. particle) and a presumed der. of *1555; not expounded* in full, i.e. *indescribable:*—unspeakable {1x}.

The stress of this word is that the object is inexpressible; i.e. adequate words cannot be found to correctly describe the object, which is in 2 Cor 9:15 the unspeakable of the gift of God—His Son, Jesus: "Thanks *be* unto God for His unspeakable gift." Some scholars feel this "gift" may be the Holy Spirit. Syn.: 412, 731. See: BAGD—64b; THAYER—44a.

412. **ἀνεκλάλητος** {1x} **anĕklalētŏs**, *an-ek-lal'-ay-tos;* from *1* (as a neg. particle) and a presumed der. of *1583; not spoken out,* i.e. (by impl.) *unutterable:*—unspeakable {1x}.

With this word, the words can be found, but due to joy, they are overwhelmed and not spoken: "Whom having not seen, ye love; in whom, though now ye see *Him* not, yet believing, ye rejoice with joy unspeakable and full of glory" (1 Pet 1:8). Syn.: 411, 731. See: BAGD—64b; THAYER—44a.

413. **ἀνέκλειπτος** {1x} **anĕklĕiptŏs**, *an-ek'-lipe-tos;* from *1* (as a neg. particle) and a presumed der. of *1587; not left out,* i.e. (by impl.) *inexhaustible:*—not to fail {1x}.

This word means "unfailing" and is rendered "that faileth not": "Sell that ye have, and give alms; provide yourselves bags which wax not old, a treasure in the heavens that faileth not (*anakleiptos*), where no thief approacheth, neither moth corrupteth" (Lk 12:33). See: BAGD—64b; THAYER—44a.

414. **ἀνεκτότερος** {6x} **anĕktŏtĕrŏs**, *an-ek-tot'-er-os;* comp. of a der. of *430; more endurable:*—more tolerable {6x}.

This word is used in its comparative form, *anektoteros:* "KJV Matthew 10:15 Verily I say unto you, It shall be more tolerable for the land of Sodom and Gomorrha in the day of judgment, than for that city" (Mt 10:15; cf 11:22, 24; Mar 6:11; Lk 10:12, 14). See: TDNT—1:359,*; BAGD—64c; THAYER—44a.

415. **ἀνελεήμων** {1x} **anĕlĕēmōn**, *an-eleh-ay'-mone;* from *1* (as a neg. particle) and *1655; merciless:*—unmerciful {1x}.

This word means "without mercy" [*a,* negative, *n,* euphonic, *eleemon,* "merciful"] and occurs in Rom 1:31: "Without understanding, covenantbreakers, without natural affection, implacable, unmerciful (*aneleemon*) . . ." See: TDNT—2:487, 222; BAGD—64c; THAYER—44a.

416. **ἀνεμίζω** {1x} **anemizō**, *an-em-id'-zo;* from *417;* to *toss with the wind:*—drive with the wind {1x}.

Anemizo means "to drive by the wind" [*anemos,* "wind"] and is used in Jas 1:6: "But let him ask in faith, nothing wavering. For he that wavereth is like a wave of the sea driven with the wind and tossed." See: BAGD—64c; THAYER—44b.

417. **ἄνεμος** {31x} **anĕmŏs**, *an'-em-os;* from the base of *109; wind;* (plur.) by impl. (the four) *quarters* (of the earth):—wind {31x}.

Anemos, **(1)** besides its literal meaning of a strong often tempestuous wind: "And the rain descended, and the floods came, and the winds (*anemos*) blew, and beat upon that house; and it fell not: for it was founded upon a rock" (Mt 7:25; cf. Jn 6:18; Acts 27:14; Jas 3:4), is used **(2)** metaphorically of variable teaching: "That we *henceforth* be no more children, tossed to and fro, and carried about with every wind of doctrine, by the sleight of men, *and* cunning craftiness, whereby they lie in wait to deceive" (Eph 4:14 – No one ever seen the wind; only its devastating after effects. God's gifted men are to be pro-active, preventing the winds from inflicting damage). **(3)** The four winds stand for the four cardinal points of the compass: "And He shall send His angels with a great sound of a trumpet, and they shall gather together His elect from the four winds, from one end of heaven to the other" (Mt 24:31; cf. Mk 13:27; Rev 7:1). **(4)** The contexts indicate that these are connected with the execution of divine judgments. Syn.: 2366, 2978, 4151, 4157. See: BAGD—64c; THAYER—44b.

418. **ἀνένδεκτος** {1x} **anĕndĕktŏs**, *an-en'-dek-tos;* from *1* (as a neg. particle) and a der. of the same as *1735; unadmitted,* i.e. (by impl.) *not supposable:*—impossible {1x}.

Anendektos signifies "inadmissible" [*a,* negative, *n,* euphonic, and *endechomai,* "to admit, allow"], of occasions of stumbling, where the meaning is "it cannot be but that they will come": "Then said He unto the disciples, It is impossible but that offences will come: but woe *unto him,* through whom they come!" (Lk 17:1). Syn.: 101, 102. See: BAGD—65a; THAYER—44b.

419. **ἀνεξερεύνητος** {1x} **anĕxĕrĕunētŏs**, *an-ex-er-yoo'-nay-tos;* from *1* (as a neg. particle) and a presumed der. of *1830; not searched out,* i.e. (by impl.) *inscrutable:*—unsearchable {1x}.

Anexereunetos, as an adjective [*a,* negative, *n,* euphonic, *ex* (*ek*), "out," *eraunao,* "to search, examine,"] is used in Rom 11:33, of the judgments of God: "O the depth of the riches both of the wisdom and knowledge of God! how unsearchable *are* His judgments, and His ways past finding out!" Syn.: 421. See: TDNT—1:357, 58; BAGD—65a; THAYER—44c.

420. **ἀνεξίκακος** {1x} **anĕxikakŏs**, *an-ex-ik'-ak-os;* from *430* and *2556; enduring of ill,* i.e. *forbearing:*—patient {1x}.

Anexikakos denotes "patiently forbearing evil," literally "patient of wrong," [from *anecho* and *kakos,* "evil"], "enduring"; it is rendered "forbearing": "And the servant of the Lord must not strive; but be gentle unto all *men,* apt to teach, patient (*anexikakos*)" (2 Ti 2:24). Syn.: 420, 430, 447, 463, 1933, 4722, 5339. See: TDNT—3:486, 391; BAGD—65a; THAYER—44c.

421. **ἀνεξιχνίαστος** {2x} **anĕxichniastŏs**, *an-ex-ikh-nee'-as-tos;* from *1* (as a neg. particle) and a presumed der. of a comp. of *1537* and a der. of *2487; not tracked out,* i.e. (by impl.) *untraceable:*—past finding out {1x}, unsearchable {1x}.

This word is rendered **(1)** "past finding out": "O the depth of the riches both of the wisdom and knowledge of God! how unsearchable *are* His judgments, and His ways past finding out!" (Rom 11:33) and **(2)** "unsearchable": "Unto me, who am less than the least of all saints, is this grace given, that I should preach among the Gentiles the unsearchable riches of Christ" (Eph 3:8). **(3)** The stress is on the fact that God's ways are not ways that leave a trail behind; they are unique for each situation. See: TDNT—1:358, 58; BAGD—65a; THAYER—44c.

422. **ἀνεπαίσχυντος** {1x} **anĕpaischuntŏs**, *an-ep-ah'-ee-skhoon-tos;* from *1* (as a neg. particle) and a presumed der. of a comp. of *1909* and *153; not ashamed,* i.e. (by impl.) *irreprehensible:*—that needeth not to be ashamed {1x}. See: BAGD—65a; THAYER—44c.

423. **ἀνεπίληπτος** {3x} **anĕpilēptŏs**, *an-ep-eel'-ape-tos;* from *1* (as a neg. particle) and a der. of *1949; not arrested,* i.e. (by impl.) *inculpable:*—blameless {2x}, unrebukeable {1x}.

Anepileptos, as an adjective, literally means "that cannot be laid hold of"; hence, "not open to censure, irreproachable" and is translated **(1)** "blameless": "A bishop then must be blameless, the husband of one wife, vigilant, sober, of good behaviour, given to hospitality, apt to teach" (1 Ti 3:2; cf. 5:7) and **(2)** "unrebukeable": "That thou keep *this* commandment without spot, unrebukeable, until the appearing of our Lord Jesus Christ" (1 Ti 6:14). Syn.: 273, 274, 298, 299, 338, 410, 2607, 3201, 3469. See: TDNT—4:9, 495; BAGD—65b; THAYER—44c.

424. **ἀνέρχομαι** {3x} **anĕrchŏmai**, *an-erkh'-om-ahee;* from *303* and *2064;* to *ascend:*—go up {3x}.

Anerchomai means "to go up" and occurs in Jn 6:3: "And Jesus went up (*anerchomai*) into a mountain, and there He sat with his disciples" (cf. Gal 1:17, 18). See: BAGD—65b; THAYER—44c.

425. **ἄνεσις** {5x} **anĕsis**, *an'-es-is;* from *447; relaxation* or (fig.) *relief:*—eased {1x}, liberty {1x}, rest {3x}.

Anesis denotes a letting loose, relaxation, easing and signifies rest, not from toil, but from endurance and suffering. Thus it is said **(1)** of a less vigorous condition in imprisonment: "And he commanded a centurion to keep Paul, and to let *him* have liberty (*anesis*), and that he should forbid none of his acquaintance to minister or come unto him" (Acts 24:23), **(2)** relief from anxiety: "I had no rest (*anesis*) in my spirit, because I found not Titus my brother: but taking my leave of them, I went from thence into Macedonia" (2 Cor 2:13; cf. 7:5), **(3)** relief from persecutions: "And to you who are troubled rest (*anesis*) with us, when the Lord Jesus shall be revealed from heaven with His mighty angels" (2 Th 1:7), **(4)** of relief from the sufferings of poverty": "For *I mean* not that other men be eased (*anesis*), and ye burdened" (2 Cor 8:13). Syn.: 373; see esp. 372. See: TDNT—1:367, 60; BAGD—65b; THAYER—44d.

426. **ἀνετάζω** {2x} **anĕtazō**, *an-et-ad'-zo;* from *303* and ἐτάζω **ĕtazō** (to *test*); to *investigate* (judicially):—(should have) examine (-d) {2x}.

Anetazo means "to examine judicially" [*ana*, "up," *etazo*, "to test"], and is used in Acts 22:24: "The chief captain commanded him to be brought into the castle, and bade that he should be examined (*anetazo*) by scourging; that he might know wherefore they cried so against him" (cf. Acts 22:29). Syn.: 1833. See: TDNT—1:367, 60; BAGD—65c; THAYER—44d.

427. **ἄνευ** {3x} **anĕu**, *an'-yoo;* a prim. particle; *without:*—without {3x}.

This word stresses without one's will or intervention: "Are not two sparrows sold for a farthing? and one of them shall not fall on the ground without (*aneu*) your Father" (Mat 10:19; cf. 1 Pe 3:1; 4:9). See: BAGD—65c; THAYER—44d. comp. *1*.

428. **ἀνεύθετος** {1x} **anĕuthĕtŏs**, *an-yoo'-the-tos;* from *1* (as a neg. particle) and *2111; not well set,* i.e. *inconvenient:*—not commodious {1x}.

Aneuthetos means "not commodious," literally "not-well-placed" [from *a*, "not," *n*, euphonic, *eu*, "well," *thetos*, "from" *tithemi* "to put, place"] and is found in Acts 27:12, where it is said of the haven at the place called Fair Havens: "And because the haven was not commodious (*aneuthetos*) to winter in, the more part advised to depart thence also, if by any means they might attain to Phenice, *and there* to winter; *which is* an haven of Crete, and lieth toward the south west and north west." See: BAGD—65c; THAYER—44d.

429. **ἀνευρίσκω** {2x} **anĕuriskō**, *an-yoo-ris'-ko;* from *303* and *2147; to find out:*—find {2x}.

Aneurisko means "to find out" (by search), "discover" implying diligent searching and is used **(1)** in Lk 2:16, of the shepherds in searching for and "finding" Mary and Joseph and the Child: "And they came with haste, and found Mary, and Joseph, and the babe lying in a manger"; and **(2)** in Acts 21:4, of Paul and his companions, in searching for and "finding" "the disciples" at Tyre: "And finding (*aneurisko*) disciples, we tarried there seven days: who said to Paul through the Spirit, that he should not go up to Jerusalem." See: BAGD—65c; THAYER—44d.

430. **ἀνέχομαι** {15x} **anĕchŏmai**, *an-ekh'-om-ahee;* mid. voice from *303* and *2192; to hold oneself up* against, i.e. (fig.) *put up* with:—bear with {4x}, endure {2x}, forbear {2x}, suffer {7x}.

This word signifies "to hold up against a thing and so to bear with" [*ana*, "up," and *echomai*, the middle voice of *echo*, "to have, to hold"]: "Then Jesus answered and said, O faithless and perverse generation, how long shall I be with you? how long shall I suffer you? bring him hither to Me" (Mt 17:17; cf. 1 Cor 4:12; 2 Cor 11:1, 4, 19–20; Heb 13:22). See: TDNT—1:359,* BAGD—65d; THAYER—44d.

431. **ἀνέψιος** {1x} **anĕpsiŏs**, *an-eps'-ee-os;* from *1* (as a particle of union) and an obs. νέπος **nĕpŏs** (a *brood*); prop. *akin,* i.e. (spec.) a *cousin:*—sister's son {1x}.

This word denotes a nephew; hence we are to understand, therefore, that Mark was the cousin of Barnabas. See: BAGD—66a; THAYER—45a.

432. **ἄνηθον** {1x} **anēthŏn**, *an'-ay-thon;* prob. of for. or.; *dill:*—anise {1x}.

This word means "dill, anise" and was used for food and for pickling: "Woe unto you, scribes and Pharisees, hypocrites! for ye pay tithe of mint and anise and cummin, and have omitted the weightier *matters* of the law, judgment, mercy, and faith: these ought ye to have done, and not to leave the other undone" (Mt 23:23). See: BAGD—66a; THAYER—45a.

433. **ἀνήκω** {3x} **anēkō**, *an-ay'-ko;* from *303* and *2240; to attain to,* i.e. (fig.) *be proper:*—convenient {2x}, be fit {1x}.

Aneko means **(1)** primarily "to have arrived at, reached to, pertained to," came to denote "what is due to a person, one's duty, what is befitting." **(2)** It is used ethically in the NT: **(2a)** Eph 5:4: "Neither filthiness, nor foolish talking, nor jesting, which are not convenient (*aneko*): but rather giving of thanks"; **(2b)** "Wives, submit yourselves unto your own husbands, as it is fit (*aneko*) in the Lord" (Col. 3:18 concerning the duty of wives towards husbands). **(2c)** In Philem 8, the participle is used with the article, signifying "that which is convenient": "Wherefore, though I might be much bold in Christ to enjoin thee that which is convenient (*aneko*)." See: TDNT—1:359,* BAGD—66b; THAYER—45b.

434. **ἀνήμερος** {1x} **anēmĕrŏs**, *an-ay'-mer-os;* from *1* (as a neg. particle) and ἥμερος **hēmĕrŏs** (*lame, gentle*); *not tame, savage:*—fierce {1x}.

This word signifies "not tame, savage" [from *a* negative, and *hemeros*, "gentle"]: "Without natural affection, trucebreakers, false accusers, incontinent, fierce (*anemeros*), despisers of those that are good" (2 Ti 3:3). See: BAGD—66c; THAYER—45b.

435. **ἀνήρ** {215x} **anēr**, *an-ayr';* a prim. word [comp. *444*]; a *man* (prop. as an indiv. male):—fellow {1x}, husband {50x}, man {156x}, sir {6x}, not trans. {2x}.

Aner is never used of the female sex; it stands **(1)** in distinction from a woman: "But when they believed Philip preaching the things concerning the kingdom of God, and the name of Jesus Christ, they were baptized, both men and women" (Acts 8:12; cf. 1 Ti 2:12); **(2)** as a husband: "And Jacob begat Joseph the husband of Mary, of whom was born Jesus, who is called Christ" (Mt 1:16; cf. Jn 4:16; Rm 7:2); **(3)** as distinct from a boy or infant: "When I was a child, I spake as a child, I understood as a child, I thought as a child: but when I became a man, I put away childish things" (1 Cor 13:11); **(4)** metaphorically: "Till we all come in the unity of the faith, and of the knowledge of the Son of God, unto a perfect man, unto the measure of the stature of the fulness of Christ" (Eph 4:13); **(5)** denotes "a man," in relation to his sex or age; in Acts 17:5 (plural) it is rendered "fellows," as more appropriate to the accompanying description of them: "But the Jews which believed not, moved with envy, took unto them certain lewd fellows of the baser sort, and gathered a company, and set all the city on an uproar, and assaulted the house of Jason, and sought to bring them out to the people." Syn.: 444, 730, 5046. See: TDNT—1:360, 59; BAGD—66c; THAYER—45b.

436. **ἀνθίστημι** {14x} **anthistēmi**, *anth-is'-tay-mee;* from *473* and *2476;* to *stand against,* i.e. *oppose:*—resist {9x}, withstand {5x}.

Anthistemi, as a verb, means "to set against" [*anti*, "against," *histemi*, "to cause to stand"], and is used in the middle (or passive) voice and in the intransitive 2nd aorist and perfect active, signifying "to withstand, oppose, resist." It is translated **(1)** "to resist": "But I say unto you, That ye resist not evil: but whosoever shall smite thee on thy right cheek, turn to him the other also" (Mt 5:39; cf. Lk 21:15; Acts 6:10; Rom 9:19; 13:2 [twice]; **(2)** "withstand, withstood": "But Elymas the sorcerer (for so is his name by interpretation) withstood them, seeking to turn away the deputy from the faith" (Acts 13:8; cf. Gal 2:11; Eph 6:13; 2 Ti 4:15; Jas 4:7; 1 Pet 5:9); **(3)** both "to withstood" and "resist" in 2 Ti 3:8: "Now as Jannes and Jambres withstood (*anthistemi*) Moses, so do these also resist (*anthistemi*) the truth: men of corrupt minds, reprobate concerning the faith." Syn.: 478, 498. See: BAGD—67b; THAYER—45c.

437. **ἀνθομολογέομαι** {1x} **anthŏmŏlŏgĕŏmai**, *anth-om-ol-og-eh'-om-ahee;* from *473* and the mid. voice of *3670; to confess in turn,* i.e. *respond* in praise:—give thanks {1x}.

Anthomologeomai means "to acknowledge fully, to celebrate fully in praise with thanksgiving," and is used of Anna in Lk 2:35: "And she [Anna] coming in that instant gave thanks (*anthomologeomai*) likewise unto the Lord, and spake of Him to all them that looked for redemption in Jerusalem." Syn.: 1843, 2168. See: TDNT—5:199, 687; BAGD—67b; THAYER—45d.

438. **ἄνθος** {4x} **anthŏs**, *anth'-os;* a prim. word; a *blossom:*—flower {4x}.

Anthos is "a blossom, flower": "For all flesh *is* as grass, and all the glory of man as the flower of grass. The grass withereth, and the flower thereof falleth away" (1 Pe 1:24; cf. Jas 1:10). See: BAGD—67c; THAYER—45d.

439. **ἀνθρακιά** {2x} **anthrakia**, *anth-rak-ee-ah';* from *440;* a bed of burning *coals:*—fire of coals {2x}.

Anthrakia is "a heap of burning coals, or a charcoal fire": "And the servants and officers stood there, who had made a fire of coals; for it was cold: and they warmed themselves: and Peter stood with them, and warmed himself" (Jn 18:18; cf. 21:9). Syn.: 440. See: BAGD—67c; THAYER—45d.

440. **ἄνθραξ** {1x} **anthrax**, *anth'-rax;* of uncert. der.; a live *coal:*—coals of fire {1x}.

Anthrax, "a burning coal" [cf. Eng., "anthracite,"] is used in the plural in Rom 12:20, metaphorically in a proverbial expression, "thou shalt heap coals of fire on his head" [from Prov 25:22], signifying retribution by kindness, i.e., that, by conferring a favor on your enemy, you recall the wrong he has done to you, so that he repents, with pain of heart. Syn.: 439. See: BAGD—67c; THAYER—45d.

441. **ἀνθρωπάρεσκος** {2x} **anthrōparĕskŏs**, *anth-ro-par'-es-kos;* from *444* and *700; man-courting,* i.e. *fawning:*—men-pleaser {2x}.

Anthropareskos, an adjective signifying "studying to please men" [*anthropos*, "man," *aresko*, "to please"], designates, not simply one who is pleasing to men . . . , but one who endeavors to please men and not God. It is used in Eph 6:6: "Not with eyeservice, as menpleasers; but as the servants of Christ, doing the will of God from the heart" (cf. Col 3:22). See: TDNT—1:465, 77; BAGD—67d; THAYER—46a.

442. **ἀνθρώπινος** {7x} **anthrōpinŏs**, *anth-ro'-pee-nos;* from *444; human:*—man's {3x}, after the manner of man {1x}, of man {1x}, common to man {1x}, mankind + 5449 {1x}.

Anthropinos means "human, belonging to man" [from *anthropos*), and is used **(1)** of man's wisdom: "Which things also we speak, not in the words which man's wisdom teacheth, but which the Holy Ghost teacheth; comparing spiritual things with spiritual" (1 Cor 2:13); **(2)** of "man's judgment: "But with me it is a very small thing that I should be judged of you, or of man's judgment: yea, I judge not mine own self" (1 Cor 4:3); **(3)** of "mankind": "For every kind of beasts, and of birds, and of serpents, and of things in the sea, is tamed, and hath been tamed of mankind" (Jas 3:7 lit., "nature of man");

(4) of human ordinance: "Submit yourselves to every ordinance of man for the Lord's sake: whether it be to the king, as supreme" (1 Pet 2:13); **(5)** of temptation: "There hath no temptation taken you but such as is common to man: but God *is* faithful, who will not suffer you to be tempted above that ye are able; but will with the temptation also make a way to escape, that ye may be able to bear *it*" (1 Cor 10:13 "such as is common to man," i.e., such as must and does come to "men"); **(6)** of "men's" hands: "Neither is worshipped with men's hands, as though He needed any thing, seeing He giveth to all life, and breath, and all things" (Acts 17:25); **(7)** in the phrase "after the manner of men": "I speak after the manner of men because of the infirmity of your flesh" (Rom 6:19). See: TDNT—1:366, 59; BAGD—67d; THAYER—46a.

443. **ἀνθρωποκτόνος** {3x} **anthrōpŏktŏnŏs**, *anth-ro-pok-ton'-os;* from *444* and κτείνω **ktĕinō** (to *kill*); a *manslayer:*—murderer {3x}.

Anthropoktonon, an adjective, lit., "manslaying," used as a noun, "a manslayer, murderer" [*anthropos,* "a man," *kteino,* "to slay"], is used **(1)** of Satan: "Ye are of *your* father the devil, and the lusts of your father ye will do. He was a murderer from the beginning, and abode not in the truth" (Jn 8:44); **(2)** of one who hates his brother, and who, being a "murderer," has not eternal life: "Whosoever hateth his brother is a murderer: and ye know that no murderer hath eternal life abiding in him" (1Jn 3:15). *Anthropoktonos* corresponds exactly to the English manslayer and homicide. Syn.: 4607, 5406. Phoneus (5406) refers to any murderer. Sikarious (4607) is an assassin using a particular knife (sicarii). *Anthropoktonos* refers to the murder of men/males only. See: TDNT—1:366, 59; BAGD—68a; THAYER—46b.

444. **ἄνθρωπος** {559x} **anthrōpŏs**, *anth'-ro-pos;* from *435* and ὤψ **ōps** (the *countenance;* from *3700*); *man-faced,* i.e. a *human* being:—man {552x}, not tr {4x}, misc. {3x}.

Anthropos is used **(1)** generally, of a human being, male or female, without reference to sex or nationality: "But He answered and said, It is written, Man shall not live by bread alone, but by every word that proceedeth out of the mouth of God" (Mt 4:4; cf. 12:35; Jn 2:25); **(1)** in distinction from God: "Wherefore they are no more twain, but one flesh. What therefore God hath joined together, let not man put asunder" (Mt 19:6; cf. Jn 10:33); **(3)** in distinction from animals: "And so *was* also James, and John, the sons of Zebedee, which were partners with Simon. And Jesus said unto Simon, Fear not; from henceforth thou shalt catch men" (Lk 5:10); **(4)** sometimes, in the plural, of men and women, people: "Ye are the salt of the earth: but if the salt have lost his savour, wherewith shall it be salted? it is thenceforth good for nothing, but to be cast out, and to be trodden under foot of men" (Mt 5:13; cf. 5:16); **(5)** in some instances with a suggestion of human frailty and imperfection: "That your faith should not stand in the wisdom of men, but in the power of God" (1 Cor 2:5);

(6) in the phrases translated "after man," "after the manner of men," "as a man" means **(6a)** the practices of fallen humanity: "For ye are yet carnal: for whereas *there is* among you envying, and strife, and divisions, are ye not carnal, and walk as men?" (1Cor 3:3); **(6b)** anything of human origin: "But I certify you, brethren, that the gospel which was preached of me is not after man" (Gal 1:11); **(6c)** the standard generally accepted among men: "Brethren, I speak after the manner of men; Though *it be* but a man's covenant, yet *if it be* confirmed, no man disannulleth, or addeth thereto" (Gal 3:15); **(6d)** an illustration not drawn from Scripture: "Say I these things as a man? or saith not the law the same also?" (1 Cor 9:8); **(6e)** in the phrase the inward man means **(6e1)** the regenerate person's spiritual nature personified, the inner self of the believer: "For I delight in the law of God after the inward man" (Rom 7:22), **(6e2)** as the sphere of the renewing power of the Holy Spirit: "That He would grant you, according to the riches of His glory, to be strengthened with might by His Spirit in the inner man" (Eph 3:16); **(6e3)** in contrast to the outward man, the physical frame, the man as cognizable by the senses: "For which cause we faint not; but though our outward man perish, yet the inward *man* is renewed day by day" (2 Cor 4:16); **(6e4)** the inward man is identical with the hidden man of the heart: "But *let it be* the hidden man of the heart, in that which is not corruptible, *even the ornament* of a meek and quiet spirit, which is in the sight of God of great price" (1 Pet 3:4);

(7) in the expression "the old man," it stands for the unregenerate nature personified as the former self of a believer: "Knowing this, that our old man is crucified with *Him,* that the body of sin might be destroyed, that henceforth we should not serve sin" (Rom 6:6; cf. Eph 4:22; Col 3:9); **(8)** "the new man" standing for the new nature personified as the believer's regenerate self, **(8a)** a nature created in righteousness and holiness of truth: "And that ye put on the new man, which after God is created in righteousness and true holiness" (Eph 4:24), and **(8b)** having been put on at regeneration: "And have put on the new *man,* which is renewed in knowledge after the image of Him that created him" (Col 3:10); and it is to be put on in practical apprehension of these facts. **(9)** The phrase "the man of God" (2 Ti 3:17) is not used as an official designation, nor denoting a special class of believers, but specifies what every believer should be, namely, a person whose life and conduct represent the mind of God and fulfill His will: "But thou, O man of God, flee these things; and follow after righteousness, godliness, faith, love, patience, meekness" (1Ti 6:11). Syn.: 435, 730, 5046. See: TDNT—1:364, 59; BAGD—68a; THAYER—46b.

445. **ἀνθυπατεύω** {1x} **anthupatĕuō**, *anth-oo-pat-yoo'-o;* from *446;* to *act as a proconsul:*—be the deputy {1x}.

Anthupateuo means to act as a pro-consul. Syn.: 446. See: BAGD—69c; THAYER—47a.

446. **ἀνθύπατος** {4x} **anthupatŏs**, *anth-oo'-pat-os;* from *473* and a superl. of *5228; instead* of the *highest* officer, i.e. (spec.) a Roman *proconsul:*—deputy {4x}.

Anthupatos comes from *anti,* "instead of," and *hupatos,* "supreme," and **(1)** denotes "a consul, one acting in place of a consul, a proconsul, the governor of a senatorial province" [i.e., one which had no standing army]. **(2)** The "proconsuls" were of two classes, **(2a)** exconsuls, the rulers of the provinces of Asia and Africa, who were therefore "proconsuls." These are the "proconsuls" at Ephesus, Acts 19:38 ("deputies"); **(2b)** those who were ex-pretors or "proconsuls" of other senatorial provinces [a pretor being virtually the same as a consul]. These were men like Sergius Paulus in Cyprus, Acts 13:7, 8, 12, and Gallio at Corinth, 18:12. **(3)** In the NT times Egypt was governed by a prefect. Provinces in which a standing army was kept were governed by an imperial legate [e.g., Quirinius in Syria, Luke 2:2]. Syn.: 755, 1481, 2232, 3623. See: BAGD—69c; THAYER—47a.

447. **ἀνίημι** {4x} **aniēmi**, *an-ee'-ay-mee;* from *303* and ἵημι **hiēmi** (to *send*); to *let up,* i.e. (lit.) *slacken* or (fig.) *desert, desist* from:—forbear {1x}, leave {1x}, loose {2x}.

Aniemi literally means to send up or back; hence, to relax, loosen or metaphorically to desist from and is translated forbearing: "And, ye masters, do the same things unto them, forbearing threatening: knowing that your Master also is in heaven; neither is there respect of persons with him" (Eph 6:9—giving up your threatening). Syn.: 420, 430, 463, 5339. See: TDNT—1:367, 60; BAGD—69d; THAYER—47b.

448. **ἀνίλεως** {1x} **anilĕōs**, *an-ee'-leh-oce;* from *1* (as a neg. particle) and *2436; inexorable:*—without mercy {1x}

Anileos "unmerciful, merciless" [*a,* negative, *n,* euphonic, and *eleos,* "mercy"], occurs in Jas 2:13, said of judgment on him who shows no mercy: "For he shall have judgment without mercy, that hath shewed no mercy; and mercy rejoiceth against judgment." See: TDNT—2:487,*; BAGD—69d; THAYER—47b.

449. **ἄνιπτος** {3x} **aniptŏs**, *an'-ip-tos;* from *1* (as a neg. particle) and a presumed der. of *3538; without ablution:*—unwashen {3x}.

Aniptos means "unwashed" [*a,* negative, *nipto,* "to wash"] and occurs in Mt 15:20: "These are *the things* which defile a man: but to eat with unwashen hands defileth not a man" (cf. Mk 7:2, 5). See: TDNT—4:947, 635; BAGD—69d; THAYER—47b.

450. **ἀνίστημι** {112x} **anistēmi**, *an-is'-tay-mee;* from *303* and *2476;* to *stand up* (lit. or fig., trans. or intr.):—arise {38x}, rise {19x}, rise up {16x}, rise again {13x}, raise up {11x}, stand up {8x}, raise up again {2x}, misc. {5x} = lift up, stand upright.

Anistemi, as a verb, means "to stand up or to make to stand up," according as its use is intransitive or transitive and is used **(1)** of a physical change of position **(1a)** of "rising" from sleep (Mk 1:35); **(1b)** rising from a meeting in a synagogue (Lk 4:29); **(1c)** of the illegal "rising" of the high priest in the tribunal in Mt 26:62; **(1d)** of an invalid "rising" from his couch (Lk 5:25); **(1e)** the "rising" up of a disciple from his vocation to follow Christ (Lk 5:28; cf. Jn 11:31); **(1f)** "rising" up from prayer (Lk 22:45); **(1g)** of a whole company (Acts 26:30; 1 Cor 10:7); **(2)** metaphorically, of "rising" up antagonistically against persons: **(2a)** of officials against people (Acts 5:17); **(2b)** of a seditious leader (Acts 5:36); **(2c)** of the "rising" up of Satan (Mk 3:26); **(2d)** of false teachers (Acts 20:30); **(4)** of "rising" to a position of preeminence or power: **(4a)** of Christ as a prophet (Acts 3:22; 7:37); **(4b)** as God's servant in the midst of the nation of Israel (Acts 3:26); **(4c)** as the Son of God in the midst of the nation

(Acts 13:33); **(4d)** as a priest (Heb 7:11, 15); **(4e)** as king over the nations (Rom 15:12);

(5) of a spiritual awakening from lethargy (Eph 5:14); **(6)** of resurrection from the dead: **(6a)** of the resurrection of Christ (Mt 17:9; 20:19; Mk 8:31; 9:9–10, 31; 10:34; Lk 18:33; 24:7, 46; Jn 20:9; Acts 2:24, 32; 10:41; 13:34; 17:3, 31; 1 Th 4:14); **(6b)** of believers (Jn 6:39–40, 44, 54; 11:24; 1 Th 4:16); **(6c)** of unbelievers (Mt 12:41). Syn.: Egeiro (1453) stands in contrast to *anistemi* (450 - when used with reference to resurrection) in this respect, that egeiro is frequently used both in the transitive sense of "raising up" and the intransitive of "rising," whereas *anistemi* is comparatively infrequent in the transitive use. See also: 305, 393, 1096, 1326, 1453, 1525, 1817, 4911. See: TDNT—1:368, 60; BAGD—70a; THAYER—47b.

451. **Ἄννα** {1x} **Anna**, *an'-nah;* of Heb. or. [2584]; *Anna,* an Israelitess:—*Anna* {1x}. See: BAGD—70c; THAYER—47d.

452. **Ἄννας** {4x} **Annas**, *an'-nas;* of Heb. or. [2608]; *Annas* (i.e. *367*), an Isr.:—*Annas* {4x}. See: BAGD—70c; THAYER—47d.

453. **ἀνόητος** {6x} **anŏētŏs**, *an-o'-ay-tos;* from *1* (as a neg. particle) and a der. of *3539; unintelligent;* by impl. *sensual:*—fool {1x}, foolish {4x}, unwise {1x}.

Anoetos means not understanding, not applying the mind it signifies **(1)** senseless, an unworthy lack of understanding: "Then He said unto them, O fools (*anoetos*), and slow of heart to believe all that the prophets have spoken" (Lk 24:25; cf. Rom 1:14; Gal 3:1, 3); or **(2)** sometimes it carries a moral reproach and describes one who does not govern his lusts: "For we ourselves also were sometimes foolish (*anoetos*), disobedient, deceived, serving divers lusts and pleasures, living in malice and envy, hateful, *and* hating one another" (Titus 3:3; cf. 1 Ti 6:9). Syn.: 801, 877, 878, 3471, 3472, 3474, 3912. See: TDNT—4:961, 636; BAGD—70d; THAYER—48a.

454. **ἄνοια** {2x} **anŏia**, *an'-oy-ah;* from a comp. of *1* (as a neg. particle) and *3563 stupidity;* by impl. *rage:*—folly {1x}, madness {1x}.

Anoia literally signifies "without understanding" [*a,* negative, *nous,* "mind"]; hence, "folly," or, rather, **(1)** "senselessness": "But they shall proceed no further: for their folly (*anoia*) shall be manifest unto all *men,* as theirs also was" (2 Ti 3:9); and **(2)** in Lk 6:11 it denotes violent or mad rage, "madness": "And they were filled with madness; and communed one with another what they might do to Jesus." See: TDNT—4:962, 636; BAGD—70d; THAYER—48a.

455. **ἀνοίγω** {77x} **anŏigō**, *an-oy'-go;* from *303* and οἴγω **ŏigō** (to *open*); to *open up* (lit. or fig., in various applications):—open {77x}.

Anoigo is used **(1)** transitively, **(1a)** literally, **(1a1)** of a door or gate (Acts 5:19); **(1a2)** graves (Mt 27:52); **(1a3)** a sepulcher (Rom 3:13); **(1a4)** a book (Lk 4:17; Rev. 5:2–5); **(1a5)** the seals of a roll (Rev. 5:9; 6:1); **(1a6)** the eyes (Acts 9:40); **(1a7)** the mouth of a fish (Mt 17:27); **(1a8)** the pit of the abyss (Rev 9:2); **(1a9)** heaven and the heavens (Mt 3:16; Lk 3:21; Acts 10:11); **(1b)** metaphorically,: "Ask, and it shall be given you; seek, and ye shall find; knock, and it shall be opened unto you: For every one that asketh receiveth; and he that seeketh findeth; and to him that knocketh it shall be opened" (Mt 7:7–8; cf. 25:11; Rev 3:7); **(2)** intransitively **(2a)** literally, of the heaven: "And He saith unto him [Nathanael], Verily, verily, I say unto you, Hereafter ye shall see heaven open, and the angels of God ascending and descending upon the Son of man" (Jn 1:51); **(2b)** metaphorically, of speaking freely: "O *ye* Corinthians, our mouth is open unto you, our heart is enlarged" (2 Cor 6:11). Syn.: 457, 1272, 3692. See: BAGD—70d; THAYER—48a.

456. **ἀνοικοδομέω** {2x} **anŏikŏdŏmĕō**, *an-oy-kod-om-eh'-o;* from *303* and *3618;* to *rebuild:*—build again {2x}.

Anoikodomeo signifies "to build again": "After this I will return, and will build again (*anoikodomeo*) the tabernacle of David, which is fallen down; and I will build again (*anoikodomeo*) the ruins thereof, and I will set it up" (Acts 15:16). Syn.: 2026, 4925. See: BAGD—71c; THAYER—48c.

457. **ἄνοιξις** {} **anŏixis**, *an'-oix-is;* from *455; opening* (throat):—that (one) may open + 1722 {1x}.

Anoixis is "an opening" and is used in Eph 6:19, metaphorically of the "opening" of the mouth: "And for me [Paul], that utterance may be given unto me, that I may open my mouth boldly, to make known the mystery of the gospel." Syn.: 455, 1272, 3692. See: BAGD—71c; THAYER—48c.

458. **ἀνομία** {15x} **anŏmia**, *an-om-ee'-ah;* from *459; illegality,* i.e. *violation of law* or (gen.) *wickedness:*—iniquity {12x}, unrighteousness {1x}, transgress the law + 4160 {1x}, transgression of the law {1x}.

Anomia **(1)** refers **(1a)** not to one living without law, **(1b)** but to one who acts contrary to law; **(1c)** where there is no law given there can be hamartia (266) but not *anomia;* an error against adopted law. **(2)** Its usual rendering is iniquity, which lit. means unrighteousness and it is used **(2a)** of iniquity in general: "And then will I profess unto them, I never knew you: depart from Me, ye that work iniquity" (Mt 7:23; cf. 13:41; Rom 6:19); and **(2b)** in the plural, of acts or manifestations of lawlessness: "*Saying,* Blessed *are* they whose iniquities are forgiven, and whose sins are covered" (Rom 4:7; cf. Heb 10:17). Syn.: 51, 92, 93, 265, 266, 2275, 3847, 3876, 3892, 3900, 4189. See: TDNT—4:1085, 646; BAGD—71d; THAYER—48c.

459. **ἄνομος** {10 x} **anŏmŏs**, *an'-om-os;* from *1* (as a neg. particle) and *3551; lawless,* i.e. (neg.) *not subject to* (the Jewish) *law;* (by impl. a *Gentile*), or (pos.) *wicked:*—without law {4x}, transgressor {2x}, wicked {2x}, lawless {1x}, unlawful {1x}.

Anomos signifies "without law, having no existing law" and has this meaning in 1 Cor 9:21: "To them that are without law (*anomos*), as without law (*anomos*), [being not without law (*anomos*), to God, but under the law to Christ,] that I might gain them that are without law (*anomos*)." See: TDNT—4:1086, 646; BAGD—72a; THAYER—48d.

460. **ἀνόμως** {2x} **anŏmōs**, *an-om'-oce;* adv. from *459; lawlessly,* i.e. (spec.) *not amenable to* (the Jewish) *law:*—without law {2x}.

Anomos, as an adverb, means without law and is used **(1)** in Rom 2:12: "For as many as have sinned without law (*anomos*) shall also perish without law (*anomos*): and as many as have sinned in the law shall be judged by the law"; **(2)** where "have sinned without law" means in the absence of some specifically revealed law, like the law of Sinai; and **(3)** "shall perish without law" predicates that the absence of such a law will not prevent their doom. Syn.: 459. See: BAGD—72b; THAYER—48d.

461. **ἀνορθόω** {3x} **anŏrthŏō**, *an-orth-ŏ'-o;* from *303* and a der. of the base of *3717;* to *straighten up; to set upright:*—lift up {1x}, set up {1x}, make straight {1x}.

Anorthoo, as a verb, means "to set upright" [*ana,* "up," *orthos,* "straight"] and is used **(1)** metaphorically, **(1a)** of "lifting" up "hands that hang down": "Wherefore lift up the hands which hang down, and the feeble knees" (Heb 12:12); **(1b)** of setting up a building, restoring ruins: "After this I [God] will return, and will build again the tabernacle of David, which is fallen down; and I will build again the ruins thereof, and I will set it up" (Acts 15:16); **(2)** literally, of the healing of the woman with a spirit of infirmity: "And He laid *His* hands on her: and immediately she was made straight, and glorified God" (Lk 13:13 "was made straight"). See: BAGD—72c; THAYER—49a.

462. **ἀνόσιος** {2x} **anŏsiŏs**, *an-os'-ee-os;* from *1* (as a neg. particle) and *3741; wicked:*—unholy {2x}.

Anosios, as an adjective [*a,* negative, *n,* euphonic, *hosios,* "holy"] means "unholy, profane": "Knowing this, that the law is not made for a righteous man, but for the lawless and disobedient, for the ungodly and for sinners, for unholy (*anosios*) and profane, for murderers of fathers and murderers of mothers, for manslayers" (1 Ti 1:9; cf. 2 Ti 3:2). Syn.: 2839. See: TDNT—5:492, 734; BAGD—72c; THAYER—49a.

463. **ἀνοχή** {2x} **anŏchē**,*an-okh-ay';* from *430; self-restraint,* i.e. *tolerance:*—forbearance {2x}.

Anoche means a holding back and denotes forbearance, a delay of punishment, a demonstration of God's forbearance with men used **(1)** in Rom 2:4 where it represents a suspension of wrath which must eventually be exercised unless the sinner accepts God's conditions: "Or despisest thou the riches of his goodness and forbearance and longsuffering; not knowing that the goodness of God leadeth thee to repentance?"; and **(2)** in Rom 3:25 it is connected with the passing over of sins in times past, previous to the atoning work of Christ: "Whom God hath set forth *to be* a propitiation through faith in His blood, to declare His righteousness for the remission of sins that are past, through the forbearance of God." His forbearance is the ground, not of His forgiveness, but of His pretermission of sins, His withholding punishment. Syn.: 420, 1933, 3115, 5281. See: TDNT—1:359, 58; BAGD—72c; THAYER—49a.

464. **ἀνταγωνίζομαι** {1x} **antagōnizŏmai**, *an-tag-o-nid'-zom-ahee;* from *473* and *75;* to *struggle against* (fig.) ["antagonize"]:—strive against {1x}.

Antagonizomai means "to struggle against": "Ye have not yet resisted unto blood, striving against sin" (Heb 12:4 "striving against"). Syn.: 4865, 4866. See: TDNT—1:134, 20; BAGD—72d; THAYER—49a.

465. **ἀντάλλαγμα** {2x} **antallagma**, *an-tal'-lag-mah;* from a comp. of *473* and *236;* an *equivalent* or *ransom:*—in exchange {2x}.

Antallagma is the price received as an equivalent of, or in exchange for, an article, an exchange; hence, it denotes the price at which the exchange is effected: "For what is a man profited, if he shall gain the whole world, and lose his own soul? or what shall a man give in exchange (*antallagma*) for his soul?" (Mt 16:26; cf. Mk 8:37). Syn.: 3337. See: TDNT—1:252, 40; BAGD—72d; THAYER—49a.

466. **ἀνταναπληρόω** {1x} **antanaplērŏō**, *an-tan-ap-lay-rŏ'-o;* from *473* and *378;* to *supplement:*—fill up {1x}.

Antanapleroo means to fill up in turn and is used in Col 1:24, of the apostle's responsive devotion to Christ in "filling" up, or undertaking on his part a full share of, the sufferings which follow after the sufferings of Christ, and are experienced by the members of His Body, the church: "Who now rejoice in my sufferings for you, and fill up that which is behind of the afflictions of Christ in my flesh for His body's sake, which is the church." The point of the apostle's boast is that Christ, the sinless Master, should have left something for Paul, the unworthy servant, to suffer. Syn.: 4845. See: TDNT—1:252, 40; BAGD—72d; THAYER—49b.

467. **ἀνταποδίδωμι** {7x} **antapŏdidōmi**, *an-tap-od-ee'-do-mee;* from *473* and *591;* to *requite* (good or evil):—recompense {3x}, recompense again {1x}, render {1x}, repay {1x}.

Antapodidomi means "to give back as an equivalent, to requite, recompense" [the *anti* expressing the idea of a complete return] and is translated **(1)** "render": "For what thanks can we render to God again for you, for all the joy wherewith we joy for your sakes before our God" (1 Th 3:9 here only in the NT of thanksgiving to God); elsewhere it is used of **(2)** "recompense" **(2a)** whether between men: "See that none render (apodidomi) evil for evil unto any *man;* but ever follow that which is good, both among yourselves, and to all *men*" (1 Th 5:15; cf. Lk 14:14 see the corresponding noun in v. 12); or **(2b)** between God and evil-doers: "Dearly beloved, avenge not yourselves, but *rather* give place unto wrath: for it is written, Vengeance *is* mine; I will repay (apodidomi), saith the Lord" (Rom 12:19; cf. Heb 10:30); or **(2c)** between God and those who do well: "And thou shalt be blessed; for they cannot recompense (apodidomi) thee: for thou shalt be recompensed (apodidomi) at the resurrection of the just" (Lk 14:14; cf. Rom 11:35); **(2d)** in 2 Th 1:6 retribution are in view: "Seeing *it is* a righteous thing with God to recompense (apodidomi) tribulation to them that trouble you." Syn.: 469, 591. See: TDNT—2:169, 166; BAGD—73a; THAYER—49b.

468. **ἀνταπόδομα** {2x} **antapŏdŏma**, *an-tap-od'-om-ah;* from *467;* a *requital* (prop. the thing):—recompense {2x}.

Antapodoma means "a recompense," lit., "a giving back in return," a requital, recompence, and is used **(1)** in a favorable sense: "Then said He also to him that bade Him, When thou makest a dinner or a supper, call not thy friends, nor thy brethren, neither thy kinsmen, nor *thy* rich neighbours; lest they also bid thee again, and a recompence (*antapodoma*) be made thee" (Lk 14:12); **(2)** in an unfavorable sense: "And David saith, Let their table be made a snare, and a trap, and a stumblingblock, and a recompence (*antapodoma*) unto them" (Rom 11:9) indicating that the present condition of the Jewish nation is the retributive effect of their transgressions, on account of which that which was designed as a blessing ("their table") has become a means of judgment. Syn.: 459, 489. See: TDNT—2:169, 166; BAGD—73a; THAYER—49b.

469. **ἀνταπόδοσις** {1x} **antapŏdŏsis**, *an-tap-od'-os-is;* from *467;* *requital* (prop. the act):—reward {1x}.

Antapodosis is rendered "reward" in Col 3:24: "Knowing that of the Lord ye shall receive the reward of the inheritance: for ye serve the Lord Christ." Syn.: 468, 489. See: TDNT—2:169, 166 BAGD—73a; THAYER—49b.

470. **ἀνταποκρίνομαι** {2x} **antapŏkrinŏmai**, *an-tap-ok-ree'-nom-ahee;* from *473* and *611;* to *contradict* or *dispute:*—answer again {1x}, reply against {1x}.

This word is a strengthened form and means "to answer by contradiction, to reply against": "And they could not answer (*antapokrinomai*) Him again to these things" (Lk 14:6; cf. Rom 9:20). See: TDNT—3:944, 469; BAGD—73b; THAYER—49c.

471. **ἀντέπω** {2x} **antĕpō**, *an-tep'-o;* from *473* and *2036;* to *refute* or *deny:*—gainsay {1x}, say against {1x}.

(1) This word means to say against, to weigh in [gain] against; to declare weighty matters against someone to gain advantage. **(2)** *Antepo*, as a verb, means serves as an aorist tense of *antilego* (483) and is rendered **(2a)** "gainsay": "For I will give you a mouth and wisdom, which all your adversaries shall not be able to gainsay nor resist" (Lk 21:15); and **(2b)** "say against": "And beholding the man which was healed standing with them, they could say nothing against it" (Acts 4:14). Syn.: 368, 369, 483, 485. See: BAGD—73b; THAYER—49c.

472. **ἀντέχομαι** {4x} **antĕchŏmai**, *an-tekh'-om-ahee;* from *473* and the mid. voice of *2192;* to *hold* oneself *opposite* to, i.e. (by impl.) *adhere to;* by extens. to *care for:*—hold fast {1x}, hold to {2x}, support {1x}.

This word signifies in **(1)** the middle voice, **(1a)** "to hold firmly to, cleave to," of "holding" or cleaving to a person: "No man can serve two masters: for either he will hate the one, and love the other; or else he will hold to the one, and despise the other" (Mt 6:24; cf. Lk 16:13); **(1b)** of "holding fast" to the faithful word: "Holding fast the faithful word as he hath been taught, that he may be able by sound doctrine both to exhort and to convince the gainsayers" (Titus 1:9); **(2)** "to support": "Now we exhort you, brethren, warn them that are unruly, comfort the feebleminded, support the weak, be patient toward all *men*" (1 Th 5:14 the weak). Syn.: See: TDNT—2:827, 286; BAGD—73b; THAYER—49c.

473. **ἀντί** {22x} **anti**, *an-tee';* a prim. particle; *opposite,* i.e. *instead* or *because* of (rarely *in addition* to):—for {15x}, because + 3639 {4x}, for . . . cause {1x}, therefore + 3639 {1x}, in the room of {1x}.

This preposition is first of equivalence and then of exchange, stressing being in the place where another should be; total replacement. Syn.: 528. See: TDNT—1:372, 61; BAGD—73c; THAYER—49d.

474. **ἀντιβάλλω** {1x} **antiballō**, *an-tee-bal'-lo;* from *473* and *906;* to *bandy:*—have {1x}.

Antiballo, as a verb, means literally "to throw in turn, exchange, to cast back and forth from one to another; one has and gives to another"; hence, metaphorically, "to exchange thoughts": "And He said unto them, What manner of communications *are* these that ye have (*antiballo*) one to another, as ye walk, and are sad?" (Lk 24:17). See: BAGD—74a; THAYER—50a.

475. **ἀντιδιατίθεμαι** {1x} **antidiatithĕmai**, *an-tee-dee-at-eeth'-em-ahee;* from *473* and *1303;* to *set oneself opposite,* i.e. *be disputatious:*—that oppose themselves {1x}.

This word signifies "to place oneself in opposition, oppose": "In meekness instructing those that oppose themselves; if God peradventure will give them repentance to the acknowledging of the truth" (2 Ti 2:25). See: BAGD—74a; THAYER—50a.

476. **ἀντίδικος** {5x} **antidikŏs**, *an-tid'-ee-kos;* from *473* and *1349;* an *opponent* (in a lawsuit); spec. *Satan* (as the arch-enemy):—adversary {5x}.

Antidikos, firstly means **(1)** "an opponent in a lawsuit": "Agree with thine adversary (*antidikos*) quickly, whiles thou art in the way with him; lest at any time the adversary (*antidikos*) deliver thee to the judge, and the judge deliver thee to the officer, and thou be cast into prison" (Mt 5:25; cf. Lk 12:58; 18:3), and is also used **(2)** to denote "an adversary or an enemy," without reference to legal affairs, and this is perhaps its meaning in 1 Pet 5:8 where it is used of the Devil. Some would regard the word as there used in a legal sense, since the Devil accuses men before God. See: TDNT—1:373, 62; BAGD—74a; THAYER—50a.

477. **ἀντίθεσις** {1x} **antithĕsis**, *an-tith'-es-is;* from a comp. of *473* and *5087;* *opposition,* i.e. a *conflict* (of theories):—opposition {1x}.

This word means "a contrary position" [*anti,* "against," *tithemi,* "to place"; Eng., "*antithesis*"]: "O Timothy, keep that which is committed to thy trust, avoiding profane *and* vain babblings, and oppositions (*antithesis*) of science falsely so called" (1 Ti 6:20). See: TDNT—1:373,*; BAGD—74b; THAYER—50a.

478. **ἀντικαθίστημι** {1x} **antikathistēmi**, *an-tee-kath-is'-tay-mee;* from *473* and *2525;* to *set down* (troops) *against,* i.e. *withstand:*—resist {1x}.

This word stresses taking a stand firm against [*anti,* "against," *kathistemi,* "to set down," *kata*] and is translated "ye have (not) resisted": "Ye have not yet resisted unto blood, striving against sin" (Heb 12:4). Syn.: 496, 498. See: BAGD—74b; THAYER—50b.

479. **ἀντικαλέω** {1x} **antikalĕō**, *an-tee-kal-eh'-o;* from *473* and *2564;* to *invite in return:*—bid again {1x}.

Antikaleo means "to bid again, invite in turn": "Then said He also to him that bade Him, When thou makest a dinner or a supper, call not thy friends, nor thy brethren, neither thy kinsmen, nor *thy* rich neighbours; lest they also bid thee again, and a recompence be made thee" (Lk 14:12). See: TDNT—3:496, 394; BAGD—74b; THAYER—50b.

480. **ἀντίκειμαι** {8x} **antikĕimai**, *an-tik'-i-mahee;* from *473* and *2749;* to *lie opposite,* i.e. *be adverse* (fig. *repugnant*) to:—adversary {5x}, be contrary {2x}, oppose {1x}.

(1) This word literally means "to lie opposite to, to be set over against." **(2)** In addition to its legal sense it signifies "to withstand"; the present participle of the verb with the article, which is equivalent to a noun, signifies "an adversary": "And when He had said these things, all His adversaries (*antikeimai*) were ashamed: and all the people rejoiced for all the glorious things that were done by Him" (Lk 13:17; cf. 21:15; 1 Cor 16:9; Phil 1:28; 1 Ti 5:14). **(3)** This construction is used of the Man of Sin, in 2 Th. 2:4, and is translated "He that opposeth," where, adopting the noun form, we might render by "the opponent and self-exalter against. . . ." **(4)** In Gal 5:17 it is used of the antagonism between ["contrary to"] the Holy Spirit and the flesh in the believer; **(5)** in 1 Ti 1:10, of anything, in addition to persons, that is opposed to the doctrine of Christ: "For whoremongers, for them that defile themselves with mankind, for menstealers, for liars, for perjured persons, and if there be any other thing that is contrary to (*antikeimai*) sound doctrine." See: TDNT—3:655, 425; BAGD—74b; THAYER—50b.

481. **ἀντικρύ** {1x} **antikru**, *an-tee-kroo';* prol. from *473; opposite:*—over against {1x}. See: BAGD—74c; THAYER—50b.

482. **ἀντιλαμβάνομαι** {3x} **antilambanŏmai**, *an-tee-lam-ban'-om-ahee;* from *473* and the mid. voice of *2983;* to *take* hold of *in turn,* i.e. *succor;* also to *participate:*—help {1x}, partaker {1x}, support {1x}.

This word literally means "to take instead of, or in turn" and is used in the middle voice, and rendered **(1)** "He hath holpen": "He hath holpen His servant Israel, in remembrance of *His* mercy" (Lk 1:54; "holpen" is an aorist participle stressing that God characteristically always helped His servant Israel); **(2)** "to support": "I have shewed you all things, how that so labouring ye ought to support (*antilambanomai*) the weak" (Acts 20:35); and **(3)** "partakers of": "And they that have believing masters, let them not despise *them,* because they are brethren; but rather do *them* service, because they are faithful and beloved, partakers of the benefit" (1 Ti 6:2). See: TDNT—1:375, 62; BAGD—74c; THAYER—50b.

483. **ἀντίλεγω** {10x} **antilĕgō**, *an-til'-eg-o;* from *473* and *3004;* to *dispute, refuse:*—speak against {5x}, deny {1x}, contradict {1x}, gainsay {1x}, gainsayer {1x}, answer again {1x}.

This word means "to speak against" and is rendered "answering again": "*Exhort* servants to be obedient unto their own masters, *and* to please *them* well in all *things;* not answering again" (Titus 2:9). See: BAGD—74d; THAYER—50c.

484. **ἀντίληψις** {1x} **antilēpsis**, *an-til'-ape-sis;* from *482; relief:*—help {1x}.

Antilepsis properly signifies "a laying hold of, an exchange." It is mentioned in 1 Cor 12:28, as one of the ministrations in the local church, by way of rendering assistance, perhaps especially of "help" ministered to the weak and needy. These are not official functionaries are in view in the term "helps," but rather the functioning of those who, like the household of Stephanas, devote themselves to minister to the saints; anything that would be done for poor or weak or outcast brethren. See: TDNT—1:375, 62; BAGD—75a; THAYER—50c.

485. **ἀντιλογία** {4x} **antilŏgia**, *an-tee-log-ee'-ah;* from a der. of *483; dispute, disobedience:*—contradiction {2x}, gainsaying {1x}, strife {1x}.

This word literally means to speak against in order to gain advantage for one's self and is translated "contradiction" (Heb 7:7; 12:3), "strife" (Heb 6:16), and **(3)** "gainsaying" (Jude 11). See: BAGD—75a; THAYER—50c.

486. **ἀντιλοιδορέω** {1x} **antilŏidŏrĕō**, *an-tee-loy-dor-eh'-o;* from *473* and *3058;* to *rail in reply:*—revile again {1x}.

Antiloidoreo means "to revile back or again" and is found in 1 Pet 2:23: "Who, when He was reviled, reviled not again; when He suffered, He threatened not; but committed *Himself* to Him that judgeth righteously." See: TDNT—4:293, 538; BAGD—75a; THAYER—50d.

487. **ἀντίλυτρον** {1x} **antilutrŏn**, *an-til'-oo-tron;* from *473* and *3083;* a *redemption-price:*—ransom {1x}.

This word stresses what is given in exchange for another as the price of his redemption, ransom: "Who gave Himself a ransom (*antilutron*) for (*uper* – 5228) all, to be testified in due time." The preposition, *anti,* stresses a substitutionary "ransom." The preposition is huper, "on behalf of," and the statement is made that He "gave Himself a ransom for all," indicating that the "ransom" was provisionally universal, while being of a vicarious character. See: TDNT—4:349, 543; BAGD—75b; THAYER—50d.

488. **ἀντιμετρέω** {2x} **antimĕtrĕō**, *an-tee-met-reh'-o;* from *473* and *3354;* to *mete in return:*—measure again {2x}.

Antimetreo, as a verb, means "to measure in return," is used in the passive voice, and found in Mt 7:2: "For with what judgment ye judge, ye shall be judged: and with what measure ye mete, it shall be measured to you again (*antimetreo*)" (cf. Lk 6:38). Syn.: 280, 943, 2884, 3313, 3354, 3358, 4057, 4568, 5234, 5249, 5518. See: BAGD—75b; THAYER—50d.

489. **ἀντιμισθία** {2x} **antimisthia**, *an-tee-mis-thee'-ah;* from a comp. of *473* and *3408; requital, correspondence:*—recompense {2x}.

Antimisthia means "a reward, requital" [*anti,* "in return," *misthos,* "wages, hire"] and is used **(1)** in a good sense: "Now for a recompence in the same, (I speak as unto *my* children,) be ye also enlarged" (2 Cor 6:13); **(2)** in a bad sense: "And likewise also the men, leaving the natural use of the woman, burned in their lust one toward another; men with men working that which is unseemly, and receiving in themselves that recompence of their error which was meet" (Rom 1:27). See: TDNT—4:695, 599; BAGD—75b; THAYER—50d.

490. **Ἀντιόχεια** {18x} **Antiŏchĕia**, *an-tee-okh'-i-ah;* from Ἀντίοχυς **Antiŏchus** (a Syrian king); *Antiochia,* a place in Syria:—Antioch {18x}. See: BAGD—75b; THAYER—50d.

491. **Ἀντιοχεύς** {1x} **Antiŏchĕus**, *an-tee-okh-yoos';* from *490;* an *Antiochian* or inhab. of Antiochia:—of Antioch {1x}. See: BAGD—75c; THAYER—51a.

492. **ἀντιπαρέρχομαι** {2x} **antiparĕrchŏmai**, *an-tee-par-er'-khom-ahee;* from *473* and *3928;* to *go along opposite:*—pass by on the other side {2x}.

This word denotes "to pass by opposite to": "And by chance there came down a certain priest that way: and when he saw him, he passed by on the other side (*antiparerchomai*). And likewise a Levite, when he was at the place, came and looked *on him,* and passed by on the other side (*antiparerchomai*)" (Lk 10:31, 32). See: BAGD—75c; THAYER—51a.

493. **Ἀντίπας** {1x} **Antipas**, *an-tee'-pas;* contr. for a comp. of *473* and a der. of *3962; Antipas,* a Chr.:—*Antipas* {1x}. See: BAGD—75d; THAYER—51b.

494. **Ἀντιπατρίς** {1x} **Antipatris**, *an-tip-at-rece';* from the same as *493; Antipatris,* a place in Pal.:—*Antipatris* {1x}. See: BAGD—75d; THAYER—51b.

495. **ἀντιπέραν** {1x} **antipĕran**, *an-tee-per'-an;* from *473* and *4008; on the opposite side:*—over against {1x}.

This word occurs only in Lk 8:26: "And they arrived at the country of the Gadarenes, which is over against Galilee." See: BAGD—75d; THAYER—51b.

496. **ἀντιπίπτω** {1x} **antipiptō**, *an-tee-pip'-to;* from *473* and *4098* (incl. its alt.); to *oppose:*—resist {1x}.

This word literally and primarily means "to fall against or upon" [*anti,* "against," *pipto,* "to fall"], then by extension, "to strive against, resist" and is used in Acts 7:51 of "resisting" the Holy Spirit. See: BAGD—75d; THAYER—51b.

497. **ἀντιστρατεύομαι** {1x} **antistratĕuŏmai**, *an-tee-strat-yoo'-om-ahee;* from *473* and *4754;* (fig.) to *attack,* i.e. (by impl.) *destroy:*—war against {1x}.

This word means to make a military expedition, or take the field, against anyone, to oppose, war against (Rom 7:23). See: BAGD—75d; THAYER—51b.

498. **ἀντιτάσσομαι** {5x} **antitassŏmai**, *an-tee-tas'-som-ahee;* from *473* and the mid. voice of *5021;* to *range oneself against,* i.e. *oppose:*—oppose themselves {1x}, resist {4x}.

This word is used in the middle voice in the sense of setting oneself against [*anti,* "against," *tasso,* "to order, set"], and denotes **(1)** "opposing oneself to": "And when they opposed themselves, and blasphemed, he (Paul) shook *his* raiment, and said unto them, Your blood *be* upon your own heads; I *am* clean: from henceforth I will go unto the Gentiles" (Acts 18:6); and **(2)** elsewhere rendered by the verb "to resist": (Rom 13:2; Jas 4:6; 5:6; 1 Pet 5:5). Syn.: 475, 480. See: BAGD—76a; THAYER—51b.

499. **ἀντίτυπον** {2x} **antitupŏn**, *an-teet'-oo-pon;* neut. of a comp. of *473* and *5179; corresponding* ["antitype"], i.e. a *representative, counterpart:*—figure {1x}, like figure whereunto {1x}.

Antitupos, an adjective, used as a noun, denotes, lit., "a striking back"; metaphorically, "resisting, adverse"; then, in a passive sense, "struck back"; in the NT metaphorically, "corresponding to," **(1)** a copy of an archetype, i.e., the event or person or circumstance corresponding to the type, Heb 9:24, "the figure of", of the tabernacle, which, with its structure and appurtenances, was a pattern of that "holy place," "Heaven itself," "the true," into which Christ entered, "to appear before the face of God for us." The earthly tabernacle anticipatively represented what is now made good in Christ; it was a "figure" or "parable" (9:9), "for the time now present"; **(2)** "a corresponding type," 1 Pet 3:21, said of baptism; the circumstances of the flood, the ark and its occupants, formed a type, and baptism forms "a corresponding type," each setting forth the spiritual realities of the death, burial, and resurrection of believers in their identification with Christ. It is not a case of type and antitype, but of two types, that in Genesis, the type, and baptism, the corresponding type. Syn.: 3850, 5179. See: TDNT—8:246, 1193; BAGD—76a; THAYER—51c.

500. **ἀντίχριστος** {5x} **antichristŏs**, *an-tee'-khris-tos;* from *473* and *5547;* an *opponent of, an imposter for the Messiah:*—antichrist {5x}.

Antichristos can mean either "against Christ" or "instead of Christ," or perhaps, combining the two, "one who, assuming the guise of Christ, opposes Christ and takes His place. Syn.: 5580. The *antichristos* denies Jesus in the flesh is the Christ (2 Jn 2:7); the pseudochristos (5580) affirms himself to be the Christ. See: TDNT—9:493, 1322; BAGD—76b; THAYER—51c.

501. **ἀντλέω** {4x} **antlĕō**, *ant-leh-o;* from ἄντλος **antlŏs** (the *hold* of a ship); to *bale* up (prop. bilge water), i.e. *dip* water (with a bucket, pitcher, etc.):—draw {3x}, draw out {1x}.

Antleo, as a verb, signified primarily, "to draw out a ship's bilgewater, to bale or pump out"; hence, "to draw water" in any way: "And He saith unto them, Draw out (*antleo*) now, and bear unto the governor of the feast. And they bare *it*. When the ruler of the feast had tasted the water that was made wine, and knew not whence it was: but the servants which drew (*antleo*) the water knew . . ." (Jn 2:8–9; cf. 4:7, 15). Syn.: 307, 385, 392, 502, 645, 868, 1096, 1670, 1448, 1828, 2020, 2464, 4317, 4334, 4358, 4685, 4951, 5288, 5289. See: TDNT—9:493, 1322; BAGD—76b; THAYER—51d.

502. **ἄντλημα** {1x} **antlēma**, *ant'-lay-mah;* from *501;* a *baling-vessel:*—nothing to draw with + 3777 {1x}.

In John 4:11, "to draw with" translates the corresponding noun *antlema*, "a bucket for drawing water by a rope." Syn.: 307, 385, 392, 501, 645, 868, 1096, 1670, 1448, 1828, 2020, 2464, 4317, 4334, 4358, 4685, 4951, 5288, 5289. See: TDNT—9:493, 1322; BAGD—76c; THAYER—52a.

503. **ἀντοφθαλμέω** {1x} **antŏphthalmĕō**, *ant-of-thal-meh'-o;* from a compound of *473* and *3788;* to *face:*—bear up into {1x}.

This word literally means to look against or straight at; and hence, metaphorically, to bear up against, withstand, "to face": "And when the ship was caught, and could not bear up into (*antophthalmeo*) the wind, we let *her* drive" (Acts 27:15. See: BAGD—76c; THAYER—52a.

504. **ἄνυδρος** {4x} **anudrŏs**, *an'-oo-dros;* from *1* (as a neg. particle) and *5204;* *waterless*, i.e. *dry:*—dry {2x}, without water {2x}.

Anudros literally means "waterless" and is rendered **(1)** "dry" in Mt 12:43 and Lk 11:24, and **(2)** "without water" in 2 Pet 2:17 and Jude 12. See: BAGD—76c; THAYER—52a.

505. **ἀνυπόκριτος** {6x} **anupŏkritŏs**, *an-oo-pok'-ree-tos;* from *1* (as a neg. particle) and a presumed der. of *5271;* *undissembled*, i.e. *sincere:*—without dissimulation {1x}, without hypocrisy {1x}, unfeigned {4x}.

This word signifies "true, unfeigned, without hypocrisy": **(1)** of love (2 Cor 6:6; 1 Pet 1:22; Rom 12:9 "without dissimulation); **(2)** of faith (1 Ti 1:5; 2 Tim 1:5); **(3)** of the wisdom that is from above (Jas 3:17 "without hypocrisy"). See: TDNT—8:570, 1235; BAGD—76d; THAYER—52a.

506. **ἀνυπότακτος** {4x} **anupŏtaktŏs**, *an-oo-pot'-ak-tos;* from *1* (as a neg. particle) and a presumed der. of *5293;* *unsubdued*, i.e. *insubordinate* (in fact or temper):—disobedient {1x}, that is not put under {1x}, unruly {2x}.

This word stresses "not subject to rule" and is used **(1)** of things: "Thou hast put all things in subjection under His feet. For in that He put all in subjection under Him, He left nothing *that is* not put under (*anupotaktos*) Him. But now we see not yet all things put under Him" (Heb 2:8 "not put under"); **(2)** of persons: "Knowing this, that the law is not made for a righteous man, but for the lawless and disobedient (*anupotaktos*), for the ungodly and for sinners . . ." (1 Ti 1:9; cf. Titus 1:6, 10). Syn.: 814. See: TDNT—8:47, 1156; BAGD—76d; THAYER—52b.

507. **ἄνω** {9x} **anō**, *an'-o;* adv. from *473;* *upward* or *on the top; in a higher place:*—above {5x}, brim {1x}, high {1x}, up {2x}.

This word denotes **(1)** "above, in a higher place"(Acts 2:19). **(2)** With the article it means "that which is above" (Gal 4:26; Phil 3:14 "the high calling"); **(3)** with the plural article, "the things above" (Jn 8:23, lit., "from the things above"; Col 3:1–2). **(4)** With *heos*, "as far as," it is translated "up to the brim" (Jn 2:7). **(5)** It has the meaning "upwards" (Jn 11:41; Heb 12:15). See: TDNT—1:376, 63; BAGD—76d; THAYER—52b.

508. **ἀνώγεον** {2x} **anōgĕōn**, *an-ogue'-eh-on* (or, ἀνάγαιον *an-ag-ahee'-on;* from *507* and *1093;* *above* the *ground*, i.e. (prop.) the *second floor* of a building; used for a *dome* or a *balcony* on the upper story:—upper room {2x}.

Anogeon is "an upper room" and occurs in Mk 14:15; Lk 22:12, "a chamber," often over a porch, or connected with the roof, where meals were taken and privacy obtained. See: BAGD—77a; THAYER—52b.

509. **ἄνωθεν** {13x} **anōthĕn**, *an'-o-then;* from *507; from above;* by anal. *from the first;* by impl. *anew:*—from above {5x}, top {3x}, again {2x}, from the first {1x}, from the beginning {1x}, not tr {1x}.

This word literally means "from above" and is used **(1)** of place **(1a)** with the meaning "from the top" (Mt 27:51; Mk 15:38 of the temple veil); **(1b)** in Jn 19:23 of the garment of Christ, lit., "from the upper parts" (plural); **(2)** of things which come from heaven, or from God in Heaven (Jn 3:31; 19:11; Jas 1:17; 3:15, 17). It is also used in the sense of "again" (Jn 3:3). See: TDNT—1:378, 63; BAGD—77a; THAYER—52b.

510. **ἀνωτερικός** {1x} **anōtĕrikŏs**, *an-o-ter-ee-kos';* from *511;* *superior*, i.e. (locally) *more remote:*—upper {1x}.

Anoterikos means "upper" and is used in the plural in Acts 19:1 to denote "upper regions, coast"; i.e., the high central plateau, in contrast to the roundabout way by the river through the valley. See: BAGD—77c; THAYER—52c.

511. **ἀνώτερος** {2x} **anōtĕrŏs**, *an-o'-ter-os;* comparative degree of *507;* *upper*, i.e. (neut. as adv.) to a *more conspicuous* place, in a *former* part of the book:—above {1x}, higher {1x}.

It is used **(1)** of motion to a higher place, "higher," Lk 14:10; **(2)** of location in a higher place, i.e., in the preceding part of a passage, "above" Heb 10:8. See: TDNT—1:376,*; BAGD—77c; THAYER—52c.

512. **ἀνωφέλες** {2x} **anōphĕlĕs**, *an-o-fel'-ace;* from *1* (as a neg. particle) and the base of *5624;* *useless* or (neut.) *inutility:*—unprofitable {1x}, unprofitableness {1x}.

Anopheles, as an adjective, means "not beneficial or serviceable" and is rendered **(1)** "unprofitable": "But avoid foolish questions, and genealogies, and contentions, and strivings about the law; for they are unprofitable and vain" (Titus 3:9); **(2)** "unprofitableness": "For there is verily a disannulling of the commandment going before for the weakness and unprofitableness thereof" (Heb 7:18 in the neuter, used as a noun) said of the Law as not accomplishing that which the "better hope" could alone bring. Syn.: 255, 888, 889, 890. See: BAGD—77c; THAYER—52d.

513. **ἀξίνη** {2x} **axinē**, *ax-ee'-nay;* prob. from ἄγνυμι **agnumi** (to *break;* comp. *4486*); an *axe:*—axe {2x}.

This word is found in Mt 3:10, and Lk 3:9. See: BAGD—77d; THAYER—52d.

514. **ἄξιος** {41x} **axiŏs**, *ax'-ee-os;* prob. from *71;* *deserving, being of worth, comparable* or *suitable* (as if *drawing* praise):—worthy {35x}, meet {4x}, due reward {1x}, unworthy + 3756 {1x}.

Axios has the meaning of being of "weight, value, worth"; also "befitting, becoming, right on the ground of fitness" (Mt 3:8 "meet"; Acts 26:20; Lk 3:8 "worthy"; 23:41 "due reward"). See: TDNT—1:379, 63; BAGD—78a; THAYER—52d.

515. **ἀξιόω** {7x} **axiŏō**, *ax-ee-ŏ'-o;* from *514;* to *deem entitled* or *fit:*—count worthy {3x}, think worthy {2x}, think good {1x}, desire {1x}.

This word means **(1)** "to think meet, fit, right (Acts 15:38; 28:22); or **(2)** to judge worthy, deem, deserving (Lk 7:7; 2 Th 1:11; 1 Ti 5:17; Heb 3:3; 10:29). See: TDNT—1:380, 63; BAGD—78c; THAYER—53a.

516. **ἀξίως** {6x} **axiōs**, *ax-ee'-oce;* adv. from *514;* *appropriately:*—worthy {3x}, as becometh {2x}, after a godly sort + 2316 {1x}.

This word means **(1)** "worthily" and is translated in **(1a)** "worthily of God" (1 Th 2:12 of the Christian walk as it should be; 3 John 6 of assisting servants of God in a way which reflects God's character and thoughts); **(1b)** "worthily of the Lord" (Col. 1:10); **(2)** of the calling of believers (Eph 4:1 in regard to their "walk" or manner of life); **(3)** "worthy of the gospel of Christ" (Phil 1:27 of a manner of life in accordance with what the gospel declares); **(4)** "worthily of the saints" (Rom 16:2 of receiving a fellow believer in such a manner as befits those who bear the name of "saints"). See: BAGD—78d; THAYER—53a.

517. **ἀόρατος** {5x} **aŏratŏs**, *ah-or'-at-os;* from *1* (as a neg. particle) and *3707;* *invisible:*—invisible {4x}, invisible things {1x}.

This word literally means "unseen" and is translated "invisible" **(1)** in Rom 1:20 of the power and divinity of God; **(2)** of God Himself (Col 1:15; 1 Ti 1:17; Heb 11:27); **(3)** of things unseen (Col 1:16). See: TDNT—5:368, 706; BAGD—79a; THAYER—53b.

518. **ἀπαγγέλλω** {45x} **apaggĕllō**, *ap-ang-el'-lo;* from *575* and the base of *32;* to *announce:*—tell {26x}, show {10x}, declare {3x}, report {2x}, bring word {1x}, bring word again {1x}, show again {1x}, vr show {1x}.

Apangello, as a verb, means "to announce" and is translated "bring word" in Mt 2:8: "And he [Herod] sent them [the magi] to Bethlehem, and said, Go and search diligently for the young child; and when ye have found *him*, bring me word again [apangello], that I may come and worship him also" (cf. Mt 28:8). See: TDNT—1:64, 10; BAGD—79b; THAYER—53b.

519. **ἀπάγχομαι** {1x} **apagchŏmai**, *ap-ang'-khom-ahee* from *575* and ἄγχω **agchō** (to *choke;* akin to the base of *43*); to *strangle oneself off* (i.e. to death):—hang himself {1x}.

Apagchomai signifies "to strangle" and in the middle voice means to "hang" one's self (Mt 27:5). See: BAGD—79c; THAYER—53c.

520. **ἀπάγω** {16x} **apagō**, *ap-ag'-o;* from *575* and *71;* to *take off* (in various senses):—lead away {10x}, lead {2x}, put to death {1x}, bring {1x}, take away {1x}, carry away {1x}.

(1) *Apago*, as a verb, means "to lead away, bring forth, bring unto": "Then Paul called one of the centurions unto *him*, and said, Bring this young man unto (*apago*) the chief captain: for he hath a certain thing to tell him" (Acts 23:17). **(2)** *Apago* is used especially in a judicial sense, "to put to death," e.g., Acts 12:19. Syn.: 336, 337, 520, 1935, 2288, 2289, 5054. See: BAGD—79c; THAYER—53c.

521. **ἀπαίδευτος** {1x} **apaidĕutŏs**, *ap-ah'-ee-dyoo-tos;* from *1* (as a neg. particle) and a der. of *3811; uninstructed,* i.e. (fig.) *stupid:*—unlearned {1x}.

Apaideutos, as an adjective, means "uninstructed" (3811 - paideuo, "to train, teach") and is translated "unlearned": "But foolish and unlearned questions avoid, knowing that they do gender strifes" (2 Ti 2:23). Syn.: 62, 261. See: TDNT—5:596, 753; BAGD—79d; THAYER—53c.

522. **ἀπαίρω** {3x} **apairō**, *ap-ah'-ee-ro;* from *575* and *142;* to *lift off,* i.e. *remove:*—take {1x}, take away {2x}.

Apairo means "to lift off" and is used, in the passive voice, of Christ, metaphorically as the Bridegroom taken from His followers (Mt 9:15; Mk 2:20; Lk 5:35). See: BAGD—79d; THAYER—53d.

523. **ἀπαιτέω** {2x} **apaitĕō**, *ap-ah'-ee-teh-o;* from *575* and *154;* to *demand back:*—ask again {1x}, require {1x}.

Apaiteo means "to ask back, demand back" and is translated **(1)** "shall be required" in Lk 12:20, lit. "do they require," in the impersonal sense; and **(2)** "to ask again" in Lk 6:30: "Give to every man that asketh of thee; and of him that taketh away thy goods ask *them* not again." It is used in the papyri frequently in the sense of "demanding, making demands." See: TDNT—1:193, 30; BAGD—80a; THAYER—53d.

524. **ἀπαλγέω** {1x} **apalgĕō**, *ap-alg-eh'-o;* from *575* and ἀλγέω **algĕō** (to *smart*); to *grieve out,* i.e. *become apathetic:*—be past feeling {1x}.

Apalgeo signifies to cease to feel pain for [*apo* "from," *algeo,* "to feel pain"; cf. Eng., "neuralgia"]; hence, to be callous, "past feeling," insensible to honor and shame: "Who being past feeling have given themselves over unto lasciviousness, to work all uncleanness with greediness" (Eph 4:19). See: BAGD—80a; THAYER—53d.

525. **ἀπαλλάσσω** {3x} **apallassō**, *ap-al-las'-so;* from *575* and *236;* to *change away,* i.e. *release,* (refl.) *remove:*—deliver {2x}, depart {1x}.

Apallasso, as a verb, means literally "to change from" [apo, "from," allasso, "to change"], "to free from, release" and is **(1)** translated "deliver": "And deliver them who through fear of death were all their lifetime subject to bondage" (Heb 2:15); **(2)** in Lk 12:58, it is used in a legal sense of being quit of a person, i.e., the opponent being appeased and withdrawing his suit: "When thou goest with thine adversary to the magistrate, *as thou art* in the way, give diligence that thou mayest be delivered (*apallasso*) from him; lest he hale thee to the judge, and the judge deliver thee to the officer, and the officer cast thee into prison." Syn.: 325, 629, 591, 859, 1325, 1560, 1659, 1807, 1929, 3086, 3860, 4506, 5483. See: TDNT—1:252, 40; BAGD—80a; THAYER—53d.

526. **ἀπαλλοτριόω** {3x} **apallŏtriŏō**, *ap-al-lot-ree-ŏ'-o;* from *575* and a der. of *245;* to *estrange away,* i.e. (pass. and fig.) to *be non-participant:*—be alienated with + 5607 {2x}, be alien {1x}.

This word signifies "to be rendered an alien, to be alienated." **(1)** In Eph 2:12: "That at that time ye were without Christ, being aliens (*apallotrioo*) from the commonwealth of Israel, and strangers from the covenants of promise"; **(2)** elsewhere in Eph 4:18 and Col 1:21 the condition of the unbeliever is presented in a threefold state of "alienation," **(2a)** from the commonwealth of Israel, **(2b)** from the life of God, **(2c)** from God Himself. See: TDNT—1:265, 43; BAGD—80b; THAYER—54a.

527. **ἁπαλός** {2x} **hapalŏs**, *hap-al-os';* of uncert. der.; *soft:*—tender {2x}.

This word means "soft, tender" and is used of the branch of a tree which is full of sap (Mt 24:32; Mk 13:28). See: BAGD—80b; THAYER—54a.

528. **ἀπαντάω** {7x} **apantaō**, *ap-an-tah'-o;* from *575* and a der. of *473;* to *meet away,* i.e. *encounter:*—meet {7x}.

Apantao means to go to meet, to meet with a purpose, to meet with, come face to face with and is used in Mk 14:13; Lk 17:12; Mt 28:9; Mk 5:2; Lk 14:31; Jn 4:51; Acts 16:16. See: BAGD—80c; THAYER—54a.

529. **ἀπάντησις** {4x} **apantēsis**, *ap-an'-tay-sis;* from *528;* a (friendly) *encounter:*—to meet + 1519 {4x}.

This word means "a meeting" and occurs in Mt 25:1, 6; Acts 28:15; 1 Th 4:17. It is used in the papyri of a newly arriving magistrate. It seems that the special idea of the word was the official welcome of a newly arrived dignitary. See: TDNT—1:380, 64; BAGD—80c; THAYER—54a.

530. **ἅπαξ** {15x} **hapax**, *hap'-ax;* prob. from *537; one* (or a *single*) *time* (numerically or conclusively):—once {15x}.

This word denotes **(1)** "once, one time" (2 Cor 11:25; Heb 9:7, 26–27; 12:26–27; in the phrase "once and again," lit., "once and twice" Phil 4:16; 1 Th 2:18); **(2)** "once, once for all" of what is of perpetual validity, not requiring repetition (Heb 6:4; 9:28; 10:2; 1 Pet 3:18; Jude 3 & 5 "once"; 1 Pet 3:20). See: TDNT—1:381, 64; BAGD—80c; THAYER—54a.

531. **ἀπαράβατος** {1x} **aparabatŏs**, *ap-ar-ab'-at-os;* from *1* (as a neg. particle) and a der. of *3845; not passing away,* i.e. *untransferable* (perpetual):—unchangeable {1x}.

This word means unviolated, not to be violated, inviolable, unchangeable and therefore not liable to pass to a successor and is used of the priesthood of Christ in Heb 7:24. See: TDNT—5:742, 772; BAGD—80d; THAYER—54b.

532. **ἀπαρασκεύαστος** {1x} **aparaskĕuastŏs**, *ap-ar-ask-yoo'-as-tos;* from *1* (as a neg. particle) and a der. of *3903; unready:*—unprepared {1x}.

This word means unprepared and occurs in 2 Cor 9:4: "Lest haply if they of Macedonia come with me, and find you unprepared, we (that we say not, ye) should be ashamed in this same confident boasting." See: BAGD—80d; THAYER—54b.

533. **ἀπαρνέομαι** {13x} **aparnĕŏmai**, *ap-ar-neh'-om-ahee;* from *575* and *720;* to *deny utterly,* i.e. *disown, abstain:*—deny {13x}.

This word means **(1)** "to deny utterly," to abjure, to affirm that one has no connection with a person, **(1a)** as in Peter's denial of Christ (Mt 26:34–35, 75; Mk 14:30–31, 72; Lk 22:34, 61; Jn 13:38). **(1a1)** This stronger form is used in the Lord's statements foretelling Peter's "denial," and in Peter's assurance of fidelity; **(1a2)** the simple verb (arneomai - 720) is used in all the records of his actual denial. **(1b)** The strengthened form is the verb used in the Lord's warning as to being "denied" in the presence of the angels (Lk 12:9); **(1b1)** in the preceding clause, "he that denieth Me," the simple verb *arneomai* is used; **(1b2)** the rendering therefore should be understood as "he that denieth Me in the presence of men, shall be utterly denied in the presence of the angels of God"; **(2)** "to deny oneself" as a follower of Christ (Mt 16:24; Mk 8:34; Lk 9:23). See: TDNT—1:471,*; BAGD—81a; THAYER—54b.

534. **ἀπάρτι** {1x} **aparti**, *ap-ar'-tee;* from *575* and *737; from now,* i.e. *henceforth* (*already*):—from henceforth {1x}.

This word means from this point in time and forward without end. See: BAGD—81a; THAYER—54c.

535. **ἀπαρτισμός** {1x} **apartismŏs**, *ap-ar-tis-mos';* from a der. of *534; completion:*—finish {1x}. See: BAGD—81b; THAYER—54c.

536. **ἀπαρχή** {8x} **aparchē**, *ap-ar-khay';* from a compound of *575* and *756;* a *beginning* of sacrifice, i.e. the (Jewish) *first-fruit* (fig.):—firstfruits {8x}.

Aparche denotes, primarily, "an offering of firstfruits." **(1)** Though the English word is plural in each of its occurrences save Rom. 11:16, **(1a)** the Greek word is always singular. **(1b)** Two Hebrew words are thus translated, **(1b1)** one meaning the "chief" or "principal part," e.g., Num 18:12; Prov 3:9; **(1b2)** the other, "the earliest ripe of the crop or of the tree," e.g., Ex 23:16; Neh 10:35; **(1b3)** they are found together, e.g., in Ex 23:19, "the first of the firstfruits." **(2)** The term is applied in things spiritual, **(2a)** to the presence of the Holy Spirit with the believer as the firstfruits of the full harvest of the Cross, Rom 8:23; **(2b)** to Christ Himself in resurrection in relation to all believers who have fallen asleep, 1 Cor 15:20, 23; **(2c)** to the earliest believers in a country in relation to those of their countrymen subsequently converted, Rom 16:5; 1 Cor 16:15; **(2d)** to the believers of this age in relation to the whole of the redeemed, 2 Th 2:13; Jas 1:18; Rev 14:4. See: TDNT—1:484, 81; BAGD—81b; THAYER—54c.

537. **ἅπας** {44x} **hapas**, *hap'-as;* from *1* (as a particle of union) and *3956;* absolutely *all* or (sing.) *every* one:—all {34x}, all things {5x}, whole {3x}, every one {1x}, every {1x}.

This is a strengthened form of *pas* (3956) and signifies "quite all, the whole," and, in the plural, "all, all things." Preceded by an article and followed by a noun it means "the whole of." In 1 Ti 1:16 the significance is "the whole of His longsuffering," or "the fulness of His longsuffering. See: TDNT—5:886, 795; BAGD—81d; THAYER—54d, 55a.

538. **ἀπατάω** {4x} **apataō**, *ap-at-ah'-o;* of uncert. der.; to *cheat,* i.e. *delude:*—deceive {4x}. Syn.: 1185, 1818. See: TDNT—1:384, 65; BAGD—81d; THAYER—55a.

539. **ἀπάτη** {7x} **apatē**, *ap-at'-ay;* from *538; delusion:*—deceitfulness {3x}, deceitful {1x}, deceit {1x}, deceivableness {1x}, deceivings {1x}.

Apate means **(1)** "deceit or deceitfulness, that which gives a false impression, whether by appearance, statement or influence" and is said **(1a)** of riches (Mt 13:22; Mk 4:19); **(1b)** of sin (Heb 3:13). **(2)** The phrase in Eph 4:22 "deceitful lusts" signifies lusts excited by "deceit," of which "deceit" is the source of strength, not lusts "deceitful" in themselves. **(3)** In 2 Th 2:10 "all deceivableness of unrighteousness" signifies all manner of unscrupulous words and deeds designed to "deceive" (see Rev 13:13–15). **(4)** In Col 2:8, "vain deceit" suggests that "deceit" is void of anything profitable. Syn.: 538, 1386, 1388, 1818, 5422. See: TDNT—1:385, 65; BAGD—82a; THAYER—55a.

540. **ἀπάτωρ** {1x} **apatōr**, *ap-at'-ore;* from *1* (as a neg. particle) and *3962; fatherless,* i.e. *of unrecorded paternity:*—without father {1x}.

Apator signifies in Heb 7:3 with no recorded genealogy. See: TDNT—5:1019, 805; BAGD—82b; THAYER—55b.

541. **ἀπαύγασμα** {1x} **apaugasma**, *ap-ŏw'-gas-mah;* from a compound of *575* and *826;* an *off-flash,* i.e. *effulgence:*—brightness {1x}.

This word means "a shining forth" [*apo,* "from," *augo,* "brightness"], of a light coming from a luminous body, is said of Christ in Heb 1:3, i.e., shining forth (not a reflected brightness). See: TDNT—1:508, 87; BAGD—82b; THAYER—55b.

542. **ἀπείδω** {1x} **apĕidō**, *ap-i'-do;* from *575* and the same as *1492;* to *see* fully:—see {1x}.

This word is used in Phil 2:23 and means to wait and perceive how things unfold before making a decision: "Him [Timotheus] therefore I hope to send presently, so soon as I shall see how it will go with me." See: BAGD—82c; THAYER—55b.

543. **ἀπείθεια** {7x} **apĕithĕia**, *ap-i'-thi-ah;* from *545; disbelief* (obstinate and rebellious):—disobedience {3x}, unbelief {4x}.

This word literally means "the condition of being unpersuadable" and denotes "obstinacy, obstinate rejection of the will of God"; hence, "disobedience, unbelief" (Eph 2:2; 5:6; Col 3:6; Rom 11:30, 32; Heb 4:6, 11). See: TDNT—6:11, 818; BAGD—82c; THAYER—55c.

544. **ἀπειθέω** {16x} **apĕithĕō**, *ap-i-theh'-o;* from *545;* to *disbelieve* (wilfully and perversely):—believe not {8x}, disobedient {4x}, obey not {3x}, unbelieving {1x}.

This word means "to refuse to be persuaded, to refuse belief, to be disobedient" and is translated **(1)** "believeth not" (Jn 3:36); **(2)** "unbelieving" (Acts 14:2), **(3)** "believed not" (Acts 17:5; 19:9; Heb 3:18; 11:31), **(4)** "do not obey" (Rom 2:8), **(5)** "disobedient" (Rom 10:21), **(6)** "have not believed" (Rom 11:3, 31), **(7)** "do not believe" (Rom 15:31), **(8)** "disobedient" (1 Pet 2:7, 8; 3:20), **(9)** "obey not" (1 Pet 3:1; 4:17). See: TDNT—6:10, 818; BAGD—82c; THAYER—55c.

545. **ἀπειθής** {6x} **apĕithēs**, *ap-i-thace';* from *1* (as a neg. particle) and *3982; unpersuadable,* i.e. *contumacious:*—disobedient {6x}.

This word signifies "unwilling to be persuaded, spurning belief, disobedient" (Lk 1:17; Acts 26:19; Rom 1:30; 2 Ti 3:2; Titus 1:16; 3:3). See: TDNT—6:10, 818; BAGD—82d; THAYER—55c.

546. **ἀπειλέω** {2x} **apĕilĕō**, *ap-i-leh'-o;* of uncert. der.; to *menace;* by impl. to *forbid:*—threaten {2x}.

Apeileo is **(1)** used of Christ, negatively, in 1 Pet 2:23: "Who, when He was reviled, reviled not again; when He suffered, He threatened not; but committed *Himself* to Him that judgeth righteously"; and **(2)** in the middle voice, "But that it spread no further among the people, let us straitly threaten (apeilo) them, that they speak henceforth to no man in this name" (Acts 4:17 lit., "let us threaten . . . with threatening). See: BAGD—82d; THAYER—55d.

547. **ἀπειλή** {4x} **apĕilē**, *ap-i-lay';* from *546;* a *menace:*—× straitly {1x}, threatening {3x}.

This word means a strong threatening (Acts 4:17, 29; 9:1; Eph 6:9). See: BAGD—83a; THAYER—55d.

548. **ἄπειμι** {7x} **apĕimi**, *ap'-i-mee;* from *575* and *1510;* to *be away:*—be absent {1x}, absent {6x}.

This word means to go away, depart, and hence to be absent (1 Cor 5:3; 2 Cor 10:1, 11; 13:2, 10; Phil 1:27; Col 2:5). See: BAGD—83a; THAYER—55d. comp. *549.*

549. **ἄπειμι** {1x} **apĕimi**, *ap'-i-mee;* from *575* and **εἶμι ĕimi** (to go), to go away: go {1x}.

This word means "to go away, depart" (Acts 17:10). See: BAGD—83a; THAYER—55d. comp. *548.*

550. **ἀπειπόμην** {1x} **apĕipŏmēn**, *ap-i-pom'-ane;* refl. past of a compound of *575* and *2036;* to *say off* for oneself, i.e. *disown:*—renounce {1x}.

This word literally means "to tell from" and signifies "to renounce" (2 Cor 4:2 middle voice, of disowning "the hidden things of shame"). In the Sept. of 1 Kin 11:2 it signifies "to forbid," a meaning found in the papyri. The meaning "to renounce" may therefore carry with it the thought of forbidding the approach of the things disowned. See: BAGD—83b; THAYER—55d.

551. **ἀπείραστος** {1x} **apĕirastŏs**, *ap-i'-ras-tos;* from *1* (as a neg. particle) and a presumed der. of *3987; untried,* i.e. *not temptable:*—not to be tempted + 2076.

This word means "untempted, untried" and occurs in Jas 1:13: "Let no man say when he is tempted, I am tempted of God: for God cannot be tempted (*apeirastos*) with evil, neither tempteth He any man" [with *eimi-* 2076, "to be," "cannot be tempted," "untemptable"]. See: TDNT—6:23, 822; BAGD—83b; THAYER—55d.

552. **ἄπειρος** {1x} **apĕirŏs**, *ap'-i-ros;* from *1* (as a neg. particle) and *3984; inexperienced,* i.e. *ignorant:*—unskillful {1x}.

This word means "without experience, inexperienced" [*a,* negative, *peira,* "a trial, experiment"]: "For every one that useth milk *is* unskilful in the word of righteousness: for he is a babe" (Heb 5:13). See: BAGD—83b; THAYER—56a.

553. **ἀπεκδέχομαι** {7x} **apĕkdĕchŏmai**, *ap-ek-dekh'-om-ahee;* from *575* and *1551;* to *expect fully:*—look for {2x}, wait for {5x}.

This word means "to await or expect eagerly" and is rendered "to wait for" (Rom 8:19, 23, 25; 1 Cor 1:7; Gal 5:5; Phil. 3:20 "look for"; Heb 9:28 "look for"; 1 Pet 3:20). See: TDNT—2:56, 146; BAGD—83c; THAYER—56a.

554. **ἀπεκδύομαι** {2x} **apĕkduŏmai**, *ap-ek-doo'-om-ahee;* mid. voice from *575* and *1562;* to *divest wholly* oneself, or (for oneself) *despoil:*—put off {1x}, spoil {1x}.

This word means "to strip off clothes or armaments" and is used in the middle voice: **(1)** Col 2:15: "*And* having spoiled (*apekduomai*) principalities and powers, He made a shew of them openly, triumphing over them in it"; and **(2)** Col 3:9: "ye have put off" of "the old man." See: TDNT—2:318,*; BAGD—83c; THAYER—56a.

555. **ἀπέκδυσις** {1x} **apĕkdusis**, *ap-ek'-doo-sis;* from *554; divestment:*—putting off {1x}.

This word means "a putting off, a stripping off, a laying aside" and is used in Col 2:11 of "the body of the flesh." See: TDNT—2:321, 192; BAGD—83c; THAYER—56a.

556. **ἀπελαύνω** {1x} **apĕlaunō**, *ap-el-ŏw'-no;* from *575* and *1643;* to *dismiss:*—drive {1x}.

This word means "to drive from, to drive off" and is used in Acts 18:16: "And he drave them from the judgment seat." See: BAGD—83c; THAYER—56a.

557. **ἀπελεγμός** {1x} **apĕlĕgmŏs**, *ap-el-eg-mos';* from a compound of *575* and *1651; refutation,* i.e. (by impl.) *contempt:*—nought {1x}.

Apelegmos denotes "censure, repudiation" [of something shown to be worthless], hence, "contempt, disrepute": "So that not only this our craft is in danger to be set at nought (*apelegmos*); but also that the temple of the great goddess Diana should be despised, and her magnificence should be destroyed, whom all Asia and the world worshippeth" (Acts 19:27). See: BAGD—83d; THAYER—56a.

558. **ἀπελεύθερος** {1x} **apĕlĕuthĕrŏs**, *ap-el-yoo'-ther-os;* from *575* and *1658;* one *freed away from slavery,* i.e. a *freedman:*—freeman {1x}.

An *apeleutheros* is a slave that has been released from servitude, a "freeman, a freed man" and is used in 1 Cor 7:22: "For he that is called in the Lord, *being* a servant, is the Lord's freeman: likewise also he that is called, *being* free, is Christ's servant." Here the fuller word brings out the spiritual emancipation in contrast to the natural "freedman." See: TDNT—2:487, 224; BAGD—83d; THAYER—56b.

559. **Ἀπελλῆς** {1x} **Apĕllēs**, *ap-el-lace';* of Lat. or.; *Apelles,* a Chr.:—*Apelles* {1x}. See: BAGD—83d; THAYER—56b.

560. **ἀπελπίζω** {1x} **apĕlpizō**, *ap-el-pid'-zo;* from *575* and *1679;* to *hope out,* i.e. *fully expect:*—hope for again {1x}.

This word means literally "to give up in despair, to despair" and is used in Lk 6:35: "But love ye your enemies, and do good, and lend, hoping for nothing again (*apelpizo*); and your reward shall be great, and ye shall be the children of the Highest: for He is kind unto the unthankful and *to* the evil." "Hoping for nothing again" is a wonderful phrase which stresses that a believer, when anticipating the future, rests without anxiety as to the result, or not "despairing" of the recompense from God. See: TDNT—2:533, 229; BAGD—83d; THAYER—56b.

561. **ἀπέναντι** {6x} **apĕnanti**, *ap-en'-an-tee;* from *575* and *1725; from in front,* i.e. *opposite, before* or *against:*—before {2x}, contrary {1x}, over against {2x}, in the presence of {1x}.

This word denotes **(1)** "opposite": "And there was Mary Magdalene, and the other Mary, sitting over against the sepulchre" (Mt 27:61); **(2)** "in the sight of, before": "When Pilate saw that he could prevail nothing, but *that* rather a tumult was made, he took water, and washed *his* hands before (*apenanti*) the multitude, saying, I am innocent of the blood of this just person: see ye *to it*" (Mt 27:24; Acts 3:16; Rom 3:18); **(1)** "contrary, against": "Whom Jason hath received: and these all do contrary (*apenanti*) to the decrees of Caesar, saying that there is another king, *one* Jesus" (Acts 17:7). See: BAGD—84a; THAYER—56b.

ἀπέπω apĕpō. See *550.*

562. **ἀπέραντος** {1x} **apĕrantŏs**, *ap-er'-an-tos;* from *1* (as a neg. particle) and a second. der. of *4008; unfinished,* i.e. (by impl.) *interminable:*—endless {1x}.

Aperantos means "to complete, finish" and signifies "interminable, endless"; it is said of genealogies: "Neither give heed to fables and endless genealogies, which minister questions, rather than godly edifying which is in faith: *so do*" (1 Tim 1:4). Syn.: 179. See: BAGD—84a; THAYER—56b.

563. **ἀπερισπάστως** {1x} **apĕrispastōs**, *ap-er-is-pas-toce';* adv. from a compound of *1* (as a neg. particle) and a presumed der. of *4049; undistractedly,* i.e. *free from* (domestic) *solicitude:*—without distraction {1x}.

This word means without distraction, without solicitude or anxiety or care: "And this I speak for your own profit; . . . that ye may attend upon the Lord without distraction." See: BAGD—84b; THAYER—56c.

564. **ἀπερίτμητος** {1x} **apĕritmētŏs**, *ap-er-eet'-may-tos;* from *1* (as a neg. particle) and a presumed der. of *4059; uncircumcised* (fig.):—uncircumcised {1x}.

Aperitmetos, as an adjective, means "uncircumcised" is used in Acts 7:51, metaphorically, of "heart and ears." Syn.: 203, 1986, 4059, 4061. See: TDNT—6:72, 831; BAGD—84b; THAYER—56c.

565. **ἀπέρχομαι** {120x} **apĕrchŏmai**, *ap-erkh'-om-ahee;* from *575* and *2064;* to *go off* (i.e. *depart*), *aside* (i.e. *apart*) or *behind* (i.e. *follow*), lit. or fig.:—go {53x}, depart {27x}, go (one's) way {16x}, go away {14x}, come {4x}, misc. {6x} = pass away, be past. See: TDNT—2:675, 257; BAGD—84c; THAYER—56c.

566. **ἀπέχει** {1x} **apĕchĕi**, *ap-ekh'-i;* third pers. sing. pres. ind. act. of *568* used impers.; *it is sufficient:*—it is enough {1x}. See: BAGD—84d; THAYER—57a.

567. **ἀπέχομαι** {6x} **apĕchŏmai**, *ap-ekh'-om-ahee;* mid. voice (refl.) of *568;* to *hold oneself off,* i.e. *refrain:*—abstain {6x}.

This word invariably refers to abstaining from evil practices, moral and ceremonial: "But that we write unto them, that they abstain (*apechomai*) from pollutions of idols, and *from* fornication, and *from* things strangled, and *from* blood" (Acts 15:20, 29; 1 Th 4:3; 5:22; 1 Ti 4:3; 1 Pet 2:11). See: BAGD—84d; THAYER—57a.

568. **ἀπέχω** {11x} **apĕchō**, *ap-ekh'-o;* from *575* and *2192;* (act.) to *have out,* i.e. *receive in full;* (intr.) to *keep* (oneself) *away,* i.e. *be distant* (lit. or fig.):—be {5x}, have {4x}, receive {2x}.

Apecho, as a verb, denotes **(1)** transitively, **(1a)** "to have in full, to have received": "Therefore when thou doest *thine* alms, do not sound a trumpet before thee, as the hypocrites do in the synagogues and in the streets, that they may have glory of men. Verily I say unto you, They (*apecho*) have their reward" (Mt 6:2; cf. 6:5, 16; Lk 6:24). **(1b)** In all these instances the present tense has a perfective force, consequent upon the combination with the prefix apo ["from"], not that it stands for the perfect tense, but that it views the action in its accomplished result; **(1c)** so in Phil 4:18: "But I have all, and abound: I am full, having received of Epaphroditus the things *which were sent* from you, an odour of a sweet smell, a sacrifice acceptable, well-pleasing to God"; **(1c)** in Philem 15, "(that) thou shouldest receive (have him for ever)" **(2)** intransitively, **(2a)** "to be away, distant"; "This people draweth nigh unto me with their mouth, and honoureth me with *their* lips; but their heart is far from me" (Mt 15:8; cf. Mk 7:6); **(2b)** "far off, afar": "Then Jesus went with them. And when He was now not far from the house, the centurion sent friends to Him, saying unto Him, Lord, trouble not thyself: for I am not worthy that thou shouldest enter under my roof" (Lk 7:6; 15:20); **(2c)** without an accompanying adverb, "which was from": "And, behold, two of them went that same day to a village called Emmaus, which was from Jerusalem *about* threescore furlongs" (Lk 24:13). Syn.: 324, 353, 354, 588, 618, 1209, 1523, 1926, 2210, 2865, 2975, 2983, 3028, 3335, 3336, 3858, 3880, 3970, 4327, 4355, 4356, 4380, 4381, 4382, 5562, 5264, 5274. See: TDNT—2:828, 286; BAGD—84d; THAYER—57a.

569. **ἀπιστέω** {7x} **apistĕō**, *ap-is-teh'-o;* from *571;* to *be unbelieving,* i.e. (trans.) *disbelieve,* or (by impl.) *disobey:*—believe not {7x}.

This word is used in Mk 16:11, 16; Lk 24:11, 41; Acts 28:24; Rom 3:3; 2 Ti 2:13 and is translated disbelieve implying that the unbeliever has had a full opportunity of believing and has rejected it. See: TDNT—6:174, 849; BAGD—85b; THAYER—57b.

570. **ἀπιστία** {12x} **apistia**, *ap-is-tee'-ah;* from *571; faithlessness,* i.e. (neg.) *disbelief* (*want* of Chr. *faith*), or (pos.) *unfaithfulness* (*disobedience*):—unbelief {12x}. See: TDNT—6:174, 849; BAGD—85c; THAYER—57b.

571. **ἄπιστος** {23x} **apistŏs**, *ap'-is-tos;* from *1* (as a neg. particle) and *4103;* (act.) *disbelieving,* i.e. *without* Chr. *faith* (spec. a *heathen*); (pass.) *untrustworthy* (person), or *incredible* (thing):—that believe not {6x}, unbelieving {5x}, faithless {4x}, unbeliever {4x}, infidel {2x}, thing incredible {1x}, which believe not {1x}.

Apistos is used with meanings somewhat parallel to apistia (570): **(1)** "untrustworthy, not worthy of confidence or belief, is said of things "incredible": "Why should it be thought a thing incredible (*apistos*) with you, that God should raise the dead?" (Acts 26:8); **(2)** "unbelieving, distrustful" used as a noun, "unbeliever" (Lk 12:46; 1 Ti 5:8 "infidel"; in Titus 1:15 and Rev 21:8 "unbelieving"); **(3)** "faithless" (Mt 17:17; Mk 9:19; Lk 9:41; Jn 20:27). **(4)** The word is most frequent in 1 and 2 Corinthians. See: TDNT—6:174, 849; BAGD—85d; THAYER—57b.

572. **ἁπλότης** {8x} **haplŏtēs**, *hap-lot'-ace;* from *573; singleness,* i.e. (subj.) *sincerity* (*without dissimulation* or *self-seeking*), or (obj.) *generosity* (*copious bestowal*):—bountifulness {1x}, liberal {1x}, liberalty {1x}, simplicity {3x}, singleness {2x}.

This word means "simple, single" and is **(1)** translated "bountifulness" (2 Cor 9:11; cf. 8:2; 9:13); from sincerity of mind springs "liberality." **(2)** The thought of sincerity is present in (Rom 12:8; 2 Cor 11:3; Eph 6:5; Col 3:22). See: TDNT—1:386, 65; BAGD—85d; THAYER—57c.

573. **ἁπλοῦς** {2x} **haplŏus**, *hap-looce';* prob. from *1* (as a particle of union) and the base of *4120;* prop. *folded together,* i.e. *single* (fig. *clear*):—single {2x}.

This word means "simple, single" and is used in a moral sense in Mt 6:22 and Lk 11:34, said of the eye; "singleness" of purpose keeps us from the snare of having a double treasure and consequently a divided heart. Syn.: As the akakos (172) has no harmfulness in him, and the adolos (97) no guile, so the akeraios (185) no foreign mixture, and the *haplous* (573) no folds within which to hide something. See: TDNT—1:386, 65; BAGD—86a; THAYER—57c.

574. **ἁπλῶς** {1x} **haplōs**, *hap-loce';* adv. from *573* (in the obj. sense of *572*); *bountifully:*—liberally {1x}.

This word means liberally, with singleness of heart" and is used in Jas 1:5 of God as the gracious and "liberal" giver. The word may be taken either (a) in a logical sense, signifying unconditionally, simply, or (b) in a moral sense, generously. See: BAGD—86b; THAYER—57d.

575. **ἀπό** {669x} **apŏ**, *apŏ';* a primary particle; *"off,"* i.e. *away* (from something near), in various senses (of place, time, or relation; lit. or fig.):—from {392x}, of {129x}, out of {48x}, for {10x}, off {10x}, by {9x}, at {9x}, in {6x}, since + 3739 5, on {5x}, not tr. {15x}, misc. {31x} = (X here-) after, ago, because of, before, by the space of, forth, upon, once, with. See: BAGD—86c; THAYER—57d. In composition (as a prefix) it usually denotes *separation, departure, cessation, completion, reversal,* etc.

576. **ἀποβαίνω** {4x} **apŏbainō**, *ap-ob-ah'-ee-no;* from *575* and the base of *939;* lit. to *disembark;* fig. to *eventuate:*—become {1x}, go out {1x}, turn {2x}.

This word **(1)** literally means to come down from, i.e. a ship (Lk 5:2; Jn 21:9); or **(2)** to turn out, result, to be the outcome (Lk 21:13; Phil 1:19). See: BAGD—88c; THAYER—59d.

577. **ἀποβάλλω** {2x} **apŏballō**, *ap-ob-al'-lo;* from *575* and *906;* to *throw off;* fig. to *lose:*—cast away {2x}.

Apoballo means "to throw off from, to lay aside, to cast away" **(1)** a garment (Mk 10:50 twice); or **(2)** "confidence" (Heb 10:35). See: BAGD—88D; THAYER—60a.

578. **ἀποβλέπω** {1x} **apŏblĕpō**, *ap-ob-lep'-o;* from *575* and *991;* to *look away* from everything else, i.e. (fig.) intently *regard:*—have respect {1x}.

Apoblepo, as a verb, signifies "to look away from" all else at one object; hence, "to look steadfastly": "Esteeming the reproach of Christ greater riches than the treasures in Egypt: for he [Moses] had respect (*apoblepo*) unto the recompence of the reward" (Heb 11:26). Syn.: 308, 352, 816, 872, 991, 1689, 1896, 1914, 1980, 1983, 2300, 2334, 3706, 3708, 3879, 4017, 4648. See: BAGD—89a; THAYER—60a.

579. **ἀπόβλητος** {1x} **apŏblētŏs**, *ap-ob'-lay-tos;* from *577; cast off,* i.e. (fig.) such as to *be rejected:*—be refused {1x}.

This word means to be thrown away, rejected, despised, abominated as unclean: "For every creature of God *is* good, and nothing to be refused, if it be received with thanksgiving" (1 Ti 4:4). See: BAGD—89a; THAYER—60a.

580. **ἀποβολή** {2x} **apŏbŏlē**, *ap-ob-ol-ay';* from *577; rejection;* fig. *loss:*—casting away {1x}, loss {1x}.

This word literally means "casting away" and is translated **(1)** "loss" in Acts 27:22; and **(2)** in Rom 11:15 "casting away" of the temporary exclusion of the nation of Israel from its position of divine favor involving the reconciling of the world (i.e., the provision made through the gospel, which brings the world within the scope of reconciliation). See: BAGD—89a; THAYER—60a.

581. **ἀπογενόμενος** {1x} **apŏgĕnŏmĕnŏs**, *ap-og-en-om'-en-os;* past part. of a compound of *575* and *1096; absent,* i.e. *deceased* (fig. *renounced*):—being dead {1x}.

This word literally means "to be away from" [*apo* here signifies "separation"] and is used in 1 Pet 2:24 of the believer's attitude towards sin as the result of Christ's having borne our sins in His body on the tree. BAGD—89b; THAYER—60a.

582. **ἀπογραφή** {2x} **apŏgraphē**, *ap-og-raf-ay';* from *583;* an *enrollment;* by impl. an *assessment:*—taxing {2x}.

This word means primarily a written copy (Luke 2:2; Acts 5:37). Taxing means an enrollment or registration in the public records of persons together with their income and property, as the basis of a census or valuation, i.e. that it might appear how much tax should be levied upon each one. See: BAGD—89b; THAYER—60a.

583. **ἀπογράφω** {4x} **apŏgraphō**, *ap-og-raf'-o;* from *575* and *1125;* to *write off* (a copy or list), i.e. *enroll:*—tax {3x}, write {1x}.

This is the verb for 582 and means to enter in a register or records specifically to enter in public records the names of men, their property and income. See: BAGD—89c; THAYER—60b.

584. **ἀποδείκνυμι** {4x} **apŏdĕiknumi**, *ap-od-ike'-noo-mee;* from *575* and *1166;* to *show off,* i.e. *exhibit;* fig. to *demonstrate,* i.e. *accredit:*—approve {1x}, prove {1x}, set forth {1x}, shew {1x}.

This word means to point away from one's self, to point out, show forth, to expose to view, exhibit, to declare, to show, to prove what kind of person anyone is, to prove by arguments, and is used once in the sense of proving by demonstration, and so bringing about an "approval." The Lord Jesus was "a Man approved of God by mighty works and wonders and signs" (Acts 2:22). See: BAGD—89c; THAYER—60b.

585. **ἀπόδειξις** {1x} **apŏdĕixis**, *ap-od'-ike-sis;* from *584;* *manifestation:*—demonstration {1x}.

This word literally means "a pointing out, a showing" or demonstrating by argument and is found in 1 Cor 2:4, where the apostle speaks of a proof, a "showing" forth or display, by the operation of the Spirit of God in him, as affecting the hearts and lives of his hearers, in contrast to the attempted methods of proof by rhetorical arts and philosophic arguments. See: BAGD—89d; THAYER—60b.

586. **ἀποδεκατόω** {4x} **apŏdĕkatŏō**, *ap-od-ek-at-ŏ'-o;* from *575* and *1183;* to *tithe* (as debtor or creditor):—give tithe {1x}, pay tithe {1x}, take tithe {1x}, tithe {1x}.

This word means one-tenth and denotes **(1)** "to pay tithe of" (Mt 23:23; Lk 11:42; Lk 18:12); or **(2)** "to exact tithes" (Heb 7:5). See: BAGD—89d; THAYER—60c.

587. **ἀπόδεκτος** {2x} **apŏdĕktŏs**, *ap-od'-ek-tos;* from *588;* *accepted,* i.e. *agreeable:*—acceptable {2x}.

This word denotes that which is pleasing and welcome (1 Ti 2:3; 5:4). See: TDNT—2:58, 146; BAGD—90a; THAYER—60c.

588. **ἀποδέχομαι** {6x} **apŏdĕchŏmai**, *ap-od-ekh'-om-ahee;* from *575* and *1209;* to *take fully,* i.e. *welcome* (persons), *approve* (things):—accept {1x}, receive {3x}, receive gladly {2x}.

Apodechomai, as a verb, means "to welcome, to accept gladly, to receive without reserve" and is used **(1)** literally: "And it came to pass, that, when Jesus was returned, the people *gladly* received Him: for they were all waiting for Him" (Lk 8:40; cf. Acts 18:27; 28:30); and **(2)** metaphorically: "Then they that gladly received his [Peter's] word were baptized: and the same day there were added *unto them* about three thousand souls" (Acts 2:41; cf. 24:3, "we accept," in the sense of acknowledging, the term being used in a tone of respect). Syn.: 324, 353, 354, 568, 618, 1209, 1523, 1926, 2210, 2865, 2975, 2983, 3028, 3335, 3336, 3858, 3880, 3970, 4327, 4355, 4356, 4380, 4381, 4382, 5562, 5264, 5274. See: TDNT—2:55, 146; BAGD—90a; THAYER—60c.

589. **ἀποδημέω** {6x} **apŏdēmĕō**, *ap-od-ay-meh'-o;* from *590;* to *go abroad,* i.e. *visit a foreign land:*—go into a far country {3x}, take (one's) journey {2x}, travel into a far country {1x}.

This word signifies "to go or travel into a far country," literally "to be away from one's people" (Mt 21:33; 25:14; in v. 15 the verb is translated "took his journey"; Mk 12:1; Lk 15:13 "took his journey" "into a far country"; 20:9). See: BAGD—90a; THAYER—60d.

590. **ἀπόδημος** {1x} **apŏdēmŏs**, *ap-od'-ay-mos;* from *575* and *1218;* *absent from* one's own *people,* i.e. a *foreign traveller:*—taking a far journey {1x}.

This word means "gone abroad" and signifies "taking a far journey " (Mk 13:34). Syn.: 3927, 3941. See: BAGD—90b; THAYER—60d.

591. **ἀποδίδωμι** {48x} **apŏdidōmi**, *ap-od-eed'-o-mee;* from *575* and *1325;* to *give away,* i.e. *up, over, back,* etc. (in various applications):—pay {9x}, give {9x}, render {9x}, reward {7x}, sell {3x}, yield {2x}, misc. {9x} = deliver, deliver again, repay, payment be made, perform, recompense, requite, restore.

Apodidomi, as a verb, means literally "to give away"; hence, "to give back or up" is used **(1)** in Pilate's command for the Lord's body to be "given up": "He went to Pilate, and begged the body of Jesus. Then Pilate commanded the body to be delivered" (Mt 27:58); **(2)** in the sense of "giving back": "And as he was yet a coming, the devil threw him down, and tare *him.* And Jesus rebuked the unclean spirit, and healed the child, and delivered him again to his father" (Lk 9:42 of the Lord's act in giving a healed boy back to his father). Syn.: 325, 525, 629, 859, 1325, 1560, 1659, 1807, 1929, 3086, 3860, 4506, 5483. See: TDNT—2:167, 166; BAGD—90b; THAYER—60d.

592. **ἀποδιορίζω** {1x} **apŏdiŏrizō**, *ap-od-ee-or-id'-zo;* from *575* and a compound of *1223* and *3724;* to *disjoin, to make separations* (by a boundary, fig. a party):—separate {1x}.

This word means "to mark off", hence denotes metaphorically to make "separations": "These be they who separate themselves, sensual, having not the Spirit" (Jude 19); of persons who make divisions (in contrast with v. 20); there is no pronoun in the original representing "themselves." See: TDNT—5:455, 728; BAGD—90d; THAYER—61b.

593. **ἀποδοκιμάζω** {9x} **apŏdŏkimazō**, *ap-od-ok-ee-mad'-zo;* from *575* and *1381;* to *disapprove,* i.e. (by impl.) to *repudiate:*—disallow {2x}, reject {7x}.

This word means "to reject as the result of disapproval" is **(1)** always translated "to reject" (Mt 21:42; Mk 8:31; 12:10; Lk9:22; 17:25; 20:17; Heb 12:17); except in **(2)** 1 Pet 2:4 and 7. See: TDNT—2:255, 181; BAGD—90d; THAYER—61b.

594. **ἀποδοχή** {2x} **apŏdŏchē**, *ap-od-okh-ay';* from *588;* *acceptance:*—acceptation {2x}.

This word denotes worthy to be received (1 Tim 1:15; 4:9). See: TDNT—2:55, 146; BAGD—91a; THAYER—61b.

595. **ἀπόθεσις** {2x} **apŏthĕsis**, *ap-oth'-es-is;* from *659;* a *laying aside* (lit. or fig.):—putting away {1x}, must put off + 2076 {1x}.

This word denotes a "putting off or away" and is used metaphorically **(1)** in 1 Pet 3:21 of the "putting" away of the filth of the flesh; and **(2)** in 2 Pet 1:14 of "the putting off" of the body (as a tabernacle) at death. See: BAGD—91a; THAYER—61b.

596. **ἀποθήκη** {6x} **apŏthēkē**, *ap-oth-ay'-kay;* from *659;* a *repository,* i.e. *granary:*—barn {4x}, garner {2x}.

This word designates a place where anything is stored [Eng., "apothecary"] hence denoting a garner, granary, barn (Mt 3:12; 6:26; 13:30; Lk 3:17; 12:18, 24). Syn.: 597. See: BAGD—91a; THAYER—61b.

597. **ἀποθησαυρίζω** {1x} **apŏthēsaurizō**, *ap-oth-ay-sŏw-rid'-zo;* from *575* and *2343;* to *treasure away:*—lay up in store {1x}.

This word means "to treasure up, store away" and is used in 1 Ti 6:19 of "laying up in store" a good foundation for the hereafter by being rich in good works. Syn.: 596. See: BAGD—91b; THAYER—61b.

598. **ἀποθλίβω** {1x} **apŏthlibō**, *ap-oth-lee'-bo;* from *575* and *2346;* to *crowd* (from every side):—press {1x}.

This is a strengthened form of *thlibo,* ["to throng" *apo,* intensive] and is used in Lk 8:45 "press" of the multitude who were pressing around Christ. See: BAGD—91b; THAYER—61c.

599. **ἀποθνήσκω** {112x} **apŏthnēskō**, *ap-oth-nace'-ko;* from *575* and *2348;* to *die* off (lit. or fig.):—die {98x}, be dead {29x}, be at the point of death + 3195 {1x}, perish {1x}, lie a dying {1x}, be slain + 5408 {1x}, vr dead {1x}.

Apothnesko, as a verb, means lit., "to die off or out" and is used **(1)** of the separation of the soul from the body, i.e., the natural "death" of human beings (e.g., Mt 9:24; Rom 7:2); **(1a)** by reason of descent from Adam (1 Cor 15:22); or **(1b)** of violent "death" whether of men or animals; with regard to the latter it is once translated "perished," Mt 8:32; of vegetation, Jude 12; of seeds, Jn 12:24; 1 Cor 15:36; **(1c)** it is used of "death" as a punishment in Israel under the Law, in Heb 10:28; **(2)** of the separation of man from God, **(2a)** all who are descended from Adam not only "die" physically, owing to sin, see **(1a)** above, but **(2b)** are naturally in the state of separation from God, 2 Cor 5:14. **(2c)** From this believers are freed both now and eternally, Jn 6:50; 11:26, through the "death" of Christ, Rom 5:8, e.g.; **(2d)** unbelievers, who "die" physically as such, remain in eternal separation from God, Jn 8:24. **(3)** Believers have spiritually "died" **(3a)** to the Law as a means of life, Gal 2:19; Col 2:20; **(3b)** to sin, Rom 6:2, and in general **(3c)** to all spiritual association with the world and with that which pertained to their unregenerate state, Col 3:3, because of their identification with the "death" of Christ, Rom 6:8. **(4)** As life never means mere existence, so "death," the opposite of life, never means nonexistence; but separation always. Syn.: 2348, 2837, 4880, 5053. See: TDNT—3:7, 312; BAGD—91b; THAYER—61c.

600. **ἀποκαθίστημι** {8x} **apŏkathistēmi**, *ap-ok-ath-is'-tay-mee;* from *575* and *2525;* to *reconstitute* (in health, home or organization):—restore {7x}, restore again {1x}.

This word is used **(1)** of "restoration" to a former condition of health (Mt 12:13; Mk 3:5; 8:25; Lk 6:10); **(2)** of the divine "restoration" of Israel and conditions affected by it, including the renewal of the covenant broken by them (Mt 17:11; Mk 9:12; Acts 1:6); **(3)** of "giving" or "bringing" a person back: "But I beseech *you* the rather to do this, that I may be restored to you the sooner" (Heb 13:19). See: TDNT—1:387, 65; BAGD—91d; THAYER—62a.

601. **ἀποκαλύπτω** {26x} **apŏkaluptō**, *ap-ok-al-oop'-to;* from *575* and *2572;* to take *off the cover,* i.e. *disclose:*—reveal {26x}.

Apokalupto, as a verb, signifies "to uncover, unveil" **(1)** The subjective use of *apokalupto* is that in which something is presented to the mind directly, as, **(1a)** the meaning of the acts of God (Mt 11:25; Lk 10:21); **(1b)** the secret of the Person of the Lord Jesus (Mt 16:17; Jn 12:38); **(1c)** the character of God as Father (Mt 11:27; Lk 10:22); **(1d)** the will of God for the conduct of His children (Phil 3:15); **(1e)** the mind of God to the prophets of Israel (1 Pet 1:12), and of the Church (1 Cor 14:30; Eph 3:5). **(2)** The objective use is that in which something is presented to the senses, sight or hearing, as, referring to the past **(2a)** the truth declared to men in the gospel (Rom 1:17; 1 Cor 2:10; Gal 3:23); **(2b)** the Person of Christ to Paul on the way to Damascus (Gal 1:16); **(2c)** thoughts before hidden in the heart (Lk 2:35); **(2d)** referring to the future, **(2d1)** the coming in glory of the Lord Jesus (Lk 17:30); **(2d2)** the salvation and glory that await the believer (Rom 8:18; 1 Pet 1:5; 5:1); **(2d3)** the true value of service (1 Cor 3:13); **(2d4)** the wrath of God [at the Cross, against sin, and, at the revelation of the Lord Jesus, against the sinner] (Rom 1:18); **(2d5)** the Lawless One (2 Th 2:3, 6, 8). Syn.: 5537. See: TDNT—3:563, 405; BAGD—92a; THAYER—62a.

602. **ἀποκάλυψις** {18x} **apŏkalupsis**, *ap-ok-al'-oop-sis;* from *601; disclosure:*—revelation {12x}, be revealed {2x}, to lighten + 1519 {1x}, manifestation {1x}, coming {1x}, appearing {1x}.

This word is more comprehensive than epiphaneia (2015) and depicts the progressive and immediate unveiling of the otherwise unknown and unknowable God to His church. Syn.: 2015, 5321. See: TDNT—3:563, 405; BAGD—92b; THAYER—62c.

603. **ἀποκαραδοκία** {2x} **apŏkaradŏkia**, *ap-ok-ar-ad-ok-ee'-ah;* from a compound of *575* and a comp. of κάρα **kara** (the *head*) and *1380* (in the sense of *watching*); *intense anticipation:*—earnest expectation {2x}.

This word primarily means "a watching with outstretched head" and signifies "strained expectancy, eager longing," the stretching forth of the head indicating an "expectation" of something from a certain place, Rom 8:19 and Phil 1:20. The prefix *apo* suggests "abstraction and absorption" i.e., abstraction from anything else that might engage the attention, and absorption in the object expected till the fulfillment is realized. The intensive character of the noun is clear from the contexts: in Rom 8:19 it is said figuratively of the creation as waiting for the revealing of the sons of God. In Phil 1:20 the apostle states it as his "earnest expectation" and hope, that, instead of being put to shame, Christ shall be magnified in his body, "whether by life, or by death," suggesting absorption in the person of Christ, abstraction from aught that hinders. See: BAGD—92c; THAYER—62d.

604. **ἀποκαταλλάσσω** {3x} **apŏkatallassō**, *ap-ok-at-al-las'-so;* from *575* and *2644;* to *reconcile fully:*—reconcile {3x}.

This word means to change from one condition to another so as to remove all enmity and leave no impediment to unity and peace and is used in Eph 2:16, of the "reconciliation" of believing Jew and Gentile in one body unto God through the cross. In Col 1:21 not the union of Jew and Gentile is in view, but the change wrought in the individual believer from alienation and enmity, on account of evil works, to "reconciliation" with God; in v. 20 the word is used of the divine purpose to "reconcile" through Christ "all things unto Himself . . . whether things upon the earth, or things in the heavens," the basis of the change being the peace effected "through the blood of His Cross." It is the divine purpose, on the ground of the work of Christ accomplished on the cross, to bring the whole universe, except rebellious angels and unbelieving man, into full accord with the mind of God, Eph 1:10. Things "under the earth," Phil 2:10, are subdued, not "reconciled. See: TDNT—1:258, 40; BAGD—92c; THAYER—63a.

605. **ἀποκατάστασις** {1x} **apŏkatastasis**, *ap-ok-at-as'-tas-is;* from *600; reconstitution:*—restitution {1x}.

This word means "to set in order" and is used in Acts 3:21: "Whom the heaven must receive until the times of restitution of all things, which God hath spoken by the mouth of all his holy prophets since the world began." See: TDNT—1:258, 40; BAGD—92d; THAYER—63a.

606. **ἀπόκειμαι** {4x} **apŏkĕimai**, *ap-ok'-i-mahee;* from *575* and *2749;* to *be reserved;* fig. to *await:*—be appointed {1x}, (be) laid up {3x}.

Apokeimai, as a verb, signifies **(1)** "to be laid, reserved": "And another came, saying, Lord, behold, *here is* thy pound, which I have kept laid (*apokeimai*) up in a napkin" (Lk 19:20; cf. Col 1:5; 2 Ti 4:8); **(2)** to be "appointed": "And as it is appointed unto men once to die, but after this the judgment" (Heb 9:27 where it is said of death and the judgment following). See: TDNT—3:655, 425; BAGD—92d; THAYER—63a.

607. **ἀποκεφαλίζω** {4x} **apŏkĕphalizō**, *ap-ok-ef-al-id'-zo;* from *575* and *2776;* to *decapitate:*—beheaded {4x}.

This word means to cut off the head (Mt 14:10; Mk 6:16, 27; Lk 9:9). See: BAGD—93a; THAYER—63b.

608. **ἀποκλείω** {1x} **apŏklĕiō**, *ap-ok-li'-o;* from *575* and *2808;* to *close fully:*—shut up {1x}.

This word is used in Lk 13:25 and expresses the impossibility of entrance after the closing. See: BAGD—93a; THAYER—63b.

609. **ἀποκόπτω** {6x} **apŏkŏptō**, *ap-ok-op'-to;* from *575* and *2875;* to *amputate;* refl. (by irony) to *mutilate* (the privy parts):—cut off {6x}.

This word means "to cut off, or cut away" and is used **(1)** literally, **(1a)** of members of the body: "And if thy hand offend thee, cut it off: it is better for thee to enter into life maimed, than having two hands to go into hell, into the fire that never shall be quenched" (Mk 9:43; cf. 9:45; Jn 18:10, 26); **(1b)** of ropes (Acts 27:32); **(2)** metaphorically, in the middle voice, of "cutting off oneself," to excommunicate, Gal 5:12, of the Judaizing teachers, with a sarcastic reference, no doubt, to the "cutting away" of the Juadaizers themselves. See: TDNT—3:852, 453; BAGD—93a; THAYER—63b. comp. *2699.*

610. **ἀπόκριμα** {1x} **apŏkrima**, *ap-ok'-ree-mah;* from *611* (in its orig. sense of *judging*); a judicial *decision:*—sentence {1x}.

Apokrima denotes a judicial "sentence" and in 2 Cor 1:9 it is the answer of God to the apostle's appeal, giving him strong confidence: "But we had the sentence of death in ourselves, that we should not trust in ourselves, but in God which raiseth the dead." See: TDNT—3:945, 469; BAGD—93b; THAYER—63b.

611. **ἀποκρίνομαι** {250x} **apŏkrinŏmai**, *ap-ok-ree'-nom-ahee;* from *575* and κρίνω **krinō**; to *conclude for oneself,* i.e. (by impl.) to *respond;* by Heb. [comp. 6030] to *begin to speak* (where an address is expected):—answer {250x}.

Apokrinomai signifies either **(1)** "to give an answer to a question" (its more frequent use) or **(2)** "to begin to speak," but always where something has preceded, either statement or act to which the remarks refer (Mt 11:25; Lk 14:3; Jn 2:18). It is translated by "answered" (Mt 28:5; Mk 12:35; Lk 3:16 where some have suggested "began to say" or "uttered solemnly," whereas the speaker is replying to the unuttered thought or feeling of those addressed by him). See: TDNT—3:944,*; BAGD—93b; THAYER—63b.

612. **ἀπόκρισις** {4x} **apŏkrisis**, *ap-ok'-ree-sis;* from *611;* a *response:*—answer {4x}.

This word literally means "a separation or distinction" and is the regular word for "answer" (Lk 2:47; 20:26; Jn 1:22; 19:9). See: TDNT—3:946, 469; BAGD—93c; THAYER—63d.

613. **ἀποκρύπτω** {6x} **apŏkruptō**, *ap-ok-roop'-to;* from *575* and *2928;* to *conceal away* (i.e. *fully*); fig. to *keep secret:*—hide {6x}.

This word means "to conceal from, to keep secret" and is used metaphorically **(1)** in Lk 10:21 of truths "hidden" from the wise and prudent and revealed to babes (cf. Mt 11:25); **(1a)** in 1 Cor 2:7 of God's wisdom; **(1b)** in Eph 3:9 of the mystery of the unsearchable riches of Christ, revealed through the gospel; Col 1:26, of the mystery associated with the preceding. **(2)** It is used literally of hiding an object (Mt 25:18). See: TDNT—3:957, 476; BAGD—93d; THAYER—63d.

614. **ἀπόκρυφος** {3x} **apŏkruphŏs**, *ap-ok'-roo-fos;* from *613; secret;* by impl. *treasured:*—hid, kept secret {3x}.

This word means "hidden away from" and is translated **(1)** "kept secret" (Mk 4:22; Lk 8:17 "hid"; Col 2:3 "hid"). See: TDNT—3:957, 476; BAGD—93d; THAYER—64a.

615. **ἀποκτείνω** {75x} **apŏktĕinō**, *ap-ok-ti'-no;* from *575* and κτείνω **ktĕinō** (to *slay*); to *kill* outright; fig. to *destroy:*—put to death {6x}, kill {55x}, slay {14x}.

Apokteino, as a verb, means "to kill, put to death" and is so translated in Mk 14:1; Lk 18:33; Jn 11:53; 12:10; 18:31. Syn.: 336, 337, 520, 1935, 2288, 2289, 5054. See: BAGD—93d; THAYER—64a.

616. **ἀποκυέω** {2x} **apŏkuĕō**, *ap-ok-oo-eh'-o;* from *575* and the base of *2949;* to *breed forth, to give birth to,* i.e. (by transf.) to *generate* (fig.):—beget {1x}, bring forth {1x}.

Apokueo, as a verb, means "to give birth to, to bring forth, to begat" and is used metaphorically **(1)** of spiritual birth by means of the Word of God: "Of His own will begat (*apokueo*) He us with the word of truth" (Jas 1:18), and **(2)** of death as the offspring of sin: "Then when lust hath conceived, it bringeth forth (tikto – 5088) sin: and sin, when it is finished, bringeth forth (*apokueo*) death" (Jas 1:15). Syn.: 313, 738, 1080, 1084, 1085, 1626, 5088. See: BAGD—94a; THAYER—64b.

617. **ἀποκυλίω** {4x} **apŏkuliō**, *ap-ok-oo-lee'-o;* from *575* and *2947;* to *roll away:*—roll away {3x}, roll back {1x}.

This word means "to roll away" and is used of the sepulchre stone (Mt 28:2; Mk 16:3, 4; Lk 24:2). See: BAGD—94b; THAYER—64b.

618. **ἀπολαμβάνω** {12x} **apŏlambanō**, *ap-ol-am-ban'-o;* from *575* and *2983;* to *receive* (spec. in *full,* or as a host); also to *take aside:*—receive {10x}, take aside {1x}, receive again {1x}.

Apolambano, as a verb, signifies "to receive from another," **(1)** to "receive" as one's due: "And we indeed justly; for we receive (*apolambano*) the due reward of our deeds: but this Man hath done nothing amiss" (Lk 23:41; cf. Rom 1:27; Col 3:24; 2 Jn 8); **(2)** without the indication of what is due: "But Abraham said, Son, remember that thou in thy lifetime receivedst (*apolambano*) thy good things, and likewise Lazarus evil things: but now he is comforted, and thou art tormented" (Lk 16:25; cf. Gal 4:5); **(3)** to receive back: "And if ye lend *to them* of whom ye hope to receive (*apolambano*), what thank have ye? for sinners also lend to sinners, to receive (*apolambano*) as much again" (Lk 6:34; cf. 15:27). **(4)** It also means "to take apart": "And He took him aside from the multitude, and put His fingers into his ears, and He spit, and touched his tongue" (Mk 7:33). Syn.: 324, 353, 354, 568, 588, 1209, 1523, 1926, 2210, 2865, 2975, 2983, 3028, 3335, 3336, 3858, 3880, 3970, 4327, 4355, 4356, 4380, 4381, 4382, 5562, 5264, 5274. See: BAGD—94b; THAYER—64b.

619. **ἀπόλαυσις** {2x} **apŏlausis**, *ap-ol'-ow-sis;* from a compound of *575* and λαύω **lauō** (to *enjoy*); full *enjoyment:*—to enjoy + 1519 {1x}, enjoy the pleasures + 2192 {1x}.

This word means "enjoyment" and suggests the advantage or pleasure to be obtained from a thing. **(1)** It is used with the preposition *eis,* in 1 Ti 6:17: "Charge them that are rich in this world, that they be not highminded, nor trust in uncertain riches, but in the living God, who giveth us richly all things to enjoy", lit., "unto enjoyment" rendered "to enjoy"; **(2)** with *echo,* "to have" in Heb 11:25 lit., means "to have pleasure (of sin)" and is translated "to enjoy the pleasures." See: BAGD—94d; THAYER—64c.

620. **ἀπολείπω** {6x} **apŏlĕipō**, *ap-ol-ipe'-o;* from *575* and *3007;* to *leave* behind (pass. *remain*); by impl. to *forsake:*—leave {3x}, remain {3x}.

This word means "to leave behind" and is used **(1)** in the active voice, of **(1a)** "leaving" behind a cloak (2 Ti 4:3); **(1b)** a person (2 Ti 4:20); **(1c)** of "abandoning" a principality [by angels] (Jude 6); and **(2)** in the passive voice, "to be reserved, to remain" (Heb 4:6, 9; 10:26). See: BAGD—94d; THAYER—64c.

621. **ἀπολείχω** {1x} **apŏlĕichō**, *ap-ol-i'-kho;* from *575* and λείχω **lĕichō** (to "*lick*"); to *lick* clean:—lick {1x}.

This word is used only in Lk 16:21 of the dogs licking Lazarus' wounds. See: BAGD—95a; THAYER—64c.

622. **ἀπόλλυμι** {92x} **apŏllumi**, *ap-ol'-loo-mee;* from *575* and the base of *3639;* to *destroy* fully (refl. to *perish,* or *lose*), lit. or fig.:—perish {33x}, destroy {26x}, lose {22x}, be lost {5x}, lost {4x}, misc. {2x} = die, mar.

Apollumi signifies **(1)** "to destroy utterly"; **(1a)** in middle voice, "to perish." **(1b)** The idea is not extinction but ruin, loss, not of being, but of well-being. **(2)** This is clear from its use, as, e.g., **(2a)** of the marring of wine skins (Lk 5:37); **(2b)** of lost sheep, i.e., lost to the shepherd, metaphorical of spiritual destitution (Lk 15:4, 6); **(2c)** the lost son (Lk 15:24); **(2c)** of the perishing of food (Jn 6:27); **(2d)** of gold (1 Pet 1:7). **(3)** So of persons: **(3a)** Mt 2:13 "destroy"; **(3b)** Mt 8:25 "perish" (cf. 22:7; 27:20); **(3c)** of the loss of well-being in the case of the unsaved hereafter (Mt 10:28; Lk 13:3, 5; Jn 3:15, 16; 10:28; 17:12; Rom 2:12; 1 Cor 15:18; 2 Cor 2:15 "are perishing"; 4:3; 2 Th 2:10; Jas 4:12; 2 Pet 3:9). See: TDNT—1:394, 67; BAGD—95a; THAYER—64c.

623. **Ἀπολλύων** {1x} **Apŏlluōn**, *ap-ol-loo'-ohn;* act. part. of *622;* a *destroyer* (i.e. *Satan*):—Apollyon {1x}. See: TDNT—1:397, 67; BAGD—95c; THAYER—65a.

624. **Ἀπολλωνία** {1x} **Apŏllōnia**, *ap-ol-lo-nee'-ah;* from the pagan deity Ἀπόλλων **Apŏllōn** (i.e. the *sun;* from *622*); *Apollonia,* a place in Macedonia:—*Apollonia* {1x}. See: BAGD—95c; THAYER—65a.

625. **Ἀπολλώς** {10x} **Apŏllōs**, *ap-ol-loce';* prob. from the same as *624; Apollos,* an Isr.:—*Apollos* {10x}. See: BAGD—95c; THAYER—65b.

626. **ἀπολογέομαι** {10x} **apŏlŏgĕŏmai**, *ap-ol-og-eh'-om-ahee;* mid. voice from a compound of *575* and *3056;* to give an *account* (legal *plea*) of oneself, i.e. *exculpate* (self):—answer {3x}, answer for (one's) self {3x}, make defence {1x}, excuse {1x}, excuse (one's) self {1x}, speak for (one's) self {1x}.

The English word "excuse" means to give cogent reasons why one acts with the goal of clearing charges. Syn.: See 627 for an explanation. See: BAGD—95d; THAYER—65b.

627. **ἀπολογία** {8x} **apŏlŏgia**, *ap-ol-og-ee'-ah;* from the same as *626;* a *plea* ("apology"):—defence {3x}, answer {3x}, answer for (one's) self {1x}, clearing of (one's) self {1x}.

(1) This does not mean saying "I'm sorry. I apologize." **(2)** The root means to give a cogent explanation for one's beliefs. **(3)** The word means "to talk one's self off from" i.e. to explain one's basis for operation, explain the basis upon which and from which one makes his decisions. **(4)** Making a defense is not to escape punishment nor trial but to explain forcefully and completely why one does what he does. **(5)** It is translated: **(5a)** "to answer, give an answer" (Acts 25:16; 1 Cor 9:3; 2 Ti 4:16; 1 Pet 3:15), **(5b)** "defense" (Acts 22:1; Phil 1:7, 17), and **(5c)** "clearing of [yourselves]" (2 Cor 7:11). See: BAGD—96a; THAYER—65c.

628. **ἀπολούω** {2x} **apŏlŏuō**, *ap-ol-oo'-o;* from *575* and *3068;* to *wash* fully, i.e. (fig.) *have remitted* (refl.):—wash {1x}, wash away {1x}.

Apolouo means "to wash off or away," is used **(1)** in the middle voice, metaphorically, "to wash oneself," in Acts 22:16, where the command to Saul of Tarsus to "wash away" his sins indicates that by his public confession, he would testify to the removal of his sins, and to the complete change from his past life; this "washing away" was not in itself the actual remission of his sins, which had taken place at his conversion; the middle voice implies his own particular interest in the act (as with the preceding verb "baptize," lit., "baptize thyself," i.e., "get thyself baptized"); the aorist tenses mark the decisiveness of the acts; **(2)** in 1 Cor. 6:11, lit., "ye washed yourselves clean"; here the middle voice (rendered in the passive) again indicates that the converts at Corinth, by their obedience to the faith, voluntarily gave testimony to the complete spiritual change divinely wrought in them. See: TDNT—4:295, 538; BAGD—96a; THAYER—65c.

629. **ἀπολύτρωσις** {10x} **apŏlutrōsis**, *ap-ol-oo'-tro-sis;* from a compound of *575* and *3083;* (the act) *ransom* in full, i.e. (fig.) *riddance,* or (spec.) Chr. *salvation:*—deliverance {1x}, redemption {9x}.

Summary: This word means to be purchased from the slave market of sin, totally set free, never to sold again. *Apolutrosis,* as a noun, is a strengthened form of lutrosis (3085), and means lit., "a releasing, for (i.e., on payment of) a ransom." It is used of **(1)** "deliverance" from physical torture (Heb 11:35); and **(2)** the deliverance of the tribulation saints at the coming of Christ with His glorified saints, **(2a)** "in a cloud with power and great glory," (Lk 21:28), a "redemption" to be accomplished at the "outshining of His Parousia" (2 Th 2:8), **(2b)** i.e., at His second advent;

(3) It is used of forgiveness and justification, **(3a)** "redemption" as the result of propitiation and expiation, **(3b)** deliverance from the guilt of sins (Rom 3:24), **(3c)** "through the redemption that is in Christ Jesus" (Eph 1:7), **(3d)** defined as "the forgiveness of sins" (cf. Col 1:14), **(3e)** indicating both the liberation from the guilt and doom of sin and the introduction into a life of liberty, "newness of life" (Rom 6:4); and **(3f)** "for the redemption of the transgressions that were under the first testament," (Heb 9:15 - here "redemption of" is equivalent to "redemption from," the genitive case being used of the object from which the "redemption" is effected, not from the consequence of the transgressions, but from the transgressions themselves); **(4)** It is used of the deliverance of the believer from the presence and power of sin, and of his body from bondage to corruption, at the coming (the Parousia in its inception) of the Lord Jesus (Rom 8:23; cf. 1 Cor 1:30; Eph 1:4; 4:30). Syn.: 2434, 2643. See: TDNT—4:351,*; BAGD—96b; THAYER—65c.

630. **ἀπολύω** {69x} **apŏluō**, *ap-ol-oo'-o;* from *575* and *3089;* to *free* fully, i.e. (lit.) *relieve, release, dismiss* (refl. *depart*), or (fig.) *let die, pardon* or (spec.) *divorce:*—release {17x}, put away {14x}, send away {13x}, let go {13x}, set at liberty {2x}, let depart {2x}, dismiss {2x}, misc. 6x} = divorce, forgive, loose.

This word means **(1)** to set free; **(2)** to let go, dismiss, (to detain no longer): **(2a)** a petitioner to whom liberty to depart is given by a decisive answer (Mt 15:25; Lk 2:29), **(2b)** to bid depart, send away (Mt 14:15; Mk 6:36); **(3)** to let go free, release: **(3a)** a captive i.e. to loose his bonds and bid him depart, to give him liberty to depart (Lk 22:68; 23:22), **(3b)** to acquit one accused of a crime and set him at liberty (Jn 19:12; Acts 3:13), **(3c)** indulgently to grant a prisoner leave to depart (Acts 4:21, 23), **(3d)** to release a debtor, i.e. not to press one's claim against him, to remit his debt (Mt 18:27); **(4)** used of divorce, to dismiss from the house, to repudiate (Mt 1:19); and **(5a)** to send one's self away, to depart (Acts 28:25). See: BAGD—96c; THAYER—65d.

631. **ἀπομάσσομαι** {1x} **apŏmassŏmai**, *ap-om-as'-som-ahee;* mid. voice from *575* and **μάσσω** **massō** (to *squeeze, knead, smear*); to *scrape away:*—wipe off {1x}.

This word means "to wipe off, wipe clean" and is used in the middle voice, of "wiping" dust from the feet (Lk 10:11). Syn.: 1591, 1813. See: BAGD—96d; THAYER—66b.

632. **ἀπονέμω** {1x} **apŏnĕmō**, *ap-on-em'-o;* from *575* and the base of *3551;* to *apportion,* i.e. *bestow:*—give {1x}.

This word means "to assign, apportion" and is rendered "giving" in 1 Pet 3:7 of giving honor to the wife. See: BAGD—97a; THAYER—66b.

633. **ἀπονίπτω** {1x} **apŏniptō**, *ap-on-ip'-to;* from *575* and *3538;* to *wash off* (refl. one's own hands symb.):—wash {1x}.

This word means "to wash off" and is used in the middle voice in Mt 27:24. See: BAGD—97a; THAYER—66c.

634. **ἀποπίπτω** {1x} **apŏpiptō**, *ap-op-ip'-to;* from *575* and *4098;* to *fall off:*—fall {1x}.

This word means "to fall from, to slip down from" and is used in Acts 9:18 of the scales which "fell" from the eyes of Saul of Tarsus. Syn.: 1601. See: BAGD—97b; THAYER—66c.

635. **ἀποπλανάω** {2x} **apŏplanaō**, *ap-op-lan-ah'-o;* from *575* and *4105;* to *lead astray* (fig.); pass. to *stray* (from truth):—err {1x}, seduce {1x}.

This word means "to cause to wander away from the truth, to lead astray from the truth" and is used **(1)** metaphorically of leading into error (Mk 13:22 "seduce"); and **(2)** in 1 Ti 6:10, in the passive voice, "have erred" [by being led astray]. See: TDNT—6:228, 857; BAGD—97b; THAYER—66c.

636. **ἀποπλέω** {4x} **apŏplĕō**, *ap-op-leh'-o;* from *575* and *4126;* to *set sail:*—sail away {4x}.

This word means "to sail away from, depart by ship" and occurs in Acts 13:4; 14:26; 20:15; 27:1. See: BAGD—97c; THAYER—66c.

637. **ἀποπλύνω** {1x} **apŏplunō**, *ap-op-loo'-no;* from *575* and *4150;* to *rinse off:*—wash {1x}.

This word means to wash off and is used of nets in Lk 5:2. See: BAGD—97c; THAYER—66c.

638. **ἀποπνίγω** {3x} **apŏpnigō**, *ap-op-nee'-go;* from *575* and *4155;* to *stifle* (by drowning or overgrowth):—choke {3x}.

This word is used **(1)** metaphorically, of "thorns crowding out seed sown and preventing its growth" (Mt 13:7; Lk 8:7). **(2)** It is Luke's word for "suffocation by drowning": "Then went the devils out of the man, and entered into the swine: and the herd ran violently down a steep place into the lake, and were choked [*apopnigo*]" (Lk 8:33). See: TDNT—6:455, 895 BAGD—97c; THAYER—66d.

639. **ἀπορέω** {4x} **apŏrĕō**, *ap-or-eh'-o;* from a compound of *1* (as a neg. particle) and the base of *4198;* to *have no way* out, i.e. *be at a loss* (mentally):—stand in doubt {1x}, doubt {2x}, be perplexed {1x}.

(1) This word is always used in the middle voice, lit. means "to be without a way, to be without resources, embarrassed, in doubt, perplexity, at a loss" **(1a)** as was Herod regarding John the Baptist (Mk 6:20); **(1b)** as the disciples were, **(1b1)** regarding the Lord's betrayal, (Jn 13:22 "doubting"); and **(1b2)** regarding the absence of His body from the tomb (Lk 24:4 "were perplexed"); **(1c)** as was Festus, about the nature of the accusations brought against Paul (Acts 25:20 "doubted"); **(1d1)** as Paul was, in his experiences of trial (2 Cor 4:8 "perplexed"); and, **(1d2)** as to his attitude towards the believers of the churches in Galatia concerning Judaistic errors (Gal 4:20 "I stand in doubt"). **(2)** Perplexity is the main idea. See: BAGD—97c; THAYER—66d.

640. **ἀπορία** {1x} **apŏria**, *ap-or-ee'-a;* from the same as *639;* a (state of) *quandary; at a loss for a way:*—perplexity {1x}.

This word is translated "perplexity" in Lk 21:25 (lit., "at a loss for a way,"), of the distress of nations, finding no solution to their embarrassments; papyri illustrations are in the sense of being at one's wit's end, at a loss how to proceed, without resources. See: BAGD—97d; THAYER—66d.

641. **ἀποῤῥίπτω** {1x} **apŏrrhiptō**, *ap-or-hrip'-to;* from *575* and *4496;* to *hurl off,* i.e. *precipitate* (oneself):—cast one's self {1x}.

This word means "to cast off," Acts 27:43, of shipwrecked people in throwing themselves into the water. See: TDNT—6:991,*; BAGD—97d; THAYER—66d.

642. **ἀπορφανίζω** {1x} **apŏrphanizō**, *ap-or-fan-id'-zo;* from *575* and a der. of *3737;* to *bereave wholly,* i.e. (fig.) *separate* (from intercourse):—taken {1x}.

This word means taken from, literally, to be rendered an orphan" and is used metaphorically in 1 Th. 2:17 ("taken from"), in the sense of being "bereft" of the company of the saints through being compelled to leave them (cf. the similes in 7 and 11). The word has a wider meaning than that of being an orphan. See: BAGD—98a; THAYER—67a.

643. **ἀποσκευάζω** {1x} **apŏskĕuazō**, *ap-osk-yoo-ad'-zo;* from *575* and a der. of *4632;* to *pack up* (one's) *baggage:*—take up (one's) carriages {1x}.

This word means "to furnish with things necessary"; in the middle voice, "to furnish for oneself"; it was used of equipping baggage animals for a journey; in Acts 21:15, it is translated "we took up our carriages.". The form is the 1st aorist participle, and lit. means "having made ready (the things that were necessary for the journey)." Bags are containers in which things are carried; hence, "carriages." See: BAGD—98a; THAYER—67a.

644. **ἀποσκίασμα** {1x} **apŏskiasma**, *ap-os-kee'-as-mah;* from a compound of *575* and a der. of *4639;* a *shading off,* i.e. *obscuration:*—shadow {1x}.

This word means "a shadow," and denotes a "shadow that is cast" in Jas 1:17. The probable significance of this word is "overshadowing" or "shadowing-over" (which *apo* may indicate), and this with the genitive case of *trope,* "turning," yields the meaning "shadowing-over of mutability" implying an alternation of "shadow" and light; of this there are two alternative explanations, namely, "overshadowing" (a) not caused by mutability in God, or (b) caused by change in others, i.e., no changes in this lower world can cast a shadow on the unchanging Fount of light. The meaning of the passage will then be, God is alike incapable of change and incapable of being changed by the action of others. See: TDNT—7:399, 1044; BAGD—98a; THAYER—67a.

645. **ἀποσπάω** {4x} **apŏspaō**, *ap-os-pah'-o;* from *575* and *4685;* to *drag forth,* i.e. (lit.) *unsheathe* (a sword), or rel. (with a degree of force impl.) *retire* (pers. or factiously):—draw {1x}, withdraw {1x}, draw away {1x}, be gotten {1x}.

Apospao, as a verb, means "to draw away," lit., "to wrench away from" and is used **(1)** of a sword: "And, behold, one of them which were with Jesus stretched out *his* hand, and drew his sword" (Mt 26:51); **(2)** of "drawing" away disciples into error: "Also of your own selves shall men arise, speaking perverse things, to draw away disciples after them" (Acts 20:30); **(3)** of Christ's "withdrawal" from the disciples in Gethsemane (Lk 22:41); **(4)** of "parting" from a company: "And it came to pass, that after we were gotten (*apospao*) from them, and had launched, we came with a straight course unto Coos" (Acts 21:1). Syn.: 307, 385, 392, 501, 502, 868, 1096, 1670, 1448, 1828, 2020, 2464, 4317, 4334, 4358, 4685, 4951, 5288, 5289. See: BAGD—98a; THAYER—67a.

646. **ἀποστασία** {2x} **apŏstasia**, *ap-os-tas-ee'-ah;* fem. of the same as *647; defection* from truth (prop. the state) ["apostasy"]:—to forsake + 575 {1x}, falling away {1x}.

This word means "a defection, revolt, apostasy" and is used in the NT of religious apostasy; **(1)** in Acts 21:21, it is translated "to forsake," lit., "thou teachest apostasy from Moses." **(2)** In 2 Th 2:3 "the falling away" signifies apostasy from the faith. **(3)** In papyri documents it is used politically of rebels. See: TDNT—1:513, 88; BAGD—98b; THAYER—67b.

647. **ἀποστάσιον** {3x} **apŏstasiŏn**, *ap-os-tas'-ee-on;* neut. of a (presumed) adj. from a der. of *868;* prop. something *separative,* i.e. (spec.) *divorce:*—divorcement {2x}, writing of divorcement {1x}.

This word primarily means "a defection," lit., "a standing off" and denotes, in the NT, "a writing or bill of divorcement" (Mt 5:31; 19:7; Mk 10:4). See: BAGD—98b; THAYER—67b.

648. **ἀποστεγάζω** {1x} **apŏstĕgazō**, *ap-os-teg-ad'-zo;* from *575* and a der. of *4721;* to *unroof:*—uncover {1x}.

This word signifies "to unroof" [*apo,* from, *stege,* "a roof"] (Mk 2:4). See: BAGD—98c; THAYER—67b.

649. **ἀποστέλλω** {133x} **apŏstĕllō**, *ap-os-tel'-lo;* from *575* and *4724; set apart,* i.e. (by impl.) to *send out* (prop. on a mission) lit. or fig.:—send {110x}, send forth {15x}, send away {4x}, send out {2x}, misc. {2x} = put in, set [at liberty].

This word means **(1)** to order (one) to go to a place appointed: **(1)** Jesus sent by the Father (Mt 10:40), **(1b)** the apostles sent by Jesus (Mk 6:7), **(1c)** messengers are sent (Lk 7:3), **(1d)** servants are sent (Mk 6:27), **(1e)** angels (Mk 12:27), **(1f)** things are sent (Mt 21:3); **(2)** to send away, dismiss: **(2a)** to allow one to depart, that he may be in a state of liberty (Lk 4:18), **(2b)** to order one to depart, send off (Mk 8:26), **(2c)** to drive away (Mk 5:10). See: TDNT—1:398, 67; BAGD—98c; THAYER—67b.

650. **ἀποστερέω** {6x} **apŏstĕrĕō**, *ap-os-ter-eh'-o;* from *575* and στερέω **stĕrĕō** (to *deprive*); to *despoil:*—defraud {4x}, destitute {1x}, keep back by fraud {1x}.

This word means "to rob, defraud, deprive" and is used in 1 Ti 6:5, in the passive voice, of being deprived or "bereft, destitute" (of the truth), with reference to false teachers (cf. Mk 10:19; 1 Cor 6:7, 8; 7:5; Jas 5:4). See: BAGD—99a; THAYER—68a.

651. **ἀποστολή** {4x} **apŏstŏlē**, *ap-os-tol-ay';* from *649; commission,* i.e. (spec.) *apostolate:*—apostleship {4x}.

This word signifies "a sending, a mission, a commission," an apostleship (Acts 1:25; Rom 1:5; 1 Cor 9:2; Gal 2:8). See: TDNT—1:446, 67; BAGD—99b; THAYER—68a.

652. **ἀπόστολος** {81x} **apŏstŏlŏs**, *ap-os'-tol-os;* from *649;* a *delegate;* spec. an *ambassador* of the Gospel; officially a *commissioner* of Christ ["*apostle*"] (with miraculous powers):—apostle {78x}, messenger {2x}, he that is sent {1x}.

Apostolos is, lit., "one sent forth" [*apo,* "from," *stello,* "to send"]. **(1)** The word is used of the Lord Jesus to describe His relation to God (Heb 3:1; see Jn 17:3). **(2)** The twelve disciples chosen by the Lord for special training were so called (Lk 6:13; 9:10). **(3)** Paul, though he had seen the Lord Jesus, 1 Cor 9:1; 15:8, had not 'companied with' the Twelve 'all the time' of His earthly ministry, and hence was not eligible for a place among them, according to Peter's description of the necessary qualifications, Acts 1:22. Paul was commissioned directly, by the Lord Himself, after His Ascension, to carry the gospel to the Gentiles. **(4)** The word has also a wider reference. **(4a)** In Acts 14:4, 14, it is used of Barnabas as well as of Paul; **(4b)** in Rom 16:7 of Andronicus and Junias. **(4b)** In 2 Cor 8:23 two unnamed brethren are called 'messengers [apostles – sent ones] of the churches'; **(4c)** in Phil 2:25 Epaphroditus is referred to as "your messenger [apostle – sent one]." **(4d)** It is used in 1 Th 2:6 of Paul, Silas and Timothy, to define their relation to Christ." See: TDNT—1:407, 67; BAGD—99c; THAYER—68b.

653. **ἀποστοματίζω** {1x} **apŏstŏmatizō**, *ap-os-tom-at-id'-zo;* from *575* and a (presumed) der. of *4750;* to *speak off-hand* (prop. *dictate*), i.e. to *catechize* (in an invidious manner):—provoke to speak {1x}.

This word in **(1)** classical Greek meant "to speak from memory, to dictate to a pupil"; in **(2)** later Greek, "to catechize"; and in **(3)** Lk 11:53 "to provoke (Him) to speak." Jesus's enemies were tempting Him to speak systematically concerning the doctrine of God in order to trap Him into blasphemy; a false charge that eventually accomplished. See: BAGD—100b; THAYER—68c.

654. **ἀποστρέφω** {10x} **apŏstrĕphō**, *ap-os-tref'-o;* from *575* and *4762;* to *turn away* or *back* (lit. or fig.):—turn away {4x}, turn away from {2x}, put up again {1x}, turn from {1x}, bring again {1x}, pervert {1x}.

This word means **(1)** to turn away (2 Ti 4:4): **(1a)** to remove anything from anyone (Rom 11:26), **(1b)** to turn him away from allegiance to any one, tempt to defect (Lk 23:14); **(2)** to turn back, return, bring back: **(2a)** of putting a sword back in its sheath (Mt 26:52), **(2b)** of Judas returning money to temple (Mt 27:3); **(3)** to turn one's self away, turn back, return (Acts 3:26); **(4)** to turn one's self away from, deserting (2 Ti 1:15). See: TDNT—7:719, 1093; BAGD—100b; THAYER—68c.

655. **ἀποστυγέω** {1x} **apŏstugĕō**, *ap-os-toog-eh'-o;* from *575* and the base of *4767;* to *detest* utterly:—abhor {1x}.

This word means "to shudder" [*apo*, "from," here used intensively, *stugeo*, "to hate"]; hence, "to abhor, dislike intensely" (Rom. 12:9). See: BAGD—100c; THAYER—68d.

656. **ἀποσυνάγωγος** {3x} **apŏsunagōgŏs**, *ap-os-oon-ag'-o-gos;* from *575* and *4864; excommunicated:*—be put out of the synagogue + 1096 {2x}, put out of the synagogue + 4160 {1x}.

This word is an adjective denoting "expelled from the congregation, excommunicated," is used **(1)** with *ginomai*, "to become, be made [out of the synagogue]" (Jn 9:22; 12:42); and **(2)** with *poieo*, "to make [one go from the synagogue]" (Jn 16:2). **(3)** This excommunication involved prohibition not only from attendance at the "synagogue," but from all fellowship with Israelites. See: TDNT—7:848, 1107; BAGD—100d; THAYER—68d.

657. **ἀποτάσσομαι** {6x} **apŏtassŏmai**, *ap-ot-as'-som-ahee;* mid. voice from *575* and *5021;* lit. to *say adieu* (by departing or dismissing); fig. to *renounce:*—bid farewell {2x}, take leave {2x}, send away {1x}, forsake {1x}.

This word is **(1)** used in the middle voice to signify "to bid adieu to a person." **(2)** It primarily means **(2a)** "to set apart, separate"; then, **(2b)** "to take leave of, to bid farewell to" (Mk 6:46; Lk 9:61), **(2c)** "to give parting instructions to" (Acts 18:18, 21; 2 Cor 2:13); **(2d)** "to forsake, renounce" (Lk 14:33). See: TDNT—8:33,*; BAGD—100d; THAYER—69a.

658. **ἀποτελέω** {1x} **apŏtĕlĕō**, *ap-ot-el-eh'-o;* from *575* and *5055;* to *complete entirely*, i.e. *consummate:*—finish {1x}.

This word means "to bring to an end, accomplish, to perfect" and is translated "I do" in Lk 13:32. See: BAGD—100d; THAYER—69a.

659. **ἀποτίθημι** {8x} **apŏtithēmi**, *ap-ot-eeth'-ay-mee;* from *575* and *5087;* to *put away* (lit. or fig.):—put off {2x}, lay aside {2x}, lay down {1x}, cast off {1x}, put away {1x}, lay apart {1x}.

This word means "to put off, lay aside," denotes, in the middle voice, "to put off from oneself, cast off" and is used figuratively of works of darkness (Rom 13:12 "let us cast off'" cf. Acts 7:58; Eph 4:22; 4:25; Col 3:8; Heb 12:1; Jas 1:21; 1 Pet 2:1). See: BAGD—101a; THAYER—69a.

660. **ἀποτινάσσω** {2x} **apŏtinassō**, *ap-ot-in-as'-so;* from *575* and τινάσσω **tinassō** (to *jostle*); to *brush off:*—shake off {2x}.

This word means "to shake off" and is used **(1)** in Lk 9:5, of dust from the foot; and **(2)** Acts 28:5 of a viper from the hand. See: BAGD—101b; THAYER—69b.

661. **ἀποτίνω** {1x} **apŏtinō**, *ap-ot-ee'-no;* from *575* and *5099;* to *pay* in full:—repay {1x}.

This word signifies "to pay off" and is used in Philem 19 of Paul's promise to "repay" whatever Onesimus owed Philemon, or to whatever extent the runaway slave had wronged his master. See: BAGD—101b; THAYER—69b.

662. **ἀποτολμάω** {1x} **apŏtŏlmaō**, *ap-ot-ol-mah'-o;* from *575* and *5111;* to *venture* plainly:—be very bold {1x}.

This word means "to be very bold, to speak out boldly" and is used in Rom. 10:20. See: TDNT—8:181, 1183; BAGD—101b; THAYER—69b.

663. **ἀποτομία** {2x} **apŏtŏmia**, *ap-ot-om-ee'-ah;* from the base of *664;* (fig.) *decisiveness*, i.e. *rigor:*—severity {2x}.

This word means "steepness, sharpness" and is used metaphorically in Rom 11:22 (twice) of "the severity of God," which lies in His temporary retributive dealings with Israel. In the papyri it is used of exacting to the full the provisions of a statute. See: TDNT—8:106, 1169; BAGD—101c; THAYER—69b.

664. **ἀποτόμως** {2x} **apŏtŏmōs**, *ap-ot-om'-oce;* adv. from a der. of a compound of *575* and τέμνω **tĕmnō** (to *cut*); *abruptly*, i.e. *peremptorily:*—sharpness {1x}, sharply {1x}.

This word signifies "abruptly, curtly," lit., "in a manner that cuts"; hence "sharply, severely": **(1)** 2 Cor 13:10: ""Therefore I write these things being absent, lest being present I should use sharpness, according to the power which the Lord hath given me to edification, and not to destruction"; the pronoun "you" is to be understood, i.e., "that I may not use (or deal with) . . . sharply *with you*"; **(2)** Titus 1:13 of rebuking: "This witness is true. Wherefore rebuke them sharply, that they may be sound in the faith . . ." See: TDNT—8:106, 1169; BAGD—101c; THAYER—69b.

665. **ἀποτρέπω** {1x} **apŏtrĕpō**, *ap-ot-rep'-o;* from *575* and the base of *5157;* to *deflect*, i.e. (refl.) *avoid:*—turn away {1x}.

This word means "to cause to turn away" (*apo*), is used in the middle voice in 2 Tim. 3:5: "Having a form of godliness, but denying the power thereof: from such turn away." See: BAGD—101c; THAYER—69c.

666. **ἀπουσία** {1x} **apŏusia**, *ap-oo-see'-ah;* from the part. of *548;* a *being away:*—absence {1x}.

This word means lit., "a being away from," is used in Phil 2:12, of the apostle's absence from Philippi, in contrast to his parousia, his presence with the saints there ("parousia") does not signify merely "a coming," it includes or suggests "the presence" which follows the arrival. See: BAGD—101d; THAYER—69c.

667. **ἀποφέρω** {5x} **apŏphĕrō**, *ap-of-er'-o;* from *575* and *5342;* to *bear off* (lit. or rel.):—carry away {3x}, carry {1x}, bring {1x}.

Apophero, as a verb, means "to carry forth" and is rendered "bring": "And when I come, whomsoever ye shall approve by *your* letters, them will I send to bring your liberality unto Jerusalem" (1 Cor 16:3; cf. Acts 19:12). Syn.: 399, 1533. See: BAGD—101d; THAYER—69c.

668. **ἀποφεύγω** {3x} **apŏphĕugō**, *ap-of-yoo'-go;* from *575* and *5343;* (fig.) to *escape:*—escape {2x}, escape from {1x}.

This word means "to flee away from, escape from" and is used in 2 Pet 1:4: "Whereby are given unto us exceeding great and precious promises: that by these ye might be partakers of the divine nature, having escaped the corruption that is in the world through lust" (cf. 2:18, 20). Syn.: 1628. See: BAGD—101d; THAYER—69c.

669. **ἀποφθέγγομαι** {3x} **apŏphthĕggŏmai**, *ap-of-theng'-om-ahee;* from *575* and *5350;* to *enunciate* plainly, i.e. *declare:*—utterance {1x}, speak forth {1x}, say {1x}.

This word means **(1)** "to speak forth, said" (Acts 2:14; 26:25). **(2)** In Acts 2:4 it denotes to give utterance: "And they were all filled with the Holy Ghost, and began to speak with other tongues, as the Spirit gave them utterance." **(3)** This is not a word of everyday speech but one "belonging to dignified and elevated discourse. See: TDNT—1:447, 75; BAGD—102a; THAYER—69c.

670. **ἀποφορτίζομαι** {1x} **apŏphŏrtizŏmai**, *ap-of-or-tid'-zom-ahee;* from *575* and the mid. voice of *5412;* to *unload:*—unlade {1x}.

This word means "to discharge a cargo" and is used in Acts 21:3. See: BAGD—102a; THAYER—69d.

671. **ἀπόχρησις** {1x} **apŏchrēsis**, *ap-okh'-ray-sis;* from a compound of *575* and *5530;* the act of *using up*, i.e. *consumption:*—using {1x}.

This word is a strengthened form of *chresis* (5540), "a using," signifies "a misuse" and is translated "using" in Col 2:22; the clause may be rendered "by their using up." The unusual word was chosen for its expressiveness; the *chresis* here was an *apochresis;* the things could not be used without rendering them unfit for further use. See: BAGD—102a; THAYER—69d.

672. **ἀποχωρέω** {3x} **apŏchōrĕō**, *ap-okh-o-reh'-o;* from *575* and *5562;* to *go away:*—depart {3x}.

This word means "to depart from" and is so translated in Mt 7:23; Lk 9:39; Acts 13:13. Syn.: 1633. See: BAGD—102a; THAYER—70a.

673. **ἀποχωρίζω** {2x} **apŏchōrizō**, *ap-okh-o-rid'-zo;* from *575* and *5563;* to *rend apart;* refl. to *separate:*—depart asunder {1x}, depart {1x}.

This word signifies "to separate off" and **(1)** in the middle voice means "to depart from, depart asunder" (Acts 15:39); and **(2)** in Rev 6:14 it is translated "departed." See: BAGD—102b; THAYER—70a.

674. **ἀποψύχω** {1x} **apŏpsuchō**, *ap-ops-oo'-kho;* from *575* and *5594;* to *breathe out,* i.e. *faint:*—heart failing {1x}.

This word means to breathe out life, expire, to faint or swoon away (Lk 21:26). See: BAGD—102b; THAYER—70a.

675. **Ἄππιος** {1x} **ʾAppiŏs**, *ap'-pee-os;* of Lat. or.; (in the gen., i.e. possessive case) of *Appius,* the name of a Rom.:—Appii {1x}. See: BAGD—102b; THAYER—70a.

676. **ἀπρόσιτος** {1x} **aprŏsitŏs**, *ap-ros'-ee-tos;* from *1* (as a neg. particle) and a der. of a compound of *4314* and εἶμι **ĕimi** (to *go*); *inaccessible:*—which no man can approach unto {1x}.

This word means "unapproachable, inaccessible" and is used in 1 Ti 6:16 of the light in which God dwells. See: BAGD—102c; THAYER—70a.

677. **ἀπρόσκοπος** {3x} **aprŏskŏpŏs**, *ap-ros'-kop-os;* from *1* (as a neg. particle) and a presumed der. of *4350;* act. *inoffensive,* i.e. *not leading into sin;* pass. *faultless,* i.e. *not led into sin:*—void of offense {1x}, none offence {1x}, without offence {1x}.

This word is used **(1)** in the active sense, "not causing to stumble, none offence" (1 Cor 10:32 metaphorically of "refraining from doing anything to lead astray" either Jews or Greeks or the church of God i.e., the local church); **(2)** in the passive sense, "blameless, without stumbling, void of offense" (Acts 24:16 "a conscience void of offense"; Phil 1:10 "without offense"). See: TDNT—6:745, 946; BAGD—102c; THAYER—70b.

678. **ἀπροσωπολήπτως** {1x} **aprŏsōpŏlēptōs**, *ap-ros-o-pol-ape'-toce;* adv. from a compound of *1* (as a neg. particle) and a presumed der. of a presumed comp. of *4383* and *2983* [comp. *4381*]; in a way *not accepting* the *person,* i.e. *impartially:*—without respect of persons {1x}.

This word only occurs in 1 Pet 1:17. See: TDNT—6:779, 950; BAGD—102c; THAYER—70b.

679. **ἄπταιστος** {1x} **aptaistŏs**, *ap-tah'-ees-tos;* from *1* (as a neg. particle) and a der. of *4417; not stumbling,* i.e. (fig.) *without sin:*—keep from falling + 5442 {1x}.

This word means not stumbling, standing firm and is used in Jude 1:24. See: BAGD—102c; THAYER—70b.

680. **ἅπτομαι** {36x} **haptŏmai**, *hap'-tom-ahee;* refl. of *681;* prop. to *attach* oneself to, i.e. to *touch* (in many impl. relations):—touch {36x}. See: BAGD—102d; THAYER—70b.

681. **ἅπτω** {4x} **haptō**, *hap'-to;* a primary verb; prop. to *fasten* to, i.e. (spec.) to *set* on fire:—light {3x}, kindle {1x}.

This word means primarily "to fasten to," hence, of fire, "to kindle," denotes, in the middle voice **(1)** "to touch" (Mt 8:3, 15; 9:20, 21, 29); **(2)** "to cling to, lay hold of" (Jn 20:17; here the Lord's prohibition as to clinging to Him was indicative of the fact that communion with Him would, after His ascension, be by faith, through the Spirit; **(3)** "to have carnal intercourse with a woman" (1 Cor 7:1); **(4)** "to have fellowship and association with unbelievers" (2 Cor 6:17); **(5)** (negatively) "to adhere to certain Levitical and ceremonial ordinances," in order to avoid contracting external defilement, or to practice rigorous asceticism, all such abstentions being of "no value against the indulgence of the flesh" (Col 2:21); **(6)** "to assault," in order to sever the vital union between Christ and the believer, said of the attack of the Evil One (1 Jn 5:18). See: BAGD—102d; THAYER—70b.

682. **Ἀπφία** {1x} **Apphia**, *ap-fee'-a;* prob. of for. or.; *Apphia,* a woman of Collosæ:—*Apphia* {1x}. See: BAGD—103b; THAYER—70d.

683. **ἀπωθέομαι** {6x} **apōthĕŏmai**, *ap-o-theh'-om-ahee;* or ἀπώθομαι **apōthŏmai**, *ap-o'-thom-ahee;* from *575* and the mid. voice of ὠθέω **ōthĕō** or ὤθω **ōthō** (to *shove*); to *push off,* fig. to *reject:*—cast away {2x}, thrust away {1x}, put from {1x}, thrust from {1x}, put away {1x}.

This word means "to thrust away" and in the NT used in the middle voice, signifying "to thrust from oneself, to cast off, by way of rejection" (Acts 7:27, 39; 13:46; Rom 11:1–2; 1 Ti 1:19). See: TDNT—1:448,*; BAGD—103b; THAYER—70d.

684. **ἀπώλεια** {20x} **apōlĕia**, *ap-o'-li-a;* from a presumed der. of *622; ruin* or *loss* (phys. spiritual or eternal):—perdition {8x}, destruction {5x}, waste {2x}, damnable {1x}, to die + 1519 {1x}, perish + 1498 + 1519 {1x}, pernicious {1x}.

Apoleia means "loss of well-being, not of being" and is used **(1)** of things, signifying their waste, or ruin; **(1a)** of ointment (Mt 26:8; Mk 14:4); **(1b)** of money (Acts 8:20 "perish"); **(2)** of persons, signifying their spiritual and eternal perdition (Mt 7:13; Jn 17:12); 2 Th 2:3 where "son of perdition" signifies the proper destiny of the person mentioned; metaphorically of men persistent in evil; Rom 9:22, where "fitted" is in the middle voice, indicating that the vessels of wrath fitted themselves for "destruction", **(2a)** of the adversaries of the Lord's people (Phil 1:28 "perdition"); **(2b)** of professing Christians, really enemies of the cross of Christ (Phil 3:19); **(1e)** of those who are subjects of foolish and hurtful lusts (1 Ti. 6:9); **(2c)** of professing Hebrew adherents who shrink back into unbelief (Heb 10:39); **(2d)** of false teachers (2 Pet 2:1, 3); **(2e)** of ungodly men (2 Pet 3:7); **(2f)** of those who wrest the Scriptures (2 Pet 3:16); **(2g)** of the Beast, the final head of the revived Roman Empire (Rev 17:8, 11); **(3)** of impersonal subjects, as heresies (2 Pet 2:1, where "damnable heresies" is lit., "heresies of destruction"). See: TDNT—1:396, 67; BAGD—103b; THAYER—70d.

685. **ἀρά** {1x} **ara**, *ar-ah';* prob. from *142;* prop. *prayer* (as *lifted* to Heaven), i.e. (by impl.) *imprecation:*—curse {1x}.

Ara, as a noun, in its most usual meaning, "a malediction, cursing" is used in Rom. 3:14: "Whose mouth *is* full of cursing and bitterness." Syn.: 331, 332, 944, 2552, 2652, 2653, 2671, 2672. See: TDNT—1:448, 75; BAGD—103d; THAYER—71d.

686. **ἄρα** {51x} **ara**, *ar'-ah;* prob. from *142* (through the idea of *drawing* a conclusion); a particle denoting an *inference* more or less decisive (as follows):—therefore + 3767 {7x}, so then + 3767 {4x}, now therefore + 3767 {1x}, then + 1065 {2x}, wherefore + 1065 {1x}, haply + 1065 {1x}, not tr {7x}, misc. {7x} = (what) manner (of man), no doubt, perhaps, truly. Often used in connection with other particles, esp. *1065* or *3767* (after) or *1487* (before). See: BAGD—103d; THAYER—71a. comp. also *687.*

687. **ἆρα** {3x} **ara**, *ar'-ah;* a form of *686,* denoting an *interrogation* to which a negative answer is presumed:—therefore {1x}, not tr {2x}. See: BAGD—104a; THAYER—71c.

688. **Ἀραβία** {2x} **Arabia**, *ar-ab-ee'-ah;* of Heb. or. [6152]; *Arabia,* a region of Asia:—*Arabia* {2x}. See: BAGD—104a; THAYER—71d.

ἄραγε **aragĕ**. See *686* and *1065.*

689. **Ἀράμ** {3x} **Aram**, *ar-am';* of Heb. or. [7410]; *Aram* (i.e. *Ram*), an Isr.:—*Aram* {3x}. See: BAGD—104b; THAYER—71d.

690. **Ἄραψ** {1x}} **ʾAraps**, *ar'-aps;* from *688;* an *Arab* or native of Arabia:—Arabians {1x}. See: BAGD—104c; THAYER—72a.

691. **ἀργέω** {1x} **argĕō**, *arg-eh'-o;* from *692;* to *be idle,* i.e. (fig.) to *delay:*—linger {1x}.

This word means "to be idle, inactive, to linger, delay" and is used in 2 Pet 2:3: "And through covetousness shall they with feigned words make merchandise of you: whose judgment now of a long time lingereth not, and their damnation slumbereth not." See: BAGD—104c; THAYER—72a.

692. **ἀργός** {8x} **argŏs**, *ar-gos';* from *1* (as a neg. particle) and *2041; inactive,* i.e. *unemployed;* (by impl.) *lazy, useless:*—barren {1x}, idle {6x}, slow {1x}.

This word denotes "idle, barren, yielding no return, because of inactivity" is rendered **(1)** "barren" (2 Pet 1:8); **(2)** "idle" (Mt 12:36 the "idle word" means the word that is thoughtless or profitless; cf. 20:3, 6 [twice]; 1 Ti 5:13 [twice]); and **(3)** "slow" (Titus 1:12). Syn.: 1021, 3576. See: TDNT—1:452, 76; BAGD—104c; THAYER—72a.

693. **ἀργύρεος** {3x} **argurĕŏs**, *ar-goo'-reh-os;* from *696;* made *of silver:*—of silver {1x}, silver {2x}.

This word signifies "silver, made of silver," (Acts 19:24; 2 Ti 2:20; Rev 9:20). See: BAGD—104d; THAYER—72b.

694. **ἀργύριον** {20x} **arguriŏn**, *ar-goo'-ree-on;* neut. of a presumed der. of *696; silvery,* i.e. (by impl.) *cash;* spec. a *silverling* (i.e. *drachma* or *shekel*):—money {11x}, piece of silver {5x}, silver {3x}, silver piece {1x}.

This word means properly "a piece of silver" and denotes **(1)** "silver," e.g., Acts 3:6; **(2)** a "silver coin," often in the plural, "pieces of silver," e.g., Mt 26:15; so 28:12, where the meaning is "many pieces of silver"; **(3)** "money"; it has this meaning in Mt 25:18, 27; 28:15; Mk 14:11; Lk 9:3; 19:15, 23; 22:5; Acts 8:20. See: BAGD—104d; THAYER—72b.

695. **ἀργυροκόπος** {1x} **argurŏkŏpŏs**, *ar-goo-rok-op'-os;* from *696* and *2875;* a *beater* (i.e. *worker*) *of silver:*—silversmith {1x}.

This word means "to beat" occurs in Acts 19:24 of the one who smoothes the silver through tapping. See: BAGD—105a; THAYER—72b.

696. **ἄργυρος** {5x} **argurŏs**, *ar'-goo-ros;* from ἀργός **argŏs** (*shining*); *silver* (the metal, in the articles or coin):—silver {5x}.

This word denotes "silver" and in each occurrence in the NT it follows the mention of gold, Mt 10:9; Acts 17:29; Jas 5:3; Rev 18:12. See: BAGD—105a; THAYER—72b.

697. Ἄρειος Πάγος {2x} **Arĕiŏs Pagŏs,** *ar'-i-os pag'-os;* from Ἄρης **Arēs** (the name of the Greek deity of war) and a der. of *4078; rock of Ares,* a place in Athens:—Areopagus {1x}, Mars' Hill {1x}. See: BAGD—105b; THAYER—72c.

698. Ἀρεοπαγίτης {1x} **Arĕŏpagitēs,** *ar-eh-op-ag-ee'-tace;* from *697;* an *Areopagite* or member of the court held on Mars' Hill:—Areopagite {1x}. See: BAGD—105b; THAYER—72c.

699. ἀρέσκεια {1x} **arĕskĕia,** *ar-es'-ki-ah;* from a der. of *700; complaisance:*—pleasing {1x}.

This word means a "pleasing," a giving pleasure, Col 1:10, of the purpose Godward of a walk worthy of the Lord (cf. 1 Thess. 4:1). See: TDNT—1:456, 77; BAGD—105c; THAYER—72c.

700. ἀρέσκω {17x} **arĕskō,** *ar-es'-ko;* prob. from *142* (through the idea of *exciting* emotion); to *be agreeable* (or by impl. to seek to be so):—please {17x}.

This word signifies **(1)** "to be pleasing to, be acceptable to," Mt 14:6; Mk 6:22; Acts 6:5; Rom 8:8; 15:2; 1 Cor 7:32–34; Gal 1:10; 1 Th 2:15; 4:1 where the preceding *kai,* "and," is epexegetical, "even," explaining the "walking," i.e., Christian manner of life as "pleasing" God; 2 Tim. 2:4; **(2)** "to endeavor to please," and so, "to render service," **(2a)** doing so evilly in one's own interests, Rom 15:1, which Christ did not, v. 3; or **(2b)** unselfishly, 1 Cor 10:33; 1 Th 2:4. See: TDNT—1:455, 77; BAGD—105c; THAYER—72d.

701. ἀρεστός {4x} **arĕstŏs,** *ar-es-tos';* from *700; agreeable;* by impl. *fit:*—those things that please {1x}, reason {1x}, please + 2076 {1x}, those things that are pleasing {1x}. See: TDNT—1:456, 77; BAGD—105d; THAYER—72d.

702. Ἀρέτας {1x} **Arĕtas,** *ar-et'-as;* of for. or.; *Aretas,* an Arabian:—*Aretas* {1x}. See: BAGD—105d; THAYER—72d.

703. ἀρέτη {5x} **arĕtē,** *ar-et'-ay;* from the same as *730;* prop. *manliness* (*valor*), i.e. *excellence* (intrinsic or attributed):—praise {1x}, virtue {4x}.

This word properly denotes whatever procures preeminent estimation for a person or thing; hence, "intrinsic eminence, moral goodness, virtue," **(1)** of God, **(1a)** 1 Pet 2:9 "praises"; here the original and general sense seems to be blended with the impression made on others, i.e., renown, excellence or praise; **(1b)** in 2 Pet 1:3, "by His own glory and virtue" i.e., the manifestation of His divine power; **(2)** of any particular moral excellence, Phil 4:8; 2 Pet 1:5 [twice] where virtue is enjoined as an essential quality in the exercise of faith." See: TDNT—1:457, 77; BAGD—105d; THAYER—73a.

704. ἀρήν {1x} **arēn,** *ar-ane';* perh. the same as *730;* a *lamb* (as a *male*):—lamb {1x}.

Aren, a noun, the nominative case of which is found only in early times occurs in Lk 10:3. Syn.: The *aren* is a little older than the arnion (721). See discussion under 721. See: TDNT—1:340, 54; BAGD—106a; THAYER—73b.

705. ἀριθμέω {3x} **arithmĕō,** *ar-ith-meh'-o;* from *706;* to *enumerate* or *count:*—number {3x}.

This word means "to number" and is found in Mt 10:30; Lk 12:7; Rev 7:9. See: TDNT—1:461, 78; BAGD—106b; THAYER—73b.

706. ἀριθμός {18x} **arithmŏs,** *ar-ith-mos';* from *142;* a *number* (as reckoned *up*):—number {18x}.

This word means "a number" [Eng., "arithmetic"] and occurs in Lk 22:3; Jn 6:10; Rom 9:27; elsewhere five times in Acts, ten times in the Apocalypse. See: TDNT—1:461, 78; BAGD—106b; THAYER—73b.

707. Ἀριμαθαία {4x} **Arimathaia,** *ar-ee-math-ah'-ee-ah;* of Heb. or. [7414]; *Arimathæa* (or *Ramah*), a place in Pal.:—Arimathæa {4x}. See: BAGD—106c; THAYER—73b.

708. Ἀρίσταρχος {5x} **Aristarchŏs,** *ar-is'-tar-khos;* from the same as *712* and *757; best ruling; Aristarchus,* a Macedonian:—Aristarchus {5x}. See: BAGD—106c; THAYER—73c.

709. ἀριστάω {3x} **aristaō,** *ar-is-tah'-o;* from *712; to take the principle meal:*—dine {3x}.

This word means primarily, "to breakfast" was later used also with the meaning "to dine," e.g., Lk 11:37; in Jn 21:12, 15; obviously there it was the first meal in the day. See: BAGD—106c; THAYER—73c.

710. ἀριστερός {3x} **aristĕrŏs,** *ar-is-ter-os';* appar. a comparative of the same as *712;* the *left* hand (as *second-best*):—left hand {1x}, left {1x}, on the left {1x}.

This word is used **(1)** of the "left" hand **(1a)** in Mt 6:3, the word "hand" being understood; **(1b)** in connection with the armor of righteousness, in 2 Cor 6:7, "(on the right hand and) on the left," lit., "(of the weapons . . . the right and) the left"; **(2)** in the phrase "on the left," formed by *ex* (for *ek*), "from," and the genitive plural of this adjective, Mk 10:37. See: BAGD—106c; THAYER—73c.

711. Ἀριστόβουλος {1x} **Aristŏbŏulŏs,** *ar-is-tob'-oo-los;* from the same as *712* and *1012; best counselling; Aristobulus,* a Chr.:—Aristobulus {1x}. See: BAGD—106d; THAYER—73c.

712. ἄριστον {3x} **aristŏn,** *ar'-is-ton;* appar. neut. of a superl. from the same as *730;* the *best* meal [or *breakfast;* perh. from ἦρι **ēri** ("*early*")], i.e. *luncheon:*—dinner {3x}.

This word means primarily, "the first food," taken early in the morning before work; the meal in the Pharisee's house, in Lk 11:37, was a breakfast or early meal. It also became known as any meal during the day. See: BAGD—106d; THAYER—73c.

713. ἀρκετός {3x} **arkĕtŏs,** *ar-ket-os';* from *714; satisfactory:*—enough {1x}, suffice {1x}, sufficient {1x}.

This word means "sufficient" and is rendered **(1)** "enough" in Mt 10:25; **(2)** "sufficient" in Mt 6:34; and **(3)** "suffice" in 1 Pet 4:3 lit. "(is) sufficient." See: TDNT—1:464, 78; BAGD—107a; THAYER—73d.

714. ἀρκέω {8x} **arkĕō,** *ar-keh'-o;* appar. a primary verb [but prob. akin to *142* through the idea of *raising* a barrier]; prop. to *ward off,* i.e. (by impl.) to *avail* (fig. *be satisfactory*):—be content {3x}, be sufficient {2x}, be enough {1x}, suffice {1x}, content {1x}.

Arkeo, as a verb, primarily signifies "to be sufficient, to be possessed of sufficient strength, to be strong, to be enough for a thing"; hence, "to defend, ward off"; in the middle voice, "to be satisfied, contented with": **(1)** Lk 3:14 with wages; **(2)** 1 Ti 6:8 with food and raiment; **(3)** Heb 13:5 with "such things as ye have"; **(4)** negatively of Diotrephes in 3 Jn 10, "not content therewith." Syn.: 841, 842, 2425, 4909. See: TDNT—1:464, 78; BAGD—107a; THAYER—73d.

715. ἄρκτος {1x} **arktŏs,** *ark'-tos;* prob. from *714;* a *bear* (as *obstructing* by ferocity):—bear {1x}.

This word denotes the animal and is found only in Rev 13:2. See: BAGD—107b; THAYER—73d.

716. ἅρμα {4x} **harma,** *har'-mah;* prob. from *142* [perh. with *1* (as a particle of union) prefixed]; a *chariot* (as *raised* or fitted *together* [comp. *719*]):—chariot {4x}.

This word denotes "a war chariot with two wheels," Acts 8:28, 29, 38; Rev 9:9. Syn.: 4480. See: BAGD—107b; THAYER—73d.

717. Ἀρμαγεδδών {1x} **Armagĕddōn,** *ar-mag-ed-dohn';* of Heb. or. [2022 and 4023]; *Armageddon* (or *Har-Meggiddon*), a symbol. name:—*Armageddon* {1x}. See: TDNT—1:468, 79; BAGD—107c; THAYER—73d.

718. ἁρμόζω {1x} **harmŏzō,** *har-mod'-zo;* from *719;* to *joint,* i.e. (fig.) to *woo* (refl. to *betroth*):—espouse {1x}.

This word is used in the middle voice, of marrying or giving in marriage; in 2 Cor 11:2 and is rendered "espoused," metaphorically of the relationship established between Christ and the local church, through the apostle's instrumentality. The thought may be that of "fitting" or "joining" to one husband, the middle voice expressing the apostle's interest or desire in doing so. Syn.: 3423. See: BAGD—107c; THAYER—74a.

719. ἁρμός {1x} **harmŏs,** *har-mos';* from the same as *716;* an *articulation* (of the body):—joint {1x}.

This word means "a joining, joint" and is found in Heb 4:12, figuratively (with the word "marrow") of the inward moral and spiritual being of man, as just previously expressed literally in the phrase "soul and spirit." Syn.: 860. See: BAGD—107d; THAYER—74b.

720. ἀρνέομαι {29x} **arnĕŏmai,** *ar-neh'-om-ahee;* perh. from *1* (as a neg. particle) and the mid. voice of *4483;* to *contradict,* i.e. *disavow, reject, abnegate:*—deny {29x}, refuse {2x}.

This word signifies **(1)** "to say . . . not, to contradict," e.g., Mk 14:70; Jn 1:20; 18:25, 27; 1 Jn 2:22; **(2)** "to deny" by way of disowning a person, as, **(2a)** e.g., the Lord Jesus as master, e.g., Mt 10:33; Lk 12:9; 2 Ti 2:12; or, on the other hand, **(2b)** of Christ Himself, "denying" that a person is His follower, Mt 10:33; 2 Ti 2:12; or **(2c)** to "deny" the Father and the Son, by apostatizing and by disseminating pernicious teachings, **(2d)** to "deny" Jesus Christ as master and Lord by immorality under a cloak of religion, 2 Pet 2:1; Jude 4; **(3)** "to deny oneself," either **(3a)** in a good sense, by disregarding one's own interests, Lk 9:23, or **(3b)** in a bad sense, to prove false to oneself, to act quite unlike oneself, 2 Ti 2:13; **(4)** to "abrogate, forsake, or renounce a thing," **(4a)** whether evil, Titus 2:12, or **(4b)** good, 1 Ti 5:8; 2 Ti 3:5; Rev 2:13; 3:8; **(5)** "not to accept, to reject" something offered, Acts 3:14; 7:35, "refused"; Heb. 11:24 "refused." See: TDNT—1:469, 79; BAGD—107d; THAYER—74b.

721. ἀρνίον {30x} **arniŏn,** *ar-nee'-on;* dimin. from *704;* a *lambkin:*—lamb {2x}, Lamb, i.e. Christ {28x}.

Arnion is a diminutive in form of aren (704). **(1)** It is used only by the apostle John, **(1a)** in the plural, in the Lord's command to Peter: "He saith unto him, Feed my lambs" (Jn 21:15, with symbolic reference to young converts); **(1b)** in the singular, in the Apocalypse, some 28 times, of Christ as the "Lamb" of God, the symbolism having reference to His character and His vicarious Sacrifice, as the basis both of redemption and of divine vengeance. **(1c)** He is seen in the position of sovereign glory and honor, (e.g., Rev 7:17, which He shares equally with the Father, 22:1, 3), **(1d)** the center of angelic beings and of the redeemed and the object of their veneration (e.g. 5:6, 8, 12, 13; 15:3), **(1e)** the Leader and Shepherd of His saints (e.g., 7:17; 14:4), **(1f)** the Head of his spiritual bride (e.g., 21:9), **(1g)** the luminary of the heavenly and eternal city (21:23), **(1h)** the One to whom all judgment is committed (e.g., 6:1, 16; 13:8), **(1i)** the Conqueror of the foes of God and His people (17:14); **(1j)** the song that celebrates the triumph of those who "gain the victory over the Beast," is the song of Moses . . . and the song of the Lamb (15:3).

(2) His sacrifice, the efficacy of which avails for those who accept the salvation thereby provided, forms the ground of the execution of divine wrath for the rejector, and the defier of God (14:10); **(3)** in the description of the second "Beast" (Rev 13:11), seen in the vision "like a lamb," suggestive of his acting in the capacity of a false messiah, a travesty of the true. Syn.: The contrast between *arnion* and amnos (286) does not lie in the diminutive character of the former as compared with the latter. The contrast lies in the manner in which Christ is presented in the two respects. The use of amnos points directly to the fact, the nature and character of His sacrifice; *arnion* (only in the Apocalypse) presents Him, on the ground, indeed, of His sacrifice, but in His acquired majesty, dignity, honor, authority and power. See: TDNT—1:340,*; BAGD—108b; THAYER—74c.

722. **ἀροτριόω** {3x} **arŏtriŏō**, *ar-ot-ree-o'-o;* from *723;* to *plough:*—plow {3x}.

This verb "to plow" and occurs in Lk 17:7 and 1 Cor 9:10 [twice]. See: BAGD—108b; THAYER—74c.

723. **ἄροτρον** {1x} **arŏtrŏn**, *ar'-ot-ron;* from ἀρόω **arŏō** (to *till*); a *plow:*—plow {1x}.

This noun means "a plough" and occurs in Lk 9:62. See: BAGD—108b; THAYER—74c.

724. **ἁρπαγή** {3x} **harpagē**, *har-pag-ay';* from *726; pillage* (prop. abstr.):—extortion {1x}, ravening {1x}, spoiling {1x}.

This word denotes "pillage, plundering, robbery, extortion" [akin to *harpazo,* "to seize, carry off by force," and *harpagmos,* "a thing seized, or the act of seizing"; from the root *arp,* seen in Eng., "rapacious"; an associated noun, with the same spelling, denoted a rake, or hook for drawing up a bucket] and is translated **(1)** "extortion" in Mt 23:25; **(2)** "ravening" in Lk 11:39; and **(3)** "spoiling" in Heb 10:34. See: BAGD—108b; THAYER—74d.

725. **ἁρπαγμός** {1x} **harpagmŏs**, *har-pag-mos';* from *726; plunder* (prop. concr.):—robbery {1x}.

Harpagmos, as a verb, means "to seize, carry off by force" and is **(1)** found in Phil 2:6, "thought it not robbery" to be equal with God. **(2)** Christ possessed equality with God prior to His Incarnation, and then for a time veiled that glory, being always God in all of the co-equal attributes, but in the incarnation never using His Godly powers to better Himself. **(2)** He was fully God, fully man, God taking on the likeness of sinful flesh (Rom 8:3), not a man adding Godliness. **(3)** His glory was all that was veiled, present but veiled (cf. His transfiguration – Mt 17:2). **(3a)** He prayed for its restoration (Jn 17:5). **(3b)** It was restored after His ascension (cf. His appearing to Saul on the Damascus road, Act 9:3; and John's vision of Him in the midst of the candlesticks, Rev 1:13f). **(4)** The middle/passive sense gives meaning to the passage as the purpose of the passage is to set forth Christ as the supreme example to the Philippians (and us) of humility and self-renunciation: "Who though He was subsisting in the essential form of God, yet did not regard His being on an equality of glory and majesty with God as a prize and a treasure to be held fast. He would not feel as if He had been robbed to give up His shared glory." See: TDNT—1:473, 80; BAGD—108c; THAYER—74d.

726. **ἁρπάζω** {13x} **harpazō**, *har-pad'-zo;* from a der. of *138;* to *seize* (in various applications):—catch up {4x}, take by force {3x}, catch away {2x}, pluck {2x}, catch {1x}, pull {1x}.

Harpazo means **(1)** to snatch or catch away and is said of **(1a)** the act of the Spirit of the Lord in regard to Philip (Acts 8:39); **(1b)** of Paul caught up to paradise (2 Cor 12:2, 4); **(1c)** of the rapture of the saints to meet the Lord (1 Th 4:17); **(1d)** of the rapture of the man child in the vision of Rev 12:5. **(2)** This verb conveys the idea of force suddenly exercised (Mt 11:12; 12:29; Jn 6:15). Syn.: 4815, 4884. See: TDNT—1:472, 80; BAGD—109a; THAYER—74d.

727. **ἅρπαξ** {5x} **harpax**, *har'-pax;* from *726; rapacious:*—extortioner {4x}, ravening {1x}.

This word means "rapacious" and is translated as **(1)** a noun, "extortioners," in Lk 18:11; 1 Cor 5:10–11; 6:10; and **(2)** in Mt 7:15 "ravening" (of wolves). See: BAGD—109b; THAYER—75a.

728. **ἀῤῥαβών** {3x} **arrhabōn**, *ar-hrab-ohn';* of Heb. or. [6162]; a *pledge,* i.e. part of the purchase-money or property given in advance as *security* for the rest:—earnest {3x}.

(1) This word meant originally, "earnest-money" deposited by the purchaser and forfeited if the purchase was not completed. **(2)** In general usage it came to denote "a pledge" or "earnest" of any sort; in the NT it is used only of that which is assured by God to believers; it is said **(2a)** of the Holy Spirit as the divine "pledge" of all their future blessedness, 2 Cor 1:22; 5:5; and **(2b)** in Eph 1:14, particularly of their eternal inheritance. See: TDNT—1:472, 80; BAGD—109b; THAYER—75a.

729. **ἄῤῥαφος** {1x} **arrhaphŏs**, *ar'-hraf-os;* from *1* (as a neg. particle) and a presumed der. of the same as *4476; unsewed,* i.e. of a single piece:—without seam {1x}.

Arrhaphos denotes "without seam" [*a,* negative, and *rhapto,* "to sew"] in Jn 19:23. See: BAGD—109c; THAYER—75a.

730. **ἄῤῥην** {9x} **arrhēn**, *ar'-hrane;* or

ἄρσην **arsēn**, *ar'-sane;* prob. from *142; male* (as stronger for *lifting*):—male {4x}, man {3x}, man child {1x}, man child + 5207 {1x}.

Arsen is translated **(1)** "men" in Rom 1:27 [three times]; **(2)** "man child" in Rev 12:5, 13; and **(3)** "male" in Mt 19:4; Mk 10:6; Lk 2:23; Gal 3:28 "there is neither male nor female," i.e. sex distinction does not obtain benefits in Christ; nor is sex a barrier either to salvation or the development of Christian graces. See: BAGD—109c; THAYER—75b.

731. **ἄῤῥητος** {1x} **arrhētŏs**, *ar'-hray-tos;* from *1* (as a neg. particle) and the same as *4490; unsaid,* i.e. (by impl.) *inexpressible:*—unspeakable {1x}.

Unspeakable due to their sacredness or that which is observed cannot be adequately describe by presently known human words (2 Cor 12:4). See: BAGD—109c; THAYER—75b.

732. **ἄῤῥωστος** {5x} **arrhōstŏs**, *ar'-hroce-tos;* from *1* (as a neg. particle) and a presumed der. of *4517; infirm:*—sick {2x}, sick folk {1x}, be sick {1x}, sickly {1x}.

This word means "feeble, sickly" [*a,* negative, *rhonnumi,* "to be strong"], is translated **(1)** "sick" in Mt 14:14; Mk 16:18; **(2)** "sick folk" in Mk 6:5; **(3)** "that were sick" in Mk 6:13; and **(4)** "sickly" in 1 Cor 11:30, here also of the physical state. See: BAGD—109d; THAYER—75b.

733. **ἀρσενοκοίτης** {2x} **arsĕnŏkoitēs**, *ar-sen-ok-oy'-tace;* from *730* and *2845;* a *sodomite:*—abuser of (one's) self with mankind {1x}, defile (one's) self with mankind {1x}.

This word means one who lies with a male as with a female; he is a sodomite, a homosexual (1 Cor 6:9; 1 Ti 1:10). See: BAGD—109d; THAYER—75b.

734. **Ἀρτεμᾶς** {1x} **Artĕmas**, *ar-tem-as';* contr. from a compound of *735* and *1435; gift of Artemis; Artemas* (or *Artemidorus*), a Chr.:—*Artemas* {1x}. See: BAGD—110a; THAYER—75b.

735. **Ἄρτεμις** {5x} **Artĕmis**, *ar'-tem-is;* prob. from the same as *736; prompt; Artemis,* the name of a Grecian goddess borrowed by the Asiatics for one of their deities:—Diana {5x}. See: BAGD—110a; THAYER—75b.

736. **ἀρτέμων** {1x} **artĕmōn**, *ar-tem'-ohn;* from a der. of *737;* prop. something *ready* [or else more remotely from *142* (comp. *740*); something *hung* up], i.e. (spec.) the *topsail* (rather *foresail* or *jib*) of a vessel:—mainsail {1x}.

Artemon is rendered "mainsail" in Acts 27:40. As to the particular kind of sail there mentioned, Sir William Ramsay, quoting from Juvenal concerning the entrance of a disabled ship into harbor by means of a prow-sail, indicates that the *artemon* would be a sail set on the bow. See: BAGD—110a; THAYER—75c.

737. **ἄρτι** {36x} **arti**, *ar'-tee;* adv. from a der. of *142* (comp. *740*) through the idea of *suspension;* just *now:*—now {24x}, henceforth + 575 {2x}, hereafter + 575 {2x}, this present {2x}, hitherto + 2193 {2x}, misc. {4x} = this day (hour), hither, (even) now.

(1) *Arti* expresses "coincidence," and denotes "strictly present time." **(2)** It signifies "just now, this moment," in contrast **(2a)** to the past, e.g., Mt 11:12; Jn 2:10; 9:19, 25; 13:33; Gal 1:9–10; **(2b)** to the future, e.g., Jn 13:37; 16:12, 31; 1 Cor 13:12; 2 Th 2:7; 1 Pet 1:6, 8; **(2c)** sometimes without necessary reference to either, e.g., Mt 3:15; 9:18; 26:53; Gal 4:20; Rev 12:10. See: TDNT—4:1106, 658; BAGD—110b; THAYER—75c.

738. **ἀρτιγέννητος** {1x} **artigĕnnētŏs**, *ar-teeg-en'-nay-tos;* from *737* and *1084; just born,* i.e. (fig.) a *young convert:*—newborn {1x}.

Artigennetos, as an adjective, [arti, "newly, recently"] is translated "newborn": "As newborn babes, desire the sincere milk of the word, that ye may grow thereby" (1 Pet 2:2). Syn.: 313, 616, 1080, 1084, 1085, 1626, 5088. See: TDNT—1:672, 114; BAGD—110c; THAYER—75d.

739. **ἄρτιος** {1x} **artiŏs**, *ar'-tee-os;* from *737; fresh,* i.e. (by impl.) *complete:*—perfect {1x}. Syn.: 3648, 5046.

This word stresses that in which nothing is maimed. It refers not only to the presence of all the parts that are necessary for completeness but also to the further adaptation and aptitude of these parts for their designed purpose (2 Ti 3:17). See: TDNT—1:475, 80; BAGD—110c; THAYER—75d.

740. **ἄρτος** {99x} **artos**, *ar'-tos;* from *142; bread* (as *raised*) or a *loaf:*—bread {72x}, loaf {23x}, shewbread + 4286 + 3588 {4x}.

Artos, as a noun, means "bread" and signifies **(1)** "a small loaf or cake" **(1a)** composed of flour and water, and baked, **(1b)** in shape either oblong or round, and about as thick as the thumb; **(1c)** these were not cut, but broken and were consecrated to the Lord every Sabbath and called the "shewbread" [loaves of presentation], Mt 12:4; **(1d)** when the "shewbread" was reinstituted by Nehemiah (Neh 10:32) a poll-tax of ⅓ shekel was laid on the Jews, Mt 17:24; **(2)** "the bread at the Lord's Supper," e.g., Mt 26:26; **(2a)** the breaking of "bread" became the name for this institution, Acts 2:42; 20:7; 1 Cor 10:16; 11:23; **(3)** "bread of any kind," Mt 16:11; **(4)** metaphorically, "of Christ as the Bread of God, and of Life," John 6:33, 35; **(5)** "food in general," the necessities for the sustenance of life, Mt 6:11; 2 Cor. 9:10. Syn.: 106. See: TDNT—1:477, 80; BAGD—110c; THAYER—75d.

741. **ἀρτύω** {3x} **artuō**, *ar-too'-o;* from a presumed der. of *142; to prepare,* i.e. *spice* (with *stimulating* condiments):—to season {3x}.

This word is used of "seasoning" Mk 9:50; Lk 14:34; Col 4:6. See: BAGD—111a; THAYER—76a.

742. **Ἀρφαξάδ** {1x} **Arphaxad**, *ar-fax ad';* of Heb. or. [775]; *Arphaxad,* a post-diluvian patriarch:—*Arphaxad* {1x}. See: BAGD—111a; THAYER—76b.

743. **ἀρχάγγελος** {2x} **archaggĕlŏs**, *ar-khang'-el-os;* from *757* and *32;* a *chief angel:*—archangel {2x}.

Archaggelos is **(1)** not found in the OT, and in the NT only in 1 Th 4:16 and Jude 9, where it is used of Michael, who in Daniel is called 'one of the chief princes,' and 'the great prince', 10:13, 21; 12:1. Cf. also Rev 12:7. . . . **(2)** Whether there are other beings of this exalted rank in the heavenly hosts, Scripture does not say, though the description 'one of the chief princes' suggests that this may be the case. **(3)** In 1 Th 4:16 the meaning seems to be that the voice of the Lord Jesus will be of the character of an "archangelic" shout. See: TDNT—1:87, 12; BAGD—111a; THAYER—76b.

744. **ἀρχαῖος** {12x} **archaiŏs**, *ar-khah'-yos;* from *746; original* or *primeval:*—old {8x}, of old time {3x}, a good while ago + 575 + 2250 {1x}.

Archaios, means "original, ancient" and is used **(1)** of persons belonging to a former age, "(to) them of old time," Mt 5:21, 27, 33; **(1a)** of prophets, Lk 9:8, 19; **(1b)** of time long gone by, Acts 15:21; **(2)** of days gone by in a person's experience, Acts 15:7, "a good while ago," lit., "from old (days)," i.e., from the first days onward in the sense of originality, not age; **(3)** of Mnason, "an old disciple," Acts 21:16,not referring to age, but to his being one of the first who had accepted the gospel from the beginning of its proclamation; **(4)** of things which are "old" in relation to the new, earlier things in contrast to things present, 2 Cor 5:17, i.e., of what characterized and conditioned the time previous to conversion in a believer's experience, i.e., they have taken on a new complexion and are viewed in an entirely different way; **(5)** of the world (i.e., the inhabitants of the world) just previous to the Flood, 2 Pet 2:5; **(6)** of the Devil, as "that old serpent," Rev 12:9; 20:2, "old," not in age, but as characterized for a long period by the evils indicated. Syn.: 1088, 4246. Syn.: Archaios designates something that is both ancient and venerable and stresses going back to the beginning. Palaios (3820) stresses old and worn out; it has existed a long time and has suffered from the wrongs and injuries of time. See: TDNT—1:486, 81; BAGD—111b; THAYER—76b.

745. **Ἀρχέλαος** {1x} **Archĕlaŏs**, *ar-khel'-ah-os;* from *757* and *2994; people-ruling; Archelaus,* a Jewish king:—Archelaus {1x}. See: BAGD—111a; THAYER—76a.

746. **ἀρχή** {58x} **archē**, *ar-khay';* from *756;* (prop. abstr.) a *commencement,* or (concr.) *chief* (in various applications of order, time, place, or rank):—beginning {40x}, principality {8x}, corner {2x}, first {2x}, misc. {6x} = first estate, magistrate, power, principle, rule.

Arche, as a noun, means "a beginning." **(1)** The root arch primarily indicated what was of worth. Hence the verb **(1a)** archo meant "to be first," and archon denoted "a ruler." **(1b)** So also arose the idea of "a beginning," the origin, the active cause, whether a person or thing, e.g., Col 1:18. **(2)** In Heb 2:3 the phrase "having at the first been spoken" is, lit., "having received a beginning to be spoken." **(3)** In Heb 6:1, where the word is rendered "first principles," the original has "let us leave the word of the beginning of Christ," i.e., the doctrine of the elementary principles relating to Christ. **(4)** In Jn 8:25, Christ's reply to the question "Who art Thou?," "Even that which I have spoken unto you from the beginning," does not mean that He had told them before; He declares that He is consistently the unchanging expression of His own teaching and testimony from the first, the immutable embodiment of His doctrine. Syn.: 756, 4412. See: TDNT—1:479, 81; BAGD—111d; THAYER—76a, 77b.

747. **ἀρχηγός** {4x} **archēgŏs**, *ar-khay-gos';* from *746* and *71;* a *chief leader:*—prince {2x}, captain {1x}, author {1x}.

Archegos, **(1)** primarily signifies one who takes a lead in, or provides the first occasion of anything. **(1a)** It is translated "Prince" (Acts 3:15; 5:31), but **(1b)** "Author" (Heb 2:10; 12:2), **(1c)** primarily signifies "one who takes a lead in, or provides the first occasion of, anything." **(1d)** In Heb 2:10, the word suggests a combination of the meaning of leader with that of the source from whence a thing proceeds. **(1e)** That Christ is the Prince of life signifies the life He had was not from another; the Prince or Author of life must be He who has life from Himself. **(2)** But the word does not necessarily combine the idea of the source or originating cause with that of leader. **(2a)** In Heb 12:2 where Christ is called the "Author and Perfecter of faith," He is represented as the one who takes precedence in faith and is thus the perfect exemplar of it. **(2b)** Christ in the days of His flesh trod undeviatingly the path of faith, and as the Perfecter has brought it to a perfect end in His own person. **(2c)** Thus He is the leader of all others who tread that path. **(3)** Jesus, being the Author of faith wrote the first and last chapters in the life of faith. Syn.: 159. See: TDNT—1:487, 81; BAGD—112c; THAYER—77b.

748. **ἀρχιερατικός** {1x} **archiĕratikŏs**, *ar-khee-er-at-ee-kos';* from *746* and a der. of *2413; high-priestly:*—of the high priest {1x}. See: BAGD—112d; THAYER—77c.

749. **ἀρχιερεύς** {123x} **archiĕrĕus**, *ar-khee-er-yuce';* from *746* and *2409;* the *high-priest* (lit. of the Jews, typ. Christ); by extens. a *chief priest:*—chief priest {64x}, high priest {58x}, chief of the priest {1x}.

This word means **(1)** "a chief priest, high priest" and is **(2)** frequent in the gospels, Acts and Hebrews, but there only in the NT. **(3)** It is used of Christ, e.g., in Heb 2:17; 3:1; **(4)** of "chief" priests, including ex-high priests and members of their families, e.g., Mt 2:4; Mk 8:31. See: TDNT—3:265, 349; BAGD—112d; THAYER—77c.

750. **ἀρχιποίμην** {1x} **archipŏimēn**, *ar-khee-poy'-mane;* from *746* and *4166;* a *head shepherd:*—chief shepherd {1x}.

This word means "a chief shepherd" and is said of Christ only, 1 Pet 5:4. See: TDNT—6:485, 901; BAGD—113a; THAYER—78a.

751. **Ἄρχιππος** {2x} **Archippŏs**, *ar'-khip-pos;* from *746* and *2462; horse-ruler; Archippus,* a Chr.:—Archippus {2x}. See: BAGD—113a; THAYER—78b.

752. **ἀρχισυνάγωγος** {9x} **archisunagōgŏs**, *ar-khee-soon-ag'-o-gos;* from *746* and *4864; director of* the *synagogue* services:—ruler of the synagogue {7x}, chief ruler of the synagogue {2x}.

This word means "a ruler of a synagogue," translated "chief ruler of the synagogue," in Acts 18:8, 17. He was the administrative officer supervising the worship. See: TDNT—6:844, 1107; BAGD—113b; THAYER—78b.

753. **ἀρχιτέκτων** {1x} **architĕktōn**, *ar-khee-tek'-tone;* from *746* and *5045;* a *chief constructor,* i.e. "*architect*":—masterbuilder {1x}.

This word means "a principal artificer" and is used figuratively by the apostle in 1 Cor 3:10, of his work in laying the foundation of the local church in Corinth, inasmuch as the inception of the spiritual work there devolved upon him. The examples from the papyri and from inscriptions show that the word had a wider application than our "architect," and confirm the rendering "masterbuilder" in this passage, which is of course borne out by the context. See: BAGD—113b; THAYER—78b.

754. **ἀρχιτελώνης** {1x} **architĕlōnēs**, *ar-khee-tel-o'-nace;* from *746* and *5057;* a *principle tax-gatherer:*—chief among the publicans {1x}.

This word denotes "a chief tax-collector, or publican," Lk 19:2. See: BAGD—113b; THAYER—78b.

755. **ἀρχιτρίκλινος** {3x} **architriklinŏs**, *ar-khee-tree'-klee-nos;* from *746* and a compound of *5140* and *2827* (a *dinner-bed,* because composed of three couches); *director of* the *entertainment:*—governor of the feast {2x}, ruler of the feast {1x}.

This word means literally "a room with three couches" and denotes "the governor of a feast," Jn 2:8, a man appointed to see that the table and couches were duly placed and the courses arranged, and to taste the food and wine. The center couch was most prominent with the adjoining side couches bearing significance; hence, the desire of the two apostles (Mk 10:37). See: BAGD—113b; THAYER—78c.

756. **ἄρχομαι** {84x} **archŏmai**, *ar'-khom-ahee;* mid. voice of *757* (through the impl. of *precedence*); to *commence* (in order of

time):—begin {83x}, rehearse from the beginning {1x}.

Archomai, as a verb, denotes "to begin." **(1)** In Lk 3:23 the present participle is used in a condensed expression, lit., "And Jesus Himself was beginning about thirty years." **(2)** Some verb is to be supplied in English. **(3)** The meaning seems to be that He was about thirty years when He "began" His public career (cf. Acts 1:1). See: TDNT—1:478,*; BAGD—113c; THAYER—77b.

757. **ἄρχω** {2x} **archō,** *ar'-kho;* a primary verb; to be *first* (in political rank or power):—rule over {1x}, reign over {1x}. See: TDNT—1:478, 81; BAGD—113c; THAYER—78c.

758. **ἄρχων** {37x} **archōn,** *ar'-khone;* pres. part. of *757;* a *first* (in rank or power):—ruler {22x}, prince {11x}, chief {2x}, magistrate {1x}, chief ruler {1x}. See: TDNT—1:488, 81; BAGD—113d; THAYER—79a.

759. **ἄρωμα** {4x} **"arōma,"** *ar'-o-mah;* from *142* (in the sense of *sending* off scent); an *aromatic:*—spices {3x}, sweet spices {1x}.

This word means "sweet spice" and occurs in Mk 16:1; Lk 23:56; 24:1; Jn 19:40. See: BAGD—114b; THAYER—79b.

760. **Ἀσά** {2x} **Asa,** *as-ah';* of Heb. or. [609]; *Asa,* an Isr.:—*Asa* {2x}. See: BAGD—114b; THAYER—79b.

761. **ἀσάλευτος** {2x} **asalĕutŏs,** *as-al'-yoo-tos;* from *1* (as a neg. particle) and a der. of *4531; unshaken,* i.e. (by impl.) *immovable* (fig.):—unmoveable {1x}, which cannot be moved {1x}.

Asaleutos, as an adjective, means "unmoved, immoveable" and is translated **(1)** "unmoveable": "And falling into a place where two seas met, they ran the ship aground; and the forepart stuck fast, and remained unmoveable, but the hinder part was broken with the violence of the waves" (Acts 27:41); and **(2)** "which cannot be moved": "Wherefore we receiving a kingdom which cannot be moved, let us have grace, whereby we may serve God acceptably with reverence and godly fear" (Heb 12:28). Syn.: 277, 383, 2795, 2796, 3334, 4525, 4531, 4579, 4787, 5342. See: BAGD—114b; THAYER—79c.

762. **ἄσβεστος** {4x} **asbĕstŏs,** *as'-bes-tos;* from *1* (as a neg. particle) and a der. of *4570; not extinguished,* i.e. (by impl.) *perpetual:*—unquenchable {2x}, never shall be quenched {2x}.

This word means "not quenched" and is used of the doom **(1)** of persons described figuratively as "chaff" into "unquenchable" fire, Mt 3:12 and Luke 3:17; **(2)** of the fire of Gehenna, Mk 9:43, 45. See: BAGD—114b; THAYER—79c.

763. **ἀσέβεια** {6x} **asĕbĕia,** *as-eb'-i-ah;* from *765; impiety,* i.e. (by impl.) *wickedness:*—ungodliness {4x}, ungodly {2x}.

Asebeia means impiety, ungodliness and is used of **(1)** general impiety (Rom 1:18; 11:26; 2 Ti 2:16; Titus 2:12); **(2)** ungodly deeds (Jude 15); **(3)** of lusts or desires after evil things (Jude 18). **(4)** It is the opposite of eusebeia (2150 – godliness). Syn.: Anomia (458) is disregard for, or defiance of, God's laws; asebeia is the same attitude towards God's Person. See: TDNT—7:185, 1010; BAGD—114c; THAYER—79c.

764. **ἀσεβέω** {2x} **asĕbĕō,** *as-eb-eh'-o;* from *765;* to *be* (by impl. *act*) *impious* or *wicked:*—live ungodly {1x}, commit ungodly {1x}.

Asebeo signifies **(1)** "to be or live ungodly," 2 Pet 2:6; **(2)** "to commit ungodly deeds," Jude 15. See: TDNT—7:185, 1010; BAGD—114c; THAYER—79d.

765. **ἀσεβής** {9x} **asĕbēs,** *as-eb-ace';* from *1* (as a neg. particle) and a presumed der. of *4576; irreverent,* i.e. (by extens.) *impious* or *wicked:*—ungodly {8x}, ungodly men {1x}.

This word means "impious, ungodly, without reverence for God," not merely irreligious, but acting in contravention of God's demands, Rom 4:5; 5:6; 1 Ti 1:9; 1 Pet 4:18; 2 Pet 2:5; 3:7; Jude 4, 15 [twice]. See: TDNT—7:185, 1010; BAGD—114c; THAYER—79d.

766. **ἀσέλγεια** {9x} **asĕlgĕia,** *as-elg'-i-a;* from a compound of *1* (as a neg. particle) and a presumed σελγής **sĕlgēs** (of uncert. der., but appar. mean. *continent*); *licentiousness* (sometimes incl. other vices):—lasciviousness {6x}, wantonness {2x}, filthy {1x}.

Aselgeia is best described as wanton, lawless insolence; a disposition of the soul not having or bearing a struggle with remorse; no restraints and is translated "filthy (conversation)," in 2 Pet. 2:7. Syn.: 810. See: TDNT—1:490, 83; BAGD—114d; THAYER—79d.

767. **ἄσημος** {1x} **asēmŏs,** *as'-ay-mos;* from *1* (as a neg. particle) and the base of *4591; unmarked,* i.e. (fig.) *ignoble:*—mean {1x}.

This word stresses that someone or something is not made special by any distinguishing marks; lit., "without mark", i.e., "undistinguished, obscure," was applied by the apostle Paul negatively, to his native city, Tarsus, Acts 21:39. See: TDNT—7:267, 1015; BAGD—115a; THAYER—80a.

768. **Ἀσήρ** {2x} **Asēr,** *as-ayr';* of Heb. or. [836]; *Aser* (i.e. *Asher*), an Isr. tribe:—*Aser* {2x}. See: BAGD—115a; THAYER—80a.

769. **ἀσθένεια** {24x} **asthĕnĕia,** *as-then'-i-ah;* from *772; feebleness* (of body or mind); by impl. *malady;* mor. *frailty:*—infirmity {17x}, weakness {5x}, diseases {1x}, sickness {1x}.

This word means lit., "lacking strength, weakness, infirmity" and is translated **(1)** "infirmities" in Mt 8:17; its most used rendering; **(2)** "diseases" in Acts 28:9; **(3)** "sickness" in Jn 11:4; and **(4)** "weakness" in 1 Cor 2:3; 15:43; 2 Cor 12:9 [first mention]; 13:4; Heb 11:34. See: TDNT—1:490, 83; BAGD—115a; THAYER—80a.

770. **ἀσθενέω** {36x} **asthĕnĕō,** *as-then-eh'-o;* from *772;* to *be feeble* (in any sense):—be weak {12x}, be sick {10x}, sick {7x}, weak {3x}, impotent man {1x}, be diseased {1x}, be made weak {1x}.

This word means to be weak, feeble, to be without strength, powerless. See: TDNT—1:490, 83; BAGD—115b; THAYER—80b.

771. **ἀσθένημα** {1x} **asthĕnēma,** *as-then'-ay-mah;* from *770;* a *scruple* of conscience:—infirmity {1x}.

This word is found in the plural in Rom 15:1, "infirmities," i.e., those scruples which arise through weakness of faith. The strong must support the infirmities of the weak (adunatos) by submitting to self-restraint. See: TDNT—1:490, 83; BAGD—115c; THAYER—80c.

772. **ἀσθενής** {25x} **asthĕnēs,** *as-then-ace';* from *1* (as a neg. particle) and the base of *4599; strengthless* (in various applications, lit., fig. and mor.):—weak {12x}, sick {6x}, weakness {2x}, weaker {1x}, weak things {1x}, impotent {1x}, more feeble {1x}, without strength {1x}. See: TDNT—1:490, 83; BAGD—115c; THAYER—80c.

773. **Ἀσία** {19x} **Asia,** *as-ee'-ah;* of uncert. der.; *Asia,* i.e. *Asia Minor,* or (usually) only its western shore:—*Asia* {19x}. See: BAGD—116a; THAYER—80c.

774. **Ἀσιανός** {1x} **Asianŏs,** *as-ee-an-os';* from *773;* an *Asian* (i.e. *Asiatic*) or an inhabitant of Asia:—of Asia {1x}. See: BAGD—116a; THAYER—80d.

775. **Ἀσιάρχης** {1x} **Asiarchēs,** *as-ee-ar'-khace;* from *773* and *746;* an *Asiarch* or president of the public festivities in a city of Asia Minor:—chief of Asia {1x}.

An "Asiarch" was one of certain officers elected by various cities in the province of Asia, whose function consisted in celebrating, partly at their own expense, the public games and festivals; in Acts 19:31, "chief of Asia". It seems probable that they were "the high priests of the temples of the Imperial worship in various cities of Asia"; further, that "the Council of the Asiarchs sat at stated periods in the great cities alternately . . . and were probably assembled at Ephesus for such a purpose when they sent advice to St. Paul to consult his safety. A festival would have brought great crowds to the city. See: BAGD—116a; THAYER—80d.

776. **ἀσιτία** {1x} **asitia,** *as-ee-tee'-ah;* from *777; fasting* (the state):—abstinence {1x}.

Asitia stresses abstinence from food whether voluntary or inforced, Acts 27:21. See: BAGD—116a; THAYER—81a.

777. **ἄσιτος** {1x} **asitŏs,** *as'-ee-tos;* from *1* (as a neg. particle) and *4621; without* (taking) *food:*—fasting {1x}.

This word means fasting, without having eaten, Acts 27:33. Syn.: 3521. See: BAGD—116b; THAYER—81a.

778. **ἀσκέω** {1x} **askĕō,** *as-keh'-o;* prob. from the same as *4632;* to *elaborate,* i.e. (fig.) *train* (by impl. *strive*):—exercise {1x}.

Askeo signifies to form by art, to adorn, to work up raw material with skill; hence, in general, to take pains, endeavor, exercise by training or discipline with a view to a conscience void of offense (Acts 24:16). See: TDNT—1:494, 84; BAGD—116b; THAYER—81a.

779. **ἀσκός** {12x} **askŏs,** *as-kos';* from the same as *778;* a leathern (or skin) *bag* used as a bottle:—bottle {12x}.

This word means **(1)** "a leather bottle, wineskin," occurs in Mt 9:17 [four times]; Mk 2:22 [four times]; Lk 5:37 [three times], 38. **(2)** A whole goatskin, for example, would be used with the apertures bound up, and when filled, tied at the neck. **(3)** They were tanned with acacia bark and left hairy on the outside. New wines, by fermenting, would rend old skins (cf. Josh 9:13; Job 32:19). **(4)** Hung in the smoke to dry, the skin-bottles become shriveled (see Ps 119:83). **(5)** The English word "bottle" has a root which signifies "a container for liguids" usually with a somewhat long, narrow neck for pouring. See: BAGD—116c; THAYER—81a.

780. **ἀσμένως** {2x} **asmĕnōs,** *as-men'-oce;* adv. from a der. of the base of *2237; with pleasure:*—gladly {2x}.

Asmenos, as an adverb, means "with delight, delightedly, gladly," and is found in 21:17: "And when we were come to Jerusalem, the brethren received us gladly" (cf. Acts 2:41). Syn.: 2234, 2236. See: BAGD—116c; THAYER—81a.

781. **ἄσοφος** {1x} **asŏphŏs**, *as'-of-os;* from *1* (as a neg. particle) and *4680; unwise:*—fool {1x}.

This word means "unwise, foolish," Eph 5:15. Syn.: 3471. See: BAGD—116c; THAYER—81a.

782. **ἀσπάζομαι** {60x} **aspazŏmai**, *as-pad'-zom-ahee;* from *1* (as a particle of union) and a presumed form of *4685;* to *enfold* in the arms, i.e. (by impl.) to *salute,* (fig.) to *welcome:*—embrace {2x}, greet {15x}, salute {42x}, take leave {1x}.

This word lit. **(1)** signifies "to draw to oneself"; hence, **(1a)** "to greet, salute, welcome," the ordinary meaning, **(1b)** e.g., in Rom16, where it is used 21 times. **(2)** It also signifies "embraced to bid farewell," e.g., Acts 20:1. A "salutation or farewell" was generally made by embracing and kissing (see Lk 10:4, which indicates the possibility of delay on the journey by frequent salutation). **(3)** In Heb 11:13 it is said of those who greeted/embraced the promises from afar. See: TDNT—1:496, 84; BAGD—116c; THAYER—81a.

783. **ἀσπασμός** {10x} **aspasmŏs**, *as-pas-mos';* from *782;* a *greeting* (in person or by letter):—greeting {3x}, salutation {7x}.

This word means a salutation, is rendered "greetings" in Mt 23:7; Lk 11:43; 20:46, and is used **(1)** orally in those instances and in Mk 12:38; Lk 1:29, 41, 44; and **(2)** in written salutations, 1 Cor 16:21; Col 4:18; 2 Th 3:17. See: TDNT—1:496, 84; BAGD—117a; THAYER—81b.

784. **ἄσπιλος** {4x} **aspilŏs**, *as'-pee-los;* from *1* (as a neg. particle) and *4695; unblemished* (phys. or mor.):—without spot {3x}, unspotted {1x}.

This word means "unspotted, unstained" and is used **(1)** of a lamb, 1 Pet 1:19; **(2)** metaphorically, of keeping a commandment without alteration and in the fulfillment of it, 1 Ti 6:14; **(3)** of the believer **(3a)** in regard to the world, Jas 1:27, and **(3b)** free from all defilement in the sight of God, 2 Pet 3:14. See: TDNT—1:502, 85; BAGD—117a; THAYER—81b.

785. **ἀσπίς** {1x} **aspis**, *as-pece';* of uncert. der.; a *buckler* (or *round* shield); used of a serpent (as *coiling* itself), prob. the *"asp"*:—asp {1x}.

A small and very venomous serpent, the bite of which is fatal, unless the part affected is at once cut away. In Rom 3:13 is said, metaphorically, of the conversation of the ungodly. See: BAGD—117b; THAYER—81c.

786. **ἄσπονδος** {2x} **aspŏndŏs**, *as'-pon-dos;* from *1* (as a neg. particle) and a der. of *4689;* lit. *without libation* (which usually accompanied a treaty), i.e. (by impl.) *truceless:*—implacable {1x}, truce-breaker {1x}.

This word denotes **(1)** "without a libation", i.e., **(2)** "without a truce," as a libation accompanied the making of treaties and compacts; then, **(3)** "one who cannot be persuaded to enter into a covenant," "implacable, trucebreakers" 2 Ti 3:3 and Rom. 1:31. Syn.: Asunthetos (802) presumes a state of peace interrupted by the unrighteous, *aspondos* (786) a state of war, which the implacable refuse to terminate equitably. The words are clearly not synonymous. See: BAGD—117b; THAYER—81c.

787. **ἀσσάριον** {2x} **assariŏn**, *as-sar'-ee-on;* of Lat. or.; an *assarius* or *as,* a Roman coin:—farthing {2x}.

An *assarion* was one-tenth of a drachma, or one-sixteenth of a Roman *denarius,* i.e., about three farthings, Mt 10:29; Lk 12:6. Syn.: 2835. See: BAGD—117b; THAYER—81c.

788. **ἆσσον** {1x} **assŏn**, *as'-son;* neut. comparative of the base of *1451; more nearly,* i.e. *very near:*—close {1x}.

This word is found in Acts 27:13, of sailing "close" by a place. See: BAGD—117b; THAYER—81d.

789. **Ἆσσος** {2x} **Assŏs**, *as'-sos;* prob. of for. or.; *Assus,* a city of Asia Minor:—*Assos* {2x}. See: BAGD—117b; THAYER—81d.

790. **ἀστατέω** {1x} **astatĕō**, *as-tat-eh'-o;* from *1* (as a neg. particle) and a der. of *2476; to be non-stationary,* i.e. (fig.) *homeless:*—have no certain dwelling-place {1x}.

This word means to wander about, to have no fixed dwelling-place" and is used in 1 Cor 4:11. See: TDNT—1:503, 86; BAGD—117b; THAYER—81d.

791. **ἀστεῖος** {2x} **astĕiŏs**, *as-ti'-os;* from ἄστυ **astu** (a *city*); *urbane,* i.e. (by impl.) *handsome:*—fair {1x}, proper {1x}.

This word stresses **(1)** "city-bred," polished (cf. πολις, Eng. polite). **(2)** It is found in the NT only of Moses, **(2a)** Acts 7:20, "(exceeding) fair," lit., "fair (to God)," and **(2b)** Heb 11:23, "proper". **(3)** Fair in the English means all things treated equally; hence, Moses' parents saw him as a normal child, yet one who if dedicated to God by them would fulfill God's particular calling for him. **(4)** They were probably unaware of the specifics. **(5)** He was also considered proper which means fitted for a particular service. **(6)** Moses' mother, Jochebed, much like Mary, the mother of Jesus, pondered God's consecration of her son and released his care unto Him. Syn.: 2570, 5611. See: BAGD—117c; THAYER—81d.

792. **ἀστήρ** {24x} **astēr**, *as-tare';* prob. from the base of *4766;* a *star* (as *strown* over the sky), lit. or fig.:—star {24x}.

Aster is **(1)** a literal heavenly body, a star (Mt 2:2–10; 24:29; 1 Cor 15:41) and is used **(2)** metaphorically, **(2a)** of Christ as the morning star, figurative of the approach of the day when He will appear as the sun of righteousness to govern the earth in peace; an event to be preceded by the rapture of the Church (Rev 2:28; 22:16); **(2b)** of the angels of the seven churches (Rev 1:16, 20); and **(2c)** of certain false teachers, described as wandering stars (Jude 13), as if the stars intended for light and guidance, became the means of deceit by irregular movements. Syn.: 798. See: TDNT—1:503, 86; BAGD—117c; THAYER—81d.

793. **ἀστήρικτος** {2x} **astēriktŏs**, *as-tay'-rik-tos;* from *1* (as a neg. particle) and a presumed der. of *4741; unfixed,* i.e. (fig.) *vacillating:*—unstable {2x}.

This word means not fixed, not fastened and is used in 2 Pet. 2:14; 3:16, "unstable." See: TDNT—7:653, 1085; BAGD—118a; THAYER—82a.

794. **ἄστοργος** {2x} **astŏrgŏs**, *as'-tor-gos;* from *1* (as a neg. particle) and a presumed der. of στέργω **stĕrgō** (to *cherish* affectionately); *hard-hearted* toward kindred:—without natural affection {2x}.

This word means without natural affection [*a,* negative, and *storge,* "love of kindred,"] especially of parents for children and children for parents, Rom 1:31; 2 Tim 3:3. See: BAGD—118a; THAYER—82a.

795. **ἀστοχέω** {3x} **astŏchĕō**, *as-tokh-eh'-o;* from a compound of *1* (as a neg. particle) and στόιχος **stŏichŏs** (an *aim*); to *miss* the mark, i.e. (fig.) *deviate* from truth:—err {2x}, swerve {1x}.

This word means "to miss the mark, fail" and is used only in the Pastoral Epistles, 1 Ti 1:6, "having swerved"; 6:21 and 2 Ti 2:18, "have erred." See: BAGD—118a; THAYER—82a.

796. **ἀστραπή** {9x} **astrapē**, *as-trap-ay';* from *797; lightning;* by anal. *glare:*—lightning {8x}, bright shining {1x}.

Astrape denotes **(1)** "lightning", Mt 24:27; 28:3; Lk 10:18; 17:24; in the plural, Rev 4:5; 8:5; 11:19; 16:18; **(2)** "bright shining," or "shining brightness," Lk 11:36. See: TDNT—1:505, 86; BAGD—118a; THAYER—82b.

797. **ἀστράπτω** {2x} **astraptō**, *as-trap'-to;* prob. from *792;* to *flash* as lightning:—lighten {1x}, shine {1x}.

This word means "to flash forth, lighten," is said **(1)** of lightning, Lk 17:24, and **(2)** "shining" of the apparel of the two men by the Lord's sepulchre, 24:4. Syn.: 1823. See: BAGD—118b; THAYER—82b.

798. **ἄστρον** {4x} **astrŏn**, *as'-tron;* neut. from *792;* prop. a *constellation;* put for a single *star* (nat. or artif.):—star {4x}.

This word means "star" and is used **(1)** in the sing. in Acts 7:43, "the star of the god Remphan," probably of Saturn, worshiped as a god, apparently the same as Chiun in Amos 5:26. Remphan being the Egyptian deity corresponding to Saturn, Chiun the Assyrian; **(2)** in the plur., of literal stars, Lk 21:25; Acts 27:20; Heb 11:12. See: TDNT—1:503, 86; BAGD—118b; THAYER—82b.

799. **Ἀσύγκριτος** {1x} **Asugkritŏs**, *as-oong'-kree-tos;* from *1* (as a neg. particle) and a der. of *4793; incomparable; Asyncritus,* a Chr.:—Asyncritus {1x}. See: BAGD—118b; THAYER—82b.

800. **ἀσύμφωνος** {1x} **asumphōnŏs**, *as-oom'-fo-nos;* from *1* (as a neg. particle) and *4859; inharmonious* (fig.):—agree not + 5607 {1x}.

This word means not agreeing in sound, dissonant, inharmonious, at variance and is used in Acts 28:25, "they agreed not." See: BAGD—118c; THAYER—82b.

801. **ἀσύνετος** {5x} **asunĕtŏs**, *as-oon'-ay-tos;* from *1* (as a neg. particle) and *4908; unintelligent;* by impl. *wicked:*—foolish {2x}, without understanding {3x}.

This word denotes "without discernment, unintelligent, stupid" or **(1)** "without understanding" Mt 15:16; Mk 7:8; Rom 1:31; and **(2)** "senseless/foolish," Rom 1:21 of the heart; 10:19. See: TDNT—7:888, 1119; BAGD—118c; THAYER—82b.

802. **ἀσύνθετος** {1x} **asunthĕtŏs**, *as-oon'-thet-os;* from *1* (as a neg. particle) and a der. of *4934;* prop. *not agreed,* i.e. *treacherous* to compacts:—covenant-breaker {1x}.

This word stresses one who is in a covenant/treaty and refuses to abide by the terms stipulated, Rom 1:31. Syn.: *Asunthetos* (802) presumes a state of peace interrupted by the unrighteous, aspondos (786) a state of war, which the implacable refuse to terminate equitably. The words are clearly not synonymous. See: BAGD—118d; THAYER—82c.

803. **ἀσφάλεια** {3x} **asphalĕia**, *as-fal'-i-ah;* from *804; security* (lit. or fig.):—certainty {1x}, safety {2x}.

Asphaleia primarily means not liable to fall, steadfast, firm; hence, denoting safety (Acts 5:23; 1 Th 5:3) and has the further meaning of certainty (Lk 1:4). See: TDNT—1:506, 87; BAGD—118d; THAYER—82c.

804. **ἀσφαλής** {5x} **asphalēs**, *as-fal-ace';* from *1* (as a neg. particle) and σφάλλω

sphallō (to "*fail*"); *secure* (lit. or fig.):—certain {1x}, certainty {2x}, safe {1x}, sure {1x}.

This word means safe and is translated **(1)** "certainty" Acts 21:34; 22:30; **(2)** "certain," Acts 25:26; **(3)** "safe," Phil 3:1; **(4)** "sure," Heb 6:19. See: TDNT—1:506, 87; BAGD—119a; THAYER—82c.

805. **ἀσφαλίζω** {4x} **asphalizō**, *as-fal-id'-zo;* from *804;* to *render secure:*—make fast {1x}, make sure {3x}.

This word means "to make secure, safe, firm" is translated **(1)** "make . . . fast," in Acts 16:24, of prisoners' feet in the stocks. **(2)** In Matt. 27:64, 65, 66, it is rendered "to make sure." See: TDNT—1:506, 87; BAGD—119a; THAYER—82c.

806. **ἀσφαλῶς** {3x} **asphalōs**, *as-fal-oce';* adv. from *804; securely* (lit. or fig.):—assuredly {1x}, safely {2x}.

This adverb means **(1)** "safely," Mk 14:44; Acts 16:23; and **(2)** "assuredly," Acts 2:36; the knowledge there enjoined involves freedom from fear of contradiction, with an intimation of the impossibility of escape from the effects. See: TDNT—1:506, 87; BAGD—119a; THAYER—82d.

807. **ἀσχημονέω** {2x} **aschēmŏnĕō**, *as-kay-mon-eh'-o;* from *809; to be* (i.e. *act*) *unbecoming:*—behave (one's) self uncomely {1x}, behave (one's) self unseemly {1x}.

This word means "to be unseemly" and is used **(1)** in 1 Cor 7:36, "behave (himself) unseemly," i.e., so as to run the risk of bringing the virgin daughter into danger or disgrace, and **(2)** in 1 Cor 13:5, "doth (not) behave itself unseemly." See: BAGD—119b; THAYER—82d.

808. **ἀσχημοσύνη** {2x} **aschēmŏsunē**, *as-kay-mos-oo'-nay;* from *809;* an *indecency;* by impl. the *pudenda:*—shame {1x}, that which is unseemly {1x}.

Aschemosune, as a noun, denotes **(1)** "unseemliness": "And likewise also the men, leaving the natural use of the woman, burned in their lust one toward another; men with men working that which is unseemly (*aschemosune*), and receiving in themselves that recompence of their error which was meet." (Rom 1:27); **(2)** "shame, nakedness": Behold, I come as a thief. Blessed *is* he that watcheth, and keepeth his garments, lest he walk naked, and they see his shame (*aschemosune*) (Rev 16:15). Syn.: 150, 152, 818, 819, 1788, 1791, 2617, 3856. See: BAGD—119b; THAYER—82d.

809. **ἀσχήμων** {1x} **aschēmōn**, *as-kay'-mone;* from *1* (as a neg. particle) and a presumed der. of *2192* (in the sense of its congener *4976*); prop. *shapeless,* i.e. (fig.) *inelegant:*—uncomely {1x}.

This word means does not seem to fit, to not correspond to the rest of the form and is used in 1 Cor 12:23. See: BAGD—119b; THAYER—82d.

810. **ἀσωτία** {3x} **asōtia**, *as-o-tee'-ah;* from a compound of *1* (as a neg. particle) and a presumed der. of *4982;* prop. *unsavedness,* i.e. (by impl.) *profligacy:*—excess {1x}, riot {2x}.

Asotia denotes "prodigality, profligacy, riot" and is translated **(1)** "excess" in Eph 5:18 and **(2)** "riot" in Titus 1:6 and 1 Pet 4:4. Syn.: see discussion under 766. See: TDNT—1:506, 87; BAGD—119c; THAYER—82d.

811. **ἀσώτως** {1x} **asōtōs**, *as-o'-toce;* adv. from the same as *810; wastefully, dissolutely:*—riotous {1x}.

Asotos, as an adverb, means "wastefully," "in riotous living" (Lk 15:13). A synonymous noun is aselgeia (766) "lasciviousness, outrageous conduct, wanton violence." See: TDNT—1:506, 87 BAGD—119c; THAYER—83a.

812. **ἀτακτέω** {1x} **ataktĕō**, *at-ak-teh'-o;* from *813; to be* (i.e. *act*) *irregular:*—behave (one's) self disorderly {1x}. See: TDNT—8:47, 1156; BAGD—119c; THAYER—83a.

813. **ἄτακτος** {1x} **ataktŏs**, *at'-ak-tos;* from *1* (as a neg. particle) and a der. of *5021; unarranged, not keeping order,* i.e. (by impl.) *insubordinate* (religiously):—unruly {1x}.

Ataktos signifies "not keeping order"; it was especially a military term, denoting "not keeping rank, insubordinate" and is used in 1 Th 5:14, describing certain church members who manifested an insubordinate spirit, whether by excitability or officiousness or idleness. See: TDNT—8:47, 1156; BAGD—119c; THAYER—83a.

814. **ἀτάκτως** {2x} **ataktōs**, *at-ak'-toce;* adv. from *813; irregularly* (mor.):—disorderly {2x}.

Ataktos signifies disorderly, with slackness, like soldiers not keeping rank (2 Th 3:6, 11). See: TDNT—8:47, 1156; BAGD—119d; THAYER—83a.

815. **ἄτεκνος** {3x} **atĕknŏs**, *at'-ek-nos;* from *1* (as a neg. particle) and *5043; childless:*—childless {1x}, without children {2x}. See: BAGD—119d; THAYER—83a.

816. **ἀτενίζω** {14x} **atĕnizō**, *at-en-id'-zo;* from a compound of *1* (as a particle of union) and τείνω **tĕinō** (to *stretch*); to *gaze* intently:—look steadfastly {2x}, behold steadfastly {2x}, fasten (one's) eyes {2x}, look earnestly on {1x}, look earnestly upon {1x}, look up steadfastly {1x}, behold earnestly {1x}, misc. {4x} = look earnestly, set eyes.

Atenizo, as a verb, means "to look fixedly, gaze," is translated **(1)** "earnestly looked": "But a certain maid beheld him [Peter] as he sat by the fire, and earnestly looked upon him, and said, This man was also with him" (Lk 22:56; cf. Acts 3:12); **(2)** "looked steadfastly": "And while they looked stedfastly toward heaven as He went up, behold, two men stood by them in white apparel" (Acts 1:10); **(3)** "fasten . . . eyes": "And Peter, fastening his eyes upon him with John, said, Look on us" (Acts 3:4; cf. 11:6); **(4)** "looked up steadfastly": "But he [Stephen], being full of the Holy Ghost, looked up stedfastly into heaven, and saw the glory of God, and Jesus standing on the right hand of God" (Acts 7:55); **(5),** "earnestly beholding": "And Paul, earnestly beholding the council, said, Men *and* brethren, I have lived in all good conscience before God until this day" (Act 23:1); **(6)** "steadfastly behold": "But if the ministration of death, written *and* engraven in stones, was glorious, so that the children of Israel could not stedfastly behold the face of Moses for the glory of his countenance; which *glory* was to be done away" (2 Cor 3:7); and **(7)** in Lk 4:20, "eyes . . . were fastened": "And He closed the book, and He gave *it* again to the minister, and sat down. And the eyes of all them that were in the synagogue were fastened on Him." Syn. for **(1) - (7):** 308, 352, 578, 872, 991, 1689, 1896, 1914, 1980, 1983, 2300, 2334, 3706, 3708, 3879, 4017, 4648. **(8)** *Atenizo* [from atenes, "strained, intent"], also denotes "to gaze upon," "beholding earnestly," or "steadfastly": "The same heard Paul speak: who stedfastly beholding (*atenizo*) him, and perceiving that he had faith to be healed" (Acts 14:9; cf. 23:1). Syn.for **(8):** 333, 991, 1689, 1896, 2029, 2300, 2334, 2657, 2734, 3708. See: BAGD—119d; THAYER—83b.

817. **ἄτερ** {2x} **atĕr**, *at'-er;* a particle prob. akin to *427; aloof,* i.e. *apart* from (lit. or fig.):—in the absence of {1x}, without {1x}.

This word means **(1)** "without" in Lk 22:35, "without purse"; and **(2)** in Lk 22:6 "in the absence of the multitude." See: BAGD—120a; THAYER—83b.

818. **ἀτιμάζω** {6x} **atimazō**, *at-im-ad'-zo;* from *820;* to *render infamous,* i.e. (by impl.) *contemn* or *maltreat:*—despise {1x}, dishonour {3x}, suffer shame {1x}, treat shamefully {1x}.

Atimazo, as a verb, means "to dishonor, put to shame. **(1)** It is translated "treat shamefully": "And again he sent another servant: and they beat him also, and entreated *him* shamefully, and sent *him* away empty" (Lk 20:11). **(2)** *Atimazo* signifies to dishonour, treat shamefully, insult, whether **(2a)** in word: "Jesus answered, I have not a devil; but I honour my Father, and ye do dishonour me." (Jn 8:49) or **(2a)** deed: "And again he sent unto them another servant; and at him they cast stones, and wounded *him* in the head, and sent *him* away shamefully handled." (Mk 12:4). Syn.: 150, 152, 808, 819, 1788, 1791, 2617, 3856. See: BAGD—120a; THAYER—83b.

819. **ἀτιμία** {7x} **atimia**, *at-ee-mee'-ah;* from *820; infamy,* i.e. (subj.) comparative indignity, (obj.) *disgrace:*—dishonour {4x}, reproach {1x}, shame {1x}, vile {1x}.

(1) This word means to lower down from a place of honor. *Atimia,* as a noun, signifies **(2)** "shame, disgrace": "For this cause God gave them up unto vile affections (*aitimia*): for even their women did change the natural use into that which is against nature:" (Rom 1:26, lit., "(passions) of shame"); cf. 1 Cor 11:14; **(3)** "dishonor": "But in a great house there are not only vessels of gold and of silver, but also of wood and of earth; and some to honour, and some to dishonour (*aitimia*)." (2 Ti 2:20), **(3a)** where the idea of disgrace or "shame" does not attach to the use of the word; **(3b)** the meaning is that while in a great house some vessels are designed for purposes of honor, others have no particular honor attached to their use (the prefix "a" simply negates the idea of honor). Syn.: 150, 152, 808, 818, 1788, 1791, 2617, 3856. See: BAGD—120a; THAYER—83b.

820. **ἄτιμος** {4x} **atimŏs**, *at'-ee-mos;* from *1* (as a neg. particle) and *5092;* (neg.) *unhonoured* or (pos.) *dishonoured:*—despised {1x}, without honour {2x}, less honourable {1x} [*comparative degree*].

(1) This word stresses that no honor is present to lower. **(2)** It means "without honor" and is translated **(2a)** as a verb in 1 Cor 4:10 "are despised"; lit., "(we are) without honor"; and **(2b)** "without honor" in Mt 13:57; Mk 6:4; and **(2c)** "less honourable" in 1 Cor 12:23. Syn.: 819. See: BAGD—120b; THAYER—83c.

821. **ἀτιμόω** {1x} **atimŏō**, *at-ee-mŏ'-o;* from *820;* used like *818,* to *maltreat:*—handle shamefully {1x}.

This word means to dishonour, mark with disgrace, Mk 12:4. See: BAGD—120b; THAYER—83c.

822. **ἀτμίς** {2x} **atmis**, *at-mece';* from the same as *109; mist:*—vapour {2x}.

Atmis is used **(1)** of "smoke," Acts 2:19; **(2)** figuratively of human life, Jas 4:14. See: BAGD—120b; THAYER—83c.

823. **ἄτομος** {1x} **atŏmŏs**, *at'-om-os;* from *1* (as a neg. particle) and the base

of *5114; uncut,* i.e. (by impl.) *indivisible* [an "*atom*" of time]:—moment {1x}.

This word means lit. "indivisible" [from *a,* negative, and *temno,* "to cut"; Eng., "atom"]; hence it denotes "a moment," 1 Cor 15:52. See: BAGD—120b; THAYER—83c.

824. **ἄτοπος** {3x} **atŏpŏs**, *at'-op-os;* from *1* (as a neg. particle) and *5117; out of place,* i.e. (fig.) *improper, injurious, wicked:*—amiss {1x}, harm {1x}, unreasonable {1x}.

(1) This word means lit., "out of place" and denotes unbecoming, not befitting. **(2)** It is rendered "amiss" in the malefactor's testimony of Christ, Lk 23:41; **(2)** "harm"in Acts 28:6, of the expected effect of the viper's attack upon Paul; and **(3)** "unreasonable" in 2 Th 3:2 of men capable of outrageous conduct. See: BAGD—120c; THAYER—83c.

825. **Ἀττάλεια** {1x} **Attalĕia**, *at-tal'-i-ah;* from Ἄτταλος **Attalŏs** (a king of Pergamus); *Attaleia,* a place in Pamphylia:—Attalia {1x}. See: BAGD—120c; THAYER—83d.

826. **αὐγάζω** {1x} **augazō**, *ŏw-gad'-zo;* from *827;* to *beam* forth (fig.):—shine {1x}.

This word means "to shine" and is used metaphorically of the light of dawn, in 2 Cor 4:4. See: TDNT—1:507, 87; BAGD—120c; THAYER—83d.

827. **αὐγή** {1x} **augē**, *ŏwg'-ay;* of uncert. der.; a *ray* of light, i.e. (by impl.) *radiance, dawn:*—break of day {1x}.

This word means "brightness, bright, shining, as of the sun"; hence, "the beginning of daylight" and is translated "break of day" in Acts 20:11. See: BAGD—120d; THAYER—83d.

828. **Αὔγουστος** {1x} **Augŏustŏs**, *ŏw'-goos-tos;* from Lat. ["august"]; *Augustus,* a title of the Rom. emperor:—Augustus {1x}. See: BAGD—120d; THAYER—83d.

829. **αὐθάδης** {2x} **authadēs**, *ŏw-thad'-ace;* from *846* and the base of *2237; self-pleasing,* i.e. *arrogant:*—self-willed {2x}.

Authades means self-pleasing and denotes one who, dominated by self-interest, and inconsiderate of others, arrogantly asserts his own will. He asserts his own rights, regardless of the rights of others. With no motive at all he is quick to act contrary to the feelings of others. (Titus 1:7; 2 Pet 2:10). Syn.: 5367. See: TDNT—1:508, 87; BAGD—120d; THAYER—83d.

830. **αὐθαίρετος** {2x} **authairĕtŏs**, *ŏw-thah'-ee-ret-os;* from *846* and the same as *140; self-chosen,* i.e. (by impl.) *voluntary:*—willing of (one's)self {2x}.

This word means "to choose, self-chosen, voluntary, of one's own accord" and occurs **(1)** in 2 Cor 8:3 of the churches of Macedonia as to their gifts for the poor saints in Judea, and **(2)** of Titus in his willingness to go and exhort the church in Corinth concerning the matter 2 Cor 8:17. See: BAGD—121a; THAYER—84a.

831. **αὐθεντέω** {1x} **authĕntĕō**, ἕντης **hĕntēs** *aw-than-teh'-o* (a *worker*); to *act of oneself,* i.e. (fig.) *dominate:*—usurp authority over {1x}.

This word means "to exercise authority on one's own account, to domineer over" and is used in 1 Ti 2:12 "to usurp authority over." See: BAGD—121a; THAYER—84a.

832. **αὐλέω** {3x} **aulĕō**, *ŏw-leh'-o;* from *836;* to play the *flute:*—to pipe {3x}.

This word means "to play on an *aulos*" [a flute-like instrument] and is used in Mt 11:17; Lk 7:32; 1 Cor 14:7. See: BAGD—121b; THAYER—84a.

833. **αὐλή** {12x} **aulē**, *ŏw-lay';* from the same as *109;* a *yard* (as open to the *wind*); by impl. a *mansion:*—palace {7x}, hall {2x}, sheepfold + 4163 {1x}, fold {1x}, court {1x}.

Aule is primarily an uncovered space around a house, enclosed by a wall, where the stables were; hence, describes **(1)** the courtyard of a house (Rev 11:2); **(2)** the courts in the dwellings of well-to-do folk, which usually had two: **(2a)** one exterior, between the door and the street (Mk 14:68), and the other **(2b)** interior, surrounded by the buildings of the dwellings (Mt 26:69; Mk 14:66). Syn.: 60. See: BAGD—121b; THAYER—84a.

834. **αὐλητής** {2x} **aulētēs**, *ŏw-lay-tace';* from *832;* a *flute-player:*—minstrel {1x}, piper {1x}.

This word means "a flute-player" and occurs **(1)** in Mt 9:23 "minstrel" and **(2)** Rev 18:22 "pipers." See: BAGD—121b; THAYER—84b.

835. **αὐλίζομαι** {2x} **aulizŏmai**, *ŏw-lid'-zom-ahee;* mid. voice from *833;* to *pass the night* (prop. in the open air):—abide {1x}, lodge {1x}.

This word means "to lodge," originally "to lodge in the *aule,* or courtyard" and is said of shepherds and flocks; hence, **(1)** to pass the night in the open air, as did the Lord, Lk 21:37; and **(2)** "to lodge in a house," [in the courtyard?] as of His visit to Bethany, Mt 21:17. See: BAGD—121c; THAYER—84b.

836. **αὐλός** {1x} **aulos**, *ŏw-los';* from the same as *109;* a *flute* (as *blown*):—a pipe {1x}.

This word means "a flute" and occurs in 1 Cor 14:7. Syn.: 832, 834. See: BAGD—121c; THAYER—84c.

837. **αὐξάνω** {22x} **auxanō**, *ŏwx-an'-o;* a prol. form of a primary verb; to *grow* ("*wax*"), i.e. *enlarge* (lit. or fig., act. or pass.):—grow {12x}, increase {7x}, give the increase {2x}, grow up {1x}.

This word means "to grow or increase" of the growth of that which lives, naturally or spiritually, and is used transitively, signifying to make to increase, said **(1)** of giving the increase, 1 Cor 3:6, 7; 2 Cor 9:10, the effect of the work of God, according to the analogy of His operations in nature; **(2)** "to grow, become greater" e.g. of plants and fruit, Mt 6:28; **(3)** used in the passive voice in Mt 13:32 and Mk 4:8, "increase"; **(4)** in the active in Lk 12:27; 13:19; **(4a)** of the body, Lk 1:80; 2:40; **(4b)** of Christ, Jn 3:30, "increase"; **(4c)** of the work of the gospel of God, Acts 6:7, "increased"; 12:24; 19:20; **(4d)** of people, Acts 7:17; **(4e)** of faith, 2 Cor 10:15 (passive voice, "is increased"); **(4f)** of believers individually, Eph 4:15; Col 1:6; 1 Pet 2:2; 2 Pet 3:18; **(4g)** of the church, Col 2:19; **(4h)** of churches, Eph 2:21. See: TDNT—8:517,*; BAGD—121c; THAYER—84c.

838. **αὔξησις** {2x} **auxēsis**, *ŏwx'-ay-sis;* from *837; growth:*—increase {2x}.

This word expresses growth in the "body of Christ", the church, Eph 4:16, Col 2:9. See: BAGD—122a; THAYER—84d.

839. **αὔριον** {15x} **auriŏn**, *ŏw'-ree-on;* from a der. of the same as *109* (mean. a *breeze,* i.e. the morning *air*); prop. *fresh,* i.e. (adv. with ellipsis of *2250*) *to-morrow:*—tomorrow {9x}, morrow {5x}, next day {1x}.

Aurion is an adverb denoting "tomorrow," is used **(1)** with this meaning in Mt 6:30; Lk 12:28; 13:32, 33; Acts 23:15, 20; 25:22; 1 Cor 15:32; Jas 4:13, **(2)** with the word *hemera,* "day," understood and translated as a noun, "(the) morrow," Mt 6:34 [twice]; Lk 10:35; Acts 4:3 "next day"; 4:5; Jas 4:14. See: BAGD—122a; THAYER—84d.

840. **αὐστηρός** {2x} **austērŏs**, *ŏw-stay-ros';* from a (presumed) der. of the same as *109* (mean. *blown*); *rough* (prop. as a *gale*), i.e. (fig.) *severe:*—austere {2x}.

Austeros means to dry up [Eng., "austere"] and primarily denotes stringent to the taste, like new wine not matured by age, unripe fruit; hence, harsh, severe, Lk 19:21–22. Syn.: Synonymous with *austeros,* but to be distinguished from it, is skleros (4642 from *skello,* "to be dry"). It was applied to that which lacks moisture, and so is rough and disageeable to the touch, and hence came to denote "harsh, stern, hard." It is used by Mt 25:24 to describe the unprofitable servant's remark concerning his master. *Austeros* (840) is derived from a word having to do with the taste, skleros "with the touch." *Austeros* is not necessarily a term of reproach, whereas skleros is always so, and indicates a harsh, even inhuman character. *Austeros* is "rather the exaggeration of a virtue pushed too far, than an absolute vice." Skleros is used of the character of a man, Mt 25:24; of a saying, Jn 6:60; of the difficulty and pain of kicking against the ox-goads, Acts 9:5; 26:14; of rough winds, Jas 3:4 and of harsh speeches, Jude 15. See: BAGD—122b; THAYER—84d.

841. **αὐτάρκεια** {2x} **autarkeia**, *ŏw-tar'-ki-ah;* from *842; self-satisfaction,* i.e. (abstr.) *contentedness,* or (concr.) a *competence:*—contentment {1x}, sufficiency {1x}.

Autarkeia, as a noun, means **(1)** "contentment, satisfaction with what one has": "But god liness with contentment is great gain" (1 Ti 6:6); or **(2)** "sufficiency": "And God *is* able to make all grace abound toward you; that ye, always having all sufficiency in all *things,* may abound to every good work" (2 Cor 9:8). Syn.: 714, 842, 2425, 4909. See: TDNT—1:466, 78; BAGD—122b; THAYER—84d.

842. **αὐτάρκης** {1x} **autarkēs**, *ŏw-tar'-kace;* from *846* and *714; self-complacent,* i.e. *contented:*—content {1x}.

Autarkes, as an adjective, means "self-sufficient, adequate, needing no assistance"; hence, "content": "Not that I speak in respect of want: for I have learned, in whatsoever state I am, *therewith* to be content" (Phil 4:11). Syn.: 714, 841, 2425, 4909. See: TDNT—1:466, 78; BAGD—122b; THAYER—85a.

843. **αὐτοκατάκριτος** {1x} **autŏkatakritŏs**, *ŏw-tok-at-ak'-ree-tos;* from *846* and a der. or *2632; self-condemned:*—condemned of self {1x}.

Autokatakritos, as an adjective, means "self-condemned" i.e., on account of doing himself what he condemns in others: "Knowing that he that is such is subverted, and sinneth, being condemned of himself" (Titus 3:11). Syn.: 176, 2607, 2613, 2631, 2632, 2633, 2917, 2919, 2920. See: TDNT—3:952, 469; BAGD—122c; THAYER—85a.

844. **αὐτόματος** {2x} **autŏmatŏs**, *ŏw-tom'-at-os;* from *846* and the same as *3155; self-moved; moved by one's own impulse* ["automatic"], i.e. *spontaneous:*—of (one's) self {1x}, of (one's) own accord {1x}.

(1) This word comes from "self," and a root *ma*—, signifying "desire" and denotes of oneself, moved by one's own impulse. **(2)** It occurs in **(2a)** Mk 4:28, of the power of the earth to produce plants and fruits of itself; **(2b)** Acts 12:10, of the door which opened of its own accord. Syn.: 4861. See: BAGD—122c; THAYER—85a.

845. **αὐτόπτης** {1x} **autŏptēs**, *ŏw-top'-tace;* from *846* and *3700; self-seeing,* i.e. an *eyewitness:*—eye-witness {1x}.

This word signifies "seeing with one's own eyes", Lk 1:2. See: TDNT—5:373, 706; BAGD—122c; THAYER—85a.

846. **αὐτός** {5118x} **autŏs**, *av-rŏs';* αὖ **au** [perh. akin to the base of *109* through the idea of a *baffling* wind] (*backward*); the refl. pron. *self,* used (alone or in the comp. *1438*) of the third pers., and (with the proper pers. pron.) of the other persons:—him {1947x}, them {1148x}, her {195x}, it {152x}, not tr. {36x}, misc. {1676x} = itself, one, the other, (mine) own, said, ([self-], the) same, ([him-, my-, thy-]) self, [your-] selves, she, that, their (-s), themselves, there [-at, -by, -in, -into, -of, -on, -with], they, (these) things, this (man), those, together, very, which. See: BAGD—122c; THAYER—85b. comp. *848.*

847. **αὐτοῦ** {4x} **autŏu**, *ŏw-too';* gen. (i.e. possessive) of *846,* used as an adv. of location; prop. belonging to the *same* spot, i.e. *in this* (or *that*) *place:*—there {3x}, here {1x}.

This word is the genitive case of *autos,* "self," and signifies **(1)** "here" in Mt 26:36 and **(2)** "there" in Acts 15:34; 18:19; 21:4. See: BAGD—124a; THAYER—87b.

848. **αὑτοῦ** {5x} **hautŏu**, *how-too';* contr. for *1438; self* (in some oblique case or refl. relation):—himself {3x}, themself {1x}, them {1x}. See: BAGD—212c; THAYER—87b.

849. **αὐτόχειρ** {1x} **autŏchĕir**, *ŏw-tokh'-ire;* from *846* and *5495; self-handed,* i.e. doing *personally:*—with . . . own hands {1x}.

Autocheir is a noun and is used in the plural in Acts 27:19, "with their own hands." See: BAGD—124a; THAYER—87d.

850. **αὐχμηρός** {1x} **auchmērŏs**, *owkh-may-ros';* αὐχμός **auchmŏs** [prob. from a base akin to that of *109*] (*dust,* as *dried* by wind); prop. *dirty,* i.e. (by impl.) *obscure:*—dark {1x}.

Auchmeros means a dry, murky, dark, squalid (2 Pet 1:19). Syn.: 2217, 4652, 4653, 4654, 4655, 4656.

See: BAGD—124b; THAYER—87d.

851. **ἀφαιρέω** {10x} **aphairĕō**, *af-ahee-reh'-o;* from *575* and *138; to remove* (lit. or fig.):—cut off {2x}, smite off {1x}, take away {7x}.

This word means "to take away, remove," is translated **(1)** "cut off" in Mk 14:47; and Lk 22:50; **(2)** "smote off" in Mt 26:51; and **(3)** "take away" in Lk. 1:25; 10:42; 16:3; Rom 11:27; Heb 10:4; Rev 22:19 (twice). See: BAGD—124b; THAYER—87d.

852. **ἀφανής** {1x} **aphanēs**, *af-an-ace';* from *1* (as a neg. particle) and *5316; non-apparent, hidden, unseen:*—that is not manifest {1x}.

This word denotes "unseen, hidden," Heb 4:13, "not manifest." See: BAGD—124c; THAYER—88a.

853. **ἀφανίζω** {5x} **aphanizō**, *af-an-id'-zo;* from *852; to render unapparent,* i.e. (act.) *consume* (*becloud*), or (pass.) *disappear* (*be destroyed*):—corrupt {2x}, disfigure {1x}, perish {1x}, vanish away {1x}.

This word means lit., "to cause to disappear, put out of sight," came to mean "to do away with" and is **(1)** said of the destructive work of moth and rust, to deprive of lustre, render unsightly, corrupt, Mt 6:19–20. It is also rendered **(2)** "perish" in Acts 13:41; **(3)** "disfigure" in Mt 6:16; and **(4)** "vanish away" in Jas 4:14. See: BAGD—124c; THAYER—88a.

854. **ἀφανισμός** {1x} **aphanismŏs**, *af-an-is-mos';* from *853; disappearance,* i.e. (fig.) *abrogation:*—vanish away {1x}.

This word means "to cause to appear" and in the negative [*a,* negative, *phaino*] to "vanish away" and occurs in Heb 8:13; the word is suggestive of abolition. See: BAGD—124d; THAYER—88a.

855. **ἄφαντος** {1x} **aphantŏs**, *af'-an-tŏs;* from *1* (as a neg. particle) and a der. of *5316; non-manifested,* i.e. *invisible:*—vanished out of sight + 575 {1x}.

This word means lit., "to cause to disappear, put out of sight," came to mean "to do away with" [*a,* negative, *phaino,* "to cause to appear"], said of the destructive work of moth and rust, Mt 6:19–20; the corruption being complete. See: BAGD—124d; THAYER—88a.

856. **ἀφεδρών** {2x} **aphĕdrōn**, *af-ed-rone';* from a compound of *575* and the base of *1476;* a place of *sitting apart,* i.e. a *privy:*—draught {2x}.

This word means "a latrine, a sink, drain," a place where the human waste discharges are dumped, a privy, sink, toilet and is found in Mt 15:17 and Mk 7:19. See: BAGD—124d; THAYER—88b.

857. **ἀφειδία** {1x} **aphĕidia**, *af-i-dee'-ah;* from a compound of *1* (as a neg. particle) and *5339; unsparingness,* i.e. *austerity* (*ascetism*):—neglecting {1x}.

Apheidia stresses unsparing treatment, severity, ascetic discipline (Col 2:23). See: BAGD—124d; THAYER—88b.

858. **ἀφελότης** {1x} **aphĕlŏtēs**, *af-el-ot'-ace;* from a compound of *1* (as a neg. particle) and φέλλος **phĕllŏs** (in the sense of a *stone* as *stubbing* the foot); *smoothness,* i.e. (fig.) *simplicity:*—singleness {1x}.

This word denotes "simplicity," Acts 2:46, "singleness, unworldly simplicity"; the idea here is that of an unalloyed benevolence expressed in act. See: BAGD—124d; THAYER—88b.

859. **ἄφεσις** {17x} **aphĕsis**, *af'-es-is;* from *863; freedom;* (fig.) *pardon:*—deliverance {1x}, forgiveness {6x}, liberty {1x}, remission {9x}.

(1) *Aphesis* denotes a release, from bondage, imprisonment, liberation from captivity and remission of debt. **(2)** *Aphesis,* as a noun, denotes "a release, from bondage, imprisonment" and in Lk 4:18 it is used of "liberation" from captivity: "The Spirit of the Lord *is* upon me, because He hath anointed me to preach the gospel to the poor; He hath sent me to heal the brokenhearted, to preach deliverance to the captives, and recovering of sight to the blind, to set at liberty (*aphesis*) them that are bruised." **(3)** It also means forgiveness or pardon, of sins (letting them go as if they had never been committed), remission of the penalty, Mt 26:28; Eph 1:7. Syn.: 325, 525, 629, 591, 1325, 1560, 1659, 1807, 1929, 3086, 3860, 4506, 5483. Syn.: 3929. See: TDNT—1:509, 88; BAGD—125a; THAYER—88b.

860. **ἁφή** {2x} **haphē**, *haf-ay';* from *680;* prob. a *ligament* (as *fastening*):—joint {2x}.

This word means "a ligature, joint, a place where a ligament joins muscle to bone, and occurs in Eph 4:16 and Col 2:19. See: BAGD—125a; THAYER—88c.

861. **ἀφθαρσία** {8x} **aphtharsia**, *af-thar-see'-ah;* from *862; incorruptibility;* gen. *unending existence;* (fig.) *genuineness:*—immortality {2x}, incorruption {4x}, sincerity {2x}.

This word means "incorruption," and is used **(1)** of the resurrection body, 1 Cor 15:42, 50, 53–54; **(2)** of a condition associated with glory and honor and life, including perhaps a moral significance, immortality, Rom 2:7; 2 Ti 1:10; **(3)** of love to Christ, that which is sincere and undiminishing, "sincerity" Eph 6:24 and Titus 2:7. See: TDNT—9:93, 1259; BAGD—125b; THAYER—88c.

862. **ἄφθαρτος** {7x} **aphthartŏs**, *af'-thar-tos;* from *1* (as a neg. particle) and a der. of *5351; undecaying* (in essence or continuance):—not corruptible {1x}, incorruptible {4x}, uncorruptible {1x}, immortal {1x}.

This word means "not liable to corruption or decay, incorruptible" and is used **(1)** God, Rom 1:23; 1 Ti 1:17 "immortal"; **(2)** the raised dead, 1 Cor 15:52; **(3)** rewards given to the saints hereafter, metaphorically described as a "crown," 1 Cor 9:25; **(4)** the eternal inheritance of the saints, 1 Pet 1:4; **(5)** the Word of God, as "incorruptible" seed, 1 Pet 1:23; **(6)** a meek and quiet spirit, metaphorically spoken of as "incorruptible" apparel, 1 Pet 3:4. See: TDNT—9:93, 1259; BAGD—125b; THAYER—88c.

863. **ἀφίημι** {146x} **aphiēmi**, *af-ee'-ay-mee;* from *575* and ἵημι **hiēmi** (to *send;* an intens. form of εἶμι **ĕimi**, to *go*); to *send forth,* in various applications (as follow):—leave {52x}, forgive {47x}, suffer {14x}, let {8x}, forsake {6x}, let alone {6x}, misc. {13x} = cry, lay aside, omit, put (send) away, remit, yield up.

This word means **(1)** to send away: **(1a)** to bid going away or depart, **(1a1)** a crowd (Mt 13:36), **(1a2)** of a husband divorcing his wife (1 Cor 7:11–13); **(1b)** to send forth, yield up, to expire (Mt 27:50; Mk 15:37); **(1c)** to let go, let alone, let be: **(1c1)** to disregard (Mt 15:14), **(1c2)** to leave, not to discuss now, (a topic), used of teachers, writers and speakers (Heb 6:1), **(1c3)** to omit, neglect (Mt 23:23); **(1d)** to let go, give up a debt, forgive, to remit (Jn 20:23); **(1e)** to give up, keep no longer (Rev 2:4); **(2)** to permit, allow, not to hinder, to give up a thing to a person (Mk 10:14; Lk 18:16; Jn 11:34); **(3)** to leave, go way from one: **(3a)** in order to go to another place (Mt 22:22; 26:44), **(3b)** to depart from any one (Mt 4:11), **(3c)** to depart from one and leave him to himself so that all mutual claims are abandoned (Mt 4:22; Mk 1:20), **(3d)** to desert wrongfully (Mt 26:56; Mk 14:50); **(3e)** to go away leaving something behind (Mt 5:24; Jn 4:28); **(3f)** to leave one by not taking him as a companion (Mt 24:40; Lk 17:34); **(3g)** to leave one dying, leave behind one (Mt 22:25); **(3h)** to leave so that what is left may remain, leave remaining (Mt 24:2; Mk 13:2); **(3i)** abandon, leave destitute (Acts 14: 17). See: TDNT—1:509, 88; BAGD—125c; THAYER—88d.

864. **ἀφικνέομαι** {1x} **aphiknĕŏmai**, *af-ik-neh'-om-ahee;* from *575* and the base of *2425;* to *go* (i.e. *spread*) *forth* (by rumor):—come abroad {1x}.

This word means "to arrive at a place," is used in Rom 16:19, "come abroad" (of the obedience of the saints): "For your obedience is come abroad unto all *men.* I am glad therefore on your behalf: but yet I would have you wise unto that which is good, and simple concerning evil." See: BAGD—126c; THAYER—89c.

865. **ἀφιλάγαθος** {1x} **aphilagathŏs**, *af-il-ag'-ath-os;* from *1* (as a neg. particle) and *5358; hostile to virtue:*—despiser of those that are good {1x}.

This word means opposed to goodness and good men, 2 Ti 3:3. See: TDNT—1:18, 3; BAGD—126c; THAYER—89c.

866. **ἀφιλάργυρος** {2x} **aphilargurŏs**, *af-il-ar'-goo-ros;* from *1* (as a neg.

particle) and *5366; unavaricious; free from the love of money:*—without covetousness {1x}, not covetous.

This word means "without covetousness, free from the love of money" in Heb 13:5 and 1 Ti 3:3. See: BAGD—126c; THAYER—89c.

867. **ἄφιξις** {1x} **aphixis**, *af'-ix-is;* from *864;* prop. *arrival,* i.e. (by impl.) *departure:*—departing {1x}.

Etymologically, this word means to come far enough, reach; the departure being regarded in relation to the end in view (Acts 20:29). See: BAGD—126d; THAYER—89d.

868. **ἀφίστημι** {15x} **aphistēmi**, *af-is'-tay-mee;* from *575* and *2476; to remove,* i.e. (act.) *instigate* to revolt; usually (refl.) to *desist, desert,* etc.:—depart {10x}, draw away {1x}, fall away {1x}, away {1x}, refrain {1x}, withdraw self {1x}.

This word means in the active voice, **(1)** used transitively, signifies "to cause to depart, to cause to revolt," Acts 5:37; **(2)** used intransitively, "to stand off, or aloof, or to depart from anyone," Lk 4:13; 13:27; Acts 5:38 "refrain from"; 12:10; 15:38; 19:9; 22:29; 2 Cor 12:8; **(3)** metaphorically, "to fall away," 2 Ti 2:19; **(3a)** in the middle voice, "to withdraw or absent oneself from," Lk 2:37; **(3b)** to "apostatize," Lk 8:13; 1 Tim 4:1; Heb 3:12. **(4)** Aphistem also means "depart": "And she *was* a widow of about fourscore and four years, which departed not from the temple, but served *God* with fastings and prayers night and day" (Lk 2:37). Syn.: 307, 385, 392, 501, 502, 645, 1096, 1670, 1448, 1828, 2020, 2464, 4317, 4334, 4358, 4685, 4951, 5288, 5289. See: TDNT—1:512, 88; BAGD—126d; THAYER—89d.

869. **ἄφνω** {3x} **aphnō**, *af'-no;* adv. from *852* (contr.); *unawares,* i.e. *unexpectedly:*—suddenly {3x}.

Aphno, as an adverb, means "suddenly": "And suddenly there came a sound from heaven as of a rushing mighty wind, and it filled all the house where they were sitting" (Acts 2:2; cf. 16:26; 28:6). Syn.: 160, 1810, 1819. See: BAGD—127a; THAYER—89d.

870. **ἀφόβως** {4x} **aphŏbōs**, *af-ob'-oce;* adv. from a compound of *1* (as a neg. particle) and *5401; fearlessly:*—without fear {4x}.

This word means "without fear" and is found in Lk 1:74; 1 Co 16:10; Phil 1:14; Jude 12. See: BAGD—127a; THAYER—89d.

871. **ἀφομοιόω** {1x} **aphŏmŏiŏō**, *af-om-oy-ŏ'-o;* from *575* and *3666;* to *assimilate* closely:—make like {1x}.

This word means "to make like" and is used in Heb 7:3, of Melchizedek as "made like" the Son of God, i.e., in the facts related and withheld in the Genesis record. See: TDNT—5:198, 684; BAGD—127b; THAYER—89d.

872. **ἀφοράω** {2x} **aphŏraō**, *af-or-ah'-o;* from *575* and *3708;* to *consider* attentively:—see {1x}, look {1x}.

Aphorao, as a verb, means "to look away from one thing so as to see another," "to concentrate the gaze upon": "Looking (*aphorao*) unto Jesus the author and finisher of *our* faith" (Heb 12:2; cf. Phil 2:23). Syn.: 308, 352, 578, 816, 991, 1689, 1896, 1914, 1980, 1983, 2300, 2334, 3706, 3708, 3879, 4017, 4648. See: BAGD—127b; THAYER—90a.

873. **ἀφορίζω** {10x} **aphŏrizō**, *af-or-id'-zo;* from *575* and *3724;* to *set off* by boundary, i.e. (fig.) *limit, exclude, appoint,* etc.:—divide {1x}, separate {8x}, sever {1x}.

This word means lit., "to mark off by boundaries or limits" [*apo,* "from," *horizo,* "to determine, mark out"] and denotes **(1)** "to separate", Mt 25:32 (first occurrence); Lk 6:22; Acts 13:2; 19:9; Rom 1:1; 2 Cor 6:17; Gal 1:15; 2:12; **(2)** "to sever", Mt 13:49; and **(3)** "to divide", Mt 25:32 (second occurrence). See: TDNT—5:454, 728; BAGD—127b; THAYER—90a.

874. **ἀφορμή** {7x} **aphŏrmē**, *af-or-may';* from a compound of *575* and *3729;* a *starting*-point, i.e. (fig.) an *opportunity:*—occasion {7x}.

Aphorme properly is a starting point and was used to denote a base of operations in war. It is used of **(1)** the Law providing sin with a base of operations for its attack upon the soul (Rom 7:8, 11); **(2)** the irreproachable conduct of the Apostle providing his friends with a base of operations against his detractors (2 Cor 5:12); **(3)** by refusing temporal support at Corinth he deprived these detractors of their base of operations against him (2 Cor 11:12); **(4)** Christian freedom is not to provide a base of operations for the flesh (Gal 5:13); **(5)** unguarded behavior on the part of young widows would provide Satan with a base of operations against the faith (1 Ti 5:14). See: TDNT—5:472, 730; BAGD—127c; THAYER—90b.

875. **ἀφρίζω** {2x} **aphrizō**, *af-rid'-zo;* from *876;* to *froth* at the mouth (in epilepsy):—foam {2x}.

This word denotes "to foam at the mouth", Mk 9:18, 20. Syn.: 1890. See: BAGD—127c; THAYER—90b.

876. **ἀφρός** {1x} **aphrŏs**, *af-ros';* appar. a primary word; *froth,* i.e. *slaver:*—the one foameth again + 3326 {1x}.

This word means "foam," and occurs in Lk 9:39, where it is used with the preposition *meta,* "with," lit., "(teareth him) with (accompanied by) foam." See: BAGD—127d; THAYER—90b.

877. **ἀφροσύνη** {4x} **aphrŏsunē**, *af-ros-oo'-nay;* from *878; senselessness,* i.e. (euphem.) *egotism;* (mor.) *recklessness:*—foolishly + 1722 {2x}, foolishness {1x}, folly {1x}.

This word means "senselessness," is translated **(1)** "foolishness" in Mk 7:22; **(2)** "folly" in 2 Cor 11:1; and **(3)** "foolishly" in 2 Cor 11:17, 21. See: TDNT—9:220, 1277; BAGD—127d; THAYER—90b.

878. **ἄφρων** {11x} **aphrōn**, *af'-rone;* from *1* (as a neg. particle) and *5424;* prop. *mindless,* i.e. *stupid,* (by impl.) *ignorant,* (spec.) *egotistic,* (practically) *rash,* or (mor.) *unbelieving:*—fool {8x}, foolish {2x}, unwise {1x}.

Aphron signifies without reason, want of mental sanity and sobriety, a reckless and inconsiderate habit of mind; the lack of common sense perception of the reality of things natural and spiritual or the imprudent ordering of one's life in regard to salvation. It is translated **(1)** "foolish" or "foolish ones" in Rom 2:20; 1 Cor 15:36; 2 Cor 11:16 (twice); 19 (contrasted with *phronimos,* "prudent"); 12:6, 11; 1 Pet 2:15; **(2)** "fool/fools" in Lk 11:40; 12:20; and **(3)** "unwise" in Eph 5:17. Syn.: 453, 801, 877, 3472, 3474. See: TDNT—9:220, 1277; BAGD—127d; THAYER—90b.

879. **ἀφυπνόω** {1x} **aphupnŏō**, *af-oop-nŏ'-o;* from a compound of *575* and *5258;* prop. to *become awake,* i.e. (by impl.) to *drop* (off) in slumber:—fall asleep {1x}.

This word means "to fall asleep" and is used of natural "sleep," Lk 8:23, of the Lord's falling "asleep" in the boat on the lake of Galilee. See: TDNT—8:545, 1233; BAGD—127d; THAYER—90c.

880. **ἄφωνος** {4x} **aphōnŏs**, *af'-o-nos;* from *1* (as a neg. particle) and *5456; voiceless,* i.e. *mute* (by nature or choice); fig. *unmeaning:*—dumb {3x}, without signification {1x}.

Aphonos, as an adjective, literally means "voiceless, or soundless" [*a,* negative, and *phone,* "a sound"], and has reference **(1)** to voice: "The place of the scripture which He read was this, He was led as a sheep to the slaughter; and like a lamb dumb before his shearer, so opened he not his mouth" (Acts 8:32; cf. 1 Cor 12:2; 2 Pet 2:16). **(2)** In 1 Cor 14:10 it is used metaphorically of the significance of voices or sounds, "without signification": "There are, it may be, so many kinds of voices in the world, and none of them *is* without signification." Syn.: *Aphonos* (880), lit., "voiceless, or soundless" has reference to voice, while alalos (216) has reference to words. See also: 216, 2974, 4623. See: BAGD—128a; THAYER—90c.

881. **Ἀχάζ** {2x} **Achaz**, *akh-adz';* of Heb. or. [271]; *Achaz,* an Isr.:—*Achaz* {2x}. See: BAGD—128a; THAYER—90c.

882. **Ἀχαΐα** {11x} **Achaïa**, *ach-ah-ee'-ah;* of uncert. der.; *Achaia* (i.e. *Greece*), a country of Europe:—*Achaia* {11x}. See: BAGD—128a; THAYER—90d.

883. **Ἀχαϊκός** {2x} **Achaïkŏs**, *ach-ah-ee-kos';* from *882;* an *Achaïan; Achaïcus,* a Chr.:—Achaicus {2x}. See: BAGD—128b; THAYER—90d.

884. **ἀχάριστος** {2x} **acharistŏs**, *ach-ar'-is-tos;* from *1* (as a neg. particle) and a presumed der. of *5483; thankless,* i.e. *ungrateful:*—unthankful {2x}.

This word denotes "ungrateful, thankless", Lk 6:35; 2 Ti 3:2. See: TDNT—9:372, 1298; BAGD—128b; THAYER—90d.

885. **Ἀχείμ** {2x} **Achĕim** or Ἀχίμ **Achim**, *akh-ime';* prob. of Heb. or. [comp. 3137]; *Achim,* an Isr.:—*Achim* {2x}. See: BAGD—128b; THAYER—90d.

886. **ἀχειροποίητος** {3x} **achĕirŏpŏiētŏs**, *akh-i-rop-oy'-ay-tos;* from *1* (as a neg. particle) and *5499; unmanufactured,* i.e. *inartificial:*—made without hands {2x}, not made with hands {1x}.

This word means "not made by hands" and is said **(1)** of an earthly temple, Mk 14:58; **(2)** of the resurrection body of believers, metaphorically as a house, 2 Cor 5:1; **(3)** metaphorically, of spiritual circumcision, Col 2:11. See: TDNT—9:436, 1309; BAGD—128b; THAYER—90d.

887. **ἀχλύς** {1x} **achlus**, *akh-looce';* of uncert. der.; *dimness* of sight, i.e. (prob.) a *cataract:*—mist {1x}.

This word means "a mist," especially a dimness of the eyes, is used in Acts 13:11. "In the single place of its NT use it attests the accuracy in the selection of words, and not least of medical words, which 'the beloved physician' so often displays. For him it expresses the mist of darkness . . . which fell on the sorcerer Elymas, being the outward and visible sign of the inward spiritual darkness which would be his portion for a while in punishment for his resistance to the truth. See: BAGD—128b; THAYER—90d.

888. **ἀχρεῖος** {2x} **achrĕiŏs**, *akh-ri'-os;* from *1* (as a neg. particle) and a der. of

5534 [comp. 5532]; *useless,* i.e. (euphem.) *unmeritorious:*—unprofitable {2x}.

Achreios, as an adjective, means "useless" [5532 - chreia, "use"], "unprofitable": "And cast ye the unprofitable servant into outer darkness: there shall be weeping and gnashing of teeth" (Mt 25:30; cf. Lk 17:10). Syn.: *Achreios,* positively hurtful, is more distinctly negative than achrestos (890). See also: 255, 512, 889, 890. See: BAGD—128c; THAYER—91a.

889. **ἀχρειόω** {1x} **achrĕiŏō**, *akh-ri-ŏ'-o;* from *888;* to *render useless,* i.e. *spoil:*—become unprofitable {1x}.

Achreoo, or *achreioo,* as a verb, means "to make useless": "They are all gone out of the way, they are together become unprofitable; there is none that doeth good, no, not one" (Rom 3:12, in the passive voice). Syn.: 255, 512, 888, 890. See: BAGD—128c; THAYER—91a.

890. **ἄχρηστος** {1x} **achrēstŏs**, *akh'-race-tos;* from *1* (as a neg. particle) and *5543; inefficient,* i.e. (by impl.) *detrimental:*—unprofitable {1x}.

Achrestos, as an adjective, means "unprofitable, unserviceable" (5543 - chrestos, "serviceable"), is said of Onesimus, antithetically to (2173 - euchrestos, "profitable"): "Which in time past was to thee unprofitable (*achrestos*), but now profitable (euchrestos) to thee and to me" (Philem 11). Syn.: Achreios (888), positively hurtful, is more distinctly negative than *achrestos.* See also: 255, 512, 888, 889. See: BAGD—128c; THAYER—91a.

891. **ἄχρι** {49x} **achri**, *akh'-ree;* or ἄχρις **achris**, *akh'-rece;* akin to *206* (through the idea of a *terminus*); (of time) *until* or (of place) *up to:*—until {14x}, unto {13x}, till {3x}, till + 3739 + 302 {3x}, until + 3739 {2x}, while + 3739 {2x}, even to {2x}, misc. {7x} = as far as, for, in, into. See: BAGD—128d; THAYER—91b. comp. *3360.*

892. **ἄχυρον** {2x} **achurŏn**, *akh'-oo-ron;* perh. remotely from χέω **chĕō** (to *shed* forth); *chaff* (as *diffusive*):—chaff {2x}.

Chaff is the stalk of the grain from which the kernels have been beaten out, or the straw broken up by a threshing machine (Mt 3:12; Lk 3:17). See: BAGD—129a; THAYER—91d.

893. **ἀψευδής** {1x} **apsĕudēs**, *aps-yoo-dace';* from *1* (as a neg. particle) and *5579; veracious; free from falsehood:*—that cannot lie {1x}.

This word denotes "free from falsehood" truthful, Titus 1:2, of God, "who cannot lie." See: TDNT—9:594, 1339; BAGD—129c; THAYER—91d.

894. **ἄψινθος** {2x} **apsinthŏs**, *ap'-sin-thos;* of uncert. der.; *wormwood* (as a type of *bitterness,* i.e. [fig.] *calamity*):—wormwood {2x}.

This word means a plant both bitter and deleterious, and growing in desolate places, figuratively suggestive of "calamity" (Lam 3:15) and injustice (Amos 5:7), and is used in Rev 8:11 (twice; in the 1st part as a proper name). See: BAGD—129c; THAYER—91d.

895. **ἄψυχος** {1x} **apsuchŏs**, *ap'-soo-khos;* from *1* (as a neg. particle) and *5590; lifeless,* i.e. *inanimate* (mechanical):—without life {1x}.

This word means denotes "lifeless inanimate" "without life": "And even things without life giving sound, whether pipe or harp, except they give a distinction in the sounds, how shall it be known what is piped or harped?"(1 Cor 14:7). See: BAGD—129c; THAYER—91d.

B

896. **Βάαλ** {1x} **Baal**, *bah'-al;* of Heb. or. [1168]; *Baal,* a Phœnician deity (used as a symbol of idolatry):—*Baal* {1x}. See: BAGD—129b; THAYER—92a.

897. **Βαβυλών** {12x} **Babulōn**, *bab-oo-lone';* of Heb. or. [894]; *Babylon,* the capital of Chaldæa (lit. or fig. [as a type of tyranny]):—Babylon {12x}. See: TDNT—1:514, 89; BAGD—129b; THAYER—92b.

898. **βαθμός** {1x} **bathmŏs**, *bath-mos';* from the same as *899;* a *step,* i.e. (fig.) *grade* (of dignity):—degree {1x}.

This word means denotes "a step," primarily of a threshold or stair, and figuratively, means "a standing, a stage in a career, position, degree," 1 Ti 3:13, of faithful deacons. See: BAGD—130a; THAYER—92d.

899. **βάθος** {9x} **bathŏs**, *bath'-os;* from the same as *901; profundity,* i.e. (by impl.) *extent;* (fig.) *mystery:*—depth {5x}, deep {1x}, deep + 2596 {1x}, deepness {1x}, deep thing {1x}.

Bathos is used **(1)** naturally, in Mt 13:5: "Some fell upon stony places, where they had not much earth: and forthwith they sprung up, because they had no deepness of earth"; (cf. Mk 4:5; Lk 5:4, of "deep" water; Rom 8:39 contrasted with "height"); **(2)** metaphorically, in **(2a)** Rom 11:33, of God's wisdom and knowledge; in **(2b)** 1 Cor 2:10, of God's counsels; in **(3)** Eph 3:18 of the dimensions of the sphere of the activities of God's counsels, and of the love of Christ which occupies that sphere; in **(4)** 2 Cor 8:2, of "deep" poverty; and in **(5)** Rev 2:24 of the depths of Satan. Syn.: 1037. See: TDNT—1:517, 89; BAGD—130a; THAYER—92d.

900. **βαθύνω** {1x} **bathunō**, *bath-oo'-no;* from *901;* to *deepen:*—dig deep + 4626 {1x}.

This word means "to deepen, make deep," is used in Lk 6:48 ("digged deep"). The original has two separate verbs, *skapto,* "to dig," and *bathuno;* therefore, "digged and went deep." See: BAGD—130b; THAYER—92d.

901. **βαθύς** {3x} **bathus**, *bath-oos';* from the base of *939; profound* (as *going* down), lit. or fig.:—deep {2x}, very early in the morning + 3722 {1x}.

Bathus is said **(1)** in Jn 4:11, of a deep well; **(2)** in Acts 20:9, of deep sleep; and **(3)** in Lk 24:1 of very early [deep in darkness, the early hours of] the morning. See: BAGD—130b; THAYER—93a.

902. **βαΐον** {1x} **baïŏn**, *bah-ee'-on;* a diminutive of a der. prob. of the base of *939;* a palm *twig* (as *going* out far):—branch {1x}.

This word means "a branch of the palm tree," Jn 12:13. See: BAGD—130c; THAYER—93a.

903. **Βαλαάμ** {3x} **Balaam**, *bal-ah-am';* of Heb. or. [1109]; *Balaam,* a Mesopotamian (symbolic of a false teacher):—*Balaam* {3x}. See: TDNT—1:524, 91; BAGD—130c; THAYER—93a.

904. **Βαλάκ** {1x} **Balak**, *bal-ak';* of Heb. or. [1111]; *Balak,* a Moabite:—Balac {1x}. See: BAGD—130c; THAYER—93b.

905. **βαλάντιον** {4x} **balantiŏn**, *bal-an'-tee-on;* prob. remotely from *906* (as a *depository*); a *pouch* (for money):—purse {3x}, bag {1x}.

This word means "a money-box or purse" and is found in Luke's gospel, four times, 10:4; 12:33 ("bag"); 22:35–36. See: TDNT—1:525, 91; BAGD—130d; THAYER—93b.

906. **βάλλω** {125x} **ballō**, *bal'-lo;* a primary verb; to *throw* (in various applications, more or less violent or intense):—cast {86x}, put {13x}, thrust {5x}, cast out {4x}, lay {3x}, lie {2x}, misc. {12x} = arise, × dung, pour, send, strike, throw (down).

This word means **(1)** with force and effort: **(1a)** to smite someone with slaps, to buffet (Mk 14:65); and **(1b)** to apprehend someone (Jn 7:44); **(2)** without force and effort: **(2a)** to throw or let go of a thing without caring where it falls: to scatter, to throw, cast into (Mt 27:35; Mk 15:24); **(2b)** to give over to one's care uncertain about the result (Mt 25:27); **(2c)** to pour (Mt 19:17; Mk 2:22: Lk 5:37). See: TDNT—1:526, 91; BAGD—130d; THAYER—93b. comp. *4496.*

907. **βαπτίζω** {80x} **baptizō**, *bap-tid'-zo;* from a der. of *911;* to *make overwhelmed* (i.e. *fully wet*); used only (in the N.T.) of ceremonial *ablution,* espec. (tech.) of the ordinance of Chr. *baptism:*—baptize {76x}, wash {2x}, baptist {1x}, baptized + 2258 {1x}.

Baptizo means to baptize and is used of **(1)** washing oneself (Lk 11:38); **(2)** the rite performed by John the Baptist who called upon the people to repent that they might receive remission of sins. Those who obeyed came confessing their sins, thus acknowledging their unfitness to be in the Messiah's coming kingdom (Acts 1:5; 11:16; 19:4). **(3)** Distinct from **(2)** is the baptism enjoined by Christ (Mt 28:19), a baptism to be undergone by believers, thus witnessing to their identification with Him in death, burial and resurrection (Acts 19:5; 1 Cor 1:13–17). **(4)** The phrase in Mt 28:19, "baptizing them into the Name" would indicate that the baptized person was closely bound to, or became the property of, the one into whose name he was baptized. **(5)** In Acts 22:16 it is used in the middle voice, in the command given to Saul of Tarsus, "arise and be baptized," the significance of the middle voice form being "get thyself baptized."

(6) The experience of those who were in the ark at the time of the Flood was a figure or type of the facts of spiritual death, burial, and resurrection, Christian baptism being an antitupon, "a corresponding type," a "like figure," (1 Pet 3:21). **(7)** Likewise the nation of Israel was figuratively baptized (1 Cor 10:2). **(8)** The verb is used metaphorically also in two distinct senses: **(8a)** of baptism by the Holy Spirit, which took place on the Day of Pentecost, showing eternal association with and bound to the Holy Spirit; **(8b)** of the calamity which would come upon the nation of the Jews, a baptism of the fire of divine judgment for rejection of the will and word of God (Mt 3:11; Lk 3:16). See: TDNT—1:529, 92; BAGD—131c; THAYER—94a.

908. **βάπτισμα** {22x} **baptisma**, *bap'-tis-mah;* from *907; baptism* (tech. or fig.):—baptism {22x}.

Baptisma means baptism consisting of the processes of immersion, submersion and emergence and is used **(1)** of John's baptism **(2)** of Christian baptism; **(3)** of the overwhelming afflictions and judgments to which the Lord voluntarily submitted on the cross (Lk 12:50); **(4)** of the sufferings His followers would experience, not of a vicarious character, but in fellowship with the sufferings of their Master (Mk 10:38–39).

Syn.: 909, 910. See: TDNT—1:545, 92; BAGD—132c; THAYER—94d.

909. **βαπτισμός** {4x} **baptismŏs**, *bap-tis-mos';* from *907; ablution* (cerem. or Chr.):—washing {3x}, baptism {1x}.

Baptismos, as distinct from baptisma (908 - the ordinance), is used **(1)** of the ceremonial washing of articles (Mk 7:4, 8; Heb 9:10). It is translated "baptisms" in Heb 6:2. Syn.: 908. See: TDNT—1:545, 92; BAGD—132d; THAYER—95a.

910. **Βαπτιστής** {14x} **Baptistēs**, *bap-tis-tace';* from *907; a baptizer,* as an epithet of Christ's forerunner:—Baptist {14x}.

This word is used only of John the Baptist, and only in the Synoptists. See: TDNT—1:545, 92; BAGD—132d; THAYER—95b.

911. **βάπτω** {3x} **baptō**, *bap'-to;* a primary verb; to *overwhelm,* i.e. cover wholly with a fluid; in the N.T. only in a qualified or special sense, i.e. (lit.) to *moisten* (a part of one's person), or (by impl.) to *stain* (as with dye):—dip {3x}.

This word means "to immerse, dip" and also signified "to dye," which is suggested in Rev 19:13, of the Lord's garment "dipped (i.e. dyed) in blood." It is elsewhere translated "to dip," Lk 16:24; Jn 13:26. See: TDNT—1:529, 92; BAGD—132d; THAYER—95b.

912. **Βαραββᾶς** {11x} **Barabbas**, *bar-ab-bas';* of Chald. or. [1347 and 5]; *son of Abba; Bar-abbas,* an Isr.:—*Barabbas* {11x}. See: BAGD—133a; THAYER—95b.

913. **Βαράκ** {1x} **Barak**, *bar-ak';* of Heb. or. [1301]; *Barak,* an Isr.:—*Barak* {1x}. See: BAGD—133a; THAYER—95c.

914. **Βαραχίας** {1x} **Barachias**, *bar-akh-ee'-as;* of Heb. or. [1296]; *Barachias* (i.e. *Berechijah*), an Isr.:—*Barachias* {1x}. See: BAGD—133a; THAYER—95c.

915. **βάρβαρος** {6x} **barbarŏs**, *bar'-bar-os;* of uncert. der.; a *foreigner* (i.e. *non-Greek*):—barbarian {5x}, barbarous {1x}.

Barbaros properly meant **(1)** "one whose speech is rude, or harsh"; the word is onomatopoeic, indicating in the sound the uncouth character represented by the repeated syllable "bar-bar." **(2)** Hence it signified one who speaks a strange or foreign language (1 Cor 14:11). **(3)** It then came to denote any foreigner ignorant of the Greek language and culture. **(4)** After the Persian war it acquired the sense of rudeness and brutality. **(5)** In Acts 28:2, 4, it is used unreproachfully of the inhabitants of Malta, who were of Phoenician origin. **(6)** So in Rom 1:14, where it stands in distinction from Greeks, and in implied contrast to both Greeks and Jews. **(7)** Cf. the contrasts in Col 3:11, where all such distinctions are shown to be null and void in Christ. See: TDNT—1:546, 94; BAGD—133b; THAYER—95c.

916. **βαρέω** {6x} **barĕō**, *bar-eh'-o;* from *926;* to *weigh* down (fig.):—be heavy {3x}, be pressed {1x}, be burdened {1x}, be charged {1x}.

Bareo is used of **(1)** the effects of drowsiness: "And He came and found them asleep again: for their eyes were heavy (bareo)" (Mt 26:43; cf. Mk 14:40; Lk 9:32); **(2)** of the believer's present physical state in the body: "For we that are in *this* tabernacle do groan, being burdened: not for that we would be unclothed, but clothed upon, that mortality might be swallowed up of life" (2 Cor 5:4 "burdened"); **(3)** of persecution: "For we would not, brethren, have you ignorant of our trouble which came to us in Asia, that we were pressed out of measure, above strength, insomuch that we despaired even of life" (2 Cor 1:8 "pressed" out of measure); and **(4)** of a charge upon material resources: "If any man or woman that believeth have widows, let them relieve them, and let not the church be charged; that it may relieve them that are widows indeed" (1 Ti 5:16 "charged"). Syn.: 922, 1912, 2599, 2655. See: TDNT—1:558, 95; BAGD—133c; THAYER—95d.

917. **βαρέως** {2x} **barĕōs**, *bar-eh'-oce;* adv. from *926; heavily, with difficulty* (fig.):—dull {2x}.

This word means "heavily, with difficulty" and is used with *akouo,* "to hear," in Mt 13:15, and Acts 28:27 [from Is 6:10], lit., "to hear heavily, to be dull of hearing." See: BAGD—133c; THAYER—95d.

918. **Βαρθολομαῖος** {4x} **Barthŏlŏmaiŏs**, *bar-thol-om-ah'-yos;* of Chald. or. [1247 and 8526]; *son of Tolmai; Bar-tholomæus,* a Chr. apostle:—Bartholomew {4x}. See: BAGD—133d; THAYER—95d.

919. **Βαριησοῦς** {1x} **Bariēsŏus**, *bar-ee-ay-sooce';* of Chald. or. [1247 and 3091]; *son of Jesus* (or *Joshua*); *Bar-jesus,* an Isr.:—Barjesus {1x}. See: BAGD—133d; THAYER—96a.

920. **Βαριωνᾶς** {1x} **Bariōnas**, *bar-ee-oo-nas';* of Chald. or. [1247 and 3124]; *son of Jonas* (or *Jonah*); *Bar-jonas,* an Isr.:—Barjona {1x}. See: BAGD—133d; THAYER—96a.

921. **Βαρνάβας** {30x} **Barnabas**, *bar'-nub'-as;* of Chald. or. [1247 and 5029]; *son of Nabas* (i.e. *prophecy*); *Barnabas,* an Isr.:—*Barnabas* {29x}. See: BAGD—133d; THAYER—96a.

922. **βάρος** {6x} **barŏs**, *bar'-os;* prob. from the same as *939* (through the notion of *going* down; comp. *899*); *weight;* in the N.T. only fig. a *load, abundance, authority:*—burden {4x}, burdensome + 1722 {1x}, weight {1x}.

This word means denotes **(1)** "a weight, anything pressing on one physically," Mt 20:12, or **(2)** "that makes a demand on one's resources," whether **(2a)** material, 1 Th 2:6 (to be burdensome), or **(2b)** spiritual, Gal 6:2; Rev 2:24, or **(2c)** religious, Acts 15:28. **(3)** In one place it metaphorically describes the future state of believers as "an eternal weight of glory," 2 Cor 4:17. See: TDNT—1:553, 95; BAGD—133d; THAYER—96a.

923. **Βαρσαβᾶς** {2x} **Barsabas**, *bar-sab-as';* of Chald. or. [1247 and prob. 6634]; *son of Sabas* (or *Tsaba*); *Bar-sabas,* the name of two Isr.:—Joseph {1x}, Judas {1x}. See: BAGD—134a; THAYER—96b.

924. **Βαρτιμαῖος** {1x} **Bartimaiŏs**, *bar-tim-ah'-yos;* of Chald. or. [1247 and 2931]; *son of Timæus* (or the *unclean*); *Bartimæus,* an Isr.:—Bartimaeus {1x}. See: BAGD—134a; THAYER—96b.

925. **βαρύνω** {1x} **barunō**, *bar-oo'-no;* from *926;* to *burden, weighed down* (fig.):—be overcharged {1x}.

This word means to weigh down, overcharge and is used in Lk 21:34: "And take heed to yourselves, lest at any time your hearts be overcharged (*baruno*) with surfeiting, and drunkenness, and cares of this life, and *so* that day come upon you unawares." See: BAGD—134b; THAYER—96b.

926. **βαρύς** {6x} **barus**, *bar-ooce';* from the same as *922; weighty,* i.e. (fig) *burdensome, grave:*—grievous {3x}, heavy {1x}, weighty {1x}, weightier {1x}.

This word means **(1)** denotes "heavy, burdensome"; **(2)** it is always used metaphorically in the NT, and is **(3)** translated **(3a)** "heavy" in Mt 23:4, of Pharisaical ordinances; **(3b)** in the comparative degree "weightier," Mt 23:23, of details of the law of God; **(3c)** "grievous," metaphorically **(3c1)** of wolves, in Acts 20:29; **(3c2)** of charges, Acts 25:7; **(3c3)** negatively of God's commandments, 1 Jn 5:3 (causing a burden on him who fulfills them); and **(4)** in 2 Cor. 10:10, "weighty," of Paul's letters. See: TDNT—1:556, 95; BAGD—134b; THAYER—96b.

927. **βαρύτιμος** {1x} **barutimŏs**, *bar-oo'-tim-os;* from *926* and *5092;* highly *valuable:*—very precious {1x}.

This word means "of great value, exceeding precious" [*barus,* "weighty," *time,* value] and is used in Mt 26:7. See: BAGD—134b; THAYER—96b.

928. **βασανίζω** {12x} **basanizō**, *bas-an-id'-zo;* from *931;* to *torture:*—torment {8x}, pain {1x}, toss {1x}, vex {1x}, toil {1x}.

Basanizo, as a verb, properly signifies in Greek **(1)** "to test by rubbing on the touchstone" [basanos, "a touchstone"], then, **(1a)** "to question by applying torture"; hence **(1b)** "to vex, torment"; **(2)** in the NT in the passive voice, **(2a)** "to be harassed, **(2b)** distressed"; **(2c)** it is said of men struggling in a boat against wind and waves: "But the ship was now in the midst of the sea, tossed (*basanizo*) with waves: for the wind was contrary" (Mt 14:24; Mk 6:48, toiling). Syn.: 318, 2347, 2669, 4660, 4729, 4730, 4928. See: TDNT—1:561, 96; BAGD—134c; THAYER—96c.

929. **βασανισμός** {6x} **basanismŏs**, *bas-an-is-mos';* from *928; torture:*—torment {6x}.

This word describes the results of divine judgments, torment, in Rev 9:5 (twice); 14:11; 18:7, 10, 15. See: TDNT—1:561, 96; BAGD—134c; THAYER—96c.

930. **βασανιστής** {1x} **basanistēs**, *bas-an-is-tace';* from *928;* a *torturer:*—tormentor {1x}.

One who elicits information by torture and is used of jailors (Mt 18:34). See: TDNT—1:561, 96; BAGD—134d; THAYER—96d.

931. **βάσανος** {3x} **basanŏs**, *bas'-an-os;* perh. remotely from the same as *939* (through the notion of *going* to the bottom); a *touch-stone,* i.e. (by anal.) *torture:*—torment {3x}.

This word means **(1)** a touchstone, which is a black siliceous stone used to test the purity of gold or silver by the color of the streak produced on it by rubbing it with either metal; hence **(2)** "torment" because of strong force being exerted and was used of the rack or instrument of torture by which one is forced to divulge the truth. **(3)** In the NT it speaks of torture, torment, acute pains of the pains **(3a)** of physical diseases, Mt 4:24; and **(3b)** of those in hell after death, Lk 16:23, 28. See: TDNT—1:561, 96; BAGD—134d; THAYER—96d.

932. **βασιλεία** {162x} **basilĕia**, *bas-il-i'-ah;* from *935;* prop. *royalty,* i.e. (abstr.) *rule,* or (concr.) a *realm* (lit. or fig.):—kingdom (of God) {71x}, kingdom (of heaven) {32x}, kingdom (general or evil) {20x}, (Thy or Thine) kingdom {6x}, His kingdom {6x}, the kingdom {5x}, (My) kingdom {4x}, misc. {18x} = kingdom, + reign.

Basileia is primarily an abstract noun, **(1)** denoting **(1a)** "sovereignty, royal power, dominion," e.g., Rev 17:18: "And the woman which thou sawest is that great city, which reigneth over the kings of the earth"; then, **(1b)** by metonymy, a concrete noun, denoting the territory or people over whom a king rules: "Again, the devil taketh Him up into an exceeding high mountain, and sheweth Him all the kingdoms of the world, and the glory of them" (Mt 4:8; Mk 3:24).

(2) It is used especially of the "kingdom" of God and of Christ. The Kingdom of God is **(2a)** the sphere of God's rule: "For the kingdom *is* the LORD'S: and He *is* the governor among the nations" (Ps 22:28; cf. 145:13; Dan 4:25; Lk 1:52; Rom 13:1, 2). **(2b)** Since, however, this earth is the scene of universal rebellion against God, (e.g., Lk 4:5, 6; 1 Jn 5:19; Rev 11:15–18), the "kingdom" of God is the sphere in which, at any given time, His rule is acknowledged. **(2c)** God has not relinquished His sovereignty in the face of rebellion, demoniac and human, but has declared His purpose to establish it: "And in the days of these kings shall the God of heaven set up a kingdom, which shall never be destroyed: and the kingdom shall not be left to other people, *but* it shall break in pieces and consume all these kingdoms, and it shall stand for ever" (Dan 2:44; cf. 7:14; 1 Cor 15:24, 25). **(2d)** Meantime, seeking willing obedience, He gave His law to a nation and appointed kings to administer His "kingdom" over it, 1 Chr 28:5. **(2e)** Israel, however, though declaring still a nominal allegiance shared in the common rebellion, Is 1:2–4, and, after they had rejected the Son of God, Jn 1:11 (cf. Mt 21:33–43), were "cast away," Rom 11:15, 20, 25. **(2e)** Henceforth God calls upon men everywhere, without distinction of race or nationality, to submit voluntarily to His rule. **(2f)** Thus the "kingdom" is said to be "in mystery" now, Mk 4:11, that is, it does not come within the range of the natural powers of observation, Lk 17:20, but is spiritually discerned, Jn 3:3 (cf. 1 Cor 2:14). **(2g)** When, hereafter, God asserts His rule universally, Christ will return to establish His earthly rule; then the "kingdom" will be in glory of the rebuilt Davidic, Messianic Kingdom, that is, it will be manifest to all; cf. Mt 25:31–34; Phil 2:9–11; 2 Ti 4:1, 18.

(3) Thus, speaking generally, references to the Kingdom fall into two classes, **(3a)** the first, in which it is viewed as present and involving suffering for those who enter it, 2 Th 1:5; **(3b)** the second, in which it is viewed as future and is associated with reward, Mt 25:34, and glory, 13:43. See also Acts 14:22. **(4)** The fundamental principle of the Kingdom is declared in the words of the Lord spoken in the midst of a company of Pharisees, "the Kingdom of God is in the midst of you," Lk 17:21, that is, where the King is, there is the Kingdom. **(5)** Thus at the present time and so far as this earth is concerned, where the King is and where His rule is acknowledged, is, **(5a)** first, in the heart of the individual believer, Acts 4:19; Eph 3:17; 1 Pet 3:15; and **(5b)** then in the churches of God, 1 Cor. 12:3, 5, 11; 14:37; cf. Col. 1:27. **(6)** Now, the King and His rule being refused, **(6a)** those who enter the Kingdom of God are brought into conflict with all who disown its allegiance, as well as with the desire for ease, and the dislike of suffering and unpopularity, natural to all. **(6b)** On the other hand, subjects of the Kingdom are the objects of the care of God, Mt 6:33, and of the rejected King, Heb 13:5.

(7) Entrance into the Kingdom of God is by the new birth, Mt 18:3; Jn 3:5, for nothing that a man may be by nature, or can attain to by any form of self-culture, avails in the spiritual realm. **(7a)** And as the new nature, received in the new birth, is made evident by obedience, **(7b)** it is further said that only such as do the will of God shall enter into His Kingdom, Mt 7:21, where, **(7c)** however, the context shows that the reference is to the future, as in 2 Pet 1:10, 11. Cf. also 1 Cor 6:9, 10; Gal 5:21; Eph 5:5. **(8)** The expression "Kingdom of God" occurs four times in Matthew, "Kingdom of [from] the Heavens" usually taking its place. **(8a)** The latter (cf. Dan 4:26) does not occur elsewhere in NT, but **(8b)** see 2 Ti 4:18, "His heavenly Kingdom." **(9)** This Kingdom is identical with **(9a)** the Kingdom of the Father (cf. Mt 26:29 with Mk 14:25), and **(9b)** with the Kingdom of the Son (cf. Lk 22:30).

(10) Thus there is but one Kingdom, variously described: **(10a)** of the Son of Man, Mt 13:41; **(10b)** of Jesus, Rev 1:9; **(10c)** of Christ Jesus, 2 Ti 4:1; **(10d)** "of Christ and God," Eph 5:5; **(10e)** "of our Lord, and of His Christ," Rev 11:15; **(10f)** "of our God, and the authority of His Christ," Rev 12:10; **(10g)** "of the Son of His love," Col 1:13. **(11)** Concerning the future, the Lord taught His disciples to pray, "Thy Kingdom come," Mt 6:10, where the verb is in the point tense, precluding the notion of gradual progress and development, and implying a sudden establishment of the kingdom as declared in 2 Th 2:8. **(12)** Concerning the present, that a man is of the Kingdom of God is not shown in the punctilious observance of ordinances, which are external and material, but in the deeper matters of the heart, which are spiritual and essential, viz., "righteousness, and peace, and joy in the Holy Spirit," Rom 14:17."

(13) With regard to the expressions "the Kingdom of God" and the "Kingdom of the Heavens," while they are often used interchangeably, it does not follow that in every case they mean exactly the same and are quite identical. **(13a)** The Apostle Paul often speaks of the Kingdom of God, not dispensationally but morally, e.g., in Rom 14:17; 1 Cor 4:20, but never so of the Kingdom of Heaven. **(13b)** "God" is not the equivalent of "the heavens." He is everywhere and above all dispensations, whereas 'the heavens' are distinguished from the earth, until the Kingdom comes in judgment and power and glory (Rev 11:15) when rule in heaven and on earth will be one. **(13c)** While, then, the sphere of the Kingdom of God and the Kingdom of Heaven are at times identical, yet the one term cannot be used indiscriminately for the other. **(13d)** In the 'Kingdom of Heaven' (32 times in Mt), heaven is in antithesis to earth, and the phrase is stressing the originating point for the kingdom. It will come from heaven (Jn 18:36), not raised up from the earth. **(13e)** In the 'Kingdom of God', in its broader aspect, God is in antithesis to 'man' or 'the world,' and **(13e1)** the term signifies the entire sphere of God's rule and action in relation to the world. **(13e2)** It has a moral and spiritual force and is a general term for the Kingdom at any time. The Kingdom of [from, genitive of source] Heaven is always the Kingdom of God, but the Kingdom of God is not limited to the Kingdom of Heaven, until in their final form, they become identical, e.g., Jn 3:5; Rev 11:15; Rev 12:10. See: TDNT—1:579, 97; BAGD—134d; THAYER—96d.

933. **βασίλειον** {1x} **basilĕiŏn**, *bas-il'-i-on;* neut. of *934;* a *palace:*—king's court + 3588 {1x}.

Basileion is an adjective meaning "royal" and signifies, in the neuter plural, "a royal palace," translated "kings' courts" in Lk 7:25. See: BAGD—136a; THAYER—98a.

934. **βασίλειος** {1x} **basilĕiŏs**, *bas-il'-i-os;* from *935; kingly* (in nature):—royal {1x}.

This word means royal, kingly, regal and occurs in 1 Pet 2:9: "But ye *are* a chosen generation, a royal priesthood, an holy nation, a peculiar people; that ye should shew forth the praises of Him who hath called you out of darkness into His marvelous light." See: TDNT—1:591, 97; BAGD—136a; THAYER—98a.

935. **βασιλεύς** {118x} **basilĕus**, *bas-il-yooce';* prob. from *939* (through the notion of a *foundation* of power); a *sovereign* (abstr., rel., or fig.):—king {82x}, King (of Jews) {21x}, King (God or Christ) {11x}, King (of Israel) {4x}.

Basileus, as a noun, means **(1)** "a king" e.g., **(1a)** Mt 1:6, and is used of the Roman emperor in 1 Pet 2:13, 17 (a command of general application); **(1b)** of Herod the Tetrarch, Mt 14:9; **(1c)** of Christ, **(1c1)** as the "King" of the Jews, e.g., Mt 2:2; 27:11, 29, 37; **(1c2)** as the "King" of Israel, Mk 15:32; Jn 1:49; 12:13; **(1c3)** as "King of kings," Rev 17:14; 19:16; **(1c4)** as "the King" in judging nations and men at the establishment of the millennial kingdom, Mt 25:34, 40; **(2)** of God, **(2a)** "the great King," Mt 5:35; **(2b)** "the King eternal, incorruptible, invisible," 1 Tim 1:17; **(2c)** "King of kings" 1 Ti 6:15. **(3)** Christ's "kingship" **(3a)** was predicted in the OT, e.g., Ps 2:6, and **(3b)** in the NT, e.g., Lk 1:32, 33; **(3c)** He came as such e.g., Mt 2:2; Jn 18:37; **(3d)** was rejected and died as such, Lk 19:14; Mt 27:37; **(3e)** is now a "King" Priest, after the order of Melchizedek, Heb 5:6; 7:1, 17; and **(3f)** will reign for ever and ever, Rev 11:15. Syn.: 934, 937. See: TDNT—1:576, 97; BAGD—136a; THAYER—98a.

936. **βασιλεύω** {21x} **basilĕuō**, *bas-il-yoo'-o;* from *935;* to *rule* (lit. or fig.):—reign {20x}, king {1x}.

Basileuo, as a verb, means "to reign" and is used **(1)** literally, **(1a)** of God, Rev 11:17; 19:6, in each of which the aorist tense (in the latter, translated "reigneth") is "ingressive," stressing the point of entrance; **(1b)** of Christ, Lk 1:33; 1 Cor 15:25; Rev 11:15; as rejected by the Jews, Lk 19:14, 27; **(1c)** of the saints, hereafter, 1 Cor 4:8 (2nd part), where the apostle, casting a reflection upon the untimely exercise of authority on the part of the church at Corinth, anticipates the due time for it in the future; Rev 5:10; 20:4, where the aorist tense is not simply of a "point" character, but "constative," that is, regarding a whole action as having occurred, without distinguishing any steps in its progress (in this instance the aspect is future); 5:6; 22:5; **(1d)** of earthly potentates, Mt 2:22; 1 Ti 6:15, where "kings" is, lit., "them that reign"; **(2)** metaphorically, **(2a)** of believers, Rom 5:17, where "shall reign in life" indicates the activity of life in fellowship with Christ in His sovereign power, reaching its fullness hereafter; 1 Cor 4:8 (1st part), of the carnal pride that laid claim to a power not to be exercised until hereafter; **(2b)** of divine grace, Rom 5:21; **(2c)** of sin, Rom 5:21; 6:12; **(2d)** of death, Rom 5:14, 17. Syn.: 4821. See: TDNT—1:590, 97; BAGD—136c; THAYER—98b.

937. **βασιλικός** {5x} **basilikŏs**, *bas-il-ee-kos';* from *935; regal* (in relation), i.e. (lit.) belonging to (or befitting) the sovereign (as land, dress, or a *courtier*), or (fig.) *preeminent:*—nobleman {2x}, royal {2x}, king's country + 3588 {1x}.

This word means "royal, belonging to a king," is used **(1)** in Acts 12:20 with "country" understood, "their country was fed from the king's," lit., "the royal [country], the "king's country." **(2)** It is also translated "nobleman," Jn 4:46, 49; and **(3)** "royal" (robes), Acts 12:21; "royal [law]", Jas 2:8.

See: TDNT—1:591, 97; BAGD—136d; THAYER—98c.

938. **βασίλισσα** {4x} **basilissa**, *bas-il'-is-sah;* fem. from *936;* a *queen:*—queen {4x}.

Basilissa is the feminine of *basileus,* "a king," is used **(1)** of the "Queen of Sheba," Mt 12:42; Lk 11:31; **(2)** of "Candace," Acts 8:27; **(3)** metaphorically, of "Babylon," Rev 18:7. See: TDNT—1:590, 97; BAGD—137a; THAYER—98c.

939. **βάσις** {1x} **basis**, *bas'-ece;* from βαίνω **bainō** (to *walk*); a *pace* ("base"), i.e. (by impl.) the *foot:*—foot (sole of) {1x}.

This word means lit., "a step"; hence denotes that with which one steps, "a foot," and is used in the plural in Acts 3:7. See: BAGD—137a; THAYER—98d.

940. **βασκαίνω** {1x} **baskainō**, *bas-kah'-ee-no;* akin to *5335;* to *malign,* i.e. (by extens.) to *fascinate* (by false representations):—bewitch {1x}.

This word means primarily, "to slander, to prate about anyone"; then "to bring evil on a person by feigned praise, or mislead by an evil eye, and so to charm, bewitch" [Eng., "fascinate" is connected] and is used figuratively in Gal 3:1, of leading into evil doctrine. See: TDNT—1:594, 102; BAGD—137a; THAYER—98d.

941. **βαστάζω** {27x} **bastazō**, *bas-tad'-zo;* perh. remotely der. from the base of *939* (through the idea of *removal*); to *lift,* lit. or fig. (*endure, declare, sustain, receive,* etc.):—bear {23x}, carry {3x}, take up {1x}.

Bastazo signifies "to support as a burden." It is used with the meaning **(1)** "to take up," as in picking up anything stones, Jn 10:31; **(2)** "to carry" **(2a)** something, Mt 3:11; Mk 14:13; Lk 7:14; 22:10; Acts 3:2; 21:35; Rev 17:7; **(2b)** "to carry" on one's person, Lk 10:4; Gal 6:17; **(2c)** in one's body, Lk 11:27; **(2d)** "to bear" a name in testimony, Acts 9:15; **(2e)** metaphorically, of a root "bearing" branches, Rom 11:18; **(3)** "to bear" a burden, whether **(3a)** physically, as of the cross, Jn 19:17, or **(3b)** metaphorically in respect of sufferings endured in the cause of Christ, Lk 14:27; Rev 2:3; **(3c)** it is said of physical endurance, Mt 20:12; **(3d)** of sufferings "borne" on behalf of others, Mt 8:17; Rom 15:1; Gal 6:2; **(3e)** of spiritual truths not able to be "borne," Jn 16:12; **(3f)** of the refusal to endure evil men, Rev 2:2; **(3g)** of religious regulations imposed on others, Acts 15:10; **(3h)** of the burden of the sentence of God to be executed in due time, Gal 5:10; **(3i)** of the effect at the judgment seat of Christ, to be "borne" by the believer for failure in the matter of discharging the obligations of discipleship, Gal 6:5; **(4)** to "bear" by way of carrying off, Jn 12:6; 20:15. Syn.: 4064, 5342. See: TDNT—1:596, 102; BAGD—137b; THAYER—98d.

942. **βάτος** {5x} **batŏs**, *bat'-os;* of uncert. der.; a *brier* shrub:—bush {4x}, bramble bush {1x}.

Batos denotes **(1)** "a bramble bush," as in Lk 6:44. **(2)** In Mk 12:26 and Lk 20:37 the phrase "in the place concerning the Bush" signifies in that part of the book of Exodus concerning the "burning bush." See also Acts 7:30, 35. See: BAGD—137c; THAYER—99b.

943. **βάτος** {1x} **batŏs**, *bat'-os;* of Heb. or. [1324]; a *bath,* or measure for liquids:—measure {1x}.

Batos, as a noun, denotes a bath, a Jewish liquid measure (the equivalent of an ephah), containing between 8 and 9 gallons, Lk 16:6. Syn.: 280, 488, 2884, 3313, 3354, 3358, 4057, 4568, 5234, 5249, 5518. See: BAGD—137c; THAYER—99b.

944. **βάτραχος** {1x} **batrachŏs**, *bat'-rakh-os;* of uncert. der.; a *frog:*—frog {1x}.

Batrachos is mentioned in Rev 16:13 only. See: BAGD—137d; THAYER—99b.

945. **βαττολογέω** {1x} **battŏlŏgĕō**, *bat-tol-og-eh'-o;* from Βάττος **Battŏs** (a proverbial stammerer) and *3056;* to *stutter,* i.e. (by impl.) to *prate* tediously:—use vain repetitions {1x}.

This word means "to repeat idly" and is used in Mt 6:7, "use (not) vain repetitions"; the meaning "to stammer" is scarcely to be associated with this word. It denotes meaningless and mechanically repeated phrases, the reference being to pagan (not Jewish) modes of prayer. See: TDNT—1:597, 103; BAGD—137d; THAYER—99b.

946. **βδέλυγμα** {6x} **bdĕlugma**, *bdel'-oog-mah;* from *948;* a *detestation,* i.e. (spec.) *idolatry:*—abomination {6x}.

Bdelugma denotes **(1)** an "object of disgust, an abomination." **(2)** This is said of the image to be set up by Antichrist, Mt 24:15; Mk 13:14; **(3)** of that which is highly esteemed amongst men, in contrast to its real character in the sight of God, Lk 16:15. The constant association with idolatry suggests that what is highly esteemed among men constitutes an idol in the human heart. **(4)** In Rev 21:27, entrance is forbidden into the Holy City on the part of the unclean, or one who "maketh an abomination and a lie." **(5)** It is also used of the contents of the golden cup in the hand of the evil woman described in Rev 17:4, and of the name ascribed to her in the following verse. See: TDNT—1:598, 103; BAGD—137d; THAYER—99b.

947. **βδελυκτός** {1x} **bdĕluktŏs**, *bdel-ook-tos';* from *948; detestable,* i.e. (spec.) *idolatrous:*—abominable {1x}.

Bdeluktos is used in Titus 1:16 and is said of deceivers who profess to know God, but deny Him by their works. See: TDNT—1:598, 103; BAGD—138a; THAYER—99c.

948. **βδελύσσω** {2x} **bdĕlussō**, *bdel-oos'-so;* from a (presumed) der. of βδέω **bdĕō** (to *stink*); to *be disgusted,* i.e. (by impl.) *detest* (esp. of idolatry):—abhor {1x}, abominable {1x}.

This word means "to render foul" [from *bdeo,* "to stink"], "to cause to be abhorred" and is used in the middle voice, signifying "to turn oneself away from" (as if from a stench); hence, **(1)** "to detest, abhor" Rom 2:22. **(2)** In Rev 21:8 it denotes "to be abominable." See: TDNT—1:598,*; BAGD—138a; THAYER—99d.

949. **βέβαιος** {9x} **bĕbaiŏs**, *beb'-ah-yos;* from the base of *939* (through the idea of *basality*); *stable* (lit. or fig.):—stedfast {4x}, sure {2x}, firm {1x}, of force {1x}, more sure {1x}.

This word means "firm, steadfast, secure" and is translated **(1)** "firm" in Heb 3:6, of the maintenance of the boldness of the believer's hope; and **(2)** "steadfast" in Heb 3:14 "the beginning of our confidence"; 2 Cor 1:7; Heb 2:2; 6:19. It is also translated **(3)** "sure" in Rom 4:16; **(4)** "of force" in Heb 9:17; and **(5)** "more sure" in 2 Pet 1:10, 19. Syn.: 4731. See: TDNT—1:600, 103; BAGD—138b; THAYER—99d.

950. **βεβαιόω** {8x} **bĕbaiŏō**, *beb-ah-yŏ'-o;* from *949;* to *stabilitate* (fig.):—confirm {5x}, establish {2x}, stablish {1x}.

This word means "to make firm, establish, make secure" (the connected adjective *bebaios* signifies "stable, fast, firm"), and is used of "confirming, stalishing, establishing" **(1)** a word, Mk 16:20; **(2)** promises, Rom 15:8; **(3)** the testimony of Christ, 1 Cor 1:6; **(4)** the saints by the Lord Jesus Christ, 1 Cor 1:8; **(5)** the saints by God, 2 Cor 1:21 ("stablisheth"); **(6)** in faith, Col 2:7; **(7)** the salvation spoken through the Lord and "confirmed" by the apostles, Heb 2:3; **(8)** the heart by grace, Heb 13:9 ("stablished"). "Establish" means to build up from without; "stablish" means to build up from within. See: TDNT—1:600, 103; BAGD—138c; THAYER—99d.

951. **βεβαίωσις** {2x} **bĕbaiōsis**, *beb-ah'-yo-sis;* from *950; stabiliment:*—confirmation {2x}.

Bebaiosis is used in two senses **(1)** "of firmness, establishment," said of the "confirmation" of the gospel, Phil 1:7; and **(2)** "of authoritative validity imparted," said of the settlement of a dispute by an oath to produce confidence, Heb 6:16. The word is found frequently in the papyri of the settlement of a business transaction. See: TDNT—1:600, 103; BAGD—138d; THAYER—100a.

952. **βέβηλος** {5x} **bĕbēlŏs**, *beb'-ay-los;* from the base of *939* and βηλός **bēlŏs** (a *threshold*); *accessible* (as by *crossing the doorway*), i.e. (by impl. of Jewish notions) *heathenish, wicked:*—profane {4x}, profane person {1x}.

(1) This word suggests a trodden and trampled spot that is open to the causal step of every intruder or careless passer-by. **(2)** This word means primarily, "permitted to be trodden, accessible"; hence, "unhallowed, profane" [opposite to *hieros,* "sacred"], and is used of **(2a)** persons, 1 Ti 1:9; Heb 12:16; **(2b)** things, 1 Ti 4.7; 6:20; 2 Ti 2:16. **(3)** The natural antagonism between the profane and the holy or divine grew into a moral antagonism. . . . Accordingly *bebelos* is that which lacks all relationship or affinity to God." Syn.: 2839. See: TDNT—1:604, 104; BAGD—138d; THAYER—100a.

953. **βεβηλόω** {2x} **bĕbēlŏō**, *beb-ay-lŏ'-o;* from *952;* to *desecrate:*—profane {2x}.

This word means primarily, "to cross the threshold"; hence, "to profane, pollute" and occurs in Mt 12:5 and Acts 24:6. See: TDNT—1:605, 104; BAGD—138d; THAYER—100a.

954. **Βεελζεβούλ** {7x} **Bĕĕlzĕbŏul**, *beh-el-zeb-ool';* of Chald. or. [by parody on 1176]; *dung-god; Beelzebul,* a name of Satan:—Beelzebub {7x}. See: TDNT—1:605, 104; BAGD—139a; THAYER—100a.

955. **Βελίαλ** {1x} **Bĕlial**, *bel-ee'-al;* or Βελιάρ **Beliar**, *bel-ee'-ar* of Heb. or. [1100]; *worthlessness; Belial,* as an epithet of Satan:—*Belial* {1x}.

Belial (955) is a word **(1)** frequently used in the Old Testament, with various meanings, especially in the books of Samuel, where it is found nine times. See also Deut 13:13; Judg 19:22; 20:13; 1 Kin 21:10, 13; 2 Chr 13:7. **(2)** Its original meaning was either "worthlessness" or "hopeless ruin." **(3)** It also had the meanings of "extreme wickedness and destruction," the latter indicating the destiny of the former. **(4)** In the period between the OT and the NT it came to be a proper name for Satan. There may be an indication of this in Nahum 1:15, where the word translated "the wicked one" is *Belial.* **(5)** The oldest form of the word is "Beliar," possibly from a phrase signifying "Lord of the forest," or perhaps simply a corruption of the form "*Belial.*" **(6)** In the NT, in 2 Cor 6:15, it is set in contrast to Christ and represents a personification of the system of impure worship connected especially with the cult of Aphrodite. See: TDNT—1:607, 104; BAGD—139a; THAYER—100c.

956. **βέλος** {1x} **bĕlŏs**, *bel'-os;* from *906;* a *missile,* i.e. *spear* or *arrow:*—dart {1x}.

Belos denotes "a missile, an arrow, javelin, dart", Eph 6:16. See: TDNT—1:608, 104; BAGD—139b; THAYER—100c.

957. **βελτίον** {1x} **bĕltiŏn**, *bel-tee'-on;* neut. of a comparative of a der. of *906* (used for the comparative of *18*); *better:*—very well {1x}. See: BAGD—139b.100c.

958. **Βενιαμίν** {4x} **Bĕniamin**, *ben-ee-am-een';* of Heb. or. [1144]; *Benjamin,* an Isr.:—Benjamin {4x}. See: BAGD—139b; THAYER—100c.

959. **Βερνίκη** {3x} **Bĕrnikē**, *ber-nee'-kay;* from a provincial form of *5342* and *3529; victorious; Bernicè, a member of the Herodian family:*- Bernice {3x}. See: BAGD—139c; THAYER—100c.

960. **Βέροια** {2x} **Bĕrŏia**, *ber'-oy-ah;* perh. a provincial from a der. of *4008* [*Peræa,* i.e. the region *beyond* the coast-line]; *Berœa,* a place in Macedonia:—Berea {2x}. See: BAGD—139c; THAYER—100c.

961. **Βεροιαῖος** {1x} **Bĕrŏiaiŏs**, *ber-oy-ah'-yos;* from *960;* a *Berœœan* or native of Beræa:—of Berea {1x}. See: BAGD—139c; THAYER—100c.

962. **Βηθαβαρά** {1x} **Bēthabara**, *bay-thab-ar-ah';* of Heb. or. [1004 and 5679]; *ferry-house; Bethabara* (i.e. *Bethabarah*), a place on the Jordan:—Bethabara {1x}. See: BAGD—139c; THAYER—100d.

963. **Βηθανία** {11x} **Bēthania**, *bay-than-ee'-ah;* of Chald. or.; *date-house; Bethany,* a place in Pal.:—Bethany {11x}. See: BAGD—139d; THAYER—100d.

964. **Βηθεσδά** {1x} **Bēthĕsda**, *bay-thes-dah';* of Chald. or. [compound of 1004 and 2617]; *house of kindness; Beth-esda,* a pool in Jerusalem:—*Bethesda* {1x}. See: BAGD—139d; THAYER—100d.

965. **Βηθλεέμ** {8x} **Bēthlĕĕm**, *bayth-leh-em';* of Heb. or. [1036]; *Bethleem* (i.e. *Beth-lechem*), a place in Pal.:—Bethlehem {8x}. See: BAGD—140a; THAYER—101a.

966. **Βηθσαϊδά** {7x} **Bēthsaïda**, *bayth-sahee-dah';* of Chald. or. [compound of 1004 and 6719]; *fishing-house; Bethsaïda,* a place in Pal.:—*Bethsaida* {7x}. See: BAGD—140a; THAYER—101a.

967. **Βηθφαγή** {3x} **Bēthphagē**, *bayth-fag-ay';* of Chald. or. [compound of 1004 and 6291]; *fig-house; Beth-phage',* a place in Pal.:—*Bethphage* {3x}. See: BAGD—140b; THAYER—101b.

968. **βῆμα** {12x} **bēma**, *bay'-ma;* from the base of *939;* a *step,* i.e. *foot-breath;* by impl. a *rostrum,* i.e. a *tribunal:*—judgment seat {10x}, throne {1x}, to set (one's) foot on + 4128 {1x}.

Bema primarily means a step, a pace (Acts 7:5) and was used **(1)** to denote a raised place or platform, reached by steps, where was the place of assembly; from the platform orations were made. **(2)** It is used of the divine tribunal before which all believers are hereafter to stand (Rom 14:10). **(3)** In 2 Cor 5:10 it is called the judgment seat of Christ, to whom the Father has given all judgment (Jn 5:22, 27). **(3a)** At this *bema* believers are to be made manifest, that each may "receive the things done in (or through) the body," according to what he has done, "whether it be good or bad." **(3b)** There they will receive rewards for their faithfulness to the Lord. For all that has been contrary in their lives to His will they will suffer loss (1 Cor 3:15). **(3c)** This judgment seat is to be distinguished from **(3c1)** the premillennial, earthly throne of Christ (Mt 25:31), and **(3c2)** the postmillennial Great White Throne (Rev 20:11), at which only "the unsaved dead" will appear. See: BAGD—140b; THAYER—101b.

969. **βήρυλλος** {1x} **bērullŏs**, *bay'-rool-los;* of uncert. der.; a *"beryl":*—beryl {1x}.

Beryl is a precious stone of a sea-green color (Rev. 21:20; cf. Ex 28:20). See: BAGD—140b; THAYER—101c.

970. **βία** {4x} **bia**, *bee'-ah;* prob. akin to *979* (through the idea of *vital* activity); *force:*—violence {4x}.

This word denotes "force, violence" and is said **(1)** of men, Acts 5:26; 21:35; 24:7; and **(2)** of waves, Acts 27:41. See: BAGD—140c; THAYER—101c.

971. **βιάζω** {2x} **biazō**, *bee-ad'-zo;* from *970;* to *force,* i.e. (refl.) to *crowd oneself* (into), or (pass.) to *be seized:*—suffer violence {1x}, press {1x}.

Biazo, in the middle voice "means to press violently" or "force one's way into" and is translated **(1)** "presseth" in Lk 16:16, "entereth violently," a meaning confirmed by the papyri, speaking of "those who (try to) force their way in" and in Mt 11:12 "suffereth violence": "And from the days of John the Baptist until now the kingdom of heaven suffereth violence, and the violent take it by force." See: TDNT—1:609,*; BAGD—140b; THAYER—101c.

972. **βίαιος** {1x} **biaiŏs**, *bee'-ah-yos;* from *970; violent:*—mighty {1x}.

This word is translated "mighty" in Acts 2:2: "And suddenly there came a sound from heaven as of a rushing mighty (*biaios*) wind, and it filled all the house where they were sitting." See: BAGD—141a; THAYER—101d.

973. **βιαστής** {1x} **biastēs**, *bee-as-tace';* from *971;* a *forceful man,* i.e. (fig.) *energetic:*—violent {1x}.

This word means "a forceful or violent man" and is used in Mt 11:12. See: TDNT—1:613, 105; BAGD—141a; THAYER—101d.

974. **βιβλιαρίδιον** {4x} **bibliaridiŏn**, *bib-lee-ar-id'-ee-on;* a dimin. of *975;* a *booklet:*—little book {4x}.

Bibliaridion is diminutive of *bibliov* (975) and is always rendered "little book" in Rev 10:2, 8, 9–10. See: BAGD—141a; THAYER—101d.

975. **βιβλίον** {32x} **bibliŏn**, *bib-lee'-on;* a dimin. of *976;* a *roll:*—book {29x}, bill {1x}, scroll {1x}, writing {1x}.

This word means primarily "a small book, a scroll, or any sheet on which something has been written"; hence, in connection with *apostasion,* "divorce," signifies "a writing of divorcement," Mt 19:7; Mk 10:4. See: TDNT—1:617, 106; BAGD—141b; THAYER—101d.

976. **βίβλος** {13x} **biblŏs**, *bib'-los;* prop. the inner *bark* of the papyrus plant, i.e. (by impl.) a *sheet* or *scroll* of writing:—book {13x}.

Biblos was the inner part, or rather the cellular substance, of the stem of the papyrus (Eng. "paper"). It came to denote the paper made from this bark in Egypt, and then a written "book," roll, or volume. It is used in referring to **(1)** "books" of Scripture, the "book," or scroll, of Matthew's Gospel, Mt 1:1; **(2)** the Pentateuch, as the "book" of Moses, Mk 12:26; **(3)** Isaiah, as "the book of the words of Isaiah," Lk 3:4; **(4)** the Psalms, Lk 20:42 and Acts 1:20; **(5)** "the prophets," Acts 7:42; **(6)** to "the Book of Life," Phil 4:3; Rev 3:5; 20:15. **(7)** Once only it is used of secular writings, Acts 19:19. See: TDNT—1:615, 106; BAGD—141c; THAYER—102a.

977. **βιβρώσκω** {1x} **bibrōskō**, *bib-ro'-sko;* a redupl. and prol. form of an obs. primary verb [perh. caus. of *1006*]; to *eat:*—eat {1x}.

This word means "to eat" and is derived from a root, *bor,* "to devour." Syn.: In Jn 6:5 phago (5315) intimates nothing about a full supply; whereas, *bibrosko* (6:13), indicates that the people had been provided with a big meal, of which they had partaken eagerly. See also: 1089, 2068, 2719, 2880, 5176, 5315. See: BAGD—141c; THAYER—102a.

978. **Βιθυνία** {2x} **Bithunia**, *bee-thoo-nee'-ah;* of uncert. der.; *Bithynia,* a region of Asia:—Bithynia {2x}. See: BAGD—141d; THAYER—102a.

979. **βίος** {11x} **biŏs**, *bee'-os;* a primary word; *life,* i.e. (lit.) the present state of existence; by impl. the means of *livelihood:*—life {5x}, living {5x}, good {1x}.

Bios denotes **(1)** "life, lifetime", Lk 8:14; 1 Ti 2:2; 2 Ti 2:4; 1 Pet 4:3; 1 Jn 2:16; **(2)** "livelihood, living, means of living", Mk 12:44; Lk 8:43; 15:12, 30; 21:4; and is translated **(3)** "good" in 1 Jn 3:17: "But whoso hath this world's good, and seeth his brother have need, and shutteth up his bowels *of compassion* from him, how dwelleth the love of God in him?" Syn.: 2222. See: TDNT—2:832, 290; BAGD—141d; THAYER—102b.

980. **βιόω** {1x} **biŏō**, *bee-ŏ'-o;* from *979;* to *spend* existence:—live {1x}.

Bioo, as a verb, means "to spend life, to pass one's life": "That he no longer should live the rest of *his* time in the flesh to the lusts of men, but to the will of God" (1 Pet 4:2). Syn.: 326, 390, 1236, 2198, 2225, 4176, 4800, 5225. See: TDNT—2:832, 280; BAGD—142a; THAYER—102b.

981. **βίωσις** {1x} **biōsis**, *bee'-o-sis;* from *980; living* (prop. the act, by impl. the mode):—manner of life {1x}.

This word means "to spend one's life, to live" and denotes "a manner of living and acting, way of life," Acts 26:4. See: BAGD—142a; THAYER—102b.

982. **βιωτικός** {3x} **biōtikŏs**, *bee-o-tee-kos';* from a der. of *980; relating to* the present *existence:*—things pertaining to this life {1x}, things that pertain to this life {1x}, of this life {1x}.

Biotikos means "pertaining to life" (*bios*) and is translated **(1)** "of this life" in Lk 21:34; **(2)** with reference to cares; in 1 Cor 6:3 "(things) that pertain to this life"; and **(3)** 1 Cor 6: 4, "(things) pertaining to this life," i.e., matters of this world, concerning which Christians at Corinth were engaged in public lawsuits one with another; such matters were to be regarded as relatively unimportant in view of the great tribunals to come under the jurisdiction of saints hereafter. See: BAGD—142a; THAYER—102b.

983. **βλαβερός** {1x} **blabĕrŏs**, *blab-er-os';* from *984; injurious:*—hurtful {1x}.

Blaberos signifies "hurtful" in 1 Ti 6:9, said of lusts. See: BAGD—142b; THAYER—102b.

984. **βλάπτω** {2x} **blaptō**, *blap'-to;* a primary verb; prop. to *hinder,* i.e. (by impl.) to *injure, mar do damage to:*—hurt {2x}.

Blapto signifies **(1)** "to injure, mar, do damage to," Mk 16:18, "shall (in no wise) hurt (them)";

and **(2)** in Lk 4:35, "hurt him not." Syn.: *Adikeo* (91) stresses the unrighteousness of the act, *blapto* stresses the injury done. See: BAGD—142b; THAYER—102c.

985. **βλαστάνω** {4x} **blastanō**, *blas-tan'-o;* from βλαστός **blastŏs** (a *sprout*); to *germinate;* by impl. to *yield* fruit:—spring up {2x}, bud {1x}, bring forth {1x}.

Blastano, as a verb, means "to bud, spring up" and is translated "brought forth" [i.e., "caused to produce"] in Jas 5:18: "And he [Elijah] prayed again, and the heaven gave rain, and the earth brought forth her fruit." Cf. Mt 13:26; Mk 4:27; Heb 9:4. See: BAGD—142b; THAYER—102c.

986. **Βλάστος** {1x} **Blastŏs**, *blas'-tos; perh.* the same as the base of *985; Blastus,* an officer of Herod Agrippa:—Blastus {1x}. See: BAGD—142c; THAYER—102c.

987. **βλασφημέω** {35x} **blasphēmĕō**, *blas-fay-meh'-o;* from *989;* to *vilify;* spec. to *speak impiously:*—blaspheme {17x}, speak evil of {10x}, rail on {2x}, blasphemer {1x}, speak blasphemy {1x}, blasphemously {1x}, misc. {3x} = defame, revile.

(1) This word means to use speech to bring down another's value, honor, due-respect; to injure another's reputation in the eyes of others. **(1a)** *Blasphemeo,* as a verb, means "to blaspheme, rail at or revile" and is used **(1b)** in a general way, of any contumelious speech, reviling, calumniating, railing at, etc., as of those who railed at Christ, e.g., Mt 27:39; Mk 15:29; Lk 22:65; 23:39; **(2)** of those who speak contemptuously of God or of sacred things, e.g., Mt 9:3; Mk 3:28; Rom 2:24; 1 Ti 1:20; 6:1; Rev 13:6; 16:9, 11, 21; **(2a)** "hath spoken blasphemy," Mt 26:65; **(2b)** "rail at," 2 Pet 2:10; Jude 8, 10; **(2c)** "railing," 2 Pet 2:12; **(2d)** "slanderously reported," Rom 3:8; **(2e)** "be evil spoken of," Rom 14:16; 1 Cor 10:30; 2 Pet 2:2; **(2f)** "speak evil of," Titus 3:2; 1 Pet 4:4; **(2g)** "being defamed," 1 Cor 4:13. **(3)** The verb (in the present participial form) is translated **(3a)** "blasphemers" in Acts 19:37; **(3b)** in Mk 2:7, "speaketh blasphemies." **(4)** As to Christ's teaching concerning "blasphemy" against the Holy Spirit, e.g., Mt 12:32, that anyone, with the evidence of the Lord's power before His eyes, should declare it to be Satanic, exhibited a condition of heart beyond divine illumination and therefore hopeless. Divine forgiveness would be inconsistent with the moral nature of God. As to the Son of Man, in His state of humiliation, there might be misunderstanding, but not so with the Holy Spirit's power demonstrated. This sin can not be committed today; only during the days of His incarnation. See: TDNT—1:621, 107; BAGD—142c; THAYER—102c.

988. **βλασφημία** {19x} **blasphēmia**, *blas-fay-me'-ah;* from *989; vilification* (espec. against God):—blasphemy {16x}, railing {2x}, evil speaking {1x}.

Blasphemia is **(1)** translated **(1a)** "blasphemy, blasphemies" sixteen times; **(1b)** "a railing, railings" in 1 Ti 6:4, Jude 9; and **(1c)** "evil speaking" in Eph 4:31. **(2)** The word "blasphemy" is practically confined to speech defamatory of the Divine Majesty. See: TDNT—1:621, 107; BAGD—143a; THAYER—102d.

989. **βλάσφημος** {5x} **blasphēmŏs**, *blas'-fay-mos;* from a der. of *984* and *5345; scurrilous,* i.e. *calumnious* (against man), or (spec.) *impious* (against God):—blasphemous {2x}, blasphemer {2x}, railing {1x}.

Blasphemos means "abusive, speaking evil" and is translated **(1)** "blasphemous," in Acts 6:11, 13; **(2)** "a blasphemer," 1 Ti 1:13; 2 Ti 3:2; and **(3)** "railing." 2 Pet 2:11. See: TDNT—1:621, 107; BAGD—143a; THAYER—103a.

990. **βλέμμα** {1x} **blemma**, *blem'-mah;* from *991; vision* (prop. concr.; by impl. abstr.):—seeing {1x}.

This word means primarily, "a look, a glance" and denotes "sight, seeing," 2 Pet 2:8. See: BAGD—143b; THAYER—103a.

991. **βλέπω** {135x} **blĕpō**, *blep'-o;* a primary verb; to *look* at (lit. or fig.):—see {90x}, take heed {12x}, behold {10x}, beware {4x}, look on {4x}, look {3x}, beware of {3x}, misc. {9x} = lie, perceive, regard, sight.

Blepo, as a verb, means primarily, "to have sight, to see," then, "observe, discern, perceive," frequently implying special contemplation, and is rendered **(1)** "to looking back" (Lk 9:62); **(2)** Jn 13:22 "(the disciples) looked (one on another)"; **(3)** "beheld" (Acts 1:9); **(4)** Acts 3:4 "look (on us)"; **(5)** Eph 5:15 "see (that ye walk circumspectly)"; **(6)** Rev 11:9 and 18:9 "shall see." Syn.for **(1) - (5):** 308, 352, 578, 816, 872, 1689, 1896, 1914, 1980, 1983, 2300, 2334, 3706, 3708, 3879, 4017, 4648.

(7) *Blepo,* is used of bodily, mental vision, and also, **(7a)** "to perceive": "Therefore speak I to them in parables: because they seeing (*blepo*) see not (*blepo*); and hearing they hear not, neither do they understand" (e.g., Mt 13:13); and **(7b)** "to take heed": "But take ye heed (*blepo*): behold, I have foretold you all things" (e.g., Mk 13:23, 33). **(7c)** It indicates greater vividness than horao (3708), expressing a more intent, earnest contemplation **(7d)** in Lk 6:41 of "beholding" the mote in a brother's eye; **(7e)** in Lk 24:12 of "beholding" the linen clothes in the empty tomb; **(7f)** in Acts 1:9 of the gaze of the disciples when the Lord ascended; **(7g)** The greater earnestness is sometimes brought out by the rendering "regardest": "And they [Pharisees] sent out unto Him their disciples with the Herodians, saying, Master, we know that thou art true, and teachest the way of God in truth, neither carest thou for any *man:* for thou regardest (*blepo*) not the person of men" (Mt 22:16). Syn. for **(7a-g):** 333, 816, 1689, 1896, 2029, 2300, 2334, 2657, 2734, 3708. See: TDNT—5:315, 706; BAGD—143b; THAYER—103a. comp. *3700.*

992. **βλητέος** {2x} **blētĕŏs**, *blay-teh'-os;* from *906;* fit *to be cast* (i.e. *applied*):—must be put {2x}.

Bleteos means that which must be put, placed specifically: "And no man putteth (*bleteos*) new wine into old bottles: else the new wine doth burst the bottles, and the wine is spilled, and the bottles will be marred: but new wine must be put into new bottles" (cf. Lk 5:38). See: BAGD—144a; THAYER—103d.

993. **Βοανεργές** {1x} **Bŏanĕrgĕs**, *bŏ-an-erg-es';* of Chald. or. [1123 and 7266]; *sons of commotion; Boänerges,* an epithet of two of the Apostles:—*Boanerges* {1x}. See: BAGD—144a; THAYER—103d.

994. **βοάω** {11x} **bŏaō**, *bŏ-ah'-o;* appar. a prol. form of a primary verb; to *halloo,* i.e. *shout* (for help or in a tumultuous way):—cry {11x}.

Boao, as a verb, signifies **(1)** "to raise a cry" whether **(1a)** of joy (Gal 4:27), or **(1b)** vexation (Acts 8:7); **(2)** "to speak with a strong voice" (Mt 3:3; Mk 1:3; 15:34; Lk 3:4; Jn 1:23; Acts 17:6); **(3)** "to cry out for help" (Lk 18:7, 38). Syn.: Kaleo (2564), denotes "to call out for any purpose," *boao* (994), "to cry out as an expression of feeling," krazo (2896), to cry out loudly." Kaleo suggests intelligence, *boao,* sensibilities, krazo, instincts. See also: 310, 349, 994, 995, 1916, 2019, 2896, 2905, 2906, 5455. See: TDNT—1:625, 108; BAGD—144b; THAYER—103d.

995. **βοή** {1x} **bŏē**, *bŏ-ay';* from *994;* a *halloo,* i.e. *call* (for aid, etc.):—cry {1x}.

Boe, as a noun, means especially "a cry for help" and is found in Jas 5:4: "Behold, the hire of the labourers who have reaped down your fields, which is of you kept back by fraud, crieth (krazo – 2896): and the cries (*boe*) of them which have reaped are entered into the ears of the Lord of sabaoth." Syn.: 310, 349, 994, 1916, 2019, 2896, 2905, 2906, 5455. See: BAGD—144c; THAYER—104a.

996. **βοήθεια** {2x} **bŏēthĕia**, *bŏ-ay'-thi-ah;* from *998; aid;* spec. a rope or chain for *frapping* a vessel:—help {2x}.

Boetheia denotes **(1)** "an answer to a cry for help": "Let us therefore come boldly unto the throne of grace, that we may obtain mercy, and find grace to help (*boetheia*) in time of need", Heb. 4:16 literally, "(grace) unto (timely) help"; and **(2)** in Acts 27:17, where the plural is used, the term is nautical, "frapping": "Which when they had taken up, they used helps (*boetheia*), undergirding the ship; and, fearing lest they should fall into the quicksands, strake sail, and so were driven." Frapping means to use ropes or chains to wrap around a ship to prevent its demise. See: TDNT—1:628, 108; BAGD—144c; THAYER—104a.

997. **βοηθέω** {8x} **bŏēthĕō**, *bŏ-ay-theh'-o;* from *998;* to *aid* or *relieve:*—help {6x}, succour {2x}.

This word means "to come to the aid of anyone, to succour" and is used in Mt 15:25; Mk 9:22, 24; Acts 16:0; 21:28; 2 Cor 6.2, "did I succour"; Heb 2:18, "to succour"; Rev 12:16. See: TDNT—1:628, 108; BAGD—144c; THAYER—104a.

998. **βοηθός** {1x} **bŏēthŏs**, *bŏ-ay-thos';* from *995* and θέω **thĕō** (to *run*); a *succorer:*—helper {1x}.

Boethos is an adjective and is used as a noun in Heb 13:6 of God as the helper of His saints: "So that we may boldly say, The Lord *is* my helper, and I will not fear what man shall do unto me." See: TDNT—1:628, 108; BAGD—144d; THAYER—104b.

999. **βόθυνος** {3x} **bŏthunŏs**, *both'-oo-nos;* akin to *900;* a *hole* (in the ground); spec. a *cistern:*—ditch {2x}, pit {1x}.

Bothunos is any kind of "deep hole or pit" and is translated **(1)** "ditch" in Mt 15:14 and Lk 6:39, and **(2)** "pit" in Mt 12:11. See: BAGD—144d; THAYER—104b.

1000. **βολή** {1x} **bŏlē**, *bol-ay';* from *906;* a *throw* (as a measure of distance):—cast {1x}.

This word means a short throw, cast: "And He was withdrawn from them about a stone's cast, and kneeled down, and prayed . . ." (Lk 22:41). See: BAGD—144d; THAYER—104b.

1001. **βολίζω** {2x} **bŏlizō**, *bol-id'-zo;* from *1002;* to *heave* the lead:—sound {2x}.

This word means "to heave the lead, sounding-lead" to take soundings, occurs in Acts 27:28 (twice). See: BAGD—144d; THAYER—104b.

1002. **βολίς** {1x} **bŏlis**, *bol-ece';* from *906;* a *missile,* i.e. *javelin:*—dart {1x}. See: BAGD—144d; THAYER—104b.

1003. **Βοόζ** {3x} **Bŏŏz**, *bŏ-oz';* of Heb. or. [1162]; *Boöz,* (i.e. *Boäz*), an Isr.:—*Booz* {3x}. See: BAGD—145a; THAYER—104b.

1004. **βόρβορος** {1x} **bŏrbŏrŏs**, *bor'-bor-os;* of uncert. der.; *mud:*—mire {1x}.

This word means "mud, filth" and occurs in 2 Pet. 2:22. See: BAGD—145a; THAYER—104c.

1005. **βοῤῥᾶς** {2x} **borrhas**, *bor-hras';* of uncert. der.; the *north* (prop. wind):—north {2x}.

This word means primarily Boreas, the North Wind and came to denote the "north" (cf. "Borealis"), Lk 13:29; Rev 21:13. See: BAGD—145b; THAYER—104c.

1006. **βόσκω** {9x} **bŏskō**, *bos'-ko;* a prol. form of a primary verb [comp. *977, 1016*]; to *pasture;* by extens. to, *fodder;* refl. to *graze:*—feed {2x}, keep {1x}.

This word means "to feed" and is primarily used of a herdsman [from *boo,* "to nourish," the special function being to provide food; the root is *bo,* found in *boter,* "a herdsman or herd," and *botane,* "fodder, pasture"]. Its uses are **(2)** literal, Mt 8:30; 33; Mk. 5:14; Lk 8:34; in Mk 5:11 and Lk 8:32, "feeding"; Lk 15:15; **(3)** metaphorical, of spiritual ministry, Jn 21:15, 17. Syn.: 4165. *Bosko* simply means to feed; whereas, poimein (4165) refers to the whole office of shepherd: guiding, guarding, folding, and providing pasture (Rev 2:27; 19:15). See: BAGD—145b; THAYER—104c.

1007. **Βοσόρ** {1x} **Bŏsŏr**, *bos-or';* of Heb. or. [1160]; *Bosor* (i.e. *Beör*), a Moabite:—*Bosor* {1x}. See: BAGD—145b; THAYER—104c.

1008. **βοτάνη** {1x} **bŏtanē**, *bot-an'-ay;* from *1006; herbage* (as if for *grazing*):—herb {1x}.

This word means an herb fit for fodder, green herb, growing plant, Heb 6:7. See: BAGD—145b; THAYER—104c.

1009. **βότρυς** {1x} **bŏtrus**, *bot'-rooce;* of uncert. der.; a *bunch* (of grapes):—(vine) cluster (of the vine) {1x}.

This word means "a cluster, or bunch, bunch of grapes" and is found in Rev 14:18. Syn.: *Staphule,* (4718) "a bunch of grapes, the ripe cluster," stresses the individual grapes themselves within the cluster; whereas *botrus* stresses the cluster. See: BAGD—145c; THAYER—104d.

1010. **βουλευτής** {2x} **bŏulĕutēs**, *bool-yoo-tace';* from *1011;* an *adviser,* i.e. (spec.) a *councillor* or member of the Jewish Sanhedrin:—counsellor {2x}.

Joseph of Arimathaea is described as "a councillor of honorable estate," Mk 15:43; cf. Lk 23:50. See: BAGD—145c; THAYER—104d.

1011. **βουλεύω** {8x} **bŏulĕuō**, *bool-yoo'-o;* from *1012;* to *advise,* i.e. (refl.) *deliberate,* or (by impl.) *resolve:*—consult {2x}, take counsel {1x}, determine {1x}, be minded {2x}, purpose {2x}.

Bouleuo, used in the middle voice, means **(1)** "to consult, consider," Lk 14:31; Jn 12:10; **(2)** "take counsel", Act 5:33; **(3)** "determine", Acts 15:37; **(4)** "be minded", Acts 27:39; and **(5)** "purpose", 2 Cor 1:17. See: BAGD—145c; THAYER—104d.

1012. **βουλή** {12x} **bŏulē**, *boo-lay';* from *1014; volition,* i.e. (obj.) *advice,* or (by impl.) *purpose:*—+ advise + 5087 {1x}, counsel {10x}, will {1x}.

Boule comes from a root meaning "a will," hence "a counsel, a piece of advice." The word is used **(1)** of the counsel of God in Lk 7:30; Acts 2:23; 4:28; 13:36; 20:27; Eph 1:11; Heb 6:17; and in other passages, **(2)** of the counsel of men, Lk 23:51; Acts 27:12, 42; 1 Cor 4:5. See: BAGD—145d; THAYER—104d. Syn.: *Boule* is to be distinguished from *gnome* (1106); *boule* is the result of determination, *gnome* is the result of knowledge.

1013. **βούλημα** {2x} **bŏulēma**, *boo'-lay-mah;* from *1014;* a *resolve:*—purpose {1x}, will {1x}.

This word means "a purpose or will, a deliberate intention" and occurs **(1)** as "purpose" in Acts 27:43: "But the centurion, willing to save Paul, kept them from *their* purpose; and commanded that they which could swim should cast *themselves* first *into the sea,* and get to land"; and **(2)** "will" in Rom 9:19: "Thou wilt say then unto me, Why doth He yet find fault? For who hath resisted His will?" See: TDNT—1:636, 108; BAGD—145d; THAYER—105a.

1014. **βούλομαι** {34x} **bŏulŏmai**, *boo'-lom-ahee;* mid. voice of a primary verb.; to "*will,*" i.e. (refl.) *be willing:*—will {15x}, would {11x}, be minded {2x}, intend {2x}, be disposed {1x}, be willing {1x}, list {1x}, of his own will {1x}.

This word means "to wish, to will deliberately," and expresses strongly the deliberate exercise of the will. See: TDNT—1:629, 108; BAGD—146a; THAYER—105a. comp. *2309.*

1015. **βουνός** {2x} **bŏunŏs**, *boo-nos';* prob. of for. or.; a *hillock:*—hill {2x}.

Bounos means "a mound, heap, height," is translated **(1)** "hill" in Lk 3:5; **(2)** "hills" in Lk 23:30. See: BAGD—146c; THAYER—105b.

1016. **βοῦς** {8x} **bŏus**, *booce;* prob. from the base of *1006;* an *ox* (as *grazing*), i.e. an animal of that species ("beef"):—ox {8x}.

This word means denotes an "ox" or "a cow," Lk 13:15; 14:5, 19; Jn 2:14–15; 1 Cor 9:9 (twice); 1 Ti 5:18. Syn.: 5022. See: BAGD—146c; THAYER—105b.

1017. **βραβεῖον** {2x} **braběiŏn**, *brab-i'-on;* from βραβεύς **braběus** (an *umpire;* of uncert. der.); an *award* (of arbitration), i.e. (spec.) a *prize* in the public games:—prize {2x}.

Brabeion is "a prize bestowed in connection with the games." **(1)** In 1 Cor 9:24, is used metaphorically of "the reward" to be obtained hereafter by the faithful believer; and **(2)** in Phil 3:14; the preposition *eis,* "unto," indicates the position of the goal. The "prize" is not "the high calling," but will be bestowed in virtue of, and relation to, it, the heavenly calling, (cf. Heb 3:1), which belongs to all believers and directs their minds and aspirations heavenward; for the "prize" see especially 2 Ti 4:7, 8. See: TDNT—1:638, 110; BAGD—146d; THAYER—105b.

1018. **βραβεύω** {1x} **braběuō**, *brab-yoo'-o;* from the same as *1017;* to *arbitrate,* i.e. (gen.) to *govern* (fig. *prevail*):—rule {1x}.

This word properly means to act as an umpire (*brabeus*); hence, generally, to arbitrate, decide (Col 3:15) representing "the peace of God" as deciding all matters in the hearts of believers; some regard the meaning as that of simply directing, controlling, "ruling." See: TDNT—1:637, 110; BAGD—146d; THAYER—105c.

1019. **βραδύνω** {2x} **bradunō**, *brad-oo'-no;* from *1021;* to *delay; to be slow:*—be slack {1x}, tarry {1x}.

Braduno used intransitively signifies "to be slow, to tarry" and is said **(1)** negatively of God, 2 Pet 3:9, "is (not) slack"; and **(2)** in 1 Ti 3:15 is translated "(if) I tarry." See: BAGD—147a; THAYER—105c.

1020. **βραδυπλοέω** {1x} **braduplŏĕō**, *brad-oo-plŏ-eh'-o;* from *1021* and a prol. form of *4126;* to *sail slowly:*—sail slowly {1x}.

Bradupleoo means "to sail slowly" (*bradus,* "slow," *plous,* "a voyage") and occurs in Acts 27:7: "And when we had sailed slowly many days, and scarce were come over against Cnidus, the wind not suffering us, we sailed under Crete, over against Salmone . . ." See: BAGD—147a; THAYER—105c.

1021. **βραδύς** {3x} **bradus**, *brad-ooce';* of uncert. aff.; *slow;* fig. *dull:*—slow {3x}. Syn.: 692, 3576.

Bradus is used **(1)** twice in Jas 1:19, in an exhortation to "be slow to speak" and "slow to wrath"; and **(2)** in Lk 24:25, metaphorically of the understanding. Syn.: *Bradus* means slow, nothros (3576) means sluggish, and argos (692) means idle. See: BAGD—147a; THAYER—105c.

1022. **βραδύτης** {1x} **bradutēs**, *brad-oo'-tace;* from *1021; tardiness:*—slackness {1x}.

This word means "slowness" and is rendered "slackness" in 2 Pet 3:9. See: BAGD—147a. 105d.

1023. **βραχίων** {3x} **brachiōn**, *brakh-ee'-own;* prop. comp. of *1024,* but appar. in the sense of βράσσω **brassō** (to *wield*); the *arm,* i.e. (fig.) *strength:*—arm {3x}.

Brachion is the shorter part of the arm, from the shoulder to the elbow and is used metaphorically to denote strength, power; always in the NT of the power of God (Lk 1:51; Jn 12:38; Acts 13:17). See: TDNT—1:639, 110; BAGD—147b; THAYER—105d.

1024. **βραχύς** {7x} **brachus**, *brakh-ooce';* of uncert. aff.; *short* (of time, place, quantity, or number):—few words {1x}, a little {4x}, a little space {1x}, a little while {1x}.

Brachus denotes **(1)** "short," **(1a)** in regard to time, e.g., Heb 2:7; or **(1b)** distance, Acts 27:28; **(2)** "few," in regard to quantity, Heb 13:22, lit., "by means of few," i.e., "in few words." See: BAGD—147b; THAYER—105d.

1025. **βρέφος** {8x} **brĕphŏs**, *bref'-os;* of uncert. affin.; an *infant* (prop. unborn) lit. or fig.:—babe {5x}, young child {1x}, child {1x}, infant {1x}.

Brephos denotes **(1)** "an unborn child," as in Lk 1:41, 44; **(2)** "a newborn child, or an infant still older," Lk 2:12, 16; 18:15; Acts 7:19; 2 Ti 3:15; 1 Pet 2:2. Syn.: 3516. See: TDNT—5:636, 759; BAGD—147b; THAYER—105d.

1026. **βρέχω** {7x} **brĕchō**, *brekh'-o;* a primary verb; to *moisten* (espec. by a shower):—send rain {1x}, rain + 5205 {1x}, rain {3x}, wash {2x}.

Brecho signifies **(1)** "to wash," Lk 7:38, 44; **(2)** "to send rain," Mt 5:45; **(3)** to rain, Lk 17:29 (of fire and brimstone); **(4)** Jas 5:17, used literally (twice); **(5)** Rev 11:6, lit., "(that) rain rain (not)." See: BAGD—147c; THAYER—105d.

1027. **βροντή** {12x} **brŏntē**, *bron-tay';* akin to βρέμω **brĕmō** (to *roar*); *thunder:*—thunder {8x}, thundering {4x}.

Bronte means **(1)** literal thunder signaling a storm, Rev. 4:5; 6:1; 8:5; 10:3, 4; 11:19; 14:2; 16:18; 19:6. **(2)** In Mk 3:17 "sons of thunder" is the interpretation of Boanerges, the name applied by the Lord to James and John; their fiery disposition is seen in 9:38 and Lk 9:54. See: TDNT—1:640, 110; BAGD—147d; THAYER—106a.

1028. **βροχή** {2x} **brŏchē**, *brokh-ay';* from *1026; rain:*—rain {2x}.

This word means lit., "a wetting," hence, "rain" and is used in Mt 7:25, 27. See: BAGD—147d; THAYER—106a.

1029. **βρόχος** {1x} **brŏchŏs**, *brokh'-os;* of uncert. der.; a *noose:*—snare {1x}.

Brochos is "a noose, slipknot, halter," is used metaphorically in 1 Cor 7:35, "a snare." See: BAGD—147d; THAYER—106a.

1030. **βρυγμός** {7x} **brugmŏs**, *broog-mos';* from *1031;* a *grating* (of the teeth):—gnashing {7x}.

Brugmos denotes "gnashing" ("of teeth" being added), Mt 8:12; 13:42, 50; 22:13; 24:51; 25:30; Lk 13:28. See: TDNT—1:641, 110; BAGD—147d; THAYER—106a.

1031. **βρύχω** {1x} **bruchō**, *broo'-kho;* a primary verb; to *grate* the teeth (in pain or rage):—gnash {1x}.

Brucho means primarily, "to bite or eat greedily" and denotes "to grind or gnash with the teeth," Acts 7:54. See: TDNT—1:641, 110; BAGD—148a; THAYER—106b.

1032. **βρύω** {1x} **bruō**, *broo'-o;* a primary verb; to be full to bursting, *to swell* out, i.e. (by impl.) to *gush:*—send forth {1x}.

Bruo means "to be full to bursting," was used of the earth in producing vegetation, of plants in putting forth buds; in Jas 3:11 it is said of springs gushing with water, "(doth the fountain) send forth . . . ?" See: BAGD—148a; THAYER—106b.

1033. **βρῶμα** {17x} **brōma**, *bro'-mah;* from the base of *977; food* (lit. or fig.), espec. (cer.) articles allowed or forbidden by the Jewish law:—meat {16x}, victuals {1x}.

Broma frequently translated "meat," and always so except in Mt 14:15, "victuals." See: TDNT—1:642, 111; BAGD—148a; THAYER—106b.

1034. **βρώσιμος** {1x} **brōsimŏs**, *bro'-sim-os;* from *1035; eatable:*—meat {1x}.

Brosimos signifying "eatable," is found in Lk 24:41: "And while they yet believed not for joy, and wondered, He said unto them, Have ye here any meat?" "Meat" is defined in vs. 42 as broiled fish and honeycomb. See: BAGD—148b; THAYER—106c.

1035. **βρῶσις** {11x} **brōsis**, *bro'-sis;* from the base of *977;* (abstr.) *eating* (lit. or fig.); by extens. (concr.) *food* (lit. or fig.):—eating {1x}, morsel of meat {1x}, food {1x}, meat {6x}, rust {2x}.

Brosis denotes **(1)** "the act of eating," e.g., Rom 14:17; **(2)** is said of rust, Mt 6:19–20; or, more usually **(3)** "that which is eaten, food, meat," Jn 4:32; 6:27, 55; Col 2:16; Heb 12:16 ("morsel of meat"); **(4)** "food," 2 Cor 9:10; **(5)** "eating," 1 Cor 8:4. See: TDNT—1:642, 111; BAGD—148b; THAYER—106c.

1036. **βυθίζω** {2x} **buthizō**, *boo-thid'-zo;* from *1037;* to *sink;* by impl. to *drown:*—begin to sink {1x}, drown {1x}.

This word means "to plunge into the deep, to sink" [*buthos*, "bottom, the deep, the sea", akin to *bathos*, "depth," and *abussos*, "bottomless," and Eng., "bath,"] and is used **(1)** in Lk 5:7 of the "sinking" of a boat; and **(2)** metaphorically in 1 Ti 6:9, of the effect of foolish and hurtful lusts, which "drown men in destruction and perdition." See: BAGD—148c; THAYER—106c.

1037. **βυθός** {1x} **buthŏs**, *boo-thos';* a var. of *899; depth,* i.e. (by impl.) the *sea:*—deep {1x}.

Buthos, "a depth," is used in the NT only in the natural sense, of the sea 2 Cor 11:25. See: BAGD—148c; THAYER—106c.

1038. **βυρσεύς** {3x} **bursĕus**, *boorce-yooce';* from βύρσα **bursa** (a *hide*); a *tanner:*—tanner {1x}.

Burseus is "a tanner" (from *bursa*, "a hide"), and occurs in Acts 9:43; 10:6, 32. See: BAGD—148d; THAYER—106d.

1039. **βύσσινος** {4x} **bussinŏs**, *boos'-see-nos;* from *1040;* made of *linen* (neut. a linen *cloth*):—fine linen {4x}.

Bussinos is an adjective denoting "made of fine linen." This is used **(1)** of the clothing of the mystic Babylon, Rev 18:12; 16, and **(2)** of the suitable attire of the Lamb's wife, Rev 19:8, 14, figuratively describing "the righteous acts of the saints. The presumption of Babylon is conspicuous in that she arrays herself in that which alone befits the bride of Christ. See: BAGD—148d; THAYER—106d.

1040. **βύσσος** {2x} **bussŏs**, *boos'-sos;* of Heb. or. [948]; white *linen:* fine linen {2x}.

Bussos is "fine linen," made from a special species of flax. **(1)** In Lk 16:19 it is the clothing of the "rich man"; and **(2)** it is one of the products of mystery Babylon, Rev 18:12. See: BAGD—148d; THAYER—106d.

1041. **βῶμος** {1x} **bōmŏs**, *bo'-mos;* from the base of *939;* prop. a *stand,* i.e. (spec.) an *altar:*—altar {1x}.

Bomos is properly, "an elevated place" and always denotes either a pagan "altar" or an "altar" reared without divine appointment. In the NT the only place where this is found is Acts 17:23, as this is the only mention of such. Syn.: *Bomos* refers to the heathen altar and thysiasterion (2379) refers to the altar of the true God. See: BAGD—148d; THAYER—106d.

Γ

1042. **γαββαθά** {1x} **gabbatha**, *gab-bath-ah';* of Chald. or. [comp. 1355]; *the knoll; gabbatha,* a vernacular term for the Roman tribunal in Jerusalem:—*Gabbatha* {1x}. See: BAGD—149a; THAYER—107a.

1043. **Γαβριήλ** {2x} **Gabriēl**, *gab-ree-ale';* of Heb. or. [1403]; *Gabriel,* an archangel:—*Gabriel* {2x}. See: BAGD—149a; THAYER—107b.

1044. **γάγγραινα** {1x} **gaggraina**, *gang'-graheenah;* from γραίνω **grainō** (to *gnaw*); an *ulcer* ("gangrene"); an eating sore:—canker {1x}.

Gaggraina is "an eating sore," spreading corruption and producing mortification, is used, in 2 Ti 2:17, of errorists in the church, who, pretending to give true spiritual food, produce spiritual gangrene ("canker"). See: BAGD—149a; THAYER—107b.

1045. **Γάδ** {1x} **Gad**, *gad;* of Heb. or. [1410]; *Gad,* a tribe of Isr.:—*Gad* {1x}. See: BAGD—149a; THAYER—107b

1046. **Γαδαρηνός** {3x} **Gadarēnŏs**, *gad-aray-nos';* from Γαδαρά (a town E. of the Jordan); a *Gadarene* or inhab. of Gadara:—Gadarene {3x}. See: BAGD—149a; THAYER—107b.

1047. **γάζα** {1x} **gaza**, *gad'-zah;* of for. or.; a *treasure:*—treasure {1x}.

Gaza signifies "royal treasure" and occurs in Acts 8:27. See: BAGD—149b; THAYER—107c.

1048. **Γάζα** {1x} **Gaza**, *gad'-zah;* of Heb. or. [5804]; *Gazah* (i.e. *Azzah*), a place in Pal.:—*Gaza* {1x}. See: BAGD—149b; THAYER—107c.

1049. **γαζοφυλάκιον** {5x} **gazŏphulakiŏn**, *gad-zof-oo-lak'-ee-on;* from *1047* and *5438;* a *treasure-house,* i.e. a court in the temple for the collection-boxes:—treasury {5x}.

This word comes from *gaza*, "a treasure," *phulake*, "a guard," is used by Josephus for a special room in the women's court in the Temple in which gold and silver bullion was kept. This seems to be referred to in Jn 8:20; in Mk 12:41 (twice), 43 and Lk 21:1. It is used of the trumpet-shaped or ram's-horn-shaped chests, into which the temple offerings of the people were cast. There were 13 chests, six for such gifts in general, seven for distinct purposes. Syn.: 2878. See: BAGD—149b; THAYER—107d.

1050. **Γάϊος** {5x} **Gaïŏs**, *gah'-ee-os;* of Lat. or.; *Gâus* (i.e. *Caius*), a Chr.:—Gaius (of Corinth) {2x}, Gaius (of Macedonia) {1x}, Gaius (of Derbe) {1x}, Gaius (a Christian) {1x}. See: BAGD—149c; THAYER—108a.

1051. **γάλα** {5x} **gala**, *gal'-ah;* of uncert. aff.; *milk* (fig.):—milk {5x}.

Gala is used **(1)** literally (1 Cor 9:7) and **(2)** metaphorically, **(2a)** of rudimentary spiritual teaching (1 Cor 3:2, Heb 5:12, 13; 1 Pet 2:2). **(2b)** The nourishment may be understood as of that spiritually rational nature which, acting through the regenerate mind, develops spiritual growth. God's Word is not given so that it is impossible to understand it, or that it requires a special class of men to interpret it; its character is such that the Holy Spirit who gave it can unfold its truths even to the young convert (cf. 1 Jn 2:27). See: TDNT—1:645, 111; BAGD—149c; THAYER—108b.

1052. **Γαλάτης** {2x} **Galatēs**, *gal-at'-ace;* from *1053;* a *Galatian* or inhab. of Galatia:—Galatians {2x}. See: BAGD—149d; THAYER—108b.

1053. **Γαλατία** {4x} **Galatia**, *gal-at-ee'-ah;* of for. or.; *Galatia,* a region of Asia:—Galatia {4x}. See: BAGD—149d; THAYER—108b.

1054. **Γαλατικός** {2x} **Galatikŏs**, *gal-at-ee-kos';* from *1053; Galatic* or relating to Galatia:—of Galatia {2x}. See: BAGD—150a; THAYER—108b.

1055. **γαλήνη** {3x} **Galēnē**, *gal-ay'-nay;* of uncert. der.; *tranquillity:*—calm {3x}. See: BAGD—150b; THAYER—108b.

1056. **Γαλιλαία** {63x} **Galilaia**, *gal-il-ah'-yah,* of Heb. or. [1551]; *Galilœa* (i.e. the heathen *circle*), a region of Pal.:—Galilee {63x}. See: BAGD—150b; THAYER—108c.

1057. **Γαλιλαῖος** {11x} **Galilaiŏs**, *gal-ee-lah'-yos;* from *1056; Galilœan* or belonging to Galilæa:—Galilæan {8x}, of Galilee {3x}. See: BAGD—150c; THAYER—108c.

1058. **Γαλλίων** {3x} **Galliōn**, *gal-lee'-own;* of Lat. or.; *Gallion* (i.e. *Gallio*), a Roman officer:—Gallio {3x}. See: BAGD—150c; THAYER—108d.

1059. **Γαμαλιήλ** {2x} **Gamaliēl**, *gam-al-ee-ale';* of Heb. or. [1583]; *Gamaliel* (i.e. *Gamliel*), an Isr.:—*Gamaliel* {2x}. See: BAGD—150c; THAYER—108d.

1060. **γαμέω** {29x} **gamĕō**, *gam-eh'-o;* from *1062;* to *wed* (of either sex):—marry {24x}, married {3x}, marry a wife {2x}.

This word means "to marry" and is used **(1)** of "the man," Mt 5:32; 19:9, 10; 22:25 ("married a wife"); v. 30; 24:38; Mk 6:17; 10:11; 12:25; Lk 14:20; 16:18; 17:27, ("married wives"); 20:34, 35; 1 Cor 7:28 (1st part); v. 33; **(2)** of "the woman," **(2a)** in the active voice, Mk 10:12; 1 Cor 7:28 (last part); ver. 34; 1 Ti 5:11, 14; **(2b)** in the passive voice, 1 Cor 7:39; **(3)** of "both sexes," 1 Cor 7:9, 10, 36; 1 Ti 4:3. See: TDNT—1:648, 111; BAGD—150d; THAYER—108d.

1061. **γαμίσκω** {1x} **gamiskō**, *gam-is'-ko;* from *1062;* to *espouse* (a daughter to a husband):—give in marriage {1x}. See: BAGD—151b; THAYER—109a.

1062. **γάμος** {16x} **gamŏs**, *gam'-os;* of uncert. aff.; *nuptials:*—marriage {9x}, wedding {6x}.

This word means "a wedding," especially a wedding "feast." It is used **(1)** in the plural in the following passages: Mt 22:2, 3, 4, 9 (in verses 11, 12, it is used in the singular, in connection with the wedding garment); 25:10; Lk 12:36; 14:8; **(2)** in the following it signifies a wedding itself, Jn 2:1, 2; Heb 13:4; and **(3)** figuratively in Rev 19:7, of the marriage of the Lamb; in v. 9 it is used in connection with the supper, the wedding supper, not the wedding itself, as in v. 7. See: TDNT—1:648, 111; BAGD—151b; THAYER—109b.

1063. **γάρ** {1067x} **gar**, *gar;* a primary particle; prop. assigning a *reason* (used in argument, explanation or intensification; often with other particles):—for {1027x}, not tr {12x}, misc. {28x}, = and, as, because (that), but, even, indeed, no doubt, seeing, then, therefore, verily, what, why, yet. See: BAGD—151c; THAYER—109b.

1064. **γαστήρ** {9x} **gastēr**, *gas-tare';* of uncert. der.; the *stomach;* by anal. the *matrix;* fig. a *gourmand:*—be with child + 1722 + 2192 {5x}, with child + 1722 + 2192 {2x}, womb {1x}, belly {1x}.

This word means womb or be with child. But in Titus 1:12, by synecdoche (a figure of speech in which the part is put for the whole, or vice versa), it is used to denote "gluttons" ("bellies"). See: BAGD—152c; THAYER—110d.

1065. **γέ** {11x} **gĕ**, *gheh;* a primary particle of *emphasis* or *qualification* (often used with other particles pref.):—yet {2x}, at least {1x}, beside {1x}, doubtless {1x}, not tr {6x}. See: BAGD—152d; THAYER—110d.

1066. **Γεδεών** {1x} **Gĕdĕōn**, *ghed-eh-own';* of Heb. or. [1439]; *Gedeon* (i.e. *Gid[e]on*), an Isr.:—*Gedeon* (Gideon) {1x}. See: BAGD—153b; THAYER—111c.

1067. **γέεννα** {12x} **gĕĕnna**, *gheh'-en-nah;* of Heb. or. [1516 and 2011]; *valley of* (the son of) *Hinnom; ge-henna* (or *Ge-Hinnom*), a valley of Jerusalem, used (fig.) as a name for the place (or state) of everlasting punishment:—hell {9x}, hell fire + 3588 + 4442 {3x}.

Geenna **(1)** represents the Hebrew Ge-Hinnom (the valley of Tophet); **(2)** it is found twelve times in the NT, eleven of which are in the Synoptists, in every instance as uttered by the Lord Himself. **(2a)** He who says to his brother, Thou fool will be in danger of "the hell of fire," Mt 5:22; **(2b)** it is better to pluck out (a metaphorical description of irrevocable law) an eye that causes its possessor to stumble, than that his "whole body be cast into hell," Mt 5:29; similarly with the hand, v. 30; **(2c)** in Mt 18:8, 9, the admonitions are repeated, with an additional mention of the foot; here, too, the warning concerns the person himself (for which obviously the "body" stands in chapt. 5); **(2d)** in Mt 18: 8, "the eternal fire" is mentioned as the doom, the character of the region standing for the region itself, the two being combined in the phrase "the hell of fire," Mt 18: 9. **(2e)** To the passage in Matt. 18, that in Mark 9:43–47, is parallel; here to the word "hell" are applied the extended descriptions "the unquenchable fire" and "where their worm dieth not and the fire is not quenched."

(3) That God, "after He hath killed, hath power to cast into hell," **(3a)** is assigned as a reason why He should be feared with the fear that keeps from evil doing, Lk 12:5; **(3b)** the parallel passage to this in Mt 10:28 declares, not the casting in, but the doom which follows, namely, the destruction (not the loss of being, but of well-being) of "both soul and body." **(4)** In Mt 23 the Lord denounces the scribes and Pharisees, who in proselytizing a person "make him two-fold more a son of hell" than themselves (v. 15), **(4a)** the phrase here being expressive of moral characteristics, and **(4b)** declares the impossibility of their escaping "the judgment of hell," v. 33. **(5)** In Jas 3:6 "hell" is described as the source of the evil done by misuse of the tongue; here the word stands for the powers of darkness, whose characteristics and destiny are those of "hell." **(6)** For terms descriptive of "hell," see e.g., Mt 13:42; 25:46; Phil 3:19; 2 Th 1:9; Heb 10:39; 2 Pet 2:17; Jude 13; Rev 2:11; 19:20; 20:6, 10, 14; 21:8. **(7)** The verb tartaroo, translated "cast down to hell" in 2 Pet 2:4, signifies to consign to Tartarus, which is neither Sheol nor hades nor hell, but the place where those angels whose special sin is referred to in that passage are confined "to be reserved unto judgment"; the region is described as "pits of darkness." See: TDNT—1:657, 113; BAGD—153; THAYER—111c.

1068. **Γεθσημανῆ** {2x} **Gĕthsēmanē**, *gheth-say-man-ay';* of Chald. or. [comp. 1660 and 8081]; *oil-press; Gethsemane,* a garden near Jerusalem:—*Gethsemane* {2x}. See: BAGD—153b.111d.

1069. **γείτων** {4x} **gĕitōn**, *ghi'-tone;* from *1093;* a *neighbour* (living in the same land and probably adjoining one's *ground*); by impl. a *friend:*—neighbour {4x}.

Geiton is literally "one living in the same land" and denotes "a neighbor," always plural in the NT, Lk 14:12; 15:6, 9; Jn 9:5. See: BAGD—153c; THAYER—112a.

1070. **γελάω** {2x} **gĕlaō**, *ghel-ah'-o;* of uncert. aff.; to *laugh* (as a sign of joy or satisfaction):—laugh {2x}.

Gelao means "to laugh," is found in Lk 6:21, 25. This signifies loud laughter in contrast to demonstrative weeping. Syn.: 1071, 2606. See: TDNT—1:658, 113; BAGD—153c; THAYER—112a.

1071. **γέλως** {1x} **gĕlōs**, *ghel'-oce;* from *1070; laughter* (as a mark of gratification):—laughter {1x}. Syn.: 1070, 2606. See: TDNT—1:658, 113; BAGD—153c; THAYER—112a.

1072. **γεμίζω** {9x} **gĕmizō**, *ghem-id'-zo;* tran. from *1073;* to *fill* entirely:—fill {7x}, be full {1x}, fill . . . fill {1x}.

Gemizo means "to fill or load full" and is **(1)** used of a boat, Mk 4:37; **(2)** a sponge, Mk 15:36; **(3)** a house, Lk 14:23; **(4)** the belly, Lk 15:16; **(5)** waterpots, Jn 2:1; **(6)** baskets, 6:13; **(7)** bowls, with fire, Rev 8:5; **(8)** the temple, with smoke, Rev 15:8. See: BAGD—153c; THAYER—112a.

1073. **γέμω** {11x} **gĕmō**, *ghem'-o;* a primary verb; to *swell* out, i.e. *be full:*—be full {3x}, full {8x}.

Gemo means **(1)** "to be full, to be heavily laden with," was primarily used of a ship; **(2)** it is chiefly used in the NT of evil contents, such as **(2a)** extortion and excess, Mt 23:25; **(2b)** dead men's bones, Mt 23:27; **(2c)** extortion and wickedness, Lk 11:39; **(2d)** cursing, Rom 3:14; **(2e)** blasphemy, Rev 17:3; **(2f)** abominations, Rev 17: 4; **(2g)** of divine judgments, Rev 15:7; 21:9; **(2h)** of good things, Rev 4:6, 8; 5:8. See: BAGD—153d; THAYER—112a.

1074. **γενεά** {42x} **gĕnĕa**, *ghen-eh-ah';* from (a presumed der. of) *1085;* a *generation;* by impl. an *age* (the period or the persons):—age {2x}, generation {37x}, nation {1x}, time {2x}.

Genea, connected with ginomai (1096), "to become," primarily **(1)** signifies "a begetting, or birth"; hence, that which has been begotten, a family; **(1a)** or successive members of a genealogy (Mt 1:17), or **(1b)** of a race of people, possessed of similar characteristics, pursuits, etc., of a bad character: "Then Jesus answered and said, O faithless and perverse generation (1074), how long shall I be with you?" (Mt 17:17; cf. Mk 9:19; Lk 9:41; 16:8; Acts 2:40); or **(1c)** of the whole multitude of men living at the same time: "Verily I say unto you, This generation shall not pass, till all these things be fulfilled" (Mt 24:34; cf. Mk 13:30; Lk 1:48; 21:32; Phil 2:15), and **(1d)** especially of those of the Jewish race living at the same period: "But whereunto shall I liken this generation? It is like unto children sitting in the markets, and calling unto their fellows" (Mt 11:16). **(2)** Transferred from people to the time in which they lived, the word came to mean "an age," i.e., a period ordinarily occupied by each successive generation, say, of thirty or forty years: "Who in times (*genea*) past suffered all nations to walk in their own ways" (Acts 14:16; cf. 15:21; Eph 3:5; Col 1:26). **(3)** In Eph 3:21 *genea* is combined with aion (165) in a remarkable phrase in a doxology: **(3a)** "Unto him *be* glory in the church by Christ Jesus throughout all ages, world without end. Amen." **(3b)** The word *genea* is to be distinguished from aion, as not denoting a period of unlimited duration. Syn.: 165, 166, 2244, 2250, 5046, 5230. See: TDNT—1:662, 114; BAGD—153d; THAYER—112b.

1075. **γενεαλογέω** {1x} **gĕnĕalŏgĕō**, *ghen-eh-al-og-eh'-o;* from *1074* and *3056;* to *reckon by generations,* i.e. *trace in genealogy:*—count (one's) descent {1x}.

This word means "to reckon or trace a genealogy" and is used, in the passive voice, of Melchizedek in Heb 7:6 "whose descent' is not counted." See: TDNT—1:665, 114; BAGD—154b; THAYER—112c.

1076. **γενεαλογία** {2x} **gĕnĕalŏgia**, *ghen-eh-al-og-ee'-ah;* from the same as *1075; tracing by generations,* i.e. *"genealogy"*:—genealogy {2x}.

This word is used in 1 Ti 1:4 and Tit 3:9, with reference to such "genealogies" as are found in Philo, Josephus and the book of Jubilees, by which Jews traced their descent from the patriarchs and their families, and perhaps also to Gnostic "genealogies" and orders of aeons and spirits. Amongst the Greeks, as well as other nations, mythological stories gathered round the birth and "genealogy" of their heroes. Probably Jewish "genealogical" tales crept into Christian communities. Hence the warnings to Timothy and Titus. See: TDNT—1:663, 114; BAGD—154b; THAYER—112c.

1077. γενέσια {2x} **gĕnĕsia**, *ghen-es'-ee-ah;* neut. plur. of a der. of *1078; birthday* ceremonies:—birthday {2x}.

This word primarily denoted "the festivities of a birthday, a birthday feast," and is found in Mt 14:6 and Mk 6:21. See: BAGD—154c; THAYER—112d.

1078. γένεσις {3x} **genesis**, *ghen'-es-is;* from the same as *1074; nativity;* fig. *nature:*—generation {1x}, nature {1x}, natural {1x}.

Genesis denotes "an origin, a lineage, or birth" **(1)** translated "generation" in Mt 1:1; **(2)** "nature" in Jas 3:6; and **(3)** "natural" in Jas 1:23, describing the face with which one is born. See: BAGD—154d; THAYER—112d.

1079. γενετή {1x} **gĕnĕtē**, *ghen-et-ay;* fem. of a presumed der. of the base of *1074; birth:*—birth {1x}.

This word means "a being born, or the hour of birth" and is used in Jn 9:1 of a man born blind. See: BAGD—155a; THAYER—112d.

1080. γεννάω {97x} **gĕnnaō**, *ghen-nah'-o;* from a var. of *1085;* to *procreate* (prop. of the father, but by extens. of the mother); fig. to *regenerate:*—begat {49x}, be born {39x}, bear {2x}, gender {2x}, bring forth {1x}, be delivered {1x}, conceive {1x}, make {1x}, spring {1x}.

Gennao, as a verb, **(1)** means "to beget" and in the passive voice means "to be born." **(2)** It is chiefly used of men "begetting" children (Mt 1:2–16). **(3)** A woman "brings forth" a child, "is delivered" (Lk 1:57) or "bares" the child (Lk 1:13; 23:29). **(4)** The child is said to "be born" (Jn 16:21). **(5)** In Gal 4:24, it is used allegorically, to contrast Jews under bondage to the Law, and spiritual Israel to contrast the natural birth of Ishmael and the supernatural birth of Isaac. **(6)** In Mt 1:20 it is used of conception, "that which is conceived in her." **(7)** It is used of the act of God in the birth of Christ, (Acts 13:33; Heb 1:5; 5:5, quoted from Ps 2:7, none of which indicate that Christ became the Son of God at His birth). **(8)** It is used metaphorically **(8a)** in the writings of the apostle John, of the gracious act of God in conferring upon those who believe the nature and disposition of "children," imparting to them spiritual life (Jn 3:3, 5, 7; 1 Jn 2:29; 3:9; 4:7; 5:1, 4, 18); **(8b)** of one who by means of preaching the gospel becomes the human instrument in the impartation of spiritual life (1 Cor 4:15; Philem 10); **(8c)** in 2 Pet 2:12 with reference to the evil men whom the apostle describes as "natural brute beasts"; **(9)** in the sense of gendering strife (2 Ti 2:23). **(10)** Beget in English means to bring into a special relationship. The "be" is intensive and "get" means to bring to one's self. Jesus, as the "only begotten of the Father" means that even though He had the unique and equal relationship within the trinity in eternity past, He took upon Himself the likeness of sinful flesh, dwelt among men, was tempted in all ways, yet without sin, submitted to the death on the cross, was raised on the third day, and ascended to the right hand of the Father. He was always uniquely related to the Father, but even more so now as He is the only unique Son of God, the only sacrifice to remove sins and restore fallen man to God. **(10)** In John 3:3, 5, 7, the adverb anothen (509) "anew, or from above," accompanies the simple verb *gennao.* Syn.: 313, 616, 738, 1084, 1085, 1626, 5088. See: TDNT—1:665, 114; BAGD—155b; THAYER—113a.

1081. γέννημα {9x} **gĕnnēma**, or γένημα **gĕnēma**, *ghen'-nay-mah;* from *1080; offspring;* by anal. *produce* (lit. or fig.):—fruit {5x}, generation {4x}.

This word means "to beget" and denotes "the offspring of men and animals," Mt 3:7; 12:34; 23:33; Lk 3:7. See: TDNT—1:672, 114; BAGD—155d; THAYER—113c.

1082. Γεννησαρέτ {3x} **Gĕnnēsarĕt**, *ghen-nay-sar-et';* of Heb. or. [comp. 3672]; *Gennesaret* (i.e. *Kinnereth*), a lake and plain in Pal.:—*Gennesaret* {3x}. See: BAGD—156a; THAYER—113c.

1083. γέννησις {2x} **gĕnnēsis**, *ghen'-nay-sis;* from *1080; nativity:*—birth {2x}.

Gennesis is "a birth, begetting, producing" and is used in Mt 1:18 and Lk 1:14. See: BAGD—156a.113d.

1084. γεννητός {2x} **gĕnnētŏs**, *ghen-nay-tos';* from *1080; born:*—that is born {2x}.

Gennetos, as an adjective, is translated "born" and is used in Mt 11:11: "Verily I say unto you, Among them that are born of women there hath not risen a greater than John the Baptist" (cf. Lk 7:28 - a periphrasis for "men," and suggestive of frailty). Syn.: 313, 616, 738, 1080, 1085, 1626, 5088. See: TDNT—1:672, 114; BAGD—156a; THAYER—113d.

1085. γένος {21x} **gĕnŏs**, *ghen'-os;* from *1096; "kin"* (abstr. or concr., lit. or fig., indiv. or collect.):—kind {5x}, kindred {3x}, offspring {3x}, nation {2x}, stock {2x}, born {2x}, diversity {1x}, country {1x}, countryman {1x}, generation {1x}.

Genos, as a noun, means "a generation, kind, stock," is used in the dative case, with the article, to signify "by race": "And found a certain Jew named Aquila, born (*genos*) in Pontus" (Acts 18:2; cf. vs 24). Syn.: 313, 616, 738, 1080, 1084, 1626, 5088. See: TDNT—1:684, 117; BAGD—156b; THAYER—113d.

1086. Γεργεσηνός {1x} **Gĕrgĕsēnŏs**, *gher-ghes-ay-nos';* of Heb. or. [1622]; a *Gergesene* (i.e. *Girgashite*) or one of the aborigines of Pal.:—Gergesenes {1x}. See: BAGD—156d; THAYER—114a.

1087. γερουσία {1x} **gĕrŏusia**, *gher-oo-see'-ah;* from *1088;* the *eldership,* i.e. (collect.) the Jewish *Sanhedrin:*—senate {1x}.

This word means "a council of elders" (from *geron,* "an old man," a term which early assumed a political sense among the Greeks, the notion of age being merged in that of dignity), is used in Acts 5:21, apparently epexegetically of the preceding word *sunedrion,* "council," the Sanhedrin. See: BAGD—156d; THAYER—114b.

1088. γέρων {1x} **gĕrōn**, *gher'-own;* of uncert. aff. [comp. *1094*]; *aged:*—old {1x}.

Geron denotes "an old man", Jn 3:4. See: BAGD—157a; THAYER—114b.

1089. γευομαι {15x} **gĕuŏmai**, *ghyoo'-om-ahee;* a primary verb; to *taste;* by impl. to *eat;* fig. to *experience* (good or ill):—eat {3x}, taste {12x}.

Geuomai means primarily, "to cause to taste, to give one a taste of," is used in the middle voice and denotes **(1)** "to taste," its usual meaning; **(2)** "to take food, to eat," Acts 10:10; 20:11; 23:14. See: TDNT—1:675, 117; BAGD—157a; THAYER—114b.

1090. γεωργέω {1x} **gĕōrgĕō**, *gheh-or-gheh'-o;* from *1092;* to *till* (the soil):—dress {1x}.

This word means "to till the ground," is used in the passive voice in Heb 6:7, ". . . dressed. See: BAGD—157b; THAYER—114c.

1091. γεώργιον {1x} **gĕōrgiŏn**, *gheh-ore'-ghee-on;* neut. of a (presumed) der. of *1092; cultivable,* i.e. a *farm:*—husbandry {1x}.

Georgion denotes "tillage, cultivation, husbandry," 1 Cor 3:9, where the local church is described under this metaphor ("tillage"), suggestive of the diligent toil of the apostle and his fellow missionaries, both in the ministry of the gospel, and the care of the church at Corinth; suggestive, too, of the effects in spiritual fruitfulness. See: BAGD—157b; THAYER—114c.

1092. γεωργός {19x} **gĕōrgŏs**, *gheh-ore-gos';* from *1093* and the base of *2041;* a *land-worker,* i.e. *farmer:*—husbandman {19x}.

Georgos from *ge,* "land, ground," and *ergo* (or *erdo*), "to do" [Eng., "George"], denotes **(1)** "a husbandman," a tiller of the ground, 2 Ti 2:6; Jas 5:7; **(2)** "a vinedresser," Mt 21:33–35, 38, 40, 41; Mk 12:1, 2, 7, 9; Lk 20:9, 10, 14, 16; Jn 15:1, where Christ speaks of the Father as the "Husbandman," Himself as the Vine, His disciples as the branches, the object being to bear much fruit, life in Christ producing the fruit of the Spirit, i.e., character and ways in conformity to Christ. See: BAGD—157b; THAYER—114c.

1093. γῆ {252x} **gē**, *ghay;* contr. from a primary word; *soil;* by extension a *region,* or the solid part or the whole of the *terrene* globe (incl. the occupants in each application):—earth 188, land {42x}, ground {18x}, country {2x}, world {1x}, earthly + 1537 + 3588 {1x}.

Ge denotes **(1)** "earth as arable land," e.g., Mt 13:5, 8, 23; **(2)** in 1 Cor 15:47 it is said of the "earthly" material of which "the first man" was made, suggestive of frailty; **(3)** "the earth as a whole, the world," **(3a)** in contrast, whether to the heavens, e.g., Mt 5:18, 35, or **(3b)** to heaven, the abode of God, e.g., Mt 6:19, where the context suggests the "earth" as a place characterized by mutability and weakness; **(3c)** in Col 3:2 the same contrast is presented by the word "above"; **(4)** in Jn 3:31 ("of the earth, earthly") it describes one whose origin and nature are "earthly" and whose speech is characterized thereby, in contrast with Christ as the One from heaven; **(5)** in Col 3:5 the physical members are said to be "upon the earth," as a sphere where, as potential instruments of moral evils, they are, by metonymy, spoken of as the evils themselves; **(6)** "the inhabited earth," e.g., Lk 21:35; Acts 1:8; 8:33; 10:12; 11:6; 17:26; 22:22; Heb 11:13; Rev 13:8. **(7)** In the following the phrase "on the earth" signifies "among men," Lk 12:49; 18:8; Jn 17:4, **(8)** "a country, territory," e.g. Lk 4:25; Jn 3:22; **(9)** "the ground," e.g., Mt 10:29; Mk 4:26, "(into the) ground"; **(10)** "land," e.g., Mk 4:1; Jn 21:8–9, 11. **(11)** Cf. Eng. words beginning with ge–, e.g., "geodetic," "geodesy," "geology," "geometry," "geography." Syn.: 3625. See: TDNT—1:677, 116; BAGD—157c; THAYER—114d.

1094. γῆρας {1x} **gēras**, *ghay'-ras;* akin to *1088; senility:*—old age {1x}. See: BAGD—157d; THAYER—115a.

1095. γηράσκω {2x} **gēraskō**, *ghay-ras'-ko;* from *1094;* to *be senescent:*—be old {1x}, wax old {1x}.

Gerasko signifies **(1)** "to grow old," Jn 21:18 ("when thou shalt be old") and **(2)** Heb 8:13 ("that which . . . waxeth old"). See: BAGD—158a; THAYER—115a.

1096. γίνομαι {678x} **ginŏmai**, *ghin'-om-ahee;* a prol. and mid. voice form of a primary verb; to *cause to be* ("*gen*"-erate), i.e. (refl.) to *become* (*come into being*), used with great latitude (lit., fig., intens., etc.):—be {255x}, come to pass {82x}, be made {69x}, be done {63x}, come {52x}, become {47x}, God forbid + 3361 {15x}, arise {13x}, have {5x}, be fulfilled {3x}, be married to {3x}, be preferred {3x}, not tr {14x}, vr done {2x}, misc. {4x} = be assembled, befall, behave self, be brought (to pass), continue, be divided, draw, be ended, fall, be finished, follow, be found, grow, happen, be kept, be ordained to be, partake, pass, be performed, be published, require, seem, be showed, × soon as it was, sound, be taken, be turned, use, wax, will, would, be wrought.

Ginomai, as a verb, means "to become, to come into existence" and is used in the sense of **I. "taking place after"** and translated **(1)** "there followed" (Rev 8:7; cf. 11:15, 19). **(2)** It is translated "by means of [a death] having taken place": "And for this cause He is the mediator of the new testament, that by means of death, for the redemption of the transgressions *that were* under the first testament, they which are called might receive the promise of eternal inheritance" (Heb 9:15), referring, not to the circumstances of a testamentary disposition, but to the sacrifice of Christ as the basis of the New Covenant. Syn.: 190, 201, 402, 1377, 1502, 1811, 1837, 1872, 2614, 2628, 3877, 4042, 4870, 5117, 5247, 5564, 5602. **II. It can also be translated "arise": (1)** of a great tempest on the sea (Mt 8:24; Mk 4:37); **(2)** of persecution (Mt 13:21; Mk 4:17, this might be translated "taketh place"); **(3)** of a tumult (Mt 27:24, kjv, "made"); **(4)** of a flood (Lk 6:48); **(5)** a famine (Lk 15:14); **(6)** a questioning (Jn 3:25); **(7)** a murmuring (Acts 6:1); **(8)** a stir in the city (Acts 19:23); **(9)** a dissension (Acts 23:7); **(10)** a great clamor (Acts 23:9). Syn.: 305, 393, 450, 1326, 1453, 1525, 1817, 4911. See: TDNT—1:681, 117; BAGD—158a; THAYER—115b.

1097. **γινώσκω** {223x} **ginōskō**, *ghin-oce'-ko;* a prol. form of a primary verb; to "*know*" (absolutely) in a great variety of applications and with many impl. (as follow, with others not thus clearly expressed):—know {196x}, perceive {9x}, understand {8x}, misc.10x} = allow, be aware (of), feel, have knowledge, be resolved, can speak, be sure.

Ginosko (1097) signifies **(1)** "to be taking in knowledge, to come to know, recognize, understand," or "to understand completely," e.g., Mk 13:28, 29; Jn 13:12; 15:18; 21:17; 2 Cor 8:9; Heb 10:34; 1 John 2:5; 4:2, 6 (twice), 7, 13; 5:2, 20; **(2)** in its past tenses it frequently means "to know in the sense of realizing," the aorist or point tense usually indicating definiteness, Mt 13:11; Mk 7:24; Jn 7:26; in 10:38 "that ye may know (aorist tense) and understand, (present tense)"; 19:4; Acts 1:7; 17:19; Rom 1:21; 1 Cor 2:11 (2nd part), 14; 2 Cor 2:4; Eph 3:19; 6:22; Phil 2:19; 3:10; 1 Th 3:5; 2 Ti 2:19; Jas 2:20; 1 Jn 2:13 (twice), 14; 3:6; 4:8; 2 John 1; Rev 2:24; 3:3, 9. **(3)** In the passive voice, it often signifies "to become known," e.g., Mt 10:26; Phil 4:5. **(4)** In the sense of complete and absolute understanding on God's part, it is used, e.g., in Lk 16:15; Jn 10:15 (of the Son as well as the Father); 1 Cor 3:20. **(5)** In Lk 12:46 it is rendered "He is . . . aware."

(6) In the NT *ginosko* frequently indicates a relation between the person "knowing" and the object known; in this respect, what is "known" is of value or importance to the one who knows, and hence the establishment of the relationship, e.g., especially **(6a)** of God's "knowledge," 1 Cor 8:3, "if any man love God, the same is known of Him"; **(6b)** Gal 4:9, "to be known of God"; here the "knowing" suggests approval and bears the meaning "to be approved"; so in 2 Ti 2:19; cf. Jn 10:14, 27; **(6c)** The same idea of appreciation as well as "knowledge" underlies several statements concerning the "knowledge" of God and His truth on the part of believers, e.g., Jn 8:32; 14:20, 31; 17:3; Gal 4:9 (1st part); 1 Jn 2:3–13, 14; 4:6, 8, 16; 5:20; **(6c1)** such "knowledge" is obtained, not by mere intellectual activity, but by operation of the Holy Spirit consequent upon acceptance of Christ. **(6c2)** Nor is such "knowledge" marked by finality; see e.g., 2 Pet 3:18. **(7)** The verb is also used to convey the thought of connection or union, as between man and woman, Matt 1:25; Luke 1:34. **(8)** *Ginosko,* as a verb, means "to know by observation and experience" is translated "to know" (to learn - Mk 15:45; Jn 12:9). Syn.: See discussion under oida (1492); epiginosko (1921). See also: 198, 1097, 1107, 1110, 1492, 1921, 1467, 1922, 1987, 3129, 3453. See: TDNT—1:689, 119; BAGD—160d; THAYER—117b.

1098. **γλεῦκος** {1x} **glĕukŏs**, *glyoo'-kos;* akin to *1099; sweet* wine, i.e. (prop.) *must* (fresh juice), but used of the more saccharine (and therefore highly inebriating) fermented *wine:*—new wine {1x}.

Gleukos denotes sweet "new wine," or must, Acts 2:13, where the accusation shows that it was intoxicant and must have been undergoing fermentation some time. See: BAGD—162a; THAYER—118c.

1099. **γλυκύς** {4x} **glukus**, *gloo-koos';* of uncert. aff.; *sweet* (i.e. not bitter nor salt)[cf. glucose]:—sweet {3x}, fresh {1x}.

This word occurs in Jas 3:11, 12 ("fresh" in this verse); Rev 10:9, 10. See: BAGD—162a; THAYER—118c.

1100. **γλῶσσα** {50x} **glōssa**, *gloce-sah';* of uncert. aff.; the *tongue;* by impl. a *language* (spec., one naturally unacquired):—tongue {50x}.

Glossa is used of **(1)** the "tongues . . . like as of fire" which appeared at Pentecost; **(2)** "the tongue," as an organ of speech, e.g., Mk 7:33; Rom 3:13; 14:11; 1 Cor 14:9; Phil 2:11; Jas 1:26; 3:5, 6, 8; 1 Pet 3:10; 1 Jn 3:18; Rev 16:10;

(3) "a language," **(3a)** coupled with phule, "a tribe," laos, "a people," ethnos, "a nation," seven times in the Apocalypse, 5:9; 7:9; 10:11; 11:9; 13:7; 14:6; 17:15; **(3b)** the supernatural gift of speaking in another language without its having been learnt; in Acts 2:4–13 the circumstances are recorded from the viewpoint of the hearers; to those in whose language the utterances were made it appeared as a supernatural phenomenon; to others, the stammering of drunkards; what was uttered was not addressed primarily to the audience but consisted in recounting "the mighty works of God"; cf. 2:46; **(3c)** in 1 Cor., chapters 12 and 14, the use of the gift of "tongues" is mentioned as exercised in the gatherings of local churches; 12:10 speaks of the gift in general terms, and couples with it that of "the interpretation of tongues"; chapt. 14 gives instruction concerning the use of the gift, the paramount object being the edification of the church; unless the "tongue" was interpreted the speaker would speak "not unto men, but unto God,"; 14:2; he would edify himself alone, v. 4, unless he interpreted, v. 5, in which case his interpretation would be of the same value as the superior gift of prophesying, as he would edify the church, vv. 4–6; he must pray that he may interpret, v. 13; if there were no interpreter, he must keep silence, v. 28, for all things were to be done "unto edifying," v. 26. "If I come . . . speaking with tongues, what shall I profit you," says the apostle (expressing the great object in all oral ministry), "unless I speak to you either by way of revelation, or of knowledge, or of prophesying, or of teaching?" (v. 6). "Tongues" were for a sign, not to believers, but to unbelievers, v. 22, and especially to unbelieving Jews (see v. 21): cf. the passages in the Acts.

(4) There is no evidence of the continuance of this gift after apostolic times nor indeed in the later times of the apostles themselves; this provides confirmation of the fulfillment in this way of 1 Cor 13:8, that this gift would cease in the churches, just as would "prophecies" and "knowledge" in the sense of knowledge received by immediate supernatural power (cf. 14:6). The completion of the Holy Scriptures has provided the churches with all that is necessary for individual and collective guidance, instruction, and edification. Syn.: 1258, 2804. See: TDNT—1:689, 119; BAGD—162b; THAYER—118c.

1101. **γλωσσόκομον** {2x} **glōssŏkŏmŏn**, *glocesok'-om-on;* from *1100* and the base of *2889;* prop. a *case* (to keep mouthpieces of wind-instruments in) i.e. (by extens.) a *casket* or (spec.) *purse:*—bag {2x}.

This word denotes "a small box" for any purpose, but especially a "casket or purse," to keep money in. It is used of the "bag" which Judas carried, Jn 12:6; 13:29. See: BAGD—162d; THAYER—119a.

1102. **γναφεύς** {1x} **gnaphĕus**, *gnaf-yuce';* by var. for a der. from κνάπτω **knaptō** (to *tease* cloth); a cloth-*dresser:*—fuller {1x}. See: BAGD—162d; THAYER—119a.

1103. **γνήσιος** {4x} **gnēsiŏs**, *gnay'-see-os;* from the same as *1077; legitimate* (of birth), i.e. *genuine:*—own {2x}, sincerity {1x}, true {1x}.

Gnesios, as an adjective, means primarily "lawfully begotten"; hence, "true, genuine, sincere" and is used **(1)** in the apostle's exhortation to his "true yoke-fellow": "And I intreat thee also, true yokefellow, help those women which laboured with me in the gospel, with Clement also, and *with* other my fellow-labourers, whose names *are* in the book of life" (Phil 4:3). It also speaks of **(2)** the "sincerity of love", 2 Cor 8:8; and **(3)** "one's own son", 1 Ti 1:2 and Titus 1:4. Syn.: 225, 226, 227, 228, 230, 1104. See: TDNT—1:727, 125; BAGD—162d; THAYER—119a.

1104. **γνησίως** {1x} **gnēsiōs**, *gnay-see'-oce;* adv. from *1103; genuinely,* i.e. *really:*—naturally {1x}.

Gnesios, as an adverb, means "sincerely, honorably" and is rendered "naturally": "For I have no man likeminded, who will naturally care for your state" (Phil 2:20). Syn.: 225, 226, 227, 228, 230, 1103. See: BAGD—163a; THAYER—119a.

1105. **γνόφος** {1x} **gnŏphŏs**, *gnof'-os;* akin to *3509; gloom* (as of a storm):—blackness {1x}.

Ghophos in Heb 12:18 denotes "blackness, gloom," seems to have been associated with the idea of a tempest and is related to *skotos,* "darkness." Syn.: 887, 2217, 4655. See: BAGD—163a; THAYER—119b.

1106. **γνώμη** {9x} **gnōmē**, *gno'-may; from 1097; cognition,* i.e. (subj.) *opinion,* or (obj.) *resolve* (*counsel, consent,* etc.):—judgment {3x}, mind {2x}, purpose + 1096 {1x}, advice {1x}, will {1x}, agree + 4160 + 3391 {1x}.

This word comes from "to know, perceive" and **(1)** firstly means "the faculty or knowledge, reason"; then, **(2)** "that which is thought or known, one's mind." **(3)** Under this heading there are various meanings: **(3a)** a view, judgment, opinion, 1 Cor 1:10; Philem 14; Rev 17:13, 17; **(3b)** an opinion as to what ought to be done, either **(3b1)** by oneself, and so a resolve, or purpose, Acts 20:3; or **(3b2)** by others, and so, judgment, advice, 1 Cor 7:25, 40; 2 Cor 8:10. Syn.: *Boule* (1012) is to be distinguished from *gnome; boule* is the result of determination, *gnome* is the result of knowledge. See: TDNT—1:717, 119; BAGD—163a.; THAYER—119b.

1107. **γνωρίζω** {24x} **gnōrizō**, *gno-rid'-zo;* from a der. of *1097;* to *make known;* subj. to *know:*—make known {16x}, declare {4x}, certify {1x}, give to understand {1x}, do to wit {1x}, wot {1x}.

Gnorizo signifies **(1)** "to come to know, discover, know," Phil 1:22, "I wot (not)," i.e., "I know not," "I have not come to know"; **(2)** "to make known," whether **(2a)** communicating things before "unknown," Lk 2:15; Jn 15:15, "I have made known"; 17:26; Acts 2:28; 7:13 (1st part); Rom 9:22, 23; 16:26 (passive voice); 2 Cor 8:1, "we do (you) to wit"; Eph 1:9; 3:3, 5, 10 (all three in the passive voice); 6:19, 21; Col 1:27; 4:7, 9, "shall declare"; 2 Pet 1:16; or **(2b)** reasserting things already "known," 1 Cor 12:3, "I give (you) to understand" (the apostle reaffirms what they knew); 15:1, **(2b1)** of the gospel; Gal 1:11 (he reminds them of what they well knew, the ground of his claim to apostleship); **(2b2)** Phil 4:6 (passive voice), of requests to God. This word signifies **(3)** to come to know, discover, know (Phil 1:22) and **(4)** to make known (Lk 2:15, 17). Syn.: 1097, 1110, 1492, 1921, 1467, 1922, 1987. See: TDNT—1:718, 119; BAGD—163b; THAYER—119b

1108. **γνῶσις** {29x} **gnōsis**, *gno'-sis;* from *1097; knowing* (the act), i.e. (by impl.) *knowledge:*—knowledge {28x}, science {1x}.

This word means primarily "a seeking to know, an enquiry, investigation" and denotes, in the NT, "knowledge," especially of spiritual truth; it is used **(1)** absolutely, in Lk 11:52; Rom 2:20; 15:14; 1 Cor 1:5; 8:1 (twice), 7, 10, 11; 13:2, 8; 14:6; 2 Cor 6:6; 8:7; 11:6; Eph 3:19; Col 2:3; 1 Pet 3:7; 2 Pet 1:5, 6; **(2)** with an object: in respect of **(2a)** God, 2 Cor 2:14; 10:5; **(2b)** the glory of God, 2 Cor 4:6; **(2c)** Christ Jesus, Phil 3:8; 2 Pet 3:18; **(2d)** salvation, Lk 1:77; **(3)** subjectively, **(3a)** of God's "knowledge," Rom 11:33; **(3b)** the word of "knowledge," 1 Cor 12:8; **(3c)** "knowledge" falsely so called, 1 Ti 6:20. Syn.: Epignosis (1903) is the complete comprehension after the first knowledge [*gnosis*]. Something that is known before is now more familiar; a more exact viewing of an object previously seen from a distance. The small portion of knowledge [*gnosis*] is improved upon and it is seen more strongly and clearly. See also: 1922, 4678, 4907, 5428, 5826. See: TDNT—1:689, 119; BAGD—163d; THAYER—119c.

1109. **γνώστης** {1x} **gnōstēs**, *gnoce'-tace;* from *1097;* a *knower:*—expert {1x}.

A *gnostes* is "one who knows" and denotes "an expert, a connoisseur," Acts 26:3. See: BAGD—164b; THAYER—119d.

1110. **γνωστός** {12x} **gnōstŏs**, *gnoce-tos';* from *1097;* well-*known:*—acquaintance {2x}, (which may be) known {12x}, notable {1x}.

Gnostos signifies "known, or knowable"; hence, "one's acquaintance"; it is used in this sense, in the plural, in Lk 2:44 and 23:49. See: TDNT—1:718, 119; BAGD—164b; THAYER—119d.

1111. **γογγύζω** {8x} **gŏgguzō**, *gong-good'-zo;* of uncert. der.; to *grumble:*—murmur {8x}. Syn.: 1112, 1234, 1690.

This word means "to mutter, murmur, grumble, say anything in a low tone", an onomatopoeic word, representing the significance by the sound of the word, as in the word "murmur" itself, **(1)** is used of the laborers in the parable of the householder, Mt 20:11; **(2)** of the scribes and Pharisees, against Christ, Lk 5:30; **(3)** of the Jews, Jn 6:41, 43; **(4)** of the disciples, Jn 6:61; **(5)** of the people, Jn 7:32 (of debating secretly); **(6)** of the Israelites, 1 Cor 10:10 (twice), where it is also used in a warning to believers. See: TDNT—1:728, 125; BAGD—164b; THAYER—120a.

1112. **γογγυσμός** {4x} **gŏggusmŏs**, *gong-goos-mos';* from *1111;* a *grumbling:*—grudging {1x}, murmuring {3x}.

This word means "a murmuring, muttering" and is used **(1)** in the sense of secret debate among people, Jn 7:12; **(2)** of displeasure or complaining (more privately than in public), said of Grecian Jewish converts against Hebrews, Acts 6:1; **(3)** in general admonitions, Phil 2:14; 1 Pet 4:9, "grudging." Syn.: 1234, 1690. See: TDNT—1:735, 125; BAGD—164c; THAYER—120a.

1113. **γογγυστής** {1x} **gŏggustēs**, *gong-goos-tace';* from *1111;* a *grumbler:*—murmurer {1x}.

A *goggustes* is "a murmurer", i.e. "one who complains" and is used in Jude 16, especially perhaps of utterances against God (see v. 15). See: TDNT—1:737, 125; BAGD—164c; THAYER—120b.

1114. **γόης** {1x} **gŏēs**, *go'-ace;* from γοάω **gŏaō** (to *wail*); prop. a *wizard* (as *muttering* spells), i.e. (by impl.) an *imposter:*—seducer {1x}.

Goes primarily denotes "a wailer"; hence, from the howl in which spells were chanted, "a wizard, sorcerer, enchanter," and hence, "a juggler, cheat, impostor," rendered "impostors" in 2 Ti 3:13 "seducers"; possibly the false teachers referred to practiced magical arts, cf. v. 8. See: TDNT—1:737, 126; BAGD—164d; THAYER—120b.

1115. **Γολγοθᾶ** {3x} **Golgŏtha**, *gol-goth-ah';* of Chald. or. [comp. 1538]; *the skull; Golgotha,* a knoll near Jerusalem:—*Golgotha* {3x}. See: BAGD—164d; THAYER—120b.

1116. **Γόμορρα** {5x} **Gŏmŏrrha**, *gom'-or-hrhah;* of Heb. or. [6017]; *Gomorrha* (i.e. *'Amorah*), a place near the Dead Sea:—*Gomorrha* {5x}. See: BAGD—164d; THAYER—120b.

1117. **γόμος** {3x} **gŏmŏs**, *gom'-os;* from *1073;* a *load* (as *filling*), i.e. (spec.) a *cargo,* or (by extens.) *wares:*—burden {1x}, merchandise {2x}.

This word means "full, or heavy," and denotes **(1)** "the lading of freight of a ship," Acts 21:3, or **(2)** "merchandise conveyed in a ship," and so "merchandise in general," Rev 18:11–12. See: BAGD—164d; THAYER—120c.

1118. **γονεύς** {19x} **gŏnĕus**, *gon-yooce';* from the base of *1096;* a *parent:*—parents {19x}.

A *goneus* is "a begetter, a father" and is used **(1)** in the plural in the NT, Mt 10:21; Mk 13:12; **(2)** six times in Lk (in Lk 2:43 "Joseph and His mother"); **(3)** six in Jn; **(4)** elsewhere, Rom 1:30; 2 Cor 12:14 (twice); Eph 6:1; Col 3:20; 2 Ti 3:2. See: BAGD—165a; THAYER—120c.

1119. **γόνυ** {12x} **gŏnu**, *gon-oo';* of uncert. aff.; the "*knee*":—knee {7x}, kneel + 5087 + 3588 {5x}.

A *gonu* is "a knee" (Latin, *genu* cf. genuflect) and is used **(1)** metaphorically in Heb 12:12, where the duty enjoined is that of "courageous self-recovery in God's strength;" **(2)** literally, **(2a)** of the attitude of a suppliant, Lk 5:8; Eph 3:14; **(2b)** of veneration, Rom 11:4; 14:11; Phil 2:10; **(2c)** in mockery, Mk 15:19. See: TDNT—1:738, 126; BAGD—165a; THAYER—120c.

1120. **γονυπετέω** {4x} **gŏnupĕtĕō**, *gon-oo-pet-eh'-o;* from a compound of *1119* and the alt. of *4098;* to *fall* on the *knee:*—kneel down to {2x}, bow the knee {1x}, kneel to {1x}.

This word denotes **(1)** "to bow the knees, kneel," from *gonu* (see above) and *pipto,* "to fall prostrate," the act of one imploring aid, Mt 17:14; Mk 1:40; **(2)** of one expressing reverence and honor, Mk 10:17; **(3)** in mockery, Mt 27:29. See: TDNT—1:738, 126; BAGD—165b; THAYER—120c.

1121. **γράμμα** {15x} **gramma**, *gram'-mah;* from *1125;* a *writing,* i.e. a *letter, note, epistle, book,* etc.; plur. *learning:*—letter {9x}, bill {2x}, writing {1x}, learning {1x}, scripture {1x}, written + 1722 {1x}. See: TDNT—1:761, 128; BAGD—165b; THAYER—120d.

1122. **γραμματεύς** {67x} **grammatĕus**, *gram-mat-yooce';* from *1121;* a *writer,* i.e. (professionally) *scribe* or *secretary:*—scribe {66x}, town-clerk {1x}.

Grammateus **(1)** denotes a scribe, a man of letters, a teacher of the law. **(2)** They are connected with the Pharisees, **(2a)** with whom they virtually formed one party (Lk 5:21), **(2b)** sometimes with the chief priests (Mt 2:4; Mk 8:31; 10:33). **(3)** They were considered naturally qualified to teach in the synagogues (Mk 1:22). **(4)** They were ambitious of honor (Mt 23:5–11), **(4a)** which they demanded especially from their pupils, and **(4b)** which was readily granted them, as well as by the people generally. **(5)** Like Ezra (cf. Ezra 7:12), the scribes were found originally among the priests and Levites. **(6)** The priests being the official interpreters of the Law, the scribes became an independent company. **(7)** Though they never held political power, they became leaders of the people. **(8)** Their functions regarding the Law were **(8a)** to teach it, **(8b)** develop it, and **(8c)** use it in connection with the Sanhedrin and various local courts. **(9)** They also occupied themselves with the sacred writings both historical and didactic. **(10)** They attached the utmost importance to ascetic elements, by which the nation was especially separated from the Gentiles. **(10a)** In their regime piety was reduced to external formalism. **(10b)** Only that was of value which was governed by external precept. **(10c)** Life under them became a burden; **(10c1)** they themselves sought to evade certain of their own precepts (Mt 23:16; Luke 11:46); **(10c2)** by their traditions the Law, instead of being a help in moral and spiritual life, became an instrument for preventing true access to God (Lk 11:52). See: TDNT—1:740, 127; BAGD—165d; THAYER—121a.

1123. **γραπτός** {1x} **graptŏs**, *grap-tos';* from *1125; inscribed* (fig.):—written {1x}. See: BAGD—166a; THAYER—121b.

1124. **γραφή** {51x} **graphē**, *graf-ay';* from *1125;* a *document,* i.e. holy *Writ* (or its contents or a statement in it):—scripture {51x}.

Graphe, as a verb, means "to write" [Eng., "graph," "graphic," etc.], primarily denotes "a drawing, painting"; then "a writing," **(1)** of the OT Scriptures, **(1a)** in the plural, **(1a1)** the whole, e.g., Mt 21:42; 22:29; Jn 5:39; Acts 17:11; 18:24; **(1a2)** Rom 1:2, where "the prophets" comprises the OT writers in general; 15:4; **(1a3)** Rom 16:26, lit., "prophetic writings," expressing the character of all the Scriptures; **(1b)** in the singular in reference to a particular passage, e.g., Mk 12:10; Lk 4:21; Jn 2:22; 10:35 (though applicable to all); 19:24, 28, 36, 37; 20:9; Acts 1:16; 8:32, 35; Rom 4:3; 9:17; 10:11; 11:2; Gal 3:8, 22; 4:30; 1 Ti 5:18, where the 2nd quotation is from Lk 10:7, from which it may be inferred that the apostle included Luke's gospel as "Scripture" alike with Deuteronomy, from which the first quotation is taken; **(1c)** in reference to the whole, e.g. Jas 4:5; **(1c1)** in 2 Pet 1:20, "no prophecy of Scripture," a description of all, **(1c2)** with special application to the OT in the next verse;

(2) of the OT Scriptures (those accepted by the Jews as canonical) and all those of the NT which were to be accepted by Christians as authoritative, 2 Ti 3:16; these latter were to be discriminated from the many forged epistles and other religious "writings" already produced and circulated in Timothy's time. Such discrimination would be directed by the fact that "all Scripture," is inspired by God, and is profitable for the purposes mentioned. **(3)** The Scriptures are frequently personified by the NT writers (as by the Jews, Jn 7:42), **(3a)** as speaking with divine authority, e.g., Jn 19:37; Rom 4:3; 9:17, where the Scripture is said to speak to Pharaoh, giving the message actually sent previously by God to him through Moses; Jas 4:5; **(3b)** as possessed of the sentient quality of foresight, and the active power of preaching, Gal 3:8, where the Scripture mentioned was written more than four centuries after the words were spoken. **(4)** The Scripture, in such a case, stands for its divine Author with an intimation that it remains perpetually characterized as the living voice of God. **(5)** This divine agency is again illustrated in Gal 3:22 (cf. v. 10 and Mt 11:13). Syn.: 1121. See: TDNT—1:749, 128; BAGD—166a; THAYER—121b.

1125. **γράφω** {209x} **graphō**, *graf'-o;* a primary verb; to *"grave,"* espec. to *write;* fig. to *describe:*—write {206x}, writing {1x}, describe {1x}, vr write {1x}. See: TDNT—1:742, 128; BAGD—166c; THAYER—121c.

1126. **γραώδης** {1x} **graōdēs**, *grah-o'-dace;* from γραῦς **graus** (an *old woman*) and *1491; crone-like,* i.e. *silly:*—old wives' {1x}.

Graodes is an adjective, signifying "old-womanish" and is said of fables, in 1 Ti 4:7. See: BAGD—167b; THAYER—122b.

1127. **γρηγορέω** {23x} **grēgŏrĕuō**, *gray-gor-yoo'-o;* from *1453;* to *keep awake,* i.e. *watch* (lit. or fig.):—watch {21x}, wake {1x}, be vigilant {1x}.

Gregoreo, as a verb, has **(1)** the meaning of vigilance and expectancy as contrasted with laxity and indifference. **(2)** It translated "wake" in 1 Th 5:10. **(2a)** It is not used in the metaphorical sense of "to be alive"; here **(2b)** it is set in contrast with katheudo, "to sleep," which is never used by the apostle with the meaning "to be dead." **(3)** All believers will live together with Christ from the time of the Rapture described in ch. 4; **(3a)** for all have spiritual life now, **(3b)** though their spiritual condition and attainment vary considerably. **(4)** Those who are lax and fail to be watchful will suffer loss (1 Cor 3:15; 9:27; 2 Cor 5:10, e.g.), but the apostle is not here dealing with that aspect of the subject. **(5)** What he does make clear is that **(5a)** the Rapture of believers seven years before the second coming of Christ will depend solely on the death of Christ for them, and not upon their spiritual condition. **(5b)** The Rapture is not a matter of reward, but of salvation. See: TDNT—2:338, 195; BAGD—167b; THAYER—122b.

1128. **γυμνάζω** {4x} **gumnazō**, *goom-nad'-zo;* from *1131;* to *practise naked* (in the games), i.e. *train* (fig.):—exercise {4x}.

Gumnazo **(1)** primarily means to exercise naked (from gumnos, "naked"); then, **(2)** generally, of **(2a)** exercise, training the body or mind [Eng., "gymnastic"] with a view to godliness (1 Ti 4:7); **(2b)** of exercising the senses, so as to discern good and evil (Heb 5:14); **(2c)** of the effect of chastening, the spiritual "exercise producing the fruit of righteousness" (Heb 2:11); **(2d)** of certain evil teachers with hearts exercised in covetousness (2 Pet 2:14). Syn.: 1129. See: TDNT—1:775, 133; BAGD—167c; THAYER—1128c.

1129. **γυμνασία** {1x} **gumnasia**, *goom-nas-ee'-ah;* from *1128; training,* i.e. (fig.) *asceticism:*—exercise {1x}.

Gumnasia primarily denotes "gymnastic exercise", 1 Ti 4:8, where the immediate reference is probably not to mere physical training for games but to discipline of the body such as that to which the apostle refers in 1 Cor 9:27, though there may be an allusion to the practices of asceticism and/or separtion. See: TDNT—1:775, 133; BAGD—167d; THAYER—122c.

1130. **γυμνητεύω** {1x} **gumnētĕuō**, *goom-nayt-yoo'-o* or γυμνιτεύω **gumniteuo**, *goom-niyt-yoo'-o;* from a der. of *1131;* to *strip,* i.e. (refl.) *go poorly clad:*—be naked {1x}.

This word means "to be naked or scantily clad" and is used in 1 Cor. 4:11: "Even unto this present hour we [the apostles] both hunger, and thirst, and are naked, and are buffeted, and have no certain dwelling place." See: BAGD—167d; THAYER—122d.

1131. **γυμνός** {15x} **gumnŏs**, *goom-nos';* of uncert. aff.; *nude* (absol. or rel., lit. or fig.):—naked {14x}, bare {1x}.

Gumnos, "naked," is once translated "bare," 1 Cor 15:37, where, used of grain, the meaning is made clearer by understanding the phrase by "a bare grain." See: TDNT—1:773, 133; BAGD—167d; THAYER—122d.

1132. **γυμνότης** {3x} **gumnŏtēs**, *goom-not'-ace;* from *1131; nudity* (absol. or comp.):—nakedness {3x}.

Gumnotes, "nakedness" is used **(1)** of "want of sufficient clothing," Rom 8:35; 2 Cor 11:27; and **(2)** metaphorically, of "the nakedness of the body," said of the condition of a local church, Rev 3:18. See: TDNT—1:775, 133; BAGD—168a; THAYER—122d.

1133. **γυναικάριον** {1x} **gunaikariŏn**, *goo-na-hee-kar'-ee-on;* a dimin. from *1135;* a *little* (i.e. *foolish*) *woman:*—silly woman {1x}.

Gunaikarion, a diminutive of *gune* (1135), a "little woman," is used contemptuously in 2 Ti 3:6, "a silly woman." See: BAGD—168b; THAYER—123a.

1134. **γυναικεῖος** {1x} **gunaikĕiŏs**, *goo-nahee-ki'-os;* from *1135; feminine:*—wife {1x}.

Gunaikeios, an adjective denoting "womanly, female," is used as a noun in 1 Pet 3:7, "wife." See: BAGD—168b; THAYER—123a.

1135. **γυνή** {221x} **gunē**, *goo-nay';* prob. from the base of *1096;* a *woman;* spec. a *wife:*—wife {129x}, woman {92x}.

Gune, is **(1)** a woman of any age, whether a virgin, or married, or a widow; or **(2)** a "wife," e.g., Mt. 1:20; 1 Cor 7:3, 4; and **(3)** in 1 Tim 3:11, "women," the reference is to the "wives" of deacons. See: TDNT—1:776, 134; BAGD—168b; THAYER—123a.

1136. **Γώγ** {1x} **Gōg**, *gogue;* of Heb. or. [1463]; *Gog,* a symb. name for some future Antichrist:—*Gog* {1x}. See: TDNT—1:789, 136; BAGD—168d; THAYER—123c.

1137. **γωνία** {9x} **gōnia**, *go-nee'-ah;* prob. akin to *1119;* an *angle:*—corner {8x}, quarter {1x}.

Gonia, "an angle", signifies **(1)** "an external angle," as **(1a)** of the "corner" of a street, Mt 6:5; or **(1b)** of a building, Mt 21:42; Mk 12:10; Lk 20:17; Acts 4:11; 1 Pet 2:7, "the corner stone or headstone of the corner"; or **(1c)** the four extreme limits of the earth, Rev 7:1; 20:8; **(2)** "an internal corner," a secret place, Acts 26:26. See: TDNT—1:791, 137; BAGD—168d; THAYER—123c.

Δ

1138. **Δαβίδ** {59x} **Dabid**, *dab-eed';* of Heb. or. [1732]; *Dabid* (i.e. *David*), the Isr. king:—David {59x}. See: TDNT—8:478,*; BAGD—169a; THAYER—123b.

1139. **δαιμονίζομαι** {13x} **daimŏnizŏmai**, *da-hee-mon-id'-zom-ahee;* mid. voice from *1142;* to *be exercised by a demon:*—possessed with devils {4x}, possessed with the devil {3x}, of the devils {2x}, vexed with a devil {1x}, possessed with a devil {1x}, have a devil {1x}. See: TDNT—2:19, 137; BAGD—169a; THAYER—123b.

1140. **δαιμόνιον** {60x} **daimŏniŏn**, *dahee-mon'-ee-on;* neut. of a der. of *1142;* a *demonic being;* by extens. a *deity:*—devil {59x}, god {1x}. See: TDNT—2:1, 137; BAGD—169a; THAYER—123d.

1141. **δαιμονιώδης** {1x} **daimŏniōdēs**, *dahee-mon-ee-o'-dace;* from *1140* and *1142; demon-like:*—devilish {1x}. See: TDNT—2:20, 137; BAGD—169d; THAYER—124b.

1142. **δαίμων** {5x} **daimōn**, *dah'-ee-mown;* from δαίω **daiō** (to *distribute* fortunes); a *demon* or supernatural spirit (of a bad nature):—devils {4x}, devil {1x}. See: TDNT—2:1, 137; BAGD—169d; THAYER—124d.

1143. **δάκνω** {1x} **daknō**, *dak'-no;* a prol. form of a primary root; to *bite,* i.e. (fig.) *thwart:*—bite {1x}. See: BAGD—169d; THAYER—124c.

1144. **δάκρυ** {11x} **dakru**, *dak'-roo;* or **δάκρυον** **dakruŏn**, *dak'-roo-on;* of uncert. affin.; a *tear:*—tear {11x}. Tear drops from the eyes. See: BAGD—170a; THAYER—124c.

1145. **δακρύω** {1x} **dakruō**, *dak-roo'-o;* from *1144;* to *shed tears:*—weep {1x}. See: BAGD—170a; THAYER—124c. comp. *2799.*

1146. **δακτύλιος** {1x} **daktuliŏs**, *dak-too'-lee-os;* from *1147;* a *finger*-ring:—ring {1x}. See: BAGD—170a; THAYER—124c.

1147. **δάκτυλος** {8x} **daktulŏs**, *dak'-too-los;* prob. from *1176;* a *finger:*—finger {8x}. See: TDNT—2:20, 140; BAGD—170a; THAYER—124c.

1148. **Δαλμανουθά** {1x} **Dalmanŏutha**, *dal-man-oo-thah';* prob. of Chald. or.; *Dalmanūtha,* a place in Pal.:—Dalmanutha {1x}. See: BAGD—170b; THAYER—124c.

1149. **Δαλματία** {1x} **Dalmatia**, *dal-mat-ee'-ah;* prob. of for. der.; *Dalmatia,* a region of Europe:—*Dalmatia* {1x}. See: BAGD—170b; THAYER—124d.

1150. **δαμάζω** {4x} **damazō**, *dam-ad'-zo;* a var. of an obs. primary of the same mean.; to *tame:*—tame {4x}. See: BAGD—170b; THAYER—124d.

1151. **δάμαλις** {1x} **damalis**, *dam'-al-is;* prob. from the base of *1150;* a *heifer* (as *tame*):—heifer {1x}. See: BAGD—170a; THAYER—124d.

1152. **Δάμαρις** {1x} **Damaris**, *dam'-ar-is;* prob. from the base of *1150;* perh. *gentle; Damaris,* an Athenian woman:—*Damaris* {1x}. See: BAGD—170c; THAYER—124d.

1153. **Δαμασκηνός** {1x} **Damaskēnŏs**, *dam-as-kay-nos';* from *1154;* a *Damascene* or inhab. of Damascus:—Damascenes {1x}. See: BAGD—170c; THAYER—124d.

1154. **Δαμασκός** {15x} **Damaskŏs**, *dam-as-kos';* of Heb. or. [1834]; *Damascus,* a city of Syria:—Damascus {15x}. See: BAGD—170c; THAYER—125a.

1155. **δανείζω** {4x} **danĕizō**, *dan-ayd'-zo;* or **δανίζω** **danizō**, *dan-ide'-zo* from *1156;* to *loan* on interest; refl. to *borrow:*—lend {3x}, borrow {1x}. See: BAGD—170d; THAYER—125a.

1156. **δάνειον** {1x} **danĕiŏn**, *dan'-i-on;* from δάνος **danŏs** (a *gift*); prob. akin to the base of *1325;* a *loan:*—debt {1x}. See: BAGD—170d; THAYER—125a.

1157. **δανειστής** {1x} **danĕistēs**, *dan-ice-tace';* or **δανιστής** **danistēs**, *dan-iys-tace'* from *1155;* a *lender:*—creditor {1x}

This is one who lends money to another on credit. See: BAGD—170d; THAYER—125a.

1158. **Δανιήλ** {2x} **Daniēl**, *dan-ee-ale';* of Heb. or. [1840]; *Daniel,* an Isr.:—*Daniel* {2x}. See: BAGD—170d; THAYER—125b.

1159. **δαπανάω** {5x} **dapanaō**, *dap-an-ah'-o;* from *1160;* to *expend,* i.e. (in a good sense) to *incur cost,* or (in a bad one) to *waste:*—spend {3x}, be at charges with {1x}, consume {1x}. See: BAGD—171a; THAYER—125b.

1160. **δαπάνη** {1x} **dapanē**, *dap-an'-ay;* from δάπτω **daptō** (to *devour*); *expense* (as *consuming*):—cost {1x}. See: BAGD—171a; THAYER—125b.

1161. **δέ** {2870x} **dĕ**, *deh;* a primary particle (adversative or continuative); *but, and,* etc.:—but {1237x}, and {935x}, now {166x}, then {132x}, also {18x}, yet {16x}, yea {13x}, so {13x}, moreover {13x}, nevertheless {11x}, for {4x}, even {3x}, misc. {9x}, not tr {300x}. See: BAGD—171c; THAYER—125b.

1162. **δέησις** {19x} **dĕēsis**, *deh'-ay-sis;* from *1189;* a *petition:*—prayer {12x}, supplication {6x}, request {1x}. Syn.: 155, 1783, 2171, 2428, 5335.

Deesis is prayer for particular benefits and *proseuche* (4335) is prayer in general. See: TDNT—2:40, 144; BAGD—171d; THAYER—126a.

1163. **δεῖ** {106x} **dĕi**, *die;* third pers. sing. act. present of *1210;* also δεόν **dĕŏn**, *deh-on';* neut. act. part. of the same; both used impers.; *it is* (*was,* etc.) *necessary* (as *binding*):—must {58x}, ought {32x}, must needs {5x}, should {4x}, misc. {7x} = behoved, be meet, (be) need (-ful). See: TDNT—2:21, 140; BAGD—172a; THAYER—126b.

1164. **δεῖγμα** {1x} **dĕigma**, *dīgh'-mah;* from the base of *1166;* a *specimen* (as *shown*):—example {1x}. See: BAGD—172c; THAYER—126d.

1165. **δειγματίζω** {1x} **dĕigmatizō**, *dīgh-mat-id'-zo;* from *1164;* to *exhibit:*—make a show {1x}. See: TDNT—2:31, 141; BAGD—172c; THAYER—126d.

1166. **δεικνύω** {31x} **dĕiknuō**, *dike-noo'-o;* a prol. form of an obs. primary of the same mean.; to *show* (lit. or fig.):—show {31x}. Syn.: 322, 1731. See: TDNT—2:25,*; BAGD—172d; THAYER—126d.

1167. **δειλία** {1x} **dĕilia**, *di-lee'-ah;* from *1169; timidity:*—fear {1x}.

The word denotes cowardice, unmanliness, and timidity (2 Ti 1:7). Syn.: 2124, 5401. See: BAGD—173a; THAYER—127a.

1168. **δειλιάω** {1x} **dĕiliaō**, *di-lee-ah'-o;* from *1167;* to *be timid:*—be afraid {1x}. See: BAGD—173a; THAYER—127a.

1169. **δειλός** {3x} **dĕilŏs**, *di-los';* from δέος **dĕŏs** (*dread*); *timid,* i.e. (by impl.) *faithless:*—fearful {3x}. See: BAGD—173a; THAYER—127a.

1170. **δεῖνα** {1x} **dĕina**, *di'-nah;* prob. from the same as *1171* (through the idea of forgetting the name as *fearful,* i.e. *strange*); *so and so* (when the person is not specified):—such a man {1x}. See: BAGD—173a; THAYER—127b.

1171. **δεινῶς** {2x} **dĕinōs**, *di-noce';* adv. from a der. of the same as *1169; terribly,* i.e. *excessively:*—grievously {1x}, vehemently {1x}. See: BAGD—173b, THAYER—127b.

1172. **δειπνέω** {4x} **dĕipnĕō**, *dipe-neh'-o;* from *1173;* to *dine,* i.e. take the principal (or evening) meal:—sup {3x}, supper {1x}. See: TDNT—2:34, 143; BAGD—173b; THAYER—127b.

1173. **δεῖπνον** {16x} **dĕipnŏn**, *dipe'-non;* from the same as *1160; dinner,* i.e. the chief meal (usually in the evening):—supper {13x}, feast {3x}. See: TDNT—2:34, 143; BAGD—173b; THAYER—127b.

1174. **δεισιδαιμονέστερος** {1x} **dĕisidaimŏnĕstĕrŏs**, *dice-ee-dahee-mon-es'-ter-os;* the comparative of a der. of the base of *1169* and *1142; more religious* than others:—too superstitious {1x}.

This person has a conceit that God is well-pleased by an overdoing in external things and observances and laws of men's own making. Syn.: 2126, 2152, 2318, 2357. See: TDNT—2:20; BAGD—173d; THAYER—127c.

1175. **δεισιδαιμονία** {1x} **dĕisidaimŏnia**, *dice-ee-dahee-mon-ee'-ah;* from the same as *1174; relig.:*—superstition {1x}. See: TDNT—2:20, 137; BAGD—173c; THAYER—127c.

1176. **δέκα** {27x} **dĕka**, *dek'-ah;* a primary number; *ten:*—ten {24x}, eighteen + 2532 + 3638 {3x}. See: TDNT—2:36, 143; BAGD—173d; THAYER—127d.

1177. **δεκαδύο** {2x} **dĕkaduŏ**, *dek-ad-oo'-o;* from *1176* and *1417; two* and *ten,* i.e. *twelve:*—twelve {2x}. See: BAGD—174a; THAYER—127d.

1178. **δεκαπέντε** {3x} **dĕkapĕntĕ**, *dek-ap-en'-teh;* from *1176* and *4002; ten* and *five,* i.e. *fifteen:*—fifteen {3x}. See: BAGD—174a; THAYER—127d.

1179. **Δεκάπολις** {3x} **Dĕkapŏlis**, *dek-ap'-ol-is;* from *1176* and *4172;* the *ten-city* region; the *Decapolis,* a district in Syria:—Decapolis {3x}. See: BAGD—174a; THAYER—127d.

1180. **δεκατέσσαρες** {5x} **dĕkatĕssarĕs**, *dek-at-es'-sar-es;* from *1176* and *5064; ten* and *four,* i.e. *fourteen:*—fourteen {5x}. See: BAGD—174a; THAYER—128a.

1181. **δεκάτη** {4x} **dĕkatē**, *dek-at'-ay;* fem. of *1182;* a *tenth,* i.e. as a percentage or (tech.) *tithe:*—tithe {2x}, tenth part {1x}, tenth {1x}. See: BAGD—174a; THAYER—128a.

1182. **δέκατος** {3x} **dĕkatŏs**, *dek'-at-os;* ordinal from *1176; tenth:*—tenth {3x}. See: BAGD—174a; THAYER—128a.

1183. **δεκατόω** {2x} **dĕkatŏō**, *dek-at-ŏ'-o;* from *1181;* to *tithe,* i.e. to *give* or *take a tenth:*—receive tithes {1x}, pay tithes {1x}. See: BAGD—174b; THAYER—128a.

1184. **δεκτός** {5x} **dĕktŏs**, *dek-tos';* from *1209; approved;* (fig.) *propitious:*—accepted {3x}, acceptable {2x}. See: TDNT—2:58, 146; BAGD—174b; THAYER—128a.

1185. **δελεάζω** {3x} **dĕlĕazō**, *del-eh-ad'-zo;* from the base of *1388;* to *entrap,* i.e. (fig.) *delude:*—entice {1x}, beguile {1x}, allure {1x}.

This word means to catch using bait. See: BAGD—174b; THAYER—128b.

1186. **δένδρον** {26x} **dĕndrŏn**, *den'-dron;* prob. from δρῦς **drus** (an *oak*); a *tree:*—tree {26x}. See: BAGD—174c; THAYER—128b.

1187. **δεξιολάβος** {1x} **dĕxiŏlabŏs**, *dex-ee-ol-ab'-os;* from *1188* and *2983;* a *guardsman* (as if *taking the right hand*) or light-armed soldier:—spearmen {1x}. See: BAGD—174c; THAYER—128b.

1188. **δεξιός** {53x} **dĕxiŏs**, *dex-ee-os';* from *1209;* the *right* side or (fem.) hand (as that which usually *takes*):—right hand {39x}, right {12x}, right side {2x}. See: TDNT—2:37, 143; BAGD—174c; THAYER—128c.

1189. **δέομαι** {22x} **dĕŏmai**, *deh'-om-ahee;* mid. voice of *1210;* to *beg* (as *binding oneself*), i.e. *petition:*—pray {12x}, beseech {9x}, make request {1x}. See: TDNT—2:40, 144; BAGD—175a; THAYER—129a. comp. *4441.*

δεόν **dĕŏn**. See *1163.*

1190. **Δερβαῖος** {1x} **Dĕrbaiŏs**, *der-bah'-ee-os;* from *1191;* a *Derbæan* or inhab. of Derbe:—of Derbe {1x}. See: BAGD—175c; THAYER—129b.

1191. **Δέρβη** {3x} **Dĕrbē**, *der-bay';* of for. or.; *Derbe',* a place in Asia Minor:—*Derbe* {3x}. See: BAGD—175c; THAYER—129b.

1192. **δέρμα** {1x} **dĕrma**, *der'-mah;* from *1194;* a *hide:*—skin + 122 {1x}. See: BAGD—175c; THAYER—129b.

1193. **δερμάτινος** {2x} **dĕrmatinŏs**, *der-mat'-ee-nos;* from *1192;* made of *hide:*—leathern {1x}, of a skin {1x}. See: BAGD—175c; THAYER—129b.

1194. **δέρω** {15x} **dĕrō**, *der'-o;* a primary verb; prop. to *flay,* i.e. (by impl.) to *scourge,* or (by anal.) to *thrash:*—beat {12x}, smite {3x}. See: BAGD—175d; THAYER—129b.

1195. **δεσμεύω** {2x} **dĕsmĕuō**, *des-myoo'-o;* from a (presumed) der. of *1196;* to *be a binder* (*captor*), i.e. to *enchain* (a prisoner), to *tie on* (a load):—bind {2x}. See: BAGD—175d; THAYER—129c.

1196. **δεσμέω** {1x} **děsmĕō**, *des-meh'-o;* from *1199;* to *tie,* i.e. *shackle:*—bind {1x}. See: BAGD—175d; THAYER—129c.

1197. **δέσμη** {1x} **děsmē**, *des-may';* from *1196;* a *bundle:*—bundle {1x}. See: BAGD—176a; THAYER—129c.

1198. **δέσμιος** {16x} **děsmiŏs**, *des'-mee-os;* from *1199;* a *captive* (as *bound*):—prisoner {14x}, be in bonds {1x}, in bonds {1x}.

Desmios, as a noun, means "a binding" and **(1)** denotes "a prisoner in bonds" (Acts 25:14; Heb 13:3, "them that are in bonds"). **(2)** Paul speaks of himself as a prisoner of Christ (Eph 3:1; 2 Ti 1:8; Philem 1, 9; Eph 4:1 "in the Lord"). Syn.: 254, 1199, 4886. See: TDNT—2:43, 145; BAGD—176a; THAYER—129c.

1199. **δεσμόν** {20x} **děsmŏn**, *des-mon';* or

δεσμός **děsmŏs**, *des-mos';* neut. and masc. respectively from *1210;* a *band,* i.e. *ligament* (of the body) or *shackle* (of a prisoner); fig. an *impediment* or *disability:*—bond {15x}, band {3x}, string {1x}, chain {1x}.

Desmos, as a noun, **(1)** is usually found in the plural, either masculine or neuter; **(1a)** it stands thus for the actual "bonds" which bind a prisoner (Lk 8:29; Acts 16:26; 20:23 the only three places where the neuter plural is used; 22:30); **(1b)** the masculine plural stands frequently in a figurative sense for "a condition of imprisonment:" "Even as it is meet for me to think this of you all, because I have you in my heart; inasmuch as both in my bonds (*demos*), and in the defence and confirmation of the gospel, ye all are partakers of my grace" (Phil 1:7; cf. vss 13–16, i.e., "so that my captivity became manifest as appointed for the cause of Christ"; Col 4:18; 2 Ti 2:9; Philem 10, 13; Heb 10:34). **(2)** In Mk 7:35 "the bond (kjv, string)" stands metaphorically for "the infirmity which caused an impediment in his speech." **(3)** So in Lk 13:16, of the infirmity of the woman who was bowed together. Syn.: 254, 1198, 4886. See: TDNT—2:43; BAGD—176a; THAYER—129d.

1200. **δεσμοφύλαξ** {3x} **děsmŏphulax**, *des-mof-oo'-lax;* from *1199* and *5441;* a *jailer* (as *guarding* the *prisoners*):—keeper of the prison {2x}, jailor {1x}. See: BAGD—176b; THAYER—129d.

1201. **δεσμωτήριον** {4x} **děsmōtēriŏn**, *des-mo-tay'-ree-on;* from a der. of *1199* (equiv. to *1196); a place of bondage,* i.e. a *dungeon:*—prison {4x}. See: BAGD—176b; THAYER—130a.

1202. **δεσμώτης** {2x} **děsmōtēs**, *des-mo'-tace;* from the same as *1201;* (pass.) a *captive:*—prisoner {2x}. See: BAGD—176b; THAYER—130a.

1203. **δεσπότης** {10x} **děspŏtēs**, *des-pot'-ace;* perh. from *1210* and πόσις **pŏsis** (a *husband*); an absolute *ruler* ("despot"):—Lord {5x}, master {5x}.

A man is a *despotes* to his slaves, but a kurios (2962) to his wife and children. He exercises an unrestricted power and domination, with no limitations or restraints. Syn.: 2962. See: TDNT—2:44, 145; BAGD—176c; THAYER—130a.

1204. **δεῦρο** {9x} **děurŏ**, *dyoo'-ro;* of uncert. aff.; *here;* used also imperative *hither!;* and of time, *hitherto:*—come {6x}, come hither {2x}, hitherto + 891 + 3588 {1x}. See: BAGD—176c; THAYER—130a.

1205. **δεῦτε** {13x} **děutě**, *dyoo'-teh;* from *1204* and an imper. form of εἶμι **ĕimi** (to *go*); *come hither!:*—come {12x}, follow + 3694 {1x}. See: BAGD—176d; THAYER—130b.

1206. **δευτεραῖος** {1x} **děutěraiŏs**, *dyoo-ter-ah'-yos;* from *1208; secondary,* i.e. (spec.) on the *second* day:—next day {1x}. See: BAGD—177a; THAYER—130b.

1207. **δευτερόπρωτος** {1x} **děutěrŏprōtŏs**, *dyoo-ter-op'-ro-tos;* from *1208* and *4413; second-first,* i.e. (spec.) a designation of the Sabbath immediately after the Paschal week (being the *second* after Passover day, and the *first* of the seven Sabbaths intervening before Pentecost):—second . . . after the first {1x}. See: BAGD—177a; THAYER—130b.

1208. **δεύτερος** {47x} **děutěrŏs**, *dyoo'-ter-os;* as the comp. of *1417;* (ordinal) *second* (in time, place, or rank; also adv.):—second {34x}, the second time + 1537 {4x}, the second time {4x}, again + 1537 {2x}, again {1x}, secondarily {1x}, afterward {1x}. See: BAGD—177a; THAYER—130c.

1209. **δέχομαι** {59x} **děchŏmai**, *dekh'-om-ahee;* mid. voice of a primary verb; to *receive* (in various applications, lit. or fig.):—receive {52x}, take {4x}, accept {2x}, take up {1x}.

This word signifies to accept by a deliberate and ready reception of what is offered (1 Th 2:13). *Dechomai,* as a verb, means "to receive by deliberate and ready reception of what is offered" and is used of **(1)** taking with the hand, taking hold, taking hold of or up: "Then took (*dechomai*) he (Simeon) Him up in his arms, and blessed God, and said" (Lk 2:28; cf. 16:6, 7; 22:17; Eph 6:17); **(2)** "receiving," said **(2a)** of a place "receiving" a person, of Christ into the Heavens: "Whom the heaven must receive until the times of restitution of all things, which God hath spoken by the mouth of all his holy prophets since the world began" (Acts 3:21); or **(2b)** of persons in giving access to someone as a visitor: "Then when He was come into Galilee, the Galilaeans received Him, having seen all the things that He did at Jerusalem at the feast: for they also went unto the feast" (Jn 4:45; cf. 2 Cor 7:15; Gal 4:14; Col 4:10);

(3) by way of giving hospitality: "And whosoever shall not receive (*dechomai*) you, nor hear your words, when ye depart out of that house or city, shake off the dust of your feet" (Mt 10:14; cf. 10: 40 [four times], 41 [twice]; 18:5; Mk 6:11; 9:37; Lk 9:5, 48, 53; 10:8, 10; 16:4, 9 of reception "into the eternal tabernacles," said of followers of Christ who have used "the mammon of unrighteousness" to render assistance to "make . . . friends of" others); **(4)** of Rahab's reception of the spies: "By faith the harlot Rahab perished not with them that believed not, when she had received (*dechomai*) the spies with peace" (Heb 11:31); **(5)** of the reception, by the Lord, of the spirit of a departing believer: "And they stoned Stephen, calling upon *God,* and saying, Lord Jesus, receive my spirit" (Acts 7:59); **(6)** of "receiving" a gift: "Praying us with much intreaty that we would receive the gift, and *take upon us* the fellowship of the ministering to the saints" (2 Cor 8:4);

(7) of the favorable reception of testimony and teaching: **(7a)** "They on the rock *are they,* which, when they hear, receive the word with joy; and these have no root, which for a while believe, and in time of temptation fall away" (Lk 8:13; cf. Acts 8:14; 11:1; 17:11; 1 Cor 2:14; 2 Cor 8:17; 1 Th 1:6; 2:13, where *paralambano* (3880) is used in the 1st part, "ye received," *dechomai* in the 2nd part, "ye accepted," rv (kjv, "received"), the former refers to the ear, the latter, adding the idea of appropriation, to the heart; Jas 1:21); **(7b)** in 2 Th 2:10 receiving "the love of the truth, i.e., love for the truth (cf. Mt 11:14 "if ye are willing to receive it" an elliptical construction frequent in Greek writings); **(8)** of "receiving," by way of bearing with, enduring: "I say again, Let no man think me a fool; if otherwise, yet as a fool receive me, that I may boast myself a little" (2 Cor 11:16);

(9) of "receiving" by way of getting: "As also the high priest doth bear me witness, and all the estate of the elders: from whom also I received letters unto the brethren, and went to Damascus, to bring them which were there bound unto Jerusalem, for to be punished" (Acts 22:5; cf. 28:21, of becoming partaker of benefits, Mk 10:15; Lk 18:17; Acts 7:38; 2 Cor 6:1; 11:4; Phil 4:18). Syn.: There is a certain distinction between *lambano* (2983) and *dechomai* (1209) in that in many instances *lambano* suggests a self-prompted taking, whereas *dechomai* more frequently indicates "a welcoming or an appropriating reception." See also: 324, 353, 354, 568, 588, 618, 1523, 1926, 2210, 2865, 2975, 2983, 3028, 3335, 3336, 3858, 3880, 3970, 4327, 4355, 4356, 4380, 4381, 4382, 5562, 5264, 5274. See: TDNT—2:50, 146; BAGD—177b; THAYER—130d.

1210. **δέω** {44x} **děō**, *deh'-o;* a primary verb; to *bind* (in various applications, lit. or fig.):—bind {37x}, be in bonds {1x}, knit {1x}, tie {4x}, wind {1x}. See: TDNT—2:60, 148; BAGD—177c; THAYER—131b. See also *1163, 1189.*

1211. **δή** {6x} **dē**, *day;* prob. akin to *1161;* a particle of emphasis or explicitness; *now, then,* etc.:—also {1x}, and {1x}, doubtless {1x}, now {1x}, therefore {1x}, not tr {1x}. See: BAGD—178b; THAYER—131c.

1212. **δῆλος** {4x} **dēlŏs**, *day'-los;* of uncert. der.; *clear:*—bewray + 4160 {1x}, certain {1x}, evident {1x}, manifest {1x}.

This word signifies visible, clear to the mind, evident (Gal. 3:11; 1 Cor 15:27). See: BAGD—178b; THAYER—131d.

1213. **δηλόω** {7x} **dēlŏō**, *day-lŏ'-o;* from *1212;* to *make plain* (by words):—declare {3x}, show {1x}, signify {3x}. See: TDNT—2:61, 148; BAGD—178c; THAYER—131d.

1214. **Δημᾶς** {3x} **Dēmas**, *day-mas';* prob. for *1216; Demas,* a Chr.:—*Demas* {3x}. See: BAGD—178c; THAYER—132a.

1215. **δημηγορέω** {1x} **dēmēgŏrĕō**, *day-may-gor-eh'-o;* from a compound of *1218* and *58;* to *be a people-gatherer,* i.e. to *address* a public assembly:—make an oration {1x}. See: BAGD—178d; THAYER—132a.

1216. **Δημήτριος** {3x} **Dēmētriŏs**, *day-may'-tree-os;* from Δημήτηρ **Dēmētēr** (*Ceres*); *Demetrius,* the name of an Ephesian and of a Chr.:—Demetrius {3x}. See: BAGD—178d; THAYER—132a.

1217. **δημιουργός** {1x} **dēmiŏurgŏs**, *day-me-oor-gos';* from *1218* and *2041;* a *worker* for the *people,* i.e. *mechanic* (spoken of the *Creator*):—maker {1x}.

This word emphasizes the power of a Divine creator. Syn.: 5079. See: TDNT—2:62, 149; BAGD—178d; THAYER—132a.

1218. **δῆμος** {4x} **dēmŏs**, *day'-mos;* from *1210;* the *public* (as *bound* together socially):—people {4x}.

Demos is an assembly of people gathered together with consent of the law and for mutual benefit; an assembled group of people actively exercising their rights as citizens. Syn.: 1484, 2992, 3793. See: TDNT—2:63, 149; BAGD—179a; THAYER—132b.

1219. **δημόσιος** {4x} **dēmŏsiŏs**, *day-mos'ee-os;* from *1218; public;* (fem. sing. dat. case as adv.) *in public:*—common {1x}, openly {1x}, publicly {2x}. See: BAGD—179a; THAYER—132b.

1220. **δηνάριον** {16x} **dēnariŏn**, *day-nar'-ee-on;* of Lat. or.; a *denarius* (or *ten asses*):—pence {9x}, penny {5x}, pennyworth {2x}. See: BAGD—179b; THAYER—132b.

1221. **δήποτε** {1x} **dēpŏtĕ**, *day'-pot-eh;* from *1211* and *4218;* a particle of generalization; *indeed, at any time:*—whatsoever + 3769 {1x}. See: BAGD—179b; THAYER—132b.

1222. **δήπου** {1x} **dēpŏu**, *day'-poo;* from *1211* and *4225;* a particle of asseveration; *indeed doubtless:*—verily {1x}. See: BAGD—179b; THAYER—132c.

1223. **διά** {647x} **dia**, *dee-ah';* a primary prep. denoting the *channel* of an act; *through* (in very wide applications, local, causal, or occasional):—by {241x}, through {88x}, with {16x}, for {58x}, for . . . sake {47x}, therefore + 5124 {44x}, for this cause + 5124 {14x}, because {53x}, misc. {86x} = after, always, among, at, to avoid, briefly, fore, from, in, by occasion of, of, by reason of, that, thereby, though, throughout, to, wherefore, within. In composition it retains the same general import. See: TDNT—2:65, 149; BAGD—179b; THAYER—132c.

Δία Dia. See *2203*.

1224. **διαβαίνω** {3x} **diabainō**, *dee-ab-ah'-ee-no;* from *1223* and the base of *939;* to *cross:*—come over {1x}, pass {1x}, pass through {1x}. See: BAGD—181c; THAYER—135a.

1225. **διαβάλλω** {1x} **diaballō**, *dee-ab-al'-lo;* from *1223* and *906;* (fig.) to *traduce:*—accuse {1x}.

Diaballo, as a verb, is used in Lk 16:1, in the passive voice, literally **(1)** signifies "to hurl across" (dia, "through," ballo, "to throw"), and suggests a verbal assault: "And he said also unto his disciples, There was a certain rich man, which had a steward; and the same was accused unto him that he had wasted his goods." **(2)** It stresses the act rather than the author of the accusation, as in the case of aitia (156) and kategoria (2724). Syn.: 156, 157, 1458, 1462, 1908, 2723, 2724, 4811. See: TDNT—2:71, 150; BAGD—181d; THAYER—135a.

1226. **διαβεβαιόομαι** {2x} **diabĕbaiŏŏmai**, *dee-ab-eb-ahee-ŏ'-om-ahee;* mid. voice of a compound of *1223* and *950;* to *confirm thoroughly* (by words), i.e. *asseverate:*—affirm {1x}, affirm constantly {1x}. See: BAGD—181d; THAYER—135a.

1227. **διαβλέπω** {2x} **diablĕpō**, *dee-ab-lep'-o;* from *1223* and *991;* to *look through,* i.e. *recover* full *vision:*—see clearly {2x}. See: BAGD—181d; THAYER—135b.

1228. **διάβολος** {38x} **diabŏlŏs**, *dee-ab'-ol-os;* from *1225;* a *traducer;* spec. *Satan* [comp. 7854]:—false accuser {2x}, devil {35x}, slanderer {1x}. See: TDNT—2:72, 150; BAGD—182a.135b.

1229. **διαγγέλλω** {3x} **diaggĕllō**, *de-ang-gel'-lo;* from *1223* and the base of *32;* to *herald thoroughly:*—declare {1x}, preach {1x}, signify {1x}. See: TDNT—1:67, 10; BAGD—182b; THAYER—135c.

1230. **διαγίνομαι** {3x} **diaginŏmai**, *dee-ag-in'-om-ahee;* from *1223* and *1096;* to *elapse meanwhile:*—after {1x}, be past {1x}, be spent {1x}. See: BAGD—182b; THAYER—135c.

1231. **διαγινώσκω** {2x} **diaginōskō**, *dee-ag-in-o'-sko;* from *1223* and *1097;* to *know thoroughly,* i.e. *ascertain exactly:*—(would) enquire {1x}, know the uttermost {1x}. See: BAGD—182b; THAYER—135c.

1232. **διαγνωρίζω** {1x} **diagnōrizō**, *dee-ag-no-rid'-zo;* from *1123* and *1107;* to *tell abroad:*—make known abroad {1x}. See: BAGD—182b; THAYER—135d.

1233. **διάγνωσις** {1x} **diagnōsis**, *dee-ag'-no-sis;* from *1231;* (magisterial) *examination* ("diagnosis"):—hearing {1x}. See: BAGD—182c; THAYER—135d.

1234. **διαγογγύζω** {2x} **diagŏgguzō**, *dee-ag-ong-good'-zo;* from *1223* and *1111;* to *complain throughout* a crowd:—murmur {2x}. See: TDNT—1:735, 125; BAGD—182c; THAYER—135d.

1235. **διαγρηγορέω** {1x} **diagrēgŏrĕō**, *dee-ag-ray-gor-eh'-o;* from *1223* and *1127;* to *waken thoroughly:*—be awake {1x}. See: BAGD—182c; THAYER—135d.

1236. **διάγω** {2x} **diagō**, *dee-ag'-o;* from *1223* and *71;* to *pass* time or life:—lead a life + 979 {1x}, living {1x}.

Diago is used of time in the sense of passing a life: **(1)** 1 Ti 2:2 "[prayer] For kings, and *for* all that are in authority; that we may lead (*diago*) a quiet and peaceable life in all godliness and honesty"; and **(2)** in Titus 3:3 "For we ourselves also were sometimes foolish, disobedient, deceived, serving divers lusts and pleasures, living (*diago*) in malice and envy, hateful, *and* hating one another." Syn.: 326, 390, 980, 2198, 2225, 4176, 4800, 5225. See: BAGD—182c; THAYER—135d.

1237. **διαδέχομαι** {1x} **diadĕchŏmai**, *dee-ad-ekh'-om-ahee;* from *1223* and *1209;* to *receive in turn,* i.e. (fig.) *succeed to:*—come after {1x}. See: BAGD—182c; THAYER—136a.

1238. **διάδημα** {3x} **diadēma**, *dee-ad'-ay-mah;* from a compound of *1223* and *1210;* a "*diadem*" (as *bound about* the head):—crown {3x}.

It is always the symbol of kingly or imperial dignity; whereas a *stephanos* (4735) is the victor's crown. See: BAGD—182d; THAYER—136a. comp. *4735*.

1239. **διαδίδωμι** {5x} **diadidōmi**, *dee-ad-id'-o-mee;* from *1223* and *1325;* to *give throughout* a crowd, i.e. *deal out;* also to *deliver* over (as to a successor):—make distribution {1x}, distribute {2x}, divide {1x}, give {1x}. See: BAGD—182d; THAYER—136a.

1240. **διάδοχος** {1x} **diadŏchŏs**, *dee-ad'-okh-os;* from *1237;* a *successor* in office:—come into (one's) room {1x}. See: BAGD—182d; THAYER—136b.

1241. **διαζώννυμι** {3x} **diazōnnumi**, *dee-az-own'-noo-mee;* from *1223* and *2224;* to *gird tightly:*—gird {3x}.

Diazonnumi, as a verb, means "to gird round," i.e., firmly [dia, "throughout," used intensively], is used **(1)** of the Lord's act in "girding" Himself with a towel: "He riseth from supper, and laid aside His garments; and took a towel, and girded (*diazonnumi*) Himself. 5 After that He poureth water into a bason, and began to wash the disciples' feet, and to wipe *them* with the towel wherewith He was girded (*diazonnimi*)" (Jn 13:4–5), and **(2)** of Peter's girding himself with his coat: "Therefore that disciple whom Jesus loved saith unto Peter, It is the Lord. Now when Simon Peter heard that it was the Lord, he girt (*diazonnumi*) *his* fisher's coat *unto him,* (for he was naked,) and did cast himself into the sea" (Jn 21:7). Syn.: 328, 2224, 4024. See: TDNT—5:302, 702; BAGD—182d; THAYER—136b.

1242. **διαθήκη** {33x} **diathēkē**, *dee-ath-ay'-kay;* from *1303;* prop. a *disposition,* i.e. (spec.) a *contract* (espec. a devisory *will*):—covenant {20x}, testament {13x}. See: TDNT—2:106, 157; BAGD—183a; THAYER—136b.

1243. **διαίρεσις** {3x} **diairĕsis**, *dee-ah'-ee-res-is;* from *1244;* a *distinction* or (concr.) *variety:*—difference {1x}, diversity {2x}. See: TDNT—1:184, 27; BAGD—1243c; THAYER—137a.

1244. **διαιρέω** {2x} **diairĕō**, *dee-ahee-reh'-o;* from *1223* and *138;* to *separate,* i.e. *distribute:*—divide {2x}.

Diaireo means to divide into parts, to distribute (Lk 15:12; 1 Cor 12:11). See: TDNT—1:184, 27; BAGD—183c; THAYER—137b.

1245. **διακαθαρίζω** {2x} **diakatharizō**, *dee-ak-ath-ar-id'-zo;* from *1223* and *2511;* to *cleanse perfectly, completely,* i.e. (spec.) *winnow:*—thoroughly purged {2x}. See: BAGD—183d; THAYER—137b.

1246. **διακατελέγχομαι** {1x} **diakatĕlĕgchŏmai**, *dee-ak-at-el-eng'-khom-ahee;* mid. voice from *1223* and a compound of *2596* and *1651;* to *prove downright,* i.e. *confute:*—convince {1x}. See: BAGD—184a; THAYER—137b.

1247. **διακονέω** {37x} **diakŏnĕō**, *dee-ak-on-eh'-o;* from *1249;* to *be an attendant,* i.e. *wait upon* (menially or as a host, friend, or [fig.] teacher); techn. to *act as a* Chr. *deacon:*—minister unto {15x}, serve {10x}, minister {7x}, misc. {5x} = administer, use the office of a deacon. See: TDNT—2:81, 152; BAGD—184a; THAYER—137b.

1248. **διακονία** {34x} **diakŏnia**, *dee-ak-on-ee'-ah;* from *1249; attendance* (as a servant, etc.); fig. (eleemosynary) *aid,* (official) *service* (espec. of the Chr. teacher, or techn. of the *diaconate*):—ministry {16x}, ministration {6x}, ministering {3x}, misc. {9x} = administer, office, relief, servicing. See: TDNT—2:87, 152; BAGD—184b; THAYER—137d.

1249. **διάκονος** {31x} **diakŏnŏs**, *dee-ak'-on-os;* prob. from an obs. διάκω **diakō** (to *run* on errands; comp. *1377*); an *attendant,* i.e. (gen.) a *waiter* (at table or in other menial duties); spec. a Chr. *teacher* and *pastor* (tech. a *deacon* or *deaconess*):—deacon {3x}, minister {20x}, servant {8x}.

This word focuses on the servant in his activity for the work and not his relation to a person. Doulos (1401) stresses relationship. Syn.: 1401, 2324, 3610, 5257. See: TDNT—2:88, 152; BAGD—184c; THAYER—138a.

1250. **διακόσιοι** {8x} **diakŏsiŏi**, *dee-ak-os'-ee-oy;* from *1364* and *1540; two hundred:*—two hundred {8x}. See: BAGD—185a; THAYER—138c.

1251. **διακούομαι** {1x} **diakŏuŏmai**, *dee-ak-oo'-om-ahee;* mid. voice from *1223* and *191;* to *hear throughout,* i.e. *patiently listen* (to a prisoner's plea):—hear {1x}.

Diakouo, as a verb, means "to hear through, hear fully" and is used technically, of "hearing" judicially (Acts 23:35 of Felix in regard to the charges against Paul). Syn.: 189, 191, 1522, 1873, 1874, 3878, 4257. See: BAGD—185; THAYER—138c.

1252. **διακρίνω** {19x} **diakrinō**, *dee-ak-ree'-no;* from *1223* and *2919;* to *separate thoroughly,* i.e. (lit. and refl.) to *withdraw* from, or (by impl.) *oppose;* fig. to *discriminate* (by impl. *decide*), or (refl.) *hesitate:*—doubt {5x}, judge {3x}, discern {2x}, contend {2x}, waver {2x}, misc. {5x} = make (to) differ, difference, be partial, stagger.

Diakrino is rendered "to waver" (Rom 4:20; Jas 1:6 twice). See: TDNT—3:946, 469; BAGD—185a; THAYER—138c.

1253. **διάκρισις** {3x} **diakrisis**, *dee-ak'-ree-sis;* from *1252;* judicial *estimation:*—discern {1x}, discerning {1x}, disputation {1x}. See: TDNT—3:949, 469; BAGD—185b; THAYER—139a.

1254. **διακωλύω** {1x} **diakōluō**, *dee-ak-o-loo'-o;* from *1223* and *2967;* to *hinder altogether,* i.e. *utterly prohibit:*—forbid {1x}. See: BAGD—185c; THAYER—139a.

1255. **διαλαλέω** {2x} **dialalĕō**, *dee-al-al-eh'-o;* from *1223* and *2980;* to *talk throughout* a company, i.e. *converse* or (gen.) *publish:*—commune {1x}, noise abroad {1x}. See: BAGD—185c; THAYER—139a.

1256. **διαλέγομαι** {13x} **dialĕgŏmai**, *dee-al-eg'-om-ahee;* mid. voice from *1223* and *3004;* to *say thoroughly,* i.e. *discuss* (in argument or exhortation):—dispute {6x}, preach {1x}, preach unto {1x}, reason {2x}, reason with {2x}, speak {1x}.

Dialegomai primarily denotes to ponder, resolve in one's mind. See: TDNT—2:93, 155; BAGD—185c; THAYER—139a.

1257. **διαλείπω** {1x} **dialĕipō**, *dee-al-i'-po;* from *1223* and *3007;* to *leave off in the middle,* i.e. *intermit:*—cease {1x}. See: TDNT—4:194; BAGD—185d; THAYER—139b.

1258. **διάλεκτος** {6x} **dialĕktŏs**, *dee-al'-ek-tos;* from *1256;* a (mode of) discourse, i.e. "*dialect*":—language {1x}, tongue {5x}. See: BAGD—185d; THAYER—139b.

1259. **διαλλάσσω** {1x} **diallassō**, *dee-al-las'-so;* from *1223* and *236;* to *change thoroughly,* i.e. (ment.) to *conciliate:*—reconcile {1x}. See: TDNT—1:253, 40; BAGD—186a; THAYER—139b.

1260. **διαλογίζομαι** {16x} **dialŏgizŏmai**, *dee-al-og-id'-zom-ahee;* from *1223* and *3049;* to *reckon thoroughly,* i.e. (gen.) to *deliberate* (by reflection or discussion):—reason {11x}, dispute {1x}, cast in the mind {1x}, muse {1x}, think {1x}, consider {1x}. See: TDNT—2:95, 155; BAGD—186a; THAYER—139c.

1261. **διαλογισμός** {14x} **dialŏgismŏs**, *dee-al-og-is-mos';* from *1260;* *discussion,* i.e. (internal) *consideration* (by impl. *purpose*), or (external) *debate:*—dispute {1x}, doubtful {1x}, doubting {1x}, imagination {1x}, reasoning {9x}, thought {1x}. See: TDNT—2:96, 155; BAGD—186a; THAYER—139c.

1262. **διαλύω** {1x} **dialuō**, *dee-al-oo'-o;* from *1223* and *3089;* to *dissolve utterly:*—scatter {1x}. See: BAGD—186b; THAYER—139d.

1263. **διαμαρτύρομαι** {15x} **diamarturŏmai**, *dee-am-ar-too'-rom-ahee;* from *1223* and *3140;* to *attest* or *protest earnestly,* or (by impl.) *hortatively:*—charge {3x}, testify (unto) {11x}, witness {1x}. See: TDNT—4:510, 564; BAGD—186c; THAYER—139d.

1264. **διαμάχομαι** {1x} **diamachŏmai**, *dee-am-akh'-om-ahee;* from *1223* and *3164;* to *fight fiercely* (in altercation):—strive {1x}. See: BAGD—186c; THAYER—140a.

1265. **διαμένω** {5x} **diamĕnō**, *dee-am-en'-o;* from *1223* and *3306;* to *stay constantly* (in being or relation):—continue {3x}, remain {2x}. See: BAGD—186c; THAYER—140a.

1266. **διαμερίζω** {12x} **diamĕrizō**, *dee-am-er-id'-zo;* from *1223* and *3307;* to *partition thoroughly* (lit. in distribution, fig. in dissension):—cloven {1x}, divide {5x}, part {6x}. See: BAGD—186d; THAYER—140b.

1267. **διαμερισμός** {1x} **diamĕrismŏs**, *dee-am-er-is-mos';* from *1266;* *disunion* (of opinion and conduct):—division {1x}. See: BAGD—186d; THAYER—140b.

1268. **διανέμω** {1x} **dianĕmō**, *dee-an-em'-o;* from *1223* and the base of *3551;* to *distribute,* i.e. (of information) to *disseminate:*—spread {1x}. See: BAGD—186d; THAYER—140b.

1269. **διανεύω** {1x} **dianĕuō**, *dee-an-yoo'-o;* from *1223* and *3506;* to *nod* (or *express* by signs) *across* an intervening space:—beckoned + 2258 {1x}. See: BAGD—187a; THAYER—140b.

1270. **διανόημα** {1x} **dianŏēma**, *dee-an-o'-ay-mah;* from a compound of *1223* and *3539;* something *thought through,* i.e. a *sentiment:*—thought {1x}. See: TDNT—4:968, 636; BAGD—187a; THAYER—140c.

1271. **διάνοια** {13x} **dianŏia**, *dee-an'-oy-ah;* from *1223* and *3563;* *deep thought,* prop. the faculty (*mind* or its *disposition*), by impl. its exercise:—imagination {1x}, mind {9x}, understanding {3x}. See: TDNT—4:963, 636; BAGD—187a; THAYER—140c.

1272. **διανοίγω** {8x} **dianŏigō**, *dee-an-oy'-go;* from *1223* and *455;* to *open thoroughly,* lit. (as a first-born) or fig. (to *expound*):—open {8x}. See: BAGD—187b; THAYER—140c.

1273. **διανυκτερεύω** {1x} **dianuktĕrĕuō**, *dee-an-ook-ter-yoo'-o;* from *1223* and a der. of *3571;* to *sit up the whole night:*—continued all night + 2258 {1x}. See: BAGD—187b; THAYER—140d.

1274. **διανύω** {1x} **dianuō**, *dee-an-oo'-o;* from *1223* and ἀνύω **anuō** (to *effect*); to *accomplish thoroughly:*—finish {1x}. See: BAGD—187b; THAYER—140d.

1275. **διαπαντός** {7x} **diapantŏs**, *dee-ap-an-tos';* from *1223* and the genit. of *3956;* *through all* the time, i.e. (adv.) *constantly:*—alway {2x}, always {3x}, continually {2x}. See: BAGD—187c; THAYER—140d.

1276. **διαπεράω** {6x} **diapĕraō**, *dee-ap-er-ah'-o;* from *1223* and a der. of the base of *4008;* to *cross entirely:*—go over {1x}, pass {1x}, pass over {3x}, sail over {1x}. See: BAGD—187c; THAYER—140d.

1277. **διαπλέω** {1x} **diaplĕō**, *dee-ap-leh'-o;* from *1223* and *4126;* to *sail through, across:*—sail over {1x}. See: BAGD—187c; THAYER—141a.

1278. **διαπονέω** {2x} **diapŏnĕō**, *dee-ap-on-eh'-o;* from *1223* and a der. of *4192;* to *toil through,* i.e. (pass.) *be worried:*—be grieved {2x}. See: BAGD—187c; THAYER—141a.

1279. **διαπορεύομαι** {5x} **diapŏrĕuŏmai**, *dee-ap-or-yoo'-om-ahee;* from *1223* and *4198;* to *travel through:*—went through {3x}, in (one's) journey {1x}, pass by {1x}. See: BAGD—187d; THAYER—141a.

1280. **διαπορέω** {5x} **diapŏrĕō**, *dee-ap-or-eh'-o;* from *1223* and *639;* to *be thoroughly nonplussed:*—be in doubt {1x}, doubt {2x}, be much perplexed {1x}, be perplexed {1x}.

Diaporeo signifies to be thoroughly perplexed, amounting to despair, at a loss as to what to do; without resources to solve the problem. See: BAGD—187d; THAYER—141a.

1281. **διαπραγματεύομαι** {1x} **diapragmatĕuŏmai**, *dee-ap-rag-mat-yoo'-om-ahee;* from *1223* and *4231;* to *thoroughly occupy oneself,* i.e. (tran. and by impl.) to *earn* in business:—gain by trading {1x}. See: TDNT—6:641, 927; BAGD—187d; THAYER—141b.

1282. **διαπρίω** {2x} **diapriō**, *dee-ap-ree'-o;* from *1223* and the base of *4249;* to *saw asunder,* i.e. (fig.) to *exasperate:*—cut {1x}, be cut to the heart {1x}. See: BAGD—187d; THAYER—141b.

1283. **διαρπάζω** {4x} **diarpazō**, *dee-ar-pad'-zo;* from *1223* and *726;* to *seize asunder,* i.e. *plunder:*—spoil {4x}. See: BAGD—188a; THAYER—141b.

1284. **διαῤῥήσσω** {5x} **diarrhēssō**, *dee-ar-hrayce'-so;* from *1223* and *4486;* to *tear asunder:*—break {2x}, rend {3x}. See: BAGD—188a; THAYER—141b.

1285. **διασαφέω** {1x} **diasaphĕō**, *dee-as-af-eh'-o;* from *1223* and σαφής **saphēs** (*clear*); to *clear thoroughly, explain fully,* i.e. (fig.) *declare:*—tell unto {1x}. See: BAGD—188b; THAYER—141c.

1286. **διασείω** {1x} **diasĕiō**, *dee-as-i'-o;* from *1223* and *4579;* to *shake thoroughly, violently,* i.e. (fig.) to *intimidate:*—do violence to {1x}. See: BAGD—188b; THAYER—141c.

1287. **διασκορπίζω** {9x} **diaskŏrpizō**, *dee-as-kor-pid'-zo;* from *1223* and *4650;* to *dissipate,* i.e. (gen.) to *rout* or *separate;* spec., to *winnow;* fig. to *squander:*—disperse {1x}, scatter {2x}, scatter abroad {2x}, strew {2x}, waste {2x}. See: TDNT—7:418, 1048; BAGD—188b; THAYER—141c.

1288. **διασπάω** {2x} **diaspaō**, *dee-as-pah'-o;* from *1223* and *4685;* to *draw apart,* i.e. *sever* or *dismember:*—pluck asunder {1x}, pull in pieces {1x}. See: BAGD—188c; THAYER—141d.

1289. **διασπείρω** {3x} **diaspĕirō**, *dee-as-pi'-ro;* from *1223* and *4687;* to *sow throughout,* i.e. (fig.) *distribute* in foreign lands:—scatter abroad {3x}. See: BAGD—188c; THAYER—141d.

1290. **διασπορά** {3x} **diaspŏra**, *dee-as-por-ah';* from *1289;* *dispersion,* i.e. (spec. and concr.) the (converted) Isr. *resident* in Gentile countries:—dispersed {1x}, which are scattered abroad {1x}, scattered {1x}. See: TDNT—2:98, 156; BAGD—188c; THAYER—141d.

1291. **διαστέλλομαι** {8x} **diastĕllŏmai**, *dee-as-tel'-lom-ahee;* mid. voice from *1223* and *4724;* to *set* (oneself) *apart* (fig. *distinguish*), i.e. (by impl.) to *enjoin:*—charge {6x}, give commandment {1x}, be commanded {1x}. See: TDNT—7:591; BAGD—188d; THAYER—142a.

1292. **διάστημα** {1x} **diastēma**, *dee-as'-tay-mah;* from *1339;* an *interval:*—space {1x}. See: BAGD—188d; THAYER—142a.

1293. **διαστολή** {3x} **diastŏlē**, *dee-as-tol-ay';* from *1291;* a *variation:*—difference {2x}, distinction {1x}. See: TDNT—7:592, 1074; BAGD—188d; THAYER—142a.

1294. **διαστρέφω** {7x} **diastrĕphō**, *dee-as-tref'-o;* from *1223* and *4762;* to *distort, twist,* i.e. (fig.) *misinterpret,* or (morally) *corrupt:*—perverse {4x}, pervert {2x}, turn away {1x}. See: TDNT—7:717, 1093; BAGD—189a; THAYER—142a.

1295. **διασώζω** {8x} **diasōzō**, *dee-as-odze'-o;* from *1223* and *4982;* to *save thoroughly,* i.e. (by impl. or anal.) to *cure, preserve, rescue,* etc.:—escape {2x}, save {2x}, make perfectly whole {1x}, escape safe {1x}, bring safe {1x}, heal {1x}. See: BAGD—189a; THAYER—142b.

1296. **διαταγή** {2x} **diatagē**, *dee-at-ag-ay';* from *1299; arrangement,* i.e. *institution:*—disposition {1x}, ordinance {1x}. See: TDNT—8:36, 1156; BAGD—189b; THAYER—142b.

1297. **διάταγμα** {1x} **diatagma**, *dee-at'-ag-mah;* from *1299;* an *arrangement,* i.e. (authoritative) *edict:*—commandment {1x}.

Diatagma signifies that which is imposed by decree or law (Heb 11:23). It stresses the concrete character of the commandment. See: BAGD—189b; THAYER—142c.

1298. **διαταράσσω** {1x} **diatarassō**, *dee-at-ar-as'-so;* from *1223* and *5015;* to *disturb wholly,* i.e. *agitate* (with alarm):—trouble {1x}. See: BAGD—189b; THAYER—142c.

1299. **διατάσσω** {16x} **diatassō**, *dee-at-as'-so;* from *1223* and *5021;* to *arrange thoroughly,* i.e. (spec.) *institute, prescribe,* etc.:—command {7x}, appoint {4x}, ordain {3x}, set in order {1x}, give order {1x}.

Diatasso, a verb, a strengthened form of *tasso* (5021) [*dia*, "through," intensive], frequently denotes "to arrange, appoint, prescribe" **(1)** what was "appointed" for tax collectors to collect: "And he said unto them, Exact no more than that which is appointed you" (Lk 3:13); **(2)** of the tabernacle, as "appointed" by God for Moses to make: "Our fathers had the tabernacle of witness in the wilderness, as He had appointed, speaking unto Moses, that he should make it according to the fashion that he had seen" (Acts 7:11), **(3)** of the arrangements "appointed" by Paul with regard to himself and his travelling companions: "And we went before to ship, and sailed unto Assos, there intending to take in Paul: for so had he appointed, minding himself to go afoot" (Acts 20:13);

(4) of what the apostle "ordained" in all the churches in regard to marital conditions: "But as God hath distributed to every man, as the Lord hath called every one, so let him walk. And so ordain I in all churches" (1 Cor 7:17); **(5)** of what the Lord "ordained" in regard to the support of those who proclaimed the gospel: "Even so hath the Lord ordained that they which preach the gospel should live of the gospel" (1 Cor 9:14); **(6)** of the Law as divinely "ordained," or administered, through angels, by Moses,: "Wherefore then *serveth* the law? It was added because of transgressions, till the seed should come to whom the promise was made; *and it was* ordained by angels in the hand of a mediator" (Gal 3:19). See: TDNT—8:34, 1156; BAGD—189c; THAYER—142c.

1300. **διατελέω** {1x} **diatĕlĕō**, *dee-at-el-eh'-o;* from *1223* and *5055;* to *accomplish thoroughly,* i.e. (subj.) to *persist:*—continue {1x}.

Diatelo means to bring through to an end. See: BAGD—189c; THAYER—142d.

1301. **διατηρέω** {2x} **diatērĕō**, *dee-at-ay-reh'-o;* from *1223* and *5083;* to *watch thoroughly,* i.e. (pos. and tran.) to *observe* strictly, or (neg. and refl.) to *avoid* wholly:—keep {2x}. See: TDNT—8:151, 1174; BAGD—189d; THAYER—142d.

1302. **διατί** {27x} **diati**, *dee-at-ee';* from *1223* and *5101; through what* cause?, i.e. *why?:*—wherefore {4x}, why {23x}. See: BAGD—189d; THAYER—142d.

1303. **διατίθεμαι** {7x} **diatithĕmai**, *dee-at-ith'-em-ahee;* mid. voice from *1223* and *5087;* to *put apart,* i.e. (fig.) *dispose* (by assignment, compact, or bequest):—appoint {2x}, make {3x}, testator {2x}.

Diatithemi, a verb, a strengthened form of tithemi (5087) [*dia*, "through," intensive], is **(1)** used in the middle voice only. **(2)** It means to arrange, dispose of, one's own affairs **(2a)** of something that belongs to one: The Lord used it of His disciples with reference to the kingdom which is to be theirs hereafter, and of Himself in the same respect, as that which has been "appointed" for Him by His Father: "And I appoint (*diatithemi*) unto you a kingdom, as My Father hath appointed (*diatithemi*) unto Me" (Lk 22:29); **(2b)** to make a covenant, enter into a covenant, with one, Acts 3:25; Heb 8:10; 10:16; **(3)** be the person who disposes of through covenant, a testator, Heb 9:16, 17. See: TDNT—2:104, 157; BAGD—189d; THAYER—142d.

1304. **διατρίβω** {10x} **diatribō**, *dee-at-ree'-bo;* from *1223* and the base of *5147;* to *wear through* (time), i.e. *remain:*—abide {5x}, be {1x}, continue {2x}, tarry {2x}.

Diatribo means lit., "to wear through by rubbing, to wear away" and **(1)** when used of time, "to spend or pass time, to stay, continue" Jn 11:54; Acts 15:35; elsewhere it means **(2)** "abiding, abode" Acts 12:19; 14:3, 28; 16:12; 20:6; **(3)** "had been" Acts 25:14; **(4)** "tarry" Jn 3:22; Acts 25:6. See: BAGD—190a; THAYER—143a.

1305. **διατροφή** {1x} **diatrŏphē**, *dee-at-rof-ay';* from a compound of *1223* and *5142; nourishment:*—food {1x}.

This word means "sustenance, food," suggesting a sufficient supply and is used in 1 Ti 6:8. See: BAGD—190a; THAYER—143a.

1306. **διαυγάζω** {1x} **diaugazō**, *dee-ow-gad'-zo;* from *1223* and *826;* to *glimmer* (*through*), i.e. *break* (as day):—dawn {1x}.

Diaugazo describes the breaking of daylight upon the darkness of night, metaphorically in 2 Pet 1:19, of the shining of spiritual light into the heart. A probable reference is to the day to be ushered in at the second coming of Christ: "until the Day gleam through the present darkness, and the Light-bringer dawn in your hearts." See: BAGD—190a; THAYER—143a.

1307. **διαφανής** {1x} **diaphanēs**, *dee-af-an-ace';* from *1223* and *5316; appearing through,* i.e. "*diaphanous*":—transparent {1x}. See: BAGD—190b; THAYER—143a.

1308. **διαφέρω** {13x} **diaphĕrō**, *dee-af-er'-o;* from *1223* and *5342;* to *bear through,* i.e. (lit.) *transport;* usually to *bear apart,* i.e. (obj.) to *toss about* (fig. *report*); subj. to "*differ,*" or (by impl.) *surpass:*—be better {3x}, be of more value {2x}, differ from {2x}, should carry {1x}, publish {1x}, drive up and down {1x}, misc. {3x} = be (more) excellent, make matter.

This word used **(1)** transitively, means "to carry through", Mk 11:16; Acts 13:49; 27:27 ("driven to and fro"); **(2)** intransitively, **(2a)** "to differ," Rom 2:18; Gal 2:6; Phil 1:10; **(2b)** "to excel, be better," e.g., Mt 6:26; 10:31 ("of more value"); 12:12; Lk 12:7, 24; Rom 2:18; 1 Cor 15:41; Gal 4:1; Phil 1:10. See: BAGD—190b; THAYER—143b.

1309. **διαφεύγω** {1x} **diaphĕugō**, *dee-af-yoo'-go;* from *1223* and *5343;* to *flee through,* i.e. *escape:*—escape {1x}.

Diapheugo means lit., "to flee through," is used of the "escaping" of prisoners from a ship, Acts 27:42. See: BAGD—190c; THAYER—143c.

1310. **διαφημίζω** {3x} **diaphēmizō**, *dee-af-ay-mid'-zo;* from *1223* and a der. of *5345;* to *report thoroughly,* i.e. *divulgate:*—spread abroad (one's) fame {1x}, be commonly reported {1x}, blaze abroad {1x}.

This word means "to spread broad, commonly reported" (*dia*, "throughout," *phemizo*, "to speak"), and is so translated in Mt 9:31; 28:15 ("commonly reported"), Mk 1:45 ("blaze abroad"). See: BAGD—190c; THAYER—143c.

1311. **διαφθείρω** {6x} **diaphthĕirō**, *dee-af-thi'-ro;* from *1225* and *5351;* to *rot thoroughly,* i.e. (by impl.) to *ruin* (pass. *decay* utterly, fig. *pervert*):—corrupt {2x}, destroy {3x}, perish {1x}.

This word, derived from *dia*, "through," intensive, and *phtheiro* (5351), "to corrupt utterly, through and through," is **(1)** said of men "of corrupt in mind," whose wranglings result from the doctrines of false teachers, 1 Ti 6:5. **(2)** It is translated "corrupteth," in Lk 12:33, of the work of a moth; **(3)** in Rev 8:9, of the effect of divine judgments hereafter upon navigation; **(4)** in 11:18, of the divine retribution of destruction upon those who have destroyed the earth; **(5)** in 2 Cor 4:16 it is translated "perish," said of the human body. See: TDNT—9:93, 1259; BAGD—190c; THAYER—143c.

1312. **διαφθορά** {6x} **diaphthŏra**, *dee-af-thor-ah';* from *1311; decomposition and decay:*—corruption {6x}.

Diaphthora, an intensified form of *phtheiro* (5351), "utter or thorough corruption," referring in the NT to physical decomposition and decay, is used **(1)** six times, five of which refer, negatively, to the body of God's "Holy One," after His death, which body, by reason of His absolute holiness, could not see "corruption," Acts 2:27, 31; 13:34–35, 37; **(2)** once it is used of a human body, that of David, which, by contrast, saw "corruption," Acts 13:36. See: TDNT—9:93, 1259; BAGD—190d; THAYER—143d.

1313. **διάφορος** {4x} **diaphŏrŏs**, *dee-af'-or-os;* from *1308; varying;* also *surpassing:*—differing {1x}, divers {1x}, more excellent {2x}.

Diaphoros signifies "varying in kind, different, diverse." It is used **(1)** of spiritual gifts, Rom 12:6; and **(2)** of ceremonial washings, Heb 9:10 ("divers"); and in the **(3)** comparative degree of *diaphoros*, "excellent," it is used twice, **(3a)** in Heb 1:4, "more excellent (name)," and **(3b)** Heb

8:6, "more excellent (ministry)." See: TDNT—9:62, 1259; BAGD—190d; THAYER—143d.

1314. **διαφυλάσσω** {1x} **diaphulassō**, *dee-af-oo-las'-so;* from *1223* and *5442;* to *guard thoroughly,* i.e. *protect:*—keep {1x}.

Diaphulasso, a strengthened form of *phulasso* (5442), (*dia,* "through," used intensively), "to guard carefully, defend, to keep" is found in Lk 4:10. See: BAGD—191a; THAYER—143d.

1315. **διαχειρίζομαι** {2x} **diachĕirizŏmai**, *dee-akh-i-rid'-zom-ahee;* from *1223* and a der. of *5495;* to *handle thoroughly,* i.e. *lay* violent *hands* upon:—kill {1x}, slay {1x}.

This word means primarily, "to have in hand, manage" and is used in the middle voice, in the sense of "laying hands on" with a view to "kill," or of actually "killing," Acts 5:30, "ye slew"; 26:21, "to kill." See: BAGD—191a; THAYER—143d.

1316. **διαχωρίζομαι** {1x} **diachōrizŏmai**, *dee-akh-o-rid'-zom-ahee;* from *1223* and the mid. voice of *5563;* to *remove* (oneself) *wholly,* i.e. *retire:*—depart {1x}.

This word means lit., "to unloose, undo" and signifies "to depart," in the sense of "departing" from life, Phil 1:23, a metaphor drawn from loosing moorings preparatory to setting sail, or, according to some, from breaking up an encampment, or from the unyoking of baggage animals. See: BAGD—191a; THAYER—144a.

1317. **διδακτικός** {2x} **didaktikŏs**, *did-ak-tik-os';* from *1318; instructive* ("didactic"):—This word means apt to teach {2x}. "skilled in teaching" and is translated "apt to teach" in 1 Tim 3:2; 2 Ti 2:24. See: TDNT—2:165, 161; BAGD—191b; THAYER—144a.

1318. **διδακτός** {3x} **didaktŏs**, *did-ak-tos';* from *1321;* (subj.) *instructed,* or (obj.) *communicated* by teaching:—taught {1x}, which . . . teacheth {2x}.

This word means primarily "what can be taught," then, "taught," is used **(1)** of persons, Jn 6:45; **(2)** of things, 1 Cor 2:13 (twice), "(not in words which man's wisdom) teacheth, (but which the Spirit) teacheth," lit., "(not in words) taught (of man's wisdom, but) taught (of the Spirit)." See: TDNT—2:165, 161; BAGD—191b; THAYER—144a.

1319. **διδασκαλία** {21x} **didaskalia**, *did-as-kal-ee'-ah;* from *1320; instruction* (the function or the information; that which is taught):—doctrine {19x}, learning {1x}, teaching {1x}.

This word denotes **(1)** "that which is taught, doctrine," Mt 15:9; Mk 7:7; Eph 4:14; Col 2:22; 1 Ti 1:10; 4:1, 6; 6:1, 3; 2 Ti 4:3; Titus 1:9 ("doctrine," in last part of verse); 2:1, 10; **(2)** "teaching, instruction," Rom 12:7, "teaching"; 15:4, "learning", 1 Ti 4:13 "doctrine"; v. 16 "the doctrine,"; 5:17 "doctrine"; 2 Ti 3:10, 16 (ditto); Titus 2:7, "thy doctrine." See: TDNT—2:160, 161; BAGD—191c; THAYER—144a.

1320. **διδάσκαλος** {58x} **didaskalŏs**, *did-as'-kal-os;* from *1321;* an *instructor* (gen. or spec.):—Master (Jesus) {40x}, teacher {10x}, master {7x}, doctor {1x}.

This word means a teacher and in the NT one who teaches concerning the things of God, and the duties of man **(1)** one who is fitted to teach, or thinks himself so, Heb 5:12; Rom 2:20; **(2)** the teachers of the Jewish religion, Lk 2:46; Jn 3:10; **(3)** of those who by their great power as teachers draw crowds around them **(3a)** John the Baptist, Lk 3:12, **(3b)** Jesus, Jn 1:38; 3:2; 8:4; **(4)** of the apostles, and of Paul, 1 Ti 2:7; 2 Ti 1:11; **(5)** of those who in the religious assemblies of the Christians, undertook the work of teaching, with the special assistance of the Holy Spirit, 1 Cor 12:28; Eph 4:11; Acts 13:1; **(6)** of false teachers among Christians, 2 Ti 4:3. See: TDNT—2:148, 161; BAGD—191c; THAYER—144b.

1321. **διδάσκω** {97x} **didaskō**, *did-as'-ko;* a prol. (caus.) form of a primary verb δάω **daō** (to *learn*); to *teach* (in the same broad application):—teach {93x}, taught + 2258 {4x}.

This word denotes to cause to learn, to effect learning. This word means is used **(1)** absolutely, "to give instruction," e.g., Mt 4:23; 9:35; Rom 12:7; 1 Cor 4:17; 1 Ti 2:12; 4:11; **(2)** transitively, with an object, whether **(2a)** persons, e.g., Mt 5:2; 7:29, and frequently in the Gospels and Acts, or **(2b)** things "taught," e.g., Mt 15:9; 22:16; Acts 15:35; 18:11; **(2c)** both persons and things, e.g., Jn 14:26; Rev 2:14, 20. See: TDNT—2:135, 161; BAGD—192a; THAYER—144b.

1322. **διδαχή** {30x} **didachē**, *did-akh-ay';* from *1321; instruction* (the act or the matter):—doctrine {29x}, hath been taught {1x}.

This word denotes "teaching," either **(1)** that which is taught, e.g., Mt 7:28 "doctrine"; Titus 1:9; Rev 2:14–15, 24, or **(2)** the act of teaching, instruction, e.g., Mk 4:2 "doctrine"; Rom 16:17. See: TDNT—2:163, 161; BAGD—192b; THAYER—144d.

1323. **δίδραχμον** {2x} **didrachmŏn**, *did'-rakh-mon;* from *1364* and *1406;* a *double drachma* (*didrachm*):—tribute {1x}, tribute money {1x}.

This word means "a half-shekel" (i.e., *dis,* "twice," *drachme,* "a drachma," the coin mentioned in Lk 15:8, 9), was the amount of the tribute in the 1st cent., A.D., due from every adult Jew for the maintenance of the Temple services, Mt 17:24 (twice). See: BAGD—192c; THAYER—145a.

1324. **Δίδυμος** {3x} **Didumŏs**, *did'-oo-mos;* prol. from *1364; double,* i.e. *twin; Didymus,* a Chr.:—Didymus {1x}. See: BAGD—192c; THAYER—145a.

1325. **δίδωμι** {413x} **didōmi**, *did'-o-mee;* a prol. form of a primary verb (which is used as an altern. in most of the tenses); to *give* (used in a very wide application, prop. or by impl., lit. or fig.; greatly modified by the connection):—give {365x}, grant {10x}, put {5x}, shew {4x}, deliver {2x}, make {2x}, misc. {25x} = adventure, bestow, bring forth, commit, hinder, minister, number, offer, have power, receive, set, smite (+ with the hand), strike (+ with the palm of the hand), suffer, take, utter, yield. See: TDNT—2:166, 166; BAGD—192c; THAYER—145a.

1326. **διεγείρω** {7x} **diĕgĕirō**, *dee-eg-i'-ro;* from *1223* and *1453;* to *wake fully;* i.e. *arouse* (lit. or fig.):—arise {2x}, awake {2x}, raise {1x}, stir up {2x}.

Degeiro, as a verb, signifies "to rouse, to awaken from sleep." **(1)** In Mt 1:24, "Joseph being raised from sleep," the passive participle is, lit., "being aroused." **(2)** In Mk 4:39 "he arose," the lit. rendering is "he being awakened." **(3)** In Jn 6:18 "the sea arose" the imperfect tense of the passive voice is used, and is understood as "the sea was being aroused." Syn. for **(1) - (3):** 305, 393, 450, 1096, 1453, 1525, 1817, 4911. **(4)** *Diegeiro* also means "stir up": "Yea, I think it meet, as long as I am in this tabernacle, to stir you up by putting *you* in remembrance" (2 Pet 1:13; cf. 3:1). Syn. for **(4):** 329, 383, 387, 1892, 2042, 3947, 3951, 4531, 4579, 4787, 4797, 5017. See: BAGD—193d; THAYER—147a.

1327. **διέξοδος** {1x} **diĕxŏdŏs**, *dee-ex'-od-os;* from *1223* and *1841;* an *outlet through,* i.e. prob. an open *square* (from which roads diverge):—highway + 3598 + 3588 {1x}. In Mt 22:9, the word is translated "highways," "the partings of the highways, the crossroads." See: TDNT—5:103, 666; BAGD—194a; THAYER—147b.

1328. **διερμηνευτής** {1x} **diĕrmēnĕutēs**, *dee-er-main-yoo-tace';* from *1329;* an *explainer:*—interpreter {1x}. See: TDNT—2:661, 256; BAGD—194b; THAYER—147c.

1329. **διερμηνεύω** {6x} **diĕrmēnĕuō**, *dee-er-main-yoo'-o;* from *1223* and *2059;* to *explain thoroughly,* by impl. to *translate:*—expound {1x}, interpret {4x}, interpretatioin {1x}.

This word means "to interpret fully" (*dia* "through," intensive, *hermeneuo,* "to interpret"); (Eng., "hermeneutics"), and is translated, **(1)** "He expounded" in Lk 24:27; **(2)** in Acts 9:36, "by interpretation," lit., "being interpreted"; see also **(3)** 1 Cor 12:30; 14:5, 13, 27. See: TDNT—2:661, 256; BAGD—194b; THAYER—147c.

1330. **διέρχομαι** {43x} **diĕrchŏmai**, *dee-er'-khom-ahee;* from *1223* and *2064;* to come or go through; to *traverse* (lit.):—pass {8x}, pass through {7x}, go {7x}, go over {3x}, go through {2x}, walk {2x}, vr to go {1x}, misc. {13x} come, depart, go about, go abroad, go everywhere, go throughout, pass (by, over, throughout), pierce through, travel.

This word means to go through, pass through **(1)** to go, walk, journey, pass through a place, Mt 12:43; 19:24; **(2)** to travel the road which leads through a place, go, pass, travel through a region, Lk 19:1; Acts 12:10; 13:6; **(3)** to go to different places, of people, to go abroad, Acts 8:4, 40; 13:14; **(4)** of a report, to spread, go abroad, Lk 5:15. See: TDNT—2:676, 257; BAGD—194c; THAYER—147c.

1331. **διερωτάω** {1x} **diĕrōtaō**, *dee-er-o-tah'-o;* from *1223* and *2065;* to *question throughout,* i.e. *ascertain* by interrogation:—make enquiry for {1x}.

Dierotao means "to find by inquiry, to inquire through to the end" (*dia,* intensive, *erotao,* "to ask") and is used in Acts 10:17. See: BAGD—194d; THAYER—148a.

1332. **διετής** {1x} **diĕtēs**, *dee-et-ace';* from *1364* and *2094;* of *two years* (in age):—two years old {1x}. See: BAGD—194d; THAYER—148a.

1333. **διετία** {2x} **diĕtia**, *dee-et-ee'-a;* from *1332;* a space of *two years* (*biennium*):—two years {2x}. See: BAGD—194d; THAYER—148a.

1334. **διηγέομαι** {8x} **diēgĕŏmai**, *dee-ayg-eh'-om-ahee;* from *1223* and *2233;* to *relate fully:*—declare {3x}, shew {1x}, tell {4x}.

This word means to conduct a narration through to the end; hence, denotes to recount, to relate in full (Mk 5:16; Lk 8:39; 9:10). See: BAGD—195a; THAYER—148a.

1335. **διήγεσις** {1x} **diēgĕsis**, *dee-ayg'-es-is;* or διήγησις **diēgēsis** *dee-ayg'-es-is;* from *1334;* a *recital:*—declaration {1x}.

Diegesis is translated "a declaration" in Lk 1:1 and denotes a "narrative," ("to set out in detail, recount). See: TDNT—2:909, 303; BAGD—195a; THAYER—148b.

1336. **διηνεκές** {4x} **diēnĕkĕs**, *dee-ay-nek-es';* neut. of a compound of *1223* and a der. of an alt. of *5342; carried through,* i.e. (adv. with *1519* and *3588* pref.) *perpetually:*—+ continually + 1519 {2x}, for ever + 1591 {2x}. See: BAGD—195a; THAYER—148b.

1337. **διθάλασσος** {1x} **dithalassŏs**, *dee-thal'-as-sos;* from *1364* and *2281; having two seas,* i.e. a *sound* with a double outlet:—where two seas meet {1x}.

This word means primarily "divided into two seas," then, "dividing the sea," as of a reef or rocky projection running out into the "sea," Acts 27:41. See: BAGD—195a; THAYER—148b.

1338. **διϊκνέομαι** {1x} **diïknĕŏmai**, *dee-ik-neh'-om-ahee;* from *1223* and the base of *2425;* to *reach through,* i.e. *penetrate:*—pierce {1x}.

This word means "to go through, penetrate" and is used of the power of the Word of God, in Heb 4:12, "piercing." See: BAGD—195b; THAYER—148b.

1339. **διΐστημι** {3x} **diïstēmi**, *dee-is'-tay-mee;* from *1223* and *2476;* to *stand apart,* i.e. (refl.) to *remove, intervene:*—after the space of . . . {1x}, go further {1x}, be parted {1x}.

Diistemi means "to set apart, separate" (*dia*, "apart," *histemi*, "to cause to stand"), and is used **(1)** in the active voice in Lk 24:51, "was parted"; and is translated **(2)** "after the space of . . .", Lk 22:59; and **(3)** "gone . . . further", Acts 27:28). See: BAGD—195b; THAYER—148b.

1340. **διϊσχυρίζομαι** {2x} **diïschurizŏmai**, *dee-is-khoo-rid'-zom-ahee;* from *1223* and a der. of *2478;* to *stout* it *through,* i.e. *asseverate:*—confidently affirm {1x}, constantly affirm {1x}.

This word primarily signifies "to lean upon," hence, "to affirm stoutly, assert vehemently," Lk 22:59; Acts 12:15. See: BAGD—195b; THAYER—140c.

1341. **δικαιοκρισία** {1x} **dikaiŏkrisia**, *dik-ah-yok-ris-ee'-ah;* from *1342* and *2920;* a *just sentence:*—righteous judgment {1x}. See: TDNT—2:224, 168; BAGD—195c; THAYER—148c.

1342. **δίκαιος** {81x} **dikaiŏs**, *dik'-ah-yos;* from *1349; equitable* (in character or act); by impl. *innocent, holy* (absol. or rel.):—righteous {41x}, just {33x}, right {5x}, meet {2x}.

Dikaios denotes **(1)** righteous, a state of being right, or right conduct, judged whether by the divine standard, or according to human standards, of what is right. **(2)** Said of God, it designates the perfect agreement between His nature and His acts (in which He is the standard for all men). It is used in the broad sense, **(3)** of persons: **(3a)** of God (Jn 17:25; Rom 3:26; 1 Jn 1:9; 2:29); **(3b)** of Christ (Acts 3:14; 7:52; 2 Ti 4:8; 1 Pet 3:18); **(3c)** of men (Mt 1:19; Lk 1:6; Rom 1:17); **(4)** of things: **(4a)** blood [metaphorical] (Mt 23:35); **(4b)** Christ's judgment (Jn 5:30); **(4c)** any circumstance, fact or deed (Mt 20:4; Lk 12:57; Acts 4:19); **(4d)** the commandment [the Law] (Rom 7:12); **(4d)** works (1 Jn 3:12); **(4e)** the ways of God (Rev 15:3). Syn.: 1346, 1738. See: TDNT—2:182, 168; BAGD—195c; THAYER—148c.

1343. **δικαιοσύνη** {92x} **dikaiŏsunē**, *dik-ah-yos-oo'-nay;* from *1342; equity* (of character or act); spec. (Chr.) *justification:*—righteousness {92x}.

Dikaiosune is the character or quality of being right or just. **(1)** It denotes an attribute of God (Rom 3:5). **(2)** It is found in the sayings of the Lord Jesus **(2a)** of whatever is right or just in itself that conforms to the revealed will of God (Mt 5:6, 10, 20; Jn 16:8, 10); **(2b)** whatever has been appointed by God to be acknowledged and obeyed by man (Mt 3:15; 21:32); **(2c)** the sum total of the requirements of God (Mt 6:33); **(2d)** religious duties (Mt 6:1–15): distinguished as **(2d1)** almsgiving, man's duty to his neighbor (6: 2–4), **(2d2)** prayer—his duty to God (vv. 5–15), and **(2d3)** fasting—the duty of self-control (vv. 16–18).

(3) It is used of that gracious gift of God to men **(3a)** whereby all who believe on the Lord Jesus Christ are brought into right relationship with God. **(3b)** This righteousness is unattainable by obedience to any law, or by any merit of man's own, or any other condition than that of faith in Christ. **(3c)** The man who trusts in Christ becomes 'the righteousness of God in Him,' (2 Cor 5:21), i.e., becomes in Christ all that God requires a man to be, all that he could never be in himself. **(4)** Righteousness is not said to be imputed to the believer save in the sense that faith is imputed (reckoned) for righteousness (Rom 4:6, 11). **(5)** The faith thus exercised brings the soul into vital union with God in Christ, and inevitably produces righteousness of life, that is, conformity to the will of God. Syn.: 1345. See: TDNT—2:192, 168; BAGD—196b; THAYER—149b.

1344. **δικαιόω** {40x} **dikaiŏō**, *dik-ah-yŏ'-o;* from *1342;* to *render* (i.e. *show* or *regard* as) *just* or *innocent:*—be freed {1x}, justify {37x}, justifier {1x}, be righteous {1x}.

Dikaioo, as a verb, means primarily "to deem to be right," and signifies, in the NT, **(1)** "to show to be right or righteous"; in the passive voice, to be justified, Mt 11:19; Lk 7:35; Rom 3:4; 1 Ti 3:16; **(2)** "to declare to be righteous, to pronounce righteous," **(2a)** by man, **(2a1)** concerning God, Lk 7:29; **(2a2)** concerning himself, Lk 10:29; 16:15; **(2b)** by God concerning men, who are declared to be righteous before Him on certain conditions laid down by Him.

(3) Ideally the complete fulfillment of the law of God would provide a basis of "justification" in His sight, Rom 2:13. **(3a)** But no such case has occurred in mere human experience, and therefore no one can be "justified" on this ground, Rom 3:9–20; Gal 2:16; 3:10, 11; 5:4. **(3b)** From this negative presentation in Rom 3, the apostle proceeds to show that, consistently with God's own righteous character, and with a view to its manifestation, He is, through Christ, as "a propitiation . . . by (en, "instrumental") His blood," 3:25, "justification" being the legal and formal acquittal from guilt by God as Judge, the pronouncement of the sinner as righteous, who believes on the Lord Jesus Christ. **(3c)** In v. 24, "being justified" is in the present continuous tense, indicating the constant process of "justification" in the succession of those who believe and are "justified." **(3d)** In 5:1, "being justified" is in the aorist, or point, tense, indicating the definite time at which each person, upon the exercise of faith, was justified. **(3e)** In 8:1, "justification" is presented as "no condemnation." That "justification" is in view here is confirmed by the preceding chapters and by verse 34. **(3f)** In 3:26, the word rendered "Justifier" is the present participle of the verb, lit., "justifying"; similarly in 8:33 (where the artide is used), "God that justifieth," is, more lit., "God is the (One) justifying," with stress upon the word "God."

(4) "Justification" is primarily and gratuitously by faith, subsequently and evidentially by works. **(4a)** In regard to "justification" by works, the so-called contradiction between James and the apostle Paul is only apparent. There is harmony in the different views of the subject. **(4a1)** Paul has in mind Abraham's attitude toward God, his acceptance of God's word. This was a matter known only to God. The Romans epistle is occupied with the effect of this Godward attitude, not upon Abraham's character or actions, but upon the contrast between faith and the lack of it, namely, unbelief, cf. Rom 11:20. **(4a2)** James (2:21–26) is occupied with the contrast between faith that is real and faith that is false, a faith barren and dead, which is not faith at all. **(4b)** Again, the two writers have before them different epochs in Abraham's life—**(4b1)** Paul, the event recorded in Gen 15, **(4b2)** James, that in Gen 22. **(4c)** Contrast the words "believed" in Gen. 15:6 and "obeyed" in 22:18. **(4d)** Further, the two writers use the words "faith" and "works" in somewhat different senses. **(4d1)** With Paul, faith is acceptance of God's word; with **(4d2)** James, it is acceptance of the truth of certain statements about God, (v. 19), which may fail to affect one's conduct. **(4e)** Faith, as dealt with by Paul, results in acceptance with God., i.e., "justification," and is bound to manifest itself. If not, as James says "Can that faith save him?" (v. 14). **(4f)** With Paul, works are dead works, with James they are life works. The works of which Paul speaks could be quite independent of faith: those referred to by James can be wrought only where faith is real, and they will attest its reality. **(4g)** So with righteousness, or "justification": Paul is occupied with a right relationship with God, James, with right conduct. Paul testifies that the ungodly can be "justified" by faith, James that only the right-doer is "justified." See: TDNT—2:211, 168; BAGD—197c; THAYER—150b.

1345. **δικαίωμα** {10x} **dikaiōma**, *dik-ah'-yo-mah;* from *1344;* an *equitable deed;* by impl. a *statute* or *decision:*—judgment {2x}, justification {1x}, ordinance {3x}, righteousness {4x}.

Dikaioma has three distinct meanings, and seems best described comprehensively as "a concrete expression of righteousness"; it is a declaration that a person or thing is righteous, and hence, broadly speaking, it represents the expression and effect of dikaiosis (1347). It signifies **(1)** "an ordinance, judgment", Lk 1:6; **(1a)** Rom 1:32, judgment, i.e., what God has declared to be right, referring to His decree of retribution; **(1b)** Rom 2:26, "righteousness of the Law" (i.e., righteous requirements enjoined by the Law); **(1c)** so 8:4, collectively, the precepts of the Law, all that it demands as right; **(1d)** in Heb. 9:1, 10, ordinances connected with the tabernacle ritual;

(2) "a sentence of acquittal," by which God acquits men of their guilt, on the conditions **(2a)** of His grace in Christ, through His expiatory sacrifice, **(2b)** the acceptance of Christ by faith, Rom 5:16; **(2c)** "a righteous act," Rom 5:18, "(through one) act of righteousness," **(2c1)** not the act of "justification," nor **(2c2)** the righteous character of Christ (*dikaioma* does not signify character, as does *dikaiosune,* righteousness), but **(2c3)** the death of Christ, as an act accomplished consistently with God's character and counsels; **(2c4)** this is clear as being in antithesis to the "one trespass" in the preceding statement. **(2d)** Some take the word here as meaning a decree of righteousness, as in v. 16; the death of Christ could indeed be regarded as fulfilling such a decree, but as the apostle's argument proceeds, the word, as is frequently the case, passes from one shade of meaning to another, and **(2d1)** here stands not for a decree, but **(2d2)** an act; so in Rev 15:4, "righteous judgments", and 19:8, "righteousness (acts) of the saints." See: TDNT—2:219, 168; BAGD—198a; THAYER—151b.

1346. **δικαίως** {5x} **dikaiōs**, *dik-ah'-yoce;* adv. from *1342; equitably:*—justly {2x}, to righteousness {1x}, righteously {2x}.

This adverb means "justly, righteously, in accordance with what is right," and is said **(1)** of God's judgment, 1 Pet 2:23; **(2)** of men, Lk 23:41, "justly;" 1 Cor 15:34 "righteousness"; 1 Th 2:10; Titus 2:12. See: BAGD—198b; THAYER—151c.

1347. **δικαίωσις** {2x} **dikaiōsis**, *dik-ah'-yo-sis;* from *1344; acquittal* (for Christ's sake):—justification {2x}.

Dikaiosis denotes "the act of pronouncing righteous, justification, acquittal"; its precise meaning is determined by that of the verb dikaioo, "to justify" (1344); **(1)** it is used twice in Romans, and there alone in the NT, signifying the establishment of a person as just by acquittal from guilt. **(2)** In Rom 4:25 the phrase "for our justification," is, lit., "because of our justification" (parallel to the preceding clause "for our trespasses," i.e., because of trespasses committed), and means, not with a view to our "justification," but because all that was necessary on God's part for our "justification" had been effected in the death of Christ. On this account He was raised from the dead. The propitiation being perfect and complete, His resurrection was the confirmatory counterpart. **(3)** In 5:18, "justification of life" means "justification which results in life" (cf. v. 21). That God "justifies" the believing sinner on the ground of Christ's death, involves His free gift of life. See: TDNT—2:223, 168; BAGD—198b; THAYER—151c.

1348. **δικαστής** {3x} **dikastēs**, *dik-as-tace';* from a der. of *1349;* a *judger:*—judge {3x}.

Dikastes denotes "a judge", Lk 12:14; Acts 7:27, 35. Syn.: While *dikastes* is a forensic term, *krites* (2923) "gives prominence to the mental process." The *dikastes* acted as a juryman, the *krites* being the presiding "judge." See: BAGD—198b; THAYER—151c.

1349. **δίκη** {4x} **dikē**, *dee'-kay;* prob. from *1166; right* (as self-*evident*), i.e. *justice* (the principle, a decision, or its execution):—judgment {1x}, punish + 5099 {1x}, vengeance {2x}.

Dike means primarily "custom, usage," came to denote "what is right"; then, "a judicial hearing"; hence, "the execution of a sentence," **(1)** "punished," 2 Th 1:9; **(2)** "judgment", Acts 25:15; **(3)** Jude 7, "vengeance". Some feel that in Acts 28:4 ("vengeance") should be personified to denote the goddess Justice or Nemesis (Lat., *Justitia*), who the Melita folk supposed was about to inflict the punishment of death upon Paul by means of the viper. See: TDNT—2:178, 168; BAGD—198c; THAYER—151d.

1350. **δίκτυον** {12x} **diktuŏn**, *dik'-too-on;* prob. from a primary verb δίκω **dikō** (to *cast*); a *seine* (for fishing):—net {12x}.

Diktuon, a general term for a "net," occurs in Mt 4:20–21; Mk 1:18–19; Lk 5:2, 4–6; Jn 21:6, 8, 11 [twice]. Syn.: 293, 4522. See 293 for discussion. See: BAGD—198c; THAYER—151d.

1351. **δίλογος** {1x} **dilŏgŏs**, *dil'-og-os;* from *1364* and *3056; equivocal,* i.e. telling a different story:—double-tongued {1x}.

Dilogos primarily means saying the same thing twice, or given to repetition; hence, saying a thing to one person and giving a different view of it to another, double-tongued (1 Ti 3:8). See: BAGD—198d; THAYER—151d.

1352. **διό** {53x} **diŏ**, *dee-ŏ';* from *1223* and *3739; through which* thing, i.e. *consequently:*—for which cause {2x}, therefore {10x}, wherefore {41x}. See: BAGD—198d; THAYER—152a.

1353. **διοδεύω** {2x} **diŏdĕuō**, *dee-od-yoo'-o;* from *1223* and *3593; to travel through:*—go throughout {1x}, pass through {1x}.

Diodeuo means "to travel throughout or along" and is used in **(1)** Lk 8:1, of "going throughout" cities and villages; and **(2)** of "passing through" towns, Acts 17:1. See: BAGD—198d; THAYER—152a.

1354. **Διονύσιος** {1x} **Diŏnusiŏs**, *dee-on-oo'-see-os;* from Διόνυσος **Diŏnusŏs** (*Bacchus*); *reveller; Dionysius,* an Athenian:—Dionysius {1x}. See: BAGD—199a; THAYER—152a.

1355. **διόπερ** {3x} **diŏpĕr**, *dee-op'-er;* from *1352* and *4007; on which very account:*—wherefore {3x}. See: BAGD—199a; THAYER—152a.

1356. **διοπετής** {1x} **diŏpĕtēs**, *dee-op-et'-ace;* from the alt. of *2203* and the alt. of *4098; sky-fallen* (i.e. an *aerolite*):—which fell down from Jupiter {1x}. See: BAGD—199a; THAYER—152a.

1357. **διόρθωσις** {1x} **diŏrthōsis**, *dee-or'-tho-sis;* from a compound of *1223* and a der. of *3717,* mean. to *straighten thoroughly; rectification,* i.e. (spec.) the Messianic *restoration:*—reformation {1x}.

Diorthosis means properly **(1)** "a making straight" and denotes a "reformation" or reforming, Heb 9:10. **(2)** The word has the meaning of a right arrangement, right ordering, and what is here indicated is a time when the imperfect, the inadequate, would be superseded by a better order of things. See: TDNT—5:450, 727; BAGD—199a; THAYER—152b.

1358. **διορύσσω** {4x} **diŏrussō**, *dee-or-oos'-so;* from *1223* and *3736;* to *penetrate* burglariously:—break through {2x}, be broken up {1x}, be broken through {1x}.

This word means lit., "to dig through" and is used of the act of thieves in "breaking" into a house, Mt 6:19, 20; 24:43; Lk 12:39. See: BAGD—199b; THAYER—152b.

Διός **Diŏs**. See *2203*.

1359. **Διόσκουροι** {1x} **Diŏskŏurŏi**, *dee-os'-koo-roy;* from the alt. of *2203* and a form of the base of *2877; sons of Jupiter,* i.e. the twins *Dioscuri:*—Castor and Pollux {1x}. See: BAGD—199b; THAYER—152b.

1360. **διότι** {22x} **diŏti**, *dee-ot'-ee;* from *1223* and *3754; on the very account that,* or *inasmuch as:*—because {10x}, for {8x}, because that {3x}, therefore {1x}. See: BAGD—199b; THAYER—152c.

1361. **Διοτρεφής** {1x} **Diŏtrĕphēs**, *dee-ot-ref-ace';* from the alt. of *2203* and *5142; Jove-nourished; Diotrephes,* an opponent of Christianity:—*Diotrephes* {1x}. See: BAGD—199c; THAYER—152c.

1362. **διπλοῦς** {4x} **diplŏus**, *dip-looce';* or διπλόος **diploos**, *dip-loce'* from *1364* and (prob.) the base of *4119; two-fold:*—double {3x}, two-fold more {1x}.

Diplous denotes **(1)** "twofold, double," 1 Ti 5:17; Rev 18:6 (twice). **(2)** The comparative degree *diploteron* (neuter) is used adverbially in Mt 23:15, "twofold more." See: BAGD—199c; THAYER—152c.

1363. **διπλόω** {1x} **diplŏō**, *dip-lŏ'-o;* from *1362;* to *render two-fold:*—double {1x}.

Diploo signifies "to double, to repay or render twofold," Rev 18:6. See: BAGD—199d; THAYER—152c.

1364. **δίς** {6x} **dis**, *dece;* adv. from *1417; twice:*—again {2x}, twice {4x}.

Dis, the ordinary numeral adverb signifying twice, is rendered **(1)** "again" in Phil 4:16, "ye sent once and again unto my need," and **(2)** in 1 Th 2:18, where Paul states that he would have come to the Thessalonians "once and again," that is, twice at least he had attempted to do so. See: BAGD—199d; THAYER—152d.

Δίς **Dis**. See *2203*.

1365. **διστάζω** {2x} **distazō**, *dis-tad'-zo;* from *1364;* prop. to *duplicate,* i.e. (ment.) to *waver* (in opinion):—doubt {2x}.

Distazo means to stand in two ways implying uncertainty which way to take (Mt 14:31; 28:17). See: BAGD—200a; THAYER—152d.

1366. **δίστομος** {3x} **distŏmŏs**, *dis'-tom-os;* from *1364* and *4750; double-edged:*—with two edges {1x}, two-edged {2x}.

Distomos, lit., "double-mouthed, two-edged," is used of a sword with two edges, Heb. 4:12; Rev. 1:16; 2:12. See: BAGD—200a; THAYER—152d.

1367. **δισχίλιοι** {1x} **dischiliŏi**, *dis-khil'-ee-oy;* from *1364* and *5507; two thousand:*—two thousand {1x}. See: BAGD—200a; THAYER—153a.

1368. **διυλίζω** {1x} **diulizō**, *dee-oo-lid'-zo;* from *1223* and ὑλίζω **hulizō**, *hoo-lid'-zo* (to *filter*); to *strain out:*—strain at {1x}.

Diulizo primarily denotes "to strain thoroughly" (*dia,* "through," intensive, *hulizo,* "to strain"), then, "to strain at," as through a sieve or strainer, as in the case of wine, so as to remove the unclean midge, Mt 23:24. It is correctly translated "strain at" and not "strained out" as the stress is on the point of focus. The Pharisees habitually focused not on the life and joy in the wine itself, but focused on the insignificant (cf. tithing the mint, anise, and cumin, Mt 23:23. Their focus was the gnat so they strained at the gnat, not strain the wine to enjoy the immenseness of its purity. See: BAGD—200d; THAYER—153a.

1369. **διχάζω** {1x} **dichazō**, *dee-khad'-zo;* from a der. of *1364;* to *make apart,* i.e. *sunder* (fig. *alienate*):—set at variance {1x}.

Dichazo, "to cut apart, divide in two," is used metaphorically in Mt 10:35, "to set at variance." See: BAGD—200b; THAYER—153a.

1370. **διχοστασία** {3x} **dichŏstasia**, *dee-khos-tas-ee'-ah;* from a der. of *1364* and *4714; disunion,* i.e. (fig.) *dissension:*—division {2x}, sedition {1x}.

Dichostasia means lit., "a standing apart" (*dicha,* "asunder, apart," *stasis,* "a standing"), hence "a dissension, division," is translated **(1)** "seditions" in Gal 5:20; and "divisions" in Rom 16:17; 1 Cor 3:3. See: TDNT—1:514, 88; BAGD—200b; THAYER—153a.

1371. **διχοτομέω** {2x} **dichŏtŏmĕō**, *dee-khot-om-eh'-o;* from a compound of a der. of *1364* and a der. of τέμνω **tĕmnō** (to *cut*); to *bisect,* i.e. (by extens.) to *flog* severely:—cut asunder {1x}, cut in sunder {1x}.

This word means lit., to cut into two parts": **(1)** Mt 24:51, "to cut asunder," and **(2)** Lk 12:46, "cut in sunder." **(2a)** Some take the reference to be to the mode of punishment by which criminals and captives were "cut" in two; others, on account of the fact that in these passages the delinquent is still surviving after the treatment, take the verb to denote "to cut up" by scourging, to scourge severely, the word being used figuratively, denoting "cutting" future recurrences of the crime from the criminal. **(2b)** As to Mt 24:51, it has been remarked that the "cutting asunder" was an appropriate punishment for one who had lived a double life. **(2c)** In both passages the latter part of the sentence applies to retribution beyond this life. See: TDNT—2:225, 177; BAGD—200c; THAYER—153a.

1372. **διψάω** {16x} **dipsaō**, *dip-sah'-o;* from a var. of *1373;* to *thirst* for (lit. or fig.):—(be, be athirst {3x}, thirst {10x}, thirsty {3x}.

Dipsao is used **(1)** in the natural sense, e.g., Mt 25:35, 37, 42; in v. 44, "athirst" (lit., "thirsting"); Jn 4:13, 15; 19:28; Rom 12:20; 1 Cor 4:11; Rev 7:16; **(2)** figuratively, of spiritual "thirst," Mt 5:6; Jn 4:14; 6:35; 7:37; in Rev 21:6 and 22:17, "that is athirst." See: TDNT—2:226, 177; BAGD—200c; THAYER—153b.

1373. **δίψος** {1x} **dipsŏs**, *dip'-sos;* of uncert. aff.; *thirst:*—thirst {1x}.

This word means "thirst" and occurs in 2 Cor 11:27. See: TDNT—2:226; BAGD—200d; THAYER—153b.

1374. **δίψυχος** {2x} **dipsuchŏs**, *dip'-soo-khos;* from *1364* and *5590; two-spirited,* i.e. *vacillating* (in opinion or purpose):—double minded {2x}.

Dipsuchos lit. means "two-souled", hence, "double-minded," Jas 1:8; 4:8. This person lives one life for himself and lives another for God. See: TDNT—9:665, 1342; BAGD—201a; THAYER—153b.

1375. **διωγμός** {10x} **diōgmŏs**, *dee-ogue-mos';* from *1377; persecution:*—persecution {10x}.

Diogmos means persecution and occurs in Mt 13:21; Mk 4:17; 10:30; Acts 8:1; 13:50; Rom 8:35; 2 Cor 12:10; 2 Th 1:4; 2 Ti 3:11 (twice). See: BAGD—201a; THAYER—153c.

1376. **διώκτης** {1x} **diōktēs**, *dee-oke'-tace;* from *1377;* a *persecutor:*—persecutor {1x}. See: TDNT—2:229; BAGD—201b; THAYER—153c.

1377. **διώκω** {44x} **diōkō**, *dee-o'-ko;* a prol. (and caus.) form of a primary verb δίω **diō** (to *flee;* comp. the base of *1169* and *1249*); to *pursue* (lit. or fig.); by impl. to *persecute:*—persecute {28x}, follow after {6x}, follow {4x}, suffer persecution {3x}, ensue {1x}, given to {1x}, press toward {1x}.

Dioko, as a verb, denotes **(1)** "to drive away" (Mt 23:34); **(2)** "to pursue without hostility, to follow, follow after," said **(2a)** of righteousness (Rom 9:30); **(2b)** the Law (Rom 9:31; 12:13); **(3)** literally, "pursuing" (as one would a calling), **(3a)** the things which make for peace (Rom 14:19); **(3b)** love (1 Cor 14:1); **(3c)** that which is good (1 Th 5:15); **(3d)** righteousness, godliness, faith, love, patience, meekness (1 Ti 6:11); **(3e)** righteousness, faith, love, peace (2 Ti 2:22); **(3f)** peace and sanctification (Heb 12:14); **(3g)** peace (1 Pet 3:11). Syn.: 190, 1096, 1811, 1872, 2614, 2628, 3877, 4870. See: TDNT—2:229, 177; BAGD—201b; THAYER—153c.

1378. **δόγμα** {5x} **dŏgma**, *dog'-mah;* from the base of *1380;* a *law* (civil, cerem. or eccl.):—decree {3x}, ordinance {2x}.

Dogma is transliterated in English, primarily denoting an opinion or judgment; hence, an opinion expressed with authority, a doctrine, ordinance, decree (Lk 2:1; Acts 16:4; 17:7; Eph 2:15; Col 2:14). See: TDNT—2:230, 178; BAGD—201c; THAYER—153d.

1379. **δογματίζω** {1x} **dŏgmatizō**, *dog-mat-id'-zo;* from *1378;* to *prescribe* by statute, i.e. (refl.) to *submit* to cer. *rule:*—be subject to ordinances {1x}.

This word means "to decree," and signifies, in the middle voice, "to subject oneself to an ordinance," Col 2:20. See: TDNT—2:230, 178; BAGD—201d; THAYER—154a.

1380. **δοκέω** {63x} **dŏkĕō**, *dok-eh'-o,* a prol. form of a primary verb, δόκω **dŏkō**, *dok'-o* (used only in an alt. in certain tenses; comp. the base of *1166*) of the same mean.; to *think;* by impl. to *seem* (truthfully or uncertainly):—think {33x}, seem {13x}, suppose {7x}, seem good {3x}, please {2x}, misc. {5x} = be accounted, of own pleasure, be of reputation, trow.

This refers to a person's subjective mental estimate or opinion about something. A person's *doxa* (1391) may be right or wrong since it always involves the possibility of error [except when used of Jesus]. It always signifies a subjective estimate of a thing, not the objective appearance and qualities the thing actually possesses. Syn.: 5316. See: TDNT—2:232, 178; BAGD—201d; THAYER—154b.

1381. **δοκιμάζω** {23x} **dŏkimazō**, *dok-im-ad'-zo;* from *1384;* to *test* (lit. or fig.); by impl. to *approve:*—prove {10x}, try {4x}, approve {3x}, discern {2x}, allow {2x}, like {1x}, examine {1x}.

This word means "to prove with a view to approving," and is **(1)** twice translated by the verb "to allow" in Rom 14:22, and **(2)** "have been approved," 1 Th 2:4, of being qualified to be entrusted with the gospel; **(3)** in Rom 1:28, with the negative. Syn.: 3985. See: TDNT—2:255, 181; BAGD—202c; THAYER—154c.

1382. **δοκιμή** {7x} **dŏkimē**, *dok-ee-may';* from the same as *1384; test* (abstr. or concr.); by impl. *trustiness:*—proof {3x}, experience {2x}, trial {1x}, experiment {1x}.

Dokime means **(1)** "the process of proving"; it is **(2)** rendered "experiment" in 2 Cor 9:13; **(3)** in 2 Cor 8:2 "trial"; **(4)** "the effect of proving, approval, experience," Rom 5:4 (twice); **(5)** "proof" in 2 Cor 2:9; 13:3 and Phil 2:22. See: TDNT—2:255, 181; BAGD—202d; THAYER—154d.

1383. **δοκίμιον** {2x} **dŏkimiŏn**, *dok-im'-ee-on;* neut. of a presumed der. of *1382;* a *testing;* by impl. *trustworthiness:*—trial {1x}, trying {1x}.

Dokimion, "a test, a proof," is rendered **(1)** "trying" in Jas 1:3; **(2)** the same phrase is used in 1 Pet 1:7 "the trial of your faith," where the meaning probably is "that which is approved [i.e., as genuine] in your faith." See: TDNT—2:255, 181; BAGD—203a; THAYER—155a.

1384. **δόκιμος** {7x} **dŏkimŏs**, *dok'-ee-mos;* from *1380;* prop. *acceptable* (*current* after assayal), i.e. *approved:*—approved {6x}, tried {1x}. See: TDNT—2:255, 183; BAGD—203a; THAYER—155a.

1385. **δοκός** {6x} **dŏkŏs**, *dok-os';* from *1209* (through the idea of *holding* up); a *stick* of timber:—beam {6x}.

Dokos, "a beam," was the heavy rafters holding up the ceiling. The Lord used it metaphorically, in contrast to a mote, "of a great fault, or vice," Matt. 7:3–5; Luke 6:41–42. See: BAGD—203a; THAYER—155a.

δόκω **dŏkō**. See *1380*.

1386. **δόλιος** {1x} **dŏliŏs**, *dol'-ee-os;* from *1388; guileful:*—deceitful {1x}.

Dolios, "deceitful," is used in 2 Cor 11:13, of false apostles as "deceitful workers." See: BAGD—203b; THAYER—155a.

1387. **δολιόω** {1x} **dŏliŏō**, *dol-ee-ŏ'-o;* from *1386;* to *be guileful:*—use deceit {1x}.

Dolioo means to lure using bait and is translated "have used deceit" in Rom. 3:13. See: BAGD—203b; THAYER—155b.

1388. **δόλος** {12x} **dŏlŏs**, *dol'-os;* from an obs. primary verb, δέλλω **dĕllō** (prob. mean. to *decoy;* comp. *1185*); a *trick* (*bait*), i.e. (fig.) *wile:*—craft {1x}, deceit {2x}, guile {7x}, subtilty {2x}.

Dolos, primarily, "a bait," is rendered **(1)** "craft" in Mk 14:1; **(2)** "guile" Jn 1:47; 2 Co 12:16; 1 Th 2:3; 1 Pet 2:1; 2:22; 3:10; Rev 14:5 and **(3)** "subtilty" in Mt 26:4; Acts 13:10; and **(4)** "deceit" in Mk 7:22; Rom 1:29. See: BAGD—203b; THAYER—155b.

1389. **δολόω** {1x} **dŏlŏō**, *dol-ŏ'-o;* from *1388;* to *ensnare,* i.e. (fig.) *adulterate:*—handle deceitfully {1x}.

Doloo signifies to ensnare; hence, to corrupt, especially by mingling the truths of the Word of God with false doctrines or notions, and so handling it deceitfully (2 Cor. 4:2). It focuses on the falsifying, not the motives for falsifying. See: BAGD—203b; THAYER—155b.

1390. **δόμα** {4x} **dŏma**, *dom'-ah;* from the base of *1325;* a *present:*—gift {4x}.

Doma lends greater stress to the concrete character of the gift than to its beneficent nature (Mt 7:11; Lk 11:13; Eph 4:8; Phil 4:17). See: BAGD—203c; THAYER—155b.

1391. **δόξα** {168x} **dŏxa**, *dox'-ah;* from the base of *1380; glory* (as very *apparent*), in a wide application (lit. or fig., obj. or subj.):—dignity {2x}, glory {145x}, glorious {10x}, honour {6x}, praise {4x}, worship {1x}.

Doxa, "glory" primarily signifies an opinion, estimate, and hence, the honor resulting from a good opinion. It is used **(1)** of the nature and acts of God in self-manifestation, i.e., **(1a)** what He essentially is and does, as exhibited in whatever way he reveals Himself in these respects, and particularly in the person of Christ, in whom essentially His "glory" has ever shone forth and ever will do, Jn 17:5, 24; Heb 1:3; **(1b)** it was exhibited in the character and acts of Christ in the days of His flesh, Jn 1:14; Jn 2:11; at Cana both His grace and His power were manifested, and these constituted His "glory", so also in the resurrection of Lazarus, Jn 11:4, 40; **(1c)** the "glory" of God was exhibited **(1c1)** n the resurrection of Christ, Rom 6:4, and **(1c2)** in His ascension and exaltation, 1 Pet 1:21, **(1c3)** likewise on the Mount of Transfiguration, 2 Pet 1:17. **(1d)** In Rom 1:23 His "everlasting power and Divinity" are spoken of as His "glory," i.e., His attributes and power as revealed through creation; **(1e)** in Rom 3:23 the word denotes the manifested perfection of His character, especially His righteousness, of which all men fall short; **(1f)** in Col 1:11 "the might of His glory" signifies the might which is characteristic of His "glory"; **(1g)** in Eph 1:6, 12, 14, "the praise of the glory of His grace" and "the praise of His glory" signify the due acknowledgement of the exhibition of His attributes and ways; **(1h)** in Eph 1:17, "the Father of glory" describes Him as the source from whom all divine splendor and perfection proceed in their manifestation, and to whom they belong;

(2) of the character and ways of God as exhibited through Christ to and through believers, 2 Cor 3:18 and 4:6; **(3)** of the state of blessedness into which believers are to enter hereafter through being brought into the likeness of Christ, e.g., Rom 8:18, 21; Phil 3:21; 1 Pet 5:1, 10; Rev 21:11; **(4)** brightness or splendor, **(4a)** supernatural, **(4a1)** emanating from God (as in the *shekinah* "glory," in the pillar of cloud and in the Holy of Holies, e.g., Ex 16:10; 25:22), Lk 2:9; Acts 22:11; Rom 9:4; 2 Cor 3:7; Jas 2:1; **(4a2)** in Titus 2:13 it is used of Christ's return, "the appearing of the glory of the great God and our Savior Jesus Christ"; **(4b)** natural, as of the heavenly bodies, 1 Cor 15:40, 41; **(5)** of good reputation, praise, honor, Lk 14:10 "worship"; Jn 5:41 "honor"; 7:18; 8:50; 12:43 "praise"; 2 Cor 6:8 "honor"; Phil 3:19; Heb 3:3; **(5a)** in 1 Cor 11:7, of man as representing the authority of God, and of woman as rendering conspicuous the authority of man; **(5b)** in 1 Th 2:6, "glory" probably stands, by metonymy, for material gifts, an honorarium, since in human estimation "glory" is usually expressed in things material.

(6) The word is used in **(6a)** ascriptions of praise to God, e.g. Lk 17:18; Jn 9:24, "praise"; Acts 12:23; **(6b)** as in doxologies (lit., "glory-words"), e.g., Lk 2:14; Rom 11:36; 16:27; Gal 1:5; Rev 1:6. **(7)** *Doxa* also denotes always a good opinion, praise, honor, glory, an appearance commanding respect, magnificence, excellence, manifestation of glory; hence, of angelic powers, in respect of their state as commanding recognition (dignities—2 Pet 2:10; Jude 8). Syn.: 1741. See: TDNT—2:233, 178; BAGD—203c; THAYER—155c.

1392. **δοξάζω** {62x} **dŏxazō**, *dox-ad'-zo;* from *1391;* to *render* (or *esteem*) *glorious* (in a wide application):—glorify {54x}, honour {3x}, have glory {2x}, magnify {1x}, make glorious {1x}, full of glory {1x}.

Doxazo, as a verb, primarily denotes in the NT **(1)** "to magnify, extol, praise", especially of "glorifying"; **(1a)** God, i.e., ascribing honor to Him, acknowledging Him as to His being, attributes and acts, i.e., His glory, e.g., Mt 5:16; 9:8; 15:31; Rom 15:6, 9; Gal 1:24; 1 Pet 4:16; **(1b)** the Word of the Lord, Acts 13:48; **(1c)** the Name of the Lord, Rev 15:4; **(1c)** also of "glorifying" oneself, Jn 8:54; Rev. 18:7; **(2)** "to do honor to, to make glorious," e.g., Rom 8:30; 2 Cor 3:10; 1 Pet 1:8, "full of glory," passive voice (lit., "glorified"); **(2a)** said of Christ, e.g., Jn 7:39; 8:54 "honor" and "honoreth"; **(2b)** of the Father, e.g., Jn 13:31, 32; 21:19; 1 Pet 4:11; **(2c)** of "glorifying" one's ministry, Rom 11:13, "magnify"); **(2d)** of a member of the body, 1 Cor 12:26, "be honored."

(3) As the glory of God is the revelation and manifestation of all that He has and is . . . , it is said of a Self-revelation in which God manifests all the goodness that is His, Jn 12:28. **(3a)** So far it is Christ through whom this is made manifest, He is said to glorify the Father, Jn 17:1, 4; or the Father is glorified in Him, 13:31; 14:13; **(3b)** and Christ's meaning is analogous when He says to His disciples, "Herein is My Father glorified, that ye bear much fruit; and so shall ye be My disciples," Jn 15:8. **(3c)** When *doxazo* is predicated of Christ . . . , it means simply that His innate glory is brought to light, is made manifest; cf. Jn 11:4; so 7:39; 12:16, 23; 13:31; 17:1, 5. **(3d)** It is an act of God the Father in Him. . . . As the revelation of the Holy Spirit is connected with the glorification of Christ, Christ says regarding Him, 'He shall glorify Me," Jn 16:14. Syn.: 1740, 4888. See: TDNT—2:253, 178; BAGD—204c; THAYER—157a.

1393. **Δορκάς** {2x} **Dŏrkas**, *dor-kas';* *gazelle; Dorcas,* a Chr. woman:—*Dorcas* {2x}. See: BAGD—204d; THAYER—157b.

1394. **δόσις** {2x} **dŏsis**, *dos'-is;* from the base of *1325;* a *giving;* by impl. (concr.) a *gift:*—gift {1x}, giving {1x}.

Dosis denotes, properly, **(1)** "the act of giving," Phil 4:15, euphemistically referring to "gifts" as a matter of debt and credit accounts; then, **(2)** objectively, "a gift," Jas. 1:17. See: BAGD—204d; THAYER—157b.

1395. **δότης** {1x} **dŏtēs**, *dot'-ace;* from the base of *1325;* a *giver:*—giver {1x}.

Dotes is used in 2 Cor 9:7 of him who gives cheerfully (hilariously) and is thereby loved of God. See: BAGD—205a; THAYER—157c.

1396. **δουλαγωγέω** {1x} **dŏulagōgĕō**, *doo-lag-ogue-eh'-o;* from a presumed compound of *1401* and *71;* to *be a slave-driver,* i.e. to *enslave* (fig. *subdue*):—bring into subjection {1x}.

This word means "to bring into bondage" and is used in 1 Cor 9:27, concerning the body. The stress is on mastery of the body's carnal desires; hence, subjection. See: TDNT—2:279, 182; BAGD—205a; THAYER—157c.

1397. **δουλεία** {5x} **dŏulĕia**, *doo-li'-ah;* from *1398; slavery* (cerem. or fig.):—bondage {5x}.

Douleia, primarily "the condition of being a slave," came to denote any kind of bondage, as, e.g., **(1)** of the condition of creation, Rom 8:21; **(2)** of that fallen condition of man himself which makes him dread God, Rom 8:15, and **(3)** fear death, Heb 2:15; and **(4)** of the condition imposed by the Mosaic Law, Gal. 4:24; 5:1. See: TDNT—2:261, 182; BAGD—205a; THAYER—157c.

1398. **δουλεύω** {25x} **dŏulĕuō**, *dool-yoo'-o;* from *1401; to be a slave* to (lit. or fig., invol. or vol.):—serve {18x}, be in bondage {4x}, do service {3x}.

Douleus, "to serve as a slave, to be a slave, to be in bondage," is frequently used without any association of slavery, e.g., Acts 20:19; Rom 6:6; 7:6; 12:11; Gal 5:13. See: TDNT—2:261, 182; BAGD—205a; THAYER—157d.

1399. **δούλη** {3x} **dŏulē**, *doo'-lay;* fem. of *1401;* a *female slave* (invol. or vol.):—handmaid {1x}, handmaiden {2x}. See: TDNT—2:261, 182; BAGD—205c; THAYER—157d.

1400. **δοῦλον** {2x} **dŏulŏn**, *doo'-lon;* neut. of *1401; subservient:*—servant {1x}. See: BAGD—205c; THAYER—157d.

1401. **δοῦλος** {125x} **dŏulŏs**, *doo'-los;* from *1210;* a *slave* (lit. or fig., invol. or vol.; frequently, therefore in a qualified sense of *subjection* or *subserviency*):—bond {6x}, bondman {1x}, servant {118x}.

(1) The *doulos* was properly the "bond man," one who was in a permanent relation of servitude to another one whose will was completely subject to the will of another. **(2)** He was a *doulos* apart from any service he rendered at any given moment. The focus is on the relationship, not the service. [see 1249]. **(3)** This word means "a slave," originally the lowest term in the scale of servitude, came also to mean **(3a)** "one who gives himself up to the will of another," e.g., 1 Cor 7:23; Rom 6:17, 20, and **(3b)** became the most common and general word for "servant," as in Mt 8:9, without any idea of bondage. **(4)** In calling himself, however, a "bondslave of Jesus Christ," e.g., Rom 1:1, the apostle Paul intimates **(4a)** that he had been formerly a "bondslave" of Satan, and **(4b)** that, having been bought by Christ, he was now a willing slave, bound to his new Master. Syn.: *Diakonos* (1249) is, generally speaking, to be distinguished from *doulos* (1401), "a bondservant, slave"; *diakonos* views a servant in relationship to his work, *doulos* views him in relationship to his master. See, e.g., Mt 22:2–14; those who bring in the guests (vv. 3–4, 6, 8, 10) are douloi those who carry out the king's sentence (v. 13) are diakonoi. See also: 2324, 3610, 5257. See: TDNT—2:261, 182; BAGD—205c; THAYER—157d.

1402. **δουλόω** {8x} **dŏulŏō**, *doo-lŏ'-o;* from *1401;* to *enslave* (lit. or fig.):—become servant {2x}, bring into bondage {2x}, be under bondage {1x}, given {1x}, make servant {1x}, in bondage {1x}.

Douloo signifies **(1)** "to make a slave of, to bring into bondage," Acts 7:6; 1 Cor 9:19; **(2)** in the passive voice, "to be brought under bondage," 2 Pet 2:19; **(3)** "to be held in bondage," Gal 4:3 (lit., "were reduced to bondage"); **(4)** Titus 2:3, "of being enslaved to wine"; **(5)** Rom 6:18, "of service to righteousness" (lit., "were made bondservants"). **(6)** As with the purchased slave there were no limitations either in the kind or the time of service, so the life of the believer is to be lived in continuous obedience to God. See: TDNT—2:279, 182; BAGD—206b; THAYER—158b.

1403. **δοχή** {2x} **dŏchē**, *dokh-ay';* from *1209;* a *reception,* i.e. convivial *entertainment:*—feast {2x}.

Doche is "a reception feast, a banquet", Lk 5:29; 14:13. See: TDNT—2:54, 146; BAGD—206b; THAYER—158b.

1404. **δράκων** {13x} **drakōn**, *drak'-own;* prob. from an alt. form of δέρκομαι **dĕrkŏmai** (to *look*); a fabulous kind of *serpent* (perh. as supposed to *fascinate*):—dragon {13x}.

Drakon denoted also a large serpent, so called because of its keen power of sight (from a root *derke,* signifying "to see"). Thirteen times in the Apocalypse it is used of the devil 12:3–4, 7, 9, 13, 16–17; 13:2, 4, 11; 16:13; 20:2. See: TDNT—2:281, 186; BAGD—206b; THAYER—158b.

1405. **δράσσομαι** {1x} **drassŏmai**, *dras'-som-ahee;* perh. akin to the base of *1404* (through the idea of *capturing*); to *grasp,* i.e. (fig.) *entrap:*—take {1x}.

This word means "to grasp with the hand, take hold of," and is used metaphorically in 1 Cor 3:19, "taketh (the wise in their craftiness)." See: BAGD—206c; THAYER—158c.

1406. **δραχμή** {3x} **drachmē**, *drakh-may';* from *1405;* a *drachma* or (silver) coin (as *handled*):—piece {2x}, piece of silver {1x}.

A *drachma,* firstly, is **(1)** as much as one can hold in the hand (connected with *drassomai,* "to grasp with the hand, lay hold of," 1 Cor 3:19), then, **(2)** "a coin," nearly equal to the Roman *denarius,* is translated **(2a)** "pieces of silver" in Lk 15:8, 1st part; **(2b)** "piece," Lk 15:8, 2nd part and v. 9. See: BAGD—206c; THAYER—158c.

δρέμω **drĕmō**. See *5143*.

1407. **δρέπανον** {8x} **drĕpanŏn**, *drep'-an-on;* from δρέπω **drĕpō** (to *pluck*); a gathering *hook* (espec. for harvesting):—sickle {8x}.

A *drepanon* is "a pruning hook, a sickle, a hooked vine knife" and occurs in Mk 4:29; Rev 14:14, 15, 16, 17, 18 (twice), 19. See: BAGD—206d; THAYER—158c.

1408. **δρόμος** {3x} **drŏmŏs**, *drom'-os;* from the alt. of *5143;* a *race*, i.e. (fig.) *career:*—course {3x}.

Dromos properly means a running, a race; hence, metaphorically, denotes a career, course of occupation, or of life (Acts 13:25; 20:24; 2 Ti 4:7). See: TDNT—8:233, 1189; BAGD—206d; THAYER—158c.

1409. **Δρούσιλλα** {1x} **Drŏusilla**, *droo'-sil-lah;* a fem. dimin. of *Drusus* (a Rom. name); *Drusilla*, a member of the Herodian family:—*Drusilla* {1x}. See: BAGD—207a; THAYER—158c.

δῦμι **dumi**. See *1416*.

1410. **δύναμαι** {210x} **dunamai**, *doo'-nam-ahee;* of uncert. aff.; to *be able* or *possible:*—can (could) {100x}, cannot + 3756 {45x}, be able {37x}, may (might) {18x}, able {3x}, misc. {7x} = be possible, be of power.

Dunamai means to be able, to have power, whether by **(1)** virtue of one's own ability and resources (Rom 15:14); or **(2)** through a state of mind, or through favorable circumstances (1 Th 2:6); or **(3)** by permission of law or custom (Acts 24:8, 11); or **(4)** simply to be able, powerful (Mt 3:9; 2 Ti 3:15). See: TDNT—2:284, 186; BAGD—207a; THAYER—158d.

1411. **δύναμις** {120x} **dunamis**, *doo'-nam-is;* from *1410; force* (lit. or fig.); spec. miraculous *power* (usually by impl. a *miracle* itself):—power {77x}, mighty work {11x}, strength {7x}, miracle {7x}, might {4x}, virtue {3x}, mighty {2x}, misc. {9x} = ability, abundance, meaning, mightily, worker of miracles, violence.

Dunamis almost always points to new and higher forces that have entered and are working in this lower world of ours. It is **(2)** "power, ability," physical or moral, as residing in a person or thing; **(3)** "power in action," as, e.g., when put forth in performing miracles. **(4)** It occurs 118 times in the NT. **(5)** It is sometimes used of the miracle or sign itself, the effect being put for the cause, e.g., Mk 6:5, frequently in the Gospels and Acts. **(6)** In 1 Cor 14:11 it is rendered "meaning." Syn.: 1741, 2297, 3167, 3861, 4592, 5059. See: TDNT—2:284, 186; BAGD—207b; THAYER—159a.

1412. **δυναμόω** {1x} **dunamŏō**, *doo-nam-ŏ'-o;* from *1411;* to *enable:*—strengthen {1x}.

This word means "to make strong, confirm, strengthen" and occurs in Col 1:11. See: TDNT—2:284, 186; BAGD—208c; THAYER—160a.

1413. **δυνάστης** {3x} **dunastēs**, *doo-nas'-tace;* from *1410;* a *ruler* or *officer:*—of great authority {1x}, mighty {1x}, Potentate {1x}.

Dunastes signifies "a potentate, a high officer"; **(1)** in Acts 8:27, of a high officer, it is rendered "of great authority"; **(2)** in Lk 1:52, "the mighty"; **(3)** in 1 Ti 6:15 it is said of God ("Potentate"). See: TDNT—2:284, 186; BAGD—208c; THAYER—160a.

1414. **δυνατέω** {1x} **dunatĕō**, *doo-nat-eh'-o;* from *1415;* to *be efficient* (fig.):—be mighty {1x}.

Dunateo signifies "to be mighty, to show oneself powerful," Rom 4:14; 2 Cor 9:8; 13:3. See: TDNT—2:284, 186; BAGD—208c; THAYER—160a.

1415. **δυνατός** {35x} **dunatŏs**, *doo-nat-os';* from *1410; powerful* or *capable* (lit. or fig.); neut. *possible:*—possible {13x}, able {10x}, mighty {6x}, strong {3x}, could {1x}, power {1x}, mighty man {1x}.

Dunatos signifies "powerful." See, e.g., Rom 4:21; 9:22; 11:23; 12:18; 15:1; 1 Cor 1:26; 2 Cor 9:8. See: TDNT—2:284, 186; BAGD—208c; THAYER—160b.

1416. **δύνω** {2x} **dunō**, *doo'-no;* or

δῦμι **dumi**, *doo'-mee;* prol. forms of an obsolete primary δύω **duō**, *doo'-o* (to *sink*); to *go "down"*:—set {2x}.

Dumi, "to sink into," is used **(1)** of the "setting" of the sun, Mk 1:32, "did set"; **(2)** Lk 4:40, "was setting." The sun, moon and stars were conceived of as sinking into the sea when they set. See: TDNT—2:318, 192; BAGD—209a; THAYER—160b.

1417. **δύο** {135x} **duŏ**, *doo'-ŏ;* a primary numeral; *"two"*:—two {122x}, twain {10x}, both {2x}, two and two + 303 {1x}.

Duo is rendered **(1)** "twain" in Mt 5:41; 19:5, 6; 21:31; 27:21, 51; Mk 10:8 (twice); 15:38; Eph 2:15; **(2)** in 1 Cor 6:16 and Eph 5:31 "two"; **(3)** in Jn 20:4; Rev 19:20. See: BAGD—209a; THAYER—160c.

1418. **δυς-** {0x} **dus-**, *doos;* a primary inseparable particle of uncert. der.; used only in composition as a pref.; *hard*, i.e. *with difficulty:*—+ hard, + grievous, *etc.*; THAYER—160d.

1419. **δυσβάστακτος** {2x} **dusbastaktŏs**, *doos-bas'-tak-tos;* from *1418* and a der. of *941; oppressive:*—grievous to be borne {2x}.

This word means "hard to be borne" (from *dus*, an inseparable prefix, like Eng. "mis-," and "un-," indicating "difficulty, injuriousness, opposition," etc., and *bastazo*, "to bear"), is used in Lk 11:46 and Mt 23:4, "grievous to be borne." See: BAGD—209b; THAYER—160d.

1420. **δυσεντερία** {1x} **dusĕntĕria**, *doos-en-ter-ee'-ah;* from *1418* and a comp. of *1787* (mean. a *bowel*); a *"dysentery"*:—bloody flux {1x}.

Dusenteria, [whence Eng., "dysentery"] is translated "bloody flux" in Acts 28:8. (*enteron* denotes an "intestine"). See: BAGD—209c; THAYER—160d.

1421. **δυσερμήνευτος** {1x} **dusĕrmēnĕutŏs**, *doos-er-mane'-yoo-tos;* from *1418* and a presumed der. of *2059; difficult of explanation:*—hard to be uttered {1x}. See: BAGD—209c; THAYER—160d.

1422. **δύσκολος** {1x} **duskŏlŏs**, *doos'-kol-os;* from *1418* and κόλον **kŏlŏn** (*food*); prop. *fastidious about eating* (*peevish*), i.e. (gen.) *impracticable:*—hard {1x}.

This word means primarily means "hard to satisfy with food, difficulty, opposition, injuriousness"; hence, "difficult," Mk 10:24, of the "difficulty," for those who trust in riches, to enter into the Kingdom of God. See: BAGD—209c; THAYER—161a.

1423. **δυσκόλως** {3x} **duskŏlōs**, *doos-kol'-oce;* adv. from *1422; impracticably:*—hardly {3x}.

Duskolos, the adverbial form of HARD, is used in Mt 19:23; Mk 10:23; Lk 18:24 of the danger of riches. See: BAGD—209d; THAYER—161a.

1424. **δυσμή** {5x} **dusmē**, *doos-may';* from *1416;* the sun-*set*, i.e. (by impl.) the *western* region:—west {5x}.

Dusme, "the quarter [north, south, east, west] where sun sets"; hence, "the west," occurs in Mt. 8:11; 24:27; Lk 12:54 (some regard this as the sunset); 13:29; Rev 21:13. See: BAGD—209d; THAYER—161a.

1425. **δυσνόητος** {1x} **dusnŏētŏs**, *doos-no'-ay-tos;* from *1418* and a der. of *3539; difficult of perception:*—hard to be understood {1x}. See: TDNT—4:963, 636; BAGD—209d; THAYER—161b.

1426. **δυσφημία** {1x} **dusphēmia**, *doos-fay-mee'-ah;* from a compound of *1418* and *5345; defamation:*—evil report {1x}. See: BAGD—209d; THAYER—161b.

δύω **duō**. See *1416*.

1427. **δώδεκα** {72x} **dōdĕka**, *do'-dek-ah;* from *1417* and *1176; two* and *ten*, i.e. a *dozen:*—twelve {72x}.

Dodeka is used **(1)** frequently in the Gospels for the twelve apostles, and in Acts 6:2; 1 Cor 15:5; Rev 21:14b; **(2)** of the tribes of Israel, Mt 19:28; Lk 22:30; Jas 1:1; Rev 21:12c (cf. 7:5–8; 12:1); **(3)** in various details relating to the heavenly Jerusalem, Rev 21:12–21; 22:2. **(4)** The number in general is regarded as suggestive of divine administration. See: TDNT—4:963, 636; BAGD—210a; THAYER—161b.

1428. **δωδέκατος** {1x} **dōdĕkatŏs**, *do-dek'-at-os;* from *1427; twelfth:*—twelfth {1x}. See: TDNT—2:321, 192; BAGD—210b; THAYER—161b.

1429. **δωδεκάφυλον** {1x} **dōdĕkaphulŏn**, *do-dek-af'-oo-lon;* from *1427* and *5443;* the *commonwealth* of Israel:—twelve tribes {1x}. See: TDNT—2:321, 192; BAGD—210b; THAYER—161b.

1430. **δῶμα** {7x} **dōma**, *do'-mah;* from δέμω **dĕmō** (to *build*); prop. an *edifice*, i.e. (spec.) a *roof:*—housetop {7x}.

Doma denotes a housetop. **(1)** The housetop was flat, and **(2)** guarded by a low parapet wall (cf. Deut 22:8). **(3)** It was much frequented and used for: **(3a)** for proclamations (Mt 10:27; Lk 12:3); **(3b)** for prayer (Acts 10:9). **(4)** The housetop could be reached by stairs outside the building. **(5)** External flight from the housetop in time or danger is enjoined (Mt 24:17; Mk 13:15; Lk 17:31). See: BAGD—210b; THAYER—161c.

1431. **δωρεά** {11x} **dōrĕa**, *do-reh-ah';* from *1435;* a *gratuity:*—gift {11x}.

Dorea denotes a free gift, stressing its gratuitous character and it is always used in the NT of a spiritual or supernatural gift (Jn 4:10; Acts 8:20; 11:17; Rom 5:15; 2 Cor 9:15; Eph 3:7; Heb 6:4). See: TDNT—2:166, 166; BAGD—210b; THAYER—161c.

1432. **δωρεάν** {9x} **dōrĕan**, *do-reh-an';* acc. of *1431* as adv.; *gratuitously* (lit. or fig.):—freely {6x}, without a cause {1x}, in vain {1x}, for nought {1x}.

Dorean, lit., "as a gift, gratis," (connected with *doron*, "a gift"), is rendered **(1)** "without a cause," Jn 15:25; **(2)** "for nought," 2 Cor 11:7; Gal 2:21; 2 Th 3:8; **(3)** "freely," Mt 10:8; Rom 3:24; Rev 21:6; 22:17. See: TDNT—2:167, 166; BAGD—210c; THAYER—161d.

1433. **δωρέομαι** {3x} **dōrĕŏmai**, *do-reh'-om-ahee;* mid. voice from *1435;* to *bestow* gratuitously:—give {3x}.

Doreomai, used in the middle voice means "to bestow, make a gift of": "And when he [Pilate] knew *it* of the centurion, he gave the body [of Jesus] to Joseph." (Mk 15:45; cf. 2 Pet 1:3, 4). See: TDNT—2:166, 166; BAGD—210d; THAYER—161d.

1434. **δώρημα** {2x} **dōrēma**, *do'-ray-mah;* from *1433; a bestowment:*—gift {2x}.

Dorema, translated "gift" in Jas 1:17 is thus distinguished, as the thing given, from the preceding word in the verse, *dosis* (1394), "the act of giving"; **(2)** elsewhere in Rom 5:16. Syn.: *Dorema* is the thing given; whereas, *dosis* (1394) is the act of giving. See: TDNT—2:166, 166; BAGD—210d; THAYER—161d.

1435. **δῶρον** {19x} **dōrŏn**, *do'-ron; a present;* spec. a *sacrifice:*—gift {18x}, offering {1x}.

Doron means to give and is used of gifts **(1)** presented as an expression of honor (Mt 2:11); **(2)** for the support of the temple and the needs of the poor (Mt 15:5; Mk 7:11; Lk 21:1, 4); **(3)** offered to God (Mt 5:23, 24; 8:4; Heb 5:1; 8:3); **(4)** of salvation by grace as the gift of God (Eph 2:8); **(5)** of presents for mutual celebration of an occasion (Rev 11:10). Syn.: 1390, 1394, 1431, 1434, 5486. See: TDNT—2:166, 166; BAGD—210d; THAYER—161d.

E

1436. **ἔα** {2x} **ĕa**, *eh'-ah;* appar. imper. of *1439;* prop. *let* it *be,* i.e. (as interj.) *aha!:*—let alone {2x}.

An interjection of surprise, fear and anger, was the cry of the man with the spirit of an unclean demon (Lk 4:34). See: BAGD—211a; THAYER—162a.

1437. **ἐάν** {275x} **ĕan**, *eh-an';* from *1487* and *302;* a *conditional* particle; *in case* that, *provided,* etc.; often used in connection with other particles to denote *indefiniteness* or *uncertainty:*—if {200x}, whosoever + 3769 {14x}, whatsoever + 3739 {16x}, though {14x}, misc. {31x} = before, but, except, whithersoever, whensoever), whether (or), to whom, soever. See: BAGD—211a; THAYER—162a. See *3361.*

ἐάν μή **ĕan mē**. See *3361* and *3362.*

1438. **ἑαυτοῦ** {339x} **hĕautŏu**, *heh-ow-too'* (incl. all other cases); from a refl. pron. otherwise obs. and the gen. (dat. or acc.) of *846; him-* (*her-, it-, them-,* also [in conjunction with the pers. pron. of the other persons] *my-, thy-, our-, your-*) *self* (*selves*), etc.:—himself {110x}, themselves {57x}, yourselves {36x}, ourselves {20x}, his {19x}, their {15x}, itself {9x}, misc. {73x} = alone, her (own, -self), his (own), itself, one (to) another, our (thine) own (-selves), + that she had, their (own, own selves), they, thyself, you, your (own, own conceits, own selves). See: BAGD—211d; THAYER—163b.

1439. **ἐάω** {13x} **ĕaō**, *eh-ah'-o;* of uncert. aff.; to *let be,* i.e. *permit* or *leave* alone:—suffer {9x}, let alone {1x}, leave {1x}, let {1x}, commit {1x}.

Eao signifies **(1)** "let alone", Acts 5:38; **(2)** "to leave," Acts 23:32, of "leaving" horsemen; **(3)** Acts 27:40, of "committing (themselves)" unto the sea; **(4)** "to suffer" in Mt 24:43; Lk 4:41; 22:51; Acts 14:16; 16:7; 19:30; 28:4; 1 Cor 10:13; Rev 2:20; **(5)** "to let" Acts 27:32. See: BAGD—212c; THAYER—163c. See also *1436.*

1440. **ἑβδομήκοντα** {5x} **hĕbdŏmēkŏnta**, *heb-dom-ay'-kon-tah;* from *1442* and a modified form of *1176; seventy:*—seventy {2x}, three score and ten {1x}, three score and fifteen + 4002 {1x}. See: TDNT—2:627, 249; BAGD—212d; THAYER—163d.

1441. **ἑβδομηκοντακίς** {1x} **hĕbdŏmēkŏntakis**, *heb-dom-ay-kon-tak-is;* multiple adv. from *1440; seventy times:*—seventy times {1x}.

Having a possible *allusion* to the Genesis story (4:24) is highly probable: Jesus pointedly sets against the natural man's craving for seventy-sevenfold revenge the spiritual man's ambition to exercise the privilege of seventy-sevenfold forgiveness". The Lord's reply "until seventy times seven" was indicative of completeness, the absence of any limit, and was designed to turn away Peter's mind from a merely numerical standard. God's forgiveness is limitless; so should man's be. See: TDNT—2:627, 249; BAGD—213a; THAYER—163d.

1442. **ἕβδομος** {9x} **hĕbdŏmŏs**, *heb'-dom-os;* ord. from *2033; seventh:*—seventh {9x}. This word occurs in Jn 4:52; Heb 4:4 (twice); Jude 14; Rev 8:1; 10:7; 11:15; 16:17; 21:20. See: TDNT—2:627, 249; BAGD—213a.163d; THAYER—163d.

1443. **Ἐβέρ** {1x} **Ĕbĕr**, *eb'-er;* of Heb. or. [5677]; *Eber,* a patriarch:—*Eber* {1x}. See: BAGD—213a; THAYER—163d.

1444. **Ἑβραϊκός** {1x} **Hĕbraïkŏs**, *heb-rah-ee-kos';* from *1443; Hebraïc* or the *Jewish* language:—Hebrew (Aramaic) {1x}. See: TDNT—3:356, 372; BAGD—213a; THAYER—163d.

1445. **Ἑβραῖος** {5x} **Hĕbraiŏs**, *heb-rah'-yos;* from *1443;* a *Hebræan* (i.e. Hebrew) or *Jew:*—Hebrew {5x}. See: TDNT—3:356, 372; BAGD—213b; THAYER—163d.

1446. **Ἑβραΐς** {3x} **Hĕbraïs**, *heb-rah-is';* from *1443;* the *Hebraistic* (i.e. *Hebrew*) or *Jewish* (*Chaldee*) language:—Hebrew (Aramaic) {3x}. See: TDNT—3:356, 372; BAGD—213b; THAYER—163d.

1447. **Ἑβραϊστί** {6x} **Hĕbraïsti**, *heb-rah-is-tee';* adv. from *1446; Hebraistically* or in the Jewish (Chaldee) language:—in the Hebrew tongue {3x}, in the Hebrew {2x}, in Hebrew {1x}. See: TDNT—3:356, 372; BAGD—213c; THAYER—164b.

1448. **ἐγγίζω** {43x} **ĕggizō**, *eng-id'-zo;* from *1451;* to make *near,* i.e. (refl.) *approach:*—draw nigh {12x}, be at hand {9x}, come nigh {8x}, come near {5x}, draw near {4x}, misc. {5x} = approach, be nigh.

Engizo, as a verb, means "to come near draw nigh" and is translated **(1)** "approacheth ": "Sell that ye have, and give alms; provide yourselves bags which wax not old, a treasure in the heavens that faileth not, where no thief approacheth, neither moth corrupteth" (Lk 12:33); **(2)** "approaching": "Not forsaking the assembling of ourselves together, as the manner of some *is;* but exhorting *one another:* and so much the more, as ye see the day approaching" (Heb 10:25; cf. Lk 18:35; 19:29, 37); **(3)** "was come nigh": "And it came to pass, that, as I made my journey, and was come nigh unto Damascus about noon . . ." (Acts 22:6); **(4)** "came nigh": "Now when He came nigh to the gate of the city" (Lk 7:12); **(5)** "came near": "And as he journeyed, he came near Damascus . . ." (Acts 9:3). **(6)** It also means "to draw near, to approach," and is used **(6a)** of place and position, **(6a1)** literally and physically, Mt 21:1; Mk 11:1; Lk 12:33; 15:25; **(6a2)** figuratively, of drawing near to God, Mt 15:8; Heb 7:19; Jas 4:8; **(6b)** of time, with reference to things that are imminent, as **(6b1)** the kingdom of heaven, Mt 3:2; 4:17; 10:7; **(6b2)** the kingdom of God, Mk 1:15; Lk 10:9, 11; **(6b3)** the time of fruit, Mt 21:34; **(6b4)** the desolation of Jerusalem, Lk 21:8; **(6b5)** redemption, Lk 21:28; **(6b6)** the fulfillment of a promise, Acts 7:17; **(6b7)** the Day of Christ in contrast to the present night of the world's spiritual darkness, Rom 13:12; Heb 10:25; **(6b8)** the coming of the Lord, Jas 5:8; **(6b9)** the end of all things, 1 Pet 4:7. **(7)** It is also said of one who was drawing near to death, Phil 2:30. Syn.: 307, 385, 392, 501, 502, 645, 868, 1670, 1828, 2020, 2464, 4317, 4334, 4358, 4685, 4951, 5288, 5289. See: TDNT—2:330, 194; BAGD—213c; THAYER—164b.

1449. **ἐγγράφω** {2x} **ĕggraphō**, *eng-graf'-o;* from *1722* and *1125;* to *"engrave,"* i.e. *inscribe:*—write (in) {2x}.

Eggrapho denotes "to write in," Lk 10:20; 2 Cor 3:2, 3. See: TDNT—1:769, 128; BAGD—213d; THAYER—164c.

1450. **ἔγγυος** {1x} **ĕgguŏs**, *eng'-goo-os;* from *1722* and γυῖον **guiŏn** (a *limb*); *pledged* (as if *articulated* by a member), i.e. a *bondsman:*—surety {1x}.

Enguos primarily signifies the bail who personally answers for anyone, whether with his life or his property. In Heb 7:22 it refers to Jesus, the personal guarantee of the terms of the new and better covenant, secured on the ground of His perfect sacrifice (v. 27). See: TDNT—2:329, 194; BAGD—214a; THAYER—164d.

1451. **ἐγγύς** {30x} **ĕggus**, *eng-goos';* from a primary verb ἄγχω **agchō** (to *squeeze* or *throttle;* akin to the base of *43*); *near* (lit. or fig., of place or time):—nigh {13x}, at hand {6x}, nigh at hand {4x}, near {4x}, from {1x}, nigh unto {1x}, ready {1x}.

Engus means "near, nigh" and is translated **(1)** "nigh": **(1a)** of a place: "And as they heard these things, He added and spake a parable, because He was nigh to Jerusalem" (Lk 19:11; Jn 6:19, 23; metaphorically in Rom 10:8; Eph 2:13, 17); **(1b)** of time: "Now learn a parable of the fig tree; When his branch is yet tender, and putteth forth leaves, ye know that summer *is* nigh" (Mt 24:32–33; cf. Lk 21:30–31); **(1c)** as a preposition **(1c1)** Heb 6:8 "nigh unto (a curse)" and **(1c2)** Heb 8:13 "nigh unto (vanishing away)." **(2)** It is translated "near" [of place] in Jn 3:23 and 11:54. **(3)** The difference between "near" and "nigh" is one of focus. **(3a)** When the speaker is focusing on the two objects, and not the distance separating the two objects, he uses "near." The listener focuses on the two objects becoming closer to each other. **(3b)** When the speaker is focusing on the distance separating the two objects as lessening, he uses "nigh." The listener/reader focuses on the distance lessening, not the two objects. Syn.: 316, 1448, 1452, 4139, 4317, 4334. See: TDNT—2:330, 194; BAGD—214a; THAYER—164d.

1452. **ἐγγύτερον** {1x} **ĕggutĕrŏn**, *eng-goo'-ter-on;* neut. of the comp. of *1451; nearer:*—nearer {1x}.

Enguteron is the comparative degree of engus (1451) and the neuter of the adjective engut-eros and is used adverbially in Rom 13:11: "And that, knowing the time, that now *it is* high time to awake out of sleep: for now *is* our salvation nearer (*enguteron*) than when we believed." Syn.: 316, 1451, 1448, 1451, 4139, 4317, 4334. See: BAGD—214a; THAYER—165a.

1453. **ἐγείρω** {141x} **ĕgĕirō**, *eg-i'-ro;* prob. akin to the base of *58* (through the idea of *collecting* one's faculties); to *waken* (tran. or intr.), i.e. *rouse* (lit. from sleep, from sitting or lying, from disease, from death; or fig. from obscurity, inactivity, ruins, nonexistence):—rise {36x}, raise {28x}, arise {27x}, raise up {23x}, rise up {8x}, rise again {5x}, raise again {4x}, misc. {10x} awake, lift up, rear up, arise, stand, take up.

Egeiro, as a verb, is frequently used in the NT in the sense **(1)** of "raising" (active voice), or "rising" (middle and passive voices): **(1a)** from sitting, lying, sickness: "When he arose, he took the young child and his mother by night, and departed into Egypt" (Mt 2:14; cf. 9:5, 7, 19; Jas 5:15; Rev 11:1); **(1b)** of causing to appear, or, in the passive, appearing, or raising up so as to occupy a place in the midst of people: "And think not to say within yourselves, We have Abraham to *our* father: for I say unto you, that God is able of these stones to raise up children unto Abraham" (Mt 3:9; cf. Mk 13:22; Acts 13:22). **(3)** It is thus said of Christ in Acts 13:23: "Of this man's seed hath God according to *His* promise raised unto Israel a Saviour, Jesus"; **(4)** of rousing, stirring up, or "rising" against: "For nation shall rise against nation, and kingdom against kingdom:" (Mt 24:7; cf. Mk 13:8;

(5) of "raising buildings" (Jn 2:19–20); **(6)** of "raising or rising" from the dead: **(6a)** of Christ (Mt 16:21); and **(6b)** of Christ's "raising" the dead (Mt 11:5; cf. Mk 5:41; Lk 7:14; Jn 12:1, 9, 17); **(6c)** of the act of the disciples (Mt 10:8); **(6d)** of the resurrection of believers (Mt 27:52; Jn 5:21; 1 Cor 15:15–16, 29, 32, 35, 42–44 52; 2 Cor 1:9; 4:14); **(6e)** of unbelievers(Mt 12:42). Syn.: *Egeiro* (1453) stands in contrast to anistemi (450 - when used with reference to resurrection) in this respect, that egeiro is frequently used both in the transitive sense of "raising up" and the intransitive of "rising," whereas anistemi is comparatively infrequent in the transitive use. See also: 305, 393, 450, 1096, 1326, 1525, 1817, 4911. See: TDNT—2:333, 195; BAGD—214c; THAYER—165a.

1454. **ἔγερσις** {1x} **ĕgĕrsis**, *eg'-er-sis;* from *1453;* a *resurgence* (from death):—resurrection {1x}.

Egersis, "a rousing, an excitation", is used of the "resurrection" of Christ, in Mt 27:53. See: TDNT—2:337, 195; BAGD—215b; THAYER—165d.

1455. **ἐγκάθετος** {1x} **ĕgkathĕtŏs**, *eng-kath'-et-os;* from *1722* and a der. of *2524; subinduced,* i.e. surreptitiously *suborned* as a lier-in-wait:—spy {1x}.

Egkathetos, an adjective denoting "suborned to lie in wait, one who is bribed by others to entrap a man by crafty words" is used as a plural noun in Lk 20:20, "spies." See: BAGD—215a; THAYER—165d.

1456. **ἐγκαίνια** {1x} **ĕgkainia**, *eng-kah'-ee-nee-ah;* neut. plur. of a presumed compound from *1722* and *2537; innovatives,* i.e. (spec.) *renewal* (of relig. services after the Antiochian interruption):—feast of dedication {1x}.

Egkainia, in the sense of "dedication," became used particularly for the annual eight days' feast beginning on the 25th of Chisleu (mid. of Dec.), instituted by Judas Maccabaeus, 164, B.C., to commemorate the cleansing of the Temple from the pollutions of Antiochus Epiphanes; hence it was called the Feast of the Dedication, Jn 10:22. This feast could be celebrated anywhere. The lighting of lamps was a prominent feature; hence the description "Feast of Lights." John 9:5 may also refer to this. See: BAGD—215b; THAYER—165d.

1457. **ἐγκαινίζω** {2x} **ĕgkainizō**, *eng-kahee-nid'-zo;* from *1456;* to *renew,* i.e. *inaugurate:*—consecrate {1x}, dedicate {1x}.

Egkainizo, primarily means "to make new, to renew"; then, **(1)** to initiate or "dedicate," Heb 9:18, with reference to the first covenant, as not "dedicated" without blood; **(2)** in Heb 10:20, of Christ's "consecration" of the new and living way ("consecrated"). See: TDNT—3:453, 388; BAGD—215b; THAYER—166a.

1458. **ἐγκαλέω** {7x} **ĕgkalĕō**, *eng-kal-eh'-o;* from *1722* and *2564;* to *call in* (as a debt or demand), i.e. *bring to account* (*charge, criminate,* etc.):—accuse {4x}, implead {1x}, call in question {1x}, lay anything to the charge {1x}.

Egkaleo, as a verb, means **(1)** "to bring a charge against, or **(2)** to come forward as an accuser against." **(3)** It literally denotes "to call in" (en, "in," kaleo, "to call"), **(3a)** i.e., "to call (something) in or against (someone)"; hence, **(3b)** "to call to account, to accuse, to implead": "Wherefore if Demetrius, and the craftsmen which are with him, have a matter against any man, the law is open, and there are deputies: let them implead (enkaleo) one another" (Acts 19:38); **(3c)** "accused": "For we are in danger to be called in question (enkaleo) for this day's uproar, there being no cause whereby we may give an account of this concourse." (Acts 19:40; 23:28–29; 26:2, 7); **(3d)** "shall lay to the charge": "Who shall lay any thing to the charge (enkaleo) of God's elect? *It is* God that justifieth." (Rom 8:33). Syn.: 156, 157, 1225, 1462, 1908, 2723, 2724, 4811. See: TDNT—3:496, 394; BAGD—215c; THAYER—166b.

1459. **ἐγκαταλείπω** {9x} **ĕgkatalĕipō**, *eng-kat-al-i'-po;* from *1722* and *2641;* to *leave behind in* some place, i.e. (in a good sense) *let remain over,* or (in a bad sense) to *desert:*—forsake {7x}, leave {2x}.

Egkataleipo denotes **(1)** "to leave behind, among, leave surviving," Rom 9:29; **(2)** "to forsake, abandon, leave in straits, or helpless," said **(2a)** by, or of, Christ, Mt 27:46; Mk 15:34; Acts 2:27; **(2b)** of men, 2 Cor 4:9; 2 Tim 4:10, 16; **(2c)** by God, Heb 13:5, **(2d)** of things, by Christians (negatively), Heb. 10:25. See: BAGD—215d; THAYER—166b.

1460. **ἐγκατοικέω** {1x} **ĕgkatŏikĕō**, *eng-kat-oy-keh'-o;* from *1722* and *2730;* to *settle down in* a place, i.e. *reside:*—dwell among {1x}. See: BAGD—216a; THAYER—166c.

1461. **ἐγκεντρίζω** {6x} **ĕgkĕntrizō**, *eng-ken-trid'-zo;* from *1722* and a der. of *2759;* to *prick in,* i.e. *ingraft:*—graff {1x}, graff in {4x}, graff into {1x}.

Egkentrizo denotes "to graff in" to insert a slip of a cultivated tree into a wild one. In Rom 11:17, 19, 23, 24, however, the metaphor is used "contrary to nature" (v. 24), of grafting a wild olive branch (the Gentile) into the good olive tree (the Jews); that unbelieving Jews (branches of the good tree) were broken off that Gentiles might be grafted in, afforded no occasion for glorying on the part of the latter. Jew and Gentile alike must enjoy the divine blessings by faith alone. So Jews who abide not in unbelief shall, as "the natural branches, be grafted into their own olive tree." See: BAGD—216a; THAYER—166c.

1462. **ἔγκλημα** {2x} **ĕgklēma**, *eng'-klay-mah;* from *1458;* an *accusation,* i.e. *offence* alleged:—laid to (one's) charge {1x}, crime laid against (one) {1x}.

Egklema is "an accusation made in public," but not necessarily before a tribunal. **(1)** That is the case in Acts 23:29: "Whom I perceived to be accused of questions of their law, but to have nothing laid to his charge (*enklema*) worthy of death or of bonds." **(2)** In Acts 25:16 it signifies a matter of complaint, a crime: "To whom I answered, It is not the manner of the Romans to deliver any man to die, before that he which is accused have the accusers face to face, and have licence to answer for himself concerning the crime (*enklema*) laid against him." Syn.: 156, 157, 1225, 1458, 1908, 2723, 2724, 4811. See: TDNT—3:496, 394; BAGD—216b; THAYER—166c.

1463. **ἐγκομβόομαι** {1x} **ĕgkŏmbŏŏmai**, *eng-kom-bŏ'-om-ahee;* mid. voice from *1722* and κομβόω **kŏmbŏō** (to *gird*); to *engirdle* oneself (for labor), i.e. fig. (the apron being a badge of servitude) to *wear* (in token of mutual deference):—be clothed with {1x}.

Enkomboomai, "to gird oneself with a thing, be clothed with": "Likewise, ye younger, submit yourselves unto the elder. Yea, all *of you* be subject one to another, and be clothed with humility: for God resisteth the proud, and giveth grace to the humble"(1 Pet 5:5). Syn.: 294, 1737, 1746, 1902, 2439, 4016. See: TDNT—2:339, 196; BAGD—216b; THAYER—166d.

1464. **ἐγκοπή** {1x} **ĕgkŏpē**, *eng-kop-ay';* from *1465;* a *hindrance:*—× hinder {1x}.

Egkope is literally a cut in a road to impede an enemy's advance and is used in 1 Cor 9:12, with *didomi,* "to give," "(lest) we should hinder." See: TDNT—3:855, 453; BAGD—216b; THAYER—166d.

1465. **ἐγκόπτω** {4x} **ĕgkŏptō**, *eng-kop'-to;* from *1722* and *2875;* to *cut into,* i.e. (fig.) *impede, detain:*—hinder {3x}, be tedious unto {1x}.

Egkepto, lit., "to cut into" (*en,* "in," *kopto,* "to cut"), was used of "impeding" persons by breaking up the road, or by placing an obstacle sharply in the path; hence, **(1)** metaphorically, of "detaining" a person unnecessarily, Acts 24:4; **(2)** of "hindrances" in the way of reaching others, Rom 15:22; **(3)** or returning to them, 1 Th 2:18; **(4)** of "hindering" progress in the Christian life, Gal 5:7, where the significance virtually is "who broke up the road along which you were travelling so well?"; **(5)** of "hindrances" to the prayers of husband and wife, through low standards of marital conduct, 1 Pet 3:7. See: TDNT—3:855, 453; BAGD—216c; THAYER—166d.

1466. **ἐγκράτεια** {4x} **ĕgkratĕia**, *eng-krat'-i-ah;* from *1468; self-control* (espec. *continence*):—temperance {4x}.

(1) *Egkrateia* is the virtue of one who masters his desires and passions, esp. his sensual appetites. **(1)** It comes from *kratos,* "strength," and occurs in Acts 24:25; Gal 5:23; 2 Pet 1:6 (twice), in all of which it is rendered "temperance." **(2)** To render it self-control in Gal 5:23 is contradictory. If one has contol of self, the Spirit's ministry is needless. **(3)** The various powers bestowed by God upon man are capable of abuse; the right use demands the controlling power of the will under the operation of the Spirit of God. **(4)** In Acts 24:25 the word follows "righteousness," which represents God's claims, self-control, even in the non-Christian, being man's response thereto. **(5)** In 2 Pet 1:6, it follows "knowledge," suggesting that what is learned requires to be put into practice. See: TDNT—2:339, 196; BAGD—216c; THAYER—166d.

1467. **ἐγκρατεύομαι** {2x} **ĕgkratĕuŏmai**, *eng-krat-yoo'-om-ahee;* mid. voice from *1468;* to *exercise self-restraint* (in diet and chastity):—can not contain {1x}, be temperate {1x}.

This is the opposite of 1466. *Egkrateuomai,* "power, strength," lit., "to have power over oneself," is rendered **(1)** "(if) they have (not) continency, can not contain" (i.e., are lacking in self-control), in 1 Cor 7:9; **(2)** in 1 Cor 9:25, "is temperate." See: TDNT—2:339, 196; BAGD—216c; THAYER—167a.

1468. **ἐγκρατής** {1x} **ĕgkratēs**, *eng-krat-ace';* from *1722* and *2904; strong in* a thing (*masterful*), i.e. (fig. and refl.) *self-controlled* (in appetite, etc.):—temperate {1x}.

Egkrates denotes "exercising self-control," and is rendered "temperate" in Titus 1:8. See: TDNT—2:339, 196; BAGD—216d; THAYER—167a.

1469. **ἐγκρίνω** {1x} **ĕgkrinō**, *eng-kree'-no;* from *1722* and *2919; to judge in,* i.e. *count* among:—make of the number {1x}.

(1) *Egkrino* means to judge one worthy of being admitted to a certain class. **(2)** *Egkrino,* "to reckon among" is translated "to number . . . (ourselves) with" in 2 Cor 10:12 of the apostle's dissociation of himself and his fellow missionaries from those who commended themselves. See: TDNT—3:951, 469; BAGD—216d; THAYER—167a.

1470. **ἐγκρύπτω** {2x} **ĕgkruptō**, *eng-kroop'-to;* from *1722* and *2928; to conceal in,* i.e. *incorporate, mingle with:*—hid in {2x}. See: BAGD—216d; THAYER—167b.

1471. **ἔγκυος** {1x} **ĕgkuŏs**, *eng'-koo-os;* from *1722* and the base of *2949; swelling inside,* i.e. *pregnant:*—great with child {1x}. See: BAGD—216d; THAYER—167b.

1472. **ἐγχρίω** {1x} **ĕgchriō**, *eng-khree'-o;* from *1722* and *5548;* to *rub in* (oil), i.e. *besmear:*—anoint {1x}.

Enchrio, as a verb, means primarily "to rub in," hence, "to besmear, to anoint," and is used metaphorically in the command to the church in Laodicea to "anoint" their eyes with eye salve (Rev 3:18). Syn.: 218, 2025, 3462, 5545, 5548. See: BAGD—217a; THAYER—167b.

1473. **ἐγώ** {370x} **ĕgō**, *eg-o';* a primary pron. of the first pers. *I* (only expressed when emphatic):—I {365x}, my {2x}, me {2x}, not tr {1x}. For the other cases and the plur. see *1691, 1698, 1700, 2248, 2249, 2254, 2257,* etc. See: TDNT—2:343, 196; BAGD—217a.; THAYER—167b.

1474. **ἐδαφίζω** {1x} **ĕdaphizō**, *ed-af-id'-zo;* from *1475;* to *raze:*—lay even with the ground {1x}. See: BAGD—217c; THAYER—167d.

1475. **ἔδαφος** {1x} **ĕdaphŏs**, *ed'-af-os;* from the base of *1476;* a *basis* (*bottom*), i.e. the *soil:*—ground {1x}.

Edaphos, "a bottom, base," is used of the "ground" in Acts 22:7, suggestive of that which is level and hard. See: BAGD—217d; THAYER—168a.

1476. **ἑδραῖος** {3x} **hĕdraiŏs**, *hed-rah'-yos;* from a der. of ἕζομαι **hĕzŏmai** (to *sit*); *sedentary,* i.e. (by impl.) *immovable:*—settled {2x}, stedfast {1x}.

Hedraios primarily denotes "seated"; hence, "steadfast," metaphorical of moral fixity, 1 Cor 7:37; 15:58; Col 1:23. See: TDNT—2:362, 200; BAGD—217d; THAYER—168a.

1477. **ἑδραίωμα** {1x} **ĕdraiōma**, *hed-rah'-yo-mah;* from a der. of *1476;* a *support,* i.e. (fig.) *basis:*—ground {1x}.

Edraioma, "a support, bulwark, stay" (from *hedraios,* "steadfast, firm"; from *hedra,* "a seat"), is translated "ground" in 1 Ti 3:15 (said of a local church; that upon which one can build because it dispenses Christ's words, the rock, upon which one builds his life, cf. Mt 7:24–25; 16:18; Lk 6:48; 8:6). See: TDNT—2:362, 200; BAGD—218a; THAYER—168a.

1478. **Ἐζεκίας** {2x} **ezĕkias**, *ed-zek-ee'-as;* of Heb. or. [2396]; *Ezekias* (i.e. *Hezekiah*), an Isr.:—*Ezekias* {2x}. See: BAGD—218a; THAYER—168a.

1479. **ἐθελοθρησκεία** {1x} **ethĕlŏthrēskĕia**, *eth-el-oth-race-ki'-ah;* from *2309* and *2356; voluntary* (*arbitrary* and *unwarranted*) *piety,* i.e. *sanctimony:*—will worship {1x}.

Ethelothreskeia occurs in Col 2:23 and means voluntarily adopted worship, not that which is imposed by others, but which one affects himself. See: TDNT—3:155, 337; BAGD—218a; THAYER—168a.

ἐθέλω **ĕthĕlō**. See *2309*.

1480. **ἐθίζω** {1x} **ethizō**, *eth-id'-zo;* from *1485;* to *accustom,* i.e. (neut. pass. part.) *customary:*—custom {1x}.

Ethizo signifies "to accustom," or in the passive voice, "to be accustomed." In the participial form it is equivalent to a noun, "custom, Lk 2:27. See: BAGD—218b; THAYER—168b.

1481. **ἐθνάρχης** {1x} **ethnarchēs**, *eth-nar'-khace;* from *1484* and *746;* the *governor* [not king] *of a district:*—governor {1x}.

Ethnarches is translated "governor" in 2 Cor 11:32. It describes normally the ruler of a nation possessed of separate laws and customs among those of a different race. Eventually it denoted a ruler of a province, superior to a tetrarch, but inferior to a king (e.g., Aretas). See: BAGD—218b; THAYER—168b.

1482. **ἐθνικός** {2x} **ĕthnikŏs**, *eth-nee-kos';* from *1484; national* ("*ethnic*"), i.e. (spec.) a *Gentile:*—heathen {1x}, heathen man {1x}.

Ethnikos is used as noun, and translated **(1)** "heathen" in Mt 6:7; **(2)** "an heathen man" in Mt 18:17. TDNT—2:372, 201; BAGD—218b; THAYER—168b.

1483. **ἐθνικῶς** {1x} **ĕthnikōs**, *eth-nee-koce';* adv. from *1482; as a Gentile:*—after the manner of Gentiles {1x}. See: BAGD—218b; THAYER—168c.

1484. **ἔθνος** {164x} **ĕthnŏs**, *eth'-nos;* prob. from *1486;* a *race* (as of the same *habit*), i.e. a *tribe;* spec. a *foreign* (*non-Jewish*) one (usually by impl. *pagan*):—Gentiles {93x}, heathen {5x}, nation {64x}, people {2x}.

Ethnos denotes, firstly, "a multitude or company"; then, "a multitude of people of the same nature or genus, a nation, people"; **(1)** it is used in the singular, of the Jews, e.g., Lk 7:5; 23:2; Jn 11:48, 50–52; **(2)** in the plural, of nations (Heb., *goiim*) other than Israel, e.g., Mt 4:15; Rom 3:29; 11:11; 15:10; Gal 2:8; **(3)** occasionally it is used of gentile converts in distinction from Jews, e.g., Rom 11:13; 16:4; Gal 2:12, 14; Eph 3:1. See: TDNT—2:364, 201; BAGD—218b; THAYER—168c.

1485. **ἔθος** {12x} **ĕthŏs**, *eth'-os;* from *1486;* a *usage* (prescribed by habit or law):—custom {7x}, manner {4x}, be wont {1x}.

Ethos, as a noun, means "a habit, custom" and is translated **(1)** "manner": "Then took they the body of Jesus, and wound it in linen clothes with the spices, as the manner of the Jews is to bury" Jn 19:40; cf. Acts 15:1; 25:16; Heb 10:25. It denotes **(2)** "a custom, usage, prescribed by law," Lk 1:9; 2:42; Acts 6:14; 16:21; 21:21; 26:2; 28:17; **(3)** "wont", Lk 22:39. Syn.: 195, 2239, 3634, 3668, 3697, 3779, 4169, 4187, 4217, 4459, 5158, 5159, 5179, 5615. See: TDNT—2:372, 202; BAGD—218d; THAYER—168d.

1486. **ἔθω** {4x} **ĕthō**, *eth'-o;* a primary verb; to *be used* (by habit or conventionality); neut. perfect part. *usage:*—be wont {2x}, -as his custom was + 2596 + 3588 {1x}, as his manner was + 2596 + 3588 {1x}.

Etho, "to be accustomed" is used **(1)** in the passive participle as a noun, signifying "a custom, a manner" Lk 4:16; Acts 17:2; and **(2)** in Mt 7:15 and Mk 10:1, "was wont." See: BAGD—219a; THAYER—168d.

1487. **εἰ** {{290x} **ĕi**, *i;* a primary particle of conditionality; *if, whether, that,* etc.:—if {242x}, whether {20x}, that {6x}, not tr {19x}, forasmuch as {1x}, although {1x}, whether {1x}. Often used in connection or composition with other particles, espec. as in *1489, 1490, 1499, 1508, 1509, 1512, 1513, 1536, 1537*. See also *1437*. See: BAGD—219a; THAYER—169a.

1488. **εἶ** {92x} **ĕi**, *i;* second pers. sing. present of *1510;* thou *art:*—art {81x}, be {11x}. See: BAGD—223a [under 1510]; THAYER—175c [1510].

1489. **εἴγε** {5x} **ĕigĕ**, *i'-gheh;* from *1487* and *1065; if indeed, seeing that, unless,* (with neg.) *otherwise:*—if {2x}, if so be that {2x}, yet {1x}. See: BAGD—220a; THAYER—172c.

1490. **εἰ δὲ μή(γε)** {14x} **ĕi dĕ mē(gĕ)** *i deh may'-(gheh);* from *1487, 1161,* and *3361* (sometimes with *1065* added); *but if not:*—or else {3x}, else {4x}, if not {2x}, if otherwise {2x}, if not {1x}, or else {1x}, otherwise {1x}. See: BAGD—220a; THAYER—111b.

1491. **εἶδος** {5x} **ĕidŏs**, *i'-dos;* from *1492;* a *view,* i.e. *form* (lit. or fig.):—appearance {1x}, fashion {1x}, shape {2x}, sight {1x}.

Eidos, as a noun, means properly "that which strikes the eye, that which is exposed to view," signifies **(1)** the "external appearance, form, or shape," and in this sense is used **(1a)** of the Holy Spirit in taking bodily form, as a dove, Lk 3:22; **(1b)** of Christ, Lk 9:29, "And as He prayed, the fashion (*eidos*) of His countenance was altered, and His raiment *was* white *and* glistering" (Lk 9:29); **(1c)** Christ used it, negatively, of God the Father, when He said "Ye have neither heard His voice at any time, nor seen His form," Jn 5:37. **(1d)** Thus it is used with reference to each person of the Trinity. **(1e)** Probably the same meaning attaches to the word in the apostle's statement, "We walk by faith, not by sight (*eidos*)," 2 Cor 5:7, **(1f)** where *eidos* can scarcely mean the act of beholding, but the visible "appearance" of things which are set in contrast to that which directs faith. **(1g)** The believer is guided, then, not only by what he beholds but by what he knows to be true though it is invisible. **(2)** It has a somewhat different significance in 1 Th 5:22, in the exhortation, "Abstain from every appearance of evil," i.e., every sort or kind of evil, even that which can allow onlookers to think one is participating in evil. See: TDNT—2:373, 202; BAGD—221b; THAYER—172d.

1492. **εἴδω** {666x} **ĕidō**, *i'-do;* a primary verb; used only in certain past tenses, the others being borrowed from the equiv. *3700* and *3708;* prop. to *see* (lit. or fig.); by impl. (in the perf. only) to *know by perception:*—know {282x}, cannot tell + 3756 {8x}, know how {7x}, wist {6x}, see {314x}, behold {16x}, look {5x}, perceive {5x}, vr see {3x}, vr know {1x}, misc. {19x}, be aware, consider, have knowledge, knowledge, be sure, tell, understand, wot.

Oida (Perf. of *eido*), as a verb, "to see,"**(1)** is a perfect tense with a present meaning, **(2)** signifying, primarily, "to have seen or perceived"; hence, "to know, to have knowledge of," whether absolutely, **(2a)** as in divine knowledge, e.g., Mt 6:8, 32; Jn 6:6, 64; 8:14; 11:42; 13:11; 18:4; 2 Cor 11:31; 2 Pet 2:9; Rev 2:2, 9, 13, 19; 3:1, 8, 15; **(2b)** or in the case of human "knowledge," to know from observation, e.g., 1 Th 1:4, 5; 2:1; 2 Th 3:7. Syn.: The differences between *ginosko* (1097) and *oida* (1492) demand consideration: **(A)** *ginosko,* frequently suggests inception or progress in "knowledge," while *oida* suggests fullness of "knowledge," e.g., **(A1)** Jn 8:55, "ye have not known Him" (*ginosko*), i.e., begun to "know," "but I know Him" (*oida*), i.e., "know Him perfectly"; **(A2)** Jn 13:7, "What I do thou knowest not now," i.e. Peter did not yet perceive (oida) its significance, "but thou shalt understand," i.e., "get to know (*ginosko*), hereafter"; **(A3)** Jn14:7, "If ye had known Me" (*ginosko*), i.e., "had definitely come to know Me," "ye would have known My Father also" (*oida*), i.e., "would have had perception of": "from henceforth ye know Him" (*ginosko*), i.e., having unconsciously been coming to the Father, as the One who was in Him, they would now consciously be in the constant and progressive experience of "knowing" Him; **(A4)** in Mk 4:13, "Know ye not (*oida*) this parable? and how shall ye know (*ginosko*) all the parables?"; the intimation being that the first parable is a leading and testing one; **(B)** while ginosko frequently implies an active relation between the one who "knows" and the person or thing "known" oida expresses the fact that the object has simply come within the scope of the "knower's" perception; **(B1)** thus in Mt 7:23 "I never knew you" (*ginosko*) suggests "I have never been in approving connection with you," whereas **(B2)** in Mt 25:12, "I know you not" (oida) suggests "you stand in no relation to Me." See also: 1097, 1107, 1110, 1492, 1921, 1467, 1922, 1987. See: TDNT—5:116, 673; BAGD—220c; THAYER—172d. comp. *3700*.

1493. **εἰδωλεῖον** {1x} **ĕidōlĕiŏn**, *i-do-li'-on;* neut. of a presumed der. of *1497;* an *image-fane:*—idol's temple {1x}. See: TDNT—2:379, 202; BAGD—221b; THAYER—174c.

1494. **εἰδωλόθυτον** {10x} **ĕidōlŏthutŏn**, *i-do-loth'-oo-ton;* neut. of a compound of *1497* and a presumed der. of *2380;* an *image-sacrifice,* i.e. part of an *idolatrous offering:*—things offered unto idols {4x}, things offered in sacrifice to idols {3x}, things sacrificed unto idols {2x}, meats offered to idols {1x}.

This word is an adjective signifying "sacrificed to idols" (*eidolon* – 1497, and *thuo* – 2380, "to sacrifice"), Acts 15:29; 21:25; 1 Cor 8:1, 4, 7, 10; 10:19, 28; Rev 2:14, 20 (in these the RV and KJV both have "sacrificed"). See: TDNT—2:378, 202; BAGD—221b; THAYER—174c.

1495. **εἰδωλολατρεία** {4x} **ĕidōlŏlatrĕia**, *i-do-lol-at-ri'-ah;* from *1497* and *2999; image-worship* (lit. or fig.):—idolatry {4x}.

Eidololatreia, whence Eng., "idolatry," and **(1)** is found in 1 Cor 10:14; Gal 5:20; Col 3:5; and, in the plural, in 1 Pet 4:3. **(2)** Heathen sacrifices were sacrificed to devils, 1 Cor 10:19. **(2a)** There was a dire reality in the cup and table of devils and in the involved communion with devils. **(2b)** In Rom 1:22–25, "idolatry," the sin of the mind against God (Eph 2:3), and immorality, sins of the flesh, are associated, and are traced to lack of the acknowledgment of God and of gratitude to Him. **(2c)** An "idolater" is a slave to the depraved ideas his idols represent, Gal 4:8, 9; and thereby, to divers lusts, Titus 3:3. See: TDNT—2:379, 202; BAGD—221c; THAYER—174c.

1496. **εἰδωλολάτρης** {7x} **ĕidōlŏlatrēs**, *i-do-lol-at'-race;* from *1497* and the base of *3000;* an *image-*(*servant* or) *worshipper* (lit. or fig.):—idolater {7x}.

Eidololatres, an "idolater" (from *eidolon,* and *latris,* "a hireling"), is **(1)** found in 1 Cor 5:10, 11; 6:9, 10:7. **(2)** The warning is to believers against turning away from God to idolatry, whether openly or secretly, consciously or unconsciously; Eph 5:5; Rev 21:8; 22:15. See: TDNT—2:379, 202; BAGD—221c; THAYER—174c.

1497. **εἴδωλον** {11x} **ĕidōlŏn**, *i'-do-lon;* from *1491;* an *image* (i.e. for worship); by impl. a heathen *god,* or (plur.) the *worship* of such:—idol {11x}.

Eidolon, primarily **(1)** "a phantom or likeness" (from eidos, "an appearance"), means **(1a)** lit., "that which is seen", or **(1b)** "an idea, fancy," **(2)** denotes in the NT **(2a)** "an idol," an image to represent a false god, Acts 7:41; 1 Cor 12:2; Rev 9:20; **(2b)** "the false god" worshipped in an image, Acts 15:20; Rom 2:22; 1 Cor 8:4, 7; 10:19; 2 Cor 6:16; 1 Th 1:9; 1 Jn 5:21. **(3)** The corresponding Heb. word denotes 'vanity,' cf. Jer 14:22; 18:15; "thing of nought," Lev 19:4, cf. Eph 4:17. **(4)** Hence what represented a deity to the Gentiles, was to Paul a 'vain thing,' Acts 14:15; 'nothing in the world,' 1 Cor 8:4; 10:19. **(5)** Jeremiah describes the idol, 10:5; cf. Is 44:9–20; Hab 2:18, 19; and the Psalmist, 115:4–8, etc., are all equally scathing. **(6)** It is important to notice, however, that in each case the people of God are addressed. **(7)** When he speaks to idolaters, Paul, knowing that no man is won by ridicule, adopts a different line, Acts 14:15–18; 17:16, 21–31." See: TDNT—2:375, 202; BAGD—221c; THAYER—174d.

1498. **εἴην** {12x} **ĕiēn**, *i'-ane;* optative (i.e. English subjunctive) present of *1510* (incl. the other pers.); *might* (*could, would,* or *should*) *be:*—should be {3x}, be {3x}, meant {2x}, might be {1x}, should mean {1x}, wert {1x}, not tr {1x}. See: BAGD—222d; THAYER—175c.

1499. **εἰ καί** {22x} **ĕi kai**, *i kahee;* from *1487* and *2532; if also* (or *even*):—though {14x}, if {4x}, and if {2x}, if that {1x}, if also {1x}. See: BAGD—220a; THAYER—171b.

1500. **εἰκῆ** {7x} **ĕikē**, *i-kay';* prob. >From *1502* (through the idea of *failure*); *idly,* i.e. *without a reason* (or *effect*):—in vain {5x}, without a cause {1x}, vainly {1x}.

Eike denotes **(1)** "without cause," Mt 5:22; **(2)** "vainly," Col 2:18; **(3)** "to no purpose," "in vain," Rom 13:4; 1 Cor 15:2; Gal 3:4 (twice); 4:11 See: TDNT—2:380, 203; BAGD—221d; THAYER—174d.

1501. **εἴκοσι** {12x} **ĕikŏsi**, *i'-kos-ee;* of uncert. aff.; a *score:*—twenty {12x}. See: BAGD—222a; THAYER—174d.

1502. **εἴκω** {1x} **ĕikō**, *i'-ko;* appar. a primary verb; prop. to *be weak,* i.e. *yield:*—give place {1x}.

Eiko, as a verb, means "to yield, give way" and is rendered "gave place": "To whom we gave place by subjection, no, not for an hour; that the truth of the gospel might continue with you" (Gal 2:5). Syn.: 201, 402, 1096, 3837, 4042, 5117, 5247, 5564, 5602. See: BAGD—222b; THAYER—175a.

1503. **εἴκω** {2x} **ĕikō**, *i'-ko;* appar. a primary verb [perh. akin to *1502* through the idea of *faintness* as a copy]; to *resemble:*—be like {2x}. See: BAGD—222b; THAYER—175a.

1504. **εἰκών** {23x} **ĕikōn**, *i-kone';* from *1503;* a *likeness,* i.e. (lit.) *statue, profile,* or (fig.) *representation, resemblance:*—image {23x}.

(1) This word always refers to a prototype that it resembles and from which it is drawn; an imitation of an archtype. **(1a)** *Eikon* denotes "an image"; **(1b)** the word involves the two ideas of representation and manifestation. **(2)** The idea of a perfect likeness does not lie in the word itself, but must be sought from the context; the following instances clearly show any distinction between the imperfect and the perfect likeness. **(3)** The word is used **(3a)** of an "image" or a coin (not a mere likeness), Mt 22:20; Mk 12:16; Lk 20:24; **(3b)** so of a statue or similar representation (more than a resemblance), Rom 1:23; Rev 13:14, 15 (thrice); 14:9, 11; 15:2; 16:2; 19:20; 20:4; **(3c)** of the descendants of Adam as bearing his image, 1 Cor 15:49, each a representation derived from the prototype; **(3d)** of subjects relative to things spiritual, Heb 10:1, negatively of the Law as having "a shadow of the good things to come, not the very image of the things," i.e., not the essential and substantial form of them; the contrast has been likened to the difference between a statue and the shadow cast by it;

(4) of the relations between God the Father, Christ, and man, **(4a)** of man as he was created as being a visible representation of God, 1 Cor 11:7, a being corresponding to the original; **(4a1)** the condition of man as a fallen creature has not entirely effaced the "image"; **(4a2)** he is still suitable to bear responsibility, he still has God-like qualities, such as love of goodness and beauty, none of which are found in a mere animal; **(4a3)** in the Fall man ceased to be a perfect vehicle for the representation of God; **(4a4)** God's grace in Christ will yet accomplish more than what Adam lost; **(4b)** of regenerate persons, in being moral representations of what God is, Col 3:10; cf. Eph 4:24; **(4c)** of believers, in their glorified state, not merely as resembling Christ but representing Him, Rom 8:29; 1 Cor 15:49; here the perfection is the work of divine grace; believers are yet to represent, not something like Him, but what He is in Himself, both in His spiritual body and in His moral character;

(5) of Christ in relation to God, **(5a)** 2 Cor. 4:4, "the image of God," i.e., essentially and absolutely the perfect expression and representation of the Archetype, God the Father; **(5b)** in Col 1:15, "the image of the invisible God" gives the additional thought suggested by the word "invisible," that Christ is the visible representation and manifestation of God to created beings; **(5c)** the likeness expressed in this manifestation is involved in the essential relations in the Godhead, and is therefore unique and perfect; "he that hath seen Me hath seen the Father," John 14:9. **(5d)** The epithet 'invisible' . . . must not be confined to the apprehension of the bodily senses, but will include the cognizance of the inward eye also. Syn.: 3667, 3669. See: TDNT—2:381, 203; BAGD—222b; THAYER—175a.

1505. **εἰλικρίνεια** {3x} **ĕilikrinĕia**, *i-lik-ree'-ni-ah;* from *1506; clearness,* i.e. (by impl.) *purity* (fig.):—sincerity {3x}.

Eilikrineia denotes "sincerity, purity"; it is described **(1)** metaphorically in 1 Cor 5:8 as "unleavened (bread)"; in **(2)** 2 Cor 1:12, "(godly) sincerity," it describes a quality possessed by God, as that which is to characterize the conduct of believers; **(3)** in 2 Cor 2:17 it is used of the rightful ministry of the Scriptures. See: TDNT—2:397, 206; BAGD—222d; THAYER—175b.

1506. **εἰλικρινής** {2x} **ĕilikrinēs**, *i-lik-ree-nace';* from εἵλη **hĕilē** (the sun's *ray*) and *2919; judged by sunlight,* i.e. tested as *genuine* (fig.):—pure {1x}, sincere {1x}.

Eilikrines, signifies "unalloyed, pure"; and it was used of unmixed substances; **(1)** in the NT it is used of moral and ethical "purity," Phil 1:10, "sincere"; and **(2)** in 2 Pet 3:1 "pure." **(3)** Some regard the etymological meaning as "tested by the sunlight" Syn.: This Christian virtue will exclude all double-mindedness (Jas 1:8; 4:8), the eye that is not single (Mt 6:22), and all hypocrisies (1 Pet 2:1). It refers to the Christian freedom from falsehoods, while katharos (2513) refers to the Christian's freedom from defilements of the flesh and the world. See: TDNT—2:397, 206; BAGD—222d; THAYER—175b

1507. **εἱλίσσω** {1x} **hĕilissō**, *hi-lis'-so;* a prol. form of a primary but defective verb εἵλω **hĕilō** (of the same mean.); to *coil* or *wrap:*—roll together {1x}. See: BAGD—222d; THAYER—175b. See also *1667.*

1508. **εἰ μή** {91x} **ĕi mē**, *i-may';* from *1487* and *3361; if not:*—but {53x}, save {16x}, except {6x}, if not {5x}, not tr {1x}, misc. {1x}. See: BAGD—220a; THAYER—171c.

1509. **εἰ μή τι** {3x} **ĕi mē ti**, *i-may'-tee;* from *1508* and the neut. of *5100; if not somewhat:*—except {3x}. See: BAGD—220b; THAYER—172a.

1510. **εἰμί** {146x} **ĕimi**, *i-mee';* the first pers. sing. present ind.; a prol. form of a primary and defective verb; I *exist* (used only when emphatic):—I am + 1473 {74x}, am {55x}, it is I + 1473 {6x}, be {2x}, I was + 1473 {1x}, have been {1x}, not tr {7x}. See: BAGD—222d; THAYER—175c. See also *1488, 1498, 1511, 2258, 2071, 2070, 2075, 2076, 2771, 2468, 5600, 5607.*

1511. **εἶναι** {126x} **ĕinai**, *i'-nahee;* present infin. from *1510;* to *exist:*—to be {33x}, be {28x}, was {15x}, is {14x}, am {7x}, are {6x}, were {4x}, not tr {11x}, misc. {8x} = come, × lust after, × please well, there is. See: BAGD—223a; THAYER—176c.

εἵνεκεν **hĕinĕkĕn**. See *1752.*

1512. **εἴ περ** {6x} **ĕi pĕr**, *i-per;* from *1487* and *4007; if perhaps:*—if so be that {3x}, though {1x}, seeing {1x}, if so be {1x}. See: BAGD—226a; 220b; THAYER—180c; 172a.

1513. **εἴ πως** {4x} **ĕi pōs**, *i-poce;* from *1487* and *4458; if somehow:*—if by any means {4x} See: BAGD—220b; THAYER—172a.

1514. **εἰρηνεύω** {4x} **ĕirēnĕuō**, *i-rane-yoo'-o;* from *1515; to be (act) peaceful:*—have peace {1x}, live peaceably {1x}, live in peace {1x}, be at peace {1x}.

Eireneuo means primarily, "to bring to peace, reconcile" and denotes in the NT, "to keep peace or to be at peace": in **(1)** Mk 9:50 the Lord bids the disciples "be at peace" with one another, gently rebuking their ambitious desires; **(2)** in Rom 12:18 "live peaceably", the limitation "if it be possible, as much as in you lieth," seems due to the phrase "with all men," but is not intended to excuse any evasion of the obligation imposed by the command; **(3)** in 2 Cor 13:11 it is rendered "live in peace," a general exhortation to believers; **(4)** in 1 Th 5:13, "be at peace (among yourselves). See: TDNT—2:417, 207; BAGD—227a; THAYER—182a.

1515. **εἰρήνη** {92x} **ĕirēnē**, *i-ray'-nay;* prob. from a primary verb εἴρω **ĕirō** (to *join*); *peace* (lit. or fig.); by impl. *prosperity:*—one {1x}, peace {89x}, quietness {1x}, rest {1x}.

Eirene **(1)** occurs in each of the books of the NT, save 1 Jn and save in Acts 7:26 ['(at) one again']. **(2)** It describes **(2a)** harmonious relationships between men, Mt 10:34; Rom 14:19; **(2b)** between nations, Lk 14:32; Acts 12:20; Rev 6:4; **(2c)** friendliness, Acts 15:33; 1 Cor 16:11; Heb 11:31; **(2d)** freedom from molestation, Lk 11:21; 19:42; Acts 9:31 "rest"; 16:36; **(2e)** order, in the State, Acts 24:2 "quietness"; **(2f)** order in the churches, 1 Cor 14:33; **(2g)** the harmonized relationships between God and man, accomplished through the gospel, Acts 10:36; Eph 2:17; **(2h)** the sense of rest and contentment consequent thereon, Mt 10:13; Mk 5:34; Lk 1:79; 2:29; Jn 14:27; Rom 1:7; 3:17; 8:6; **(2i)** in certain passages this idea is not distinguishable from the last, Rom 5:1. See: TDNT—2:400, 207; BAGD—227b; THAYER—182a.

1516. **εἰρηνικός** {2x} **ĕirēnikŏs**, *i-ray-nee-kos';* from *1515; pacific;* by impl. *salutary:*—peaceable {2x}.

Eirenikos denotes "peaceful." It is used **(1)** of the fruit of righteousness, Heb 12:11, "peaceable" (or "peaceful") because it is produced in communion with God the Father, through His chastening; and **(2)** of "the wisdom that is from above," Jas 3:17. See: TDNT—2:418, 207; BAGD—228a; THAYER—182d.

1517. **εἰρηνοποιέω** {1x} **ĕirēnŏpŏiĕō**, *i-ray-nop-oy-eh'-o;* from *1518;* to *be a peace-maker,* i.e. (fig.) to *harmonize:*—make peace {1x}.

This word means to go away or to go slowly away, to depart, withdraw oneself, often with the idea of going without noise or notice: Jas 2:16; 1 Jn 2:11; Rev 10:8; 13:10; 14:4; 16:1; 17:8, 11. It is frequently rendered "go your (thy) way." See: TDNT—2:419, 207; BAGD—228a; THAYER—183a.

1518. **εἰρηνοποιός** {1x} **ĕirēnŏpŏiŏs**, *i-ray-nop-oy-os';* from *1515* and *4160; pacificatory,* i.e. (subj.) *peaceable:*—peacemakers {1x}. See: TDNT—2:419, 207; BAGD—228a; THAYER—183a.

εἴρω **ĕirō**. See *1515, 4483, 5346.*

1519. **εἰς** {1773x} **ĕis**, *ice;* a primary prep.; *to* or *into* (indicating the point reached or entered), of place, time, or (fig.) purpose (result, etc.); also in adv. phrases:—into {573x}, to {281x}, unto {207x}, for {140x}, in {138x}, on {58x}, toward {29x}, against {26x}, misc. {321x} = [abundant-] ly, among, as, at, [back-] ward, before, by, concerning, continual, far more exceeding, for [intent, purpose], fore, forth, in (among, at, unto, so much that,), to the intent that, of one mind, never, of, upon, perish, set at one again, (so) that, therefore (unto), throughout, till, to be, to the end, (here) until, [where] fore, with. Often used in composition with the same general import, but only with verbs (etc.) expressing motion (lit. or fig.). See: TDNT—2:420, 211; BAGD—228a; THAYER—183a.

1520. **εἷς** {271x} **hĕis**, *hice;* (incl. the neut. [etc.] ἕν **hĕn**); a primary numeral; *one:*—one {229x}, a {9x}, other {6x}, some {6x}, not tr {4x}, misc. {17x} any, a certain, + abundantly, man, one another, only.

Heis, the first cardinal numeral, masculine (feminine and neuter nominative forms are *mia* and *hen,* respectively), is used to signify **(1)** "one" in contrast to many, e.g., Mt 25:15; Rom 5:18, "the offense of one", Adam's transgression, in contrast to the "one act of righteousness," i.e., the death of Christ; **(2)** metaphorically, "union" and "concord," e.g., Jn 10:30; 11:52; 17:11, 21–22; Rom 12:4–5; Phil 1:27; **(3)** emphatically, **(3a)** a single ("one"), to the exclusion of others, e.g., Mt 21:24; Rom 3:10; 1 Cor 9:24; 1 Ti 2:5 (twice); **(3b)** "one, alone," e.g., Mk 2:7, "only"; 10:18; Lk 18:19; **(3c)** "one and the same," e.g., Rom 3:30, "God is one," i.e., there is not "one" God for the Jew and one for the Gentile; **(3c)** cf. Gal 3:20, which means that in a promise there is no other party; 1 Cor 3:8; 11:5; 12:11; 1 Jn 5:8 (lit., "and the three are into one," i.e., united in "one" and the same witness);

(4) a certain "one," **(4a)** in the same sense as the indefinite pronoun tis, e.g., Mt 8:19, "a certain (scribe)"; 19:16, "one;" in Rev 8:13 "one (eagle)"; **(4b)** *heis* tis are used together in Lk 22:50; Jn 11:49; **(5)** distributively, with *hekastos,* **(5a)** "each," i.e., "every one," e.g., Lk 4:40; Acts 2:6, "every man" (lit., "every one"); **(5b)** in the sense of "one . . . and one," e.g., Jn 20:12; **(5c)** or "one" . . . followed by *allos* or *heteros,* "the other," e.g., Mt 6:24; **(5d)** or by a second *heis,* e.g., Mt 24:40; Jn 20:12; in Rom 12:5 heis is preceded by *kata* (*kath* in the sense of "severally (members) one (of another)," "every one . . . one"); cf. Mk 14:19; **(5e)** in 1 Th 5:11 the phrase in the 2nd part, "each other," "one another", is, lit., "one the one"; **(6)** as an ordinal number, equivalent to *protos,* "first," in the phrase "the first day of the week," lit. and idiomatically, "one of sabbaths," signifying "the first day after the sabbath," e.g., Mt 28:1; Mk 16:2; Acts 20:7; 1 Cor 16:2. See: TDNT—2:434, 214; BAGD—230d; THAYER—186b.

1521. **εἰσάγω** {10x} **ĕisagō**, *ice-ag'-o;* from *1519* and *71;* to *introduce* (lit. or fig.):—bring in {5x}, bring {4x}, lead {1x}. See: BAGD—232b; THAYER—187c.

1522. **εἰσακούω** {5x} **ĕisakŏuō**, *ice-ak-oo'-o;* from *1519* and *191;* to *listen to:*—hear {5x}.

Eisakouo, as a verb, means "to listen to" and has two meanings: **(1)** "to hear and to obey" (1 Cor 14:21 - "they will not hear"); **(2)** "to hear so as to answer" of God's answer to prayer (Mt 6:7; Lk 1:13; Acts 10:31; Heb 5:7). Syn.: 189, 191, 1251, 1873, 1874, 3878, 4257. See: TDNT—1:222, 34; BAGD—232b; THAYER—187c.

1523. **εἰσδέχομαι** {1x} **ĕisdĕchŏmai**, *ice-dekh'-om-ahee;* from *1519* and *1209;* to *take into* one's favor:—receive {1x}.

Eisdechomai, as a verb, means "to receive into" and is used only in 2 Cor 6:17, where the verb does not signify "to accept," but "to admit": "Wherefore come out from among them, and be ye separate, saith the Lord, and touch not the unclean *thing;* and I will receive (*eisdechomai*) you" [as antithetic to "come ye out" cf. Is 52:11 with Zeph 3:20]. Syn.: 324, 353, 354, 568, 588, 618, 1209, 1926, 2210, 2865, 2975, 2983, 3028, 3335, 3336, 3858, 3880, 3970, 4327, 4355, 4356, 4380, 4381, 4382, 5562, 5264, 5274. See: TDNT—2:57, 146; BAGD—232c; THAYER—187c.

1524. **εἴσειμι** {4x} **ĕisĕimi**, *ice'-i-mee;* from *1519* and εἶμι **ĕimi** (to *go*); to *enter:*—entered {1x}, went {2x}, went into {1x}.

Eiseimi, means **(1)** "to go into" Acts 3:3; **(2)** "entered" Acts 21:26; and **(3)** "went" Acts 21:18. Heb 9:6. See: BAGD—232c; THAYER—187d.

1525. **εἰσέρχομαι** {198x} **ĕisĕrchŏmai**, *ice-er'-khom-ahee;* from *1519* and *2064;* to *enter* (lit. or fig.):—enter {107x}, go {22x}, come in {19x}, go in {18x}, enter in {17x}, come {14x}, arise {1x}.

Eiserchomai, as a verb, means **(1)** literally "to go in, to enter" and is **(2)** once rendered "arose," metaphorically, with reference to a reasoning among the disciples which of them should be the greatest" (Lk 9:46). Syn.: 305, 393, 450, 1096, 1326, 1453, 1817, 4911. See: TDNT—2:676, 257; BAGD—232d; THAYER—187d.

1526. **εἰσί** {163x} **ĕisi**, *i-see';* third pers. plur. present ind. of *1510;* they *are:*—are {135x}, be {14x}, were {7x}, have {2x}, not tr {1x}, misc. {4x} = agree, is. See: BAGD—223a; THAYER—175c.

1527. **εἷς καθ' εἷς** {2x} **hĕis kath hĕis**, *hice kath hice;* from *1520* repeated with *2596* inserted; *severally:*—one by one {2x}.

This phrase means "one by one, one after the other", Mr 14:19; Jn 8:9. See: BAGD—232b; THAYER—187b.

1528. **εἰσκαλέω** {1x} **ĕiskalĕō**, *ice-kal-eh'-o;* from *1519* and *2564;* to *invite* in:—call in {1x}. See: TDNT—3:496, 394; BAGD—233b; THAYER—188c.

1529. **εἴσοδος** {5x} **ĕisŏdŏs**, *ice'-od-os;* from *1519* and *3598;* an *entrance* (lit. or fig.):—coming {1x}, entering in {1x}, entrance in {1x}, to enter into + 1519 {1x}, entrance {1x}.

Eisodos, "an entrance, an entering in," is **(1)** once translated "coming," Acts 13:24, of the coming of Christ into the nation of Israel. For its meaning "entrance" **(2)** see 1 Th 1:9; 2:1; Heb 10:19; 2 Pet 1:11. See: TDNT—5:103, 666; BAGD—233b; THAYER—189c.

1530. **εἰσπηδάω** {2x} **ĕispedao**, *ice-pay-dah'-o;* from *1519* and πηδάω **pēdaō** (to *leap*); to *rush in:*—ran in {1x}, sprang in {1x}.

Eispedao means **(1)** "sprang in," occurs in Acts 16:29; and **(2)** "ran in" in Acts 14:14. See: BAGD—233c; THAYER—188c.

1531. **εἰσπορεύομαι** {17x} **ĕispŏrĕuŏmai**, *ice-por-yoo'-om-ahee;* from *1519* and *4198;* to *enter* (lit. or fig.):—enter {9x}, enter in {5x}, come in {3x}.

Eisporeuomai, "to go into," found only in the Synoptists and Acts, is translated **(1)** "entered, entereth" in Mt 15:16; Mk 1:21; 6:56; 7:19; 11:2; Lk 8:16; 22:10; Acts 3:2; **(2)** "entering in" Mk 4:19; 5:40; 7:15; 7:18; Lk 19:20; Acts 8:3; **(3)** "come in" Lk 11:33; Acts 9:28; 28:30. See: TDNT—6:578, 915; BAGD—233c; THAYER—188c.

1532. **εἰστρέχω** {1x} **ĕistrĕchō**, *ice-trekh'-o;* from *1519* and *5143;* to *hasten inward:*—run in {1x}. See: BAGD—233d; THAYER—188d.

1533. **εἰσφέρω** {7x} **ĕisphĕrō**, *ice-fer'-o;* from *1519* and *5342;* to *carry inward* (lit. or fig.):—bring {3x}, bring in {2x}, lead into {2x}.

Eisphero denotes **(1)** "to bring to", Lk 5:19; Acts 17:20; **(2)** "to bring into", Lk 5:18; 1 Ti 6:7; Heb 13:11; and **(3)** "lead into", Mt 6:13; Lk 11:4. See: TDNT—9:64, 1252; BAGD—233d; THAYER—188d.

1534. **εἶτα** {16x} **ĕita**, *i'-tah;* of uncert. aff.; a particle of *succession* (in time or logical enumeration), *then, moreover:*—then {11x}, after that {3x}, afterward {1x}, furthermore {1x}.

Eita which is chiefly used of time or enumerations, signifying "then" or "next," is once used in argument, signifying furthermore, Heb. 12:9. See: BAGD—233d; THAYER—188d. See also *1899.*

1535. **εἴτε** {65x} **ĕitĕ**, *i'-teh;* from *1487* and *5037; if too:*—or {33x}, whether {28x}, or whether {3x}, if {1x}. See: BAGD—234a; 220b; THAYER—172c.

1536. **εἴ τις** {79x} **ĕi tis**, *i tis;* from *1487* and *5100; if any:*—if any man {35x}, if any {19x}, if a man {8x}, if any thing {6x}, if ought {3x}, whosoever {2x}, misc. {6x} he that, whether any. See: BAGD—220b; THAYER—172c.

1537. **ἐκ** {921x} **ĕk**, *ek* or

ἐξ **ĕx**, *ex;* a primary prep. denoting *origin* (the point *whence* motion or action proceeds), *from, out* (of place, time, or cause; lit. or fig.; direct or remote):—of {367x}, from {181x}, out of {162x}, by {55x}, on {34x}, with {25x}, misc. {97x} = after, among, are, at, betwixt, beyond, by the means of, exceedingly, (abundantly above), for (th), grudgingly, heartily, heavenly, hereby, very highly, in, . . . ly, (because, by reason) of, off (from), out among, out from, over, since, thenceforth, through, unto, vehemently, without. Often used in composition, with the same general import; often of completion. See: BAGD—234b; THAYER—189a.

1538. **ἕκαστος** {83x} **hĕkastŏs**, *hek'-as-tos;* as if a superl. of ἕκας **hĕkas** (*afar*); *each* or *every:*—every man {39x}, every one {20x}, every {17x}, misc. {7x} any, both, each (one), every woman, particularly.

This word means "each" or "every," is used of any number separately, either **(1)** as an adjective qualifying a noun, **(1a)** e.g., Lk 6:44; Jn 19:23; Heb 3:13, where "day by day," is, lit., "according to each day"; **(1b)** or, more emphatically with *heis,* "one," in Mt 26:22; Lk 4:40; 16:5; Acts 2:3, 6, 20:31; 1 Cor 12:18; Eph 4:7, 16 "every"; Col 4:6; 1 Th. 2:11; 2 Th 1:3; **(2)** as a distributive pronoun, **(2a)** e.g., Acts 4:35; Rom 2:6; Gal 6:4; in Phil 2:4, it is used in the plural; Rev 6:11. **(2b)** The repetition in Heb 8:11 is noticeable "every man" (i.e., everyone). **(3)** Prefixed by the preposition **(3a)** *ana,* "apiece" (a colloquialism), it is used, with stress on the individuality, in Rev 21:21, of the gates of the heavenly city, "every several gate"; **(3b)** in Eph 5:33, preceded by *kath' hena,* "by one," it signifies "each (one) his own." See: BAGD—236c; THAYER—192a.

1539. **ἑκάστοτε** {1x} **hĕkastŏtĕ**, *hek-as'-tot-eh;* as if from *1538* and *5119;* at *every time:*—always {1x}.

Ekastote, "each," is used in 2 Pet. 1:15. "Always" stresses "all ways, in all manners"; and "alway" stresses "all the time, all along the way without interruption." See: BAGD—236d; THAYER—192b.

1540. **ἑκατόν** {17x} **hĕkatŏn**, *hek-at-on';* of uncert. aff.; a *hundred:*—hundred {15x}, hundredfold {2x}.

Ekaton is an indeclinable numeral, denotes **(1)** "a hundred," e.g., Mt 18:12, 28; **(2)** it also signifies "a hundredfold," Mt 13:8, 23, signifying the complete productiveness of sown seed. **(3)** In the passage in Mk 4:8, 20 the phrase is, lit., "in thirty and in sixty and in a hundred." **(4)** In Mk 6:40 it is used with the preposition *kata,* in the phrase "by hundreds." **(5)** It is followed by other numerals in Jn 21:11; Acts 1:15; Rev 7:4; 14:1, 3; 21:17. See: BAGD—236d; THAYER—192b.

1541. **ἑκατονταετης** {1x} **hĕkatŏntaĕtēs**, *hek-at-on-tah-et'-ace;* from *1540* and *2094; centenarian:*—hundred years old {1x}. See: BAGD—236d; THAYER—192b.

1542. **ἑκατονταπλασίων** {3x} **hĕkatŏntaplasiōn**, *hek-at-on-ta-plah-see'-own;* from *1540* and a presumed der. of *4111;* a *hundred times, a hundred times as much:*—hundredfold {3x}. See: BAGD—237a; THAYER—192c.

1543. **ἑκατοντάρχης** {21x} **hĕkatŏntarchēs**, *hek-at-on-tar'-khace;* or

ἑκατόνταρχος **hĕkatŏntarchŏs**, *hek-at-on'-tar-khos;* from *1540* and *757;* the *captain of one hundred men:*—centurion {21x}. See: BAGD—237a; THAYER—192c.

1544. **ἐκβάλλω** {82x} **ĕkballō**, *ek-bal'-lo;* from *1537* and *906;* to *eject* (lit. or fig.):—cast out {45x}, cast {11x}, bring forth {3x}, pull out {3x}, send forth {3x}, misc. {17x} = drive (out), expel, leave, pluck, take out, thrust out, put forth, put out, send away, send out. See: TDNT—1:527, 91; BAGD—237b; THAYER—192d.

1545. **ἔκβασις** {2x} **ĕkbasis**, *ek'-bas-is;* from a compound of *1537* and the base of *939* (mean. to *go out*); an *exit* (lit. or fig.):—end {1x}, way to escape {1x}.

Ekbasis denotes **(1)** "a way out", 1 Cor 10:13, "way of escape"; or **(2)** an "end", Heb 13:7. See: BAGD—237d; THAYER—193b.

1546. **ἐκβολή** {1x} **ĕkbŏlē**, *ek-bol-ay';* from *1544; ejection,* i.e. (spec.) a *throwing overboard* of the cargo:—lighten the ship + 4060 {1x}.

Ekbasis, lit., "a throwing out" denotes "a jettison, a throwing out of cargo," Acts 27:18, lit., "they made a throwing out." See: BAGD—238a; THAYER—193b.

1547. **ἐκγαμίζω** {5x} **ĕkgamizō**, *ek-gam-id'-zo;* from *1537* and a form of *1061* [comp. *1548*]; to *marry off* a daughter:—give in marriage {5x}. See: BAGD—238a; THAYER—193b.

1548. **ἐκγαμίσκω** {2x} **ĕkgamiskō**, *ek-gam-is'-ko;* from *1537* and *1061;* the same as *1547:*—give in marriage {2x}. See: BAGD—238a; THAYER—193b.

1549. **ἔκγονον** {1x} **ĕkgŏnŏn**, *ek'-gon-on;* neut. of a der. of a compound of *1537* and *1096;* a *descendant,* i.e. (spec.) *grandchild:*—nephew {1x}.

Ekgonon, an adjective, denoting "born of" (*ek,* "from," *ginomai,* "to become or be born"), was used as a noun, signifying "a child"; in the plural, descendants, "nephews" 1 Ti 5:4. See: BAGD—238a; THAYER—193c.

1550. **ἐκδαπανάω** {1x} **ĕkdapanaō**, *ek-dap-an-ah'-o;* from *1537* and *1160;* to *expend* (wholly), i.e. (fig.) *exhaust:*—spend {1x}.

Ekdapanao lit., "to spend out", "to spend entirely," is used in 2 Cor 12:15, in the passive voice, with reflexive significance, "to spend oneself out (for others)," "will . . . be spent." See: BAGD—238b; THAYER—193c.

1551. **ἐκδέχομαι** {8x} **ĕkdĕchŏmai**, *ek-dekh'-om-ahee;* from *1537* and *1209;* to *accept from* some source, i.e. (by impl.) to *await:*—wait for {3x}, look for {2x}, tarry for {1x}, expect {1x}, wait {1x}.

Ekdechomai lit. and primarily means **(1)** "to take or receive from"; hence **(2)** denotes "to await, expect," the only sense of the word in the NT; **(3)** it suggests a reaching out in readiness to receive something; **(3a)** "expecting," Heb 10:13;

(3b) to wait for, Jn 5:3; Acts 17:16; Jas 5:7; **(3c)** "tarry for", 1 Cor 11:33; **(3d)** "wait", 1 Pet 3:20; **(3e)** "look for," 1 Cor 16:11; Heb. 11:10. See: TDNT—2:56, 146; BAGD—238b; THAYER—193c.

1552. **ἔκδηλος** {1x} **ĕkdēlŏs**, *ek'-day-los;* from *1537* and *1212; wholly evident:*—manifest {1x}. See: BAGD—238b; THAYER—192c.

1553. **ἐκδημέω** {3x} **ĕkdēmĕō**, *ek-day-meh'-o;* from a compound of *1537* and *1218;* to *emigrate; to be away from people,* i.e. (fig.) *vacate* or *quit:*—be absent {3x}.

Ekdemeo, lit., "to be away from people" (*ek,* "from," or "out of," *demos,* "people"), came to mean "to go abroad, depart, be absent." The apostle Paul uses it to speak of departing from the body as the earthly abode of the spirit, 2 Cor 5:6–9: **(1)** of being here in the body and absent from the Lord (v. 6), or **(2)** of being absent from the body and present with the Lord (v. 8). **(3)** Its other occurrence is in v. 9. See: TDNT—2:63, 149; BAGD—238b; THAYER—193d.

1554. **ἐκδίδωμι** {4x} **ĕkdidōmi**, *ek-did-o'-mee;* from *1537* and *1325; to give forth for one's advantage,* i.e. (spec.) to *lease:*—let forth {1x}, let out {1x}.

Ekdidomi, primarily, "to give out, give up, surrender" denotes "to let out for hire." In the NT it is used, in the middle voice, with the meaning in the parable of the husbandman and his vineyard **(1)** "to let out to one's advantage", Mt 21:33, 41; Mk 12:1; or **(2)** "let forth . . ." Lk 20:9. See: BAGD—238c; THAYER—193d.

1555. **ἐκδιηγέομαι** {2x} **ĕkdiēgĕŏmai**, *ek-dee-ayg-eh'-om-ahee;* from *1537* and a compound of *1223* and *2233; to narrate* through wholly:—declare {2x}.

Ekdiegeomai, properly means "to narrate in full," and came to denote, "to tell, declare wholly", Acts 13:41; 15:3. See: BAGD—238c; THAYER—193d.

1556. **ἐκδικέω** {6x} **ĕkdikĕō**, *ek-dik-eh'-o;* from *1558; to vindicate, retaliate, punish:*—avenge {5x}, revenge {1x}.

Ekdikeo, (*ek,* "from," *dike,* "justice") i.e., that which proceeds from justice, means **(1)** "to vindicate a person's right" in the parable of the unjust judge, Lk 18:3, 5, of the "vindication" of the rights of the widow; **(2)** with the meaning **(2a)** "to avenge a thing," it is used in Rev 6:10 and 19:2, of the act of God in "avenging" the blood of the saints; **(2b)** in 2 Cor 10:6, of the apostle's readiness to use his apostolic authority in punishing disobedience on the part of his readers; **(2c)** in Rom 12:19 of "avenging" oneself, against which the believer is warned. See: TDNT—2:442, 215; BAGD—238c; THAYER—193d.

1557. **ἐκδίκησις** {9x} **ĕkdikēsis**, *ek-dik'-ay-sis;* from *1556; vindication, retribution:*—vengeance {4x}, avenge + 4060 {3x}, revenge {1x}, punishment {1x}.

Ekdikesis, "vengeance," is used **(1)** with the verb *poieo,* "to make," i.e., to avenge, in Lk 18:7–8; Acts 7:24; **(2)** twice it is used in statements that "vengeance" belongs to God, Rom 12:19; Heb 10:30. **(3)** In 2 Th 1:8 it is said of the act of divine justice which will be meted out to those who know not God and obey not the gospel, when the Lord comes in flaming fire at His second advent. In the divine exercise of judgment there is no element of vindictiveness, nothing by way of taking revenge. **(4)** In Lk 21:22, it is used of the "days of vengeance" upon the Jewish people; **(5)** in 1 Pet 2:14, of civil governors as those who are sent of God "for punishment on evildoers"; **(6)** in 2 Cor 7:11, of the "revenge" of believers, in their godly sorrow for wrong doing. See: TDNT—2:445, 215; BAGD—238d; THAYER—194a.

1558. **ἔκδικος** {2x} **ĕkdikŏs**, *ek'-dik-os;* from *1537* and *1349;* carrying *justice out,* i.e. a *punisher:*—revenger {1x}, avenger {1x}.

Ekdikos, primarily, "without law," then, "one who exacts a penalty from a person, an avenger, a punisher," is used **(1)** in Rom 13:4 of a civil authority in the discharge of his function of executing wrath on the evildoer, a "revenger"; **(2)** in 1 Th 4:6, of God as the avenger of the one who wrongs his brother, here particularly in the matter of adultery. See: TDNT—2:444, 215; BAGD—238d; THAYER—194a.

1559. **ἐκδιώκω** {2x} **ĕkdiōkō**, *ek-dee-o'-ko;* from *1537* and *1377; to pursue out, to chase away,* i.e. *expel* or *persecute* implacably:—persecute {2x}.

Edkioko, to chase away, drive out," oppress with calamities, **(1)** is used in 1 Th 2:15 "have persecuted"; and **(2)** Lk 11:49 of the persecution of God's prophets. See: BAGD—239a; THAYER—194a.

1560. **ἔκδοτος** {1x} **ĕkdŏtŏs**, *ek'-dot-os;* from *1537* and a der. of *1325; given out* or *over,* i.e. *surrendered:*—delivered {1x}.

Ekdotos, as a verbal adjecive [participle] means literally "given up" [*ek,* "out of," *didomi,* "to give"], "delivered up" (to enemies, or to the power or will of someone), is used of Christ in Acts 2:23: "Him, being delivered by the determinate counsel and foreknowledge of God, ye have taken, and by wicked hands have crucified and slain." Syn.: 325, 525, 629, 591, 859, 1325, 1659, 1807, 1929, 3086, 3860, 4506, 5483. See: BAGD—239a; THAYER—194b.

1561. **ἐκδοχή** {1x} **ĕkdŏchē**, *ek-dokh-ay';* from *1551; expectation:*—looking for {1x}.

Ekdoche, "looking for expectedly" is used in Heb 10:27 "looking for" judgment. See: BAGD—239a; THAYER—194b.

1562. **ἐκδύω** {5x} **ĕkduō**, *ek-doo'-o;* from *1537* and the base of *1416;* to cause to *sink out* of, i.e. (spec. as of clothing) to *divest:*—strip {2x}, take off from {2x}, unclothe {1x}.

Ekduo, "to take off, strip off," is used especially of clothes, and rendered **(1)** "to strip" in Mt 27:28; Lk 10:30, **(2)** to take off, Mt 27:31; Mk 15:20; and **(3)** figuratively, 2 Cor 5:4, "unclothed" (middle voice), of putting off the body at death (the believer's state of being unclothed does not refer to the body in the grave but to the spirit, which awaits the "body of glory" at the resurrection). See: TDNT—2:318, 192; BAGD—239a; THAYER—194b.

1563. **ἐκεῖ** {98x} **ĕkĕi**, *ek-i';* of uncert. aff.; *there;* by extens. *thither:*—there {86x}, thither {7x}, not tr {3x}, misc. {3x} thitherward, (to) yonder (place). "There" has reference to a specific location away from the speaker; whereas, "thither" is a non-specific location somewhere away from the speaker. See: BAGD—239b; THAYER—194b.

1564. **ἐκεῖθεν** {27x} **ĕkĕithĕn**, *ek-i'-then;* from *1563; thence:*—thence {16x}, from thence {9x}, from that place {1x}, there {1x}.

"Thence" denotes time and place; "from thence" stresses place, with a hint of no return. See: BAGD—239b; THAYER—194c.

1565. **ἐκεῖνος** {251x} **ĕkĕinŏs**, *ek-i'-nos;* from *1563; that* one (or [neut.] thing); often intensified by the art. prefixed:—that {99x}, those {40x}, he {40x}, the same {20x}, they {14x}, misc. {38x} it, the other, selfsame, their, them, this.

Ekeinos denotes "that one, that person"; its use marks special distinction, favorable or unfavorable; this form of emphasis should always be noted; e.g., **(1)** Jn 2:21 "(But) He (spake)"; **(2)** 5:19, "(what things soever) He (doeth)"; 7:11; 2 Cor 10:18, lit., "for not he that commendeth himself, he (*ekeinos*) is approved"; **(3)** 2 Ti 2:13, "He (in contrast to "we") abideth faithful"; **(4)** 1 Jn 3:3, "(even as) He (is pure)"; **(5)** 1 Jn 5:5, "He (was manifested)"; **(6)** 1 Jn 5:7, "He (is righteous)"; **(7)** 1 Jn 5:16, "He laid down"; **(8)** 1 Jn 4:17, "(as) He (is)." See: BAGD—239b; THAYER—194c. See also *3778.*

1566. **ἐκεῖσε** {2x} **ĕkĕisĕ**, *ek-i'-seh;* from *1563; thither:*—there {2x}. See: BAGD—240; THAYER—195b.

1567. **ἐκζητέω** {7x} **ĕkzētĕō**, *ek-zay-teh'-o;* from *1537* and *2212; to search out,* i.e. (fig.) *investigate, crave, demand,* (by Heb.) *worship:*—require {2x}, seek after {2x}, diligently {1x}, seek carefully {1x}, enquire {1x}.

Ekzeteo, as a verb, signifies **(1)** "to seek out (ek) or after, to search for": **(1a)** "There is none that understandeth, there is none that seeketh after God" (Rom 3:11); **(1b)** the Lord: "That the residue of men might seek after the Lord, and all the Gentiles, upon whom My name is called, saith the Lord, who doeth all these things" (Acts 15:17; cf. Heb 11:6; 12:17; 1 Pet 1:10, followed by exeraunao, "to search diligently"; **(2)** "to require or demand": "That the blood of all the prophets, which was shed from the foundation of the world, may be required (*ekzeteo*) of this generation; from the blood of Abel unto the blood of Zacharias, which perished between the altar and the temple: verily I say unto you, It shall be required (*ekzeteo*) of this generation" (Lk 11:50, 51). Syn.: 327, 1934, 2206, 2212, 3713. See: TDNT—2:894, 300; BAGD—240a; THAYER—195b.

1568. **ἐκθαμβέω** {4x} **ĕkthambĕō**, *ek-tham-beh'-o;* from *1569; to astonish* utterly:—be affrighted {2x}, sore amazed {1x}, greatly amazed {1x}.

This word means to throw into terror or amazement; to alarm thoroughly, to terrify or astound and is used in the passive sense, **(1)** "to be amazed, affrighted," Mk 16:5–6; **(2)** Mk 9:15, "were greatly amazed"; **(3)** Mk 14:33, "to be sore amazed." See: TDNT—3:4,*; BAGD—240b; THAYER—195c.

1569. **ἔκθαμβος** {1x} **ĕkthambŏs**, *ek'-tham-bos;* from *1537* and *2285; utterly astounded:*—greatly wondering {1x}.

A strengthened form of *thambos* is found in Acts 3:11. The intensive force of the word is brought out by the rendering "greatly wondering. See: TDNT—3:4, 312; BAGD—240b; THAYER—195c.

1570. **ἔκθετος** {1x} **ĕkthĕtŏs**, *ek'-thet-os;* from *1537* and a der. of *5087; put out,* i.e. *exposed* to perish:—cast out {1x}. See: BAGD—240b; THAYER—195c.

1571. **ἐκκαθαίρω** {2x} **ĕkkathairō**, *ek-kath-ah'-ee-ro;* from *1537* and *2508;* to *cleanse thoroughly:*—purge {1x}, purge out {1x}.

Ekkathairo, "to cleanse out, cleanse thoroughly," is said **(1)** of "purging" out leaven, 1 Cor 5:7; and **(2)** in 2 Ti 2:21, of "purging" oneself from those who utter "profane babblings," vv. 16–18. See: TDNT—3:430, 381; BAGD—240b; THAYER—195c.

1572. **ἐκκαίω** {1x} **ĕkkaiō**, *ek-kah'-yo;* from *1537* and *2545;* to *inflame* deeply:—burn {1x}.

Ekkaio, lit., "to burn out," in the passive voice, "to be kindled, burn up," is used of the lustful passions of men, Rom 1:27. See: BAGD—240c; THAYER—195d.

1573. **ἐκκακέω** {6x} **ĕkkakĕō**, *ek-kak-eh'-o* or ἐγκακέω **egkakeō** *eng-kak-eh'-o;* from *1537* and *2556;* to *be* (*bad* or) *weak,* i.e. (by impl.) to *fail* (in heart); to lose courage:—faint {4x}, be weary {2x}.

Ekkakeo, "to lack courage, lose heart, be fainthearted", is said **(1)** of prayer, Lk 18:1; **(2)** of gospel ministry, 2 Cor 4:1, 16; **(3)** of the effect of tribulation, Eph 3:13; **(4)** as to well doing, 2 Th 3:13, "be not weary"; **(5)** as to reaping, Gal 6:9. See: TDNT 3:486,*; BAGD—240c; THAYER—195d.

1574. **ἐκκεντέω** {2x} **ĕkkĕntĕō**, *ek-ken-teh'-o;* from *1537* and the base of *2759;* to *transfix:*—pierce {2x}.

Ekkenteo "to pierce" [Christ], Jn 19:37; Rev 1:7. See: TDNT—2:446, 216; BAGD—240c; THAYER—195d.

1575. **ἐκκλάω** {3x} **ĕkklaō**, *ek-klah'-o;* from *1537* and *2806;* to *exscind:*—break off {3x}.

Ekklao, "to break off," is used metaphorically of branches, Rom 11:17, 19–20. See: BAGD—240c; THAYER—195d.

1576. **ἐκκλείω** {2x} **ĕkklĕiō**, *ek-kli'-o;* from *1537* and *2808;* to *shut out* (lit. or fig.):—exclude {2x}.

Ekkleio, "to shut out" is said **(1)** of glorying in works as a means of justification, Rom 3:27; **(2)** of Gentiles, who by Judaism would be "excluded" from salvation and Christian fellowship, Gal 4:17. See: BAGD—240d; THAYER—195d.

1577. **ἐκκλησία** {118x} **ĕkklēsia**, *ek-klay-see'-ah;* from a compound of *1537* and a der. of *2564;* a *calling out,* i.e. (concr.) a popular *meeting,* espec. a religious *congregation* (Jewish *synagogue,* or Chr. community of members on earth or saints in heaven or both):—assembly {3x}, church {115x}.

(1) This word stresses a group of people called out for a special purpose. **(1a)** It designated the new society of which Jesus was the founder, being as it was a society knit together by the closest spiritual bonds and altogether independent of space. **(1b)** *Ekklesia,* from ek, "out of," and klesis, "a calling" (*kaleo,* "to call"), was used among the Greeks of a body of citizens "gathered" to discuss the affairs of state, Acts 19:39. **(2)** In Acts 7:38 it is used of Israel; in 19:32, 41, of a riotous mob. **(3)** It has two applications to companies of Christians, **(3a)** to the whole company of the redeemed throughout the present era, the company of which Christ said, "I will build My Church," Mt 16:18, and which is further described as "the Church which is His Body," Eph 1:22; 5:23, **(3b)** in the singular number (e.g., Mt 18:17), to a company consisting of professed believers, e.g., Acts 20:28; 1 Cor 1:2; Gal 1:13; 1 Th 1:1; 2 Th 1:1; 1 Ti 3:5, and in the plural, with reference to churches in a district. **(4)** In Acts 9:31 "churches" point to a district. Syn.: 3831, 4864. See: TDNT—3:501, 394; BAGD—40d; THAYER—195d.

1578. **ἐκκλίνω** {3x} **ĕkklinō**, *ek-klee'-no;* from *1537* and *2827;* to *deviate,* i.e. (absolutely) to *shun* (lit. or fig.), or (rel.) to *decline* (from piety):—avoid {1x}, eschew {1x}, go out of the way {1x}.

Ekklino, "to turn away from, to turn aside," lit., "to bend out of" (*ek,* "out," *klino,* "to bend"), is **(1)** used in Rom 3:12, of the sinful condition of mankind, "gone out of the way"; **(2)** in Rom 16:17, of turning away from those who cause offenses and occasions of stumbling "avoid"; **(3)** in 1 Pet 3:11 of turning away from evil, "eschew." See: BAGD—240c; THAYER—196c.

1579. **ἐκκολυμβάω** {1x} **ĕkkŏlumbaō**, *ek-kol-oom-bah'-o;* from *1537* and *2860;* to *escape* by *swimming:*—swim out {1x}. See: BAGD—241d; THAYER—196c.

1580. **ἐκκομίζω** {1x} **ĕkkŏmizō**, *ek-kom-id'-zo;* from *1537* and *2865;* to *bear forth* (to burial):—carry out {1x}. See: BAGD—241d; THAYER—196c.

1581. **ἐκκόπτω** {11x} **ĕkkŏptō**, *ek-kop'-to;* from *1537* and *2875;* to *exscind;* fig. to *frustrate:*—cut off {4x}, hewn down {3x}, cut down {2x}, cut out {1x}, be hindered {1x}.

Ekkopto, "to cut down," is used **(1)** literally, **(1a)** "hewn down", Mt 3:10; 7:19; Lk 3:9; **(1b)** "cut down", Lk 13:7, 9; **(2)** metaphorically, **(2a)** of "cutting off" from spiritual blessing, Rom 11:22, 24; **(2b)** of "cutting off" an offending body part, Mt 5:30; 18:8 **(3)** of depriving persons of an occasion for something, 2 Cor 11:12; and **(4)** "to hinder" prayers ["cut off" from reaching God] 1 Pet 3:7. See: TDNT—3:857, 453; BAGD—241d; THAYER—196c.

1582. **ἐκκρέμαμαι** {1x} **ĕkkrĕmamai**, *ek-krem'-am-ahee;* mid. voice from *1537* and *2910;* to *hang upon* the lips of a speaker, i.e. *listen closely:*—be very attentive {1x}. See: TDNT—3:915, 468; BAGD—242a; THAYER—196d.

1583. **ἐκλαλέω** {1x} **ĕklalĕō**, *ek-lal-eh'-o;* from *1537* and *2980;* to *divulge:*—tell {1x}.

Eklaleo, "to speak out" is translated "tell" in Acts 23:22. See: BAGD—242a; THAYER—196d.

1584. **ἐκλάμπω** {1x} **ĕklampō**, *ek-lam'-po;* from *1537* and *2989;* to *be resplendent:*—shine forth {1x}. See: TDNT—4:16, 497; BAGD—242a; THAYER—196d.

1585. **ἐκλανθάνομαι** {1x} **ĕklanthanŏmai**, *ek-lan-than'-om-ahee;* mid. voice from *1537* and *2990;* to *be* utterly *oblivious* of:—forget {1x}. See: BAGD—242b; THAYER—196d.

1586. **ἐκλέγομαι** {21x} **ĕklĕgŏmai**, *ek-leg'-om-ahee;* mid. voice from *1537* and *3004* (in its primary sense); to *select:*—make choice {1x}, choose {19x}, choose out {1x}.

(1) *Eklegomai,* "to pick out, select," means, in the middle voice, "to choose for oneself," not necessarily implying the rejection of what is not chosen, but "choosing" with the subsidiary ideas of kindness or favor or love, Mk 13:20; Lk 6:13; 10:42; 14:7; Jn 6:70; 13:18; 15:16, 19; Acts 1:2, 24; 6:5; 13:17; 15:7 "made choice"; 15:22, 25; 1 Cor 1:27–28; Eph 1:4; Jas 2:5. See: TDNT—4:144, 505; BAGD—242b; THAYER—196d.

1587. **ἐκλείπω** {3x} **ĕklĕipō**, *ek-li'-po;* from *1537* and *3007;* to *omit,* i.e. (by impl.) *cease* (*die*):—fail {3x}.

Ekleipo, "to leave out", used intransitively, means "to leave off, cease, fail"; **(1)** it is said of the cessation of earthly life, Lk 16:9; **(2)** of faith, Lk 22:32; **(3)** of the years of Christ, Heb 1:12. See: BAGD—242c; THAYER—197a.

1588. **ἐκλεκτός** {23x} **ĕklĕktŏs**, *ek-lek-tos';* from *1586; select, chosen out;* by impl. *favorite:*—chosen {16x}, elect {7x}.

Eklektos, signifies "chosen out, select," **(1)** e.g., Mt 22:14; Lk 23:35; Rom 16:13; Rev 17:14; 1 Pet 2:4, 9. See: TDNT—4:181, 505; BAGD—242d; THAYER—197b.

1589. **ἐκλογή** {7x} **ĕklŏgē**, *ek-log-ay';* from *1586;* (divine) *selection* (abstr. or concr.):—chosen {1x}, election {6x}.

Ekloge, "a picking out, choosing", is translated **(1)** "chosen" in Acts 9:15, lit., "he is a vessel of choice unto Me." **(2)** In the six other places where this word is found it is translated "election", Rom 9:11; 11:5; 11:7; 11:28; 1:4; 2 Pet 1:10. See: TDNT—4:176, 505; BAGD—243a; THAYER—197c.

1590. **ἐκλύω** {6x} **ĕkluō**, *ek-loo'-o;* from *1537* and *3089;* to *relax* (lit. or fig.):—faint {5x}, faint + 2258 {1x}.

Ekluo, denotes (a) "to loose, release" (*ek,* "out," *luo,* "to loose"); (b) "to unloose," as a bow-string, "to relax," and so, "to enfeeble," and is used in the passive voice with the significance "to be faint, grow weary," **(1)** of the body, Mt 9:36; 15:32; Mk 8:3; **(2)** of the soul, Gal 6:9 (last clause), in discharging responsibilities in obedience to the Lord; **(3)** in Heb 12:3, of becoming weary in the strife against sin; **(4)** in Heb 13:5, under the chastening hand of God. See: BAGD—243b; THAYER—197d.

1591. **ἐκμάσσω** {5x} **ĕkmassō**, *ek-mas'-so;* from *1537* and the base of *3145;* to *knead out,* i.e. (by anal.) to *wipe dry:*—wipe {5x}.

Ekmasso, "to wipe out" (*ek*), "wipe dry," is used **(1)** of "wiping" tears from Christ's feet, Lk 7:38, 44; Jn 11:2; 12:3; **(2)** of Christ's "wiping" the disciples' feet, Jn 13:5. See: BAGD—243b; THAYER—198a.

1592. **ἐκμυκτηρίζω** {2x} **ĕkmuktĕrizō**, *ek-mook-ter-id'-zo;* from *1537* and *3456;* to *sneer* outright at:—deride {2x}.

Ekmukterizo, "to hold up the nose in derision at" (*ek,* "from," used intensively, *mukterizo,* "to mock"; from *mukter,* "the nose"), is translated "derided" **(1)** in Lk 16:14, of the Pharisees in their derision of Christ on account of His teaching; **(2)** in Lk 23:35, of the mockery of Christ on the cross by the rulers of the people. See: TDNT—4:176, 505; BAGD—243b; THAYER—198a.

1593. **ἐκνεύω** {1x} **ĕknĕuō**, *ek-nyoo'-o;* from *1537* and *3506;* (by anal.) to *slip off,* i.e. quietly *withdraw:*—convey self away {1x}.

Ekneuo, primarily, "to bend to one side, to turn aside"; then "to take oneself away, withdraw," is found in Jn 5:13, of Christ's "conveying" Himself away from one place to another. Some have regarded the verb as having the same meaning as *ekneo,* "to escape," as from peril, "slip away secretly"; but the Lord did not leave the place where He had healed the paralytic in order to escape danger, but to avoid the applause of the throng. See: BAGD—243b; THAYER—198a.

1594. **ἐκνήφω** {1x} **ĕknēphō**, *ek-nay'-fo;* from *1537* and *3525;* (fig.) to *rouse* (oneself) *out* of stupor:—awake {1x}.

In 1 Cor 15:34 *eknepho* means to awake up righteously and sin not, suggesting a return to soberness of mind from the stupor consequent upon the influence of evil doctrine. TDNT—4:941, 633; BAGD—243b; THAYER—198b.

1595. **ἑκούσιον** {1x} **hĕkŏusiŏn**, *hek-oo'-see-on;* neut. of a der. from *1635; voluntariness:*—willingly + 2596 {1x}. See: TDNT—2:470; BAGD—243b; THAYER—198b.

1596. **ἑκουσίως** {2x} **hĕkŏusiōs**, *hek-oo-see'-oce;* adv. from the same as *1595; voluntarily:*—wilfully {1x}, willingly {1x}.

Hekousios denotes "voluntarily, willingly," **(1)** Heb 10:26, (of sinning) "willfully"; and **(2)** in 1 Pet 5:2, "willingly" (of exercising oversight over the flock of God). See: TDNT—221; BAGD—243c; THAYER—198b.

1597. **ἔκπαλαι** {2x} **ĕkpalai**, *ek'-pal-ahee;* from *1537* and *3819; long ago, for a long while:*—of a long time {1x}, of old {1x}.

Ekpalai, is translated **(1)** "from of old" in 2 Pet 3:5; and **(2)** "of a long time" in 2 Pet 2:3. See: BAGD—243c; THAYER—198b.

1598. **ἐκπειράζω** {4x} **ĕkpĕirazō**, *ek-pi-rad'-zo;* from *1537* and *3985; to test thoroughly:*—tempt {4x}.

Ekpeirazo, an intensive form, is used **(1)** in Christ's quotation from Deut 6:16, in reply to the devil, Mt 4:7; Lk 4:12; **(2)** in 1 Cor 10:9 "Christ": "Neither let us tempt Christ, as some of them also tempted, and were destroyed of serpents"; **(3)** of the lawyer who "tempted" Christ, Lk 10:25. See: TDNT—6:23, 822; BAGD—243c; THAYER—198b.

1599. **ἐκπέμπω** {2x} **ĕkpĕmpō**, *ek-pem'-po;* from *1537* and *3992; to despatch:*—sent away {1x}, being sen forth {1x}.

Ekpempo denotes "to send forth", **(1)** Acts 13:4, "being sent forth"; and **(2)** Acts 17:10, "sent away." See: BAGD—243c; THAYER—198c.

ἐκπερισσοῦ **ĕkpĕrissŏu**. See *1537* and *4053*.

1600. **ἐκπετάννυμι** {1x} **ĕkpĕtannumi**, *ek-pet-an'-noo-mee;* from *1537* and a form of *4072; to fly out like a sail,* i.e. (by anal.) to *extend:*—stretch forth {1x}.

Ekpetannumi, "to spread out" (as a sail), is rendered in Rom 10:21, "I have stretched forth". See: BAGD—243d; THAYER—198c.

1601. **ἐκπίπτω** {14x} **ĕkpiptō**, *ek-pip'-to;* from *1537* and *4098; to drop away;* spec., *be driven out* of one's course; fig. to *lose, become inefficient:*—fall {7x}, fall off {2x}, be cast {1x}, take none effect {1x}, fall away {1x}, fail {1x}, vr fallen {1x}.

This word means literally **(1)** to fall out of, to fall down from, to fall off Acts 12:7; **(2)** metaphorically, **(2a)** to fall from a thing, to lose it Gal 5:4; 2 Pet 3:17; **(2b1)** to perish, to fall from a place from which one cannot keep; fall from its position, 1 Cor 13:8; **(2b2)** to fall powerless, to fall to the ground, be without effect; of the divine promise of salvation Rom 9:6. See: TDNT—6:167, 846; BAGD—243d; THAYER—198c.

1602. **ἐκπλέω** {3x} **ĕkplĕō**, *ek-pleh'-o;* from *1537* and *4126; to depart* by ship:—sail {1x}, sail away {1x}, sail thence {1x}.

This means to depart by ship, Acts 15:39; 18:18; 20:6. See: BAGD—244a; THAYER—198d.

1603. **ἐκπληρόω** {1x} **ĕkplērŏō**, *ek-play-rŏ'-o;* from *1537* and *4137; to accomplish* entirely:—fulfill {1x}. See: TDNT—6:307, 867; BAGD—244a; THAYER—198d.

1604. **ἐκπλήρωσις** {1x} **ĕkplērōsis**, *ek-play'-ro-sis;* from *1603; completion:*—accomplishment {1x}. See: TDNT—6:308, 867; BAGD—244b; THAYER—198d.

1605. **ἐκπλήσσω** {13x} **ĕkplēssō**, *ek-place'-so;* from *1537* and *4141; to strike* with astonishment:—be amazed {3x}, be astonished {10x}.

Ekplesso, signifies "to be exceedingly struck in mind, to be astonished", e.g., Mt 19:25; Lk 2:48; 9:43. Syn.: **(A)** *Ekplesso* (1605) means "to be astonished", prop. to be struck with terror, of a sudden and startling alarm; but like our "astonish" in popular use, often employed on comparatively slight occasions. **(B)** *Ptoeo* (4422) signifies "to terrify", to agitate with fear. **(C)** Tremo (5141) "to tremble", predominately physical; and **(D)** *phobeo* (5399) denotes "to fear", the general term; often used of a protracted state. See: BAGD—244b; THAYER—198d.

1606. **ἐκπνέω** {3x} **ĕkpnĕō**, *ek-pneh'-o;* from *1537* and *4154;* to *expire:*—give up the ghost {3x}.

Ekpneo, lit., "to breathe out", "to expire," is used in the NT, without an object, "soul" or "life" being understood, Mk 15:37, 39, and Lk 23:46, of the death of Christ. In Mt 27:50 and Jn 19:30, where different verbs are used, the act is expressed in a way which stresses it as of His own volition. See: TDNT—6:452, 876; BAGD—244b; THAYER—199a.

1607. **ἐκπορεύομαι** {35x} **ĕkpŏrĕuŏmai**, *ek-por-yoo'-om-ahee;* from *1537* and *4198; to depart, be discharged, proceed, project:*—proceed {10x}, go out {6x}, go {5x}, come {4x}, depart {3x}, go forth {2x}, vr go forth {1x}, misc. {4x} come (forth, out of), issue.

Ekporeuomai, "from," in the middle and passive, "to proceed from or forth," more expressive of a definite course than simply "to go forth," is translated **(1)** "departed," in Mt 20:29; Mk 6:11; Acts 25:4; **(2)** "that which cometh" in Mk 7:20; **(3)** It is frequently translated by the verb "to proceed," and is often best so rendered Eph 4:29; Rev 11:5; and **(4)** "issued" in Rev 9:17–18. See: TDNT—6:578, 915; BAGD—244b; THAYER—199a.

1608. **ἐκπορνεύω** {1x} **ĕkpŏrnĕuō**, *ek-porn-yoo'-o;* from *1537* and *4203;* to *be utterly unchaste:*—give self over to fornication {1x}.

Ekporneuo, (a strengthened form of *porneuo*, *ek*, used intensively), "to give oneself up to fornication," implies excessive indulgence, Jude 7. See: 6:579, 918; BAGD—244d; THAYER—199b.

1609. **ἐκπτύω** {1x} **ĕkptuō**, *ek-ptoo'-o;* from *1537* and *4429; to spit out,* i.e. (fig.) *spurn:*—reject {1x}.

Ekptuo, "to spit out" i.e., "to abominate, loathe," is used in Gal 4:14, "rejected" where the sentence is elliptical: "although my disease repelled you, you did not refuse to hear my message." See: TDNT—2:448, 216; BAGD—244d; THAYER—199b.

1610. **ἐκριζόω** {4x} **ĕkrizŏō**, *ek-rid-zŏ'-o;* from *1537* and *4492;* to *uproot:*—pluck up by the root {2x}, root up {2x}.

Ekrizoo, "to pluck up by the roots" (*ek*, "out," *rhiza*, "a root"), is so translated **(1)** in Jude 12 (figuratively), Lk 17:6; **(2)** "root up," Mt 13:29; "shall be rooted up," 15:13. See: TDNT—6:991, 985; BAGD—244d; THAYER—199c.

1611. **ἔκστασις** {7x} **ĕkstasis**, *ek'-stas-is;* from *1839;* a *displacement* of the mind, i.e. *bewilderment, "ecstasy":*—be amazed + 3083 {2x}, amazement {1x}, astonishment {1x}, trance {3x}.

Ekstasis is, lit., a standing out [Eng. "ecstasy"] and was said of any displacement, and especially, with reference to the mind, of that alteration of the normal condition by which the person is thrown into a state of surprise or fear, or both; **(1)** or again, in which a person is so transported out of his natural state that he falls into a trance (Acts 10:10; 11:5; 22:17). As to the other meanings: **(2)** "astonishment", see Mk 5:42 and Luke 5:26; but **(3)** "amazed"in Mk 16:8; Lk 5:26; and **(4)** "amazement" in Acts 3:10. Syn.: 1568, 1569, 2285. See: TDNT—2:449, 217; BAGD—245a; THAYER—199c.

1612. **ἐκστρέφω** {1x} **ĕkstrĕphō**, *ek-stref'-o;* from *1537* and *4762; to pervert* (fig.):—subvert {1x}.

The word means to turn inside out, to change entirely and is used metaphorically in Titus 3:11. See: BAGD—245b; THAYER—199d.

1613. **ἐκταράσσω** {1x} **ĕktarassō**, *ek-tar-as'-so;* from *1537* and *5015; to disturb wholly:*—exceedingly trouble {1x}. See: BAGD—245b; THAYER—199d.

1614. **ἐκτείνω** {16x} **ĕktĕinō**, *ek-ti'-no;* from *1537* and τείνω **tĕinō** (to *stretch*); to *extend:*—cast {1x}, put forth {3x}, stretch forth {10x}, stretch out {2x}.

Ekteino means **(1)** "to stretch forth," is so rendered in Mt 12:13 (twice), 49; 14:31; Mk 3:5 (first part), Lk 6:10; Lk 22:53; Jn 21:18; Acts 4:30; 26:1 **(2)** "put forth" in Mt 8:3; Mk 1:41; Lk 5:13; **(3)** "cast" in Acts 27:30; and **(4)** "stretch out" in Mt 26:51; Mk 3:5 (second part). See: TDNT—2:460, 219; BAGD—245b; THAYER—199d.

1615. **ἐκτελέω** {2x} **ĕktĕlĕō**, *ek-tel-eh'-o;* from *1537* and *5055; to complete* fully:—finish {2x}.

Ekteleo, literally means, "to finish out," i.e., "completely" (*ek*, "out," intensive), and is used in Lk 14:29, 30. See: BAGD—245c; THAYER—200a.

1616. **ἐκτένεια** {1x} **ĕktĕnĕia**, *ek-ten-i'-ah;* from *1618; intentness (of mind):*—instantly + 1722 {7x}. See: TDNT—2:464, 219; BAGD—245c; THAYER—200a.

1617. **ἐκτενέστερον** {1x} **ĕktĕnĕstĕrŏn**, *ek-ten-es'-ter-on;* neut. of the comparative of *1618; more intently:*—more earnestly {1x}.

Ektenesteron, the comparative degree, used as an adverb in this neuter form, denotes "more earnestly, fervently," Lk 22:44. See: TDNT—2:463, 219; BAGD—245c; THAYER—200a.

1618. **ἐκτενής** {2x} **ĕktĕnēs**, *ek-ten-ace';* from *1614; intent:*—without ceasing {1x}, fervent {1x}.

Ektenes denotes "strained, stretched out"; hence, **(1)** metaphorically, "fervent," 1 Pet 4:8; and **(2)** the adverb, "without ceasing" in Acts 12:5. See: TDNT—2:463, 219; BAGD—245c; THAYER—200a.

1619. **ἐκτενῶς** {1x} **ĕktĕnōs**, *ek-ten-oce';* adv. from *1618; intently:*—fervently {1x}.

In 1 Pet. 1:22, "fervently"; the idea suggested is that of not relaxing in effort and acting in a right spirit. See: BAGD—245d; THAYER—200a.

1620. **ἐκτίθημι** {4x} **ĕktithēmi**, *ek-tith'-ay-mee;* from *1537* and *5087;* to *expose;* fig. to *declare:*—cast out {1x}, expound {3x}.

Ektithemi, "to set out, expose" is used **(1)** literally, Acts 7:21; **(2)** metaphorically, in the middle voice, to set forth, "expound," **(2a)** of circumstances, Acts 11:4; **(2b)** of the way of God, Acts 18:26; **(2c)** of the kingdom of God, Acts 28:23. See: BAGD—245d; THAYER—200a.

1621. **ἐκτινάσσω** {4x} **ĕktinassō**, *ek-tin-as'-so;* from *1537* and τινάσσω **tinassō** (to *swing*); to *shake* violently:—shake {1x}, shake off {3x}.

Ektinasso, "to shake out," is used **(1)** of "shaking off" the dust from the feet, Mt 10:14; Mk

6:11; Acts 13:51; **(2)** of "shaking out" one's raiment, Acts 18:6. See: BAGD—245d; THAYER—200b.

1622. **ἐκτός** {9x} **ěktŏs**, *ek-tos';* from *1537;* the *exterior;* fig. (as a prep.) *aside from, besides:*—out of {2x}, outside {1x}, other than {1x}, without {1x}, be excepted {1x}, except + 1508 {1x}, unless + 1508 {1x}, but + 1508 {1x}.

Ektos, an adverb, lit., "outside," is used with *ei me,* as an extended conjunction signifying **(1)** "except", in 1 Cor 14:5; **(2)** in 1 Cor 15:2 "unless"; **(3)** in 1 Ti 5:19 "but." **(4)** It has the force of a preposition in the sense of **(4)** "without" in 1 Cor 6:18; **(4)** "out of" in 2 Cor 12:2–3; **(4)** "other than" in Acts 26:22; **(4)** in 1 Cor 15:27 "excepted." **(5)** For its use as a noun see Mt 23:26, "(the) outside of." See: BAGD—246a; THAYER—200b.

1623. **ἕκτος** {14x} **hěktŏs**, *hek'-tos;* ordinal from *1803; sixth:*—sixth {14x}. See: BAGD—246a; THAYER—200b.

1624. **ἐκτρέπω** {5x} **ěktrěpō**, *ek-trep'-o;* from *1537* and the base of *5157;* to *deflect,* i.e. *turn away* (lit. or fig.):—turn aside {2x}, avoid {1x}, turn {1x}, turn out of the way {1x}.

Ektrepo, lit., "to turn or twist out," is used **(1)** in the passive voice in Heb 12:13, "that which is lame be not turned out of the way" (or rather, "put out of joint"); **(2)** in the sense of the middle voice (though passive in form) of turning aside, or turning away from, 2 Ti 4:4 "shall be turned unto fables; **(3)** in 1 Ti 1:6, of those who, having swerved from the faith, have turned aside unto vain talking; **(4)** in 1 Ti 5:15, of those who have turned aside after satan; **(5)** in 6:20, of "avoiding" profane babblings and oppositions of the knowledge which is falsely so called. See: BAGD—246b; THAYER—200c.

1625. **ἐκτρέφω** {2x} **ěktrěphō**, *ek-tref'-o;* from *1537* and *5142; to rear up* to maturity, i.e. (gen.) to *cherish* or *train:*—bring up {1x}, nourish {1x}.

This word means **(1)** "to nourish (up to maturity)" Eph 5:29; or **(2)** "bring up (to maturity)", Eph 6:4. See: BAGD—246c; THAYER—200c.

1626. **ἔκτρωμα** {1x} **ěktrōma**, *ek'-tro-mah;* from a compound of *1537* and τιτρώσκω **titrōskō** (to *wound*); a *miscarriage* (*abortion*), i.e. (by anal.) *untimely birth:*—born out of due time {1x}.

Ektroma, as a noun, denotes "an abortion, an untimely birth": "And last of all He was seen of me also, as of one born out of due time" (1 Cor 15:8). The apostle likens himself to "one born out of due time"; i.e., in point of time, inferior to the rest of the apostles, as an immature birth comes short of a mature one. Syn.: 313, 616, 738, 1080, 1084, 1085, 5088. See: TDNT—2:465, 220; BAGD—246c; THAYER—200d.

1627. **ἐκφέρω** {7x} **ěkphěrō**, *ek-fer'-o;* from *1537* and *5342; to bear out* (lit. or fig.):—bear {1x}, bring forth {2x}, carry forth {1x}, carry out {3x}.

Ekphero is used, literally, **(1)** "of carrying something forth, or out," **(1a)** e.g., a garment, Lk 15:22; **(1b)** sick folk, Acts 5:15; **(1c)** a corpse, Acts 5:6; 9–10; **(1d)** of the impossibility of "carrying" anything out from this world at death, 1 Ti 6:7. **(2)** It is also used of the earth, in "bringing forth" produce, Heb. 6:8. See: BAGD—246d; THAYER—200d.

1628. **ἐκφεύγω** {7x} **ěkphěugō**, *ek-fyoo'-go;* from *1537* and *5343; to flee out:*—escape {5x}, flee {2x}.

This word means "to flee out of a place" and is said **(1)** of the "escape" of prisoners, Acts 16:27; **(2)** of Sceva's sons, "fleeing" from the man with an evil spirit, Acts 19:16; **(3)** of Paul's escape from Damascus, 2 Cor 11:33; **(4)** elsewhere with reference to the judgments of God, Lk 21:36; Rom 2:3; Heb 2:3; 12:25; 1 Th 5:3. See: BAGD—246d; THAYER—200d.

1629. **ἐκφοβέω** {1x} **ěkphŏběō**, *ek-fob-eh'-o;* from *1537* and *5399; to frighten utterly away:*—terrify {1x}. See: BAGD—247a; THAYER—201a.

1630. **ἔκφοβος** {2x} **ěkphŏbŏs**, *ek'-fob-os;* from *1537* and *5401; frightened out* of one's wits: sore afraid {1x}, exceedingly fear + 1510 {1x}.

Ekphobos signifies "frightened outright" **(1)** Heb. 12:21 (with *eimi,* "I am"), "I exceedingly fear"; **(2)** Mk 9:6, "sore afraid." See: BAGD—247a; THAYER—201a.

1631. **ἐκφύω** {2x} **ěkphuō**, *ek-foo'-o;* from *1537* and *5453;* to *sprout up:*—put forth {2x}.

This word means "to cause to grow out, put forth" (*ek,* "out," *phuo,* "to bring forth, produce, beget"), and is used of the leaves of a tree, Mt 24:32; Mk 13:28, "putteth forth." See: BAGD—247b; THAYER—201a.

1632. **ἐκχέω** {28x} **ěkchěō**, *ek-kheh'-o;* or (by var.)

ἐκχύνω **ěkchunō**, *ek-khoo'-no;* from *1537;* and χέω **chěō** (to *pour*); to *pour forth;* fig. to *bestow:*—pour out {12x}, shed {4x}, shed forth {1x}, spill {1x}, run out {1x}, shed {5x}, run greedily {1x}, shed abroad {1x}, gush out {1x}, spill {1x}.

This word means "to pour out" and is used **(1)** of Christ's act as to the changers' money, Jn 2:15; **(2)** of the Holy Spirit, Acts 2:17, 18, 33, "He hath . . . shed forth"); Titus 3:6 "shed"), **(3)** of the emptying of the contents of the "vials" of divine wrath, Rev 16:1–4, 8, 10, 12, 17; **(4)** of the shedding of the blood of saints by the foes of God, Acts 22:20; Rev 16:6 "shed"). See: TDNT—2:467, 220; BAGD—247b; THAYER—201a.

1633. **ἐκχωρέω** {1x} **ěkchōrěō**, *ek-kho-reh'-o;* from *1537* and *5562;* to *depart:*—depart out {1x}.

Ekchoreo signifies "to depart out", "to leave a place" in the sense of fleeing from," Luke 21:21 (twice). See: BAGD—247c; THAYER—201c.

1634. **ἐκψύχω** {3x} **ěkpsuchō**, *ek-psoo'-kho;* from *1537* and *5594;* to *expire:*—give up the ghost {2x}, yield up the ghost {1x}.

Ekpsucho means "to expire," lit., "to breathe out the soul (or life), to give up the ghost" (*ek,* "out," *psuche,* "the soul"), and is used in Acts 5:5, 10; 12:23. See: BAGD—247c; THAYER—201c.

1635. **ἑκών** {2x} **hěkōn**, *hek-own';* of uncert. aff.; *voluntary:*—willingly {2x}.

Hekon "of free will, willingly," occurs **(1)** in Rom 8:20 "willingly"; **(2)** 1 Cor 9:17 "willingly." See: TDNT—2:469, 221; BAGD—247d; THAYER—201c.

1636. **ἐλαία** {15x} **ělaia**, *el-ah'-yah;* fem. of a presumed der. from an obsolete primary; an *olive* (the tree or the fruit):—olives {11x}, olive tree {3x}, olive berries {1x}.

This word denotes **(1)** "an olive tree," Rom 11:17, 24; Rev 11:4 (plural); **(2)** the Mount of Olives was so called from the numerous olive trees there, and indicates the importance attached to such; the Mount is mentioned in the NT in connection only with the Lord's life on earth, Mt 21:1; 24:3; 26:30; Mk 11:1; 13:3; 14:26; Lk 19:37; 22:39; Jn 8:1; **(3)** "an olive," Jas 3:12 "olive berries." See: BAGD—247d; THAYER—201c.

1637. **ἔλαιον** {11x} **ělaiŏn**, *el'-ah-yon;* neut. of the same as *1636;* olive *oil:*—oil {11x}.

In the NT the uses mentioned were **(1)** for lamps, in which the "oil" is a symbol of the Holy Spirit, Mt 25:3–4, 8; **(2)** as a medicinal agent, for healing, Lk 10:34; **(3)** for anointing at feasts, Lk 7:46; **(4)** on festive occasions, Heb 1:9, where the reference is probably to the consecration of kings; **(5)** as an accompaniment of miraculous power, Mk 6:13, or of the prayer of faith, Jas 5:14. **(6)** For its general use in commerce, see Lk 16:6; Rev 6:6; 18:13. Syn.: **(A)** Muron, denotes "ointment." **(A1)** The distinction between this and *elaion,* "oil," is observable in Lk 7:46 in Christ's reproof of the Pharisee who, while desiring Him to eat with him, failed in the ordinary marks of courtesy; **(A2)** "My head with oil (1637 - *elaion*) thou didst not anoint (*aleipho*), but she hath anointed (aleipho) My feet with ointment" (3464 - muron). **(B)** It is used of normal, yet inexpensive courtesies; whereas, *myron* (3464) is seen as costly and rare. See also: 218, 3464, 5548. See: TDNT—2:470, 221; BAGD—247d; THAYER—201d.

1638. **ἐλαιών** {1x} **ělaiōn**, *el-ah-yone';* from *1636;* an *olive-orchard,* i.e. (spec.) the *Mt. of Olives:*—Olivet {1x}. See: BAGD—248a; THAYER—201d.

1639. **Ἐλαμίτης** {1x} **Ělamitēs**, *el-am-ee'-tace;* of Heb. or. [5867]; an *Elamite* or Persian:—*Elamites* {1x}. See: BAGD—248a; THAYER—202a.

1640. **ἐλάσσων** {4x} **ělassōn**, *el-as'-sone;* or

ἐλάττων **ělattōn** *el-at-tone';* comparative of the same as *1646; smaller* (in size, quantity, age or quality):—less {1x}, under {1x}, worse {1x}, younger {1x}.

Elatton serves as a comparative degree of *mikros,* "little" and denotes "less" in **(1)** quality, as of wine, Jn 2:10, "worse;" **(2)** age, Rom 9:12, "younger"; **(3)** 1 Ti 5:9, "under" neuter, adverbially; **(4)** rank, Heb 7:7. See: TDNT—4:648, 593; BAGD—248b; THAYER—202a.

1641. **ἐλαττονέω** {1x} **ělattŏněō**, *el-at-ton-eh-o;* from *1640;* to *diminish,* i.e. *fall short:*—have lack {1x}.

This word means "to be less" (from *elatton,* "less"), is translated "had no lack," 2 Cor 8:15, the circumstance of the gathering of the manna being applied to the equalizing nature of cause and effect in the matter of supplying the wants of the needy. See: BAGD—248d; THAYER—202a.

1642. **ἐλαττόω** {3x} **ělattŏō**, *el-at-tŏ'-o;* from *1640;* to *lessen* (in rank or influence):—decrease {1x}, make lower {2x}.

Elattoo signifies "to make less or inferior, in quality, position or dignity"; **(1)** "madest . . . lower" and "hast made . . . lower," in Heb 2:7, 9. **(2)** In Jn 3:30, it is used in the middle voice, in John the Baptist's "I must decrease," indicating the special interest he had in his own "decrease," i.e., in authority and popularity. See: BAGD—248b; THAYER—202b.

1643. **ἐλαύνω** {5x} **ělaunō**, *el-ŏw'-no;* a prol. form of a primary verb (obsolete except in certain tenses as an altern. of this) of uncert. affin; to *push, drive, impel, urge on* (as wind, oars or demoniacal power):—carry {1x}, drive {2x}, row {2x}.

Elauno signifies "to drive, impel,. urge on." It is used **(1)** of "rowing," Mk 6:48 and Jn 6:19;

(2) of the act of a demon upon a man, Lk 8:29; **(3)** of the power of winds upon ships, Jas 3:4; and **(4)** of storms upon mists, 2 Pet 2:17 "carried." See: BAGD—248c; THAYER—202b.

1644. **ἐλαφρία** {1x} **ĕlaphria**, *el-af-ree'-ah;* from *1645; levity, not taking things seriously* (fig.), i.e. *fickleness:*—lightness {1x}. See: BAGD—248c; THAYER—202b.

1645. **ἐλαφρός** {2x} **ĕlaphrŏs**, *el-af-ros';* prob. akin to *1643* and the base of *1640; light,* i.e. *easy; not heavy:*—light {2x}.

This word means "light in weight, easy to bear," is used **(1)** of the burden imparted by Christ, Mt. 11:30; **(2)** of affliction, 2 Cor 4:17. See: BAGD—248c; THAYER—202b.

1646. **ἐλάχιστος** {13x} **ĕlachistŏs**, *el-akh'-is-tos;* superl. of ἔλαχυς **ĕlachus** (*short*); used as equiv. to *3398; least* (in size, amount, dignity, etc.):—least {9x}, very little {1x}, very small {2x}, smallest {1x}.

Elachistos, "least," is a superlative degree formed from the word *elachus,* "little," the place of which was taken by *mikros* (the comparative degree being *elasson,* "less"); it is used of **(1)** size, Jas 3:4; **(2)** amount; of the management of affairs, Lk 16:10 (twice), 19:17, "very little"; **(3)** importance, 1 Cor 6:2, "smallest (matters)"; **(4)** authority: of commandments, Mt 5:19; **(5)** estimation, **(5a)** as to persons, Mt 5:19 (2nd part); 25:40, 45; 1 Cor 15:9; **(5b)** as to a town, Mt 2:6; **(5c)** as to activities or operations, Lk 12:26; 1 Cor 4:3, "a very small thing." See: TDNT—4:648, 593; BAGD—248d; THAYER—202b.

1647. **ἐλαχιστότερος** {1x} **ĕlachistŏtĕrŏs**, *el-akh-is-tot'-er-os;* comparative of *1646; far less:*—less than the least {1x}. See: BAGD—248d; THAYER—202c.

1648. **Ἐλεάζαρ** {2x} **Ĕlĕazar**, *el-eh-ad'-zar;* of Heb. or. [499]; *Eleazar,* an Isr.:—*Eleazar* {2x}. See: BAGD—249a; THAYER—202c.

1649. **ἔλεγξις** {1x} **ĕlĕgxis**, *el'-eng-xis;* from *1651; refutation,* i.e. *reproof:*—rebuke + 2192 {1x}. See: TDNT—2:476, 221; BAGD—249a; THAYER—202c.

1650. **ἔλεγχος** {2x} **ĕlĕgchŏs**, *el'-eng-khos;* from *1651; proof, conviction:*—evidence {1x}, reproof {1x}.

Elegchos, "a reproof", is found in 2 Ti 3:16 and in Heb 11:1, "evidence." See: TDNT—2:476, 221; BAGD—249a; THAYER—202d.

1651. **ἐλέγχω** {17x} **ĕlĕgchō**, *el-eng'-kho;* of uncert. aff.; to *confute, admonish:*—reprove {6x}, rebuke {5x}, convince {4x}, tell (one's) fault {1x}, convict {1x}.

(1) This word means to rebuke another with the truth so that the person confesses, or at least is convicted of his sin. Although convicted, he may not be convinced. **(2)** The world will be convicted by the Holy Spirit (Jn 16:8) but not all will change. **(3)** Jesus was charged with sin (Mt 9:3; Jn 9:16) but none convicted nor convinced Him of sin (Jn 8:46). It signifies **(4)** "to convict, confute, refute," usually with the suggestion of putting the convicted person to shame; **(5)** see Mt 18:15, where more than telling the offender his fault is in view; **(6)** it is used of "convicting" of sin, Jn 8:46; **(6a)** gainsayers in regard to the faith, Titus 1:9; **(6b)** transgressors of the Law, Jas 2:9; Jn 8:9; **(7)** "to convince," 1 Cor 14:24, for the unbeliever is there viewed as being reproved for, or "convicted" of, his sinful state; **(6c)** so in Lk 3:19; **(6d)** it is used of reproving works, Jn 3:20; Eph 5:11, 13; 1 Ti 5:20; 2 Ti 4:2; Titus 1:13; 2:15; all these speak of reproof by word of mouth. **(6e)** In Heb 12:5 and Rev 3:19, the word is used of reproving by action. Syn.: 156, 1650, 2008. See: TDNT—2:473, 221; BAGD—249b; THAYER—202d.

1652. **ἐλεεινός** {2x} **ĕlĕĕinŏs**, *el-eh-i-nos';* from *1656; pitiable:*—miserable {2x}.

Here the idea is probably that of a combination of "misery" and pitiableness. Misearable comes from "miser," one who has the means available to relieve his pain, but chooses not to take advantage of it; hence, miserable, and one to be pitied. See: BAGD—249c; THAYER—203a.

1653. **ἐλεέω** {31x} **ĕlĕĕō**, *el-eh-eh'-o;* from *1656;* to *compassionate* (by word or deed, spec., by divine grace):—have mercy on {14x}, obtain mercy {8x}, shew mercy {2x}, have compassion {1x}, have compassion on {1x}, have pity on {1x}, have mercy {1x}, have mercy upon {1x}, receive mercy {1x}.

Eleeo (1653), as a verb, signifies, **(1)** in general, "to feel sympathy with the misery of another," and especially sympathy manifested in act, **(1a)** in the active voice, "to have pity or mercy on, to show mercy" to, e.g., Mt 9:27; 15:22; 17:15; 18:33; 20:30, 31; Rom 9:15, 16, 18; 11:32; 12:8; Phil 2:27; Jude 22, 23; **(1b)** in the passive voice, "to have pity or mercy shown one, to obtain mercy," Mt 5:7; Rom 11:30, 31; 1 Cor 7:25; 2 Cor 4:1; 1 Ti 1:13, 16; 1 Pet 2:10. Syn.: *Eleeo* means to feel sympathy with the misery of another, esp. such sympathy as manifests itself in act, less freq. in word. *Oiktirmos* (3628) denotes the inward feeling of compassion which abides in the heart. A criminal begs 1653 of his judge; but hopeless suffering is often the object of 3628. See also: 1655, 1656, 2433, 2436, 3627, 3628, 3629, 4698. See: TDNT—2:477, 222; BAGD—249c; THAYER—203a.

1654. **ἐλεημοσύνη** {14x} **ĕlĕēmŏsunē**, *el-eh-ay-mos-oo'-nay;* from *1656; compassionateness,* i.e. (as exercised toward the poor) *beneficence,* or (concr.) a *benefaction:*—alms {13x}, almsdeeds {1x}.

Eleemosune, connected with *eleemon,* "merciful," signifies **(1)** "mercy, pity, particularly in giving alms," Mt 6:1, 2–4; Acts 10:2; 24:17; **(2)** the benefaction itself, the "alms" (the effect for the cause), Lk 11:41; 12:33; Acts 3:2–3, 10; 9:36, "alms-deeds"; 10:2, 4, 31. See: TDNT—2:485, 222; BAGD—249d; THAYER—203b.

1655. **ἐλεήμων** {2x} **ĕlĕēmōn**, *el-eh-ay'-mone;* from *1653; compassionate* (actively):—merciful {2x}.

Eleemon, as an adjective, means "merciful," not simply possessed of pity but actively compassionate, is used **(1)** of Christ as a High Priest, Heb 2:17, and **(2)** of those who are like God, Mt 5:7. Syn.: 1653, 1656, 2433, 2436, 3627, 3628, 3629, 4698. See: TDNT—2:485, 222; BAGD—250a; THAYER—203c.

1656. **ἔλεος** {28x} **ĕlĕŏs**, *el'-eh-os;* of uncert. aff.; *compassion* (human or divine, espec. active):—mercy {28x}.

Summary: *Eleos* is the free gift for the forgiveness of sins and is related to the misery that sins brings. God's tender sense of our misery displays itself in His efforts to lessen and entirely remove it—efforts that are hindered and defeated only by man's continued perverseness. Grace removes guilt, mercy removes misery. *Eleos* **(1)** is the outward manifestation of pity; it assumes need on the part of him who receives it, and resources adequate to meet the need on the part of him who shows it. **(2)** It is used **(2a)** of God, **(2a1)** who is rich in mercy, Eph 2:4, and **(2a2)** who has provided salvation for all men, Titus 3:5, for Jews, Lk 1:72, and Gentiles, Rom 15:9. **(3)** He is merciful to those who fear him, Lk 1:50, for they also are compassed with infirmity, and He alone can succor them. **(4)** Hence they are to pray boldly for mercy, **(4a)** Heb 4:16, and if for themselves, **(4b)** it is seemly that they should ask for mercy for one another, Gal 6:16; 1 Ti 1:2.

(5) When God brings His salvation to its issue at the Second Coming of Christ, His people will obtain His mercy, 2 Ti 1:16; Jude 21; **(6)** It is used of men; for since God is merciful to them, He would have them show mercy to one another, Mt 9:13; 12:7; 23:23; Lk 10:37; Jas 2:13. **(7)** Wherever the words mercy and peace are found together they occur in that order, except in Gal 6:16. Mercy is the act of God, peace is the resulting experience in the heart of man. Grace describes God's attitude toward the lawbreaker and the rebel; mercy is His attitude toward those who are in distress." **(8)** In the order of the manifestation of God's purposes of salvation grace must go before mercy . . . only the forgiven may be blessed. . . . From this it follows that in each of the apostolic salutations where these words occur, grace precedes mercy, 1 Ti 1:2; 2 Ti 1:2; Titus 1:4; 2 Jn 3. Syn.: 1653, 1655, 2433, 2436, 3627, 3628, 3629, 4698. See: TDNT—2:477, 222; BAGD—250a; THAYER—203c.

1657. **ἐλευθερία** {11x} **ĕlĕuthĕria**, *el-yoo-ther-ee'-ah;* from *1658; freedom* (legitimate or licentious, chiefly mor. or cerem.):—liberty {11x}.

Eleutheria, as a noun, means "liberty" and is **(1)** so rendered in Gal 5:1, "in the liberty wherewith Christ hath made us free." **(2)** The combination of the noun with the verb stresses the completeness of the act. **(3)** Not to bring us into another form of bondage did Christ liberate us from that in which we were born, but in order to make us free from bondage. **(4)** The word is twice rendered "liberty" in Gal. 5:13. The phraseology is that of manumission from slavery, which among the Greeks was effected by a legal fiction, according to which the manumitted slave was purchased by a god; as the slave could not provide the money, the master paid it into the temple treasury in the presence of the slave, a document being drawn up containing the words "for freedom." No one could enslave him again, as he was the property of the god. Hence the word *apeleutheros,* "a freed man." **(5)** The word is also translated "liberty" in 1 Pet 2:16. **(6)** In 2 Cor 3:17 the word denotes "liberty" of access to the presence of God. See: TDNT—2:487, 224; BAGD—250c; THAYER—204a.

1658. **ἐλεύθερος** {23x} **ĕlĕuthĕrŏs**, *el-yoo'-ther-os;* prob. from the alt. of *2064; unrestrained* (to *go* at pleasure), i.e. (as a citizen) *not a slave* (whether *freeborn* or *manumitted*), or (gen.) *exempt* (from obligation or liability):—free {18x}, freeman {1x}, free woman {3x}, at liberty {1x}.

Eleutheros, as an adjtive, means primarily of "freedom to go wherever one likes," is used of **(1)** "freedom from restraint and obligation" in general, Mt 17:26; Rom 7:3; 1 Cor 7:39, of the second marriage of a woman; 9:1, 19; 1 Pet 2:16; **(2)** from the Law, Gal 4:26; **(3)** from sin, Jn 8:36; **(4)** with regard to righteousness, Rom 6:20 (i.e., righteousness laid no sort of bond upon them, they had no relation to it); **(5)** in a civil sense, "free" from bondage or slavery, Jn 8:33; 1 Cor 7:21, 22, second part; 12:13; Gal 3:28; Eph 6:8; Rev 13:16; 19:18; **(6)** as a noun, "free (man)," Col 3:11; Rev

6:15; **(7)** "freewoman," Gal 4:22, 23, 30, 31. See: TDNT—2:487, 224; BAGD—250d; THAYER—204a.

1659. **ἐλευθερόω** {7x} **ĕlĕuthĕrŏō**, *el-yoo-ther-ŏ'-o;* from *1658;* to *liberate*, i.e. (fig.) to *exempt* (from mor., cerem. or mortal liability):—deliver {1x}, make free {6x}.

Eleutheroo, as a verb, means "to set free" is translated **(1)** "deliver": "Because the creature itself also shall be delivered from the bondage of corruption into the glorious liberty of the children of God" (Rom 8:21). **(2)** In six other places it is translated "make free": "And ye shall know the truth, and the truth shall make you free" (Jn 8:32; cf. 8:36; Rom 6:18, 22; 8:2; Gal 5:1). **(3)** *Eleutheroo*, as a verb, means "to make free" and is used of deliverance from **(3a)** sin, Jn 8:32, 36; Rom 6:18, 22; **(3b)** the Law, Rom 8:2; Gal 5:1; **(3c)** the bondage of corruption, Rom 8:21. Syn.: 325, 525, 629, 591, 859, 1325, 1560, 1659, 1807, 1929, 3086, 3860, 4506, 5483. See: TDNT—2:487, 224; BAGD—250d; THAYER—204b.

ἐλεύθω **ĕlĕuthō**. See *2064*.

1660. **ἔλευσις** {1x} **ĕlĕusis**, *el'-yoo-sis;* from the alt. of *2064;* an *advent:*—coming {1x}. See: TDNT—2:675, 257; BAGD—251a; THAYER—204c.

1661. **ἐλεφάντινος** {1x} **ĕlĕphantinŏs**, *el-ef-an'-tee-nos;* from ἔλεφας **ĕlĕphas** (an "*elephant*"); *elephantine*, i.e. (by impl.) composed of *ivory:*—of ivory {1x}. See: BAGD—251a; THAYER—204c.

1662. **Ἐλιακείμ** {3x} **Ĕliakĕim**, *el-ee-ak-ehm'* or Ἐλιακίμ **Ĕliakim** *el-ee-ak-ime';* of Heb. or. [471]; *Eliakim*, an Isr.:—Eliakim {3x}. See: BAGD—251b; THAYER—204c.

1663. **Ἐλιέζερ** {1x} **Ĕliĕzĕr**, *el-ee-ed'-zer;* of Heb. or. [461]; *Eliezer*, an Isr.:—*Eliezer* {1x}. See: BAGD—251b; THAYER—204c.

1664. **Ἐλιούδ** {2x} **Ĕliŏud**, *el-ee-ood';* of Heb. or. [410 and 1935]; *God of majesty; Eliud*, an Isr.:—Eliud {2x}. See: BAGD—251b; THAYER—204c.

1665. **Ἐλισάβετ** {9x} **Ĕlisabĕt**, *el-ee-sab'-et;* of Heb. or. [472]; *Elisabet*, an Israelitess:—Elisabeth {9x}. See: BAGD—251b; THAYER—204c.

1666. **Ἐλισσαῖος** {1x} **Ĕlissaiŏs**, *el-is-sah'-yos;* of Heb. or. [477]; *Elissæus*, an Isr.:—Elissæus {1x}. See: BAGD—251b; THAYER—204c.

1667. **ἑλίσσω** {1x} **hĕlissō**, *hel-is'-so;* a form of *1507;* to *coil* or *wrap:*—fold up {1x}. See: BAGD—251b; THAYER—204d.

1668. **ἕλκος** {3x} **hĕlkŏs**, *hel'-kos;* prob. from *1670;* an *ulcer* (as if drawn together):—sore {3x}.

Elkos, "a sore" or "ulcer" (primarily a wound with a discharge), occurs in Lk 16:21; Rev 16:2, 11. See: BAGD—251c; THAYER—204d.

1669. **ἑλκόω** {1x} **hĕlkŏō**, *hel-kŏ'-o;* from *1668;* to *cause to ulcerate*, i.e. (pass.) *be ulcerous:*—full of sores {1x}.

Helkoo, "to wound, to ulcerate," is used in the passive voice, signifying "to suffer from sores," to be "full of sores," Lk 16:20 (perfect participle). See: BAGD—251c; THAYER—204d.

1670. **ἑλκύω** {8x} **hĕlkuō**, *hel-koo'-o;* or **ἕλκω** **hĕlkō**, *hel'-ko;* prob. akin to *138;* to *drag* (lit. or fig.):—draw {8x}.

Helko, as a verb, is translated **(1)** "to draw": "And all the city was moved, and the people ran together: and they took Paul, and drew him out of the temple: and forthwith the doors were shut" (Acts 21:30; cf. Jas 2:6). **(2)** It differs from *suro* (4951), as "drawing" does from violent "dragging." **(2a)** This less violent significance, **(2b)** usually present in *helko*, but always absent from suro, **(3)** is seen in the metaphorical use of *helko*, to signify "drawing" by inward power, by divine impulse, Jn 6:44; 12:32. **(4)** It is used of a more vigorous action, **(4a)** in Jn 18:10, of "drawing" a sword; **(4b)** in Acts 16:19; 21:30, of forcibly "drawing" men to or from a place; so in Jas 2:6. Syn.: It is used of "drawing" a net, Jn 21:6, 11. **(A)** At vv. 6 and 11 *helko* (or *helkuo*) is used; for there a drawing of the net to a certain point is intended; by the disciples to themselves in the ship, by Peter to himself upon the shore. **(B)** But at v. 8 *helko* gives place to *suro* (4951): for nothing is there intended but the dragging of the net, which had been fastened to the ship, after it through the water. Syn.: 307, 385, 392, 501, 502, 645, 868, 1448, 1828, 2020, 2464, 4317, 4334, 4358, 4685, 4951, 5288, 5289. See: TDNT—2:503, 227; BAGD—251c; THAYER—204d. comp. *1667*.

1671. **Ἑλλάς** {1x} **Hĕllas**, *hel-las';* of uncert. aff.; *Hellas* (or *Greece*), a country of Europe:—Greece {1x}. See: TDNT—2:504, 227; BAGD—251d; THAYER—205a.

1672. **Ἕλλην** {27x} **Hĕllēn**, *hel'-lane;* from *1671;* a *Hellen* (*Grecian*) or inhab. of Hellas; by extens. a *Greek-speaking* person, espec. a *non-Jew:*—Gentile {7x}, Greek {20x}.

Hellen **(1)** originally denoted the early descendants of Thessalian Hellas; then, **(2)** Greeks as opposed to barbarians, Rom 1:14. **(3)** It became applied to such Gentiles as spoke the Greek language, e.g., Gal 2:3; 3:28. **(4)** Since that was the common medium of intercourse in the Roman Empire, Greek and Gentile became more or less interchangeable terms, "Gentiles," e.g., Jn 7:35; Rom 2:9, 10; 3:9; 1 Cor 10:32, where the local church is distinguished from Jews and Gentiles; 12:13. See: TDNT—2:504, 227; BAGD—251d; THAYER—205a.

1673. **Ἑλληνικός** {2x} **Hĕllēnikŏs**, *hel-lay-nee-kos';* from *1672; Hellenic*, i.e. *Grecian* (in language):—Greek {2x}. See: TDNT—2:504, 227; BAGD—252a; THAYER—205b.

1674. **Ἑλληνίς** {2x} **Hĕllēnis**, *hel-lay-nis';* fem. of *1672;* a *Grecian* (i.e. *non-Jewish*) woman:—Greek {2x}. See: TDNT—2:504, 227; BAGD—252a; THAYER—205b.

1675. **Ἑλληνιστής** {3x} **Hĕllēnistēs**, *hel-lay-nis-tace';* from a der. of *1672;* a *Hellenist* or Greek-speaking Jew:—Grecian {3x}. See: TDNT—2:504, 227; BAGD—252b; THAYER—205b.

1676. **Ἑλληνιστί** {2x} **Hĕllēnisti**, *hel-lay-nis-tee';* adv. from the same as *1675; Hellenistically*, i.e. in the Grecian language:—Greek {2x}. See: TDNT—2:504, 227; BAGD—252b; THAYER—205b.

1677. **ἐλλογέω** {2x} **ĕllŏgĕō**, *el-log-eh'-o;* from *1722* and *3056* (in the sense of account); to *reckon in*, i.e. *attribute:*—impute {1x}, put on (one's) account {1x}.

Ellogeo, **(1)** "to put to a person's account," Philem 18, is used **(2)** of sin in Rom 5:13, "impute." See: TDNT—2:516, 229; BAGD—252b; THAYER—205b.

ἔλλομαι **hĕllŏmai**. See *138*.

1678. **Ἐλμωδάμ** {1x} **Ĕlmōdam**, *el-mo-dam';* of Heb. or. [perh. for 486]; *Elmodam*, an Isr.:—*Elmodam* {1x}. See: BAGD—252c; THAYER—205c.

1679. **ἐλπίζω** {32x} **ĕlpizō**, *el-pid'-zo;* from *1680;* to *expect* or *confide:*—trust {18x}, hope {10x}, hope for {2x}, things hoped for {1x}, vr hope {1x}.

Elpizo, as a verb, means **(1)** "to hope," e.g., **(1a)** Jn 5:45, "Moses, on whom ye have set your hope"; **(1b)** 2 Cor 1:10, "on whom we have set our hope"; so in 1 Ti 4:10; 5:5; 6:17; see also, e.g., Mt 12:21; Lk 24:21; Rom 15:12, 24. **(2)** The verb is followed by three prepositions: **(2a)** *eis*, rendered "on" in Jn 5:45; the meaning is really "in" as in 1 Pet 3:5, "who hoped in God"; the "hope" is thus said to be directed to, and to center in, a person; **(2b)** *epi*, "on," Rom 15:12, "in Him shall the Gentiles trust (hope)"; so 1 Ti 4:10; 5:5; **(2c)** *en*, "in," 1 Cor 15:19, "we have hoped in Christ," the preposition expresses that Christ is not simply the ground upon whom, but the sphere and element in whom, the "hope" is placed. The form of the verb (the perfect participle with the verb to be, lit., "are having hoped") stresses the character of those who "hope," more than the action; "hope" characterizes them, showing what sort of persons they are. Syn.: 560, 1680, 4276. See: BAGD—252c; THAYER—205c.

1680. **ἐλπίς** {54x} **ĕlpis**, *el-pece';* from a primary ἔλπω **ĕlpō** (to *anticipate*, usually with pleasure); *expectation* (abstr. or concr.) or *confidence:*—faith {1x}, hope {53x}.

Elpis (1680), as a noun in the NT, "favorable and confident expectation, a forward look with assurance." **(1)** It has to do with the unseen and the future, Rom 8:24, 25. **(2)** "Hope" describes **(2a)** the anticipation of good (the most frequent significance), e.g., Titus 1:2; 1 Pet 1:21; **(2b)** the ground upon which "hope" is based, Acts 16:19; Col 1:27, "Christ in you the hope of glory"; **(2c)** the object upon which the "hope" is fixed, e.g., 1 Ti 1:1.

(3) Various phrases are used with the word "hope," in Paul's epistles and speeches: **(3a)** Acts 23:6, "the hope and resurrection of the dead"; this has been regarded as a *hendiadys* (one by means of two), i.e., the "hope" of the resurrection; but the kai, "and," is epexegetic, defining the "hope," namely, the resurrection; **(3b)** Acts 26:6, 7, "the hope of the promise (i.e., the fulfillment of the promise) made unto the fathers"; **(3c)** Gal 5:5, "the hope of righteousness"; i.e., the believer's complete conformity to God's will, at the coming of Christ; **(3d)** Col 1:23, "the hope of the Gospel," i.e., the "hope" of the fulfillment of all the promises presented in the gospel; cf. 1:5; **(3e)** Rom 5:2, "(the) hope of the glory of God," i.e., as in Titus 2:13, "the blessed hope and appearing of the glory of our great God and Savior Jesus Christ"; cf. Col 1:27; **(3f)** 1 Th 5:8, "the hope of salvation," i.e., of the rapture of believers, to take place at the opening of the Parousia of Christ; **(3g)** Eph 1:18, "the hope of His (God's) calling," i.e., the prospect before those who respond to His call in the gospel; **(3h)** Eph 4:4, "the hope of your calling," regarded from the point of view of the called; **(3i)** Titus 1:2, and 3:7, "the hope of eternal life," i.e., the full manifestation and realization of that life which is already the believer's possession; **(3j)** Acts 28:20, "the hope of Israel," i.e., the expectation of the coming of the Messiah.

(4) In Eph 1:18; 2:12 and 4:4, the "hope" is objective. **(5)** The objective and subjective use of the word need to be distinguished, in Rom 15:4, e.g., the use is subjective. **(6)** In the NT three adjectives are descriptive of "hope": **(6a)** "good," 2 Th 2:16; **(6b)** "blessed," Titus 2:13; **(6c)** "living,"

1 Pet 1:3; **(6d)** Heb 7:19, "a better hope," i.e., additional to the commandment, which became disannulled (v. 18), a hope centered in a new priesthood. **(7)** In Rom 15:13 God is spoken of as "the God of hope," i.e., He is the author, not the subject, of it. **(8)** "Hope" is a factor in endurance, Rom 8:24; it finds its expression in endurance under trial, which is the effect of waiting for the coming of Christ, 1 Th 1:3; **(9)** it is "an anchor of the soul," staying it amidst the storms of this life, Heb 6:18, 19; **(10)** it is a purifying power, "every one that hath this hope set on Him (Christ) purifieth himself, even as He is pure," 1 Jn 3:3 (the apostle John's one mention of "hope"). **(11)** The phrase "full assurance of hope," Heb 6:11 expresses the completeness of its activity in the soul. Syn.: 560, 1679, 4276. See: TDNT—2:517, 229; BAGD—252d; THAYER—205d.

1681. **Ἐλύμας** {1x} **Ělumas**, *el-oo'-mas;* of for. or.; *Elymas*, a wizard:—Elymas {1x}. See: BAGD—253c; THAYER—206b.

1682. **ἐλοΐ** {2x} **ĕlōï**, *el-o-ee';* of Chald. or. [426 with pron. suff.] *my God:—Eloi* {2x} See: BAGD—253d.; THAYER—206c.

1683. **ἐμαυτοῦ** {37x} **ĕmautŏu**, *em-ŏw-too';* gen. compound of *1700* and *846; of myself* (so likewise the dat.

ἐμαυτῷ **ĕmautŏi**, *em-ow-to';* and acc.

ἐμαυτόν **ĕmautŏn**, *em-ow-ton':*—myself {29x}, me {4x}, mine own self {2x}, mine own {1x}, I myself {1x}. See: BAGD—253d; THAYER—206c.

1684. **ἐμβαίνω** {18x} **ĕmbainō**, *em-ba'-hee-no;* from *1722* and the base of *939;* to *walk on,* i.e. *embark* (aboard a vessel), *reach* (a pool):—enter {8x}, come {2x}, get {2x}, go {2x}, take + 1519 {2x}, go up {1x}, step in {1x}. See: BAGD—254a; THAYER—206c.

1685. **ἐμβάλλω** {1x} **ĕmballō**, *em-bal'-lo;* from *1722* and *906;* to *throw on,* i.e. (fig.) *subject to* (eternal punishment):—cast into {1x}. See: BAGD—254a; THAYER—206c.

1686. **ἐμβάπτω** {3x} **ĕmbaptō**, *em-bap'-to;* from *1722* and *911;* to *whelm on,* i.e. *wet* (a part of the person, etc.) by contact with a fluid:—dip {3x}. See: BAGD—254b; THAYER—206d.

1687. **ἐμβατεύω** {1x} **ĕmbatĕuō**, *em-bat-yoo'-o;* from *1722* and a presumed der. of the base of *939;* equiv. to *1684;* to *intrude on* (fig.):—intrude into {1x}.

Embateuo, in Col 2:18 perhaps used in this passage as a technical term of the mystery religions, denoting the entrance of the initiated into the new life. See: TDNT—2:535, 232; BAGD—254b; THAYER—206d.

1688. **ἐμβιβάζω** {1x} **ĕmbibazō**, *em-bib-ad'-zo;* from *1722* and βιβάζω **bibazō** (to *mount;* caus. of *1684*); to *place on,* i.e. *transfer* (aboard a vessel):—put in {1x}. See: BAGD—254c; THAYER—207a.

1689. **ἐμβλέπω** {12x} **ĕmblĕpō**, *em-blep'-o;* from *1722* and *991;* to *look on,* i.e. (rel.) to *observe* fixedly, or (absolutely) to *discern* clearly:—behold {5x}, look upon {4x}, see {1x}, gaze up {1x}, can see {1x}.

Emblepo, as a verb, means "to look at" and **(1)** is translated "to look upon": "And Jesus looking upon them saith, With men *it is* impossible, but not with God" (Mk 10:27; cf. 14:67; Lk 22:61; Jn 1:36). **(2)** This verb implies a close, penetrating "look," as distinguished from *epiblepo* (1914) and *epeidon* (1896). Syn.for **(1) - (2):** 308, 352, 578, 816, 872, 991, 1896, 1914, 1980, 1983, 2300, 2334, 3706, 3708, 3879, 4017, 4648. *Emblepo,* **(3)** [en, "in" (intensive)], expresses "earnest looking" e.g., in the Lord's command to "behold" the birds of the heaven, with the object of learning lessons of faith from them: "Behold the fowls of the air: for they sow not, neither do they reap, nor gather into barns; yet your heavenly Father feedeth them. Are ye not much better than they?" (Mt 6:26. cf. 19:26; Mk 8:25; 10:21, 27; 14:67; Lk 20:17; 22:61; Jn 1:36; of the Lord's looking upon Peter, Jn 1:42; Acts 1:11; 22:11). Syn. for **(3):** 333, 816, 991, 1896, 2029, 2300, 2334, 2657, 2734, 3708. See: BAGD—254c; THAYER—207a.

1690. **ἐμβριμάομαι** {5x} **ĕmbrimaŏmai**, *em-brim-ah'-om-ahee;* from *1722* and βριμάομαι **brimaŏmai** (to *snort* with anger); to have *indignation on,* i.e. (tran.) to *blame,* (intr.) to *sigh* with chagrin, (spec.) to sternly *enjoin:*—straitly charge {2x}, groan {2x}, murmur against {1x}.

Embrimaomai, from *en,* "in," intensive, and *brime,* "strength," **(1)** primarily signifies "to snort with anger, as of horses." **(2)** Used of men it signifies "to fret, to be painfully moved"; then, **(3)** "to express indignation against"; hence, "to rebuke sternly, to charge strictly," Mt 9:30; Mk 1:43; **(4)** it is rendered "murmured against" in Mk 14:5; and **(5)** "groaned" in Jn 11:33; "groaning" in v. 38. See: BAGD—254d; THAYER—207a.

1691. **ἐμέ** {88x} **ĕmĕ**, *em-eh';* a prol. form of *3165; me:*—me {83x}, I {2x}, my {2x}, myself {1x}. See: BAGD—217a; [see 1423]; THAYER—207 bottom.

1692. **ἐμέω** {1x} **ĕmĕō**, *em-eh'-o;* of uncert. aff.; to *vomit:*—(will) spue {1x}. See: BAGD—254d; THAYER—207b.

1693. **ἐμμαίνομαι** {1x} **ĕmmainŏmai**, *em-mah'-ee-nom-ahee;* from *1722* and *3105;* to *rave on, furious, exceedingly mad against,* i.e. *rage at:*—be mad against {1x}. See: BAGD—255a; THAYER—207b.

1694. **Ἐμμανουήλ** {1x} **Ěmmanŏuēl**, *em-man-oo-ale';* of Heb. or. [6005]; *God with us; Emmanuel,* a name of Christ:—Emmanuel {1x}. See: BAGD—255a; THAYER—207b.

1695. **Ἐμμαούς** {1x} **Ěmmaŏus**, *em-mah-ooce';* prob. of Heb. or. [comp. 3222]; *Emmaüs,* a place in Pal.:—Emmaus {1x}. See: BAGD—255a; THAYER—207b.

1696. **ἐμμένω** {3x} **ĕmmĕnō**, *em-men'-o;* from *1722* and *3306;* to *stay in* the same place, i.e. (fig.) *persevere:*—continue {3x}.

Emmeno, "to remain in", is used of "continuing" **(1)** in the faith, Acts 14:22; **(2)** in the Law, Gal 3:10; **(3)** in God's covenant, Heb 8:9. See: TDNT—4:576, 581; BAGD—255b; THAYER—207c.

1697. **Ἐμμόρ** {1x} **Ěmmŏr**, *em-mor';* of Heb. or. [2544]; *Emmor* (i.e. *Chamor*), a Canaanite:—*Emmor* {1x}. See: BAGD—255b; THAYER—207c.

1698. **ἐμοί** {95x} **ĕmŏi**, *em-oy';* a prol. form of *3427; to me:*—I {6x}, me {86x}, mine {2x}, my {1x}. See: BAGD—217a, c; [1473]; THAYER—207c.

1699. **ἐμός** {78x} **ĕmŏs**, *em-os';* from the oblique cases of *1473* (*1698, 1700, 1691*); *my:*—my {50x}, mine {12x}, mine own {11x}, of me {4x}, I {1x}. See: BAGD—255c; THAYER—207c.

1700. **ἐμοῦ** {109x} **ĕmŏu**, *em-oo';* a prol. form of *3450; of me:*—me {97x}, mine {1x}, my {11x}. See: BAGD—255c; THAYER—207c.

1701. **ἐμπαιγμός** {1x} **ĕmpaigmŏs**, *emp-aheeg-mos';* from *1702; derision:*—mocking {1x}. See: TDNT—5:635, 758; BAGD—255d; THAYER—207d.

1702. **ἐμπαίζω** {13x} **ĕmpaizō**, *emp-aheed'-zo;* from *1722* and *3815;* to *jeer at,* i.e. *deride:*—mock {13x}.

Empaizo, a compound of *paizo,* "to play like a child" (*pais*), "to sport, jest," prefixed by *en,* "in" or "at," is used **(1)** only in the Synoptists, and, in every instance, of the "mockery" of Christ, **(1a)** except in Mt 2:16 (there in the sense of deluding, or deceiving, of Herod by the wise men) and **(1b)** in Lk 14:29, of ridicule cast upon the one who after laying a foundation of a tower is unable to finish it. **(2)** The word is used **(2a)** prophetically by the Lord, of His impending sufferings, Mt 20:19; Mk 10:34; Lk 18:32; **(2b)** of the actual insults inflicted upon Him by the men who had taken Him from Gethsemane, Lk 22:63; **(2b1)** by Herod and his soldiers, Lk 23:11; **(2b2)** by the soldiers of the governor, Mt 27:29, 31; Mk 15:20; Lk 23:36; **(2b3)** by the chief priests, Mt 27:41; Mk 15:31. See: TDNT—5:630, 758; BAGD—255d; THAYER—207d.

1703. **ἐμπαίκτης** {2x} **ĕmpaiktēs**, *emp-aheek-tace';* from *1702;* a *derider,* i.e. (by impl.) a *false teacher:*—mockers {1x}, scoffers {1x}.

Empaiktes, "a mocker" is used **(1)** in 2 Pet 3:3, "scoffers"; and **(2)** Jude 18, "mockers." See: TDNT—5:635, 758; BAGD—255d; THAYER—208a.

1704. **ἐμπεριπατέω** {1x} **ĕmpĕripatĕō**, *em-per-ee-pat-eh'-o;* from *1722* and *4043;* to *perambulate on* a place, i.e. (fig.) to *be occupied among* persons:—walk in {1x}.

Emperipateo, "to walk about in, or among" is used in 2 Cor 6:16, of the activities of God in the lives of believers. See: TDNT—5:940, 804; BAGD—256a; THAYER—208a.

1705. **ἐμπίπλημι** {5x} **ĕmpiplēmi**, *em-pip'-lay-mee;* or

ἐμπλήθω **ĕmplēthō**, *em-play'-tho;* from *1722* and the base of *4118;* to *fill in (up),* i.e. (by impl.) to *satisfy* (lit. or fig.):—fill {4x}, be full {1x}.

Empletho, "to fill full, to satisfy," is used **(1)** of "filling" the hungry, Lk 1:53; Jn 6:12; **(2)** "filling hearts", Acts 14:17; **(3)** of the abundance of the rich, Lk 6:25; **(4)** metaphorically, of a company of friends, Rom 15:24, "filled." See: TDNT—6:128, 840; BAGD—256a; THAYER—208a.

1706. **ἐμπίπτω** {7x} **ĕmpiptō**, *em-pip'-to;* from *1722* and *4098;* to *fall on,* i.e. (lit.) to *be entrapped by,* or (fig.) *be overwhelmed with:*—fall among (into) {7x}.

Empipto, "to fall into, or among" is used **(1)** literally, Mt 12:11; 10:36; 14:5; **(2)** metaphorically, **(2a)** into condemnation, 1 Ti 3:6; **(2b)** reproach, 3:7; **(2c)** temptation and snare, 6:9; **(2d)** the hands of God in judgment, Heb 10:13. See: BAGD—256b; THAYER—208b.

1707. **ἐμπλέκω** {2x} **ĕmplĕkō**, *em-plek'-o;* from *1722* and *4120;* to *entwine,* i.e. (fig.) *involve* with:—entangle (one's) self with {1x}, entangle therein + 5125 {1x}.

Empleko, "to weave in" (*en,* "in," *pleko,* "to weave"), hence, metaphorically, to be involved, entangled in, is used **(1)** in the passive voice in 2 Ti 2:4, "entangleth himself;" **(2)** 2 Pet 2:20, "are entangled." See: BAGD—256c; THAYER—208b.

ἐμπλήθω **ĕmplēthō**. See *1705*.

1708. **ἐμπλοκή** {1x} **ĕmplŏkē**, *em-plok-ay';* from *1707;* elaborate *braiding* of the hair:—plaiting {1x}. See: BAGD—256c; THAYER—208b.

1709. **ἐμπνέω** {1x} **ĕmpnĕō**, *emp-neh'-o;* from *1722* and *4154;* to *inhale*, i.e. (fig.) to *be animated by* (*bent upon*):—breathe out {1x}.

Empneo, lit., "to breathe in, or on," is used in Acts 9:1, indicating that threatening and slaughter were, so to speak, the elements from which Saul drew and expelled his breath. See: TDNT—6:452, 876; BAGD—256c; THAYER—208b.

1710. **ἐμπορεύομαι** {2x} **ĕmpŏrĕuŏmai**, *em-por-yoo'-om-ahee;* from *1722* and *4198;* to *travel in* (a country as a pedlar), i.e. (by impl.) to *trade:*—buy and sell {2x}, make merchandise {1x}.

This word primarily signifies "to travel," especially for business; then, **(1)** "to traffic, trade," Jas 4:13; then, **(2)** "to make a gain of, make merchandise of," 2 Pet 2:3. See: BAGD—256d; THAYER—208c.

1711. **ἐμπορία** {1x} **ĕmpŏria**, *em-por-ee'-ah;* fem. from *1713; commerce, business, trade, traffic:*—merchandise {1x}. That which is sold in an *emporion* (1712). See: BAGD—256d; THAYER—208c.

1712. **ἐμπόριον** {1x} **ĕmpŏriŏn**, *em-por'-ee-on;* neut. from *1713;* a *mart* ("*emporium*"):—merchandise {1x}.

Emporion denotes "a trading place, exchange" (Eng., "emporium"), Jn 2:16, "(a house) of merchandise." See: BAGD—257a; THAYER—208c.

1713. **ἔμπορος** {5x} **ĕmpŏrŏs**, *em'-por-os;* from *1722* and the base of *4198;* a (wholesale) *tradesman:*—merchant {5x}.

Emporos denotes "a person on a journey" (*poros*, "a journey"), "a passenger on shipboard"; then, "a merchant," Mt 13:45; Rev 18:3, 11, 15, 23. See: BAGD—257a; THAYER—208c.

1714. **ἐμπρήθω** {1x} **ĕmprēthō**, *em-pray'-tho;* from *1722* and πρήθω **prēthō** (to *blow* a flame); to *enkindle*, i.e. *set on fire:*—burn up {1x}. See: BAGD—no listing; THAYER—208d.

1715. **ἔμπροσθεν** {48x} **ĕmprŏsthĕn**, *em'-pros-then;* from *1722* and *4314; in front of* (in place [lit. or fig.] or time):—before {41x}, in (one's) sight {2x}, of {1x}, against {1x}, in the sight of {1x}, in the presence of {1x}, at {1x}. See: BAGD—257a; THAYER—208d.

1716. **ἐμπτύω** {6x} **ĕmptuō**, *emp-too'-o;* from *1722* and *4429;* to *spit at* or *on:*—spit upon {2x}, spit on {2x}, spit {2x}. See: BAGD—257c; THAYER—209a.

1717. **ἐμφανής** {2x} **ĕmphanēs**, *em-fan-ace';* from a compound of *1722* and *5316; apparent in* self:—show openly + 1325 + 1096 {1x}, manifest {1x}.

Emphanes is used **(1)** literally in Acts 10:40; and **(2)** metaphorically in Rom 10:20, "(I was made) manifest." See: BAGD—257c; THAYER—209b.

1718. **ἐμφανίζω** {10x} **ĕmphanizō**, *em-fan-id'-zo;* from *1717;* to *exhibit* (in person) or *disclose* (by words):—inform {3x}, be manifest {2x}, appear {2x}, signify {1x}, show {1x}, declare plainly {1x}.

Emphanizo, from *en*, "in," intensive, and *phaino*, "to shine," is used, either **(1)** of "physical manifestation," Mt. 27:53; Heb 9:24; cf. Jn 14:22, or, **(2)** metaphorically, of "the manifestation of Christ" by the Holy Spirit in the spiritual experience of believers who abide in His love, Jn 14:21. **(3)** It has another, secondary meaning, "to make known, signify, inform." This is confined to the Acts, where it is used five times, 23:15, 22; 24:1; 25:2, 15. **(4)** There is perhaps a combination of the two meanings in Heb 11:14, i.e., to declare by oral testimony and to "manifest" by the witness of the life. See: TDNT—9:7, 1244; BAGD—257d; THAYER—209b.

1719. **ἔμφοβος** {6x} **ĕmphŏbŏs**, *em'-fob-os;* from *1722* and *5401; in fear*, i.e. *alarmed:*—afraid {3x}, affrighted {2x}, tremble + 1096 {1x}.

Emphobos, lit., "in fear" means **(1)** "afraid" Lk 24:5; Acts 10:4; 22:9; **(2)** "affrighted" Lk 24:37; Rev 11:13; and **(3)** "trembled" Acts 24:25. See: BAGD—257d; THAYER—209b.

1720. **ἐμφυσάω** {1x} **ĕmphusaō**, *em-foo-sah'-o;* from *1722* and φυσάω **phusaō** (to *puff*) [comp. *5453*]; to *blow at* or *on:*—breathe on {1x}. See: TDNT—2:536, 232; BAGD—258a; THAYER—209b.

1721. **ἔμφυτος** {1x} **ĕmphutŏs**, *em'-foo-tos;* from *1722* and a der. of *5453; implanted* (fig.):—engrafted {1x}. See: BAGD—258a; THAYER—209c.

1722. **ἐν** {{2782x} **ĕn**, *en;* a primary prep. denoting (fixed) *position* (in place, time or state), and (by impl.) *instrumentality* (medially or constructively), i.e. a relation of *rest* (intermediate between *1519* and *1537*); "*in*," *at*, (up-) *on, by*, etc.:—in {1874x}, by {141x}, with {134x}, among {117x}, at {112x}, on {46x}, through {37x}, misc. {321x} about, after, against, almost, altogether, as, before, between, hereby, by all means, for (. . . sake of), give self wholly to, herein, into, inwardly, mightily, (because) of, upon, [open-] ly, outwardly, one, quickly, shortly, [speedi-] ly, that, there (-in, -on), throughout, (un-) to (-ward), under, when, where (-with), while, within. Often used in compounds, with substantially the same import; rarely with verbs of motion, and then not to indicate direction, except (elliptically) by a separate (and different) prep. See: TDNT—2:537, 233; BAGD—258b; THAYER—209c.

1723. **ἐναγκαλίζομαι** {2x} **ĕnagkalizŏmai**, *en-ang-kal-id'-zom-ahee;* from *1722* and a der. of *43;* to *take in* one's *arms*, i.e. *embrace:*—take in (one's) arms {1x}, take up in (one's) arms {1x}. See: BAGD—261c; THAYER—213b.

1724. **ἐνάλιος** {1x} **ĕnaliŏs**, *en-al'-ee-os;* from *1722* and *251; in the sea*, i.e. *marine:*—things in the sea {1x}.

Enalios, "in the sea," lit., "of, or belonging to, the salt water" (from *hals*, "salt"), occurs in Jas 3:7. See: BAGD—261d; THAYER—213b.

1725. **ἔναντι** {1x} **ĕnanti**, *en'-an-tee;* from *1722* and *473; in front* (i.e. fig. *presence*) *of:*—before {1x}. See: BAGD—261d; THAYER—213b.

1726. **ἐναντίον** {5x} **ĕnantiŏn**, *en-an-tee'-on;* neut. of *1727;* (adv.) *in* the *presence* (*view*) *of:*—before {4x}, in the sight of {1x}.

Enantion, virtually an adverb, is used as a preposition signifying **(1)** "in the presence of, in the sight of," Mk 2:12; Lk 20:26; Acts 7:10; 8:32; **(2)** "in the judgment of," Lk 24:9. See: BAGD—261d; THAYER—213b.

1727. **ἐναντίος** {8x} **ĕnantiŏs**, *en-an-tee'-os;* from *1725; opposite;* fig. *antagonistic:*—(over) against {2x}, contrary {6x}.

Enantios, "over against" is used primarily **(1)** of place, Mk 15:39; **(2)** of an opposing wind, Mt 14:24; Mk 6:48; Acts 27:4; **(3)** metaphorically, opposed as an adversary, antagonistic, Acts 26:9; 1 Th 2:15; Titus 2:8; Acts 28:17, "against." See: BAGD—262a; THAYER—213b.

1728. **ἐνάρχομαι** {2x} **ĕnarchŏmai**, *en-ar'-khom-ahee;* from *1722* and *756;* to *commence on:*—begun {2x}.

This word means lit., "to begin in" is used in **(1)** Gal 3:3 ("having begun in the Spirit"), to refer to the time of conversion; **(2)** similarly in Phil 1:6, "He which began a good work in you." The *en* may be taken in its literal sense in these places. See: BAGD—262b; THAYER—213c.

1729. **ἐνδεής** {1x} **ĕndĕēs**, *en-deh-ace';* from a compound of *1722* and *1210* (in the sense of *lacking*); *deficient in:*—lacked {1x}. See: BAGD—262c; THAYER—213d.

1730. **ἔνδειγμα** {1x} **ĕndĕigma**, *en'-dighe-mah;* from *1731;* an *indication* (concr.):—manifest token {1x}.

Endeigma, "a plain token, a proof" is used in 2 Th 1:5 "a manifest token," said of the patient endurance and faith of the persecuted saints at Thessalonica, affording proof to themselves of their new life, and a guarantee of the vindication by God of both Himself and them. See: BAGD—262c; THAYER—213d.

1731. **ἐνδείκνυμι** {12x} **ĕndĕiknumi**, *en-dike'-noo-mee;* from *1722* and *1166;* to *indicate* (by word or act):—show {9x}, show forth {1x}, do {1x}, vr show {1x}.

This word signifies **(1)** "to show forth, prove" (middle voice), said **(1a)** of God as to **(1a1)** His power, Rom 9:17; **(1a2)** His wrath, 9:22; **(1a3)** the exceeding riches of His grace, Eph 2:7; **(1b)** of Christ, as to His longsuffering, 1 Tim 1:16; **(1c)** of Gentiles, as to "the work of the Law written in their hearts," Rom. 2:15; **(1d)** of believers, as to the proof of **(1d1)** their love, 2 Cor. 8:24; **(1d2)** all good fidelity, Titus 2:10; **(1d3)** meekness, 3:2; **(1d4)** love toward God's Name, Heb 6:10; **(1d5)** diligence in ministering to the saints, v. 11; **(2)** "to manifest by evil acts," 2 Ti 4:14, "did (me much evil)." See: BAGD—262c; THAYER—213d.

1732. **ἔνδειξις** {4x} **ĕndĕixis**, *en'-dike-sis;* from *1731; a pointing out; indication* (abstr.):—to declare + 1519 {1x}, to declare + 4214 {1x}, proof {1x}, evident token {1x}.

Endeixis, "a showing, pointing out" is translated **(1)** "to declare" God's righteousness, in Rom 3:25–26; **(2)** "proof" in 2 Cor. 8:24; and **(3)** in Phil 1:28, "an evident token." See: BAGD—262d; THAYER—213d.

1733. **ἕνδεκα** {6x} **hĕndĕka**, *hen'-dek-ah;* from (the neut. of) *1520* and *1176; one* and *ten*, i.e. *eleven:*—eleven {6x}. See: BAGD—262d; THAYER—213d.

1734. **ἑνδέκατος** {3x} **hĕndĕkatŏs**, *hen-dek'-at-os;* ord. from *1733; eleventh:*—eleventh {3x}. See: BAGD—262d; THAYER—214a.

1735. **ἐνδέχεται** {1x} **ĕndĕchĕtai**, *en-dekh'-et-ahee;* third pers. sing. present of a compound of *1722* and *1209;* (impers.) *it is accepted in*, i.e. *admitted* (*possible*); *is* (*not*) *admissible:*—it can be {1x}. See: BAGD—262d; THAYER—214a.

1736. **ἐνδημέω** {3x} **ĕndēmĕō**, *en-day-meh'-o;* from a compound of *1722* and *1218;* to *be in* one's own *country*, i.e. *home* (fig.):—be at home {1x}, be present {1x}, present {1x}.

Endemeo, lit., "to be among one's people" (*en,* "in," *demos,* "people"; *endemos,* "one who is in his own place or land"), is used **(1)** metaphorically of the life on earth of believers, 2 Cor 5:6, "at home (in the body)"; **(2)** in v. 8 of the life in Heaven of the spirits of believers, after their decease, "present (with the Lord)"; **(3)** in v. 9, "present" refers again to the life on earth. **(4)** In each verse the verb is contrasted with *ekdemeo,* "to be away from home, to be absent"; **(4a)** in v. 6, "we are absent," i.e., away from "home" (from the Lord); **(4b)** in v. 8, "to be absent" (i.e., away from the "home" of the body); **(4c)** so in v. 9, "absent." **(5)** The implication in being "at home with the Lord" after death is a testimony against the doctrine of the unconsciousness of the spirit, when freed from the natural body. See: TDNT—2:63, 149 BAGD—263a; THAYER—214a.

1737. **ἐνδιδύσκω** {2x} **ĕndiduskō**, *en-did-oos'-ko;* a prol. form of *1746;* to *invest* (with a garment):—clothed in {1x}, wear {1x}.

Endidusko, as a verb, means "to wear clothes, be clothed" [the termination,—*sko* suggests the beginning or progress of the action]. The verb is used **(1)** in the middle voice in Lk 16:19: "There was a certain rich man, which was clothed in purple and fine linen, and fared sumptuously every day." **(2)** It is used in Lk 8:27 of a devil-possessed man: "And when He (Jesus) went forth to land, there met Him out of the city a certain man, which had devils long time, and ware no clothes, neither abode in *any* house, but in the tombs." Syn.: 294, 1463, 1746, 1902, 2439, 4016. See: BAGD—263a; THAYER—214a.

1738. **ἔνδικος** {2x} **ĕndikŏs**, *en'-dee-kos;* from *1722* and *1349; in the right,* i.e. *equitable:*—just {2x}.

Endikos is said **(1)** of the condemnation of those who say "Let us do evil, that good may come," Rom 3:8; **(2)** of the recompense of reward of transgressions under the Law, Heb 2:2. See: BAGD—263b; THAYER—214a.

1739. **ἐνδόμησις** {1x} **ĕndŏmēsis**, *en-dom'-ay-sis;* from a compound of *1722* and a der. of the base of *1218;* a *housing in* (*residence*), i.e. *structure:*—building {1x}. See: BAGD—263b; THAYER—214a.

1740. **ἐνδοξάζω** {2x} **ĕndŏxazō**, *en-dox-ad'-zo;* from *1741;* to *glorify:*—glorify {2x}.

Endoxazo signifies, in the passive voice, "to be glorified," i.e., to exhibit one's glory; it is said **(1)** of God, regarding His saints in the future, 2 Th 1:10, and **(2)** of the name of the Lord Jesus as "glorified" in them in the present, v. 12. See: TDNT—2:254, 178; BAGD—263b; THAYER—214.

1741. **ἔνδοξος** {4x} **ĕndŏxŏs**, *en'-dox-os;* from *1722* and *1391; in glory,* i.e. *splendid,* (fig.) *noble:*—glorious {2x}, gorgeously {1x}, honourable {1x}.

Endoxos signifies **(1)** "held in honor", "of high repute," 1 Cor 4:10, "are honorable"); **(2)** "splendid, glorious," said **(2a)** of apparel, Lk 7:25, "gorgeously"; **(2b)** of the works of Christ, Lk 13:17; **(2c)** of the church, Eph 5:27. See: TDNT—2:254, 178; BAGD—263b; THAYER—214b.

1742. **ἔνδυμα** {8x} **ĕnduma**, *en'-doo-mah;* from *1746; apparel* (espec. the outer *robe*):—clothing {1x}, garment {2x}, raiment {5x}.

In the NT it is used **(1)** of John the Baptist's raiment, Mt 3:4; **(2)** of raiment in general, Mt 6:25, 28; Lk 12:23; **(3)** metaphorically, **(3a)** of sheep's clothing, Mt 7:15; **(3b)** of a wedding garment, Mt 22:11–12; **(3c)** of the raiment of the angel at the tomb of the Lord after His resurrection, Mt 28:3. See: BAGD—263c.214b.

1743. **ἐνδυναμόω** {8x} **ĕndunamŏō**, *en-doo-nam-ŏ'-o;* from *1722* and *1412;* to *empower:*—be strong {2x}, was strong {1x}, strengthen {2x}, increase in strength {1x}, enable {1x}, be made strong {1x}.

Endunamoo, "to make strong" (*en,* "in," *dunamis,* "power"), "to strengthen," is rendered **(1)** "was strong" in Rom 4:20; **(2)** "be strong," Eph 6:10; 2 Ti 2:1; **(3)** "were made strong," Heb 11:34; **(4)** "increased . . . in strength" in Acts 9:22; **(5)** "which strengtheneth" in Phil 4:13; 2 Ti 4:17 "strengthened"; **(6)** "hath enabled" in 1 Ti 1:12, more lit., "instrengthened," "inwardly strengthened," suggesting strength in soul and purpose. See: TDNT—2:284, 186; BAGD—263d; THAYER—214b.

1744. **ἐνδύνω** {1x} **ĕndunō**, *en-doo'-no;* from *1772* and *1416;* to *sink* (by impl. *wrap* [comp. *1746*]) *on,* i.e. (fig.) *sneak:*—creep {1x}.

Enduno means properly, "to envelop in" (*en,* "in," *duno,* "to enter"), "to put on," as of a garment, has the secondary and intransitive significance of "creeping into, insinuating oneself into," and is found with this meaning in 2 Tim 3:6. See: BAGD—263d; THAYER—214c.

1745. **ἔνδυσις** {1x} **ĕndusis**, *en'-doo-sis;* from *1746; investment* with clothing:—putting on {1x}. See: BAGD—263d; THAYER—214d.

1746. **ἐνδύω** {29x} **ĕnduō**, *en-doo'-o;* from *1722* and *1416* (in the sense of *sinking* into a garment); to *invest* with clothing (lit. or fig.):—put on {18x}, clothed with {2x}, clothed in {2x}, have on {2x}, clothe with {1x}, be endued {1x}, arrayed in {1x}, be clothed {1x}, vr put on {1x}.

Enduo, as a verb, signifies "to enter into, get into," as into clothes, "to put on" (Mk 1:6; 24:49; 2 Cor 5:3; Rev 1:13; 19:14). This word means literally to sink into (clothing), put on, clothe one's self. Syn.: 294, 1463, 1737, 1902, 2439, 4016. See: TDNT—2:319, 192; BAGD—264a; THAYER—214d.

ἐνέγκω **ĕnĕgkō**. See *5342*.

1747. **ἐνέδρα** {1x} **ĕnĕdra**, *en-ed'-rah;* fem. from *1722* and the base of *1476;* an *ambuscade, lying in wait, an ambush,* i.e. (fig.) murderous *purpose:*—a laying wait + 4060 {1x}. See: BAGD—264c; THAYER—215a. See also *1749*.

1748. **ἐνεδρεύω** {2x} **ĕnĕdrĕuō**, *en-ed-ryoo'-o;* from *1747;* to *lurk,* i.e. (fig.) *plot a trap or plan for* assassination:—to lay in wait for {1x}, lay wait for {1x}. Cf. Lk 11:54; Acts 23:21. See: BAGD—264c; THAYER—215a.

1749. **ἔνεδρον** {1x} **ĕnĕdrŏn**, *en'-ed-ron;* neut. of the same as *1747;* an *ambush,* i.e. (fig.) murderous *design:*—lying in wait {1x}. See: BAGD—264C; THAYER—215a.

1750. **ἐνειλέω** {1x} **ĕnĕilĕō**, *en-i-leh'-o;* from *1772* and the base of *1507;* to *enwrap:*—wrap in {1x}.

Eneileo, "to roll in, wind in," is used in Mk 15:46, of "winding" the cloth around the Lord's body, "wrapped." See: BAGD—264C; THAYER—215a.

1751. **ἔνειμι** {1x} **ĕnĕimi**, *en'-i-mee;* from *1772* and *1510;* to *be within* (neut. part. plur.):—such things as (one) has {1x}. See: BAGD—264c; THAYER—215a. See also *1762*.

1752. **ἕνεκα** {25x} **hĕnĕka**, *hen'-ek-ah;* or **ἕνεκεν** **hĕnĕkĕn**, *hen'-ek-en;* or **εἵνεκεν** **hĕinĕkĕn**, *hi'-nek-en;* of uncert. aff.; *on account of:*—for . . . sake {14x}, for . . . cause {5x}, for {2x}, because + 3739 {1x}, wherefore + 5101 {1x}, by reason of {1x}, that . . . might {1x}. See: BAGD—264d; THAYER—215b.

1753. **ἐνέργεια** {8x} **ĕnĕrgĕia**, *en-erg'-i-ah;* from *1756; efficiency* ("energy"):—operation {1x}, strong {1x}, effectual working {2x}, working {4x}.

Energeia (Eng., "energy") is used **(1)** of the "power" of God, **(1a)** in the resurrection of Christ, Eph 1:19; Col 2:12, "operation"; **(1b)** in the call and enduement of Paul, Eph 3:7; Col 1:29; **(1c)** in His retributive dealings in sending "strong delusion, a working of error" upon those under the rule of the Man of Sin who receive not the love of the truth, but have pleasure in unrighteousness, 2 Th 2:11; **(2)** of the "power" of Christ **(2a)** generally, Phil 3:21; **(2b)** in the church, individually, Eph 4:16; **(2c)** of the power of Satan in energizing the Man of Sin in his "parousia," 2 Th 2:9, "coming." See: TDNT—2:652, 251; BAGD—265a; THAYER—215b.

1754. **ἐνεργέω** {21x} **ĕnĕrgĕō**, *en-erg-eh'-o;* from *1756;* to *be active, efficient:*—work {12x}, show forth (one's) self {2x}, wrought {1x}, be effectual {1x}, effectually work {1x}, effectual fervent {1x}, work effectually in {1x}, be might in {1x}, to do {1x}.

Energeo, lit., "to work in", "to be active, operative," is used of **(1)** God, 1 Cor 12:6; Gal 2:8; 3:5; Eph 1:11, 20; 3:20; Phil 2:13a; Col 1:29; **(2)** the Holy Spirit, 1 Cor 12:11; **(3)** the Word of God, 1 Th 2:13 (middle voice; "effectually worketh"); **(4)** supernatural power, undefined, Mt 14:2; Mk 6:14; **(5)** faith, as the energizer of love, Gal 5:6; **(6)** the example of patience in suffering, 2 Cor 1:6; **(7)** death (physical) and life (spiritual), 2 Cor 4:12; **(8)** sinful passions, Rom 7:5; **(9)** the spirit of the Evil One, Eph 2:2; **(10)** the mystery of iniquity, 2 Th 2:7. See: TDNT—2:652, 251; BAGD—265b; THAYER—215c.

1755. **ἐνέργημα** {2x} **ĕnĕrgēma**, *en-erg'-ay-mah;* from *1754;* an *effect; what is wrought:*—operation {1x}, working {1x}. See: TDNT—2:652, 251; BAGD—265c; THAYER—215d.

1756. **ἐνεργής** {3x} **ĕnĕrgēs**, *en-er-gace';* from *1722* and *2041; active, operative:*—effectual {2x}, powerful {1x}.

Energes, lit., "in work" (cf. Eng., "energetic"), is used **(1)** of the Word of God, Heb. 4:12, "powerful"; **(2)** of a door for the Gospel, 1 Cor 16:9, "effectual"; **(3)** of faith, Philem 6, "effectual." See: TDNT—2:652, 251; BAGD—265d; THAYER—215d.

1757. **ἐνευλογέω** {2x} **ĕnĕulŏgĕō**, *en-yoo-log-eh'-o;* from *1722* and *2127;* to *confer a benefit on:*—bless {2x}. Cf. Acts 3:25, and Gal 3:8. See: TDNT—2:765, 275; BAGD—265d; THAYER—215d.

1758. **ἐνέχω** {3x} **ĕnĕchō**, *en-ekh'-o;* from *1722* and *2192;* to *hold in* or *upon,* i.e. *ensnare;* by impl. to *keep a grudge:*—entangle with {1x}, have a quarrel against {1x}, urge {1x}.

Enecho, "to hold in," is said **(1)** of being "entangled" in a yoke of bondage, such as Judaism, Gal 5:1; **(2)** with the meaning to set oneself against, be urgent against, said of the plotting of Herodias against John the Baptist, Mk 6:19, "had a quarrel against"; **(3)** of the effort of the scribes and Pharisees to provoke the Lord to say something which would provide them with a ground of accusation against Him, Lk 11:53, "to urge." See: TDNT—2:828, 286; BAGD—265d; THAYER—216a.

1759. **ἐνθάδε** {8x} **ĕnthadĕ**, *en-thad'-eh;* from a prol. form of *1722;* prop. *within,* i.e. (of place) *here, hither:*—there {1x}, hither {4x}, here {3x}. See: BAGD—266a; THAYER—216a.

1760. **ἐνθυμέομαι** {3x} **ĕnthumĕŏmai**, *en-thoo-meh'-om-ahee;* from a compound of *1722* and *2372;* to *be inspirited,* i.e. *think on, ponder:*—think {3x}.

Enthumeomai, "to reflect on, ponder," is used in Mt 1:20; 9:4; Acts 10:19. Syn.: 3541. See: TDNT—3:172, 339; BAGD—266a; THAYER—216b.

1761. **ἐνθύμησις** {4x} **ĕnthumēsis**, *en-thoo'-may-sis;* from *1760; deliberation:*—device {1x}, thoughts {3x}.

This word denotes a cogitation, an inward reasoning and intentions, strong feelings, passion; generally, with evil surmising or supposition. The word is translated **(1)** "device" in Acts 17:29, of man's production of images; elsewhere, **(2)** "thoughts," Mt 9:4; 12:25; Heb 4:12. Syn.: 3540. See: TDNT—3:172, 339; BAGD—266b; THAYER—216b.

1762. **ἔνι** {6x} **ĕni**, *en'-ee;* contr. for the third pers. sing. pres. ind. of *1751;* impers. *there is* in or among:—be {1x}, there is {4x}. Cf. Gal 3:28 (thrice); Col 3:11; Jas 1:17. See: BAGD—266b; THAYER—216b.

1763. **ἐνιαυτός** {14x} **ĕniautŏs**, *en-ee-ŏw-tos';* prol. from a primary **ἔνος ĕnŏs** (a *year*); a *year:*—year {14x}.

Eniautos, originally "a cycle of time," is used **(1)** of a particular time marked by an event, e.g., Lk 4:19; Jn 11:49, 51; 18:13; Gal 4:10; Rev 9:15; **(2)** to mark a space of time, Acts 11:26; 18:11; Jas 4:13; 5:17; **(3)** of that which takes place every year, Heb 9:7; with *kata* Heb 9:25; 10:1, 3. See: BAGD—266b; THAYER—216c.

1764. **ἐνίστημι** {7x} **ĕnistēmi**, *en-is'-tay-mee;* from *1722* and *2476;* to *place on* hand, i.e. (refl.) *impend,* (part.) be *instant:*—come {1x}, be at hand {1x}, present {3x}, things present {2x}.

Enistemi, "to set in," or, in the middle voice and perfect tense of the active voice, "to stand in, be present," is used of the present **(1)** in contrast with the past, Heb 9:9; **(2)** in contrast to the future, Rom 8:38; 1 Cor 3:22; Gal 1:4, "present"; **(3)** 1 Cor 7:26, where "the present distress" is set in contrast to both the past and the future; **(4)** 2 Th 2:2, "is at hand"; the saints at Thessalonica, owing to their heavy afflictions were possessed of the idea that "the day of (the) Christ" had begun; this mistake the apostle corrects; 2 Tim. 3:1, "shall come." **(5)** It is also understood as "to be present or to be imminent," and is rendered "shall come" in 2 Ti 3:1; here expressing permanence, "shall settle in (upon you). See: TDNT—2:543, 234; BAGD—266d; THAYER—216c.

1765. **ἐνισχύω** {2x} **ĕnischuō**, *en-is-khoo'-o;* from *1722* and *2480;* to *invigorate* (tran. or refl.):—strengthen {2x}. Cf. Lk 22:43 and Acts 9:19. See: BAGD—266d; THAYER—216d.

1766. **ἔννατος** {10x} **ĕnnatŏs**, *en'-nat-os;* ord. from *1767; ninth:*—ninth {10x}.

The ninth hour corresponds to our 3 o'clock in the afternoon for the sixth hour of the Jews coincides with the twelfth of the day as divided by our method, and the first hour of the day is 6 A.M. to us. See: BAGD—267a; THAYER—216d.

1767. **ἐννέα** {1x} **ĕnnĕa**, *en-neh'-ah;* a primary number; *nine:*—nine {1x}. See: BAGD—267a; THAYER—216d.

1768. **ἐννενηκονταεννέα** {4x} **ĕnnĕnēkŏntaĕnnĕa**, *en-nen-ay-kon-tah-en-neh'-ah;* from a (tenth) multiple of *1767* and *1767* itself; *ninety-nine:*—ninety and nine {4x}. See: BAGD—267a; THAYER—216b.

1769. **ἐννεός** {1x} **ĕnnĕŏs**, *en-neh-os';* from *1770; dumb* (as *making signs*), i.e. *silent* from astonishment:—speechless {1x}. See: BAGD—267a; THAYER—217a.

1770. **ἐννεύω** {1x} **ĕnnĕuō**, *en-nyoo'-o;* from *1722* and *3506;* to *nod at,* i.e. *beckon* or *communicate by gesture:*—make signs {1x}. See: BAGD—267a; THAYER—217a.

1771. **ἔννοια** {2x} **ĕnnŏia**, *en'-noy-ah;* from a compound of *1722* and *3563; thoughtfulness,* i.e. moral *understanding:*—intent {1x}, mind {1x}.

This word primarily means a thinking, idea, consideration and denotes purpose, intention, design (Heb. 4:12-"intents;" 1 Pet 4:1- "mind"). See: TDNT—4:968, 636; BAGD—267a; THAYER—217a.

1772. **ἔννομος** {2x} **ĕnnŏmŏs**, *en'-nom-os;* from *1722* and *3551;* (subj.) *legal,* or (obj.) *subject* to:—lawful {1x}, under law {1x}.

This word means what is within the range of law and is translated **(1)** "lawful" in Acts 19:39, of the legal tribunals in Ephesus; and **(2)** "under the law" in relation to Christ, 1 Cor 9:21, where it is contrasted with *anomos.* The word as used by the apostle suggests not merely the condition of being under "law," but the intimacy of a relation established in the loyalty of a will devoted to his Master. See: TDNT—4:1087, 646; BAGD—267b; THAYER—217b.

1773. **ἔννυχον** {1x} **ĕnnuchŏn**, *en'-noo-khon;* neut. of a compound of *1722* and *3571;* (adv.) *by night; very early, still night:*—a great while before day + 3129 {1x}. See: BAGD—267b; THAYER—217b.

1774. **ἐνοικέω** {6x} **ĕnŏikĕō**, *en-oy-keh'-o;* from *1722* and *3611;* to *inhabit* (fig.):—dwell in {6x}.

This word means literally to dwell in and is used, with a spiritual significance only, of the indwelling of **(1)** God in believers (2 Cor 6:16); **(2)** the Holy Spirit (Rom 8:11; 2 Ti 1:14); **(3)** the Word of Christ (Col 3:16); **(4)** faith (2 Ti 1:5); **(5)** sin in the believer (Rom 7:17). See: BAGD—267b; THAYER—217b.

1775. **ἑνότης** {2x} **hĕnŏtēs**, *hen-ot-ace';* from *1520; oneness,* i.e. (fig.) *unanimity:*—unity {2x}. Cf. Eph 4:3, 13. See: BAGD—267c; THAYER—217c.

1776. **ἐνοχλέω** {1x} **ĕnŏchlĕō**, *en-okh-leh'-o;* from *1722* and *3791;* to *crowd in,* i.e. (fig.) to *annoy:*—trouble {1x}. See: BAGD—267d; THAYER—217c.

1777. **ἔνοχος** {10x} **ĕnŏchŏs**, *en'-okh-os;* from *1758; liable* to (a condition, penalty or imputation):—in danger of {5x}, guilty of {4x}, subject to {1x}. See: TDNT—4:1087, 646; BAGD—267d; THAYER—217c.

1778. **ἔνταλμα** {3x} **ĕntalma**, *en'-tal-mah;* from *1781;* an *injunction,* i.e. relig. *precept:*—commandment {3x}.

Entalma marks more especially "the thing commanded, a commission"; in Mt 15:9; Mk 7:7; Col 2:22, "commandments." Syn.: *Entole* (1785), the most frequent term, denotes an injunction, charge, precept, commandment and is used of moral and religious precepts (Mt 5:19; Acts 17:15; Rom 7:8–13). *Diatagma* (1297) signifies that which is imposed by decree or law (Heb 11:23) and stresses the concrete character of the commandment more than *epitage* (2003). Epitage stresses the authoritativeness of the command (Rom 16:26; 1 Cor 7:6, 25). *Entalma* (1778) marks more especially the thing commanded, a commission (Mt 15:9; Mk 7:7; Col 2:22). See: BAGD—268b; THAYER—218a.

1779. **ἐνταφιάζω** {2x} **ĕntaphiazō**, *en-taf-ee-ad'-zo;* from a compound of *1722* and *5028;* to *inswathe* with cerements for interment:—bury {1x}, burial {1x}.

Entaphiazo, "to prepare a body for burial," is used of any provision for this purpose, Mt 26:12; Jn 19:40 "to bury." See: BAGD—268b; THAYER—218a.

1780. **ἐνταφιασμός** {2x} **ĕntaphiasmŏs**, *en-taf-ee-as-mos';* from *1779; preparation* for interment:—burying {2x}.

Entahiasmos, lit. "an entombing" (from *en,* "in," *taphos,* "a tomb"), "burying," occurs in Mk 14:8; Jn 12:7. See: BAGD—268b; THAYER—218a.

1781. **ἐντέλλομαι** {17x} **ĕntĕllŏmai**, *en-tel'-lom-ahee;* from *1722* and the base of *5056;* to *enjoin:*—command {10x}, give commandment {3x}, give charge {2x}, enjoin {1x}, charge {1x}.

Entellomai signifies "to enjoin upon, to charge with"; it is used in the middle voice in the sense **(1)** of commanding, Mt 19:7; 28:20; Mk 10:3; 13:34; Jn 8:5; 15:14, 17; Acts 13:47; Heb 9:20; 11:22, "gave commandment." **(2)** It is translated by the verb "to charge, to give charge", Mt 4:6; 17:9; Lk 4:10. See: TDNT—2:544, 234; BAGD—268b; THAYER—218a.

1782. **ἐντεῦθεν** {13x} **ĕntĕuthĕn**, *ent-yoo'-then;* from the same as *1759; hence* (lit. or fig.); (repeated) *on both sides:*—hence {6x}, on either side + 2534 {4x}, from hence {3x}. See: BAGD—268c; THAYER—218b.

1783. **ἔντευξις** {2x} **ĕntĕuxis**, *ent'-yook-sis;* from *1793;* an *interview,* i.e. (spec.) *supplication:*—intercession {1x}, prayer {1x}.

Enteuxis primarily denotes a lighting upon, a meeting with; then, a conversation; and hence, a petition. It is a technical term for approaching a king, and so for boldy approaching God in intimate intercession and prayer [seeking the presence and hearing of God on behalf of others] (1 Ti 2:1; 4:5). Syn.: 155, 1162, 1793, 2169, 2171, 2428, 4335, 5241. See: TDNT—8:244, 1191; BAGD—268d; THAYER—218b.

1784. **ἔντιμος** {5x} **ĕntimŏs**, *en'-tee-mos;* from *1722* and *5092; valued* (fig.):—dear {1x}, more honourable {1x}, precious {2x}, in reputation {1x}.

Entimos, "held in honor", **(1)** "precious, dear," is found in Lk 7:2, of the centurion's servant; **(2)** Lk 14:8, "more honorable"; **(3)** Phil 2:29, "reputation", **(4)** of devoted servants of Christ, in 1 Pet. 2:4, 6, "precious," of stones, metaphorically. See: BAGD—268d; THAYER—218b.

1785. **ἐντολή** {71x} **ĕntŏlē**, *en-tol-ay';* from *1781; injunction,* i.e. an authoritative *prescription:*—commandment {69x}, precept {2x}. See: TDNT—2:545, 234; BAGD—269a; THAYER—218c.

1786. **ἐντόπιος** {1x} **ĕntŏpiŏs**, *en-top'-ee-os;* from *1722* and *5117;* a *res-*

ident:—of that place {1x}. See: BAGD—269b; THAYER—218d.

1787. **ἐντός** {2x} **ĕntŏs**, *en-tos';* from *1722; inside* (adverb or noun):—within {2x}.

Entos, an adverb denoting "within," is once used with the article, as a noun, **(1)** of "the inside (of the cup and of the platter)," Mt 23:26, "that which is within etc."; elsewhere, **(2)** "among, in your midst," Lk 17:21. See: BAGD—269b; THAYER—218d.

1788. **ἐντρέπω** {9x} **ĕntrĕpō**, *en-trep'-o;* from *1722* and the base of *5157;* to *invert,* i.e. (fig. and refl.) in a good sense, to *respect;* or in a bad one, to *confound:*—reverence {4x}, regard {2x}, be ashamed {2x}, shame {1x}.

Entrepo, "to turn in" (*en,* "in," *trepo,* "to turn"), is **(1)** metaphorically used of "putting to shame," e.g., 1 Cor 4:14; **(2)** in the middle voice, "to reverence," in Mt 21:37; Mk 12:6; Lk 20:13; Heb 12:9; **(3)** "to regard" Lk 18:2, 4; **(4)** "to put to shame," in the passive voice, to be ashamed, that is, to turn one upon himself and so produce a feeling of "shame," a wholesome "shame" which involves a change of conduct, 1 Cor 4:14; 2 Th 3:14; Titus 2:8, the only places where it has this meaning. See: BAGD—269c; THAYER—219a.

1789. **ἐντρέφω** {1x} **ĕntrĕphō**, *en-tref'-o;* from *1722* and *5142;* (fig.) to *educate:*—nourish up in {1x}.

Entrepho, "to train up, nurture," is used metaphorically, in the passive voice, in 1 Ti 4:6, of being "nourished" in the faith. See: BAGD—269d; THAYER—219a.

1790. **ἔντρομος** {3x} **ĕntrŏmŏs**, *en'-trom-os;* from *1722* and *5156; terrified:*—tremble + 1096 {1x}, trembling {1x}, quake {1x}.

Entromos, "trembling with fear" (*en,* "in," intensive, and *tremo,* "to tremble, quake"; Eng., "tremor," etc.), is **(1)** in Acts 7:32, "trembled"; **(2)** Acts 16:29, "trembling (for fear)"; **(3)** in Heb 12:21, "quake." See: BAGD—269d; THAYER—219a.

1791. **ἐντροπή** {2x} **ĕntrŏpē**, *en-trop-ay';* from *1788; confusion:*—shame {2x}.

Entrope is a turning in upon oneself producing a recoil—based on a wholesome shame—from what is unseemly or vile (1 Cor 6:5; 15:34). Syn.: 127, 152. See: BAGD—269d; THAYER—219b.

1792. **ἐντρυφάω** {1x} **ĕntruphaō**, *en-troo-fah'-o;* from *1722* and *5171;* to *revel in; live in luxury:*—sporting themselves {1x}.

Entruphao means to live in luxury, live delicately or luxuriously, to revel in, to take delight in; 2 Pe 2:13. See: BAGD—270a; THAYER—219b.

1793. **ἐντυγχάνω** {5x} **ĕntugchanō**, *en-toong-khan'-o;* from *1722* and *5177;* to *chance upon,* i.e. (by impl.) *confer with;* by extens. to *entreat* (in favor or against):—deal with {1x}, make intercession {4x}.

Entugchano means primarily to fall in with, meet with in order to converse; then, to make petition, especially to make intercession, plead with a person **(1)** either for others: **(1a)** the Holy Spirit for the saints (8:27); **(1b)** Christ praying for the saints (Rom 8:34; Heb 7:25); or **(2)** against others: **(2a)** Paul (Acts 25:24); **(2b)** Israel by Elijah (Rom 11:2). Syn.: 1792, 5241. See: TDNT—8:242, 1191; BAGD—270a; THAYER—219b.

1794. **ἐντυλίσσω** {3x} **ĕntulissō**, *en-too-lis'-so;* from *1722* and τυλίσσω **tulissō** (to *twist;* prob. akin to *1507*); to *entwine,* i.e. *wind* up in; roll up:—wrap in {2x}, wrap together {1x}.

Entulisso, "to wrap up, roll round or about," is translated **(1)** "wrapped together" in Jn 20:7, of the cloth or "napkin" that had been wrapped around the head of the Lord before burial. "Wrapped together," might suggest that this cloth had been "rolled" or wrapped up and put in a certain part of the tomb at the Lord's resurrection, whereas, as with the body wrappings, the head cloth was lying as it had been "rolled" round His head, an evidence, to those who looked into the tomb, of the fact of His resurrection without any disturbance of the wrappings either by friend or foe or when the change took place. **(2)** It is followed by *en,* "in," and translated "wrapped" in Mt 27:59; Lk 23:53. See: BAGD—270b; THAYER—219b.

1795. **ἐντυπόω** {1x} **ĕntupŏō**, *en-too-pŏ'-o;* from *1722* and a der. of *5179;* to *enstamp,* i.e. *engrave:*—engrave {1x}. See: BAGD—270b; THAYER—219c.

1796. **ἐνυβρίζω** {1x} **ĕnubrizō**, *en-oo-brid'-zo;* from *1722* and *5195;* to *insult:*—do despite unto {1x}.

This word means to treat insultingly; to insult; the insulting disdain of one who considers himself superior (Heb 10:29). See: TDNT—8:295, 1200; BAGD—270b; THAYER—219c.

1797. **ἐνυπνιάζομαι** {2x} **ĕnupniazŏmai**, *en-oop-nee-ad'-zom-ahee;* mid. voice from *1798;* to *dream:*—dreams {1x}, filthy dreamers {1x}.

This word means **(1)** in the passive voice in a phrase which means shall be given up to dream by dreams [shall dream dreams] and is used in Acts 2:17; **(2)** metaphorically in Jude 8, of being given over to sensuous dreamings and so defiling the flesh. See: TDNT—8:545, 1233; BAGD—270b; THAYER—219c.

1798. **ἐνύπνιον** {1x} **ĕnupniŏn**, *en-oop'-nee-on;* from *1722* and *5258;* something seen *in sleep,* i.e. a *dream* (*vision* in a dream):—dream {1x}. See: TDNT—8:545, 1233; BAGD—270c; THAYER—219c.

1799. **ἐνώπιον** {97x} **ĕnōpiŏn**, *en-o'-pee-on;* neut. of a compound of *1722* and a der. of *3700; in* the *face* of (lit. or fig.):—before {64x}, in the sight of {16x}, in the presence of {7x}, in (one's) sight {5x}, in (one's) presence {2x}, to {1x}, not tr {2x}. See: BAGD—270c; THAYER—219c.

1800. **Ἐνώς** {1x} **Ĕnōs**, *en-oce';* of Heb. or. [583]; *Enos* (i.e. *Enosh*), a patriarch:—*Enos* {1x}. See: BAGD—271a; THAYER—220b.

1801. **ἐνωτίζομαι** {1x} **ĕnōtizŏmai**, *en-o-tid'-zom-ahee;* mid. voice from a compound of *1722* and *3775;* to take *in one's ear,* i.e. to *listen:*—hearken {1x}. See: TDNT—5:559, 744; BAGD—271a; THAYER—220a.

1802. **Ἐνώχ** {3x} **Ĕnōch**, *en-oke';* of Heb. or. [2585]; *Enoch* (i.e. *Chanok*), an antediluvian:—*Enoch* {3x}. See: TDNT—2:556, 237; BAGD—271a; THAYER—220c.

ἐξ **ĕx**.See *1537*.

1803. **ἕξ** {13x} **hĕx**, *hex;* a primary numeral; *six:*—six {13x}. See: BAGD—271b; THAYER—220c.

1804. **ἐξαγγέλλω** {1x} **ĕxaggĕllō**, *ex-ang-el'-lo;* from *1537* and the base of *32;* to *publish,* i.e. *celebrate:*—shew forth {1x}.

This word means to tell out, proclaim abroad, to publish completely; it indicates a complete proclamation and is rendered "show forth" in 1 Pet 2:9. See: TDNT—1:69, 10; BAGD—271b; THAYER—220d.

1805. **ἐξαγοράζω** {4x} **ĕxagŏrazō**, *ex-ag-or-ad'-zo;* from *1537* and *59;* to *buy up,* i.e. *ransom;* fig. to *rescue* from loss (*improve* opportunity):—redeem {4x}.

Exagorazo, as a verb, is a strengthened form of agorazo (59 - "to buy"), and denotes "to buy out," especially of purchasing a slave with a view to his freedom. **(1)** It is used in Gal 3:13 and 4:5, **(1a)** of the deliverance by Christ of Christians from the Law and its curse. **(1b)** Christ paid the ransom to God in order to satisfy the demands of His holy character. **(2)** It is used in the middle voice, "to buy up for oneself": "Redeeming the time, because the days are evil" (Eph 5:16). **(2a)** "Redeeming the time," where "time" is kairos, "a season," a time in which something is seasonable, i.e., **(2b)** making the most of every opportunity, turning each to the best advantage since none can be recalled if missed (Col 4:5). Syn.: **(A)** Agorazo (59) means to purchase; the slave has a new owner but is still unsure of his future. **(B)** *Exagorazo* means to purchase out implying a new master and at least the slave knows he will not be sold again. **(C)** Apolutrosis (629) means to purchase and set totally free. See also: 3084, 3085. See: TDNT—1:124, 19; BAGD—271b.

1806. **ἐξάγω** {13x} **ĕxagō**, *ex-ag'-o;* from *1537* and *71;* to *lead forth:*—lead out {6x}, bring out {5x}, bring forth {1x}, fetch out {1x}. See: BAGD—271c; THAYER—220d.

1807. **ἐξαιρέω** {8x} **ĕxairĕō**, *ex-ahee-reh'-o;* from *1537* and *138;* act. to *tear out;* mid. voice to *select;* fig. to *release:*—deliver {5x}, pluck out {2x}, rescue {1x}.

Exaireo, as a verb, means literally **(1)** "to take out" and denotes, in the middle voice, "to take out for oneself," hence, "to deliver, to rescue," the person who does so having a special interest in the result of his act. Thus it is used, in Gal. 1:4, of the act of God in "delivering" believers "out of this present evil world" the middle voice indicating His pleasure in the issue of their "deliverance": "Who gave Himself for our sins, that He might deliver (*exaireo*) us from this present evil world, according to the will of God and our Father." **(2)** It signifies to "deliver" by rescuing **(2a)** from danger: "And when Peter was come to himself, he said, Now I know of a surety, that the Lord hath sent his angel, and hath delivered me out of the hand of Herod, and *from* all the expectation of the people of the Jews" (Acts 12:11; cf. 23:27; 26:17); **(2b)** from bondage: "And delivered him [Joseph] out of all his afflictions, and gave him favour and wisdom in the sight of Pharaoh king of Egypt; and he made him governor over Egypt and all his house" (Acts 7:10; cf. 7:34. **(3)** It also means "to pluck out of": "And if thy right eye offend thee, pluck it out, and cast *it* from thee: for it is profitable for thee that one of thy members should perish, and not *that* thy whole body should be cast into hell" (Mt 5:29; cf. 18:9). Syn.: 325, 525, 629, 591, 859, 1325, 1560, 1659, 1929, 3086, 3860, 4506, 5483. See: BAGD—271d.; THAYER—221a.

1808. **ἐξαίρω** {2x} **ĕxairō**, *ex-ah'-ee-ro;* from *1537* and *142;* to *remove:*—put away {1x}, take away {1x}.

Exairo means to put away from the midst of and is used of church discipline (1 Cor 5:2, 13). See: BAGD—272a; THAYER—221a.

1809. **ἐξαιτέομαι** {1x} **ĕxaitĕŏmai**, *ex-ahee-teh'-om-ahee;* mid. voice from *1537* and *154;* to *demand* (for trial):—desire {1x}. See: TDNT—1:194,*; BAGD—272a; THAYER—221a.

1810. **ἐξαίφνης** {5x} **ĕxaiphnēs**, *ex-ah'-eef-nace;* from *1537* and the base of *160; of a sudden* (*unexpectedly*):—suddenly {5x}.

Exaiphnes, as and adverb, a strengthened form, is translated "suddenly": "Lest coming suddenly he find you sleeping" (Mk 13:36; cf. Lk 2:13; 9:39; Acts 9:3; 22:6). Syn.: 160, 869, 1819. See: BAGD—272b; THAYER—220b. comp. *1819.*

1811. **ἐξακολουθέω** {3x} **ĕxakŏlŏuthĕō**, *ex-ak-ol-oo-theh'-o;* from *1537* and *190;* to *follow out the end,* i.e. (fig.) to *imitate, obey,* yield to:—follow {3x}.

Exakoloutheo, as a verb, means "to follow up, or out to the end" and is used metaphorically, and only by the apostle Peter in his second epistle: **(1)** in 1:16, of cunningly devised fables; **(2)** 2:2 of lascivious doings; **(3)** 2:15, of the way of Balaam. Syn.: 190, 1096, 1377, 1872, 2614, 2628, 3877, 4870. See: TDNT—1:215, 33; BAGD—272b; THAYER—221b.

1812. **ἑξακόσιοι** {2x} **hĕxakŏsiŏi**, *hex-ak-os'-ee-oy;* plur. ordinal from *1803* and *1540; six hundred:*—six hundred {2x}. See: BAGD—272b; THAYER—221c.

1813. **ἐξαλείφω** {5x} **ĕxalĕiphō**, *ex-al-i'-fo;* from *1537* and *218;* to *smear out,* i.e. *obliterate* (*erase* tears, fig. *pardon* sin):—blot out {3x}, wipe away {2x}.

This word means to wipe and signifies to wash, or to smear completely; hence, metaphorically, in the sense of removal, to wipe away, wipe off, obliterate: **(1)** sins (Acts 3:19); **(2)** writing (Col 2:14); **(3)** of a name in a book (Rev 3:5); and **(4)** of tears (Rev 7:17; 21:4). See: BAGD—272c; THAYER—221c.

1814. **ἐξάλλομαι** {1x} **ĕxallŏmai**, *ex-al'-lom-ahee;* from *1537* and *242;* to *spring forth:*—leap up {1x}. See: BAGD—272c; THAYER—221c.

1815. **ἐξανάστασις** {1x} **ĕxanastasis**, *ex-an-as'-tas-is;* from *1817;* a *rising from* death:—resurrection {1x}. See: TDNT—1:371, 60; BAGD—272d; THAYER—221c.

1816. **ἐξανατέλλω** {2x} **ĕxanatĕllō**, *ex-an-at-el'-lo;* from *1537* and *393;* to *start up out* of the ground, i.e. *germinate:*—spring up {2x}. Cf. Mt. 13:5; Mk 4:5. See: BAGD—272d; THAYER—221c.

1817. **ἐξανίστημι** {3x} **ĕxanistēmi**, *ex-an-is'-tay-mee;* from *1537* and *450;* obj. to *produce,* i.e. (fig.) *beget;* subj. to *arise,* i.e. (fig.) *object:*—raise up {2x}. rise up {1x}.

Exanistemi, as a verb, is a strengthened form of anistemi (450) and signifies **(1)** "to raise up": "Master, Moses wrote unto us, If a man's brother die, and leave *his* wife *behind him,* and leave no children, that his brother should take his wife, and raise up seed unto his brother" (Mk 12:19; Lk 20:28); **(2)** intransitively, "to rise up": "But there rose up certain of the sect of the Pharisees which believed, saying, That it was needful to circumcise them" (Acts 15:5). Syn.: 305, 393, 450, 1096, 1326, 1453, 1525, 4911. See: TDNT—1:368, 60; BAGD—272d; THAYER—221d.

1818. **ἐξαπατάω** {5x} **ĕxapataō**, *ex-ap-at-ah'-o;* from *1537* and *538;* to *seduce wholly:*—beguile {1x}, deceive {4x}.

Exapatao, a strengthened form, is rendered **(1)** "beguile," 2 Cor 11:3; literally "as the serpent thoroughly beguiled Eve." It is translated **(2)** "deceive" and speaks **(2a)** of the influence of sin, Rom 7:11; **(2b)** of self-deception, 1 Cor 3:18; **(2c)** of evil men who cause divisions, Rom 16:18; **(2d)** of deceitful teachers, 2 Th 2:3. See: TDNT—1:384, 65; BAGD—273a; THAYER—221d.

1819. **ἐξάπινα** {1x} **ĕxapina**, *ex-ap'-ee-nah;* from *1537* and a der. of the same as *160; of a sudden,* i.e. *unexpectedly:*—suddenly {1x}.

Exapina, as an adverb, occurs in Mk 9:8: "And suddenly (*exapina*), when they had looked round about, they saw no man any more, save Jesus only with themselves." Syn.: 160, 869, 1810. See: BAGD—273a; THAYER—221d. comp. *1810.*

1820. **ἐξαπορέομαι** {2x} **ĕxapŏrĕŏmai**, *ex-ap-or-eh'-om-ahee;* mid. voice from *1537* and *639;* to *be utterly at a loss,* i.e. *despond:*—in despair {1x}, despair {1x}.

Exaporeomai means to be utterly without a way, without a way through, to be quite at a loss, without resource, in despair. It is used **(1)** in 2 Cor 1:8 to despair of life; and **(2)** in 2 Cor 4:8, in the sentence "perplexed, yet not unto in despair." See: BAGD—273a; THAYER—221d.

1821. **ἐξαποστέλλω** {11x} **ĕxapŏstĕllō**, *ex-ap-os-tel'-lo;* from *1537* and *649;* to *send away forth,* i.e. (on a mission) to *despatch,* or (peremptorily) to *dismiss:*—send {2x}, send away {4x}, send forth {4x}, send out {1x}.

Exapostello denotes **(1)** "to send forth": **(1a)** of the Son by God the Father, Gal 4:4; **(1b)** of the Holy Spirit, Gal 4:6; **(1c)** an angel, Acts 12:11; **(1d)** the ancestors of Israel, Acts 7:12; **(1e)** Paul to the Gentiles, Acts 22:21; **(2)** "to send away," Lk 1:53; 20:10, 11; Acts 9:30; 11:22; 17:14. See: TDNT—1:406, 67; BAGD—273a; THAYER—221d.

1822. **ἐξαρτίζω** {2x} **ĕxartizō**, *ex-ar-tid'-zo;* from *1537* and a der. of *739;* to *finish out* (time); fig. to *equip fully* (a teacher):—accomplish + 1096 {1x}, thoroughly furnish {1x}.

Exartizo, "to fit out," means **(1)** "to furnish completely," 2 Ti 3:17, or **(2)** "to accomplish," Acts 21:5, there said of a number of days, as if to render the days complete by what was appointed for them. See: TDNT—1:475, 80; BAGD—273c; THAYER—222a.

1823. **ἐξαστράπτω** {1x} **ĕxastraptō**, *ex-as-trap'-to;* from *1537* and *797;* to *lighten forth,* i.e. (fig.) to *be radiant* (of very white garments):—glistening {1x}.

Exastrapto stresses the source of light is from Christ Himself; He was not reflecting light (Lk 9:29). See: BAGD—273d; THAYER—222a.

1824. **ἐξαυτῆς** {6x} **ĕxautēs**, *ex-ow'-tace;* from *1537* and the gen. sing. fem. of *846* (*5610* being understood); *from that* hour, i.e. *instantly:*—by and by {1x}, immediately {3x}, presently {1x}, straightway {1x}. See: BAGD—273d; THAYER—222b.

1825. **ἐξεγείρω** {2x} **ĕxĕgĕirō**, *ex-eg-i'-ro;* from *1537* and *1453;* to *rouse fully,* i.e. (fig.) to *resuscitate* (from death), *release* (from infliction):—raise up {2x}.

Exegeiro, is used **(1)** of the "resurrection" of believers, 1 Cor 6:14 [2nd part]; **(2)** of "raising" a person to public position, Rom. 9:17, said of Pharaoh by God. See: TDNT—2:338, 195; BAGD—273d; THAYER—222b.

1826. **ἔξειμι** {4x} **ĕxĕimi**, *ex'-i-mee;* from *1537* and εἶμι **ĕimi** (to *go*); to *issue,* i.e. *leave* (a place), *escape* (to the shore):—depart {2x}, get [*to land*]{1x}, gone out {1x}.

Exeimi, "to go out" is rendered **(1)** "gone out" in Acts 13:42; **(2)** in Acts 27:43, "get," of mariners getting to shore; **(3)** in Acts 17:15, "departed"; and in Acts 20:7, "to depart." See: BAGD—273d; THAYER—222b.

1827. **ἐξελέγχω** {1x} **ĕxĕlĕgchō**, *ex-el-eng'-kho;* from *1537* and *1651;* to *convict fully,* i.e. (by impl.) to *punish:*—convince {1x}.

Exelegcho, an intensive form, "to convince thoroughly," is used of the Lord's future "conviction" of the ungodly, Jude 15. A person can be convicted by a court, but not convinced within himself that he is guilty. A person can also be convinced of wrong doing, but no outside power convicts. See: BAGD—274a; THAYER—222b.

1828. **ἐξέλκω** {1x} **ĕxĕlkō**, *ex-el'-ko;* from *1537* and *1670;* to *drag forth,* i.e. (fig.) to *entice* (to sin):—draw away {1x}.

Exelko, as a verb, means "to draw away, or lure forth" and is used metaphorically in Jas 1:14, of being "drawn away" by lust. As in hunting or fishing the game is "lured" from its haunt, so man's lust "allures" him from the safety of his self-restraint. Syn.: 307, 385, 392, 501, 502, 645, 868, 1448, 1670, 2020, 2464, 4317, 4334, 4358, 4685, 4951, 5288, 5289. See: BAGD—274a; THAYER—222b.

1829. **ἐξέραμα** {1x} **ĕxĕrama**, *ex-er'-am-ah;* from a compound of *1537* and a presumed ἐράω **ĕraō** (to *spue*); *vomit,* i.e. *food disgorged:*—vomit {1x}. See: BAGD—274b; THAYER—222c.

1830. **ἐξερευνάω** {1x} **ĕxĕrĕunaō**, *ex-er-yoo-nah'-o;* from *1537* and *2045;* to *explore* (fig.):—search diligently {1x}. See: TDNT—2:655, 255; BAGD—274b; THAYER—222c.

1831. **ἐξέρχομαι** {222x} **ĕxĕrchŏmai**, *ex-er'-khom-ahee;* from *1537* and *2064;* to *issue* (lit. or fig.):—go out {60x}, come {34x}, depart {28x}, go {25x}, go forth {25x}, come out {23x}, come forth {9x}, misc. {18x} = escape, get out, go (abroad, away, thence), proceed (forth), spread abroad. See: TDNT—2:678, 257; BAGD—274b; THAYER—222c.

1832. **ἔξεστι** {32x} **ĕxĕsti**, *ex'-es-tee* or ἔξεστιν **exestin**, *ex'-es-teen;* third pers. sing. pres. ind. of a compound of *1537* and *1510;* so also

ἐξόν **ĕxŏn**, *ex-on';* neut. pres. part. of the same (with or without some form of *1510* expressed); impers. *it is right* (through the fig. idea of *being out* in public):—be lawful {29x}, let {1x}, × mayest {2x}.

Exesti, an impersonal verb, signifying **(1)** "it is permitted, it is lawful" (or interrogatively, "is it lawful?"), **(2)** occurs most frequently in the synoptic Gospels and the Acts; **(2a)** elsewhere in Jn 5:10; 18:31; 1 Cor 6:12; 10:23; 2 Cor 12:4; Acts 2:29 it is rendered "let me (speak)," lit., "it being permitted"; **(2b)** in Acts 8:37, "thou mayest," lit., "it is permitted;" 16:21; **(2c)** in 21:37, "may I," lit., "is it permitted?" See: TDNT—2:560, 238; BAGD—275b; THAYER—223c.

1833. **ἐξετάζω** {3x} **ĕxĕtazō**, *ex-et-ad'-zo;* from *1537* and ἐτάζω **ĕtazō** (to *examine*); to searach out; *test thoroughly* (by questions), i.e. *ascertain* or *interrogate:*—ask {1x}, enquire {1x}, search {1x}.

Exetazo, "to search out" (*ek,* "out," intensive, *etazo,* "to examine"), is translated **(1)** "ask," in Jn 21:12; **(2)** in Mt 2:8, "search"; and **(3)** Mt 10:11 "inquire." See: BAGD—275c; THAYER—223d.

1834. **ἐξηγέομαι** {6x} **ĕxēgĕŏmai**, *ex-ayg-eh'-om-ahee;* from *1537* and *2233;* to *consider out* (aloud), i.e. *rehearse, unfold:*—declare {5x}, tell {1x}.

This word means **(1)** to lead out and signifies to make known, rehearse declare, tell (Lk 24:35; Acts 10:8; 15:12, 14; 21:19). **(2)** In John 1:18, in the sentence "He hath declared Him," means to unfold in teaching, to declare by making known. See: TDNT—2:908, 303; BAGD—275d; THAYER—223d.

1835. **ἑξήκοντα** {9x} **hĕxēkŏnta**, *hex-ay'-kon-tah;* the tenth multiple of *1803; sixty:*—sixty {3x}, sixtyfold {1x}, threescore {5x}. See: BAGD—276a; THAYER—223d.

1836. **ἑξῆς** {5x} **hĕxēs**, *hex-ace';* from *2192* (in the sense of *taking hold of,* i.e. *adjoining*); *successive:*—next {1x}, next day {1x}, day after {1x}, day following {1x}, morrow {1x}.

Hexes denotes "after" with the significance of a succession of events, an event following next in order after another, Lk 7:11; 9:37; Acts 21:1; 25:17; 27:18. See: BAGD—276a; THAYER—223d.

1837. **ἐξηχέομαι** {1x} **ĕxēchĕŏmai**, *ex-ay-kheh'-om-ahee;* mid. voice from *1537* and *2278;* to "*echo*" *forth,* i.e. *resound* (*be* generally *reported*):—sound forth {1x}.

Execheomai, "to sound forth as a trumpet" or "thunder" is used in 1 Th 1:8, "sounded forth," passive voice, lit., "has been sounded out." See: BAGD—276a; THAYER—224a.

1838. **ἕξις** {1x} **hĕxis**, *hex'-is;* from *2192; habit,* i.e. (by impl.) *experience, practice:*—use {1x}. See: BAGD—276b; THAYER—224a.

1839. **ἐξίστημι** {17x} **ĕxistēmi**, *ex-is'-tay-mee;* from *1537* and *2476;* to *put* (*stand*) *out* of wits, i.e. *astound,* or (refl.) *become astounded, insane:*—be amazed {5x}, be astonished {6x}, bewitch {2x}, be beside (one's) self {2x}, make astonished {1x}, wonder {1x}.

This word means to throw out of position, displace: **(1)** to amaze, Mt 12:23; Mk 2:12; 6:51; Acts 2:7; 9:21; **(2)** be astonished, Mk 5:42; Lk 2:47; 8:56; Acts 2:12; 10:45; 12:16 **(3)** bewitch, Acts 8:9, 11; **(4)** make astonished, Lk 24:22; **(5)** wonder, throw into wonderment, Act 8:13; and **(6)** to be out of one's mind, besides one's self, insane, Mk 3:21; 2 Cor 5:13. Syn.: 1611, 2285. See: TDNT—2:459, 217; BAGD—276b; THAYER—224a.

1840. **ἐξισχύω** {1x} **ĕxischuō**, *ex-is-khoo'-o;* from *1537* and *2480;* to *have full strength,* i.e. *be entirely competent:*—be able {1x}. See: BAGD—276c; THAYER—224b.

1841. **ἔξοδος** {3x} **ĕxŏdŏs**, *ex'-od-os;* from *1537* and *3598;* an *exit,* i.e. (fig.) *death:*—decease {2x}, departing {1x}.

Exodos, lit. signifies "a way out" (*ex,* "out," *hodos,* "a way"); hence, "a departure," especially from life, **(1)** "a decease"; **(1a)** in Lk 9:31, of the Lord's death, "which He was about to accomplish"; **(1b)** in 2 Pet. 1:15, of Peter's death; **(3)** "departure" from Egypt in Heb 11:22. See: TDNT—5:103, 666; BAGD—276c; THAYER—224b.

1842. **ἐξολοθρεύω** {1x} **ĕxŏlŏthrĕuō**, *ex-ol-oth-ryoo'-o;* from *1537* and *3645;* to *extirpate:*—destroy {1x}.

Exolothreuo, "to destroy utterly to slay wholly," is found in Acts 3:23, to the "destruction" of one who would refuse to hearken to the voice of God through Christ. See: TDNT—5:170, 681; BAGD—276b; THAYER—224b.

1843. **ἐξομολογέω** {11x} **ĕxŏmŏlŏgĕō**, *ex-om-ol-og-eh'-o;* from *1537* and *3670;* to *acknowledge* or (by impl. of *assent*) *agree fully:*—confess {8x}, thank {2x}, promise {1x}.

Exomologeo, intensive, "to confess forth," i.e., "freely, openly," is used **(1)** "of a public acknowledgment or confession of sins," Mt 3:6; Mk 1:5; Acts 19:18; Jas 5:16; **(2)** "to profess or acknowledge openly," Mt 11:25 (translated "thank," but indicating the fuller idea); Phil 2:11; Rev 3:5; **(3)** "to confess by way of celebrating, giving praise," Rom 14:11; 15:9. **(4)** In Lk 10:21, it is translated "I thank," the true meaning being "I gladly acknowledge." **(5)** In Lk 22:6 it signifies "promised." See: TDNT—5:199, 687; BAGD—277a; THAYER—224c.

ἐξόν **ĕxŏn**. See *1832*.

1844. **ἐξορκίζω** {1x} **ĕxŏrkizō**, *ex-or-kid'-zo;* from *1537* and *3726;* to *extract an oath,* i.e. *conjure:*—adjure {1x}. See: TDNT—5:464, 729; BAGD—277b; THAYER—224c.

1845. **ἐξορκιστής** {1x} **ĕxŏrkistēs**, *ex-or-kis-tace';* from *1844; one that binds by an oath* (or *spell*), i.e. (by impl.) an "*exorcist*" (*conjurer*):—exorcist {1x}. See: TDNT—5:464, 729; BAGD—277b; THAYER—224d.

1846. **ἐξορύσσω** {2x} **ĕxŏrussō**, *ex-or-oos'-so;* from *1537* and *3736;* to *dig out,* i.e. (by extens.) to *extract* (an eye), *remove* (roofing):—break up {1x}, pluck out {1x}.

Exorusso, "to dig out" is used **(1)** of the "breaking up" of part of a roof, Mk 2:4, and, **(2)** in a vivid expression, of plucking out the eyes, Gal 4:15. See: BAGD—277c; THAYER—224c.

1847. **ἐξουδενόω** {1x} **ĕxŏudĕnŏō**, *ex-oo-den-ŏ'-o;* from *1537* and a der. of the neut. of *3762;* to *make utterly nothing of,* i.e. *despise:*—set at nought {1x}. See: BAGD—277c. See also *1848;* THAYER—224d.

1848. **ἐξουθενέω** {11x} **ĕxŏuthĕnĕō**, *ex-oo-then-eh'-o;* a var. of *1847* and mean. the same:—contemptible {1x}, despise {6x}, least esteemed {1x}, set at nought {3x}.

Exoutheneo, "to make of no account" (*ex,* "out," *oudeis,* "nobody") means "to regard as nothing, to despise utterly, to treat with contempt." This is usually translated to **(1)** "set at nought," Lk 23:11; Acts 4:11; Rom 14:10; **(2)** "despise", Lk 18:9; Rom 14:3; 1 Cor 1:28; 16:11; Gal 4:14; 1 Th 5:20; **(3)** "contemptible", 2 Cor 10:10; and **(4)** "least esteemed", 1 Cor 6:4. **(4a)** It is used, not in a contemptuous sense, **(4b)** but of gentile judges, before whom the saints are not to go to law with one another, such magistrates having no place, and therefore being "of no account" in the church. **(4c)** The apostle is not speaking of any believers as "least esteemed." See: BAGD—277c; THAYER—225a.

1849. **ἐξουσία** {103x} **ĕxŏusia**, *ex-oo-see'-ah;* from *1832* (in the sense of *ability*); *privilege,* i.e. (subj.) *force, capacity, competency, freedom,* or (obj.) *mastery* (concr. *magistrate, superhuman, potentate, token of control*), delegated *influence:*—power {69x}, authority {29x}, right {2x}, liberty {1x}, jurisdiction {1x}, strength {1x}.

Exousia, as a noun, denotes **(1)** "authority" (from the impersonal verb exesti, "it is lawful"). **(2)** From the meaning of "leave or permission," or liberty of doing as one pleases, **(2a)** it passed to that of "the ability or strength with which one is endued," **(2c)** then to that of the "power of authority," the right to exercise power, e.g., Mt 9:6; 21:23; 2 Cor 10:8; **(2d)** or "the power of rule or government," the power of one whose will and commands must be obeyed by others, e.g., Mt 28:18; Jn 17:2; Jude 25; Rev 12:10; 17:13; **(2e)** more specifically of apostolic "authority," 2 Cor 10:8; 13:10; **(3)** the "power" **(3a)** of judicial decision, Jn 19:10; **(3b)** of "managing domestic affairs," Mk 13:34. **(4)** By metonymy, or name-change (the substitution of a suggestive word for the name of the thing meant), it stands for "that which is subject to authority or rule," Lk 4:6 "power"; **(5)** or, as with the English "authority," "one who possesses authority, a ruler, magistrate," Rom 13:1–3; Lk 12:11; Titus 3:1; **(6)** or "a spiritual potentate," e.g., Eph 3:10; 6:12; Col 1:16; 2:10, 15; 1 Pet 3:22. **(7)** In 1 Cor 11:10 it is used of the veil with which a woman is required to cover herself in an assembly or church, as a sign of the Lord's "authority" over the church. See: TDNT—2:562, 238; BAGD—277d; THAYER—225a.

1850. **ἐξουσιάζω** {4x} **ĕxŏusiazō**, *ex-oo-see-ad'-zo;* from *1849;* to *control:*—exercise authority upon {1x}, bring under the power of {1x}, have power of {2x}.

Exousiazo, as a verb, means **(1)** exercise authority upon, Gentile rulers, Lk 22:25; **(2)** bring under the power of a thing, 1 Cor 6:12, All are within my power; but I will not put myself under the power of any one of all things; **(3)** have power of one's body in proper marital relationships, 1 Cor 7:4 (twice). See: TDNT—2:574, 238; BAGD—279a; THAYER—225d.

1851. **ἐξοχή** {1x} **ĕxŏchē**, *ex-okh-ay';* from a compound of *1537* and *2192* (mean. to *stand out*); *prominence* (fig.):—principal + 2596 {1x}.

Exoche describes men of eminence, excellence, superiority, Acts 25:23. See: BAGD—279a; THAYER—226a.

1852. **ἐξυπνίζω** {1x} **ĕxupnizō**, *ex-oop-nid'-zo;* from *1853;* to *waken:*—awake out of sleep {1x}. See: TDNT—8:545, 1233; BAGD—279b; THAYER—226a.

1853. **ἔξυπνος** {1x} **ĕxupnŏs**, *ex'-oop-nos;* from *1537* and *5258; fully awake:*—wake out of sleep + 1096 {1x}. See: TDNT—8:545, 1233; BAGD—279b; THAYER—226a.

1854. **ἔξω** {65x} **ĕxō**, *ex'-o;* adv. from *1537; out* (*-side, of doors*), lit. or fig.:—without {23x}, out {16x}, out of {15x}, forth {8x}, outward {1x}, strange {1x}, away {1x}. See: TDNT—2:575, 240; BAGD—279b; THAYER—226a.

1855. **ἔξωθεν** {11x} **ĕxōthĕn**, *ex'-o-then;* from *1854; external* (*-ly*):—without {4x}, outside {2x}, from without {2x}, outward {2x}, outwardly {1x}.

Exothen is an adverb and properly signifies "from without." See: BAGD—279d; THAYER—226b.

1856. **ἐξωθέω** {2x} **ĕxōthĕō**, *ex-o-theh'-o;* or

ἐξώθω **ĕxōthō**, *ex-o'-tho;* from *1537* and ὠθέω **ōthĕō** (to *push*); to *expel;* by impl. to *propel:*—drive out {1x}, thrust in {1x}. Cf. Acts 7:45, 27:39. See: BAGD—280a; THAYER—226c.

1857. **ἐξώτερος** {3x} **ĕxōtĕrŏs**, *ex-o'-ter-os;* comp. of *1854; exterior:*—outer {3x}. Cf. Mt 8:12; 22:13; 25:30. See: BAGD—280a; THAYER—226c.

1858. **ἑορτάζω** {1x} **hĕŏrtazō**, *heh-or-tad'-zo;* from *1859;* to *observe a festival:*—keep the feast {1x}.

Heortazo in 1 Cor 5:8 is not the Lord's Supper, nor the Passover, but has reference to the continuous life of the believer as a festival or holy-day, in freedom from "the leaven of malice and wickedness, but with the unleavened bread of sincerity and truth." See: BAGD—280a; THAYER—226c.

1859. **ἑορτή** {27x} **hĕŏrtē**, *heh-or-tay';* of uncert. aff.; a *festival, especially of the Jews:*—feast {26x}, holyday {1x}.

Heorte, "a feast or festival," is used **(1)** especially of those of the Jews, and particularly of the Passover; **(2)** the word is found mostly in John's gospel (seventeen times); apart from the Gospels it is used in this way only in Acts 18:21; **(3)** in a more general way, in Col 2:16, "holy day." See: BAGD—280b; THAYER—226c.

1860. **ἐπαγγελία** {53x} **ĕpaggĕlia**, *ep-ang-el-ee'-ah;* from *1861;* an *announcement* (for information, assent or pledge; espec. a divine *assurance* of good):—message {52x}, promise {1x}.

Epangelia, as a noun, is **(1)** primarily a law term, **(1a)** denoting "a summons" and **(1b)** also meant "an undertaking to do or give something, a promise." **(2)** Except in Acts 23:21 it is used only of the "promises" of God. **(3)** It frequently stands for the thing "promised," and so signifies a gift graciously bestowed, not a pledge secured by negotiation; thus, **(3a)** in Gal 3:14, "the promise of the Spirit" denotes "the promised Spirit", cf. Lk 24:49; Acts 2:33 and Eph 1:13; **(3b)** in Heb 9:15, "the promise of the eternal inheritance" is "the promised eternal inheritance." **(3c)** On the other hand, in Acts 1:4, "the promise of the Father," is the "promise" made by the Father. **(4)** In Gal 3:16, the plural "promises" is used because **(4a)** the one "promise" to Abraham was variously repeated (cf. Gen 12:1–3; 13:14–17; 15:18; 17:1–14; 22:15–18), and because **(4b)** it contained the germ of all subsequent "promises"; cf. Rom 9:4; Heb 6:12; 7:6; 8:6; 11:17; **(4c)** Gal 3 is occupied with showing that the "promise" was conditional upon faith and not upon the fulfillment of the Law. The Law was later than, and inferior to, the "promise," and did not annul it, v. 21; cf. 4:23, 28.

(5) Again, in Eph 2:12, "the covenants of the promise" does not indicate different covenants, but a covenant often renewed, all centering in Christ as the "promised" Messiah-Redeemer, and comprising the blessings to be bestowed through Him. **(6)** In 2 Cor 1:20 the plural is used of every "promise" made by God: cf. Heb 11:33; in 7:6, of special "promises" mentioned. **(7)** For other applications of the word, see, e.g., Eph 6:2; 1 Ti 4:8; 2 Ti 1:1; Heb 4:1; 2 Pet 3:4, 9; 1 Jn 1:5. **(8)** The occurrences of the word in relation to Christ and what centers in Him, may be arranged under the headings **(8a)** the contents of the "promise," e.g., Acts 26:6; Rom 4:20; 1 Jn 2:25; **(8b)** the heirs, e.g., Rom 9:8; 15:8; Gal 3:29; Heb 11:9; **(8c)** the conditions, e.g., Rom 4:13, 14; Gal 3:14–22; Heb 10:36. See: TDNT—2:576, 240; BAGD—280c; THAYER—226d.

1861. **ἐπαγγέλλω** {15x} **ĕpaggĕllō**, *ep-ang-el'-lo;* from *1909* and the base of *32;* to *announce upon* (refl.), i.e. (by impl.) to *engage* to do something, to *assert* something respecting oneself:—profess {2x}, make promise {2x}, promise {11x}.

Epangello, as a verb, means "to announce, proclaim," has in the NT the two meanings "to profess" and "to promise," each used in the middle voice; **(1)** "to promise" **(1a)** of "promises" of God, Acts 7:5; Rom 4:21; in Gal 3:19, passive voice; Titus 1:2; Heb 6:13; 10:23; 11:11; 12:26; Jas 1:12; 2:5; 1 Jn 2:25; **(2)** made by men, Mk 14:11; 2 Pet 2:19. See: TDNT—2:576, 240; BAGD—280d; THAYER—227b.

1862. **ἐπάγγελμα** {2x} **ĕpaggĕlma**, *ep-ang'-el-mah;* from *1861;* a *self-committal* (by *assurance* of conferring some good):—a promise {2x}.

Epangelma denotes "a promise made," 2 Pet 1:4; 3:13. See: TDNT—2:585, 240; BAGD—281a; THAYER—227c.

1863. **ἐπάγω** {3x} **ĕpagō**, *ep-ag'-o;* from *1909* and *71;* to *superinduce,* i.e. *inflict* (an evil), *charge* (a crime):—bring {1x}, bring upon {1x}, bring in upon {1x}.

This word means to cause something to befall one, usually something evil, Acts 5:28; 2 Pet 2:1, 5. See: BAGD—281b; THAYER—227c.

1864. **ἐπαγωνίζομαι** {1x} **ĕpagōnizŏmai**, *ep-ag-o-nid'-zom-ahee;* from *1909* and *75;* to *struggle for:*—earnestly contend for {1x}.

This word signifies to contend about a thing, as a combatant. The word "earnestly" is added to convey the intensive force of the preposition (Jude 3). See: TDNT—1:134, 20; BAGD—281b; THAYER—227c.

1865. **ἐπαθροίζω** {1x} **ĕpathrŏizō**, *ep-ath-roid'-zo;* from *1909* and ἀθροίζω **athrŏizō** (to *assemble*); to *accumulate:*—gather thick together {1x}. See: BAGD—281b; THAYER—227c.

1866. **Ἐπαίνετος** {1x} **Ĕpainĕtŏs**, *ep-a'-hee-net-os;* from *1867; praised; Epænetus,* a Chr.:—Epenetus {1x}. See: BAGD—281c; THAYER—227d.

1867. **ἐπαινέω** {6x} **ĕpainĕō**, *ep-ahee-neh'-o;* from *1909* and *131;* to *applaud:*—commend {1x}, laud {1x}, praise {4x}. See: BAGD—281c; THAYER—227d.

1868. **ἔπαινος** {11x} **ĕpainŏs**, *ep'-ahee-nos;* from *1909* and the base of *134; laudation;* concr. a *commendable* thing:—praise {11x}.

Epainos, denotes "approbation, commendation, praise"; it is used **(1)** of those on account of, and by reason of, whom as God's heritage, "praise" is to be ascribed to God, in respect of His glory (the exhibition of His character and operations), Eph 1:12; **(1a)** in 1:14, of the whole company, the church, viewed as "God's own possession"; **(1b)** in 1:6, with particular reference to the glory of His grace towards them; **(1c)** in Phil 1:11, as the result of "the fruits of righteousness" manifested in them through the power of Christ; **(2)** of "praise" bestowed by God, **(2a)** upon the Jew spiritually (Judah = "praise"), Rom 2:29; **(2b)** bestowed upon believers hereafter at the judgment seat of Christ, 1 Cor 4:5 (where the definite article indicates that the "praise" will be exactly in accordance with each person's actions); **(2c)** as the issue of present trials, "at the revelation of Jesus Christ," 1 Pet 1:7; **(3)** of whatsoever is "praiseworthy," Phil 4:8; **(4)** of the approbation by churches of those who labor faithfully in the ministry of the gospel, 2 Cor 8:18; **(5)** of the approbation of well-doers by human rulers, Rom 13:3; 1 Pet 2:14. Syn.: 133. See: TDNT—2:586, 242; BAGD—281c; THAYER—227d.

1869. **ἐπαίρω** {19x} **ĕpairō**, *ep-ahee'-ro;* from *1909* and *142;* to *raise up* (lit. or fig.):—lift up {15x}, exalt (one's) self {2x}, take up {1x}, hoisted up {1x}.

Epairo, as a verb, means "to lift up" and is said **(1)** literally, **(1a)** of a sail, Acts 27:40; **(1b)** hands, Lk 24:50; 1 Ti 2:8; **(1c)** heads, Lk 21:28; **(1d)** eyes, Mt 17:8; Lk 6:20; 16:23, 18:13; Jn 4:35; 6:5; 17:1; **(1e)** the voice, Lk 11:27; Acts 2:14; 14:11; 22:22; **(1f)** a foresail, Acts 27:40; **(2)** metaphorically, **(2a)** of "exalting" oneself, being "lifted up" with pride, 2 Cor 10:5; 11:20"exalteth himself"; **(2b)** of the heel, Jn 13:18, as of one "lifting" up the foot before kicking; the expression indicates contempt and violence; **(3)** in the passive voice, Acts 1:9, of Christ's ascension, "was taken up." See: TDNT—1:186, 28; BAGD—281d; THAYER—227d.

1870. **ἐπαισχύνομαι** {11x} **ĕpaischunŏmai**, *ep-ahee-skhoo'-nom-ahee;* from *1909* and *153;* to *feel shame for* something.—be ashamed {11x}.

Epaischunomai, as a verb, means "the feeling of shame arising from something that has been done." It is said of being "ashamed" **(1)** of persons, Mk 8:38; Lk 9:26; **(2)** the gospel, Rom 1:16; **(3)** former evil doing, Rom 6:21; **(4)** "the testimony of our Lord," 2 Ti 1:8; **(5)** suffering for the gospel, 2 Ti 1:12; **(6)** rendering assistance and comfort to one who is suffering for the gospel's sake, 2 Ti 1: 16. **(7)** It is used in Hebrews of Christ **(7a)** in calling those who are sanctified His brethren, Heb 2:11; and **(7b)** of God in His not being "ashamed" to be called the God of believers, Heb 11:16. See: TDNT—1:189,*; BAGD—282a; THAYER—228a.

1871. **ἐπαιτέω** {1x} **ĕpaitĕō**, *ep-ahee-teh'-o;* from *1909* and *154;* to *ask for:*—beg {1x}. See: BAGD—282b; THAYER—228b.

1872. **ἐπακολουθέω** {4x} **ĕpakŏlŏuthĕō**, *ep-ak-ol-oo-theh'-o;* from *1909* and *190;* to *accompany:*—follow {3x}, follow after {1x}.

Epakoloutheo (1872), as a verb, means "to follow after, close upon" and is used of signs "following" the preaching of the gospel (Mk 16:20); **(2)** of "following" good works (1 Ti 5:10); **(3)** of sins "following" after those who are guilty of them (1 Ti 5:24); **(4)** of "following" the steps of Christ (1 Pet 2:21). Syn.: 190, 1096, 1377, 1811, 2614, 2628, 3877, 4870. See: TDNT—1:215, 33; BAGD—282b; THAYER—228b.

1873. **ἐπακούω** {1x} **ĕpakŏuō**, *ep-ak-oo'-o;* from *1909* and *191;* to *hearken* (favorably) *to:*—hear {1x}.

Epakouo, as a verb, means "to listen to, hear with favor, at or upon an occasion" and is used in 2 Cor 6:2: "For he saith, I have heard (*epakouo*) thee in a time accepted, and in the day of salvation have I succoured thee: behold, now *is* the accepted time; behold, now *is* the day of salvation." Syn.: 189, 191, 1251, 1522, 1874, 3878, 4257. See: TDNT—1:222, 34; BAGD—282c; THAYER—228b.

1874. **ἐπακροάομαι** {1x} **ĕpakrŏaŏmai**, *ep-ak-rŏ-ah'-om-ahee;* from *1909* and the base of *202;* to *listen* (intently) *to:*—hear {1x}.

Epakroaomai, as a verb, means "to listen attentively to" and is used in Acts 16:25: "(the prisoners) were listening to (them)." Syn.: 189, 191, 1251, 1522, 1873, 3878, 4257. See: BAGD—282c; THAYER—228b.

1875. **ἐπάν** {3x} **ĕpan**, *ep-an';* from *1909* and *302;* a particle of indef. contemporaneousness; *whenever, as soon as:*—when {3x}. See: BAGD—282c; THAYER—228c.

1876. **ἐπάναγκες** {1x} **ĕpanagkĕs**, *ep-an'-ang-kes;* neut. of a presumed compound of *1909* and *318;* (adv.) *on necessity,* i.e. *necessarily:*—necessary {1x}. See: BAGD—282d; THAYER—228c.

1877. **ἐπανάγω** {3x} **ĕpanagō**, *ep-an-ag'-o;* from *1909* and *321;* to *lead up on,* i.e. (tech.) to *put out* (to sea); (intr.) to *return:*—launch out {1x}, thrust out {1x}, return {1x}.

Epanago, as a verb, means **(1)** "to bring up or back" [primarily a nautical term for "putting to sea"], (cf. Lk 5:3, 4); and **(2)** is used intransitively in Mt 21:18: "Now in the morning as He returned into the city, He hungered." Syn.: 344, 360, 390, 1880, 1994, 5290. See: BAGD—282d; THAYER—228c.

1878. **ἐπαναμιμνήσκω** {1x} **ĕpanamimnēskō,** *ep-an-ah-mim-nace'-ko;* from *1909* and *363;* to *remind of again,* to *recall to mind again:*—put in mind {1x}. See: BAGD—282d; THAYER—228c.

1879. **ἐπαναπαύομαι** {2x} **ĕpanapauŏmai,** *ep-an-ah-pŏw'-om-ahee;* mid. voice from *1909* and *373;* to *settle on;* lit. (*remain*) or fig. (*rely*):—rest in {1x}, rest upon {1x}.

Epanapauomai, "to cause to rest," is used in the middle voice, metaphorically, signifying **(1)** "to rest upon" in Lk 10:6 and **(2)** "rest in" in Rom 2:17. See: TDNT—1:351,*; BAGD—282d; THAYER—228c.

1880. **ἐπανέρχομαι** {{2x} **ĕpanĕrchŏmai,** *ep-an-er'-khom-ahee;* from *1909* and *424;* to *come up on,* i.e. *return:*—come (back) again {1x}, return {1x}.

In Lk 19:15, *epanerchomai,* as a verb, means "returned": "And it came to pass, that when he was returned, having received the kingdom. . . ." (cf. Lk 10:35). Syn.: 344, 360, 390, 1877, 1994, 5290. See: BAGD—283a; THAYER—228d.

1881. **ἐπανίσταμαι** {2x} **ĕpanistamai,** *ep-an-is'-tam-ahee;* mid. voice from *1909* and *450;* to *stand up on,* i.e. (fig.) to *attack:*—rise up against {2x}. Cf. Mt 10:31; Mk 13:12. See: BAGD—283a; THAYER—228d.

1882. **ἐπανόρθωσις** {1x} **ĕpanŏrthōsis,** *ep-an-or'-tho-sis;* from a compound of *1909* and *461;* a *straightening up again,* i.e. (fig.) *rectification* (*reformation*):—correction {1x}.

Epanorthosis, lit., "a restoration to an upright or right state", hence, "correction," is used of the Scripture in 2 Ti 3:16, referring to improvement of life and character. See: TDNT—5:450, 727; BAGD—283a; THAYER—228d.

1883. **ἐπάνω** {20x} **ĕpanō,** *ep-an'-o;* from *1909* and *507;* *up above,* i.e. *over* or *on* (of place, amount, rank, etc.):—over {6x}, on {4x}, thereon + 846 {3x}, upon {3x}, above {3x}, more than {1x}. See: BAGD—283b; THAYER—228d.

1884. **ἐπαρκέω** {3x} **ĕparkĕō,** *ep-ar-keh'-o;* from *1909* and *714;* to *avail for,* i.e. *help:*—relieve {3x}.

Eparkeo signifies to be strong enough for and so to ward off or to aid, to relieve (1 Tim 5:10, 16, 16). See: BAGD—283c; THAYER—229a.

1885. **ἐπαρχία** {2x} **ĕparchia,** *ep-ar-khee'-ah* or ἐπαρχεία **ĕparchĕia,** *ep-ar-khi'-ah;* from a compound of *1909* and *757* (mean. a *governor* of a district, "eparch"); a special *region* of government, i.e. a Roman *præfecture:*—province {2x}.

Eparcheia, or *eparchia,* was a technical term for the administrative divisions of the Roman Empire. The original meaning was the district within which a magistrate, whether consul or pretor, exercised supreme authority. The "province" mentioned in Acts 23:34 and 25:1 was assigned to the jurisdiction of an eparchos, "a prefect or governor." See: BAGD—283c; THAYER—229a.

1886. **ἔπαυλις** {1x} **ĕpaulis,** *ep'-ŏw-lis;* from *1909* and an equiv. of *833;* a *hut over* the head, i.e. a *dwelling:* —habitation {1x}. See: BAGD—283d; THAYER—229b.

1887. **ἐπαύριον** {17x} **ĕpauriŏn,** *ep-ow'-ree-on;* from *1909* and *839;* occurring *on* the *succeeding* day, i.e. (*2250* being implied) *to-morrow:*—morrow {7x}, next day {6x}, day following {2x}, next day after {1x}, morrow after {1x}. See: BAGD—283d; THAYER—229b.

1888. **ἐπαυτοφώρῳ** {1x} **ĕpautŏphōrōi,** *ep-ow-tof-o'-ro;* from *1909* and *846* and (the dat. sing. of) a der. of φώρ **phōr** (a *thief*); *in theft itself,* i.e. (by anal.) *in actual crime:*—in the very act {1x}. See: BAGD—124a; THAYER—229b.

1889. **Ἐπαφρᾶς** {3x} **Ĕpaphras,** *ep-af-ras';* contr. from *1891; Epaphras,* a Chr.:—*Epaphras* {3x}. See: BAGD—283d; THAYER—229b.

1890. **ἐπαφρίζω** {1x} **ĕpaphrizō,** *ep-af-rid'-zo;* from *1909* and *875;* to *foam upon,* i.e. (fig.) to *exhibit* (a vile passion):—foam out {1x}.

This word is used metaphorically in Jude 13, of the impious libertines, who had crept in among the saints, and "foamed" out their own shame with swelling words; i.e. the refuse borne on the crest of waves and cast up on the beach. See: BAGD—283d; THAYER—229b.

1891. **Ἐπαφρόδιτος** {3x} **Ĕpaphrŏditŏs,** *ep-af-rod'-ee-tos;* from *1909* (in the sense of *devoted* to) and Ἀφροδίτη **Aphrŏditē** (*Venus*); *Epaphroditus,* a Chr.:—Epaphroditus {3x}. See: BAGD—284a; THAYER—229c. comp. *1889.*

1892. **ἐπεγείρω** {2x} **ĕpĕgĕirō,** *ep-eg-i'-ro;* from *1909* and *1453;* to *rouse upon,* i.e. (fig.) to *excite* against:—raise {1x}, stir up {1x}.

Epegeiro, as a verb, means "stirred up": "But the unbelieving Jews stirred up the Gentiles, and made their minds evil affected against the brethren" (Acts 14:2). Syn.: 329, 383, 387, 1326, 2042, 3947, 3951, 4531, 4579, 4787, 4797, 5017. See: BAGD—284a; THAYER—229c.

1893. **ἐπεί** {27x} **ĕpĕi,** *ep-i';* from *1909* and *1487;* *thereupon,* i.e. *since* (of time or cause):—because {7x}, otherwise {4x}, for then {3x}, else {3x}, seeing {3x}, forasmuch as {2x}, for that {1x}, misc. {4x} = seeing that, since, when. See: BAGD—284a; THAYER—229c.

1894. **ἐπειδή** {11x} **ĕpĕidē,** *ep-i-day';* from *1893* and *1211;* *since now,* i.e. (of time) *when,* or (of cause) *whereas:*—for {3x}, because {2x}, seeing {2x}, forasmuch as {1x}, after that {1x}, since {1x}, for that {1x}. See: BAGD—284b; THAYER—229c.

1895. **ἐπειδήπερ** {1x} **ĕpĕidēpĕr,** *ep-i-day'-per;* from *1894* and *4007;* *since indeed* (of cause):—forasmuch {1x}. See: BAGD—284b; THAYER—229d.

1896. **ἐπεῖδον** {2x} **ĕpĕidŏn,** *ep-i'-don;* and other moods and persons of the same tense; from *1909* and *1492;* to *regard* (favorably or otherwise):—behold {1x}, look upon {1x}.

Epeidon, as a verb, denotes "to look upon" **(1)** favorably: "Thus hath the Lord dealt with me in the days wherein He looked on *me,* to take away my reproach among men" (Lk 1:25); or **(2)** unfavorably: "And now, Lord, behold (*epeidon*) their threatenings: and grant unto thy servants, that with all boldness they may speak thy word" (Acts 4:29). Syn.: 308, 352, 578, 816, 872, 991, 1689, 1914, 1980, 1983, 2300, 2334, 3706, 3708, 3879, 4017, 4648. See: BAGD—284b; THAYER—229d.

1897. **ἐπείπερ** {1x} **ĕpĕipĕr,** *ep-i'-per;* from *1893* and *4007;* *since* indeed (of cause):—seeing {1x}. See: BAGD—284c; THAYER—229d.

1898. **ἐπεισαγωγή** {1x} **ĕpĕisagōgē,** *ep-ice-ag-o-gay';* from a compound of *1909* and *1521;* a *superintroduction, a bringing in besides, in addition:*—bringing in {1x}.

The word literally means to bring something in and upon (Heb 7:19). See: BAGD—284c; THAYER—230a.

1899. **ἔπειτα** {16x} **ĕpĕita,** *ep'-i-tah;* from *1909* and *1534;* *thereafter:*—after that {4x}, afterward(s) {3x}, then {9x}. See: BAGD—284c; THAYER—230a.

1900. **ἐπέκεινα** {1x} **ĕpĕkĕina,** *ep-ek'-i-nah;* from *1909* and (the acc. plur. neut. of) *1565;* *upon those* parts of, i.e. *on the further side of:*—beyond {1x}. See: BAGD—284d; THAYER—230b.

1901. **ἐπεκτείνομαι** {1x} **ĕpĕktĕinŏmai,** *ep-ek-ti'-nom-ahee;* mid. voice from *1909* and *1614;* to *stretch* (oneself) forward *upon:*—reach forth unto {1x}. See: BAGD—284d; THAYER—230b.

1902. **ἐπενδύομαι** {2x} **ĕpĕnduŏmai,** *ep-en-doo'-om-ahee;* mid. voice from *1909* and *1746;* to *invest upon* oneself:—be clothed upon {2x}.

Ependuo, as a verb, used in the middle voice, "to cause to be put on over, to be clothed upon": "For in this we groan, earnestly desiring to be clothed upon with our house which is from heaven" (2 Cor 5:2; cf, vs 4, of the future spiritual body of the redeemed). Syn.: 294, 1463, 1737, 1746, 2439, 4016. See: TDNT—2:320,*; BAGD—284d; THAYER—230b.

1903. **ἐπενδύτης** {1x} **ĕpĕndutēs,** *ep-en-doo'-tace;* from *1902;* a *wrapper,* i.e. outer garment:—fisher's coat {1x}. See: BAGD—285a; THAYER—230b.

1904. **ἐπέρχομαι** {10x} **ĕpĕrchŏmai,** *ep-er'-khom-ahee;* from *1909* and *2064;* to *supervene,* i.e. *arrive, occur, impend, attack,* (fig.) *influence:*—come {6x}, come upon {2x}, come on {1x}, come thither {1x}. See: TDNT—2:680, 257; BAGD—285a; THAYER—230b.

1905. **ἐπερωτάω** {59x} **ĕpĕrōtaō,** *ep-er-o-tah'-o;* from *1909* and *2065;* to *ask for,* i.e. *inquire, seek:*—ask {53x}, demand {2x}, desire {1x}, ask question {1x}, question {1x}, ask after {1x}.

Due to the prefixed preposition (επι) the asking is intensified and approximates a demand (Lk 2:46; 3:14; 6:9; 17:20). See: TDNT—2:687, 262; BAGD—285b; THAYER—230c.

1906. **ἐπερώτημα** {1x} **ĕpĕrōtēma,** *ep-er-o'-tay-mah;* from *1905;* an *inquiry:*—answer {1x}. See: TDNT—2:688, 262; BAGD—285c; THAYER—230d.

1907. **ἐπέχω** {5x} **ĕpĕchō,** *ep-ekh'-o;* from *1909* and *2192;* to *hold upon,* i.e. (by impl.) to *retain;* (by extens.) to *detain;* (with impl. of *3563*) to *pay attention to:*—mark {1x}, give heed unto {1x}, stay {1x}, hold forth {1x}, take heed unto {1x}.

(1) This word literally means to hold upon; then to direct towards, to give attention to; so thus is rendered "gave heed" (Acts 3:5; 1 Ti 4:16). **(2)** It also signifies "to hold out" **(2a)** Phil 2:16, of the word of life; then, **(2b)** "to hold one's mind towards, to observe," translated "marked" in Lk

14:7, of the Lord's observance of those who chose the chief seats. See: BAGD—285c; THAYER—231a.

1908. **ἐπηρεάζω** {3x} **ĕpērĕazō**, *ep-ay-reh-ad'-zo;* from a comp. of *1909* and (prob.) ἀρειά **arĕia** (*threats*); to *insult, slander:*—despitefully use {2x}, falsely accuse {1x}.

Epereazo, as a verb, has its **(1)** more ordinary meaning "to insult, treat abusively, despitefully": "Bless them that curse you, and pray for them which despitefully use you" (Lk 6:28), and **(2)** has the forensic significance "to accuse falsely": "Having a good conscience; that, whereas they speak evil of you, as of evildoers, they may be ashamed that falsely accuse (*epereazo*) your good conversation in Christ" (1 Pet 3:16). Syn.: 156, 157, 1225, 1458, 1462, 2723, 2724, 4811. See: BAGD—285d; THAYER—221b.

1909. **ἐπί** {895x} **ĕpi**, *ep-ee';* a primary prep.; prop. mean. *superimposition* (of time, place, order, etc.), as a relation of *distribution* [with the gen.], i.e. *over, upon,* etc.; of *rest* (with the dat.) *at, on,* etc.; of *direction* (with the acc.) *toward, upon,* etc.:—on {196x}, in {120x}, upon {159x}, unto {41x}, to {41x}, misc. {338x} = about (the times), above, after, against, among, as long as (touching), at, beside, × have charge of, (be-, [where-])fore, into, (because) of, over, (by, for) the space of, through (-out), toward, with. In compounds it retains essentially the same import, *at, upon,* etc. (lit. or fig.). See: BAGD—285d; THAYER—221b.

1910. **ἐπιβαίνω** {6x} **ĕpibainō**, *ep-ee-bah'-ee-no;* from *1909* and the base of *939;* to *walk upon,* i.e. *mount, ascend, embark, arrive:*—sit {1x}, come {1x}, go aboard {1x}, take + 1519 {1x}, come into {1x}, enter into {1x}.

Epibaino, as a verb, means "sitting upon": "Tell ye the daughter of Sion, Behold, thy King cometh unto thee, meek, and sitting upon an ass, and a colt the foal of an ass" (Mt 21:5). Cf. Acts 20:18; 221:2, 6; 25:1; 27:2. Syn.: 339, 345, 347, 377, 2516, 2521, 2621, 2523, 2625, 4775, 4776, 4873. See: BAGD—289d; THAYER—236a.

1911. **ἐπιβάλλω** {18x} **ĕpiballō**, *ep-ee-bal'-lo;* from *1909* and *906;* to *throw upon* (lit. or fig., tran. or refl.; usually with more or less force); spec. (with *1438* implied) to *reflect;* impers. to *belong to:* lay {8x}, put {3x}, lay on {1x}, beat {1x}, cast on {1x}, think thereon {1x}, fall {1x}, stretch forth {1x}, cast upon {1x}. See: TDNT—1:528, 91; BAGD—289d; THAYER—236b.

1912. **ἐπιβαρέω** {3x} **ĕpibarĕō**, *ep-ee-bar-eh'-o;* from *1909* and *916; to be heavy upon,* i.e. (pecuniarily) to *be expensive to;* fig. to *be severe toward:*—be chargeable to {1x} be chargeable unto {1x}, overcharge {1x}.

Epibareo, "to burden heavily," is said **(1)** of material resources, **(1a)** "be chargeable unto", 1 Th 2:9; **(1b)** "be chargeable to", 2 Th 3:8; **(3)** of the effect of spiritual admonition and discipline, 2 Cor 2:5, "overcharge." See: BAGD—290b; THAYER—236c.

1913. **ἐπιβιβάζω** {3x} **ĕpibibazō**, *ep-ee-bee-bad'-zo;* from *1909* and a redupl. deriv. of the base of *939* [comp. *307*]; to *cause to mount* (an animal):—set on {2x}, set thereon {1x}.

Epibibazo, "to place upon," is used of causing persons to mount animals for riding, Lk 10:34; 19:35; Acts 23:24. See: BAGD—290b; THAYER—236c.

1914. **ἐπιβλέπω** {3x} **ĕpiblĕpō**, *ep-ee-blep'-o;* from *1909* and *991;* to *gaze at* (with favor, pity or partiality):—look upon {1x}, regard {1x}, have respect to {1x}.

Epiblepo, as a verb, means "to look upon" and is used **(1)** of favorable regard: "For He hath regarded the low estate of His handmaiden: for, behold, from henceforth all generations shall call me blessed" (Lk 1:48 of the low estate of the Virgin Mary); **(2)** in a request to the Lord to "look" upon an afflicted son: "And, behold, a man of the company cried out, saying, Master, I beseech thee, look upon my son: for he is mine only child" (Lk 9:38); **(3)** of having a partial regard, respect, for the well-to-do: "And ye have respect to him that weareth the gay clothing, and say unto him, Sit thou here in a good place; and say to the poor, Stand thou there, or sit here under my footstool" (Jas 2:3). Syn.: 308, 352, 578, 816, 872, 991, 1689, 1896, 1980, 1983, 2300, 2334, 3706, 3708, 3879, 4017, 4648. See: BAGD—290b; THAYER—236c.

1915. **ἐπίβλημα** {4x} **ĕpiblēma**, *ep-ib'-lay-mah;* from *1911; a patch:*—piece {4x}.

Epiblema primarily denotes "that which is thrown over, a cover" (*epi*, "over," *ballo*, "to throw"); then, "that which is put on, or sewed on, to cover a rent, a patch," Mt 9:16; Mk 2:21; Lk 5:36 (twice). See: BAGD—290c; THAYER—236d.

1916. **ἐπιβοάω** {1x} **ĕpibŏaō**, *ep-ee-bo-ah'-o;* from *1909* and *994; to exclaim against:*—cry {1x}.

Epiboao, as a verb, [epi, "upon," intensive], means "to cry out, exclaim vehemently" and is used in Acts 25:24: "And Festus said, King Agrippa, and all men which are here present with us, ye see this man, about whom all the multitude of the Jews have dealt with me, both at Jerusalem, and *also* here, crying that he ought not to live any longer." Syn.: 310, 349, 994, 995, 2019, 2896, 2905, 2906, 5455. See: BAGD—290c; THAYER—236d.

1917. **ἐπιβουλή** {4x} **ĕpibŏulē**, *ep-ee-boo-lay';* from a presumed compound of *1909* and *1014;* a *plan against* someone, i.e. a *plot:*—lying in wait {1x}, lay wait for + 1096 {1x}, lay wait + 3195 + 2071 {1x}, - laying await {1x}.

Epiboule, lit., "a plan against" (*epi*, "against," *boule*, "a counsel, plan"), is translated "laying await" and "lying in wait" in Acts 9:24; 20:3, 19; 23:30. See: BAGD—290c; THAYER—236d.

1918. **ἐπιγαμβρεύω** {1x} **ĕpigambrĕuō**, *ep-ee-gam-bryoo'-o;* from *1909* and a der. of *1062;* to *form affinity with,* i.e. (spec.) in a levirate way:—marry {1x}.

Epigambreuo, "to take to wife after" (*epi*, "upon," *gambros*, "a connection by marriage"), signifies "to marry" (of a deceased husband's next of kin, Mt 22:24). See: BAGD—290c; THAYER—236d.

1919. **ἐπίγειος** {7x} **ĕpigĕiŏs**, *ep-ig'-i-os;* from *1909* and *1093; worldly* (phys. or mor.):—earthly {4x}, in earth {1x}, terrestrial {2x}.

Epigeios, "on earth" (*epi*, "on," *ge*, "the earth"), is rendered **(1)** "earthly" in Jn 3:12; 2 Cor 5:1; Phil 3:19; Jas 3:15; **(2)** in Phil 2:10, "in earth"; and **(3)** "terrestrial" in 1 Cor 15:40 (twice). See: TDNT—1:680, 116; BAGD—290c; THAYER—236d.

1920. **ἐπιγίνομαι** {1x} **ĕpiginŏmai**, *ep-ig-in'-om-ahee;* from *1909* and *1096;* to *arrive upon,* i.e. *spring up* (as a wind):—blew {1x}.

In Acts 28:13, *epiginomai*, "to come on," is used of the springing up of a wind, "blew." See: BAGD—290d; THAYER—236a.

1921. **ἐπιγινώσκω** {42x} **ĕpiginōskō**, *ep-ig-in-oce'-ko;* from *1909* and *1097;* to *know upon* some mark, i.e. *recognize;* by impl. to *become fully acquainted with,* to *acknowledge:*—know {30x}, acknowledge {5x}, perceive {3x}, take knowledge of {2x}, have knowledge of {1x}, know well {1x}.

Epiginosko denotes **(1)** "to observe, fully perceive, notice attentively, discern, recognize"; **(1a)** it suggests generally a directive, a more special, recognition of the object "known" than does ginosko (1097); **(1b)** it also may suggest advanced "knowledge" or special appreciation; thus, in Rom 1:32, "knowing the ordinance of God" (*epiginosko*) means "knowing full well," whereas in verse 21 "knowing God" (ginosko) simply suggests that they could not avoid the perception. **(1c)** Sometimes *epiginosko* implies a special participation in the object "known," and gives greater weight to what is stated; thus in Jn 8:32, "ye shall know the truth," ginosko is used, whereas in 1 Ti 4:3, "them that believe and know the truth," *epiginosko* lays stress on participation in the truth. **(1d)** Cf. the stronger statement in Col 1:6 (*epiginosko*) with that in 2 Cor 8:9 (ginosko), and the two verbs in 1 Cor 13:12, "now I know in part (ginosko); but then shall I know (*epiginosko*) even as also I have been known (*epiginosko*)," "a knowledge" which perfectly unites the subject with the object; **(1e)** It also signifies **(1a1)** "to know thoroughly" (*epi* "intensive," *ginosko*, "to know"); **(1a2)** "to recognize a thing to be what it really is, to acknowledge," 1 Cor 14:37; 16:18; 2 Cor 1:13–14;

(2) "to discover, ascertain, determine," **(2a)** e.g., Lk 7:37; 23:7; Acts 9:30; 19:34; 22:29; 28:1; **(2b)** epignosis is "knowledge directed towards a particular object, perceiving, discerning," whereas gnosis (1108) is knowledge in the abstract. Syn.: 1097, 1107, 1110, 1492, 1467, 1922, 1987, 4267. See: TDNT—1:689, 119; BAGD—291a; THAYER—237a.

1922. **ἐπίγνωσις** {20x} **ĕpignōsis**, *ep-ig'-no-sis;* from *1921; recognition,* i.e. (by impl.) full *discernment, acknowledgement:*—knowledge {16x}, acknowledging {3x}, acknowledgement {1x}.

(1) *Epignosis* is the complete comprehension after the first knowledge (gnosis - 1108) of a matter. **(1a)** It is bringing one to be better acquainted with something known previously; a more exact viewing of something beheld before. *Epignosis* denotes **(1b)** "exact or full knowledge, discernment, recognition," and **(1c)** is a strengthened form gnosis expressing a fuller or a full "knowledge," **(1d)** a greater participation by the "knower" in the object "known," thus more powerfully influencing him. **(1e)** It is not found in the Gospels and Acts. **(1f)** Paul uses it 15 times (16 if Heb. 10:26 is included) out of the 20 occurrences; Peter 4 times, all in his 2nd Epistle. **(1g)** Contrast Rom 1:28 (*epignosis*) with the simple verb in v. 21. **(2)** It is used with reference **(2a)** to God in Rom 1:28; 10:2; Eph 1:17; Col 1:10; 2 Pet 1:3; **(2b)** God and Christ, 2 Pet 1:2; **(2c)** Christ, Eph 4:13; 2 Pet 1:8; 2:20; **(2d)** the will of the Lord, Col 1:9; **(2e)** every good thing, Philem 6 "acknowledging"; **(2f)** the truth, 1 Ti 2:4; Col 2:2 "to the acknowledgment of"), lit., "into a full knowledge." **(3)** It is used without the mention of an object in Phil 1:9; Col 3:10. Syn.: 1097, 1107, 1108, 1110, 1492, 1921, 1467, 1922, 1987, 4678, 5428. See: TDNT—1:689, 119; BAGD—291b; THAYER—237b.

1923. **ἐπιγραφή** {5x} **ĕpigraphē**, *ep-ig-raf-ay';* from *1924;* an *inscription:*—superscription {5x}.

Epigraphe, lit., "an overwriting" (epi, "over," grapho, "to write") (the meaning of the anglicized Latin word "superscription"), denotes **(1)** "an inscription, a title." **(2)** On Roman coins the emperor's name was inscribed, Mt 22:20; Mk 12:16; Lk 20:24. **(3)** In the Roman Empire, in the case of a criminal on his way to execution, a board on which was inscribed the cause of his condemnation, was carried before him or hung round his neck; the inscription was termed a "title" (titlos). **(3a)** The four Evangelists state that at the crucifixion of Christ the title was affixed to the cross, Mk 15:26, and Lk (23:38), call it a "superscription"; Mk says it was "written over" (epigrapho, the corresponding verb). Matthew calls it "His accusation"; John calls it "a title" (a technical term). **(3b)** The wording varies: the essential words are the same, and the variation serves to authenticate the narratives, showing that each evangelist wrote separate but complementary details of the account to present a complete picture. See: BAGD—291c; THAYER—237c.

1924. **ἐπιγράφω** {5x} **ĕpigraphō**, *ep-ee-graf'-o;* from *1909* and *1125;* to *inscribe* (phys. or ment.):—write {2x}, write over {1x}, write thereon {1x}, with this inscription + 1722 + 3639 {1x}.

Epigrapho, "to write upon, inscribe" (*epi,* "upon," *grapho,* "to write"), is usually rendered **(1)** by the verb "to write upon, over, or in," Mk 15:26; Heb 8:10; 10:16; Rev 21:12; **(2)** it is translated by a noun phrase in Acts 17:23, "(with this) inscription," lit., "(on which) had been inscribed." See: BAGD—291c; THAYER—237c.

1925. **ἐπιδείκνυμι** {9x} **ĕpidĕiknumi**, *ep-ee-dike'-noo-mee;* from *1909* and *1166;* to *exhibit* (phys. or ment.):—shew {9x}.

(1) This words means to bring forth to view, to show, to furnish to be looked at, to produce what may looked at. **(2)** It signifies **(2a)** "to exhibit, display," Mt 16:1; 22:19; 24:1; Lk 17:14; 24:40; **(2b)** in the middle voice, "to display," with a special interest in one's own action, Acts 9:39; **(3)** "to point out, prove, demonstrate," Acts 18:28; Heb 6:17. See: BAGD—291d; THAYER—237d.

1926. **ἐπιδέχομαι** {2x} **ĕpidĕchŏmai**, *ep-ee-dekh'-om-ahee;* from *1909* and *1209;* to *admit* (as a guest or [fig.] teacher):—receive {2x}.

Epidechomai, as a verb, means literally "to accept besides, to receive" and is used in the sense **(1)** of accepting in 3 Jn 9: "I wrote unto the church: but Diotrephes, who loveth to have the preeminence among them, receiveth (*epidechomai*) us not"; **(2)** and in 3 Jn 10 in the sense of "receiving" with hospitality: "Wherefore, if I come, I will remember his [Diotrephes'] deeds which he doeth, prating against us with malicious words: and not content therewith, neither doth he himself receive (*epidechomai*) the brethren, and forbiddeth them that would, and casteth *them* out of the church." Syn.: 324, 353, 354, 568, 588, 618, 1209, 1523, 2210, 2865, 2975, 2983, 3028, 3335, 3336, 3858, 3880, 3970, 4327, 4355, 4356, 4380, 4381, 4382, 5562, 5264, 5274. See: BAGD—292a; THAYER—237d.

1927. **ἐπιδημέω** {2x} **ĕpidēmĕō**, *ep-ee-day-meh'-o;* from a compound of *1909* and *1218;* to *make oneself at home,* i.e. (by extens.) to *reside* (in a foreign country):—[be] dwelling (which were) there {1x}, stranger {1x}.

Epidemeo means to be a sojourner of a foreign resident, among any people, in any country, Acts 2:10; 17:21. See: BAGD—292a; THAYER—237d.

1928. **ἐπιδιατάσσομαι** {1x} **ĕpidiatassŏmai**, *ep-ee-dee-ah-tas'-som-ahee;* mid. voice from *1909* and *1299;* to *appoint besides,* i.e. *supplement* (as a codicil):—add to {1x}.

Epidiatassomai, lit., "to arrange in addition" (*epi,* "upon," *dia,* "through," *tasso,* "to arrange"), is used in Gal 3:15 ("addeth," or rather, "ordains something in addition"). If no one does such a thing in the matter of a human covenant, how much more is a covenant made by God inviolable! The Judaizers by their "addition" violated this principle, and, by proclaiming the divine authority for what they did, they virtually charged God with a breach of promise. He gave the Law, indeed, but neither in place of the promise nor to supplement it. See: BAGD—292b; THAYER—238a.

1929. **ἐπιδίδωμι** {11x} **ĕpididōmi**, *ep-ee-did'-o-mee;* from *1909* and *1325;* to *give over* (by hand or surrender):—give {7x}, deliver {1x}, offer {1x}, let drive + 5342 {1x}, deliver unto {1x}.

Epididomi signifies **(1)** "to give by handing, to hand" (*epi,* "over"), e.g., Mt 7:9, 10; Lk 11:11 (twice), 12; **(1a)** cf. Lk 4:17; 24:30, here of the Lord's act in "handing" the broken loaf to the two at Emmaus, an act which was the means of the revelation of Himself as the crucified and risen Lord; **(2)** of the "delivering" of the epistle from the elders at Jerusalem to the church at Antioch, Acts 15:30; **(3)** in Lk 11:12, "to give" (*epi,* "over," in the sense of "instead of"), is translated "will he offer"; **(4)** "to give in, give way," Acts 27:15, "let drive" of the ship by the wind; **(5)** "to give upon or in addition," as from oneself to another, hence, "to deliver over unto," is used of the "delivering" of the roll of Isaiah to Christ in the synagogue, "And there was delivered unto Him the book of the prophet Esaias. And when He had opened the book, He found the place where it was written" (Lk 4:17). Syn.: 325, 525, 629, 591, 859, 1325, 1560, 1659, 1807, 3086, 3860, 4506, 5483. See: BAGD—292b; THAYER—238a.

1930. **ἐπιδιορθόω** {1x} **ĕpidiŏrthŏō**, *ep-ee-dee-or-thŏ'-o;* from *1909* and a der. of *3717;* to *straighten further,* i.e. (fig.) *arrange additionally:*—set in order {1x}.

This word is used in Titus 1:5, in the sense of setting right again what was defective, a commission to Titus, not to add to what the apostle himself had done, but to restore what had fallen into disorder since the apostle had labored in Crete; this is suggested by the *epi.* See: BAGD—292b; THAYER—238a

1931. **ἐπιδύω** {1x} **ĕpiduō**, *ep-ee-doo'-o;* from *1909* and *1416;* to *set* fully (as the sun):—go down {1x}.

Epiduo, signifies "to go down," and is said of the sun in Eph 4:26; i.e., put wrath away before sunset. See: BAGD—292c; THAYER—238a.

1932. **ἐπιείκεια** {2x} **ĕpiĕikĕia**, *ep-ee-i'-ki-ah;* from *1933; suitableness,* i.e. (by impl.) *equity, mildness:*—clemency {1x}, gentleness {1x}.

This word suggests "sweet reasonableness", is translated "clemency" in Acts 24:4; elsewhere, in 2 Cor 10:1, of the gentleness of Christ. It refers to the sort of moderation that recognizes that it is impossible for formal laws to anticipate and provide for all possible cases. It rectifies and redresses the injustices of justice; a correction of the law where law falls short on account of generalities. God remembers we are but dust and deals with us accordingly [cf. Ps 103:10]; expecting us to treat others as He has treated us (Mt 18:23; Eph 4:32). Syn.: 4236. See: TDNT—2:588, 243; BAGD—292c; THAYER—238a.

1933. **ἐπιεικής** {5x} **ĕpiĕikēs**, *ep-ee-i-kace';* from *1909* and *1503; appropriate,* i.e. (by impl.) *mild:*—gentle {3x}, moderation {1x}, patient {1x}.

Epieikes, an adjective (from *epi,* used intensively, and *eikos,* "reasonable"), denotes **(1)** "seemly, fitting"; hence, "equitable, fair, moderate, forbearing, not insisting on the letter of the law"; **(2)** it expresses that considerateness that looks "humanely and reasonably at the facts of a case"; **(3)** it is rendered **(3a)** "patient" in 1 Ti 3:3, in contrast to contentiousness; **(3b)** "gentle," **(3b1)** in Titus 3:2, in association with meekness, **(3b2)** in Jas 3:17, as a quality of the wisdom from above, and **(3b3)** in 1 Pet 2:18, in association with the good; **(4)** it is used as a noun with the article in Phil 4:5, and translated "moderation," not going to the extremes. See: TDNT—2:588, 243; BAGD—292c; THAYER—238b.

1934. **ἐπιζητέω** {14x} **ĕpizētĕō**, *ep-eed-zay-teh'-o;* from *1909* and *2212;* to *search* (*inquire*) *for;* intens. to *demand,* to *crave:*—seek after {5x}, seek {3x}, desire {3x}, seek for {2x}, enquire {1x}.

Epizeteo, as a verb, means "to seek after" (directive, *epi,* "towards"), and is translated: **(1)** "to seek after", Mt 6:32; 12:39; 16:4; Mk 8:12; Lk 12:30; **(2)** "to seek", Lk 11:29; Heb 11:14; 13:14; **(3)** "desired": **(3a)** "Which was with the deputy of the country, Sergius Paulus, a prudent man; who called for Barnabas and Saul, and desired (*epizeteo*) to hear the word of God" (Acts 13:7); **(3b)** "desire": "Not because I desire a gift: but I desire fruit that may abound to your account" Phil 4:17 (twice); **(4)** "seeketh for", Rom 11:7; Acts 12:19 "sought"; **(5)** "enquire": "But if ye enquire (*epizeteo*) any thing concerning other matters, it shall be determined in a lawful assembly" (Acts 19:39). Syn.: 327, 1567, 2206, 2212, 3713. See: TDNT—2:895, 300; BAGD—292d; THAYER—238b.

1935. **ἐπιθανάτιος** {1x} **ĕpithanatiŏs**, *ep-ee-than-at'-ee-os;* from *1909* and *2288;* doomed to *death:*—appointed to death {1x}.

Epithanatios, as an adjective, means "appointed to death" and is said of the apostles (1 Cor 4:9): "For I think that God hath set forth us the apostles last, as it were appointed to death: for we are made a spectacle unto the world, and to angels, and to men." Syn.: 336, 337, 520, 2288, 2289, 5054. See: BAGD—292d; THAYER—238b.

1936. **ἐπίθεσις** {4x} **ĕpithĕsis**, *ep-ith'-es-is;* from *2007;* an *imposition* (of hands officially):—laying on {3x}, putting on {1x}.

Epithesis means a laying on, and is used **(1)** of the laying on of the apostles' hands accompanied by the impartation of the Holy Spirit in outward demonstration, **(1a)** in the cases of those in Samaria who had believed (Acts 8:18); **(1b)** such supernatural manifestations were signs especially intended to give witness to Jews as to the facts of Christ and the faith, **(1c)** they were thus temporary; **(1d)** there is no record of their continuance after the time and circumstances narrated in Acts 19, **(1e)** nor was the gift delegated by the apostles to others; **(2)** of the similar act by the elders of a church on occasions when a member of a church was set apart for a particular work, having given evidence of qualifications necessary for it, as in the case of Timothy (1 Ti 4:14); **(3)** of the impartation of a spiritual gift through the laying on of the hands of the apostle Paul (2 Ti 1:6). **(4)** The principle underlying the act was that of identification on the part of him who did it with the animal or person upon whom the hands were laid. See: TDNT—8:159, 1176; BAGD—293a; THAYER—238b.

1937. **ἐπιθυμέω** {16x} **ĕpithumĕō**, *ep-ee-thoo-meh'-o;* from *1909* and *2372;* to set the *heart upon,* i.e. *long* for (rightfully or otherwise):—covet {3x}, desire {8x}, would fain {1x}, lust {1x}, lust after {1x}.

Epithumeo, "to fix the desire upon" (*epi,* "upon," used intensively, *thumos,* "passion"), whether things good or bad; hence, translated **(1)** "desire", "to desire earnestly" stresses the inward impulse rather than the object desired, Mt 13:17 of good men, for good things; Lk 16:21 "desiring"; 17:22; 22:15 of the Lord Jesus, "I have desired"; 1 Ti 3:1; Heb 6:11; 1 Pet 1:12 of the holy angels; Rev 9:6 of men to die; **(2)** "covet", "to fix the desire upon" whether things good or bad; hence, "to long for, lust after, covet," is used with the meaning "to covet evilly" in Acts 20:33, of "coveting money and apparel"; cf. Rom 7:7; 13:9 a Ten Commandment; **(3)** "lust", 1 Cor 10:6; Gal 5:17 used of the Holy Spirit against the flesh; Jas 4:2; **(4)** "lust after", Mt 5:28; **(5)** "fain", "to set one's heart upon, desire," is translated "would fain" in Lk 15:16, of the Prodigal Son. See: TDNT—3:168, 339; BAGD—293a; THAYER—238c.

1938. **ἐπιθυμητής** {1x} **ĕpithumētēs**, *ep-ee-thoo-may-tace';* from *1937;* a *craver:*—lust after + 1510 {1x}.

Epithumetes, literally is "a luster after" and is translated in 1 Cor 10:6, in verbal form, "should not lust after." See: TDNT—3:172, 339; BAGD—293b; THAYER—238d.

1939. **ἐπιθυμία** {38x} **ĕpithumia**, *ep-ee-thoo-mee'-ah;* from *1937;* a *longing* (espec. for what is forbidden):—concupiscence {3x}, desire {3x}, lust {31x}, lust after {1x}.

(1) This word stresses the lust, craving, longing, or desire for what is usually forbidden. It refers to the whole world of active lusts and desires—to all that the sarx (4561) as the seat of desires and the natural appetites impels. **(2)** Concupiscence is an irrational longing for pleasure, "unbridled lust." *Epithumia,* as a noun, means "a desire, craving, longing, mostly of evil desires," frequently translated "lust," is used in the following, **(3)** of good "desires": **(3a)** of the Lord's "wish" concerning the last Passover, Lk 22:15, **(3b)** of Paul's "desire" to be with Christ, Phil 1:23; **(3c)** of his "desire" to see the saints at Thessalonica again, 1 Th 2:17. **(4)** With regard to evil "desires," **(4a)** "concupiscence" in Rom 7:8; Col 3:5; 1 Th 4:5; **(4b)** In Rom 6:12 the injunction against letting sin reign in our mortal body to obey the "lust" thereof, refers to those evil desires which are ready to express themselves in bodily activity. **(4c)** They are equally the "lusts" of the flesh, Rom 13:14; Gal 5:16, 24; Eph 2:3; 2 Pet 2:18; 1 Jn 2:16, a phrase which describes the emotions of the soul, the natural tendency towards things evil. **(4d)** Such "lusts" are not necessarily base and immoral, they may be refined in character, but are evil if inconsistent with the will of God.

(5) Other descriptions besides those already mentioned are:—lusts: **(5a)** "of the mind," Eph 2:3; **(5b)** "evil (desire)," Col. 3:5; **(5c)** "the passion of," 1 Th 4:5; **(5d)** "foolish and hurtful," 1 Ti 6:9; **(5e)** "youthful," 2 Ti 2:22; **(5f)** "divers," 2 Ti 3:6 and Titus 3:3; **(5g)** "their own," 2 Ti 4:3; 2 Pet 3:3; Jude 16; **(5h)** "worldly," Titus 2:12; **(5i)** "his own," Jas 1:14; **(5j)** "your former," 1 Pet 1:14; **(5k)** "fleshly," 1 Pet 2:11; **(5l)** "of men," 1 Pet 4:2; **(5m)** "of defilement," 2 Pet 2:10; **(5n)** "of the eyes," 1 Jn 2:16; **(5o)** of the world ("thereof"), Jn 2:17; **(5p)** "their own ungodly," Jude 18. Syn.: *Epithumia* is the more comprehensive term, including all manner of "lusts and desires"; pathema (3804) denotes suffering; in the passage in Gal 5:17f the sufferings are those produced by yielding to the flesh; pathos points more to the evil state from which "lusts" spring. See: TDNT—3:168, 339; BAGD—293b; THAYER—238d.

1940. **ἐπικαθίζω** {2x} **ĕpikathizō**, *ep-ee-kath-id'-zo;* from *1909* and *2523;* to cause to sit upon; *seat upon:*—set on {2x}. See: BAGD—293d; THAYER—239a.

1941. **ἐπικαλέομαι** {32x} **ĕpikalĕŏmai**, *ep-ee-kal-eh'-om-ahee;* mid. voice from *1909* and *2564;* to *entitle;* by impl. to *invoke* (for aid, worship, testimony, decision, etc.):—call on {7x}, be (one's) surname {6x}, be surnamed {5x}, call upon {4x}, appeal unto {4x}, call {4x}, appeal to {1x}, appeal {1x}.

Epikaleomai means to call upon and has the meaning **(1)** "appeal" in the middle voice, which suggests a special interest on the part of the doer of an action in that in which he is engaged; Stephen died "calling upon the Lord" (Acts 7:59). **(2)** In the more strictly legal sense the word is used only of Paul's appeal to Caesar (Acts 25:11–12, 21, etc.). See: TDNT—3:496,*; BAGD—294a; THAYER—239a.

1942. **ἐπικάλυμα** {1x} **ĕpikaluma**, *ep-ee-kal'-oo-mah;* from *1943;* a *covering,* i.e. (fig.) *pretext:*—cloke {1x}. See: BAGD—294b; THAYER—239c.

1943. **ἐπικαλύπτω** {1x} **ĕpikaluptō**, *ep-ee-kal-oop'-to;* from *1909* and *2572;* to *conceal,* i.e. (fig.) *forgive:*—cover {1x}. See: BAGD—294c; THAYER—239c.

1944. **ἐπικατάρατος** {3x} **ĕpikataratŏs**, *ep-ee-kat-ar'-at-os;* from *1909* and a der. of *2672; imprecated,* i.e. *execrable:*—accursed {3x}.

Epikataratos, as an adjective, means "cursed, accursed accursed, exposed to divine vengeance, lying under God's curse": "For as many as are of the works of the law are under the curse (katara - 2671): for it is written, Cursed (*epikataratos*) *is* every one that continueth not in all things which are written in the book of the law to do them." (Gal 3:10; cf. vs 13; Jn 7:49). Syn.: 331, 332, 685, 2551, 2652, 2653, 2671, 2672. See: TDNT—1:451, 75; BAGD—294c; THAYER—239d.

1945. **ἐπίκειμαι** {7x} **ĕpikĕimai**, *ep-ik'-i-mahee;* from *1909* and *2749;* to *rest upon* (lit. or fig.):—press upon {1x}, be instant {1x}, lie {1x}, be laid thereon {1x}, lie on {1x}, be laid upon {1x}, be imposed on {1x}.

Epikeimai denotes "to be placed on, to lie on," **(1)** literally, **(1a)** as of the stone on the sepulchre of Lazarus, Jn 11:38; **(1b)** of the fish on the fire of coals, Jn 21:9; **(2)** figuratively, **(2a)** of a tempest (to press upon), Acts 27:20; **(2b)** of a necessity laid upon the apostle Paul, 1 Cor 9:16; **(2c)** of the pressure of the multitude upon Christ to hear Him, Lk 5:1, "pressed upon"; **(2d)** of the insistence of the chief priests, rulers and people that Christ should be crucified, Lk 23:23, "were instant"; **(2e)** of carnal ordinances "imposed" under the Law until a time of reformation, brought in through the High Priesthood of Christ, Heb 9:10. See: TDNT—3:655, 425; BAGD—294c; THAYER—239d.

1946. **Ἐπικούρειος** {1x} **Ĕpikŏurĕiŏs**, *ep-ee-koo'-ri-os* or Ἐπικούριος **Ĕpikŏuriŏs**, *ep-ee-koo'-ree-os;* from Ἐπίκουρος **Ĕpikŏurŏs** [comp. *1947*] (a noted philosopher); an *Epicurean* or follower of Epicurus:—Epicurea {1x}. See: BAGD—294d; THAYER—239d.

1947. **ἐπικουρία** {1x} **ĕpikŏuria**, *ep-ee-koo-ree'-ah;* from a compound of *1909* and a (prol.) form of the base of *2877* (in the sense of *servant*); *assistance:*—help {1x}.

This word strictly denotes such aid as is rendered by an *epikouros,* "an ally, an auxiliary"; Paul uses it in his testimony to Agrippa, "having therefore obtained the help that is from God" (Acts 26:22). See: BAGD—294d; THAYER—239d.

1948. **ἐπικρίνω** {1x} **ĕpikrinō**, *ep-ee-kree'-no;* from *1909* and *2919;* to *adjudge:*—give sentence {1x}. See: BAGD—295a; THAYER—240a.

1949. **ἐπιλαμβάνομαι** {19x} **ĕpilambanŏmai**, *ep-ee-lam-ban'-om-ahee;* mid. voice from *1909* and *2983;* to *seize* (for help, injury, attainment, or any other purpose; lit. or fig.):—take {7x}, take by {3x}, catch {2x}, take on {2x}, lay hold on {2x}, take hold of {2x}, lay hold upon {1x}.

Epilambanomai, **(1)** in the middle voice, "to lay hold of, take hold of," is used **(1a)** literally, e.g., Mk 8:23; Lk 9:47; 14:4; **(1b)** metaphorically, e.g., **(1b1)** Heb 8:9, "(I, God) took them (by the hand)"; **(1b2)** Lk 20:20, 26, of taking "hold" of Christ's words; **(1b3)** in Lk 23:26 and Acts 21:33, of laying "hold" of persons; **(1b4)** in 1 Ti 6:12, 19, of laying "hold" on eternal life, i.e., practically appropriating all the benefits, privileges and responsibilities involved in the possession of it; **(1b5)** in Heb 2:16, "He took on"; **(2)** it is translated "caught" in Acts 16:19. See: TDNT—4:9,*; BAGD—295a; THAYER—240a.

1950. **ἐπιλανθάνομαι** {8x} **ĕpilanthanŏmai**, *ep-ee-lan-than'-om-ahee;* mid. voice from *1909* and *2990;* to *lose out* of mind; by impl. to *neglect:*—be forgetful of {1x}, forget {7x}.

Epilanthanomai, "to forget, or neglect" (*epi,* "upon," used intensively), is said **(1)** negatively **(1a)** of God, indicating His remembrance of sparrows, Lk 12:6, and **(1b)** of the work and labor of love of His saints, Heb 6:10; **(2)** of the disciples regarding taking bread, Mt 16:5: Mk 8:14; **(3)** of Paul regarding "the things which are behind," Phil 3:13; **(4)** of believers, **(4a)** as to entertaining strangers, Heb 13:2; **(4b)** and as to doing good and communicating, Heb13:16; **(5)** of a person who after looking at himself in a mirror, forgets what kind of person he is, Jas 1:24. See: BAGD—295b; THAYER—240b.

1951. **ἐπιλέγομαι** {2x} **ĕpilĕgŏmai**, *ep-ee-leg'-om-ahee;* mid. voice from *1909* and *3004;* to *surname, select:*—call {1x}, choose {1x}.

This word means "to call in addition," i.e., by another name besides that already intimated (John 5:2). By extension, in Acts 15:40 Paul named Silas as his traveling companion in the place of Timothy. See: BAGD—295c; THAYER—240b.

1952. **ἐπιλείπω** {1x} **ĕpilĕipō**, *ep-ee-li'-po;* from *1909* and *3007;* to *leave upon,* i.e. (fig.) to *be insufficient for:*—fail {1x}.

This word means not enough to suffice for a purpose and is said of insufficient time (Heb 11:32). See: BAGD—295c; THAYER—240b.

1953. **ἐπιλησμονή** {1x} **ĕpilēsmŏnē**, *ep-ee-lace-mon-ay';* from a der. of *1950; negligence:*—× forgetful {1x}.

(1) This word implies that the person has the necessary information to accomplish a task, but fails to recall it in time to act on it. **(2)** It means "forgetfulness" and is used in Jas 1:25, "a forgetful hearer", "a hearer that forgetteth," lit., "a hearer of forgetfulness," i.e., a hearer characterized by "forgetfulness." See: BAGD—295d; THAYER—240c.

1954. **ἐπίλοιπος** {1x} **ěpilŏipŏs**, *ep-il'-oy-pos;* from *1909* and *3062; left over,* i.e. *remaining:*—rest {1x}.

Epiloipos, signifying "still left, left over", is used in the neuter with the article in 1 Pet 4:2, "the rest (of your time)." See: BAGD—295d; THAYER—240c.

1955. **ἐπίλυσις** {1x} **ěpilusis**, *ep-il'-oo-sis;* from *1956; explanation,* i.e. *application:*—interpretation {1x}.

This word means to loose, solve, explain and denotes a solution, explanation, lit., "a release." In 2 Pet 1:20, "(of private) interpretation"; i.e., the writers of Scripture did not put their own construction upon the "Godbreathed" words they wrote. See: TDNT—4:337, 543; BAGD—295d; THAYER—240c.

1956. **ἐπιλύω** {2x} **ěpiluō**, *ep-ee-loo'-o;* from *1909* and *3089; to solve further,* i.e. (fig.) to *explain, decide:*—determine {1x}, expound {1x}.

Literally, this word means to loosen upon, and denotes **(1)** to solve, expound in Mk 4:34; and **(2)** to settle a controversy in Acts 19:39. See: TDNT—4:337, 543; BAGD—295d; THAYER—240c.

1957. **ἐπιμαρτυρέω** {1x} **ěpimarturěō**, *ep-ee-mar-too-reh'-o;* from *1909* and *3140; to attest further,* i.e. *corroborate:*—testify {1x}.

Epimartureo, to bear witness to, establish by testimony, is rendered "testifying" in 1 Pet 5:12. See: TDNT—4:508, 564; BAGD—296a; THAYER—240c.

1958. **ἐπιμέλεια** {1x} **ěpimělěia**, *ep-ee-mel'-i-ah;* from *1959; carefulness,* i.e. kind *attention* (*hospitality*):—refresh (one's) self + 5177 {1x}.

Epimelei, in the middle voice, means to care for, give attention to one's self, Acts 27:3. See: BAGD—296a; THAYER—240d.

1959. **ἐπιμελέομαι** {3x} **ěpimělěŏmai**, *ep-ee-mel-eh'-om-ahee;* mid. voice from *1909* and the same as *3199; to care for* (phys. or otherwise):—take care of {3x}.

This word signifies to take care of, involving forethought and provision (*epi* indicating "the direction of the mind toward the object cared for"). **(1)** Lk 10:34–35 of the Good Samaritan's care for the wounded man; **(2)** and in 1 Ti 3:5 of a bishop's (or overseer's) care of a church—a significant association of ideas. See: BAGD—296a; THAYER—240d.

1960. **ἐπιμελῶς** {1x} **ěpimělōs**, *ep-ee-mel-oce';* adv. from a der. of *1959; carefully:*—diligently {1x}. See: BAGD—296a; THAYER—240d.

1961. **ἐπιμένω** {18x} **ěpiměnō**, *ep-ee-men'-o;* from *1909* and *3306; to stay over,* i.e. *remain* (fig. *persevere*):—tarry {7x}, continue in {5x}, continue {2x}, abide {2x}, abide in {1x}, abide still {1x}.

Epimeno is a strengthened form of *meno* [3306] (*epi,* "intensive"), indicating **(1)** perseverance in continuing, whether **(1a)** in evil (Rom 6:1; 11:23), or **(1b)** good (Rom 11:22; 1 Ti 4:16). **(2)** It also means to abide, continue, and is translated "to tarry" in Acts 10:48; 21:4, 10; 28:12, 14; 1 Cor 16:7, 8; Gal. 1:18, "abode"; **(3)** It also "to remain on," i.e., in addition to (*epi,* "upon," and No. 3), "to continue long, still to abide," is used of "continuing"**(3a)** to ask, Jn 8:7; **(3b)** to knock, Acts 12:16; **(3c)** in the grace of God, Acts 13:43; **(3d)** in sin, Rom 6:1; **(3e)** in God's goodness, Rom 11:22; **(3f)** in unbelief, Rom 11:23 "abide"); **(3g)** in the flesh, Phil 1:24; **(3h)** in the faith, Col 1:23; **(3i)** in doctrine, 1 Ti 4:16. See: BAGD—296b; THAYER—240d.

1962. **ἐπινεύω** {1x} **ěpiněuō**, *ep-een-yoo'-o;* from *1909* and *3506; to nod at,* i.e. (by impl.) to *assent:*—consent {1x}. See: BAGD—296c; THAYER—241a.

1963. **ἐπίνοια** {1x} **ěpinŏia**, *ep-in'-oy-ah;* from *1909* and *3563; attention* of the mind, i.e. (by impl.) *purpose:*—thought {1x}. See: BAGD—296c; THAYER—241a.

1964. **ἐπιορκέω** {1x} **ěpiŏrkěō**, *ep-ee-or-keh'-o;* from *1965; to commit perjury:*—forswear (one's) self {1x}.

Epiorkeo signifies "to swear falsely, to undo one's swearing, forswear oneself", Mt 5:33. Forswear means to take an oath to fulfill an event before the event occurs, yet being unable to fulfill the vow when the event does happen. Do not swear ahead of time what you may not be able to fulfill. Cf. 1965. See: TDNT—5:466, 729; BAGD—296d; THAYER—241a.

1965. **ἐπίορκος** {1x} **ěpiŏrkŏs**, *ep-ee'-or-kos;* from *1909* and *3727; on oath,* i.e. (falsely) a *forswearer:*—perjured person {1x}. Cf. 1964 for discussion. See: TDNT—5:466, 729; BAGD—296d; THAYER—241a.

1966. **ἐπιοῦσα** {5x} **ěpiŏusa**, *ep-ee-oo'-sah;* fem. sing. part. of a compound of *1909* and εἶμι **ěimi** (to *go*); *supervening,* i.e. (*2250* or *3571* being expressed or implied) the *ensuing* day or night:—following {2x}, next day {2x}, next {1x}. See: BAGD—96d; THAYER—241a.

1967. **ἐπιούσιος** {2x} **ěpiŏusiŏs**, *ep-ee-oo'-see-os;* perh. from the same as *1966; tomorrow's;* but more prob. from *1909* and a der. of the pres. part. fem. of *1510; for subsistence,* i.e. *needful:*—daily {2x}.

This word is derived from [1909] *epi,* and [1510] *eimi,* "to go" and means (bread) for going on, i.e., for the morrow and after, or (bread) coming (for us). The added *semeron* [4594] "today," i.e., the prayer is to be for bread that suffices for this day and next, so that the mind may conform to Christ's warning against anxiety for the morrow. See: TDNT—2:590, 243; BAGD—296d; THAYER—241a.

1968. **ἐπιπίπτω** {13x} **ěpipiptō**, *ep-ee-pip'-to;* from *1909* and *4098; to embrace* (with affection) or *seize* (with more or less violence; lit. or fig.):—fall {10x}, fall on {1x}, press {1x}, lie {1x}.

Epipipto, "to fall upon", is used **(1)** literally, Mk 3:10, "pressed upon"; Acts 20:10, 37; **(2)** metaphorically, **(2a)** of fear, Lk 1:12; Acts 19:17; Rev. 11:11; **(2b)** reproaches, Rom 15:3; **(2c)** of the Holy Spirit, Acts 8:16; 10:44; 11:15. See: BAGD—297c; THAYER—241c.

1969. **ἐπιπλήσσω** {1x} **ěpiplēssō**, *ep-ee-place'-so;* from *1909* and *4141;* to *chastise,* i.e. (with words) to *upbraid:*—rebuke {1x}.

Epiplesso, "to strike at" (*epi,* "upon" or "at," *plesso*), "to strike, smite", to strike upon, beat upon, to chastise with words, to chide, upbraid, rebuke and is used in the injunction against "rebuking" an elder, 1 Ti 5:1. See: BAGD—297d; THAYER—241d.

1970. **ἐπιπνίγω** {1x} **ěpipnigō**, *ep-ee-pnee'-go;* from *1909* and *4155;* to *throttle upon,* i.e. (fig.) *overgrow:*—choke {1x}. See: BAGD—679d [4155]; THAYER—231b [1901] + 524a [4155].

1971. **ἐπιποθέω** {9x} **ěpipŏthěō**, *ep-ee-poth-eh'-o;* from *1909* and ποθέω **pŏthěō** (to *yearn*); to *dote upon,* i.e. *intensely crave* possession (lawfully or wrongfully):—greatly desire {2x}, long {1x}, earnestly desire {1x}, long after {1x}, greatly long after {1x}, lust {1x}, desire {1x}, longed after + 2258 {1x}.

Epipotheo, "to long for greatly", is translated **(1)** "I long," in Rom 1:11; **(2)** in 2 Cor 5:2, "earnestly desiring"; **(3)** in 1 Th 3:6 and 2 Ti 1:4, "desiring greatly"; **(4)** to long after, in 2 Cor 9:14; Phil 1:8; 2:26; **(5)** to long for, in 1 Pet 2:2, "desire"; **(6)** Jas 4:5, "long." See: BAGD—297d; THAYER—241d.

1972. **ἐπιπόθησις** {2x} **ěpipŏthēsis**, *ep-ee-poth'-ay-sis;* from *1971;* a *longing for:*—earnestly desire {1x}, vehemently desire {1x}. Cf. 2 Cor 7:7, 11. See: BAGD—298a; THAYER—242a.

1973. **ἐπιπόθητος** {1x} **ěpipŏthētŏs**, *ep-ee-poth'-ay-tos;* from *1909* and a der. of the latter part of *1971; yearned upon,* i.e. *greatly loved:*—longed for {1x}. See: BAGD—298a; THAYER—242a.

1974. **ἐπιποθία** {1x} **ěpipŏthia**, *ep-ee-poth-ee'-ah;* from *1971; intense longing:*—great desire {1x}. See: BAGD—298a; THAYER—242a.

1975. **ἐπιπορεύομαι** {1x} **ěpipŏrěuŏmai**, *ep-ee-por-yoo'-om-ahee;* from *1909* and *4198; to journey further,* i.e. *travel on* (reach):—come {1x}.

Epiporeuomai, "to travel or journey to a place" is translated "were come [resorted]" in Lk 8:4. See: BAGD—298a; THAYER—242a.

1976. **ἐπιῤῥάπτω** {1x} **ěpirrhaptō**, *ep-ir-hrap'-to;* from *1909* and the base of *4476; to stitch upon,* i.e. *fasten* with the needle:—sew on {1x}. See: BAGD—298a; THAYER—242a.

1977. **ἐπιῤῥίπτω** {2x} **ěpirrhiptō**, *ep-ir-hrip'-to;* from *1909* and *4496;* to *throw upon* (lit. or fig.):—cast upon {2x}.

Epirrhipto, "to cast upon," means **(1)** lit., "of casting garments on a colt," Lk 19:35; **(2)** figuratively, "of casting care upon God," 1 Pet 5:7. See: TDNT—6:991, 987; BAGD—298b; THAYER—242a.

1978. **ἐπίσημος** {2x} **ěpisēmŏs**, *ep-is'-ay-mos;* from *1909* and some form of the base of *4591; remarkable,* i.e. (fig.) *eminent:*—notable {1x}, of note {1x}.

This word means having a mark on it, marked, stamped, coined; **(1)** in a good sense [of note, illustrious]; **(2)** in a bad sense [notorious, infamous]. *Episemos,* primarily meant "bearing a mark," e.g., of money "stamped, coined"; it is used in the NT, metaphorically, **(1)** in a good sense, Rom 16:7, "of note, illustrious," said of Andronicus and Junias; **(2)** in a bad sense, Mt 27:16, "notable," of the prisoner Barabbas. See: TDNT—7:267, 1015; BAGD—298b; THAYER—242a.

1979. **ἐπισιτισμός** {1x} **ěpisitismŏs**, *ep-ee-sit-is-mos';* from a compound of *1909* and a der. of *4621;* a *provisioning,* i.e. (concr.) *food:*—victuals {1x}. See: BAGD—298c; THAYER—242b.

1980. **ἐπισκέπτομαι** {10x} **ěpiskěptŏmai**, *ep-ee-skep'-tom-ahee;* mid. voice from *1909* and the base of *4649; to inspect,* i.e. (by impl.) to *select;* by extens. to *go to see, relieve:*—look out {1x}, visit {10x}.

Episkeptomai, as a verb, means "to visit," and has the meaning of "seeking out," and is rendered "look ye out": primarily, "to inspect" ("to look upon, care for, exercise oversight"), and **(1)** signifies **(1a)** "to visit" with help, of the act of God, Lk 1:68, 78; 7:16; Acts 15:14; Heb 2:6; **(1b)** "to visit" the sick and afflicted, Mt 25:36, 43; Jas 1:27; **(1c)** "to go and see," "pay a visit to," Acts 7:23; 15:36; **(1d)** "to look out" certain men for a purpose, Acts 6:3; **(2)** it has the meaning of "seeking out," and is rendered "look ye out" in Acts 6:3 "Wherefore, brethren, look ye out among you seven men of honest report, full of the Holy Ghost and wisdom" (Acts 6:3). Syn.: 308, 352, 578, 816, 872, 991, 1689, 1896, 1914, 1983, 2300, 2334, 3706, 3708, 3879, 4017, 4648. See: TDNT—2:599, 244; BAGD—298d; THAYER—242b.

1981. **ἐπισκηνόω** {1x} **ĕpiskēnŏō**, *ep-ee-skay-nŏ'-o;* from *1909* and *4637;* to *tent upon,* i.e. (fig.) *abide with:*—rest upon {1x}.

Episkenoo "to spread a tabernacle over" (*epi,* "upon," *skene,* "a tent"), is used metaphorically in 2 Cor 12:9, "may rest upon (me)", "cover," "spread a tabernacle over." See: TDNT—7:386, 1040; BAGD—298d; THAYER—242c.

1982. **ἐπισκιάζω** {5x} **ĕpiskiazō**, *ep-ee-skee-ad'-zo;* from *1909* and a der. of *4639;* to *cast a shade upon,* i.e. (by anal.) to *envelop* in a haze of brilliancy; fig. to *invest* with preternatural influence:—overshadow {5x}.

From a vaporous cloud that casts a shadow the word is transferred to a shining cloud surrounding and enveloping persons with brightness. **(1)** Used of the Holy Spirit exerting creative energy upon the womb of the virgin Mary and impregnating it (Lk 1:35); a use of the word which seems to have been drawn from the familiar OT idea of a cloud as symbolising the immediate presence and power of God. It is used **(2)** of the bright cloud at the Transfiguration, Mt 17:5; Mk 9:7; Lk 9:34; **(3)** of the apostle Peter's shadow upon the sick, Acts 5:15. See: TDNT—7:399, 1044; BAGD—298d; THAYER—242c.

1983. **ἐπισκοπέω** {2x} **ĕpiskŏpĕō**, *ep-ee-skop-eh'-o;* from *1909* and *4648;* to *oversee;* by impl. to *beware:*—look diligently {1x}, take the oversight {1x}.

Episkopeo, as a verb, means literally "to look upon" and is rendered **(1)** "looking carefully/diligently": "Looking diligently lest any man fail of the grace of God" (Heb 12:15, epi being probably intensive here); and **(2)** "to exercise the oversight, to visit, care for": "Feed the flock of God which is among you, taking the oversight *thereof,* not by constraint, but willingly" (1 Pet 5:2). Syn.: 308, 352, 578, 816, 872, 991, 1689, 1896, 1914, 1980, 2300, 2334, 3706, 3708, 3879, 4017, 4648. See: TDNT—2:599, 244; BAGD—298d; THAYER—242d.

1984. **ἐπισκοπή** {4x} **ĕpiskŏpē**, *ep-is-kop-ay';* from *1980; inspection* (for relief); by impl. *superintendence;* spec., the Chr. "*episcopate*":—the office of a bishop {1x}, bishoprick {1x}, visitation {2x}.

(1) This word expresses that act by which God looks into and searches out the ways, deeds, and character of men in order to adjudge them their lot accordingly, whether joyous or sad; and by extension the role of the bishop within the local church. Besides its meaning, **(2)** "visitation," e.g., 1 Pet 2:12, it is rendered **(3)** "office," in Acts 1:20, "bishoprick"; and **(4)** in 1 Tim 3:1 "the office of a bishop," lit., "(if any one seeketh) overseership." See: TDNT—2:606, 244; BAGD—299a; THAYER—242d.

1985. **ἐπίσκοπος** {7x} **ĕpiskŏpŏs**, *ep-is'-kop-os;* from *1909* and *4649* (in the sense of *1983*); a *superintendent,* i.e. Chr. officer in general charge of a (or the) church (lit. or fig.):—bishop {6x}, overseer {1x}.

Episkopos is translated **(1)** "bishop" in Phil 1:1; 1 Ti 3:2; Titus 1:7; 3:15; 1 Pet 2:25; and **(2)** "overseer" in Acts 20:28. See: TDNT—2:608, 244; BAGD—299b; THAYER—243a.

1986. **ἐπισπάομαι** {1x} **ĕpispaŏmai**, *ep-ee-spah'-om-ahee;* from *1909* and *4685;* to *draw over,* i.e. (with *203* impl.) *efface* the mark of *circumcision* (by recovering with the foreskin):—become uncircumcised {1x}. See: BAGD—299d; THAYER—243a.

1987. **ἐπίσταμαι** {14x} **ĕpistamai**, *ep-is'-tam-ahee;* appar. a mid. voice of *2186* (with *3563* implied); to *put* the mind *upon,* i.e. *comprehend,* or *be acquainted with:*—know {13x}, understand {1x}.

Epistamai, "to know, know of, understand" is used **(1)** in Mk 14:68, "understand," which follows oida "I (neither) know"; and translated **(2)** "know" most frequently in the Acts, 10:28; 15:7; 18:25; 19:15, 25; 20:18; 22:19; 24:10; 26:26; **(3)** elsewhere, 1 Ti 6:4; Heb 11:8; Jas 4:14; Jude 10. Syn.: 1097, 1107, 1110, 1492, 1921, 1467, 1922, 1987. See: BAGD—300a; THAYER—243b.

1988. **ἐπιστάτης** {7x} **ĕpistatēs**, *ep-is-tat'-ace;* from *1909* and a presumed der. of *2476;* an *appointee over,* i.e. *commander* (*teacher*):—Master {7x}.

It is used by the disciples in addressing the Lord, in recognition of His authority rather than His instruction, Lk 5:5; 8:24 (twice), 45; 9:33, 49; 17:13. See: TDNT—2:622, 248; BAGD—300b; THAYER—243c.

1989. **ἐπιστέλλω** {3x} **ĕpistĕllō**, *ep-ee-stel'-lo;* from *1909* and *4724;* to *enjoin* (by writing), i.e. (gen.) to *communicate by letter* (for any purpose):—write {1x}, write unto {1x}, write a letter unto {1x}.

Epistello denotes "to send a message by letter, to write word" (*stello,* "to send"; Eng., "epistle"), Acts 15:20; 21:25; Heb. 13:22. See: TDNT—7:593, 1074; BAGD—300c; THAYER—243c.

1990. **ἐπιστήμων** {1x} **ĕpistēmōn**, *ep-ee-stay'-mone;* from *1987; intelligent:*—endued with knowledge {1x}.

This person is intelligent, experienced, and one having the knowledge of an expert, Jas 3:13. See: BAGD—300c; THAYER—243d.

1991. **ἐπιστηρίζω** {4x} **ĕpistērizō**, *ep-ee-stay-rid'-zo;* from *1909* and *4741;* to *support further,* i.e. *reestablish:*—confirm {3x}, strengthen {1x}.

(1) This word means to make to lean upon, and thus to strengthen through support. It is used of **(2)** "confirming" souls, Acts 14:22, **(2)** brethren, Acts 15:32; **(3)** churches, Acts 15:41; **(4)** disciples, Acts 18:23. See: TDNT—7:653, 1085; BAGD—300d; THAYER—243d.

1992. **ἐπιστολή** {24x} **ĕpistŏlē**, *ep-is-tol-ay';* from *1989;* a *written message:*—epistle {15x}, letter {9x}.

Epistole, primarily "a message" (from epistello, "to send to"), hence, "a letter, an epistle," is used **(1)** in the singular, e.g., Acts 15:30; **(2)** in the plural, e.g., Acts 9:2; 2 Cor 10:10. **(3)** Epistle is a less common word for a letter. A letter affords a writer more freedom, both in subject and expression, than does a formal treatise. A letter is usually occasional, that is, it is written in consequence of some circumstance which requires to be dealt with promptly. The style of a letter depends largely on the occasion that calls it forth. **(4)** A broad line is to be drawn between the letter and the epistle. The letter is essentially a spontaneous product dominated throughout by the image of the reader, his sympathies and interests, instinct also with the writer's own soul: it is virtually one half of an imaginary dialogue, the suppressed responses of the other party shaping the course of what is actually written. The epistle has a general aim, addressing all and sundry whom it may concern: it is like a public speech and looks towards publication. **(5)** In 2 Pet 3:16 the apostle includes the Epistles of Paul as part of the God-breathed Scriptures. See: TDNT—7:593, 1074; BAGD—300d; THAYER—243d.

1993. **ἐπιστομίζω** {1x} **ĕpistŏmizō**, *ep-ee-stom-id'-zo;* from *1909* and *4750;* to put something *over* the *mouth,* i.e. (fig.) to *silence:*—stop mouths {1x}. See: BAGD—301a; THAYER—243d.

1994. **ἐπιστρέφω** {39x} **ĕpistrĕphō**, *ep-ee-stref'-o;* from *1909* and *4762;* to *revert* (lit., fig. or mor.):—turn {16x}, be converted {6x}, return {6x}, turn about {4x}, turn again {3x}, misc. {4x} = come (go) again.

Epistrepho, as a verb, means "to turn about," or "towards" and is translated **(1)** "to return": "Then he [a demon] saith, I will return into my house from whence I came out; and when he is come, he findeth *it* empty, swept, and garnished", Mt 12.44, cf. 24:18; Mk 13:16 "turn back again"; Lk 2:39; 8:55, "came again"; 17:31; Acts 15:36 "go again." **(2)** It also denotes **(2a)** "to make to turn towards", Lk 1:16, 17; Jas 5:19, 20 (to convert); **(2b)** intransitively, "to turn oneself round," e.g., **(2b1)** in the passive voice, Mk 5:30; **(2b2)** in the active voice, Mt 13:15, "be converted"; Acts 11:21; 14:15; 15:19; 1 Th 1:9, "ye turned," indicating an immediate and decisive change, consequent upon a deliberate choice; conversion is a voluntary act in response to the presentation of truth. Syn.: 344, 360, 390, 1880, 1877, 5290. See: TDNT—7:722, 1093; BAGD—301a; THAYER—243d.

1995. **ἐπιστροφή** {1x} **ĕpistrŏphe**, *ep-is-trof-ay';* from *1994; reversion,* i.e. mor. *revolution:*—conversion {1x}.

This word means a turning about, or round, conversion (Acts 15:3). The word implies a turning and a turning from; corresponding to these are faith and repentance; cf. "turned to God from idols" (1 Th 1:9). Divine grace is the efficient cause, human agency the responding effect. See: TDNT—7:722, 1093; BAGD—301c; THAYER—244a.

1996. **ἐπισυνάγω** {7x} **ĕpisunagō**, *ep-ee-soon-ag'-o;* from *1909* and *4863;* to *collect upon* the same place:—gather {2x}, gather together {5x}.

Episunago "to gather together," suggesting stress upon the place at which the "gathering" is made, is said **(1)** of a hen and her chickens, Mt 23:37; and so of the Lord's would-be protecting care of the people of Jerusalem; cf. Lk 13:34; **(2)** of the "gathering" together of the elect, Mt 24:31; Mk 13:27; **(3)** of the "gathering" together of a crowd, Mk 1:33; Lk 12:1. See: BAGD—301c; THAYER—244b.

1997. **ἐπισυναγωγή** {2x} **ĕpisunagōgē**, *ep-ee-soon-ag-o-gay';* from *1996;* a complete *collection;* spec. a Chr. *meeting* (for worship):—assembling together {1x}, gathering together {1x}.

Episunagoge, "a gathering together," is used in **(1)** 2 Th 2:1, of the "rapture" of the saints; and for **(2)** Heb 10:25, of the "gatherings" of believers on earth during the present period. See: TDNT—7:841, 1107; BAGD—301d; THAYER—244b.

1998. **ἐπισυντρέχω** {1x} **ĕpisuntrĕchō**, *ep-ee-soon-trekh'-o;* from *1909* and *4936;* to *hasten together upon* one place (or a particular occasion):—come running together {1x}. See: BAGD—301d; THAYER—244b.

1999. **ἐπισύστασις** {2x} **ĕpisustasis**, *ep-ee-soo'-stas-is;* from the mid. voice of a compound of *1909* and *4921;* a *conspiracy,* i.e. *concourse* (riotous or friendly):—that which comes upon {1x}, a raising up + 4060 {1x}.

This word primarily means a stopping, halting (as of soldiers), then, **(1)** an incursion, onset, rush, pressure, a coming upon, 2 Cor 11:28, "Beside those things that are without, that which cometh upon me daily, the care of all the churches" describing the "pressure" or onset due to the constant call upon the apostle for all kinds of help, advice, counsel, exhortation, decisions as to difficulties, disputes, etc. **(2)** The other occurrence of the word is in Acts 24:12, "stirring up, raising", lit. "making a stir." See: BAGD—301d; THAYER—244b.

2000. **ἐπισφαλής** {1x} **ĕpisphalēs**, *ep-ee-sfal-ace';* from a compound of *1909* and σφάλλω **sphallō** (to *trip*); fig. *insecure:*—dangerous {1x}.

This word literally means "prone to fall"; hence, "insecure, dangerous" as in Acts 27:9. See: BAGD—302a; THAYER—244b.

2001. **ἐπισχύω** {1x} **ĕpischuō**, *ep-is-khoo'-o;* from *1909* and *2480;* to *avail further,* i.e. (fig.) *insist stoutly:*—be the more fierce {1x}. See: BAGD—302a; THAYER—244c.

2002. **ἐπισωρεύω** {1x} **ĕpisōrĕuō**, *ep-ee-so-ryoo'-o;* from *1909* and *4987;* to *accumulate further,* i.e. (fig.) *seek* additionally:—heap {1x}.

Episoreuo, "to heap upon" or "together" is used metaphorically in 2 Ti 4:3 of appropriating a number of teachers to suit the liking of those who do the gathering. See: TDNT—7:1094, 1150; BAGD—302a; THAYER—244c.

2003. **ἐπιταγή** {7x} **ĕpitagē**, *ep-ee-tag-ay';* from *2004;* an *injunction* or *decree;* by impl. *authoritativeness:*—authority {1x}, commandment {6x}.

Epitage stresses "the authoritativeness of the command"; **(1)** it is used in Rom 16:26; 1 Cor 7:6, 25; 2 Cor 8:8; 1 Ti 1:1; Titus 1:3; 2:15. It is also **(2)** an injunction (from *epi*, "upon," *tasso*, "to order"), and is once rendered "authority," Titus 2:15. See: TDNT—8:36, 1156; BAGD—302a; THAYER—244c.

2004. **ἐπιτάσσω** {10x} **ĕpitassō**, *ep-ee-tas'-so;* from *1909* and *5021;* to *arrange upon,* i.e. *order:*—charge {1x}, command {8x}, enjoin {1x}.

This word signifies to appoint over, put in charge; then, "to put upon one as a duty, to enjoin" and is translated **(1)** "charge" in Mk 9:25; **(2)** "command" in Mk 1:27; 6:27; 6:39; Lk 4:36; 8:25, 31; 14:22; Acts 23:2; and **(3)** "enjoin" in Philem 8. See: BAGD—302b; THAYER—244c.

2005. **ἐπιτελέω** {11x} **ĕpitĕlĕō**, *ep-ee-tel-eh'-o;* from *1909* and *5055;* to *fulfill further* (or *completely*), i.e. *execute;* by impl. to *terminate, undergo:*—perform {3x}, perfect {2x}, accomplish {2x}, finish {1x}, performance {1x}, make {1x}, do {1x}.

Epiteleo, intensive, is a strengthened form in the sense of "accomplishing." **(1)** The fuller meaning is "to accomplish perfectly"; **(1a)** "performed" in Rom 15:28; **(1b)** "perfecting" in 2 Cor 7:1; **(1c)** "complete" in 2 Cor 8:6 and 11; **(1d)** "performance" in the latter part of this 11th verse; **(1d)** "perfected" in Gal 3:3; **(1e)** "perfect" in Phil 1:6. **(2)** In Heb 8:5 "make," with regard to the tabernacle. **(3)** In Heb 9:6 and in 1 Pet 5:9 it is translated "accomplish." See: TDNT—8:61, 1161; BAGD—302b; THAYER—244c.

2006. **ἐπιτήδειος** {1x} **ĕpitēdĕiŏs**, *ep-ee-tay'-di-os;* from ἐπιτηδές **ĕpitēdēs** (*enough*); *serviceable,* i.e. (by impl.) *requisite:*—things which are needful {1x}.

Epitedeios denotes needful, esp. of the necessities of life, Jas 2:16. See: BAGD—302d; THAYER—244d.

2007. **ἐπιτίθημι** {42x} **ĕpitithēmi**, *ep-ee-tith'-ay-mee;* from *1909* and *5087;* to *impose* (in a friendly or hostile sense):—lay on {10x}, lay {7x}, put {6x}, lay upon {4x}, put on {3x}, put upon {2x}, set {2x}, not tr {1x}, misc. {7x} = add unto, lade, + surname, × wound.

Epitithemi, as a verb, means **(1)** "to add to, lay upon," and is used of **(1a)** "laying" hands on the sick, for healing, Mt 9:18; 19:13, "put"; 19:15; Mk 5:23; 6:5; 7:32; 8:23, "put"; so in v. 25; 16:18; Lk 4:40; 13:13; Acts 6:6; 8:17, 19; 9:12 and 17, "putting"; 13:3; 19:6; 28:8; Rev. 1:17; **(1b)** of "laying" hands on a person by way of public recognition, 1 Ti 5:22; **(1c)** of a shepherd's "laying" a sheep on his shoulders, Lk 15:5; **(1d)** of laying" the cross on Christ's shoulders, Lk 23:26; **(1e)** of "laying" on stripes, Acts 16:23; **(1f)** wood on a fire, Acts 28:3; **(1g)** metaphorically, **(1g1)** of "laying" burden's on men's shoulders, Mt 23:4; **(1g2)** similarly of "giving" injunctions, Acts 15:28 (cf. "put . . . upon" in v. 10). **(2)** In Acts 28:10 it is translated "they laded (us) with" [put on board with us]. **(3)** It is also translated "to put, or set" and is used **(3a)** of the placing over the head of Christ on the cross "His accusation," Mt 27:37, "set up"; **(3b)** of attacking a person, Acts 18:10, "shall set on." **(4)** It has a secondary and somewhat infrequent meaning, "to add to," and is found in this sense in **(4a)** Mk 3:16–17, lit., "He added the name Peter to Simon," "He added to them the name Boanerges," and **(4b)** Rev 22:18, where the word is set in contrast to "take away from" (v. 19). See: TDNT—8:159, 1176; BAGD—302a; THAYER—244d.

2008. **ἐπιτιμάω** {29x} **ĕpitimaō**, *ep-ee-tee-mah'-o;* from *1909* and *5091;* to *tax upon,* i.e. *censure* or *admonish;* by impl. *forbid:*—straitly charge {1x}, charge {4x}, rebuke {24x}.

Epitimao, as a verb, signifies **(1)** to put honour upon (*epi*, upon, *time*, honour); honor being derived from the root "to be heavy" hence to weigh down upon someone, to exert pressure upon. **(2)** To judge, to find fault with, rebuke; hence to charge, or rather, to charge strictly (*epi*, intensive), **(2a)** e.g., Mt 12:16; Mk 3:12, "charged much"; Mk 8:30; 10:48; **(2b)** "to rebuke"; except for 2 Ti 4:2 and Jude 9, it is confined in the NT to the Synoptic Gospels, where it is frequently used of the Lord's rebukes to **(2b1)** evil spirits, e.g., Mt 17:18; Mk 1:25; 9:25; Lk 4:35, 41; 9:42; **(2b2)** winds, Mt 8:26; Mk 4:39; Lk 8:24; **(2b3)** fever, Lk 4:39; **(2b4)** disciples, Mk 8:33; Lk 9:55; contrast Lk 19:39. **(2c)** For rebukes by others see Mt 16:22; 19:13; 20:31; Mk 8:32; 10:13; 10:48, "charged"; Lk 17:3; 18:15, 39; 23:40. **(3)** One may rebuke a person without convicting that person of any fault. In such a case either there is no fault (so the rebuke is unnecessary or unjust), or although there is a fault, the rebuke does not cause the offender to admit it. Syn.: Thus the distinction between *epitimao* and elencho (1651) lies in the possibility of rebuking for sin without convincing of sin. See also: 156, 1650, 1651. See: TDNT—2:623, 249 BAGD—303b; THAYER—245b.

2009. **ἐπιτιμία** {1x} **ĕpitimia**, *ep-ee-tee-mee'-ah;* from a compound of *1909* and *5092;* prop. *esteem,* i.e. *citizenship;* used (in the sense of *2008*) of a *penalty:*—punishment {1x}.

(1) *Epitimia* in the NT denotes "penalty, punishment," 2 Cor 2:6. **(2)** Originally it signified the enjoyment of the rights and privileges of citizenship; then it became used of the estimate fixed by a judge on the infringement of such rights, and hence, in general, a "penalty." See: TDNT—2:627, 249; BAGD—303c; THAYER—245c.

2010. **ἐπιτρέπω** {19x} **ĕpitrĕpō**, *ep-ee-trep'-o;* from *1909* and the base of *5157;* to *turn over* (*transfer*), i.e. *allow:*—suffer {10x}, permit {4x}, give leave {2x}, give liberty {1x}, give license {1x}, let {1x}.

Epitrepo, as a verb, lit. denotes "to turn to" (*epi*, "upon, to," *trepo*, "to turn"), and so **(1)** "to permit, give leave, send," **(1a)** of Christ's permission to the unclean spirits to enter the swine, Mk 5:13; in Lk 8:32, "suffer" and "suffered"); **(1b)** in Jn 19:38, of Pilate's permission to Joseph to take away the body of the Lord; **(1c)** in Acts 21:39, of Paul's request to the chief captain to permit him to address the people, "suffer"; **(1d)** in Acts 21:40, "he had given him licence"; **(2)** "to entrust," signifies "to permit," Acts 26:1; 1 Cor 14:34; 16:7; 1 Ti 2:12, "suffer"; Heb 6:3; **(3)** is rendered "to suffer" in Mt 8:21; Mk 10:4; Lk 9:59; Acts 28:16; Lk 9:61 "let"; Acts 21:39; Mt 8:31. See: BAGD—303c; THAYER—245c.

2011. **ἐπιτροπή** {1x} **ĕpitrŏpē**, *ep-ee-trop-ay';* from *2010; permission,* i.e. (by impl.) full *power:*—commission {1x}.

This word denotes a turning over (to another), a referring of a thing to another, and so a committal of full powers, a commission (Acts 26:12). See: BAGD—303d; THAYER—245c.

2012. **ἐπίτροπος** {3x} **ĕpitrŏpŏs**, *ep-it'-rop-os;* from *1909* and *5158* (in the sense of *2011*); a *commissioner,* i.e. domestic *manager, guardian:*—steward {2x}, tutor {1x}.

An *epitropos*, literally, is one to whose care something is committed and is rendered **(1)** "tutors" in Gal 4:2; and **(2)** "steward" Mt 20:8 and Lk 8:3. See: BAGD—303d; THAYER—245c.

2013. **ἐπιτυγχάνω** {5x} **ĕpitugchanō**, *ep-ee-toong-khan'-o;* from *1909* and *5177;* to *chance upon,* i.e. (by impl.) to *attain:*—obtain {1x}. Cf. Rom 11:7 (twice); Heb 6:15; 11:33; Jas 4:2. See: BAGD—303d.

2014. **ἐπιφαίνω** {4x} **ĕpiphainō**, *ep-ee-fah'-ee-no;* from *1909* and *5316;* to *shine upon,* i.e. *become* (lit.) *visible* or (fig.) *known:*—appear {3x}, give light {1x}.

Epiphaino is used **(1)** in the active voice with the meaning "to give light," Lk 1:79; **(2)** in the passive voice, "to appear, become visible." It is said of heavenly bodies, e.g., the stars, Acts 27:20; **(3)** metaphorically, of things spiritual, **(3a)** the grace of God, Titus 2:11; **(3b)** the kindness and the love of God, Titus 3:4. See: TDNT—9:7, 1244; BAGD—304a; THAYER—245d.

2015. **ἐπιφάνεια** {6x} **ĕpiphanĕia**, *ep-if-an'-i-ah;* from *2016;* a *manifestation,* i.e. (spec.) the *advent* of Christ (past or future):—appearing {5x}, brightness {1x}.

(1) Often used of the glorious manifestation of Christ, —not only that which has already taken place and by which His presence and power appear in the saving light He has shed upon mankind, but also that illustrious return from heaven to earth to occur in the future. **(2)** "Epiphany," lit., "a shining forth," was used of the "appearance" of a god to men, and of an enemy to an army in the field, etc. In the NT it occurs of **(1)** the advent of the Savior when the Word became flesh, 2 Ti 1:10; **(2)** the coming of the Lord Jesus into the air to the meeting with His saints, 1 Ti 6:14; 2 Ti 4:1, 8; **(3)** the shining forth of the glory of the Lord Jesus "as the lightning cometh forth from the east, and is seen even unto the west," Mt 24:27, immediately consequent on the unveiling, *apokalupsis,* of His *Parousia,* His return, in the air with His saints, 2 Th 2:8; Titus 2:13. Syn.: 602, 5321. See: TDNT—9:7, 1244; BAGD—304a; THAYER—245d.

2016. **ἐπιφανής** {1x} **ĕpiphanēs**, *ep-if-an-ace';* from *2014; conspicuous,* i.e. (fig.) *memorable:*—notable {1x}.

Epiphanes denotes conspicuous, manifest, illustrious is translated "notable" in Acts 2:20, of the great Day of the Lord. See: TDNT—9:7, 1244; BAGD—304b; THAYER—246a.

2017. **ἐπιφαύω** {1x} **ĕpiphauō**, *ep-ee-fŏw'-o;* a form of *2014;* to *illuminate* (fig.):—give light {1x}.

This word means to shine forth and is rendered "shall give . . . light," in Eph 5:14 of the glory of Christ, illumining the believer who fulfills the conditions, so that being guided by His "light" he reflects His character. See: TDNT—9:310,*; BAGD—304a; THAYER—246a.

2018. **ἐπιφέρω** {5x}} **ĕpiphĕrō**, *ep-ee-fer'-o;* from *1909* and *5342;* to *bear upon* (or *further*), i.e. *adduce* (pers. or judicially [*accuse, inflict*]), *superinduce:*—add {1x}, bring {2x}, bring against {1x}, take {1x}.

Epiphero signifies **(1)** "to bring upon, or to bring against," Acts 25:18; Jude 9; **(2)** "to impose, inflict, visit upon," Rom 3:5; **(3)** "to bring", Acts 19:12; and **(4)** "to add", Phil 1:16. See: BAGD—304c; THAYER—246a.

2019. **ἐπιφωνέω** {3x} **ĕpiphōnĕō**, *ep-ee-fo-neh'-o;* from *1909* and *5455;* to *call at* something, i.e. *exclaim:*—cry {1x}, cry against {1x}, give a shout {1x}.

Epiphoneo, as a verb, signifies "to shout" either **(1)** against: "But they cried, saying, Crucify *him,* crucify him"(Lk 23:21; 22:24), or **(2)** in acclamation: "And the people gave a shout, *saying, It is* the voice of a god, and not of a man" (Acts 12:22). Syn.: 310, 349, 994, 995, 1916, 2896, 2905, 2906, 5455. See: BAGD—304d; THAYER—246b.

2020. **ἐπιφώσκω** {2x} **ĕpiphōskō**, *ep-ee-foce'-ko;* a form of *2017;* to begin to *grow light:*—begin to dawn {1x}, × draw on {1x}.

Epiphosko, as a verb, means "to dawn" (lit., "to make to shine upon"), and is said of the approach of the Sabbath: "And that day was the preparation, and the sabbath drew on" (Lk 23:54 – "drew on/began to dawn"; cf. Mt 28:1). Syn.: 307, 385, 392, 501, 502, 645, 868, 1448, 1670, 1828, 2464, 4317, 4334, 4358, 4685, 4951, 5288, 5289. See: TDNT—9:310, 1293; BAGD—304d; THAYER—246b.

2021. **ἐπιχειρέω** {3x} **ĕpichĕirĕō**, *ep-ee-khi-reh'-o;* from *1909* and *5495;* to put the *hand upon,* i.e. *undertake:*—go about {1x}, take in hand {1x}, take upon {1x}.

This word occurs **(1)** in Lk 1:1, "have taken in hand"; **(2)** in Acts 9:29, "they went about"; **(3)** in Acts 19:13, "took upon them." See: BAGD—304d; THAYER—246b.

2022. **ἐπιχέω** {1x} **ĕpichĕō**, *ep-ee-kheh'-o;* from *1909* and χέω **chĕō** (to pour);—to *pour upon:*—pour in {1x}.

The wounds being deep needed ointment poured "in" in order to cleanse. See: BAGD—305a; THAYER—246b.

2023. **ἐπιχορηγέω** {5x} **ĕpichŏrēgĕō**, *ep-ee-khor-ayg-eh'-o;* from *1909* and *5524;* to *furnish besides,* i.e. fully *supply,* (fig.) *aid* or *contribute:*—add {1x}, minister {2x}, minister nourishment {1x}, minister unto {1x}.

This word means "to supply, to minister" and is translated **(1)** "add to" in 2 Pet 1:5; and **(2)** "minister", 2 Cor 9:10; Gal 3:5; Col 2:19; 2 Pet 1:5, "add"; 1:11. See: BAGD—305a; THAYER—246b.

2024. **ἐπιχορηγία** {2x} **ĕpichŏrēgia**, *ep-ee-khor-ayg-ee'-ah;* from *2023; contribution:*—supply {1x}.

Epichoregia, "a full supply," occurs in **(1)** Eph 4:16, "supplieth," lit., "by the supply of every joint," metaphorically of the members of the church, the body of which Christ is the Head, and **(2)** Phil 1:19, "the supply (of the Spirit of Jesus Christ)," i.e., "the bountiful supply"; here "of the Spirit" may be taken either in the subjective sense, the Giver, or the objective, the Gift. See. BAGD—305b; THAYER—246c.

2025. **ἐπιχρίω** {2x} **ĕpichriō**, *ep-ee-khree'-o;* from *1909* and *5548;* to *smear over:*—anoint {1x}, anoint + 1909 {1x}.

Epichrio, as a verb, means primarily, "to rub on" and is used of the blind man whose eyes Christ "anointed," and indicates the manner in which the "anointing" was done: "When He had thus spoken, He spat on the ground, and made clay of the spittle, and He anointed the eyes of the blind man with the clay" (Jn 9:6; cf. vs 11). Syn.: 218, 1472, 3462, 5545, 5548. See: BAGD—305b; THAYER—246c.

2026. **ἐποικοδομέω** {8x} **ĕpŏikŏdŏmĕō**, *ep-oy-kod-om-eh'-o;* from *1909* and *3618;* to *build upon,* i.e. (fig.) to *rear up:*—build up {3x}, build thereon {1x}, build thereupon {2x}, build {2x}. Cf. 1 Cor 3:10 (twice), 12, 14; Eph 2:20; Jude 20; or up, Acts 20:32; Col 2:7. See: TDNT—5:147, 674; BAGD—305b; THAYER—246c.

2027. **ἐποκέλλω** {1x} **ĕpŏkĕllō**, *ep-ok-el'-lo;* from *1909* and ὀκέλλω **ŏkĕllō** (to *urge*); to *drive upon* the shore, i.e. to *beach* a vessel:—run aground {1x}. See: BAGD—305c; THAYER—246d.

2028. **ἐπονομάζω** {1x} **ĕpŏnŏmazō**, *ep-on-om-ad'-zo;* from *1909* and *3687;* to *name further,* to surname, i.e. *denominate:*—call {1x}. See: TDNT—5:282, 694; BAGD—305c; THAYER—246d.

2029. **ἐποπτεύω** {2x} **ĕpŏptĕuō**, *ep-opt-yoo'-o;* from *1909* and a der. of *3700;* to *inspect,* i.e. *watch:*—behold {2x}.

Epopteuo, [from epi, "upon," and a form of horao], "to see," is used of "witnessing as a spectator, or overseer": "Having your conversation honest among the Gentiles: that, whereas they speak against you as evildoers, they may by *your* good works, which they shall behold (eporteuo), glorify God in the day of visitation" (1 Pet 2:12; cf. 3:2). Syn.: 333, 816, 991, 1689, 1896, 2300, 2334, 2657, 2734, 3708. See: TDNT—5:373, 706; BAGD—305c; THAYER—246d.

2030. **ἐπόπτης** {1x} **ĕpŏptēs**, *ep-op'-tace;* from *1909* and a presumed der. of *3700;* a *looker-on:*—eye-witness {1x}.

Epoptes, as a noun, means "an eye-witness": "For we have not followed cunningly devised fables, when we made known unto you the power and coming of our Lord Jesus Christ, but were eyewitnesses (*epoptes*) of His majesty" (2 Pet 1:16). Syn.: 333, 816, 991, 1689, 1896, 2029, 2300, 2334, 2657, 2734, 3708. See: TDNT—5:373, 706; BAGD—305d; THAYER—246d.

2031. **ἔπος** {1x} **ĕpŏs**, *ep'-os;* from *2036;* a *word:*—say + 2036 {1x}. See: BAGD—305d; THAYER—246d.

2032. **ἐπουράνιος** {20x} **ĕpŏuraniŏs**, *ep-oo-ran'-ee-os;* from *1909* and *3772; above* the *sky:*—celestial {2x}, in heaven {1x}, heavenly {16x}, high {1x}.

Epouranios (2032), as a noun, means "heavenly," what pertains to, or is in, heaven (epi, in the sense of "pertaining to," not here, "above"). It is used **(1)** of God the Father, Mt 18:35; **(2)** of the place where Christ "sitteth at the right hand of God" (i.e., in a position of divine authority), Eph 1:20; and **(2a)** of the present position of believers in relationship to Christ, Eph 2:6; **(2b)** where they possess "every spiritual blessing," 1:3; **(3)** of Christ as "the Second Man," and all those who are related to Him spiritually, 1 Cor 15:48; **(4)** of those whose sphere of activity or existence is above, or in contrast to that of earth, **(4a)** of "principalities and powers," Eph 3:10; **(4b)** of "spiritual hosts of wickedness," Eph 6:12, "in high places"; **(5)** of the Holy Spirit, Heb 6:4;

(6) of "heavenly things," **(6a)** as the subjects of the teaching of Christ, Jn 3:12, and **(6b)** as consisting of the spiritual and "heavenly" sanctuary and "true tabernacle" and all that appertains thereto in relation to Christ and His sacrifice as antitypical of the earthly tabernacle and sacrifices under the Law, Heb 8:5; 9:23; **(7)** of the "calling" of believers, Heb 3:1; **(8)** of heaven as the abode of the saints, **(8a)** "a better country" than that of earth, Heb 11:16, and **(8b)** of the spiritual Jerusalem, Heb 12:22; **(9)** of the kingdom of Christ in its future manifestation, 2 Ti 4:18; **(10)** of all beings and things, animate and inanimate, that are "above the earth," Phil 2:10; **(11)** of the resurrection and glorified bodies of believers, 1 Cor 15:49; **(12)** of the "heavenly orbs," 1 Cor 15:40 ("celestial," twice, and so rendered here only). Syn.: 3321, 3770, 3771, 3772. See: TDNT—5:538, 736; BAGD—305d; THAYER—247a.

2033. **ἑπτά** {87x} **hĕpta**, *hep-tah';* a primary number; *seven:*—seven {86x}, seventh {1x}. See: TDNT—2:627, 249; BAGD—306b; THAYER—247b.

2034. **ἑπτακίς** {4x} **hĕptakis**, *hep-tak-is';* adv. from *2033; seven times:*—seven times {4x}. See: TDNT—2:627, 249; BAGD—306b; THAYER—247b.

2035. **ἑπτακισχίλιοι** {1x} **hĕptakischiliŏi**, *hep-tak-is-khil'-ee-oy;* from *2034* and *5507; seven times a thousand:*—seven thousand {1x}. See: TDNT—2:627, 249; BAGD—306c; THAYER—247b.

2036. **ἔπω** {977x} **ĕpō**, *ep'-o;* a primary verb (used only in the def. past tense, the others being borrowed from *2046, 4483,* and *5346*); to *speak* or *say* (by word or writing):—

say {859x}, speak {57x}, tell {41x}, command {8x}, bid {5x}, vr say {1x}, misc. {6x} = answer, bring word, call, grant. See: BAGD—468a; THAYER—247b. Comp. *3004*.

2037. Ἔραστος {3x} **Ĕrastŏs**, *er'-as-tos;* from ἐράω **ĕraō** (to *love*); *beloved; Erastus,* a Chr.:—Erastus {3x}. See: BAGD—306c; THAYER—247b.

ἐραυνάω **ĕraunaō.** See *2045.*

2038. ἐργάζομαι {39x} **ĕrgazŏmai**, *er-gad'-zom-ahee;* mid. voice from *2041;* to *toil* (as a task, occupation, etc.), (by impl.) *effect, be engaged in* or *with,* etc.:—work {22x}, wrought {7x}, do {3x}, minister about {1x}, forbear working + 3361 {1x}, labour for {1x}, labour {1x}, commit {1x}, trade by {1x}, trade {1x}.

This word is used **(1)** intransitively, e.g., Mt 21:28; Jn 5:17; 9:4 (2nd part); Rom 4:4, 5; 1 Cor 4:12; 9:6; 1 Th 2:9; 4:11; 2 Th 3:8, 10–12; **(2)** transitively, **(2a)** "to work something, produce, perform," e.g., Mt 26:10, "she hath wrought"; Jn 6:28, 30; 9:4 (1st part); Acts 10:35; 13:41; Rom 2:10; 13:10; 1 Cor 16:10; Gal 6:10; Eph 4:28; Heb 11:33; 2 Jn 8; **(2b)** "to earn by working, work for," Jn 6:27, "labor"; **(3)** it is translated by the verb "to commit" (of committing sin), in Jas 2:9. See: TDNT—2:635, 251; BAGD—306d; THAYER—247b.

2039. ἐργασία {6x} **ĕrgasia**, *er-gas-ee'-ah;* from *2040; occupation, a business;* by impl. *profit, pains:*—craft {1x}, diligence {1x}, gain {3x}, work {1x}.

Ergasia, **(1)** lit., "a working" (akin to *ergon,* "work"), is indicative of a process, in contrast to the concrete, *ergon,* e.g., Eph 4:19, lit., "unto a working" (contrast *ergon* in v. 12); **(2)** "craft," Acts 19:25; **(3)** or gain got by "work," Acts 16:16, 19; 19:24; **(4)** endeavor, pains, "diligence," Lk 12:58. See: TDNT—2:635, 251; BAGD—307c; THAYER—247d.

2040. ἐργάτης {16x} **ĕrgatēs**, *er-gat'-ace;* from *2041;* a *toiler;* fig. a *teacher:*—labourer {10x}, worker {3x}. workmen {3x}.

An *ergates* (2040), akin to ergazomai, "to work," and ergon, "work," denotes **(1)** "a field laborer, a husbandman," Mt 9:37, 38; 20:1, 2, 8; Lk 10:2 (twice); Jas 5:4; **(2)** "a workman, laborer," in a general sense, Mt 10:10; Lk 10:7; Acts 19:25; 1 Ti 5:18; and it is used **(3)** of false apostles and evil teachers, 2 Cor 11:13; Phil 3:2, **(4)** of a servant of Christ, 2 Ti 2:15; **(5)** of evildoers, Lk 13:27. See: TDNT—2:635, 251; BAGD—307c; THAYER—248a.

2041. ἔργον {176x} **ĕrgŏn**, *er'-gon;* from a primary (but obs.) ἔργω **ĕrgō** (to *work*); *toil* (as an effort or occupation); by impl. an *act:*—deed {22x}, doing {1x}, labour {1x}, work {152x}. See: TDNT—2:635, 251; BAGD—307d; THAYER—248a.

2042. ἐρεθίζω {2x} **ĕrĕthizō**, *er-eth-id'-zo;* from a presumed prol. form of *2054;* to *stimulate* (espec. to anger):—provoke {2x}.

Erethizo, as a verb, means "to excite, stir up, provoke," is used **(1)** in a good sense in 2 Cor 9:2, "hath provoked"; **(2)** in an evil sense in Col 3:21, "provoke." Syn.: 329, 383, 387, 1326, 1892, 3947, 3951, 4531, 4579, 4787, 4797, 5017. See: BAGD—308d; THAYER—249a.

2043. ἐρείδω {1x} **ĕrĕidō**, *er-i'-do;* of obscure aff.; to *prop,* i.e. (refl.) *get fast:*—stick fast {1x}. See: BAGD—308d; THAYER—249a.

2044. ἐρεύγομαι {1x} **ĕrĕugŏmai**, *er-yoog'-om-ahee;* of uncert. aff.; to *belch,* i.e. (fig.) to *speak outloud:*—utter {1x}. See: BAGD—308d; THAYER—249a.

2045. ἐρευνάω {6x} **ĕrĕunaō**, *er-yoo-nah'-o* or ἐραυνάω **ĕraunaō**, *er-ouw-nah'-o;* appar. from *2046* (through the idea of *inquiry*); to *seek,* i.e. (fig.) to *investigate:*—search {6x}.

Ereunao, "to search, examine," is used **(1)** of God, as "searching" the heart, Rom 8:27; **(2)** of Christ, similarly, Rev 2:23; **(3)** of the Holy Spirit, as "searching" all things, 1 Cor 2:10, acting in the spirit of the believer; **(4)** of the OT prophets, as "searching" their own writings concerning matters foretold of Christ, testified by the Spirit of Christ in them, 1 Pet 1:11; **(5)** of the Jews, as commanded by the Lord to "search" the Scriptures, Jn 5:39; **(6)** of Nicodemus as commanded similarly by the chief priests and Pharisees, Jn 7:52. See: TDNT—2:655, 255; BAGD—306c; THAYER—249a.

2046. ἐρέω {71x} **ĕrĕō**, *er-eh'-o;* prob. a fuller form of *4483;* an alternate for *2036* in cert. tenses; to *utter,* i.e. *speak* or *say:*—call {1x}, say {57x}, speak {7x}, speak of {2x}, tell {4x}. See: TDNT—2:655, 255; BAGD—468a; 735a; THAYER—562a [4483].

2047. ἐρημία {4x} **ĕrēmia**, *er-ay-mee'-ah;* from *2048; solitude* (concr.):—desert {1x}, wilderness {3x}.

Eremia, primarily "a solitude, an uninhabited place," in contrast to a town or village, is **(1)** translated "deserts" in Heb 11:38; **(2)** "the wilderness" in Mt 15:33, "a desert place," in Mk 8:4; **(3)** "wilderness" in 2 Cor 11:26. **(4)** It does not always denote a barren region, void of vegetation; it is often used of a place uncultivated, but fit for pasturage. See: TDNT—2:657, 255; BAGD—308d; THAYER—249b.

2048. ἔρημος {50x} **ĕrēmŏs**, *er'-ay-mos;* of uncert. aff.; *lonesome,* i.e. (by impl.) *waste* (usually as a noun, *5561* being implied):—desert {13x}, desolate {4x}, solitary {1x}, wilderness {32x}. See: TDNT—2:657, 255; BAGD—309a; THAYER—249b.

2049. ἐρημόω {5x} **ĕrēmŏō**, *er-ay-mŏ'-o;* from *2048;* to *lay waste* (lit. or fig.):—bring to desolation {2x}, desolate {1x}, come to nought {1x}, make desolate {1x}.

Eremoo signifies "to make desolate, lay waste." From the primary sense of "making quiet" comes that of "making lonely." It is used only in the passive voice in the NT; **(1)** in Rev 17:16, "shall make desolate" is, lit., "shall make her desolated"; in **(2)** Rev 18:17, 19, "is made desolate"; **(3)** in Mt 12:25 and Lk 11:17, "is brought to desolation." See: TDNT—2:657, 255; BAGD—309b; THAYER—249c.

2050. ἐρήμωσις {3x} **ĕrēmōsis**, *er-ay'-mo-sis;* from *2049; despoliation:*—desolation {3x}.

Eremosis denotes "desolation," **(1)** in the sense of "making desolate," e.g., in the phrase "the abomination of desolation," Mt 24:15; Mk 13:14; the genitive is objective, "the abomination that makes desolate"; **(2)** with stress upon the effect of the process, Lk 21:20, with reference to the "desolation" of Jerusalem. See: TDNT—2:660, 255; BAGD—309b; THAYER—249c.

2051. ἐρίζω {1x} **ĕrizō**, *er-id'-zo;* from *2054;* to *wrangle:*—strive {1x}.

Erizo means to wrangle, engage in strife used to describe the calm temper of Jesus in contrast with the vehemence of the Jewish doctors wrangling together about tenets and practices in Mt 12:19. See: BAGD—309b; THAYER—249c.

2052. ἐριθεία {7x} **ĕrithĕia**, *er-ith-i'-ah;* perh. as the same as *2042;* prop. *intrigue,* i.e. (by impl.) *faction:*—contention {1x}, contentious {1x}, strife {5x}.

Eritheia denotes **(1)** "ambition, self-seeking, rivalry," self-will being an underlying idea in the word; hence it denotes "party-making." **(1a)** Seeking to win followers creates factions. **(1b)** Factions are the result of jealousy. **(1c)** It is derived, not from eris, "strife," but from erithos, "a hireling"; hence the meaning of "seeking to win followers," "strifes, factions," 2 Cor 12:20; not improbably the meaning here is rivalries, or base ambitions (all the other words in the list express abstract ideas rather than factions); cf. Gal 5:20; Phil 1:17,(v. 16, "contention"); Phil 2:3 "strife"; Jas 3:14, 16; **(2)** in Rom 2:8 it is translated as an adjective, "contentious." **(2a)** The order "strife, jealousy, wrath, faction," is the same in 2 Cor 12:20 and **(2b)** Gal 5:20. See: TDNT—2:660, 256; BAGD—309b; THAYER—249c.

2053. ἔριον {2x} **ĕriŏn**, *er'-ee-on;* of obscure aff.; *wool:*—wool {2x}. Cf. Heb 9:19; Rev 1:14. See: BAGD—309c; THAYER—249d.

2054. ἔρις {9x} **ĕris**, *er'-is;* of uncert. aff.; a *quarrel,* i.e. (by impl.) *wrangling:*—contention {2x}, debate {2x}, strife {4x}, variance {1x}.

Eris, "strife, contention," is the **(1)** expression of "enmity," Rom 1:29, "debate"; 13:13; 1 Cor 1:11, "contentions"; 3:3; 2 Cor 12:20, "debates"; Gal 5:20, "variance"; Phil 1:15; 1 Ti 6:4; Titus 3:9, "contentions". **(2)** The stress in this word is on rivalry. See: BAGD—309c; THAYER—249d.

2055. ἐρίφιον {1x} **ĕriphiŏn**, *er-if'-ee-on;* from *2056;* a *kidling,* i.e. (gen.) *goat* (symbol. *wicked* person):—goat {1x}.

This diminutive of eriphos [2056] is in Mt 25:33. Its use is purely figurative and where the application is made, though metaphorically, the change to the diminutive is suggestive of the contempt which those so described bring upon themselves by their refusal to assist the needy. See: BAGD—309d; THAYER—249d.

2056. ἔριφος {2x} **ĕriphŏs**, *er'-if-os;* perh. from the same as *2053* (through the idea of *hairiness*); a *kid* or (gen.) *goat:*—goat {1x}, kid {1x}. Cf. Mt 25:32; Lk 15:29. See: BAGD—309d; THAYER—249d.

2057. Ἑρμᾶς {1x} **Hĕrmas**, *her-mas';* prob. from *2060; Hermas,* a Chr.:—*Hermas* {1x}. See: BAGD—309d; THAYER—250a.

2058. ἑρμηνεία {2x} **hĕrmēnĕia**, *her-may-ni'-ah;* from the same as *2059; translation:*—interpretation {2x}.

Hermeneia is interpretation of what has been spoken more or less obscurely by others, 1 Cor 12:10; 14:26. See: TDNT—2:661, 256; BAGD—310a; THAYER—250a.

2059. ἑρμηνεύω {4x} **hĕrmēnĕuō**, *her-mayn-yoo'-o;* from a presumed der. of *2060* (as the god of language); to *translate:*—by interpretation {3x}, being interpreted {1x}.

(1) *Hermes,* the Greek name of the pagan god Mercury, was regarded as the messenger of the gods. **(2)** *Hermeneuo,* denotes "to explain, interpret" (Eng., "hermeneutics"), and is used of explaining the meaning of words in a different language: **(2a)** Jn 1:38, "Siloam," interpreted as "sent"; **(2b)** Heb 7:2, Melchizedec, "by interpretation," lit., "being interpreted," King of righteousness; **(2c)** Jn 1:42, "Cephas, which is by interpretation, a stone"; and **(2d)** Jn 1:38, "rabbi . . . being interpreted master." See: TDNT—2:661, 256; BAGD—310a; THAYER—250a.

2060. ῾Ερμῆς {2x} **Hĕrmēs**, *her-mace';* perh. from *2046; Hermes,* the name of the messenger of the Gr. deities; also of a Chr.:—*Hermes* {1x}, Mercurious {1x}.

See 2059 for why Paul, being the chief speaker, was called *Hermes* by those at Lystra, Acts 14:12. See: BAGD—310a; THAYER—250a.

2061. ῾Ερμογένης {1x} **Hĕrmŏgĕnēs**, *her-mog-en'-ace;* from *2060* and *1096; born of Hermes; Hermogenes,* an apostate Chr.:—*Hermogenes* {1x}. See: BAGD—310b; THAYER—250a.

2062. ἑρπετόν {4x} **hĕrpĕtŏn**, *her-pet-on';* neut. of a der. of ἕρπω **hĕrpō** (to *creep*); a *reptile,* i.e. (by Heb. [comp. 7431]) a small *animal:*—creeping thing {3x}, serpent {1x}.

Herpeton signifies "a creeping thing" and is translated **(1)** "serpents" in Jas 3:7 (which form only one of this genus); **(2)** it is set in contrast to quadrupeds and birds, Acts 10:12; 11:6; Rom 1:23. See: BAGD—310b; THAYER—250b.

2063. ἐρυθρός {2x} **ĕruthrŏs**, *er-oo-thros';* of uncert. aff.; *red,* i.e. (with *2281*) the *Red* Sea:—red {2x}. Cf. Acts 7:36; Heb 11:29. See: BAGD—310b; THAYER—250b.

2064. ἔρχομαι {643x} **ĕrchŏmai**, *er'-khom-ahee;* mid. voice of a primary verb (used only in the present and imperfect tenses, the others being supplied by a kindred [mid. voice]

ἐλεύθομαι **ĕlĕuthŏmai**, *el-yoo'-thom-ahee;* or [act.]

ἔλθω **ĕlthō**, *el'-tho;* which do not otherwise occur); to *come* or *go* (in a great variety of applications, lit. and fig.):—come {616x}, go {13x}, vr come {1x}, misc. {13x} = accompany, appear, bring, enter, fall out, grow, × light, × next, pass, resort, be set. See: TDNT—2:666, 257; BAGD—310b; THAYER—250b.

2065. ἐρωτάω {58x} **ĕrōtaō**, *er-o-tah'-o;* appar. from *2046* [comp. *2045*]; to *interrogate;* by impl. to *request:*—ask {23x}, beseech {14x}, pray {14x}, desire {16x}, intreat {1x}.

Erotao more frequently suggests **(1)** that the petitioner is on a footing of equality or familiarity that lends authority to the request with the person whom he intreats. It is used **(1a)** of a king in making request from another king (Lk 14:32); **(1b)** of the Pharisee who desired Christ that He would eat with him, indicating the inferior conception he had of Christ (Lk 7:36). **(2)** It is significant that the Lord Jesus never used aiteo (154) in the matter of making request to the Father. The consciousness of His equal dignity, of His potent and prevailing intercession, speaks out in this, that as often as He asks, or declares that He will ask anything of the Father, it is always *erotao,* an asking, that is, upon equal terms, (Jn 14:16; 16:26; 17:9, 15, 20). **(2)** Martha, on the contrary, plainly reveals her poor unworthy conception of His person, that . . . she ascribes that aiteo to Him which He never ascribes to Himself (Jn 11:22). Syn.: 154, 1833, 1905, 4441. See: TDNT—2:685, 262; BAGD—311d; THAYER—252b.

2066. ἐσθής {7x} **ĕsthēs**, *es-thace';* from ἕννυμι **hĕnnumi** (to *clothe*); *dress:*—apparel {3x}, clothing {2x}, raiment {1x}, robe {1x}.

This word usually suggests good clothing as compared to common. See: BAGD—312b; THAYER—252c.

2067. ἔσθησις {1x} **ĕsthēsis**, *es'-thay-sis;* from a der. of *2066; clothing* (concr.):—garment {1x}. See: BAGD—312b; THAYER—252c; THAYER—252c.

2068. ἐσθίω {65x} **ĕsthiō**, *es-thee'-o;* strengthened for a primary ἔδω **ĕdō** (to *eat*); used only in certain tenses, the rest being supplied by *5315;* to *eat* (usually lit.):—devour {1x}, eat {63x}, live {1x}. See: TDNT—2:689, 262; BAGD—312b; THAYER—252c.

2069. ᾿Εσλί {1x} **Ĕsli**, *es-lee';* of Heb. or. [prob. for 454]; *Esli,* an Isr.:—*Esli* {1x}. See: BAGD—313b; THAYER—253b.

2070. ἐσμέν {53x} **ĕsmĕn**, *es-men';* first pers. plur. ind. of *1510;* we *are:*—are {49x}, have hope + 1679 {1x}, was {1x}, be {1x}, have our being {1x}. See: BAGD—222d [1510]; THAYER—175c [1510].

2071. ἔσομαι {188x} **ĕsŏmai**, *es'-om-ahee;* future of *1510; will be:*—shall be {151x}, will be {9x}, be {6x}, shall have {6x}, shall come to pass {4x}, shall {4x}, not tr {1x}, misc. {7x} = should be, × may have, × fall, what would follow, × live long, × sojourn. See: BAGD—223a [1510]; THAYER—175c [1510].

2072. ἔσοπτρον {2x} **ĕsŏptrŏn**, *es'-op-tron;* from *1519* and a presumed der. of *3700;* a *mirror* (for *looking into*):—glass {2x}. Cf. 1 Cor 13:12 and Jas 1:23. See: TDNT—2:696, 27/264; BAGD—313b; THAYER—253b. Syn.: ????.

2073. ἑσπέρα {3x} **hĕspĕra**, *hes-per'-ah;* fem. of an adj. ἑσπερός **hĕspĕrŏs** (*evening*); the *eve* (*5610* being implied):—evening {2x}, eventide {1x}. Cf. Lk 24:29; Acts 4:3, "eventide"; 28:23. See: BAGD—313c; THAYER—253b.

2074. ᾿Εσρώμ {3x} **Ĕsrōm**, *es-rome';* of Heb. or. [2696]; *Esrom* (i.e. *Chetsron*), an Isr.:—*Esrom* {3x}. See: BAGD—313d; THAYER—253b.

2075. ἐστέ {92x} **ĕstĕ**, *es-teh';* second pers. plur. pres. ind. of *1510;* ye *are:*—are {82x}, be {5x}, is {2x}, belong to {1x}, have been {1x}, not tr {1x}. See: BAGD—222d [1510]; THAYER—175c [1510].

2076. ἐστί {910x} **ĕsti**, *es-tee';* third pers. sing. pres. ind. of *1510;* he (she or it) *is;* also (with neut. plur.) they *are:*—is {752x}, are {51x}, was {29x}, be {25x}, have {11x}, not tr {15x}, vr is {1x}, misc. {27x} = belong, call, × can [-not], come, consisteth, × dure for a while, + follow, (that) is (to say), make, meaneth, × must needs, + profit, + remaineth, + wrestle. See: BAGD—222d [1510]; THAYER—175c [1510].

2077. ἔστω {16x} **ĕstō**, *es'-to;* second pers. sing. pres. imper. of *1510; be* thou; also

ἔστωσαν **ĕstōsan**, *es'-to-san;* third pers. of the same; *let* them *be:*—let be {10x}, be {5x}, not tr {1x}. See: BAGD—222d [1510]; THAYER—175c [1510].

2078. ἔσχατος {54x} **ĕschatŏs**, *es'-khat-os;* a superl. prob. from *2192* (in the sense of *contiguity*); *farthest, final* (of place or time):—last {46x}, lowest {2x}, uttermost {2x}, last state {2x}, ends {1x}, latter end {1x}.

Eschatos, "last, utmost, extreme," is used **(1)** of place, e.g., Lk 14:9, 10, "lowest;" Acts 1:8 and 13:47, "uttermost part;" **(2)** of rank, e.g., Mk 9:35; **(3)** of time, relating either to persons or things, e.g., Mt 5:26, "the uttermost (farthing)"; **(4)** of apostles as "last" in the program of a spectacular display, Mt 20:8, 12, 14; Mk 12:6, 22; 1 Cor 4:9; **(5)** 1 Cor 15:45, "the last Adam"; **(6)** of the "last" state of persons, Rev 2:19; Mt 12:45; Lk 11:26; 2 Pet 2:20, "the latter end"; **(7)** of Christ as the Eternal One, Rev 1:11, 17; 2:8; 22:13; **(8)** in eschatological phrases as follows: **(8a)** "the last day," a comprehensive term including both **(8a1)** the time of the resurrection of the redeemed, Jn 6:39, 40, 44, 54 and 11:24, and **(8a2)** the ulterior time of the judgment of the unregenerate, at the Great White Throne, Jn 12:48; **(8b)** "the last days," Acts 2:17, a period relative to the supernatural manifestation of the Holy Spirit at Pentecost and the resumption of the divine interpositions in the affairs of the world at the end of the present age, before "the great and notable Day of the Lord," which will usher in the messianic kingdom; **(8c)** in 2 Ti 3:1, "the last days" refers to the close of the present age of world conditions; **(8d)** in Jas 5:3, the phrase "for the last days" refers both to the period preceding the Roman overthrow of the city and the land in A.D. 70, and to the closing part of the age in consummating acts of gentile persecution including "the time of Jacob's trouble" (cf. verses 7, 8); **(8e)** in 1 Pet 1:5, "the last time" refers to the time of the Lord's second advent; **(8f)** in 1 Jn 2:18,"the last time" and, in Jude 18, "the last time" signify the present age previous to the Second Advent.

(9) In Heb 1:2, "in these last days", the reference is to the close of the period of the testimony of the prophets under the Law, terminating with the presence of Christ and His redemptive sacrifice and its effects, **(9a)** the perfect tense "hath spoken" indicating the continued effects of the message embodied in the risen Christ; **(9b)** so in 1 Pet 1:20, "in these last times." See: TDNT—2:697, 264; BAGD—313d; THAYER—253b.

2079. ἐσχάτως {1x} **ĕschatōs**, *es-khat'-oce;* adv. from *2078; finally,* i.e. (with *2192*) *at the extremity* of life:—point of death + 2292 {1x}.

This word means extreme, to be in the last gasp, at the point of death, Mk 5:23. See: BAGD—314; THAYER—254a.

2080. ἔσω {8x} **ĕsō**, *es'-o;* from *1519; inside* (as prep. or adj.):—within {3x}, in {1x}, inner {1x}, into {1x}, inward {1x}, not tr. {1x}.

Eso is an adverb connected with *eis,* "into," and is translated **(1)** "inner" in Eph 3:16; **(2)** after verbs of motion, it denotes "into," Mk 15:16; **(3)** after verbs of rest, "within," Jn 20:26; Acts 5:23; 1 Cor 5:12 (i.e., "within" the church); **(4)** "in", Mt 26:58; **(5)** "inward", Rom 7:22. See: TDNT—2:698, 265; BAGD—314b; THAYER—254a.

2081. ἔσωθεν {14x} **ĕsōthĕn**, *es'-o-then;* from *2080; from inside;* also used as equiv. to *2080* (*inside*):—within {7x}, from within {3x}, inward part {1x}, inwardly {1x}, inward man {1}, without {1x}.

Esothen is an adverb denoting "from within," or "within," and is **(1)** used with the article, as a noun, of the inner being, the secret intents of the heart, which, the Lord declared, God made, as well as the visible physical frame, Lk 11:40. **(2)** In Lk 11:39, it is rendered "inward part"; **(3)** in Mt 7:15 it has its normal use as an adverb, "inwardly"; also translated **(4)** "within", Mt 23:25, 27, 28; 2 Cor 7:5; Rev 4:8; 5:1; **(5)** "from within," Mk 7:21, 23; Lk 11:7; "inward man", 2 Cor 4:16. See: BAGD—314b; THAYER—254a.

2082. ἐσώτερος {2x} **ĕsōtĕrŏs**, *es-o'-ter-os;* comparative of *2080; interior:*—inner {1x}, within {1x}.

Esoteros the comparative degree, denotes **(1)** "inner," Acts 16:24 (of a prison); **(2)** Heb 6:19, with the article, and practically as a noun, "that which is within (the veil)," lit., "the inner (of the veil)." See: BAGD—314c; THAYER—254b.

2083. **ἑταῖρος** {4x} **hĕtairŏs**, *het-ah'-ee-ros;* from ἔτης **ĕtēs** (a *clansman*); a *comrade:*—fellow {1x}, friend {3x}.

Hetairos, "a companion, comrade," is translated **(1)** "fellows" in Mt 11:16. The word is used only by Matthew and is translated "friend" in 20:13; 22:12; 26:50. See: TDNT—2:699, 265; BAGD—314c; THAYER—254b.

2084. **ἑτερόγλωσσος** {1x} **hĕtĕrŏglōssŏs**, *het-er-og'-loce-sos;* from *2087* and *1100; other-tongued,* i.e. a *foreigner:*—other tongue {1x}. See: TDNT—1:726, 123; BAGD—314d; THAYER—254b.

2085. **ἑτεροδιδασκαλέω** {2x} **hĕtĕrŏdidaskalĕō**, *het-er-od-id-as-kal-eh'-o;* from *2087* and *1320;* to *instruct differently:*—teach other doctrine {1x}, teach otherwise {1x}.

This word means to teach a different doctrine (*heteros,* different, to be distinguished from *allos,* another of the same kind), and is used in 1 Ti 1:3; 6:3 of what is contrary to the faith. See: TDNT—2:163, 161; BAGD—314d; THAYER—254b.

2086. **ἑτεροζυγέω** {1x} **hĕtĕrŏzugĕō**, *het-er-od-zoog-eh'-o;* from a compound of *2087* and *2218;* to *yoke* up *differently,* i.e. (fig.) to *associate discordantly:*—unequally yoked together with {1x}. See: TDNT—2:901, 301; BAGD—314d; THAYER—254b.

2087. **ἕτερος** {99x} **hĕtĕrŏs**, *het'-er-os;* of uncert. aff.; (an-, the) *other* or *different:*—another {43x}, other {42x}, other thing {3x}, some {2x}, next day {2x}, misc. {7x} = altered, else, one, strange.

This word means "another": i.e. one not of the same nature, form, class, kind, different. See: TDNT—2:702, 265; BAGD—315a; THAYER—254b.

2088. **ἑτέρως** {1x} **hĕtĕrōs**, *het-er'-oce;* adv. from *2087; differently:*—otherwise {1x}. See: BAGD—315c; THAYER—254d.

2089. **ἔτι** {117x} **ĕti**, *et'-ee;* perh. akin to *2094;* "*yet,*" *still* (of time or degree):—yet {52x}, more {34x}, any more {5x}, still {4x}, further {4x}, longer {3x}, misc. {15x} = after that, also, ever, (t-) henceforth (more), hereafter, anyone), now. See: BAGD—315c; THAYER—254d.

2090. **ἑτοιμάζω** {40x} **hĕtŏimazō**, *het-oy-mad'-zo;* from *2092;* to *prepare:*—prepare {29x}, provide {1x}, make ready {10x}.

Hetoimazo, as a verb, means "to prepare, make ready," is used **(1)** absolutely, e.g., Mk 14:15; Lk 9:52; **(2)** with an object, e.g., of those things which are ordained **(2a)** by God, such as future positions of authority, Mt 20:23; **(2a1)** the coming Kingdom, 25:34; **(2a2)** salvation personified in Christ, Lk 2:31; **(2a3)** future blessings, 1 Cor 2:9; **(2a4)** a city, Heb 11:16; **(2a5)** a place of refuge for the Jewish remnant, Rev 12:6; **(2a6)** Divine judgments on the world, Rev 8:6; 9:7, 15; 16:12; **(2a7)** eternal fire, for the Devil and his angels, Mt 25:41; **(2b)** by Christ: a place in Heaven for His followers, Jn 14:2, 3; **(3)** of human "preparation" for the Lord, e.g., Mt 3:3; 26:17, 19; Lk 1:17 ("make ready"), 76; 3:4; 9:52 ("to make ready"); 23:56; Rev 19:7; 21:2; **(4)** in 2 Ti 2:21, of "preparation" of oneself for "every good work"; **(5)** of human "preparations" for human objects, e.g., Lk 12:20, "thou hast provided"; Acts 23:23; Philem 22. See: TDNT—2:704, 266; BAGD—316a; THAYER—255b. comp. *2680.*

2091. **ἑτοιμασία** {1x} **hĕtŏimasia**, *het-oy-mas-ee'-ah;* from *2090; preparation:*—preparation {1x}.

In Eph 6:15, the gospel itself is to be the firm footing of the believer, his walk being worthy of it and therefore a testimony in regard to it. See: TDNT—2:704, 266; BAGD—316c; THAYER—255c.

2092. **ἕτοιμος** {17x} **hĕtŏimŏs**, *het'-oy-mos;* from an old noun ἕτεος **hĕtĕŏs** (*fitness*); *adjusted,* i.e. *ready:*—ready {14}, prepared {1x}, readiness {1x}, make ready to (one's) hand {1x}.

Hetoimos denotes **(1)** "preparation"; it is found in Eph 6:15, of having the feet shod with the "preparation" of the gospel of peace; it also has the meaning of firm footing (foundation); if that is the meaning in Eph 6:15, the gospel itself is to be the firm footing of the believer, his walk being worthy of it and therefore a testimony in regard to it. It also means **(2)** "ready" and is used **(2a)** of persons, Mt 24:44; 25:10; Lk 12:40; 22:33; Acts 23:15, 21; Titus 3:1; 1 Pet 3:15; **(2b)** of things, Mt 22:4 (2nd part), 8; Mk 14:15, "prepared"; Lk 14:17; Jn 7:6; 2 Cor 9:5; 10:16, "things made ready"; 1 Pet 1:5. See: TDNT—2:704, 266; BAGD—316c; THAYER—255c.

2093. **ἑτοίμως** {3x} **hĕtŏimōs**, *het-oy'-moce;* adv. from *2092; in readiness:*—ready {3x}. Cf. Acts 21:13; 2 Cor. 12:14; 1 Pet. 4:5. See: BAGD—316d; THAYER—256d.

2094. **ἔτος** {49x} **ĕtŏs**, *et'-os;* appar. a primary word; a *year:*—year {4x}. See: BAGD—316d; THAYER—256d.

2095. **εὖ** {6x} **ĕu**, *yoo;* neut. of a primary εὖς **ĕus** (*good*); (adv.) *well:*—good {1x}, well {3x}, well done {2x}. See: BAGD—317b; THAYER—256a.

2096. **Εὖα** {2x} **Ĕua**, *yoo'-ah;* of Heb. or. [2332]; *Eua* (or *Eva,* i.e. *Chavvah*), the first woman:—Eve {2x}. See: BAGD—317b; THAYER—256b.

2097. **εὐαγγελίζω** {55x} **ĕuaggĕlizō**, *yoo-ang-ghel-id'-zo;* from *2095* and *32;* to *announce good* news ("evangelize") espec. the gospel:—preach {23x}, preach the Gospel {22x}, bring good tidings {2x}, show glad tidings {2x}, bring glad tidings {1x}, declare {1x}, declare glad tidings {1x}, misc. {3x}.

Euangelizo, as a verb, means "to bring or announce glad tidings" (Eng., "evangelize"), is used **(1)** in the active voice in Rev 10:7, "declared" and 14:6, "to preach"; **(2)** in the passive voice, **(2a)** of matters to be proclaimed as "glad tidings," Lk 16:16; Gal 1:11; 1 Pet 1:25; **(2b)** of persons to whom the proclamation is made, Mt 11:5; Lk 7:22; Heb 4:2, 6; 1 Pet 4:6; **(3)** in the middle voice, especially of the message of salvation, **(3a)** with a personal object, either **(3a1)** of the person preached, e.g., Acts 5:42; 11:20; Gal 1:16, or, **(3a2)** with a preposition, of the persons evangelized, e.g., Acts 13:32, "declare glad tidings"; Rom 1:15; Gal 1:8; **(3b)** with an impersonal object, e.g., **(3b1)** "the word," Acts 8:4; **(3b2)** "good tidings," Acts 8:12; **(3b3)** "the word of the Lord," Acts 15:35; **(3b4)** "the gospel," 1 Cor 15:1; 2 Cor 11:7; **(3b5)** "the faith," Gal 1:23; **(3b6)** "peace," Eph 2:17; **(3b7)** "the unsearchable riches of Christ, 3:8. Syn.: 4283. See: TDNT—2:707,*; BAGD—317b; THAYER—256b.

2098. **εὐαγγέλιον** {77x} **ĕuaggĕliŏn**, *yoo-ang-ghel'-ee-on;* from the same as *2097;* a *good message,* i.e. the *gospel:*—gospel {46x}, gospel of Christ {11x}, gospel of God {7x}, gospel of the Kingdom {3x}, misc. {10x}.

Euangelion **(1)** originally denoted a reward for good tidings; **(1a)** later, the idea of reward dropped, and **(1b)** the word stood for "the good news" itself. **(1c)** The Eng. word "gospel," i.e. "good message," is the equivalent of euangelion (Eng., "evangel"). **(1d)** In the NT it denotes the "good tidings" of the kingdom of God and of salvation through Christ, to be received by faith, on the basis of His expiatory death, His burial, resurrection, and ascension, e.g., Acts 15:7; 20:24; 1 Pet 4:17; **(1e)** Apart from those references and those in the gospels of Matthew and Mark, and Rev 14:6, the noun is confined to Paul's epistles. **(2)** The apostle uses it of two associated yet distinct things, **(2a)** of the basic facts of the death, burial and resurrection of Christ, e.g., 1 Cor 15:1–3; the "gospel" is viewed historically; **(2b)** of the interpretation of these facts, e.g., Rom 2:16; Gal 1:7, 11; 2:2; the gospel is viewed doctrinally, with reference to the interpretation of the facts, as is sometimes indicated by the context.

(3) The following phrases describe the subjects or nature or purport of the message; it is the "gospel" of **(3a)** God, Mk 1:14; Rom 1:1; 15:16; 2 Cor 11:7; 1 Th 2:2, 9; 1 Pet 4:17; **(3b)** God, concerning His Son, Rom 1:1–3; **(3c)** His Son, Rom 1:9; **(3d)** Jesus Christ, the Son of God, Mk 1:1; **(3e)** our Lord Jesus, 2 Th 1:8; **(3f)** Christ, Rom 15:19, etc.; **(3g)** the glory of Christ, 2 Cor 4:4; **(3h)** the grace of God, Acts 20:24; **(3i)** the glory of the blessed God, 1 Ti 1:11; **(3j)** your salvation, Eph 1:13; **(3k)** peace, Eph 6:15. **(4)** Cf. also **(4a)** "the gospel of the Kingdom," Mt 4:23; 9:35; 24:14; **(4b)** "an eternal gospel," Rev 14:6. **(5)** In Gal 2:14, "the truth of the gospel" denotes, not the true "gospel," but the true teaching of it, in contrast to perversions of it. See: TDNT—2:721, 267; BAGD—317d; THAYER—257a.

2099. **εὐαγγελιστής** {3x} **ĕuaggĕlistēs**, *yoo-ang-ghel-is-tace';* from *2097;* a *preacher* of the gospel:—evangelist {3x}.

Euaggelistes denotes a "preacher of the gospel," Acts 21:8; Eph 4:11, which makes clear the distinctiveness of the function in the churches; 2 Ti 4:5. See: TDNT—2:736, 267; BAGD—318c; THAYER—257c.

2100. **εὐαρεστέω** {3x} **ĕuarĕstĕō**, *yoo-ar-es-teh'-o;* from *2101;* to *gratify entirely:*—please {2x}, be well pleased {1x}

Euaresteo, **(1)** in the active voice, Heb 11:5, "he pleased"; **(2)** so 11: 6; in the passive voice, Heb 13:16. See: TDNT—1:456, 77; BAGD—318c; THAYER—257d.

2101. **εὐάρεστος** {9x} **ĕuarĕstŏs**, *yoo-ar'-es-tos;* from *2095* and *701; fully agreeable:*—acceptable {4x}, well pleasing {3x}, please well + 1510 {1x}, accepted {1x}.

Euarestos is translated **(1)** "acceptable" Rom 12:1, 2; 14:8; Eph 5:10; Heb 13:1; **(2)** "well pleasing" Phil 4:18; Col 3:20; **(3)** "please well" Titus 2:9; **(4)** "accepted" 2 Cor 5:9. See: TDNT—1:456, 77; BAGD—318d; THAYER—257d.

2102. **εὐαρέστως** {1x} **ĕuarĕstōs**, *yoo-ar-es'-toce;* adv. from *2101; quite agreeably:*—acceptably {1x}.

Euarestos means in a manner well pleasing to one, acceptable, so as to please, Heb 12:28. See: BAGD—318d; THAYER—257d.

2103. **Εὔβουλος** {1x} **Ĕubŏulŏs**, *yoo'-boo-los;* from *2095* and *1014; good-willer; Eubulus,* a Chr.:—Eubulus {1x}. See: BAGD—319a; THAYER—257d.

2104. **εὐγένης** {3x} **ĕugĕnēs**, *yoog-en'-ace;* from *2095* and *1096; well born,* i.e. (lit.) *high* in rank, or (fig.) *generous:*—nobleman + 444 {1x}, more noble {1x}, noble {1x}.

Eugenes, an adjective, lit., "well born" (*eu,* "well," and *genos,* "a family, race"), **(1)** signifies "more noble," Acts 17:11; 1 Cor 1:26; and **(2)** is used with *anthropos*, "a man," i.e., "a nobleman," in Lk 19:12. See: BAGD—319a; THAYER—257d.

2105. **εὐδία** {1x} **ĕudia**, *yoo-dee'-ah;* fem. from *2095* and the alternate of *2203* (as the god of the weather); a *clear sky,* i.e. *fine weather:*—fair weather {1x}. See: BAGD—319a; THAYER—258a.

2106. **εὐδοκέω** {21x} **ĕudŏkĕō**, *yoo-dok-eh'-o;* from *2095* and *1380;* to *think well* of, i.e. *approve* (an act); spec., to *approbate* (a person or thing):—be well pleased {7x}, please {5x}, have pleasure {4x}, be willing {2x}, be (one's) good pleasure {1x}, take pleasure {1x}, think good {1x}.

Eudokeo signifies **(1)** "to be well pleased, to think it good" not merely an understanding of what is right and good as in *dokeo*, but stressing the willingness and freedom of an intention or resolve regarding what is good, e.g., Lk 12:32, "it is (your Father's) good pleasure"; so Rom 15:26, 27; 1 Cor 1:21; Gal 1:15; Col 1:19; 1 Th 2:8, "we were willing"; **(2)** "to be well pleased with," or "take pleasure in," e.g., Mt 3:17; 12:18; 17:5; 1 Cor 10:5; 2 Cor 12:10; 2 Th 2:12; Heb 10:6, 8, 38; 2 Pet 1:17. See: TDNT—2:738, 273; BAGD—319b; THAYER—258a.

2107. **εὐδοκία** {9x} **ĕudŏkia**, *yoo-dok-ee'-ah;* from a presumed compound of *2095* and the base of *1380; satisfaction,* i.e. (subj.) *delight,* or (obj.) *kindness, wish, purpose:*—good pleasure {4x}, good will {2x}, seem good + 1096 {2x}, desire {1x}.

Eudokia, lit., "good pleasure", implies a gracious purpose, a good object being in view, with the idea of a resolve, showing the willingness with which the resolve is made. It is often translated **(1)** "good pleasure," e.g., Eph 1:5, 9; Phil 2:13; **(2)** in Phil 1:15, "good will"; **(3)** in Rom 10:1, "desire"; **(4)** in 2 Th 1:11, "good pleasure." **(4)** It is used of God in Mt 11:26 "seemed good"; Lk 2:14; 10:21; Eph 1:5, 9; Phil 2:13. See: TDNT—2:742, 273; BAGD—319c; THAYER—258b.

2108. **εὐεργεσία** {2x} **ĕuĕrgĕsia**, *yoo-erg-es-ee'-ah;* from *2110; beneficence* (gen. or spec.):—benefit {1x}, good deed done {1x}. Cf. Acts 4:9, "good deed," and 1 Ti 6:2, "benefit." See: TDNT—2:654, 251; BAGD—319d; THAYER—258c.

2109. **εὐεργετέω** {1x} **ĕuĕrgĕtĕō**, *yoo-erg-et-eh'-o;* from *2110; to be philanthropic:*—doing good {1x}.

Euergeteo, as a verb, means "to bestow a benefit, to do good": "How God anointed Jesus of Nazareth with the Holy Ghost and with power: Who went about doing good, and healing all that were oppressed of the devil; for God was with Him" (Acts 10:38). See: TDNT—2:654, 251; BAGD—320a; THAYER—258c.

2110. **εὐεργέτης** {1x} **ĕuĕrgĕtēs**, *yoo-erg-et'-ace;* from *2095* and the base of *2041;* a *worker of good,* i.e. (spec.) a *philanthropist:*—benefactor {1x}. See: TDNT—2:654, 251; BAGD—320a; THAYER—258c.

2111. **εὔθετος** {3x} **ĕuthĕtŏs**, *yoo'-thet-os;* from *2095* and a der. of *5087; well placed,* i.e. (fig.) *appropriate:*—fit {2x}, meet {1x}.

Euthetos means "ready for use, fit, well adapted," lit., "well placed" (*eu,* "well," *tithemi,* "to place"), and is used **(1)** of persons, Lk 9:62, negatively, of one who is not fit for the kingdom of God; **(2)** of things, **(2a)** Lk 14:35, of salt that has lost its savor; **(2b)** rendered "meet" in Heb 6:7, of herbs. See: BAGD—320b; THAYER—258c.

2112. **εὐθέως** {80x} **ĕuthĕōs**, *yoo-theh'-oce;* adv. from *2117; directly,* i.e. *at once* or *soon:*—immediately {35x}, straightway {32x}, forthwith {7x}, misc. {6x} = anon, as soon as, shortly. See: BAGD—320b; THAYER—258d.

2113. **εὐθυδρομέω** {2x} **ĕuthudrŏmĕō**, *yoo-thoo-drom-eh'-o;* from *2117* and *1408;* to *lay a straight course,* i.e. *sail direct:*—(come) with a straight course {2x}. Cf. Acts 16:11; 21:1. See: BAGD—320d; THAYER—258d.

2114. **εὐθυμέω** {3x} **ĕuthumĕō**, *yoo-thoo-meh'-o;* from *2115;* to *cheer up,* i.e. (intr.) *be cheerful;* neut. comparative (adv.) *more cheerfully:*—be of good cheer {2x}, be merry {1x}. Euthumeo signifies, in the active voice, "to put in good spirits, to make cheerful" (*eu,* "well," *thumos,* "passion"); or **(1)** intransitively, "to be cheerful", Acts 27:22, 25; and **(2)** Jas 5:13 "merry". See: BAGD—320d; THAYER—258d.

2115. **εὔθυμος** {2x} **ĕuthumŏs**, *yoo'-thoo-mos;* from *2095* and *2372;* in *fine spirits,* i.e. *cheerful:*—of good cheer {1x}, the more cheerfully {1x}. Cf. Act 24:10; 27:36. See: BAGD—320d; THAYER—258d.

2116. **εὐθύνω** {2x} **ĕuthunō**, *yoo-thoo'-no;* from *2117;* to *straighten* (*level*); tech. to *steer:*—governor + 3588 {1x}, make straight {1x}.

Euthuno is used **(1)** of the directing of a ship by the steersman, Jas 3:4 (A governor is one who guides straight); **(2)** metaphorically, of making "straight" the way of the Lord, Jn 1:23. See: BAGD—320d; THAYER—258d.

2117. **εὐθύς** {16x} **ĕuthus**, *yoo-thoos';* perh. from *2095* and *5087; straight,* i.e. (lit.) *level,* or (fig.) *true;* adv. (of time) *at once:*—straight {5x}, right {3x}, immediately {3x}, straightway {2x}, anon {1x}, by and by {1x}, forthwith {1x}. See: BAGD—321a,b; THAYER—259a.

2118. **εὐθύτης** {1x} **ĕuthutēs**, *yoo-thoo'-tace;* from *2117; rectitude:*—righteousness {1x}. See: BAGD—321b; THAYER—259a.

2119. **εὐκαιρέω** {3x} **ĕukairĕō**, *yoo-kahee-reh'-o;* from *2121;* to *have good time,* i.e. *opportunity* or *leisure:*—have leisure {1x}, have convenient time {1x}, spend time {1x}.

Eukaireo, as a verb, means "to have time or leisure or convenient time" and is translated **(1)** "he shall have convenient time": "As touching *our* brother Apollos, I greatly desired him to come unto you with the brethren: but his will was not at all to come at this time; but he will come when he shall have convenient time" (1 Cor 16:12). It is also translated **(2)** "they had . . . leisure" in Mk 6:31; and **(3)** in Acts 17:21, "spent their time." Syn.: 170, 2120, 2540, 5117. See: BAGD—321b; THAYER—259a.

2120. **εὐκαιρία** {2x} **ĕukairia**, *yoo-kahee-ree'-ah;* from *2121;* a favorable *occasion:*—opportunity {2x}.

Eukairia, as a noun, means "a fitting time, opportunity": "And from that time he sought opportunity to betray him" (Mt 26:16; cf. Lk 22:6). Syn.: 170, 2119, 2540, 5117. See: TDNT—3:462, 389; BAGD—321; THAYER—259b.

2121. **εὔκαιρος** {2x} **ĕukairŏs**, *yoo'-kahee-ros;* from *2095* and *2540; well-timed,* i.e. *opportune:*—convenient {1x}, in time of need {1x}.

Eukairos, lit., "well-timed" (*eu,* "well," *kairos,* "a time, season"), hence signifies "timely, opportune, convenient"; it is said **(1)** of a certain day, Mk 6:21; elsewhere, **(2)** Heb 4:16, "in time of need." See: TDNT—3:462, 389; BAGD—321c; THAYER—259b.

2122. **εὐκαίρως** {2x} **ĕukairōs**, *yoo-kah'-ee-roce;* adv. from *2121; opportunely:*—conveniently {1x}, in season {1x}.

Eukairos, as an adverb, means **(1)** "in season": "Preach the word; be instant in season, out of season (akairos); reprove, rebuke, exhort with all longsuffering and doctrine" (2 Ti 4:2); or **(2)** "conveniently": "And when they heard *it,* they were glad, and promised to give him money. And he sought how he might conveniently betray him" (Mk 14:11). Syn.: 171, 2540, 3641, 4340, 5550, 5610. See: BAGD—321c; THAYER—259b.

2123. **εὐκοπώτερος** {7x} **ĕukŏpōtĕrŏs**, *yoo-kop-o'-ter-os;* comp. of a compound of *2095* and *2873; better for toil,* i.e. *more facile:*—easier {7x}.

Eukopoteros, the comparative degree of *eukopos,* "easy, with easy labor" (*eu,* "well," *kopos,* "labor"), hence, of that which is "easier to do," is found in the Synoptics only, Mt 9:5; 19:24; Mk 2:9; 10:25; Lk 5:23; 16:17; 18:25. See: BAGD—321d; THAYER—259b.

2124. **εὐλάβεια** {2x} **ĕulabĕia**, *yoo-lab'-i-ah;* from *2126;* prop. *caution,* i.e. (religiously) *reverence* (*piety*); by impl. *dread* (concr.):—godly fear {1x}, feared {1x}.

In general, this word means apprehension, but especially holy fear, that mingled fear and love which, combined, constitute the piety of man toward God; the OT places its emphasis on the fear, the NT . . . on the love, though there was love in the fear of God's saints then, as there must be fear in their love now. It signifies, firstly, "caution"; then, **(1)** "fear", Heb 5:7; and **(2)** "godly fear," Heb 12:28, "apprehension, but especially holy fear." Syn.: 1167, 5401. See: TDNT—2:751, 275; BAGD—321d; THAYER—259b.

2125. **εὐλαβέομαι** {2x} **ĕulabĕŏmai**, *yoo-lab-eh'-om-ahee;* mid. voice from *2126;* to *be circumspect,* i.e. (by impl.) to *be apprehensive;* religiously to *reverence:*—moved with fear {1x}, fear {1x}.

This word means to be cautious, to beware and signifies to act with the reverence produced by holy fear (Heb 11:7); moved with godly fear. It also speaks of human fear of something happening, Acts 23:10. See: TDNT—2:751,*; BAGD—321d; THAYER—259c.

2126. **εὐλαβής** {3x} **ĕulabēs**, *yoo-lab-ace';* from *2095* and *2983; taking well* (*carefully*), i.e. *circumspect* (religiously, *pious*):—devout {3x}.

Literally, this word means taking hold well, cautious; and signifies careful as to the realization of the presence and claims of God, reverencing God, pious, devout (Lk 2:25; Acts 2:5; 8:2) which manifests itself in caution and carefulness in human relationships. This one is a anxious and scrupulous worshipper who never changes or omits anything because he is afraid of offending. Syn.: 1174, 2152, 2318, 2357. See: TDNT—2:751,*; BAGD—322a; THAYER—259c.

2127. **εὐλογέω** {44x} **ĕulŏgĕō**, *yoo-log-eh'-o;* from a compound of *2095* and *3056;* to *speak well of,* i.e. (religiously) to *bless* (*thank* or *invoke a benediction upon, prosper*):—bless {43x}, praise {1x}.

Eulogeo literally means to speak well of and signifies **(1)** to praise, to celebrate with praises, of that which is addressed to God, acknowledging His goodness, with desire for His glory (Lk 1:64; 2:28; Jas 3:9); **(2)** to invoke blessings upon a person (Lk 6:28; Rom 12:14); **(3)** to consecrate/

bless a thing with solemn prayers, to ask God's blessing on a thing (Lk 9:16; 1 Cor 10:16); **(4)** to cause to prosper, to make happy, to bestow blessings on, said of God (Acts 3:26; Gal 3:9; Eph 1:3). Syn.: 1757, 2128, 2129. See: TDNT—2:754, 275; BAGD—322b; THAYER—259d.

2128. **εὐλογητός** {8x} **ĕulŏgētŏs**, *yoo-log-ay-tos'*; from *2127; adorable:*—blessed (said of God) {8x}. This word is only applied to God, Mk 14:61; Lk 1:68; Rom 1:25; 9:5; 2 Cor 1:3; 11:31; Eph 1:3; 1 Pet 1:3. See: TDNT—2:764, 275; BAGD—322c; THAYER—260a.

2129. **εὐλογία** {16x} **ĕulŏgia**, *yoo-log-ee'-ah;* from the same as *2127; fine speaking,* i.e. *elegance of language; commendation* ("*eulogy*"), i.e. (reverentially) *adoration;* religiously *benediction;* by impl. *consecration;* by extens. *benefit* or *largess:*—blessing {11x}, bounty {2x}, bountifully + 1909 {2x}, fair speech {1x}.

Eulogia, lit., "good speaking, praise," is used of **(1)** God and Christ, Rev 5:12–13; 7:12; **(2)** of the invocation of blessings, benediction, Heb 12:17; Jas 3:10; **(3)** of the giving of thanks, 1 Cor 10:16; **(4)** of a blessing, a benefit bestowed, Rom 15:29; Gal 3:14; Eph 1:3; Heb 6:7; **(5)** of a monetary gift sent to needy believers, 2 Cor 9:5–6; **(6)** in a bad sense, of fair speech, Rom 16:18, where it is joined with *chrestologia,* "smooth speech," the latter relating to the substance, *eulogia* to the expression. See: TDNT—2:754, 275; BAGD—322d; THAYER—260b.

2130. **εὐμετάδοτος** {1x} **ĕumĕtadŏtŏs**, *yoo-met-ad'-ot-os;* from *2095* and a presumed der. of *3330; good at imparting,* i.e. *liberal:*—ready to distribute {1x}. See: BAGD—323a; THAYER—260c.

2131. **Εὐνίκη** {1x} **Ĕunikē**, *yoo-nee'-kay;* from *2095* and *3529; victorious; Eunice,* a Jewess:—Eunice {1x}. See: BAGD—323b; THAYER—260c.

2132. **εὐνοέω** {1x} **ĕunŏĕō**, *yoo-no-eh'-o;* from a compound of *2095* and *3563;* to *be well-minded, well disposed, of a peaceable spirit,* i.e. *reconcile:*—agree {1x}. See: TDNT—4:971, 636; BAGD—323b; THAYER—260c.

2133. **εὔνοια** {2x} **ĕunŏia**, *yoo'-noy-ah;* from the same as *2132; kindness;* euphem. *conjugal duty:*—benevolence {1x}, good will {1x}.

Eunoia, "good will" is rendered **(1)** "benevolence" in 1 Cor 7:3; and **(2)** "good will" in Eph 6:7, "good will." See: TDNT—4:971, 636; BAGD—323b; THAYER—260c.

2134. **εὐνουχίζω** {2x} **ĕunŏuchizō**, *yoo-noo-khid'-zo;* from *2135;* to *castrate* (fig. *live unmarried*):—make . . . eunuch {2x}. Cf. Mt 19:12 (thrice). See: TDNT—2:765, 277; BAGD—323c; THAYER—260d.

2135. **εὐνοῦχος** {8x} **ĕunŏuchŏs**, *yoo-noo'-khos;* from εὐνή **ĕunē** (a *bed*) and *2192;* a *castrated* person (such being employed in Oriental bed-chambers); by extens. an *impotent* or *unmarried* man; by impl. a *chamberlain* (*state-officer*):—eunuch {8x}.

Eunouchos denotes **(1)** "an emasculated man, a eunuch," Mt 19:12; **(2)** in the 3rd instance in that Mt 19:12, "one naturally incapacitated for, or voluntarily abstaining from, wedlock"; **(3)** one such, in a position of high authority in a court, "a chamberlain," Acts 8:27–39 (5 times). See: TDNT—2:765, 277; BAGD—323c; THAYER—260d.

2136. **Εὐοδία** {1x} **Ĕuŏdia**, *yoo-od-ee'-ah;* from the same as *2137; fine travelling; Euodia,* a Chr. woman:—Euodias {1x}. See: BAGD—323d; THAYER—260d.

2137. **εὐοδόω** {4x} **ĕuŏdŏō**, *yoo-od-ŏ'-o;* from a compound of *2095* and *3598;* to *help* on the *road,* i.e. (pass.) *succeed in reaching;* fig. to *succeed* in business affairs:—prosper {3x}, have a prosperous journey {1x}.

Euodoo, "to help on one's way" (*eu,* "well," and *hodos*), is used in the passive voice with the meaning **(1)** "to have a prosperous journey"; so Rom 1:10; and **(2)** "to prosper", 1 Cor 16:2; 3 Jn 2. See: TDNT—5:109, 666; BAGD—323d; THAYER—260d.

2138. **εὐπειθής** {1x} **ĕupĕithēs**, *yoo-pi-thace';* from *2095* and *3982; good* for *persuasion,* i.e. (intr.) *compliant:*—easy to be intreated {1x}.

Eupeithes, "well persuaded" (*eu,* "well," *peithomai,* "to obey, to be persuaded"), "compliant," is translated "easy to be intreated" in Jas 3:17, said of the wisdom that is from above. Heavenly wisdom is unchanging, well-persuaded of its own unchangeableness (cf. wisdom in the Prov). Heavenly wisdom can be freely approached, is not rigid, but is open to discussion (compliant), will not waver but will attempt in gentleness to persuade. See: BAGD—324a; THAYER—261a.

2139. **εὐπερίστατος** {1x} **ĕupĕristatŏs**, *yoo-per-is'-tat-os;* from *2095* and a der. of a presumed compound of *4012* and *2476; well standing around,* i.e. (a *competitor*) *thwarting* (a racer) in every direction (fig. of sin in gen.):—which doth so easily beset {1x}.

It describes the sin of unbelief skillfully surrounding and as having advantage in favor of its prevailing, Heb 12:1. See: BAGD—324a; THAYER—261a.

2140. **εὐποιΐα** {1x} **ĕupŏiïa**, *yoo-poy-ee'-ah;* from a compound of *2095* and *4160; well-doing,* i.e. *beneficence:*—to do good {1x}.

Eupoiia, means "beneficence, doing good," and is translated as a verb, "to do good" in Heb 13:16: "But to do good and to communicate forget not: for with such sacrifices God is well pleased." See: BAGD—324a; THAYER—261a.

2141. **εὐπορέω** {1x} **ĕupŏrĕō**, *yoo-por-eh'-o;* from a compound of *2090* and the base of *4197;* (intr.) to *be good* for *passing* through, i.e. (fig.) *have* pecuniary *means:*—his ability + 5100 {1x}.

Euporeo, lit., "to journey well" (*eu,* "well," *poreo,* "to journey"), hence, "to prosper," is translated "according to (his) ability", "as he has been blessed in his life's journey", in Acts 11:29. See: BAGD—324b; THAYER—261b.

2142. **εὐπορία** {1x} **ĕupŏria**, *yoo-por-ee'-ah;* from the same as *2141;* pecuniary *resources:*—wealth {1x}. See: BAGD—324b; THAYER—261b.

2143. **εὐπρέπεια** {1x} **ĕuprĕpĕia**, *yoo-prep'-i-ah;* from a compound of *2095* and *4241; good suitableness,* i.e. *gracefulness:*—grace {1x}.

This word means outward comeliness, goodly appearance, shapeliness, and beauty and is said of the outward appearance of the flower of the grass (Jas 1:11). See: BAGD—324b; THAYER—261b.

2144. **εὐπρόσδεκτος** {5x} **ĕuprŏsdĕktŏs**, *yoo-pros'-dek-tos;* from *2095* and a der. of *4327; well-received,* i.e. *approved, favorable:*—acceptable {2x}, accepted {3x}.

This word is a strong form and signifies a very favorable acceptance (Rom 15:16, 31; 2 Cor 6:2; 8:12; 1 Pet 2:5). See: TDNT—2:58, 146; BAGD—324c; THAYER—261b.

2145. **εὐπρόσεδρος** {1x} **ĕuprŏsĕdrŏs**, *yoo-pros'-ed-ros;* from *2095* and the same as *4332; sitting well toward,* i.e. (fig.) *assiduous* (neut. *diligent service*):—that (one) may attend upon + 4314 + 3588 {1x}.

Euprosedros, lit., "sitting well beside", i.e., sitting constantly by, and so applying oneself diligently to, anything, is used in 1 Cor 7:35, with *pros,* "upon," "that ye may attend upon." See: BAGD—324c; THAYER—261b.

2146. **εὐπροσωπέω** {1x} **ĕuprŏsōpĕō**, *yoo-pros-o-peh'-o;* from a compound of *2095* and *4383;* to *be of good countenance,* i.e. (fig.) to *make a display:*—make a fair show {1x}.

Euprosopeo denotes "to look well, make a fair show" (*eu,* "well," *prosopon,* "a face"), and is used in Gal 6:12, "to make a fair show (in the flesh)," i.e., "to make a display of religious zeal." See: TDNT—6:779, 950; BAGD—324d; THAYER—261b.

2147. **εὑρίσκω** {178x} **hĕuriskō**, *hyoo-ris'-ko;* a prol. form of a primary **εὕρω hĕurō**, *hyoo'-ro;* which (together with another cognate form **εὑρέω hĕurĕō**, *hyoo-reh'-o*) is used for it in all the tenses except the present and imperfect; to *find* (lit. or fig.):—find {174x}, get {1x}, obtain {1x}, perceive {1x}, see {1x}. See: TDNT—2:769,*; BAGD—324d; THAYER—261c.

2148. **Εὐροκλύδων** {1x} **Ĕurŏkludōn**, *yoo-rok-loo'-dohn;* from Εὖρος **Ĕurŏs** (the *east* wind) and *2830;* a *storm from the East* (or Southeast), i.e. (in modern phrase) a *Levanter:*—Euroklydon {1x}. See: BAGD—325d; THAYER—262b.

2149. **εὐρύχωρος** {1x} **ĕuruchōrŏs**, *yoo-roo'-kho-ros;* from εὐρύς **ĕurus** (*wide*) and *5561; spacious:*—broad {1x}. See: BAGD—326a; THAYER—262c.

2150. **εὐσέβεια** {15x} **ĕusĕbĕia**, *yoo-seb'-i-ah;* from *2152; piety;* spec. the *gospel* scheme:—godliness {14x}, holiness {1x}.

(1) It is from *eu,* "well," and *sebomai,* "to be devout," denotes that piety which, characterized by a Godward attitude, does that which is well-pleasing to Him. **(1a)** This and the corresponding verb and adverb are frequent in the Pastoral Epistles, but do not occur in previous epistles of Paul. **(1b)** The apostle Peter has the noun four times in his 2nd Epistle, 1:3, 6, 7; 3:11. **(1c)** Elsewhere it occurs in Acts 3:12; 1 Ti 2:2; 3:16; 4:7, 8; 6:3, 5, 6, 11; 2 Ti 3:5; Titus 1:1. **(2)** In 1 Ti 6:3 "the doctrine which is according to godliness" signifies that which is consistent with "godliness," in contrast to false teachings; **(3)** in Titus 1:1, "the truth which is according to godliness" is that which is productive of "godliness"; **(4)** in 1 Ti 3:16, "the mystery of godliness" is "godliness" as embodied in, and communicated through, the truths of the faith concerning Christ; **(5)** in 2 Pet 3:11, the word is in the plural, signifying acts of "godliness." See: TDNT—7:175, 1010; BAGD—326a; THAYER—262c.

2151. **εὐσεβέω** {2x} **ĕusĕbĕō**, *yoo-seb-eh'-o;* from *2152;* to *be pious,* i.e. (toward God) to *worship,* or (toward parents) to *respect* (*support*):—show piety {1x}, worship {1x}.

Eusebeo, "to reverence, to show piety" towards any to whom dutiful regard is due and is used **(1)** in 1 Ti 5:4 of the obligation on the part

Greek

of children to express in a practical way their dutifulness "towards their own family"; **(2)** in Acts 17:23 of worshiping God. See: TDNT—7:175, 1010; BAGD—326b; THAYER—262c.

2152. **εὐσεβής** {4x} **ĕusĕbēs**, *yoo-seb-ace';* from *2095* and *4576; well-reverent,* i.e. *pious:*—devout {3x}, godly {1x}.

The root of this word—seb—signifies sacred awe and describes reverence exhibited especially in actions; reverence or awe well directed. In the NT it is used **(1)** "devout", of a pious attitude towards God, Acts 10:2, 7; 22:12; **(2)** "godly," in 2 Pet 2:9. Syn.: 1174, 2126, 2318, 2357. See: TDNT—7:175, 1010; BAGD—326b; THAYER—262d.

2153. **εὐσεβῶς** {2x} **ĕusĕbōs**, *yoo-seb-oce';* adv. from *2152; piously:*—godly {2x}.

This word denotes "piously, godly"; it is used with the verb "to live" (of manner of life) in 2 Ti 3:12; Titus 2:12. See: BAGD—326c; THAYER—262d.

2154. **εὔσημος** {1x} **ĕusēmŏs**, *yoo'-say-mos;* from *2095* and the base of *4591; well indicated,* i.e. (fig.) *significant:*—easy to be understood {1x}.

Eusemos primarily denotes "conspicuous" or "glorious", then, "distinct, clear to understanding," "easy to be understood" well marked, clear and definite, distinct, 1 Cor 14:9. See: TDNT—2:770, 278; BAGD—32c; THAYER—262d.

2155. **εὔσπλαγχνος** {2x} **ĕusplagchnŏs**, *yoo'-splangkh-nos;* from *2095* and *4698; well compassioned,* i.e. *sympathetic:*—pitiful {1x}, tender-hearted {1x}.

This word denotes "compassionate, tender hearted," lit., "of good heartedness" and is translated **(1)** "pitiful" in 1 Pet. 3:8, and **(2)** "tender-hearted" in Eph 4:32. See: TDNT—7:548, 1067; BAGD—320d; THAYER—262d.

2156. **εὐσχημόνως** {3x} **ĕuschēmŏnōs**, *yoo-skhay-mon'-oce;* adv. from *2158; decorously:*—decently {1x}, honestly {2x}.

This word denotes "gracefully, becomingly, in a seemly manner" (*eu,* "well," *schema,* "a form, figure"); and is translated **(1)** "honestly," **(1a)** in Rom 13:13, in contrast to the shamefulness of Gentile social life; and **(1b)** in 1 Th 4:12, the contrast is to idleness and its concomitant evils and the resulting bad testimony to unbelievers; **(2)** in 1 Cor 14:40, "decently," where the contrast is to disorder in oral testimony in the churches. See: BAGD—327a; THAYER—262d.

2157. **εὐσχημοσύνη** {1x} **ĕuschēmŏsunē**, *yoo-skhay-mos-oo'-nay;* from *2158; decorousness:*—comeliness {1x}.

This word depicts charm or elegance of figure, external beauty, decorum, modesty, seemliness, of external charm, comeliness, 1 Cor 12:23. See: BAGD—327a; THAYER—262d.

2158. **εὐσχήμων** {5x} **ĕuschēmōn**, *yoo-skhay'-mone;* from *2095* and *4976; well-formed,* i.e. (fig.) *decorous, noble* (in rank):—comely {2x}, honourable {3x}.

This word stresses **(1)** "comely", elegant figure, shapely, graceful, bearing one's self becomingly in speech or behaviour; or by extension, 1 Cor 7:35; 12:24; and **(2)** "honourable", of good standing, influential, wealthy, respectable, Mk 15:43; Acts 13:50; 17:12. See: TDNT—2:770, 278; BAGD—327a; THAYER—263a.

2159. **εὐτόνως** {2x} **ĕutŏnōs**, *yoo-ton'-oce;* adv. from a compound of *2095* and a der. of τείνω **tĕinō** (to *stretch*); *in a well-strung manner,* i.e. (fig.) *intensely* (in a good sense, *cogently;* in a bad one, *fiercely*):—mightily {1x}, vehemently {1x}.

This word means "vigorously, vehemently" and is translated **(1)** "mightily" in Acts 18:28, of the power of Apollos in "confuting" the Jews; and **(2)** in Lk 23:10 it is rendered "vehemently." See: BAGD—327b; THAYER—263a.

2160. **εὐτραπελία** {1x} **ĕutrapĕlia**, *yoo-trap-el-ee'-ah;* from a compound of *2095* and a der. of the base of *5157* (mean. *well-turned,* i.e. *ready at repartee, jocose*); *witticism,* i.e. (in a vulgar sense) *ribaldry:*—jesting {1x}.

Paul did not use this method which in its common, worldly sense means something that turns easily, of something that adapts itself to the shifting circumstances of the hour, to the moods and conditions of those around it, Eph 5:4. Syn.: 148, 3437. See: BAGD—327c; THAYER—263a.

2161. **Εὔτυχος** {1x} **Ĕutuchŏs**, *yoo'-too-khos;* from *2095* and a der. of *5177; well-fated,* i.e. *fortunate; Eutychus,* a young man:—Eutychus {1x}. See: BAGD—327c; THAYER—263b.

2162. **εὐφημία** {1x} **ĕuphēmia**, *yoo-fay-mee'-ah;* from *2163; good language* ("*euphemy*"), i.e. *praise* (*repute*):—good report {1x}. See: BAGD—327c; THAYER—263b.

2163. **εὔφημος** {1x} **ĕuphēmŏs**, *yoo'-fay-mos;* from *2095* and *5345; well spoken of,* i.e. *reputable:*—of good report {1x}. See: BAGD—327c; THAYER—263b.

2164. **εὐφορέω** {1x} **ĕuphŏrĕō**, *yoo-for-eh'-o;* from *2095* and *5409; to bear well,* i.e. *be fertile:*—bring forth plentifully {1x}. See: BAGD—327c; THAYER—263b.

2165. **εὐφραίνω** {14x} **ĕuphrainō**, *yoo-frah'-ee-no;* from *2095* and *5424; to put* (mid. or pass. *be*) *in a good* frame of *mind,* i.e. *rejoice:*—rejoice {6x}, be merry {3x}, make merry {3x}, fare {1x}, make glad {1x}.

Euphraino, as a verb, means "to cheer, gladden," is translated **(1)** "rejoice", Acts 2:26; 7:41; Rom 15:10; Gal 4:7; Rev 12:12; 18:20; **(2)** "be merry", Lk 12:19; 15:23, 24; **(3)** "make merry", Lk 15:29, 32; Rev 11:10; **(4)** "fared", Lk 16:19; **(5)** "make glad", 2 Cor 2:2. Syn.: 21, 5463. See: TDNT—2:772, 278; BAGD—327c; THAYER—263b.

2166. **Εὐφράτης** {2x} **Ĕuphratēs**, *yoo-frat'-ace;* of for. or. [comp. 6578]; *Euphrates,* a river of Asia:—*Euphrates* {2x}. See: BAGD—328a; THAYER—263c.

2167. **εὐφροσύνη** {2x} **ĕuphrŏsunē**, *yoo-fros-oo'-nay;* from the same as *2165; joyfulness:*—gladness {1x}, joy {1x}.

Euphrosune, "good cheer, joy, mirth, gladness of heart" is rendered **(1)** "joy" in Acts 2:28, and **(2)** "gladness in Acts 14:17. See: TDNT—2:772, 278; BAGD—328a; THAYER—263c.

2168. **εὐχαριστέω** {39x} **ĕucharistĕō**, *yoo-khar-is-teh'-o;* from *2170; to be grateful,* i.e. (act.) to *express gratitude* (toward); spec. to *say grace* at a meal:—give thanks {26x}, thank {12x}, be thankful {1x}.

Eucharisteo, as a verb, means "to give thanks," **(1)** is said of Christ, Mt 15:36; 26:27; Mk 8:6; 14:23; Lk 22:17, 19; Jn 6:11, 23; 11:41; 1 Cor 11:24; **(2)** of the Pharisee in Lk 18:11 in his self-complacent prayer; **(3)** "giving thanks" is used by Paul **(3a)** at the beginning of all his epistles, except 2 Cor, Gal, 1 Ti, 2 Tim, and Titus, **(3b)** for his readers, Rom 1:8; Eph 1:16; Col 1:3; 1 Thess 1:2; 2 Th 1:3 (cf. 2:13); virtually so in Philem 4; **(3c)** for fellowship shown, Phil 1:3; **(3d)** for God's gifts to them, 1 Cor 1:4; **(4)** is recorded **(4a)** of Paul elsewhere, Acts 27:35; 28:15; Rom 7:25; 1 Cor 1:14; 14:18; **(4b)** of Paul and others, Rom 16:4; 1 Th 2:13; **(4c)** of himself, representatively, as a practice, 1 Cor 10:30; **(4d)** of others, Lk 17:16; Rom 14:6 (twice); 1 Cor 14:17; Rev 11:17; **(4e)** is used in admonitions to the saints, the Name of the Lord Jesus suggesting His character and example, Eph 5:20; Col 1:12; 3:17; 1 Th 5:18; **(4f)** as the expression of a purpose, 2 Cor 1:11; **(4g)** negatively of the ungodly, Rom 1:21. **(5)** "Thanksgiving" is the expression of joy Godward, and is therefore the fruit of the Spirit (Gal 5:22); believers are encouraged to abound in it (e.g., Col 2:7). Syn.: 437, 1843, 2169. See: TDNT—9:407, 1298; BAGD—328a; THAYER—263c.

2169. **εὐχαριστία** {15x} **ĕucharistia**, *yoo-khar-is-tee'-ah;* from *2170; gratitude;* act. *grateful language* (to God, as an act of worship):—thanksgiving {9x}, giving of thanks {3x}, thanks {2x}, thankfulness {1x}.

(1) This prayer expresses the grateful acknowledgement of past mercies as distinct from seeking future ones. *Eucharistia* denotes **(2)** "gratitude," "thankfulness," Acts 24:3; **(3)** "giving of thanks, thanksgiving," 1 Cor 14:16; 2 Cor 4:15; 9:11, 12 (plur.); Eph 5:4; Phil 4:6; Col 2:7; 4:2; 1 Th 3:9 ("thanks"); 1 Ti 2:1 (plur.); 4:3, 4; Rev 4:9, "thanks"; 7:12. Syn.: 155, 1162, 1783, 2171, 2428. See: TDNT—9:407, 1298; BAGD—328c; THAYER—264a.

2170. **εὐχάριστος** {1x} **ĕucharistŏs**, *yoo-khar'-is-tos;* from *2095* and a der. of *5483; well favored,* i.e. (by impl.) *grateful:*—thankful {1x}.

(1) This word stresses mindful of favours. **(2)** It means primarily, "gracious, agreeable" then "grateful, thankful," and is so used in Col 3:15. See: TDNT—9:407, 1298; BAGD—329a; THAYER—264a.

2171. **εὐχή** {3x} **ĕuchē**, *yoo-khay';* from *2172;* prop. a *wish,* expressed as a *petition* to God, or in *votive* obligation:—prayer {1x}, vow {2x}.

(1) The concept of the vow or dedicated thing is more present than prayer in this word. *Euche* denotes **(2)** "a prayer," Jas 5:15; and **(2)** "a vow," Acts 18:18 and 21:23. See: TDNT—2:775, 279; BAGD—329b; THAYER—264a.

2172. **εὔχομαι** {7x} **ĕuchŏmai**, *yoo'-khom-ahee;* mid. voice of a primary verb; to *wish;* by impl. to *pray* to God:—wish {3x}, pray {2x}, can wish {1x}, I would to God {1x}.

Euchomai, **(1)** "to pray (to God)," is used with this meaning in 2 Cor 13:7, Jas 5:16. Even when it is translated **(2)** "wish", Acts 27:29; 2 Cor 13:9; 3 Jn 1:2; **(3)** "can wish", Rom 9:3; **(4)** "I would to God," Acts 26:29, the indication is that "prayer" is involved. See: TDNT—2:775, 279; BAGD—329b; THAYER—264b.

2173. **εὔχρηστος** {3x} **ĕuchrēstŏs**, *yoo'-khrays-tos;* from *2095* and *5543; easily used,* i.e. *useful:*—profitable {2x}, meet for use {1x}.

This word means easy to make use of, useful and is translated **(1)** "profitable", 2 Ti 4:11; Philem 11; and **(2)** "meet for use", 2 Ti 2:21. See: BAGD—329c; THAYER—264b.

2174. **εὐψυχέω** {1x} **ĕupsuchĕō**, *yoo-psoo-kheh'-o;* from a compound of *2095* and *5590;* to *be in good spirits,* i.e. *feel encouraged:*—be of good comfort {1x}.

This word means to be of good courage, to be of a cheerful spirit, Phil 2:19. See: BAGD—329d; THAYER—264b.

2175. **εὐωδία** {3x} **ĕuōdia**, *yoo-o-dee'-ah;* from a compound of *2095* and a der. of *3605; good-scentedness,* i.e. *fragrance:*—sweet savour {1x}, sweet smell {1x}, sweet smelling {1x}.

Euodia, "fragrance" is used metaphorically **(1)** of those who in the testimony of the gospel are to God "a sweet savor of Christ," 2 Cor 2:15; **(2)** of the giving up of His life by Christ for us, an offering and a sacrifice to God for an odor of "a sweet smelling savor," Eph 5:2; and **(3)** of material assistance sent to Paul from the church at Philippi "(an odor) of a sweet smell," Phil 4:18. In all three instances the fragrance is that which ascends to God through the person, and as a result of the sacrifice, of Christ. See: TDNT—2:808, 285; BAGD—329d; THAYER—264b.

2176. **εὐώνυμος** {10x} **ĕuōnumŏs**, *yoo-o'-noo-mos;* from *2095* and *3686;* prop. *well-named* (*good-omened*), i.e. the *left* (which was the *lucky* side among the pagan Greeks); neut. as adv. *at the left* hand:—left {5x}, on the left hand {4x}, left foot {1x}. See: BAGD—39d; THAYER—264c.

2177. **ἐφάλλομαι** {1x} **ĕphallŏmai**, *ef-al'-lom-ahee;* from *1909* and *242;* to *spring upon:*—leap on {1x}. See: BAGD—330a; THAYER—264c.

2178. **ἐφάπαξ** {5x} **ĕphapax**, *ef-ap'-ax;* from *1909* and *530; upon one occasion* (only):—(at) once (for all) {5x}.

Ephapax a strengthened form signifies **(1)** "once (for all)," Rom 6:10; Heb 7:27; 9:12; 10:10; **(2)** "at once," 1 Cor 15:6. See: TDNT—1:383, 64; BAGD—330a; THAYER—264d.

2179. **Ἐφεσῖνος** {1x} **Ĕphĕsinŏs**, *ef-es-ee'-nos;* from *2181; Ephesine,* or situated at Ephesus:—of Ephesus {1x}. See: BAGD—330a; THAYER—264d.

2180. **Ἐφέσιος** {7x} **Ĕphĕsiŏs**, *ef-es'-ee-os;* from *2181;* an *Ephesian* or inhab. of Ephesus:—Ephesian {6x}, of Ephesus {1x}. See: BAGD—330b; THAYER—264d.

2181. **Ἔφεσος** {15x} **Ĕphĕsŏs**, *ef'-es-os;* prob. of for. or.; *Ephesus,* a city of Asia Minor:—Ephesus {15x}. See: BAGD—330b; THAYER—264d.

2182. **ἐφευρέτης** {1x} **ĕphĕurĕtēs**, *ef-yoo-ret'-ace;* from a compound of *1909* and *2147;* a *discoverer,* i.e. *contriver:*—inventor {1x}. See: BAGD—330b; THAYER—265a.

2183. **ἐφημερία** {2x} **ĕphēmĕria**, *ef-ay-mer-ee'-ah;* from *2184; diurnality,* i.e. (spec.) the quotidian *rotation* or *class* of the Jewish priests' service at the Temple, as distributed by families:—course {2x}. Cf. Lk 1:5, 8. See: BAGD—330c; THAYER—265a.

2184. **ἐφήμερος** {1x} **ĕphēmĕrŏs**, *ef-ay'-mer-os;* from *1909* and *2250; for a day* ("ephemeral"), i.e. *diurnal (happening each day):*—daily {1x}. See: BAGD—330c; THAYER—265a.

2185. **ἐφικνέομαι** {2x} **ĕphiknĕŏmai**, *ef-ik-neh'-om-ahee;* from *1909* and a cognate of *2240;* to *arrive upon,* i.e. *extend to:*—reach {2x}. Cf. 2 Cor. 10:13, 14. See: BAGD—330c; THAYER—265b.

2186. **ἐφίστημι** {21x} **ĕphistēmi**, *ef-is'-tay-mee;* from *1909* and *2476;* to *stand upon,* i.e. *be present* (in various applications, friendly or otherwise, usually lit.);—come upon {6x}, come {4x}, stand {3x}, stand by {3x}, misc. {5x} = assault, be at hand (instant), present. See: BAGD—330d; THAYER—265b.

2187. **Ἐφραΐμ** {1x} **Ĕphraïm**, *ef-rah-im';* of Heb. or. [669 or better 6085]; *Ephraïm,* a place in Pal.:—*Ephraim* {1x}. See: BAGD—331a; THAYER—265b.

2188. **ἐφφαθά** {1x} **ĕphphatha**, *ef-fath-ah';* of Chald. or. [6606]; *be opened!:*—*Ephphatha* {1x}. See: BAGD—331b; THAYER—265c.

2189. **ἔχθρα** {6x} **ĕchthra**, *ekh'-thrah;* fem. of *2190; hostility;* by impl. a reason for *opposition:*—enmity {5x}, hatred {1x}.

Echthra is rendered **(1)** "enmity" in Lk 23:12; Rom 8:7; Eph 2:15–16; Jas 4:4; and **(2)** "hatred", Gal 5:20. **(3)** It is the opposite of *agape,* "love." See: TDNT—2:815, 285; BAGD—331b; THAYER—265c.

2190. **ἐχθρός** {32x} **ĕchthrŏs**, *ekh-thros';* from a primary ἔχθω **ĕchthō** (to *hate*); *hateful* (pass. *odious,* or act. *hostile*); usually as a noun, an *adversary* (espec. *Satan*):—enemy {30x}, foe {2x}.

Echthros, an adjective, primarily denoting "hated" or "hateful" hence, in the active sense, denotes "hating, hostile." It is used as a noun signifying an "enemy," adversary, and is said **(1)** of the Devil, Mt 13:39; Lk 10:19; **(2)** of death, 1 Cor 15:26; **(3)** of the professing believer who would be a friend of the world, thus making himself an enemy of God, Jas 4:4; **(4)** of men who are opposed **(4a)** to Christ, Mt 13:25, 28; 22:44; Mk 12:36; Lk 19:27; 20:43; Acts 2:35; Rom 11:28; Phil 3:18; Heb 1:13; 10:13; or **(4b)** to His servants, Rev 11:5, 12; **(4c)** to the nation of Israel, Lk 1:71, 74; 19:43; **(5)** of one who is opposed to righteousness, Acts 13:10; **(6)** of Israel in its alienation from God, Rom 11:28; **(7)** of the unregenerate in their attitude toward God, Rom 5:10; Col 1:21; **(8)** of believers in their former state, 2 Th 3:15; **(9)** of foes, Mt 5:43–44; 10:36; Lk 6:27, 35; Rom 12:20; 1 Cor 15:25; **(10)** of the apostle Paul because he told converts "the truth," Gal 4:16. See: TDNT—2:811, 285; BAGD—331b; THAYER—265c.

2191. **ἔχιδνα** {5x} **ĕchidna**, *ekh'-id-nah;* of uncert. or.; an *adder* or other poisonous snake (lit. or fig.):—viper {5x}.

Echidna is probably a generic term for "poisonous snakes." It is rendered "viper" **(1)** of the actual creature, Acts 28:3; **(2)** metaphorically in Mt 3:7; 12:34; 23:33; Lk 3:7. See: TDNT—2:815, 286; BAGD—331d; THAYER—265d.

2192. **ἔχω** {712x} **ĕchō**, *ekh'-o;* (incl. an alt. form **σχέω** **schĕō**, *skheh'-o;* used in certain tenses only); a primary verb; to *hold* (used in very various applications, lit. or fig., direct or remote; such as *possession; ability, contiguity, relation,* or *condition*):—have {613x}, be {22x}, need + 5532 {12x}, vr have {2x}, misc {63x} = accompany, + begin to amend, can (+ -not), × conceive, count, diseased, do + eat, + enjoy, + fear, following, hold, keep, + lack, + go to law, lie, + must needs, + of necessity, next, + recover, + reign, + rest, return, × sick, take for, + tremble, + uncircumcised, use.

This word stresses that one has the means to accomplish a task. See: TDNT—2:816, 286; BAGD—331d; THAYER—365d.

2193. **ἕως** {148x} **hĕōs**, *heh'-oce;* of uncert. aff.; a conjunc., prep. and adv. of continuance, *until* (of time and place):—till {28x}, unto {27x}, until {25x}, to {16x}, till + 3739 {11x}, misc. {41x} = even (until, unto), (as) far (as), how long, (hither-, up) to, while (-s). See: BAGD—334b; THAYER—268a.

Z

2194. **Ζαβουλών** {3x} **Zabŏulōn**, *dzab-oo-lone';* of Heb. or. [2074]; *Zabulon* (i.e. *Zebulon*), a region of Pal.:—Zabulon {3x}. See: BAGD—335b; THAYER—269a.

2195. **Ζακχαῖος** {3x} **Zakchaiŏs**, *dzak-chah'-ee-yos;* of Heb. or. [comp. 2140]; *Zacchœus,* an Isr.:—Zacchæus {3x}. See: BAGD—335b; THAYER—269a.

2196. **Ζαρά** {1x} **Zara**, *dzar-ah';* of Heb. or. [2226]; *Zara,* (i.e. *Zerach*), an Isr.:—*Zara* {1x}. See: BAGD—335d; THAYER—269a.

2197. **Ζαχαρίας** {11x} **Zacharias**, *dzakh-ar-ee'-as;* of Heb. or. [2148]; *Zacharias* (i.e. *Zechariah*), the name of two Isr.:—*Zacharias* {11x}. See: BAGD—335d; THAYER—269a.

2198. **ζάω** {143x} **zaō**, *dzah'-o;* a primary verb; to *live* (lit. or fig.):—live {117x}, be alive {9x}, alive {6x}, quick {4x}, lively {3x}, not tr {1x}, vr live {1x}, life {1x}, lifetime {1x}.

Zao, as a verb, means "to live, be alive" and is used in the NT of **(1)** God: "And Simon Peter answered and said, Thou art the Christ, the Son of the living God" Mt 16:16; cf. Jn 6:57; Rom 14:11; **(2)** the Son in Incarnation: "He that eateth My flesh, and drinketh My blood, dwelleth in Me, and I in him" (Jn 6:57); **(3)** the Son in Resurrection: "Yet a little while, and the world seeth Me no more; but ye see Me: because I live, ye shall live also" (Jn 14:19; cf. Acts 1:3; Rom 6:10; 2 Cor 13:4; Heb 7:8); **(4)** spiritual life: "As the living Father hath sent Me, and I live by the Father: so he that eateth Me, even he shall live by Me" (Jn 6:57; cf. Rom 1:17; 8:13b; Gal 2:19, 20; Heb 12:9); **(5)** the present state of departed saints: "For He is not a God of the dead, but of the living: for all live unto Him" (Lk 20:38; 1 Pet 4:6); **(6)** the hope of resurrection: "Blessed *be* the God and Father of our Lord Jesus Christ, which according to His abundant mercy hath begotten us again unto a lively hope by the resurrection of Jesus Christ from the dead" (1 Pet 1:3);

(7) the resurrection **(7a)** of believers: "Who died for us, that, whether we wake or sleep, we should live together with Him" (1 Th 5:10; cf. Jn 5:25; Rev 20:4), and **(7b)** of unbelievers: "But the rest of the dead lived not again until the thousand years were finished. This *is* the first resurrection" (Rev 20:5); **(8)** the way of access to God through the Lord Jesus Christ: "By a new and living way, which He hath consecrated for us, through the veil, that is to say, His flesh" (Heb 10:20); **(9)** the manifestation of divine power in support of divine authority; "For though He was crucified through weakness, yet He liveth by the power of God. For we also are weak in Him, but we shall live with Him by the power of God toward you" (2 Cor 13:4b; cf. 12:10; 1 Cor 5:5); **(10)** bread: "I am the living bread which came down from heaven: if any man eat of this bread, he shall live for ever: and the bread that I will give is my flesh, which I will give for the life of the world" (Jn 6:51 figurative of the Lord Jesus); **(11)** a stone "To Whom coming, *as unto* a living stone, disallowed indeed of men, but chosen of God, *and* precious" (1 Pet 2:4 figurative of the Lord Jesus);

(12) water: "Jesus answered and said unto her, If thou knewest the gift of God, and who it is that saith to thee, Give me to drink; thou wouldest have asked of him, and he would have given thee living water" (Jn 4:10 figurative of the Holy Spirit; 7:38); **(13)** a sacrifice: "I beseech you therefore, brethren, by the mercies of God, that ye present your bodies a living sacrifice, holy, acceptable unto God, *which is* your reasonable service" (Rom 12:1 figurative of the believer); **(14)** stones: "Ye also, as lively stones, are built up a spiritual house, an holy priesthood, to offer up spiritual sacrifices, acceptable to God by Jesus Christ" (1 Pet 2:5 figurative of the believer); **(15)** the oracles, logion, word, logos, of God: "This is he [Moses], that was in the church in the wilderness with the angel which spake to him in the mount Sina, and *with* our fathers: who received the lively oracles to give unto us"(Acts 7:38; cf. Heb 4:12; 1 Pet 1:23);

(16) the physical life of men: "For this we say unto you by the word of the Lord, that we which are alive *and* remain unto the coming of the Lord shall not prevent them which are asleep" (1 Th 4:15; Mt 27:63; Acts 25:24; Rom 14:9; Phil 1:21 in the infinitive mood used as a noun with the article, 'living', 22; 1 Pet 4:5); **(17)** the maintenance of physical life: "But He answered and said, It is written, Man shall not live by bread alone, but by every word that proceedeth out of the mouth of God" (Mt 4:4; cf. 1 Cor 9:14); **(18)** the duration of physical life: "And deliver them who through fear of death were all their lifetime subject to bondage" (Heb 2:15); **(19)** the enjoyment of physical life: "For now we live, if ye stand fast in the Lord" (1 Th 3:8); **(20)** the recovery of physical life from the power of disease: "And besought Him greatly, saying, My little daughter lieth at the point of death: *I pray thee,* come and lay thy hands on her, that she may be healed; and she shall live" (Mk 5:23; cf. Jn 4:50);

(21) the recovery of physical life from the power of death: "While He spake these things unto them, behold, there came a certain ruler, and worshipped Him, saying, My daughter is even now dead: but come and lay thy hand upon her, and she shall live" (Mt 9:18; cf. Acts 9:41; Rev 20:5); **(22)** the course, conduct, and character of men: **(22a)** good: "Which knew me from the beginning, if they would testify, that after the most straitest sect of our religion I lived a Pharisee" (Acts 26:5; cf. 2 Ti 3:12; Titus 2:12); **(22b)** evil: "And not many days after the younger son gathered all together, and took his journey into a far country, and there wasted his substance with riotous living" (Lk 15:13; cf. Rom 6:2; 8:13a; 2 Cor 5:15b; Col 3:7); **(22c)** undefined: "For I was alive without the law once: but when the commandment came, sin revived, and I died" (Rom 7:9; 14:7; Gal 2:14); **(22d)** restoration after alienation: "It was meet that we should make merry, and be glad: for this thy brother was dead, and is alive again; and was lost, and is found" (Lk 15:32).

(23) Note: In 1 Th 5:10, to live means to experience that change, 1 Cor 15:51, which is to be the portion of all in Christ who will be alive upon the earth at the Parousia of the Lord Jesus, cf. Jn 11:25, and which corresponds to the resurrection of those who had previously died in Christ, 1 Cor 15:52–54. **(24)** Note: *Zao* is translated **(24a)** "quick": "And He commanded us to preach unto the people, and to testify that it is He which was ordained of God *to be* the Judge of quick and dead" (Acts 10:42; cf. 2 Tim 4:1; 1 Pet 4:5); and **(24b)** "living": "For the word of God *is* quick, and powerful, and sharper than any two-edged sword, piercing even to the dividing asunder of soul and spirit, and of the joints and marrow, and *is* a discerner of the thoughts and intents of the heart" (Heb 4:12). Quick implies the ability to respond immediately to God's word and living stresses the ongoing nature of His word; it is just as effective today as tomorrow. Syn.: 326, 390, 980, 1236, 2225, 4176, 4800, 5225. See: TDNT—2:832, 290; BAGD—336a; THAYER—269c.

2199. **Ζεβεδαῖος** {12x} **Zĕbĕdaiŏs**, *dzeb-ed-ah'-yos;* of Heb. or. [comp. 2067]; *Zebedœus,* an Isr.:—Zebedee {12x}. See: BAGD—337b; THAYER—270d.

2200. **ζεστός** {3x} **zĕstŏs**, *dzes-tos';* from *2204; boiled,* i.e. (by impl.) *calid* (fig. *fervent*):—hot {3x}.

Zestos means "boiling hot" (from *zeo,* "to boil, be hot, fervent"; cf. Eng., "zest"), and is used, metaphorically, in Rev 3:15 (twice), 16. See: TDNT—2:876, 296; BAGD—337b; THAYER—270d.

2201. **ζεῦγος** {2x} **zĕugŏs**, *dzyoo'-gos;* from the same as *2218;* a *couple,* i.e. a *team* (of oxen yoked together) or *brace* (of birds tied together):—yoke {1x}, pair {1x}.

Zeugos "a yoke" is used **(1)** of beasts, Lk 14:19; and **(2)** of a pair of anything; in Lk 2:24, of turtledoves. See: BAGD—337b; THAYER—270d.

2202. **ζευκτηρία** {1x} **zĕuktēria**, *dzook-tay-ree'-ah;* fem. of a der. (at the second stage) from the same as *2218;* a *fastening* (*tiller-rope*):—band {1x}. See: BAGD—337b; THAYER—271a.

2203. **Ζεύς** {2x} **Zĕus**, *dzyooce;* of uncert. aff.; in the oblique cases there is used instead of it a (prob. cognate) name.

Δίς **Dis**, *deece,* which is otherwise obs.; *Zeus* or *Dis* (among the Latins *Jupiter* or *Jove*), the supreme deity of the Greeks:—Jupiter {2x}. Cf. Acts 14:12, 13. See: BAGD—337c, THAYER—271a.

2204. **ζέω** {2x} **zĕō**, *dzeh'-o;* a primary verb; to *be hot* (*boil,* of liquids; or *glow,* of solids), i.e. (fig.) *be fervid* (*earnest*):—be fervent {1x}, fervent {1x}.

Zeo "to be hot, to boil" (Eng. "zeal" is akin), is metaphorically used of "fervency" of spirit, Acts 18:25; Rom. 12:11. See: TDNT—2:875, 296; BAGD—337c; THAYER—271a.

2205. **ζῆλος** {17x} **zēlŏs**, *dzay'-los;* from *2204;* prop. *heat,* i.e. (fig.) *"zeal"* (in a favorable sense, *ardor;* in an unfavorable one, *jealousy,* as of a husband [fig. of God], or an enemy, *malice*):—zeal {6x}, envying {5x}, indignation {2x}, envy {1x}, fervent mind {1x}, jealousy {1x}, emulation {1x}.

Zelos may be a favorable term but usually is used of evil. When considering good it is an honorable emulation and consequent imitation of that which is excellent. In an evil sense envy is tormented by another's good fortune and is active and aggressive to diminish the good in another; usually accompanied by petty complaining and fault finding. See: TDNT—2:877, 297; BAGD—337d; THAYER—271a.

2206. **ζηλόω** {12x} **zēlŏō**, *dzay-lŏ'-o* or ζηλεύω **zēlĕuō** *dzay-loo'-o;* from *2205;* to *have warmth* of feeling for or against:—zealously affect {2x}, move with envy {2x}, envy {1x}, be zealous {1x}, affect {1x}, desire {1x}, covet {1x}, covet earnestly {1x}, misc. {2x}.

Zeloo, as a verb, in Gal 4:17, 18 means "they zealously seek," "ye may seek," "to be zealously sought": "They zealously affect (*zeloo*) you, *but* not well; yea, they would exclude you, that ye might affect them. 18 But *it is* good to be zealously (*zeloo*) affected always in *a* good *thing,* and not only when I am present with you." Syn.: 327, 1567, 1934, 2212, 3713. See: TDNT—2:882, 297; BAGD—338a; THAYER—271b.

2207. **ζηλωτής** {5x} **zēlōtēs**, *dzay-lo-tace';* from *2206;* a *"zealot"*:—zealous {5x}.

Zelotes is used adjectivally, of "being zealous" **(1)** "of the Law," Acts 21:20; **(2)** "toward God," lit., "of God," Acts 22:3; **(3)** "of spiritual gifts," 1 Cor 14:12, i.e., for exercise of spiritual gifts; **(4)** "of/for the traditions of my fathers," Gal 1:14, of Paul's loyalty to Judaism before his conversion; **(5)** "of good works," Titus 2:14. See: TDNT—2:882, 297; BAGD—338a; THAYER—271c.

2208. **Ζηλωτής** {2x} **Zēlōtēs**, *dzay-lo-tace';* the same as *2208;* a *Zealot,* i.e. (spec.) *partisan* for Jewish political independence:—*Zelotes* {2x}. See: TDNT—2:882, 297; BAGD—338b; THAYER—271c.

2209. **ζημία** {4x} **zēmia**, *dzay-mee'-ah;* prob. akin to the base of *1150* (through the idea of *violence*); *detriment:*—damage {1x}, loss {3x}.

Zemia is used **(1)** in Acts 27:10, "damage", and "loss", Acts 27:21, of ship and cargo; **(2)** in Phil 3:7, 8 of the apostle's estimate of the things which he formerly valued, and of all things on account of "the excellency of the knowledge of Christ Jesus." **(3)** This is loss actively incurred. See: TDNT—2:888, 299; BAGD—338c; THAYER—271d.

2210. **ζημιόω** {6x} **zēmiŏō**, *dzay-mee-ŏ'-o;* from *2209;* to *injure,* i.e. (refl. or pass.) to *experience detriment:*—be cast away {1x}, receive damage {1x}, lose {2x}, suffer loss {2x}.

(1) What is in view here is the act of forfeiting what is of the greatest value, not the casting away by divine judgment, though that is involved, but losing or penalizing one's own self, with spiritual and eternal loss: "For what is a man profited, if he shall gain the whole world, and lose his own soul? or what shall a man give in exchange for his soul?" (Mt 16:26; cf. Mk 8:36; Lk 9:25; cf. Phil 3:8). **(2)** In 2 Cor 7:9 *zemioo* is translated "ye might receive damage": "Now I rejoice, not that ye were made sorry, but that ye sorrowed to repentance: for ye were made sorry after a godly manner, that ye might receive damage by us in nothing"; also **(3)** "to suffer loss", 1 Cor 3:15. Syn.: 324, 353, 354, 568, 588, 618, 1209, 1523, 1926, 2865, 2975, 2983, 3028, 3335, 3336, 3858, 3880, 3970, 4327, 4355, 4356, 4380, 4381, 4382, 5562, 5264, 5274. See: TDNT—2:888, 299; BAGD—338c; THAYER—272a.

2211. **Ζηνᾶς** {1x} **Zēnas**, *dzay-nas';* prob. contr. from a poetic form of *2203* and *1435; Jove-given; Zenas,* a Chr.:—*Zenas* {1x}. See: BAGD—338c; THAYER—272a.

2212. **ζητέω** {119x} **zētĕō**, *dzay-teh'-o;* of uncert. aff., to *seek* (lit. or fig.); spec. (by Heb.) to *worship* (God), or (in a bad sense) to *plot* (against life):—seek {100x}, seek for {5x}, go about {4x}, desire {3x}, misc. {7x} = be about, endeavour, enquire (for), require.

Zeteo, as a verb, signifies **(1)** "to seek, to seek for": "Ask, and it shall be given you; seek, and ye shall find; knock, and it shall be opened unto you" (Mt 7:7; cf. 7:88; 13:45; Lk 24:5; Jn 6:24); **(1a)** of plotting against a person's life: "Saying, Arise, and take the young Child and His mother, and go into the land of Israel: for they are dead which sought the young Child's life" (Mt 2:20; Acts 21:31; Rom 11:3); **(1b)** metaphorically, to "seek" by thinking, to "seek" how to do something, or what to obtain: "And the scribes and chief priests heard *it,* and sought how they might destroy Him: for they feared Him, because all the people was astonished at His doctrine" (Mk 11:18; Lk 12:29; **(1c)** to "seek" to ascertain a meaning: "Now Jesus knew that they were desirous to ask him, and said unto them, Do ye enquire (*zeteo*) among yourselves of that I said, A little while, and ye shall not see me: and again, a little while, and ye shall see me?" (Jn 16:19); **(1d)** to "seek" God: "That they should seek the Lord, if haply they might feel after him, and find him, though he be not far from every one of us" (Acts 17:27; Rom 10:20);

(2) "to seek or strive after, endeavor, to desire": "While He yet talked to the people, behold, *his* mother and his brethren stood without, desiring (*zeteo*) to speak with him" (Mt 12:46, 47; Lk 9:9; Jn 7:19; Rom 10:3); **(2b)** of "seeking" the kingdom of God and His righteousness, in the sense of coveting earnestly, striving after: "But seek ye first the kingdom of God, and his righteousness; and all these things shall be added unto you" (Mt 6:33; Col 3:1; 1 Pet 3:11); **(3)** "to require or demand": "And He sighed deeply in His spirit, and saith, Why doth this generation seek after a sign? verily I say unto you, There shall no sign be given unto this generation" (Mk 8:12; Lk 11:29; 1 Cor 4:2; 2 Cor 13:3). Syn.: 327, 1567, 1934, 2206, 3713, 4441. See: TDNT—2:892, 300; BAGD—338d; THAYER—272a.

2213. **ζήτημα** {5x} **zētēma**, *dzay'-tay-mah;* from *2212;* a *search* (prop. concr.), i.e. (in words) a *debate:*—question {5x}. This word denotes questions about the Law, Acts 15:2; 18:15; 23:29; 25:19; 26:3. See: BAGD—339b; THAYER—272c.

2214. **ζήτησις** {6x} **zētēsis**, *dzay'-tay-sis;* from *2212;* a *searching* (prop. the act), i.e. a *dispute* or its *theme:*—question {6x}.

Zetesis denotes, firstly, "a seeking" (*zeteo*, "to seek"), then, "a debate, dispute, questioning, questions", Jn 3:25; Acts 15:2, 7; Acts 25:20; 1 Ti 1:4; 6:4; 2 Ti 2:23; Titus 3:9. See: TDNT—2:893, 300; BAGD—339b; THAYER—272c.

2215. **ζιζάνιον** {8x} **zizaniŏn**, *dziz-an'-ee-on;* of uncert. or.; *darnel* or false grain:—tares {8x}.

Zizanion is a kind of darnel growing in the grain fields, as tall as wheat and barley, and resembling wheat in appearance, except the seeds are black. It was credited among the Jews with being degenerate wheat. The seeds are poisonous to man and herbivorous animals, producing sleepiness, nausea, convulsions and even death (they are harmless to poultry). The plants can be separated out, but the custom, as in the parable, is to leave the cleaning out till near the time of harvest (Mt 13:25–27, 29, 30, 36, 38, 40). See: BAGD—339c; THAYER—272c.

2216. **Ζοροβάβελ** {3x} **Zŏrŏbabĕl**, *dzor-ob-ab'-el;* of Heb. or. [2216]; *Zorobabel* (i.e. *Zerubbabel*), an Isr.:—*Zorobabel* {3x}. See: BAGD—339c; THAYER—272d.

2217. **ζόφος** {4x} **zŏphŏs**, *dzof'-os;* akin to the base of *3509; gloom of the netherworld* (as shrouding like a *cloud*):—blackness {1x}, darkness {2x}, mist {1x}.

Zophos always signifies the darkness of that shadowy land where there is no light, but only visible darkness, and translated **(1)** "blackness", Jude 13; **(2)** "darkness", 2 Pet 2:4; Jude 6; and **(3)** "mist", 2 Pet 2:17. See: TDNT—2:893, 300; BAGD—339d; THAYER—272d.

2218. **ζυγός** {6x} **zugŏs**, *dzoo-gos';* from the root of ζεύγνυμι **zĕugnumi** (to *join,* espec. by a "yoke"); a *coupling,* i.e. (fig.) *servitude* (a *law* or *obligation*); also (lit.) the *beam* of the balance (as *connecting* the scales):—pair of balances {1x}, yoke {5x}.

Zugos is "a yoke," serving to couple two things together, is used **(1)** metaphorically, **(1a)** of submission to authority, Mt 11:29, 30, of Christ's "yoke," not simply imparted by Him but shared with Him; **(1b)** of bondage, Acts 15:10 and Gal 5:1, of bondage to the Law as a supposed means of salvation; **(1c)** of bond service to masters, 1 Tim 6:1; **(2)** to denote "a balance, a pair of scales," Rev. 6:5. See: TDNT—2:896, 301; BAGD—339d; THAYER—272d.

2219. **ζύμη** {13x} **zumē**, *dzoo'-may;* prob. from *2204; ferment* (as if *boiling* up):—leaven {13x}.

Zume is leaven, sour dough, in a high state of fermentation and was used in making bread. It required time to fulfill the process. Leaven paints the picture of being bred of corruption, coming from previous evil, and spreading through the mass of that in which it is mixed; and therefore, symbolizing the pervasive character of evil. It is used **(1)** metaphorically **(1a)** of corrupt doctrine, of error as mixed with the truth (Mt 16:6; Lk 13:21; 1 Cor 5:7, 8 twice); **(1b)** of the kingdom of heaven (Mt 13:33; 16:11, 12; Mk 8:15 twice; Lk 12:1), but does not mean that the kingdom is leaven. The same statement, as made in other parables, shows that it is the whole parable which constitutes the similitude of the kingdom; the history of Christendom confirms the fact that the pure meal of the doctrine of Christ has been adulterated with error; **(1c)** of corrupt practices (Mk 8:15; 1 Cor 5:7, 8); and **(2)** literally, **(2a)** of leaven (Lk 13:21; 1 Cor 5:6); **(2b)** of corrupt practice (Mt 16:12; 1 Cor 5:6), and **(2c)** corrupt doctrine (Gal 5:9). Syn.: 2220. See: TDNT—2:902, 302; BAGD—340a; THAYER—273a.

2220. **ζυμόω** {4x} **zumŏō**, *dzoo-mŏ'-o;* from *2219;* to *cause to ferment:*—to leaven {4x}.

(1) This verb stresses mixing leaven with dough so as to make it ferment. **(2)** It signifies "to leaven, to act as leaven," **(2a)** passive voice in Mt 13:33 and Lk 13:21; **(2b)** active voice in 1 Cor 5:6 and Gal 5:9. See: TDNT—2:902, 302; BAGD—340a; THAYER—273b.

2221. **ζωγρέω** {2x} **zōgrĕō**, *dzogue-reh'-o;* from the same as *2226* and *64;* to *take alive* (*make a prisoner of war*), i.e. (fig.) to *capture* or *ensnare:*—take captive {1x}, catch {1x}.

Zogreo, as a verb, (from zoos, "alive," and agreuo, "to hunt or catch"), **(1)** literally signifies "to take men alive": "And so *was* also James, and John, the sons of Zebedee, which were partners with Simon. And Jesus said unto Simon, Fear not; from henceforth thou shalt catch men" (Lk 5:10 - there of the effects of the work of the gospel). **(2)** In 2 Ti 2:26 it is said of the power of Satan to lead men astray: "and that they may recover themselves out of the snare of the Devil (having been taken captive by him)." Syn.: 161, 162, 163, 164. See: BAGD—340b; THAYER—273b.

2222. **ζωή** {134x} **zōē**, *dzo-ay';* from *2198; life* (lit. or fig.):—life {133x}, lifetime {1x}.

Zoe means **(1)** life in the absolute sense, **(1a)** life as God has it, which the Father has in Himself, and **(1a1)** which He gave to the Incarnate Son to have in Himself (Jn 5:26), and **(1a2)** which the Son manifested in the world (1 Jn 1:2). **(1a3)** From this life man has become alienated in consequence of the Fall (Eph 4:18), and **(1a4)** of this life men become partakers through faith in the Lord Jesus Christ (Jn 3:15), **(1a4i)** who becomes its Author to all such as trust in Him (Acts 3:15), and **(1a4ii)** who is therefore said to be 'the life' of the believer (Col 3:4), because **(1a4iii)** the life that He gives He maintains (Jn 6:35, 63). **(1b)** Eternal life is **(1b1)** the present actual possession of the believer because of his relationship with Christ (Jn 5:24; 1 Jn 3:14), and **(1b2)** that it will one day extend its domain to the sphere of the body is assured by the resurrection of Christ (2 Cor 5:4; 2 Ti 1:10). **(1c)** This life is not merely a principle of power and mobility, however, for it has moral associations which are inseparable from it: holiness and righteousness. *Zoe* also means

(2) life as a principle of that **(2a)** which is the common possession of all animals and men by nature (Acts 17:25; 1 Jn 5:16), and of that **(2b)** describing the present sojourn of man upon the earth with reference to its duration (Lk 16:25; 1 Cor 15:19). **(3)** 'This life' is a term equivalent to 'the gospel,' 'the faith,' 'Christianity' (Acts 5:20). Syn.: 979, 5590. While *zoe* is life intensive, bios (979) is life extensive; and psuche (5590) is the individual life, the living being, whereas *zoe* is the life of that being (cf. Ps 66:9; Jn 10:10–11). See: TDNT—2:832, 290; BAGD—340; THAYER—273b. comp. *5590.*

2223. **ζώνη** {8x} **zōnē**, *dzo'-nay;* prob. akin to the base of *2218;* a *belt;* by impl. a *pocket:*—girdle {6x}, purse {2x}. Zone denotes **(1)** "a belt or girdle," Mt 3:4; Mk 1:6; Acts 21:11; Rev 1:13; 15:6; **(2)** it was often hollow, and hence served as a purse, Mt 10:9; Mk 6:8. See: TDNT—5:302, 702; BAGD—341b; THAYER—274c.

2224. **ζώννυμι** {2x} **zōnnumi**, *dzone'-noo-mi;* from *2223;* to *bind about* (espec. with a belt):—gird {2x}.

Zonnumi, as a verb, means "to gird" in the middle voice, "to gird oneself," is used of the long garments worn in the east: "Verily, verily, I say unto thee, When thou wast young, thou girdedst (*zonnumi*) thyself, and walkedst whither thou wouldest: but when thou shalt be old, thou shalt stretch forth thy hands, and another shall gird (*zonnumi*) thee, and carry *thee* whither thou wouldest not" (Jn 21:18). Syn.: 328, 1241, 4024. See: TDNT—5:302, 702; BAGD—341c; THAYER—274c.

2225. **ζωογονέω** {2x} **zōŏgŏnĕō**, *dzo-og-on-eh'-o;* from the same as *2226* and a der. of *1096;* to *engender alive,* i.e. (by anal.) to *rescue* (pass. *be saved*) from death:—live {1x}, preserve {1x}.

Zoogoneo, as a verb, denotes **(1)** "to preserve alive": "Whosoever shall seek to save his life shall lose it; and whosoever shall lose his life shall preserve it" (Lk 17:33); and **(2)** in Acts 7:19 "live," negatively of the efforts of Pharaoh to destroy the babes in Israel: "The same dealt subtilly with our kindred, and evil entreated our fathers, so that they cast out their young children, to the end they might not live." Syn.: 326, 390, 980, 1236, 2198, 4176, 4800, 5225. See: TDNT—2:873, 290; BAGD—341c; THAYER—274c.

2226. **ζῷον** {23x} **zōŏn**, *dzo'-on;* neut. of a der. of *2198;* a *live* thing, i.e. an *animal:*—beast {23x}.

(1) All creatures that live on earth, including man are *zoon.* **(1a)** This word primarily denotes "a living being" (*zoe,* "life"). **(1b)** The Eng., "animal," is the equivalent, stressing the fact of life as the characteristic feature. **(2)** In Heb 13:11 it is translated it "beasts." (cf. 2 Pet 2:12 and Jude 10). **(3)** In the Apocalypse, where the word is found some 20 times, and always of those beings which stand before the throne of God, who give glory and honor and thanks to Him, 4:6, and act in perfect harmony with His counsels, 5:14; 6:1–7, e.g., the word "beasts" is signifying that not only are these creatures "living" they are also on the upper end of the life scale; neither small animals, nor men. Syn.: 2342. See: TDNT—2:873, 290; BAGD—341c; THAYER—274c.

2227. **ζωοποιέω** {12x} **zōŏpŏiĕō**, *dzo-op-oy-eh'-o;* from the same as *2226* and *4160;* to *(re-) vitalize* (lit. or fig.):—make alive {1x}, give life {2x}, quicken {9x}.

Zoopoieo, as a verb, means "to make alive, cause to live, quicken" (from zoe, "life," and poieo, "to make"), is used as follows: **(1)** of God as the bestower **(1a)** of every kind of life in the universe, 1 Ti 6:13; and, particularly, **(1b)** of resurrection life, Jn 5:21; Rom 4:17; **(2)** of Christ, who also is the bestower of resurrection life, Jn 5:21 (2nd part); 1 Cor 15:45; cf. v. 22; **(3)** of the resurrection of Christ in "the body of His glory," 1 Pet 3:18; **(4)** of the power of reproduction inherent in seed, which presents a certain analogy with resurrection, 1 Cor 15:36; **(5)** of the 'changing,' or 'fashioning anew,' of the bodies of the living, which corresponds with, and takes place at the same time as, the resurrection of the dead in Christ, Rom 8:11; **(6)** of the impartation of spiritual life, and the communication of spiritual sustenance generally, Jn 6:63; 2 Cor 3:6; Gal 3:2. **(7)** "Quicken" means to enable to respond to His voice immediately. Once born again and indwelt by the Holy Ghost, one does not have to wait to be able to respond. Response comes fully and instaneously. Syn.: 979, 981, 982, 2222. See: TDNT—2:874, 290; BAGD—341d; THAYER—274d.

H

2228. **ἤ** {357x} **ē**, *ay;* a primary particle of distinction between two connected terms; disjunctive, *or;* comparative, *than:*—or {259x}, than {38x}, either {8x}, or else {5x}, nor {5x}, not tr {22x}, misc. {20x} = and, but (either), neither, except it be, rather, save, that, what, yea. Often used in connection with other particles. See: BAGD—342a; THAYER—275a. comp. especially *2235, 2260, 2273.*

2229. **ἦ** {1x} **ē**, *ay;* an adv. of *confirmation;* perh. intens. of *2228;* used only (in the N.T.) before *3303; assuredly:*—surely + 3375 {1x}. See: BAGD—343a; THAYER—275a.

ἡ **hē**. See *3588.*

ἥ **hē** See *3739.*

ᾗ ${}_i$ē${}_i$ See *5600.*

2230. **ἡγεμονεύω** {2x} **hēgĕmŏnĕuō**, *hayg-em-on-yoo'-o;* from *2232;* to *act as ruler:*—be governor {2x}.

The root of this word stresses leading the way, Lk 2:2; 3:1. See: BAGD—343a; THAYER—275d.

2231. **ἡγεμονία** {1x} **hēgĕmŏnia**, *hayg-em-on-ee'-ah;* from *2232; government,* i.e. (in time) official *term:*—reign {1x}. See: BAGD—343b; THAYER—275d.

2232. **ἡγεμών** {22x} **hēgĕmōn**, *hayg-em-ohn';* from *2233;* a *leader,* i.e. *chief* person (or fig. place) of a province:—governor {19x}, prince {1x}, ruler {2x}.

Hegemon is a term used **(1)** for rulers generally [leader of any kind, a guide, ruler, prefect, chief, general, commander, sovereign] (Mk 13:9; 1 Pet 2:14); or **(2)** for the Roman procurators, referring, in the gospels to **(2a1)** Pontius Pilate (Mt 27:2; Lk 20:20); **(2a2)** Felix (Acts 23:26). **(2b)** Technically the procurator was **(2b1)** a financial official under a proconsul or proprietor, for collecting the imperial revenues, but **(2b2)** entrusted also with magisterial powers for decisions of questions relative to the revenues. **(2b2)** In certain provinces, of which Judea was one (the procurator of which was dependent on the legate of Syria), he was the general administrator and supreme judge, with sole power of life and death. **(2c)** Such a governor was a person of high social standing. Felix, however, was an ex-slave, a freedman, and his appointment to Judea could not but be regarded by the Jews as an insult to the nation. **(2d)** The headquarters of the governor of Judea was Caesarea, which was made a garrison town. Syn.: 1481, 2233, 3623. See: BAGD—343b; THAYER—275d.

2233. **ἡγέομαι** {28x} **hēgĕŏmai**, *hayg-eh'-om-ahee;* mid. voice of a (presumed) strengthened form of *71;* to *lead,* i.e. *command* (with official authority); fig. to *deem,* i.e. *consider:*—count {10x}, think {4x}, esteem {3x}, have rule over {3x}, be governor {2x}, misc. {6x} = account, (be) chief, judge, suppose. See: TDNT—2:907, 303; BAGD—343c; THAYER—276a.

2234. **ἡδέως** {3x} **hēdĕōs**, *hay-deh'-oce;* adv. from a der. of the base of *2237; sweetly,* i.e. (fig.) *with pleasure:*—gladly {3x}.

Hedeos, as an adverb, means "gladly" and is used in Mk 6:20, 12:37; and 2 Cor 11:19. Syn.: 780, 2236. See: BAGD—343d; THAYER—276c.

2235. **ἤδη** {59x} **ēdē**, *ay'-day;* appar. from *2228* (or possibly *2229*) and *1211; even now:*—now {37x}, already {17x}, yet {2x}, even now {1x}, by this time {1x}, now already {1x}.

Ede is always used of time and means now, at (or by) this time, sometimes in the sense of now already. See: BAGD—344a; THAYER—276c.

2236. **ἥδιστα** {2x} **hēdista**, *hay'-dis-tah;* neut. plur. of the superl. of the same as *2234; with great pleasure:*—most gladly {1x}, very gladly {1x}.

Hedista, as an adverb, means "most gladly, most delightedly, with great relish," and is rendered **(1)** "most gladly" in 2 Cor 12:9, and **(2)** "very gladly" in 2 Cor 12:15. Syn.: 780, 2234. See: BAGD—344a; THAYER—276c.

2237. **ἡδονή** {5x} **hēdŏnē**, *hay-don-ay';* from ἁνδάνω **handanō** (to *please*); sensual *delight;* by impl. *desire:*—lusts {2x}, pleasure {3x}.

Hedone, "pleasure," is used of the gratification of the natural desire or sinful desires and is translated **(1)** "lusts" Jas 4:1, 3; and **(2)** "pleasure", Lk 8:14 plural; Titus 3:3 plural; 2 Pet 2:13. See: TDNT—2:909, 303; BAGD—344b; THAYER—276c.

2238. **ἡδύοσμον** {2x} **hēduŏsmŏn**, *hay-doo'-os-mon;* neut. of the compound of the same as *2234* and *3744;* a *sweet-scented* plant, i.e. *mint:*—mint {2x}. Cf. Mt 23:23; Lk 11:42. See: BAGD—344b; THAYER—276d.

2239. **ἦθος** {1x} **ēthŏs**, *ay'-thos;* a strengthened form of *1485; usage,* i.e. (plur.) moral *habits:*—manners {1x}.

'Athos, as a noun, means "a custom, manner" and occurs in the plural in 1 Cor 15:33: "Be not deceived: evil communications corrupt good manners" [i.e., ethical conduct, morals]. Syn.: 195, 1485, 3634, 3668, 3697, 3779, 4169, 4187, 4217, 4459, 5158, 5159, 5179, 5615. See: BAGD—344c; THAYER—276d.

2240. **ἥκω** {27x} **hēkō**, *hay'-ko;* a primary verb; to *arrive,* i.e. *be present* (lit. or fig.):—to come {27x}.

Heko means **(1)** "to come, to be present" **(2)** "to come upon, of time and events," Mt 24:14; Jn 2:4; 2 Pet 3:10; Rev 18:8; **(3)** metaphorically, "to come upon one, of calamitous times, and evils," Mt 23:36; Lk 19:43. See: TDNT—2:926, 306; BAGD—344c; THAYER—276d.

2241. **ἠλί** {2x} **ēli**, *ay-lee'* or ἐλοι **ĕloi** *ay-lo'-ee;* of Heb. or. [410 with pron. suff.]; *my God:*—*Eli* {2x}. See: BAGD—345a; THAYER—277a.

2242. **Ἡλί** {1x} **Hēli**, *hay-lee';* of Heb. or. [5941]; *Heli* (i.e. *Eli*), an Isr.:—*Heli* {1x}. See: BAGD—345a; THAYER—277a.

2243. **Ἡλίας** {30x} **Hēlias**, *hay-lee'-as;* of Heb. or. [452]; *Helias* (i.e. *Elijah*), an Isr.:—Elias {30x}. See: TDNT—2:928, 306; BAGD—345a; THAYER—277a.

2244. **ἡλικία** {8x} **hēlikia**, *hay-lik-ee'-ah;* from the same as *2245; maturity* (in years or size):—age {3x}, stature {5x}.

Helikia, as a noun, primarily "an age," as a certain length of life, came to mean **(1)** "a particular time of life," as when a person is said to be "of age": **(1a)** "But by what means he now seeth, we know not; or who hath opened his eyes, we know not: he is of age; ask him: he shall speak for himself" (Jn 9:21, cf. vs 23), or **(1b)** beyond a certain stage of life: "Through faith also Sara herself received strength to conceive seed, and was delivered of a child when she was past age, because she judged him faithful who had promised" (Heb 11:11); **(2)** elsewhere only "of stature": "Which of you by taking thought can add one cubit unto his stature (*helikia*)?" (Mt 6:27; cf. Lk 2:52; 12:25; 19:3; Eph 4:13). Syn.: 165, 166, 1074, 2250, 5046, 5230. See: TDNT—2:941, 308; BAGD—345a; THAYER—277b.

2245. **ἡλίκος** {2x} **hēlikŏs**, *hay-lee'-kos;* from ἧλιξ **hēlix** (a *comrade,* i.e. one of the same age); *as big as,* i.e. (interjectively) *how much:*—how great {1x}, what great {1x}.

Helikos primarily denotes "as big as, as old as"; then, as an indirect interrogation, "what, what size, how great, how small" (the context determines the meaning), said **(1)** of a spiritual conflict, Col. 2:1, "what great (conflict) I have"; **(2)** of much wood as kindled by a little fire, Jas 3:5 "how great a matter (wood is kindled by) how small (a fire)." See: BAGD—345c; THAYER—277c.

2246. **ἥλιος** {32x} **hēliŏs**, *hay'-lee-os;* from ἕλη **hĕlē** (a *ray;* perh. akin to the alt. of *138*); the *sun;* by impl. *light:*—+ east {2x}, sun {30x}.

Helios is used **(1)** as a means of the natural benefits of light and heat (Mt 5:45) and power (Rev 1:16), **(2)** of its qualities of brightness and glory (Mt 13:43; 17:2; Acts 26:13; 1 Cor 15:41; Rev 10:1; 12:1); **(3)** as a means of destruction (Mt 13:6; Jas 1:11); **(4)** of physical misery (Rev 7:16); and **(4)** as a means of judgment (Mt 24:29; Mk 13:24; Lk 21:25; 23:45; Acts 2:20; Rev 6:12; 8:12; 9:2; 16:8). See: BAGD—345c; THAYER—277c.

2247. **ἧλος** {2x} **hēlŏs**, *hay'-los;* of uncert. aff.; a *stud,* i.e. *spike:*—nails {2x}. Cf. Jn 20:25 twice. See: BAGD—345d; THAYER—277c.

2248. **ἡμᾶς** {178x} **hēmas**, *hay-mas';* acc. plur. of *1473; us:*—us {148x}, we {25x}, our {2x}, us-ward + 1519 {2x}, not tr {1x}. See: BAGD—217a [1473]; THAYER—167b [1473].

2249. **ἡμεῖς** {127x} **hēmĕis**, *hay-mice';* nom. plur. of *1473; we* (only used when emphat.):—us {3x}, we {123x}, we ourselves {1x}. See: BAGD—217a [1473]; THAYER—277c; 167b [1473].

2250. **ἡμέρα** {389x} **hēmĕra**, *hay-mer'-ah;* fem. (with *5610* impl.) of a der. of ἧμαι **hēmai** (to *sit;* akin to the base of *1476*) mean. *tame,* i.e. *gentle; day,* i.e. (lit.) the time space between dawn and dark, or the whole 24 hours (but several days were usually reckoned by the Jews as inclusive of the parts of both extremes); fig. a *period* (always defined more or less clearly by the context):—day {355x}, daily + 2596 {15x}, time {3x}, not tr {2x}, misc. {14x} = age, + alway, midday, + for ever, judgment, while, years.

Hemera, as a noun, means "a day," is rendered "age," "of a great age" (lit., "advanced in many days") in Lk 2:36: "And there was one Anna, a prophetess, the daughter of Phanuel, of the tribe of Aser: she was of a great age, and had lived with an husband seven years from her virginity." Syn.: 165, 166, 1074, 2244, 5046, 5230. See: TDNT—2:943, 309; BAGD—345d; THAYER—277c.

2251. **ἡμέτερος** {9x} **hēmĕtĕrŏs**, *hay-met'-er-os;* from *2349; our:*—our {8x}, your {1x}. See: BAGD—347d; THAYER—279b.

2252. **ἤμην** {16x} **ēmēn**, *ay'-mane;* a prol. form of *2349; I was:*—was {13x}, I imprisoned + 1473 + 5439 {1x}, I was + 1473 {1x}, should be {1x}. See: BAGD—343a [2229]; THAYER—279c. [*Sometimes unexpressed*].

2253. **ἡμιθανής** {1x} **hēmithanēs**, *hay-mee-than-ace';* from a presumed compound of the base of *2255* and *2348; half dead,* i.e. *entirely exhausted:*—half dead {1x}. See: BAGD—348a; THAYER—279c.

2254. **ἡμῖν** {177x} **hēmin**, *hay-meen';* dat. plur. of *1473; to* (or *for, with, by*) *us:*—us {161x}, we {13x}, our {2x}, for us {1x}. See: BAGD—217a; THAYER—167b [1473].

2255. **ἥμισυ** {5x} **hēmisu**, *hay'-mee-soo;* neut. of a der. from an inseparable pref. akin to *260* (through the idea of *partition* involved in *connection*) and mean. *semi-;* (as noun) *half:*—half {5x}.

Hemisu, an adjective, is used **(1)** as such in the neuter plural, in Lk 19:8, lit., "the halves (of my goods)"; **(2)** as a noun, in the neuter sing., "the half," Mk 6:23; "half (a time)," Rev. 12:14; "half," 11:9, 11. See: BAGD—348a; THAYER—279c.

2256. **ἡμιώριον** {1x} **hēmiōriŏn**, *hay-mee-o'-ree-on;* from the base of *2255* and *5610;* a *half-hour:*—half an hour {1x}. See: BAGD—348a; THAYER—279d.

2257. **ἡμῶν** {410x} **hēmōn**, *hay-mone';* gen. plur. of *1473; of* (or *from*) *us:*—our {313x}, us {82x}, we {12x}, not tr {1x}, misc. {2x}. See: BAGD—217a; THAYER—167b [1473].

2258. **ἦν** {455x} **ēn**, *ane;* imperf. of *1510; I* (*thou,* etc.) *was* (*wast* or *were*):—was {266x}, were {115x}, had been {12x}, had {11x}, taught + 1321 {4x}, stood + 2476 {4x}, vr was {1x}, misc {41x} = + agree, be, × have (+ charge of), hold, use. See: BAGD—222d; THAYER—175c [1510].

2259. **ἡνίκα** {2x} **hēnika**, *hay-nee'-kah;* of uncert. aff.; *at which time:*—when {2x}. Cf. 2 Cor 3:15, 16. See: BAGD—348b; THAYER—279d.

2260. **ἤπερ** {1x} **ēpĕr**, *ay'-per;* from *2228* and *4007; than at all* (or *than perhaps, than indeed*):—than {1x}. See: BAGD—348b; THAYER—279d.

2261. **ἤπιος** {2x} **ēpiŏs**, *ay'-pee-os;* prob. from *2031;* prop. *affable,* i.e. *mild* or *kind:*—gentle {2x}.

(1) In 1 Th 2:7, the apostle uses *epios* of the conduct of himself and his fellow missionaries towards the converts at Thessalonica (cf. 2 Cor. 11:13, 20); and **(2)** in 2 Ti 2:24, of the conduct requisite for a servant of the Lord. See: BAGD—348b; THAYER—279d.

2262. **Ἤρ** {1x} **Ēr**, *ayr;* of Heb. or. [6147]; *Er,* an Isr.:—Er {1x}. See: BAGD—348b; THAYER—279d.

2263. **ἤρεμος** {1x} **ērĕmŏs**, *ay'-rem-os; perh.* by transposition from *2048* (through the idea of *stillness*); *tranquil:*—quiet {1x}.

Eremos means quiet, tranquil, occurs in 1 Ti 2:2 and indicates tranquility arising from without. See: BAGD—348b; THAYER—279d.

2264. **Ἡρώδης** {44x} **Hērōdēs**, *hay-ro'-dace;* compound of ἥρως **hērōs** (a "*hero*") and *1491; heroic; Herod,* the name of four Jewish kings:—Herod, Antipas {27x}, Herod, the Great {11x}, Herod Agrippa {6x}. See: BAGD—348c; THAYER—280a.

2265. **Ἡρωδιανοί** {3x} **Hērōdianŏi**, *hay-ro-dee-an-oy';* plur. of a der. of *2264; Herodians,* i.e. partisans of Herod:—Herodians {3x}. See: BAGD—348d; THAYER—280d.

2266. **Ἡρωδιάς** {6x} **Hērōdias**, *hay-ro-dee-as';* from *2264; Herodias,* a woman of the Herodian family:—*Herodias* {6x}. See: BAGD—348d; THAYER—280d.

2267. **Ἡρωδίων** {1x} **Hērōdiōn**, *hay-ro-dee'-ohn;* from *2264; Herodion,* a Chr.:—*Herodion* {1x}. See: BAGD—348d; THAYER—281a.

2268. **Ἡσαΐας** {21x} **Hēsaïas**, *hay-sah-ee'-as;* of Heb. or. [3470]; *Hesaias* (i.e. *Jeshajah*), an Isr.:—Esaias {21x}. See: BAGD—348d; THAYER—281a.

2269. **Ἠσαῦ** {3x} **Ēsau**, *ay-sow';* of Heb. or. [6215]; *Esau,* an Edomite:—*Esau* {3x}. See: TDNT—2:953, 311; BAGD—349a; THAYER—281b.

2270. **ἡσυχάζω** {5x} **hēsuchazō**, *hay-soo-khad'-zo;* from the same as *2272;* to *keep still* (intr.), i.e. *refrain* from labor, meddlesomeness or speech:—cease {1x}, hold (one's) peace {1x}, be quiet {1x}, rest {1x}.

Hesuchazo, "to be quiet, still, at rest," is said **(1)** of Paul's friends in Caesarea, in "ceasing" to persuade him not to go to Jerusalem, Acts 21:14; **(2)** it is used of silence ("held their peace") in Lk 14:4 and Acts 11:18. It is translated **(3)** "rested" in Lk 23:56 and **(4)** "quiet" in 1 Th 4:11. See: BAGD—349a; THAYER—281b.

2271. **ἡσυχία** {4x} **hēsuchia**, *hay-soo-khee'-ah;* fem. of *2272;* (as noun) *stillness,* i.e. desistance from bustle or language:—quietness {1x}, silence {3x}.

Hesuchia denotes **(1)** "quietness," 2 Th 3:12; it is translated **(2)** "silence" **(2a)** 1 Ti 2:11, 12; and **(2b)** in Acts 22:2, "(they kept the more) silence," lit., "they kept quietness the more." See: BAGD—349b; THAYER—281b.

2272. **ἡσύχιος** {2x} **hēsuchiŏs**, *hay-soo'-khee-os;* a prol. form of a compound prob. of a der. of the base of *1476* and perh. *2192;* prop. *keeping* one's *seat* (*sedentary*), i.e. (by impl.) *still* (*undisturbed, undisturbing*):—peaceable {1x}, quiet {1x}.

(1) This word indicates tranquility arising from within, causing no disturbance to others. **(2)** It is translated **(2a)** "peaceable" in 1 Ti 2:2; and **(2b)** "quiet" in 1 Pet 3:4, where it is associated with "meek," and is to characterize the spirit or disposition. See: BAGD—349c; THAYER—281c.

2273. **ἤτοι** {1x} **ētŏi**, *ay'-toy;* from *2228* and *5104; either indeed:*—whether {1x}. See: BAGD—349c; THAYER—281c.

2274. **ἡττάω** {3x} **hēttaō**, *hayt-tah'-o;* from the same as *2276;* to *make worse,* i.e. *vanquish* (lit. or fig.); by impl. to *rate lower:*—be inferior {1x}, overcome {2x}.

Hettao, "to be less or inferior," is used in the passive voice, and translated **(1)** "ye were inferior," in 2 Cor 12:13, i.e., were treated with less consideration than other churches, through his independence in not receiving gifts from them. **(2)** In 2 Pet 2:19, 20 it signifies to be overcome, in the sense of being subdued and enslaved. See: BAGD—349c; THAYER—281c.

2275. **ἥττημα** {2x} **hēttēma**, *hayt'-tay-mah;* from *2274;* a *deterioration,* i.e. (obj.) *failure* or (subj.) *loss:*—diminishing {1x}, fault {1x}.

Hettema primarily means "a lessening, a decrease, diminution," denotes "a loss." **(1)** It is used of the "loss" sustained by the Jewish nation in that they had rejected God's testimonies and His Son and the gospel, **(1a)** Rom 11:12, the reference being not only to national diminution but to spiritual "loss"; "diminishing." **(1b)** Here the contrasting word is *pleroma,* "fullness." **(2)** In 1 Cor 6:7 the reference is to the spiritual "loss" sustained by the church at Corinth because or their discord and their litigious ways in appealing to the world's judges, "fault." **(2a)** The preceding adverb "altogether" shows the comprehensiveness of the "defect"; **(2b)** the "fault" affected the whole church, and was "an utter detriment." See: BAGD—349c; THAYER—281d.

2276. **ἧττον** {2x} **hēttŏn**, *hate'-ton;* neut. of comp. of ἧκα **hēka** (*slightly*) used for that of *2556; worse* (as noun); by impl. *less* (as adv.):—less {1x}, worse {1x}.

Hetton, "less, inferior," used in the neuter, after *epi,* "for," is translated **(1)** "worse" in 1 Cor 11:17; and **(2)** in 2 Cor 12:15 the neuter, used adverbially, is translated "the less." See: BAGD—397c; THAYER—281d.

2277. **ἤτω** {2x} **ētō**, *ay'-to;* third pers. sing. imper. of *1510; let him* (or *it*) *be:*—let . . . be {2x}. See: BAGD—222d; THAYER—175c [1510].

2278. **ἠχέω** {2x} **ēchĕō**, *ay-kheh'-o;* from *2279;* to *make a* loud *noise,* i.e. *reverberate:*—roaring {1x}, sounding {1x}.

Echeo, occurs **(1)** in 1 Cor 13:1, "sounding (brass)"; and **(2)** "a noise" or "sound" (Eng., "echo"), is used of the "roaring" of the sea in Lk 21:25, "(the sea and the waves) roaring." See: BAGD—349c; THAYER—281d,

2279. **ἦχος** {3x} **ēchŏs**, *ay'-khos;* of uncert. aff.; a loud or confused *noise* ("*echo*"), i.e. *roar;* fig. a *rumor:*—fame {1x}, sound {2x}.

Echos, "a noise, report, sound," is translated "fame," in Lk 4:37; and **(2)** "sound" in Acts 2:2; Heb 12:19. See: BAGD—349d; THAYER—281d.

Θ

2280. **Θαδδαῖος** {2x} **Thaddaiŏs**, *thad-dah'-yos;* of uncert. or.; *Thaddæus,* one of the Apostles:—Thaddæus {2x}. See: BAGD—350a; THAYER—282a.

2281. **θάλασσα** {92x} **thalassa**, *thal'-as-sah;* prob. prol. from *251;* the *sea* (gen. or spec.):—sea {92x}.

Thalassa, as a noun, is used **(1)** chiefly literally, e.g., **(1a)** "the Red Sea," Acts 7:36; 1 Cor 10:1; Heb 11:29; **(1b)** the "sea" of Galilee or Tiberias, Mt 4:18; 15:29; Mk 6:48, 49, where the acts of Christ testified to His deity; Jn 6:1; 21:1; **(1c)** in general, e.g., Lk 17:2; Acts 4:24; Rom 9:27; Rev 16:3; 18:17; 20:8, 13; 21:1; **(1d)** in combination, Mt 18:6; **(2)** metaphorically, of "the ungodly men" described in Jude 13 (cf. Is 57.20), **(3)** symbolically, **(3a)** in the apocalyptic vision of "a glassy sea like unto crystal," Rev 4:6, emblematic of the fixed purity and holiness of all that appertains to the authority and judicial dealings of God; **(3b)** in 15:2, the same, "mingled with fire," and, standing on it, those who had "come victorious from the beast" (ch. 13); **(3c)** of the wild and restless condition of nations, Rev 13:1 (see 17:1, 15), where "he stood" refers to John; **(3d)** from the midst of this state arises the beast, symbolic of the final gentile power dominating the federated nations of the Roman world (see Dan, chs. 2, 7, etc.). Syn.: 989, 1337, 1724, 3864, 3882. See: BAGD—350a; THAYER—282a.

2282. **θάλπω** {2x} **thalpō**, *thal'-po;* prob. akin to θάλλω **thallō** (to *warm*); to *brood,* i.e. (fig.) to *foster:*—cherish {2x}.

Thalpo primarily means **(1)** "to heat, to soften by heat"; **(1a)** then, "to keep warm," as of birds covering their young with their feathers, cf. Deut 22:6t.; **(2)** metaphorically, "to cherish with tender love, to foster with tender care," **(2a)** in Eph 5:29 of Christ and the church; **(2b)** in 1 Th 2:7 of the care of the saints at Thessalonica by the apostle and his associates, as of a nurse for her children. See: BAGD—350b; THAYER—282b.

2283. **Θάμαρ** {1x} **Thamar**, *tham'-ar;* of Heb. or. [8559]; *Thamar* (i.e. *Tamar*), an Israelitess:—*Thamar* {1x}. See: BAGD—350c; THAYER—282c.

2284. **θαμβέω** {4x} **thambĕō**, *tham-beh'-o;* from *2285;* to *stupefy* (with surprise), i.e. *astound:*—be amazed {2x}, be astonished {2x}.

Thambeo is translated **(1)** "be amazed" in Mk 1:27; 10:32; and **(2)** "be astonished" Mk 10:24; Acts 9:6. **(3)** Amazement comes first, then settled amazement equals astonished, and settle astonishment equals astonied, cf. 2285. See: TDNT—3:4, 312; BAGD—350c; THAYER—282c.

2285. **θάμβος** {3x} **thambŏs**, *tham'-bos;* akin to an obs. τάφω **taphō** (to *dumbfound*); *stupefaction* (by surprise), i.e. *astonishment:*—be amazed + 1096 {1x}, be astonished + 4023 {1x}, wonder {1x}.

This word means amazement, wonder and is probably connected with a root signifying to render immovable; it is frequently associated with terror as well as astonishment (Lk 4:36; 5:9; Acts 3:10). See: TDNT—3:4, 312; BAGD—350c; THAYER—282c.

2286. **θανάσιμος** {1x} **thanasimŏs**, *than-as'-ee-mos;* from *2288; fatal,* i.e. *poisonous:*—deadly {1x}.

This word means belonging to death, or partaking of the nature of death: "They shall take up serpents; and if they drink any deadly thing, it shall not hurt them; they shall lay hands on the sick, and they shall recover" (Mk 16:18). See: BAGD—350d; THAYER—282c.

2287. **θανατήφορος** {1x} **thanatēphŏrŏs**, *than-at-ay'-for-os;* from (the fem. form of) *2288* and *5342; death-bearing,* i.e. *fatal:*—deadly {1x}.

This word means death-bearing, deadly: "But the tongue can no man tame; *it is* an unruly evil, full of deadly poison" (Jas 3:8). See: BAGD—350d; THAYER—282c.

2288. **θάνατος** {119x} **thanatŏs**, *than'-at-os;* from *2348;* (prop. an adj. used as a noun) *death* (lit. or fig.):—X deadly {2x}, (be . . .) death {117x}.

Thanatos, death, has the basic meaning of separation of **(1)** the soul (the spiritual part of man) from the body (the material part), the latter ceasing to function and turning to dust (Jn 11:13; Heb 2:15; 5:7; 7:23); **(2)** man from God; **(2a)** Adam died on the day he disobeyed God (cf. Gen 2:17); and hence **(2b)** all mankind are born in the same spiritual condition (Rom 5:12, 14, 17, 21), **(2c)** from which, however, those who believe in Christ are delivered (Jn 5:24; 1 Jn 3:14). **(3)** Death is the opposite of life; it never denotes nonexistence. **(4)** As spiritual life is conscious existence in communion with God, so spiritual death is conscious existence in separation from God. **(5)** Death, in whichever of the above-mentioned senses it is used, is **(5a)** always, in Scripture, viewed as the penal consequence of sin, and **(5b)** since sinners alone are subject to death (Rom 5:12), **(5c)** it was as the Bearer of sin that the Lord Jesus submitted thereto on the Cross (1 Pet 2:24). **(5d)** And while the physical death of the Lord Jesus was of the essence of His sacrifice, it was not the whole. **(5e)** The darkness symbolized, and His cry expressed, the fact that He was left alone in the universe, He was forsaken (Mt 27:45–46). Syn.: 336, 615, 1935, 2289, 5054. See: TDNT—3:7, 312; BAGD—350d; THAYER—282d.

2289. **θανατόω** {11x} **thanatŏō**, *than-at-ŏ'-o;* from *2288;* to *kill* (lit. or fig.):—put to death {4x}, cause to be put to death {3x}, kill {2x}, become dead {1x}, mortify {1x}.

Thanatoo, as a verb, means **(1)** "to put to death" (Mt 10:21; cf. Mk 13:12; Lk 21:16) and is translated "shall . . . cause (them) to be put to death" literally, "shall put (them) to death." **(2)** It is used of the death of Christ in Mt 26:59; 27:1; Mk 14:55 and 1 Pet 3:18. **(3)** In Rom 7:4 (passive voice) it is translated "ye . . . are become dead," with reference to the change from bondage to the Law to union with Christ; **(3a)** cf. in 8:13, "mortify" of the act of the believer in regard to the deeds of the body; **(3b)** in 8:36, "are killed" (so in 2 Cor 6:9). Syn.: 336, 337, 520, 1935, 2288, 5054. See: TDNT—3:21, 312; BAGD—351c; THAYER—283c.

θάνω **thanō**. See *2348.*

2290. **θάπτω** {11x} **thaptō**, *thap'-to;* a primary verb; to *celebrate funeral rites,* i.e. *inter:*—bury {11x}.

Thapto occurs **(1)** generally, in Mt. 8:21, 22, Lk 9:59, 60; **(2)** of the rich man, Lk 16:22; **(3)** of David, Acts 2:29; **(4)** of Ananias, Acts 5:6, and Sapphira, 9–10; **(5)** of John the baptizer, Mt. 14:12; **(6)** of Christ's "burial," 1Cor 15:4. See: BAGD—351d; THAYER—283d.

2291. **Θάρα** {1x} **Thara**, *thar'-ah;* of Heb. or. [8646]; *Thara* (i.e. *Terach*), the father of Abraham:—*Thara* {1x}. See: BAGD—351d; THAYER—283d.

2292. **θαῤῥέω** {6x} **tharrhĕō**, *thar-hreh'-o;* another form for *2293;* to *exercise courage:*—be bold {2x}, be confident {1x}, confident {1x}, have confidence {1x}, boldly {1x}.

The root of this word means to be warm" [warmth of temperament being associated with confidence; cf. Eng. "he had cold feet" implying a lack of courage]; hence, **(1)** "to be confident", 2 Cor 5:6, 8; **(2)** 2 Cor 7:16 "to have confidence"; **(3)** 2 Cor 10:1, 2 "to be bold"; **(4)** Heb 13:6 "boldly"; (lit., "being courageous"). See: TDNT—3:25, 315; BAGD—352a; THAYER—283d. comp. *5111.*

2293. **θαρσέω** {8x} **tharsĕō**, *thar-seh'-o;* from *2294;* to *have courage:*—be of good cheer {5x}. be of good comfort {3x}.

This word means "to be of good courage, of good cheer" (*tharsos,* "courage, confidence"), and is used only in the imperative mood, in the NT; **(1)** "be of good cheer", Mt 9:2; 14:27; Mk 6:50; Jn 16:33; Acts 23:11; and **(2)** "be of good comfort", Mt 9:22; Mk 10:49; Lk 8:48. See: TDNT—3:25, 315; BAGD—352a; THAYER—283d. Comp. *2292.*

2294. **θάρσος** {1x} **tharsŏs**, *thar'-sos;* akin (by transp.) to θράσος **thrasŏs** (*daring*); *boldness* (subj.):—courage {1x}. See: BAGD—352a; THAYER—283d.

2295. **θαῦμα** {1x} **thauma**, *thŏu'-mah;* appar. from a form of *2300; wonder* (prop. concr.); but by impl. abstr.):—admiration {1x}.

Thauma, "a wonder" (akin to *theaomai,* "to gaze in wonder"), is found in Rev 17:6 "admiration", said of John's astonishment at the vision of the woman described as Babylon the Great. See: TDNT—3:27, 316; BAGD—352a; THAYER—283d.

2296. **θαυμάζω** {47x} **thaumazō**, *thŏu-mad'-zo;* from *2295;* to *wonder;* by impl. to *admire:*—marvel {29x}, wonder {14x}, have in admiration {1x}, admire {1x}, marvelled + 2258 {1x}, vr wonder {1x}.

This word means to wonder, wonder at, marvel, to be wondered at, and hence, to be had in admiration. See: TDNT—3:27, 316; BAGD—352b; THAYER—284a.

2297. **θαυμάσιος** {1x} **thaumasiŏs**, *thŏw-mas'-ee-os;* from *2295; wondrous,* i.e. (neut. as noun) a *miracle:*—wonderful thing {1x}.

Thaumasios is admiration and astonishment provoked by a miracle: "And when the chief priests and scribes saw the wonderful things that He did, and the children crying in the temple, and saying, Hosanna to the Son of David; they were sore displeased" (Mt 21:15). Syn.: 1411, 1741, 3167, 3861, 4592, 5259. See: TDNT—3:27, 316; BAGD—352d; THAYER—284b.

2298. **θαυμαστός** {7x} **thaumastŏs**, *thŏw-mas-tos';* from *2296; wondered* at, i.e. (by impl.) *wonderful:*—marvel {1x}, marvellous {5x}, marvelous thing {1x}.

Thaumastos, is translated **(1)** "marvellous" and is said **(1a)** of the Lord's doing in making the rejected Stone the Head of the corner, Mt 21:42; Mk 12:11; **(1b)** of the spiritual light into which believers are brought, 1 Pet 2:9; **(1c)** of the vision of the seven angels having the seven last plagues, Rev 15:1; **(1d)** of the works of God, Rev 15:3; **(2)** "a marvellous thing", of the erstwhile [former] blind man's astonishment that the Pharisees knew not from whence Christ had come, and yet He had given him sight, Jn 9:30 and translated **(3)** "marvel": "And no marvel; for Satan himself is transformed into an angel of light", 2 Cor 11:14. See: TDNT—3:27, 316; BAGD—352d; THAYER—284b.

2299. **θεά** {3x} **thĕa**, *theh-ah';* fem. of *2316;* a female *deity:*—goddess {3x}. Cf. Acts 19:27, 35, 37. See: BAGD—353a; THAYER—284c.

2300. **θεάομαι** {24x} **thĕaŏmai**, *theh-ah'-om-ahee;* a prol. form of a primary verb; to *look* closely at, i.e. (by impl.) *perceive* (lit. or fig.); by extens. to *visit:*—see {20x}, behold {2x}, look {1x}, look upon {1x}.

(1) *Theaomai*, as a verb, means "to behold" [of careful contemplation], and is translated **(1a)** "looking" (Jn 4:35, of "looking" on the fields); and **(1b)** "looked upon" (1 Jn 1:1, of the apostles' personal experiences of Christ in the days of His flesh, and the facts of His Godhood and Manhood). **(2)** *Theaomai* also means "to behold, view attentively, contemplate," in the sense of a wondering regard. **(2a)** It signifies a more earnest contemplation than the ordinary verbs for "to see," "a careful and deliberate vision which interprets . . . its object," and **(2b)** is more frequently rendered "behold": "And the women also, which came with him from Galilee, followed after, and beheld the sepulchre, and how His body was laid" (Lk 23:55; cf. Jn 1:14; 1:32; Acts 1:11; 1 Jn 1:1(more than merely seeing); 4:12, 14). Syn.: 308, 333, 352, 578, 816, 872, 991, 1689, 1896, 1914, 1980, 1983, 2029, 2334, 2657, 2734, 3700, 3706, 3708, 3879, 4017, 4648. See: TDNT—5:315, 706; BAGD—353a; THAYER—284c.

2301. **θεατρίζω** {1x} **thĕatrizō**, *theh-at-rid'-zo;* from *2302;* to *expose as a spectacle:*—make a gazing stock {1x}.

This word means to bring upon the stage, to set forth as a spectacle, and to expose to contempt, Heb 10:33. See: TDNT—3:42,*; BAGD—353c; THAYER—284d.

2302. **θέατρον** {3x} **thĕatrŏn**, *theh'-at-ron;* from *2300;* a *place for public show* ("*theatre*"), i.e. general *audience-room;* by impl. a *show* itself (fig.):—spectacle {1x}, theatre {2x}.

Theatron, akin to *theaomai*, "to behold," denotes **(1)** "a theater" (used also as a place of assembly), Acts 19:29, 31; and **(2)** "a spectacle, a show," metaphorically in 1 Cor 4:9. See: TDNT—3:42, 318; BAGD—353c; THAYER—284d.

2303. **θεῖον** {7x} **thĕiŏn**, *thi'-on;* prob. neut. of *2304* (in its orig. sense of *flashing*); *sulphur:*—brimstone {7x}.

Theion originally denoted "fire from heaven." It is connected with sulphur. Places touched by lightning were called *theia*, and, as lightning leaves a sulphurous smell, and sulphur was used in pagan purifications, it received the name of *theion* Lk 17:29; Rev 9:17–18; 14:10; 19:20; 20:10; 21:8. See: TDNT—3:122,*; BAGD—353c; THAYER—284d.

2304. **θεῖος** {3x} **thĕiŏs**, *thi'-os;* from *2316; god-like* (neut. as noun, *divinity*):—divine {2x}, Godhead {1x}.

Theios means **(1)** divine and is used **(1a)** of the power of God (2 Pet 1:3), and **(1b)** of His nature (2 Pet 1: 4), both of which proceed from Himself. **(2)** In Acts 17:29 it is used as a noun with the definite article, to denote the Godhead, the Deity, the one true God. See: TDNT—3:122, 322; BAGD—353d; THAYER—285a.

2305. **θειότης** {1x} **thĕiŏtēs**, *thi-ot'-ace;* from *2304; divinity* (abstr.):—Godhead {1x}.

Theiotes (2305 - Rom 1:20), Godhead, is derived from theios (2304), and is to be distinguished from theotes (2320 - Col 2:9). In Rom 1:20 the apostle is declaring how much of God may be known from the revelation of Himself which He has made in the creation, from those vestiges of Himself which men may everywhere trace in the world around them. Yet it is not the personal God whom any man may learn to know by these aids; He can be known only by the revelation of Himself in His Son. In Col 2:9, Paul is declaring that in the Son there dwells all the fullness of absolute Godhead; they were no mere rays of Divine glory which gilded Him, lighting up His Person for a season and with a splendor not His own; but He was, and is, absolute and perfect God; and the apostle uses theotes (2320) to express this essential and personal Godhead of the Son. Theotes (2320) indicates the divine essence of Godhood, the personality of God; *theiotes* (2305), the attributes of God, His divine nature and properties. See: TDNT—3:123, 322; BAGD—354a; THAYER—285a.

2306. **θειώδης** {1x} **thĕiōdēs**, *thi-o'-dace;* from *2303* and *1491; sulphur-like*, i.e. *sulphurous:*—brimstone {1x}. See: BAGD—354a; THAYER—285a.

θελέω **thĕlĕō**. See *2309*.

2307. **θέλημα** {64x} **thĕlēma**, *thel'-ay-mah;* from the prol. form of *2309;* a *determination* (prop. the thing), i.e. (act.) *choice* (spec. *purpose, decree;* abstr. *volition*) or (pass.) *inclination:*—desire {1x}, pleasure {1x}, will {62x}.

(1) What one wishes or has determined shall be done, Lk 12:47, Jn 5:30; 1 Cor 7:37; and speaks **(1a)** of the purpose of God to bless mankind through Christ, Acts 22:14; Eph 1:9; Col 1:9; **(1b)** of what God wishes to be done by us, **(1b1)** Rom 12:2; Col 4:12; 1 Pet 4:2; **(1b2)** especially His commands, precepts, Acts 13:22; **(2)** of one's will, choice, inclination, desire, pleasure. Jn 1:13; Eph 2:13 plural. See: TDNT—3:52, 318; BAGD—354b; THAYER—285a.

2308. **θέλησις** {1x} **thĕlēsis**, *thel'-ay-sis;* from *2309; determination* (prop. the act), i.e. *option:*—will {1x}.

Thelesis denotes "a willing, a wishing", Heb. 2:4. See: TDNT—3:62, 318; BAGD—354c; THAYER—285c.

2309. **θέλω** {210x} **thĕlō**, *thel'-o;* or ἐθέλω **ĕthĕlō**, *eth-el'-o;* in certain tenses θελέω **thĕlĕō**, *thel-eh'-o;* and ἐθελέω **ĕthĕlĕō**, *eth-el-eh'-o;* which are otherwise obs.; appar. strengthened from the alt. form of *138;* to *determine* (as an act. *option* from subj. impulse; whereas *1014* prop. denotes rather a pass. *acquiescence* in obj. considerations), i.e. *choose* or *prefer* (lit. or fig.); by impl. to *wish*, i.e. *be inclined* to (sometimes adv. *gladly*); impers. for the future tense, to *be about to;* by Heb. to *delight in:*—will/would {159x}, will/would have {16x}, desire {13x}, desirous {3x}, list {3x}, to will {2x}, misc. {4x}.

This word stresses to will, to wish, implying volition and purpose, frequently a determination, have in mind, intend, to be resolved or determined; usually rendered "to will." See: TDNT—3:44, 318; BAGD—354d; THAYER—285c.

2310. **θεμέλιος** {16x} **thĕmĕliŏs**, *them-el'-ee-os;* from a der. of *5087;* something *put* down, i.e. a *substruction* (of a building, etc.), (lit. or fig.):—foundation {16x}.

Themelios is properly an adjective denoting "belonging to a foundation" (connected with *tithemi*, "to place"). It is used **(1)** as a noun, with *lithos*, "a stone," understood, in Lk 6:48, 49; 14:29; Heb 11:10; Rev 21:14, 19; **(2)** as a neuter noun in Acts 16:26, and metaphorically, **(2a)** of "the ministry of the gospel and the doctrines of the faith," Rom 15:20; 1 Cor 3:10, 11, 12; Eph 2:20, where the "of" is not subjective (i.e., consisting of the apostles and prophets), but objective, (i.e., laid by the apostles, etc.); so in 2 Ti 2:19, where "the foundation of God" is "the foundation laid by God,"—not the Church (which is not a "foundation"), but Christ Himself, upon whom the saints are built; Heb 6:1; **(2b)** "of good works, 1 Ti 6:19. See: TDNT—3:63, 322; BAGD—355d; THAYER—286d.

2311. **θεμελιόω** {6x} **thĕmĕliŏō**, *them-el-ee-ŏ'-o;* from *2310;* to *lay a basis* for, i.e. (lit.) *erect*, or (fig.) *consolidate:*—lay the foundation {1x}, found {2x}, ground {2x}, settle {1x}.

Themelioo, "to lay a foundation, to found" is used **(1)** literally, **(1a)** "lay the foundation", Heb 1:10; **(1b)** "founded", Mt 7:25; Lk 6:48; and **(2)** metaphorically, **(2a)** "grounded", Eph 3:17 in love; Col 1:23 in the faith; **(2b)** "settle" 1 Pet 5:10. See: TDNT—3:63, 322; BAGD—356a; THAYER—287a.

2312. **θεοδίδακτος** {1x} **thĕŏdidaktŏs**, *theh-od-id'-ak-tos;* from *2316* and *1321; divinely instructed:*—taught of God {1x}.

Theodidaktos, "God-taught" occurs in 1 Th 4:9, lit., "God-taught (persons)"; while the missionaries had "taught" the converts to love one another, God had Himself been their Teacher. See: TDNT—3:121, 322; BAGD—356b; THAYER—287b.

2312. **θεολόγος** {1x} **thĕŏlŏgŏs**, *theh-ol-og'-os;* from *2316* and *3004;* a "*theologian*":—divine {1x}. See: BAGD—356b; THAYER—287b.

2313. **θεομαχέω** {1x} **thĕŏmachĕō**, *theh-o-makh-eh'-o;* from *2314;* to *resist deity:*—fight against God {1x}. See: TDNT—4:528, 573; BAGD—356c; THAYER—287b.

2314. **θεόμαχος** {1x} **thĕŏmachŏs**, *theh-om'-akh-os;* from *2316* and *3164;* an *opponent of deity:*—to fight against God {1x}.

Theomachos, "to fight against God" occurs in Acts 5:39 and literally means "god-fighters" (Acts 5:39). See: TDNT—4:528, 573; BAGD—356c; THAYER—287b.

2315. **θεόπνευστος** {1x} **thĕŏpnĕustŏs**, *theh-op'-nyoo-stos;* from *2316* and a presumed der. of *4154; divinely breathed* in:—given by inspiration of God {1x}.

This word means "inspired by God" (*theos*, "God," *pneuo*, "to breathe"), is used in 2 Ti 3:16, of the Scriptures as distinct from non-inspired writings. See: TDNT—6:453, 876; BAGD—356c; THAYER—287c.

2316. **θεός** {1343x} **thĕŏs**, *theh'-os;* of uncert. aff.; a *deity*, espec. (with *3588*) the supreme *Divinity;* fig. a *magistrate;* by Heb. *very:*—God {1320x}, god {13x}, godly {3x}, Godward + 4214 {2x}, misc. {5x} = × exceeding.

Theos, as a noun, means **I.** in the polytheism of the Greeks, denoted "a god or deity," e.g., Acts 14:11; 19:26; 28:6; 1 Cor 8:5; Gal 4:8. **II.** **(1)** Hence the word was appropriated by Jews and retained by Christians to denote "the one true God." **(1a)** In the OT "God" comes from the Hebrew words Elohim and Jehovah, the former indicating His power and preeminence, the latter His unoriginated, immutable, eternal and self-sustained existence. **(1b)** In the NT, these and all the other divine attributes are predicated of Him. To Him are ascribed, e.g., **(1b1)** His unity, or monism, e.g., Mk 12:29; 1 Ti 2:5; **(1b2)** self-existence, Jn 5:26; **(1b3)** immutability, Jas 1:17; **(1b4)** eternity, Rom 1:20; **(1b5)** universality, Mt 10:29; Acts 17:26–28; **(1b6)** almighty power Mt 19:26; **(1b7)** infinite knowledge, Acts 2:23; 15:18; Rom 11:33; **(1b8)** creative power, Rom 11:36; 1 Cor 8:6; Eph 3:9; Rev 4:11; 10:6; **(1b9)** absolute holiness, 1 Pet 1:15; 1 Jn 1:5; **(1b10)** righteousness, Jn 17:25; **(1b11)** faithfulness, 1 Cor 1:9; 10:13; 1 Th 5:24; 2 Th 3:3; 1 Jn 1:9; **(1b12)** love, 1 Jn 4:8, 16; **(1b13)** mercy, Rom 9:15, 18; **(1b14)** truthfulness, Titus 1:2; Heb 6:18.

(2) The divine attributes are likewise indicated or definitely predicated of Christ, e.g., Mt 20:18–19; Jn 1:1–3; 1:18; 5:22–29; 8:58; 14:6; 17:22–24; 20:28; Rom 1:4; 9:5; Phil 3:21; Col 1:15; 2:3; Titus 2:13; Heb 1:3; 13:8; 1 Jn 5:20; Rev 22:12, 13. **(3)** Also of the Holy Spirit, e.g., Mt 28:19; Lk 1:35; Jn 14:16; 15:26; 16:7–14; Rom 8:9, 26; 1 Cor 12:11; 2 Cor 13:14.

(4) *Theos* is used **(4a)** with the definite article, **(4b)** without (i.e., as an anarthrous noun). **(4c)** The English may or may not have need of the article in translation. But that point cuts no figure in the Greek idiom. Thus in Acts 27:23 ("of [the] God whose I am,") the article points out the special God whose Paul is, and is to be preserved in English. In the very next verse (ho *theos*) we in English do not need the article. **(4c) John 1:1** As to this latter it is usual to employ the article with a proper name, when mentioned a second time. **(4c)** There are, of course, exceptions to this, as when the absence of the article serves to lay stress upon, or give precision to, the character or nature of what is expressed in the noun. **(4c1)** A notable instance of this is in Jn 1:1, "and the Word was God"; here a double stress is on *theos*, by the absence of the article and by the emphatic position. To translate it literally, "a god was the Word," is entirely misleading. Moreover, that "the Word" is the subject of the sentence, exemplifies the rule that the subject is to be determined by its having the article when the predicate is anarthrous (without the article). **(4c2)** In Rom 7:22, in the phrase "the law of God," both nouns have the article; in v. 25, neither has the article. This is in accordance with a general rule that if two nouns are united by the genitive case (the "of" case), either both have the article, or both are without. Here, in the first instance, both nouns, "God" and "the law" are definite, whereas in v. 25 the word "God" is not simply titular; the absence of the article stresses His character as lawgiver. **(4c3)** Where two or more epithets are applied to the same person or thing, one article usually serves for both (the exceptions being when a second article lays stress upon different aspects of the same person or subject, e.g., Rev. 1:17).

(5) Titles: In the following titles God is described by certain of His attributes; the God **(5a)** of glory, Acts 7:2; **(5b)** of peace, Rom 15:33; 16:20; Phil 4:9; 1 Th 5:23; Heb 13:20; **(5c)** of love and peace, 2 Cor 13:11; **(5d)** of patience and comfort, Rom 15:5; **(5e)** of all comfort, 2 Cor 1:3; **(5f)** of hope, Rom 15:13; **(5g)** of all grace, 1 Pet 5:10. **(5h)** These describe Him, not as in distinction from other persons, but as the source of all these blessings; hence the employment of the definite article. **(5i)** In such phrases as "the God of a person," e.g., Mt 22:32, the expression marks the relationship in which the person stands to God and God to him. **(6)** The phrase "the things of God" (translated literally or otherwise) stands for **(6a)** His interests, Mt 16:23; Mk 8:33; **(6b)** His counsels, 1 Cor 2:11; **(6c)** things which are due to Him, Mt 22:21; Mk 12:17; Lk 20:25. **(7)** The phrase "things pertaining to God," Rom 15:17; Heb 2:17; 5:1, describes, in the Heb passages, the sacrificial service of the priest; in the Rom passage the gospel ministry as an offering to God. **III. (1)** The word is used of divinely appointed judges in Israel, as representing God in His authority, Jn 10:34, quoted from Ps 82:6, which indicates that God Himself sits in judgment on those whom He has appointed. **(2)** The application of the term to **(2a)** the Devil, 2 Cor 4:4, and **(2b)** the belly, Phil 3:19, virtually places these instances under **I.** See: TDNT—3:65, 322; BAGD—356d; THAYER—287c.

2317. **θεοσέβεια** {1x} **thĕŏsĕbĕia**, *theh-os-eb'-i-ah;* from *2318; devoutness,* i.e. *piety:*—godliness {1x}.

Theosebia denotes "the fear or reverence of God, a reverence for God's goodness", 1 Ti 2:10. See: TDNT—3:123, 331; BAGD—358b; THAYER—288c.

2318. **θεοσεβής** {1x} **thĕŏsĕbēs**, *theh-os-eb-ace';* from *2316* and *4576; reverent of God,* i.e. *pious:*—worshipper of God {1x}.

Theosebes denotes "reverencing God" (*theos*, "God," *sebomai*), and is rendered "a worshipper of God" in John 9:35. Syn.: 1174, 2126, 2152, 2357. See: TDNT—3:123, 331; BAGD—358b; THAYER—288c.

2319. **θεοστυγής** {1x} **thĕŏstugēs**, *theh-os-too-gace';* from *2316* and the base of *4767; hateful to God,* i.e. *impious:*—haters of God {1x}.

These people are exceptionally impious and wicked and act out their wickedness by hating God, Rom 1:30. See: BAGD—358c; THAYER—288c.

2320. **θεότης** {1x} **thĕŏtēs**, *theh-ot'-ace;* from *2316; divinity* (abstr.): godhead {1x}.

This word stresses deity, the state of being God [see 2305 for full discussion]. See: TDNT—3:119, 322; BAGD—358c; THAYER—288c.

2321. **Θεόφιλος** {2x} **Thĕŏphilŏs**, *theh-of'-il-os;* from *2316* and *5384; friend of God; Theophilus,* a Chr.:—Theophilus {2x}. See: BAGD—358d; THAYER—288d.

2322. **θεραπεία** {4x} **thĕrapĕia**, *ther-ap-i'-ah;* from *2323; attendance* (spec. medical, i.e. *cure*); fig. and collec. *domestics:*—healing {2x}, household {2x}.

Therapeia primarily denotes **(1)** "household", a place where one's render constant care and attention, Mt 24:45; Lk 12:42; and then, **(2)** "medical service, healing" (Eng., "therapy"), Lk 9:11; Rev 22:2, of the effects of the leaves of the tree of life, perhaps here with the meaning "health." See: TDNT—3:131, 331; BAGD—358d; THAYER—288d.

2323. **θεραπεύω** {44x} **thĕrapĕuō**, *ther-ap-yoo'-o;* from the same as *2324;* to *wait upon* menially, i.e. (fig.) to *adore* (God), or (spec.) to *relieve* (of disease):—cure {5x}, heal {38x}, worship {1x}.

Therapeuo primarily signifies "to serve as a *therapon*, an attendant"; then, "to care for the sick, to treat, cure, heal" (Eng., "therapeutics"). It is translated **(1)** many times "heal" and chiefly used in Mt and Lk, once in Jn (5:10), and, after the Acts, only Rev 13:3, 12. **(2)** Taking the idea of service, it is translated "worshipped", Acts 17:25. **(3)** Applying the healing aspect it is translated "cure", Mt 17:16, 18; Lk 7:21; 9:1; Jn 5:10; Acts 28:9. See: TDNT—3:128, 331; BAGD—359a; THAYER—288d.

2324. **θεράπων** {1x} **thĕrapōn**, *ther-ap'-ohn;* appar. a part. from an otherwise obs. der. of the base of *2330;* a menial *attendant* (as if *cherishing*):—servant {1x}.

Therapon means to serve, be an attendant, a servant, and is a term used of Moses (Heb 3:5) discharging the duties committed to him by God from a more confidential position, offering a freer service, and possessing a higher dignity than a doulos (1401). Syn.: 1401, 1249, 3610, 5257. See: TDNT—3:132, 331; BAGD—359b; THAYER—289a.

2325. **θερίζω** {21x} **thĕrizō**, *ther-id'-zo;* from *2330* (in the sense of the *crop*); to *harvest:*—reap {21x}.

Therizo, "to reap" (akin to theros, "summer, harvest"), is used **(1)** literally, Mt 6:26; 25:24, 26; Lk 12:24; 19:21, 22; Jas 5:4 2nd part), "have reaped"; **(2)** figuratively or in proverbial expressions, **(2a)** Jn 4:36 (twice), 37, 38, with immediate reference to bringing Samaritans into the kingdom of God, in regard to which the disciples would enjoy the fruits of what Christ Himself had been doing in Samaria; the Lord's words are, however, of a general application in respect of such service; **(2b)** in 1 Cor 9:11, with reference to the right of the apostle and his fellow missionaries to receive material assistance from the church, a right which he forbore to exercise; **(2c)** in 2 Cor 9:6 (twice), with reference to rendering material help to the needy, either "sparingly" or "bountifully," the "reaping" being proportionate to the sowing; **(2d)** in Gal 6:7, 8 (twice), of "reaping" corruption, **(2d1)** with special reference, according to the context, to that which is naturally short-lived, transient (though the statement applies to every form of sowing to the flesh), and **(2d2)** of "reaping" eternal life (characteristics and moral qualities being in view), **(2d3)** as a result of sowing "to the Spirit," the reference probably being to the new nature of the believer, which is, however, under the controlling power of the Holy Spirit, v. 9, **(2d4)** the "reaping" (the effect of well doing) being accomplished, to a limited extent, in this life, but in complete fulfillment at and beyond the judgment seat of Christ; **(2d5)** diligence or laxity here will then produce proportionate results; **(2e)** in Rev 14:15 (twice), 16, figurative of the discriminating judgment divinely to be fulfilled at the close of this age, when the wheat will be separated from the tares (see Mt 13:30). See: TDNT—3:132, 332; BAGD—359b; THAYER—289a.

2326. **θερισμός** {13x} **thĕrismŏs**, *ther-is-mos';* from *2325; reaping,* i.e. the *crop:*—harvest {13x}.

Therismos, akin to *therizo,* "to reap," is used **(1)** of "the act of harvesting," Jn 4:35; **(2)** "the time of harvest," figuratively, Mt 13:30, 39; Mk 4:29; **(3)** "the crop," figuratively, Mt 9:37, 38; Lk 10:2; Rev 14:15. **(4)** The beginning of "harvest" varied according to natural conditions, but took place on the average about the middle of April in the eastern lowlands of Palestine, in the latter part of the month in the coast plains and a little later in high districts. **(4a)** Barley "harvest" usually came first and then wheat. **(4b)** "Harvesting" lasted about seven weeks, and was the occasion of festivities. See: TDNT—3:133, 332; BAGD—359c; THAYER—289b.

2327. **θεριστής** {2x} **thĕristēs**, *ther-is-tace';* from *2325;* a *harvester:*—reaper {2x}.

Theristes, "a reaper" (akin to *therizo,* see above), is used of angels in Mt 13:30, 39. See: BAGD—359c; THAYER—289b.

2328. **θερμαίνω** {6x} **thĕrmainō**, *ther-mah'-ee-no;* from *2329;* to *heat* (oneself):—warm (one's) self {5x}, be warmed {1x}.

Thermaino, "to warm, heat" (Eng. "thermal," etc.), when used in the middle voice, signifies **(1)** "to warm oneself," Mk 14:54, 67; Jn 18:18 (twice), 25; and **(2)** "be warmed", Jas 2:16. See: BAGD—359c; THAYER—289b.

2329. **θέρμη** {1x} **thĕrmē**, *ther'-may;* from the base of *2330; warmth:*—heat {1x}. See: BAGD—359c; THAYER—289c.

2330. **θέρος** {3x} **thĕrŏs**, *ther'-os;* from a primary θέρω **thĕrō** (to *heat*); prop. *heat,* i.e. *summer:*—summer {3x}.

Theros, akin to *thero,* "to heat," occurs in Mt 24:32; Mk 13:28; Lk 21:30. See: BAGD—359d; THAYER—289c.

2331. **Θεσσαλονικεύς** {6x} **Thĕssalŏnikĕus**, *thes-sal-on-ik-yoos';* from *2332;* a *Thessalonican,* i.e. inhab. of Thessalonice:—Thessalonians {5x}, of Thessalonica {1x}. See: BAGD—359d; THAYER—289c.

2332. **Θεσσαλονίκη** {5x} **Thĕssalŏnikē**, *thes-sal-on-ee'-kay;* from Θεσσαλός **Thĕssalŏs** (a *Thessalian*) and *3529; Thessalonice,* a place in Asia Minor:—Thessalonica {5x}. See: BAGD—359d; THAYER—289c.

2333. **Θευδᾶς** {1x} **Thĕudas**, *thyoo-das';* of uncert. or.; *Theudas,* an Isr.:—Theudas {1x}. See: BAGD—359d; THAYER—289c.

θέω **thĕō**. See *5087.*

2334. **θεωρέω** {57x} **thĕōrĕō**, *theh-o-reh'-o;* from a der. of *2300* (perh. by add. of *3708*); to *be a spectator* of, i.e. *discern,* (lit., fig. [*experience*] or intens. [*acknowledge*]):—see {40x}, behold {11x}, perceive {4x}, consider {1x}, look on {1x}.

This word means **(1)** to be a spectator, look at, behold, view attentively, take a view of, survey, to view mentally, consider; and **(2)** to see, to perceive with the eyes, to enjoy the presence of one, to discern, to ascertain, find out by seeing. **(3)** *Theoreo,* as a verb, means "to look at, gaze at, behold" and is translated "looking on": "There were also women looking on afar off" (Mk 15:40). Syn.for **(1) - (3):** 308, 352, 578, 816, 872, 991, 1689, 1896, 1914, 1980, 1983, 2300, 3706, 3708, 3879, 4017, 4648. *Theoreo,* also[from theoros, "a spectator,"], as a verb, is used **(4)** of one who looks at a thing with interest and for a purpose, usually indicating the careful observation of details: "And Mary Magdalene and Mary *the mother* of Joses beheld where He was laid" (Mk 15:47; cf. Lk 10:18; 23:35; Jn 20:6; so in verses 12 and 14); **(5)** "consider": "Now consider how great this man *was,* unto whom even the patriarch Abraham gave the tenth of the spoils" (Heb 7:4). **(6)** It is used of experience, in the sense of partaking of: "Verily, verily, I say unto you, If a man keep my saying, he shall never see (*theoreo*) death" (Jn 8:51; cf. 17:24). Syn.for **(4) - (6):** 333, 816, 991, 1689, 1896, 2029, 2300, 2657, 2734, 3700, 3708. See: TDNT—5:315, 706; BAGD—360a; THAYER—289d.

2335. **θεωρία** {1x} **thĕōria**, *theh-o-ree'-ah;* from the same as *2334; spectatorship,* i.e. (concr.) a *spectacle:*—sight {1x}.

Theoria, as a noun, denotes "a spectacle, a sight": "And all the people that came together to that sight (*theoria*), beholding the things which were done, smote their breasts, and returned" (Lk 23:48 - the crucifixion). See: BAGD—360b; THAYER—290b.

2336. **θήκη** {1x} **thēkē**, *thay'-kay;* from *5087;* a *receptacle,* i.e. *scabbard:*—sheath {1x}.

Theke, "a place to put something in", "a receptacle, chest, case," is used of the "sheath" of a sword, Jn 18:11. See: BAGD—360b; THAYER—290b.

2337. **θηλάζω** {6x} **thēlazō**, *thay-lad'-zo;* from θηλή **thēlē** (the *nipple*); to *suckle,* (by impl.) to *suck:*—give suck {4x}, suck {1x}, suckling {1x}.

Thelazo, from *thele,* "a breast," is used **(1)** of the mother, "to suckle, give suck" Mt 24:19; Mk 13:17; Lk 21:23; 23:29; **(2)** of the young, "sucklings," Mt 21:16; and **(3)** "to suck", Lk 11:27, "hast sucked." See: BAGD—60c; THAYER—290b.

2338. **θῆλυς** {5x} **thēlus**, *thay'-loos;* from the same as *2337; female:*—female {3x}, woman {2x}.

Thelus, an adjective (from *thele,* "a breast"), is used in the form *thelu* (grammatically neuter) **(1)** as a noun, "female," in Mt 19:4; Mk 10:6; Gal 3:28; **(2)** in the feminine form *theleia,* in Rom 1:26, "women"; v. 27 "woman." See: BAGD—360c; THAYER—290b.

2339. **θήρα** {1x} **thēra**, *thay'-rah;* from θήρ **thēr** (a wild *animal,* as *game*); *hunting,* i.e. (fig.) *destruction:*—trap {1x}.

This word denotes a hunting, chase, then, a prey; hence, figuratively, of preparing destruction by a net or trap (Rom 11:9). See: BAGD—360d; THAYER—290b.

2340. **θηρεύω** {1x} **thērĕuō**, *thay-ryoo'-o;* from *2339;* to *hunt* (an animal), i.e. (fig.) to *carp at:*—catch {1x}.

Thereuo, "to hunt or catch wild beasts" (*therion,* "a wild beast"), is used by Luke metaphorically, of the Pharisees and Herodians in seeking to catch Christ in His talk, Lk 11:54. See: BAGD—360d; THAYER—290c.

2341. **θηριομαχέω** {1x} **thēriŏmachĕō**, *thay-ree-om-akh-eh'-o;* from a compound of *2342* and *3164;* to *be a beast-fighter* (in the gladiatorial show), i.e. (fig.) to *encounter* (furious men):—fight with wild beasts {1x}.

This word signifies "to fight with wild beasts", 1 Cor 15:32. Some think that the apostle was condemned to fight with wild beasts; if so, he would scarcely have omitted it from 2 Cor 11:23–end. Moreover, he would have lost his status as a Roman citizen. Probably he uses the word figuratively of contending with ferocious men. Ignatius so uses it in his Ep. to the Romans. See: BAGD—360d; THAYER—290c.

2342. **θηρίον** {46x} **thēriŏn**, *thay-ree'-on;* dimin. from the same as *2339;* a *dangerous animal:*—beast {42x}, venomous beast {1x}, wild beast {3x}.

Therion, **(1)** to be distinguished from *zoon,* almost invariably denotes "a wild beast." **(2)** In Acts 28:4, "venomous beast" is used of the viper which fastened on Paul's hand. **(3)** The idea of a "beast" of prey is not always present. Once, in Heb 12:20, it is used of the animals in the camp of Israel, such, e.g., as were appointed for sacrifice. *Therion,* in the sense of wild "beast," is used in the Apocalypse for the two antichristian potentates who are destined to control the affairs of the nations with Satanic power in the closing period of the present era, 11:7; 13:1–18; 14:9, 11; 15:2; 16:2, 10, 13; 17:3–17; 19:19–20; 20:4, 10. Syn.: Zoon (2226) means a living creature; whereas, *therion* means a beast. *Zoon* stresses the vital element, *therion* the bestial. See: TDNT—3:133, 333; BAGD—361a; THAYER—290c.

2343. **θησαυρίζω** {8x} **thēsaurizō**, *thay-sŏw-rid'-zo;* from *2344;* to *amass* or *reserve* (lit. or fig.):—lay up {3x}, in store {1x}, lay up treasure {1x}, treasure up {1x}, heap treasure together {1x}, keep in store {1x}.

Thesaurizo, "to lay up, store up" (akin to *thesauros,* "a treasury, a storehouse, a treasure"), is used **(1)** of "laying" up treasures, **(1a)** on earth, Mt 6:19; **(1b)** in Heaven, Mt 16: 20; **(1c)** in the last days, Jas 5:3, "ye have heaped treasure together"); **(2)** in Lk 12:21, "that layeth up treasure (for himself)"; **(3)** in 1 Cor 16:2, of money for needy ones (here the present participle is translated "in store," lit. "treasuring" or "storing," the "laying by" translating the preceding verb *tithemi*); **(4)** in 2 Cor 12:14, negatively, of children for parents; **(5)** metaphorically, of "laying" up wrath, Rom 2:5, "treasurest up." **(6)** In 2 Pet 3:7 the passive voice is used of the heavens and earth as "stored up" for fire, "kept in store." See: TDNT—3:138, 333; BAGD—361b; THAYER—290d.

2344. **θησαυρός** {18x} **thēsaurŏs**, *thay-sow-ros';* from *5087;* a *deposit,* i.e. *wealth* (lit. or fig.):—treasure {18x}.

This word denotes **(1)** "a place of safe keeping" (possibly akin to *tithemi,* "to put"), **(1a)** "a casket," Mt 2:11; **(1b)** "a storehouse," Mt 13:52; **(1c)** used metaphorically of the heart, Mt 12:35, twice, "out of the treasure"; Lk 6:45; **(2)** "a treasure," Mt 6:19, 20, 21; 13:44; Lk 12:33, 34; Heb 11:26; **(2a)** "treasure" (in heaven or the heavens), Mt 19:21; Mk 10:21; Lk 18:22; **(2b)** in these expressions (which are virtually equivalent to that in Mt 6:1, "with your Father which is in Heaven") the promise does not simply refer to the present life, but looks likewise to the hereafter; **(3)** in 2 Cor 4:7 it is used of "the light of the knowledge of the glory of God in the face of Jesus Christ," descriptive of the gospel, as deposited in the earthen vessels of the persons who proclaim it (cf. v. 4); **(4)** in Col 2:3, of the wisdom and knowledge hidden in Christ. See: TDNT—3:136, 333; BAGD—361c; THAYER—290d.

2345. **θιγγάνω** {3x} **thigganō**, *thing-gan'-o;* a prol. form of an obs. primary θίγω **thigō** (to *finger*); to *manipulate,* i.e. *have to do with;* by impl. to *injure:*—handle {1x}, touch {2x}.

This word signifies "to touch, to handle" and is translated **(1)** "handle" in Col 2:21: "Touch (hapto) not; taste not; handle (*thiggano*) not". It is translated **(2)** "touch" in **(2a)** Heb 12:20, of a beast's touching Mount Sinai; and **(2b)** "to touch by way of injuring," Heb 11:28. See: BAGD—361d; THAYER—291a.

2346. **θλίβω** {10x} **thlibō**, *thlee'-bo;* akin to the base of *5147;* to *crowd* (lit. or fig.):—afflict {3x}, narrow {1x}, throng {1x}, suffer tribulation {1x}, trouble {4x}.

Thlibo, "to suffer affliction, to be troubled," has reference to sufferings due to the pressure of circumstances, or the antagonism of persons. It is translated **(1)** "afflict", 2 Cor 1:6; 1 Ti 5:10; Heb 11:37; **(2)** "narrow", Mt 7:14; **(3)** "throng", Mk 3:9; **(4)** "suffer tribulation", 1 Th 3:4; **(5)** "trouble", 2 Cor 4:8; 7:5; 2 Th 1:6, 7. **(6)** Both the verb and the noun, when used of the present experience of believers, refer almost invariably to that which comes upon them from without. See: TDNT—3:139, 334; BAGD—362a; THAYER—291a.

2347. **θλίψις** {45x} **thlipsis**, *thlip'-sis;* from *2346; pressure* (lit. or fig.):—tribulation {21x}, affliction {17x}, trouble {3x}, anguish {1x}, persecution {1x}, burdened {1x}, to be afflicted + 1519 {1x}.

This word primarily means "a pressing, pressure", anything which burdens the spirit. **(1)** In two passages in Paul's Epistles it is used of future retribution, in the way of "affliction," Rom 2:9; 2 Th 1:6. **(2)** In Mt 24:9 "to be afflicted". **(3)** It is coupled **(3a)** with *stenochoria* (4730), "anguish," in Rom 2:9; 8:35; **(3b)** with *ananke* (318), "distress," 1 Th 3:7; **(3c)** with *diogmos* (1375), "persecution," Mt 13:21; Mk 4:17; 2 Th 1:4. **(4)** It is used of the calamities of war, Mt 24:21, 29;

Mk 13:19, 24; **(5)** of want, 2 Cor 8:13, lit., "distress for you"; Phil 4:14 (cf. 1:16); Jas 1:27; **(6)** of the distress of woman in childbirth, Jn 16:21; **(7)** of persecution, Acts 11:19; 14:22; 20:23; 1 Th 3:3, 7; Heb 10:33; Rev 2:10; 7:14; **(8)** of the "afflictions" of Christ, from which (His vicarious sufferings apart) His followers must not shrink, whether sufferings of body or mind, Col 1:24; **(9)** of sufferings in general, 1 Cor 7:28; 1 Th 1:6. Syn.: 4730. See: TDNT—3:139, 334; BAGD—362b; THAYER—291a.

2348. **θνήσκω** {13x} **thnesko**, *thnay'-sko;* a strengthened form of a simpler primary θάνω **thanō**, *than'-o* (which is used for it only in certain tenses); to *die* (lit. or fig.):—be dead {10x}, die {1x}, dead man {1x}, dead {1x}.

(1) This word means to die (in the perf. tense, "to be dead"), and **(1a)** is always used of physical death, **(1b)** except in 1 Ti 5:6, where it is metaphorically used of the loss of spiritual life. **(2)** The noun *thanatos* (2288) and the verb *thanatoo* (2230) are connected; the root probably signifying the breathing out of the last breath. See: TDNT—3:7, 312; BAGD—362c; THAYER—291b.

2349. **θνητός** {6x} **thnētŏs**, *thnay-tos';* from *2348; liable to die:*—mortal {5x}, mortality + 3588 {1x}.

Thnetos, "subject or liable to death, mortal" (akin to thnesko, "to die"), is translated **(1)** "mortal" **(1a)** in Rom 6:12, of the body, where it is called "mortal," not simply because it is liable to death, but because it is the organ in and through which death carries on its death-producing activities; **(1b)** in Rom 8:11 where the stress is on the liability to death, and the quickening is not reinvigoration but the impartation of life at the time of the Rapture, as in 1 Cor 15:53, 54; and **(1c)** in 2 Cor 4:11, it is applied to the flesh, which stands, not simply for the body, but the body as that which consists of the element of decay, and is thereby death-doomed. **(3a)** Christ's followers are in this life delivered unto death, that His life may be manifested in that which naturally is the seat of decay and death. **(3b)** That which is subject to suffering is that in which the power of Him who suffered here is most manifested. **(4)** It is translated "mortality" in 2 Cor 5:4. See: TDNT—3:21, 312; BAGD—362d; THAYER—291c.

2350. **θορυβέω** {4x} **thŏrubĕō**, *thor-oo-beh'-o;* from *2351;* to *be in tumult,* i.e. *disturb, clamor:*—make ado {1x}, make a noise {1x}, set on an uproar {1x}, trouble (one's) self {1x}.

"To make an uproar, to throw into confusion, or to wail tumultuously," is rendered **(1)** "make . . . ado," in Mk 5:39; **(2)** "making a noise" in Mt. 9:23; **(3)** "set . . . on an uproar" in Acts 17:5; and **(4)** "trouble . . . yourselves" in Acts 20:10. See: BAGD—362d; THAYER—291c.

2351. **θόρυβος** {7x} **thŏrubŏs**, *thor'-oo-bos;* from the base of *2360;* a *disturbance:*—tumult {4x}, uproar {3x}.

Thorubos, "a noise, uproar, tumult," is rendered **(1)** "tumult" in Mt 27:24; Mk 5:38; Acts 21:34; 24:18; and **(2)** "uproar" in Mt 26:5; Mk 14:2; Acts 20:1. See: BAGD—363a; THAYER—291c.

2352. **θραύω** {1x} **thrauō**, *thrŏw'-o;* a primary verb; to *crush:*—bruise {1x}.

This word means to smite through, shatter and in Lk 4:18, "them that are bruised," i.e., broken by calamity. See: BAGD—363; THAYER—291d. Syn.: 4486.

2353. **θρέμμα** {1x} **thrĕmma**, *threm'-mah;* from *5142; stock* (as *raised* on a farm):—cattle {1x}.

The word means whatever is fed or nourished, raised by man (Jn 4:12). See: BAGD—363b; THAYER—291d.

2354. **θρηνέω** {4x} **thrēnĕō**, *thray-neh'-o;* from *2355;* to *bewail:*—lament {2x}, mourn {2x}.

(1) This word means to break out into a wailing composed of unstudied words or may take a more elaborate form like a poem (cf. 2 Sa 1:17). *Threneo,* "to lament, wail" (akin to *threnos,* "a lamentation, a dirge"), is translated **(2)** "lament" **(2a)** in a general sense, of the disciples during the absence of the Lord, Jn 16:20; and **(2b)** of those who sorrowed for the sufferings and the impending crucifixion of the Lord, Lk 23:27. It is translated **(3)** "mourn, mourning" as for the dead, Mt 11:17, "have mourned"; Lk 7:32. Syn.: 2857, 3076, 3996. See: TDNT—3:148, 335; BAGD—363b; THAYER—291d.

2355. **θρῆνος** {1x} **thrēnŏs**, *thray'-nos;* from the base of *2360; wailing:*—lamentation {1x}. See: TDNT—3:148, 335; BAGD—363b; THAYER—291d.

2356. **θρησκεία** {4x} **thrēskĕia**, *thrace-ki'-ah;* from a der. of *2357;* ceremonial *observance:*—religion {3x}, worshipping {1x}.

Threskeia signifies religion in its external aspect, religious worship, especially the ceremonial service of religion. It is used of the religion **(1)** of the Jews (Acts 26:5); **(2)** of the worshiping of angels (Col 2:18) **(2a)** which they themselves repudiate (Rev 22:8, 9); **(2b)** there was an officious parade of humility in selecting these lower beings as intercessors rather than appealing directly to the throne of grace; **(3)** in Jas 1:26, 27 the contrast is set forth between that which is unreal and deceptive, and the pure religion which consists in visiting the fatherless and widows in their affliction and in keeping oneself unspotted from the world. He is not herein affirming . . . these offices to be the sum total, nor yet the great essentials, of true religion, but declares them to be the body, the *threskeia,* of which godliness, or the love of God, is for the informing soul. See: TDNT—3:155, 337; BAGD—363b; THAYER—292a.

2357. **θρῆσκος** {1x} **thrēskŏs**, *thrace'-kos;* prob. from the base of *2360; ceremonious* in worship (as *demonstrative*), i.e. *pious:*—religious {1x}.

This word denotes religious, careful of the externals of divine service (Jas 1:26). Syn.: 1174, 2126, 2152, 2318, 2356. See: TDNT—3:155, 337; BAGD—363d; THAYER—292a.

2358. **θριαμβεύω** {2x} **thriambĕuō**, *three-am-byoo'-o;* from a prol. compound of the base of *2360;* and a der. of *680* (mean. a *noisy iambus,* sung in honor of Bacchus); to *make an acclamatory procession,* i.e. (fig.) to *conquer* or (by Heb.) to *give victory:*—cause to triumph {1x},triumph over {1x}.

Thriambeuo (2358) denotes **(1)** "to cause to triumph," used of a conqueror with reference to the vanquished, 2 Cor 2:14. Theodoret paraphrases it "He leads us about here and there and displays us to all the world." This is in agreement with evidences from various sources. Those who are led are not captives exposed to humiliation, but are displayed as the glory and devoted subjects of Him who leads (see the context). This is so even if there is a reference to a Roman "triumph." On such occasions the general's sons, with various officers, rode behind his chariot (Livy, xlv. 40). But there is no necessary reference here to a Roman "triumph." The main thought is that of the display, "in Christ" being the sphere; its evidences are the effects of gospel testimony. **(2)** In Col 2:15 ("triumph over") the circumstances and subjects are quite different, and relate to Christ's victory over spiritual foes at the time of His death; accordingly the reference may be to the triumphant display of the defeated. See: TDNT—3:159, 337; BAGD—363d; THAYER—292b.

2359. **θρίξ** {15x} **thrix**, *threeks;* gen. τριχός **trichŏs**, etc.; of uncert. der.; *hair:*—hair {15x}.

Thrix denotes the "hair," whether of beast, as of the camel's "hair" **(1)** which formed the raiment of John the Baptist, Mt 3:4; Mk 1:6; **(2)** or of man. Regarding the latter **(2a)** it is used to signify the minutest detail, as that which illustrates the exceeding care and protection bestowed by God upon His children, Mt 10:30; Lk 12:7; 21:18; Acts 27:34; **(2b)** as the Jews swore by the "hair," the Lord used the natural inability to make one "hair" white or black, as one of the reasons for abstinence from oaths, Matt 5:36; **(2c)** while long "hair" is a glory to a woman, and to wear it loose or disheveled is a dishonor, yet the woman who wiped Christ's feet with her "hair" (in place of the towel which Simon the Pharisee omitted to provide), despised the shame in her penitent devotion to the Lord (slaves were accustomed to wipe their masters' feet), Lk 7:38, 44; see also Jn 11:2; 12:3; **(2d)** the dazzling whiteness of the head and "hair" of the Son of Man in the vision of Rev. 1: 14 is suggestive of the holiness and wisdom of "the Ancient of Days"; **(2e)** the long "hair" of the spirit-beings described as locusts in Rev 9:8 is perhaps indicative of their subjection to their satanic master (cf. 1 Cor 11:10); **(2f)** Christian women are exhorted to refrain from adorning their "hair" for outward show, 1 Pet 3:3.

(3) Goat's hair was used in tentmaking, as, e.g., in the case of Paul's occupation, Acts 18:3; the haircloth of Cilicia, his native province, was noted, being known in commerce as cilicium. Syn.: 2863, 2864, 5155. See: BAGD—363d; THAYER—292b.

2360. **θροέω** {3x} **thrŏĕō**, *thrŏ-eh'-o;* from θρέομαι **thrĕŏmai** to *wail;* to *clamor, to cry aloud,* i.e. (by impl.) to *frighten:*—trouble {3x}.

Throeo, "to make an outcry" (*throos,* "a tumult"), is used in the passive voice, Mt 24:6; Mk 13:7; Lk 24:37; 2 Th 2:2. See: TDNT—3:159, 337; BAGD—364a; THAYER—292b.

2361. **θρόμβος** {1x} **thrŏmbŏs**, *throm'-bos;* perh. from *5142* (in the sense of *thickening*); a *clot:*—great drop {1x}.

Thrombos, "a large, thick drop of clotted blood" (etymologically akin to *trepho,* "to curdle"), is used in Lk 22:44, in the plural, in the narrative of the Lord's agony in Gethsemane. See: BAGD—364a; THAYER—292c.

2362. **θρόνος** {61x} **thrŏnŏs**, *thron'-os;* from θράω **thraō** (to *sit*); a stately *seat* ("*throne*"); by impl. *power or authority* or (concr.) a *potentate:*—seat {7x}, throne {54x}.

Thronos, as a noun, means "a throne, a seat of authority," is used of the "throne" **(1)** of God, e.g., Mt 5:34; 23:22; Acts 7:49; Heb 4:16, "the throne of grace," i.e., from which grace proceeds; 8:1; 12:2; Rev 1:4; 3:21 (2nd part); 4:2 (twice); 5:1; frequently in Rev.; 21:3; **(2)** of Christ, e.g. **(2a)** Heb 1:8; Rev 3:21 (1st part); 22:3; **(2b)** His seat of authority in the Millennium, Mt 19:28 (1st part); **(3)** by metonymy for angelic powers,

Col 1:16; **(4)** of the Apostles in millennial authority, Mt 19:28 (2nd part); Lk 22:30; **(5)** of the elders in the heavenly vision, Rev 4:4 (2nd and 3rd parts), "seats"); so 11:16; **(6)** of David, Lk 1:32; Acts 2:30; **(7)** of Satan, Rev 2:13, "seat"; **(8)** of "the beast," the final and federal head of the revived Roman Empire, Rev 13:2; 16:10. See: TDNT—3:160, 338; BAGD—364b; THAYER—292c.

2363. **Θυάτειρα** {4x} **Thuatĕira**, *thoo-at'-i-rah;* of uncert. der.; *Thyatira,* a place in Asia Minor:—Thyatira {4x}. See: BAGD—364c; THAYER—292d.

2364. **θυγάτηρ** {29x} **thugatēr**, *thoo-gat'-air;* appar. a primary word [comp. "daughter"]; a *female child,* or (by Heb.) *descendant* (or *inhabitant*):—daughter {29x}.

Thugater means a daughter and is used of **(1)** the natural relationship; **(2)** spiritual relationship to God (2 Cor 6:18); **(3)** the inhabitants of a city or region (Mt 21:5; Jn 12:15); **(4)** the women who followed Christ to Calvary (Lk 23:28); **(5)** women of Aaron's posterity (Lk 1:5); **(6)** a female descendant of Abraham (Lk 13:16). Syn.: 2365, 3933. See: BAGD—364d; THAYER—292d.

2365. **θυγάτριον** {2x} **thugatriŏn**, *thoo-gat'-ree-on;* diminutive from *2364;* a *daughterling:*—little daughter {1x}, young daughter {1x}. Cf. Mk 5:23; 7:25. See: BAGD—365a; THAYER—293a.

2366. **θύελλα** {1x} **thuĕlla**, *thoo'-el-lah;* from *2380* (in the sense of *blowing*) a sudden storm, a whirlwind:—tempest {1x}.

(1) This word often refers to a wilder and fiercer natural phenomenon that lailaps (2978) and refers to the conflicted mingling of many opposing winds; **(2)** a sudden storm, tempest, whirlwind, Heb 12:18. Syn.: 417, 2978, 4151, 4157. See: BAGD—365a; THAYER—293a.

2367. **θΰϊνος** {1x} **thuïnŏs**, *thoo'-ee-nos;* from a der. of *2380* (in the sense of *blowing;* denoting a certain *fragrant* tree); made of *citron*-wood:—thyine {1x}.

Thumos is akin to *thuia,* or *thua,* an African aromatic and coniferous tree; in Rev 18:12 it describes a wood which formed part of the merchandise of Babylon; it was valued by Greeks and Romans for tables, being hard, durable and fragrant ("sweet"). See: BAGD—365a; THAYER—293a.

2368. **θυμίαμα** {6x} **thumiama**, *thoo-mee'-am-ah;* from *2370;* an *aroma,* i.e. fragrant *powder* burnt in relig. service; by impl. the *burning* itself:—incense {4x}, odour {2x}.

This word denotes "fragrant stuff for burning, incense" (from *thuo,* "to offer in sacrifice"). It is translated **(1)** "incense" Lk 1:10, 11; Rev 8:3, 4 signifying "frankincense"; and **(2)** by metonomy ["odour" for what produces it], Rev 5:8; 18:13 both times in plural. **(3)** In connection with the tabernacle, the "incense" was to be prepared from stacte, onycha, and galbanum, with pure frankincense, an equal weight of each; imitation for private use was forbidden. See: BAGD—365a; THAYER—293a.

2369. **θυμιαστήριον** {1x} **thumiastēriŏn**, *thoo-mee-as-tay'-ree-on;* or

θυμιατήριον **thumiatērion**, *thoo-mee-a-tay'-ree-on;* from a der. of *2370;* a *place of fumigation,* i.e. the *altar of incense* (in the Temple):—censer {1x}. This is a vessel for burning incense (Heb 9:4). See: BAGD—365b; THAYER—293a.

2370. **θυμιάω** {1x} **thumiaō**, *thoo-mee-ah'-o;* from a der. of *2380* (in the sense of *smoking*); to *fumigate,* i.e. *offer* aromatic *fumes:*—burn incense {1x}. See: BAGD—365b; THAYER—293b.

2371. **θυμομαχέω** {1x} **thumŏmachĕō**, *thoo-mom-akh-eh'-o;* from a presumed compound of *2372* and *3164;* to *be in a furious fight,* i.e. (fig.) to *be exasperated:*—be highly displeased {1x}.

Thumomacheo, means lit., "to fight with great animosity," "to be very angry, to be highly displeased," is said of Herod's "displeasure" with the Tyrians and Sidonians in Acts 12:20. See: BAGD—365b; THAYER—293b.

2372. **θυμός** {18x} **thumŏs**, *thoo-mos';* from *2380; passion* (as if *breathing* hard):—fierceness {2x}, indignation {1x}, wrath {15x}.

Thumos, "hot anger, wrath, passion," is translated **(1)** "wrath" in Lk 4:28; Acts 19:28; Gal 5:20; Eph 4:31; Col 3:8; Heb 11:27; Rev 12:12; 14:8, 10, 19; 15:1, 7; 16:1; 18:3; "wraths" in 2 Cor 12:20; **(2)** "fierceness" in Rev. 16:19; 19:15; of the wrath of God; and **(3)** "indignation" Rom 2:8. Syn.: *Thumos* is incipient displeasure fermenting in the mind. Orge (3709) take over when *thumos* has subsided and longs for revenge and desires to injure the one causing the harm. See also: 3950. See: TDNT—3:167, 339; BAGD—365b; THAYER—293b. comp. *5590.*

2373. **θυμόω** {1x} **thumŏō**, *tho-mŏ'-o;* from *2372;* to *put in a passion,* i.e. *enrage:*—be wroth {1x}.

Thumoo signifies "to be very angry" (from *thumos,* "wrath, hot anger"), "to be stirred into passion," Mt 2:16, of Herod (passive voice). See: BAGD—365c; THAYER—293c.

2374. **θύρα** {39x} **thura**, *thoo'-rah;* appar. a primary word [comp. "door"]; a *portal* or entrance (the opening or the closure, lit. or fig.):—door {38x}, gate {1x}.

Thura, "a door, gate" is used **(1)** literally, e.g., Mt. 6:6; 27:60; **(2)** metaphorically, **(2a)** of Christ, Jn 10:7, 9; **(2b)** of faith, by acceptance of the gospel, Acts 14:27; **(2c)** of "openings" for preaching and teaching the Word of God, 1 Cor 16:9; 2 Cor 2:12; Col 4:3; Rev 3:8; **(2d)** of "entrance" into the Kingdom of God, Mt 25:10; Lk 13:24–25; **(2e)** of Christ's "entrance" into a repentant believer's heart, Rev 3:20; **(2f)** of the nearness of Christ's second advent, Mt 24:33; Mk 13:29; **(2g)** of "access" to behold visions relative to the purposes of God, Rev 4:1. It is translated "gate" in Acts 3:2. See: TDNT—3:173, 340; BAGD—365d; THAYER—293d.

2375. **θυρεός** {1x} **thurĕŏs**, *thoo-reh-os';* from *2374;* a large oblong *shield* (as *door*-shaped):—shield {1x}.

Thureos formerly meant "a stone for closing the entrance of a cave"; then, "a shield," large and oblong, protecting every part of the soldier; the word is used metaphorically of faith, Eph 6:16, which the believer is to take up "in (*en* in the original) all" (all that has just been mentioned), i.e., as affecting the whole of his activities. See: TDNT—5:312, 702; BAGD—366a; THAYER—294a.

2376. **θυρίς** {2x} **thuris**, *thoo-rece';* a diminutive from *2374;* an *aperture,* i.e. *window:*—window {2x}.

Thuris, a diminutive of *thura* (2374), "a door," occurs in Acts 20:9; 2 Cor 11:33. See: BAGD—366a; THAYER—294a.

2377. **θυρωρός** {4x} **thurōrŏs**, *thoo-ro-ros';* from *2374* and οὖρος **ŏurŏs** (a *watcher*); a *gate-warden:*—that keeps the door {2x}, porter {2x}.

A *thuroros,* "a door-keeper" (*thura,* "a door," *ouros,* "a guardian"), is translated **(1)** "porter" in Mk 13:34; Jn 10:3; and **(2)** it is used of a female in Jn 18:16, 17, translated "(her) that kept the door." See: BAGD—366a; THAYER—294a.

2378. **θυσία** {29x} **thusia**, *thoo-see'-ah;* from *2380; sacrifice* (the act or the victim, lit. or fig.):—sacrifice {29x}.

Thusia primarily denotes "the act of offering"; then, objectively, "that which is offered" **(1)** of idolatrous "sacrifice," Acts 7:41; **(2)** of animal or other "sacrifices," as offered under the Law, Mt 9:13; 12:7; Mk 9:49; 12:33; Lk 2:24; 13:1; Acts 7:42; 1 Cor 10:18; Heb 5:1; 7:27; 8:3; 9:9; 10:1, 5, 8, 11; 11:4; **(3)** of Christ, in His "sacrifice" on the cross, Eph 5:2; Heb 9:23, where the plural anti-typically comprehends the various forms of Levitical "sacrifices" in their typical character; Heb 9:26; 10:12, 26; **(4)** metaphorically, **(4a)** of the body of the believer, presented to God as a living "sacrifice," Rom 12:1; **(4b)** of faith, Phil 2:17; **(4c)** of material assistance rendered to servants of God, Phil 4:18; **(4d)** of praise, Heb 13:15; **(4e)** of doing good to others and communicating with their needs, Heb 13:16; **(4f)** of spiritual "sacrifices" in general, offered by believers as a holy priesthood, 1 Pet 2:5. Syn.: 2380. See: TDNT—3:180, 342; BAGD—366b; THAYER—

2379. **θυσιαστήριον** {23x} **thusiastēriŏn**, *thoo-see-as-tay'-ree-on;* from a der. of *2378;* a *place of sacrifice,* i.e. an *altar* (spec. or gen., lit. or fig.):—altar {23x}.

(1) This word is derived from *thuciazo,* "to sacrifice." **(2)** Accordingly it denotes an "altar" for the sacrifice of victims, though it was also used for the "altar" of incense, e.g., Lk 1:11. **(3)** In the NT this word is reserved for the "altar" of the true God, Mt 5:23–24; 23:18–20, 35; Lk 11:51; 1 Cor 9:13; 10:18, in contrast to *bomos* (1041). Syn.: This is the altar to the one true God; whereas, bomos (1041) is a heathen altar. See: TDNT—3:180, 342; BAGD—366c; THAYER—294c.

2380. **θύω** {14x} **thuō**, *thoo'-o;* a primary verb; prop. to *rush* (*breathe* hard, *blow, smoke*), i.e. (by impl.) to *sacrifice* (prop. by fire, but gen.); by extens. to *immolate* (*slaughter* for any purpose):—kill {8x}, sacrifice {3x}, do sacrifice {2x}, slay {1x}.

This word primarily denotes "to offer firstfruits to a god"; then **(1)** "to sacrifice by slaying a victim," Acts 14:13, 18, to do sacrifice; 1 Cor 10:20, to sacrifice; 1 Cor 5:7, "hath been sacrificed," of the death of Christ as our Passover; **(2)** "to slay, kill," Mt 22:4; Mk 14:12; Lk 15:23, 27, 30; 22:7; Jh 10:10; Acts 10:13; 11:7. See: TDNT—3:180, 342; BAGD—367a; THAYER—294c.

2381. **Θωμᾶς** {12x} **Thōmas**, *tho-mas';* of Chald. or. [comp. 8380]; *the twin; Thomas,* a Chr.:—*Thomas* {12x}. See: BAGD—367c; THAYER—294d.

2382. **θώραξ** {5x} **thōrax**, *tho'-rax;* of uncert. aff.; the *chest* ("*thorax*"), i.e. (by impl.) a *corslet:*—breast-plate {5x}.

Thorax, primarily, "the breast," denotes "a breastplate or corselet," consisting of two parts and protecting the body on both sides, from the neck to the middle. **(1)** It is used metaphorically **(1a)** of righteousness, Eph 6:14; **(1b)** of faith and love, 1 Th 5:8, with perhaps a suggestion of the two parts, front and back, which formed the coat of mail (an alternative term for the word in the NT sense); **(2)** elsewhere in Rev 9:9, 17. See: TDNT—5:308, 702; BAGD—367c; THAYER—294d.

I

2383. **Ἰάειρος** {2x} **Iaĕirŏs**, *ee-ah'-i-ros;* or **Ἰάϊρος** **Iairŏs**, *ee-ahee'-ros;* of Heb. or. [2971]; *Jaïrus* (i.e. *Jair*), an Isr.:—Jairus {2x}. See: BAGD—367b; THAYER—295b.

2384. **Ἰακώβ** {27x} **Iakōb**, *ee-ak-obe';* of Heb. or. [3290]; *Jacob* (i.e. *Ja'akob*), the progenitor of the Isr.:—also an Isr.:—Jacob {27x}. See: TDNT—*, 344; BAGD—367b; THAYER—295b.

2385. **Ἰάκωβος** {42x} **Iakōbŏs**, *ee-ak'-o-bos;* the same as *2384* Græcized; *Jacobus*, the name of three Isr.:—James (son of Zebedee) {21x}, James (son of Alphaeus) {16x}, James (half-brother of Jesus) {1x}5. See: BAGD—367d; THAYER—295b.

2386. **ἴαμα** {3x} **iama**, *ee'-am-ah;* from *2390;* a *cure* (the effect):—healing {3x}.

Iama formerly signified "a means of healing"; in the NT, "a healing" (the result of the act), used in the plural, in 1 Cor 12:9, 28 plural, 30; of divinely imparted gifts in the churches in apostolic times. See: TDNT—3:194, 344; BAGD—368a; THAYER—295d.

2387. **Ἰαμβρῆς** {1x} **Iambrēs**, *ee-am-brace';* of Eg. or.; *Jambres*, an Eg.:—Jambres {1x}. See: TDNT—3:192, 344; BAGD—368b; THAYER—295d.

2388. **Ἰαννά** {1x} **Ianna**, *ee-an-nah';* prob. of Heb. or. [comp. 3238]; *Janna*, an Isr.:—Janna {1x}.368b; THAYER—296a.

2389. **Ἰαννῆς** {1x} **Iannēs**, *ee-an-nace';* of Eg. or.; *Jannes*, an Eg.:—Jannes {1x}. See: TDNT—3:192, 344; BAGD—368b; THAYER—296a.

2390. **ἰάομαι** {28x} **iaŏmai**, *ee-ah'-om-ahee;* mid. voice of appar. a primary verb; to *cure* (lit. or fig.):—heal {26x}, make whole {2x}.

Iaomai, "to heal," is used **(1)** of physical treatment **(1a)** 22 times; **(1b)** in Mt 5:28; Acts 9:34, "made whole"; **(2)** figuratively, of spiritual "healing," Mt 13:15; Jn 12:40; Acts 28:27; Heb 12:13; 1 Pet 2:24; possibly, Jas 5:16 includes both **(1)** and **(2)**. **(3)** Luke, the physician, uses the word fifteen times. See: TDNT—3:194, 344; BAGD—368b; THAYER—296a.

2391. **Ἰάρεδ** {1x} **Iarĕd**, *ee-ar'-ed* or **Ἰάρετ** **Iaret**, *ee-ar'-et;* of Heb. or. [3382]; *Jared* (i.e. *Jered*), an antediluvian:—Jared {1x}. See: BAGD—368c; THAYER—296b.

2392. **ἴασις** {3x} **iasis**, *ee'-as-is;* from *2390; curing* (the act):—cures {1x}, to heal + 1519 {1x}, healing {1x}.

Iasis, "a healing, a cure" (akin to *iaomai*, "to heal," and *iatros*, "a physician"), is **(1)** used in the plural, "cures", in Lk 13:32; **(2)** in Acts 4:22, "healing", **(3)** in Acts 4:30 with the preposition *eis* "unto," lit., "unto healing," translated "to heal." See: TDNT—3:194, 344; BAGD—368c; THAYER—296b.

2393. **ἴασπις** {4x} **iaspis**, *ee'-as-pis;* prob. of for. or. [see 3471]; *"jasper,"* a gem:—jasper {4x}.

Jasper is a precious stone of various colours (some are purple, others blue, others green, and others the colour of brass (Rev 4:3; 21:11, 18, 19). See: BAGD—368d; THAYER—296b.

2394. **Ἰάσων** {5x} **Iasōn**, *ee-as'-oan;* future act. part. masc. of *2390; about to cure; Jason*, a Chr.:—Jason {5x}. See: BAGD—368d; THAYER—296b.

2395. **ἰατρός** {7x} **iatrŏs**, *ee-at-ros';* from *2390;* a *physician:*—physician {7x}.

Iatros, akin to *iaomai*, "to heal," "a physician," occurs in Mt 9:12; Mk 2:17; 5:26; Lk 4:23; 5:31; 8:43; Col 4:14. See: TDNT—3:194, 344; BAGD—368d; THAYER—296b.

2396. **ἴδε** {27x} **idĕ**, *id'-eh;* second pers. sing. imper. act. of *1492;* used as an interj. to denote *surprise; lo!:*—behold {22x}, lo {3x}, look {1x}, see {1x}.

Ide and idou (2396 and 2400) are imperative moods, active and middle voices, respectively, of eidon (1492), to see, calling attention to what may be seen or heard or mentally apprehended in any way, **(1)** regularly rendered "behold." **(2)** It is used as an interjection, addressed either to one or many persons, e.g., Mt 25:20, 22, 25; Jn 1:29, 36, 47; Gal 5:2, the only occurrence outside Matthew, Mark and John. See: BAGD—369b; THAYER—296b.

2397. **ἰδέα** {1x} **idĕa**, *id-eh'-ah;* from *1492;* a *sight* [comp. fig. "idea"], i.e. *aspect:*—countenance {1x}.

This word is concerned with outward form, external appearance, one's aspect, one's looks. It is the sight occurring to the eyes, not to the thing itself but to the thing as it is seen. Syn.: Morphe (3444) means form, schema (4976) means fashion, and *idea* means appearance. See: TDNT—2:373, 202, BAGD—369c; THAYER—296c.

2398. **ἴδιος** {113x} **idiŏs**, *id'-ee-os;* of uncert. aff.; *pertaining to self*, i.e. one's *own;* by impl. *private* or *separate:*—his own {48x}, their own {13x}, privately {8x}, apart {7x}, your own {6x}, his {5x}, own {5x}, not tr {1x}, misc. {20x} = × his acquaintance, when they were alone, aside, due, his (proper, several), home, (her, our, thine) own (business), proper, severally. See: BAGD—369c; THAYER—296d.

2399. **ἰδιώτης** {5x} **idiōtēs**, *id-ee-o'-tace;* from *2398;* a *private* person, i.e. (by impl.) an *ignoramus* (comp. "idiot"):—ignorant {1x}, rude {1x}, unlearned {3x}.

Idiotes, as a noun, primarily means **(1)** "a private person" in contrast to a state official, hence, "a person without professional knowledge, unskilled, uneducated, unlearned," is translated **(1a)** "unlearned" in 1 Cor 14:16, 23, 24, of those who have no knowledge of the facts relating to the testimony borne in and by a local church; **(1b)** "rude" in 2 Cor 11:6, of the apostle's mode of speech in the estimation of the Corinthians;

(3) "ignorant men" in Acts 4:13, of the speech of the apostle Peter and John in the estimation of the rulers, elders and scribes in Jerusalem. Syn.: While agrammatoi (62) refers to being unacquainted with rabbinical book learning, idiotai would signify laymen, in contrast with the religious officials. The apostles were accused of not having that learning gained by mingling with people who have important affairs to transact. Sources of learning are from God Himself or from books and people (literature and politics). One is agrammatos when he has not shared in the first; he is *idiotes* when not sharing in the second. The word became a derogatory word because the Greeks felt one's highest education consisted in public life and to purposely withdraw from it was unthinkable. See also: 50, 51, 52, 56, 2990. See: TDNT—3:215, 348; BAGD—370c; THAYER—297b.

2400. **ἰδού** {219x} **idŏu**, *id-oo';* second pers. sing. imper. mid. voice of *1492;* used as imper. *lo!;*—behold {181x}, lo {29x}, see {3x}.

Ide and *idou* (2396 and 2400) are imperative moods, active and middle voices, respectively, of eidon (1492), to see, calling attention to what may be seen or heard or mentally apprehended in any way, regularly rendered "behold." See: BAGD—370d; THAYER—297c.

2401. **Ἰδουμαία** {1x} **Idŏumaia**, *id-oo-mah'-yah;* of Heb. or. [123]; *Idumæa* (i.e. *Edom*), a region E. (and S.) of Pal.:—Idumæa {1x}. See: BAGD—371b; THAYER—297d.

2402. **ἱδρώς** {1x} **hidrōs**, *hid-roce';* a strengthened form of a primary ἴδος **idŏs** (*sweat*); *perspiration:*—sweat {1x}. See: BAGD—371c; THAYER—298a.

2403. **Ἰεζαβήλ** {1x} **Iĕzabēl**, *ee-ed-zab-ale';* of Heb. or. [348]; *Jezabel* (i.e. *Jezebel*), a Tyrian woman (used as a synonym of a termagant or false teacher):—Jezabel {1x}. See: TDNT—3:217, 348; BAGD—371c; THAYER—298a.

2404. **Ἱεράπολις** {1x} **Hiĕrapŏlis**, *hee-er-ap'-ol-is;* from *2413* and *4172; holy city; Hierapolis*, a place in Asia Minor:—*Hierapolis* {1x}. See: BAGD—371c; THAYER—298a.

2405. **ἱερατεία** {2x} **hiĕratĕia**, *hee-er-at-i'-ah;* from *2407; priestliness*, i.e. the *sacerdotal function:*—office of the priesthood {1x}, priest's office {1x}. Cf. Lk 1:9; Heb 7:5. See: TDNT—3:251, 349; BAGD—371d; THAYER—298b.

2406. **ἱεράτευμα** {2x} **hiĕratĕuma**, *hee-er-at'-yoo-mah;* from *2407;* the *priestly fraternity*, i.e. *sacerdotal order* (fig.):—priesthood {2x}.

This word means a body of priests consisting of all believers, the whole church (not a special order from among them), called "a holy priesthood," (1 Pet 2:5); "a royal priesthood," (1 Pet 2:9); the former term is associated with offering spiritual sacrifices, the latter with the royal dignity of showing forth the Lord's excellencies. See: TDNT—3:249, 349; BAGD—371d; THAYER—298b.

2407. **ἱερατεύω** {1x} **hiĕratĕuō**, *hee-er-at-yoo'-o;* prol. from *2409;* to *be a priest*, i.e. *perform his functions:*—execute the priest's office {1x}. See: TDNT—3:248, 349; BAGD—371d; THAYER—298b.

2408. **Ἱερεμίας** {2x} **Hiĕrĕmias**, *hee-er-em-ee'-as;* of Heb. or. [3414]; *Hieremias* (i.e. *Jermijah*), an Isr.:—Jeremias {1x}, Jeremy {1x}. See: TDNT—3:218,*; BAGD—371d; THAYER—298b.

2409. **ἱερεύς** {32x} **hiĕrĕus**, *hee-er-yooce';* from *2413;* a *priest* (lit. or fig.):—high priest {1x}, priest {31x}.

Hiereus refers to one who offers sacrifice and has the charge of things pertaining thereto and is used **(1)** of a priest of the pagan god Zeus (Acts 14:13); **(2)** of Jewish priests (Mt 8:4; 12:4, 5; Lk 1:5); **(3)** of believers (Rev 1:6; 5:10; 1 Pet 2:5, 9), **(3a)** constituting **(3a1)** a kingdom of priests (Rev 1:6), **(3a2)** a holy priesthood (1 Pet 2:5), and **(3a2)** royal (1 Pet 2: 9), **(3b)** not a special sacerdotal class in contrast to the laity; **(3c)** all believers are commanded to offer the sacrifices

(Rom 12:1; Phil 2:17; 4:18; Heb 13:15, 16; 1 Pet 2:5); **(4)** of Christ (Heb 5:6; 7:11, 15, 17, 21; 8:4); **(5)** of Melchizedek, as the foreshadower of Christ (Heb 7:1, 3). Syn.: 749. See: TDNT—3:257, 349; BAGD—372a; THAYER—298c.

2410. **Ἱεριχώ** {7x} **Hiĕrichō**, *hee-er-ee-kho'*; of Heb. or. [3405]; *Jericho*, a place in Pal.:—Jericho {7x}. See: BAGD—372b; THAYER—298c.

2411. **ἱερόν** {71x} **hiĕrŏn**, *hee-er-on'*; neut. of *2413*; a *sacred* place, i.e. the entire precincts (whereas *3485* denotes the central *sanctuary* itself) of the *Temple* (at Jerusalem or elsewhere):—temple {71x}

Hieron, the neuter of the adjective *hieros,* "sacred," is used as a noun denoting "a sacred place, a temple," **(1)** that of Artemis (Diana), Acts 19:27; **(2)** that in Jerusalem, Mk 11:11, signifying the entire building with its precincts, or some part thereof, as distinct from the *naos,* "the inner sanctuary"; **(3)** apart from the Gospels and Acts, it is mentioned only in 1 Cor 9:13. **(4)** Christ taught in one of the courts, to which all the people had access. **(5)** *Hieron* is never used figuratively. **(6)** The Temple mentioned in the Gospels and Acts was begun by Herod in 20 B.C., and destroyed by the Romans in A.D. 70. Syn.: 3485. See: TDNT—3:230, 349; BAGD—372b; THAYER—298d.

2412. **ἱεροπρεπής** {1x} **hiĕrŏprĕpēs**, *hee-er-op-rep-ace'*; from *2413* and the same as *4241*; *reverent*:—as becometh holiness {1x}.

Hieroprepes, from *hieros,* "sacred," with the adjectival form of *prepo,* denotes "suited to a sacred character, that which is befitting in persons, actions or things consecrated to God," Titus 2:3, "as becometh holiness." Syn.: 38, 40, 41, 42, 3741, 3742, 3743. See: TDNT—3:253, 349; BAGD—372d; THAYER—299b.

2413. **ἱερός** {2x} **hiĕrŏs**, *hee-er-os'*; of uncert. aff.; *sacred*:—holy {2x}.

This word means sacred, consecrated to deity, pertaining to God; the sacred Scriptures, because inspired by God, treating of divine things and therefore to be devoutly revered, translated "holy" (1 Cor 9:13; 2 Ti 3:15). See: TDNT—3:221, 349; BAGD—372d; THAYER—299b.

2414. **Ἱεροσόλυμα** {59x} **Hiĕrŏsŏluma**, *hee-er-os-ol'-oo-mah*; of Heb. or. [3389]; *Hierosolyma* (i.e. *Jerushalaïm*), the capital of Pal.:—Jerusalem {5x}. See: TDNT—7:292, 1028; BAGD—372d; THAYER—299b. comp. *2419*.

2415. **Ἱεροσολυμίτης** {2x} **Hiĕrŏsŏlumitēs**, *hee-er-os-ol-oo-mee'-tace*; from *2414*; a *Hierosolymite*, i.e. inhab. of Hierosolyma:—of Jerusalem {2x}. See: TDNT—7:292, 1028; BAGD—373b; THAYER—299d.

2416. **ἱεροσυλέω** {1x} **hiĕrŏsulĕō**, *hee-er-os-ool-eh'-o*; from *2417*; to *be a temple-robber* (fig.):—commit sacrilege {1x}.

This word means to commit sacrilege, to rob a temple and in Rom 2:22, the meaning is, thou who abhorrest idols and their contamination, doest yet not hesitate to plunder their shrines and copy their ways. See: TDNT—3:255, 349; BAGD—373c; THAYER—299d.

2417. **ἱερόσυλος** {1x} **hiĕrŏsulŏs**, *hee-er-os'-oo-los*; from *2411* and *4813*; a *temple-despoiler*:—robber of churches {1x}.

In Acts 19:37 this word is used by the Roman town clerk generally of an assembly of religious people and not to the gathering of Christians. See: TDNT—3:256, 349; BAGD—373c; THAYER—300a.

2418. **ἱερουργέω** {1x} **hiĕrŏurgĕō**, *hee-er-oorg-eh'-o*; from a compound of *2411* and the base of *2041*; to *be a temple-worker,* i.e. *officiate as a priest* (fig.):—minister {1x}.

Hierourgeo means to minister in priestly service, a sacrificing priest and is used by Paul metaphorically of his ministry of the Gospel (Rom 15:16); the offering connected with his priestly ministry is "the offering up of the Gentiles," i.e., the presentation of Gentile converts to God. Syn.: 1247, 1249, 3011. See: TDNT—3:251, 349; BAGD—373c; THAYER—300a.

2419. **Ἱερουσαλήμ** {83x} **Hiĕrŏusalēm**, *hee-er-oo-sal-ame'*; of Heb. or. [3389]; *Hierusalem* (i.e. *Jerushalem*), the capital of Pal.:—Jerusalem {83x}. See: TDNT—7:292, 1028; BAGD—373c; THAYER—300a. comp. *2414*.

2420. **ἱερωσύνη** {4x} **hiĕrōsunē**, *hee-er-o-soo'-nay*; from *2413*; *sacredness*, i.e. (by impl.) the *priestly office*:—priesthood {4x}.

Hierosune, "a priesthood," signifies the office, quality, rank and ministry of "a priest," Heb 7:11, 12, 14, 24, where the contrasts between the Levitical "priesthood" and that of Christ are set forth. See: TDNT—3:247, 349; BAGD—373c; THAYER—300a.

2421. **Ἰεσσαί** {5x} **Iĕssai**, *es-es-sah'-ee*; of Heb. or. [3448]; *Jessae* (i.e. *Jishai*), an Isr.:—Jesse {5x}. See: BAGD—373d; THAYER—300a.

2422. **Ἰεφθάε** {1x} **Iĕphthaĕ**, *ee-ef-thah'-eh*; of Heb. or. [3316]; *Jephthaë* (i.e. *Jiphtach*), an Isr.:—Jephthah {1x}. See: BAGD—373d; THAYER—300b.

2423. **Ἰεχονίας** {2x} **Iĕchŏnias**, *ee-ekh-on-ee'-as*; of Heb. or. [3204]; *Jechonias* (i.e. *Jekonjah*), an Isr.:—Jechonias {2x}. See: BAGD—373d; THAYER—300b.

2424. **Ἰησοῦς** {975x} **Iēsŏus**, *ee-ay-sooce'*; of Heb. or. [3091]; *Jesus* (i.e. *Jehoshua*), the name of our Lord and two (three) other Isr.:—Jesus {972x}, Jesus (Joshua) {2x}, Jesus (Justus) {1x}. See: TDNT—3:284, 360; BAGD—373d; THAYER—300b.

2425. **ἱκανός** {41x} **hikanŏs**, *hik-an-os'*; from ἵκω **hikō** [ἱκάνω **hikanō** or ἱκνέομαι **hiknĕŏmai**, akin to *2240*] (to *arrive*); *competent* (as if *coming* in season), i.e. *ample* (in amount) or *fit* (in character):—many}, much {6x}, worthy {5x}, long {4x}, sufficient {3x}, misc. {12x} = able, + content, enough, good, great, large, meet, security, sore.

(1) *Hikanos,* as an adjective, means "sufficient" and is used with poieo (4160 - "to do") in Mk 15:15 and is translated "to content (the multitude)," i.e., to do sufficient to satisfy them: "And *so* Pilate, willing to content the people, released Barabbas unto them, and delivered Jesus, when he had scourged *him,* to be crucified." **(2)** This word translated "able," is to be distinguished from dunatos (1415) which means possessing power; *hikanos* means sufficient power. **(3)** When said of things it signifies enough: "And they said, Lord, behold, here *are* two swords. And he said unto them, It is enough." (Lk 22:38); **(4)** when said of persons, it means competent, worthy: "To the one *we are* the savour of death unto death; and to the other the savour of life unto life. And who *is* sufficient for these things?" (2 Cor 2:16; cf. 3:5; 2 Ti 2:2). Syn.: 714, 841, 842, 4909. See: TDNT—3:293, 361; BAGD—374b; THAYER—300c.

2426. **ἱκανότης** {1x} **hikanŏtēs**, *hik-an-ot'-ace*; from *2425*; *ability*:—sufficiency {1x}.

This word means sufficient power, ability or competency to do a thing (2 Cor 3:5). See: TDNT—3:293, 361; BAGD—374d; THAYER—300d.

2427. **ἱκανόω** {2x} **hikanŏō**, *hik-an-ŏ'-o*; from *2425*; to *enable*, i.e. *qualify*:—make able {1x}, make meet {1x}.

Hidanoo, "to render fit, meet, to make sufficient," is translated **(1)** "hath made . . . meet" in Col 1:12; and **(2)** "hath made able" in 2 Cor 3:6. See: TDNT—3:293, 361; BAGD—374d; THAYER—300d.

2428. **ἱκετηρία** {1x} **hikĕtēria**, *hik-et-ay-ree'-ah*; from a der. of the base of *2425* (through the idea of *approaching* for a favor); *intreaty*:—supplication {1x}.

Hiketeria is the feminine form of the adjective *hiketerios,* denoting "of a suppliant," and used as a noun, formerly "an olive branch" carried by a suppliant (*hiketes*), then later, "a supplication," used in Heb 5:7. See: TDNT—3:296, 362; BAGD—375a; THAYER—301a.

2429. **ἰκμάς** {1x} **hikmas**, *hik-mas'*; of uncert aff.; *dampness*:—moisture {1x}. See: BAGD—375a; THAYER—301a.

2430. **Ἰκόνιον** {6x} **Ikŏniŏn**, *ee-kon'-ee-on*; perh. from *1504*; *image-like*; *Iconium*, a place in Asia Minor:—Iconium {6x}. See: BAGD—375b; THAYER—30a.

2431. **ἱλαρός** {1x} **hilarŏs**, *hil-ar-os'*; from the same as *2436*; *propitious* or *merry* ("*hilarious*"), i.e. *prompt* or *willing*:—cheerful {1x}.

This word signifies that readiness of mind, that joyousness, which is prompt to do anything (2 Cor 9:7). See: TDNT—3:297, 362; BAGD—375b; THAYER—301a.

2432. **ἱλαρότης** {1x} **hilarŏtēs**, *hil-ar-ot'-ace*; from *2431*; *alacrity*:—cheerfulness {1x}. See: TDNT—3:297, 362; BAGD—375b; THAYER—301b.

2433. **ἱλάσκομαι** {2x} **hilaskŏmai**, *hil-as'-kom-ahee*; mid. voice from the same as *2436*; to *conciliate*, i.e. (tran.) to *atone* for (sin), or (intr.) *be propitious*:—be merciful {1x}, make reconciliation for {1x}.

Hilaskomai **(1)** was used amongst the Greeks with the significance "to make the gods propitious, to appease, propitiate," inasmuch as their good will was not conceived as their natural attitude, but something to be earned first. **(2)** This use of the word is foreign to the Greek Bible, with respect to God whether in the Sept. or in the NT. **(3)** It is never used of any act whereby man brings God into a favorable attitude or gracious disposition. **(4)** It is God who is "propitiated" by the vindication of His holy and righteous character, whereby through the provision He has made in the vicarious and expiatory sacrifice of Christ, He has so dealt with sin that He can show mercy to the believing sinner in the removal of his guilt and the remission of his sins. **(5)** Thus in Lk 18:13 it signifies "to be propitious" or "merciful to" (with the person as the object of the verb), and in Heb 2:17 "to expiate, to make reconciliation" (the object of the verb being sins). **(6)** Through the "propitiatory" sacrifice of Christ, he who believes upon Him is by God's own act delivered from justly deserved wrath, and comes under the covenant of grace.

(7) Never is God said to be reconciled, a fact itself indicative that the enmity exists on man's part alone, and that it is man who needs to be reconciled to God, and not God to man. **(8)** God is always the same and, since He is Himself immutable, His relative attitude does change towards those who change. **(9)** He can act differently towards those who come to Him by faith, and solely on the ground of the "propitiatory" sacrifice of Christ, not because He has changed, but because He ever acts according to His unchanging righteousness. **(10)** The expiatory work of the Cross is therefore the means whereby the barrier which sin interposes between God and man is broken down. **(11)** By the giving up of His sinless life sacrificially, Christ annuls the power of sin to separate between God and the believer. **(12)** Man has forfeited his life on account of sin and God has provided the one and only way whereby eternal life could be bestowed, namely, by the voluntary laying down of His life by His Son, under divine retribution. Of this the former sacrifices appointed by God were foreshadowings. Syn.: 1653, 1655, 1656, 2436, 3627, 3628, 3629, 4698. See: TDNT—3:301, 362; BAGD—375c; THAYER—301b.

2434. **ἱλασμός** {2x} **hilasmŏs**, *hil-as-mos';* *atonement,* i.e. (concr.) an *expiator:*—propitiation {2x}.

Hilasmos (2434), akin to hileos ("merciful, propitious"), signifies "an expiation, a means whereby sin is covered and remitted." **(1)** It is used in the NT of Christ Himself as "the propitiation," in 1 Jn 2:2 and 4:10, **(1a)** signifying that He Himself, through Him alone, the violated holiness and righteousness of God by man's sin has been propitiated [satisfied]. This is the personal means through which God shows mercy to the sinner who believes on Christ as the One thus provided. **(1b)** In the former passage He is described as "the propitiation for our sins; and not for ours only, but also for *the sins of* the whole world." **(1c)** Provision is made for the whole world, so that no one is, by divine predetermination, excluded from the scope of God's mercy; **(1d)** the efficacy of the "propitiation," however, is made actual for those who believe. **(1e)** In 4:10, the fact that God "sent His Son to be the propitiation for our sins," is shown to be the great expression of God's love toward man, and the reason why Christians should love one another. See: TDNT—3:301, 362; BAGD—375c; THAYER—301b.

2435. **ἱλαστήριον** {2x} **hilastēriŏn**, *hil-as-tay'-ree-on;* neut. of a der. of *2433;* an *expiatory* (place or thing), i.e. (concr.) an atoning *victim,* or (spec.) the *lid* of the Ark (in the Temple):—mercyseat {1x}, propitiation {1x}.

Hilasterion (2435), is regarded as the neuter of an adjective signifying "propitiatory." **(1)** It is used for the lid of the ark in Heb 9:5. **(2)** Elsewhere in the NT it occurs only in Rom 3:25, where it is used of Christ Himself. **(3)** Christ, through His expiatory death, is the personal means by whom God shows the mercy of His justifying grace to the sinner who believes. **(4)** His "blood" stands for the voluntary giving up of His life, by the shedding of His blood in expiatory sacrifice under divine judgment righteously due to us as sinners, faith being the sole condition on man's part. **(5)** Note: By metonymy, 'blood' is sometimes put for 'death,' inasmuch as, blood being essential to life, Lev 17:11, when the blood is shed life is given up, that is, death takes place. The fundamental principle on which God deals with sinners is expressed in the words 'apart from shedding of blood,' i.e., unless a death takes place, 'there is no remission' of sins, Heb 9:22.

(6) But whereas the essential of the type lay in the fact that blood was shed, the essential of the antitype lies in this, that the blood shed was that of Christ. Hence, in connection with Jewish sacrifices, 'the blood' is mentioned without reference to the victim from which it flowed, but in connection with the great antitypical sacrifice of the NT the words 'the blood' never stand alone; the One Who shed the blood is invariably specified, for it is the Person that gives value to the work; the saving efficacy of the Death depends entirely upon the fact that He Who died was the Son of God. See: TDNT—3:318, 362; BAGD—375d.301c.

2436. **ἵλεως** {2x} **hilĕōs**, *hil'-eh-oce;* perh. from the alt. form of *138; cheerful* (as *attractive*), i.e. *propitious;* adv. (by Heb.) God be *gracious!,* i.e. (in averting some calamity) *far* be it:—be it far {1x}, merciful {1x}.

Hileos, as an adjective, means "propitious, merciful." **(1)** The quality expressed by it there essentially appertains to God, though man is undeserving of it. **(2)** It is used only of God, Heb 8:12; **(3)** in Mt 16:22, "Be it far from Thee" (Peter's word to Christ) may have the meaning, "(God) have mercy on Thee," lit., "propitious to Thee" so that what You said will not happen. Syn.: 1653, 1655, 1656, 2433, 3627, 3628, 3629, 4698. See: TDNT—3:300, 362; BAGD—376a; THAYER—301d.

2437. **Ἰλλυρικόν** {1x} **Illurikŏn**, *il-loo-ree-kon';* neut. of an adj. from a name of uncert. der.: (the) *Illyrican* (shore), i.e. (as a name itself) *Illyricum,* a region of Europe:—Illyricum {1x}. See: BAGD—376a.301d.

2438. **ἱμάς** {4x} **himas**, *hee-mas';* perh. from the same as *260;* a *strap,* i.e. (spec.) the *tie* (of a sandal) or the *lash* (of a scourge):—latchet {3x}, thong {1x}.

Himas denotes "a thong, strap," whether **(1)** for binding prisoners, Acts 22:25, "(the) thongs" or **(2)** for fastening sandals, Mk 1:7; Lk 3:16; Jn 1:27. Among the Orientals everything connected with the feet and shoes is defiled and debasing, and the stooping to unfasten the dusty latchet is the most insignificant in such service. See: BAGD—376b; THAYER—302a.

2439. **ἱματίζω** {2x} **himatizō**, *him-at-id'-zo;* from *2440;* to *dress:*—clothe {2x}.

Himatizo as a verb, means "to put on raiment": "And they come to Jesus, and see him that was possessed with the devil, and had the legion, sitting, and clothed (*himatizo*), and in his right mind: and they were afraid" (Mk 5:15; cf. Lk 8:35). Syn.: 294, 1463, 1737, 1746, 1902, 4016. See: BAGD—376b; THAYER—302a.

2440. **ἱμάτιον** {61x} **himatiŏn**, *him-at'-ee-on;* neut. of a presumed der. of ἕν-νυμι **ĕnnumi** (*to put on*), a *dress* (inner or outer):—garment {30}, raiment {12x}, clothes {12x}, cloke {2x}, robe {2x}, vesture {2x}, apparel {1x}.

Himation, a diminutive of *heima,* "a robe," was used especially of an outer cloak or mantle thrown over the *chiton* (5509), and in **(1)** general of raiment, "apparel" in 1 Pet 3:3; **(2)** in the plural, "clothes" (the "cloke" and the tunic), e.g., Mt 17:2; 26:65; 27:31, 35; **(3)** "an outer garment," is rendered "vesture" in Rev 19:13, 16. See: BAGD—376b; THAYER—302a.

2441. **ἱματισμός** {6x} **himatismŏs**, *him-at-is-mos';* from *2439; clothing:*—vesture {2x}, apparel {2x}, raiment {1x}, array {1x}.

Himatismos, in form a collective word, denoting "vesture, garments," is used **(1)** generally of "costly or stately raiment," the apparel of kings, of officials, etc. **(1a)** See Lk 7:25, where "gorgeously apparelled" is, lit., "in gorgeous vesture." **(1b)** See also Acts 20:33 and 1 Ti 2:9, "costly raiment." **(2)** This is the word used of the Lord's white and dazzling raiment on the Mount of Transfiguration, Lk 9:29. **(3)** It is also used of His *chiton* (5509), His undergarment for which the soldiers cast lots, Jn 19:23–24; **(4)** "vesture" in Mt 27:35. See: BAGD—376d; THAYER—302b.

2442. **ἱμείρομαι** {1x} **himĕirŏmai**, *him-i'-rom-ahee;* mid. voice from ἵμερος **himĕrŏs** (a *yearning;* of uncert. aff.); to *long for:*—be affectionately desirous {1x}.

Himeiromai, "to have a strong affection for, a yearning after," is found in 1 Th 2:8, "being affectionately desirous of you." It is probably derived from a root indicating remembrance. See: TDNT—5:176,*; BAGD—376d; THAYER—302b.

2443. **ἵνα** {621x} **hina**, *hin'-ah;* prob. from the same as the former part of *1438* (through the *demonstrative* idea; comp. *3588*); in order *that* (denoting the *purpose* or the *result*):—that {536x}, to {69x}, for to {8x}, not translated {1x}, misc. {7x} = albeit, because, lest, so as. See: TDNT—3:323, 366; BAGD—376d; THAYER—302b. comp. *3363.*

ἵνα μή **hina mē**. See *3363.*

2444. **ἱνατί** {6x} **hinati**, *hin-at-ee';* from *2443* and *5101; for what* reason?, i.e. *why?:*—wherefore {1x}, why {5x}. See: BAGD—378c; THAYER—305a.

2445. **Ἰόππη** {10x} **Iŏppē**, *ee-op'-pay;* of Heb. or. [3305]; *Joppe* (i.e. *Japho*), a place in Pal.:—Joppa {10x}. See: BAGD—378d; THAYER—305a.

2446. **Ἰορδάνης** {15x} **Iŏrdanēs**, *ee-or-dan'-ace;* of Heb. or. [3383]; the *Jordanes* (i.e. *Jarden*), a river of Pal.:—Jordan {15x}. See: TDNT—6:608, 921; BAGD—378d; THAYER—305b.

2447. **ἰός** {3x} **iŏs**, *ee-os';* perh. from εἶμι **ĕimi** (*to go*) or ἵημι **hiēmi** (*to send*); *rust* (as if *emitted* by metals); also *venom* (as *emitted* by serpents):—poison {2x}, rust {1x}.

This word denotes something active as **(1)** rust, as acting on metals, affecting their nature (Jas 5:3); **(2)** poison, as of asps, acting destructively on living tissues, figuratively **(2a)** of the evil use of the lips as the organs of speech (Rom 3:13); **(2b)** so of the tongue (Jas 3:8). See: TDNT—3:334, 368; BAGD—378d; THAYER—305b.

2448. **Ἰουδά** {1x} **Iŏuda**, *ee-oo-dah';* of Heb. or. [3063 or perh. 3194]; *Judah* (i.e. *Jehudah* or *Juttah*), a part of (or place in) Pal.:—Judah {1x}. See: BAGD—379b; THAYER—305b.

2449. **Ἰουδαία** {44x} **Iŏudaia**, *ee-oo-dah'-yah;* fem. of *2453* (with *1093* impl.); the *Judæan* land (i.e. *Judæa*), a region of Pal.:—Judæa {42x}, Jewry {2x}. See: TDNT—3:356, 372; BAGD—379a; THAYER—305c.

2450. **Ἰουδαΐζω** {1x} **Iŏudaïzō**, *ee-oo-dah-id'-zo;* from *2453;* to *become a Judæan,* i.e. "*Judaize*":—live as the Jews {1x}.

This word means to adopt Jewish customs and rites, practices and manners, imitate the Jews, Judaise, observe the ritual law of the Jews (Gal 14). See: TDNT—3:356, 372; BAGD—379b; THAYER—305d.

2451. **Ἰουδαϊκός** {1x} **Iŏudaïkŏs**, *ee-oo-dah-ee-kos';* from *2453; Judaïc,* i.e. *resembling a Judæan:*—Jewish {1x}. See: TDNT—3:356, 372; BAGD—379b; THAYER—305d.

2452. **Ἰουδαϊκῶς** {1x} **Iŏudaïkōs**, *ee-oo-dah-ee-koce';* adv. from *2451; Judaïcally* or *in a manner resembling a Judæan:*—as do the Jews {1x}. See: BAGD—379b; THAYER—305d.

2453. **Ἰουδαῖος** {198x} **Iŏudaiŏs**, *ee-oo-dah'-yos;* from *2448* (in the sense of *2455* as a country); *Judæan,* i.e. belonging to *Jehudah:*—Jew {193x}, of Judea {3x}, Jewess {2x}.

This word means Jewish, **(1)** belonging to the Jewish race, or **(1a)** Jewish as respects to birth, race, religion. *Ioudaios* is used **(1b)** adjectivally, with the lit. meaning, "Jewish," **(1c)** sometimes with the addition **(1c1)** of aner, "a man," Acts 10:28; 22:3; **(1c2)** in Acts 21:39 with anthropos; **(1c3)** in Acts 13:6, lit., "a Jewish false-prophet"; **(1c4)** in Jn 3:22, with the word chora, "land" or "country," signifying "Judean," lit., "Judean country"; used by metonymy for the people of the country; **(2)** as a noun, "a Jew, Jews," e.g., Mt 2:2; Mk 7:3. **(2a)** The name "Jew" is primarily tribal (from Judah). **(2b)** It is first found in 2 Kin 16:6, as distinct from Israel, of the northern kingdom. **(2c)** After the Captivity it was chiefly used to distinguish the race from Gentiles, e.g., Jn 2:6; Acts 14:1; Gal 2:15, where it denotes Christians of "Jewish" race; **(2d)** it distinguishes Jews **(2d1)** from Samaritans, in Jn 4:9; **(2d2)** from proselytes, in Acts 2:10. **(2e)** The word is most frequent in John's gospel and the Acts; in the former it especially denotes the typical representatives of Jewish thought contrasted with believers in Christ . . . or with other Jews of less pronounced opinions, e.g., Jn 3:25; 5:10; 7:13; 9:22; **(2f)** such representatives were found, generally, in opposition to Christ; in the Acts they are chiefly those who opposed the apostles and the gospel. **(3)** In Rom 2:28, 29 the word is used of ideal "Jews," i.e., "Jews" in spiritual reality, believers, whether "Jews" or Gentiles by natural birth. **(4)** The feminine, "Jewess," is found in Acts 16:1; 24:24. **(5)** It also denotes Judea, e.g., Mt 2:1; Lk 1:5; Jn 4:3, the word "country" being understood. **(6)** In Lk 23:5 and Jn 7:1, "Jewry." See: TDNT—3:356, 372; BAGD—379b; THAYER—305d.

2454. **Ἰουδαϊσμός** {2x} **Iŏudaismŏs**, *ee-oo-dah-is-mos';* from *2450; "Judaism",* i.e. the *Jewish faith* and usages:—Jews' religion {2x}.

This word denotes the Jews religion (Gal 1:13, 14) and stands, not for their religious beliefs, but for their religious practices, not as instituted by God, but as developed and extended from these by the traditions of the Pharisees and scribes. See: TDNT—3:356, 372; BAGD—379d; THAYER—306b.

2455. **Ἰουδάς** {45x} **Iŏudas**, *ee-oo-das';* of Heb. or. [3063]; *Judas* (i.e. *Jehudah*), the name of ten Isr.; also of the posterity of one of them and its region:—Judas (Iscariot) {22x}, Juda (Son of Jacob) {7x}, Judah (Son of Jacob) {1x}, Judas (Son of Jacob) {2x}, Judas (Brother of James) {3x}, Jude (Brother of James) {1x}, Judas Barsabas {3x}, Juda (Ancestors of Jesus {2x}, misc. {4x}. See: BAGD—379d; THAYER—306b.

2456. **Ἰουλία** {1x} **Iŏulia**, *ee-oo-lee'-ah;* fem. of the same as *2457; Julia,* a Chr. woman:—Julia {1x}. See: BAGD—380b; THAYER—306d.

2457. **Ἰούλιος** {2x} **Iŏuliŏs**, *ee-oo'-lee-os;* of Lat. or.; *Julius,* a centurion:—Julius {2x}. See: BAGD—380b; THAYER—306d.

2458. **Ἰουνίας** {1x} **Iŏunias**, *ee-oo-nee'-as;* of Lat. or.; *Junias,* a Chr.:—Junias {1x}. See: BAGD—380b; THAYER—306d.

2459. **Ἰοῦστος** {3x} **Iŏustŏs**, *ee-ooce'-tos;* of Lat. or. (*"just"*); *Justus,* the name of three Chr.:—Justus (of Corinth) {1x}, Justus (surnamed Barabbas) {1x}, Justus (Jesus, a fellow worker of Paul) {1x}. See: BAGD—380b; THAYER—306d.

2460. **ἱππεύς** {2x} **hippĕus**, *hip-yooce';* from *2462;* an *equestrian,* i.e. member of a *cavalry* corps.:—horseman {2x}. Cf. Acts 23:23, 32. See: BAGD—306d; THAYER—380c.

2461. **ἱππικόν** {1x} **hippikŏn**, *hip-pee-kon';* neut. of a der. of *2462;* the *cavalry* force:—horsemen {1x}.

Hippikon is an adjective signifying "of a horse" or "of horsemen, equestrian," is used as a noun denoting "horsemen," in Rev 9:16, "horsemen," numbering "two hundred thousand thousand." See: BAGD—380c; THAYER—306d.

2462. **ἵππος** {16x} **hippŏs**, *hip'-pos;* of uncert. aff.; a *horse:*—horse {16x}.

Hippos, **(1)** has fifteen occurrences in the Apocalypse, **(1a)** seen in visions in 6:2, 4, 5, 8; 9:7, 9, 17 (twice); 14:20; 19:11, 14, 19, 21; and **(1b)** otherwise in 18:13; 19:18. **(2)** It also occurs in Jas 3:3. See: TDNT—3:336, 369; BAGD—380c; THAYER—306d.

2463. **ἶρις** {2x} **iris**, *ee'-ris;* perh. from *2046* (as a symbol of the female *messenger* of the pagan deities); a *rainbow* (*"iris"*):—rainbow {2x}.

(1) This rainbow "round about the throne, like an emerald to look upon (Rev 4:3) is emblematic of the fact that, in the exercise of God's absolute sovereignty and perfect counsels, He will remember His covenant concerning the earth (cf. Gen 9:9–17). **(2)** In Rev 10:1, "a rainbow," suggests a connection with the scene in 4:3. See: TDNT—3:339, 369; BAGD—380d; THAYER—306d.

2464. **Ἰσαάκ** {20x} **Isaak**, *ee-sah-ak';* of Heb. or. [3327]; *Isaac* (i.e. *Jitschak*), the son of Abraham:—Isaac {20x}. See: TDNT 3:191,*; BAGD—380d; THAYER—306d.

2465. **ἰσάγγελος** {1x} **isaggĕlŏs**, *ee-sang'-el-los;* from *2470* and *32; like an angel,* i.e. *angelic:*—equal unto the angels {1x}. See: TDNT—1:87, 12; BAGD—380d; THAYER—307a.

2466. **Ἰσαχάρ** {1x} **Isachar**, *ee-sakh-ar';* of Heb. or. [3485]; *Isachar* (i.e. *Jissaskar*), a son of Jacob (fig. his desc.):—Issachar {1x}. See: BAGD—381d; THAYER—307a.

2467. **ἴσημι** {2x} **isēmi**, *is'-ay-mee;* assumed by some as the base of cert. irreg. forms of *1492;* to *know:*—know {2x}. See: BAGD—220c; THAYER—307a.

2468. **ἴσθι** {5x} **isthi**, *is'-thee;* second pers. imper. present of *1510; be* thou:—be thou {1x}, be {1x}, agree + 2132 {1x}, give thyself wholly to + 1722 {1x}, not tr {1x}. See: BAGD—380d; THAYER—175c [see 1510].

2469. **Ἰσκαριώτης** {11x} **Iskariōtēs**, *is-kar-ee-o'-tace;* of Heb. or. [prob. 377 and 7149]; *inhabitant of Kerioth; Iscariotes* (i.e. *Keriothite*), an epithet of Judas the traitor:—Iscariot {11x}. See: BAGD—380d; THAYER—307a.

2470. **ἴσος** {8x} **isŏs**, *ee'-sos;* prob. from *1492* (through the idea of *seeming*); *similar* (in amount and kind):—equal {4x}, agree together + 2258 {2x}, as much {1x}, like {1x}.

This word, translated "equal," is used with the verb "to be," signifying "to agree" (Mk 14:56, 59); lit., "their thought was not equal one with the other. See: TDNT—3:343, 370; BAGD—381a; THAYER—307b.

2471. **ἰσότης** {3x} **isŏtēs**, *ee-sot'-ace; likeness* (in condition or proportion); by impl. *equity:*—equal {1x}, equality {2x}.

Isotes, "equality", is translated **(1)** "equality" in 2 Cor 8:14, twice; and **(2)** in Col 4:1, with the article, "that which is . . . equal," (lit., "the equality,"), i.e., equity, fairness, what is equitable. See: TDNT—3:343, 370; BAGD—381b; THAYER—307b.

2472. **ἰσότιμος** {1x} **isŏtimŏs**, *ee-sot'-ee-mos;* from *2470* and *5092; of equal value* or *honor:*—like precious {1x}.

Isotimos, "of equal value, held in equal honor" (*isos,* "equal," and *time,* is used in 2 Pet 1:1, "a like precious (faith)." See: TDNT—3:343, 370; BAGD—381b; THAYER—307b.

2473. **ἰσόψυχος** {1x} **isŏpsuchŏs**, *ee-sop'-soo-khos;* from *2470* and *5590; of similar spirit:*—likeminded {1x}.

Isopsuchos, lit., "of equal soul" (*isos,* "equal," *psuche,* "the soul"), is rendered "likeminded" in Phil 2:20. See: BAGD—381b; THAYER—307b.

2474. **Ἰσραήλ** {70x} **Israēl**, *is-rah-ale';* of Heb. or. [3478]; *Israel* (i.e. *Jisrael*), the adopted name of Jacob, incl. his desc. (lit. or fig.):—Israel {70x}. See: TDNT—3:356, 372; BAGD—381c; THAYER—307b.

2475. **Ἰσραηλίτης** {9x} **Israēlitēs**, *is-rah-ale-ee'-tace;* from *2474;* an *"Israelite",* i.e. desc. of Israel (lit. or fig.):—Israel {5x}, Israelite {4x}.

Syn.: Hebraios (1445) refers to a Hebrew-speaking as contrasted to a Greek-speaking or Hellenizing Jew, and Ioudaios (2453) refers to the Jew nationalistically in distinction from Gentiles, and *Israelites,* the most majestic title of all, refers to a Jew as a member of the theocracy and heir of the promises. The first word refers to his language, the second to his nationality, and the third to his theocratic privileges and glorious vocation. See: TDNT—3:356, 372; BAGD—381d; THAYER—307c.

2476. **ἵστημι** {158x} **histēmi**, *his'-tay-mee;* a prol. form of a primary στάω **staō**, *stah'-o* (of the same mean., and used for it in certain tenses); to *stand* (tran. or intr.), used in various applications (lit. or fig.):—stand {116x}, set {11x}, establish {5x}, stand still {4x}, stand by {3x}, vr stand {2x}, misc. {17x} = abide, appoint, bring, continue, covenant, hold up, lay, present, stanch.

Histemi, as a verb, means "to make to stand," means "to appoint": "Because He hath appointed (*histemi*) a day, in the which He will judge the world in righteousness by *that* man whom He hath ordained; *whereof* he hath given assurance unto all *men,* in that he hath raised Him from the dead" (Acts 17:31 of the day in which God will judge the world by Christ). **(2)** In Acts 1:23, with reference to Joseph and Barnabas, were simply singled out, in order that it might be made known which of them the Lord had chosen: "And they appointed two, Joseph called Barsabas, who was surnamed Justus, and Matthias." The Lord then chose by lots which one He wanted. See: TDNT—7:638, 1082; BAGD—381d; THAYER—307d. comp. *5087.*

2477. ἱστορέω {1x} **histŏrĕō**, *his-tor-eh'-o;* from a der. of *1492;* to *be knowing* (*learned*), i.e. (by impl.) to *visit* for information (*interview*):—see {1x}.

Historeo, from *histor,* "one learned in anything," denotes "to visit" in order to become acquainted with, "to see", Gal 1:18. See: TDNT—3:391, 377; BAGD—383a; THAYER—308d.

2478. ἰσχυρός {27x} **ischurŏs**, *is-khoo-ros';* from *2479; forcible* (lit. or fig.):—mighty {10x}, strong {9x}, strong man {5x}, boisterous {1x}, powerful {1x}, valiant {1x}.

Ischuros, "strong, mighty," as an adjective, is used of **(1)** persons: **(1a)** God, Rev 18:8; **(1b)** angels, Rev 5:2; 10:1; 18:21; **(1c)** men, Mt 12:29 (twice) and parallel passages; Heb 11:34, "valiant"; 19:18, "mighty"; metaphorically, **(1d)** the church at Corinth, 1 Cor 4:10, where the apostle reproaches them ironically with their unspiritual and self-complacent condition; **(1e)** of young men in Christ spiritually strong, through the Word of God, to overcome the evil one, 1 Jn 2:14; of **(2)** things: **(2a)** wind, Mt 14:30 "boisterous"; **(2b)** famine, Lk 15:14; **(2c)** things in the mere human estimate, 1 Cor 1:27; **(2d)** Paul's letters, 2 Cor 10:10; **(2e)** the Lord's crying and tears, Heb 5:7; **(2f)** consolation, Heb 6:18; **(2g)** Babylon, Rev 18:10; **(2h)** thunderings, Rev 19:6. It is translated "boisterous" in Mt 14:30. See: TDNT—3:397, 378; BAGD—383a; THAYER—309a.

2479. ἰσχύς {11x} **ischus**, *is-khoos';* from a der. of ἰς **is** (*force;* comp. ἔσχον **ĕschŏn**, a form of *2192*); *forcefulness* (lit. or fig.):—strength {1x}, power {2x}, might {2x}, ability {1x}, mightily + 1722 {1x}, mighty {1x}.

Ischus, "to have, to hold" denotes "ability, force, strength"; **(1)** "strength" in 1 Pet 4:11. **(2)** In Eph 1:19 and 6:10, it is said of the strength of God bestowed upon believers, the phrase "the power of His might" indicating strength afforded by power. **(3)** In 2 Th 1:9, "the glory of His might" signifies the visible expression of the inherent personal power of the Lord Jesus. It is said of angels in 2 Pet 2:11 (cf. Rev 18:2, "mightily"). **(4)** It is ascribed to God in Rev 5:12 and 7:12. **(5)** In Mk 12:30, 33, and Lk 10:27 it describes the full extent of the power wherewith we are to love God. Syn.: 970, 1411, 1753, 1849, 2904. See: TDNT—3:397, 378; BAGD—383c; THAYER—309b.

2480. ἰσχύω {29x} **ischuō**, *is-khoo'-o;* from *2479;* to *have* (or *exercise*) *force* (lit. or fig.):—can (could) {9x}, be able {6x}, avail {3x}, prevail {3x}, be whole {2x}, cannot + 3756 {1x}, can do {1x}, may {1x}, be good {1x}, be of strength {1x}, + much work {1x}.

(1) *Ischuo,* means "to be strong, to have efficacy, force or value" and is said of salt, negatively, "it is good for nothing". "Ye are the salt of the earth: but if the salt have lost his savour, wherewith shall it be salted? it is thenceforth good (2480) for nothing, but to be cast out, and to be trodden under foot of men." (Mt 5:13). **(2)** This word denotes to be strong, to prevail and indicates a more forceful strength or ability than dunamai (1410) and in Jas 5:16 it is rendered "availeth much" (i.e., "prevails greatly"). See: TDNT—3:397, 378; BAGD—383d; THAYER—309b.

2481. ἴσως {1x} **isōs**, *ee'-soce;* adv. from *2470; likely,* i.e. *perhaps:*—it may be {1x}. See: BAGD—384a; THAYER—309c.

2482. Ἰταλία {5x} **Italia**, *ee-tal-ee'-ah;* prob. of for. or.; *Italia,* a region of Europe:—Italy {5x}. See: BAGD—384a; THAYER—309c.

2483. Ἰταλικός {1x} **Italikŏs**, *ee-tal-ee-kos';* from *2482; Italic,* i.e. belonging to Italia:—Italian {1x}. See: BAGD—384a; THAYER—309c.

2484. Ἰτουραΐα {1x} **Itŏuraia**, *ee-too-rah'-yah;* of Heb. or. [3195]; *Ituræa* (i.e. *Jetur*), a region of Pal.:—Ituræa {1x}. See: BAGD—384a; THAYER—309c.

2485. ἰχθύδιον {2x} **ichthudiŏn**, *ikh-thoo'-dee-on;* dimin. from *2486;* a *petty fish:*—little little fish {1x}, small fish {1x}. Cf. Mt 15:34; Mk 8:7. See: BAGD—384b; THAYER—309d.

2486. ἰχθύς {20x} **ichthus**, *ikh-thoos';* of uncert. aff.; a *fish:*—fish {20x}. Ichthus denotes "a fish," Mt 7:10; Mk 6:38, etc.; apart from the Gospels, only in 1 Cor 15:39. See: BAGD—384b; THAYER—309d.

2487. ἴχνος {3x} **ichnŏs**, *ikh'-nos;* from ἰκνέομαι **iknĕŏmai** (to *arrive;* comp. *2240*); a *track* (fig.):—step {3x}.

This word denotes a footstep, a track and is used metaphorically of the steps **(1)** of Christ's conduct (1 Pet 2:21); **(2)** of Abraham's faith (Rom 4:12); **(3)** of identical conduct in carrying on the work of the gospel (2 Cor 12:18). See: TDNT—3:402, 379; BAGD—384b; THAYER—309d.

2488. Ἰωάθαμ {2x} **Iōatham**, *ee-o-ath'-am;* of Heb. or. [3147]; *Joatham* (i.e. *Jotham*), an Isr.:—Joatham {2x}. See: BAGD—384c; THAYER—309d.

2489. Ἰωάννα {2x} **Iōanna**, *ee-o-an'-nah;* fem. of the same as *2491; Joanna,* a Chr.:—Joanna {2x}. See: BAGD—384c; THAYER—309d.

2490. Ἰωαννᾶς {1x} **Iōannas**, *ee-o-an-nas';* a form of *2491; Joannas,* an Isr.:—Joannas {1x}. See: BAGD—384c; THAYER—309d.

2491. Ἰωάννης {133x} **Iōannēs**, *ee-o-an'-nace;* of Heb. or. [3110]; *Joannes* (i.e. *Jochanan*), the name of four Isr.:—John (the Baptist) {92x}, John (the apostle) {36x}, John (Mark) {4x}, John (the chief priest) {1x}. See: BAGD—384d; THAYER—309d.

2492. Ἰώβ {1x} **Iōb**, *ee-obe';* of Heb. or. [347]; *Job* (i.e. *Ijob*), a patriarch:—Job {1x}. See: BAGD—385a; THAYER—310c.

2493. Ἰωήλ {1x} **Iōēl**, *ee-o-ale';* of Heb. or. [3100]; *Joel,* an Isr.:—Joel {1x}. See: BAGD—385b; THAYER—310c.

2494. Ἰωνάν {1x} **Iōnan**, *ee-o-nan'* or Ιωναμ **Ionam**, *ee-o-nam';* prob. for *2491* or *2495; Jonan,* an Isr.:—Jonan (Jonam) {1x}. See: BAGD—385b; THAYER—310c.

2495. Ἰωνᾶς {13x} **Iōnas**, *ee-o-nas';* of Heb. or. [3124]; *Jonas* (i.e. *Jonah*), the name of two Isr.:—Jonas (the prophet) {9x}, Jona (father of Peter) {4x}. See: TDNT—3:406, 380; BAGD—385b; THAYER—310d.

2496. Ἰωράμ {2x} **Iōram**, *ee-o-ram';* of Heb. or. [3141]; *Joram,* an Isr.:—Joram {2x}. See: BAGD—385c; THAYER—310d.

2497. Ἰωρείμ {1x} **Iōrĕim**, *ee-o-rime'* or Ἰωρίμ **Iōrim**, *ee-o-reem';* perh. for *2496; Jorim,* an Isr.:—Jorim {1x}. See: BAGD—385c; THAYER—310d.

2498. Ἰωσαφάτ {2x} **Iōsaphat**, *ee-o-saf-at';* of Heb. or. [3092]; *Josaphat* (i.e. *Jehoshaphat*), an Isr.:—Josaphat {2x}. See: BAGD—385c; THAYER—310d.

2499. Ἰωσή {1x} **Iōsē**, *ee-o-say';* gen. of *2500; Jose,* an Isr.:—Jose (son of Eliezer) {1x}. See: BAGD—385c; THAYER—310d.

2500. Ἰωσῆς {6x} **Iōsēs**, *ee-o-sace';* perh. for *2501; Joses,* the name of two Isr.:—Joses (brother of James) {3x}, Joses (Brother of Jesus) {2x}, Joses (Barnabas) {1x}. See: BAGD—385d; THAYER—310d. comp. *2499.*

2501. Ἰωσήφ {35x} **Iōsēph**, *ee-o-safe';* of Heb. or. [3130]; *Joseph,* the name of seven Isr.:—Joseph (husband of Mary) {16x}, Joseph (son of Jacob) {9x}, Joseph of Arimathaea {6x}, Joseph (son of Judas) {1x}, Joseph of Barsabas {1x}, Joseph son of Jonan {1x}, Joseph (son of Mattathias) {1x}. See: BAGD—385d; THAYER—311a.

2502. Ἰωσίας {2x} **Iōsias**, *ee-o-see'-as;* of Heb. or. [2977]; *Josias* (i.e. *Joshiah*), an Isr.:—Josias {2x}. See: BAGD—386a; THAYER—311c.

2503. ἰῶτα {1x} **iōta**, *ee-o'-tah;* of Heb. or. [the tenth letter of the Heb. alphabet]; "*iota,*" the name of the eighth letter of the Greek alphabet, put (fig.) for a very small part of anything:—jot {1x}.

Iota is from the Heb. *yod,* the smallest Hebrew letter, and is mentioned by the Lord in Mt 5:18, together with keraia (2762) a little horn, a tittle, the point or extremity which distinguishes certain Hebrew letters from others, to express the fact that not a single item of the Law will pass away or remain unfulfilled. See: BAGD—386a; THAYER—311c.

K

2504. κἀγώ {72x} **kago**, *kag-o';* from *2532* and *1473* (so also the dat.)

κἀμοί **kamŏi**, *kam-oy';* and acc.

κἀμέ **kamĕ**, *kam-eh'; and* (or *also, even,* etc.) *I,* (*to*) *me:*—and I {34x}, I also {17x}, so I {4x}, I {4x}, even I {3x}, me also {3x}, misc. {7x} = (even so) I (in like wise), both me. See: BAGD—386a; THAYER—311b.

2505. καθά {1x} **katha**, *kath-ah';* from *2596* and the neut. plur. of *3739; according to which* things, i.e. *just as:*—as {1x}. See: BAGD—386b; THAYER—311d.

2506. καθαίρεσις {3x} **kathairĕsis**, *kath-ah'-ee-res-is;* from *2507; demolition;* fig. *extinction:*—destruction {2x}, pulling down {1x}.

Kathairesis, "a taking down, a pulling down," is used three times in 2 Cor and is translated **(1)** "destruction" in 10:8; 13:10; and **(2)** "pulling down" in 10:4. See: TDNT—3:412, 381; BAGD—386b; THAYER—311d.

2507. καθαιρέω {9x} **kathairĕō**, *kath-ahee-reh'-o;* from *2596* and *138* (incl. its alt.); to *lower* (or with violence) *demolish* (lit. or fig.):—take down {4x}, destroy {2x}, put down {1x}, pull down {1x}, cast down {1x}.

Kathaireo, kata, "down," *haireo,* means **(1)** "to take, to cast down, demolish," in 2 Cor 10:5, of strongholds and imaginations; **(2)** and "He hath put down down" the mighty in Lk 1:52. **(3)** It is translated "to destroy" in Acts 13:19; and in Acts 19:27, "should be destroyed." **(4)** It is translated "I will pull down" in Lk 12:18. **(5)** It denotes "to take down" (*kata*), besides its meaning of "putting down by force," was the technical term for the "removal" of the body after crucifixion, Mk 15:36, 46; Lk 23:53; Acts 13:29. See: TDNT—3:411, 380; BAGD—386c; THAYER—311d.

2508. **καθαίρω** {2x} **kathairō**, *kath-ah'-ee-ro;* from *2513;* to *cleanse,* i.e. (spec.) to *prune;* fig. to *expiate:*—purge {2x}.

Kathairo means to cleanse, of filth impurity, **(1)** to prune trees and vines from useless shoots, Jn 15:2 "purgeth"; and **(2)** metaphorically purging worshippers from guilt, Heb 10:2. See: TDNT—3:413, 381; BAGD—386d; THAYER—312a.

2509. **καθάπερ** {13x} **kathapĕr**, *kath-ap'-er;* from *2505* and *4007; exactly as:*—as {7x}, even as {5x}, as well as {1x}. See: BAGD—387a; THAYER—312a.

2510. **καθάπτω** {1x} **kathaptō**, *kath-ap'-to;* from *2596* and *680;* to *seize upon:*—fasten on {1x}.

Kathapto, "to fasten on, lay hold of, attack," is used of the serpent which fastened on Paul's hand, Acts 28:3. See: BAGD—387a; THAYER—312b.

2511. **καθαρίζω** {30x} **katharizō**, *kath-ar-id'-zo;* from *2513;* to *cleanse* (lit. or fig.):—cleanse {16x}, make clean {5x}, be clean {3x}, purge {3x}, purify {3x}.

Katharizo signifies to **(1)** make clean, to cleanse **(1a)** literally, from **(1a1)** physical stains and dirt (Mt 23:25); **(1a2)** disease (Mt 8:2); **(1b)** in a moral sense, from **(1b1)** the defilement of sin (Acts 15:9; 2 Cor 7:1; Heb 9:14; Jas 4:8), **(1b2)** the guilt of sin (Eph 5:26; 1 Jn 1:7); **(2)** to pronounce clean in a Levitical sense (Mk 7:19; Acts 10:15; 11:9); **(3)** to consecrate by cleansings (Heb 9:22, 23; 10:2). Syn.: 1245, 2512, 2514. See: TDNT—3:413, 381; BAGD—387b; THAYER—312b.

2512. **καθαρισμός** {7x} **katharismŏs**, *kath-ar-is-mos';* from *2511;* a *washing* off, i.e. (cer.) *ablution,* (mor.) *expiation:*—cleansing {2x}, purifying {2x}, be purged {1x}, purge + 4060 {1x}, purification {1x}.

This word denotes "cleansing," **(1)** both the action and its results, in the Levitical sense, Mk 1:44; Lk 2:22, "purification"; Lk 5:14, "cleansing"; Jn 2:6; 3:25, "purifying"; **(2)** in the moral sense, from sins, Heb 1:3; 2 Pet 1:9. See: TDNT—3:429, 381; BAGD—387d; THAYER—312c.

2513. **καθαρός** {28x} **katharŏs**, *kath-ar-os';* of uncert. aff.; *clean* (lit. or fig.):—clean {10x}, clear {1x}, pure {17x}.

Katharos means free from impure admixture, without blemish, spotless and is used **(1)** physically (Mt 23:26; 27:59); **(2)** figuratively, (Jn 13:10) where the Lord teaches that one who has been entirely cleansed needs not radical renewal, but only to be cleansed from every sin into which he may fall (Jn 15:3; Heb 10:22); **(3)** in a Levitical sense (Rom 14:20; Titus 1:15 – pure); **(4)** ethically, with the significance free from corrupt desire, from guilt (Mt 5:8; Jn 13:10–11; 1 Ti 1:5; 3:9); and **(5)** in a combined Levitical and ethical sense ceremonially (Lk 11:41). Syn.: *Eilikrines* (1506) refers to the Christian's freedom from falsehoods. *Katharos* refers to the Christian's freedom from the defilements of the flesh and the world. See: TDNT—3:413, 381; BAGD—388a; THAYER—312d.

2514. **καθαρότης** {1x} **katharŏtēs**, *kath-ar-ot'-ace;* from *2513; cleanness* (cer.):—purifying {1x}.

This word means "cleanness, purity," and is used in the Levitical sense in Heb 9:13. See: TDNT—3:413, 381; BAGD—388b; THAYER—313a.

2515. **καθέδρα** {3x} **kathĕdra**, *kath-ed'-rah;* from *2596* and the same as *1476;* a *bench* (lit. or fig.):—seat {3x}.

(1) This word is used of the exalted seat occupied by men of eminent rank or influence. [cf. Eng. cathedral]. *Kathedra,* from *kata,* "down," and *hedra,* "a seat," denotes "a seat", Mt 21:12; Mk 11:15; of teachers, Mt 23:2. See: BAGD—388b; THAYER—313a.

2516. **καθέζομαι** {6x} **kathĕzŏmai**, *kath-ed'-zom-ahee;* from *2596* and the base of *1476;* to *sit down:*—sit {6x}.

Kathezomai, as a verb, means "to sit (down)": "In that same hour said Jesus to the multitudes, Are ye come out as against a thief with swords and staves for to take me? I sat daily (*kathezomai*) with you teaching in the temple, and ye laid no hold on me" (Mt 26:55; cf. Lk 2:46; Jn 4:6; 11:20; 20:12; Acts 6:15). Syn.: 339, 345, 347, 377, 1910, 2521, 2621, 2523, 2625, 4775, 4776, 4873. See: TDNT—3:440, 386; BAGD—388c; THAYER—313a.

2517. **καθεξῆς** {5x} **kathĕxēs**, *kath-ex-ace';* from *2596* and *1836; thereafter,* i.e. *consecutively;* as a noun (by ellip. of noun) a *subsequent* person or time:—in order {2x}, afterward {1x}, after {1x}, by order {1x}.

Kathexes means one after another, successively, in order, Lk 1:3; 8:1; Acts 3:24; 11:4; 18:23. See: BAGD—388d; THAYER—313a.

2518. **καθεύδω** {22x} **kathĕudō**, *kath-yoo'-do;* from *2596* and εὕδω **hĕudō** (to *sleep*); to lie *down* to *rest,* i.e. (by impl.) to *fall asleep* (lit. or fig.):—(be a-) sleep {22x}.

Katheudo means to go to sleep and is **(1)** chiefly used of natural sleep (1 Th 5:7); **(2)** figuratively of death: "He said unto them, Give place: for the maid is not dead, but sleepeth. And they laughed Him to scorn", (Mt 9:24; cf. Mk 5:39; Lk 8:52); **(3)** of carnal indifference to spiritual things on the part of believers (Eph 5:14; 1 Th 5:6, 10); **(4)** and in Mk 13:36 of a condition of insensibility to divine things involving conformity to the world. Syn.: 2837. See: TDNT—3:431, 384; BAGD—388d; THAYER—313b.

2519. **καθηγητής** {3x} **kathēgētēs**, *kath-ayg-ay-tace';* from a compound of *2596* and *2233;* a *guide,* i.e. (fig.) a *teacher:*—master {3x}.

This word is properly a guide and denotes a master, a teacher, one who can guide the learner (Mt 23:8, 10 twice). See: BAGD—388d; THAYER—313b.

2520. **καθήκω** {2x} **kathēkō**, *kath-ay'-ko;* from *2596* and *2240;* to *reach to,* i.e. (neut. of pres. act. part., fig. as adj.) *becoming:*—convenient {1x}, fit {1x}.

Katheko, "to be fitting, [not] convenient" is so translated **(1)** in Rom 1:28; "(not) convenient"; and **(2)** in Acts 22:22, "it is (not) fit." See: TDNT—3:437, 385; BAGD—389a; THAYER—313b.

2521. **κάθημαι** {89x} **kathēmai**, *kath'-ay-mahee;* from *2596;* and ἧμαι **hēmai** (to *sit;* akin to the base of *1476*); to *sit down;* fig. to *remain, reside:*—sit {82x}, sit down {3x}, sit by {2x}, be set down {1x}, dwell {1x}.

Kathemai, as a verb, is used **(1)** of the natural posture: "And as Jesus passed forth from thence, he saw a man, named Matthew, sitting at the receipt of custom: and He saith unto him, Follow Me. And he arose, and followed Him" (Mt 9:9, most frequently in the Apocalypse, some 32 times; frequently in the Gospels and Acts; elsewhere only in 1 Cor 14:30; Jas 2:3 [twice]; **(2)** and of Christ's position of authority on the throne of God: "If ye then be risen with Christ, seek those things which are above, where Christ sitteth on the right hand of God" (Col 3:1; cf. Heb 1:13; Mt 22:44; 26:64 and parallel passages in Mark and Luke, and Acts 2:34); **(3)** often as antecedent or successive to, or accompanying, another act: "And Jesus departed from thence, and came nigh unto the sea of Galilee; and went up into a mountain, and sat down there" (Mt 15:29; 27:36; Mk 2:14; 4:1); **(4)** metaphorically in Mt 4:16: "The people which sat in (*kathemai*) darkness saw great light; and to them which sat (*kathemai*) in the region and shadow of death light is sprung up"; **(5)** of inhabiting a place (translated "dwell"): "For as a snare shall it come on all them that dwell on the face of the whole earth" (Lk 21:35; cf. Lk 1:79). Syn.: 339, 345, 347, 377, 1910, 2516, 2621, 2523, 2625, 4775, 4776, 4873. See: TDNT—3:440, 386; BAGD—389b; THAYER—313b.

2522. **καθημερινός** {1x} **kathēmĕrinŏs**, *kath-ay-mer-ee-nos';* from *2596* and *2250; quotidian:*—daily {1x}.

This word means, lit., "according to" (*kata*) "the day" (*hemera*), "day by day, daily," Acts 6:1. See: BAGD—389d; THAYER—313d.

2523. **καθίζω** {48x} **kathizō**, *kath-id'-zo;* another (act.) form for *2516;* to *seat down,* i.e. *set* (fig. *appoint*); intr. to *sit* (down); fig. to *settle* (*hover, dwell*):—. sit {26x}, sit down {14x}, set {2x}, be set {2x}, be set down {2x}, continue {1x}, tarry {1x}.

Kathizo, as a verb, is used **(1)** transitively, "to make sit down": "Therefore being a prophet, and knowing that God had sworn with an oath to him [David], that of the fruit of his loins, according to the flesh, he would raise up Christ to sit on his throne" (Acts 2:30); **(2)** intransitively, "to sit down, was set": "And seeing the multitudes, He went up into a mountain: and when He was set, His disciples came unto Him" (Mt 5:1; 19:28; 20:21, 23; 23:2; 25:31; 26:36; Mk 11:2, 7; 12:41; Lk 14:28, 31; 16:6; Jn 19:13; Acts 2:3, of the tongues of fire; 8:31; 1 Cor 10:7; 2 Th 2:4, "he takes his seat" as, e.g., in Mk 16:19; Rev 3:21 [twice]). Syn.: 339, 345, 347, 377, 1910, 2516, 2521, 2621, 2625, 4775, 4776, 4873. See: TDNT—3:440, 386; BAGD—389d; THAYER—313d.

2524. **καθίημι** {4x} **kathiēmi**, *kath-ee'-ay-mee;* from *2596;* and ἵημι **hiēmi** (to *send*); to *lower:*—let down {4x}.

Kathiemi, "to send," or "let down" (*kata,* "down," *hiemi,* "to send"), is translated "to let down," with reference to **(1)** the paralytic in Lk 5:19; **(2)** Saul of Tarsus, Acts 9:25; **(3)** the great sheet in Peter's vision, 10:11 and 11:5. See: BAGD—390b; THAYER—314a.

2525. **καθίστημι** {22x} **kathistēmi**, *kath-is'-tay-mee;* from *2596* and *2476;* to *place down* (permanently), i.e. (fig.) to *designate, constitute, convoy:*—make {8x}, make ruler {6x}, ordain {3x}, be {2x}, appoint {1x}, conduct {1x}, set {1x}.

Kathistemi, as a verb, a strengthened form of *histemi* (2476), **(1)** usually signifies "to appoint a person to a position." **(2)** In this sense the verb is often translated "to make" or "to set," in appointing a person to a place of authority, **(2a)** a servant over a household: "Who then is a faithful and wise servant, whom his lord hath made ruler (*kathistemi*) over his household, to give them meat in due season?" (Mt 24:45; cf. 25:47; 25:21, 23; Lk 12:42, 44); **(2b)** a judge: "And he said unto him, Man, who made me a judge or a divider over you?" (Lk 12:14; cf. Acts 7:27, 35); **(2c)** a governor: "And delivered him (Joseph) out of all his afflictions, and gave him favour and wisdom in the sight of Pharaoh king of Egypt; and he made him governor over Egypt and all his house" (Acts 7:10); **(2d)** man by God over the work of His hands: "Thou madest him a little lower than the angels; thou crownedst him with glory and honour, and didst set him over the works of thy hands" (Heb 2:7).

(3) It is rendered "appoint," with reference to the so-called seven deacons in Acts 6:3: "Wherefore, brethren, look ye out among you seven men of honest report, full of the Holy Ghost and wisdom, whom we may appoint over this business." **(4)** Titus was to "ordain" elders in ever city in Crete where there were churches: "For this cause left I thee in Crete, that thou shouldest set in order the things that are wanting, and ordain elders in every city, as I had appointed thee" (Titus 1:5). Not a formal ecclesiastical ordination is in view, but the "appointment," for the recognition of the churches, of those who had already been raised up and qualified by the Holy Spirit, and had given evidence of this in their life and service. **(4)** It is used of the priests of old: "For every high priest taken from among men is ordained (*kathistemi*) for men in things *pertaining* to God, that he may offer both gifts and sacrifices for sins" (Heb 5:1; cf. 7:28; 8:3). See: TDNT—3:444, 387; BAGD—390b; THAYER—314b.

2526. **καθό** {4x} **kathŏ**, *kath-o'; from 2596* and *3739; according to which* thing, i.e. *precisely as, in proportion as*:—according to {2x}, as {1x}, inasmuch as {1x}. See: BAGD—390d; THAYER—314c.

2526. **καθολικός** {2x} **kathŏlikŏs**, *kath-ol-ee-kos'; from 2527; universal*:—general {2x}. See: BAGD—390d; THAYER—314c.

2527. **καθόλου** {1x} **kathŏlŏu**, *kath-ol' oo;* from *2596* and *3650; on the whole,* i.e. *entirely*:—at all {1x}.

This word means wholly, entirely, at all: "And they called them, and commanded them not to speak at all (*katholikos*) nor teach in the name of Jesus", Acts 4:18. See: BAGD—391a; THAYER—314c.

2528. **καθοπλίζω** {1x} **kathŏplizō**, *kath-op-lid'-zo;* from *2596;* and *3695;* to *equip fully* with armor:—arm {1x}.

Kathoplizo is an intensive form, "to furnish fully with arms," *kata,* "down," intensive, *hoplon,* "a weapon," Lk 11:21, lit., "a strong man fully armed." See: BAGD—391a; THAYER—314d.

2529. **καθοράω** {1x} **kathŏraō**, *kath-or-ah'-o;* from *2596* and *3708;* to *behold fully,* i.e. (fig.) *distinctly apprehend*:—clearly see {1x}.

This word literally means to look down, see from above, view from on high; and hence, to see thoroughly, perceive clearly, understand, Rom 1:20. See: TDNT—5:379, 706; BAGD—391a; THAYER—314d.

2530. **καθότι** {5x} **kathŏti**, *kath-ot'-ee;* from *2596;* and *3739* and *5100; according to which certain* thing, i.e. *as far* (or *inasmuch*) *as*:—because {2x}, forsomuch as {1x}, as {1x}, according as {1x}.

Kathoti, from *kata,* "according to," and *hoti,* "that," lit., **(1)** "because that," Lk 1:7; **(2)** "forasmuch as", Lk 19:9; **(3)** "because", Acts 2:24; **(4)** "as", Acts 2:45; and **(5)** "according as", Acts 4:35. See: BAGD—319b; THAYER—314d.

2531. **καθώς** {182x} **kathōs**, *kath-oce';* from *2596* and *5613; just* (or *inasmuch*) *as, that*:—as {138x}, even as {36x}, according as {4x}, when {1x}, according to {1x}, how {1x}, as well as + 2532 {1x}. See: BAGD—391b; THAYER—314d.

2532. **καί** {9280x} **kai**, *kahee;* appar. a primary particle, having a *copulative* and sometimes also a *cumulative* force; *and, also, even, so, then, too,* etc.; often used in connection (or composition) with other particles or small words:—and {8182x}, also {515x}, even {108x}, both {43x}, then {20x}, so {18x}, likewise {13x}, not tr. {354x}, vr and {1x}, misc. {46x} = but, for, if, indeed, moreover, or, that, therefore, when, yet. See: BAGD—391d; THAYER—315b.

2533. **Καϊάφας** {9x} **Kaïaphas**, *kah-ee-af'-as;* of Chald. or.; *the dell; Câaphas* (i.e. *Cajepha*), an Isr.:—Caiaphas {9x}. See: BAGD—393d; THAYER—317a.

2534. **καίγε** {1x} **kaigĕ**, *kah'-ee-gheh;* from *2532* and *1065; and at least* (or *even, indeed*):—and at least {1x}. See: BAGD—394a;153a; THAYER—317c.

2535. **Κάϊν** {3x} **Kaïn**, *kah'-in;* of Heb. or. [7014]; *Cân,* (i.e. *Cajin*), the son of Adam:—Cain {3x}. See: TDNT—1:6,*; BAGD—394a; THAYER—317c.

2536. **Καϊνάν** {2x} **Kaïnan**, *kah-ee-nan'* or **Καϊνάμ** **Kaïnam** *kah-ee-nam';* of Heb. or. [7018]; *Cânan* (i.e. *Kenan*), the name of two patriarchs:—Cainan {2x}. See: BAGD—394a; THAYER—317d.

2537. **καινός** {44x} **kainŏs**, *kahee-nos';* of uncert. aff.; *new* (espec. in *freshness;* while *3501* is prop. so with respect to *age*:—new {44x}.

Kainos denotes **(1)** "new," of that which is unaccustomed or unused, not "new" in time, recent, but "new" as to form or quality, of different nature from what is contrasted as old. **(2)** The new tongues,' *kainos,* of Mk 16:17 are the 'other tongues,' *heteros,* of Acts 2:4. These languages, however, were 'new' and 'different,' not in the sense that they had never been heard before, or that they were new to the hearers, for it is plain from v. 8 that this is not the case; they were new languages to the speakers, different from those in which they were accustomed to speak. **(3)** The new things that the Gospel brings for present obedience and realization are: **(3a)** a new covenant, Mt 26:28; **(3b)** a new commandment, Jn 13:34; **(3c)** a new creative act, Gal 6:15; **(3d)** a new creation, 2 Cor 5:17; **(3e)** a new man, i.e., a new character of manhood, spiritual and moral, after the pattern of Christ, Eph 4:24; **(3f)** a new man, i.e., 'the Church which is His (Christ's) body,' Eph 2:15.

(4) The new things that are to be received and enjoyed hereafter are: **(4a)** a new name, the believer's, Rev 2:17; **(4b)** a new name, the Lord's, Rev 3:12; **(4c)** a new song, Rev 5:9; **(4d)** a new Heaven and a new Earth, Rev 21:1; **(4e)** the new Jerusalem, Rev 3:12; 21:2; **(4f)** 'And He that sitteth on the Throne said, Behold, I make all things new,' Rev 21:5. Syn.: *Kainos* denotes new primarily in reference to quality, the fresh, unworn, a condition; whereas, *neos* (3501) denotes the new primarily in reference to time, the young, recent, appearing for the first time. See: TDNT—3:447, 388; BAGD—394a; THAYER—317d.

2538. **καινότης** {2x} **kainŏtēs**, *kahee-not'-ace;* from *2537; renewal* (fig.):—newness {2x}.

Kainotes, akin to *kainos,* is used in the phrases **(1)** "newness of life," Rom 6:4, i.e., life of a new quality; the believer, being a new creation (2 Cor 5:17), is to behave himself consistently with this in contrast to his former manner of life; **(2)** "newness of spirit," RV, Rom 7:6, said of the believer's manner of serving the Lord. While the phrase stands for the new life of the quickened spirit of the believer, it is impossible to dissociate this (in an objective sense) from the operation of the Holy Spirit, by whose power the service is rendered. See: TDNT—3:450, 388; BAGD—394c; THAYER—318a.

2539. **καίπερ** {6x} **kaipĕr**, *kah'-ee-per;* from *2532* and *4007;* and *indeed,* i.e. *nevertheless* or *notwithstanding*:—and yet {1x}, although {5x}. See: BAGD—394c; THAYER—318a.

2540. **καιρός** {87x} **kairŏs**, *kahee-ros';* of uncert. aff.; an *occasion,* i.e. *set* or *proper* time:—time {64x}, season {13x}, opportunity {2x}, due time {2x}, always + 1722 + 3956 {2x}, not tr {1x}, a while {3x}.

Kairos, as a noun, means **(1)** primarily, "due measure, fitness, proportion," **(2)** is used in the NT to signify "a season, a time, a period" possessed of certain characteristics, **(3)** and is frequently rendered **(3a)** "time" or "times": "At that time Jesus answered and said, I thank thee, O Father, Lord of heaven and earth, because thou hast hid these things from the wise and prudent, and hast revealed them unto babes" (Mt 11:25; 12:1; 14:1; 21:34; Mk 11:13; Acts 3:19; 7:20; 17:26; Rom 3:26; 5:6; 9:9; 13:11; 1 Cor 7:5; Gal 4:10; 1 Th 2:17); **(3b)** literally, "for a season (of an hour)". "And now ye know what withholdeth that he might be revealed in his time [*kairos*]" (2 Th 2:6); **(3c)** "always" [lit. "at all seasons"]: "Praying always (*kairos*) with all prayer and supplication in the Spirit, and watching thereunto with all perseverance and supplication for all saints" (Eph 6:18); **(3d)** "in due times": "But hath in due times manifested his word through preaching, which is committed unto me according to the commandment of God our Saviour" (Titus 1:3).

(4) The characteristics of a period are exemplified in the use of the term with regard **(4a)** to harvest (Mt 13:30); **(4b)** reaping (Gal 6:9); **(4c)** punishment (Mt 8:29); **(4d)** discharging duties (Lk 12:42); **(4e)** opportunity for doing anything, whether **(4e1)** good (Mt 26:18; cf. Gal 6:10 ("opportunity"); Eph 5:16); or **(4e2)** evil (Rev 12:12); **(4f)** the fulfillment of prophecy (Lk 1:20; Acts 3:19; 1 Pet 1:11); **(4g)** a time suitable for a purpose (Lk 4:13, lit., "until a season"; cf. 2 Cor 6:2). Syn.: *Chronos* (5550) is simply time as such or the succession of moments together, length. *Kairos* is a favorable opportunity, time as it brings forth its several events. See also: 171, 2122, 3641, 4340, 5550, 5610. See: TDNT—3:455, 389; BAGD—394c; THAYER—318b.

2541. **Καῖσαρ** {30x} **Kaisar**, *kah'-ee-sar;* of Lat. or.; *Cæsar,* a title of the Rom. emperor:—Cæsar {30x}. See: BAGD—395d; THAYER—319c.

2542. **Καισάρεια** {17x} **Kaisarĕia**, *kahee-sar'-i-a;* from *2541; Cæsaria,* the name of two places in Pal.:—Caesarea (of Palestine) {15x}, Caesarea (Philippi) {2x}. See: BAGD—396a; THAYER—319b.

2543. **καίτοι** {1x} **kaitŏi**, *kah'-ee-toy;* from *2532* and *5104; and yet,* i.e. *nevertheless*:—although {1x}. See: BAGD—396a; THAYER—319c.

2544. **καίτοιγε** {3x} **kaitŏigĕ**, *kah'-ee-toyg-eh;* from *2543* and *1065; and yet indeed,* i.e. *although really*:—nevertheless {1x}, though {2x}. See: BAGD—396b; THAYER—319c.

2545. **καίω** {12x} **kaiō**, *kah'-yo;* appar. a primary verb; to *set on fire*, i.e. *kindle* or (by impl.) *consume:*—burn {10x}, did burn + 2258 {1x}, light {1x}.

Kaio, "to set fire to, to light"; **(1)** in the passive voice, "to be lighted, to burn," Mt 5:15; Jn 15:6; Heb 12:18; Rev 4:5; 8:8, 10; 19:20; 21:8; 1 Cor 13:3; **(2)** is used metaphorically of the heart, Lk 24:32; **(3)** of spiritual light, Lk 12:35; Jn 5:35; **(4)** it is translated "do (men) light" in Mt 5:15. See: TDNT—3:464, 390; BAGD—396b; THAYER—319c.

2546. **κἀκεῖ** {11x} **kakĕi**, *kak-i';* from *2532* and *1563; likewise in that place:*—and there {9x}, there also {1x}, thither also {1x}. See: BAGD—396c; THAYER—319d.

2547. **κἀκεῖθεν** {9x} **kakĕithĕn**, *kak-i'-then;* from *2532* and *1564; likewise from that place* (or *time*):—and from thence {5x}, and thence {2x}, and afterward {1x}, thence also {1x}. See: BAGD—396d; THAYER—319d.

2548. **κἀκεῖνος** {23x} **kakĕinŏs**, *kak-i'-nos;* from *2532* and *1565; likewise that* (or *those*):—and he {4x}, and they {3x}, he also {3x}, and them {2x}, and the other {2x}, and him {2x}, they also {2x}, him also {1x}, misc. {4x}. See: BAGD—396d; THAYER—319d.

2549. **κακία** {11x} **kakia**, *kak-ee'-ah;* from *2556; badness*, i.e. (subj.) *depravity*, or (act.) *malignity*, or (pass.) *trouble:*—malice {6x}, maliciousness {2x}, evil {1x}, wickedness {1x}, naughtiness {1x}.

This word basically means badness in quality, an evil mindset, and works itself out **(1)** in malignity, malice [the shrewd and deceitful calculation of doing harm], ill-will, desire to injure; **(2)** wickedness, depravity that is not ashamed to break laws; and **(3)** evil, trouble; it denotes **(4)** "wickedness, depravity, malignity," e.g., Acts 8:22, "wickedness"; **(4b)** Rom. 1:29, "maliciousness"; **(4c)** in Jas 1:21, "naughtiness"; **(4d)** "the evil of trouble, affliction," Mt 6:34, only, and here alone translated "evil." **(5)** "badness in quality" (the opposite of *arete*, "excellence"), "the vicious character generally" is also translated "malice" in 1 Cor 5:8; 14:20; Eph 4:31; Col 3:8; Titus 3:3; 1 Pet 2:1; 1 Pet 2:16. Syn.: 4190, 5337. See: TDNT—3:482, 391; BAGD—397a; THAYER—320a.

2550. **κακοήθεια** {1x} **kakŏēthĕia**, *kak-ŏē-ay'-thi-ah;* from a compound of *2556* and *2239; bad character*, i.e. (spec.) *mischievousness:*—malignity {1x}.

Lit., this word means bad manner or character; hence, an evil disposition that tends to put the worst construction on everything, malice, malevolence, craftiness (Rom 1:29). This *kakoetheia,* the evil that we find in ourselves, makes us ready to suspect that evil exists in others. See: TDNT—3:485, 391; BAGD—397b; THAYER—320a.

2551. **κακολογέω** {4x} **kakŏlŏgĕō**, *kak-ol-og-eh'-o;* from a compound of *2556* and *3056;* to *revile:*—curse {2x}, speak evil of {2x}.

Kakologeo, as a verb, means "to speak evil" and is translated **(1)** "to curse": "For God commanded, saying, Honour thy father and mother: and, He that curseth father or mother, let him die the death." (Mt 15:4; cf. Mk 7:10); and **(2)** "to speak evil of father and mother," not necessarily "to curse," is what the Lord intended; Mk 9:39 and Acts 19:9. Syn.: 331, 332, 685, 1944, 2652, 2653, 2671, 2672.See: TDNT—3:468, 391; BAGD—397b; THAYER—320a.

2552. **κακοπάθεια** {1x} **kakŏpathĕia**, *kak-op-ath'-i-ah;* from a compound of *2556* and *3806; hardship:*—suffering affliction {1x}.

This word, from *kakos,* "evil," and *pascho,* "to suffer" is rendered "suffering affliction" in Jas 5:10. See: TDNT—5:936, 798; BAGD—397b; THAYER—320b.

2553. **κακοπαθέω** {4x} **kakŏpathĕō**, *kak-op-ath-eh'-o;* from the same as *2552;* to *undergo hardship:*—endure hardness {1x}, suffer trouble {1x}, endure affliction {1x}, be afflicted {1x}.

This word from *kakos,* "evil," *pathos,* "suffering," signifies "to suffer hardship." It is translated **(1)** "endure hardness', 2 Ti 2:3; **(2)** "suffer trouble", 2 Ti 2:9; **(3)** "endure afflictions", 2 Ti 4:5; and **(4)** "afflicted", Jas 5:13. See: TDNT—5:936, 798; BAGD—397c; THAYER—320b.

2554. **κακοποιέω** {4x} **kakŏpŏiĕō**, *kak-op-oy-eh'-o;* from *2555;* to *be a bad-doer*, i.e. (obj.) to *injure*, or (gen.) to *sin:*—do evil {3x}, evil doing {1x}.

This word signifies **(1)** "to do evil", Mk 3:4; Lk 6:9; 3 Jn 11, "doeth evil"; and **(2)** in 1 Pet 3:17, "evil doing." See: TDNT—3:485, 391; BAGD—397c; THAYER—320b.

2555. **κακοποιός** {5x} **kakŏpŏiŏs**, *kak-op-oy-os';* from *2556* and *4160;* a *bad-doer;* (spec.) a *criminal:*—evil-doer {4x}, malefactor {1x}.

Kakopoios, properly the masculine gender of the adjective, denotes an **(1)** "evil-doer" (*kakon,* "evil," *poieo,* "to do"), 1 Pet 2:12, 14; 3:16; 4:15; and **(2)** "malefactor" in Jn 18:30. See: TDNT—3:485, 391; BAGD—397c; THAYER—320c.

2556. **κακός** {51x} **kakŏs**, *kak-os';* appar. a primary word; *worthless* (*intrinsically,* such; whereas *4190* prop. refers to *effects*), i.e. (subj.) *depraved*, or (obj.) *injurious:*—evil {40x}, evil things {3x}, harm {2x}, that which is evil + 3458 {2x}, wicked {1x}, ill {1x}, bad {1x}, noisome {1x}.

Kakos indicates the lack in a person or thing of those qualities which should be possessed and means bad in character **(1)** morally, by way of thinking, feeling or acting (Mk 7:21; 1 Cor 15:33; Col 3:5; 1 Ti 6:10; 1 Pet 3:9); **(2)** in the sense of what is injurious or baneful: **(2a)** the tongue as a restless evil (Jas 3:8); **(2b)** evil beasts (Titus 1:12); **(3)** harm (Acts 16:28). **(4)** *Kakon,* the neuter adjective, is used with the article, as a noun, e.g., Acts 23:9; Rom 7:21; Heb 5:14; in the plural, "evil things," e.g., 1 Cor 10:6; 1 Ti 6:10, "all kinds of evil."

(5) It stands for "whatever is evil in character, base," its use broadly divided as follows: **(5a)** of what is morally or ethically "evil," whether **(5b)** of persons, e.g., Mt 21:41; 24:48; Phil 3:2; Rev 2:2, or **(5c)** qualities, emotions, passions, deeds, e.g., Mk 7:21; Jn 18:23, 30; Rom 1:30; 3:8; 7:19, 21; 13:4; 14:20; 16:19; 1 Cor 13:5; 2 Cor 13:7; 1 Th 5:15; 1 Ti 6:10; 2 Ti 4:14; 1 Pet 3:9, 12; **(5d)** of what is injurious, destructive, baneful, pernicious, e.g., Lk 16:25; Acts 16:28; 28:5; Titus 1:12; Jas 3:8; Rev 16:2. Syn.: *Kakos,* in distinction (wherever the distinction is observable) from *poneros* (4190), which indicates "what is evil in influence and effect, malignant." *Kakos* is the wider term and often covers the meaning of poneros. *Kakos* is antithetic to *kalos* (2570), "fair, advisable, good in character," and to *agathos* (18), "beneficial, useful, good in act"; hence it denotes what is useless, incapable, bad; poneros is essentially antithetic to *chrestos* (5543), "kind, gracious, serviceable"; hence it denotes what is destructive, injurious, evil. As evidence that *poneros* and *kakos* have much in common, though still not interchangeable, each is used of thoughts, cf. Mt 15:19 with Mk 7:21; of speech, Mt 5:11 with 1 Pet 3:10; of actions, 2 Ti 4:18 with 1 Th 5:15; of man, Mt 18:32 with 24:48. See also: 2554, 2559, 2560. See: TDNT—3:469, 391; BAGD—397d; THAYER—320c.

2557. **κακοῦργος** {4x} **kakŏurgŏs**, *kak-oor'-gos;* from *2556* and the base of *2041;* a *wrong-doer*, i.e. *criminal:*—evil-doer {1x}, malefactor {3x}.

Kakourgos, an adjective, lit., "evil-working" (*kakos,* "evil," *ergon,* "work"), is used as a noun, translated **(1)** "malefactor(-s)" in Luke 23:32, 33, 39, and **(2)** in 2 Ti 2:9, "evil doer." See: DNT - 3:484, 391; BAGD—398b; THAYER—320d.

2558. **κακουχέω** {2x} **kakŏuchĕō**, *kak-oo-kheh'-o;* from a presumed compound of *2556* and *2192;* to oppress, plague, *maltreat:*—which suffer adversity {1x}, torment {1x}.

Kakoucheo, from *kakos,* "evil," and *echo,* "to have," signifies, in the passive voice, **(1)** "to suffer ill, to be maltreated, tormented," Heb 11:37, "tormented"; and **(2)** Heb 13:3, "suffer adversity." See: BAGD—398b; THAYER—320d.

2559. **κακόω** {6x} **kakŏō**, *kak-ŏ'-o;* from *2556;* to *injure;* fig. to *exasperate:*—make evil affected {1x}, entreat evil {2x}, harm {1x}, hurt {1x}, vex {1x}.

Kakoo, as a verb, means "to ill-treat", and is rendered "to entreat evil" in Acts 7:6, 19; "made (them) evil affected," 14:2. See: TDNT—3:484, 391; BAGD—398b; THAYER—320d.

2560. **κακῶς** {16x} **kakōs**, *kak-oce';* from *2556; badly* (phys. or mor.):—be sick + 2192 {7x}, be diseased + 2192 {2x}, evil {2x}, grievously {1x}, sore {1x}, miserable {1x}, amiss {1x}, sick people + 2192 {1x}.

Kakos, "badly, evilly," is used in the physical sense, **(1)** "to be sick," e.g., Mt 4:24; Mk 1:32, 34; Lke 5:31. **(2)** In Mt 21:41 this adverb is used with the adjective, "He will miserably destroy those miserable men," more lit., "He will evilly destroy those men (evil as they are)," with stress on the adjective; **(3)** in the moral sense, "to speak evilly," Jn 18:23; Acts 23:5. It is translated **(4)** "amiss" "evil," is translated "amiss, evilly" in Jas 4:3. **(5)** It denotes "badly, ill," is translated "grievously (vexed)," in Mt 15:22. See: TDNT—4:1091,*; BAGD—398c; THAYER—321a.

2561. **κάκωσις** {1x} **kakōsis**, *kak'-o-sis;* from *2559; maltreatment:*—affliction {1x}. See: BAGD—398c; THAYER—321a.

2562. **καλάμη** {1x} **kalamē**, *kal-am'-ay;* fem. of *2563;* a *stalk* of grain after the ears have been cut off, i.e. (collect.) *stubble:*—stubble {1x}. See: BAGD—398c; THAYER—321a.

2563. **κάλαμος** {12x} **kalamŏs**, *kal'-am-os;* or uncert. aff.; a *reed* (the plant or its stem, or that of a similar plant); by impl. a *pen:*—pen {1x}, reed {11x}.

This word denotes **(1)** "the reed" mentioned in Mt 11:7; 12:20; Lk 7:24; the same as the Heb., *qaneh* (among the various reeds in the OT), e.g., Is 42:3, from which Matt. 12:20 is quoted (cf. Job 40:21; Eze 29:6, "a reed with jointed, hollow stalk"); **(2)** "a reed staff, staff," Mt. 27:29, 30, 48; Mk 15:19; **(3)** "a measuring reed or rod," Rev 11:1; 21:15, 16; **(4)** "a writing reed, a pen," 3Jn 13. See: BAGD—398d; THAYER—321a.

2564. **καλέω** {146x} **kalĕō**, *kal-eh'-o;* akin to the base of *2753;* to "*call*" (prop. aloud, but used in a variety of applications, dir. or otherwise):—call {125x}, bid {16x}, be so named {1x}, named + 3686 {1x}, misc. {3x} = (whose, whose sur-) name (was [called]).

Kaleo is used **(1)** with a personal object, **(1a)** "to call anyone, summon," e.g., Mt 20:8; 25:14; **(1b)** it is used particularly of the divine call to partake of the blessings of redemption, e.g., Rom 8:30; 1 Cor 1:9; 1 Th 2:12; Heb 9:15; **(2)** of nomenclature or vocation, "to call by a name, to name"; in the passive voice, "to be called by a name, to bear a name." Thus it suggests either vocation or destination; the context determines which, e.g., Rom 9:25–26; **(3)** it is also translated "surname," in Acts 15:37. **(4)** This word means to call and often means to bid in the sense of invite (Mt 22:3–4, 8, 9; Lk 14:7–10, 13). Syn.: *Boao* (994) means to cry out as a manifestation of feeling, esp. a cry for help; *kaleo* (2564) to cry out for a purpose; *krazo* (2896) means to cry out harshly, often of inarticulate and brutish sound; and *kraugazo* (2905), an intensive of (2896) and denotes to cry coarsely, in contempt. (2564) suggests intelligence; (994) sensibilities; and (2896) instincts. See: TDNT—3:487, 394; BAGD—398d; THAYER—321b.

2565. **καλλιέλαιος** {1x} **kalliĕlaiŏs**, *kal-le-el'-ah-yos;* from the base of *2566* and *1636;* a *cultivated olive* tree, i.e. a *domesticated* or *improved* one:—good olive tree {1x}.

Kallielaios is the garden olive as opposed to the wild olive, Rom 11:24. See: BAGD—400a; THAYER—322a.

2566. **κάλλιον** {1x} **kalliŏn**, *kal-lee'-on;* neut. of the (irreg.) comp. of *2570;* (adv.) *better* than many:—very well {1x}.

Being in the comparative form it is to be understood as "better." See: BAGD—400a; THAYER—322a.

2567. **καλοδιδάσκαλος** {1x} **kalŏdidaskalŏs**, *kal-od-id-as'-kal-os;* from *2570* and *1320;* a *teacher* of the *right:*—teacher of good things {1x}. See: TDNT—2:159, 161; BAGD—400a; THAYER—322b.

2568. **Καλοὶ Λιμένες** {1x} **Kalŏi Limĕnĕs**, *kal-oy' lee-men'-es;* plur. of *2570* and *3040; Good Harbors,* i.e. *Fairhaven,* a bay of Crete:—Fair Havens {1x}. See: BAGD—400a; THAYER—322a.

2569. **καλοποιέω** {1x} **kalŏpŏiĕō**, *kal-op-oy-eh'-o;* from *2570* and *4160;* to *do well,* i.e. live virtuously:—well doing {1x}.

Kalopoieo,"to do well, excellently, act honorably, act uprightly" (*kalos,* "good," *poieo,* "to do"), occurs in 2 Th 3:13. See: BAGD—400b; THAYER—322b.

2570. **καλός** {102x} **kalŏs**, *kal-os';* of uncert. aff.; prop. *beautiful,* but chiefly (fig.) *good* (lit. or mor.), i.e. *valuable* or *virtuous* (for *appearance* or *use,* and thus distinguished from *18,* which is prop. *intrinsic*):—good {83x}, better {7x}, honest {5x}, meet {2x}, goodly {2x}, fair {1x}, well {1x}, worthy {1x}.

Introduction: This word denotes something is **(1)** beautiful, handsome to look at, shapely, magnificent; **(2)** good, excellent in its nature and characteristics, and therefore well adapted to its ends, praiseworthy, noble; **(3)** beautiful by reason of purity of heart and life, and hence praiseworthy; morally good, noble; or **(4)** honourable, conferring honour which effects the mind agreeably, comforting and confirming.

Definition: *Kalos,* as an adjective, denotes that which is intrinsically "good," and so, "goodly, fair, beautiful," as **(1)** of that which is well adapted to its circumstances or ends: **(1a)** fruit: "And now also the axe is laid unto the root of the trees: therefore every tree which bringeth not forth good fruit is hewn down, and cast into the fire" (Mt 3:10); **(1b)** a tree: "Either make the tree good, and his fruit good; or else make the tree corrupt, and his fruit corrupt: for the tree is known by *his* fruit." (Mt 12:33); **(1c)** ground: "But other fell into good ground, and brought forth fruit, some an hundredfold, some sixtyfold, some thirtyfold." (Mt 13:8; cf. vs 23); **(1d)** fish: "Which, when it was full, they drew to shore, and sat down, and gathered the good into vessels, but cast the bad away." (Mt 13:48); **(1e)** the Law: "If then I do that which I would not, I consent unto the Law that *it is* good." (Rom 7:16; cf. 1 Ti 1:8); **(1f)** every creature of God: "For every creature of God *is* good, and nothing to be refused, if it be received with thanksgiving:" (1 Ti 4:4); **(1g)** a faithful minister of Christ and the doctrine he teaches: "If thou put the brethren in remembrance of these things, thou shalt be a good minister of Jesus Christ, nourished up in the words of faith and of good doctrine, whereunto thou hast attained." (1 Ti 4:6);

(2) of that which is ethically good, right, noble, honorable: "But *it is* good to be zealously affected always in *a* good *thing,* and not only when I am present with you." (Gal 4:18; cf. 1 Ti 5:10, 25; 6:18; Titus 2:7, 14; 3:8, 14). **(3)** Christians are to **(3a)** "take thought for things honest" (*kalos*): "Providing for honest things, not only in the sight of the Lord, but also in the sight of men." (2 Cor 8:21); **(3b)** not to be weary in well doing (Gal 6:9); **(3c)** to hold fast "that which is good" (1 Th 5:21); **(3d)** to be zealous of good works (Titus 2:14); **(3d1)** to maintain them (Titus 3:8); **(3d2)** to provoke to them (Heb 10:24); **(3d3)** to bear testimony by them (1 Pt 2:12).

Syn.: **(A)** *Kalos* and *agathos* (18) occur together in Lk 8:15: "But that on the good (*kalos*) ground are they, which in an honest (*kalos*) and good (*agathos*) heart, having heard the word, keep *it,* and bring forth fruit with patience." An "honest" (*kalos*) heart is one that has a right attitude before God and a "good" (*agathos*) heart is one that, instead of working ill to a neighbor, acts beneficially towards him. **(B)** In Rom 7:18, "in me . . . dwelleth no good thing" (*agathos*) signifies that in him is nothing capable of doing "good," and hence he lacks the power "to do that which is good" (*kalos*). **(C)** In 1 Th 5:15, "follow after that which is good" (*agathos*), the "good" is that which is beneficial; in v. 21, "hold fast that which is good (*kalos*)," the "good" describes the intrinsic value of the teaching. See also: 5543. See: TDNT—3:536, 402; BAGD—400b; THAYER—322b.

2571. **κάλυμμα** {4x} **kaluma**, *kal'-oo-mah;* from *2572;* a *cover,* i.e. *vail:*—vail {4x}.

Kaluma, "a covering," is used **(1)** of the "vail" which Moses put over his face when descending Mount Sinai, thus preventing Israel from beholding the glory, 2 Cor 3:13; **(2)** metaphorically of the spiritually darkened vision suffered retributively by Israel, until the conversion of the nation to their Messiah takes place, 2 Cor 3:14, 15, 16. See: TDNT—3:558, 405; BAGD—400d; THAYER—322d.

2572. **καλύπτω** {8x} **kaluptō**, *kal-oop'-to;* akin to *2813* and *2928;* to *cover* up (lit. or fig.):—cover {5x}, hide {3x}.

Kalupto signifies **(1)** "to cover," Mt 8:24; 10:26; Lk 8:16; 23:30; 1 Pet. 4:8; **(2)** to hide in Jas 5:20; 2 Cor 4:3 (twice). See: TDNT—3:536, 405; BAGD—401a; THAYER—323a.

2573. **καλῶς** {37x} **kalōs**, *kal-oce';* adv. from *2570; well* (usually mor.):—well {30x}, good {2x}, full well {1x}, very well {1x}, misc. {3x} = in a good place {1x}, honestly {1x}, recover {1x}.

Kalos, "finely", is usually translated **(1)** "well," indicating what is done rightly, in the Epistles it is most frequent in 1 Ti (3:4, 12, 13; 5:17); **(2)** twice it is used as an exclamation of approval, Mk 12:32; Rom 11:20. See: BAGD—401b; THAYER—323a.

2574. **κάμηλος** {6x} **kamēlŏs**, *kam'-ay-los;* of Heb. or. [1581]; a "*camel*":—camel {6x}.

Kamelos, from a Hebrew word signifying "a bearer, carrier," is used in proverbial statements to indicate **(1)** "something almost or altogether impossible," Mt 19:24; Mk 10:25; Lk 18:25; and **(2)** "the acts of a person who is careful not to sin in trivial details, but pays no heed to more important matters," Mt 23:24; **(3)** its hair being used for clothing, Mt3:4; Mk 1:7. See: TDNT—3:592, 413; BAGD—401c; THAYER—323b.

2575. **κάμινος** {4x} **kaminŏs**, *kam'-ee-nos;* prob. from *2545;* a *furnace:*—furnace {4x}.

Kaminos, "an oven, furnace, kiln" (whence Lat. *caminus,* Eng., chimney), used for smelting, or for burning earthenware, occurs in Mt 13:42, 50; Rev 1:15; 9:2. See: BAGD—401d; THAYER—323c.

2576. **καμμύω** {2x} **kammuo**, *kam-moo'-o;* from a compound of *2596* and the base of *3466;* to *shut down,* i.e. *close* the eyes:—close {2x}.

This word denotes "to close down", hence, "to shut the eyes," Mt 13:15 and Acts 28:27, in each place of the obstinacy of Jews in their opposition to the gospel. See: BAGD—402a; THAYER—323c.

2577. **κάμνω** {3x} **kamnō**, *kam'-no;* appar. a primary verb; prop. to *toil,* i.e. (by impl.) to *tire* (fig. *faint, sicken*):—faint {1x}, sick {1x}, be wearied {1x}.

This word primarily signifies to work; then, as the effect of continued labor, to be weary. It is used **(1)** in Heb 12:3 of becoming weary; **(2)** in Jas 5:15 of sickness; and **(3)** in Rev 2:3 of fainting. See: BAGD—402a; THAYER—323c.

2578. **κάμπτω** {4x} **kamptō**, *kamp'-to;* appar. a primary verb; to *bend:*—bow {4x}.

Kampto means to bend, bow, the knee (the knees) or one's self and is used of worshippers who bend in honour of one in religious veneration (Rom 11:4; 14:11; Eph 3:14; Phil 2:10). See: TDNT—3:594, 413; BAGD—402b; THAYER—323d.

2579. **κἄν** {13x} **kan**, *kan;* from *2532* and *1437; and* (or *even*) *if:*—though {4x}, and if {3x}, if but {2x}, also if {1x}, at the least {1x}, and if so much as {1x}, yet {1x}. See: BAGD—402c; THAYER—323d.

2580. **Κανᾶ** {4x} **Kana**, *kan-ah';* of Heb. or. [comp. 7071]; *Cana,* a place in Pal.:—Cana {4x}. See: BAGD—402c; THAYER—324a.

2581. **Κανανίτης** {2x} **Kananitēs**, *kan-an-ee'-tace;* of Chald. or. [comp. 7067]; *zealous; Cananitēs,* an epithet:—Canaanite {2x}. See: BAGD—402d; THAYER—324a, 324b.

2582. **Κανδάκη** {1x} **Kandakē**, *kan-dak'-ay;* of for. or.; *Candacē,* an Eg. queen:—

Candace {1x}. See: BAGD—402d; THAYER—324b.

2583. **κανών** {5x} **kanōn**, *kan-ohn';* from κάνη **kanē** (a straight *reed,* i.e. *rod*); a *rule* ("*canon*"), i.e. (fig.) a *standard* (of faith and practice); by impl. a *boundary,* i.e. (fig.) a *sphere* (of activity):—line {4x}, rule {1x}.

Kanon **(1)** originally denoted a straight rod used as a ruler or measuring instrument, or, in rare instances, the beam of a balance; **(2)** the secondary notion being either **(2a)** of keeping anything straight, as of a rod used in weaving, or **(2b)** of testing straightness, as a carpenter's rule; hence, **(2c)** its metaphorical use to express what serves to measure or determine anything. **(3)** In general the word thus came to serve for anything regulating the actions of men, as a standard or principle, Phil 3:16; **(3a)** In Gal 6:16 are those who make what is stated in vv. 14 and 15 their guiding line in the matter of salvation through faith in Christ alone, apart from works, whether following the principle themselves or teaching it to others. **(3b)** In 2 Cor 10:13, 15, 16, province signifies the limits of the responsibility in gospel service as measured and appointed by God. See: TDNT—3:596, 414; BAGD—403a; THAYER—324b.

2584. **Καπερναούμ** {16x} **Kapĕrnaŏum**, *kap-er-nah-oom';* of Heb. or. [prob. 3723 and 5151]; *Capernaüm* (i.e. *Caphanachum*), a place in Pal.:—Capernaum {16x}. See: BAGD—403a; 426b; THAYER—324c.

2585. **καπηλεύω** {1x} **kapēlĕuō**, *kap-ale-yoo'-o;* from κάπηλος **kapēlŏs** (a *huckster*); to *retail,* i.e. (by impl.) to *adulterate* (fig.):—corrupt {1x}.

This word means to be a retailer, to peddle, to hucksterize; hence, intentionally to get base gain by dealing in anything, to do anything for sordid personal advantage (2 Cor 2:17). Syn.: 1389. See: TDNT—3:603, 415; BAGD—403a; THAYER—324d.

2586. **καπνός** {13x} **kapnŏs**, *kap-nos';* of uncert. aff.; *smoke:*—smoke {13x}.

Kapnos, "smoke," occurs in Acts 2:19 and 12 times in the Apocalypse. See: BAGD—403b; THAYER—325a.

2587. **Καππαδοκία** {2x} **Kappadŏkia**, *kap-pad-ok-ee'-ah;* of for. or.; *Cappadocia,* a region of Asia Minor:—Cappadocia {2x}. See: BAGD—403b; THAYER—325a.

2588. **καρδία** {160x} **kardia**, *kar-dee'-ah;* prol. from a primary κάρ **kar** (Lat. *cor,* "*heart*"); the *heart,* i.e. (fig.) the *thoughts* or *feelings* (*mind*); also (by anal.) the *middle:*—heart {159x}, broken hearted + 4937 {1x}.

Kardia is the heart, **(1)** the chief organ of physical life, and occupies the most important place in the human system. **(2)** By an easy transition the word came to stand for man's entire mental and moral activity, both the rational and the emotional elements. **(3)** It is used figuratively for the hidden springs of the personal life: **(3a)** the seat of total depravity, the principle in the center of man's inward life that defiles all he does (Mt 15:19, 20; and **(3b)** it is the sphere of Divine influence (Rom 2:15; Acts 15:9; 'the hidden man,' 1 Pet 3:4, the real man). It represents the true character but conceals it. **(4)** It denotes **(4a)** the seat of physical life (Acts 14:17; Jas 5:5); **(4b)** the seat of moral nature and spiritual life: **(4b1)** the seat of grief (Jn 14:1; Rom 9:2; 2 Cor 2:4); **(4b2)** joy (Jn 16:22; Eph 5:19); **(4b3)** the desires (Mt 5:28; 2 Pet 2:14); **(4b4)** the affections (Lk 24:32; Acts 21:13); **(4b5)** the perceptions (Jn 12:40; Eph 4:18); **(4b6)** the thoughts (Mt 9:4; Heb 4:12); **(4b7)** the understanding (Mt 13:15; Rom 1:21); **(4b7)** the reasoning powers (Mk 2:6; Lk 24:38); **(4b8)** the imagination (Lk 1:51); **(4b9)** conscience (Acts 2:37; 1 Jn 3:20); **(4b10)** the intentions (Heb 4:12, cf. 1 Pet 4:1); **(4b11)** purpose (Acts 11:23; 2 Cor 9:7); **(4b12)** the will (Rom 6:17; Col 3:15); and **(4b13)** faith (Mk 11:23; Rom 10:10; Heb 3:12). (cf. Eng., "cardiac,") See: TDNT—3:605, 415; BAGD—403b; THAYER—325a.

2589. **καρδιογνώστης** {2x} **kardiŏgnōstēs**, *kar-dee-og-noce'-tace;* from *2588* and *1097;* a *heart-knower:*—which knowest the hearts {2x}.

Kardiognostes, "a knower of hearts" (*kardia* and *ginosko,* "to know"), is used in Acts 1:24; 15:8. See: TDNT—3:613, 415; BAGD—404c; THAYER—326b.

2590. **καρπός** {66x} **karpŏs**, *kar-pos';* prob. from the base of *726; fruit* (as *plucked*), lit. or fig.:—fruit {66x}.

Karpos, as a noun, means "fruit" and is used **(1)** of the fruit of trees, fields, the earth, that which is produced by the inherent energy of a living organism (Mt 7:17; Jas 5:7, 18; **(2)** plural (Lk 12:17; 2 Tim 2:6; **(3)** of the human body: "And she spake out with a loud voice, and said, Blessed *art* thou among women, and blessed *is* the fruit of thy womb" Lk 1:42; Acts 2:30); **(4)** metaphorically, **(4a)** of works or deeds, "fruit" being the visible expression of power working inwardly and invisibly, the character of the "fruit" being evidence of the character of the power producing it: "Ye shall know them by their fruits. Do men gather grapes of thorns, or figs of thistles?" (Mt 7:16). **(4b)** As the visible expressions of hidden lusts are the works of the flesh, so the invisible power of the Holy Spirit in those who are brought into living union with Christ (Jn 15:2–8, 16) produces "the fruit of the Spirit" (Gal 5:22 the singular form suggesting the unity of the character of the Lord as reproduced in them, namely, "love, joy, peace, longsuffering, kindness, goodness, faithfulness, meekness, temperance," all in contrast with the confused and often mutually antagonistic "works of the flesh"). **(5)** So in Phil 1:11 "fruit of righteousness." In Heb. 12:11, "the fruit of righteousness" is described as "peaceable fruit," the outward effect of divine chastening;

(6) "the fruit of righteousness is sown in peace" (Jas 3:18, i.e., the seed contains the fruit; those who make peace, produce a harvest of righteousness); **(7)** "fruit of the light" (Eph 5:9 is seen in "goodness and righteousness and truth," as the expression of the union of the Christian with God; **(7a)** for God is good (Mk 10:18), **(7b)** the Son is "the righteous One" (Acts 7:52), **(7c)** the Spirit is "the Spirit of truth" (Jn 16:13); **(8)** Fruit speaks of advantage, profit, consisting **(8a)** of converts as the result of evangelistic ministry (Jn 4:36; Rom 1:13; Phil 1:22; **(8b)** of sanctification, through deliverance from a life of sin and through service to God (Rom 6:22), in contrast to **(8c)** the absence of anything regarded as advantageous as the result of former sins (Rom 6: 21); **(8d)** of the reward for ministration to servants of God (Phil 4:17); **(8e)** of the effect of making confession to God's Name by the sacrifice of praise (Heb 13:15). Syn.: 175, 2592, 2593, 3703, 5352. See: TDNT—3:614, 416; BAGD—404c; THAYER—326b; THAYER—326b.

2591. **Κάρπος** {1x} **Karpŏs**, *kar'-pos;* perh. for *2590; Carpus,* prob. a Chr.:—Carpus {1x}. See: BAGD—404b; THAYER—326b.

2592. **καρποφορέω** {8x} **karpŏphŏrĕō**, *kar-pof-or-eh'-o;* from *2593;* to *be fertile* (lit. or fig.):—bring forth fruit {6x}, bear fruit {1x}, be fruitful {1x}.

Karpophoreo, as a verb, "to bear or bring forth fruit" is used in the natural sense, of the "fruit of the earth," **(1)** "bring forth fruit", metaphorically, of conduct, or that which takes effect in conduct, ": "And these are they which are sown on good ground; such as hear the word, and receive *it,* and bring forth fruit, some thirtyfold, some sixty, and some an hundred" (Mk 4:20, 28; cf. Lk 8:15; Rom 7:4, 5 the latter, of evil "fruit," borne "unto death," of activities resulting from a state of alienation from God; Col 1:6 (in the middle voice); **(2)** "to bear fruit", Mt 13:23; and **(3)** "to be fruitful", Col 1:10. See: TDNT—3:616, 416; BAGD—405a; THAYER—326c.

2593. **καρποφόρος** {1x} **karpŏphŏrŏs**, *kar-pof-or'-os;* from *2590* and *5342; fruitbearing* (fig.):—fruitful {1x}.

Karpophoros, as an adjective, denotes "fruitful": "Nevertheless he left not himself without witness, in that he did good, and gave us rain from heaven, and fruitful seasons, filling our hearts with food and gladness" (Acts 14:17). Syn.: 175, 2590, 2592, 3703, 5352. See: BAGD—405b; THAYER—326d.

2594. **καρτερέω** {1x} **kartĕrĕō**, *kar-ter-eh'-o;* from a der. of *2904* (transp.); to *be strong,* i.e. (fig.) *steadfast* (*patient*):—endure {1x}.

Kartereo, "to be steadfast, patient," is used in Heb 11:27, "endured," of Moses in relation to Egypt. See: TDNT—3:617, 417; BAGD—405b; THAYER—326d.

2595. **κάρφος** {6x} **karphŏs**, *kar'-fos;* from κάρφω **karphō** (to *wither*); a dry *twig* or *straw:*—mote {6x}.

Karphos, "a small, dry stalk, a twig, a bit of dried stick", or "a tiny straw or bit of wool," such as might fly into the eye, is used metaphorically of a minor fault, Mt 7:3, 4, 5; Lk 6:41, 42 (twice), in contrast with *dokos* (1385), "a beam supporting the roof of a building." See: BAGD—405c; THAYER—326d.

2596 **κατά** {480x} **kata**, *kat-ah';* a primary particle; (prep.) *down* (in place or time), in varied relations (according to the case [gen., dat. or acc.] with which it is joined):—according to {107x}, after {61x}, against {58x}, in {36x}, by {27x}, daily + 2250 {15x}, as {11x}, misc. {165x} = about, (when they were) × alone, among, and, × apart, (even, like) as (concerning, pertaining to touching), × aside, at, before, beyond, by, to the charge of, [charita-] bly, concerning, + covered, down, every, (+ far more) exceeding, × more excellent, for, from . . . to, godly, after the manner of, + by any means, beyond (out of) measure, × mightily, more, × natural, of (up-) on (× part), out (of every), over against, (+ your) × own, + particularly, so, through (-oughout, oughout every), thus, (un-) to (-gether, -ward), × uttermost, where (-by), with. In composition it retains many of these applications, and frequently denotes *opposition, distribution,* or *intensity.* See: BAGD—405c; THAYER—326d.

2597. **καταβαίνω** {81x} **katabainō**, *kat-ab-ah'-ee-no;* from *2596* and the base of *939;* to *descend* (lit. or fig.):—come down {41x}, descend {18x}, go down {17x}, fall down {1x}, step down {1x}, get down {1x}, fall {1x}, vr come down {1x}.

Inherent within this word is someone or something leaving a positionally higher position and arriving at a lower one. See: TDNT—1:522, 90; BAGD—408b; THAYER—329c.

2598. **καταβάλλω** {3x} **kataballō**, *kat-ab-al'-lo;* from *2596* and *906;* to *throw down:*—cast down {2x}, lay {1x}.

Kataballo, signifies **(1)** "cast down," **(1a)** 2 Cor 4:9: "Persecuted, but not forsaken; cast down, but not destroyed"; **(1b)** "the casting down of satan", Rev 12:10; and **(2)** Heb 6:1: "Therefore leaving the principles of the doctrine of Christ, let us go on unto perfection; not laying [down] again the foundation of repentance from dead works, and of faith toward God"; and See: BAGD—408d; THAYER—329d.

2599. **καταβαρέω** {1x} **katabarĕō**, *kat-ab-ar-eh'-o;* from *2596* and *916;* to *impose upon:*—burden {1x}.

Katabareo means to weigh down, to overload and is used of material weight (metaphorically, 2 Cor 12:16). See: BAGD—408d; THAYER—330a.

2600. **κατάβασις** {1x} **katabasis**, *kat-ab'-as-is;* from *2597;* a *declivity:*—a descent {1x}.

Katabasis stresses the "way down," Lk 19:37; whereas, *katabaino* (2597) stresses the activity of descending. See: BAGD—409a; THAYER—330a.

2601. **καταβιβάζω** {2x} **katabibazō**, *kat-ab-ib-ad'-zo;* from *2596* and a der. of the base of *939;* to *cause to go down,* i.e. *precipitate:*—bring down {1x}, thrust down {1x}.

Katabibazo, as a verb, means in the active voice, "to cause to go down" and is used in the passive in the sense of **(1)** "being brought down, thrust down": "And thou, Capernaum, which art exalted to heaven, shalt be thrust down to hell" (Lk 10:15); **(2)** "go down": "And thou, Capernaum, which art exalted unto heaven, shalt be brought down (*katabibazo*) to hell: for if the mighty works, which have been done in thee, had been done in Sodom, it would have remained until this day" (Mt 11:23). See: BAGD—409a; THAYER—330a.

2602. **καταβολή** {11x} **katabŏlē**, *kat-ab-ol-ay';* from *2598;* a *deposition,* i.e. *founding;* fig. *conception:*—to conceive + 1519 {1x}, foundation {10x}.

Literally, *katabole* means "a casting down," is used **(1)** of "conceiving seed," the injection or depositing of the virile semen in the womb, Heb. 11:11; **(2)** of "a foundation," as that which is laid down, or in the sense of founding; metaphorically, of "the foundation of the world"; in this respect two phrases are used, **(2a)** "from the foundation of the world," Mt 13:35; 25:34; Lk 11:50; Heb 4:3; 9:26; Rev 13:8; 17:8; **(2b)** "before the foundation of the world," Jn 17:24; Eph 1:4; 1 Pet 1:20. The latter phrase looks back to the past eternity. See: TDNT—3:620, 418; BAGD 409a; THAYER—330a.

2603. **καταβραβεύω** {1x} **katabrabĕuō**, *kat-ab-rab-yoo'-o;* from *2596* and *1018* (in its orig. sense); to *award* the price *against,* i.e. (fig.) to *defraud* (of salvation):—beguile of (one's) reward {1x}.

Katabrabeuo means to defraud or beguile of the prize of victory; occurs in Col 2:18, said of false teachers who would frustrate the faithful adherence of the believers to the truth, causing them to lose their reward. See: BAGD—409b; THAYER—330b.

2604. **καταγγελεύς** {1x} **kataggĕlĕus**, *kat-ang-gel-yooce';* from *2605;* a *proclaimer:*—setter forth {1x}.

Kataggeleus, "a proclaimer, herald" (akin to *katangello,* "to proclaim"), is used in Acts 17:18, "a setter forth (of strange gods)." See: TDNT—1:70, 10; BAGD—409b; THAYER—330c.

2605. **καταγγέλλω** {17x} **kataggĕllō**, *kat-ang-gel'-lo;* from *2596* and the base of *32;* to *proclaim, promulgate:*—declare {2x}, preach {10x}, shew {3x}, speak of {1x}, teach {1x}.

Kataggello, lit., "to report down" (*kata,* intensive), means to lay it down firmly, accurately, and in order. It is translated **(1)** "to preach" in Acts 4:2; 13:5, 38; 15:36; 17:3, 13; 1 Cor 9:14; Col 1:28; **(2)** "to declare" in Acts 17:23; 1 Cor 2:1; **(3)** "to shew" Acts 16:17; 26:23; 1 Cor 11:26, "shew"; in the last passage the partaking of the elements at the Lord's Supper is a "showing forth" of His death, a "visual" detailing of it; **(4)** "to teach", Acts 16:21; and **(5)** "speak of" in Rom 1:8. See: TDNT—1:70, 10; BAGD—409b; THAYER—330c.

2606. **καταγελάω** {3x} **katagĕlaō**, *kat-ag-el-ah'-o;* to *laugh down,* i.e. *deride:*—laugh to scorn {3x}.

Katagelao denotes "to laugh scornfully at," (*kata,* "down," used intensively), and signifies derisive laughter, Mt 9:24; M 5:40; Lk 8:53. See: TDNT—1:658, 113; BAGD—409c; THAYER—330c.

2607. **καταγινώσκω** {3x} **kataginōskō**, *kat-ag-in-o'-sko;* from *2596* and *1097,* to *note against,* i.e. *find fault with:*—blame {1x}, condemn {2x}.

Kataginosko, as a verb, means "to know something against" (*kata,* "against," *ginosko,* "to know by experience"), hence, "to think ill of, to condemn" and is said, **(1)** in Gal 2:11, of Peter's conduct, he being "self-condemned" as the result of an exercised and enlightened conscience, and "condemned" in the sight of others: "But when Peter was come to Antioch, I withstood him to the face, because he was to be blamed." **(2)** so of "self-condemnation" due to an exercise of heart: "For if our heart condemn us, God is greater than our heart, and knoweth all things. 21 Beloved, if our heart condemn us not, *then* have we confidence toward God" (1 Jn 3:20–21). 2607 *Kataginosko,* as a verb, in Gal 2:11 can be understood as "stood condemned": "But when Peter was come to Antioch, I withstood him to the face, because he was to be blamed." Syn.: 176, 273, 274, 298, 299, 338, 410, 423, 843, 2613, 2631, 2632, 2633, 2917, 2919, 2920, 3201, 3469. See: TDNT—1:714, 119; BAGD—409d; THAYER—330c.

2608. **κατάγνυμι** {4x} **katagnumi**, *kat-ag'-noo-mee;* from *2596* and the base of *4486;* to *rend in pieces,* i.e. *crack apart:*—break {4x}.

Katagnumi, (*kata,* "down", intensive), is used **(1)** of the "breaking" of a bruised reed, Mt 12:20, and **(2)** of the "breaking" of the legs of those who were crucified, Jn 19:31, 32, 33. See: BAGD—409d; THAYER—330d.

2609. **κατάγω** {10x} **katagō**, *kat-ag'-o;* from *2596* and *71;* to *lead down;* spec. to *moor* a vessel:—bring down {5x}, land {2x}, bring {1x}, bring forth {1x}, touch {1x}.

Katago, as a verb, means **(1)** "to bring down": "*Which* when the brethren knew, they brought him down (*katago*) to Caesarea, and sent him forth to Tarsus" (Acts 9:30; cf. 22:30; 23:15, 20; Rom 10:6); **(2)** "to bring forth": "And when I would have known the cause wherefore they accused him, I brought him forth (*katago*) into their council" (Acts 23:28); **(3)** of ships, "to bring to land": "And when they had brought their ships to land, they forsook all, and followed Him" (Lk 5:11); **(4)** "to land", Acts 21:3 (make land, arrive at land); and **(5)** "to touch", Acts 27:3 (to briefly land). See: BAGD—410a; THAYER—330d.

2610. **καταγωνίζομαι** {1x} **katagōnizŏmai**, *kat-ag-o-nid'-zom-ahee;* from *2596* and *75;* to *struggle against,* i.e. (by impl.) to *overcome:*—subdue {1x}.

This word means primarily, "to struggle against" (*kata,* "against," *agon,* "a contest"), came to signify "to conquer," Heb 11:33, "subdued." See: TDNT—1:134, 20; BAGD—410a; THAYER—330d.

2611. **καταδέω** {1x} **katadĕō**, *kat-ad-eh'-o;* from *2596* and *1210;* to *tie down,* i.e. *bandage* (a wound):—bind up {1x}.

Katadeo, (*kata,* "down," *deo* "to bind or tie down, or bind up"), is used in Lk 10:34 of the act of the good Samaritan: "And went to *him,* and bound up (*katadeo*) his wounds, pouring in oil and wine, and set him on his own beast, and brought him to an inn, and took care of him". The man evidently had broken bones which were "bound" in a sort of cast. See: BAGD—410b; THAYER—331a.

2612. **κατάδηλος** {1x} **katadēlŏs**, *kat-ad'-ay-los;* from *2596* intens. and *1212; manifest:*—far more evident {1x}.

Kadadelos, "quite manifest, evident, thoroughly clear, plain" is used in Heb 7:15, "more evident". See: BAGD—410b; THAYER—331a.

2613. **καταδικάζω** {5x} **katadikazō**, *kat-ad-ik-ad'-zo;* from *2596* and a der. of *1349;* to *adjudge against,* i.e. *pronounce guilty:*—condemn {5x}.

Katadikazo, as a verb, signifies "to exercise right or law against anyone"; hence, "to pronounce judgment, to condemn": "But if ye had known what *this* meaneth, I will have mercy, and not sacrifice, ye would not have condemned the guiltless" (Mt 12:7; cf. 12: 37; Lk 6:37 twice; Jas 5:6). Syn.: 176, 843, 2607, 2631, 2632, 2633, 2917, 2919, 2920. See: TDNT—3:621, 418; BAGD—410b; THAYER—331a.

2614. **καταδιώκω** {1x} **katadiōkō**, *kat-ad-ee-o'-ko;* from *2596* and *1377;* to *hunt down,* i.e. *search for:*—follow after {1x}.

Katadioko, as a verb, means "to follow up or closely," with the determination to find (*kata,* "down," intensive, giving the idea of a hard, persistent search, and *dioko* - 1377), "followed after (Him)," is said of the disciples in going to find the Lord who had gone into a desert place to pray (Mk 1:36). Syn.: 190, 1096, 1377, 1811, 1872, 2628, 3877, 4870. See: BAGD—410c; THAYER—331a.

2615. **καταδουλόω** {2x} **katadŏulŏō**, *kat-ad-oo-lŏ'-o;* from *2596* and *1402;* to *enslave utterly:*—bring into bondage {2x}. Cf. 2 Cor 11:20; Gal 2:4. See: TDNT—2:279, 182; BAGD—410c; THAYER—331b.

2616. **καταδυναστεύω** {2x} **katadunastĕuō**, *kat-ad-oo-nas-tyoo'-o;* from *2596* and a der. of *1413;* to *exercise dominion against,* i.e. *oppress:*—oppress {2x}.

This word denotes "to exercise power over" (*kata,* "down," *dunastes,* "a potentate": *dunamai* "to have power"), "to oppress," is used, **(1)** in the passive voice, in Acts 10:38; **(2)** in the active, in Jas 2:6. See: BAGD—410c; THAYER—331b.

2617. **καταισχύνω** {13x} **kataischunō**, *kat-ahee-skhoo'-no;* from *2596* and *153;* to *shame down,* i.e. *disgrace* or (by impl.)

put to the blush:—ashamed {7x}, confound {3x}, dishonour {2x}, shame {1x}.

Kataischuno, as a verb, means **(1)** "to put to shame": "What? have ye not houses to eat and to drink in? or despise ye the church of God, and shame (*kataischuno*) them that have not? What shall I say to you? shall I praise you in this? I praise *you* not" (1 Cor 11:22; cf. Lk 13:17; Rom 5:5; 9:33; 10:11; 1 Cor 11:22; 2 Cor 7:14; 9:4; 1 Pet 3:16). It is translated **(2)** "confound": "But God hath chosen the foolish things of the world to confound the wise; and God hath chosen the weak things of the world to confound the things which are mighty" (1 Cor 1:27 twice; cf. 1 Pet 2:6); "dishonour", 1 Cor 11:4, 5 Syn.: 150, 152, 181, 808, 818, 819, 1788, 1791, 3856, 4797, 4799. See: TDNT—1:189, 29; BAGD—410d; THAYER—331b.

2618. **κατακαίω** {12x} **katakaiō**, *kat-ak-ah'-ee-o;* from *2596* and *2545;* to *burn down* (to the ground), i.e. *consume wholly:*—burn {7x}, burn up {4x}, burn utterly {1x}.

Katakaio, signifies "to burn up, burn utterly," as of **(1)** chaff, Mt 3:12; Lk 3:17; **(2)** tares, Mt 13:30, 40; **(3)** the earth and its works, 2 Pet 3:10; **(4)** trees and grass, Rev 8:7 twice. **(5)** This form should be noted in Acts 19:19; 1 Cor 3:15; Heb 13:11, Rev 17:16. In each place the full rendering "burn utterly" might be used, as in Rev 18:8. See: BAGD—411a; THAYER—331c.

2619. **κατακαλύπτω** {3x} **katakaluptō**, *kat-ak-al-oop'-to;* from *2596* and *2572;* to *cover wholly,* i.e. *veil:*—cover {3x}.

In 1 Cor 11:4 "having his head covered" is, lit., "having (something) down the head" signifying that hair that hangs down is too long for a man, and consequently hair that does not hang down on a woman is too short. See: TDNT—3:561, 405; BAGD—411a; THAYER—331c.

2620. **κατακαυχάομαι** {4x} **katakauchaŏmai**, *kat-ak-ŏw-khah'-om-ahee;* from *2596* and *2744;* to *exult against* (i.e. *over*):—boast {1x}, boast against {1x}, glory {1x}, rejoice against {1x}.

(1) This word means to glory against, to exult over, to boast one's self to the injury of a person. **(2)** It signifies **(2a)** "to boast against, exult over," Rom 11:18 twice; **(2b)** "rejoiceth against" Jas. 2:13; **(2c)** Jas 3:14, "glory (not)." See: TDNT—3:653, 423; BAGD—411b; THAYER—331c.

2621. **κατάκειμαι** {11x} **katakĕimai**, *kat-ak'-i-mahee;* from *2596* and *2749;* to *lie down,* i.e. (by impl.) *be sick;* spec. to *recline* at a meal:—lie {6x}, sit at meat {3x}, keep {1x}, sat down + 2258 {1x}.

Katakeimai, as a verb, means "to lie down" and is used **(1)** of "reclining at a meal", Mk 2:15; 14:3; Lk 5:29; 1 Cor 8:10; **(2)** "to lie down" is used of the sick, Mk 1:30; 2:4; Lk 5:25; Jn 5:3, 6; Acts 28:8; **(3)** in Acts 9:33 it is rendered "had kept (his bed)," lit., "lying (on a bed)." Syn.: 339, 345, 347, 377, 1910, 2516, 2521, 2523, 2625, 4775, 4776, 4873. See: TDNT—3:655, 425; BAGD—411c; THAYER—331a.

2622. **κατακλάω** {2x} **kataklaō**, *kat-ak-lah'-o;* from *2596* and *2806;* to *break down,* i.e. *divide into pieces:*—break {2x}.

Kataklao is used in Mk 6:41 and Lk 9:16, of Christ's "breaking" loaves for the multitudes. See: BAGD—411c; THAYER—331d.

2623. **κατακλείω** {2x} **kataklĕiō**, *kat-ak-li'-o;* from *2596* and *2808;* to *shut down* (in a dungeon), i.e. *incarcerate:*—shut up {2x}.

Kartakleio, lit., to shut down" (the *kata* has, however, an intensive use; cf. Eng. "lock down"), signifies "to shut up in confinement," Lk 3:20; Acts 26:10. See: BAGD—411c; THAYER—331d.

2624. **κατακληροδοτέω** {1x} **kataklērŏdŏtĕō**, *kat-ak-lay-rod-ot-eh'-o;* from *2596* and a der. of a compound of *2819* and *1325;* to *be a giver of lots to each,* i.e. (by impl.) to *apportion an estate:*—divide by lot {1x}. See: BAGD—411d; THAYER—331d.

2625. **κατακλίνω** {3x} **kataklinō**, *kat-ak-lee'-no;* from *2596* and *2827;* to *recline down,* i.e. (spec.) to *take a place* at table:—sit down {1x}, sit at meat {1x}, make sit down {1x}.

Kataklino, as a verb, is used only in connection with meals **(1)** in the active voice, "to make recline": "For they were about five thousand men. And He said to His disciples, Make them sit down by fifties in a company" (Lk 9:14); **(2)** in the passive voice, "to recline, sat down to meat": "When thou art bidden of any *man* to a wedding, sit not down (*kakaklino*) in the highest room; lest a more honourable man than thou be bidden of him" (Lk 14:8; cf. 24:30). Syn.: 339, 345, 347, 377, 1910, 2516, 2521, 2621, 2523, 4775, 4776, 4873. See: BAGD—411d; THAYER—332a.

2626. **κατακλύζω** {1x} **katakluzō**, *kat-ak-lood'-zo;* from *2596* and the base of *2830;* to *dash* (*wash*) *down,* i.e. (by impl.) to *deluge:*—overflow {1x}.

Katakluzo, "to inundate, to submerge, deluge, overwhelm with water" (*kata,* "down," *kluzo,* "to wash" or "dash over," said, e.g., of the sea), is used in the passive voice in 2 Pet 3:6, of the Flood. See: BAGD—411d; THAYER—332a.

2627. **κατακλυσμός** {4x} **kataklusmŏs**, *kat-ak-looce-mos';* from *2626;* an *inundation:*—flood {4x}.

This word is used of the "flood" in Noah's time, Mt 24:38, 39; Lk 17:27; 2 Pet 2:5; 2 Pet 3:6. See: BAGD—411d; THAYER—332a.

2628. **κατακολουθέω** {2x} **katakŏlŏuthĕō**, *kat-ak-ol-oo-theh'-o;* from *2596* and *190;* to *accompany closely:*—follow {1x}, follow after {1x}.

Katakoloutheo, as a verb, means "to follow behind or intently after" and is used **(1)** of the women on their way to Christ's tomb (Lk 23:55); **(2)** of the demon-possessed maid in Philippi in "following" the missionaries (Acts 16:17). Syn.: 190, 1096, 1377, 1811, 1872, 2614, 3877, 4870. See: BAGD—412a; THAYER—332b.

2629. **κατακόπτω** {1x} **katakŏptō**, *kat-ak-op'-to;* from *2596* and *2875;* to *chop down,* i.e. *mangle:*—cut {1x}.

Katakopto, lit., to cut down, cut in pieces" (*kata,* "down," intensive), Mk 5:5, of the devil possessed man, who had many deep wounds/cuts from stumbling among the sharp stones of the graveyard. See: BAGD—412a; THAYER—332b.

2630. **κατακρημνίζω** {1x} **katakrēmnizō**, *kat-ak-rame-nid'-zo;* from *2596* and a der. of *2911;* to *precipitate down:*—cast down headlong {1x}.

Katakremnizo signifies "to throw over a precipice" (*kata,* "down," *kremnos,* "a steep bank," etc.), said of the purpose of the people of Nazareth to destroy Christ, Lk 4:29. See: BAGD—412a; THAYER—332b.

2631. **κατάκριμα** {3x} **katakrima**, *kat-ak'-ree-mah;* from *2632;* an *adverse sentence* (the verdict):—condemnation {3x}.

Katakrima, as a noun, is "the sentence pronounced, the condemnation" with a suggestion of the punishment following: "And not as *it was* by one that sinned, *so is* the gift: for the judgment *was* by one to condemnation (*katakrima*), but the free gift *is* of many offences unto justification" (Rom 5:16; cf. 5:18; 8:1). Syn.: 176, 843, 2607, 2613, 2632, 2633, 2917, 2919, 2920. See: TDNT—3:951, 469; BAGD—412a; THAYER—332b.

2632. **κατακρίνω** {19x} **katakrinō**, *kat-ak-ree'-no;* from *2596* and *2919;* to *judge against,* i.e. *sentence:*—condemn {17x}, damn {2x}.

Katakrino, as a verb, **(1)** signifies "to give judgment against, pass sentence upon"; hence, "to condemn," implying **(1a)** the fact of a crime (Rom 2:1; 14:23; 2 Pet 2:6); **(1b)** the imputation of a crime, as in the "condemnation" of Christ by the Jews (Mt 20:18; Mk 14:64). **(2)** It is used metaphorically of "condemning" by a good example: "The men of Nineveh shall rise in judgment with this generation, and shall condemn it: because they repented at the preaching of Jonas; and, behold, a greater than Jonas *is* here. 42 The queen of the south shall rise up in the judgment with this generation, and shall condemn it: for she came from the uttermost parts of the earth to hear the wisdom of Solomon; and, behold, a greater than Solomon *is* here" (Mt 12:41–42; cf. Lk 11:31–32; Heb 11:7). **(3)** In Rom 8:3, God's "condemnation" of sin is set forth in that Christ, His own Son, sent by Him to partake of human nature (sin apart) and to become an offering for sin, died under the judgment due to our sin. Syn.: 176, 843, 2607, 2613, 2631, 2633, 2917, 2919, 2920. See: TDNT—3:951, 469; BAGD—412a; THAYER—332b.

2633. **κατάκρισις** {2x} **katakrisis**, *kat-ak'-ree-sis;* from *2632; sentencing adversely* (the act):—condemn {1x}, condemnation {1x}.

Katakrisis, as a noun, denotes "a judgment against, condemnation," with the suggestion of the process leading to it, as **(1)** of "the ministration of condemnation" (2 Cor 3:9); **(2)** in 2 Cor 7:3 "to condemn," more lit., "with a view to condemnation." Syn.: 176, 843, 2607, 2613, 2631, 2632, 2917, 2919, 2920. See: TDNT—3:951, 469; BAGD—332c; THAYER—332c.

2634. **κατακυριεύω** {4x} **katakuriĕuō**, *kat-ak-oo-ree-yoo'-o;* from *2596* and *2961;* to *lord against,* i.e. *control, subjugate:*—exercise dominion over {1x}, overcome {1x}, be lord over {1x}, exercise lordship over {1x}.

Katakurieul, "to exercise, or gain, dominion over, to lord it over," is used of **(1)** the "lordship" of Gentile rulers, Mt 20:25, "exercise dominion"; **(2)** Mk 10:42, "exercise lordship over"; **(3)** the power of devils over men, Acts 19:16, "overcame"; **(4)** of the evil of elders in "lording" it over the saints under their spiritual care, 1 Pet 5:3. See: TDNT—3:1098, 486; BAGD—412c; THAYER—332c.

2635. **καταλαλέω** {5x} **katalalĕō**, *kat-al-al-eh'-o;* from *2637;* to *be a traducer,* i.e. to *slander:*—speak against {1x}, speak evil of {4x}.

This word means to speak against one, to criminate, and is translated **(1)** "speak against", 1 Pet 2:12; 3:16; and **(2)** "speak evil of", Jas 4:1 thrice. See: TDNT—4:3, 495; BAGD—412c; THAYER—332c.

2636. **καταλαλιά** {2x} **katalalia**, *kat-al-al-ee'-ah;* from *2637; defamation:*—backbiting {1x}, evil speaking {1x}.

Katalalia is translated **(1)** "evil speaking" in 1 Pet 2:1; **(2)** "backbiting" in 2 Cor 12:20. See: TDNT—4:3, 495; BAGD—412d; THAYER—332d.

2637. **κατάλαλος** {1x} **katalalŏs**, *kat-al'-al-os;* from *2596* and the base of *2980; talkative against,* i.e. a *slanderer:*—backbiter {1x}. See: TDNT—4:3, 495; BAGD—412d; THAYER—332d.

2638. **καταλαμβάνω** {15x} **katalambanō**, *kat-al-am-ban'-o;* from *2596* and *2983;* to *take eagerly,* i.e. *seize, possess,* etc. (lit. or fig.):—take {3x}, apprehend {3x}, comprehend {2x}, come upon {1x}, attain {1x}, find {1x}, overtake {1x}, obtain {1x}.

Katalambano properly signifies to lay hold of; then, to lay hold of so as to possess as one's own, to appropriate. Hence it has the twofold meaning of to apprehend: **(1)** to seize upon, take possession of **(1a)** with a beneficial effect **(1a1)** laying hold of the righteousness which is of faith (Rom 9:30 - not there a matter of attainment, but of appropriation); **(1a2)** of the obtaining of a prize (1 Cor 9:24); **(1a3)** of the apostle's desire to apprehend, or lay hold of that for which he was apprehended by Christ (Phil 3:12–13); **(1b)** with a detrimental effect **(1b1)** of demon power (Mk 9:18); **(1b2)** of human action in seizing upon a person (Jn 8:3–4); **(1b3)** metaphorically, with the added idea of overtaking, **(1b3a)** of spiritual darkness in coming upon people (Jn 12:35); **(1b3b)** of the Day of the Lord, in suddenly coming upon unbelievers as a thief (1 Th 5:4); **(2)** to lay hold of with the mind, to understand, perceive **(2a)** metaphorically, **(2a1)** of darkness with regard to light (Jn 1:5); **(2a2)** of mental perception (Acts 4:13; 10:34; 25:25; Eph 3:18). Syn.: 4084. See: TDNT—4:9, 495; BAGD—412d; THAYER—332d.

2639. **καταλέγω** {1x} **katalĕgō**, *kat-al-eg'-o;* from *2596* and *3004* (in its orig. mean.); to *lay down,* i.e. (fig.) to *enroll:*—take into the number {1x}. See: BAGD—413b; THAYER—333a.

2640. **κατάλειμμα** {1x} **katalĕimma**, *kat-al'-ime-mah;* from *2641;* a *remainder,* i.e. (by impl.) a *few:*—remnant {1x}. See: TDNT—4:194, 523; BAGD—413c; THAYER—333a.

2641. **καταλείπω** {25x} **katalĕipō**, *kat-al-i'-po;* from *2596* and *3007;* to *leave down,* i.e. *behind;* by impl. to *abandon, have remaining:*—forsake {2x}, leave {22x}, reserve {1x}.

(1) This word usually denotes to forsake, to purposely leave a person or thing by ceasing to care for it, to abandon, leave in the lurch. *Kataleipo,* a strengthened form of *leipo,* signifies **(2)** "to leave", **(2a)** "to leave behind", e.g., Mt 4:13; **(2b)** "to leave remaining, reserve", e.g., Lk 10:40; **(2c)** "to leave," in the sense of "abandoning", Mk 10:7; 14:52; Lk 15:4; Eph 5:31; **(3)** "to forsake," in the sense of abandoning, in Heb 11:27; 2 Pet. 2:15; **(4)** "reserved", in the sense of permanently set aside; left, Rom 11:4. See: TDNT—4:194, 523; BAGD—413c; THAYER—333a.

2642. **καταλιθάζω** {1x} **katalithazō**, *kat-al-ith-ad'-zo;* from *2596* and *3034;* to *stone down,* i.e. *to death:*—stone {1x}.

Katalithazo, an intensive form of lithazo, "to cast stones at, overwhelm with stones" occurs in Lk 20:6. See: TDNT—4:267, 533; BAGD—413d; THAYER—333b.

2643. **καταλλαγή** {4x} **katallagē**, *kat-al-lag-ay';* from *2644; exchange* (fig. *adjustment*), i.e. *restoration* to (the divine) favor:—atonement {1x}, reconciliation {2x}, reconciling {1x}.

(1) This word denotes an adjustment of a difference, reconciliation, restoration to favour, especially the restoration of the favour of God to sinners that repent and put their trust in the expiatory/propitiatory death of Christ. Man changes and is reconciled. God does not change. **(2)** It is translated **(2a)** "atonement" in Rom 5:11, signifying that sinners are made "at one" with God; and in the NT so much more is given the believer in Christ; **(2b)** "reconciliation" 2 Cor 5:18, 19; **(2c)** "reconciling", Rom 11:15. **(3)** Man receives Christ as his Saviour, he is reconciled, has received the reconciliation, and is "at one" with God. Reconciliation stresses the process, atonement stresses the end result of the process. Syn.: *Hilasmos* (2434), [expiation and propitiation] and *apolytrosis* (629) have fundamentally a single benefit—namely, the restitution of a lost sinner. It is *apoltrosis* in reference to an enemy, and *katallage* in respect to God. And here these terms *hilasmos* and *katallage,* again differ. *Hilasmos* (propitiation) removes an offense against God; *katallage* (reconciliation) has two fronts and removes (a) God's displeasure toward us (2 Cor 5:19) and (b) our alienation from God (2 Cor 5:20). See: TDNT—1:258, 40; BAGD—414a; THAYER—333b.

2644. **καταλλάσσω** {6x} **katallassō**, *kat-al-las'-so;* from *2596* and *236;* to *change mutually,* i.e. (fig.) to *compound* a difference:—reconcile {6x}.

Katallasso properly denotes **(1)** to change, exchange; hence, of persons, to change from enmity to friendship, to reconcile. **(2)** With regard to the relationship between God and man, **(2a)** reconciliation is what God accomplishes, **(2a1)** exercising His grace towards sinful man **(2a2)** on the ground of the death of Christ in propitiatory sacrifice under the judgment due to sin (2 Cor. 5:18–20). **(2b)** By reason of this **(2b1)** men in their sinful condition and alienation from God **(2b2)** are invited to be reconciled to Him; that is to say, to change their attitude, and accept the provision God has made, **(2b3)** whereby their sins can be remitted and they themselves be justified in His sight in Christ. **(2c)** What we do receive is the result, namely, reconciliation.

(3) The removal of God's wrath does not contravene His immutability. **(3a)** He always acts according to His unchanging righteousness and lovingkindness, and **(3b)** it is because He changes not that His relative attitude does change towards those who change. **(4)** Not once is God said to be reconciled. **(4a)** The enmity is alone on our part. **(4b)** It was we who needed to be reconciled to God, not God to us, and **(4c)** it is propitiation, which His righteousness and mercy have provided, that makes the reconciliation possible to those who receive it. **(5)** The hostility is not on the part of God, but of man. Syn.: 604, 1259, 2643. *Diallasso* (1259 - only in Mt 5:24) is never used in this connection, but always *katallasso,* because the former word denotes mutual concession after mutual hostility, an idea absent from *katallasso.* See: TDNT—1:254, 40; BAGD—414a; THAYER—333c.

2645. **κατάλοιπος** {1x} **katalŏipŏs**, *kat-al'-oy-pos;* from *2596* and *3062; left down* (*behind*), i.e. *remaining* (plur. the *rest*):—residue {1x}.

Kataloipos, an adjective denoting "left remaining" (*kata,* "after, behind," *leipo,* "to leave"), is translated "residue" in Acts 15:17, cf. Amos 9:12. See: BAGD—414b; THAYER—333d.

2646. **κατάλυμα** {3x} **kataluma**, *kat-al'-oo-mah;* from *2647;* prop. a *dissolution* (breaking up of a journey), i.e. (by impl.) a *lodging-place:*—guest chamber {2x}, inn {1x}.

Kataluma signifies **(1)** an inn, lodging-place (Lk 2:7); or **(2)** a guest-room (Mk 14:14; Lk 22:11). The word lit. signifies a loosening down, used of the place where travelers and their beasts untied their packages, belts and sandals. See: TDNT—4:338, 543; BAGD—414b; THAYER—333d.

2647. **καταλύω** {17x} **kataluō**, *kat-al-oo'-o;* from *2596* and *3089;* to *loosen down* (*disintegrate*), i.e. (by impl.) to *demolish* (lit. or fig.); spec. [comp. *2646*] to *halt* for the night:—destroy {9x}, throw down {3x}, lodge {1x}, guest {1x}, come to nought {1x}, overthrow {1x}, dissolve {1x}.

Kataluo, "to destroy utterly, to overthrow completely," is rendered **(1)** "destroy," **(1a)** the Law, in Mt 5:17, twice; **(1b)** the Temple, in Mt 26:61; 27:40; Mk 13:2; 14:58; 15:29; Lk 21:6; **(1c)** Jerusalem, (temple only) in Acts 6:14; **(1d)** the Law as a means of justification, in Gal 2:18; **(1e)** in Rom 14:20, of the marring of a person's spiritual well-being; **(1f)** in Acts 5:38 and 39 of the failure of purposes; **(1g)** in 2 Cor 5:1, of the death of the body ("dissolved"). It is also translated **(2)** "throw down", Mt 24:2; Mk 13:2; **(3)** "lodge", Lk 9:12, of a traveler "throwing down" his luggage; **(4)** "guest", Lk 19:7, one who has "thrown down" his luggage in a lodge; **(5)** "come to nought", Acts 5:38; **(6)** "overthrow", Acts 5:39; and **(7)** "dissolve", 2 Cor 5:1, the earthly body. See: TDNT—4:338, 543; BAGD—414b; THAYER—334a.

2648. **καταμανθάνω** {1x} **katamanthanō**, *kat-am-an-than'-o;* from *2596* and *3129;* to *learn thoroughly,* i.e. (by impl.) to *note carefully:*—consider {1x}.

This word means to note accurately, consider well, to learn thoroughly through careful examination (Mt 6:28). See: TDNT—4:414, 552; BAGD—414d; THAYER—334b.

2649. **καταμαρτυρέω** {4x} **katamarturĕō**, *kat-am-ar-too-reh'-o;* from *2596* and *3140;* to *testify against:*—witness against {4x}.

Katamartureo, as a verb, denotes "to witness against": "And the high priest arose, and said unto Him, Answerest thou nothing? what *is it which* these witness against thee?" (Mt 26:62; cf. 27:13; Mk 14:60; 15:4). Syn.: 267, 3140, 3141, 3142, 3143, 3144, 4828, 4901, 5571, 5576, 5577. See: TDNT—4:508, 564; BAGD—414d; THAYER—334b.

2650. **καταμένω** {1x} **katamĕnō**, *kat-am-en'-o;* from *2596* and *3306;* to *stay fully,* i.e. *reside:*—abide + 2258 {1x}.

Katameno is used in Acts 1:13 and may signify "constant residence," but more probably indicates "frequent resort." See: BAGD—414d; THAYER—334b.

2651. **καταμόνας** {2x} **katamŏnas**, *kat-am-on'-as;* from *2596* and acc. plur. fem. of *3441* (with *5561* impl.); *according to sole* places, i.e. (adv.) *separately:*—alone {2x}.

Katamonas signifies apart, in private, alone (Mk 4:10; Lk 9:18). See: BAGD—414d; THAYER—334b.

2652. **κατανάθεμα** {1x} **katanathĕma**, *kat-an-ath'-em-ah;* from *2596* (intens.) and *331;* an *imprecation:*—a curse {1x}.

Katathema, as a noun, is stronger than *anathema* (331), and denotes, by metonymy, "an accursed thing" (the object "cursed" being put for the "curse" pronounced): "And there shall be no more curse: but the throne of God and of the

Lamb shall be in it; and His servants shall serve Him:"(Rev 22:3). Syn.: 331, 332, 685, 1944, 2552, 2653, 2671, 2672.See: TDNT—1:354,*; BAGD—414d; THAYER—334b.

2653. **καταναθεματίζω** {1x} **katanathĕmatizō,** *kat-an-ath-em-at-id'-zo;* from *2596* (intens.) and *332;* to *imprecate:*—to curse {1x}.

Katanathematizo, a strengthened form of *anathematizo* (332), as a verb, denotes "to utter curses against": "Then began he [Peter] to curse and to swear, *saying,* I know not the man." (Mt 26:74). Syn.: 331, 332, 685, 1944, 2551, 2652, 2671, 2672. See: TDNT—1:355,*; BAGD—414d; THAYER—334b.

2654. **καταναλίσκω** {1x} **katanaliskō,** *kat-an-al-is'-ko;* from *2596* and *355;* to *consume utterly:*—consume {1x}.

Katanalisko, "to consume utterly, wholly" (*kata,* intensive), is said, in Heb 12:29, of God as "a consuming fire." See: BAGD—414d; THAYER—334b.

2655. **καταναρκάω** {3x} **katanarkaō,** *kat-an-ar-kah'-o;* from *2596* and *ναρκάω* **narkaō** (to *be numb*); to *grow utterly torpid,* i.e. (by impl.) *slothful* (fig. *expensive*):—be burdensome {2x}, be chargeable {1x}.

This word means to be a burden, to be burdensome, primarily signifying to be numbed or torpid, to grow stiff (*narke* is the torpedo or cramp fish, which benumbs anyone who touches it); hence, to be idle to the detriment of another person, like a useless limb. It is translated **(1)** "be chargeable", 2 Cor 11:9; and **(2)** "be burdensome", 2 Cor 12:13–14. See: BAGD—414d; THAYER—334b.

2656. **κατανεύω** {1x} **katanĕuō,** *kat-an-yoo'-o;* from *2596* and *3506;* to *nod down* (*toward*), i.e. (by anal.) to *make signs* to:—beckon {1x}.

Kataneuo means to nod to, make a sign, to indicate to another by a nod and is used of the fishermen-partners in Lk 5:7, as they held the full nets with both hands they beckoned with frantic nods of their heads for their friends to assist them. See: BAGD—415a; THAYER—334c.

2657. **κατανοέω** {14x} **katanŏĕō,** *kat-an-o-eh'-o;* from *2596* and *3539;* to *observe fully:*—behold {4x}, consider {7x}, discover {1x}, perceive {2x}.

Katanoeo, as a verb, a strengthened form of *noeo,* "to perceive, understand fully, consider closely" (*kata,* intensive), denotes "the action of the mind in apprehending certain facts about a thing"; hence, translated **(1)** "behold," Acts 7:31–32; Jas 1:23–24; **(2)** "consider" **(2a)** the beam in one's own eye, Mt 7:3; **(2b)** of carefully "considering" the ravens, Lk 12:24; **(2c)** the lilies, Lk 12:27; **(2d)** of Peter's full "consideration" of his vision, Acts 11:6; **(2e)** of Abraham's careful "considering" of his own body, and Sarah's womb, as dead, and yet accepting by faith God's promise, Rom. 4:19; **(2f)** of "considering" fully the Apostle and High Priest of our confession, Heb. 3:1; **(2g)** of thoughtfully "considering" one another to provoke unto love and good works, Heb. 10:24; **(3)** "discover," Acts 27:39; **(4)** "perceive," **(4a)** the beam in one's eye, Lk 6:41; **(4b)** of Jesus' perceiving the chief priests' craftiness, Lk 20:23. Syn.: 333, 816, 991, 1689, 1896, 2029, 2300, 2334, 2734, 3708. See: TDNT—4:973, 636; BAGD—415a; THAYER—334c.

2658. **καταντάω** {13x} **katantaō,** *kat-an-tah'-o;* from *2596* and a der. of *473;* to *meet against,* i.e. *arrive* at (lit. or fig.):—attain {2x}, come {11x}.

Katantao, "to come to, arrive at", is translated **(1)** "to come", **(1a)** literally, of locality, Acts 16:1;18:19, 24; 20:15; 21:7; 25:13; 26:7; 28:13; **(1b)** metaphorically, **(1b1)** in 1 Cor 10:11 "upon whom the ends of the world are come", the metaphor is apparently that of an inheritance as coming down or descending to an heir, the "ends" (*tele* being the spiritual revenues (cf. Mt 17:25, revenues derived from taxes, and Rom. 13:7, where the singular, *telos,* "custom," is used); the inheritance metaphor is again seen in 1 Cor 14:36, of the coming (or descending) of the Word of God to the Corinthians; and **(1b2)** to come in the sense of attain, Eph 4:13, of "attaining" to the unity of the faith and of the knowledge of the Son of God. It is also translated **(2)** "to attain", in the sense of arriving completely at, **(2a)** in Acts 27:12, to the city of Phinece; **(2b)** Phil 3:11, of the paramount aims of the apostle's life, "if by any means," he says, "I might attain unto the resurrection from the dead," not the physical resurrection, which is assured to all believers hereafter, but to the present life of identification with Christ in His resurrection. See: TDNT—3:623, 419; BAGD—415d; THAYER—334c.

2659. **κατάνυξις** {1x} **katanuxis,** *kat-an'-oox-is;* from *2660;* a *prickling* (sensation, as of the limbs *asleep*), i.e. (by impl. [perh. by some confusion with *3506* or even with *3571*]) *stupor* (*lethargy*):—slumber {1x}.

Katanuxis, literally means "a pricking" (akin to *katanusso,* "to strike" or "prick violently," Acts 2:37), and is used in Rom. 11:8, "slumber." This word describes the prickly, numb, tingling feeling one has when a limb [hand, foot, leg, etc.] "falls asleep." In the Jews' case their eyes and ears slumber. The Jews are still "wide awake" but their abilities to respond through their eyes and ears is hampered by "being asleep, slumbering, a deep sleep." See: TDNT—3:626, 419; BAGD—415c; THAYER—334d.

2660. **κατανύσσω** {1x} **katanussō,** *kat-an-oos'-so;* from *2596* and *3572;* to *pierce thoroughly,* i.e. (fig.) to *agitate* violently ("sting to the quick"):—prick {1x}.

Katanusso, primarily, "to strike or prick violently, to stun," is used of strong emotion, in Acts 2:37 (passive voice), "they were pricked (in their heart)." See: TDNT—3:626, 419; BAGD—415c; THAYER—334d.

2661. **καταξιόω** {4x} **kataxiŏō,** *kat-ax-ee-ŏ'-o;* from *2596* and *515;* to *deem entirely deserving:*—account worthy {2x}, count worthy {2x}.

Kataxioo denotes "to account worthy" (*kata,* "intensive," *axios,* "worthy"), "to judge, account worthy," Lk 20:35; 21:36; Acts 5:41; 2 Th 1:5. See: TDNT—1:380, 63; BAGD—415c; THAYER—335a.

2662. **καταπατέω** {5x} **katapatĕō,** *kat-ap-at-eh'-o;* from *2596* and *3961;* to *trample down;* fig. to *reject* with disdain:—trample {1x}, tread down {1x}, tread underfoot {2x}, tread {1x}.

Katapateo, "to tread down, trample under foot," is used **(1)** literally, Mt 5:13; 7:6; Lk 8:5; 12:1; **(2)** metaphorically, of "treading under foot" the Son of God, Heb 10:29, i.e., turning away from Him, to indulge in willful sin. See: TDNT—5:940, 804; BAGD—415d; THAYER—335a.

2663. **κατάπαυσις** {9x} **katapausis,** *kat-ap'-ow-sis;* from *2664;* *reposing down,* i.e. (by Heb.) *abode:*—rest {9x}.

Katapausis, "rest, repose"; is used **(1)** of God's "rest," Acts 7:49; Heb 3:11, 18; 4:1, 3 (twice), 5, 11; **(2)** in a general statement, applicable to God and man, Heb 4:10. **(3)** God's rest is entered when the believer is confidently assured within and outwardly lives peaceably in the assurance of God's daily provisions. See: TDNT—3:628, 419; BAGD—415d; THAYER—335a.

2664. **καταπαύω** {4x} **katapauō,** *kat-ap-ŏw'-o;* from *2596* and *3973;* to *settle down,* i.e. (lit.) to *colonize,* or (fig.) to (*cause to*) *desist:*—cease {1x}, give rest {1x}, rest {1x}, restrain {1x}.

Katapauo, signifies "to cause to cease, restrain", and is translated **(1)** "restrained in Acts 14:18; **(2)** "rest" in Heb 4:4; **(2)** "give rest" in Heb 4:8; and **(3)** intransitively, "ceased" in Heb 4:10. See: TDNT—3:627, 419; BAGD—416a; THAYER—334b.

2665. **καταπέτασμα** {6x} **katapĕtasma,** *kat-ap-et'-as-mah;* from a compound of *2596* and a congener of *4072;* something *spread thoroughly,* i.e. (spec.) the door *screen* (to the Most Holy Place) in the Jewish Temple:—veil {6x}.

Katapetasma, lit., "that which is spread out" (*petannumi*) "before" (*kata*), hence, "a veil," is used **(1)** of the inner "veil" of the tabernacle, Heb 6:19; 9:3; **(2)** of the corresponding "veil" in the Temple, Mt 27:51; Mk 15:38; Lk 23:45; **(3)** metaphorically of the "flesh" of Christ, Heb 10:20, i.e., His body which He gave up to be crucified, thus by His expiatory death providing a means of the spiritual access of believers, the "new and living way," into the presence of God. See: TDNT—3:628, 420; BAGD—416b; THAYER—335b.

2666. **καταπίνω** {7x} **katapinō,** *kat-ap-ee'-no;* from *2596* and *4095;* to *drink down,* i.e. *gulp entire* (lit. or fig.):—devour {1x}, drown {1x}, swallow {4x}, swallow up {1x}.

Katapino, from *kato,* "down," intensive, *pino,* "to drink," **(1)** in 1 Pet 5:8 is translated "devour," of Satan's activities against believers. **(2)** The meaning "to swallow" is found in Mt 23:24; 1 Cor 15:54; 2 Cor 2:7; 5:4; Heb 11:29; Rev 12:16. See: TDNT—6:158, 841; BAGD—416b; THAYER—335c.

2667. **καταπίπτω** {2x} **katapiptō,** *kat-ap-ip'-to;* from *2596* and *4098;* to *fall down:*—fall {1x}, fall down {1x}. Cf. Acts 26:14; 28:6. See: TDNT—6:169, 846; BAGD—416c; THAYER—335d.

2668. **καταπλέω** {1x} **kataplĕō,** *kat-ap-leh'-o;* from *2596* and *4126;* to *sail down from the high seas* upon a place, i.e. to *land* at:—arrive {1x}.

Katapleo denotes "to sail down" (*kata,* "down," *pleo,* "to sail"), i.e., from the high sea to the shore, Lk 8:26. See: BAGD—416d; THAYER—335d.

2669. **καταπονέω** {2x} **katapŏnĕō,** *kat-ap-on-eh'-o;* from *2596* and a der. of *4192;* to *labor down,* i.e. *wear with toil* (fig. *harass*):—oppress {1x}, vex {1x}.

Kataponeo, as a verb, means primarily, **(1)** "to tire down with toil, exhaust with labor" [*kata,* "down," *ponos,* "labor"], hence signifies **(1a)** "to afflict, oppress"; **(1b)** in the passive voice, "to be oppressed, much distressed." **(2)** It is translated **(2a)** "oppressed": "And seeing one *of them* suffer wrong, he (Moses) defended *him,* and avenged him that was oppressed, and smote the Egyptian" (Acts 7:24), and **(2b)** "sore distressed/vexed": "And delivered just Lot, vexed with the filthy conversation of the wicked" (2 Pet 2:7). Syn.: 318, 928, 2347, 4660, 4729, 4730, 4928. See: BAGD—416d; THAYER—335d.

2670. **καταποντίζω** {2x} **katapŏntizō**, *kat-ap-on-tid'-zo;* from *2596* and a der. of the same as *4195;* to *plunge down,* i.e. *submerge:*—drown {1x}, sink {1x}.

Katapontizo, "to throw into the sea" (*kata,* "down," *pontos,* "the open sea"), in the passive voice, "to be sunk in, to be drowned," is translated **(1)** "were drowned," in Mt 18:6; and in **(2)** Mt 14:30, "(beginning) to sink." See: BAGD—417a; THAYER—335d.

2671. **κατάρα** {6x} **katara**, *kat-ar'-ah;* from *2596* (intens.) and *685; imprecation, execration:*—curse {3x}, cursed {2x}, cursing {1x}.

Katara, (*kata,* "down," intensive), denotes **(1)** an "execration, imprecation, curse," uttered out of malevolence, Jas 3:10; 2 Pet 2:14; or **(2)** pronounced by God in His righteous judgment, as upon a land doomed to barrenness, Heb 6:8; **(3)** upon those who seek for justification by obedience, in part or completely, to the Law, Gal 3:10, 13; in this 13th verse it is used concretely of Christ, as having "become a curse" for us, i.e., by voluntarily undergoing on the cross the appointed penalty of the "curse." He thus was identified, on our behalf, with the doom of sin. See: TDNT—1:449, 75; BAGD—417a; THAYER—335d.

2672. **καταράομαι** {6x} **kataraŏmai**, *kat-ar-ah'-om-ahee;* mid. voice from *2671;* to *execrate;* by anal. to *doom:*—curse {6x}.

Kataraomai, as a verb, primarily signifies "to pray against, to wish evil against a person or thing"; hence "to curse": "Then shall he say also unto them on the left hand, Depart from me, ye cursed, into everlasting fire, prepared for the devil and his angels:" (Mt 25:41; cf. Mk 11:21; Lk 6:28; Rom 12:14; Jas 3:9). Syn.: 331, 332, 685, 1944, 2551, 2652, 2653, 2671. See: TDNT—1:448, 75; BAGD—417a; THAYER—336a.

2673. **καταργέω** {27x} **katargĕō**, *kat-arg-eh'-o;* from *2596* and *691;* to *be* (*render*) *entirely* idle (*useless*), lit. or fig.:—destroy {5x}, do away {3x}, abolish {3x}, cumber {1x}, loose {1x}, cease {1x}, fall {1x}, deliver {1x}, misc. {11x} = become (make) of no (none, without) effect, bring (come) to nought, put away (down), vanish away, make void.

Katargeo, as a verb, means lit., "to reduce to inactivity" (*kata,* "down," *argos,* "inactive"), is translated **(1)** "abolish" in Eph 2:15; 2 Ti 1:10; 2 Cor 3:13. In this and similar words not loss of being is implied, but loss of well being. **(1a)** The barren tree was cumbering the ground, making it useless for the purpose of its existence, Lk 13:7; **(1b)** the unbelief of the Jews could not "make of none effect" the faithfulness of God, Rom. 3:3; **(1c)** the preaching of the gospel could not "make of none effect" the moral enactments of the Law, Rom 3:31; **(1d)** the Law could not make the promise of "none effect," Rom 4:14; Gal 3:17; **(1e)** the effect of the identification of the believer with Christ in His death is to render inactive his body in regard to sin, Rom 6:6; **(1f)** the death of a woman's first husband discharges her from the law of the husband, that is, it makes void her status as his wife in the eyes of the law, Rom 7:2; **(1g)** in that sense the believer has been discharged from the Law, Rom 7:6; **(1h)** God has chosen things that are not "to bring to nought things that are," i.e., to render them useless for practical purposes, 1 Cor 1:28; **(1i)** the princes of this world are "brought to nought," i.e., their wisdom becomes ineffective, Rom 2:6; **(1j)** the use for which the human stomach exists ceases with man's death, Rom 6:13; **(1k)** knowledge, prophesyings, and that which was in part were to be "done away," 1 Cor 13:8, 10, i.e., they were to be rendered of no effect after their temporary use was fulfilled; **(1l)** when the apostle became a man he did away with the ways of a child, 1 Cor 13:11; **(1m)** God is going to abolish all rule and authority and power, i.e., He is going to render them inactive, 1 Cor 15:24; **(1n)** the last enemy that shall be abolished, or reduced to inactivity, is death, 1 Cor 15: 26; **(1o)** the glory shining in the face of Moses, "was passing away," 2 Cor 3:7, **(1p)** the transitoriness of its character being of a special significance; 2 Cor 3:11, 13; **(1q)** the veil upon the heart of Israel is "done away" in Christ, 2 Cor 3:14; **(1r)** those who seek justification by the Law are "severed" from Christ, they are rendered inactive in relation to Him, Gal 5:4; **(1s)** the essential effect of the preaching of the Cross would become inoperative by the preaching of circumcision, 2 Cor 5:11; **(1t)** by the death of Christ the barrier between Jew and Gentile is rendered inoperative as such, Eph 2:15; **(1u)** the Man of Sin is to be reduced to inactivity by the manifestation of the Lord's Parousia with His people, 2 Th 2:8; **(1v)** Christ has rendered death inactive for the believer, 2 Tim 1:10, death becoming the means of a more glorious life, with Christ; **(1w)** the Devil is to be reduced to inactivity through the death of Christ, Heb 2:14. **(2)** It is translated "cumber" in Lk 13:7. See: TDNT—1:452, 76; BAGD—417b; THAYER—336a.

2674. **καταριθμέω** {1x} **katarithmĕō**, *kat-ar-ith-meh'-o;* from *2596* and *705;* to *reckon among:*—number with {1x}. See: BAGD—417c; THAYER—336b.

2675. **καταρτίζω** {13x} **katartizō**, *kat-ar-tid'-zo;* from *2596* and a der. of *739;* to *complete thoroughly,* i.e. *repair* (lit. or fig.) or *adjust:*—perfect {2x}, make perfect {2x}, mend {2x}, be perfect {2x}, fit {1x}, frame {1x}, prepare {1x}, restore {1x}, perfectly joined together {1x}.

Katartizo, "to render fit, complete" (*artios*), "is used **(1)** of mending nets, Mt 4:21; Mk 1:19, and is translated **(2)** "restore" in Gal 6:1. **(3)** It does not necessarily imply, however, that that to which it is applied has been damaged, though it may do so, as in these passages; it signifies, rather, right ordering and arrangement, Heb 11:3, "framed"; **(4)** it points out the path of progress, as in Mt 21:16; Lk 6:40; cf. 2 Cor 13:9; Eph 4:12, where corresponding nouns occur. **(5)** It indicates the close relationship between character and destiny, Rom 9:22, "fitted", where the middle voice signifies that those referred to "fitted" themselves for destruction, as illustrated in the case of Pharaoh, who self-hardened his own heart. **(6)** It expresses the pastor's desire for the flock, **(6a)** in prayer, Heb 13:21, and **(6b)** in exhortation, 1 Cor 1:10, "perfectly joined"; 2 Cor 13:11, **(6c)** as well as his conviction of God's purpose for them, 1 Pet 5:10. **(7)** It is used of the Incarnation of the Word in Heb 10:5, "prepare" quoted from Ps 40:6, where it is apparently intended to describe the unique creative act involved in the Virgin Birth, Lk 1:35. **(8)** In 1 Th 3:10 it means to supply what is necessary, as the succeeding words show. See: TDNT—1:475, 80; BAGD—417d; THAYER—336c.

2676. **κατάρτισις** {1x} **katartisis**, *kat-ar'-tis-is;* from *2675; thorough equipment* (subj.):—perfection {1x}.

This word means making a fit and is used figuratively in an ethical sense in 2 Cor 13:9, implying a process leading to consummation. See: TDNT—1:475, 80; BAGD—418a; THAYER—336d.

2677. **καταρτισμός** {1x} **katartismŏs**, *kat-ar-tis-mos';* from *2675; complete furnishing* (obj.):—perfecting {1x}.

This word means "a fitting or preparing fully," Eph 4:12. See: TDNT—1:475, 80; BAGD—418a; THAYER—336d.

2678. **κατασείω** {4x} **katasĕiō**, *kat-as-i'-o;* from *2596* and *4579;* to *sway downward,* i.e. *make a signal usually with the hand:* beckon {4x}.

Kataseio, lit., "to shake down" (*kata,* "down," *seio,* "to shake"), of shaking the hand, of waving, expresses a little more vigorously the act of "beckoning," Acts 12:17; 13:16; 19:33; 21:40. Syn.: *Neuo* and its compounds have primary reference to a movement of the head; *kataseio,* to that of the hand. See also 2656. See: BAGD—418a; THAYER—336d.

2679. **κατασκάπτω** {2x} **kataskaptō**, *kat-as-kap'-to;* from *2596* and *4626;* to *undermine,* i.e. (by impl.) *destroy:*—dig down {1x}, ruin {1x}.

This verb means to dig under, dig down under the foundation so as to topple, demolish, and destroy and is found **(1)** in Rom 11:3, of altars, and in **(2)** Acts 15:16, "ruins," lit., "the things dug down." See: BAGD—418b; THAYER—336d.

2680. **κατασκευάζω** {11x} **kataskĕuazō**, *kat-ask-yoo-ad'-zo;* from *2596* and a der. of *4632;* to *prepare thoroughly* (prop. by extern. *equipment;* whereas *2090* refers rather to intern. *fitness*); by impl. to *construct, create:* build {3x}, make {1x}, ordain {1x}, prepare {6x}.

Kataskeuazo, "to prepare, make ready" (*kata,* used intensively, *skeue,* "equipment"), and is translated **(1)** "prepare" in Mt 11:10; Mk 1:2; Lk 1:17; 7:27; Heb11:7; 1 Pet 3:20; **(2)** "were . . . ordained" in Heb 9:6; and **(3)** "made" in Heb 9:2; and **(4)** "build" in Heb 3:3, 4 twice. See: BAGD—418b; THAYER—336d.

2681. **κατασκηνόω** {4x} **kataskēnŏō**, *kat-as-kay-nŏ'-o;* from *2596* and *4637;* to *camp down,* i.e. *haunt;* fig. to *remain:*—lodge {3x}, rest {1x}.

Literally, *kataskenoo* means to pitch one's tent, and is translated **(1)** "lodge" (Mt 13.32, Mk 4:32; Lk 13:19); and **(2)** "rest" in Acts 2:26. See: TDNT—7:387, 1040; BAGD—418c; THAYER—337a.

2682. **κατασκήνωσις** {2x} **kataskēnōsis**, *kat-as-kay'-no-sis;* from *2681;* an *encamping,* i.e. (fig.) a *perch:*—nest {2x}.

This word means properly "an encamping, taking up one's quarters," then, "a lodging, abode" (*kata,* "down over," *skene,* "a tent"), is used of birds' "nests" in Mt 8:20 and Lk 9:58. See: BAGD—418c; THAYER—337a.

2683. **κατασκιάζω** {1x} **kataskiazō**, *kat-as-kee-ad'-zo;* from *2596* and a der. of *4639;* to *overshade,* i.e. *cover:*—shadow {1x}.

Kataskiazo, lit., "to shadow down," is used of the cherubim of glory above the mercy seat casting their shadow down upon it, Heb 9:5, "shadowing." See: BAGD—418d; THAYER—337a.

2684. **κατασκοπέω** {1x} **kataskŏpĕō**, *kat-as-kop-eh'-o;* from *2685;* to *be a sentinel,* i.e. to *inspect* insidiously:—spy out {1x}.

This word means to view closely, spy out, search out with a view to plotting against and overthrowing (Gal 2:4). See: TDNT—7:416, 1047; BAGD—418d; THAYER—337b.

2685. **κατάσκοπος** {1x} **kataskŏpŏs**, *kat-as'-kop-os;* from *2596* (intens.) and *4649* (in the sense of a *watcher*); a *reconnoiterer:*—a spy {1x}.

One who does 2684 is a *kataskopos,* Heb 11:31. See: TDNT—7:417, 1047; BAGD—418d; THAYER—337b.

2686. **κατασοφίζομαι** {1x} **katasŏphizŏmai**, *kat-as-of-id'-zom-ahee;* mid. voice from *2596* and *4679; to be crafty against,* i.e. *circumvent:*—deal subtilly (subtly) with {1x}.

This word means to circumvent by artifice or fraud, to conquer by subtle devices; to outwit, to deal craftily with (Acts 7:19). See: BAGD—418d; THAYER—337b.

2687. **καταστέλλω** {2x} **katastĕllō**, *kat-as-tel'-lo;* from *2596* and *4724;* to *put down,* i.e. *quell:*—appease {1x}, quiet {1x}.

Katastello means to put or keep down one who is roused or incensed, to repress, restrain, appease, quiet and is translated **(1)** in the passive voice, "to be quiet, or to be quieted" in Acts 19:36, lit., "to be quieted"; and **(2)** in the active voice in Acts 19:35, "appeased. See: TDNT—7:595, 1074; BAGD—419a; THAYER—337b.

2688. **κατάστημα** {1x} **katastēma**, *kat-as'-tay-mah;* from *2525;* prop. a *position* or *condition,* i.e. (subj.) *demeanor:*—behaviour {1x}.

Katastema denotes "a condition, or constitution of anything, or deportment", Titus 2:3. See: BAGD—419a; THAYER—337b.

2689. **καταστολή** {1x} **katastŏlē**, *kat-as-tol-ay';* from *2687;* a *deposit,* i.e. (spec.) *costume:*—apparel {1x}.

Katastole, "to send or let down, to lower", connected with *katastello* (*kata,* "down," *stello,* "to send"), was primarily a garment let down; hence, "dress, attire," in general (cf. *stole,* a loose outer garment worn by kings and persons of rank,—Eng., "stole"); 1 Ti 2:9, "apparel." See: TDNT—7:595, 1074; BAGD—419a; THAYER—337b.

2690. **καταστρέφω** {2x} **katastrĕphō**, *kat-as-tref'-o;* from *2596* and *4762;* to *turn* upside *down,* i.e. *upset:*—overthrow {2x}.

Katastrepho, lit. and primarily, "to turn down" or "turn over," as, e.g., the soil, denotes to "overturn, overthrow," Mt 21:12; Mk 11:15. See: TDNT—7:715, 1093; BAGD—419a; THAYER—337c.

2691. **καταστρηνιάω** {1x} **katastrēniaō**, *kat-as-tray-nee-ah'-o;* from *2596* and *4763; to become voluptuous against:*—begin to wax wanton against {1x}.

Used only once, 1 Tim 5:11: "But the younger widows refuse: for when they have begun to wax wanton against Christ, they will marry . . ." Wanton means to be undiscipline [to the vows of widowhood and receiving care from being on the church's support list]. These young widows will slowly over time ["wax"] desire support from a husband [not condemned, just stated] and they will beome undisciplined in their vows contained in being put on the list; hence, against Christ as their sole support through His church. To prevent this natural desire leading to an uncomfortable situation for the local church, let the younger widows marry. See: TDNT—3:631, 420; BAGD—419b; THAYER—337c.

2692. **καταστροφή** {2x} **katastrŏphē**, *kat-as-trof-ay';* from *2690;* an *overturn* ("*catastrophe*"), i.e. *demolition;* fig. *apostasy:*—overthrow {1x}, subverting {1x}.

Katastrophe, lit., "a turning down" (*kata,* "down," *strophe,* "a turning"; Eng., "catastrophe"), is used **(1)** literally, 2 Pet 2:6, "overthrow" (of cities); and **(2)** metaphorically, 2 Tim 2:14 "subverting," i.e., the "overthrowing" of faith. See: TDNT—7:715, 1093; BAGD—419b; THAYER—337c.

2693. **καταστρώννυμι** {1x} **katastrōnnumi**, *kat-as-trone'-noo-mee;* from *2596* and *4766; to strew down,* i.e. (by impl.) to *prostrate* (*slay*):—overthrow {1x}.

These unbelieving Israelites were slain (*katastronnumi*) and strewn over the wilderness [and buried] over the forty years (1 Cor 10:5). See: BAGD—419b; THAYER—337c.

2694. **κατασύρω** {1x} **katasurō**, *kat-as-oo'-ro;* from *2596* and *4951; to drag down,* i.e. *arrest* judicially:—hale {1x}.

Katasuro means to pull down and drag away forcibly to stand before a judge (Lk 12:58). See: BAGD—419b; THAYER—337d.

2695. **κατασφάττω** {1x} **katasphattō**, *kat-as-fat'-to;* from *2596* and *4969; to kill down,* i.e. *slaughter:*—slay {1x}.

This word stresses to kill off, to slaughter all the disobedient (Lk 19:27). See: BAGD—419c; THAYER—337d.

2696. **κατασφραγίζω** {1x} **katasphragizō**, *kat-as-frag-id'-zo;* from *2596* and *4972; to seal closely and securely:*—to seal {1x}.

In Rev 5:1 the book/scroll is securely sealed (*kata,* intensive) by seven seals. See: TDNT—7:939, 1127; BAGD—419c; THAYER—337d.

2697. **κατάσχεσις** {2x} **kataschĕsis**, *kat-as'-khes-is;* from *2722;* a *holding down,* i.e. *occupancy:*—possession {2x}.

Kataschesis, primarily "a holding back", then, "a holding fast," denotes "a possession," Acts 7:5, or "taking possession," v. 45, with the article, lit., "in the (i.e., their) taking possession." See: BAGD—419c; THAYER—337d.

2698. **κατατίθημι** {3x} **katatithēmi**, *kat-at-ith'-ay-mee;* from *2596* and *5087; to place down,* i.e. *deposit* (lit. or fig.):—do {1x}, lay {1x}, shew {1x}.

This word means to deposit, lay up, to lay down, (*kata*), is translated **(1)** "lay" in Mk 15:46 of the act of Joseph of Arimathaea in "laying" Christ's body in the tomb; **(2)** "do", Acts 25:9, doing the Jews a pleasure; and **(3)** "shew", Acts 24:27, to shew the Jews a pleasure. See: BAGD—419c; THAYER—337d.

2699. **κατατομή** {1x} **katatŏmē**, *kat-at-om-ay';* from a compound of *2596* and τέμνω **tĕmnō** (to *cut*); a *cutting down* (*off*), i.e. *mutilation* (ironically):—concision {1x}.

Katatome, lit., "a cutting off" (*kata,* "down," *temno,* "to cut"), "a mutilation," is a term found in Phil 3:2, there used by the apostle, by a *paranomasia* (play on words), contemptuously, for the Jewish circumcision with its Judaistic influence, in contrast to the true spiritual circumcision. See: TDNT—8:109, 1169; BAGD—419d; THAYER—338a. comp. *609.*

2700. **κατατοξεύω** {1x} **katatŏxĕuō**, *kat-at-ox-yoo'-o;* from *2596* and a der. of *5115; to shoot down* with an arrow or other missile:—thrust through {1x}. See: BAGD—419d; THAYER—338a.

2701. **κατατρέχω** {1x} **katatrĕchō**, *kat-at-rekh'-o;* from *2596* and *5143;* to *run down,* i.e. *hasten* from a tower:—run down (from) {1x}. See: BAGD—419d; THAYER—338a.

καταφάγω kataphagō. See *2719.*

2702. **καταφέρω** {3x} **kataphĕrō**, *kat-af-er'-o;* from *2596* and *5342* (incl. its alt.); to *bear down,* i.e. (fig.) *overcome* (with drowsiness); spec. to *cast* a vote:—fall {1x}, give {1x}, sink down {1x}.

Kataphero, "to bring down or against" (*kata,* "down"), **(1)** of Eutychus **(1a)** "fallen down" into a deep sleep, Acts 26:10 (first reference), and **(2)** being "borne down" with sleep, Acts 20:9 (second reference), he fell from the window to the street below; and **(3)** it is used of casting a ballot or "giving" a vote in Acts 26:10. See: BAGD—419d; THAYER—338a.

2703. **καταφεύγω** {2x} **kataphĕugō**, *kat-af-yoo'-go;* from *2596* and *5343;* to *flee down* (*away*):—flee {2x}.

Katapheugo, "to flee for refuge" (*kata,* used intensively), is used **(1)** literally in Acts 14:6; and **(2)** metaphorically in Heb 6:18, of "fleeing" for refuge to lay hold upon hope. See: BAGD—420a; THAYER—338b.

2704. **καταφθείρω** {2x} **kataphthĕirō**, *kat-af-thi'-ro;* from *2596* and *5351;* to *spoil entirely,* i.e. (lit.) to *destroy;* or (fig.) to *deprave:*—corrupt {1x}, utterly perish {1x}.

Kataphtheiro is said **(1)** of men who are reprobate concerning the faith, "corrupt in mind", 2 Ti 3:8; and **(2)** men who will "utterly perish", 2 Pet 2:12. See: TDNT—9:93, 1259; BAGD—420a; THAYER—338b.

2705. **καταφιλέω** {6x} **kataphilĕō**, *kat-af-ee-leh'-o;* from *2596* and *5368;* to *kiss earnestly:*—kiss {6x}.

Kataphileo denotes "to kiss fervently" (*kata,* intensive); the stronger force of this verb has been called in question, but the change from *phileo* to *kataphileo* in Mt 26:49 and Mk 14:45 can scarcely be without significance, and the act of the traitor was almost certainly more demonstrative than the simple kiss of salutation. So with the kiss of genuine devotion, Lk 7:38, 45; 15:20; Acts 20:37, in each of which this verb is used. See: TDNT—9:114, 1262; BAGD—420b; THAYER—338b.

2706. **καταφρονέω** {9x} **kataphrŏnĕō**, *kat-af-ron-eh'-o;* from *2596* and *5426;* to *think against,* i.e. *disesteem:*—despise {9x}.

This verb denotes to think little of, slightly of, or nothing of another lit., "to think down upon or against anyone" (*kata,* "down," *phren,* "the mind"), hence signifies "to think slightly of, to despise," Mt 6:24; 18:10; Lk 16:13; Rom 2:4; 1 Cor 11:22; 1 Ti 4:12; 6:2; Heb 12:2; 2 Pet 2:10. See: TDNT—3:631, 421; BAGD—420b; THAYER—338c.

2707. **καταφρονητής** {1x} **kataphrŏntēs**, *kat-af-ron-tace';* from *2706;* a *contemner:*—despiser {1x}.

Kataphrontes, lit., "one who thinks down against," hence, "a despiser" is found in Acts 13:41. See: TDNT—3:632, 421; BAGD—420c; THAYER—338c.

2708. **καταχέω** {2x} **katachĕō**, *kat-akh-eh'-o;* from *2596* and χέω **chĕō** (to *pour*); to *pour down* (*out*):—pour {2x}.

Katacheo, "to pour down upon" (*kata,* "down," *cheo,* "to pour"), is used in Mt 26:7 and Mk 14:3, of ointment. See: BAGD—420c; THAYER—338c.

2709. **καταχθόνιος** {1x} **katachthŏniŏs**, *kat-akh-thon'-ee-os;* from *2596* and χθών **chthōn** (the *ground*); *subterranean,* i.e. *infernal* (belonging to the world of departed spirits):—under the earth {1x}. See: TDNT—3:633, 421; BAGD—420d; THAYER—338c.

2710. **καταχράομαι** {2x} **katachraŏmai**, *kat-akh-rah'-om-ahee;* from *2596* and *5530;* to *overuse,* i.e. *misuse:*—abuse {2x}.

Katachraomai, lit., "to use overmuch" (*kata,* "down," intensive, *chraomai,* "to use"), is found in 1 Cor 7:31, with reference to the believer's use [over use] of the world, and 1 Cor 9:18, "abuse." See: BAGD—420d; THAYER—338d.

2711. **καταψύχω** {1x} **katapsuchō**, *kat-ap-soo'-kho;* from *2596* and *5594;* to *cool down* (*off*), i.e. *refresh:*—cool {1x}. See: BAGD—421a; THAYER—338d.

2712. **κατείδωλος** {1x} **katĕidōlŏs**, *kat-i'-do-los;* from *2596* (intens.) and *1497; utterly idolatrous:*—wholly given to idolatry {1x}. See: TDNT—2:379, 202; BAGD—412a; THAYER—338d.

κατελεύθω **katĕlĕuthō**. See *2718.*

2713. **κατέναντι** {5x} **katĕnanti**, *kat-en'-an-tee;* from *2596* and *1725; directly opposite:*—before {1x}, over against {4x}.

Katenanti, (*kata,* "down," lit., "down over against"), is used **(1)** of locality, "over against", e.g., Mk 11:2; 13:3; Lk 19:30; **(2)** as "before", "in the sight of", Rom 4:17. See: BAGD—421b; THAYER—338d.

κατενέγκω **katĕnĕgkō**. See *2702.*

2714. **κατενώπιον** {5x} **katĕnōpiŏn**, *kat-en-o'-pee-on;* from *2596* and *1799; dir. in front of:*—before {2x}, in sight of {1x}, in (one's) sight {1x}, before the presence of {1x}.

Katenopion signifies "right over against, opposite", always in reference to God: **(1)** "before", **(1a)** "before (God)", 2 Cor 12:19; **(1b)** "before" (God as Judge), Eph 1:4; **(2)** "in the sight of (God), 2 Cor 2:17 **(3)** "in His sight", Col. 1:22; **(4)** "before the presence of (His glory), Jude 24. See: BAGD—421b; THAYER—339a.

2715. **κατεξουσιάζω** {2x} **katĕxŏusiazō**, *kat-ex-oo-see-ad'-zo;* from *2596* and *1850;* to *have* (*wield*) *full privilege over:*—exercise authority upon {2x}. Cf. Mt 20:25; Mk 10:42. See: TDNT—2:575, 238; BAGD—421c; THAYER—339a.

2716. **κατεργάζομαι** {24x} **katĕrgazŏmai**, *kat-er-gad'-zom-ahee;* from *2596* and *2038;* do *work fully,* i.e. *accomplish;* by impl. to *finish, fashion:*—work {15x}, do {5x}, do deed {1x}, to perform {1x}, cause {1x}, work out {1x}.

(1) This word usually means to work out, i.e. to do that from which something results, to bring about, to result in. **(2)** It is an emphatic form and signifies "to work out, achieve, effect by toil," rendered "to work" (past tense, "wrought") in Rom 1:27; 4:15 (the Law brings men under condemnation and so renders them subject to divine wrath); 5:3; 7:8, 13; 15:18; 2 Cor 4:17; 5:5; 7:10, 11; 12:12; Phil 2:12, where "your own salvation" refers especially to freedom from strife and vainglory; Jas 1:3, 20; 1 Pet 4:3. **(3)** It has various translations of "do": **(3a)** Rom 2:9 "doeth", **(3b)** Rom 7:15, 17, "I do", **(3c)** Rom 7:20, "I that do", **(3d)** 1 Cor 5:3, "done." **(6)** In Eph 6:13 "having done (all). See: TDNT—3:634, 421; BAGD—421c; THAYER—339a.

2717. Because of some changes in the numbering system (while the original work was in progress) no Greek words were cited for *2717* or *3203-3302.* These numbers were dropped altogether. This will not cause any problems in Strong's numbering system. No Greek words have been left out. Because so many other reference works use this numbering system, it has not been revised. If it were revised, much confusion would certainly result.

2718. **κατέρχομαι** {13x} **katĕrchŏmai**, *kat-er'-khom-ahee;* from *2596* and *2064* (incl. its alt.); to *come* (or *go*) *down* (lit. or fig.):—come down {5x}, come {3x}, go down {2x}, depart {1x}, descend {1x}, land {1x}.

This word means "to come down" (*kata,* "down"), and is translated **(1)** "come down", Lk 4:31; 9:37; Acts 9:32; 15:1; 21:10; **(2)** "come", Acts 11:27; 18:5; 27:5; **(3)** "go down", Acts 8:5; 12:19; **(4)** "depart", Acts 13:4; **(5)** "descend", Jas 3:15; **(6)** "landed", Acts 18:22. See: BAGD—422a; THAYER—339b.

2719. **κατεσθίω** {15x} **katĕsthiō**, *kat-es-thee'-o;* from *2596* and *2068* (incl. its alt.); to *eat down,* i.e. *devour* (lit. or fig.):—devour {10x}, eat up {3x}, devour up {2x}.

Katesthio denotes **(1)** "to consume by eating, to devour," said of birds, Mt 13:4, Mk 4:4, Lk 8:5, **(1a)** of the Dragon, Rev 12:4; **(1b)** of a prophet, "eating" up a book, suggestive of spiritually "eating" and digesting its contents, Rev 10:9 (cf. Eze 2:8; 3:1–3; Jer 15:16); **(2)** metaphorically, **(2a)** "to squander, to waste," Lk 15:30; **(2b)** "to consume" one's physical powers by emotion, Jn 2:17; **(2c)** "to devour" by forcible appropriation, as of widows' property, Mt 23:14; Mk 12:40; **(2d)** "to demand maintenance," as false apostles did to the church at Corinth, 2 Cor 11:20; **(2e)** "to exploit or prey on one another," Gal 5:15, where "bite . . . devour . . . consume" form a climax, the first two describing a process, the last the act of swallowing down; **(2f)** to "destroy" by fire, Rev 11:5; 20:9. See: BAGD—422a; THAYER—339b.

2720. **κατευθύνω** {3x} **katĕuthunō**, *kat-yoo-thoo'-no;* from *2596* and *2116;* to *straighten fully,* i.e. (fig.) *direct:*—guide {1x}, direct {2x}.

This word means to make straight, remove all hindrances in order to guide or direct (Lk 1:79; 1 Th. 3:11; 2Th 3:5). See: BAGD—422b; THAYER—339c.

2721. **κατεφίστημι** {1x} **katĕphistēmi**, *kat-ef-is'-tay-mee;* from *2596* and *2186;* to *stand over against,* i.e. *rush upon* (*assault*):—make insurrection against {1x}. See: BAGD—422c; THAYER—339d.

2722. **κατέχω** {19x} **katĕchō**, *kat-ekh'-o;* from *2596* and *2192;* to *hold down* (*fast*), in various applications (lit. or fig.):—hold {3x}, hold fast {3x}, keep {2x}, possess {2x}, stay {1x}, take {1x}, have {1x}, make {1x}, misc. {5x} = let, retain, seize on, withhold.

(1) This word stresses holding fast in order to hinder the course or progress of something or someone. This word means "to hold firmly, hold fast" and is rendered **(1)** "keep" in 1 Cor 11:2; **(2)** "hold fast" in 1 Th 5:21; Heb 3:6; 10:23; **(3)** "hold" in Heb 3:14; Rom. 1:18, of unrighteous men who restrain the spread of truth by their unrighteousness, **(4)** "held" in Rom 7:6 of the Law as that which had "held" in bondage those who through faith in Christ were made dead to it as a means of life; **(5)** "to hold fast, hold back," signifies "to possess," in 1 Cor 7:30 and 2 Cor 6:10. See: TDNT—2:829, 286; BAGD—422c; THAYER—339d.

2723. **κατηγορέω** {22x} **katēgŏrĕō**, *kat-ay-gor-eh'-o;* from *2725;* to *be a plaintiff,* i.e. to *charge* with some offence:—accuse {21x}, object {1x}.

Kategoreo, as a verb, means "to speak against, accuse" is used **(1)** in a general way, "to accuse": "Which shew the work of the law written in their hearts, their conscience also bearing witness, and *their* thoughts the mean while accusing or else excusing one another;" (Rom 2:15); and more specifically **(2)** before a judge: "And, behold, there was a man which had *his* hand withered. And they asked him, saying, Is it lawful to heal on the sabbath days? that they might accuse him" (Mt 12:10). Syn.: *Aitiama* (157) means to accuse with primary reference to the ground of the accusation; the crime, *egklema* (1462) means to make a verbal assault which reaches its goal, and *katagoreo* (2723) means to accuse formally before a tribunal, bring a charge against publicly. See also: 156, 157, 1225, 1458, 1462, 1908, 2724, 4811. See: TDNT—3:637, 422; BAGD—423a; THAYER—340a.

2724. **κατηγορία** {4x} **katēgŏria**, *kat-ay-gor-ee'-ah;* from *2725;* a *complaint* ("category"), i.e. criminal *charge:*—accusation {3x}, accused {1x}.

Kategoria (2724), means **(1)** "an accusation": "Pilate then went out unto them, and said, What accusation bring ye against this man?" (Jn 18:29; cf. 1 Ti 5:19; Titus 1:6). **(2)** This noun and the verb *kategoreo* (2723 - "to accuse")," and the participle *kategoros* (from 2723 - "an accuser"), all have chiefly to do with judicial procedure, as distinct from *diaballo* (1225 - "to slander"). **(3)** It is derived from *agora,* "a place of public speaking," prefixed by *kata,* "against"; hence, it signifies a speaking against a person before a public tribunal. It is the opposite to *apologia* (626), "a defense." Syn.: 156, 157, 1225, 1458, 1462, 1908, 2723, 4811. See: TDNT—3:637, 422; BAGD—423c; THAYER—340c.

2725. **κατήγορος** {7x} **katēgŏrŏs**, *kat-ay'-gor-os;* from *2596* and *58; against* one in the *assembly,* i.e. a *complainant* at law; spec. *Satan:*—accuser {7x}.

A *kategoros* is "an accuser," and is used in Jn 8:10; Acts 23:30, 35; 24:8; 25:16, 18. In Rev 12:10, it is used of Satan. See: TDNT—3:636, 422; BAGD—423c; THAYER—340c.

2726. **κατήφεια** {1x} **katēphĕia**, *kat-ay'-fi-ah;* from a compound of *2596* and perh. a der. of the base of *5316* (mean. *downcast* in look); *demureness,* i.e. (by impl.) *sadness:*—heaviness {1x}.

Katapheia denotes a downcast look, expressive of sorrow; hence, "dejection, heaviness"; it is used in Jas. 4:9. See: BAGD—423c; THAYER—340c.

2727. **κατηχέω** {8x} **katēchĕō**, *kat-ay-kheh'-o;* from *2596* and *2279;* to *sound down* into the ears, i.e. (by impl.) to *indoctrinate* ("catechize") or (gen.) to *apprise* of:—inform {2x}, instruct {3x}, teach {3x}.

(1) This word indicates verbal instruction which is "sounded down into the student's ears, and then repeated by the student to assure learning has taken place [cf. Eng. catechize]. *Katecheo* primarily denotes "to resound" (*kata,* "down," *echos* "a sound"); then, "to sound down the ears, to teach by word of mouth, instruct, inform" (Eng., "catechize, catechumen"); it is rendered,

(2) in the passive voice, by the verb "to inform," in Acts 21:21, 24. Here it is used of the large numbers of Jewish believers at Jerusalem whose zeal for the Law had been stirred by information of accusations made against the Apostle Paul, as to certain anti-Mosaic teaching he was supposed to have given the Jews. **(3)** It also denotes "to teach orally, inform, instruct," is translated by the verb "to instruct" in Lk 1:4; Acts 18:25; Rom 2:18; **(4)** is rendered to teach" in 1 Cor 14:19; Gal 6:6 (twice). See: TDNT—3:638, 422; BAGD—423d; THAYER—340d.

2728. **κατιόω** {1x} **katiŏō**, *kat-ee-ŏ'-o;* from *2596* and a der. of *2447;* to *rust down,* i.e. *corrode:*—canker {1x}.

A canker is an ulcer-like sore, erupting from below the surface, like rust erupts in metal. See: TDNT—3:334; BAGD—424a; THAYER—340d.

2729. **κατισχύω** {2x} **katischuō**, *kat-is-khoo'-o;* from *2596* and *2480;* to *overpower:*—prevail {1x}, prevail against {1x}.

(1) This word means to be strong to another's detriment, to prevail against, to be superior in strength, to overcome, to prevail. **(2)** *Katischus,* "to be strong against" is used **(1)** in Mt 16:18, negatively of the gates of hades not "prevailing against" Christ's church; and **(2)** in Lk 23:23, of the voices of the chief priests, rulers and people "prevailed" over Pilate regarding the crucifixion of Christ. See: TDNT—3:397, 378; BAGD—424a; THAYER—340d.

2730. **κατοικέω** {47x} **katŏikĕō**, *kat-oy-keh'-o;* from *2596* and *3611;* to *house permanently,* i.e. *reside* (lit. or fig.):—dwell {42x}, dweller {2x}, inhabitant {1x}, inhabiters {2x}

This frequent verb properly signifies "to settle down in a dwelling, to dwell fixedly in a place." Besides its literal sense, it is used of **(1)** the "indwelling" of the totality of the attributes and powers of the Godhead in Christ, Col 1:19; 2:9; **(2)** the "indwelling" of Christ in the hearts of believers ("may make a home in your hearts"), Eph 3:17; **(3)** the "dwelling" of Satan in a locality, Rev 2:13; **(4)** the future "indwelling" of righteousness in the new heavens and earth, 2 Pet 3:13. It is translated **(5)** "dwellers" in Acts 1:19; 2:9; **(6)** "inhabitants" in Rev 17:2; and **(7)** "inhabiters" in Rev 8:13 and 12:12. See: TDNT—5:153, 674; BAGD—424a; THAYER—341a.

2731. **κατοίκησις** {1x} **katŏikēsis**, *kat-oy'-kay-sis;* from *2730; residence* (prop. the act; but by impl. concr. the mansion):—a dwelling {1x}. See: BAGD—424c; THAYER—341b.

2732. **κατοικητήριον** {2x} **katŏikētēriŏn**, *kat-oy-kay-tay'-ree-on;* from a der. of *2730;* a *dwelling-place:*—habitation {2x}.

Katoiketerion, (*kata,* "down," used intensively), implying permanency, is used **(1)** in Eph 2:22 of the church as the dwelling place of the Holy Spirit; **(2)** in Rev 18:2 of Babylon, figuratively, as the dwelling place of devils. See: TDNT—5:155, 674; BAGD—424c; THAYER—341b.

2733. **κατοικία** {1x} **katŏikia**, *kat-oy-kee'-ah; residence* (prop. the condition; but by impl. the abode itself):—habitation {1x}.

Kakoikia is "a settlement, colony, dwelling" (*kata,* and *oikos,* see above), is used in Acts 17:26, of the localities divinely appointed as the dwelling places of the nations. See: BAGD—424c; THAYER—341b.

2734. **κατοπτρίζομαι** {1x} **katŏptrizŏmai**, *kat-op-trid'-zom-ahee;* mid. voice from a compound of *2596* and a der. of *3700* [comp. *2072*]; to *mirror oneself,* i.e. to *see reflected* (fig.):—behold as in a glass {1x}.

Katoptrizo, as a verb, signifies in the middle voice "beholding as in a glass ": "But we all, with open face beholding as in a glass the glory of the Lord, are changed into the same image from glory to glory, *even* as by the Spirit of the Lord" (2 Co 3:18). Syn.: 333, 816, 991, 1689, 1896, 2029, 2300, 2334, 2657, 3708. See: TDNT—2:696, 264; BAGD—424d; THAYER—341c.

2735. **κατόρθωμα** {1x} **katŏrthōma**, *kat-or'-tho-mah;* from a compound of *2596* and a der. of *3717* [comp. *1357*]; something *made fully upright,* i.e. (fig.) *rectification* (spec. *good* public *administration*):—a very worthy deed {1x}. See: BAGD—424d; THAYER—341c.

2736. **κάτω** {11x} **katō**, *kat'-o;* also (comparative)

κατωτέρω **katōtĕrō**, *kat-o-ter'-o;* [comp. *2737*]; adv. from *2596; downwards:*—beneath {3x}, bottom {2x}, down {5x}, under {1x}. See: TDNT—3:640, 422; BAGD—425a; THAYER—341c.

2737. **κατώτερος** {1x} **katōtĕrŏs**, *kat-o'-ter-os;* comparative from *2736; inferior* (locally, of Hades):—lower {1x}. See: TDNT—3:640, 422; BAGD—425a; THAYER—341d.

2738. **καῦμα** {2x} **kauma**, *kŏw'-mah;* from *2545;* prop. a *burn* (concr.), but used (abstr.) of a *glow:*—heat {2x}.

This word denotes painful and hurtful heat and signifies "the result of burning," or "the heat produced," Rev 7:16; 16:9. See: TDNT—3:642, 423; BAGD—425a; THAYER—341d.

2739. **καυματίζω** {4x} **kaumatizō**, *kŏw-mat-id'-zo;* from *2738;* to *burn:*—scorch {4x}.

This word means "to scorch" (from *kauma,* "heat"), and is used **(1)** of seed that had not much earth, Mt 13:6; Mk 4:6; **(2)** of men, stricken retributively by the sun's heat, Rev 16:8, 9. See: TDNT—3:643, 423; BAGD—341d.

2740. **καῦσις** {1x} **kausis**, *kŏw'-sis;* from *2545; burning* (the act):—be burned + 1519 {1x}. See: TDNT—3:643, 423; BAGD—425b; THAYER—341d.

2741. **καυσόω** {2x} **kausŏō**, *kŏw-sŏ'-o;* from *2740;* to *set on fire:*—with fervent heat {2x}.

Kausoo was used as a medical term, of "a fever"; in the NT, "to burn with great heat", and is said of the future destruction of the natural elements, 2 Pet. 3:10, 12, "with fervent heat," passive voice, lit. "being burned." See: TDNT—3:644,*; BAGD—425b; THAYER—342a.

2742. **καύσων** {3x} **kausōn**, *kŏw'-sone;* from *2741;* a *glare:*—(burning) heat {3x}.

Kauson denotes "a burning heat" (from *kaio,* "to burn"; cf. Eng., "caustic," "cauterize"), Mt 20:12; Lk 12:55 "heat"; in Jas 1:11, "a burning heat." See: TDNT—3:644, 423; BAGD—425c; THAYER—342a.

2743. **καυτηριάζω** {1x} **kautēriazō**, *kŏw-tay-ree-ad'-zo* or

καυστηριάζω **kaustēriazō** *kŏws-tay-ree-ad'-zo;* from a der. of *2545;* to *brand* ("*cauterize*"), i.e. (by impl.) to *render unsensitive* (fig.):—sear with a hot iron {1x}.

This word means "to burn in with a branding iron" (cf. Eng., "caustic") and is found in 1 Tim 4:2. The reference is to apostates whose consciences are "branded" with the effects of their sin. See: TDNT—3:644,*; BAGD—425c; THAYER—342a.

2744. **καυχάομαι** {38x} **kauchaŏmai**, *kŏw-khah'-om-ahee;* from some (obsolete) base akin to that of αὐχέω **auchĕō** (to *boast*) and *2172;* to *vaunt* (in a good or a bad sense):—glory {23x}, boast {8x}, rejoice {4x}, make boast {2x}, joy {1x}.

Kauchaomai means "to boast or glory," is translated **(1)** "to boast" (see, e.g., Rom 2:17, 23; 2 Cor 7:14; 9:2; 10:8, 13, 15, 16); **(2)** it is used **(2a)** of "vainglorying," e.g., 1 Cor 1:29; 3:21; 4:7; 2 Cor 5:12; 11:12, 18; Eph 2:9; **(2b)** of "valid glorying," e.g., Rom 5:2, "rejoice"; 5:3; 1 Cor 1:31; 2 Cor 9:2; 10:8, 12:9; Gal 6:14; Phil 3:3 and Jas 1:9, "rejoice". See: TDNT—3:645, 423; BAGD—425c; THAYER—342b.

2745. **καύχημα** {11x} **kauchēma**, *kŏw'-khay-mah;* from *2744;* a *boast* (prop. the obj.; by impl. the act) in a good or a bad sense:—rejoicing {4x}, to glory {3x}, glorying {2x}, boasting {1x}, rejoice {1x}.

Kauchema denotes **(1)** "that in which one glories, a matter or ground of glorying," Rom 4:2 and Phil 2:16; **(2)** in the following the meaning is likewise "a ground of glorying": 1 Cor 5:6; 9:15, "glorying," 16, "to glory of"; Gal 6:4, "rejoicing"; Phil 1:26; Heb 3:6. **(3)** In 2 Cor 5:12 and 9:3 the word denotes the boast itself, yet as distinct from the act. See: TDNT—3:645, 423; BAGD—426a; THAYER—342c.

2746. **καύχησις** {12x} **kauchēsis**, *kŏw'-khay-sis;* from *2744; boasting* (prop. the act; by impl. the obj.), in a good or a bad sense:—boasting {6x}, whereof I may glory {1x}, glorying {1x}, rejoicing {4x}.

Kauchesis denotes "the act of boasting," Rom 3:27; 15:17, "whereof I may glory"; 1 Cor 15:31; 2 Cor 1:12; 7:4, 14 "boasting"; 8:24; 11:10, and 17; 1 Th 2:19 "rejoicing"; Jas 4:16. See: TDNT—3:645, 423; BAGD—426b; THAYER—342d.

2747. **Κεγχρεαί** {3x} **Kĕgchrĕai**, *keng-khreh-a'-hee;* prob. from κέγχρος **kĕgchrŏs** (*millet*); *Cenchreæ,* a port of Corinth:—Cenchrea {3x}. See: BAGD—426c; THAYER—342d.

2748. **Κεδρών** {1x} **Kĕdrōn**, *ked-rone';* of Heb. or. [6939]; *Cedron* (i.e. *Kidron*), a brook near Jerusalem:—Cedron {1x}. See: BAGD—426c; THAYER—342d.

2749. **κεῖμαι** {26x} **kĕimai**, *ki'-mahee;* mid. voice of a primary verb; to *lie* outstretched (lit. or fig.):—lie {9x}, be laid {6x}, be set {6x}, be appointed {1x}, be {1x}, be made {1x}, laid up {1x}, there {1x}.

Keimai, as a verb, means "to lie" and is used **(1)** in 1 Th 3:3 of the "appointment" of affliction for faithful believers: "That no man should be moved by these afflictions: for yourselves know that we are appointed (*keima*) thereunto." **(2)** It is rendered "set" in Lk 2:34: "And Simeon blessed them, and said unto Mary his mother, Behold, this *child* is set (*keima*) for the fall and rising again of many in Israel; and for a sign which shall be spoken against" (cf. Phil 1:17; The verb is a perfect tense, used for the perfect passive of *tithemi,* "to place," "I have been placed," i.e., "I lie."). See: TDNT—3:654, 425; BAGD—426c; THAYER—343a. comp. *5087.*

2750. **κειρία** {1x} **kĕiria**, *ki-ree'-ah;* of uncert. aff.; a *swathe,* i.e. *winding-sheet:*—graveclothes {1x}.

Keiria denotes, firstly, "a band" either for a bed girth, or bed sheets themselves; then, "the swathings wrapped round a corpse"; it is used in the plural in Jn 11:44. See: BAGD—427a; THAYER—343b.

2751. **κείρω** {4x} **kĕirō**, *ki'-ro;* a primary verb; to *shear:*—shear {3x}, shearer {1x}.

Keiro is used **(1)** of "shearing sheep," Acts 8:32, "shearer," lit., "the (one) shearing": **(2)** in the middle voice, "to have one's hair cut off, be shorn," Acts 18:18; 1 Cor 11:6 (twice). See: BAGD—427a; THAYER—343b.

2752. **κέλευμα** {1x} **kĕlĕuma**, *kel'-yoo-mah* or **κέλευσμα** **kĕlĕusma**, *kel'-yoos-mah;* from *2753;* a *cry* of incitement:—shout {1x}.

This word means "a call, summons, shout of command" (akin to *keleuo,* "to command"), is used in 1 Th 4:16 of the "shout" with which the Lord will descend from heaven at the time of the rapture of the saints to meet Him in the air. The "shout" is not here said to be His actual voice, though this indeed will be so (Jn 5:28). See: TDNT—3:656,*; BAGD—427b; THAYER—343b.

2753. **κελεύω** {27x} **kĕlĕuō**, *kel-yoo'-o;* from a primary κέλλω **kĕllō** (to *urge* on); "hail;" to *incite* by word, i.e. *order:*—command {24x}, at (one's) command {1x}, give commandment {1x}, bid {1x}.

This word means "to urge, incite, order," Mt 14:9, 19; 15:35; 18:25; 27:58, 64; Lk 18:40; Acts 4:15. See: BAGD—427b; THAYER—343b.

2754. **κενοδοξία** {1x} **kĕnŏdŏxia**, *ken-od-ox-ee'-ah;* from *2755; empty glorying,* i.e. *self-conceit:*—vain-glory {1x}.

This word stresses groundless, self esteem, empty pride, a vain opinion. See: TDNT—3:662, 426; BAGD—427c; THAYER—343d.

2755. **κενόδοξος** {1x} **kĕnŏdŏxŏs**, *ken-od'-ox-os;* from *2756* and *1391; vainly glorifying,* i.e. *self-conceited:*—desirous of vain-glory {1x}.

This word denotes one who is glorying without reason, conceited, vain glorious, eager for empty glory, Phil 2:3. See: TDNT—3:662, 426; BAGD—427d; THAYER—343d.

2756. **κενός** {18x} **kĕnŏs**, *ken-os';* appar. a primary word; *empty* (lit. or fig.):—vain {9x}, in vain {4x}, empty {4x}, vain things {1x}.

Summary: This word denotes that which is empty, implies hollowness, and is devoid of contents. There is the absence of good, but also the presence of evil because man's moral nature permits no vacuum (Jas 2:20). *Kenos* expresses the "hollowness" of anything, the "absence" of that which otherwise might be possessed. It is used **(1)** literally, Mk 12:3; Lu 1:53; 20:10–11; **(2)** metaphorically, **(2a)** of imaginations, Acts 4:25; **(2b)** of words which convey erroneous teachings, Eph. 5:6; **(2c)** of deceit, Col 2:8; **(2d)** of a person whose professed faith is not accompanied by works, Jas 2:20; **(2e)** negatively, concerning the grace of God, 1 Cor 15:10; **(2f)** of refusal to receive it, 2 Cor 6:1; **(2g)** of faith, 1 Cor 15:14; **(2h)** of preaching and other forms of Christian activity and labor, 1 Cor 15:58; Gal 2:2; Phil 2:16; 1 Th 2:1; 3:5. Syn.: The synonymous word *mataios* (3152), "vain," signifies "void" of result, it marks the aimlessness of anything. The vain (*kenos*) man in Jas 2:20 is one who is "empty" of divinely imparted wisdom; in 1:26 the vain (*mataios*) religion is one that produces nothing profitable. *Kenos* stresses the absence of quality, *mataios,* the absence of useful aim or effect. See: TDNT—3:659, 426; BAGD—427d; THAYER—343d.

2757. **κενοφωνία** {2x} **kĕnŏphōnia**, *ken-of-o-nee'-ah;* from a presumed compound of *2756* and *5456; empty sounding,* i.e. *fruitless discussion:*—vain babblings {2x}.

This word signifies empty discussion, discussion on useless subjects (1 Ti 6:20; 2 Ti 2:16). See: BAGD—428a; THAYER—343d.

2758. **κενόω** {5x} **kĕnŏō**, *ken-ŏ'-o;* from *2756;* to *abase, neutralize:*—make void {2x}, make of none effect {1x}, make of no reputation {1x}, be in vain {1x}.

(1) *Kenoo* means to neutralize or to take that which has positivie effects and renders them neutral; making negative is not within the definition of the word. It is translated **(2)** "should be made of none effect" in 1 Cor 1:17, to neutralize the effects of preaching the Cross of Christ; **(3)** of Christ, "making Himself of no reputation", Phil 2:7, He did not effect His own reputation, but left it up to God; **(3)** of faith, being made "void", of no effect, if the promise of salvation is earned by works of the Law, Rom 4:14; **(4)** of the apostle Paul's glorying in the gospel ministry, 1 Cor. 9:15; **(5)** of his glorying on behalf of the church at Corinth, 2 Cor 9:3, would "be in vain", of no effect, if the Corinthians failed in the offering. See: TDNT—3:661, 426; BAGD—428a; THAYER—344a.

2759. **κέντρον** {5x} **kĕntrŏn**, *ken'-tron;* from κεντέω **kĕntĕō** (to *prick*); a *point* ("centre"), i.e. a *sting* (fig. *poison*) or *goad* (fig. divine *impulse*):—prick {2x}, sting {3x}.

Kentron from *kenteo,* "to prick," denotes **(1)** "a sting," **(1a)** literally, Rev 9:10; **(1b)** metaphorically, of sin as the "sting" of death, 1 Cor 15:55, 56; **(2)** "a prick," Acts 9:5; 26:14, said of the promptings and conscience "stings" which Saul of Tarsus felt before conversion, possibly at approving and witnessing the stoning death of Stephen. See: TDNT—3:663, 427; BAGD—428b; THAYER—344a.

2760. **κεντυρίων** {3x} **kĕnturiōn**, *ken-too-ree'-ohn;* of Lat. or.; a *centurion,* i.e. *captain* of one hundred soldiers:—centurion {3x}. Cf. Mk 14: 39, 44–45. See: BAGD—428c; THAYER—344a.

2761. **κενῶς** {1x} **kĕnōs**, *ken-oce';* adv. from *2756; vainly,* i.e. *to no purpose:*—in vain {1x}. See: BAGD—428c; THAYER—344a.

2762. **κεραία** {2x} **kĕraia**, *ker-ah'-yah;* fem. of a presumed der. of the base of *2768;* something *horn-like,* i.e. (spec.) the *apex* of a Heb. letter (fig. the least *particle*):—tittle {2x}.

Keraia, "a little horn" (*keras,* "a horn"), was used to denote the small stroke distinguishing one Hebrew letter from another. The rabbis attached great importance to these; hence the significance of the Lord's statements in Mt 5:18 and Lk 16:17, charging the Pharisees with hypocrisy, because, while professing the most scrupulous reverence to the Law, they violated its spirit. See: BAGD—428d; THAYER—344b.

2763. **κεραμεύς** {3x} **kĕramĕus**, *ker-am-yooce';* from *2766;* a *potter:*—potter {3x}.

Kerameus, "a potter" is used **(1)** in connection with the "potter's field," Mt 27:7, 10; and **(2)** illustratively of the "potter's" right over the clay, Rom 9:21, where the introductory "or" suggests the alternatives that either there must be a recognition of the absolute discretion and power of God, or a denial that the "potter" has power over the clay. There is no suggestion of the creation of sinful beings, or of the creation of any simply in order to punish them. What the passage sets forth is God's right to deal with sinful beings according to His own counsel. See: BAGD—428d; THAYER—344b.

2764. **κεραμικός** {1x} **kĕramikŏs**, *ker-am-ik-os';* from *2766; made of clay,* i.e. *earthen:*—of a potter {1x}. See: BAGD—428; THAYER—344b.

2765. **κεράμιον** {2x} **kĕramiŏn**, *ker-am'-ee-on;* neut. of a presumed der. of *2766;* an *earthenware* vessel, i.e. *jar:*—pitcher {2x}.

Keramion, "an earthen vessel", "a jar" or "jug," occurs in Mk 14:13; Lk 22:10. See: BAGD—428d; THAYER—344b.

2766. **κέραμος** {1x} **kĕramŏs**, *ker'-am-os;* prob. from the base of *2767* (through the idea of *mixing* clay and water); *earthenware,* i.e. a *tile* (by anal. a thin *roof* or *awning*):—tiling {1x}.

This word means "potter's clay," or "an earthen vessel," denotes in the plural "tiling" in Lk 5:19. See: BAGD—429a; THAYER—344b.

2767. **κεράννυμι** {3x} **kĕrannumi**, *ker-an'-noo-mee;* a prol. form of a more primary κεράω **kĕraō**, *ker-ah'-o* (which is used in certain tenses); to *mingle,* i.e. (by impl.) to *pour* out (for drinking):—fill {2x}, pour out {1x}.

Kerannumi, "to mix, to mingle," chiefly of the diluting of wine, implies "a mixing of two things, so that they are blended and form a compound, as in wine and water. It is translated "fill, filled" in Rev 18:6 (twice); and "poured out" in Rev 14:10. See: BAGD—429a; THAYER—344c. comp. *3396.*

2768. **κέρας** {11x} **kĕras**, *ker'-as;* from a primary κάρ **kar** (the *hair* of the head); a *horn* (lit. or fig.):—horn {11x}.

Keras, "a horn," is used in the plural, as the symbol of strength, **(1)** in the apocalyptic visions; **(1a)** on the head of the Lamb as symbolic of Christ, Rev 5:6; **(1b)** on the heads of beasts as symbolic of national potentates, Rev 12:3; 13:1, 11; 17:3, 7, 12, 16 (cf. Dan 7:8; 8:9; Zech 1:18, etc.); **(1c)** at the corners of the golden altar, Rev 9:13 (cf. Ex 30:2; the horns were of one piece with the altar, as in the case of the brazen altar, 27:2, and were emblematic of the efficacy of the ministry connected with it); **(2)** metaphorically, in the singular, "a horn of salvation," Lk 1:69. See: TDNT—3:669, 428; BAGD—429b; THAYER—344d.

2769. **κεράτιον** {1x} **kĕratiŏn**, *ker-at'-ee-on;* neut. of a presumed der. of *2768;* something *horned,* i.e. (spec.) the *pod* of the carob-tree:—husk {1x}.

Keraton, used in the plural in Lk 15:16, of carob pods, given to swine, and translated "husks." See: BAGD—429b; THAYER—344d.

κεράω **kĕraō**. See *2767.*

2770. **κερδαίνω** {17x} **kĕrdainō**, *ker-dah'-ee-no;* from *2771;* to *gain* (lit. or fig.):—gain {13x}, win {2x}, get gain {1x}, vr gain {1x}.

Kerdaino signifies **(1)** literally, **(1a)** "to gain something," Mt 16:26; 25:17, 20, 22; Mk 8:36; Lk 9:25; **(1b)** "to get gain, make a profit," Jas 4:13; **(2)** metaphorically, "to win persons," said **(2a)** of "gaining" an offending brother who by being told privately of his offense, and by accepting the representations, is won from alienation and from the consequences of his fault, Mt 18:15; **(2b)** of winning souls into the kingdom of God **(2b1)** by the gospel, 1 Cor 9:19, 20 (twice), 21, 22, or **(2b2)** by godly conduct, 1 Pet 3:1; **(2c)** of so practically appropriating Christ to oneself that He becomes the dominating power in and over one's whole being and circumstances, Phil 3:8; **(3)** "to gain things," said of getting injury and loss, Acts 27:21. See: TDNT—3:672, 428; BAGD—429c; THAYER—345a.

2771. **κέρδος** {3x} **kĕrdŏs**, *ker'-dos;* of uncert. aff.; *gain* (pecuniary or gen.):—gain {2x}, lucre {1x}.

Kerdos, "gain", is translated "gain" in Phil 1:21; 3:7; and **(2)** "lucre" in Titus 1:11. See: TDNT—3:672, 428; BAGD—429c; THAYER—345a.

2772. **κέρμα** {1x} **kĕrma**, *ker'-mah;* from *2751;* a *clipping* (*bit*), i.e. (spec.) a *coin:*—money {1x}.

Kerma, primarily "a slice", hence, "a small coin, change," is used in the plural in Jn 2:15, "the changers' money," probably considerable heaps of small coins for making change. See: BAGD—429d; THAYER—345b.

2773. **κερματιστής** {1x} **kĕrmatistēs**, *ker-mat-is-tace';* from a der. of *2772;* a *handler of coins,* i.e. *money-broker:*—changer of money {1x}.

In the court of the Gentiles, in the temple precincts, were the seats of those who sold selected and approved animals for sacrifice, and other things. The magnitude of this traffic had introduced the bankers' or brokers' business, Jn 2:14. See: BAGD—429d; THAYER—345b.

2774. **κεφάλαιον** {2x} **kĕphalaiŏn**, *kef-al'-ah-yon;* neut. of a der. of *2776;* a *principal* thing, i.e. *main point;* spec. an *amount* (of money):—sum {2x}.

This word, akin to the adjective *kephalaios,* "belonging to the head," and *kephale,* "the head," denotes **(1)** the chief point, principal thing, or the "total of what has been said to this point" in a subject, Heb 8:1; and **(2)** in Acts 22:28 (of principal, as to money), "(a great) sum." See: BAGD—429d; THAYER—345b.

2775. **κεφαλαιόω** {1x} **kĕphalaiŏō**, *kef-al-ahee-ŏ'-o;* from the same as *2774;* (spec.) to *strike on the head:*—wound in the head {1x}. See: BAGD—430a; THAYER—345c.

2776. **κεφαλή** {76x} **kĕphalē**, *kef-al-ay';* prob. from the primary κάπτω **kaptō** (in the sense of *seizing*); the *head* (as the part most readily *taken* hold of), lit. or fig.:—head {76x}.

Kephale, besides its natural significance, is used figuratively **(1)** in Rom 12:20, of heaping coals of fire on a "head"; **(2)** in Acts 18:6, "Your blood be upon your own heads," i.e., "your blood-guiltiness rest upon your own persons," a mode of expression frequent in the OT, and perhaps here directly connected with Eze 3:18, 20; 33:6, 8; see also Lev 20:16; 2 Sa 1:16; 1 Kin 2:37; **(3)** of Christ in relation to the Church, Eph 1:22; 4:15; 5:23; Col 1:18; 2:19; **(4)** of Christ in relation to principalities and powers, Col 2:10. **(5)** metaphorically, of the authority or direction of God in relation to Christ, of Christ in relation to believing men, of the husband in relation to the wife, 1 Cor 11:3; **(6)** it is used of Christ as the foundation of the spiritual building set forth by the Temple, with its "corner stone," Mt 21:42; **(7)** symbolically also of the imperial rulers of the Roman power, as seen in the apocalyptic visions, Rev 13:1, 3; 17:3, 7, 9. See: TDNT—3:673, 429; BAGD—430a; THAYER—345c.

2777. **κεφαλίς** {1x} **kĕphalis**, *kef-al-is';* from *2776;* prop. a *knob,* i.e. (by impl.) a *roll* (by extens. from the *end* of a stick on which the MS. was rolled):—volume {1x}. See: BAGD—430c; THAYER—345d.

2778. **κῆνσος** {4x} **kēnsŏs**, *kane'-sos;* of Lat. or.; prop. an *enrollment* ("*census*"), i.e. (by impl.) a *tax:*—tribute {4x}.

Kensos is literally a census (among the Romans, denoting a register and valuation of property in accordance with which taxes were paid), in the NT the tax or tribute levied on individuals and to be paid yearly, Mt 17:25; 22:17, 19; Mk 12:14. Taxes were collected from all to fund the normal expenses of the government. Custom was charged to strangers in the land. Tribute was paid by a conquered people in order to remain in good standing with the conquering army. It is above the normal levied taxes. Taxes are levied, tribute is paid somewhat ironically to the conquerors to maintain favor. See: BAGD—430d; THAYER—345d.

2779. **κῆπος** {5x} **kēpŏs**, *kay'-pos;* of uncert. aff.; a *garden:*—garden {5x}.

Kepos, "a garden," occurs **(1)** in Lk 13:19, in one of the Lord's parables; **(2)** in Jn 18:1, 26, of the garden of Gethsemane; **(3)** in Jn 19:41, of the garden near the place of the Lord's crucifixion. See: BAGD—430d; THAYER—346a.

2780. **κηπουρός** {1x} **kēpŏurŏs**, *kay-poo-ros';* from *2779* and οὖρος **ŏurŏs** (a *warden*); a *garden-keeper,* i.e. *gardener:*—gardener {1x}. See: BAGD—430d; THAYER—346a.

2781. **κηρίον** {7} **kēriŏn**, *kay-ree'-on;* dimin. from κηός **kēŏs** (*wax*); a *cell* for honey, i.e. (collect.) the *comb:*—honeycomb + 3193 {1x}. See: BAGD—430d; THAYER—346a.

2782. **κήρυγμα** {8x} **kērugma**, *kay'-roog-mah;* from *2784;* a *proclamation* (espec. of the gospel; by impl. the *gospel* itself):—preaching {8x}.

Kerugma, as a noun, means "a proclamation by a herald" and denotes "a message, a preaching" (the substance of what is "preached" as distinct from the act of "preaching"), Mt 12:41; Lk 11:32; Rom 16:25; 1 Cor 1:21; 2:4; 15:14; 2 Ti 4:17; Titus 1:3. See: TDNT—3:714, 430; BAGD—430d; THAYER—346a.

2783. **κῆρυξ** {3x} **kērux**, *kay'-roox;* from *2784;* a *herald,* i.e. of divine truth (espec. of the gospel):—preacher {3x}.

Kerux, "a herald", is used **(1)** of the "preacher" of the gospel, 1 Ti 2:7; 2 Ti 1:11; and **(2)** of Noah, as a "preacher" of righteousness, 2 Pet 2:5. See: TDNT—3:683, 430; BAGD—431a; THAYER—346b.

2784. **κηρύσσω** {61x} **kērussō**, *kay-roos'-so;* of uncert. aff.; to *herald* (as a public *crier*), espec. divine truth (the gospel):—preach {51x}, publish {5x}, proclaim {2x}, preached + 2258 {2x}, preacher {1x}.

Kerusso signifies **(1)** "to be a herald," or, in general, "to proclaim," e.g., Mt 3:1; Mk 1:45, "publish"; in Lk 4:18, "to preach"; so verse 19; Lk 12:3; Acts 10:37; Rom 2:21; Rev 5:2. **(2)** "to preach the gospel as a herald," e.g., Mt 24:14; Mk 13:10, "be published"; 14:9; 16:15, 20; Lk 8:1; 9:2; 24:47; Acts 8:5; 19:13; 28:31; Rom 10:14, present participle, lit., "(one) preaching," "a preacher"; 10:15 (1st part); 1 Cor 1:23; 15:11, 12; 2 Cor 1:19; 4:5; 11:4; Gal 2:2; Phil 1:15; Col 1:23; 1 Th 2:9; 1 Ti 3:16; **(3)** "to preach the word," 2 Ti 4:2 (of the ministry of the Scriptures, with special reference to the gospel). Syn.: 2097, 2782, 3955, 4283, 4296. See: TDNT—3:697, 430; BAGD—431b; THAYER—346b.

2785. **κῆτος** {1x} **kētŏs**, *kay'-tos;* prob. from the base of *5490;* a huge *fish* (as *gaping* for prey):—whale {1x}. See: BAGD—431d; THAYER—346d.

2786. **Κηφᾶς** {6x} **Kēphas**, *kay-fas';* of Chald. or. [comp. 3710]; *the Rock; Cephas* (i.e. *Kepha*), a surname of Peter:—Cephas {6x}. See: TDNT—6:100, 835; BAGD—431d.

2787. **κιβωτός** {6x} **kibōtŏs**, *kib-o-tos';* of uncert. der.; a *box,* i.e. the sacred *ark* and that of Noah:—ark {6x}.

Kibotos, "a wooden box, a chest," is used of **(1)** Noah's vessel, Mt 24:38; Lk 17:27; Heb 11:7; 1 Pet 3:20; **(2)** the "ark" of the covenant in the tabernacle, Heb 9:4; **(3)** the "ark" seen in vision in the heavenly temple, Rev 11:19. See: BAGD—431d; THAYER—346d.

2788. **κιθάρα** {4x} **kithara**, *kith-ar'-ah;* of uncert. aff.; a *lyre:*—harp {4x}.

Kithara denotes "a lyre" or "harp"; it is described by Josephus as an instrument of ten strings, played by a plectrum (a smaller instrument was played by the hand); it is mentioned in 1 Cor 14:7; Rev 5:8; 14:2; 15:2. See: BAGD—432a; THAYER—347a.

2789. **κιθαρίζω** {2x} **kitharizō**, *kith-ar-id'-zo;* from *2788;* to *play on a lyre:*—to harp {2x}.

Kitharizo signifies "to play on the harp," 1 Cor 14:7; Rev 14:2. See: BAGD—432a; THAYER—347a.

2790. **κιθαρῳδός** {2x} **kitharōidŏs**, *kith-ar-o'-dos;* from *2788* and a der. of the same as *5603;* a *lyre-singer* (*-player*), i.e. *harpist:*—harper {2x}.

Kitharodos denotes "one who plays and sings to the lyre" (from *kithara,* "a lyre," and *aoidos,* "a singer"), Rev 14:2; 18:22. See: BAGD—432a; THAYER—347a.

2791. **Κιλικία** {8x} **Kilikia**, *kil-ik-ee'-ah;* prob. of for. or.; *Cilicia,* a region of Asia Minor:—Cilicia {8x}. See: BAGD—432a; THAYER—346a.

2792. **κινάμωμον** {1x} **kinamōmŏn**, *kin-am'-o-mon;* of for. or. [comp. 7076]; *cinnamon:*—cinnamon {1x}. See: BAGD—432a; THAYER—347b.

2793. **κινδυνεύω** {4x} **kinduneuō**, *kin-doon-yoo'-o;* from *2794;* to *undergo peril:*—be in danger {2x}, be in jeopardy {1x}, stand in jeopardy {1x}.

Kinduneuo properly signifies "to run a risk, face danger," but is used in the NT in the sense of **(1)** "being in danger," Acts 19:27, 40. It is translated **(2)** "were in jeopardy" in Lk 8:23, and **(3)** "stand we in jeopardy," 1 Cor 15:30. See: BAGD—432b; THAYER—347b.

2794. **κίνδυνος** {9x} **kindunŏs**, *kin'-doo-nos;* of uncert. der.; *danger:*—peril {9x}. Cf. Rom 8:35; 2 Cor 11:26. See: BAGD—432b; THAYER—347b.

2795. **κινέω** {8x} **kinĕō**, *kin-eh'-o;* from κίω-κιο (poetic for εἶμι **ĕimi**, to *go*); to *stir* (tran.), lit. or fig.:—move {4x}, wag {2x}, remove {1x}, mover {1x}.

Kineo, as a verb, means "to set in motion, move" and is used **(1)** of wagging the head (Mt 27:39; Mk 15:29); **(2)** of the general activity of the human being: "For in him we live, and move (2795), and have our being" (Acts 17:28); **(3)** of the "moving" of mountains: "And the heaven departed as a scroll when it is rolled together; and every mountain and island were moved out of their places" (Rev 6:14, in the sense of removing, as in Rev 2:5, of removing a lampstand [there figuratively of causing a local church to be discontinued]; **(4)** figuratively, of exciting, stirring up feelings and passions: "And all the city was moved, and the people ran together: and they took Paul, and drew him out of the temple: and forthwith the doors were shut" (Acts 21:30 [passive voice]; cf. 24:5, "a mover"); **(5)** of "moving burdens": "For they bind heavy burdens and grievous to be borne, and lay *them* on men's shoulders; but they *themselves* will not move them with one of their fingers" (Mt 23:4). Syn.: 277, 383, 761, 2796, 3334, 4525, 4531, 4579, 4787, 5342. See: TDNT—3:718, 435; BAGD—432c; THAYER—347b.

2796. **κίνησις** {1x} **kinēsis**, *kin'-ay-sis;* from *2795; a stirring:*—moving {1x}.

Kinesis, as a noun, means "a moving" and is found in Jn 5:3: "In these lay a great multitude of impotent folk, of blind, halt, withered, waiting for the moving of the water." Syn.: 277, 383, 761, 2795, 3334, 4525, 4531, 4579, 4787, 5342. See: BAGD—432d; THAYER—347c.

2797. **Κίς** {1x} **Kis**, *kis;* of Heb. or. [7027]; *Cis* (i.e. *Kish*), an Isr.:—Cis {1x}. See: BAGD—432d; THAYER—347c.

κίχρημι **kichrēmi**. See *5531.*

2798. **κλάδος** {11x} **kladŏs**, *klad'-os;* from *2806;* a small tender *twig* or *bough* (as if broken off):—branch {11x}.

Klados properly a young tender shoot, "broken off" for grafting, is used for any kind of branch, Mt 13:32; 21:8; 24:32; Mk 4:32; 13:28; Lk 13:19; the descendants of Israel, Rom 11:16–19, 21. See: TDNT—3:720,*; BAGD—433a; THAYER—347c.

2799. **κλαίω** {40x} **klaiō**, *klah'-yo;* of uncert. aff.; to *sob,* i.e. *wail* aloud (whereas *1145* is rather to *cry* silently):—bewail {1x}, weep {39x}.

Klaio is used of **(1)** "any loud expression of grief," especially in mourning for the dead, Mt 2:18; Mk 5:38, 39; 16:10; Lk 7:13; 8:52 (twice); Jn 11:31, 33 (twice); 20:11 (twice), 13, 15; Acts 9:39; **(2)** otherwise, e.g., in exhortations, Lk 23:28; Rom 12:15; Jas 4:9; 5:1; **(3)** negatively, "weep not," Lk 7:13; 8:52; 23:28; Rev 5:5 (cf. Acts 21:13); **(4)** in Acts 18:9, "bewail." Syn.: *Alalazo* (214) means to wail in oriental style, to howl in a consecrated, semi-liturgical fashion. *Dakruo* (1145) means to shed tears, weep silently. *Threneo* (2354) means to give formal expression to grief, to sing a dirge. *Klaio* (2799) means to weep audibly, cry as a child. *Odurmos* (3602) means to give verbal expression to grief, to lament. *Stenazo* (4727) means to express grief by inarticulate or semi-articulate sounds, to groan. See: TDNT—3:722, 436; BAGD—433a.

2800. **κλάσις** {2x} **klasis**, *klas'-is;* from *2806; fracture* (the act):—breaking {2x}.

Klasis, "a breaking", is used in Lk 24:35 and Acts 2:42, of the "breaking" of bread. See: TDNT—3:726, 437; BAGD—433b; THAYER—347d.

2801. **κλάσμα** {9x} **klasma**, *klas'-mah;* from *2806; a piece* (*bit*):—broken {2x}, fragment {7x}.

Klasma is always used of remnants of food and translated **(1)** "broken", Mt 5:37; Mk 8:8; and **(2)** "fragments", Mt 14:20; Mk 6:43; 8:19, 20; Lk 9:17; Jn 6:12, 13. See: TDNT—3:726, 437; BAGD—433b; THAYER—347d.

2802. **Κλαύδη** {1x} **Klaudē**, *klŏw'-day* or **Καύδη** **Kaudē** *kŏw'-day;* of uncert. der.; *Claude,* an island near Crete:—Clauda (Cauda) {1x}. See: BAGD—433b; THAYER—347d.

2803. **Κλαυδία** {1x} **Klaudia**, *klŏw-dee'-ah;* fem. of *2804; Claudia,* a Chr. woman:—Claudia {1x}. See: BAGD—433c; THAYER—348a.

2804. **Κλαύδιος** {3x} **Klaudiŏs**, *klŏw'-dee-os;* of Lat. or.; *Claudius,* the name of two Romans:—Claudius (Caesar) {2x}, Claudius (Lysias) {1x}. See: BAGD—433c; THAYER—348a.

2805. **κλαυθμός** {9x} **klauthmŏs**, *klŏwth-mos';* from *2799; lamentation:*—wailing {2x}, weeping {6x}, wept {1x}.

This word denotes "weeping, crying," Mt 2:18; 8:12; 13:42, "wailing"; 13:50, "wailing"; 22:13; 24:51; 25:30; Lk 13:28; Acts 20:37, "wept." See: TDNT—3:725, 436; BAGD—433c; THAYER—348a.

2806. **κλάω** {15x} **klaō**, *klah'-o;* a primary verb; to *break* (spec. of bread):—break {15x}.

This word means "to break, to break off pieces," is used of "breaking bread," **(1)** of the Lord's act in providing for people, Mt 14:19; 15:36; Mk 8:6, 19; **(2)** of the "breaking of bread" in the Lord's Supper, Mt 26:26; Mk 14:22; Lk 22:19; Acts 20:7; 1 Cor 10:16; 11:24; **(3)** of an ordinary meal, Acts 2:46; 20:11; 27:35; **(4)** of the Lord's act in giving evidence of His resurrection, Lk 24:30. See: TDNT—3:726, 437; BAGD—433d; THAYER—348a.

2807. **κλείς** {6x} **klĕis**, *klice;* from *2808; a key* (as *shutting* a lock), lit. or fig.:—key {6x}.

Kleis, "a key," is used metaphorically **(1)** of "the keys of the kingdom of heaven," which the Lord committed to Peter, Mt 16:19, by which he would open the door of faith, as he did to Jews at Pentecost, and to Gentiles in the person of Cornelius, acting as one commissioned by Christ, through the power of the Holy Spirit; he had precedence over his fellow disciples, not in authority, but in the matter of time, on the ground of his confession of Christ (v. 16); equal authority was committed to them (18:18); **(2)** of "the key of knowledge," Lk 11:52, i.e., knowledge of the revealed will of God, by which men entered into the life that pleases God; this the religious leaders of the Jews had presumptuously "taken away," so that they neither entered in themselves, nor permitted their hearers to do so; **(3)** of "the keys of death and of Hades," Rev 1:18, indicative of the authority of the Lord over the bodies and souls of men;

(4) of "the key of David," Rev 3:7, a reference to Is 22:22, speaking of the deposition of Shebna and the investiture of Eliakim, in terms evidently messianic, the metaphor being that of the right of entrance upon administrative authority; the mention of David is symbolic of complete sovereignty; **(5)** of "the key of the pit of the abyss," Rev 9:1; here the symbolism is that of competent authority; the pit represents a shaft or deep entrance into the region, from whence issued smoke, symbolic of blinding delusion; **(6)** of "the key of the abyss," Rev 20:1; this is to be distinguished from (5) the symbolism is that of the complete supremacy of God over the region of the lost, in which, by angelic agency, Satan is destined to be confined for a thousand years. See: TDNT—3:744, 439; BAGD—433d; THAYER—348b.

2808. **κλείω** {16x} **klĕiō**, *kli'-o;* a primary verb; to *close* (lit. or fig.):—shut {12x}, shut up {4x}.

Kleio is used **(1)** of things material, Mt 6:6; 25:10; Lk 11:7; Jn 20:19, 26; Acts 5:23; 21:30; Rev 20:3; figuratively, 21:25; **(2)** metaphorically, **(2a)** of the kingdom of heaven, Mt 23:13; **(2b)** of heaven, with consequences of famine, Lk 4:25; Rev 11:6; **(2c)** of compassion, 1 Jn 3:17, "bowels *of compassion*"; **(2d)** of the blessings accruing from the promises of God regarding David, Rev 3:7; **(2e)** of a door for testimony, Rev 3:8. See: BAGD—434a; THAYER—348b.

2809. **κλέμμα** {1x} **klĕmma**, *klem'-mah;* from *2813; stealing* (prop. the thing stolen, but used of the act):—theft {1x}. See: BAGD—434b; THAYER—348c.

2810. **Κλεόπας** {1x} **Klĕŏpas**, *kleh-op'-as;* prob. contr. from Κλεόπατρος **Klĕŏpatrŏs** (compound of *2811* and *3962*); *Cleopas,* a Chr.:—Cleopas {1x}. See: BAGD—434b; THAYER—348c.

2811. **κλέος** {1x} **klĕŏs**, *kleh'-os;* from a short. form of *2564; renown* (as if *being called*):—glory {1x}.

The word is derived from a root signifying hearing; hence, the meaning reputation, good report, fame, renown (1 Pet 2:20). See: BAGD—434b; THAYER—348c.

2812. **κλέπτης** {16x} **klĕptēs**, *klep'-tace;* from *2813;* a *stealer* (lit. or fig.):—thief {16x}.

Kleptes is used **(1)** literally, Mt 6:19, 20; 24:43; Lk 12:33, 39; Jn 10:1, 10; 12:6; 1 Cor 6:10; 1 Pet 4:15; **(2)** metaphorically of "false teachers," Jn 10:8; **(3)** figuratively, **(3a)** of the personal coming of Christ, in a warning to a local church, with most of its members possessed of mere outward profession and defiled by the world, Rev 3:3; **(3b)** in retributive intervention to overthrow the foes of God, 16:15, **(4)** of the Day of the Lord, in divine judgment upon the world, 2 Pet 3:10 and 1 Th 5:2, 4; there is no reference to the time of the coming, only to the manner of it. The use of the present tense instead of the future emphasizes the certainty of the coming. . . . The unexpectedness of the coming of the thief, and the unpreparedness of those to whom He comes, are the essential elements in the figure. Syn.: A *kleptes* uses deception while the lestes (3027) is a robber who plunders, audaciously snatching away that which is another's. See: TDNT—3:754, 441; BAGD—434b; THAYER—348c.

2813. **κλέπτω** {13x} **klĕptō**, *klep'-to;* a primary verb; to *filch:*—steal {13x}.

Klepto, "to steal," akin to *kleptes,* "a thief" (cf. Eng., "kleptomania"), occurs in Mt 6:19, 20; 19:18; 27:64; 28:13; Mk 10:19; Lk 18:20; Jn 10:10; Rom 2:21 (twice); 13:9; Eph 4:28 (twice). See: TDNT—3:754, 441; BAGD—434c; THAYER—348c.

2814. **κλῆμα** {4x} **klēma**, *klay'-mah;* from *2806;* a *limb* or *shoot* (as if *broken* off):—branch {4x}.

Klema denotes a tender, flexible branch, especially the shoot of a vine, a vine sprout (Jn 15:2, 4, 5, 6). See: TDNT—3:757, 441; BAGD—434c, THAYER—348d.

2815. **Κλήμης** {1x} **Klēmēs**, *klay'-mace;* of Lat. or.; *merciful; Clemes* (i.e. *Clemens*), a Chr.:—Clement {1x}. See: BAGD—434c; THAYER—348d.

2816. **κληρονομέω** {18x} **klērŏnŏmĕō**, *klay-ron-om-eh'-o;* from *2818;* to *be* an *heir* to (lit. or fig.):—be heir {2x}, obtain by inheritance {1x}, inherit {15x}.

Introduction: *Kleronomeo* strictly means "to receive by lot" (*kleros,* "a lot," *nemomai,* "to possess"); then, in a more general sense, "to possess oneself of, to receive as one's own, to obtain." The following list shows how in the NT the idea of inheriting broadens out to include all spiritual good provided through and in Christ, and particularly all that is contained in the hope grounded on the promises of God. The verb is used of the following objects: **(1)** birthright, that into the possession of which one enters in virtue of sonship, not because of a price paid or of a task accomplished, Gal 4:30; Heb 1:4; 12:17; **(2)** that which is received as a gift, in contrast with that which is received as the reward of law-keeping, Heb 1:14; 6:12 ("through," i.e., "through experiences that called for the exercise of faith and patience,' but not 'on the ground of the exercise of faith and patience.'); **(3)** that which is received on condition of obedience to certain precepts, 1 Pet 3:9, and of faithfulness to God amidst opposition, Rev 21:7; **(4)** the reward of that condition of soul which forbears retaliation and self-vindication, and expresses itself in gentleness of behavior. . . ; Mt 5:5. The phrase "inherit the earth," or "land," occur several times in OT. See especially Ps 37:11, 22;

(5) the reward (in the coming age, Mk 10:30) of the acknowledgment of the paramountcy of the claims of Christ, Mt 19:29. In the three accounts given of this incident, see Mk 10:17–31; Lk 18:18–30, the words of the question put to the Lord are, in Matthew, "that I may have," in Mark and Luke, "that I may inherit." In the report of the Lord's word to Peter in reply to his subsequent question, Matthew has "inherit eternal life," while Mark and Luke have "receive eternal life." It seems to follow that the meaning of the word "inherit" is here ruled by the words "receive" and "have," with which it is interchanged in each of the three Gospels, i.e., the less common word "inherit" is to be regarded as equivalent to the more common words "receive" and "have." Cf. Luke 10:25: Note: In regard to (5), the word clearly signifies entrance into eternal life without any previous title; it will not bear the implication that a child of God may be divested of his "inheritance" by the loss of his right of succession. **(6)** the reward of those who have shown kindness to the "brethren" of the Lord in their distress during the tribulatioin, Mt 25:34; **(7)** the kingdom of God, which the morally corrupt cannot "inherit," 1 Cor 6:9, 10, the "inheritance" of which is likewise impossible to the present physical constitution of man, 1 Cor 15:50; **(8)** incorruption, impossible of "inheritance" by corruption, 1 Cor 15:50. See: TDNT—3:767, 442; BAGD—434d; THAYER—348d.

2817. **κληρονομία** {14x} **klērŏnŏmia**, *klay-ron-om-ee'-ah;* from *2818; heirship,* i.e. (concr.) a *patrimony* or (gen.) a *possession:*—inheritance {14x}.

Kleronomia, "a lot", properly "an inherited property, an inheritance." **(1)** It is always rendered inheritance in NT, but only in a few cases in the Gospels has it the meaning ordinarily attached to that word in English, i.e., that into possession of which the heir enters only on the death of an ancestor. **(2)** The NT usage may be set out as follows: **(2a)** that property in real estate which in ordinary course passes from father to son on the death of the former, Mt 21:38; Mk 12:7; Lk 12:13; 20:14; **(2b)** a portion of an estate made the substance of a gift, Acts 7:5; Gal 3:18, which also is to be included under (2c); In Gal 3:18, "if the inheritance is of the Law," the word "inheritance" stands for "the title to the inheritance." **(2c)** the prospective condition and possessions of the believer in the new order of things to be ushered in at the return of Christ, Acts 20:32; Eph 1:14; 5:5; Col 3:24; Heb 9:15; 1 Pet 1:4; **(2d)** what the believer will be to God in that age, Eph 1:18. See: TDNT—3:767, 442; BAGD—435a; THAYER—349a.

2818. **κληρονόμος** {15x} **klērŏnŏmŏs**, *klay-ron-om'-os;* from *2819* and the base of *3551* (in its orig. sense of *partitioning,* i.e. [refl.] *getting* by apportionment); a *sharer by lot,* i.e. *inheritor* (lit. or fig.); by impl. a *possessor:*—heir {15x}. See: TDNT—3:767, 442; BAGD—435b; THAYER—349b.

2819. **κλῆρος** {13x} **klērŏs**, *klay'-ros;* prob. from *2806* (through the idea of using *bits* of wood, etc., for the purpose); a *die* (for drawing chances); by impl. a *portion* (as if so secured); by extens. an *acquisition* (espec. a *patrimony,* fig.):—heritage {1x}, inheritance {2x}, lot {8x}, part {2x}.

Kleros, (whence Eng., "clergy"), denotes **(1)** "a lot," given or cast (the latter as a means of obtaining divine direction), Mt 27:35 twice; Mk 15:24; Lk 23:24; Jn 19:24; Acts 1:26 twice; **(2)** "a person's share" in anything, Acts 1:17, "part"; 8:21, "lot"; **(3)** "a charge" (lit., "charges") "allotted," to elders, 1 Pet 5:3, "(God's) heritage"; the figure is from portions of lands allotted to be cultivated; **(4)** "an inheritance"; Acts 26:18; Col 1:12. See: TDNT—3:758, 442; BAGD—435b; THAYER—349c.

2820. **κληρόω** {1x} **klērŏō**, *klay-rŏ'-o;* from *2819;* to *allot,* i.e. (fig.) to *assign* (a privilege):—obtain an inheritance {1x}. See: TDNT—3:764, 442; BAGD—435d; THAYER—349d.

2821. **κλῆσις** {11x} **klēsis**, *klay'-sis;* from a shorter form of *2564;* an *invitation* (fig.):—calling {10x}, vocation {1x}.

Klesis, "a calling", **(1)** is always used in the NT of that "calling" the origin, nature and destiny of which are heavenly (the idea of invitation being implied); **(2)** it is used especially of God's invitation to man to accept the benefits of salvation, Rom 11:29; 1 Cor 1:26; 7:20 (said there of the condition in which the "calling" finds one); Eph 1:18, "His calling"; Phil 3:14, the "high calling"; 2 Th 1:11 and 2 Pet 1:10, "your calling"; 2 Ti 1:9, a "holy calling"; Heb 3:1, a "heavenly calling"; Eph 4:1, "the vocation wherewith ye were called"; 4:4, "in one hope of your calling." See: TDNT—3:491, 394; BAGD—435d; THAYER—349d.

2822. **κλητός** {11x} **klētŏs**, *klay-tos';* from the same as *2821; invited,* i.e. *appointed,* or (spec.) a *saint:*—called {11x}.

Kletos, "called, invited," is used, **(1)** "of the call of the gospel," Mt 20:16; 22:14, not there "an effectual call," as in the Epistles, Rom 1:1, 6–7; 8:28; 1 Cor 1:2, 24; Jude 1; Rev 17:14; **(2)** in Rom 1:7 and 1 Cor 1:2 the meaning is "saints by calling"; **(3)** of "an appointment to apostleship," Rom 1:1; 1 Cor 1:1. See: TDNT—3:494, 394; BAGD—436a; THAYER—350a.

2823. **κλίβανος** {2x} **klibanŏs**, *klib'-an-os;* of uncert. der.; an earthen *pot* used for baking in:—oven {2x}.

Klibanos is mentioned in Mt 6:30 and Lk 12:28. The form of "oven" commonly in use in the east indicates the kind in use as mentioned in Scripture. A hole is sunk in the ground about 3 feet deep and somewhat less in diameter. The walls are plastered with cement. A fire is kindled inside, the fuel being grass, or dry twigs, which heat the oven rapidly and blacken it with smoke and soot (see Lam 5:10). When sufficiently heated the surface is wiped, and the dough is molded into broad thin loaves, placed one at a time on the wall of the "oven" to fit its concave inner circle. The baking takes a few seconds. Such ovens are usually outside the home, and often the same "oven" serves for several families (Lev 26:26). An "oven" of this sort is doubtless referred to in Ex 8:3. See: BAGD—436b; THAYER—350b.

2824. **κλίμα** {3x} **klima**, *klee'-mah;* from *2827;* a *slope,* i.e. (spec.) a "*clime*" or *tract* of country:—part {1x}, region {2x}.

Klima, primarily "an incline, slope" (Eng., "clime, climate"), is used **(1)** of "parts", Rom 15:23; and **(2)** of "regions", 2 Cor 11:10; Gal 1:21. See: BAGD—436b; THAYER—350b.

2825. **κλίνη** {10x} **klinē**, *klee'-nay;* from *2827;* a *couch* (for sleep, sickness, sitting or eating):—bed {9x}, table {1x}.

Kline, akin to *klino,* "to lean" (Eng., "recline, incline" etc.), **(1)** "a bed," e.g., Mk 7:30, also denotes **(2)** a "couch" **(2a)** for reclining at meals, Mk 4:21, or **(2b)** a "couch" for carrying the sick, Mt 9:2, 6. **(3)** The metaphorical phrase "to cast into a bed," Rev 2:22, signifies to afflict with disease (or possibly, to lay on a bier); **(4)** in Mk 7:4, "tables." See: BAGD—436b; THAYER—350c.

2826. **κλινίδιον** {2x} **klinidiŏn**, *kleen-eed'-ee-on;* neut. of a presumed der. of *2825;* a *pallet* or *little couch:*—bed {2x}.

Klinidion, "a small bed," a diminutive form of *kline,* "a bed" (from *klino,* "to incline, recline"), is used in Luke 5:19, 24 of the "bed" (*kline,* in v. 18) on which the palsied man was brought. See: BAGD—436c; THAYER—350c.

2827. **κλίνω** {7x} **klinō**, *klee'-no;* a primary verb; to *slant* or *slope,* i.e. *incline* or *recline* (lit. or fig.):—bow {1x}, bow down {1x}, be far spent {1x}, lay {2x}, turn to flight {1x}, wear away {1x}.

Klino, "to incline, to bow down," is used **(1)** of the women who in their fright "bowed" their faces to the earth at the Lord's empty tomb, Lk 24:5; **(2)** of the act of the Lord on the cross immediately before giving up His Spirit. What is indicated in the statement "He bowed His head," is not the helpless dropping of the head after death, but the deliberate putting of His head into a position of rest, Jn 19:30. The verb is deeply significant here. The Lord reversed the natural order. The same verb is used in His statement in Mt 8:20 and Lk 9:58, "the Son of Man hath not where to lay His head." **(3)** It is used, too, of the decline of day, Lk 9:12; 24:29; **(4)** of turning enemies to flight, Heb 11:34. See: BAGD—436c; THAYER—350c.

2828. **κλισία** {1x} **klisia**, *klee-see'-ah;* from a der. of *2827;* prop. *reclination,* i.e. (concr. and spec.) a *party* at a meal:—company {1x}.

It is found in the plural in Lk 9:14 signifying companies reclining at a meal. See: BAGD—436d; THAYER—350d.

2829. **κλοπή** {2x} **klŏpē**, *klop-ay';* from *2813; stealing:*—theft {2x}. Cf. Matt. 15:19; Mark 7:22. See: BAGD—436d; THAYER—350d.

2830. **κλύδων** {2x} **kludōn**, *kloo'-dohn;* from κλύζω **kluzō** (to *billow* or *dash* over); a *surge* of the sea (lit. or fig.):—raging {1x}, wave {1x}.

Kludon "a billow, a dashing or surging wave, a surge, a violent agitation" (akin to *kluzo,* "to wash over"), said of the sea; translated **(1)** "raging" in Lk 8:24; and **(2)** "wave" in Jas 1:6. Syn.: *Kludon* (2949) denotes a wave, suggesting uninterrupted successions; and *kuma* (2830) denotes a billow, surge, suggesting size and extension. Both are figuratively used of words suggesting the same definitions. See: BAGD—436d; THAYER—350d.

Greek

2831. **κλυδωνίζομαι** {1x} **kludōnizŏmai,** *kloo-do-nid'-zom-ahee;* mid. voice from *2830;* to *surge,* i.e. (fig.) to *fluctuate:*—toss to and fro {1x}.

This word signifies "to be tossed by billows" (*kludon,* "a billow"); metaphorically, in Eph 4:14 it speaks of an unsettled condition of mind influenced and agitated by one false teaching and another, and characterized by that immaturity which lacks the firm conviction begotten by the truth. See: BAGD—436d; THAYER—350d.

2832. **Κλωπᾶς** {1x} **Klōpas,** *klo-pas';* of Chald. or. (corresp. to *256*); *Clopas,* an Isr.:—Clopas {1x}. See: BAGD—436d; THAYER—351a.

2833. **κνήθω** {1x} **knēthō,** *knay'-tho;* from a primary κνάω **knaō** (to *scrape*); to *scratch,* i.e. (by impl.) to *tickle:*—× itching {1x}.

Knetho, "to scratch, tickle," is used in the passive voice, metaphorically, of an eagerness to hear, in 2 Ti 4:3, lit., "itched (as to the hearing)," of those who, not enduring sound doctrine, heap to themselves teachers who teach what they are "itching" to hear." See: BAGD—437a; THAYER—351a.

2834. **Κνίδος** {1x} **Knidŏs,** *knee'-dos;* prob. of for. or.; *Cnidus,* a place in Asia Minor:—Cnidus {1x}. See: BAGD—437a; THAYER—351a.

2835. **κοδράντης** {2x} **kŏdrantēs,** *kod-ran'-tace;* of Lat. or.; a *quadrans,* i.e. the fourth part of an as:—farthing {2x}.

This coin equals about ⅜ of a cent, Mt 5:26; Mk 12:42. See: BAGD—437a; THAYER—351a.

2836. **κοιλία** {23x} **kŏilia,** *koy-lee'-ah;* from κοῖλος **kŏilŏs** ("*hollow*"); a *cavity,* i.e. (spec.) the *abdomen;* by impl. the *matrix;* fig. the *heart:*—belly {11x}, womb {12x}.

Koilia, from *koilos,* "hollow", denotes the entire physical cavity, but most frequently was used to denote **(1)** "the womb", Mt 19:12; Lk 1:15, 41, 42, 44; 2:21; 11:27; 23:29; Jn 3:4; Acts 3:2; 14:8; Gal 1:15; **(2)** When translated "belly" it represents the whole belly, the entire cavity, the upper [i.e. stomach] and the lower belly being distinguished; **(2a)** the lower belly, the lower region, the receptacle of the excrement, Mt 15:17; Mk 7:19; **(2b)** the gullet, Mt 12:40; Lk 15:16; and **(3)** to be given up to the pleasures of the palate, to gluttony, Rom 16:18; Phil 3:19; it also **(4)** stands metaphorically for the innermost part of man, the soul, the heart, seat of thought, feeling, choice, Jn 7:38. See: TDNT—3:786, 446; BAGD—437b; THAYER—351b.

2837. **κοιμάω** {18x} **kŏimaō,** *koy-mah'-o;* from *2749;* to *put to sleep,* i.e. (pass. or refl.) to *slumber;* fig. to *decease:*—sleep {10x}, fall asleep {4x}, be asleep {2x}, fall on sleep {1x}, be dead {1x}.

Koimaomai is used of **(1)** natural sleep (Mt 28:13; Lk 22:45; Jn 11:12); **(2)** the death of the body, but only of such as are Christ's; **(3)** yet never of Christ Himself, though He is the firstfruits of them that have fallen asleep (1 Cor 15:20); **(4)** of saints who departed before Christ came (Mt 27:52; Acts 13:36); **(5)** of Lazarus, while Christ was yet upon the earth (Jn 11:11); **(6)** of believers since the ascension (1 Th 4:13–15; Acts 7:60; 1 Cor 7:39; 11:30; 15:6, 18, 51; 2 Pet 3:4). **(7)** This metaphorical use of the word sleep is appropriate, because of the similarity in appearance between a sleeping body and a dead body; restfulness and peace normally characterize both. As the sleeper does not cease to exist while his body sleeps, so the dead person continues to exist despite his absence from the region in which those who remain can communicate with him, and that, as sleep is known to be temporary, so the death of the body will be found to be. See: BAGD—437c; THAYER—351b.

2838. **κοίμησις** {1x} **kŏimēsis,** *koy'-may-sis;* from *2837; sleeping,* i.e. (by impl.) *repose:*—taking of rest {1x}.

Koimesis, "a resting, reclining", is used in Jn 11:13, of natural sleep, translated "taking of rest." See: BAGD—437d; THAYER—351c.

2839. **κοινός** {12x} **kŏinŏs,** *koy-nos';* prob. from *4862; common,* i.e. (lit.) shared by all or several, or (cer.) *profane:*—common {7x}, defiled {1x}, unclean {3x}, unholy {1x}.

(1) This word means "common" from the idea of coming into contact with everything, not separated in the least. **(2)** *Koinos,* as an adjective, means "common," and is translated "unclean": "I know, and am persuaded by the Lord Jesus, that *there is* nothing unclean of itself: but to him that esteemeth any thing to be unclean, to him *it is* unclean" (Rom 14:14 (thrice). *Koinos* (2834) denotes "common, belonging to several" (Lat., *communis*), said **(3)** of things had in common, Acts 2:44; 4:32; **(3a)** of faith, Titus 1:4; **(3b)** of salvation, Jude 3; it stands in contrast to idios, "one's own"; **(4)** "ordinary, belonging to the generality, as distinct from what is peculiar to the few", hence the application to religious practices of Gentiles in contrast with those of Jews; **(4a)** or of the ordinary people in contrast with those of the Pharisees; hence the meaning "unhallowed, profane," Levitically unclean (Lat., *profanus*), said **(4b)** of hands, Mk 7:2, "defiled"; **(4c)** of animals, ceremonially unclean, Acts 10:14; 11:8; **(4d)** of a man, Acts 10:28; **(4e)** of meats, Rom 14:14, "unclean"; **(4f)** of the blood of the covenant, as viewed by an apostate, Heb 10:29, "unholy"; **(4g)** of everything unfit for the holy city, Rev 21:27.

Syn.: 167, 169, 952, 2840, 3394. See: TDNT—3:789, 447; BAGD—438a; THAYER—351c.

2840. **κοινόω** {15x} **kŏinŏō,** *koy-nŏ'-o;* from *2839;* to *make* (or *consider*) *profane* (ceremon.):—call common {2x}, defile {11x}, pollute {1x}, unclean {1x}.

Koinoo, as a verb, means **(1)** to make *koinos* a (2839), "to defile," **(2)** is translated "unclean": "For if the blood of bulls and of goats, and the ashes of an heifer sprinkling the unclean, sanctifieth to the purifying of the flesh:" (Heb 9:13), **(3)** where the perfect participle, passive, is used with the article, hence "them that have been defiled." Syn.: 167, 169, 2839, 3394. See: TDNT—3:809, 447; BAGD—438b; THAYER—351d.

2841. **κοινωνέω** {8x} **kŏinōnĕō,** *koy-no-neh'-o;* from *2844;* to *share* with others (obj. or subj.):—communicate {2x}, distribute {1x}, be partaker {5x}.

Koinoneo is used in two senses, **(1)** "to have a share in," Rom 15:27; 1 Tim 5:22; Heb 2:14; 1 Pet 4:13; 2 Jn 11; **(2)** "to give a share to, go shares with," Rom 12:13, "distributing"; Gal 6:6, "communicate"; Phil 4:15, "did communicate"; it is also translated **(3)** "to be partaker of" **(3a)** in 1 Ti 5:22; Heb 2:14, 1st part, "are partakers of"; **(3b)** 1 Pet 4:13; 2 Jn 11, "is partaker of"; **(3c)** in the passive voice in Rom 15:27, "have been made partakers of." See: TDNT—3:797, 447; BAGD—438c; THAYER—351d.

2842. **κοινωνία** {20x} **kŏinōnia,** *koy-nohn-ee'-ah;* from *2844; partnership,* i.e. (lit.) *participation,* or (social) *intercourse,* or (pecuniary) *benefaction:*—fellowship {12x}, communion {4x}, communication {1x}, distribution {1x}, contribution {1x}, to communicate {1x}.

Koinonia, "a having in common (*koinos*), partnership, fellowship" denotes **(1)** the share which one has in anything, a participation, fellowship recognized and enjoyed; thus it is used of the common experiences and interests of Christian men, Acts 2:42; Gal 2:9; **(2)** of participation in the knowledge of the Son of God, 1 Cor 1:9; **(3)** of sharing in the realization of the effects of the blood (i.e., the death) of Christ and the body of Christ, as set forth by the emblems in the Lord's Supper, 1 Cor 10:16; **(4)** of participation in what is derived from the Holy Spirit, 2 Cor 13:14; Phil 2:1; **(5)** of participation in the sufferings of Christ, Phil 3:10; **(6)** of sharing in the resurrection life possessed in Christ, and so of fellowship with the Father and the Son, 1 Jn 1:3, 6–7; **(7)** negatively, of the impossibility of "communion" between light and darkness, 2 Cor 6:14; **(8)** fellowship manifested in acts, the practical effects of fellowship with God, **(8a)** wrought by the Holy Spirit in the lives of believers as the outcome of faith, Philem 6, and **(8b)** finding expression in joint ministration to the needy, Rom 15:26; 2 Cor 8:4; 9:13; Heb 13:16, and **(8c)** in the furtherance of the Gospel by gifts, Phil 1:5. **(9)** It is translated **(9a)** "fellowship", Acts 2:42; 1 Cor 1:9; 2 Cor 8:4; Gal 2:9; Eph 3:9; Phil 1:5; 2:1; 3:10; 1 Jn 1:3 twice; 1:6, 7; **(9b)** "communion", 1 Cor 10:16 twice; 2 Cor 6:14; 13:14; **(9c)** "communication", Philem 6; **(9d)** "distribution", 2 Cor 9:13, **(9e)** "contribution", Rom 15:26; **(9f)** "to communicate", Heb 13:16. See: TDNT—3:797, 447; BAGD—438d; THAYER—352a.

2843. **κοινωνικός** {1x} **kŏinōnikŏs,** *koy-no-nee-kos';* from *2844; communicative,* i.e. (pecuniarily) *liberal:*—willing to communicate {1x}.

This word denotes social, sociable, ready and apt to form and maintain communion and fellowship; inclined to make others sharers in one's possessions, inclined to impart, free in giving, liberal, 1 Ti 6:18. See: TDNT—3:809, 447; BAGD—439c; THAYER—352b.

2844. **κοινωνός** {10x} **kŏinōnŏs,** *koy-no-nos';* from *2839;* a *sharer,* i.e. *associate:*—companion {1x}, × fellowship {1x}, partaker {5x}, partner {3x}.

Koinonos, "having in common," is rendered **(1)** "are partakers with (the altar),"—the altar standing by metonymy for that which is associated with it—in 1 Cor 10:18, and **(2)** in 10: 20, "have fellowship with (devils)." **(3)** It is translated **(3a)** "companion", Heb 10:33; **(3b)** "× fellowship", 1 Cor 10:20; **(3c)** "partaker", Mt 23:30; 1 Cor 10:18; 2 Cor 1:7; 1 Pet 5:1; 2 Pet 1:4; **(3d)** "partner", Lk 5:10; 2 Cor 8:23; Philemon 7. See: TDNT—3:797, 447; BAGD—439d; THAYER—352b.

2845. **κοίτη** {4x} **kŏitē,** *koy'-tay;* from *2749;* a *couch;* by extens. *cohabitation;* by impl. the male *sperm:*—bed {2x}, chambering {1x}, × conceive {1x}.

Koite, primarily "a place for lying down", denotes **(1)** a "bed," Lk 11:7; the marriage "bed," Heb 13:4; **(2)** in Rom 13:13, it is used of sexual intercourse. **(3)** By metonymy, the cause standing for the effect, it denotes conception, Rom 9:10. See: BAGD—440a; THAYER—352c.

2846. **κοιτών** {1x} **kŏitōn,** *koy-tone';* from *2845;* a *bedroom:*—+ chamberlain + 1909 {1x}.

Koiton, denotes the officer who is over the bed chamber, the chamberlain, Acts 12:20. See: BAGD—440b; THAYER—352d.

2847. **κόκκινος** {6x} **kŏkkinŏs**, *kok'-kee-nos;* from *2848* (from the *kernel*-shape of the insect); *crimson*-colored:—scarlet {4x}, scarlet colour {1x}, scarlet coloured {1x}.

Kokkinos is derived from *kokkos,* used of the "berries" (clusters of the eggs of an insect) collected from the *ilex coccifera;* the color, however, is obtained from the *cochineal* insect, which attaches itself to the leaves and twigs of the *coccifera* oak; another species is raised on the leaves of the *cactus ficus.* The Arabic name for this insect is *qirmiz,* whence the word "crimson." It is used **(1)** of "scarlet" wool, Heb 9:19; **(1a)** cf. in connection with the cleansing of a leper, Lev 14:4, 6, "scarlet"; **(1b)** with the offering of the red heifer, cf. Num 19:6; **(2)** of the robe put on Christ by the soldiers, Mt 27:28; **(3)** of the "beast" seen in symbolic vision in Rev 17:3, "scarlet-colored"; **(4)** of the clothing of the "woman" as seen sitting on the "beast," Rev 17:4; **(5)** of part of the merchandise of Babylon, Rev 18:12; **(6)** figuratively, of the glory of the city itself, Rev 18:16; the neuter is used in the last three instances. See: TDNT—3:812, 450; BAGD—440b; THAYER—352d.

2848. **κόκκος** {6x} **kŏkkŏs**, *kok'-kos;* appar. a primary word; a *kernel* of seed:—corn {1x}, grain {6x}.

Kokkos denotes "a grain," Mt 13:31; 17:20; Mk 4:31; Lk 13:19; 17:6; Jn 12:24 "corn"; 1 Cor 15:37. See: TDNT—3:810, 450; BAGD—440c; THAYER—352d.

2849. **κολάζω** {2x} **kŏlazō**, *kol-ad'-zo;* from κόλος **kŏlos** (*dwarf*); prop. to *curtail,* i.e. (fig.) to *chastise* (or *reserve* for infliction):—punish {2x}.

Kolos, primarily denotes "to curtail, prune, dock" (from *kolos,* "docked"); then, "to check, restrain, punish"; it is used in the **(1)** middle voice in Acts 4:21; **(2)** passive voice in 2 Pet. 2:9, "to be punished", "being punished", a futurative present tense. See: TDNT—3:814, 451; BAGD—440c; THAYER—352d.

2850. **κολακεία** {1x} **kŏlakĕia**, *kol-ak-i'-ah;* from a der. of κόλαξ **kŏlax** (a *fawner*); *flattery:*—X flattering {1x}.

Kolakeia is used in 1 Th 2:5 of flattering words, adopted as a cloke of coveousness, i.e., words which flattery uses, not simply as an effort to give pleasure, but with motives of self-interest. See: TDNT—3:817, 451; BAGD—440d; THAYER—353a.

2851. **κόλασις** {2x} **kŏlasis**, *kol'-as-is;* from *2849;* penal *infliction:*—punishment {1x}, torment {1x}.

(1) *Kolasis* stresses the punishment aspect of judgment. **(2)** *Kolasis,* "punishment," is used in **(2a)** Mt 25:46, "(eternal) punishment," and **(2b)** 1 Jn 4:18, "(fear hath) torment", which there describes a process, not merely an effect; this kind of fear is expelled by perfect love; where God's love is being perfected in us, it gives no room for the fear of meeting with His reprobation; the "torment/punishment" referred to is the immediate consequence of the sense of sin, not a holy awe but a slavish fear, the negation of the enjoyment of love. Syn.: 5098. See: TDNT—3:816, 451; BAGD—440d; THAYER—353a.

2852. **κολαφίζω** {5x} **kŏlaphizō**, *kol-af-id'-zo;* from a der. of the base of *2849;* to *rap* with the fist:—buffet {5x}.

Kolaphizo signifies "to strike with clenched hands, to buffet with the fist" (*kolaphos,* "a fist"), Mt 26:67; Mk 14:65; 1 Cor 4:11; 2 Cor 12:7; 1 Pet 2:20. See: TDNT—3:818, 451; BAGD—441a; THAYER—353b.

2853. **κολλάω** {11x} **kŏllaō**, *kol-lah'-o;* from κόλλα **kŏlla** ("*glue*"); to *glue,* i.e. (pass. or refl.) to *stick* (fig.):—join (one's) self {4x}, cleave {3x}, be joined {2x}, keep company {1x}, vr reach {1x}.

Kollao, "to join fast together, to glue, cement," is **(1)** primarily said of metals and other materials (from *kolla,* "glue"). **(2)** In the NT it is used only in the passive voice, with reflexive force, in the sense of **(2a)** "cleaving unto," as of cleaving to one's wife, Mt 19:5; 1 Cor. 6:16–17, "joined." **(2b)** In Lk 10:11 it is used of the "cleaving" of dust to the feet; **(2c)** in Acts 5:13; 8:29; 9:26; 10:28; 17:34, in the sense of becoming associated with a person so as to company with him, or be on his side, said, in the last passage, of those in Athens who believed; **(2d)** in Rom 12:9, ethically, of"cleaving" to that which is good; **(2e)** in Rev 18:5, metaphorically, Babylon "has sinned to high heaven", so severe are her sins they, "when piled high" reach and cleave even unto heaven itself. See: TDNT—3:822, 452; BAGD—441c; THAYER—353b.

2854. **κολλούριον** {1x} **kŏllŏuriŏn**, *kol-loo'-ree-on;* neut. of a presumed der. of κολλύρα **kŏllura** (a *cake;* prob akin to the base of *2853*); prop. a *poultice* (as made of or in the form of *crackers*), i.e. (by anal.) a *plaster:*—eyesalve {1x}.

Kollourion, an "eye-salve," shaped like a roll, is used in Rev 3:18, of the true knowledge of one's condition and of the claims of Christ. See: BAGD—441d; THAYER—353c.

2855. **κολλυβιστής** {3x} **kŏllubistēs**, *kol-loo-bis-tace';* from a presumed der. of κόλλυβος **kŏllubŏs** (a small *coin;* prob. akin to *2854*); a *coin-dealer:*—moneychanger {2x}, changer {1x}.

A *kollubos* is a "a small coin or rate of change" (*koloboo* signifies "to cut off, to clip, shorten," Mt 24:22), and denotes "a money-changer," lit., money-clipper, Mt 21:12; Mk 11:15; Jn 2:15 "changers." See: BAGD—442a; THAYER—353c.

2856. **κολοβόω** {4x} **kŏlŏbŏō**, *kol-ob-ŏ'-o;* from a der. of the base of *2849;* to *dock,* i.e. (fig.) *abridge:*—shorten {4x}.

Koloboo denotes to cut off, amputate; hence, to curtail, shorten, said of the shortening by God of the time of the great tribulation (Mt 24:22 twice; Mk 13:20 twice). See: TDNT—3:823, 452; BAGD—442a; THAYER—353d.

2857. **Κολοσσαί** {1x} **Kŏlŏssai**, *kol-os-sah'-ee;* appar. fem. plur. of κολοσσός **kŏlŏssŏs** ("*colossal*"); *Colossæ,* a place in Asia Minor:—Colosse {1x}. See: BAGD—442b; THAYER—353d.

2858. **Κολοσσαεύς** {1x} **Kŏlŏssaĕus**, *kol-os-sayoos';* from *2857;* a *Colossæan,* (i.e. inhab. of Colossæ:—Colossian {1x}. See: BAGD—442a; THAYER—353d.

2859. **κόλπος** {6x} **kŏlpŏs**, *kol'-pos;* appar. a primary word; the *bosom;* by anal. a *bay:*—bosom {5x}, creek {1x}.

Kolpos signifies **(1)** "the front of the body between the arms"; hence, to recline in the "bosom" was said of one who so reclined at table that his head covered, as it were, the "bosom" of the one next to him, Jn 13:23. Hence, **(2)** figuratively, **(2a)** it is used of a place of blessedness with another, as with Abraham in paradise, Lk 16:22–23 (plural in v. 23), from the custom of reclining at table in the "bosom," a place of honor; **(2b)** of the Lord's eternal and essential relation with the Father, in all its blessedness and affection as intimated in the phrase, "The Only-begotten Son, which is in the bosom of the Father" (Jn 1:18); **(3)** "of the bosom of a garment, the hollow formed by the upper forepart of a loose garment, bound by a girdle and used for carrying or keeping things"; thus figuratively of repaying one liberally, Lk 6:38; cf. Is 65:6; Jer 39:18; **(4)** "of an inlet of the sea," because of its shape, like a bosom, Acts 27:39. By analogy a creek is a small inlet as seen from the sea that narrows by the "arms" of the land on each of its sides. See: TDNT—3:824, 452; BAGD—442b; THAYER—353d.

2860. **κολυμβάω** {1x} **kŏlumbaō**, *kol-oom-bah'-o;* from κόλυμβος **kŏlumbŏs** (a *diver*); to *plunge* into water:—swim {1x}. See: BAGD—442c; THAYER—354b.

2861. **κολυμβήθρα** {5x} **kŏlumbēthra**, *kol-oom-bay'-thrah;* from *2860;* a *diving-place,* i.e. *pond* for bathing (or swimming):—pool {5x}.

This word denotes "a pool large enough to swim in, a swimming pool," (akin to *kolumbao,* "to swim," Acts 27:43), Jn 5:2, 4, 7; 9:7, 11. See: BAGD—442c; THAYER—354b.

2862. **κολωνία** {1x} **kŏlōnia**, *kol-o-nee'-ah;* of Lat. or.; a Rom. "*colony*" for veterans:—colony {1x}.

Philippi was a Roman military colony (Acts 16:12), a watch tower of the Roman state. It possessed the right of Roman freedom, and of holding the soil under Roman law, as well as exemption from poll-tax and tribute. See: BAGD—442c; THAYER—354b.

2863. **κομάω** {2x} **kŏmaō**, *kom-ah'-o;* from *2864;* to *wear tresses* of hair:—have long hair {2x}.

Komao signifies "to let the hair grow long, to wear long hair," a glory to a woman, a dishonor to a man (as taught by nature), 1 Cor 11:14, 15. See: BAGD—442d; THAYER—354b.

2864. **κόμη** {1x} **kŏmē**, *kom'-ay;* appar. from the same as *2865;* the *hair* of the head (*locks,* as *ornamental,* and thus differing from *2359;* which prop. denotes merely the *scalp*):—hair {1x}.

Kome is used only of "human hair," but not in the NT of the ornamental. The word is found in 1 Cor 11:15, where the context shows that the "covering" provided in the long "hair" of the woman is as a veil, a sign of subjection to authority, as indicated in the headships spoken of in vv. 1–10. Syn.: *Thrix* (2359) is the anatomical or physical term for hair; whereas, *kome* (2864) designates the hair as an ornament, the notion of length being only secondary and suggested. See: BAGD—442d; THAYER—354b.

2865. **κομίζω** {10x} **kŏmizō**, *kom-id'-zo;* from a primary κομέω **kŏmĕō** (to *tend,* i.e. take care of); prop. to *provide* for, i.e. (by impl.) to *carry* off (as if from harm; generally *obtain*):—bring {1x}, receive {10x}.

Komizo, as a verb, denotes **(1)** "to bear, carry": "And, behold, a woman in the city, which was a sinner, when she knew that *Jesus* sat at meat in the Pharisee's house, brought an alabaster box of ointment" (Lk 7:37); **(2)** in the middle voice, "to bear for oneself" hence **(2a)** "to receive": "For ye have need of patience, that, after ye have done the will of God, ye might receive (*komizo*) the promise" (Heb 10:36; cf. 11:39; 1 Pet 1:9; 5:4; 2 Pet 2:13); **(2b)** "to receive back, recover": "Thou oughtest therefore to have put my money to the exchangers, and *then* at my coming I should have received (*komizo*) mine own with usury" (Mt 25:27; cf. Heb 11:19; metaphorically, of requital 2 Cor 5:10; Col 3:25); **(2c)** of "receiving back again" by the believer at the judgment seat of Christ hereafter, for wrong done in this life: "But he that doeth wrong shall receive for the wrong which he hath done: and there is no respect of persons" (Col 3:25); **(2d)** Eph 6:8 of "receiving," on the same occasion, "whatsoever good thing each one doeth": "Knowing that whatsoever good thing any man doeth, the same shall he receive of the Lord, whether *he be* bond or free." Syn.: 324, 353, 354, 568, 588, 618, 1209, 1523, 1926, 2210, 2975, 2983, 3028, 3335, 3336, 3858, 3880, 3970, 4327, 4355, 4356, 4380, 4381, 4382, 5562, 5264, 5274. See: BAGD—442d; THAYER—354c.

2866. **κομψότερον** {1x} **kŏmpsŏtĕrŏn**, *komp-sot'-er-on;* neut. comparative of a der. of the base of *2865* (mean. prop. *well dressed,* i.e. *nice*); fig. *convalescent:*—began to amend + 2192 {1x}. See: BAGD—443a; THAYER—354d.

2867. **κονιάω** {2x} **kŏniaō**, *kon-ee-ah'-o;* from κονία **kŏnia** (*dust;* by anal. *lime*); to *whitewash:*—whiten {2x}.

Koniao, from *konia,* "dust, lime," denotes "to whiten, whitewash," **(1)** of tombs, Mt 23:27; **(2)** figuratively of a hypocrite, Acts 23:3. See: TDNT—3:827, 453; BAGD—443a; THAYER—354d.

2868. **κονιορτός** {5x} **kŏniŏrtŏs**, *kon-ee-or-tos';* from the base of *2867* and ὄρνυμι **ŏrnumi** (to "*rouse*"); *pulverulence* (as *blown* about):—dust {5x}.

Koniortos, "raised or flying dust" (*konia,* "dust," *ornumi,* "to stir up"), is found in Mt 10:14; Lk 9:5; 10:11; Acts 13:51; 22:23. See: BAGD 443b; THAYER—355a.

2869. **κοπάζω** {3x} **kŏpazō**, *kop-ad'-zo;* from *2873;* to *tire,* i.e. (fig.) to *relax:*—cease {3x}.

Kopazo, "to cease through being spent with toil, to cease raging" (from *kopos,* "labor, toil," *kopiao,* "to labor"), is said of the wind only, Mt 14:32; Mk 4:39; 6:51. See: BAGD—443b; THAYER—355a.

2870. **κοπετός** {1x} **kŏpĕtŏs**, *kop-et-os';* from *2875; mourning* (prop. by *beating* the breast):—lamentation {1x}. See: TDNT—3:830, 453; BAGD—443b; THAYER—355a.

2871. **κοπή** {1x} **kŏpē**, *kop-ay';* from *2875; cutting,* i.e. *carnage:*—slaughter {1x}.

Kope, "a stroke" (akin to *kopto,* "to strike, to cut"), signifies "a decisive smiting in battle," in Heb 7:1. See: BAGD—443c; THAYER—355a.

2872. **κοπιάω** {23x} **kŏpiaō**, *kop-ee-ah'-o;* from a der. of *2873;* to *feel fatigue;* by impl. to *work hard:*—bestow labour {3x}, labour {16x}, toil {3x}, be wearied {1x}.

This word **(1)** means **(1a)** to grow weary, tired, exhausted with toil or burdens or grief and **(1b)** to labour with wearisome effort, bodily labour, toiling and is translated: **(2)** "bestow labour", Jn 4:38; Rom 16:6; Gal 4:11; **(3)** "labour", Mt 11:28; Jn 4:38 (2nd part); Acts 20:35; Rom 16:12 (twice); 1 Cor 4:12; 15:10; 16:16; Eph 4:28; Phil 2:16; Col 1:29; 1 Th 5:12; 1 Ti 4:10; 5:17; 2 Ti 2:6; Rev 2:3; **(4)** "toil", Mt 6:28; Lk 5:5; 12:27; **(5)** "be wearied", Jn 4:6. See: TDNT—3:827, 453; BAGD—443c; THAYER—355a.

2873. **κόπος** {19x} **kŏpŏs**, *kop'-os;* from *2875;* a *cut,* i.e. (by anal.) *toil* (as *reducing* the strength), lit. or fig.; by impl. *pains:*—labour {13x}, trouble + 3830 {5x}, weariness {1x}.

Kopos means "a striking, beating", then, "toil resulting in weariness, laborious toil, trouble"; **(2)** it is translated **(2a)** "labor" or "labors" in Jn 4:38; 1 Cor 3:8; 15:58; 2 Cor 6:5; 10:15; 11:23; 1 Th 1:3; 2:9; 3:5; 2 Th 3:8; Heb 6:10; Rev 2:2; 14:13. **(2b)** In the following the noun is used as the object of the verb *parecho,* "to afford, give, cause," the phrase being rendered "to trouble," lit., "to cause toil or trouble," to embarrass a person by giving occasion for anxiety, as some disciples did to the woman with the ointment, perturbing her spirit by their criticisms, Mt 26:10; Mk 14:6; or by distracting attention or disturbing a person's rest, as the importunate friend did, Lk 11:7; 18:5; in Gal 6:17, "let no man trouble me," the apostle refuses, in the form of a peremptory prohibition, to allow himself to be distracted further by the Judaizers, through their proclamation of a false gospel and by their malicious attacks upon himself; and **(2c)** "weariness", 2 Cor 11:27. Syn.: *Kopos* (4192) gives prominence to the effort, work as requiring force, which begins the weariness from excessive labor. *Mochthos* (3449) refers to the final state of fatigue. *Ponos* (4192) refers to the hardship. See: TDNT—3:827, 453; BAGD—443d; THAYER—355b.

2874. **κοπρία** {2x} **kŏpria**, *kop-ree'-ah;* from κόπρος **kŏprŏs** (*ordure;* perh. akin to *2875*); *manure:*—dung + 906 {1x}, dunghill {1x}.

Kopria, "manure," **(1)** Lk 13:8, used in the plural with *ballo,* "to throw," is translated by the verb "to dung" and **(2)** in Lk 14:35 "a dunghill,." See: TDNT—3:827, 453; BAGD—443d; THAYER 355c.

2875. **κόπτω** {8x} **kŏptō**, *kop'-to;* a primary verb; to "*chop;*" spec. to *beat* the breast in grief:—cut down {2x}, lament {2x}, mourn {2x}, bewail {1x}, wail {1x}.

Kopto, primarily, "to beat, smite"; then, "to cut off," is translated **(1)** literally to "cut down" branches from trees, Mt 21:8; Mk 11:8; also **(2)** in the middle voice, of beating oneself, beating the breast, as a token of grief; hence, "lamented," Mt 11:17; Rev. 18:9; and **(3)** "mourn", Mt 24:30; **(4)** "bewail", in Lk 8:52; 23:27; and **(5)** in Rev 1:7 "wail." Syn.: 2354, 3079, 3996. See: TDNT—3:830, 453; BAGD—444a; THAYER—355d. comp. the base of *5114*.

2876. **κόραξ** {1x} **kŏrax**, *kor'-ax;* perh. from *2880;* a *crow* (from its *voracity*):—raven {1x}. See: BAGD—444b; THAYER—355d.

2877. **κοράσιον** {8x} **kŏrasiŏn**, *kor-as'-ee-on;* neut. of a presumed der. of κόρη **kŏrē** (a *maiden*); a (little) *girl:*—damsel {6x}, maid {2x}.

Koarion, a diminutive of *kore,* "a girl," denotes "a little girl"; in the NT it is used only in familiar conversation: **(1)** "damsel", Mt 14:11; Mark 5:41–42; 6:22, 28 twice; and **(2)** "maid", Mt 9:24–25. See: BAGD—444b; THAYER—355d.

2878. **κορβᾶν** {2x} **kŏrban**, *kor-ban';* and **κορβανᾶς** **kŏrbanas**, *kor-ban-as';* of Heb. and Chald. or. respectively [7133]; a votive *offering* and *the offering;* a *consecrated present* (to the Temple fund); by extens. (the latter term) the *Treasury* itself, i.e. the room where the contribution boxes stood:—Corban {1x}, treasury {1x}.

Korban signifies **(1)** "an offering," and was a Hebrew term for any sacrifice, whether by the shedding of blood or otherwise [not used in the NT]; **(2)** "a gift offered to God," Corban, Mk 7:11; and **(3)** "treasury", the place where offerings were stored, Mt 27:6. **(4)** Jews were much addicted to rash vows; a saying of the rabbis was, "It is hard for the parents, but the law is clear, vows must be kept." See: TDNT—3:860, 459; BAGD—444b; THAYER—355d.

2879. **Κορέ** {1x} **Kŏrĕ**, *kor-eh';* of Heb. or. [7141]; *Corë* (i.e. *Korach*), an Isr.:—Core {1x}. See: BAGD—444c; THAYER—356a.

2880. **κορέννυμι** {2x} **kŏrĕnnumi**, *kor-en'-noo-mee;* a primary verb; to *cram,* i.e. *glut* or *sate:*—eat enough {1x}, full {1x}.

This word means "to satiate, to satisfy," as with food, is used in the middle voice **(1)** in Acts 27:38, "had eaten enough"; and **(2)** in 1 Cor 4:8, "ye are filled." See: BAGD—444c; THAYER—356a.

2881. **Κορίνθιος** {4x} **Kŏrinthiŏs**, *kor-in'-thee-os;* from *2882;* a *Corinthian,* i.e. inhab. of Corinth:—Corinthian {4x}. See: BAGD—444d; THAYER—356a.

2882. **Κόρινθος** {7x} **Kŏrinthŏs**, *kor'-in-thos;* of uncert. der.; *Corinthus,* a city of Greece:—Corinth {7x}. See: BAGD—444d; THAYER—356a.

2883. **Κορνήλιος** {10x} **Kŏrnēliŏs**, *kor-nay'-lee-os;* of Lat. or.; *Cornelius,* a Rom.:—Cornelius {10x}. See: BAGD—444d; THAYER—356b.

2884. **κόρος** {1x} **kŏrŏs**, *kor'-os;* of Heb. or. [3734]; a *cor,* i.e. a spec. measure:—measure {1x}.

Koros, as a noun, denotes a "cor", the largest Hebrew dry measure (ten *ephahs*), containing about 11 bushels, Lk 16:7; the hundred "measures" amounted to a very considerable quantity. Syn.: 280, 488, 943, 3313, 3354, 3358, 4057, 4568, 5234, 5249, 5518. See: BAGD—444d; THAYER—356b.

2885. **κοσμέω** {10x} **kŏsmĕō**, *kos-meh'-o;* from *2889;* [cf. Eng. cosmetic]; to *put in* proper *order,* i.e. *decorate* (lit. or fig.); spec. to *snuff* (a wick):—adorn {5x}, garnish {4x}, trim {1x}.

Kosmeo, primarily "to arrange, to put in order" (Eng., "cosmetic"), hence, **(1)** "to adorn, to ornament," **(1a)** one's person, 1 Ti 2:9; 1 Pet 3:5; Rev. 21:2; **(1b)** metaphorically, of "adorning a doctrine, Titus 2:10; **(1c)** the "temple", Lk 21:5; it is also **(2)** translated by the verb "to garnish" **(2a)** "rooms" in Mt 12:44; **(2b)** "tombs", Mt 23:29; **(2c)** "buildings", Lk 11:25; Rev 21:19; and denotes **(3)** trimming lamps, Mt 25:7. See: TDNT—3:867, 459; BAGD—445a; THAYER—356b.

2886. **κοσμικός** {2x} **kŏsmikŏs**, *kos-mee-kos';* from *2889* (in its second sense); *terrene* ("*cosmic*"), lit. (*mundane*) or fig. (*corrupt*):—worldly {2x}.

Kosmikos is used **(1)** in Heb 9:1 of the tabernacle as worldly (i.e., made of mundane materials, adapted to this visible world, local and transitory); and **(2)** in Titus 2:12, ethically, of worldly lusts or desires which have the character of this present corrupt age. See: TDNT—3:897, 459; BAGD—445b; THAYER—356c.

2887. **κόσμιος** {2x} **kŏsmiŏs**, *kos'-mee-os;* from *2889* (in its primary sense); *orderly,* i.e. *decorous:*—of good behaviour {1x}, modest {1x}.

(1) This word stresses well-ordered in earthly life, seemly, modest. **(2)** The stress is outward appearance and is translated **(2a)** "of good behavior" in 1 Ti 3:2 and **(2)** "modest" in 1 Ti 2:9. See: TDNT—3:895, 459; BAGD—445c; THAYER—356c.

2888. **κοσμοκράτωρ** {1x} **kŏsmŏkratōr**, *kos-mok-rat'-ore;* from *2889* and *2902;* a *world-ruler,* an epithet of Satan:—ruler {1x}.

Kosmokrator, plural in its only use, denotes rulers of this world and the context of Eph 6:12 ("the rulers of the darkness of this world") shows that not earthly potentates are indicated, but spirit powers, who, under the permissive will of God, and in consequence of human sin, exercise satanic and therefore antagonistic authority over the world in its present condition of spiritual darkness and alienation from God. Syn.: 746, 758, 4173. See: TDNT—3:913, 466; BAGD—445c; THAYER—356d.

2889. **κόσμος** {187x} **kŏsmŏs**, *kos'-mos;* prob. from the base of *2865;* orderly *arrangement,* i.e. *decoration;* by impl. the *world* (in a wide or narrow sense, incl. its inhab., lit. or fig. [mor.]):—adorning {1x}, world {186x}.

Summary: *Kosmos* is first a harmonious arrangement or order, then by extension, adornment or decoration, and came to denote the world, or the universe, as that which is divinely arranged. It came to mean anyone not of the *ekklasia* (1577). *Kosmos,* primarily "order, arrangement, ornament, adornment" is used to denote **(1)** the "earth," e.g., Mt 13:35; Jn 21:25; Acts 17:24; Rom 1:20 (probably here the universe: it had this meaning among the Greeks, owing to the order observable in it); 1 Ti 6:7; Heb 4:3; 9:26; **(2)** the "earth" in contrast with Heaven, 1 Jn 3:17 (perhaps also Rom 4:13); **(3)** by metonymy, the "human race, mankind," e.g., Mt 5:14; Jn 1:9, 10; 3:16, 17 (thrice), 19; 4:42, and frequently in Rom, 1 Cor and 1 John; **(4)** "Gentiles" as distinguished from Jews, e.g., Rom 11:12, 15; **(5)** the "present condition of human affairs," in alienation from and opposition to God, e.g., Jn 7:7; 8:23; 14:30; 1 Cor 2:12; Gal 4:3; 6:14; Col 2:8; Jas 1:27; 1 Jn 4:5 (thrice); 5:19; **(6)** the "sum of temporal possessions," Mt 16:26; 1 Cor 7:31 (1st part); **(7)** metaphorically, of the "tongue" as "a world (of iniquity)," Jas 3:6, expressive of magnitude and variety. Syn.: 165, 3625. See: TDNT—3:868, 459; BAGD—445d; THAYER—356d.

2890. **Κούαρτος** {1x} **Kŏuartŏs**, *koo'-ar-tos;* of Lat. or. (*fourth*); *Quartus,* a Chr.:—Quartus {1x}. See: BAGD—447b; THAYER—358a.

2891. **κοῦμι** {1x} **kŏumi**, *koo'-mee* or κουμ **koum**, *koom';* of Chald. origin [6966]; *cumi* (i.e. *rise!*):—cumi {1x}. See: BAGD—447b; THAYER—358a.

2892. **κουστωδία** {3x} **kŏustōdia**, *koos-to-dee'-ah;* of Lat. or.; "*custody,*" i.e. a Rom. *sentry:*—watch {3x}.

Koustodia, "a guard," (Latin, *custodia,* Eng., "custodian"), is used of the soldiers who "guarded" Christ's sepulchre, Mt 27:65, 66 and 28:11, and is translated, ". . . a watch," "(setting a) watch," and ". . . the watch." This was the Temple guard, stationed under a Roman officer in the tower of Antonia, and having charge of the high priestly vestments. Hence the significance of Pilate's words "Ye have a guard." A Roman guard was made up of four to sixteen soldiers. In combat, they would form a square, and were able to hold off a much larger force. See: BAGD—447b; THAYER—358a.

2893. **κουφίζω** {1x} **kŏuphizō**, *koo-fid'-zo;* from κοῦφος **kŏuphŏs** (*light* in weight); to *unload:*—lighten {1x}.

Kouphizo, "to make light, lighten", denotes "slight, light, empty", and is used of "lightening" the ship, in Acts 27:38. See: BAGD—447b; THAYER—358a.

2894. **κόφινος** {6x} **kŏphinŏs**, *kof'-ee-nos;* of uncert. der.; a (small) *basket:*—basket {6x}.

A *kophinos* was "a wicker basket," originally containing a certain measure of capacity, Mt 14:20; 16:9; Mk 6:43; 8:19; Lk 9:17; Jn 6:13. See: BAGD—447c; THAYER—358a.

2895. **κράββατος** {12x} **krabbatŏs**, *krab'-bat-os;* prob. of for. or.; a *mattress:*—bed {11x}, couch {1x}.

This word denotes a small, one-person pallet or mattress for the poor (Mk 2:4, 9, 11–12; 6:55; Jn 5:8–11). See: BAGD—447c; THAYER—358a.

2896. **κράζω** {59x} **krazō**, *krad'-zo;* a primary verb; prop. to "*croak*" (as a raven) or *scream,* i.e. (gen.) to *call* aloud (*shriek, exclaim, intreat*):—cry {40x}, cry out {19x}.

Krazo, as a verb, means "to cry out," used especially of the "cry" of the raven; then, **(1)** of any inarticulate cries, from fear, pain etc.and in the NT **(1a)** of the shouts of the children in the Temple: "And when the chief priests and scribes saw the wonderful things that he did, and the children crying in the temple, and saying, Hosanna to the Son of David; they were sore displeased" (Mt 21:15); **(1b)** of the people who shouted for Christ to be crucified (Mat 27:23; Mk 15:13–14); **(1c)** of the "cry" of Christ on the Cross at the close of His sufferings (Mt 27:50; Mk 15:39). **(2)** Elsewhere: **(2a)** In John's gospel it is used three times, out of the six, of Christ's utterances, 7:28, 37; 12:44. **(2b)** In the Acts it is not used of "cries" of distress, but chiefly of the shouts of opponents; **(2c)** in the Apocalypse, chiefly of the utterances of heavenly beings concerning earthly matters; **(2d)** in Rom 8:15 and Gal 4:6, of the appeal of believers to God the Father; **(2c)** in Rom 9:27, of a prophecy concerning Israel; **(2d)** in Jas 5:4, metaphorically, of hire kept back by fraud. Syn.: *Kaleo* (2564), denotes "to call out for any purpose," *boao* (994), "to cry out as an expression of feeling," *krazo* (2896), to cry out loudly." *Kaleo* suggests intelligence, *boao,* sensibilities, *krazo,* instincts. See also: 310, 349, 994, 995, 1916, 2019, 2905, 2906, 5455. See: TDNT—3:898, 465; BAGD—447c; THAYER—358b.

2897. **κραιπάλη** {1x} **kraipalē**, *krahee-pal'-ay;* prob. from the same as *726;* prop. a *headache* (as a *seizure* of pain) from drunkenness, i.e. (by impl.) a *debauch* (by anal. a *glut*):—surfeiting {1x}.

This word signifies the giddiness and headache resulting from excessive wine-bibbing, a drunken nausea; the disguist and loathing that arises from drinking to much wine", "surfeiting", Lk 21:34. Syn.: 239. See: BAGD—448a; THAYER—358c.

2898. **κρανίον** {4x} **kraniŏn**, *kran-ee'-on;* dimin. of a der. of the base of *2768;* a *skull* ("*cranium*"):—Calvary {1x}, skull {3x}.

Kranion is a head (Eng., cranium) and denotes a skull (Latin *calvaria*) with the corresponding Aramaic word being *Golgotha* (Mt 27:33; Mk 15:22; Lk 23:33; Jn 19:17). See: BAGD—448a; THAYER—358d.

2899. **κράσπεδον** {5x} **kraspĕdŏn**, *kras'-ped-on;* of uncert. der.; a *margin,* i.e. (spec.) a *fringe* or *tassel:*—border {3x}, hem {2x}.

Kraspedon was primarily the extremity or prominent part of a thing, an edge; hence the fringe of a garment, or a little fringe hanging down from the edge of the mantle or cloak. The Jews had these attached to their mantles to remind them of the Law (cf. Num 15:38–39; Deut 22:12; Zec 8:23). It is translated **(1)** of the edge of Christ's garment, **(1a)** "hem", in Mt 9:20; 14:36; and **(1b)** "border" in Mk 6:56; Lk 8:44; **(2)** it refers to the edge of the scribes and Pharisees' garments in Mt 23:5. See: TDNT—3:904, 466; BAGD—448b; THAYER—358d.

2900. **κραταιός** {1x} **krataiŏs**, *krat-ah-yos';* from *2904; powerful:*—mighty {1x}. See: TDNT—3:912, 466; BAGD—448b; THAYER—358d.

2901. **κραταιόω** {4x} **krataiŏō**, *krat-ah-yŏ'-o;* from *2900;* to *empower,* i.e. (pass.) *increase in vigor:*—be strengthened {1x}, be strong {1x}, wax strong {2x}.

Krataioo, "to strengthen," is rendered **(1)** "to be strengthened" in Eph 3:16; **(2)** "be strong" in 1 Cor 16:30; and **(3)** "wax strong" in Lk 1:80; 2:40.

Wax denotes growing strong slowly; not a sudden influx of power. See: TDNT—3:912, 466; BAGD—448b; THAYER—358d.

2902. **κρατέω** {47x} **kratĕō**, *krat-eh'-o;* from *2904;* to *use strength,* i.e. *seize* or *retain* (lit. or fig.):—hold {12x}, take {9x}, lay hold on {8x}, hold fast {5x}, take by {4x}, lay hold upon {2x}, lay hand on {2x}, misc. {5x} = keep, obtain, retain.

Krateo, as a verb, means "to be strong, mighty, to prevail," **(1)** is most frequently rendered "to lay or take hold on" **(1a)** literally, e.g., Mt 12:11; 14:3; 18:28 and 21:46, "laid hands on"; 22:6, "took"); 26:55, took); 28:9, "held by"; Mk 3:21; 6:17; 12:12; 14:51; Act 24:6, "took"; Rev 20:2; **(1b)** metaphorically, of "laying hold of the hope of the Lord's return," Heb 6:18; **(2)** also signifies "to hold" or "hold fast," i.e., firmly, **(2a)** literally, Mt 26:48; Acts 3:11; Rev. 2:1; **(2b)** metaphorically, of "holding fast a tradition or teaching," **(2b1)** in an evil sense, Mk 7:3, 4, 8; Rev 2:14, 15; **(2b2)** in a good sense, 2 Th 2:15; Rev 2:25; 3:11; **(2c)** of "holding" Christ, i.e., practically apprehending Him, as the head of His church, Col 2:19; **(2d)** a confession, Heb 4:14; **(2e)** the name of Christ, i.e., abiding by all that His name implies, Rev 2:13; **(2f)** of restraint, Lk 24:16, "(their eyes) were holden"; **(2g)** of the winds, Rev 7:1; **(2h)** of the impossibility of Christ's being "holden" of death, Acts 2:24. Syn.: 1949, 2192, 2722, 4912. See: TDNT—3:910, 466; BAGD—448c; THAYER—359a.

2903. **κράτιστος** {4x} **kratistŏs**, *krat'-is-tos;* superl. of a der. of *2904; strongest,* i.e. (in dignity) *very honorable:*—most excellent {2x}, most noble {2x}.

Kratistos, "mightiest, noblest, best," the superlative degree of *kratus* (2904), "strong", is used as a title of honor and respect, **(1)** "most excellent," Lk 1:3 (Theophilus was quite possibly a man of high rank); and "most noble" (Acts 23:26; 24:3; 26:25). See: BAGD—449a; THAYER—359b.

2904. **κράτος** {12x} **kratŏs**, *krat'-os;* perh. a primary word; *vigor* ["great"] (lit. or fig.):—dominion {4x}, might + 2596 {1x}, power {6x}, strength {1x}.

Kratos, "force, strength, might," more especially "manifested power," is derived from a root which means "to perfect, to complete"; "creator" is probably connected. It signifies **(1)** "dominion," and is so rendered frequently in doxologies, 1 Pet 4:11; 5:11; Jude 25; Rev 1:6; **(2)** "mightily" in Acts 19:20; **(3)** "power" in Eph 1:19 (last part); 6:10; Col 1:11; 1 Ti 6:16; Heb 2:14; Rev 5:13; and **(4)** "strength" in Lk 1:51. Syn.: *Bia* (970) means force, effective, often oppressive power exhibiting itself in single deeds of violence. *Dunamis* (1411) expresses power, natural ability, general and inherent. *Energeia* (1753) denotes working, power in exercise, operative power. *Exousia* (1849) is primarily liberty of action; then authority — either as delegated power, or as unrestrained, arbitrary power. *Ischus* (2479) expresses strength, power, (especially physical) as an endowment. *Kratos* (2904) means might, relative and manifested power —chiefly of God. See: TDNT—3:905, 466; BAGD—449a; THAYER—358a.

2905. **κραυγάζω** {7x} **kraugazō**, *krŏw-gad'-zo;* from *2906;* to *clamor:*—cry {4x}, cry out {3x}.

Kraugazo, a stronger form of *krazo* (2896), means "to make a clamor or outcry": "He shall not strive, nor cry (*kraugazo*); neither shall any man hear his voice in the streets" (Mt 12:19, in a prophecy from Isaiah of Christ; Jn 11:43; 18:40; 19:6, 15; Acts 22:23). Syn.: 310, 349, 994, 995, 1916, 2019, 2896, 2906, 5455. See: TDNT—3:898, 465; BAGD—449b; THAYER—359c.

2906. **κραυγή** {6x} **kraugē**, *krŏw-gay';* from *2896;* an *outcry* (in notification, tumult or grief):—clamour {1x}, cry {3x}, crying {2x}.

Krauge, as a noun, is translated **(1)** "cry, crying": "And at midnight there was a cry made, Behold, the bridegroom cometh; go ye out to meet him" (Mt 25:6; cf. Acts 23:9; Heb 5:7; Rev 14:18; 21:4); and **(2)** "clamor" (Eph 4:31). Syn.: 310, 349, 994, 995, 1916, 2019, 2896, 2905, 5455. See: 2896 for discussion. See: TDNT—3:898, 465; BAGD—449c; THAYER—359d.

2907. **κρέας** {2x} **krĕas**, *kreh'-as;* perh. a primary word; (butcher's) *meat:*—flesh {2x}.

Kreas denotes flesh in the sense of animal meat and may only refer to animals sacrificed to idols. It is used only in the plural (Rom 14:21; 1 Cor 8:13). See: BAGD—449c; THAYER—359d.

2908. **κρεῖσσον** {1x} **krĕissŏn**, *krice'-son;* neut. of an alt. form of *2909;* (as noun) *better,* i.e. *greater advantage:*—better {1x}. See: BAGD—449d; THAYER—359d.

2909. **κρείττων** {19x} **krĕittōn**, *krite'-tohn;* comparative of a der. of *2904;* *stronger,* i.e. (fig.) *better,* i.e. *nobler:*—best {1x}, better {18x}.

Kreitton, from *kratos* (2904) means strong (which denotes power in activity and effect), is used 12 times in Hebrews, and indicates what is **(1)** advantageous or useful (1 Cor 7:9, 38; 11:17; Heb 11:40; 12:24); or **(2)** excellent (Heb. 1:4; 6:9; 7:7, 19, 22; 8:6; 9:23; 10:34; 11:16, 35). See: BAGD—449d; THAYER—359d.

2910. **κρεμάννυμι** {7x} **krĕmannumi**, *krem-an'-noo-mee;* a prol. form of a primary verb; to *hang:*—hang {7x}.

Kremannumi is used **(1)** transitively in Acts 5:30; 10:39 of Jesus being hanged on a tree; **(2)** in the passive voice, **(2a)** in Mt 18:6, of a millstone about a neck, and **(2b)** in Lk 23:39, of the malefactors hanging on crosses beside Jesus; **(3)** intransitively, in the middle voice, **(3a)** in Mt 22:40, of the dependence of "the Law and the prophets" (i.e., that which they enjoin) upon the one great principle of love to God and one's neighbor (as a door "hangs" on a hinge, or as articles "hang" on a nail); **(3b)** in Acts 28:4, of the serpent "hanging" from Paul's hand; **(3c)** in Gal 3:13 with reference to Christ's hanging on a tree (Deut 21:23). Syn.: 1582. See: TDNT—3:915, 468; BAGD—450a; THAYER—359d.

2911. **κρημνός** {3x} **krēmnŏs**, *krame-nos';* from *2910; overhanging,* i.e. a *precipice:*—steep place {3x}.

Kremnos, "a steep bank" (akin to *kremannumi,* "to hang"), occurs in Mt 8:32; Mk 5:13; Lk 8:33, "a steep place." See: BAGD—450b; THAYER—360a.

2912. **Κρής** {3x} **Krēs**, *krace;* from *2914;* a *Cretan,* i.e. inhab. of Crete:—Crete {1x}, Cretians {2x}. See: BAGD—450b; THAYER—360a.

2913. **Κρήσκης** {1x} **Krēskēs**, *krace'-kace;* of Lat. or.; *growing; Cresces* (i.e. *Crescens*), a Chr.:—Crescens {1x}. See: BAGD—450a; THAYER—360a.

2914. **Κρήτη** {5x} **Krētē**, *kray'-tay;* of uncert. der.; *Cretē,* an island in the Mediterranean:—Crete {5x}. See: BAGD—450c; THAYER—360b.

2915. **κριθή** {1x} **krithē**, *kree-thay';* of uncert. der.; *barley:*—barley {1x}. See: BAGD—450c; THAYER—360b.

2916. **κρίθινος** {2x} **krithinŏs**, *kree'-thee-nos;* from *2915;* consisting of *barley:*—barley {2x}. See: BAGD—450c; THAYER—360b.

2917. **κρῖμα** {28x} **krima**, *kree'-mah;* from *2919;* a *decision* (the function or the effect, for or against ["crime"]):—judgment {13x}, damnation {7x}, condemnation {5x}, be condemned {1x}, go to law + 2192 {1x}, avenge + 2919 {1x}.

Krima, as a noun, denotes **(1)** "the sentence pronounced, a verdict, a condemnation, the decision resulting from an investigation" (Mk 12:40; Lk 23:40; 1 Tim 3:6; Jude 4); it is used **(1a)** of a decision passed on the faults of others, Mt 7:2; **(1b)** of "judgment" by man upon Christ, Lk 24:20; **(1c)** of God's "judgment" upon men, e.g., Rom 2:2, 3; 3:8; 5:16; 11:33; 13:2; 1 Cor 11:29; Gal 5:10; Heb 6:2; Jas 3:1; through Christ, e.g., Jn 9:39; **(1d)** of the right of "judgment," Rev 20:4; **(2)** "the process of judgment leading to a decision" (1 Pet 4:17). **(3)** In Lk 24:20, "to be condemned" translates the phrase *eis krima,* "unto condemnation" (i.e., unto the pronouncement of the sentence of "condemnation"). **(4)** In these (Rom 11:33; 1 Cor 11:34; Gal 5:10; Jas 3:1) the **(4a)** the process leading to a decision and **(4b)** the pronouncement of the decision, the verdict, are to be distinguished. **(5)** In 1 Cor 6:7 the word means a matter for judgment, a lawsuit: "Now therefore there is utterly a fault among you, because ye go to law (*krima*) one with another. Why do ye not rather take wrong? why do ye not rather *suffer yourselves to* be defrauded?" Syn.: 176, 843, 2607, 2613, 2631, 2632, 2633, 2919, 2920. See: TDNT—3:942, 469; BAGD—450c; THAYER—360b.

2918. **κρίνον** {2x} **krinŏn**, *kree'-non;* perh. a prim word; a *lily:*—lily {2x}.

Krinon occurs in Mt 6:28 and Lk 12:27; in the former the Lord speaks of "the lilies of the field"; the "lily" referred to was a flower of rich color, probably including the gladiolus and iris species. The former "grow among the grain, often overtopping it and illuminating the broad fields with their various shades of pinkish purple to deep violet purple and blue. . . . Anyone who has stood among the wheat fields of Galilee . . . will see at once the appropriateness of our Savior's allusion. They all have a reedy stem, which, when dry, would make such fuel as is used in the ovens. The beautiful irises . . . have gorgeous flowers, and would suit our Savior's comparison even better than the above. But they are plants of pasture grounds and swamps, and seldom found in grain fields. If, however, we understand by 'lilies of the field' simply wild lilies, these would also be included in the expression. Our Savior's comparison would then be like a 'composite photograph,' a reference to all the splendid colors and beautiful shapes of the numerous wild plants comprehended under the name 'lily'. See: BAGD—451a; THAYER—60d.

2919. **κρίνω** {114x} **krinō**, *kree'-no;* prop. to distinguish, i.e. *decide* (mentally or judicially); by impl. to *try, condemn, punish:*—judge {88x}, determine {7x}, condemn {5x}, go to law {2x}, call in question {2x}, esteem {2x}, misc. {8x} = avenge, conclude, damn, decree, ordain, sentence to, think.

Krino, as a verb, means "to distinguish, choose, give an opinion upon, judge," sometimes denotes "to condemn": "For they that dwell at Jerusalem, and their rulers, because they knew him not, nor yet the voices of the prophets which are read every sabbath day, they have fulfilled *them* in condemning *him*" (Acts 13:27; cf. Rom 2:27). To separate, put asunder, to pick out, select, choose, hence, **(1)** to approve, esteem, to prefer, Rom 14:5; **(2)** to be of opinion, deem, think, to be of opinion, Lk 7:43; Acts 15:19; 1 Cor 11:13; 2 Cor 5:14; **(3)** to determine, resolve, decree, 1 Cor 7:37; Acts 16:4; **(4)** to judge, **(4a)** to pronounce an opinion concerning right and wrong, **(4a1)** in a forensic sense, Jn 7:51; 18:31; Acts 23:3: 24:6; **(4a2)** to pronounce judgment, to subject to censure, Jn 8:16, 26; 1 Cor 10:15; **(5)** to rule, govern; Mt 19:28; Lk 22:30. Syn.: 176, 843, 2607, 2613, 2631, 2632, 2633, 2917, 2920. See: TDNT—3:921, 469; BAGD—451b; THAYER—360d.

2920. **κρίσις** {48x} **krisis**, *kree'-sis;* decision (subj. or obj., for or against); by extens. a *tribunal;* by impl. *justice* (spec. divine *law*):—accusation {2x}, condemnation {2x}, damnation {3x}, judgment {41x}.

Krisis, as a noun, **(1)** denotes "the process of investigation, the act of distinguishing and separating" [as distinct from *krima* (2917)]; hence "a judging, a passing of judgment upon a person or thing." **(2)** It has a variety of meanings, such as **(2a)** judicial authority (Jn 5:22, 27); **(2b)** justice (Acts 8:33); **(2c)** a tribunal (Mt 5:21–22); **(2d)** a trial (Jn 5:24; 2 Pet 2:4); **(2e)** a judgment (2 Pet 2:11; Jude 9); **(2f)** by metonymy, the standard of judgment, just dealing (Mt 12:18, 20; 23:23; Lk 11:42); **(2g)** divine judgment executed (2 Th 1:5; Rev 16:7). **(3)** Sometimes it has the meaning "condemnation," and is virtually equivalent to *krima* (2917) - see Mt 23:33; Jn 3:19; Jas 5:12. Syn.: 176, 843, 2607, 2613, 2631, 2632, 2633, 2917, 2919. See: TDNT—3:941, 469; BAGD—452c; THAYER—361d.

2921. **Κρίσπος** {2x} **Krispŏs**, *kris'-pos;* of Lat. or.; *"crisp"; Crispus,* a Corinthian:—Crispus {2x}. See: BAGD—453b; THAYER—362b.

2922. **κριτήριον** {3x} **kritēriŏn**, *kree-tay'-ree-on;* neut. of a presumed der. of *2923;* a *rule* of judging (*"criterion"*), i.e. (by impl.) a *tribunal:*—to judge {1x}, judgment {1x}, judgment seat {1x}.

Kriterion is primarily "a means of judging" (akin to *krino,* "to judge": Eng., "criterion"), then, a tribunal, law court, or "lawsuit," and is translated **(1)** "to judge" in 1 Cor 6:2; **(2)** "judgment" in 1 Cor 6:4; and **(3)** "(human) judgment seats" in Jas 2:6. See: TDNT—3:943, 469; BAGD—453b; THAYER—362b.

2923. **κριτής** {1x} **kritēs**, *kree-tace';* from *2919;* a *judge* (gen. or spec.):—judge {1x}.

Krites, "a judge", is used **(1)** of God, Heb 12:23, where the order in the original is "to a

Judge who is God of all"; this is really the significance; it suggests that He who is the Judge of His people is at the same time their God; that is the order in 10:30; the word is also used of God in Jas. 4:12; **(2)** of Christ, Acts 10:42; 2 Ti 4:8; Jas 5:9; **(3)** of a ruler in Israel in the times of the Judges, Acts 13:20; **(4)** of a Roman procurator, Acts 24:10; **(5)** of those whose conduct provides a standard of "judging," Mt 12:27; Lk 11:19; **(6)** in the forensic sense, of one who tries and decides a case, Mt 5:25 (twice); 12:58 (twice); 18:2; 18:6 (lit., "the judge of unnghteousness," expressing subjectively His character); Acts 18:15; **(7)** of one who passes, or arrogates to himself, judgment on anything, Jas 2:4; 4:11. Syn.: *Dikastes* (1348) is the more dignified and official term; whereas, *krites* (2923) gives prominence to the mental process, whether the judge is a magistrate or not. See: TDNT—3:943, 469; BAGD—453c; THAYER—362b.

2924. **κριτικός** {1x} **kritikŏs**, *krit-ee-kos';* from *2923; decisive* ("*critical*"), i.e. *discriminative:*—discerner {1x}.

Kritikos signifies that which relates to judging, fit for, or skilled in, judging (Eng., critical), and found in Heb 4:12, of the Word of God as quick to discern the thoughts and intents of the heart, i.e., discriminating and passing judgment on the thoughts, intents, and feelings. See: TDNT—3:943, 469; BAGD—453d; THAYER—362c.

2925. **κρούω** {9x} **krŏuō**, *kroo'-o;* appar. a primary verb; to *rap:*—knock.

Krouo, "to strike, knock," is used in the NT of "knocking" at a door, **(1)** literally, Lk 12:36; Acts 12:13, 16; **(2)** figuratively, Mt 7:7, 8; Lk 11:9, 10 (of importunity in dealing with God); 13:25; Rev 3:20. See: TDNT—3:954, 475; BAGD—453d; THAYER—362c.

2926. **κρυπτή** {1x} **kruptē**, *kroop-tay';* fem. of *2927;* a *hidden* place, i.e. *cellar* ("*crypt*"):—secret place {1x}.

Krupte, (Eng., "crypt"), "a covered way or vault" (akin to *kruptos*, "hidden, secret"), is used in Lk 11:33, of lighting a lamp and putting it "in a cellar." See: TDNT—3:957, 476; BAGD—454a; THAYER—362c.

2927. **κρυπτός** {19x} **kruptŏs**, *kroop-tos';* from *2928; concealed,* i.e. *private:*—secret {12x}, hid {3x}, hidden {3x}, inwardly {1x}.

Kruptos, "secret, hidden" (akin to *krupto*, "to hide"), Eng., "crypt," "cryptic," etc., is used as an adjective and rendered **(1)** "secret" **(1a)** in Lk 8:17, in the neuter, with *en*, "in," as an adverbial phrase, "in secret," **(1b)** with the article, Mt 6:4, 6, 18 twice in each verse, **(1c)** without the article, Jn 7:4, 10; 18:20; **(1d)** in the neuter plural, with the article, "the secrets **(1d1)** (of men)," Rom 2:16; **(1d2)** of the heart, 1 Cor 14:25; **(1e)** in Lk 11:33, "a secret place"; and is translated **(2)** "hid" in Mt 10:26; Mk 4:22; Lk 12:2 (last part); **(3)** "hidden" in **(3a)** 1 Cor 4:5, "hidden (things of darkness)"; **(3b)** 2 Cor 4:2, "hidden (things of shame)"; **(3c)** 1 Pet 3:4, "hidden (man of the heart)"; and **(4)** "inwardly" in Rom 2:29. See: TDNT—3:957, 476; BAGD—454a; THAYER—362d.

2928. **κρύπτω** {16x} **kruptō**, *kroop'-to;* a primary verb; to *conceal* (prop. by *covering*):—hide {11x}, hide (one's) self {2x}, keep secret {1x}, secretly {1x}, hidden {1x}.

Krupto, "to cover, conceal, keep secret" (Eng., "crypt," "cryptic," etc.), is translated **(1)** "hide, hid" **(1a)** literally, Mt 5:14; 13:44 twice; 25:18; 25:25; Heb 11:23; Rev 6:15, 16; **(1b)** metaphorically, e.g., Lk 18:34; 19:42; Col 3:3; 1 Ti 5:25; **(2)** "hid himself", Jn 8:59; 12:36; **(3)** "kept secret" in Mt 13:35; **(4)** "secretly" in Jn 19:38 [perfect participle, passive voice, lit., "(but) having been hidden"], referring to Nicodemus as having been a "secret" disciple of Christ; and **(5)** "hidden" in Rev 2:17. See: TDNT—3:957, 476; BAGD—454b; THAYER—362d.

2929. **κρυσταλλίζω** {1x} **krustallizō**, *kroos-tal-lid'-zo;* from *2930;* to *make* (i.e. intr. *resemble*) *ice* ("crystallize"):—be clear as crystal {1x}. See: BAGD—454d; THAYER—363a.

2930. **κρύσταλλος** {2x} **krustallŏs**, *kroos'-tal-los;* from a der. of κρύος **kruos** (*frost*); *ice,* i.e. (by anal.) rock, a precious stone, "*crystal*":—crystal {2x}. See: BAGD—454d; THAYER—363a.

2931. **κρυφῆ** {1x} **kruphē**, *kroo-fay';* adv. from *2928; privately:*—in secret {1x}. See: TDNT—3:957, 476; BAGD—454d; THAYER—363a.

2932. **κτάομαι** {7x} **ktaŏmai**, *ktah'-om-ahee;* a primary verb; to *get,* i.e. *acquire* (by any means; *own*):—obtain {1x}, possess {3x}, provide {1x}, purchase {2x}.

Ktaomai means "to procure for oneself, acquire, obtain,"and is translated **(1)** "obtained" in Acts 22:28; **(2)** "to possess" in Lk 18:12; 21:19 where the probable meaning is "ye shall gain the mastery over your souls," i.e., instead of giving way to adverse circumstances.; 1 Th 4:4; **(3)** "provide" in Mt 10:9; and **(4)** "purchased", "to procure for oneself, get, gain, acquire" in Acts 1:18, 8:20. See: BAGD—455a; THAYER—363b.

2933. **κτῆμα** {4x} **ktēma**, *ktay'-mah;* from *2932;* an *acquirement,* i.e. *estate:*—possession {4x}.

Ktema denotes "a possession, property," Mt 19:22; Mk 10:22; Acts 2:45; 5:1. See: BAGD—455b; THAYER—363b.

2934. **κτῆνος** {4x} **ktēnŏs**, *ktay'-nos;* from *2932; property,* i.e. (spec.) a domestic *animal:*—beast {4x}.

Ktenos signifies, **(1)** a "beast" of burden, Lk 10:34; Acts 23:24; and **(2)** "beasts" of any sort, apart from those signified by *therion* (2432), 1 Cor 15:39; Rev 18:13. Syn.: 2432. See: BAGD—455b; THAYER—363b.

2935. **κτήτωρ** {1x} **ktētōr**, *ktay'-tore;* from *2932;* an *owner:*—possessor {1x}. See: BAGD—455c; THAYER—363b.

2936. **κτίζω** {14x} **ktizō**, *ktid'-zo;* prob. akin to *2932* (through the idea of *proprietorship* of the *manufacturer*); to *fabricate,* i.e. *found* (*form* orig.):—create {12x}, Creator {1x}, make {1x}.

Ktizo signifies, in Scripture, "to create," always of the act of God, whether **(1)** in the natural creation, Mk 13:19; Rom 1:25 (where the title "The Creator" translates the article with the aorist participle of the verb); 1 Cor 11:9; Eph 3:9; Col 1:16; 1 Ti 4:3; Rev 4:11; 10:6, or **(2)** in the spiritual creation, Eph 2:10, 15; 4:24; Col 3:10. See: TDNT—3:1000, 481; BAGD—455c; THAYER—363b.

2937. **κτίσις** {19x} **ktisis**, *ktis'-is;* from *2936;* orig. *formation* (prop. the act; by impl. the thing, lit. or fig.):—building {1x}, creation {6x}, creature {11x}, ordinance {1x}.

Ktisis, primarily "the act of creating," or "the creative act in process," and is translated **(1)** "building" in Heb 9:11; **(2)** "creation" in Mk 10:16; 13:19; Rom 1:20; 8:22; Gal 6:15 the creative act of God, whereby a man is introduced into the blessing of salvation, in contrast to circumcision done by human hands, which the Judaizers claimed was necessary to that end; 2 Cor 5:17 the reference is to what the believer is in Christ; in consequence of the creative act he has become a new creature; 2 Pet 3:4; Rev 3:14; **(3)** "creature" in Mk 16:15 mankind in general; Rom 1:25; 8:19, 20, 21, 39; Gal 6:15; Col 1:15; 23 mankind in general; Heb 4:13; **(4)** "ordinance" in 1 Pet 2:13 used of human actions. See: TDNT—3:1000, 481; BAGD—455d; THAYER—363c.

2938. **κτίσμα** {4x} **ktisma**, *ktis'-mah;* from *2936;* an orig. *formation* (concr.), i.e. *product* (created thing):—creature {4x}.

Ktisma has the concrete sense, "the created thing, the creature, the product of the creative act," 1 Ti 4:4; Jas 1:18; Rev 5:13; 8:9. See: TDNT—3:1000, 481; BAGD—456b; THAYER—363d.

2939. **κτιστής** {1x} **ktistēs**, *ktis-tace';* from *2936;* a *founder,* i.e. *God* (as author of all things):—Creator {1x}. See: TDNT—3:1000, 481; BAGD—456b; THAYER—364a.

2940. **κυβεία** {1x} **kubĕia**, *koo-bi'-ah;* from κύβος **kubŏs** (a "*cube,*" i.e. *die* for playing); *gambling,* i.e. (fig.) *artifice* or *fraud:*—sleight {1x}.

Metaph., *kubos* is used for the deception of men, because dice players sometimes cheated and defrauded their fellow players. It denotes "dice playing" (from *kubos,* "a cube, a die as used in gaming"); hence, metaphorically, "trickery, sleight," Eph 4:14. The Eng. word is connected with "sly" ("not with slight"). See: BAGD—456c; THAYER—364a.

2941. **κυβέρνησις** {1x} **kubĕrnēsis**, *koo-ber'-nay-sis;* from κυβερνάω **kubĕrnaō** (of Lat. or., to *steer*); *pilotage,* i.e. (fig.) *directorship* (in the church):—government {1x}.

Kubernesis means to guide (whence Eng., "govern") and denotes **(1)** steering, pilotage; and **(2)** metaphorically, governments or governings, said of those who act as guides in a local church (1 Cor 12:28). See: TDNT—3:1035, 486; BAGD—456c; THAYER—364a.

2942. **κυβερνήτης** {2x} **kubĕrnētēs**, *koo-ber-nay'-tace;* from the same as *2941; helmsman,* i.e. (by impl.) *captain:*—shipmaster {1x}, master {1x}.

Kubernetes, "the pilot or steersman of a ship," or, metaphorically, "a guide or governor" (akin to *kubernao,* "to guide": Eng., "govern" is connected; cf. *kubernesis,* "a steering, pilotage," 1 Cor 12:28, "governments"), is translated **(1)** "master" in Acts 27:11; and **(2)** "shipmaster" in Rev 18:17. See: BAGD—456c; THAYER—364a.

2943. **κυκλόθεν** {4x} **kuklŏthĕn**, *koo-kloth'-en;* adv. from the same as *2945; from* the *circle,* i.e. *all around:*—round about {3x}, about {1x}.

Kuklothen, "round about, or all round" (from *kuklos,* "a circle, cycle"), is found in the Apocalypse only: **(1)** "round about", Rev 4:3, 4; 5:11; and **(2)** "about" 4: 8. See: BAGD—456c; THAYER—364a.

κυκλός kuklŏs. See *2945*.

2944. **κυκλόω** {5x} **kuklŏō**, *koo-klŏ'-o;* from the same as *2945;* to *encircle,* i.e. *surround:*—compass about {2x}, compass {1x}, come round about {1x}, stand round about {1x}.

Kukloo, "to compass, to encircle, surround" (Eng., "cycle"), is translated **(1)** "compassed about" in **(1a)** Rev 20:9, of a camp surrounded by foes;

(1b) Heb 11:30 of Jericho; **(2)** "compassed" in Lk 21:20 as of a city "compassed" by armies, Luke 21:20; Heb. 11:30; **(3)** "came round about," in Jn 10:24; and **(4)** "stood round about" in Acts 14:20. See: BAGD—456d; THAYER—364b.

2945. **κύκλῳ** {7x} **kuklōi**, *koo'-klo;* as if dat. of κύκλος **kuklŏs** (a *ring, "cycle"*; akin to *2947*); i.e. *in a circle* (by impl. of *1722*), i.e. (adv.) *all around:*—round about {7x}.

Kuklo, the dative case of *kuklos* (2945), means "round about," lit., "in a circle", Mk 3:34; 6:6, 36; Lk 9:12; Rom 15:19; Rev 4:6; 5:11; 7:11. See: BAGD—456d; THAYER—364b.

2946. **κύλισμα** {1x} **kulisma**, *koo'-lis-mah;* from *2947;* a *wallow* (the effect of *rolling*), i.e. *filth:*—wallowing {1x}. See: BAGD—457b; THAYER—364b.

2947. **κυλίω** {1x} **kuliŏō**, *koo-lee-ŏ'-o;* from the base of *2949* (through the idea of *circularity;* comp. *2945, 1507*); to *roll* about; roll along:—wallow {1x}. See: BAGD—457b; THAYER—364c.

2948. **κυλλός** {4x} **kullŏs**, *kool-los';* from the same as *2947; rocking* about, i.e. *crippled* (*maimed,* in feet or hands):—maimed {4x}.

Kullos denotes "crooked crippled"; translated "maimed" in Mt 15:30, 31; 18:8; Mk 9:43. See: BAGD—457b; THAYER—364c.

2949. **κῦμα** {5x} **kuma**, *koo'-mah;* from κύω **kuō** (to *swell* [with young], i.e. *bend, curve*); a *billow* (as *bursting* or *toppling*):—wave {5x}.

Kuo, "to be pregnant, to swell, swelling in order to break forth with force", is used **(1)** literally in the plural, Mt 8:24; 14:24; Mk 4:37; Acts 27:41; **(2)** figuratively, Jude 13 of the impulse of restless men, tossed to and fro by their raging passions. Syn.: *Kludon* (2949) denotes a wave, suggesting uninterrupted successions; and *kuma* (2830) denotes a billow, surge, suggesting size and extension. Both are figuratively used of words suggesting the same definitions. See: BAGD—457c; THAYER—364c.

2950. **κύμβαλον** {1x} **kumbalŏn**, *koom'-bal-on;* from a der. of the base of *2949;* a *"cymbal"* (as *hollow*):—cymbal {1x}.

Kumbalon, "a cymbal," was so called from its shape (akin to *kumbos,* "a hollow basin," *kumbe,* "a cup"), and was made of bronze, two being struck together, 1 Cor 13:1. It was noted for its loud, sharp, attention-getting sound. See: TDNT—3:1037, 486; BAGD—457c; THAYER—364c.

2951. **κύμινον** {1x} **kuminŏn**, *koo'-min-on;* of for. or. [comp. *3646*]; *dill* or *fennel* ("cummin"):—cummin {1x}.

Cummin is a cultivated plant in Palestine with seeds that have a bitter warm taste and an aromatic flavour. See: BAGD—457c; THAYER—364d.

2952. **κυνάριον** {4x} **kunariŏn**, *koo-nar'-ee-on;* neut. of a presumed der. of *2965;* a *puppy:*—dog {4x}.

Kunarion, "a little dog, a puppy," is used in Mt 15:26–27; Mk 7:27, 28. See: TDNT—3:1104, 494; BAGD—457d; THAYER—364d.

2953. **Κύπριος** {3x} **Kupriŏs**, *koo'-pree-os;* from *2954;* a *Cyprian* (*Cypriot*), i.e. inhab. of Cyprus:—of Cyprus {3x}. See: BAGD—457d; THAYER—364d.

2954. **Κύπρος** {5x} **Kuprŏs**, *koo'-pros;* of uncert. or.; *Cyprus,* an island in the Mediterranean:—Cyprus {5x}. See: BAGD—457d; THAYER—364d.

2955. **κύπτω** {3x} **kuptō**, *koop'-to;* prob. from the base of *2949;* to *bend* forward:—stoop {2x}, stoop down {1x}.

Kupto, "to bow the head, stoop down," occurs in Mk 1:7; Jn 8:6, 8. See: BAGD—458a; THAYER—364d.

2956. **Κυρηναῖος** {6x} **Kurēnaiŏs**, *koo-ray-nah'-yos;* from *2957;* i.e. *Cyrenæan,* i.e. inhab. of Cyrene:—of Cyrene {3x}, Cyrenian {3x}. See: BAGD—458a; THAYER—364d.

2957. **Κυρήνη** {1x} **Kurēnē**, *koo-ray'-nay;* of uncert. der.; *Cyrenē,* a region of Africa:—Cyrene {1x}. See: BAGD—458a; THAYER—364d.

2958. **Κυρήνιος** {1x} **Kurēniŏs**, *koo-ray'-nee-os;* of Lat. or.; *Cyrenius* (i.e. *Quirinus*), a Rom.:—Cyrenius {1x}. See: BAGD—458b; THAYER—365a.

2959. **Κυρία** {2x} **Kuria**, *koo-ree'-ah;* fem. of *2962; Cyria,* a Chr. woman:—lady {2x}.

Kuria, is the person addressed in 2 Jn 1 and 5. This is probably a reference to the church itself. See: TDNT—3:1095, 486; BAGD—458b; THAYER—365b.

2960. **κυριακός** {2x} **kuriakŏs**, *koo-ree-ak-os';* from *2962; belonging to* the *Lord* (Jehovah or Jesus):—Lord's {2x}

Kuriakos, from *kurios,* signifies "pertaining to a lord or master"; in the NT, is used only of Christ; **(1)** in 1 Cor 11:20, of the Lord's Supper, or the Supper of the Lord; and **(2)** in Rev 1:10, of the Day of the Lord; which may be a reference to Sunday, the day observed by the early church in honor of the resurrection. See: TDNT—3:1095, 486; BAGD—458c; THAYER—365b.

2961. **κυριεύω** {7x} **kuriĕuō**, *koo-ree-yoo'-o;* from *2962;* to *rule:*—have dominion over {4x}, exercise lordship over {1x}, be Lord of {1x}, lords {1x}.

Kurieus, "to be lord over, rule over, have dominion over" is used of **(1)** divine authority over men, Rom 14:9, "(He might) be Lord"; **(2)** human authority over men, Lk 22:25, "exercise lordship over"; **(3)** 1 Ti 6:15, "lords"; **(4)** the permanent immunity of Christ from the "dominion" of death, Rom 6:9; **(5)** the deliverance of the believer from the "dominion" of sin, Rom 6:14; **(6)** the "dominion" of law over men, Rom 7:1; **(7)** the "dominion" of a person over the faith of other believers, 2 Cor 1:24. See: BAGD—458d; THAYER—365b.

2962. **κύριος** {748x} **kuriŏs**, *koo'-ree-os;* from κῦρος **kurŏs** (*supremacy*); *supreme* in authority, i.e. (as noun) *controller;* by impl. *Mr.* (as a respectful title):—Lord {667x}, lord {54x}, master {11x}, sir {6x}, Sir {6x}, God {4x}.

Summary: The *kurios* wielded a limited moral authority which took into consideration the good of those over whom it is exercised. *Kurios,* properly an adjective, signifying "having power" (*kuros*) or "authority," is used as a noun, variously translated in the NT, "Lord, master, Master, owner, Sir, a title of wide significance, occurring in each book of the NT save Titus and the Epistles of John. It is used **(1)** of an owner, as in Lk 19:33, cf. Mt 20:8; Acts 16:16; Gal 4:1; or **(2)** of one who has the disposal of anything, as the Sabbath, Mt 12:8; **(3)** of a master, i.e., one to whom service is due on any ground, Mt 6:24; 24:50; Eph 6:5; **(4)** of an Emperor or King, Acts 25:26; Rev 17:14; **(5)** of idols, ironically, 1 Cor 8:5, cf. Is 26:13; **(6)** as a title of respect addressed to **(6a)** a father, Mt. 21:30, **(6b)** a husband, 1 Pet 3:6, **(6c)** a master, Mt 3:27; Lk 13:8, **(6d)** a ruler, Mt 27:63, **(6e)** an angel, Acts 10:4; Rev 7:14; **(7)** as a title of courtesy addressed to a stranger, Jn 12:21; 20:15; Acts 16:30; **(8)** from the outset of His ministry this was a common form of address to the Lord Jesus, alike **(8a)** by the people, Matt 8:2; Jn 4:11, and **(8b)** by His disciples, Mt 8:25; Lk 5:8; Jn 6:68; **(9)** kurios is the NT representative of Heb. Jehovah ('LORD' in Eng. versions), see Mt 4:7; Jas 5:11, e.g., **(9a)** of adon, Lord, Mt 22:44, and **(9b)** of Adonay, Lord, Mt 1:22; **(9c)** it also occurs for Elohim, God, 1 Pet 1:25.

(10) "Christ Himself assumed the title, Mt 7:21, 22; 9:38; 22:41–45; Mk 5:19 (cf. Ps 66:16; the parallel passage, Lk 8:39, has "God"); Lk 19:31; Jn 13:13, apparently intending it in the higher senses of its current use, and at the same time suggesting its OT associations. **(11)** His purpose did not become clear to the disciples until after His resurrection, and the revelation of His Deity consequent thereon. Thomas, when he realized the significance of the presence of a mortal wound in the body of a living man, immediately joined with it the absolute title of Deity, saying, "My Lord and my God," Jn 20:28. Thereafter, except in Acts 10:4 and Rev. 7:14, there is no record that *kurios* was ever again used by believers in addressing any save God and the Lord Jesus; cf Acts 2:47 with 4:29, 30. **(12)** How soon and how completely the lower meaning had been superseded is seen in Peter's declaration in his first sermon after the resurrection, "God hath made Him—Lord," Acts 2:36, and that in the house of Cornelius, "He is Lord of all," Acts 10:36, cf. Deut 10:14; Mt 11:25; Acts 17:24. **(12)** In Peter's writings the implications of his early teaching are confirmed and developed. **(12a)** Thus Ps 34:8, 'O taste and see that Jehovah is good,' is applied to the Lord Jesus, 1 Pet 2:3, and **(12b)** "Jehovah of Hosts, Him shall ye sanctify," Is 8:13, becomes "sanctify in your hearts Christ as Lord," 1 Pet 3:15.

(13) So also James who uses *kurios* alike of God, Jas 1:7 (cf. v. 5); 3:9; 4:15; 5:4, 10, 11, and of the Lord Jesus, 1:1 (where the possibility that kai is intended epexegetically, i.e. = even, cf. 1 Th 3:11, should not be overlooked); 2:1 (lit., "our Lord Jesus Christ of glory,' cf. Ps 24:7; 29:3; Acts 7:2; 1 Cor 2:8); 5:7, 8, while the language of 4:10; 5:15, is equally applicable to either. **(14)** Jude, v. 4, speaks of "our only—Lord, Jesus Christ,' and immediately, v. 5, uses "Lord" of God as he does later, vv. 9, 14. **(15)** Paul ordinarily uses *kurios* of the Lord Jesus, 1 Cor 1:3, e.g., but also on occasion of God, in quotations from the OT, 1 Cor 3:20, e.g., and in his own words, 1 Cor 3:5, cf. v. 10. It is equally appropriate to either in 1 Cor 7:25; 2 Cor 3:16; 8:21; 1 Th 4:6, and if 1 Cor 11:32 is to be interpreted by 10:21, 22, the Lord Jesus is intended, but if by Heb 12:5–9, then *kurios* here also = God. 1 Ti 6:15, 16 is probably to be understood of the Lord Jesus, cf. Rev 17:14.

(16) Though John does not use "Lord" in his Epistles, and though, like the other Evangelists, he ordinarily uses the personal Name in his narrative, yet he occasionally speaks of Him as "the Lord," Jn 4:1; 6:23; 11:2; 20:20; 21:12. The full significance of this association of Jesus with God under the one appellation, "Lord," is seen when it is remembered that these men belonged to the only monotheistic race in the world. To associate with the Creator one known to be a creature, however exalted, though possible to Pagan philosophers, was quite impossible to a Jew. It is not recorded that in the days of His flesh any of His disciples either addressed the Lord, or spoke of Him, by His personal Name. Where Paul has occasion to refer to the facts of the gospel history he speaks of what the Lord Jesus said, Acts 20:35, and did, 1 Cor 11:23, and suffered, 1 Th 2:15; 5:9, 10. It is our Lord Jesus who is coming, 1 Th 2:19, etc. In prayer also the title is given, 3:11; Eph 1:3; the sinner is invited to believe on the Lord Jesus, Acts 16:31; 20:21, and the saint to look to the Lord Jesus for deliverance, Rom 7:24, 25, and in the few exceptional cases in which the personal Name stands alone a reason is always discernible in the immediate context.

(17) The title "Lord," as given to the Savior, in its full significance rests upon the resurrection, Acts 2:36; Rom 10:9; 14:9, and is realized only in the Holy Spirit, 1 Cor 12:3. Syn.: There is a degree of truth in the saying "a man is a *despot* (1203) to his slaves, but a *kurios* to his wife and children." See also: 1203, 3175. See: TDNT—3:1039, 486; BAGD—458d; THAYER—365b.

2963. **κυριότης** {4x} **kuriŏtēs**, *koo-ree-ot'-ace;* from *2962; mastery,* i.e. (concr. and collect.) *rulers:*—dominion {3x}, government {1x}.

Kuriotes denotes "lordship" (*kurios,* "a lord"), "power, dominion," whether angelic or human and is translated **(1)** "dominion" Eph 1:21; Col 1:16; Jude 1:8; and **(2)** "government" 2 Pet 2:10. In Eph. and Col. it indicates a grade in the angelic orders, in which it stands second. See: TDNT—3:1039, 486; BAGD—460d; THAYER—366c.

2964. **κυρόω** {2x} **kurŏō**, *koo-rŏ'-o;* from the same as *2962;* to *make authoritative,* i.e. *ratify:*—confirm {2x}.

Kuroo, "to make valid, ratify, impart authority or influence" (from *kuros,* "might," *kurios,* "mighty, a head, as supreme in authority"), is translated "confirm" and used of confirming **(1)** love, 2 Cor 2:8; and **(2)** a human covenant, Gal. 3:15. See: TDNT—3:1098, 486; BAGD—461a; THAYER—366d.

2965. **κύων** {5x} **kuōn**, *koo'-ohn;* a primary word; a *dog* ["*hound*"] (lit. or fig.):—dog {5x}.

Kuon is used in two senses, **(1)** natural, Mt 7:6; Lk 16:21; 2 Pet 2:22; and **(2)** metaphorically, dogs are ungodly men with impure minds exercising immoral ways which will exclude them from the New Jerusalem, Phil 3:2; Rev 22:15. **(3)** The Jews used the term of Gentiles, under the idea of ceremonial impurity. See: TDNT—3:1101,; BAGD—461b; THAYER—366d.

2966. **κῶλον** {1x} **kōlŏn**, *ko'-lon;* from the base of *2849;* a *limb* of the body (as if *lopped*):—carcase (carcass) {1x}.

Kolon **(1)** specifically is a member of a body, particularly the more external and prominent members esp. the feet and **(2)** extension a dead body, corpse, inasmuch as the members of a corpse are loose and fall apart (Heb 3:17). See: BAGD—461b; THAYER—366d.

2967. **κωλύω** {23x} **kōluō**, *ko-loo'-o;* from the base of *2849;* to *estop,* i.e. *prevent* (by word or act):—forbid {17x}, hinder {2x}, withstand {1x}, keep from {1x}, let {1x}, not suffer {1x}.

Koluo, "to hinder, restrain, withhold, forbid" (akin to *kolos,* "docked, lopped, clipped"), is most usually translated **(1)** "to forbid" in Mt 19:14; Mk 9:38, 39; Mk 10:14; Lk 6:29; 9:49, 50; 18:16; 23:2; Acts 10:47; 16:6; 24:23; 1 Cor 14:39; 1 Th 2:16; 1 Ti 4:3; 2 Pet 2:16; 3 Jn 1:10; **(2)** "to hinder" in Lk 11:52; Acts 8:36; **(3)** "withstand" in Acts 11:17; **(4)** "kept (them) from" in Acts 27:43; **(5)** "was let" in Rom 1:13; and **(6)** "were not suffered" in Heb 7:23. See: BAGD—461b; THAYER—366d.

2968. **κώμη** {28x} **kōmē**, *ko'-may;* from *2749;* a *hamlet* (as if *laid* down):—town {11x}, village {17x}.

A hamlet is a few small houses in the country. A village is a larger group of houses in the country, loosely organized, and without walls. A country town is larger than a village, usually somewhat isolated, more organized, having city officials or representatives, a synagogue, and usually has no walls. Normally a town is somewhat near a city. A city is usually organized and walled and increases in complexity as the population increases. In the scriptures there are villages, towns, and cities. Syn.: 2969. See: BAGD—461d; THAYER—367a.

2969. **κωμόπολις** {1x} **kōmŏpŏlis**, *ko-mop'-ol-is;* from *2968* and *4172;* an unwalled *city:*—town {1x}.

Komopolis is a larger village, still unwalled, and loosely organized, Mk 1:38. Syn.: 2968. See: BAGD—461d; THAYER—367b.

2970. **κῶμος** {3x} **kōmŏs**, *ko'-mos;* from *2749;* a *carousal* (as if *letting loose*):—revelling {2x}, rioting {1x}.

Summary: *Komos* unites the concepts of rioting and revelry and usually involves a nocturnal and riotous procession of half drunken and frolicsome fellows who after supper parade through the streets with torches and music in honour some deity, and sing and play before houses of male and female friends; hence used generally of feasts and drinking parties that are protracted till late at night and indulge in revelry. It is used **(1)** in the plural, Rom 13:13, translated by the singular, "rioting"; and translated **(2)** "reveling" in Gal 5:21 and 1 Pet 4:3, "revelings." Syn.: 2897, 3178, 3632, 4224. See: BAGD—461d; THAYER—462a.

2971. **κώνωψ** {1x} **kōnōps**, *ko'-nopes;* appar. a der. of the base of *2759* and a der. of *3700;* a *mosquito* (from its *stinging proboscis*):—gnat {1x}.

Konops probably denotes the winegnat or midge which breeds in fermenting or evaporating wine (Mt 23:24). See: BAGD—462a.

2972. **Κῶς** {1x} **Kōs**, *koce;* of uncert. or.; *Cos,* an island in the Mediterranean:—Coos {1x}. See: BAGD—462a; THAYER—367c.

2973. **Κωσάμ** {1x} **Kōsam**, *ko-sam';* of Heb. or. [comp. 7081]; *Cosam* (i.e. *Kosam*) an Isr.:—Cosam {1x}. See: BAGD—367c; THAYER—462a.

2974. **κωφός** {14x} **kōphŏs**, *ko-fos';* from *2875; blunted,* i.e. (fig.) of hearing (*deaf*) or speech (*dumb*):—deaf {5x}, dumb {8x}, speechless {1x}.

Kophos, as an adjective, (akin to *kopto,* "to beat," and *kopiao*), "to be tired" signifies "blunted, dull," as of a weapon; it denotes **(1)** "blunted or dulled in tongue", and is translated "dumb": "As they went out, behold, they brought to Him a dumb man possessed with a devil" in Mt 9:32, 33; 12:22 twice; 15:30, 31;. The man had his ability to speak "blunted" by the devil. When **(2)** "blunted in hearing" it is translated "deaf," Mt 11:5; Mk 7:32, 37; Mk 9:25; Lk 7:22; 11:14 twice. It is also translated **(3)** "speechless" in Lk 1:22. Syn.: 216, 880, 4623. See: BAGD—462a; THAYER—367d.

Λ

2975. **λαγχάνω** {4x} **lagchanō**, *lang-khan'-o;* a prol. form of a primary verb, which is only used as an alt. in certain tenses; to *lot,* i.e. *determine* (by impl. *receive*) espec. by lot:—his lot be {1x}, cast lots {1x}, obtain {2x}.

Lagchano, as a verb, means "to obtain by lot" in Acts 1:17: "For he [Judas Iscariot] was numbered with us, and had obtained part of this ministry." *Lagchano* denotes "to draw lots, to obtain by casting lots" and is translated **(1)** "his lot" in Lk 1:9; lit., "he received by lot," i.e., by divine appointment; **(2)** "cast lots" in Jn 19:24; and **(3)** "obtained" in **(3a)** Acts 1:17, of the portion "allotted" by the Lord to His apostles in their ministry; and in **(3b)** 2 Pet 1:1, "that have obtained (a like precious faith)," i.e., by its being "allotted" to them, not by acquiring it for themselves, but by divine grace (an act independent of human control, as in the casting of "lots"). Syn.: 324, 353, 354, 568, 588, 618, 1209, 1523, 1926, 2210, 2865, 2983, 3028, 3335, 3336, 3858, 3880, 3970, 4327, 4355, 4356, 4380, 4381, 4382, 5562, 5264, 5274. See: TDNT—4:1, 495; BAGD—462a; THAYER—367b.

2976. **Λάζαρος** {15x} **Lazarŏs**, *lad'-zar-os;* prob. of Heb. or. [499]; *Lazarus* (i.e. *Elazar*), the name of two Isr.:—Lazarus {11x}, Lazarus (the poor man) {4x}. See: BAGD—462b.

2977. **λάθρα** {4x} **lathra**, *lath'-rah;* adv. from *2990; privately:*—privily {3x}, secretly {1x}.

Lathra means "secretly, covertly" (from a root *lath*— indicating "unnoticed, unknown," seen in *lanthano,* "to escape notice," *lethe,* "forgetfulness"), and is translated **(1)** "privily" in Mt 1:19; 2:7; Acts 16:37; and **(2)** "secretly" in Jn 11:28. See: BAGD—462c; THAYER—367d.

2978. **λαῖλαψ** {3x} **lailaps**, *lah'-ee-laps;* of uncert. der.; a *whirlwind* (*squall*):—storm {2x}, tempest {1x}.

Lailaps refers to a forminable squall, a storm raging back and forth unstably, breaking forth from dark clouds and accompanied by torrential rains and is translated **(1)** "storm" in Mk 4:37; Lk 8:23; and **(2)** "tempest" in 2 Pet 2:17. Syn.: 417, 2366, 4151, 4157. See: BAGD—462d; THAYER—368a.

2979. **λακτίζω** {2x} **laktizō**, *lak-tid'-zo;* from adv. λάξ **lax** (*heelwise*); to *recalcitrate:*—kick {2x}.

This word means to kick forcefully with the heal (Acts 9:5; 26:14). See: TDNT—4:3, 495; BAGD—463a; THAYER—368a.

2980. **λαλέω** {296x} **lalĕō**, *lal-eh'-o;* a prol. form of an otherwise obs. verb; to *talk,* i.e. *utter* words:—speak {244x}, say {15x}, tell {12x}, talk {11x}, preach {6x}, utter {4x}, vr speak {1x}, misc. {3x}.

This word focuses on the articulated, distinct sound of the formed word in human language. Syn.: 2981, 3004. See: TDNT—4:69, 505; BAGD—463a; THAYER—368a. comp. *3004.*

2981. **λαλιά** {4x} **lalia**, *lal-ee-ah';* from *2980; talk:*—saying {1x}, speech {3x}.

(1) *Lalia* focuses not on the speaker but on the condition of the hearer to receive the word spoken. **(2)** *Lalia* requires an open heart to receive the spoke word. **(3)** It denotes "talk, a particular dialect of speech" and is translated **(1)** "speech" Mt 26:73; Mk 14:70; Jn 8:43; and **(2)** "saying" Jn 4:42. Syn.: 2980, 3004. See: BAGD—464a; THAYER—369b.

2982. **λαμά** {2x} **lama**, *lam-ah';* or **λαμμᾶ** **lamma**, *lam-mah';* or **λεμά** **lĕma**, *leh-mah';* of Heb. or Aramaic orig. [4100 with prep. pref.]; *lama* (i.e. *why*):—*lama* {2x}. See: BAGD—464a; THAYER—370a.

2983. **λαμβάνω** {263x} **lambanō**, *lam-ban'-o;* a prol. form of a primary verb, which is use only as an alt. in certain tenses; to *take* (in very many applications, lit. and fig. [properly obj. or act., to *get hold* of; whereas *1209* is rather subj. or pass., to *have offered* to one; while *138* is more violent, to *seize* or *remove*]):—receive {133x}, take {106x}, have {3x}, catch {3x}, not tr {1x}, misc. {7x} = accept, + be amazed, assay, attain, bring, × when I call, come on (× unto), + forget, hold, obtain.

Lambano, as a verb, denotes either "to take" or "to receive," **(1)** literally, **(1a)** without an object, in contrast to asking: "For every one that asketh receiveth (*lambano*); and he that seeketh findeth; and to him that knocketh it shall be opened" (Mt 7:8; cf. Mk 11:24); **(1b)** in contrast to giving: "" (Mt 10:8; cf. Acts 20:35); **(1c)** with objects, whether **(1c1)** things: "But he shall receive (*lambano*) an hundredfold now in this time, houses, and brethren, and sisters, and mothers, and children, and lands, with persecutions; and in the world to come eternal life" (Mk 10:30; cf. Jn 13:30; Acts 9:19; 1 Cor 9:25); or **(1c2)** persons: "Then they willingly received Him into the ship. and immediately the ship was at the land whither they went" (Jn 6:21; cf. 13:20; 16:14; 2 Jn 10; Mk 14:65);

(2) metaphorically, **(2a)** of the word of God: "But he that received the seed into stony places, the same is he that heareth the word, and *anon* with joy receiveth it" (Mt 13:20; cf. Mk 4:16); **(2c)** of the sayings of Christ: "He that rejecteth me, and receiveth not My words, hath one that judgeth him: the word that I have spoken, the same shall judge him in the last day" (Jn 12:48); **(2d)** of the witness of Christ: "Verily, verily, I say unto thee, We speak that we do know, and testify that we have seen; and ye receive not our witness" (Jn 3:11); **(2e)** of a hundredfold in this life, and eternal life in the world to come: "But he shall receive an hundredfold now in this time, houses, and brethren, and sisters, and mothers, and children, and lands, with persecutions; and in the world to come eternal life" (Mk 10:30); **(2f)** of mercy: "Let us therefore come boldly unto the throne of grace, that we may obtain mercy, and find grace to help in time of need" (Heb 4:16); **(2g)** of a person: "And they asked Him, saying, Master, we know that thou sayest and teachest rightly, neither acceptest (*lambano*) thou the person *of any*, but teachest the way of God truly" (Lk 20:21; cf. Gal 2:6 "accepteth," an expression used in the OT either in the sense of being gracious or kind to a person [Gen 19:21; 32:20], or negatively in the sense of being impartial [Lev 19:15; Deut 10:17]. Syn.: There is a certain distinction between *lambano* (2983) and *dechomai* (1209) in that in many instances *lambano* suggests a self-prompted taking, whereas *dechomai* more frequently indicates "a welcoming or an appropriating reception." See also: 324, 353, 354, 568, 588, 618, 1209, 1523, 1926, 2210, 2865, 2975, 3028, 3335, 3336, 3858, 3880, 3970, 4327, 4355, 4356, 4380, 4381, 4382, 5562, 5264, 5274. See: TDNT—4:5, 495; BAGD—464a; THAYER—371c.

2984. **Λάμεχ** {1x} **Lamĕch**, *lam'-ekh;* of Heb. or. [3929]; *Lamech* (i.e. *Lemek*), a patriarch:—*Lamech* {1x}. See: BAGD—465c; THAYER—371c.

λαμμᾶ **lamma**. See *2982*.

2985. **λαμπάς** {9x} **lampas**, *lam-pas';* from *2989;* a "*lamp*" or *flambeau:*—lamp {7x}, light {1x}, torch {1x}.

(1) *Lampas* denotes a light, frequently fed, like a lamp with oil from a little vessel used for that purpose; they held little oil and would frequently need replenishing. **(2)** It is translated **(2a)** "lamp" in Mt 25:1, 3, 4, 7, 8; Rev 4:5; 8:10; **(2)** "light" in Acts 20:8; and **(3)** "torch" in Jn 18:3 i.e. larger lamps. Syn.: 3088, 5338, 5457, 5458. See: TDNT—4:16, 497; BAGD—465c; THAYER—371c.

2986. **λαμπρός** {9x} **lamprŏs**, *lam-pros';* from the same as *2985; radiant;* by anal. *limpid;* fig. *magnificent* or *sumptuous* (in appearance):—bright {2x}, goodly {2x}, white {2x}, gorgeous {1x}, gay {1x}, clear {1x}.

Lampros, "shining, brilliant, bright," is used **(1)** of the clothing of an angel, Acts 10:30 and Rev 15:6; **(2)** symbolically, "white" of the clothing **(2a)** of the saints, Rev 19:8; and angels, Rev 15:6; **(3)** of Christ **(3a)** as the Morning Star, Rev 22:16 "bright"; and of His appearance to Saul on the Damascus road, Acts 10:30 "bright"; **(4)** of the water of life, Rev 22:1, "clear." It is translated **(4)** "gorgeous" of the robe put on Jesus by Herod, Lk. 23:11. **(5)** The clothing of the favored rich man is described as **(5a)** "gay", Jas 2.2, and **(5b)** "goodly", Jas 2:3. **(6)** "Goodly" also refers to the destroyed merchandise of Babylon, Rev 18:14. See: TDNT—4:16, 497; BAGD—465d; THAYER—371c.

2987. **λαμπρότης** {1x} **lamprŏtēs**, *lam-prot'-ace;* from *2986; brilliancy:*—brightness {1x}. See: BAGD—466a; THAYER—371c.

2988. **λαμπρῶς** {1x} **lamprōs**, *lam-proce';* adv. from *2986; brilliantly,* i.e. fig. *luxuriously:*—sumptuously {1x}. See: BAGD—466a; THAYER—371d.

2989. **λάμπω** {7x} **lampō**, *lam'-po;* a primary verb; to *beam,* i.e. *radiate* brilliancy (lit. or fig.):—give light {1x}, shine {6x}.

Lampo, "to give the light of a torch," is rendered **(1)** "giveth light" in Mt 5:15; and **(2)** "to shine (as a torch)" in Mt 5:16, 17:2; Lk 17:24; Acts 12:7; 2 Cor 4:6 (twice). See: TDNT—4:16, 497; BAGD—466a; THAYER—371d.

2990. **λανθάνω** {6x} **lanthanō**, *lan-than'-o;* a prol. form of a primary verb, which is used only an alt. in certain tenses; to *lie hid* (lit. or fig.); often used adv. *unwittingly:*—be hid {3x}, be ignorate of {2x}, unawares {1x}.

Lanthano, "to escape notice, to be hidden from," is rendered **(1)** "be hid" in **(1a)** Mk 7:24 "(could not) be hid", of Christ; "was (not) hid"; **(1b)** Lk 8:47, of the woman with the issue of blood; "was (not) hid"; and **(1c)** Acts 26:26, of the facts concerning Christ; the sentence might be rendered "none of these things has escaped (are hidden from) the king's notice"; **(2)** "be ignorant of" in **(2a)** 2 Pet 3:5, "they willingly are ignorant of": "For this they willingly are ignorant of, that by the word of God the heavens were of old, and the earth standing out of the water and in the water", **(2b)** 2 Pet 3:8, "be not ignorant of", "let this one thing not escape your notice"; and **(3)** "unawares" in Heb 13:2 of entertaining angels unawares. Syn.: 50, 51, 52, 56, 2399. See: TDNT—4:16, 497; BAGD—371d; THAYER—466b.

2991. **λαξευτός** {1x} **laxĕutŏs**, *lax-yoo-tos';* from a compound of **λᾶς** **las** (a *stone*) and the base of *3584* (in its orig. sense of *scraping*); *rock-quarried:*—hewn in stone {1x}. See: BAGD—466c; THAYER—371d.

2992. **λαός** {143x} **laŏs**, *lah-os';* appar. a primary word; a *people* (in general; thus differing from *1218*, which denotes one's *own* populace):—people {143x}.

Laos is used of **(1)** "the people at large," especially of people assembled, e.g., Mt 27:25; Lk 1:21; 3:15; Acts 4:27; **(2)** "a people of the same race and language," e.g., **(2a)** Rev 5:9; in the plural, e.g., Lk 2:31; Rom 15:11; Rev 7:9; 11:9; **(2b)** especially of Israel, e.g., Mt 2:6; 4:23; Jn 11:50; Acts 4:8; Heb 2:17; **(2b1)** in distinction from their rulers and priests, e.g., Mt 26:5; Lk 20:19; Heb 5:3; **(2b2)** in distinction from Gentiles, e.g., Acts 26:17, 23; Rom 15:10; **(3)** of Christians as the people of God, e.g., Acts 15:14; Titus 2:14; Heb 4:9; 1 Pet. 2:9. Syn.: 1218, 1484, 3793. See: TDNT—4:29, 499; BAGD—466c; THAYER—372a.

2993. **Λαοδίκεια** {6x} **Laŏdikĕia**, *lah-od-ik'-i-ah;* from a compound of *2992* and *1349; Laodicia,* a place in Asia Minor:—Laodicea {6x}. See: BAGD—466c; THAYER—371d.

2994. **Λαοδικεύς** {2x} **Laŏdikĕus**, *lah-od-ik-yooce';* from *2993;* a *Laodicean,* i.e. inhab. of Laodicia:—Laodicean {2x}. See: BAGD—466c; THAYER—372a.

2995. **λάρυγξ** {1x} **larugx**, *lar'-oongks;* of uncert. der.; the *throat* ("*larynx*"):—throat {1x}.

This word is used metaphorically of the instrument or organ of speech (Rom 3:13). See: TDNT—4:57, 503; BAGD—467b; THAYER—372b.

2996. **Λασαία** {1x} **Lasaia**, *las-ah'-yah;* of uncert. or.; *Lasæa*, a place in Crete:—Lasea {1x}. See: BAGD—467b; THAYER—372c.

2997. **λάσκω** {1x} **laschō**, *las'-kho;* a strengthened form of a primary verb, which only occurs in this and another prol. form as alt. in certain tenses; to *crack* open (from a fall):—burst asunder {1x}.

Lascho primarily means to crack, or crash and denotes to burst asunder with a crack, crack open, always of making a noise (Acts 1:18). See: BAGD—467b; THAYER—372c.

2998. **λατομέω** {2x} **latŏmĕō**, *lat-om-eh'-o;* from the same as the first part of *2991* and the base of *5114;* to hew out stones, *to quarry:*—hew {2x}.

Latomeo signifies "to hew out stones" (from *latomos*, "a stone-cutter"; *las*, "a stone," *temno*, "to cut"), and is used of the sepulchre which Joseph of Arimathaea had "hewn" out of a rock for himself, where the body of the Lord was buried, Mt 27:60; Mk 15:46. See: BAGD—467b; THAYER—372c.

2999. **λατρεία** {5x} **latrĕia**, *lat-ri'-ah;* from *3000; ministration* of God, i.e. *worship:*—divine service {1x}, service {4x}.

Latreia means to serve primarily and denotes **(1)** specifically, the service of God according to the requirements of the Levitical Law ("divine service - Rom 9:4; Heb 9:1, 6); and **(2)** generally, a sense of service to God (Jn 16:2; Rom 12:1). Syn.: 3000, 3008. See: TDNT—4:58, 503; BAGD—467b; THAYER—372d.

3000. **λατρεύω** {21x} **latrĕuō**, *lat-ryoo'-o;* from λάτρις **latris** (a hired *menial*); to *minister* (to God), i.e. *render,* relig. *homage:*—serve {16x}, do the service {1x}, worship {3x}, worshipper {1x}.

Latreuo, primarily "to work for hire" (akin to *lataris,* "a hired servant"), signifies **(1)** to worship, **(2)** to "serve"; in the latter sense it is used of service **(2a)** to God, Mt 4:10; Lk 1:74 ("without fear"); 4:8; Acts 7:7; 24:14, "worship"; 26:7; 27:23; Rom 1:9 ("with my spirit"); 2 Ti 1:3; Heb 9:14; 12:28, "we may serve"; Rev 7:15; **(2b)** to God and Christ ("the Lamb"), Rev 22:3; **(2c)** in the tabernacle, Heb 8:5; 13:10; **(2d)** to "the host of heaven," Acts 7:42, "to worship"; **(2e)** to "the creature," instead of the Creator, Rom 1:25, of idolatry. It is translated **(3)** "to worship" in Phil 3:3, "(which) worship (God in the spirit)"; "to worship" in Acts 7:42; 24:14; and **(4)** "(the) worshipers" in Heb 10:2, present participle, lit., "(the ones) worshiping. Syn.: 2999, 3008. See: TDNT—4:58, 503; BAGD—467c; THAYER—372d.

3001. **λάχανον** {4x} **lachanŏn**, *lakh'-an-on;* from λαχαίνω **lachainō** (to *dig*); a *vegetable:*—herb {4x}.

Lachanon denotes a garden herb, a vegetable, in contrast to wild plants (Mt 13:32; Mk 4:32; Lk 11:42; Rom 14:2). See: TDNT—4:65, 504; BAGD—467d; THAYER—373a.

3002. **Λεββαῖος** {1x} **Lĕbbaiŏs**, *leb-bah'-yos;* of uncert. or.; *Lebbæus,* a Chr.:—Lebbæus {1x}. See: BAGD—467d; THAYER—373a.

3003. **λεγεών** {4x} **lĕgĕōn**, *leg-eh-ohn'* or **λεγιών** **lĕgiōn**, *leg-ee-ohn';* of Lat. or.; a "*legion,*" i.e. Rom. *regiment* (fig.):—legion {4x}.

This word means **(1)** specifically, a *legion,* a body of soldiers whose number differed at different times, and in the time of Augustus seems to have consisted of 6826 men: 6100 foot soldiers, and 726 horsemen (Mt 26:53); and **(2)** more generally a large number (Mk 5:9, 15; Lk 8:30). See: TDNT—4:68, 505; BAGD—467d; THAYER—373a.

3004. **λέγω** {1343x} **lĕgō**, *leg'-o;* a primary verb; prop. to "*lay*" forth, i.e. (fig.) *relate* (in words [usually of systematic or set *discourse;* whereas *2036* and *5346* generally refer to an *individual* expression or speech respectively; while *4483* is prop. to *break silence* merely, and *2980* means an *extended* or random harangue]); by impl. to *mean:*—say {1184x}, speak {61x}, call {48x}, tell {33x}, misc. {17x} = ask, bid, boast, describe, give out, name, put forth, shew, utter.

(1) *Lego* focuses on the words that are uttered, the thought of the mind which is correlative to the spoken word as their necessary condition; the bringing together of words into a sentence. **(2)** *Lego* occasionally signifies "to ask," as of an inquiry, the reason being that *lego* is used for every variety of speaking, e.g., Acts 25:20, "I asked whether he would come to Jerusalem." Syn.: 154, 155, 350, 1833, 1905, 2065, 2980, 2981, 4441. See: TDNT—4:69, 505; BAGD—468a; THAYER—373b.

3005. **λεῖμμα** {1x} **lĕimma**, *lime'-mah;* from *3007;* a *remainder:*—remnant {1x}.

Leimma "that which is left" (akin to *leipo,* "to leave"), "a remnant," is used in Rom 11:5, "there is a remnant," more lit., "there has come to be a remnant," i.e., there is a spiritual "remnant" saved by the gospel from the midst of apostate Israel. While in one sense there has been and is a considerable number, yet, compared with the whole nation, past and present, the "remnant" is small, and as such is an evidence of God's electing grace (see v. 4). See: TDNT—4:194, 523; BAGD—470b; THAYER—375b.

3006. **λεῖος** {1x} **lĕiŏs**, *li'-os;* appar. a primary word; *smooth,* i.e. "*level*":—smooth {1x}.

Leios literally means "smooth" and occurs in Lk 3:5, prophetically and figuratively (or literally) of the topographical changes that incur to insure the full view of the Messiah; mountains lowered, valleys filled. It may speak of the lowering of spiritual pride and the raising of false humility necessary to receive Him. See: TDNT—4:193, 523; BAGD—470b; THAYER—375b.

3007. **λείπω** {6x} **lĕipō**, *li'-po;* a primary verb; to *leave,* i.e. (intr. or pass.) to *fail* or *be absent:*—lack {2x}, be wanting {2x}, want + 1722 {1x}, be destitute {1x}.

Leipo, "to leave," denotes **(1)** transitively, **(1a)** in the passive voice, "to be left behind, to lack," **(1a1)** Jas 1:4, "ye may be wanting in (nothing)"; **(1a2)** Jas 1:5, "lacketh"; **(1a3)** Jas 2:15, "be . . . destitute"); **(2)** intransitively, **(2a)** active voice, **(2a1)** Lk 18:22, "(one thing thou) lackest," is, lit., "(one thing) is lacking (to thee)"; **(2a2)** Titus 1:5, "(the things) that were wanting"; **(2a3)** Titus 3:13, "(that nothing) be wanting." See: BAGD—470b; THAYER—375c.

3008. **λειτουργέω** {3x} **lĕitŏurgĕō**, *li-toorg-eh'-o;* from *3011;* to be a *public servant,* i.e. (by anal.) to *perform* relig. or charitable *functions* (*worship, obey, relieve*):—minister {3x}.

(1) Basically, this word means to serve at one's own expense; free service, nothing expected in return. The service is the focus and then the office. **(2)** In the NT it is used **(2a)** of the prophets and teachers in the church at Antioch, who "ministered to the Lord," Acts 13:2; **(2b)** of the duty of churches of the Gentiles to "minister" in "carnal things" to the poor Jewish saints at Jerusalem, in view of the fact that the former had "been made partakers" of the "spiritual things" of the latter, Rom 15:27; **(2c)** of the official service of priests and Levites under the Law, Heb 10:11. See: TDNT—4:215, 526; BAGD—470c; THAYER—375c.

3009. **λειτουργία** {6x} **lĕitŏurgia**, *li-toorg-ee'-ah;* from *3008; public function* (as priest ["liturgy"] or almsgiver):—ministration {1x}, ministry {2x}, service {3x}.

Leitourgia is used in the NT of "sacred ministrations," **(1)** priestly, Lk 1:23; Heb 8:6; 9:21; **(2)** figuratively, of the practical faith of the members of the church at Philippi regarded as priestly sacrifice, upon which the apostle's life-blood might be poured out as a libation, Phil 2:17; **(3)** of the "ministration" of believers one to another, regarded as priestly service, 2 Cor 9:12; Phil 2:30. See: TDNT—4:215, 526; BAGD—471a; THAYER—375d.

3010. **λειτουργικός** {1x} **lĕitŏurgikŏs**, *li-toorg-ik-os';* from the same as *3008; functional publicly* ("liturgic"); i.e. *beneficent:*—ministering {1x}.

Leitourgikos is related to the performance of service, employed in ministering, Heb 1:14. See: TDNT—4:231, 526; BAGD—471b; THAYER—376a.

3011. **λειτουργός** {5x} **lĕitŏurgŏs**, *li-toorg-os';* from a der. of *2992* and *2041;* a *public servant,* i.e. a *functionary* in the Temple or Gospel, or (gen.) a *worshipper* (of God) or *benefactor* (of man):—minister {4x}, he that ministers {1x}.

In the NT it is used **(1)** of Christ, as a "Minister of the sanctuary" (in the Heavens), Heb 8:2; **(2)** of angels, Heb 1:7 (Ps 104:4); **(3)** of the apostle Paul, in his evangelical ministry, fulfilling it as a serving priest, Rom 15:16; that he used it figuratively and not in an ecclesiastical sense, is obvious from the context; **(4)** of Epaphroditus, as ministering to Paul's needs on behalf of the church at Philippi, Phil 2:25; here, representative service is in view; **(5)** of earthly rulers, who though they do not all act consciously as servants of God, yet discharge functions which are the ordinance of God, Rom 13:6. See: TDNT—4:229, 526; BAGD—471b; THAYER—377c.

3012. **λέντιον** {2x} **lĕntiŏn**, *len'-tee-on;* of Lat. or.; a "*linen*" cloth, i.e. *apron:*—towel {2x}.

Lention denotes "a linen cloth or towel" (Lat., *linteum*), as used by the Lord, Jn 13:4, 5; it was commonly used by servants in a household. See: BAGD—471c; THAYER—376b.

3013. **λεπίς** {1x} **lĕpis**, *lep-is';* from λέπω **lĕpō** (to *peel*); a *flake:*—scale {1x}. See: TDNT—4:232, 529; BAGD—471c; THAYER—376b.

3014. **λέπρα** {4x} **lĕpra**, *lep'-rah;* from the same as *3013; scaliness,* i.e. "*leprosy*":—leprosy {4x}.

Lepra, akin to *lepros* (3015), **(1)** is mentioned in Mt 8:3; Mk 1:42; Lk 5:12, 13. **(2)** In the removal of other maladies the verb "to heal" (*iaomai*) is used, but in the removal of "leprosy," the verb "to cleanse" (*katharizo*), save in the statement concerning the Samaritan, Lk 17:15, "when he saw that he was healed." Mt 10:8 and Lk 4:27 indicate that the disease was common in the nation. Only twelve cases are recorded in the NT, but these are especially selected. For the Lord's commands to the leper mentioned in Mt 8 and to the ten in Lk 17, see Lev 14:2–32. See: TDNT—4:233, 529; BAGD—471d; THAYER—376b.

3015. **λεπρός** {9x} **lĕprŏs**, *lep-ros';* from the same as *3014; scaly,* i.e. *leprous* (a *leper*):—leper {9x}.

Lepros, an adjective, characterized by an eruption of rough scaly patches; later, "*leprous,*" but chiefly used as a noun, "a leper," Mt 8:2; 10:8; 11:5; Mk 1:40; Lk 4:27; 7:22; 17:12; especially of Simon mentioned in Mt 26:6; Mk 14:3. See: TDNT—4:233, 529; BAGD—472a; THAYER—376b.

3016. **λεπτόν** {3x} **lĕptŏn**, *lep-ton';* neut. of a der. of the same as *3013;* something *scaled* (*light*), i.e. a small *coin:*—mite {3x}.

Lepton denotes a small copper coin, proverbially the smallest Jewish coin. It was valued at 1/8th of the Roman *as,* and the 1/128th part of the *denarious:* its legal value was about one third of an English farthing, ½ cent American money. See: TDNT—4:233,*; BAGD—472a; THAYER—376c.

3017. **Λευΐ** {5x} **Lĕuï**, *lyoo-ee';* of Heb. or. [3878]; *Levi,* the name of three Isr.:—Levi {5x}. See: TDNT—4:234, 529; BAGD—472; THAYER—376c. comp. *3018.*

3018. **Λευΐς** {3x} **Lĕuïs**, *lyoo-is';* a form of *3017; Lewis* (i.e. *Levi*), a Chr.:—Levi {3x}. See: TDNT—4:234, 529; BAGD—472a; THAYER—376c.

3019. **Λευΐτης** {3x} **Lĕuïtēs**, *lyoo-ee'-tace;* from *3017;* a *Levite,* i.e. desc. of Levi:—Levite {3x}. See: TDNT—4:239, 530; BAGD—472b; THAYER—376d.

3020. **Λευϊτικός** {1x} **Lĕuïtikŏs**, *lyoo-it-ee-kos';* from *3019; Levitic,* i.e.

relating to the Levites:—Levitical {1x}. See: BAGD—472b; THAYER—376d.

3021. **λευκαίνω** {2x} **lĕukainō**, *lyoo-kah'-ee-no;* from *3022;* to *whiten:*—make white {1x}, whiten {1x}.

Leukaino, "to whiten, make white", is used in Mk 9:3; figuratively in Rev 7:14. See: TDNT—4:241, 530; BAGD—472b; THAYER—376d.

3022. **λευκός** {25x} **lĕukŏs**, *lyoo-kos';* from λύκη **lukē**, ("*light*"); *white:*—white {25x}.

Luke is used of **(1)** clothing (sometimes in the sense of "bright"), Mt 17:2; 28:3; Mk 9:3; 16:5; Lk 9:29; Jn 20:12; Acts 1:10; symbolically, Rev 3:4, 5, 18; 4:4; 6:11; 7:9, 13; 19:14 (2nd part); **(2)** hair, Mt 5:36; Christ's head and hair (in a vision; cf. Dan 7:9), Rev 1:14 (twice); **(3)** ripened grain, Jn 4:35; **(4)** a stone, Rev 2:17, an expression of the Lord's special delight in the overcomer, the new name on it being indicative of a secret communication of love and joy; **(5)** a horse (in a vision), Rev 6:2; 19:11–14 (1st part); **(6)** a cloud, Rev 14:14; **(7)** the throne of God, Rev 20:11. See: TDNT—4:241, 530; BAGD—472b; THAYER—376d.

3023. **λεών** {9x} **lĕōn**, *leh-ohn';* a primary word; a "*lion*":—lion {9x}.

Leon occurs **(1)** in 2 Ti 4:17, **(1a)** probably figurative of the imminent peril of death, the figure being represented by the whole phrase, not by the word "lion" alone; **(1b)** some suppose the reference to be to the lions of the amphitheater; **(1c)** the Greek commentators regarded the "lion" as Nero; **(1d)** others understand it to be Satan. **(1e)** The language not improbably recalls that of Ps 22:21, and Dan 6:20. **(2)** The word is used metaphorically, too, in Rev 5:5, where Christ is called "the Lion of the tribe of Judah." **(3)** Elsewhere it has the literal meaning, Heb 11:33; 1 Pet 5:8, Rev 4:7; 9:8, 17; 10:3; 13:2. **(4)** Taking the OT and NT occurrences the allusions are to the three great features of the "lion," **(4a)** its majesty and strength, indicative of royalty, e.g., Prov 30:30, **(4b)** its courage, e.g., Prov 28:1, **(4c)** its cruelty, e.g., Ps 22:13. See: TDNT—4:251, 531; BAGD—472d; THAYER—377a.

3024. **λήθη** {1x} **lēthē**, *lay'-thay;* from *2990; forgetfulness:*—forget + 3083 {1x}. See: BAGD—472d; THAYER—377a.

3025. **ληνός** {5x} **lēnŏs**, *lay-nos';* appar. a primary word; a *trough,* i.e. wine-*vat:*—winepress {4x}, winepress + 3631 {1x}.

Lenos denotes "a trough or vat," used especially for the treading of grapes, Matt. 21:33. Not infrequently they were dug out in the soil or excavated in a rock, as in the rock vats in Palestine today. In Rev. 14:19, 20 (twice) and 19:15 (where *oinos* is added, lit. "the winepress of the wine") the word is used metaphorically with reference to the execution of divine judgment upon the gathered foes of the Jews at the close of this age preliminary to the establishment of the millennial kingdom. See: TDNT—4:254, 531; BAGD—473a.

3026. **λῆρος** {1x} **lērŏs**, *lay'-ros;* appar. a primary word; *twaddle,* i.e. an *incredible* story:—idle tale.

Leros denotes an incredible tale in that it is foolish talk, nonsense, lacking credibility (Lk 24:11). See: BAGD—473a; THAYER—377b.

3027. **λῃστής** {15x} **lēistēs**, *lace-tace';* from ληΐζομαι **leizomai** (to *plunder*); a *brigand:*—robber {4x}, thief {11x}.

Lestes, "a robber, brigand" (akin to *leia,* "booty"), "one who plunders openly and by violence" (in contrast to *kleptes,* "a thief"), is translated **(1)** "robber" or "robbers", Jn 10:1, 8, 18:40; 2 Cor 11:26; and **(2)** "thief" or "thieves" in Mt 21:13; 26:55; 27:38, 44; Mk 11:17; 14:48; 15:27; Lk 10:30, 36; 19:46; 22:52. Syn.: A *lestes* is a robber, a brigand, one who plunders openly and by violence; whereas the *kleptes,* (2812), a thief, denotes one who steals by stealth. See: TDNT—4:257, 532; BAGD—473a; THAYER—377b.

3028. **λῆμψις** {1x} **lēmpsis**, *lemp'-sis;* from *2983; receipt* (the act):—a receiving {1x}.

Lempsis, as a noun, means "a receiving" and is used in Phil 4:15: "Now ye Philippians know also, that in the beginning of the gospel, when I departed from Macedonia, no church communicated with me as concerning giving and receiving (*lempsis*), but ye only." Syn.: 324, 353, 354, 568, 588, 618, 1209, 1523, 1926, 2210, 2865, 2975, 2983, 3335, 3336, 3858, 3880, 3970, 4327, 4355, 4356, 4380, 4381, 4382, 5562, 5264, 5274. See: BAGD—473a; THAYER—377b.

3029. **λίαν** {14x} **lian**, *lee'-an;* of uncert. aff.; *much* (adv.):—exceeding {5x}, greatly {4x}, very chiefest + 5228 {2x}, great {1x}, sore {1x}, very {1x}.

Lian, "very, exceedingly," is translated **(1)** "exceeding" in Mt 2:16; 4:8; 8:28; Mk 9:3; Lk 23:8; **(2)** "greatly" **(2a)** in Mt 27:14, of wonder, **(2b)** 2 Ti 4:15, of opposition; **(2c)** 2 Jn 3 and 3 Jn 4, of joy; **(3)** "very chiefest" in 2 Cor 11:5; 12:11; **(4)** "great" in Mk 1:35; **(5)** "sore" in Mk 6:51 of amazement; and **(6)** "very" in Mk 16:2. See: BAGD—473a; THAYER—377b.

3030. **λίβανος** {2x} **libanŏs**, *lib'-an-os;* of for. or. [3828]; the *incense*-tree, i.e. (by impl.) *incense* itself:—frankincense {2x}. Cf. Mt 2:11; Rev 18:13. See: TDNT—4:263, 533; BAGD—473c; THAYER—377c.

3031. **λιβανωτός** {2x} **libanōtŏs**, *lib-an-o-tos';* from *3030; frankincense,* i.e. (by extens.) a *censer* for burning it:—censer {2x}.

A *libanotos* is a vessel in which to burn incense," Rev 8:3, 5. See: TDNT—4:263, 533; BAGD—473d; THAYER—317a.

3032. **Λιβερτῖνος** {1x} **Libĕrtinŏs**, *lib-er-tee'-nos;* of Lat. or.; a Rom. *freedman:*—Libertine {1x}. See: TDNT—4:265, 533; BAGD—473d; THAYER—377c.

3033. **Λιβύη** {1x} **Libuē**, *lib-oo'-ay;* prob. from *3047; Libye,* a region of Africa:—Libya {1x}. See: BAGD—473d; THAYER—377d.

3034. **λιθάζω** {8x} **lithazō**, *lith-ad'-zo;* from *3037;* to *lapidate:*—to stone {8x}.

This word [cf. 3036] is used for throwing stones at someone, to pelt one in order to wound, frighten away, or kill him; most contexts seem to indicate intent to kill, Jn 10:31–33; 11:8; Acts 5:26; 14:19; 2 Cor 11:25; Heb 11:37. See: TDNT—4:267, 533; BAGD—473d; THAYER—377d.

3035. **λίθινος** {3x} **lithinŏs**, *lith-ee'-nos;* from *3037; stony,* i.e. made of *stone:*—of stone {3x}. Cf. Jn 2:6; 2 Cor 3:3; Rev 9:20. See: TDNT—4:268, 534; BAGD—474a; THAYER—378a.

3036. **λιθοβολέω** {9x} **lithŏbŏlĕō**, *lith-ob-ol-eh'-o;* from a compound of *3037* and *906;* to *throw stones,* i.e. *lapidate:*—stone {8x}, cast stones {1x}.

Lithoboleo, "to pelt with stones", "to stone to death." This word seems to carry the idea of casting stones to kill (exception – Mk 12:4), not just frighten or hurt [cf. 3034]. It occurs in Mt 21:35; 23:37; Lk 13:34; Jn 8:5; Acts 7:58, 59; 14:5; Heb 12:20. See: TDNT—4:267, 533; BAGD—474a; THAYER—378a.

3037. **λίθος** {60x} **lithŏs**, *lee'-thos;* appar. a primary word; a *stone* (lit. or fig.):—stone {49x}, one stone {4x}, another {4x}, stumbling stone + 4348 {2x}, mill stone + 3457 {1x}.

Lithos is used **(1)** literally, of **(1a)** the "stones" of the ground, e.g., Mt 4:3, 6; 7:9; **(1b)** "tombstones," e.g., Mt 27:60, 66; **(1c)** "building stones," e.g., Mt 21:42; **(1d)** "a millstone," Lk 17:2; cf. Rev 18:21; **(1e)** the "tables (or tablets)" of the Law, 2 Cor. 3:7, **(1f)** "idol images," Acts 17:29; **(1g)** the "treasures" of commercial Babylon, Rev 18:12, 16; **(2)** metaphorically, of **(2a)** Christ, Rom 9:33; 1 Pet 2:4, 6, 8; **(2b)** believers, 1 Pet 2:5; **(2c)** spiritual edification by scriptural teaching, 1 Cor 3:12; **(2d)** the adornment of the foundations of the wall of the spiritual and heavenly Jerusalem, Rev 21:19; **(2e)** the adornment of religious Babylon, Rev 17:4; **(3)** figuratively, of Christ, Rev 4:3; 21:11, where "light" stands for "Light-giver." It is also translated **(1)** one stone, Mt 24:2 first reference; Mk 13:2 first reference; Lk 19:44; 21:6 both first reference; **(2)** another, Mt 24:2 second reference; Mk 13:2 second reference; Lk 19:44; 21:6 both second reference; **(3)** stumbling stone + 4348, Rom 9:32, 33; **(4)** mill stone + 3457, Mk 9:42. See: TDNT—4:268, 534; BAGD—474b; THAYER—378a.

3038. **λιθόστρωτος** {1x} **lithŏstrōtŏs**, *lith-os'-tro-tos;* from *3037* and a der. of *4766; stone-strewed,* i.e. a tessellated *mosaic* on which the Rom. tribunal was placed:—Pavement {1x}.

This word is an adjective, denoting "paved with stones" (*lithos,* "a stone," and *stronnuo,* "to spread"), especially of tessellated work, is used as a noun in Jn 19:13, of a place near the Praetorium in Jerusalem, called *Gabbatha,* a Greek transliteration of an Aramaic word. See: BAGD—474d; THAYER—378b.

3039. **λικμάω** {2x} **likmaō**, *lik-mah'-o;* from λικμός **likmŏs**, the equiv. of λίκνον **liknŏn** (a winnowing *fan* or basket); to *winnow,* i.e. (by anal.) to *triturate:*—grind to powder {2x}.

Likmao, as a verb, means "to winnow," as of grain, by throwing it up against the wind, to scatter the chaff and straw; hence has the meaning "to scatter," as chaff or dust, and is translated "will grind . . . to powder" (Mt 21:44; Lk 20:18). See: TDNT—4:280, 535; BAGD—474d; THAYER—378c.

3040. **λιμήν** {3x} **limēn**, *lee-mane';* appar. a primary word; a *harbor:*—haven {2x}, the fair havens + 2570 {1x}.

This is a place called "Fair Haven", Acts 27:8, 12. See: BAGD—475a; THAYER—378c. comp. *2568.*

3041. **λίμνη** {10x} **limnē**, *lim'-nay;* prob. from *3040* (through the idea of nearness of shore); a *pond* (large or small):—lake {10x}.

This word, "a lake," is used **(1)** in the Gospels, only by Lk, of the Sea of Galilee, Lk 5:2; 8:22, 23, 33, called Gennesaret in 5:1 (Mt and Mk use *thalassa,* "a sea"); **(2)** of the "lake" of fire, Rev 19:20; 20:10, 14, 15; 21:8. Lake Gennesaret is the western most "indention" of the Sea of Galilee. See: BAGD—475a; THAYER—378c.

3042. **λιμός** {12x} **limŏs**, *lee-mos';* prob. from *3007* (through the idea of *destitution*); a *scarcity* of food:—dearth {2x}, famine {7x}, hunger {3x}.

Limos has the meanings "famine" and "hunger" and is translated **(1)** "dearth", Acts 7:11; 11:28; **(2)** "famine", Mt 24:7; Mk 13:8; Lk 4:25; 15:14; 21:11; Rom 8:35; Rev 18:8; **(3)** hunger" Lk 15:17; 2 Cor 11:27; Rev 6:8. See: TDNT—6:12, 820; BAGD—475a; THAYER—378c.

3043. **λίνον** {2x} **linŏn**, *lee'-non;* prob. a primary word; *flax,* i.e. (by impl.) *"linen"*:—flax {1x}, linen {1x}.

Linon primarily denotes **(1)** "flax" (Eng., "linen"); then, that which is made of it, "a wick of a lamp," Mt 12:20; and **(2)** "linen" in Rev 15:6. See: BAGD—475b; THAYER—378d.

3044. **Λῖνος** {1x} **Linŏs**, *lee'-nos;* perh. from *3043; Linus,* a Chr.:—Linus {1x}. See: BAGD—475c; THAYER—378d.

3045. **λιπαρός** {1x} **liparŏs**, *lip-ar-os';* from λίπος **lipŏs** (*grease*); *fat,* i.e. (fig.) *sumptuous:*—dainty {1x}.

Liparos properly signifies "oily, or anointed with oil" (from *lipos,* "grease," connected with *aleipho,* "to anoint"); it is said of things which pertain to delicate and sumptuous living; hence, "dainty," Rev 18:14. See: BAGD—475c; THAYER—378d.

3046. **λίτρα** {2x} **litra**, *lee'-trah;* of Lat. or. [*libra*]; a *pound* in weight:—pound {2x}.

In the NT it is used as a measure of weight, a pound, Jn 12:3; 19:39. See: BAGD—475d; THAYER—378d.

3047. **λίψ** {1x} **lips**, *leeps;* prob. from λείβω **lĕibō** (to *pour* a "libation"); the *south* (-west) wind (as bringing rain, i.e. (by extens.) the *south* quarter):—southwest {1x}.

Lips denotes "the S.W. wind," Acts 27:12, which blows towards the N.E. See: BAGD—475d; THAYER—378d.

3048. **λογία** {2x} **lŏgia**, *log-ee'-ah* or **λογεία** **lŏgĕia**, *log-i'-ah;* from *3056* (in the commercial sense); a *contribution:*—collection {1x}, gathering {1x}.

Logeia, to collect," is translated **(1)** "collection" in 1 Cor 16:1 and **(2)** "gathering" in 1 Cor 16:2. See: TDNT—4:282,*; BAGD—475d; THAYER—379a.

3049. **λογίζομαι** {41x} **lŏgizŏmai**, *log-id'-zom-ahee;* mid. voice from *3056;* to *take an inventory,* i.e. *estimate* (lit. or fig.):—think {9x}, impute {8x}, reckon {6x}, count {5x}, account {4x}, suppose {2x}, reason {1x}, number {1x}, misc. {5x} = conclude, + despise, esteem, lay.

Logizomai primarily signifies **(1)** "to reckon," whether by calculation or imputation, e.g., Gal 3:6; then, **(2)** to deliberate, and so to "account," Rom 8:36; "esteemeth"; Jn 11:50; 1 Cor 4:1; Heb 11:19; "consider"; Acts 19:27; 1 Pet 5:12. **(3)** It is used of love in 1 Cor 13:5, as not "thinking" of evil. **(4)** In 2 Cor 3:5 the apostle uses it in repudiation of the idea that he and fellow-servants of God are so self-sufficient as to "think anything" as from themselves, i.e., as to attribute anything to themselves. Cf. 12:6. **(5)** In 2 Ti 4:16 it is used of laying to, charging a person's "account" as a charge against him. **(6)** Imputation has three steps: **(6a)** the collecting of all charges and remissions; **(6b)** the totaling of these debits and credits; **(6c)** the placing of the balance or credit on one's account. See: TDNT—4:284, 536; BAGD—475d; THAYER—379a.

3050. **λογικός** {2x} **lŏgikŏs**, *log-ik-os';* from *3056; rational* ("*logical*"):—reasonable {1x}, of the word {1x}.

Logikos pertains to the reasoning faculty, reasonable, rational and is used **(1)** of the service rendered by believers in presenting their bodies a living sacrifice. The sacrifice is to be in accordance with the spiritual intelligence of those who are new creatures in Christ and are mindful of the mercies of God; in contrast to those offered by ritual and compulsion (Rom 12:1). **(2)** The word signifies a rationale affecting the soul (1 Pet 2:2). **(3)** It pertains to "the reasoning faculty, reasonable, rational," and is used **(3a)** in Rom. 12:1, of the service (*latreia*) to be rendered by believers in presenting their bodies "a living sacrifice, holy, acceptable to God." The sacrifice is to be intelligent, in contrast to those offered by ritual and compulsion; the presentation is to be in accordance with the spiritual intelligence of those who are new creatures in Christ and are mindful of "the mercies of God." **(3b)** It is found also in 1 Pet 2:2, "(milk) of the word" and so here the nourishment may be understood as of that spiritually rational nature which, acting through the regenerate mind, develops spiritual growth. God's Word is not given so that it is impossible to understand it, or that it requires a special class of men to interpret it; its character is such that the Holy Spirit who gave it can unfold its truths even to the young convert. See: TDNT—4:142, 505; BAGD—476c; THAYER—379c.

3051. **λόγιον** {4x} **lŏgiŏn**, *log'-ee-on;* neut. of *3052;* an *utterance* (of God):—oracle {4x}.

Logion, "a word, narrative, statement," denotes "a divine response or utterance, an oracle"; it is used of **(1)** the contents of the Mosaic Law, Acts 7:38; **(2)** all the written utterances of God through OT writers, Rom 3:2; **(3)** the substance of Christian doctrine, Heb 5:12; **(4)** the utterances of God through Christian teachers, 1 Pet 4:11. See: TDNT—4:137, 505; BAGD—476c; THAYER—379c.

3052. **λόγιος** {1x} **lŏgiŏs**, *log'-ee-os;* from *3056; fluent,* i.e. an *orator:*—eloquent {1x}.

Logios, from *logos,* "a word," primarily meant "learned, a man skilled in literature and the arts." In Acts 18:24, it is translated "eloquent," said of Apollos, who had stores of "learning" and could express it convincingly. See: TDNT—4:136, 505; BAGD—476d; THAYER—379d.

3053. **λογισμός** {2x} **lŏgismŏs**, *log-is-mos';* from *3049; computation,* i.e. (fig.) *reasoning* (*conscience, conceit*):—imagination {1x}, thought {1x}.

Logismos, "a reasoning, a thought" (akin to *logizomai,* "to count, reckon"), is translated **(1)** "thoughts" in Rom 2:15, suggestive of evil intent, not of mere reasonings; **(2)** "imaginations" in 2 Cor 10:5. The word suggests the contemplation of actions as a result of the verdict of conscience. See: TDNT—4:284, 536; BAGD—476d; THAYER—380a.

3054. **λογομαχέω** {1x} **lŏgŏmachĕō**, *log-om-akh-eh'-o;* from a compound of *3056* and *3164;* to *be disputatious* (on trifles):—to strive about words {1x}.

This word means to wrangle about empty and trifling matters, 2 Ti 2:14. See: TDNT—4:143, 505; BAGD—477a; THAYER—380a.

3055. **λογομαχία** {1x} **lŏgŏmachia**, *log-om-akh-ee'-ah;* from the same as *3054; disputation* about trifles ("*logomachy*"):—a strife of words {1x}.

Logomachia denotes "a dispute about words" (*logos,* "a word," *mache,* "a fight"), or about trivial things, 1 Ti 6:4, "strifes." See: TDNT—4:143, 505; BAGD—477a; THAYER—380a.

3056. **λόγος** {330x} **lŏgŏs**, *log'-os;* from *3004;* something *said* (incl. the *thought*); by impl. a *topic* (subject of discourse), also *reasoning* (the mental faculty) or *motive;* by extens. a *computation;* spec. (with the art. in John) the Divine *Expression* (i.e. *Christ*):—word {218x}, saying {50x}, account {8x}, speech {8x}, Word (Christ) {7x}, thing {5x}, not tr {2x}, misc. {32x} = cause, communication, × concerning, doctrine, fame, × have to do, intent, matter, mouth, preaching, question, reason, + reckon, remove, shew, × speaker, talk, + none of these things move me, tidings, treatise, utterance, work.

Logos denotes **I.** "the expression of thought"—not the mere name of an object—**(1)** as embodying a conception or idea, e.g., Lk 7:7; 1 Cor 14:9, 19; **(2)** a saying or statement, **(2a)** by God, e.g., Jn 15:25; Rom 9:9; 9:28, "work"; Gal 5:14; Heb 4:12; **(2b)** by Christ, e.g., Mt 24:35 (plur.); Jn 2:22; 4:41; 14:23 (plur.); 15:20. In connection with (2a) and (2b) the phrase "the word of the Lord," i.e., the revealed will of God (very frequent in the OT), is used **(2b1)** of a direct revelation given by Christ, 1 Th 4:15; **(2b2)** of the gospel, Acts 8:25; 13:49; 15:35, 36; 16:32; 19:10; 1 Th 1:8; 2 Th 3:1; **(2b3)** in this respect it is the message from the Lord, delivered with His authority and made effective by His power (cf. Acts 10:36); **(2b4)** for other instances relating to the gospel see Acts 13:26; 14:3; 15:7; 1 Cor 1:18; 2 Cor 2:17; 4:2; 5:19; 6:7; Gal 6:6; Eph 1:13; Phil 2:16; Col 1:5; Heb 5:13; **(2b5)** sometimes it is used as the sum of God's utterances, e.g., Mk 7:13; Jn 10:35; Rev 1:2, 9; **(3)** discourse, speech, of instruction, etc., e.g., Acts 2:40; 1 Cor 2:13; 12:8; 2 Cor 1:18; 1 Th 1:5; 2 Th 2:15; Heb 6:1; **(4)** doctrine, e.g., Mt 13:20; Col 3:16; 1 Ti 4:6; 2 Ti 1:13; Titus 1:9; 1 Jn 2:7.

II. "The Personal Word," a title of the Son of God; this identification is substantiated by the statements of doctrine in Jn 1:1–18, declaring in verses 1 and 2 **(1)** His distinct and super-finite Personality, **(2)** His relation in the Godhead (pros, "with," not mere company, but the most intimate communion), **(3)** His deity; in v. 3 His creative power; in v. 14 His incarnation ("was made flesh," expressing His voluntary act), the reality and totality of His human nature, and His glory "as of the only begotten from the Father", the absence of the article in each place lending stress to the nature and character of the relationship; His was the *shekinah* glory in open manifestation; v. 18 consummates the identification: "the only-begotten Son, which is in the bosom of the Father, He hath declared Him," thus fulfilling the significance of the title "*Logos,*" the "Word," the personal manifestation, not of a part of the divine nature, but of the whole deity (see image). The title is used also in 1 Jn 1, "the Word of life" combining the two declarations in Jn 1:1 and 4 and Rev 19:13. Syn.: The significance of *rhema* (4487) as distinct from *logos* is exemplified in the injunction to take "the sword of the Spirit, which is the word of God," Eph 6:17; here the reference is not to the whole Bible as such, but to the individual scripture which the Spirit brings to our remembrance for use in time of need, a prerequisite being the regular storing of the mind with Scripture. See: TDNT—4:69, 505; BAGD—477a; THAYER—380a.

3057. **λόγχη** {1x} **lŏgchē**, *long'-khay;* perh. a primary word; a "*lance*":—spear {1x}.

Logche is primarily "a spearhead," then, "a lance or spear," and occurs in John 19:34. See: BAGD—479b; THAYER—382a.

3058. **λοιδορέω** {4x} **lŏidŏrĕō**, *loy-dor-eh'-o;* from *3060;* to *reproach,* i.e. *vilify:*—revile {4x}.

Loidoreo denotes "to abuse, revile," Jn 9:28; Acts 23:4; 1 Cor 4:12; 1 Pet 2:23 (1st clause). See: TDNT—4:293, 538; BAGD—479c.

3059. **λοιδορία** {3x} **lŏidŏria**, *loy-dor-ee'-ah;* from *3060; slander* or *vituperation:*—railing {2x}, to speak reproachfully + 5484 {1x}.

Loidoria, "abuse, railing, reviling," is rendered **(1)** "railing" in 1 Pet 3:9 (twice); and "to speak reproachfully" in 1 Ti 5:14. See: TDNT—4:293, 538; BAGD—479c; THAYER—382b.

3060. **λοίδορος** {2x} **lŏidŏrŏs**, *loy'-dor-os;* from λοιδός **lŏidŏs** (*mischief*); *abusive,* i.e. a *blackguard:*—railer {1x}, reviler {1x}.

Loidoros, an adjective denoting "reviling, railing" is used as a noun, **(1)** "a railer," 1 Cor 5:11 and **(2)** "railers" in 1 Cor 6:10. See: TDNT—4:293, 538; BAGD—479c; THAYER—382b.

3061. **λοιμός** {3x} **lŏimŏs**, *loy'-mos;* of uncert. aff.; a *plague* (lit. the *disease,* or fig. a *pest*):—pestilence {1x}, pestilent {1x}.

This word denotes **(1)** a pestilence, any deadly infectious malady (Lk 21:11; Mt 24:7); and **(2)** metaphorically, a pestilent fellow, one who spreads a deadly infection (Acts 24:5). See: BAGD—479d; THAYER—382b.

3062. **λοιποί** {41x} **lŏipŏi**, *loy-poy';* masc. plur. of a der. of *3007; remaining* ones:—other {15x}, rest {12x}, others {7x}, remnant {4x}, residue {1x}, which remains {1x}, other things {1x}. **(1)** other, in Mt 25:11; Lk 18:11; 24:10; Acts 17:9; Rom 1:13; 1 Cor 9:5; 15:37; 2 Cor 12:13, 13:2; Gal 2:13; Eph 4:17; Phil 1:13; 4:3; 2 Pet 3:16; Rev 8:13; **(2)** rest, in Mt 27:49; Lk 12:26; 24:9; Acts 2:37; 5:13; 27:44; Rom 11:7; 1 Cor 7:12; 11:34; Rev 2:24; 9:20; 20:5; **(3)** others, in Lk 8:9; Acts 28:9; Eph 2:3; 1 Th 4:13; 5:6; 1 Ti 5:20; **(4)** remnant, in Mt 22:6; Rev 11:13; 12:17; 19:21; **(5)** residue {1x}, in Mk 16:13, plural; **(6)** which remains, in Rev 3:2; and **(7)** other things, in Mk 4:19. See: BAGD—479d; THAYER—382b.

3063. **λοιπόν** {14x} **lŏipŏn**, *loy-pon';* neut. sing. of the same as *3062;* something *remaining* (adv.):—finally {5x}, now {2x}, then {1x}, besides {1x}, moreover + 1161 + 3739 {1x}, it remains + 2076 {1x}, furthermore {1x}, henceforth {1x}, from henceforth {1x}.

Loipon is the neuter of the adjective *loipos,* remaining (which is used in its different genders as a noun, "the rest"), and is used either with the article or without, to signify "finally," lit., "for the rest." The apostle Paul uses it frequently in the concluding portion of his epistles, introducing practical exhortations, not necessarily implying that the letter is drawing to a close, but marking a transition in the subject-matter, as in Phil 3:1, where the actual conclusion is for the time postponed and the farewell injunctions are resumed in 4:8. It is translated **(1)** finally, in 2 Cor 13:11; Eph 6:10; Phil 3:1; 4:8; 2 Th 3:1; **(2)** now, in Mt 26:45; Mk 14:41; **(3)** then, in Acts 27:20; **(4)** besides, in 1 Cor 1:16; **(5)** moreover + 1161 + 3739, in 1 Cor 4:2; **(6)** it remains + 2076, in 1 Cor 7:29; **(7)** furthermore, in 1 Th 4:1; **(8)** henceforth, in 2 Ti 4:8; **(9)** from henceforth, in Heb 10:13. See: BAGD—479d; THAYER—382b.

3064. **λοιποῦ** {1x} **lŏipŏu**, *loy-poo';* gen. sing. of the same as *3062; remaining* time:—from henceforth {1x}.

Loipou means hereafter, for the future, Gal 6:17. See: BAGD—480a; THAYER—382b.

3065. **Λουκᾶς** {4x} **Lŏukas**, *loo-kas';* contr. from Lat. *Lucanus; Lucas,* a Chr.:—Lucas {2x}, Luke {2x}. See: BAGD—480b; THAYER—382c.

3066. **Λούκιος** {2x} **Lŏukiŏs**, *loo'-kee-os;* of Lat. or.; *illuminative; Lucius,* a Chr.:—Lucius {2x}. See: BAGD—480c; THAYER—382d.

3067. **λουτρόν** {2x} **lŏutrŏn**, *loo-tron';* from *3068;* a *bath,* i.e. (fig.), *baptism:*—washing {2x}.

Loutron, "a bath, a laver" (akin to *louo* – 3068), is used **(1)** metaphorically of the Word of God, as the instrument of spiritual cleansing, Eph 5:26; and **(2)** in Titus 3:5, of "the washing of regeneration". Syn.: 2354, 2875, 3996. See: TDNT—4:295, 538; BAGD—480c; THAYER—382d.

3068. **λούω** {6x} **lŏuō**, *loo'-o;* a primary verb; to *bathe* (the *whole* person; whereas *3538* means to wet a *part* only, and *4150* to wash, cleanse *garments* exclusively):—wash {6x}. Syn.: 3538, 4150.

Louo, signifies "to bathe, to wash the body," **(1)** active voice, Acts 9:37; 16:33; **(2)** passive voice, Jn 13:10, "washed" [completely]; Heb 10:22, lit., "having been washed as to the body," metaphorical of the effect of the Word of God upon the activities of the believer; **(3)** middle voice, 2 Pet 2:22; **(4)** Rev 1:5, we are washed from our sins by His blood. See: TDNT—4:295, 538; BAGD—480d; THAYER—382d.

3069. **Λύδδα** {3x} **Ludda**, *lud'-dah;* of Heb. or. [3850]; *Lydda* (i.e. *Lod*), a place in Pal.:—Lydda {3x}. See: BAGD—481a; THAYER—383a.

3070. **Λυδία** {2x} **Ludia**, *loo-dee'-ah;* prop. fem. of Λύδιος **Ludiŏs** [of for. or.] (a *Lydian,* in Asia Minor); *Lydia,* a Chr. woman:—Lydia {2x}. See: BAGD—481b; THAYER—383a.

3071. **Λυκαονία** {1x} **Lukaŏnia**, *loo-kah-on-ee'-ah;* perh. remotely from *3074; Lycaonia,* a region of Asia Minor:—Lycaonia {1x}. See: BAGD—481b; THAYER—383a.

3072. **Λυκαονιστί** {1x} **Lukaŏnisti**, *loo-kah-on-is-tee';* adv. from a der. of *3071; Lycaonistically,* i.e. in the language of the Lycaonians:—in the speech of Lycaonia {1x}. See: BAGD—481b; THAYER—383b.

3073. **Λυκία** {1x} **Lukia**, *loo-kee'-ah;* prob. remotely from *3074; Lycia,* a province of Asia Minor:—Lycia {1x}. See: BAGD—481b; THAYER—383b.

3074. **λύκος** {6x} **lukŏs**, *loo'-kos;* perh. akin to the base of *3022* (from the *whitish* hair); a *wolf:*—wolf {6x}.

Lukos is **(1)** figuratively literal in Jn 10:12 twice; and **(2)** metaphorically, *lukos* speaks of cruel, greedy, rapacious, destructive men (Mt 7:15; 10:16; Lk 10:3; Acts 20:29). See: TDNT—4:308, 540; BAGD—481b; THAYER—383b.

3075. **λυμαίνομαι** {1x} **lumainŏmai**, *loo-mah'-ee-nom-ahee;* mid. voice from a prob. der. of *3089* (mean. *filth*); prop. to *soil,* i.e. (fig.) *insult* (*maltreat*):—make havock of {1x}.

This word means to affix a stigma to, to dishonour, spot, defile, to treat shamefully or with injury, to ravage, devastate, ruin, Acts 8:3. See: TDNT—4:312, 540; BAGD—481c; THAYER—383b.

3076. **λυπέω** {26x} **lupĕō**, *loo-peh'-o;* from *3077;* to *distress;* refl. or pass. to *be sad:*—be sorrowful {6x}, grieve {6x}, make sorry {6x}, be sorry {3x}, sorrow {3x}, cause grief {1x}, be in heaviness {1x}.

Lupeo denotes **(1)** in the active voice, **(1a)** "to cause pain, or grief, to distress, grieve," e.g., 2 Cor 2:2 (twice, active and passive voices); **(1b)** 2 Cor 2:5 (twice), "have caused grief," and "grieved"; **(1c)** 2 Cor 7:8, "made (you) sorry"; **(1d)** Eph 4:30, of grieving the Holy Spirit of God (as indwelling the believer); **(2)** in the passive voice, **(2a)** "to be grieved, to be made sorry, to be sorry, sorrowful," e.g., Mt 14:9, "(the king was sorry"); **(2b)** Mk 10:22, "(went away grieved"); **(2c)** Jn 21:17, "(Peter) was grieved"; **(2d)** Rom 14:15, "(if . . . thy brother) is grieved"; **(2e)** 2 Cor 2:4, "(not that) ye should be grieved." See: TDNT—4:313, 540; BAGD—481c; THAYER—383b.

3077. **λύπη** {16x} **lupē**, *loo'-pay;* appar. a primary word; *sadness:*—sorrow {11x}, heaviness {2x}, grievous {1x}, grudging + 1537 {1x}, grief {1x}.

Lupe, as a noun, means "grief, sorrow" and is translated **(1)** "sorrow": "And when he rose up from prayer, and was come to his disciples, he found them sleeping for sorrow," (Lk 22:45; cf. Jn 16:6, 20–22; 2 Cor 2:3, 7; 7:10 [twice]; Phil. 2:27 [twice] or **(2)** "heaviness": "That I have great heaviness (*lupe*) and continual sorrow (3601 – *odune*) in my heart" (Rom 9:2; cf. 2 Co 2:1). Syn.: 253, 3076, 3600, 3601, 3997, 4036, 5604.See: TDNT—4:313, 540; BAGD—482a; THAYER—383c.

3078. **Λυσανίας** {1x} **Lusanias**, *loo-san-ee'-as;* from *3080* and ἀνία **ania** (*trouble*); *grief-dispelling; Lysanias,* a governor of Abilene:—Lysanias {1x}. See: BAGD—482b; THAYER—383c.

3079. **Λυσίας** {3x} **Lusias**, *loo-see'-as;* of uncert. aff.; *Lysias,* a Rom.:—Lysias {3x}. See: BAGD—482b; THAYER—384a.

3080. **λύσις** {1x} **lusis**, *loo'-sis;* from *3089;* a *loosening,* i.e. (spec.) *divorce:*—to be loosed {1x}. See: BAGD—482b; THAYER—384a.

3081. **λυσιτελεῖ** {1x} **lusitĕlĕi**, *loo-sit-el-i';* third pers. sing. pres. ind. act. of a der. of a compound of *3080* and *5056;* impers. it *answers* the *purpose,* i.e. *is advantageous:*—it is better {1x}.

Lusitelei signifies "to indemnify, pay expenses, pay taxes" (from *luo,* "to loose," *telos,* "toll, custom"); hence, "to be useful, advantageous, to be better" Lk 17:2. See: BAGD—482b; THAYER—384a.

3082. **Λύστρα** {6x} **Lustra**, *loos'-trah;* of uncert. or.; *Lystra,* a place in Asia Minor:—Lystra {6x}. See: BAGD—482c; THAYER—384a.

3083. **λύτρον** {2x} **lutrŏn**, *loo'-tron;* from *3089;* something to *loosen* with, i.e. a redemption *price* (fig. *atonement*):—ransom {2x}.

Lutron, lit., "a means of loosing" (from *luo,* "to loose"), and **(1)** in the OT where it is always used to signify "equivalence." Thus it is used of the "ransom" **(1)** for a life, e.g., Ex 21:30, **(1b)** of the redemption price of a slave, e.g., Lev 19:20, **(1c)** of land, Lev 25:24, **(1d)** of the price of a captive, Is 45:13.

(2) In the NT it **(2a)** occurs in Mt 20:28 and Mk 10:45, where it is used of Christ's gift of Himself as "a ransom for many." **(2b)** Christ paid the ransom to God, to satisfy violated holiness and righteousness. He did not pay the ransom to Satan or to some impersonal power such as death, or evil. That Christ gave up His life in expiatory sacrifice under God's judgment upon sin and thus provided a "ransom" whereby those who receive Him on this ground obtain deliverance from the penalty due to sin, is what Scripture teaches. **(2c)** What the Lord states in the two passages mentioned involves this essential character of His death. In these passages the preposition is *anti,* which has a vicarious significance, indicating that the "ransom" holds good for those who, accepting it as such, no longer remain in death since Christ suffered death in their stead. **(2d)** The change of preposition in 1 Ti 2:6, where the word *antilutron.* a substitutionarv "ransom," is used, is significant. There the preposition is *huper,* "on behalf of," and the statement is made that He "gave Himself a ransom for all," indicating that the "ransom" was provisionally universal, while being of a vicarious character. **(2e)** Thus the three passages consistently show that while the provision was universal, for Christ died for all men, yet it is actual for those only who accept God's conditions, and who are described in the Gospel statements as "the many." **(2f)** The giving of His life was the giving of His entire person, and while His death under divine judgment was alone expiatory, it cannot be dissociated from the character of His life which, being sinless, gave virtue to His death and was a testimony to the fact that His death must be of a vicarious nature. See: TDNT—4:328 & 4:340, 543; BAGD—482c; THAYER—384a.

3084. **λυτρόω** {3x} **lutrŏō**, *loo-trŏ'-o;* from *3083;* to *ransom* (lit. or fig.):—redeem {3x}.

Lutroo, as a verb, means "to release on receipt of ransom" and **(1)** is used **in the middle voice,** signifying "to release by paying a ransom price, to redeem" **(1a)** in the natural sense of delivering: "But we trusted that it had been He which should have redeemed Israel: and beside all this, to day is the third day since these things were done." (Lk 24:21 - of setting Israel free from the Roman yoke); **(1b)** in a spiritual sense: "Who gave Himself for us, that He might redeem us from all iniquity, and purify unto Himself a peculiar people, zealous of good works." (Titus 2:14 - of the work of Christ in "redeeming" men "from all iniquity" (*anomia* – 459 "lawlessness," the bondage of self-will which rejects the will of God); **(1c) in the passive voice,** "ye were redeemed," from a vain manner of life, i.e., from bondage to tradition: "Forasmuch as ye know that ye were not redeemed with corruptible things, *as* silver and gold, from your vain conversation *received* by tradition from your fathers;" (1 Pet 1:18). **(2)** In both instances the death of Christ is stated as the means of "redemption." Syn.: *Exagorazo* (1805) does not signify the actual "redemption," but the price paid with a view to it. *Lutroo* signifies the actual "deliverance," the setting at liberty. See also: 629, 3085. See: TDNT—4:349, 543; BAGD—482d; THAYER—384a.

3085. **λύτρωσις** {3x} **lutrōsis**, *loo'-tro-sis;* from *3084;* a *ransoming* (fig.):—redeemed + 4160 {1x}, redemption {2x}.

Lutrosis, as a noun, means "a redemption" and is used **(1)** in the general sense of "deliverance," of the nation of Israel (Lk 1:68; 2:38; and **(2)** of "the redemptive work" of Christ (Heb 9:12), bringing deliverance through His death, from the guilt and power of sin. Syn.: 625. See: TDNT—4:351, 543; BAGD—483; THAYER—384b.

3086. **λυτρωτής** {1x} **lutrōtēs**, *loo-tro-tace';* from *3084;* a *redeemer* (fig.):—deliverer {1x}.

Lutrotes, as a noun, means "a redeemer, one who releases" and is translated "deliverer" in Acts 7:35: "This Moses whom they refused, saying, Who made thee a ruler and a judge? the same did God send *to be* a ruler and a deliverer by the hand of the angel which appeared to him in the bush." Syn.: 325, 525, 629, 591, 859, 1325, 1560, 1659, 1807, 1929, 3860, 4506, 5483. See: TDNT—4:351, 543; BAGD—483a; THAYER—384b.

3087. **λυχνία** {12x} **luchnia**, *lookh-nee'-ah;* from *3088;* a *lamp-stand* (lit. or fig.):—candlestick {12x}.

This is the stand ["the stick"] upon which a portable light sits [is stuck]; not the candle [the light producer] itself [see 3088]. See: TDNT—4:324, 542; BAGD—483a; THAYER—384b.

3088. **λύχνος** {14x} **luchnŏs**, *lookh'-nos;* from the base of *3022;* a portable *lamp* or other *illuminator* (lit. or fig.):—candle {8x}, light {6x}.

Luchnos, "candle," is a portable "lamp" usually set on a stand (see 3087); the word is used **(1)** literally, Mt 5:15; Mk 4:21; Lk 8:16; 11:33, 36; 15:8; Rev 18:23; 22:5; **(2)** metaphorically, **(2a)** of Christ as the Lamb, Rev 21:23, "the light"; **(2b)** of John the Baptist, Jn 5:35, "a . . . light"; **(2c)** "light" of the eye/body, Mt 6:22, and Lk 11:34; **(2d)** of spiritual readiness, Lk 12:35 "lights be burning"; **(2e)** of "the word of prophecy," 2 Pet 1:19 "a light shining". See: TDNT—4:324, 542; BAGD—483b; THAYER—384c.

3089. **λύω** {43x} **luō**, *loo'-o;* a primary verb; to "*loosen*" (lit. or fig.):—loose {27x}, break {5x}, unloose {3x}, destroy {2x}, dissolve {2x}, put off {1x}, melt {1x}, break up {1x}, break down {1x}.

Luo denotes **(1)** "to loose, unbind, release," **(1a1)** of things, e.g., in Mk 1:7 "shoes"; **(1a2)** of animals, e.g., Mt 21:2; **(1a3)** of persons, e.g., Jn 11:44; Acts 22:30; **(1a4)** of Satan, Rev 20:3, 7; and **(1a5)** angels, Rev 9:14, 15; **(1b)** metaphorically, of one diseased, Lk 13:16; **(1b2)** of the marriage tie, 1 Cor 7:27; **(1c)** "to loosen, break up, dismiss, dissolve, destroy"; in this sense it is translated "to loose" in **(1c1)** Acts 2:24, of the pains of death; **(1c2)** in Rev 5:2, of the seals of a roll; **(2)** "breaking, destructively," e.g., **(2a)** of "breaking" commandments, not only infringing them, but loosing the force of them, rendering them not binding, Mt 5:19; Jn 5:18; **(2b)** of "breaking" the Law of Moses, Jn 7:23; **(2c)** Scripture, Jn 10:35; **(2d)** non-destructively, a congregation, Acts 13:43; **(3)** "unloose" in Mk 1:7; Lk 3:16; Jn 1:27; **(4)** "destroy" in **(4a)** in 1 Jn 3:8, of the works of the Devil; and **(4b)** Jn 2:19 of Christ's body figuratively called "temple"; **(5)** "dissolve" in 2 Pet 3:11–12, of the earth and its elements; **(6)** "put off" in Acts 7:33; **(7)** "melt" in 2 Pet 3:10; **(8)** "break up" in Acts 27:41, of the "breaking up" of a ship; **(9)** "break down" in Eph 2:14, of the "breaking down" of the middle wall of partition, Eph. 2:14. See: TDNT—2:60 & 4:328, 543; BAGD—483c; THAYER—384d. comp. *4486.*

3090. **Λωΐς** {1x} **Lōïs**, *lo-ece';* of uncert. or.; *Loïs,* a Chr. woman:—*Lois* {1x}. See: BAGD—484c; THAYER—385c.

3091. **Λώτ** {4x} **Lōt**, *lote;* of Heb. or. [3876]; *Lot,* a patriarch:—*Lot* {4x}. See: BAGD—484c; THAYER—385c.

M

3092. **Μαάθ** {1x} **Maath**, *mah-ath';* prob. of Heb. or.; *Maath,* an Isr.:—*Maath* {1x}. See: BAGD—484b; THAYER—385b.

3093. **Μαγδαλά** {1x} **Magdala**, *mag-dal-ah';* of Chald. or. [comp. 4026]; *the tower; Magdala* (i.e. *Migdala*), a place in Pal.:—*Magdala* {1x}. See: BAGD—484b; THAYER—385b.

3094. **Μαγδαληνή** {12x} **Magdalēnē**, *mag-dal-ay-nay';* fem. of a der. of *3093;* a female *Magdalene,* i.e. inhab. of Magdala:—*Magdalene* {12x}. See: BAGD—484b; THAYER—385d.

3095. **μαγεία** {1x} **magĕia**, *mag-i'-ah;* from *3096;* "*magic*":—sorcery {1x}.

Mageia, "the magic art," is used in the plural in Acts 8:11, "sorceries. See: TDNT—4:359, 547; BAGD—484b; THAYER—385d.

3096. **μαγεύω** {1x} **magĕuō**, *mag-yoo'-o;* from *3097;* to *practice magic:*—use sorcery {1x}.

Mageuo, "to practice magic," Acts 8:9, "used sorcery," is used as in 3095, of Simon Magus. See: TDNT—4:359, 547; BAGD—484d; THAYER—385d.

3097. **μάγος** {6x} **magŏs**, *mag'-os;* of for. or. [7248]; a *Magian,* i.e. Oriental astrologer, *scientist;* by impl. a *magician:*—sorcerer {2x}, wise man {4x}.

Magos, denotes **(1)** "a wizard, sorcerer, a pretender to magic powers, a professor of the arts of witchcraft," Acts 13:6, 8, where Bar-Jesus was the Jewish name, *Elymas,* an Arabic word meaning "wise." Hence the name Magus, "the magician," originally applied to Persian priests. **(2)** It also denotes "a Magian," one of a sacred caste, originally Median, who apparently conformed to the Persian religion while retaining their old beliefs; it is used in the plural, Mt 2:1, 7, 16 (twice), "wise men.". See: TDNT—4:356, 547; BAGD—484d; THAYER—385d.

3098. **Μαγώγ** {1x} **Magōg**, *mag-ogue';* of Heb. or. [4031]; *Magog,* a for. nation, i.e. (fig.) an Antichristian party:—*Magog* {1x}. See: TDNT—1:789,*; BAGD—485b; THAYER—386a.

3099. **Μαδιάν** {1x} **Madian**, *mad-ee-on'* or **Μαδιάμ** **Madiam**, *mad-ee-on';* of Heb. origin [4080]; *Madian* (i.e. *Midian*), a region of Arabia:—*Madian* {1x}. See: BAGD—485b; THAYER—386a.

3100. **μαθητεύω** {4x} **mathētĕuō**, *math-ayt-yoo'-o;* from *3101;* intr. to *become a pupil;* tran. to *disciple,* i.e. enroll as scholar:—be disciple {1x}, instruct {1x}, teach {2x}.

Matheteuo is used **(1)** in the active voice, intransitively, in some mss., in Mt 27:57, in the sense of being the "disciple" of a person; **(2)** Mt 13:52, "which is instructed." **(3)** It is used in this transitive sense in the active voice in **(3a)** Mt 28:19, "teach", and **(3b)** Acts 14:21, "taught." See: TDNT—4:461, 552; BAGD—485c; THAYER—386a.

3101. **μαθητής** {269x} **mathētēs**, *math-ay-tes';* from *3129;* a *learner,* i.e. *pupil:*—disciple {269x}.

Mathetes, lit., "a learner" (from *manthano,* "to learn," from a root math—, indicating thought accompanied by endeavor), in contrast to *didaskalos,* "a teacher"; hence it denotes "one who follows one's teaching," as **(1)** the "disciples" **(1a)** of John, Mt 9:14; **(1b)** of the Pharisees, Mt 22:16; **(1c)** of Moses, Jn 9:28; **(2)** it is used of the "disciples" of Jesus **(2a)** in a wide sense, of Jews who became His adherents, Jn 6:66; Lk 6:17, some being secretly so, Jn 19:38; **(2b)** especially of the twelve apostles, Mt 10:1; Lk 22:11, e.g.; **(3)** of all who manifest that they are His "disciples" by abiding in His Word, Jn 8:31, cf. 13:35; 15:8; **(4)** in the Acts, of those who believed upon Him and confessed Him, 6:1–2, 7; 14:20, 22, 28; 15:10; 19:1, etc. **(5)** A "disciple" was not only a pupil, but an adherent; hence they are spoken of as imitators of their teacher; cf. Jn 8:31; 15:8. Syn.: 3102, 4827. See: TDNT—4:415, 552; BAGD—485c; THAYER—386a.

3102. **μαθήτρια** {1x} **mathētria**, *math-ay'-tree-ah;* fem. from *3101;* a female *pupil:*—disciple {1x}.

Mathatria, "a female disciple," is said of Tabitha, Acts 9:36. See: TDNT—4:460, 552; BAGD—486a; THAYER—386b.

3103. **Μαθουσάλα** {1x} **Mathŏusala**, *math-oo-sal' ah;* of Heb. or. [4968]; *Mathusala* (i.e. *Methushelach*), an antediluvian:—Mathusala {1x}. See: BAGD—486b; THAYER—386b.

3104. **Μαϊνάν** {1x} **Maïnan**, *mahee-nan';* prob. of Heb. or.; *Maïnan,* an Isr.:—*Mainan* {1x}. See: BAGD—486b; THAYER—386b.

3105. **μαίνομαι** {5x} **mainŏmai**, *mah'-ee-nom-ahee;* mid. voice from a primary μάω **maō** (to *long* for; through the idea of insensate *craving*); to *rave* as a "maniac":—be mad {4x}, be beside (one's) self {1x}. **(1)**

Mainomai, "to be mad, to rave", is said **(1)** of one who so speaks that he appears to be out of his mind, out of himself, beside himself, Acts 26:24, translated "thou art beside thyself"; **(2)** of one is said "to be mad" in Jn 10:20; Acts 12:15; 26:24, 25; 1 Cor 14:23. See: TDNT—4:360, 548; BAGD—486b; THAYER—386c.

3106. **μακαρίζω** {2x} **makarizō**, *mak-ar-id'-zo;* from *3107;* to *beatify,* i.e. *pronounce* (or *esteem*) *fortunate:*—call blessed {1x}, count happy {1x}.

Makarizo, from a root *mak,* meaning "large, lengthy," found also in *makros,* "long," *mekos,* "length," hence denotes "to pronounce happy, blessed", Lk 1:48 and Jas 5:11. See: TDNT—4:362, 548; BAGD—486a; THAYER—386c.

3107. **μακάριος** {50x} **makariŏs**, *mak-ar'-ee-os;* a prol. form of the poet. μάκαρ **makar** (mean. the same); supremely *blest;* by extens. *fortunate, well off:*—blessed {44x}, happy {5x}, happier {1x}.

Makarios is used **(1)** in the beatitudes in Mt 5 and Lk 6, is especially frequent in the Gospel of Luke, and is found seven times in Revelation, 1:3; 14:13; 16:15; 19:9; 20:6; 22:7, 14. **(2)** It is said of God twice, 1 Ti 1:11; 6:15. **(3)** In the beatitudes the Lord indicates not only the characters that are "blessed," but the nature of that which is the highest good. See: TDNT—4:362, 548; BAGD—486c; THAYER—386c.

3108. **μακαρισμός** {3x} **makarismŏs**, *mak-ar-is-mos';* from *3106; beatification,* i.e. *attribution of good fortune:*—blessedness {3x}.

Mararismos denotes "a declaration of blessedness, a felicitation"; it is translated **(1)** "blessedness" in Gal 4:15; the Galatian converts had counted themselves happy when they heard and received the gospel from Paul; he asks them rhetorically what had become of that spirit which had animated them; **(2)** the word is rendered "blessing" in Rom 4:6, 9. See: TDNT—4:362, 548; BAGD—487a; THAYER—386c.

3109. **Μακεδονία** {24x} **Makĕdŏnia**, *mak-ed-on-ee'-ah;* from *3110; Macedonia,* a region of Greece:—Macedonia {24x}. See: BAGD—487b; THAYER—386c.

3110. **Μακεδών** {5x} **Makĕdōn**, *mak-ed'-ohn;* of uncert. der.; a *Macedon* (*Macedonian*), i.e. inhab. of Macedonia:—of Macedonia {4x}, Macedonian {1x}. See: BAGD—487b; THAYER—386b.

3111. **μάκελλον** {1x} **makĕllŏn**, *mak'-el-lon;* of Lat. or. [*macellum*]; a *butcher's stall, meat market* or *provision-shop:*—shambles {1x}.

Due to the unkempt nature of the slaughter house, the benches upon which the meat was sold [Lat. shambles] became synonymous with anything disorderly. A plan, drawn by Lietzmann, of a forum in Pompeii, shows both the slaughterhouse and the meat shop next to the chapel of Caesar. Some of the meat which had been used for sacrificial purposes was afterwards sold in the markets. The apostle enjoins upon the believer to enter into no inquiry, so as to avoid the troubling of conscience, 1 Cor 10:25; (contrast v. 28). See: TDNT—4:370, 549; BAGD—487b; THAYER—386d.

3112. **μακράν** {10x} **makran**, *mak-ran';* fem. acc. sing. of *3117* (*3598* being impl.); *at a distance* (lit. or fig.):—far {4x}, afar off {2x}, good way off {1x}, far hence {1x}, great way off {1x}, far off {1x}.

Makran, a feminine adjective, from *macros,* **(1)** "far," Mt 8:20 "a good way"; **(2)** "a long way off," is used with *eis,* "unto," in Acts 2:39, "afar off." **(3)** With the article, in Eph 2:13, 17, it signifies "the (ones) far off." It also denotes **(4)** "a long way, far," **(4a)** literally, Mt 8:30; Lk 7:6; 15:20; Jn 21:8; Acts 17:27; 22:21; **(4b)** metaphorically, "far (from the kingdom of God)," Mk 12:34; **(4c)** in spiritual darkness, Acts 2:39; Eph 2:13, 17; **(5)** "a good (or great) way off," Mt 8:30; Lk 15:20. See: TDNT—4:372, 549; BAGD—487c; THAYER—386b.

3113. **μακρόθεν** {14x} **makrŏthĕn**, *mak-roth'-en;* adv. from *3117; from a distance* or *afar:*—afar off {13x}, from far {1x}. See: TDNT—4:372, 549; BAGD—487d; THAYER—387a.

3114. **μακροθυμέω** {10x} **makrŏthumĕō**, *mak-roth-oo-meh'-o;* from the same as *3116;* to *be long-spirited,* i.e. (obj.) *forbearing* or (subj.) *patient:*—be patient {3x}, have patience {2x}, have long patience {1x}, bear long {1x}, suffer long {1x}, be longsuffering {1x}, patiently endure {1x}.

Summary: *Makrothumeo* is **(1)** to be of a long spirit, not to lose heart; **(2)** to persevere patiently and bravely in enduring misfortunes and troubles; **(3)** to be patient in bearing the offenses and injuries of others and to be mild and slow in avenging **(4)** to be longsuffering, slow to anger, slow to punish. **(5)** It means "to be long-tempered" (*makros,* "long," *thumos,* "temper"), and is translated **(5a)** "to be patient" in 1 Th 5:14; Jas 5:7 first part; Jas 5:8; **(5b)** "to have patience," Mt 18:26, 29; **(5c)** "have long patience" in Jas 5:7, second part; **(5d)** "bear long with " in Lk 18:7; **(5e)** "suffereth long" in 1 Cor 13:4; **(5f)** "be longsuffering" in 2 Pet 3:9; **(5g)** "after he had patiently endured" in Heb 6:15. See: TDNT—4:374, 550; BAGD—488a; THAYER—387a.

3115. **μακροθυμία** {14x} **makrŏthumia**, *mak-roth-oo-mee'-ah;* from the same as *3116; longanimity,* i.e. (obj.) *forbearance* or (subj.) *fortitude:*—longsuffering {12x}, patience {2x}. "forbearance, patience, longsuffering" (*makros,* "long," *thumos,* "temper"), is usually rendered **(1)** "longsuffering," Rom 2:4; 9:22; 2 Cor 6:6; Gal 5:22; Eph 4:2; Col 1:11; 3:12; 1 Ti 1:16; 2 Ti 3:10; 4:2; 1 Pet 3:20; 2 Pet 3:15; **(2)** "patience" in Heb. 6:12 and Jas. 5:10. **(3)** One who possesses *makrothumia* has the power to avenge but refrains from doing so. Syn.: 463, 5281. See: TDNT—4:374, 550; BAGD—488b; THAYER—387b.

3116. **μακροθυμώς** {1x} **makrŏthumōs**, *mak-roth-oo-moce';* adv. of a compound of *3117* and *2372; with long* (*enduring*) *temper,* i.e. *leniently:*—patiently {1x}. See: TDNT—4:387, 550; BAGD—488b; THAYER—387c.

3117. **μακρός** {5x} **makrŏs**, *mak-ros';* from *3372; long* (in place [*distant*] or time [neut. plur.]):—far {2x}, long {3x}.

Makros is used **(1)** of space and time, long, said of prayers, in Mt 23:14, Mk 12:40; Lk 20:47; **(2)** of distance, "far, far" distant, Lk 15:13; 19:12. See: BAGD—488c; THAYER—387c.

3118. **μακροχρόνιος** {1x} **makrŏchrŏniŏs**, *mak-rokh-ron'-ee-os;* from *3117* and *5550; long-timed,* i.e. *long-lived:*—live long {1x}. See: BAGD—488c; THAYER—387d.

3119. **μαλακία** {3x} **malakia**, *mal-ak-ee'-ah;* from *3120; softness,* i.e. *enervation* (*debility*):—disease {3x}.

Malakia means infirmity, debility, bodily weakness, sickness found in Matthew only (4:23; 9:35; 10:1). See: TDNT—4:1091, 655; BAGD—488c; THAYER—387b.

3120. **μαλακός** {4x} **malakŏs**, *mal-ak-os';* of uncert. aff.; *soft,* i.e. *fine* (clothing); fig. a *catamite:*—effeminate {1x}, soft {3x}.

Malakos is used **(1)** of raiment, Mt 11:8 (twice); Lk 7:25; **(2)** metaphorically, in a bad sense, 1 Cor 6:9, "effeminate," not simply of a male who practices forms of lewdness, but persons in general, who are guilty of addiction to sins of the flesh, voluptuous. See: BAGD—488d; THAYER—387d.

3121. **Μαλελεήλ** {1x} **Malĕlĕēl**, *mal-el-eh-ale';* of Heb. or. [4111]; *Maleleēl* (i.e. *Mahalalel*), an antediluvian:—*Maleleel* {1x}. See: BAGD—488d; THAYER—387d.

3122. **μάλιστα** {12x} **malista**, *mal'-is-tah;* neut. plur. of the superl. of an appar. primary adv. μάλα **mala** (*very*); (adv.) *most* (*in the greatest degree*) or *particularly:*—specially {5x}, especially {4x}, chiefly {2x}, most of all {1x}.

Malista, "most, most of all, above all", "very, very much," is the superlative of *mala,* "very much" and is translated **(1)** "specially," Acts 25:26; 1 Ti 4:10; 5:8; Titus 1:10; Philem 16; **(2)** "especially" in Acts 26:3; Gal 6:10; 1 Ti 5:17; 2 Ti 4:13; **(3)** "chiefly" in 2 Pet 2:10; Phil 4:22; **(4)** in Acts 20:38, "most of all." "Specially" and "especially" both describe something as distinct, attention-getting and unique in relation to another. Especially is an intensified form which may, according to context, denote pre-eminence. Both draw attention to source; special having to do within a circle of influence; whereas, especially implies an outside influence. See: BAGD—488d; THAYER—387d.

3123. **μᾶλλον** {85x} **mallŏn**, *mal'-lon;* neut. of the comparative of the same as *3122;* (adv.) *more* (*in a greater degree*) or *rather:*—more {34x}, rather {33x}, the more {12x}, better + 2570 {2x}, misc. {4x}.

Mallon, the comparative degree of *mala,* "very, very much," is used **(1)** of increase, "more," **(1a)** with qualifying words, with *pollo,* "much," e.g., Mk 10:48, "the more (a great deal)"; Rom 5:15, 17, "(much) more"; Phil 2:12 (ditto); **(1b)** with *poso,* "how much," e.g., Lk 12:24; Rom 11:12; **(1c)** with *tosouto,* "by so much," Heb 10:25; **(2)** without a qualifying word, by way of comparison, "the more," e.g., **(2a)** Lk 5:15, "so much the more"; **(2b)** Jn 5:18, "the more"; Acts 5:14; Phil 1:9; 1 Th 4:1, 10, "more and more"; **(2c)** in Acts 20:35, by a periphrasis, it is translated "more (blessed)"; **(2d)** in Gal 4:27, "more (than)," lit., "rather (than)"; **(3)** with qualifying words, similarly to, e.g., Mk 7:36. **(4)** It is also translated "rather": e.g., Mt 10:6, 28; 1 Cor 14:1, 5; **(4a)** sometimes followed by "than," with a connecting particle, e.g., Mt 18:13 ("more than"); **(4b)** or without, e.g., Jn 3:19; Acts 4:19, "more"; **(4c)** in 1 Cor 9:12, "rather"; 12:22, "more"; 2 Cor. 3:9; Philem 16; **(4d)** in 2Pet 1:10, "the rather." See: BAGD—489a; THAYER—387d.

3124. **Μάλχος** {1x} **Malchŏs**, *mal'-khos;* of Heb. or. [4429]; *Malchus,* an Isr.:—Malchus {1x}. See: BAGD—489d; THAYER—388c.

3125. **μάμμη** {1x} **mammē**, *mam'-may;* of nat. or. ["mammy"]; a *grandmother:*—grandmother {1x}. See: BAGD—490a; THAYER—388c.

3126. **μαμμωνᾶς** {4x} **mammōnas** *mam-mo-nas',* or

μαμωνᾶς **mamōnas** *mam-o-nas';* of Chald. or. (*confidence,* i.e. *wealth,* personified); *mammonas,* i.e. *avarice* (deified):—mammon {4x}.

Mamonas, a common Aramaic word for "riches," akin to a Hebrew word signifying "to be firm, steadfast" (whence "Amen"), hence, "that which is to be trusted"; it is personified in Mt 6:24; Lk 16:9, 11, 13. See: TDNT—4:388, 552; BAGD—490a; THAYER—388d.

3127. **Μαναήν** {1x} **Manaēn**, *man-ah-ane';* of uncert. or.; *Manaën,* a Chr.:—*Manaen* {1x}. See: BAGD—490a; THAYER—388d.

3128. **Μανασσῆς** {3x} **Manassēs**, *man-as-sace';* of Heb. or. [4519]; *Mannasses* (i.e. *Menashsheh*), an Isr.:—*Manasses* {3x}. See: BAGD—490b; THAYER—388d.

3129. **μανθάνω** {25x} **manthanō**, *man-than'-o;* prol. from a primary verb, another form of which, μαθέω **mathĕō**, is used as an alt. in cert. tenses; to *learn* (in any way):—learn {24x}, understand {1x}.

Manthano, as a verb, denotes **(1)** "to learn" [akin to mathetes - 3101, "a disciple"), "to increase one's knowledge," or "be increased in knowledge," frequently "to learn by inquiry, or observation" (e.g., Mt 9:13; 11:29; 24:32; Mk 13:28; Jn 7:15; Rom 16:17; 1 Cor 4:6; 14:35; Phil 4:9; 2 Ti 3:14; Rev 14:3); **(2)** said of "learning" Christ (Eph 4:20), not simply the doctrine of Christ, but Christ Himself, a process not merely of getting to know the person but of so applying the knowledge as to walk differently from the rest of the Gentiles; **(3)** "to ascertain" (Acts 23:27 kjv, "understood"); **(4)** Gal 3:2, "This only would I learn from you," perhaps with a tinge of irony in the enquiry, the answer to which would settle the question of the validity of the new Judaistic gospel they were receiving; **(4)** "to learn by use and practice, to acquire the habit of, be accustomed to," (e.g., Phil 4:11; 1 Ti 5:4, 13; Titus 3:14; Heb 5:8). Syn.: 198, 1097, 3453. See: TDNT—4:390, 552; BAGD—490b; THAYER—388d.

3130. **μανία** {1x} **mania**, *man-ee'-ah;* from *3105; craziness:*—[+ make] × mad {1x}.

Mania, transliterated into English, denotes "frenzy, madness," Acts 26:24 "(thy much learning doth make thee) mad." See: BAGD—490d; THAYER—389b.

3131. **μάννα** {5x} **manna**, *man'-nah;* of Heb. or. [4478]; *manna* (i.e. *man*), an edible wafer:—*manna* {5x}.

Manna, as a noun, means **(1)** the supernaturally provided food for Israel during their wilderness journey (for details see Ex 16 and Num 11). **(2)** It is described in Ps 78:24, 25 as "the corn of heaven" and "angels' food" and in 1 Cor 10:3, as "spiritual meat." **(3)** The vessel appointed to contain it as a perpetual memorial, was of gold, Heb 9:4, with Ex 16:33. **(4)** The Lord speaks of it as being typical of Himself, the true Bread from Heaven, imparting eternal life and sustenance to those who by faith partake spiritually of Him, Jn 6:31–35. **(5)** The "hidden manna" is promised as one of the rewards of the overcomer, Rev 2:17; it is thus suggestive of the moral excellence of Christ in His life on earth, hid from the eyes of men, by whom He was "despised and rejected"; the path of the overcomer is a reflex of His life. See: TDNT—4:462, 563; BAGD—490d; THAYER—389b.

3132. **μαντεύομαι** {1x} **mantĕuŏmai**, *mant-yoo'-om-ahee;* from a der. of *3105* (mean. a *prophet,* as supposed to *rave* through *inspiration*); to *divine,* i.e. *utter spells* (under pretense of foretelling:—by soothsaying {1x}.

This word refers to the tumult of the mind, to the fury or temporary madness of those who were supposedly possessed by the god during the time they uttered their message. It is the art of heathen divination, Acts 16:16. Syn.: 4395. See: BAGD—491a; THAYER—389c.

3133. **μαραίνω** {1x} **marainō**, *mar-ah'-ee-no;* of uncert. aff.; to *extinguish* (as fire), i.e. (fig. and pass.) to *pass away:*—fade away {1x}.

Maraino, as a verb, in the active voice, means "to quench, waste, wear out"; in the passive, "to waste away" Jas 1:11, of the "fading" away of a rich man, as illustrated by the flower of the field. Syn.: 262, 263. See: BAGD—491b; THAYER—389d.

3134. **μαρὰν ἀθά** {1x} **maran atha**, *mar-an' ath-ah';* of Chald. or. (mean. *our Lord has come*); *maranatha,* i.e. an exclamation of the approaching *divine judgment:*—*Maran-atha* {1x}.

Maran-atha, **(1)** an expression used in 1 Cor 16:22, **(2)** is the Greek spelling for two Aramaic words, **(3)** formerly supposed by some to be an imprecatory utterance or "a curse reinforced by a prayer," an idea contrary to the intimations conveyed by its use in early Christian documents, e.g., "The Teaching of the Apostles," a document of the beginning of the 2nd cent., and in the "Apostolic Constitutions" (vii. 26), where it is used as follows: "Gather us all together into Thy Kingdom which Thou hast prepared. *Maranatha,* Hosanna to the Son of David; blessed is He that cometh, etc." **(4)** The first part, ending in 'n,' signifies "Lord"; as to the second part, the Fathers regarded it as a past tense, "has come." Modern expositors take it as equivalent to a present, "cometh," or future, "will come." Certain Aramaic scholars regard the last part as consisting of *tha,* and regard the phrase as an ejaculation, "Our Lord, come," or "O Lord, come."

(5) The character of the context, however, indicates that the apostle is making a statement rather than expressing a desire or uttering a prayer. **(6)** As to the reason why it was used, most probably it was a current proclamation among early Christians, as embodying the consummation of their desires. **(7)** At first the title *Marana* or *Maran,* used in speaking to and of Christ was no more than the respectful designation of the Teacher on the part of the disciples. After His resurrection they used the title of or to Him as applied to God, but it must here be remembered that the Aramaic-speaking Jews did not, save exceptionally, designate God as "Lord"; so that in the 'Hebraist' section of the Jewish Christians the expression "our Lord" (*Marana*) was used in reference to Christ only." See: TDNT—4:466, 563; BAGD—491b; THAYER—389d.

3135. **μαργαρίτης** {9x} **margaritēs**, *mar-gar-ee'-tace;* from μάργαρος **margarŏs** (a pearl-*oyster*); a *pearl:*—pearl {9x}.

Margarite, "a pearl" (Eng., Margaret), occurs in Mt 7:6 (proverbially and figuratively); 13:45, 46; 1 Tim. 2:9; Rev. 17:4; 18:12, 16; 21:21 (twice). See: TDNT—4:472, 564; BAGD—91c; THAYER—389d.

3136. **Μάρθα** {13x} **Martha**, *mar'-thah;* prob. of Chald. or. (mean. *mistress*); *Martha,* a Chr. woman:—*Martha* {13x}. See: BAGD—491c; THAYER—389d.

3137. **Μαρία** {54x} **Maria**, *mar-ee'-ah;* or

Μαριάμ **Mariam**, *mar-ee-am';* of Heb. or. [4813]; *Maria* or *Mariam* (i.e. *Mirjam*), the name of six Chr. females:—Mary the mother of Jesus {19x}, Mary Magdalene {13x}, Mary the sister of Martha {11x}, Mary the mother of James {9x}, Mary the mother of John Mark {1x}, Mary of Rome {1x}. See: BAGD—491d; THAYER—389d.

3138. **Μάρκος** {5x} **Markŏs**, *mar'-kos;* of Lat. or.; *Marcus,* a Chr.:—Marcus {3x}, Mark {5x}. See: BAGD—492b; THAYER—390b.

3139. **μάρμαρος** {1x} **marmarŏs**, *mar'-mar-os;* from μαρμαίρω **marmairō**, (to *glisten*); *marble* (as sparkling *white*):—marble {1x}.

Marmaros primarily denoted any "glistering stone" (from *maraino,* "to glisten"); hence, "marble," Rev. 18:12. See: BAGD—492c; THAYER—390c.

μάρτυρ **martur**.See *3144.*

3140. **μαρτυρέω** {79x} **marturĕō**, *mar-too-reh'-o;* from *3144;* to *be a witness,* i.e. *testify* (lit. or fig.):—bear witness {25x}, testify {19x}, bear record {13x}, witness {5x}, be a witness {2x}, give testimony {2x}, have a good report {2x}, misc. {11x} = charge, give [*evidence*], (obtain, of) good (honest) report, be well reported of.

Martureo, as a verb, denotes **(1)** "to be a *martus*" (3144), or "to bear witness to," sometimes rendered "to testify"; **(1a)** It means to affirm that one has seen or heard or experienced something, or **(1b)** that he knows it because taught by divine revelation or inspiration. **(2)** It is used of the witness **(2a)** of God the Father **(2a1)** to Christ: "There is another that beareth witness of me; and I know that the witness which he witnesseth of me is true" (Jn 5:32, cf. vs 37; 8:18; 1 Jn 5:9, 10; **(2a2)** to others: "And when He had removed him, He raised up unto them David to be their king; to whom also He gave testimony, and said, I have found David the *son* of Jesse, a man after mine own heart, which shall fulfill all my will" (Acts 13:22; cf. 15:8; Heb 11:2, 4 [twice], 5, 39);

(3) of Christ: "Verily, verily, I say unto thee, We speak that we do know, and testify that we have seen; and ye receive not our witness" (Jn 3:11, cf. vs 32; 4:44; 5:31; 7:7; 8:13, 14, 18; 13:21; 18:37; Acts 14:3; 1 Ti 6:13; Rev 22:18, 20); **(4)** of the Holy Spirit to Christ: "But when the Comforter is come, whom I will send unto you from the Father, *even* the Spirit of truth, which proceedeth from the Father, He shall testify of me" (Jn 15:26; cf. Heb 10:15; 1 Jn 5:7, 8); **(5)** of the

Scriptures, to Christ: "Search the scriptures; for in them ye think ye have eternal life: and they are they which testify of me" (Jn 5:39; cf. Heb 7:8, 17); **(6)** of the works of Christ, to Himself, and of the circumstances connected with His death: "But I have greater witness than *that* of John: for the works which the Father hath given me to finish, the same works that I do, bear witness of me, that the Father hath sent me" (Jn 5:36; cf. 10:25; 1 Jn 5:8);

(7) of prophets and apostles, **(7a)** to the righteousness of God: "But now the righteousness of God without the law is manifested, being witnessed by the law and the prophets" (Rom 3:21); **(7b)** to Christ: "The same [John the baptizer] came for a witness, to bear witness of the Light, that all *men* through him might believe" (Jn 1:7, 8, 15, 32, 34; 3:26; 15:27; 19:35; 21:24; Acts 10:43; 23:11; 1 Cor 15:15; 1 Jn 1:2; 4:14; Rev 1:2); **(7c)** to doctrine: "Having therefore obtained help of God, I continue unto this day, witnessing both to small and great, saying none other things than those which the prophets and Moses did say should come" (Acts 26:22); **(7d)** to the Word of God: "[John, the apostle] Who bare record of the word of God, and of the testimony of Jesus Christ, and of all things that he saw" (Rev 1:2); **(7e)** of others, concerning Christ: "And all bare Him witness, and wondered at the gracious words which proceeded out of His mouth. And they said, Is not this Joseph's son?" (Lk 4:22; cf. Jn 4:39; 12:17); **(7f)** of believers to one another: "Ye yourselves bear me [John the baptizer] witness, that I said, I am not the Christ, but that I am sent before Him" (Jn 3:28; cf. 2 Cor 8:3; Gal 4:15; Col 4:13; 3 Jn 3, 6, 12); **(7g)** of the apostle Paul concerning Israel (Rom 10:2); **(7h)** of an angel, to the churches (Rev 22:16); **(7i)** of unbelievers, **(7i1)** concerning themselves: "Wherefore ye be witnesses unto yourselves, that ye are the children of them which killed the prophets" (Mt 23:31); **(7i2)** concerning Christ: "Jesus answered him, If I have spoken evil, bear witness of the evil: but if well, why smitest thou me?" (Jn 18:23); **(7i3)** concerning others: "And needed not that any should testify of man: for He knew what was in man" (Jn 2:25; cf. Acts 22:5; 26:5);

(8) *Martureo* means "to give a good report, to approve of": "Wherefore, brethren, look ye out among you seven men of honest report (*martureo*), full of the Holy Ghost and wisdom, whom we may appoint over this business" (Acts 6:3; cf. 10:22; 16:2; 22:12; 1 Ti 5:10; 3 Jn 12). Syn.: 267, 2649, 3141, 3142, 3143, 3144, 4828, 4901, 5571, 5576, 5577. See: TDNT—4:474, 564; BAGD—492c; THAYER—390c.

3141. **μαρτυρία** {37x} **marturia**, *mar-too-ree'-ah; from 3144; evidence* given (judicially or gen.):—record {7x}, report {1x}, testimony {14x}, witness {15x}.

Marturia, as a noun, means "witness, evidence, testimony," is rendered **(1)** "record" in Jn 1:19; 8:13, 14; 19:35; 1 Jn 5:10b, 11, 12; **(2)** "report" in 1 Ti 3:7; **(3)** "testimony" in Jn 3:32, 33; 5:34; 8:17; 21:24; Acts 22:18; Rev 1:2, 9; 6:9; 11:7; 12:11, 17; 19:10 (twice); and **(4)** "witness" in Mk 14:55, 56, 59; Lk 22:71; Jn 1:7; 3:11, 32; 5:31, 32, 36; Titus 1:13; 1 Jn 5:9 (thrice), 10a; 20:4. **(5)** In Rev 19:10, "the testimony of Jesus" is objective, the "testimony" or witness given to Him (cf. 1:2, 9; as to those who will bear it, see Rev 12:17). The statement "the testimony of Jesus is the spirit of prophecy," is to be understood in the light, e.g., of the "testimony" concerning Christ and Israel in the Psalms, which will be used by the godly Jewish remnant in the coming time of "Jacob's Trouble." All such "testimony" centers in and points to Christ. Syn.: 267, 2649, 3142, 3140, 3143, 3144, 4828, 4901, 5571, 5576, 5577. See: TDNT—4:474, 564; BAGD—493c; THAYER—391c.

3142. **μαρτύριον** {20x} **marturiŏn**, *mar-too'-ree-on;* neut. of a presumed der. of *3144;* something *evidential,* i.e. (gen.) *evidence* given or (spec.) the *Decalogue* (in the sacred Tabernacle):—to be testified {1x}, testimony {15x}, witness {4x}.

Marturion, as a noun, means "a testimony, witness," and is translated "to be testified" in 1 Ti 2:6; **(2)** predominantly "testimony"; and **(3)** "witness" in Mt 24:14; Acts 4:33; 7:44; Jas 5:3. **(4)** In 2 Th 1:10, "our testimony among you," refers to the fact that the missionaries, besides proclaiming the truths of the gospel, had borne witness to the power of these truths. **(4a)** *Kerugma,* "the thing preached, the message," is objective, having especially to do with the effect on the hearers; *marturion* is mainly subjective, having to do especially with the preacher's personal experience. **(5)** In 1 Ti 2:6 "to be testified in due time", i.e., in the times divinely appointed for it, namely, the present age, from Pentecost till the church is complete. **(6)** In Rev 15:5, in the phrase, "the temple of the tabernacle of the testimony in Heaven," the "testimony" is the witness to the rights of God, denied and refused on earth, but about to be vindicated by the exercise of the judgments under the pouring forth of the seven bowls or vials of divine retribution. Syn.: 267, 2649, 3140, 3141, 3143, 3144, 4828, 4901, 5571, 5576, 5577. See: TDNT—4:474, 564; BAGD—493d; THAYER—391d.

3143. **μαρτύρομαι** {3x} **marturŏmai**, *mar-too'-rom-ahee;* mid. voice from *3144; to be adduced* as *a witness,* i.e. (fig.) to *obtest* (in affirmation or exhortation).—take to record {1x}, testify {2x}.

Marturomai, as a verb, strictly meaning "to summon as a witness," signifies "to affirm solemnly, adjure," and is used in the middle voice only, rendered **(1)** "I take . . . to record" (Acts 20:26); and **(2)** "testify" (Gal 5:3; Eph. 4:17). Syn.: 267, 2649, 3140, 3141, 3142, 3144, 4828, 4901, 5571, 5576, 5577. See: TDNT—4:510, 564; BAGD—494a; THAYER—392b.

3144. **μάρτυς** {34x} **martus**, *mar'-toos;* of uncert. aff.; a *witness* (lit. [judicially] or fig. [gen.]); by anal. a *"martyr"*:—martyr {3x}, record {2x}, witness {29x}.

Martus or *martur* (whence Eng., "martyr," one who bears "witness" by his death) **(1)** denotes "one who can or does aver what he has seen or heard or knows"; it is used **(2)** of God: "For God is my witness, whom I serve with my spirit in the gospel of his Son, that without ceasing I make mention of you always in my prayers" (Rom 1:9; cf. 2 Cor 1:23; Phil 1.8, 1 Th 2:5, 10); of Christ, Rev. 1:5; 3:14; **(3)** of those who "witness" for Christ by their death (Acts 22:20; Rev 2:13; Rev 17:6); **(4)** of the interpreters of God's counsels, yet to "witness" in Jerusalem in the times of the Antichrist (Rev 11:3); **(5)** in a forensic sense: "But if he will not hear *thee, then* take with thee one or two more, that in the mouth of two or three witnesses every word may be established" (Mt 18:16; 26:65; Mk 14:63; Acts 6:13; 7:58; 2 Cor 13:1; 1 Ti 5:19; Heb 10:28); **(6)** in a historical sense: "Truly ye bear witness that ye allow the deeds of your fathers: for they indeed killed them, and ye build their sepulchres" (Lk 11:48; cf. 24:48; Acts 1:8, 22; 2:32; 3:15; 5:32; 10:39, 41; 13:31; 22:15; 26:16; 1 Th 2:10; 1 Ti 6:12; 2 Ti 2:2; Heb 12:1, "[a cloud] of witnesses," here of those mentioned in ch. 11, those whose lives and actions testified to the worth and effect of faith, and whose faith received "witness" in Scripture; 1 Pet 5:1). Syn.: 267, 2649, 3140, 3141, 3142, 3143, 4828, 4901, 5571, 5576, 5577. See: TDNT—4:474, 564; BAGD—494b; THAYER—392b.

3145. **μασσάομαι** {1x} **massaŏmai**, *mas-sah'-om-ahee;* from a primary μάσσω **massō** (to *handle* or *squeeze*); to bite or *chew:*—gnaw {1x}. See: TDNT—4:514, 570; BAGD—392c; THAYER—392c.

3146. **μαστιγόω** {7x} **mastigŏō**, *mas-tig-ŏ'-o;* from *3148;* to *flog* (lit. or fig.):—to scourge {7x}.

Matigoo is used of **(1)** Jewish "scourgings" of **(1a)** Christ, in Mt 20:19; Mk 10:34; Lk 18:33; Jn 19:1; **(1b)** "apostles", in Mt 10:17; and **(1c)** "prophets", in Mt 23:34; **(1d)** "believers", metaphorically, in Heb 12:6, of the "chastening" by the Lord administered in love to His spiritual sons. **(2)** The Jewish method of "scourging," as described in the *Mishna,* was by the use of three thongs of leather, the offender receiving thirteen stripes on the bare breast and thirteen on each shoulder, the "forty stripes save one," as administered to Paul five times (2 Cor. 11:24). See: TDNT—4:515, 571; BAGD—495a; THAYER—392c.

3147. **μαστίζω** {1x} **mastizō**, *mas-tid'-zo;* from *3149;* to *whip* (lit.):—to scourge {1x}. See: TDNT—4:515, 571; BAGD—495a; THAYER—392d.

3148. **μάστιξ** {6x} **mastix**, *mas'-tix;* prob. from the base of *3145* (through the idea of *contact*); a *whip* (lit. the Rom. *flagellum* for criminals; fig. a *disease*):—plague {4x}, scourging {2x}.

Mastix is "a whip, scourge," is used **(1)** literally, with the meaning **(1a)** "scourging," in Acts 22:24, of the Roman method, **(1b)** in Heb 11:36, of the "sufferings" of saints in the OT times. Among the Hebrews the usual mode, legal and domestic, was that of beating with a rod (2 Cor 11:25); **(2)** metaphorically, of "disease" or "suffering, a scourge, plague, a calamity, misfortune", Mk 3:10; 5:29, 34; Lk 7:21. See: TDNT—4:518, 571; BAGD—495c; THAYER—392d.

3149. **μαστός** {3x} **mastŏs**, *mas-tos';* from the base of *3145;* a (prop. female) *breast* (as if *kneaded* up):—pap {3x}. Cf. Lk 11:27; 23:29; Rev 1:13. See: BAGD—495b; THAYER—392d.

3150. **ματαιολογία** {1x} **mataiŏlŏgia**, *mat-ah-yol-og-ee'-ah;* from *3151; random talk,* i.e. *babble:*—vain jangling {1x}. See: TDNT—4:524, 571; BAGD—495c; THAYER—392d.

3151. **ματαιολόγος** {1x} **mataiŏlŏgŏs**, *mat-ah-yol-og'-os;* from *3152* and *3004;* an *idle* (i.e. *senseless* or *mischievous*) *talker,* i.e. a *wrangler:*—vain talker {1x}.

This one is an idle talker, one who utters empty senseless things, 1 Ti 1:6. See: TDNT—4:524, 571; BAGD—495c; THAYER—392d.

3152. **μάταιος** {6x} **mataiŏs**, *mat'-ah-yos;* from the base of *3155; empty,* i.e. (lit.) *profitless,* or (spec.) an *idol:*—vain {5x}, vanities {1x}.

(1) *Mataios* denotes communication that is devoid of force, truth, success, result; it is useless, of no purpose. **(2)** It stresses aimlessness and vanity of anything that does not have God. **(3)** It means "void of result," is used of **(3a)** idolatrous practices, Acts 14:15, "vanities"; **(3b)** the thoughts of the wise, 1 Cor 3:20, "vain"; **(3c)**

faith, if Christ is not risen, 1 Cor 15:17; **(3e)** questionings, strifes, etc., Titus 3:9; **(3f)** religion, with an unbridled tongue, Jas 1:26; **(3g)** manner of life, 1 Pet 1:18. Syn.: *Mataios* (3152), "vain," signifies "void" of result, it marks the aimlessness of anything. The vain (*kenos* - 2756) man in Jas 2:20 is one who is "empty" of divinely imparted wisdom; in 1:26 the vain (*mataios*) religion is one that produces nothing profitable. *Kenos* stresses the absence of quality, *mataios*, the absence of useful aim or effect. See: TDNT—4:519, 571; BAGD—495c; THAYER—392d.

3153. **ματαιότης** {3x} **mataiŏtēs**, *mat-ah-yot'-ace;* from *3152; inutility;* fig. *transientness;* mor. *depravity:*—vanity {3x}.

This word stresses emptiness as to results and is used **(1)** of the creation (Rom 8:20) as failing of the results designed, owing to sin; **(2)** of the mind which governs the manner of life of the Gentiles (Eph 4:17); and **(3)** of the great swelling words of false teachers (2 Pet 2:18). See: TDNT—4:523, 571; BAGD—495d; THAYER—393a.

3154. **ματαιόω** {1x} **mataiŏō**, *mat-ah-yŏ'-o;* from *3152;* to *render* (pass. *become*) *foolish, empty,* i.e. (mor.) *wicked* or (spec.) *idolatrous:*—become vain {1x}. See: TDNT—4:523, 571; BAGD—495d; THAYER—393a.

3155. **μάτην** {2x} **matēn**, *mat'-ane;* accus. of a der. of the base of *3145* (through the idea of tentative *manipulation,* i.e. unsuccessful *search,* or else of *punishment*); *folly,* i.e. (adv.) to *no purpose:*—in vain {2x}.

Maten, "a fault, a folly," signifies "in vain, to no purpose," Mt 15:9; Mk 7:7. See: TDNT—4:523, 571; BAGD—495d; THAYER—393a.

3156. **Ματθαῖος** {5x} **Matthaiŏs**, *mat-thah'-yos;* or

Μαθθαῖος **Maththaiŏs**, *math-thah'-yos;* a short. form of *3161; Matthæus* (i.e. *Matthitjah*), an Isr. and a Chr.:—Matthew {5x}. See: BAGD—496a; THAYER—393b.

3157. **Ματθάν** {2x} **Matthan**, *mat-than';* of Heb. or. [4977]; *Matthan* (i.e. *Mattan*), an Isr.:—*Matthan* {2x}. See: BAGD—496a; THAYER—393b.

3158. **Ματθάτ** {2x} **Matthat**, *mat-that';* or

Μαθθάτ **Maththat**, *math-that';* prob. a short. form of *3161; Matthat* (i.e. *Mattithjah*), the name of two Isr.:—Mathat {2x}. See: BAGD—496a; THAYER—393c.

3159. **Ματθίας** {2x} **Matthias** *mat-thee'-as,* or Μαθθίας **Maththias**, *math-thee'-as;* appar. a short. form of *3161; Matthias* (i.e. *Mattithjah*), an Isr.:—*Matthias* {2x}. See: BAGD—496a; THAYER—393c.

3160. **Ματταθά** {1x} **Mattatha**, *mat-tah-thah';* prob. a short. form of *3161* [comp. 4992]; *Mattatha* (i.e. *Mattithjah*), an Isr.:—*Mattatha* {1x}. See: BAGD—496a; THAYER—393c.

3161. **Ματταθίας** {2x} **Mattathias**, *mat-tath-ee'-as;* of Heb. or. [4993]; *Mattathias* (i.e. *Mattithjah*), an Isr. and a Chr.:—*Mattathias* {2x}. See: BAGD—496b; THAYER—393c.

3162. **μάχαιρα** {29x} **machaira**, *makh'-ahee-rah;* prob. fem. of a presumed der. of *3163;* a *knife,* i.e. *dirk;* fig. *war,* judicial *punishment:*—sword {29x}.

Machaira is a short sword, long knife, or dagger (Mt 26:47, 51, 52) and is used metaphorically and by metonomy **(1)** for ordinary violence, or dissensions, that destroy peace (Mt 10:34); **(2)** as the instrument of a magistrate or judge (Rom 13:4); **(3)** of the Word of God, "the sword of the Spirit," (Eph 6:17). Syn.: *Rhomphaia* (4501) denotes a large sword occuring **(a)** literally (Rev 6:8); **(b)** metaphorically, as the instrument **(b1)** of anguish (Lk 2:35); **(b2)** of judgment (Rev 1:16; 2:12, 16; 19:15, 21), probably figurative of the Lord's judicial utterances. See: TDNT—4:524, 572; BAGD—496b; THAYER—393c.

3163. **μάχη** {4x} **machē**, *makh'-ay;* from *3164;* a *battle,* i.e. (fig.) *controversy:*—fighting {2x}, strife {1x}, striving {1x}.

(1) *Mache* are contentions that may involve armed conflict, but usually do not. *Mache,* "a fight, strife", is always used in the plural in the NT, and translated **(1)** "fightings" in 2 Cor 7:5; Jas 4:1; **(2)** "strivings" in Titus 3:9; and **(3)** "strifes" in 2 Ti 2:23. Syn.: *Mache* is the battle and *polemos* (4171) is the war. See: TDNT—4:527, 573; BAGD—496c; THAYER—394a.

3164. **μάχομαι** {4x} **machŏmai**, *makh'-om-ahee;* mid. voice of an appar. primary verb; to *war,* i.e. (fig.) to *quarrel, dispute:*—fight {1x}, strive {3x}.

Machomai, "to fight," is rendered **(1)** "fightings," in Jas 4:2; and **(2)** "strive": **(2a)** "strive" in 2 Ti 2:24; **(2b)** "strove" in Jn 6:52; Acts 7:26. See: TDNT—4:527, 573; BAGD—496c; THAYER—394a.

3165. **μέ** {301x} **mĕ**, *meh;* a short. (and prob. orig.) form of *1691; me:*—*me* {262x}, I {37x}, my {1x}, not tr {1x}. See: BAGD—[1473] 217a; THAYER—167b.

3166. **μεγαλαυχέω** {1x} **mĕgalauchĕō**, *meg-al-ow-kheh'-o;* from a compound of *3173* and αὐχέω **auchĕō**, (to *boast;* akin to *837* and *2744*); to *talk big,* i.e. *be grandiloquent* (*arrogant, egotistic*):—boast great things {1x}.

This word means to lift up the neck; hence, to boast and indicates any kind of haughty speech which stirs up strife or provokes others (Ja 3:5). See: BAGD—496c; THAYER—394a.

3167. **μεγαλεῖος** {2x} **mĕgalĕiŏs**, *meg-al-i'-os;* from *3173; magnificent,* i.e. (neut, plur. as noun) a conspicuous *favor,* or (subj.) *perfection:*—great things {1x}, wonderful works {1x}.

(1) *Megaleois* are outpourings of the greatness of God's power and glory leaving the observer full of wonder. **(2)** In Acts 2:11, the adjective *megaleios,* "magnificent," in the neuter plural with the article, is rendered "the wonderful works" (of God). **(3)** In Lk 1:49 Mary proclaims what "great things" God had done for her. Syn.: 1411, 1741, 2297, 3861, 4192, 5259. See: TDNT—4:541, 573; BAGD—496d; THAYER—394b.

3168. **μεγαλειότης** {3x} **mĕgalĕiŏtēs**, *meg-al-i-ot'-ace;* from *3167; superbness,* i.e. *glory* or *splendor:*—magnificence {1x}, majesty {1x}, mighty power {1x}.

Megaleiotes denotes "splendor, magnificence" (from *megaleios,* "magnificent," mighty," Acts 2:11, *megas,* "great"), and is translated **(1)** "magnificence" in Acts 19:27, of the splendor of the goddess Diana. **(2)** In Lk 9:43, "mighty power"; and **(3)** in 2 Pet 1:16, "majesty." See: TDNT—4:541, 573; BAGD—496d; THAYER—394b.

3169. **μεγαλοπρεπής** {1x} **mĕgalŏprĕpēs**, *meg-al-op-rep-ace';* from *3173* and *4241; befitting greatness* or *magnificence* (*majestic*):—excellent {1x}.

Megaloprepes signifies "magnificent, majestic, that which is becoming to a great man" (from *megas,* "great," and *prepo,* "to be fitting or becoming"), in 2 Pet 1:17, "excellent." See: TDNT—4:542, 573; BAGD—497a; THAYER—394a.

3170. **μεγαλύνω** {8x} **mĕgalunō**, *meg-al-oo'-no;* from *3173;* to *make* (or *declare*) *great,* i.e. *increase* or (fig.) *extol:*—enlarge {2x}, magnify {5x}, shew great {1x}.

Megaluno denotes "to make great" (from *megas,* "great"), and is translated in **(1)** "enlarge" in Mt 23:5; 2 Cor 10:15; **(2)** "to magnify" in Lk 1:46; Acts 5:13; 10:46; 19:17; Phil 1:20; and **(3)** "shew great" in Lk 1:58 "had showed great (mercy). See: TDNT—4:543, 573; BAGD—497b; THAYER—394b.

3171. **μεγάλως** {1x} **mĕgalōs**, *meg-al'-oce;* adv. from *3173; much:*—greatly {1x}. See: BAGD—497b; THAYER—394b.

3172. **μεγαλωσύνη** {3x} **mĕgalōsunē**, *meg-al-o-soo'-nay;* from *3173; greatness,* i.e. (fig.) *divinity* (often *God* himself):—Majesty {2x}, majesty {1x}.

Megalosune, from *megas,* "great," denotes "greatness, majesty"; it is used of God the Father, signifying **(1)** His greatness and dignity, in **(1a)** Heb 1:3, "the Majesty (on high)", **(1b)** Heb 8:1, "the Majesty (in the Heavens)"; and **(2)** in an ascription of praise acknowledging the attributes of God in Jude 25. See: TDNT—4:544, 573; BAGD—497b; THAYER—394c.

3173. **μέγας** {195x} **mĕgas**, *meg'-as;* [incl. the prol. forms, fem.

μεγάλη **mĕgalē**, plur.

μεγάλοι **mĕgalŏi**, etc.; comp. also *3176, 3187*]; *big* (lit. or fig. in a very wide application):—great {150x}, loud {33x}, misc. {12x} = (+ fear) exceedingly, high, large, mighty, + (be) sore (afraid), strong, × to years.

Metas is used **(1)** of external form, size, measure, e.g., of **(1a)** a stone, Mt 27:60; **(1b)** fish, Jn 21:11; **(2)** of degree and intensity, e.g., **(2a)** of fear, Mk 4:41; **(2b)** wind, Jn 6:18; Rev. 6:13, "mighty"; **(3)** of a circumstance, 1 Cor 9:11; 2 Cor 11:15; **(4)** in Rev 5:2, 12, "loud", of a voice; **(5)** of rank, whether of persons, e.g., **(5a)** God, Titus 2:13; **(5b)** Christ as a "great Priest," Heb 10:21; **(5c)** Diana, Acts 19:27, **(5d)** Simon Magus, Acts 8:9 "(some) great one"; **(5e)** in the plural "great ones," Mt 20:25; Mk 10:42, those who hold positions of authority in Gentile nations; **(6)** or of things, e.g., a mystery, Eph 5:32; Acts 8:8, of joy; **(7)** of intensity, as, e.g., **(7a)** of the force of a voice, e.g., Mt 27:46, 50; **(7b)** "loud" in Rev. 5:2, 12; 6:10; 7:2, 10; 8:13; 10:3; 12:10; 14:7, 9, 15, 18. See: TDNT—4:529, 573; BAGD—497c; THAYER—394c.

3174. **μέγεθος** {1x} **mĕgĕthŏs**, *meg'-eth-os;* from *3173; magnitude* (fig.):—greatness {1x}. See: TDNT—4:544, 573; BAGD—498c; THAYER—395c.

3175. **μεγιστᾶνες** {3x} **mĕgistanĕs**, *meg-is-tan'-es;* plur. from *3176; grandees:*—great men {2x}, lords {1x}.

Megistanes, akin to *megistos,* "greatest," the superlative degree of *megas,* "great," denotes "chief men, nobles", it is rendered **(1)** "lords" in Mk 6:21, of nobles in Herod's entourage; **(2)** "great men" in Rev 6:15 and 18:23. See: BAGD—498c; THAYER—395c.

3176. **μέγιστος** {1x} **mĕgistŏs**, *meg'-is-tos;* superl. of *3173; greatest* or *very great:*—exceeding great {1x}. See: BAGD—498d; THAYER—395c.

3177. **μεθερμηνεύω** {7x} **mĕthĕrmēnĕuō**, *meth-er-mane-yoo'-o;* from *3326* and *2059;* to *explain over,* i.e. *translate:*—being interpreted {6x}, be by interpretation {1x}.

Methermeneuo, "to change or translate from one language to another, to interpret," is always used in the passive voice in the NT, "being interpreted," of interpreting **(1)** names, **(1a)** Immanuel, Mt 1:23, "God with us"; **(1b)** Golgotha, Mk 15:22, "the place of a skull"; **(1c)** Barnabas, Acts 4:36, "the son of consolation"; **(1d)** in Acts 13:8, of *Elymas,* the verb is rendered "is . . . by interpretation," lit., "is interpreted"; **(1e)** Jn 1: 41 Messiah, interpreted as "Christ"; **(2)** it is used of interpreting or translating sentences in Mk 5:41; 15:34. See: BAGD—498c; THAYER—395c.

3178. **μέθη** {3x} **mĕthē**, *meth'-ay;* appar. a primary word; an *intoxicant,* i.e. (by impl.) *intoxication:*—drunkenness {3x}.

Methe"strong drink" (akin to *methu,* "wine"), denotes "drunkenness, habitual intoxication," Lk 21:34; Rom 13:13; Gal 5:21. Syn.: 2897, 2970, 3632, 4224. See: TDNT—4:545, 576; BAGD—498d; THAYER—395d.

3179. **μεθίστημι** {5x} **mĕthistēmi**, *meth-is'-tay-mee;* or (1 Cor. 13:2)

μεθιστάνω **mĕthistanō**, *meth-is-tan'-o;* from *3326* and *2476;* to *transfer,* i.e. *carry away, depose* or (fig.) *exchange, seduce:*—put out {1x}, remove {2x}, translate {1x}, turn away {1x}.

This word means to transpose, transfer, remove from one place to another, is used transitively in the sense of causing "to remove", specifically **(1)** of change of situation or place, in 1 Cor 13:2, of "removing" mountains; **(2)** to remove from the office of a steward, Lk 16:4; or **(3)** to depart from life, to die, in Acts 13:22, of the "removing" of King Saul, by bringing about his death. See: BAGD—498d; THAYER—395d.

3180. **μεθοδεία** {2x} **mĕthŏdĕia**, *meth-od-i'-ah;* from a compound of *3326* and *3593* [comp. "method"]; *travelling over,* i.e. *travesty* (*trickery*):—wile {1x}, lie in wait {1x}.

Methodeia denotes "craft, deceit" (*meta,* "after," *hodos,* "a way"), "a cunning device, a wile," and is translated **(1)** "wiles (of error)" in Eph 4:14, "they lie in wait (to deceive)", lit., "with a view to the craft (singular) of deceit"; **(2)** in Eph 6:11, "the wiles (plural) of the Devil. See: TDNT—5:102, 666; BAGD—499a; THAYER—395d.

3181. **μεθόριος** {1x} **mĕthŏriŏs**, *meth-or'-ee-os;* from *3326* and *3725; bounded alongside,* i.e. *contiguous* (neut. plur. as noun, *frontier*):—border {1x}. See: BAGD—499b; THAYER—396a.

3182. **μεθύσκω** {3x} **mĕthuskō**, *meth-oos'-ko;* a prol. (tran.) form of *3184;* to *intoxicate:*—be drunk {1x}, be drunken {2x}.

Methusko signifies "to make drunk, or to grow drunk" (an inceptive verb, marking the process of the state), "to become intoxicated," Lk 12:45; Eph 5:18; 1 Th 5:7*a.* See: TDNT—4:545,*; BAGD—499b; THAYER—396a.

3183. **μέθυσος** {2x} **mĕthusŏs**, *meth'-oo-sos;* from *3184; tipsy,* i.e. (as noun) a *sot:*—drunkard {2x}.

Methusos, "drunken", is used as noun, **(1)** in the singular, in 1 Cor 5:11, "drunkard", and **(2)** in the plural, in 1 Cor 6:10, "drunkards." See: TDNT—4:545, 576; BAGD—499b; THAYER—396a.

3184. **μεθύω** {7x} **mĕthuō**, *meth-oo'-o;* from another form of *3178;* to *drink* to *intoxication,* i.e. *get drunk:*—be drunken {5x}, have well drunk {1x}, be made drunk {1x}.

Metheuo, is used **(1)** in Jn 2:10 in the passive voice, and is translated "have well drunk." **(2)** It signifies "to be drunk with wine", originally it denoted simply "a pleasant drink." **(2a)** The verb is used of "being intoxicated" in Mt 24:49; Acts 2:15; 1 Cor 11:21; 1 Th 5:7b; **(2b)** metaphorically, of the effect upon men of partaking of the abominations of the Babylonish system, Rev 17:2; **(2c)** of being in a state of mental "intoxication," through the shedding of men's blood profusely, Rev 17:6. See: TDNT—4:545, 576; BAGD—499c; THAYER—396a.

3185. **μεῖζον** {1x} **mĕizŏn**, *mide'-zon;* neut. of *3187;* (adv.) in *greater* degree:—the more {1x}. See: BAGD—499d; THAYER—394b [3173].

3186. **μειζότερος** {1x} **mĕizŏtĕrŏs**, *mide-zot'-er-os;* continued comparative of *3187; still larger* (fig.):—greater {1x}. See: BAGD—499d; THAYER—396b.

3187. **μείζων** {45x} **mĕizōn**, *mide'-zone;* irreg. comparative of *3173; larger* (lit. or fig. spec. in age):—greater {34x}, greatest {9x}, elder {1x}, more {1x}.

Meizon is the comparative degree of *megas,* translated **(1)** "greater", e.g., Mt 11:11; in Jas 3:1, "the greater condemnation"; it is used in the neuter plural in John 1:50, "greater things"; in 14:12, "greater works" (lit., "greater things." **(2)** It is used of age, and translated "elder" in Rom 9:12, with reference to Esau and Jacob. **(3)** In Mt 20:31, the neuter of *meizon,* used as an adverb, is translated "the more." It also expresses the superlative and is translated **(4)** "greatest" in Mt 13:32, "the greatest among"; cf. Matt. 18:1, 4; 23:11; Mk 9:34; Lk 9:46; 22:24, 26; 1 Cor 13:13. See: BAGD—499d; THAYER—396b.

3188. **μέλαν** {3x} **mĕlan**, *mel'-an;* neut. of *3180* as noun; *ink:*—ink {3x}.

Melan, the neuter of the adjective *melas,* "black" (3189), denotes "ink," 2 Cor 3:3; 2 Jn 12; 3Jn 13. See: BAGD—499d; THAYER—396b.

3189. **μέλας** {3x} **mĕlas**, *mel'-as;* appar. a primary word; *black:*—black {3x}; Cf. Mt 5:36; Rev 6:5, 12. See: BAGD—499d; THAYER—396b.

3190. **Μελεᾶς** {1x} **Mĕlĕas**, *mel-eh-as';* of uncert. or.; *Meleas,* an Isr.:—*Meleas* {1x}. See: BAGD—500a; THAYER—396b.

μέλει **mĕlĕi**. See *3199.*

3191. **μελετάω** {3x} **mĕlĕtaō**, *mel-et-ah'-o;* from a presumed der. of *3199;* to *take care of,* i.e. (by impl.) *revolve* in the mind:—imagine {1x}, premeditate {1x}, meditate {1x}.

Meletao signifies "to care for, attend carefully" (from *melete,* "care"); **(1)** in 1 Ti 4:15, "meditate"; **(2)** in Acts 4:25, "imagine"; **(3)** in Mk 13:11, "premediate." See. BAGD—500b; THAYER—396b.

3192. **μέλι** {4x} **mĕli**, *mel'-ee;* appar. a primary word; *honey:*—honey {4x}.

Meli occurs with the adjective *agrios,* **(1)** "wild," in Mt 3:4; Mk 1:6; **(2)** in Rev 10:9, 10, as an example of sweetness. **(2)** As "honey" is liable to ferment, it was precluded from offerings to God, Lev 2:11. The liquid "honey" mentioned in Ps 19:10 and Prov 16:24 is regarded as the best; a cruse of it was part of the present brought to Ahijah by Jeroboam's wife, 1 Kin 14:3. See: TDNT—4:552, 577; BAGD—500c; THAYER—396c.

3193. **μελίσσιος** {1x} **mĕlissiŏs**, *mel-is'-see-os;* from *3192; relating to honey,* i.e. *bee* (comb):—honeycomb + 2781 {1x}. See: BAGD—500d; THAYER—396c.

3194. **Μελίτη** {1x} **Mĕlitē**, *mel-ee'-tay;* of uncert. or.; *Melita,* an island in the Mediterranean:—Melita {1x}. See: BAGD—500d; THAYER—396c.

3195. **μέλλω** {110x} **mĕllō**, *mel'-lo;* a strengthened form of *3199* (through the idea of *expectation*); to *intend,* i.e. *be about* to be, do, or suffer something (of persons or things, espec. events; in the sense of *purpose, duty, necessity, probability, possibility,* or *hesitation*):—shall {25x}, should {20x}, would {9x}, to come {9x}, will {7x}, things to come {4x}, not tr {3x}, misc. {33x} = about, after that, be (almost), intend, was to (be), mean, mind, be at the point, (be) ready, + return, tarry, which was for, be yet.

Mello signifies **(1)** "of intention, to be about to do something," e.g., Acts 3:3; 18:14; 20:3; Heb 8:5; **(2)** "of certainty, compulsion or necessity, to be certain to act," e.g., Jn 6:71. It is used **(3)** used of purpose. It is rendered simply by "shall" or "should" (which frequently represent elsewhere part of the future tense of the verb) in the following: Mt 16:27 (1st part), lit., "is about to come"; 17:12, 22; 20:22; 24:6; Mk 13:4 (2nd part); Lk 9:44; 21:7 (2nd part); v. 36; Acts 23:3; 24:15; 26:2; Rom 4:24; 8:13 (1st part); v. 18; 2 Ti 4:1; Heb 1:14; 10:27; Jas 2:12; 1 Pet 5:1; Rev 1:19; 2:10 (1st and 2nd parts); 3:10; 17:8 (1st part); **(4)** "should" e.g., Mk 10:32; Lk 19:11; 22:23; 24:21; Jn 6:71; 7:39; 11:51; 12:4, 33; 18:32; Acts 11:28; 23:27; 1Th 3:4; Rev 6:11. See: BAGD—500d; THAYER—396d.

3196. **μέλος** {34x} **mĕlŏs**, *mel'-os;* of uncert. aff.; a *limb* or *part* of the body:—member {34x}.

Melos, as a noun, means "a limb of the body," is used **(1)** literally, Mt 5:29–30; Rom 6:13 (twice), 19 (twice); 7:5, 23 (twice); 12:4 (twice); 1 Cor 12:12 (twice), 14, 18–20, 22, 25–26 (twice); Jas 3:5, 6; 4:1; **(2)** in Col. 3:5, "mortify therefore your members which are upon the earth"; since our bodies and their "members" belong to the earth, and are the instruments of sin, they are referred to as such (cf. Mt 5:29–30; Rom 7:5, 23); **(2a)** the putting to death is not physical, but ethical; as the physical "members" have distinct individualities, so those evils, of which the physical "members" are agents, are by analogy regarded as examples of the way in which the "members" work if not put to death; **(2b)** this is not precisely the same as "the old man," v. 9, i.e., the old nature, though there is a connection;

(3) metaphorically, of believers **(3a)** as members of Christ, 1 Cor 6:15 (1st part); of one another, Rom. 12:5 (as with the natural illustration, so with the spiritual analogy, there is not only vital unity, and harmony in operation, but diversity, all being essential to effectivity; the unity is not due to external organization but to common and vital union in Christ); there is stress in v. 5 upon "many" and "in Christ" and "members;" **(3b)** 1 Cor 12:27 of the "members" of a local church as a body; **(3c)** Eph 4:25 of the "members" of the whole Church as the mystical body of Christ; **(3d)** in 1 Cor 6:15 (2nd part), of one who practices fornication. See: TDNT—4:555, 577; BAGD—501d; THAYER—397b.

3197. **Μελχί** {2x} **Mĕlchi**, *mel-khee';* of Heb. or [4428 with pron. suffix *my king*]; *Melchi* (i.e. *Malki*), the name of two Isr.:—*Melchi* {2x}. See: BAGD—502a; THAYER—397b.

3198. **Μελχισεδέκ** {9x} **Mĕlchisĕdĕk**, *mel-khis-ed-ek';* of Heb. or. [4442]; *Melchisedek* (i.e. *Malkitsedek*), a patriarch:—Melchisedec {9x}. See: TDNT—4:568,*; BAGD—502a; THAYER—397b.

3199. **μέλω** {10x} **mĕlō**, *mel'-o;* a primary verb; to *be of interest* to, i.e. to *concern* (only third pers. sing. pres. ind. used impers. *it matters*):—take care {1x}, care {9x}.

Melo, the third person sing. of *melo,* used impersonally, **(1)** signifies that "something is an object of care," especially the care of forethought and interest, rather than anxiety, Mt 22:16; Mk 4:38; 12:14; Lk 10:40; Jn 10:13; 12:6; Acts 18:17; 1 Cor 7:21, 9:9, (God does "care" for oxen, but there was a divinely designed significance in the OT passage, relating to the service of preachers of the gospel); 1Pet 5:7. See: BAGD—500d [3195]; THAYER—396b.

3200. **μεμβράνα** {1x} **mĕmbrana**, *mem-bran'-ah;* of Lat. or. ("*membrane*"); a (written) sheep-*skin:*—parchment {1x}.

Membrana is a Latin word, properly an adjective, from *membrum,* "a limb," but denoting "skin, parchment." The Eng. word "parchment" is a form of *pergamena,* an adjective signifying "of Pergamum," the city in Asia Minor where "parchment" was either invented or brought into use. The word *membrana* is found in 2 Ti 4:13, where Timothy is asked to bring to the apostle "the books, especially the parchments." The writing material was prepared from the skin of the sheep or goat. The skins were first soaked in lime for the purpose of removing the hair, and then shaved, washed, dried, stretched and ground or smoothed with fine chalk or lime and pumice stone. The finest kind is called "vellum," and is made from the skins of calves or kids. See: BAGD—502a; THAYER—397c.

3201. **μέμφομαι** {3x} **mĕmphŏmai**, *mem'-fom-ahee;* mid. voice of an appar. primary verb; to *blame:*—find fault {3x}.

Memphomai, as a verb, means "to find fault": "And when they saw some of his disciples eat bread with defiled, that is to say, with unwashen, hands, they found fault" (Mk 7:2; cf. Rom 9:19; Heb 8:8). Syn.: 273, 274, 298, 299, 338, 410, 423, 2607, 3469. See: TDNT—4:571, 580; BAGD—502b; THAYER—397c.

3202. **μεμψίμοιρος** {1x} **mĕmpsimŏirŏs**, *mem-psim'-oy-ros;* from a presumed der. of *3201* and μοῖρα **mŏira**, (*fate;* akin to the base of *3313*); *blaming fate,* i.e. *querulous* (*discontented*):—complainer {1x}.

This word denotes one who complains of his lot, his station in life; hence, discontented, querulous, repining, blaming someone else (Jude 16). See: TDNT—4:571, 580; BAGD—502c; THAYER—397c.

3203–3302. Because of some changes in the numbering system (while the original work was in progress) no Greek words were cited for *2717* or *3203–3302*. These numbers were dropped altogether. This will not cause any problems in Strong's numbering system. No Greek words have been left out. Because so many other reference works use this numbering system, it has not been revised. If it were revised, much confusion would certainly result.

3303. **μέν** {194x} **mĕn**, *men;* a primary particle; prop. ind. of *affirmation* or *concession* (*in fact*); usually followed by a *contrasted* clause with *1161* (*this* one, the *former,* etc):—indeed {22x}, verily {14x}, truly {12x}, not tr {142x}, misc. {4x}.

Often compounded with other particles in an *intens.* or *asseverative* sense. *Men,* a conjunctive particle (originally a form of *men,* "verily, truly," found in Heb 6:14 is usually related to an adversative conjunction or particle, like *de,* in the following clause, which is placed in opposition to it. Frequently it is untranslatable; sometimes it is rendered "indeed," e.g., Mt 3:11; 13:32; 17:11 "truly"; 20:23; 26:41; Mk 1:8; 9:12 "verily." See: BAGD—502c; THAYER—397c.

3304. **μενοῦνγε** {4x} **mĕnŏungĕ**, *men-oon'-geh* or

μενοῦν **mĕnŏun**, *men-oon'* or

μενοῦν γε **mĕnŏun ge** *men-oon' geh;* from *3203* and *3767* and *1065; so then at least:*—yea rather {1x}, nay but {1x}, yea verily {1x}, yea doubtless {1x}.

Menounge, "nay rather," is rendered **(1)** "yea rather" in Lk 11:28; **(2)** "nay but" in Rom 9:20; **(3)** "yea verily" in Rom 10:18; and "yea doubtless" in Phil 3:8. See: BAGD—503c; THAYER—399a.

3305. **μέντοι** {8x} **mĕntŏi**, *men'-toy;* from *3303* and *5104; indeed though,* i.e. *however:*—yet {2x}, nevertheless {2x}, howbeit {1x}, but {1x}, not tr {2x}.

This word is translated **(1)** "yet", in Jn 4:27; 20:5; **(2)** "nevertheless", in Jn 12:42; 2 Ti 2:19; **(3)** "howbeit", in Jn 7:13; **(4)** "but," in Jn 21:4; **(5)** not tr in Jas 2:8; Jude 8. See: BAGD—593c; THAYER—399a.

3306. **μένω** {120x} **mĕnō**, *men'-o;* a primary verb; to *stay* (in a given place, state, relation or expectancy):—abide {61x}, remain {16x}, dwell {15x}, continue {11x}, tarry {9x}, endure {3x}, misc. {5x} = "to abide," be present, stand, × thine own.

It is translated "abide" and used **(1)** of place, **(1a)** literally, e.g., Mt 10:11, **(1b)** metaphorically, is said **(1b1)** of God, 1 Jn 4:15; **(1b2)** Christ, Jn 6:56; 15:4, etc.; **(1b3)** the Holy Spirit, Jn 1:32–33; 14:17; **(1b4)** believers, Jn 6:56; 15:4; 1 Jn 4:15, etc.; **(1b5)** the Word of God, 1 Jn 2:14; **(1b6)** the truth, 2 Jn 2, etc.; **(2)** of time; it is said **(2a)** of believers, Jn 21:22–23; Phil 1:25; 1 Jn 2:17; **(2b)** Christ, Jn 12:34; Heb 7:24; **(2c)** the Word of God, 1 Pet 1:23; **(2d)** sin, Jn 9:41; **(2e)** cities, Mt 11:23; Heb 13:14; **(2f)** bonds and afflictions, Acts 20:23; **(3)** of qualities; **(3a)** faith, hope, love, 1 Cor 13:13; **(3b)** Christ's love, Jn 15:10; **(3c)** afflictions, Acts 20:23; **(3d)** brotherly love, Heb 13:1; **(3e)** the love of God, 1 Jn 3:17; **(3f)** the truth, 2 Jn 2. **(4)** It is translated "to remain," e.g., Mt 11:23; Lk 10:7; Jn 1:33; 9:41; 15:16; 19:31; Acts 5:4 (twice); 27:41; 1 Cor 7:11; 15:6; 2 Cor 3:11, 14; 9:9; Heb 12:27; 1 Jn 3:9. **(5)** It is translated "to dwell," in Jn 1:38–39; 6:56; 14:10, 17; Acts 28:16. **(6)** It is translated "to tarry," in Mt 26:38; Mk 14:34; Lk 24:29; Jn 4:40; Acts 9:43; 18:20; 20:5, 15. See: TDNT—4:574, 581; BAGD—503c; THAYER—399b.

3307. **μερίζω** {14x} **mĕrizō**, *mer-id'-zo;* from *3313; to part,* i.e. (lit.) to *apportion, bestow, share,* or (fig.) to *disunite, differ:*—divide {9x}, distribute {2x}, deal {1x}, be difference between {1x}, give part {1x}.

Merizo, akin to *meros,* hence, "to distribute, divide out, deal out to, a part, to part, divide into," in the middle voice means "to divide anything with another, to share with." The usual meaning is **(1)** "to divide," Mt 12:25 twice, 26; Mk 3:24–26 thrice; 6:41; Lk 12:13; 1 Cor 1:13; **(2)** "hath distributed" in 1 Cor 7:17; 2 Cor 10:13; **(3)** "hath dealt" in Rom 12:3;

(4) "be difference between" in 1 Cor 7:34; **(5)** "gave a part" in Heb 7:2. See: BAGD—504c; THAYER—399d.

3308. **μέριμνα** {6x} **mĕrimna**, *mer'-im-nah;* from *3307* (through the idea of *distraction*); *solicitude:*—care {6x}.

Merimna, probably connected with *merizo,* "to draw in different directions, distract," hence signifies "that which causes this, a care, especially an anxious care," Mt 13:22; Mk 4:19; Lk 8:14; 21:34; 2 Cor 11:28; 1 Pet 5:7. See: TDNT—4:589, 584; BAGD—504d; THAYER—400a.

3309. **μεριμνάω** {19x} **mĕrimnaō**, *mer-im-nah'-o;* from *3308; to be anxious* about:—take thought {11x}, care {5x}, be careful {2x}, have care {1x}.

Merimnao signifies **(1)** "to be anxious about, to have a distracting care," e.g., Mt 6:25, 27, 28, 31, 34; Lk 12:11, 22, 25, 26 "take thought"; 10:19; Lk 10:41 "careful"; 12:11; **(2)** to be careful for, 1 Cor 7:32–34; **(3)** to have a care for, 1 Cor 12:25; **(4)** to care for, Phil 2:20; **(5)** "be anxious", Phil 4:6. See: TDNT—4:589, 584; BAGD—505a; THAYER—400b.

3310. **μερίς** {5x} **mĕris**, *mer-ece';* fem. of *3313;* a *portion,* i.e. *province, share* or (abstr.) *participation:*—part {4x}, to be partaker + 1519 {1x}.

Meris, denotes **(1)** "a part" or "portion," **(1a)** Lk 10:42; Acts 8:21; 2 Cor 6:15; **(1b)** "a district" or "division," Acts 16:12; **(2)** in Col 1:12, "partakers," lit., "unto the part of." See: BAGD—505a; THAYER—400b.

3311. **μερισμός** {2x} **mĕrismŏs**, *mer-is-mos';* from *3307;* a *separation* or *distribution:*—dividing asunder {1x}, gift {1x}.

Merismos primarily denotes "a division, partition" (*meros,* "a part"); hence, **(1)** "a distribution," Heb 2:4, "gifts"; **(2)** "a dividing or separation", Heb 4:12, "dividing asunder." See: BAGD—505c; THAYER—400c.

3312. **μεριστής** {1x} **mĕristēs**, *mer-is-tace';* from *3307;* an *apportioner* (*administrator*):—divider {1x}. See: BAGD—505d; THAYER—400c.

3313. **μέρος** {43x} **mĕrŏs**, *mer'-os;* from an obs. but more primary form of μείρομαι **mĕirŏmai** (to *get* as a *section* or *allotment*); a *division* or *share* (lit. or fig. in a wide application):—part {24x}, portion {3x}, coast {3x}, behalf {2x}, respect {2x}, misc. {9x} = course, craft, particular (+ -ly), partly, piece, side, some sort (-what).

Meros denotes **(1)** "a part, portion," **(1a)** of the whole, e.g., Jn 13:8; Rev 20:6; 22:19; **(1b)** hence, "a lot" or "destiny," e.g., Rev 21:8; **(1c)** in Mt 24:51 and Lk 12:46, "portion"; **(2)** "a part" as opposite to the whole, e.g., Lk 11:36; Jn 19:23; 21:6, "side"; Acts 5:2; 23:6; Eph 4:16; Rev 16:19; **(2a)** a party, Acts 23:9; the divisions of a province, e.g., Mt 2:22; Acts 2:10; **(2b)** the regions belonging to a city, e.g., Mt 15:21, "coasts"; 16:13; Acts 19:1; Mk 8:10; **(2c)** "the lower parts of the earth," Eph 4:9; this phrase means the regions beneath the earth; **(3)** "a class," or "category" (with *en,* in, "in respect of"), Col 2:16; "in this respect," 2 Cor 3:10; 9:3; 1 Pet 4:16, "in this behalf"; **(4)** used with the preposition *apo,* "from," with the meaning "in some sort": "Nevertheless, brethren, I have written the more boldly unto you in some sort (*meros*), as putting you in mind, because of the grace that is given to me of God" (Rom 15:15). Syn.: 280, 488, 943, 2884, 3354, 3358, 4057, 4568, 5234, 5249, 5518. See: TDNT—4:594, 585; BAGD—505d; THAYER—400d.

3314. **μεσημβρία** {2x} **mĕsēmbria**, *mes-ame-bree'-ah;* from *3319* and *2250; midday;* by impl. the *south:*—noon {1x}, south {1x}.

The south, Acts 8:26, is the direction from which the most glaring sunlight comes; like the noon, Acts 22:6, day sun. See: BAGD—506d; THAYER—401a.

3315. **μεσιτεύω** {1x} **mĕsitĕuō**, *mes-it-yoo'-o;* from *3316;* to *interpose* (as arbiter), i.e (by impl.) to *ratify* (as surety):—confirm {1x}.

Mesiteuo means to act as a mediator between litigating or covenanting parties, to accomplish something by interposing between two parties, and then seeing the agreement is carried out; hence, to confirm, make firm between them, Heb 6:17. See: TDNT—4:598, 585; BAGD—506d; THAYER—401b.

3316. **μεσίτης** {6x} **mĕsitēs**, *mes-ee'-tace;* from *3319;* a *go-between,* i.e. (simply) an *internunciator,* or (by impl.) a *reconciler* (*intercessor*):—mediator {6x}.

Mesites, as a noun, means lit., "a go-between" (from *mesos,* "middle," and *eimi,* "to go"), is used in two ways in the NT, **(1)** "one who mediates" between two parties with a view to producing peace, as in 1 Ti 2:5, **(1a)** though more than mere "mediatorship" is in view, **(1b)** for the salvation of men necessitated that the Mediator should Himself possess the nature and attributes of Him towards whom He acts, and should likewise participate in the nature of those for whom He acts (sin apart); **(1c)** only by being possessed both of deity and humanity could He comprehend the claims of the one and the needs of the other; **(1d)** further, the claims and the needs could be met only by One who, Himself being proved sinless, would offer Himself an expiatory sacrifice on behalf of men; **(1e)** "one who acts as a guarantee" so as to secure something which otherwise would not be obtained. **(1f)** Thus in Heb 8:6; 9:15; 12:24 Christ is the Surety of "the better covenant," "the new covenant," guaranteeing its terms for His people.

(2) In Gal 3:19 Moses is spoken of as a "mediator," and the statement is made that "a mediator is not a mediator of one," v. 20, that is, of one party. **(2a)** Here the contrast is between the promise given to Abraham and the giving of the Law. **(2b)** The Law was a covenant enacted between God and the Jewish people, requiring fulfillment by both parties. **(2c)** But with the promise to Abraham, all the obligations were assumed by God, which is implied in the statement, "but God is one." See: TDNT—4:598, 585; BAGD—506d; THAYER—401b.

3317. **μεσονύκτιον** {4x} **mĕsŏnuktiŏn**, *mes-on-ook'-tee-on;* neut. of compound of *3319* and *3571; midnight* (espec. as a watch):—midnight {4x}.

Mesonuktion, an adjective denoting "at, or of, midnight," is used as a noun in Mk 13:35; Lk 11:5; Acts 16:25; 20:7. See: BAGD—507a; THAYER—401c.

3318. **Μεσοποταμία** {2x} **Mĕsŏpŏtamia**, *mes-op-ot-am-ee'-ah;* from *3319* and *4215; Mesopotamia* (as lying between the Euphrates and the Tigris; comp. *763*), a region of Asia:—Mesopotamia {2x}. See: BAGD—507b; THAYER—401c.

3319. **μέσος** {61x} **mĕsŏs**, *mes'-os;* from *3326; middle* (as an adj. or [neut.] noun):—midst {41x}, among {6x}, from among + 1537 {5x}, midnight + 3571 {2x}, × before them {1x}, between {1x}, + forth {1x}, midday {1x}, way {1x}.

Mesos, an adjective denoting "middle, in the middle or midst," is used in the following, in which the English requires a phrase, and the adjectival rendering must be avoided: **(1)** Lk 22:55, "Peter sat in the midst of them," lit., "a middle one of (them)"; **(2)** Lk 23:45, of the rending of the veil "in the midst"; here the adjective idiomatically belongs to the verb "was rent," and is not to be taken literally, as if it meant "the middle veil"; **(3)** Jn 1:26, "in the midst of you (standeth One)", lit., "a middle One"; **(4)** Acts 1:18, where the necessity of avoiding the lit. rendering is obvious. See: BAGD—507b; THAYER—401c.

3320. **μεσότοιχον** {1x} **mĕsŏtŏichŏn**, *mes-ot'-oy-khon;* from *3319* and *5109;* a *partition* (fig.):—middle wall {1x}.

Mesotoichon, "a partition wall" (*mesos,* "middle"), occurs in Eph 2:14, figuratively of the separation of Gentile from Jew in their unregenerate state, a partition demolished by the Cross for both on acceptance of the gospel. See: TDNT—4:625, 589; BAGD—508a; THAYER—402b.

3321. **μεσουράνημα** {3x} **mĕsŏuranēma**, *mes-oo-ran'-ay-mah;* from a presumed compound of *3319* and *3772; mid-sky:*—midst of heaven {3x}.

This word denotes the highest point in the heavens, which the sun occupies at noon, where what is done can be seen and heard by all (Rev 8:13; 14:6; 19:17). See: BAGD—508a; THAYER—402b.

3322. **μεσόω** {1x} **mĕsŏō**, *mes-ŏ'-o;* from *3319;* to *form* the *middle,* i.e. (in point of time), to *be half-way* over:—be about the midst {1x}.

Mesoo, "to be in the middle," is used of time in Jn 7:14, translated "when it was . . . the midst (of the feast)," lit., "(the feast) being in the middle" or about half over. See: BAGD—508b; THAYER—402b.

3323. **Μεσσίας** {2x} **Mĕssias**, *mes-see'-as;* of Heb. or. [4899]; the *Messias* (i.e. *Mashiach*), or Christ:—*Messias* {2x}. See: TDNT 9:493, 1322; BAGD—508b; THAYER—402c.

3324. **μεστός** {8x} **mĕstŏs**, *mes-tos';* of uncert. der.; *replete* (lit. or fig.):—full {8x}.

Mestos, probably akin to a root signifying "to measure," hence conveys the sense of "having full measure," **(1)** of material things, **(1a)** a vessel, Jn 19:29; **(1b)** a net, 21:11; **(2)** metaphorically, of thoughts and feelings, exercised **(2a)** in evil things, hypocrisy, Mt 23:28; **(2b)** envy, murder, strife, deceit, malignity, Rom 1:29; **(2c)** the utterances of the tongue, Jas 3:8; **(2d)** adultery, 2 Pet 2:14; **(3)** in virtues, **(3a)** goodness, Rom 15:14; **(3b)** mercy, etc, Jas 3:17. See: BAGD—508b; THAYER—402c.

3325. **μεστόω** {1x} **mĕstŏō**, *mes-tŏ'-o;* from *3324;* to *replenish,* i.e. (by impl.) to *intoxicate:*—fill {1x}. See: BAGD—508c; THAYER—402c.

3326. **μετά** {473x} **mĕta**, *met-ah';* a primary prep. (often used adv.); prop. denoting *accompaniment; "amid"* (local or causal); modif. variously according to the case (gen. *association,* or acc. *succession*) with which it is joined; occupying an intermediate position between *575* or *1537* and *1519* or *4314;* less intimate than *1722* and less close than *4862*):—with {345x}, after {88x}, among {5x}, hereafter + 5023 {4x}, afterward + 5023 {4x}, against {4x}, not tr {1x}, misc {32x} = × that he again, × and, + follow, hence, in, of, (up-) on, + our, × and setting, since, (un-) to, + together, when, without. Often used in composition, in substantially the same relations of *participation* or *proximity,* and *transfer* or *sequence.* See: TDNT—7:766, 1102; BAGD—508c; THAYER—402c.

3327. **μεταβαίνω** {12x} **mĕtabainō**, *met-ab-ah'-ee-no;* from *3326* and the base of *939;* to *change place:*—depart {7x}, go {1x}, pass {2x}, remove {2x}.

Metabaino is rendered "to depart" in Mt 8:34; 11:1; 12:9; 15:29; Jn 7:3; 13:1; Acts 18:7; **(2)** "go" in Lk 10:7; **(3)** "pass" in Jn 5:24; 1Jn 3:14; **(4)** "remove" in Mt 17:20 twice. See: TDNT—1:523, 90; BAGD—510c; THAYER—404d.

3328. **μεταβάλλω** {1x} **mĕtaballō**, *met-ab-al'-lo;* from *3326* and *906;* to *throw over,* i.e. (mid. voice fig.) to *turn about* in opinion:—change (one's) mind {1x}.

The emphasis of this word seems to be on the quickness of the change; literally, "thrown over with" (Acts 28:6). See: BAGD—510d; THAYER—404d.

3329. **μετάγω** {2x} **mĕtagō**, *met-ag'-o;* from *3326* and *71;* to *lead over,* i.e. *transfer* (*direct*):—turn about {2x}.

Metago literally means "to move from one side to another," is rendered "to turn about" in Jas. 3:3, 4. See: BAGD—510d; THAYER—404d.

3330. **μεταδίδωμι** {5x} **mĕtadidōmi**, *met-ad-id'-o-mee;* from *3326* and *1325;* to *give over,* i.e. *share:*—give {2x}, impart {3x}.

(1) This word stresses giving something that is part of and precious to the giver, as if part of the giver resides within the gift. **(2)** It means "to give a share of, impart" (*meta,* "with"), as distinct from "giving." **(2a)** The apostle Paul speaks of "sharing" some spiritual gift with Christians at Rome, Rom 1:11, "that I may impart," and exhorts those who minister in things temporal, to do so as "sharing," and **(2b)** that generously, 12:8, "he that giveth"; so in Eph 4:28; Lk 3:11; **(3)** in 1 Th 2:8 he speaks of himself and his fellow missionaries as having been well pleased to impart to the converts both God's gospel and their own souls (i.e., so "sharing" those with them as to spend themselves and spend out their lives for them). See: BAGD—510d; THAYER—404d.

3331. **μετάθεσις** {3x} **mĕtathĕsis**, *met-ath'-es-is;* from *3346; transp.,* i.e. *transferral* (to heaven), *disestablishment* (of a law):—change {1x}, removing {1x}, translation {1x}.

(1) This word stresses the permanency of the change. **(2)** *Metathesis,* "a transposition, or a transference from one place to another" (from *meta,* implying "change," and *tithemi* "to put"), **(2a)** has the meaning of "change" in Heb 7:12, **(2b)** in connection with the necessity of a "change" of the Law (or, as margin, law), if the priesthood is changed. **(3)** It is rendered "translation" in Heb 11:5, and **(4)** "removing" in Heb 12:27. See: TDNT—8:161, 1176; BAGD—511a; THAYER—405a.

3332. **μεταίρω** {2x} **mĕtairō**, *met-ah'-ee-ro;* from *3326* and *142;* to *betake* oneself, i.e. *remove* (locally):—depart {2x}.

(1) A permanent removal without returning is implied. *Metairo,* "to make a distinction, to remove, to lift away" (in its transitive sense), is used intransitively in the NT, signifying **(2)** "to depart," and is said **(2a)** of Christ, in Mt 13:53; 19:1. It could be well understood as "removed." See: BAGD—511a; THAYER—405a.

3333. **μετακαλέω** {4x} **mĕtakalĕō**, *met-ak-al-eh'-o;* from *3326* and *2564;* to *call elsewhere,* i.e. *summon:*—call {1x}, call for {1x}, call hither {1x}, call to (one's) self {1x}.

Metakaleo stresses calling someone from one place to another, especially to summon, to call to one's self (Acts 7:14; 10:32; 20:17; 24:25). See: TDNT—3:496, 394; BAGD—511a; THAYER—405a.

3334. **μετακινέω** {1x} **mĕtakinĕō**, *met-ak-ee-neh'-o;* from *3326* and *2795;* to *stir* to a place *elsewhere,* i.e. *remove* (fig.):—move away {1x}.

Metakineo, as a verb, in the middle voice, means **(1)** "to remove oneself, shift" and is translated in the passive in Col 1:23: "be . . . not moved away (from the hope of the gospel)." **(2)** This word literally means to be stirred by an external stimuli and then moving from one place or position to another. Syn.: 277, 383, 761, 2795, 2796, 4525, 4531, 4579, 4787, 5342. See: TDNT—3:720, 435; BAGD—511b; THAYER—405a.

3335. **μεταλαμβάνω** {6x} **mĕtalambanō**, *met-al-am-ban'-o;* from *3326* and *2983;* to *participate;* generally to *accept* (and use):—eat {1x}, have {1x}, be partaker {2x}, receive {1x}, take {1x}.

Metalambano, as a verb, means "to have or get a share of, partake of" and is rendered **(1)** "receiveth": "For the earth which drinketh in the rain that cometh oft upon it, and bringeth forth herbs meet for them by whom it is dressed, receiveth (*metalambano*) blessing from God" (Heb 6:7). It also is translated **(2)** "did eat," in Acts 2:46; **(3)** "have" in Acts 24:25; **(4)** "be partaker" in 2 Ti 2:6; Heb 12:10; and **(5)** "take" in Acts 27:23. Syn.: 324, 353, 354, 568, 588, 618, 1209, 1523, 1926, 2210, 2865, 2975, 2983, 3028, 3336, 3858, 3880, 3970, 4327, 4355, 4356, 4380, 4381, 4382, 5562, 5264, 5274. See: TDNT—4:10, 495; BAGD—511b; THAYER—405b.

3336. **μετάληψις** {1x} **mĕtalēmpsis**, *met-al'-ampe-sis;* from *3335;* *participation:*—to be received + 1519 {1x}.

Metalempsis, as a noun, means "a participation, taking, receiving" and is used in 1 Ti 4:3, in connection with food, "to be received," literally, "with a view to [*eis*] reception: "Forbidding to marry, *and commanding* to abstain from meats, which God hath created to be received (*metalempsis*) with thanksgiving of them which believe and know the truth." Syn.: 324, 353, 354, 568, 588, 618, 1209, 1523, 1926, 2210, 2865, 2975, 2983, 3028, 3335, 3858, 3880, 3970, 4327, 4355, 4356, 4380, 4381, 4382, 5562, 5264, 5274. See: TDNT—4:10, 495; BAGD—511c; THAYER—405b.

3337. **μεταλλάσσω** {2x} **mĕtallassō**, *met-al-las'-so;* from *3326* and *236;* to *exchange:*—change {2x}.

This word means totally to surrender one thing for another; hence, change—give one thing for another, and exchange meaning a supposedly equivalent swap (Rom 1:25–26). See: TDNT—1:259, 40; BAGD—511c; THAYER—405b.

3338. **μεταμέλλομαι** {6x} **mĕtamĕllŏmai**, *met-am-el'-lom-ahee;* from *3326* and the mid. voice of *3199;* to *care afterwards,* i.e. *regret:*—repent {5x}, repent (one's) self {1x}.

Metamelomai, as a verb, means "to regret, to repent one," stresses a change of the will which results in change in single individual actions and is translated "to repent": "For though I made you sorry with a letter, I do not repent, though I did repent: for I perceive that the same epistle hath made you sorry, though *it were* but for a season" (2 Cor 7:8 twice). Syn.: 278. cf. 3340 for discussion. See: TDNT—4:626, 589; BAGD—511c; THAYER—405b.

3339. **μεταμορφόω** {4x} **mĕtamŏrphŏō**, *met-am-or-fŏ'-o;* from *3326* and *3445;* to *transform* (lit. or fig. "metamorphose"):—change {1x}, transfigure {2x}, transform {1x}.

Metamorphoo, as a verb, means "to change into another form" (*meta,* implying change, and *morphe,* "form", is used in the passive voice **(1)** of Christ's "transfiguration," Mt 17:2; Mk 9:2; Lk (in 9:29) avoids this term, which might have suggested to Gentile readers the metamorphoses of heathen gods, and uses the phrase *egeneto heteron,* "was altered", lit., "became (*ginomai*) different (*heteros*)"; **(2)** of believers, Rom 12:2, "be ye transformed," the obligation being to undergo a complete change which, under the power of God, will find expression in character and conduct; *morphe* lays stress on the inward change, *schema* (see the preceding verb in that verse, *suschematizo*) lays stress on the outward; the present continuous tenses indicate a process; **(3)** 2 Cor 3:18 describes believers as being "are changed into the same image" (i.e., of Christ in all His moral excellencies), the change being effected by the Holy Spirit. See: TDNT—4:755, 607; BAGD—511d; THAYER—405c.

3340. **μετανοέω** {34x} **mĕtanŏĕō**, *met-an-ŏ-eh'-o;* from *3326* and *3539;* to *think differently* or *afterwards,* i.e. *reconsider* (mor. *feel compunction*):—repent {34x}.

Metanoeo, lit., "to perceive afterwards" (*meta,* "after," implying "change," *noeo,* "to perceive"; *nous,* "the mind, the seat of moral reflection"), in contrast to *pronoeo,* "to perceive beforehand," hence signifies **(1)** "to change one's mind or purpose," **(1a)** always, in the NT, involving a change for the better, an amendment, and always, **(1b)** except in Lk 17:3, 4, of "repentance" from sin. **(2)** The word is found in the Synoptic Gospels (in Lk, nine times), in Acts five times, in the Apocalypse twelve times, eight in the messages to the churches, 2:5 (twice), 16, 21 (twice), "she repented not" (2nd part); 3:3, 19 (the only churches in those chapters which contain no exhortation in this respect are those at Smyrna and Philadelphia); **(3)** elsewhere only in 2 Cor 12:21. **(4)** The three steps found in *metanoeo* is **(4a)** new knowledge, **(4b)** regret for the previous course, displeasure with self, and **(4c)** a change of action. Syn.: *Metamellomai* (3338) refers to an emotional change, *metanoeo* to a change of choice; (3338) has reference to particulars, (3340) to the entire life, (3338) signifies nothing but regret even amounting to remorse, (3340) that reversal of moral purpose known as repentance. See: TDNT—4:975, 636; BAGD—511d; THAYER—405c.

3341. **μετάνοια** {24x} **mĕtanŏia**, *met-an'-oy-ah;* from *3340;* (subj.) *compunction* (for guilt, incl. *reformation*); by impl. *reversal* (of [another's] decision):—repentance {24x}.

Metanoia, as a noun, means "afterthought, change of mind, repentance," and **(1)** is used of "repentance" from sin or evil, except in Heb 12:17, where the word "repentance" seems to mean, not simply a change of Isaac's mind, but such a change as would reverse the effects of his own previous state of mind. Esau's birthright-bargain could not be recalled; it involved an irretrievable loss. **(2)** As regards "repentance" from sin, **(2a)** the requirement by God on man's part is set forth, e.g., in Mt 3:8; Lk 3:8; Acts 20:21; 26:20; **(2b)** the mercy of God in giving "repentance" or leading men to it is set forth, e.g., in Acts 5:31; 11:18; Rom 2:4; 2 Ti 2:25.

(3) NOTE: In the OT, "repentance" **(3a)** with reference to sin is not so prominent as that change of mind or purpose, out of pity for those who have been affected by one's action, or in whom the results of the action have not fulfilled expectations, a "repentance" attributed both to God and to man, e.g., Gen 6:6; Ex 32:14 (that this does not imply anything contrary to God's immutability, but that the aspect of His mind is changed toward an object that has itself changed. **(3b)** In the NT the subject chiefly has reference to "repentance" from sin, and this change of mind involves both a turning from sin and a turning to God. **(3b1)** The parable of the Prodigal Son is an outstanding illustration of this. **(3b2)** Christ began His ministry with a call to "repentance," Mt 4:17, but the call is addressed, not as in the OT to the nation, but to the individual. **(3b3)** In the Gospel of John, as distinct from the Synoptic Gospels, referred to above, "repentance" is not mentioned, even in connection with John the Baptist's preaching; in John's gospel and 1st epistle the effects are stressed, e.g., in the new birth, and, generally, in the active turning from sin to God by the exercise of faith (Jn 3:3; 9:38; 1 Jn 1:9), as in the NT in general. See: TDNT—4:975, 636; BAGD—512c; THAYER—405d.

3342. **μεταξύ** {9x} **mĕtaxu**, *met-ax-oo';* from *3326* and a form of *4862;* *betwixt* (of place or pers.); (of time) as adj. *intervening,* or (by impl.) *adjoining:*—between {6x}, mean while {2x}, next {1x}.

Metaxu, "in the midst, or between", is used as a preposition, **(1)** of mutual relation, Mt 18:15; Acts 15:9; Rom 2:15, "the meanwhile" lit., "between one another"; **(2)** of place, Mt 23:35; Lk 11:51; 16:26; Acts 12:6; **(3)** of time, "meanwhile," Jn 4:31. **(4)** In Acts 13:42, "the next Sabbath" implies "in the week between," the literal rendering. See: BAGD—512d; THAYER—406b.

3343. **μεταπέμπω** {8x} **mĕtapĕmpō**, *met-ap-emp'-o;* from *3326* and *3992;* to *send* from *elsewhere,* i.e. (mid. voice) to *summon* or *invite:*—call for {2x}, send for {6x}.

Metapempo, "to send after or for" (*meta,* "after," *pempo,* "to send"), in the middle voice, understood as "to fetch": **(1)** Peter, Acts 10:5, "call for", 22, "send for"; 29, "sent for"; 11:13, "call for"; and **(1)** Paul, Acts 24:24, "sent for"; 24:26, "sent for"; Acts 25:3, "send for." See: BAGD—513b; THAYER—406b.

3344. **μεταστρέφω** {3x} **mĕtastrĕphō**, *met-as-tref'-o;* from *3326* and *4762;* to *turn across,* i.e. *transmute* or (fig.) *corrupt:*—pervert {1x}, turn {2x}.

This word means to transform into something of an opposite character: **(1)** the Judaizers perverting the gospel of Christ (Gal 1:7); **(2)** the sun into darkness (Acts 2:20); **(3)** laughter into mourning and joy to heaviness (Jas 4:9). See: TDNT—7:729, 1093; BAGD—513b; THAYER—406b.

3345. **μετασχηματίζω** {5x} **mĕtaschēmatizō**, *met-askh-ay-mat-id'-zo;* from *3326* and a der. of *4976;* to *transfigure* or *disguise;* fig. to *apply* (by accommodation):—transform {2x}, transfer in a figure {1x}, transform (one's) self {1x}, change {1x}.

Metaschematizo, "to change in fashion or appearance" (*meta,* "after," here implying change, *schema*), is rendered **(1)** "shall change" in Phil 3:21, of the bodies of believers as changed or raised at the Lord's return; **(2)** in 2 Cor 11:13, 14, 15, to transform, of Satan and his human ministers, false apostles; **(3)** in 1 Cor 4:6 it is used by way of a rhetorical device, with the significance of transferring by a figure. Syn.: *Metamorphoo* (3339) refers to the permanent state to which a change takes place; whereas, *metaschematizo* (3345) refers to the transient condition from which a change happens. See: TDNT—7:957, 1129; BAGD—513b; THAYER—406c.

3346. **μετατίθημι** {6x} **mĕtatithēmi**, *met-at-ith'-ay-mee;* from *3326* and *5087;* to *transfer,* i.e. (lit.) *transport,* (by impl.) *exchange* (refl.) *change sides,* or (fig.) *pervert:*—carry over {1x}, change {1x}, remove {1x}, translate {2x}, turn {1x}.

Metatithemi, "to place among, put in another place" (*meta,* implying "change," and *tithemi,* "to put"), **(1)** "to remove a person or thing from one place to another", e.g., in Acts 7:16, "were carried over." It is also translated: **(2)** "to change", is said of priesthood, Heb 7:12; **(3)** "to change oneself," signifies, in the middle voice, and is so used in Gal. 1:6 "(I marvel that) ye are . . . removed"; the present tense suggests that the defection of the Galatians from the truth was not yet complete and would continue unless they changed their views. The middle voice indicates that they were themselves responsible for their decision, rather than the Judaizers who had influenced them. **(4)** "to translate" in Heb 11:5 (twice); and **(5)** "turning (the grace of God)" in Jude 4. See: TDNT—8:161, 1176; BAGD—513c; THAYER—406d.

3347. **μετέπειτα** {1x} **mĕtĕpĕita**, *met-ep'-i-tah;* from *3326* and *1899; thereafter:*—afterward {1x}.

Metepeita, "afterwards," without necessarily indicating an order of events is found in Heb 12:17. See: BAGD—514a; THAYER—406d.

3348. **μετέχω** {8x} **mĕtĕchō**, *met-ekh'-o;* from *3326* and *2192;* to *share* or *participate;* by impl. *belong* to, *eat* (or *drink*):—be partaker {5x}, pertain {1x}, take part {1x}, use {1x}.

Metecho, "to partake of, share in" (*meta,* "with," *echo,* "to have"), is translated **(1)** "be partaker of", **(1a)** lit "of partaking" in 1 Cor 9:10; **(1b)** "be partakers of" in 9:12; so in 10:17, 21; **(1c)** in 10:30 "partake"; **(2)** in Heb 2:14, "took part of", Christ "partook of" flesh and blood; **(3)** in Heb 5:13, metaphorically, of receiving elementary spiritual teaching, "useth of (milk)"; **(4)** in Heb 7:13, it is said of Christ (the antitype of Melchizedek) as "pertaineth to" another tribe than that of Levi. See: TDNT—2:830, 286; BAGD—514a; THAYER—406d.

3349. **μετεωρίζω** {1x} **mĕtĕōrizō**, *met-eh-o-rid'-zo;* from a compound of *3326* and a collat. form of *142* or perh. rather *109* (comp. "meteor"); to *raise in mid-air,* i.e. (fig.) *suspend* (pass. *fluctuate* or *be anxious*):—be of doubtful mind {1x}.

Meteorizo, from *meteoros* (Eng., "meteor"), signifying "in mid air, raised on high," was primarily used of putting a ship out to sea, or of "raising" fortifications, or of the "rising" of the wind. In the OT., it is used, e.g., in Mic 4:1, of the "exaltation" of the Lord's house; in Eze 10:16, of the "lifting" up of the wings of the cherubim; in Obad 4, of the "mounting" up of the eagle; in the NT metaphorically, of "being anxious," through a "distracted" state of mind, of "wavering" between hope and fear, Lk 12:29, "neither be ye of doubtful mind", addressed to those who have little faith. See: TDNT—4:630,*; BAGD—514a; THAYER—407a.

3350. **μετοικεσία** {4x} **mĕtŏikĕsia**, *met-oy-kes-ee'-ah;* from a der. of *3326* and *3624;* a *change of abode by force,* i.e. (spec.) *expatriation:*—carrying away into {2x}, carried away to {1x}, be brought to {1x}.

Metoikesia, "a change of abode, or a carrying away by force" (*meta,* implying "change," *oikia,* "a dwelling"), is used only of the carrying away to Babylon, Mt 1:11–12, 17. See: BAGD—514b; THAYER—407b.

3351. **μετοικίζω** {2x} **mĕtŏikizō**, *met-oy-kid'-zo;* from the same as *3350;* to *transfer* as a *settler* or *captive,* i.e *colonize* or *exile:*—carry away {1x}, remove into {1x}.

Metoikizo is used of the removal of Abraham into Canaan, Acts 7:4, and of the carrying of Judah into Babylon, 7:43. See: BAGD—514b; THAYER—407b.

3352. **μετοχή** {1x} **mĕtŏchē**, *met-okh-ay';* from *3348; participation,* i.e. *intercourse:*—fellowship {1x}. a sharing, communion, fellowship in 2 Cor 6:4. See: BAGD—514c; THAYER—407c.

3353. **μέτοχος** {6x} **mĕtŏchŏs**, *met'-okh-os;* from *3348; participant,* i.e. (as noun) a *sharer;* by impl. an *associate:*—fellow {1x}, partaker {4x}, partner {1x}.

Metochos, properly an adjective, signifying "sharing in, partaking of," is translated **(1)** "partners" in Lk 5:7; **(2)** "partakers" in Heb 3:1, 14; 6:4; 12:8; and **(3)** "fellows" in Heb 1:9, of those who share in a heavenly calling, or have held, or will hold, a regal position in relation to the earthly, messianic kingdom. See: TDNT—2:830, 286; BAGD—514c; THAYER—407c.

3354. **μετρέω** {10x} **mĕtrĕō**, *met-reh'-o;* from *3358;* to *measure* (i.e. ascertain in size by a fixed standard); by impl. to *admeasure* (i.e, allot by rule); fig. to *estimate:*—measure {7x}, mete {3x}.

Metreo, as a verb, means "to measure" and is used **(1)** of space, number, value: "And there was given me a reed like unto a rod: and the angel stood, saying, Rise, and measure the temple of God, and the altar, and them that worship therein" (Rev 11:1, cf. 11:2; 21:15, 16, 17); **(2)** metaphorically: **(2a)** "measuring [one's] self": "For we dare not make ourselves of the number, or compare ourselves with some that commend themselves: but they measuring themselves by themselves, and comparing themselves among themselves, are not wise" (2 Cor 10:12); **(2b)** in the sense of "measuring" out, giving by "measure": "For with what judgment ye judge, ye shall be judged: and with what measure ye mete (*metreo*), it shall be measured to you again" (Mt 7:2; cf. Mk 4:24; Lk 6:38). Syn.: 280, 488, 943, 2884, 3313, 3358, 4057, 4568, 5234, 5249, 5518. See: TDNT—4:632, 590; BAGD—514c; THAYER—497c.

3355. **μετρητής** {1x} **mĕtrētēs**, *met-ray-tace';* from *3354;* a *measurer,* i.e. (spec.) a certain standard *measure* of capacity for liquids:—firkin {1x}.

A liquid measure containing somewhat less the nine English gallons or about 40 liters, Jn 2:6. See: BAGD—514d; THAYER—407d.

3356. **μετριοπαθέω** {1x} **mĕtriŏpathĕō**, *met-ree-op-ath-eh'-o;* from a compound of the base of *3357* and *3806;* to *be moderate in passion,* i.e. *gentle* (to *treat indulgently*):—have compassion {1x}.

(1) This word means to be affected moderately or in due measure, yet preserving moderation in the passions, especially anger or grief. **(2)** This word means "to treat with mildness, or moderation, to bear gently with" (*metrios,* "moderate," and *pascho,* "to suffer"), is used in Heb. 5:2. **(3)** The idea is that of not being unduly disturbed by the faults and ignorance of others or rather perhaps of feeling in some measure, in contrast to the full feeling with expressed in the verb *sumpatheo* in 4:15, with reference to Christ as the High Priest. See: TDNT—5:938, 798; BAGD—514d; THAYER—407d.

3357. **μετρίως** {1x} **mĕtriōs**, *met-ree'-oce;* adv. from a der. of *3358; moderately,* i.e. *slightly:*—a little {1x}. See: BAGD—515a; THAYER—407d.

3358. **μέτρον** {13x} **mĕtrŏn**, *met'-ron;* an appar. primary word; a *measure* ("*metre*"), lit. or fig.; by impl. a limited *portion* (*degree*):—a measure {13x}.

Metron denotes **(1)** "that which is used for measuring, a measure," **(1a)** of "a vessel" figuratively: "Fill ye up then the measure of your fathers" (Mt 23: 32; cf. Lk 6:38 [twice]; **(1b)** in Jn 3:34, with the preposition *ek,* "He giveth not the Spirit *unto Him*" by measure." **(1b1)** Not only had Christ the Holy Spirit without "measure," but God so gives the Spirit through Him to others. **(1b2)** It is the ascended Christ who gives the Spirit to those who receive His testimony and set their seal to this, that God is true. **(1b3)** The Holy Spirit is imparted neither by degrees, nor in portions, as if He were merely an influence, He is bestowed personally upon each believer, at the time of the New Birth; **(2)** of "a graduated rod or rule for measuring," **(2a)** figuratively: "For with what judgment ye judge, ye shall be judged: and with what measure ye mete, it shall be measured to you again" (Mt 7:2; cf. Mk 4:24); **(2b)** literally: "And He that talked with me had a golden reed to measure the city, and the gates thereof, and the wall thereof" (Rev 21:15);

(3) "that which is measured, a determined extent, a portion measured off": **(3a)** of faith: "For I say, through the grace given unto me, to every man that is among you, not to think *of himself* more highly than he ought to think; but to think soberly, according as God hath dealt to every man the measure of faith" (Rom 12:3; cf. 2 Cor 10:13 [twice]; **(3b)** of grace: "But unto every one of us is given grace according to the measure of the gift of Christ" (Eph 4:7), the gift of grace is "measured" and given according to the will of Christ; whatever the endowment, His is the bestowment and the adjustment; **(3c)** Eph 4:13 "the measure (of the stature of the fullness of Christ)," the standard of spiritual stature being the fullness which is essentially Christ's; **(3d)** Eph 4:16, "according to the working in due measure of each several part," i.e., according to the effectual working of the ministration rendered in due "measure" by every part. Syn.: 280, 488, 943, 2884, 3313, 3354, 4057, 4568, 5234, 5249, 5518. See: TDNT—4:632, 590; BAGD—515a; THAYER—408a.

3359. **μέτωπον** {8x} **mĕtōpŏn**, *met'-o-pon;* from *3326* and ὤψ **ōps** (the *face*); the *forehead* (as *opposite,* the *countenance*):—forehead {8x}.

Metopon, from *meta,* "with," and *opo,* "an eye," occurs only in the Apocalypse, 7:3; 9:4; 13:16; 14:1, 9; 17:5; 20:4; 22:4. See: TDNT—4:635, 591; BAGD—515b; THAYER—408a.

3360. **μέχρι** {17x} **mĕchri** *mekh'-ree;* or **μεχρίς** **mĕchris**, *mekh-ris';* from *3372; as far as,* i.e. *up to* a certain point (as a prep. of extent [denoting the *terminus,* whereas *891* refers espec. to the *space* of time or place intervening] or a conjunc.):—unto {7x}, until {7x}, till {1x}, to {1x}, till + 3739 {1x}. See: BAGD—515b; THAYER—408b.

3361. **μή** {674x} **mē**, *may;* a primary particle of qualified *negation* (whereas *3756* expresses an absolute denial); (adv.) *not,* (conjunc.) *lest;* also (as an interrog. implying a *neg.*

answer [whereas *3756* expects an *affirmative* one]) *whether:*—not {487x}, no {44x}, that not {21x}, God forbid + 1096 {15x}, lest {14x}, neither {7x}, no man + 5100 {6x}, but {3x}, none {3x}, not translated {51x}, misc. {23x} = any, × forbear, + lack, never, nor, nothing, untaken, without. Often used in compounds in substantially the same relations. See also *3362, 3363, 3364, 3372, 3373, 3375, 3378.* See: BAGD—515d; THAYER—408b.

3362. **ἐὰν μή** {60x} **ĕan mē**, *eh-an' may;* i.e. *1437* and *3361; if not,* i.e. *unless:*—except {33x}, if not {16x}, whosoever not + 3739 {5x}, but {3x}, if no {1x}, not {1x}, before {1x}. See: BAGD—515d; 211c [1437]; THAYER—408d.

3363. **ἵνα μή** {97x} **hina mē** *hin'-ah may;* i.e. *2443* and *3361; in order* (or *so*) *that not:*—that not {45x}, lest {43x}, that . . . no {6x}, that nothing + 5100 {1x}, albeit not {1x}, so that not {1x}. See: BAGD—516a; THAYER—302c.

3364. **οὐ μή** {94x} **ŏu mē**, *oo may;* i.e. *3756* and *3361;* a double neg. streng. the denial; *not at all:*—not {56x}, in no wise {6x}, no {6x}, never + 1519 + 165 + 3588 {6x}, no more at all + 2089 {5x}, not tr. {1x}, misc. {14x} = any more, by any (no) means, neither, in no case, nor ever. See: BAGD—517c; THAYER—411b. comp. *3378.*

3365. **μηδαμῶς** {2x} **mēdamōs**, *may-dam-oce';* adv. from a compound of *3361* and ἀμός **amŏs** (*somebody*); *by no means:*—not so {2x}. See: BAGD—517d; THAYER—411b.

3366. **μηδέ** {57x} **mēdĕ**, *may-deh';* from *3361* and *1161; but not, not even;* in a continued negation, *nor:*—neither {32x}, nor {18x}, not {3x}, nor yet {1x}, not once {1x}, no not {1x}, not so much as {1x}. See: BAGD—517d; THAYER—411b.

3367. **μηδείς** {91x} **mēdĕis**, *may-dice';* incl. the irreg. fem. μηδεμία **mēdĕmia** *may-dem-ee'-ah;* and the neut. μηδέν **mēdĕn**, *may-den';* from *3361* and *1520; not even one* (man, woman, thing):—no man {32x}, nothing {27x}, no {16x}, none {6x}, not {1x}, anything {2x} misc. {7x} = not (at all, any man, a whit), + without delay.

This form is found, not in direct negative statements, but **(1)** in warnings, prohibitions, etc., e.g., Mt 27:19; Acts 19:36; **(2)** in expressions conveying certain impossibilities, e.g., Acts 4:21; **(3)** comparisons, e.g., 2 Cor 6:10; **(4)** intimating a supposition to the contrary, 1 Ti 6:4; **(5)** adverbially, e.g., 2 Cor 11:5, "not a whit." See: BAGD—518a; THAYER—411c.

3368. **μηδέποτε** {1x} **mēdĕpŏtĕ**, *may-dep'-ot-eh;* from *3366* and *4218; not even ever:*—never {1x}. See: BAGD—518b; THAYER—412a.

3369. **μηδέπω** {1x} **mēdĕpō**, *may-dep'-o;* from *3366* and *4452; not even yet:*—not as yet {1x}. See: BAGD—518b; THAYER—412a.

3370. **Μῆδος** {1x} **Mēdŏs**, *may'-dos;* of for. or. [comp. 4074]; a *Median,* or inhab. of Media:—Mede {1x}. See: BAGD—518b; THAYER—412a.

3371. **μηκέτι** {21x} **mēkĕti**, *may-ket'-ee;* from *3361* and *2089; no further:*—no more {7x}, no longer {4x}, henceforth not {2x}, no {1x}, no . . . henceforward {1x}, hereafter {1x}, misc. {5x} = any longer, not any more.

Meketi means "no more, no longer," but generally **(1)** suggests what is a matter of thought or supposition, whereas *eti* refers to what is a matter of fact. **(2)** It is rendered **(2a)** "any longer" in Acts 25:24; **(2b)** "no longer," in Mk 2:2, "no (room)"; **(2c)** 2 Cor 5:15, "not henceforth"; **(2d)** Eph 4:14, "no more"; 4:17, "henceforth . . . not"; **(2e)** "no longer", 1 Th 3:1, 5; 1 Tim. 5:23; 1 Pet 4:2. See: BAGD—518c; THAYER—412a.

3372. **μῆκος** {3x} **mēkŏs**, *may'-kos;* prob. akin to *3173; length* (lit. or fig.):—length {3x}.

Mekos, "length," from the same root as *makros,* "long", occurs in Eph 3:18 and Rev 21:16 (twice). See: BAGD—518c; THAYER—412b.

3373. **μηκύνω** {1x} **mēkunō**, *may-koo'-no;* from *3372;* to *lengthen,* i.e. (mid. voice) to *enlarge:*—grow up {1x}.

Mekuno, "to grow long, lengthen, extend" (from *mekos,* "length"), is used of the "growth" of plants, in Mk 4:27. See: BAGD—518d; THAYER—412b.

3374. **μηλωτή** {1x} **mēlōtē**, *may-lo-tay';* from μῆλον **mēlŏn**, (a *sheep*); a *sheepskin:*—sheepskin {1x}. See: TDNT—4:637, 591; BAGD—518d; THAYER—412b.

3375. **μήν** {1x} **mēn**, *mane;* a stronger form of *3303;* a particle of affirmation (only with *2229*); *assuredly:*—surely + 2229 {1x}. See: BAGD—518d; THAYER—412c.

3376. **μήν** {18x} **mēn**, *mane;* a primary word; a *month:*—month {18x}.

Men, connected with *mene,* "the moon," akin to a Sanskrit root ma—, "to measure" (the Sanskrit *masa* denotes both moon and month, cf, e.g., Lat. *mensis,* Eng., "moon" and "month," the moon being in early times the measure of the "month"). **(1)** The interval between the 17th day of the second "month" (Gen 7:11) and the 17th day of the seventh "month," is said to be 150 days (8:3, 4), i.e., five months of 30 days each; hence the year would be 360 days (cf. Dan 7:25; 9:27; 12:7 with Rev 11:2–3; 12:6, 14; 13:5; whence we conclude that 3½ years or 42 months = 1260 days, i.e., one year = 360 days); this was the length of the old Egyptian year; later, five days were added to correspond to the solar year. The Hebrew year was as nearly solar as was compatible with its commencement, coinciding with the new moon, or first day of the "month." This was a regular feast day, Num 10:10; 28:11–14; the Passover coincided with the full moon (the 14th of the month Abib). **(2)** Except in Gal 4:10; Jas 5:17; Rev 9:5, 10, 15; 11:2; 13:5; 22:2, the word is found only in Luke's writings, Lk 1:24, 26, 36, 56; 4:25; Acts 7:20; 18:11; 19:8; 20:3; 28:11, examples of Luke's care as to accuracy of detail. Syn.: 5072, 5150. See: TDNT—4:638, 591; BAGD—518d; THAYER—412c.

3377. **μηνύω** {4x} **mēnuō**, *may-noo'-o;* prob. from the same base as *3145* and *3415* (i.e. μάω **maō**, to *strive*); to *disclose* (through the idea of ment. *effort* and thus calling to *mind*), i.e. *report, declare, intimate:*—shew {3x}, tell {1x}.

Menuo, "to disclose, make known" (what was secret), is rendered **(1)** "to show" in Lk 20:37; 1 Cor 10:28; in a forensic sense, Jn 11:57; and **(2)** Acts 23:30, "it was told." See: BAGD—519a; THAYER—412c.

3378. **μὴ οὐκ** {6x} **mē ŏuk**, *may ook;* i.e. *3361* and *3756;* as interrog. and neg. *is it not that?:*—not {6x}. See: BAGD—519b; 517b; THAYER—412c. comp. *3364.*

3379. **μήποτε** {25x} **mēpŏtĕ**, *may'-pot-eh;* or **μή ποτε** **mē pŏtĕ**, *may pot'-eh;* from *3361* and *4218; not ever;* also *if* (or *lest*) *ever* (or *perhaps*):—lest {12x}, lest at any time {7x}, whether or not {1x}, lest haply + 2443 {1x}, if peradventure {1x}, no . . . not at all {1x}, not tr {1x}.

Mepote, lit., "lest ever," **(1)** "lest haply," e.g., Lk 14:29, of laying a foundation, with the possibility of being unable to finish the building; **(2)** Acts 5:39, of the possibility of being found fighting against God; **(3)** Heb 3:12, "lest " of the possibility of having an evil heart of unbelief; **(4)** "lest at any time", e.g., Mt 4:6; 5:25; 13:15; Mk 4:12; Lk 4:11; 21:34; Heb 2:1; **(5)** in 2 Ti 2:25, "if peradventure"; **(6)** in Jn 7:26, "Do." See: BAGD—519b; THAYER—412d.

3380. **μήπω** {2x} **mēpō**, *may'-po;* from *3361* and *4452; not yet:*—not yet {2x}. Cf. Rom 9:11; Heb 9:8. See: BAGD—519c; THAYER—413b.

3381. **μήπως** {12x} **mēpōs**, *may'-poce;* or **μή πως** **mē pōs**, *may poce;* from *3361* and *4458; lest somehow:*—lest {5x}, lest by any means {3x}, lest perhaps {1x}, lest haply {1x}, lest by some means {1x}, lest that by any means {1x}. See: BAGD—519c; THAYER—413b.

3382. **μηρός** {1x} **mērŏs**, *may-ros';* perh. a primary word; a *thigh:*—thigh {1x}.

Meros occurs in Rev 19:16; Christ appears there in the manifestation of His judicial capacity and action hereafter as the executor of divine vengeance upon the foes of God; His name is spoken of figuratively as being upon His "thigh" (where the sword would be worn; cf. Ps 45:3), emblematic of His strength to tread down His foes, His action being the exhibition of His divine attributes of righteousness and power. See: BAGD—519d; THAYER—413c.

3383. **μήτε** {37x} **mētĕ**, *may'-teh;* from *3361* and *5037; not too,* i.e. (in continued negation) *neither* or *nor;* also, *not even:*—neither {20x}, nor {15x}, so much as {1x}, or {1x}. See: BAGD—519d; THAYER—413c.

3384. **μήτηρ** {85x} **mētēr**, *may'-tare;* appar. a primary word; a "*mother*" (lit. or fig., immed. or remote):—mother {85x}.

Meter is used **(1)** of the natural relationship (e.g., Mt 1:18; 2 Ti 1:5); **(2)** figuratively, **(2a)** of "one who takes the place of a mother," (Mt 12:49, 50; Mk 3:34, 35; Jn 19:27; Rom 16:13; 1 Ti 5:2); **(2b)** of "the heavenly and spiritual Jerusalem" (Gal 4:26, which is "free" not bound by law imposed externally, as under the Law of Moses), "which is our mother", i.e., of Christians, the metropolis, mother-city, used allegorically, just as the capital of a country is "the seat of its government, the center of its activities, and the place where the national characteristics are most fully expressed; **(3)** symbolically, of "Babylon" (Rev 17:5), as the source from which has proceeded the religious harlotry of mingling pagan rites and doctrines with the Christian faith. **(4)** Note: In Mk 16:1 the article, followed by the genitive case of the name "James," the word "mother" being omitted, is an idiomatic mode of expressing the phrase "the mother of James." See: TDNT—4:642, 592; BAGD—520a; THAYER—413d.

3385. **μήτι** {15x} **mēti**, *may'-tee;* from *3361* and the neut. of *5100; whether at all:*—not {2x}, not tr. {13x} [*the particle usually not expressed, except by the form of the question*]. See: BAGD—520b; THAYER—413d.

3386. **μήτιγε** {1x} **mētigĕ**, *may'-tig-eh;* from *3385* and *1065; not at all then,* i.e. *not to say* (*the rather still*):—how much more {1x}. See: BAGD—520b; THAYER—414a.

3387. **μήτις** {4x} **mētis**, *may'-tis;* or

μή τις **mē tis** *may tis;* from *3361* and *5100; whether any:*—any {2x}, any man {1x}, not tr. {1x} [*sometimes unexpressed except by the simple interrogative form of the sentence*]. See: BAGD—517b [3361]; THAYER—414a.

3388. **μήτρα** {2x} **mētra**, *may'-trah;* from *3384;* the *matrix:*—womb {2x}.

Metra, the matrix (akin to *meter* "a mother"), occurs in Lk 2:23; Rom. 4:19. See: BAGD—520b; THAYER—414a.

3389. **μητραλῴας** {1x} **mētralōias**, *may-tral-o'-as* or

μετρολῴας **mĕtrolōias**, *may-trol-o'-as;* from *3384* and the base of *257;* a *mother-thresher,* i.e. *matricide:*—murderers of mothers {1x}.

Metroloas, or *metraloas* denotes "a matricide" (1 Tim 1:9 "murderers of mothers"). See: BAGD—520c; THAYER—414a.

3390. **μητρόπολις** {1x} **mētrŏpŏlis**, *may-trop'-ol-is;* from *3384* and *4172;* a *mother city,* i.e. "*metropolis*":—chiefest city {1x}. See: BAGD—520c; THAYER—414a.

3391. **μία** {79x} **mia**, *mee'-ah;* irreg. fem. of *1520; one* or *first:*—one {62x}, first {8x}, a certain {4x}, a {3x}, the other {1x}, agree + 4160 + 1106 {1x}. See: BAGD—230d [1520]; THAYER—414a.

3392. **μιαίνω** {5x} **miainō**, *me-ah'-ee-no;* perh. a primary verb; to *sully* or *taint,* i.e. *contaminate* (cer. or mor.):—defile {5x}.

Miaino, primarily, "to stain, to tinge or dye with another color," as in the staining of a glass, hence, "to pollute, contaminate, soil, defile," is used **(1)** of "ceremonial defilement," Jn 18:28; cf. Lev 22.5, 8; Num 19:13, 20; **(2)** of "moral defilement," Titus 1:15 (twice); **(3)** Heb 12:15; "of moral and physical defilement," Jude 8. Syn.: *Miaino* (3392) means to stain, and differs from *moluno* (3435), to smear, not only in its primary and outward sense, but in the circumstance that (like Eng. "stain") it may be used in good part, while 3435 has no worthy reference. See: TDNT—4:644, 593; BAGD—520d; THAYER—414a.

3393. **μίασμα** {1x} **miasma**, *mee'-as-mah;* from *3392* ("*miasma*"); (mor.) *foulness* (prop. the effect):—pollution {1x}.

Miasma denotes the vices of the ungodly which contaminate a person in his interaction with the world, 2 Pet 2:20. See: TDNT—4:646, 593; BAGD—521a; THAYER—414b.

3394. **μιασμός** {1x} **miasmŏs**, *mee-as-mos';* from *3392;* (mor.) *contamination* (prop. the act of defiling):—uncleanness {1x}.

Miasmos, **(1)** primarily denotes "the act of defiling," the process, in contrast to the "defiling" thing (3393). **(2)** *Miasmos,* as a noun, is rendered "uncleanness" in 2 Pet 2:10: "But chiefly them that walk after the flesh in the lust of uncleanness (*miasmos*), and despise government. Presumptuous *are they,* self-willed, they are not afraid to speak evil of dignities." Syn.: 167, 169, 2839, 2840. See: TDNT—4:647, 593; BAGD—521a; THAYER—414b.

3395. **μίγμα** {1x} **migma**, *mig'-mah;* from *3396;* a *compound:*—mixture {1x}. See: BAGD—521a; THAYER—414c.

3396. **μίγνυμι** {4x} **mignumi**, *mig'-noo-mee;* a primary verb; to *mix:*—mingle {4x}.

Mignumi, "to mix, mingle" (from a root *mik;* Eng., "mix" is akin), is always in the NT translated "to mingle," Mt 27:34; Lk 13:1; Rev 8:7; 15:2. Syn.: *Keramos* (2766) denotes in a strict sense, mixing as combines the ingredients into a new compound, chemical mixture, inseparable. *Mignumi* denotes such a mixture as merely blending or intermingling of them promiscuously, as in a mechanical mixture; hence, separable. See: BAGD—521a; 499c; THAYER—414c.

3397. **μικρόν** {16x} **mikrŏn**, *mik-ron';* masc. or neut. sing. of *3398* (as noun); a *small* space of *time* or *degree:*—a little while {9x}, a little {6x}, a while {1x}.

Mikron, the neuter of *mikros* (3398) is used adverbially **(1)** of distance, Mt 26:39; Mk 14:35; **(2)** of quantity, 2 Cor 11:1, 16; **(3)** of time, Mt 26:73, "a while"; Mk 14:70; Jn 13:33, "a little while", 14:19; 16:16–19; Heb 10:37, with the repeated *hoson,* "how very," lit., "a little while, how little, how little!" See: BAGD—521b; THAYER—414c.

3398. **μικρός** {30x} **mikrŏs**, *mik-ros';* incl. the comp.

μικρότερος **mikrŏtĕrŏs**, *mik-rot'-er-os;* appar. a primary word; *small* (in size, quantity, number or (fig.) dignity):—least {6x}, less {2x}, little {14x}, small {6x}.

Mikron, "little, small" (the opposite of *megos,* "great"), is used **(1)** of persons, with regard to **(1a)** station, or age, in the singular, Mk 15:40, of James "the less", possibly referring to age; Lk 19.3, in the plural, "little" ones, Mt 18:6, 10, 14; Mk 9:42; **(1b)** rank or influence, e.g., Mt 10:42 (see context); Acts 8:10; 26:22, "small," as in Rev 11:18; 13:16; 19:5, 18; 20:12; **(2)** of things, with regard to **(2a)** size, e.g., Jas. 3:5; **(2b)** quantity, Lk 12:32; 1 Cor 5:6; Gal 5:9; Rev 3:8; **(2c)** time, Jn 7:33; 12:35; Rev 6:11; 20:3. See: TDNT—4:648, 593; BAGD—521b; THAYER—414c.

3399. **Μίλητος** {3x} **Milētŏs**, *mil'-ay-tos;* of uncert. or.; *Miletus,* a city of Asia Minor:—Miletus {2x}, Miletum {1x}. See: BAGD—521d; THAYER—414d.

3400. **μίλιον** {1x} **miliŏn**, *mil'-ee-on;* of Lat. or.; a *thousand* paces, i.e. a "*mile*":—mile {1x}.

A mile, among the Romans, is the distance of a thousand paces or eight stadia, about 1.5 km [somewhat less than our mile], Mt 5:41. See: BAGD—521d; THAYER—414d.

3401. **μιμέομαι** {4x} **mimĕŏmai**, *mim-eh'-om-ahee;* mid. voice from μῖμος **mimŏs** (a "*mimic*"); to *imitate:*—follow {4x}.

(1) This verb is always used in exhortations, and always in the continuous tense, suggesting a constant habit or practice. **(2)** *Mimeomai,* "a mimic, an actor" (Eng., "mime," etc.), is translated "to follow," **(2a)** of imitating the conduct of missionaries, 2 Th 3:7, 9; **(2b)** the faith of spiritual guides, Heb 13:7; **(2c)** that which is good, 3 Jn 11. See: TDNT—4:659, 594; BAGD—521d; THAYER—414d.

3402. **μιμητής** {7x} **mimētēs**, *mim-ay-tace';* from *3401;* an *imitator:*—follower {7x}.

Mimetes, "a follower," is always used in a good sense in the NT. **(1)** In 1 Cor 4:16; 11:1; Eph 5:1; Heb 6:12, it is used in exhortations, accompanied by the verb *ginomai,* "to be, become," and in the continuous tense (except in Heb 6:12, where the aorist or momentary tense indicates a decisive act with permanent results); **(2)** in 1 Th 1:6; 2:14, the accompanying verb is in the aorist tense, referring to the definite act of conversion in the past. **(3)** These instances, coupled with the continuous tenses referred to, teach that what we became at conversion we must diligently continue to be thereafter. See: TDNT—4:659, 594; BAGD—522a; THAYER—415a.

3403. **μιμνήσκω** {2x} **mimnēskō**, *mim-nace'-ko;* a prol. form of *3415* (from which some of the tenses are borrowed); to *remind,* i.e. (mid. voice) to *recall to mind:*—be mindful {1x}, remember {1x}.

Mimnesko, from the older form *mnaomai,* in the active voice signifies "to remind"; in the middle voice, "to remind oneself of," hence, "to remember, to be mindful of"; the later form is found only in the present tense, **(1)** in Heb 2:6, "are mindful of," and **(2)** 13:3, "remember." **(3)** By comparison, the perfect tense in 1 Cor 11:2 and in 2 Ti 1:4, "being mindful of", is used with a present meaning. **(4)** See also **(4a)** Lk 1:54, "in remembrance of"; **(4b)** 2 Pet 3:2, "be mindful of"; **(4c)** Rev 16:19 (passive voice), "came in remembrance". **(4d)** The passive voice is used also in Acts 10:31, "are had in remembrance." See: BAGD—522b; THAYER—415a.

3404. **μισέω** {42x} **misĕō**, *mis-eh'-o;* from a primary μῖσος **misŏs** (*hatred*); to *detest* (espec. to *persecute*); by extens. to *love less:*—hate {41x}, hateful {1x}.

Summary: *Miseo* basically means having a relative preference for one thing over another, by way of expressing either aversion from, or disregard for, the claims of one person or thing relatively to those of another. It may work itself in strong emotion, but not necessarily (Mt 6:24; Lk 16:13; Lk 14:26; Jn 12:25). *Miseo,* as a verb, means "to hate," is used especially **(1)** of malicious and unjustifiable feelings towards others, whether towards the innocent or by mutual animosity, e.g., Mt 10:22; 24:10; Lk 6:22, 27; 19:14; Jn 3:20, of "hating" the light (metaphorically); 7:7; 15:18, 19, 23–25; Titus 3:3; 1 Jn 2:9, 11; 3:13, 15; 4:20; Rev 18:2, where "hateful" translates the perfect participle passive voice of the verb, lit., "hated," or "having been hated"; **(2)** of a right feeling of aversion from what is evil; **(2a)** said of wrongdoing, Rom 7:15; **(2b)** iniquity, Heb 1:9; **(2c)** "the garment (figurative) spotted by the flesh," Jude 23; **(2d)** "the works of the Nicolaitans," Rev 2:6, 15;

(3) of relative preference for one thing over another, by way of expressing either aversion from, or disregard for, the claims of one person or thing relatively to those of another, **(3a)** Mt 6:24, and Lk 16:13, as to the impossibility of serving two masters; **(3b)** Lk 14:26, as to the claims of parents relatively to those of Christ; **(3c)** Jn 12:25, of disregard for one's life relatively to the claims of Christ; **(3d)** Eph 5:29, negatively, of one's flesh, i.e. of one's own, and therefore a man's wife as one with him; **(3e)** Rom 9:13, of God "hating" Esau. No emotions are involved here, just God's sovereign choice. **(4)** In 1 Jn 3:15, he who "hates" his brother is called a murderer; for the sin lies in the inward disposition, of which the act is only the outward expression. Syn.: 2189, 2319, 4767. See: TDNT—4:683, 597; BAGD—522c; THAYER—415b.

3405. **μισθαποδοσία** {3x} **misthapŏdŏsia**, *mis-thap-od-os-ee'-ah;* from *3406; requital* (good or bad):—recompence of reward {3x}.

This noun stands for payment of wages due, recompence. Cf. Heb 22:2; 10:35; 11:26. See: TDNT—4:695, 599; BAGD—523a; THAYER—415c.

3406. **μισθαποδότης** {1x} **misthapŏdŏtēs**, *mis-thap-od-ot'-ace;* from *3409* and *591;* a *renumerator:*—rewarder {1x}.

See: TDNT—4:695, 599; BAGD—523a; THAYER—415c.

3407. **μίσθιος** {2x} **misthiŏs**, *mis'-thee-os;* from *3408;* a *wage-earner:*—hired servant {2x}.

Misthios, an adjective, signifying "a hired servant," is used in Lk 15:17, 19. See: TDNT—4:695, 599; BAGD—523a; THAYER—415c.

3408. **μισθός** {29x} **misthŏs**, *mis-thos';* appar. a primary word; *pay* for services (lit. or fig.), good or bad:—hire {3x}, reward {24x}, wages {2x}.

Misthos, primarily "wages, hire," and then, generally, "reward," **(1)** received in this life, Mt 5:46; 6:2, 5, 16; Rom 4:4; 1 Cor 9:17, 18; of evil "rewards," Acts 1:18; **(2)** to be received hereafter, Mt 5:12; 10:41 (twice), 42; Mk 9:41; Lk 6:23, 35; 1 Cor 3:8, 14; 2 Jn 8; Rev 11:18; 22:12. See: TDNT—4:695, 599; BAGD—523b; THAYER—415c.

3409. **μισθόω** {2x} **misthŏō**, *mis-thŏ'-o;* from *3408;* to *let* out for wages, i.e. (mid. voice) to *hire:*—hire {2x}.

Misthoo, "to let out for hire," is used in the middle voice, signifying "to hire, to engage the services of anyone by contract," Mt 20:1, 7. See: TDNT—4:695, 599; BAGD—523d; THAYER—415d.

3410. **μίσθωμα** {1x} **misthōma**, *mis'-tho-mah;* from *3409;* a *rented* building:—hired house {1x}.

Misthoma, primarily, "a price, a hire" (akin to *misthos,* "wages, hire" and *misthoo,* "to let out for hire") is used in Acts 28:30 to denote "a hired dwelling." See: BAGD—523d; THAYER—415d.

3411. **μισθωτός** {4x} **misthōtŏs**, *mis-tho-tos';* from *3409;* a *wage-worker* (good or bad):—hired servant {1x}, hireling {3x}.

Misthotos, an adjective denoting "hired," is used as a noun, signifying "one who is hired," **(1)** "hired servants," Mk 1:20; **(2)** "hireling," Jn 10:12, 13 twice; here, it expresses, not only one who has no real interest in his duty (that may or may not be present in its use in Mk 1:20), but one who is unfaithful in the discharge of it; that sense attaches always to the word rendered "hireling." See: TDNT—4:695, 599; BAGD—523d; THAYER—415d.

3412. **Μιτυλήνη** {1x} **Mitulēnē**, *mit-oo-lay'-nay;* for μυτιλήνη **mutilēnē**, (*abounding in shell-fish*); *Mitylene* (or *Mytilene*), a town on the island of Lesbos:—Mitylene {1x}. See: BAGD—524a; THAYER—415d.

3413. **Μιχαήλ** {2x} **Michaēl**, *mikh-ah-ale';* of Heb. or. [4317]; *Michaël,* an archangel:—*Michael* {2x}. See: BAGD—524a; THAYER—415d.

3414. **μνᾶ** {9x} **mna**, *mnah;* of Lat. or.; a *mna* (i.e. *mina*), a certain *weight:*—pound {9x}.

In the NT, a weight and sum of money equal to 100 drachmae, one talent was 100 pounds, a pound equaled 10⅓ oz. (300 gm) and occurs in Lk 19:13, 16 (twice), 18 (twice), 20, 24 (twice), 25. See: BAGD—524a; THAYER—416a.

3415. **μνάομαι** {21x} **mnaŏmai**, *mnah'-om-ahee;* mid. voice of a der. of *3306* or perh. of the base of *3145* (through the idea of *fixture* in the mind or of mental *grasp*); to *bear in mind,* i.e. *recollect;* by impl. to *reward* or *punish:*—remember {16x}, be mindful {2x}, be had in remembrance {1x}, in remembrance {1x}, come in remembrance {1x}. See: BAGD—524b; THAYER—416a. comp. *3403.*

3416. **Μνάσων** {1x} **Mnasōn**, *mnah'-sohn;* of uncert. or.; *Mnason,* a Chr.:—*Mnason* {1x}. See: BAGD—524b; THAYER—416a.

3417. **μνεία** {7x} **mnĕia**, *mni'-ah;* from *3415* or *3403; recollection;* by impl. *recital:*—mention {4x}, remembrance {3x}.

Mneia, "remembrance, mention" (akin to *mimnesko,* "to remind, remember"), is always used in connection with prayer, and translated **(1)** "mention" in Rom 1:9; Eph 1:16; 1 Th 1:2; Philem 4, in each of which it is preceded by the verb to make; **(2)** "remembrance" in Phil 1:3; 1 Th 3:6; 2 Ti 1:3. See: TDNT—4:678, 596; BAGD—524b; THAYER—416a.

3418. **μνῆμα** {7x} **mnēma**, *mnay'-mah;* from *3415;* a *memorial,* i.e. sepulchral *monument* (*burial-place*):—grave {1x}, sepulchre {4x}, tomb {2x}.

This word first signified "a memorial" or "record of a thing or a dead person," then "a sepulchral monument," and hence "a tomb"; **(1)** it is rendered "graves" in Rev 11:9; **(2)** "tomb" or "tombs" in Mk 5: 5; Lk 8:27; and **(3)** "sepulcher" in Lk 23:53; 24:1; Acts 2:29; 7:16. See: TDNT—4:679, 596; BAGD—524c; THAYER—416a.

3419. **μνημεῖον** {42x} **mnēmĕiŏn**, *mnay-mi'-on;* from *3420;* a *remembrance,* i.e. *cenotaph* (*place of interment*):—grave {8x}, sepulchre {29x}, tomb {5x}.

Mnemeion, primarily denotes **(1)** "a memorial" (akin to *mnaomai,* "to remember"), then, **(1a)** "a monument" (the significance of the word rendered "sepulchres," in Lk 11:47), **(1b)** anything done to preserve the memory of things and persons; **(2)** it usually denotes a tomb, and is translated either "tomb" or "sepulchre" or "grave." **(3)** Apart from the Gospels, it is found only in Acts 13:29. Among the Hebrews it was generally a cavern, closed by a door or stone, often decorated. Cf. Mt 8:28; 27:60; 23:29; Mk 5:2; 6:29. Syn.: In English, a sepulchre is a general term designating a place for safekeeping, especially for safe keeping a dead body and may be decorated with something as a memorial, Mt 23:29. A grave is also a general word for a place where a dead is placed, but usually implying going/digging down into the earth, Mt 27:52. [cf. "the sea was his grave"]. A tomb is secured grave, usually implying something above ground, like a cave, where the body is sealed and lain with some kind of "memorial" marker placed upon it, Mt 27:60. See: TDNT—4:680, 596; BAGD—524c; THAYER—416b.

3420. **μνήμη** {1x} **mnēmē**, *mnay'-may;* from *3403; memory:*—remembrance {1x}.

Mneme denotes "a memory" (akin to *mnaomai*), "remembrance, mention," 2 Pet 1:15, "remembrance"; here, however, it is used with *poieo,* "to make" (middle voice), and some suggest that the meaning is "to make mention." See: TDNT—4:679, 596; BAGD—524d; THAYER—416b.

3421. **μνημονεύω** {21x} **mnēmŏnĕuō**, *mnay-mon-yoo'-o;* from a der. of *3420;* to *exercise memory,* i.e. *recollect;* by impl. to *punish;* also to *rehearse:*—make mention {1x}, be mindful {1x}, remember {19x}.

Mnemoneul signifies **(1)** "to call to mind, remember"; **(1a)** it is used absolutely in Mk 8:18; **(1b)** everywhere else it has an object, **(2)** persons, Lk 17:32; Gal 2:10; **(2a)** 2 Ti 2:8; Paul was not reminding Timothy (nor did he need to) that Christ was raised from the dead, **(2b)** what was needful for him was to "remember" (to keep in mind) the One who rose, the Source and Supplier of all his requirements; **(3)** things, e.g., Mt 16:9; Jn 15:20; 16:21; Acts 20:35; Col 4:18; 1 Th 1:3; 2:9; Heb 11:15, "had been mindful of"; 13:7; Rev 18:5; **(4)** a clause, representing a circumstance, etc., Jn 16:4; Acts 20:31; Eph 2:11; 2 Th 2:5; Rev 2:5; 3:3; **(5)** in Heb 11:22 it signifies "to make mention of." See: TDNT—4:682, 596; BAGD—525a; THAYER—416b.

3422. **μνημόσυνον** {3x} **mnēmŏsunŏn**, *mnay-mos'-oo-non;* from *3421;* a *reminder* (*memorandum*), i.e. *record:*—memorial {3x}.

This noun denotes a memorial, that which keeps alive the memory of someone or something (Mt 26:13; Mk 14:9; Acts 10:4). See: BAGD—525b; THAYER—416c.

3423. **μνηστεύω** {3x} **mnēstĕuō**, *mnace-tyoo'-o;* from a der. of *3415;* to *give a souvenir* (engagement present), i.e. *betroth:*—espouse {3x}.

Mneustos, in the active voice, signifies "to woo a woman and ask for her in marriage"; in the NT, only in the passive voice, "to be promised in marriage, to be betrothed," Mt 1:18; Lk 1:27; 2:5, "espoused". See: BAGD—525c; THAYER—416c.

3424. **μογιλάλος** {1x} **mŏgilalŏs**, *mog-il-al'-os;* from *3425* and *2980; hardly talking,* i.e. *dumb* (*tongue-tied*):—having an impediment in his speech.

Mogilalos denotes "speaking with difficulty" (*mogis,* "hardly," *laleo,* "to talk"), "stammering," Mk 7:32. See: BAGD—525c; THAYER—416d.

3425. **μόγις** {1x} **mŏgis**, *mog'-is;* adv. from a primary μόγος **mŏgŏs**, (*toil*); *with difficulty:*—hardly {1x}.

Mogis, "with labor, pain, trouble" (akin to *mogos,* "toil"), Lk 9:39. See: TDNT—4:735, 606; BAGD—525d; THAYER—416d.

3426. **μόδιος** {3x} **mŏdiŏs**, *mod'-ee-os;* of Lat. or.; a *modius,* i.e. certain measure for things dry (the quantity or the utensil):—bushel {3x}.

Modios was a dry measure containing about a peck, Mt 5:15; Mk 4:21; Lk 11:33. See: BAGD—525d; THAYER—416d.

3427. **μοί** {240x} **mŏi**, *moy;* the simpler form of *1698; to me:*—me {218x}, my {11x}, I {10x}, mine {1x}. See: BAGD—255b [1698]; THAYER—207c [1698].

3428. **μοιχαλίς** {7x} **mŏichalis**, *moy-khal-is';* a prol. form of the fem. of *3432;* an *adulteress* (lit. or fig.):—adulterous {3x}, adulteress {3x}, adultery {1x}.

Moichalis, "an adulteress," is used **(1)** in the natural sense, 2 Pet 2:14; Rom 7:3; **(2)** in the spiritual sense, Jas 4:4. **(3)** As in Israel the breach of their relationship with God through their idolatry, was described as "adultery" or "harlotry" (e.g., Eze 16:15; 23:43), so believers who cultivate friendship with the world, thus breaking their spiritual union with Christ, are spiritual "adulteresses," having been spiritually united to Him as wife to husband, Rom 7:4. **(4)** It is used adjectivally to describe the Jewish people in transferring their affections from God, Mt 12:39; 16:4; Mk 8:38. **(5)** In 2 Pet 2:14, "adultery." See: TDNT—4:729, 605; BAGD—526a; THAYER—416d.

3429. **μοιχάω** {6x} **mŏichaō**, *moy-khah'-o;* from *3432;* (mid. voice) to *commit adultery:*—commit adultery {6x}.

Moichao, used in the middle voice in the NT, is said **(1)** of men in Mt 5:32; 19:9; Mk 10:11; **(2)** of women in Mk 10:12. See: TDNT—4:729, 605; BAGD—526a; THAYER—417a.

3430. **μοιχεία** {4x} **mŏichĕia**, *moy-khi'-ah;* from *3431; adultery:*—adultery {4x}. Mt 15:19; Mk 7:21; Jn 8:3; Gal 5:19. See: TDNT—4:729, 605; BAGD—526b; THAYER—417a.

3431. **μοιχεύω** {14x} **mŏichĕuō**, *moy-khyoo'-o;* from *3432; to commit adultery:*—commit adultery {13x}, in adultery {1x}.

Moicheuo, is used in Mt 5:27–28; 19:18; Mk 10:19; Lk 16:18; 18:20; Jn 8:4; Rom 2:22; 13:9; Jas 2:11; in Rev 2:22, metaphorically, of those who are by a Jezebel's solicitations drawn away to idolatry. See: TDNT—4:729, 605; BAGD—526a; THAYER—417b.

3432. **μοιχός** {4x} **mŏichŏs**, *moy-khos';* perh. a primary word; a (male) *paramour;* fig. *apostate:*—adulterer {4x}.

Moichos denotes one "who has unlawful intercourse with the spouse of another" **(1)** literally, Lk 18:11; 1 Cor 6:9; Heb 13:4; **(2)** metaphorically, Jas 4:4. See: TDNT—4:729, 605; BAGD—526d; THAYER—417b.

3433. **μόλις** {6x} **mŏlis**, *mol'-is;* prob. by var. for *3425; with difficulty:*—scarce {2x}, scarcely {2x}, hardly {1x}, have much work + 2480 {1x}.

Molis signifies "with difficulty, hardly" (from *molos,* "toil"). **(1)** In Lk 9:39, it is rendered "hardly," of the "difficulty" in the departure of a devil. **(2)** In Acts 27:7, 8, 16, it has three different renderings, "scarce," "hardly," and "much work," respectively. **(3)** For its other meanings, "scarce, scarcely," see Acts 14:18; Rom 5:7; 1 Pet 4:18. See: TDNT—4:735, 606; BAGD—526d; THAYER—417b.

3434. **Μολόχ** {1x} **Mŏlŏch**, *mol-okh';* of Heb. or. [1132]; *Moloch* (i.e. *Molek*), an idol:—*Moloch* {1x}. See: BAGD—526d; THAYER—417b.

3435. **μολύνω** {3x} **mŏlunō**, *mol oo' no;* prob. from *3189;* to *soil* (fig.):—defile {3x}.

(1) Both the literal and figurative meanings of *moluno* are negative. **(2)** It properly denotes "to besmear," as with mud or filth, "to befoul." **(3)** It is used in the figurative sense, **(3a)** of a conscience "defiled" by sin, 1 Cor 8:7; **(3b)** of believers who have kept themselves (their "garments") from "defilement," Rev 3:4, and **(3c)** of those who have not "soiled" themselves by adultery or fornication, Rev 14:4. See: TDNT—4:736, 606; BAGD—526d; THAYER—417c.

3436. **μολυσμός** {1x} **mŏlusmŏs**, *mol-oos-mos';* from *3435;* a *stain;* i.e. (fig.) *immorality:*—filthiness {1x}.

Molsumos denotes "defilement," in the sense of an action by which anything is "defiled," 2 Cor 7:1. See: TDNT—4:737, 606; BAGD—527a; THAYER—417c.

3437. **μομφή** {1x} **mŏmphē**, *mom-fay';* from *3201; blame,* i.e. (by impl.) a *fault:*—quarrel {1x}.

Momphe denotes "blame" (akin to *memphomai*), "an occasion of complaint," Col 3:13, "quarrel." See: TDNT—4:571, 580; BAGD—527a; THAYER—417d.

3438. **μονή** {2x} **mŏnē**, *mon-ay';* from *3306;* a *staying,* i.e. *residence* (the act or the place):—abode {1x}, mansion {1x}.

Mone, "an abode", is found in **(1)** Jn 14:2, "mansions" (cf. Eng. "manse", a dwelling place for a minister), and **(2)** Jn 14:23, "abode." See: TDNT—4:579, 581; BAGD—527a; THAYER—417d.

3439. **μονογενής** {9x} **mŏnŏgĕnēs**, *mon-og-en-ace';* from *3441* and *1096; only-born,* i.e. *sole:*—only {2x}, only begotten {6x}, only child {1x}.

Monogenes is translated **(1)** "only" in **(1a)** Lk 7:12 of the widow of Nain's son; **(1b)** Lk 8:42 of Jairus' daughter; **(2)** "only begotten" **(2a)** of Jesus in Jn 1:14, 18; 3:16, 18; 1 Jn 4:9; **(2)** of Isaac in Heb 11:17; and **(3)** "only child" in Lk 9:38 of the devil-possessed child. **(4)** With reference to Christ, the phrase "the only begotten of (from) the Father," Jn 1:14, indicates that as the Son of God He was the sole representative of the Being and character of the One who sent Him. **(4a)** In the original the definite article is omitted both before "only begotten" and before "Father," and its absence in each case serves to lay stress upon the characteristics referred to in the terms used. **(4b)** The apostle's object is to demonstrate what sort of glory it was that he and his fellow apostles had seen. **(4c)** That he is not merely making a comparison with earthly relationships is indicated by *para,* "from." **(4d)** The glory was that of a unique relationship and the word "begotten" does not imply a beginning of His Sonship. **(4e)** It suggests relationship indeed, but must be distinguished from generation as applied to man.

(5) We can only rightly understand the term "the only begotten" when used of the Son, in the sense of un-originated relationship. **(5a)** The begetting is not an event of time, however remote, but a fact irrespective of time. **(5b)** The Christ did not become, but necessarily and eternally is the Son. He, a Person, possesses every attribute of pure Godhood. **(5c)** This necessitates eternity, absolute being; in this respect He is not 'after' the Father. **(6)** The expression also suggests the thought of the deepest affection, as in the case of the OT word *yachid,* variously rendered, **(6a)** "only one," Gen 22:2, 12; **(6b)** "only son," Jer 6:26; Amos 8:10; Zec 12:10; **(6c)** "only beloved," Prov 4:3, and **(6d)** "darling," Ps 22:20; 35:17. **(7)** In Jn 1:18 the clause "the only begotten son, which is in the bosom of the Father," expresses both His eternal union with the Father in the Godhead and the ineffable intimacy and love between them, the Son sharing all the Father's counsels and enjoying all His affections.

(8) In Jn 3:16 the statement, "God so loved the world that He gave His only begotten son," must not be taken to mean that Christ became the only begotten son by incarnation. **(8a)** The value and the greatness of the gift lay in the Sonship of Him who was given. **(8b)** His Sonship was not the effect of His being given. **(9)** In Jn 3:18 the phrase "the name of the only begotten son of God" lays stress upon the full revelation of God's character and will, His love and grace, as conveyed in the name of One who, being in a unique relationship to Him, was provided by Him as the object of faith. **(10)** In 1 Jn 4:9 the statement "God hath sent His only begotten son into the world" **(10a)** does not mean that God sent out into the world one who at His birth in Bethlehem had become His Son. **(10b)** Cf. the parallel statement, "God sent forth the Spirit of His Son," Gal 4:6, which could not mean that God sent forth One who became His Spirit when He sent Him. See: TDNT—4:737, 606; BAGD—527b; THAYER—417d.

3440. **μόνον** {66x} **mŏnŏn**, *mon'-on;* neut. of *3441* as adv.; *merely:*—alone {3x}, but {1x}, only {62x}. See: BAGD—527c, 528a; THAYER—418b.

3441. **μόνος** {47x} **mŏnŏs**, *mon'-os;* prob. from *3306; remaining,* i.e. *sole* or *single;* by impl. *mere:*—alone {21x}, only {24x}, by themselves {2x}. See: BAGD—527c; THAYER—418b.

3442. **μονόφθαλμος** {2x} **mŏnŏphthalmŏs**, *mon-of'-thal-mos;* from *3441* and *3788; one-eyed:*—with one eye {2x}.

Monophthalmos, "one-eyed, deprived of one eye", is used in the Lord's warning in Mt 18:9; Mk 9:47. See: BAGD—528b; THAYER—418c.

3443. **μονόω** {1x} **mŏnŏō**, *mon-ŏ'-o;* from *3441;* to *isolate,* i.e. *bereave:*—be desolate {1x}.

Monoo, "to leave alone" (akin to *monos,* "alone"), is used in 1 Ti 5:5, in the passive voice, but translated "desolate," lit., "was made desolate" or "left desolate." See: BAGD—528b; THAYER—418c.

3444. **μορφή** {3x} **mŏrphē**, *mor-fay';* perh. from the base of *3313* (through the idea of *adjustment* of parts); *shape;* fig. *nature:*—form {3x}.

Morphe denotes **(1)** "the special or characteristic form or feature" of a person or thing; **(2)** it is used with particular significance in the NT, only of Christ, **(2a)** in Phil 2:6, "being in the form of God," and **(2b)** 2:7 "taking the form of a servant." **(3)** An excellent definition of the word is: *morphe* is therefore properly the nature or essence, not in the abstract, but as actually subsisting in the individual, and retained as long as the individual itself exists. . . . **(3a)** Thus in the passage before us *morphe Theou* is the Divine nature actually and inseparably subsisting in the Person of Christ. . . . **(3b)** For the interpretation of 'the form of God' it is sufficient to say that **(3b1)** it includes the whole nature and essence of Deity, and is inseparable from them, since they could have no actual existence without it; and **(3b2)** that it does not include in itself anything 'accidental' or separable, such as particular modes of manifestation, or conditions of glory and majesty, which may at one time be attached to the 'form,' at another separated from it. . . . **(4)** The true meaning of *morphe* in the expression "form of God" is confirmed by its recurrence in the corresponding phrase, "form of a servant." It is universally admitted that the two phrases are directly antithetical, and that 'form' must therefore have the same sense in both. **(5)** The definition above mentioned applies to its use in Mark 16:12, as to the particular ways in which the Lord manifested Himself. Syn.: 2397. *Morphe* (3444) is intrinsic and essential; *schema* (4976) is that which is outward. See: TDNT—4:742, 607; BAGD—528b; THAYER—418c.

3445. **μορφόω** {1x} **mŏrphŏō**, *mor-fŏ'-o;* from the same as *3444;* to *fashion* (fig.):—form {1x}.

Morphoo refers, not to the external and transient, but to the inward and real; it is used in Gal 4:19, expressing the necessity of a change in character and conduct to correspond with inward spiritual condition, so that there may be moral conformity to Christ. See: TDNT—4:752, 607; BAGD—528c; THAYER—418d.

3446. **μόρφωσις** {2x} **mŏrphōsis**, *mor'-fo-sis;* from *3445; formation,* i.e. (by impl.) *appearance* (an outward *semblance* or [concr.] *formula*):—form {2x}.

Morphosis, "a form or outline," denotes, in the NT, "an image or impress, an outward semblance," **(1)** Rom 2:20, of knowledge of the truth; **(2)** 2 Ti 3:5, of godliness. Syn.: It is thus to be distinguished from *morphe;* it is used in almost the same sense as *schema,* "fashion", but is not so purely the outward "form" as *schema* is. See: TDNT—4:754, 607; BAGD—528c; THAYER—419a.

3447. **μοσχοποιέω** {1x} **mŏschŏpŏiĕō**, *mos-khop-oy-eh'-o;* from *3448* and *4160;* to *fabricate* the image of a *bullock:*—make a calf {1x}. See: BAGD—528c; THAYER—419a.

3448. **μόσχος** {6x} **mŏschŏs**, *mos'-khos;* prob. strengthened for ὄσχος **ŏschŏs** (a *shoot*); a young *bullock:*—calf {6x}.

Moschos primarily denotes "anything young," whether plants or the offspring of men or animals, the idea being that which is tender and delicate; hence "a calf, young bull, heifer," Lk 15:23, 27, 30; Heb 9:12, 19; Rev 4:7. See: TDNT—4:760, 610; BAGD—528c; THAYER—419a.

3449. **μόχθος** {3x} **mŏchthŏs**, *mokh'-thos;* from the base of *3425; toil,* i.e. (by impl.) *sadness:*—painfulness {1x}, travail {2x}.

Mochtos, "labor, involving painful effort," is rendered **(1)** "travail" in 1 Th 2:9 and 2 Th 3:8 where it stresses the toil involved in the work; and **(2)** "painfulness" in 2 Cor 11:27. Syn.: 2873, 4192. See: BAGD—528d; THAYER—419a.

3450. **μοῦ** {587x} **mŏu**, *moo;* the simpler form of *1700; of me:*—my {501x}, me {52x}, mine {19x}, I {11x}, mine own {4x}. See: BAGD—255c [1700]; THAYER—167b [1473].

3451. **μουσικός** {1x} **mŏusikŏs**, *moo-sik-os';* from Μοῦσα **Mŏusa**, (a *Muse*); "*musical*", i.e. (as noun) a *minstrel:*—musician {1x}.

Mousikos is found in Rev 18:22, "musicians"; inasmuch as other instrumentalists are mentioned, some word like "musicians" is necessary to make the distinction. Primarily the word denoted "devoted to the Muses" (the nine goddesses who presided over the principal departments of letters), and was used of anyone devoted to or skilled in arts and sciences, or "learned" implying the skill necessary to play an instrument; to make music. See: BAGD—528d; THAYER—419a.

3452. **μυελός** {1x} **muĕlŏs**, *moo-el-os';* perh. a primary word; the *marrow:*—marrow {1x}.

Muelos, "marrow," occurs in Heb 4:12, where, by a natural metaphor, the phraseology changes from the material to the spiritual. See: BAGD—528d; THAYER—419b.

3453. **μυέω** {1x} **muĕō**, *moo-eh'-o;* from the base of *3466;* to *initiate,* i.e. (by impl.) to *teach:*—instruct {1x}.

Mueo, as a verb, means "to initiate into mysteries" is translated "I am instructed" [passive voice, perfect tense] (Phil 4:12). Mysteries are not only for the initiated or special privileged people. In the NT it denotes one to whom God has revealed further details of His plan for all times; details previously only known to Him. Syn.: 198, 1097, 3129. See: TDNT—4:828, 615; BAGD—529a; THAYER—419b.

3454. **μῦθος** {5x} **muthŏs**, *moo'-thos;* perh. from the same as *3453* (through the idea of *tuition*); a *tale,* i.e. *fiction* ("*myth*"):—fable {5x}.

(1) *Muthos* is that which is a simple account which attempts to explain reality; yet is unreal and fabricated having only the appearance of truth, no truth actually contained therein. **(2)** It primarily signifies "speech, conversation." The first syllable comes from a root *mu*—, signifying "to close, keep secret, be dumb"; whence, *muo,* "to close" (eyes, mouth) and *musterion,* "a secret, a mystery"; hence, "a story, narrative, fable, fiction" (Eng., "myth"). **(3)** The word is used of gnostic errors and of Jewish and profane fables and genealogies, "fables", in 1 Ti 1:4; 4:7; 2 Ti 4:4; Titus 1:14; of fiction, in 2 Pet 1:16. See: TDNT—4:762, 610; BAGD—529a; THAYER—419b.

3455. **μυκάομαι** {1x} **mukaŏmai**, *moo-kah'-om-ahee;* from a presumed der. of μύζω **muzō** (to "*moo*"); to *bellow* (*roar*):—roar {1x}.

This word formerly was used of oxen, an onomatopoeic word, "to low, bellow," is used of a lion, Rev 10:3, roaring as a sign of conquering and to instill fear. See: BAGD—529b; THAYER—419b.

3456. **μυκτηρίζω** {1x} **muktērizō**, *mook-tay-rid'-zo;* from a der. of the base of *3455* (mean. *snout,* as that whence *lowing* proceeds); to *make mouths* at, i.e. *ridicule:*—mock {1x}.

Mukterizo, from *mukter,* "the nose," hence, "to turn up the nose at, sneer at, treat with contempt," is used in the passive voice in Gal 6:7, where the statement "God is not mocked" does not mean that men do not mock Him, they do; the apostle vividly contrasts the essential difference between God and man. It is impossible to impose upon Him who discerns the thoughts, the mockings and intents of the heart. See: TDNT—4:796, 614; BAGD—529b; THAYER—419c.

3457. **μυλικός** {1x} **mulikŏs**, *moo-lee-kos';* from *3458; belonging to a mill:*—millstone + 3037 {1x}. See: BAGD—529b; THAYER—419c.

3458. **μύλος** {4x} **mulŏs**, *moo'-los;* prob. ultimately from the base of *3433* (through the idea of *hardship*); a "*mill*", i.e. (by impl.) a *grinder* (*millstone*):—millstone + 3684 {2x}, millstone {2x}.

Mulos denotes **(1)** "a handmill," consisting of two circular stones, one above the other, the lower being fixed. >From the center of the lower a wooden pin passes through a hole in the upper, into which the grain is thrown, escaping as flour between the stones and falling on a prepared material below them. The handle is inserted into the upper stone near the circumference. Small stones could be turned by one woman (millgrinding was a work deemed fit only for women and slaves; cf. Judg 16:21); larger ones were turned by two (cf. Mt 24:41, under mill), or more. **(2)** Still larger ones were turned by an ass (*onikos*), **(2a)** Mt 18:6, "a millstone" ("a millstone turned by an ass"), indicating the immediate and overwhelming drowning of one who causes one young believer to stumble; **(2b)** "a stone of a mill," as in Lk 17:2; Rev 18:22. See: BAGD—529b; THAYER—419c.

3459. **μύλων** {1x} **mulōn**, *moo'-lone;* from *3458;* a *mill-house:*—mill {1x}.

Mulon denotes "a mill house," where the millstone is, Mt 24:41. See: BAGD—529c; THAYER—419c.

3460. **Μύρα** {1x} **Mura**, *moo'-rah;* of uncert. der.; *Myra,* a place in Asia Minor:—Myra {1x}. See: BAGD—529c; THAYER—419d.

3461. **μυρίας** {9x} **murias**, *moo-ree'-as;* from *3463;* a *ten-thousand;* by extens. a "*myriad*" or indef. number:—ten thousand times ten thousand {2x}, two hundred thousand thousand + 1417 {2x}, innumerable multitude {1x}, ten thousand {1x}, innumerable company {1x}, fifty thousand + 3902 {1x}, thousands {1x}.

Murias denotes either "ten thousand," or, "indefinitely, a myriad, a numberless host," in the plural, Acts 19:19; lit. "five ten-thousands," Rev 5:11; 9:16; in the following, used of vast numbers, Lk 12:1, "an innumerable multitude"; Acts 21:20, "thousands"; Heb 12:22, "innumerable hosts"; Jude 14, "ten thousands." See: BAGD—529c; THAYER—419d.

3462. **μυρίζω** {1x} **murizō**, *moo-rid'-zo;* from *3464;* to *apply* (perfumed) *unguent* to:—anoint {1x}.

Murizo, as a verb, is used of "anointing" the body for burial: (Mk 14:8). Syn.: 218, 1472, 1637, 2025, 3464, 5545, 5548. See: TDNT—4:800, 615; BAGD—529d; THAYER—419d.

3463. **μύριοι** {3x} **muriŏi**, *moo'-ree-oi;* plur. of an appar. primary word (prop. mean. *very many*); *ten thousand;* by extens. *innumerably* many:—ten thousand {3x}. See: BAGD—529d; THAYER—419d.

3464. **μύρον** {14x} **murŏn**, *moo'-ron;* prob. of for. or. [comp. 4753, *4666*]; "*myrrh*", i.e. (by impl.) fragrent and *perfumed oil:*—ointment {14x}.

Muron, a word derived by the ancients from *muro,* "to flow," or from *murra,* "myrrh-oil" (it is probably of foreign origin; see myrrh). The "ointment" is mentioned in the NT in connection with **(1)** the anointing of the Lord on the occasions recorded in Mt 26:7, 9, 12; Mk 14:3–4; Lk 7:37–38, 46; Jn 11:2; 12:3 (twice), 5. **(2)** The alabaster cruse mentioned in the passages in Mt, Mk and Lk was the best of its kind, and the spikenard was one of the costliest of perfumes. **(3)** "Ointments" were used in preparing a body for burial, Lk 23:56 ("ointments"). **(4)** Of the act of the woman mentioned in Mt 26:6–13, the Lord said, "she did it to prepare Me for burial"; her devotion led her to antedate the customary ritual after death, by showing both her affection and her understanding of what was impending. **(5)** For the use of the various kinds of "ointments" as articles of commerce, see Rev 18:13. Syn.: *Muron,* denotes "ointment." The distinction between this and *elaion,* "oil," is observable in Lk 7:46 in Christ's reproof of the Pharisee who, while desiring Him to eat with him, failed in the ordinary marks of courtesy; "My head with oil (1637 - *elaion*) thou didst not anoint (*aleipho*), but she hath anointed (*aleipho*) My feet with ointment" (3464 - *muron*). Syn. 3462. See: TDNT—4:800, 615; BAGD—529d; THAYER—419d.

3465. **Μυσία** {2x} **Musia**, *moo-see'-ah;* of uncert. or.; *Mysia,* a region of Asia Minor:—Mysia {2x}. See: BAGD—530a; THAYER—429a.

3466. **μυστήριον** {27x} **mustēriŏn**, *moos-tay'-ree-on;* from a der. of μύω **muō** (to *shut* the mouth); a *secret* or "*mystery*" (through the idea of *silence* imposed by *initiation* into relig. rites):—mystery {27x}.

Musterion, **(1)** In the NT it denotes, not the mysterious (as with the Eng. word), but that which, being outside the range of unassisted natural apprehension, can be made known only by divine revelation, and is made known in a manner and at a time appointed by God, and to those only who are illumined by His Spirit. **(1a)** In the ordinary sense a "mystery" implies knowledge withheld; **(1b)** its Scriptural significance is truth revealed. Hence the terms especially associated with the subject are "made known," "manifested," "revealed," "preached," "understand," "dispensation." **(2)** The definition given above may be best illustrated by the following passage: "*Even* the mystery which hath been hid from ages and from generations, but now is made manifest to His saints."

(3) It is used of: **(3a)** spiritual truth generally, as revealed in the gospel, 1 Cor 13:2; 14:2 [cf.

1 Ti 3:9]. **(3a1)** Among the ancient Greeks 'the mysteries' were religious rites and ceremonies practiced by secret societies into which any one who so desired might be received. **(3a2)** Those who were initiated into these 'mysteries' became possessors of certain knowledge, which was not imparted to the uninitiated, and were called 'the perfected,' cf. 1 Cor 2:6–16 where the Apostle has these 'mysteries' in mind and presents the gospel in contrast thereto; here 'the perfected' are, of course the believers, who alone can perceive the things revealed; **(3b)** Christ, who is God Himself revealed under the conditions of human life, Col 2:2; 4:3, and submitting even to death, 1 Cor 2:1, 7, but raised from among the dead, 1 Ti 3:16, that the will of God to coordinate the universe in Him, and subject it to Him, might in due time be accomplished, Eph 1:9 (cf. Rev 10:7), as is declared in the gospel Rom 16:25; Eph 6:19; **(3c)** the Church, which is Christ's Body, i.e., the union of redeemed men with God in Christ, Eph 5:32 [cf. Col 1:27]; **(3d)** the rapture into the presence of Christ of those members of the Church which is His Body who shall be alive on the earth at His Parousia, 1 Cor 15:51; **(3e)** the operation of those hidden forces that either retard or accelerate the Kingdom of Heaven (i.e., of God), Mt 13:11; Mk 4:11; **(3f)** the cause of the present condition of Israel, Rom 11:25; **(3g)** the spirit of disobedience to God, 2 Th 2:7; Rev 17:5, 7, cf. Eph 2:2. **(3h)** To these may be added the seven local churches, and their angels, seen in symbolism, Rev 1:20; **(3l)** the ways of God in grace, Eph 3:9. **(3j)** The word is used in a comprehensive way in 1 Cor 4:1. See: TDNT—4:802, 615; BAGD—530a; THAYER—420a.

3467. **μυωπάζω** {1x} **muōpazō**, *moo-ope-ad'-zo;* from a compound of the base of *3466* and ὤψ **ōps** (the *face;* from *3700*); to *shut* the *eyes,* i.e. *blink* (*see indistinctly*):—cannot see far off {1x}.

Muopazo, "to be short-sighted" (*muo,* "to shut," *ops,* "the eye"; cf. Eng., "myopy," "myopic"), occurs in 2Pet 1:9, "and cannot see afar off"; this does not contradict the preceding word "blind," it qualifies it; he of whom it is true is blind in that he cannot discern spiritual things, he is near-sighted in that he is occupied in regarding worldly affairs. See: BAGD—531a; THAYER—420c.

3468. **μώλωψ** {1x} **mōlōps**, *mo'-lopes;* from μῶλος **mōlŏs**, ("*moil;*" prob. akin to the base of *3433*) and prob. ὤψ **ōps**, (the *face;* from *3700*); a *mole* ("black eye") or *blow-mark:*—stripe {1x}.

Molops, "a bruise, a wound from a stripe," is used in 1 Pet 2:24 (from the OT of Is 53:5), lit., in the original, "by whose bruise," not referring to Christ's scourging, but figurative of the stroke of divine judgment administered vicariously to Him on the cross (a comforting reminder to these Christian servants, who were not infrequently buffeted, v. 20, by their masters). See: TDNT—4:829, 619; BAGD—531a; THAYER—420c.

3469. **μωμάομαι** {2x} **mōmaŏmai**, *mo-mah'-om-ahee;* from *3470;* to *carp* at, i.e. *censure* (*discredit*):—blame {2x}.

Momaomai, as a verb, means "to find fault with, to blame, or calumniate" is used **(1)** of the ministry of the gospel: "Giving no offence in any thing, that the ministry be not blamed [*momaomai*]" (2 Cor 6:3); and **(2)** of the ministration of financial help: "Avoiding this, that no man should blame [*momaomai*] us in this abundance which is administered by us" (2 Co 8:20). Syn.: 273, 274, 298, 299, 338, 410, 423, 2607, 3201. See: BAGD—531a; THAYER—420c.

3470. **μῶμος** {1x} **mōmŏs**, *mo'-mos;* perh. from *3201;* a *flaw* or *blot,* i.e. (fig.) *disgraceful* person:—blemish {1x}.

Momos signifies "a shame, a moral disgrace," metaphorical of the licentious, 2 Pet 2:13. See: TDNT—4:829, 619; BAGD—531a; THAYER—420c.

3471. **μωραίνω** {4x} **mōrainō**, *mo-rah'-ee-no;* from *3474;* to *become insipid;* fig. to *make* (pass. *act*) as a *simpleton:* become a fool {1x}, make foolish {1x}, lose savour {2x}.

Moraino is used **(1)** in the causal sense, "to make foolish," 1 Cor 1:20; **(2)** in the passive sense, "to become foolish," Rom 1:22; **(3)** in Mt 5:13 and Lk 14:34 it is said of salt that has lost its flavor, becoming tasteless, having lost the ability to make thirsty for spiritual truth and to preserve from further corruption. When salt is damp it clumps and looses its properties, much like when the believers "clump" and fail to give thirst to the world for Christ and fail to stop its ever-encroaching evil. See: TDNT—4:832, 620; BAGD—531b; THAYER—420c.

3472. **μωρία** {5x} **mōria**, *mo-ree'-ah;* from *3474; silliness,* i.e. *absurdity:*—foolishness {5x}.

Moria denotes "foolishness", and is used in 1 Cor 1:18, 21, 23; 2:14; 3:19. See: TDNT—4:832, 620; BAGD—531b; THAYER—420d.

3473. **μωρολογία** {1x} **mōrŏlŏgia**, *mo-rol-og-ee'-ah;* from a compound of *3474* and *3004; silly talk,* i.e. *buffoonery:*—foolish talking {1x}.

Morologia, (from *moros,* "foolish, dull, stupid," and *lego*), is used in Eph 5:4; it denotes more than mere idle "talk"; it is "that talk of fools which is foolishness and sin together." **(2)** Even though foolish, what is said, is still sin. Syn.: 148, 2160. See: TDNT—4:832, 620; BAGD—531b; THAYER—420d.

3474. **μωρός** {13x} **mōrŏs**, *mo-ros';* prob. from the base of *3466; dull* or *stupid* (as if *shut* up), i.e. *heedless,* (mor.) *blockhead,* (appar.) *absurd:*—fool {5x}, foolish {7x}, foolishness {1x}.

Moros primarily denotes **(1)** "dull, sluggish" (from a root *muh,* "to be silly"); hence, "stupid, foolish"; **(2)** it is used **(2a)** of persons, **(2a1)** Mt 5:22, "Thou fool"; here the word means morally worthless, a scoundrel, a more serious reproach than "*Raca*"; the latter scorns a man's mind and calls him stupid; *moros* scorns his heart and character; hence the Lord's more severe condemnation; **(2a2)** in Mt 7:26, "a foolish man"; 23:17, 19, "fools"; 25:2, 3, 8, "foolish"; **(2a3)** in 1 Cor 3:18, "a fool"; **(2a4)** the apostle Paul uses it of himself and his fellow-workers, in 1 Cor 4:10, "fools" (i.e., in the eyes of opponents); **(2b)** of things, **(2b1)** 2 Ti 2:23, "foolish and ignorant questionings"; so Titus 3:9; **(2b2)** in 1 Cor 1:25, "the foolishness of God," not *moria,* "foolishness" as a personal quality, but adjectivally, that which is considered by the ignorant as a "foolish" policy or mode of dealing, lit., "the foolish (thing)"; so in v. 27, "the foolish (things) of the world." See: TDNT—4:832, 620; BAGD—531c; THAYER—420d.

3475. **Μωσεύς** {80x} **Mōsĕus**, *moce-yoos';* or

Μωσῆς **Mōsēs**, *mo-sace';* or

Μωϋσῆς **Mōësēs**, *mo-oo-sace';* of Heb. or.; [4872]; *Moseus, Moses,* or *Moüses* (i.e. *Mosheh*), the Heb. lawgiver:—*Moses* {80x}. See: TDNT—4:848, 622; BAGD—531d; THAYER—420d.

N

3476. **Ναασσών** {3x} **Naassōn**, *nah-as-sone';* of Heb. or. [5177]; *Naasson* (i.e. *Nachshon*), an Isr.:—*Naasson.* See: BAGD—532a; THAYER—421b.

3477. **Ναγγαί** {1x} **Naggai**, *nang-gah'-ee;* prob. of Heb. or. [comp. *5052*]; *Nangæ* (i.e. perh. *Nogach*), an Isr.:—Nagge {1x}. See: BAGD—532a; THAYER—421b.

3478. **Ναζαρέθ** {12x} **Nazarĕth**, *nad-zar-eth';* or

Ναζαρέτ **Nazarĕt**, *nad-zar-et';* of uncert. der.; *Nazareth* or *Nazaret,* a place in Pal.:—*Nazareth* {12x}. See: BAGD—532a; THAYER—421b.

3479. **Ναζαρηνός** {4x} **Nazarēnŏs**, *nad-zar-ay-nos';* from *3478;* a *Nazarene,* i.e. inhab. of Nazareth:—of Nazareth {4x}. See: TDNT—4:874, 625; BAGD—532b; THAYER—422a.

3480. **Ναζωραῖος** {15x} **Nazōraiŏs**, *nad-zo-rah'-yos;* from *3478;* a *Nazoræan,* i.e. inhab. of Nazareth; by extens. a *Christian:*—Nazarene {2x}, of Nazareth {13x}. See: TDNT—4:874, 625; BAGD—532b; THAYER—422a.

3481. **Ναθάν** {1x} **Nathan**, *nath-an',* or

Ναθάμ **Natham**, *nath-am';* of Heb. or. [5416]; *Nathan,* an Isr.:—*Nathan* {1x}. See: BAGD—532d; THAYER—422b.

3482. **Ναθαναήλ** {6x} **Nathanaēl**, *nath-an-ah-ale';* of Heb. or. [5417]; *Nathanaël* (i.e. *Nathanel*), an Isr. and Chr.:—*Nathanael* {6x}. See: BAGD—532d; THAYER—422b.

3483. **ναί** {34x} **nai**, *nahee;* a primary particle of strong affirmation; *yes:*—yea {23x}, even so {5x}, yes {3x}, truth {1x}, verily {1x}, surely {1x}.

Nai, a particle of strong affirmation, is used **(1)** in answer to a question, Mt 9:28; 11:9; 13:51; 17:25; 21:16; Lk 7:26; Jn 11:27; 21:15, 16; Acts 5:8; 22:27; Rom 3:29; **(2)** in assent to an assertion, Mt 15:27, "truth"; Mk 7:28; Rev 14:13; 16:7, "even so"; **(3)** in confirmation of an assertion, Mt 11:26 and Lk 10:21 "even so"; Lk 11:51, "verily"; 12:5; Philem 20; **(4)** in solemn asseveration, Rev. 1:7 "even so"; 22:20, "surely"; **(5)** in repetition for emphasis, Mt 5:37; 2 Cor 1:17; Jas 5:12; **(6)** singly in contrast to *ou,* "nay," 2 Cor 1:18, 19 (twice), 20, "(the) yea." See: BAGD—532d; THAYER—422b.

3484. **Ναΐν** {1x} **Naïn**, *nah-in';* prob. of Heb. or. [comp. 4999]; *Naïn,* a place in Pal.:—*Nain* {1x}. See: BAGD—533b; THAYER—422c.

3485. **ναός** {46x} **naŏs**, *nah-os';* from a primary ναίω **naiō** (to *dwell*); a *fane, shrine, temple:*—shrine {1x}, temple {45x}.

Naos, "a shrine or sanctuary," was used **(1)** among the heathen, to denote the shrine containing the idol, Acts 17:24; 19:24 (in the latter, miniatures); **(2)** among the Jews, the sanctuary in the "Temple," **(2a)** into which only the priests could lawfully enter, e.g., Lk 1:9, 21, 22; **(2b)** Christ, as being of the tribe of Judah, and thus not being a priest while upon the earth (Heb 7:13, 14; 8:4), did not enter the *naos;* **(2c)** by Christ metaphorically, of His own physical body, Jn 2:19, 21; **(3)** in apostolic teaching, metaphorically, **(3a)** of the church, the mystical body of

Christ, Eph 2:21; **(3b)** of a local church, 1 Cor 3:16, 17; 2 Cor. 6:16; **(3c)** of the present body of the individual believer, 1 Cor 6:19; **(3d)** of the "Temple" seen in visions in the Apocalypse, 3:12; 7:15; 11:19; 14:15, 17; 15:5, 6, 8; 16:1, 17; **(3e)** of the Lord God Almighty and the Lamb, as the "Temple" of the new and heavenly Jerusalem, Rev 21:22. Syn.: *Hieron* (2411) refers to the whole sacred enclosure including the outer courts, porches, and porticoes (Mt 26:55; Lk 21:37; Jn 8:20). *Naos* refers to the temple itself, the proper habitation of God (Acts 7:38; 17:24; Mt 27:5). See: TDNT—4:880, 625; BAGD—533b; THAYER—422c. Comp *2411*.

3486. **Ναούμ** {1x} **Naŏum**, *nah-oom';* of Heb. or. [5151]; *Naüm* (i.e. *Nachum*), an Isr.:—Naum {1x}. See: BAGD—534a; THAYER—422d.

3487. **νάρδος** {2x} **nardŏs**, *nar'dos;* of for. or. [comp. 5373]; *"nard"*:—spikenard + 4101 {2x}.

Nardos, is "a fragrant oil," procured from the stem of an Indian plant. The Arabs call it the "Indian spike [hence, spike nard]." The adjective *pistikos* is attached to it in the NT, Mk 14:3; Jn 12:3; *pistikos,* i.e., the *Pistacia Terebinthus,* which grows in Cyprus, Syria, Palestine, etc., and yields a resin of very fragrant odor, and in such inconsiderable quantities as to be very costly. *Nard* was frequently mixed with aromatic ingredients . . . so when scented with the fragrant resin of the *pistake* it would quite well be called *nardos pistakes*. The oil used for the anointing of the Lord's head was worth about L/12, and must have been of the most valuable kind. See: BAGD—534a; THAYER—423a.

3488. **Νάρκισσος** {1x} **Narkissŏs**, *nar'-kis-sos;* a flower of the same name, from νάρκη **narkē** (*stupefaction,* as a "narcotic"); *Narcissus,* a Rom.:—Narcissus {1x}. See: BAGD—534b; THAYER—423a.

3489. **ναυαγέω** {2x} **nauagĕō**, *nŏw-ag-eh'-o;* from a compound of *3491* and *71;* to *be shipwrecked* (*stranded,* "navigate"), lit. or fig.:—make shipwreck {1x}, suffer shipwreck {1x}.

Nauageo signifies **(1)** literally, "to suffer shipwreck" (*naus,* "a ship," *agnumi,* "to break"), 2 Cor 11:25; **(2)** metaphorically, "to make shipwreck," 1 Ti 1:19, "concerning the faith," as the result of thrusting away a good conscience. See: TDNT—4:891, 627; BAGD—534b; THAYER—423a.

3490. **ναύκληρος** {1x} **nauklērŏs**, *nŏw'-klay-ros;* from *3491* and *2819* ("clerk"); a *captain:*—owner of a ship {1x}. See: BAGD—534b; THAYER—423b.

3491. **ναῦς** {1x} **naus**, *nŏwce;* from νάω **naō** or νέω **nĕō** (to *float*); a *boat* (of any size):—ship {1x}. See: BAGD—534c; THAYER—423b.

3492. **ναύτης** {3x} **nautēs**, *now'-tace;* from *3491;* a *boatman,* i.e. *seaman:*—sailor {1x}, shipman {1x}.

Nautes, "a seaman, mariner, sailor" (from *naus,* "a ship," Eng., "nautical"), is translated **(1)** "shipmen" in Acts 27:27, 30; and **(2)** "sailors" in Rev 18:17. See: BAGD—534c; THAYER—423b.

3493. **Ναχώρ** {1x} **Nachōr**, *nakh-ore';* of Heb. or. [5152]; *Nachor,* the grandfather of Abraham:—*Nachor* {1x}. See: BAGD—534c; THAYER—423b.

3494. **νεανίας** {5x} **nĕanias**, *neh-an-ee'-as;* from a der. of *3501;* a *youth* (up to about forty years):—young man {5x}.

Neanias, "a young man," occurs in Acts 7:58; 20:9; 23:17, 18; 23:22. See: BAGD—534c; THAYER—423b.

3495. **νεανίσκος** {10x} **nĕaniskŏs**, *neh-an-is'-kos;* from the same as *3494;* a *youth* (under forty):—young man {10x}.

*Neaniskos,*a diminutive of 3494, "a youth, a young man," occurs in Mt 19:20, 22; Mk 14:51 twice; 16:5; Lk 7:14; Acts 2:17; 5:10 (i.e., attendants); 1 Jn 2:13, 14, of the second branch of the spiritual family. See: BAGD—534c; THAYER—423b.

3496. **Νεάπολις** {1x} **Nĕapŏlis**, *neh-ap'-ol-is;* from *3501* and *4172; new town; Neäpolis,* a place in Macedonia:—*Neapolis* {1x}. See: BAGD—534c, 536b; THAYER—423c.

3497. **Νεεμάν** {1x} **Nĕĕman**, *neh-eh-man'* or **Ναιμάν** **Naïman**, *nah-ee-man';* of Heb. or. [5283]; *Neëman* (i.e. *Naaman*), a Syrian:—Naaman {1x}. See: BAGD—534d, 533b; THAYER—423c.

3498. **νεκρός** {132x} **nĕkrŏs**, *nek-ros';* from an appar. primary νέκυς **nĕkus** (a *corpse*); *dead* (lit. or fig.; also as noun):—dead {132x}.

Nekros is used of **(1)** the death of the body, cf. Jas 2:26, its most frequent sense; **(2)** the actual spiritual condition of unsaved men, Mt 8:22; Jn 5:25; Eph 2:1, 5; 5:14; Phil 3:11; Col 2:13; cf. Lk 15:24; **(3)** the ideal spiritual condition of believers in regard to sin, Rom 6:11; **(4)** a church in declension, inasmuch as in that state it is inactive and barren, Rev 3:1; **(5)** sin, which apart from law cannot produce a sense of guilt, Rom 7:8; **(6)** the body of the believer in contrast to his spirit, Rom 8:10; **(7)** the works of the Law, inasmuch as, however good in themselves, Rom 7:13, they cannot produce life, Heb 6:1; 9:14; **(8)** the faith that does not produce works, Jas 2:17, 26; cf. v. 20. See: TDNT—4:892, 627; BAGD—534d.

3499. **νεκρόω** {3x} **nĕkrŏō**, *nek-rŏ'-o;* from *3498;* to *deaden,* i.e. (fig.) to *subdue:*—be dead {2x}, mortify {1x}.

Nekroo, "to put to death," is used **(1)** in the active voice in the sense of destroying the strength of, depriving of power, with reference to the evil desires which work in the body, Col 3:5. **(2)** In the passive voice it is used of Abraham's body as being "as good as dead," Rom 4:19 with Heb 11:12. Syn.: 2289. See: TDNT—4:894, 627; BAGD—533c; THAYER—424a.

3500. **νέκρωσις** {2x} **nĕkrōsis**, *nek'-ro-sis;* from *3499; decease;* fig. *impotency:*—deadness {1x}, dying {1x}.

Nekrosis, "a putting to death", is rendered **(1)** "dying" in 2 Cor 4:10; **(2)** "deadness" in Rom 4:19, i.e., the state of being virtually "dead." See: TDNT—4:895, 627; BAGD—535c; THAYER—424a.

3501. **νέος** {24x} **nĕŏs**, *neh'-os;* incl. the comparative νεώτερος **nĕōtĕrŏs**, *neh-o'-ter-os;* a primary word; *"new"*, i.e. (of persons) *youthful,* or (of things) *fresh;* fig. *regenerate:*—new {11x}, younger {7x}, young man {2x}, new man {1x}, young women {1x}, younger man {1x}, young {1x}.

Neos (3501) signifies **(1)** "new" in respect of time, that which is recent; it is used **(1a)** of the young, and so translated, especially the comparative degree "younger"; **(1b)** accordingly what is *neos* may be a reproduction of the old in quality or character. **(2)** *Neos* and *kainos* (2537) are sometimes used of the same thing, but there is a difference, as already indicated. **(2a)** Thus the "new man" in Eph 2:15 (*kainos*) is "new" in differing in character; so in 4:24; **(2b)** but the "new man" in Col 3:10 (*neos*) stresses the fact of the believer's "new" experience, recently begun, and still proceeding. **(2c)** The old man in him . . . dates as far back as Adam; a new man has been born, who therefore is fitly so called" [i.e., *neos*].

(3) The "New" Covenant in Heb 12:24 is "new" (*neos*) compared with the Mosaic, nearly fifteen hundred years before; it is "new" (*kainos*) compared with the Mosaic, which is old in character, ineffective, 8:8, 13; 9:15. **(4)** The "new" wine of Mt 9:17; Mk 2:22; Lk 5:37–39, is *neos,* as being of recent production; the "new" wine of the kingdom, Mt 26:29; Mk 14:25, is *kainos,* since it will be of a different character from that of this world. **(5)** The rendering "new" (*neos*) is elsewhere used metaphorically in 1 Cor 5:7, "a new lump." **(6)** This word in the feminine plural, denotes "young women," Titus 2:4. Syn.: *Kainos* (2537) denotes the new primarily in reference to quality, the fresh, unworn; whereas, *neos* denotes the new primarily in reference to time, the young, recent. See: TDNT—4:896, 628; BAGD—535d; THAYER—424b.

3502. **νεοσσός** {1x} **nĕŏssŏs**, *neh-os-sos'* or **νοσσός** **nossos**, *nos-sos';* from *3501;* a *youngling* (*nestling*):—young {1x}. See: BAGD—536c, 543d; THAYER—424b.

3503. **νεότης** {5x} **nĕŏtēs**, *neh-ot'-ace;* from *3501; newness,* i.e. *youthfulness:*—youth {5x}.

Neotes, from *neos,* "new," occurs in Mk 10:20; Lk 18:21; Acts 26:4; 1 Ti 4:12; Mt 19:20). See: BAGD—536c; THAYER—424b.

3504. **νεόφυτος** {1x} **nĕŏphutŏs**, *neh-of'-oo-tos;* from *3501* and a der. of *5453; newly planted,* i.e. (fig.) a *young convert* (*"neophyte"*):—novice {1x}.

Neophutos, an adjective, lit., "newly-planted" (from *neos,* "new," and *phuo,* "to bring forth, produce"), denotes "a new convert, *neophyte,* novice," 1 Ti 3:6, of one who by inexperience is unfitted to act as a bishop or overseer in a church. See: BAGD—536c; THAYER—424b.

3505. **Νέρων** {1x} **Nĕrōn**, *ner'-ohn;* of Lat. or.; *Neron* (i.e. *Nero*), a Rom. emperor:—Nero {1x}. See: BAGD—536c; THAYER—424c.

3506. **νεύω** {2x} **nĕuō**, *nyoo'-o;* appar. a primary verb; to *"nod,"* i.e. (by anal.) *signal:*—beckon {2x}.

Literally, *neuo* means to give a nod, to signify by a nod and **(1)** is used in Jn 13:24 of Peter's beckoning to John to ask the Lord of whom He had been speaking; and **(2)** in Acts 24:10 of the intimation given by Felix to Paul to speak. See: BAGD—536d; THAYER—424c.

3507. **νεφέλη** {26x} **nĕphĕlē**, *nef-el'-ay;* from *3509;* prop. *cloudiness,* i.e. (concr.) a *cloud:*—cloud {26x}.

Nephele, "a definitely shaped cloud, or masses of clouds possessing definite form," is used, besides the physical element, **(1)** of the "cloud" on the mount of transfiguration, Mt 17:5; **(2)** of the "cloud" which covered Israel in the Red Sea, 1 Cor 10:1–2; **(3)** of "clouds" seen in the Apocalyptic visions, Rev 1:7; 10:1; 11:12; 14:14–16; **(4)** metaphorically in 2 Pet 2:17, of the evil workers there mentioned. See: TDNT—4:902, 628; BAGD—536d; THAYER—424c.

3508. **Νεφθαλείμ** {3x} **Nĕphthalĕim**, *nef-thal-ime';* of Heb. or. [5321]; *Nephthaleim* (i.e. *Naphthali*), a tribe in Pal.:—Nephthalim {3x}. See: BAGD—537a; THAYER—424c.

3509. **νέφος** {1x} **něphŏs**, *nef'-os;* appar. a primary word; a *cloud:*—cloud {1x}.

Nephos denotes "a cloudy, shapeless mass covering the heavens"; hence, metaphorically, of "a dense multitude, a throng," Heb 12:1. See: TDNT—4:902, 628; BAGD—537a; THAYER—424d.

3510. **νεφρός** {1x} **něphrŏs**, *nef-ros';* of uncert. aff.; a *kidney* (plur.), i.e. (fig.) the inmost *mind:*—reins {1x}.

Nephros is literally a kidney, usually in the plural, and is used metaphorically of the inmost thoughts, feelings, purposes, and will of the soul (Rev 2:23). So called because the two ureters from the kidneys to the bladder resemble reins (cf. Ps 7:9; Jer 11:20; 17:10; 20:12). See: TDNT—4:911, 630; BAGD—537a; THAYER—424d.

3511. **νεωκόρος** {1x} **něōkŏrŏs**, *neh-o-kor'-os;* from a form of *3485* and κορέω **kŏrěō** (to *sweep*); a *temple-servant,* i.e. (by impl.) a *votary:*—worshipper {1x}.

This word appears from coins still extant, it was an honourary title [temple-keeper or temple-warden] of certain cities, esp. in Asia Minor, or in which some special worship of some deity or even some deified human ruler had been established; used of Ephesus (Acts 19:35). See: BAGD—537b; THAYER—424d.

3512. **νεωτερικός** {1x} **něōtěrikŏs**, *neh-o-ter'-ik-os;* from the comparative of *3501; appertaining to younger* persons, i.e. *juvenile:*—youthful {1x}. See: BAGD—537b; THAYER—425a.

νεώτερος **něōtěrŏs**. See *3501*.

3513. **νή** {1x} **nē**, *nay;* prob. an intens. form of *3483;* a particle of attestation (accompanied by the obj. invoked or appealed to in confirmation); *as sure as:*—I protest by {1x}. See: BAGD—537b; THAYER—425a.

3514. **νήθω** {2x} **nēthō**, *nay'-tho;* from νέω **něō** (of like mean.); to *spin:*—spin {2x}.

This word means to spin as in making cloth, and is found in Mt 6:28 and Lk 12:27, of the lilies of the field. See: BAGD—537c; THAYER—425b.

3515. **νηπιάζω** {1x} **nēpiazō**, *nay-pee-ad'-zo;* from *3516; to act* as a *babe,* i.e. (fig.) *innocently:*—be a child {1x}. See: TDNT—4:912, 631; BAGD—537c; THAYER—425b.

3516. **νήπιος** {14x} **nēpiŏs**, *nay'-pee-os;* from an obs. particle νη- **nē-** (implying *negation*) and *2031; not speaking,* i.e. an *infant* (*minor*); fig. a *simple-minded* person, an *immature* Christian:—babe {6x}, child {7x}, childish {1x}.

(1) Literally, a *napios* was one without the power of speech, a little child; he can make sounds but not articulate speech. **(1a)** *Nepios,* lit., "without the power of speech," denotes "a little child," the literal meaning having been lost in the general use of the word. It is used **(1b)** of "infants," Mt 21:16; **(2)** metaphorically, of the unsophisticated in mind and trustful in disposition, Mt 11:25 and Lk 10:21, where it stands in contrast to the wise; **(2a)** of those who are possessed merely of natural knowledge, Rom 2:20; **(2b)** of those who are carnal, and have not grown, as they should have done, in spiritual understanding and power, the spiritually immature, 1 Cor 3:1; **(2c)** those who are so to speak partakers of milk, and "without experience of the word of righteousness," Heb 5:13; **(2d)** of the Jews, who, while the Law was in force, were in a state corresponding to that of childhood, or minority, just as the word "infant" is used of a minor, in English law, Gal 4:3, "children"; **(2e)** of believers in an immature condition, impressionable and liable to be imposed upon instead of being in a state of spiritual maturity, Eph 4:14, "children." **(3)** "Immaturity" is always associated with this word. Syn.: 1025. See: TDNT—4:912, 631; BAGD—537c; THAYER—425b.

3517. **Νηρεύς** {1x} **Nērěus**, *nare-yoos';* appar. from a der. of the base of *3491* (mean. *wet*); *Nereus,* a Chr.:—*Nereus* {1x}. See: BAGD—538a; THAYER—425b.

3518. **Νηρί** {1x} **Nēri**, *nay-ree';* of Heb. or. [5374]; *Neri* (i.e. *Nerijah*), an Isr.:—*Neri* {1x}. See: BAGD—538a; THAYER—425b.

3519. **νησίον** {1x} **nēsiŏn**, *nay-see'-on;* dimin. of *3520;* a small island, an *islet:*—island {1x}.

This is a small island, Cauda (Acts 27:16). See: BAGD—538a; THAYER—425b.

3520. **νῆσος** {9x} **nēsŏs**, *nay'-sos;* prob. from the base of *3491;* an *island:*—island {6x}, isle {3x}.

Nasos, "an island," occurs in Acts 13:6 "isle"; 27:26; 28:1, 7, 9, 11 "isle"; Rev 1:9 "isle"; 6:14; 16:20. See: BAGD—538a; THAYER—425b.

3521. **νηστεία** {8x} **nēstěia**, *nace-ti'-ah;* from *3522; abstinence* (from lack of food, or vol. and relig.); spec. the *fast* of the Day of Atonement:—fast {7x}, fasting {1x}.

Nesteia, "a fasting, fast" (from *ne,* a negative prefix, and *esthio,* "to eat"), is used **(1)** of voluntary abstinence from food, Mt 17:21; Mk 9:29; Lk 2:37; Acts 14:23; **(1a)** "fasting" had become a common practice among Jews, and **(1b)** was continued among Christians; **(2)** in Acts 27:9, "the Fast" refers to the Day of Atonement, Lev 16:29; that time of the year would be one of dangerous sailing; **(3)** of involuntary abstinence (perhaps voluntary is included), consequent upon trying circumstances, 2 Cor 6:5; 11:27. See: TDNT—4:924, 632; BAGD—538; THAYER—425b.

3522. **νηστεύω** {21x} **nēstěuō**, *nace-tyoo'-o;* from *3523;* to *abstain* from food (relig.):—fast {21x}.

Nesteuo, as a verb, means "to fast, to abstain from eating", and is used **(1)** of voluntary "fasting," Mt. 4:2; 6:16, 17, 18; 9:14, 15; Mk 2:18, 19, 20; Lk 5:33, 34, 35; 18:12; Acts 13:2, 3. **(2)** Some of these passages show that teachers to whom scholars or disciples were attached gave them special instructions as to "fasting." Christ taught the need of purity and simplicity of motive. **(3)** The answers of Christ to the questions of the disciples of John and of the Pharisees reveal His whole purpose and method. No doubt He and His followers observed such a fast as that on the Day of Atonement, but He imposed no frequent "fasts" in addition. What He taught was suitable to the change of character and purpose which He designed for His disciples. His claim to be the Bridegroom, Mt 9:15, and the reference there to the absence of "fasting," virtually involved a claim to be the Messiah (cf. Zec 8:19). Syn.: 777, 3521, 3523. See: TDNT—4:924, 632; BAGD—538b; THAYER—425c.

3523. **νῆστις** {2x} **nēstis**, *nace'-tis;* from the insep. neg. particle νη- **nē-**, (*not*) and *2068; not eating,* i.e. *abstinent* from food (relig.):—fasting {2x}.

Nestis, "not eating", "fasting," is used of lack of food, Mt 15:32; Mk 8:3. See: TDNT—4:924, 632; BAGD—538c; THAYER—425d.

3524. **νηφάλεος** {3x} **nēphalěŏs**, *nay-fal'-eh-os;* or

νηφάλιος **nēphaliŏs**, *nay-fal'-ee-os;* from *3525; sober,* i.e. (fig.) *circumspect:*—sober {2x}, vigilant {1x}.

Naphalios means **(1)** to abstain from wine or any substance that could cloud one's judgment. It is translated **(2)** "vigilant" in 1 Ti 3:2; and **(2)** in 1 Ti 3:11 and Titus 2:2, "sober." Syn.: 3525. See: TDNT—4:939, 633; BAGD—538d; THAYER—425d.

3525. **νήφω** {6x} **nēphō**, *nay'-fo;* of uncert. aff.: to *abstain* from wine (*keep sober*), i.e. (fig.) *be discreet:*—be sober {4x}, watch {2x}.

Nepho signifies **(1)** "to be free from the influence of intoxicants"; **(2)** in the NT, metaphorically, it does not in itself imply watchfulness, but is used **(3)** in association with it, 1 Th 5:6, 8; 2 Ti 4:5; 1 Pet 1:13; 4:7, "watch"; 5:8. See: TDNT—4:936, 633; BAGD—538d; THAYER—425d.

3526. **Νίγερ** {1x} **Nigěr**, *neeg'-er;* of Lat. or.; *black; Niger,* a Char.:—*Niger* {1x}. See: BAGD—539a; THAYER—425D.

3527. **Νικάνωρ** {1x} **Nikanōr**, *nik-an'-ore;* prob. from *3528; victorious; Nicanor,* a Chr.:—Nicanor {1x}. See: BAGD—539a; THAYER—425d.

3528. **νικάω** {28x} **nikaō**, *nik-ah'-o;* from *3529;* to *subdue* (lit. or fig.):—overcome {24x}, conquer {2x}, prevail {1x}, get the victory {1x}.

Nikao is used **(1)** of God, Rom 3:4 (a law term); **(2)** of Christ, Jn 16:33; Rev 3:21; 5:5; 17.14, **(3)** of His followers, Rom 12:21 (2nd part); 1 Jn 2:13–14; 4:4; 5:4–5; Rev 2:7, 11, 17, 26; 3:5, 12, 21; 12:11; 15:2; 21:7; **(4)** of faith, 1 Jn 5:4; **(5)** of evil (passive voice), Rom 12:21; **(6)** of predicted human potentates, Rev 6:2; 11:7; 13:7. See: TDNT—4:942, 634; BAGD—539a. THAYER—425d.

3529. **νίκη** {1x} **nikē**, *nee'-kay;* appar. a primary word; *conquest* (abstr.), i.e. (fig.) the *means of success:*—victory {1x}. See: TDNT—4:942, 634; BAGD—539c; THAYER—426a.

3530. **Νικόδημος** {5x} **Nikŏdēmŏs**, *nik-od'-ay-mos;* from *3534* and *1218; victorious* among his *people; Nicodemus,* an Isr.:—Nicodemus {5x}. See: TDNT—4:942, 634; BAGD—539c; THAYER—426b.

3531. **Νικολαΐτης** {2x} **Nikŏlaïtēs**, *nik-ol-ah-ee'-tace;* from *3532;* a *Nicolaïte,* i.e. adherent of *Nicolaüs:*—Nicolaitans {2x}. See: BAGD—539; THAYER—426b.

3532. **Νικόλαος** {1x} **Nikŏlaŏs**, *nik-ol'-ah-os;* from *3534* and *2992; victorious* over the *people; Nicolaüs,* a heretic:—Nicolaus {1x}. See: BAGD—539d; THAYER—426b.

3533. **Νικόπολις** {2x} **Nikŏpŏlis**, *nik-op'-ol-is;* from *3534* and *4172; victorious city; Nicopolis,* a place in Macedonia:—Nicopolis {2x}. See: BAGD—539d; THAYER—426b.

3534. **νῖκος** {4x} **nikŏs**, *nee'-kos;* from *3529;* a *conquest* (concr.), i.e. (by impl.) *triumph:*—victory {4x}.

Nikos, as a noun, means victory, utterly vanquished one's foes, is used in Mt 12:20; 1 Cor 15:54, 55, 57. See: TDNT—4:942, 634; BAGD—539d; THAYER—426c.

3535. **Νινευΐ** {1x} **Niněuï**, *nin-yoo-ee';* of Heb. or. [5210]; *Ninevi* (i.e. *Nineveh*), the capital of Assyria:—Nineve {1x}. See: BAGD—540a; THAYER—426c.

3536. **Νινευΐτης** {2x} **Niněuïtēs**, *nin-yoo-ee'-tace;* from *3535;* a *Ninevite,* i.e. inhab. of Nineveh:—of Nineve {1x}, Ninevite {1x}. See: BAGD—540a; THAYER—429d.

3537. **νιπτήρ** {1x} **niptēr**, *nip-tare';* from *3538;* a *ewer:*—bason {1x}.

Nipter, the vessel into which the Lord poured water to wash the disciples' feet, was "a large ewer," Jn 13:5. The word is connected with the verb *nipto,* "to wash." See: BAGD—540a; THAYER—426d.

3538. **νίπτω** {17x} **niptō**, *nip'-to;* to *cleanse* (espec. the hands or the feet or the face); cerem. to *perform ablution:*—wash {17x}.

(1) This word is only used of washing part of the body, **(1a)** literally, Jn 13:5–6, 8, 12, 14 (twice); **(1b)** in 1 Ti 5:10, including the figurative sense; **(3)** in the middle voice, to wash oneself, Mt 6:17; 15:2; Mk 7:3; Jn 9:7, 11, 15; 13:10. Syn.: 3068, 4150. See: TDNT—4:946, 635; BAGD—540B; THAYER—426D. comp. *3068*.

3539. **νοιέω** {14x} **nŏiěō**, *noy-eh'-o;* from *3563* **νοέω** **nŏěō** *no-eh'-o;* to *exercise* the *mind,* (*observe*), i.e. (fig.) to *comprehend, heed:*—consider {1x}, perceive {2x}, think {1x}, understand {10x}.

Noieo, "to perceive with the mind," as distinct from perception by feeling, is so used **(1)** in Mt 15:17, "understand"; 16:9, 11; 24:15 (here rather perhaps in the sense of considering) and parallels in Mk (not in Lk); Jn 12:40; Rom 1:20; 1 Ti 1:7; Heb 11:3; **(2)** in Eph 3:4, "may understand"; 3:20, "think"; 2 Ti 2:7, "consider." See: TDNT—4:948, 636; BAGD—540B; THAYER—426D.

3540. **νόημα** {8x} **nŏēma**, *nŏ'-ay-mah;* from *3539;* a *perception,* i.e. *purpose,* or (by impl.) the *intellect, disposition,* itself:—device {1x}, mind {8x}, thought {1x}.

Noema denotes "thought, that which is thought out" (cf. *noeo,* "to understand"); hence, "a purpose, device"; translated **(1)** "devices" in 2 Cor 2:11; **(2)** "minds" in 2 Cor 3:14; 4:4; 11:3; **(3)** in 2 Cor 10:5, "thought"; **(4)** in Phil 4:7, "minds." See: TDNT—4:960, 636; BAGD—540d; THAYER—427a.

3541. **νόθος** {1x} **nŏthŏs**, *noth'-os;* of uncert. aff.; a *spurious* or *illegitimate* son:—bastard {1x}.

Nothos denotes an illegitimate child, one born out of lawful wedlock (Heb 12:8). See: BAGD—540d. See: TDNT—4:960, 636; BAGD—427a; THAYER—427a.

3542. **νομή** {2x} **nŏmē**, *nom-ay';* fem. from the same as *3551; pasture,* i.e. (the act) *feeding* (fig. *spreading* of a gangrene), or (the food) *pasturage:*—eat + 2192 {1x}, pasture {1x}.

Noma denotes **(1)** "pasture, pasturage," figuratively in Jn 10:9; **(2)** "grazing, feeding," figuratively in 2 Ti 2:17, of the doctrines of false teachers, lit., "their word will have feeding as a gangrene." See: BAGD—541a; THAYER—427a.

3543. **νομίζω** {15x} **nŏmizō**, *nom-id'-zo;* from *3551;* prop. to *do* by *law* (*usage*), i.e. to *accustom* (pass. *be usual*); by extens. to *deem* or *regard:*—suppose {9x}, think {5x}, be wont {1x}.

Nomizo, to consider, suppose, think," is rendered **(1)** "to suppose" in Mt 20:10; Lk 2:34; 3:23; Acts 7:25; 14:19; 16:27; 21:29; 1 Ti 6:5; in 1 Cor 7:26; Acts 16:13, "to suppose," "(where) we supposed (there was a place of prayer)"; **(3)** this word also signifies "to practice a custom" (*nomos*) and is commonly so used by Greek writers; "was wont (to be made)" in Acts 16:13; **(4)** it is rendered "to think" in Mt 5:17; 10:34; Acts 8:20; 17:29; 1 Cor 7:36. See: BAGD—541a; THAYER—427b.

3544. **νομικός** {9x} **nŏmikŏs**, *nom-ik-os';* from *3551; according* (or *pertaining*) *to law,* i.e. *legal* (cer.); as noun, an *expert in* the (Mosaic) *law:*—about the law {1x}, lawyer {8x}.

Nomikos, an adjective, "learned in the law", is used as a noun, **(1)** "a lawyer," Mt 22:35; Lk 7:30; 10:25; 11:45, 46, 52; 14:3; Titus 3:13, where Zenas is so named. **(2)** As there is no evidence that he was one skilled in Roman jurisprudence, the term may be regarded in the usual NT sense as applying to one skilled in the Mosaic Law. **(3)** The usual name for a scribe is *grammateus,* a man of letters; for a doctor of the law, *nomo didaskalos,* a comparison of Lk 5:17 with v. 21 and Mk 2:6 and Mt 9:3 shows that the three terms were used synonymously, and did not denote three distinct classes. **(3a)** The scribes were originally simply men of letters, students of Scripture, and the name first given to them contains in itself no reference to the law; in course of time, however, they devoted themselves mainly, though by no means exclusively, to the study of the law. They became jurists rather than theologians, and received names which of themselves called attention to that fact. **(3b)** Some would doubtless devote themselves more to one branch of activity than to another; but a "lawyer" might also be a 'doctor,' and the case of Gamaliel shows that a "doctor" might also be a member of the Sanhedrin, Acts 5:34. See: TDNT—4:1088, 646; BAGD—541b.

3545. **νομίμως** {2x} **nŏmimōs**, *nom-im'-oce;* adv. from a der. of *3551; legitimately* (spec. agreeably to the rules of the lists):—lawfully {2x}.

Nomimos, "lawfully," is used **(1)** in 1 Ti 1:8, "the Law is good, if a man use it lawfully," i.e., agreeably to its design; the meaning here is that, while no one can be justified or obtain eternal life through its instrumentality, the believer is to have it in his heart and to fulfill its requirements; walking "not after the flesh but after the spirit," Rom. 8:4, he will "use it lawfully." **(2)** In 2 Ti 2:5 it is used of contending in the games and adhering to the rules. See: TDNT—4:1088, 646; BAGD—541c; THAYER—427b.

3546. **νόμισμα** {1x} **nŏmisma**, *nom'-is-mah;* from *3543; what is reckoned* as of value (after the Lat. *numisma*), i.e. current *coin:*—money {1x}.

Nomisma, primarily "that which is established by custom" (*nomos,* "a custom, law"), hence, "the current coin of a state, currency," is found in Mt 22:19, "(tribute) money." See: BAGD—541d; THAYER—427b.

3547. **νομοδιδάσκαλος** {3x} **nŏmŏdidaskalŏs**, *nom-od-id-as'-kal-os;* from *3551* and *1320;* an *expounder of* the (Jewish) *law,* i.e. a *Rabbi:*—doctor of the law {2x}, teacher of the law {1x}.

This word means **(1)** "a teacher of the Law", with reference to the doctors of the Mosaic Law, Lk 5:17; Acts 5:34; **(2)** also of those who went about among Christians, professing to be instructors of the Law, 1 Ti 1:7. See: TDNT—2:159, 161; BAGD—541d; THAYER—427c.

3548. **νομοθεσία** {1x} **nŏmŏthĕsia**, *nom-oth-es-ee'-ah;* from *3550; legislation* (spec. the *institution of* the Mosaic *code*):—giving of the law {1x}.

This word denotes "legislation, lawgiving", Rom 9:4, "(the) giving of the law." See: TDNT—4:1089, 646; BAGD—541d; THAYER—427c.

3549. **νομοθετέω** {2x} **nŏmŏthĕtĕō**, *nom-oth-et-eh'-o;* from *3550;* to *legislate,* i.e. (pass.) to *have* (the Mosaic) *enactments* injoined, *be sanctioned* (by them):—establish {1x}, receive the law {1x}.

This word means "to ordain by law, to enact" (*nomos,* "a law," *tithemi,* "to put"), is used in the passive voice, and rendered **(1)** "established" in Heb 8:6; **(2)** in 7:11, used intransitively, it is rendered "received the Law." See: TDNT—4:1090, 646; BAGD—541d; THAYER—427c.

3550. **νομοθέτης** {1x} **nŏmŏthĕtēs**, *nom-oth-et'-ace;* from *3551* and a der. of *5087;* a *legislator:*—lawgiver {1x}.

This word means "a lawgiver" and occurs in Jas 4:12, of God, as the sole "Lawgiver"; therefore, to criticize the Law is to presume to take His place, with the presumption of enacting a better law. See: TDNT—4:1090, 646; BAGD—542a; THAYER—427c.

3551. **νόμος** {197x} **nŏmŏs**, *nom'-os;* from a primary νέμω **němō**, (to *parcel* out, espec. *food* or *grazing* to animals); *law* (through the idea of prescriptive *usage*), gen. (*regulation*), spec. (of Moses [incl. the volume]; also of the Gospel), or fig. (a *principle*):—law {197x}.

Nomos, in the NT is used **(1)** of "law" in general, **(1a)** e.g., Rom 2:12, 13, expressing a general principle relating to "law"; **(1b)** 3:27, "By what manner of law?" i.e., "by what sort of principle (has the glorying been excluded)?"; **(1c)** 5:13, referring to the period between Adam's trespass and the giving of the Law; **(1d)** 7:1 against those graces which constitute the fruit of the Spirit "there is no law," Gal 5:23; **(1e)** the ostensible aim of the law is to restrain the evil tendencies natural to man in his fallen estate, yet in experience law finds itself not merely ineffective, it actually provokes those tendencies to greater activity. The intention of the gift of the Spirit is to constrain the believer to a life in which the natural tendencies shall have no place, and to produce in him their direct contraries. Law, therefore, has nothing to say against the fruit of the Spirit; hence the believer is not only not under law, ver. 18, the law finds no scope in his life, inasmuch as, and in so far as, he is led by the Spirit. **(2)** of a force or influence impelling to action, Rom 7:21, 23 (1st part), "a different law";

(3) of the Mosaic Law, the "law" of Sinai, **(3a)** with the definite article, e.g., Mt 5:18; Jn 1:17; Rom 2:15, 18, 20, 26, 27; 3:19; 4:15; 7:4, 7, 14, 16, 22; 8:3, 4, 7; Gal 3:10, 12, 19, 21, 24; 5:3; Eph 2:15; Phil 3:6; 1 Ti 1:8; Heb 7:19; Jas 2:9; **(3b)** without the article, thus stressing the Mosaic Law in its quality as "law," e.g., Rom 2:14 (1st part); 5:20; 7:9, where the stress in the quality lies in this, that "the commandment which was unto (i.e., which he thought would be a means of) life," he found to be "unto (i.e., to have the effect of revealing his actual state of) death"; 10:4; 1 Cor 9:20; Gal 2:16, 19, 21; 3:2, 5, 10 (1st part), 11, 18, 23; 4:4, 5, 21 (1st part); 5:4, 18; 6:13; Phil 3:5, 9; Heb 7:16; 9:19; Jas 2:11; 4:11; (in regard to the statement in Gal 2:16, that "a man is not justified by the works of the Law," the absence of the article before *nomos* indicates the assertion of a principle, "by obedience to law," but evidently the Mosaic Law is in view. Here the apostle is maintaining that submission to circumcision entails the obligation to do the whole "Law." Circumcision belongs to the ceremonial part of the "Law," but, while the Mosaic Law is actually divisible into the ceremonial and the moral, no such distinction is made or even assumed in Scripture. The statement maintains the freedom of the believer from the "law" of Moses in its totality as a means of justification);

(4) by metonymy, of the books which contain the "law," **(4a)** of the Pentateuch, e.g., Mt 5:17; 12:5; Lk 16:16; 24:44; Jn 1:45; Rom 3:21; Gal 3:10; **(4b)** of the Psalms, Jn 10:34; 15:25; **(4c)** of the Psalms, Isaiah, Ezekiel and Daniel, 12:34, the Psalms and Isaiah, Rom 3:19 (with vv. 10–18); Isaiah, 1 Cor 14:21; **(5)** from all this it may be inferred that "the law" in the most comprehensive sense was an alternative title to "The Scriptures."

(6) The following phrases specify "laws" of various kinds; **(6a)** "the law of Christ," Gal 6:2, i.e., **(6a1)** either given by Him (as in the Sermon on the Mount and in Jn 13:14, 15; 15:4), or **(6a2)** the "law" or principle by which Christ Himself lived (Mt 20:28; Jn 13:1); these are not actual alternatives, for the "law" imposed by Christ was always that by which He Himself lived in the "days of His flesh." He confirmed the "Law" as being of divine authority (cf. Mt 5:18); yet He presented a higher standard of life than perfunctory obedience to the current legal rendering of the "Law," a standard which, without annulling the "Law," He embodied in His own character and life (see, e.g., Mt 5:21–48; this breach with legalism is especially seen in regard to the ritual or ceremonial part of the "Law" in its wide scope); He showed Himself superior to all human interpretations of it; **(6b)** "a law of faith," Rom 3:27, i.e., a principle which demands only faith on man's part; **(6c)** "the law of my mind," Rom 7:23, that principle which governs the new nature in virtue of the new birth; **(6d)** "the law of sin," Rom 7:23, the principle by which sin exerts its influence and power despite the desire to do what is right; **(6e)** "of sin and death," 8:2, death being the effect; **(6f)** "the law of liberty," Jas 1:25; 2:12, a term comprehensive of all the Scriptures, not a "law" of compulsion enforced from without, but meeting with ready obedience through the desire and delight of the renewed being who is subject to it; into it he looks, and in its teaching he delights; he is "under law (*ennomos,* "in law," implying union and subjection) to Christ," 1 Cor 9:21; cf, e.g., Ps 119:32, 45, 97; 2 Cor 3:17; **(6g)** "the royal law," Jas 2:8, i.e., the "law" of love, royal in the majesty of its power, the "law" upon which all others hang, Mt 22:34–40; Rom 13:8; Gal 5:14; **(6h)** "the law of the Spirit of life," Rom 8:2, i.e., the animating principle by which the Holy Spirit acts as the imparter of life (cf. Jn 6:63); **(6i)** "a law of righteousness," Rom 9:31, i.e., a general principle presenting righteousness as the object and outcome of keeping a "law," particularly the "Law" of Moses (cf. Gal 3:21); **(6j)** "the law of a carnal commandment," Heb 7:16, i.e., the "law" respecting the Aaronic priesthood, which appointed men conditioned by the circumstances and limitations of the flesh.

(7) In the Epistle to the Hebrews the "Law" is treated of especially in regard to the contrast between the Priesthood of Christ and that established under the "law" of Moses, and in regard to access to God and to worship. In these respects the "Law" "made nothing perfect," 7:19. There was "a disannulling of a foregoing commandment . . . and a bringing in of a better hope." This is established under the "new Covenant," a covenant instituted on the basis of "better promises," 8:6. **(8)** In Gal 5:3, the statement that to receive circumcision constitutes a man a debtor to do "the whole Law," views the "Law" as made up of separate commands, each essential to the whole, and predicates the unity of the "Law"; in v. 14, the statement that "the whole law" is fulfilled in the one commandment concerning love, views the separate commandments as combined to make a complete "law." **(9)** In Rom 8:3, "what the law could not do," is lit., "the inability (*adunaton,* the neuter of the adjective *adunatos,* 'unable,' used as a noun) of the Law"; this may mean either "the weakness of the Law" or "that which was impossible for the Law"; the latter is preferable; the significance is the same in effect; the "Law" could neither give freedom from condemnation nor impart life. See: TDNT—4:1022, 646; BAGD—542b; THAYER—427d.

3552. **νοσέω** {1x} **nŏsĕō**, *nos-eh'-o;* from *3554;* to *be sick,* i.e. (by impl. of a diseased appetite) to *hanker* after (fig. to *harp* upon):—dote {1x}.

Noseo signifies "to be ill, to be ailing," whether in body or mind; hence, "to be taken with such a morbid interest in a thing as is tantamount to a disease, to dote," 1 Ti 6:4. The primary meaning of "*dote*" is to be foolish (cf. Jer 50:36), the evident meaning of *noseo,* in this respect, is "to be unsound." See: TDNT—4:1091, 655; BAGD—543c; THAYER—429c.

3553. **νόσημα** {1x} **nŏsēma**, *nos'-ay-ma;* from *3552;* an *ailment:*—disease {1x}. See: TDNT—4:1091, 655; BAGD—543c; THAYER—429a.

3554. **νόσος** {12x} **nŏsŏs**, *nos'-os;* of uncert. aff.; a *malady* (rarely fig. of mor. *disability*):—disease {6x}, infirmity {1x}, sickness {5x}.

Nosos is the regular word for **(1)** "sickness" in Mt 4:23; 8:17; 9:35; 10:1; Mk 3:15; **(2)** "disease" in Mt 4:24; Mk 1:34; Lk 4:40; 6:17; 9:1; Acts 19:12; and **(3)** "infirmities" in Lk 7:21. See: TDNT—4:1091, 655; BAGD—543c; THAYER—429a.

3555. **νοσσιά** {1x} **nŏssia**, *nos-see-ah';* from *3502;* a *brood* (of chickens):—brood {1x}.

Nossia is primarily, "a nest" and denotes "a brood," Lk 13:34. See: BAGD—543d; THAYER—429a.

3556. **νοσσίον** {1x} **nŏssiŏn**, *nos-see'-on;* dimin. of *3502;* a *birdling:*—chicken {1x}. See: BAGD—543d; THAYER—429a.

3557. **νοσφίζομαι** {3x} **nŏsphizŏmai**, *nos-fid'-zom-ahee;* mid. voice from νοσφί **nŏsphi** (*apart* or *clandestinely*); to *sequestrate,* for oneself, i.e. *embezzle:*—keep back {2x}, purloin {1x}.

This word means "to set apart, remove," signifies, **(1)** in the middle voice, "to set apart for oneself, to purloin," and is rendered "purloining" in Titus 2:10; **(2)** "kept back" (and "keep") in Acts 5.2, 3, of the act of Ananias and his wife in "retaining" part of the price of the land. See: BAGD—543d; THAYER—429b.

3558. **νότος** {7x} **nŏtŏs**, *not'-os;* of uncert. aff.; the *south (-west) wind;* by extens. the *southern quarter* itself:—south {4x}, south wind {3x}.

Notos denotes **(1)** the south wind (Lk 12:55; Acts 27:13; 28:13); **(2)** south as a direction (Lk 13:29; Rev 21:13); **(3)** the South as a region (Mt 12:42; Lk 11:31). See: BAGD—544a; THAYER—429b.

3559. **νουθεσία** {3x} **nŏuthĕsia**, *noo-thes-ee'-ah;* from *3563* and a der. of *5087;* calling *attention* to, i.e. (by impl.) mild *rebuke* or *warning:*—admonition {3x}.

Literally, this word means a putting in mind, and is used of **(1)** the purpose of the Scriptures (1 Cor 10:11); **(2)** of that which is ministered by the Lord (Eph 6:4); and **(3)** of that which is to be administered for the correction of one who creates trouble in the church (Titus 3:10). Syn.: *Nouthesia* is the training by word, whether of encouragement, or, if necessary, by reproof or remonstrance. *Paideia* (3809) stresses training by act, though both words are used in each respect. See: TDNT—4:1019, 636; BAGD—544b; THAYER—429b.

3560. **νουθετέω** {8x} **nŏuthĕtĕō**, *noo-thet-eh'-o;* from the same as *3559;* to *put in mind,* i.e. (by impl.) to *caution* or *reprove* gently:—admonish {4x}, warn {4x}.

Noutheteo (3560) means "to put in mind, admonish," **(1)** "to warn" in Acts 20:31; 1 Cor 4:14; Col 1:28 "warning"; 1 Th 5:14 "warn"; and **(2)** "to admonish" in Rom 15:14; Col 3:16; 1 Th 5:12; 2 Th 3:15. **(3)** The difference between "admonish" and "teach" seems to be that, whereas the former has mainly in view the things that are wrong and call for warning, the latter has to do chiefly with the impartation of positive truth, cf. Col 3:16; they were to let the Word of Christ dwell richly in them, so that they might be able **(3a)** to teach and 'admonish' one another, and **(3b)** to abound in the praises of God. **(4)** Admonition differs from remonstrance, in that the former is warning based on instruction; the latter may be little more than expostulation. For example, though Eli remonstrated with his sons, 1 Sa 2:24, he failed to admonish them, 3:13. Pastors and teachers in the churches are thus themselves admonished, i.e., instructed and warned, by the Scriptures, 1 Cor 10:11, so to minister the Word of God to the saints, that, naming the Name of the Lord, they shall depart from unrighteousness, 2 Ti 2:19. Syn.: 3560, 3867, 5537. See: TDNT—4:1019, 636; BAGD—544b; THAYER—429b.

3561. **νουμηνία** {1x} **nŏumēnia**, *noo-may-nee'-ah;* fem. of a compound of *3501* and *3376* (as noun by impl. of *2250*); the festival of *new moon:*—new moon {1x}.

This word, denoting "a new moon" (*neos,* "new," *men,* "a month"), is **(1)** used in Col 2:16, of a Jewish festival. **(2)** Judaistic tradition added special features in the liturgy of the synagogue in connection with the observance of the first day of the month, the new "moon" time. **(3)** In the OT see Num 29:6; 1 Sam 20:27; Hos 5:7. **(4)** For the connection with feast days see Lev 23:24; Num 10:10; 29:1; Ps 81:31. See: TDNT—4:638,*; BAGD—544b; THAYER—429b.

3562. **νουνεχῶς** {1x} **nŏunĕchōs**, *noon-ekh-oce';* adv. from a comp. of the acc. of *3563* and *2192;* in a *mind-having* way, i.e. *prudently:*—discreetly {1x}.

Nounechos, lit., "mindpossessing" (*nous,* "mind, understanding," *echo,* "to have"), hence denotes "discreetly, sensibly prudently." Mk 12:34. See: TDNT—2:816,*; BAGD—544b; THAYER—429c.

3563. **νοῦς** {24x} **nŏus**, *nooce;* prob. from the base of *1097;* the *intellect,* i.e. *mind* (divine or human; in thought, feeling, or will); by impl. *meaning:*—mind {21x}, understanding {3x}.

Nous, as a noun, means "mind," denotes, **(1)** speaking generally, the seat of reflective consciousness, comprising the faculties of perception and understanding, and those of feeling, judging and determining. **(2)** Its use in the NT may be analyzed as follows: it denotes **(2a)** the faculty of knowing, the seat of the understanding, Lk 24:45; Rom 1:28; 14:5; 1 Cor 14:15, 19; Eph 4:17; Phil 4:7; Col 2:18; 1 Ti 6:5; 2 Ti 3:8; Titus 1:15; Rev 13:18; 17:9; **(2b)** counsels, purpose, Rom 11:34 (of the "mind" of God); **(2b1)** Rom 12:2; 1 Cor 1:10; 2:16, twice of the thoughts and counsels of God, **(2b2)** of Christ, a testimony to His Godhood; Eph. 4:23; **(2b3)** 2 Th 2:2, where it stands for the determination to be steadfast amidst afflictions, through the confident expectation of the day of rest and recompense mentioned in the first chapter; **(3)** the new nature, which belongs to the believer by reason of the new birth, Rom 7:23, 25, where it is contrasted with "the flesh," the principle of evil which dominates fallen man. Syn.: 363, 1271, 1771, 3540, 5279, 5436, 5427. See: TDNT—4:951, 636; BAGD—544c; THAYER—429c. comp. *5590*.

3564. **Νυμφᾶς** {1x} **Numphas**, *noom-fas';* prob. contr. for a compound of *3565* and *1435; nymph-given* (i.e. *-born*); *Nymphas*, a Chr.:—Nymphas {1x}. See: BAGD—545a; THAYER—429d.

3565. **νύμφη** {8x} **numphē**, *noom-fay';* from a primary but obs. verb νύπτω **nuptō**, (to *veil* as a bride; comp. Lat. "*nupto*," to *marry*); a young *married* woman (as *veiled*), incl. a *betrothed* girl; by impl. a *son's wife:*—bride {5x}, daughter in law {3x}.

Numphe means a bride, or young wife (Jn 3:29; Rev 18:23; 21:2, 9; 22:17) who was led veiled from her home to the bridegroom; hence, the secondary meaning of daughter-in-law (Mt 10:35; Lk 12:53). See: TDNT—4:1099, 657; BAGD—545b; THAYER—429d.

3566. **νυμφίος** {16x} **numphiŏs**, *noom-fee'-os;* from *3565;* a *bride-groom* (lit. or fig.):—bridegroom {16x}. See: TDNT—4:1099, 657; BAGD—545b; THAYER—429d.

3567. **νυμφών** {3x} **numphōn**, *noom-fohn';* from *3565;* the *bridal* room:—bridechamber {3x}.

Numphion signifies **(1)** "the room or dining hall in which the marriage ceremonies were held," Mt 22:10; **(2)** "the chamber containing the bridal bed," "the sons of the bridechamber" being the friends of the bridegroom, who had the charge of providing what was necessary for the nuptials, Mt 9:15; Mk 2:19; Lk 5:34. See: BAGD—545b; THAYER—430a.

3568. **νῦν** {139x} **nun**, *noon;* a primary particle of present time; "*now*" (as adv. of date, a transition or emphasis); also as noun or adj. *present* or *immediate:*—now {121x}, present {4x}, henceforth {4x}, this + 3588 {3x}, this time {2x}, misc. {5x} = + hereafter, of late, soon.

Nun is used **(1)** of time, the immediate present, whether in contrast **(1a)** to the past, e.g., Jn 4:18; Acts 7:52, or **(1b)** to the future, e.g., Jn 12:27; Rom 11:31; **(1c)** sometimes with the article, singular or plural, e.g., Acts 4:29; 5:38; **(2)** of logical sequence, often partaking also of the character of (1), "now therefore, now however," as it is, e.g., Lk 11:39; Jn 8:40; 9:41; 15:22, 24; 1 Cor 5:11. See: TDNT—4:1106, 658; BAGD—545c; THAYER—430a. See also *3569, 3570*.

3569. **τανῦν** {5x} **tanun**, *tan-oon';* or

τὰ νῦν **ta nun** *tah noon;* from neut. plur. of *3588* and *3568; the* things *now,* i.e. (adv.) *at present:*—but now {1x}, now {4x}. See: BAGD—546a; THAYER—430a.

3570. **νυνί** { {20x} **nuni**, *noo-nee';* a prol. form of *3568* for emphasis; *just now:*—now {20x}.

Nuni, a strengthened form of *nun* (3569) is used **(1)** of time, e.g., Acts 24:13; Rom 6:22; 15:23, 25; **(2)** with logical import, e.g., Rom 7:17. See: BAGD—546b; THAYER—430d.

3571. **νύξ** {65x} **nux**, *noox;* a primary word; "*night*" (lit. or fig.):—night {63x}, midnight + 3319 {2x}.

Nux is used **(1)** literally, **(1a)** of "the alternating natural period to that of the day," e.g., Mt 4:2; 12:40; 2 Ti 1:3; Rev 4:8; **(1b)** of "the period of the absence of light," the time in which something takes place, e.g., Mt 2:14; 27:64; Lk 2:8; Jn 3:2; 7:50; Acts 5:19; 9:25; **(1c)** of "point of time," e.g., Mt 14:30; Lk 12:20; Acts 27:23; **(1d)** of "duration of time," e.g., Lk 2:37; 5:5; Acts 20:31; 26:7; **(2)** metaphorically, **(2a)** of "the period of man's alienation from God," Rom 13:12; 1 Th 5:5, lit., "not of night," where "of" means 'belonging to;' cf. "of the Way"; Acts 9:2; **(2b)** "of shrinking back" and "of faith," Heb 10:39, marg.; **(2c)** of "death," as the time when work ceases, Jn 9:4. See: TDNT—4:1123, 661; BAGD—546b; THAYER—431a.

3572. **νύσσω** {1x} **nussō**, *noos'-so;* appar. a primary word; to *prick* ("nudge"):—pierce {1x}.

Nusso means to pierce or pierce through often of inflicting severe or deadly wounds, is used of the piercing of the side of Christ (Jn 19:34). See: BAGD—547a; THAYER—431c.

3573. **νυστάζω** {2x} **nustazō**, *noos-tad'-zo;* from a presumed der. of *3506;* to *nod,* i.e. (by impl.) to *fall asleep;* fig. to *delay:*—slumber {2x}.

Nustazo denotes "to nod in sleep" (akin to *neuo,* "to nod"), "fall asleep," and is used **(1)** of natural slumber, Mt 25:5; **(2)** metaphorically in 2 Pet 2:3, negatively, of the destruction awaiting false teachers. See: BAGD—547a; THAYER—431c.

3574. **νυχθήμερον** {1x} **nuchthēmĕrŏn**, *nookh-thay'-mer-on;* from *3571* and *2250;* a *day*-and-*night,* i.e. full *day* of twenty-four hours:—a night and day {1x}.

This word is an adjective denoting "lasting a night and a day" (from *nux,* "night," and *hemera,* "a day"), and is used in 2 Cor 11:25, in the neuter gender, as a noun, the object of the verb *poieo,* to do, lit., 'I have done a night-and-a-day. See: BAGD—547a; THAYER—431c.

3575. **Νῶε** {8x} **Nōĕ**, *no'-eh;* of Heb. or. [5146]; *Noë,* (i.e. *Noäch*), a patriarch:—Noe {5x}, Noah {3x}. See: BAGD—547c; THAYER—431c.

3576. **νωθρός** {2x} **nōthrŏs**, *no-thros';* from a der. of *3541; sluggish,* i.e. (lit.) *lazy,* or (fig.) *stupid:*—dull {1x}, slothful {1x}.

Nothros, "slow, sluggish, indolent, dull" is translated **(1)** "dull" in Heb 5:11 (in connection with the noun, *akoe,* "hearing"; lit., "in hearings"); **(2)** "slothful," in Heb 6:12. Syn.: In Lk 24:25 "slow (of heart)" translates the synonymous word *bradus* (917). *Bradus* differs from *nothros* in that no moral fault or blame is necessarily involved in it; so far indeed is it from this, that of the three occasions on which it is used in the NT two are in honor; for to be 'slow' to evil things, to rash speaking, or to anger (Jas 1:19, twice), is a grace, and not the contrary. . . . There is a deeper, more inborn sluggishness implied in *nothros,* and this bound up as it were in the very life. Syn.: 692, 1021. See: TDNT—4:1126, 661; BAGD—547c; THAYER—431d.

3577. **νῶτος** {1x} **nōtŏs**, *no'-tos;* of uncert. aff.; the *back:*—back {1x}.

Notos, "the back," signifying "to bend, curve" is used in Rom 11:10. See: BAGD—547c; THAYER—431d.

Ξ

3578. **ξενία** {2x} **xĕnia**, *xen-ee'-ah;* from *3581;* hospitality, i.e. (by impl.) a *place of entertainment:*—lodging {2x}.

Xenia denotes "hospitality, entertainment" and by metonymy, "a place of entertainment, a lodging-place," Acts 28:23; Philemon 22. See: TDNT—5:1, 661; BAGD—547b; THAYER—3578b.

3579. **ξενίζω** {10x} **xĕnizō**, *xen-id'-zo;* from *3581;* to *be a host* (pass. a *guest*); by impl. *be* (*make, appear*) *strange:*—entertain {1x}, lodge {6x}, think it strange {2x}, strange {1x}.

This word signifies to receive as a guest, rendered **(1)** lodged (Acts 28:7); **(2)** have entertained (Heb 13:2); and **(3)** to be astonished by the strangeness of a thing (Acts 17:20; 1 Pet 4:4, 12). When one lodges in a place the host sees that the guests are entertained, i.e. have no thoughts for needs. The root for entertain means to hold and in order to take the traveler's mind off his cares the host provides that which is new and unfamiliar to the guest; hence, strange. See: TDNT—5:1, 661; BAGD—547d; THAYER—431d.

3580. **ξενοδοχέω** {1x} **xĕnŏdŏchĕō**, *xen-od-okh-eh'-o;* from a compound of *3581* and *1209;* to *be hospitable:*—lodge strangers {1x}. See: TDNT—5:1, 661; BAGD—548a; THAYER—432a.

3581. **ξένος** {14x} **xĕnŏs**, *xen'-os;* appar. a primary word; *for.* (lit. *alien,* or fig. *novel*); by impl. a *guest* or (vice-versa) *entertainer:*—host {1x}, strange {3x}, stranger {10x}.

Xenos denotes **(1)** one who receives and entertains another hospitably, the one with whom he stays or lodges, a host, Rom 16:23; **(2)** "stranger" in Mt 25:35, 38, 43, 44; 27:7; Acts 17:21 plural; Eph 2:12, 19; Heb 11:13; 3 Jn 1:5; and **(3)** "strange" in Acts 17:18; Heb 13:9; 1 Pet 4:2, "served" by the "host". See: TDNT—5:1, 661; BAGD—548a; THAYER—432a.

3582. **ξέστης** {2x} **xĕstēs**, *xes'-tace;* as if from ξέω **xĕō**, (prop. to *smooth;* by impl. [of *friction*] to *boil* or *heat*); a *vessel* (as *fashioned* or for *cooking*) [or perh. by corruption from the Lat. *sextarius,* the *sixth* of a modius, i.e. about a *pint*], i.e. (spec.) a *measure* for liquids or solids, (by anal. a *pitcher*):—pot {2x}. See: BAGD—548b; THAYER—432b.

3583. **ξηραίνω** {16x} **xērainō**, *xay-rah'-ee-no;* from *3584;* to *desiccate;* by impl. to *shrivel,* to *mature:*—wither away {6x}, wither {5x}, dry up {3x}, pine away {1x}, be ripe {1x}.

Xeraino means "to dry up, wither" and is translated "to wither," **(1)** of plants, Mt 13:6; 21:19, 20; Mk 4:6; 11:20, "dried up", 21; Lk 8:6; Jn 15:6; Jas 1:11; 1 Pet 1:24; **(2)** of the body, Mk 3:1, 3, a "withered hand"; 5:29 of blood; **(3)** of "ripened" crops: "And another angel came out of the temple, crying with a loud voice to him that sat on the cloud, Thrust in thy sickle, and reap: for the time is come for thee to reap; for the harvest of the earth is ripe" (Rev 14:15); **(4)** "pineth away" in Mk 9:18; and **(5)** "dried up" of the Euphrates river, Rev 16:12. Syn.: 187, 3860. See: BAGD—548c; THAYER—432b.

3584. **ξηρός** {7x} **xērŏs**, *xay-ros';* from the base of *3582* (through the idea of *scorching*); *arid;* by impl. *shrunken, earth* (as opposed to water):—withered {4x}, dry {1x}, dry land {1x}, land {1x}.

Xeros is used **(1)** naturally, of "dry" land, Heb 11:29; or of land in general, Mt 23:15, "land"; or **(2)** of physical infirmity, "withered," Mt 12:10; Lk 6:6, 8; Jn 5:3; **(3)** figuratively, in Lk 23:31, "dry", with reference to the spiritual "barrenness" of the Jews, in contrast to the character of the Lord. Cf. Ps 1:3; Is 56:3; Eze 17:24; 20:47. See: BAGD—548c; THAYER—432c.

3585. **ξύλινος** {2x} **xulinŏs**, *xoo'-lin-os;* from *3586;* wooden:—of wood {2x}. See: BAGD—549a; THAYER—432c.

3586. **ξύλον** {19x} **xulŏn**, *xoo'-lon;* from another form of the base of *3582;* timber (as fuel or material); by impl. a *stick, club* or *tree* or other wooden art. or substance:—staff {5x}, stocks {1x}, tree {10x}, wood {3x}.

Xulon, "wood, a piece of wood, anything made of wood" is used, with the rendering **(1)** "tree," in Lk 23:31, where "the green tree" refers either to Christ, figuratively of all His living power and excellencies, or to the life of the Jewish people while still inhabiting their land, in contrast to "the dry," a figure fulfilled in the horrors of the Roman massacre and devastation in A.D. 70 (cf. the Lord's parable in Lk 13:6–9; see Eze 20:47, and cf. 21:3); **(2)** of "the cross," the tree being the *stauros,* the upright pale or stake to which Romans nailed those who were thus to be executed, Acts 5:30; 10:39; 13:29; Gal 3:13; 1 Pet 2:24; **(3)** of "the tree of life," Rev. 2:7; 22:2 (twice), 14, 19, "book"; and "a cudgel" or **(4)** "staff," the plural being "staves" in Mt 26:47, 55; Mk 14:43, 48; Lk 22:52. See: TDNT—5:37, 665; BAGD—549a; THAYER—432c.

3587. **ξυράω** {3x} **xuraō**, *xoo-rah'-o;* from a der. of the same as *3586* (mean. a *razor*); to *shave* or *"shear"* the hair:—shave {3x}.

Xurao, a late form of *xureo,* or *xuro,* from *xuron,* "a razor," occurs in Acts 21:24 (middle voice), in connection with a vow (cf. Num 6:2–18; Acts 18:18); 1 Cor 11:5, 6 (2nd part in each). See: BAGD—549c; THAYER—432d.

O

3588. **ὁ** {543x} **hŏ**, *hŏ;* incl. the fem.

ἡ **hē**, *hay;* and the neut.

τό **tŏ**, *tŏ;* in all their inflections; the def. art.; *the* (sometimes to be supplied, at others omitted, in English idiom):—which {413x}, who {79x}, the things {11x}, the son {8x}, misc. {32x} = the, this, that, one, he, she, it, etc. See: BAGD—549b; THAYER—433a.

ὅ **hŏ**. See *3739*.

3589. **ὀγδοήκοντα** {2x} **ŏgdŏēkŏnta**, *og-dŏ-ay'-kon-tah;* from *3590; ten times eight:*—fourscore {2x}. Cf. Luke 2:37; 16:7. See: BAGD—552d; THAYER—437b.

3590. **ὄγδοος** {5x} **ŏgdŏŏs**, *og'-dŏ-os;* from *3638;* the *eighth:*—eighth {5x}. Cf. Lk 1:59; Acts 7:8; 2 Pet 2:5; Rev 17:11; 21:20. See: BAGD—552d; THAYER—437b.

3591. **ὄγκος** {1x} **ŏgkŏs**, *ong'-kos;* prob. from the same as *43;* a *mass* (as *bending* or *bulging* by its load), i.e. *burden* (*hindrance*):—weight {1x}. Syn.:

Baros (922) refers to weight, *ogkos* (3591) to bulk, and either may be oppressive; 922 is a load in so far as it is heavy, *phortion,* (5413) a burden in so far as it is borne; hence 5413 may be either heavy or light. See: TDNT—5:41, 666; BAGD—553a; THAYER—437b.

3592. **ὅδε** {12x} **hŏdĕ**, *hod'-eh;* incl. the fem.

ἥδε **hēdĕ**, *hay'-deh;* and the neut.

τόδε **tŏdĕ**, *tod'-e;* from *3588* and *1161;* the *same,* i.e. *this* or *that* one (plur. *these* or *those*); often used as pers. pron.:—these things {7x}, thus {1x}, after this manner {1x}, he {1x}, she {1x}, such {1x}. See: BAGD—553a; THAYER—437b.

3593. **ὁδεύω** {1x} **hŏdĕuō**, *hod-yoo'-o;* from *3598;* to *travel:*—journey {1x}.

Hodeuo, "to be on the way, journey" (from *hodos,* "a way"), the simplest form of the verbs denoting "to journey," is used in the parable of the good samaritan, Lk 10:33. See: BAGD—553b; THAYER—437c.

3594. **ὁδηγέω** {5x} **hŏdēgĕō**, *hod-ayg-eh'-o;* from *3595;* to *show* the *way* (lit. or fig. [*teach*]):—guide {2x}, lead {3x}.

This word means "to lead the way", and is used **(1)** literally, "lead", **(1a)** of "guiding" the blind, in Mt 15:14; Lk 6:39; **(1b)** of "guiding" unto fountains of waters of life, Rev 7:17; **(2)** figuratively, in **(2a)** Jn 16:13, of "guidance" into the truth by the Holy Spirit; **(2b)** in Acts 8:31, of the interpretation of Scripture. See: TDNT—5:97, 666; BAGD—553b; THAYER—437c.

3595. **ὁδηγός** {5x} **hŏdēgŏs**, *hod-ayg-os';* from *3598* and *2233;* a *conductor* (lit. or fig. [*teacher*]):—guide {4x}, leader {1x}.

Hodegos, "a leader on the way" (*hodos,* "a way," *hegeomai,* "to lead"), "a guide," is used **(1)** literally, in Acts 1:16; **(2)** figuratively, Mt 15:14, "leaders"; Mt 23:16, 24, "guides"; Rom 2:19, "a guide." See: TDNT—5:97, 666; BAGD—553c; THAYER—437d.

3596. **ὁδοιπορέω** {1x} **hŏdŏipŏrĕō**, *hod-oy-por-eh'-o;* from a compound of *3598* and *4198;* to *be a wayfarer,* i.e. *travel:*—go on (one's) journey {1x}. See: BAGD—553d; THAYER—437d.

3597. **ὁδοιπορία** {2x} **hŏdŏipŏria**, *hod-oy-por-ee'-ah;* from the same as *3596; travel:*—journey {1x}, journeyings {1x}.

Hodoiporia, "a wayfaring, journeying" (*hodos,* and *poros,* "a way, a passage"), is used **(1)** of the Lord's journey to Samaria, Jn 4:6, and **(2)** of Paul's "journeyings," 2 Cor 11:26. See: BAGD—553d; THAYER—437d.

3598. **ὁδός** {102x} **hŏdŏs**, *hod-os';* appar. a primary word; a *road;* by impl. a *progress* (the route, act or distance); fig. a *mode* or *means:*—way {83x}, way side {8x}, journey {6x}, highway {3x}, misc. {2x}.

Hodos denotes **(1)** "a natural path, road, way," **(1a)** frequent in the Synoptic Gospels; **(1b)** elsewhere, e.g., Acts 8:26; 1 Th 3:11; Jas 2:25; Rev. 16:12; **(2)** "a traveler's way" (see journey); **(3)** metaphorically, of a course of conduct, or way of thinking," e.g., **(3a)** of righteousness, Mt. 21:32; 2 Pet 2:21; **(3b)** of God, Mt 22:16, and parallels, i.e., **(3b1)** the "way" instructed and approved by God; so Acts 18:26 and Heb 3:10, **(3b2)** "My ways" (cf. Rev 15:3); **(3c)** of the Lord, Acts 18:25; **(3d)** that leads **(3d1)** "that leadeth to destruction," Mt 7:13; **(3d2)** ". . . unto life," 7:14; **(3d3)** of peace, Lk 1:79; Rom. 3:17; **(4)** of Paul's "ways" in Christ, 1 Cor 4:17 (plural); **(5)** "more excellent" **(5a)** of love, 1 Cor 12:31; **(5b)** of truth, 2 Pet 2:2; **(6)** of the right "way," 2 Pet 2:15; **(7)** of Balaam (id.), of Cain, Jude 11; **(8)** of a "way" consisting in what is from God, e.g., **(8a)** of life, Acts 2:28 (plural); **(8b)** of salvation, Acts 16:17; **(9)** personified, of Christ as the means of access to the Father, Jn 14:6; **(10)** of the course followed and characterized by the followers of Christ, Acts 9:2; 19:9, 23; 24:22. See: TDNT—5:42, 666; BAGD—553d; THAYER—437d.

3599. **ὀδούς** {12x} **ŏdŏus**, *od-ooce;* perh. from the base of *2068;* a *"tooth":*—tooth {12x}.

Odous is used in the **(1)** sing. in Mt 5:38 (twice); **(2)** elsewhere in the plural, **(2a)** of "the gnashing of teeth," the gnashing being expressive of anguish and indignation, Mt 8:12; 13:42, 50; 22:13; 24:51; 25:30; Mk 9:18; Lk 13:28; Acts 7:54; and **(2b)** in Rev 9:8, of the beings seen in a vision and described as locusts. See: BAGD—555a; THAYER—437d.

3600. **ὀδυνάω** {4x} **ŏdunaō**, *od-oo-nah'-o;* from *3601;* to *grieve:*—sorrow {2x}, torment {2x}.

Odunao, as a verb, means "to cause pain" and is used in the middle voice: "And when they saw him, they were amazed: and his mother said unto him, Son, why hast thou thus dealt with us? behold, thy father and I have sought thee sorrowing (*odunao*)" (Lk 2:48; cf. Lk 16:24–25 "tormented", Acts 20:38 "sorrowing"). Syn.: 253, 3076, 3077, 3601, 3997, 4036, 5604. See: TDNT—5:115,*; BAGD—555a; THAYER—438c.

3601. **ὀδύνη** {2x} **ŏdunē**, *od-oo'-nay;* from *1416; grief* (as *dejecting*):—sorrow {2x}.

Odune, as a noun, means "pain, consuming grief, distress" **(1)** of heart: "That I have great heaviness and continual sorrow in my heart" (Rom 9:2); or **(2)** "sorrows" as a result of loving money: "For the love of money is the root of all evil: which while some coveted after, they have erred from the faith, and pierced themselves through with many sorrows" (1 Ti 6:10). Syn.: 253, 3076, 3077, 3600, 3997, 4036, 5604. See: TDNT—5:115, 673; BAGD—555b; THAYER—438d.

3602. **ὀδυρμός** {2x} **ŏdurmŏs**, *od-oor-mos';* from a der. of the base of *1416; moaning,* i.e. *lamentation:*—mourning {2x}.

Odurmos, "lamentation, mourning," is translated "mourning" in Mt 2:18 and 2 Cor 7:7. See: TDNT—5:116, 673; BAGD—555b.438d; THAYER—438d.

3603. **ὅ ἐστι** {11x} **hŏ esti**, *hŏ es-tee'* or

ὅ ἐστιν **hŏ estin**, *hŏ es-teen';* from the neut. of *3739* and the third pers. sing. pres. ind. of *1510; which is:*—which is {5x}, that is {3x}, that is to say {1x}, which make {1x}, called {1x}. See: BAGD—596b [3603]; THAYER—455b [3739].

3604. **Ὀζίας** {2x} **Ŏzias**, *od-zee'-as;* of Heb. or. [5818]; *Ozias* (i.e. *Uzziah*), an Isr.:—*Ozias* {2x}. See: BAGD—555b; THAYER—438d.

3605. **ὄζω** {1x} **ŏzō**, *od'-zo;* a primary verb (in a strengthened form); to *scent* (usually an ill "odor"):—stink {1x}. See: BAGD—555c; THAYER—438d.

3606. **ὅθεν** {15x} **hŏthĕn**, *hoth'-en;* from *3739* with the directive enclitic of source; *from which* place or source or cause (adv. or conjunc.):—wherefore {4x}, from whence {3x}, whereupon {3x}, where {2x}, whence {1x}, from thence {1x}, whereby {1x}. See: BAGD—555c; THAYER—439a.

3607. **ὀθόνη** {2x} **ŏthŏnē**, *oth-on'-ay;* of uncert. aff.; a *linen* cloth, i.e. (espec.) a *sail:*—sheet {2x}.

Othone primarily denoted "fine linen," later, "a sheet," Acts 10:11; 11:5. See: BAGD—555c; THAYER—439a.

3608. **ὀθόνιον** {5x} **ŏthŏniŏn**, *oth-on'-ee-on;* neut. of a presumed der. of *3607;* a linen *bandage:*—linen clothes {5x}.

Othonion, "a piece of fine linen," is used **(1)** in the plural, of the strips of cloth with which the body of the Lord was bound, Lk 24:12; Jn 19:40; 20:5, 6, 7. **(2)** The word is a diminutive of *othone* (3607) "a sheet." See: BAGD—555c; THAYER—439a.

3609. **οἰκεῖος** {3x} **ŏikĕiŏs**, *oy-ki'-os;* from *3624; domestic,* i.e. (as noun), a *relative, adherent:*—of the household {2x}, of (one's) own house {1x}.

Oikeios primarily signifies "of, or belonging to, a house," hence, "of persons, one's household, or kindred," as in **(1)** 1 Ti 5:8 "house"; in **(2)** Eph 2:19, "the household of God" denotes the company of the redeemed; in **(3)** Gal 6:10, it is called "the household of the faith." See: TDNT—5:134, 674; BAGD—556d; THAYER—439a.

3610. **οἰκέτης** {5x} **ŏikĕtēs**, *oy-ket'-ace;* from *3611;* a fellow *resident,* i.e. menial *domestic:*—household servant {1x}, servant {4x}.

An *oiketes* was one of the family, of the household, but not necessarily born in the home and translated **(1)** "household servant" in Acts 10:7; and **(2)** "servant" in Lk 16:13; Rom 14:4; Philemon 25; 1 Pet 2:18. Syn.: 1249, 1401, 2324, 5257. See: BAGD—557a; THAYER—439b.

3611. **οἰκέω** {9x} **ŏikĕō**, *oy-keh'-o;* from *3624;* to *occupy a house,* i.e. *reside* (fig. *inhabit, remain, inhere*); by impl. to *cohabit:*—dwell {9x}.

Oikeo, "to dwell" (from *oikos,* "a house"), "to inhabit as one's abode." It is used **(1)** of God as "dwelling" in light, 1 Ti 6:16; **(2)** of the "indwelling" of the Spirit of God in the believer, Rom 8:9, 11, or in a church, 1 Cor 3:16; **(3)** of the "indwelling" of sin, Rom 7:17, 20; **(4)** of the absence of any good thing in the flesh of the believer, Rom 7:18; **(5)** of the "dwelling" together of those who are married, 1 Cor 7:12–13. See: TDNT—5:135, 674; BAGD—557a; THAYER—439b. See also *3625.*

3612. **οἴκημα** {1x} **ŏikēma**, *oy'-kay-mah;* from *3611;* a *tenement,* i.e. (spec.) a *jail:*—prison {1x}. See: BAGD—557a; THAYER—439c.

3613. **οἰκητήριον** {2x} **ŏikētēriŏn**, *oy-kay-tay'-ree-on;* neut. of a presumed der. of *3611* (equiv. to *3612*); a *residence* (lit. or fig.):—habitation {1x}, house {1x}.

Oiketerion, "a habitation" (from *oiketer,* "an inhabitant," and *oikos,* "a dwelling"), is used in **(1)** Jude 6, of the heavenly region appointed by God as the dwelling place of angels; **(2)** in 2 Cor 5:2, "house," figuratively of the spiritual bodies of believers when raised or changed at the return of the Lord. See: TDNT—5:155, 674; BAGD—357b; THAYER—439c.

3614. **οἰκία** {95x} **ŏikia**, *oy-kee'-ah;* from *3624;* prop. *residence* (abstr.), but usually (concr.) an *abode* (lit. or fig.); by impl. a *family* (espec. *domestics*):—house {92x}, at home {1x}, household {1x}, from the house {1x}.

(1) *Oikos* denoted the whole estate, *oikia* stood for the dwelling only; this distinction was largely lost in later Greek. In the NT it denotes **(2)** "a house, a dwelling," e.g., **(2a)** Mt 2:11; 5:15; 7:24–27; 2 Ti 2:20; 2 Jn 10; **(2b)** it is not used of the Tabernacle or the Temple; **(3)** metaphorically, the heavenly abode, spoken of by the Lord as "My Father's house," Jn 14:2, the eternal dwelling place of believers; **(4)** the body as the dwelling place of the soul, 2 Cor 5:1; **(5)** similarly the resurrection body of believers 2 Cor 5:1; **(6)** property, e.g., Mk 12:40; **(7)** by metonymy, the inhabitants of a house, a household, e.g., Mt 12:25; Jn 4:53; 1 Cor 16:15. See: TDNT—5:131, 674; BAGD—557b; THAYER—439c.

3615. **οἰκιακός** {2x} **ŏikiakŏs**, *oy-kee-ak-os';* from *3614; familiar,* i.e. (as noun) *relatives:*—they (them) of (his own) household {2x}. Cf. Matt. 10:25, 36. See: BAGD—557d; THAYER—439d.

3616. **οἰκοδεσποτέω** {1x} **ŏikŏdĕspŏtĕō**, *oy-kod-es-pot-eh'-o;* from *3617;* to *be* the *head of* (i.e. *rule*) *a family:*—guide the house {1x}. See: TDNT—2:49, 145; BAGD—558a; THAYER—439d.

3617. **οἰκοδεσπότης** {12x} **ŏikŏdĕspŏtēs**, *oy-kod-es-pot'-ace;* from *3624* and *1203; the head of a family:*—householder {4x}, goodman of the house {4x}, master of the house {3x}, goodman {1x}.

The goodman, master of the house, oversees all of the goods in a house and is translated **(1)** "householder" in Mt 13:27; 13:52; 20:1; 21:13; **(2)** "goodman of the house" in Mt 20:11; 24:43; Mk 14:14; Lk 12:39; **(3)** "master of the house" in Mt 10:25; Lk 13:25; 14:21; and **(4)** "goodman" in Lk 22:11. See: TDNT—2:49, 145; BAGD—558a; THAYER—439d.

3618. **οἰκοδομέω** {39x} **ŏikŏdŏmĕō**, *oy-kod-om-eh'-o;* from the same as *3619;* to *be* a *house-builder,* i.e. *construct* or (fig.) *confirm:*—build {24x}, edify {7x}, builder {5x}, build up {1x}, be in building {1x}, embolden {1x}.

Oikodomeo, as a verb, means lit., "to build a house" (*oikos,* "a house," *domeo,* "to build"), hence, to build anything, **(1)** e.g., Mt 7:24; Lk 4:29; 6:48; Jn 2:20; **(1a)** usually signifies "to build," whether literally, or figuratively; **(1b)** the present participle, lit., "the (ones) building," is used as a noun, "the builders," in Mt 21:42; Mk 12:10; Lk 20:17; Acts 4:11; 1 Pet 2:7; **(2)** is used metaphorically, in the sense of "edifying," promoting the spiritual growth and development of character of believers, by teaching or by example, suggesting such spiritual progress as the result of patient labor. It is said **(2a)** of the effect of this upon local churches, Acts 9:31; 1 Cor 14:4; **(2b)** of the individual action of believers towards each other, 1 Cor 8:1; 10:23; 14:17; 1 Th 5:11; **(3)** of an individual in regard to himself, 1 Cor 14:4. **(4)** In 1 Cor 8:10, where it is translated "emboldened," the apostle uses it with pathetic irony, of the action of a brother in "building up" his brother who had a weak conscience, causing him to compromise his scruples; "strengthened," or "confirmed," would be suitable renderings. See: TDNT—5:136, 674; BAGD—558a; THAYER—439d.

3619. **οἰκοδομή** {18x} **ŏikŏdŏmē**, *oy-kod-om-ay';* fem. (abstr.) of a compound of *3624* and the base of *1430; architecture,* i.e. (concr.) a *structure;* fig. *confirmation:*—edifying {7x}, building {6x}, edification {4x}, wherewith (one) may edify {1x}.

Oikodome denotes "a building, or edification" and is used **(1)** literally, e.g., Mt 24:1; Mk 13:1–2; **(2)** figuratively, e.g., **(2a)** Rom. 14:19 (lit., "the things of building up"); Rom 15:2; **(2b)** of a local church as a spiritual building, 1 Cor 3:9, or **(2c)** the whole church, the body of Christ, Eph 2:21. **(3)** It expresses the strengthening effect **(3a)** of teaching, 1 Cor 14:3, 5, 12, 26; 2 Cor 10:8; 12:19; 13:10, or **(3b)** other ministry, Eph 4:12, 16, 29 (the idea conveyed is progress resulting from patient effort). **(4)** It is also used of the believer's resurrection body, 2 Cor 5:1. See: TDNT—5:144, 674; BAGD—558d; THAYER—440b.

3620. **οἰκοδομία** {1x} **ŏikŏdŏmia**, *oy-kod-om-ee'-ah;* from the same as *3619; confirmation:*—edifying {1x}.

Oidodomia is used of building up another, edifying, 1 Ti 1:4. See: BAGD—559c; THAYER—440c.

3621. **οἰκονομέω** {1x} **ŏikŏnŏmĕō**, *oy-kon-om-eh'-o;* from *3623;* to *manage* (a house, i.e. an estate):—be steward {1x}. See: BAGD—559c; THAYER—440c.

3622. **οἰκονομία** {7x} **ŏikŏnŏmia**, *oy-kon-om-ee'-ah;* from *3623; administration* (of a household or estate); spec. a (relig.) "*economy*":—dispensation {4x}, stewardship {3x}.

Oikonomia (3622) **(1)** primarily signifies "the management of a household or of household affairs" (*oikos,* "a house," *nomos,* "a law"); **(1a)** then the management or administration of the property of others, and so **(1b)** "a stewardship," Lk 16:2–4; **(2)** elsewhere only in the epistles of Paul, who applies it **(2a)** to the responsibility entrusted to him of preaching the gospel, 1 Cor 9:17 "dispensation"; **(2b)** to the stewardship committed to him "to fulfill the Word of God," the fulfillment being the unfolding of the completion of the divinely arranged and imparted cycle of truths which are consummated in the truth relating to the church as the body of Christ, Col 1:25 "dispensation"; **(2c)** so in Eph 3:2, of the grace of God given him as a stewardship ("dispensation") in regard to the same "mystery"; **(3)** in Eph 1:10 and 3:2, it is used of the arrangement or administration by God, by which in "the fullness of the times" (or seasons) God will sum up all things in the heavens and on earth in Christ. **(4)** A "dispensation" is not a period or epoch, but a mode of dealing, an arrangement or administration of affairs; but by metonomy, dispensation is applied to that period of time (not clearly demarked in the Scriptures) wherein God deals specifically with man, giving him a special stewardship to administer. **(5)** A steward oversees another's goods and dispenses them in accordance with the Master's desires. See: TDNT—5:151, 674; BAGD—559c; THAYER—440d.

3623. **οἰκονόμος** {10x} **ŏikŏnŏmŏs**, *oy-kon-om'-os;* from *3624* and the base of *3551;* a *house-distributor* (i.e. *manager*), or *overseer,* i.e. an employee in that capacity; by extens. a fiscal *agent* (*treasurer*); fig. a *preacher* (of the Gospel):—chamberlain {1x}, governor {1x}, steward {8x}.

Oikonomos primarily denoted "the manager of a household or estate" (*oikos,* "a house," *nemo,* "to arrange"), **(1)** "a steward" (such were usually slaves or freedmen), Lk 12:42; 16:1, 3, 8; 1 Cor 4:2; Gal 4:2, "governors"; **(2)** in Rom 16:23, the "the chamberlain" of a city; **(3)** it is used metaphorically, in the wider sense, of a "steward" in general, **(3a)** of preachers of the gospel and teachers of the Word of God, 1 Cor 4:1; **(3b)** of elders or bishops in churches, Titus 1:7; **(3c)** of believers generally, 1 Pet 4:10. See: TDNT—5:149, 674; BAGD—560a; THAYER—440d.

3624. **οἶκος** {114x} **ŏikŏs**, *oy'-kos;* of uncert. aff.; a *dwelling* (more or less extens., lit. or fig.); by impl. a *family* (more or less related, lit. or fig.):—house {104x}, household {3x}, home + 1519 {2x}, at home + 1722 {2x}, temple {3x}.

Oikos denotes **(1)** "a house, a dwelling," e.g., Mt 9:6, 7; 11:8; it is used of **(1a)** the Tabernacle, as the House of God, Mt 12:4, and the Temple similarly, e.g., Mt 21:13; Lk 11:51, "temple"; Jn 2:16, 17; **(1b)** called by the Lord "your house" in

Mt 23:38 and Lk 13:35; **(2)** metaphorically of Israel as God's house, Heb 3:2, 5, where "His house" is not Moses', but God's; **(3)** of believers, similarly, Heb 3:6, where Christ is spoken of as "over God's House"; Heb 10:21; 1 Pet 2:5; 4:17; **(4)** of the body, Mt 12:44; Lk 11:24; **(5)** by metonymy, of the members of a household or family, e.g., Lk 10:5; Acts 7:10; 11:14; 1 Ti 3:4, 5, 12; 2 Ti 1:16; 4:19, "household"; Titus 1:11 (plural); **(6)** of a local church, 1 Ti 3:15; **(7)** of the descendants of Jacob (Israel) and David, e.g., Mt 10:6; Lk 1:27, 33; Acts 2:36; 7:42. See: TDNT—5:119, 674; BAGD—560b; THAYER—441a.

3625. **οἰκουμένη** {15x} **ŏikŏumĕnē**, *oy-kou-men'-ay;* fem. part. pres. pass. of *3611* (as noun, by impl. of *1093*); *land,* i.e. the (terrene part of the) *globe;* spec. the Rom. *empire:*—earth {1x}, world {14x}.

Oidouomene, **(1)** "the inhabited earth", is used **(1a)** of the whole inhabited world, Mt 24:14; Lk 4:5; 21:26; Rom 10:18; Heb 1:6; Rev 3:10; 16:14; **(1b)** by metonymy, of its inhabitants, Acts 17:31; Rev 12:9; **(2)** of the Roman Empire, **(2a)** the world as viewed by the writer or speaker, Lk 2:1; Acts 11:28; 24:5; **(2b)** by metonymy, of its inhabitants, Acts 17:6; 19:27; **(3)** the inhabited world in a coming age, Heb 2:5. See: TDNT—5:157, 674; BAGD—561b; THAYER—441d.

3626. **οἰκουρός** {1x} **ŏikŏurŏs**, *oy-koo-ros'* or **οἰκουργός** **ŏikŏurgŏs**, *oy-koor-gos';* from *3624* and οὖρος **ŏurŏs** (a *guard,* be "ware"); a *stayer at home,* i.e. *domestically inclined* (a "good housekeeper"):—keeper at home {1x}.

This word means "working at home" (*oikos,* and a root of *ergon,* "work"), is used in Titus 2:5, "workers at home", in the injunction given to elder women regarding the training of the young women. See: BAGD—561c; THAYER—442a.

3627. **οἰκτείρω** {2x} **ŏiktĕirō**, *oyk-ti'-ro;* also (in certain tenses) prol. **οἰκτερέω** **ŏiktĕrĕō**, *oyk-ter-eh'-o;* from οἶκτος **ŏiktŏs**, (*pity*); to *exercise pity:*—have compassion on {1x}, have compassion {1x}.

This verb means to have pity, a feeling of distress through the ills of others, Rom 9:15. See: TDNT—5:159,*; BAGD—561d; THAYER—442a.

3628. **οἰκτιρμός** {5x} **ŏiktirmŏs**, *oyk-tir-mos';* from and stronger than *3627; pity:*—mercy {5x}.

This word means "the viscera, the inward parts," as the seat of emotion, **(1)** the "heart," Phil 2:1; Col 3:12, "bowels of mercies". **(2)** In Heb 10:28 it is used with *choris,* "without," (lit., "without compassions"). **(3)** It is translated "mercies" in Rom 12:1 and 2 Cor 1:3. Syn.: *Eleeo* (1653) means to feel sympathy with the misery of another, esp. such sympathy as manifests itself in act, less freq. in word. *Oiktirmos* (3628) denotes the inward feeling of compassion which abides in the heart. A criminal begs 1653 of his judge; but hopeless suffering is often the object of 3628. See: TDNT—5:159, 680; BAGD—561d; THAYER—442b. See also: 1653, 1655, 1656, 2433, 2436, 3627, 3629, 4698.

3629. **οἰκτίρμων** {3x} **ŏiktirmōn**, *oyk-tir'-mone;* from *3627; compassionate:*—merciful {2x}, of tender mercy {1x}.

This word means "pitiful, compassionate for the ills of others" and is used **(1)** twice in Lk 6:36, "merciful" (of the character of God, to be expressed in His people); and **(2)** Jas 5:11, "of tender mercy." See: TDNT—5:159, 680; BAGD—561d; THAYER—442b. Syn.: 1653, 1655, 1656, 2433, 2436, 3627, 3628, 4698.

οἶμαι **ŏimai**. See *3633.*

3630. **οἰνοπότης** {2x} **ŏinŏpŏtēs**, *oy-nop-ot'-ace;* from *3631* and a der. of the alt. of *4095;* a *tippler:*—winebibber {2x}.

Oinopotes designates a wine drinker (Mt 11:19; Lk 7:34). See: BAGD—562a; THAYER—442b.

3631. **οἶνος** {33x} **ŏinŏs**, *oy'-nos;* a primary word (or perh. of Heb. origin [3196]); "*wine*" (lit. or fig.):—wine {32x}, winepress + 3125 {1x}.

Oinos is the general word for "wine." **(1)** The mention of the bursting of the wineskins, Mt 9:17; Mk 2:22; Lk 5:37, implies fermentation. See also Eph 5:18 (cf. Jn 2:10; 1 Ti 3:8; Titus 2:3). **(2)** In Mt 27:34 it is translated "vinegar" the result of complete fermentation. **(3)** The drinking of "wine" could be a stumbling block and the apostle enjoins abstinence in this respect, as in others, so as to avoid giving an occasion of stumbling to a brother, Rom 14:21. Contrast 1 Ti 5:23, which has an entirely different connection. **(4)** The word is used metaphorically **(4a)** of the evils ministered to the nations by religious Babylon, 14:8; 17:2; 18:3; **(4b)** of the contents of the cup of divine wrath upon the nations and Babylon, Rev 14:10; 16:19; 19:15. See: TDNT—5:162, 680; BAGD—562a; THAYER—442b.

3632. **οἰνοφλυγία** {1x} **ŏinŏphlugia**, *oy-nof-loog-ee'-ah;* from *3631* and a form of the base of *5397;* an *overflow* (or surplus) of *wine,* i.e. *vinolency* (*drunkenness*):—excess of wine {1x}.

(1) This word means an insatiate desire for wine and refers to debauchery, an extravagant indulgence on alcoholic beverages that may permanently damage the body. **(2)** In 1 Pet 4:3, *oinophlugia,* means "drunkenness, debauchery" [from *oinos,* "wine," *phluo,* "to bubble up, overflow"] and is rendered "excess of wine": "For the time past of *our* life may suffice us to have wrought the will of the Gentiles, when we walked in lasciviousness, lusts, excess of wine, revellings, banquetings, and abominable idolatries." Syn.: 2897, 2970, 3178, 4224. See: BAGD—562c; THAYER—442c.

3633. **οἴομαι** {3x} **ŏiŏmai**, *oy'-om-ahee;* or (shorter) **οἶμαι** **ŏimai**, *oy'-mahee;* mid. voice appar. from *3634;* to *make like* (oneself), i.e. *imagine* (*be of* the *opinion*):—suppose {2x}, think {1x}.

Oimai signifies "to expect, imagine, suppose"; it is rendered **(1)** "to suppose" in Jn 21:25; and **(2)** "think" in Jas 1:7; Phil 1:16, "thinking." Syn.: *Dokeo* (1380) refers to the subjective judgment, which may or may not conform to the fact. *Hegeomai* (2233) refers to the actual external appearance, generally correct, but possibly deceptive. *Hegeomai* (2233) and *nomizo* (3543) denote a belief resting not on one's inner feeling or sentiment, but on the due consideration of external grounds, and the weighing and comparing of facts. *Dokeo* (1380) and *oiomai* (3633) on the other hand, describe a subjective judgment growing out of inclination or a view of facts in their relation to us. *Hegeomai* denotes a more deliberate and careful judgment than *nomizo* (3543); *oiomai* (3633) having a subjective judgment which has feeling rather than thought (*dokeo* –1380) for its ground. See: BAGD—562c; THAYER—442c.

3634. **οἷος** {15x} **hŏiŏs**, *hoy'-os;* prob. akin to *3588, 3739,* and *3745; such* or *what sort* of (as a correl. or exclamation); espec. the neut. (adv.) with neg. not *so:*—such as {6x}, as {3x}, which {2x}, what manner {1x}, so as {1x}, what manner of man {1x}, what {1x}.

Hoios, a relative pronoun, signifying "what sort of or manner of" (1 Th 1:5; Lk 9:55). Syn.: 195, 1485, 2239, 3668, 3697, 3779, 4169, 4187, 4217, 4459, 5158, 5159, 5179, 5615. See: BAGD—561c; THAYER—442c.

οἴω **ŏiō**. See *5342.*

3635. **ὀκνέω** {1x} **ŏknĕō**, *ok-neh'-o;* from ὄκνος **ŏknŏs**, (*hesitation*); to *be slow* (fig. *loath*):—delay {1x}.

Okneo, as a verb, means "to shrink, to be loath or slow to do a thing, to hesitate, delay": ". . . the disciples had heard that Peter was there, they sent unto him two men, desiring *him* that he would not delay to come to them" (Acts 9:38). Syn.: 311, 5549. See: BAGD—563a; THAYER—442d.

3636. **ὀκνηρός** {3x} **ŏknērŏs**, *ok-nay-ros';* from *3635; tardy,* i.e. *indolent;* (fig.) *irksome:*—grievous {1x}, slothful {2x}.

This word means "shrinking, timid" (from *okneo,* "to shrink, delay"), is used **(1)** negatively in Phil 3:1, "grievous", i.e., "I do not hesitate"; and **(2)** in Mt 25:26, and Rom 12:11, "slothful." See: TDNT—5:166, 681; BAGD—563a; THAYER—442d.

3637. **ὀκταήμερος** {1x} **ŏktaēmĕrŏs**, *ok-tah-ay'-mer-os;* from *3638* and *2250;* an *eight-day* old person or act:—the eighth day {1x}.

Oktaemeros, an adjective, signifying an "eighth-day" person or thing, "eight days old" (*okto,* and *hemera,* "a day"), is used in Phil 3:5. This, and similar numerical adjectives not found in the NT, indicate duration rather than intervals. The apostle shows by his being an "eighth-day" person as to circumcision, that his parents were neither Ishmaelites (circumcised in their thirteenth year) nor other Gentiles, converted to Judaism (circumcised on becoming Jews). See: BAGD—563a; THAYER—442d.

3638. **ὀκτώ** {9x} **ŏktō**, *ok-to';* a primary numeral; "*eight*":—eight {6x}, eighteen + 1176 + 2532 {3x}. See: BAGD—563a; THAYER—443a.

3639. **ὄλεθρος** {4x} **ŏlĕthrŏs**, *ol'-eth-ros;* from a primary ὄλλυμι **ŏllumi** (to *destroy;* a prol. form); *ruin,* i.e. *death, punishment:*—destruction {4x}.

Olethros, "ruin, destruction," always translated "destruction," is used **(1)** in 1 Cor 5:5, of the effect upon the physical condition of an erring believer for the purpose of his spiritual profit; **(2)** in 1 Th 5:3 and 2 Th 1:9, of the effect of the divine judgments upon men at the ushering in of the Day of the Lord and the revelation of the Lord Jesus; **(3)** in 1 Ti 6:9, of the consequences of the indulgence of the flesh, referring to physical "ruin" and possibly that of the whole being, the following word *apoleia* stressing the final, eternal and irrevocable character of the ruin. See: TDNT—5:168, 681; BAGD—563b; THAYER—443a.

3640. **ὀλιγόπιστος** {5x} **ŏligŏpistŏs**, *ol-ig-op'-is-tos;* from *3641* and *4102; incredulous,* i.e. *lacking confidence* (in Christ):—of little faith {5x}.

Literally, this word means little of faith and is used only by the Lord as a tender rebuke **(1)** for anxiety (Mt 6:30; Lk 12:28); or **(2)** for fear (Mt 8:26; 14:31; 16:8). See: TDNT—6:174, 849; BAGD—563b; THAYER—443a.

3641. **ὀλίγος** {43x} **ŏligŏs**, *ol-ee'-gos;* of uncert. aff.; *puny* (in extent, degree, number, duration or value); espec. neut. (adv.) *somewhat:*—few {14x}, (a) little {7x}, small {5x}, few things {4x}, almost + 1722 {2x}, a while {2x}, misc. {9x} = brief [-ly], + long, a season, short.

Oligon, as an adverb, is used of number quantity, and size, and denotes **(1)** "few, little, small, slight," e.g., Mt 7:14; 9:37; 15:34; 20:16; **(2)** neuter plural, "a few things," Mt 25:21, 23; Rev 2:14, 20; **(3)** in Eph 3:3, the phrase *en oligo,* in brief, is translated "in a few words"; also translated **(4)** "for a season": "Wherein ye greatly rejoice, though now for a season, if need be, ye are in heaviness through manifold temptations" (1 Pet 1:6). Syn.: 171, 2122, 2540, 4340, 5550, 5610. See: TDNT—5:171, 682; BAGD—563c; THAYER—443a.

3642. **ὀλιγόψυχος** {1x} **ŏligŏpsuchŏs**, *ol-ig-op'-soo-khos;* from *3641* and *5590; little-spirited,* i.e. *faint-hearted:*—feebleminded {1x}.

Oligopsuchos, lit., "small-souled" (*oligos,* "small," *psuche,* "the soul"), denotes "despondent"; then, "fainthearted," 1 Th 5:14, "feebleminded." See: TDNT—9:665, 1342; BAGD—564a; THAYER—443b.

3643. **ὀλιγωρέω** {1x} **ŏligōrĕō**, *ol-ig-o-reh'-o;* from a compound of *3641* and ὥρα **ōra** ("*care*"); to *have little regard,* for, i.e. to *disesteem:*—despise {1x}. See: BAGD—564a; THAYER—443b.

3644. **ὀλοθρευτής** {1x} **ŏlŏthrĕutēs**, *ol-oth-ryoo-tace';* from *3645;* a *ruiner,* i.e. (spec.) a venomous *serpent:*—destroyer {1x}. See: TDNT—5:169, 681; BAGD—564b; THAYER—443c.

3645. **ὀλοθρεύω** {1x} **ŏlŏthrĕuō**, *ol-oth-ryoo'-o;* from *3639;* to *spoil,* i.e. *slay:*—destroy {1x}. See: TDNT—5:167,*; BAGD—564b; THAYER—443c.

3646. **ὁλοκαύτωμα** {3x} **hŏlŏkautōma**, *hol-ok-ŏw'-to-mah;* from a der. of a compound of *3650* and a der. of *2545;* a *wholly-consumed* sacrifice ("holocaust"):—(whole) burnt offering {3x}.

This word denotes "a whole burnt offering" (*holos,* "whole," *kautos,* for *kaustos,* a verbal adjective from *kaio,* "to burn"), i.e., "a victim," the whole of which is burned (cf. Ex 30:20; Lev 5:12; 23:8, 25, 27). It is used in Mk 12:33, by the scribe who questioned the Lord as to the first commandment in the Law and in Heb 10:6, 8. See: BAGD—564b; THAYER—443c.

3647. **ὁλοκληρία** {1x} **hŏlŏklēria**, *hol-ok-lay-ree'-ah;* from *3648; integrity,* i.e. phys. *wholeness:*—perfect soundness {1x}.

This word speaks of an unimpaired condition of the body, in which all its members are healthy and fit for use; good health, Acts 3:16. See: TDNT—3:767, 442; BAGD—564c; THAYER—443c.

3648. **ὁλόκληρος** {2x} **hŏlŏklērŏs**, *hol'-ok'-lay-ros;* from *3650* and *2819; complete* in every *part,* i.e. perfectly *sound* (in body):—entire {1x}, whole {1x}.

This word refers to that which retains all that was initially allotted to it and implies completion and wholeness in all its parts and is used ethically in 1 Th 5:23, indicating that every grace present in Christ should be manifested in the believer; so Jas 1:4. Syn.: 739, 5046. See: TDNT—3:766, 442; BAGD—564c; THAYER—443d.

3649. **ὀλολύζω** {1x} **ŏlŏluzō**, *ol-ol-ood'-zo;* a redupl. primary verb; to "*howl*" or "*halloo*", i.e. *shriek:*—howl {1x}.

Ololuzo is an onomatopoeic verb (expressing its significance in its sound) meaning to cry aloud [Eng., howl] and was primarily used of crying aloud to the gods with Jas 5:1 being an exhortation to the godless rich. See: TDNT—5:173, 682; BAGD—564c; THAYER—443d.

3650. **ὅλος** {112x} **hŏlŏs**, *hol'-os;* a primary word; "*whole*" or "*all*", i.e. *complete* (in extent, amount, time or degree), espec. (neut.) as noun or adv.:—all {65x}, whole {43x}, every whit {2x}, altogether {1x}, throughout + 1223 {1x}. See: TDNT—5:174, 682; BAGD—564c; THAYER—443d.

3651. **ὁλοτελής** {1x} **hŏlŏtĕlēs**, *hol-ot-el-ace';* from *3650* and *5056; complete* to the *end,* i.e. *absolutely perfect:*—wholly {1x}.

Holoteles, "wholly," 1 Th 5:23, is lit., "whole-complete", i.e., "through and through"; the apostle's desire is that the sanctification of the believer may extend to every part of his being. See: TDNT—5:175, 682; BAGD—565a.; THAYER—444b.

3652. **Ὀλυμπᾶς** {1x} **Olumpas**, *ol-oom-pas';* prob. a contr. from Ὀλυμπιόδωρος **Olumpiŏdōrŏs**, (*Olympian-bestowed,* i.e. *heaven-descended*); *Olympas,* a Chr.:—Olympas {1x}. See: BAGD—565a; THAYER—444b.

3653. **ὄλυνθος** {1x} **ŏlunthŏs**, *ol'-oon-thos;* of uncert. der.; an *unripe* (because out of season) *fig:*—untimely fig {1x}. See: TDNT—7:751, 1100; BAGD—565a; THAYER—444b.

3654. **ὅλως** {4x} **hŏlōs**, *hol'-oce;* adv. from *3650; completely,* i.e. *altogether;* (by anal.) *everywhere;* (neg.) not *by any means:*—at all {2x}, commonly {1x}, utterly {1x}.

Holos, "all, whole," is translated **(1)** "commonly" in 1 Cor 5:1; **(2)** in 1 Cor 6:7 it is translated "utterly"; **(3)** in 1 Cor 15:29, "at all" as in Mt 5:34. See: BAGD—565b; THAYER—444b.

3655. **ὄμβρος** {1x} **ŏmbrŏs**, *om'-bros;* of uncert. aff.; a thunder *storm:*—shower {1x}.

Ombros denotes a heavy shower, a storm of rain (Lk 12:54). See: BAGD—565b; THAYER—444b.

3656. **ὁμιλέω** {4x} **hŏmilĕō**, *hom-il-eh'-o;* from *3658;* to *be in company* with, i.e. (by impl.) to *converse:*—commune {1x}, commune with {1x}, talk {2x}. Cf. Lk 24:14, 15; Acts 20:11; 24:26. See: BAGD—565c; THAYER—444c.

3657. **ὁμιλία** {1x} **hŏmilia**, *hom-il-ee'-ah;* from *3658; companionship* ("homily"), i.e. (by impl.) *intercourse:*—communication {1x}.

Homilia, "an association of people, those who are of the same company" (*homos,* "same"), is used in 1 Cor 15:33, "(evil) communications." See: BAGD—565c; THAYER—444d.

3658. **ὅμιλος** {1x} **hŏmilŏs**, *hom'-il-os;* from the base of *3674* and a der. of the alt. of *138* (mean. a *crowd*); *association together,* i.e. a *multitude:*—company {1x}. See: BAGD—565d; THAYER—444d.

3659. **ὄμμα** {1x} **ŏmma**, *om'-mah;* from *3700;* a *sight,* i.e. (by impl.) the *eye:*—eye {1x}. See: BAGD—565d; THAYER—444d.

3660. **ὀμνύω** {27x} **ŏmnuō**, *om-noo'-o;* a prol. form of a primary but obsolete ὄμω **ŏmō**, for which another prol. form ὀμόω **ŏmŏō** *om-ŏ'-o* is used in certain tenses; to *swear,* i.e. *take* (or *declare on*) *oath:*—swear {27x}.

Omnuo is used of "affirming or denying by an oath," **(1)** e.g., Mt 26:74; Mk 6:23; Lk 1:73; Heb 3:11, 18; 4:3; 7:21; accompanied by that by which one swears, **(2)** e.g., Mt. 5:34, 36; 23:16; Heb 6:13, 16; Jas 5:12; Rev. 10:6. See: TDNT—5:176, 683; BAGD—565d; THAYER—444d.

3661. **ὁμοθυμαδόν** {12x} **hŏmŏthumadŏn**, *hom-oth-oo-mad-on';* adv. from a compound of the base of *3674* and *2372; unanimously:*—with one accord {11x}, with one mind {1x}.

Homothumadon, "of one accord" (from *homos,* "same," *thumos,* "mind"), **(1)** occurs eleven times, **(1)** ten in the Acts, 1:14; 2:46; 4:24; 5:12; 7:57; 8:6; 12:20; 15:25; 18:12, 19:29, and the other **(2)** in Rom 15:6, "with one mind." See: TDNT—5:185, 684; BAGD—566c; THAYER—445a.

3662. **ὁμοιάζω** {1x} **hŏmŏiazō**, *hom-oy-ad'-zo;* from *3664;* to *resemble:*—agree thereto {1x}. See: BAGD—566c; THAYER—445a.

3663. **ὁμοιοπαθής** {2x} **hŏmŏiŏpathēs**, *hom-oy-op-ath-ace';* from *3664* and the alt. of *3958; similarly affected:*—of like passions {1x}, subject to like passions {1x}.

Homoiopathes, "of like feelings or affections", is rendered **(1)** "of like passions" in Acts 14:15; and **(2)** in Jas 5:17, "subject to like passions." See: TDNT—5:938, 798; BAGD—566c; THAYER—445a.

3664. **ὅμοιος** {47x} **hŏmŏiŏs**, *hom'-oy-os;* from the base of *3674; similar* (in appearance or character):—like {47x}.

Homios, "like, resembling, such as, the same as," is used **(1)** of appearance or form Jn 9:9; Rev 1:13, 15; 2:18; 4:3 (twice), 6, 7; 9:7 (twice), 10, 19; 11:1; 13:2, 11; 14:14; **(2)** of ability, condition, nature, Mt 22:39; Acts 17:29; Gal 5:21, "such like," lit., "and the (things) similar to these"; 1 Jn 3:2; Rev 13:4; 18:18; 21:11, 18; **(3)** of comparison in parables, Mt 13:31, 33, 44, 45, 47; 20:1; Lk 13:18, 19, 21; **(4)** of action, thought, etc. Mt 11:16; 13:52; Lk 6:47, 48, 49; 7:31, 32; 12:36; Jn 8:55; Jude 7. See: TDNT—5:186, 684; BAGD—566; THAYER—445b.

3665. **ὁμοιότης** {2x} **hŏmŏiŏtēs**, *hom-oy-ot'-ace;* from *3664; resemblance:*—like as + 2596 {1x}, similitude {1x}. Cf. Heb 4:15; 7:15. See: TDNT—5:189, 684; BAGD—567a; THAYER—445b.

3666. **ὁμοιόω** {15x} **hŏmŏiŏō**, *hom-oy-ŏ'-o;* from *3664;* to *assimilate,* i.e. *compare;* pass. to *become similar:*—liken {9x}, make like {2x}, be like {2x}, in the likeness of {1x}, resemble {1x}.

Homioo, "to make like", is used **(1)** especially in the parables, **(1a)** with the significance of comparing, "likening," or, in the passive voice, "being likened," Mt 7:24, 26; 11:16; 13:24; 18:23; 22:2; 25:1; Mk 4:30; Lk 7:31; 13:18, "resemble"; v. 20; **(1b)** in several of these instances the point of resemblance is not a specific detail, but the whole circumstances of the parable; **(2)** of making "like," or, in the passive voice, of being made or becoming "like," Mt 6:8; Acts 14:11, "in the likeness of (men)," lit., "being made like" (aorist participle, passive); Rom 9:29; Heb 2:17, of Christ in being "made like" unto His brethren, i.e., in partaking of human nature, apart from sin (cf. v. 14). See: TDNT—5:188, 684; BAGD—567b; THAYER—445c.

3667. **ὁμοίωμα** {6x} **hŏmŏiōma**, *hom-oy'-o-mah;* from *3666;* a *form;* abstr. *resemblance:*—made like to {1x}, likeness {3x}, shape {1x}, similitude {1x}.

(1) The main stress of this word is on the outward similarities with nothing being considered about the inward realities. **(2)** This resemblance is an accidental one like two eggs and not a derived resemblance like a statue resembles its model (see *eikon* – 1504). The key word is similar, like in appearance without considering the essence. **(3)** This word denotes "that which is made like something, a resemblance," **(3a)** in the concrete sense, Rev 9:7, "shapes"; **(3b)** in the abstract sense, Rom 1:23, "(into an image) made like to"; **(3b1)** the association here of the two words *homoioma* and *eikon* serves to enhance the contrast between the idol and "the glory of the incorruptible God," and **(3b2)** is expressive of contempt; **(3c)** in Rom 5:14, "(the) similitude of Adam's transgression"; **(3d)** in Rom 6:5, "(the) likeness (of His death); **(3d)** in Rom 8:3, "(the) likeness (of sinful flesh); **(3e)** in Phil 2:7, "the likeness of men." **(3f)** The expression "likeness of men" does not of itself imply, still less does it exclude or diminish, the reality of the nature which Christ assumed. That . . . is declared in the words "form of a servant." Paul justly says *in the likeness of men,* because, in fact, Christ, although certainly perfect Man (Rom 5:15; 1 Cor 15:21; 1 Ti 2:5), was, by reason of the Divine nature present in Him, not simply and merely man . . . but the Incarnate Son of God. Syn.: 1504, 3669. See: TDNT—5:191, 684; BAGD—567c; THAYER—445c.

3668. **ὁμοίως** {30x} **hŏmŏiōs**, *hom-oy'-oce;* adv. from *3664; similarly:*—likewise {28x}, moreover + 1161 {1x}, so {1x}.

Homoios, signifies "likewise, in like manner, equally" in Mt 26:35; 27:41; Mk 4:16; Lk 5:33; 6:31; 10:32; 10:37; 17:28, 31; 22:36; Jn 5:19; 6:11; 21:13; Rom 1:27; Jas 2:25; 1 Pet 5:5. Syn.: 195, 1485, 2239, 3634, 3697, 3779, 4169, 4187, 4217, 4459, 5158, 5159, 5179, 5615. See: BAGD—568d; THAYER—445c. Matt. 26:35; Luke 5:33; 6:31; 10:37; 17:28, 31; 22:36; John 6:11; 21:13; Rom 1:27; 1 Pet. 5:5

3669. **ὁμοίωσις** {1x} **hŏmŏiōsis**, *hom-oy'-o-sis;* from *3666; assimilation,* i.e. *resemblance:*—similitude {1x}. Syn.: 3667, 1504. See: TDNT—5:190, 684; BAGD—568a; THAYER—445d.

3670. **ὁμολογέω** {24x} **hŏmŏlŏgĕō**, *hom-ol-og-eh'-o;* from a compound of the base of *3674* and *3056;* to *assent,* i.e. *covenant, acknowledge:*—confess {17x}, profess {3x}, promise {1x}, give thanks {1x}, confession is made {1x}, acknowledgeth {1x}.

Homologeo, lit., "to speak the same thing" (*homos,* "same," *lego,* "to speak"), "to assent, accord, agree with," denotes, **(1)** "to confess, declare, admit," Jn 1:20; e.g., Acts 24:14; Heb 11:13; **(2)** "to confess by way of admitting oneself guilty of what one is accused of, the result of inward conviction," 1 Jn 1:9; **(3)** "to declare openly by way of speaking out freely, such confession being the effect of deep conviction of facts," Mt 7:23; 10:32 (twice) and Lk 12:8; Jn 9:22; 12:42; Acts 23:8; Rom 10:9–10 ("confession is made"); 1 Ti 6:12; Titus 1:16; 1 Jn 2:23; 4:2, 15; 2 Jn 7; **(4)** "to confess by way of celebrating with praise," Heb 13:15; **(5)** "to promise," Mt 14:7.

(6) In Mt 10:32 and Lk 12:8 the construction of this verb with *en,* "in," followed by the dative case of the personal pronoun, has a special significance, namely, to "confess" in a person's name, the nature of the "confession" being determined by the context, the suggestion being to make a public "confession." Thus the statement, "every one . . . who shall confess Me (lit. "in Me," i.e., in My case) before men, him (lit., "in him," i.e., in his case) will I also confess before My Father . . . ," conveys the thought of "confessing" allegiance to Christ as one's Master and Lord, and, on the other hand, of acknowledgment, on His part, of the faithful one as being His worshipper and servant, His loyal follower; this is appropriate to the original idea in *homologeo* of being identified in thought or language. See: TDNT—5:199, 687; BAGD—568a; THAYER—446a.

3671. **ὁμολογία** {6x} **hŏmŏlŏgia**, *hom-ol-og-ee'-ah;* from the same as *3670; acknowledgment:*—confession {1x}, profession {4x}, professed {1x}.

Homologia denotes "confession, by acknowledgment of the truth," 2 Cor 9:13; 1 Ti 6:12–13; Heb 3:1; 4:14; 10:23; 1 Ti 6:13). See: TDNT—5:199, 687; BAGD—568d; THAYER—446b.

3672. **ὁμολογουμένως** {1x} **hŏmŏlŏgŏumĕnōs**, *hom-ol-og-ŏw-men'-oce;* adv. of pres. pass. part. of *3670; confessedly:*—without controversy {1x}. See: TDNT—5:199, 687; BAGD—569a; THAYER—446c.

3673. **ὁμότεχνος** {1x} **hŏmŏtĕchnŏs**, *hom-ot'-ekh-nos;* from the base of *3674* and *5078;* a *fellow-artificer:*—of the same craft {1x}. See: BAGD—569b; THAYER—446c.

3674. **ὁμοῦ** {3x} **hŏmŏu**, *hom-oo';* gen. of ὁμός **hŏmŏs**, (the *same;* akin to *260*) as adv.; *at the same* place or time:—together {3x}.

Homou, used in connection with place, and is used with the idea of together at the same place: "So they ran both together: and the other disciple did outrun Peter, and came first to the sepulchre" (Jn 20:4); **(2)** without reference to place, Jn 4:36; 21:2. Syn.: *Hama* (260) stresses the temporal, being together at the same time. See: BAGD—569b; THAYER—446c.

3675. **ὁμόφρων** {1x} **hŏmŏphrōn**, *hom-of'-rone;* from the base of *3674* and *5424; like-minded,* i.e. *harmonious:*—of one mind {1x}. See: BAGD—569c; THAYER—446c.

ὁμόω **ŏmŏō**. See *3660.*

3676. **ὅμως** {3x} **hŏmōs**, *hom'-oce;* adv. from the base of *3674; at the same* time, i.e. (conjunc.) *notwithstanding, yet still:*—and even {1x}, nevertheless {1x}, though it be but {1x}.

Homos, "yet, nevertheless," is translated **(1)** "and even" in 1 Cor 14:7; **(2)** elsewhere **(2a)** Jn 12:42, "nevertheless"; **(2b)** Gal 3:15, "nevertheless." See: BAGD—569c; THAYER—446c.

3677. **ὄναρ** {6x} **ŏnar**, *on'-ar;* of uncert. der.; a *dream:*—dream {6x}.

An *onar* is a vision in sleep in distinction from a waking vision (Mt. 1:20; 2:12–13, 19, 22; 27:19). See: TDNT—5:220, 690; BAGD—569d; THAYER—446d.

3678. **ὀνάριον** {1x} **ŏnariŏn**, *on-ar'-ee-on;* neut. of a presumed der. of *3688;* a *little ass:*—young ass {1x}. See: TDNT—5:283, 700; BAGD—570a; THAYER—446d.

ὀνάω **ŏnaō**. See *3685.*

3679. **ὀνειδίζω** {10x} **ŏnĕidizō**, *on-i-did'-zo;* from *3681;* to *defame,* i.e. *rail at, chide, taunt:*—upbraid {3x}, reproach {3x}, revile {2x}, cast in (one's) teeth {1x}, suffer reproach {1x}.

Oneidizo signifies **(1)** in the active voice, "to reproach, upbraid," Mt 5:11, "shall revile"; 11:20, "to upbraid"; 27:44, "cast . . . in (His) teeth"; Mk 15:32, "reviled"; 16:14 "upbraided"; Lk 6:22 "shall reproach", Rom 15:3; Jas 1:5, "upbraideth"; **(2)** in the passive voice, "to suffer reproach, be reproached," 1 Ti 4:10; 1 Pet 4:14. See: TDNT—5:239, 693; BAGD—570a; THAYER—446d.

3680. **ὀνειδισμός** {5x} **ŏnĕidismŏs**, *on-i-dis-mos';* from *3679; contumely:*—reproach {5x}.

This word means "a reproach, defamation" and is used in Rom 15:3; 1 Ti 3:7; Heb 10:33; 11:26; 13:13. See: TDNT—5:241, 693; BAGD—570b; THAYER—446d.

3681. **ὄνειδος** {1x} **ŏnĕidŏs**, *on'-i-dos;* prob. akin to the base of *3686; notoriety,* i.e. a *taunt* (*disgrace*):—a reproach {1x}. See: TDNT—5:238, 693; BAGD—570b; THAYER—447a.

3682. **Ὀνήσιμος** {4x} **Ŏnēsimŏs**, *on-ay'-sim-os;* from *3685; profitable; Onesimus,* a Chr.:—Onesimus {4x}. See: BAGD—570c; THAYER—447a.

3683. **Ὀνησίφορος** {2x} **Ŏnēsiphŏrŏs**, *on-ay-sif'-or-os;* from a der. of *3685* and *5411; profit-bearer; Onesiphorus,* a Chr.:—Onesiphorus {2x}. See: BAGD—570c; THAYER—447a.

3684. **ὀνικός** {2x} **ŏnikŏs**, *on-ik-os';* from *3688; belonging to* an *ass,* i.e. *large* (so as to be turned by an ass):—millstone + 3458 {2x}. See: BAGD—570c; THAYER—447a.

3685. **ὀνίνημι** {1x} **ŏninēmi**, *on-in'-ay-mee;* a prol. form of an appar. primary verb

ὄνομαι **ŏnŏmai**, to *slur*); for which another prol. form (ὀνάω **ŏnaō**) is used as an alt. in some tenses [unless indeed it be ident. with the base of *3686* through the idea of *notoriety*]; to *gratify,* i.e. (mid. voice) to *derive pleasure* or *advantage* from:—have joy {1x}.

Oninemi, "to benefit, profit," in the middle voice, "to have profit, derive benefit," is translated "let me have joy" in Philem 20; the apostle is doubtless continuing his credit and debit metaphors and using the verb in the sense of "profit." See: BAGD—570d; THAYER—447a.

3686. **ὄνομα** {230x} **ŏnŏma**, *on'-om-ah;* from a presumed der. of the base of *1097* (comp. *3685*); a *"name"* (lit. or fig.) [*authority, character*]:—name {194x}, named {28x}, called {4x}, surname + 2007 {2x}, named + 2564 {1x}, not tr {1x}.

Onoma, as a noun, is used **I.** in general of the "name" by which a person or thing is called, e.g., **(1)** Mk 3:16, 17, "(He) surnamed," lit., "(He added) the name"; **(2)** Mk 14:32, lit., "(of which) the name (was)"; Lk 1:63; Jn 18:10; **(2a)** sometimes translated "named," e.g., **(2a1)** Lk 8:5, "named (Zacharias)," lit., "by name"; **(2a2)** in the same verse, "named (Elizabeth)," lit., "the name of her," an elliptical phrase, with "was" understood; **(3)** Acts 8:9, "called," 10:1; **(4)** the "name" is put for the reality in Rev 3:1; **(5)** in Phil 2:9, the "Name" represents "the title and dignity" of the Lord, as in Eph 1:21 and Heb 1:4; **II.** for all that a "name" implies, of authority, character, rank, majesty, power, excellence, etc., of everything that the "name" covers: **(1)** of the "Name" of God as expressing His attributes, etc., e.g., Mt 6:9; Lk 1:49; Jn 12:28; 17:6, 26; Rom 15:9; 1 Ti 6:1; Heb 13:15; Rev 13:6; **(2)** of the "Name" of Christ, e.g., Mt 10:22; 19:29; Jn 1:12; 2:23; 3:18; Acts 26:9; Rom 1:5; Jas 2:7; 1 Jn 3:23; 3 Jn 7; Rev 2:13; 3:8;

(3) also the phrases rendered "in the name"; these may be analyzed as follows: **(3a)** representing the authority of Christ, e.g., Mt 18:5 (with *epi,* "on the ground of My authority"); **(3b1)** so Mt 24:5 (falsely) and parallel passages; **(3b2)** as substantiated by the Father, Jn 14:26; 16:23; **(3b)** in the power of (with *en,* "in"), e.g.,

Mk 16:17; Lk 10:17; Acts 3:6; 4:10; 16:18; Jas 5:14; **(3c)** in acknowledgement or confession of, e.g., Acts 4:12; 8:16; 9:27, 28; **(3d)** in recognition of the authority of (sometimes combined with the thought of relying or resting on), Mt 18:20; cf. 28:19; Acts 8:16; 9:2 (*eis,* "into"); Jn 14:13; 15:16; Eph 5:20; Col 3:17; **(3e)** owing to the fact that one is called by Christ's "Name" or is identified with Him, e.g. **(3e1)** 1 Pet 4:14 (with *en,* "in"); **(3e2)** with *heneken,* "for the sake of," e.g., Mt 19:29; **(3e3)** with *dia,* "on account of," Mt 10:22; 24:9; Mk 13:13; Lk 21:17; Jn 15:21; 1 Jn 2:12; Rev 2:3; **III.** as standing, by metonymy, for "persons," Acts 1:15; Rev 3:4; 11:13. Syn.: 3687. See: TDNT—5:242, 694; BAGD—570d; THAYER—447a.

3687. **ὀνομάζω** {10x} **ŏnŏmazō**, *on-om-ad'-zo;* from *3686;* to *name,* i.e. *assign an appellation;* by extens. to *utter, mention, profess:*—call {2x}, name {8x}.

Onomazo denotes **(1)** "to name," "mention," or "address by name," **(1a)** Acts 19:13, "to call"; **(1b)** in the passive voice, Rom 15:20; Eph 1:21; 5:3; to make mention of the "Name" of the Lord in praise and worship, 2 Ti 2:19; **(2)** "to name, call, give a name to," **(2a)** Lk 6:13, 14; **(2b)** passive voice, 1 Cor 5:11, "is called"; **(2c)** Eph 3:15; 1 Cor 5:1, "is named." See: TDNT—5:282, 694; BAGD—573d; THAYER—448d.

3688. **ὄνος** {6x} **ŏnŏs**, *on'-os;* appar. a primary word; a *donkey:*—an ass {6x}. See: TDNT—5:283, 700; BAGD—574a; THAYER—448d.

3689. **ὄντως** {10x} **ŏntōs**, *on'-toce;* adv. of the oblique cases of *5607; really:*—certainly {1x}, clean {1x}, indeed {6x}, of a truth {1x}, verily {1x}. See: BAGD—574a; THAYER—448d.

3690. **ὄξος** {7x} **ŏxŏs**, *ox-os;* from *3691; vinegar,* i.e. *sour* wine:—vinegar {7x}.

Oxos denotes "sour wine," the ordinary drink of laborers and common soldiers; it is used in the four Gospels of the "vinegar" offered to the Lord at His crucifixion, Mt 27:34, 48; Mk 15:36; Lk 23:36; Jn 19:29, 30. This, which the soldiers offered before crucifying, was refused by Him, as it was designed to alleviate His sufferings. See: TDNT—5:288, 701; BAGD—574b; THAYER—449a.

3691. **ὀξύς** {8x} **ŏxus**, *ox-oos';* prob. akin to the base of *188* ["*acid*"]; *keen;* by anal. *rapid:*—sharp {7x}, swift {1x}.

Oxus denotes **(1)** "sharp", said **(1)** of a sword, Rev 1:16; 2:12; 19:15; **(2)** of a sickle, Rev 14:14, 17, 18 (twice); and **(2)** of motion, "swift," Rom 3:15. See: BAGD—574a; THAYER—449a.

3692. **ὀπή** {2x} **ŏpē**, *op-ay';* prob. from *3700;* a *hole* (as if for light), i.e. *cavern;* by anal. a *spring* (of water):—cave {1x}, place {1x}.

Ope denotes "a hole, an opening," **(1)** such as a fissure in a rock, Heb 11:38, a "cave"; and in **(2)** Jas 3:11, the "place" of the orifice of a fountain. See: BAGD—574d; THAYER—449a.

3693. **ὄπισθεν** {7x} **ŏpisthĕn**, *op'-is-then;* from ὄπις **ŏpis**, (*regard;* from *3700*) with enclitic of source; *from the rear* (as a secure *aspect*), i.e. *at* the *back* (adv. and prep. of place or time):—after {2x}, backside {1x}, behind {4x}.

Opisthen, "behind," is used only of place, e.g., **(1)** "behind" in Mt 9:20; Mk 5:27; Lk 8:44; Rev 4:6; **(2)** as a preposition, **(2a)** Mt 15:23; Lk 23:26, "after"; **(2b)** in Rev 5:1, "backside." See: TDNT—5:289, 702; BAGD—574d; THAYER—449b.

3694. **ὀπίσω** {36x} **ŏpisō**, *op-is'-o;* from the same as *3693* with enclitic of direction; *to* the *back,* i.e. *aback* (as adv. or prep. of time or place; or as noun):—after {22x}, behind {6x}, back + 1519 + 3588 {5x}, back {1x}, follow {1x}, backward + 1519 + 3588 {1x}.

Opiso, connected with *hepomai,* "to follow," is used adverbially, of place, with the meaning "back," "backward," in the phrase *eis ta opiso,* lit., "unto the things behind," in Mk 13:16; Lk 9:62; 17:31; Jn 6:66; 18:6; 20:14. Cf. Phil 3:13, "the things which are behind. See: TDNT—5:289, 702; BAGD—575a; THAYER—449b.

3695. **ὁπλίζω** {1x} **hŏplizō**, *hop-lid'-zo;* from *3696;* to *equip* (with weapons [mid. voice and fig.]):—arm (one's) self with {1x}.

Hopilizo, "to arm oneself," is used in 1 Pet 4:1, in an exhortation "to arm" ourselves with the same mind as that of Christ in regard to His sufferings. See: TDNT—5:294, 702; BAGD—575c; THAYER—449c.

3696. **ὅπλον** {6x} **hŏplŏn**, *hop'-lon;* prob. from a primary ἕπω **hĕpō** (to be *busy* about); an *implement,* or *utensil* or *tool* (lit. or fig., espec. offensive for war):—armour {2x}, instrument {2x}, weapon {2x}.

Hoplon, originally any tool or implement for preparing a thing, became used in the plural for "weapons of warfare." **(1)** Once in the NT it is used of actual weapons, Jn 18:3; elsewhere, **(2)** metaphorically, of **(2a)** the members of the body as instruments of unrighteousness and as instruments of righteousness, Rom 6:13; **(2b)** the "armor" of light, Rom 13:12; **(2c)** the "armor" of righteousness, 2 Cor 6:7; **(2d)** the weapons of the Christian's warfare, 2 Cor 10:4. See: TDNT—5:292, 702; BAGD—575c; THAYER—449d.

3697. **ὁποῖος** {5x} **hŏpŏiŏs**, *hop-oy'-os;* from *3739* and *4169;* of *what* kind *that,* i.e. *how* (*as*) *great* (*excellent*) (spec. as an indef. correl. to the antecedent def. *5108* of quality):—what manner of {1x}, such as {1x}, of what sort {1x}, whatsoever + 4118 {1x}, what manner of man {1x}.

Hopoios is rendered **(1)** "what manner of" in 1 Th 1:9; **(2)** "of what sort" in 1 Cor 3:13; **(3)** "such as" in Acts 26:29; **(4)** "whatsoever" in Gal 2:6; and **(5)** "what manner of man" in Jas 1:24. Syn.: 195, 1485, 2239, 3634, 3668, 3779, 4169, 4187, 4217, 4459, 5158, 5159, 5179, 5615. See: BAGD—575d; THAYER—449d.

3698. **ὁπότε** {1x} **hŏpŏtĕ**, *hop-ot'-eh;* from *3739* and *4218; what* (-ever) *then,* i.e. (of time) *as soon as:*—when {1x}. See: BAGD—576a; THAYER—449d.

3699. **ὅπου** {82x} **hŏpŏu**, *hop'-oo;* from *3739* and *4225; what* (-ever) *where,* i.e. *at whichever* spot:—where {58x}, whither {9x}, wheresoever + 302 {3x}, whithersoever + 302 {4x}, wheresoever + 1437 {2x}, whereas {2x}, not tr {1x}, in what place {3x}. See: BAGD—576a; THAYER—449d.

3700. **ὀπτάνομαι** {58x} **ŏptanŏmai**, *op-tan'-om-ahee;* a (mid. voice) prol. form of the primary (mid. voice)

ὄπτομαι **ŏptŏmai**, *op'-tom-ahee;* which is used for it in certain tenses; and both as alternate of *3708;* to *gaze* (i.e. with wide-open eyes, as at something remarkable; and thus differing from *991,* which denotes simply *voluntary* observation; and from *1492,* which expresses merely mechanical, passive or casual vision; while *2300,* and still more emphatically its intensive *2334,* signifies an earnest but more continued *inspection;* and *4648* a watching *from a distance*):—see {37x}, appear {17x}, look {2x}, show (one's) self {1x}, being seen {1x}.

Optomai, "to see" (from *ops,* "the eye"; cf. Eng. "optical," etc.), in the passive sense, "to be seen, to appear," is used **(1)** objectively, with reference to the person or thing seen, e.g., 1 Cor 15:5–8, "was seen"; **(2)** subjectively, with reference **(2a)** to an inward impression or a spiritual experience, Jn 3:36, or **(2b)** a mental occupation, Acts 18:15, "look to it"; **(3)** cf. Mt 27:4, 24, "see (thou) to it," "see (ye) to it," throwing responsibility on others. **(4)** *Optomai* is to be found in dictionaries under the word *horao,* "to see"; it supplies some forms that are lacking in that verb. See: TDNT—5:315, 706; BAGD—576c; THAYER—450b.

3701. **ὀπτασία** {4x} **ŏptasia**, *op-tas-ee'-ah;* from a presumed der. of *3700; visuality,* i.e. (concr.) an *apparition:*—vision {4x}.

Optasia, from *optano,* "to see, a coming into view," denotes a "vision" in Lk 1:22; 24:23; Acts 26:19; 2 Cor 12:1. See: TDNT—5:372, 706; BAGD—576c; THAYER—450b.

ὄπτομαι **ŏptŏmai**. See *3700*.

3702. **ὀπτός** {1x} **ŏptŏs**, *op-tos';* from an obs. verb akin to ἕψω **hĕpsō** (to "*steep*"); *cooked,* i.e. *roasted:*—broiled {1x}.

Optos, (from *optao,* "to cook, roast"), is said of food prepared by fire, Luke 24:42. See: BAGD—576c; THAYER—450b.

3703. **ὀπώρα** {1x} **ŏpōra**, *op-o'-rah;* appar. from the base of *3796* and *5610;* prop. *even-tide* of the (summer) season (*dog-days*), i.e. (by impl.) *ripe* fruit:—fruit {1x}.

Opora as a noun, primarily denotes "late summer or early autumn," i.e., late July, all August and early September. Since that is the time of "fruit-bearing," the word was used, by metonymy, for the "fruits" themselves: "And the fruits that thy soul lusted after are departed from thee, and all things which were dainty and goodly are departed from thee, and thou shalt find them no more at all" (Rev 18:14). Syn.: 175, 2590, 2592, 2593, 5352. See: BAGD—576c; THAYER—450b.

3704. **ὅπως** {56x} **hŏpōs**, *hop'-oce;* from *3739* and *4459; what* (-ever) *how,* i.e. *in* the *manner that* (as adv. or conjunc. of coincidence, intentional or actual):—that {45x}, how {4x}, to {4x}, so that {1x}, when {1x}, because {1x}. See: BAGD—576d; THAYER—450c.

3705. **ὅραμα** {12x} **hŏrama**, *hor'-am-ah;* from *3708; something gazed at,* i.e. a *spectacle* (espec. supernatural):—sight {1x}, vision {11x}.

Horama, as a noun, signifies "that which is seen" and denotes **(1)** "a spectacle, sight," Mt 17:9; Acts 7:31 ("sight"); **(2)** "an appearance, vision," Acts 9:10, 12; 10:3, 17, 19; 11:5; 12:9; 16:9, 10; 18:9. Syn.: *Horama* (3705) the noun, signifies that which is seen, *horasis* (3706) the act of seeing. See: TDNT—5:371, 706; BAGD—577b; THAYER—451a.

3706. **ὅρασις** {4x} **hŏrasis**, *hor'-as-is;* from *3708;* the act of *gazing,* i.e. (external) an *aspect* or (intern.) an inspired *appearance:*—in sight {1x}, look upon {1x}, vision {2x}.

Horasis, as a noun, denotes **(1)** a vision: "And thus I saw the horses in the vision, and them that sat on them" (Rev 9:17; cf. Acts 2:17); and **(2)** to look upon [in appearance], in sight: "And He that sat was to look upon (*horasis*) like a jasper and a sardine stone: and *there was* a rainbow round about the throne, in sight (*horasis*) like unto an emerald" (Rev 4:3). Syn.: *Horama* (3705) the noun, signifies that which is seen, *hor-*

asis, the verb, (3706) the act of seeing. See also: 308, 352, 578, 816, 872, 991, 1689, 1896, 1914, 1980, 1983, 2300, 2334, 3708, 3879, 4017, 4648. See: TDNT—5:370, 706; BAGD—577c; THAYER—451a.

3707. **ὁρατός** {1x} **hŏratŏs**, *hor-at-os'*; from *3708; gazed at*, i.e. (by impl.) *capable of being seen:*—visible {1x}. See: TDNT—5:368, 706; BAGD—577c.

3708. **ὁράω** {59x} **hŏraō**, *hor-ah'-o;* prop. to *stare* at [comp. *3700*], i.e. (by impl.) to *discern* clearly (phys. or ment.); by extens. to *attend* to; by Heb. to *experience;* pass. to *appear:*—behold {1x}, perceive {1x}, see {51x}, take heed {5x}. not tr. {1x}.

Horao, as a verb, is said **(1)** of bodily vision: "He saith unto them, How many loaves have ye? go and see" (e.g., Mk 6:38; Jn 1:18, 46); **(2)** of mental perception: "But as it is written, To whom He was not spoken of, they shall see (*horao*): and they that have not heard shall understand" (e.g., Rom 15:21; Col 2:18); **(3)** of taking heed: "And Jesus saith unto him, See (*horao*) thou tell no man; but go thy way, shew thyself to the priest, and offer the gift that Moses commanded, for a testimony unto them" (e.g., Mt 8:4; 1 Th 5:15); **(4)** of experience, as **(4a)** of death: "And it was revealed unto him by the Holy Ghost, that he should not see (*horao*) death, before he had seen the Lord's Christ" (Lk 2:26; cf. Heb 11:5), **(4b)** life: "He that believeth on the Son hath everlasting life: and he that believeth not the Son shall not see (*horao*) life, but the wrath of God abideth on him" (Jn 3:36); **(4c)** corruption: "Because thou wilt not leave My soul in hell, neither wilt thou suffer thine Holy One to see (*horao*) corruption" (Acts 2:27); **(5)** of caring for: "Saying, I have sinned in that I have betrayed the innocent blood. And they said, What *is that* to us? see (*horao*) thou *to that*" (Mt 27:4). Syn.: 333, 816, 991, 1689, 1896, 2029, 2300, 2334, 2657, 2734. See: TDNT—5:368, 706; BAGD—577d; THAYER—451b.

3709. **ὀργή** {36x} **ŏrgē**, *or-gay';* from *3713;* prop. *desire* (as a *reaching* forth or *excitement* of the mind), i.e. (by anal.) violent *passion* (*ire*, or [justifiable] *abhorrence*); by impl. *punishment:*—anger {3x}, indignatio {1x}, vengeance {1x}, wrath {31x}.

Orge, originally any "natural impulse, or desire, or disposition," came to signify "anger," as the strongest of all passions. It is used of **(1)** the wrath of man, Eph 4:31; Col 3:8; 1 Ti 2:8; Jas 1:19–20; **(2)** the displeasure of human governments, Rom 13:4–5; **(3)** the sufferings of the Jews at the hands of the Gentiles, Lk 21:23; **(4)** the terrors of the Law, Rom 4:15; **(5)** "the anger" of the Lord Jesus, Mk 3:5; **(6)** God's "anger" with Israel in the wilderness, in a quotation from the OT, Heb 3:11; 4:3; **(7)** God's present "anger" with the Jews nationally, Rom 9:22; 1 Th 2:16; **(8)** His present "anger" with those who disobey the Lord Jesus in His gospel, Jn 3:36; **(9)** God's purposes in judgment, Mt. 3:7; Lk 3:7; Rom 1:18; 2:5, 8; 3:5; 5:9; 12:19; Eph 2:3; 5:6; Col 3:6; 1 Th 1:10; 5:9. Syn.: cf. 2372 for discussion; 3950. See: TDNT—5:382, 716; BAGD—578d; THAYER—452a.

3710. **ὀργίζω** {8x} **ŏrgizō**, *or-gid'-zo;* from *3709;* to *provoke* or *enrage*, i.e. (pass.) *become exasperated:*—be angry {5x}, be wroth {3x}.

Orgizo, "to provoke, to arouse to anger," is used in the middle voice in the eight places where it is found, and signifies "to be angry, wroth." It is said **(1)** of individuals, in Mt 5:22; 18:34; 22:7; Lk 14:21; 15:28, and Eph 4:26; **(2)** of nations, Rev 11:18; **(3)** of Satan as the Dragon, Rev 12:17. See: TDNT—5:382,*; BAGD—579c; THAYER—452c.

3711. **ὀργίλος** {1x} **ŏrgilŏs**, *org-ee'-los;* from *3709; irascible:*—soon angry {1x}. See: TDNT—5:382, 716; BAGD—579d; THAYER—452c.

3712. **ὀργυιά** {2x} **ŏrguia**, *org-wee-ah';* from *3713;* a *stretch* of the arms, i.e. a *fathom:*—fathom {2x}.

A fathom is the distance across the chest from the tip of one middle finger to the tip of the other when the arms are outstretched, 5 to 6 feet (2 m), Acts 27:28 twice. See: BAGD—579d; THAYER—452c.

3713. **ὀρέγομαι** {3x} **ŏrĕgŏmai**, *or-eg'-om-ahee;* mid. voice of appar. a prol. form of an obs. primary [comp. *3735*]; to *stretch* oneself, i.e. *reach* out after (*long* for):—covet after {1x}, desire {2x}.

Oregomai, as a verb, means "to reach out, or after," is used in the middle voice, and is translated "desireth": "This *is* a true saying, If a man desire the office of a bishop, he desireth a good work" (1 Ti 3:1; cf. 6:10; Heb 11:16). Syn.: 327, 1567, 1934, 2206, 2212. See: TDNT—5:447, 727; BAGD—579d; THAYER—452d.

3714. **ὀρεινός** {2x} **ŏrĕinŏs**, *or-i-nos;* from *3735; mountainous*, i.e. (fem. by impl. of *5561*) the *Highlands* (of Judæa):—hill country {2x}.

Oreinos, "hilly" (from *oros*, "a hill, mountain"), is translated "hill country" in Lk 1:39, 65. See: BAGD—580a; THAYER—452d.

3715. **ὄρεξις** {1x} **ŏrĕxis**, *or'-ex-is;* from *3713; excitement* of the mind, i.e. *longing* after:—lust {1x}.

Orexis denotes an irrational longing, "a reaching" or "stretching after" (akin to *oregomai*, "to stretch oneself out, reach after"), a general term for every kind of desire, is used in Rom 1:27, "lust." Syn.: 1939, 3730, 3806. See: TDNT—5:447, 727; BAGD—580a; THAYER—452d.

3716. **ὀρθοποδέω** {1x} **ŏrthŏpŏdĕō**, *or-thop-od-eh'-o;* from a compound of *3717* and *4228;* to *be straight-footed*, i.e. (fig.) to *go directly* forward:—walk uprightly {1x}. See: TDNT—5:451, 727; BAGD—580a; THAYER—452d.

3717. **ὀρθός** {2x} **ŏrthŏs**, *or-thos';* prob. from the base of *3735; right* (as *rising*), i.e. (perpendicularly) *erect* (fig. *honest*), or (horizontally) *level* or *direct:*—straight {1x}, upright {1x}.

Orthos, "to walk in a straight path" (*orthos*, "straight," *pous*, "a foot"), is used **(1)** metaphorically in Gal 2:14, signifying a "course of conduct" by which one leaves a straight track for others to follow ("walked . . . uprightly"); and **(2)** Peter's command to the cripple to not only stand but to walk in a straight line, without staggering, signifying complete healing. See: TDNT—5:449, 727; BAGD—580b; THAYER—453a.

3718. **ὀρθοτομέω** {1x} **ŏrthŏtŏmĕō**, *or-thot-om-eh'-o;* from a compound of *3717* and the base of *5114*, to *make* a *straight cut*, i.e. (fig.) to *dissect* (*expound*) *correctly* (the divine message):—rightly divide {1x}.

Orthotomeo, lit., "to cut straight" (*orthos*, "straight," *temno*, "to cut"), is found in 2 Ti. 2:15, "rightly dividing" (the word of truth); the meaning passed from the idea of cutting or "dividing," to the more general sense of "rightly dealing with a thing." What is intended here is not "dividing" Scripture from Scripture, but teaching Scripture accurately, carefully discerning each nuance. See: TDNT—8:111, 1169; BAGD—580b; THAYER—453a.

3719. **ὀρθρίζω** {1x} **ŏrthrizō**, *or-thrid'-zo;* from *3722;* to *use* the *dawn*, i.e. (by impl.) to *repair betimes:*—come early in the morning {1x}.

Orthizo, "to do anything early in the morning," is translated "came early in the morning," in Lk 21:38. See: BAGD—580c; THAYER—453a.

3720. **ὀρθρινός** {1x} **ŏrthrinŏs**, *or-thrin-os';* from *3722; relating to* the *dawn*, i.e. *matutinal* (as an epithet of Venus, espec. brilliant in the early day):—morning {1x}. See: BAGD—580c; THAYER—453b.

3721. **ὄρθριος** {1x} **ŏrthriŏs**, *or'-three-os;* from *3722; in the dawn*, i.e. up *at daybreak:*—early {1x}. See: BAGD—580c; THAYER—453b.

3722. **ὄρθρος** {3x} **ŏrthrŏs**, *or'-thros;* from the same as *3735; dawn* (as *sun-rise, rising* of light); by extens. *morn:*—early in the morning {3x}.

Orthros, "daybreak," denotes "early in the morning," Lk 24:1; Jn 8:2; and Acts 5:21. See: BAGD—580c; THAYER—453b.

3723. **ὀρθῶς** {4x} **ŏrthōs**, *or-thoce';* adv. from *3717; in a straight* manner, i.e. (fig.) *correctly* (also mor.):—plain {1x}, right {1x}, rightly {2x}. See: BAGD—580d; THAYER—453b.

3724. **ὁρίζω** {8x} **hŏrizō**, *hor-id'-zo;* from *3725*, to *mark* out or *bound* ("horizon"), i.e. (fig.) to *appoint, decree, specify:*—determine {2x}, ordain {2x}, as it was determined + 2596 + 3588 {1x}, declare {1x}, limit {1x}, determine {1x}.

Horizo, [Eng., "horizon"], as a verb, means literally "to mark by a limit," hence, "to determine, ordain" and is used **(1)** of Christ as ordained of God to be a judge of the living and the dead: "Because He hath appointed a day, in the which He will judge the world in righteousness by *that* man whom He hath ordained (*horizo*); *whereof* He hath given assurance unto all *men*, in that He hath raised him from the dead" (Acts 17:31); **(2)** of His being "marked out" as the Son of God: "And declared (*horizo*) *to be* the Son of God with power, according to the spirit of holiness, by the resurrection from the dead" (Rom 1:4); **(3)** of divinely appointed seasons: "And hath made of one blood all nations of men for to dwell on all the face of the earth, and hath determined (*horizo*) the times before appointed, and the bounds of their habitation" (Acts 17:26). See: TDNT—5:452, 728; BAGD—580d; THAYER—453b.

3725. **ὅριον** {11x} **hŏriŏn**, *hor'-ee-on;* neut. of a der. of an appar. primary ὅρος **hŏrŏs** (a *bound* or *limit*); a *boundary*-line, i.e. (by impl.) a *frontier* (*region*):—border {1x}, coast {10x}.

Horion, "the border of a country or district" (cf. Eng., "horizon"), is always used in the plural and translated **(1)** "borders" in Mt 4:13; **(2)** "coasts" in Mt 2:16; 4:13; 8:34; 15:22, 39; 19:1; Mk 5:17; 7:31 (twice); 10:1; Acts 13:50. See: BAGD—581b; THAYER—453c.

3726. **ὁρκίζω** {3x} **hŏrkizō**, *hor-kid'-zo;* from *3727;* to *put on oath*, i.e. *make swear;* by anal. to solemnly *enjoin:*—adjure {2x}, charge {1x}.

Orkizo, "to cause to swear, to lay under the obligation of an oath", **(1)** "adjure" in Mk 5:7; Acts 19:13, and **(2)** "charge" in 1 Th 5:27. See: TDNT—5:462, 729; BAGD—581b; THAYER—453c.

3727. **ὅρκος** {10x} **hŏrkŏs**, *hor'-kos;* from ἕρκος **hĕrkŏs**, (a *fence;* perh. akin to *3725*);

a *limit,* i.e. (sacred) *restraint* (spec. an *oath*):—oath {10x}.

Horkos is primarily equivalent to *herkos,* "a fence, an enclosure, that which restrains a person"; hence, "an oath." **(1)** The Lord's command in Mt 5:33 was a condemnation of the minute and arbitrary restrictions imposed by the scribes and Pharisees in the matter of adjurations, by which God's Name was profaned. **(2)** The injunction is repeated in Jas 5:12. **(3)** The language of the apostle Paul, e.g., in Gal 1:20 and 1 Th. 5:27 was not inconsistent with Christ's prohibition, read in the light of its context. **(4)** Contrast the "oaths" mentioned in Mt 14:7, 9; 26:72; Mk 6:26. **(5)** Heb 6:16 refers to the confirmation of a compact among men, guaranteeing the discharge of liabilities; in their disputes "the oath is final for confirmation." This is referred to in order to illustrate the greater subject of God's "oath" to Abraham, confirming His promise; cf. Lk 1:73; Acts 2:30. See: TDNT—5:457, 729; BAGD—581c; THAYER—453d.

3728. **ὁρκωμοσία** {4x} **hŏrkōmŏsia**, *hor-ko-mos-ee'ah;* from a compound of *3727* and a der. of *3660; asseveration on oath:*—oath {4x}.

This word denotes "an affirmation on oath." **(1)** This is used in Heb 7:20–21 (twice), 28, of the establishment of the Priesthood of Christ, the Son of God, appointed a Priest after the order of Melchizedek, and "perfected for evermore." See: TDNT—5:463, 729; BAGD—581d; THAYER—453d.

3729. **ὁρμάω** {5x} **hŏrmaō**, *hor-mah'-o;* from *3730;* to *start, spur* or *urge* on, i.e. (refl.) to *dash* or *plunge:*—run violently {3x}, run {1x}, rush {1x}.

Hormao, "to set in motion, urge on," but intransitively, "to hasten on, rush," is always translated **(1)** "ran violently," Mt 8:32; Mk 5:13; Lk 8:33; **(2)** "ran," Acts 7:57; **(3)** "rushed", Acts 19:29. See: TDNT—5:467, 730; BAGD—581d; THAYER—453d.

3730. **ὁρμή** {2x} **hŏrmē**, *hor-may';* of uncert. aff.; a violent *impulse,* i.e. *onset:*—assault {1x}, not tr. {1x}.

This word stresses the purpose and intention, an impulse of the mind or soul, a person's reason compelling him to act; sometimes the action going unfulfilled, Acts 14:5. Syn.: 1939, 3715, 3806. See: TDNT—5:467, 730; BAGD—581d; THAYER—453d.

3731. **ὅρμημα** {1x} **hŏrmēma**, *hor'-may-mah;* from *3730;* an *attack,* i.e. (abstr.) *precipitancy:*—violence {1x}. See: TDNT—5:467, 730; BAGD—581d; THAYER—453d.

3732. **ὄρνεον** {3x} **ŏrnĕŏn**, *or'-neh-on;* neut. of a presumed der. of *3733;* a *birdling:*—bird {1x}, fowl {2x}. Cf. Rev. 18:2; 19:17, 21. See: BAGD—581d; THAYER—454a.

3733. **ὄρνις** {2x} **ŏrnis**, *or'-nis;* prob. from a prol. form of the base of *3735;* a *bird* (as *rising* in the air), i.e. (spec.) a *hen* (or female domestic fowl):—hen {2x}. Cf. Matt. 23:37; Luke 13:34. See: BAGD—582a; THAYER—454a.

3734. **ὁροθεσία** {1x} **hŏrŏthĕsia**, *hor-oth-es-ee'-ah;* from a compound of the base of *3725* and a der. of *5087;* a *limit-placing,* i.e. (concr.) *boundary-line:*—bound {1x}. See: BAGD—582a; THAYER—454a.

3735. **ὄρος** {65x} **ŏrŏs**, *or'-os;* prob. from an obs. ὄρω **ŏrō** (to *rise* or "*rear;*" perh. akin to *142;* comp. *3733*); a *mountain* (as *lifting* itself above the plain):—hill {3x}, mount {21x}, mountain {41x}

Oros is used **(1)** without specification, e.g., Lk 3:5 (distinct from *bounos,* "a hill"); Jn 4:20; **(2)** of "the Mount of Transfiguration," Mt 17:1, 9; Mk 9:2, 9; Lk 9:28, 37, "hill"; 2 Pet 1:18; **(3)** of "Zion," Heb 12:22; Rev 14:1; **(4)** of "Sinai," Acts 7:30, 38; Gal 4:24, 25; Heb 8:5; 12:20; **(5)** of "the Mount of Olives," Mt 21:1; 24:3; Mk 11:1; 13:3; Lk 19:29, 37; 22:39; Jn 8:1; Acts 1:12; **(6)** of "the hill districts as distinct from the lowlands," especially of the hills above the Sea of Galilee, e.g., Mt 5:1; 8:1; 18:12; Mk 5:5; **(7)** of "the mountains on the east of Jordan" and "those in the land of Ammon" and "the region of Petra," etc., Mt 24:16; Mk 13:14; Lk 21:21; **(8)** proverbially, "of overcoming difficulties, or accomplishing great things," 1 Cor 13:2; cf. Mt 17:20; 21:21; Mk 11:23; **(9)** symbolically, of "a series of the imperial potentates of the Roman dominion, past and future," Rev 17:9. See: TDNT—5:475, 732; BAGD—582b; THAYER—454a.

3736. **ὀρύσσω** {3x} **ŏrussō**, *or-oos'-so;* appar. a primary verb; to "*burrow*" in the ground, i.e. *dig:*—dig {3x}. Orusso, "to dig, dig up soil, dig a pit," is said **(1)** of a place for a winepress, Mt 21:33; Mk 12:1; **(2)** of "digging" a pit for hiding something, Mt 25:15. See: BAGD—582d; THAYER—454b.

3737. **ὀρφανός** {2x} **ŏrphanŏs**, *or-fan-os';* of uncert. aff.; *bereaved* ("*orphan*"), i.e. *parentless:*—comfortless {1x}, fatherless {1x}.

Orphanos, (Eng., "orphan"), signifies "bereft of parents or of a father." **(1)** In Jas 1:27 it is translated "fatherless." **(2)** It was also used in the general sense of being "friendless or desolate." In Jn 14:18 the Lord uses it of the relationship between Himself and His disciples, He having been their guide, teacher and protector; "comfortless." See: TDNT—5:487, 734; BAGD—583a; THAYER—454b.

3738. **ὀρχέομαι** {4x} **ŏrchĕŏmai**, *or-kheh'-om-ahee;* mid. voice from ὄρχος **ŏrchŏs** (a *row* or *ring*); to *dance,* (from the *rank-like* or *regular* motion):—dance {4x}.

Orcheomai, (cf. Eng., "orchestra"), probably originally signified "to lift up," as of the feet; hence, "to leap with regularity of motion." **(1)** It is always used in the middle voice, Mt 11:17; 14:6; Mk 6:22; Lk 7:32. **(2)** The performance by the daughter of Herodias is the only clear instance of artistic dancing. See: BAGD—583b; THAYER—454b.

3739. **ὅς** {1393x} **hŏs**, *hos;* incl. fem.

ἥ **hē**, *hay;* and neut.

ὅ **hŏ** *hŏ;* prob. a primary word (or perh. a form of the art. *3588*); the rel. (sometimes demonstr.) pron., *who, which, what, that:*—which {395x}, whom {262x}, that {129x}, who {84x}, whose {53x}, what {42x}, that which {20x}, whereof {13x}, misc. {430x} = one, (an-, the) other, some, etc. See: BAGD—583b; THAYER—454b. See also *3757*.

3740. **ὁσάκις** {3x} **hŏsakis**, *hos-ak'-is;* multiple adv. from *3739; how* (i.e. with *302, so*) *many times* as:—as often as + 302 {1x}, as often as + 1437 {1x}, as oft as + 302 {1x}. See: BAGD—585b; THAYER—456b.

3741. **ὅσιος** {8x} **hŏsiŏs**, *hos'-ee-os;* of uncert. aff.; prop. *right* (by intrinsic or divine character; thus distinguished from *1342,* which refers rather to *human* statutes and relations; from *2413,* which denotes formal *consecration;* and from *40,* which relates to *purity* from defilement), i.e. *hallowed* (*pious, sacred, sure*):—holy {4x}, Holy One {2x}, mercies {1x}, shall be {1x}.

(1) *Hosios* means undefiled by sin, free from wickedness, religiously observing every moral obligation, pure holy, pious. **(2)** This is one who reverences God's everlasting ordinances and admits his obligations to them. **(3)** *Hosios,* as an adjective, signifies "religiously right, holy," as opposed to what is unrighteous or polluted. **(4)** It is commonly associated with righteousness. **(5)** It is used **(5a)** of God (Rev 15:4; 16:5); and **(5b)** of the body of the Lord Jesus (Acts 2:27; 13:35, citations from Ps 16:10); **(5c)** and of certain promises made to David, which could be fulfilled only in the resurrection of the Lord Jesus (Acts 13:34). **(6)** In 1 Tim 2:8 and Titus 1:8, it is used of the character of Christians. Syn.: 38, 40, 41, 42, 3742, 3743. See: TDNT—5:489, 734; BAGD—585c; THAYER—456b.

3742. **ὁσιότης** {2x} **hŏsiŏtēs**, *hos-ee-ot'-ace;* from *3741; piety:*—holiness {2x}.

Hosiotes denotes that quality of "holiness" **(1)** which is manifested in those who have regard equally to grace and truth; **(1a)** it involves a right relation to God; **(2)** it is used in Lk 1:75 and Eph 4:24, and in each place is associated with righteousness. Syn.: 38, 40, 41, 42, 2412, 3741, 3743.See: TDNT—5:493, 734; BAGD—585d; THAYER—456c.

3743. **ὁσίως** {1x} **hŏsiōs**, *hos-ee-oce';* adv. from *3741; piously:*—holily {1x}.

Hosios, as an adverb, means **(1)** pure from evil conduct, and observant of God's will. **(2)** It is used in 1 Th 2:10 of the conduct of the apostle and his fellow missionaries: "Ye *are* witnesses, and God *also,* how holily and justly and unblameably we behaved ourselves among you that believe." Syn.: 38, 40, 41, 42, 2412, 3741, 3742. See: TDNT—5:489, 734; BAGD—585d; THAYER—456c.

3744. **ὀσμή** {6x} **ŏsmē**, *os-may';* from *3605; fragrance* (lit. or fig.):—odour {2x}, savour {4x}.

Osme, "a smell, an odor", is translated **(1)** "odour" in Jn 12:3; **(2)** it is used metaphorically in Eph 5:2, "a sweet smelling savor," of the effects God-ward of the sacrifice of Christ; **(3)** in Phil 4:18 of the effect of sacrifice, on the part of those in the church at Philippi, who sent material assistance to the apostle in his imprisonment. **(4)** The word is translated "savor" in 2 Cor 2:14, 16 (twice). See: TDNT—5:493, 735; BAGD—586a; THAYER—456c.

3745. **ὅσος** {115x} **hŏsŏs**, *hos'-os;* by redupl. from *3739; as* (*much, great, long,* etc.) *as:*—as many as {24x}, whatsoever {9x}, that {9x}, whatsoever things {8x}, whatsoever + 302 {7x} as long as {5x}, how great things {5x}, what {4x}, misc. {37x} = all (that), as much as, how great (many, much), [in-] as much as, so many as, that (ever), the more, those things, wheresoever, wherewithsoever, which, × while, who (-soever). See: BAGD—586b; THAYER—456c.

3746. **ὅσπερ** {1x} **hŏspĕr**, *hos'-per;* from *3739* and *4007; who especially:*—whomsoever {1x}. See: BAGD—586c; 585a; THAYER—457a.

3747. **ὀστέον** {5x} **ŏstĕŏn**, *os-teh'-on;* or contr.

ὀστοῦν **ŏstŏun**, *os-toon';* of uncert. aff.; a *bone:*—bone {5x}. Cf. Mt 23:27; Lk 24:39; Jn 19:36; Heb 11:22. See: BAGD—586c; THAYER—457a.

3748. **ὅστις** {154x} **hŏstis**, *hos'-tis;* incl. the fem.

ἥτις **hētis**, *hay'-tis;* and the neut.

ὅ,τι **hŏ,ti**, *hot'-ee;* from *3739* and *5100; which some,* i.e. *any that;* also (def.) *which same:*—which {82x}, who {30x}, whosoever {12x}, that {8x}, whatsoever + 302 {4x}, whosoever + 302 {3x}, whatsoever + 3956 + 302 {2x}, misc {13x} = X and (they), (such) as, (they) that, in that they, whereas ye, they which. See: BAGD—586d; THAYER—457b. comp. *3754*.

3749. **ὀστράκινος** {2x} **ŏstrakinŏs**, *os-tra'-kin-os;* from ὄστρακον **ŏstrakŏn**, ["oyster"] (a *tile,* i.e. *terra cotta*); *earthen*-ware, i.e. *clayey;* by impl. *frail:*—of earth {1x}, earthen {1x}.

Ostrakinos signifies "made of earthenware or clay" (from *ostrakon,* "baked clay, potsherd, shell"; akin to *osteon,* "a bone"), translated **(1)** 2 Ti 2:20, "of earth"; **(2)** 2 Cor 4:7, "earthen." See: BAGD—587c; THAYER—457d.

3750. **ὄσφρησις** {1x} **ŏsphrēsis**, *os'-fray-sis;* from a der. of *3605; smell* (the sense):—smelling {1x}. See: BAGD—587c; THAYER—457d.

3751. **ὀσφύς** {8x} **ŏsphus**, *os-foos';* of uncert. aff.; the *loin* (extern.), i.e. the *hip;* intern. (by extens.) *procreative power:*—loins {8x}.

(1) The loins are the hips plus the lower abdomen regarded as the center of strength and procreative power. **(2)** It is used **(2a)** in the natural sense in Mt 3:4; Mk 1:6; **(2b)** as "the seat of generative power," Heb 7:5, 10; **(3)** metaphorically in Acts 2:30; **(4)** metaphorically, **(4a)** of girding the "loins" in readiness for active service for the Lord, Lk 12:35; **(4b)** the same, with truth, Eph 6:14, i.e., bracing up oneself so as to maintain perfect sincerity and reality as the counteractive in Christian character against hypocrisy and falsehood; **(4c)** of girding the "loins" of the mind, 1 Pet 1:13, suggestive of the alertness necessary for sobriety and for setting one's hope perfectly on "the grace to be brought . . . at the revelation of Jesus Christ" (the present participle, "girding," is introductory to the rest of the verse). See: TDNT—5:496, 736; BAGD—587d; THAYER—457d.

3752. **ὅταν** {123x} **hŏtan**, *hot'-an;* from *3753* and *302; whenever* (implying *hypothesis* or more or less *uncertainty*); also caus. (conjunc.) *inasmuch as:*—when {116x}, as soon as {2x}, as long as {1x}, that {1x}, whensoever {1x}, while {1x}, till + 1508 {1x}. See: BAGD—587d; THAYER—458a.

3753. **ὅτε** {105x} **hŏtĕ**, *hot'-eh;* from *3739* and *5037;* at *which* (thing) *too,* i.e. *when:*—when {97x}, while {2x}, as soon as {2x}, after that {2x}, after {1x}, that {1x}. See: BAGD—588b; THAYER—458c.

ὅ, τε **hŏ, tĕ**, *hŏ,t'-eh;* also fem.

ἥ, τε **hē, tĕ**, *hay'-teh;* and neut.

τό, τε **tŏ, tĕ**, *tot'-eh;* simply the art. *3588* followed by *5037;* so written (in some editions) to distinguish them from *3752* and *5119*.

3754. **ὅτι** {1293x} **hŏti**, *hot'-ee;* neut. of *3748* as conjunc.; demonst. *that* (sometimes redundant); caus. *because:*—that {612x}, for {264x}, because {173x}, how that {21x}, how {11x}, misc. {212x} = as concerning that, as though, because that, for that, in that, though, why. See: BAGD—588c; THAYER—458d.

3755. **ὅτου** {6x} **hŏtŏu**, *hot'-oo;* for the gen. of *3748* (as adverb); during *which same* time, i.e. *whilst:*—not tr. {6x}. See: BAGD—587c; THAYER—460a.

3756. **οὐ** {1453x} **ŏu**, *oo;* also (before a vowel)

οὐκ **ŏuk**, *ook;* and (before an aspirate)

οὐχ **ŏuch**, *ookh;* a primary word; the absolute neg. [comp. *3361*] adv.; *no* or *not:*—not {1214x}, no {136x}, cannot + 1410 {55x}, misc. {48x} = + long, nay, neither, never, no man, none, + nothing, + special, unworthy, when, + without, + yet but. See: BAGD—589a; THAYER—460b. See also *3364, 3372*.

3757. **οὗ** {27x} **hŏu**, *hoo;* gen. of *3739* as adv.; at *which* place, i.e. *where:*—where {22x}, whither {2x}, when {1x}, wherein {1x}, whithersoever + 1437 {1x}. See: BAGD—589d; THAYER—460b.

3758. **οὐά** {1x} **ŏua**, *oo-ah';* a primary exclamation of surprise; "*ah*":—ah {1x}.

Oua, an interjection of derision and insult, is translated "Ha!" in Mk 15:29. See: BAGD—591a; THAYER—461c.

3759. **οὐαί** {47x} **ŏuai**, *oo-ah'-ee;* a primary exclamation of grief; "*woe*":—alas {6x}, woe {41x}.

Ouai, **(1)** an interjection, is used **(1a)** in denunciation, Mt. 11:21; 18:7 (twice); eight times in ch. 23; 24:19; 26:24; Mk 13:17; 14:21; Lk 6:24, 25 (twice), 26; 10:13; six times in ch. 11; 17:1; 21:23; 22:22; 1 Cor 9:16; Jude 11; Rev 8:13 (thrice); 12:12; **(1b)** as a noun, Rev 9:12 (twice); 11:14 (twice); **(2)** in grief, "alas," Rev 18:10, 16, 19 (twice in each). See: BAGD—591a; THAYER—461c.

3760. **οὐδαμῶς** {1x} **ŏudamōs**, *oo-dam-oce';* adv. from (the fem.) of *3762; by no means:*—not {1x}.

This word denotes "by no means, in no wise," Mt 2:6. See: BAGD—591b; THAYER—461d.

3761. **οὐδέ** {137x} **ŏudĕ**, *oo-deh';* from *3756* and *1161; not however,* i.e. *neither, nor, not even:*—neither {69x}, nor {31x}, not {10x}, no not {8x}, not so much as {2x}, then not {1x}, not tr. {1x}, misc {14x} = neither indeed, never, no more, no not, + nothing, so much as. See: BAGD—591c; THAYER—461d.

3762. **οὐδείς** {236x} **ŏudĕis**, *oo-dice';* incl. fem.

οὐδεμία **ŏudĕmia**, *oo-dem-ee'-ah;* and neut.

οὐδέν **ŏudĕn**, *oo-den';* from *3761* and *1520; not even one* (man, woman or thing), i.e. *none, nobody, nothing:*—no man {94x}, nothing {68x}, none {27x}, no {24x}, any man {3x}, any {3x}, man {2x}, neither any man {2x}, misc. {13x} = aught, man, neither any (thing), never (man), none of these things), not (any, at all), nought. See: BAGD—591d; THAYER—462b.

3763. **οὐδέποτε** {16x} **ŏudĕpŏtĕ**, *oo-dep'-ot-eh;* from *3761* and *4218; not even at any time,* i.e. *never at all:*—never {14x}, neither at any time {1x}, nothing at any time + 3856 {1x}.

This word, (from *oude,* "not even," and *pote,* "at any time"), is used **(1)** in definite negative statements, e.g., Mt 7:23; 1 Cor 13:8; Heb 10:1, 11, or **(2)** questions, e.g., Mt 21:16, 42; **(3)** in Lk 15:29 (1st part), "neither . . . at any time"; "never" (2nd part). See: BAGD—592b; THAYER—462d.

3764. **οὐδέπω** {5x} **ŏudĕpō**, *oo-dep'-o;* from *3761* and *4452; not even yet:*—never before {1x}, never yet {1x}, nothing yet {1x}, not yet {1x}, as yet not {1x}. See: BAGD—592c; THAYER—462d.

3765. **οὐκέτι** {47x} **ŏukĕti**, *ook-et'-ee;* also (separately)

οὐκ ἔτι **ŏuk ĕti**, *ook et'-ee;* from *3756* and *2089; not yet, no longer:*—no more {29x}, any more {3x}, now not {2x}, misc. {13x} = after that (not), not any more, henceforth (hereafter) not, no longer, not as yet (now), now no more, yet (not).

Ouketi, "no more, no longer", is rendered **(1)** "no more" in Mk 7:12, **(2)** Jn 15:15, "henceforth not", **(3)** Rom 14:15, "now . . . not", **(4)** Gal 2:20, "yet not", **(5)** Gal 3:25; 4:7, "no more", and **(6)** Philem 16, "not now". See: BAGD—592c; THAYER—462d.

3766. **οὐκοῦν** {1x} **ŏukŏun**, *ook-oon';* from *3756* and *3767;* is it *not therefore* that, i.e. (affirmatively) *hence* or *so:*—then {1x}. See: BAGD—592d; THAYER—463a.

3767. **οὖν** {526x} **ŏun**, *oon;* appar. a primary word; (adv.) *certainly,* or (conjunc.) *accordingly:*—therefore {263x}, then {197x}, so {18x}, and {11x}, now {9x}, wherefore {8x}, but {5x}, not tr. {9x}, misc. {6x} = but, so likewise then, verily. See: BAGD—592d; THAYER—463b.

3768. **οὔπω** {23x} **ŏupō**, *oo'-po;* from *3756* and *4452; not yet:*—not yet {20x}, hitherto . . . not {1x}, as yet {1x}, no . . . as yet {1x}. See: BAGD—593c; THAYER—464b

3769. **οὐρά** {5x} **ŏura**, *oo-rah';* appar. a primary word; a *tail:*—tail {5x}.

Oura, "the tail of an animal," occurs in Rev 9:10 (twice), 19; 12:4. See: BAGD—593c; THAYER—464b.

3770. **οὐράνιος** {6x} **ŏuraniŏs**, *oo-ran'-ee-os;* from *3772; celestial,* i.e. *belonging to* or *coming from* the *sky:*—heavenly {6x}.

Ourainos, signifying "of heaven, heavenly," is used **(1)** as an appellation of God the Father, **(1a)** Mt 6:14, 26, 32, "your heavenly Father"; **(1b)** 15:13, "My heavenly Father"; **(2)** as descriptive of the holy angels, Lk 2:13; **(3)** of the vision seen by Paul, Acts 26:19. See: TDNT—5:536, 736; BAGD—593c; THAYER—464b.

3771. **οὐρανόθεν** {2x} **ŏuranŏthĕn**, *oo-ran-oth'-en;* from *3772* and the enclitic of source; *from* the *sky:*—from heaven {2x}.

Ouranothen, denoting "from heaven," is used of **(1)** the aerial heaven, Acts 14:17; **(2)** heaven, as the uncreated sphere of God's abode, Acts 26:13. See: TDNT—5:542, 736; BAGD—593d; THAYER—464c.

3772. **οὐρανός** {284x} **ŏuranŏs**, *oo-ran-os';* perh. from the same as *3735* (through the idea of *elevation*); the *sky;* by extens. *heaven* (as the abode of God); by impl. *happiness, power, eternity;* spec. the *Gospel* (*Christianity*):—heaven {268x}, air {10x}, sky {5x}, heavenly + 1537 {1x}.

Ouranos, is used in the NT **(1)** of "the aerial heavens," e.g., Mt 6:26; 8:20; Acts 10:12; 11:6 "air"; Jas 5:18; **(2)** "the sidereal" (i.e. the starry heavens), e.g., Mt 24:29, 35; Mk 13:25, 31; Heb 11:12, "sky"; Rev 6:14; 20:11; **(3)** they, (1) and (2), **(3a)** were created by the Son of God, Heb 1:10, as also **(3b)** by God the Father, Rev 10:6; **(4)** "the eternal dwelling place of God," Mt 5:16; 12:50; Rev 3:12; 11:13; 16:11; 20:9. **(5)** From thence the Son of God descended to become incarnate, Jn 3:13, 31; 6:38, 42. **(6)** In His ascension Christ "passed through the heavens," Heb 4:14, **(6)** He "ascended far above all the heavens," Eph 4:10, and was "made higher than the heavens," Heb 7:26; **(7)** He "sat down on the right hand of the throne of the Majesty in the heavens," Heb 8:1; **(8)** He is "on the right hand of God," having gone into heaven, 1 Pet 3:22. **(9)** Since His ascension it is the scene of His present life and activity, e.g., Rom 8:34; Heb 9:24.

(10) From thence the Holy Spirit descended at Pentecost, 1 Pet 1:12. **(11)** It is the abode of the angels, e.g., Mt 18:10; 22:30; cf. Rev 3:5. **(12)** Thither Paul was "caught up," whether in the body or out of the body, he knew not, 2 Cor 12:2. **(13)** It is to be the eternal dwelling place of the saints in resurrection glory, 2 Cor 5:1. **(14)** From thence Christ will descend to the air **(14a)** to receive His saints at the Rapture, 1 Th 4:16; Phil 3:20, 21, and **(14b)** will subsequently come with His saints and with His holy angels at His second advent, Mt 24:30; 2 Th 1:7. **(15)** In the present life "heaven" is the region of the spiritual citizenship of believers, Phil 3:20. **(16)** The present "heavens," with the earth, are to pass away, 2 Pet 3:10, "being on fire," v. 12 (see v. 7); Rev 20:11, and **(17)** new "heavens" and earth are to be created, 2 Pet 3:13; Rev 21:1, with Is 65:17. **(18)** In Lk 15:18, 21, "heaven" is used, by metonymy, for God. See: TDNT—5:497, 736 BAGD—593d; THAYER—464c.

3773. **Οὐρβανός** {1x} **Ŏurbanŏs**, *oor-ban-os';* of Lat. or.; *Urbanus* (*of the city, "urbane"*), a Chr.:—Urbane {1x}. See: BAGD—595c; THAYER—465d.

3774. **Οὐρίας** {1x} **Ŏurias**, *oo-ree'-as;* of Heb. or. [223]; *Urias* (i.e. *Urijah*), a Hittite:—Urias {1x}. See: TDNT—3:1,*; BAGD—595c; THAYER—465d.

3775. **οὖς** {37x} **ŏus**, *ooce;* appar. a primary word; the *ear* (phys. or ment.):—ear {37x}.

Ous is used **(1)** of the physical organ (Lk 4:21; Acts 7:57); **(1a)** in Acts 11:22, in the plural with *akouo*, "to hear," lit., "was heard into the ears of someone," i.e., came to the knowledge of, similarly, in the singular, Mt 10:27, in familiar private conversation; **(1b)** in Jas 5:4 the phrase is used with *eiserchomai* (1525), "to enter into"; **(1c)** in Lk 1:44, with *ginomai* (1096), "to become, to come"; **(1d)** in Lk 12:3, with *lalein* (2980), "to speak" and pros, "to"; **(2)** metaphorically, of the faculty of perceiving with the mind, understanding and knowing (Mt 13:16);

(3) frequently with *akouo* (191), "to hear" (Mt 11:15; 13:9, 43); **(3a)** Rev 2 and 3, at the close of each of the messages to the churches; **(3b)** in Mt 13:15 and Acts 28:27, with *bareos* (917), "heavily," of being slow to understand and obey; **(3c)** with a negative: "Having eyes, see ye not? and having ears, hear ye not? and do ye not remember?" (Mk 8:18; cf. Rom 11:8); **(3d)** in Lk 9:44 the lit. meaning is "put those words into your ears," i.e., take them into your mind and keep them there; **(3e)** in Acts 7:51 it is used with *aperitmetos* (564), "uncircumcised." **(4)** As seeing is metaphorically associated with conviction, so hearing is with obedience [*hupakoe* - 5219, lit., "hearing under"; the Eng., "obedience" is etymologically "hearing over against," i.e., with response in the hearer]. Syn.: 189, 5621. See: TDNT—5:543, 744; BAGD—595c; THAYER—465d.

3776. **οὐσία** {2x} **ŏusia**, *oo-see'-ah;* from the fem. of *5607; substance*, i.e. *property* (*possessions*):—goods {1x}, substance {1x}.

Ousia, derived from a present participial form of *eimi*, "to be," denotes "substance, property," and is translated **(1)** Lk 15:12, "goods", and **(2)** 15:13, "substance." See: BAGD—596a; THAYER—466a.

3777. **οὔτε** {94x} **ŏutĕ**, *oo'-teh;* from *3756* and *5037; not too*, i.e. *neither* or *nor;* by anal. *not even:*—neither {44x}, nor {40x}, nor yet {4x}, no not {1x}, not {1x}, yet not {1x}, misc. {3x} = none, nothing. See: BAGD—596a; THAYER—466b.

3778. **οὗτος** {355x} **hŏutŏs**, *hoo'-tos;* incl. nom. masc. plur.

οὗτοι **hŏutŏi**, *hoo'-toy;* nom. fem. sing.

αὕτη **hautē**, *hŏw'-tay;* and nom. fem. plur.

αὗται **hautai**, *hŏw'-tahee;* from the art. *3588* and *846; the he* (*she* or it), i.e. *this* or *that* (often with art. repeated):—this {157x}, these {59x}, he {31x}, the same {28x}, this man {25x}, she {12x}, they {10x}, misc. {33x} = he it was that, hereof, it, such as, this (same, woman), which, who. See: BAGD—596b; THAYER—466c.

3779. **οὕτω** {213x} **hŏutō**, *hoo'-to;* or (before a vowel)

οὕτως **hŏutōs**, *hoo'-toce;* adv. from *3778; in this way* (referring to what precedes or follows):—so {164x}, thus {17x}, even so {9x}, on this wise {6x}, likewise {4x}, after this manner {3x}, misc. {10x} = after that, in this manner, as, for all that, no more, on this fashion, so in like manner, what.

Houtos or *houto*, as an averb, means "thus, in this way" and is rendered "after this manner" (Mt 6:9; 1 Pet 3:5; Rev 11:5). Syn.: 195, 1485, 2239, 3634, 3668, 3697, 4169, 4187, 4217, 4459, 5158, 5159, 5179, 5615. See: BAGD—597c; THAYER—468a.

3780. **οὐχί** {56x} **ŏuchi**, *oo-khee';* intens. of *3756; not indeed:*—not {46x}, nay {5x}, not {4x}, not so {1x}. See: BAGD—598b; THAYER—469a.

3781. **ὀφειλέτης** {7x} **ŏphĕilĕtēs**, *of-i-let'-ace;* from *3784;* an *ower*, i.e. person *indebted;* fig. a *delinquent;* mor. a *transgressor* (against God):—debtor {5x}, which owed {1x}, sinner {1x}.

This word means one who owes anything to another," primarily in regard to money; **(1)** in Mt 18:24, "who owed" (lit., "one was brought, a debtor to him of ten thousand talents"). The slave could own property, and so become a "debtor" to his master, who might seize him for payment. **(2)** It is used metaphorically, **(2a)** of a person who is under an obligation, Rom 1:14, **(2a1)** of Paul, in the matter of preaching the gospel; **(2a2)** in Rom 8:12, of believers, to mortify the deeds of the body; **(2a3)** in Rom 15:27, of gentile believers, to assist afflicted Jewish believers; **(2a4)** in Gal 5:3, of those who would be justified by circumcision, to do the whole Law; **(2b)** of those who have not yet made amends to those whom they have injured, Mt 6:12, "our debtors"; **(2c)** of some whose disaster was liable to be regarded as a due punishment, Lk 13:4, "sinners." See: TDNT—5:565, 746; BAGD—598b; THAYER—469a.

3782. **ὀφειλή** {2x} **ŏphĕilē**, *of-i-lay';* from *3784; indebtedness*, i.e. (concr.) a *sum* owed; fig. *obligation*, i.e. (conjugal) *duty:*—debt {1x}, due {1x}.

Opheile, "that which is owed", is translated **(1)** "debt" in Mt 18:32; **(2)** in the plural, "dues", Rom 13:7. See: TDNT—5:564, 746; BAGD—598c; THAYER—469b.

3783. **ὀφείλημα** {2x} **ŏphĕilēma**, *of-i'-lay-mah;* from (the alt. of) *3784; something owed*, i.e. (fig.) a *due;* mor. a *fault:*—debt {2x}.

Opheilema, expressing a "debt" more concretely, is used **(1)** literally, of that which is legally due, Rom 4:4; **(2)** metaphorically, of sin as a "debt," because it demands expiation, and thus payment by way of punishment, Mt. 6:12. See: TDNT—5:565, 746; BAGD—598c; THAYER—469b.

3784. **ὀφείλω** {36x} **ŏphĕilō**, *of-i'-lo;* or (in certain tenses) its prol. form

ὀφειλέω **ŏphĕilĕō**, *of-i-leh'-o;* prob. from the base of *3786* (through the idea of *accruing*); to *owe* (pecuniarily); fig. to *be under obligation* (*ought, must, should*); mor. to *fail* in duty:—ought {15x}, owe {7x}, be bound {2x}, be (one's) duty {2x}, be a debtor {1x}, be guilty {1x}, be indebted 1, misc. {7x} = behove, (must) need (-s), should. Syn.: *Dei* (1165) expresses a logical necessity, *opheilo* (3784), a moral obligation; cf. *chre* (5534), Jas 3:10, "ought," which expresses a need resulting from the fitness of things. See: TDNT—5:559, 746; BAGD—598d; THAYER—469b. See also *3785*.

3785. **ὄφελον** {4x} **ŏphĕlŏn**, *of'-el-on;* first pers. sing. of a past tense of *3784; I ought* (*wish*), i.e. (interj.) *oh that!:*—I would {2x}, I would to God {1x}, would to God {1x}. See: BAGD—599a; THAYER—469c.

3786. **ὄφελος** {3x} **ŏphĕlŏs**, *of'-el-os;* from ὀφέλλω **ŏphĕllō**, (to *heap* up, i.e. *accumulate* or *benefit*); *gain:*—it advantageth {1x}, it profiteth {2x}.

Ophello, "to increase," comes from a root signifying "to increase"; hence, "advantage, profit"; it is rendered as a verb in its three occurrences, **(1)** 1 Cor 15:32, "advantageth"; **(2)** Jas 2:14, 16, "What (is) the profit?" See: BAGD—599b; THAYER—469d.

3787. **ὀφθαλμοδουλεία** {2x} **ŏphthalmŏdŏulĕia**, *of-thal-mod-oo-li'-ah;* from *3788* and *1397; sight-labor*, i.e. that needs watching (*remissness*):—eye-service {2x}.

This is service performed [only] under the master's eyes for the master's eye usually stimulates to greater diligence and his absence, on the other hand, renders sluggish, Eph 6:6 and Col 3:22. See: TDNT—2:280, 182; BAGD—599b; THAYER—469d.

3788. **ὀφθαλμός** {101x} **ŏphthalmŏs**, *of-thal-mos';* from *3700;* the *eye* (lit. or fig.); by impl. *vision;* fig. *envy* (from the jealous side-glance):—eye {101x}, sight {1x}.

Ophthalmos, akin to *opsis*, "sight," probably from a root signifying "penetration, sharpness", (cf. Eng., "ophthalmia," etc.), is used **(1)** of the physical organ, e.g., Mt 5:38; **(1a)** of restoring sight, e.g., Mt 20:33; **(1b)** of God's power of vision, Heb 4:13; 1 Pet 3:12; **(1c)** of Christ in vision, Rev 1:14; 2:18; 19:12; **(1d)** of the Holy Spirit in the unity of Godhood with Christ, Rev 5:6; **(2)** metaphorically, **(2a)** of ethical qualities, evil, Mt 6:23; Mk 7:22 (by metonymy, for envy); **(2b)** singleness of motive, Mt 6:22; Lk 11:34; **(2c)** as the instrument of evil desire, "the principal avenue of temptation," 1 Jn 2:16; **(2d)** of adultery, 2 Pet 2:14; **(3)** metaphorically, **(3a)** of mental vision, Mt 13:15; Jn 12:40; Rom 11:8; Gal 3:1; **(3b)** by gospel-preaching Christ had been, so to speak, placarded before their "eyes"; **(3c)** the question may be paraphrased, "What evil teachers have been malignly fascinating you?"; **(3d)** Eph 1:18, of the "eyes of the heart," as a means of knowledge. See: TDNT—5:375, 706; BAGD—599b; THAYER—470a.

3789. **ὄφις** {14x} **ŏphis**, *of'-is;* prob. from *3700* (through the idea of *sharpness* of vision); a *snake,* fig. (as a type of sly cunning) an artful *malicious* person, espec. *Satan:*—serpent {14x}.

(1) The characteristics of the "serpent" as alluded to in Scripture **(1a)** are mostly evil (though Mt 10:16 refers to its caution in avoiding danger); **(1b)** its treachery, cf. Gen. 49:17; 2 Cor 11:3; **(1c)** its venom, cf. Ps 58:4; 1 Cor 10:9; Rev 9:19; **(1d)** its skulking, cf. Job 26:13; **(1e)** its murderous proclivities, e.g., Ps 58:4; Prov 23:32; Eccl 10:8, 11; Amos 5:19; Mk 16:18; Lk 10:19; **(2)** the Lord used the word metaphorically of the scribes and Pharisees, Mt 23:33 (cf. *echidna,* "viper," in Mt 3:7; 12:34). **(3)** The general aspects of its evil character are intimated in the Lord's rhetorical question in Mt 7:10 and Lk 11:11. **(4)** Its characteristics are concentrated in the archadversary of God and man, the Devil, metaphorically described as the serpent, 2 Cor 11:3; Rev 12:9, 14, 15; 20:2. **(5)** The brazen "serpent" lifted up by Moses was symbolical of the means of salvation provided by God, in Christ and His vicarious death under the divine judgment upon sin, Jn 3:14. **(6)** While the living "serpent" symbolizes sin in its origin, hatefulness, and deadly effect, the brazen "serpent" symbolized the bearing away of the curse and the judgment of sin; the metal was itself figurative of the righteousness of God's judgment. See: TDNT—5:566, 748; BAGD—600a; THAYER—470b.

3790. **ὀφρύς** {1x} **ŏphrus**, *of-roos';* perh. from *3700* (through the idea of the shading or proximity to the organ of *vision*); the eye-"*brow*" or *forehead,* i.e. (fig.) the *brink* of a precipice:—brow {1x}. See: BAGD—600b; THAYER—470c.

3791. **ὀχλέω** {2x} **ŏchlĕō**, *okh-leh'-o;* from *3793;* to *mob,* i.e. (by impl.) to *harass:*—vex {2x}.

Ochleo means to disturb, trouble and is used in the passive voice, of being troubled, molested, vexed by evil spirits (Lk 6:18; Acts 5:16). See: BAGD—600c; THAYER—470c.

3792. **ὀχλοποιέω** {1x} **ŏchlŏpŏiĕō**, *okh-lop-oy-eh'-o;* from *3793* and *4160;* to *make a crowd,* i.e. *raise a* public *disturbance:*—gather a company {1x}. See: BAGD—600c; THAYER—470c.

3793. **ὄχλος** {175x} **ŏchlŏs**, *okh'los;* from a der. of *2192* (mean. a *vehicle*); a disorganized *throng* (as *borne* along); by impl. the *rabble;* by extens. a *class* of people; fig. a *riot:*—people {82x}, multitude {79x}, press {5x}, company {7x}, number of people {1x}, number {1x}.

Ochlos is used **(1)** frequently in the four Gospels and the Acts; elsewhere only in Rev. 7:9; 17:15; 19:1, 6; **(2)** it denotes **(2a)** "a crowd or multitude of persons, a throng," e.g., Mt 14:14, 15; 15:33; **(2b)** often in the plural, e.g., Mt 4:25; 5:1; **(2c)** with *polus,* "much" or "great," it signifies **(2c1)** "a great multitude," e.g., Mt 20:29, or **(2c2)** "the common people," Mk 12:37, perhaps preferably "the mass of the people." The mass of the people was attracted to Him (for the statement "heard Him gladly" cf. what is said in Mk 6:20 of Herod Antipas concerning John the Baptist; **(2c3)** in Jn 12:9, "the people" stands in contrast with their leaders (v. 10); Acts 24:1 "crowd"; **(3)** "the populace, an unorganized multitude," in contrast to *demos,* "the people as a body politic," e.g., Mt 14:5; 21:26; Jn 7:12 (2nd part); **(4)** in a more general sense, **(4a)** "the company of His disciples" e.g., Lk 6:17; **(4b)** Acts 1:15, "the number of names"; **(4c)** Acts 24:18, "multitude." Syn.: 1218, 1484, 2992, 3793. See: TDNT—5:582, 750; BAGD—600c; THAYER—470c.

3794. **ὀχύρωμα** {1x} **ŏchurōma**, *okh-oo'-ro-mah;* from a remote der. of *2192* (mean. to *fortify,* through the idea of *holding* safely); a *castle* (fig. *argument*):—stronghold {1x}.

Ochurmoa, "a stronghold, fortress" (akin to *ochuroo,* "to make firm"), is used metaphorically in 2 Cor 10:4, of those things in which mere human confidence is imposed. See: TDNT—5:590, 752; BAGD—601a; THAYER—471a.

3795. **ὀψάριον** {5x} **ŏpsariŏn**, *op-sar'-ee-on;* neut. of a presumed der. of the base of *3702;* a *relish* to other food (as if cooked *sauce*), i.e. (spec.) *fish* (presumably salted and dried as a condiment):—fish {4x}, small fish {1x}.

Opsarion is a diminutive of *opson* (3702 - cooked meat), or a relish, a dainty dish, especially of fish or little fish (Jn 6:9, "small fishes"; 6:11; 21:9, 10, 13). See: BAGD—601b; THAYER—471a.

3796. **ὀψέ** {3x} **ŏpsĕ**, *op-seh';* from the same as *3694* (through the idea of *backwardness*); (adv.) *late* in the day; by extens. *after the close* of the day:—in the end {1x}, even {1x}, at even {1x}.

Opse, "long after, late, late in the day, at evening" (in contrast to *proi,* "early," e.g., Mt 20:1), is used **(1)** practically as a noun in Mk 11:11, lit., "the hour being at eventide", 11:19; 13:35; **(2)** in Mt 28:1 it is rendered "in the end of." See: BAGD—601b; THAYER—471b.

3797. **ὄψιμος** {1x} **ŏpsimŏs**, *op'-sim-os;* from *3796; later,* i.e. *vernal* (showering):—latter {1x}.

Opsimos denotes "late," or "latter," and is used of "the latter rain" in Jas 5:7; this rain falls in March and April, just before the harvest, in contrast to the early rain, in October. See: BAGD—601c; THAYER—471c.

3798. **ὄψιος** {15x} **ŏpsiŏs**, *op'-see-os;* from *3796; late;* fem. (as noun) *afternoon* (early eve) or *nightfall* (later eve):—even {8x}, evening {4x}, in the evening + 1096 {1x}, eventide + 5610 {1x}, at even + 1096 {1x}.

Opsios, the feminine of the adjective *opsios,* "late," **(1)** used as a noun, denoting "evening," with *hora,* "understood", is found seven times in Mt, five in Mk, two in Jn, and in these places only in the NT. **(2)** The word really signifies the "late evening," the latter of the two "evenings" as reckoned by the Jews, the first from 3 p.m. to sunset, the latter after sunset; this is the usual meaning. It is used, however, of both, e.g., Mk 1:32. See: BAGD—601c; THAYER—471c.

3799. **ὄψις** {3x} **ŏpsis**, *op'-sis;* from *3700;* prop. *sight* (the act), i.e. (by impl.) the *visage,* an extern. *show:*—appearance {1x}, countenance {1x}, face {1x}.

Opsis, (from *ops,* "the eye," connected with *horao,* "to see", primarily denotes "seeing, sight"; hence, **(1)** "the face, the countenance," Jn 11:44 ("face"); **(2)** Rev 1:16 ("countenance"); **(3)** the outward "appearance," the look, Jn 7:24, only here, of the outward aspect of a person. See: BAGD—601d; THAYER—471d.

3800. **ὀψώνιον** {4x} **ŏpsōniŏn**, *op-so'-nee-on;* neut. of a presumed der. of the same as *3795; rations* for a soldier, i.e. (by extens.) his *stipend* or *pay:*—wages {3x}, charges {1x}.

Opsonion, (from *opson,* "meat," and *oneomai,* "to buy"), primarily signified whatever is brought to be eaten with bread provisions, supplies for an army, soldier's pay, translated **(1)** "charges," 1 Cor 9:7, of the service of a soldier. **(2)** It is rendered "wages" in Lk 3:14; Rom 6:23; 2 Cor 11:8. See: TDNT—5:591, 752; BAGD—602a; THAYER—471d.

3801. **ὁ ὢν καί ὁ ἦν καί ὁ ἐρχόμενος** {15x} **hŏ ōn kai hŏ ēn kai hŏ ĕrchŏmĕnŏs**, *hŏ own kahee hŏ ane kahee hŏ er-khom'-en-os;* a phrase combining *3588* with the pres. part. and imperf. of *1510* and the pres. part. of *2064* by means of *2532; the* one *being and the* one that *was and the* one *coming,* i.e. *the Eternal,* as a divine epithet of Christ:—which is {2x}, and which was {2x}, and which is to come {2x}, which art {2x}, and wast {2x}, which was {1x}, and is {1x}, and is to come {1x}, and art to come {1x}, and shall be {1x}. See: BAGD—not listed; THAYER—not listed.

Π

3802. **παγιδεύω** {1x} **pagidĕuō**, *pag-id-yoo'-o;* from *3803,* to *ensnare* (fig.):—entangle {1x}.

Pagideuo, "to entrap, lay snares for" (from *pagis,* "anything which fixes or grips," hence, "a snare"), is used in Mt 22:15, of the efforts of the Pharisees to "entangle" the Lord in His speech. **(2)** Metaphorically, *pagideuo* speaks of the attempt to elicit from one some remark which can be turned into an accusation against him. See: TDNT—5:595, 752; BAGD—602a; THAYER—472a.

3803. **παγίς** {5x} **pagis**, *pag-ece';* from *4078;* a *trap* (as *fastened* by a noose or notch); fig. a *trick* or *statagem* (*temptation*):—snare {5x}.

Pagis, "a trap, a snare" (akin to *pegnumi,* "to fix," and *pagideuo,* "to ensnare", is used metaphorically of **(1)** the allurements to evil by which the Devil "ensnares" one, 1 Ti 3:7; 2 Ti 2:26; **(2)** seductions to evil, which "ensnare" those who "desire to be rich," 1 Ti 6:9; **(3)** the evil brought by Israel upon themselves by which the special privileges divinely granted them and centering in Christ, became a "snare" to them, their rejection of Christ and the Gospel being the retributive effect of their apostasy, Rom 11:9; **(4)** of the sudden judgments of God to come upon those whose hearts are "overcharged with surfeiting, and drunkenness, and cares of this life," Lk 21:35. See: TDNT—5:593, 752; BAGD—602a; THAYER—472a.

Πάγος **Pagŏs**. See *697*.

3804. **πάθημα** {16x} **pathēma**, *path'-ay-mah;* from a presumed der. of *3806;* something *undergone,* i.e. *hardship* or *pain;* subj. an *emotion* or *influence:*—affection {1x}, affliction {3x}, motion {1x}, suffering {11x}.

Pathema, from *pathos,* "suffering," signifies "affliction." **(1)** The word is frequent in Paul's epistles and is found three times in Hebrews, four in 1 Pet; and it is used **(2)** of "afflictions", Rom 8:18, etc.; **(3)** of Christ's "sufferings", 1 Pet 1:11; 5:1; Heb 2:9; **(4)** of those as shared by believers, 2 Cor 1:5; Phil 3:10; 1 Pet 4:13; 5:1; **(5)** of "an evil emotion, passion", Rom 7:5; Gal 5:24. **(6)** The connection between the two meanings is that the emotions, whether good or evil, **(6a)** were regarded as consequent upon external influences exerted on the mind (cf. the two meanings of the English "passion"). It expresses in sense **(6b)** the uncontrolled nature of evil desires, in contrast to *epithumia,* the general and comprehensive term, lit., "what you set your heart upon." **(7)** Its concrete character is seen in

Heb. 2:9. See: TDNT—5:930, 798; BAGD—602b; THAYER—472a.

3805. **παθητός** {1x} **pathētŏs**, *path-ay-tos';* from the same as *3804; liable* (i.e. *doomed*) to experience *pain:*—suffer {1x}.

Pathetos denotes "one who has suffered," or "subject to suffering," or "destined to suffer", endued with the capacity of suffering, capable of feeling; and hence, subject to the necessity of suffering; it is used in the last sense of the "suffering" of Christ, Acts 26:23. See: TDNT—5:924, 798; BAGD—602d; THAYER—472b.

3806. **πάθος** {3x} **pathŏs**, *path'-os;* from the alt. of *3958;* prop. *suffering* ("*pathos*"), i.e. (subj.) a *passion* (espec. *concupiscence*):—inordinate affection {1x}, affection {1x}, lust {1x}.

(1) This word primarily denotes whatever one experiences in any way which affects him; hence, an affection of the mind which stimulates a passionate desire, capricious delight, the disease of passion, and is always used in a bad sense; primarily denotes whatever one suffers or experiences in any way; hence, "an affection of the mind, a passionate desire." **(2)** Used by the Greeks of either good or bad desires, it is always used in the NT of the latter, **(2a)** Rom 1:26, "(vile) affections"; **(2b)** Col 3:5, "inordinate affection"; **(2c)** 1 Th 4:5, "lust." Syn.: 1939, 3715, 3730. See: TDNT—5:926, 798; BAGD—602d; THAYER—472c.

πάθω **pathō**. See *3958*.

3807. **παιδαγωγός** {3x} **paidagōgŏs**, *pahee-dag-o-gos';* from *3816* and a redupl. form of *71;* a *boy-leader,* i.e. a servant whose office it was to take the children to school; (by impl. [fig.] a *tutor* ["*pædagogue*"]):—instructor {1x}, schoolmaster {2x}.

This word means "a guide," or "guardian" or "trainer of boys," lit., "a child-leader" (*pais,* "a boy, or child," *ago,* "to lead"), "a tutor," is translated **(1)** "instructors" in 1 Cor 4:15; here the thought is that of pastors rather than teachers; **(2)** in Gal 3:24, 25, "schoolmaster", but here the idea of instruction is absent. **(2a)** In this and allied words the idea is that of training, discipline, not of impartation of knowledge. **(2b)** The *paidagogos* was not the instructor of the child; he exercised a general supervision over him and was responsible for his moral and physical wellbeing. **(2c)** Thus understood, *paidagogos* is appropriately used with "kept in ward" and "shut up," whereas to understand it as equivalent to "teacher" introduces, an idea entirely foreign to the passage, and throws the Apostle's argument into confusion. See: TDNT—5:596, 753; BAGD—603a; THAYER—472d.

3808. **παιδάριον** {2x} **paidariŏn**, *pahee-dar'-ee-on;* neut. of a presumed der. of *3816;* a *little boy:*—child {1x}, lad {1x}.

Paidarion, a diminutive of *pais,* is used **(1)** of "boys and girls," in Mt 11:16, and **(2)** a "lad" in Jn 6:9. Syn.: *Paidarion* (3808) refers to a child up to his first school years. *Paidion* (3813) refers exclusively to little children. *Paidiske* (3814) refers to female in late childhood and early youth. *Pais* (3816) refers to a child of any age. *Teknon* (5043) gives prominence to physical and outward aspects of parentage. *Huios* (5207) gives prominence to the inward, ethical, legal aspects of parentage. *Pais* (3816) and *teknon* (5043) denote a child as respects to descent and age, reference to the later being more prominent in the former word, to descent in *paidion* (3813); but the period *pais* (3816) covers is not sharply defined. See: TDNT—5:636, 759; BAGD—603b; THAYER—472d.

3809. **παιδεία** {6x} **paidĕia**, *pahee-di'-ah;* from *3811; tutorage,* i.e. *education* or *training;* by impl. disciplinary *correction:*—chastening {3x}, chastisement {1x}, instruction {1x}, nurture {1x}.

Paideia denotes "the training of a child, including instruction"; hence, "discipline, correction," "chastening," and is translated **(1)** in Eph 6:4, "nurture", suggesting the Christian discipline that regulates character; and **(2)** "chastening" in Heb12:5, 7; **(3)** "chastisement" in Heb 12:8; and **(4)** in 2 Tim. 3:16, "instruction. Syn.: 3559. See: TDNT—5:596, 753; BAGD—603b; THAYER—472d.

3810. **παιδευτής** {2x} **paidĕutēs**, *pahee-dyoo-tace';* from *3811;* a *trainer,* i.e. *teacher* or (by impl.) *discipliner:*—which corrected {1x}, instructor {1x}.

Paideutes has two meanings, corresponding to the two meanings of the verb *paideuo* (3811) from which it is derived, **(1)** "a teacher, preceptor, corrector," Rom 2:20, "instructor", and **(2)** [the one] "which corrected", "a chastiser," Heb 12:9. See: TDNT—5:596, 753; BAGD—603d; THAYER—473a.

3811. **παιδεύω** {13x} **paidĕuō**, *pahee-dyoo'-o;* from *3816;* to *train* up a child, i.e. *educate,* or (by impl.) *discipline* (by punishment):—chasten {6x}, chastise {2x}, instruct {1x}, learn {2x}, teach {2x}.

Paideuo primarily denotes "to train children," suggesting the broad idea of education (*pais,* "a child"), and is translated **(1)** "learned" in Acts 7:22; **(2)** "taught" in Acts 22:3; **(3)** "teaching" in Titus 2:12, here of a training gracious and firm; grace, which brings salvation, employs means to give us full possession of it; hence, **(4)** "to chastise," this being part of the training, whether **(4a)** by correcting with words, reproving, and admonishing, 1 Ti 1:20; 2 Ti 2:25, or **(4b)** by "chastening" by the infliction of evils and calamities, 1 Cor 11:32; 2 Cor. 6:9; Heb 12:6–7, 10; Rev 3:19. **(5)** The verb also has the meaning "to chastise with blows, to scourge," said of the command of a judge, Lk 23:16, 22. See: TDNT—5:596, 753; BAGD—603d; THAYER—473a.

3812. **παιδιόθεν** {1x} **paidiŏthĕn**, *pahee-dee-oth'-en;* adv. (of *source*) from *3813; from infancy:*—of a child {1x}. See: BAGD—604a; THAYER—473b.

3813. **παιδίον** {51x} **paidiŏn**, *pahee-dee'-on;* neut. dimin. of *3816;* a *childling* (of either sex), i.e. (prop.) an infant, or (by extens.) a half-grown *boy* or girl; fig. an *immature* Chr.:—child {25x}, little child {12x}, young child {10x}, damsel {4x}.

Paidion, a diminutive of *pais,* **(1)** signifies "a little or young child"; **(1a)** it is used of an infant just born, Jn 16:21, **(1b)** of a male child recently born, e.g., Mt 2:8; Heb 11:23; **(1c)** of a more advanced child, Mk 9:24; **(1d)** of a son, Jn 4:49; **(1e)** of a girl, Mk 5:39, 40, 41; **(1f)** in the plural, of "children," e.g., Mt 14:21. **(2)** It is used metaphorically **(2a)** of believers who are deficient in spiritual understanding, 1 Cor 14:20, and **(2b)** in affectionate and familiar address by the Lord to His disciples, almost like the Eng., "lads," Jn 21:5; **(2c)** by the apostle John to the youngest believers in the family of God, 1 Jn 2:13, 18; there it is to be distinguished from *teknia,* which term he uses in addressing all his readers. Syn.: *Paidarion* (3808) refers to a child up to his first school years. *Paidion* (3813) refers exclusively to little children. *Paidiske* (3814) refers to a female in late childhood and early youth. *Pais* (3816) refers to a child of any age. *Teknon* (5043) gives prominence to physical and outward aspects of parentage. *Huios* (5207) gives prominence to the inward, ethical, legal aspects of parentage. *Pais* (3816) and *teknon* (5043) denote a child as respects to descent and age, reference to the later being more prominent in the former word, to descent in *paidion* (3813); but the period *pais* (3816) covers is not sharply defined. See: TDNT—5:636, 759; BAGD—604a; THAYER—473b.

3814. **παιδίσκη** {13x} **paidiskē**, *pahee-dis'-kay;* fem. dimin. of *3816;* a *girl,* i.e. (spec.) a *female slave* or *servant:*—damsel {4x}, bondwomen {4x}, maid {3x}, maiden {1x}, bondmaid {1x}.

Syn.: *Paidarion* (3808) refers to a child up to his first school years. *Paidion* (3813) refers exclusively to little children. *Paidiske* (3814) refers to a female in late childhood and early youth. *Pais* (3816) refers to a child of any age. *Teknon* (5043) gives prominence to physical and outward aspects of parentage. *Huios* (5207) gives prominence to the inward, ethical, legal aspects of parentage. *Pais* (3816) and *teknon* (5043) denote a child as respects to descent and age, reference to the later being more prominent in the former word, to descent in *paidion* (3813); but the period *pais* (3816) covers is not sharply defined. See: BAGD—604b; THAYER—473c.

3815. **παίζω** {1x} **paizō**, *paheed'-zo;* from *3816;* to *sport* (to play as a boy):—play {1x}.

Paizo, properly, "to play as a child" (*pais*), hence denotes "to play" as in dancing and making merry, 1 Cor 10:7. See: TDNT—5:625, 758; BAGD—604c; THAYER—473c.

3816. **παῖς** {24x} **pais**, *paheece;* perh. from *3817;* a *boy* (as often *beaten* with impunity), or (by anal.) a *girl,* and (gen.) a *child;* spec. a *slave* or *servant* (espec. a *minister* to a king; and by eminence to God):—servant {10x}, child {7x}, son (Christ) {2x}, son {1x}, manservant {1x}, maid {1x}, maiden {1x}, young man {1x}.

Syn.: *Paidarion* (3808) refers to a child up to his first school years; *paidion* (3813) refers exclusively to little children; *paidiske* (3814) refers to late childhood and early youth; *pais* (3816) stresses the age of the child and refers to a child of any age, not clearly defined; *teknon* (5043) stresses descent and gives prominence to physical and outward aspects of parentage; *huios* (5207) gives prominence to the inward, ethical, legal aspects of parentage. See: BAGD—604c; THAYER—473d.

3817. **παίω** {5x} **paiō**, *pah'-yo;* a primary verb; to *hit* (as if by a single blow and less violently than *5180*); spec. to *sting* (as a scorpion):—smite {4x}, strike {1x}.

(1) This verb means to strike, not kill. **(2)** All who are killed are smitten, but not all who are smitten are killed. **(3)** This word signifies "to strike or smite" **(3a)** with the hand or fist, Mt 26:68; Lk 22:64; **(3b)** with a sword, Mk 14:47; Jn 18:10, "struck"; **(3c)** with a sting, Rev 9:5, "striketh." See: BAGD—605b; THAYER—474a.

3818. **Πακατιανή** {1x} **Pakatianē**, *pak-at-ee-an-ay';* fem. of an adj. of uncert. der.; *Pacatianian,* a section of Phrygia:—Pacatiana {1x}. See: BAGD—605c; THAYER—474b.

3819. **πάλαι** {6x} **palai**, *pal'-ahee;* prob. another form for *3825* (through the idea of *retrocession*); (adv.) *formerly,* or (by rel.) *sometime since;* (ellip. as adj.) *ancient:*—long ago {1x}, any while {1x}, a great while ago {1x}, old {1x}, in time past {1x}, of old {1x}.

Palai denotes "long ago, of old," **(1)** Heb 1:1, "in time past"; **(2)** in Jude 4, "of old"; **(3)** it is used as an adjective in 2 Pet 1:9, "(his) old (sins)," lit., "his sins of old"; **(4)** "long ago" in Mt 11:12; **(5)** "any while" Mk 15:44; **(6)** "a great while ago" Lk 10:13. See: TDNT—5:717, 769; BAGD—605c; THAYER—474b.

3820. **παλαιός** {19x} **palaiŏs**, *pal-ah-yos'*; from *3819; antique,* i.e. *not recent, worn out:*—old {18x}, old wine {1x}.

Palaios, (Eng., "paleontology," etc.), **(1)** "of what is of long duration, old in years," etc., **(1)** a garment, wine (in contrast to *neos,* new), Mt 9:16:17; Mk 2:21–22 (twice); Lk 5:36–37, 39 (twice); **(2)** of the treasures of divine truth, Mt 13:52 (compared with *kainos*); **(3)** of what belongs to the past, e.g., the believer's former self before his conversion, his "old man," "old" because it has been superseded by that which is new, Rom 6:6; Eph 4:22 (in contrast to *kainos*); Col 3:9 (in contrast to *neos*); **(4)** of the covenant in connection with the Law, 2 Cor 3:14; **(5)** of leaven, metaphorical of moral evil, 1 Cor 5:7, 8 (in contrast to *neos*); **(6)** of that which was given long ago and remains in force, an "old" commandment, 1 Jn 2:7 (twice), that which was familiar and well known in contrast to that which is fresh. Syn.: In *palaios* (3820) the simple idea of time dominates, while *archaios* (744) often carries with it a suggestion of nature or original character. *Palaios* is out of date, antiquated; and arachaios is old in the sense of more or less worn out (Mt. 9:16–17). See: TDNT—5:717, 769; BAGD—605d; THAYER—474b.

3821. **παλαιότης** {1x} **palaiŏtēs**, *pal-ah-yot'-ace;* from *3820; antiquatedness:*—oldness {1x}.

This word occurs in Rom 7:6 of the letter of the law with its rules of conduct, mere outward conformity to which has yielded place in the believer's service to a response to the inward operation of the Holy Spirit. The word is contrasted with *kainotes* (2538 – newness). See: TDNT—5:720, 769; BAGD—606a; THAYER—474c.

3822. **παλαιόω** {4x} **palaiŏō**, *pal-ah-yŏ'-o;* from *3820;* to *make* (pass. *become*) *worn out,* or *declare obs.:*—decay {1x}, make old {1x}, wax old {2x}.

(1) As wax candles are dipped layer upon layer, this word expresses graduality. **(2)** *Palaioo* "to make old" (*palaios*), is translated in **(2a)** Heb 8:13, first use **(2a1)** "hath made . . . old," **(2a2)** second use (passive voice), "decayeth"; and **(3)** "wax old" in Lk 12:33 and Heb 1:11. See: TDNT—5:720, 769; BAGD—606a.

3823. **πάλη** {1x} **palē**, *pal'-ay;* from πάλλω **pallō**, (to *vibrate;* another form for *906*); *wrestling:*—+ wrestle {1x}.

Pallo, "a wrestling" (akin to *pallo,* "to sway, vibrate"), is used figuratively in Eph 6:12, of the spiritual conflict engaged in by believers, "(we) wrestle." See: TDNT—5:721, 770; BAGD—606a; THAYER—474c.

3824. **παλιγγενεσία** {2x} **paliggĕnĕsia**, *pal-ing-ghen-es-ee'-ah;* from *3825* and *1078;* (spiritual) *rebirth* (the state or the act), i.e. (fig.) spiritual *renovation;* spec. Messianic *restoration:*—regeneration {2x}.

(1) The new birth and regeneration do not represent successive stages in spiritual experience, they refer to the same event but view it in different aspects. **(2)** The new birth stresses the communication of spiritual life in contrast to antecedent spiritual death; regeneration stresses the inception of a new state of things in contrast with the old.

(3) This word means "new birth" (*palin,* "again," *genesis,* "birth"), and is used of "spiritual regeneration," **(3a)** Titus 3:5, involving the communication of a new life, the two operating powers to produce which are **(3a1)** "the word of truth," Jas 1:18; 1 Pet 1:23, and **(3a2)** the Holy Spirit, Jn 3:5, 6; **(3b)** the *loutron,* "the laver, the washing," is explained in Eph. 5:26, "having cleansed it by the washing (*loutron*) of water with the word." Syn.: *Anakainosis* (342) is the result of *paliggenesia.* The *paliggenesia* is that free act of God's mercy and power by which He removes the sinner from the kingdom of darkness and places him in the kingdom of light; it is that act by which God brings him from death to life. In the act itself (rather than the preparations for it), the recipient is passive, just as a child has nothing to do with his own birth. *Anakainos,* by contrast, is the gradual conforming of the person to the new spiritual world in which he now lives, the restoration of the divine image. In this process the person is not passive but is a fellow worker with God. See: TDNT—1:686, 117; BAGD—606a; THAYER—474d.

3825. **πάλιν** {142x} **palin**, *pal'-in;* prob. from the same as *3823* (through the idea of *oscillatory* repetition); (adv.) *anew,* i.e. (of place) *back,* (of time) *once more,* or (conjunc.) *furthermore* or *on the other hand:*—again {142x}.

Palin, the regular word for "again," is used chiefly in two senses, **(1)** with reference to repeated action; **(2)** rhetorically, in the sense **(2a)** of "moreover" or "further," indicating a statement to be added in the course of an argument, e.g., Mt 5:33; or **(2b)** with the meaning "on the other hand, in turn," Lk 6:43; 1 Cor 12:21; 2 Cor 10:7; 1 Jn 2:8. **(3)** In the first chapter of Hebrews, **(3a)** v. 5, *palin* simply introduces an additional quotation; in **(3b)** v. 6 this is not so. That is to say, *palin* is here set in contrast to the time when God *first* brought His Son into the world. This statement, then, refers to the future second advent of Christ. **(4)** The word is used far more frequently in the Gospel of John than in any other book in the New Testament. See: BAGD—606c; THAYER—475a.

3826. **παμπληθεί** {1x} **pamplēthĕi**, *pam-play-thi';* dat. (adv.) of a compound of *3956* and *4128; in full multitude,* i.e. *concertedly* or *simultaneously:*—all at once {1x}. See: BAGD—607b; THAYER—475c.

3827. **πάμπολυς** {1x} **pampŏlus**, *pam-pol-ooce;* from *3956* and *4183; full many,* i.e. *immense:*—very great {1x}. See: BAGD—607b; THAYER—475c.

3828. **Παμφυλία** {5x} **Pamphulia**, *pam-fool-ee'-ah;* from a compound of *3956* and *5443; every-tribal,* i.e. *heterogeneous* (*5561* being impl.); *Pamphylia,* a region of Asia Minor:—Pamphylia {5x}. See: BAGD—607b; THAYER—475c.

3829. **πανδοχεῖον** {1x} **pandŏchĕiŏn**, *pan-dokh-i'-on;* neut. of a presumed compound of *3956* and a der. of *1209; all-receptive,* i.e. a public *lodging*-place (*caravanserai* or *khan*):—inn {1x}.

Pandocheion, lit., "a place where all are received" (*pas,* "all," *dechomai,* "to receive"), denotes "a house for the reception of strangers," a *caravanserai,* translated "inn," in Lk 10:34, in the parable of the good samaritan. Cattle and beasts of burden could be sheltered there. See: BAGD—607c; THAYER—475d.

3830. **πανδοχεύς** {1x} **pandŏchĕus**, *pan-dokh-yoos';* from the same as *3829;* an *innkeeper* (*warden of a caravanserai*):—host {1x}.

Pandocheus, lit., "one who receives all" (*pas,* "all," *dechomai,* "to receive"), denotes "an innkeeper, host," Lk 10:35. See: BAGD—475d; THAYER—607d.

3831. **πανήγυρις** {1x} **panēguris**, *pan-ay'-goo-ris;* from *3956* and a der. of *58;* a *mass-meeting,* i.e. (fig.) *universal companionship:*—gen. assembly {1x}.

The *paneguris* refers to that solemn assembly gathered for festal rejoicing used in Heb 12:23 to represent the church in heaven whose earthly toil and suffering has forever passed away (cf. Rev 21:4). See: TDNT—5:722, 770; BAGD—607d.

3832. **πανοικί** {1x} **panŏiki**, *pan-oy-kee'* or **πανοικεί** **panŏikei**, *pan-oy-ki'* adv. from *3956* and *3624; with* the *whole family:*—with all his house {1x}. See: BAGD—607d; THAYER—475d.

3833. **πανοπλία** {3x} **panŏplia**, *pan-op-lee'-ah;* from a compound of *3956* and *3696; full armor* ("*panoply*"):—all . . . armour {1x}, whole armour {2x}.

Panoplia, lit., "all armor, full armor," (*pas,* "all," *hoplon,* "a weapon"), is used **(1)** of literal "armor," Lk 11:22; **(2)** of the spiritual helps supplied by God for overcoming the temptations of the Devil, Eph 6:11, 13. See: TDNT—5:295, 702; BAGD—607d.

3834. **πανουργία** {5x} **panŏurgia**, *pan-oorg-ee'-ah;* from *3835; adroitness,* i.e. (in a bad sense) *trickery* or *sophistry:*—cunning craftiness {1x}, craftiness {3x}, subtilty (subtlety) {1x}.

Panourgia literally means all-working, able to do everything; hence, high discerning which works itself out in unscrupulous conduct, craftiness. It is always used in a bad sense, Lk 20:23; 1 Cor 3:19; 2 Cor 4:2; 11:3; Eph 4:14, "cunning craftiness." See: TDNT—5:722, 770; BAGD—608a; THAYER—476a.

3835. **πανοῦργος** {1x} **panŏurgŏs**, *pan-oor'-gos;* from *3956* and *2041; all-working,* i.e. *adroit* (*shrewd*):—crafty {1x}.

Panourgos, "cunning, crafty," is found in 2 Cor 12:16, where the apostle speaks ironically or is really quoting an accusation made against him by his detractors. Syn.: 3834 for discussion. See: TDNT—5:722, 770; BAGD—608a; THAYER—476a.

3836. **πανταχόθεν** {1x} **pantachŏthĕn**, *pan-takh-oth'-en;* adv. (of *source*) from *3837; from all* directions:—from every quarter {1x}. See: BAGD—608b; THAYER—476b.

3837. **πανταχοῦ** {7x} **pantachŏu**, *pan-takh-oo';* gen. (as adv. of *place*) of a presumed der. of *3956; universally:*—in all places {1x}, everywhere {6x}.

Pantachou, as an adverb is translated **(1)** "everywhere" in **(1a)** Mk 16:20, of preaching; **(1b)** Lk 9:6, of healing; **(1c)** Acts 17:30, of a divine command for repentance; **(1d)** Acts 28:22, of disparagement of Christians; **(1e)** 1 Cor 4:17, of apostolic teaching; **(2)** in Acts 24:3, it is rendered "in all places": "We accept *it* always, and in all places, most noble Felix, with all thankfulness." Syn.: 201, 402, 1096, 1502, 4042, 5117, 5247, 5564, 5602. See: BAGD—608b; THAYER—476b.

3838. **παντελής** {2x} **pantĕlēs**, *pan-tel-ace';* an adverb of manner from *3956* and *5056; full-ended,* i.e. *entire* (neut. as noun, *completion*):—in no wise + 1519 + 3588 {1x}, uttermost {1x}.

Panteles, the neuter of the adjective *panteles,* "complete, perfect," used with *eis to* ("unto the"), is translated **(1)** "to the uttermost" in Heb 7:25, where the meaning is "finally and completely in all ways"; **(2)** in Lk 13:11 (negatively), "in no wise." See: TDNT—8:66, 1161; BAGD—608c; THAYER—476b.

3839. **πάντη** {1x} **pantē**, *pan'-tay;* adv. (of *manner*) from *3956; wholly:*—always {1x}.

This word means everywhere, wholly, in all respects, in every way and is found in Acts 24:3. See: BAGD—608d; THAYER—476b.

3840. **παντόθεν** {2x} **pantŏthĕn**, *pan-toth'-en;* adv. (of *source*) from *3956; from* (i.e. *on*) *all* sides:—on every side {1x}, round about {1x}.

Pantothen, "from all sides," is translated **(1)** in Lk 19:43, "on every side"; and **(2)** in Heb 9:4, "round about." See: BAGD—608d; THAYER—476b.

3841. **παντοκράτωρ** {10x} **pantŏkratōr**, *pan-tok-rat'-ore;* from *3956* and *2904;* the *all-ruling,* i.e. *God* (as absolute and universal *sovereign*):—Almighty {9x}, Omnipotent {1x}.

Pantokrator, "almighty, or ruler of all" (*pas,* "all," *krateo,* "to hold, or to have strength"), is used of God only, and is found, **(1)** in the Epistles, only in 2 Cor 6:18, where the title is suggestive in connection with the context; **(2)** elsewhere only in the Apocalypse, 1:8; 4:8; 11:17; 15:3; 16:7, 14; 19:6, "omnipotent"; 19:15; 21:22. See: TDNT—3:914, 466; BAGD—608d; THAYER—476b.

3842. **πάντοτε** {42x} **pantŏtĕ**, *pan'-tot-eh;* from *3956* and *3753; every when,* i.e. *at all* times:—always {29x}, ever {6x}, alway {5x}, evermore {2x}.

Pantote, "at all times, always" (akin to *pas,* "all"), is translated **(1)** "always", Mt 26:11; Mk 14:7 twice; Lk 18:1; Jn 8:29; 11:42; 12:8 twice; 18:20 second part; Rom 1:9; 1 Cor 1:4; 15:58; 2 Cor 2:14; 4:10; 5:6; 9:8; Gal 4:18; Eph 5:20; Phil 1:4, 20; 2:12; Col 1:3; 4:12; 1 Th 1:2; 3:6; 2 Th 1:3, 11; Philemon 4; **(2)** "always", Phil 4:4; Col 4:6; 1 Th 2:16; 2 Th 2:13; **(3)** "ever", Lk 15:31; Jn 18:20 first part; 1 Th 4:7; 5:15; 2 Ti 3:7; Heb 7:25; and **(4)** "evermore", Jn 6:34; 7:6, 1 Th 5:16. **(5) NOTE: (5a)** "Always" stresses manner: "all ways, all means" and **(5b)** "alway" stresses time, "all the way." See: BAGD—609b; THAYER—476c.

3843. **πάντως** {9x} **pantōs**, *pan'-toce;* adv. from *3956; entirely;* spec. *at all events,* (with neg. following) *in* no *event:*—by all means {2x}, altogether {2x}, surely {1x}, must needs + 1163 {1x}, no doubt {1x}, in no wise {1x}, at all {1x}.

Pantos, when used **(1)** without a negative, signifies **(1a)** "wholly, entirely, by all means," Acts 18:21; 1 Cor 9:22; **(1b)** "altogether," 1 Cor 9:10; **(1c)** "surely," Lk 4:23; Acts 28:4. **(1d)** In Acts 21:22 it is translated "needs" (lit., "by all means"). **(2)** With a negative it signifies "in no wise," Rom 3:9; 1 Cor 5:10; 16:12 (at all). See: BAGD—609b; THAYER—476c.

3844. **παρά** { {200x} **para**, *par-ah';* a primary prep.; prop. *near;* i.e. (with gen.) *from beside* (lit. or fig.), (with dat.) *at* (or *in*) the *vicinity* of (object or subject), (with acc.) to the *proximity* with (local [espec. *beyond* or *opposed* to] or causal [*on account* of]):—of {51x}, with {42x}, from {24x}, by . . . side {15x}, at {12x}, than {11x}, misc. {45x} = above, against, among, before, by, contrary to, × friend, + give [such things as they], + that [she] had, × his, in, more than, nigh unto, out of, past, save, in the sight of, then, [there-] fore.

(1) In compounds it retains the same variety of application. **(2)** It has the meaning "contrary to" in Acts 18:13; Rom 11:24; 16:17; **(3)** "other than" in Gal 1:8. See: TDNT—5:727, 771; BAGD—609c; THAYER—476d.

3845. **παραβαίνω** {4x} **parabainō**, *par-ab-ah'-ee-no;* from *3844* and the base of *939;* to *go contrary* to, i.e. *violate* a command:—transgression {3x}, fall by transgression {1x}.

Parabaino, lit., "to go aside" (*para*), hence "to go beyond," **(1)** is chiefly used metaphorically **(1a)** of "transgressing" the tradition of the elders, Mt 15:2; **(1b)** the commandment of God, Mt 15:3; and **(2)** in Acts 1:25, of Judas, "by transgression fell." **(3)** *Parabaino* means to overstep, disregard an accepted boundary either on purpose or neglect; to violate. Syn.: 3847. See: TDNT—5:736, 772; BAGD—611c; THAYER—478c.

3846. **παραβάλλω** {2x} **paraballō**, *par-ab-al'-lo;* from *3844* and *906;* to *throw alongside,* i.e. (refl.) to *reach* a place, or (fig.) to *liken:*—arrive {1x}, compare {1x}.

Paraballo, "to place side by side, to set forth," and the noun *parabole* (Eng., "parable"), **(1)** occur in Mk 4:30, "with what comparison shall we compare it?" **(2)** This word means to put one thing by the side of another for the sake of comparison. See: BAGD—611d; THAYER—478d.

3847. **παράβασις** {7x} **parabasis**, *par-ab'-as-is;* from *3845; violation:*—breaking {1x}, transgression {6x}.

(1) *Parabasis* is the act of excessive and enormous transgression of a stated law or a given commandment. **(2)** This word means primarily "a going aside," then, "an overstepping," is used metaphorically to denote "transgression" (always of a breach of law): **(2a)** of Adam, Rom 5:14; **(2b)** of Eve, 1 Ti 2:14; **(2c)** negatively, where there is no law, since "transgression" implies the violation of law, none having been enacted between Adam's "transgression" and those under the Law, Rom 4:15; **(2d)** of "transgressions" of the Law, Gal 3:19, where the statement "it was added because of transgressions" is best understood according to Rom 4:15; 5:13 and 5:20; the Law does not make men sinners, but makes them "transgressors"; hence sin becomes "exceeding sinful," Rom 7:7, 13. Conscience thus had a standard external to itself; by the Law men are taught their inability to yield complete obedience to God, that thereby they may become convinced of their need of a Savior; **(3)** in Rom 2:23, "breaking (the Law)"; Heb 2:2; 9:15. Syn.: 51, 265, 266, 458, 2275, 3876, 3892, 3900. See: TDNT—5:739, 772; BAGD—611d; THAYER—478d.

3848. **παραβάτης** {5x} **parabatēs**, *par-ab-at'-ace;* from *3845;* a *violator:*—breaker {1x}, transgress {1x}, transgressor {3x}.

A *parabates* is "a transgressor", and is translated **(1)** "breaker," Rom 2:25. **(2)** in Rom 2:27 "dost transgress"; and **(3)** "transgressor" in Gal 2:18; Jas 2:9, plural, 11. Syn.: 3847. See: TDNT—5:740, 772; BAGD—612a; THAYER—479a.

3849. **παραβιάζομαι** {2x} **parabiazŏmai**, *par-ab-ee-ad'-zom-ahee;* from *3844* and the mid. voice of *971;* to *force contrary* to (nature), i.e. *compel* (by entreaty):—constrain {2x}.

Parabiazomai, as a verb, primarily denotes "to employ force contrary to nature and right, to compel by using force" [*para,* "alongside," intensive, *biazo,* "to force"], and is used only of "constraining" by entreaty, **(1)** as the two going to Emmaus did to Christ: "But they constrained Him, saying, Abide with us: for it is toward evening, and the day is far spent. And He went in to tarry with them" (Lk 24:29); and **(2)** as Lydia did to Paul and his companions: "And when she was baptized, and her household, she besought *us,* saying, If ye have judged me to be faithful to the Lord, come into my house, and abide *there.* And she constrained us" (Acts 16:15). Syn.: 315, 317, 4912. See: BAGD—612a; THAYER—479a.

3850. **παραβολή** {50x} **parabŏlē**, *par-ab-ol-ay';* from *3846;* a *similitude* ("*parable*"), i.e. (symbol.) *fictitious narrative* (of common life conveying a mor.), *apothegm* or *adage:*—comparison {1x}, figure {2x}, parable {46x}, proverb {1x}.

Parabole, as a noun, lit. denotes "a placing beside" (akin to *paraballo,* "to throw" or "lay beside, to compare"). **(1)** It signifies "a placing of one thing beside another" with a view to comparison (some consider that the thought of comparison is not necessarily contained in the word). **(2)** In the NT it is found outside the gospels, only in Heb 9:9 and 11:19. **(3)** It is generally used of a somewhat lengthy utterance or narrative drawn from nature or human circumstances, the object of which is to set forth a spiritual lesson, e.g., those in Mt 13 and Synoptic parallels; **(3a)** sometimes it is used of a short saying or proverb, e.g., Mt 15:15; Mk 3:23; 7:17; Lk 4:23; 5:36; 6:39. **(3b)** It is the lesson that is of value; the hearer must catch the analogy if he is to be instructed (this is true also of a proverb). **(3c)** Such a narrative or saying, dealing with earthly things with a spiritual meaning, is distinct from a fable, which attributes to things what does not belong to them in nature.

(4) Christ's "parables" most frequently convey truths connected with the subject of the kingdom of God. **(4a)** His withholding the meaning from His hearers as He did from the multitudes, Mt 13:34, was a divine judgment upon the unworthy. A parable hides the truth from unbelievers and reveals the truth to the soft hearted, the fourth soil in the parable of "the sower", Mt 13:1f. **(5)** Two dangers are to be avoided in seeking to interpret the "parables" in Scripture, **(5a)** that of ignoring the important features, and **(5b)** that of trying to make all the details mean something. Syn.: 3942. See: TDNT—5:744, 773; BAGD—612b; THAYER—479b.

3851. **παραβουλεύομαι** {1x} **parabŏulĕuŏmai**, *par-ab-ool-yoo'-om-ahee* or

παραβολεύομαι **parabŏlĕuŏmai**, *par-ab-ol-yoo'-om-ahee* from *3844,* and the mid. voice of *1011;* to *misconsult,* i.e. *disregard:*—not (to) regard (-ing) {1x}.

Literally, this verb means to throw aside; hence, to expose oneself to danger, to hazard one's life as said of Ephaphroditis, (Phil 2:30). See: BAGD—613a; THAYER—479c.

3852. **παραγγελία** {5x} **paraggĕlia**, *par-ang-gel-ee'-ah;* from *3853;* a *mandate:*—charge {2x}, commandment {2x}, straitly {1x}.

This word means "a proclamation, a command or commandment," and is strictly used of commands received from a superior and transmitted to others. It is rendered **(1)** "charge" in Acts 16:24; 1 Ti 1:18; **(2)** "commandment" in 1 Ti 1:5; 1 Th 4:2, plural; and **(3)** "straitly" in Acts 5:28, literally meaning "Did we not command you with a command?" See: TDNT—5:761, 776; BAGD—613a; THAYER—479d.

3853. **παραγγέλλω** {31x} **paraggĕllō**, *par-ang-gel'-lo;* from *3844* and the base of *32;* to *transmit a message,* i.e. (by impl.) to *enjoin:*—command {20x}, charge {6x}, give commandment {1x}, give charge {1x}, declare {1x}, give in charge {1x}, vr. command {1x}.

This word means "to announce beside" (*para,* "beside," *angello,* "to announce"), "to pass on an announcement," hence denotes "to give the word, order, give a charge, command", e.g., Mk 6:8; Lk 8:29; 9:21; Acts 5:28; 2 Th 3:4, 6, 10, 12. Syn.: *Entellomai* (1781) means to enjoin, is used esp. of those whose office or position invests them with claims, and points rather to the contents of the command, cf our instruction. *Keleuo* (2753) means to command and designates verbal orders, coming usually from a superior. *Paraggello* (3853) means to charge, and is used esp. of the order of a military commander to his troops. *Tasso* (5021) means to assign a post to, with a suggestion of duties connected with it, often used of military appointments. *Paraggello* (3853) differs from *entellomai* (1781) in denoting fixed and abiding obligations rather than specific or occasional instructions, duties arising from the office rather than coming from the personal will of a superior. See: TDNT—5:761, 776; BAGD—613b; THAYER—479d.

3854. **παραγίνομαι** {37x} **paraginŏmai**, *par-ag-in'-om-ahee;* from *3844* and *1096;* to *become near,* i.e. *approach* (*have arrived*); by impl. to *appear* on the scene publicly:—come {35x}, go {1x}, be present {1x}.

This word means to come forth, make one's public appearance such as John the baptizer, Mt 3:1. See: BAGD—613c; THAYER—479d.

3855. **παράγω** {10x} **paragō**, *par-ag'-o;* from *3844* and *71;* to *lead near,* i.e. (refl. or intr.) to *go along* or *away:*—pass by {5x}, pass away {2x}, pass forth {1x}, depart {1x}, pass {1x}.

Parago, used intransitively, means **(1)** "to pass by" (*para,* "by, beside"), and is so translated everywhere in the Gospels, except in Mt 9:27, "departed." **(2)** Outside the Gospels it is used in its other meaning, "to pass away," 1 Cor 7:31; 1 Jn 2:8 "past", 17. **(3)** It also means "to pass by, pass away," in Mt 9:9, "passed forth", and **(4)** is used in the middle voice in 1 Jn 2:8, "is past", **(4a)** of the "passing" of spiritual darkness through the light of the gospel, and **(4b)** in 1 Jn 2:17 of the world. See: TDNT—1:129, 20; BAGD—613d; THAYER—480a.

3856. **παραδειγματίζω** {2x} **paradĕigmatizō**, *par-ad-igue-mat-id'-zo;* from *3844* and *1165;* to *show alongside* (the public), i.e. *expose to infamy:*—make a public example {1x}, put to an open shame {1x}.

Paradeigmatizo, as a verb, signifies "to set forth as an example" (*para,* "beside," *deiknumi,* "to show"), and is used **(1)** in Mt 1:19: "Then Joseph, her husband, being a just *man,* and not willing to make her a public example (*paradeigmatizo*), was minded to put her away privily." It is also used in Heb 6:6, "put (Christ) to open shame" by the apostate Christians. Syn.: 150, 152, 808, 818, 819, 1788, 1791, 2617. See: TDNT—2:32, 141; BAGD—614a; THAYER—480b.

3857. **παράδεισος** {3x} **paradĕisŏs**, *par-ad'-i-sos;* of Oriental or. [comp. 6508]; a *park,* i.e. (spec.) an *Eden* (place of future happiness, "*paradise*"):—paradise {3x}.

Paradeisos, "paradise" is found: **(1)** In Lk 23:43, the promise of the Lord to the repentant robber was fulfilled the same day; **(1a)** Christ, at His death, having committed His spirit to the Father, went in spirit immediately into Heaven itself, the dwelling place of God. **(1b)** The Lord's mention of the place as "paradise" must have been a great comfort to the malefactor because it expressed the sum total of blessedness. **(2)** Thither the apostle Paul was caught up, 2 Cor 12:4, spoken of as "the third heaven" (v. 3 does not introduce a different vision), **(2a)** beyond the heavens of the natural creation. **(2b)** The same region is mentioned in Rev 2:7, where the "tree of life," the figurative antitype of that in Eden, held out to the overcomer, is spoken of as being in "the Paradise of God" as in Gen 2:8. **(3)** In the OT see **(3a)** Neh 2:8; Eccl 2:5; Song 4:13. **(3b)** It is also used of **(3b1)** the garden of Eden, Gen 2:8, and **(3b2)** in other respects, e.g., Num 24:6; Is 1:30; Jer 29:5; Eze 31:8–9. See: TDNT—5:765, 777; BAGD—614a; THAYER—480b.

3858. **παραδέχομαι** {5x} **paradĕchŏmai**, *par-ad-ekh'-om-ahee;* from *3844* and *1209;* to *accept near,* i.e. receive with approval, *admit* or (by impl.) *delight* in:—receive {5x}.

Paradechomai, as a verb, means "to receive or admit with approval" and is used **(1)** of persons: "For whom the Lord loveth He chasteneth, and scourgeth every son whom He receiveth" (Heb. 12:6); **(2)** of things: "And these are they which are sown on good ground; such as hear the word, and receive *it,* and bring forth fruit, some thirtyfold, some sixty, and some an hundred" (Mk 4:20; cf. Acts 16:21; 22:18; 1 Ti 5:9). Syn.: 324, 353, 354, 568, 588, 618, 1209, 1523, 1926, 2210, 2865, 2975, 2983, 3028, 3335, 3336, 3880, 3970, 4327, 4355, 4356, 4380, 4381, 4382, 5562, 5264, 5274. See: BAGD—614b; THAYER—480d.

3859. **παραδιατριβή** {1x} **paradiatribē**, *par-ad-ee-at-ree-bay';* from a compound of *3844* and *1304; misemployment,* i.e. *meddlesomeness:*—perverse disputing {1x}.

This word denotes a constant or incessant wrangling, to wear out, suggesting the attrition or wearing effect of contention, "perverse disputings", 1 Ti 6:5. See: BAGD—614b; THAYER—480d.

3860. **παραδίδωμι** {121x} **paradidōmi**, *par-ad-id'-o-mee;* from *3844* and *1325;* to *surrender,* i.e. to deliver over to another to keep, *yield up, intrust, transmit:*—deliver {53x}, betray {40x}, deliver up {10x}, give {4x}, give up {4x}, give over {2x}, commit {2x}, misc. {6x} = bring forth, cast, hazard, put in prison, recommend.

Paradidomi, as a verb, means "to deliver over": **(1)** "But God be thanked, that ye were the servants of sin, but ye have obeyed from the heart that form of doctrine which was delivered you" (Rom 6:17). **(2)** In Rom 8:32 it is used of God in "delivering" His Son to expiatory death: "He that spared not His own Son, but delivered Him up for us all, how shall He not with Him also freely give us all things?" (cf. Rom 4:25; Mk 9:31); **(3)** of Christ in "delivering" Himself up: "I am crucified with Christ: nevertheless I live; yet not I, but Christ liveth in me: and the life which I now live in the flesh I live by the faith of the Son of God, who loved me, and gave Himself for me" (Gal 2:20; cf. Eph 5:2, 25).

(4) *Pardidomi* also means "to give over, commit, deliver" and also signifies "is brought forth": "But when the fruit is brought forth, immediately he putteth in the sickle, because the harvest is come" (Mk 4:29 – the grain is ready to be given over the table as food). **(5)** It is also translated "to betray" (*para,* "up," *didomi,* "to give"), lit., "to give over," and is used either **(5a)** in the sense of delivering a person or thing to be kept by another, to commend, e.g., Acts 28:16; **(5b)** to deliver to prison or judgment, e.g., Mt 4:12; 1 Ti 1:20; **(5c)** to deliver over treacherously by way of "betrayal," Mt 17:22; 26:16; Jn 6;64 etc.; **(5d)** to hand on, deliver, e.g., 1 Cor 11:23; **(5e)** to allow of something being done, said of the ripening of fruit, Mk 4:29. Syn.: 187, 325, 525, 629, 591, 859, 1325, 1560, 1659, 1807, 1929, 3583, 4506, 5483. See: TDNT—2:169, 166; BAGD—614b; THAYER—480d.

3861. **παράδοξος** {1x} **paradŏxŏs**, *par-ad'-ox-os;* from *3844* and *1391* (in the sense of *seeming*); *contrary to expectation,* i.e. *extraordinary* ("*paradox*"):—strange {1x}.

Paradoxos (Lk 5:26) describes miracles not previously seen (cf. Mk 2:12); hence "strange" and thus they are beside and beyond people's opinions and expectations. Syn.: 1411, 1741, 2297, 3167, 6592, 5059. See: TDNT—2:255, 178; BAGD—615d; THAYER—481d.

3862. **παράδοσις** {13x} **paradŏsis**, *par-ad'-os-is;* from *3860; transmission,* i.e. (concr.) a *precept;* spec. the Jewish *traditionary law:*—ordinance {1x}, tradition {12x}.

Paradosis, "a handing down or on" (akin to *paradidomi,* "to hand over, deliver"), denotes "a tradition," and hence, by metonymy, **(1)** "the teachings of the rabbis," interpretations of the Law, which was thereby made void in practice, Mt 15:2, 3, 6; Mk 7:3, 5, 8, 9, 13; Gal 1:14; Col 2:8; **(2)** of "apostolic teaching," 1 Cor 11:2, "ordinances", of instructions concerning the gatherings of believers (instructions of wider scope than ordinances in the limited sense); **(3)** in 2 Thess. 2:15, of Christian doctrine in general, where the apostle's use of the word constitutes a denial that what he preached originated with himself, and a claim for its divine authority; **(4)** in 2 Th 3:6, it is used of instructions concerning everyday conduct. See: TDNT—2:172, 166; BAGD—615d; THAYER—481d.

3863. **παραζηλόω** {4x} **parazēlŏō**, *par-ad-zay-lŏ'-o;* from *3844* and *2206;* to *stimulate alongside,* i.e. *excite to rivalry:*—provoke to emulation {1x}, provoke to jealousy {3x}.

Parazeloo, "to provoke to jealousy" (*para,* "beside," used intensively, is found **(1)** in Rom 10:19 and 11:11, of God's dealings with Israel through his merciful dealings with Gentiles; **(2)** in Rom 11:14, "I may provoke to emulation", of the apostle's evangelical ministry to Gentiles with a view to stirring his fellow nationals to a sense of their need and responsibilities regarding the gospel; **(3)** in 1 Cor 10:22, of the provocation of God on the part of believers who compromise their divine relationship by partaking of the table of demons; **(4)** in Gal 5:20, of the works of the flesh. See: TDNT—2:881, 297; BAGD—616a; THAYER—482a.

3864. **παραθαλάσσιος** {1x} **parathalassiŏs**, *par-ath-al-as'-see-os;* from *3844* and *2281; along the sea,* i.e. *maritime* (*lacustrine*):—upon the sea coast {1x}. See: BAGD—616a; THAYER—482a.

3865. **παραθεωρέω** {1x} **parathĕōrĕō**, *par-ath-eh-o-reh'-o;* from *3844* and *2334;* to *overlook* or *disregard:*—neglect {1x}.

Paratheoreo, primarily, "to examine side by side, compare" (*para,* "beside," *theoreo,* "to look at"), hence, "to overlook, to neglect," is used in Acts 6:1, of the "neglect" of widows in the daily ministration in Jerusalem. See: BAGD—616b; THAYER—482a.

3866. **παραθήκη** {1x} **parathēkē**, *par-ath-ay'-kay;* from *3908;* a *deposit,* i.e. (fig.) *trust:*—that . . . committed {1x}.

Paratheke, "a putting with, a deposit" (*para,* "with," *tithemi,* "to put"), is found in 2 Ti 1:12, "that which I have committed unto Him." See: TDNT—8:162, 1176; BAGD—616b; THAYER—482b.

3867. **παραινέω** {2x} **parainĕō**, *par-ahee-neh'-o;* from *3844* and *134;* to *mispraise,* i.e. *recommend* or *advise* (a different course):—admonish {1x}, exhort {1x}.

Paraineo, "to admonish by way of exhorting or advising," is found in Acts 27:9, "Paul admonished them", and v. 22, "and now I exhort you", based on the admonition to put what I said into action. See: BAGD—616b; THAYER—482b.

3868. **παραιτέομαι** {11x} **paraitĕŏmai**, *par-ahee-teh'-om-ahee;* from *3844* and the mid. voice of *154;* to *beg off,* i.e. *deprecate, decline, shun:*—avoid {1x}, make excuse {1x}, excuse {2x}, intreat {1x}, refuse {1x}, reject {1x}.

Pariteomai, lit., "to ask aside" (*para,* "aside," *aiteo,* "to ask"), signifies **(1)** "to entreat (that) not," Heb 12:19; **(2)** "to refuse, decline, avoid," 1 Ti 4:7; 5:11; 2 Ti 2:23; Titus 3:10; Heb 12:25; **(3)** "to beg off, ask to be excused," Lk 14:18–19. See: TDNT—1:195, 30; BAGD—616c; THAYER—482b.

3869. **παρακαθίζω** {1x} **parakathizō**, *par-ak-ath-id'-zo;* from *3844* and *2523;* to *sit down near:*—sit {1x}.

Parakathezomai, as a verb, means "to sit down beside"and in a passive voice form occurs in Lk 10:39: "And she had a sister called Mary, which also sat (*parakathezomai*) at Jesus' feet, and heard His word." Syn.: 339, 345, 347, 377, 1910, 2516, 2521, 2621, 2523, 2625, 4775, 4776, 4873. See: BAGD—616d; THAYER—482c.

3870. **παρακαλέω** {109x} **parakalĕō**, *par-ak-al-eh'-o;* from *3844* and *2564;* to *call near,* i.e. *invite, invoke* (by *imploration, hortation* or *consolation*):—beseech {43x}, comfort {23x}, exhort {21x}, desire {8x}, pray {6x}, intreat {3x}, vr besought {1x}, misc. {4x} = call for, (give) exhort (-ation).

Parakaleo, the most frequent word with this meaning, lit. denotes "to call to one's side," hence, "to call to one's aid." It is used for every kind of calling to a person which is meant to produce a particular effect, hence, with various meanings, such as "comfort, exhort, desire, call for," in addition to its significance "to beseech," which has a stronger force than *aiteo.* See: TDNT—5:773, 778; BAGD—617a; THAYER—482c.

3871. **παρακαλύπτω** {1x} **parakaluptō**, *par-ak-al-oop'-to;* from *3844* and *2572;* to *cover alongside,* i.e. *veil* (fig.):—hide {1x}.

Parakalupto, "to conceal thoroughly" (*para,* "beside," intensive, *kalupto,* "to hide"), is found in Lk 9:45, of "concealing" from the disciples the fact of the delivering up of Christ. See: BAGD—617d; THAYER—483b.

3872. **παρακαταθήκη** {2x} **parakatathēkē**, *par-ak-at-ath-ay'-kay;* from a compound of *3844* and *2698;* something *put down alongside,* i.e. a *deposit* (sacred *trust*):—that (thing) which is committed (un-) to (trust) + 3588 {2x}.

A deposit, a trust or thing consigned to one's faithful keeping; used of the correct knowledge and pure doctrine of the gospel, to be held firmly and faithfully, and to be conscientiously delivered unto others; 1 Ti 6:20; 2 Ti 1:14. See: TDNT—8:162, 1176; BAGD—617d; THAYER—483b.

3873. **παράκειμαι** {2x} **parakĕimai**, *par-ak'-i-mahee;* from *3844* and *2749;* to *lie near,* i.e. *be at hand* (fig. *be prompt* or *easy*):—be present {2x}.

Parakeimai, "to lie beside" (*para,* and *keimai,* "to lie"), "to be near," is translated "is present" in Rom 7:18, 21. See: TDNT—3:656, 425; BAGD—617d; THAYER—483b.

3874. **παράκλησις** {29x} **paraklēsis**, *par-ak'-lay-sis;* from *3870; imploration, hortation, solace:*—comfort {6x}, consolation {14x}, exhortation {8x}, intreaty {1x}.

Paraklesis, means "a calling to one's side" (*para,* "beside," *kaleo,* "to call"); hence, **(1)** either "an exhortation, or consolation, comfort," e.g., Lk 2:25 (here "looking for the consolation of Israel" is equivalent to waiting for the coming of the Messiah); 6:24; Acts 9:31; Rom 15:4–5; 1 Cor 14:3, "exhortation"; 2 Cor 1:3, 4–7; 7:4, 7, 13; 2 Th 2:16; Philem 7. **(2)** In 2 Th 2:16 it combines encouragement with alleviation of grief; **(3)** "consolation", Lk 2:25; 6:24; Acts 4:36; 15:31; Heb 6:18; in Acts 4:36. See: TDNT—5:773, 778; BAGD—618a; THAYER—483b.

3875. **παράκλητος** {5x} **paraklētŏs**, *par-ak'-lay-tos;* an *intercessor, consoler:*—advocate {1x}, comforter {4x}.

Parakletos is the one summoned, called to one's side, esp. called to one's aid and is used of **(1)** Christ in his exaltation at God's right hand, pleading with God the Father for the pardon of our sins (1 Jn 2:1); and **(2)** the Holy Spirit destined to take the place of Christ with the apostles (after Christ's ascension to the Father), to lead them to a deeper knowledge of the gospel truth, and give them divine strength needed to enable them to undergo trials and persecutions on behalf of the divine kingdom (Jn 14:16;14:26; 15:26; 16:7). See: TDNT—5:800, 782; BAGD—618b; THAYER—483c.

3876. **παρακοή** {3x} **parakŏē**, *par-ak-ŏ-ay';* from *3878; inattention,* i.e. (by impl.) *disobedience:*—disobedience {3x}.

(1) Carelessness in attitude is the precursor of actual disobedience, the mind and will both wavering. Primarily, *parakoe,* means "hearing amiss" (*para,* "aside," *akouo,* "to hear"), hence signifies "a refusal to hear"; hence, **(2)** "an act of disobedience," Rom 5:19; 2 Cor 10:6; Heb 2:2. Syn.: It is broadly to be distinguished from *apeitheia* as an act from a condition, though *parakoe* itself is the effect, in transgression, of the condition of failing or refusing to hear. **(3)** In the OT "disobedience" is frequently described as "a refusing to hear," e.g., Jer 11:10; 35:17; cf. Acts 7:57. Syn.: 51, 265, 266, 458, 2275, 3847, 3892, 3900. See: TDNT—1:223, 34; BAGD—618d; THAYER—483d.

3877. **παρακολουθέω** {4x} **parakŏlouthĕō**, *par-ak-ol-oo-theh'-o;* from *3844* and *190;* to *follow near,* i.e. (fig.) *attend* (as a result), *trace out, conform* to:—attain {1x}, follow {1x}, fully know {1x}, have understanding {1x}.

Parakoloutheo, as a verb, literally signifies "to follow close up, or side by side," hence, "to accompany, to conform to" and is used of **(1)** signs accompanying "them that believe" (Mk 16:17); **(2)** of tracing the course of facts (Lk 1:3); **(3)** of "following" good doctrine (1 Ti 4:6); **(3)** similarly of "following" teaching so as to practice it: "But thou hast fully known (*parakoloutheo*) my doctrine, manner of life, purpose, faith, longsuffering, charity, patience," (2 Ti 3:10). Syn.: 190, 1096, 1377, 1811, 1872, 2614, 2628, 4870. See: TDNT—1:215, 33; BAGD—618d; THAYER—484a.

3878. **παρακούω** {2x} **parakŏuō**, *par-ak-oo'-o;* from *3844* and *191;* to *mishear,* i.e. (by impl.) to *disobey:*—neglect to hear {2x}.

Parakouo primarily signifies "to overhear, hear amiss or imperfectly" (*para,* "beside, amiss"); **(1)** then (in the NT) "to hear without taking heed, to neglect to hear," Mt 18:17 (twice). It seems obvious that the Lord paid no attention to those from the ruler's house and their message that his daughter was dead. Syn.: 189, 191, 1251, 1522, 1873, 1874, 3876, 4257. See: TDNT—1:223, 34; BAGD—619a; THAYER—484a.

3879. **παρακύπτω** {5x} **parakuptō**, *par-ak-oop'-to;* from *3844* and *2955;* to *bend beside,* i.e. *lean over* (so as to *peer within*):—look (into) {2x}, stoop down {3x}.

Parakupto, as a verb, means literally and primarily "to stoop sideways" and denotes **(1)** "to stoop to look into": "Then arose Peter, and ran unto the sepulchre; and stooping down, he beheld the linen clothes . . ." (Lk 24:12 "stooping and looking in"); **(2)** metaphorically in Jas 1:25, of "looking" into the perfect law of liberty; and **(3)** in 1 Pet 1:12 of things which the angels desire "to look into." Syn.: 308, 352, 578, 816, 872, 991, 1689, 1896, 1914, 1980, 1983, 2300, 2334, 3706, 3708, 4017, 4648. See: TDNT—5:814, 784; BAGD—619b; THAYER—484a.

3880. **παραλαμβάνω** {50x} **paralambanō**, *par-al-am-ban'-o;* from *3844* and *2983;* to *receive near,* i.e. *associate with* oneself (in any familiar or intimate act or relation); by anal. to *assume* an office; fig. to *learn:*—take {30x}, receive {15x}, take unto {2x}, take up {2x}, take away {1x}.

Paralambano, "to receive from another" (*para,* "from beside"), signifies **(1)** "to receive," e.g., in Mk 7:4; Jn 1:11; 14:3; 1 Cor 11:23; 15:1, 3; Gal 1:9, 12; Phil 4:9; Col 2:6; 4:17; 1 Th 2:13 (1st part); 4:1; 2 Th 3:6; Heb 12:28. It also denotes **(2)** "to take to (or with) oneself," **(2a)** of "taking" a wife, e.g., Mt 1:20, 24; **(2b)** of "taking" a person or persons with one, e.g., Mt 2:13, 14, 20, 21; 4:5, 8; **(2c)** of devils, Mt 12:45; **(2d)** of Christ and His disciples, Mt17:1; 20:17; Mk 9:2; 10:32; 14:33; **(2e)** of witnesses, Mt 18:16; **(2f)** of the removal of persons from the earth in judgment, when "the Son of Man is revealed," Mt 24:40, 41; Lk 17:34, 35 (cf. the means of the removal of corruption, in v. 37); **(2g)** of the "taking" of Christ by the soldiers for scourging, Mt 27:27, and to crucifixion, Jn 19:16; **(2h)** see also Acts 15:39; 16:33; 21:24, 26, 32; 23:18. See: TDNT—4:11, 495; BAGD—619b; THAYER—484b.

3881. **παραλέγομαι** {2x} **paralĕgŏmai**, *par-al-eg'-om-ahee;* from *3844* and the mid. voice of *3004* (in its orig. sense); (spec.) to *lay* one's course *near,* i.e. *sail past:*—pass {1x}, sail by {1x}.

This word is used, in the middle voice, as a nautical term, **(1)** "to sail past," Acts 27:8, **(2)** "coasting along"; Acts 27:13, "sailed by." See: BAGD—619d; THAYER—484d.

3882. **παράλιος** {1x} **paraliŏs**, *par-al'-ee-os;* from *3844* and *251; beside* the *salt* (*sea*), i.e. *maritime:*—sea coast {1x}. See: BAGD—620a; THAYER—484d.

3883. **παραλλαγή** {1x} **parallagē**, *par-al-lag-ay';* from a compound of *3844* and *236; transmutation* (of phase or orbit), i.e. (fig.) *fickleness:*—variableness {1x}.

Parallage denotes, in general, "a change" (Eng., "parallax," the difference between the directions of a body as seen from two different points), "a transmission" from one condition to another; it occurs in Jas 1:17, "variableness", and speaks of God's immutability. See: BAGD—620a; THAYER—484d.

3884. **παραλογίζομαι** {2x} **paralŏgizŏmai**, *par-al-og-id'-zom-ahee;* from *3844* and *3049;* to deceive by false reasoning, *misreckon,* i.e. *delude:*—beguile {1x}, deceive {1x}.

Paralogizomai means lit. and primarily, "to reckon wrong," hence means "to reason falsely" (*para,* "from, amiss," *logizomai,* "to reason") or "to deceive by false reasoning"; translated **(1)** "beguile" in Col 2:4, and **(2)** Jas 1:22 "deceive." See: BAGD—620b; THAYER—484d.

3885. **παραλυτικός** {10x} **paralutikŏs**, *par-al-oo-tee-kos';* from a der. of *3886;* as if *dissolved,* i.e. "*paralytic*":—sick of palsy {9x}, (one) that has the palsy {1x}.

This one is suffering from the relaxing of the nerves of one's side; hence, disabled, weak of limb "paralytic, sick of the palsy," is found in Mt 4:24; 8:6; 9:2 (twice), 6; Mk 2:3, 4, 5, 9, 10. See: BAGD—620b; THAYER—484d.

3886. **παραλύω** {5x} **paraluō**, *par-al-oo'-o;* from *3844* and *3089;* to *loosen beside,* i.e. *relax* (perf. pass. part. *paralyzed* or *enfeebled*):—sick of the palsy {2x}, taken with palsy {2x}, feeble {1x}.

Paraluo, lit., "to loose from the side," hence, "to set free," is used in the passive voice of "being enfeebled by a paralytic stroke, palsied," **(1)** Lk 5:18, "taken with a palsy"; 5:24 (ditto); Acts 8:7 (ditto); **(2)** Lk 9:33, "was sick of the palsy"; **(3)** Heb 12:12, "feeble." Syn.: 3885. See: BAGD—620b; THAYER—484d.

3887. **παραμένω** {3x} **paramĕnō**, *par-am-en'-o;* from *3844* and *3306;* to *stay near,* i.e. *remain beside* (lit. *tarry;* or fig. *be permanent, persevere*):—abide {1x}, continue {2x}.

Parameno, "to remain beside" (*para,* "beside"), "to continue near," came to signify simply "to continue," **(1)** e.g., negatively, of the Levitical priests, Heb 7:23. **(2)** In 1 Cor 16:6 the apostle uses this word to express his desire to winter with the Corinthians. **(3)** In Jas 1:25, of steadfast continuance in the law of liberty. See: TDNT—4:577, 581; BAGD—620c; THAYER—485a.

3888. **παραμυθέομαι** {4x} **paramuthĕŏmai**, *par am oo-theh'-om-ahee;* from *3844* and the mid. voice of a der. of *3454;* to *relate near,* i.e. (by impl.) *encourage, console:*—comfort {4x}

This word means "to soothe, console, encourage," and is translated "comfort" in Jn 11:19, 31; 1 Th 2:11 and 5:14, as the sense there is that of stimulating to the earnest discharge of duties. See: TDNT—5:816, 784; BAGD—620d; THAYER—485a.

3889. **παραμυθία** {1x} **paramuthia**, *par-am-oo-thee'-ah;* from *3888; consolation* (prop. abstr.):—comfort {1x}.

Primarily, *paramutha* is an address spoken closely to someone; hence, denoting consolation and comfort with a great degree of tenderness (1 Cor 14:3). See: TDNT—5:816, 784; BAGD—620d; THAYER—485a.

3890. **παραμύθιον** {1x} **paramuthiŏn**, *par-am-oo'-thee-on;* neut. of *3889; consolation* (prop. concr.):—comfort {1x}.

Paramuthion stresses the instrument as used by the agent, Phil 2:1. Syn.: *Paramuthion* (3890) has the same meaning as 3889, the difference being that *paramuthia* (3889) stresses the process or progress of the act, *paramuthion* emphasizing the instrument of comfort used by the agent. See: TDNT—5:816, 784; BAGD—620d; THAYER—485b.

3891. **παρανομέω** {1x} **paranŏmĕō**, *par-an-om-eh'-o;* from a compound of *3844* and *3551;* to *be opposed to law,* i.e. to *transgress:*—contrary to law {1x}.

Paranomeo, "to transgress law" (*para,* "contrary to," and *nomos*), is used in the present participle in Acts 23:3, and translated "contrary to the law," lit., "transgressing the law." See: TDNT—4:1091, 646; BAGD—621a; THAYER—485b.

3892. **παρανομία** {1x} **paranŏmia**, *par-an-om-ee'-ah;* from the same as *3891; transgression:*—iniquity {1x}.

A person who commits *paranomia* is one living contrary to a stated law, not one who has no law as a guide (2 Pet 2:16). Syn.: 51, 265, 266, 458, 2275, 3847, 3876, 3900. See: TDNT—4:1090, 646; BAGD—621a; THAYER—485b.

3893. **παραπικραίνω** {1x} **parapikrainō**, *par-ap-ik-rah'-ee-no;* from *3844* and *4087;* to *embitter alongside,* i.e. (fig.) to *exasperate:*—provoke {1x}.

Parapikraino, "to embitter, provoke", occurs in Heb 3:16 of provoking God. See: TDNT—6:125, 839; BAGD—621a; THAYER—485b.

3894. **παραπικρασμός** {2x} **parapikrasmŏs**, *par-ap-ik-ras-mos';* from *3893; irritation:*—provocation {2x}.

Parapikrasmos, from *para,* "amiss" or "from," used intensively, and *pikraino,* "to make bitter" (*pikros,* "sharp, bitter"), "provocation," occurs in Heb 3:8, 15. See: TDNT—6:125, 839; BAGD—621b; THAYER—485b.

3895. **παραπίπτω** {1x} **parapiptō**, *par-ap-ip'-to;* from *3844* and *4098;* to *fall aside,* i.e. (fig.) to *apostatize:*—fall away {1x}.

Parpipto means properly, "to fall in one's way" (*para,* "by"), and signifies "to fall away" (from adherence to the realities and facts of the faith), Heb 6:6. See: TDNT—6:170, 846; BAGD—621b; THAYER—485c.

3896. **παραπλέω** {1x} **paraplĕō**, *par-ap-leh'-o;* from *3844* and *4126;* to *sail near:*—sail by {1x}. See: BAGD—621; THAYER—485c.

3897. **παραπλήσιον** {1x} **paraplēsiŏn**, *par-ap-lay'-see-on;* neut. of a compound of *3844* and the base of *4139* (as adv.); *close by,* i.e. (fig.) *almost:*—nigh unto {1x}.

This word denotes beside, near, nearly resembling and has reference to death because it stresses the person is drawing near to that state when the body is lifeless (Phil 2:27). See: BAGD—621c; THAYER—485c.

3898. **παραπλησίως** {1x} **paraplēsiōs**, *par-ap-lay-see'-oce;* adv. from the same as *3897; in a manner near by,* i.e. (fig.) *similarly:*—likewise {1x}.

Paraplesios, from *para,* "beside," and the adjective *plesios,* "near" (akin to the adverb *pelas,* "near, hard by"), is used in Heb 2:14, "likewise", expressing the true humanity of Christ in partaking of flesh and blood. See: BAGD—621c; THAYER—485c.

3899. **παραπορεύομαι** {5x} **parapŏĕruŏmai**, *par-ap-or-yoo'-om-ahee;* from *3844* and *4198;* to *travel near:*—go {1x}, pass {1x}, pass by {3x}.

This word means primarily, "to go beside, accompany" (*para,* "beside," *poreuomai,* "to proceed"), and denotes **(1)** "to go past, pass by," Mt 27:39; **(2)** Mk 9:30, "passed through"; 11:20; 15:29; **(3)** in Mk 2:23, "going . . . through." See. BAGD—621d; THAYER—485c.

3900. **παράπτωμα** {23x} **paraptōma**, *par-ap'-to-mah;* from *3895;* a *side-slip* (*lapse* or *deviation*), i.e. (unintentional) *error* or (willful) *transgression:*—fall {2x}, fault, {2x} offence {7x}, sin {3x}, trespass {9x}.

(1) Primarily, this word means a false step, a blunder; hence, a lapse from uprightness, a sin, a moral trespass, misdeed; a downfall, a falling down along side of the correct path (Rom 11:11–12). **(1a)** *Paraptoma,* as a noun, (akin to *parapipto,* "to fall away," Heb 6:6), means lit., "a fall beside," used ethically, denotes **(1b)** "a trespass," a deviation, from uprightness and truth, Mt 6:14, 15 (twice); 18:35; Mk 11:25, 26; **(2)** in Romans **(2a)** 4:25, "for (i.e., because of) our trespasses"; **(2b)** 5:15 (twice), where the trespass is that of Adam (in contrast to the free gift of righteousness), **(2c)** 5:16, where "of many trespasses" expresses a contrast of quantity; the condemnation resulted from one "trespass," the free gift is "of (*ek,* expressing the origin, and throwing stress upon God's justifying grace in Christ) many trespasses"; **(2d)** 5:17, introducing a contrast between legal effects and those of divine grace; **(2e)** 5:18, "through one offense," is contrasted with "one act of righteousness"; this is important, the difference is not between one man's "trespass" and Christ's righteousness, but between two acts, that of Adam's "trespass" and the vicarious death of Christ. Syn.: *Paraptoma,* and *hamartema* (264 -"a sinful deed") are closely associated, with regard to their primary meanings: *parabasis* seems to be a stronger term, as the breach of a known law. Syn.: 51, 265, 266, 458, 2275, 3847, 3876, 3892. See: TDNT—6:170, 846; BAGD—621d; THAYER—485d.

3901. **παραῤῥυέω** {1x} **pararrhuĕō**, *par-ar-hroo-eh'-o;* from *3844* and the alternate of *4482;* to glide by, *flow by,* i.e. (fig.) carelessly *pass* (*miss*):—let slip {1x}.

(1) The significance of this word is to find oneself flowing, gliding, or passing by without giving due heed to a thing. **(2)** It means lit., "to flow past, glide by" (*para,* "by," *rheo,* "to flow"), and is used in Heb 2:1, where the significance is to find oneself "flowing" or "passing by," without giving due heed to a thing, here "the things that were heard," or perhaps the salvation of which they spoke; "let them slip." See: BAGD—621d; THAYER—485d.

3902. **παράσημος** {1x} **parasēmŏs**, *par-as'-ay-mos;* from *3844* and the base of *4591; side-marked,* i.e. *labelled* (with a *badge* [*figure-head*] of a ship):—sign {1x}.

Parasmos, an adjective meaning "marked at the side" (*para,* "beside," *sema,* "a mark"), is used in Acts 28:11 as a noun denoting the figurehead of a vessel. See: BAGD—622a; THAYER—486a.

3903. **παρασκευάζω** {4x} **paraskĕuazō**, *par-ask-yoo-ad'-zo;* from *3844* and a der. of *4632;* to *furnish aside,* i.e. *get ready:*—make ready {1x}, prepare oneself {1x}, be ready {1x}, ready {1x}.

This word means "to prepare, make ready" (*para,* "beside"), is used **(1)** of making ready a meal, Acts 10:10; **(2)** in the middle voice, of "preparing" oneself for war, 1 Cor 14:8; **(3)** in the passive voice, of **(3a)** "preparing" an offering for the needy, 2 Cor 9:2, "was ready"; **(3b)** 2 Cor 9:3, "ye may be ready." See: BAGD—622a; THAYER—486a.

3904. **παρασκευή** {6x} **paraskĕuē**, *par-ask-yoo-ay';* as if from *3903; readiness:*—preparation.

Paraskeue denotes "preparation, equipment." **(1)** The day on which Christ died is called **(1a)** "the Preparation" in Mk 15:42; Jn 19:31; **(1b)** in Jn 19:42 "the Jews' Preparation"; **(1c)** in 19:14 it is described as "the Preparation of the Passover"; **(1d)** in Lk 23:54, RV, "the day of the preparation (and the sabbath drew on)." **(2)** The same day is in view in Mt 27:62, where the events recorded took place on "that followed the day of the preparation." The reference would be to the 6th day of the week. The title arose from the need of preparing food etc. for the Sabbath. Apparently it was first applied only to the afternoon of the 6th day; later, to the whole day. **(3)** In regard to the phraseology in Jn 19:14, many hold this to indicate the "preparation" for the paschal feast. It probably means "the Preparation day," and thus falls in line with the Synoptic Gospels. See: TDNT—7:1, 989; BAGD—622b; THAYER—486a.

3905. **παρατείνω** {1x} **paratĕinō**, *par-at-i'-no;* from *3844* and τείνω **tĕinō** (to stretch); to *extend along,* i.e. *prolong* (in point of time):—continue {1x}.

Parateino, "to stretch out along" (*para,* "along," *teino,* "to stretch"), is translated "continued" in Acts 20:7, of Paul's discourse. See: BAGD—622c; THAYER—486b.

3906. **παρατηρέω** {6x} **paratērĕō**, *par-at-ay-reh'-o;* from *3844* and *5083;* to *inspect alongside,* i.e. *note insidiously* or *scrupulously:*—watched {4x}, observe {1x}, watched + 2258 {1x}.

Paratereo, to observe," especially with sinister intent, is rendered "to watch" in Mk 3:2; Lk 6:7; 14:1; 20:20; Acts 9:24. **(2)** This verb also means to watch closely, observe narrowly, used in Gal 4:10, where the middle voice suggests that their religious observance of days, etc. was not from disinterested motives, but with a view to their own advantage. See: TDNT—8:146, 1174; BAGD—622c; THAYER—486b.

3907. **παρατήρησις** {1x} **paratērēsis**, *par-at-ay'-ray-sis;* from *3906; inspection,* i.e. *ocular evidence:*—observation {1x}.

Parateresis is attentive watching and is used in Lk 17:20, of the manner in which the kingdom of God (i.e., the operation of the spiritual kingdom in the hearts of men) does not come in such a manner that it can be watched with the eyes; not with outward show. See: TDNT—8:148, 1174; BAGD—622d; THAYER—486c.

3908. **παρατίθημι** {19x} **paratithēmi**, *par-at-ith'-ay-mee;* from *3844* and *5087;* to *place alongside,* i.e. *present* (food, truth); by impl. to *deposit* (as a trust or for protection):—set before {9x}, commit {3x}, commend {3x}, put forth {2x}, commit the keeping of {1x}, allege {1x}.

Paratithemi means **(1)** "to place beside", "to put forth," **(1a)** of a parable, Mt 13:24, 31; **(1b)** "to set before," of food, Mk 6:41; 8:6 (twice), 7; Lk 9:16; 10:8; 11:6; Acts 16:34; 1 Cor 10:27. It is also translated **(2)** "to entrust, commit to one's charge," in Lk 12:48, "committed"; 1 Ti 1:18; 2 Ti 2:2; 1 Pet 4:19, "commit the keeping"; **(3)** "to commend" in Lk 23:46; Acts 14:23; 20:32; and **(4)** "alleging" in Acts 17:3. See: TDNT—8:162, 1176; BAGD—622d; THAYER—486c.

3909. **παρατυγχάνω** {1x} **paratugchanō**, *par-at-oong-khan'-o;* from *3844* and *5177;* to *chance near,* i.e. *fall in with:*—meet with {1x}.

Paratugchano, "to happen to be near or present, to chance to be by" (*para,* "beside, near," *tunchano,* "to happen"), occurs in Acts 17:17, "met with (him)." See: BAGD—623a; THAYER—486d.

3910. **παραυτίκα** {1x} **parautika**, *par-ŏw-tee'-kah;* from *3844* and a der. of *846; at* the *very* instant, i.e. *momentary:*—but for a moment {1x}.

Parautika, "at the same circumstances," is used adjectivally in 2 Cor 4:17 and translated "which is but for a moment"; the meaning is not, however, simply that of brief duration, but that which is present with us now or immediate (*para,* "beside with"), in contrast to the future glory; the clause is, lit., "for the present lightness (i.e., 'light burden,' the adjective *elaphron,* 'light,' being used as a noun) of (our) affliction." See: BAGD—623b; THAYER—486b.

3911. **παραφέρω** {3x} **paraphĕrō**, *par-af-er'-o;* from *3844* and *5342* (incl. its alt. forms); to *bear along* or *aside,* i.e. *carry off* (lit. or fig.); by impl. to *avert:*—remove {1x}, take away {2x}.

Paraphero, lit., "to bring to or before" (*para,* "beside," *phero,* "to carry"), "to take or carry away," is translated "take away" in the Lord's prayer in Gethsemane, Mk 14:36; Lk 22:42. See: BAGD—623b; THAYER—486d.

3912. **παραφρονέω** {1x} **paraphrŏnĕō**, *par-af-ron-eh'-o;* from *3844* and *5426;* to *misthink,* i.e. *be insane* (*silly*):—as a fool {1x}.

This word literally means to be beside oneself, to be deranged, out of one's senses, void of understanding, insane (2 Cor 11:23). See: BAGD—623c; THAYER—486d.

3913. **παραφρονία** {1x} **paraphrŏnia**, *par-af-ron-ee'-ah;* from *3912; insanity,* i.e. *foolhardiness:*—madness {1x}.

This word means madness; literally, contrary to the mind, speaking as mindless (2 Pet 2:16). See: BAGD—623c; THAYER—486d.

3914. **παραχειμάζω** {4x} **parachĕimazō**, *par-akh-i-mad'-zo;* from *3844* and *5492;* to *winter near,* i.e. *stay* with over the *rainy* season:—to winter {4x}.

Paracheimazo denotes "to winter at a place", Acts 27:12 (2nd part); 28:11; 1 Cor 16:6; Titus 3:12. See: BAGD—623c; THAYER—487a.

3915. **παραχειμασία** {1x} **parachĕimasia**, *par-akh-i-mas-ee'-ah;* from *3914;* a *wintering* over:—winter in {1x}. See: BAGD—623d; THAYER—487a,

3916. **παραχρῆμα** {19x} **parachrēma**, *par-akh-ray'-mah;* from *3844* and *5536* (in its orig. sense); *at the thing* itself, i.e. *instantly:*—immediately {13x}, straight way {3x}, forthwith {1x}, presently {1x}, soon {1x}.

Parachrema, lit., "with the matter (or business) itself" (*para,* "with," *chrema,* "a business," or "event"), and so, **(1)** "immediately," Lk 1:64; 4:39; 5:25; 8:44, 47; 13:13; 18:43; 19:11; 22:60; Acts 3:7; 12:23; 13:11; 16:26; it is thus used by Luke only, save for the two instances in Matthew. **(2)** It is also rendered "presently" in Mt 21:19; **(3)** "forthwith" in Acts 9:18; **(4)** "soon" in Mt 21:20; and **(5)** "straightway" in Lk 8:55; Acts 5:10; 16:33. See: BAGD—623d; THAYER—487a.

3917. **πάρδαλις** {1x} **pardalis**, *par'-dal-is;* fem. of πάρδος **pardŏs** (a *panther*); a *leopard:*—leopard {1x}.

Pardalis denotes "a leopard or a panther," an animal characterized by swiftness of movement and sudden spring, in Dan 7:6 symbolic of the activities of Alexander the Great, and the formation of the Grecian kingdom, the third seen in the vision there recorded. In Rev 13:2 the imperial power, described there also as a "beast," is seen to concentrate in himself the characteristics of those mentioned in Dan 7. See: BAGD—623d; THAYER—487a.

3918. **πάρειμι** {23x} **parĕimi**, *par'-i-mee;* from *3844* and *1510* (incl. its various forms); to *be near,* i.e. *at hand;* neut. pres. part. (sing.) *time being,* or (plural) *property:*—be present {9x}, come {7x}, present {3x}, be present here {1x}, be here {1x}, such things as one hath + 3588 {1x}, he that lacketh + 3361 + 3739 {1x}.

Pareimi signifies **(1)** "to be by, at hand or present," **(1a)** of persons, e.g., Lk 13:1; Acts 10:33; 24:19; 1 Cor 5:3; 2 Cor 10:2, 11; Gal 4:18, 20; **(1b)** of things, **(1b1)** Jn 7:6, of a particular season in the Lord's life on earth, "is (not yet) come," or "is not yet at hand"; **(1b2)** Heb 12:11, of chastening "(for the) present" (the neuter of the present participle, used as a noun); **(1b3)** in Heb 13:5 "such things as ye have" is, lit., "the things that are present"; **(1b4)** 2 Pet 1:12, of the truth "the present truth," i.e. the truth which is now with you, not as if of special doctrines applicable to a particular time; **(1b5)** in 2 Pet 1:9 "he that lacketh" is lit., "to whom are not present"; **(2)** "to have arrived or come," Mt 26:50, "thou art come"; Jn 11:28; Acts 10:21; Col 1:6. See: TDNT—5:858, 791; BAGD—624a; THAYER—487b.

3919. **παρεισάγω** {1x} **parĕisagō**, *par-ice-ag'-o;* from *3844* and *1521;* to *lead in aside,* i.e. *introduce surreptitiously:*—privily bring in {1x}.

Pareisago, as a verb, means "to bring in privily" [lit., "to bring in beside"], "to introduce secretly": "But there were false prophets also among the people, even as there shall be false teachers among you, who privily shall bring in (*pareisago*) damnable heresies, even denying the Lord that bought them, and bring upon themselves swift destruction" (2 Pet 2:1). See: TDNT—5:824, 786; BAGD—624c; THAYER—487c.

3920. **παρείσακτος** {1x} **parĕisaktŏs**, *par-ice'-ak-tos;* from *3919; smuggled in:*—unawares brought in {1x}. *Pareisaktos,* See: TDNT—5:824, 786; BAGD—624c; THAYER—487c.

3921. **παρεισδύνω** {1x} **parĕisdunō**, *par-ice-doo'-no;* from *3844* and a compound of *1519* and *1416;* to *settle in alongside,* i.e. *lodge stealthily:*—creep in unawares {1x}. See: BAGD—624d; THAYER—487c.

3922. **παρεισέρχομαι** {2x} **parĕisĕrchŏmai**, *par-ice-er'-khom-ahee;* from *3844* and *1525;* to *come in alongside,* i.e. *supervene additionally* or *stealthily:*—come in privily {1x}, enter {1x}.

This word means lit., "to come in" (*eis*) "beside or from the side" (*para*) so as to be present with, and is used **(1)** in the literal sense, of the "coming" in of the Law in addition to sin, Rom 5:20; **(2)** in Gal 2:4, of false brethren, suggesting their "coming" in by stealth. See: TDNT—2:682, 257; BAGD—624d; THAYER—487c.

3923. **παρεισφέρω** {1x} **parĕisphĕrō**, *par-ice-fer'-o;* from *3844* and *1533;* to *bear in alongside,* i.e. *introduce simultaneously:*—give {1x}.

This word means "to bring in besides" (*para,* "besides," *eis,* "in," *phero,* "to bring"), means "to add," 2 Pet 1:5, "giving" (all your diligence) representing the intensive force of the verb. See: BAGD—625a; THAYER—487d.

3924. **παρεκτός** {3x} **parĕktŏs**, *par-ek-tos';* from *3844* and *1622; near outside,* i.e. *besides:*—except {1x}, saving {1x}, without {1x}.

Parektos, (a strengthened form *ektos,* and *para,* beside), is used **(1)** as an adverb, signifying "without," 2 Cor 11:28; lit., "the things without," i.e., the things happening without; **(2)** as a preposition signifying **(2a)** "except" in Mt 5:32, and **(2b)** "saving" in Acts 26:29 except. See: BAGD—625a; THAYER—487d.

3925. **παρεμβολή** {10x} **parĕmbŏlē**, *par-em-bol-ay';* from a compound of *3844* and *1685;* a *throwing in beside* (*juxtaposition*), i.e. (spec.) *battle-array, encampment* or *barracks* (tower Antonia):—army {1x}, camp {3x}, castle {6x}.

This word means lit., "a casting in among, an insertion" (*para,* "among," *ballo,* "to throw"), and was a military term. **(1)** In the NT it denotes the distribution of troops in army formation, "armies," **(1a)** Heb 11:34; a camp, as of the Israelites, Ex 19:17; 29:14; 32:17; hence, **(1b)** in Heb 13:11, 13, of Jerusalem, since the city was to the Jews what the camp in the wilderness had been to the Israelites; **(1c)** in Rev 20:9, the "armies" or camp of the saints, at the close of the Millennium. **(2)** It also denoted a castle or barracks, the defensible part of the royal estate: Acts 21:34, 37; 22:24; 23:10, 16, 32. See: BAGD—625b; THAYER—487d.

3926. **παρενοχλέω** {1x} **parĕnŏchlĕō**, *par-en-okh-leh'-o;* from *3844* and *1776;* to *harass further,* i.e. *annoy:*—trouble {1x}. See: BAGD—625c; THAYER—488a.

3927. **παρεπίδημος** {3x} **parepidēmŏs**, *par-ep-id'-ay-mos;* from *3844* and the base of *1927;* an *alien alongside,* i.e. a *resident foreigner:*—pilgrim {2x}, stranger {1x}.

This word is an adjective signifying "sojourning in a strange place, away from one's own people" (*para,* "from," expressing a contrary condition, and *epidemeo,* "to sojourn"; *demos,* "a people"), and is used **(1)** of OT saints, Heb 11:13, "pilgrims" (coupled with *xenos,* "a foreigner"); **(2)** of Christians, 1 Pet 1:1, "strangers scattered"; the word is stressing those Christians scattered in Pontus, etc., and applied metaphorically of those to whom Heaven is their own country, and who are sojourners on earth. See: TDNT—2:64, 49; BAGD—625d; THAYER—488a.

3928. **παρέρχομαι** {31x} **parĕrchŏmai**, *par-er'-khom-ahee;* from *3844* and *2064;* to *come near* or *aside,* i.e. to *approach* (*arrive*), *go by* (or *away*), (fig.) *perish* or *neglect,* (caus.) *avert:*—pass away {12x}, pass {10x}, pass by {3x}, pass over {1x}, transgress {1x}, past {1x}, go {1x}, come forth {1x}, come {1x}.

Parerchomai, from *para,* "by," *erchomai,* "to come" or "go," denotes **(1)** literally, "to pass, pass by," **(1a)** of persons, Mt 8:28; Mk 6:48; Lk 18:37; Acts 16:8; **(1b)** of things, Mt 26:39, 42; **(1c)** of time, Mt 14:15; Mk 14:35; Acts 27:9, "past"; 1 Pet 4:3; **(2)** metaphorically, **(2a)** "to pass away, to perish," Mt 5:18; 24:34, 35; Mk 13:30, 31; Lk 16:17; 21:32, 33; 2 Cor 5:17; Jas 1:10; 2 Pet 3:10; **(2b)** "to pass by, disregard, neglect, pass over," Lk 11:42; 15:29, "transgressed." **(3)** For the meaning "to come forth or come," see Lk 12:37; 17:7. See: TDNT—2:681, 257; BAGD—625d; THAYER—488b.

3929. **πάρεσις** {1x} **parĕsis**, *par'-es-is;* from *2935; prætermission,* i.e. *toleration:*—remission {1x}.

Paresis primarily means a letting go, a dismissal and denotes a passing by, a suspension of judgment or withholding of punishment (Rom 3:25) with reference to sins committed previously up to the propitiatory sacrifice of Christ; the passing by not being a matter of divine disregard but of forbearance. Syn.: 859. See: TDNT—1:509, 88; BAGD—626b; THAYER—488c.

3930. **παρέχω** {16x} **parĕchō**, *par-ekh'-o;* from *3844* and *2192;* to *hold near,* i.e. *present, afford, exhibit, furnish occasion:*—trouble + 2873 {5x}, give {3x}, bring {2x}, shew {2x}, do for {1x}, keep {1x}, minister {1x}, offer {1x}.

Parecho, as a verb, means usually, "to offer, furnish, supply" [lit., "to have near"], **(1)** "to bring, in the sense of supplying": "And it came to pass, as we went to prayer, a certain damsel possessed with a spirit of divination met us, which brought (*parecho*) her masters much gain by soothsaying" (Acts 16:16; cf. 19:24). **(2)** In the active voice, signifies "to afford, furnish, provide, supply" (lit., "to hold out or towards"; and is translated **(2a)** "hath given" in Acts 17:31; **(2b)** "giveth" in 1 Ti 6:17 (in the sense of affording); and **(2c)** in Col 4:1, "give." See: BAGD—626b; THAYER—488c.

3931. **παρηγορία** {1x} **parēgŏria**, *par-ay-gor-ee'-ah;* from a compound of *3844* and a der. of *58* (mean. to *harangue* an assembly); an *address alongside,* i.e. (spec.) *consolation:*—comfort {1x}.

This word primarily means an addressing, an address; hence, denotes a soothing, a solace (Col 4:11). A verbal form of the word signifies medicines which allay irritation (Eng., paregoric). See: BAGD—626d; THAYER—488d.

3932. **παρθενία** {1x} **parthĕnia**, *par-then-ee'-ah;* from *3933; maidenhood:*—virginity {1x}. See: BAGD—626d; THAYER—489a.

3933. **παρθένος** {14x} **parthĕnŏs**, *par-then'-os;* of unknown or.; a *maiden;* by impl. an unmarried *daughter:*—virgin {14x}.

Parthenos is used **(1)** of "the Virgin Mary," Mt 1:23; Lk 1:27; **(2)** of the ten "virgins" in the parable, Mt 25:1, 7, 11; **(3)** of the "daughters" of Philip the evangelist, Acts 21:9; **(4)** those concerning whom the apostle Paul gives instructions regarding marriage, 1 Cor 7:25, 28, 34; in vv. 36, 37, 38, the subject passes to that of "virgin daughters", which almost certainly formed one of the subjects upon which the church at Corinth sent for instructions from the apostle; one difficulty was relative to the discredit which might be brought upon a father (or guardian), if he allowed his daughter or ward to grow old unmarried. The interpretation that this passage refers to a man and woman already in some kind of relation by way of a spiritual marriage and living together in a vow of virginity and celibacy, is untenable if only in view of the phraseology of the passage; **(5)** figuratively, of "a local church" in its relation to Christ, 2 Cor 11:2; **(6)** literally of virgin young men," Rev 14:4. See: TDNT—5:826, 786; BAGD—627a; THAYER—489a.

3934. **Πάρθος** {1x} **Parthŏs**, *par'-thos;* prob. of for. or.; a *Parthian,* i.e. inhab. of Parthia:—Parthian {1x}. See: BAGD—627b; THAYER—489b.

3935. **παρίημι** {1x} **pariēmi**, *par-ee'-ay-mi;* from *3844* and ἵημι **hiēmi**, (to *send*); to *let by,* i.e. *relax:*—hang down {1x}.

Pareiemi means relaxed, unstrung, weakened, exhausted; hence, hanging down, Heb 12:12. See: TDNT—1:509, 88; BAGD—627c.

3936. **παρίστημι** {42x} **paristēmi**, *par-is'-tay-mee;* or prol.

παριστάνω **paristanō** *par-is-tan'-o;* from *3844,* and *2476;* to *stand beside,* i.e. (tran.) to *exhibit, proffer,* (spec.) *recommend,* (fig.) *substantiate;* or (intr.) to *be at hand* (or *ready*), *aid:*—stand by {13x}, present {9x}, yield {5x}, shew {2x}, stand {2x}, misc. {11x} = assist, bring before, command, commend, give presently, prove, provide.

Paristano, **(1)** intransitively, denotes **(1a)** "to stand by or beside" in Mk 14:47, 69, 70; 15:35, 39; Lk 19:24; Jn 18:22; 19:26; Acts 1:10; 9:39; 23:2, 4; 27:23; **(1b)** in Acts 27:24, "stand before"; **(1c)** in Acts 4:10, "doth . . . stand here"; **(1d)** in Lk 1:19, "stand"; **(1e)** Rom 14:10, "we shall . . . stand before" (middle voice); **(1f)** 2 Ti 4:17, "stood with"; **(2)** used transitively, "to place beside" (*para,* "by," *histemi,* "to set"), **(2a)** "to present," e.g., Lk 2:22; Acts 1:3, "He shewed (Himself)"; 9:41; 23:33; Rom. 6:13 (2nd part), "yield"; so 6:19 (twice); 12:1; 2 Cor 4:14; 11:2; Eph 5:27; Col 1:22, 28; 2 Ti 2:15, "show." See: TDNT—5:837, 788; BAGD—627c; THAYER—489b.

3937. **Παρμενᾶς** {1x} **Parmĕnas**, *par-men-as';* prob. by contr. for Παρμενίδης **Parmĕnidēs** (a der. of a compound of *3844* and *3306*); *constant; Parmenas,* a Chr.:—*Parmenas* {1x}. See: BAGD—628c; THAYER—489d.

3938. **πάροδος** {1x} **parŏdŏs**, *par'-od-os;* from *3844* and *3598;* a *by-road,* i.e. (act.) a *route:*—way {1x}. See: BAGD—628d; THAYER—488b.

3939. **παροικέω** {2x} **parŏikĕō**, *par-oy-keh'-o;* from *3844* and *3611;* to *dwell near,* i.e. *reside* as a *foreigner:*—sojourn in {1x}, be a stranger {1x}.

Paroikeo denotes "to dwell beside, among or by" (*para,* "beside," *oikeo,* "to dwell"); then, "to dwell in a place as a *paroikos,* a stranger" (3941), **(1)** Lk 24:18, "art thou (only) a stranger?" [*monos,* "alone," is an adjective, not an adverb]; **(2)** in Heb 11:9, "he sojourned." See: TDNT—5:841, 788; BAGD—628d; THAYER—489d.

3940. **παροικία** {2x} **parŏikia**, *par-oy-kee'-ah;* from *3941; foreign residence:*—sojourning here {1x}, dwelt as strangers {1x}.

Paroikia denotes **(1)** "a sojourning," Acts 13:17, lit., "in the sojourning," translated "dwelt as strangers"; and **(2)** in 1 Pet 1:17, "sojourning here." See: TDNT—5:841, 788; BAGD—629a; THAYER—490a.

3941. **πάροικος** {4x} **parŏikŏs**, *par'-oy-kos;* from *3844* and *3624;* having a *home near,* i.e. (as noun) a *by-dweller* (*alien resident*):—foreigner {1x}, sojourn {1x}, stranger {2x}.

Paroidos, as a noun, "a sojourner," is **(1)** used with *eimi,* "to be," in Acts 7:6, "should sojourn"; **(2)** in Acts 7:29, "stranger"; in 1 Pet 2:11, "strangers"; **(3)** in Eph 2:19, "foreigners." See: TDNT—5:841, 788; BAGD—629a; THAYER—490a.

3942. **παροιμία** {5x} **parŏimia**, *par-oy-mee'-ah;* from a compound of *3844* and perh. a der. of *3633;* appar. a state *alongside* *of supposition,* i.e. (concr.) an *adage;* spec. an enigmatical or fictitious *illustration:*—parable {1x}, proverb {4x}.

Paraoimia is **(1)** a saying out of the usual course or deviating from the usual manner of speaking; **(2)** any dark saying **(2a)** which shadows forth some didactic truth, esp. a symbolic or figurative saying; **(2b)** speech or discourse in which a thing is illustrated by the use of similes and comparisons. **(3)** It is translated "parable" in Jn 10:6; and "proverb" in Jn 16:25 twice; 16:29; 2 Pet 2:2. See: TDNT—5:854, 790; BAGD—629b; THAYER—490b.

3943. **πάροινος** {2x} **parŏinŏs**, *par'-oy-nos;* from *3844* and *3631;* staying *near wine,* i.e. *tippling* (a *toper*):—given to wine {2x}.

Paroinos, as an adjective, literally means "tarrying at wine, given to wine" (1 Ti 3:3; Titus 1:7with the secondary sense, of the effects of wine-bibbing, viz., abusive brawling). Syn.: 269. See: BAGD—629b; THAYER—490b.

3944. **παροίχομαι** {1x} **parŏichŏmai**, *par-oy'-khom-ahee;* from *3844* and οἴχομαι **ŏichŏmai** (to *depart*); to *escape along,* i.e. *be gone:*—past {1x}.

Paroichomai, "to have passed by, to be gone by," is used in Acts 14:16, of past generations, "(in times) past." See: BAGD—629b; THAYER—490b.

3945. **παρομοιάζω** {1x} **parŏmŏiazō**, *par-om-oy-ad'-zo;* from *3946;* to *resemble:*—be like unto {1x}.

This word is used in Mt 23:27 (perhaps with intensive force), in the Lord's comparison of the scribes and Pharisees to whitened sepulchers. See: TDNT—5:199, 684; BAGD—629b; THAYER—490b.

3946. **παρόμοιος** {2x} **parŏmŏiŏs**, *par-om'-oy-os;* from *3844* and *3664;* *alike nearly,* i.e. *similar:*—like things {2x}.

Paromoios "much like" is used in Mark 7:8, 13, in the neuter plural, "(many such) like things." See: TDNT—5:198, 684; BAGD—629b; THAYER—490c.

3947. **παροξύνω** {2x} **parŏxunō**, *par-ox-oo'-no;* from *3844* and a der. of *3691;* to *sharpen alongside,* i.e. (fig.) to *exasperate:*—easily provoked {1x}, stir {1x}.

Paroxuno, as a verb, primarily, means "to sharpen" and is used metaphorically, signifying "to rouse to anger, to provoke," **(1)** in the passive voice, in Acts 17:16: "Now while Paul waited for them at Athens, his spirit was stirred in him, when he saw the city wholly given to idolatry"; and **(2)** "was stirred" in 1 Cor 13:5. Syn.: 329, 383, 387, 1326, 1892, 2042, 3951, 4531, 4579, 4787, 4797, 5017. See: TDNT—5:857, 791; BAGD—629c; THAYER—490c.

3948. **παροξυσμός** {2x} **parŏxusmŏs**, *par-ox-oos-mos';* from *3947* ("*par-oxysm*"); *incitement* (to good), or *dispute* (in anger):—contention . . . so sharp {1x}, provoke unto + 1519 {1x}.

Paroxusmos, lit., "a sharpening," hence "a sharpening of the feeling, or action" (*para,* "beside," intensive, *oxus,* "sharp"), denotes **(1)** an incitement, a sharp contention, Acts 15:39, the effect of irritation; and **(2)** elsewhere in Heb 10:24, "provoke," unto love. See: TDNT—5:857, 791; BAGD—629c; THAYER—490c.

3949. **παροργίζω** {2x} **parŏrgizō**, *par-org-id'-zo;* from *3844* and *3710;* to *anger alongside,* i.e. *enrage:*—anger {1x}, provoke to wrath {1x}.

Parorgizo is "to arouse to wrath, provoke"; **(1)** Rom 10:19, "will I anger"; **(2)** Eph 6:4, "provoke to wrath." See: TDNT—5:382, 716; BAGD—62d; THAYER—490c.

3950. **παροργισμός** {1x} **parŏrgismŏs**, *par-org--is-mos';* from *3949; rage:*—wrath {1x}.

Parorgismos occurs when irritation, exasperation, and embitterment attaches themselves to righteous anger and makes it sin (Eph 4:26). Syn.: 2372, 3209. See: TDNT—5:382, 716; BAGD—629d; THAYER—490d.

3951. **παροτρύνω** {1x} **parŏtrunō**, *par-ot-roo'-no;* from *3844* and ὀτρύνω **ŏtrunō** (to *spur*); to *urge along,* i.e. *stimulate* (to hostility):—stir up {1x}.

Parotruno, as a verb, [from *para,* used intensively, beyond measure, and *otruno*], means "to urge on, rouse": "But the Jews stirred up the devout and honourable women, and the chief men of the city, and raised persecution against Paul and Barnabas, and expelled them out of their coasts" (Acts 13:50). Syn.: 329, 383, 387, 1326, 1892, 2042, 3947, 4531, 4579, 4787, 4797, 5017. See: BAGD—629d; THAYER—490d.

3952. **παρουσία** {24x} **parŏusia**, *par-oo-see'-ah;* from the present part. of *3918;* a *being near,* i.e. *advent* (often, *return;* spec. of Christ to punish Jerusalem, or finally the wicked); (by impl.) phys. *aspect:*—coming {22x}, presence {2x}.

Parousia is used **(1)** to describe the presence of Christ with His disciples on the Mount of Transfiguration (2 Pet 1:16). **(2)** When used of the return of Christ, at the rapture of the church, it signifies, not merely His momentary coming for His saints in the rapture, but His presence with them from that moment until His revelation and manifestation to the world in His second coming. **(3)** In some passages the word **(3a)** gives prominence to the beginning of that period, the course of the period being implied (1 Cor 15:23; 1 Th 4:15; 5:23; 2 Th 2:1; Jas 5:7–8; 2 Pet 3:4). **(3b)** In some, the course is prominent (Mt 24:3, 37; 1 Th 3:13; 1 Jn 2:28); **(3c)** in others the conclusion of the period (Mt 24:27; 2 Th 2:8). See: TDNT—5:858, 791; BAGD—629d; THAYER—490d.

3953. **παροψίς** {2x} **parŏpsis**, *par-op-sis';* from *3844* and the base of *3795;* a *side-dish* (the receptacle):—platter {2x}.

This word, (*para,* "beside," *opson,* "cooked"), means **(1)** firstly, "a side dish of dainties" in Mt 23:26; **(2)** then, "the dish itself" in Mt 23:25. See: BAGD—630b; THAYER—491a.

3954. **παῤῥησία** {31x} **parrhēsia**, *par-rhay-see'-ah;* from *3956* and a der. of *4483; all* out-*spokenness,* i.e. *frankness, bluntness, publicity;* by impl. *assurance:*—boldness {8x}, confidence {6x}, openly {4x}, plainly {4x}, openly + 1722 {2x}, boldly + 1722 {1x}, misc. {6x} = × freely, plainness.

This word (from *pas,* "all," *rhesis,* "speech") denotes **(1)** primarily, **(1a)** "freedom of speech, unreservedness of utterance," Acts 4:29, 31; 2 Cor 3:12; 7:4; Philem 8; or **(1b)** "to speak without ambiguity, plainly," Jn 10:24; **(1c)** or "without figures of speech," Jn 16:25; **(2)** "the absence of fear in speaking boldly; hence, confidence, cheerful courage, boldness, without any connection necessarily with speech"; "boldness" in the following; Acts 4:13; Eph 3:12; 1 Ti 3:13; Heb 3:6; 4:16; 10:19, 35; 1 Jn 2:28; 3:21; 4:17; 5:14; **(3)** the deportment by which one becomes conspicuous, Jn 7:4; 11:54, acts openly, or secures publicity, Col 2:15. See: TDNT—5:871, 794; BAGD—639c; THAYER—491a.

3955. **παῤῥησιάζομαι** {9x} **parrhēsiazŏmai**, *par-hray-see-ad'-zom-ahee;* mid. voice from *3954;* to *be frank* in utterance, or *confident* in spirit and demeanor:—speak boldly {4x}, preach boldly {1x}, be bold {1x}, wax bold {1x}, boldly {1x}, freely {1x}.

This word means "to speak boldly, or freely," and primarily had reference to speech, but acquired the meaning of "being bold, or waxing bold," 1 Th 2:2; in Acts 13:46, the aorist participle here signifies "waxing bold"; Acts 9:27, 29, "preached boldly"; 18:26, "speak boldly"; 19:8, "spake boldly; 26:26, "speak freely." See: TDNT—5:871, 794; BAGD—631a; THAYER—491b.

3956. **πᾶς** {1243x} **pas** *pas;* incl. all the forms of declension; appar. a primary word; *all, any, every,* the *whole:*—all {748x}, all things {170x}, every {117x}, all men {41x}, whosoever {31x}, everyone {28x}, whole {12x}, all manner of {11x}, every man {11x}, no + 3756 {9x}, every thing {7x}, any {7x}, whatsoever {6x}, whosoever + 3739 + 302 {3x}, always + 1223 {3x}, daily + 2250 {2x}, any thing {2x}, no + 3361 {2x}, not tr {7x}, misc. {26x} = all means, any one, × daily, + ever, every-way, as many as, × thoroughly, whole. See: TDNT—5:886, 795; BAGD—631b; THAYER—491b.

3957. **πάσχα** {29x} **pascha**, *pas'-khah;* of Chald. or. [comp. 6453]; the *Passover* (the meal, the day, the festival or the special sacrifices connected with it):—Easter {1x}, Passover {28x}.

Pascha is the Greek spelling o the Aramaic word for the Passover, from the Hebrew *pasach,* "to pass over, to spare," a feast instituted by God in commemoration of the deliverance of Israel from Egypt, and anticipatory of the expiatory sacrifice of Christ. The word signifies **(1)** "the Passover Feast," e.g., Mt 26:2; Jn 2:13, 23; 6:4; 11:55; 12:1; 13:1; 18:39; 19:14; Acts 12:4; Heb 11:28; **(2)** by metonymy, **(2a)** "the Paschal Supper," Mt 26:18, 19; Mk 14:16; Lk 22:8, 13; **(2b)** "the Paschal lamb," e.g., Mk 14:12 (cf. Ex 12:21); Lk 22:7; **(2c)** "Christ Himself," 1 Cor 5:7. **(3)** It is also translated "Easter" which etymologically arises from the Anglo-Saxon *eastre* which is derived from *east* which means "to shine, to dawn, to spring forth" and is an excellent designation for the resurrection of Jesus Christ. Unfortunately the pagans also had a holiday which corresponded. See: TDNT—5:896, 797; BAGD—633b; THAYER—493d.

3958. **πάσχω** {42x} **paschō**, *pas'-kho;* incl. the forms

πάθω (**pathō**, *path'-o*) and

πένθω (**pěnthō**, *pen'-tho*), used only in certain tenses for it; appar. a primary verb; to *experience* a sensation or impression (usually painful):—suffer {39x}, be vexed {1x}, passion + 3588 {1x}, feel {1x}.

Pascho, "to suffer," is used **I.** of the "sufferings" of Christ **(1)** at the hands of men, e.g., Mt 16:21; 17:12; 1 Pet 2:23; **(2)** in His expiatory and vicarious sacrifice for sin, Heb 9:26; 13:12; 1 Pet 2:21; 3:18; 4:1; **(3)** including both (1) and (2), Lk 22:15; 24:26, 46; Acts 1:3, "passion"; 3:18; 17:3; Heb 5:8; **(4)** by the antagonism of the evil one, Heb 2:18; **II.** of human "suffering" **(1)** of followers of Christ, Acts 9:16; 2 Cor 1:6; Gal 3:4; Phil 1:29; 1 Th 2:14; 2 Th. 1:5; 2 Ti 1:12; 1 Pet 3:14, 17; 5:10; Rev 2:10; **(1a)** in identification with Christ in His crucifixion, as the spiritual ideal to be realized, 1 Pet 4:1; **(1b)** in a wrong way, 4:15; **(2)** of others, physically, **(2a)** as the result of demoniacal power, Mt 17:15, "is (sore) vexed"; cf. Mk 5:26; **(2b)** in a dream, Mt 27:19; **(2c)** through maltreatment, Lk 13:2; 1 Pet 2:19, 20; **(2d)** by a serpent (negatively), Acts 28:5, "felt"; **(3)** of the effect upon the whole body through the "suffering" of one member, 1 Cor 12:26, with application to a church. See: TDNT—5:904, 798; BAGD—633d; THAYER—494b.

3959. **Πάταρα** {1x} **Patara**, *pat'-ar-ah;* prob. of for. or.; *Patara*, a place in Asia Minor:—*Patara* {1x}. See: BAGD—634c; THAYER—494c.

3960. **πατάσσω** {10x} **patassō**, *pat-as'-so;* prob. prol. from *3817;* to *knock* (gently or with a weapon or fatally):—smite {9x}, strike {1x}.

Patasso, "to strike, smite," is used **I.** literally, of giving a blow with the hand, or fist or a weapon, Mt 26:51, "struck"; Lk 22:49, 50; Acts 7:24; 12:7; **II.** metaphorically, **(1)** of judgment meted out to Christ, Mt 26:31; Mk 14:27; **(2)** of the infliction of disease, by an angel, Acts 12:23; **(3)** of plagues to be inflicted upon men by two divinely appointed witnesses, Rev 11:6; **(4)** of judgment to be executed by Christ upon the nations, Rev 19:15, the instrument being His Word, described as a sword. See: TDNT—5:939, 804; BAGD—634d; THAYER—494c. comp. *5180.*

3961. **πατέω** {5x} **patĕō**, *pat-eh'-o;* from a der. prob. of *3817* (mean. a *"path"*); to *trample* (lit. or fig.):—tread {3x}, tread down {1x}, tread under foot {1x}.

Pateo is used **(1)** intransitively and figuratively, of "treading" upon serpents, Lk 10:19; **(2)** transitively, of "treading" on, down or under, **(2a)** of the desecration of Jerusalem by its foes, Lk 21:24; Rev. 11:2; **(2b)** of the avenging, by the Lord in Person hereafter, of this desecration and of the persecution of the Jews, in divine retribution, metaphorically spoken of as the "treading" of the winepress of God's wrath, Rev 14:20; 19:15 (cf. Is 63:2, 3). See: TDNT—5:940, 804; BAGD—634d; THAYER—494d.

3962. **πατήρ** {419x} **patēr**, *pat-ayr';* appar. a primary word; a *"father"* (lit. or fig., near or more remote):—Father {268x}, father {150x}.

Pater, from a root signifying "a nourisher, protector, upholder" (Lat., *pater,* Eng., "father," are akin), is used **(1)** of the nearest ancestor, e.g., Mt 2:22; **(2)** of a more remote ancestor, the progenitor of the people, a "forefather," e.g., Mt 3:9; 23:30; 1 Cor 10:1; the patriarchs, 2 Pet 3:4; **(3)** one advanced in the knowledge of Christ, 1 Jn 2:13; **(4)** metaphorically, of the originator of a family or company of persons animated by the same spirit as himself, as **(4a)** of Abraham, Rom 4:11, 12, 16, 17, 18, or **(4b)** of Satan, John 8:38, 41, 44; **(5)** of one who, as a preacher of the gospel and a teacher, stands in a "father's" place, caring for his spiritual children, 1 Cor 4:15 (not the same as a mere title of honor, which the Lord prohibited, Mt. 23:9); **(6)** of the members of the Sanhedrin, as of those who exercised religious authority over others, Acts 7:2; 22:1;

(7) of God in relation **(7a)** to those who have been born anew (Jn 1:12, 13), and **(7b)** so are believers, Eph 2:18; 4:6 (cf. 2 Cor 6:18), and **(7c)** imitators of their "Father," Mt 5:45, 48; 6:1, 4, 6, 8, 9, etc. **(7d)** Christ never associated Himself with them by using the personal pronoun "our"; **(7d1)** He always used the singular, "My Father," His relationship being unoriginated and essential, whereas theirs is by grace and regeneration, e.g., Mt 11:27; 25:34; Jn 20:17; Rev 2:27; 3:5, 21; **(7d2)** so the apostles spoke of God as the "Father" of the Lord Jesus Christ, e.g., Rom 15:6; 2 Cor 1:3; 11:31; Eph 1:3; Heb 1:5; 1 Pet 1:3; Rev 1:6;

(8) of God, as the "Father" **(8a)** of lights, i.e., the Source or Giver of whatsoever provides illumination, physical and spiritual, Jas 1:17; **(8b)** of mercies, 2 Cor 1:3; **(8c)** of glory, Eph 1:17; **(9)** of God, as Creator, Heb 12:9 (cf. Zec 12:1). **(10)** *Note:* Whereas the everlasting power and divinity of God are manifest in creation, His "Fatherhood" in spiritual relationship through faith is the subject of NT revelation, and waited for the presence on earth of the Son, Mt 11:27; Jn 17:25. The spiritual relationship is not universal, Jn 8:42, 44 (cf. Jn 8:12 and Gal 3:26). See: TDNT—5:945, 805; BAGD—635a; THAYER—494d.

3963. **Πάτμος** {1x} **Patmŏs**, *pat'-mos;* of uncert. der.; *Patmus*, an islet in the Mediterranean:—*Patmos* {1x}. See: BAGD—636c; THAYER—495c.

3964. **πατραλῴας** {1x} **patralōias**, *pat-ral-o'-as* πατρολῴας **patrŏlōias**, *pat-rol-o'-as;* from *3962* and the same as the latter part of *3389;* a *parricide:*—murderer of fathers {1x}. See: BAGD—636c; THAYER—495d.

3965. **πατριά** { 3x} **patria**, *pat-ree-ah';* as if fem. of a der. of *3962;* paternal *descent*, i.e. (concr.) a *group* of families or a whole *race* (*nation*):—family {1x}, kindred {1x}, lineage {1x}.

Patria, primarily "an ancestry, lineage," signifies in the NT "a family or tribe"; it is used **(1)** of the "family" of David, Lk 2:4, "lineage"; **(2)** in the wider sense of "nationalities, races," Acts 3:25, "kindreds"; **(3)** in Eph 3:15, "the whole family," the reference being to all those who are spiritually related to God the Father, He being the Author of their spiritual relationship to Him as His children, they being united to one another in "family" fellowship. See: TDNT—5:1015, 805; BAGD—636d; THAYER—495d.

3966. **πατριάρχης** {4x} **patriarchēs**, *pat-ree-arkh'-ace;* from *3965* and *757;* a *progenitor* ("patriarch"):—patriarch {4x}. See: BAGD—636d; THAYER—496a.

3967. **πατρικός** {1x} **patrikŏs**, *pat-ree-kos';* from *3962; paternal*, i.e. *ancestral:*—of (one's) fathers {1x}.

Patrikos, from *patria,* "a family," and *archo,* "to rule," is found in Acts 2:29; 7:8, 9; Heb. 7:4. See: TDNT—5:1021, 805; BAGD—636d; THAYER—496a.

3968. **πατρίς** {8x} **patris**, *pat-rece';* from *3962;* a *father-land*, i.e. *native town;* (fig.) heavenly *home:*—of (one's) own country {5x}, country {3x}.

Patris, primarily signifies "one's fatherland, native country, of one's own town," Mt 13:54, 57; Mk 6:1, 4; Lk 4:23–24; Jn 4:44; Heb 11:14. See: BAGD—636d; THAYER—496a.

3969. **Πατρόβας** {1x} **Patrŏbas**, *pat-rob'-as;* perh. contr. for Πατρόβιος **Patrŏbiŏs** (a compound of *3962* and *979*); *father's life; Patrobas*, a Chr.:—*Patrobas* {1x}. See: BAGD—637a; THAYER—496a.

3970. **πατροπαράδοτος** {1x} **patrŏparadŏtŏs**, *pat-rop-ar-ad'-ot-os;* from *3962* and a der. of *3860* (in the sense of *handing over* or *down*); *traditionary:*—received by tradition from (one's) fathers {1x}.

Patroparadotos, as a verb, means in 1 Pet 1:18 "received by tradition from your fathers": "Forasmuch as ye know that ye were not redeemed with corruptible things, *as* silver and gold, from your vain conversation *received* by tradition from your fathers." Syn.: 324, 353, 354, 568, 588, 618, 1209, 1523, 1926, 2210, 2865, 2975, 2983, 3028, 3335, 3336, 3858, 3880, 4327, 4355, 4356, 4380, 4381, 4382, 5562, 5264, 5274. See: BAGD—637a; THAYER—496b.

3971. **πατρῷος** {3x} **patrōiŏs**, *pat-ro'-os;* from *3962; paternal*, i.e. *hereditary:*—of (one's) fathers {2x}, of the fathers {1x}.

Patroos signifies "of one's fathers," or "received from one's fathers" in Acts 22:3; 24:14; 28:17. See: TDNT—5:1014,*; BAGD—637b; THAYER—496b.

3972. **Παῦλος** {164x} **Paulŏs**, *pŏw'-los;* of Lat. or.; (*little;* but remotely from a der. of *3973,* mean. the same); *Paulus*, the name of a Rom. and of an apostle:—Paul {163x}, Paulus (the deputy) {1x}. See: BAGD—637b; THAYER—496b.

3973. **παύω** {15x} **pauō**, *pŏw'-o;* a primary verb ("*pause*"); to *stop* (tran. or intr.), i.e. *restrain, quit, desist, come to an end:*—cease {15x}, leave {2x}, refrain {1x}.

Pauo, "to stop, to make an end," is used chiefly in the middle voice in the NT, signifying "to come to an end, to take one's rest, a willing cessation" (in contrast to the passive voice which denotes a forced cessation), **(1)** Lk 5:4, of a discourse; **(2)** Lk 8:24, of a storm; **(3)** Lk 11:1, of Christ's prayer; **(4)** Acts 5:42, of teaching and preaching; **(5)** Acts 6:13, of speaking against; **(6)** Acts 13:10, of evil doing; **(7)** Acts 20:1, of an uproar; **(8)** Acts 20:31, of admonition; **(9)** Acts 21:32, of a scourging; **(10)** 1 Cor 13:8, of tongues; **(11)** Eph 1:16, of giving thanks; **(12)** Col 1:9, of prayer; **(13)** Heb 10:2, of sacrifices; **(14)** 1 Pet 4:1, of "ceasing" from sin. **(15)** It is used in the active voice in 1 Pet 3:10, "let him cause his tongue to cease from evil." See: BAGD—638a; THAYER—496d.

3974. **Πάφος** {2x} **Paphŏs**, *paf'-os;* of uncert. der.; *Paphus*, a place in Cyprus:—*Paphos* {2x}. See: BAGD—638b; THAYER—497a.

3975. **παχύνω** {2x} **pachunō**, *pakh-oo'-no;* from a der. of *4078* (mean. *thick*); to *thicken*, i.e. (by impl.) to *fatten* (fig. *stupefy* or *render callous*):—wax gross {2x}.

Pachuno, from *pachus,* "thick," signifies "to thicken, fatten"; **(1)** in the passive voice, "to grow fat"; metaphorically said of the heart, to wax gross or dull, Mt 13:15; Acts 28:27. **(2)** "Wax" denotes slowly, thin layer by thin layer, until thick and hardened. See: TDNT—5:1022, 816; BAGD—638b; THAYER—497a.

3976. **πέδη** {3x} **pĕdē**, *ped'-ay;* ultimately from *4228;* a *shackle* for the feet:—fetter {3x}.

Pede, "a fetter" (akin to *peza,* "the instep," and *pous,* "a foot"; cf. Eng. prefix *ped-*), occurs in Mk 5:4, twice, and Lk 8:29. See: BAGD—638c; THAYER—497b.

3977. **πεδινός** {1x} **pĕdinŏs**, *ped-ee-nos';* from a der. of *4228* (mean. the *ground*); *level* (as easy for the *feet*):—plain + 5117 {1x}. See: BAGD—638c; THAYER—497b.

3978. **πεζεύω** {1x} **pĕzĕuō**, *ped-zyoo'-o;* from the same as *3979;* to *foot* a journey, i.e. *travel* by land:—go afoot {1x}.

Pezeuo is to travel on foot (not on horseback or in carriage), or (if opp. to going by sea) by land, Acts 20:13. See: BAGD—638d; THAYER—497b.

3979. **πεζῇ** {2x} **pĕzēi**, *ped-zay';* dat. fem. of a der. of *4228* (as adv.); *foot-wise*, i.e.

by *walking:*—afoot {1x}, on foot {1x}. See: BAGD—638d; THAYER—497b.

3980. **πειθαρχέω** {4x} **pĕitharchĕō**, *pi-tharkh-eh'-o;* from a compound of *3982* and *757;* to *be persuaded* by a *ruler,* i.e. (gen.) to *submit* to authority; by anal. to *conform* to advice:—hearken {1x}, obey {2x}, to obey magistrates {1x}.

This word means "to obey one in authority" and is translated **(1)** "obey" in Acts 5:29, 32; **(2)** Titus 3:1, "to obey magistrates"; and **(3)** in Acts 27:21, "hearkened." See: TDNT—6:9, 818; BAGD—638d; THAYER—497b.

3981. **πειθός** {1x} **pĕithŏs**, *pi-thos';* from *3982; persuasive:*—enticing {1x}.

Peithos, "apt to persuade" (from *peitho,* "to persuade"), is used in 1 Cor 2:4, "enticing." See: TDNT—6:8, 818; BAGD—639a; THAYER—497c.

3982. **πείθω** {55x} **pĕithō**, *pi'-tho;* a primary verb; to *convince* (by argument, true or false); by anal. to *pacify* or *conciliate* (by other fair means); refl. or pass. to *assent* (to evidence or authority), to *rely* (by inward certainty):—persuade {22x}, trust {8x}, obey {7x}, have confidence {6x}, believe {3x}, be confident {2x}, misc. {7x} = agree, assure, wax confident, make friend, yield.

Peitho, **(1)** in the active voice, signifies **(1a)** "to apply persuasion, to prevail upon or win over, to persuade," bringing about a change of mind by the influence of reason or moral considerations, e.g., in Mt 27:20; 28:14; Acts 13:43; 19:8; **(1b)** in the passive voice, "to be persuaded, believe", e.g., Lk 16:31; 20:6; Acts 17:4, "believed"; 21:14; 26:26; Rom 8:38; 14:14; 15:14; 2 Ti 1:5, 12; Heb 6:9; 11:13; 13:18, "trust." **(2)** *Peitho,* intransitively, in the perfect and pluperfect active, "to have confidence, trust," is rendered "to trust" in Mt 27:43; Mk 10:24; Lk 11:22; 18:9; 2 Cor 1:9; 10:7; Phil 2:24; 3:4; Heb 2:13; in the present middle, Heb 13:18. **(3)** It also means "to persuade, to win over," in the passive and middle voices, "to be persuaded, to listen to, to obey," is **(3a)** so used with this meaning, in the middle voice, e.g., in Acts 5:36–37 (in v. 40, passive voice, "they agreed"); Rom 2:8; Gal 5:7; Heb 13:17; Jas 3:3. **(3b)** The "obedience" suggested is not by submission to authority, but resulting from persuasion. Syn.: *Peitho* and *pisteuo,* "to trust," **(1)** are closely related etymologically; **(2)** the difference in meaning is that the former implies the obedience that is produced by the latter, cf. Heb 3:18–19, where the disobedience of the Israelites is said to be the evidence of their unbelief Faith is of the heart, invisible to men; **(3)** obedience is of the conduct and may be observed. **(4)** When a man obeys God he gives the only possible evidence that in his heart he believes God. **(5)** Of course it is persuasion of the truth that results in faith (we believe because we are persuaded that the thing is true, a thing does not become true because it is believed), **(6)** but *peitho,* in NT suggests an actual and outward result of the inward persuasion and consequent faith. See: TDNT—6:1, 818; BAGD—639a; THAYER—497c.

3983. **πεινάω** {23x} **pĕinaō**, *pi-nah'-o;* from the same as *3993* (through the idea of pinching *toil;* "*pine*"); to *famish* (absol. or comp.); fig. to *crave:*—hunger {10x}, be an hungred {9x}, be hungry {3x}, hungry {1x}.

Peinao, "to hunger, be hungry, hungered," is used **(1)** literally, **(1a)** e.g., Mt 4:2; 12:1; 21:18; Rom 12:20; 1 Cor 11:21, 34; Phil 4:12; Rev 7:16; **(1b)** Christ identifies Himself with His saints in speaking of Himself as suffering in their sufferings in this and other respects, Mt 25:35, 42; **(2)** metaphorically, Mt 5:6; Lk 6:21, 25; Jn 6:35. See: TDNT—6:12, 820; BAGD—640a; THAYER—498a.

3984. **πεῖρα** {2x} **pĕira**, *pi'-rah;* from the base of *4008* (through the idea of *piercing*); a *test,* i.e. *attempt, experience:*—assay + 2983 {1x}, trial {1x}.

Peira, "a making trial, an experiment," is used with *lambano,* "to receive or take," **(1)** in Heb 11:29, rendered "assaying," and **(2)** Heb 11:36, in the sense of "having experience of" (akin to *peirao,* "to assay, to try"), "had trial." See: TDNT—6:23, 822; BAGD—640a; THAYER—498b.

3985. **πειράζω** {39x} **pĕirazō**, *pi-rad'-zo;* from *3984; to test* (obj.), i.e. *endeavor, scrutinize, entice, discipline:*—assay {1x}, examine {1x}, go about {1x}, prove {1x}, tempt {29x}, tempter {2x}, try {4x}.

(1) Testing will cause its recipients to appear as what they always have been. This is predominantly, though not exclusively, the sense of *peirazo.* **(2)** Nothing in the word requires it to refer to a trial given with the intention of entangling the person in sins. **(3)** *Peirazo* properly means to make an experience of, to pierce or search into, or to attempt (Acts 16:7, 24:6). **(4)** It also signifies testing whose intention was to discover whether a person or thing was good or evil or strong or weak (Mt 16:1; 19:3; 22:18); or **(5)** if the outcome is already was known to the tester, to reveal the same to the one being tested (2 Cor 13:5). **(5)** Sinners are said to tempt God, when they put Him to the test by refusing to believe His word until He manifests His power. **(6)** God tempts people only in the sense of self-knowledge and so that they may and often do emerge from testing holier, humbler, and stronger than they were before. **(7)** *Peirazo* applied also to the solicitations and suggestions of satan, the tempter (Mt 4:3; 1 Th 3:5), putting one to a test with the intentions and the desire that the proved may not turn out approved, but reprobate, and break down under the test. Satan never proves in order to approve, nor tests that he may accept. Syn.: 1381. See: TDNT—6:23, 822; BAGD—640b; THAYER—498b.

3986. **πειρασμός** {21x} **pĕirasmŏs**, *pi-ras-mos';* from *3985;* a putting to *proof* (by experiment [of good], *experience* [of evil], solicitation, discipline or provocation); by impl. *adversity:*—temptation {19x}, temptations {1x}, × try {1x}.

Peirasmos is used of **I.** "trials" with a beneficial purpose and effect, **(1)** of "trials" or "temptations," divinely permitted or sent, Lk 22:28; Acts 20:19; Jas 1:2; 1 Pet 1:6; 4:12, "to try"; 2 Pet 2:9 (singular); Rev 3:10, "temptation"; **(2)** in Jas 1:12, "temptation" used in the widest sense; **(2a)** with a good or neutral significance, Gal 4:14, of Paul's physical infirmity, "a temptation" to the Galatian converts, of such a kind as to arouse feelings of natural repugnance; **(3)** of "trials" of a varied character, **(3a)** Mt 6:13 and Lk 11:4, where believers are commanded to pray not to be led into such by forces beyond their own control; **(3b)** Mt 26:41; Mk 14:38; Lk 22:40, 46, where they are commanded to watch and pray against entering into "temptations" by their own carelessness or disobedience; in all such cases God provides "the way of escape"; **(3c)** 1 Cor 10:13 (where *peirasmos* occurs twice). **II.** Of "trial" definitely designed to lead to wrong doing, "temptation," Lk 4:13; 8:13; 1 Ti 6:9; **III.**of "trying" or challenging God, by men, Heb 3:8. See: TDNT—6:23, 822; BAGD—640d; THAYER—498d.

3987. **πειράω** {3x} **pĕiraō**, *pi-rah'-o;* from *3984;* to *test* (subj.), i.e. (refl.) to *attempt:*—assay {1x}, go about {1x}, vr tempted {1x}.

(1) to make a trial of, to attempt, Acts 9:26, of Saul [Paul] attempting to join himself to the Jerusalem disciples; **(2)** to test, to make trial of one, put him to proof, Acts 26:21, of the Jews attempting to gain a case against Paul that would allow for them to kill him; and **(3)** in particular, to attempt to induce one to commit some (esp. carnal) crime, Heb 4:15, of Christ being tempted in all points as we are.See: TDNT—6:23, 822; BAGD—641a; THAYER—499a.

3988. **πεισμονή** {1x} **pĕismŏnē**, *pice-mon-ay';* from a presumed der. of *3982; persuadableness,* i.e. *credulity:*—persuasion {1x}.

In Gal 5:8 the meaning is this influence that has won you over, or that seems likely to do so. See: TDNT—6:9, 818; BAGD—641b; THAYER—499b.

3989. **πέλαγος** {2x} **pĕlagŏs**, *pel'-ag-os;* of uncert. aff.; deep or open *sea,* i.e. the *main:*—depth {1x}, sea {1x}.

Pelagos is the vast uninterrupted expanse of open water as distinguished from a sea broken by islands and shut in by coasts and headlines. It primarily suggests the breadth of the open sea, Acts 27:5, and sometimes its depth, Mt18:6. Syn.: 2281. See: BAGD—641b; THAYER—499b.

3990. **πελεκίζω** {1x} **pĕlĕkizō**, *pel-ek-id'-zo;* from a der. of *4141* (mean. an *axe*); to *chop* off (the head), i.e. *truncate:*—behead {1x}. See: BAGD—641c; THAYER—499b.

3991. **πέμπτος** {4x} **pĕmptŏs**, *pemp'-tos;* from *4002; fifth:*—fifth {4x}. See: BAGD—641c; THAYER—499c.

3992. **πέμπω** {81x} **pĕmpō**, *pem'-po;* appar. a primary verb; to *dispatch* (from the subj. view or point of *departure,* whereas ἵημι **hiēmi** [as a stronger form of εἶμι **ĕimi**] refers rather to the obj. point or *terminus ad quem,* and *4724* denotes prop. the *orderly* motion involved), espec. on a temporary errand; also to *transmit, bestow,* or *wield:*—send {77x}, thrust in {2x}, again send {2x}.

Pempo, "to send," is used **(1)** of persons: **(1a)** Christ, by the Father, Lk 20:13; Jn 4:34; 5:23, 24, 30, 37; 6:38, 39, (40), 44; 7:16, 18, 28, 33; 8:16, 18, 26, 29; 9:4; 12:44, 45, 49; 13:20 (2nd part); 14:24; 15:21; 16:5; Rom 8:3; **(1b)** the Holy Spirit, Jn 14:26; 15:26; 16:7; **(1c)** Elijah, Lk 4:26; **(1d)** John the Baptist, Jn 1:33; **(1e)** disciples and apostles, e.g., Mt 11:2; Jn 20:21; **(1f)** servants, e.g., Lk 20:11, 12; **(1g)** officials, Mt 14:10; **(1h)** messengers, e.g., Acts 10:5, 32, 33; 15:22, 25; 2 Cor 9:3; Eph 6:22; Phil 2:19, 23, 25; 1 Th 3:2, 5; Titus 3:12; **(1i)** a prisoner, Acts 25:25, 27; **(1k)** *potentates,* by God, 1 Pet 2:14; **(1l)** an angel, Rev 22:16; **(1m)** demons, Mk 5:12; **(2)** of things, Acts 11:29; Phil 4:16; 2 Th 2:11; Rev 1:11; 11:10; 14:15, 18, "thrust in." Syn.: *Pempo* is a more general term than *apostello; apostello* usually suggests official or authoritative sending. A comparison of the usages mentioned above shows how nearly (in some cases practically quite) interchangeably they are used, and yet on close consideration the distinction just mentioned is discernible; in the Gospel of John, cf. *pempo* in 5:23, 24, 30, 37, *apostello* in 5:33, 36, 38; *pempo* in 6:38, 39, 44, *apostello* in 6:29, 57; the two are not used simply for the sake of variety of expression. *Pempo* is not used in the

Lord's prayer in Jn 17, whereas *apostello* is used six times. See: TDNT—1:398, 67; BAGD—641d; THAYER—499c.

3993. **πένης** {1x} **pĕnēs**, *pen'-ace;* from a primary πένω **pĕnō**, (to *toil* for daily subsistence); *starving,* i.e. *indigent:*—poor {1x}.

Penes, "a laborer" (akin to *penomai,* "to work for one's daily bread"), is translated "poor" in 2 Cor 9:9. Syn.: *Penes* is one who is so poor he earns his bread by daily labour; whereas, *ptochos* (4434) is one who only obtains his living by begging. See; TDNT—6:37, 824; BAGD—642c; THAYER—499d. comp. *4434.*

3994. **πενθερά** {6x} **pĕnthĕra**, *pen-ther-ah';* fem. of *3995;* a *wife's mother:*—mother in law {3x}, wife's mother {3x}.

Penthera, the feminine of *pentheros* ("a father-in-law"), is translated **(1)** "mother in law" Mt 8:14; 10:35; Lk 12:53 twice; and **(2)** "wife's mother" in Mk 1:30; Lk 4:38. See: BAGD—642c; THAYER—500a.

3995. **πενθερός** {1x} **pĕnthĕrŏs**, *pen-ther-os';* of uncert. aff.; a *wife's father:*—father in law {1x}. See: BAGD—642c; THAYER—500a.

3996. **πενθέω** {10x} **pĕnthĕō**, *pen-theh'-o;* from *3997;* to *grieve* (the feeling or the act):—mourn {7x}, bewail {1x}, wail {2x}.

(1) *Pentheo* means to mourn, bewail primarily for the dead, but also includes any other passionate lamenting; a grief so all-emcompassing that it cannot be hidden. This word means "to mourn for, lament," and is used **(1)** of mourning in general, Mt 5:4; 9:15; Lk 6:25; **(2)** of sorrow for the death of a loved one, Mk 16:10; **(3)** of "mourning" for the overthrow of Babylon and the Babylonish system, Rev 18:11, 15, "wailing"; v. 19 wailing; **(4)** of sorrow for sin or for condoning it, Jas 4:9; 1 Cor 5:2; **(5)** of grief for those in a local church who show no repentance for evil committed, 2 Cor 12:21, "bewail." Syn.: 2354, 2875, 3076. See: TDNT—6:40, 825; BAGD—642c; THAYER—500a.

3997. **πένθος** {5x} **pĕnthŏs**, *pen'-thos;* strengthened from the alt. of *3958; grief:*—mourning {2x}, sorrow {3x}.

Penthos, is translated **(1)** "mourning" in Jas 4:9; Rev. 18:8; and **(2)** "sorrow": "How much she hath glorified herself, and lived deliciously, so much torment and sorrow [*penthos*] give her: for she saith in her heart, I sit a queen, and am no widow, and shall see no sorrow [*penthos*]" (Rev 18:7 twice; cf. 21:4). Syn.: 253, 3076, 3077, 3600, 3601, 4036, 5604. See: TDNT—6:40, 825; BAGD—642d; THAYER—500a.

3998. **πενιχρός** {1x} **pĕnichrŏs**, *pen-ikh-ros';* prol. from the base of *3993, necessitous:*—poor {1x}. See: TDNT—6:40, 824; BAGD—642d; THAYER—500a.

3999. **πεντακίς** {1x} **pĕntakis**, *pen-tak-ece';* mult. adv. from *4002; five times:*—five times {1x}. See: BAGD—643a; THAYER—500b.

4000. **πεντακισχίλιοι** {6x} **pĕntakischiliŏi**, *pen-tak-is-khil'-ee-oy;* from *3999* and *5507; five times a thousand:*—five thousand {6x}. See: BAGD—643a; THAYER—500b.

4001. **πεντακόσιοι** {2x} **pĕntakŏsiŏi**, *pen-tak-os'-ee-oy;* from *4002* and *1540; five hundred:*—five hundred {2x}. See: BAGD—643a; THAYER—500b.

4002. **πέντε** {38x} **pĕntĕ**, *pen'-teh;* a primary number; "*five*":—five {36x}, three score and fifteen + 1440 {1x}, fifty thousand + 3461 {1x}. See: BAGD—643a; THAYER—500b.

4003. **πεντεκαιδέκατος** {1x} **pĕntĕkaidĕkatŏs**, *pen-tek-ahee-dek'-at-os;* from *4002* and *2532* and *1182; five and tenth:*—fifteenth {1x}. See: BAGD—643a; THAYER—500b.

4004. **πεντήκοντα** {7x} **pĕntēkŏnta**, *pen-tay'-kon-tah;* mult. of *4002; fifty:*—fifty {7x}. See: BAGD—643b; THAYER—500a.

4005. **πεντηκοστή** {3x} **pĕntēkŏstē**, *pen-tay-kos-tay';* fem. of the ord. of *4004; fiftieth* (*2250* being impl.) from Passover, i.e. the festival of "*Pentecost*":—Pentecost {3x}.

Pentekoste, an adjective denoting "fiftieth," is used as a noun, with "day" understood, i.e., the "fiftieth" day after the Passover, counting from the second day of the Feast, Acts 2:1; 20:16; 1 Cor 16:8. See: TDNT—6:44, 826; BAGD—643b; THAYER—500b.

4006. **πεποίθησις** {6x} **pĕpŏithēsis**, *pep-oy'-thay-sis;* from the perfect of the alt. of *3958; reliance:*—confidence {5x}, trust {1x}.

Pepoitesis, akin to *peitho,* denotes "persuasion, assurance, confidence," and is translated **(1)** "confidence" in 2 Cor 1:15; 8:22; 10:2; Eph 3:12; Phil 3:4, and **(2)** "trust" in 2 Cor 3:4. See: TDNT—6:7, 818; BAGD—643b; THAYER—500b.

4007. **περ** {4x} **pĕr**, *per;* from the base of *4008;* an enclitic particle significant of *abundance* (*thoroughness*), i.e. *emphasis; much, very* or *ever:*—whomsoever + 3739 {1x}, not tr {3x}. See: BAGD—643c; THAYER—500c.

4008. **πέραν** {23x} **pĕran**, *per'-an;* appar. acc. of an obs. der. of πείρω **pĕirō**, (to "*pierce*"); *through* (as adv. or prep.), i.e. *across:*—other side {10x}, beyond {7x}, over {3x}, on the other side {2x}, farther side {1x}.

This word means "on the other side, across," is **(1)** used with the definite article, signifying the regions "beyond," the opposite shore, Mt 8:18 etc. **(2)** With verbs of going it denotes direction towards and "beyond" a place, e.g., Jn 10:40. **(3)** It frequently indicates "beyond," of locality, without a verb of direction, Mt 16:5; Mk 10:1; Jn 1:28; 3:26. **(4)** As an adverb, it signifies "beyond, on the other side" and is used **(4a)** as a preposition and translated "on the other side of," e.g., in Mk 5:1; Lk 8:22; Jn 6:1; 6:22, 25; **(4b)** as a noun with the article, e.g., Mt 8:18, 28; 14:22; 16:5. See: BAGD—643d; THAYER—500c.

4009. **πέρας** {4x} **pĕras**, *per'-as;* from the same as *4008;* an *extremity:*—end {2x}, utmost part {1x}, uttermost part {1x}.

Peras, "a limit, boundary" (from *pera,* "beyond"), is used **(1)** of space, chiefly in the plural, in **(1a)** Mt 12:42, "uttermost parts"; **(1b)** Lk 11:31, "utmost"; **(1c)** Rom 10:18 "ends"; **(2)** of the termination of something occurring in a period, Heb 6:16, "an end" said of strife. See: BAGD—644a; THAYER—500d.

4010. **Πέργαμος** {2x} **Pĕrgamŏs**, *per'-gam-os;* from *4444; fortified; Pergamus,* a place in Asia Minor:—Pergamos {2x}. See: BAGD—644b; THAYER—500d.

4011. **Πέργη** {3x} **Pĕrgē**, *perg'-ay;* prob. from the same as *4010;* a *tower; Perga,* a place in Asia Minor:—Perga {3x}. See: BAGD—644b; THAYER—501a.

4012. **περί** {331x} **pĕri**, *per-ee';* from the base of *4008;* prop. *through* (all over), i.e. *around;* fig. *with respect* to; used in various applications, of place, cause or time (with the gen. denoting the *subject* or *occasion* or *superlative* point; with the acc. the *locality, circuit, matter, circumstance* or general *period*):—of {148x}, for {61x}, concerning {40x}, about {31x}, as touching {8x}, touching {3x}, whereof + 3739 {3x}, not tr {4x}, misc {33x} = (there-) about, above, against, at, on behalf of, × and his company, which concern, × how it will go with, there of, on, over, pertaining (to), for sake, × (e-) state, whereby, wherein, with. In composition it retains substantially the same meaning of circuit (*around*), excess (*beyond*), or completeness (*through*). See: TDNT—6:53, 827; BAGD—644b; THAYER—501a.

4013. **περιάγω** {6x} **pĕriagō**, *per-ee-ag'-o;* from *4012* and *71;* to *take around* (as a companion); refl. to *walk around:*—compass {1x}, go about {3x}, go round about {1x}, lead about {1x}.

Periago, **(1)** "to lead about" is found in 1 Cor 9:5; or **(2)** intransitively, "to go about, to go up and down" and is so used in Mt 4:23; 9:35; Mk 6:6 "go round about"; Acts 13:11; **(3)** "to compass regions" Mt 23:15. See: BAGD—645c; THAYER—502a.

4014. **περιαιρέω** {4x} **pĕriairĕō**, *per-ee-ahee-reh'-o;* from *4012* and *138* (incl. its alt.); to *remove* all *around,* i.e. *unveil, cast off* (anchor); fig. to *expiate:*—take away {3x}, take up {1x}.

Periaireo, "to take away that which surrounds" is used **(1)** literally, of "having taken up" the anchors from the different sides of the ship, Acts 27:40; **(2)** metaphorically, **(2a)** of "taking away" the veil off the hearts of Israel, 2 Cor 3:16; **(2b)** of hope of rescue, Acts 27:20; **(2c)** of sins (negatively), Heb 10:11. See: BAGD—645d; THAYER—502b.

4015. **περιαστράπτω** {2x} **pĕriastraptō**, *per-ee-as-trap'-to;* from *4012* and *797;* to *flash* all *around,* i.e. *to envelop in light:*—shine round {1x}, shine round about {1x}.

Periastrapto, "to flash around, shine round about" (*peri,* and *astrape,* "shining brightness"), is used in Acts 9:3 and 22:6 of the same circumstance as in 26:13, of the heavenly light shine around Saul [Paul] on the Damascus road. See: BAGD—645d; THAYER—502b.

4016. **περιβάλλω** {24x} **pĕriballō**, *per-ee-bal'-lo;* from *4012* and *906;* to *throw* all *around,* i.e. *invest* (with a palisade or with clothing):—clothe {7x}, clothed with {4x}, array {3x}, array in {3x}, clothe in {3x}, cast about {3x}, put on {1x}.

Periballo, as a verb, (in 23 of the 24 uses) means **(1)** "to cast around or about, to put on, array," or, in the middle and passive voices, "to clothe oneself": "Naked, and ye clothed me: I was sick, and ye visited me" (Mt 25:36; cf. vss 38, 43). **(2)** It is most frequent in the Apocalypse, where it is found some 12 times. **(3)** In Lk 19:43 it is used of "casting" up a bank or palisade against a city, "shall cast a trench about thee." A palisade is built by digging a large trench. Syn.: 294, 1463, 1737, 1746, 1902, 2439. See: BAGD—646a; THAYER—502b.

4017. **περιβλέπω** {7x} **pĕriblĕpō**, *per-ee-blep'-o;* from *4012* and *991;* to *look* all *around:*—look round about {3x}, look round about upon {2x}, look round about on {2x}.

Periblepo, as a verb, means "to look about, or round about, on" and is used in the middle voice: "And when He had looked round about on them with anger" (Mk 3:5; cf. 3:34, 5:32; 9:8; 10:23; 11:11; Lk 6:10). Syn.: 308, 352, 578, 816, 872, 991, 1689, 1896, 1914, 1980, 1983, 2300, 2334, 3706, 3708, 3879, 4648. See: BAGD—646b; THAYER—502c.

4018. **περιβόλαιον** {2x} **pĕribŏlaiŏn**, *per-ib-ol'-ah-yon;* neut. of a presumed der. of *4016;* something *thrown around* one, i.e. a *mantle, veil:*—covering {1x}, vesture {1x}.

Peribolaion, lit. denotes "something thrown around" (*peri,* "around," *ballo,* "to throw"); hence, **(1)** "a veil, covering," 1 Cor 11:15; or **(2)** "a mantle around the body, a vesture," Heb 1:12. See: BAGD—646c; THAYER—502c.

4019. **περιδέω** {1x} **pĕridĕō**, *per-ee-deh'-o;* from *4012* and *1210;* to *bind around* one, i.e. *enwrap:*—bind about {1x}.

Perodeo, (*peri,* "around," with "to bind around"), is used in Jn 11:44 of the napkin around the face of Lazarus. See: BAGD—646c; THAYER—502d.

περιδρέμω **pĕridrĕmō**. See *4063*.

περιέλλω **pĕriĕllō**. See *4014*.

περιέλθω **pĕriĕlthō**. See *4022*.

4020. **περιεργάζομαι** {1x} **pĕriĕrgazŏmai**, *per-ee-er-gad'-zom-ahee;* from *4012* and *2038;* to *work* all *around,* i.e. *bustle about* (*meddle*):—be a busybody {1x}.

This word literally means to be working round about, instead of at one's own business and signifies to take more pains than enough about a thing, to waste one's labor, to be meddling with, trifling in needless useless matters, or bustling about, overbusied in other people's matters (2 Th 3:11). See: BAGD—646d; THAYER—502d.

4021. **περίεργος** {2x} **pĕriĕrgŏs**, *per-ee'-er-gos;* from *4012* and *2041;* *working all around,* i.e. *officious* (*meddlesome,* neut. plur. *magic*):—busybody {1x}, curious arts {1x}.

This word means busy **(1)** about trifles and neglectful of important matters, esp. busy about other folks' affairs, a busybody (1 Ti 5:13); and **(2)** with things that are impertinent and superfluous, the curious arts (Acts 19:9). "Curious" is derived from "care" and means devoting much time and energy to learn and master matters that are less than eternal. Syn.: 4020. See: BAGD—646d; THAYER—502b.

4022. **περιέρχομαι** {4x} **pĕriĕrchŏmai**, *per-ee-er'-khom-ahee;* from *4012* and *2064* (incl. its alt.); to *come* all *around,* i.e. *stroll, vacillate, veer:*—fetch a compass {1x}, vagabond {1x}, wandering about {2x}.

Perierchomai means "to go about" (*peri,* "about," *erchomai,* "to go"), and is said **(1)** of "navigating a ship under difficulty owing to contrary winds," Acts 28:13, "we fetched a compass." **(2)** In 1 Ti 5:13 and Heb 11:37, *perierchomai* means "to go about or around," is translated "to wander about." It is also translated "vagabond", one who wanders about, Acts 19:13. See: TDNT—2:682, 257; BAGD—646d; THAYER—502d.

4023. **περιέχω** {3x} **pĕriĕchō**, *per-ee-ekh'-o;* from *4012* and *2192;* to *hold* all *around,* i.e. *include, clasp* (fig.):—be astonished + 2285 {1x}, after this manner + 5126 + 5176 {1x}, be contained {1x}.

Pericho literally means to have all around, to completely hold all around, and denotes **(1)** to contain, enclose (1 Pet 2:6); **(2)** after this manner, completely following this manner, lit. "having this form" (Acts 23:25); and **(3)** astonished, as the person is completely seized by an event (Lk 5:9). See: BAGD—647a; THAYER—502d.

4024. **περιζώννυμι** {7x} **pĕrizōnnumi**, *per-id-zone'-noo-mee;* from *4012* and *2224;* to *gird* all *around,* i.e. (middle or passive voice) to *fasten on one's belt* (lit. or fig.):—gird (one's) self {3x}, be girded about {1x}, have girded {1x}, have girded about {1x}, be girt {1x}.

Perizonnumi, as a verb, means "to gird around or about," and is used **(1)** literally, **(1a)** of "girding" oneself for service: "Blessed *are* those servants, whom the lord when he cometh shall find watching: verily I say unto you, that he shall gird himself, and make them to sit down to meat, and will come forth and serve them" (Lk 12:37; 17:8); **(2)** for rapidity of movement: "And the angel said unto him, Gird thyself, and bind on thy sandals" (Acts 12:8); **(2)** figuratively, of the condition for service on the part of the followers of Christ: "Let your loins be girded about, and *your* lights burning" (Lk 12:35; cf. Eph 6:14); **(3)** emblematically, **(3a)** of Christ's priesthood: "And in the midst of the seven candlesticks *one* like unto the Son of man, clothed with a garment down to the foot, and girt about the paps with a golden girdle" (Rev 1:13, indicative of majesty of attitude and action, the middle voice suggesting the particular interest taken by Christ in "girding" Himself thus); and **(3b)** so of the action of the angels: "KJV Revelation 15:6 And the seven angels came out of the temple, having the seven plagues, clothed in pure and white linen, and having their breasts girded with golden girdles" (Rev 15:6). Syn.: 328, 1241, 2224. See: TDNT—5:302, 702; BAGD—647b; THAYER—503a.

4025. **περίθεσις** {1x} **pĕrithĕsis**, *per-ith'-es-is;* from *4060;* a *putting* all *around,* i.e. *decorating* oneself with:—wearing {1x}.

Perithesis, "a putting around or on" (*peri,* "around," *tithemi,* "to put"), is used in 1 Pet 3:3 of "wearing" of gold. See: BAGD—647; THAYER—503b.

4026. **περιΐστημι** {4x} **pĕriistēmi**, *per-ee-is'-tay-mee;* from *4012* and *2476;* to *stand* all *around,* i.e. (near) to *be a bystander,* or (aloof) to *keep away* from:—avoid {1x}, shun {1x}, stand by {1x}, stand round about {1x}.

Periistemi **(1)** in the active voice means to stand by or around about (Jn 11:42; Acts 25:7); and **(2)** in the middle voice means to turn oneself about for the purpose of avoiding or shunning something: **(2a)** profane babblings (2 Ti 2:16); **(2b)** foolish questions, genealogies, strife, etc. (Titus 3:9). See: BAGD—647c; THAYER—503b.

4027. **περικάθαρμα** {1x} **pĕrikatharma**, *per-ee-kath'-ar-mah;* from a compound of *4012* and *2508;* something *cleaned* off all *around,* i.e. *refuse* (fig.):—filth {1x}.

This word denotes "offscouring, refuse" (lit., "cleanings," i.e., that which is thrown away in cleansing; from *perikathairo,* "to purify all around," i.e., completely. It is used in 1 Cor 4:13 "the filth of the world" representing the most abject and despicable men, the scum or rubbish of humanity. See: TDNT—3:430, 381; BAGD—647d; THAYER—503b.

4028. **περικαλύπτω** {3x} **pĕrikaluptō**, *per-ee-kal-oop'-to;* from *4012* and *2572;* to *cover* all *around,* i.e. *entirely* (the face, a surface):—blindfold {1x}, cover {1x}, overlay {1x}.

This word means "to cover around" (*peri,* "around"), e.g., the face, and so, to blindfold, is translated **(1)** "cover" in Mk 14:65, of the face of Jesus in His scourging and mocking by the soldiers; **(2)** "blindfold" in Lk 22:64 of the same event; and **(3)** in Heb 9:4, it signifies "to overlay" of the gold on the ark of the covenant. See: BAGD—647d; THAYER—503c.

4029. **περίκειμαι** {5x} **pĕrikĕimai**, *per-ik'-i-mahee;* from *4012* and *2749;* to *lie* all *around,* i.e. *enclose, encircle, hamper* (lit. or fig.):—be hanged {2x}, be bound with {1x}, be compassed with {1x}, be compassed about with + 2192 {1x}.

Perikeimai, lit., "to lie around" (*peri,* "around," *keimai,* "to lie"), "to be compassed," is used **(1)** of binding fetters around a person, Acts 28:20; **(2)** in Mk 9:42, and Lk 17:2, to hang about a person's neck; **(3)** in Heb 5:2, to compass about, metaphorically of infirmities; and **(4)** in Heb 12:1, of those who have witness borne to their faith. See: TDNT—3:656, 425; BAGD—647d; THAYER—503c.

4030. **περικεφαλαία** {2x} **pĕrikĕphalaia**, *per-ee-kef-al-ah'-yah;* fem. of a compound of *4012* and *2776;* *encirclement of* the *head,* i.e. a *helmet:*—helmet {2x}.

This word (from *peri,* "around," and *kephale,* "a head") is used **(1)** figuratively in Eph 6:17, with reference to salvation, and **(2)** 1 Th 5:8, where it is described as "the hope of salvation." **(3)** The head is regarded here as standing for the seat of the intellect which has been enlightened by the Holy Spirit to comprehend all the aspects of salvation portrayed in the others parts of the armor. **(3a)** In Eph 6:17 salvation is a present experience of the Lord's deliverance of believers as those who are engaged in spiritual conflict; **(3b)** in 1 Th 5:8, the hope is that of the Lord's return, which encourages the believer to resist the spirit of the age in which he lives. See: TDNT—5:314, 702; BAGD—648a; THAYER—503d.

4031. **περικρατής** {1x} **pĕrikratēs**, *per-ee-krat-ace';* from *4012* and *2904;* *strong* all *around,* i.e. a *master* (*manager*):—+ come by {1x}.

This adjective signifies having full command of; it is used with *ginomai* (1096 —to become) and translated "to come by" (Acts 27:16). [cf. Eng. "How did you come by that new home?]. See: BAGD—648b; THAYER—503d.

4032. **περικρύπτω** {1x} **pĕrikruptō**, *per-ee-kroop'-to;* from *4012* and *2928;* to *conceal* all *around,* i.e. *entirely:*—hide {1x}.

Perikrupto signifies "to hide by placing something around, to conceal entirely, to keep hidden" (*peri,* "around," used intensively), Lk 1:24, where Elizabeth "hid" her pregnancy by wearing large clothing. See: BAGD—648b; THAYER—503d.

4033. **περικυκλόω** {1x} **pĕrikuklŏō**, *per-ee-koo-klŏ'-o;* from *4012* and *2944;* to *encircle* all *around,* i.e. *blockade completely:*—compass round {1x}. See: BAGD—648b; THAYER—503d.

4034. **περιλάμπω** {2x} **pĕrilampō**, *per-ee-lam'-po;* from *4012* and *2989;* to *illuminate* all *around,* i.e. *invest with a halo:*—shine round about {2x}.

Perilampo, "to shine around", is used **(1)** in Lk 2:9, "shone round about," of the glory of the Lord; so **(2)** in Acts 26:13, of the light from Heaven upon Saul of Tarsus. See: TDNT—4:16, 497; BAGD—648c; THAYER—503d.

4035. **περιλείπω** {2x} **pĕrilĕipō**, *per-ee-li'-po;* from *4012* and *3007;* to *leave* all *around,* i.e. (pass.) *survive:*—remain {2x}.

Perileipo, "to leave over," used in the middle voice, is translated "remain" in 1 Th 4:15, 17, where it stands for the living believers at the coming (the beginning of the Parousia) of Christ. See: TDNT—4:194,*; BAGD—648c; THAYER—503d.

4036. **περίλυπος** {5x} **pĕrilupŏs**, *per-il'-oo-pos;* from *4012* and *3077;* *grieved* all *around,* i.e. *intensely sad:*—exceeding sorrowful {2x}, very sorrowful {2x}, exceeding sorry {1x}.

Perilupos, as an adjective, means "very sad, deeply grieved" and is translated "exceedingly sorrowful": "Then saith He unto them, My soul is exceeding sorrowful, even unto death: tarry ye here, and watch with Me" (Mt 26:38; cf. Mk 14:34; Mk 6:26; Lk 18:23, 24). Syn.: 253, 3076, 3077, 3600, 3601, 3997, 5604. See: TDNT—4:323, 540; BAGD—648c; THAYER—503d.

4037. **περιμένω** {1x} **pĕrimĕnō**, *per-ee-men'-o;* from *4012* and *3306;* to *stay around,* i.e. *await:*—wait for {1x}.

Perimeno means to await an event, Acts 1:4, of "waiting" for the Holy Spirit, "the promise of the Father." See: TDNT—4:578, 581; BAGD—648c; THAYER—503d.

4038. **πέριξ** {1x} **pĕrix**, *per'-ix;* adv. from *4012;* all *around,* i.e. (as an adj.) *circumjacent:*—round about {1x}.

This word means round about: the neighbouring cities, Acts 5:16. See: BAGD—648d; THAYER—504a.

4039. **περιοικέω** {1x} **pĕriŏikĕō**, *per-ee-oy-keh'-o;* from *4012* and *3611;* to *reside around,* i.e. *be a neighbor:*—dwell round about {1x}. See: BAGD—648d; THAYER—504a.

4040. **περίοικος** {1x} **pĕriŏikŏs**, *per-ee'-oy-kos;* from *4012* and *3624;* *housed around,* i.e. *neighboring* (ellip. used as a noun):—neighbour {1x}. See: BAGD—648d; THAYER—504a.

4041. **περιούσιος** {1x} **pĕriŏusiŏs**, *per-ee-oo'-see-os;* from the pres. part. fem. of a compound of *4012* and *1510;* *being beyond* usual, i.e. *special* (one's *own possession*):—peculiar {1x}.

Periousios, "of one's own possession, one's own," qualifies the noun *laos,* "people," in Titus 2:14, "peculiar", a people selected by God from the other nations for His own possession. See: TDNT—6:57, 828; BAGD—648d; THAYER—504a.

4042. **περιοχή** {1x} **pĕriŏchē**, *per-ee-okh-ay';* from *4023;* a *being held around,* i.e. (concr.) a *passage* (of Scripture, as *circumscribed*):—a place {1x}.

Perioche, as a noun, in reference to a writing or book, "a portion or passage of its contents": "The place of the scripture which he read was this, He was led as a sheep to the slaughter; and like a lamb dumb before his shearer, so opened he not his mouth" (Acts 8:32). Syn.: 201, 402, 1096, 1502, 3837, 5117, 5247, 5564, 5602. See: BAGD—648d; THAYER—504a.

4043. **περιπατέω** {96x} **pĕripatĕō**, *per-ee-pat-eh'-o;* from *4012* and *3961;* to *tread* all *around,* i.e. *walk* at large (espec. as proof of ability); fig. to *live, deport oneself, follow* (as a companion or votary):—walk {93x}, go {1x}, walk about {1x}, be occupied {1x}. See: TDNT—5:940, 804; BAGD—649a; THAYER—504b.

4044. **περιπείρω** {1x} **pĕripĕirō**, *per-ee-pi'-ro;* from *4012* and the base of *4008;* to *penetrate entirely,* i.e. *transfix* (fig.):—pierce through {1x}.

Peripeiro means to put on a spit; hence, to pierce and is used metaphorically in 1 Tim 6:10 of torturing one's soul with many sorrows, "have pierced (themselves) through." See: BAGD—649d; THAYER—504d.

4045. **περιπίπτω** {3x} **pĕripiptō**, *per-ee-pip'-to;* from *4012* and *4098;* to *fall* into something all *around,* i.e. *light among* or *upon, be surrounded with:*—fall among {1x}, fall into {2x}.

Peripipto, "to fall around", hence signifies to "fall" in with, or among, to light upon, come across, and is translated **(1)** "fall among" in Lk 10:30, "among (robbers)"; and **(2)** "fall into" in Acts 27:41, **(2a)** "falling into", a part of a shore; and **(2b)** "fall into" in Jas 1:2, into temptation (i.e., trials). See: TDNT—6:173, 846; BAGD—649d; THAYER—504d.

4046. **περιποιέομαι** {2x} **pĕripŏiĕŏmai**, *per-ee-poy-eh'-om-ahee;* mid. voice from *4012* and *4160;* to *make around oneself,* i.e. *acquire* (*buy*):—purchase {2x}.

This word signifies "to gain" or "get for oneself, purchase"; middle voice in Acts 20:28 and 1 Ti 3:13. See: BAGD—650a; THAYER—504d.

4047. **περιποίησις** {5x} **pĕripŏiēsis**, *per-ee-poy'-ay-sis;* from *4046;* *acquisition* (the act or the thing); by extens. *preservation:*—purchased possession {1x}, to obtain + 1519 {1x}, obtaining {1x}, saving {1x}, peculiar + 1519 {1x}.

Peripoiesis, lit., "a making around" (*peri,* "around," *poieo,* "to do or make"), denotes **(1)** "the act of obtaining" anything, **(1a)** "to obtain", as of salvation, deliverence; 1 Th 5:9; **(1b)** "obtaining" salvation in its completeness, the glory of Christ; **(2)** "a thing acquired, an acquisition, possession," Eph 1:14, "(*God's* own) possession"; **(3)** 1 Pet 2:9, "a peculiar (people)"; cf. Is 43:21; **(4)** preservation, this may be the meaning in Heb 10:39, "saving." See: BAGD—650a; THAYER—504d.

4048. **περιρρήγνυμι** {1x} **pĕrirrhēgnumi**, *per-ir-hrayg'-noo mee;* from *4012* and *4486;* to *tear* all *around,* i.e. *completely away:*—rend off {1x}.

This word means "to tear off all round" and is said of garments in Acts 16:22. See: BAGD—650b; THAYER—505a.

4049. **περισπάω** {1x} **pĕrispaō**, *per-ee-spah'-o;* from *4012* and *4685;* to *drag* all *around,* i.e. (fig.) to *distract* (with care):—cumber {1x}.

Perispao literally means to draw around, to draw away, to distract and is used in the passive voice in the sense of being overoccupied about a thing; cumbered (Lk 10:40). See: BAGD—650b; THAYER—505a.

4050. **περισσεία** {4x} **pĕrissĕia**, *per-is-si'-ah;* from *4052;* *surplusage,* i.e. *superabundance:*—abundance {2x}, abundantly {1x}, superfluity {1x}.

Perisseia is an exceeding measure, something above the ordinary and is used **(1)** of the abundance of grace (Rom 5:17); **(2)** of the abundance of joy (2 Cor 8:2); **(3)** of the extension of the apostle's sphere of service through the practical fellowship of the saints at Corinth (2 Cor 10:15); and **(4)** metaphorically in Jas 1:21 of overflowing ["superfluity of"] wickedness. See: TDNT—6:63, 828; BAGD—650c; THAYER—505a.

4051. **περίσσευμα** {5x} **pĕrissĕuma**, *per-is'-syoo-mah;* from *4052;* a *surplus,* or *superabundance:*—abundance {4x}, that was left over and above {1x}.

Perisseuma denotes **(1)** "abundance" in a slightly more concrete form, **(1a)** 2 Cor 8:13–14, where it stands for the gifts in kind supplied by the saints. **(1b)** In Mt 12:34 and Lk 6:45 it is used of the "abundance" of the heart; **(2)** in Mk 8:8, of the broken pieces left after feeding the multitude "that was left"). See: TDNT—6:63, 828; BAGD—650c; THAYER—505b.

4052. **περισσεύω** {39x} **pĕrissĕuō**, *per-is-syoo'-o;* from *4053;* to *superabound* (in quantity or quality), *be in excess, be superfluous;* also (tran.) to *cause to superabound* or *excel:*—abound {17x}, abundance {3x}, remain {3x}, exceed {2x}, increase {2x}, be left {1x}, redound {1x}, misc. {10x} = be more abundant, be the better, enough and to spare, excel.

Perisseuo is used **I.** intransitively **(1)** "of exceeding a certain number, or measure, to be over, to remain," of the fragments after feeding the multitude (cf. *perisseuma*), Lk 9:17; Jn 6:12–13; **(2)** "to exist in abundance"; **(2a)** as of wealth, Lk 12:15; 21:4; **(2b)** of food, Lk 15:17. In this sense it is used also **(2c)** of consolation, 2 Cor 1:5; **(2d)** of the effect of a gift sent to meet the need of saints, 2 Cor 9:12; **(2d)** of rejoicing, Phil 1:26; **(3)** of what comes or falls to the lot of a person in large measure, **(3a)** as of the grace of God and the gift by the grace of Christ, Rom 5:15, **(3b)** of the sufferings of Christ, 2 Cor 1:5. **(3c)** In Mk 12:44 and Lk 21:4, "abundance." **(4)** "to redound to, or to turn out abundantly for something," as **(4a)** of the liberal effects of poverty, 2 Cor 8:2; **(4b)** in Rom 3:7, argumentatively of the effects of the truth of God, as to whether God's truthfulness becomes more conspicuous and His glory is increased through man's untruthfulness; **(4c)** of numerical increase, Acts 16:5. **(5)** "to be abundantly furnished, to abound in a thing," **(5a)** as of material benefits, Lk 12:15; **(5b)** Phil 4:18 of spiritual gifts; **(6)** 1 Cor 14:12, or "to be pre-eminent, to excel, to be morally better off," as regards partaking of certain meats; **(7)** 1 Cor 8:8, "are we the better"; **(8)** "to abound" **(8a)** in hope, Rom 15:13; **(8b)** the work of the Lord, 1 Cor 15:58; **(8c)** faith and grace, 2 Cor 8:7; **(8d)** thanksgiving, Col 2:7; **(8e)** walking so as to please God, Phil 1:9; 1 Th 4:1, 10; **(8f)** of righteousness, Mt 5:20; **(8g)** of the Gospel, as the ministration of righteousness 2 Cor 3:9, "exceed." **II.** It is used transitively, in the sense of **(1)** "to make to abound," e.g., to provide a person richly so that he has "abundance," as **(1a)** of spiritual truth, Mt 13:12; **(1b)** the right use of what God has entrusted to us, Mt 25:29; **(1c)** the power of God in conferring grace, 2 Cor 9:8; **(2)** Eph 1:8; to "make abundant" or to cause to excel, **(2a)** as of the effect of grace in regard to thanksgiving, 2 Cor 4:15; **(2b)** His power to make us "to abound" in love, 1 Th 3:12. See: TDNT—6:58, 828; BAGD—650c; THAYER—505b.

4053. **περισσός** {10x} **pĕrissŏs**, *per-is-sos';* from *4012* (in the sense of *beyond*); *superabundant* (in quantity) or *superior* (in quality); by impl. *excessive;* adv. (with *1537*) *violently;* neut. (as noun) *preeminence:*—more {2x}, beyond measure {1x}, vehemently + 1537 {1x}, more abundantly {1x}, advantage {1x}, superfluous {1x}, very highly + 5228 + 1537 {1x}, exceeding abundantly above + 5228 + 1537 {1x}, exceeding + 5228 + 1537 {1x}.

Perissos, "abundant," is translated **(1)** "advantage" in Rom 3:1; **(2)** "superfluous" in 2 Cor 9:1. **(3)** It also means "what is above and over, superadded," hence came to denote "what is superior and advantageous," Rom 3:1, "advantage" in a comparison between Jew and Gentile; only here with this meaning. **(4)** It is translated "more," e.g., in Mt 5:37–47 and **(5)** in Jn 10:10 the neuter form is rendered "more abundantly." See: TDNT—6:61, 828; BAGD—651b; THAYER—505d.

4054. **περισσότερον** {4x} **pĕrissŏtĕrŏn**, *per-is-sot'-er-on;* neut. of *4055* (as adv.); in a *more superabundant* way:—more abundantly {2x}, a great deal {1x}, far more {1x}.

This word is the neuter of the comparative degree of *perissos*, "more abundant," is translated **(1)** "more abundantly" in 1 Cor 15:10; Heb 6:17; **(2)** "a great deal" in Mk 7:36; **(3)** "far more" in Heb 7:15. See: BAGD—651c; THAYER—506a.

4055. **περισσότερος** {12x} **pĕrissŏtĕrŏs**, *per-is-sot'-er-os;* comp. of *4053; more superabundant* (in number, degree or character):—more {4x}, greater {3x}, more abundant {3x}, much more {1x}, overmuch {1x}.

Perissoteros, the comparative degree of *perissos* (4053) is translated as follows: **(1)** "more" in Mt 11:9; Lk 12:4, 48; 2 Cor 10:8; **(2)** "greater" in Mt 23:14; Mk 12:40; Lk 20:47; **(3)** in 1 Cor 12:23 twice, 24, "more abundant"; **(4)** in 2 Cor 2:7, "overmuch"; and **(5)** "much more" in Lk 7:26. See: BAGD—651c; THAYER—506 bottom of page; go to 505d [4053].

4056. **περισσοτέρως** {13x} **pĕrissŏtĕrōs**, *per-is-sot-er'-oce;* adv. from *4055; more superabundantly:*—more abundantly {4x}, more exceedingly {2x}, more abundant {2x}, much more {1x}, more frequent {1x}, the rather {1x}, exceedingly {1x}, the more earnest {1x}. See: BAGD—651d; THAYER—506 bottom of page; go to 505d [4053].

4057. **περισσῶς** {3x} **pĕrissōs**, *per-is-soce';* adv. from *4053; superabundantly:*—exceedingly {1x}, out of measure {1x}, the more {1x}.

Perissos, as an adverb, is translated **(1)** "exceedingly" in Acts 26:11; **(2)** "the more" in Mt 27:23; and **(3)** "out of measure": "And they were astonished out of measure, saying among themselves, Who then can be saved?" (Mk 10:26). Syn.: 280, 488, 943, 2884, 3313, 3354, 3358, 4568, 5234, 5249, 5518. See: BAGD—651d; THAYER—506a.

4058. **περιστερά** {10x} **pĕristĕra**, *per-is-ter-ah';* of uncert. der.; a *pigeon:*—dove {9x}, pigeon {1x}.

Peristera denotes "a dove or pigeon," Mt 3:16; 10:16 (indicating its proverbial harmlessness); 21:12; Mk 1:10; 11:15; Lk 2:24 (pigeons"); 3:22; Jn 1:32; 2:14, 16. See: TDNT—6:63, 830; BAGD—651d; THAYER—506b.

4059. **περιτέμνω** {18x} **pĕritĕmnō**, *per-ee-tem'-no;* from *4012* and the base of *5114; to cut around,* i.e. (spec.) to *circumcise:*—circumcise {18x}.

Peritemno, as a verb, means "to circumcise" and is used **(1)** literally, **(1a)** being circumcised (Lk 1:59; 2:21); **(1b)** of receiving circumcision (Gal 5:2–3; 6:13); **(2)** metaphorically, of spiritual circumcision (Col 2:11). Syn.: 203, 564, 1986, 4061. See: TDNT—6:72, 831; BAGD—652b; THAYER—506b.

4060. **περιτίθημι** {8x} **pĕritithēmi**, *per-ee-tith'-ay-mee;* from *4012* and *5087;* to *place around;* by impl. to *present:*—put on {3x}, put upon {1x}, set about {1x}, put about {1x}, bestow upon {1x}, hedge around + 5318 {1x}. See: BAGD—652c; THAYER—506b.

4061. **περιτομή** {36x} **pĕritŏmē**, *per-it-om-ay';* from *4059; circumcision* (the rite, the condition or the people, lit. or fig.):—× circumcised {1x}, circumcision {35x}.

Peritome, as a noun, literally means "a cutting round, circumcision" and **(1)** was a rite enjoined by God upon Abraham and his male descendants and dependents, as a sign of the covenant made with him (Gen 17; Acts 7:8; Rom. 4:11). **(2)** Hence Israelites termed Gentiles "the uncircumcised" (cf. Judg 15:18; 2 Sa 1:20). So in the NT, but without the suggestion of contempt (e.g., Rom 2:26; Eph 2:11). **(3)** The rite had a moral significance (cf. Ex 6:12, 30, where it is metaphorically applied to the lips; so to the ear, Jer 6:10, and the heart, Deut 30:6; Jer 4:4. Cf. Jer 9:25–26). **(3a)** It refers to the state of "circumcision" (Rom. 2:25–28; 3:1; 4:10; 1 Cor 7:19; Gal 5:6; 6:15; Col 3:11). **(3b)** In the economy of grace no account is taken of any ordinance performed on the flesh; the old racial distinction is ignored in the preaching of the gospel, and faith is the sole condition upon which the favor of God in salvation is to be obtained (Rom 10:11–13; 1 Cor 7:19; cf. Rom 4:9–12).

(4) Upon the preaching of the gospel to, and the conversion of, Gentiles, a sect of Jewish believers arose who argued that the gospel, without the fulfillment of "circumcision," would make void the Law and make salvation impossible (Acts 15:1). **(4a)** Hence this party was known as "the circumcision" (Acts 10:45; 11:2; Gal 2:12; Col 4:11; Titus 1:10 - the term being used by metonymy, the abstract being put for the concrete, as with the application of the word to Jews generally, Rom 3:30; 4:9, 12; 15:8; Gal 2:7–9; Eph 2:11). **(4b)** It is used metaphorically and spiritually of believers with reference **(4b1)** to the act (Col 2:11; Rom 2:29); **(4b2)** to the condition (Phil 3:3). Syn.: 203, 564, 1986, 4059. See: TDNT—6:72, 831; BAGD—652d; THAYER—506c.

4062. **περιτρέπω** {1x} **pĕritrĕpō**, *per-ee-trep'-o;* from *4012* and the base of *5157;* to *turn around,* i.e. (ment.) to *craze:*—make mad + 3130 + 1519 {1x}. See: BAGD—653a; THAYER—506d.

4063. **περιτρέχω** {1x} **pĕritrĕchō**, *per-ee-trekh'-o;* from *4012* and *5143* (incl. its alt.); to *run around,* i.e. *traverse:*—run through {1x}. See: BAGD—653a; THAYER—506d.

4064. **περιφέρω** {5x} **pĕriphĕrō**, *per-ee-fer'-o;* from *4012* and *5342;* to *convey around,* i.e. *transport hither and thither:*—bear about {1x}, carry about {4x}.

Periphero, "about," signifies "to carry about, or bear about," and is used **(1)** literally, **(1a)** of carrying the sick Mk 6:55; or **(1b)** of physical sufferings endured in fellowship with Christ, 2 Cor 4:10; **(2)** metaphorically, of being "carried" about by different evil doctrines, Eph 4:14; Heb 13:9; Jude 12. See: BAGD—653b; THAYER—506d.

4065. **περιφρονέω** {1x} **pĕriphrŏnĕō**, *per-ee-fron-eh'-o;* from *4012* and *5426;* to *think beyond,* i.e. *depreciate* (*contemn*):—despise {1x}.

Literally, this word means **(1)** to think round a thing, to turn over in the mind, to have thoughts beyond, to consider or examine on all sides, i.e. carefully, thoroughly; **(2)** to exalt one's self in thought above a person or a thing; hence, **(3)** to feel contempt for, to despise (Titus 2:15). See: TDNT—3:663, 421; BAGD—653b; THAYER—507a.

4066. **περίχωρος** {10x} **pĕrichōrŏs**, *per-ikh'-o-ros;* from *4012* and *5561; around* the *region,* i.e. *circumjacent* (as noun, with *1093* impl. *vicinity*):—region round about {5x}, country round about {3x}, country about {1x}, region that lieth around about {1x}.

Perochoros, signifies **(1)** "country round about," Lk 8:37; **(2)** "country about," Lk 3:3; **(3)** in Mt 14:35 and Lk 4:37, "country round about"; **(4)** Mt 3:5; Mk 1:28; Lk 4:14; 7:17; Acts 14:6. See: BAGD—653c; THAYER—507a.

4067. **περίψωμα** {1x} **pĕripsōma**, *per-ip'-so-mah* or

περίψημα **pĕripsēma**, *per-ip'-say-mah;* from a compound of *4012* and ψάω *psaō* (to *rub*); something *brushed* all *around,* completely wiped off all around, i.e. *off-scrapings* (fig. *scum*):—offscouring {1x}.

Peripsema, "that which is wiped off" (akin to *peripsao*, "to wipe off all round"; *peri*, "around," *psao*, "to wipe"), hence, "offscouring," is used metaphorically in 1 Cor 4:13. This and the synonymous word *perikatharma*, "refuse, rubbish," "were used especially of condemned criminals of the lowest classes, who were sacrificed as expiatory offerings because of their degraded life. See: TDNT—6:84,*; BAGD—653c; THAYER—507a.

4068. **περπερεύομαι** {1x} **pĕrpĕrĕuŏmai**, *per-per-yoo'-om-ahee;* mid. voice from πέρπερος **pĕrpĕrŏs** (*braggart;* perh. by redupl. of the base of *4008*); to *boast:*—vaunt itself {1x}.

This word means to boast one's self, give a self display, employing rhetorical embellishments in extolling one's self excessively, "to boast or vaunt oneself" and is used in 1 Cor 13:4, negatively of love. See: TDNT—6:93, 833; BAGD—653d; THAYER—507b.

4069. **Περσίς** {1x} **Pĕrsis**, *per-sece';* a *pers.* woman; *Persis,* a Chr. female:—Persis {1x}. See: BAGD—653d; THAYER—507b.

4070. **πέρυσι** {2x} **pĕrusi**, *per'-oo-si;* adv. from *4009;* the *by-gone,* i.e. (as noun) *last year:*—a year ago + 572 {2x}. Cf. 2 Cor 8:10; 9:2. See: BAGD—653d; THAYER—507b.

πετάομαι **pĕtaŏmai**. See *4072*.

4071. **πετεινόν** {14x} **pĕtĕinŏn**, *pet-i-non';* neut. of a der. of *4072;* a *flying* animal, i.e. *bird:*—bird {5x}, fowl {9x}. See: BAGD—654a; THAYER—507c.

4072. **πέτομαι** {5x} **pĕtŏmai**, *pet'-om-ahee;* or prol.

πετάομαι **pĕtaŏmai**, *pet-ah'-om-ahee;* or contr. πτάομαι **ptaŏmai**, *ptah'-om-ahee;* mid. voice of a primary verb; to *fly:*—fly {3x}, flying {2x}. See: BAGD—654a; THAYER—507c.

4073. **πέτρα** {16x} **pĕtra**, *pet'-ra;* fem. of the same as *4074;* a (mass of) *rock* (lit. or fig.):—rock {16x}.

Petra denotes **(1)** a mass of rock (Mt 7:24, 25; 27:51, 60; Mk 15:46; Lk 6:48) as distinct from **(2)** *petros* (4074), **(2a)** a detached stone or boulder, or **(2a)** a stone that might be thrown or easily moved. See: TDNT—6:95, 834; BAGD—654a; THAYER—507c.

4074. **Πέτρος** {162x} **Pĕtrŏs**, *pet'-ros;* appar. a primary word; a (piece of) *rock* (larger than *3037*); as a name, *Petrus,* an apostle:—Peter {161x}, rock {1x}. See: TDNT—6:100, 835; BAGD—654d; THAYER—507d. comp. *2786.*

4075. **πετρώδης** {4x} **pĕtrōdēs**, *pet-ro'-dace;* from *4073* and *1491; rock-like,* i.e. *rocky:*—stony place {2x}, stony ground {2x}.

Petrodes, "rock-like" (*petra,* "a rock," *eidos,* "a form, appearance"), is used of "rock" underlying shallow soil, **(1)** Mt 13:5, 20, "stony places"; **(2)** Mk 4:5, 16, "stony ground." See: BAGD—655c; THAYER—508b.

4076. **πήγανον** {1x} **pēganŏn**, *pay'-gan-on;* from *4078; rue* (from its *thick* or *fleshy* leaves):—rue {1x}.

Peganon is a shrubby plant with yellow flowers and a heavy smell, cultivated for medicinal purposes (Lk 11:42). See: BAGD—655d; THAYER—508b.

4077. **πηγή** {12x} **pēgē**, *pay-gay';* prob. from *4078* (through the idea of *gushing* plumply); a *fount* (lit. or fig.), i.e. *source* or *supply* (of water, blood, enjoyment) (not necessarily the orig. spring):—fountain {8x}, well {4x}.

Pege, "a spring or fountain," is used of **(1)** "an artificial well," fed by a spring, Jn 4:6; **(2)** metaphorically (in contrast to such a well), "the indwelling Spirit of God," Jn 4:14; **(3)** "springs," metaphorically in 2 Pet. 2:17, "wells" (without water, spoken of apostate teachers); **(4)** "natural fountains or springs," Jas 3:11, 12; Rev 8:10; 14:7; 16:4; **(5)** metaphorically, "eternal life and the future blessings accruing from it," Rev 7:17; 21:6; **(6)** "a flow of blood," Mk 5:29. See: TDNT—6:112, 837; BAGD—655d; THAYER—508b.

4078. **πήγνυμι** {1x} **pēgnumi**, *payg'-noo-mee;* a prol. form of a primary verb (which in its simpler form occurs only as an alt. in certain tenses); to *fix* ("*peg*"), i.e. (spec.) to *set up* (a tent):—to pitch {1x}. See: BAGD—656a; THAYER—508b.

4079. **πηδάλιον** {2x} **pēdaliŏn**, *pay-dal'-ee-on;* neut. of a (presumed) der. of πηδόν **pēdŏn** (the *blade* of an oar; from the same as *3976*); a "*pedal,*" i.e. *helm:*—rudder {1x}, helm {1x}.

Pedalion, "a rudder" (akin to *pedos,* "the blade of an oar"), occurs in **(1)** Jas 3:4, "helm"; and **(2)** Acts 27:40, plural, "the rudder (bands)." **(3)** The *pedalia* were actually steering paddles, two of which were used as "rudders" in ancient ships. See: BAGD—656a; THAYER—508b.

4080. **πηλίκος** {2x} **pēlikŏs**, *pay-lee'-kos;* a quantitative form (the fem.) of the base of *4225; how much* (as an indef.), i.e. in size or (fig.) dignity:—how great {1x}, how large {1x}.

Pelikos, primarily a direct interrogative, "how large? how great?" is used in exclamations, indicating magnitude, in **(1)** Gal 6:11, of letter characters; in **(2)** Heb 7:4, metaphorically, of the distinguished character of Melchizedek. See: BAGD—656b; THAYER—508c.

4081. **πηλός** {6x} **pēlŏs**, *pay-los';* perh. a primary word; *clay:*—clay {6x}.

Pelos, "clay," especially such as was used by a mason or potter, is used **(1)** of moist "clay," in Jn 9:6, 11, 14–15, in connection with Christ's healing the blind man; in **(2)** Rom 9:21, of potter's "clay," as to the potter's right over it as an illustration of the prerogatives of God in His dealings with sinful men. See: TDNT—6:118, 838; BAGD—656b; THAYER—508c.

4082. **πήρα** {6x} **pēra**, *pay'-rah;* of uncert. aff.; a *wallet* or leather *pouch* for food:—scrip {6x}.

Pera, "a traveler's leather bag or pouch for holding provisions," is translated "scrip", Mt 10:10; Mk 6:8; Lk 9:3; 10:4; 22:35, 36. See: TDNT—6:119, 838; BAGD—656c; THAYER—508c.

4083. **πῆχυς** {4x} **pēchus**, *pay'-khoos;* of uncert. aff.; the *fore-arm,* i.e. (as a measure) a *cubit:*—cubit {4x}.

A *pechus* is a measure of length equal to distance from the joint of the elbow to the tip of the middle finger [i.e. about 18 inches, or.5 m] (Mt 6:27; Lk 12:25; Jn 21:8; Rev 21:17). See: BAGD—656d; THAYER—508c.

4084. **πιάζω** {12x} **piazō**, *pee-ad'-zo;* prob. another form of *971;* to *squeeze,* i.e. *seize* (gently by the hand [*press*], or officially [*arrest*], or in hunting [*capture*]):—apprehend {2x}, catch {2x}, lay hand on {1x}, take {7x}.

Poiazo, "to lay hold of," with the suggestion of firm pressure or force, **(1)** is used in John, six times of efforts to seize Christ and is always rendered "take" in 7:30, 32, 44; 10:39; 11:57. **(2)** It is translated "laid hands on" in 8:20. **(3)** In Acts 12:4 and 2 Cor. 11:32 it is translated respectively "apprehended" and "apprehend." **(4)** In Rev 19:20, "taken", it is used of the seizure of the Beast and the False Prophet. **(5)** In Jn 21:3, 10 it is used of catching fish, "caught." **(5)** Elsewhere in Acts 3:7, "took.". See: BAGD—657a; THAYER—508d. comp. *4085.*

4085. **πιέζω** {1x} **piĕzō**, *pee-ed'-zo,* another form for *4084;* to *pack:*—press down {1x}.

Piezo, "to press down together," is used in Lk 6:38, "pressed down," of the character of the measure given in return for giving. See: BAGD—657b; THAYER—508d.

4086. **πιθανολογία** {1x} **pithanŏlŏgia**, *pith-an-ol-og-ee'-ah;* from a compound of a der. of *3982* and *3056; persuasive language:*—enticing words {1x}. See: BAGD—657b; THAYER—508d.

4087. **πικραίνω** {4x} **pikrainō**, *pik-rah'-ee-no;* from *4089;* to *embitter* (lit. or fig.):—be bitter {2x}, make bitter {2x}.

Pikraino signifies, **(1)** in the active voice, "to be bitter," Col 3:19, or "to embitter, irritate, or to make bitter," Rev 10:9; **(2)** the passive voice, "to be made bitter," is used in Rev 8:11; 10:10. See: TDNT—6:122, 839; BAGD—657b; THAYER—508d.

4088. **πικρία** {4x} **pikria**, *pik-ree'-ah;* from *4089; acridity* (espec. *poison*), lit. or fig.:—bitterness {4x}.

Pikria denotes "bitterness." **(1)** It is used in Acts 8:23, metaphorically, of a condition of extreme wickedness, "gall of bitterness" or "bitter gall"; **(2)** in Rom 3:14, of evil speaking; **(3)** in Eph 4:31, of "bitter" hatred; **(4)** in Heb 12:15, in the same sense, metaphorically, of a root of "bitterness," producing "bitter" fruit. See: TDNT—6:122, 839; BAGD—657c; THAYER—509a.

4089. **πικρός** {2x} **pikrŏs**, *pik-ros';* perh. from *4078* (through the idea of *piercing*); *sharp* (*pungent*), i.e. *acrid* (lit. or fig.):—bitter {2x}.

Pikros, meaning "to cut, to prick," hence, lit., "pointed, sharp, keen, pungent to the sense of taste, smell, etc.," is found in Jas 3:11, 14. In v. 11 it has its natural sense, with reference to water; in v. 14 it is used metaphorically of jealousy. See: TDNT—6:122, 839; BAGD—657c; THAYER—509a.

4090. **πικρῶς** {2x} **pikrōs**, *pik-roce';* adv. from *4089; bitterly,* i.e. (fig.) *violently:*—bitterly {2x}.

Pikros, "bitterly," is used of the poignant grief of Peter's weeping for his denial of Christ, Mt 26:75; Lk 22:62. See: BAGD—657d; THAYER—509a.

4091. **Πιλάτος** {55x} **Pilatŏs**, *pil-at'-os;* of Lat. or.; *close-pressed,* i.e. *firm; Pilatus,* a Rom.:—Pilate {55x}. See: BAGD—657d; THAYER—509b.

πίμπλημι **pimplēmi**. See *4130*.

4092. **πίμπρημι** {1x} **pimprēmi**, *pim'-pray-mee;* a redupl. and prol. form of a primary

πρέω **prĕō**, *preh'-o;* which occurs only as an alt. in certain tenses); to *fire,* i.e. *burn* (fig. and pass. *become inflamed* with fever):—be (× should have) swollen {1x}. See: BAGD—658b; THAYER—509d.

4093. **πινακίδιον** {1x} **pinakidiŏn**, *pin-ak-id'-ee-on;* dimin. of *4094;* a *tablet* (for writing on):—writing table {1x}. See: BAGD—658b; THAYER—509d.

4094. **πίναξ** {5x} **pinax**, *pin'-ax;* appar. a form of *4109;* a *plate:*—charger {4x}, platter {1x}.

Pinax is primarily a board or plank and came to denote various articles of wood, [cf. "cutting boards"] upon which meat was sliced; hence, a wooden platter, a charger (Mt 14:8, 11; Mk 6:25, 28; Lk 11:39). See: BAGD—658c; THAYER—509d.

4095. **πίνω** {75x} **pinō**, *pee'-no;* a prol. form of

πίω **piō**, *pee'-o;* which (together with another form πόω **pŏō**, *pŏ'-o;* occurs only as an alt. in certain tenses; to *imbibe* (lit. or fig.):—drink {68x}, drink of {7x}.

Pino, as a verb, means "to drink," and is used chiefly in the Gospels and in 1 Cor, whether literally (most frequently), or figuratively, **(1)** of "drinking" of the blood of Christ, in the sense of receiving eternal life, through His death, Jn 6:53–54, 56; **(2)** of "receiving" spiritually that which refreshes, strengthens and nourishes the soul, Jn 7:37; **(3)** of "deriving" spiritual life from Christ, Jn 4:14, as Israel did typically 1 Cor 10:4; **(4)** of "sharing" in the sufferings of Christ humanly inflicted, Mt 20:22–23; Mk 10:38–39; **(5)** of "participating" in the abominations imparted by the corrupt religious and commercial systems emanating from Babylon, Rev 18:3; **(6)** of "receiving" divine judgment, through partaking unworthily of the Lord's Supper, 1 Cor 11:29; **(7)** of "experiencing" the wrath of God, Rev 14:10; 16:6; **(8)** of the earth's "receiving" the benefits of rain, Heb 6:7. Syn.: 3184, 4213, 4222, 4844, 5202. See: TDNT—6:135, 840; BAGD—658c; THAYER—510a.

4096. **πιότης** {1x} **piŏtēs**, *pee-ot'-ace;* from πίων **piōn**, (*fat;* perh. akin to the alt. of *4095* through the idea of *repletion*); *plumpness,* i.e. (by impl.) *richness* (*oiliness*):—fatness {1x}.

Piotes, from *pion,* "fat," from a root which signifies "swelling," is used metaphorically in Rom 11:17. The gentile believer had become a sharer in the spiritual life and blessing bestowed by divine covenant upon Abraham and his descendants as set forth under the figure of "the root of (not 'and') the 'fatness' of the olive tree." See: BAGD—659a; THAYER—510b.

4097. **πιπράσκω** {9x} **pipraskō**, *pip-ras'-ko;* a redupl. and prol. form of

πράω **praō**, *prah'-o;* (which occurs only as an alt. in certain tenses); contr. from περάω **pĕraō** (to *traverse;* from the base of *4008*); to *traffic* (by *travelling*), i.e. *dispose* of as merchandise or into slavery (lit. or fig.):—sell {9x}.

Piprasko, from an earlier form, *perao,* "to carry across the sea for the purpose of selling or to export," is used **(1)** literally, Mt 13:46; 18:25; 26:9; Mk 14:5; Jn 12:5; Acts 2:45; 4:34; 5:4; **(2)** metaphorically, Rom 7:14, "sold under sin," i.e., as fully under the domination of sin as a slave is under his master; the statement evinces an utter dissatisfaction with such a condition; it expresses, not the condemnation of the unregenerate state, but the evil of bondage to a corrupt nature, involving the futility of making use of the Law as a means of deliverance. See: TDNT—6:160, 846; BAGD—659a; THAYER—510b.

4098. **πίπτω** {90x} **piptō**, *pip'-to;* a redupl. and contr. form of πέτω **pĕtō**, *pet'-o;* (which occurs only as an alt. in certain tenses); prob. akin to *4072* through the idea of *alighting;* to *fall* (lit. or fig.):—fail {1x}, fall {69x}, fall down {19x}, light on {1x}.

Pipto, "to fall," is used **(1)** of descent, to "fall" down from, e.g., Mt 10:29; 13:4; **(2)** of a lot, Acts 1:26; **(3)** of "falling" under judgment, Jas 5:12 (cf. Rev 18:2); **(4)** of persons in the act of prostration, to prostrate oneself, **(4a)** e.g., Mt 17:6; Jn 18:6; Rev 1:17; **(4b)** in homage and worship, e.g., Mt 2:11; Mk 5:22; Rev 5:14; 19:4; **(5)** of things, "falling" into ruin, or failing, e.g., Mt 7:25; Heb 11:30; **(6)** of "falling" in judgment upon persons, as of the sun's heat, Rev 7:16, "light"; **(7)** of persons, in "falling" morally or spiritually, Rom 14:4; 1 Cor 10:8, 12; Rev 2:5; **(8)** Lk 16:17, "fail", of one tittle of the Law to fail. See: TDNT—6:161, 846; BAGD—659b; THAYER—510b.

4099. **Πισιδία** {2x} **Pisidia**, *pis-id-ee'-ah;* prob. of for. or.; *Pisidia,* a region of Asia Minor:—Pisidia {2x}. See: BAGD—660b; THAYER—511b.

4100. **πιστεύω** {248x} **pistĕuō**, *pist-yoo'-o;* from *4102;* to *have faith* (in, upon, or with respect to, a person or thing), i.e. *credit;* by impl. to *entrust* (espec. one's spiritual well-being to Christ):—believe {239x}, commit unto {4x}, commit to (one's) trust {1x}, be committed unto {1x}, be put in trust with {1x}, be commit to one's trust {1x}, believer {1x}.

Pisteuo means not just to believe, but also to be persuaded of; and hence, to place confidence in, to trust, and signifies, in this sense of the word, reliance upon, not mere credence, hence it is translated "commit unto", "commit to one's trust", "be committed unto", etc. See: TDNT—6:174, 849; BAGD—660b; THAYER—511b.

4101. **πιστικός** {2x} **pistikŏs**, *pis-tik-os';* from *4102; trustworthy,* i.e. *genuine* (*unadulterated*):—spikenard + 3487 {2x}.

Spikenard is the head or spike of the nard plant from which was extracted and purified a juice of delicious odour which was used (either pure or mixed) in the preparation of a most precious ointment. Pure, unmixed, unadulterated spikenard was described as *pistikos.* See: BAGD—662b; THAYER—512d.

4102. **πίστις** {244x} **pistis**, *pis'-tis;* from *3982; persuasion,* i.e. *credence;* mor. *conviction* (of *relig.* truth, or the truthfulness of God or a relig. teacher), espec. *reliance* upon Christ for salvation; abstr. *constancy* in such profession; by extension, the system of religious (Gospel) *truth* itself:—faith {239x}, assurance {1x}, believe + 1537 {1x}, belief {1x}, them that believe {1x}, fidelity {1x}.

Pistis is **(1)** conviction of the truth of anything, belief; of a conviction or belief respecting man's relationship to God and divine things, generally with the included idea of trust and holy fervour born of faith and joined with it. It is related **(1a)** to God with the conviction that God exists and is the creator and ruler of all things, the provider and bestower of eternal salvation through Christ; **(1b)** to Christ with a strong and welcome conviction or belief that Jesus is the Messiah, through whom we obtain eternal salvation in the kingdom of God. **(2)** It includes all of the religious beliefs of Christians ["the faith" - 1 Ti 1:2; 4:1]. **(3)** *Pistis* is used of belief with the predominate idea of trust (or confidence) whether in God or in Christ, springing from faith in the same. **(4)** It speaks of fidelity, faithfulness. **(5)** It describes the character of one who can be relied on. See: TDNT—6:174, 849; BAGD—662b; THAYER—512d.

4103. **πιστός** {67x} **pistŏs**, *pis-tos';* from *3982;* obj. *trustworthy;* subj. *trustful:*—faithful {53x}, believe {6x}, believe in {2x}, true {2x}, faithfully {1x}, believer {1x}, sure {1x}; not tr {1x}.

Pistos, **(1)** in the active sense means "believing, trusting" in Gal 3:9; Acts 16:1; 2 Cor 6:15; **(2)** in the passive sense, "trusty, faithful, trustworthy" in 1 Th 5:24; 2 Th 3:3. **(3)** It is translated **(3a)** "believer" in 2 Cor 6:15; **(3b)** "believers" in 1 Ti 4:12; **(3c)** in 1 Ti 5:16, "if any woman that believeth," lit. "if any believing woman." **(3d)** So in 1 Ti 6:2, "believing masters." **(3e)** In 1 Pet 1:21, "do believe in God"; **(3e)** In Jn 20:27 it is translated "believing." See: TDNT—6:174, 849; BAGD—664c; THAYER—514b.

4104. **πιστόω** {1x} **pistŏō**, *pis-tŏ'-o;* from *4103;* to *assure:*—assure of {1x}.

Pistoo, "to trust or give assurance to" has a secondary meaning, in the passive voice, "to be assured of," 2 Ti 3:14. See: TDNT—6:174, 849; BAGD—665b; THAYER—514c.

4105. **πλανάω** {39x} **planaō**, *plan-ah'-o;* from *4106;* to (prop. *cause* to) *roam* (from safety, truth, or virtue):—deceive {24x}, err {6x}, go astray {5x}, seduce {2x}, wander {1x}, be out of the way {1x}.

Planao, in the passive form sometimes means **(1)** "to go astray, wander," Mt 18:12; 1 Pet 2:25; Heb 11:38; **(2)** frequently active, "to deceive, by leading into error, to seduce," e.g., Mt 24:4, 5, 11, 24; Jn 7:12; 1 Jn 3:7. **(3)** In Rev 12:9 the present participle is used with the definite article, as a title of the Devil, "the Deceiver," lit., "the deceiving one." **(4)** Often it has the sense of "deceiving oneself," e.g., 1 Cor 6:9; 15:33; Gal 6:7; or **(5)** Jas 1:16, "do not err." See: TDNT—6:228, 857; BAGD—665b; THAYER—514d.

4106. **πλάνη** {39x} **planē**, *plan'-ay;* fem. of *4108* (as abstr.); obj. *fraudulence;* subj. a *straying* from orthodoxy or piety:—deceive {24x}, err {6x}, go astray {5x}, seduce {2x}, wander {1x}, be out of the way {1x}.

(1) Literally, plane means a wandering whereby those who are led astray roam hither and thither and is always used of mental straying, wrong opinion, error in morals or religion, 2 Th 2:11, "delusion." **(2)** It is akin to *planao,* "a wandering, a forsaking of the right path," (see Jas 5:20), whether **(2a)** in doctrine, 2 Pet 3:17; 1 Jn 4:6, or **(2b)** in morals, Rom 1:27; 2 Pet 2:18; Jude 11; **(3)** though, in Scripture, doctrine and morals are never divided by any sharp line. **(4)** "Errors" in doctrine are not infrequently the effect of relaxed morality, and vice versa. See: TDNT—6:228, 857; BAGD—665d; THAYER—514d.

4107. **πλανήτης** {1x} **planētēs**, *plan-ay'-tace;* from *4108;* a *rover* ("planet"), i.e. (fig.) an *erratic* teacher:—wandering {1x}.

Planetes, "a wanderer" (Eng., "planet"), is used metaphorically in Jude 13, of the evil teachers there mentioned as "wandering (stars)." See: TDNT—6:228, 857; BAGD—666a; THAYER—515a.

4108. **πλάνος** {5x} **planŏs**, *plan'-os;* of uncert. aff.; *roving* (as a *tramp*), i.e. (by impl.) an *impostor* or *misleader:*—deceiver {4x}, seducing {1x}.

Planos, properly, an adjective, signifying **(1)** "wandering, or leading astray, seducing," 1 Ti 4:1, "seducing (spirits)", used as a noun, it denotes **(2)** an impostor of the vagabond type, and so any kind of "deceiver" or corrupter, Mt 27:63; 2 Cor 6:8; 2 Jn 7 (twice), in the last of which the accompanying definite article necessitates the translation "the deceiver." See: TDNT—6:228, 857; BAGD—666a; THAYER—515a.

4109. **πλάξ** {3x} **plax**, *plax;* from *4111;* a *moulding-board,* i.e. *flat* surface ("*plate*", or *tablet,* lit. or fig.):—table {3x}.

Plax primarily denotes anything flat and broad; hence, a flat stone, a small table, i.e., a tablet, 2 Cor 3:3 twice; Heb 9:4. See: BAGD—666a; THAYER—515a.

4110. **πλάσμα** {1x} **plasma**, *plas'-mah;* from *4111;* something *moulded:*—thing formed {1x}. See: TDNT—6:254, 862; BAGD—666b; THAYER—515b.

4111. **πλάσσω** {2x} **plassō**, *plas'-so;* a primary verb; to *mould,* i.e. *shape* or *fabricate:*—form {2x}.

Plasso, "to mold, to shape," was used of the artist who wrought in clay or wax (Eng., "plastic," "plasticity"), and occurs in Rom 9:20; 1 Ti 2:13. See: TDNT—6:254, 862; BAGD—666c; THAYER—515b.

4112. **πλαστός** {1x} **plastŏs**, *plas-tos';* from *4111; moulded,* i.e. (by impl.) *artificial* or (fig.) *fictitious* (*false*):—feigned {1x}.

Plastos primarily denotes formed, molded; then, metaphorically, made up, fabricated, feigned (2 Pet 2:3). See: TDNT—6:262, 862; BAGD—666c; THAYER—515b.

4113. **πλατεῖα** {9x} **platĕia**, *plat-i'-ah;* fem. of *4116;* a *wide* "*plat*" or "*place*", i.e. open *square:*—street {9x}.

Plateia, as a noun, means "a broad way, a street" (Mt 6:5; 12:19; Lk 10:10; 13:26; 14:21; Acts 5:15; Rev 11:8; 21:21; 22:2). Syn.: 296, 4505. See: BAGD—666d; THAYER—515b.

4114. **πλάτος** {4x} **platŏs**, *plat'-os;* from *4116; width:*—breadth {4x}.

This word denotes "breadth," Eph 3:18; Rev 20:9; 21:16, twice. See: BAGD—666d; THAYER—515b.

4115. **πλατύνω** {3x} **platunō**, *plat-oo'-no;* from *4116;* to *widen* (lit. or fig.):—make broad {1x}, enlarge {2x}.

Platuno, connected with *plak,* "a flat, broad surface," signifies "to make broad"; said **(1)** of phylacteries, Mt 23:5; **(2)** used figuratively in 2 Cor 6:11, 13, "to be enlarged," in the ethical sense, of the heart. See: BAGD—667a; THAYER—515b.

4116. **πλατύς** {1x} **platus**, *plat-oos';* from *4111;* spread out *"flat"* ("plot"), i.e. *broad:*—wide {1x}.

Platus denotes "breadth," Eph 3:18; Rev 20:9; 21:16 (twice). See: BAGD—667b; THAYER—515c.

4117. **πλέγμα** {1x} **plĕgma**, *pleg'-mah;* from *4120;* a *plait* (of hair):—broidered hair {1x}.

Plegma signifies what is woven and is used in 1 Ti 2:9, of broided hair. See: BAGD—667a; THAYER—515c.

πλεῖον **plĕiŏn**. See *4119*.

4118. **πλεῖστος** {3x} **plĕistŏs**, *plice'-tos;* irreg. superl. of *4183;* the *largest number* or *very large:*—very great {1x}, most {2x}.

Pleistos, the superlative degree of *polus,* is used **(1)** as an adjective in Mt 21:8, "a very great"; **(2)** in the neuter, with the article, adverbially, "at the most", Mt 11:20; 1 Cor 14:27. See: BAGD—689d; THAYER—515c.

4119. **πλείων** {56x} **plĕiōn**, *pli-own;* neut.

πλεῖον **plĕiŏn**, *pli'-on;* or

πλέον **plĕŏn**, *pleh'-on;* comparative of *4183; more* in quantity, number, or quality; also (in plur.) the *major portion:*—more {23x}, many {12x}, greater {5x}, further + 1909 {3x}, most {2x}, more part {2x}, not tr {1x}, misc. {8x} = × above, + exceed, yet but. See: BAGD—667b; THAYER—515c.

4120. **πλέκω** {3x} **plĕkō**, *plek'-o;* a primary word; to *twine* or *braid:*—plait {3x}.

Pleko, "to weave, twist, plait," is used of the crown of thorns inflicted on Christ, Mt 27:29; Mk 15:17; Jn 19:2. See: BAGD—667b; THAYER—516a.

πλέον **plĕŏn**. See *4119*.

4121. **πλεονάζω** {9x} **plĕŏnazō**, *pleh-on-ad'-zo;* from *4119;* to *do, make* or *be more,* i.e. *increase* (tran. or intr.); by extens. to *superabound:*—abound {6x}, abundant {1x}, make to increase {1x}, have over {1x}.

This word, from *pleion,* or *pleon,* "more" (greater in quantity), akin to *pleo,* "to fill," signifies, **(1)** intransitively, "to superabound," **(1a)** of a trespass or sin, Rom 5:20; **(1b)** of grace, Rom 6:1; 2 Cor 4:15; **(1c)** of spiritual fruit, Phil 4:17; **(1d)** of love, 2 Th 1:3; **(1e)** of various fruits, 2 Pet 1:8; **(1f)** of the gathering of the manna, 2 Cor 8:15, "had . . . over"; **(2)** transitively, "to make to increase," 1 Th 3:12. See: TDNT—6:263, 864; BAGD—667b; THAYER—516a.

4122. **πλεονεκτέω** {5x} **plĕŏnĕktĕō**, *pleh-on-ek-teh'-o;* from *4123;* to *be covetous,* i.e. (by impl.) to *over-reach:*—get an advantage {1x}, defraud {2x}, make a gain {2x}.

(1) This word always signifies an unfair advantage, never used positively. This word means lit., "to seek to get more" (*pleon,* "more," *echo,* "to have"); hence, "to get an advantage of, to take advantage of." **(1)** In 2 Cor 7:2, "defrauded"; **(2)** in 1 Th 4:6, "defraud." It is also translated **(3)** "get an advantage" in 2 Cor 2:11, of Satan's effort to gain an "advantage" over the church, through their neglect to restore the backslider; and **(4)** "make a gain" in 2 Cor 12:17–18. See: TDNT—6:266, 864; BAGD—667c; THAYER—516b.

4123. **πλεονέκτης** {4x} **plĕŏnĕktēs**, *pleh-on-ek'-tace;* from *4119* and *2192; holding* (*desiring*) *more,* i.e. *eager for gain* (*avaricious,* hence, a *defrauder*):—covetous {4x}.

This word means lit., "(eager) to have more", i.e., to have what belongs to others; hence, "greedy of gain, covetous" in 1 Cor 5:10–11; 6:10; Eph 5:5, "covetous man." See: TDNT—6:266, 864; BAGD—667c; THAYER—516b.

4124. **πλεονεξία** {10x} **plĕŏnĕxia**, *pleh-on-ex-ee'-ah;* from *4123; avarice,* i.e. (by impl.) *fraudulency, extortion:*—covetousness {8x}, covetous practices {1x}, greediness {1x}.

Pleonexia, "covetousness," lit., "a desire to have more" (*pleon,* "more," *echo,* "to have"), **(1)** always in a bad sense, is used in **(2)** a general way in Mk 7:22 (plural, lit., "covetings," i.e., various ways in which "covetousness" shows itself); Rom 1:29; Eph 5:3; 1 Th 2:5. **(3)** Elsewhere it is used, **(3a)** of material possessions, Lk 12:15; 2 Pet 2:3; 2 Cor 9:5, a gift which betrays the giver's unwillingness to bestow what is due; **(3b)** of sensuality, **(3b1)** Eph 4:19, "greediness"; **(3b2)** Col 3:5, where it is called "idolatry"; **(3b3)** 2 Pet 2:14, "covetous practices." Syn.: **(A)** *Pleonexia* is the more active sin, *philargyria* (5365) the more passive. *Pleonexia* refers to having more with the desire to have more, seeking to possess what is not possessed. *Philargyria* refers to seeking to retain what is possessed and, through accumulation, to multiplying what is possessed. *Pleonexia* often implies bold and aggressive methods of acquisition; it frequently refers to behavior that is as free in scattering and squandering as it was eager and unscrupulous in acquiring. *Pleonexia* often squanders what he has seized. **(B)** The main distinction between *pleonexia* (4124) and *philarguria* (5365) is being that between "covetousness" and avarice, the former having a much wider and deeper sense, being "the genus of which *philarguria* is the species." The "covetous" man is often cruel as well as grasping, while the avaricious man is simply miserly and stinting. See: TDNT—6:266, 864; BAGD—667d; THAYER—516b.

4125. **πλευρά** {5x} **plĕura**, *plyoo-rah';* of uncert. aff.; a *rib,* i.e. (by extens.) *side:*—side {5x}.

Pleura, "a side" (cf. Eng., "pleurisy"), is used **(1)** of the "side" of Christ, into which the spear was thrust, Jn 19:34; 20:20, 25, 27; **(2)** elsewhere, in Acts 12:7, of Peter's side. See: BAGD—668a; THAYER—516b.

4126. **πλέω** {5x} **plĕō**, *pleh'-o;* another form for

πλεύω **plĕuō**, *plyoo'-o;* which is used as an alt. in certain tenses; prob. a form of *4150* (through the idea of *plunging* through the water); to *pass* in a vessel:—to sail {5x}. See: BAGD—668a; THAYER—516c. See also *4130*.

4127. **πληγή** {21x} **plēgē**, *play-gay';* from *4141;* a *stroke;* by impl. a *wound;* fig. a *calamity:*—plague {12x}, stripe {5x}, wound (-ed) {4x}.

A *plege* is a stripe, wound and is used by extension of a public calamity, heavy affliction, a plague (e.g. Rev 9:20; 11:6; 15:1). See: BAGD—667a; THAYER—516c.

4128. **πλῆθος** {32x} **plēthŏs**, *play'-thos;* from *4130;* a *fulness,* i.e. a *large number, throng, populace:*—bundle {1x}, company {1x}, multitude {30x}.

Plethos, lit., "a fullness," hence, "a large company, a multitude," is used **(1)** of things: **(1a)** of fish, Lk 5:6; Jn 21:6; **(1b)** of sticks ("bundle"), Acts 28:3; **(1c)** of stars and of sand, Heb 11:12; **(1d)** of sins, Jas 5:20; 1 Pet 4:8; **(2)** of persons, **(2a)** a "multitude": **(2a1)** of people, e.g., Mk 3:7, 8; Lk 6:17; Jn 5:3; Acts 14:1; **(2a2)** of angels, Lk 2:13; **(2b)** with the article, the whole number, the "multitude," the populace, e.g., Lk 1:10; 8:37; Acts 5:16; 19:9; 23:7; **(2c)** a particular company, e.g., **(2c1)** of disciples, Lk 19:37; Acts 4:32; 6:2, 5; 15:30; **(2c2)** of elders, priests, and scribes, Acts 23:7; **(2c3)** of the apostles and the elders of the Church in Jerusalem, Acts 15:12. See: TDNT—6:274, 866; BAGD—668b; THAYER—516c.

4129. **πληθύνω** {12x} **plēthunō**, *play-thoo'-no;* from another form of *4128;* to *increase* (tran. or intr.):—abound {1x}, multiply {11x}.

Plethuno, used **(1)** transitively, denotes **(1a)** "to cause to increase, to multiply," 2 Cor 9:10; Heb 6:14 (twice); **(1b)** in the passive voice, "to be multiplied," Mt 24:12, "(iniquity) shall abound"; Acts 6:7; 7:17; 9:31; 12:24; 1 Pet 1:2; 2 Pet 1:2; Jude 2; **(2)** intransitively it denotes "to be multiplying," Acts 6:1, "was multiplied." See: TDNT—6:279, 866; BAGD—669a; THAYER—516d.

4130. **πλήθω** {24x} **plēthō**, *play'-tho;* a prol. form of a primary πλέω **plĕō**, *pleh'-o* (which appears only as an alt. in certain tenses and in the redupl. form πίμπλημι **pimplēmi**); to *"fill"* (lit. or fig. [*imbue, influence, supply*]); spec. to *fulfil* (time):—fill {18x}, accomplish {4x}, furnish {1x}, full . . . come {1x}.

This word is used **(1)** of things; **(1a)** boats, with fish, Lk 5:7; **(1b)** a sponge, with vinegar, Mt 27:48; Jn 19:29; **(1c)** a city, with confusion, Acts 19:29; **(1d)** a wedding, with guests, Mt 22:10; **(2)** of persons (only in Luke's writings). **(2a)** with the Holy Spirit, Lk 1:15, 41, 67; Acts 2:4; 4:8, 31; 9:17; 13:9; **(2b)** with emotions: **(2b1)** wrath, Lk 4:28; **(2b2)** fear, Lk 5:26; **(2b3)** madness, Lk 6:11; **(2b4)** wonder, amazement, Acts 3:10; **(2b5)** indignation, Acts 5:17; and **(2b6)** Acts 13:45. **(3)** It is translated "accomplished" in Lk 1:23; 2:6, 21–22. See: TDNT—6:128,*; BAGD 658a; THAYER—516d.

4131. **πλήκτης** {2x} **plēktēs**, *plake'-tace;* from *4141;* a *smiter,* i.e. *pugnacious* (*quarrelsome*):—striker {2x}.

This person is a bruiser, one ready to deliver a blow; a pugnacious, contentious, quarrelsome person, 1 Ti 3:3; Titus 1:7. See: BAGD—669; THAYER—519d.

4132. **πλήμμυρα** {1x} **plēmmura**, *plame-moo'-rah;* prol. from *4130; flood tide,* i.e. (by anal.) a *freshet:*—flood {1x}. See: BAGD—669b; THAYER—517a.

4133. **πλήν** {31x} **plēn**, *plane;* from *4119; moreover* (*besides*), i.e. *albeit, save that, rather, yet:*—but {14x}, nevertheless {8x}, notwithstanding {4x}, but rather {2x}, except {1x}, than {1x}, save {1x}. See: BAGD—669b; THAYER—517b.

4134. **πλήρης** {17x} **plērēs**, *play'-race;* from *4130; replete,* or *covered* over; by anal. *complete:*—full {17x}.

Pleres denotes "full," **(1)** in the sense of "being filled," **(1a)** materially, Mt 14:20; 15:37; Mk 8:19, said of baskets "full" of bread crumbs; **(1b)** of leprosy, Lk 5:12; **(1c)** spiritually, of the Holy Spirit, Lk 4:1; Acts 6:3; 7:55; 11:24; **(1d)** grace and truth, Jn 1:14; **(1e)** faith, Acts 6:5; **(1f)** grace and power, Acts 6:8; **(1g)** of the effects of spiritual life and qualities, seen in good works, Acts 9:36; **(1h)** in an evil sense, of guile and villany, Acts 13:10; **(1i)** wrath, Acts 19:28; **(2)** in the sense of "being complete," **(2a)** "full corn in the ear," Mk 4:28; **(2b)** of a reward hereafter, 2 Jn 8. See: TDNT—6:283, 867; BAGD—669d; THAYER—517b.

4135. **πληροφορέω** {5x} **plērŏphŏrĕō**, *play-rof-or-eh'-o;* from *4134* and

5409; to *carry* out *fully* (in evidence), i.e. *completely assure* (or *convince*), *entirely accomplish:*—be fully persuaded {2x}, be most surely believed {1x}, be fully known {1x}, make full proof of {1x}.

This word means "to bring in full measure, to fulfill," also signifies **(1)** "to be fully persuaded" **(1a)** Rom 4:21, of Abrahams faith. **(1b)** In Rom 14:5 it is said of the apprehension of the will of God. **(1c)** In these two places it is used subjectively, with reference to an effect upon the mind. It is also understood **(2)** "to fulfill entirely," **(2a)** of circumstances relating to Christ, Lk 1:1, "are most surely believed"; **(2b)** of evangelical ministry, 2 Ti 4:5, "make full proof"; so **(2c)** in 2 Ti 4:17, "fully known." See: TDNT—6:309, 867; BAGD—670b; THAYER—517b.

4136. **πληροφορία** {4x} **plērŏphŏria**, *play-rof-or-ee'-ah;* from *4135; entire confidence:*—full assurance {3x}, assurance {1x}.

This word means "a fullness, abundance," also means "full assurance, entire confidence"; lit., a "full-carrying" (*pleros*, "full," *phero*, "to carry"). It is translated **(1)** "full assurance" in Heb 6:11, the engrossing effect of the expectation of the fulfillment of God's promises; **(2)** In 1 Th 1:5 it describes the willingness and freedom of spirit enjoyed by those who brought the gospel to Thessalonica, "much assurance"; **(3)** in Col 2:2, the freedom of mind and confidence resulting from an understanding in Christ, "full assurance"; **(4)** in Heb 10:22, the character of the faith by which we are to draw near to God, "full assurance." See: TDNT—6:310, 867; BAGD—670c; THAYER—517c.

4137. **πληρόω** {90x} **plērŏō**, *play-rŏ'-o;* from *4134;* to *make replete,* i.e. (lit.) to *cram* (a net), *level* up (a hollow), or (fig.) to *furnish* (or *imbue, diffuse, influence*), *satisfy, execute* (an office), *finish* (a period or task), *verify* (or *coincide* with a prediction), etc.:—fulfil {51x}, fill {19x}, be full {7x}, complete {2x}, end {2x}, misc. {9x} = accomplish, × after, expire, fully preach, perfect, supply.

Pleroo signifies **(1)** "to fill" and is used **(1a)** of things: **(1a1)** a net, Mt 13:48; **(1a2)** a building, Jn 12:3; Acts 2:2; **(1a3)** a city, Acts 5:28; **(1a4)** needs, Phil 4:19, "supply"; **(1a5)** metaphorically, of valleys, Lk 3:5; **(1a6)** figuratively, of a measure of iniquity, Mt 23:32; **(1b)** of persons: **(1b1)** of the members of the church, the body of Christ, as filled by Him, Eph 1:23, "all things in all the members"; 4:10; in Eph 3:19, of their being filled "into" (*eis*), "with" (all the fullness of God); of their being "made full" in Him, Col 2:10, "complete"; **(1b2)** of Christ Himself: with wisdom, in the days of His flesh, Lk 2:40; with joy, in His return to the Father, Acts 2:28; **(1b3)** of believers: with the Spirit, Eph 5:18; with joy, Acts 13:52; 2 Ti 1:4; with joy and peace, Rom 15:13; with knowledge, Rom 15:14; with comfort, 2 Cor 7:4; with the fruits of righteousness, Phil 1:11 (Gk. "fruit"); with the knowledge of God's will, Col 1:9; with abundance through material supplies by fellow believers, Phil 4:18; **(1b4)** of the hearts of believers as the seat of emotion and volition, Jn 16:6 (sorrow); Acts 5:3 (deceitfulness); **(1b5)** of the unregenerate who refuse recognition of God, Rom 1:29;

(2) "to fulfill, complete," **(2a)** of time, e.g., **(2a1)** Mk 1:15; Lk 21:24; Jn 7:8, "full come"; **(2a2)** Acts 7:23, "he was full forty years old", lit., "the time of forty years was fulfilled to him"; **(2a3)** Acts 7:30, "were expired"; **(2a4)** Acts 9:23; 24:27, "after two years"; **(2b)** "fulfill" **(2b1)** of number, Rev 6:11; **(2b2)** of good pleasure, 2 Th 1:11; **(2b3)** of joy, Phil 2:2; **(2b4)** in the passive voice, "to be fulfilled," Jn 3:29 and 17:13; **(2b5)** of obedience, 2 Cor 10:6; **(2b6)** of works, Rev 3:2; **(2b7)** of the future Passover, Lk 22:16; **(2b8)** of sayings, prophecies, etc., e.g., Mt. 1:22 (twelve times in Mt, two in Mk, four in Lk, eight in Jn, two in Acts); Jas 2:23; **(3)** in Col 1:25 the word signifies to preach "fully," to complete the ministry of the Gospel appointed. See: TDNT—6:286, 867; BAGD—670c; THAYER—517c.

4138. **πλήρωμα** {17x} **plērōma**, *play'-ro-mah;* from *4137; repletion* or *completion,* i.e. (subj.) what *fills* (as contents, supplement, copiousness, multitude), or (obj.) what is *filled* (as container, performance, period):—fulness {13x}, full {1x}, fulfilling {1x}, which is put in to fill up {1x}, pierce that filled up {1x}.

Pleroma denotes "fullness," that of which a thing is "full"; it is thus used **(1)** of the grace and truth manifested in Christ, Jn 1:16; **(2)** of all His virtues and excellencies, Eph 4:13; Rom 15:29; **(3)** the conversion and restoration of Israel, Rom 11:12; **(4)** the completion of the number of Gentiles who receive blessing through the gospel, Rom 11:25; **(5)** the complete products of the earth, 1 Cor 10:26; **(6)** the end of an appointed period, Gal 4:4; Eph 1:10; **(7)** God, in the completeness of His Being, Eph 3:19; Col 1:19; 2:9; **(8)** the church as the complement of Christ, Eph 1:23. **(9)** In Mk 6:43, "basketfuls." See: TDNT—6:298, 867; BAGD—672a; THAYER—518c.

4139. **πλησίον** {17x} **plēsiŏn**, *play-see'-on;* neut. of a der. of πέλας **pĕlas** (near); (adv.) *close* by; as noun, a *neighbor,* i.e. *fellow* (as man, countryman, Chr. or friend):—near {16x}, neighbour {1x}.

(1) The neuter of the adjective *plesios* (from *pelas,* "near"), is used as an adverb accompanied by the article, lit., "the (one) near"; hence, one's "neighbor", "Then cometh He to a city of Samaria, which is called Sychar, near to the parcel of ground that Jacob gave to his son Joseph" (Jn 4:5). **(2)** This word has a wider range of meaning than that of the Eng. word "neighbor." There were no farmhouses scattered over the agricultural areas of Palestine; the populations, gathered in villages, went to and fro to their toil. Hence domestic life was touched at every point by a wide circle of neighborhood. The terms for neighbor were therefore of a very comprehensive scope. This may be seen from the chief characteristics of the privileges and duties of neighborhood as set forth in Scripture, **(2a)** its helpfulness, e.g., Prov 27:10; Lk 10:36; **(2b)** its intimacy, e.g., Lk 15:6, 9; Heb 8:11; **(2c)** its sincerity and sanctity, e.g., Ex 22:7, 10; Prov 3:29; 14:21; Rom 13:10; 15:2; Eph 4:25; Jas 4:12. **(3)** The NT quotes and expands the command in Lev 19:18, "to love one's neighbor as oneself"; see, e.g., Mt 5:43; 19:19; 22:39; Mk 12:31, 33; Lk 10:27; Gal 5:14; Jas 2:8; see also Acts 7:27. Syn.: 316, 1448, 1451, 1452, 4317, 4334. See: TDNT—6:311, 872; BAGD—672c; THAYER—518d.

4140. **πλησμονή** {1x} **plēsmŏnē**, *place-mon-ay';* from a presumed der. of *4130;* a *filling* up, i.e. (fig.) *gratification:*—satisfying {1x}.

This word means "a filling up, satiety" (akin to *pimplemi,* "to fill"), is translated "satisfying (of the flesh)" in Col 2:23. It can be understood as "yet not really of any value to remedy indulgence of the flesh." A possible meaning is, "of no value in attempts at asceticism." Some regard it as indicating that the ascetic treatment of the body is not of any honor to the satisfaction of the flesh (the reasonable demands of the body): this interpretation is unlikely. The following paraphrase well presents the contrast between the asceticism which "practically treats the body as an enemy, and the Pauline view which treats it as a potential instrument of a righteous life": ordinances, "which in fact have a specious look of wisdom (where there is no true wisdom), by the employment of self-chosen acts of religion and humility (and) by treating the body with brutality instead of treating it with due respect, with a view to meeting and providing against over-indulgence of the flesh. See: TDNT—6:131, 840; BAGD—673a; THAYER—519a.

4141. **πλήσσω** {1x} **plēssō**, *place'-so;* appar. another form of *4111* (through the idea of *flattening* out); to *pound,* i.e. (fig.) to *inflict* with (calamity):—smite {1x}.

This word means "a plague, stripe, wound," is used figuratively of the effect upon sun, moon and stars, after the sounding of the trumpet by the fourth angel, in the series of divine judgments upon the world hereafter, Rev 8:12. See: BAGD—673a; THAYER—519a. comp. *5180.*

4142. **πλοιάριον** {6x} **plŏiariŏn**, *ploy-ar'-ee-on;* neut. of a presumed der. of *4143;* a *boat:*—boat {3x}, little ship {2x}, small ship {1x}. See: BAGD—673b; THAYER—519b.

4143. **πλοῖον** {67x} **plŏiŏn**, *ploy'-on;* from *4126;* a *sailer,* i.e. *vessel:*—ship {66x}, shipping {1x}. See: BAGD—673b; THAYER—519b.

4144. **πλόος** {3x} **plŏŏs**, *plŏ'-os;* from *4126;* a *sail,* i.e. *navigation:*—course {1x}, sailing {1x}, voyage {1x}. See: BAGD—673c; THAYER—519b.

4145. **πλούσιος** {28x} **plŏusiŏs**, *ploo'-see-os;* from *4149; wealthy;* fig. *abounding* with:—rich {28x}.

This word means "rich, wealthy," is used **(1)** literally, **(1a)** adjectivally (with a noun expressed separately) in Mt 27:57; Lk 12:16; 14:12; 16:1, 19; (without a noun), 18:23; 19:2; **(1b)** as a noun, singular, a "rich" man (the noun not being expressed), Mt 19:23, 24; Mk 10:25; 12:41; Lk 16:21, 22; 18:25; Jas 1:10, 11, "the rich," "the rich (man)"; plural, Mk 12:41, lit., "rich (ones)"; Lk 6:24; 21:1; 1 Ti 6:17, "(them that are) rich," lit., "(the) rich"; Jas 2:6; 5:1; Rev 6:15 and 13:16; **(2)** metaphorically, **(2a)** of God, Eph 2:4, "in mercy"; **(2b)** of Christ, 2 Cor 8:9; **(2c)** of believers, Jas 2:5; **(2d)** Rev 2:9, of spiritual "enrichment" generally; **(2e)** Rev 3:17, of a false sense of "enrichment." See: TDNT—6:318, 873; BAGD—673c; THAYER—519b.

4146. **πλουσίως** {4x} **plŏusiōs**, *ploo-see'-oce;* adv. from *4145; copiously:*—abundantly {2x}, richly {2x}.

Plousios, connected with *ploutos,* "riches," is used of **(1)** the gift of the Holy Spirit, "abundantly, Titus 3:6; **(2)** entrance into the coming kingdom, "abundantly" in 2 Pet 1:11; **(3)** the indwelling of the Word of Christ, "richly" in Col 3:16; and of **(4)** material benefits, "richly" in 1 Ti 6:17. See: BAGD—673d; THAYER—519c.

4147. **πλουτέω** {12x} **plŏutĕō**, *ploo-teh'-o;* from *4148;* to *be* (or *become*) *wealthy* (lit. or fig.):—be rich {7x}, be made rich {2x}, rich {1x}, wax rich {1x}, be increased with goods {1x}.

This word means "to be rich," in the aorist or point tense, "to become rich," is used **(1)** literally, Lk 1:53, "the rich," present participle, lit., "(ones or those) being rich"; 1 Ti 6:9, 18; Rev 18:3, 15, 19; **(2)** metaphorically, **(2a)** of Christ, Rom 10:12, the passage stresses the fact that Christ is Lord; **(2b)** of the "enrichment" of believers through His poverty, 2 Cor 8:9, expressing completeness, with permanent results; **(2c)** so in Rev 3:18, where the spiritual "enrichment" is conditional upon righteousness of life and conduct; **(2d)** of a false sense of "enrichment," 1 Cor 4:8, "ye are rich"; Rev 3:17, perfect tense, "I am . . . increased with goods." See: TDNT—6:318, 873; BAGD—673d; THAYER—519c.

4148. **πλουτίζω** {3x} **plŏutizō**, *ploo-tid'-zo;* from *4149;* to *make wealthy* (fig.):—enrich {2x}, make rich {1x}.

This word means "to make rich" (from *ploutos,* "wealth, riches"), is used metaphorically, **(1)** of spiritual "riches," in 1 Cor 1:5, "ye were enriched"; **(2)** 2 Cor 6:10, "making rich"; **(3)** 2 Cor 9:11, "being enriched." See: TDNT—6:318, 873; BAGD—674a; THAYER—519c.

4149. **πλοῦτος** {22x} **plŏutŏs**, *ploo'-tos;* from the base of *4130; wealth* (as *fulness*), i.e. (lit.) *money, possessions,* or (fig.) *abundance, richness,* (spec.) valuable *bestowment:*—riches {22x}.

Ploutos is used in the singular **(1)** of material "riches," used evilly, Mt 13:22: Mk 4:19; Lk 8:14; 1 Ti 6:17; Jas 5:2; Rev 18:17; **(2)** of spiritual and moral "riches," **(2a)** possessed by God and exercised towards men, **(2a1)** Rom 2:4, "of His goodness and forbearance and longsuffering"; **(2a2)** Rom 9:23 and Eph 3:16, "of His glory" (i.e., of its manifestation in grace towards believers); **(2a3)** Rom 11:33, of His wisdom and knowledge; **(2a4)** Eph 1:7 and 2:7, "of His grace"; **(2a5)** Eph 1:18, "of the glory of His inheritance in the saints"; **(2a6)** Eph 3:8, "of Christ"; **(2a7)** Phil 4:19, "in glory in Christ Jesus"; **(2b)** to be ascribed to Christ, Rev 5:12; **(2c)** of the effects of the gospel upon the Gentiles, Rom 11:12 (twice), **(2d)** of the full assurance of understanding in regard to the mystery of God, even Christ, Col 2:2; **(2e)** of the liberality of the churches of Macedonia, 2 Cor 8:2, where "the riches" stands for the spiritual and moral value of their liberality; **(2f)** of "the reproach of Christ" in contrast to this world's treasures, Heb 11:26. See: TDNT—6:318, 873; BAGD—674b; THAYER—519c.

4150. **πλύνω** {1x} **plunō**, *ploo'-no;* a prol. form of an obs. πλύω **pluō**, (to *"flow"*); to *"plunge,"* i.e. *launder* clothing:—wash {1x}.

Pluno is used of washing only inanimate objects, garments (Rev 7:14). Syn.: 3068, 3538. See: BAGD—674c; THAYER—519d.

4151. **πνεῦμα** {385x} **pnĕuma**, *pnyoo'-mah;* from *4154;* a *current* of air, i.e. *breath* (*blast*) or a *breeze;* by anal. or fig. a *spirit,* i.e. (human) the rational *soul,* (by impl.) *vital principle,* ment. *disposition,* etc., or (superhuman) an *angel, demon,* or (divine) *God,* Christ's *spirit,* the Holy *Spirit:*—Spirit {111x}, Holy Ghost {89x}, Spirit (of God) {13x}, Spirit (of the Lord) {5x}, (My) Spirit {3x}, Spirit (of truth) {3x}, Spirit (of Christ) {2x}, human (spirit) {49x}, (evil) spirit {47x}, spirit (general) {26x}, spirit {8x}, (Jesus' own) spirit {6x}, (Jesus' own) ghost {2x}, misc. {21x} = life, spiritual, spiritually, wind.

Syn.: This word is rarely used of wind, but when so used it is known for its strength, vigor, and force (Jn 3:8; Acts 2:2; 27:40). *Pnoe* (4157) by contrast is a gentle breeze, a quiet and calm exhalation. Comp. 417, 2366, 2978, 4157, 5590. See: TDNT—6:332, 876; BAGD—674c; THAYER—520a.

4152. **πνευματικός** {26x} **pnĕumatikŏs**, *pnyoo-mat-ik-os';* from *4151; non-carnal,* i.e. (humanly) *ethereal* (as opposed to gross), or (demoniacally) a *spirit* (concr.), or (divinely) *supernatural, regenerate, religious:*—spiritual {26x}.

Pneumatikos always connotes the ideas of invisibility and of power. It does not occur in the OT or in the Gospels; it is in fact an after-Pentecost word. In the NT it is used as follows: **(1)** the angelic hosts, lower than God but higher in the scale of being than man in his natural state, are "spiritual hosts," Eph 6:12; **(2)** things that have their origin with God, and which, therefore, are in harmony with His character, as His law is, are "spiritual," Rom 7:14; **(3)** "spiritual" is prefixed to the material type in order to indicate that what the type sets forth, not the type itself, is intended, 1 Cor 10:3, 4; **(4)** the purposes of God **(4a)** revealed in the gospel by the Holy Spirit, 1 Cor 2:13a; and the words in which that revelation is expressed, are "spiritual"; matching, or combining, spiritual things with spiritual words; **(4b)** "spiritual songs" are songs of which the burden is the things revealed by the Spirit, Eph 5:19; Col 3:16; **(4c)** "spiritual wisdom and understanding" is wisdom in, and understanding of, those things, Col 1:9;

(5) men in Christ who walk so as to please God are "spiritual," Gal 6:1; 1 Cor 2:13b, 15; 3:1; 14:37; **(6)** the whole company of those who believe in Christ is a "spiritual house," 1 Pet 2:5a; **(7)** the blessings that accrue to regenerate men at this present time are called "spiritualities," Rom 15:27; 1 Cor 9:11; **(8)** "spiritual blessings," Eph 1:3; **(9)** "spiritual gifts," Rom 1:11; **(10)** the activities Godward of regenerate men are "spiritual sacrifices," 1 Pet 2:5b; **(11)** their appointed activities in the churches are also called "spiritual gifts," lit., "spiritualities," 1 Cor 12:1; 14:1; **(11)** the resurrection body of the dead in Christ is "spiritual," i.e., such as is suited to the heavenly environment, 1 Cor 15:44;

(12) all that is produced and maintained among men by the operations of the Spirit of God is "spiritual," 1 Cor 15:46. . . . The spiritual man is one who walks by the Spirit both in the sense of Gal 5:16 and in that of 5:25, and who himself manifests the fruit of the Spirit in his own ways. According to the Scriptures, the "spiritual" state of soul is normal for the believer, but to this state all believers do not attain, nor when it is attained is it always maintained. Thus the apostle, in 1 Cor 3:1–3, suggests a contrast between this spiritual state and that of the babe in Christ, i.e., of the man who because of immaturity and inexperience has not yet reached spirituality, and that of the man who by permitting jealousy, and the strife to which jealousy always leads, has lost it. The spiritual state is reached by diligence in the Word of God and in prayer; it is maintained by obedience and self-judgment. Such as are led by the Spirit are spiritual, but, of course, spirituality is not a fixed or absolute condition, it admits of growth; indeed growth in "the grace and knowledge of our Lord and Savior Jesus Christ," 2 Pet 3:18, is evidence of true spirituality. See: TDNT—6:332, 876; BAGD—678b; THAYER—523c. comp. *5591.*

4153. **πνευματικῶς** {2x} **pnĕumatikōs**, *pnyoo-mat-ik-oce';* adv. from *4152; non-physical,* i.e. *divinely, figuratively:*—spiritually {2x}. Cf. 1 Cor 2:14; Rev. 11:8. See: BAGD—679b; THAYER—523d.

4154. **πνέω** {7x} **pnĕō**, *pneh'-o;* a primary word; to *breathe* hard, i.e. *breeze:*—to blow {6x}, wind {1x}. See: TDNT—6:452, 876; BAGD—679c; THAYER—524a. comp. *5594.*

4155. **πνίγω** {2x} **pnigō**, *pnee'-go;* strengthened from *4154;* to *wheeze,* i.e. (cause. by impl.) to *throttle* or *strangle* (*drown*):—choke {1x}, take by the throat {1x}.

Pnigo is used, in the passive voice, **(1)** of "perishing by drowning," Mk 5:13; **(2)** in the active, "to seize a person's throat, to throttle," Mt 18:28. See: TDNT—6:455, 895; BAGD—679d; THAYER—524a.

4156. **πνικτός** {3x} **pniktŏs**, *pnik-tos';* from *4155; throttled,* i.e. (neut. concr.) an animal *choked* to death (*not bled*):—strangled {3x}. See: TDNT—6:455, 895; BAGD—679d; THAYER—524a.

4157. **πνοή** {2x} **pnŏē**, *pno-ay';* from *4154; respiration,* a *breeze:*—breath {1x}, wind {1x}.

Pnoe, akin to *pneo,* "to blow," lit., "a blowing," signifies **(1)** "breath, the breath of life," Acts 17:25; and **(2)** "wind," Acts 2:2. Syn.: *Pneuma* (4151) stresses strength, vigor, and force (Jn 3:8; Acts 2:2; 27:40). *Pnoe* (4157) by contrast is a gentle breeze, a quiet and calm exhalation. Comp. 417, 2366, 2978, 4151, 5590. See: TDNT—6:453, 876; BAGD—680b; THAYER—524a.

4158. **ποδήρης** {1x} **pŏdērēs**, *pod-ay'-race;* from *4228* and another element of uncert. aff.; a *dress* (*2066* impl.) *reaching* the *ankles:*—garment down to the foot {1x}. Syn.: 2440, 2441, 4749, 5509, 5511. See: BAGD—680b; THAYER—524a.

4159. **πόθεν** {28x} **pŏthĕn**, *poth'-en;* from the base of *4213* with enclitic adverb of origin; *from which* (as interr.) or *what* (as rel.) place, state, source or cause:—whence {28x}. See: BAGD—680b; THAYER—524b.

4160. **ποιέω** {579x} **pŏiĕō**, *poy-eh'-o;* appar. a prol. form of an obs. primary; to *make* or *do* (in a very wide application, more or less dir.):—do {357x}, make {113x}, bring forth {14x}, commit {9x}, cause {9x}, work {8x}, shew {5x}, bear {4x}, keep {4x}, fulfil {3x}, deal {2x}, perform {2x}, not tr {3x}, misc, {43x}, vr do {3x} = abide, + agree, appoint, × avenge, + band together, be, + bewray, cast out, + content, continue, + without any delay, doing, execute, exercise, gain, give, have, hold, × journeying, + lay wait, + lighten the ship, × mean, + none of these things move me, observe, ordain, provide, + have purged, purpose, put, + raising up, × secure, shew, × shoot out, spend, take, tarry, + transgress the law, yield.

Poieo, as a verb, means "to make, to do" and is used of the bringing forth of fruit: "Bring forth therefore fruits meet for repentance" (Mt 3:8, cf. 10; 7:17, 18). Syn.: cf. 4238 for discussion. See: TDNT—6:458, 895; BAGD—680d; THAYER—524b.

4161 **ποίημα** {2x} **pŏiēma**, *poy'-ay-mah;* from *4160;* a *product,* i.e. *fabric* (lit. or fig.):—thing that is made {1x}, workmanship {1x}. Cf. Rom 1:20; Eph 2:10. See: TDNT—6:458, 895; BAGD—683b; THAYER—527b.

4162. **ποίησις** {1x} **pŏiēsis**, *poy'-ay-sis;* from *4160; action,* i.e. *performance* (of the law):—deed {1x}. See: TDNT—6:458, 895; BAGD—683b; THAYER—527b.

4163. **ποιητής** {6x} **pŏiētēs**, *poy-ay-tace';* from *4160;* a *performer;* spec. a *"poet"*:—doer {5x}, poet {1x}.

Poietes signifies **(1)** "a doer," Rom 2:13; Jas 1:22–23, 25; 4:11. **(2)** Its meaning "poet" is found in Acts 17:28. A poet is one who "makes" a writing, not just reports or narrates. See: TDNT—6:458, 895; BAGD—683b; THAYER—527b.

4164. **ποικίλος** {10x} **pŏikilŏs**, *poy-kee'-los;* of uncert. der.; *motley,* i.e. *various* in character:—divers {8x}, manifold {2x}.

Poikilos denotes "particolored, variegated" hence **(1)** "divers," Mt 4:24; Mk 1:34; Lk 4:40;

2 Ti 3:6; Titus 3:3; Heb 2:4; 13:9; Jas 1:2; and **(2)** in 1 Pet 1:6 and 4:10, "manifold." See: TDNT–6:484, 901; BAGD–683c; THAYER–527b.

4165. **ποιμαίνω** {11x} **pŏimainō**, *poy-mah'-ee-no;* from *4166;* to *tend* as a shepherd (or fig. *superviser*):—feed {6x}, feed cattle {1x}, rule {4x}.

(1) *Poimaino* refers to the whole process of shepherding: guiding, guarding, folding, and providing pasture. It means "to act as a shepherd" (from *poimen,* "a shepherd"), is used **(1)** literally, Lk 17:7, "feeding cattle"; 1 Cor 9:7, **(2)** metaphorically, "to tend, to shepherd"; said **(2a)** of Christ Mt 2:6, "shall rule"; **(2b)** of those who act as spiritual shepherds under Him, Jn 21:16, "feed", so 1 Pet 5:2; Acts 20:28, "to feed"; **(2c)** of base shepherds, Jude 12. **(3)** It is also translated "to rule" in Rev 2:27; 12:5; 19:15, all indicating that the governing power exercised by the Shepherd is to be of a firm character. **(4)** Cattle is the word for any four-footed beast, usually domesticated. THAYER–1006. See: TDNT–6:485, 901; BAGD–683d; THAYER–527c.

4166. **ποιμήν** {18x} **pŏimēn**, *poy-mane';* of uncert. aff.; a *shepherd* (lit. or fig.):—shepherd {15x}, Shepherd {2x}, pastor {1x}.

Poimen, "a shepherd, one who tends herds or flocks" (not merely one who feeds them), is used **(1)** metaphorically of Christian "pastors," Eph 4:11. **(2)** "Pastors" guide as well as feed the flock, cf. Acts 20:28, which with 20:17, indicates that this was the service committed to elders (overseers or bishops); so also in 1 Pet 5:1, 2, "tend the flock . . . exercising the oversight"; this involves tender care and vigilant superintendence. See: TDNT–6:485, 901; BAGD–684a; THAYER–527c.

4167. **ποίμνη** {5x} **pŏimnē**, *poym'-nay;* contr. from *4165;* a *flock* (lit. or fig.):—flock {4x}, fold {1x}.

A flock is a group of animals, possibly mixed [sheep and goats] but a fold contains only one kind of animal. See: TDNT–6:499, 901; BAGD–684c; THAYER–527d.

4168. **ποίμνιον** {5x} **pŏimniŏn**, *poym'-nee-on;* neut. of a presumed der. of *4167;* a *flock,* i.e. (fig.) *group* (of believers):—flock {5x}. Syn.: 4167. See: TDNT–6:499, 901; BAGD–684c; THAYER–527d.

4169. **ποῖος** {34x} **pŏiŏs**, *poy'-os;* from the base of *4226* and *3634;* individualizing interr. (of character) *what* sort of, or (of number) *which* one:—what {27x}, which {4x}, what things {1x}, what way {1x}, what manner of {1x}.

Poios, as an adjective, means "of what sort" is translated **(1)** "by what [manner of] death" (Jn 21:19); **(2)** "what [manner of] house" (Acts 7:49); **(3)** "what [manner of] law" (Rom 3:27); **(4)** "what [manner of] body" (1 Cor 15:35). Syn.: 195, 1485, 2239, 3634, 3668, 3697, 3779, 4187, 4217, 4459, 5158, 5159, 5179, 5615. See: BAGD–684c; THAYER–527d.

4170. **πολεμέω** {7x} **pŏlĕmĕō**, *pol-em-eh'-o;* from *4171;* to *be* (engaged) in *warfare,* i.e. to *battle* (lit. or fig.):—fight {3x}, make war {3x}, war {1x}.

Polemeo, (Eng., "polemics"), "to fight, to make war," is used **(1)** literally, "fought", Rev 12:7 (twice); 13:4; 17:14; 19:11; **(2)** metaphorically, Rev 2:16; and **(3)** hyperbolically, Jas 4:2. Syn.: *Polemeo* is the war and *mache* (3163) refers to the battles of which *polemeo* is made. See: TDNT–6:502, 904; BAGD–685a; THAYER–527d.

4171. **πόλεμος** {18x} **pŏlĕmŏs**, *pol'-em-os;* from πέλομαι **pĕlŏmai**, (to *bustle*); *warfare* (lit. or fig.; a single encounter or a series):—battle {5x}, fight {1x}, war {12x}. See: TDNT–6:502, 904; BAGD–685a; THAYER–528a.

4172. **πόλις** {164x} **pŏlis**, *pol'-is;* prob. from the same as *4171,* or perh. from *4183;* a *town* (prop. with walls, of greater or less size):—city {164x}.

(1) A *polis* is primarily a town enclosed with a wall. **(2)** It is used of the heavenly Jerusalem, the abode and community of the redeemed, Heb 11:10, 16; 12:22; 13:14. **(3)** In the Apocalypse it signifies the visible capital of the heavenly kingdom, as destined to descend to earth in a coming age e.g., Rev 3:12; 21:2, 14, 19. **(4)** By metonymy the word stands for the inhabitants, as in the English use, e.g., Mt 8:34; 12:25; 21:10; Mk 1:33; Acts 13:44. See: TDNT–6:516, 906; BAGD–685b; THAYER–528a.

4173. **πολιτάρχης** {2x} **pŏlitarchēs**, *pol-it-ar'-khace;* from *4172* and *757;* a *town-officer,* i.e. *magistrate:*—ruler of the city {2x}.

This word means "a ruler of a city" (*polis,* "a city," *archo,* "to rule"), "a politarch," is used in Acts 17:6, 8, of the magistrates in Thessalonica, before whom the Jews, with a mob of market idlers, dragged Jason and other converts, under the charge of showing hospitality to Paul and Silas, and of treasonable designs against the emperor. Thessalonica was a "free" city and the citizens could choose their own politarchs. The accuracy of Luke has been vindicated by the use of the term, for while classical authors use the terms *poliarchos* and *politarchos* of similar "rulers," the form used by Luke is supported by inscriptions discovered at Thessalonica. See: BAGD–686a; THAYER–528c.

4174. **πολιτεία** {2x} **pŏlitĕia**, *pol-ee-ti'-ah;* from *4177* ("*polity*"); *citizenship;* concr. a *community:*—commonwealth {1x}, freedom {1x}.

Politeia signifies **(1)** "the relation in which a citizen stands to the state, the condition of a citizen, citizenship," Acts 22:28, "with a great sum obtained I this freedom." While Paul's "citizenship" of Tarsus was not of advantage outside that city, yet his Roman "citizenship" availed throughout the Roman Empire and, besides private rights, included **(1a)** exemption from all degrading punishments; **(1b)** a right of appeal to the emperor after a sentence; **(1c)** a right to be sent to Rome for trial before the emperor if charged with a capital offense. It is also **(2)** "a civil polity, the condition of a state, a commonwealth," said of Israel, Eph. 2:12. See: TDNT–6:516, 906; BAGD–686a; THAYER–528c.

4175. **πολίτευμα** {1x} **pŏlitĕuma**, *pol-it'-yoo-mah;* from *4176;* a *community,* i.e. (abstr.) *citizenship* (fig.):—conversation {1x}.

To converse is go back and forth with another; hence, by extension how one goes back in forth in life, Phil 3:20. See: TDNT–6:516, 906; BAGD–686b; THAYER–528c.

4176. **πολιτεύομαι** {2x} **pŏlitĕuŏmai**, *pol-it-yoo'-om-ahee;* mid. voice of a der. of *4177;* to *behave* as a citizen (fig.):—let (one's) conversation be {1x}, live {1x}.

Politeuo, as a verb, means "to be a citizen (polites), to live as a citizen" and is used metaphorically of conduct as in accordance with the characteristics of the heavenly community; **(1)** in Acts 23:1: "And Paul, earnestly beholding the council, said, Men *and* brethren, I have lived (*politeuo*) in all good conscience before God until this day"; and **(2)** in Phil 1:27 "Only let your conversation (*politeuo*) be as it becometh the gospel of Christ: that whether I come and see you, or else be absent, I may hear of your affairs, that ye stand fast in one spirit, with one mind striving together for the faith of the gospel." Syn.: 326, 390, 980, 1236, 2198, 2225, 4800, 5225. See: TDNT–6:516, 906; BAGD–686c; THAYER–528d.

4177. **πολίτης** {3x} **pŏlitēs**, *pol-ee'-tace;* from *4172;* a *townsman:*—citizen {3x}.

Polites, "a member of a city or state, or the inhabitant of a country or district," Lk 15:15, is used elsewhere in Lk 19:14, Acts 21:39. See: TDNT–6:516, 906; BAGD–686d; THAYER–528d.

4178. **πολλάκις** {18x} **pŏllakis**, *pol-lak'-is;* mult. adv. from *4183; many times,* i.e. *frequently:*—often {7x}, oft {5x}, ofttimes {3x}, oftentimes {3x}. See: BAGD–686d; THAYER–529a.

4179. **πολλαπλασίων** {1x} **pŏllaplasiōn**, *pol-lap-las-ee'-ohn;* from *4183* and prob. a der. of *4120; manifold,* i.e. (neut. as noun) *very much more:*—manifold more {1x}. See: BAGD–686d; THAYER–529a.

4180. **πολυλογία** {1x} **pŏlulŏgia**, *pol-oo-log-ee'-ah;* from a compound of *4183* and *3056; loquacity,* i.e. *prolixity:*—much speaking {1x}. See: TDNT–6:545, 911; BAGD–687b; THAYER–529a.

4181. **πολυμέρως** {1x} **pŏlumĕrōs**, *pol-oo-mer'-oce;* adv. from a compound of *4183* and *3313; in many portions,* i.e. *variously* as to time and agency (*piecemeal*):—at sundry times {1x}.

This word means by many portions, by many times and in many ways, yet all connected. It is related to "asunder" to break one item into many pieces; hence, all of God's means of revelation still have Him, the One God, as their source. See: BAGD–687b; THAYER–529a.

4182. **πολυποίκιλος** {1x} **pŏlupŏikilŏs**, *pol-oo-poy'-kil-os;* from *4183* and *4164; much variegated,* i.e. *multifarious:*—manifold {1x}. See: TDNT–6:485, 901; BAGD–687b; THAYER–529a.

4183. **πολύς** {365x} **pŏlus**, *pol-oos';* incl. the forms from the alt. πολλός **pŏllŏs;** (sing.) *much* (in any respect) or (plural) *many;* neut. (sing.) as adv. *largely;* neut. (plural) as adv. or noun *often, mostly, largely:*—many {210x}, much {73x}, great {59x}, misc {23x} = abundant, + altogether, common, + far (passed, spent), long, oft (-en [-times]), plenteous, sore, straitly. See: TDNT–6:536,*; BAGD–687c; THAYER–529a. comp. *4118, 4119.*

4184. **πολύσπλαγχνος** {1x} **pŏlusplagchnŏs**, *pol-oo'-splankh-nos;* from *4183* and *4698* (fig.); full of pity, *extremely compassionate:*—very pitiful {1x}.

This word denotes "very pitiful" or "full of pity" (*polus,* "much," *splanchnon,* "the heart"; in the plural, "the affections"), occurs in Jas 5:11. See: TDNT–7:548, 1067; BAGD–689d; THAYER–530b.

4185. **πολυτελής** {3x} **pŏlutĕlēs**, *pol-oo-tel-ace';* from *4183* and *5056; extremely expensive:*—costly {1x}, very precious {1x}, of great price {1x}.

This word means primarily, "the very end or limit" (from *polus,* "much," *telos,* "revenue"), with reference to price, of highest "cost," very expensive, is said **(1)** of spikenard, Mk 14:3, "very pressure"; **(2)** raiment, 1 Ti 2:9, "costly"; and **(3)** metaphorically, of a meek and quiet spirit, 1 Pet 3:4, "of great price." See: BAGD—690a; THAYER—530b.

4186. **πολύτιμος** {2x} **pŏlutimŏs**, *pol-oot'-ee-mos;* from *4183* and *5092; extremely valuable:*—very costly {1x}, of great price {1x}.

This word means lit., "of great value" and is used **(1)** of a pearl, Mt 13:46, "of great price"; and **(2)** of spikenard, Jn 12:3, "very costly." See: BAGD—690a; THAYER—530b.

4187. **πολυτρόπως** {1x} **pŏlutrŏpōs**, *pol-oot-rop'-oce;* adv. from a compound of *4183* and *5158; in many ways,* i.e. *variously* as to method or form:—in divers manners {1x}.

Polutropos, as an adverb, literally means "much turning, in many ways (or manners)" and is rendered "in divers manners" (Heb 1:1). Syn.: 195, 1485, 2239, 3634, 3668, 3697, 3779, 4169, 4217, 4459, 5158, 5159, 5179, 5615. See: BAGD—690b; THAYER—530b.

4188. **πόμα** {2x} **pŏma**, *pom'-ah;* from the alt. of *4095;* the thing drunk, a *beverage:*—a drink {2x}.

Poma denotes "the thing drunk" in 1 Cor 10:4; Heb 9:10. See: TDNT—6:145, 840; BAGD—690b; THAYER—530b.

4189. **πονηρία** {7x} **pŏnēria**, *pon-ay-ree'-ah;* from *4190; depravity,* i.e. (spec.) *malice;* plur. (concr.) *plots, sins:*—iniquity {1x}, wickedness {6x}.

Poneria denotes **(1)** "wickedness," and is so translated in Mt 22:18; Mk 7:22 (plural); Lk 11:39; Rom 1:29; 1 Cor 5:8; Eph 6:12; and **(2)** in Acts 3:26, "iniquities." Syn.: *Kakia* (2549) denotes a vicious disposition; whereas, *poneria* (4189) denotes the active exercise of a vicious disposition. See: TDNT—6:562, 912; BAGD—690c; THAYER—530b.

4190. **πονηρός** {76x} **pŏnērŏs**, *pon-ay-ros';* from a der. of *4192; hurtful,* i.e. *evil* (prop. in effect or influence, and thus differing from *2556,* which refers rather to *essential* character, as well as from *4550,* which indicates *degeneracy* from original virtue); fig. *calamitous;* also (pass.) *ill,* i.e. *diseased;* but especially (mor.) *culpable,* i.e. *derelict, vicious, facinorous;* neut. (sing.) *mischief, malice,* or (plural) *guilt;* masc. (sing.) the *devil,* or (plural) *sinners:*—evil {51x}, wicked {10x}, wicked one {6x}, evil things {2x}, misc. {7x} = bad, grievous, harm, lewd, malicious, wickedness.

Poneros is connected with *ponos* (4192) and means labor and expresses especially **(1)** the active form of evil. It is used **(1a)** of thoughts (Mt 15:19); **(1b)** of speech (Mt 5:11); **(1c)** of acts (2 Ti 4:18). **(2)** *Poneros* alone is used **(2a)** of Satan (Mt 5:37); and **(2b)** of demons (Lk 7:21). This word also denotes "labor, toil," and denotes "evil that causes labor, pain, sorrow, malignant evil" being used **(3)** with the meaning bad, worthless, **(3a)** in the physical sense, Mt 7:17–18; **(3b)** in the moral or ethical sense, "evil," wicked; **(3b1)** of persons, e.g., Mt 7:11; Lk 6:45; Acts 17:5; 2 Th 3:2; 2 Ti 3:13; **(3b2)** of "evil" spirits, e.g., Mt 12:45; Lk 7:21; Acts 19:12–13, 15–16; **(3b3)** of a generation, Mt 12:39, 45; 16:4; Lk 11:29; **(3b4)** of things, e.g., Mt 5:11; 6:23; 20:15; Mk 7:22; Lk 11:34; Jn 3:19; 7:7; Acts 18:14; Gal 1:4; Col 1:21; 1 Ti 6:4; 2 Ti 4:18; Heb 3:12; 10:22; Jas 2:4; 4:16; 1 Jn 3:12; 2 Jn 11; 3 Jn 10; **(4)** with the meaning toilsome, painful, Eph 5:16; 6:13; Rev 16:2. Syn.: Where *kakos* (2556) and *poneros* are put together, *kakos* is always put first and signifies bad in character, base and *poneros* means bad in effect, malignant (1 Cor 5:8; Rev 16:2). *Kakos* has a wider meaning, *poneros* a stronger meaning. Comp. 5337. See: TDNT—6:546, 912; BAGD—690d; THAYER—650c. See also *4191.*

4191. **πονηρότερος** {2x} **pŏnērŏtĕrŏs**, *pon-ay-rot'-er-os,* comp. of *4190; more evil:*—more wicked {2x}. See: BAGD—690d; THAYER—650c.

4192. **πόνος** {3x} **pŏnŏs**, *pon'-os;* from the base of *3993; toil,* i.e. (by impl.) *anguish:*—pain {3x}.

Ponos refers to labor that demands the greatest exertion if one is to accomplish a task. It denotes "the consequence of toil," viz., distress, suffering, pain, Rev 16:10, 11; 21:4. Syn.: 2873, 3449. See: BAGD—691c; THAYER—531a.

4193. **Ποντικός** {1x} **Pŏntikŏs**, *pon-tik-os';* from *4195;* a *Pontican,* i.e. native of Pontus:—born in Pontus {1x}. See: BAGD—691d; THAYER—531a.

4194. **Πόντιος** {4x} **Pŏntiŏs**, *pon'-tee-os;* of Lat. or.; appar. *bridged; Pontius,* a Rom.:—Pontius [Pilate]{4x}. See: BAGD—691d; THAYER—531a.

4195. **Πόντος** {2x} **Pŏntŏs**, *pon'-tos;* a *sea; Pontus,* a region of Asia Minor:—Pontus {2x}. See: BAGD—691d; THAYER—531a.

4196. **Πόπλιος** {2x} **Pŏpliŏs**, *pop'-lee-os;* of Lat. or.; appar. *"popular"*; *Poplius* (i.e. *Publius*), a Rom.:—Publius {2x}. See: BAGD—692a; THAYER—530a.

4197. **πορεία** {2x} **pŏrĕia**, *por-i'-ah;* from *4198; travel* (by land); fig. (plural) *proceedings,* i.e. *career:*—journeying + 4160 {1x}, ways {1x}.

This word refers **(1)** to a purposeful journey, Lk 13:22; and **(2)** describes the purposeful ways a rich man lives his life, Jas 1:11. See: BAGD—692a; THAYER—531b.

4198. **πορεύομαι** {154x} **pŏrĕuŏmai**, *por-yoo'-om-ahee;* mid. voice from a der. of the same as *3984;* to *traverse,* i.e. *travel* (lit. or fig.; espec. to *remove* [fig. *die*], *live,* etc.);—go {117x}, depart {11x}, walk {9x}, go (one's) way {8x}, misc. {9x} = (make a, take a) journey.

Syn.: **(A)** *Erchomai* (2064) denotes motion or progress generally, and of any sort, hence to "come" and arrive at, as well as "to go." **(B)** *Bathmos* (898) primarily signifies "to walk", "take steps", picturing the mode of motion; to "go away." **(C)** *Poreuomai* (4198) expresses motion in general, often confined within certain limits, or giving prominence to the bearing; hence the regular word for the march of an army. **(D)** *Choreo* (5562) always emphasizes the idea of separation, change of place, and does not, like e.g. 4198, note the external and perceptible motion. See: TDNT—6:566, 915; BAGD—692b; THAYER—531b.

4199. **πορθέω** {3x} **pŏrthĕō**, *por-theh'-o;* prol. from πέρθω **pĕrthō**, (to *sack*); to *ravage* (fig.):—destroy {2x}, waste {1x}.

Portheo, "to destroy, ravage, lay waste," is used of the persecution inflicted by Saul of Tarsus on the church in Jerusalem, **(1)** Acts 9:21, and Gal 1:23, "destroyed"; **(2)** Gal 1:13, "wasted." See: BAGD—693a; THAYER—531d.

4200. **πορισμός** {2x} **pŏrismŏs**, *por-is-mos';* from a der. of πόρος **pŏrŏs** (a *way,* i.e. *means*); *furnishing,* (*procuring*), i.e. (by impl.) *money-getting* (*acquisition*):—gain {2x}.

This word primarily denotes "a providing" (akin to *porizo,* "to procure"), then, "a means of gain," 1 Ti 6:5; 6:6. See: BAGD—693a; THAYER—531d.

4201. **Πόρκιος** {1x} **Pŏrkiŏs**, *por'-kee-os;* of Lat. or.; appar. *swinish; Porcius,* a Rom.:—Porcius {1x}. See: BAGD—693a; THAYER—531d.

4202. **πορνεία** {26x} **pŏrnĕia**, *por-ni'-ah;* from *4203; harlotry* (incl. *adultery* and *incest*); fig. *idolatry:*—fornication {26x}.

Porneis is used **(1)** of "illicit sexual intercourse," in Jn 8:41; Acts 15:20, 29; 21:25; 1 Cor 5:1; 6:13, 18; 2 Cor 12:21; Gal 5:19; Eph 5:3; Col 3:5; 1 Th 4:3; Rev 2:21; 9:21; in the plural in 1 Cor 7:2; **(2)** in Mt 5:32 and 19:9 it stands for, or includes, adultery; it is distinguished from it in 15:19 and Mk 7:21; **(3)** metaphorically, of "the association of pagan idolatry with doctrines of, and professed adherence to, the Christian faith," Rev 14:8; 17:2, 4; 18:3; 19:2. See: TDNT—6:579, 918; BAGD—693b; THAYER—531d.

4203. **πορνεύω** {8x} **pŏrnĕuō**, *porn-yoo'-o;* from *4204;* to *act* the *harlot,* i.e. (lit.) *indulge* unlawful *lust* (of either sex), or (fig.) *practice idolatry:*—commit {1x}, commit fornication {7x}.

Porneuo, "to commit fornication," is used **(1)** literally, Mk 10:19; 1 Cor 6:18; 10:8; Rev 2:14, 20; **(2)** metaphorically, Rev 17:2; 18:3, 9. See: TDNT—6:579, 918; BAGD—693c; THAYER—532a.

4204. **πόρνη** {12x} **pŏrnē**, *por'-nay;* fem. of *4205;* a *strumpet;* fig. an *idolater:*—harlot {8x}, whore {4x}.

(1) A woman who sells her body for sexual uses is **(1a)** a prostitute, a harlot (a hirelot), one who yields herself to defilement for the sake of gain; or **(1b)** any woman indulging in unlawful sexual intercourse, usually driven by lust, maybe for gain. **(2)** Metaphorically, it is used of Babylon, the chief seat of idolatry. See: TDNT—6:579, 918; BAGD—693c; THAYER—532b.

4205. **πόρνος** {10x} **pŏrnŏs**, *por'-nos;* from πέρνημι **pĕrnēmi**, (to *sell;* akin to the base of *4097*); a (male) *prostitute* (as *venal*), i.e. (by anal.) a *debauchee* (*libertine*):—fornicator {5x}, whoremonger {5x}.

Pornos denotes "a man who indulges in fornication, **(1)** a fornicator" 1 Cor 5:9, 10, 11; 6:9; Heb. 12:16; or **(2)** a "whoremonger" in Eph 5:5; 1 Ti 1:10; Heb 13:4; Rev. 21:8; 22:15. See: TDNT—6:579, 918; BAGD—693d; THAYER—532b.

4206. **πόῤῥω** {3x} **pŏrrhō**, *por'-rho;* adv. from *4253; forwards,* i.e. *at a distance:*—far {2x}, a great way off {1x}. Cf. Mt 15:8; Lk 14:32; 24:28. See: BAGD—693d; THAYER—532c. See also *4207.*

4207. **πόῤῥωθεν** {2x} **pŏrrhōthĕn**, *por'-rho-then;* from *4206* with adv. enclitic of source; *from far,* or (by impl.) *at a distance,* i.e. *distantly:*—afar off {2x}. Cf. Lk 17:12; Heb 11:13. See: BAGD—693d; THAYER—532c.

4208. **ποῤῥωτέρω** {1x} **pŏrrhōtĕrō**, *por-rho-ter'-o;* adv. comparative of *4206; further,* i.e. *a greater distance:*—farther {1x}. See: BAGD—694a; 693d; THAYER—532c.

4209. **πορφύρα** {5x} **pŏrphura**, *por-foo'-rah;* of Lat. or.; the *"purple"* mussel, i.e. (by impl.) the *red-blue* color itself, and finally a garment dyed with it:—purple {5x}. Cf.

Mk 15:17, 20; Lk 16:19; Rev 18:12. See: BAGD—694a; THAYER—532c.

4210. **πορφυρόπωλις** {1x} **pŏrphurŏpōlis**, *por-foo-rop'-o-lis;* fem. of a compound of *4209* and *4453;* a *female trader in purple* cloth:—seller of purple {1x}. See: BAGD—694a; THAYER—532c.

4211. **πορφυροῦς** {3x} **pŏrphurŏus**, *por-foo-rooce';* from *4209; purpureal,* i.e. *bluish red:*—purple {3x}. Cf. Jn 19:2, 5; Rev 18:16. See: BAGD—694b; THAYER—532c.

4212. **ποσάκις** **pŏsakis**, *pos-ak'-is;* mult. from *4214; how many times:*—how oft {1x}, how often {2x}. Cf. Mt 18:21; 23:37; Lk 13:34. See: BAGD—694b; THAYER—532c.

4213. **πόσις** {3x} **pŏsis**, *pos'-is;* from the alt. of *4095;* a *drinking* (the act), i.e. (concr.) a *draught:*—drink {3x}.

Posis suggests "the act of drinking and that which is drunk," Jn 6:55; Rom 14:17; Col 2:16. See: TDNT—6:145, 841; BAGD—694b; THAYER—532d.

4214. **πόσος** {27x} **pŏsŏs**, *pos'-os;* from an obs. πός **pŏs**, (*who, what*) and *3739;* interr. pron. (of amount) *how much* (*large, long* or [plural] *many*):—how much {13x}, how many {9x}, how many things {2x}, what {1x}, how long {1x}, how great {1x}. See: BAGD—694b; THAYER—532d.

4215. **ποταμός** {16x} **pŏtamŏs**, *pot-am-os';* prob. from a der. of the alt. of *4095* (comp. *4224*); a *current, brook* or *freshet* (as *drinkable*), i.e. *running water:*—flood {4x}, river {9x}, stream {2x}, water {1x}.

Potamos denotes **(1)** "a stream," Lk 6:48, 49; **(2)** "a flood or floods," Mt 7:25, 27; **(3)** "a river," **(3a)** natural, Mk 1:5; Acts 16:13; 2 Cor 11:26, "waters"; Rev 8:10; 9:14; 16:4, 12; **(3b)** symbolical, Rev 12:15 (1st part), "flood"; so 12:16; 22:1, 2 (cf. Gen 2:10; Eze 47); **(3c)** figuratively, Jn 7:38, the effects of the operation of the Holy Spirit in and through the believer. See: TDNT—6:595, 921; BAGD—694c; THAYER—532d.

4216. **ποταμοφόρητος** {1x} **pŏtamŏphŏrētŏs**, *pot-am-of-or'-ay-tos;* from *4215* and a der. of *5409; river-borne,* i.e. *overwhelmed by a stream:*—carried away of the flood {1x}. See: TDNT—6:607, 921; BAGD—694d; THAYER—532d.

4217. **ποταπός** {7x} **pŏtapŏs**, *pot-ap-os';* appar. from *4219* and the base of *4226;* interrog. *whatever,* i.e. of *what possible* sort:—what manner of {4x}, what {1x}, what manner of man {1x}, what manner of person {1x}.

Potapos, as an adjective, means primarily "what manner" **(1)** of man" (Mt 8:27); **(2)** persons (2 Pet 3:11); **(3)** Mk 13:1: "And as he went out of the temple, one of his disciples saith unto him, Master, see what manner (*potapos*) of stones and what (*potapos*) buildings *are here!*"; **(4)** salutation (Lk 1:29); **(5)** woman (Lk 7:39); **(6)** love (1 Jn 3:1). Syn.: 195, 1485, 2239, 3634, 3668, 3697, 3779, 4169, 4187, 4459, 5158, 5159, 5179, 5615. See: BAGD—694d; THAYER—532d.

4218. **πότε** {19x} **pŏtĕ**, *pot'-eh;* from the base of *4226* and *5037;* interr. adv., at *what time:*—when {12x}, how long + 2193 {7x}. See: BAGD—695a; THAYER—533a.

4219. **ποτέ** {32x} **pŏtĕ**, *pot-eh';* from the base of *4225* and *5037;* indef. adv., at *some time, ever:*—in time past {5x}, at any time {4x}, in times past {3x}, sometimes {3x}, sometime {3x}, once {2x}, not tr {3x}, misc. {9x} = at length (the last), (+ n-) ever, in the old time, when. See: BAGD—695a; THAYER—533a.

4220. **πότερον** {1x} **pŏtĕrŏn**, *pot'-er-on;* neut. of a comparative of the base of *4226;* interr. as adv., *which* (of two), i.e. *is it* this or that:—whether {1x}. See: BAGD—695b; THAYER—533b.

4221. **ποτήριον** {33x} **pŏtēriŏn**, *pot-ay'-ree-on;* neut. of a der. of the alt. of *4095;* a *drinking-vessel;* by extens. the contents thereof, i.e. a *cupful* (*draught*); fig. a *lot* or *fate:*—cup {33x}.

Poterion, a diminutive of *poter,* denotes, primarily, a "drinking vessel"; hence, "a cup" **(1)** literal, as, e.g., in Mt 10:42. **(2)** The "cup" of blessing, 1 Cor 10:16, is so named from the third "cup" in the Jewish Passover feast, over which thanks and praise were given to God. This connection is not to be rejected on the ground that the church at Corinth was unfamiliar with Jewish customs. That the contrary was the case, see 5:7; **(2)** figurative, of one's lot or experience, joyous or sorrowful **(2a)** frequent in the Psalms; cf. Ps 116:18, "cup of salvation"; **(2b)** in the NT it is used most frequently **(2b1)** of the sufferings of Christ, Mt 20:22–23; 26:39; Mk 10:38–39; 14:36; Lk 22:42; Jn 18:11; **(2b2)** also of the evil deeds of Babylon, Rev 17:4; 18:6; **(2b3)** of divine punishments to be inflicted, Rev 14:10; 16:19. See: TDNT—6:148, 841; BAGD—695b; THAYER—533b.

4222. **ποτίζω** {15x} **pŏtizō**, *pot-id'-zo;* from a der. of the alt. of *4095;* to *furnish drink, irrigate:*—give to drink {4x}, give drink {4x}, water {3x}, make to drink {2x}, watering {1x}, feed {1x}.

Potizo, "to give to drink, to make to drink," is used **(1)** in the material sense, in Mt. 10:42, 25:35, 37, 42 (here of "ministering" to those who belong to Christ and thus doing so virtually to Him); 27:48; Mk 9:41; 15:36; Lk 13:15 ("to watering"); Rom 12:20; 1 Cor 3:7–8; **(2)** figuratively, with reference to "teaching" of an elementary character, 1 Cor 3:2, "I fed (you with milk)"; **(3)** of "spiritual watering by teaching" the Word of God, 1 Cor 3:6; **(4)** of being "provided" and "satisfied" by the power and blessing of the Spirit of God, 1 Cor 12:13; **(5)** of the effect upon the nations of "partaking" of the abominable mixture, provided by Babylon, of paganism with details of the Christian faith, Rev 14:8. See: TDNT—6:159, 841; BAGD—695d; THAYER—533c.

4223. **Ποτίολοι** {1x} **Pŏtiŏlŏi**, *pot-ee'-ol-oy;* of Lat. or.; *little wells,* i.e. *mineral springs; Potioli* (i.e. *Puteoli*), a place in Italy:—Puteoli {1x}. See: BAGD—696a; THAYER—533c.

4224. **πότος** {1x} **pŏtŏs**, *pot'-os;* from the alt. of *4095;* a *drinking-bout* or *carousal:*—banqueting {1x}.

Potos is a drinking bout, a banquet; not necessarily excessiveness, though it does provide that opportunity. Syn.: 2897, 2970, 3178, 3632. See: TDNT—6:145, 841; BAGD—696a; THAYER—533d.

4225. **πού** {3x} **pŏu**, *poo;* gen. of an indef. pron. πός **pŏs** (*some*) otherwise obs. (comp. *4214*); as adv. of place, *somewhere,* i.e. *nearly:*—about {1x}, a certain place {2x}.

Pou, an indefinite particle, signifying "somewhere, somewhere about, nearly," **(1)** has a limiting force, with numerals, e.g., Rom 4:19. **(2)** In referring to a passage in the OT, it is translated in Heb 2:6 and 4:4. By not mentioning the actual passage referred to, the writer acknowledged the familiar acquaintance of his readers with the OT. Also, when Hebrews was written the Scriptures had not been broken down into chapters and verses; hence, "in a certain place." See: BAGD—696a; THAYER—533d.

4226. **ποῦ** {47x} **pŏu**, *poo;* gen. of an interr. pron. πός **pŏs**, (*what*) otherwise obs. (perh. the same as *4225* used with the rising slide of inquiry); as adv. of place; *at* (by impl. to) *what* locality:—where {10x}, whither {47x}. Where is specific, whither, non-specific. See: BAGD—696b; THAYER—533d.

4227. **Πούδης** {1x} **Pŏudēs**, *poo'-dace;* of Lat. or.; *modest; Pudes* (i.e. *Pudens*), a Chr.:—Pudens {1x}. See: BAGD—696c; THAYER—533d.

4228. **πούς** {93x} **pŏus**, *pooce;* a primary word; a "*foot*" (fig. or lit.):—foot {85x}, footstool + 5286 {8x}.

Pous, **(1)** besides its literal meaning, is used, **(2)** by metonymy, of "a person in motion," Lk 1:79; Acts 5:9; Rom 3:15; 10:15; Heb 12:13. **(3)** It is used in phrases expressing subjection, 1 Cor 15:27; **(3a)** of the humility and receptivity of discipleship, Lk 10:39; Acts 22:3; **(3b)** of obeisance and worship, e.g., Mt 28:9; **(3c)** of scornful rejection, Mt 10:14; Acts 13:51. **(4)** Washing the "feet" of another betokened the humility of the service and the comfort of the guest, and was a feature of hospitality, Lk 7:38; Jn 13:5; 1 Ti 5:10 (here figuratively). See: TDNT—6:624, 925; BAGD—696c; THAYER—534a.

4229. **πρᾶγμα** {11x} **pragma**, *prag'-mah;* from *4238;* that which has been done, a *deed;* by impl. an *affair;* by extens. an *object* (material):—business {1x}, matter {3x}, thing {6x}, work {1x}.

Pragma, akin to *prasso,* "to do," denotes **(1)** "that which has been done, a deed," translated **(1a)** "things" in Lk 1:1, **(1b)** "matter" in 2 Cor 7:11; **(2)** "that which is being done, an affair," translated "matter" in Rom 16:2, "business"; 1 Cor. 6:1, in a forensic sense, "a lawsuit"; **(3)** 1 Th 4:6, "in the matter," i.e., the "matter" under consideration, which, as the preceding words show, is here the sin of adultery. See: TDNT—6:638, 927; BAGD—697a; THAYER—534b.

4230. **πραγματεία** {1x} **pragmatĕia**, *prag-mat-i'-ah;* from *4231;* a *transaction,* i.e. *negotiation:*—affair {1x}.

Pragmateia is a deed and denotes a business, occupation, the prosecution of any affair; and in the plural, pursuits, affairs of life (2 Ti 2:4). See: TDNT—6:640, 927; BAGD—697b; THAYER—534b.

4231. **πραγματεύομαι** {1x} **pragmatĕuŏmai**, *prag-mat-yoo'-om-ahee;* from *4229;* to *busy oneself* with, i.e. to *trade:*—occupy {1x}.

This word means to be engaged in a business, hence, occupied totally, Lk 19:13. See: TDNT—6:641, 927; BAGD—697b; THAYER—534b.

4232. **πραιτώριον** {8x} **praitōriŏn**, *prahee-to'-ree-on;* of Lat. or.; the *prætorium* or governor's *court-room* (sometimes incl. the whole *edifice* and *camp*):—judgment hall {4x}, hall of judgment {1x}, common hall {1x}, praetorium {1x}, palace {1x}.

Praitorion is translated **(1)** "common hall" in Mt 27:27, "palace"; **(2)** "Praetorium" in Mk 15:16; **(3)** "hall of judgment" or "judgment hall" in Jn 18:28, 33; 19:9; Acts 23:35; **(3)** "palace", Phil 1:13. See: BAGD—697c; THAYER—534c.

4233. **πράκτωρ** {2x} **praktōr**, *prak'-tor;* from a der. of *4238;* a *practiser,* i.e. (spec.) an official *collector:*—officer {2x}.

An officer of justice of the lower order whose business it is to inflict punishment (Lk 12:58). See: TDNT—6:642, 927; BAGD—697d; THAYER—534d.

4234. **πρᾶξις** {6x} **praxis**, *prax'-is;* from *4238; practice,* i.e. (concr.) an *act;* by extens. a *function:*—deed {4x}, office {1x}, work {1x}.

Praxis denotes "a doing, transaction, a deed the action of which is looked upon as incomplete and in progress" (cf. *prasso,* "to practice"); **(1)** in Mt 16:27, "works"; and **(2)** "deed": Lk 23:51; Acts 19:18; Rom. 8:13; Col. 3:9. **(3)** In Rom. 12:4 it denotes an "action," business, or function, translated "office." See: TDNT—6:642, 927; BAGD—697d; THAYER—534d.

4235. **πρᾶος** {1x} **praiŏs**, *prah'-os;* a form of *4239,* used in certain parts; *gentle,* i.e. *humble:*—meek {1x}.

Praos is mildness of disposition, gentleness of spirit, meekness. Meekness toward God is that disposition of spirit in which we accept His dealings with us as good, and therefore without disputing or resisting. The meek man truly acknowledges himself as a sinner among sinners and this knowledge of his own sin teaches him to meekly endure the provocations of others and not to withdraw from the burdens their sins may impose on him (Gal 6:1; 2 Ti 2:25; Titus 3:2). The meek are those wholly relying on God rather than their own strength to defend them against injustice. Thus, meekness toward evil people means knowing God is permitting the injuries they inflict, that He is using them to purify His elect, and that He will deliver His elect in His time (cf. Is 41:17, Lk 10:1–0). Gentleness or meekness is the opposite to self-assertiveness and self-interest. It stems from trust in God's goodness and control over the situation. The gentle person is not occupied with self at all. This is a work of the Holy Spirit, not of the human will (Gal 5:23). Syn.: 1932, 5912. See: BAGD—698b; THAYER—534d.

4236. **πραότης** {9x} **praiŏtēs**, *prah-ot'-ace;* from *4235; gentleness,* by impl. *humility:*—meekness {9x}. See: BAGD—698b; 699a; THAYER—535a.

4237. **πρασιά** {1x} **prasia**, *pras-ee-ah';* perh. from πράσον **prasŏn** (a *leek,* and so an *onion-patch*); a *garden plot,* i.e. (by impl. of reg. *beds*) a *row* (repeated in plur. by Heb., to indicate an arrangement):—in ranks {1x}. See: BAGD—698b; THAYER—535a.

4238. **πράσσω** {38x} **prassō**, *pras'-so;* a primary verb; to *"practice"*, i.e. *perform repeatedly* or *habitually* (thus differing from *4160,* which prop. refers to a *single* act); by impl. to *execute, accomplish,* etc.; spec. to *collect* (dues), *fare* (personally):—do {28x}, commit {5x}, exact {1x}, require {1x}, deed {1x}, keep {1x}, use arts {1x}.

(1) *Prasso* signifies "to practice," though this is not always to be pressed. **(2)** The apostle John, in his epistles, uses the continuous tenses of *poieo,* to indicate a practice, the habit of doing something, e.g., 1 Jn 3:4, 8, 9, "committeth" and "commit." He uses *prasso* twice in the Gospel, 3:20 and 5:29. **(3)** Generally speaking, in Paul's epistles *poieo* denotes "an action complete in itself," while *prasso* denotes "a habit." Again, *poieo* stresses the accomplishment, e.g., "perform," in Rom. 4:21; *prasso* stresses the process leading to the accomplishment, e.g., "doer," in 2:25. In Rom. 2:3 he who does, *poieo,* the things mentioned, is warned against judging those who practice them, *prasso.* The distinction in Jn 3:20–21 is noticeable: "Every one that doeth (*prasso,* practiceth) ill . . . he that doeth (*poieo*) the truth." While we cannot draw the regular distinction, that *prasso* speaks of doing evil things, and *poieo* of doing good things, yet very often "where the words assume an ethical tinge, there is a tendency to use the verbs with this distinction. Syn.: *Poieo* (4160) denotes to do and *prasso* (4238) denotes to practice. *Poieo* (4160) designates performance, *prasso* designates an intended, earnest, and habitual performance; *poieo* denotes merely productive action, *prasso* denotes definitely directed action; *poieo* points to the action result and *prasso* points to the scope and character of the result. See: TDNT—6:632, 927; BAGD—698b; THAYER—535a.

4239. **πραΰς** {3x} **praës**, *prah-ooce';* appar. a primary word; gentle, *mild,* i.e. (by impl.) *humble:*—meek {3x}. See: TDNT—6:645, 929; BAGD—698d; THAYER—535c. See also *4235.*

4240. **πραΰτης** {3x} **praëtēs**, *prah-oo'-tace;* from *4239; mildness,* i.e. (by impl.) *humility:*—meekness {3x}.

Praetes denotes "meekness." In its use in Scripture, in which it has a fuller, deeper significance than in nonscriptural Greek writings, it consists not in a person's "outward behavior only, nor yet in his relations to his fellow-men; as little in his mere natural disposition. Rather it is an inwrought grace of the soul; and the exercises of it are first and chiefly towards God. It is that temper of spirit in which we accept His dealings with us as good, and therefore without disputing or resisting; it is closely linked with the word *tapeinophrosune* [humility], and follows directly upon it, Eph 4:2; Col 3:12. It is only the humble heart which is also the meek, and which, as such, does not fight against God and more or less struggle and contend with Him. This meekness, however, being first of all a meekness before God, is also such in the face of men, even of evil men, out of a sense that these, with the insults and injuries which they may inflict, are permitted and employed by Him for the chastening and purifying of His elect.

In Gal. 5:23 it is associated with *enkrateia,* "self-control." The meaning of *prautes* is not readily expressed in English, for the terms meekness, mildness, commonly used, suggest weakness and pusillanimity to a greater or less extent, whereas *prautes* does nothing of the kind. Nevertheless, it is difficult to find a rendering less open to objection than 'meekness'; 'gentleness' has been suggested, but as *prautes* describes a condition of mind and heart, and as 'gentleness' is appropriate rather to actions, this word is no better than that used in both English versions. It must be clearly understood, therefore, that the meekness manifested by the Lord and commended to the believer is the fruit of power. The common assumption is that when a man is meek it is because he cannot help himself; but the Lord was "meek" because he had the infinite resources of God at His command.

Described negatively, meekness is the opposite to self-assertiveness and self-interest; it is equanimity of spirit that is neither elated nor cast down, simply because it is not occupied with self at all. In 2 Cor 10:1 the apostle appeals to the "meekness . . . of Christ." Christians are charged to show "all meekness toward all men," Titus 3:2, for meekness becomes "God's elect," Col. 3:12. To this virtue the "man of God" is urged; he is to "follow after meekness" for his own sake, 1 Ti 6:11, and in his service, and more especially in his dealings with the "ignorant and erring," he is to exhibit "a spirit of meekness," 1 Cor 4:21, and Gal 6:1; even "they that oppose themselves" are to be corrected in meekness, 2 Ti 2:25. James exhorts his "beloved brethren" to "receive with meekness the implanted word," 1:21. Peter enjoins "meekness" in setting forth the grounds of the Christian hope, 1 Pet 3:15. See: TDNT—6:645, 929; BAGD—699a; THAYER—535c.

4241. **πρέπω** {7x} **prĕpō**, *prep'-o;* appar. a primary verb; to *tower* up (*be conspicuous*), i.e. (by impl.) to *be suitable* or *proper* (third pers. sing. pres. ind., often used impers., it is *fit* or *right*):—become {6x}, comely {1x}.

Prepo means "to be conspicuous among a number, to be eminent, distinguished by a thing," hence, "to be becoming, seemly, fit." **(1)** The adornment of good works "becometh women professing godliness," 1 Ti 2:10. **(2)** Those who minister the truth are to speak "the things which befit the sound doctrine," Titus 2:1. **(3)** Christ, as a High Priest "became us," Heb 7:26. **(4)** In the impersonal sense, it signifies "it is fitting, it becometh," Mt 3:15; 1 Cor 11:13; Eph 5:3; Heb 2:10. See: BAGD—699b; THAYER—535c.

4242. **πρεσβεία** {2x} **prĕsbĕia**, *pres-bi'-ah;* from *4243; seniority* (*eldership*), i.e. (by impl.) an *embassy* (concr. *ambassadors*).—ambassage {1x}, message {1x}.

Presbeia denotes **(1)** to be elder or eldest, prior in birth or age; and **(2)** to be an ambassador (2 Cor 5:20; Eph 6:20; Philem 9). There is a suggestion that to be an ambassador for Christ involves the experience suggested by the word elder. See: BAGD—699b; THAYER—535c.

4243. **πρεσβεύω** {2x} **prĕsbĕuō**, *pres-byoo'-o;* from the base of *4245;* to be a *senior,* i.e. (by impl.) *act as a representative* (fig. *preacher*):—be an ambassador {2x}.

Presbeuo, "to be an ambassador," 2 Cor 5:20, and Eph 6:20. There is a suggestion that to be an "ambassador" for Christ involves the experience suggested by the word "elder." Elder men were chosen as "ambassadors." See: TDNT—6:681, 931; BAGD—699c; THAYER—535d.

4244. **πρεσβυτέριον** {3x} **prĕsbutĕriŏn**, *presboo-ter'-ee-on;* neut. of a presumed der. of *4245;* the *order of elders,* i.e. (spec.) Isr. *Sanhedrin* or Chr. *"presbytery"*:—elders {1x}, estate of elders {1x}, presbytery {1x}.

Presbuterion, "an assembly of aged men," denotes **(1)** the Council or Senate among the Jews, Lk 22:66; Acts 22:5; **(2)** the "elders" or bishops in a local church, 1 Ti 4:14, "the presbytery." See: TDNT—6:651, 931; BAGD—699c; THAYER—535d.

4245. **πρεσβύτερος** {67x} **prĕsbutĕrŏs**, *presboo'-ter-os;* comparative of πρέσβυς **prĕsbus** (*elderly*); *older;* as noun, a *senior;* spec. an Isr. *Sanhedrist* (also fig. member of the celestial council) or Chr. *"presbyter"*:—elder {64x}, old man {1x}, eldest {1x}, elder woman {1x}.

Presbuteros, an adjective, the comparative degree of *presbus,* "an old man, an elder," is used **(1)** of age, whether **(1a)** of the "elder" of two persons, Lk 15:25, or more, Jn 8:9, "the eldest", or **(1b)** of a person advanced in life, a senior, Acts 2:17; **(1c)** in Heb 11:2, the "elders" are the forefathers in Israel so in Mt 15:2; Mk 7:3, 5; **(1d)** the feminine of the adjective is used of "elder" women in the churches, 1 Ti 5:2, not in respect of position but in seniority of age; **(2)** of rank or positions of responsibility, **(2a)** among Gentiles, as in Gen 50:7; Num 22:7, **(2b)** in the

Jewish nation, **(2b1)** firstly, those who were the heads or leaders of the tribes and families, as of the seventy who assisted Moses, Num 11:16; Deut 27:1, and those assembled by Solomon; **(2b2)** secondly, members of the Sanhedrin, consisting of the chief priests, "elders" and scribes, learned in Jewish law, e.g., Mt 16:21; 26:47; **(2c)** thirdly, those who managed public affairs in the various cities, Lk 7:3;

(3) in the Christian churches those who, being raised up and qualified by the work of the Holy Spirit, were appointed to have the spiritual care of, and to exercise oversight over, the churches. To these the term "bishops," *episkopoi*, or "overseers," is applied (see Acts 20, v. 17 with v. 28, and Titus 1:5 and 7), the latter term indicating the nature of their work *presbuteroi* their maturity of spiritual experience. The divine arrangement seen throughout the NT was for a plurality of these to be appointed in each church, Acts 14:23; 20:17; Phil 1:1; 1 Ti 5:17; Titus 1:5. The duty of "elders" is described by the verb *episkopeo*. They were appointed according as they had given evidence of fulfilling the divine qualifications, Titus 1:6 to 9; cf. 1 Ti 3:1–7 and 1 Pet 5:2; **(4)** the twenty-four "elders" enthroned in heaven around the throne of God, Rev 4:4, 10; 5:5–14; 7:11, 13; 11:16; 14:3; 19:4. The number twenty-four is representative of earthly conditions. The word "elder" is nowhere applied to angels. See: TDNT—6:651, 931; BAGD—699d; THAYER—535d.

4246. **πρεσβύτης** {3x} **prĕsbutēs**, *pres-boo'-tace;* from the same as *4245;* an *old man:*—aged {1x}, aged man {1x}, old man {1x}.

The noun is found in **(1)** Lk 1:18, "an old man"; **(2)** Titus 2:2, "aged men," and **(3)** Philem 9, "an old man." See: TDNT—6:683, 931; BAGD—700d; THAYER—536b.

4247. **πρεσβῦτις** {1x} **prĕsbutis**, *pres-boo'-tis;* fem. of *4246;* an *old woman:*—aged woman {1x}. See: BAGD—700d; THAYER—536b.

πρήθω **prēthō**. See *4092*.

4248. **πρηνής** {1x} **prēnēs**, *pray-nace';* from *4253; leaning (falling) forward* ("*prone*"), i.e. *head foremost:*—headlong {1x}. See: BAGD—700d; THAYER—536b.

4249. **πρίζω** {1x} **prizō**, *prid'-zo;* a strengthened form of a primary πρίω **priō**, (to *saw*); to *saw* in two:—saw asunder {1x}. See: BAGD—701a; THAYER—536b.

4250. **πρίν** {14x} **prin**, *prin;* adv. from *4253; prior, sooner:*—before {11x}, before that {2x}, ere {1x}. See: BAGD—701a; THAYER—536b.

4251. **Πρίσκα** {1x} **Priska**, *pris'-kah;* of Lat. or.; fem. of *Priscus, ancient; Priska,* a Chr. woman:—Prisca {1x}. See: BAGD—701b; THAYER—536c. See also *4252*.

4252. **Πρίσκιλλα** {5x} **Priskilla**, *pris'-kil-lah;* dimin. of *4251; Priscilla* (i.e. *little Prisca*), a Chr. woman:—Priscilla {5x}. See: BAGD—701d; THAYER—536c.

4253. **πρό** {48x} **prŏ**, *prŏ;* a primary prep.; "*fore*", i.e. *in front of, prior* (fig. *superior*) *to:*—before {44x}, above {2x}, above . . . ago {1x}, or ever {1x}. See: TDNT—6:683, 935; BAGD—701c; THAYER—536d. In composition it retains the same significations.

4254. **προάγω** {18x} **prŏagō**, *prŏ-ag'-o;* from *4253* and *71;* to *lead forward* (magisterially); intr. to *precede* (in place or time [part. *previous*]):—go before {14x}, bring forth {2x}, went before + 2258 {1x}, bring out {1x}.

Proago, as a verb, means "to bring, go before, or lead forth": "And when Herod would have brought him forth (*proago*), the same night Peter was sleeping between two soldiers, bound with two chains: and the keepers before the door kept the prison" (Acts 12:6; cf.16:30; 25:26). See: TDNT—1:130, 20; BAGD—702a; THAYER—537a.

4255. **προαιρέομαι** {1x} **prŏairĕŏmai**, *prŏ-ahee-reh'-om-ahee;* from *4253* and *138;* to *choose* for oneself *before* another thing (*prefer*), i.e. (by impl.) to *propose* (*intend*):—purpose {1x}.

This word means "to bring forth or forward," or, in the middle voice, "to take by choice, prefer, purpose," is translated "He purposed" in 2 Cor 9:7. See: BAGD—702b; THAYER—537b.

4256. **προαιτιάομαι** {1x} **prŏaitiaŏmai**, *prŏ-ahee-tee-ah'-om-ahee;* from *4253* and a der. of *156;* to *accuse already,* i.e. *previously charge:*—prove before {1x}.

Proaitiaomai denotes "to prove beforehand": "What then? are we better *than they*? No, in no wise: for we have before proved (*proaitiaomai*) both Jews and Gentiles, that they are all under sin;" (Rom 3:9). See: BAGD—702c; THAYER—537b.

4257. **προακούω** {1x} **prŏakŏuō**, *prŏ-ak-oo'-o;* from *4253* and *191;* to *hear already,* i.e. *anticipate:*—hear before {1x}.

Proakouo, as a verb, signifies "to hear before": "For the hope which is laid up for you in heaven, whereof ye heard before in the word of the truth of the gospel", Col 1:5 - the preposition, *pro,* contrasts what they heard before, the true gospel, with the false gospel of their recent teachers. Syn.: 189, 191, 1251, 1522, 1873, 1874, 3878. See: BAGD—702c; THAYER—537b.

4258. **προαμαρτάνω** {2x} **prŏamartanō**, *prŏ-am-ar-tan'-o;* from *4253* and *264;* to *sin previously* (to conversion):—sin already {1x}, heretofore sin {1x}.

Proamartano, as a verb, means "to sin previously": "*And* lest, when I come again, my God will humble me among you, and *that* I shall bewail many which have sinned already (*proamartano*), and have not repented of the uncleanness and fornication and lasciviousness which they have committed" (2 Cor 12:21; cf. 13:2). Syn.: 264, 265, 266, 361. See: BAGD—702c; THAYER—537c.

4259. **προαύλιον** {1x} **prŏauliŏn**, *prŏ-ŏw'-lee-on;* neut. of a presumed compound of *4253* and *833;* a *forecourt,* i.e. *vestibule* (*alley-way*):—porch {1x}.

Proaulion, "the exterior court" or "vestibule," between the door and the street, in the houses of well-to-do folk, Mk 14:68, "porch." See: BAGD—702d; THAYER—537c.

4260. **προβαίνω** {5x} **prŏbainō**, *prob-ah'-ee-no;* from *4253* and the base of *939;* to *walk forward,* i.e. *advance* (lit. or in years):—be well stricken {2x}, go on {1x}, go farther {1x}, be of . . . age + 2250 + 1722 {1x}.

Probaino, "to go on, forwards, advance," is used **(1)** of locality, Mt. 4:21; Mk 1:19; **(2)** metaphorically use with reference to age, Lk 1:7, 18; 2:36. See: BAGD—702d; THAYER—537c.

4261. **προβάλλω** {2x} **prŏballō**, *prob-al'-lo;* from *4253* and *906;* to *throw forward,* i.e. *push to the front, germinate:*—put forward {1x}, shoot forth {1x}.

It is used **(1)** of plants shooting forth leaves, Lk 21:30; and **(2)** of Paul being thrust forward to defend himself, Acts 19:33. See: BAGD—702d; THAYER—537c.

4262. **προβατικός** {1x} **prŏbatikŏs**, *prob-at-ik-os';* from *4263; relating to sheep,* i.e. (a *gate*) through which they were led into Jerusalem:—sheep (market) {1x}. See: BAGD—703a; THAYER—537d.

4263. **πρόβατον** {41x} **prŏbatŏn**, *prob'-at-on;* prob. neut. of a presumed. der. of *4260; something that walks forward* (a *quadruped*), i.e. (spec.) a *sheep* (lit. or fig.):—sheep {40x}, sheepfold + 833 {1x}.

Probaton, from *probaino,* "to go forward," i.e., of the movement of quadrupeds, was used among the Greeks of small cattle, sheep and goats; in the NT, of "sheep" only **(1)** naturally, e.g., Mt 12:11, 12; **(2)** metaphorically, **(2a)** of those who belong to the Lord, the lost ones of the house of Israel, Mt 10:6; **(2b)** of those who are under the care of the Good Shepherd, e.g., Mt 26:31; Jn 10:1, lit., "the fold of the sheep," and vv. 2–27; 21:16; Heb 13:20; **(2c)** of those who in a future day, at the introduction of the millennial kingdom, have shown kindness to His persecuted earthly people in their great tribulation, Mt 25:33; **(2d)** of the clothing of false shepherds, Mt 7:15; **(3)** figuratively, by way of simile, **(3a)** of Christ, Acts 8:32; **(3b)** of the disciples, e.g., Mt 10:16; **(3c)** of true followers of Christ in general, Rom 8:36; **(3d)** of the former wayward condition of those who had come under His Shepherd care, 1 Pet 2:25; **(3e)** of the multitudes who sought the help of Christ in the days of His flesh, Mt 9:36; Mk 6:34. See: TDNT—6:689, 936; BAGD—703a; THAYER—537d.

4264. **προβιβάζω** {2x} **prŏbibazō**, *prob-ib-ad'-zo;* from *4253* and a redupl. form of *971;* to *force forward,* i.e. *bring to the front, instigate:*—draw {1x}, before instruct {1x}.

Probibazo, as a verb, means "to draw, to bring or drag forward": "And they drew Alexander out of the multitude" (Acts 19:33). It is also used of Herodias' daughter being "before instructed," thrust forward by her mother; possibly indicating a reluctance, Mt 14:8. Syn.: 307, 385, 392, 501, 502, 645, 868, 1448, 1670, 1828, 2020, 4317, 4334, 4358, 4685, 4951, 5288, 5289. See: BAGD—703c; THAYER—538a.

4265. **προβλέπω** {1x} **prŏblĕpō**, *prob-lep'-o;* from *4253* and *991;* to *look* out *beforehand,* i.e. *furnish in advance:*—provide {1x}. See: BAGD—703c; THAYER—538a.

4266. **προγίνομαι** {1x} **prŏginŏmai**, *prog-in'-om-ahee;* from *4253* and *1096;* to *be already,* i.e. *have previously transpired:*—be past {1x}.

Proginomai, "to happen before" is used in Rom 3:25, "that are past", of sins committed in times previous to the atoning sacrifice of Christ. See: BAGD—703c; THAYER—538a.

4267. **προγινώσκω** {5x} **prŏginōskō**, *prog-in-oce'-ko;* from *4253* and *1097;* to *know beforehand,* i.e. *foresee:*—foreknow {2x}, foreordain {1x}, know {1x}, know before {1x}.

Proginosko, "to know beforehand," is used **(1)** of the divine "foreknowledge" **(1a)** concerning believers, Rom 8:29; **(1b)** Israel, 11:2; **(1c)** Christ as the Lamb of God, 1 Pet 1:20, "foreordained"; **(2)** of human previous "knowledge," **(2a)** of a person, Acts 26:5, "which knew"; **(2b)** of facts, 2 Pet 3:17. Syn.: 1097, 1107, 1110, 1492,

1921, 1467, 1922, 1987. See: TDNT—1:715, 119; BAGD—703d; THAYER—538a.

4268. **πρόγνωσις** {2x} **prŏgnōsis**, *prog'-no-sis;* from *4267; forethought:*—foreknowledge {2x}.

"Foreknowledge" is one aspect of omniscience; it is implied in God's warnings, promises and predictions. See Acts 15:18. God's "foreknowledge" involves His electing grace, but this does not preclude human will. He "foreknows" the exercise of faith which brings salvation. The apostle Paul stresses especially the actual purposes of God rather than the ground of the purposes, see, e.g., Gal 1:16; Eph 1:5, 11. The divine counsels will ever be unthwartable. See: TDNT—1:715, 119; BAGD—703d; THAYER—538b.

4269. **πρόγονος** {2x} **prŏgŏnŏs**, *prog'-on-os;* from *4266;* an *ancestor,* (*grand-*) *parent:*—forefather {1x}, parent {1x}.

This word is used as a noun in the plural, **(1)** 2 Ti 1:3, "forefathers"; **(2)** in 1 Ti 5:4, "parents." See: BAGD—704a; THAYER—538b.

4270. **προγράφω** {5x} **prŏgraphō**, *prog-raf'-o;* from *4253* and *1125;* to *write previously;* fig. to *announce, prescribe:*—write {1x}, write aforetime {1x}, write afore {1x}, evidently set forth {1x}, before ordain {1x}.

This word is used **(1)** in Rom 15:4 first time, "written aforetime"; second time, "written"; **(2)** in Gal 3:1, "evidently set forth"; **(3)** in Eph 3:3, "wrote before time"; and **(4)** in Jude 1, "before ordained." See: TDNT—1:770, 128; BAGD—704a; THAYER—538b.

4271. **πρόδηλος** {3x} **prŏdēlŏs**, *prod'-ay-los,* from *4253* and *1212; plain before* all men, i.e. *obvious:*—evident {1x}, manifest beforehand {1x}, open beforehand {1x}.

This word is used **(1)** in Heb 7:14 in the sense of "clearly evident"; **(2)** in 1 Ti 5:24, "open beforehand"; and **(3)** in 1 Ti 5:25, "manifest beforehand." See: BAGD—704b; THAYER—538c.

4272. **προδίδωμι** {1x} **prŏdidōmi**, *prod-id'-o-mee;* from *4253* and *1325;* to *give before* the other party has given:—first give {1x}. See: BAGD—704c; THAYER—538c.

4273. **προδότης** {3x} **prŏdŏtēs**, *prod-ot'-ace;* from *4272* (in the sense of *giving forward* into another's [the enemy's] hands); a *surrender:*—betrayer {1x}, traitor {2x}.

This word is translated **(1)** "betrayers" in Acts 7:52; **(2)** "traitor," in Lk 6:16; and "traitors" in 2 Ti 3:4. See: BAGD—704c; THAYER—538c.

προδρέμω **prŏdrĕmō**. See *4390.*

4274. **πρόδρομος** {1x} **prŏdrŏmŏs**, *prod'-rom-os;* from the alt. of *4390;* a *runner ahead,* i.e. *scout* (fig. *precursor*):—forerunner {1x}. See: TDNT—8:235, 1189; BAGD—704c; THAYER—538c.

4275. **προείδω** {2x} **prŏĕidō**, *pro-i'-do;* from *4253* and *1492; foresee:*—foresee {1x}, saw before {1x}.

Oreido is used **(1)** of David, as foreseeing Christ, in Acts 2:31, "seeing before"; and **(2)** in Gal 3:8 it is said of the Scripture, personified, personal activity being attributed to it by reason of its divine source (cf. v. 22). "What saith the Scripture?" was a common formula among the Rabbis. See: TDNT—5:381,*; BAGD—704c; 709a; THAYER—538d.

προειρέω **prŏĕirĕō**. See *4280.*

4276. **προελπίζω** {1x} **prŏĕlpizō**, *prŏ-el-pid'-zo;* from *4253* and *1679;* to *hope in advance* of other confirmation:—first trust {1x}. See: TDNT—2:534, 229; BAGD—705a; THAYER—538d.

4277. **προέπω** {3x} **prŏĕpō**, *prŏ-ep'-o;* from *4253* and *2036;* to say before the event, *say already,* to *predict:*—speak before {1x}, tell in time past {1x}, forewarn {1x}. See: BAGD—none listed; THAYER—none listed. comp. *4280.*

4278. **προενάρχομαι** {2x} **prŏĕnarchŏmai**, *prŏ-en-ar'-khom-ahee;* from *4253* and *1728;* to *commence already:*—begin {1x}, begin before {1x}. See: BAGD—705b; THAYER—538d.

4279. **προεπαγγέλλομαι** {1x} **prŏĕpaggĕllŏmai**, *prŏ-ep-ang-ghel'-lom-ahee;* mid. voice from *4253* and *1861;* to *promise of old:*—promise afore {1x}. See: TDNT—2:586, 240; BAGD—705b; THAYER—539a.

4280. **προερέω** {9x} **prŏĕrĕō**, *prŏ-er-eh'-o;* from *4253* and *2046;* used as alt. of *4277;* to *say already, predict:*—say before {4x}, tell before {2x}, speak before {2x}, foretell {1x}. See: BAGD—not listed; THAYER—not listed.

4281. **προέρχομαι** {9x} **prŏĕrchŏmai**, *prŏ-er'-khom-ahee;* from *4253* and *2064* (incl. its alt.); to *go onward, precede* (in place or time):—go before {5x}, go farther {1x}, go forward {1x}, outgo {1x}, pass on {1x}. See: BAGD—705b; THAYER—539a.

4282. **προετοιμάζω** {2x} **prŏĕtŏimazō**, *pro-et-oy-mad'-zo;* from *4253* and *2090;* to *fit up in advance* (lit. or fig.): ordain before {1x}, prepare afore {1x}. See: TDNT—2:704, 266; BAGD—705d; THAYER—539a.

4283. **προευαγγελίζομαι** {1x} **prŏĕuaggĕlizŏmai**, *prŏ-yoo-ang-ghel-id'-zom-ahee;* mid. voice from *4253* and *2097;* to *announce* glad news *in advance:*—preach before the gospel {1x}. See: TDNT—2:737, 267; BAGD—705d; THAYER—539b.

4284. **προέχομαι** {1x} **prŏĕchŏmai**, *prŏ-ekh-om-ahee;* mid. voice from *4253* and *2192;* to *hold* oneself *before* others, i.e. (fig.) to *excel:*—be better {1x}.

This word means to have before or in advance of another, to have pre-eminence over another, to excel, surpass; and hence, be better, to be intrinsically better before the comparison is made, Rom 3:9. See: TDNT—6:692, 937; BAGD—705d; THAYER—539b.

4285. **προηγέομαι** {1x} **prŏēgĕŏmai**, *prŏ-ay-geh'-om-ahee;* from *4253* and *2233;* to *lead the way* for others, i.e. *show deference:*—prefer {1x}.

This word is used in Rom 12:10, in the sense of taking the lead in showing deference one to another, "(in honor) preferring one another." See: TDNT—2:908, 303; BAGD—706a; THAYER—539b.

4286. **πρόθεσις** {12x} **prŏthĕsis**, *proth'-es-is;* from *4388;* a *setting forth,* i.e. (fig.) *proposal* (*intention*); spec. the *show*-bread (in the Temple) as *exposed* before God:—purpose {8x}, shewbread + 740 {4x}.

Prothesis, "a setting forth" (used of the "shewbread"), "a purpose", is used **(1)** of the "purposes of God," Rom 8:28; 9:11; Eph 1:11; 3:11; 2 Ti 1:9; **(2)** of "human purposes," as to things **(2a)** material, Acts 27:13; **(2b)** spiritual, Acts 11:23; 2 Ti 3:10. One puts forth his purpose first, then acts. God put forth the shewbread daily to demonstrate His purpose; He would provide daily bread. See: TDNT—8:164, 1176; BAGD—706a; THAYER—539a.

4287. **προθέσμιος** {1x} **prŏthĕsmiŏs**, *proth-es'-mee-os;* from *4253* and a der. of *5087; fixed beforehand,* i.e. (fem. with *2250* implied) a *designated* day:—time appointed {1x}.

Prothesmia, as a verb, means "appointed": "But is under tutors and governors until the time appointed of the father" (Gal 4:2). See: BAGD—706c; THAYER—539c.

4288. **προθυμία** {5x} **prŏthumia**, *proth-oo-mee'-ah;* from *4289; predisposition,* i.e. *alacrity:*—forwardness of mind {1x}, readiness {1x}, readiness of mind {1x}, ready mind {1x}, willing mind {1x}.

This word connotes zeal, spirit, eagerness, inclination, readiness of mind, implying action to surely follow. See: TDNT—6:697, 937; BAGD—706c; THAYER—539d.

4289. **πρόθυμος** {3x} **prŏthumŏs**, *proth'-oo-mos;* from *4253* and *2372; forward* in *spirit,* i.e. *predisposed;* neut. (as noun) *alacrity:*—ready {2x}, willing {1x}. Cf. Mt 26:41; Mk 14:38; Rom 1:15. See: TDNT—6:694, 937; BAGD—706c; THAYER—539d.

4290. **προθύμως** {1x} **prŏthumōs**, *proth-oo'-moce;* adv. from *4289; with alacrity:*—of a ready mind {1x}.

This word implies a ready mind, a desire to do what is right for the flock, and actions that follow. See: BAGD—706d; THAYER—539d.

4291. **προΐστημι** {8x} **prŏïstēmi**, *prŏ-is'-tay-mee;* from *4253* and *2476;* to *stand before,* i.e. (in rank) to *preside,* or (by impl.) to *practice:*—maintain {2x}, be over {1x}, rule {5x}. See: TDNT—6:700,*; BAGD—707a; THAYER—539d.

4292. **προκαλέομαι** {1x} **prŏkalĕŏmai**, *prok-al-eh'-om-ahee;* mid. voice from *4253* and *2564;* to *call forth to oneself* (*challenge*), i.e. (by impl.) to *irritate:*—provoke {1x}.

This word means to call forth as to a contest; hence to stir up what is evil in another (Gal 5:26). See: TDNT—3:496,*; BAGD—707b; THAYER—540a.

4293. **προκαταγγέλλω** {4x} **prŏkataggĕllō**, *prok-at-ang-ghel'-lo;* from *4253* and *2605;* to *announce beforehand,* i.e. *predict, promise:*—foretell {1x}, have notice before {1x}, shew before {1x}.

This verb implies previous verbal communication of a message. See: TDNT—1:70, 10; BAGD—707b; THAYER—540a.

4294. **προκαταρτίζω** {1x} **prŏkatartizō**, *prok-at-ar-tid'-zo;* from *4253* and *2675;* to *prepare in advance:*—make up beforehand {1x}. See: BAGD—707c; THAYER—540a.

4295. **πρόκειμαι** {5x} **prŏkĕimai**, *prok'-i-mahee;* from *4253* and *2749;* to *lie before* the view, i.e. (fig.) to *be present* (to the mind), to *stand forth* (as an example or reward):—be set before {3x}, be first {1x}, be set forth {1x}.

This word signifies **(1)** "to be set before", and is so rendered in **(1a)** Heb 6:18 of the hope of the believer; **(1b)** 12:1, of the Christian race; **(1c)** Heb 12:2. 2, of the joy "set" before Christ in the days of His flesh and at His death; **(2)** "to be set forth," said of Sodom and Gomorrah, in Jude 7. **(3)** It is used elsewhere in 2 Cor 8:12, "first" a willing mind. See: TDNT—3:656, 425; BAGD—707c; THAYER—540a.

4296. **προκηρύσσω** {2x} **prŏkērussō**, *prok-ay-rooce'-so;* from *4253* and *2784;* to *herald* (i.e. *proclaim*) *in advance:*—preach before {1x}, preach first {1x}. See: TDNT—3:717, 430; BAGD—707d; THAYER—540a.

4297. **προκοπή** {3x} **prŏkŏpē**, *prok-op-ay';* from *4298; progress,* i.e. *advancement* (subj. or obj.):—furtherance {2x}, profit {1x}. See: TDNT—6:703, 939; BAGD—707d; THAYER—540b.

4298. **προκόπτω** {6x} **prŏkŏptō**, *prok-op'-to;* from *4253* and *2875;* to *drive forward* (as if by beating), i.e. (fig. and intr.) to *advance* (in amount, to *grow;* in time, to *be well along*):—increase {2x}, proceed {1x}, profit {1x}, be far spent {1x}, wax {1x}.

(1) This word stresses a steady and incremental progress. This word means lit., "to strike forward, cut forward a way," i.e., to make progress, is translated **(1)** "increased" in Lk 2:52, of the Lord Jesus; **(2)** in Gal 1:14 "profited", of Paul's former progress in the Jews' religion; **(3)** in Rom 13:12, "is far spent," of the "advanced" state of the "night" of the world's spiritual darkness; **(4)** in 2 Ti 2:16, "will increase unto more [ungodliness]," of profane babblings; **(5)** in 2 Ti 3:9, "shall proceed no further," of the limit divinely to be put to the doings of evil men; **(6)** in 2 Ti 3:13, of the progress of evil men and impostors, "shall wax," lit., "shall advance to the worse." See: TDNT—6:703, 939 BAGD—707d; THAYER—540b.

4299. **πρόκριμα** {1x} **prŏkrima**, *prok'-ree-mah;* from a compound of *4253* and *2919;* a *prejudgment* (*prejudice*), i.e. *prepossession:*—prefer one before another {1x}.

Prokrima denotes prejudging, to judge beforehand (1 Ti 5:21), preferring one person, another being put aside by unfavorable judgment due to partiality. See: TDNT—3:953, 469; BAGD—708a; THAYER—540c.

4300. **προκυρόω** {1x} **prŏkurŏō**, *prok-oo-rŏ'-o;* from *4253* and *2964;* to *ratify previously:*—confirm before {1x}.

Prokuroo, "to confirm or ratify before," is said of the divine confirmation of a promise given originally to Abraham, Gen 12, and "confirmed" by the vision of the furnace and torch, Gen 15, by the birth of Isaac, Gen 21, and by the oath of God, Gen. 22, all before the giving of the Law, Gal 3:17. See: TDNT—3:1100, 494; BAGD—708b; THAYER—540c.

4301. **προλαμβάνω** {3x} **prŏlambanō**, *prol-am-ban'-o;* from *4253* and *2983;* to *take in advance,* i.e. (lit.) *eat before* others have an opportunity; (fig.) to *anticipate, surprise:*—come aforehand {1x}, overtake {1x}, take before {1x}.

Prolambano, "to anticipate" (*pro,* "before," *lambano,* "to take"), is used **(1)** of the act of Mary, in Mk 14:8; **(2)** of forestalling the less favored at a social meal, 1 Cor 11:21; **(3)** of being "overtaken" in any trespass, Gal 6:1, where the meaning is not that of detecting a person in the act, but of his being caught by the trespass, through his being off his guard (see 5:21 and contrast the premeditated practice of evil in 5:26). See: TDNT—4:14, 495; BAGD—708b; THAYER—540c.

4302. **προλέγω** {3x} **prŏlĕgō**, *prol-eg'-o;* from *4253* and *3004;* to *say beforehand,* i.e. *predict, forewarn:*—foretell {2x}, tell before {1x}. See: BAGD—708b; THAYER—540c.

4303. **προμαρτύρομαι** {1x} **prŏmarturŏmai**, *prom-ar-too'-rom-ahee;* from *4253* and *3143;* to *be a witness in advance,* i.e. *predict:*—testify beforehand {1x}. See: TDNT—4:510, 564; BAGD—708c; THAYER—540d.

4304. **προμελετάω** {1x} **prŏmĕlĕtaō**, *prom-el-et-ah'-o;* from *4253* and *3191;* to *premeditate:*—meditate before {1x}. See: BAGD—708c; THAYER—540d.

4305. **προμεριμνάω** {1x} **prŏmĕrimnaō**, *prom-er-im-nah'-o;* from *4253* and *3309;* to *care* (anxiously) *in advance:*—take thought beforehand {1x}. See: TDNT—4:589, 584; BAGD—708c; THAYER—540d.

4306. **προνοέω** {3x} **prŏnŏĕō**, *pron-ŏ-eh'-o;* from *4253* and *3539;* to *consider in advance,* i.e. *look* out for *beforehand* (act. by way of *maintenance* for others; mid. voice by way of *circumspection* for oneself):—provide {1x}, provide for {2x}. Cf. 1 Ti 5:8; Rom 12:17; 2 Cor 8:21. See: TDNT—4:1009, 636; BAGD—708c; THAYER—540d.

4307. **πρόνοια** {2x} **prŏnŏia**, *pron'-oy-ah;* from *4306; forethought,* i.e. provident *care* or *supply:*—providence {1x}, provision {1x}. See: TDNT—4:1011, 636; BAGD—708d; THAYER—540d.

4308. **προοράω** {2x} **prŏŏraō**, *prŏ-or-ah'-o;* from *4253* and *3708;* to *behold in advance,* i.e. (act.) to *notice* (another) *previously,* or (mid. voice) to *keep in* (one's own) *view:*—foresee {1x}, see before {1x}.

Proorao is used with reference **(1)** to the past, of seeing a person before, Acts 21:29; **(2)** to the future, in the sense of "foreseeing" a person or thing, Acts 2:25, with reference to Christ and the Father, "saw before" (here the middle voice is used). See: TDNT—5:381, 706; BAGD—709a; THAYER—540d.

4309. **προορίζω** {6x} **prŏŏrizō**, *prŏ-or-id'-zo;* from *4253* and *3724;* to *limit in advance,* i.e. (fig.) *predetermine:*—determine before {1x}, ordain {1x}, predestinate {4x}.

This word denotes "to mark out beforehand, to determine before, foreordain"; **(1)** in Acts 4:28, "determined before"; **(2)** so in 1 Cor 2:7, "ordained", **(3)** in Rom 8:29–30 and Eph 1:5, 11, "predestinate." See: TDNT—5:456, 728; BAGD—709b; THAYER—541a.

4310. **προπάσχω** {1x} **prŏpaschō**, *prop-as'-kho;* from *4253* and *3958;* to *undergo* hardship *previously:*—suffer before {1x}. See: TDNT—5:924, 798; BAGD—709b; THAYER—541a.

4311. **προπέμπω** {9x} **prŏpĕmpō**, *prop-em'-po;* from *4253* and *3992;* to *send forward,* i.e. *escort* or *aid* in travel:—bring on (one's) way {4x}, bring (forward) on (one's) journey {3x}, conduct forth {1x}, accompany {1x}.

Propempo, as a verb, means "to send forth, to bring on one's way" and means "to send forward"; hence of assisting a person on a journey **(1)** in the sense of fitting him out with the requisites for it, **(1a)** Rom 15:24 and 1 Cor 16:6, and v. 11. **(1b)** So in 2 Cor. 1:16 and Titus 3:13, and **(1c)** of John's exhortation to Gaius concerning traveling evangelists, "whom thou wilt do well to set forward on their journey worthily of God," 3 Jn 6. **(2)** While personal "accompaniment" is not excluded, practical assistance seems to be generally in view, as indicated by Paul's word to Titus to set forward Zenas and Apollos on their journey and to see "that nothing be wanting unto them." In regard to the parting of Paul from the elders of Ephesus at Miletus, personal "accompaniment" is especially in view, perhaps not without the suggestion of assistance, Acts 20:38; "accompaniment" is also indicated in 21:5; "they all with wives and children brought us on our way, till we were out of the city." In Acts 15:3, both ideas perhaps are suggested. See: BAGD—709b; THAYER—541a.

4312. **προπετής** {2x} **prŏpĕtēs**, *prop-et-ace';* from a compound of *4253* and *4098; falling forward,* i.e. *headlong* (fig. *precipitate*):—heady {1x}, rashly {1x}.

Propetes lit. means "falling forwards" (from *pro,* "forwards," and *pipto,* "to fall"); it is used metaphorically to signify "precipitate, rash, reckless," and is said **(1)** of persons, 2 Ti 3:4; "headstrong" is the appropriate understanding; **(2)** of things, Acts 19:36, "(nothing) rashly." See: BAGD—709c; THAYER—541b.

4313. **προπορεύομαι** {2x} **prŏpŏrĕuŏmai**, *prop-or-yoo'-om-ahee;* from *4253* and *4198;* to *precede* (as guide or herald):—go {1x}, go before {1x}. See: BAGD—709c; THAYER—541b.

4314. **πρός** {726x} **prŏs**, *pros;* a strengthened form of *4253;* a prep. of direction; *forward to,* i.e. *toward* (with the gen. *the side* of, i.e. *pertaining to;* with the dat. *by the side of,* i.e. *near to;* usually with the acc., the place, time, occasion, or respect, which is the *destination* of the relation, i.e. *whither* or *for* which it is predicated):—unto {340x}, to {203x}, with {43x}, for {25x}, against {24x}, among {20x}, at {11x}, not tr {6x}, vr to {1x}, misc. {53x} = about, according to, because of, before, between, ([where-]) by, × at thy house, in, for intent, nigh unto, of, which pertain to, that, to (the end that), + together, to ([you]) -ward, within. In composition it denotes essentially the same applications, namely, motion *toward,* accession *to,* or nearness *at.* See: TDNT—6:720, 942; BAGD—709c; THAYER—541b.

4315. **προσάββατον** {1x} **prŏsabbatŏn**, *pros-ab'-bat-on;* from *4253* and *4521;* a *fore-sabbath,* i.e. the *Sabbath-eve:*—day before the sabbath {1x}. See: BAGD—711a; THAYER—543c. comp. *3904.*

4316. **προσαγορεύω** {1x} **prŏsagŏrĕuō**, *pros-ag-or-yoo'-o;* from *4314* and a der. of *58* (mean to *harangue*); to *address,* i.e. salute by *name:*—call {1x}. See: BAGD—711b; THAYER—543d.

4317. **προσάγω** {4x} **prŏsagō**, *pros-ag'-o;* from *4314* and *71;* to *lead toward,* i.e. (tran.) to *conduct near* (*summon, present*), or (intr.) to *approach:*—bring {3x}, draw near {1x}.

Prosago, as a verb, used **(1)** transitively, means "to bring to": "And Jesus answering said, O faithless and perverse generation, how long shall I be with you, and suffer you? Bring thy son hither" (Lk 9:41; cf. Acts 16:20; 1 Pet 3:18); **(2)** intransitively, "to draw near": "But when the fourteenth night was come, as we were driven up and down in Adria, about midnight the shipmen deemed that they drew near to some country" (Acts 27:27). Syn.: 307, 385, 392, 501, 502, 645, 868, 1448, 1670, 1828, 2020, 4264, 4334, 4358, 4685, 4951, 5288, 5289. See: TDNT—1:131, 20; BAGD—711b; THAYER—543d.

4318. **προσαγωγή** {3x} **prŏsagōgē**, *pros-ag-ogue-ay';* from *4317* (comp. 72); *admission:*—access {3x}.

Prosagoge, lit., "a leading or bringing into the presence of" (*pros,* "to," *ago,* "to lead"), denotes "access," with which is associated the thought of freedom to enter through the assistance or favor of another. It is used three times, **(1)** Rom 5:2, of the "access" which we have by faith, through our Lord Jesus Christ, into grace; **(2)** Eph 2:18, of our "access" in one Spirit through Christ, unto the Father; **(3)** Eph 3:12, of the same "access," there said to be "in Christ," and which we have "in confidence through our faith in Him." This "access" involves the acceptance which we have in Christ with God, and the privilege of His favor towards us. See: TDNT—1:133, 20; BAGD—711c; THAYER—544a.

4319. **προσαιτέω** {3x} **prŏsaitĕō**, *pros-ahee-teh'-o;* from *4314* and *154;* to *ask repeatedly* (*importune*), i.e. *solicit:*—beg {3x}.

Prosaiteo, lit., "to ask besides" (*pros,* "towards," used intensively, and *aiteo*), "to ask earnestly, to importune, continue asking," is said of the blind beggar in Mk 10:46; Lk 18:35; Jn 9:8. See: BAGD—711c; THAYER—544a.

4320. **προσαναβαίνω** {1x} **prŏsanabainō**, *pros-an-ab-ah'-ee-no;* from *4314* and *305;* to *ascend farther,* i.e. *be promoted* (*take an upper* [*more honorable*] *seat*):—go up {1x}. See: BAGD—711c; THAYER—544a.

4321. **προσαναλίσκω** {1x} **prŏsanaliskō**, *pros-an-al-is'-ko;* from *4314* and *355;* to *expend further:*—spend {1x}. See: BAGD—711c; THAYER—544a.

4322. **προσαναπληρόω** {2x} **prŏsanaplērŏō**, *pros-an-ap-lay-ro'-o;* from *4314* and *378;* to *fill up further,* i.e. *furnish fully:*—supply {2x}.

Prosanapleroo, "to fill up by adding to, to supply fully", is translated **(1)** "supplieth" in 2 Cor 9:12; and **(2)** in 11:9, "supplied." See: BAGD—711d; THAYER—544b.

4323. **προσανατίθημι** {2x} **prŏsanatithēmi**, *pros-an-at-ith'-ay-mee;* from *4314* and *394;* to *lay up in addition,* i.e. (mid. voice and fig.) to *impart* or (by impl.) to *consult:*—in conference add {1x}, confer {1x}.

This word means lit., "to lay upon in addition," and came to be used in the sense of putting oneself before another, for the purpose of consulting him; hence simply "to consult, to take one into counsel, to confer." **(1)** With this meaning it is used only in Gal 1:16. This less intensive word may have been purposely used there by the apostle to suggest that he described to his fellow apostles the character of his teaching, not to obtain their approval or their advice concerning it, but simply that they might have the facts of the case before them on which they were shortly to adjudicate. **(2)** It was also used to signify "to communicate, to impart." With this meaning it is used only in Gal 2:6, in the middle voice, the suggestion being to "add" from one's store of things. In regard to his visit to Jerusalem the apostle says "those who were of repute in conference added" nothing to me, that is to say, they neither modified his teaching nor "added" to his authority. See: TDNT—1:353, 57; BAGD—711d; THAYER—544b.

4324. **προσαπειλέω** {1x} **prŏsapĕilĕō**, *pros-ap-i-leh'-o;* from *4314* and *546;* to *menace additionally:*—threaten further {1x}. See: BAGD—711d; THAYER—544b.

4325. **προσδαπανάω** {1x} **prŏsdapanaō**, *pros-dap-an-ah'-o;* from *4314* and *1159;* to *expend additionally:*—spend more {1x}. See: BAGD—712a; THAYER—544b.

4326. **προσδέομαι** {1x} **prŏsdĕŏmai**, *pros-deh'-om-ahee;* from *4314* and *1189;* to *require additionally,* i.e. *want further:*—need {1x}. See: TDNT—2:41, 143; BAGD—712a; THAYER—544c.

4327. **προσδέχομαι** {14x} **prŏsdĕchŏmai**, *pros-dekh'-om-ahee;* from *4314* and *1209;* to *admit* (to intercourse, hospitality, credence, or [fig.] endurance); by impl. to *await* (with confidence or patience):—look for {4x}, wait for {3x}, receive {3x}, waited for + 2258 {1x}, allow {1x}, take {1x}, accept {1x}.

Prosdechomai, as a verb, means "to receive to oneself, to receive favorably," also "to look for, wait for," is used **(1)** of "receiving": "And the Pharisees and scribes murmured, saying, This man receiveth sinners, and eateth with them" (Lk 15:2; cf. Rom 16:2; Phil 2:29). It also means "to receive favorably," denoting "to expect," and is rendered **(2)** "to look for," e.g., in Lk 2:38; 23:51; Titus 2:13; Jude 21. **(3)** It is translated "allow" in Acts 24:15. Syn.: 324, 353, 354, 568, 588, 618, 1209, 1523, 1926, 2210, 2865, 2975, 2983, 3028, 3335, 3336, 3858, 3880, 3970, 4355, 4356, 4380, 4381, 4382, 5562, 5264, 5274. See: TDNT—2:57, 146; BAGD—712b; THAYER—544c.

4328. **προσδοκάω** {16x} **prŏsdŏkaō**, *pros-dok-ah'-o;* from *4314* and δοκεύω **dŏkĕuō** (to watch); to *anticipate* (in thought, hope or fear); by impl. to *await.*—look for {8x}, waited for + 2258 {2x}, expect {1x}, be in expectation {1x}, look {1x}, look when {1x}, waiting for {1x}, tarry {1x}. See: TDNT—6:725, 943; BAGD—712c; THAYER—544c.

4329. **προσδοκία** {2x} **prŏsdŏkia**, *pros-dok-ee'-ah;* from *4328; apprehension* (of evil); by impl. *infliction* anticipated:—expectation {1x}, looking after {1x}.

Proskokia, "a watching for, expectation", is used in the NT only of the "expectation" of evil, **(1)** Lk 21:26, "looking for," regarding impending calamities; **(2)** Acts 12:11, "the expectation" of the execution of Peter. See: TDNT—6:725, 943; BAGD—712c; THAYER—544d.

προσδρέμω **prŏsdrĕmō**. See *4370.*

4330. **προσεάω** {1x} **prŏsĕaō**, *pros-eh-ah'-o;* from *4314* and *1439;* to *permit further* progress:—suffer {1x}. See: BAGD—712d; THAYER—544d.

4331. **προσεγγίζω** {1x} **prŏsĕggizō**, *pros-eng-ghid'-zo;* from *4314* and *1448;* to *approach near:*—come nigh {1x}. See: TDNT—2:330, 194; BAGD—712d; THAYER—544d.

4332. **προσεδρεύω** {1x} **prŏsĕdrĕuō**, *pros-ed-ryoo'-o;* from a compound of *4314* and the base of *1476;* to *sit near,* i.e. *attend* as a servant:—wait at {1x}. See: BAGD—712d; THAYER—544d.

4333. **προσεργάζομαι** {1x} **prŏsĕrgazŏmai**, *pros-er-gad'-zom-ahee;* from *4314* and *2038;* to *work additionally,* i.e. (by impl.) *acquire besides:*—gain {1x}. See: BAGD—713a; THAYER—544d.

4334. **προσέρχομαι** {86x} **prŏsĕrchŏmai**, *pros-er'-khom-ahee;* from *4314* and *2064* (incl. its alt.); to *approach,* i.e. (lit.) *come near, visit,* or (fig.) *worship, assent to:*—come {30x}, come to {25x}, come unto {19x}, go to {3x}, go unto {2x}, draw near {2x}, misc. {5x} = come thereunto, consent, go near.

Proserchomai, as a verb, is translated **(1)** "draw near": "Let us draw near with a true heart in full assurance of faith . . ." (Heb 10:22); **(2)** "drew near": "When Moses saw *it,* he wondered at the sight: and as he drew near to behold *it,* the voice of the Lord came unto him" (Act 7:31); **(3)** "come boldly": "Let us therefore come boldly unto the throne of grace" (Heb 4:16); and "come": "Wherefore He is able also to save them to the uttermost that come (*proserchomai*) unto God by him, seeing He ever liveth to make intercession for them" (Heb 7:25). Syn.: 307, 316, 385, 392, 501, 502, 645, 868, 1448, 1451, 1452, 1670, 1828, 2020, 4139, 4264, 4317, 4358, 4685, 4951, 5288, 5289. See: TDNT—2:683, 257; BAGD—713a; THAYER—545a.

4335. **προσευχή** {37x} **prŏsĕuchē**, *pros-yoo-khay';* from *4336; prayer* (*worship*); by impl. an *oratory* (*chapel*):—pray earnestly + 3346 {1x}, prayer {36x}.

Proseuche denotes **(1)** "prayer" (to God), the most frequent term, e.g., Mt 21:22; **(1a)** Lk 6:12, where the phrase is not to be taken literally as if it meant, "the prayer of God" (subjective genitive), but objectively, "prayer to God." **(1b)** In Jas 5:17, "He prayed with prayer [fervently]," (a Hebraistic form); Eph 6:18; Phil 4:6; 1 Tim 2:1; 5:5; **(2)** "a place of prayer," Acts 16:13, 16, a place outside the city wall. Syn.: *Deesis* (1162) is petitionary, *proseuche* (4335) is a word of sacred character, being limited to prayer to God, whereas *deesis* (1162) may also be used of a request addressed to man. *Enteuxis* (1783) expresses confiding access to God, *deesis* (1162) gives prominence to the expression of personal need. *Proseuche* (4335) refers to the element of devotion, *enteuxis* (1783) to that of childlike confidence, by representing prayer as the heart's conversation with God. Several *aitemata* (155) make up one *proseuche* (4335). See: TDNT—2:807, 279; BAGD—713b; THAYER—545b.

4336. **προσεύχομαι** {87x} **prŏsĕuchŏmai**, *pros-yoo'-khom-ahee;* from *4314* and *2172;* to *pray to* God, i.e. *supplicate, worship:*—pray {83x}, make prayer {3x}, pray for {1x}.

Proseuchomai, "to pray," is **(1)** always used of "prayer" to God, and **(2)** is the most frequent word in this respect, **(3)** especially in the Synoptists and Acts, once in **(3a)** Rom 8:26; **(3b)** in Eph 6:18; **(3c)** in Phil 1:9; **(3d)** in 1 Ti 2:8; **(3e)** in Heb13:18; **(3f)** in Jude 20. See: TDNT—2:807, 279; BAGD—713d; THAYER—545d.

4337. **προσέχω** {24x} **prŏsĕchō**, *pros-ekh'-o;* from *4314* and *2192;* (fig.) to *hold* the mind (*3563* impl.) *toward,* i.e. *pay attention to, be cautious about, apply oneself* to, *adhere to:*—beware {7x}, give heed to {5x}, take heed to {3x}, give heed unto {1x}, take heed {1x}, take heed unto {1x}, take heed whereunto + 3739 {1x}, misc. {5x} = be given to, have regard. Prosecho suggests devotion of thought and effort to a thing. See: BAGD—714b; THAYER—546a.

4338. **προσηλόω** {1x} **prŏsēlŏō**, *pros-ay-lŏ'-o;* from *4314* and a der. of *2247;* to *peg to,* i.e. *spike* fast:—nail to {1x}.

Proseloo, "to nail to", is used in Col 2:14, in which the figure of a bond (ordinances of the Law) is first described as cancelled, and then removed; the idea in the verb itself is not that of the cancellation, to which the taking out of the way was subsequent, but of nailing up the removed thing in triumph to the cross. The death of Christ not only rendered the Law useless as a means of salvation, but gave public demonstration that it was so. See: BAGD—714d; THAYER—546c.

4339. **προσήλυτος** {4x} **prŏsēlutŏs**, *pros-ay'-loo-tos;* from the alt. of *4334;* an *arriver* from a for. region, i.e. (spec.) an *acceder* (*convert*) to Judaism ("*proselyte*"):—proselyte {4x}.

Proselutos, akin to *proserchomai,* "to come to," primarily signifies "one who has arrived, a stranger"; in the NT it is used **(1)** of converts to Judaism, or foreign converts to the Jewish religion, Mt 23:15; Acts 2:10; 6:5; 13:43. **(2)** There seems to be no connection necessarily with Palestine, for in Acts 2:10 and 13:43 it is used of those who lived abroad. See: TDNT—6:727, 943; BAGD—715a; THAYER—546c.

4340. **πρόσκαιρος** {4x} **prŏskairŏs**, *pros'-kahee-ros;* from *4314* and *2540; for* the *occasion* only, i.e. *temporary:*—dureth for awhile {1x}, endure for a time {1x}, for a season {1x}, temporal {1x}.

Proskairos, as an adjective, means "temporary, transient" and is rendered "for a season": "Choosing rather to suffer affliction with the people of God, than to enjoy the pleasures of sin for a season" (Heb 11:25; cf. Mt 13:21; Mk 4:17; 2 Cor 4:18). Syn.: 171, 2122, 2540, 3641, 5550, 5610. See: TDNT—3:463, 389; BAGD—715b; THAYER—546d.

4341. **προσκαλέομαι** {30x} **prŏskalĕŏmai**, *pros-kal-eh'-om-ahee;* mid. voice from *4314* and *2564;* to *call toward oneself,* i.e. *summon, invite:*—call {7x}, call for {2x}, call to {1x}, call unto {20x}.

This word signifies **(1)** "to call to oneself, to bid to come"; it is used only in the middle voice, e.g., Mt 10:1; Acts 5:40; Jas 5:14; **(2)** "God's call to Gentiles through the gospel," Acts 2:39; **(3)** the divine call in entrusting men with the preaching of the gospel," Acts 13:2; 16:10. See: TDNT—3:500,*; BAGD—715c; THAYER—546d.

4342. **προσκαρτερέω** {10x} **prŏskartĕrĕō**, *pros-kar-ter-eh'-o;* from *4314* and *2594;* to *be earnest toward,* i.e. (to a thing) to *persevere, be constantly* diligent, or (in a place) to *attend* assiduously all the exercises, or (to a person) to *adhere* closely to (as a servitor):—continue {4x}, continue instant {1x}, continue steadfastly {1x}, attend continually {1x}, give (one's) self continually {1x}, wait on {1x}, wait on continually {1x}.

This word means lit., "to be strong towards" (*pros,* "towards," used intensively, and *kartereo,* "to be strong"), "to endure in, or persevere in, to be continually steadfast with a person or thing," is used of "continuing" **(1)** in prayer with others, Acts 1:14; Rom 12:12; Col 4:2; **(2)** in the apostles' teaching, Acts 2:42; **(3)** in the Temple, Acts 2:46, the adverb representing the intensive preposition; **(4)** in prayer and the ministry, Acts 6:4; **(5)** of Simon Magus with Philip, Acts 8:13. **(6)** In Mk 3:9 and Acts 10:7, it signifies "to wait on"; **(7)** in Rom 13:6, to attend "continually" upon. See: TDNT—3:618, 417; BAGD—715c; THAYER—547a.

4343. **προσκαρτέρησις** {1x} **prŏskartĕrēsis**, *pros-kar-ter'-ay-sis;* from *4342; persistency:*—perseverance {1x}. See: TDNT—3:619, 417; BAGD—715d; THAYER—547b.

4344. **προσκεφάλαιον** {1x} **prŏskĕphalaiŏn**, *pros-kef-al'-ahee-on;* neut. of a presumed compound of *4314* and *2776;* something *for* the *head,* i.e. a *cushion:*—pillow {1x}. See: BAGD—715d; THAYER—547b.

4345. **προσκληρόω** {1x} **prŏsklērŏō**, *pros-klay-rŏ'-o;* from *4314* and *2820;* to *give* a common *lot to,* i.e. (fig.) to *associate with:*—consort with {1x}.

Literally, *proskleroo* means to assign by lot, to allot (Acts 17:4), consorted with, imparting to the passive voice (the form of the verb there) a middle voice significance, i.e., "they joined themselves to," or "threw in their lot with." The passive voice significance can be retained by translating (in the stricter sense of the word), "they were allotted" (i.e., by God) to Paul and Silas, as followers or disciples. See: TDNT—3:765, 442; BAGD—716a; THAYER—547b.

4346. **πρόσκλισις** {1x} **prŏsklisis**, *pros'-klis-is;* from a compound of *4314* and *2827;* a *leaning toward,* i.e. (fig.) *proclivity* (*favoritism*):—partiality {1x}. See: BAGD—716a; THAYER—547c.

4347. **προσκολλάω** {4x} **prŏskŏllaō**, *pros-kol-lah'-o;* from *4314* and *2853;* to *glue to,* i.e. (fig.) to *adhere:*—cleave {2x}, be joined {1x}, join (one's) self {1x}.

Inherit within this word are two aspects with the second aspect being stressed. In order to cleave, one must first make a clean break; hence, cleave as in to cut. Then once cleanly separated a joining is easy, Mt 19:5; Mk 10:7; Acts 5:36; Eph 5:31. See: TDNT—3:823, 452; BAGD—716a; THAYER—547c.

4348. **πρόσκομμα** {6x} **prŏskŏmma**, *pros'-kom-mah;* from *4350;* a *stub,* i.e. (fig.) *occasion of apostasy:*—stumbling stone + 3037 {2x}, stumbling block {2x}, stumbling {1x}, offence {1x}.

Proskomma, "an obstacle against which one may dash his foot" (akin to *proskopto,* "to stumble" or "cause to stumble"; *pros,* "to or against," *kopto,* "to strike"), is translated **(1)** "offence" in Rom 14:20, **(2)** in Rom 14:13, "a stumblingblock," of the spiritual hindrance to another by a selfish use of liberty; so in 1 Cor 8:9. **(3)** It is used of Christ, in Rom 9:32, 33, "a stumblingstone," and **(4)** 1 Pet 2:8, "a stone of stumbling." See: TDNT—6:745, 946; BAGD—716b; THAYER—547c.

4349. **προσκοπή** { {1x} **prŏskŏpē**, *pros-kop-ay';* from *4350;* a *stumbling,* i.e. (fig. and concr.) *occasion of sin:*—offence {1x}.

Proskope occurs in 2 Cor 6:3, "offence", and means something which leads others into error or sin. See: TDNT—6:745, 946; BAGD—716b; THAYER—547d.

4350. **προσκόπτω** {8x} **prŏskŏptō**, *pros-kop'-to;* from *4314* and *2875;* to *strike at,* i.e. *surge against* (as water); spec. to *stub on,* i.e. *trip up* (lit. or fig.):—beat upon {1x}, dash {2x}, stumble {3x}, stumble at {2x}.

Proskopto, "to strike against," is used of "stumbling," **(1)** physically, Jn 11:9, 10; **(2)** metaphorically, **(2a)** of Israel in regard to Christ, whose Person, teaching, and atoning death, and the gospel relating thereto, were contrary to all their ideas as to the means of righteousness before God, Rom 9:32; 1 Pet 2:8; **(2b)** of a brother in the Lord in acting against the dictates of his conscience, Rom 14:21; **(3)** is once used of a storm "beating" upon a house, Mt 7:27; and **(4)** used once of "dash", Mt 4:6, of Christ's foot against a stone. See: TDNT—6:745, 946; BAGD—716b; THAYER—547d.

4351. **προσκυλίω** {2x} **prŏskuliō**, *pros-koo-lee'-o;* from *4314* and *2947;* to *roll toward,* i.e. *block against:*—roll (to) {2x}.

This word means "to roll up or to" and is used in Mt 27:60 and Mk 15:46 of the sepulchre stone. See: BAGD—716c; THAYER—548a.

4352. **προσκυνέω** {60x} **prŏskunĕō**, *pros-koo-neh'-o;* from *4314* and a probable der. of *2965* (mean. to *kiss,* like a dog *licking* his master's hand); to *fawn* or *crouch to,* i.e. (lit. or fig.) *prostrate* oneself in homage (do *reverence* to, *adore*):—worship {60x}.

This word means "to make obeisance, do reverence to" (from *pros,* "towards," and *kuneo,* "to kiss"), is the most frequent word rendered "to worship." It is used of an act of homage or reverence **(1)** to God, e.g., Mt 4:10; Jn 4:21–24; 1 Cor 14:25; Rev 4:10; 5:14; 7:11; 11:16; 19:10 (2nd part) and 22:9; **(2)** to Christ, e.g., Mt 2:2, 8, 11; 8:2; 9:18; 14:33; 15:25; 20:20; 28:9, 17; Jn 9:38; Heb 1:6, in a quotation from the Sept. of Deut. 32:43, referring to Christ's second advent; **(3)** to a man, Mt 18:26; **(4)** to the Dragon, by men, Rev 13:4; **(5)** to the Beast, his human instrument, Rev 13:4, 8, 12; 14:9, 11; **(6)** the image of the Beast, Rev 13:15; 14:11; 16:2; **(7)** to demons, Rev 9:20; **(8)** to idols, Acts 7:43. See: TDNT—6:758, 948; BAGD—716c; THAYER—548a.

4353. **προσκυνητής** {1x} **prŏskunētēs**, *pros-koo-nay-tace';* from *4352;* an *adorer:*—worshipper {1x}. See: TDNT—6:766, 948; BAGD—717b; THAYER—548c.

4354. **προσλαλέω** {2x} **prŏslalĕō**, *pros-lal-eh'-o;* from *4314* and *2980;* to *talk to,* i.e. *converse with:*—speak to {1x}, speak with {1x}. Cf. Acts 13:43 and 28:20. See: BAGD—717b; THAYER—548c.

4355. **προσλαμβάνω** {14x} **prŏslambanō**, *pros-lam-ban'-o;* from *4314* and *2983;* to *take to* oneself, i.e. *use* (food), *lead* (aside), *admit* (to friendship or hospitality):—receive {7x}, take {5x}, take unto {2x}.

Proslambano, as a verb, denotes "to take to oneself" or **(1)** "to receive," always in the middle voice, signifying a special interest on the part of the receiver, suggesting a welcome: "And the barbarous people shewed us no little kindness: for they kindled a fire, and received (*proslambano*) us every one, because of the present rain, and because of the cold" (Acts 28:2; cf. Rom 14:1, 3; 15:7; Philem 12, 17). It also means **(2)** "to take to oneself" and is used **(2a)** of food, Acts 27:33–36; **(2b)** of persons, **(2b1)** of Peter's act toward Christ, Mt 16:22; Mk 8:32; **(2b2)** for evil purposes, Acts 17:5; **(2b3)** for good purposes, Acts 18:26. Syn.: 324, 353, 354, 568, 588, 618, 1209, 1523, 1926, 2210, 2865, 2975, 2983, 3028, 3335, 3336, 3858, 3880, 3970, 4327, 4356, 4380, 4381, 4382, 5562, 5264, 5274. See: TDNT—4:15, 495; BAGD—717b; THAYER—548c.

4356. **πρόσληψις** {1x} **prŏslēpsis**, *pros'-lape-sis;* from *4355; admission:*—receiving {1x}.

Proslepsis, as a noun, is used in Rom 11:15 of the restoration of Israel: "For if the casting away of them *be* the reconciling of the world, what *shall* the receiving (4356) *of them be,* but life from the dead?" Syn.: 324, 353, 354, 568, 588, 618, 1209, 1523, 1926, 2210, 2865, 2975, 2983, 3028, 3335, 3336, 3858, 3880, 3970, 4327, 4355, 4380, 4381, 4382, 5562, 5264, 5274. See: TDNT—4:15, 495; BAGD—717c; THAYER—548d.

4357. **προσμένω** {6x} **prŏsmĕnō**, *pros-men'-o;* from *4314* and *3306;* to *stay further,* i.e. *remain* in a place, with a person; fig. to *adhere* to, *persevere* in:—abide still {1x}, be with {1x}, cleave unto {1x}, continue in {1x}, tarry {1x}, continue with {1x}.

Prosmeno, "to abide still longer, continue with" is used **(1)** of place, Mt 15:32; Mk 8:2, "been with"; Acts 18:18, "tarried"; 1 Ti 1:3, "abide still"; **(2)** metaphorically, "of cleaving unto a person," Acts 11:23, indicating persistent loyalty; **(3)** of continuing in a thing, 1 Ti 5:5. See: TDNT—4:579, 581; BAGD—717c; THAYER—548d.

4358. **προσορμίζω** {1x} **prŏsŏrmizō**, *pros-or-mid'-zo;* from *4314* and a der. of the same as *3730* (mean. to *tie* [*anchor*] or *lull*); to *moor to,* i.e. (by impl.) *land at:*—draw to the shore {1x}.

Prosormizo, as a verb, means "to bring a ship (or boat) to anchor, cast anchor, land at a place" is translated "drew to the shore": "And when they had passed over, they came into the land of Gennesaret, and drew to the shore" (Mk 6:53). Syn.: 307, 385, 392, 501, 502, 645, 868, 1448, 1670, 1828, 2020, 4264, 4317, 4334, 4685, 4951, 5288, 5289. See: BAGD—717d; THAYER—548d.

4359. **προσοφείλω** {1x} **prŏsŏphĕilō**, *pros-of-i'-lo;* from *4314* and *3784;* to *be indebted additionally:*—to owe besides {1x}.

This word is used in Philem 19, "thou owest (to me even thine own self) besides," i.e., "thou owest me already as much as Onesimus" debt, and in addition even thyself" (not "thou owest me much more"). See: BAGD—717d; THAYER—549a.

4360. **προσοχθίζω** {2x} **prŏsŏchthizō**, *pros-okh-thid'-zo;* from *4314* and a form of ὀχθέω **ŏchthĕō** (to *be vexed* with something irksome); to *feel indignant at:*—be grieved with {2x}.

Prosochthizo means "to be wroth or displeased with" and is used in Heb 3:10, 17. Grieved means to become inactive. God withdrew His active hand from them; yet always maintained sovereignty and providence. See: BAGD—717d; THAYER—549a.

4361. **πρόσπεινος** {1x} **prŏspĕinŏs**, *pros'-pi-nos;* from *4314* and the same as *3983; hungering further,* i.e. *intensely hungry:*—very hungry {1x}. See: BAGD—718a; THAYER—549a.

4362. **προσπήγνυμι** {1x} **prŏspēgnumi**, *pros-payg'-noo-mee;* from *4314* and *4078;* to *fasten to,* i.e. (spec. on a cross):—crucify {1x}.

Prospegnumi, "to fix or fasten to anything" (*pros,* "to," *pegnumi,* "to fix"), is used of the "crucifixion" of Christ, Acts 2:23. See: BAGD—718a; THAYER—549b.

4363. **προσπίπτω** {8x} **prŏspiptō**, *pros-pip'-to;* from *4314* and *4098;* to *fall toward,* i.e. (gently) *prostrate* oneself (in supplication or homage), or (violently) to *rush* upon (in storm):—fall down before {5x}, beat upon {1x}, fall down at {1x}, fall {1x}.

Prospipto "to fall towards anything" (*pros,* "towards"), "to strike against," is said **(1)** of "wind," Mt 7:25; **(2)** it also signifies to "fall" down at one's feet, "fall" prostrate before, Mk 3:11; 5:33; 7:25; Lk 5:8; 8:28, 47; Acts 16:29. See: BAGD—718a; THAYER—549b.

4364. **προσποιέομαι** {2x} **prŏspŏiĕŏmai**, *pros-poy-eh'-om-ahee;* mid. voice from *4314* and *4160;* to *do forward for oneself,* i.e. *pretend* (as if about to do a thing):—make as though {2x}. See: BAGD—718b; THAYER—549b.

4365. **προσπορεύομαι** {1x} **prŏspŏrĕuŏmai**, *pros-por-yoo'-om-ahee;* from *4314* and *4198;* to *journey toward,* i.e. *approach* [not the same as *4313*]:—come unto {1x}. See: BAGD—718b; THAYER—549c.

4366. **προσρήγνυμι** {2x} **prŏsrēgnumi**, *pros-rayg'-noo-mee;* from *4314* and *4486;* to *tear toward,* i.e. *burst upon* (as a tempest or flood):—beat vehemently against {1x}, beat vehemently upon {1x}. See: BAGD—not listed; THAYER—549c.

4367. **προστάσσω** {7x} **prŏstassō**, *pros-tas'-so;* from *4314* and *5021;* to *arrange toward,* i.e. (fig.) *enjoin:*—bid {1x}, command {6x}.

(1) This word is a mild command stressing that the one giving the command arranges the life of the receiver for the near future. **(2)** It denotes "to arrange or set in order towards" (*pros,* "towards," *tasso,* "to arrange"); hence "to prescribe, give command," Mt 1:24, "bidden"; 8:4; 21:6; Mk 1:44; Lk 5:14; Acts 10:33, 48. TDNT—8:37, 1156; BAGD—718c; THAYER—549c.

4368. **προστάτις** {1x} **prŏstatis**, *pros-tat'-is;* fem. of a der. of *4291;* a *patroness,* i.e. *assistant:*—succourer {1x}.

Prostatis is the feminine form of *prostates* and denotes a protectress, a patroness. It is used metaphorically of Phoebe (Rom 16:2) and is a word of dignity. It indicates the high esteem with which she was regarded, as one who had been a protectress of many. *Prostates* was the title of a citizen in Athens, who had the responsibility of seeing to the welfare of resident aliens who were without civic rights. Among the Jews it signified a wealthy patron of the community. See: BAGD—718d; THAYER—549c.

4369. **προστίθημι** {18x} **prŏstithēmi**, *pros-tith'-ay-mee;* from *4314* and *5087;* to *place additionally,* i.e. *lay beside, annex, repeat:*—add {11x}, again send + 3892 {2x}, give more {1x}, increase {1x}, proceed further {1x}, lay unto {1x}, speak to any more {1x}. See: TDNT—8:167, 1176; BAGD—718d; THAYER—549d.

4370. **προστρέχω** {3x} **prŏstrĕchō**, *pros-trekh'-o;* from *4314* and *5143* (incl. its alt.); to *run toward,* i.e. *hasten* to meet or join:—run {1x}, run thither to {1x}, run to {1x}. Cf. Mk 9:15; 10:17; Acts 8:30. See: BAGD—719b; THAYER—550a.

4371. **προσφάγιον** {1x} **prŏsphagiŏn**, *pros-fag'-ee-on;* neut. of a presumed der. of a compound of *4314* and *5315;* something *eaten in addition* to bread, i.e. a *relish* (spec. *fish;* comp. *3795*):—meat {1x}.

This word is not so broad a word as "something to eat" but stresses something small in addition to bread; hence, relish, usually small fish, Mk 8:14. See: BAGD—719c; THAYER—550a.

4372. **πρόσφατος** {1x} **prŏsphatŏs**, *pros'-fat-os;* from *4253* and a der. of *4969; previously* (*recently*) *slain* (*fresh*), i.e. (fig.) *lately made:*—new {1x}. See: TDNT—6:766, 950; BAGD—719c; THAYER—550a.

4373. **προσφάτως** {1x} **prŏsphatōs**, *pros-fat'-oce;* adv. from *4372; recently:*—lately {1x}. See: TDNT—6:766, 950; BAGD—719c; THAYER—550a.

4374. **προσφέρω** {48x} **prŏsphĕrō**, *pros-fer'-o;* from *4314* and *5342* (incl. its alt.); to *bear toward,* i.e. *lead to, tender* (espec. to God), *treat:*—offer {22x}, bring unto {10x}, bring to {4x}, bring {3x}, offer up {3x}, offer unto {1x}, offer to {1x}, deal with {1x}, do {1x}, present unto {1x}, put to {1x}.

Prosphero, as a verb, means **(1)** "to bring (in addition)": "And so he that had received five talents came and brought (*prosphero*) other five talents, saying, Lord, thou deliveredst unto me five talents: behold, I have gained beside them five talents more" (Mt 25:20); **(2)** "to bring unto": "Therefore if thou bring (*prosphero*) thy gift to the altar, and there rememberest that thy brother hath ought against thee" (Mt 5:23; Mark 10:13); **(3)** "to offer": "Leave there thy gift before the altar, and go thy way; first be reconciled to thy brother, and then come and offer (*prosphero*) thy gift" (Mt 5:24). See: TDNT—9:65, 1252; BAGD—719c; THAYER—550a.

4375. **προσφιλής** {1x} **prŏsphilēs**, *pros-fee-lace';* from a presumed compound of *4314* and *5368; friendly toward,* i.e. *acceptable:*—lovely {1x}. See: BAGD—720b; THAYER—550c.

4376. **προσφορά** {9x} **prŏsphŏra**, *pros-for-ah';* from *4374; presentation;* concr. an *oblation* (bloodless) or *sacrifice:*—offering {8x}, offering up {1x}.

Prosphora, lit., "a bringing to", hence an "offering," in the NT a sacrificial "offering," **(1)** of Christ's sacrifice, Eph 5:2; Heb 10:10 (of His body); 10:14; negatively, of there being no repetition, 10:18; **(2)** of "offerings" under, or according to, the Law, Acts 21:26; Heb 10:5, 8; **(3)** of gifts in kind conveyed to needy Jews, Acts 24:17; **(4)** of the presentation of believers themselves (saved from among the Gentiles) to God, Rom 15:16, "offering up." See: TDNT—9:68, 1252; BAGD—720b; THAYER—550c.

4377. **προσφωνέω** {7x} **prŏsphōnĕō**, *pros-fo-nch'-o;* from *4314* and *5455;* to *sound toward,* i.e. *address, exclaim, summon:*—call {2x}, call unto {1x}, call to {1x}, speak {1x}, speak to {1x}, speak unto {1x}.

Prosphoneo, "to address, call to," is rendered **(1)** "spake to" (or "to") in Lk 23:20; Acts 21:40; 22:2; **(2)** "to call unto" (or "to") in Mt 11:16; Lk 6:13; 7:32; 13:12. See: BAGD—720c; THAYER—550d.

4378. **πρόσχυσις** {1x} **prŏschusis**, *pros'-khoo-sis;* from a comp. of *4314* and χέω **chĕō** (to *pour*); a *shedding forth,* i.e. *affusion:*—sprinkling {1x}. See: BAGD—720c; THAYER—550d.

4379. **προσψαύω** {1x} **prŏspsauō**, *pros-psŏw'-o;* from *4314* and ψαύω **psauō** (to *touch slightly*); to *impinge,* i.e. *lay a finger on and touch slightly* (in order to relieve):—touch {1x}. See: BAGD—720c; THAYER—550d.

4380. **προσωποληπτέω** {1x} **prŏsōpŏlēptĕō**, *pros-o-pol-ape-teh'-o;* from *4381;* to *favor an individual,* i.e. *show partiality:*—have respect to persons {1x}.

(1) This word means to respect the person based on the external conditions of the man, i.e. his wealth, fame, looks, etc. in contrast to his inward character. **(2)** *Prosopolepto,* as a verb, means "to have respect of persons" and is found in Jas 2:9: "But if ye have respect to persons, ye commit sin, and are convinced of the law as transgressors." Syn.: 324, 353, 354, 568, 588, 618, 1209, 1523, 1926, 2210, 2865, 2975, 2983, 3028, 3335, 3336, 3858, 3880, 3970, 4327, 4355, 4356, 4381, 4382, 5562, 5264, 5274. See: TDNT—6:779, 950; BAGD—720c; THAYER—550d.

4381. **προσωπολήπτης** {1x} **prŏsōpŏlēptēs**, *pros-o-pol-ape'-tace;* from *4383* and *2983;* an *accepter* of *a face* (*individual*), i.e. (spec.) one *exhibiting partiality:*—respecter of persons {1x}.

Prosopoleptes, as a noun, means "respecter of persons" and is found in Acts 10:34: "Then Peter opened *his* mouth, and said, Of a truth I perceive that God is no respecter of persons." Syn.: 324, 353, 354, 568, 588, 618, 1209, 1523, 1926, 2210, 2865, 2975, 2983, 3028, 3335, 3336, 3858, 3880, 3970, 4327, 4355, 4356, 4380, 4382, 5562, 5264, 5274. See: TDNT—6:779, 950; BAGD—720d; THAYER—550d.

4382. **προσωποληψία** {4x} **prŏsōpŏlēpsia**, *pros-o-pol-ape-see'-ah;* from *4381; partiality,* i.e. *favoritism:*—respect of persons {4x}.

(1) *Prosopolepsia,* as a noun, means "respect of persons" and is found in Rom 2:11: "For there is no respect of persons with God" (cf. Eph 6:9; Col 3:25; Jas 2:1). **(2)** It denotes "respect of persons, partiality", the fault of one who, when responsible to give judgment, has respect to the position, rank, popularity, or circumstances of men, instead of their intrinsic conditions, preferring the rich and powerful to those who are not so. Syn.: 324, 353, 354, 568, 588, 618, 1209, 1523, 1926, 2210, 2865, 2975, 2983, 3028, 3335, 3336, 3858, 3880, 3970, 4327, 4355, 4356, 4380, 4381, 5562, 5264, 5274. See: TDNT—6:779, 950; BAGD—720d; THAYER—551a.

4383. **πρόσωπον** {78x} **prŏsōpŏn**, *pros'-o-pon;* from *4314* and ὤψ **ōps** (the *visage,* from *3700*); the *front,* (as being *toward view*), i.e. the *countenance, aspect, appearance, surface;* by impl. *presence, person:*—face {55x}, person {7x}, presence {7x}, countenance {3x}, not tr {1x}, misc. {5x} = (outward) appearance, × before, fashion.

Prosopon, (*pros,* "towards," *ops,* "an eye"), lit., "the part round the eye, the face," denotes "the countenance," lit., "the part towards the eyes" (from *pros,* "towards," *ops,* "the eye"), and is used **(1)** of the "face," Mt 6:16–17; Rev 12:14; **(1a)** 2 Cor 3:7, 2nd part, "countenance"; **(1b)** in 2 Cor 5:12; 10:7, "outward appearance", the phrase is figurative of superficial judgment; **(2)** of the look i.e., the "face," which by its various movements affords an index of inward thoughts and feelings. e g., Lk 9:51, 53; 1 Pet 3:12, used of the face of the Lord; **(3)** the presence of a person, the "face" being the noblest part, e.g., **(3a)** Acts 3:13, "in the presence of"; **(3b)** Acts 5:41; 2 Th 1:9, "presence"; **(3c)** came to signify the presentation of the whole person (translated "person," of "persons", e.g., in Mt 22:16; Mk 12:14; Lk 20:21; 2 Cor 1:11; 2 Cor 2:10; Gal 2:6; Jude 16. **(3d)** Acts 3:13; 1 Th 2:17 (first part), "presence";

(4) the person himself, e.g., Gal 1:22; 1 Th 2:17 (second part); **(5)** the appearance one presents by his wealth or poverty, his position or state, Mt 22:16; Mk 12:14; Gal 2:6; Jude 16; **(6)** the outward appearance of inanimate things, Mt 16:3; Lk 12:56; 21:35; Acts 17:26. **(7)** "To spit in a person's face" was an expression of the utmost scorn and aversion, e.g., Mt 26:67 (cf. 27:30; Mk 10:34; Luke 18:32). **(8)** Cf. the expression in OT passages, as **(8a)** Gen 19:21, where it is said by God of Lot, and **(8b)** Gen 33:10, where it is said by Jacob of Esau; **(8c)** see also Deut 10:17 ("persons"), Lev 19:15 ("person"). **(0)** It also signifies the presence of a company, Acts 5:41. See: TDNT—6:768, 950; BAGD—720d; THAYER—551a.

4384. **προτάσσω** {1x} **prŏtassō**, *prot-as'-so;* from *4253* and *5021;* to *prearrange,* i.e. *prescribe:*—before appoint {1x}.

Protasso, as a verb, means "to appoint before" and is used in Acts 17:26 of the seasons arranged by God for nations, and the bounds of their habitation: "And hath made of one blood all nations of men for to dwell on all the face of the earth, and hath determined the times before appointed, and the bounds of their habitation." See: BAGD—721d; THAYER—552a.

4385. **προτείνω** {x} **prŏtĕinō**, *prot-i'-no;* from *4253* and τείνω **tĕinō** (to *stretch*); to *protend,* i.e. *tie prostrate* (for scourging):—bind {x}.

Proteino, lit., "to stretch forth" (*pro,* "forth," *teino,* "to stretch"), is used in Acts 22:25, "they bound"; in reference to the preparations made for scourging, probably, to stretch the body forward, to make it tense for severe punishment. See: BAGD—721d; THAYER—721d; THAYER—552a.

4386. **πρότερον** {10x} **prŏtĕrŏn**, *prot'-er-on;* neut. of *4387* as adv. (with or without the art.); *previously:*—before + 3588 {3x}, first {2x}, former {2x}, before {2x}, at the first + 3588 {1x}.

Proteron, the comparative of *pro,* "before, aforetime," as being definitely antecedent to something else, is more emphatic than *pote* in this respect. See, e.g., Jn 6:62; 7:50; 9:8; 2 Cor 1:13; Gal 4:13; 1 Ti 1:13; Heb 4:6; 7:27; 10:32; 1 Pet 1:14. See: BAGD—721d; THAYER—552a.

4387. **πρότερος** {1x} **prŏtĕrŏs**, *prot'-er-os;* comp. of *4253; prior* or *previous:*—former {1x}. See: BAGD—721d; THAYER—552a.

4388. **προτίθημ** {3x} **prŏtithĕmo**, *prot-ith'-em-ahee;* mid. voice from *4253* and *5087;* to *place before,* i.e. (for oneself) to *exhibit;* (to oneself) to *propose* (*determine*):—purpose {2x}, set forth {1x}.

Protithemi, "to set before, set forth", is used **(1)** in Rom 3:25, "set forth," middle voice, which lays stress upon the personal interest which God had in so doing. **(2)** It is also found in Rom 1:13, "I purposed"; and Eph 1:9, "He purposed (in Him)." See: TDNT—8:164, 1176; BAGD—722b; THAYER—552b.

4389. **προτρέπομαι** {1x} **prŏtrĕpŏmai**, *prot-rep'-om-ahee;* mid. voice from *4253* and the base of *5157;* to *turn forward* for oneself, i.e. *encourage:*—exhort {1x}.

This word means "to urge forward, persuade," and is used in Acts 18:27 in the middle voice, "exhorting" indicating their particular interest in giving Apollos the "encouragement" mentioned. See: BAGD—722b; THAYER—552c.

4390. **προτρέχω** {2x} **prŏtrĕchō**, *prot-rekh'-o;* from *4253* and *5143* (incl. its alt.); to *run forward,* i.e. *outstrip, precede:*—outrun {1x}, run before {1x}.

Protrecho, primarily, "to run forward" (*pro,* "forward" or "before," *trecho,* "to run"), is **(1)** used with *tachion,* "more quickly," in Jn 20:4, "did outrun"), lit., "ran forward more quickly"; **(2)** in Lk 19:4, "he ran before." See: BAGD—722b; THAYER—552c.

4391. **προϋπάρχω** {2x} **prŏëparchō**, *prŏ-oop-ar'-kho;* from *4253* and *5225;* to *exist before,* i.e. (adv.) to *be* or *do* something *previously:*—be before {1x}, be beforetime {1x}.

This word means "to exist before, or be beforehand" and is found **(1)** in Lk 23:12, "be before"; and **(2)** Acts 8:9, "be beforetime." See: BAGD—722c; THAYER—552c.

4392. **πρόφασις** {7x} **prŏphasis**, *prof'-as-is;* from a compound of *4253* and *5316;* an *outward showing,* i.e. *pretext:*—cloke {2x}, colour {1x}, pretence {3x}, shew {1x}.

Prophases, either from *pro,* "before," and *phaino,* "to cause to appear, shine," or, more probably, from *pro,* and *phemi,* "to say," is rendered **(1)** "cloke" (of covetousness) in Jn 15:22; 1 Th 2:5; **(2)** "pretence" in Mt 23:14; Mk 12:40; Phil 1:18; **(3)** "shew" in Lk 20:47; and **(4)** "colour" in Acts 27:30. **(5)** It signifies the assuming of something so as to disguise one's real motives. See: BAGD—722c; THAYER—552c.

4393. **προφέρω** {2x} **prŏphĕrō**, *prof-er'-o;* from *4253* and *5342;* to *bear forward,* i.e. *produce:*—bring forth {2x}.

Prophero, as a verb, denotes "to bring forth": "A good man out of the good treasure of his heart bringeth forth that which is good; and an evil man out of the evil treasure of his heart bringeth forth that which is evil: for of the abundance of the heart his mouth speaketh" (Lk 6:45, twice). See: BAGD—722d; THAYER—552c.

4394. **προφητεία** {19x} **prŏphētĕia**, *prof-ay-ti'-ah;* from *4396* ("*prophecy*"); *prediction* (scriptural or other):—prophecy {16x}, prophesying {3x}.

(1) Prophecy is not necessarily, nor even primarily, fore-telling. **(2)** It is the declaration of that which cannot be known by natural means (Mt 26:68), **(3)** it emanates from God and is the forth-telling of the will of God, whether with reference to the past, the present, or the future (Rev 10:11; 11:3). **(4)** It signifies "the speaking forth of the mind and counsel of God" (*pro,* "forth," *phemi,* "to speak"); **(5)** in the NT it is used **(5a)** of the gift, e.g., Rom 12:6; 1 Cor 12:10; 13:2; **(5b)** either of the exercise of the gift or of that which is "prophesied," e.g., Mt 13:14; 1 Cor 13:8; 14:6, 22 and 1 Th 5:20, "prophesying (s)"; 1 Ti 1:18; 4:14; 2 Pet 1:20, 21; Rev 1:3; 11:6; 19:10; 22:7, 10, 18, 19. See: TDNT—6:781, 952; BAGD—722d; THAYER—552d.

4395. **προφητεύω** {28x} **prŏphētĕuō**, *prof-ate-yoo'-o;* from *4396;* to *foretell* events, *divine, speak* under *inspiration, exercise* the prophetic office:—prophesy {28x}. Syn.: see 3132 for discussion.

This word means "to be a prophet, to prophesy," and is used **(1)** with the primary meaning of telling forth the divine counsels, e.g., Mt 7:22; 26:68; 1 Cor 11:4, 5; 13:9; 14:1, 3–5, 24, 31, 39; Rev 11:3; **(2)** of foretelling the future, e.g., Mt 15:7; Jn 11:51; 1 Pet 1:10; Jude 14. See: TDNT—6:781, 952; BAGD—723a; THAYER—552d.

4396. **προφήτης** {149x} **prŏphētēs**, *prof-ay'-tace;* from a compound of *4253* and *5346;* a *foreteller* ("*prophet*"); by anal. an *inspired speaker;* by extens. a *poet:*—prophet {149x}.

Prophetes, "one who speaks forth or openly", "a proclaimer of a divine message." **I. In the OT,** it is the translation **(1)** of the word *roeh,* "a seer"; 1 Sa 9:9, indicating that the "prophet" was one who had immediate conversation with God. **(2)** It also translates the word *nabhi,* meaning "either one in whom the message from God springs forth" or "one to whom anything is secretly communicated." **(3)** Hence, in general, "the prophet" was one upon whom the Spirit of God rested, Num 11:17–29, one, to whom and through whom God speaks, Num 12:2; Amos 3:7, 8. **(4)** In the case of the OT prophets their messages were very largely the proclamation of the divine purposes of salvation and glory to be accomplished in the future; the "prophesying" of the NT "prophets" was both a preaching of the divine counsels of grace already accomplished and the foretelling of the purposes of God in the future.

II. In the NT the word is used **(1)** of "the OT prophets," e.g., Mt 5:12; Mk 6:15; Lk 4:27; Jn 8:52; Rom 11:3; **(2)** of "prophets in general," e.g., Mt 10:41; 21:46; Mk 6:4; **(3)** of "John the Baptist," Mt 21:26; Lk 1:76; **(4)** of "prophets in the churches," e.g., Acts 13:1; 15:32; 21:10; 1 Cor 12:28, 29; 14:29, 32, 37; Eph 2:20; 3:5; 4:11; **(5)** of "Christ, **(5a)** as the afore-promised Prophet," e.g., Jn 1:21; 6:14; 7:40; Acts 3:22; 7:37, or, **(5b)** without the article, and, without reference to the Old Testament, Mk 6:15; Lk 7:16; in Lk 24:19 it is used with aner, "a man"; Jn 4:19; 9:17; **(6)** of "two witnesses" yet to be raised up for special purposes, Rev 11:10, 18; **(7)** of "the Cretan poet Epimenides," Titus 1:12; **(8)** by metonymy, of "the writings of prophets," e.g., Lk 24:27; Acts 8:28. Syn.: 4394. See: TDNT—6:781, 952; BAGD—723b; THAYER—553b.

4397. **προφητικός** {2x} **prŏphētikŏs**, *prof-ay-tik-os';* from *4396; pertaining to a foreteller* ("*prophetic*"):—of prophecy {1x}, of the prophets {1x}

Prophetikos, "of or relating to prophecy," or "proceeding from a prophet, prophetic," is used **(1)** of the OT Scriptures, Rom 16:26, "of the prophets," lit., "(by) prophetic (Scriptures)"; **(2)** 2 Pet 1:19, "the word of prophecy (*made* more sure)," i.e., confirmed by the person and work of Christ ("a more sure, etc."), lit., "the prophetic word." Syn.: 4394. See: TDNT—6:781, 952; BAGD—724b; THAYER—554a.

4398. **προφῆτις** {2x} **prŏphētis**, *prof-ay'-tis;* fem. of *4396; a female foreteller* or an *inspired woman:*—prophetess {2x}.

Prophetis, the feminine of *prophetes,* is used of Anna, Lk 2:36; of the self-assumed title of "the woman Jezebel" in Rev 2:20. See: TDNT—6:781, 952; BAGD—724b; THAYER—554a.

4399. **προφθάνω** {1x} **prŏphthanō**, *prof-than'-o;* from *4253* and *5348;* to *get* an *earlier start of,* i.e. *anticipate:*—prevent {1x}.

Prevent is derived from Latin, *pre* – before, and *venir,* to go; hence, to go before, precede in time. See: TDNT—9:88, 1258; BAGD—724b; THAYER—554a.

4400. **προχειρίζομαι** {2x} **prŏchĕirizŏmai**, *prokh-i-rid'-zom-ahee;* mid. voice from *4253* and a der. of *5495; to handle* for oneself *in advance,* i.e. (fig.) to *purpose:*—choose {1x}, make {1x}.

Procheirizo, as a verb, signifies **(1)** in the middle voice, "to take into one's hand, to determine, appoint beforehand," translated "appointed": "And he said, The God of our fathers hath chosen (*procheirizo*) thee, that thou shouldest know his will, and see that Just One, and shouldest hear the voice of his mouth" (Acts 22:14); and **(2)** "to make, to appoint": "But rise, and stand upon thy feet: for I have appeared unto thee for this purpose, to make (*procheirizo*) thee a minister and a witness both of these things which thou hast seen, and of those things in the which I will appear unto thee" (Acts 26:16). See: TDNT—6:862,*; BAGD—724c; THAYER—554b.

4401. **προχειροτονέω** {1x} **prŏchĕirŏtŏnĕō**, *prokh-i-rot-on-eh'-o;* from *4253* and *5500;* to *elect in advance:*—choose before {1x}.

This word signifies "to choose before," Acts 10:41, where it is used of a choice made before by God. See: BAGD—724c; THAYER—554b.

4402. **Πρόχορος** {1x} **Prŏchŏrŏs**, *prokh'-or-os;* from *4253* and *5525; before* the *dance; Prochorus,* a Chr.:—*Prochorus* {1x}. See: BAGD—724c; THAYER—554b.

4403. **πρύμνα** {3x} **prumna**, *proom'-nah;* fem. of πρυμνύς **prumnus** (*hindmost*); the *stern* of a ship:—hinder part {1x}, hinder part of ship {1x}, stern {1x}. Cf. Mk 4:38; Acts 27:29, 41. See: BAGD—724d; THAYER—554b.

4404. **πρωΐ** { {1x} **prōï**, *pro-ee';* adv. from *4253;* at *dawn;* by impl. the *day-break* watch:—in the morning {5x}, early in the morning {2x}, early {2x}, morning {1x}.

(1) *Proi* is the fourth watch of the night, from 3 o'clock in the morning until 6 o'clock approximately. This word means "early in the day, at morn." **(1)** In Mk 16:2, it is translated "early in the morning"; **(2)** in Mk 16:9 and Jn 18:28; 20:1, "early"; **(3)** in Mt 16:3; 20:1; 21:18; Mk 1:35; 11:20; 13:35; 15:1, "in the morning"; **(4)** in Acts 28:23, "(from) morning." See: BAGD—724d; THAYER—554b.

4405. **πρωΐα** {4x} **prōïa**, *pro-ee'-ah;* fem. of a der. of *4404* as noun; *day-dawn:*—early {1x}, morning {3x}.

Proia, "early, at early morn" (from *pro,* "before"), is used **(1)** as a noun in the feminine form *proia,* "morning" in Mt 21:18; 27:1; Jn 18:28; 21:4. Its adjectival force is retained by regarding it as qualifying the noun *hora,* "an hour," i.e., "at an early hour." See: BAGD—724d; THAYER—554c.

4406. **πρώϊμος** {1x} **prōïmŏs**, *pro'-ee-mos;* from *4404; dawning,* i.e. (by anal.) *autumnal* (showering, the first of the rainy season in October):—early {1x}. See: BAGD—725a; 706d; THAYER—554c.

4407. **πρωϊνός** {1x} **prōïnŏs**, *pro-ee-nos';* from *4404;* pertaining to the *dawn,* i.e. *matutinal:*—morning {1x}.

This adjective qualifies *aster,* "star," in Rev 2:28. That Christ will give to the overcomer "the morning star" indicates a special interest for such in Himself. For Israel He will appear as "the sun of righteousness"; as the "morning" Star which precedes the dawn, He will appear for the rapture of the church. See: BAGD—725a; THAYER—554c.

4408. **πρῷρα** {2x} **prōra**, *pro'-ra;* fem. of a presumed der. of *4253* as noun; the *prow,* i.e. forward part of a vessel:—forepart {1x}, foreship {1x}. See: BAGD—725a; THAYER—554c.

4409. **πρωτεύω** {1x} **prōtĕuō**, *prote-yoo'-o;* from *4413;* to *be first* (in rank or influence):—have the preeminence {1x}. See: TDNT—6:881, 965; BAGD—725a; THAYER—554d.

4410. **πρωτοκαθεδρία** {4x} **prōtŏkathĕdria**, *pro-tok-ath-ed-ree'-ah;* from *4413* and *2515;* a *sitting first* (in the front row), i.e. *preeminence* in council:—chief seat {2x}, highest seat {1x}, uppermost seat {1x}.

This word means "a sitting in the first or chief seat" (*protos,* "first," *kathedra,* "a seat"), and is found in Mt 23:6; Mk 12:39; Lk 11:43; 20:46. See: TDNT—6:870, 965; BAGD—725b; THAYER—554d.

4411. **πρωτοκλισία** {5x} **prōtŏklisia**, *pro-tok-lis-ee'-ah;* from *4413* and *2828;* a *reclining first* (in the place of honor) at the dinner-bed, i.e. *preeminence* at meals:—chief room {2x}, highest room {1x}, uppermost room {2x}.

Protoklisia, "the first reclining place, the chief place at table" (from *protos,* and *klisia,* "a company reclining at a meal"; cf. *klino,* "to incline"), is found in Mt 23:6; Mk 12:39; Lk 14:7–8; 20:46. Room signifies a place or position of total and complete authority. To take over another's room is to exercise total control over what the previous one held. To be in one's stead, by comparison, is to replace another, but not with the same extent of authority. See: TDNT—6:870, 965; BAGD—725b; THAYER—554d.

4412. **πρῶτον** {60x} **prōtŏn**, *pro'-ton;* neut. of *4413* as adv. (with or without *3588*); *firstly* (in time, place, order, or importance):—first {51x}, at the first + 3588 {2x}, first of all {2x}, misc. {5x} = before, at the beginning, chiefly.

Proton, the neuter of the adjective *protos* (the superlative degree of *pro,* "before"), signifies "first, or at the first," **(1)** in order of time, e.g., Lk 10:5; Jn 18:13; 1 Cor 15:46; 1 Th 4:16; 1 Ti 3:10; **(2)** in enumerating various particulars, e.g., Rom 3:2; 1 Cor 11:18; 12:28; Heb 7:2; Jas 3:17. **(3)** It is translated "before" in Jn 15:18. See: TDNT—6:868, 965; BAGD—725b; THAYER—554d.

4413. **πρῶτος** {105x} **prōtŏs**, *pro'-tos;* contr. superl. of *4253; foremost* (in time, place, order or importance):—first {85x}, chief {9x}, first day {2x}, former {2x}, misc. {7x} = before, beginning, best.

Protos, the superlative degree of *pro,* "before," is used **I.** "of time or place," **(1)** as a noun, e.g., Lk 14:18; Rev 1:17; **(1a)** opposite to "the last," in the neuter plural, Mt 12:45; Lk 11:26; 2 Pet 2:20; **(1b)** in the neuter singular, opposite to "the second," Heb 10:9; **(1c)** in 1 Cor 15:3, *en protois,* lit., "in the first (things, or matters)" denotes "first of all"; **(2)** as an adjective, e.g., Mk 16:9, used with "day" understood, lit., "the first (day) of (i.e., after) the Sabbath," in which phrase the "of" is objective, not including the Sabbath, but following it; **(2a)** in Jn 20:4, 8; Rom 10:19, e.g., equivalent to an English adverb; **(2b)** in Jn 1:15, lit., "first of me," i.e., "before me" (of superiority); **II.** "of rank or dignity," denotes "the first," whether in time or place. **(1)** It is translated "chief" in Mk 6:21, **(1a)** of men of Galilee; **(1b)** in Acts 13:50, of men in a city; **(1c)** in Acts 28:7, of the "chief" man in the island of Melita; **(1d)** in Acts 17:4, of "chief" women in a city; **(1e)** in Acts 28:17, of Jews; **(1f)** in 1 Ti 1:15–16, of a sinner. **(1g)** Cf. Mt 20:27; Mk 10:44; Lk 19:47; Acts 16:12; 25:2. See: TDNT—6:865, 965; BAGD—725b; THAYER—554d.

4414. **πρωτοστάτης** {1x} **prōtŏstatēs**, *pro-tos-tat'-ace;* from *4413* and *2476;* one *standing first* in the ranks, i.e. a *captain* (*champion*):—ringleader {1x}.

Protostates, "one who stands first" (*protos,* "first," *histemi,* "to cause to stand"), was used of soldiers, one who stands in the front rank; hence, metaphorically, "a leader," Acts 24:5. See: BAGD—725c; THAYER—555c.

4415. **πρωτοτόκια** {1x} **prōtŏtŏkia**, *pro-tot-ok'-ee-ah;* from *4416; primogeniture* (as a privilege):—birthright {1x}.

(1) *Prototokia* is the right or advantages of the firstborn son. **(2)** This word means a birthright" (from *protos*, "first," *tikto*, "to beget"), and is found in Heb 12:16, with reference to Esau (cf. *prototokos*, firstborn). The "birthright" involved preeminence and authority, Gen 27:29; 49:3. Another right was that of the double portion, Deut 21:17; 1 Chr 5:1–2. Connected with the "birthright" was the progenitorship of the Messiah. Esau transferred his "birthright" to Jacob for a paltry mess of pottage, profanely despising this last spiritual privilege, Gen 25 and 27. In the history of the nation God occasionally set aside the "birthright," to show that the objects of His choice depended not on the will of the flesh, but on His own authority. Thus Isaac was preferred to Ishmael, Jacob to Esau, Joseph to Reuben, David to his elder brethren, Solomon to Adonijah. See: TDNT—6:871, 965; BAGD—725c; THAYER—555d.

4416. **πρωτότοκος** {9x} **prōtŏtŏkŏs**, *pro-tot-ok'-os;* from *4413* and the alt. of *5088; first-born* (usually as noun, lit. or fig.):—first begotten {2x}, firstborn {7x}.

Firstborn is used **(1)** of Christ as born of the Virgin Mary (Mt 1:25; Lk 2:7); **(2)** of His relationship to the Father, expressing His priority to, and preeminence over, creation, not in the sense of being the first to be born. It is used of superiority of position (cf. Ex 4:22; Deut 21:16, 17). **(3)** Chronologically, the four passages relating to Christ as firstborn, first begotten, may be set forth thusly: **(3a)** Col 1:15, where His eternal relationship with the Father is in view, and the clause means both that He was the firstborn before all creation and that He Himself produced creation (the genitive case being objective, as v. 16 makes clear); **(3b)** Col 1:18 and Rev 1:5, in reference to His resurrection; **(3c)** Rom 8:29, His being firstborn among those living by faith alone in God the Father; **(3d)** Heb 1:6, first begotten, stresses His superior position, His preeminence over all; His second advent in contrast to His first advent, at His birth, being implied. See: TDNT—6:871, 965; BAGD—726c; THAYER—555d.

4417. **πταίω** {5x} **ptaiō**, *ptah'-yo;* a form of *4098;* to *trip*, i.e. (fig.) to *err, sin, fail* (of salvation):—fall {1x}, offend {3x}, stumble {1x}.

Ptaio, "to cause to stumble," signifies, intransitively, "to stumble," used **(1)** metaphorically in Rom 11:11; **(2)** with moral significance in Jas 2:10 and 3:2 (twice), "offend"; **(3)** in 2 Pet 1:10, "fall." See: TDNT—6:883, 968; BAGD—727a; THAYER—556b.

4418. **πτέρνα** {1x} **ptĕrna**, *pter'-nah;* of uncert. der.; the *heel* (fig.):—heel {1x}.

Pterna is found in Jn 13:18, where the Lord quotes from Ps 41:9; the metaphor is that of tripping up an antagonist in wrestling. See: BAGD—727b; THAYER—556b.

4419. **πτερύγιον** {2x} **ptĕrugiŏn**, *pter-oog'-ee-on;* neut. of a presumed der. of *4420;* a *winglet*, i.e. (fig.) *extremity* (top corner):—pinnacle {2x}.

This wing/pinnacle has been regarded **(1)** as the apex of the sanctuary, **(2)** the top of Solomon's porch, or **(3)** the top of the Royal Portico, which Josephus describes as of tremendous height (*Antiq.* xv. 11.5). Cf. Mt 4:5; Lk 49. See: BAGD—727b; THAYER—556b.

4420. **πτέρυξ** {5x} **ptĕrux**, *pter'-oox;* from a der. of *4072* (mean. a *feather*); a *wing as of a bird:*—wing {5x}.

Pterux is used **(1)** of birds, Mt 23:37; Lk 13:34; **(2)** symbolically in Rev 12:14, "two wings of a great eagle", suggesting the definiteness of the action, the "wings" indicating rapidity and protection, an allusion, perhaps, to Ex 19:4 and Deut 32:11, 12; **(3)** of the "living creatures" in a vision, Rev 4:8; 9:9. See: BAGD—727b; THAYER—556c.

4421. **πτηνόν** {1x} **ptēnŏn**, *ptay-non';* contr. for *4071;* a *bird:*—bird {1x}. See: BAGD—727c; THAYER—556c.

4422. **πτοέω** {2x} **ptŏĕō**, *ptŏ-eh'-o;* prob. akin to the alt. of *4098* (through the idea of causing to *fall*) or to *4072* (through that of causing to *fly* away); to *scare:*—terrify {2x}.

Ptoeo, "to terrify," is used in the passive voice, Lk 21:9; 24:37. Syn.: **(A)** *Ekplesso* (1605) means "to be astonished", prop. to be struck with terror, of a sudden and startling alarm; but like our "astonish" in popular use, often employed on comparatively slight occasions. **(B)** *Ptoeo* (4422) signifies "to terrify", to agitate with fear. **(C)** *Tremo* (5141) "to tremble", predominately physical; and **(D)** *phobeo* (5399) denotes "to fear", the general term; often used of a protracted state. See: BAGD—727c; THAYER—556c.

4423. **πτόησις** {1x} **ptŏēsis**, *ptŏ'-ay-sis;* from *4422; alarm:*—amazement {1x}. See: BAGD—727c; THAYER—556c.

4424. **Πτολεμαΐς** {1x} **Ptŏlĕmaïs**, *ptol-em-ah-is';* from Πτολεμαῖος **Ptŏlĕmaiŏs** (*Ptolemy*, after whom it was named); *Ptolemaïs*, a place in Pal.:—*Ptolemais* {1x}. See: BAGD—727c; THAYER—556c.

4425. **πτύον** {2x} **ptuŏn**, *ptoo'-on;* from *4429;* a *winnowing-fork* (as *scattering* like spittle):—fan {2x}.

Ptuon denotes a winnowing shovel or fan with which grain is thrown up against the wind, in order to separate the chaff (Mt 3:12; Lk 3:17). See: BAGD—727c; THAYER—556d.

4426. **πτύρω** {1x} **pturō**, *ptoo'-ro;* from a presumed der. of *4429* (and thus akin to *4422*); to *frighten:*—terrify {1x}. See: BAGD—727d; THAYER—556d.

4427. **πτύσμα** {1x} **ptusma**, *ptoos'-mah;* from *4429; saliva:*—spittle {1x}. See: BAGD—727d; THAYER—556d.

4428. **πτύσσω** {1x} **ptussō**, *ptoos'-so;* prob. akin to πετάννυμι **pĕtannumi**, (to *spread;* and thus appar. allied to *4072* through the idea of *expansion*, and to *4429* through that of *flattening;* comp. *3961*); to *fold*, i.e. *furl, roll up* a scroll:—close {1x}.

This word means "to fold, double up," and is used of a scroll of parchment, Lk 4:20. See: BAGD—727d; THAYER—556d.

4429. **πτύω** {3x} **ptuō**, *ptoo'-o;* a primary verb (comp. *4428*); to *spit:*—spit {3x}. Cf. Mk 7:33; 8:23; Jn 9:6. See: BAGD—727d; THAYER—556d.

4430. **πτῶμα** {5x} **ptōma**, *pto'-mah;* from the alt. of *4098;* a *ruin*, i.e. (spec.) lifeless *body* (*corpse, carrion*):—dead body {3x}, carcase {1x}, corpse {1x}.

Ptoma denotes, lit., "a fall" (akin to *pipto*, "to fall"); hence, "that which is fallen, a corpse," Mt 14:12; 24:28, "carcase"; Mk 6:29; 15:45, "corpse"; Rev 11:8–9, "dead bodies." See: TDNT—6:166, 846; BAGD—727d; THAYER—557a.

4431. **πτῶσις** {2x} **ptōsis**, *pto'-sis;* from the alt. of *4098;* a *crash*, i.e. *downfall* (lit. or fig.):—fall {2x}.

Ptosos, "a fall", is used **(1)** literally, of the "overthrow of a building," Mt 7:27; **(2)** metaphorically, Lk 2:34, of the spiritual "fall" of those in Israel who would reject Christ. See: TDNT—6:167, 846; BAGD—728a; THAYER—557a.

4432. **πτωχεία** {3x} **ptōchĕia**, *pto-khi'-ah;* from *4433; beggary*, i.e. *indigence* (lit. or fig.):—poverty {3x}.

Ptocheia, "destitution" is used **(1)** of the "poverty" which Christ voluntarily experienced on our behalf, 2 Cor 8:9; **(2)** of the destitute condition of saints in Judea, 2 Cor 8:2; **(3)** of the condition of the church in Smyrna, Rev 2:9, where the word is used in a general sense. See: TDNT—6:885, 969; BAGD—728a; THAYER—557a.

4433. **πτωχεύω** {1x} **ptōchĕuō**, *pto-khyoo'-o;* from *4434;* to *be a beggar*, i.e. (by impl.) to *become indigent* (fig.):—become poor {1x}. See: TDNT—6:885, 969; BAGD—728a; THAYER—557a.

4434. **πτωχός** {34x} **ptōchŏs**, *pto-khos';* from πτώσσω **ptōssō**, to *crouch;* akin to *4422* and the alt. of *4098*); a *beggar* (as *cringing*), i.e. *pauper* (strictly denoting absolute or public *mendicancy*, although also used in a qualified or relative sense; whereas *3993* prop. means only *straitened* circumstances in private), lit. (often used as a noun) or fig. (*distressed*):—beggar {2x}, beggarly {1x}, poor {30x}, poor man {1x}.

Ptochos, an adjective describing "one who crouches and cowers," is used **(1)** as a noun, "a beggar" (from *ptosso*, "to cower down or hide oneself for fear"), e.g., Lk 14:13, 21 ("poor"); 16:20, 22; **(2)** as an adjective, "beggarly" in Gal 4:9, i.e., poverty-stricken, powerless to enrich, metaphorically descriptive of the religion of the Jews. Syn.: While **(A)** *prosaites* (4319) is descriptive of a "beggar," and stresses his "begging," *ptochos* stresses his poverty-stricken condition. **(B)** *Penes* (3993) is one who is so poor he earns his bread by daily labour; whereas, *ptochos* (4434) is one who only obtains his living by begging. See: TDNT—6:885, 969; BAGD—728b; THAYER—557b.

4435. **πυγμή** { {1x} **pugmē**, *poog-may';* from a primary πύξ **pux** (the *fist*, as a weapon); the clenched *hand*, i.e. (only in dat. as adverb) *with the fist* (hard *scrubbing*):—oft {1x}.

The dative case of *pugme* is a fist, and literally, means "with the fist" (one hand being rubbed with the clenched fist of the other, a metaphorical expression for thoroughly, diligently, oft, in contrast to what is superficial (Mk 7:3). See: TDNT—6:915, 973; BAGD—728c; THAYER—557c.

4436. **Πύθων** {1x} **Puthōn**, *poo'-thone;* from Πυθώ **Puthō** (the name of the region where Delphi, the seat of the famous *oracle*, was located); a *Python*, i.e. (by anal. with the supposed *diviner* there) *inspiration* (*soothsaying*):—divination {1x}.

Puthon, (Eng., "python"), in Greek mythology was the name of the Pythian serpent or dragon, dwelling in Pytho, at the foot of mount Parnassus, guarding the oracle of Delphi, and slain by Apollo. Thence the name was transferred to Apollo himself. Later the word was applied to diviners or soothsayers, regarded as inspired by Apollo. Since devils are the agents inspiring idolatry, 1 Cor 10:20, the young woman in Acts 16:16 was possessed by a devil instigating the cult of Apollo, and thus had "a spirit of divination." See: TDNT—6:917,*; BAGD—728d; THAYER—557c.

4437. **πυκνός** {3x} **puknŏs**, *pook-nos';* from the same as *4635; clasped* (*thick*), i.e. (fig.) *frequent;* neut. plur. (as adv.) *frequently:*—often {2x}, oftener {1x}. Cf. Lk 5:3; Acts 24:26; 1 Ti 5:23. See: BAGD—729a; THAYER—557d.

4438. **πυκτεύω** {1x} **puktĕō**, *pook-teh'-o;* from a der. of the same as *4435;* to *box* (with the fist), i.e. *contend* (as a boxer) at the games (fig.):—fight {1x}. See: BAGD—729c; THAYER—557d.

4439. **πύλη** {10x} **pulē**, *poo'-lay;* appar. a primary word; a *gate*, i.e. the leaf or wing of a folding *entrance* (lit. or fig.):—gate {10x}.

Pule is used **(1)** literally, for a larger sort of gate in the wall either of a city or palace or temple (Lk 7:12: Acts 3:10; 9:24; 12:10; Heb 13:12); and **(2)** metaphorically, of the gates at the entrances of the ways leading to life and to destruction (Mt 7:13 twice, 14; Lk 13:24). **(3)** The importance and strength of gates made them viewed as synonymous with power; figuratively of hell's power, Mt 16:18. **(4)** By metonymy, the gates stood for those who held government and administered justice there. See: TDNT—6:921, 974; BAGD—729b; THAYER—557d.

4440. **πυλών** {18x} **pulōn**, *poo-lone';* from *4439;* a *gate-way, door-way* of a building or city; by impl. a *portal* or *vestibule:*—gate {17x}, porch {1x}.

(1) *Pulon* is a large gate of a palace or the front part of a house, into which one enters through the gate, porch. **(2)** It primarily signifies **(2a)** "a porch or vestibule," e.g., Mt 26:71; Lk 16:20; Acts 10:17; 12:13, 14; **(2b)** then, the "gateway" or "gate tower" of a walled town, Acts 14:13; Rev 21:12, 13, 15, 21, 25; 22:14. See: TDNT—6:921, 974; BAGD—729c; THAYER—558a.

4441. **πυνθάνομαι** {12x} **punthanŏmai**, *poon-than'-om-ahee;* mid. voice prol. from a primary πύθω **puthō** (which occurs only as an alt. in certain tenses); to *question*, i.e. *ascertain* by inquiry (as a matter of *information* merely; and thus differing from *2065*, which prop. means a *request* as a favor; and from *154*, which is strictly a *demand* for something due; as well as from *2212*, which implies a *search* for something hidden; and from *1189*, which involves the idea of urgent *need*); by impl. to *learn* (by casual intelligence):—ask {7x}, demand {2x}, enquire {2x}, understand {1x}.

Punthanomai, as a verb, means **(1)** to ask by way of inquiry, not by way of making a request for something, **(2)** is found in the Gospels and the Acts, five times in the former, seven in the latter. **(3)** In Mt 2:4 it is translated "demanded": "And when he had gathered all the chief priests and scribes of the people together, he demanded of them where Christ should be born." (cf. Acts 21:33). **(4)** It is translated "enquired" in Mt 2:4; Jn 4:52; Acts 23:20; **(5)** in Acts 21:33, "demanded"; **(6)** in Lk 15:26; 18:36; Jn 13:24; Acts 4:7; 10:18, 29; 23:19, "asked"; and **(7)** in Acts 23:34 it denotes "when (he) understood." Syn.: 154, 155, 350, 1833, 1905, 2065, 3004. See: BAGD—729c; THAYER—558a.

4442. **πῦρ** {74x} **pur**, *poor;* a primary word; "*fire*" (lit. or fig., spec. *lightning*):—fiery {1x}, fire {73x}.

Pur is used (besides its ordinary natural significance): **(1)** of the holiness of God, which consumes all that is inconsistent therewith, Heb 10:27; 12:29; cf. Rev 1:14; 2:18; 10:1; 15:2; 19:12; **(1a)** similarly of the holy angels as His ministers, Heb 1:7; **(1b)** in Rev 3:18 it is symbolic of that which tries the faith of saints, producing what will glorify the Lord; **(2)** of the divine judgment, testing the deeds of believers, at the judgment seat of Christ 1 Cor 3:13 and 15; **(3)** of the fire of divine judgment upon the rejectors of Christ, Mt 3:11 (where a distinction is to be made between the baptism of the Holy Spirit at Pentecost and the "fire" of divine retribution; Acts 2:3 could not refer to baptism); Lk 3:16;

(4) of the judgments of God at the close of the present age previous to the establishment of the kingdom of Christ in the world, 2 Th 1:8; Rev 18:8; **(5)** of the "fire" of Hell, to be endured by the ungodly hereafter, Mt 5:22; 13:42, 50; 18:8, 9; 25:41; Mk 9:43, 48; Lk 3:17; **(6)** of human hostility both to the Jews and to Christ's followers, Lk 12:49; **(7)** as illustrative of retributive judgment upon the luxurious and tyrannical rich, Jas 5:3; **(8)** of the future overthrow of the Babylonish religious system at the hands of the Beast and the nations under him, Rev 17:16; **(9)** of turning the heart of an enemy to repentance by repaying his unkindness by kindness, Rom 12:20; **(10)** of the tongue, as governed by a "fiery" disposition and as exercising a destructive influence over others, Jas 3:6; **(11)** as symbolic of the danger of destruction, Jude 23. See: TDNT—6:928, 975; BAGD—729d; THAYER—558a.

4443. **πυρά** {2x} **pura**, *poo-rah';* from *4442;* a *fire* (concr.):—fire {2x}.

Pura denotes a heap of fuel collected to be set on fire [Eng., pyre], Acts 28:2, 3. See: BAGD—730c; THAYER—558c.

4444. **πύργος** {4x} **purgŏs**, *poor'-gos;* appar. a primary word ("*burgh*"); a *tower* or *castle:*—tower {4x}.

Purgos is used **(1)** of "a watchtower in a vineyard," Mt 21:33; Mk 12:1; **(2)** probably, too, in Lk 14:28 (cf. Is 5:2); in Lk 13:4, of the "tower in Siloam." See: TDNT—6:953, 980; BAGD—730d; THAYER—538c.

4445. **πυρέσσω** {2x} **purĕssō**, *poo-res'-so;* from *4443;* to *be on fire*, i.e. (spec.) to *have a fever:*—be sick of a fever {2x}. Cf. Matt. 8:14; Mark 1:30. See: TDNT—6:956, 981; BAGD—730d; THAYER—538c.

4446. **πυρετός** {6x} **purĕtŏs**, *poo-ret-os';* from *4445; inflamed,* i.e. (by impl.) *feverish* (as noun, *fever*):—fever {6x}.

Puretos, "feverish heat" (from *pur,* "fire"), hence, "a fever," occurs in Mt 8:15; Mk 1:31; Jn 4:52; Acts 28:8; in Lk 4:38, with *megas,* "great, a high fever"; v. 39. Luke, as a physician, uses the medical distinction by which the ancients classified fevers into great and little. See: TDNT—6:956, 981; BAGD—730d; THAYER—558c.

4447. **πύρινος** {1x} **purinŏs**, *poo'-ree-nos;* from *4443; fiery,* i.e. (by impl.) *flaming:*—of fire {1x}. See: TDNT—6:951, 975; BAGD—731a; THAYER—558d.

4448. **πυρόω** {6x} **purŏō**, *poo-rŏ'-o;* from *4442;* to *kindle*, i.e. (pass.) to *be ignited, glow* (lit.), *be refined* (by impl.), or (fig.) to *be inflamed* (with anger, grief, lust):—burn {3x}, fiery {1x}, be on fire {1x}, try {1x}.

Puroo, from *pur,* "fire, to glow with heat," is said **(1)** of the feet of the Lord, in the vision in Rev 1:15; **(2)** it is translated "fiery" in Eph 6:16 (of the darts of the evil one); **(3)** used metaphorically of the emotions, in 1 Cor 7:9; 2 Cor 11:29; **(4)** elsewhere literally, of the heavens, 2 Pet 3:12; **(5)** of gold, Rev 3:18. See: TDNT—6:948, 975; BAGD—731a; THAYER—558d.

4449. **πυρράζω** {2x} **purrhazō**, *poor-hrad'-zo;* from *4450;* to *redden* (intr.):—be red {2x}. See: BAGD—731b; THAYER—558d.

4450. **πυρρός** {2x} **purrhŏs**, *poor-hros';* from *4442; fire-like,* i.e. (spec.) *flame-colored:*—red {2x}.

This word means "to be fiery red", is used of the sky, Mt 16:2, 3. See: TDNT—6:952, 975; BAGD—731c; THAYER—559a.

4451. **πύρωσις** {3x} **purōsis**, *poo'-ro-sis;* from *4448; ignition,* i.e. (spec.) *smelting* (fig. *conflagration, calamity* as a *test*):—burning {2x}, trial {1x}.

Purosis is used **(1)** literally in Rev 18:9, 18; **(2)** metaphorically in 1 Pet 4:12, "fiery trial." See: TDNT—6:950, 975; BAGD—731c; THAYER—559a.

4452. **-πω** {0x} **-pō**, *po;* another form of the base of *4458;* an enclitic particle of indefiniteness; *yet, even;* used only in composition. See *3369, 3380, 3764, 3768, 4455*. See: BAGD—not listed; cf. 732d [4458]; THAYER—413b [3380].

4453. **πωλέω** {22x} **pōlĕō**, *po-leh'-o;* prob. ultimately from πέλομαι **pĕlŏmai** (to *be busy,* to *trade*); to *barter* (as a *pedlar*), i.e. to *sell:*—sell {21x}, whatever is sold {1x}.

Poleo, "to exchange or barter, to sell," is used in the latter sense in the NT, six times in Mt, three in Mk, six in Lk; in Jn only in connection with the cleansing of the Temple by the Lord, Jn 2:14, 16; in Acts only in connection with the disposing of property for distribution among the community of believers, 4:34, 37; 5:1; elsewhere, 1 Cor 10:25; Rev 13:17. See: BAGD—731c; THAYER—559a.

4454. **πῶλος** {12x} **pōlŏs**, *po'-los;* appar. a primary word; a "*foal*" or "*filly*", i.e. (spec.) a *young ass:*—colt {12x}.

Polos, "a foal," whether "colt or filly," had the general significance of "a young creature"; in Mt 21:2, and parallel passages, "an ass's colt." See: TDNT—6:959, 981; BAGD—731d; THAYER—559b.

4455. **πώποτε** {6x} **pōpŏtĕ**, *po'-pot-e;* from *4452* and *4218; at any time,* i.e. (with neg. particle) *at no time:*—at any time {3x}, yet never + 3762 {1x}, never {1x}, never + 3364 {1x}. See: BAGD—732a; THAYER—559b.

4456. **πωρόω** {5x} **pōrŏō**, *po-rŏ'-o;* appar. from πῶρος **pōrŏs**, (a kind of *stone*); to *petrify*, i.e. (fig.) to *indurate* (*render stupid* or *callous*):—blind {2x}, harden {3x}.

Poroo signifies "to harden" (from *poros,* "a thick skin, a hardening"), "to make hard, callous, to petrify", is used **(1)** metaphorically, **(1a)** of the heart, Mk 6:52; 8:17; Jn 12:40; **(1b)** of the mind (or thoughts), 2 Cor 3:14, of those in Israel who refused the revealed will and ways of God in the gospel, as also in Rom 11:7, "blinded", in both places. See: TDNT—5:1025, 816; BAGD—732a; THAYER—559b.

4457. **πώρωσις** {3x} **pōrōsis**, *po'-ro-sis;* from *4456; stupidity* or *callousness:*—blindness {2x}, hardness {1x}.

Porosis, primarily means "a covering with a callus," **(1)** in Rom 11:25 and Eph 4:18, "blindness"; **(2)** in Mk 3:5, "hardness." **(3)** It is metaphorical of a dulled spiritual perception. See: TDNT—5:1025, 816; BAGD—732a; THAYER—559b.

4458. **-πώς** {16x} **-pōs**, *poce;* adv. from the base of *4225;* an enclitic particle of indefiniteness of manner; *somehow* or *anyhow;* used only in composition:—be any means {8x}, by some means {1x}, perhaps {1x}, haply {1x}, not tr {5x}.

This word means "at all, somehow, in any way," and is used after the conjunction **(1)** *ei*, "if," meaning "if by any means," e.g., Acts 27:12; Rom 1:10; 11:14; Phil 3:11; **(2)** *me*, "lest, lest by any means," e.g., 1 Cor 8:9; 9:27; 2 Cor 2:7, "perhaps"; 9:4, "haply"; 11:3; 12:20; Gal 2:2; 4:11, "lest"; 3:5, "lest by some means." See: BAGD—732d; THAYER—560c. See *1513, 3381.* comp. *4459.*

4459. **πῶς** {103x} **pōs**, *poce;* adv. from the base of *4226;* an interr. particle of manner; *in what way?* (sometimes the question is indirect, *how?*); also as exclamation, *how much!:*—how {99x}, by what means {2x}, after what manner {1x}, that {1x}. [*Occasionally unexpressed in English*].

Pos (4459), "how," is translated "after what manner" in Acts 20:18. Syn.: 195, 1485, 2239, 3634, 3668, 3697, 3779, 4169, 4187, 4217, 5158, 5159, 5179, 5615. See: BAGD—732b; THAYER—559c.

P

4460. **῾Ραάβ** {2x} **Rhaab**, *hrah-ab';* of Heb. or. [7343]; *Raab* (i.e. *Rachab*), a Canaanitess:—Rahab {2x}. See: BAGD—733a; THAYER—560b. See also *4477.*

4461. **ῥαββί** {17x} **rhabbi**, *hrab-bee';* of Heb. or. [7227 with pron. suff.); *my master,* i.e *Rabbi,* as an official title of honor:—Master (Christ) {9x}, Rabbi (Christ) {5x}, rabbi {3x}. *Rhabbi* was an Aramaic word signifying "my master," a title of respectful address to Jewish teachers. The Aramaic word *rabbei*, transliterated into Greek, is explicitly recognized as the common form of address to Christ, Mt 26:25. **(1)** It is translated "Master"; Mt 26:25, 49; Mk 9:5; 11:21; 14:45; Jn 4:31; 9:2; 11:8. **(2)** In other passages, "Rabbi," Mt 23:7–8; Jn 1:38, 49; 3:2, 26; 6:25. See: TDNT—6:961, 982; BAGD—733a; THAYER—560b.

4462. **ῥαββονί** {2x} **rhabbŏni**, *hrab-bon-ee';* or

ῥαββουνί **rhabbŏuni**, *hrab-boo-nee';* of Chald. or.; corresp. to *4461:*—Lord (Christ) {1x}, Rabboni (Christ) {1x}.

(1) In its use in the NT the pronominal force of the suffix is apparently retained (contrast Rabbi - 4461); **(2)** it is found in **(2a)** Mk 10:51, "Lord"), addressed to Christ by blind Bartimaeus, and **(2b)** in Jn 20:16 by Mary Magdalene, where it is interpreted by *didaskalos*, "Master." This title is said to be Galilean; hence it would be natural in the lips of a woman of Magdala. It does not differ materially from "Rabbi." See: TDNT—6:962, 982; BAGD—733a; THAYER—560b.

4463. **ῥαβδίζω** {2x} **rhabdizō**, *hrab-did'-zo;* from *4464;* to *strike with a stick,* i.e. *bastinado:*—beat {1x}, beat with rods {1x}.

Rhabdizo is the verbal form of *rhabdos* (4464), "a rod, or staff," Acts 16:22; 2 Cor 11:25. See: TDNT—6:970, 982; BAGD—733b; THAYER—560c.

4464. **ῥάβδος** {12x} **rhabdŏs**, *hrab'-dos;* from the base of *4474;* a *stick* or *wand* (as a *cudgel,* a *cane* or a *baton* of royalty):—rod {6x}, sceptre {2x}, staff {4x}.

Rhabdos, "a staff, rod, scepter," is used **(1)** of Aaron's "rod," Heb 9:4; **(2)** a staff used on a journey, Mt 10:10, "staves"; so Lk 9:3; Mk 6:8, "staff"; Heb 11:21, "staff"; **(3)** a ruler's staff, a "scepter," Heb 1:8 (twice); elsewhere **(4)** a "rod," Rev 2:27; 12:5; 19:15; **(5)** a "rod" for chastisement (figuratively), 1 Cor 4:21; **(6)** a measuring rod, Rev 11:1. See: TDNT—6:966, 982; BAGD—733b; THAYER—560d.

4465. **ῥαβδοῦχος** {2x} **rhabdŏuchŏs**, *hrab-doo'-khos;* from *4464* and *2192;* a *rod-* (the Lat. *fasces*) *holder,* i.e. a Rom. *lictor* (*constable* or *executioner*):—serjeant {2x}. [now spelled sergeants —Acts 16:35, 38].

The duty of these officials was to attend Roman magistrates to execute their orders, especially administering punishment by scourging or beheading; they carried as their sign of office the *fasces* (whence "Fascist"), a bundle of rods with an axe inserted. See: TDNT—6:971, 982; BAGD—733c; THAYER—560d.

4466. **῾Ραγαύ** {1x} **Rhagau**, *hrag-ŏw';* of Heb. or. [7466]; *Ragaü* (i.e. *Reu*), a patriarch:—*Ragau* {1x}. See: BAGD—733c; THAYER—560d.

4467. **ῥᾳδιούργημα** {1x} **rhaᵢdiŏurgēma**, *hrad-ee-oorg'-ay-mah;* from a comp. of ῥᾴδιος **rhaᵢdiŏs** (*easy,* i.e. *reckless*) and *2041; easy-going behavior,* i.e. (by extens.) a *crime:*—lewdness {1x}.

Lewdness does not always mean public indecency. It can mean acts of villainy. See: TDNT—6:972, 983; BAGD—733c; THAYER—561a.

4468. **ῥᾳδιουργία** {1x} **rhaᵢdiŏurgia**, *hrad-ee-oorg-ee'-a;* from the same as *4467; recklessness,* i.e. (by extens.) *malignity:*—mischief {1x}. See: TDNT—6:972, 983; BAGD—733c; THAYER—561a.

4469. **ῥακά** {1x} **rhaka**, *hrak-ah';* of Chald. or. [comp. 7386]; O *empty* one, i.e. thou *worthless* (as a term of utter vilification):—*Raca* {1x}.

(1) *Rhaka* is an Aramaic word akin to the Heb. *req*, "empty," the first *a* being due to a Galilean change. **(2)** It was a word of utter contempt, signifying "empty," intellectually rather than morally, "empty-headed," like Abimelech's hirelings, Judg 9:4, and the "vain" man of Jas 2:20. **(3)** As condemned by Christ, Mt 5:22, it was worse than being angry, inasmuch as an outrageous utterance is worse than a feeling unexpressed or somewhat controlled in expression; it does not indicate such a loss of self-control as the word rendered "fool," a godless, moral reprobate. See: TDNT—6:973, 983; BAGD—733d; THAYER—561a.

4470. **ῥάκος** {2x} **rhakŏs**, *hrak'-os;* from *4486;* a *"rag,"* i.e. *piece* of cloth:—cloth {2x}.

Rakos denotes "a ragged garment, or a piece of cloth torn off, a rag"; hence, a piece of undressed "cloth," Mt 9:16; Mk 2:21. See: BAGD—734a; THAYER—561a.

4471. **῾Ραμά** {1x} **Rhama**, *hram-ah';* of Heb. or. [7414]; *Rama* (i.e. *Ramah*), a place in Pal.:—*Rama* {1x}. See: BAGD—734a; THAYER—561b.

4472. **ῥαντίζω** {4x} **rhantizō**, *hran-tid'-zo;* from a der. of ῥαίνω **rhainō** (to *sprinkle*); to *render besprinkled,* i.e. *asperse* (cerem. or fig.):—sprinkle {4x}.

Rhaino, "to sprinkle", is used **(1)** in the active voice in Heb 9:13, of "sprinkling" with blood the unclean, a token of the efficacy of the expiatory sacrifice of Christ, His blood signifying the giving up of His life in the shedding of His blood (cf. 9:22) under divine judgment upon sin (the voluntary act to be distinguished from that which took place after His death in the piercing of His side); so again in vv. 19, 21; **(2)** in Heb 10:22, passive voice, of the purging (on the ground of the same efficacy) of the hearts of believers from an evil conscience. This application of the blood of Christ is necessary for believers, in respect of their committal of sins, which on that ground receive forgiveness, 1Jn 1:9. See: TDNT—6:976, 984; BAGD—734a; THAYER—561d.

4473. **ῥαντισμός** {2x} **rhantismŏs**, *hran-tis-mos';* from *4472; aspersion* (cerem. or fig.):—sprinkling {2x}.

Rhantismos is used of the "sprinkling" of the blood of Christ, in Heb 12:24 and 1 Pet 1:2, an allusion to the use of the blood of sacrifices, appointed for Israel, typical of the sacrifice of Christ. See: TDNT—6:976, 984; BAGD—734b; THAYER—561b.

4474. **ῥαπίζω** {2x} **rhapizō**, *hrap-id'-zo;* from a der. of a primary ῥέπω **rhĕpō** (to *let fall,* "*rap*"); to *slap:*—smite {1x}, smite with the palm of the hand {1x}.

Rhapizo, primarily "to strike with a rod" (*rhapis*, "a rod"), then, "to strike the face with the palm of the hand or the clenched fist," which is its usage in Mt 5:39; 26:67. See: BAGD—734b; THAYER—561c. comp. *5180.*

4475. **ῥάπισμα** {3x} **rhapisma**, *hrap'-is-mah;* from *4474;* a *slap:*—strike with the palm of (one's) hand + 906 {1x}, strike with the palm of (one's) hand + 1325 {1x}, smite with (one's) hand + 1325 {1x}.

Rhapisma is **(1)** "a blow with a rod or staff," **(2)** "a blow with the hand, a slap or cuff," is found in three places; **(2a)** of the maltreatment of Christ by the officials or attendants of the high priest, Mk 14:65, "did strike Him with the palms of their hands"; **(2)** that they received, or took, Him would indicate their rough handling of Him; Jn 18:22 and 19:3. So with the corresponding verb *rhapizo* (4475), in Mt 26:67. The soldiers subsequently beat Him with a reed, 27:30, where *tupto*, "to beat," is used. See: BAGD—734c; THAYER—561c.

4476. **ῥαφίς** {3x} **rhaphis**, *hraf-ece';* from a primary ῥάπτω **rhaptō** (to *sew;* perh. rather akin to the base of *4474* through the idea of *puncturing*); a *needle:*—needle {3x}.

Rhapis, denotes a sharp point, hence, "a needle," Lk 18:25. *Note:* The idea of applying "the needle's eye" to small gates seems to be a modern one; there is no ancient trace of it. The Lord's object in the statement is to express human impossibility and there is no need to endeavor to soften the difficulty by taking the needle to mean anything more than the ordinary instrument. An attempt is sometimes made to explain the words as a reference to the small door, a little over 2 feet square, in the large heavy gate of a walled city. This mars the figure without materially altering the meaning, and receives no justification from the language and traditions of Palestine. See: BAGD—734c; THAYER—561c.

4477. ʽΡαχάβ {1x} **Rhachab**, *hrakh-ab';* from the same as *4460; Rachab,* a Canaanitess:—*Rachab* {1x}. See: TDNT—3:1, 311; BAGD—734c; THAYER—561c.

4478. ʽΡαχήλ {1x} **Rhachēl**, *hrakh-ale';* of Heb. or. [7354]; *Rachel,* the wife of Jacob:—Rachel {1x}. See: BAGD—734d; THAYER—561d.

4479. ʽΡεβέκκα {1x} **Rhĕbĕkka**, *hreb-bek'-kah;* of Heb. or. [7259]; *Rebecca* (i.e. *Ribkah*), the wife of Isaac:—Rebecca {1x}. See: BAGD—734d; THAYER—561d.

4480. ῥέδα {1x} **rhĕda**, *hred'-ah;* of Lat. or.; a *rheda,* i.e. four-wheeled *carriage* (*wagon* for riding):—chariot {1x}. See: BAGD—734d; THAYER—561d.

4481. ʽΡεμφάν {1x} **Rhĕmphan**, *hrem-fan'* or

ʽΡαιφάν **Rhaiphan**, *hrahee-fan';* by incorrect transliteration for a word of Heb. of [3594]; *Remphan* (i.e. *Kijun*), an Eg. idol:—*Remphan* {1x}. See: BAGD—735a; THAYER—561d.

4482. ῥέω {1x} **rhĕō**, *hreh'-o;* a primary verb; for some tenses of which a prol. form

ῥεύω **rhĕuō**, *hryoo'-o* is used; to *flow* ("*run*"; as water):—flow {1x}.

Rheo, "to flow," is used figuratively in Jn 7:38 of the Holy Spirit, acting in and through the believer. See: BAGD—735a; THAYER—561d.

4483. ῥέω {26x} **rhĕō**, *hreh'-o;* for certain tenses of which a prol. form

ἐρέω **ĕrĕō**, *er-eh'-o;* is used; and both as alt. for *2036;* perh. akin (or ident.) with *4482* (through the idea of *pouring* forth); to *utter,* i.e. *speak* or *say:*—speak {12x}, say {9x}, speak of {3x}, command {1x}, make {1x}. See: BAGD—735a; THAYER—562a. comp. *3004*.

4484. ʽΡήγιον {1x} **Rhēgiŏn**, *hrayg'-ee-on;* of Lat. or.; *Rhegium,* a place in Italy:—*Rhegium* {1x}. See: BAGD—735a; THAYER—562a.

4485. ῥῆγμα {1x} **rhēgma**, *hrayg'-mah;* from *4486;* something *torn,* i.e. a *fragment* (by impl. and abstr. a *fall*):—ruin {1x}.

Rhegma denotes "a cleavage, fracture"; by metonymy, that which is broken, "a ruin," Lk 6:49. See: BAGD—735a; THAYER—562a.

4486. ῥήγνυμι {7x} **rhēgnumi**, *hrayg'-noo-mee;* or

ῥήσσω **rhēssō**, *hrace'-so;* both prol. forms of ῥήκω **rhēkō** (which appears only in certain forms, and is itself prob. a strengthened form of ἄγνυμι **agnumi**, [see in *2608*]); to "*break*", "*wreck*" or "*crack*", i.e. (espec.) to *sunder* (by *separation* of the parts; *2608* being its intensive [with the prep. in composition], and *2352* a *shattering* to minute fragments; but not a *reduction* to the constituent particles, like *3089*) or *disrupt, lacerate;* by impl. to *convulse* (with *spasms*); fig. to *give vent* to joyful emotions:—burst {2x}, tear {1x}, rend {1x}, break {1x}, break forth {1x}, throw down {1x}.

Rhesso, "to tear, rend, as of garments, etc.," is translated **(1)** "break" in Mt 9:17, of wine-skins; **(2)** "burst" in Mk 2:22 and Lk 5:37; **(3)** "break forth" in Gal. 4:27. It is also translated **(4)** "rend" in Mt 7:6; **(5)** "teareth" in Mk 9:18; and **(6)** "throw down" in Lk 9:42. Syn.: *Thrauo* (2352) means to shatter and is suggestive of many fragments and minute dispersion. *Katagnumi* (2608) means to break and denotes the destruction of a things unity or completeness. *Rhegnumi* (4486) means to rend asunder and makes pointed reference to the separation of the parts. See: BAGD—735a; THAYER—562a.

4487. ῥῆμα {70x} **rhēma**, *hray'-mah;* from *4483;* an *utterance* (indiv., collect. or spec.); by impl. a *matter* or *topic* (espec. of narration, command or dispute); with a neg. *naught* whatever:—word {56x}, saying {9x}, thing {3x}, no thing + 3756 {1x}, not tr {1x}.

Rhema, **(1)** in the singular, "a word," e.g., Mt 12:36; 27:14; 2 Cor 12:4; 13:1; Heb 12:19; **(2)** in the plural, speech, discourse, e.g., Jn 3:34; 8:20; Acts 2:14; 6:11, 13; 11:14; 13:42; 26:25; Rom 10:18; 2 Pet 3:2; Jude 17; **(3)** it is used of the gospel in Rom 10:8 (twice), 17, "the word of God"; 10:18; 1 Pet 1:25 (twice); **(4)** of a statement, command, instruction, e.g., Mt 26:75; Lk 1:37, 38; Acts 11:16; Heb 11:3. Syn.: The significance of *rhema,* (as distinct from *logos*) is exemplified in the injunction to take "the sword of the Spirit, which is the word of God," Eph 6:17; here the reference is not to the whole Bible as such, but to the individual scripture which the Spirit brings to our remembrance for use in time of need, a prerequisite being the regular storing of the mind with Scripture. See: TDNT—4:69, 505; BAGD—735b; THAYER—562b.

4488. ʽΡησά {1x} **Rhēsa**, *hray-sah';* prob. of Heb. or. [appar. for 7509]; *Resa* (i.e. *Rephajah*), an Isr.:—*Rhesa* {1x}. See: BAGD—735d; THAYER—563a.

4489. ῥήτωρ {1x} **rhētōr**, *hray'-tore;* from *4483;* a *speaker,* i.e. (by impl.) a forensic *advocate:*—orator {1x}.

Rhetor, "to say" (cf. Eng., "rhetoric"), denotes "a public speaker, an orator," Acts 24:1, of Tertullus. Such a person, distinct from the professional lawyer, was hired, as a professional speaker, to make a skillful presentation of a case in court. His training was not legal but rhetorical. See: BAGD—735d; THAYER—563a.

4490. ῥητῶς {1x} **rhētōs**, *hray-toce';* adv. from a der. of *4483;* out-*spokenly,* i.e. *distinctly:*—expressly {1x}.

Rhetos, meaning "in stated terms" (from *rhetos,* "stated, specified"; from *rheo, or ero,* "to say"; cf. *rhema,* "a word"), is used in 1 Ti 4:1, "expressly." See: BAGD—736a; THAYER—563a.

4491. ῥίζα {17x} **rhiza**, *hrid'-zah;* appar. a primary word; a "*root*" (lit. or fig.):—root {17x}.

Rhiza is used **(1)** in the natural sense, Mt 3:10; 13:6, 21; Mk 4:6, 17, 11:20; Lk 3:9; 8:13; **(2)** metaphorically of "cause, origin, source," said **(2a)** of persons, ancestors, Rom 11:16, 17, 18 (twice); **(2b)** of things, **(2b1)** evils, 1 Ti 6:10, of the love of money as a "root" of all "evil"); **(2b2)** bitterness, Heb 12:15; **(3)** of that which springs from a "root," a shoot, said of offspring, Rom 15:12; Rev 5:5; 22:16. See: TDNT—6:985, 985; BAGD—736a; THAYER—563a.

4492. ῥιζόω {2x} **rhizŏō**, *hrid-zŏ'-o;* from *4491;* to cause to take *root* (fig. *become stable*):—root {2x}.

Rhizoo, "to cause to take root," is used metaphorically in the passive voice **(1)** in Eph 3:17, of being "rooted" in love; **(2)** Col 2:7, in Christ, i.e., in the sense of being firmly planted, or established. See: TDNT—6:990, 985; BAGD—736b; THAYER—563b.

4493. ῥιπή {1x} **rhipē**, *hree-pay';* from *4496;* a *jerk* (of the eye, i.e. [by anal.] an *instant*):—twinkling {1x}.

Rhipe, akin to *rhipto,* "to hurl," was used of any rapid movement, e.g., the throw of a javelin, the rush of wind or flame; in 1 Cor 15:52 of the "twinkling" of an eye. See: BAGD—736b; THAYER—563b.

4494. ῥιπίζω {1x} **rhipizō**, *hrip-id'-zo;* from a der. of *4496* (mean. a *fan* or *bellows*); to *breeze up,* i.e. (by anal.) to *agitate* (into waves):—toss {1x}.

Rhipizo, primarily "to fan a fire" (*rhipis,* "a fan," cf. *rhipe,* "twinkling"), then, "to make a breeze," is used in the passive voice in Jas 1:6, "tossed," of the raising of waves by the wind. See: BAGD—736b; THAYER—563b.

4495. ῥιπτέω {1x} **rhiptĕō**, *hrip-teh'-o;* from a der. of *4496;* to *toss* up:—cast off {1x}. See: TDNT—6:991,*; BAGD—736c; THAYER—563c.

4496. ῥίπτω {7x} **rhiptō**, *hrip'-to;* a primary verb (perh. rather akin to the base of *4474,* through the idea of sudden *motion*); to *fling* (prop. with a quick *toss,* thus differing from *906,* which denotes a *deliberate* hurl; and from τείνω **tĕinō**, [see in *1614*], which indicates an *extended* projection); by qualification, to *deposit* (as if a load); by extens. to *disperse:*—cast down {2x}, cast {2x}, scatter abroad {1x}, cast out {1x}, throw {1x}.

Rhipto denotes "to throw with a sudden motion, to jerk, cast forth"; **(1)** "cast down," Mt 15:30 and 27:5; **(2)** "thrown down," Lk 4:35; **(3)** "cast," Lk 17:2; **(4)** in Acts 27:19 "cast out," of the tackling of a ship; **(5)** in Acts 17:29 "cast", of anchors; **(6)** in Mt 9:36, "scattered abroad," said of sheep. See: TDNT—6:991, 987; BAGD—736c; THAYER—563c.

4497. ʽΡοβοάμ {2x} **Rhŏbŏam**, *hrob-ŏ-am';* of Heb. or. [7346]; *Roboäm* (i.e. *Rechabam*), an Isr.:—Roboam {2x}. See: BAGD—736d; THAYER—563d.

4498. ʽΡόδη {1x} **Rhŏdē**, *hrod'-ay;* prob. for ῥοδή **rhŏdē**, (a *rose*); *Rodē,* a servant girl:—Rhoda {1x}. See: BAGD—736d; THAYER—563d.

4499. ʽΡόδος {1x} **Rhŏdŏs**, *hrod'-os;* prob. from ῥόδον **rhŏdŏn**, (a *rose*); *Rhodus,* an island of the Mediterranean:—Rhodes {1x}. See: BAGD—737a; THAYER—563d.

4500. ῥοιζηδόν {1x} **rhŏizēdŏn**, *hroyd-zay-don';* adv. from a der. of ῥοῖζος **rhŏizŏs** (a *whir*); *whizzingly,* i.e. *with a crash:*—with a great noise {1x}.

Rhoizedon is from a root which means the whistling of an arrow signifying with a rushing sound, as of roaring flames, and is used in 2 Pet 3:10 of the future passing away of the heavens. See: BAGD—737a; THAYER—563d.

4501. ῥομφαία {7x} **rhŏmphaia**, *hrom-fah'-yah;* prob. of for. or.; a *sabre,* i.e. a long and broad *cutlass* (any *weapon* of the kind, lit. or fig.):—sword {7x}.

Rhomphaia denoted a sword of large size and occurs **(1)** literally in (Rev 6:8); **(2)** metaphorically, as the instrument of anguish (Lk 2:35); **(3)** of judgment (Rev 1:16; 2:12, 16; 19:15, 21), probably figurative of the Lord's judicial utterances. See: TDNT—6:993, 987; BAGD—737a; THAYER—564a.

4502. ʻΡουβήν {1x} **Rhŏubēn**, *hroo-bane';* of Heb. or. [7205]; *Ruben* (i.e. *Reuben*), an Isr.:—Reuben {1x}. See: BAGD—737b; THAYER—564a.

4503. ʻΡούθ {1x} **Rhŏuth**, *hrooth;* of Heb. or. [7327]; *Ruth,* a Moabitess:—Ruth {1x}. See: TDNT—3:1, 311; BAGD—737b; THAYER—564a.

4504. ʻΡοῦφος {2x} **Rhŏuphŏs**, *hroo'-fos;* of Lat. or.; *red; Rufus,* a Chr.:—Rufus {2x}. See: BAGD—737b; THAYER—564a.

4505. ῥύμη {4x} **rhumē**, *hroo'-may;* prol. from *4506* in its orig. sense; an *alley* or *avenue* (as crowded):—lane {1x}, street {3x}.

Rhume, "a narrow road lane or street", is translated **(1)** "streets" in Mt 6:2; "street" in Acts 9:11; 12:10; and **(2)** "lanes" in Lk 14:21, "Then the master of the house being angry said to his servant, Go out quickly into the streets and lanes of the city, and bring in hither the poor, and the maimed, and the halt, and the blind." Syn.: 296, 4113. See: BAGD—737c; THAYER—564b.

4506. ῥύομαι {18x} **rhuŏmai**, *hroo'-om-ahee;* mid. voice of an obs. verb, akin to *4482* (through the idea of a *current;* comp. *4511*); to *rush* or *draw* (for oneself), i.e. *rescue:*—deliver {17x}, Deliverer {1x}.

Rhuomai, as a verb, means **(1)** "to rescue from, to preserve from" and so, **(1a)** "to deliver," the word by which it is regularly translated, **(1b)** with the idea of "rescue from" as predominant in *rhuomai:* "He trusted in God; let him deliver him now, if he will have him: for he said, I am the Son of God" (Mt 27:43). **(2)** In Rom 11:26 the present participle is used with the article, as a noun, **(2a)** "the Deliverer": "And so all Israel shall be saved: as it is written, There shall come out of Sion the Deliverer, and shall turn away ungodliness from Jacob." **(2b)** In 1 Th. 1:10, Christ is similarly spoken of, "our Deliverer," that is, from the retributive calamities with which God will visit men at the end of the present age. From that wrath believers are to be "delivered."

(3) The verb is used **(3a)** with *apo,* "away from": "And lead us not into temptation, but deliver us from (*rhuomai apo*) evil: For thine is the kingdom, and the power, and the glory, for ever. Amen" (Mt 6:13; Lk 11:4; Rom 15:31; 2 Th 3:2; 2 Tim 4:18); and **(3b)** with *ek,* "from, out of": "That He would grant unto us, that we being delivered out of (*rhuomai ek*) the hand of our enemies might serve Him without fear" (Lk 1:74; cf. Rom 7:24; 2 Cor 1:10; Col 1:13 from bondage; in 2 Pet 2:9 from temptation; in 2 Ti 3:11 from persecution); **(3c)** but *ek* is used of ills impending: "Who delivered us from so great a death, and doth deliver: in whom we trust that He will yet deliver *us*" (2 Cor 1:10); and **(3d)** in 2 Tim 4:17 *ek* indicates that the danger was more imminent than in v. 18, where *apo* is used: "Notwithstanding the Lord stood with me, and strengthened me; that by me the preaching might be fully known, and *that* all the Gentiles might hear: and I was delivered out (*rhuomai ek*) of the mouth of the lion. 18 And the Lord shall deliver me from (*rhuomai apo*) every evil work, and will preserve *me* unto his heavenly kingdom: to whom *be* glory for ever and ever. Amen."

(4) Accordingly the meaning "out of the midst of": "And to wait for His Son from heaven, whom He raised from the dead, *even* Jesus, which delivered us from the wrath to come" (1 Th 1:10). Syn.: 325, 525, 629, 591, 859, 1325, 1560, 1659, 1807, 1929, 3086, 3860, 5483. See: TDNT—6:998, 988; BAGD—737c; THAYER—737c.

4507. ῥυπαρία {1x} **rhuparia**, *hroo-par-ee'-ah;* from *4508; dirtiness* (mor.):—filthiness {1x}.

Rhuparia means to make filthy, befoul, to defile, to dishonor (Jas 1:21). See: BAGD—738a; THAYER—564c.

4508. ῥυπαρός {1x} **rhuparŏs**, *hroo-par-os';* from *4509; dirty,* i.e. (rel.) *cheap* or *shabby;* mor. *wicked:*—vile {1x}. See: BAGD—738a; THAYER—564c.

4509. ῥύπος {1x} **rhupŏs**, *hroo'-pos;* of uncert. aff.; *dirt,* i.e. (mor.) *depravity:*—filth {1x}. See: BAGD—738a; THAYER—564c.

4510. ῥυπόω {2x} **rhupŏō**, *hroo-pŏ'-o;* from *4509; to soil,* i.e. (intr.) to *become dirty* (mor.):—be filthy {2x}. See: BAGD—738b; THAYER—564b.

4511. ῥύσις {3x} **rhusis**, *hroo'-sis;* from *4506* in the sense of its congener *4482;* a *flux* (of blood):—issue {3x}.

Rhusis, "a flowing" (akin to *rheo,* "to flow"), "an issue," is used in Mk 5:25; Lk 8:43, 44. See: BAGD—738b; THAYER—564c.

4512. ῥυτίς {1x} **rhutis**, *hroo-tece';* from *4506;* a *fold* (as *drawing* together), i.e. a *wrinkle* (espec. on the face):—wrinkle {1x}.

Rhutis, from an obsolete verb *rhuo,* signifying "to draw together," occurs in Eph 5:27, describing the flawlessness of the complete church, as the result of the love of Christ in giving Himself up for it, with the purpose of presenting it to Himself hereafter. See: BAGD—738b; THAYER—564d.

4513. ʻΡωμαϊκός {1x} **Rhōmaïkŏs**, *hro-mah-ee-kos';* from *4514; Romaïc,* i.e. *Lat.:*—Latin {1x}. See: BAGD—738c; THAYER—564d.

4514. ʻΡωμαῖος {13x} **Rhōmaiŏs**, *hro-mah'-yos;* from *4516; Romœan,* i.e. *Roman* (as noun):—Roman {12x}, of Rome {1x}.

This word occurs in Jn 11:48; Acts 2:10, ("of Rome"); 16:21, 37, 38; 22:25, 26, 27, 29; 23:27; 25:16; 28:17. See: BAGD—738c; THAYER—564d.

4515. ʻΡωμαϊστί {1x} **Rhōmaïsti**, *hro-mah-is-tee';* adv. from a presumed der. of *4516; Romaïstically,* i.e. *in* the *Latin* language:—Latin {1x}.

This word is an adverb, "in Latin," occurs in Jn 19:20. See: BAGD—738c; THAYER—564d.

4516. ʻΡώμη {14x} **Rhōmē**, *hro'-may;* from the base of *4517; strength; Roma,* the capital of Italy:—Rome {14x}. See: BAGD—738c; THAYER—564d.

4517. ῥώννυμι {2x} **rhōnnumi**, *hrone'-noo-mee;* prol. from ῥώομαι **rhōŏmai** (to *dart;* prob. akin to *4506*); to *strengthen,* i.e. (impers. pass.) *have health* (as a parting exclamation, *good-bye*):—farewell {2x}.

Rhonnumi, "to strengthen, to be strong," is used in the imperative mood as a formula at the end of letters, signifying "Farewell," Acts 15:29; 23:30. See: BAGD—738d; THAYER—565a.

Σ

4518. σαβαχθάνι {2x} **sabachthani**, *sab-akh-than-ee';* of Chald. or [7662 with pron. suff.]; *thou hast left me; sabachthani* (i.e. *shebakthani*), a cry of distress:—sabachthani {2x}.

Literally "thou hast forsaken me", Mt 27:46; Mk 15:34. See: BAGD—738b; THAYER—565b.

4519. σαβαώθ {2x} **sabaōth**, *sab-ah-owth';* of Heb. or. [6635 in fem. plur.]; *armies; sabaoth* (i.e. *tsebaoth*), a military epithet of God:—sabaoth {2x}.

Sabaoth is the transliteration of a Hebrew word which denotes "hosts" or "armies," Rom 9:29; Jas 5:4. While the word "hosts" probably had special reference to angels, the title "the LORD of hosts" became used to designate Him as the One who is supreme over all the innumerable hosts of spiritual agencies, or of what are described as "the armies of heaven." Eventually it was used as equivalent to "the LORD all-sovereign." See: BAGD—738b; THAYER—565b.

4520. σαββατισμός {1x} **sabbatismŏs**, *sab-bat-is-mos';* from a der. of *4521;* a *"sabbatism,"* i.e. (fig.) the *repose* of Christianity (as a type of heaven):—rest {1x}.

Sabbath-keeping,". is used in Heb 4:9, "a keeping of a sabbath"; here the sabbath-keeping is the perpetual sabbath "rest" to be enjoyed uninterruptedly by believers in their fellowship with the Father and the Son, in contrast to the weekly Sabbath under the Law. Because this sabbath "rest" is the "rest" of God Himself, 4:10, its full fruition is yet future, though believers now enter into it. In whatever way they enter into divine "rest," that which they enjoy is involved in an indissoluble relation with God. See: TDNT—7:34, 989; BAGD—739a; THAYER—565c.

4521. σάββατον {68x} **sabbatŏn**, *sab'-bat-on;* of Heb. or. [7676]; the *Sabbath* (i.e. *Shabbath*), or day of weekly *repose* from secular avocations (also the observance or institution itself); by extens. a *se'nnight,* i.e. the interval between two Sabbaths; likewise the plural in all the above applications:—sabbath {22x}, sabbath day {37x}, week {9x}.

(1) The root means "to cease, desist" (Heb., *shabath*); **(2)** the doubled *b* has an intensive force, implying a complete cessation or a making to cease, probably the former. **(3)** The idea is not that of relaxation or refreshment, but cessation from activity. **(4)** The observation of the seventh day of the week, enjoined upon Israel, was a sign between God and His earthly people, based upon the fact that after the six days of creative operations He rested, cf. Ex 31:16, 17, with 20:8–11. **(5)** The OT regulations were developed and systematized to such an extent that they became a burden upon the people (who otherwise rejoiced in the rest provided) and a byword for absurd extravagance. **(6)** Two treatises of the Mishna (the *Shabbath* and *Erubin*) are entirely occupied with regulations for the observance; so with the discussions in the Gemara, on rabbinical opinions.

(7) The effect upon current opinion explains the antagonism roused by the Lord's cures wrought on the "Sabbath," e.g., Mt 12:9–13; Jn 5:5–16, and explains the fact that on a "Sabbath" the sick were brought to be healed after sunset, e.g., Mk 1:32. **(8)** According to rabbinical ideas, the disciples, by plucking ears of corn (Mt 12:1; Mk 2:23), and rubbing them (Lk 6:1), broke the "sabbath" in two respects; for to pluck was to reap, and to rub was to thresh. **(9)** The Lord's attitude towards the "sabbath" was by way of freeing it from these vexatious traditional accretions by which it was made an end in itself, instead of a means to an end (Mk 2:27). **(10)** In the Epistles the only direct mentions are in **(10a)** Col 2:16, "sabbath days", where it is listed among things that were "a shadow of the things to come" (i.e., of the age introduced at Pentecost), and in **(10b)** Heb 4:4–11, where the perpetual *sabbatismos* is appointed for believers; **(10c)** inferential references are in Rom 14:5 and Gal 4:9–11. **(11)** For the first three centuries of the Christian era the first day of the week was never confounded with the "sabbath"; the confusion of the Jewish and Christian institutions was due to declension from apostolic teaching. See: TDNT—7:1, 989; BAGD—739a; THAYER—565c.

4522. **σαγήνη** {1x} **sagēnē**, *sag-ay'-nay;* from a der. of σάττω **sattō** (to *equip*) mean. *furniture,* espec. a *pack-saddle* (which in the E. is merely a bag of *netted* rope); a "*seine*" for fishing:—net {1x}.

Sagene denotes "a dragnet, a seine"; two modes were employed with this, either by its being let down into the water and drawn together in a narrowing circle, and then into the boat, or as a semicircle drawn to the shore, Mt 13:47. Syn.: 293, 1350. Syn.: **(A)** *Sagene* is the long-drawn net or sweep net. **(B)** *Diktyon* (1350) is the general terms for nets. **(C)** *Amphiblestron* (293) is the circular casting net. See: BAGD—739c; THAYER—566b.

4523. **Σαδδουκαῖος** {14x} **Saddŏukaiŏs**, *sad-doo-kah'-yos;* prob. from *4524;* a *Sadducœan* (i.e. *Tsadokian*), or follower of a certain heretical Isr.:—Sadducee {14x}. Syn.: See discussion under Pharisse, (5330). See: TDNT—7:35, 992; BAGD—739d; THAYER—566b.

4524. **Σαδώκ** {2x} **Sadōk**, *sad-oke';* of Heb. or. [6659]; *Sadoc* (i.e. *Tsadok*), an Isr.:—Sadoc {2x}. See: BAGD—739d; THAYER—566c.

4525. **σαίνω** {1x} **sainō**, *sah'-ee-no;* akin to *4579;* to *wag* (as a dog its tail fawningly), i.e. (gen.) to *shake* (fig. *disturb*):—move {1x}

Saino, as a verb, means properly, of dogs, "to wag the tail"; hence, metaphorically of persons, "to disturb, disquiet," 1 Th 3:3, passive voice, "(that no man) be moved (by these afflictions)." Syn.: 277, 383, 761, 2795, 2796, 3334, 4531, 4579, 4787, 5342. See: TDNT—7:54, 994; BAGD—740a; THAYER—566c.

4526. **σάκκος** {4x} **sakkŏs**, *sak'-kos;* of Heb. or. [8242]; "*sack*"-cloth, i.e. *mohair* (the material or garments made of it, worn as a sign of grief):—sackcloth {4x}.

Sakkos, "a warm material woven from goat's or camel's hair," and **(1)** hence of a dark color, Rev 6:12. **(2)** It was used for garments worn as **(2a)** expressing mourning or penitence, Mt 11:21; Lk 10:13, or **(2b)** for purposes of prophetic testimony, Rev 11:3. See: TDNT—7:56, 995; BAGD—740a; THAYER—566d.

4527. **Σαλά** {1x} **Sala**, *sal-ah';* of Heb. or. [7974]; *Sala* (i.e. *Shelach*), a patriarch:—*Sala* {1x}. See: BAGD—740b; THAYER—566d.

4528. **Σαλαθιήλ** {3x} **Salathiēl**, *sal-ath-ee-ale';* of Heb. or. [7597]; *Salathiël* (i.e. *Sheältiël*), an Isr.:—*Salathiel* {3x}. See: BAGD—740b; THAYER—566d.

4529. **Σαλαμίς** {1x} **Salamis**, *sal-am-ece';* prob. from *4535* (from the *surge* on the shore); *Salamis,* a place in Cyprus:—*Salamis* {1x}. See: BAGD—740b; THAYER—567a.

4530. **Σαλείμ** {1x} **Salĕim**, *sal-ime';* prob. from the same as *4531; Salim,* a place in Pal.:—Salim {1x}. See: BAGD—740d; THAYER—567a.

4531. **σαλεύω** {15x} **salĕuō**, *sal-yoo'-o;* from *4535;* to *waver,* i.e. *agitate, rock, topple* or (by impl.) *destroy;* fig. to *disturb, incite:*—shake {10x}, move {1x}, shake together {1x}, that are shaken {1x}, which cannot be shaken + 3361 {1x}, stir up {1x}.

Saleuo, as a verb, means **I.** "to shake," properly of the action of stormy wind, then, "to render insecure, stir up," is rendered **(1)** "I should (not) be moved" in Acts 2:25, in the sense of being cast down or shaken from a sense of security and happiness, said of Christ, in a quotation from Ps 16:8. **(2)** It also means "to agitate, shake," primarily of the action of stormy winds, waves, etc., is used **(2a)** literally, **(2a1)** of a reed, Mt 11:7; Lk 7:24; **(2a2)** a vessel, "shaken" in filling, Lk 6:38; **(2a3)** a building, Lk 6:48; Acts 4:31; 16:26; **(2a4)** the natural forces of the heavens and heavenly bodies, Mt 24:29; Mk 13:25; Lk 21:26; **(2a5)** the earth, Heb 12:26, "shook"; **(2b)** metaphorically, **(2b1)** of "shaking" so as to make insecure, Heb 12:27 (twice); **(2b2)** of casting down from a sense of security, Acts 2:25, "I should (not) be moved"; **(2b3)** to stir up (a crowd), Acts 17:13; **(2b4)** to unsettle, 2 Th 2:2, "(to the end that) ye be not (quickly) shaken (from your mind)," i.e., from their settled conviction and the purpose of heart begotten by it, as to the return of Christ before the Day of the Lord begins; the metaphor may be taken from the loosening of a ship from its moorings by a storm.

Syn. for **I:** 277, 383, 761, 2795, 2796, 3334, 4525, 4579, 4787, 5342. **II.** *Saleuo,* also means "stirred up": "But when the Jews of Thessalonica had knowledge that the word of God was preached of Paul at Berea, they came thither also, and stirred up the people" (Acts 17:13). Syn. for **II:** 329, 383, 387, 1326, 1892, 2042, 3947, 3951, 4579, 4787, 4797, 5017. See: TDNT—7:65, 996; BAGD—740c; THAYER—567a.

4532. **Σαλήμ** {2x} **Salēm**, *sal-ame';* of Heb. or. [8004]; *Salem* (i.e. *Shalem*), a place in Pal.:—*Salem* {2x}. See: BAGD—740d; THAYER—567b.

4533. **Σαλμών** {3x} **Salmōn**, *sal-mone';* of Heb. or. [8012]; *Salmon,* an Isr.:—*Salmon* {3x}. See: BAGD—740d; THAYER—567b.

4534. **Σαλμώνη** {1x} **Salmōnē**, *sal-mo'-nay;* perh. of similar or. to *4529; Salmone,* a place in Crete:—*Salmone* {1x}. See: BAGD—740d; THAYER—567b.

4535. **σάλος** {1x} **salŏs**, *sal'-os;* prob. from the base of *4525;* a *vibration,* i.e. (spec.) *billow:*—wave {1x}.

Salos denotes "a tossing," especially the rolling swell of the sea, Lk 21:25, "waves." See: BAGD—741a; THAYER—567c.

4536. **σάλπιγξ** {11x} **salpigx**, *sal'-pinx;* perh. from *4535* (through the idea of *quavering* or *reverberation*); a *trumpet:*—trump {2x}, trumpet {9x}.

Salpigx is used **(1)** of the natural instrument, 1 Cor 14:8; **(2)** of the supernatural accompaniment of divine interpositions, **(2a)** at Sinai, Heb 12:19; **(2b)** of the acts of angels at the second advent of Christ, Mt 24:31; **(2c)** of their acts in the period of divine judgments preceding this, Rev 8:2, 6, 13; 9:14; **(2d)** of a summons to John to the presence of God, Rev 1:10; 4:1; **(2e)** of the act of the Lord in raising from the dead the saints who have fallen asleep and changing the bodies of those who are living, at the Rapture of all to meet Him in the air, 1 Cor 15:52, where "the last trump" is a military allusion, familiar to Greek readers, and has no connection with the series in Rev 8:6 to 11:15; there is a possible allusion to Num 10:2–6, with reference to the same event, 1 Th 4:16, "the (lit., a) trump of God" (the absence of the article suggests the meaning "a trumpet such as is used in God's service"). See: BAGD—741a; THAYER—567c.

4537. **σαλπίζω** {12x} **salpizō**, *sal-pid'-zo;* from *4536;* to *trumpet,* i.e. *sound a blast* (lit. or fig.):—sound {10x}, sound of a trumpet {1x}, trumpet sounds {1x}.

Salpizo, "to sound a trumpet" (*salpinx*), occurs in Mt 6:2; 1 Cor 15:52, "the trumpet shall sound"; Rev 8:6–8, 10, 12, 13; 9:1, 13; 10:7; 11:15. See: TDNT—7:71, 997; BAGD—741a; THAYER—567c.

4538. **σαλπιστής** {1x} **salpistēs**, *sal-pis-tace';* from *4537;* a *trumpeter:*—trumpeter {1x}. See: TDNT—7:71, 997; BAGD—741b; THAYER—567d.

4539. **Σαλώμη** {2x} **Salōmē**, *sal-o'-may;* prob. of Heb. or. [fem. from 7965]; *Salome'* (i.e. *Shelomah*), an Israelitess:—*Salome* {2x}. See: BAGD—741b; THAYER—567d.

4540. **Σαμάρεια** {11x} **Samarĕia**, *sam-ar'-i-uh;* of Heb. or. [8111]; *Samaria* (i.e. *Shomeron*), a city and region of Pal.:—Samaria {11x}. See: TDNT—7:88, 999; BAGD—741b; THAYER—567d.

4541. **Σαμαρείτης** {9x} **Samarĕitēs**, *sam-ar-i'-tace* or

Σαμαρίτης **Samaritēs**, *sam-ar-ee'-tace;* from *4540;* a *Samarite,* i.e. inhab. of Samaria:—Samaritan {9x}. See: TDNT—7:88, 999; BAGD—741c; THAYER—568a.

4542. **Σαμαρεῖτις** {2x} **Samarĕitis**, *sam-ar-i'-tis* or

Σαμαρῖτις **Samaritis**, *sam-ar-ee'-tis* fem. of *4541;* a *Samaritess,* i.e. woman of Samaria:—of Samaria {2x}. See: TDNT—7:88, 999; BAGD—741d; THAYER—568c.

4543. **Σαμοθράκη** {1x} **Samŏthrakē**, *sam-oth-rak'-ay;* from *4544* and Θρᾴκη **Thrakē** (*Thrace*); *Samo-thrace'* (*Samos of Thrace*), an island in the Mediterranean:—Samothracia {1x}. See: BAGD—741d; THAYER—568c.

4544. **Σάμος** {1x} **Samŏs**, *sam'-os;* of uncert. aff.; *Samus,* an island of the Mediterranean:—*Samos* {1x}. See: BAGD—741d; THAYER—568c.

4545. **Σαμουήλ** {3x} **Samŏuēl**, *sam-oo-ale';* of Heb. or. [8050]; *Samuel* (i.e. *Shemuel*), an Isr.:—Samuel {3x}. See: BAGD—741d; THAYER—568c.

4546. **Σαμψών** {1x} **Sampsōn**, *samp-sone';* of Heb. or. [8123]; *Sampson* (i.e. *Shimshon*), an Isr.:—Samson {1x}. See: BAGD—742a; THAYER—568c.

4547. **σανδάλιον** {2x} **sandaliŏn**, *san-dal'-ee-on;* neut. of a der. of σάνδαλον **sandalŏn** (a *"sandal"*; of uncert. or.); a *slipper* or *sole-pad:*—sandal {2x}. Cf. Mark 6:9; Acts 12:8.

The sandal usually had a wooden sole bound on by straps round the instep and ankle (Mk 6:9; Acts 12:8). See: TDNT—5:310, 702; BAGD—742a; THAYER—568d.

4548. **σανίς** {1x} **sanis**, *san-ece';* of uncert. aff.; a *plank:*—board {1x}. See: BAGD—742a; THAYER—568d.

4549. **Σαούλ** {9x} **Saŏul**, *sah-ool';* of Heb. or. [7586]; *Saül* (i.e. *Shaül*), the Jewish name of *Paul:*—Saul (Paul) {8x}, Saul (son of Cis) {1x}. See: BAGD—742a; THAYER—568d. comp. *4569.*

4550. **σαπρός** {8x} **saprŏs**, *sap-ros';* from *4595; rotten,* i.e. *worthless* (lit. or mor.):—bad {8x}, corrupt {1x}.

Primarily, *sapros* speaks of vegetable and animal substances, expresses what is of poor quality, unfit for use, putrid. It is said of **(1)** a tree and its fruit (Mt 7:17–18; 12:33; Lk 6:43); **(2)** certain fish (Mt 13:48 - "bad"); and **(3)** defiling speech (Eph 4:29). See: TDNT—7:94, 1000; BAGD—742b; THAYER—568d. comp. *4190.*

4551. **Σάπφιρα** {1x} **Sapphĕirē**, *sap-fi'-ray;* fem. of *4552; Sapphirē,* an Israelitess:—Sapphira {1x}. See: BAGD—742b; THAYER—569a.

4552. **σάπιρος** {1x} **sapphĕirŏs**, *sap'-fi-ros;* of Heb. or. [5601]; a *"sapphire"* or *lapis-lazuli* gem:—sapphire {1x}.

(1) It was one of the stones in the high priest's breastplate, cf. Ex 28:18; 39:11; **(2)** as an intimation of its value see Job 28:16; Eze 28:13. **(3)** The sapphire has various shades of blue and ranks next in hardness to the diamond. See: BAGD—742c; THAYER—569a.

4553. **σαργάνη** {1x} **sarganē**, *sar-gan'-ay;* appar. of Heb. or. [8276]; a *basket* (as *interwoven* or *wicker*-work:—basket {1x}.

Sargene denotes **(1)** "a braided rope or band," **(2)** "a large basket made of ropes, or a wicker "basket" made of entwined twigs, 2 Cor 11:33. **(3)** That the "basket" in which Paul was let down from a window in Damascus is spoken of by Luke as a *spuris,* and by Paul himself as a *sargane,* is quite consistent, the two terms being used for the same article. See: BAGD—742c; THAYER—569a.

4554. **Σάρδεις** {3x} **Sardĕis**, *sar'-dice;* plur. of uncert. der.; *Sardis,* a place in Asia Minor:—Sardis {3x}. See: BAGD—742c; THAYER—569a.

4555. **σάρδινος** {1x} **sardinŏs**, *sar'-dee-nos;* from the same as *4556; sardine* (*3037* being impl.), i.e. a gem, so called:—sardine {1x}.

(1) There are two special varieties, one a yellowish brown, the other a transparent red (like a cornelian). **(2)** It denotes "the sardian stone." *Sardius,* is the word in Rev 4:3, where it formed part of the symbolic appearance of the Lord on His throne, setting forth His glory and majesty in view of the judgment to follow. **(3)** The beauty of the stone, its transparent brilliance, the high polish of which it is susceptible, made it a favorite among the ancients. **(4)** It forms the sixth foundation of the wall of the heavenly Jerusalem, Rev 21:20. See: BAGD—742c; THAYER—569a.

4556. **σάρδιον** {1x} **sardiŏs**, *sar'-dee-os;* prop. an adj. from an uncert. base; *sardian* (*3037* being impl.), i.e. (as noun) the gem so called:—sardius {1x}. See: BAGD—742d; THAYER—569b.

4557. **σαρδόνυξ** {1x} **sardŏnux**, *sar-don'-oox;* from the base of *4556* and ὄνυξ **ŏnux** (the *nail* of a finger; hence, the *"onyx"* stone); a *"sardonyx"*, i.e. the gem so called:—sardonyx {1x}.

(1) A *sardonyx* is a precious stone marked by the red colors of the carnelian (sard) and the white of the onyx. **(2)** *Saradonux,* a name which indicates the formation of the gem, a layer of sard, and a layer of onyx, marked by the red of the sard and the white of the onyx. **(3)** It was used among the Romans both for cameos and for signets. **(4)** It forms the fifth foundation of the wall of the heavenly Jerusalem, Rev 21:20. See: BAGD—742d; THAYER—569b.

4558. **Σάρεπτα** {1x} **Sarĕpta**, *sar'-ep-tah;* of Heb. or. [6886]; *Sarepta* (i.e. *Tsarephath*), a place in Pal.:—*Sarepta* {1x}. See: BAGD—742d; THAYER—569b.

4559. **σαρκικός** {11x} **sarkikŏs**, *sar-kee-kos';* from *4561; pertaining to flesh,* i.e. (by extens.) *bodily, temporal,* or (by impl.) *animal, unregenerate:*—carnal {9x}, fleshly {2x}.

Sarkikos, flesh, signifies **(1)** having the nature of flesh, **(1a)** i.e., sensual, controlled by animal appetites, governed by human nature, instead of by the Spirit of God (1 Cor 3:3); **(1b)** having its seat in the animal nature, or excited by it (1 Pet 2:11—fleshly); **(1c)** as the equivalent of human with the added idea of weakness, figuratively of the weapons of spiritual warfare: i.e. of the flesh, carnal (2 Cor 10:4); or **(1d)** with the idea of unspirituality, of human wisdom, fleshly (2 Cor 1:12); **(2)** pertaining to the flesh, i.e., the body (Rom 15:27; 1 Cor 9:11); **(3)** "pertaining to the natural, transient life of the body," Heb 7:16, "a carnal commandment"; **(4)** given up to the flesh, Rom 7:14, "I am carnal sold under sin"; 1 Cor. 3:1. **(5)** In regard to 1 Pet 2:11, *sarkikos* describes the lusts which have their source in man's corrupt and fallen nature, and the man is *sarkikos* who allows to the flesh a place which does not belong to it of right; **(6)** in 1 Cor 3:1, 3–4 *sarkios* is an accusation graver than *sarkinos* would have been. The Corinthian saints were making no progress, and they were anti-spiritual in respect of the particular point with which the apostle was there dealing. Syn.: *Sarkikos* describes the lusts which have their source in man's corrupt and fallen nature, and the man is *sarkikos* who allows to the flesh a place which does not belong to it of right (1 Pet 2:11). *Sarkinos* stresses the material; *sarkikos* the quality. Syn.: 4560, 5591. See: TDNT—7:98, 1000; BAGD—742d; THAYER—569b.

4560. **σάρκινος** {1x} **sarkinŏs**, *sar'-kee-nos;* from *4561; similar to flesh,* i.e. (by anal.) *soft:*—fleshly {1x}.

Sarkinos, means "consisting of flesh," 2 Cor 3:3, "fleshy tables of the heart." Syn.: See discussion under 4559. See: TDNT—7:98, 1000; BAGD—743a; THAYER—569c.

4561. **σάρξ** {151x} **sarx**, *sarx;* prob. from the base of *4563; flesh* (as *stripped* of the skin), i.e. (strictly) the *meat* of an animal (as food), or (by extens.) the *body* (as opposed to the soul [or spirit], or as the symbol of what is external, or as the means of kindred), or (by impl.) *human nature* (with its frailties [phys. or mor.] and passions), or (spec.) a *human being* (as such):—flesh {147x}, carnal {2x}, carnally minded + 5427 {1x}, fleshly {1x}.

Sarx means **(1)** the substance of the body whether of beasts or of men (1 Cor 15:39); **(2)** the human body (2 Cor 10:3a; Gal 2:20; Phil 1:22); **(3)** by synecdoche, of mankind, in the totality of all that is essential to manhood, i.e., spirit, soul, and body, (Mt 24:22; Jn 1:13; Rom 3:20); **(4)** by synecdoche, of the holy humanity of the Lord Jesus, in the totality of all that is essential to manhood, i.e., spirit, soul, and body (Jn 1:14; 1 Ti 3:16; 1 Jn 4:2; 2 Jn 7; in Heb 5:7, "the days of His flesh," i.e., His past life on earth in distinction from His present life in resurrection; **(5)** by synecdoche, for the complete person (Jn 6:51–57; 2 Cor 7:5; Jas 5:3);

(6) the weaker element in human nature (Mt 26:41; Rom 6:19; 8:3a); **(7)** the unregenerate state of men (Rom 7:5; 8:8, 9); **(8)** the seat of sin in man, but this is not the same thing as in the body (2 Pet 2:18; 1 Jn 2:16); **(9)** the lower and temporary element in the Christian (Gal 3:3; 6:8, and in religious ordinances, Heb 9:10); **(10)** the natural attainments of men (1 Cor 1:26; 2 Cor 10:2, 3b); **(11)** circumstances (1 Cor 7:28; the externals of life, 2 Cor 7:1; Eph 6:5; Heb 9:13); **(12)** by metonymy, the outward and seeming as contrasted with the spirit, the inward and real, (Jn 6:63; 2 Cor 5:16); **(13)** natural relationship, **(13a)** consanguine (1 Cor 10:18; Gal 4:23), or **(13b)** marital (Mt 19:5). See: TDNT—7:98, 1000; BAGD—743b; THAYER—569d.

4562. **Σαρούχ** {1x} **Sarŏuch** *sa-rooch',* or

Σερούχ **Sĕrŏuch**, *seh-rooch';* of Heb. or. [8286]; *Saruch* (i.e. *Serug*), a patriarch:—Saruch {1x}. See: BAGD—744d; 747c; THAYER—571d.

4563. **σαρόω** {3x} **sarŏō**, *sar-ŏ'-o;* from a der. of σαίρω **sairō** (to *brush* off; akin to *4951*); mean. a *broom; to sweep:*—sweep {3x}. Cf. Mt. 12:44; Lk 11:25; 15:8. See: BAGD—744d; THAYER—571d.

4564. **Σάρρα** {4x} **Sarrha**, *sar'-hrah;* of Heb. or. [8283]; *Sarra* (i.e. *Sarah*), the wife of Abraham:—Sara {2x}, Sarah {2x}. See: BAGD—744d; THAYER—571d.

4565. **Σάρων** {1x} **Sarōn**, *sar'-one;* of Heb. or. [8289]; *Saron* (i.e. *Sharon*), a district of Pal.:—*Saron* {1x}. See: BAGD—744d; THAYER—571d.

4566. **Σατάν** {1x} **Satan**, *sat-an';* of Heb. or. [7854]; *Satan,* i.e. the *devil:*—*Satan* {1x}. See: TDNT—7:151,*; BAGD—744d; THAYER—571d. comp. *4567.*

4567. **Σατανᾶς** {36x} **Satanas**, *sat-an-as';* of Chald. or. corresp. to *4566* (with the def. aff.); *the accuser,* i.e. the *devil:*—Satan {36x}.

Satanas, a Greek form derived from the Heb, *Satan*), "an adversary," is used **(1)** of an angel of Jehovah in Num 22:22 (the first occurrence of the Word in the OT); **(2)** of men, e.g., 1 Sa 29:4; Ps 38:20; 71:13; four in Ps 109; **(3)** of *"Satan,"* the Devil, some seventeen or eighteen times in the OT; in Zec 3:1, where the name receives its interpretation, "to resist him." **(4)** In the NT the word is always used of *"Satan,"* the adversary **(4a)** of God and Christ, e.g., Mt 4:10; 12:26; Mk 1:13; 3:23, 26; 4:15; Lk 4:8; 11:18; 22:3; Jn 13:27; **(4b)** of His people, e.g., Lk 22:31; Acts 5:3; Rom 16:20; 1 Cor 5:5; 7:5; 2 Cor 2:11; 11:14; 12:7; 1 Th 2:18; 1 Ti 1:20; 5:15; Rev 2:9, 13 (twice), 24; 3:9; **(4c)** of mankind, Lk 13:16; Acts 26:18; 2 Th 2:9;

Rev 12:9; 20:7. **(5)** His doom, sealed at the Cross, is foretold in its stages in Lk 10:18; Rev 20:2, 10. **(6)** Believers are assured of victory over him, Rom 16:20. **(7)** The appellation was given by the Lord to Peter, as a "*Satan*-like" man, on the occasion when he endeavored to dissuade Him from death, Mt 16:23; Mk 8:33. **(8)** "*Satan*" is not simply the personification of evil influences in the heart, for he tempted Christ, in whose heart no evil thought could ever have arisen (Jn 14:30; 2 Cor 5:21; Heb 4:15); **(9)** moreover his personality is asserted in both the OT and the NT, and especially in the latter, whereas if the OT language was intended to be figurative, the NT would have made this evident. See: TDNT—7:151, 1007; BAGD—744d; THAYER—571d.

4568. **σάτον** {2x} **satŏn**, *sat'-on;* of Heb. or. [5429]; a certain *measure* for things dry:—measure {2x}.

Saton, as a noun, is a Hebrew dry measure (Heb., *seah*), about a peck and a half, Mt 13:33; Lk 13:21; "three measures" would be the quantity for a baking (cf. Gen 18:6; Judg 6:19; 1 Sa 1:24; the "ephah" of the last two passages was equal to three *sata*). Syn.: 280, 488, 943, 2884, 3313, 3354, 3358, 4057, 5234, 5249, 5518. See: BAGD—745b; THAYER—572a.

4569. **Σαῦλος** {17x} **Saulŏs**, *sŏw'-los;* of Heb. or., the same as *4549; Saulus* (i.e. *Shaül*), the Jewish name of *Paul:*—Saul {17x}. See: BAGD—745b; THAYER—572b.

σαυτοῦ **sautŏu**.etc. See *4572*.

4570. **σβέννυμι** {8x} **sbĕnnumi**, *sben'-noo-mee;* a prol. form of an appar. primary verb; to *extinguish* (lit. or fig.):—go out {1x}, quench {7x}.

Sbennumi is used **(1)** of "quenching" fire or things on fire, Mt 12:20, quoted from Is 42:3, **(1a)** figurative of the condition of the feeble, Heb 11:34; **(1b)** in the passive voice, **(1b1)** Mt 25:8, of torches, "are gone out", lit., "are being quenched"; **(1b2)** of the retributive doom hereafter of sin unrepented of and unremitted in this life, Mk 9:44, 46, 48; **(2)** metaphorically, **(2a)** of "quenching" the fire-tipped darts of the evil one, Eph 6:16; **(2b)** of "quenching" the Spirit, by hindering His operations in oral testimony in the church gatherings of believers, 1 Th 5:19. **(2c)** The peace, order, and edification of the saints were evidence of the ministry of the Spirit among them, 1 Cor 14:26, 32, 33, 40, but if, through ignorance of His ways, or through failure to recognize, or refusal to submit to, them, or through impatience with the ignorance or self-will of others, the Spirit were quenched, these happy results would be absent. For there was always the danger that the impulses of the flesh might usurp the place of the energy of the Spirit in the assembly, and the endeavor to restrain this evil by natural means would have the effect of hindering His ministry also. Apparently then, this injunction was intended to warn believers against the substitution of a mechanical order for the restraints of the Spirit. See: TDNT—7:165, 1009; BAGD—745b; THAYER—572b.

4571. **σέ** {197x} **sĕ**, *seh;* acc. sing. of *4771; thee:*—thee {178x}, thou {16x}, thy house {1x}, not tr {2x}. See: BAGD—772a [4771]; THAYER—591c [4771].

4572. **σεαυτοῦ** {40x} **sĕautŏu**, *seh-ŏw-too';* gen. from *4571* and *846;* also dat. of the same,

σεαυτῷ **sĕautōi**, *seh-ŏw-to';* and acc.

σεαυτόν **sĕautŏn**, *seh-ŏw-ton';* likewise contr.

σαυτοῦ **sautŏu**, *sŏw-too';*

σαυτῷ **sautōi**, *sŏw-to';* and

σαυτόν **sautŏn**, *sŏw-ton';* respectively; *of (with, to) thyself:*—thyself {35x}, thine own self {2x}, thou thyself {1x}, thee {1x}, thy {1x}. See: BAGD—745c; THAYER—572b.

4573. **σεβάζομαι** {1x} **sĕbazŏmai**, *seb-ad'-zom-ahee;* mid. voice from a der. of *4576;* to *venerate,* i.e. *adore:*—worship {1x}.

This word means to worship religiously; through religious practices, Rom 1:25. See: TDNT—7:172, 1010; BAGD—745c; THAYER—572c.

4574. **σέβασμα** {3x} **sĕbasma**, *seb'-as-mah;* from *4573;* something *adored,* i.e. an *object of worship* (god, altar, etc):—devotion {1x}, that is worshipped {2x}.

(1) It denotes "an object of worship", Acts 17:23; **(2)** in 2 Th 2:4, "that is worshipped"; every object of "worship," whether the true God or pagan idols, will come under the ban of the Man of Sin. See: TDNT—7:173, 1010; BAGD—745d; THAYER—572c.

4575. **σεβαστός** {3x} **sĕbastŏs**, *seb-as-tos';* from *4573; venerable* (*august*), i.e. (as noun) a title of the Rom. *Emperor,* or (as adj.) *imperial:*—Augustus {3x}.

Sebastos, "august, reverent," the masculine gender of an adjective (from *sebas,* "reverential awe"), became used as the title of the Roman emperor, Acts 25:21, 25, "Augustus"; then, taking its name from the emperor, it became a title of honor applied to certain legions or cohorts or battalions, marked for their valor, Acts 27:1. See: TDNT—7:174, 1010; BAGD—745d; THAYER—572c.

4576. **σέβομαι** {10x} **sĕbŏmai**, *seb'-om-ahee;* mid. voice of an appar. primary verb; to feel awe, to *revere,* i.e. *adore:*—devout {3x}, religious {1x}, worship {6x}.

Sebomai, "to revere," stressing the feeling of awe or devotion, is used of **(1)** "worship" **(1a)** to God, Mt 15:9; Mk 7:7; Acts 16:14; 18:7, 13; **(1b)** to a goddess, Acts 19:27. It also denotes "to feel awe," whether before God or man, "to worship," is translated **(2)** "devout," in Acts 13:50; 17:4, 17; and **(3)** "religious" in Acts 13:43. See: TDNT—7:169, 1010; BAGD—746a; THAYER—572d.

4577. **σειρά** { {1x} **sĕira**, *si-rah';* prob. from *4951* through its congener εἴρω **ĕirō** (to *fasten;* akin to *138*); a *chain,* (as *binding* or *drawing*):—chain {1x}. See: BAGD—746b; THAYER—572d.

4578. **σεισμός** {14x} **sĕismŏs**, *sice-mos';* from *4579;* a *commotion,* i.e. (of the air) a *gale,* (of the ground) an *earthquake:*—earthquake {13x}, tempest {1x}.

Seismos, "a shaking, a shock," from *seio,* "to move to and fro, to shake," chiefly with the idea of concussion (Eng., "seismic," "seismology," "seismometry"), is used **(1)** of a "tempest" in the sea, Mt 8:24; **(2)** of "earthquakes," Mt 24:7; 27:54; 28:2; Mk 13:8; Lk 21:11; Acts 16:26; Rev 6:12; 8:5; 11:13 (twice), 19; 16:18 (twice). See: TDNT—7:196, 1014; BAGD—746b; THAYER—572d.

4579. **σείω** {5x} **sĕiō**, *si'-o;* appar. a primary verb; to *rock* (*vibrate,* prop. sideways or to and fro), i.e. (gen.) to *agitate* (in any direction; cause to *tremble*); fig. to throw into a *tremor* (of fear or concern):—move {1x}, quake {1x}, shake {3x}.

Sio, as a verb, means "to shake, move to and fro," usually of violent concussion [Eng., "seismic," "seismograph," "seismology"], and is said **(1)** of the earth as destined to be shaken by God (Heb 12:26); **(2)** of a local convulsion of the earth, at the death of Christ (Mt 27:51 "did quake"); **(3)** of a fig tree (Rev 6:13); **(4)** metaphorically, to stir up with fear or some other emotion, **(4a)** Mt 21:10 of the people of a city: "And when He was come into Jerusalem, all the city was moved, saying, Who is this?"; **(4b)** Mt 28:4 of the keepers or watchers, at the Lord's tomb ("did shake"). Syn.: 277, 383, 761, 2795, 2796, 3334, 4525, 4531, 4787, 5342. See: TDNT—7:196, 1014; BAGD—746c; THAYER—573a.

4580. **Σεκοῦνδος** {1x} **Sĕkoundŏs**, *sek-oon'-dos;* of Lat. or.; "*second*"; *Secundus,* a Chr.:—Secundus {1x}. See: BAGD—746c; THAYER—573a.

4581. **Σελεύκεια** {1x} **Sĕlĕukĕia**, *sel-yook'-i-ah;* from Σέλευκος **Sĕlĕukŏs**, (*Seleucus,* a Syrian king); *Seleuceia,* a place in Syria:—Seleucia {1x}. See: BAGD—746d; THAYER—573a.

4582. **σελήνη** {9x} **sĕlēnē**, *sel-ay'-nay;* from σέλας **sĕlas**, (*brilliancy;* prob. akin to the alt. of *138,* through the idea of *attractiveness*); the *moon:*—moon {9x}.

Selene, from *selas,* "brightness" (the Heb. words are *yareach,* "wandering," and *lebanah,* "white"), **(1)** occurs in Mt 24:29; Mk 13:24; Lk 21:25; Acts 2:20; 1 Cor 15:41; Rev 6:12; 8:12; 12:1; 21:23. **(2)** In Rev 12:1, "the moon under her feet" is suggestive of derived authority, just as her being clothed with the sun is suggestive of supreme authority, everything in the symbolism of the passage centers in Israel. In Rev 6:12 the similar symbolism of the sun and "moon" is suggestive of the supreme authority over the world, and of derived authority, at the time of the execution of divine judgments upon nations at the close of the present age. See: BAGD—746d; THAYER—573a.

4583. **σεληνιάζομαι** {2x} **sĕlēniazŏmai**, *sel-ay-nee-ad'-zom-ahee;* middle or passive voice from a presumed der. of *4582;* to *be moon-struck,* i.e. *crazy:*—be a lunatick {2x}.

Seleniazomai, lit., "to be moon struck" (from *selene,* "the moon"), is used in the passive voice with active significance, "*lunatick,*" Mt 4:24; 17:15; the corresponding English word is "lunatic." Epilepsy was supposed to be influenced by the moon. See: BAGD—746d; THAYER—573b.

4584. **Σεμεΐ** { {1x} **Sĕmĕi**, *sem-eh-ee'* or

Σεμεΐν **Sĕmĕïn**, *sem-eh-een'* of Heb. or. [8096]; *Semeï* (i.e. *Shimi*), an Isr.:—Semei {1x}. See: BAGD—746d; THAYER—573b.

4585. **σεμίδαλις** {1x} **sĕmidalis**, *sem-id'-al-is;* prob. of for. origin; fine wheaten *flour:*—fine flour {1x}. See: BAGD—746b; THAYER—573b.

4586. **σεμνός** {4x} **sĕmnŏs**, *sem-nos';* from *4576; venerable,* i.e. *honorable:*—grave {3x}, honest {1x}.

(1) One who is *semnos* is well ordered in his earthly life and has a grace and dignity derived from his heavenly citizenship. **(2)** There is something majestic and awe-inspiring about one who is *semnos;* he does not repel but invites and attracts. **(3)** It first denoted "reverend, august, venerable" (akin to *sebomai,* "to reverence"); then, **(4)** "serious, grave," whether **(4a)** of persons, 1 Ti 3:8, 11 (deacons and their wives); Titus 2:2 (aged men); or **(4b)** things, Phil 4:8, "honest." **(5)** It denotes what inspires reverence and awe. **(6)** The word points to seriousness of purpose and to self-respect in conduct. Syn.: 2412, 2887. See: TDNT—7:191, 1010; BAGD—746d; THAYER—573b.

4587. **σεμνότης** {3x} **sĕmnŏtēs**, *sem-not'-ace;* from *4586; venerableness,* i.e. *probity:*—gravity {2x}, honesty {1x}.

(1) *Semnotes* is the characteristic of a person that entitles him to reverence and respect, dignity, majesty, and sanctity. **(2)** It denotes "venerableness, dignity, honesty"; **(2a)** it is a necessary characteristic of the life and conduct of Christians, 1 Ti 2:2, "honesty" which flows from a life of gravity; **(2b)** a qualification of a bishop or overseer in a church, in regard to his children, 1 Ti 3:4, "gravity"; **(2c)** a necessary characteristic of the teaching imparted by a servant of God, Titus 2:7, "gravity." See: TDNT—7:191, 1010; BAGD—747a; THAYER—573b.

4588. **Σέργιος** {1x} **Sĕrgiŏs**, *serg'-ee-os;* of Lat. or.; *Sergius,* a Rom.:—Sergius (Paulus) {1x}. See: BAGD—747b; THAYER—573b.

4589. **Σήθ** {1x} **Sēth**, *sayth;* of Heb. or. [8352]; *Seth* (i.e. *Sheth*), a patriarch:—*Seth* {1x}. See: BAGD—747c; THAYER—573b.

4590. **Σήμ** {1x} **Sēm**, *same;* of Heb. or. [8035]; *Sem* (i.e. *Shem*), a patriarch:—*Sem* {1x}. See: BAGD—747c; THAYER—573c.

4591. **σημαίνω** {6x} **sēmainō**, *say-mah'-ee-no;* from σῆμα **sēma**, (a *mark;* of uncert. der.); to make a sign, *indicate:*—signify {6x}.

'*Semaino,* "to give a sign, indicate" (*sema,* "a sign"), "to signify," is so translated in Jn 12:33; 18:32; 21:19; Acts 11:28; 25:27; Rev 1:1, where perhaps the suggestion is that of expressing by signs. See: TDNT—7:262, 1015; BAGD—747c; THAYER—573c.

4592. **σημεῖον** {77x} **sēmĕiŏn**, *say-mi'-on;* neut. of a presumed der. of the base of *4591;* an *indication,* espec. cerem. or supernat.:—miracle {23x}, sign {50x}, token {1x}, wonder {3x}.

(1) *Semeion* is a manifest deed, having in itself an explanation of something hidden and secret. **(2)** It denotes "a sign, mark, indication, token," is used **(2a)** of that which distinguished a person or thing from others, e.g., Mt 26:48; Lk 2:12; Rom 4:11; 2 Cor 12:12 (1st part); 2 Th 3:17, "token," i.e., his autograph attesting the authenticity of his letters; **(2b)** of a "sign" as a warning or admonition, e.g., Mt 12:39, "the sign of (i.e., consisting of) the prophet Jonas"; 16:4; Lk 2:34; 11:29, 30; **(2c)** of miraculous acts, "miracles", **(2c1)** as tokens of divine authority and power, e.g., Mt 12:38, 39 (1st part); Jn 2:11, 23; 3:2; 4:54; 6:2, 14, 26; 7:31; 9:16; 10:41; 11:47; 12:18, 37; 20:30; in 1 Cor 1:22, "the Jews ask for a sign" indicates that the Apostles were met with the same demand from Jews as Christ had been. Signs were vouchsafed in plenty, signs of God's power and love, but these were not the signs which they sought. They wanted signs of an outward Messianic Kingdom, of temporal triumph, of material greatness for the chosen people. With such cravings the Gospel of a "crucified Messiah" was to them a stumblingblock indeed, 1 Cor 14:22; **(2c2)** by devils, Rev 16:14; **(2c3)** by false teachers or prophets, indications of assumed authority, e.g., Mt 24:24; Mk 13:22; **(2c4)** by Satan through his special agents, 2 Th 2:9; Rev 13:13, 14; 19:20; **(2c5)** of tokens portending future events, e. g., Mt 24:3, where "the sign of the Son of Man" signifies, subjectively, that the Son of Man is Himself the "sign" of what He is about to do; Mk 13:4; Lk 21:7, 11, 25; Acts 2:19; Rev 12:1, 3; 15:1.

(3) "Signs" confirmatory of what God had accomplished in the atoning sacrifice of Christ, His resurrection and ascension, and of the sending of the Holy Spirit, were given to the Jews for their recognition, as at Pentecost, and supernatural acts by apostolic ministry, as well as by the supernatural operations in the churches, such as the gift of tongues and prophesyings; there is no record of the continuance of these latter after the circumstances recorded in Acts 19:1–20. Syn.: 1411, 1741, 2297, 3167, 3861, 5059. See: TDNT—7:200, 1015; BAGD—747d; THAYER—573c.

4593. **σημειόω** {1x} **sēmĕiŏō**, *say-mi-ŏ'-o;* from *4592;* to *distinguish,* i.e. *mark* (for avoidance):—to note {1x}.

Semeioo means to mark, to note and being in the middle voice stresses to note for oneself; an injunction to take cautionary note of one who refuses obedience to the apostle's word (2 Th 3:14). See: TDNT—7:265, 1015; BAGD—748d; THAYER—574a.

4594. **σήμερον** {41x} **sēmĕrŏn**, *say'-mer-on;* neut. (as adv.) of a presumed compound of the art. *3588* (τ changed to ς) and *2250;* on *the* (i.e. *this*) *day* (or *night* current or just passed); gen. *now* (i.e. at *present, hitherto*):—this day {22x}, to day {18x}, this + 3588 {1x}.

Semeron, an adverb, is **(1)** used frequently in **(1a)** Mt, Lk; and **(1b)** in Acts it is always rendered "this day"; **(1c)** in Heb **(1c1)** 1:5; 5:5, "to day", in the same quotation; **(1c2)** "today" in 3:7, 13, 15; 4:7 (twice); 13:8; also Jas 4:13. **(2)** The clause containing *semeron* is **(2a)** sometimes introduced by the conjunction *hoti,* "that," e.g., Mk 14:30; Lk 4:21; 19:9; **(2b)** sometimes without the conjunction, e.g., Lk 22:34; 23:43, where "today" is to be attached to the next statement, "shalt thou be with Me"; there are no grammatical reasons for the insistence that the connection must be with the statement "Verily I say unto thee." **(3)** In Rom 11:8 and 2 Cor 3:14, 15, the lit. rendering is "unto the today day." **(4)** In Heb 4:7, the "today" of Ps 95:7 is evidently designed to extend to the present period of the Christian faith. See: TDNT—7:269, 1024; BAGD—749a; THAYER—574a.

4595. **σήπω** {1x} **sēpō**, *say'-po;* appar. a primary verb; to *putrefy,* i.e. (fig.) *perish:*—be corrupted {1x}.

(1) The verb is derived from a root signifying to rot off, drop to pieces. **(2)** It signifies "to make corrupt, to destroy"; in the passive voice with middle sense, "to become corrupt or rotten, to perish," said of riches, Jas 5:2, of the gold and silver of the luxurious rich who have ground down their laborers. See: TDNT—7:94, 1000; BAGD—749b; THAYER—574b.

4596. **σηρικός** {1x} **sērikŏs**, *say-ree-kos'* or **σιρικός** **sirikŏs**, *see-ree-kos';* from Σήρ **Sēr**, (an Indian tribe from whom *silk* was procured; hence, the name of the *silk-worm*); *Seric,* i.e. *silken* (neut. as noun, a *silky* fabric):—silk {1x}. See: BAGD—749b; 751d; THAYER—574b.

4597. **σής** {3x} **sēs**, *sace;* appar. of Heb. or. [5580]; a clothes *moth:*—moth {3x}.

Ses denotes "a clothes moth," Mt 6:19, 20; Lk 12:33. See: TDNT—7:275, 1025; BAGD—749b; THAYER—574c.

4598. **σητόβρωτος** {1x} **sētŏbrōtŏs**, *say-tob'-ro-tos;* from *4597* and a der. of *977; moth-eaten:*—motheaten {1x}. See: TDNT—7:275, 1025; BAGD—749c; THAYER—574c.

4599. **σθενόω** {1x} **sthĕnŏō**, *sthen-ŏ'-o;* from σθένος **sthĕnŏs**, (bodily *vigor;* prob. akin to the base of *2476*); to *strengthen,* i.e. (fig.) *confirm* (in spiritual knowledge and power):—strengthen {1x}. See: BAGD—749c; THAYER—574c.

4600. **σιαγών** {2x} **siagōn**, *see-ag-one';* of uncert. der.; the *jaw*-bone, i.e. (by impl.) the *cheek* or side of the face:—cheek {2x}. Cf. Mt 5:39; Lk 6:29. See: BAGD—749c; THAYER—574c.

4601. **σιγάω** {9x} **sigaō**, *see-gah'-o;* from *4602;* to *keep silent* (tran. or intr.):—hold (one's) peace {4x}, keep silence {3x}, keep close {1x}, keep secret {1x}.

Sigao signifies **(1)** used intransitively, **(1a)** "to be silent" (from *sige,* "silence"), translated "to hold one's peace," in Lk 20:26; Acts 12:17; 15:13; 1 Cor 14:34; **(1b)** "kept silence", Acts 15:12; 1 Cor 14:28, 30; **(1c)** "kept close" in Lk 9:36; **(2)** used transitively, "to keep secret"; in the passive voice, "to be kept secret," Rom 16:25. See: BAGD—749c; THAYER—574c.

4602. **σιγή** {2x} **sigē**, *see-gay';* appr. from σίζω **sizō** (to *hiss,* i.e. *hist* or *hush*); *silence:*—silence {2x}.

Sige occurs in **(1)** Acts 21:40; and **(2)** Rev 8:1, where the "silence" is introductory to the judgments following the opening of the seventh seal. See: BAGD—749d; THAYER—574c. comp. *4623.*

4603. **σιδήρεος** {5x} **sidērĕŏs**, *sid-ay'-reh-os;* from *4604;* made *of iron:*—of iron {4x}, iron {1x}.

Sidereos "of iron," occurs **(1)** in Acts 12:10, of an iron gate; and **(2)** "of iron," Rev 2:27; 9:9; 12:5; 19:15. See: BAGD—750a; THAYER—574d.

4604. **σίδηρος** {1x} **sidērŏs**, *sid'-ay-ros;* of uncert. der.; *iron:*—iron {1x}. See: BAGD—750a; THAYER—574d.

4605. **Σιδών** {11x} **Sidōn**, *sid-one';* of Heb. or. [6721]; *Sidon* (i.e. *Tsidon*), a place in Pal.:—*Sidon* {11x}. See: BAGD—750a; THAYER—574d.

4606. **Σιδώνιος** {1x} **Sidōniŏs**, *sid-o'-nee-os;* from *4605;* a *Sidonian,* i.e. inhab. of Sidon:—of Sidon {1x}. See: BAGD—750b; THAYER—574d.

4607. **σικάριος** {1x} **sikariŏs**, *sik-ar'-ee-os;* of Lat. or.; a *dagger-man* or *assassin;* a *freebooter* (Jewish *fanatic* outlawed by the Romans):—murderer {1x}.

The *sikarios* derived his name from the sica, a short sword that he wore and was prompt to use; he was a hired mercenary or swordsman. They were hired assassins. Concealing their short swords under their garments and mingling with the crowd at the great feasts, the *sicari* would stab their enemies and then join the bystanders in exclamations of horror, thus effectively averting suspicion from themselves, Acts 21:38. Syn.: 443, 5406. See: TDNT—7:278, 1026; BAGD—750b; THAYER—574d. comp. *5406*.

4608. **σίκερα** {1x} **sikĕra**, *sik'-er-ah;* of Heb. or. [7941]; an *intoxicant,* i.e. intensely fermented *liquor:*—strong drink {1x}.

Sikera is strong drink, an intoxicating beverage, different from wine; it was a artificial product, made of a mixture of sweet ingredients, whether derived from grain and vegetables, or from the juice of fruits (dates), or a decoction of honey (Lk 1:15). See: BAGD—750b; THAYER—574d.

4609. **Σίλας** {13x} **Silas**, *see'-las;* contr. for *4610; Silas,* a Chr.:—*Silas* {13x}. See: BAGD—750c; THAYER—575a.

4610. **Σιλουανός** {4x} **Silŏuanŏs**, *sil-oo-an-os';* of Lat. or.; *"silvan;" Silvanus,* a Chr.:—Silvanus {4x}. See: BAGD—750c; THAYER—575b. comp. *4609*.

4611. **Σιλωάμ** {3x} **Silōam**, *sil-o-am';* of Heb. or. [7975]; *Siloäm* (i.e. *Shiloäch*), a pool of Jerusalem:—*Siloam* {3x}. See: BAGD—750d; THAYER—575b.

4612. **σιμικίνθιον** {1x} **simikinthiŏn**, *sim-ee-kin'-thee-on;* of Lat. or.; a *semicinctium* or *half-girding,* i.e. narrow covering (*apron*):—apron {1x}.

Simikinthion, "a thing girded round half the body" (Latin, *semicinctium*), was a narrow apron, or linen covering, worn by workmen and servants, Acts 19:12. See: BAGD—751a; THAYER—575c.

4613. **Σίμων** {75x} **Simōn**, *see'-mone;* of Heb. or. [8095]; *Simon* (i.e. *Shimon*), the name of nine Isr.:—*Simon* (Peter) {49x}, *Simon* (Zelotes) {4x}, *Simon* (father of Judas) {4x}, *Simon* (Magus) {4x}, *Simon* (the tanner) {4x}, *Simon* (the Pharisee) {3x}, *Simon* (of Cyrene) {3x}, *Simon* (brother of Jesus) {2x}, *Simon* (the leper) {2x}. See: BAGD—751a; THAYER—575c. comp. *4826*.

4614. **Σινά** {4x} **Sina**, *see-nah';* of Heb. or. [5514]; *Sina* (i.e. *Sinai*), a mountain in Arabia:—*Sina* {2x}, Sinai {2x}. See: TDNT—7:282, 1026; BAGD—751c; THAYER—575d.

4615. **σίναπι** {5x} **sinapi**, *sin'-ap-ee;* perh. from σίνομαι **sinŏmai** (to *hurt,* i.e. *sting*); *mustard* (the plant):—mustard seed {5x}.

(1) *Sinapi* is mustard, the name of a plant **(1a)** which in oriental countries grows from a very small seed and attains to the height of a tree, 10 feet (3 m) and more; **(1b)** hence a very small quantity of a thing is likened to a mustard seed, and also a thing which grows to a remarkable size. **(2)** It is translated "mustard seed" in the NT. **(2a)** The conditions to be fulfilled by the mustard are that it should be a familiar plant, with a very small seed, Mt 17:20; Lk 17:6, sown in the earth, growing larger than garden herbs, Mt 13:31, having large branches, Mk 4:31, attractive to birds, Lk 13:19. **(2b)** The cultivated mustard *is sinapis nigra.* The seed is well known for its minuteness. The mustards are annuals, reproduced with extraordinary rapidity. **(3)** The translation in Mt 13:32, "greatest among herbs" should be noted. **(3a)** As the parable indicates, Christendom presents a sort of Christianity that has become conformed to the principles and ways of the world, and the world has favored this debased Christianity. **(3b)** Contrast the testimony of the NT, e.g., in Jn 17:14; Gal 6:14; 1 Pet 2:11; 1 Jn 3:1. See: TDNT—7:287, 1027; BAGD—751c; THAYER—575d.

4616. **σινδών** {6x} **sindōn**, *sin-done';* of uncert. (perh. for.) or.; *byssos,* i.e. bleached *linen* (the cloth or a garment of it):—linen cloth {3x}, linen {2x}, fine linen {1x}.

(1) *Sindon* is a linen cloth, esp. that which was fine and costly, in which the bodies of the dead were wrapped. **(2)** It was "a fine linen cloth, an article of domestic manufacture" (Prov 31:24) used **(2a)** as a garment or wrap, the "linen cloth" of Mk 14:51, 52; **(2b)** as shrouds or winding sheets, Mt 27:59; Mk 15:46, "linen"; Lk 23:53. See: BAGD—751c; THAYER—576a.

4617. **σινιάζω** {1x} **siniazō**, *sin-ee-ad'-zo;* from σινίον **siniŏn**, (a sieve); to *riddle* (fig.):—sift {1x}.

Siniazo means to sift, shake in a sieve; figuratively, by inward agitation to try one's faith to the verge of overthrow (Lk 22:31). See: TDNT—7:291, 1028; BAGD—751d; THAYER—576b.

σῖτα **sita**.See *4621*.

4618. **σιτευτός** {3x} **sitĕutŏs**, *sit-yoo-tos';* from a der. of *4621; grain-fed,* i.e. *fattened:*—fatted {3x}.

The fatted calf was one isolated and grain-fed to fatten in order to secure tender meat for feasts, Lk 15:23, 37, 30. See: BAGD—752a; THAYER—576b.

4619. **σιτιστός** {1x} **sitistŏs**, *sit-is-tos';* from a der. of *4621; grained,* i.e. *fatted:*—fatling {1x}. See: BAGD—752a; THAYER—576b.

4620. **σιτομέτρον** {1x} **sitŏmĕtrŏn**, *sit-om'-et-ron;* from *4621* and *3358; a grain-measure,* i.e. (by impl.) *ration* (*allowance* of food):—portion of meat {1x}. See: BAGD—752a; THAYER—576b.

4621. **σῖτος** {14x} **sitŏs**, *see'-tos;* plur. irreg. neut.

σῖτα **sita**, *see'-tah;* of uncert. der.; *grain,* espec. *wheat:*—corn {2x}, wheat {12x}.

(1) *Sita* speaks of any grain in which is the hard seed of any cereal plant; especially wheat; [corn in Eng. is generic for grain]. **(2)** *Sitos* is "wheat, corn"; in the plural, "grain," is translated **(2a)** "corn" in Mk 4:28; Acts 7:12; and **(2b)** "wheat" in Mt 3:12; 13:25, 29–30; Lk 3:17; 16:7; 22:31; John 12:24; Acts 27:38; 1 Cor 15:37; Rev 6:6; 18:13. See: BAGD—752b; THAYER—576b.

4622. **Σιών** {7x} **Siōn**, *see-own';* of Heb. or. [6726]; *Sion* (i.e. *Tsijon*), a hill of Jerusalem; fig. the *Church* (militant or triumphant):—*Sion* {7x}. See: TDNT—7:292, 1028; BAGD—752b; THAYER—576c.

4623. **σιωπάω** {11x} **siōpaō**, *see-o-pah'-o;* from σιωπή **siōpē**, (*silence,* i.e. a *hush;* prop. *muteness,* i.e. *involuntary* stillness, or *inability* to speak; and thus differing from *4602,* which is rather a voluntary *refusal* or *indisposition* to speak, although the terms are often used synonymously); to *be dumb* (but not *deaf* also, like *2974* prop.); fig. to *be calm* (as *quiet* water):—hold (one's) peace {9x}, peace {1x}, dumb {1x}.

Siopao, "to be silent or still, to keep silence" (from *siope,* "silence"), is translated **(1)** "to hold one's peace," in Mt 20:31; 26:63; Mk 3:4; 4:39; 10:48; 14:61; Lk 18:39; 19:40; Acts 18:9; **(2)** in the Lord's command to the sea, in Mk 4:39, it is translated "peace (be still)"; **(3)** in Lk 1:20, "dumb", is used of Zacharias' "dumbness": "And, behold, thou shalt be dumb, and not able to speak, until the day that these things shall be performed, because thou believest not my words, which shall be fulfilled in their season." Syn.: 216, 880, 2974. See: BAGD—752c; THAYER—576d.

4624. **σκανδαλίζω** {30x} **skandalizō**, *skan-dal-id'-zo* ("scandalize"); from *4625;* to *entrap,* i.e. *trip* up (fig. *stumble* [tran.] or *entice* to sin, apostasy or displeasure):—make to offend {2x}, offend {28x}.

Skandalizo means **(1)** to put a stumbling block or impediment in the way, upon which another may trip and fall; **(1a)** metaph. to offend; **(1b)** to entice to sin; **(1c)** to cause a person to begin to distrust and desert one whom he ought to trust and obey; **(1c1)** to cause to fall away; **(1c2)** to be offended in one, i.e. to see in another what I disapprove of and what hinders me from acknowledging his authority; **(1c3)** to cause one to judge unfavorably or unjustly of another. **(2)** Since one who stumbles or whose foot gets entangled feels annoyed, *skandalizo* also means **(2a)** to cause one displeasure at a thing; or **(2b)** to make indignant. **(3)** It signifies "to put a snare or stumblingblock in the way," always **(3a)** metaphorically in the NT: **(3b)** 14 times in Mt, 8 in Mk, twice in Lk, twice in Jh; **(3c)** elsewhere in 1 Cor 8:13 (twice) and 2 Cor 11:29; Rom 14:21. See: TDNT—7:339, 1036; BAGD—752d; THAYER—576d.

4625. **σκάνδαλον** {15x} **skandalŏn**, *skan'-dal-on* ("scandal"); prob. from a der. of *2578;* a *trap-stick* (*bent* sapling), i.e. *snare* (fig. *cause* of displeasure or sin):—offence {9x}, stumbling block {3x}, occasion of stumbling {1x}, occasion to fall {1x}, thing that offends {1x}.

Skandalon, **(1)** originally was "the name of the part of a trap to which the bait is attached, hence, the trap or snare itself, as **(1a)** in Rom 11:9, "stumblingblock," quoted from Ps 69:22, and **(1b)** in Rev 2:14, for Balaam's device was rather a trap for Israel than a stumblingblock to them, and **(1c)** in Mt 16:23, for in Peter's words the Lord perceived a snare laid for Him by Satan. **(2)** In NT *skandalon* is always used metaphorically, and **(2a)** ordinarily of anything that arouses prejudice, or **(2b)** becomes a hindrance to others, or **(2c)** causes them to fall by the way. **(2d)** Sometimes the hindrance is in itself good, and those stumbled by it are the wicked. Thus it is used **(2d1)** of Christ in Rom 9:33, "(a rock) of offense"; cf. 1 Pet 2:8; 1 Cor 1:23, "stumblingblock"), and **(2d2)** of His cross, Gal 5:11; **(2d3)** of the "table" provided by God for Israel, Rom 11:9; **(2e)** of that which is evil, e.g., **(2e1)** Mt 13:41, "things that offend", lit., "all stumblingblocks"; **(2e2)** Mt 18:7, "occasions of stumbling" and "occasion"; Lk 17:1; **(2e3)** Rom 14:13, "an occasion to fall", said of such a use of Christian liberty as proves a hindrance to another; **(2e4)** Rom 16:17, "offences", said of the teaching of things contrary to sound doctrine; **(2e5)** 1 Jn 2:10, "occasion of stumbling," of the absence of this in the case of one who loves his brother and thereby abides in the light. Love, then, is the best safeguard against the woes pronounced by the Lord upon those who cause others to stumble. See: TDNT—7:339, 1036; BAGD—753a; THAYER—577a.

4626. **σκάπτω** {3x} **skaptō**, *skap'-to;* appar. a primary verb; to *dig:*—dig {3x}.

Skapto, primarily, "to dig, by way of hollowing out," hence, denotes "to dig." The root *skap* is seen in *skapane,* "a spade," *skapetos,* "a ditch," *skaphe,* "a boat," and in Eng., "scoop, skiff, and ship" (i.e., something hollowed out). The verb is found in Lk 6:48; 13:8; 16:3. See: BAGD—753b; THAYER—577b.

4627. **σκάφη** {3x} **skaphē**, *skaf'-ay;* a "*skiff*" (as if *dug* out), or *yawl* (carried aboard a large vessel for landing):—boat {3x}.

Skaphe is, lit., "anything dug or scooped out" (from *skapto,* "to dig"), "as a trough, a tub, and hence a light boat, or skiff, a boat belonging to a larger vessel," Acts 27:16, 30, 32. See: BAGD—753c; THAYER—577c.

4628. **σκέλος** {3x} **skĕlŏs**, *skel'-os;* appar. from σκέλλω **skĕllō**, (to *parch;* through the idea of *leanness*); the *leg* (as *lank*):—leg {3x}.

Skello, "the leg from the hip downwards," is used only of the breaking of the "legs" of the crucified malefactors, to hasten their death, Jn 19:31–33; a customary act, not carried out in the case of Christ, in fulfillment of Ex 12:46; Num 9:12. The practice was known as *skelokopia* (from *kopto,* "to strike"), or, in Latin, *crurifragium* (from *crus,* "a leg," and *frango,* "to break"). See: BAGD—753c; THAYER—577c.

4629. **σκέπασμα** {1x} **skĕpasma**, *skep'-as-mah;* from a der. of σκέπας **skĕpas** (a *covering;* perh. akin to the base of *4649,* through the idea of *noticeableness*); *clothing:*—raiment {1x}.

Skepasma, "a covering" (*skepazo,* "to cover"), strictly, "a roofing," then, "any kind of shelter or covering," is used in the plural in 1 Ti 6:8, "raiment", outer clothing which covers others. See: BAGD—753d; THAYER—577c.

4630. **Σκευᾶς** {1x} **Skĕuas**, *skyoo-as';* appar. of Lat. or.; *left-handed; Scevas* (i.e. *Scævus*), an Isr.:—Sceva {1x}. See: BAGD—753d; THAYER—577c.

4631. **σκευή** {1x} **skĕuē**, *skyoo-ay';* from *4632; furniture,* i.e. spare *tackle:*—tackling {1x}. See: BAGD—754a; THAYER—577c.

4632. **σκεῦος** {23x} **skĕuŏs**, *skyoo'-os;* of uncert. aff.; a *vessel, implement, equipment* or *apparatus* (lit. or fig. [spec. a *wife* as contributing to the usefulness of the husband]):—goods {2x}, sail {1x}, stuff {1x}, vessel {19x}.

Skeuos is used **(1)** of "a vessel or implement" of various kinds, Mk 11:16; Lk 8:16; Jn 19:29; Acts 10:11, 16; 11:5; 27:17 (a sail); Rom 9:21; 2 Ti 2:20; Heb 9:21; Rev 2:27; 18:12; **(2)** of "goods or household stuff," Mt 12:29 and Mk 3:27, "goods"; Lk 17:31, "stuff"; **(3)** of "persons," **(3a)** for the service of God, **(3a1)** Acts 9:15, "a (chosen) vessel"; **(3a2)** 2 Ti 2:21, "a vessel (unto honor)"; **(3b)** the "subjects" of divine wrath, Rom 9:22; **(3c)** the "subjects" of divine mercy, Rom 9:23; **(3d)** the human frame, **(3d1)** 2 Cor 4:7; **(3d2)** perhaps 1 Th 4:4; **(3d3)** a husband of his wife, 1 Pet 3:7; **(3d4)** of the wife, probably, 1 Th 4:4; **(3d5)** while the exhortation to each one "to possess himself of his own vessel in sanctification and honor" is regarded by some as referring to the believer's body [cf Rom 6:13; 1 Cor 9:27], the view that the "vessel" signifies the wife, and that the reference is to the sanctified maintenance of the married state, is supported by the facts that in 1 Pet 3:7 the same word *time,* "honor," is used with regard to the wife, again in Heb 13:4, *timios,* "honorable" is used in regard to marriage; further, the preceding command in 1 Th 4 is against fornication, and the succeeding one (v. 6) is against adultery. See: TDNT—7:358, 1038; BAGD—754a; THAYER—577c.

4633. **σκηνή** {20x} **skēnē**, *skay-nay';* appar. akin to *4632* and *4639;* a *tent* or cloth hut (lit. or fig.):—habitation {1x}, tabernacle {19x}.

Skene, "a tent, booth, tabernacle," is used of **(1)** tents as dwellings, Mt 17:4; Mk 9:5; Lk 9:33; Heb 11:9, "tabernacles"; **(2)** the Mosaic tabernacle, Acts 7:44; Heb 8:5; 9:8, 21, termed "tabernacle", where the people were called to meet God; the outer part 9:2, 6; the inner sanctuary, 9:3; **(3)** the heavenly prototype, Heb 8:2; 9:11; Rev 13:6; 15:5; 21:3 (of its future descent); **(4)** the eternal abodes of the saints, Lk 16:9, "habitations"; **(5)** the Temple in Jerusalem, as continuing the service of the tabernacle, Heb 13:10; **(6)** the house of David, i.e., metaphorically of his people, Acts 15:16; **(7)** the portable shrine of the god Moloch, Acts 7:43. See: TDNT—7:368, 1040; BAGD—754c; THAYER—577d.

4634. **σκηνοπηγία** {1x} **skēnŏpēgia**, *skay-nop-ayg-ee'-ah;* from *4636* and *4078;* the *Festival of Tabernacles* (so called from the custom of erecting booths for temporary homes):—tabernacles {1x}.

Skenopegia, properly "the setting up of tents or dwellings", represents the word "tabernacles" in "the feast of tabernacles," Jn 7:2. **NOTE:** This feast, one of the three Pilgrimage Feasts in Israel, is called "the feast of ingathering" in Ex 23:16; 34:22; it took place at the end of the year, and all males were to attend at the "tabernacle" with their offerings. In Lev 23:34; Deut 16:13, 16; 31:10; 2 Chr 8:13; Ezra 3:4 (cf. Neh 8:14–18), it is called "the feast of tabernacles" (or "booths," *sukkoth*), and was appointed for seven days at Jerusalem from the 15th to the 22nd Tishri (approximately October), to remind the people that their fathers dwelt in these in the wilderness journeys. Cf. Num 29:15–38, especially v. 35–38, for the regulations of the eighth or "last day, the great day of the feast" (Jn 7:37). See: TDNT—7:390, 1040; BAGD—754d; THAYER—578b.

4635. **σκηνοποιός** {1x} **skēnŏpŏiŏs**, *skay-nop-oy-os';* from *4633* and *4160;* a *manufacturer of tents:*—tent-maker {1x}. See: TDNT—7:393, 1040; BAGD—755a; THAYER—578c.

4636. **σκῆνος** {2x} **skēnŏs**, *skay'-nos;* from *4633;* a *hut* or temporary residence, i.e. (fig.) the human *body* (as the abode of the spirit):—tabernacle {2x}.

Skenos is used metaphorically of the body as the "tabernacle" of the soul, 2 Cor 5:1, 4; stressing the temporary nature of the body. See: TDNT—7:381, 1040; BAGD—755b; THAYER—578c.

4637. **σκηνόω** {5x} **skēnŏō**, *skay-nŏ'-o;* from *4636;* to *tent* or *encamp,* i.e. (fig.) to *occupy* (as a mansion) or (spec.) to *reside* (as God did in the Tabernacle of old, a symbol of protection and communion):—dwell {5x}.

Skenoo, "to pitch a tent" (*skene*), "to tabernacle," is translated **(1)** "dwelt," in Jn 1:14; **(2)** in Rev 7:15, "shall dwell"; **(3)** in Rev 12:12; 13:6; 21:3, "dwell." See: TDNT—7:385, 1040; BAGD—755c; THAYER—578c.

4638. **σκήνωμα** {3x} **skēnōma**, *skay'-no-mah;* from *4637;* an *encampment,* i.e. (fig.) the *Temple* (as God's residence), the *body* (as a tenement for the soul):—tabernacle {3x}.

Skenoma, "a booth," or "tent pitched", is used **(1)** of the Temple as God's dwelling, as that which David desired to build, Acts 7:46, "tabernacle"; and **(2)** metaphorically of the body as a temporary tabernacle, 2 Pet 1:13, 14. See: TDNT—7:383, 1040; BAGD—755c; THAYER—578d.

4639. **σκιά** {7x} **skia**, *skee-ah';* appar. a primary word; "*shade*" or a shadow (lit. or fig. [darkness of *error* or an *adumbration*]):—shadow {7x}.

Skia, is used **(1)** of "a shadow," **(1a)** caused by the interception of light, Mk 4:32; Acts 5:15; **(1b)** metaphorically of the darkness and spiritual death of ignorance, Mt 4:16; Lk 1:79; **(2)** of "the image" or "outline" cast by an object, **(2a)** Col 2:17, of ceremonies under the Law; **(2b)** of the tabernade and its appurtenances and offerings, Heb 8:5; **(3)** of these as appointed under the Law, Heb 10:1. See: TDNT—7:394, 1044; BAGD—755d; THAYER—578d.

4640. **σκιρτάω** {3x} **skirtaō**, *skeer-tah'-o;* akin to σκαίρω **skairō**, (to *skip*); to *jump,* i.e. sympathetically *move* (as the *quickening* of a fetus):—leap {2x}, leap for joy {1x}.

Skiptao, "to leap," is found **(1)** in Lk 1:4, and 6:23, there translated "leap for joy"; **(2)** in Lk 1:44 the words "for joy" are expressed separately. See: TDNT—7:401, 1046; BAGD—755d; THAYER—578d.

4641. **σκληροκαρδία** {3x} **sklērŏkardia**, *sklay-rok-ar-dee'-ah;* fem. of a compound of *4642* and *2588; hard-heartedness,* i.e. (spec.) *destitution of* (spiritual) *perception:*—hardness of heart {3x}.

Sklerokardia, "hardness of heart" (*skleros,* "hard," and *kardia*), is used in Mt 19:8; Mk 10:5; 16:14. See: TDNT—3:613, 415; BAGD—756a; THAYER—579a.

4642. **σκληρός** {6x} **sklērŏs**, *sklay-ros';* from the base of *4628; dry,* i.e. *hard* or *tough* (fig. *harsh, severe*):—fierce {1x}, hard {5x}.

(1) *Skleros* is applied to someone who takes a serious approach to life and is rough, harsh, inhuman, uncivil and intractable in his moral nature. **(2)** *Skleros* is used **(2a)** of the character of a man, Mt 25:24; **(2b)** of a saying, Jn 6:60; **(2c)** of the difficulty and pain of kicking against the ox-goads, Acts 9:5; 26:14; **(2d)** of rough winds, Jas 3:4 and **(2e)** of harsh speeches, Jude 15. **(3)** In Jas 3:4, *skleros,* "hard, rough, violent," is said of winds, "fierce." Syn.: Synonymous with *austeros* (840) but to be distinguished from it, is *skleros* (from *skello,* "to be dry"). *Austeros* was applied to that which lacks moisture, and so is rough and disageeable to the touch, and hence came to denote "harsh, stern, hard." It is used by Matthew to describe the unprofitable servant's remark concerning his master, in the parable corresponding to that in Luke 19. *Austeros* is derived from a word having to do with the taste, *skleros,* "with the touch." *Austeros* is not necessarily a term of reproach, whereas *skleros* is always so, and indicates a harsh, even inhuman character. *Austeros* is rather the exaggeration of a virtue pushed too far, than an absolute vice. See: TDNT—5:1028, 816; BAGD—756a; THAYER—579a.

4643. **σκληρότης** {1x} **sklērŏtēs**, *sklay-rot'-ace;* from *4642; callousness,* i.e. (fig.) *stubbornness:*—hardness {1x}. See: TDNT—5:1028, 816; BAGD—756b; THAYER—579a.

4644. **σκληροτράχηλος** {1x} **sklērŏtrachēlŏs**, *sklay-rot-rakh'-ay-los;* from *4642* and *5137; hardnaped,* i.e. (fig.) *obstinate:*—stiffnecked {1x}. See: TDNT—5:1029, 816; BAGD—756b; THAYER—579a.

4645. **σκληρύνω** {6x} **sklērunō**, *sklay-roo'-no;* from *4642;* to *indurate,* i.e. (fig.) *render stubborn:*—harden {6x}.

(1) This word stresses that the nape of the neck stiffens and thus renders the head in an unbending position. *Skleruno,* "to make dry or hard", is used **(2)** in Acts 19:9 of men hardened against the gospel; **(2a)** in Rom 9:18, illustrated by the case of Pharaoh, who first persistently "hardened" his heart (see Ex 7:13, 22; 8:19, all producing the retributive "hardening" by God, after His much long-suffering, 9:12); **(2b)** in Heb 3:8, 13, 15; 4:7, warnings against the "hardening" of the heart. See: TDNT—5:1030, 816; BAGD—756b; THAYER—579b.

4646. **σκολιός** {4x} **skŏliŏs**, *skol-ee-os';* from the base of *4628; warped,* i.e. *winding;* fig. *perverse:*—crooked {2x}, froward {1x}, untoward {1x}.

Skolios, "curved, crooked," was especially used **(1)** of a way, Lk 3:5, with spiritual import; **(2)** it is set in contrast to *orthos* and *euthus,* "straight"; metaphorically, of what is morally "crooked," perverse, froward, **(2a)** of people belonging to a particular generation, Acts 2:40, "untoward"; Phil 2:15; **(2b)** of tyrannical or unjust masters, 1 Pet 2:18, "froward"; in this sense it is set in contrast to *agathos,* "good." See: TDNT—7:403, 1046; BAGD—756b; THAYER—579b.

4647. **σκόλοψ** {1x} **skŏlŏps**, *skol'-ops;* perh. from the base of *4628* and *3700; withered* at the *front,* i.e. a *point* or *prickle* (fig. a bodily *annoyance* or *disability*):—thorn {1x}.

Skolops, as a noun, originally denoted "anything pointed" and is used **(1)** 2 Cor 12:7, of the apostle's "thorn in the flesh." **(2)** His language indicates that it was physical, painful, humiliating. **(3)** It was also the effect of divinely permitted Satanic antagonism. **(4)** The verbs are in the present tense, signifying recurrent action, indicating a constantly repeated attack. **(5)** What is stressed is not the metaphorical size, but the acuteness of the suffering and its effects. **(6)** Attempts to connect this with the circumstances of Acts 14:19 and Gal 4:13 are speculative. Syn.: 173, 174.See: TDNT—7:409, 1047; BAGD—756c; THAYER—579b.

4648. **σκοπέω** {6x} **skŏpĕō**, *skop-eh'-o;* from *4649;* to take *aim* at (*spy*), i.e. (fig.) *regard:*—consider {1x}, take heed {1x}, look at {1x}, look on {1x}, mark {2x}.

Skopeo, as a verb, means "to look at, consider" [Eng., "scope"], implying mental consideration, and is rendered **(1)** "while we look . . . at": "While we look not at the things which are seen, but at the things which are not seen" (2 Cor 4:18); and **(2)** "looking on": "Look not every man on (*skopeo*) his own things, but every man also on the things of others" (Phil 2:4). **(3)** It is translated "mark" in **(3a)** Rom 16:17, of a warning against those who cause divisions, and **(3b)** in Phil 3:17, of observing those who walked after the example of the apostle and his fellow workers, so as to follow their ways. **(4)** In Lk 11:35, "to look," is translated "take heed (that)." **(5)** It is translated "consider" in Gal 6:1. Syn.: 308, 352, 578, 816, 872, 991, 1689, 1896, 1914, 1980, 1983, 2300, 2334, 3706, 3708, 3879, 4017. See: TDNT—7:414, 1047; BAGD—756d; THAYER—579a. comp. *3700.*

4649. **σκοπός** {1x} **skŏpŏs**, *skop-os'* ("scope"); from σκέπτομαι **skĕptŏmai** (to *peer* about ["skeptic"]; perh. akin to *4626* through the idea of *concealment;* comp. *4629*); a *watch* (*sentry* or *scout*), i.e. (by impl.) a *goal:*—mark {1x}.

Skopos is primarily a watcher (Eng., scope) denoting a mark on which to fix the eye and is used metaphorically of an aim or object (Phil 3:14). See: TDNT—7:413, 1047; BAGD—756d; THAYER—579c.

4650. **σκορπίζω** {5x} **skŏrpizō**, *skor-pid'-zo;* appar. from the same as *4651* (through the idea of *penetrating*); to *dissipate,* i.e. (fig.) *put to flight, waste, be liberal:*—disperse abroad {1x}, scatter {3x}, scatter abroad {1x}.

Skorpizo means "to scatter" (probably from a root, *skarp-,* signifying "to cut asunder," akin to *skorpios,* "a scorpion"), and is used **(1)** in Mt 12:30, "scattereth abroad"; **(2)** "scatter" in Lk 11:23; Jn 10:12; 16:32; **(3)** and in 2 Cor 9:9, "he hath dispersed abroad." See: TDNT—7:418, 1048; BAGD—757a; THAYER—579c.

4651. **σκορπίος** {5x} **skŏrpiŏs**, *skor-pee'-os;* prob. from an obs. σκέρπω **skĕrpō** (perh. strengthened from the base of *4649,* and mean. to *pierce*); a "*scorpion*" (from its *sting*):—scorpion {5x}.

The *skorpios* is **(1)** a small animal (the largest of the several species is 6 in. long) like a lobster, but with a long tail, at the end of which is its venomous sting; the pain, the position of the sting, and the effect are mentioned in Rev 9:3, 5, 10. **(2)** The Lord's rhetorical question as to the provision of a scorpion instead of an egg (Lk 11:12), is **(2a)** an allusion to the egg-like shape of the creature when at rest; and **(2b)** an indication of the abhorrence with which it is regarded. **(3)** In Lk 10:19 the Lord's assurance to the disciples of the authority given them by Him to tread upon serpents and scorpions **(3a)** conveys the thought of victory over spiritually antagonistic forces, the powers of darkness, **(3b)** as is shown by His reference to the power of the enemy and by the context (Lk 10:17, 20). See: BAGD—757a; THAYER—579d.

4652. **σκοτεινός** {3x} **skŏtĕinŏs**, *skot-i-nos';* from *4655; opaque,* i.e. (fig.) *benighted:*—dark {1x}, full of darkness {2x}.

Skotemos, "full of darkness, or covered with darkness," is **(1)** translated "dark" in Lk 11:36; **(2)** "full of darkness" in Mt 6:23 and Lk 11:34, where the physical condition is figurative of the moral. See: TDNT—7:423, 1049; BAGD—757b; THAYER—579d.

4653. **σκοτία** {16x} **skŏtia**, *skot-ee'-ah;* from *4655; dimness, obscurity* (lit. or fig.):—dark {2x}, darkness {14x}.

Skotia is used **(1)** of physical darkness, "dark," Jn 6:17, lit., "darkness had come on," and 20:1, lit., "darkness still being"; **(2)** of secrecy, in general, whether what is done therein is good or evil, Mt 10:27; Lk 12:3; **(3)** of spiritual or moral "darkness," emblematic of sin, as a condition of moral or spiritual depravity, Mt 4:16; Jn 1:5; 8:12; 12:35, 46; 1 Jn 1:5; 2:8–9, 11. See: TDNT—7:423, 1049; BAGD—757b; THAYER—580a.

4654. **σκοτίζω** {8x} **skŏtizō**, *skot-id-zo;* from *4655;* to deprive of light, to *obscure* (lit. or fig.):—darken {8x}.

Skotizo, "to deprive of light, to make dark," is used in the NT in the passive voice only, **(1)** of the heavenly bodies Mt 24:29; Mk 13:24; Rev 8:12; **(2)** metaphorically, **(2a)** of the mind, Rom 1:21; 11:10; Lk 23:45. See: TDNT—7:423, 1049; BAGD—757c; THAYER—580a.

4655. **σκότος** {32x} **skŏtŏs**, *skot'-os;* from the base of *4639; shadiness,* i.e. *obscurity* (lit. or fig.):—darkness {32x}.

(1) *Skotos* is the exact opposite of *phos* (5457—light). It is a neuter noun used in the NT as the equivalent of *skotia* (4653): **(1)** of "physical darkness," Mt 27:45; 2 Cor 4:6; **(2)** of "intellectual darkness," Rom 2:19; **(3)** of "blindness," Acts 13:11; **(4)** by metonymy, of the "place of punishment," e.g., Mt 8:12; 2 Pet 2:17; Jude 13; **(5)** metaphorically, of "moral and spiritual darkness," e.g., Mt 6:23; Lk 1:79; 11:35; Jn 3:19; Acts 26:18; 2 Cor 6:14; Eph 6:12; Col 1:13; 1 Th. 5:4–5; 1 Pet 2:9; 1 Jn 1:6; **(6)** by metonymy, of "those who are in moral or spiritual darkness," Eph 5:8; **(7)** of "evil works," Rom 13:12; **(8)** Eph 5:11, of the "evil powers that dominate the world"; **(9)** Lk 22:53 "of secrecy." **(10)** While *skotos* is used more than twice as many times as *skotia* in the NT, **(10a)** the apostle John uses *skotos* only once, 1 Jn 1:6, but *skotia* 15 times out of the 18. **(10b)** With the exception of the significance of secrecy, darkness is always used in a bad sense. Moreover the different forms of darkness are so closely allied, being either cause and effect, or else concurrent effects of the same cause, that they cannot always be distinguished; 1 Jn 1:5; 2:8, e.g., are passages in which both spiritual and moral darkness are intended. Syn.: 887, 1105, 2217. See: TDNT—7:423, 1049; BAGD—757c; THAYER—580b.

4656. **σκοτόω** {1x} **skŏtŏō**, *skot-ŏ'-o;* from *4655;* to *obscure* or *blind* (lit. or fig.):—be full of darkness {1x}. See: TDNT—7:423, 1049; BAGD—758a; THAYER—580c.

4657. **σκύβαλον** {1x} **skubalŏn**, *skoo'-bal-on;* neut. of a presumed der. of *1519* and *2965* and *906;* what is *thrown to* the *dogs,* i.e. *refuse* (*ordure*):—dung {1x}.

Skubalon denotes "refuse," whether **(1)** "excrement," that which is cast out from the body, or **(2)** "the leavings of a feast," that which is thrown away from the table. Judaizers counted gentile Christians as dogs, while they themselves were seated at God's banquet. The apostle, reversing the image, counts the Judaistic ordinances as refuse upon which their advocates feed, Phil 3:8. See: TDNT—7:445, 1052; BAGD—758a; THAYER—580c.

4658. **Σκύθης** {1x} **Skuthēs**, *skoo'-thace;* prob. of for. or.; a *Scythene* or *Scythian,* i.e. (by impl.) a *savage:*—Scythian {1x}. See: TDNT—7:447, 1053; BAGD—758b; THAYER—580c.

4659. **σκυθρωπός** {2x} **skuthrōpŏs**, *skoo-thro-pos';* from σκυθρός **skuthrŏs**, (*sullen*) and a der. of *3700; angry-visaged,* i.e. *gloomy* or affecting a *mournful* appearance:—of a sad countenance {1x}, sad {1x}.

This word describes **(1)** the Emmaus road travelers, Lk 24:17; and **(2)** the sad countenance of the hypocritical faster, Mt 6:16. See: TDNT—7:450, 1053; BAGD—758b; THAYER—580c.

4660. **σκύλλω** {3x} **skullō**, *skool'-lo;* appar. a primary verb; to *flay,* i.e. (fig.) to *harass:*—trouble {2x}, trouble (one's) self {1x}.

Skullo, as a verb, primarily signifies **(1)** "to skin, to flay"; then **(1a)** "to rend, mangle"; hence, **(1b)** "to vex, trouble, annoy": "While He yet spake, there came from the ruler of the synagogue's *house certain* which said, Thy daughter is dead: why troublest (*skullo*) thou the Master any further?" (Mk 5:35; cf. Lk 7:6; 8:49). Syn.: 318, 928, 2347, 2669, 4729, 4730, 4928. See: BAGD—758b; THAYER—580d.

4661. **σκῦλον** {1x} **skulŏn**, *skoo'-lon;* neut. from *4660;* something *stripped* (as a *hide*), i.e. *booty:*—spoils {1x}.

Skulon are the weapons and valuables stripped off from an enemy, "spoils", Lk 11:22. See: BAGD—758b; THAYER—580d.

4662. **σκωληκόβρωτος** {1x} **skōlēkŏbrōtŏs**, *sko-lay-kob'-ro-tos;* from *4663* and a der. of *977; worm-eaten,* i.e. *diseased with maggots:*—eaten of worms {1x}. See: TDNT—7:456, 1054; BAGD—758c; THAYER—580d.

4663. **σκώληξ** {3x} **skōlēx**, *sko'-lakes;* of uncert. der.; a *grub, maggot* or *earthworm:*—worm {3x}.

A *skolex* is a worm, specifically that kind which preys upon dead bodies (Mk 9:44, 46, 48). See: TDNT—7:452, 1054; BAGD—758c; THAYER—580d.

4664. **σμαράγδινος** {1x} **smaragdinŏs**, *smar-ag'-dee-nos;* from *4665;* consisting *of emerald:*—emerald {1x}.

This word denotes consisting of emerald green in color and character and is descriptive of the rainbow round about the throne (Rev 4:3). See: BAGD—758c; THAYER—581a.

4665. **σμάραγδος** {1x} **smaragdŏs**, *smar'-ag-dos;* of uncert. der.; the *emerald* or green gem so called:—emerald {1x}.

This is a transparent precious stone noted especially for its light green color occupying the first place in the second row on the high priest's breastplate, Ex 28:18. Tyre imported it from Syria, Eze 27:16. It is one of the foundations of the heavenly Jerusalem, Rev. 21:19. The name was applied to other stones of a similar character, such as the carbuncle. See: BAGD—758c; THAYER—581a.

4666. **σμύρνα** {2x} **smurna**, *smoor'-nah;* appar. strengthened for *3464; myrrh:*—myrrh {2x}.

Smurna, whence the name "Smyrna," a word of Semitic origin, Heb., *mor,* from a root meaning "bitter," is **(1)** a gum resin from a shrubby tree, which grows in Yemen and neighboring regions of Africa; **(2)** the fruit is smooth and somewhat larger than a pea. **(3)** The color of myrrh varies from pale reddish-yellow to reddish-brown or red. **(4)** The taste is bitter, and the substance astringent, acting as an antiseptic and a stimulant. **(5)** It was used as a perfume, Ps 45:8, where the language is symbolic of the graces of the Messiah; Prov 7:17; Song 1:13; 5:5; **(6)** it was one of the ingredients of the "holy anointing oil" for the priests, Ex 30:23; **(7)** it was used also for the purification of women, Est 2:12; **(8)** for embalming, John 19:39; **(9)** it was one of the gifts of the Magi, Mt 2:11. See: TDNT—7:457, 1055; BAGD—758d; THAYER—581a.

4667. **Σμύρνα** {1x} **Smurna**, *smoor'-nah;* the same as *4666; Smyrna,* a place in Asia Minor:—Smyrna {1x}. See: BAGD—759a; THAYER—581a.

4668. **Σμυρναῖος** {1x} **Smurnaiŏs**, *smoor-nah'-yos;* from *4667;* a *Smyrnæan:*—in Smyrna {1x}. See: BAGD—759a; THAYER—581b.

4669. **σμυρνίζω** {1x} **smurnizō**, *smoor-nid'-zo;* from *4667;* to *tincture with myrrh,* i.e. *embitter* (as a narcotic):—mingle with myrrh {1x}.

Smurnizo is used transitively in the NT, with the meaning **(1)** "to mingle or drug with myrrh," Mk 15:23; **(2)** the mixture was doubtless offered to deaden the pain; **(3)** Matthew's word "gall" suggests that "myrrh" was not the only ingredient. **(4)** Christ refused to partake of any such means of alleviation; He would retain all His mental power for the complete fulfillment of the Father's will. See: TDNT—7:458, 1055; BAGD—759a; THAYER—581b.

4670. **Σόδομα** {10x} **Sŏdŏma**, *sod'-om-ah;* plur. of Heb. or. [5467]; *Sodoma* (i.e. *Sedom*), a place in Pal.:—Sodom {9x}, Sodoma {1x}. See: BAGD—759a; THAYER—581b.

4671. **σοί** {221x} **sŏi**, *soy;* dat. of *4771; to thee:*—thee {200x}, thou {14x}, thy {4x}, thine own {1x}, not tr {2x}. See: BAGD—772a [4771]; THAYER—591c [4771].

4672. **Σολομών** or **Σολομῶν** {12x} **Sŏlŏmōn**, *sol-om-one';* of Heb. or. [8010]; *Solomon* (i.e. *Shelomoh*), the son of David:—*Solomon* {12x}. See: TDNT—7:459, 1055; BAGD—759b; THAYER—581b.

4673. **σορός** {1x} **sŏrŏs**, *sor-os';* prob. akin to the base of *4987;* a *funereal receptacle* (*urn, coffin*), i.e. (by anal.) a *bier:*—bier {1x}.

Soros **(1)** originally denoted a receptacle for containing the bones of the dead, "a cinerary urn"; **(2)** then "a coffin," Gen 50:26; Job 21:32; **(3)** then, "the funeral couch or bier" on which the Jews bore their dead to burial, Lk 7:14. See: BAGD—759b; THAYER—581c.

4674. **σός** {27x} **sŏs**, *sos;* from *4771; thine:*—thy {13x}, thine {9x}, thine own {3x}, thy goods {1x}, thy friends {1x}. See: BAGD—759b; THAYER—581c.

4675. **σοῦ** { {498x} **sŏu**, *soo;* gen. of *4771; of thee, thy:*—thy {358x}, thee {76x}, thine {50x}, thine own {7x}, thou {6x}, not tr {1x}. See: BAGD—772a [4771]; THAYER—591c [4771].

4676. **σουδάριον** {4x} **sŏudariŏn**, *soo-dar'-ee-on;* of Lat. or.; a *sudarium* (*sweat-cloth*), i.e. *towel* (for wiping the perspiration from the face, or binding the face of a corpse):—handkerchief {1x}, napkin {3x}.

Soudarion, a Latin word, *sudarium* (from *sudor,* "sweat"), denotes **(1)** "a cloth for wiping the face," etc., Lk 19:20, "napkin"; Acts 19:12, "handkerchief"; **(2)** "a headcovering for the dead," Jn 11:44, "napkin"; 20:7, "napkin." **(3)** In Lk 19:20 the reference may be to a towel or any kind of linen cloth or even a sort of headdress, any of which might be used for concealing money. See: BAGD—759c; THAYER—581c.

4677. **Σουσάννα** {1x} **Sŏusanna**, *soo-san'-nah;* of Heb. or. [7799 fem.]; *lily; Susannah* (i.e. *Shoshannah*), an Israelitess:—Susanna {1x}. See: BAGD—759c; THAYER—581d.

4678. **σοφία** {51x} **sŏphia**, *sof-ee'-ah;* from *4680; wisdom* (higher or lower, worldly or spiritual):—wisdom {51x}.

Sophia means **(1)** broad and full of intelligence; it is used of the knowledge of very diverse matters. There is **(2)** the wisdom which belongs to men, human wisdom (Lk 2:40, 52); specifically **(2a)** varied knowledge of things human and divine, acquired by acuteness and experience, and summed up in maxims and proverbs (Mt 12:42); **(2b)** science and learning (Acts 7:22); **(2c)** the act of interpreting dreams and always giving the sagest advice (Acts 7:10); **(2d)** the intelligence evinced in discovering the meaning of some mysterious number or vision (Rev 13:18; 17:9); **(2e)** skill in the management of affairs (Acts 6:3); **(2f)** devout and proper prudence in intercourse with men not disciples of Christ (Col 4:5); **(2g)** skill and discretion in imparting Christian truth (Col 1:28; 3:16); and **(2h)** the knowledge and practice of the requisites for godly and upright living (Jas 1:5; 3:13, 17). *Sophia* also includes **(3)** supreme intelligence, such as belongs **(3a)** to God (Rom 16:27), and **(3b)** to Christ (Jude 25). **(4)** This word also denotes the wisdom of God as evinced in forming and executing counsels in the formation and government of the world and the scriptures (Rom 11:33).

(5) It is used with reference **(5a)** to God, Rom 11:33; 1 Cor 1:21, 24; 2:7; Eph 3:10; Rev 7:12; **(5b)** Christ, Mt 13:54; Mk 6:2; Lk 2:40, 52; 1 Cor 1:30; Col 2:3; Rev 5:12; **(5c)** "wisdom" personified, Mt 11:19; Lk 7:35; 11:49; **(5d)** human "wisdom" **(5d1)** in spiritual things, Lk 21:15; Acts 6:3, 10; 7:10; 1 Cor 2:6 (1st part); 12:8; Eph 1:8, 17; Col 1:9, "(spiritual) wisdom," 28; 3:16; 4:5; Jas 1:5; 3:13, 17; 2 Pet 3:15; Rev 13:18; 17:9; **(5d2)** in the natural sphere, Mt 12:42; Lk 11:31; Acts 7:22; 1 Cor 1:17, 19, 20, 21 (twice), 22; 2:1, 4, 5, 6 (2nd part), 13; 3:19; 2 Cor 1:12; Col 2:23; **(5d3)** in its most debased form, Jas 3:15, "earthly, sensual, devilish." Syn.: **(A)** *Gnosis* (1108) denotes knowledge by itself, chiefly to the apprehension of truths. **(B)** *Epignosis* (1922) is greater and more accurate knowledge; complete comprehension which is intuitive and perfect (1 Cor 13:12). **(C)** *Sophia* (4678) denotes a mental excellence of the highest sense, to details with wisdom as exhibited in action, and adding the power of reasoning about wisdom's details by tracing their relationships. **(D)** *Sunesis* (4907) stresses the critical, apprehending and the bearing of things. **(E)** *Phronesis* (5428) is practical, suggesting lines of action. See also: 1922. See: TDNT—7:465, 1056; BAGD—581d; THAYER—581d.

4679. **σοφίζω** {2x} **sŏphizō**, *sof-id'-zo;* from *4680;* to *render wise;* in a sinister acceptation, to *form "sophisms",* i.e. *continue plausible error:*—cunningly devised {1x}, make wise {1x}.

Sophizo from *sophos,* "wise" **(1)** in the active voice signifies "to make wise," 2 Ti 3:15. **(2)** In the middle voice it means "to play the sophist, to devise cleverly", it is used with this meaning in the passive voice in 2 Pet 1:16, "cunningly devised fables." See: TDNT—7:527, 1056; BAGD—760b; THAYER—582c.

4680. **σοφός** {22x} **sŏphŏs**, *sof-os';* akin to σαφής **saphēs**, (*clear*); *wise* (in a most gen. application):—wise {22x}.

Sophos is used of **(1)** God, Rom 16:27; 1 Ti 1:17; Jude 25; **(2)** the comparative degree, *sophoteros,* occurs in 1 Cor 1:25, where "foolishness" is simply in the human estimate; **(3)** spiritual teachers in Israel, Mt 23:34; **(4)** believers endowed with spiritual and practical wisdom, Rom 16:19; 1 Cor 3:10; 6:5; Eph 5:15; Jas 3:13; **(4)** Jewish teachers in the time of Christ, Mt 11:25; Lk 10:21; **(5)** the naturally learned, Rom

1:14, 22; 1 Cor 1:19, 20, 26, 27; 3:15–20. Syn.: **(A)** *Sophos* denotes one who is wise, skilled, an expert. **(B)** *Sunetos* (4908) means intelligent, and denotes one who can put things together, who has insight and comprehension. **(C)** *Phronimos* (5429) means prudent, and denotes primarily one who has quick and correct perceptions; hence, discreet, circumspect. See: TDNT—7:465, 1056; BAGD—760b; THAYER—582c.

4681. **Σπανία** {2x} **Spania**, *span-ee'-ah;* prob. of for. or.; *Spania*, a region of Europe:—Spain {2x}. See: BAGD—760c; THAYER—582d.

4682. **σπαράσσω** {4x} **sparassō**, *spar-as'-so;* prol. from σπαίρω **spairō** (to *gasp;* appar. strengthened from *4685*, through the idea of *spasmodic* contraction); to *mangle*, i.e. *convulse* with epilepsy:—rend {1x}, tear {3x}.

Sparasso denotes **(1)** "to tear, convulse" in Mk 1:26; 9:20, 26; **(2)** "rent" in Lk 9:39. See: BAGD—760d; THAYER—582d.

4683. **σπαργανόω** {2x} **sparganŏō**, *spar-gan-ŏ'-o;* from σπάργανον **sparganŏn**, (a *strip;* from a der. of the base of *4682* mean. to *strap* or *wrap* with strips); to *swathe* (an infant after the Oriental custom):—wrap in swaddling clothes {2x}.

Sparganoo, "to swathe" (from *sparganon*, "a swathing band"), signifies "to wrap in swaddling clothes" in Lk 2:7, 12. The idea that the word means "rags" is without foundation. See: BAGD—760d; THAYER—582d.

4684. **σπαταλάω** {2x} **spatalaō**, *spat-al-ah'-o;* from σπατάλη **spatalē**, (*luxury*); to *be voluptuous:*—live in pleasure {1x}, be wanton {1x}.

Wanton means undisciplined. **(1)** *Spatalao* concerns extravagance and wastefulness. This word means "to live riotously," and is translated **(1)** "liveth in pleasure" in 1 Ti 5:6; **(2)** "been wanton" in Jas 5:5. Syn.: **(A)** *Spatalao* is pictured by the prodigal son (Lk 15:13); **(B)** *tryphao* (5171) by the rich man who fared sumptuously every day (Lk 16:19), and **(C)** *strenao* (4763) by the Great Whore, Babylon, who "lived deliciously", Rev 18:7, 9. See: BAGD—761a; THAYER—583a.

4685. **σπάω** {2x} **spaō**, *spah'-o;* a primary verb; to *draw:*—draw {1x}, draw out {1x}.

Spao, as a verb, means "to draw or pull" and is used, in the middle voice of "drawing" a sword from its sheath (Mk 14:47; Acts 16:27). Syn.: 307, 385, 392, 501, 502, 645, 868, 1448, 1670, 1828, 2020, 4264, 4317, 4334, 4358, 4951, 5288, 5289. See: BAGD—761a; THAYER—583a.

4686. **σπεῖρα** {7x} **spĕira**, *spi'-rah;* of immed. Lat. or., but ultimately a der. of *138* in the sense of its cognate *1507;* a *coil* (*spira*, "spire"), i.e. (fig.) a *mass* of men (a Rom. military *cohort;* also [by anal.] a *squad* of Levitical janitors):—band {7x}.

(1) Band, generically, means that which is sufficient to completely surround and accomplish the job assigned. **(2)** *Speira*, primarily "anything round," and so "whatever might be wrapped round a thing, a twisted rope," came to mean "a body of men at arms," and was the equivalent of the Roman *manipulus*. It was also used for a larger body of men, a cohort, about 600 infantry, commanded by a tribune. It is confined to its military sense. It is used for a "band" **(1)** of soldiers in Mt 27:27; Mk 15:16; Acts 10:1; 21:31; 27:1; and **(2)** of men in Jn 18:3; 18:12. See, e.g., Matt. 27:27 See: BAGD—761a; THAYER—583a.

4687. **σπείρω** {54x} **spĕirō**, *spi'-ro;* prob. strengthened from *4685* (through the idea of *extending*); to *scatter*, i.e. *sow* (lit. or fig.):—sower {44x}, sower {6x}, receive seed {4x}.

Speiro, "to sow seed," is used **(1)** literally, especially in the Synoptic Gospels; elsewhere, 1 Cor 15:36, 37; 2 Cor 9:10, "the sower", **(2)** metaphorically, **(2a)** in proverbial sayings, e.g., Mt 13:3, 4; Lk 19:21, 22; Jn 4:37; 2 Cor 9:6; **(2b)** in the interpretation of parables, e.g., Mt 13:19–23 (in these vv., "received seed"); **(2c)** otherwise as follows: **(2c1)** of "sowing" spiritual things in preaching and teaching, 1 Cor 9:11; **(2c2)** of the interment of the bodies of deceased believers, 1 Cor 15:42–44; **(2c3)** of ministering to the necessities of others in things temporal (the harvest being proportionate to the "sowing"), 2 Cor 9:6, 10; **(2c4)** of "sowing" to the flesh, Gal 6:7, 8 ("that" in v. 7 is emphatic, "that and that only," what was actually "sown"); in v. 8, *eis*, "unto," signifies "in the interests of"; **(2c5)** of the "fruit of righteousness" by peacemakers, Jas 3:18. See: TDNT—7:536, 1065; BAGD—761b; THAYER—583b.

4688. **σπεκουλάτωρ** {1x} **spĕkŏulatōr**, *spek-oo-lat'-ore;* of Lat. or.; a *speculator*, i.e. military *scout* (*spy* or [by extens.] *life-guardsman*):—executioner {1x}.

Spekoulator, primarily denotes a lookout officer, or "scout; but, under the emperors, a member of the bodyguard [one who looked out for the welfare of his superior and had the power of execution]; these were employed as messengers, watchers and executioners; ten such officers were attached to each legion; such a guard was employed by Herod Antipas, (Mk 6:27). See: BAGD—761c; THAYER—583c.

4689. **σπένδω** {2x} **spĕndō**, *spen'-do;* appar. a primary verb; to *pour* out as a libation, i.e. (fig.) to *devote* (one's life or blood, as a sacrifice) ("*spend*"):—be ready to be offered {1x}, be offered {1x}.

Spendo, "to pour out as a drink offering, make a libation," is used **(1)** figuratively in the passive voice in Phil 2:17, "be offered." **(2)** In 2 Ti 4:6, "I am already being offered", the apostle is referring to his approaching death, upon the sacrifice of his ministry. See: TDNT—7:528,*; BAGD—761c; THAYER—583d.

4690. **σπέρμα** {44x} **spĕrma**, *sper'-mah;* from *4687;* something *sown*, i.e. *seed* (incl. the male "*sperm*"); by impl. *offspring;* spec. a *remnant* (fig. as if kept over for planting):—issue {1x}, seed {43x}.

Sperma,. akin to *speiro*, "to sow" (Eng., "sperm," "spermatic," etc.), has the following usages, **(1)** agricultural and botanical, e.g., Mt 13:24, 27, 32; 1 Cor 15:38; 2 Cor 9:10; **(2)** physiological, Heb 11:11;

(3) metaphorical and by metonymy for "offspring, posterity," **(3a)** of natural offspring, e.g., Mt 22:24, 25, "issue"; Jn 7:42; 8:33, 37; Acts 3:25; Rom 1:3; 4:13, 16, 18; 9:7 (twice), 8, 29; 11:1; 2 Cor 11:22; Heb 2:16; 11:18; Rev 12:17; Gal 3:16, 19, 29; **(3b)** Gal 3:16 "He saith not, And to seeds, as of many; but as of one, And to thy seed, which is Christ," **(3b1)** quoted from Gen 13:15 and 17:7, 8, there is especial stress on the word "seed," as referring to an individual (here, Christ) in fulfillment of the promises to Abraham—a unique use of the singular. **(3b2)** While the plural form "seeds," promises to Abraham—a unique use of the singular. **(3b3)** While the plural form "seeds," neither in Hebrew nor in Greek, would have been natural any more than in English (it is not so used in Scripture of human offspring; its plural occurrence is in 1 Sa 8:15, of crops), **(3b4)** yet if the divine intention had been to refer to Abraham's natural descendants, another word could have been chosen in the plural, such as "children"; **(3b5)** all such words were, however, set aside, "seed" being selected as one that could be used in the singular, with the purpose of showing that the "seed" was Messiah. **(3b6)** Some of the rabbis had even regarded "seed," e.g., in Gen 4:25 and Is 53:10, as referring to the Coming One. **(3b7)** Descendants were given to Abraham by other than natural means, so that through him Messiah might come, and the point of the apostle's argument is that since the fulfillment of the promises of God is secured alone by Christ, they only who are "in Christ" can receive them;

(4) of spiritual offspring, **(4a)** Rom 4:16, 18; 9:8; here "the children of the promise are reckoned for a seed" points, firstly, to Isaac's birth as being not according to the ordinary course of nature but by divine promise, and, secondly, by analogy, to the fact that all believers are children of God by spiritual birth; Gal 3:29. **(4b)** As to 1 Jn 3:9, "his seed abideth in him," it is possible to understand this as meaning that children of God (His "seed") abide in Him, and "doth not commit sin." The present tense signifies continually sinning. Alternatively, the "seed" signifies the principle of spiritual life as imparted to the believer, which abides in him without possibility of removal or extinction; the child of God remains eternally related to Christ, he who lives in sin has never become so related, he has not the principle of life in him. This meaning suits the context and the general tenor of the Epistle. See: TDNT—7:536, 1065; BAGD—761d; THAYER—583d.

4691. **σπερμολόγος** {1x} **spĕrmŏlŏgŏs**, *sper-mol-og'-os;* from *4690* and *3004;* a *seed-picker* (as the crow), i.e. (fig.) a *sponger, loafer* (spec. a *gossip* or *trifler* in talk):—babbler {1x}.

This word is translated "a babbler" in Acts 17:18. Primarily an adjective, **(1)** it came to be used as a noun signifying a crow, or some other bird, picking up seeds. **(2)** Then it seems to have been used of a man accustomed to hang about the streets and markets, picking up scraps which fall from loads; hence a parasite, who lives at the expense of others, a hanger on. **(3)** Metaphorically it became used of a man who picks up scraps of information and retails them secondhand, a plagiarist, or of those who make a show, in unscientific style, of knowledge obtained from misunderstanding lectures. See: BAGD—762b; THAYER—584b.

4692. **σπεύδω** {6x} **spĕudō**, *spyoo'-do;* prob. strengthened from *4228;* to "*speed*" ("study"), i.e. *urge* on (diligently or earnestly); by impl. to *await* eagerly:—make haste {3x}, haste {1x}, haste unto {1x}, with haste {1x}.

Speudo denotes **(1)** intransitively, "with haste" in Lk 2:16; 19:5, "make haste"; 19:6, "made haste"; Acts 20:16, "he hasted"; 22:18, "Make haste"; **(2)** transitively, "to desire earnestly, hasting" in 2 Pet 3:12, "hasting unto" (the day of God), i.e., in our practical fellowship with God as those who are appointed by Him as instruments through prayer and service for the accomplishment of His purposes, purposes which will be unthwartably fulfilled both in time and manner of accomplishment. In this way the earnest desire will find its fulfillment. See: BAGD—762b; THAYER—584b.

4693. **σπήλαιον** {6x} **spēlaiŏn**, *spay'-lah-yon;* neut. of a presumed der. of σπέος **spĕŏs** (a *grotto*); a *cavern;* by impl. a *hiding-place* or *resort:*—cave {1x}, den {5x}.

Spelaion, "a grotto, cavern, den" (Lat., *spelunca*), **(1)** "cave" in Jn 11:38, is said of the grave of Lazarus; **(2)** "dens" in Heb 11:38 and Rev 6:15; **(3)** in the Lord's rebuke concerning the defilement of the Temple, Mt 21:13; Mk 11:17; Lk 19:46, "den" is used. See: BAGD—762c; THAYER—582c.

4694. **σπιλάς** {1x} **spilas**, *spee-las';* of uncert. der.; a *ledge* or *reef* of rock in the sea:—spot {1x}.

A *spilas* is a rock or reef over which the sea dashes (Jude 12), spots metaphorically stressing the quick, unsuspecting, and pointed destruction upon the life of a believer, rendered by men whose conduct is a danger to others. See: BAGD—762c; THAYER—584c.

4695. **σπίλος** {2x} **spilŏs**, *spee'-los;* of uncert. der.; a *stain* or *blemish,* i.e. (fig.) *defect, disgrace:*—spot {1x}, defile {1x}.

Spilos, "a spot or stain," is used metaphorically **(1)** of moral blemish, Eph 5:27; **(2)** of lascivious and riotous persons, 2 Pet 2:13. Syn.: *Spilas* (4695) refers to a hidden location which can destroy a life; whereas, *spilos* refers to a subtil intaking from an impure source which can equally destroy a life. Note, both externally and internally destruction can come. See: BAGD—762d; THAYER—584c.

4696. **σπιλόω** {2x} **spilŏō**, *spee-lŏ'-o;* from *4696;* to *stain* or *soil* (lit. or fig.):—defile {1x}, spot {1x}.

Spilo means to make a stain or spot and so to defile and is used **(1)** in Jas 3:6 of the defiling effects of an evil use of the tongue; and **(2)** in Jude 23 spotted refers to moral defilement. Syn.: 4696. See: BAGD—762d; THAYER—584c.

4697. **σπλαγχνίζομαι** {12x} **splagchnizŏmai**, *splangkh-nid'-zom-ahee;* mid. voice from *4698;* to have the *bowels* yearn, i.e. (fig.) *feel sympathy,* to *pity:*—have compassion {7x}, be moved with compassion {5x}.

This word means "to be moved as to one's inwards (*splanchna*), to be moved with compassion, to yearn with compassion," and is frequently recorded **(1)** of Christ towards the multitude and towards individual sufferers, Mt 9:36; 14:14; 15:32; 18:27; 20:34; Mk 1:41; 6:34; 8:2; Lk 7:13; 10:33; **(2)** Mk 9:22 of the appeal of a father for a devil-possessed son; and **(3)** of the father in the parable of the Prodigal Son, Lk 15:20. See: TDNT—7:548, 1067; BAGD—762d; THAYER—584d.

4698. **σπλάγχνον** {11x} **splagchnŏn**, *splangkh'-non;* prob. strengthened from σπλήν **splēn** (the *"spleen"*); an *intestine,* (plural); fig. *pity* or *sympathy:*—bowels {9x}, inward affection {1x}, tender mercy + 1656 {1x}.

(1) *Splagchnon* are the bowels which were regarded by the Hebrews as the seat of the tender affections. **(2)** It is used always in the plural, and properly denotes "the physical organs of the intestines," and is once used in this respect, Acts 1:18. The word is rendered **(3)** "tender mercy" in Lk 1:78; **(4)** "bowels" in 2 Cor 6:12; Phil 1:8; 2:1; Col 3:12; Philem 7, 12, 20; 1 Jn 3:17; and **(5)** "inward affection" in 2 Cor 7:15. See: TDNT—7:548, 1067; BAGD—763a; THAYER—584d.

4699. **σπόγγος** {3x} **spŏggŏs**, *spong'-gos;* perh. of for. or.; a *"sponge"*:—spunge {3x}.

Spoggos was the medium by which vinegar was carried to the mouth of Christ on the cross, Mt 27:48; Mk 15:36; Jn 19:29. See: BAGD—763b; THAYER—585a.

4700. **σποδός** {3x} **spŏdŏs**, *spod-os';* of uncert. der.; *ashes:*—ashes {3x}.

Spodos, "ashes", is found three times, **(1)** twice in association with sackcloth, Mt 11:21 and Lk 10:13, as tokens of grief (cf. Est. 4:1, 3; Is 58:5; 61:3; Jer 6:26; Jonah 3:6); **(2)** of the ashes resulting from animal sacrifices, Heb 9:13. See: BAGD—763b; THAYER—585b.

4701. **σπορά** {1x} **spŏra**, *spor-ah';* from *4687;* a *sowing,* i.e. (by impl.) *parentage:*—seed {1x}.

Spora denotes "seed sown," 1 Pet 1:23, of human offspring. See: TDNT—7:536, 1065; BAGD—763b; THAYER—585b.

4702. **σπόριμος** {3x} **spŏrimŏs**, *spor'-ee-mos;* from *4703; sown,* i.e. (neut. plur.) a planted *field:*—corn {1x}, cornfield {2x}.

(1) Corn speaks of any type grain. *Sporimos,* lit., "sown, or fit for sowing" (*speiro* "to sow, scatter seed"), denotes, in the plural, **(2)** "sown fields, fields of grain, cornfields," Mt 12:1, "corn"; Mk 2:23; Lk 6:1. See: TDNT—7:536, 1065; BAGD—763b; THAYER—585b.

4703. **σπόρος** {5x} **spŏrŏs**, *spor'-os;* from *4687;* a *scattering* (of seed), i.e. (concr.) *seed* (as sown):—seed {4x}, seed sown {1x}.

Sporos properly "a sowing," denotes "seed sown," **(1)** natural, Mk 4:26, 27; Lk 8:5, 11; **(2)** the natural being figuratively applied to the Word of God; 2 Cor 9:10 (1st part); metaphorically of material help to the needy, 2 Cor 9:10 (2nd part), "seed sown." See: TDNT—7:536, 1065; BAGD—763b; THAYER—585b.

4704. **σπουδάζω** {11x} **spŏudazō**, *spoo-dad'-zo;* from *4710;* to *use speed,* i.e. to *make effort, be prompt* or *earnest:*—endeavour {3x}, do diligence {2x}, be diligent {2x}, give diligence {1x}, be forward {1x}, labour {1x}, study {1x}.

Spoudazo signifies "to hasten to do a thing, to exert oneself, endeavor, give diligence"; **(1)** "was forward" in Gal 2:10, of remembering the poor; **(2)** "endeavoring": **(2a)** in Eph 4:3, of keeping the unity of the Spirit, **(2b)** in 1 Th 2:17, of going to see friends, "endeavored", **(2c)** in 2 Pet 1:15, of enabling believers to call Scripture truth to remembrance, "endeavour"; **(3)** "do thy diligence" in 2 Ti 4:9; 4:21; **(5)** "study" in 2 Ti 2:15; **(6)** "be diligent": **(6a)** in Titus 3:12, **(6b)** in 2 Pet. 3:14, of being found in peace without fault and blameless, when the Lord comes; **(7)** "let us labor": **(7a)** in Heb 4:11, of keeping continuous Sabbath rest, **(7b)** in 2 Pet 1:10, of making our calling and election sure. See: TDNT—7:559, 1069; BAGD—763c; THAYER—585b.

4705. **σπουδαῖος** {1x} **spŏudaiŏs**, *spoo-dah'-yos;* from *4710; prompt, energetic, earnest:*—diligent {1x}. See: TDNT—7:559, 1069; BAGD—763c; THAYER—585b.

4706. **σπουδαιότερον** {1x} **spŏudaiŏtĕrŏn**, *spoo-dah-yot'-er-on;* neut. of *4707* as adv.; *more earnestly* than others, i.e. very *promptly:*—very diligently {1x}. See: BAGD—763c; THAYER—585b.

4707. **σπουδαιότερος** {2x} **spŏudaiŏtĕrŏs**, *spoo-dah-yot'-er-os;* comparative of *4705; more prompt, more earnest:*—more diligent {1x}, more forward {1x}.

Spoudaioteros is the comparative degree of *spoude* (4710) and is translated "more diligent" in 2 Cor 8:22; and "more forward" in 2 Cor 8:17. See: BAGD—763c; THAYER—585b.

4708. **σπουδαιοτέρως** {1x} **spŏudaiŏtĕrōs**, *spoo-dah-yot-er'-oce;* adv. from *4707; more speedily,* i.e. *sooner* than otherwise:—more carefully {1x}.

This is the comparative adverb of *spoude* (4710) and signifies "the more carefully" in Phil 2:28. See: BAGD—763c; THAYER—585b.

4709. **σπουδαίως** {2x} **spŏudaiōs**, *spoo-dah'-yoce;* adv. from *4705; earnestly, promptly:*—diligently {1x}, instantly {1x}.

Spoudaios "speedily, earnestly, diligently" is translated **(1)** "instantly" in Lk 7:4; and **(2)** "diligently" in Titus 3:13. See: BAGD—763d; THAYER—585b.

4710. **σπουδή** {12x} **spŏudē**, *spoo-day';* from *4692;* *"speed"*, i.e. (by impl.) *despatch, eagerness, earnestness:*—diligence {5x}, haste {2x}, business {1x}, care {1x}, forwardness {1x}, earnest care {1x}, carefulness {1x}.

Spoude, "earnestness, zeal," or sometimes **(1)** "the haste accompanying this," Mk 6:25; Lk 1:39, is translated **(2)** "diligence" in Rom 12:8; 2 Cor 8:7; Heb. 6:11; 2 Pet 1:5; Jude 3; **(3)** "carefulness" in 2 Cor 7:11; **(4)** "care" in 2 Cor 7:12; **(5)** "business" in Rom 12:11; **(6)** "forwardness" in 2 Cor 8:8; and **(7)** "earnest care" in 2 Cor 8:16. See: TDNT—7:559, 1069; BAGD—763d; THAYER—585c.

4711. **σπυρίς** {5x} **spuris**, *spoo-rece';* from *4687* (as *woven*); a *hamper* or *lunch-receptacle:*—basket {5x}.

Spuris denotes a reed basket, plaited, a capacious kind of hamper, sometimes large enough to hold a man (Mt 15:37; 16:10; Mk 8:8, 20; Acts 9:25). See: BAGD—764a; THAYER—585c.

4712. **στάδιον** {6x} **stadiŏn**, *stad'-ee-on;* or masc. (in plur.) στάδιος **stadiŏs**, *stad'-ee-os;* from the base of *2476,* (as *fixed*); a *stade* or certain measure of distance; by impl. a *stadium* or *race-course:*—furlong {5x}, race {1x}.

Stadion denotes **(1)** a stadium, i.e., a measure of length, 600 Greek feet, or one-eighth of a Roman mile, a space or distance of about 600 feet or 185 m (Lk 24:13; Jn 6:19; 11:18; Rev 14:20; 21:16; and **(2)** a race course, the length of the Olympic course (1 Cor 9:24). See: BAGD—764a; THAYER—585c.

4713. **στάμνος** {1x} **stamnŏs**, *stam'-nos;* from the base of *2476* (as *stationary*); a *jar* or earthen *tank:*—pot {1x}. See: BAGD—764b; THAYER—585d.

4714. **στάσις** {9x} **stasis**, *stas'-is;* from the base of *2476;* a *standing* (prop. the act), i.e. (by anal.) *position* (*existence*); by impl. a popular *uprising;* fig. *controversy:*—sedition {3x}, dissension {3x}, insurrection {1x}, × standing {1x}, uproar {1x}.

Stasis, akin to *histemi,* "to stand," denotes **(1)** "a standing, stability" in Heb 9:8, "(while as the first tabernacle) is yet standing"; **(2)** "an insurrection" in Mk 15:7; **(3)** "sedition" in Lk 23:19, 25; Acts 24:5; **(4)** "uproar" in Acts 19:40; and **(5)** "a dissension, Acts 15:2; 23:7, 10. See: TDNT—7:559, 1069; BAGD—764c; THAYER—585d.

4715. **στατήρ** {1x} **statēr**, *stat-air';* from the base of *2746;* a *stander* (*standard* of value), i.e. (spec.) a *stater* or certain coin:—piece of money {1x}.

By the time recorded in Mt 17:24; the value was about three shillings, and would pay the Temple tax for two persons. See: BAGD—764c; THAYER—586a.

4716. **σταυρός** {28x} **staurŏs**, *stŏw-ros';* from the base of *2476;* a *stake* or *post* (as *set* upright), i.e. (spec.) a *pole* or *cross* (as an instrument of capital punishment), fig. *exposure to death*, i.e. *self-denial;* by impl. the *atonement* of Christ:—cross {28x}.

Stauros denotes **(1)** "the cross, or stake itself," e.g., Mt 27:32; **(2)** "the crucifixion suffered," e.g., 1 Cor 1:17–18, where "the preaching of the cross," stands for the gospel; **(3)** Gal 5:11, where crucifixion is metaphorically used of the renunciation of the world, that characterizes the true Christian life; Gal 6:12, 14; Eph 2:16; Phil 3:18. **(4)** The judicial custom by which the condemned person carried his stake to the place of execution, was applied by the Lord to those sufferings by which His faithful followers were to express their fellowship with Him, e.g., Mt 10:38. See: TDNT—7:572, 1071; BAGD—764d; THAYER—586a.

4717. **σταυρόω** {46x} **staurŏō**, *stŏw-rŏ'-o;* from *4716;* to *impale* on the cross; fig. to *extinguish* (*subdue*) passion or selfishness:—crucify {46x}.

Stauroo signifies **(1)** "the act of crucifixion," e.g., Mt 20:19; **(2)** metaphorically, "the putting off of the flesh with its passions and lusts," a condition fulfilled in the case of those who are "in Christ Jesus," Gal 5:24; **(3)** so of the relationship between the believer and the world, Gal 6:14. See: TDNT—7:581, 1071; BAGD—765b; THAYER—586b.

4718. **σταφυλή** {3x} **staphulē**, *staf-oo-lay';* prob. from the base of *4735;* a *cluster* of grapes (as if *intertwined*):—grapes {3x}.

Staphule, "a bunch of grapes, the ripe cluster," stresses the individual grapes themselves, Mt 7:16; Lk 6:44; Rev 14:18. Syn.: *Staphule,* (4718) "a bunch of grapes, the ripe cluster" stressing the individual grapes themselves within the cluster. See: BAGD—765c; THAYER—586c.

4719. **στάχυς** {5x} **stachus**, *stakh'-oos;* from the base of *2476;* a *head* of grain (as *standing* out from the stalk):—ear {2x}, ear of corn {3x}.

Stachus means "an ear of grain," Mt 12:1; Mk 2:23; 4:28; Lk 6:1. See: BAGD—765d; THAYER—586c.

4720. **Στάχυς** {1x} **Stachus**, *stakh'-oos;* the same as *4719; Stachys,* a Chr.:—Stachys {1x}. See: BAGD—765d; THAYER—586d.

4721. **στέγη** {3x} **stĕgē**, *steg'-ay;* strengthened from a primary τέγος **tĕgŏs** (a "*thatch*" or "*deck*" of a building); a *roof:*—roof {3x}.

Stege, "a covering" (*stego,* "to cover"), denotes **(1)** "a roof," Mk 2:4; **(2)** said of entering a house, Mt 8:8; Lk 7:6. See: BAGD—765d; THAYER—586d.

4722. **στέγω** {4x} **stĕgō**, *steg'-o;* from *4721;* to *roof* over, i.e. (fig.) to *cover* with silence (*endure* patiently):—can forbear {2x}, bear {1x}, suffer {1x}.

Stego means primarily to protect, or preserve by covering; hence **(1)** means to keep off something which threatens, to bear up against, to hold out against, and so to endure, bear, forbear (1 Cor 9:12). **(2)** The idea of supporting what is placed upon a thing is prominent in 1 Th 3:1, 5; 1 Cor 13:7). See: TDNT—7:585, 1073; BAGD—765d; THAYER—586d.

4723. **στεῖρος** {4x} **stĕirŏs**, *sti'-ros;* a contr. from *4731* (as *stiff* and *unnatural*); "*sterile*":—barren {4x}.

Steiros means hard, firm [Eng., "sterile"] and signifies barren, not bearing children. It is used with **(1)** the natural significance (Lk 1:7, 36; 23:29); and **(2)** a spiritual significance (Gal 4:27). See: BAGD—766a; THAYER—586d.

4724. **στέλλω** {2x} **stĕllō**, *stel'-lo;* prob. strengthened from the base of *2476;* prop. to *set* fast ("*stall*"), i.e. (fig.) to *repress* (refl. *abstain* from associating with):—avoid {1x}, withdraw (one's) self {1x}.

Stello, "to place," sometimes signifies, in the middle voice, "to take care against a thing," **(1)** "to avoid," 2 Cor 8:20; and **(2)** in 2 Th 3:6, "of withdrawing from a person." See: TDNT—7:588, 1074; BAGD—766a.

4725. **στέμμα** {1x} **stĕmma**, *stem'-mah;* from the base of *4735;* a *wreath* for show to prepare for sacrifice:—garland {1x}.

Stemma denotes "a wreath" (from *stepho,* "to put around, enwreath"), as used in sacrifices, Acts 14:13. See: BAGD—766a; THAYER—587a.

4726. **στεναγμός** {2x} **stĕnagmŏs**, *sten-ag-mos';* from *4727;* a *sigh:*—groaning {2x}.

Stenagmos, **(1)** in Acts 7:34, is used in a quote from Ex 2:24 of the children of Israel groaning in Egypt; **(2)** in Rom 8:26, in the plural, of the intercessory groanings of the Holy Spirit. See: TDNT—7:600, 1076; BAGD—766b; THAYER—587a.

4727. **στενάζω** {6x} **stĕnazō**, *sten-ad'-zo;* from *4728;* to *make* (intr. *be*) *in straits,* i.e. (by impl.) to *sigh, murmur, pray* inaudibly:—with grief {1x}, groan {3x}, grudge {1x}, sigh {1x}.

Stenazo, "to groan" (of an inward, unexpressed feeling of sorrow), is translated **(1)** "with grief" in Heb 13:17. **(2)** It is rendered "sighed" in Mk 7:34; **(3)** "groan," in Rom 8:23; 2 Cor 5:2, 4; and **(4)** "grudge" in Jas. 5:9. Syn.: **(A)** *Alalazo* (214) means to wail in oriental style, to howl in a consecrated, semi-liturgical fashion. **(B)** *Dakruo* (1145) means to shed tears, weep silently. **(C)** *Threneo* (2354) means to give formal expression to grief, to sing a dirge. **(D)** *Klaio* (2799) denotes to weep audibly, cry as a child. **(E)** *Odurmos* (3602) means to give verbal expression to grief, to lament. **(F)** *Stenazo* (4727) denotes to express grief by inarticulate or semi-articulate sounds, to groan. See: TDNT—7:600, 1076; BAGD—766b; THAYER—587a.

4728. **στενός** {3x} **stĕnŏs**, *sten-os';* prob. from the base of *2476; narrow* (from obstacles *standing* close about):—strait {3x}.

Stenos is used figuratively in Mt 7:13, 14; Lk 13:24; of the gate which provides the entrance to eternal life; narrow because it runs counter to natural inclinations. Syn.: *Stenochoreo* (4729) means to be straitened and *stenochoria* (4730) means narrowness, anguish, distress. See: TDNT—7:604, 1077; BAGD—766b; THAYER—587b.

4729. **στενοχωρέω** {3x} **stĕnŏchōrĕō**, *sten-okh-o-reh'-o;* from the same as *4730;* to *hem* in closely, i.e. (fig.) *cramp:*—distress {1x}, straiten {2x}.

This word means lit., "to crowd into a narrow space," or, in the passive voice "to be pressed for room," hence, metaphorically, **(1)** "to be straitened," 2 Cor 6:12 twice; and **(2)** "distressed" in 2 Cor 4:8. See: TDNT—7:604, 1077; BAGD—766c; THAYER—587b.

4730. **στενοχωρία** {4x} **stĕnŏchōria**, *sten-okh-o-ree'-ah;* from a compound of *4728* and *5561; narrowness of room,* i.e. (fig.) *calamity:*—anguish {1x}, distress {3x}.

(1) *Stenochoria* refers to confined space and the consequent painfulness; narrow straits. This word means lit., "narrowness of place" (*stenos,* "narrow," *chora,* "a place"), metaphorically came to mean the "distress arising from that condition, anguish." **(2)** It is used in the plural, of various forms of "distress" in 2 Cor 6:4; 12:10; Rom 8:35, and **(3)** of "anguish" in Rom 2:9. **(4)** The opposite state, is of being in a large place, and so metaphorically in a state of joy. Syn.: 2347. See: TDNT—7:604, 1077; BAGD—766c; THAYER—587b.

4731. **στερεός** {4x} **stĕrĕŏs**, *ster-eh-os';* from *2476; stiff,* i.e. *solid, stable* (lit. or fig.):—stedfast {1x}, strong {2x}, sure {1x}.

Stereos, "solid, hard, stiff," is translated **(1)** "sure" in 2 Ti 2:19, "(foundation of God standeth) sure"; **(2)** "strong (meat)" in Heb 5:12, 14; and **(3)** "steadfast" in 1 Pet 5:9. See: TDNT—7:609, 1077; BAGD—766d; THAYER—587b.

4732. **στερεόω** {3x} **stĕrĕŏō**, *ster-eh-ŏ'-o;* from *4731;* to *solidify,* i.e. *confirm* (lit. or fig.):—establish {1x}, receive strength {1x}, make strong {1x}.

Steroo, "to make firm, or solid" (akin to *stereos,* "hard, firm, solid"; cf Eng., "stereotype"), is used only in Acts, **(1)** physically, **(1a)** 3:7, "received strength"; **(1b)** 3:16, "hath made strong"; **(2)** metaphorically, of establishment in the faith, 16:5, "established." See: TDNT—7:609, 1077; BAGD—766d; THAYER—587c.

4733. **στερέωμα** {1x} **stĕrĕōma**, *ster-eh'-o-mah;* from *4732;* something *established,* i.e. (abstr.) *confirmation* (*stability*):—stedfastness {1x}.

Stereoma, primarily "a support, foundation," denotes "strength, steadfastness," Col 2:5. See: TDNT—7:609, 1077; BAGD—766d; THAYER—587c.

4734. **Στεφανᾶς** {4x} **Stĕphanas**, *stef-an-as';* prob. contr. for στεφανωτός **stĕphanōtŏs** (*crowned;* from *4737*); *Stephanas,* a Chr.:—*Stephanas* {4x}. See: BAGD—767a; THAYER—587c.

4735. **στέφανος** {18x} **stĕphanŏs**, *stef'-an-os;* from an appar. primary στέφω **stĕphō** (to *twine* or *wreathe*); a *chaplet,* (as a badge of royalty, a prize in the public games or a symbol of honor gen.; but more conspicuous and elaborate than the simple *fillet, 1238*), lit. or fig.:—crown {18x}.

Stephanos, primarily, "that which surrounds, as a wall or crowd" (from *stepho,* "to encircle"), denotes **(1)** "the victor's crown," the symbol of triumph in the games or some such contest; hence, by metonymy, a reward or prize; **(2)** "a token of public honor" for distinguished service, military prowess, etc., or of nuptial joy, or festal gladness, especially at the parousia of kings. **(3)** It was woven as a garland of oak, ivy, parsley, myrtle, or olive, or in imitation of these in gold. **(4)** In some passages the reference to the games is clear, **(4a)** 1 Cor 9:25; 2 Ti 4:8 ("crown of righteousness"); it may be so in **(4b)** 1 Pet 5:4, where the fadeless character of "the crown of glory" is set in contrast to the garlands of earth. **(5)** In other passages it stands as an emblem **(5a)** of life, joy, reward and glory, Phil 4:1; 1 Th 2:19; Jas 1:12 ("crown of life "); Rev. 2:10; 3:11; 4:4, 10; **(5b)** of triumph, Rev 6:2; 9:7; 12:1; 14:14. **(6)** It is used of "the crown of thorns" which the soldiers plaited and put on Christ's head, Mt 27:29; Mk 15:17; Jn 19:2, 5. **(6a)** At first sight this might be taken as an alternative for *diadema,* "a kingly crown", but considering the blasphemous character of that masquerade, and the materials used, obviously *diadema* would be quite unfitting and the only alternative was *stephanos.* Syn.: *Diadema* (1238) is a crown as a badge of royalty; whereas, *stephanos* is the badge of victory in the games of civic worth, of military valour, of nuptial joy, of festive gladness. See: TDNT—7:615, 1078; BAGD—767a; THAYER—587d.

4736. **Στέφανος** {7x} **Stĕphanŏs**, *stef'-an-os;* the same as *4735; Stephanus,* a Chr.:—Stephen {7x}. See: BAGD—767a; THAYER—587d.

4737. **στεφανόω** {3x} **stephanŏō**, *stef-an-ŏ'-o;* from *4735;* to *adorn with* an honorary *wreath* (lit. or fig.):—crown {3x}.

Stephanoo, "to crown," conforms in meaning to *stephanos;* **(1)** it is used of the reward of victory in the games, in 2 Ti 2:5; **(2)** of the glory and honor bestowed by God upon man in regard to his position in creation, Heb 2:7; **(3)** of the glory and honor bestowed upon the Lord Jesus in His exaltation, Heb 2:9. See: TDNT—7:615, 1078; BAGD—767c; THAYER—587d.

4738. **στῆθος** {5x} **stēthŏs**, *stay'-thos;* from *2476* (as *standing* prominently); the (entire extern.) *bosom,* i.e. *chest:*—breast {5x}.

Stethos, connected with *histemi,* "to stand," i.e., that which stands out, is used **(1)** of mourners in smiting the "breast," Lk 18:13; 23:48; **(2)** of John in reclining on the "breast" of Christ, Jn 13:25; 21:20; **(3)** of the "breasts" of the angels in Rev 15:6. See: BAGD—767d; THAYER—588a.

4739. **στήκω** {8x} **stēkō**, *stay'-ko;* from the perfect tense of *2476;* to *be stationary,* i.e. (fig.) to *persevere:*—stand {2x}, stand fast {6x}.

Steko is used **(1)** literally, Mk 11:25; **(2)** figuratively, **(2a)** Rom 14:4; **(2b)** of "standing fast," 1 Cor 16:13, "in the faith," i.e., by adherence to it; **(2c)** Gal 5:1, in freedom from legal bondage; **(2d)** Phil 1:27, "in one spirit"; **(2e)** Phil 4:1 and 1 Th 3:8, "in the Lord," i.e., in the willing subjection to His authority; **(2f)** 2 Th 2:15, in the apostle's teaching. See: TDNT—7:636, 1082; BAGD—767d; THAYER—588a.

4740. **στηριγμός** {1x} **stērigmŏs**, *stay-rig-mos';* from *4741; stability* (fig.):—stedfastness {1x}.

Sterigmos, "a setting firmly, supporting," then "fixedness, steadfastness" (akin to *sterizo,* "to establish"), is used in 2 Pet. 3:17. See: TDNT—7:653, 1085; BAGD—768a; THAYER—588b.

4741. **στηρίζω** {13x} **stērizō**, *stay-rid'-zo;* from a presumed der. of *2476* (like *4731*); to *set fast,* i.e. (lit.) to *turn resolutely* in a certain direction, or (fig.) to *confirm:*—stablish {6x}, establish {3x}, strengthen {2x}, fix {1x}, stedfastly set {1x}.

Establish is to find the source of building from without; to stablish, the source is from within. *Sterizo,* "to fix, make fast, to set" (from *sterix,* "a prop"), is used **(1)** of "establishing" or "stablishing" (i.e., the confirmation) of persons; **(1a)** the apostle Peter was called by the Lord to "establish" his brethren, Lk 22:32, translated "strengthen"; **(1b)** Paul desired to visit Rome that the saints might be "established," Rom 1:11; cf. Acts 8:23; **(1c)** so with Timothy at Thessalonica, 1 Th 3:2; **(2)** the "confirmation" of the saints is the work of God, Rom 16:25, "to stablish (you)"; 1 Th 3:13, "stablish (your hearts)"; 2 Th 2:17, "stablish them (in every good work and word)"; 1 Pet 5:10, "stablish"; **(3)** the means used to reflect the "confirmation" is the ministry of the Word of God, 2 Pet 1:12, "are established (in the truth which is with you)"; **(4)** James exhorts Christians to "stablish" their hearts, Jas 5:8; cf. Rev 3:2. **(5)** The character of this "confirmation" may be learned from its use in Lk 9:51, "steadfastly set"; 16:26, "fixed." **(6)** Neither the laying on of hands nor the impartation of the Holy Spirit is mentioned in the NT in connection with either of these words, or with the synonymous verb *bebaioo* (see 1 Cor 1:8; 2 Cor 1:21, etc.). See: TDNT—7:653, 1085; BAGD—768a; THAYER—588b.

4742. **στίγμα** {1x} **stigma**, *stig'-mah;* from a primary στίζω **stizō** (to "*stick*", i.e. *prick*); a *mark* incised or punched (for recognition of ownership), i.e. (fig.) *scar* of service:—mark {1x}.

Stigma, denotes "a tattooed mark" or "a mark burnt in, a brand", translated "marks" in Gal 6:17. **(1)** It is probable that the apostle refers to the physical sufferings he had endured since he began to proclaim Jesus as Messiah and Lord [e.g., at Lystra and Philippi]. **(2)** It is probable, too, that this reference to his scars was intended to set off the insistence of the Judaizers upon a body-mark which cost them nothing. Over against the circumcision they demanded as a proof of obedience to the law he set the indelible tokens, sustained in his own body, of his loyalty to the Lord Jesus. As to the origin of the figure, it was indeed customary for a master to brand his slaves, but this language does not suggest that the apostle had been branded by His Master. Soldiers and criminals also were branded on occasion; but to neither of these is the case of Paul as here described analogous. The religious devotee branded himself with the peculiar mark of the god whose cult he affected; so was Paul branded with the marks of his devotion to the Lord Jesus. It is true such markings were forbidden by the law, Lev 19:28, but then Paul had not inflicted these on himself. "The marks of Jesus" cannot be taken to be the marks which the Lord bears in His body in consequence of the Crucifixion; they were different in character. See: TDNT—7:657, 1086; BAGD—768c; THAYER—588c.

4743. **στιγμή** {1x} **stigmē**, *stig-may';* fem. of *4742;* a *point* of time, i.e. an *instant:*—moment {1x}. See: BAGD—768c; THAYER—588d.

4744. **στίλβω** {1x} **stilbō**, *stil'-bo;* appar. a primary verb; to *gleam,* i.e. *flash* intensely:—shining {1x}. See: TDNT—7:665, 1087; BAGD—768d; THAYER—588d.

4745. **στοά** {4x} **stŏa**, *stŏ-ah';* prob. from *2476;* a *colonnade* or interior *piazza:*—porch {4x}.

(1) A *stoa* is a portico, a covered colonnade where people can stand or walk protected from the weather and the heat of the sun. *Stoa,* "a portico," is used **(2)** of the "porches" at the pool of Bethesda, Jn 5:2; **(3)** of the covered colonnade in the Temple, called Solomon's "porch," Jn 10:23; Acts 3:11; 5:12 a portico on the eastern side of the temple. **(4)** This and the other "porches" existent in the time of Christ were almost certainly due to Herod's restoration. See: BAGD—768d; THAYER—588d.

4746. **στοιβάς** {1x} **stŏibas**, *stoy-bas'* or **στιβάς** **stibas**, *stee-bas';* from a primary στείβω **stĕibō** (to "*step*" or "*stamp*"); a *spread* (as if *tramped* flat) of loose materials for a couch, i.e. (by impl.) a *bough* of a tree so employed:—branch {1x}. See: BAGD—768d, 768b; THAYER—588d, 588c.

4747. **στοιχεῖον** {7x} **stŏichĕiŏn**, *stoy-khi'-on;* neut. of a presumed der. of the base of *4748;* something *orderly* in arrangement, i.e. (by impl.) a *serial* (*basal, fundamental, initial*) constituent (lit.), proposition (fig.):—element {4x}, principle {1x}, rudiment {2x}.

Stoicheion used in the plural, primarily signifies **(1)** any first things from which others in a series, or a composite whole take their rise. The word denotes **(1a)** an element, a first principle; or **(1b)** the letters of the alphabet, as elements of speech. **(2)** It is used of **(2a)** the substance of the material world (2 Pet 3:10, 12); **(2b)** the delusive speculations of gentile cults and of Jewish theories, **(2b1)** treated as elementary principles, "the rudiments of the world," (Col 2:8), **(2b2)** spoken of as "philosophy and vain deceit"; **(2b3)** these were presented as superior to faith in Christ; **(3)** the rudimentary principles of religion, Jewish or Gentile, also **(3a)** described as "the rudiments of the world" (Col 2:20), and **(3b)** as "weak and beggarly rudiments" (Gal 4:3, 9); **(4)** the elementary principles (the A, B, C's . .) of the OT, as a revelation from God (Heb 5:12). See: TDNT—7:670, 1087; BAGD—768d; THAYER—588d.

4748. **στοιχέω** {5x} **stŏichĕō**, *stoy-kheh'-o;* from a der. of στείχω **stĕichō** (to *range* in regular line); to *march,* in (military) rank (*keep step*), i.e. (fig.) to *conform* to virtue and piety:—walk {4x}, walk orderly {1x}.

Stoicheo, from *stoichos,* "a row," signifies "to walk in line," and is used metaphorically **(1)** of "walking" in relation to others; **(1)** in Acts 21:24, it is translated "walkest orderly"; **(2)** in Rom 4:12, "walk (in . . . steps)"; **(3)** in Gal 5:25 it is used of walking "in the Spirit", in an exhortation to keep step with one another in submission of heart to the Holy Spirit, and therefore of keeping step with Christ, the great means of unity and harmony in a church; **(4)** in Gal 6:16 it is used of walking by the rule expressed in vv. 14, 15; **(5)** in Phil 3:16 the reference is to the course pursued by the believer who makes "the prize of the high calling" the object of his ambition. See: TDNT—7:666, 1087; BAGD—769c; THAYER—589b.

4749. **στολή** {9x} **stŏlē**, *stol-ay';* from *4724;* *equipment,* i.e. (spec.) a "*stole*" or long-fitting *gown* possibility with a train (as a mark of dignity):—robe {5x}, long clothing {1x}, long garment {1x}, them + 848 {1x}, long robe {1x}. Syn.: 2440, 2441, 4158, 5509, 5511.

(1) A *stole* was a long sweeping stately robe that reached to the feet and was a garment of special solemnity, richness, and beauty. *Stole,* (Eng., "stole"), denotes any "stately robe," a long garment reaching to the feet or with a train behind. **(2)** It is used **(2a)** of the long clothing in which the scribes walked, making themselves conspicuous in the eyes of men, Mk 12:38; Lk 20:46; **(2b)** of the robe worn by the young man in the Lord's tomb, Mk 16:5; **(2c)** of the best or, rather, the chief robe, which was brought out for the returned prodigal, Lk 15:22; **(2d)** five times in the Apocalypse, as to glorified saints, 6:11; 7:9, 13–14; 22:14. See: TDNT—7:687, 1088; BAGD—769c; THAYER—589c.

4750. **στόμα** {79x} **stŏma**, *stom'-a;* prob. strengthened from a presumed der. of the base of *5114;* the *mouth* (as if a *gash* in the face); by impl. *language* (and its relations); fig. an *opening* (in the earth); spec. the *front* or *edge* (of a weapon):—edge {2x}, face {4x}, mouth {73x}.

(1) When "mouth" is used for the edge of the sword it refers, by figure, to the mouth of the river, the shallow, "sharper" edge of the water as it is emitted and flows deeper and wider, Lk 21:24; Heb 11:34. It is akin to *stomachos* (which originally meant "a throat, gullet"), is used **(2)** of "the mouth" **(2a)** of man, e.g., Mt 15:11; **(2b)** of animals, e.g., Mt 17:27; 2Ti 4:17 (figuratively); Heb 11:33; Jas 3:3; Rev 13:2 twice; **(3)** figuratively of "inanimate things," **(3a)** of the "edge" of a sword, Lk 21:24; Heb 11:34; **(3b)** of the earth, Rev 12:16; **(4)** figuratively, of the "mouth," as the organ of speech, **(4a)** of Christ's words, e.g., Mt 13:35; Lk 11:54; Acts 8:32; 22:14; 1 Pet 2:22; **(4b)** of human words, **(4b1)** e.g., Mt 18:16; 21:16; Lk 1:64; Rev 14:5; **(4b2)** as emanating from the heart, Mt 12:34; Rom 10:8, 9; **(4c)** of prophetic ministry through the Holy Spirit, Lk 1:70; Acts 1:16; 3:18; 4:25; **(4d)** of the destructive policy of two world potentates at the end of this age, Rev 13:2, 5, 6; 16:13 (twice); **(4e)** of shameful speaking, Eph 4:29 and Col 3:8; **(4f)** of the Devil speaking as a dragon or serpent, Rev 12:15, 16; 16:13; **(4g)** figuratively, in the phrase "face to face" (lit., "mouth to mouth"), 2 Jn 12; 3 Jn 14; **(4h)** metaphorically, of "the utterances of the Lord, in judgment," 2 Th 2:8; Rev 1:16; 2:16; 19:15, 21; **(4i)** of His judgment upon a local church for its lukewarmness, Rev 3:16; **(4j)** by metonymy, for "speech," Mt 18:16; Lk 19:22; 21:15; 2 Cor 13:1. Syn.: 1366. See: TDNT—7:692, 1089; BAGD—769d; THAYER—589c.

4751. **στόμαχος** {1x} **stŏmachŏs**, *stom'-akh-os;* from *4750;* an *orifice* (the *gullet*), i.e. (spec.) the "*stomach*":—stomach {1x}. See: BAGD—770b; THAYER—590a.

4752. **στρατεία** {2x} **stratĕia**, *strat-i'-ah;* from *4754;* military *service,* i.e. (fig.) the apostolic *career* (as one of hardship and danger):—warfare {2x}. Cf. 2 Cor 10:4; 1 Ti 1:18. See: TDNT—7:701, 1091; BAGD—770b; THAYER—590a.

4753. **στράτευμα** {8x} **stratĕuma**, *strat'-yoo-mah;* from *4754;* an *armament,* i.e. (by impl.) a body of *troops* (more or less extensive or systematic):—army {6x}, soldier {1x}, men of war {1x}.

Strateuma denotes **(1)** "an army" of any size, large or small, Mt 22:7; Acts 23:27; Rev 9:16; 19:14, 19 (twice); **(2)** a company of soldiers, such as Herod's bodyguard, Lk 23:11, "men of war", or **(3)** the soldiers of a garrison, Acts 23:10. See: TDNT—7:701, 1091; BAGD—770b; THAYER—590b.

4754. **στρατεύομαι** {7x} **stratĕuŏmai**, *strat-yoo'-om-ahee;* mid. voice from the base of *4756;* to *serve* in a military campaign; fig. to *execute the apostolate* (with its arduous duties and functions), to *contend* with carnal inclinations:—soldier {1x}, goeth to warfare {1x}, war {5x}.

Strateuomai, used in the middle voice, "to make war" (from *stratos,* "an encamped army"), is translated **(1)** "to war", metaphorically, of spiritual "conflict," in 2 Cor 10:3; 1 Ti 1:18; 2 Ti 2:4; Jas 4:1; 1 Pet 2:11. It is used **(2)** literally **(2a)** of "serving as a soldier," Lk 3:14, "soldiers"; **(2b)** 1 Cor 9:7, "(who) goeth a warfare." See: TDNT—7:701, 1091; BAGD—770b; THAYER—590b.

4755. **στρατηγός** {10x} **stratēgŏs**, *strat-ay-gos';* from the base of *4756* and *71* or *2233;* a *general,* i.e. (by impl. or anal.) a (military) *governor* (*prætor*), the chief (præfect) of the (Levitical) temple-wardens:—captain {5x}, magistrate {5x}.

Stragetos, originally the commander of an army (from *stratos,* "an army," and *ago,* "to lead"), came to denote **(1)** "a civil commander, a governor", the highest magistrate, or any civil officer in chief command, Acts 16:20, 22, 35–36, 38; also **(2)** the "chief captain" of the Temple, himself a Levite, having command of the Levites who kept guard in and around the Temple, Lk 22:4, 52; Acts 4:1; 5:24, 26. Cf. Jer 20:1. See: TDNT—7:701, 1091; BAGD—770c; THAYER—590b.

4756. **στρατία** {2x} **stratia**, *strat-ee'-ah;* fem. of a der. of στρατός **stratŏs**, (an *army;* from the base of *4766,* as *encamped*); *camp-likeness,* i.e. an *army,* i.e. (fig.) the *angels,* the celestial *luminaries:*—host {2x}.

Stratia, "an army," is used **(1)** of angels, Lk 2:13; **(2)** of stars, Acts 7:42. See: TDNT—7:701, 1091; BAGD—770d; THAYER—590a.

4757. **στρατιώτης** {26x} **stratiōtēs**, *strat-ee-o'-tace;* from a presumed der. of the same as *4756;* a *camper-out,* i.e. a (common) *warrior* (lit. or fig.):—soldier {26x}.

Stratiotes, "a soldier," is used **(1)** in the natural sense, e.g., Mt 8:9; 27:27; 28:12; Mk 15:16; Lk 7:8; 23:36; six times in John; thirteen times in Acts; not again in the NT; **(2)** metaphorically of one who endures hardship in the cause of Christ, 2 Ti 2:3. See: TDNT—7:701, 1091; BAGD—770d; THAYER—590c.

4758. **στρατολογέω** {1x} **stratŏlŏgĕō**, *strat-ol-og-eh'-o;* from a compound of the base of *4756* and *3004* (in its orig. sense); to *gather* (or *select*) as a *warrior,* i.e. *enlist* in the army:—choose to be a soldier {1x}. See: TDNT—7:701, 1091; BAGD—770d; THAYER—590c.

4759. **στρατοπεδάρχης** {1x} **stratŏpĕdarchēs**, *strat-op-ed-ar'-khace;* from *4760* and *757;* a *ruler of an army,* i.e. (spec.) a Prætorian *præfect:*—captain of the guard {1x}. See: BAGD—771a; THAYER—590d.

4760. **στρατόπεδον** {1x} **stratŏpĕdŏn**, *strat-op'-ed-on;* from the base of *4756* and the same as *3977;* a *camping-ground,* i.e. (by impl.) a body of *troops:*—army {1x}.

Stratopedon, from *stratos,* "a military host," *pedon,* "a plain," strictly denotes "an army encamped, a camp"; in Lk 21:20, of the soldiers which were to be encamped about Jerusalem in fulfillment of the Lord's prophecy concerning the destruction of the city; the phrase might be translated "by camps" (or encampments). See: TDNT—7:701, 1091; BAGD—771a; THAYER—590d.

4761. **στρεβλόω** {1x} **strĕblŏō**, *streb-lŏ'-o;* from a der. of *4762;* to *wrench,* i.e. (spec.) to *torture* (by the rack), but only fig. to *pervert:*—wrest {1x}.

Strebloo, "to twist, to torture" (from *streble,* "a winch" or "instrument of torture," and akin to *strepho,* "to turn"), is used metaphorically in 2 Pet 3:16, of "wresting" the Scriptures on the part of the ignorant and unsteadfast. See: BAGD—771a; THAYER—590d.

4762. **στρέφω** {19x} **strĕphō**, *stref'-o;* strengthened from the base of *5157;* to *twist,* i.e. *turn* quite around or *reverse* (lit. or fig.):—turn {11x}, turn (one's) self {2x}, turn **(one)** {1x}, turn again {1x}, turn back again {1x}, turn **(one)** about {1x}, be converted {1x}, vr turn {1x}.

Strepho denotes **(1)** in the active voice, **(1a)** "to turn" (something), Mt 5:39; **(1b)** reflexively, "to turn oneself, to turn the back to people," said of God, Acts 7:42; **(2)** "to turn one thing into another," Rev 11:6 (the only place where this word occurs after the Acts); **(3)** in the passive voice, **(3a)** used reflexively, "to turn oneself," e.g. Mt 7:6; Jn 20:14, 16; **(3b)** metaphorically, Mt 18:3, "(except) ye . . . be converted." See: TDNT—7:714, 1093; BAGD—771a; THAYER—590d.

4763. **στρηνιάω** {1x} **strēniaō**, *stray-nee-ah'-o;* from a presumed der. of *4764;* to *be luxurious:*—live deliciously {1x}.

(1) *Streniao* refers to the insolence of wealth, to the wantonness and petulance that result from being full and lacking nothing, but there is a power and vigor to this wealth. **(2)** *Streniao,* "to run riot," is rendered "lived deliciously" in Rev 18:7, 8. Syn.: 4684, 5171. See: BAGD—771c; THAYER—591a.

4764. **στρῆνος** {1x} **strēnŏs**, *stray'-nos;* akin to *4731;* a "*straining*", "*strenuousness*" or "strength", i.e. (fig.) *luxury* (*voluptuousness*):—delicacy {1x}.

Strenos stresses the results of one who strains at labor and has excess to purchase above the ordinary; hence, a delicacy. See: BAGD—771c; THAYER—591a.

4765. **στρουθίον** {4x} **strŏuthiŏn**, *stroo-thee'-on;* dimin. of στρουθός **strŏuthŏs** (a *sparrow*); a *little sparrow:*—sparrow {4x}.

Strouthion, a diminutive of *strouthos,* "a sparrow," occurs in Mt 10:29, 31; Lk 12:6, 7. Being a diminutive stresses that God takes care of even the smallest of the small. See: TDNT—7:730, 1096; BAGD—771c; THAYER—591a.

4766. **στρώννυμι** {7x} **strōnnumi**, *strone'-noo-mee;* or simpler

στρωννύω **strōnnuō**, *strone-noo'-o;* prol. from a still simpler

στρόω **strŏō**, *strŏ'-o* (used only as an alt. in certain tenses; prob. akin to *4731* through the idea of *positing*); to "*strew*", i.e. *spread* (as a carpet or couch):—make (one's) bed {1x}, furnish {2x}, spread {2x}, strew {2x}.

Stronnumi, "to spread," is used **(1)** of "furnishing a room," Mk 14:15; Lk 22:12; **(2)** of "making a bed," Acts 9:34; **(3)** "strawed" in Mt 21:8, second use; Mk 11:8, second use; and **(4)** "to spread," in Mt 21:8, first use; Mark 11:8, first use. See: BAGD—771c; THAYER—591b.

4767. **στυγνητός** {1x} **stugnētŏs**, *stoog-nay-tos';* from a der. of an obs. appar. primary στύγω **stugō** (to *hate*); *hated,* i.e. *odious:*—hateful {1x}. See: BAGD—771d; THAYER—591b.

4768. **στυγνάζω** {2x} **stugnazō**, *stoog-nad'-zo;* from the same as *4767;* to *render gloomy,* i.e. (by impl.) *glower* (*be overcast* with clouds, or *sombreness* of speech):—lower {1x}, be sad {1x}. See: BAGD—771d; THAYER—591b.

4769. **στύλος** {4x} **stulŏs**, *stoo'-los;* from στύω **stuō** (to *stiffen;* prop. akin to the base of *2476*); a *post* ("*style*"), i.e. (fig.) *support:*—pillar {4x}. See: TDNT—7:732, 1096; BAGD—772a; THAYER—591b.

4770. **Στωϊκός** {1x} **Stōïkŏs**, *sto-ik-os';* from *4745;* a "*Stoïc*" (as occupying a particular porch in Athens), i.e. adherent of a certain philosophy:—*Stoicks* {1x}. See: BAGD—772a; THAYER—591c.

4771. **σύ** {178x} **su**, *soo;* the pers. pron. of the second pers. sing.; *thou:*—thou {178x}. See: BAGD—772a; THAYER—591c. See also *4571, 4671, 4675;* and for the plur. *5209, 5210, 5213, 5216.*

4772. **συγγένεια** {3x} **suggĕnĕia**, *soong-ghen'-i-ah;* from *4773; relationship,* i.e. (concr.) *relatives:*—kindred {3x}. See: TDNT—7:736, 1097; BAGD—772c; THAYER—592a.

4773. **συγγενής** {12x} **suggĕnēs**, *soong-ghen-ace';* from *4862* and *1085;* a *relative* (by blood); by extens. a fellow *countryman:*—cousin {2x}, kin {1x}, kinsfolk {2x}, kinsman {7x}. See: TDNT—7:736, 1097; BAGD—772c; THAYER—592a.

4774. **συγγνώμη** {1x} **suggnōmē**, *soong-gno'-may;* from a compound of *4862* and *1097; fellow knowledge,* i.e. *concession:*—permission {1x}. See: TDNT—1:716, 119; BAGD—773a; THAYER—592a.

4775. **συγκάθημαι** {2x} **sugkathēmai**, *soong-kath'-ay-mahee; from 4862* and *2521;* to *seat oneself* in company *with:*—sat + 2258 {1x}, sit with {1x}.

Sunkathemai, as a verb, means "to sit with" and occurs in Mk 14:54: "And Peter followed Him afar off, even into the palace of the high priest: and he sat with the servants, and warmed himself at the fire" (cf. Acts 26:30). Syn.: 339, 345, 347, 377, 1910, 2516, 2521, 2621, 2523, 2625, 4776, 4873. See: BAGD—773a; THAYER—592b.

4776. **συγκαθίζω** {2x} **sugkathizō**, *soong-kath-id'-zo;* from *4862* and *2523;* to *give* (or *take*) *a seat* in company *with:*—make sit together {1x}, be set down together {1x}.

Sunkathizo, as a verb, denotes **(1)** transitively, "to make to sit together": "And hath raised *us* up together, and made *us* sit together in heavenly *places* in Christ Jesus" (Eph 2:6); and **(2)** intransitively, "were set down": "And when they had kindled a fire in the midst of the hall, and were set down together, Peter sat down among them" (Lk 22:55). Syn.: 339, 345, 347, 377, 1910, 2516, 2521, 2621, 2523, 2625, 4775, 4873. See: TDNT—7:787, 1102; BAGD—773b; THAYER—592b.

4777. **συγκακοπαθέω** {1x} **sugkakŏpathĕō**, *soong-kak-op-ath-eh'-o;* from *4862* and *2553;* to *suffer hardship* in company *with:*—be partaker of afflictions {1x}. See: TDNT—5:936, 798; BAGD—773b; THAYER—592b.

4778. **συγκακουχέω** {1x} **sugkakŏuchĕō**, *soong-kak-oo-kheh'-o;* from *4862* and *2558;* to *maltreat* in company *with,* i.e. (pass.) *endure persecution together:*—suffer affliction with {1x}. See: BAGD—773b; THAYER—592c.

4779. **συγκαλέω** {8x} **sugkalĕō**, *soong-kal-eh'-o;* from *4862* and *2564;* to *convoke:*—call together {8x}.

Sugkaleo signifies "to call together," Mk 15:16; Lk 9:1; 15:6, 9; 23:13; Acts 5:21; 10:24; 28:17. See: TDNT—3:496, 394; BAGD—773b; THAYER—592c

4780. **συγκαλύπτω** {1x} **sugkaluptō**, *soong-kal-oop'-to;* from *4862* and *2572;* to *conceal altogether:*—cover {1x}. See: TDNT—7:743, 1098; BAGD—773b; THAYER—592c.

4781. **συγκάμπτω** {1x} **sugkamptō**, *soong-kamp'-to;* from *4862* and *2578;* to *bend together,* i.e. (fig.) to *afflict:*—bow down {1x}.

Sugkampto signifies "to bend completely together, to bend down by compulsory force," Rom 11:10. See: BAGD—773b; THAYER—592c.

4782. **συγκαταβαίνω** {1x} **sugkatabainō**, *soong-kat-ab-ah'-ee-no;* from *4862* and *2597;* to *descend* in company *with:*—go down with {1x}. See: BAGD—773c; THAYER—592c.

4783. **συγκατάθεσις** {1x} **sugkatathĕsis**, *soong-kat-ath'-es-is;* from *4784;* a *deposition* (of sentiment) in company *with,* i.e. (fig.) *accord* with:—agreement {1x}. See: BAGD—773c; THAYER—592d.

4784. **συγκατατίθεμαι** {1x} **sugkatatithĕmai**, *soong-kat-at-ith'-em-ahee;* mid. from *4862* and *2698;* to *deposit* (one's vote or opinion) in company *with,* i.e. (fig.) to *accord* with:—consented + 2258 {1x}.

This word means lit., "to put or lay down together with" (*sun,* "with," *kata,* "down," *tithemi,* "to put"), was used of depositing one's vote in an urn; hence, "to vote for, agree with, consent to." It is said negatively of Joseph of Arimathaea, who had not "consented" to the counsel and deed of the Jews, Lk 23:51 (middle voice). See: BAGD—773c; THAYER—592d.

4785. **συγκαταψηφίζω** {1x} **sugkatapsēphizō**, *soong-kat-aps-ay-fid'-zo;* from *4862* and a compound of *2596* and *5585;* to *count down* in company *with,* i.e. *enroll among:*—number with {1x}. See: TDNT—9:604,*; BAGD—773c; THAYER—592d.

4786. **συγκεράννυμι** {2x} **sugkĕrannumi**, *soong-ker-an'-noo-mee;* from *4862* and *2767;* to *commingle,* i.e. (fig.) to *combine* or *assimilate:*—mix with {1x}, temper together {1x}. See: BAGD—773d; THAYER—592d.

4787. **συγκινέω** {1x} **sugkinĕō**, *soong-kin-eh'-o;* from *4682* and *2795;* to *move together,* i.e. (spec.) to *excite* as a mass (to sedition):—stir up {1x}.

Sunkineo, as a verb, means "to move together" [*sun,* "together," *kineo,* "to move"], "to stir up, excite," and is used metaphorically in Acts 6:12: "And they stirred up the people, and the elders, and the scribes, and came upon *him,* and caught him, and brought *him* to the council . . ." Syn.: 329, 383, 387, 1326, 1892, 2042, 3947, 3951, 4531, 4579, 4797, 5017. See: BAGD—773d; THAYER—593a.

4788. **συγκλείω** {4x} **sugklĕiō**, *soong-kli'-o;* from *4862* and *2808;* to *shut together,* i.e. *include* or (fig.) *embrace* in a common subjection to:—conclude {2x}, inclose {1x}, shut up {1x}.

Subkleio, "to shut together, shut in on all sides" (*sun,* "with," *kleio,* "to shut"), is used **(1)** of a catch of fish, Lk 5:6; **(2)** metaphorically, **(2a)** "shut up" unto faith, Gal 5:23; **(2b)** "concluded" that all are under sin, **(2b1)** Gal 5:22; and **(2b2)** in Rom 11:32, of God's dealings with Jew and Gentile, in that He has "concluded all unto disobedience, that He might have mercy upon all." **(2a)** There is no intimation in this of universal salvation. **(2b)** The meaning, from the context, is that God has ordered that all should be convicted of disobedience without escape by human merit, that He might display His mercy, and has offered the gospel without national distinction, and that when Israel is restored, He will, in the resulting Millennium, show His mercy to all nations. See: TDNT—7:744, 1098; BAGD—774a; THAYER—593a.

4789. **συγκληρονόμος** {4x} **sugklērŏnŏmŏs**, *soong-klay-ron-om'-os;* from *4862* and *2818;* a *co-heir,* i.e. (by anal.) *participant in common:*—fellow heirs {1x}, joint heirs {1x}, heirs together {1x}, heirs with {1x}.

This word means "a joint-heir, co-inheritor", and is translated **(1)** "heirs with" of Isaac and Jacob as participants with Abraham in the promises of God, Heb 11:9; **(2)** "heirs together" of husband and wife who are also united in Christ, 1 Pet 3:7; **(3)** "fellow heirs" of Gentiles who believe, as participants in the gospel with Jews who believe, Eph 3:6; and **(4)** "joint heirs", of all believers as prospective participants with Christ in His glory, as recompense for their participation in His sufferings, Rom 8:17. See: TDNT—3:767 & 7:787, 442 & 1102; BAGD—774a; THAYER—593b.

4790. **συγκοινωνέω** {3x} **sugkŏinōnĕō**, *soong-koy-no-neh'-o;* from *4862* and *2841;* to *share* in company *with,* i.e. *co-participate* in:—communicate with {1x}, have fellowship with {1x}, be partaker of {1x}.

This word means "to share together with", and is translated **(1)** "communicated with" in Phil 4:14; **(2)** "have fellowship with" in Eph 5:11; **(3)** "be . . . partakers of" in Rev 18:4. The thought is that of sharing with others what one has, in order to meet their needs. See: TDNT—3:797, 447; BAGD—774b; THAYER—593b.

4791. **συγκοινωνός** {4x} **sugkŏinōnŏs**, *soong-koy-no-nos';* from *4862* and *2844;* a *co-participant:*—companion {1x}, partaker {1x}, partaker +1096 {1x}, partaker with {1x}.

This word denotes "partaking jointly with" and is found in **(1)** Rom 11:17, "partakest"; **(2)** 1 Cor 9:23, "a partaker with"; **(3)** Phil 1:7, "partakers (of my grace)"; **(4)** Rev 1:9, "companion with (you in the tribulation, etc.)." See: TDNT—3:797, 447; BAGD—774b; THAYER—593b.

4792. **συγκομίζω** {1x} **sugkŏmizō**, *soong-kom-id'-zo;* from *4862* and *2865;* to *convey together,* i.e. *collect* or *bear* away in company *with* others:—carry {1x}. See: BAGD—774c; THAYER—593b.

4793. **συγκρίνω** {3x} **sugkrinō**, *soong-kree'-no;* from *4862* and *2919;* to *judge* of one thing in connection *with* another, i.e. *combine* (spiritual ideas with appropriate expressions) or *collate* (one person with another by way of contrast or resemblance):—compare among {1x}, compare with {2x}.

Sugkrino denotes "to join fitly, to combine", **(1)** 1 Cor 2:13, "comparing" either **(1a)** in the sense of combining spiritual things with spiritual, adapting the discourse to the subject, under the guidance of the Holy Spirit, or **(1b)** communicating spiritual things by spiritual things or words, or in the sense of interpreting spiritual things to spiritual men; **(2)** "to place together; hence, judge or discriminate by comparison, compare, with or among," 2 Cor 10:12

(twice). See: TDNT—3:953, 469; BAGD—774d; THAYER—593c.

4794. **συγκύπτω** {1x} **sugkuptō**, *soong-koop'-to;* from *4862* and *2955;* to *stoop altogether,* i.e. *be completely overcome* by:—bow together {1x}. See: BAGD—775a; THAYER—593c.

4795. **συγκυρία** {1x} **sugkuria**, *soong-koo-ree'-ah;* from a compound of *4862* and κυρέω **kurĕō**, (to *light* or *happen;* from the base of *2962*); *concurrence,* i.e. *accident:*—chance {1x}.

Sugkuria literally means a meeting together with, a coincidence of circumstances, a happening and is translated "chance" (Lk 10:31). But concurrence of events is what the word signifies, rather than chance. English chance is used here similarly to purchasing a chance on a raffle. One is seeking the ticket which concurs with the winning number. See: BAGD—775a; THAYER—593d.

4796. **συγχαίρω** {7x} **sugchairō**, *soong-khah'-ee-ro;* from *4862* and *5463;* to *sympathize in gladness, congratulate:*—rejoice in {1x}, rejoice with {6x}.

Sugchairo, "to rejoice with", is used **(1)** of "rejoicing" together in the recovery of what was lost, Lk15:6, 9; **(2)** in suffering in the cause of the gospel, Phil 2:17 (2nd part), 18; **(3)** in the joy of another, Lk 1:58; **(4)** in the honor of fellow believers, 1 Cor 12:26; **(5)** in the triumph of the truth, 1 Cor 13:6, "rejoiceth in." See: TDNT—9:359, 1298; BAGD—775a; THAYER—593d.

4797. **συγχέω** {5x} **sugchĕō**, *soong-kheh'-o;* or **συγχύνω** **sugchunō**, *soong-khoo'-no;* from *4862* and χέω **chĕō** (to *pour*) or its alt.; to *commingle,* promiscuously, i.e. (fig.) to *throw* (an assembly) *into disorder,* to *perplex* (the mind):—confound {2x}, confuse {1x}, stir up {1x}, be in an uproar {1x}.

Sugcheo, as a verb, means literally "to pour together, commingle," hence, **(1)** said of persons, means "to trouble or confuse, to stir up": "Some therefore cried one thing, and some another: for the assembly was confused (*sugcheo*); and the more part knew not wherefore they were come together" (Acts 19:32 - said of the mind); **(2)** "was in an uproar" (Acts 21:31); **(3)** "stirred up": "And when the seven days were almost ended, the Jews which were of Asia, when they saw him in the temple, stirred up all the people, and laid hands on him" (Acts 21:27); **(4)** "confounded": "Now when this was noised abroad, the multitude came together, and were confounded, because that every man heard them speak in his own language" (Acts 2:6; cf. 9:22). Syn.: 181, 329, 383, 387, 1326, 1892, 2042, 2617, 3947, 3951, 4531, 4579, 4787, 4799, 5017. See: BAGD—775a; THAYER—593d.

4798. **συγχράομαι** {1x} **sugchraŏmai**, *soong-khrah'-om-ahee;* from *4862* and *5530;* to *use jointly,* i.e. (by impl.) to *hold intercourse in common:*—have dealings with {1x}. See: BAGD—775b; THAYER—594a.

4799. **σύγχυσις** {1x} **sugchusis**, *soong'-khoo-sis;* from *4797; commixture,* i.e. (fig.) riotous *disturbance:*—confusion {1x}.

Sunchusis, as a noun, means "a pouring or mixing together"; hence "a disturbance, confusion, a tumultuous disorder, as of riotous persons": "And the whole city was filled with confusion: and having caught Gaius and Aristarchus, men of Macedonia, Paul's companions in travel, they rushed with one accord into the theatre" (Acts 19:29). Syn.: 181, 2617, 4797. See: BAGD—775c; THAYER—594a.

4800. **συζάω** {3x} **suzaō**, *sood-zah'-o;* from *4862* and *2198;* to continue to *live* in common *with,* i.e. *co-survive* (lit. or fig.):—live with {3x}.

Sunzao, as a verb, means "to live together with": "Now if we be dead with Christ, we believe that we shall also live with him" (Rom 6:8; cf. 2 Ti 2:11; 2 Cor 7:3). Syn.: 326, 390, 980, 1236, 2198, 2225, 4176, 5225. See: TDNT—7:787, 1102; BAGD—775c; THAYER—594a.

4801. **συζεύγνυμι** {2x} **suzĕugnumi**, *sood-zyoog'-noo-mee;* from *4862* and the base of *2201;* to *yoke together,* i.e. (fig.) *conjoin* (in marriage):—join together {2x}. Cf. Mt 19:6; Mk 10:9. See: BAGD—775c; THAYER—594a.

4802. **συζητέω** {10x} **suzētĕō**, *sood-zay-teh'-o;* from *4862* and *2212;* to investigate *jointly,* i.e. *discuss, controvert, cavil:*—question with {2x}, question {2x}, question one with another {1x}, enquire {1x}, dispute with {1x}, dispute {1x}, reason together {1x}, reason {1x}.

This word means "to search together", "to discuss, dispute," is translated **(1)** "question with" in Mk 8:11; 9:16; **(2)** "question" in Mk 1:27; 9:14; **(3)** "question one with another" in Mk 9:10; **(4)** "enquire" in Lk 22:23; **(5)** "dispute with" in Acts 6:9; **(6)** "dispute" in Acts 9:29; **(7)** "reason together" in Mk 12:28; and **(8)** "reason" in Lk 24:15. See: TDNT—7:747, 1099; BAGD—775d; THAYER—594a.

4803. **συζήτησις** {3x} **suzētēsis**, *sood-zay'-tay-sis;* from *4802; mutual questioning,* i.e. *discussion:*—disputation {1x}, disputing {1x}, reasoning {1x}. Cf. Acts 15:2, 7; 28:29. See: TDNT—7:748, 1099; BAGD—775d; THAYER—594b.

4804. **συζητητής** {1x} **suzētētēs**, *sood-zay-tay-tace';* from *4802;* a *disputant,* i.e. *sophist:*—disputer {1x}.

Suzetetes, from *sun,* "with," *zeteo,* "to seek," denotes "a disputer," 1 Cor 1:20, where the reference is especially to a learned "disputant," a sophist. See: TDNT—7:748, 1099; BAGD—775d; THAYER—594b.

4805. **σύζυγος** {1x} **suzugŏs**, *sood'-zoo-gos;* from *4801; co-yoked,* i.e. (fig.) as noun, a *colleague;* prob. rather as a proper name; *Syzygus,* a Chr.:—yokefellow {1x}. See: TDNT—7:748, 1099; BAGD—775a; THAYER—594b.

4806. **συζωοποιέω** {2x} **suzōŏpŏiĕō**, *sood-zo-op-oy-eh'-o;* from *4862* and *2227;* to *reanimate conjointly* with (fig.):—quicken together with {1x}, quicken together {1x}.

(1) Quicken means to make a person able to respond immediately to spiritual stimuli; neither growth nor time is necessary before one is capable of walking in the Spirit. **(2)** It is used in Eph 2:5; Col 2:13, of the spiritual life with Christ, imparted to believers at their conversion. See: TDNT—7:787, 1102; BAGD—776a; THAYER—594c.

4807. **συκάμινος** {1x} **sukaminŏs**, *soo-kam'-ee-nos;* of Heb. or. [8256] in imitation of *4809;* a *sycamore*-fig tree:—sycamine tree {1x}.

The sycamine tree has the form and foliage of the mulberry, but fruit resembling the fig; probably mimics the *sycamore* (4809) in appearance, Lk 17:6. See: TDNT—7:758, 1100; BAGD—776a; THAYER—594c.

4808. **συκῆ** {16x} **sukē**, *soo-kay';* from *4810;* a *fig-tree:*—fig tree {16x}. *Suke,* "a fig tree," is found in Mt 21:19, 20, 21; 24:32; Mk 11:13, 20, 21; 13:28; Lk 13:6, 7; 21:29; Jn 1:48, 50, Jas 3:12; Rev 6:13. ***Note:*** A "fig tree" with leaves must have young fruits already, or it will be barren for the season. The first figs ripen in late May or early June. The tree in Mk 11:13 should have had fruit, unripe indeed, but existing. In some lands "fig trees" bear the early fruit under the leaves and the later fruit above the leaves. In that case the leaves were a sign that there should have been fruit, unseen from a distance, underneath the leaves. The condemnation of this fig tree lay in the absence of any sign of fruit. See: TDNT—7:751, 1100; BAGD—776b; THAYER—594c.

4809. **συκομωραία** {1x} **sukŏmōraia**, *soo-kom-o-rah'-yah;* from *4810* and μόρον **mŏrŏn** (the *mulberry*); the "*sycamore*"-fig tree:—*sycamore* tree {1x}. See: TDNT—7:758,*; BAGD—776b; THAYER—594c. comp. *4807.*

4810. **σῦκον** {4x} **sukŏn**, *soo'-kon;* appar. a primary word; a *fig:*—fig {4x}.

Sukon denotes "the ripe fruit of a *suke,* a fig-tree" and is found in Mt 7:16; Mk 11:13; Lk 6:44; Jas 3:12. See: TDNT—7:751, 1100; BAGD—776b; THAYER—594d.

4811. **συκοφαντέω** {2x} **sukŏphantĕō**, *soo-kof-an-teh'-o;* from a compound of *4810* and a der. of *5316;* to *be a fig-informer* (reporter of the law forbidding the exportation of figs from Greece), "*sycophant*", i.e. (gen. and by extens.) to *defraud* (*exact* unlawfully, *extort*):—accuse falsely {1x}, take by false accusation {1x}.

Sukophanteo, as a verb, means **(1)** "to accuse wrongfully" in Lk 3:14; and **(2)** "to exact money wrongfully, to take anything by false accusation" in Lk 19:8. **(3)** The word is derived from *sukon,* "a fig," and *phaino,* "to show." **(3a)** At Athens a man whose business it was to give information against anyone who might be detected exporting figs out of the province, is said to have been called a *sukophantes.* **(3b)** Probably, however, the word was used to denote one who brings figs to light by shaking the tree, and then in a metaphorical sense one who makes rich men yield up their fruit by "false accusation." **(3c)** Hence in general parlance it was used to designate "a malignant informer," one who accused from love of gain. Syn.: 156, 157, 1225, 1458, 1462, 1908, 2723, 2724. See: TDNT—7:759, 1100; BAGD—776c; THAYER—594d.

4812. **συλαγωγέω** {1x} **sulagōgĕō**, *soo-lag-ogue-eh'-o;* from the base of *4813* and (the redupl. form of) *71;* to *lead* away as *booty,* i.e. (fig.) *seduce:*—spoil {1x}.

Sulagogeo means to carry off as spoil, lead captive. The false teacher, through his philosophy and vain deceit would carry them off as so much booty (Col 2:8). See: BAGD—776c; THAYER—594d.

4813. **συλάω** {1x} **sulaō**, *soo-lah'-o;* from a der. of σύλλω **sullō** (to *strip;* prob. akin to *138;* comp. *4661*); to *despoil:*—rob {1x}. See: BAGD—776c; THAYER—595a.

4814. **συλλαλέω** {6x} **sullalĕō**, *sool-lal-eh'-o;* from *4862* and *2980;* to *talk together,* i.e. *converse:*—talk with {2x}, talk {1x}, speak {1x}, commune with {1x}, confer {1x}. See: BAGD—776d; THAYER—595a.

4815. **συλλαμβάνω** {16x} **sullambanō**, *sool-lam-ban'-o;* from *4862* and *2983;* to *clasp,* i.e. *seize* (*arrest, capture*); spec. to *conceive* (lit. or fig.); by impl. to *aid:*—catch {1x}, conceive {5x}, help {2x}, take {8x}.

This word means "to seize, take," and is rendered **(1)** "to take" **(1a)** Jesus in Mt 26:55; Mk 14:48; Lk 22:54; Jn 18:12; Acts 1:16; **(1b)** a large draught of fish in Lk 5:9; **(1c)** Peter in Acts 12:3; and **(1c)** Paul in Acts 23:27; **(2)** "catch" in "Acts 26:21; **(3)** "conceive", **(3a)** Elisabeth in Lk 1:24, 36; **(3b)** Mary in Lk 1:31; **(3c)** Jesus in Lk 2:21; **(3d)** "lust" in Jas 1:15; and **(4)** "help" in Lk 5:7; Phil 4:3. See: TDNT—7:759, 1101; BAGD—776d; THAYER—595a.

4816. **συλλέγω** {8x} **sullĕgō**, *sool-leg'-o;* from *4862* and *3004* in its orig. sense; to *collect:*—gather {5x}, gather up {2x}, gather together {1x}.

(1) This word denotes to gather up, to collect in order to carry off. This word means "to collect, gather up or out" (*sun,* "with" *lego,* "to pick out"), is said **(1)** of "gathering" **(2)** grapes and figs, Mt 7:16; Lk 6:44; **(3)** tares, Mt 13:28, 29, 30, 40; **(4)** good fish, Mt 13:48; and **(5)** "all things that cause stumbling, and them that do iniquity," Mt 13:41. See: BAGD—777a; THAYER—595b.

4817. **συλλογίζομαι** {1x} **sullŏgizŏmai**, *sool-log-id'-zom-ahee;* from *4862* and *3049;* to *reckon together* (with oneself), i.e. *deliberate:*—reason with {1x}.

This word stresses to bring together accounts, reckon up, compute; and to reckon within one's self, to reason (Lk 20:5) [cf. Eng. "syllogism"]. See: BAGD—777a; THAYER—595b.

4818. **συλλυπέω** {1x} **sullupĕō**, *sool-loop-eh'-o;* from *4862* and *3076;* to *afflict jointly,* i.e. (pass.) *sorrow at* (on account of) someone:—be grieved {1x}.

Sullupeo is used in the passive voice in Mk 3:5, "to be grieved" or afflicted together with a person, said of Christ's "grief" at the hardness of heart of those who criticized His healing on the Sabbath day; it here seems to suggest the sympathetic nature of His grief because of their self-injury. Some suggest that the *sun* indicates the mingling of "grief" with His anger. See: TDNT—4:323,*; BAGD—777a; THAYER—595b.

4819. **συμβαίνω** {8x} **sumbainō**, *soom-bah'-ee-no;* from *4862* and the base of *939;* to *walk* (fig. *transpire*) *together,* i.e. *concur* (*take place*):—happen unto {4x}, happen {2x}, befell, {1x}, so it was {1x}.

(1) *Sumbaino* literally means to walk with the feet near together; hence, to walk together, come together, arrive at the same point at the same time. **(2)** Therefore, figuratively, of things which fall out at the same time, to happen, turn out, come to pass. It is translated **(1)** "happen unto" in Mk 10:32; Acts 3:10; 1 Pet 4:12; 2 Pet 2:22; **(2)** "happen" in Lk 24:14; 1 Cor 10:11; **(3)** "befell" in Acts 20:19; and **(4)** "so it was" in Acts 21:35. See: BAGD—777b; THAYER—595b.

4820. **συμβάλλω** {6x} **sumballō**, *soom-bal'-lo;* from *4862* and *906;* to *combine,* i.e. (in speaking) to *converse, consult, dispute,* (mentally) to *consider,* (by impl.) to *aid,* (personally) to *join, attack:*—confer {1x}, encounter {1x}, help {1x}, make {1x}, meet with {1x}, ponder {1x}. See: BAGD—777b; THAYER—595c.

4821. **συμβασιλεύω** {2x} **sumbasilĕuō**, *soom-bas-il-yoo'-o;* from *4862* and *936;* to *be co-regent* (fig.):—reign with {2x}.

Sumbasileuo, "to reign together with", is used of the future "reign" of believers together and with Christ in the kingdom of God in manifestation, 1 Cor 4:8 (3rd part); of those who endure, 2 Ti 2:12. See: TDNT—1:591 & 7:787, 1102; BAGD—777c; THAYER—595d.

4822. **συμβιβάζω** {6x} **sumbibazō**, *soom-bib-ad'-zo;* from *4862* and βιβάζω **bibazō** (to *force;* caus. [by redupl.] of the base of *939*); to *drive together,* i.e. *unite* (in association or affection), (mentally) to *infer, show, teach:*—compact {1x}, assuredly gather {1x}, intrust {1x}, knit together {2x}, prove {1x}. See: TDNT—7:763, 1101; BAGD—777d; THAYER—595d.

4823. **συμβουλεύω** {5x} **sumbŏulĕuō**, *soom-bool-yoo'-o;* from *4862* and *1011;* to *give* (or *take*) *advice jointly,* i.e. *recommend, deliberate* or *determine:*—consult {1x}, give counsel {1x}, take counsel {1x}, counsel together {1x}, take counsel together {1x}. See: BAGD—777d; THAYER—596a.

4824. **συμβούλιον** {8x} **sumbŏuliŏn**, *soom-boo'-lee-on;* neut. of a presumed der. of *4825; advisement;* spec. a *deliberative* body, i.e. the provincial *assessors* or lay-court:—consultation {1x}, counsel {5x}, council {2x}.

Sumboulion, "a uniting in counsel" (*sun,* "together," *boule,* "counsel, advice"), denotes **(1)** "counsel" which is given, taken and acted upon, e.g., Mt 12:14, "held a council"; 22:15; 27:1, 7; 28:12; Mk 3:6; 15:1, "consultation"; hence **(2)** "a council," an assembly of counsellors or persons in consultation, Acts 25:12, of the "council" with which Festus conferred concerning Paul. **(3)** The governors and procurators of provinces had a board of advisers or assessors, with whom they took "counsel," before pronouncing judgment. See: BAGD—778a; THAYER—596a.

4825. **σύμβουλος** {1x} **sumbŏulŏs**, *soom'-boo-los;* from *4862* and *1012;* a *consultor,* i.e. *adviser:*—counsellor {1x}. See: BAGD—778b; THAYER—596b.

4826. **Συμεών** {7x} **Sumĕōn**, *soom-eh-one';* from the same as *4613; Symeon* (i.e. *Shimon*), the name of five Isr.:—Simeon {6x}, Simon Peter {1x}. See: BAGD—778b; THAYER—596b.

4827. **συμμαθητής** {1x} **summathētēs**, *soom-math-ay-tace';* from a compound of *4862* and *3129;* a *co-learner* (of Christianity):—fellowdisciples {1x}. See: TDNT—4:460, 552; BAGD—778b; THAYER—596b.

4828. **συμμαρτυρέω** {4x} **summarturĕō**, *soom-mar-too-reh'-o;* from *4862* and *3140;* to *testify jointly,* i.e. *corroborate* by (concurrent) evidence:—testify unto {1x}, also bear witness {2x}, bear witness with {1x}.

Summartureo, as a verb, is translated **(1)** "to bear witness with" in Rom 2:15; 8:16; 9:1; and **(2)** "testify" in Rev 22:18. Syn.: 267, 2649, 3140, 3141, 3142, 3143, 3144, 4901, 5571, 5576, 5577. See: TDNT—4:508, 564; BAGD—778b; THAYER—596c.

4829. **συμμερίζομαι** {1x} **summĕrizŏmai**, *soom-mer-id'-zom-ahee;* mid. voice from *4862* and *3307;* to *share jointly,* i.e. *participate* in:—be partaker with {1x}.

This word means primarily, "to distribute in shares" (*sun,* "with," *meros,* "a part"), in the middle voice, "to have a share in," is used in 1 Cor 9:13, "are partakers with (the altar)," i.e., they feed with others on that which, having been sacrificed, has been placed upon an altar; so the believer feeds upon Christ (who is the altar in Heb 13:10). See: BAGD—778c; THAYER—596c.

4830. **συμμέτοχος** {2x} **summĕtŏchŏs**, *soom-met'-okh-os;* from *4862* and *3353;* a *co-participant:*—partaker {2x}. Cf. Eph 3:6; 5:7. See: TDNT—2:830, 286; BAGD—778c; THAYER—596c.

4831. **συμμιμητής** {1x} **summimētēs**, *soom-mim-ay-tace';* from a presumed compound of *4862* and *3401;* a *co-imitator,* i.e. *fellow votary:*—follower together {1x}. See: TDNT—4:659, 594; BAGD—778c; THAYER—596d.

4832. **σύμμορφος** {2x} **summŏrphŏs**, *soom-mor-fos';* from *4862* and *3444; jointly formed,* i.e. (fig.) *similar:*—conformed to {1x}, fashioned like unto {1x}.

Summorphos signifies "having the same form as another, conformed to"; **(1)** of the "conformity" of children of God "to the image of His Son," Rom 8:29; **(2)** of their future physical "conformity" to His body of glory, Phil 3:21. See: TDNT—7:787, 1102; BAGD—778d; THAYER—596d.

4833. **συμμορφόω** {1x} **summŏrphŏō**, *soom-mor-fŏ'-o;* from *4832;* to *render like,* i.e. (fig.) to *assimilate:*—make conformable unto {1x}.

Summorphoo, "to make of like form with another person or thing, to render like" (*sun,* "with," *morphe,* "a form"), is found in Phil 3:10 (in the passive participle of the verb), "becoming conformed" (or "growing into conformity") to the death of Christ, indicating the practical apprehension of the death of the carnal self, and fulfilling his share of the sufferings following upon the sufferings of Christ; becoming less dependent upon self and more dependent upon Him. See: BAGD—778d; THAYER—596d.

4834. **συμπαθέω** {2x} **sumpathĕō**, *soom-path-eh'-o;* from *4835;* to *feel "sympathy"* with, i.e. (by impl.) to *commiserate:*—have compassion {1x}, be touched with a feeling of {1x}. Cf. Heb 4:15; 10:34. See: TDNT—5:935, 798; BAGD—778d; THAYER—596d.

4835. **συμπαθής** {1x} **sumpathēs**, *soom-path-ace';* from *4841; having a fellow-feeling* ("*sympathetic*"), i.e. (by impl.) *mutually commiserative:*—having compassion one of another {1x}. See: TDNT—5:935, 798; BAGD—779a; THAYER—596d.

4836. **συμπαραγίνομαι** {2x} **sumparaginŏmai**, *soom-par-ag-in'-om-ahee;* from *4862* and *3854;* to *be present together,* i.e. to *convene;* by impl. to *appear in aid:*—come together {1x}, stand with {1x}. Cf. Lk 23:48; 2 Ti 4:16. See: BAGD—779a; THAYER—596d.

4837. **συμπαρακαλέω** {1x} **sumparakalĕō**, *soom-par-ak-al-eh'-o;* from *4862* and *3870;* to *console jointly:*—comfort together {1x}. See: BAGD—779a; THAYER—597a.

4838. **συμπαραλαμβάνω** {4x} **sumparalambanō**, *soom-par-al-am-ban'-o;* from *4862* and *3880;* to *take along in company:*—take with {4x}.

The word denotes "to take along with oneself," as a companion, Acts 12:25; 15:37, 38; Gal 2:1. See: BAGD—779a; THAYER—597a.

4839. **συμπαραμένω** {1x} **sumparamĕnō**, *soom-par-am-en'-o;* from *4862* and *3887;* to *remain in company,* i.e. *still live:*—continue with {1x}. See: BAGD—779a; THAYER—597a.

4840. **συμπάρειμι** {1x} **sumparĕimi**, *soom-par'-i-mee;* from *4862* and *3918;* to *be at hand together,* i.e. *now present:*—be here present with {1x}. See: BAGD—779d; THAYER—597a.

4841. **συμπάσχω** {2x} **sumpaschō**, *soom-pas'-kho;* from *4862* and *3958* (incl. its alt.); to *experience pain jointly* or of the *same kind* (spec. *persecution;* to "*sympathize*"):—suffer with {2x}.

Sumpascho, "to suffer with", is used **(1)** in Rom 8:17 of "suffering" with Christ; and **(2)** in 1 Cor 12:26 of joint "suffering" in the members of the body. See: TDNT—5:925 & 7:787, 798 & 1102; BAGD—779b; THAYER—597a.

4842. **συμπέμπω** {2x} **sumpĕmpō**, *soom-pem'-po;* from *4862* and *3992;* to *dispatch in company:*—send with {2x}. Cf. 2 Cor 8:18, 22. See: BAGD—779b; THAYER—597b.

4843. **συμπεριλαμβάνω** {1x} **sumpĕrilambanō**, *soom-per-ee-lam-ban'-o;* from *4862* and a compound of *4012* and *2983;* to *take by enclosing altogether,* i.e. *earnestly throw the arms about one:*—embrace {1x}. See: BAGD—779c; THAYER—597b.

4844. **συμπίνω** {1x} **sumpinō**, *soom-pee'-no;* from *4862* and *4095;* to *partake a beverage in company:*—drink with {1x}. See: BAGD—779c; THAYER—597b.

4845. **συμπληρόω** {3x} **sumplērŏō**, *soom-play-rŏ'-o;* from *4862* and *4137;* to *implenish completely,* i.e. (of space) to *swamp* (a boat), or (of time) to *accomplish* (pass. be *complete*):—be fully come {1x}, be come {1x}, fill up {1x}.

Sumpleroo, "to fill completely" (*sun,* "with," intensive), is used, in the passive voice, **(1)** of time to be fulfilled or completed, **(1a)** Lk 9:51, "the days were well-nigh come"; **(1b)** Acts 2:1, "the day . . . was fully come". **(2)** In Lk 8:23, it is used in the active voice, of the filling of a boat in a storm. See: TDNT—6:308, 867; BAGD—779c; THAYER—597b.

4846. **συμπνίγω** {5x} **sumpnigō**, *soom-pnee'-go;* from *4862* and *4155;* to *strangle completely,* i.e. (lit.) to *drown,* or (fig.) to *crowd:*—choke {4x}, throng {1x}.

Sumpnigo gives the suggestion of **(1)** "choking together", i.e., by crowding, Mt 13:22; Mk 4:7, 19; Lk 8:14. **(2)** It is used in Lk 8:42, of the crowd that thronged the Lord, almost, so to speak, to suffocation. See: TDNT—6:455, 895; BAGD—779d; THAYER—597b.

4847. **συμπολίτης** {1x} **sumpŏlitēs**, *soom-pol-ee'-tace;* from *4862* and *4177;* a *native of the same town,* i.e. (fig.) *co-religionist* (*fellow-Christian*):—fellow-citizens {1x}. See: BAGD—780a; THAYER—597b.

4848. **συμπορεύομαι** {4x} **sumpŏrĕuŏmai**, *soom-por-yoo'-om-ahee;* from *4862* and *4198;* to *journey together;* by impl. to *assemble:*—go with {3x}, resort {1x}.

This word means "to go together with" and is used **(1)** in Mk 10:1, "resort"; and **(2)** "go with" in Lk 7:11; 14:25; 24:15. See: BAGD—780a; THAYER—597c.

4849. **συμπόσιον** {1x} **sumpŏsiŏn**, *soom-pos'-ee-on;* neut. of a der. of the alt. of *4844;* a *drinking*-party ("*symposium*"), i.e. (by extens.) a *room* of guests:—company {1x}.

In Mk 6:39 the noun is repeated, in the plural, by way of an adverbial and distributive phrase, *sumposia sumposia,* lit., "companies-companies" (i.e., by companies). See: BAGD—780a; THAYER—579c.

4850. **συμπρεσβύτερος** {1x} **sumprĕsbutĕrŏs**, *soom-pres-boo'-ter-os;* from *4862* and *4245;* a *co-presbyter:*—presbyter, also an elder {1x}. See: TDNT—6:651, 931; BAGD—780a; THAYER—597c.

συμφάγω **sumphagō**.See *4906*.

4851. **συμφέρω** {17x} **sumphĕrō**, *soom-fer'-o;* from *4862* and *5342* (incl. its alt.); to *bear together* (*contribute*), i.e. (lit.) to *collect,* or (fig.) to *conduce;* espec. (neut. part. as a noun) *advantage:*—be expedient {7x}, profit {4x}, be profitable {3x}, bring together {1x}, be better {1x}, be good {1x}.

Sumphero, signifies **(1)** transitively, lit., "to bring together," (*sun,* "with," *phero,* "to bring"), **(2)** intransitively, "to be an advantage, profitable, expedient"; it is used mostly impersonally, **(2a)** "it is (it was) expedient", so in Mt 19:10, "it is (not) good"; Jn 11:50; 16:7; 18;14; 1 Cor 6:12; 10:23; 2 Cor 8:10; 12:1; **(2b)** "it is profitable," Mt 5:29–30; 18:6; Acts 20:20; **(2c)** "to profit withal," 1 Cor 12:7; **(2d)** in Heb 12:10, used in the neuter of the present participle with the article as a noun, "for (our) profit." See: TDNT—9:69, 1252; BAGD—780b; THAYER—597c.

4852. **σύμφημι** {1x} **sumphēmi**, *soom'-fay-mee;* from *4862* and *5346;* to *say jointly,* i.e. *assent to:*—consent unto {1x}. See: BAGD—780c; THAYER—579d.

4853. **συμφυλέτης** {1x} **sumphulĕtēs**, *soom-foo-let'-ace;* from *4862* and a der. of *5443;* a *co-tribesman,* i.e. *native of the same country:*—countryman {1x}.

Sumphuletes, lit., "a fellow-tribesman" (*sun,* "with," *phule,* "a tribe, race, nation, people"), hence, one who is of the same people, a fellow-countryman, is found in 1 Th 2:14. See: BAGD—780c; THAYER—579d.

4854. **σύμφυτος** {1x} **sumphutŏs**, *soom'-foo-tos;* from *4862* and a der. of *5453;* *grown* along *with* (*connate*), i.e. (fig.) closely *united* to:—planted together {1x}.

This word is found only in Rom 6:5, "planted together," indicating the union of the believer with Christ in experiencing spiritually "the likeness of His death." See: TDNT—7:786, 1102; BAGD—780d; THAYER—597d.

4855. **συμφύω** {1x} **sumphuō**, *soom-foo'-o;* from *4862* and *5453;* pass. to *grow jointly:*—spring up with {1x}. See: BAGD—780d; THAYER—598a.

4856. **συμφωνέω** {6x} **sumphōnĕō**, *soom-fo-neh'-o;* from *4859;* to be *harmonious,* i.e. (fig.) to *accord* (*be suitable, concur*) or *stipulate* (by compact):—agree {3x}, agree together {1x}, agree with {2x}.

Sumphoneo, lit., "to sound together" (*sun,* "together," *phone,* "a sound"), i.e., "to be in accord, primarily of musical instruments," is used in the NT of the "agreement" **(1)** of persons concerning a matter, Mt 18:19; 20:2, 13; Acts 5:9; **(2)** of the writers of Scripture, Acts 15:15; **(3)** of things that are said to be congruous in their nature, Lk 5:36. See: TDNT—9:304, 1287; BAGD—780d; THAYER—598a.

4857. **συμφώνησις** {1x} **sumphōnēsis**, *soom-fo'-nay-sis;* from *4856; accordance:*—concord {1x}.

This word literally means a sounding together, to agree (2 Cor 6:15) [Eng., symphony]. See: TDNT—9:304, 1287; BAGD—781a; THAYER—598b.

4858. **συμφωνία** {1x} **sumphōnia**, *soom-fo-nee'-ah;* from *4859; unison* of sound ("*symphony*"), i.e. a *concert* of instruments (harmonious *note*):—music {1x}. See: TDNT—9:304, 1287; BAGD—81a; THAYER—598b.

4859. **σύμφωνος** {1x} **sumphōnŏs**, *soom'-fo-nos;* from *4862* and *5456; sounding together* (*alike*), i.e. (fig.) *accordant* (neut. as noun, *agreement*):—consent {1x}. See: TDNT—9:304, 1287; BAGD—781b; THAYER—598b.

4860. **συμψηφίζω** {1x} **sumpsēphizō**, *soom-psay-fid'-zo;* from *4862* and *5585;* to *compute jointly:*—count {1x}. See: TDNT—9:604, 1341; BAGD—781b; THAYER—598b.

4861. **σύμψυχος** {1x} **sumpsuchŏs**, *soom'-psoo-khos;* from *4862* and *5590; co-spirited,* i.e. *similar in sentiment:*—like-minded {1x}. See: BAGD—781b; THAYER—598b.

4862. **σύν** {125x} **sun**, *soon;* a primary prep. denoting *union; with* or *together* (but much closer than *3326* or *3844*), i.e. by association, companionship, process, resemblance, possession, instrumentality, addition, etc.:—with {123x}, beside {1x}, accompany + 2064 {1x}. [In composition, it has similar applications, including *completeness.*] See: TDNT—7:766, 1102; BAGD—781c; THAYER—598b.

4863. **συνάγω** {62x} **sunagō**, *soon-ag'-o;* from *4862* and *71;* to *lead together,* i.e. *collect* or *convene;* spec. to *entertain* (hospitably):—gather {15x}, be gathered together {12x}, gather together {9x}, come together {6x}, be gathered {4x}, be assembled {3x}, take in {3x}, misc. {10x} = + accompany, bestow, lead into, resort, take in. See: BAGD—782a; THAYER—599d.

4864. **συναγωγή** { {57x} **sunagōgē**, *soon-ag-o-gay';* from (the redupl. form of) *4863;* an *assemblage* of persons; spec. a Jewish "*synagogue*" (the meeting or the place); by anal. a Christian *church:*—assembly {1x}, congregation {1x}, *synagogue* {55x}. Syn.: 1577, 3831.

(1) *Sunagoge* originally meant just a gathering or bringing together of people, yet in the NT it became specifically the gathering place for the Jews, Jewish proselytes, and God-fearers. **(2)** This word means properly "a bringing together" (*sun,* "together," *ago,* "to bring"), denoted **(3)** "a gathering of things, a collection," then, **(3a)** of "persons, an assembling, of Jewish religious gatherings," e.g., Acts 9:2; **(3b)** an assembly of Christian Jews, Jas 2:2; **(3c)** a company dominated by the power and activity of Satan, Rev 2:9; 3:9; **(4)** by metonymy, "the building" in which the gathering is held, e.g. Mt 6:2; Mk 1:21. **(5)** The origin of the Jewish "*synagogue*" is probably to be assigned to the time of the Babylonian exile. Having no temple, the Jews assembled on the Sabbath to hear the Law read, and the practice continued in various buildings after the return. Cf. Ps. 74:8. See:

TDNT—7:798, 1108; BAGD—782d; THAYER—600a.

4865. **συναγωνίζομαι** {1x} **sunagōnizŏmai,** *soon-ag-o-nid'-zom-ahee;* from *4862* and *75;* to *struggle* in company *with,* i.e. (fig.) to *be a partner* (*assistant*):—strive together with {1x}. See: BAGD—783b; THAYER—600c.

4866. **συναθλέω** {2x} **sunathlĕō,** *soon-ath-leh'-o;* from *4862* and *118;* to *wrestle* in company *with,* i.e. (fig.) to *seek jointly:*—labour with {1x}, strive together for {1x}. Cf. Phil 1:27; 4:3. See: TDNT—1:167, 25; BAGD—783b; THAYER—600c.

4867. **συναθροίζω** {3x} **sunathrŏizō,** *soon-ath-royd'-zo;* from *4862* and ἀθροίζω **athrŏizō** (to *hoard*); to *convene:*—call together {1x}, gather together {2x}. Acts 12:12; 19:25. See: BAGD—783b; THAYER—600c.

4868. **συναίρω** {3x} **sunairō,** *soon-ah'-ee-ro;* from *4862* and *142;* to *make up together,* i.e. (fig.) to *compute and settle* (an account):—reckon {1x}, reckon + 3056 {1x}, take {1x}. See: BAGD—783c; THAYER—600c.

4869. **συναιχμάλωτος** {3x} **sunaichmalōtŏs,** *soon-aheekh-mal'-o-tos;* from *4862* and *164;* a *co-captive:*—fellowprisoner {3x}.

Sunaichmalotos, "a fellow prisoner," primarily "one of fellow captives in war" (from *aichme,* "a spear," and *haliskomai,* "to be taken"at spear point), is used by Paul **(1)** of Andronicus and Junias, Rom 16:7; **(2)** of Epaphras, Philem 23; **(3)** of Aristarchus, Col 4:10. See: TDNT—1:195, 31; BAGD—783c; THAYER—600d.

4870. **συνακολουθέω** {2x} **sunakŏlŏuthĕō,** *soon-ak-ol-oo-theh'-o;* from *4862* and *190;* to *accompany:*—follow {2x}.

Sunakoloutheo, as a verb, means "to follow along with, to accompany a leader" and is found **(1)** in Mk 5:37: "And He suffered no man to follow Him, save Peter, and James, and John the brother of James"; **(2)** Lk 23:49, of the women who "followed with" Christ from Galilee. Syn.: 190, 1096, 1377, 1811, 1872, 2614, 2628, 3877. See: TDNT—1:216, 33; BAGD—600d; THAYER—600d.

4871. **συναλίζω** {1x} **sunalizō,** *soon-al-id'-zo;* from *4862* and ἁλίζω **halizō** (to *throng*); to *accumulate,* i.e. *convene:*—assemble together {1x}.

Sunalizo, "to gather together, to assemble," with the suggestion of a crowded meeting (*sun,* "with," *halizo,* "to crowd, or mass:" the corresponding adjective is *hales,* "thronged"), is used in Acts 1:4. See: BAGD—783d; THAYER—600d.

4872. **συναναβαίνω** {2x} **sunanabainō,** *soon-an-ab-ah'-ee-no;* from *4862* and *305;* to *ascend* in company *with:*—come up with {2x}. Cf. Mk 15:41; Acts 13:31. See: BAGD—784b; THAYER—601a.

4873. **συνανάκειμαι** {9x} **sunanakĕimai,** *soon-an-ak'-i-mahee;* from *4862* and *345;* to *recline* in company *with* (at a meal):—sit at meat with {4x}, sit with {2x}, sit together with {1x}, sit down with {1x}, sit at table with {1x}. Cf. Mt 9:10; 14:9; Mk 2:15; 6:22, 26; Lk 7:49; 14:10, 15; Jn 12:2). Syn.: 339, 345, 347, 377, 1910, 2516, 2521, 2621, 2523, 2625, 4775, 4776. See: TDNT—3:654, 425; BAGD—784b; THAYER—601a.

4874. **συναναμείγνυμι** {3x} **sunanamignumi,** *soon-an-am-ig'-noo-mee;* from *4862* and a compound of *303* and *3396;* to *mix up together,* i.e. (fig.) *associate with:*—have company with {1x}, keep company {1x}, company with {1x}. Cf. 1 Cor. 5:9, 11; 2 Thess. 3:14. See: TDNT—7:852, 1113; BAGD—784b; THAYER—601a.

4875. **συναναπαύομαι** {1x} **sunanapauŏmai,** *soon-an-ap-ŏw'-om-ahee;* mid. voice from *4862* and *373;* to *recruit oneself* in company *with:*—refresh with {1x}. See: BAGD—784b; THAYER—601a.

4876. **συναντάω** {6x} **sunantaō,** *soon-an-tah'-o;* from *4862* and a der. of *473;* to *meet with, of events;* fig. to *occur:*—befall {1x}, meet {5x}.

Sunantao, "to meet with," lit., "to meet together with" is used **(1)** literally in Lk 9:37; 22:10; Acts 10:25; Heb. 7:1, 10; **(2)** metaphorically in Acts 20:22 ("shall befall"). See: BAGD—784c; THAYER—601b.

4877. **συνάντησις** {1x} **sunantēsis,** *soon-an'-tay-sis;* from *4876;* a *meeting with:*—meet + 1519 {1x}. See: BAGD—784c; THAYER—601b.

4878. **συναντιλαμβάνομαι** {2x} **sunantilambanŏmai,** *soon-an-tee-lam-ban'-om-ahee;* from *4862* and *482;* to *take* hold of *opposite together,* i.e. *co-operate* (*assist*):—help {2x}.

This word signifies "to take hold with at the side for assistance"; hence, "to take a share in, help in bearing, to help in general." **(1)** It is used, in the middle voice in Martha's request to the Lord to bid her sister help her, Lk 10:40; **(2)** and of the ministry of the Holy Spirit in helping our infirmities, Rom 8:26. See: TDNT—1:375, 62; BAGD—784c; THAYER—601b.

4879. **συναπάγω** {3x} **sunapagō,** *soon-ap-ag'-o;* from *4862* and *520;* to *take off together,* i.e. *transport with* (*seduce,* pass. *yield*):—carry away with {1x}, lead away with {1x}, condescend {1x}.

Sunapago, "to carry away with", is used **(1)** in a bad sense, **(1a)** "was carried away" in Gal 2:13 and **(1b)** "being led away" in 2 Pet 3:17; **(2)** "condescend" in a good sense in Rom 12:16. Condescend means to lower one's self down in order to be led along with those around you. See: BAGD—784d; THAYER—601b.

4880. **συναποθνήσκω** {3x} **sunapŏthnēskō,** *soon-ap-oth-nace'-ko;* from *4862* and *599;* to *decease* (lit.) in company *with,* or (fig.) similarly *to:*—be dead with {1x}, die with {2x}.

Sunapothnesko, "to die with, to die together," is used **(1)** literally of association in physical "death," Mk 14:31; **(2)** in 2 Cor 7:3, the apostle declares that his love to the saints makes separation impossible, whether in life or in "death." **(3)** It is used once of association spiritually with Christ in His "death," 2 Ti 2:11. See: TDNT—3:7 & 7:786, 312 & 1102; BAGD—784d; THAYER—601b.

4881. **συναπόλλυμι** {1x} **sunapŏllumi,** *soon-ap-ol'-loo-mee;* from *4862* and *622;* to *destroy* (middle or passive voice *be slain*) in company *with:*—perish with {1x}. See: BAGD—785a; THAYER—601c.

4882. **συναποστέλλω** {1x} **sunapŏstĕllō,** *soon-ap-os-tel'-lo;* from *4862* and *649;* to *despatch* (on an errand) in company *with:*—send with {1x}. See: BAGD—785a; THAYER—601c.

4883. **συναρμολογέω** {2x} **sunarmŏlŏgĕō,** *soon-ar-mol-og-eh'-o;* from *4862* and a der. of a compound of *719* and *3004* (in its orig. sense of *laying*); to *render close-jointed together,* i.e. *organize compactly:*—be fitly framed together {1x}, be fitly joined together {1x}.

Sunarmologeo, "to fit or frame together" (*sun,* "with," *harmos,* "a joint, in building," and *lego,* "to choose"), is used **(1)** metaphorically of the various parts of the church as a building, Eph 2:21, "fitly framed together"; **(2)** also of the members of the church as the body of Christ, Eph 4:16, "fitly framed . . . together." See: TDNT—7:855, 1114; BAGD—785b; THAYER—601c.

4884. **συναρπάζω** {4x} **sunarpazō,** *soon-ar-pad'-zo;* from *4862* and *726;* to *snatch together,* i.e. *seize:*—catch {4x}.

Sunarpazo, (*sun,* used intensively, and *arpazo,* "to snatch, to seize, to keep a firm grip of"), is used only by Luke, and translated **(1)** "caught" in Lk 8:29, of devil-possession; **(2)** in Acts 6:12, of the act of the elders and scribes in seizing Stephen; and **(3)** of the crowd catching Gaius in Acts 19:29. **(4)** In Acts 27:15, it is used of the effects of wind upon a ship. See: BAGD—785b; THAYER—601c.

4885. **συναυξάνω** {1x} **sunauxanō,** *soon-ŏwx-an'-o;* from *4862* and *837;* to *increase* (*grow up*) *together:*—grow together {1x}. See: BAGD—785b; THAYER—601c.

4886. **σύνδεσμος** {4x} **sundĕsmŏs,** *soon'-des-mos;* from *4862* and *1199;* a *joint tie,* i.e. *ligament,* (fig.) *uniting principle, control:*—band {1x}, bond {3x}.

Sundesmos, as a noun, means "that which binds together" and is said of **(1)** "the bond of iniquity" (Acts 8:23); **(2)** "the bond of peace" (Eph 4:3); **(3)** "the bond of perfectness" (Col 3:14 figurative of the ligaments of the body); **(4)** "bands" (Col 2:19, figuratively of the bands which unite the church, the body of Christ). Syn.: 254, 1198, 1199.See: TDNT—7:856, 1114; BAGD—785b; THAYER—601d.

4887. **συνδέω** {1x} **sundĕō,** *soon-deh'-o;* from *4862* and *1210;* to *bind with,* i.e. (pass.) *be a fellow-prisoner* (fig.):—be bound with {1x}. See: BAGD—785c; THAYER—601d.

4888. **συνδοξάζω** {1x} **sundŏxazō,** *soon-dox-ad'-zo;* from *4862* and *1392;* to *exalt* to dignity in company (i.e. *similarly*) *with:*—glorify together {1x}. See: TDNT—2:253 & 7:787, 178 & 1102; BAGD—785d; THAYER—602a.

4889. **σύνδουλος** {10x} **sundŏulŏs,** *soon'-doo-los;* from *4862* and *1401;* a *co-slave,* i.e. *servitor* or *ministrant of the same master* (human or divine):—fellowservant {10x}.

Sundoulos, "a fellow servant," is used **(1)** of natural conditions, Mt 18:28, 29, 31, 33; 24:49; **(2)** of "servants" of the same divine Lord, Col 1:7; 4:7; Rev 6:11; **(3)** of angels, Rev 19:10; 22:9. See: TDNT—2:261, 182; BAGD—785d; THAYER—602a.

συνδρέμω **sundrĕmō.**See *4936.*

4890. **συνδρομή** {1x} **sundrŏmē,** *soon-drom-ay';* from (the alt. of) *4936;* a *running together,* i.e. (riotous) *concourse:*—run together + 1096 {1x}. See: BAGD—785d; THAYER—602a.

4891. **συνεγείρω** {3x} **sunĕgĕirō**, *soon-eg-i'-ro;* from *4862* and *1453;* to *rouse* (from death) in company *with*, i.e. (fig.) to *revivify* (spiritually) in resemblance to:—raise up together {1x}, rise with {2x}.

Sunergeiro, "to raise together", is used **(1)** of the believer's spiritual resurrection with Christ, Eph 2:6;**(2)** passive voice in Col 2:12, "ye are risen"; so Col 3:1. See: TDNT—7:786, 1102; BAGD—785d; THAYER—602a.

4892. **συνέδριον** {22x} **sunĕdriŏn**, *soon-ed'-ree-on;* neut. of a presumed der. of a compound of *4862* and the base of *1476;* a *joint session*, i.e. (spec.) the Jewish *Sanhedrin;* by anal. a subordinate *tribunal:*—council {22x}.

Sunedrion, properly, "a settling together" (*sun,* "together," *hedra,* "a seat"), hence, **(1)** "any assembly or session of persons deliberating or adjusting," Mt 10:17; Mk 13:9; Jn 11:47; **(2)** in particular, it denoted **(2a)** "the *Sanhedrin,*" the Great Council at Jerusalem, consisting of 71 members, namely, prominent members of the families of the high priest, elders and scribes. The Jews trace the origin of this to Num 11:16. The more important causes came up before this tribunal. The Roman rulers of Judea permitted the *Sanhedrin* to try such cases, and even to pronounce sentence of death, with the condition that such a sentence should be valid only if confirmed by the Roman procurator. **(2b)** In Jn 11:47, it is used of a meeting of the *Sanhedrin;* in Acts 4:15, of the place of meeting. See: TDNT—7:860, 1115; BAGD—786a; THAYER—602b.

4893. **συνείδησις** {32x} **sunĕidēsis**, *soon-i'-day-sis;* from a prol. form of *4894;* *co-perception*, i.e. moral *consciousness:*—conscience {32x}.

Summary: *Suneidesis* literally means "a knowing," a co-knowledge with one's self, the witness borne to one's conduct by conscience, that faculty by which we apprehend the will of God, as that which is designed to govern our lives. The word is stressing that we receive input from our surroundings [temptations, decision-making events, etc.] and we are driven to make a decision. We compare what we know with our conscience [*con* – "with", *science* – "knowledge"], our knowledge base about this input. If we follow our conscience we act according to what we know to be true about the situation and the consequences/blessings of our decision. We can violate our conscience by overriding that knowledge.

Discussion: This word means it., "a knowing with" (*sun,* "with," *oida,* "to know"), i.e., "a co-knowledge (with oneself), the witness borne to one's conduct by conscience, that faculty by which we apprehend the will of God, as that which is designed to govern our lives"; hence **(1)** the sense of guiltiness before God, Heb. 10:2; **(2)** that process of thought which distinguishes what it considers morally good or bad, commending the good, condemning the bad, and so prompting to do the former, and avoid the latter, Rom. 2:15 (bearing witness with God's law); 9:1; 2 Cor 1:12; **(3)** acting in a certain way because "conscience" requires it, Rom 13:5; **(3a)** so as not to cause scruples of "conscience" in another, 1 Cor 10:28–29; **(3b)** not calling a thing in question unnecessarily, as if conscience demanded it, 1 Cor 10:25, 27;

(4) "commending oneself to every man's conscience," 2 Cor 4:2; cf. 5:11. **(5)** There may be a "conscience" not strong enough to distinguish clearly between the lawful and the unlawful, 1 Cor 8:7, 10, 12. **(6)** The phrase "conscience toward God," in 1 Pet 2:19, signifies a "conscience" so controlled by the apprehension of God's presence, that the person realizes that griefs are to be borne in accordance with His will. **(7)** Heb 9:9 teaches that sacrifices under the Law could not so perfect a person that he could regard himself as free from guilt. **(8)** For various descriptions of "conscience" see: **(8a)** "good . . . before God" in Acts 23:1; 1 Ti 1:5, 19; Heb 13:18; 1 Pet 3:16, 21; **(8b)** "void of offence"in Acts 24:16; **(8c)** "weak" in 1 Cor 8:7, second part; **(8d)** "pure" in 1 Ti 3:9; 2 Ti 1:3; **(8e)** "seared" in 1 Ti 4:2; **(8f)** "defiled" in Titus 1:15; **(8g)** "purge . . . from dead works" in Heb 9:14; and **(8h)** "evil" in Heb 10:22. See: TDNT—7:898, 1120; BAGD—786c; THAYER—602c.

4894. **συνεῖδω** {4x} **sunĕidō**, *soon-i'-do;* from *4862* and *1492;* to *see completely;* used (like its primary) only in two past tenses, respectively mean. to *understand* or *become aware,* and to *be conscious* or (clandestinely) *informed of:*—consider {1x}, know {1x}, be privy {1x}, be ware of {1x}.

Sunoida, a perfect tense with a present meaning, denotes **(1)** "to share the knowledge of, be privy to," Acts 5:2; **(2)** "to be conscious of," especially of guilty consciousness, 1 Cor 4:4, "I know nothing by myself." It is also translated **(3)** "consider" in Acts 12:12; and **(4)** "were ware of" in Acts 14:6. Syn.: 1097, 1107, 1110, 1492, 1921, 1467, 1922, 1987. See: TDNT—7:898,*; BAGD—787a; THAYER—603b.

4895. **σύνειμι** {2x} **suneimi**, *soon'-i-mee;* from *4862* and *1510* (incl. its various inflections); to *be* in company *with,* i.e. *present* at the time;—be with {2x}. See: BAGD—787a; THAYER—603b.

4896. **σύνειμι** {1x} **sunĕimi**, *soon'-i-mee;* from *4862* and εἶμι **ĕimi** (to *go*); to *assemble:*—gather together {1x}. See: BAGD—787a; THAYER—603b.

4897. **συνεισέρχομαι** {2x} **sunĕisĕrchŏmai**, *soon-ice-er'-khom-ahee;* from *4862* and *1525;* to *enter* in company *with:*—go in with {1x}, go with into {1x}. Cf. 6:22; 18:15. See: BAGD—787a; THAYER—603b.

4898. **συνέκδημος** {2x} **sunĕkdēmŏs**, *soon-ek'-day-mos;* from *4862* and the base of *1553;* a *co-absentee* from home, i.e. *fellow-traveller:*—companion in travel {1x}, travel with {1x}. Cf. Acts 19:29; 2 Cor 8:19. See: BAGD—787a; THAYER—603b.

4899. **συνεκλεκτός** {1x} **sunĕklĕktŏs**, *soon-ek-lek-tos';* from a compound of *4862* and *1586;* *chosen* in company *with,* i.e. *co-elect* (*fellow Christian*):—elected together with {1x}. See: BAGD—787b; THAYER—603c.

4900. **συνελαύνω** {1x} **sunĕlaunō**, *soon-el-ow'-no;* from *4862* and *1643;* to *drive together,* i.e. (fig.) *exhort* (to reconciliation):—set at one again + 1515 + 1519 {1x}. See: BAGD—787b; THAYER—603c.

4901. **συνεπιμαρτυρέω** {1x} **sunĕpimarturĕō**, *soon-ep-ee-mar-too-reh'-o;* from *4862* and *1957;* to *testify further jointly,* i.e. *unite in adding evidence:*—also bear witness {1x}.

Sunepimartureo, as a verb, denotes "to join in bearing witness with others": "God also bearing *them* witness, both with signs and wonders, and with divers miracles, and gifts of the Holy Ghost, according to his own will?" (Heb 2:4). Syn.: 267, 2649, 3140, 3141, 3142, 3143, 3144, 4828, 5571, 5576, 5577.See: TDNT—4:508, 564; BAGD—787b; THAYER—603c.

4902. **συνέπομαι** {1x} **sunĕpŏmai**, *soon-ep'-om-ahee;* mid. voice from *4862* and a primary ἕπω **hĕpō** (to *follow*); to *attend* (*travel*) in company *with:*—accompany {1x}.

Sunepomai, lit., "to follow with" (*sun,* "with," *hepomai,* "to follow"), came to mean simply "to accompany," Acts 20:4, distinguishing Paul as the leader of those following/accompanying. See: BAGD—787c; THAYER—603c.

4903. **συνεργέω** {5x} **sunĕrgĕō**, *soon-erg-eh'-o,* from *4904;* to *be a fellow-worker,* i.e. *co-operate:*—work with {2x}, help with {1x}, workers together {1x}, work together {1x}. Cf. Mk 16:20; Rom 8:28; 1 Cor 16:16; 2 Cor 6:1; Jas 2:22. See: TDNT—7:871, 1116; BAGD—787c; THAYER—603c.

4904. **συνεργός** {13x} **sunĕrgŏs**, *soon-er-gos';* from a presumed compound of *4862* and the base of *2041;* a *co-laborer,* i.e. *coadjutor:*—fellowlabourer {4x}, helper {3x}, fellowhelper {2x}, fellowworkers {1x}, workfellow {1x}, labourer together with {1x}, companion in labour {1x}. Cf. Rom 16:3, 9, 21; 1 Co 3:9; 2 Co 1:24; 8:23; Phil 2:25; 4:3; Col 4:11; 1 Th 3:2; Philem 1, 24; 3 Jn 1:8. See: TDNT—7:871, 1116; BAGD—787d; THAYER—603b.

4905. **συνέρχομαι** {32x} **sunĕrchŏmai**, *soon-er'-khom-ahee;* from *4862* and *2064;* to *convene, depart* in company *with, associate* with, or (spec.) *cohabit* (conjugally):—come together {18x}, go with {4x}, come with {2x}, resort {2x}, come {2x}, come with + 2258 {1x}, company with {1x}, accompany {1x}, assemble with {1x}. See: TDNT—2:684, 257; BAGD—788a; THAYER—604a.

4906. **συνεσθίω** {5x} **sunĕsthiō**, *soon-es-thee'-o;* from *4862* and *2068* (incl. its alt.); to *take food* in company *with:*—eat with {5x}. Cf. Lk 15:2; Acts 10:41; 11:3; 1 Cor 5:11; Gal 2:12. See: BAGD—788b; THAYER—604b.

4907. **σύνεσις** {7x} **sunĕsis**, *soon'-es-is;* from *4920;* a mental *putting together,* i.e. *intelligence* or (concr.) the *intellect:*—knowledge {1x}, understanding {6x}.

(1) *Sunesis* suggests quickness of apprehension, the penetrating consideration which precedes action. *Sunesis,* "to set together, to understand," denotes **(1)** "the understanding, the mind or intelligence," Mk 12:33; Lk 2:47; 1 Cor 1:19; Eph 3:4, "knowledge"; Col 1:9; 2:2; 2 Ti 2:7. Syn.: **(A)** *Gnosis* (1108) denotes knowledge by itself and applies chiefly to the apprehension of truths. **(B)** *Sophia* (4678) denotes wisdom as exhibited in action and adds the power of reasoning about them and tracing their relationships. It is a mental excellence of the highest sense, to details. **(C)** *Sunesis* (4907) denotes critical, apprehending the bearing of things. **(D)** *Phronesis* (5428) denotes practical, suggesting lines of action. See: TDNT—7:888, 1119; BAGD—788c; THAYER—604b.

4908. **συνετός** {4x} **sunĕtŏs**, *soon-et'-os;* from *4920;* mentally *put* (or *putting*) *together,* i.e. *sagacious:*—prudent {4x}.

Sunetos, signifies "intelligent, sagacious, understanding" (akin to *suniemi,* "to perceive"), translated "prudent" in Mt 11:25; Lk 10:21; Acts 13:7; 1 Cor 1:19. Prudent is applied wisdom. Syn.: cf. 4907 for discussion. See: TDNT—7:888, 1119; BAGD—788d; THAYER—604b. comp. *5429.*

4909. **συνευδοκέω** {6x} **sunĕudŏkĕō**, *soon-yoo-dok-eh'-o;* from *4862* and *2106;* to *think well of in common,* i.e. *assent* to, *feel gratified with:*—consent unto {2x}, be pleased {2x}, allow {1x}, have pleasure in {1x}.

Suneudokeo, as a verb, means lit., "to think well with" (*sun,* "with," *eu,* "well," *dokeo,* "to think"), to take pleasure with others in anything, to approve of, to assent, is used **(1)** in Lk 11:48, of "allowing" the evil deeds of predecessors; **(2)** in Rom 1:32, of "have pleasure" in doing evil; **(3)** in Acts 8:1; 22:20, of "consenting" to the death of another. All these are cases of "consenting" to evil things. In 1 Cor 7:12–13, it is used of an unbelieving wife's "being pleased" to dwell with her converted husband, and of an unbelieving husband's "consent" to dwell with a believing wife. Syn.: 714, 841, 842, 2425. See: BAGD—788d; THAYER—604b.

4910. **συνευωχέω** {2x} **suněuōchěō,** *soon-yoo-o-kheh'-o;* from *4862* and a der. of a presumed compound of *2095* and a der. of *2192* (mean. to *be in good condition,* i.e. [by impl.] to *fare well,* or *feast*); to *entertain* sumptuously in company *with,* i.e. (middle or passive voice) to *revel together:*—feast with {2x}. Cf. 2 Pet 2:13 and Jude 12. See: BAGD—789a; THAYER—604c.

4911. **συνεφίστημι** {1x} **suněphistēmi,** *soon-ef-is'-tay-mee;* from *4862* and *2186;* to *stand up together against,* i.e. to *resist* (or *assault*) *jointly:*—rise up together {1x}.

Sunephistemi, as a verb, means "to rise up together" and is used in Acts 16:22, of the "rising up" of a multitude against Paul and Silas. Syn.: 305, 393, 450, 1096, 1326, 1453, 1525, 1817. See: BAGD—789a; THAYER—604c.

4912. **συνέχω** {12x} **suněchō,** *soon-ekh'-o;* from *4862* and *2192;* to *hold together,* i.e. to *compress* (the ears, with a crowd or siege) or *arrest* (a prisoner); fig. to *compel, perplex, afflict, preoccupy:*—be taken with {3x}, throng {1x}, straiten {1x}, keep in {1x}, hold {1x}, stop {1x}, press {1x}, lie sick of {1x}, constrain {1x}, be in a strait {1x}.

Sunecho, as a verb, means "to hold together, confine, secure, to hold fast" [*sun* "together," *echo,* "to have or hold"], "to constrain," and is said **(1)** of the effect of the word of the Lord upon Paul: "And when Silas and Timotheus were come from Macedonia, Paul was pressed in the spirit (*sunecho*), and testified to the Jews *that* Jesus *was* Christ" (Acts 18:5); **(2)** of the effect of the love of Christ: "For the love of Christ constraineth us; because we thus judge, that if one died for all, then were all dead" (2 Cor 5:14); **(3)** of being taken with a disease: "And His fame went throughout all Syria: and they brought unto Him all sick people that were taken (*sunecho*) with divers diseases and torments, and those which were possessed with devils, and those which were lunatick, and those that had the palsy; and he healed them" (Mt 4:24; cf. Lk 4:38; Acts 28:8); **(4)** taken with fear: "Then the whole multitude of the country of the Gadarenes round about besought Him to depart from them; for they were taken with great fear: and He went up into the ship, and returned back again" (Lk 8:37);

(5) of thronging or holding in a person: "And Jesus said, Who touched me? When all denied, Peter and they that were with Him said, Master, the multitude throng thee and press *thee,* and sayest thou, Who touched me?" (Lk 8:45); **(6)** being straitened: "But I have a baptism to be baptized with; and how am I straitened till it be accomplished!" (Lk 12:50); **(7)** being in a strait betwixt two: "For I am in a strait betwixt two, having a desire to depart, and to be with Christ; which is far better" (Phil 1:23); **(8)** keeping a city in on every side: "For the days shall come upon thee, that thine enemies shall cast a trench about thee, and compass thee round, and keep thee in on every side" (Lk 19:43); **(9)** keeping a tight hold on a person, as the men who seized the Lord Jesus did, after bringing Him into the High Priest's house: "And the men that held Jesus mocked him, and smote *him*" (Lk 22:63); **(10)** of stopping the ears in refusal to listen: "Then they cried out with a loud voice, and stopped their ears, and ran upon him [Stephen] with one accord" (Acts 7:57). Syn.: 315, 317, 3849. See: TDNT—7:877, 1117; BAGD—789a; THAYER—604c.

4913. **συνήδομαι** {1x} **sunēdŏmai,** *soon-ay'-dom-ahee;* mid. voice from *4862* and the base of *2237;* to *rejoice* in *with* oneself, i.e. *feel satisfaction* concerning:—delight {1x}.

Sunedomai, lit., "to rejoice with (anyone), to delight in (a thing) with (others)," signifies "to delight with oneself inwardly in a thing," in Rom 7:22. See: BAGD—789c; THAYER—604d.

4914. **συνήθεια** {2x} **sunēthěia,** *soon-ay'-thi-ah;* from a compound of *4862* and *2239; mutual habituation,* i.e. *usage:*—custom {2x}.

Sunetheia denotes **(1)** "a custom, customary usage" in Jn 18:39; 1 Cor 11:16. See: BAGD—789c; THAYER—604d.

4915. **συνηλικιώτης** {1x} **sunēlikiōtēs,** *soon-ay-lik-ee-o'-tace;* from *4862* and a der. of *2244;* a *co-aged* person, i.e. *alike* in years:—equal {1x}. See: BAGD—789d; THAYER—605a.

4916. **συνθάπτω** {2x} **sunthaptō,** *soon-thap'-to;* from *4862* and *2290;* to *inter* in company *with,* i.e. (fig.) to *assimilate* spiritually (to Christ by a sepulture as to sin):—bury with {2x}. Cf. Rom 6:4; Col 2:12. See: TDNT—7:786, 1102; BAGD—789d; THAYER—605a.

4917. **συνθλάω** {2x} **sunthlaō,** *soon-thlah'-o;* from *4862* and θλάω **thlaō** (to *crush*); to *dash together,* i.e. *shatter:*—break {2x}. Cf. Mt 21:44 and Lk 20:18. See: BAGD—790a; THAYER—605a.

4918. **συνθλίβω** {2x} **sunthlibō,** *soon-thlee'-bo;* from *4862* and *2346;* to *compress,* i.e. *crowd* on all sides:—throng {2x}. Cf. Mk 5:24, 31. See: BAGD—790a; THAYER—605a.

4919. **συνθρύπτω** {1x} **sunthruptō,** *soon-throop'-to;* from *4862* and θρύπτω **thruptō** (to *crumble*); to *crush together,* i.e. (fig.) to *dispirit:*—break {1x}. See: BAGD—790a; THAYER—605a.

4920. **συνίημι** {26x} **suniēmi,** *soon-ee'-ay-mee;* from *4862* and ἵημι **hiēmi** (to *send*); to *put together,* i.e. (mentally) to *comprehend;* by impl. to *act piously:*—consider {1x}, understand {24x}, be wise {1x}.

Suneimi, primarily, "to bring or set together," is used metaphorically **(1)** of "perceiving, understanding, uniting", so to speak, the perception with what is perceived, e.g., Mt 13:13–15, 19, 23, 51; 15:10; 16:12; 17:13, and similar passages in Mk and Lk; Acts 7:25 (twice); 28:26, 27; in Rom 3:11, the present participle, with the article, is used as a noun, lit., "there is not the understanding (one)," in a moral and spiritual sense; Rom. 15:21; 2 Cor. 10:12, "are (not) wise"; Eph. 5:17, "understand." It is translated **(2)** "consider" in Mk 6:52; and **(3)** "be wise" in 2 Cor 10:12. See: TDNT—7:888, 1119; BAGD—790a; THAYER—605b.

4921. **συνιστάω** {16x} **sunistaō,** *soon-is-tah'-o;* or (strengthened)

συνιστάνω **sunistanō,** *soon-is-tan'-o;* or

συνίστημι **sunistēmi,** *soon-is'-tay-mee;* from *4862* and *2476* (incl. its collat. forms); to *set together,* i.e. (by impl.) to *introduce* (favorably), or (fig.) to *exhibit;* intr. to *stand near,* or (fig.) to *constitute:*—commend {10x}, approve {2x}, consist {1x}, make {1x}, stand {1x}, stand with {1x}. See: TDNT—7:896, 1120; BAGD—790c; THAYER—605c.

4922. **συνοδεύω** {1x} **sunŏděuō,** *soon-od-yoo'-o;* from *4862* and *3593;* to *travel* in company *with:*—journey with {1x}. See: BAGD—791c; THAYER—605d.

4923. **συνοδία** {1x} **sunŏdia,** *soon-od-ee'-ah;* from a compound of *4862* and *3598* ("*synod*"); *companionship* on a journey, i.e. (by impl.) a *caravan:*—company {1x}.

Sunodia, lit., "a way or journey together" (*sun,* "with," *hodos,* "a way"), denotes, by metonymy, "a company of travelers", travelers bound together only by destination; in Lk 2:44, of the company from which Christ was missed by Joseph and Mary. See: BAGD—791a; THAYER—605d.

4924. **συνοικέω** {1x} **sunŏikĕō,** *soon-oy-keh'-o;* from *4862* and *3611;* to *reside together* (as a family):—dwell together {1x}. See: BAGD—791c; THAYER—605d.

4925. **συνοικοδομέω** {1x} **sunŏikŏdŏmĕō,** *soon-oy-kod-om-eh'-o;* from *4862* and *3618;* to *construct,* i.e. (pass.) to *compose* (in company with other Christians, fig.):—build together {1x}. See: TDNT—5:148, 674; BAGD—791c; THAYER—606a.

4926. **συνομιλέω** {1x} **sunŏmilĕō,** *soon-om-il-eh'-o;* from *4862* and *3656;* to *converse* mutually:—talk with {1x}. See: BAGD—791c; THAYER—606a.

4927. **συνομορέω** {1x} **sunŏmŏrĕō,** *soon-om-or-eh'-o;* from *4862* and a der. of a compound of the base of *3674* and the base of *3725;* to *border together,* i.e. *adjoin:*—join hard + 2251 {1x}. See: BAGD—791c; THAYER—606a.

4928. **συνοχή** {2x} **sunŏchē,** *soon-okh-ay';* from *4912; restraint,* i.e. (fig.) *anxiety:*—anguish {1x}, distress {1x}.

Sunoche literally means, a holding together, or compressing and was used of the narrowing of a way. It is found only in its metaphorical sense, of straits, distress, anguish **(1)** Lk 21:25—distress of nations, and **(2)** 2 Cor 2:4—anguish of heart. See: TDNT—7:886, 1117; BAGD—791d; THAYER—606a.

4929. **συντάσσω** {2x} **suntassō,** *soon-tas-so;* from *4862* and *5021;* to *arrange jointly,* i.e. (fig.) to *direct:*—appoint {2x}.

Suntasso, as a verb, means literally "to arrange together with", hence "to appoint, prescribe" and is used **(1)** Mt 26:19 of what the Lord "appointed" for His disciples: "And the disciples did as Jesus had appointed them; and they made ready the passover" and **(2)** in Mt 27:10, in a quotation concerning the price of the potter's field: "And gave them for the potter's field, as the Lord appointed me." See: BAGD—791d; THAYER—606a.

4930. **συντέλεια** {6x} **suntĕlĕia**, *soon-tel'-i-ah;* from *4931; entire completion,* i.e. *consummation* (of a dispensation):—end {6x}.

Sunteleia, signifies "a bringing to completion together" (*sun* "with," *teleo,* "to complete"), marking the "completion" or consummation of the various parts of a scheme. It is used **(1)** in Mt 13:39–40, 49; 24:3; 28:20, "the end of the world", **(1a)** not denoting a termination, but the heading up of events to the appointed climax. **(1b)** *Aion* is not the world, but a period or epoch or era in which events take place on the world. **(2)** In Heb 9:26, the word translated "world" is in the plural, and the phrase is "the end of the world." It was at the heading up of all the various epochs appointed by divine counsels that Christ was manifested (i.e., in His Incarnation) "to put away sin by the sacrifice of Himself. See: TDNT—8:64, 1161; BAGD—792a; THAYER—606b.

4931. **συντελέω** {7x} **suntĕlĕō**, *soon-tel-eh'-o;* from *4862* and *5055;* to *complete entirely;* gen. to *execute* (lit. or fig.):—end {4x}, finish {1x}, fulfil {1x}, make {1x}.

Sunteleo means to end together, bring quite to an end and is said **(1)** of the completion of a period of days (Lk 4:2; Acts 21:27); **(2)** of completing something; of the Lord ending His discourse (Mt 7:28); **(3)** of God **(3a)** in finishing a work (Rom 9:28), and **(3b)** in making a new covenant (Heb 8:8); **(4)** of the fulfillment of things foretold (Mk 13:4); **(5)** of the Devil's temptation of the Lord (Lk 4:13). See: TDNT—8:62, 1161; BAGD—792a; THAYER—606b.

4932. **συντέμνω** {2x} **suntĕmnō**, *soon-tem'-no;* from *4862* and the base of *5114;* to *contract* by cutting, i.e. (fig.) *do concisely* (*speedily*):—cut short {1x}, short {1x}.

Suntemno, lit., "to cut together" signifies "to make contract by cutting, to cut short"; thus, to bring to an end or accomplish speedily; it is said of a prophecy or decree, Rom 9:28 (twice). See: BAGD—792c; THAYER—606c.

4933. **συντηρέω** {4x} **suntērĕō**, *soon-tay-reh'-o;* from *4862* and *5083;* to *keep* closely *together,* i.e. (by impl.) to *conserve* (from ruin); ment. to *remember* (and *obey*):—keep {1x}, observe {1x}, preserve {2x}.

Suntereo denotes "to preserve, keep safe, keep close" (*sun,* "together with," used intensively), **(1)** in Lk 2:19, of the mother of Jesus in regard to the words of the shepherds; **(2)** in Mk 6:20 it is used of Herod's preservation of John the Baptist from Herodias, by "watching over/out" for him, "observed (him)"; **(3)** in Mt 9:17; Lk 5:38, of the preservation of wineskins. See: TDNT—8:151, 1174; BAGD—792c; THAYER—606c.

4934. **συντίθημι** {4x} **suntithĕmai**, *soon-tith'-em-ahee;* mid. voice from *4862* and *5087;* to *place jointly,* i.e. (fig.) to *consent* (*bargain, stipulate*), *concur:*—agree {2x}, assent {1x}, covenant {1x}.

Suntithemi, lit., "to put together" (*sun,* "with," *tithemi,* "to put"), in the middle voice, means "to make an agreement, or to assent to"; translated **(1)** "covenanted" in Lk 22:5; **(2)** "agreed" in Jn 9:22, and **(3)** Acts 23:20; "assented" in Acts 24:9. See: BAGD—72d; THAYER—606c.

4935. **συντόμως** {1x} **suntŏmōs**, *soon-tom'-oce;* adv. from a der. of *4932; concisely* (*briefly*):—a few words {1x}. See: BAGD—792d; THAYER—606d.

4936. **συντρέχω** {3x} **suntrĕchō**, *soon-trekh'-o;* from *4862* and *5143* (incl. its alt.); to *rush together* (hastily *assemble*) or *headlong* (fig.):—run {1x}, run together {1x}, run with {1x}.

Suntrecho, "to run together with", is used **(1)** literally, Mk 6:33; Acts 3:11; **(2)** metaphorically, 1 Pet 4:4, of "running" a course of evil with others. See: BAGD—793a; THAYER—606d.

4937. **συντρίβω** {8x} **suntribō**, *soon-tree'-bo;* from *4862* and the base of *5117;* to *crush completely,* i.e. to *shatter* (lit. or fig.):—bruise {3x}, break {2x}, broken to shivers {1x}, brokenhearted + 2588 {1x}, break in pieces {1x}.

(1) The stress in this word is harm inflicted by a quick blow. *Subtribo,* lit., "to rub together," and so "to shatter, shiver, break in pieces by crushing," is said **(1)** of the bruising of a reed, Mt 12:20; **(2)** the "breaking" of fetters in pieces, Mk 5:4; **(3)** the "breaking" of **(3a)** an alabaster cruse, Mk 14:3; **(3b)** an earthenware vessel, Rev 2:27; **(4)** of the physical bruising of a person possessed by a devil, Lk 9:39; **(5)** concerning Christ, "a bone of Him shall not be broken," Jn 19:36; **(6)** metaphorically of the crushed condition of a "broken-hearted" person, Lk 4:18; **(7)** of the eventual crushing of Satan, Rom 16:20. Syn.: 4938. See: TDNT—7:919, 1124; BAGD—793b; THAYER—606d.

4938. **σύντριμμα** {1x} **suntrimma**, *soon-trim'mah;* from *4937; concussion* or utter *fracture* (prop. concr.), i.e. complete *ruin:*—destruction {1x}.

This word stresses a destruction incurred through long term rubbing or wearing away. It is used metaphorically of destruction in Rom 3:16, which, in a passage setting forth the sinful state of mankind in general, suggests the wearing process of the effects of cruelty. Syn.: 4937. See: TDNT—7:919, 1124; BAGD—793c; THAYER—607a.

4939. **σύντροφος** {1x} **suntrŏphŏs**, *soon'-trof-os;* from *4862* and *5162* (in a pass. sense); a *fellow-nursling,* i.e. *comrade:*—brought up with {1x}. See: BAGD—793c; THAYER—607a.

4940. **συντυγχάνω** {1x} **suntugchanō**, *soon-toong-khan'-o;* from *4862* and *5177;* to *chance together,* i.e. *meet* with (*reach*):—come at {1x}.

Suntugchano, "to meet with" (*sun,* "with," and *tunchano,* "to reach"), is rendered "to come at" in Lk 8:19, (of the efforts of Christ's mother and brethren to get at Him through a crowd). See: BAGD—793c; THAYER—607b.

4941. **Συντύχη** {1x} **Suntuchē**, *soon-too'-khay;* from *4940;* an *accident; Syntyche,* a Chr. female:—*Syntyche* {1x}. See: BAGD—793d; THAYER—607a.

4942. **συνυποκρίνομαι** {1x} **sunupŏkrinŏmai**, *soon-oo-pok-rin'-om-ahee;* from *4862* and *5271;* to *act hypocritically* in concert *with:*—dissemble with {1x}.

Sunupokrinomai, (*sun,* "with," *hupokrinomai,* "to join in acting the hypocrite") is pretending to act from one motive, whereas another motive really inspires the act. So in Gal 2:13, Peter with other believing Jews, in separating from believing Gentiles at Antioch, pretended that the motive was loyalty to the Law of Moses, whereas really it was fear of the Judaizers. See: TDNT—8:559, 1235; BAGD—793d; THAYER—607b.

4943. **συνυπουργέω** {1x} **sunupŏurgĕō**, *soon-oop-oorg-eh'-o;* from *4862* and a der. of a compound of *5259* and the base of *2041;* to *be a co-auxiliary,* i.e. *assist:*—help together {1x}. See: BAGD—793b; THAYER—607b.

4944. **συνωδίνω** {1x} **sunōdinō**, *soon-o-dee'-no;* from *4862* and *5605;* to *have* (parturition) *pangs* in company (concert, simultaneously) *with,* i.e. (fig.) to *sympathize* (in expectation of relief from suffering):—travail in pain together {1x}. See: BAGD—793b; THAYER—607b.

4945. **συνωμοσία** {1x} **sunōmŏsia**, *soon-o-mos-ee'-ah;* from a compound of *4862* and *3660;* being leagued by oath, a *swearing together,* i.e. (by impl.) a *plot:*—conspiracy {1x}. See: BAGD—793d; THAYER—607b.

4946. **Συράκουσαι** {1x} **Surakŏusai**, *soo-rak'-oo-sahee;* plur. of uncert. der.; *Syracuse,* the capital of Sicily:—Syracuse {1x}. See: BAGD—794a; THAYER—607c.

4947. **Συρία** {8x} **Suria**, *soo-ree'-ah;* prob. of Heb. or. [6865]; *Syria* (i.e. *Tsyria* or *Tyre*), a region of Asia:—Syria {8x}. See: BAGD—794a; THAYER—607c.

4948. **Σύρος** {1x} **Surŏs**, *soo'-ros;* from the same as *4947;* a *Syran* (i.e. prob. *Tyrian*), a native of Syria:—Syrian {1x}. See: BAGD—794b; THAYER—607c.

4949. **Συροφοίνισσα** {1x} **Surŏphŏinissa**, *soo-rof-oy'-nis-sah;* fem. of a compound of *4948* and the same as *5403;* a *Syro-phœnician* woman, i.e. a female native of Phœnicia in Syria:—Syrophenician {1x}. See: BAGD—794b; THAYER—607c.

4950. **Σύρτις** {1x} **surtis**, *soor'-tis;* from *4951;* a *shoal* (from the sand *drawn* thither by the waves), i.e. the *Syrtis* Major or great bay on the N. coast of Africa:—quicksands {1x}. See: BAGD—794c; THAYER—607d.

4951. **σύρω** {5x} **surō**, *soo'-ro;* prob. akin to *138;* to *trail:*—drag {1x}, draw {3x}, hale {1x}.

Suro, as a verb, means "to drag, to hale, to draw" and is translated **(1)** "drag": "And the other disciples came in a little ship; . . . dragging the net with fishes" (Jn 21:8); **(2)** "haling, violently dragging": "As for Saul, he made havock of the church, entering into every house, and haling men and women committed *them* to prison" (Acts 8:3). It is also translated **(3)** "to draw" in Acts 14:19; 17:6; Rev 12:4. Syn.: It is used of "drawing" a net, Jn 21:6, 11: **(A)** At vv. 6 and 11 *helko* (or *helkuo*) is used; for there a drawing of the net to a certain point is intended; by the disciples to themselves in the ship, by Peter to himself upon the shore. **(B)** But at v. 8 *helko* gives place to *suro* (4951): for nothing is there intended but the dragging of the net, which had been fastened to the ship, after it through the water. See also: 307, 385, 392, 501, 502, 645, 868, 1448, 1670, 1828, 2020, 4264, 4317, 4334, 4358, 4685, 5288, 5289. See: BAGD—794c; THAYER—607d.

4952. **συσπαράσσω** {1x} **susparassō**, *soos-par-as'-so;* from *4862* and *4682;* to *rend completely,* i.e. (by anal.) to *convulse* violently:—tare (tear) {1x}. See: BAGD—794c; THAYER—608a.

4953. **σύσσημον** {1x} **sussēmŏn**, *soos'-say-mon;* neut. of a compound of *4862* and the base of *4591;* a *sign in common,* i.e. preconcerted *signal:*—token {1x}.

Sussemon, "a fixed sign or signal, agreed upon with others", is used in Mk 14:44, "a token." See: TDNT—7:269, 1015; BAGD—794d; THAYER—608a.

4954. **σύσσωμος** {1x} **sussōmŏs**, *soos'-so-mos;* from *4862* and *4983; of a joint body,* i.e. (fig.) a *fellow-member* of the Chr. community:—of the same body {1x}. See: TDNT—7:1024, 1140; BAGD—794d; THAYER—608a.

4955. **συστασιαστής** {1x} **sustasiastēs**, *soos-tas-ee-as-tace';* from a compound of *4862* and a der. of *4714; a fellow-insurgent, a rebel, a revolutionist:*—make insurrection with {1x}. See: BAGD—794d; THAYER—608a.

4956. **συστατικός** {2x} **sustatikŏs**, *soos-tat-ee-kos';* from a der. of *4921; introductory,* i.e. *recommendatory:*—of commendation {2x}. See: BAGD—795a; THAYER—608a.

4957. **συσταυρόω** {5x} **sustaurŏō**, *soos-tow-rŏ'-o;* from *4862* and *4717;* to *impale* in company *with* (lit. or fig.):—crucify with {5x}.

Sustauroo, "to crucify with" (*su-,* "for," *sun,* "with"), is used **(1)** of actual "crucifixion" in company with another, Mt 27:44; Mk 15:32; Jn 19:32; **(2)** metaphorically, of spiritual identification with Christ in His death, Rom 6:6 and Gal 2:20. See: TDNT—7:786, 1102; BAGD—795a; THAYER—608b.

4958. **συστέλλω** {2x} **sustĕllō**, *soos-tel'-lo;* from *4862* and *4724;* to *send (draw) together,* i.e. *enwrap* (*enshroud* a corpse for burial), *contract* (an interval):—short {1x}, wind up {1x}.

Sustello, is used **(1)** literally, Acts 5:6; and **(2)** metaphorically, 1 Cor 7:29. Short means to wind things up; "time is short, things are being wound up." Stress is on events winding around and upon themselves (1 Cor 7:29). See: TDNT—7:596, 1074; BAGD—795a; THAYER—608b.

4959. **συστενάζω** {1x} **sustĕnazō**, *soos-ten-ad'-zo;* from *4862* and *4727;* to *moan jointly,* i.e. (fig.) *experience a common calamity:*—groan together {1x}. See: TDNT—7:600, 1076; BAGD—795b; THAYER—608b.

4960. **συστοιχέω** {1x} **sustŏichĕō**, *soos-toy-kheh'-o;* from *4862* and *4748;* to *file together* (as soldiers in ranks), i.e. (fig.) to *correspond* to:—answer to {1x}.

Sustoicheo, lit., "to be in the same line or row with" (*sun,* "with," *stoichos,* "a row"), is translated "answereth to" in Gal 4:25. See: TDNT—7:669, 1087; BAGD—795b; THAYER—608b.

4961. **συστρατιώτης** {2x} **sustratiōtēs**, *soos-trat-ee-o'-tace;* from *4862* and *4757;* a *co-campaigner,* i.e. (fig.) an *associate* in Chr. toil:—fellowsoldier {2x}.

Sustratiotes, is used metaphorically in Phil 2:25 and Philem 2, of fellowship in Christian service. See: TDNT—7:701, 1091; BAGD—795b; THAYER—608c.

4962. **συστρέφω** {1x} **sustrĕphō**, *soos-tref'-o;* from *4862* and *4762;* to *twist together,* i.e. *collect* (a bundle, a crowd):—gather {1x}. See: BAGD—795c; THAYER—608c.

4963. **συστροφή** {2x} **sustrŏphē**, *soos-trof-ay';* from *4962;* a *twisting together,* i.e. (fig.) a secret *coalition,* riotous *crowd:*—+ band together {1x}, concourse {1x}.

Sustrophe, "a turning together" (*sun,* "with," *trepo,* "to turn"), signifies **(1)** that which is rolled together; hence, a dense mass of people, "a concourse", people bound together by a common course of action, Acts 19:40. It is translated "band together" in Acts 23:12; again a group bound together by a common course of action, to kill Paul. See: BAGD—795c; THAYER—608c.

4964. **συσχηματίζω** {2x} **suschēmatizō**, *soos-khay-mat-id'-zo;* from *4862* and a der. of *4976;* to *fashion alike,* i.e. *conform* to the same pattern (fig.):—conform to {1x}, fashion (one's) self according to {1x}.

Suschematizo, "to fashion or shape one thing like another," is translated **(1)** "conformed to" in Rom 12:2; **(2)** "fashioning ones self according to" in 1 Pet 1:14. **(3)** This word could not be used of inward transformation. Syn.: **(A)** *Summorphos* (4832) stresses inward conformity and describes what is the essence in character and thus complete or durable, not merely a form or outline. **(B)** *Suschematizo* (4964) stresses outward conformity and means to shape one thing like another and describes what is transitory, changeable, and unstable. See: BAGD—795c; THAYER—608c.

4965. **Συχάρ** {1x} **Suchar**, *soo-khar';* of Heb. or. [7941]; *Sychar* (i.e. *Shekar*), a place in Pal.:—Sychar {1x}. See: BAGD—795d; THAYER—608d.

4966. **Συχέμ** {2x} **Suchĕm**, *soo-khem';* of Heb. or. [7927]; *Sychem* (i.e. *Shekem*), the name of a Canaanite and of a place in Pal.:—Sychem (City in Ephraim) {1x}, Sychem (son of Emmor) {1x}. See: BAGD—795d; THAYER—609a.

4967. **σφαγή** {3x} **sphagē**, *sfag-ay';* from *4969; butchery* (of animals for food or sacrifice, or [fig.] of men [*destruction*]):—slaughter {3x}.

Sphage expresses slaughter **(1)** within a strain of sorrow (Acts 8:32); **(2)** within a strain of triumph (Rom 8:36); and **(3)** in Jas 5:5 the luxurious rich are getting wealth by injustice, spending it on their pleasures, and are fattening themselves like sheep unconscious of their doom. See: TDNT—7:935, 1125; BAGD—795d; THAYER—609a.

4968. **σφάγιον** {1x} **sphagiŏn**, *sfag'-ee-on;* neut. of a der. of *4967;* a *victim* (in sacrifice):—slain beast {1x}. See: BAGD—796a; THAYER—609b.

4969. **σφάζω** {10x} **sphazō**, *sfad'-zo;* a primary verb; to *butcher* (espec. an animal for food or in sacrifice) or (gen.) to *slaughter,* or (spec.) to *maim* (violently):—kill {1x}, slay {8x}, wound {1x}.

Sphazo, "to slay," especially of victims for sacrifice is used **(1)** of taking human life, 1 Jn 3:12 (twice); Rev 6:4, "kill"; in 13:3, probably of assassination, "wounded (to death)"; 18:24; **(2)** of Christ, as the Lamb of sacrifice, Rev 5:6, 9, 12; 6:9; 13:8. See: TDNT—7:925, 1125; BAGD—796a; THAYER—609b.

4970. **σφόδρα** {11x} **sphŏdra**, *sfod'-rah;* neut. plur. of σφοδρός **sphŏdrŏs**, (*violent;* of uncert. der.) as adv.; *vehemently,* i.e. in a *high degree, much:*—exceeding {4x}, very {3x}, greatly {2x}, exceedingly {1x}, sore {1x}.

Sphodra, properly the neuter plural of *sphodros,* "excessive, violent" (from a root indicating restlessness), translated **(1)** "exceeding" in Mt 2:10; 17:23; 26:22; Rev 16:21; **(2)** "very" in Mt 18:31; Mk 16:4; Lk 18:23; **(3)** "greatly" in Mt 27:54; Act 6:7; **(4)** "exceedingly" in Mt 19:25; and **(5)** "sore" in Mt 17:6. Sore means to exceed normal feelings. See: BAGD—796a; THAYER—609b.

4971. **σφοδρῶς** {1x} **sphŏdrōs**, *sfod-roce';* adv. from the same as *4970; very much:*—exceedingly {1x}. See: BAGD—796b; THAYER—609b.

4972. **σφραγίζω** {27x} **sphragizō**, *sfrag-id'-zo;* from *4973;* to *stamp* (with a signet or private mark) for security or preservation (lit. or fig.); by impl. to *keep secret,* to *attest:*—seal {22x}, set to (one's) seal {1x}, stop {1x}, seal up {1x}, set a seal {1x}, vr seal {1x}.

Spragizo, "to seal", is used to indicate **(1)** security and permanency, **(1a)** of Jesus' sepulcher, Mt 27:66; **(2)** of the doom of Satan, fixed and certain, Rev 20:3; **(2)** in Rom 15:28, "when . . . I have . . . sealed to them this fruit"; the metaphor stresses the sacred formalities of the transaction and guarantees the full complement of the contents; **(3)** secrecy and security and the postponement of disclosure, Rev 10:4; in a negative command Rev 22:10; **(4)** ownership and security, together with destination, Rev 7:3, 4, 5; **(5)** the same three indications [(1) through (3) above] are conveyed in Eph 1:13, **(5a)** in the metaphor of the "sealing" of believers by the gift of the Holy Spirit, upon believing, i.e., at the time of their regeneration; **(5b)** the idea of destination is stressed by the phrase "the Holy Spirit of promise" (see also v. 14); **(5c)** so Eph 4:30, "ye were sealed unto the day of redemption"; so in 2 Cor 1:22, where the middle voice intimates the special interest of the Sealer in His act; **(6)** authentication by the believer (by receiving the witness of the Son) of the fact that "God is true," Jn 3:33; **(7)** authentication by God in sealing the Son as the Giver of eternal life Jn 6:27. See: TDNT—7:939, 1127; BAGD—796b; THAYER—609b.

4973. **σφραγίς** {16x} **sphragis**, *sfrag-ece';* prob. strengthened from *5420;* a *signet* (as *fencing* in or protecting from misappropriation); by impl. the *stamp* impressed (as a mark of privacy, or genuineness), lit. or fig.:—seal {16x}.

Sphragis denotes **(1)** "a seal" or "signet," Rev 7:2, "the seal of the living God," **(1a)** an emblem of ownership and security, here combined with that of destination (as in Eze 9:4), **(1b)** the persons to be "sealed" being secured from destruction and marked for reward; **(2)** "the impression" of a "seal" or signet, **(2a)** literal, a "seal" on a book or roll, combining with the ideas of security and destination those of secrecy and postponement of disclosures, Rev 5:1, 2, 5, 9; 6:1, 3, 5, 7, 9, 12; 8:1; **(2b)** metaphorical, **(2b1)** Rom 4:11, said of "circumcision," as an authentication of the righteousness of Abraham's faith, and an external attestation of the covenant made with him by God; the rabbis called circumcision "the seal of Abraham"; **(2b2)** in 1 Cor 9:2, of converts as a "seal" or authentication of Paul's apostleship; **(2b3)** in 2 Ti 2:19, "the firm foundation of God standeth, having this seal, The Lord knoweth them that are His", indicating ownership, authentication, security and destination"; and, Let every one that nameth the Name of the Lord depart from unrighteousness," indicating a ratification on the part of the believer of the determining counsel of God concerning him; **(3)** Rev 9:4 distinguishes those who will be found without the "seal" of God on their foreheads. See: TDNT—7:939, 1127; BAGD—796c; THAYER—609d.

4974. **σφυρόν** {1x} **sphurŏn**, *sfoo-ron';* neut. of a presumed der. prob. of the same as σφαῖρα **sphaira** (a *ball, "sphere;"* compare the fem. σφῦρα **sphura**, a *hammer*); the *ankle* (as *globular*):—ankle bone {1x}. See: BAGD—797a; THAYER—609d.

4975. **σχεδόν** {3x} **schĕdŏn**, *skhed-on';* neut. of a presumed der. of the alt. of *2192* as adv.; *nigh*, i.e. *nearly:*—almost {3x}.

Schedon is used either **(1)** of locality, Acts 19:26, or **(2)** of degree, Acts 13:44; Heb 9:22. See: BAGD—797a; THAYER—609d.

σχέω **schĕō**. See *2192*.

4976. **σχῆμα** {2x} **schēma**, *skhay'-mah;* from the alt. of *2192;* a *figure* (as a *mode* or *circumstance*), i.e. (by impl.) extern. *condition:*—fashion {2x}.

Schema, "a figure, fashion", is translated **(1)** "fashion" in 1 Cor 7:31, of the world, signifying that which comprises the manner of life, actions, etc. of humanity in general; **(2)** in Phil 2:8 it is used of the Lord in His being found "in fashion" as a man, and signifies what He was in the eyes of men, the entire outwardly perceptible mode and shape of His existence, just as the preceding words *morphe*, "form," and *homoioma*, "likeness," describe what He was in Himself as Man. Men saw in Christ a human form, bearing, language, action, mode of life . . . in general the state and relations of a human being, so that in the entire mode of His appearance He made Himself known and was recognized as a man. Syn.: *Morphe* (3444) "form" differs from *schema* (4976) "figure, shape, fashion", as that which is intrinsic and essential, from that which is outward and accidental. In Phil 2:7 *morphe* relates to the complete form or nature of a servant; and *schema* to the external form, or human body in 2:8. See: TDNT—7:954, 1129; BAGD—797b; THAYER—610a.

4977. **σχίζω** {10x} **schizō**, *skhid'-zo;* appar. a primary verb; to *split* or *sever* (lit. or fig.):—break {1x}, divide {2x}, open {1x}, rend {5x}, make a rent {1x}.

Schizo, **(1)** "to split, to rend open," is said **(1a)** of the veil of the temple, Mt 27:51; Mk 15:38; Lk 23:45; **(1b)** the rending of rocks, Mt 27:51; **(1c)** a garment, Lk 5:36, "make a rent"; Jn 19:24; **(2)** "to break", a net, Jn 21:11; **(3)** in the passive voice, metaphorically, of a crowd being divided into factions, Acts 14:4; 23:7; **(4)** the opening of the heavens, Mk 1:10;. See: TDNT—7:959, 1130; BAGD—797b; THAYER—610a.

4978. **σχίσμα** {8x} **schisma**, *skhis'-mah;* from *4977;* a *split* or *gap* ("*schism*"), lit. or fig.:—division {5x}, rent {2x}, schism {1x}.

Schisma, (Eng., "schism"), denotes **(1)** "a cleft, a rent," Mt 9:16; Mk 2:21, then, **(2)** metaphorically, "a division dissension," Jn 7:43; 9:16; 10:19; 1 Cor 1:10; 11:18; **(3)** in 1 Cor 12:25 it is translated "schism." See: TDNT—7:963, 1130; BAGD—797c; THAYER—610a.

4979. **σχοινίον** {2x} **schŏiniŏn**, *skhoy-nee'-on;* dimin. of σχοῖνος **schŏinŏs** (a *rush* or *flag*-plant; of uncert. der.); a *rushlet*, i.e. *grass-withe* or *tie* (gen.):—small cord {1x}, rope {1x}.

Schoinion, "a cord or rope," a diminutive of *schoinos*, "a rush, bulrush," meant a "cord" made of rushes; it denotes **(1)** "a small cord," Jn 2:15 (plural), **(2)** "a rope," Acts 27:32. See: BAGD—797d; THAYER—610b.

4980. **σχολάζω** {2x} **schŏlazō**, *skhol-ad'-zo;* from *4981;* to *take a holiday*, i.e. *be at leisure* for (by impl. *devote oneself* wholly to); fig. to *be vacant* (of a house):—empty {1x}, give self {1x}.

Scholazo literally means leisure and is used **(1)** of persons who to have time for anything; hence, can consequently be totally occupied with something else (1 Cor 7:5); and **(2)** of things left empty because attention is absorbed elsewhere (Mt 12:44). See: BAGD—797d; THAYER—610b.

4981. **σχολή** {1x} **schŏlē**, *skhol-ay';* prob. fem. of a presumed der. of the alt. of *2192;* prop. *loitering* (as a *withholding* of oneself from work) or *leisure*, i.e. (by impl.) a "*school*" (as *vacation* from phys. employment):—school {1x}.

Schole, (whence Eng., "school") primarily denotes "leisure," then, "that for which leisure was employed, a disputation, lecture"; hence, by metonymy, "the place where lectures are delivered, a school," Acts 19:9. See: BAGD—798a; THAYER—610b.

4982. **σῴζω** {110x} **sōzō**, *sode'-zo;* from a primary σῶς **sōs** (contr. for obs. σάος **saŏs**, "*safe*"); to *save*, i.e. *deliver* or *protect* (lit. or fig.):—save {93x}, make whole {9x}, heal {3x}, be whole {2x}, misc. {3x} = preserve, do well.

Sozo, "to save," is used (as with the noun *soteria*, "salvation") **(1)** of material and temporal deliverance **(1a)** from danger, suffering, etc., e.g., Mt 8:25; Mk 13:20; Lk 23:35; Jn 12:27; 1 Ti 2:15; 2 Ti 4:18, "preserve"; Jude 5; **(1b)** from sickness, Mt 9:22, "made . . . whole"; so Mk 5:34; Lk 8:48; Jas 5:15; **(2)** of the spiritual and eternal salvation granted immediately by God to those who believe on the Lord Jesus Christ, **(2a)** e.g., Acts 2:47, "such as should be saved"; 16:31; Rom 8:24, "we are saved"; Eph 2:5, 8; 1 Ti 2:4; 2 Ti 1:9; Titus 3:5; **(2b)** of human agency in this, Rom 11:14; 1 Cor 7:16; 9:22; **(3)** of the present experiences of God's power to deliver from the bond age of sin, **(3a)** e.g., Mt 1:21; Rom 5:10; 1 Cor 15:2; Heb 7:25; Jas 1:21; 1 Pet 3:21; **(3b)** of human agency in this, 1 Ti 4:16;

(4) of the future deliverance of believers at the second coming of Christ for His saints, being deliverance from the wrath of God to be executed upon the ungodly at the close of this age and from eternal doom, e.g., Rom. 5:9; **(5)** of the deliverance of the nation of Israel at the second advent of Christ, e.g., Rom 11:26; **(6)** inclusively for all the blessings bestowed by God on men in Christ, e.g., Lk 19:10; Jn 10:9; 1 Cor 10:33; 1 Ti 1:15; **(7)** of those who endure to the end of the time of the Great Tribulation, Mt 10:22; Mk 13:13; **(8)** of the individual believer, who, though losing his reward at the judgment seat of Christ hereafter, will not lose his salvation, 1 Cor 3:15; 5:5; **(9)** of the deliverance of the nations at the Millennium, Rev. 21:24. See: TDNT—7:965, 1132; BAGD—798a; THAYER—610b.

4983. **σῶμα** {146x} **sōma**, *so'-mah;* from *4982;* the *body* (as a *sound* whole), used in a very wide application, lit. or fig.:—bodily {1x}, body {144x}, slave {1x}.

Soma is "the body as a whole, the instrument of life," whether **(1)** of man **(1a)** living, e.g., Mt 6:22, or **(1b)** dead, Mt 27:52; or **(1c)** in resurrection, 1 Cor 15:44; or **(2)** of beasts, Heb 13:11; **(3)** of grain, 1 Cor 15:37–38; **(4)** of the heavenly hosts, 1 Cor 15:40. **(5)** In Rev 18:13 it is translated "slaves." In its figurative uses the essential idea is preserved. **(6)** Sometimes the word stands, by *synecdoche*, for "the complete man," Mt 5:29; 6:22; Rom 12:1; Jas 3:6; Rev 18:13. **(7)** Sometimes the person is identified with his or her "body," Acts 9:37; 13:36, and this is so even of the Lord Jesus, John 19:40 with 42. **(8)** The "body" is not the man, for he himself can exist apart from his "body," 2 Cor 12:2–3. **(9)** The "body" is an essential part of the man and therefore the redeemed are not perfected till the resurrection, Heb 11:40; no man in his final state will be without his "body," Jn 5:28–29; Rev 20:13. **(10)** The word is also used for physical nature, as distinct **(10a)** from *pneuma*, "the spiritual nature," e.g., 1 Cor 5:3, and **(10b)** from *psuche*, "the soul," e.g., 1 Th 5:23. **(10c)** *Soma*, "body," and *pneuma*, "spirit," may be separated; *pneuma* and *psuche*, "soul," can only be distinguished." **(11)** It is also used metaphorically, of the mystic body of Christ, with **(11a)** reference to the whole church, e.g., Eph 1:23; Col 1:18, 22, 24; **(11b)** also of a local church, 1 Cor 12:27. See: TDNT—7:1024, 1140; BAGD—799a; THAYER—611a.

4984. **σωματικός** {2x} **sōmatikŏs**, *so-mat-ee-kos';* from *4983; corporeal* or *physical:*—bodily {2x}.

Somatikos, "bodily," is used **(1)** in Lk 3:22, of the Holy Spirit in taking a bodily shape; **(2)** in 1 Ti 4:8 of bodily exercise. See: TDNT—7:1024, 1140; BAGD—800b; THAYER—611d.

4985. **σωματικῶς** {1x} **sōmatikōs**, *so-mat-ee-koce';* adv. from *4984; corporeally* or *physically:*—bodily {1x}. See: BAGD—800b; THAYER—611d.

4986. **Σώπατρος** {1x} **Sōpatrŏs**, *so'-pat-ros;* from the base of *4982* and *3962; of a safe father; Sopatrus*, a Chr.:—*Sopater* {1x}. See: BAGD—800b; THAYER—612a. comp. *4989*.

4987. **σωρεύω** {2x} **sōrĕuō**, *sore-yoo'-o;* from another form of *4673;* to *pile* up (lit. or fig.):—heap {1x}, laden {1x}.

Soreuo, "to heap one thing on another," is said **(1)** of "heaping" coals of fire on the head, Rom 12:20; in **(2)** 2 Ti 3:6 it is used metaphorically of women "laden" (or overwhelmed) with sins. See: TDNT—7:1094, 1150; BAGD—800c; THAYER—612a.

4988. **Σωσθένης** {2x} **Sōsthĕnēs**, *soce-then'-ace;* from the base of *4982* and that of *4599; of safe strength; Sosthenes*, a Chr.:—*Sosthenes* {2x}. See: BAGD—800c; THAYER—612a.

4989. **Σωσίπατρος** {1x} **Sōsipatrŏs**, *so-sip'-at-ros;* prol. for *4986; Sosipatrus*, a Chr.:—*Sosipater* {1x}. See: BAGD—800c; THAYER—612a.

4990. **σωτήρ** {24x} **sōtēr**, *so-tare';* from *4982;* a *deliverer*, i.e. God or Christ:—Saviour {24x}.

Soter, "a savior, deliverer, preserver," is used **(1)** of God, Lk 1:47; 1 Ti 1:1; 2:3; 4:10 (in the sense of "preserver," since He gives "to all life and breath and all things"); Titus 1:3; 2:10; 3:4, Jude 25; **(2)** of Christ, Lk 2:11; Jn 4:42; Acts 5:31; 13:23 (of Israel); Eph 5:23 (the sustainer and preserver of the church, His "body"); Phil 3:20 (at His return to receive the Church to Himself); 2 Ti 1:10 (with reference to His incarnation, "the days of His flesh"); Titus 1:4 (a title shared, in the context, with God the Father); 2:13, "God and our Savior Jesus Christ"; Titus 3:6; 2 Pet 1:1, "our Savior Jesus Christ; as in the parallel in 2 Pet 1: 11, "our Lord and Savior Jesus Christ"; these passages are therefore a testimony to His deity; 2 Pet 2:20; 3:2, 18; 1 Jn 4:14. See: TDNT—7:1003, 1132; BAGD—800d; THAYER—612a.

4991. **σωτηρία** {45x} **sōtēria**, *so-tay-ree'-ah;* fem. of a der. of *4990* as (prop.

abstr.) noun; *rescue* or *safety* (phys. or mor.):—salvation {40x}, the (one) be saved {1x}, deliver + 1325 {1x}, health {1x}, saving {1x}, that (one) be saved + 1519 {1x}.

Soteria denotes "deliverance, preservation, salvation." "Salvation" is used in the NT **(1)** of material and temporal deliverance from danger and apprehension, **(1a)** national, Lk 1:69, 71; Acts 7:25, "deliverance"; **(1b)** personal, as from **(1b1)** the sea, Acts 27:34, "health"; **(1b2)** prison, Phil 1:19; **(1b3)** the flood, Heb 11:7; **(1b4)** of the spiritual and eternal deliverance granted immediately by God to those who accept His conditions of repentance and faith in the Lord Jesus, in whom alone it is to be obtained, Acts 4:12, and upon confession of Him as Lord, Rom 10:10; for this purpose the gospel is the saving instrument, Rom 1:16; Eph 1:13; **(1c)** of the present experience of God's power to deliver from the bondage of sin, e.g., **(1c1)** Phil 2:12, where the special, though not the entire, reference is to the maintenance of peace and harmony; 1 Pet 1:9; **(1c2)** this present experience on the part of believers is virtually equivalent to sanctification; **(1c3)** for this purpose, God is able to make them wise, 2 Ti 3:15; **(1c4)** they are not to neglect it, Heb 2:3; **(1d)** of the future deliverance of believers at the Parousia of Christ for His saints, a salvation which is the object of their confident hope, e.g., Rom 13:11; 1 Th 5:8, and v. 9, where "salvation" is assured to them, as being deliverance from the wrath of God destined to be executed upon the ungodly at the end of this age, 1 Th 1:10; 2 Th 2:13; Heb 1:14; 9:28; 1 Pet 1:5; 2 Pet 3:15;

(2) of the deliverance of the nation of Israel at the second advent of Christ at the time of "the epiphany (or shining forth) of His Parousia" (2 Th 2:8); Lk 1:71; Rev 12:10; **(3)** inclusively, to sum up all the blessings bestowed by God on men in Christ through the Holy Spirit, e.g., 2 Cor 6:2; Heb 5:9; 1 Pet 1:9, 10; Jude 3; **(4)** occasionally, as standing virtually for the Savior, e.g., Lk 19:9; cf. Jn 4:22; **(5)** in ascriptions of praise to God, Rev 7:10, and as that which it is His prerogative to bestow, Rev 19:1. See: TDNT—7:965, 1132; BAGD—801b; THAYER—612c.

4992. **σωτήριον** {5x} **sōtēriŏn**, *so-tay'-ree-on;* neut. of the same as *4991* as (prop. concr.) noun; *defender* or (by impl.) *defence:*—salvation {4x}, that brings salvation {1x}.

Soterion, the neuter of the adjective, is used as **(1)** a noun in Lk 2:30; 3:6; Titus 2:11, in each of which it virtually stands for the Savior as in Acts 28:28, **(2)** in Eph 6:17, for the helmet of "salvation." See: TDNT—7:1021, 1132; BAGD—801d; THAYER—612d.

4993. **σωφρονέω** {6x} **sōphrŏnĕō**, *so-fron-eh'-o;* from *4998;* to *be of sound mind,* i.e. *sane,* (fig.) *moderate:*—be in right mind {2x}, be sober {2x}, be sober minded {1x}, soberly {1x}.

Sophreno signifies **(1)** "to be of sound mind," or "in one's right mind, sober-minded" (*sozo,* "to save," *phren,* "the mind"), Mk 5:15 and Lk 8:35, "in his right mind"; 2 Cor 5:13, "we be sober"; **(2)** "to be temperate, self-controlled," Titus 2:6, "to be sober-minded"; **(3)** 1 Pet 4:7, "be ye sober"; see also Rom 12:3. See: TDNT—7:1097, 1150; BAGD—802a; THAYER—612d.

4994. **σωφρονίζω** {1x} **sōphrŏnizō**, *so-fron-id'-zo;* from *4998;* to *make of sound mind,* i.e. (fig.) to *discipline* or *correct:*—teach to be sober {1x}.

This word denotes to be of sound mind, to recall to one's senses, restore one to his senses, to moderate, control, curb, disciple, to hold one to his duty, to admonish, to exhort earnestly, Titus 2:4 encompasses the cultivation of sound judgment and prudence. See: TDNT—7:1104, 1150; BAGD—802a; THAYER—613a.

4995. **σωφρονισμός** {1x} **sōphrŏnismŏs**, *so-fron-is-mos';* from *4994; discipline,* i.e. *self-control:*—sound mind {1x}.

Literally this word means saving the mind through admonishing and calling to soundness of mind and to self-control (2 Ti 1:7). See: TDNT—7:1104, 1150; BAGD—802b; THAYER—613a.

4996. **σωφρόνως** {1x} **sōphrŏnōs**, *so-fron'-oce;* adv. from *4998; with sound mind,* i.e. *moderately:*—soberly {1x}.

Sophronos occurs in Titus 2:12 and suggests the exercise of that self-restraint that governs all passions and desires, enabling the believer to be conformed to the mind of Christ. See: BAGD—802c; THAYER—613c.

4997. **σωφροσύνη** {3x} **sōphrŏsunē**, *so-fros-oo'-nay;* from *4998; soundness of mind,* i.e. (lit.) *sanity* or (fig.) *self-control:*—soberness {1x}, sobriety {2x}.

Sophrosune refers to having complete control over the passions and desires so that they are lawful and reasonable; a certain curtailment and regulation of passions, both removing those that are improper and excessive and also arranging those that are necessary to the proper time and in morderation, Acts 26:25; 1 Ti 2:9, 15. Syn.: 127. See: TDNT—7:1097, 1150; BAGD—802c; THAYER—613c.

4998. **σώφρων** {4x} **sōphrōn**, *so'-frone;* from the base of *4982* and that of *5424; safe* (*sound*) in *mind,* i.e. *self-controlled* (*moderate* as to opinion or passion):—discreet {1x}, sober {2x}, temperate {1x}.

Sophron, "of sound mind self-controlled", is translated **(1)** "sober," in 1 Ti 3:2; Titus 1:8; **(2)** 1 Ti 2:2, "temperatve; and **(3)** in 1 Ti 2:5, "discreet." See: TDNT—7:1097, 1150; BAGD—802c.

T

τα΄ **ta**. def. art. See *3588*. See: BAGD—549b; THAYER—433a.

4999. **Ταβέρναι** {1x} **Tabĕrnai**, *tab-er'-nahee* or

Ταβερνῶν **Tabĕrnōn**, *tab-er-non';* plur. of Lat. or.; *huts* or *wooden-walled* buildings; *Tabernæ:*—taverns {1x}. See: BAGD—802b; THAYER—613b.

5000. **Ταβιθά** {2x} **Tabitha**, *tab-ee-thah';* of Chald. or. [comp. 6646]; *the gazelle; Tabitha* (i.e. *Tabjetha*), a Chr. female:—*Tabitha* {2x}. See: BAGD—802b; THAYER—613b.

5001. **τάγμα** {1x} **tagma**, *tag'-mah;* from *5021;* something orderly in *arrangement* (a *troop*), i.e. (fig.) a *series* or *succession:*—order {1x}.

Tagma, signifying "that which has been arranged in order," was especially a military term, denoting "a company"; it is used metaphorically in 1 Cor 15:23 of the various classes of those who have part in the first resurrection. See: TDNT—8:31, 1156; BAGD—802d; THAYER—613b.

5002. **τακτός** {1x} **taktŏs**, *tak-tos';* from *5021; arranged,* i.e. *appointed* or *stated:*—set {1x}.

Taktos, an adjective (from *tasso*), "ordered, fixed, set," is said of an appointed day, in Acts 12:21. See: BAGD—803a; THAYER—613d.

5003. **ταλαιπωρέω** {1x} **talaipōrĕō**, *tal-ahee-po-reh'-o;* from *5005;* to *be wretched,* i.e. *realize* one's own *misery:*—be afflicted {1x}.

Talaiporeo, "to be afflicted," is used in Jas 4:9, in the middle voice ("afflict yourselves"). It is derived from *tlao,* "to bear, undergo," and *poros,* "a hard substance, a callus," which metaphorically came to signify that which is miserable. See: BAGD—803a; THAYER—613d.

5004. **ταλαιπωρία** {2x} **talaipōria**, *tal-ahee-po-ree'-ah;* from *5005; wretchedness,* i.e. *calamity:*—misery {2x}.

Talaiporia, "hardship, suffering, distress" (akin to *talaiporos,* "wretched," Rom 7:24; Rev 3:17. See: BAGD—803b; THAYER—613d.

5005. **ταλαίπωρος** {2x} **talaipōrŏs**, *tal-ah'-ee-po-ros;* from the base of *5007* and a der. of the base of *3984; enduring trial,* i.e. *miserable:*—wretched {2x}.

Talaiporos, "distressed, miserable, wretched," is used in Rom 7:24 and Rev 3:17. See: BAGD—803b; THAYER—614a.

5006. **ταλαντιαῖος** {1x} **talantiaiŏs**, *tal-an-tee-ah'-yos;* from *5007; talent-like* in weight:—weight of a talent {1x}.

A talent of silver weighed about 100 pounds (45 kg) and a talent of gold, 200 pounds (91 kg). See: BAGD—803b; THAYER—614a.

5007. **τάλαντον** {15x} **talantŏn**, *tal'-an-ton;* neut. of a presumed der. of the orig. form of τλάω **tlaō** (to *bear;* equiv. to *5342*); a *balance* (as *supporting* weights), i.e. (by impl.) a certain *weight* (and thence a *coin* or rather *sum* of money) or "*talent*":—talent {15x}.

Talanton, originally "a balance," then, "a talent in weight," was hence "a sum of money" in gold or silver equivalent to a "talent." The Jewish "talent" contained 3,000 shekels of the sanctuary, e.g., Ex 30:13 (about 114 lbs.). In NT times the "talent" was not a weight of silver, but the Roman-Attic "talent," comprising 6,000 *denarii* or *drachmas,* and equal to about L/240. It is mentioned in Matthew only, 18:24; 25:15, 16, 20 (four times), 22 (thrice), 24, 25, 28 (twice). In 18:24 the vastness of the sum, 10,000 talents (L/2,400,000), indicates the impossibility of man's clearing himself, by his own efforts, of the guilt which lies upon him before God. See: BAGD—803c; THAYER—614a.

5008. **ταλιθά** {1x} **talitha**, *tal-ee-thah';* of Chald. or. [comp. 2924]; *the fresh,* i.e. young *girl; talitha* (*O maiden*):—*talitha* {1x}. See: BAGD—803c; THAYER—614b.

5009. **ταμεῖον** {4x} **tamĕiŏn**, *tam-i'-on;* neut. contr. of a presumed der. of ταμίας **tamias** (a *dispenser* or *distributor;* akin to τέμνω **tĕmnō**, to *cut*); a *dispensary* or *magazine,* i.e. a chamber on the ground-floor or interior of an Oriental house (gen. used for *storage* or *privacy,* a spot for retirement):—secret chamber {1x}, closet {2x}, storehouse {1x}.

Tameion denotes, firstly, "a store-chamber," then, "any private room, secret chamber," **(1)** Mt 6:6; Lk 12:3, "closet"; **(2)** Mt 24:26, "secret chambers"; **(3)** Lk 12:24, "storehouse" of birds. See: BAGD—803c; THAYER—614b.

τανῦν **tanun**.See *3568*.

5010. **τάξις** {10x} **taxis**, *tax'-is;* from *5021;* reg. *arrangement,* i.e. (in time) fixed *succession* (of rank or character), official *dignity:*—order {10x}.

Taxis, "an arranging, arrangement, order" (akin to *tasso,* "to arrange, draw up in order"), is used in **(1)** Lk 1:8 of the fixed succession of the course of the priests; **(2)** of due "order," in contrast to confusion, in the gatherings of a local church, 1 Cor 14:40; **(3)** of the general condition of the local church, Col 2:5 (some give it a military significance here); **(4)** of the divinely appointed character or nature of a priesthood, of Melchizedek, as foreshadowing that of Christ, Heb 5:6, 10; 6:20; 7:11, where also the character of the Aaronic priesthood is set in contrast also in 7:11, second part; Heb 7:17, 21. See: BAGD—803d; THAYER—614b.

5011. **ταπεινός** {8x} **tapĕinŏs**, *tap-i-nos';* of uncert. der.; *depressed,* i.e. (fig.) *humiliated* (in circumstances or disposition):—of low degree {2x}, humble {2x}, base {1x}, cast down {1x}, of low estate {1x}, lowly {1x}.

(1) Primarily *tapeinos* means that which is low, and does not rise far from the ground; hence, metaphorically, it signifies lowly, of no degree. It is translated **(1)** "of low degree" in Lk 1:52; Jas 1:9; **(2)** "humble" in Jas 4:6; 1 Pet 5:5; **(3)** "base" in 2 Cor 10:1; **(4)** "cast down" in 2 Cor 7:6; **(5)** "of low estate" in Rom 12:16; and **(6)** "lowly" in Mt 11:29. See: TDNT—8:1, 1152; BAGD—804a; THAYER—614c.

5012. **ταπεινοφροσύνη** {7x} **tapĕinŏphrŏsunē**, *tap-i-nof-ros-oo'-nay;* from a compound of *5011* and the base of *5424;* *humiliation of mind,* i.e. *modesty:*—humility {3x}, humbleness of mind {1x}, humility of mind {1x}, lowliness {1x}, lowliness of mind {1x}.

(1) This virtue, a fruit of the gospel, exists when a person through most genuine self-evaluation deems himself worthless. It involves evaluating ourselves as small because we are so. The humble person is not stressing his sinfulness, but his creatureliness, of absolute dependence, of possessing nothing and of receiving all things from God. **(2)** *Tapeinophrosune,* "lowliness of mind", is rendered **(1)** "humility of mind" in Acts 20:19; **(2)** in Eph 4:2, "lowliness"; **(3)** in Phil 2:3, "lowliness of mind"; **(4)** in Col 2:18, 23, of a false "humility"; **(5)** in Col 3:12, "humbleness of mind"; **(6)** 1 Pet 5:5, "humility." Syn.: 4236. See: TDNT—8:1, 1152; BAGD—804c; THAYER—614c.

5013. **ταπεινόω** {14x} **tapĕinŏō**, *tap-i-nŏ'-o;* from *5011;* to *depress;* fig. to *humiliate* (in condition or heart):—abase {5x}, bring low {1x}, humble {6x}, humble (one's) self {2x}.

Tapeinoo signifies "to make low, bring low," **(1)** of bringing to the ground, making level, reducing to a plain, as in Lk 3:5; **(2)** metaphorically **(2a)** in the active voice, to bring to a humble condition, "to abase," 2 Cor 11:7, and **(2b)** in the passive, "to be abased," Phil 4:12; in Mt 23:12; Lk 14:11; 18:14. **(3)** It is translated "humble yourselves" **(3a)** in the middle voice sense in Jas 4:10; 1 Pet 5:6; **(3b)** "humble," in Mt 18:4; 2 Cor 12:21 and Phil 2:8. See: TDNT—8:1, 1152; BAGD—804c; THAYER—614d.

5014. **ταπείνωσις** {4x} **tapĕinōsis**, *tap-i'-no-sis;* from *5013;* *depression* (in rank or feeling):—humiliation {1x}, be made low {1x}, low estate {1x}, vile {1x}.

Tepeinosis denotes "abasement, humiliation, low estate" (from *tapeinos,* "lowly"), **(1)** Lk 1:48, "low estate"; **(2)** Acts 8:33, "humiliation"; **(3)** Phil 3:21, "vile"; **(4)** Jas 1:10, "is made low," lit., "in his low estate. See: TDNT—8:1, 1152; BAGD—805a; THAYER—615a.

5015. **ταράσσω** {17x} **tarassō**, *tar-as'-so;* of uncert. aff.; to *stir* or *agitate* (*roil* water):—trouble {17x}.

Tarasso, akin to *tarache* (5016), is used **(1)** in a physical sense, Jn 5:4, 7; **(2)** metaphorically, **(2a)** of the soul and spirit of the Lord, Jn 11:33; **(2b)** of the hearts of disciples, Jn 14:1, 27; **(2c)** of the minds of those in fear or perplexity, Mt 2:3; 14:26; Mk 6:50; Lk 1:12; 24:38; 1 Pet 3:14; **(2d)** of subverting the souls of believers, by evil doctrine, Acts 15:24; Gal 1:7; 5:10; **(2e)** of stirring up a crowd, Acts 17:8. See: BAGD—805b; THAYER—615a.

5016. **ταραχή** {2x} **tarachē**, *tar-akh-ay';* fem. from *5015;* *disturbance,* i.e. (of water) *roiling,* or (of a mob) *sedition:*—troubles {1x}, troubling {1x}.

Tarache, "an agitation, disturbance, trouble," is found in Mk 13:8 (plur.) and Jn 5:4. See: BAGD—805c; THAYER—615b.

5017. **τάραχος** {2x} **tarachŏs**, *tar'-akh-os;* masc. from *5015;* a *disturbance,* i.e. (popular) *tumult:*—stir {2x}.

Tarachos, as a noun, is rendered "stir": "Now as soon as it was day, there was no small stir among the soldiers, what was become of Peter" (Acts 12:18; cf. 19:23). Syn.: 329, 383, 387, 1326, 1892, 2042, 3947, 3951, 4531, 4579, 1787, 1797. See: BAGD—805c; THAYER—615b.

5018. **Ταρσεύς** {2x} **Tarsĕus**, *tar-syoos';* from *5019;* a *Tarsean,* i.e. native of Tarsus:—of Tarsus {2x}. See: BAGD—805c; THAYER—615b.

5019. **Ταρσός** {3x} **Tarsŏs**, *tar-sos';* perh. the same as ταρσός **tarsŏs** (a *flat* basket); *Tarsus,* a place in Asia Minor:—Tarsus {3x}. See: BAGD—805d; THAYER—615b.

5020. **ταρταρόω** {1x} **tartarŏō**, *tar-tar-ŏ'-o;* from Τάρταρος **Tartarŏs**, (the deepest *abyss* of Hades); to *incarcerate* in eternal torment:—cast down to hell {1x}. See: BAGD—805d; THAYER—615c.

5021. **τάσσω** {8x} **tassō**, *tas'-so;* a prol. form of a primary verb (which latter appears only in certain tenses); to *arrange* in an orderly manner, i.e. *assign* or *dispose* (to a certain position or lot):—addict {1x}, appoint {3x}, determine {1x}, ordain {2x}, set {1x}.

Tasso, as a verb, means "to place in order, arrange," and signifies **(1)** "to appoint" of the place where Christ had "appointed" a meeting with His disciples after His resurrection: "Then the eleven disciples went away into Galilee, into a mountain where Jesus had appointed them" (Mt 28:16); **(1b)** of positions of military and civil authority over others, whether **(1b1)** "appointed" by men: "For I also am a man set (*tasso*) under authority, having under me soldiers, and I say unto one, Go, and he goeth; and to another, Come, and he cometh; and to my servant, Do this, and he doeth *it*" (Lk 7:8), or **(1b2)** by God: "Let every soul be subject unto the higher powers. For there is no power but of God: the powers that be are ordained of God" (Rom 13:1). It signifies

(2) to be "ordained." **(2a)** It is said of those who, having believed the gospel, "were ordained to eternal life": "And when the Gentiles heard this, they were glad, and glorified the word of the Lord: and as many as were ordained to eternal life believed" (Acts 13:48). **(2b)** The house of Stephanas at Corinth had "addicted" themselves to the ministry of the saints: "I beseech you, brethren, ye know the house of Stephanas, that it is the firstfruits of Achaia, and *that* they have addicted (*tasso*) themselves to the ministry of the saints" (1 Cor 16:15). Syn.: **(A)** *Entellomai* (1781) means to enjoin, is used esp. of those whose office or position invests them with claims, and points rather to the contents of the command, cf "our instruction." **(B)** *Keleuo* (2753) means to command, designates verbal orders, coming usually from a superior. **(C)** *Paraggello* (3853) means to charge, and is used esp. of the order of a military commander to his troops. *Tasso* means to assign a post to, with a suggestion of duties connected with it, often used of military appointments. **(D)** *Paragello* (3853) differs from *entellomai* (1781) in denoting fixed and abiding obligations rather than specific or occasional instructions, duties arising from the office rather than coming from the personal will of a superior. See: TDNT—8:27, 1156; BAGD—805d; THAYER—615c.

5022. **ταῦρος** {4x} **taurŏs**, *tow'-ros;* appar. a primary word [comp. 8450, "*steer*"]; a *bullock:*—bull {2x}, ox {2x}.

Tauros is translated **(1)** "oxen" in Mt 22:4 and Acts 14:13; **(2)** "bulls" in Heb 9:13 and 10:4. See: BAGD—806b; THAYER—615d.

5023. **ταῦτα** {247x} **tauta**, *tŏw'-tah;* nominative or acc. neut. plur. of *3778;* *these things:*—these things {158x}, these {26x}, thus {17x}, that {7x}, these words {7x}, this {6x}, afterwards + 3326 {4x}, misc. {22x} = follow, + hereafter, × him, the same, so, such, then, they, those. See: BAGD—549b [3778]; THAYER—466c [3778].

5024. **ταὐτά** {4x} **tauta**, *tŏw-tah';* neut. plur of *3588* and *846* as adv.; in *the same* way:—even thus {1x}, like {1x},like manner {1x}, so {1x}. See: BAGD—806b; THAYER—615d.

5025. **ταύταις** {21x} **tautais**, *tŏw'-taheece;* and

ταύτας **tautas**, *tŏw'-tas;* dat. and acc. fem. plur. respectively of *3778;* (*to* or *with* or *by,* etc.) *these:*—hence {1x}, that {1x}, then {1x}, these {12x}, those {6x}. See: BAGD—596b [3778]; THAYER—466c [3778].

5026. **ταύτῃ** {122x} **tautēi**, *tŏw'-tay;* and

ταύτην **tautēn**, *tŏw'-tane;* and

ταύτης **tautēs**, *tŏw'-tace;* dat., acc., and gen. respectively of the fem. sing. of *3778;* (*toward* or *of*) *this:*—this {105x}, that {4x}, the same {4x}, misc. {9x} = her, + hereof, it, + thereby. See: BAGD—596b [3778]; THAYER—466c [3778].

5027. **ταφή** {1x} **taphē**, *taf-ay';* fem. from *2290;* *burial* (the act):—bury + 1519 {1x}. See: BAGD—806b; THAYER—616a.

5028. **τάφος** {7x} **taphŏs**, *taf'-os;* masc. from *2290;* a *grave* (the place of interment):—sepulchre {6x}, tomb {1x}.

Taphos, akin to *thapto,* "to bury," originally "a burial," then, "a place for burial", **(1)** "a *sepulchre*" in Mt 23:27; 27:61, 64, 66; 28:1; **(2)** "tomb" in Mt 23:29; and **(3)** metaphorically, Rom 3:13, "*sepulchre.*" See: BAGD—806b; THAYER—616a.

5029. **τάχα** {2x} **tacha**, *takh'-ah;* as if neut. plur. of *5036* (adv.); *shortly,* i.e. (fig.) *possibly:*—peradventure {1x}, perhaps {1x}.

Tacha, primarily "quickly" (from *tachus,* "quick"), signifies **(1)** "peradventure" in Rom

5:7; and **(2)** in Philem 15, "perhaps." See: BAGD—806c; THAYER—616a.

5030. **ταχέως** {10x} **tachĕōs**, *takh-eh'-oce;* adv. from *5036; briefly,* i.e. (in time) *speedily,* or (in manner) *rapidly:*—hastily {1x}, quickly {2x}, shortly {4x}, soon {2x}, suddenly {1x}.

Tacheos in 1 Ti 5:22 carries the idea of quickly/hastily: "Lay hands suddenly (*tacheos*) on no man, neither be partaker of other men's sins: keep thyself pure." Syn.: 160, 869, 1810, 1819. See: BAGD—806d; THAYER—616a.

5031. **ταχινός** {2x} **tachinŏs**, *takh-ee-nos';* from *5034; curt,* i.e. *impending:*—shortly {1x}, swift {1x}.

Tachinos, "of swift approach," is used **(1)** in 2 Pet 1:14, "shortly", lit., "(the putting off of my tabernacle is) swift," i.e., "imminent"; **(2)** in 2 Pet 2:1, "swift (destruction)." See: BAGD—807a; THAYER—616a.

5032. **τάχιον** {5x} **tachiŏn**, *takh'-ee-on;* neut. sing. of the comp. of *5036* (as adv.); *more swiftly,* i.e. (in manner) *more rapidly,* or (in time) *more speedily:*—shortly {2x}, quickly {1x}, outrun + 4390 {1x}, the sooner {1x}.

Tachion, the comparative degree of *tachus* is translated **(1)** "quickly" in Jn 13:27; **(2)** "out(-ran)" in Jn 20:4; **(3)** "shortly" in 1 Ti 3:14 and Heb. 13:23; **(4)** in Heb 13:19, "(the) sooner." See: BAGD—807a; THAYER—616a.

5033. **τάχιστα** {1x} **tachista**, *takh'-is-tah;* neut. plur. of the superl. of *5036* (as adv.); *most quickly,* i.e. (with *5613* pref.) *as soon as possible:*—with all speed + 5613 {1x}. See: BAGD—807a; THAYER—616b.

5034. **τάχος** {7x} **tachŏs**, *takh'-os;* from the same as *5036;* a *brief* space (of time), i.e. (with *1722* pref.) in *haste:*—shortly + 1722 {4x}, quickly + 1722 {2x}, speedily + 1722 {1x}. Cf. Lk 18:8; Acts 12:7; 22:18; 25:4; Rom 16:20; Rev 1:1; 22:6. See: BAGD—807a; THAYER—616b.

5035. **ταχύ** {13x} **tachu**, *takh-oo';* neut. sing. of *5036* (as adv.); *shortly,* i.e. *without delay, soon,* or (by surprise) *suddenly,* or (by impl. of ease) *readily:*—lightly {1x}, quickly {12x}.

Tachu, the neuter of *tachus,* "swift, quick," signifies **(1)** "quickly," Mt 5:25; 28:7, 8; Lk 15:22; Jn 11:29; Rev 2:5, 16; 3:11; 11:14; 22:7, 12, 20; and **(2)** in Mk 9:39, "lightly". See: BAGD—807b; THAYER—616b.

5036. **ταχύς** {1x} **tachus**, *takh-oos';* of uncert. aff.; *fleet,* i.e. (fig.) *prompt* or *ready:*—swift {1x}. See: BAGD—807b; THAYER—616b.

5037. **τὲ** {209x} **tĕ**, *teh;* a primary particle (enclitic) of connection or addition; *both* or *also* (prop. as correl. of *2532*):—and {130x}, both {36x}, then {2x}, whether {1x}, even {1x}, also {1x}, not tr {38x}. Often used in composition, usually as the latter part. See: BAGD—807b; THAYER—616b.

5038. **τεῖχος** {9x} **tĕichŏs**, *ti'-khos;* akin to the base of *5088;* a *wall* (as *formative* of a house):—wall {9x}.

Teichos, "a wall," especially one around a town, is used **(1)** literally, Acts 9:25; 2 Cor 11:33; Heb 11:30; **(2)** figuratively, of the "wall" of the heavenly city, Rev 21:12, 14, 15, 17, 18, 19. Syn.: A *teichos* is a wall around a city and may also double as the outer wall of a house. A *toichos* (5109) is specifically a wall around a city. See: BAGD—808a; THAYER—617b.

5039. **τεκμήριον** {1x} **tĕkmēriŏn**, *tek-may'-ree-on;* neut. of a presumed der. of τεκμάρ **tĕkmar** (a *goal* or fixed *limit*); a *token,* (as *defining* a fact), i.e. *criterion* of certainty:—infallible proof {1x}.

Tekmerion denotes that from which something is surely and plainly known; indubitable evidence, a proof, Acts 1:3. See: BAGD—808a; THAYER—617b.

5040. **τεκνίον** {9x} **tĕkniŏn**, *tek-nee'-on;* dimin. of *5043;* an *infant,* i.e. (plur. fig.) *darlings* (Chr. *converts*):—little children {9x}.

(1) *Teknion,* only figuratively and always in the plural, is a term of kindly address by teachers to their disciples under circumstances requiring a tender appeal, e.g., **(1a)** of Christ to the Twelve just before His death, Jn 13:33; **(1b)** the apostle John used it in warning believers against spiritual dangers, 1 Jn 2:1, 12, 28; 3:7, 18; 4:4; 5:21; **(1c)** Paul, because of the deadly errors of Judaism assailing the Galatian churches, Gal 4:19. See: TDNT—5:636, 759; BAGD—808a; THAYER—617b.

5041. **τεκνογονέω** {1x} **tĕknŏgŏnĕō**, *tek-nog-on-eh'-o;* from a compound of *5043* and the base of *1096;* to *be a child-bearer,* i.e. *parent* (*mother*):—bear children {1x}. See: BAGD—808a; THAYER—617c.

5042. **τεκνογονία** {1x} **tĕknŏgŏnia**, *tek-nog-on-ee'-ah;* from the same as *5041; childbirth* (*parentage*), i.e. (by impl.) *maternity* (the performance of *maternal duties*):—childbearing {1x}. See: BAGD—808b; THAYER—617c.

5043. **τέκνον** {99x} **tĕknŏn**, *tek'-non;* from the base of *5098;* a *child* (as *produced*):—child {77x}, daughter {1x}, son {21x}.

Teknon, "a child" (akin to *tikto,* "to beget, bear"), is used in both the natural and the figurative senses. Figuratively, *teknon* is used of "children" of **(1)** God, Jn 1:12; **(2)** light, Eph 5:8; **(3)** obedience, 1 Pet 1:14; **(4)** a promise, Rom 9:8; Gal 4:28; **(5)** the Devil, 1 Jn 3:10; **(6)** wrath, Eph 2:3; **(7)** cursing, 2 Pet 2:14; **(8)** spiritual relationship, 2 Ti 2:1; Philem 10. Syn.: **(A)** *Paidarion* (3808) refers to a child up to his first school years. **(B)** *Paidion* (3813) refers exclusively to little children. **(C)** *Paidiske* (3814) refers to a female in late childhood and early youth. **(D)** *Pais* (3816) refers to a child of any age. **(E)** *Teknon* (5043) gives prominence to physical and outward aspects of parentage. **(F)** *Huios* (5207) gives prominence to the inward, ethical, legal aspects of parentage, the dignity and character of the relationship. *Pais* (3816) and *teknon* (5043) denote a child as respects to descent and age, reference to the later being more prominent in the former word, to descent in *paidion* (3813); but the period *pais* (3816) covers is not sharply defined. See: TDNT—5:636, 759; BAGD—808b; THAYER—617c.

5044. **τεκνοτροφέω** {1x} **tĕknŏtrŏphĕō**, *tek-not-rof-eh'-o;* from a compound of *5043* and *5142;* to *be a child-rearer,* i.e. *fulfil* the duties of a *female parent:*—bring up children {1x}. See: BAGD—808d; THAYER—618b.

5045. **τέκτων** {2x} **tĕktōn**, *tek'-tone;* from the base of *5098;* an *artificer* (as *producer* of fabrics), i.e. (spec.) a *craftsman* in wood:—carpenter {2x}. Cf. Mt 13:55; Mk 6:3. See: BAGD—809a; THAYER—618b.

5046. **τέλειος** {19x} **tĕlĕiŏs**, *tel'-i-os;* from *5056; complete* (in various applications of labor, growth, ment. and mor. character, etc.); neut. (as noun, with *3588*) *completeness:*—of full age {1x}, man {1x}, perfect {17x}.

Teleios means **(1)** brought to its end, finished; wanting nothing necessary to completeness, perfect (Jas 1:4); **(2)** consummate human integrity and virtue (Rom 12:2); **(3)** *Teleios,* as an adjective means "complete, perfect," men full grown, adult, of full age, mature [from *telos,* "an end,"] and is translated "of full age": "But strong meat belongeth to them that are of full age, *even* those who by reason of use have their senses exercised to discern both good and evil" (Heb 5:14). **(4)** It also means "perfect": signifies "having reached its end" (*telos*), "finished, complete perfect." It is used **(4a)** of persons, **(4a1)** primarily of physical development, then, with ethical import, "fully grown, mature," 1 Cor 2:6; 14:20; Eph 4:13; Phil 3:15; Col 1:28; 4:12; in Heb 5:14, "of full age"; **(4a2)** "complete," conveying the idea of goodness without necessary reference to maturity or what is expressed under (4a1) Mt 5:48; 19:21; Jas 1:4 (2nd part); 3:2. **(4a3)** It is used thus of God in Mt 5:48; **(4b)** of "things, complete, perfect," Rom 12:2; **(4b1)** 1 Cor 13:10 (referring to the complete revelation of God's will and ways, whether in the completed Scriptures or in the hereafter); **(4b2)** Jas 1:4 (of the work of patience); v. 25; 1 Jn 4:18. Syn.: **(A)** One who is *holokleros* (3648) has preserved, or regained, his completeness. **(B)** One who is *teleios* has attained the moral end for which he was intended, namely to be a man in Christ. **(C)** *Artios* (739) refers not only to the presence of all the parts that are necessary for completeness but also to the further adaptation and aptitude of these parts for their assigned purpose (2 Ti 34:17). See also: 165, 166, 739, 1074, 2244, 2250, 3648, 5230. See: TDNT—8:67, 1161; BAGD—809a; THAYER—618b.

5047. **τελειότης** {2x} **tĕlĕiŏtēs**, *tel-i-ot'-ace;* from *5046;* (the state) *completeness* (ment. or mor.):—perfection {1x}, perfectness {1x}.

Teleiotes denotes much the same as *teleiosis* (5050), but stressing perhaps the actual accomplishment of the end in view (Col 3:14, perfectness; Heb 6:1 perfection). See: TDNT—8:78, 1161; BAGD—809c; THAYER—618c.

5048. **τελειόω** {24x} **tĕlĕiŏō**, *tel-i-ŏ'-o;* from *5046;* to *complete,* i.e. (lit.) *accomplish,* or (fig.) *consummate* (in character):—make perfect {12x}, perfect {4x}, finish {4x}, fulfil {2x}, be perfect {1x}, consecrate {1x}.

The main distinction between *teleo* (5055) and *teleioo* is that *teleo* more frequently signifies to fulfill, *teleioo,* more frequently, to make perfect. See: TDNT—8:79, 1161; BAGD—809d; THAYER—618d.

5049. **τελείως** {1x} **tĕlĕiōs**, *tel-i'-oce;* adv. from *5046; completely,* i.e. (of hope) *without wavering:*—to the end {1x}.

Teleios signifies having reached its end, finished, complete perfect." See: BAGD—810b; THAYER—619a.

5050. **τελείωσις** {2x} **tĕlĕiōsis**, *tel-i'-o-sis;* from *5448;* (the act) *completion,* i.e. (of prophecy) *verification,* or (of expiation) *absolution:*—perfection {1x}, performance {1x}.

Teleiosis denotes "a fulfillment, completion, perfection, an end accomplished as the effect of a process," **(1)** Heb 7:11, "perfection"; **(2)** in Lk 1:45, "performance." See: TDNT—8:84, 1161; BAGD—810a; THAYER—619a.

5051. **τελειωτής** {1x} **tĕlĕiŏtēs**, *tel-i-o-tace';* from *5048;* a *completer,* i.e. *consummater:*—finisher {1x}.

Jesus, the one who has in His own person raised faith to its perfection and so set before us the highest example of faith, Heb 12:2. See: TDNT—8:86, 1161; BAGD—810c; THAYER—619b.

5052. **τελεσφορέω** {1x} **tĕlĕsphŏrĕō**, *tel-es-for-eh'-o;* from a compound of *5056* and *5342;* to *be a bearer to completion* (maturity), i.e. to *ripen* fruit (fig.):—bring fruit to perfection {1x}. See: BAGD—810c; THAYER—619b.

5053. **τελευτάω** {12x} **tĕlĕutaō**, *tel-yoo-tah'-o,* from a presumed der. of *5055;* to *finish* life (by impl. of *979*), i.e. *expire* (*demise*):—be dead {3x}, decease {1x}, die {8x}.

Teleutao, "to end" (from *telos,* "an end"), hence, "to end one's life," is used **(1)** of the "death" of the body, Mt 2:19; 9:18; 15:4, where "die the death" means "surely die"; Mk 7:10; Mt 22:25, "deceased"; Lk 7:2; Acts 2:29; 7:15; Heb 11:22; **(2)** of the gnawings of conscience in self reproach, under the symbol of a worm, Mk 9:44, 46, 48. See: BAGD—810c; THAYER—619b.

5054. **τελευτή** {1x} **tĕlĕutē**, *tel-yoo-tay';* from *5053; decease:*—death {1x}.

Teleute, as a noun, means "an end, limit"; hence, "the end of life, death," is used of the "death" of Herod (Mt 2:15). Syn.: 336, 337, 520, 1935, 2288, 2289. See: BAGD—810c; THAYER—619b.

5055. **τελέω** {26x} **tĕlĕō**, *tel-eh'-o;* from *5056;* to *end,* i.e. *complete, execute, conclude, discharge* (a debt):—finish {8x}, fulfil {7x}, accomplish {4x}, pay {2x}, perform {1x}, expire {1x}, make an end {1x}, fill up {1x}, go over {1x}.

Frequently this word signifies, not merely to terminate a thing, but to carry out a thing to the full. See: TDNT—8:57, 1161; BAGD—810d; THAYER—619c.

5056. **τέλος** {42x} **tĕlŏs**, *tel'-os;* from a primary τέλλω **tĕllō**, (to *set out* for a def. point or *goal*); prop. the point aimed at as a *limit,* i.e. (by impl.) the *conclusion* of an act or state (*termination* [lit., fig. or indef.], *result* [immed., ultimate or prophetic], *purpose*); spec. an *impost* or *levy* (as *paid*):—end {35x}, custom {3x}, uttermost {1x}, finally {1x}, ending {1x}, by (one's) continual + 1519 {1x}.

Telos means an end, a termination, whether of time or purpose, denotes, in its secondary significance, what is paid for public ends, a toll, tax, custom (Mt 17:25). See: TDNT—8:49, 1161; BAGD—811b; THAYER—619d. comp. *5411.*

5057. **τελώνης** {22x} **tĕlōnēs**, *tel-o'-nace;* from *5056* and *5608;* a *tax-farmer,* i.e. *collector of* public *revenue:*—publican {22x}.

(1) *Telones* primarily denoted "a farmer of the tax" (from *telos,* "toll, custom, tax"), then, as in the NT, a subsequent subordinate of such, who collected taxes in some district, "a tax gatherer"; such were naturally hated intensely by the people; **(2)** they are classed **(2a)** with "sinners," Mt 9:10, 11; 11:9; Mk 2:15, 16; Lk 5:30; 7:34; 15:1; **(2b)** with harlots, Mt 21:31, 32; **(2c)** with "the Gentile," Mt 5:47; 18:17. See also Mt 5:46; 10:3; Lk 3:12; 5:27, 29; 7:29; 18:10, 11, 13. See: TDNT—8:88, 1166; BAGD—812b; THAYER—620c.

5058. **τελώνιον** {3x} **tĕlōniŏn**, *tel-o'-nee-on;* neut. of a presumed der. of *5057;* a *tax-gatherer's* place of business:—receipt of custom {3x}.

Telonion denotes "a custom-house," for the collection of the taxes, Mt 9:9; Mk 2:14; Lk 5:27. See: BAGD—812c; THAYER—620c.

5059. **τέρας** {16x} **tĕras**, *ter'-as;* of uncert. aff.; a *prodigy* or *omen:*—wonder {16x}.

Wonders are manifested as **(1)** divine operations in thirteen occurrences (9 times in Acts); **(2)** three times they are ascribed to the work of Satan through human agents, Mt 24:24; Mk 13:22 and 2 Th 2:9. Syn.: **(A)** *Teras* denotes something strange causing the beholder to marvel and is always used in the plural, always rendered wonders, and generally follows **(B)** *semeia* (4592, signs). A sign is intended to appeal to the understanding, a wonder appeals to the imagination, **(C)** *dunamis* (1411, a power) indicates its source as supernatural. See also: 1411, 1741, 2297, 3167, 3861, 4592. See: TDNT—8:113, 1170; BAGD—812c; THAYER—620d.

5060. **Τέρτιος** {1x} **Tĕrtiŏs**, *ter'-tee-os;* of Lat. or.; *third; Tertius,* a Chr.:—Tertius {1x}. See: BAGD—813a; THAYER—620d.

5061. **Τέρτυλλος** {2x} **Tĕrtullŏs**, *ter'-tool-los;* of uncert. der.; *Tertullus,* a Rom.:—Tertullus {2x}. See: BAGD—813a; THAYER—620d.

τέσσαρα **tĕssara**. See *5064.*

5062. **τεσσαράκοντα** {22x} **tĕssarakŏnta**, *tes-sar-ak'-on-tah;* the decade of *5064; forty:*—forty {22x}. See: TDNT—8:135, 1172; BAGD—813a; THAYER—620d.

5063. **τεσσαρακονταετής** {2x} **tĕssarakŏntaĕtēs**, *tes-sar-ak-on-tah-et-ace';* from *5062* and *2094; of forty years* of age:—of forty years {1x}, forty years old {1x}. See: TDNT—8:135, 1172; BAGD—813b; THAYER—620d.

5064. **τέσσαρες** {42x} **tĕssarĕs**, *tes'-sar-es;* neut.

τέσσαρα **tĕssara**, *tes'-sar-ah;* a plur. number; *four:*—four {42x}. See: TDNT—8:127, 1172; BAGD—813b; THAYER—612a.

5065. **τεσσαρεσκαιδέκατος** {2x} **tĕssarĕskaidĕkatŏs**, *tes-sar-es-kahee-dek'-at-os;* from *5064* and *2532* and *1182; fourteenth:*—fourteenth {2x}. See: BAGD—813b; THAYER—621a.

5066. **τεταρταῖος** {1x} **tĕtartaiŏs**, *tet-ar-tah'-yos;* from *5064;* pertaining to the *fourth* day:—four days {1x}. See: TDNT—8:127, 1172; BAGD—813c; THAYER—621a.

5067. **τέταρτος** {10x} **tĕtartŏs**, *tet'-ar-tos;* ord. from *5064; fourth:*—four {1x}, fourth {9x}. See: TDNT—8:127, 1172; BAGD—813a; THAYER—621a.

5068. **τετράγωνος** {1x} **tĕtragōnŏs**, *tet-rag'-o-nos;* from *5064* and *1137; four-cornered,* i.e. *square:*—foursquare {1x}. See: BAGD—813c; THAYER—621a.

5069. **τετράδιον** {1x} **tĕtradiŏn**, *tet-rad'-ee-on;* neut. of a presumed der. of τέτρας **tĕtras** (a *tetrad;* from *5064*); a *quaternion,* or squad (picket) of four Rom. soldiers:—quaternion {1x}.

A *tetradion* is a group of four and occurs in Acts 12:4. A quaternion was a set of four men occupied in the work of a guard, two soldiers being chained to the prisoner and two keeping watch; alternatively one of the four watched while the other three slept. The night was divided into four watches of three hours each; there would be one quaternion for each watch by day and by night. See: BAGD—813d; THAYER—621b.

5070. **τετρακισχίλιοι** {5x} **tĕtrakischiliŏi**, *tet-rak-is-khil'-ee-oy;* from the mult. adv. of *5064* and *5507; four times a thousand:*—four thousand {5x}. See: BAGD—813d; THAYER—621b.

5071. **τετρακόσιοι** {4x} **tĕtrakŏsiŏi**, *tet-rak-os'-ee-oy;* neut. τετρακόσια **tĕtrakŏsia**, *tet-rak-os'-ee- ah;* plur. from *5064* and *1540; four hundred:*—four hundred {4x}. See: BAGD—813d; THAYER—621b.

5072. **τετράμηνον** {1x} **tĕtramēnŏn**, *tet-ram'-ay-non;* neut. of a compound of *5064* and *3376;* a *four months'* space:—four months {1x}. See: BAGD—813d; THAYER—621b.

5073. **τετραπλόος** {1x} **tĕtraplŏŏs**, *tet-rap-lŏ'-os;* from *5064* and a der. of the base of *4118; quadruple:*—fourfold {1x}. See: BAGD—813d; THAYER—621b.

5074. **τετράπους** {3x} **tĕtrapŏus**, *tet-rap'-ooce;* from *5064* and *4228;* a *quadruped:*—fourfooted beast {3x}. Cf. Acts 10:12; 11:6; Rom 1:23. See: BAGD—814a; THAYER—621b.

5075. **τετραρχέω** {3x} **tĕtrarchĕō**, *tet-rar-kheh'-o;* from *5076;* to *be a tetrarch:*—be tetrarch {1x}, tetrarch {2x}.

This word means to be a *tetrarch* and occurs in Lk 3:1 (thrice), of Herod Antipas, his brother Philip and Lysanias. Antipas and Philip each inherited a fourth part of his father's [Herod the Great] dominions. See: BAGD—814a; THAYER—621c.

5076. **τετράρχης** {4x} **tĕtrarchēs**, *tet-rar'-khace;* from *5064* and *757;* the *ruler of a fourth* part of a country ("*tetrarch*"):—tetrarch {4x}.

Tetarches denotes "one of four rulers" (*tetra,* "four," *arche,* "rule"), properly, "the governor of the fourth part of a region"; hence, "a dependent princeling," or "any petty ruler" subordinate to kings or ethnarchs; in the NT, Herod Antipas, Mt 14:1; Lk 3:19; 9:7; Acts 13:1. See: BAGD—814a; THAYER—621c.

τεύχω **tĕuchō**. See *5177.*

5077. **τεφρόω** {1x} **tĕphrŏō**, *tef-rŏ'-o;* from τέφρα **tephra**, (*ashes*); to *incinerate,* i.e. *consume:*—turn to ashes {1x}. See: BAGD—814b; THAYER—621c.

5078. **τέχνη** {3x} **tĕchnē**, *tekh'-nay;* from the base of *5088; art* (as *productive*), i.e. (spec.) a *trade,* or (gen.) *skill:*—art {1x}, craft {1x}, occupation {1x}.

Techne, "an art, handicraft, trade," is used **(1)** in Acts 17:29, of the art; **(2)** in Acts 18:3, of a trade or craft, "occupation"; and **(3)** in Rev 18:22, "craft" (cf. *technites,* "a craftsman," Eng., "technical"). See: BAGD—814b; THAYER—621d.

5079. **τεχνίτης** {4x} **tĕchnitēs**, *tekh-nee'-tace;* from *5078;* an *artisan;* fig. a *founder (Creator):*—builder {1x}, craftsman {3x}.

Technites, "an artificer, artisan, one who does a thing by rules of art", "a craftsman," is translated **(1)** "craftsman" in Acts 19:24, 38 and Rev 18:22. **(2)** It is found elsewhere in Heb. 11:10, "builder", viewing God as "moulding and fashioning . . . the materials which He called into existence." Syn.: *Demiourgos* (1217) recognizes God as the Maker of all things and emphasizes the power of the Divine creator. *Technites* stresses the artistic side of creation, His manifold wisdom, the infinite variety and beauty of His handiwork. See: BAGD—814b; THAYER—621d.

5080. **τήκω** {1x} **tēkō**, *tay'-ko;* appar. a primary verb; to *liquefy:*—melt {1x}. See: BAGD—814b; THAYER—621d.

5081. **τηλαυγῶς** {1x} **tēlaugōs**, *tay-lŏw-goce';* adv. from a compound of a der. of *5056* and *827;* in a *far-shining* manner, i.e. *plainly:*—clearly {1x}.

Telaugos, (from *tele,* "afar," and *auge,* "radiance"), signifies "conspicuously, or clearly," Mk 8:25, of the sight imparted by Christ to one who had been blind. See: BAGD—814c; THAYER—621d.

5082. **τηλικοῦτος** {4x} **tēlikŏutŏs**, *tay-lik-oo'-tos;* fem.

τηλικαύτη **tēlikautē**, *tay-lik-ŏw'-tay;* from a compound of *3588* with *2245* and *3778; such as this,* i.e. (in [fig.] magnitude) *so vast:*—so great {3x}, so mighty {1x}.

This word means so great and is used of things only: **(1)** "so great" **(1a)** a death (2 Cor 1:10); **(1b)** salvation (Heb 2:3); **(1c)** ships (Jas 3:4); and **(2)** "so mighty" an earthquake (Rev 16:18). See: BAGD—814c; THAYER—621d.

5083. **τηρέω** {75x} **tērĕō**, *tay-reh'-o;* from **τερός** **tĕrŏs**, (a *watch;* perh. akin to *2334*); to *guard* (from *loss* or *injury,* prop. by keeping *the eye* upon; and thus differing from *5442,* which is prop. to *prevent* escaping; and from *2892,* which implies a *fortress* or full military lines of apparatus), i.e. to *note* (a prophecy; fig. to *fulfil* a command); by impl. to *detain* (in custody; fig. to *maintain*); by extens. to *withhold* (for personal ends; fig. to *keep unmarried*):—keep {57x}, reserve {8x}, observe {4x}, watch {2x}, preserve {2x}, keeper {1x}, hold fast {1x}.

Tereo denotes **(1)** "to watch over, preserve, keep, watch," e.g., Acts 12:5, 6; 16:23; in **(1a)** in Acts 25:21, "reserved"; **(1b)** the present participle is translated "keepers" in Mt 28:4, lit. "the keeping (ones)"; **(2)** it is used of the "keeping" power of God the Father and Christ, exercised **(2a)** over His people, Jn 17:11, 12, 15; 1 Th 5:23, "preserved"; 1 Jn 5:18, where "he that is begotten of God," "keepeth himself"; Jude 1, "preserved in Jesus Christ", Rev 3:10; **(2b)** of their inheritance, 1 Pet 1:4 "reserved"; **(2c)** of judicial reservation by God in view of future doom, 2 Pet 2:4, 9, 17; 3:7; Jude 6, 13; **(3)** of "keeping" **(3a)** the faith, 2 Ti 4:7; **(3b)** the unity of the Spirit, Eph 4:3; **(3c)** oneself, 2 Cor 11:9; 1 Ti 5:22; **(3d)** Jas 1:27; figuratively, one's garments, Rev 16:15; **(4)** "to observe, to give heed to," **(4a)** as of keeping commandments, etc., e.g., Mt 19:17; Jn 14:15; 15:10; 17:6; Jas 2:10; 1 Jn 2:3, 4, 5; 3:22, 24; 5:2, 3; Rev 1:3; 2:26; 3:8, 10; 12:17; 14:12; 22:7, 9. Syn.: **(A)** *Tereo* (5083) means to watch or keep and expresses watchful care and is suggestive of present possession. **(B)** *Phulasso* (5442) means to guard and indicates safe custody and often implies assault from without; 5083 may mark the result of which 5442 is the means. See: TDNT—8:140, 1174; BAGD—814c; THAYER—622a.

5084. **τήρησις** {3x} **tērēsis**, *tay'-ray-sis;* from *5083;* a *watching,* i.e. (fig.) *observance,* or (concr.) a *prison:*—a hold {1x}, prison {1x}, keeping {1x}.

Teresis translated **(1)** "hold" in Acts 4:3, **(2)** "prison" in Acts 5:18 signifies "a watching, guarding"; hence, "imprisonment, ward" (from *tereo,* "to watch, keep"); and **(3)** "a keeping," as of commandments, 1 Cor 7:19. See: TDNT—8:146, 1174; BAGD—815c; THAYER—622c.

τῇ **te**, **τήν** **tēn**, **τῆς** **tēs**. See *3588*.

5085. **Τιβεριάς** {3x} **Tibĕrias**, *tib-er-ee-as';* from *5086; Tiberias,* the name of a town and a lake in Pal.:—*Tiberias* {3x}. See: BAGD—815c; THAYER—622c.

5086. **Τιβέριος** {1x} **Tibĕriŏs**, *tib-er'-ee-os;* of Lat. or.; prob. *pertaining to the* river *Tiberis* or *Tiber; Tiberius,* a Rom. emperor:—Tiberius {1x}. See: BAGD—815c; THAYER—622d.

5087. **τίθημι** {96x} **tithēmi**, *tith'-ay-mee;* a prol. form of a primary

θέω **thĕō**, *theh'-o* (which is used only as alt. in certain tenses); to *place* (in the widest application, lit. and fig.; prop. in a pass. or horizontal posture, and thus different from *2476,* which prop. denotes an upright and active position, while *2749* is prop. refl. and utterly prostrate):—lay {28x}, put {18x}, lay down {12x}, make {10x}, appoint {6x}, kneel down + 1119 + 3588 {5x}, misc. {17x} = + advise, bow, commit, conceive, give, ordain, purpose, set (forth), settle, sink down.

Tithemi, as a verb, means "to put" is used of "appointment" to any form of service. **(1)** Christ used it of His followers: "Ye have not chosen me, but I have chosen you, and ordained (*tithemi*) you, that ye should go and bring forth fruit, and *that* your fruit should remain: that whatsoever ye shall ask of the Father in my name, he may give it you" (Jn 15:16). **(2)** The verb is used by Paul of his service in the ministry of the gospel: "And I thank Christ Jesus our Lord, who hath enabled me, for that he counted me faithful, putting (*tithemi*) me into the ministry" (1 Ti 1:12; cf. 2:7; 2 Ti 1:11); **(3)** of the overseers, or bishops, in the local church at Ephesus, as those "appointed" by the Holy Ghost, to tend the church of God: "Take heed therefore unto yourselves, and to all the flock, over the which the Holy Ghost hath made (*tithemi*) you overseers, to feed the church of God, which he hath purchased with his own blood" (Acts 20:28);

(4) of the Son of God, as appointed Heir of all things: "Hath in these last days spoken unto us by *His* Son, whom He hath appointed (*tithemi*) heir of all things, by whom also He made the worlds" (Heb 1:2). **(5)** It is also used of "appointment" to punishment, **(5a)** as of the unfaithful servant: "And shall cut him asunder, and appoint (*tithemi*) *him* his portion with the hypocrites: there shall be weeping and gnashing of teeth" (Mt 24:51; cf. Lk 12:46); **(5b)** of unbelieving Israel: "And a stone of stumbling, and a rock of offence, *even to them* which stumble at the word, being disobedient: whereunto also they were appointed (*titnemi*)" (1 Pet 2:8; cf. 2 Pet 2:6). See: TDNT—8:152, 1176; BAGD—815d; THAYER—622d.

5088. **τίκτω** {19x} **tiktō**, *tik'-to;* a strengthened form of a primary **τέκω** **tekō**, *tek'-o* (which is used only as alt. in certain tenses); to *produce* (from seed, as a mother, a plant, the earth, etc.), lit. or fig.:—bring forth {9x}, be delivered {5x}, be born {3x}, be in travail {1x}, bear {1x}.

Tikto, as a verb, means **(1)** "to bring forth": "Now Elisabeth's full time came that she should be delivered; and she brought forth a son" (Lk 1:57; cf. Jn 16:21; Heb 11:11; Rev 12:2, 4), or **(2)** "to be born" **(2a)** said of the Child (Mt 2:2; Lk 2:11), and **(2b)** is used metaphorically in Jas 1:15 of lust as bringing forth sin. Syn.: 313, 616, 738, 1080, 1084, 1085, 1626. See: BAGD—816d; THAYER—623d.

5089. **τίλλω** {3x} **tillō**, *til'-lo;* perh. akin to the alt. of *138,* and thus to *4951;* to *pull* off:—pluck {3x}.

Tillo is used of "plucking off ears of corn," Mt 12:1; Mk 2:23; Lk 6:1. See: BAGD—817a; THAYER—623d.

5090. **Τιμαῖος** {1x} **Timaiŏs**, *tim'-ah-yos;* prob. of Chald. or. [comp. 2931]; *Timæus* (i.e. *Timay*), an Isr.:—Timæus {1x}. See: BAGD—817a; THAYER—624a.

5091. **τιμάω** {21x} **timaō**, *tim-ah'-o;* from *5093;* to *prize,* i.e. *fix* a *valuation* upon; by impl. to *revere:*—honour {19x}, value {2x}.

Timao, "to honor", is used of **(1)** valuing Christ at a price by Judas as thirty pieces of silver, Mt 27:9 twice; **(2)** "honoring" a person: **(2a)** the "honor" done by Christ to the Father, Jn 8:49; **(2b)** "honor" bestowed by the Father upon him who serves Christ, Jn 12:26; **(2c)** the duty of all to "honor" the Son equally with the Father, Jn 5:23, 4 times; **(2d)** the duty of children to "honor" their parents, Mt 15:4, 6; 19:19; Mk 7:10; 10:19; Lk 18:20; Eph 6:2; **(2e)** the duty of Christians to "honor" the king, and all men, 1 Pet 2:17 twice; **(2f)** the respect and material assistance to be given to widows "that are widows indeed," 1 Ti 5:3; **(2g)** the "honor" done to Paul and his companions by the inhabitants of Melita, Acts 28:10; **(2h)** mere lip profession of "honor" to God, Mt 15:8: Mk 7:6. See: TDNT—8:169, 1181; BAGD—817a; THAYER—624a.

5092. **τιμή** {43x} **timē**, *tee-may';* from *5099;* a *value,* i.e. *money* paid, or (concr. and collect.) *valuables;* by anal. *esteem* (espec. of the highest degree), or the *dignity* itself:—honour {35x}, precious {1x}, price {8x}, sum {1x}.

Time, primarily "a valuing," hence, objectively, **(1)** "a price paid or received," e.g., Mt 27:6, 9; Acts 4:34; 5:2, 3; 7:16, "sum"; 19:19; 1 Cor. 6:20; 7:23; **(2)** of "the preciousness of Christ" unto believers, 1 Pet 2:7, i.e., the honor and inestimable value of Christ as appropriated by believers, who are joined, as living stones, to Him the cornerstone; **(3)** in the sense of value, of human ordinances, valueless against the indulgence of the flesh, or, perhaps of no value in attempts at asceticism, Col 2:23;

(4) "honor, esteem," **(4a)** used in ascriptions of worship **(4a1)** to God, 1 Ti 1:17; 6:16; Rev 4:9, 11; 5:13; 7:12; **(4a2)** to Christ, Rev 5:12, 13; **(4b)** bestowed upon Christ by the Father, Heb 2:9; 2 Pet 1:17; **(4c)** bestowed upon man, Heb 2:7; **(4d)** bestowed upon Aaronic priests, Heb 5:4; **(4e)** to be the reward hereafter of "the proof of faith" on the part of tried saints, 1 Pet. 1:7; **(4f)** used of the believer who as a vessel is "meet for the Master's use," 2 Ti 2:21; **(4g)** to be the reward of patience in well-doing, Rom 2:7, and of working good (a perfect life to which man cannot attain, so as to be justified before God thereby), Rom 2:10; **(4h)** to be given to all to whom it is due, Rom 13:7 (see 1 Pet 2:17); **(4i)** as an advantage to be given by believers one to another instead of claiming it for self, Rom 12:10; **(4j)** to be given to elders that rule well ("double honor"), 1 Ti 5:17 (here the meaning may be an honorarium); **(4k)** to be given by servants to their master, 1 Ti 6:1; **(4l)** to be given to wives by husbands, 1 Pet 3:7; **(4m)** said of the husband's use of the wife, in contrast to the exercise of the passion of lust, 1 Th 4:4 (some regard the "vessel" here as the believer's body); **(4n)** of that bestowed upon; parts of the body, 1 Cor 12:23, 24; **(4o)** of that which belongs to the builder of a house in contrast to the house itself, Heb 3:3; **(4p)** of that which is not enjoyed by a prophet in his own country, Jn 4:44; **(4q)** of that bestowed by the inhabitants of Melita upon Paul and his fellow-passengers, in gratitude for his benefits of healing, Acts 28:10; **(4r)** of the festive honor to be possessed by nations, and brought into the Holy City, the heavenly Jerusalem, Rev. 21:24, 26; **(4s)** of honor bestowed upon things inanimate, a potters' vessel, Rom 9:21; 2 Ti 2:20. See: TDNT—8:169, 1181; BAGD—817b; THAYER—624a.

5093. **τίμιος** {14x} **timiŏs**, *tim'-ee-os;* including the comparative

τιμιώτερος timiōtĕrŏs, *tim-ee-o'- ter-os;* and the superlative

τιμιώτατος timiōtatŏs, *tim-ee-o'-tat-os;* from *5092; valuable,* i.e. (obj.) *costly,* or (subj.) *honored, esteemed,* or (fig.) *beloved:*—precious {8x}, most precious {2x}, more precious {1x}, dear {1x}, honourable {1x}, had in reputation {1x}.

Timios, from *time,* "honor, price," signifies **(1),** primarily, "accounted as of great price, precious, costly," **(1a)** 1 Cor 3:12; Rev 17:4; 18:12, 16; 21:19, and **(1b)** in the superlative degree, Rev 18:12; 21:11; **(1c)** the comparative degree is found in 1 Pet 1:7; **(2)** in the metaphorical sense, "held in honor, esteemed, very dear," **(2a)** Acts 5:34, "had in reputation"; so **(2b)** in Heb 13:4, "marriage is honorable"; **(2c)** Acts 20:24, "dear," negatively of Paul's estimate of his life; **(2d)** Jas. 5:7, "precious" (of fruit); **(2e)** 1 Pet 1:19, "precious" (of the blood of Christ); **(2e)** 2 Pet 1:4, "precious" (of God's promises). See: BAGD—818a; THAYER—624b.

5094. **τιμιότης** {1x} **timiŏtēs**, *tim-ee-ot'-ace;* from *5093; expensiveness,* i.e. (by impl.) *magnificence:*—costliness {1x}. See: BAGD—818b; THAYER—624c.

5095. **Τιμόθεος** {28x} **Timŏthĕŏs**, *tee-moth'-eh-os;* from *5092* and *2316; dear to God; Timotheus,* a Chr.:—Timotheus {19x}, Timothy {9x}. See: BAGD—818b; THAYER—624c.

5096. **Τίμων** {1x} **Timōn**, *tee'-mone;* from *5092; valuable; Timon,* a Chr.:—Timon {1x}. See: BAGD—818c; THAYER—624c.

5097. **τιμωρέω** {2x} **timōrĕō**, *tim-o-reh'-o;* from a comp. of *5092* and οὖρος **ŏurŏs** (a *guard*); prop. to *protect,* one's *honor,* i.e. to *avenge* (*inflict a penalty*):—punish {2x}.

Timoroo, primarily, "to help," then, "to avenge" (from *time,* "value, honor," and *ouros,* "a guardian"), i.e., "to help" by redressing injuries, is used **(1)** in the active voice in Acts 26:11, "I punished"; **(2)** passive voice in Acts 22:5, lit., "(that) they may be punished." See: BAGD—818c; THAYER—624c.

5098. **τιμωρία** {1x} **timōria**, *tee-mo-ree'-ah;* from *5097; vindication,* i.e. (by impl.) a *penalty:*—punishment {1x}.

Timoria emphasizes the vindictive character of punishment that satisfied the inflicter's sense of outraged justice and that defended his own honor or that of the violated law, Heb 10:29. Syn.: 2851. See: BAGD—818d; THAYER—624d.

5099. **τίνω** {1x} **tinō**, *tee'-no;* strengthened for a primary

τίω tiō, *tee'-o* (which is only used as an alt. in certain tenses); to *pay* a price, i.e. as a *penalty:*—be punished with + 1349 {1x}. See: BAGD—818d; THAYER—625d.

5100. **τὶς** {450x} **tis**, *tis;* an enclit. indef. pron.; *some* or *any* person or object:—certain {104x}, some {73x}, any man {55x}, any {38x}, one {34x}, man {34x}, anything {24x}, a {9x}, certain man {7x}, something {6x}, somewhat {6x}, ought {5x}, some man {4x}, certain thing {2x}, nothing + 3756 {2x}, divers {2x}, he {2x}, thing {2x}, another {2x}, not tr {17x}, misc. {22x} = divers, + partly, (+ that no-) thing, what (-soever), × wherewith, whom [-soever], whose ([-soever]). See: BAGD—819d; THAYER—625d.

5101. **τίς** {538x} **tis**, *tis;* prob. emphat. of *5100;* an interrog. pron., *who, which* or *what* (in direct or indirect questions):—what {260x}, who {102x}, why {67x}, whom {25x}, which {17x}, misc. {67x} = every man, how (much), + no (-ne, thing), where ([-by, -fore, -of, -unto, -with, -withal]), whether, whose. See: BAGD—818d; THAYER—624d.

5102. **τίτλος** {2x} **titlŏs**, *tit'-los;* of Lat. or.: a *titulus* or "*title*" (*placard*):—title {2x}.

Titlos is an inscription giving the accusation or crime for which a criminal suffered (Jn 19:19, 20). See: BAGD—820d; THAYER—627a.

5103. **Τίτος** {15x} **Titŏs**, *tee'-tos;* of Lat. or. but uncert. signif.; *Titus,* a Chr.:—Titus {15x}. See: BAGD—820d; THAYER—627b.

τίω tiō. See *5099.*

τό tŏ. See *3588.*

5104. **τοί** {0x} **tŏi**, *toy;* prob. for the dat. of *3588;* an enclit. particle of *asseveration* by way of contrast; *in sooth:*—[*used only with other particles in comp. as 2544, 3305, 5105, 5106, etc.*]. See: BAGD—821a; THAYER—433a [3588].

5105. **τοιγαροῦν** {2x} **tŏigarŏun**, *toy-gar-oon';* from *5104* and *1063* and *3767; truly for then,* i.e. *consequently:*—therefore {1x}, wherefore {1x}. See: BAGD—821a; THAYER—627b.

τοίγε tŏigĕ. See *2544.*

5106. **τοίνυν** {4x} **tŏinun**, *toy'-noon;* from *5104* and *3568; truly now,* i.e. *accordingly:* —then {1x}, therefore {3x}. See: BAGD—821b; THAYER—627b.

5107. **τοιόσδε** {1x} **tŏiŏsdĕ**, *toy-os'-deh;* (incl. the other inflections); from a der. of *5104* and *1161; such-like then,* i.e. *so great:*—such {1x}. See: BAGD—821b; THAYER—627c.

5108. **τοιοῦτος** {61x} **tŏiŏutŏs**, *toy-oo'-tos;* (incl. the other inflections); from *5104* and *3778; truly this,* i.e. *of this sort* (to denote character or individuality):—such {39x}, such thing {11x}, such an one {8x}, like {1x}, such a man {1x}, such a fellow {1x}. See: BAGD—821b; THAYER—627c.

5109. **τοῖχος** {1x} **tŏichŏs**, *toy'-khos;* another form of *5038;* a *wall:*—wall {1x}.

A *toichos* is especially a wall of a house, is used figuratively in Acts 23:3, "(thou whited) wall." Syn.: A *teichos* is a wall around a city and may also double as the outer wall of a house. A *toichos* (5109) is specifically a wall around a city. See: BAGD—821c; THAYER—627d.

5110. **τόκος** {2x} **tŏkŏs**, *tok'-os;* from the base of *5088; interest* on money loaned (as a *produce*):—usury {2x}.

Tokos primarily means a bringing forth, birth; then, an offspring and is used metaphorically of the produce of money lent out (Mt 25:27; Lk 19:23). Usury can imply charging an exorbitant rate of interest; not so in *tokos.* See: BAGD—821d; THAYER—627d.

5111. **τολμάω** {16x} **tŏlmaō**, *tol-mah'-o;* from τόλμα **tŏlma**, (*boldness;* prob. itself from the base of *5056* through the idea of *extreme* conduct); to *venture* (obj. or in *act;* while *2292* is rather subj. or in *feeling*); by impl. to be *courageous:*—be bold {4x}, boldly {1x}, dare {4x}, durst {7x}.

Tolmao signifies to dare to do, or to bear, something terrible or difficult; hence, to be bold, to bear oneself boldy, deal boldly. Syn.: It is translated be bold in 2 Cor 10:2 as contrasted with *tharreo* (2292) in verse 1. *Tharreo* denotes confidence in one's own powers, and has reference to character; *tolmao* denotes boldness in undertaking and has reference to manifestation. See: TDNT—8:181, 1183; BAGD—821d.

5112. **τολμηρότερον** {1x} **tŏlmērŏtĕrŏn**, *tol-may-rot'-er-on;* neut. of the comparative of a der. of the base of *5111* (as adv.); *more daringly,* i.e. *with greater confidence* than otherwise:—the more boldly {1x}. See: TDNT—8:181,*; BAGD—822a; THAYER—628a.

5113. **τολμητής** {1x} **tŏlmētēs**, *tol-may-tace';* from *5111;* a *daring* (*audacious*) man:—presumptuous {1x}.

Tolmetes means daring and is used in 2 Pet 2:10 of shameless and irreverent daring. See: TDNT—8:181, 1183; BAGD—822a; THAYER—628a.

5114. **τομώτερος** {1x} **tŏmōtĕrŏs**, *tom-o'-ter-os;* comparative of a der. of the primary τέμνω **tĕmnō** (to *cut;* more comprehensive or decisive than *2875,* as if by a *single* stroke; whereas that implies repeated blows, like *hacking*); *more keen:*—sharper {1x}. See: BAGD—822a; THAYER—628a.

5115. **τόξον** {1x} **tŏxŏn**, *tox'-on;* from the base of *5088;* a *bow* (appar. as the simplest fabric):—a bow {1x}.

Toxon is a bow as in "bow and arrow", Rev 6:2. See: BAGD—822b; THAYER—628a.

5116. **τοπάζιον** {1x} **tŏpaziŏn**, *top-ad'-zee-on;* neut. of a presumed der. (alt.) of τόπαζος **tŏpazŏs** (a "*topaz*"; of uncert. or.); a gem, prob. the *chrysolite:*—topaz {1x}.

Topazion is mentioned in Rev 21:20, as the ninth of the foundation stones of the wall of the heavenly Jerusalem, the stone is of a yellow color (though there are topazes of other colors) and is almost as hard as the diamond. It has the power of double refraction, and when heated or rubbed becomes electric. See: BAGD—822b; THAYER—628a.

5117. **τόπος** {92x} **tŏpŏs**, *top'-os;* appar. a primary word; a *spot* (gen. in *space,* but limited by occupancy; whereas *5561* is a larger but part. *locality*), i.e. *location* (as a position, home, tract, etc.); fig. *condition, opportunity;* spec. a *scabbard:*—place {80x}, room {5x}, quarter {2x}, licence {1x}, coast {1x}, where {1x}, plain + 3977 {1x}, rock + 5138 {1x}.

Topos, as a noun, [Eng., "topic," "topography"] is used of a specific "region" or "locality." It is translated **(1)** "room": **(1a)** "And she brought forth her firstborn son, and wrapped him in swaddling clothes, and laid him in a manger; because there was no room for them in the inn" (Lk 2:7; cf. 14:22); **(1b)** of a place which a person or thing occupies, a couch at table: "And he that bade thee and him come and say to thee, Give this man place; and thou begin with shame to take the lowest room" (Lk 14:9, cf. vs 10); **(2)** of the destiny of Judas Iscariot: "That he may take part of this ministry and apostleship, from which Judas by transgression fell, that he might go to his own place (*topos*)" (Acts 1:25); **(3)** of the condition of the "unlearned" or non-gifted in a church gathering: "Else when thou shalt bless with the spirit, how shall he that occupieth the room (*topos*) of the unlearned say Amen at thy giving of thanks, seeing he understandeth not what thou sayest?" (1 Cor 14:16);

(4) the sheath of a sword: "Then said Jesus unto him, Put up again thy sword into his place (*topos*): for all they that take the sword shall perish with the sword" (Mt 26:52); **(5)** a place in a book: "And there was delivered unto him the book of the prophet Esaias. And when he had opened the book, he found the place (*topos*) where it was written" (Lk 4:17; cf. Rev 2:5; 6:14; 12:8); **(6)** metaphorically, of **(6a)** "condition, occasion, opportunity, licence": "To whom I answered, It is not the manner of the Romans to deliver any man to die, before that he which is accused have the accusers face to face, and have licence (*topos*) to answer for himself concerning the crime laid against him" (Acts 25:16; cf. Rom 12:19; Eph 4:27). Syn.: **(A)** *Topos* is a place, indefinite; a portion of space viewed in reference to its occupancy, or as appropriated to itself. **(B)** *Chora* (5561) is region, country, extensive; space, yet unbounded. **(C)** *Chorion* (5564) parcel of ground, circumscribed; a definite portion of space viewed as enclosed or complete in itself. See also: 170, 201, 402, 1096, 1502, 2119, 2120, 2540, 3837, 4042, 5247, 5561, 5564, 5602. See: TDNT—8:187, 1184; BAGD—822b; THAYER—628a.

5118. **τοσοῦτος** {21x} **tŏsŏutŏs**, *tos-oo'-tos;* from τόσος **tŏsŏs**, (*so much;* appar. from *3588* and *3739*) and *3778* (including its variations); so *vast as this,* i.e. *such* (in quantity, amount, number or space):—so much {7x}, so great {5x}, so many {4x}, so long {2x}, as large {1x}, these many {1x}, so many things {1x}. See: BAGD—823b; THAYER—628d.

5119. **τότε** {159x} **tŏtĕ**, *tot'-eh;* from (the neut. of) *3588* and *3753; the when,* i.e. *at the time* that (of the past or future, also in consecution):—then {149x}, that time {4x}, when {1x}, not tr {5x}.

Tote, a demonstrative adverb of time, denoting "at that time," is used **(1)** of concurrent events, e.g., Mt 2:17; Gal 4:8, "at that time"; v. 29, "then"; 2 Pet 3:6,"(the world) that then was," lit., "(the) then (world)"; **(2)** of consequent events, "then, thereupon," e.g., Mt 2:7; Lk 11:26; 16:16, "since" that time"; Jn 11:14; Acts 17:14; **(3)** of things future, e.g., Mt 7:23; 24:30 (twice), 40; eight times in ch. 25; 1 Cor 4:5; Gal 6:4; 1 Th 5:3; 2 Th 2:8. **(4)** It occurs 90 times in Matthew, more than in all the rest of the NT together. See: BAGD—823d; THAYER—629a.

5120. **τοῦ** **tŏu**, *too;* prop. the gen. of *3588;* sometimes used for *5127; of this person:*—his {1x}. See: BAGD—549b [3588]; THAYER—433a [3588].

5121. **τοὐναντίον** {3x} **tŏunantiŏn**, *too-nan-tee'-on;* contr. for the neut. of *3588* and *1726; on the contrary:*—contrariwise {3x}. Cf. 2 Cor 2:7; Gal 2:7; 1 Pet 3:9. See: BAGD—824a; THAYER—629c.

5122. **τοὔνομα** {1x} **tŏunŏma**, *too'-no-mah;* contr. for the neut. of *3588* and *3686; the name* (is):—named {1x}.

Literally, translated this word is "of the name" = named. See: BAGD—824a; THAYER—629c.

5123. **τουτέστι** {17x} **tŏutĕsti**, *toot-es'-tee;* contr. for *5124* and *2076; that is:*—that is {12x}, that is to say {5x}. See: BAGD—824a; THAYER—629c.

5124. **τοῦτο** {320x} **tŏutŏ**, *too'-tŏ;* neut. sing. nom. or acc. of *3778; that thing:*—this {199x}, therefore + 1223 {44x}, that {25x}, for this cause + 1223 {14x}, wherefore + 1223 {7x}, it {5x}, not tr. {1x}, misc. {25x} = here [-unto], partly, self [-same], so, the same, thereunto], thus. See: BAGD—549b [3588]; THAYER—466c [3778].

5125. **τούτοις** {19x} **tŏutŏis**, *too'-toice;* dat. plur. masc. or neut. of *3778; to* (*for, in, with* or *by*) these (persons or things):—these {7x}, these things {3x}, this {2x}, such {1x}, them {1x}, therein {1x}, therewith {1x}, those {1x}, therewith + 1909 {1x}, not tr. {1x} = such, them, there [-in, -with], these, those. See: BAGD—549b [3588]; THAYER—466c [3778].

5126. **τοῦτον** {64x} **tŏutŏn**, *too'-ton;* acc. sing. masc. of *3778; this* (person, as obj. of verb or prep.):—this {39x}, him {18x}, that {4x}, this fellow {2x}, the same {1x}. See: BAGD—549b [3778]; THAYER—466c [3778].

5127. **τούτου** {7x} **tŏutŏu**, *too'-too;* gen. sing. masc. or neut. of *3778; of* (*from* or *concerning*) *this* (person or thing):—this {64x}, that {4x}, him {2x}, thus {1x}, thereabout + 4012 {1x}, it {1x}, thenceforth {1x}, hereby {1x}, here {1x}, + such manner of {1x}. See: BAGD—549b [3778]; THAYER—466c [3778].

5128. **τούτους** {27x} **tŏutŏus**, *too'-tooce;* acc. plur. masc. of *3778; these* (persons, as obj. of verb or prep.):—these {17x}, them {7x}, these men {1x}, this {1x}, such {1x}. See: BAGD—549b [3778]; THAYER—466c [3778].

5129. **τούτῳ** {89x} **tŏutōᵢ**, *too'-to;* dat. sing. masc. or neut. of *3778; to* (*in, with* or *by*) *this* (person or thing):—this {59x}, him {10x}, hereby + 1722 {8x}, herein + 1722 {7x}, misc. {5x} = one, the same, there [-in], this. See: BAGD—549b [3778]; THAYER—466c [3778].

5130. **τούτων** {69x} **tŏutōn**, *too'-tone;* gen. plur. masc. or neut. of *3778; of* (*from* or *concerning*) *these* (persons or things):—these {38x}, these things {21x}, such {2x}, these matters {1x}, such matters {1x}, those {1x}, not tr {1x}, their {1x}, they {1x}, this {1x}, sort {1x}. See: BAGD—549b [3778]; THAYER—466c [3778].

5131. **τράγος** {4x} **tragŏs**, *trag'-os;* from the base of *5176;* a *he-goat* (as a *gnawer*):—goat {4x}.

Tragos denotes "a hegoat," Heb 9:12, 13, 19; 10:4, the male prefiguring the strength by which Christ laid down His own life in expiatory sacrifice. See: BAGD—824b; THAYER—629c.

5132. **τράπεζα** {15x} **trapĕza**, *trap'-ed-zah;* prob. contr. from *5064* and *3979;* a *table* or *stool* (as being *four-legged*), usually for food (fig. a *meal*); also a *counter* for money (fig. a broker's *office* for loans at interest):—table {13x}, bank {1x}, meat {1x}.

Trapeza is used of **(1)** "a dining table," Mt 15:27; Mk 7:28; Lk 16:21; 22:21, 30; **(2)** "the table of shewbread," Heb 9:2; **(3)** by metonymy, of "what is provided on the table" (the word being used of that with which it is associated), Acts 16:34; **(3a)** Rom 11:9 (figurative of the special privileges granted to Israel and centering in Christ); **(3b)** 1 Cor 10:21 (twice), "the Lord's table," denoting all that is provided for believers in Christ on the ground of His death (and thus expressing something more comprehensive than the Lord's Supper); **(3c)** "the table of demons," denoting all that is partaken of by idolaters as the result of the influence of demons in connection with their sacrifices; **(4)** "a moneychanger's table," Mt 21:12; Mk 11:15; Jn 2:15; **(5)** "a bank," Lk 19:23; **(6)** by metonymy for "the distribution of money," Acts 6:2. See: TDNT—8:209, 1187; BAGD—824b; THAYER—629c.

5133. **τραπεζίτης** {1x} **trapĕzitēs**, *trap-ed-zee'-tace;* from *5132;* a *money-broker* or *banker:* —exchanger {1x}. See: BAGD—824d; THAYER—629d.

5134. **τραῦμα** {1x} **trauma**, *trŏw'-mah;* from the base of τιτρώσκω **titrōskō**, (to *wound;* akin to the base of *2352, 5147, 5149,* etc.); a *wound:*—wound {1x}. See: BAGD—824d; THAYER—629d.

5135. **τραυματίζω** {2x} **traumatizō**, *trŏw-mat-id'-zo;* from *5134;* to *inflict a wound:*—to wound {2x}.

Traumatizo occurs in Lk 20:12 and Acts 19:16. See: BAGD—824d; THAYER—629d.

5136. **τραχηλίζω** {1x} **trachĕlizō**, *trakh-ay-lid'-zo;* from *5137;* to *seize* by *the throat* or *neck,* i.e. to *expose* the *gullet* of a victim for killing (gen. to *lay bare*):—opened {1x}.

Trachelizo, "to seize and twist the neck" (from *trachelos,* "the throat"), was used of wrestlers, in the sense of taking by the throat. The word is found in Heb 4:13, "opened." The literal sense of the word seems to be "with the head thrown back and the throat exposed." See: BAGD—824d; THAYER—629d.

5137. **τράχηλος** {7x} **trachēlŏs**, *trakh'-ay-los;* prob. from *5143* (through the idea of *mobility*); the *throat* (*neck*), i.e. (fig.) *life:*—neck {7x}.

Trachelos is used **(1)** literally **(1a)** of that which holds up the head (Mt 18:6; Mk 9:42; Lk 17:2); **(1b)** of being embraced (Lk 15:20; Acts 20:37); **(2)** metaphorically, in Acts 15:10 of putting a yoke upon; **(3)** figuratively, in Rom 16:4, singular in the original, "laid down their neck," indicating that Prisca and Aquila in some way had risked their lives for the apostle. See: BAGD—825a; THAYER—630a.

5138. **τραχύς** {2x} **trachus**, *trakh-oos';* perh. strengthened from the base of *4486* (as if *jagged* by rents); *uneven, rocky* (*reefy*):—rock + 5117 {1x}, rough {1x}.

Trachus, **(1)** "rough, uneven," is used of paths, Lk 3:5; **(2)** of rocky places, Acts 27:29. See: BAGD—825a; THAYER—630a.

5139. **Τραχωνῖτις** {1x} **Trachōnitis**, *trakh-o-nee'-tis;* from a der. of *5138; rough* district; *Trachonitis,* a region of Syria:—*Trachonitis* {1x}. See: BAGD—825b; THAYER—630a.

5140. **τρεῖς** {69x} **trĕis**, *trice;* neut.

τρία **tria**, *tree'-ah;* or

τριῶν **triōn**, *tree-on';* a primary (plural) number; "*three*":—three {69x}. See:

TDNT—8:216, 1188; BAGD—825b; THAYER—630a.

5141. **τρέμω** {4x} **trĕmō**, *trem'-o;* strengthened from a primary τρέω **trĕō** (to *"dread," "terrify"*); to *"tremble"* or *fear:*—be afraid {1x}, trembling {3x}.

Tremo, "to tremble, especially with fear," is used in Mk 5:33; Lk 8:47; Acts 9:6; 2 Pet 2:10, "they are (not) afraid." Syn.: **(A)** *Ekplesso* (1605) means "to be astonished", prop. to be struck with terror, of a sudden and startling alarm; but like our "astonish" in popular use, often employed on comparatively slight occasions. **(B)** *Ptoeo* (4422) signifies "to terrify", to agitate with fear. **(C)** *Tremo* (5141) "to tremble", predominately physical; and **(D)** *phobeo* (5399) denotes "to fear", the general term; often used of a protracted state. See: BAGD—825b; THAYER—630a.

5142. **τρέφω** {8x} **trĕphō**, *tref'-o;* a primary verb (prop. θρέφω **thrĕphō**; but perhaps strengthened from the base of *5157* through the idea of *convolution*); prop. to *stiffen,* i.e. *fatten* (by impl. to *cherish* [with food, etc.], *pamper, rear*):—bring up {1x}, feed {4x}, nourish {3x}.

Trepho, as a verb, means "to rear, bring up" and signifies **(1)** "to make to grow, bring up, rear," Lk 4:16, "brought up"; **(2)** "to nourish, feed," Mt 6:26; 25:37; Lk 12:24; Acts 12:20; Rev 12:6, 14; **(3)** "to fatten," as of fattening animals, Jas 5:5, "ye have nourished (your hearts)." See: BAGD—825c; THAYER—630a.

5143. **τρέχω** {20x} **trĕchō**, *trekh'-o;* appar. a primary verb (prop. θρέχω **thrĕchō**; comp. *2359*); which uses δρέμω **drĕmō**, *drem'-o* (the base of *1408*) as alt. in certain tenses; to *run* or *walk hastily* (lit. or fig.):—have course {1x}, run {19x}.

Trecho, "to run," is used **(1)** in the Gospels the literal meaning alone is used, **(1a)** e.g., Mt 27:48 (*dramon,* an aorist participle, from an obsolete verb *dramo,* but supplying certain forms absent from *trecho,* lit., "having run, running," expressive of the decisiveness of the act); **(1b)** the same form in the indicative mood is used, e.g., in Mt 28:8; **(2)** elsewhere in 1 Cor 9:24 (twice in 1st part); Rev 9:9, "running";

(3) metaphorically, **(3a)** from the illustration of "runners" in a race, of either swiftness or effort to attain an end, Rom 9:16, indicating that salvation is not due to human effort, but to God's sovereign right to exercise mercy; **(3b)** of persevering activity in the Christian course with a view to obtaining the reward, **(3b1)** 1 Cor 9:24 (2nd part), and v. 26, **(3b2)** so Heb 12:1; **(3c)** in Gal 2:2 **(3c1)** (1st part), "(lest) I should run," continuous present tense referring to the activity of the special service of his mission to Jerusalem; **(3c2)** (2nd part), "had run," aorist tense, expressive of the continuous past, referring to the activity of his antagonism to the Judaizing teachers at Antioch, and his consent to submit the case to the judgment of the church in Jerusalem; **(3d)** in Gal 5:7 of the erstwhile faithful course doctrinally of the Galatian believers; **(3e)** in Phil 2:16, of the apostle's manner of life among the Philippian believers; **(3f)** in 2 Th 3:1, of the free and rapid progress of "the word of the Lord." See: TDNT—8:226, 1189; BAGD—825d; THAYER—630b.

5144. **τριάκοντα** {11x} **triakŏnta**, *tree-ak'-on-tah;* the decade of *5140; thirty:*—thirty {9x}, thirtyfold {2x}. See: BAGD—826a; THAYER—630b.

5145. **τριακόσιοι** {2x} **triakŏsiŏi**, *tree-ak-os'-ee-oy;* plur. from *5140* and *1540; three hundred:*—three hundred {2x}.

Triakosioi occurs in Mk 14:5 and Jn 12:5. See: BAGD—826a; THAYER—630c.

5146. **τρίβολος** {2x} **tribŏlŏs**, *trib'-ol-os;* from *5140* and *956;* prop. a *crow-foot* (*three-pronged* obstruction in war), i.e. (by anal.) a *thorny* plant (*caltrop*):—brier {1x}, thistle {1x}.

Tribolos occurs in **(1)** Mt 7:16 "thistle" and **(2)** Heb 6:8 "briers." Thistle is the plant which produces the briers. See: BAGD—826a; THAYER—630c.

5147. **τρίβος** {3x} **tribŏs**, *tree'-bos;* from τρίβω **tribō** (to *"rub"*; akin to τείρω **tĕirō**, τρύω **truō**, and the base of *5131, 5134*); a *rut,* or worn *track:*—path {3x}.

Tribos, "a beaten track" (akin to *tribo,* "to rub, wear down"), "a path," is used in Mt 3:3; Mk 1:3; Lk 3:4. See: BAGD—826b; THAYER—630c.

5148. **τριετία** {1x} **triĕtia**, *tree-et-ee'-ah;* from a compound of *5140* and *2094;* a *three years' period* (*triennium*):—space of three years {1x}. See: BAGD—826b; THAYER—630c.

5149. **τρίζω** {1x} **trizō**, *trid'-zo;* appar. a primary verb; to *creak* (*squeak*), i.e. (by anal.) to *grate* the teeth (in frenzy):—gnash {1x}.

Trizo, as a verb, primarily used of the sounds of animals, "to chirp, cry, squeak," came to signify "to grind or gnash with the teeth," Mk 9:18. Then the teeth are ground in gnashing they produce a squeaking sound. See: BAGD—826b; THAYER—630c.

5150. **τρίμηνον** {1x} **trimēnŏn**, *trim'-ay-non;* neut. of a compound of *5140* and *3376* as noun; a *three months'* space:—three months {1x}. See: BAGD—826b; THAYER—630c.

5151. **τρίς** {12x} **tris**, *trece;* adv. from *5140; three times:*—three times {1x}, thrice {11x}. See: TDNT—8:216, 1188; BAGD—826b; THAYER—630c.

5152. **τρίστεγον** {1x} **tristĕgŏn**, *tris'-teg-on;* neut. of a compound of *5140* and *4721* as noun; a *third roof* (*story*):—third loft {1x}. See: BAGD—826c; THAYER—630d.

5153. **τρισχίλιοι** {1x} **trischiliŏi**, *tris-khil'-ee-oy;* from *5151* and *5507; three times a thousand:*—three thousand {1x}. See: BAGD—826c; THAYER—630d.

5154. **τρίτος** {57x} **tritŏs**, *tree'-tos;* ord. from *5140; third;* neut. (as noun) a *third part,* or (as adv.) a (or the) *third* time, *thirdly:*—third {56x}, thirdly {1x}. See: TDNT—8:216, 1188; BAGD—826c; THAYER—630d.

τρίχες **trichĕs**, etc. See *2359*.

5155. **τρίχινος** {1x} **trichinŏs**, *trikh'-ee-nos;* from *2359; hairy,* i.e. made of *hair* (*mohair*):—of hair {1x}. See: BAGD—827a; THAYER—630d.

5156. **τρόμος** {5x} **trŏmŏs**, *trom'-os;* from *5141;* a *"trembling"*, i.e. quaking with *fear:* —tremble + 2192 {1x}, trembling {4x}.

(1) *Tromos* means to be with fear and trembling, used to describe the anxiety of one who distrusts his ability completely to meet all requirements, but religiously does his utmost to fulfill his duty. This word means "a trembling", and occurs in Mk 16:8; 1 Cor 2:3; 2 Cor 7:15; Eph 6:5; Phil 2:12. See: BAGD—827a; THAYER—630d.

5157. **τροπή** {1x} **trŏpē**, *trop-ay';* from an apparent primary τρέπω **trĕpō**, to *turn*); a *turn* (*"trope"*), i.e. the revolving of a planet, a *revolution* (fig. *variation*):—turning {1x}. See: BAGD—827a; THAYER—631a.

5158. **τρόπος** {13x} **trŏpŏs**, *trop'-os;* from the same as *5157;* a *turn,* i.e. (by impl.) *mode* or *style* (espec. with prep. or rel. pref. as adv. *like*); fig. *deportment* or *character:*—as + 3739 {3x}, even as + 2596 + 3739 {2x}, way {2x}, means {2x}, even as + 3739 {1x}, in like manner as + 3639 {1x}, manner {1x}, conversation {1x}.

Tropos, as a noun, means "a turning, fashion, manner, character, way of life" and is translated "manner" **(1)** in Acts 1:11, with reference to the Lord's ascension and return, and **(2)** in Jude 7, of the similarity of the evil of those mentioned in vv. 6 and 7. Syn.: 195, 1485, 2239, 3634, 3668, 3697, 3779, 4169, 4187, 4217, 4459, 5159, 5179. See: BAGD—827b; THAYER—631a.

5159. **τροποφορέω** {1x} **trŏpŏphŏrĕō**, *trop-of-or-eh'-o;* from *5158* and *5409;* to *endure* one's *habits:*—suffer (one's) manners {1x}.

Tropophoreo, as a verb, means "to bear another's manners" is translated "suffered He (their) manners" in Acts 13:18. Syn.: 195, 1485, 2239, 3634, 3668, 3697, 3779, 4169, 4187, 4217, 4459, 5158, 5179, 5615. See: BAGD—827c; THAYER—631a.

5160. **τροφή** {16x} **trŏphē**, *trof-ay';* from *5142; nourishment* (lit. or fig.); by impl. *rations* (*wages*):—meat {11x}, food {2x}, some meat {2x}, not tr {1x}.

Trophe denotes "nourishment, food" (akin to *trepho,* "to rear, nourish, feed"); **(1)** it is used literally, in the Gospels, Acts and Jas 2:15; **(2)** metaphorically, in Heb 5:12, 14, "(strong) meat," i.e., deeper subjects of the faith than that of elementary instruction. **(3)** The word is rendered "meat"; e.g., Mt 3:4; 6:25; 10:10; 24:45; Lk 12:23; Jn 4:8; Acts 2:46, "did eat their meat"; 27:33, 34, 36; and **(4)** "food" in Acts 9:19; 14:17 and Jas 2:15. Food is the general term for all nourishments [soups, liquids, gelatins, etc]. Meat refers to solid food which requires chewing. See: BAGD—827d; THAYER—631b.

5161. **Τρόφιμος** {3x} **Trŏphimŏs**, *trof'-ee-mos;* from *5160; nutritive; Trophimus,* a Chr.:—Trophimus {3x}. See: BAGD—827d; THAYER—631b.

5162. **τροφός** {1x} **trŏphŏs**, *trof-os';* from *5142;* a *nourisher,* i.e. *nurse:*—nurse {1x}.

Trophos translated "nurse" in 1 Th 2:7, there denotes a "nursing" mother, as is clear from the statement "cherisheth her own children"; this is also confirmed by the word *epios,* "gentle" (in the same verse), which was commonly used of the kindness of parents towards children. See: BAGD—827d; THAYER—631b.

5163. **τροχιά** {1x} **trŏchia**, *trokh-ee-ah';* from *5164;* a *track* (as a wheel-*rut*), i.e. (fig.) a *course* of conduct:—path {1x}.

Trochia, "the track of a wheel" (*trochos,* "a wheel"; *trecho,* "to run") hence, "a track, path," is used figuratively in Heb 12:13. See: BAGD—828a; THAYER—631b.

5164. **τροχός** {1x} **trŏchŏs**, *trokh-os';* from *5143;* a *wheel* (as a *runner*), i.e. (fig.) a *circuit* of phys. effects:—course {1x}.

Trochos is literally a wheel is translated "course" in Jas 3:6 with metaphorical reference to the round of human activity, as a glowing axle would set on fire the whole wooden wheel. See: BAGD—828a; THAYER—631b.

5165. **τρύβλιον** {2x} **trubliŏn**, *troob'-lee-on;* neut. of a presumed der. of uncert. aff.; a *bowl somewhat deep:*—dish {2x}.

Trublion denotes "a bowl," somewhat deep, Mt 26:23; Mk 14:20; See: BAGD—828b; THAYER—631b.

5166. **τρυγάω** {3x} **trugaō**, *troo-gah'-o;* from a der. of τρύγω **trugō** (to *dry*) mean. ripe *fruit* (as if *dry*); to *collect* the vintage:—gather {3x}.

Truago signifies "to gather in," of harvest, vintage, ripe fruits (*truge* denotes "fruit," etc., gathered in autumn), **(1)** Lk 6:44, of grapes (last part); **(2)** metaphorically, **(2a)** of the clusters of "the vine of the earth," Rev 14:18; **(2b)** of that from which they are "gathered", Rev 14:19. See: BAGD—828b; THAYER—631c.

5167. **τρυγών** {1x} **trugōn**, *troo-gone';* from τρύζω **truzō** (to *murmur;* akin to *5149,* but denoting a *duller* sound); a *turtledove* (as *cooing*):—turtle-dove {1x}. See: TDNT—6:63, 830; BAGD—828b; THAYER—631c.

5168. **τρυμαλιά** {2x} **trumalia**, *troo-mal-ee-ah';* from a der. of τρύω **truō** (to *wear,* away; akin to the base of *5134, 5147* and *5176*); an *orifice,* i.e. needle's *eye:*—eye {2x}. Cf. Mk 10:25; Lk 18:25. See: BAGD—828b; THAYER—631c. comp. *5169.*

5169. **τρύπημα** {1x} **trupēma**, *troo'-pay-mah;* from a der. of the base of *5168;* an *aperture,* i.e. a needle's *eye:*—eye {1x}. This "eye" is smaller than in 5168. See: BAGD—828c; THAYER—631c.

5170. **Τρύφαινα** {1x} **Truphaina**, *troo'-fahee-nah;* from *5172; luxurious; Tryphœna,* a Chr. woman:—Tryphena {1x}. See: BAGD—828c; THAYER—631c.

5171. **τρυφάω** {1x} **truphaō**, *troo-fah'-o;* from *5172;* to *indulge in luxury:*—live in pleasure {1x}.

Truphao concerns itself with the softness of a luxurious life. Syn.: 4684, 4763. See: BAGD—828c; THAYER—631c.

5172. **τρυφή** {2x} **truphē**, *troo-fay';* from θρύπτω **thruptō** (to *break,* up or [fig.] *enfeeble,* espec. the mind and body by indulgence); *effeminacy,* i.e. *luxury* or *debauchery:*—delicately {1x}, riot {1x}.

Truphe is used **(1)** with *en,* in the phrase *en truphe,* "luxuriously," "delicately," Lk 7:25, and denotes effeminacy, softness; **(2)** "to riot" in 2 Pet. 2:13, lit., "counting reveling in the day time a pleasure." See: BAGD—828d; THAYER—631d.

5173. **Τρυφῶσα** {1x} **Truphōsa**, *troo-fo'-sah;* from *5172; luxuriating; Tryphosa,* a Chr. female:—Tryphosa {1x}. See: BAGD—828d; THAYER—631d.

5174. **Τρῳάς** {6x} **Trōas**, *tro-as';* from Τρός **Trŏs** (a *Trojan*); the *Troad* (or plain of Troy), i.e. *Troas,* a place in Asia Minor:—*Troas* {6x}. See: BAGD—829a; THAYER—631d.

5175. **Τρωγύλλιον** {1x} **Trōgulliŏn**, *tro-gool'-lee-on;* of uncert. der.; *Trogyllium,* a place in Asia Minor:—Trogyllium {1x}. See: BAGD—829a; THAYER—631d.

5176. **τρώγω** {6x} **trōgō**, *tro'-go;* probably strengthened from a collateral form of the base of *5134* and *5147* through the idea of *corrosion* or *wear;* or perh. rather of a base of *5167* and *5149* through the idea of a *crunching* sound; to *gnaw* or *chew,* i.e. (gen.) to *eat:*—eat {6x}.

Trogo, primarily, "to gnaw, to chew," **(1)** stresses the slow process; it is used **(2)** metaphorically of the habit of spiritually feeding upon Christ, Jn 6:54, 56–58 (the aorists here do not indicate a definite act, but view a series of acts seen in perspective); **(2)** of the constant custom of "eating" in certain company, Jn 13:18; **(3)** of a practice unduly engrossing the world, Mt 24:38. **(4)** In Jn 6, the change in the Lord's use from the verb *esthio (phago)* to the stronger verb *trogo,* is noticeable. The more persistent the unbelief of His hearers, the more difficult His language and statements became. In vv. 49 to 53 the verb *phago* is used; in 54, 58, *trogo* (in v. 58 it is put into immediate contrast with *phago*). See: TDNT—8:236, 1191; BAGD—829b; THAYER—631d.

5177. **τυγχάνω** {13x} **tugchanō**, *toong-khan'-o;* prob. for an obs. τύχω **tuchō** (for which the mid. voice of another alt. τεύχω **tĕuchō** [to *make ready* or *bring to pass*] is used in certain tenses; akin to the base of *5088* through the idea of *effecting;* prop. to *affect;* or (spec.) to *hit* or *light upon* (as a mark to be reached), i.e. (tran.) to *attain* or *secure* an object or end, or (intr.) to *happen* (as if *meeting* with); but in the latter application only impers. (with *1487*), i.e. *perchance;* or (pres. part.) as adj. *usual* (as if commonly *met with,* with *3756, extraordinary*), neut. (as adv.) *perhaps;* or (with another verb) as adv. by *accident* (*as it were*):—obtain {5x}, be {1x}, chance {1x}, little {1x}, enjoy {1x}, may be {1x}, not tr {1x}, misc. {2x} = × refresh . . . self, + special.

Tugchano, "to meet with, light upon," also signifies "to obtain, attain to, reach, get" (with regard to things), translated "to obtain" **(1)** in Acts 26:22, of "the help that is from God"; **(2)** 2 Ti 2:10, of "the salvation which is in Christ Jesus with eternal glory"; **(3)** Heb 8:6, of the ministry obtained by Christ; **(4)** Heb 11:35, of "a better resurrection." See: TDNT—8:238, 1191; BAGD—829b; THAYER—632a. comp. *5180.*

5178. **τυμπανίζω** {1x} **tumpanizō**, *toom-pan-id'-zo;* from a der. of *5180* (mean. a *drum,* "*tympanum*"); to stretch on an instrument of *torture* resembling a drum, and thus *beat* to death:—torture {1x}.

Tumpanizo, primarily denotes "to beat a drum" (*tumpanon,* "a kettledrum," Eng., "tympanal," "tympanitis," "tympanum"), hence, "to torture by beating, to beat to death," Heb 11:35. See: BAGD—829; THAYER—632b.

5179. **τύπος** {16x} **tupŏs**, *too'-pos;* from *5180;* a *die* (as *struck*), i.e. (by impl.) a *stamp* or *scar;* by anal. a *shape,* i.e. a *statue,* (fig.) *style* or *resemblance;* spec. a *sampler* ("*type*"), i.e. a *model* (for imitation) or *instance* (for warning):—ensample {5x}, print {2x}, figure {2x}, example {2x}, pattern {2x}, fashion {1x}, manner {1x}, form {1x}.

Tupos, primarily denoted "a blow" (from a root *tupto,* "to strike"), and is translated **(1)** "ensample" in 1 Cor 10:11; Phil 3:17; 1 Th 1:7; 2 Th 3:9; 1 Pet 5:3; **(2)** "print" in Jn 20:25 twice; **(3)** "figure" in Acts 7:43; Rom 5:14; **(4)** "example" in 1 Cor 10:6; 1 Ti 4:2; **(5)** "pattern" in Titus 2:7; Heb 8:5; **(6)** "fashion" in Acts 7:44; **(7)** "manner" in Acts 23:25; and **(8)** "form" in Rom 6:17. Syn.: 195, 1485, 2239, 3634, 3668, 3697, 3779, 4169, 4187, 4217, 4459, 5158, 5159, 5615. See: TDNT—8:246, 1193; BAGD—829d; THAYER—632b.

5180. **τύπτω** {14x} **tuptō**, *toop'-to;* a primary verb (in a strengthened form); to "*thump*", i.e. *cudgel* or *pummel* (prop. with a stick or *bastinado*), but in any case by *repeated* blows; thus differing from *3817* and *3960,* which denote a [usually single] blow with the hand or any instrument, or *4141* with the *fist* [or a *hammer*], or *4474* with the *palm;* as well as from *5177,* an *accidental* collision); by impl. to *punish;* fig. to *offend* (the conscience):—beat {3x}, smite {9x}, strike {1x}, wound {1x}.

Tupto, (from a root *tup,* meaning "a blow," *tupos,* "a figure or print:" Eng., "type") denotes "to smite, strike, or beat," **(1)** usually not with the idea of giving a thrashing as with *dero.* **(2)** It frequently signifies a "blow" of violence, and, when used in a continuous tense, indicates a series of "blows." **(2a)** In Mt 27:30 the imperfect tense signifies that the soldiers kept on striking Christ on the head. **(2b)** So Mk 15:19; Lk 22:64. In that verse the word *paio,* "to smite," is used of the treatment given to Christ (*dero* in the preceding verse). **(2c)** The imperfect tense of the verb is again used in Acts 18:17, of the beating given to Sosthenes. Cf. Acts 21:32, which has the present participle. **(3)** It is used in the metaphorical sense of "wounding," in 1 Cor 8:12. **(4)** It is also translated "to strike, smite, beat," is rendered "to smite" in Mt 24:49; 27:30; Mk 15:19; Lk 6:29; 18:13; 22:64 (1st part); 23:48; Acts 23:2, 3 (twice). See: TDNT—8:260, 1195; BAGD—830b; THAYER—632d.

5181. **Τύραννος** {1x} **Turannŏs**, *too'-ran-nos;* a provincial form of the der. of the base of *2962;* a "*tyrant*"; *Tyrannus,* an Ephesian:—Tyrannus {1x}. See: BAGD—830c; THAYER—632d.

5182. **τυρβάζω** {1x} **turbazō**, *toor-bad'-zo;* from τύρβη **turbē**, (Lat. *turba,* a *crowd;* akin to *2351*); to *make* "*turbid*", i.e. *disturb:*—trouble {1x}. See: BAGD—830d; THAYER—632d.

5183. **Τύριος** {1x} **Turiŏs**, *too'-ree-os;* from *5184;* a *Tyrian,* i.e. inhab. of Tyrus:—of Tyre {1x}. See: BAGD—830d; THAYER—632d.

5184. **Τύρος** {11x} **Turŏs**, *too'-ros;* of Heb. or. [6865]: *Tyrus* (i.e. *Tsor*), a place in Pal.:—Tyre {11x}. See: BAGD—830d; THAYER—633a.

5185. **τυφλός** {53x} **tuphlŏs**, *toof-los';* from *5187; opaque* (as if *smoky*), i.e. (by anal.) *blind* (phys. or ment.):—blind {44x}, blind man {9x}.

Tuphlos, "blind," is **(1)** used both physically and metaphorically, chiefly in the Gospels; **(2)** elsewhere four times; **(2a)** physically, Acts 13:11; **(2b)** metaphorically, Rom 2:19; 2 Pet 1:9; Rev 3:17. **(3)** The word is frequently used as a noun, signifying "a blind man." See: TDNT—8:270, 1196; BAGD—830d; THAYER—633a.

5186. **τυφλόω** {3x} **tuphlŏō**, *toof-lŏ'-o;* from *5185;* to *make blind,* i.e. (fig.) to *obscure:*—to blind {3x}.

Tuphloo, "to blind" (from a root *tuph—,* "to burn, smoke"; cf. *tuphos,* "smoke"), is used metaphorically, of the dulling of the intellect, Jn 12:40; 2 Cor 4:4; 1 Jn 2:11. Cf. "cloudy thinking, not thinking clearly." See: TDNT—8:270, 1196; BAGD—831a; THAYER—633a.

5187. **τυφόω** {3x} **tuphŏō**, *toof-ŏ'-o;* from a der. of *5188;* to envelop with *smoke,* i.e. (fig.) to *inflate* with self-conceit:—high-minded {1x}, be lifted up with pride {1x}, be proud {1x}.

Tuphoo, properly means "to wrap in smoke" (from *tuphos,* "smoke"; metaphorically, for "conceit"); it is used in the passive voice, metaphorically **(1)** in 1 Ti 3:6, "lifted up with pride"; **(2)** so 1 Ti 6:4, "proud," and **(3)** 2 Ti 3:4, "highminded." Cf. "having one's head in the clouds, minding heavenly directives." See: BAGD—831a; THAYER—633c.

5188. **τύφω** {1x} **tuphō**, *too'-fo;* appar. a primary verb; to make a *smoke,* i.e. slowly *consume* without flame:—smoke {1x}.

Tupho, "to raise a smoke" (akin to *tuphoo,* "to puff up with pride), is used in the passive voice in Mt 12:20, "smoking (flax)," lit., "caused to smoke," of the wick of a lamp which has ceased to burn clearly, about to go out, figurative of mere nominal religiousness without the Spirit's power. See: BAGD—831c; THAYER—633c.

5189. **τυφωνικός** {1x} **tuphōnikŏs**, *too-fo-nee-kos';* from a der. of *5188; stormy* (as if *smoky*):—tempestuous {1x}. See: BAGD—831c; THAYER—633c.

5190. **Τυχικός** {7x} **Tuchikŏs**, *too-khee-kos';* from a der. of *5177; fortuitous,* i.e. *fortunate; Tychicus,* a Chr.:—Tychicus {7x}. See: BAGD—831c; THAYER—633c.

Υ

5191. **ὑακίνθινος** {1x} **huakinthinŏs**, *hoo-ak-in'-thee-nos;* from *5192; "hyacinthine"* or *"jacinthine",* i.e. deep *blue:*—jacinth {1x}. See: BAGD—831b; THAYER—633b.

5192. **ὑάκινθος** {1x} **huakinthŏs**, *hoo-ak'-in-thos;* of uncert. der.; the *"hy acinth"* or *"jacinth"*, i.e. some gem of a deep *blue* color, prob. the *zirkon:*—jacinth {1x}. See: BAGD—831b; THAYER—633b.

5193. **ὑάλινος** {3x} **hualinŏs**, *hoo-al'-ee-nos;* from *5194; glassy,* i.e. *transparent:*—of glass {3x}. See: BAGD—831d; THAYER—633b.

5194. **ὕαλος** {2x} **hualŏs**, *hoo'-al-os;* perh. from the same as *5205* (as being transparent like *rain*); *glass:*—glass {2x}.

Hualos signifies "glassy, made of glass", Rev 4:6; 15:2 (twice). See: BAGD—831d; THAYER—633b.

5195. **ὑβρίζω** {5x} **hubrizō**, *hoo-brid'-zo;* from *5196;* to *exercise violence,* i.e. *abuse:*—use despitefully {1x}, reproach {1x}, entreat shamefully {1x}, entreat spitefully {2x}.

Hubrizo means **(1)** to be insolent, to behave insolently, wantonly, outrageously; **(2)** to act insolently and shamefully towards one, to treat shamefully (Mt 22:6, "entreated spitefully"; Lk 18:32, "spitefully entreated"; Acts 14:5, "use despitefully"); **(3)** of one who injures another by speaking evil of him (Lk 11:45, "reproachest"; but in this case Jesus spoke the truth, which the lawyers took as reproach); and **(4)** 1 Th 2:2, "shamefully treated." See: TDNT—8:295, 1200; BAGD—831d; THAYER—633d.

5196. **ὕβρις** {3x} **hubris**, *hoo'-bris;* from *5228; insolence* (as *over*-bearing), i.e. *insult, injury:*—harm {1x}, hurt {1x}, reproach {1x}.

Hubris primarily denotes "wantonness, insolence": then, "an act of wanton violence, an outrage, injury," **(1)** 2 Cor 12:10, "reproaches" (more than reproach is conveyed by the term); **(2)** metaphorically **(2a)** of a loss by sea, Acts 27:10, "hurt," and **(2b)** Acts 27:21, "harm." See: TDNT—8:295, 1200; BAGD—832a; THAYER—633d.

5197. **ὑβριστής** {2x} **hubristēs**, *hoo-bris-tace';* from *5195;* a violent, insolent man; an *insulter,* i.e. *maltreater:*—despiteful {1x}, injurious {1x}.

(1) *Hubristes* denotes insolent wrongdoing for the sheer pleasure of inflicting pain on others, not out of revenge or a similar motive. **(2)** His contempt for others results in acts of wantonness and outrage. It is translated **(1)** "despiteful" in Rom 1:30; and **(2)** "injurious" in 1 Ti 1:13. Syn.: 213, 5244. See: TDNT—8:295, 1200; BAGD—832a; THAYER—633d.

5198. **ὑγιαίνω** {12x} **hugiainō**, *hoog-ee-ah'-ee-no;* from *5199;* to *have* sound *health,* i.e. *be well* (in body); fig. to be *uncorrupt* (*true* in doctrine):—sound {6x}, be sound {1x}, be whole {1x}, whole {1x}, wholesome {1x}, be in health {1x}, safe and sound {1x}.

Hugiaino, "to be healthy, sound in health" (Eng., "hygiene," etc.), translated **(1)** "safe and sound" in Lk 15:27, is used **(2)** metaphorically **(2a)** of doctrine, 1 Ti 1:10; 2 Ti 4:3; Titus 1:9; 2:1; **(2b)** of words, 1 Ti 6:3, "wholesome"; 2 Ti 1:13; **(2c)** "in the faith," Titus 1:13; **(2d)** "in faith," Titus 2:2. See: TDNT—8:308, 1202; BAGD—832b; THAYER—634a.

5199. **ὑγιής** {14x} **hugiēs**, *hoog-ee-ace';* from the base of *837; healthy,* i.e. *well* (in body); fig. *true* (in doctrine):—sound {1x}, whole {13x}.

Hugies is used **(1)** especially in the Gospels of making sick folk "whole," Mt 12:13; 15:31; Mk 3:5; 5:34; Lk 6:10; Jn 5:4, 6, 9, 11, 14, 15; 7:23; **(2)** also Acts 4:10; **(3)** of "sound (speech)," Titus 2:8. See: TDNT—8:308, 1202; BAGD—832c; THAYER—634a.

5200. **ὑγρός** {1x} **hugrŏs**, *hoo-gros';* from the base of *5205; wet* (as if with *rain*), i.e. (by impl.) *sappy* (*fresh*):—green {1x}.

Hugros denotes "wet, moist" (the opposite of *xeros,* "dry"); said of wood, sappy, "green," Lk 23:31, i.e., if they thus by the fire of their wrath treated Christ, the guiltless, holy, the fruitful, what would be the fate of the perpetrators, who were like the dry wood, exposed to the fire of divine wrath. See: BAGD—832c; THAYER—634b.

5201. **ὑδρία** {3x} **hudria**, *hoo-dree-ah';* from *5204;* a *water-jar,* i.e. *receptacle* for family supply:—water-pot {3x}. Cf. John 2:6, 7; 4:28. See: BAGD—832c; THAYER—634b.

5202. **ὑδροποτέω** {1x} **hudrŏpŏtĕō**, *hoo-drop-ot-eh'-o;* from a compound of *5204* and a der. of *4095;* to *be a water-drinker,* i.e. to *abstain from vinous beverages:*—drink water {1x}. See: BAGD—832d; THAYER—634b.

5203. **ὑδρωπικός** {1x} **hudrōpikŏs**, *hoo-dro-pik-os';* from a compound of *5204* and a der. of *3700* (as if *looking watery*); to *be "dropsical":*—have the dropsy {1x}.

Hudropikos, "dropsical, suffering from dropsy" (*hudrops,* "dropsy"), is found in Lk 14:2, the only instance recorded of the healing of this disease by the Lord. See: BAGD—832d; THAYER—634b.

5204. **ὕδωρ** {79x} **hudōr**, *hoo'-dore;* gen., **ὕδατος** **hudatŏs**, *hoo'-dat-os,* etc.; from the base of *5205; water* (as if *rainy*) lit. or fig.:—water {79x}.

Hudor, whence Eng. prefix, "hydro-," is used **(1)** of the natural element, **(1a)** frequently in the Gospels; **(1b)** in the plural especially in the Apocalypse; **(1c)** elsewhere, e.g., Heb 9:19; Jas 3:12; **(2)** in 1 Jn 5:6, that Christ "came by water and blood," refers to, in view of the order of the words and the prepositions here used, to His baptism in Jordan and His death on the cross. Jesus the Son of God came on His mission by, or through, "water" and blood, namely, at His baptism, when He publicly entered upon His mission and was declared to be the Son of God by the witness of the Father, and at the cross, when He publicly closed His witness; the apostle's statement thus counteracts the doctrine of the Gnostics that the divine *Logos* united Himself with the Man Jesus at His baptism, and left him at Gethsemane. On the contrary, He who was baptized and He who was crucified was the Son of God throughout in His combined deity and humanity.

(3) The word "water" is in Jn 3:5, in view of the preposition *ek,* "out of," the truth conveyed by baptism, this being the expression, not the medium, the symbol, not the cause, of the believer's identification with Christ in His death, burial and resurrection. So the New Birth is, in one sense, the setting aside of all that the believer was according to the flesh, for it is evident that there must be an entirely new beginning. **(4)** "The water of life," Rev 21:6 and 22:1, 17, is emblematic of the maintenance of spiritual life in perpetuity. **(5)** In Rev 17:1 "the waters" are symbolic of nations, peoples, etc. See: TDNT—8:314, 1203; BAGD—832d; THAYER—634b.

5205. **ὑετός** {6x} **huĕtŏs**, *hoo-et-os';* from a primary ὕω **huō**, (to *rain*); *rain,* espec. a *shower:*—rain {6x}.

Huetos, from *huo,* "to rain," is used especially, but not entirely, of "showers," and is found in Acts 14:17; 28:2; Heb 6:7; Jas 5:7; 5:18; Rev 11:6. See: BAGD—833b; THAYER—634c.

5206. **υἱοθεσία** {5x} **huiŏthĕsia**, *hwee-oth-es-ee'-ah;* from a presumed compound of *5207* and a der. of *5087;* the *placing* as a *son,* i.e. *adoption* (fig. Chr. *sonship* in respect to God):—adoption {3x}, adoption of children {1x}, adoption of sons {1x}.

Huiothesia, (from *huios,* "a son," and *thesis,* "a placing," akin to *tithemi*), "to place," **(1)** signifies the place and condition of a son given to one to whom it does not naturally belong. **(2)** The word is used by the apostle Paul only. **(3)** In Rom 8:15, believers are said to have received "the Spirit of adoption," that is, the Holy Spirit who, given as the Firstfruits of all that is to be theirs, produces in them the realization of sonship and the attitude belonging to sons. **(4)** In Gal 4:5 they are said to receive "the adoption of sons," i.e., sonship bestowed in distinction from a relationship consequent merely upon birth; here two contrasts are presented, **(4a)** between the sonship of the believer and the unoriginated sonship of Christ, **(4b)** between the freedom enjoyed by the believer and bondage, whether of Gentile natural condition, or of Israel under the Law.

(5) In Eph 1:5 they are said to have been foreordained unto "adoption as sons" through Jesus Christ, "adoption of children." God does "adopt" believers as children and they are begotten as such by His Holy Spirit through faith. **(6)** "Adoption" is a term involving the dignity of the relationship of believers as sons; it is not a putting into the family by spiritual birth, but a putting into the position of sons. **(7)** In Rom 8:23 the "adoption" of the believer is set forth as still future, as it there includes the redemption of the body, when the living will be changed and those who have fallen asleep will be raised. **(8)** In Rom 9:4 "adoption" is spoken of as belonging to Israel, in accordance with the statement in Ex 4:12, "Israel is My Son." Cf. Hos 11:1. Israel was brought into a special relation with God, a collective relationship, not enjoyed by other nations, cf. Deut 14:1; Jer 31:9. See: TDNT—8:397, 1206; BAGD—833b; THAYER—634c.

5207. **υἱός** {382x} **huiŏs**, *hwee-os';* appar. a primary word; a "*son*" (sometimes of animals), used very widely of immed. remote or fig. kinship:—son(s) {85x}, Son of Man + 444 {87x}, Son of God + 2316 {49x}, child(ren) {49x}, Son {42x}, his Son + 848 {21x}, Son of David + 1138 {15x}, my beloved Son + 27 + 3350 {7x}, thy Son + 4575 {5x}, only begotten Son + 3339 {3x}, his (David's) son + 846 {3x}, firstborn son + 4316 {2x}, foal {4x}.

(1) Primarily this word stresses the quality and essence of one so resembling another that distinctions between the two are indiscernible (Heb 1:2–3). It is used in the NT of **(2)** male offspring, Jn 9:18–20; Gal. 4:30; **(2a)** legitimate, as opposed to illegitimate offspring, Heb 12:8; **(2c)** descendants, without reference to sex, Rom 9:27; **(2d)** friends attending a wedding, Mt 9:15; **(2e)** those who enjoy certain privileges, Acts 3:25; **(2f)** those who act in a certain way, whether **(2f1)** evil, Mt 23:31, or **(2f2)** good, Gal 3:7; **(2g)** those who manifest a certain character, whether **(2g1)** evil, Acts 13:10; Eph 2:2, or **(2g2)** good, Lk 6:35; Acts 4:36; Rom 8:14; **(2h)** the destiny that corresponds with the character, whether **(2h1)** evil, Mt 23:15; Jn 17:12; 2 Th 2:3, or **(2h2)** good, Lk 20:36; **(2i)** the dignity of the relationship with God whereinto men are brought by the Holy Spirit when they believe on the Lord Jesus Christ, Rom 8:19; Gal 3:26.

(3) The Apostle John does not use *huios,* "son," of the believer, he reserves that title for the Lord; but he does use *teknon,* "child," as in his Gospel, Jn 1:12; 1 Jn 3:1, 2; Rev 21:7 (*huios*) is a quotation from 2 Sa 7:14. **(4)** The Lord Jesus used *huios* in a very significant way, as **(4a)** in Mt 5:9, "Blessed are the peacemakers, for they shall be called the sons of God," and **(4b)** vv. 44, 45, "Love your enemies, and pray for them that persecute you; that ye may be (become) sons of your Father which is in heaven." **(4c)** The disciples were to do these things, not in order that they might become children of God, but that, being children (note "your Father" throughout), they might make the fact manifest in their character, might "become sons." See also 2 Cor 6:17, 18. **(5)** As to moral characteristics, the following phrases are used: **(5a)** sons of God, Mt 5:9, 45; Lk 6:35; **(5b)** sons of the light, Lk 16:8; Jn 12:36; **(5c)** sons of the day, 1 Th 5:5; **(5d)** sons of peace, Lk 10:6; **(5e)** sons of this world, Lk 16:8; **(5f)** sons of disobedience, Eph 2:2; **(5g)** sons of the evil one, Mt 13:38, cf. "of the devil," Acts 13:10; **(5h)** son of perdition, Jn 17:12; 2 Th 2:3.

(6) It is also used to describe characteristics other than moral, as: **(6a)** sons of the resurrection, Lk 20:36; **(6b)** sons of the Kingdom, Mt 8:12; 13:38; **(6c)** sons of the bridechamber, Mk 2:19; **(6d)** sons of exhortation, Acts 4:36; **(6e)** sons of thunder, *Boanerges,* Mk 3:17. Syn.: **(A)** *Paidarion* (3808) refers to a child up to his first school years. **(B)** *Paidion* (3813) refers exclusively to little children. **(C)** *Paidiske* (3814) refers to a female in late childhood and early youth. **(D)** *Pais* (3816) refers to a child of any age. **(E)** *Teknon* (5043) gives prominence to physical and outward aspects of parentage. **(F)** *Huios* (5207) gives prominence to the inward, ethical, legal aspects of parentage. *Pais* (3816) and *teknon* (5043) denote a child as respects to descent and age, reference to the later being more prominent in the former word, to descent in *paidion* (3813); but the period *pais* (3816) covers is not sharply defined. See: TDNT—8:334, 1206; BAGD—833c; THAYER—634d.

5208. **ὕλη** {1x} **hulē**, *hoo'-lay;* perh. akin to *3586; a forest,* spec. of felled wood, i.e. (by impl.) *fuel:*—matter {1x}.

Matter is derived from "material" and signifies any combustible substance. See: BAGD—836a; THAYER—636d.

5209. **ὑμᾶς** {437x} **humas**, *hoo-mas';* acc. pl. of *5210; you* (as the obj. of a verb or prep.):—you {376x}, ye {42x}, for your sakes + 1223 {9x}, not tr {1x}, misc. {9x} = youward, your (+ own). See: BAGD—772a [4771]; THAYER—636d; 591c [4771].

5210. **ὑμεῖς** {243x} **humĕis**, *hoo-mice';* irreg. plur. of *4771; you* (as subj. of verb):—ye {236x}, ye yourselves {1x}, you {1x}, not tr {5x}. See: BAGD—836a; 772a [4771]; THAYER—636d; 591c [4771].

5211. **Ὑμέναιος** {2x} **Humĕnaiŏs**, *hoo-men-ah'-yos;* from Ὑμήν **Humēn**, (the god of *weddings*); "*hymenæal*"; *Hymenæus,* an opponent of Christianity:—Hymenæus {2x}. See: BAGD—836a; THAYER—636d.

5212. **ὑμέτερος** {10x} **humĕtĕrŏs**, *hoo-met'-er-os;* from *5210; yours,* i.e. *pertaining to you:*—your {7x}, yours {2x}, your own {1x}. See: BAGD—836a; THAYER—637a.

5213. **ὑμῖν** {621x} **humin**, *hoo-min';* irreg. dat. pl. of *5210; to* (*with* or *by*) *you:*—you {597x}, ye {14x}, your {6x}, not tr {1x}, yourselves {3x}. See: BAGD—772a [4771; THAYER—637a; 591c [4771].

5214. **ὑμνέω** {4x} **humnĕō**, *hoom-neh'-o;* from *5215; to hymn,* i.e. sing a relig. ode; by impl. to *celebrate* (God) in song:—sing a hymn {2x}, sing praise unto {2x}.

Humneo is used **(1)** transitively, Mt 26:30; Mk 14:26, where the "hymn" was that part of the *Hallel* consisting of Psalms 113—118; **(2)** intransitively, where the verb itself is rendered "to sing praises" or "praise," Acts 16:25; Heb 2:12. See: TDNT—8:489, 1225; BAGD—836b; THAYER—637a.

5215. **ὕμνος** {2x} **humnŏs**, *hoom'-nos;* appar. from a simpler (obs.) form of ὕδέω **hudĕō**, (to *celebrate;* prob. akin to *103;* comp. *5567*); a "*hymn*" or relig. ode (one of the Psalms):—hymn {2x}.

Humnos denotes "a song of praise addressed to God" (Eng., "hymn"), Eph 5:19; Col 3:16. Syn.: *Ode* (5603) is the generic term containing praises, exhortations and other admonitions. *Psalmos* (5568) and *humnos* (5215) are specific, the former designating a song which took its general character from the OT Psalms and is usually accompanied by some musical instrument, although not restricted to them; the later a song of praise with or without instrumental accompaniment; the generic term for a song; hence the accompanying adjective "spiritual." See: TDNT—8:489, 1225; BAGD—836b; THAYER—637b.

5216. **ὑμῶν** {583x} **humōn**, *hoo-mone';* gen. pl. of *5210;* of (*from* or *concerning*) *you:*—your {348x}, you {203x}, ye {9x}, yours {5x}, not tr {1x}, misc. {17x}. See: BAGD—772a [4771]; THAYER—637b; 591c [4771].

5217. **ὑπάγω** {81x} **hupagō**, *hoop-ag'-o;* from *5259* and *71;* to *lead* (oneself) *under,* i.e. *withdraw* or *retire* (as if *sinking* out of sight), lit. or fig.:—go {55x}, go (one's) way {17x}, go away {3x}, get thee {3x}, depart {2x}, get thee hence {1x}. See: TDNT—8:504, 1227; BAGD—836c; THAYER—637b.

5218. **ὑπακοή** {15x} **hupakŏē**, *hoop-ak-ŏ-ay';* from *5219; attentive hearkening,* i.e. (by impl.) *compliance* or *submission:*—obedience {11x}, obedient {1x}, to make obedient + 1519 {1x}, to obey + 1519 {1x}, obeying {1x}.

Hupakoe, "obedience" (*hupo,* "under," *akouo,* "to hear"), is used **(1)** in general, Rom 6:16 (1st part), "(to) obey"; here "obedience" is not personified, as in the next part of the verse, "servants . . . of obedience", but is simply shown to be the effect of the presentation mentioned; **(2)** of the fulfillment of apostolic counsels, 2 Cor 7:15; 10:6; Philem 21; **(3)** of the fulfillment of God's claims or commands, **(3a)** Rom 1:5 and 16:26, "obedience of faith," which grammatically is objective, obedient to the faith. Faith is one of the main subjects of the Epistle, and is the initial act of obedience in the new life [justification], as well as an essential characteristic thereof [sanctification]; **(3b)** Rom 6:16 (2nd part); **(3c)** Rom 15:18, "(to make) obedient"; 16:19; **(3d)** 1 Pet 1:2, 14, "obedient (children)", characterized by "obedience"; **(3e)** 1 Pet 1:22, "obeying (the truth)"; **(4)** of "obedience" to Christ (objective), 2 Cor 10:5; **(5)** of Christ's "obedience," **(5a)** Rom 5:19 (referring to His death; cf. Phil 2:8); **(5b)** Heb. 5:8, which refers to His delighted experience in constant "obedience" to the Father's will (not to be understood in the sense that He learned to obey). "Learned" means to experience firsthand and by experience make it one's own. See: TDNT—1:224, 34; BAGD—837a; THAYER—637d.

5219. **ὑπακούω** {21x} **hupakŏuō**, *hoop-ak-oo'-o;* from *5259* and *191;* to *hear under* (as a *subordinate*), i.e. to *listen attentively;* by impl. to *heed* or *conform* to a command or authority:—hearken {1x}, be obedient to {2x}, obey {18x}.

Hupakouo, "to listen, attend" (as in Acts 12:13), and so, "to submit, to obey," is used of "obedience" **(1)** to God, Heb 5:9; 11:8; **(2)** to Christ, by natural elements, Mt 8:27; Mk 1:27; 4:41; Lk 8:25; **(3)** to disciples of Christ, Lk 17:6; **(4)** to the faith, Acts 6:7; **(5)** to the gospel, Rom 10:16; 2 Th 1:8; **(6)** to Christian doctrine, Rom 6:17 (as to a form or mold of teaching); **(7)** to apostolic injunctions, Phil 2:12; 2 Th 3:14; **(8)** to Abraham by Sarah, 1 Pet 3:6; **(9)** to parents by children, Eph 6:1; Col 3:20; **(10)** to masters by servants, Eph 6:5; Col 3:22; **(11)** to sin, Rom 6:12; **(12)** in general, Rom 6:16. See: TDNT—1:223, 34; BAGD—837b; THAYER—638a.

5220. **ὕπανδρος** {1x} **hupandrŏs**, *hoop'-an-dros;* from *5259* and *435;* in subjection *under* a man, i.e. a *married* woman:—which hath an husband {1x}.

Hupandros, lit., "under (i.e. subject to) a man," married, and therefore, according to Roman law under the legal authority of the husband, occurs in Rom 7:2, "that hath a husband." See: BAGD—837c; THAYER—638a.

5221. **ὑπαντάω** {5x} **hupantaō**, *hoop-an-tah'-o;* from *5259* and a der. of *473;* to *go opposite* (*meet*) *under* (*quietly*), i.e. to *encounter, fall in with:*—go and meet {1x}, meet {4x}.

(1) *Hupantao* means to go to meet, to meet and may imply in military reference, a hostile meeting. **(2)** It is used in Mt 8:28; Lk 8:27; Jn 11:20, 30; 12:18. See: TDNT—3:625, 419; BAGD—837d; THAYER—638a.

5222. **ὑπάντησις** {1x} **hupantēsis**, *hoop-an'-tay-sis;* from *5221;* an *encounter* or *concurrence* (with *1519* for infin. in order to *fall in with*):—meeting + 1519 {1x}. See: TDNT—3:625, 419; BAGD—837d; THAYER—638b.

5223. **ὕπαρξις** {2x} **huparxis**, *hoop'-arx-is;* from *5225; existency* or *proprietorship,* i.e. (concr.) *property, wealth:*—goods {1x}, substance {1x}.

Huparix primarily, "subsistence," then, "substance, property, goods" (akin to *huparcho,* "to exist, be, belong to"), is translated **(1)** "goods" in Acts 2:45; **(2)** "substance" in Heb 10:34. See: BAGD—837d; THAYER—638b.

5224. **ὑπάρχοντα** {14x} **huparchŏnta**, *hoop-ar'-khon-tah;* neut. plur. of pres. part. act. of *5225* as noun; things *extant* or *in hand,* i.e. *property* or *possessions:*—goods {7x}, that (one) has {4x}, things which (one) possesses {2x}, substance {1x}. See: BAGD—838a; THAYER—638b.

5225. **ὑπάρχω** {48x} **huparchō**, *hoop-ar'-kho;* from *5259* and *756;* to *begin under* (*quietly*), i.e. *come into existence* (*be present* or *at hand*); expletively, to *exist* (as copula or subordinate to an adj., part., adv. or prep., or as auxil. to principal verb):—be {42x}, have {2x}, live {1x}, after {1x}, not tr {2x}.

Huparcho, as a verb, **(1)** means "to be in existence, to be" and is translated "live (delicately)": "But what went ye out for to see? A man clothed in soft raiment? Behold, they which are gorgeously apparelled, and live delicately (*huparcho*), are in kings' courts" (Lk 7:25). **(2)** *Huparacho* is highlighted in Phil 2:6, concerning the deity of Christ. The phrase "being (existing) in the form (*morphe* - 3444, the essential and specific form and character) of God," carries with it two facts: **(2a)** of the antecedent Godhood of Christ, previous to His incarnation, and **(2b)** the continuance of His Godhood at and after the event of His Birth. **(3)** It is translated "there be" in 1 Cor 11:18. Cf. Lk 16:14; 23:50; Acts 2:30; 3:2; 17:24; 22:3. Syn.: 326, 390, 980, 1236, 2198, 2225, 4176, 4800. See: BAGD—838a; THAYER—638b.

5226. **ὑπείκω** {1x} **hupĕikō**, *hoop-i'-ko;* from *5259* and εἴκω **ĕikō** (to *yield,* be "*weak*"); to *surrender:*—submit (one's) self {1x}.

Hupeiko, "to retire, withdraw" (*hupo,* under, *eiko,* "to yield"), hence, "to yield, submit, to pull one's self back in order to submit," is used metaphorically in Heb 13:17, of "submitting" to spiritual guides in the churches. See: BAGD—838b; THAYER—638c.

5227. **ὑπεναντίος** {2x} **hupĕnantiŏs**, *hoop-en-an-tee'-os;* from *5259* and *1727; under* (*covertly*) *contrary to,* i.e. *opposed* or (as noun) an *opponent:*—adversaries, contrary {1x}.

(1) The intensive force is due to the preposition *hupo.* **(2)** It is translated **(2a)** "contrary to," in Col 2:14, of ordinances; and **(2b)** in Heb 10:27, "adversaries." In each place a more violent form of opposition is suggested than in the case of *enantios* (1727). See: BAGD—838b; THAYER—638c.

5228. **ὑπέρ** {160x} **hupĕr**, *hoop-er';* a primary prep.; "*over*", i.e. (with the gen.) of place, *above, beyond, across,* or causal, *for* the sake of, *instead, regarding;* with the acc. *superior to,* more *than:*—for {104x}, of {12x}, above {12x}, for (one's) sake {8x}, on (one's) behalf {3x}, more than {3x}, in (one's) stead {2x}, than {2x}, very chiefest + 3029 {2x}, beyond {1x}, to {1x}, over {1x}, more {1x}, exceedingly abundantly + 1537 + 4053 {1x}, exceedingly + 1537 + 4053 {1x}, very highly + 1537 + 4053 {1x}, misc. {5x} = by, concerning, + very highly, to (-ward), very. [In composition, it retains many of the above applications.] See: BAGD—838b; THAYER—638d.

5229. **ὑπεραίρομαι** {3x} **hupĕrairŏmai**, *hoop-er-ah'-ee-rom-ahee;* mid. voice from *5228* and *142;* to *raise* oneself *over,* i.e. (fig.) to *become haughty:*—exalt (one's) self {1x}, be exalted above measure {2x}.

Huperairomai is used in the middle voice, of exalting oneself exceedingly (2 Cor 12:7; 2 Th 2:4). See: BAGD—839d; THAYER—640a.

5230. **ὑπέρακμος** {1x} **hupĕrakmŏs**, *hoop-er'-ak-mos;* from *5228* and the base of *188; beyond* the "*acme*", i.e. fig. (of a daughter) *past* the *bloom* (*prime*) of youth:—+ pass the flower of (her) age + 5610 {1x}.

Huperakmos as an adjective in 1 Cor 7:36 is rendered "past the flower of her age"; more lit., "beyond the bloom or flower (acme) of life." Syn.: 165, 166, 1074, 2244, 2250, 5046. See: BAGD—839d; THAYER—640b.

5231. **ὑπεράνω** {3x} **hupĕranō**, *hoop-er-an'-o;* from *5228* and *507; above upward,* i.e. *greatly higher* (in place or rank):—far above {2x}, over {1x}. Cf. Eph 1:21; 4:10; Heb 9:5. See: BAGD—840a; THAYER—640b.

5232. **ὑπεραυξάνω** {1x} **hupĕrauxanō**, *hoop-er-ŏwx-an'-o;* from *5228* and *837;* to *increase above* ordinary degree:—grow exceedingly {1x}.

Huperauxano, "to increase beyond measure", is used of faith and love, in their living and practical effects, 2 Th 1:3. Syn.: *Huperauxano* implies an internal, organic growth, as of a tree; whereas, *pleonazo* (4121) at the end of 2 Th 1:3, implies a diffusive or expansive character, as of a flood irrigating the land. See: TDNT—8:517, 1229; BAGD—840a; THAYER—640b.

5233. **ὑπερβαίνω** {1x} **hupĕrbainō**, *hoop-er-bah'-ee-no;* from *5228* and the base of *939;* to *transcend,* i.e. (fig.) to *overreach:*—go beyond {1x}.

Huperbaino is used metaphorically and rendered go beyond in 1 Th 4:6, i.e., of overstepping the limits separating chastity from licentiousness, sanctification from sin. See: TDNT—5:743, 772; BAGD—840a; THAYER—640b.

5234. **ὑπερβαλλόντως** {1x} **hupĕrballŏntōs**, *hoop-er-bal-lon'-toce;* adv. from pres. part. act. of *5235; excessively:*—above measure {1x}.

Huperballontos, as an adverb, means "beyond measure" and is rendered "above measure": "Are they ministers of Christ? (I speak as a fool) I *am* more; in labours more abundant, in stripes above measure, in prisons more frequent, in deaths oft" (2 Cor 11:23). Syn.: 280, 488, 943, 2884, 3313, 3354, 3358, 4057, 4568, 5249, 5518. See: TDNT—8:520, 1230; BAGD—840a; THAYER—640b.

5235. **ὑπερβάλλω** {5x} **hupĕrballō**, *hoop-er-bal'-lo;* from *5228* and *906;* to *throw beyond* the usual mark, i.e. (fig.) to *surpass* (only act. part. *supereminent*):—exceeding {3x}, excel {1x}, pass {1x}.

Huperballo, "to throw over or beyond" (*huper,* "over," *ballo,* "to throw"), is translated **(1)** "exceeding" in 2 Cor 9:14; Eph 1:19; Eph 2:19; **(2)** "excel" in 2 Cor 3:10; and **(3)** "pass" in Eph 3:19. See: TDNT—8:520, 1230; BAGD—840b; THAYER—640c.

5236. **ὑπερβολή** {7x} **hupĕrbŏlē**, *hoop-er-bol-ay';* from *5235;* a *throwing beyond* others, i.e. (fig.) *supereminence;* adv. (with *1519* or *2596*) *pre-eminently:*—exceeding + 2596 {1x}, more excellent +2596 {1x}, out of measure + 2596 {1x}, beyond measure + 2596 {1x}, excellency {1x}, abundance {1x}, exceeding + 1519 {1x}.

Huperbole, "a throwing beyond" (*huper,* "over," *ballo,* "to throw"), denotes "excellence, exceeding greatness," **(1)** "excellency"of the power of God in His servants, 2 Cor 4:7; **(2)** "abundance" of the revelations given to Paul, 2 Cor12:7; **(3)** with the preposition *kata,* the phrase signifies "exceeding," Rom 7:13; **(4)** "more excellent," 1 Cor 12:31; **(5)** "out of measure," 2 Cor 1:8; **(6)** "beyond measure," Gal 1:13; and, in a more extended phrase, **(7)** "far more exceedingly," 2 Cor 4:17. See: TDNT—8:520, 1230; BAGD—840b; THAYER—640c.

5237. **ὑπερείδω** {1x} **hupĕrĕidō**, *hoop-er-i'-do;* from *5228* and *1492;* to *overlook,* i.e. *not punish:*—wink at {1x}.

Hupereido, "to overlook" is used in Acts 17:30, "winked at", i.e., God bore with them without interposing by way of punishment, though the debasing tendencies of idolatry necessarily developed themselves, means to overlook momentarily. See: BAGD—840c; 841d; THAYER—640c.

5238. **ὑπερέκεινα** {1x} **hupĕrĕkĕina**, *hoop-er-ek'-i-nah;* from *5228* and the neut. plur. of *1565; above those* parts, i.e. *still farther:*—beyond {1x}.

Huperekeina means beyond: the regions lying beyond the country of one's residence, 2 Cor 10:16. See: BAGD—840c; THAYER—640c.

5239. **ὑπερεκτείνω** {1x} **hupĕrĕktĕinō**, *hoop-er-ek-ti'-no;* from *5228* and *1614;* to *extend inordinately:*—stretch beyond {1x} See: TDNT—2:465, 219; BAGD—840d; THAYER—640d.

5240. **ὑπερεκχύνω** {1x} **hupĕrĕkchunō**, *hoop-er-ek-khoo'-no;* from *5228* and the alt. form of *1632;* to *pour out over,* i.e. (pass.) to *overflow:*—run over {1x}. See: BAGD—840d; THAYER—640d.

ὑπερεκπερισσοῦ **hupĕrĕkpĕrissŏu**. See *5228* and *1537* and *4053*.

5241. **ὑπερεντυγχάνω** {1x} **hupĕrĕntugchanō**, *hoop-er-en-toong-khan'-o;* from *5228* and *1793;* to *intercede in behalf of:*—make intercession for {1x}. See: TDNT—8:238, 1191; BAGD—840d; THAYER—640d.

5242. **ὑπερέχω** {5x} **hupĕrĕchō**, *hoop-er-ekh'-o;* from *5228* and *2192;* to *hold* oneself *above,* i.e. (fig.) to *excel;* part. (as adj. or neut. as noun) *superior, superiority:*—better {1x}, excellency {1x}, higher {1x}, pass {1x}, supreme {1x}.

Huperecho lit. means "to hold or have above" (*huper,* "above," *echo,* "to hold"); hence, metaphorically, to be superior to, **(1)** to be better than, Phil 2:3; **(2)** 1 Pet 2:13, "supreme," in reference to kings; **(3)** in Rom 13:1, "higher"; **(4)** Phil 3:8, "excellency," more strictly "the surpassing thing, (namely, the knowledge of Christ)"; **(5)** in

Phil 4:7, passeth. See: TDNT—8:523, 1230; BAGD—840d; THAYER—640d.

5243. **ὑπερηφανία** {1x} **hupĕrēphania**, *hoop-er-ay-fan-ee'-ah;* from *5244; haughtiness:*—pride {1x}.

Huperephania describes the character of one who, with a swollen estimate of his own powers or merits, looks down on others and even treats them with insolence and contempt (Mk 7:22). See: TDNT—8:525, 1231; BAGD—841a; THAYER—640a.

5244. **ὑπερήφανος** {5x} **hupĕrēphanŏs**, *hoop-er-ay'-fan-os;* from *5228* and *5316; appearing above* others (*conspicuous*), i.e. (fig.) *haughty:*—proud {5x}.

(1) *Huperephanos* is one who compares himself (secretly or openly) with others and lifts himself above them. **(2)** His arrogance consists in claiming honor for himself. His comparing himself is not the sin, it is his sin that causes him to compare. **(3)** This word is always used in the evil sense of arrogant, disdainful, haughty (Rom 1:30; 2 Ti 3:2; Lk 1:51). **(4)** In Jas 4:6 and 1 Pet 5:5 it is in opposition to *tapeinos* (5012 - humble, lowly). Syn.: 213, 5197. See: TDNT—8:525, 1231; BAGD—841b; THAYER—641a.

ὑπερλίαν hupĕrlian. See *5228* and *3029*.

5245. **ὑπερνικάω** {1x} **hupĕrnikaō**, *hoop-er-nik-ah'-o;* from *5228* and *3528;* to *vanquish beyond,* i.e. *gain* a decisive *victory:*—more than conquer {1x}.

Hupernikao, "to be more than conqueror", "to gain a surpassing victory," is found in Rom 8:37, lit., "we are hyper-conquerors," i.e., we are pre-eminently victorious. See: TDNT—4:942, 634; BAGD—841c; THAYER—641b.

5246. **ὑπέρογκος** {2x} **hupĕrŏgkŏs**, *hoop-er'-ong-kos;* from *5228* and *3591; bulging over,* i.e. (fig.) *insolent:*—great swelling {2x}.

Huperogkos, an adjective denoting "of excessive weight or size," is used metaphorically in the sense of "immoderate," especially of arrogant speech, in the neuter plural, virtually as a noun, 2 Pet 2:18; Jude 16, "great swelling words." See: BAGD—841c; THAYER—641b.

5247. **ὑπεροχή** {2x} **hupĕrŏchē**, *hoop-er-okh-ay';* from *5242; prominence,* i.e. (fig.) *superiority* (in rank or character):—authority {1x}, excellency {1x}.

Huperoche, primarily, "a projection, eminence," as a mountain peak, hence, metaphorically, "pre-eminence, superiority, excellency," is once rendered **(1)** "authority," 1 Ti 2:2, of the position of magistrates; **(2)** in 1 Cor 2:1, "excellency" (of speech). Syn.: 201, 402, 1096, 1502, 3837, 4042, 5117, 5564, 5602. See: TDNT—8:523, 1230; BAGD—841d; THAYER—641b.

5248. **ὑπερπερισσεύω** {2x} **hupĕrpĕrissĕuō**, *hoop-er-per-is-syoo'-o;* from *5228* and *4052;* to *super-abound:*—abound much more {1x}, exceeding {1x}.

Huperperisseuo signifies **(1)** "to abound exceedingly," Rom. 5:20, of the operation of grace; **(2)** 2 Cor 7:4, in the middle voice, of the apostle's joy in the saints. See: TDNT—6:58, 828; BAGD—841d; THAYER—641b.

5249. **ὑπερπερισσῶς** {1x} **hupĕrpĕrissōs**, *hoop-er-per-is-soce';* from *5228* and *4057; superabundantly,* i.e. *exceedingly:*—beyond measure {1x}.

Huperperissos, as an adverb, and is translated "beyond measure": "And were beyond measure astonished, saying, He hath done all things well: he maketh both the deaf to hear, and the dumb to speak" (Mk 7:37). Syn.: 280, 488, 943, 2884, 3313, 3354, 3358, 4057, 4568, 5234, 5518. See: BAGD—842a; THAYER—641c.

5250. **ὑπερπλεονάζω** {1x} **hupĕrplĕŏnazō**, *hoop-er-pleh-on-ad'-zo;* from *5228* and *4121;* to *superabound:*—be exceeding abundant {1x}. See: TDNT—6:263, 864; BAGD—842a; THAYER—641c.

5251. **ὑπερυψόω** {1x} **hupĕrupsŏō**, *hoop-er-oop-so'-o;* from *5228* and *5312;* to *elevate above* others, i.e. *raise* to the *highest* position:—highly exalt {1x}. See: TDNT—8:606, 1241; BAGD—842a; THAYER—641c.

5252. **ὑπερφρονέω** {1x} **hupĕrphrŏnĕō**, *hoop-er-fron-eh'-o;* from *5228* and *5426;* to *esteem* oneself *overmuch,* i.e. *be vain* or *arrogant:*—think more highly {1x}. See: BAGD—842a; THAYER—641c.

5253. **ὑπερῷον** {4x} **hupĕrōiŏn**, *hoop-er-o'-on;* neut. of a der. of *5228;* a *higher* part of the house, i.e. apartment in the *third story:*—upper chamber {3x}, upper room {1x}. Cf. Acts 1:13; 9:37, 39; 20:8. See: BAGD—842b; THAYER—641a.

5254. **ὑπέχω** {1x} **hupĕchō**, *hoop-ekh'-o;* from *5259* and *2192;* to *hold* oneself *under,* i.e. *endure* with patience:—suffer {1x}. See: BAGD—842b; THAYER—641d.

5255. **ὑπήκοος** {3x} **hupēkŏŏs**, *hoop-ay'-kŏ-os;* from *5219; attentively listening,* i.e. (by impl.) *submissive:*—obedient {2x}, obey + 1096 {1x}.

Hupekoos, "obedient" "giving ear, subject," occurs **(1)** in Acts 7:39, "(would not) obey"; **(2)** 2 Cor 2:9, "obedient"; **(3)** Phil 2:8, where "obedience" was not to death but to the Father. See: TDNT—1:224, 34; BAGD—842b; THAYER—641d.

5256. **ὑπηρετέω** {3x} **hupērĕtĕō**, *hoop-ay-ret-eh'-o;* from *5257;* to *be a subordinate,* i.e. (by impl.) *subserve:*—minister {1x}, minister unto {1x}, serve {1x}.

Hupereteo, "to do the service of a *huperetes*", properly, "to serve as a rower on a ship," is used **(1)** of David, as serving the counsel of God in his own generation, Acts 13:36, "served"; expressive of the lowly character of his service for God; **(2)** of Paul's toil in working with his hands, and his readiness to avoid any pose of ecclesiastical superiority, Acts 20:34, "ministered unto"; **(3)** of the service permitted to Paul's friends to render to him, Acts 24:23, "minister." See: TDNT—8:530, 1231; BAGD—842c; THAYER—641d.

5257. **ὑπηρέτης** {20x} **hupērĕtēs**, *hoop-ay-ret'-ace;* from *5259* and a der. of ἐρέσσω **ĕrĕssō** (to *row*); an *under-oarsman,* i.e. (gen.) *subordinate* (*assistant, sexton, constable*):—minister {5x}, officer {11x}, servant {4x}.

Hupertes, properly "an under rower" (*hupo,* "under," *eretes,* "a rower"), as distinguished from *nautes,* "a seaman" (a meaning which lapsed from the word), hence came to denote "any subordinate acting under another's direction"; **(1)** in Lk 4:20, "minister" signifies the attendant at the synagogue service; **(2)** in Acts 13:5, it is said of Jn Mark, "minister;" **(3)** in Acts 26:16, "a minister," it is said of Paul as a servant of Christ in the gospel; so **(4)** in 1 Cor 4:1, where the apostle associates others with himself, as Apollos and Cephas, as "ministers of Christ." **(5)** It is translated "servants" in Mt 26:58; Mk 14:54, 65; Jn 18:36. Syn.: **(A)** *Diakonos* (1249) represents the servant in his activity for the work; not in his relation, either servile, as that of the **(B)** *douloo* (1402), or more voluntary, as in the case of **(C)** *therapon* (2324), to a person. A *douloo* is opposed to a *diakonos* and denotes a bondman, one who sustains a permanent servile relation to another. A *therapon* is the voluntary performer of services, whether as a freeman or a slave; it is a nobler tenderer word than *douloo.* **(D)** A *huperetes* (5257) suggests subordination. *Oiketes* (3610) is a household servant. See: TDNT—8:530, 1231; BAGD—842c; THAYER—641d.

5258. **ὕπνος** {6x} **hupnŏs**, *hoop'-nos;* from an obs. primary (perh. akin to *5259* through the idea of *subsilience*); *sleep,* i.e. (fig.) spiritual *torpor:*—sleep {6x}.

(1) *Hupnos* is never used of death. **(2)** In five places in the NT it is used of physical "sleep", Mt 1:24; Lk 9:32; Jn 11:13; Acts 20:9; and **(3)** in Rom 13:11, metaphorically, of a slumbering state of soul, i.e., of spiritual conformity to the world, out of which believers are warned to awake. See: TDNT—8:545, 1233; BAGD—843a; THAYER—642a.

5259. **ὑπό** {230x} **hupŏ**, *hoop-ŏ';* a primary prep.; *under,* i.e. (with the gen.) of place (*beneath*), or with verbs (the agency or means, *through*); (with the acc.) of place (whither [*underneath*] or where [*below*] or time (when [*at*]):—of {116x}, by {42x}, under {48x}, with {14x}, in {1x}, not tr {6x}, misc. {3x} = among, from. [In composition, it retains the same general applications, espec. of *inferior* position or condition, and spec. *covertly* or *moderately.*] See: BAGD—843a; THAYER—642a.

5260. **ὑποβάλλω** {1x} **hupŏballō**, *hoop-ob-al'-lo;* from *5259* and *906;* to *throw* in *stealthily,* i.e. *introduce* by collusion:—suborn {1x}.

Hupoballo primarily means to throw or put under, to subject, denoting to suggest, whisper, prompt; hence, to instigate, suborn (Acts 6:11). To suborn in the legal sense is to procure a person who will take a false oath. The idea of making suggestions is probably present in this use of the word. See: BAGD—843d; THAYER—642d.

5261. **ὑπογραμμός** {1x} **hupŏgrammŏs**, *hoop-og-ram-mos';* from a compound of *5259* and *1125;* an *underwriting,* i.e. *copy* for imitation (fig.):—example {1x}.

This word literally means an under-writing, to trace letters for copying by scholars; hence, a writing-copy, including all the letters of the alphabet, given to beginners as an aid in learning to draw them; an example. In 1 Pet 2:21 it is said of what Christ left for believers, by His sufferings (not expiatory, but exemplary), that they might "follow His steps." See: TDNT—1:772, 128; BAGD—843d; THAYER—642d.

5262. **ὑπόδειγμα** {6x} **hupŏdĕigma**, *hoop-od'-igue-mah;* from *5263;* an *exhibit* for imitation or warning (fig. *specimen, adumbration*):—ensample {1x}, example {4x}, pattern {1x}.

Hupodeigma, (from *hupo,* "under," *deiknumi,* "to show"), properly denotes "what is shown below or privately"; it is translated **(1)** "example," **(1a)** Heb 8:5; a sign suggestive of anything, the delineation or representation of a thing, and so, a figure, "copy"; **(1b)** an example **(1b1)** for imitation, Jn 13:15; Jas 5:10; **(1b2)** for warning, Heb 4:11; **(3)** in Heb 9:23, "patterns"; and **(4)** in 2 Pet 2:6, "ensample." An "example" is a sample taken from without the group; an "ensample" from within the group. See: TDNT—2:32, 141; BAGD—844a; THAYER—642d.

5263. **ὑποδείκνυμι** {6x} **hupŏdĕiknumi**, *hoop-od-ike'-noo-mee;* from *5259* and *1166;* to *exhibit under* the eyes, i.e. (fig.) to *exemplify* (*instruct, admonish*):—show {3x}, forewarn {1x}, warn {2x}.

Hupodeinumi primarily means **(1)** to show by placing under (i.e. before) the eyes; **(2)** to show by words and arguments, i.e. to teach/warn **(2a)** with the infinitive of the thing (Mt 3:7, Lk 3:7); **(2b)** by use of figure followed by indirect discourse (Lk 6:47; 12:5); **(2c)** to show or teach by one's example (Acts 20:35); and **(3)** to show by make known future things, Acts 9:16. See: BAGD—844b; THAYER—643a.

5264. **ὑποδέχομαι** {4x} **hupŏdĕchŏmai**, *hoop-od-ekh'-om-ahee;* from *5259* and *1209;* to *admit under* one's roof, i.e. *entertain* hospitably:—receive {4x}.

Hupodechomai, as a verb, denotes "to receive under one's roof, receive as a guest, entertain hospitably": "Now it came to pass, as they went, that he entered into a certain village: and a certain woman named Martha received (*hupodechomai*) Him into her house" (Lk 10:38; cf. 19:6; Acts 17:7; Jas 2:25). Syn.: 324, 353, 354, 568, 588, 618, 1209, 1523, 1926, 2210, 2865, 2975, 2983, 3028, 3335, 3336, 3858, 3880, 3970, 4327, 4355, 4356, 4380, 4381, 4382, 5562, 5274. See: BAGD—844b; THAYER—643a.

5265. **ὑποδέω** {3x} **hupŏdĕō**, *hoop-od-eh'-o;* from *5259* and *1210;* to *bind under* one's feet, i.e. *put on* shoes or sandals:—bind on {1x}, be shod with {1x}, shod {1x}.

Hupodeo, "to bind underneath," is used **(1)** of binding of sandals, Acts 12:8; rendered **(2)** "shod" in Mk 6:9 and Eph 6:15. See: TDNT—5:310, 702; BAGD—844b; THAYER—643a.

5266. **ὑπόδημα** {10x} **hupŏdēma**, *hoop-od'-ay-mah;* from *5265;* something *bound under* the feet, i.e. a *shoe* or *sandal:*—shoe {10x}. See: TDNT—5:310, 702; BAGD—844c; THAYER—643b.

5267. **ὑπόδικος** {1x} **hupŏdikŏs**, *hoop-od'-ee-kos;* from *5259* and *1349; under sentence,* i.e. (by impl.) *condemned:*—guilty {1x}.

Hupodikos, "brought to trial, answerable to" (*hupo,* "under," *dike,* "justice"), Rom 3:19, is translated "guilty", the decision of the court. See: TDNT—8:557, 1235; BAGD—844c; THAYER—643b.

5268. **ὑποζύγιον** {2x} **hupŏzugiŏn**, *hoop-od-zoog'-ee-on;* neut. of a compound of *5259* and *2218;* an animal *under* the *yoke* (*draught-beast*), i.e. (spec.) a *donkey:*—ass {2x}.

Hupozugion, lit., "under a yoke" (*hupo,* "under," *zugos,* "a yoke"), is used **(1)** as an alternative description of the same animal, in Mt 21:5, where both words are found together, "Behold, thy king cometh unto thee, meek and riding upon an ass (*onos*), and upon a colt the foal of an ass (*hupozugion*)." It was upon the colt that the Lord sat, John 12:14. **(2)** In 2 Pet 2:16, it is used of Balaam's "ass." See: BAGD—844d; THAYER—643b.

5269. **ὑποζώννυμι** {1x} **hupŏzōnnumi**, *hoop-od-zone'-noo-mee;* from *5259* and *2224;* to *gird under,* i.e. *frap* (a vessel with cables across the keel, sides and deck):—undergirding {1x}.

Hupozonnumi is used in Acts 27:17 of bracing the timbers of a vessel by means of strong ropes. See: BAGD—844d; THAYER—643b.

5270. **ὑποκάτω** {9x} **hupŏkatō**, *hoop-ok-at'-o;* from *5259* and *2736; down under,* i.e. *beneath:*—under {9x}.

Hupokato, an adverb signifying "under," is used as a preposition and rendered "under" in Mk 6:11; 7:28; Lk 8:16; Heb 2:8; Rev 5:3, 13; 6:9; 12:1; "underneath" in Mt 22:44; Jn 1:50, "under." See: BAGD—844d; THAYER—643c.

5271. **ὑποκρίνομαι** {1x} **hupŏkrinŏmai**, *hoop-ok-rin'-om-ahee;* mid. voice from *5259* and *2919;* to *decide* (*speak* or *act*) *under* a false part, i.e. (fig.) *dissemble* (*pretend*):—feign {1x}.

Hupokrinomai primarily denotes "to answer"; then, "to answer on the stage, play a part," and so, metaphorically, "to feign, pretend," Lk 20:20. See: TDNT—8:559, 1235; BAGD—845a; THAYER—643c.

5272. **ὑπόκρισις** {7x} **hupŏkrisis**, *hoop-ok'-ree-sis;* from *5271; acting under* a feigned part, i.e. (fig.) *deceit* ("*hypocrisy*"):—condemnation {1x}, dissimulation {1x}, hypocrisy {5x}.

(1) *Hupokrisis* is primarily, a reply and came to mean the acting of a stage player because such a one answered another in prepared dialogue; hence the meaning dissembling or pretence (Gal 2:13). It primarily denotes "a reply, an answer" (akin to *hupokrinomai,* "to answer"); then, "play-acting," as the actors spoke in dialogue; hence, "pretence, hypocrisy"; it is translated **(2)** "hypocrisy" in Mt 23:28; Mk 12:15; Lk 12:1; 1 Ti 4:2; the plural in 1 Pet 2:1; and **(3)** "condemnation" in Jas 5:12. See: TDNT—8:559, 1235; BAGD—845a; THAYER—643c.

5273. **ὑποκριτής** {20x} **hupŏkritēs**, *hoop-ok-ree-tace';* from *5271;* an *actor under* an assumed character (*stage-player*), i.e. (fig.) a *dissembler* ("*hypocrite*"):—hypocrite {20x}. See: TDNT—8:559, 1235; BAGD—845b; THAYER—643c.

5274. **ὑπολαμβάνω** {4x} **hupŏlambanō**, *hoop-ol-am-ban'-o;* from *5259* and *2983;* to *take* from *below,* i.e. *carry upward;* fig. to *take up,* i.e. *continue* a discourse or topic; ment. to *assume* (*presume*):—answer {1x}, receive {1x}, suppose {2x}.

This word means to take up in order to raise, to bear on high; **(1)** to take up and carry away: "And when He had spoken these things, while they beheld, He was taken up; and a cloud received Him out of their sight" (Acts 1:9); **(2)** to take up where another left off, follow in speech, in order either to reply to or controvert or supplement what another has said: "And Jesus answering (*hupolambano*) said, A certain *man* went down from Jerusalem to Jericho, and fell among thieves, which stripped him of his raiment, and wounded *him,* and departed, leaving *him* half dead" (Lk 10:30); **(4)** to take up in the mind, to assume, suppose: "Simon answered and said, I suppose that *he,* to whom he forgave most. And He said unto him, Thou hast rightly judged" (Lk 7:43; Acts 2:15). Syn.: 324, 353, 354, 568, 588, 618, 1209, 1523, 1926, 2210, 2865, 2975, 2983, 3028, 3335, 3336, 3858, 3880, 3970, 4327, 4355, 4356, 4380, 4381, 4382, 5562, 5264. See: TDNT—4:15, 495; BAGD—845b; THAYER—643d.

5275. **ὑπολείπω** {1x} **hupŏlĕipō**, *hoop-ol-i'-po;* from *5295* and *3007;* to *leave under* (*behind*), i.e. (pass.) to *remain* (*survive*):—be left {1x}.

Hupoleipo, "to leave remaining"; lit., "to leave under", is used in the passive voice in Rom 1:13, of a survivor. See: TDNT—4:194,*; BAGD—845c; THAYER—643d.

5276. **ὑπολήνιον** {1x} **hupŏlēniŏn**, *hoop-ol-ay'-nee-on;* neut. of a presumed compound of *5259* and *3025;* vessel or receptacle *under* the *press,* i.e. lower *winevat:*—winefat {1x}.

Hupolenion denotes "a vessel or trough beneath a winepress," to receive the juice, Mk 12:1, "a place for . . . the wine-fat." See: TDNT—4:254, 531; BAGD—845c; THAYER—643d.

5277. **ὑπολιμπάνω** {1x} **hupŏlimpanō**, *hoop-ol-im-pan'-o;* a prol. form for *5275;* to *leave behind,* i.e. *bequeath:*—leave {1x}. See: BAGD—845d; THAYER—644a.

5278. **ὑπομένω** {17x} **hupŏmĕnō**, *hoop-om-en'-o;* from *5259* and *3306;* to *stay under* (*behind*), i.e. *remain;* fig. to *undergo,* i.e. *bear* (trials), *have fortitude, persevere:*—endure {11x}, take patiently {2x}, tarry behind {1x}, abide {1x}, patient {1x}, suffer {1x}.

Hupomeno denotes "to abide under, to bear up courageously" **(1)** under suffering, Mt 10:22; 24:13; Mk 13:13; Rom 12:12, translated "patient"; 1 Cor 13:7; 2 Ti 2:10, 12, "suffer"; Heb 10:32; 12:2–3, 7; Jas 1:12; 5:11; 1 Pet 2:20, "ye shall take it patiently." It has its other significance, **(2)** "to tarry, wait for, await," in Lk 2:43; Acts 17:14. See: TDNT—4:581, 581; BAGD—845d; THAYER—644a.

5279. **ὑπομιμνήσκω** {7x} **hupŏmimnēskō**, *hoop-om-im-nace'-ko;* from *5259* and *3403;* to *remind quietly,* i.e. *suggest* to the (mid. voice, one's own) memory:—put in remembrance {3x}, remember {2x}, bring to remembrance {1x}, put in mind {1x}. See: BAGD—846a; THAYER—644b.

5280. **ὑπόμνησις** {3x} **hupŏmnēsis**, *hoop-om'-nay-sis;* from *5279;* a *reminding* or (refl.) *recollection:*—remembrance {2x}, put in remembrance {1x}.

Syn.: *Anamnesis* (364) denotes an unassisted recalling, *hupomnesis* (5280) a remembrance prompted by another. See: TDNT—1:348, 56; BAGD—846b; THAYER—644b.

5281. **ὑπομονή** {32x} **hupŏmŏnē**, *hoop-om-on-ay';* from *5278;* cheerful (or hopeful) *endurance, constancy:*—patience {29x}, enduring {1x}, patient continuance {1x}, patient waiting {1x}.

Hupomone, lit., "an abiding under" (*hupo,* "under," *meno,* "to abide"), is almost invariably rendered "patience." "Patience", which **(1)** grows only in trial, Jas 1:3 may be passive, i.e., = "endurance," as, **(1a)** in trials, generally, Lk 21:19 (which is to be understood by Mt 24:13), cf. Rom 12:12; Jas 1:12; **(1b)** in trials incident to service in the gospel, 2 Cor 6:4; 12:12; 2 Ti 3:10; **(1c)** under chastisement, which is trial viewed as coming from the hand of God our Father, Heb 12:7; **(1d)** under undeserved affliction, 1 Pet 2:20; or active, i.e. = "persistence, perseverance," as **(1e)** in well doing, Rom 2:7, "patient continuance"; **(1f)** in fruit bearing, Lk 8:15; **(1g)** in running the appointed race, Heb 12:1.

(2) Patience perfects Christian character, **(2a)** Jas 1:4, and **(2b)** fellowship in the patience of Christ is therefore the condition upon which believers are to be admitted to reign with Him, 2 Ti 2:12; Rev 1:9. **(2c)** For this patience believers are "strengthened with all power," Col 1:11, "through His Spirit in the inward man," Eph. 3:16. **(3)** In 2 Th 3:5, the phrase "the patience waiting for Christ." **(4)** In Rev 3:10, "the word of My patience" is the word which tells of Christ's patience, and its effects in producing "patience" on the part of those who are His (see above on 2 Th 3:5). Syn.: *Hupomone* (5281) is the temper which does not easily succumb under suffering, *makrothumia* (3115) is the self restraint which does not hastily retaliate a wrong. *Hupomone* is opposed to cowardice or despondency, *makrothumia* to wrath and revenge. See: TDNT—4:581, 581; BAGD—846b; THAYER—644c.

5282. **ὑπονοέω** {3x} **hupŏnŏĕō**, *hoop-on-ŏ-eh'-o;* from *5259* and *3539;* to *think under* (*privately*), i.e. to *surmise* or *conjec.:*—think {1x}, suppose {1x}, deem {1x}.

Huponoeo, "to suppose, conjecture, surmise," is translated **(1)** "deemed" in Acts 27:27; **(2)** in Acts 13:25, "think ye"; and **(3)** in Acts 25:18, "supposed." See: TDNT—4:1017, 636; BAGD—846d; THAYER—644c.

5283. **ὑπόνοια** {1x} **hupŏnŏia**, *hoop-on'-oy-ah;* from *5282; suspicion:*—surmising {1x}. See: TDNT—4:1017, 636; BAGD—846d; THAYER—644d.

5284. **ὑποπλέω** {2x} **hupŏplĕō**, *hoop-op-leh'-o;* from *5259* and *4126;* to *sail under* the lee of:—sail under {2x}. Cf 27:4, 7. See: BAGD—846d; THAYER—644d.

5285. **ὑποπνέω** {1x} **hupŏpnĕō**, *hoop-op-neh'-o;* from *5259* and *4154;* to *breathe gently,* i.e. *breeze:[a1[—blow softly {1x}. See: BAGD—846d; THAYER—644d.*

5286. **ὑποπόδιον** {9x} **hupŏpŏdiŏn**, *hoop-op-od'-ee-on;* neut. of a compound of *5259* and *4228;* something *under* the *feet,* i.e. a *foot-rest* (fig.):—footstool + 4228 {8x}, footstool {1x}.

Huupopodion, (from *hupo,* "under," and *pous,* "a foot"), is used **(1)** literally in Jas 2:3, **(2)** metaphorically, **(2a)** of the earth as God's "footstool," Mt 5:35; **(2b)** of the foes of the Lord, Mt. 22:44; Mk 12:36, Lk 20:43; Acts 2:35; 7:49; Heb 1:13; 10:13. See: BAGD—846d; THAYER—644d.

5287. **ὑπόστασις** {5x} **hupŏstasis**, *hoop-os'-tas-is;* from a compound of *5259* and *2476;* a *setting under* (*support*), i.e. (fig.) concr. *essence,* or abstr. *assurance* (obj. or subj.):—confidence {2x}, confident {1x}, person {1x}, substance {1x}.

Hupostasis, lit., "a standing under" (*hupo,* "under," *stasis,* "a standing"), "that which stands, or is set, under, a foundation, beginning"; hence, **(1)** the quality of confidence which leads one to stand under, endure, or undertake anything, 2 Cor 9:4; 11:17; Heb 3:14. **(2)** In Heb it signifies "substance" in Heb 11:1; and **(3)** "Person" in Heb 1:3. This Person is the Lord Jesus, the substance, the essence, of God Himself, the One in whom all confidence resides. See: TDNT—8:572, 1237; BAGD—847a; THAYER—644d.

5288. **ὑποστέλλω** {4x} **hupŏstĕllō**, *hoop-os-tel'-lo;* from *5259* and *4724;* to *withhold under* (*out of sight*), i.e. (refl.) to *cower* or *shrink,* (fig.) to *conceal* (*reserve*):—draw back {1x}, keep back {1x}, shun {1x}, withdraw {1x}.

Hupostello, as a verb, means "to draw back, withdraw," [the prefix *hupo,* "underneath," suggestive of stealth]. **(1)** It is perhaps a metaphor from lowering a sail and so slackening the course, and hence of being remiss in holding the truth; **(2)** in the active voice, rendered "withdrew/draw back": "For before that certain came from James, he did eat with the Gentiles: but when they were come, he [Peter] withdrew and separated himself, fearing them which were of the circumcision" (Gal 2:12); **(3)** in the middle voice, "draw back": "Now the just shall live by faith: but if *any man* draw back, My soul shall have no pleasure in him" (Heb 10:38). Syn.: 307, 385, 392, 501, 502, 645, 868, 1448, 1670, 1828, 2020, 4264, 4317, 4334, 4358, 4685, 4951, 5289. See: TDNT—7:597, 1074; BAGD—847b; THAYER—645a.

5289. **ὑποστολή** {1x} **hupŏstŏlē**, *hoop-os-tol-ay';* from *5288; shrinkage* (*timidity*), i.e. (by impl.) *apostasy:*—of them that draw back {1x}.

Hupostole, as a noun, is translated "of them who draw back": "But we are not of them who draw back unto perdition; but of them that believe to the saving of the soul" (Heb 10:39). Syn.: 307, 385, 392, 501, 502, 645, 868, 1448, 1670, 1828, 2020, 4264, 4317, 4334, 4358, 4685, 4951, 5288. See: TDNT—7:599, 1074; BAGD—847c; THAYER—645b.

5290. **ὑποστρέφω** {35x} **hupŏstrĕphō**, *hoop-os-tref'-o;* from *5259* and *4762;* to *turn under* (*behind*), i.e. to *return* (lit. or fig.):—return {28x}, return again {3x}, turn back {1x}, turn again {1x}, return back again {1x}, come again {1x}.

Hupostrepho, as a verb, means "to turn behind or back" and is translated "to return": "And when He returned, He found them asleep again, (for their eyes were heavy,) neither wist they what to answer Him" (Mk 14:40; Lk 1:56; 2:20, 43; v. 45 "turned back again", 4:1, 14; 7:10; 8:37; 10:17; 11:24 "I will turn back"; 17:18; 19:12; 23:48, 56; Acts 1:12; 12:25; 13:13; 13:34; 20:3; 21:6; 22:17, "was come again"; 23:32; Gal 1:17; Heb 7:1). Syn.: 344, 360, 390, 1880, 1877, 1994. See: BAGD—847c; THAYER—645b.

5291. **ὑποστρώννυμι** {1x} **hupŏstrōnnumi**, *hoop-os-trone'-noo-mee;* from *5259* and *4766;* to *strew underneath* (the feet as a carpet):—spread {1x}. See: BAGD—847d; THAYER—645c.

5292. **ὑποταγή** {4x} **hupŏtagē**, *hoop-ot-ag-ay';* from *5293; subordination:*—subjection {4x}.

Hupotage, "subjection," occurs in 2 Cor 9:13; Gal 2:5; 1 Ti 2:11; 3:4. See: TDNT—8:46, 1156; BAGD—847d; THAYER—645c.

5293. **ὑποτάσσω** {40x} **hupŏtassō**, *hoop-ot-as'-so;* from *5259* and *5021;* to *subordinate;* refl. to *obey:*—put under {6x}, be subject unto {6x}, be subject to {5x}, submit (one's) self unto {5x}, submit (one's) self to {3x}, be in subjection unto {2x}, put in subjection under {1x}, misc. {12x} = be under obedience (obedient), subdue unto.

(1) This was originally a Greek military term meaning to arrange [troop divisions] in a military fashion under the command of a leader. **(2)** In non-military use, it was a voluntary attitude of giving in, cooperating, assuming responsibility, and carrying a burden. **(3)** It denotes **(3a)** "to put in subjection, to subject, to put under" in Rom 8:20 (twice); 1 Cor 15:27 (thrice), 28 (3rd clause); Eph 1:22; Heb 2:8 (4th clause); **(3b)** in 1 Cor 15:28 (1st clause), "be subdued"; **(3c)** in Phil 3:21, "subdue"; **(3d)** in Heb 2:5, "hath . . . put in subjection"; **(4)** in the middle or passive voice, to subject oneself, to obey, be subject to, **(4a)** Lk 2:51; 10:17, 20; **(4b)** Rom 8:7; 10:3, "have (not) submitted themselves"; 13:1, 5; **(4c)** 1 Cor 14:34, "be under obedience"; 15:28 (2nd clause); 16:16, "submit, etc."; so Col 3:18; **(4d)** Eph 5:21, "submitting, etc."; 5:22, 24, "is subject"; **(4e)** Titus 2:5, 9,"be obedient"; 3:1, "to be subject"; **(4f)** Heb 12:9, "be in subjection"; Jas 4:7, "submit yourselves"; so **(4g)** 1 Pet 2:13, 18; so 3:1, 5, 22, "being made subject"; 5:5, "submit yourselves"; also in the 2nd part. See: TDNT—8:39, 1156; BAGD—847d; THAYER—645c.

5294. **ὑποτίθημι** {2x} **hupŏtithēmi**, *hoop-ot-ith'-ay-mee;* from *5259* and *5087;* to *place underneath,* i.e. (fig.) to *hazard,* (refl.) to *suggest:*—lay down {1x}, put in remembrance {1x}.

Hupotithemi, "to place under, lay down", is used metaphorically **(1)** in Rom 16:4, of risking one's life, "laid down" (their own necks). **(2)** In the middle voice in 1 Ti 4:6 it is used of "putting" persons in mind, "in remembrance." See: BAGD—848b; THAYER—645d.

5295. **ὑποτρέχω** {1x} **hupŏtrĕchō**, *hoop-ot-rekh'-o;* from *5259* and *5143* (incl. its alt.); to *run under,* i.e. (spec.) to *sail past:*—run under {1x}. See: BAGD—848b; THAYER—645d.

5296. **ὑποτύπωσις** {2x} **hupŏtupōsis**, *hoop-ot-oop'-o-sis;* from a compound of *5259* and a der. of *5179; typification under* (*after*), i.e. (concr.) a *sketch* (fig.) for imitation:—form {1x}, pattern {1x}.

Hupotuposis, "an outline, sketch," akin to *hupotupoo,* "to delineate," is used metaphorically to denote **(1)** a "pattern," in 1 Ti 1:16; and **(2)** 2 Ti 1:13, "form." See: TDNT—8:246, 1193; BAGD—848c; THAYER—645d.

5297. **ὑποφέρω** {3x} **hupŏphĕrō**, *hoop-of-er'-o;* from *5259* and *5342;* to *bear* from *underneath,* i.e. (fig.) to *undergo* hardship:—bear {1x}, endure {2x}.

Hupophero, lit., "to bear up under," is rendered by **(1)** "bear," as 1 Cor 10:13; and **(2)** of "enduring" **(2a)** persecutions, 2 Ti 3; **(2b)** grief, 1 Pet 2:19. See: BAGD—848c; THAYER—645d.

5298. **ὑποχωρέω** {2x} **hupŏchōrĕō**, *hoop-okh-o-reh'-o;* from *5259* and *5562;* to *vacate down,* i.e. *retire* i.e. *retire* quietly suggesting privacy:—go aside {1x}, withdraw self + 2258 {1x}.

Hupochoreo, "to go back, retire" (*hupo,* "under," suggesting privacy), **(1)** "withdraw" in Lk 5:16; and **(2)** "went aside" in Lk 9:10. See: BAGD—848c; THAYER—646a.

5299. **ὑπωπιάζω** {2x} **hupōpiazō**, *hoop-o-pee-ad'-zo;* from a compound of *5259* and a der. of *3700;* to hit *under* the *eye* (*buffet* or *disable* an antagonist as a pugilist), i.e. (fig.) to *tease* or *annoy* (into compliance), *subdue* (one's passions):—keep under {1x}, weary {1x}.

Hupopiazo, lit., "to strike under the eye" (from *hupopion,* "the part of the face below the eye"; *hupo,* "under," *ops,* "an eye"), hence, to beat the face black and blue (to give a black eye), is used metaphorically, and translated **(1)** "keep under" in 1 Cor 9:27, of Paul's suppressive treatment of his body, in order to keep himself spiritually fit; and **(2)** in Lk 18:5, of the persistent widow, "weary." See: TDNT—8:590, 1239; BAGD—848d; THAYER—646a.

5300. **ὗς** {1x} **hus**, *hoos;* appar. a primary word; a *hog* ("*swine*"):—sow {1x}. See: BAGD—848d; THAYER—646a.

5301. **ὕσσωπος** {2x} **hussōpŏs**, *hoos'-so-pos;* of for. or. [231]; *"hyssop"*:—hyssop {2x}. See: BAGD—848d; THAYER—646a.

5302. **ὑστερέω** {16x} **hustĕrĕō**, *hoos-ter-eh'-o;* from *5306;* to *be later,* i.e. (by impl.) to *be inferior;* gen. to *fall short* (*be deficient*):—lack {3x}, be behind {2x}, want {2x}, come short {1x}, be in want {1x}, fail {1x}, come behind {1x}, be destitute {1x}, misc. {4x} = suffer need, be the worse. See: TDNT—8:592, 1240; BAGD—849a; THAYER—646b.

5303. **ὑστέρημα** {9x} **hustĕrēma**, *hoos-ter'-ay-mah;* from *5302;* a *deficit;* spec. *poverty:*—which is lacking {3x}, want {3x}, which is behind {1x}, lack {1x}, penury {1x}.

Husterema denotes **(1)** "that which is lacking, deficiency, shortcoming" (akin to *hustereo,* "to be behind, in want"), 1 Cor 16:17; Phil 2:30; Col 1:24, "that which is behind" (of the afflictions of Christ)], where the reference is not to the vicarious sufferings of Christ but to those which He endured previously, and those which must be endured by His faithful servants; **(2)** 1 Th 3:10, where "that which is lacking" means that which Paul had not been able to impart to them, owing to the interruption of his spiritual instruction among them; **(3)** "need, want, poverty," Lk 21:4, "penury"; 2 Cor 8:14 (twice) "want;" 2 Cor 9:12, "want"; 11:9, "that which was lacking (to me)." See: TDNT—8:592, 1240; BAGD—849b; THAYER—646c.

5304. **ὑστέρησις** {2x} **hustĕrēsis**, *hoos-ter'-ay-sis* from *5302;* a *falling short,* i.e. (spec.) *penury:*—want {2x}. Cf. Mk 12:14 and Phil 4:11. See: TDNT—8:592, 1240; BAGD—849c; THAYER—646c.

5305. **ὕστερον** {12x} **hustĕrŏn**, *hoos'-ter-on;* neut. of *5306* as adv.; *more lately,* i.e. *eventually:*—afterward {8x}, last {2x}, at the last {1x}, last of all {1x}.

Husterion, "afterwards," with the suggestion of at length, is found in Mt 4:2; 21:29, 32, 37, "last of all"); 22:27; 25:11; 26:60, "at the last", Mk 16:14; Lk 4:2; 20:32, "last", Jn 13:36; Heb 12:11. See: TDNT—8:592, 1240; BAGD—849c; THAYER—646c.

5306. **ὕστερος** {1x} **hustĕrŏs**, *hoos'-ter-os;* comparative from *5259* (in the sense of *behind*); *later:*—latter {1x}. See: TDNT—8:592, 1240; BAGD—849c; THAYER—646c.

5307. **ὑφαντός** {1x} **huphantŏs**, *hoo-fan-tos';* from ὑφαίνω **huphainō**, to *weave; woven,* i.e. (perh.) *knitted:*—woven {1x}. See: BAGD—849d; THAYER—646d.

5308. **ὑψηλός** {11x} **hupsēlŏs**, *hoop-say-los';* from *5311; lofty* (in place or character):—high {8x}, higher {1x}, highly esteemed {1x}, high things {1x}.

Hupselos, "high, lofty," is used **(1)** naturally, **(1a)** of mountains, Mt 4:8; 17:1; Mk 9:2; Rev 21:10; **(1b)** of a wall, Rev 21:12; **(2)** figuratively, **(2a)** of the arm of God, Acts 13:17; **(2b)** of heaven, "on high," plural, lit., "in high (places)," Heb 1:3; **(3)** metaphorically, **(3a)** Lk 16:15, "highly esteemed"; **(3b)** Rom 12:16, "high things." See: BAGD—849d; THAYER—646d.

5309. **ὑψηλοφρονέω** {2x} **hupsēlŏphrŏnĕō**, *hoop-say-lo-fron-eh'-o;* from a compound of *5308* and *5424;* to *be lofty in mind,* i.e. *arrogant:*—be highminded {2x}. See: BAGD—850a; THAYER—646d.

5310. **ὕψιστος** {13x} **hupsistŏs**, *hoop'-sis-tos;* superl. from the base of *5311; highest,* i.e. (masc. sing.) the *Supreme* (God), or (neut. plur.) the *heavens:*—most high {5x}, highest {8x}.

Hupistos is used in the plural in the phrase **(1)** "in the highest," i.e., in the "highest" regions, the abode of God, Mt 21:9; Mk 11:10; Lk omits the article, Lk 2:14; 19:38; **(2)** for its use as a title of God, **(2a)** "most high," is a superlative degree, the positive not being in use; **(2b)** it is used of God in Lk 1:32, 35, 76; 6:35, "the highest", see also Mk 5:7; Lk 8:28; Acts 7:48; 16:17; Heb 7:1. See: TDNT—8:614, 1241; BAGD—850b; THAYER—647a.

5311. **ὕψος** {6x} **hupsŏs**, *hoop'-sos;* from a der. of *5228; elevation,* i.e. (abstr.) *altitude,* (spec.) the *sky,* or (fig.) *dignity:*—on high {2x}, height {2x}, high {1x}, be exalted {1x}.

Hupsos, signifying "height," is rendered **(1)** in Jas 1:9, "in that he is exalted"; **(2)** "on high," Lk 1:78; 24:49; Eph 4:8; **(3)** "height" in Eph 3:18; Rev 21:16. See: TDNT—8:602, 1241; BAGD—850c; THAYER—647a.

5312. **ὑψόω** {20x} **hupsŏō**, *hoop-sŏ'-o;* from *5311;* to *elevate* (lit. or fig.):—exalt {14x}, lift up {6x}.

Hupsoo, "to lift up" (akin to *hupsos,* "height"), is used **(1)** literally **(1a)** of the "lifting" up of Christ in His crucifixion, Jn 3:14; 8:28; 12:32, 34; **(1b)** illustratively, of the serpent of brass, Jn 3:14; **(2)** figuratively, "to exalt" **(2a)** of spiritual privileges bestowed on a city, Mt 11:23; Lk 10:15; **(2b)** of "raising" to dignity and happiness, Lk 1:52; Acts 13:17; **(2c)** of haughty self-exaltation, and, contrastingly, of being "raised" to honor, as a result of self-humbling, Mt 23.12, Lk 14:11; 18:14; **(2d)** of spiritual "uplifting" and revival, Jas 4:10; 1 Pet 5:6; **(2e)** of bringing into the blessings of salvation through the gospel, 2 Cor 11:7; **(3)** with a combination of the literal and metaphorical, of the "exaltation" of Christ by God the Father, Acts 2:33; 5:31. See: TDNT—8:606, 1241; BAGD—850d; THAYER—647a.

5313. **ὕψωμα** {2x} **hupsōma**, *hoop'-so-mah;* from *5312;* an *elevated* place or thing, i.e. (abstr.) *altitude,* or (by impl.) a *barrier* (fig.):—height {1x}, high thing {1x}.

Hupsoma is used **(1)** of "a height," as a mountain or anything definitely termed a "height," Rom 8:39 (metaphorically); **(2)** of "a high thing" lifted up as a barrier or in antagonistic exaltation, 2 Cor 10:5. See: TDNT—8:613, 1241; BAGD—851c; THAYER—647c.

Φ

5314. **φάγος** {2x} **phagŏs**, *fag'-os;* from *5315;* a *glutton:*—gluttonous {2x}. Cf. Mt 11:19; Lk 7:34. See: BAGD—851a; THAYER—647b.

5315. **φάγω** {97x} **phagō**, *fag'-o;* a primary verb (used as an alt. of *2068* in certain tenses); to *eat* (lit. or fig.):—eat {94x}, meat {3x}. See: BAGD—851a; 312b; THAYER—647b.

φαιλόνης **phailŏnēs**, *fahee-lohn'-ace;* an alt. spelling of *5341* which see; found only in 2 Tim. 4:13.

5316. **φαίνω** {31x} **phainō**, *fah'-ee-no;* prol. for the base of *5457;* to *lighten* (*shine*), i.e. *show* (tran. or intr., lit. or fig.):—appear {17x}, seem {1x}, be seen {2x}, shine {10x}, × think {1x}.

(1) *Phaino* refers to the actual external appearance, generally correct, but possibly deceptive. **(2)** It signifies, in the active voice, "to shine"; in the passive, "to be brought forth into light, to become evident, to appear." **(3)** In Rom 7:13, concerning sin, "appear." **(4)** It is used of the "appearance" of Christ to the disciples, Mk 16:9; **(5)** of His future "appearing" in glory as the Son of Man, spoken of as a sign to the world, Mt 24:30; there the genitive is subjective, the sign being the "appearing" of Christ Himself; **(6)** of Christ as the light, Jn 1:5; **(7)** of John the Baptist, Jn 5:35; **(8)** of the "appearing" of an angel of the Lord, either **(8a)** visibly, Mt 1:20, or **(8b)** in a dream, Mt 2:13; **(9)** of a star, Mt 2:7; **(10)** of men who make an outward show, Matt. 6:5; 6:18; 23:27–28; 2 Cor 13:7; **(11)** of tares, Mt 13:26; **(12)** of a vapor, Jas 4:14; **(13)** of things physical in general, Heb 11:3; **(14)** used impersonally **(14a)** in Mt 9:33, "it was never so seen"; **(14b)** also of what appears to the mind, and so in the sense of to think, Mk 14:64, or **(14c)** to seem, Lk 24:11. Syn.: **(A)** *Hegeomai* (2233) and **(B)** *nomizo* (3543) denote a belief resting not on one's inner feeling or sentiment, but on the due consideration of external grounds, and the weighing and comparing of facts. **(C)** *Dokeo* (1380) and **(D)** *oiomai* (3633) on the other hand, describe a subjective judgment growing out of inclination or a view of facts in their relation to us. *Hegeomai* (2233) denotes a more deliberate and careful judgment than *nomizo* (3543); *oiomai* (3633) is a subjective judgment which has feeling rather than thought (*dokeo*—1380) for its ground. See: TDNT—9:1, 1244, BAGD—851b; THAYER—647d.

5317. **Φάλεκ** {1x} **Phalĕk**, *fal'-ek;* of Heb. or. [6389]; *Phalek* (i.e. *Peleg*), a patriarch:—Phalec {1x}. See: BAGD—852b; THAYER—648b.

5318. **φανερός** {21x} **phanĕrŏs**, *fan-er-os';* from *5316; shining,* i.e. *apparent* (lit. or fig.); neut. (as adv.) *publicly, extern.:*—manifest {9x}, openly + 1722 + 3588 {3x}, known {3x}, abroad + 1519 {2x}, spread abroad {1x}, outwardly + 1722 + 3588 {1x}, outward {1x}, appear {1x}.

Phaneros, "open to sight, visible, manifest" (the root *phan,* signifying "shining"), is translated **(1)** "manifest" in Lk 8:17 first part; Acts 4:16; Rom 1:19; 1 Cor. 3:13; 11:19; 14:25; Gal 5:19; Phil 1:13; 1 Jn 3:10; **(2)** "known" in Mt 12:26; Mk 3:12; Acts 7:13; **(3)** "appear" in 1 Ti 4:15; **(4)** "openly" in Mt 6:4, 6, 18; **(5)** "abroad" in Mk 4:22; Lk 8:17 second part; **(6)** "spread abroad" in Mk 6:14; **(7)** "outwardly" in Rom 2:28 first part; and **(8)** "outward" in Rom 2:28 second part. See: TDNT—9:2, 1244; BAGD—852b; THAYER—648b.

5319. **φανερόω** {49x} **phanĕrŏō**, *fan-er-ŏ'-o;* from *5318;* to *render apparent* (lit. or fig.):—make manifest {19x}, appear {12x}, manifest {9x}, show {3x}, be manifest {2x}, show (one's) self {2x}, manifestly declare {1x}, manifest forth {1x}.

(1) *Phaneroo* means manifest, as opp. to what is concealed and invisible. **(2)** It signifies, in the active voice, "to manifest"; in the passive voice, "to be manifested." **(3)** It is translated "to appear" in 2 Cor 7:12; Col 3:4; Heb 9:26; 1 Pet 5:4; 1 Jn 2:28; 3:2; Rev 3:18. **(4)** To be manifested, in the Scriptural sense of the word, is more than to "appear." **(4a)** A person may "appear" in a false guise or without a disclosure of what he truly is; **(4b)** to be manifested is to be revealed in one's true character; **(4c)** this is especially the meaning of *phaneroo,* see, e.g., Jn 3:21; 1 Cor 4:5; 2 Cor 5:10–11; Eph 5:13. Syn.: **(A)** *Phaneroo* (5319) is thought to describe an external manifestation, to the senses hence open to all, single or isolated. **(B)** *Apokalupto* (601) is an internal disclosure, to the thinking believer, and abiding. The *apolalupto* (601) or unveiling precedes and produces the *phaneroo* (5319) or manifestation; the former looks toward the object revealed, the latter toward the persons to whom the revelation is made. **(C)** *Delos* (1212) means what is evident, what is known and understood and points rather to inner perception; whereas *phaneroo* (5319) points to outward appearance. See: TDNT—9:3, 1244; BAGD—852d; THAYER—648b.

5320. **φανερῶς** {3x} **phanĕrōs**, *fan-er-oce';* adv. from *5318; plainly,* i.e. *clearly* or *publicly:*—evidently {1x}, openly {2x}.

Phaneros, manifestly, is rendered **(1)** "openly" in Mk 1:45; Jn 7:10; and "evidently" in Acts 10:3. See: BAGD—853a; THAYER—649a.

5321. **φανέρωσις** {2x} **phanĕrōsis**, *fan-er'-o-sis;* from *5319; exhibition,* i.e. (fig.) *expression,* (by extens.) a *bestowment:*—manifestation {2x}. Cf. 1 Cor 12:7 and 2 Cor 4:2. See: TDNT—9:6, 1244; BAGD—853b; THAYER—649a.

5322. **φανός** {1x} **phanŏs**, *fan-os';* from *5316;* a *lightener,* i.e. *light; lantern:*—lantern {1x}. See: BAGD—853b; THAYER—649a.

5323. **Φανουήλ** {1x} **Phanŏuēl**, *fan-oo-ale';* of Heb. or. [6439]; *Phanuël* (i.e. *Penuël*), an Isr.:—Phanuel {1x}. See: BAGD—853b; THAYER—649a.

5324. **φαντάζω** {1x} **phantazō**, *fan-tad'-zo;* from a der. of *5316;* to *make apparent* i.e. (pass.) to *appear* (neut. part. as noun, a *spectacle*):—a sight {1x}.

Phantazo, as a verb, means "to make visible" and is used in the present participle as a noun, with the article, translated "(the) sight": "And so terrible was the sight, *that* Moses said, I exceedingly fear and quake" (Heb 12:21). See: TDNT—9:6, 1244; BAGD—853b; THAYER—649a.

5325. **φαντασία** {1x} **phantasia**, *fan-tas-ee'-ah;* from a der. of *5324;* (prop. abstr.) a (vain) *show* ("fantasy"):—pomp {1x}.

Phantasia, as a philosophic term, denoted an imagination; then, an appearance, an apparition; later, a show, display, pomp (Acts 25:23). See: BAGD—853b; THAYER—649a.

5326. **φάντασμα** {2x} **phantasma**, *fan'-tas-mah;* from *5324;* (prop. concr.) a (mere) *show* ("phantasm"), i.e. *spectre:*—spirit {2x}. Cf. Mt 14:26 and Mk 6:49. See: TDNT—9:6, 1244; BAGD—853c; THAYER—649b.

5327. **φάραγξ** {1x} **pharagx**, *far'-anx;* prop. streng. from the base of *4008* or rather of *4486;* a *gap* or *chasm,* i.e. *ravine* (*winter-torrent*):—valley {1x}. See: BAGD—853c; THAYER—649b.

5328. **Φαραώ** {5x} **Pharaō**, *far-ah-o';* of for. or. [6547]; *Pharaö* (i.e. *Pharoh*), an Eg. king:—Pharaoh {5x}. See: BAGD—853c; THAYER—649b.

5329. **Φαρές** {3x} **Pharĕs**, *far-es';* of Heb. or. [6557]; *Phares* (i.e. *Perets*), an Isr.:—*Phares* {3x}. See: BAGD—853c; THAYER—649b.

5330. **Φαρισαῖος** {100x} **Pharisaiŏs**, *far-is-ah'-yos;* of Heb. or. [comp. 6567]; a *separatist,* i.e. exclusively *relig.;* a *Pharisæan,* i.e. Jewish sectary:—Pharisee {100x}.

Pharisaios comes from an Aramaic word *peras* (found in Dan 5:28) and signifies to separate, owing to a different manner of life from that of the general public. The Pharisees and Sadducees appear as distinct parties in the latter half of the 2nd cent. B.C., though they represent tendencies traceable much earlier in Jewish history, tendencies which became pronounced after the return from Babylon (537 B.C.). The immediate progenitors of the two parties were, respectively, the Hasidaeans and the Hellenizers; the latter, the antecedents of the Sadducees, aimed at removing Judaism from its narrowness and sharing in the advantages of Greek life and culture. The Hasidaeans, a transcription of the Hebrew *chasidim,* i.e., "pious ones," were a society of men zealous for religion, who acted under the guidance of the scribes, in opposition to the godless Hellenizing party; they scrupled to oppose the legitimate high priest even when he was on the Greek side.

Thus the Hellenizers were a political sect, while the Hasidaeans, whose fundamental principle was complete separation from non-Jewish elements, were the strictly legal party among the Jews, and were ultimately the more popular and influential party. In their zeal for the Law they almost deified it and their attitude became merely external, formal, and mechanical. They laid stress, not upon the righteousness of an action, but upon its formal correctness. Consequently their opposition to Christ was inevitable; His manner of life and teaching was essentially a condemnation of theirs; hence His denunciation of them, e.g., Matt. 6:2, 5, 16; 15:7 and chapter 23. See: TDNT—9:11, 1246; BAGD—853b; THAYER—649b.

5331. **φαρμακεία** {3x} **pharmakĕia**, *far-mak-i'-ah;* from *5332; medication* ("pharmacy"), i.e. (by extens.) *magic* (lit. or fig.):—sorcery {2x}, witchcraft {1x}.

Primarily *pharmakeia* signified the use of medicine, drugs, spells; then, poisoning; then, witchcraft (Gal 5:20; Rev 9:21; 18:23). In sorcery the use of drugs, whether simple or potent, was generally accompanied by incantations and appeals to occult powers, with the provision of various charms, amulets, etc., professedly designed to keep the applicant or patient from the attention and power of devils, but actually to impress the applicant with the mysterious resources and powers of the sorcerer. See: BAGD—854a; THAYER—649d.

5332. **φαρμακεύς** {1x} **pharmakĕus**, *far-mak-yoos';* from φάρμακον **pharmakŏn**, (a *drug,* i.e. spell-giving *potion*); a *druggist* ("pharmacist") or *poisoner,* i.e. (by extens.) a *magician:*—sorcerer {1x}. See: BAGD—854a; THAYER—649d.

5333. **φαρμακός** {1x} **pharmakŏs**, *far-mak-os';* the same as *5332:*—sorcerer {1x}. See: BAGD—854b; THAYER—650a.

5334. **φάσις** {1x} **phasis**, *fas'-is;* from *5346* (not the same as "phase", which is from *5316*); a *saying,* i.e. *report:*—tidings {1x}.

Phasis denotes "information," especially against fraud or other delinquency, and is rendered "tidings" in Acts 21:31. See: BAGD—854b; THAYER—650a.

5335. **φάσκω** {4x} **phaskō**, *fas'-ko;* prol. from the same as *5346;* to *assert:*—affirm {1x}, profess {1x}, say {2x}.

Phasko denotes "to allege, to affirm by way of alleging or professing," and is translated **(1)** "saying" in Acts 24:9; Rev 2:2, "say"; **(2)** "affirm" in Acts 25:19; and **(3)** "professing" in Rom 1:22. See: BAGD—854b; THAYER—650a.

5336. **φάτνη** {4x} **phatnē**, *fat'-nay;* from πατέομαι **patĕŏmai** (to *eat*); a *crib* (for fodder):—manger {3x}, stall {1x}.

Phatne is **(1)** "a manger," Lk 2:7, 12, 16; and also denotes **(2)** "a stall," Lk 13:15. See: TDNT—9:49, 1251; BAGD—854b; THAYER—650a.

5337. **φαῦλος** {4x} **phaulŏs**, *fŏw'-los;* appar. a primary word; *"foul"* or *"flawy"*, i.e. (fig.) *wicked:*—evil {4x}.

(1) This word means slight, ordinary, mean, worthless, of no account and ethically, bad, base, wicked. **(2)** It primarily denotes "slight, trivial, blown about by every wind"; then, "mean, common, bad," in the sense of being worthless, paltry or contemptible, belonging to a low order of things; **(3)** in Jn 5:29, those who have practiced "evil" things, (*phaula*), are set in contrast to those who have done good things (*agatha*); **(4)** he who practices "evil" things hates the light, Jn 3:20; **(5)** jealousy and strife are accompanied by "every evil work," Jas 3:16. **(6)** It is also in Titus 2:8 of an evil report. See: BAGD—854c; THAYER—650a.

5338. **φέγγος** {3x} **phĕggŏs**, *feng'-gos;* prob. akin to the base of *5457* [comp. *5350*]; *brilliancy:*—light {3x}.

Pheggos, "brightness, luster," is used of **(1)** the "light" of the moon, Mt 24:29; Mk 13:24; **(2)** of a lamp, Lk 11:33. Syn.: **(A)** *Phos* (5457) is the general term for light: light of a fire. **(B)** *Pheggos* (5338) is a more concrete and emphatic term: the bright sunshine, the beam of light. **(C)** *Auge* (827) is a still stronger term, suggesting the fiery nature of light; used of shooting, heating rays. See: BAGD—854c; THAYER—650b.

5339. **φείδομαι** {10x} **phĕidŏmai**, *fi'-dom-ahee;* of uncert. aff.; to *be chary* of, i.e. (subj.) to *abstain* or (obj.) to *treat leniently:*—forbear {1x}, spare {9x}.

Pheidomai, as a verb, means "to spare" (its usual meaning), "to refrain from doing something," is rendered **(1)** "I forbear" in 2 Cor 12:6; and **(2)** "to spare," i.e., "to forego" the infliction of that evil or retribution which was designed, is **(2a)** used with a negative, in Acts 20:29, Rom 8:32; 11:21 (twice); 2 Cor 13:2; 2 Pet 2:4, 5; **(2b)** positively, in 1 Cor 7:28; 2 Cor 1:3. See: BAGD—854d; THAYER—650b.

5340. **φειδομένως** {2x} **phĕidŏmĕnōs**, *fi-dom-en'-oce;* adv. from part. of *5339; abstemiously,* i.e. *stingily:*—sparingly {2x}.

This word occurs in 2 Cor. 9:6 twice. See: BAGD—854d; THAYER—650b.

5341. **φελόνης** {1x} **phĕlŏnēs**, *fel-on'-ace* or

φαιλόνης **phailnŏnēs**, *fayl-on'-ace;* by transp. for a der. prob. of *5316* (as *showing* outside the other garments); a *mantle* (*surtout*):—cloke {1x}.

This garment is a traveling *cloke,* used for protection against stormy weather, 2 Ti 4:13. See: BAGD—854d; 851b; THAYER—650c.

5342. **φέρω** {64x} **phĕrō**, *fer'-o;* a primary verb (for which other and appar. not cognate ones are used in certain tenses only; namely,

οἴω **ŏiō**, *oy'-o;* and

ἐνέγκω **ĕnĕgkō**, *en-eng'-ko;* to "*bear*" or *carry* (in a very wide application, lit. and fig. as follows):—bring {34x}, bear {8x}, bring forth {5x}, come {3x}, reach {2x}, endure {2x}, carry {1x}, be {1x}, + let her drive {1x}, be driven {1x}, go on {1x}, lay {1x}, lead {1x}, move {1x}, rushing {1x}, uphold {1x}.

Phero, as a verb, means **(1)** "to bear, carry," and is rendered "being moved" in 2 Pet 1:21, signifying that they were "borne along," or impelled, by the Holy Spirit's power, not acting according to their own wills, or simply expressing their own thoughts, but expressing the mind of God in words provided and ministered by Him. **(2)** It is used also of "bearing or bringing forth fruit": "And other fell on good ground, and did yield fruit that sprang up and increased; and brought forth, some thirty, and some sixty, and some an hundred" (Mk 4:8; cf. Jn 15:5). Syn.: 277, 383, 761, 2795, 2796, 3334, 4525, 4531, 4579, 4787. See: TDNT—9:56, 1252; BAGD—854d; THAYER—650c.

5343. **φεύγω** {31x} **phĕugō**, *fyoo'-go;* appar. a primary verb; to *run away* (lit. or fig.); by impl. to *shun;* by anal. to *vanish:*—escape {3x}, flee {26x}, flee away {2x}.

Pheugo, "to flee from or away" (Eng., "fugitive"), besides its literal significance, is used metaphorically, **(1)** transitively, **(1a)** of "fleeing" fornication, 1 Cor 6:18; **(1b)** idolatry, 1 Cor 10:14; **(1c)** evil doctrine, questionings, disputes of words, envy, strife, railings, evil surmisings, wranglings, and the love of money, 1 Ti 6:11; **(1d)** youthful lusts, 2 Ti 2:22; **(2)** intransitively, of the "flight" **(2a)** of physical matter, Rev 16:20; 20:11; **(2b)** of death, Rev 9:6. **(3)** It is also rendered "escape" in Mt 23:33; Heb 11:34; 12:25. See: BAGD—855d; THAYER—651a.

5344. **Φῆλιξ** {9x} **Phēlix**, *fay'-lix;* of Lat. or.; *happy; Phelix* (i.e. *Felix*), a Rom.:—Felix {9x}. See: BAGD—856a; THAYER—651b.

5345. **φήμη** {2x} **phēmē**, *fay'-may;* from *5346;* a *saying,* i.e. *rumor* ("fame"):—fame {2x}.

Pheme, originally denoted "a divine voice, an oracle"; hence, "a saying or report" (akin to *phemi,* "to say," from a root meaning "to shine, to be clear"; hence, Lat., *fama,* Eng., "fame"), is rendered "fame" in Mt 9:26 and Lk 4:14. See: BAGD—856b; THAYER—651c.

5346. **φημί** {58x} **phēmi**, *fay-mee';* prop. the same as the base of *5457* and *5316;* to *show* or *make known* one's thoughts, i.e. *speak* or *say:*—affirm {1x}, say {57x}. See: BAGD—856b; THAYER—651c. comp. *3004.*

5347. **Φῆστος** {13x} **Phēstŏs**, *face'-tos;* of Lat. der.; *festal; Phestus* (i.e. *Festus*), a Rom.:—Festus {13x}. See: BAGD—856c; THAYER—651d.

5348. **φθάνω** {7x} **phthanō**, *fthan'-o;* appar. a primary verb; to *be beforehand,* i.e. *anticipate* or *precede;* by extens. to *have arrived* at:—already attain {1x}, attain {1x}, come {4x}, prevent {1x}.

Phthano denotes "to anticipate, to come sooner than expected," and is translated **(1)** "come": **(1a)** "is come upon" 1 Th 2:16, of divine wrath; **(1b)** or the kingdom is to "come" in a different manner from what was expected, Mt 12:28; Lk 11:20; **(1c)** "are come" in 2 Cor 10:14; **(2)** "already attain" in Phil 3:16; **(3)** "attain" in Rom 9:31; and **(4)** "prevent" in 1 Th 415. See: TDNT—9:88, 1258; BAGD—856d; THAYER—652a.

5349. **φθαρτός** {6x} **phthartŏs**, *fthar-tos';* from *5351; decayed,* i.e. (by impl.) *perishable:*—corruptible {6x}.

Phthartos, "corruptible", is used **(1)** of man as being mortal, liable to decay (in contrast to God), Rom 1:23; **(2)** of man's body as death-doomed, 1 Cor 15:53–54; **(3)** of a crown of reward at the Greek games, 1 Cor 9:25; **(4)** of silver and gold, as specimens or "corruptible" things, 1 Pet 1:18; **(5)** of natural seed, 1 Pet 1:23. See: TDNT—9:93, 1259; BAGD—857a; THAYER—652b.

5350. **φθέγγομαι** {3x} **phthĕggŏmai**, *ftheng'-gom-ahee;* prob. akin to *5338* and thus to *5346;* to *utter* a clear sound, i.e. (gen.) to *proclaim:*—speak {3x}.

Phtheggomai, "to utter a clear, authoritative sound or voice with an intention of swaying the hearer," is translated "to speak" in Acts 4:18; 2 Pet 2:16, 18. See: BAGD—857a; THAYER—652b.

5351. **φθείρω** {8x} **phthĕirō**, *fthi'-ro;* probably strengthened from φθίω **phthiō** (to *pine* or *waste*); prop. to *shrivel,* or *wither,* i.e. to *spoil* (by any process) or (gen.) to *ruin* (espec. fig., by mor. influences, to *deprave*):—corrupt {4x}, corrupt (one's) self {1x}, be corrupt {1x}, defile {1x}, destroy {1x}.

Phtheiro signifies **(1)** "to destroy by means of corrupting," and so "bringing into a worse state"; **(1a)** with this significance it is used of the effect of evil company upon the manners of believers, and so of the effect of association with those who deny the truth and hold false doctrine, 1 Cor 15:33; **(1b)** in 2 Cor 7:2, of the effects of dishonorable dealing by bringing people to want (a charge made against the apostle); **(1c)** in 2 Cor 11:3, of the effects upon the minds (or thoughts) of believers by "corrupting" them "from the simplicity and the purity that is toward Christ"; **(1d)** in Eph 4:22, intransitively, of the old nature in waxing "corrupt," morally decaying, on the way to final ruin", "after the lusts of deceit"; **(1e)** in Rev 19:2, metaphorically, of the Babylonish harlot, in "corrupting" the inhabitants of the earth by her false religion. **(2)** With the significance of destroying, it is used **(2a)** of marring a local church **(2a1)** by leading it away from that condition of holiness of life and purity of doctrine in which it should abide, 1 Cor 3:17, "defile", and **(2a2)** of God's retributive destruction of the offender who is guilty of this sin (id.); **(2b)** of the effects of the work of false and abominable teachers upon themselves, Jude 10, "corrupt themselves." See: TDNT—9:93, 1259; BAGD—857b; THAYER—652b.

5352. **φθινοπωρινός** {1x} **phthinŏpōrinŏs**, *fthin-op-o-ree-nos';* from der. of φθίνω **phthinō** (to *wane;* akin to the base of *5351*) and *3703* (mean. *late autumn*); *autumnal* (as *stripped* of leaves):—whose fruit withereth {1x}.

Phthinoporinos, "autumnal," in Jude 12, "autumn trees," bearing no "fruit" when "fruit" should be expected: "These are spots in your feasts of charity, when they feast with you, feeding themselves without fear: clouds *they are* without water, carried about of winds; trees whose fruit withereth, without fruit, twice dead, plucked up by the roots." Syn.: 175, 2590, 2592, 2593, 3703. See: BAGD—857c; THAYER—652c.

5353. **φθόγγος** {2x} **phthŏggŏs**, *fthong'-gos;* from *5350; utterance,* i.e. a *musical* note (vocal or instrumental):—sound {2x}.

Phthoggos, "to utter a voice," occurs in Rom 10:18; 1 Cor 14:7. See: BAGD—857c; THAYER—652d.

5354. **φθονέω** {1x} **phthŏnĕō**, *fthon-eh'-o;* from *5355;* to *be jealous* of:—envy {1x}. See: BAGD—857c; THAYER—652d.

5355. **φθόνος** {9x} **phthŏnŏs**, *fthon'-os;* prob. akin to the base of *5351; ill-will* (as *detraction*), i.e. *jealousy* (*spite*):—envy {8x}, envying {1x}.

Envy is the feeling of displeasure produced by witnessing or hearing of the advantage or prosperity of others; an evil sense always attaches to this word (Mt. 27:18; Mk 15:10; Rom 1:29; Gal 5:21; Phil 1:15; 1 Ti 6:4; Titus 3:3; 1 Pet. 2:1). See: BAGD—857d; THAYER—652d.

5356. **φθορά** {9x} **phthŏra**, *fthor-ah';* from *5351; decay,* i.e. *ruin* (spontaneous or inflicted, lit. or fig.):—corruption {7x}, destroy {1x}, perish + 1519 {1x}.

Phthora, connected with *phtheiro,* signifies "a bringing or being brought into an inferior or worse condition, a destruction or corruption." It is used **(1)** physically, **(1a)** of the condition of creation, as under bondage, Rom 8:21; **(1b)** of the effect of the withdrawal of life, and so of the condition of the human body in burial, 1 Cor 15:42; **(1c)** by metonymy, of anything which is liable to "corruption," 1 Cor 15:50; **(1d)** of the physical effects of merely gratifying the natural desires and ministering to one's own needs or lusts, Gal 6:8, to the flesh in contrast to the Spirit, "corruption" being antithetic to "eternal life"; **(1e)** of that which is naturally short-lived and transient, Col 2:22, "perish"; **(2)** of the death and decay of beasts, 2 Pet 2:12, "destroyed" (first part of verse; lit., "unto . . . destruction"); **(3)** ethically, with a moral significance, **(3a)** of the effect of lusts, 2 Pet 1:4; **(3b)** of the effect upon themselves of the work of false and immoral teachers, 2 Pet 2:12, "corruption," and verse 19. See: TDNT—9:93, 1259; BAGD—858a; THAYER—652d.

5357. **φιάλη** {12x} **phialē**, *fee-al'-ay;* of uncert. aff.; a broad shallow *cup* ("phial").—vial {12x}.

Phiale denotes **(1)** "a vial" in Rev 5:8; 15:7; 16:1–4, 8, 10, 12, 17; 17:1; 21:9; **(2)** the word is suggestive of rapidity in the emptying of the contents. **(3)** While the seals (ch. 6) give a general view of the events of the last "week" or "*hebdomad,*" in the vision given to Daniel, Dan 9:23–27, **(3a)** the "trumpets" refer to the judgments which, in a more or less extended period, are destined to fall especially, though not only, upon apostate Christendom and apostate Jews. **(3b)** The emptying of the "vials" betokens the final series of judgments in which this exercise of the wrath of God is "filled up" (Rev 15:1). **(3c)** These are introduced by the 7th trumpet. **(3d)** See Rev. 11:15 and the successive order in v. 18, "the nations were wroth, and Thy wrath came . . ."; see also 6:17; 14:19, 20; 19:11–12. See: BAGD—858b; THAYER—653a.

5358. **φιλάγαθος** {1x} **philagathŏs**, *fil-ag'-ath-os;* from *5384* and *18; fond to good,* i.e. a *promoter of virtue:*—lover of good men {1x}. See: TDNT—1:18, 3; BAGD—858b; THAYER—653a.

5359. **Φιλαδέλφεια** {2x} **Philadĕlphĕia**, *fil-ad-el'-fee-ah;* from Φιλάδελφος **Philadĕlphŏs** (the same as *5361*), a king of Pergamos; *Philadelphia,* a place in Asia Minor:—Philadelphia {2x}. See: TDNT—1:144,*; BAGD—858b; THAYER—653a.

5360. **φιλαδελφία** {6x} **philadĕlphia**, *fil-ad-el-fee'-ah;* from *5361; fraternal affection:*—brotherly love {3x}, brotherly kindness {2x}, love of the brethren {1x}.

Philadelphia, is translated **(1)** "brotherly love" in Rom 12:10; 1 Th 4:9; Heb 13:1; **(2)** "love of the brethren," 1 Pet 1:22; and **(3)** "brother kindness" in 2 Pet 1:7 twice. See: TDNT—1:144, 22; BAGD—858c; THAYER—653b.

5361. **φιλάδελφος** {1x} **philadělphŏs**, *fil-ad'-el-fos;* from *5384* and *80; fond of brethren,* i.e. *fraternal:*—love as brethren {1x}. See: TDNT—1:144, 22; BAGD—858c; THAYER—653b.

5362. **φίλανδρος** {1x} **philandrŏs**, *fil'-an-dros;* from *5384* and *435; fond of man,* i.e. *affectionate* as a wife:—love their husbands {1x}. See: BAGD—858c; THAYER—653b.

5363. **φιλανθρωπία** {2x} **philanthrōpia**, *fil-an-thro-pee'-ah;* from the same as *5364; fondness of mankind,* i.e. *benevolence* ("*philanthropy*"):—kindness {1x}, love toward man {1x}.

Philanthropia, (from *philos* "loving," *anthropos,* "man", Eng., "philanthropy"), denotes **(1)** "kindness," and is so translated in Acts 28:2, of that which was shown by the inhabitants of Melita to the shipwrecked voyagers; **(2)** in Titus 3:4, of the "kindness" of God, translated "(His) love toward man." See: TDNT—9:107, 1261; BAGD—858d; THAYER—653b.

5364. **φιλανθρώπως** {1x} **philanthrōpōs**, *fil-an-thro'-poce;* adv. from a compound of *5384* and *444; fondly to man* ("philanthropically"), i.e. *humanely:*—courteously {1x}. See: TDNT—9:107, 1261; BAGD—858d; THAYER—653b.

5365. **φιλαργυρία** {1x} **philarguria**, *fil-ar-goo-ree'-ah;* from *5366; avarice:*—love of money {1x}.

Syn.: The main distinction between *pleonexia* (4124) and *philarguria* (5365) is being that between "covetousness" and avarice, the former having a much wider and deeper sense, being "the genus of which *philarguria* is the species." The "covetous" man is often cruel as well as grasping, while the avaricious man is simply miserly and stinting. See: BAGD—859a; THAYER—653b.

5366. **φιλάργυρος** {2x} **philargurŏs**, *fil-ar'-goo-ros;* from *5384* and *696; fond of silver* (*money*), i.e. *avaricious:*—covetous {2x}.

Philarguros, lit., "money-loving," is rendered "covetous" in Lk 16:14 and 2 Ti 3:2. See: BAGD—859a; THAYER—653b.

5367. **φίλαυτος** {1x} **philautŏs**, *fil'-ŏw-tos;* from *5384* and *846; fond of self,* i.e. *selfish:*—lover of (one's) own self {1x}. See: BAGD—859a; THAYER—653b.

5368. **φιλέω** {25x} **philĕō**, *fil-eh'-o;* from *5384; to be a friend to* (*fond of* [an indiv. or an obj.]), i.e. *have affection* for (denoting *personal* attachment, as a matter of sentiment or feeling; while *25* is wider, embracing espec. the judgment and the *deliberate* assent of the will as a matter of principle, duty and propriety: the two thus stand related very much as *2309* and *1014,* or as *2372* and *3563* respectively; the former being chiefly of the *heart* and the latter of the *head;* spec. to *kiss* (as a mark of tenderness):—kiss {2x}, love {23x}.

(1) *Phileo* is never used in a command to men to "love" God; **(1a)** it is, however, used as a warning in 1 Cor 16:22; **(1b)** *agapao* is used instead, e.g., Mt 22:37; Lk 10:27; Rom 8:28; 1 Cor 8:3; 1 Pet 1:8; 1 Jn 4:21. **(1c)** The distinction between the two verbs finds a conspicuous instance in the narrative of Jn 21:15–17. **(1d)** The context itself indicates that *agapao* in the first two questions suggests the "love" that values and esteems (cf. Rev 12:11). It is an unselfish "love," ready to serve. **(1e)** The use of *phileo* in Peter's answers and the Lord's third question, conveys the thought of cherishing the Object above all else, of manifesting an affection characterized by constancy, from the motive of the highest veneration. **(2)** Again, to "love" (*phileo*) life, from an undue desire to preserve it, forgetful of the real object of living, meets with the Lord's reproof, Jn 12:25.

(3) On the contrary, to "love" life (*agapao*) as used in 1 Pet 3:10, is to consult the true interests of living. Here the word *phileo* would be quite inappropriate, is to be distinguished from *agapao* in this, that *phileo* more nearly represents "tender affection." **(4)** The two words are used for the "love" of the Father **(4a)** for the Son, Jn 3:35, and **(4b)** Jn 5:20, for the believer; **(4c)** Jn 14:21 and 16:27, both, of Christ's "love" for a certain disciple, 13:23, and 20:2. **(5)** Yet the distinction between the two verbs remains, and they are never used indiscriminately in the same passage; if each is used with reference to the same objects, as just mentioned, each word retains its distinctive and essential character. Syn.: See 25 for discussion. See: TDNT—9:114, 1262; BAGD—859b; THAYER—653c.

5369. **φιλήδονος** {1x} **philēdŏnŏs**, *fil-ay'-don-os;* from *5384* and *2237; fond of pleasure,* i.e. *voluptuous:*—lover of pleasure {1x}. See: TDNT—2:909, 303; BAGD—859c; THAYER—654a.

5370. **φίλημα** {7x} **philēma**, *fil'-ay-mah;* from *5368;* a *kiss:*—kiss {7x}.

(1) *Philema,* "a kiss", Lk 7:45; 22:48, **(1a)** was a token of Christian brotherhood, whether by way of welcome or farewell, **(1a1)** "a holy kiss," Rom 16:16; 1 Cor 16:20; 2 Cor 13:12; 1 Th 5:26, "holy" (*hagios*), as free from anything inconsistent with their calling as saints (*hagioi*); **(1b)** "a kiss of charity," 1 Pet 5:14. There was to be an absence of formality and hypocrisy, a freedom from prejudice arising from social distinctions, from discrimination against the poor, from partiality towards the well-to-do. **(1c)** In the churches masters and servants would thus salute one another without any attitude of condescension on the one part or disrespect on the other. **(1d)** The "kiss" took place thus between persons of the same sex. See: TDNT—9:114, 1262; BAGD—859c; THAYER—654a.

5371. **Φιλήμων** {2x} **Philēmōn**, *fil-ay'-mone;* from *5368; friendly; Philemon,* a Chr.:—*Philemon* {2x}. See: BAGD—859d; THAYER—654a.

5372. **Φιλητός** {1x} **Philētŏs**, *fil-ay-tos';* from *5368; amiable; Philetus,* an opposer of Christianity:—Philetus {1x}. See: BAGD—859d; THAYER—654a.

5373. **φιλία** {1x} **philia**, *fil-ee'-ah;* from *5384; fondness:*—friendship {1x}.

Philia, akin to *philos,* "a friend", is rendered in Jas 4:4, "the friendship (of the world)." It involves "the idea of loving as well as being loved." See: TDNT—9:146, 1262; BAGD—859d; THAYER—654a.

5374. **Φιλιππήσιος** {2x} **Philippēsiŏs**, *fil-ip-pay'-see-os;* from *5375;* a *Philippesian* (*Philippian*), i.e. native of Philippi:—Philippian {2x}. See: BAGD—859d; THAYER—654b.

5375. **Φίλιπποι** {6x} **Philippŏi**, *fil'-ip-poy;* plur. of *5376; Philippi,* a place in Macedonia:—Philippi {6x}. See: BAGD—860a; THAYER—654b.

5376. **Φίλιππος** {38x} **Philippŏs**, *fil'-ip-pos;* from *5384* and *2462; fond of horses; Philippus,* the name of four Isr.:—Philip (the apostle) {16x}, Philip (the evangelist) {16x}, Philip (Herod) {3x}, Philippi (an adjunct of Caesarea) {2x}, Philip (the tetrarch) {1x}. See: BAGD—860a; THAYER—654b.

5377. **φιλόθεος** {1x} **philŏthĕŏs**, *fil-oth'-eh-os;* from *5384* and *2316; fond of God,* i.e. *pious:*—lover of God {1x}. See: BAGD—860c; THAYER—654c.

5378. **Φιλόλογος** {1x} **Philŏlŏgŏs**, *fil-ol'-og-os;* from *5384* and *3056; fond of words,* i.e. *talkative* (*argumentative, learned, "philological"*); *Philologus,* a Chr.:—Philologus {1x}. See: BAGD—860c; THAYER—654c.

5379. **φιλονεικία** {1x} **philŏnĕikia**, *fil-on-i-kee'-ah;* lit. to love strife, from *5380; quarrelsomeness,* i.e. a *dispute:*—strife {1x}.

Philoneikia, lit., "love of strife" (*phileo,* "to love," *neikos,* "strife"), signifies "eagerness to contend"; hence, a "contention," said of the disciples, Lk 22:24. See: BAGD—860c; THAYER—654c.

5380. **φιλόνεικος** {1x} **philŏnĕikŏs**, *fil-on'-i-kos;* from *5384* and νεῖκος **nĕikŏs** (a *quarrel;* prob. akin to *3534*); *fond of strife,* i.e. *disputatious:*—contentious {1x}. See: BAGD—860d; THAYER—654d.

5381. **φιλονεξία** {2x} **philŏnĕxia**, *fil-on-ex-ee'-ah;* from *5382; hospitableness:*—entertain strangers {1x}, hospitality {1x}.

Philonexia, "love of strangers" (*philos,* "loving," *xenos,* "a stranger"), is used in Rom 12:13; Heb 13:2, lit. "be not forgetful of hospitality. See: TDNT—5:1,*; BAGD—860d; THAYER—654d.

5382. **φιλόξενος** {3x} **philŏxĕnŏs**, *fil-ox'-en-os;* from *5384* and *3581; fond of guests,* i.e. *hospitable:*—given to hospitality {1x}, lover of hospitality {1x}, use hospitality {1x}.

Plioxenos, "hospitable," occurs in **(1)** 1 Ti 3:2, "given to hospitality"; **(2)** Titus 1:8, "lover of hospitality"; and **(3)** 1 Pet 4:9, "use hospitality." See: TDNT—5:1, 661; BAGD—860d; THAYER—654d.

5383. **φιλοπρωτεύω** {1x} **philŏprōtĕuō**, *fil-op-rote-yoo'-o;* from a compound of *5384* and *4413; to be fond of being first,* i.e. *ambitious* of distinction:—love to have the preeminence {1x}. See: BAGD—860d; THAYER—654d.

5384. **φίλος** {29x} **philŏs**, *fee'-los;* prop. *dear,* i.e. a *friend;* act. *fond,* i.e. *friendly* (still as a noun, an *associate, neighbor,* etc.):—friend {29x}.

Philos, primarily an adjective, denoting "loved, dear, or friendly," became used as a noun, **(1)** masculine, **(1a)** Mt 11:19; **(1b)** fourteen times in Lk (once feminine, 15:9); **(1c)** six in John; **(1d)** three in Acts; **(1e)** two in James, **(1e1)** 2:23, "the friend of God"; **(1e2)** 4:4, "a friend of the world"; **(1f)** 3 Jn 14 (twice); **(2)** feminine, Lk 15:9, "her friends." See: TDNT—9:146, 1262; BAGD—861a; THAYER—654d.

5385. **φιλοσοφία** {1x} **philŏsŏphia**, *fil-os-of-ee'-ah;* from *5386; "philosophy",* i.e. (spec.) Jewish *sophistry:*—philosophy {1x}.

Used once in the NT of the theology, or rather theosophy, of certain Jewish Christian ascetics, which busied itself with refined and speculative enquiries into the nature and classes of angels, into the ritual of the Mosaic law and the regulations of Jewish tradition respecting practical life (Col 2:8). See: TDNT—9:172, 1269; BAGD—861b; THAYER—655a.

5386. **φιλόσοφος** {1x} **philŏsŏphŏs**, *fil-os'-of-os;* from *5384* and *4680; fond of wise* things, i.e. a *"philosopher"*:—philosopher {1x}.

This word denotes a philosopher, one given to the pursuit of wisdom or learning and in a narrower sense, one who investigates and discusses the cause of things and the highest good (Acts 17:18). See: TDNT—9:172, 1269; BAGD—861b; THAYER—655a.

5387. **φιλόστοργος** {1x} **philŏstŏrgŏs**, *fil-os'-tor-gos;* from *5384* and στοργή **stŏrgē** (*cherishing* one's kindred, espec. parents or children); *fond of* natural *relatives,* i.e. *fraternal* toward fellow Chr.:—kindly affectioned {1x}. See: BAGD—861c; THAYER—655b.

5388. **φιλότεκνος** {1x} **philŏtĕknŏs**, *fil-ot'-ek-nos;* from *5384* and *5043; fond of* one's *children,* i.e. *maternal:*—love their children {1x}. See: BAGD—861c; THAYER—655b.

5389. **φιλοτιμέομαι** {3x} **philŏtimĕŏmai**, *fil-ot-im-eh'-om-ahee;* mid. voice from a compound of *5384* and *5092;* to be *fond of honor,* i.e. *emulous* (*eager* or *earnest* to do something):—labour {1x}, strive {1x}, study {1x}.

Literally, this word means to be fond of honor, and so, actuated by this motive, to strive to bring something to pass; hence, to be ambitious, to make it one's aim: **(1)** Rom 15:20, of Paul's striving in gospel pioneering; **(2)** 2 Cor 5:9, of the labor of believers to be well-pleasing unto the Lord; and **(3)** in 1 Th 4:11, of the studying of believers to be quiet, do their own business and work with their own hands. See: BAGD—861c; THAYER—655b.

5390. **φιλοφρόνως** {1x} **philŏphrŏnōs**, *fil-of-ron'-oce;* adv. from *5391; with friendliness of mind,* i.e. *kindly:*—courteously {1x}.

Philophronos, lit., "friendly," or, more fully, "with friendly thoughtfulness" (*philos,* "friend," *phren,* "the mind"), is found in Acts 28:7, of the hospitality showed by Publius to Paul and his fellow-shipwrecked travelers. See: BAGD—861d; THAYER—655b.

5391. **φιλόφρων** {1x} **philŏphrōn**, *fil-of'-rone;* from *5384* and *5424; friendly of mind,* i.e. *kind:*—courteous {1x}. See: BAGD—861d; THAYER—655b.

5392. **φιμόω** {8x} **phimŏō**, *fee-mŏ'-o;* from φιμός **phimŏs**, (a *muzzle*); to *muzzle:*—put to silence {2x}, hold (one's) peace {2x}, muzzle {2x}, be speechless {1x}, be still {1x}.

Phimoo, "to close the mouth with a muzzle" (*phimos*), is used **(1)** of "muzzling the mouth of" the ox when it treads out the corn, with the lesson that those upon whom spiritual labor is bestowed should not refrain from ministering to the material needs of those who labor on their behalf, 1 Cor 9:9; 1 Ti 5:18; **(2)** metaphorically, of putting to silence, or subduing to stillness: **(2a)** Mt 22:12, "speechless"; **(2b)** Mt 22:34; 1 Pet 2:15, "put to silence"; **(2c)** Mk 1:25; Lk 4:35, "hold thy peace"; and **(2d)** Mk 4:39, "be still"; Lk 4:35; 1 Pet 2:15. See: BAGD—861d; THAYER—655b.

5393. **Φλέγων** {1x} **Phlĕgōn**, *fleg'-one;* act. part. of the base of *5395; blazing; Phlegon,* a Chr.:—Phlegon {1x}. See: BAGD—862a; THAYER—655c.

5394. **φλογίζω** {2x} **phlŏgizō**, *flog-id'-zo;* from *5395;* to *cause a blaze,* i.e. *ignite* (fig. to *inflame* with passion):—set on fire {2x}.

Phlogizo, "to set on fire, burn up," is used figuratively, in both active and passive voices, in Jas 3:6, of the tongue, firstly of its disastrous effects upon the whole round of the circumstances of life; secondly, of satanic agency in using the tongue for this purpose. See: BAGD—862a; THAYER—655c.

5395. **φλόξ** {7x} **phlŏx**, *flox;* from a primary φλέγω **phlĕgō**, (to *"flash"* or *"flame"*); a *blaze:* —flame {6x}, flaming {1x}.

Phlego, "to shine," is used apart from *pur,* "fire," **(1)** in Lk 16:24; with *pur,* it signifies "a fiery flame," lit., "a flame of fire," (cf. Acts 7:30; 2 Th 1:8 ("flaming), where the fire is to be understood as the instrument of divine judgment); **(2)** Heb 1:7, where the is that God makes His angels as active and powerful as a "flame" of fire; **(3)** in Rev 1:14; 2:18; 19:12, of the eyes of the Lord Jesus as emblematic of penetrating judgment, searching out evil. See: BAGD—862b; THAYER—655c.

5396. **φλυαρέω** {1x} **phluarĕō**, *floo-ar-eh'-o;* from *5397;* to *be a babbler* or *trifler,* i.e. (by impl.) to *berate* idly or mischievously:—prate against {1x}.

This word means to utter nonsense, talk idly (1 Jn 1:10). See: BAGD—862b; THAYER—655c.

5397. **φλύαρος** {1x} **phluarŏs**, *floo'-ar-os;* from φλύω **phluo**, (to *bubble*); a *garrulous* person, i.e. *prater:*—tattler {1x}. See: BAGD—862b; THAYER—655d.

5398. **φοβερός** {3x} **phŏbĕrŏs**, *fob-er-os';* from *5401; frightful,* i.e. (obj.) *formidable:*—fearful {2x}, terrible {1x}.

(1) *Phoberos* denotes inspiring fear, terrible, formidable, used in a good or bad sense. *Phoberos,* "fearful," is used **(2)** only in the active sense in the NT, i.e., causing "fear," terrible, and is translated **(2a)** "fearful" in Heb 10:27, 31; **(2b)** "terrible" [terror causing] in Heb 12:21. Syn.: **(A)** *Deilia* (1167) denotes timidity, fearfulness, cowardice and is always used in a bad sense. **(B)** *Eulabeia* (2124) is usually used in a good sense and means caution, circumspection, discretion, avoidance, a reasonable shunning; used of reverence toward God, godly fear, piety. See: BAGD—862b; THAYER—655d.

5399. **φοβέω** {93x} **phŏbĕō**, *fob-eh'-o;* from *5401;* to *frighten,* i.e. (pass.) to *be alarmed;* by anal. to *be in awe* of, i.e. *revere:*—fear {62x}, be afraid {23x}, be afraid of {5x}, reverence {1x}, misc. {2x}.

Phobeo, in the NT is always in the passive voice, has the meanings either **(1)** "to fear, be afraid," its most frequent use, e.g., Mt 1:20; 17:6; or **(2)** "to show reverential fear", **(2a)** of men, Mk 6:20; Eph 5:33, "reverence"; **(2b)** of God, e.g., Acts 10:2, 22; 13:16, 26; Col 3:22; 1 Pet 2:17; Rev 14:7; 15:4; 19:5; **(2c)** (2a) and (2b) are combined in Lk 12:4, 5, where Christ warns His followers not to be afraid of men, but to "fear" God. Syn.: **(A)** *Ekplesso* (1605) means "to be astonished", prop. to be struck with terror, of a sudden and startling alarm; but like our "astonish" in popular use, often employed on comparatively slight occasions. **(B)** *Ptoeo* (4422) signifies "to terrify", to agitate with fear. **(C)** *Tremo* (5141) "to tremble", predominately physical; and **(D)** *phobeo* (5399) denotes "to fear", the general term; often used of a protracted state. See: BAGD—862b; THAYER—655d.

5400. **φόβητρον** {1x} **phŏbētrŏn**, *fob'-ay-tron;* neut. of a der. of *5399;* a *frightening* thing, i.e. *terrific* portent:—fearful sight {1x}.

Phobetron, as a noun, in the plural, is translated "fearful sights": "And great earthquakes shall be in divers places, and famines, and pestilences; and fearful sights and great signs shall there be from heaven" (Lk 21:11). See: BAGD—863c; THAYER—656b.

5401. **φόβος** {47x} **phŏbŏs**, *fob'-os;* from a primary φέβομαι **phĕbŏmai** (to *be put in fear*), *alarm,* or *fright:*—fear {41x}, terror {3x}, misc. {3x} = be afraid, + exceedingly.

Phobos first had the meaning of "flight," that which is caused by being scared; then, "that which may cause flight," **(1)** "fear, dread, terror," **(1a)** always with this significance in the four Gospels; also e.g., in Acts 2:43; 19:17; 1 Cor 2:3; 1 Ti 5:20 (lit., "may have fear"); Heb 2:15; 1 Jn 4:18; Rev 11:11; 18:10, 15; **(1b)** by metonymy, that which causes "fear," Rom 13:3; 1 Pet 3:14, "(their) terror," an adaptation of Is 8:12, "fear not their fear"; hence some take it to mean, as there, "what they fear," but in view of Mt 10:28, e.g., it seems best to understand it as that which is caused by the intimidation of adversaries;

(2) "reverential fear," **(2a)** of God, **(2a1)** as a controlling motive of the life, in matters spiritual and moral, **(2a2)** not a mere "fear" of His power and righteous retribution, **(2a3)** but a wholesome dread of displeasing Him, a "fear" which banishes the terror that shrinks from His presence, Rom 8:15, and **(2a4)** which influences the disposition and attitude of one whose circumstances are guided by trust in God, **(2a5)** through the indwelling Spirit of God, Acts 9:31; Rom 3:18; 2 Cor 7:1; Eph 5:21; Phil 2:12; 1 Pet 1:17 (a comprehensive phrase: the reverential "fear" of God will inspire a constant carefulness in dealing with others in His "fear"); 3:2, 15; **(2a6)** the association of "fear and trembling," as, e.g., in Phil 2:12, (cf. Gen 9:2; Ex 15:16; Deut 2:25; 11:25; Ps 55:5; Is 19:16); **(2b)** of superiors, e.g., Rom 13:7; 1 Pet 2:18. See: TDNT—9:189, 1272; BAGD—863c; THAYER—656b.

5402. **Φοίβη** {2x} **Phŏibē**, *foy'-bay;* fem. of φοῖβος **phŏibŏs**, (*bright;* prob. akin to the base of *5457*); *Phœbe,* a Chr. woman:—Phebe {2x}. See: BAGD—864a; THAYER—656d.

5403. **Φοινίκη** {3x} **Phŏinikē**, *foy-nee'-kay;* from *5404; palm*-country; *Phœnice* (or *Phœnicia*), a region of Pal.:—Phenice {2x}, Phenicia {1x}. See: BAGD—864a; THAYER—656d.

5404. **φοῖνιξ** {2x} **phŏinix**, *foy'-nix;* of uncert. der.; a *palm*-tree:—palm {1x}, palm tree {1x}.

Phoinix denotes "the date palm"; it is used of **(1)** "palm" trees in Jn 12:13, from which branches were taken; **(2)** of the branches themselves in Rev 7:9. See: BAGD—864b; THAYER—656d.

5405. **Φοῖνιξ** {1x} **Phŏinix**, *foy'-nix;* prob. the same as *5404; Phœnix,* a place in Crete:—Phenice {1x}. See: BAGD—864c; THAYER—not listed.

5406. **φονεύς** {7x} **phŏnĕus**, *fon-yooce';* from *5408;* a *murderer* (always of *criminal* [or at least *intentional*] homicide; which *443* does not necessarily imply; while *4607* is a special term for a *public* bandit):—murderer {7x}.

Phoneus is used **(1)** in a general sense, **(1a)** in the singular, 1 Pet 4:15; **(1b)** in the plural, Rev 21:8; 22:15; **(2)** of those guilty of particular acts, Mt 22:7; Acts 3:14, lit. "a man (*aner*), a murderer"; 7:52; 28:4. See: BAGD—864c; THAYER—657a.

5407. **φονεύω** {12x} **phŏnĕuō**, *fon-yoo'-o;* from *5406;* to *be a murderer* (of):—kill {10x}, do murder {1x}, slay {1x}.

Phoneuo, "to murder," akin to *phoneus,* "a murderer," is rendered by the verb **(1)** "to kill", Mt 5:21 (twice); 23:31; Mk 10:19; Lk 18:20; Rom 13:9; Jas. 2:11 (twice); 4:2; 5:6; **(2)** "do . . . murder" in Mt 19:18; and **(3)** "ye slew" in Mt 23:35. See: BAGD—864c; THAYER—657a.

5408. **φόνος** {10x} **phŏnŏs**, *fon'-os;* from an obs. primary φένω **phĕnō** (to *slay*); *murder:*—murder {8x}, be slain with + 599 {1x}, slaughter {1x}.

Phonos is used **(1)** of a special act, Mk 15:7; Lk 23:19, 25; **(2)** of "murders" in general, **(2a)** in the plural, Mt 15:19; Mk 7:21; Gal 5:21; Rev 9:21; **(2b)** in the singular, Rom 1:29; **(3)** in the sense of "slaughter," **(3a)** Heb 11:37, "they were slain with the sword," lit., "(they died by) slaughter (of the sword)"; **(3b)** in Acts 9:1, "slaughter." See: BAGD—864d; THAYER—657a.

5409. **φορέω** {6x} **phŏrĕō**, *for-eh'-o;* from *5411;* to *have a burden,* i.e. (by anal.) to *wear* as clothing or a constant accompaniment:—bear {3x}, wear {3x}.

(1) This word stresses not a simple act of bearing, but a continuous or habitual condition. **(2)** A frequentative form of *phero* (5342, "to bear") and denoting "repeated or habitual action," is chiefly used **(2a)** of clothing, **(2a1)** of soft raiment, Mt 11:8; **(2a2)** fine clothing, Jas 2:3; **(2a3)** the crown of thorns, Jn 19:5; **(2b)** of weapons, of the civil authority in "bearing" the sword as symbolic of execution, Rom 13:4; **(2c)** of a natural state of bodily existence in this life, spoken of as "the image of the earthy," and the spiritual body of the believer hereafter, "the image of the heavenly," 1 Cor 15:49, the word "image" denoting the actual form and not a mere similitude. See: TDNT—9:83, 1252; BAGD—864d; THAYER—657a.

5410. **Φόρον** {1x} **Phŏrŏn**, *for'-on;* of Lat. or.; a *forum* or market-place; only in comparison with *675;* a *station* on the Appian road:—forum {1x}.

Appius Forum, a town in Italy, 43 Roman miles (70 km) from Rome on the Appian Way, Acts 28:15. See: BAGD—865a; 102b [675]; THAYER—657b.

5411. **φόρος** {5x} **phŏrŏs**, *for'-os;* from *5342;* a *load* (as *borne*), i.e. (fig.) a *tax* (prop. an indiv. *assessment* on persons or property; whereas *5056* is usually a gen. *toll* on goods or travel):—tribute {5x}.

Phoros denotes tribute paid by a subjugated nation (Lk 20:22; 23:2; Rom 13:6, 7). See: TDNT—9:78, 1252; BAGD—865a; THAYER—657b.

5412. **φορτίζω** {2x} **phŏrtizō**, *for-tid'-zo;* from *5414;* to *load* up (prop. as a vessel or animal), i.e. (fig.) to *overburden* with cerem. (or spiritual anxiety):—lade {1x}, be heavy laden {1x}.

Phortizo, "to load" (akin to *phero,* 5342, "to bear"), is used **(1)** in the active voice in Lk 11:46, "ye lade"; **(2)** in the passive voice, metaphorically, in Mt 11:28, "heavy laden." See: TDNT—9:86, 1252; BAGD—865a; THAYER—657b.

5413. **φορτίον** {5x} **phŏrtiŏn**, *for-tee'-on;* dimin. of *5414;* an *invoice* (as part of *freight*), i.e. (fig.) a *task* or *service:*—burden {5x}.

Phortion literally, is something carried and is used metaphorically (except in Acts 27:10, of the lading of a ship); **(1)** of that which, though light is involved in discipleship of Christ (Mt 11:30); **(2)** of tasks imposed by the scribes, Pharisees and lawyers (Mt 23:4; Lk 11:46); **(3)** of that which will be the result, at the judgment-seat of Christ, of each believer's work (Gal 6:5). Syn.: **(A)** *Baros* (922) refers to weight, **(B)** *ogkos* (3591) to bulk, and either may be oppressive; *baros* (922) is a load in so far as it is heavy, *phortion* (5413) a burden in so far as it is borne; hence *phortion* (5413) may be either heavy or light. See: TDNT—9:84, 1252; BAGD—865a; THAYER—657b.

5414. **φόρτος** {1x} **phŏrtŏs**, *for'-tos;* from *5342;* something *carried,* i.e. the *cargo* of a ship:—lading {1x}. See: BAGD—865b; THAYER—657c.

5415. **Φορτουνᾶτος** {2x} **Phŏrtŏunatŏs**, *for-too-nat'-os;* of Lat. or.; *"fortunate," Fortunatus,* a Chr.:—Fortunatus {2x}. See: BAGD—865b; THAYER—657c.

5416. **φραγέλλιον** {1x} **phragĕlliŏn**, *frag-el'-le-on;* neut. of a der. from the base of *5417;* a *whip,* i.e. Rom. *lash* as a public punishment:—scourge {1x}.

Phragellion, "a whip" (from Latin, *flagellum*), is used of the "scourge" of small cords which the Lord made and employed before cleansing the Temple, Jn 2:15. However He actually used it, the whip was in itself a sign of authority and judgment. See: BAGD—865b; THAYER—657c.

5417. **φραγελλόω** {2x} **phragĕllŏō**, *frag-el-lŏ'-o;* from a presumed equiv. of the Lat. *flagellum;* to *whip,* i.e. *lash* as a public punishment:—scourge {2x}.

Phragello is the word used in Mt 27:26 and Mk 15:15 of the scourging endured by Christ and administered by the order of Pilate. Under the Roman method of scourging the person was stripped and tied in a bending posture to a pillar, or stretched on a frame. The scourge was made of leather thongs, weighted with sharp pieces of bone or lead, which tore the flesh of both the back and the breast (cf. Ps 22:17). Eusebius (*Chron.*) records his having witnessed the suffering of martyrs who died under this treatment. See: BAGD—865b; THAYER—657c.

5418. **φραγμός** {4x} **phragmŏs**, *frag-mos';* from *5420;* a *fence,* or inclosing *barrier* (lit. or fig.):—hedge {2x}, hedge around about + 4060 {1x}, partition {1x}.

Phragmos denotes any sort of fence, hedge, palings or wall (akin to *phrasso,* "to fence in, stop"). It is used **(1)** in its literal sense, in Mt 21:33, lit. "(he put) a hedge (around)"; Mk 12:1; Lk 14:23; **(2)** metaphorically, of the "partition" which separated Gentile from Jew, which was broken down by Christ through the efficacy of His expiatory sacrifice, Eph 2:14. See: BAGD—865c; THAYER—657c.

5419. **φράζω** {2x} **phrazō**, *frad'-zo;* prob. akin to *5420* through the idea of *defining;* to *indicate* (by word or act), i.e. (spec.) to *expound:*—declare {2x}.

Phrazo means to indicate plainly, make known, declare, whether by gesture or by writing or speaking, or in some other ways, to explain, Mt 13:36; 15:15. See: BAGD—865c; THAYER—657c.

5420. **φράσσω** {3x} **phrassō**, *fras'-so;* appar. a streng. form of the base of *5424;* to *fence* or inclose, i.e. (spec.) to *block* up (fig. to *silence*):—stop {3x}.

Phrasso, "to fence in" (akin to *phragmos,* "a fence"), "close, stop," is used **(1)** metaphorically, passive voice, **(1a)** in Rom 3:19, of "preventing" all excuse from Jew and Gentile, as sinners; **(1b)** in 2 Cor 11:10, lit., "this boasting shall not be stopped to me"; **(2)** physically, active voice, of the mouths of lions, Heb 11:33. See: BAGD—865c; THAYER—657d.

5421. **φρέαρ** {7x} **phrĕar**, *freh'-ar;* of uncert. der.; a *hole* in the ground (dug for obtaining or holding water or other purposes), i.e. a *cistern* or *well;* fig. an *abyss* (as a *prison*):—well {2x}, pit {5x}.

Phrear, "a well, dug for water" (distinct from *pege,* "a fountain"), denotes **(1)** "a pit", **(1a)** in Rev 9:1, 2, thrice, "(bottomless) pit", "the pit (of the abyss)," "the pit," i.e., the shaft leading down to the abyss; **(1b)** in Lk 14:5; and **(2)** in Jn 4:11, 12, "well." See: BAGD—865d; THAYER—657d.

5422. **φρεναπατάω** {1x} **phrĕnapataō**, *fren-ap-at-ah'-o;* from *5423;* to *be a mind-misleader,* i.e. *delude:*—deceive {1x}.

Literally, this word means to deceive in one's mind, to deceive by fancies, and is used in Gal 6:3 with reference to self-conceit, which is self-deceit, a sin against common sense. See: BAGD—865d; THAYER—657d.

5423. **φρεναπάτης** {1x} **phrĕnapatēs**, *fren-ap-at'-ace;* from *5424* and *539; a mind-misleader,* i.e. *seducer:*—deceiver {1x}. See: BAGD-865d; THAYER—658a.

5424. **φρήν** {2x} **phrēn**, *frane;* prob. from an obs. φράω **phraō** (to *rein* in or *curb;* comp. *5420*); the *midrif* (as a *partition* of the body), i.e. (fig. and by impl. of sympathy) the *feelings* (or sensitive nature; by extens. [also in the plur.] the *mind* or cognitive faculties):—understanding {2x}. See: TDNT—9:220, 1277; BAGD—865d; THAYER—658a.

5425. **φρίσσω** {1x} **phrissō**, *fris'-so;* appar. a primary verb; to "*bristle*" or *chill,* i.e. *shudder* (*fear*):—tremble {1x}.

Phrisso, primarily, "to be rough, to bristle," then, "to shiver, shudder, tremble," is said of devils, Jas 2:19, "tremble." See: BAGD—866a; THAYER—658a.

5426. **φρονέω** {29x} **phrŏnĕō**, *fron-eh'-o;* from *5424;* to *exercise* the *mind,* i.e. *entertain* or *have* a *sentiment* or *opinion;* by impl. to *be* (mentally) *disposed* (more or less earnestly in a certain direction); intens. to *interest oneself* in (with concern or obedience):—think {5x}, regard {4x}, mind {3x}, be minded {3x}, savour {2x}, be of the same mind + 846 {2x}, be like minded + 846 {2x}, misc. {8x} = set the affection on, (be) care (-ful), (+ be of one, + let this) mind (-ed).

Phroneo, "to be minded in a certain way" (*phren,* "the mind"), is rendered **(1)** "to think," **(1a)** in Rom 12:3 (2nd and 3rd occurrences), "not to think of himself more highly (*huperphroneo*) than he ought to think (*phroneo*); but to think (*phroneo*) soberly"; the play on words may be expressed by a literal rendering somewhat as follows: "not to over-think beyond what it behoves him to think, but to think unto sober-thinking"; **(1b)** in 1 Cor 4:6, "to think"; lit., the sentence is "that ye might learn the (i.e., the rule) not beyond what things have been written"; "not to go beyond the terms of a teacher's commission, thinking more of himself than the character of his commission allows"; this accords with the context and the whole passage, 3:1–4:5. **(2)** It is also means "to think, set the mind on," implying moral interest and reflection, and is translated "to regard" in Rom 14:6 (twice).

(3) It also signifies **(3a)** "to think, to be minded in a certain way"; implying moral interest or reflection, not mere unreasoning opinion. It is rendered by the verb "to mind" in the following: **(3b)** Rom. 8:5, "(they that are after the flesh) do mind (the things of the flesh)"; **(3c)** Rom 12:16, "be of (the same) mind," lit., "minding the same," and "set (not) your mind on", "mind (not)"; **(3d)** Rom 15:5, "to be likeminded"); **(3e)** 2 Cor 13:11, "be of (one) mind"; **(3f)** Gal 5:10, "ye will be (none otherwise) minded"; **(3g)** in Phil **(3g1)** Phil 1:7, "to think (this)"; **(3g2)** Phil 2:2, "be likeminded," and "being . . . of (one) mind," lit., "minding (the one thing)"; **(3g3)** Phil 2:5, "let (this) mind be," lit., "mind this"; **(3g4)** Phil 3:15, "let us . . . be (thus) minded," and "(if) . . . ye are (otherwise) minded"; **(3g5)** Phil 3:16, "let us mind"; **(3g6)** Phil 3:19, "(who) mind (earthly things)"; **(3g7)** Phil 4:2, "be of (the same) mind"; **(3h)** Col 3:2, "set your affection." See: TDNT—9:220, 1277; BAGD—866a; THAYER—658a.

5427. **φρόνημα** {4x} **phrŏnēma**, *fron'-ay-mah;* from *5426;* (mental) *inclination* or *purpose:* —mind {2x}, carnally minded + 4561 {1x}, spiritually minded + 4151 {1x}.

Phronema denotes "what one has in the mind, the thought" (the content of the process expressed in *phroneo,* "to have in mind, to think"); or "an object of thought"; and is translated **(1)** in Rom. 8:6, "to be carnally minded" and "to be spiritually minded", in vv. 6 and 7, and "the mind of the spirit," in v. 6. **(2)** In Rom 8:27 the word is used of the "mind" of the Holy Spirit. See: TDNT—9:220, 1277; BAGD—866c; THAYER—658c.

5428. **φρόνησις** {2x} **phrŏnēsis**, *fron'-ay-sis;* from *5426;* mental *action* or *activity,* i.e. intellectual or mor. *insight:*—prudence {1x}, wisdom {1x}.

Phronesis means to have understanding and denotes practical wisdom, prudence in the management of affairs. It is translated **(1)** wisdom in Lk 1:17 and **(2)** prudence in Eph 1:8. See: TDNT—9:220, 1277; BAGD—866c; THAYER—658c.

5429. **φρόνιμος** {14x} **phrŏnimŏs**, *fron'-ee-mos;* from *5424; thoughtful,* i.e. *sagacious* or *discreet* (implying a *cautious* character; while *4680* denotes *practical* skill or acumen; and *4908* indicates rather *intelligence* or mental acquirement); in a bad sense *conceited* (also in the comparative):—wise {13x}, wiser {1x}.

Phronimos, means "prudent, sensible, practically wise," and is **(1)** found in Mt 7:24; 10:16; 24:45; 25:2, 4, 8, 9; Lk 12:42; 16:8 ("wiser", comparative degree, *phronimoteros*); 1 Cor 10:15; in an evil sense, "wise (in your own conceits)," lit., "wise (in yourselves)," i.e., "judged by the standard of your self-complacency," Rom 11:25; 12:16; ironically, 1 Cor 4:10; 2 Cor 11:19. See: TDNT—9:220, 1277; BAGD—866d; THAYER—658c.

5430. **φρονίμως** {1x} **phrŏnimōs**, *fron-im'-oce;* adv. from *5429; prudently:*—wisely {1x}. See: BAGD—866d; THAYER—658d.

5431. **φροντίζω** {1x} **phrŏntizō**, *fron-tid'-zo;* from a der. of *5424;* to *exercise thought,* i.e. *be anxious:*—be careful {1x}. See: BAGD—866d; THAYER—658d.

5432. **φρουρέω** {4x} **phrŏurĕō**, *froo-reh'-o;* from a compound of *4253* and *3708;* to *be a watcher in advance,* i.e. to *mount guard* as a sentinel (*post spies* at gates); fig. to *hem in, protect:*—keep {3x}, keep with a garrison {1x}.

Phroureo is a military term meaning to keep by guarding, to keep under guard as with a garrison. It is used **(1)** of blocking up every way of escape, as in a siege; **(2)** of providing protection against the enemy, as a garrison does (2 Cor 11:32). **(3)** It is used of the security of the Christian until the end (1 Pet 1:5); and of the sense of that security that is his when he puts all his matters into the hand of God (Phil 4:7). In these passages the idea is not merely that of protection, but of inward garrisoning as by the Holy Spirit (Gal 3:23; it means rather a benevolent custody and watchful guardianship in view of worldwide idolatry. See: BAGD—867b; THAYER—658d. comp. *5083.*

5433. **φρυάσσω** {1x} **phruassō**, *froo-as'-so;* akin to *1032, 1031;* to *snort* (as a spirited horse), i.e. (fig.) to *make a tumult:*—rage {1x}.

This word was primarily used of the snorting, neighing and prancing of horses; hence, metaphorically, of the haughtiness and insolence of men (Acts 4:25). See: BAGD—867b; THAYER—658d.

5434. **φρύγανον** {1x} **phruganŏn**, *froo'-gan-on;* neut. of a presumed der. of φρύγω **phrugō** (to *roast* or *parch;* akin to the base of *5305*); something *desiccated,* i.e. a dry *twig:*—a stick {1x}. See: BAGD—867b; THAYER—659a.

5435. **Φρυγία** {4x} **Phrugia**, *froog-ee'-ah;* prob. of for. or.; *Phrygia,* a region of Asia Minor:—Phrygia {4x}. See: BAGD—867c; THAYER—659a.

5436. **Φύγελλος** {1x} **Phugĕllŏs**, *foog'-el-los;* prob. from *5343; fugitive; Phygellus,* an apostate Chr.:—Phygellus {1x}. See: BAGD—867c; THAYER—659a.

5437. **φυγή** {2x} **phugē**, *foog-ay';* from *5343;* a *fleeing,* i.e. *escape:*—flight {2x}. Cf. Mt 24:20; Mk 13:18. See: BAGD—867c; THAYER—659a.

5438. **φυλακή** {47x} **phulakē**, *foo-lak-ay';* from *5442; a guarding* or (concr. *guard*), the act, the person; fig. the place, the condition, or (spec.) the time (as a division of day or night), lit. or fig.:—prison {36x}, watch {6x}, imprisonment {2x}, hold {1x}, cage {1x}, ward {1x}.

Phulake, from *phulasso,* "to guard," denotes **(1)** "a watching, keeping watch," Lk 2:8; **(2)** "persons keeping watch, a guard," Acts 12:10; **(3)** "a period during which watch is kept," e.g., Mt 24:43. **(4)** The word is almost invariably translated prison, e.g., Mt 14:10; Mk 6:17; Acts 5:19; 2 Cor 11:23; **(4a)** in 2 Cor 6:5 and Heb 11:36 it stands for the condition of imprisonment; **(4b)** "a prison, a hold", Rev 2:10, Babylon is described figuratively, first as a "hold" and then as a "cage" (Rev 18:2) of every unclean and hateful bird. See: TDNT—9:241, 1280; BAGD—867d; THAYER—659a.

5439. **φυλακίζω** {1x} **phulakizō**, *foo-lak-id'-zo;* from *5441;* to *incarcerate:*—to imprison {1x}. See: BAGD—868a; THAYER—659c.

5440. **φυλακτήριον** {1x} **phulaktēriŏn**, *foo-lak-tay'-ree-on;* neut. of a der. of *5442;* a *guard-case,* i.e. "*phylactery*" for wearing slips of Scripture texts:—phylactery {1x}.

This word primarily means an outpost or fortification; then, any kind of safeguard and became used especially to denote an amulet. In the NT it denotes a prayer fillet, a *phylactery,* a small strip of parchment, with portions of the Law written on it; it was fastened by a leather strap either to the forehead or to the left arm over against the heart, to remind the wearer of the duty of keeping the commandments of God in the head and in the heart (cf. Ex 13:16; Deut 6:8; 11:18). It was supposed to have potency as a charm against evils and demons. The Pharisees broadened their phylacteries to render conspicuous their superior eagerness to be mindful of God's Law (Mt 23:5). See: BAGD—868a; THAYER—659c.

5441. **φύλαξ** {3x} **phulax**, *foo'-lax;* from *5442;* a *watcher* or *sentry:*—keeper {3x}. Cf. Acts 5:23; 12:6, 19. See: BAGD—868b; THAYER—659d.

5442. **φυλάσσω** {30x} **phulassō**, *foo-las'-so;* prob. from *5443* through the idea of *isolation;* to *watch,* i.e. *be on guard* (lit. or fig.); by impl. to *preserve, obey, avoid:*—keep {23x}, observe {2x}, beware {2x}, keep (one's) self {1x}, save {1x}, be . . . ware {1x}.

Phulasso denotes "to guard, watch, keep watch," e.g., Lk 2:8; **(1)** in the passive voice, **(1a)** Lk 8:29; **(1b)** "to keep by way of protection," e.g., Lk 11:21; Jn 12:25; 17:12, 2nd part; **(2)** metaphorically, "to keep a law or precept," etc., e.g., Mt 19:20 and Lk 18:21, "have observed"; Lk 11:28; Acts 7:53; 16:4; 21:24; Rom 2:26; Gal 6:13; 1 Ti 5:21, "observe"; **(3)** in the middle voice, Mk 10:20, "have observed"; **(4)** in the middle voice, "to keep oneself from," Acts 21:25. **(5)** It is also translated by the verb "to beware": **(5a)** in the middle voice, of being "on one's guard against" (the middle voice stressing personal interest in the action), **(5a1)** Lk 12:15, "beware of", **(5a2)** as in Acts 21:25; **(5b)** in 2 Ti 4:15, "be thou ware"; and **(5c)** in 2 Pet. 3:17, "beware." Syn.: *Tereo* (5083) means to watch or keep and expresses watchful care and is suggestive of present possession; whereas, *phulasso* (5442) indicates safe custody and often implies assault from without. *Tereo* (5083) may mark the result of which *phulasso* (5442) is the means. See: TDNT—9:236, 1280; BAGD—868b; THAYER—659d.

5443. **φυλή** {31x} **phulē**, *foo-lay';* from *5453* (comp. *5444*); an *offshoot,* i.e. *race* or *clan:*—kindred {6x}, tribe {25x}.

Phule, "a company of people united by kinship or habitation, a clan, tribe," is used **(1)** of the peoples of the earth, Mt 24:30; **(2)** of "kindred(-s)": Rev 1:7; 5:9; 7:9; 11:9; 13:7; 14:6; **(3)** of the "tribes" of Israel, Mt 19:28, Lk 2:36; 22:30; Acts 13:21; Rom 11:1; Phil 3:5; Heb 7:13, 14; Jas 1:1; Rev 5:5; 7:4–8; 21:12. See: TDNT—9:245, 1280; BAGD—868d; THAYER—660b.

5444. **φύλλον** {6x} **phullŏn**, *fool'-lon;* from the same as *5443;* a *sprout,* i.e. *leaf:*—leaf {6x}. Cf. Mt 21:19; 24:32; Mk 11:13 (twice); 13:28; Rev 22:2. See: BAGD—869a; THAYER—660b.

5445. **φύραμα** {5x} **phurama**, *foo'-ram-ah;* from a prol. form of φύρω **phurō** (to *mix* a liquid with a solid; perh. akin to *5453* through the idea of *swelling* in bulk), mean to *knead;* a *mass* of dough:—lump {5x}.

Phurama denotes "that which is mixed or kneaded" (*phurao,* "to mix") hence, "a lump," either **(1)** of dough, Rom 11:16 (cf. Num 15:21);

1 Cor 5:6, 7; Gal 5:9; or **(2)** of potter's clay, Rom 9:21. See: BAGD–869a; THAYER–660b.

5446. **φυσικός** {3x} **phusikŏs**, *foo-see-kos';* from *5449; "physical"*, i.e. (by impl.) *instinctive:*—natural {3x}.

Phuskios originally signified produced by nature, inborn but in the NT denotes **(1)** according to nature (Rom 1:26, 27); **(2)** governed by mere natural instincts (2 Pet 2:12). See: TDNT–9:251, 1283; BAGD–869b; THAYER–660b. comp. *5591*.

5447. **φυσικῶς** {1x} **phusikōs**, *foo-see-koce';* adv. from *5446; "physically"*, i.e. (by impl.) *instinctively:*—naturally {1x}. See: TDNT–9:251, 1283; BAGD–869b; THAYER–660c.

5448. **φυσιόω** {7x} **phusiŏō**, *foo-see-ŏ'-o;* from *5449* in the primary sense of *blowing;* to *inflate*, i.e. (fig.) *make proud* (*haughty*):—puff up {7x}.

Phusioo means to puff up, blow up, inflate and is used metaphorically of being puffed up with pride (1 Cor 4:6, 18, 19; 5:2; 8:1; 13:4; Col 2:18). See: BAGD–869b; THAYER–660c.

5449. **φύσις** {14x} **phusis**, *foo'-sis;* from *5453; growth* (by *germination* or *expansion*), i.e. (by impl.) natural *production* (lineal *descent*); by extens. a *genus* or *sort;* fig. native *disposition, constitution* or *usage:*—nature {10x}, natural + 2596 {2x}, kind {1x}, mankind + 442 {1x}.

Phusis, (from *phuo*, "to bring forth, produce"), signifies **(1)** "the nature" (i.e., the natural powers or constitution) of a person or thing, Eph 2:3; Jas 3:7 ("kind"); 2 Pet 1:4; **(2)** "origin, birth," Rom 2:27, one who by birth is a Gentile, uncircumcised, in contrast to one who, though circumcised, has become spiritually uncircumcised by his iniquity; Gal 2:15; **(3)** "the regular law or order of nature," **(3a)** Rom 1:26, against "nature" (*para*, "against"); **(3b)** Rom 2:14, adverbially, "by nature", (cf. 11:21 "natural", and 11:24, "by nature" twice, "natural" once); 1 Cor 11:14; **(3c)** Gal 4:8, "by nature (are no gods)," here "nature" is the emphatic word, and the phrase includes devils, men regarded as deified, and idols; these are gods only in name (the negative, *me*, denies not simply that they were gods, but the possibility that they could be). See: TDNT–9:251, 1283; BAGD–869b; THAYER–660c.

5450. **φυσίωσις** {1x} **phusiōsis**, *foo-see'-o-sis;* from *5448; inflation*, i.e. (fig.) *haughtiness, swelling with pride:*—swelling {1x}. See: BAGD–870a; THAYER–661a.

5451. **φυτεία** {1x} **phutĕia**, *foo-ti'-ah;* from *5452;* trans-*planting*, i.e. (concr.) a *shrub* or *vegetable:*—plant {1x}. See: BAGD–870a; THAYER–661a.

5452. **φυτεύω** {11x} **phutĕuō**, *foot-yoo'-o;* from a der. of *5453;* to *set out* in the earth, i.e. *implant;* fig. to *instil* doctrine:—to plant {11x}.

Phuteuo "to plant," is used **(1)** literally, Mt 21:33; Mk 12:1; Lk 13:6; 17:6, 28; 20:9; 1 Cor 9:7; **(2)** metaphorically, Mt 15:13; 1 Cor 3:6, 7, 8. See: BAGD–870a; THAYER–661a.

5453. **φύω** {3x} **phuō**, *foo'-o;* a primary verb; prob. orig. to *"puff"* or *blow*, i.e. to *swell* up; but only used in the impl. sense, to *germinate* or *grow* (*sprout, produce*), lit. or fig.:—spring up {1x}, spring {1x}, as soon as it be sprung up {1x}.

Phuo, used transitively, "to bring forth, produce," denotes, **(1)** in the passive voice, "to spring up, grow," of seed, Luke 8:6, 8, "was sprung up" and "sprang up"; **(2)** in the active voice, intransitively, in Heb 12:15, of a root of bitterness. See: BAGD–870b; THAYER–661b.

5454. **φωλεός** {2x} **phōlĕŏs**, *fo-leh-os';* of uncert. der.; a *burrow* or *lurking-place:*—hole {2x}.

Pholeos, "a lair, burrow, den or hole," is used of foxes in Mt 8:20 and Lk 9:58. See: BAGD–870b; THAYER–661b.

5455. **φωνέω** {42x} **phōnĕō**, *fo-neh'-o;* from *5456;* to emit a *sound* (animal, human or instrumental); by impl. to *address* in words or by name, also in imitation:—call {23x}, crow {12x}, cry {5x}, call for {2x}.

Phoneo, as a verb, means "to sound" (Eng.,"phone"), is used **(1)** of the crowing of a cock, e.g., Mt 26:34; Jn 13:38; **(2)** of "calling" out with a clear or loud voice, to cry out, Acts 16:28; **(3)** of "calling" to come to oneself, e.g., Mt 20:32; Lk 19:15; **(4)** of "calling" forth, as of Christ's call to Lazarus to come forth from the tomb, Jn 12:17; **(5)** of inviting, e.g., Lk 14:12; **(6)** of "calling" by name, with the implication of the pleasure taken in the possession of those "called," e.g., Jn 10:3; 13:13; **(7)** of animals, Mt 26:34; or **(8)** persons, Lk 8:8; 16:24. **(9)** This is the word which Luke uses to describe the "cry" of the Lord at the close of His sufferings on the cross (Lk 23:46). Syn.: 310, 349, 994, 995, 1916, 2019, 2896, 2905, 2906. See: TDNT–9:301, 1287; BAGD–870b; THAYER–661b.

5456. **φωνή** {141x} **phōnē**, *fo-nay';* prob. akin to *5316* through the idea of *disclosure;* a *tone* (articulate, bestial or artif.); by impl. an *address* (for any purpose), *saying* or *language:*—voice {131x}, sound {8x}, be noised abroad + 1096 {1x}, noise {1x}.

Phone, most frequently **(1)** "a voice," it is also translated **(2)** "sound" in Mt 24:31; Jn 3:8; 1 Cor 14:7 (1st part), 8; Rev 1:15; 9:9 (twice); 18:22 (2nd part); and **(3)** in Acts 2:6, "(this) was noised abroad." See: TDNT–9:278, 1287; BAGD–870c; THAYER–661c.

5457. **φῶς** {70x} **phōs**, *foce;* from an obs. φάω **phaō** (to *shine*, or make *manifest*, espec. by *rays;* comp. *5316, 5346*); *luminousness* (in the widest application, nat. or artif., abstr. or concr., lit. or fig.):—fire {2x}, light {68x}.

Phos, (akin to *phao*, "to give light", from roots *pha*— and *phan*—, expressing "light as seen by the eye," and, metaphorically, as "reaching the mind," whence *phaino*, "to make to appear," *phaneros*, "evident," etc.; cf. Eng., "phosphorus", lit., "light-bearing"), is usually used of light. **(1)** Primarily light is a luminous emanation, probably of force, from certain bodies, which enables the eye to discern form and color. **(1a)** Light requires an organ adapted for its reception (Mt 6:22). **(1b)** Where the eye is absent, or where it has become impaired from any cause, light is useless. **(1c)** Man, naturally, is incapable of receiving spiritual light inasmuch as he lacks the capacity for spiritual things, 1 Cor 2:14. **(2)** Hence believers are called "sons of light," Lk 16:8, not merely because they have received a revelation from God, but because in the New Birth they have received the spiritual capacity for it.

(3) Apart from natural phenomena, light is used in Scripture of **(3a)** the glory of God's dwelling-place, 1 Ti 6:16; **(3b)** the nature of God, 1 Jn 1:5; **(3c)** the impartiality of God, Jas 1:17; **(3d)** the favor **(3d1)** of God, cf. Ps 4:6; **(3d2)** of the King, cf. Prov 16:15; **(3d3)** of an influential man, cf. Job 29:24; **(3e)** God, as the illuminator of His people, cf. Is 60:19, 20; **(3f)** the Lord Jesus as the illuminator of men, Jn 1:4, 5, 9; 3:19; 8:12; 9:5; 12:35, 36, 46; Acts 13:47; **(3g)** the illuminating power of the Scriptures, **(3g1)** Ps 119:105; **(3g2)** and of the judgments and commandments of God, cf. Is 51:4; Prov 6:23, Ps 43:3; **(3h)** the guidance **(3h1)** of God, cf. Job 29:3; Ps 112:4; Is 58:10; and, **(3h2)** ironically, of the guidance of man, Rom 2:19; **(3i)** salvation, 1 Pet 2:9; **(3j)** righteousness, Rom 13:12; 2 Cor 11:14, 15; 1 Jn 2:9, 10; **(3k)** witness for God, Mt 5:14, 16; Jn 5:35; **(3l)** prosperity and general well-being, cf. Est 8:16; Job 18:18; Is 58:8–10. See: TDNT–9:310, 1293; BAGD–871c.

5458. **φωστήρ** {2x} **phōstēr**, *foce-tare';* from *5457;* an *illuminator*, i.e. (concr.) a *luminary*, or (abstr.) *brilliancy:*—light {2x}.

Phoster denotes "a luminary, light," or "light-giver"; it is used **(1)** figuratively of believers, as shining in the spiritual darkness of the world, Phil 2:15; and **(2)** in Rev 21:11 it is used of Christ as the "Light" reflected in and shining through the heavenly city (cf. v. 23). See: TDNT–9:310, 1293; BAGD–872c; THAYER–663a.

5459. **φωσφόρος** {1x} **phōsphŏrŏs**, *foce-for'-os;* from *5457* and *5342; light-bearing* ("phosphorus"), i.e. (spec.) the *morning-star* (fig.):—day star {1x}.

Phosphoros, (Eng., "phosphorus," lit., "light-bearing" *phos*, "light," *phero*, "to bear"), is used of the morning star, as the light-bringer, 2 Pet 1:19, where it indicates the arising of the light of Christ as the personal fulfillment, in the hearts of believers, of the prophetic Scriptures concerning His coming to receive them to Himself. See: TDNT–9:310, 1293; BAGD–872d; THAYER–663a.

5460. **φωτεινός** {5x} **phōtĕinŏs**, *fo-ti-nos';* from *5457; lustrous*, i.e. *transparent* or *well-illuminated* (fig.):—bright {1x}, full of light {4x}.

Photeinos, (from *phos*, "bright"), is rendered **(1)** literally, "full of light" in Mt 6:22; Lk 11:34, 36 (twice); **(2)** figuratively, of the single-mindedness of the eye, which acts as the lamp of the body; and **(3)** in Mt 17:5, "bright," of a cloud. See: TDNT–9:310, 1293; BAGD–872d; THAYER–663a.

5461. **φωτίζω** {11x} **phōtizō**, *fo-tid'-zo;* from *5457; to shed rays*, i.e. to *shine* or (tran.) to *brighten* up (lit. or fig.):—give light {2x}, bring to light {2x}, lighten {2x}, enlighten {2x}, light {1x}, illuminate {1x}, make to see {1x}.

Photizo, from *phos*, "light," used **(1)** intransitively, signifies "to shine, give light," Rev 22:5; **(2)** transitively, **(2a)** "to illumine, to light, enlighten, to be lightened," Lk 11:36; Rev 21:23; **(2a1)** in the passive voice, Rev 18:1; **(2a2)** metaphorically, of spiritual enlightenment, Jn 1:9; Eph 1:18; 3:9, "to make . . . see;" Heb 6:4; 10:32, "ye were illuminated"; **(2b)** "to bring to light," **(2b1)** 1 Cor 4:5 (of God's act in the future); **(2b2)** 2 Ti 1:10 (of God's act in the past). See: TDNT–9:310, 1293; BAGD–872d; THAYER–663b.

5462. **φωτισμός** {2x} **phōtismŏs**, *fo-tis-mos';* from *5461; illumination* (fig.):—light {2x}.

Photismos, "an illumination, light," is used metaphorically in **(1)** 2 Cor 4:4, of the "light" of the gospel, and in **(2)** 2 Cor 4:6, of the knowledge of the glory of God. See: TDNT–9:310, 1293; BAGD–873c; THAYER–663c.

X

5463. **χαίρω** {74x} **chairō**, *khah'-ee-ro;* a primary verb; to be "*cheer*"*ful*, i.e. calmly *happy* or well-off; impers. espec. as salutation (on meeting or parting), *be well:*—rejoice {42x}, be glad {14x}, joy {5x}, hail {5x}, greeting {3x}, God speed {2x}, all hail {1x}, joyfully 1, farewell {1x}.

Chairo, "to rejoice," is most frequently so translated. **(1)** As to this verb, the following are grounds and occasions for "rejoicing," on the part of believers: **(1a)** in the Lord, Phil 3:1; 4:4; **(1b)** His incarnation, Lk 1:14; **(1c)** His power, Lk 13:17; **(1d)** His presence with the Father, Jn 14:28; **(1e)** His presence with them, Jn 16:22; 20:20; **(1f)** His ultimate triumph, Jn 8:56; **(1g)** hearing the gospel, Acts 13:48; **(1h)** their salvation, Acts 8:39; **(1i)** receiving the Lord, Lk 19:6; **(1j)** their enrollment in Heaven, Lk 10:20; **(1k)** their liberty in Christ, Acts 15:31; **(1l)** their hope, Rom 12:12 (cf. Rom 5:2; Rev 19:7); **(1m)** their prospect of reward, Mt 5:12; **(1n)** the obedience and godly conduct of fellow believers, 2 Cor 7:7, 9; 13:9; Col 2:5; 1 Th 3:9; 2 Jn 4; 3 Jn 3; **(1o)** the proclamation of Christ, Phil 1:18; **(1p)** the gospel harvest, Jn 4:36; **(1q)** suffering with Christ, Acts 5:41; 1 Pet 4:13; **(1r)** suffering in the cause of the gospel, 2 Cor 13:9 (1st part); Phil 2:17 (1st part); Col 1:24; **(1s)** in persecutions, trials and afflictions, Mt 5:12; Lk 6:23; 2 Cor 6:10; **(1t)** the manifestation of grace, Acts 11:23; **(1u)** meeting with fellow believers, 1 Cor 16:17; Phil 2:28; **(1v)** receiving tokens of love and fellowship, Phil 4:10; **(1w)** the "rejoicing" of others, Rom 12:15, 2 Cor 7:13, **(1x)** learning of the wellbeing of others, 2 Cor 7:16.

(2) It is also the usual word for "being glad" and is so rendered in Mk 14:11; Lk 15:32; 22:5; 23:8; Jn 8:56; 11:15; 20:20; Acts 11:23; 13:48; Rom 16:19; 1 Cor 16:17; 2 Cor 13:9; 1 Pet 4:13; Rev 19:7. Syn.: 21, 2165. See: TDNT—9:359, 1298; BAGD—873b; THAYER—663b.

5464. **χάλαζα** {4x} **chalaza**, *khal'-ad-zah;* prob. from *5465; hail:*—hail {4x}.

Chalaza, akin to *chalao,* "to let loose, let fall," is always used as an instrument of divine judgment, translated "hail" [balls of frozen rain] and is found in the NT in Rev 8:7; 11:19; 16:21. See: BAGD—874b; THAYER—664a.

5465. **χαλάω** {7x} **chalaō**, *khal-ah'-o;* from the base of *5490;* to *lower* (as into a *void*):—let down {6x}, strike {1x}.

Chalao, "to slacken, loosen, let loose," **(1)** denotes "to let down, to lower"; it is used with reference to **(1a)** the paralytic, in Mk 2:4; **(1b)** Paul/Saul: **(1b1)** Saul of Tarsus, Acts 9:25; **(1b2)** Paul, 2 Cor 11:33, "was I let down" (passive voice); **(1c)** "nets" in Lk 5:4, and "a net" in 5:5; **(1d)** a ship's boat, Acts 27:30, "let down." **(2)** In Acts 27:17, "they strake (sail)"; i.e. they lowered the sail, unfurling it; thus, "striking" out into the wind. See: BAGD—874b; THAYER—664b.

5466. **Χαλδαῖος** {1x} **Chaldaiŏs**, *khal-dah'-yos;* prob. of Heb. or [3778]; a *Chaldæan* (i.e. *Kasdi*), or native or the region of the lower Euphrates:—Chaldæan {1x}. See: BAGD—874c; THAYER—664b.

5467. **χαλεπός** {2x} **chalĕpŏs**, *khal-ep-os';* perh. from *5465* through the idea of *reducing* the strength; *difficult,* i.e. *dangerous,* or (by impl.) *furious:*—fierce {1x}, perilous {1x}.

This word means hard to do or deal with, difficult, fierce, perilous and is said **(1)** of the Gadarene devils (Mt 8:28); and **(2)** of the last times (2 Ti 3:1). See: BAGD—874c; THAYER—664b.

5468. **χαλιναγωγέω** {2x} **chalinagōgĕō**, *khal-in-ag-ogue-eh'-o;* from a compound of *5469* and the redupl. form of *71;* to *be a bit-leader,* i.e. to *curb* (fig.):—bridle {2x}.

Chalinagogeo, from *chalinos* and *ago,* "to lead," signifies "to lead by a bridle, to bridle, to hold in check, restrain"; it is used metaphorically of the tongue and of the body in Jas 1:26 and 3:2. See: BAGD—874c; THAYER—664b.

5469. **χαλινός** {2x} **chalinŏs**, *khal-ee-nos';* from *5465;* a *curb* or *head-stall* (as *curbing* the spirit):—bit {1x}, bridle {1x}.

Chalinos, **(1)** "bits" is used in Jas 3:3, and "bridles" in Rev 14:20. The primitive bridle was simply a loop on the haltercord passed round the lower jaw of the horse. See: BAGD—874d; THAYER—664b.

5470. **χάλκεος** {1x} **chalkĕŏs**, *khal'-keh-os;* from *5475; coppery:*—brass {1x}. See: BAGD—875b; THAYER—664c.

5471. **χαλκεύς** {1x} **chalkĕus**, *khalk-yooce';* from *5475;* a *copper-worker* or *brazier:*—coppersmith {1x}. See: BAGD—874d; THAYER—664c.

5472. **χαλκηδών** {1x} **chalkēdōn**, *khal-kay-dohn';* from *5475* and perh. *1491; copper-like,* i.e. "*chalcedony*":—chalcedony {1x}.

Chalcedony is a precious stone of misty grey colour, or green, clouded with blue, yellow, or purple. See: BAGD—874d, THAYER—664c.

5473. **χαλκίον** {1x} **chalkiŏn**, *khal-kee'-on;* dimin. from *5475;* a *brazen dish:* brazen vessel {1x}. See: BAGD—874d; THAYER—664c.

5474. **χαλκολίβανον** {2x} **chalkŏlibanŏn**, *khal-kol-ib'-an-on;* neut. of a compound of *5475* and *3030* (in the impl. mean of *whiteness* or *brilliancy*); *burnished copper,* an alloy of copper (or gold) and silver having a brilliant lustre:—fine brass {2x}.

Chalkolibanon is used of "white or shining copper or bronze," and describes the feet of the Lord, in Rev 1:15 and 2:18. See: BAGD—875a; THAYER—664c.

5475. **χαλκός** {5x} **chalkŏs**, *khal-kos';* perh. from *5465* through the idea of *hollowing* out as a vessel (this metal being chiefly used for that purpose); *copper* (the substance, or some implement or coin made of it):—brass {3x}, money {2x}.

Chalkos, primarily "brass," became used for metals in general, later was applied to bronze, a mixture of copper and tin, then, by metonymy, to any article made of these metals, e.g., **(1)** money, Mt 10:9, ["brass" used for money]; Mk 6:8; 12:41; **(2)** a sounding instrument, 1 Cor 13:1, figurative of a person destitute of love; and **(3)** the metal itself in Rev 18:12. See: BAGD—875a; THAYER—664d.

5476. **χαμαί** {2x} **chamai**, *kham-ah'-ee;* adv. perh. from the base of *5490* through the idea of a *fissure* in the soil; *earthward,* i.e. *prostrate:*—on the ground {1x}, to the ground {1x}.

Chamai, signifies "on the ground," **(1)** Jn 9:6, of the act of Christ in spitting on the "ground" before anointing the eyes of a blind man; and **(2)** in Jn 18:6, "to the ground," of the fall of the rabble that had come to seize Christ in Gethsemane. See: BAGD—875b; THAYER—664d.

5477. **Χανάαν** {2x} **Chanaan**, *khan-ah'-an;* of Heb. or. [3667]; *Chanaan* (i.e. *Kenaan*), the early name of Pal.:—*Chanaan* {2x}. See: BAGD—875b; THAYER—664d.

5478. **Χαναναῖος** {1x} **Chanaanaiŏs**, *khan-ah-an-ah'-yos;* from *5477;* a *Chanaanæan* (i.e. *Kenaanite*), or native of Gentile Pal.:—of Canaan {1x}. See: BAGD—875b; THAYER—664d.

5479. **χαρά** {59x} **chara**, *khar-ah';* from *5463; cheerfulness,* i.e. calm *delight:*—joy {51x}, gladness {3x}, joyful {1x}, joyous {1x}, joyfulness {1x}, joyfully + 3326 {1x}, greatly {1x}.

Chara, "joy, delight," is akin to *chairo,* "to rejoice." **(1)** The word is sometimes used, by metonymy, of the occasion or cause of "joy": **(1a)** Lk 2:10 (lit., "I announce to you a great joy"); **(1b)** Phil 4:1, where the readers are called the apostle's "joy"; so 1 Th 2:19, 20; **(1c)** Heb 12:2, of the object of Christ's "joy"; **(1d)** Jas 1:2, where it is connected with falling into trials; **(1e)** perhaps also in Mt 25:21, 23, where some regard it as signifying, concretely, the circumstances attending cooperation in the authority of the Lord. **(2)** In Heb 12:11, "joyous" represents the phrase *meta,* "with," followed by *chara,* lit., "with joy", so in Heb 10:34, "joyfully"; **(3)** in 2 Cor 7:4 the noun is used with the middle voice of *huperperisseuo,* "to abound more exceedingly," and translated "(I am exceeding joyful"). See: TDNT—9:359, 1298; BAGD—875c; THAYER—664d.

5480. **χάραγμα** {9x} **charagma**, *khar'-ag-mah;* from the same as *5482;* a *scratch* or *etching,* i.e. *stamp* (as a *badge* of servitude), or *sculptured* figure (*statue*):—graven {1x}, mark {8x}.

Charagma, "to engrave", denotes **(1)** "a mark" or "stamp," e.g., Rev 13:16, 17; 14:9, 11; 15:2; 16:2; 19:20; 20:4; **(2)** "a thing graven," Acts 17:29. See: TDNT—9:416, 1308; BAGD—876a; THAYER—665b.

5481. **χαρακτήρ** {1x} **charaktēr**, *khar-ak-tare';* from the same as *5482;* a *graver* (the tool or the person), i.e. (by impl.) *engraving* (["*character*"], the *figure* stamped, i.e. an exact *copy* or [fig.] *representation*):—express image {1x}.

Charakter, denotes, firstly, **(1)** "a tool for graving" (from *charasso,* "to cut into, to engross"; cf. Eng., "character," "characteristic"); then, "a stamp" or "impress," as on a coin or a seal, in which case the seal or die which makes an impression bears the "image" produced by it, and, *vice versa,* all the features of the "image" correspond respectively with those of the instrument producing it. **(2)** In the NT it is used metaphorically in Heb 1:3, of the Son of God as "the express image of His substance." The phrase expresses the fact that the Son "is both personally distinct from, and yet literally equal to, Him of whose essence He is the imprint. The Son of God is not merely his "image" (His *charakter*), He is the "image" or impress of His substance, or essence. It is the fact of complete similarity which this word stresses. See: TDNT—9:418, 1308; BAGD—876b; THAYER—665b.

5482. **χάραξ** {1x} **charax**, *khar'-ax;* from χαράσσω **charassō** (to *sharpen,* to a point; akin to *1125* through the idea of *scratching*); a *stake,* i.e. (by impl.) a *palisade* or *rampart* (military *mound* for circumvallation in a siege):—trench {1x}.

The dirt for making the siege mound came from digging a trench. See: BAGD—876b; THAYER—665c.

5483. **χαρίζομαι** {23x} **charizŏmai**, *khar-id'-zom-ahee;* mid. voice from *5485;* to grant as a *favor,* i.e. gratuitously, in kindness, pardon or rescue:—forgive {11x}, give {6x}, freely give {2x}, deliver {2x}, grant {1x}, frankly forgive {1x}.

Charizomai, as a verb, means "to bestow a favor unconditionally," is used **(1)** of the act of "forgiveness," whether **(1a)** divine, Eph 4:32; Col 2:13; 3:13; or **(1b)** human, Lk 7:42, 43 (debt); 2 Cor 2:7, 10; 12:13; Eph 4:32 (1st mention). **(2)** It also means "to gratify, to do what is pleasing to anyone" and is translated "deliver": "For if I be an offender, or have committed any thing worthy of death, I refuse not to die: but if there be none of these things whereof these accuse me, no man may deliver me unto them. I appeal unto Caesar" (Acts 25:11 to give Paul over to the Jews so as to gratify their wishes; cf. 25:16). Syn.: 325, 525, 629, 591, 859, 1325, 1560, 1659, 1807, 1929, 3086, 3860, 4506. See: TDNT—9:372, 1298; BAGD—876c; THAYER—665c.

5484. **χάριν** {9x} **charin**, *khar'-in;* acc. of *5485* as prep.; through *favor* of, i.e. *on account* of:—for this cause + 5127 {3x}, because of {2x}, wherefore + 3739 {1x}, wherefore 5101 {1x}, for . . . sake {1x}, to speak reproachfully + 3059 {1x}. Cf. Lk 7:47; Gal 3:19; Eph 3:1; 3:14; 1 Ti 5:14; Titus 1:5, 11; 1 Jn 3:12; Jude 16. See: BAGD—877a; THAYER—665d.

5485. **χάρις** {156x} **charis**, *khar'-ece;* from *5463; graciousness* (as *gratifying*), of manner or act (abstr. or concr.; lit., fig., or spiritual; espec. the divine influence upon the heart, and its reflection in the life; incl. *gratitude*):—grace {130x}, favour {6x}, thanks {4x}, thank {4x}, thank + 2192 {3x}, pleasure {2x}, misc. {7x} = acceptable, benefit, gift, gracious, joy, liberality.

(1) Grace indicates favor on the part of the giver, thanks on the part of the receiver. **(2)** Although *charis* is related to sins and is the attribute of God that they evoke, God's *eleos* (1656), the free gift for the forgiveness of sins, is related to the misery that sin brings. **(3)** God's tender sense of our misery displays itself in his efforts to lessen and entirely remove it—efforts that are hindered and defeated only by man's continued perverseness. **(4)** Grace removes guilt; mercy removes misery. It has various uses, **(5)** objective, that which bestows or occasions pleasure, delight, or causes favorable regard; it is applied, e.g., **(5a)** to beauty, or gracefulness of person, Lk 2:40; **(5b)** an act, 2 Cor 8:6, or **(5c)** speech, Lk 4:22, "gracious words"; Col 4:6;

(6) subjective, **(6a)** on the part of the bestower, **(6a1)** the friendly disposition from which the kindly act proceeds, graciousness, loving-kindness, goodwill generally, e.g., Acts 7:10; **(6a2)** especially with reference to the divine favor or "grace," e.g., Acts 14:26; **(6a3)** in this respect there is stress on its freeness and universality, its spontaneous character, as in the case of God's redemptive mercy, and the pleasure or joy He designs for the recipient; **(6a4)** thus it is set in contrast with debt, Rom 4:4, 16, with works, 11:6, and with law, Jn 1:17; see also, e.g., Rom 6:14, 15; Gal 5:4; **(6b)** on the part of the receiver, **(6b1)** a sense of the favor bestowed, a feeling of gratitude, e.g., Rom 6:17 ("thanks"); **(6b2)** in this respect it sometimes signifies "to be thankful," e.g., Lk 17:9 ("doth he thank the servant?" lit., "hath he thanks to"); 1 Ti 1:12; **(6c)** in another objective sense, the effect of "grace," the spiritual state of those who have experienced its exercise, whether **(6c1)** a state of "grace," e.g., Rom 5:2; 1 Pet 5:12; 2 Pet 3:18, or **(6c2)** a proof thereof in practical effects, deeds of "grace," e.g., 1 Cor 16:3, "liberality"; 2 Cor 8:6, 19; **(6c3)** in 2 Cor 9:8 it means the sum of earthly blessings; **(6c4)** the power and equipment for ministry, e.g., Rom 1:5; 12:6; 15:15; 1 Cor 3:10; Gal 2:9; Eph 3:2, 7.

(7) To be in favor with is to find "grace" with, e.g., Acts 2:47; **(7a)** hence it appears in this sense at the beginning and the end of several epistles, where the writer desires "grace" from God for the readers, e.g., Rom 1:7; 1 Cor 1:3; **(7)** in this respect it is connected with the imperative mood of the word *chairo,* "to rejoice," a mode of greeting among Greeks, e.g., Acts 15:23; 2 Jn 10, 11, "God speed." **(8)** The fact that "grace" is received **(8a)** both from God the Father, 2 Cor 1:12, and from Christ, Gal 1:6; Rom 5:15 (where both are mentioned), is a testimony to the deity of Christ. **(8b)** See also 2 Th 1:12, where the phrase "according to the grace of our God and the Lord Jesus Christ" is to be taken with each of the preceding clauses, "in you," "and ye in Him." **(9)** In Jas 4:6, "But He giveth more grace", the statement is to be taken in connection with the preceding verse, which contains two remonstrating, rhetorical questions, "Think ye that the Scripture speaketh in vain?" and "Doth the Spirit (the Holy Spirit) which He made to dwell in us long unto envying?" The implied answer to each is "it cannot be so." Accordingly, if those who are acting so flagrantly, as if it were so, will listen to the Scripture instead of letting it speak in vain, and will act so that the Holy Spirit may have His way within, God will give even "a greater grace," namely, all that follows from humbleness and from turning away from the world. See: TDNT—9:372, 1298; BAGD—877b; THAYER—665d.

5486. **χάρισμα** {17x} **charisma**, *khar'-is-mah;* from *5483;* a (divine) *gratuity,* i.e. *deliverance* (from danger or passion); (spec.) a (spiritual) *endowment,* i.e. (subj.) relig. *qualification,* or (obj.) miraculous *faculty:*—free gift {2x}, gift {15x}.

(1) *Charisma* is a favor which one receives without any merit of his own. **(2)** It is "a gift of grace, a gift involving grace" (*charis*) on the part of God as the donor, is used **(3)** of His free bestowments upon sinners, Rom 5:15, 16; 6:23; 11:29; **(4)** of His endowments upon believers by the operation of the Holy Spirit in the churches, Rom 12:6; 1 Cor 1:7; 12:4, 9, 28, 30, 31; 1 Ti 4:14; 2 Ti 1:6; 1 Pet 4:10; **(5)** of that which is imparted through human instruction, Rom 1:11; **(6)** of the natural "gift" of continence, consequent upon the grace of God as Creator, 1 Cor 7:7; **(7)** of gracious deliverances granted in answer to the prayers of fellow believers, 2 Cor 1:11. See: TDNT—9:402, 1298; BAGD—878d; THAYER—667a.

5487. **χαριτόω** {2x} **charitŏō**, *khar-ee-tŏ'-o;* from *5485;* to *grace,* i.e. indue with special *honor:*—make accepted {1x}, be highly favoured {1x}.

Charitoo, to endow with *charis,* primarily signified "to make graceful or gracious," and came to denote, "to cause to find favor," **(1)** Lk 1:28, "highly favored" (i.e., "endued with grace"); **(2)** in Eph 1:6, it is translated "freely bestowed"; it does not here mean to endue with grace. Grace implies more than favor; grace is a free gift, favor may be deserved or gained. See: TDNT—9:372, 1298; BAGD—879a; THAYER—667a.

5488. **Χαρράν** {2x} **Charrhan**, *khar-hran';* of Heb. or. [2771]; *Charrhan* (i.e. *Charan*), a place in Mesopotamia:—Charran {2x}. See: BAGD—879b; THAYER—667b.

5489. **χάρτης** {1x} **chartēs**, *khar'-tace;* from the same as *5482;* a *sheet* ("chart") of writing-material (as to be *scribbled* over):—paper {1x}.

Chartes, "a sheet of paper made of strips of papyrus" (whence Eng., "paper", Eng., "chart," "charter," etc.), the word is used in 2 Jn 12. The papyrus reed grew in ancient times in great profusion in the Nile and was used as a material for writing. From Egypt its use spread to other countries and it was the universal material for writing in general in Greece and Italy during the most flourishing periods of their literature. The pith of the stem of the plant was cut into thin strips, placed side by side to form a sheath. Another layer was laid upon this at right angles to it. The two layers were united by moisture and pressure and frequently with the addition of glue. The sheets, after being dried and polished, were ready for use. Normally, the writing is on that side of the papyrus on which the fibers lie horizontally, parallel to the length of the roll, but where the material was scarce the writer used the other side also (cf. Rev 5:1). Papyrus continued to be used until the seventh cent., A.D., when the conquest of Egypt by the Arabs led to the disuse of the material for literary purposes and the use of vellum till the 12th century. See: BAGD—879b; THAYER—667b.

5490. **χάσμα** {1x} **chasma**, *khas'-mah;* from a form of an obs. primary χάω **chaō**, (to "*gape*" or "*yawn*"); a "*chasm*" or *vacancy* (impassable *interval*):—gulf {1x}. See: BAGD—879b; THAYER—667b.

5491. **χεῖλος** {7x} **chĕilŏs**, *khi'-los;* from a form of the same as *5490;* a *lip* (as a *pouring* place); fig. a *margin* (of water):—lip {6x}, shore {1x}.

Cheilos is used **(1)** of the organ of speech, **(1a)** Mt 15:8 and Mk 7:6, where "honoring with the lips," besides meaning empty words, may have reference to a Jewish custom of putting to the mouth the tassel of the *tallith* (the woollen scarf wound round the head and neck during prayer), as a sign of acceptance of the Law from the heart; **(1b)** Rom 3:13; 1 Cor 14:21 (from Is 28:11, 12, speaking of the Assyrian foe as God's message to disobedient Israel); Heb 13:15; 1 Pet 3:10; **(2)** metaphorically, of "the brink or edge of things," as of the sea shore, Heb 11:12, lit., "the shore (of the sea)." See: BAGD—879c; THAYER—667b.

5492. **χειμάζω** {1x} **chĕimazō**, *khi-mad'-zo;* from the same as *5494;* to *storm,* i.e. (pass.) to *labor under a gale:*—be tossed with tempest {1x}.

Cheimazo, from *cheima,* "winter cold," primarily, "to expose to winter cold," signifies "to drive with a storm"; in the passive voice, "to be driven with storm, to be tempest-tossed," Acts 27:18, "being . . . tossed with a tempest." See: BAGD—879c; THAYER—667c.

5493. **χείμαρρος** {1x} **chĕimarrhŏs**, *khi'-mar-hros;* from the base of *5494* and *4482;* a *storm-runlet,* i.e. *winter-torrent:*—brook {1x}.

Cheimarrhos, lit., "winter-flowing" (from *cheima,* "winter," and *rheo,* "to flow"), a stream which runs only in winter or when swollen with rains, a "brook" John 18:1. See: BAGD—879c; THAYER—667c.

5494. **χειμών** {6x} **chĕimōn**, *khi-mone';* from a der. of χέω **chĕō**, (to *pour;* akin to the base of *5490* through the idea of a *channel*), mean. a *storm* (as *pouring* rain); by impl. the *rainy* season, i.e. *winter:*—tempest {1x}, foul weather {1x}, winter {4x}.

Cheimon denotes "winter," in Mt 24:20; Mk 13:18; Jn 10:22; 2 Ti 4:21. See: BAGD—879d; THAYER—667c.

5495. **χείρ** {179x} **chĕir**, *khire;* perh. from the base of *5494* in the sense of its congener the base of *5490* (through the idea of *hollowness* for grasping); the *hand* (lit. or fig. [*power*]; espec. [by Heb.] a *means* or *instrument*):—hand {179x}.

Cheir is used, besides its ordinary significance, **(1)** in the idiomatic phrases, "by the hand of," "at the hand of," etc., to signify "by the agency of," Acts 5:12; 7:35; 17:25; 14:3; Gal 3:19 (cf. Lev 26:46); Rev 19:2; **(2)** metaphorically, for the power of God, e.g., Lk 1:66; 23:46; Jn 10:28, 29; Acts 11:21; 13:11; Heb 1:10; 2:7; 10:31; **(3)** by metonymy, for power, e.g., Mt 17:22; Lk 24:7; Jn 10:39; Acts 12:11. See: TDNT—9:424, 1309; BAGD—879d; THAYER—667c.

5496. **χειραγωγέω** {2x} **chĕiragōgĕō**, *khi-rag-ogue-eh'-o;* from *5497;* to be a *hand-leader,* i.e. to *guide* (a blind person):—lead by the hand {2x}. Cf. Acts 9:8; 22:11. See: TDNT—9:435, 1309; BAGD—880d; THAYER—668a.

5497. **χειραγωγός** {1x} **chĕiragōgŏs**, *khi rag-o-gos';* from *5495* and a redupl. form of *71;* a *hand-leader,* i.e. personal *conductor* (of a blind person):—some to lead by the hand {1x}. See: TDNT—9:435, 1309; BAGD—880d; THAYER—668a.

5498. **χειρόγραφον** {1x} **chĕirŏgraphŏn**, *khi-rog'-raf-on;* neut. of a compound of *5495* and *1125;* something *handwritten* ("*chirograph*"), i.e. a *manuscript* (spec. a legal *document* or *bond* [fig.]):—handwriting {1x}. See: TDNT—9:435, 1309; BAGD—880d; THAYER—668.

5499. **χειροποίητος** {6x} **chĕirŏpŏiētŏs**, *khi-rop-oy'-ay-tos;* from *5495* and a der. of *4160; manufactured,* i.e. of *human construction:*—made by hands {1x}, made with hands {6x}

Cheiropoietos, "made by hand," of human handiwork (*cheir,* and *poieo,* "to make"), is said **(1)** of the temple in Jerusalem, Mk 14:58; **(2)** temples in general, Acts 7:48; 17:24; **(3)** negatively, of the heavenly and spiritual tabernacle, Heb 9:11; **(4)** of the holy place in the earthly tabernacle, Heb 9:24; **(5)** of circumcision, Eph 2:11. See: TDNT—9:436, 1309; BAGD—880d; THAYER—668b.

5500. **χειροτονέω** {4x} **chĕirŏtŏnĕō**, *khi-rot-on-eh'-o;* from a comp. of *5495* and τείνω **tĕinō** (to *stretch*); to be a *hand-reacher,* or *voter* (by raising the hand), i.e. (gen.) to *select* or *appoint:*—choose {1x}, ordain {3x}.

Cheirotoneo, as a verb, **(1)** primarily used of voting in the Athenian legislative assembly and meaning "to stretch forth the hands" [*cheir,* "the hand," *teino,* "to stretch"], is not to be taken in its literal sense. **(2)** *Cheirotoneo* is said of "the appointment, the ordaining" of elders by apostolic missionaries in the various churches which they revisited, Acts 14:23, "had appointed," i.e., by the recognition of those who had been manifesting themselves as gifted of God to discharge the functions of elders. **(3)** It is also said of those who were "appointed" (not by voting, but with general approbation) by the churches in Greece to accompany the apostle in conveying their gifts to the poor saints in Judea, 2 Cor 8:19. **(4)** The KJV of 1611 had an addendum added to the books detailing the theme or date of the letter. This word is so used in the ending to 2 Timothy and Titus. See: TDNT—9:437, 1309; BAGD—881a; THAYER—668b.

5501. **χείρων** {11x} **chĕirōn**, *khi'-rone;* irreg. comp. of *2556;* from an obs. equiv. χέρης **chĕrēs** (of uncert. der.); *more evil* or *aggravated* (phys., ment. or mor.):—worse {7x}, sorer {1x}, worse + 1519 + 3588 {1x}, worse and worse + 1909 + 3588 {1x}, a worse thing + 5100 {1x}.

Cheiron, used as the comparative degree of *kakos,* "evil," describes **(1)** the condition of certain men, Mt 12:45; Lk 11:26; 2 Pet 2:20; **(2)** evil men themselves and seducers, 2 Ti. 3:13; **(3)** indolent men who refuse to provide for their own households, and are worse than unbelievers, 1 Ti 5:8; **(4)** a rent in a garment, Mt 9:16; Mk 2:21; **(5)** an error, Mt 27:64; **(6)** a person suffering from a malady, Mk 5:26; **(7)** a possible physical affliction, Jn 5:14; **(8)** a punishment, Heb 10:29, "sorer." See: BAGD—881b; THAYER—668c.

5502. **χερουβίμ** {1x} **chĕrŏubim**, *kher-oo-beem';* plur. of Heb. or. [3742]; "*cherubim*" (i.e. *cherubs* or *kerubim*):—cherubims {1x}.

Cherubim, are regarded by some as the ideal representatives of redeemed animate creation. In the tabernacle and Temple they were represented by the two golden figures of two-winged living creatures. They were all of one piece with the golden lid of the ark of the covenant in the Holy of Holies signifying that the prospect of approaching the Living God by any human means other than through a blood sacrifice was protected by the angels just as the angels protected sinful man from approaching the tree of life in the Garden of Eden after he and Eve sinned. The *cherubim* faces were towards this mercy seat, suggesting a longing on their behalf to "look into" this salvation, 1 Pet 1:12.

The first reference to the "*cherubim*" is in Gen 3:24, which should read ". . . at the East of the Garden of Eden He caused to dwell in a tabernacle the *cherubim,* and the flaming sword which turned itself to keep the way of the Tree of Life." This was not simply to keep fallen human beings out; the presence of the "*cherubim*" suggests that redeemed men, restored to God on God's conditions, would have access to the Tree of Life. (See Rev. 22:14). In the NT the word is found in Heb 9:5, where the reference is to the ark in the tabernacle, and the thought is suggested of those who minister to the manifestation of the glory of God. Between these figures God was regarded as having fixed his dwelling place. See: TDNT—9:438, 1312; BAGD—881b; THAYER—668c.

5503. **χήρα** {27x} **chēra**, *khay'-rah;* fem. of a presumed der. appar. from the base of *5490* through the idea of *deficiency;* a *widow* (as *lacking* a husband), lit. or fig.:—widow {27x}.

Chera is a widow, one whose husband is dead. **(1)** It is found in Mk 12:40, 42, 43; Lk 2:37; 4:25, 26, lit., "a woman a widow"; 7:12; 18:3, 5; 20:47; 21:2, 3; Acts 6:1; 9:39, 41; 1 Ti 5:3 (twice), 4, 5, 11, 16 (twice); Jas 1:27. **(2)** 1 Ti 5:9 refers to elderly "widows" (not an ecclesiastical "order"), recognized, for relief or maintenance by the church (cf. vv. 3, 16), as those who had fulfilled the conditions mentioned; where relief could be ministered by those who had relatives that were "widows" (a likely circumstance in large families), the church was not to be responsible; there is an intimation of the tendency to shelve individual responsibility at the expense of church funds. **(3)** In Rev 18:7, it is used figuratively of a city forsaken. See: TDNT—9:440, 1313; BAGD—881c; THAYER—668d.

5504. **χθές** {3x} **chthĕs**, *khthes;* of uncert. der.; *"yesterday";* by extens. *in time past* or *hitherto:*—yesterday {3x}. Cf. John 4:52; Acts 7:28; Heb. 13:8. See: BAGD—881d; THAYER—668d.

5505. **χιλιάς** {23x} **chilias**, *khil-ee-as';* from *5507;* one *thousand* ("*chiliad*"):—thousand {23x}. See: TDNT—9:466, 1316; BAGD—882a; THAYER—669a.

5506. **χιλίαρχος** {22x} **chiliarchŏs**, *khil-ee'-ar-khos;* from *5507* and *757;* the *commander of a thousand* soldiers ("*chiliarch*"), i.e. *colonel:*—chief captain {19x}, captain {2x}, high captain {1x}.

Chiliarchos, **(1)** denoting "a commander of 1000 soldiers" (from *chilios,* "a thousand," and *archo,* "to rule"), was the Greek word for the Persian vizier, and for the Roman military tribune, the commander of a Roman cohort, e.g., Jn 18:12; Acts 21:31–33, 37. **(2)** One such commander was constantly in charge of the Roman garrison in Jerusalem. **(3)** The word became used also for any military commander, e.g., a "captain" or "chief captain," Mk 6:21; Rev 6:15; 19:18. See: BAGD—881d; THAYER—668d.

5507. **χίλιοι** {11x} **chiliŏi**, *khil'-ee-oy;* plur. of uncert. aff.; a *thousand:*—thousand {11x}. See: TDNT—9:466, 1316; BAGD—882a; THAYER—669a.

5508. **Χίος** {1x} **Chiŏs**, *khee'-os;* of uncert. der.; *Chios,* an island in the Mediterranean:—*Chios* {1x}. See: BAGD—882b; THAYER—669a.

5509. **χιτών** {11x} **chitōn**, *khee-tone';* of for. or. [3801]; a *tunic* or *shirt:*—clothes {1x}, coat {9x}, garment {1x}.

(1) A *chiton* was a tunic, an undergarment, usually worn next to the skin, a garment, a vestment. **(2)** It denotes "the inner vest or undergarment," and is to be distinguished, as such, from the *himation.* **(2a)** The distinction is made, for instance, in the Lord's command in Mt 5:40: "If any man would go to law with thee, and take away thy coat (*chiton*), (*himation*) also." **(2b)** The order is reversed in Lk 6:29, and the difference lies in this, that in Mt 5:40 the Lord is referring to a legal process, so the claimant is supposed to claim the inner garment, the less costly. The defendant is to be willing to let him have the more valuable one too. In the passage in Luke an act of violence is in view, and there is no mention of going to law. So the outer garment is the first one which would be seized. When the soldiers had crucified Jesus they took His garments (*himation,* in the plural), His outer garments, and the "coat," the *chiton,* the inner garment, which was without seam, woven from the top throughout, Jn 19:23. The outer garments were easily divisible among the four soldiers, but they could not divide the *chiton* without splitting it, so they cast lots for it.

(3) Dorcas was accustomed to make coats (*chiton*) and garments (*himation*), Acts 9:39, that is, the close fitting undergarments and the long, flowing outer robes. **(4)** A person was said to be "naked" (*gumnos*), whether he was without clothing, or had thrown off his outer garment, e.g., his *ependutes,* (1903), and was clad in a light undergarment, as was the case with Peter, in Jn 21:7 and the young man in Mk 14:51–52, (Mark himself?). **(5)** The high priest, in rending his clothes after the reply the Lord gave him in answer to his challenge, rent his undergarments (*chiton*), the more forcibly to express his assumed horror and indignation, Mk 14:63. **(6)** In Jude 23, "the garment spotted by the flesh" is the *chiton,* the metaphor of the undergarment being appropriate; for it would be that which was brought into touch with the pollution of the flesh.

Syn.: **(A)** *Himation* (2440) refers to garments in a general sense (Mt 11:8; 26:65); or when used specifically, it refers to the large outer garment that a man could sleep in (cf. Ex 22:26). **(B)** The *chlamys* (5511) refers to a garment of dignity and office. **(C)** A *stole* (4749) is any stately robe, especially a long sweeping garment that reaches to the feet or a garment that has a train that sweeps the ground; a garment of special solemnity, richness, and beauty. **(D)** *Poderes* (4158) refers, like stole, to a long garment reaching the ankles. With reference to the high priestly garments, the *poderes* only refers to the robe; *stole* refers to the whole array. See: BAGD—882b; THAYER—669a.

5510. **χιών** {3x} **chiōn**, *khee-one';* perh. akin to the base of *5490* (*5465*) or *5494* (as *descending* or *empty*); *snow:*—snow {3x}. Cf. Mt 28:3; Mk 9:3; Rev 1:14. See: BAGD—882b; THAYER—669a.

5511. **χλαμύς** {2x} **chlamus**, *khlam-ooce';* of uncert. der.; a military *cloak:*—robe {2x}.

A *chlamus* was an outer garment usually worn over the tunic (Mt 27: 28, 31). Syn.: cf. 5509 for discussion. See: BAGD—882b; THAYER—669b.

5512. **χλευάζω** {2x} **chlĕuazō**, *khlyoo-ad'-zo;* from a der. prob. of *5491;* to *throw out* the *lip,* i.e. *jeer* at:—mock {2x}. See: BAGD—882c; THAYER—669b.

5513. **χλιαρός** {1x} **chliarŏs**, *khlee-ar-os';* from χλίω **chliō**, (to *warm*); *tepid:*—lukewarm {1x}. See: TDNT—2:876, 296; BAGD—882c; THAYER—669b.

5514. **Χλόη** {1x} **Chlŏē**, *khlŏ'-ay;* fem. of appar. a primary word; "*green*"; *Chloë,* a Chr. female:—*Chloe* {1x}. See: BAGD—882c; THAYER—669b.

5515. **χλωρός** {4x} **chlōrŏs**, *khlo-ros';* from the same as *5514; greenish,* i.e. *verdant, dun-colored:*—green {3x}, pale {1x}.

Chloros, (akin to *chloe,* "tender foliage", cf. the name "Chloe," 1 Cor 1:11, and Eng., "chlorine"), denotes **(1)** "pale green," the color of young grass, Mk 6:39; Rev 8:7; 9:4, "green thing"; hence, **(2)** "pale," Rev 6:8, the color of the horse whose rider's name is Death. See: BAGD—882d; THAYER—669b.

5516. **χξς** {1x} **chi xi stigma**, *khee xee stig'-ma;* the 22nd, 14th and an obs. letter (*4742* as a *cross*) of the Greek alphabet (intermediate between the 5th and 6th), used as numbers; denoting respectively 600, 60 and 6; 666 as a numeral:—six hundred threescore and six {1x}. See: BAGD—882d; THAYER—669b.

5517. **χοϊκός** {4x} **chŏïkŏs**, *khŏ-ik-os';* from *5522; dusty* or *dirty* (*soil*-like), i.e. (by impl.) *terrene:*—earthy {4x}.

Choikos denotes "earthy," made of earth, from *chous,* "soil, earth thrown down or heaped up," 1 Cor 15:47–49. See: TDNT—9:472, 1318; BAGD—883a; THAYER—669c.

5518. **χοῖνιξ** {2x} **chŏinix**, *khoy'-nix;* of uncertain der.; a *chœnix* or certain dry measure:—measure {2x}.

Choinix, as a noun, means a dry "measure" of rather less than a quart, about "as much as would support a person of moderate appetite for a day," occurs in Rev 6:6 (twice). Usually eight *choenixes* could be bought for a *denarius* (about 9 1/2d.); this passage predicts circumstances in which the *denarius* is the price of one *choenix*. Syn.: 280, 488, 943, 2884, 3313, 3354, 3358, 4057, 4568, 5234, 5249. See: BAGD—883b; THAYER—669c.

5519. **χοῖρος** {14x} **chŏirŏs**, *khoy'-ros;* of uncert. der.; a *hog:*—swine {14x}.

Choiros, "a swine," is used in the plural, in the Synoptic Gospels only, Mt 7:6; 8:30, 31, 32; Mk 5:11, 13, 16; Lk 8:32, 33; 15:15, 16. See: BAGD—883b; THAYER—669c.

5520. **χολάω** {1x} **chŏlaō**, *khol-ah'-o;* from *5521; to be bilious,* i.e. (by impl.) *irritable* (*enraged,* "choleric"):—be angry {1x}.

Cholao, connected with *chole,* "gall, bile," which became used metaphorically to signify bitter anger, means "to be enraged," Jn 7:23, in the Lord's remonstrance with the Jews on account of their indignation at His having made a man whole on the Sabbath Day. See: BAGD—883b; THAYER—669c.

5521. **χολή** {2x} **chŏlē**, *khol-ay';* fem. of an equiv. perh. akin to the same as *5514* (from the *greenish* hue); "*gall*" or *bile,* i.e. (by anal.) *poison* or an *anodyne* (wormwood, poppy, etc.):—gall {2x}.

Chole, a word probably connected with *chloe,* "yellow," denotes "gall," **(1)** literal, Mt 27:34 (cf. Ps 69:21); some regard the word here as referring to myrrh, on account of Mk 15:23; **(2)** metaphorical, Acts 8:23, where "gall of bitterness" stands for extreme wickedness, productive of evil fruit. See: BAGD—883b; THAYER—669c.

5522. **χόος** {2x} **chŏŏs**, *khŏ'-os;* from the base of *5494;* a *heap* (as *poured* out), i.e. *rubbish;* loose *dirt:*—dust {2x}. Cf. Mk 6:11 and Rev 18:19. See: BAGD—883c, 884b; THAYER—669d.

5523. **Χοραζίν** {2x} **Chŏrazin**, *khor-ad-zin';* of uncert. der.; *Chorazin,* a place in Pal.:—*Chorazin* {2x}. See: BAGD—883c; THAYER—883c; THAYER—669d.

5524. **χορηγέω** {2x} **chŏrēgĕō**, *khor-ayg-eh'-o;* from a compound of *5525* and *71;* to be a *dance-leader,* i.e. (gen.) to *furnish:*—give {1x}, minister {1x}.

Choregeo, primarily, among the Greeks, signified **(1)** "to lead a stage chorus or dance" (*choros,* and *hegeomai,* "to lead"), then, **(2)** "to defray the expenses of a chorus"; hence, later, **(3)** metaphorically, "to supply," **(3a)** 2 Cor 9:10 (2nd part, "to minister"); **(3b)** 1 Pet 4:11, "giveth." See: BAGD—883d; THAYER—670a.

5525. **χορός** {1x} **chŏrŏs**, *khor-os';* of uncert. der.; a *ring,* i.e. round *dance* ("choir"):—dancing {1x}. See: BAGD—883d; THAYER—670a.

5526. **χορτάζω** {15x} **chŏrtazō**, *khor-tad'-zo;* from *5528;* to *fodder,* i.e. (gen.) to *gorge* (*supply food* in abundance):—feed {1x}, be full {1x}, fill {12x}, satisfy {1x}. See: BAGD—883d; THAYER—670a.

5527. **χόρτασμα** {1x} **chŏrtasma**, *khor'-tas-mah;* from *5526; forage,* i.e. *food:*—sustenance {1x}.

Chortasma refers to food, (vegetable) sustenance, whether for men or flocks, Acts 7:11. See: BAGD—884a; THAYER—670b.

5528. **χόρτος** {15x} **chŏrtŏs**, *khor'-tos;* appar. a primary word; a "*court*" or "*garden*", i.e. (by impl. of *pasture*) *herbage* or *vegetation:*—blade {2x}, grass {12x}, hay {1x}.

Chortos primarily denoted "a feeding enclosure"; then, "food," especially grass for feeding cattle; it is translated **(1)** "grass" in Mt 6:30; 14:19; Mk 6:39 (where "the green grass" is the first evidence of early spring); Lk 12:28; Jn 6:10; Jas 1:10, 11; 1 Pet 1:24; Rev 8:7; 9:4; **(2)** "blade" in Mt 13:26; Mk 4:28; **(3)** "hay" in 1 Cor 3:12, used figuratively. See: BAGD—884a; THAYER—670b.

5529. **Χουζᾶς** {1x} **Chŏuzas**, *khood-zas';* of uncert. or.: *Chuzas,* an officer of Herod:—Chuza {1x}. See: BAGD—884b; THAYER—670b.

5530. **χράομαι** {11x} **chraŏmai**, *khrah'-om-ahee;* mid. voice of a primary verb (perh. rather from *5495,* to *handle*); to *furnish* what is needed; (give an *oracle,* "*graze*" [touch slightly], *light* upon, etc.), i.e. (by impl.) to *employ* or (by extens.) to *act toward* one in a given manner:—entreat {1x}, use {10x}.

Chraomai, denotes **(1)** "to use," Acts 27:17; 1 Cor 7:21, where "use it rather" means "use your bond-service rather"; 7:31, where "they that use (this world)" is followed by the strengthened form *katachraomai,* rendered "abusing," or "using to the full"; 9:12, 15; 2 Cor 1:17; 3:12; 13:10; 1 Ti 1:8, of "using" the Law lawfully, i.e., agreeably to its designs; 1 Ti 5:23; **(2)** "deal with," Acts 27:3. See: BAGD—884b; THAYER—670c. comp. *5531; 5534.*

5531. **χράω** {1x} **chraō**, *khrah'-o;* prob. the same as the base of *5530;* to *loan:*—lend {1x}. Syn.: *Daneizo* (1155) means to lend on interest, as a business transaction; whereas, *chrao* means to lend, grant the use of, as a friendly act. See: BAGD—884d, 433a; THAYER—670d.

5532. **χρεία** {49x} **chrĕia**, *khri'-ah;* from the base of *5530* or *5534; employment,* i.e. an *affair;* also (by impl.) *occasion, demand, requirement* or *destitution:*—need {25x}, need + 2192 {14x}, necessity {3x}, use {2x}, needful {1x}, necessary {1x}, business {1x}, lack {1x}, wants {1x}. See: BAGD—884d; THAYER—670d.

5533. **χρεωφειλέτης** {2x} **chrĕōphĕilĕtēs**, *khreh-o-fi-let'-ace;* from a der. of *5531* and *3781;* a *loan-ower,* i.e. *indebted* person:—debtor {2x}. Cf. Lk 7:41; 16:5. See: BAGD—885b; THAYER—671b.

5534. **χρή** {1x} **chrē**, *khray;* third pers. sing. of the same as *5530* or *5531* used impers.; it *needs* (*must* or *should*) be:—ought {1x}.

Syn.: *Dei* (1165) expresses a logical necessity, *opheilo* (3784), a moral obligation; cf. *chre* (5534), Jas 3:10, "ought," which expresses a need resulting from the fitness of things. See: BAGD—885b; THAYER—671b.

5535. **χρῄζω** {5x} **chrē̦zō**, *khrade'-zo;* from *5532;* to *make* (i.e. *have*) *necessity,* i.e. *be in want* of:—need {2x}, have need {3x}.

Chrezo, "to need, to have need of" (akin to *chre,* "it is necessary, fitting"), is used in Mt 6:32;

Lk 11:8; 12:30; Rom 16:2, "hath need"; 2 Cor 3:1. See: BAGD—885b; THAYER—671b.

5536. **χρῆμα** {7x} **chrēma**, *khray'-mah;* something *useful* or *needed,* i.e. *wealth, price:*—money {4x}, riches {3x}.

Chrema, "what one uses or needs" (*chraomai,* "to use"), "a matter, business," hence denotes **(1)** "riches," Mk 10:23, 24; Lk 18:24. It also means lit., "a thing that one uses", hence, **(2)** "money," **(2a)** Acts 4:37, singular number, "a sum of money"; **(2b)** plural in Acts 8:18, 20; 24:26. See: TDNT—9:480, 1319; BAGD—885c; THAYER—671b.

5537. **χρηματίζω** {9x} **chrēmatizō**, *khray-mat-id'-zo;* from *5536;* to *utter an oracle* (comp. the orig. sense of *5530*), i.e. divinely *intimate;* by impl. (comp. the secular sense of *5532*) to constitute a *firm* for business, i.e. (gen.) *bear* as a *title:*—be warned of God {3x}, call {2x}, be admonished of God {1x}, reveal {1x}, speak {1x}, be warned from God {1x}.

Chrematizo means primarily, "to transact business," then, "to give advice to enquirers" (especially of official pronouncements of magistrates), or "a response to those consulting an oracle," came to signify the giving of a divine "admonition" or instruction or warning, in a general way; translated **(1)** "admonished" in Heb 8:5. Elsewhere it is translated **(2)** by the verb "to warn" in Mt 2:12, 22; Acts 10:22; 11:7. **(3)** It is also translated "spake" in Acts 12:25. **(4)** Occasionally it means "to be called or named", **(4a)** Rom 7:3; and **(4b)** Acts 11:26, of the name "Christians." Its primary significance, "to have business dealings with," led to this. They "were (publicly) called" Christians, because this was their chief business, following the Christ. See: TDNT—9:480, 1319; BAGD—885c; THAYER—671b.

5538. **χρηματισμός** {1x} **chrēmatismŏs**, *khray-mat-is-mos';* from *5537;* a divine *response* or *revelation:*—answer of God {1x}.

Chrematismos, "a divine response, an oracle," is used in Rom 11:4, of the answer given by God to Elijah's complaint against Israel. See: TDNT—9:482, 1319; BAGD—885d; THAYER—671c.

5539. **χρήσιμος** {1x} **chrēsimŏs**, *khray'-see-mos;* from *5540; serviceable:*—profit {1x}.

Chresimos means fit for use, useful, 2 Tim 2:14. See: BAGD—885d; THAYER—671d.

5540. **χρῆσις** {2x} **chrēsis**, *khray'-sis;* from *5530; employment,* i.e. (spec.) sexual *intercourse* (as an *occupation* of the body):—use {2x}. Cf. Rom 1:26, 27. See: BAGD—885d; THAYER—671d.

5541. **χρηστεύομαι** {1x} **chrēstĕuŏmai**, *khraste-yoo'-om-ahee;* mid. voice from *5543;* to *show oneself useful,* i.e. *act benevolently:*—be kind {1x}.

To be kind is to treat one as one's kin, one's own family, 1 Cor 13:4. See: TDNT—9:491, 1320; BAGD—886a; THAYER—671d.

5542. **χρηστολογία** {1x} **chrēstŏlŏgia**, *khrase-tol-og-ee'-ah;* from a compound of *5543* and *3004; fair speech,* i.e. *plausibility:*—good words {1x}.

This word means fair speaking, the smooth and plausible address which sounds good, easily received; yet deceptive. See: TDNT—9:492, 1320; BAGD—886a; THAYER—671d.

5543. **χρηστός** {7x} **chrēstŏs**, *khrase-tos';* from *5530; employed,* i.e. (by impl.) *useful* (in manner or morals):—better {1x}, easy {1x}, good {1x}, goodness {1x}, gracious {1x}, kind {2x}.

Chrestos, as an adjective, is said **(1)** of things, **(1a)** Mt 11:30, Christ's yoke being "easy"; **(1b)** of things, as wine, Lk 5:39, "better"; **(2)** of believers, Eph 4:32, "kind"; **(3)** of manners, "good", 1 Cor 15:33; **(4)** "goodness", Rom 2:4, of God. It is said **(4)** of the character of God as "kind", Lk 6:35, and "gracious", 1 Pet 2:3. See: TDNT—9:483, 1320; BAGD—886a; THAYER—671d.

5544. **χρηστότης** {10x} **chrēstŏtēs**, *khray-stot'-ace;* from *5543; usefulness,* i.e. mor. *excellence* (in character or demeanor):—gentleness {1x}, good {1x}, goodness {4x}, kindness {4x}.

Introduction: This word refers not to a virtue of a person that encompasses only to a person's words and countenance, it refers to the virtue that pervades and penetrates the whole nature, that mellows anything harsh and austere. It is that virtue that is gentle, charming, and calm, suited to the company of all good people, attracting their friendship, delightful in encouragement and moderate in manners. *Chrestotes,* as a noun, denotes **(1)** "good" **(1a)** in the sense of what is upright, righteous: "They are all gone out of the way, they are together become unprofitable; there is none that doeth good (*chrestotes*), no, not one." (Rom 3:12); **(1b)** in the sense of goodness of heart or act, said of God: "Behold therefore the goodness (*chrestotes*) and severity of God: on them which fell, severity, but toward thee, goodness (*chrestotes*), if thou continue in *his* goodness (*chrestotes*): otherwise thou also shalt be cut off." (Rom 11:22); **(2)** "kindness" (Eph 2:7; Titus 3:4; 2 Cor 6:6; Col 3:12; Gal 5:22). **(3)** It signifies "not merely goodness as a quality, rather it is goodness in action, goodness expressing itself in deeds; yet not goodness expressing itself in indignation against sin, for it is contrasted with severity in Rom 11:22, but in grace and tenderness and compassion." Syn.: 19. See: TDNT—9:489, 1320; BAGD—886b.

5545. **χρίσμα** {3x} **chrisma**, *khris'-mah;* from *5548;* an *unguent* or *smearing,* i.e. (fig.) the spec. *endowment* ("chrism") of the Holy Spirit:—anointing {2x}, unction {1x}.

Chrisma, as a verb, signifies "an unguent, or an anointing." **(1)** It was prepared from oil and aromatic herbs. **(2)** It is used only metaphorically in the NT; by metonymy, of the Holy Spirit: **(2a)** "But ye have an unction from the Holy One, and ye know all things" (1 Jn 2:20) and **(2b)** "But the anointing which ye have received of Him abideth in you, and ye need not that any man teach you: but as the same anointing teacheth you of all things, and is truth, and is no lie, and even as it hath taught you, ye shall abide in Him" (1 Jn 2:27). **(2b1)** That believers have "an anointing from the Holy One" indicates that this anointing renders them holy, separating them to God. **(2b2)** The passage teaches that the gift of the Holy Spirit is the all efficient means of enabling believers to possess a knowledge of the truth. Syn.: 218, 1472, 2025, 3462, 5548. See: TDNT—9:493, 1322; BAGD—886c; THAYER—672a.

5546. **Χριστιανός** {3x} **Christianŏs**, *khris-tee-an-os';* from *5547;* a *Christian,* i.e. follower of Christ:—Christian {3x}. See: TDNT—9:493, 1322; BAGD—886c; THAYER—672b.

5547. **Χριστός** {569x} **Christŏs**, *khris-tos';* from *5548; anointed,* i.e. the *Messiah,* an epithet of Jesus:—Christ {569x}. See: TDNT—9:493, 1322; BAGD—886d; THAYER—672b.

5548. **χρίω** {5x} **chriō**, *khree'-o;* prob. akin to *5530* through the idea of *contact;* to *smear* or *rub* with oil, i.e. (by impl.) to *consecrate* to an office or relig. service:—anoint {5x}.

Chrio, as a verb, is **(1)** more limited in its use than *aleipho* (218); **(2)** it is confined to "sacred and symbolical anointings"; **(2a)** of Christ as the "Anointed" of God (Lk 4:18; cf. Acts 4:27; 10:38), and **(2b)** Heb 1:9, where it is used metaphorically in connection with "the oil of gladness." **(3)** The title Christ signifies "The Anointed One." The word (*Christos*) is rendered **(3a)** "(His) Christ" (Acts 4:26). **(3b)** Once it is said of believers: "Now He which stablisheth us with you in Christ, and hath anointed us, *is* God" (2 Cor 1:21). Syn.: 218, 1472, 1637, 2025, 3462, 3464, 5545. See: TDNT—9:493, 1322; BAGD—887c; THAYER—673a.

5549. **χρονίζω** {5x} **chrŏnizō**, *khron-id'-zo;* from *5550;* to *take time,* i.e. *linger:*—delay {2x}, tarry {2x}, tarry so long {1x}.

Chronizo, as a verb, means literally means "to while away time" i.e., by way of "lingering, tarrying, delaying" and is translated **(1)** "delayeth" in Mt 24:48; Lk 12:45; or **(2)** "tarry, tarried" in **(2a)** Mt 25:5, "tarried", **(2b)** Lk 1:21, "tarried so long"; **(2c)** Heb 10:37, "will (not) tarry"). Syn.: 311, 3635. See: BAGD—887d; THAYER—673b.

5550. **χρόνος** {53x} **chrŏnŏs**, *khron'-os;* of uncert. der.; a space of *time* (in gen., and thus prop. distinguished from *2540,* which designates a *fixed* or special occasion; and from *165,* which denotes a particular *period*) or *interval;* by extens. an indiv. *opportunity;* by impl. *delay:*—time {33x}, season {4x}, while {2x}, a while {2x}, space {2x}, oftentimes + 4183 {1x}, not tr {5x}, misc. {4x}.

Chronos (5550), whence Eng. words beginning with "chron"—, as a noun, **(1)** denotes "a space of time," whether long or short: **(1a)** it implies duration, whether longer: **(1a1)** Acts 1:21, "(all the) time"; **(1a2)** Acts 13:18; 20:18, "at all seasons"; or **(1b)** shorter: Lk 4:5; **(1b)** It sometimes refers to the date of an occurrence, **(1b1)** whether past (Mt 2:7), or **(1b2)** future (Acts 3:21; 7:17). Syn.: **(A)** Broadly speaking, *chronos* expresses the duration of a period, *kairos* (2540) stresses it as marked by certain features; **(A1)** thus in Acts 1:7, "the Father has set within His own authority" both the times (*chronos*), the lengths of the periods, and the "seasons" (*kairos*), epochs characterized by certain events; **(A2)** in 1 Th 5:1, "times" refers to the length of the interval before the *Parousia* takes place (the presence of Christ with the saints when He comes to receive them to Himself at the Rapture), and to the length of time the *Parousia* will occupy; **(B)** "seasons" refers to the special features of the period before, during, and after the *Parousia.* **(C)** *Chronos* marks quantity, *kairos,* quality. **(D)** *Kairos* (2540) means a definitely limited portion of time with the added notion of suitableness; whereas, *chronos* refers to time in general. See also: 171, 2122, 2540, 3641, 4340, 5610. See: TDNT—9:581, 1337; BAGD—887d.

5551. **χρονοτριβέω** {1x} **chrŏnŏtribĕō**, *khron-ot-rib-eh'-o;* from a presumed compound of *5550* and the base of *5147;* to be a *time-wearer,* i.e. to *procrastinate* (*linger*):—

spend time {1x}. See: BAGD—888c; THAYER—673d.

5552. **χρύσεος** {15x} **chrusĕŏs**, *khroo'-seh-os;* from *5557;* made of *gold:*—of gold {15x}, golden {3x}. See: BAGD—888c, 888d; THAYER—673d.

5553. **χρυσίον** {9x} **chrusiŏn**, *khroo-see'-on;* dimin. of *5557;* a *golden* article, i.e. gold plating, ornament, or coin:—gold {9x}.

Chrusion, a diminutive of *chrusos,* (5557), is used **(1)** of "coin," primarily small but valuable coins, Acts 3:6; 20:33; 1 Pet 1:18; **(2)** of "ornaments," 1 Pet 3:3; **(3)** of "the metal in general," Heb 9:4; 1 Pet 1:7; Rev 21:18, 21; **(4)** metaphorically, **(4a)** of "sound doctrine and its effects," 1 Cor 3:12; **(4b)** of "righteousness of life and conduct," Rev 3:18. See: BAGD—888c; THAYER—673d.

5554. **χρυσοδακτύλιος** {1x} **chrusŏdaktuliŏs**, *khroo-sod-ak-too'-lee-os;* from *5557* and *1146; gold-ringed,* i.e. *wearing* a golden finger-ring or similar *jewelry:*—with a gold ring {1x}. See: BAGD—888c; THAYER—674a.

5555. **χρυσόλιθος** {1x} **chrusŏlithŏs**, *khroo-sol'-ee-thos;* from *5557* and *3037; gold-stone,* i.e. now called a topaz, a *yellow gem* ("*chrysolite*"):—chrysolite {1x}.

Chrusolithos, lit., "a gold stone" (*chrusos,* "gold," *lithos,* "a stone"), is the name of a precious stone of a gold color, now called "a topaz," Rev 21:20. See: BAGD—888c; THAYER—674a.

5556. **χρυσόπρασος** {1x} **chrusŏprasŏs**, *khroo-sop'-ras-os;* from *5557* and πράσον **prasŏn** (a *leek*); a *greenish-yellow* gem ("*chrysoprase*"):—chrysoprase {1x}.

Chrusoprasos, from (*chrusos,* "gold," and *prasos,* "a leek"), is a precious stone like a leek in color, a translucent, golden green. The word occurs in Rev 21:20. See: BAGD—888d; THAYER—674a.

5557. **χρυσός** {13x} **chrusŏs**, *khroo-sos';* perh. from the base of *5530* (through the idea of the *utility* of the metal); *gold;* by extens. a *golden* article, as an ornament or coin:—gold {13x}.

Chrusos is used **(1)** of "coin," Mt 10:9; Jas 5:3; **(2)** of "ornaments," Mt 23:16, 17; 1 Cor 3:12; Jas 5:3 (perhaps both coin and ornaments); Rev 18:12; **(3)** of "images," Acts 17:29; **(4)** of "the metal in general," Mt 2:11; Rev 9:7; Rev. 18:16. See: BAGD—888d; THAYER—674a.

5558. **χρυσόω** {2x} **chrusŏō**, *khroo-sŏ'-o;* from *5557;* to *gild,* i.e. *bespangle* with golden ornaments:—deck {2x}.

Chrusoo, lit., "to gild with gold" (*chrusos,* "gold"), is used in Rev. 17:4; 18:16. See: BAGD—889a; THAYER—674a.

5559. **χρώς** {1x} **chrōs**, *khroce;* prob. akin to the base of *5530* through the idea of *handling;* the *body* (prop. its *surface* or *skin*):—body {1x}.

Chros signifies "the surface of a body," especially of the human body, Acts 19:12, with reference to the handkerchiefs carried from Paul's body to the sick. See: BAGD—889b; THAYER—674b.

5560. **χωλός** {15x} **chōlŏs**, *kho-los';* appar. a primary word; "*halt,*" i.e. *limping:*—cripple {1x}, halt {4x}, lame {10x}.

Cholos, "lame," is translated **(1)** "halt" in Mt 18:8; Mk 9:45; Lk 14:21; Jn 5:3; **(2)** in Acts 14:8, "cripple"; and **(3)** "lame" in Mt 11:5; 15:30, 31; 21:14: Lk 7:22; 14:13; Acts 3:2; 3:11, "the lame man"; 8:7; Heb 12:13. See: BAGD—889a; THAYER—674b.

5561. **χώρα** {27x} **chōra**, *kho'-rah;* fem. of a der. of the base of *5490* through the idea of *empty* expanse; *room,* i.e. a space of *territory* (more or less extens.; often incl. its inhab.):—country {15x}, region {5x}, land {3x}, field {2x}, ground {1x}, coast {1x}.

Chora properly denotes "the space lying between two limits or places"; accordingly it has a variety of meanings: **(1)** "country," Mt 2:12; 8:28; Mk 1:5, "land"; 5:1, 10; Lk 2:8; 8:26; 15:13–14, "land", 15; 19:12; 21:21; Acts 10:39, "land"; 12:20; 26:20, "coasts"; 27:27; Acts 18:23. Syn.: **(A)** *Topos* (5117) is a place, indefinite; a portion of space viewed in reference to its occupancy, or as appropriated to itself. **(B)** *Chora* (5561) is region, country, an extensive; space, yet unbounded. **(C)** *Chorion* (5564) is a parcel of ground, circumscribed; a definite portion of space viewed as enclosed or complete in itself. See: BAGD—889b; THAYER—674b.

5562. **χωρέω** {10x} **chōrĕō**, *kho-reh'-o;* from *5561;* to *be* in (*give*) *space,* i.e. (intr.) to *pass, enter,* or (tran.) to *hold, admit* (lit. or fig.):—receive {3x}, contain {2x}, come {1x}, go {1x}, have place {1x}, cannot receive + 3756 {1x}, be room to receive {1x}.

Choreo, as a verb, means "to give space, make room for" [*chora,* "a place"], and is used metaphorically, of **(1)** "receiving" **(1a)** cannot with the mind, Mt 19:11, 12; **(1b)** into the heart, 2 Cor 7:2. It is also translated **(2)** "contain" Jn 2:6; 21:25; **(3)** "come" 2 Pet 3:9; **(4)** "go" in Mt 15:17; **(5)** "have place" Jn 8:37; and **(6)** "be room to receive" in Mk 2:2. Syn.: **(A)** *Bathmos* (898) primarily signifies to walk, take steps, picturing the mode of motion; to go away. **(B)** *Erchomai* (2064) denotes motion or progress generally, and of any sort; hence to come and arrive at, as well as to go. **(C)** *Poreuomai* (4198) expresses motion in general, often confined within certain limits, or giving prominence to the bearing; hence the regular word for the march of an army. **(D)** *Choreo* (5562) always emphasizes the idea of separation, change of place, and does not, like e.g. 4198, note the external and perceptible motion; it is more internal. See also: 324, 353, 354, 568, 588, 618, 1209, 1523, 1926, 2210, 2865, 2975, 2983, 3028, 3335, 3336, 3858, 3880, 3970, 4327, 4355, 4356, 4380, 4381, 4382, 5264, 5274. See: BAGD—889c; THAYER—674c.

5563. **χωρίζω** {13x} **chōrizō**, *kho-rid'-zo;* from *5561;* to *place room* between, i.e. *part;* refl. to *go away:*—depart {8x}, put asunder {2x}, separate {3x}.

Chorizo is translated **(1)** "to separate" in Rom 8:35, 39; Heb 7:26; **(2)** "to depart" in Acts 1:4; 18:1, 2; 1 Cor 7:10, 11, 15 twice; Philem 15; and **(3)** "put asunder" in Mt 19:6; Mk 10:9. See: BAGD—890a; THAYER—674d.

5564. **χωρίον** {10x} **chōriŏn**, *kho-ree'-on;* dimin. of *5561;* a *spot* or *plot* of ground:—field {3x}, land {3x}, place {2x}, parcel of ground {1x}, possession {1x}.

Chorion, as a noun, means "a region" (a diminutive of *chora* (5561), "a land, country"), and is translated **(1)** "field" in Acts 1:18, 19 twice; **(2)** "land" in Acts 4:34; 5:3, 8; **(3)** "place" in Mt 26:36; Mk 14:32, used of Gethsemane; **(4)** "parcel of ground" in Jn 4:5; and **(5)** "possession" in Acts 28:7. Syn.: 201, 402, 1096, 1502, 3837, 4042, 5117, 5247, 5602. See also: 5561 for discussion. See: BAGD—890b; THAYER—674d.

5565. **χωρίς** {39x} **chōris**, *kho-rece';* adv. from *5561;* at a *space,* i.e. *separately* or *apart* from (often as prep.):—beside {3x}, by itself {1x}, without {35x}. See: BAGD—890c; THAYER—675a.

5566. **χῶρος** {1x} **chōrŏs**, *kho'-ros;* of Lat. or.; the *north-west* wind:—north west {1x}. See: BAGD—891c; THAYER—675c.

Ψ

5567. **ψάλλω** {5x} **psallō**, *psal'-lo;* probably strengthened from ψάω **psaō**, (to *rub* or *touch* the surface; comp. *5597*); to *twitch* or *twang,* i.e. to *play* on a stringed instrument (*celebrate* the divine worship *with music* and accompanying odes):—make melody {1x}, sing {3x}, sing psalms {1x}.

Psallo, primarily "to twitch, twang," then, "to play a stringed instrument with the fingers," and hence, "to sing with a harp, sing psalms," denotes, in the NT, "to sing a hymn, sing praise" and is translated **(1)** "making melody" in Eph 5:19; **(2)** "sing" in Rom 15:9; 1 Cor 14:15 twice; and **(3)** "let him sing psalms" in Jas 5:13. See: TDNT—8:489, 1225; BAGD—891a; THAYER—675b.

5568. **ψαλμός** {7x} **psalmŏs**, *psal-mos';* from *5567;* a set piece of *music,* i.e. a sacred *ode* (accompanied with the voice, harp or other instrument; a "*psalm*"); collect. the book of the *Psalms:*—psalm {5x}, Psalm {2x}.

Psalmos primarily denoted "a striking or twitching with the fingers (on musical strings)"; then, "a sacred song, sung to musical accompaniment, a psalm." It is used **(1)** of the OT book of "Psalms," Lk 20:42; 24:44; Acts 1:20; **(2)** of a particular "psalm," Acts 13:33 (cf. v. 35); **(3)** of "psalms" in general, 1 Cor 14:26; Eph 5:19; Col 3:16. Syn.: **(A)** *Ode* (5603) is the generic term containing praises, exhortations and other admonitions. **(B)** *Psalmos* (5568) and **(C)** *humnos* (5215) are specific, the former designating a song which took its general character from the OT Psalms and is usually accompanied by some musical instrument, although not restricted to them; the later a song of praise with or without instrumental accompaniment. See: TDNT—8:489, 1225; BAGD—891b; THAYER—675b.

5569. **ψευδάδελφος** {2x} **psĕudadĕlphŏs**, *psyoo-dad'-el-fos;* from *5571* and *80;* a *spurious brother,* i.e. *pretended associate:*—false brethren {2x}. Cf. 2 Cor 11:26; Gal 2:4. See: TDNT—1:144, 22; BAGD—891b; THAYER—675d.

5570. **ψευδαπόστολος** {1x} **psĕudapŏstŏlŏs**, *psyoo-dap-os'-tol-os;* from *5571* and *652;* a *spurious apostle,* i.e. *pretended preacher:*—false apostles {1x}. See: TDNT—1:445, 67; BAGD—891b; THAYER—675d.

5571. **ψευδής** {3x} **psĕudēs**, *psyoo-dace';* from *5574; untrue,* i.e. *erroneous, deceitful, wicked:*—false {1x}, liar {2x}.

Pseudes is used of **(1)** "false witnesses," Acts 6:13; **(2)** "liars," Rev 2:2; Rev 21:8. See: TDNT—9:594, 1339; BAGD—891c; THAYER—675d.

5572. **ψευδοδιδάσκαλος** {1x} **psĕudŏdidaskalŏs**, *psyoo-dod-id-as'-kal-os;* from *5571* and *1320;* a *spurious teacher,* i.e. *propagator* of *erroneous* Chr. *doctrine:*—false teacher {1x}. See: TDNT—2:160, 161; BAGD—891d; THAYER—675d.

5573. **ψευδολόγος** {1x} **psĕudŏlŏgŏs**, *psyoo-dol-og'-os;* from *5571* and *3004; mendacious,* i.e. *promulgating erroneous* Chr. *doctrine:*—speaking lies {1x}.

Pseudologos denotes "speaking falsely" (*pseudes,* "false," *logos,* "a word") in 1 Ti 4:2, where the adjective is translated "speaking lies", and is applied to "devils," the actual utterances being by their human agents. See: BAGD—891d; THAYER—675d.

5574. **ψεύδομαι** {11x} **psĕudŏmai**, *psyoo'-dom-ahee;* mid. voice of an appar. primary verb; to *utter an untruth* or attempt to *deceive* by falsehood:—falsely {1x}, lie {11x}.

Pseudomai, "to deceive by lies," is used **(1)** in the middle voice, translated "to say . . . falsely" in Mt 5:11; and is elsewhere rendered **(2)** "to lie" in Acts 5:3–4; Rom 9:1; 2 Cor 11:31; Gal 1:20; Col 3:9; 1 Ti 2:7; Heb 6:8; Jas 3:14; 1 Jo 1:6; Rev 3:9. See: TDNT—9:594, 1339; BAGD—891d; THAYER—675d.

5575. **ψευδομάρτυρ** {3x} **psĕudŏmartur**, *psyoo-dom-ar'-toor;* from *5571* and a kindred form of *3144;* a *spurious witness,* i.e. *bearer of untrue testimony:*—false witness {3x}.

Pseudomartu, as a noun, denotes "a false witness" in Mt 26:60 twice; 1 Cor 15:15. Syn.: 267, 2649, 3140, 3141, 3142, 3143, 3144, 4828, 4901, 5576, 5577.See: TDNT—4:513,*; BAGD—892a; THAYER—676a.

5576. **ψευδομαρτυρέω** {6x} **psĕudŏmarturĕō**, *psyoo-dom-ar-too-reh'-o;* from *5575;* to *be an untrue testifier,* i.e. offer *falsehood in evidence:*—bear false witness {6x}.

Pseudomartureo, as a verb, means "to bear false witness" in Mt 19:18; Mk 10:10; 14:56, 57; Lk 18:20; Rom 13:9. Syn.: 267, 2649, 3140, 3141, 3142, 3143, 3144, 4828, 4901, 5576, 5577. See: TDNT—4:513, 564; BAGD—891d; THAYER—676a.

5577. **ψευδομαρτυρία** {2x} **psĕudŏmarturia**, *psyoo-dom-ar-too-ree'-ah;* from *5575; untrue testimony:*—false witness {2x}.

Pseudomarturia, as a noun, means "false witness" in Mt 15:19; 26:59. Syn.: 267, 2649, 3140, 3141, 3142, 3143, 3144, 4828, 4901, 5571, 5576. See: TDNT—4:513, 564; BAGD—892a; THAYER—676a.

5578. **ψευδοπροφήτης** {11x} **psĕudŏprŏphētēs**, *psyoo-dop-rof-ay'-tace;* from *5571* and *4396;* a *spurious prophet,* i.e. *pretended foreteller* or relig. *impostor:*—false prophet {11x}.

This word means "a false prophet," and is used of such **(1)** in OT times, Lk 6:26; 2 Pet 2:1; **(2)** in the present period since Pentecost, Mt 7:15; 24:11, 24; Mk 13:22; Acts 13:6; 1 Jn 4:1; **(3)** with reference to a false "prophet" destined to arise as the supporter of the "Beast" at the close of this age, Rev 16:13; 19:20; 20:10 (himself described as "another beast," 13:11. See: TDNT—6:781, 952; BAGD—892a; THAYER—676b.

5579. **ψεῦδος** {9x} **psĕudŏs**, *psyoo'-dos;* from *5574;* a *falsehood:*—lie {7x}, lying {2x}.

Pseudos, "a falsehood", is so translated in **(1)** Eph. 4:25, "lying"; 2 Th 2:9, "lying wonders" is lit. "wonders of falsehood," i.e., wonders calculated to deceive; **(3)** it is elsewhere rendered "lie" in Jn 8:44; Rom 1:25; 2 Th 2:11; 1 Jn 2:21, 27; Rev 21:27; 22:15. See: TDNT—9:594, 1339; BAGD—892b; THAYER—676b.

5580. **ψευδόχριστος** {2x} **psĕudŏchristŏs**, *psyoo-dokh'-ris-tos;* from *5571* and *5547;* a *spurious Messiah:*—false Christ {2x}.

Pseudochristos denotes "one who falsely lays claim to the name and office of the Messiah," Mt 24:24; Mk 13:22. Syn.: **(A)** The *antichristos* (500) denies that there is a Christ; **(B)** the *pseudochristos* affirms himself to be the Christ. Both make war against Christ, and though under different pretenses, each would set himself on the throne of glory. See: TDNT—9:594, 1339; BAGD—892b; THAYER—676b.

5581. **ψευδώνυμος** {1x} **psĕudōnumŏs**, *psyoo-do'-noo-mos;* from *5571* and *3686; untruly named:*—falsely so called {1x}.

Pseudonumos, "under a false name" (*pseudo* and *onoma,* "a name"; Eng., "pseudonym"), is said of the knowledge professed by the propagandists of various heretical cults, 1 Ti 6:20. See: TDNT—5:282, 694; BAGD—892c; THAYER—676b.

5582. **ψεῦσμα** {1x} **psĕusma**, *psyoos'-mah;* from *5574;* a *fabrication,* i.e. *falsehood:*—lie {1x}.

Pseusma is a falsehood or an acted lie (Rom 3:7), where "my lie" is not idolatry, but the universal false attitude of man toward God. See: TDNT—9:594, 1339; BAGD—892c; THAYER—676c.

5583. **ψεύστης** {10x} **psĕustēs**, *psyoos-tace';* from *5574;* a *falsifier:*—liar {10x}.

Pseustes, "a liar," occurs in Jn 8:44, 55; Rom 3:4; 1 Ti 1:10; Titus 1:12; 1 Jn 1:10; 2:4, 22; 4:20; 5:10. See: TDNT—9:594, 1339; BAGD—892c; THAYER—676c.

5584. **ψηλαφάω** {4x} **psēlaphaō**, *psay-laf-ah'-o;* from the base of *5567* (comp. *5586*); to *manipulate,* i.e. *verify* by contact; fig. to *search* for:—feel after {1x}, handle {2x}, touch {1x}.

Literally, this word means to feel or grope about and expresses the motion of the hands over a surface, so as to feel it. It is used **(1)** metaphorically, of seeking after God (Acts 17:27); **(2)** literally, of physical handling or touching (Lk 24:39; 1 Jn 1:1; Heb 12:18). Syn.: **(A)** *Pselaphao* never refers to handling an object in order to mold or modify it but either to feeling an object's surface (Lk 24:39; 1 Jn 1:1) perhaps to learn its composition or to feeling for or after an object without actually touching it. **(B)** *Haptomai* (680) appropriately describes the self-conscious effort of the sculptor; to touch in order to change. **(C)** *Thingano* (2345) lacks the mental effort; it refers to touching in general. See: BAGD—892c; THAYER—676c.

5585. **ψηφίζω** {2x} **psēphizō**, *psay-fid'-zo;* from *5586;* to *use pebbles* in enumeration, i.e. (gen.) to *compute:*—count {2x}.

Literally, *psephizo* means to count with pebbles, to compute, calculate, reckon, Lk 14:28; Rev 13:18. See: TDNT—9:604, 1341; BAGD—892d; THAYER—676c.

5586. **ψῆφος** {3x} **psēphŏs**, *psay'-fos;* from the same as *5584;* a *pebble* (as worn smooth by *handling*), i.e. (by impl. of use as a *counter* or *ballot*) a *verdict* (of acquittal) or *ticket* (of admission); a *vote:*—stone {2x}, voice {1x}.

Psephos, "a smooth stone, a pebble," worn smooth as by water, or polished (akin to *psao,* "to rub"), denotes **(1)** by metonymy, a vote (from the use of "pebbles" for this purpose; cf. *psephizo,* "to count"), Acts 26:10, "voice" implying one's "voice" is heard by his vote; and **(2)** a (white) "stone" to be given to the overcomer in the church at Pergamum, Rev 2:17 (twice). A white "stone" was often used in the social life and judicial customs of the ancients; festal days were noted by a white "stone," days of calamity by a black; in the courts a white "stone" indicated acquittal, a black condemnation. A host's appreciation of a special guest was indicated by a white "stone" with the name or a message written on it; this is probably the allusion here. See: TDNT—9:604, 1341; BAGD—892d; THAYER—676d.

5587. **ψιθυρισμός** {1x} **psithurismŏs**, *psith-oo-ris-mos';* from a der. of ψίθος **psithŏs** (a *whisper;* by impl. a *slander;* prob. akin to *5574*); *whispering,* i.e. secret *detraction:*—whispering {1x}.

Psithurismos, "a whispering," is used of "secret slander" in 2 Cor 12:20. See: BAGD—892d; THAYER—676d.

5588. **ψιθυριστής** {1x} **psithuristēs**, *psith-oo-ris-tace';* from the same as *5587;* a secret *calumniator:*—whisperer {1x}.

Psithuristes, "a whisperer," occurs in an evil sense in Rom 1:29. See: BAGD—893a; THAYER—676d.

5589. **ψιχίον** {3x} **psichiŏn**, *psikh-ee'-on,* dimin. from a der. of the base of *5567* (mean. a *crumb*); a *little bit* or *morsel:*—crumb {3x}.

Psichion, "a small morsel," a diminutive of *psix,* "a bit, or crumb", of bread or meat, is used in Mt 15:27; Mk 7:28; Lk 16:21. See: BAGD—893a; THAYER—677a.

5590. **ψυχή** {105x} **psuchē**, *psoo-khay';* from *5594; breath,* i.e. (by impl.) *spirit,* abstr. or concr. (the *animal* sentient principle only; thus distinguished on the one hand from *4151,* which is the rational and immortal *soul;* and on the other from *2222,* which is mere *vitality,* even of plants: these terms thus exactly correspond respectively to the Heb. 5315, 7307 and 2416):—soul {58x}, life {40x}, mind {3x}, heart {1x}, heartily + 1537 {1x}, not tr {2x}.

Psuche refers to **(1)** breath, **(1a)** the breath of life, that vital force which animates the body and shows itself in breathing (Acts 20:10), **(1a1)** of animals (Rev 8:9), or **(1a2)** of men (1 Th 5:23); **(1b)** life (Mt 6:25); **(1c)** that in which there is life, a living being, a living soul (1 Cor 15:45); **(2)** the soul, **(2a)** the seat of the feelings, desires, affections, aversions (Lk 1: 46; 2:35); **(2b)** the (human) soul in so far as it is constituted that by the right use of the aids offered it by God it can attain its highest end and secure eternal blessedness, the soul regarded as a moral being designed for everlasting life (3 Jn 2; 1 Pet 2:11); **(2c)** the soul as an essence which differs from the body and is not dissolved by death (distinguished from other parts of the body), Mt 10:28; Rev 6:9. See: TDNT—9:608, 1342; BAGD—890b; THAYER—893b.

5591. **ψυχικός** {6x} **psuchikŏs**, *psoo-khee-kos';* from *5590; sensitive,* i.e. *animate* (in distinction on the one hand from *4152,* which is the higher or *renovated* nature; and on the other from *5446,* which is the lower or *bestial* nature):—natural {4x}, sensual {2x}.

(1) The *psychikos* person is one who yields in everything to the human reasonings of the *soul* (5590), not thinking there is need for help from above. **(2)** It describes the man in Adam and what pertains to him (set in contrast to *pneumatikos* "spiritual"), and is **(3)** translated **(3a)** "natural", 1 Cor 2:14; 15:44 twice, 46 used as a noun; and **(3b)** "sensual" in Jas 3:15 and Jude 19, here relating perhaps more especially to the mind, a wisdom in accordance with, or springing from, the corrupt desires and affections. See: TDNT—9:661, 1342; BAGD—894b; THAYER—677d.

5592. **ψῦχος** {3x} **psuchŏs**, *psoo'-khos;* from *5594; coolness:*—cold {3x}.

Psuchos, "coldness, cold," appears in Jn 18:18; Acts 28:2; 2 Cor 11:27. Syn.: 5593. See: BAGD—894c; THAYER—678a.

5593. **ψυχρός** {4x} **psuchrŏs**, *psoo-chros';* from *5592; chilly* (lit. or fig.):—cold {4x}.

Psuchros, "cool, fresh, cold, chilly" (fuller in expression than *psuchos,* 5592), is used in the **(1)** natural sense in Mt 10:42, "cold water"; **(2)** metaphorically in Rev 3:15–16. Syn.: 5592. See: TDNT—2:876, 296; BAGD—894c; THAYER—678a.

5594. **ψύχω** {1x} **psuchō**, *psoo'-kho;* a primary verb; to *breathe* (*voluntarily* but *gently,* thus differing on the one hand from *4154,* which denotes prop. a *forcible* respiration; and on the other from the base of *109,* which refers prop. to an inanimate *breeze*), i.e. (by impl. of reduction of temperature by evaporation) to *chill* (fig.):—wax cold {1x}.

Psucho, "to breathe, blow, cool by blowing," passive voice, "grow cool slowly," is used metaphorically in Mt 24:12, in the sense of waning zeal or love. See: BAGD—894d; THAYER—678c.

5595. **ψωμίζω** {2x} **psōmizō**, *pso-mid'-zo;* from the base of *5596; to supply* with *bits,* i.e. (gen.) to *nourish:*—bestow to feed {1x}, feed {1x}.

Primarily, *psomizo* means to feed by putting little bits into the mouths of infants or animals and came to denote simply to give out food, to feed (1 Cor 13:3; Rom 12:20). See: BAGD—894d; THAYER—678c.

5596. **ψωμίον** {4x} **psōmiŏn**, *pso-mee'-on;* dimin. from a der. of the base of *5597;* a *crumb* or *morsel* (as if *rubbed* off), i.e. a *mouthful:*—sop {4x}.

Psomion, a diminutive of *psomos,* "a morsel," denotes "a fragment, a sop", Jn 13:26 (twice), 27, 30. It had no connection with the modern meaning of "sop," something given to pacify. See: BAGD—894d; THAYER—678c.

5597. **ψώχω** {1x} **psōchō**, *pso'-kho;* prol. from the same base as *5567; to triturate,* i.e. (by anal.) to *rub* out (kernels from husks with the fingers or hand):—rub {1x}.

Psocho, "to rub, to rub to pieces," is used in Luke 6:1. See: BAGD—894d; THAYER—678c.

Ω

5598. **Ω** {4x} **w**—, i.e. ὦμεγα **ōmĕga**, *o'-meg-ah;* the last letter of the Greek alphabet, i.e. (fig.) the *finality:*—Omega {4x}. Cf. Rev 1:8, 11; 21:6; 22:13. See: TDNT—1:1,*; BAGD—895a; THAYER—678b.

5599. **ὦ** {15x} **ō**, *o;* a primary interj.; as a sign of the voc. *O;* as a note of exclamation, *oh:*—O {15x}. See: BAGD—895a; THAYER—678b.

5600. **ὦ** {66x} **ō**, *o;* incl. the oblique forms, as well as **ᾖς** **ēs**, *ace;* **ᾖ** **ē**, *ay;* etc.; the subjunctive of *1510;* (*may, might, can, could, would, should, must,* etc.; also with *1487* and its comp., as well as with other particles) *be:*—be {22x}, may be {22x}, should be {6x}, is {5x}, might be {2x}, were {1x}, not tr {4x}, appear {1x}, have {1x}, + pass the flower of her age {1x}, should stand {1x}. See: BAGD—222d [1510] + 219a [1487]; THAYER—678b, 175c [1510].

5601. **Ὠβήδ** {3x} **Ōbēd**, *o-bade'*or **Ἰωβήδ** **Iōbēd**, *yo-bade';* of Heb. or. [5744]; *Obed,* an Isr.:—*Obed* {3x}. See: BAGD—895b, 385b; THAYER—678b.

5602. **ὧδε** {60x} **hōdĕ**, *ho'-deh;* from an adv. form of *3592; in this* same spot, i.e. *here* or *hither:*—here {44x}, hither {13x}, in this place {1x}, this place {1x}, there {1x}. Syn.: 201, 402, 1096, 1502, 3837, 4042, 5117, 5247, 5564. See: BAGD—895b; THAYER—678c.

5603. **ᾠδή** {7x} **ōidē**, *o-day';* from *103;* a *chant* or "*ode*" (the gen. term for any words sung; while *5215* denotes espec. a *relig.* metrical composition, and *5568* still more spec. a *Heb.* cantillation):—song {7x}.

Ode, "an ode, song," is **(1)** always used in the NT in praise of God or Christ; **(2)** in Eph 5:19 and Col 3:16 the adjective "spiritual" is added, because the word in itself is generic and might be used of songs anything but spiritual; **(3)** in Rev 5:9 and 14:3 (1st part) the descriptive word is "new" (*kainos,* "new," in reference to character and form), a "song," the significance of which was confined to those mentioned (v. 3, and 2nd part); **(4)** in Rev 15:3 (twice), "the song of Moses . . . and the song of the Lamb," the former as celebrating the deliverance of God's people by His power, the latter as celebrating redemption by atoning sacrifice. Syn.: **(A)** *Ode* (5603) is the generic term containing praises, exhortations and other admonitions. **(B)** *Psalmos* (5568) and **(C)** *humnos* (5215) are specific, the former designating a song which took its general character from the OT Psalms and is usually accompanied by some musical instrument, although not restricted to them; the later a song of praise with or without instrumental accompaniment. See: TDNT—1:164, 24; BAGD—895c; THAYER—679a.

5604. **ὠδίν** {4x} **ōdin**, *o-deen';* akin to *3601;* a *pang* or *throe,* espec. of childbirth:—pain {1x}, sorrow {2x}, travail {1x}.

Odin, as a noun, "a birth pang, travail pain," is rendered **(1)** "sorrows," metaphorically, in Mt 24:8 and Mk 13:8; **(2)** "travail" in 1 Th 5:3; and **(3)** "pains (of death)," Acts 2:24. Syn.: 253, 3076, 3077, 3600, 3601, 3997, 4036. See: TDNT—9:667, 1353; BAGD—895c; THAYER—679a.

5605. **ὠδίνω** {3x} **ōdinō**, *o-dee'-no;* from *5604;* to *experience* the *pains* of parturition (lit. or fig.):—travail {1x}, travail in birth {2x}.

Odino is used **(1)** negatively in Gal 4:27, "(thou) that travailest (not)," **(1a)** quoted from Is 54:1; **(1b)** the apostle applies the circumstances of Sarah and Hagar (which doubtless Isaiah was recalling) to show that, whereas the promise by grace had temporarily been replaced by the works of the Law (see Gal 3:17), this was now reversed, and, in the fulfillment of the promise to Abraham, the number of those saved by the gospel would far exceed those who owned allegiance to the Law. **(1c)** Is 54 has primary reference to the future prosperity of Israel restored to God's favor, but frequently the principles underlying events recorded in the OT extend beyond their immediate application.

(2) In Gal 4:19 the apostle uses it metaphorically of a second travailing on his part regarding the churches of Galatia; **(2a)** his first was for their deliverance from idolatry (v. 8), **(2b)** now it was for their deliverance from bondage to Judaism. **(2c)** There is no suggestion here of a second regeneration necessitated by defection. **(2d)** There is a hint of reproach, as if he was enquiring whether they had ever heard of a mother experiencing second birth pangs for her children. **(3)** In Rev 12:2 the woman is figurative of Israel; the circumstances of her birth pangs are mentioned in Is 66:7 (see also Mic 5:2, 3). **(3a)** Historically the natural order is reversed. **(3b)** The Manchild, Christ, was brought forth at His first advent; the travail is destined to take place in "the time of Jacob's trouble," the "great tribulation," Mt 24:21; Rev 7:14. **(3c)** The object in Rev 12:2 in referring to the birth of Christ is to connect Him with His earthly people Israel in their future time of trouble, from which the godly remnant, the nucleus of the restored nation, is to be delivered (Jer 30:7). See: TDNT—9:667, 1353; BAGD—895d; THAYER—679a.

5606. **ὦμος** {2x} **ōmŏs**, *o'-mos;* perh. from the alt. of *5342;* the *shoulder* (as that on which burdens are *borne*):—shoulder {2x}.

Omos occurs in Mt 23:4 and Lk 15:5, and is suggestive (as in the latter passage) of strength and safety. See: BAGD—895d; THAYER—679b.

5607. **ὤν** {154x} **ōn**, *oan;* incl. the fem. **οὖσα** **ŏusa**, *oo'-sah;* and the neut. **ὄν** **ŏn**, *on;* pres. part. of *1510; being:*—being {36x}, when . . . was {8x}, which is {12x}, that is {8x}, not tr {10x}, misc. {80x} = be, come, have. See: TDNT—2:398,*; BAGD—224d [1510]; THAYER—175c [1510].

5608. **ὠνέομαι** {1x} **ōnĕŏmai**, *o-neh'-om-ahee;* mid. voice from an appar. primary ὦνος **ōnŏs** (a *sum* or *price*); to *purchase,* (synonymous with the earlier *4092*):—buy {1x}.

Oneomai "to buy, in contradistinction to selling," is used in Acts 7:16, of the purchase by Abraham of a burying place. See: BAGD—895d; THAYER—679b.

5609. **ᾠόν** {1x} **ōŏn**, *o-on';* appar. a primary word; an "*egg*":—egg {1x}. See: BAGD—896a; THAYER—679b.

5610. **ὥρα** {108x} **hōra**, *ho'-rah;* appar. a primary word; an "*hour*" (lit. or fig.):—hour {89x}, time {11x}, season {3x}, day {1x}, instant {1x}, × short {1x}, eventide {1x}, even {1x}.

Hora, whence Lat., *hora,* Eng., "hour," primarily denoted any time or period, expecially a season. In the NT it is used to denote **(1)** "a part of the day," especially a twelfth part of day or night, an "hour," e.g., Mt 8:13; Acts 10:3, 9; 23:23; Rev 9:15; **(2)** in 1 Cor 15:30, "every hour" stands for "all the time"; **(3)** in some passages it expresses duration, e.g., Mt 20:12; 26:40; Lk 22:59; **(4)** inexactly, in such phrases as "for a season," Jn 5:35; 2 Cor 7:8; **(5)** "for an hour," Gal 2:5; **(6)** "for a short time," lit., "for the time of an hour"; 1 Th 2:17; **(7)** "a period more or less extended," e.g., 1 Jn 2:18, "it is the lasttime"; **(8)** "a definite point of time," **(8a)** e.g., Mt 26:45, "the hour is at hand"; **(8b)** Lk 1:10; 10:21; 14:17, lit., "at the hour of supper"; Acts 16:18; 22:13; Rev 3:3; 11:13; 14:7; **(9)** a point of time when an appointed action is to begin, Rev 14:15; **(10)** in Rom 13:11, "it is high time," lit., "it is already an hour," indicating that a point of time has come later than would have been the case had responsibility been realized. **(11)** In 1 Cor 4:11, it indicates a point of time previous to which certain circumstances have existed. Syn.: 171, 2122, 2540, 3641, 4340, 5550. See: TDNT–9:675, 1355; BAGD–896a; THAYER–679b.

5611. **ὡραῖος** {4x} **hōraiŏs**, *ho-rah'-yos;* from *5610; belonging* to the right *hour* or *season* (*timely*), i.e. (by impl.) *flourishing* (*beauteous* [fig.]):—beautiful {4x}.

Horaios describes "that which is seasonable, produced at the right time," as of the prime of life, or the time when anything is at its loveliest and best (from *hora,* "a season," a period fixed by natural laws and revolutions, and so the best season of the year). **(1)** It is used of the outward appearance of whited sepulchres in contrast to the corruption within Mt 23:27; **(2)** of the Jerusalem gate called "Beautiful," Acts 3:2, 10; **(3)** of the feet of those that bring glad tidings, Rom 10:15. See: BAGD–896d; THAYER–680a.

5612. **ὠρύομαι** {1x} **ōruŏmai**, *o-roo'-om-ahee;* mid. voice of an appar. primary verb; to "*roar*":—roar {1x}.

Oruomai, "to howl" or "roar," onomatopoeic, of animals or men, is used of a lion, 1 Pet 5:8, as a simile of Satan. See: BAGD–897a; THAYER–680a.

5613. **ὡς** {492x} **hōs**, *hoce;* prob. adv. of comparison from *3739; which how,* i.e. *in that manner* (very variously used, as follows):—as {342x}, when {42x}, how {18x}, as it were {20x}, about {14x}, misc. {50x} = after (that), for, like unto, since, so (that), that, to wit, unto, while, × with all speed. See: BAGD–897a; THAYER–680a.

5614. **ὡσαννά** {6x} **hōsanna**, *ho-san-nah';* of Heb. or. [3467 and 4994]; *oh save!; hosanna* (i.e. *hoshia-na*), an exclamation of adoration:—*Hosanna* {6x}.

Hosanna, in the Hebrew, means "save, we pray." The word seems to have become an utterance of praise rather than of prayer, though originally, probably, a cry for help. The people's cry at the Lord's triumphal entry into Jerusalem (Mt 21:9, 15; Mk 11:9, 10; Jn 12:13) was taken from Ps 118, which was recited at the Feast of Tabernacles in the great Hallel (Psalms 113 to 118) in responses with the priest, accompanied by the waving of palm and willow branches. "The last day of the feast" was called "the great Hosanna"; the boughs also were called "hosannas." See: TDNT–9:682, 1356; BAGD–899a; THAYER–682c.

5615. **ὡσαύτως** {17x} **hōsautōs**, *ho-sŏw'-toce;* from *5613* and an adv. from *846;* as *thus,* i.e. *in the same way:*—likewise {13x}, in like manner {2x}, even so {1x}, after the same manner {1x}.

Hosautos, a strengthened form of *hos* (5613), "thus," signifies "just so, likewise, in like manner" (1 Ti 2:9; Mk 14:31; Lk 22:20; Rom 8:26; 1 Tim 3:8; 5:25). Syn.: 195, 1485, 2239, 3634, 3668, 3697, 3779, 4169, 4187, 4217, 4459, 5158, 5159, 5179. See: BAGD–899b; THAYER–682c.

5616. **ὡσεί** {34x} **hōsĕi**, *ho-si';* from *5613* and *1487; as if:*—about {18x}, as {7x}, like {5x}, as it had been {2x}, as it were {1x}, like as {1x}. See: BAGD–899c, 595c [3775]; THAYER–682c.

5617. **Ὡσηέ** {1x} **Hōsĕĕ**, *ho-say-eh';* of Heb. or. [1954]; *Hoseë* (i.e. *Hosheă*), an Isr.:—Osee {1x}. See: BAGD–899c; THAYER–682d.

5618. **ὥσπερ** {42x} **hōspĕr**, *hoce'-per;* from *5613* and *4007; just as,* i.e. *exactly like:*—as {39x}, even as {2x}, like as {1x}. See: BAGD–899c; THAYER–682d.

5619. **ὡσπερεί** {1x} **hōspĕrĕi**, *hoce-per-i';* from *5618* and *1487; just as if,* i.e. *as it were:*—as {1x}. See: BAGD–899d; THAYER–683b.

5620. **ὥστε** {83x} **hōstĕ**, *hoce'-teh;* from *5613* and *5037; so too,* i.e. *thus therefore* (in various relations of *consecution,* as follow):—so that {25x}, wherefore {17x}, insomuch that {16x}, therefore {9x}, that {6x}, so then {5x}, to {3x}, as {1x}, insomuch as {1x}. See: BAGD–899d; THAYER–683b.

5621. **ὠτίον** {5x} **ōtiŏn**, *o-tee'-on;* dimin. of *3775;* an *earlet,* i.e. *one* of the ears, or perh. the *lobe* of the ear:—ear {5x}.

Otion, a diminutive of 3775, but without the diminutive force, it being a common tendency in everyday speech to apply a diminutive form to most parts of the body: the ear of Malchus (Mt 26:51; Mk 14:47; Lk 22:51; Jn 18:10, 26). Syn.: 189, 3775. See: TDNT–5:558, 744; BAGD–900b; THAYER–683c.

5622. **ὠφέλεια** {2x} **ōphĕlĕia**, *o-fel'-i-ah;* from a der. of the base of *5624; usefulness,* i.e. *benefit:*—advantage {1x}, profit {1x}.

Opheleia is found in **(1)** Rom 3:1, "profit," and **(2)** Jude 16, "advantage." i.e., they shew respect of persons for the sake of what they may gain from them. See: BAGD–900b; THAYER–683d.

5623. **ὠφελέω** {15x} **ōphĕlĕō**, *o-fel-eh'-o;* from the same as *5622; to be useful,* i.e. to *benefit:*—advantage {1x}, better {1x}, prevail {2x}, profit {11x}.

Opheleo signifies "to be useful, do good, profit," and is translated **(1)** "advantage" in Lk 9:25; **(2)** "better" in Mk 5:26; **(3)** "prevail" in Mt 27:24; Jn 12:19; and **(3)** "profit" in Mt 15:5; 16:26; Mk 7:11; 8:36; Jn 6:63; Rom 2:25; 1 Cor 13:3; 14:6; Gal 5:2; Heb 4:2; 13:9. See: BAGD–900c; THAYER–683d.

5624. **ὠφέλιμος** {4x} **ōphĕlimŏs**, *o-fel'-ee-mos;* from a form of *3786; helpful* or *serviceable,* i.e. *advantageous:*—profitable {3x}, profit + 2076 {1x}.

Ophelimos, "useful, profitable", is translated **(1)** "profitable" (of godliness) in 1 Ti 4:8, second time; "profiteth" in the 1st part, of physical exercise; **(2)** "profitable" in 2 Ti 3:16 of the God-breathed Scriptures; **(3)** "profitable" in Titus 3:8, of maintaining good works. See: BAGD–900d; THAYER–683d.

SUPPLEMENTS

COMPLETE TOPICAL INDEX TO THE BIBLE

SUBJECT REFERENCE

A

Aaron—*bright*

A. *Ancestry and family of:*

Descendant of Levi ... Ex. 6:16-20
Son of Amram and Jochebed ... Ex. 6:20
Moses' older brother ... Ex. 7:1, 7
Brother of Miriam ... Ex. 15:20
Husband of Elisheba ... Ex. 6:23
Father of Nadab, Abihu, Eleazar, and Ithamar ... Ex. 6:23

B. *Position of:*

Moses' helper ... Ex. 4:13-31
Becomes "prophet" to Moses ... Ex. 7:1, 2
God inspired ... Ex. 12:1
Commissioned, with Moses to deliver Israelites from Egypt ... Ex. 6:13, 26; Josh. 24:5
Inferior to that of Melchizedek ... Heb. 7:11-19

C. *Special privileges of:*

Appears before Pharaoh ... Ex. 5:1-4
Performs miracles ... Ex. 7:9, 10, 19, 20
Supports Moses' hands ... Ex. 17:10-12
Ascends Mt. Sinai ... Ex. 19:24; Ex. 24:1, 9
Sees God's glory ... Ex. 24:9, 10
Judges Israel in Moses' absence ... Ex. 24:14
Allowed inside the veil ... Lev. 16:15
Blesses the people ... Lev. 9:22
Intercedes for Miriam ... Num. 12:10-12

D. *Sins of:*

Tolerates idolatry ... Ex. 32:1-4
Permits evil ... Ex. 32:21-25
Conspires against Moses ... Num. 12:1-16
With Moses, fails at Meribah ... Num. 20:1-13, 24

E. *Character of:*

A good speaker ... Ex. 4:14
Weak in crises ... Ex. 32:1-24
Subject to jealousy ... Num. 12:1, 2
Conscious of guilt ... Num. 12:11
Submissive ... Lev. 10:1-7
A saint ... Ps. 106:16

F. *Priesthood of:*

Chosen by God ... Ex. 28:1
Sons, in office ... Lev. 8:1-36
Anointed with oil ... Ex. 30:25, 30
Duties given ... Ex. 30:7-10
Garments prescribed ... Ex. 39:27-29
Ordained to teach ... Lev. 10:8, 11
Set apart to offer sacrifices ... Lev. 9:1-24; Heb. 5:1-4
Alone enters within the holy place ... Ex. 30:10; Heb. 9:7, 25
Intercedes for others ... Num. 16:46-48
Confirmed by God ... Num. 17:8-10; Heb. 9:4
Hereditary ... Num. 20:23-28
For lifetime ... Heb. 7:23
Inferior to Melchizedek's ... Heb. 7:11-19

G. *Death and descendants of:*

Lives 123 years ... Num. 33:39
Death ... Num. 20:23, 24
Eleazar, son of, successor ... Num. 20:25-28; Deut. 10:6

Aaronites—*descendants of Aaron*

Fights with David ... 1 Chr. 12:27
Under Zadok ... 1 Chr. 27:17

Ab—*fifth month of the Jewish year*

Aaron died in ... Num. 33:38

See Jewish calendar

Ab—*father*

A part of many Hebrew names (e.g., Abinadab, Abner, Abijah) ... 1 Sam. 7:1

Abaddon—*a Hebrew word translated "destruction"*

Designates ruin in ... Job 31:12
Parallel with hell (Sheol) in ... Job 26:6
Refers to death ... Job 28:22
Personified ... Rev. 9:11

SUBJECT REFERENCE

Abagtha

A eunuch under King Ahasuerus ... Esth. 1:10

Abana—*a river flowing through Damascus*

Spoken of highly by Naaman ... 2 Kin. 5:12

Abandon—*desert*

A. *Required for:*

Safety ... Gen. 19:12-26; Acts 27:41-44
Salvation ... Phil. 3:7-10
Service ... Matt. 10:37-39
Sanctification ... 2 Cor. 6:14-18
Spiritual success ... Heb. 11:24-27

B. *Aspects of:*

Land, commanded ... Gen. 12:1-5
Idolaters, justified ... Ex. 32:1-10
One's ministry, rebuked ... 1 Kin. 19:3-18
Family, regretted ... 1 Sam. 30:1-6
The tabernacle, remembered ... Jer. 7:12
Jerusalem, lamented ... Matt. 23:37, 38

C. *Of men to judgment because of:*

Sin ... Gen. 6:5-7
Rebellion ... 1 Sam. 15:16-26
Unbelief ... Matt. 23:37-39
Rejecting God ... Rom. 1:21-32
Fornication ... 1 Cor. 5:1-5
Apostasy ... Heb. 10:26-29

Abarim—*regions beyond*

Moses sees the promised land from ... Num. 27:12

Abasement—*degradation; humiliation*

A. *As a judgment for:*

Stubbornness ... 2 Kin. 14:8-14
Defaming God ... 2 Chr. 32:1-22
Pride ... Is. 14:12-17
Hating Jews ... Esth. 7:5-10
Arrogance ... Dan. 4:33, 37; Acts 12:20-23

B. *As a virtue, seen in:*

Nineveh's repentance ... Jon. 3:1-10; Matt. 12:41
A publican's unworthiness ... Luke 18:13, 14
Paul's life ... 1 Cor. 9:19-23
Christ's humiliation ... Phil. 2:5-8

C. *Rewards of, seen in:*

Healing ... 2 Kin. 5:11-14
Elevation ... Matt. 23:12
Restoration ... Luke 15:11-24
Renewed service ... 1 Cor. 15:9, 10

Abate—*diminish, desist*

Flood waters ... Gen. 8:8, 11
Moses' natural force not ... Deut. 34:7
Anger of Ephraim ... Judg. 8:3

Abba—an Aramaic word meaning *"father"*

Used by Christ ... Mark 14:36
Expressive of sonship ... Rom. 8:15

Abda—*servant* (of God)

1. The father of Adoniram ... 1 Kin. 4:6
2. A Levite, son of Shammua ... Neh. 11:17; Called Obadiah ... 1 Chr. 9:16

Abdeel—*servant of God*

The father of Shelemiah ... Jer. 36:26

Abdi—*servant of Jehovah*

1. The grandfather of Ethan ... 1 Chr. 6:44
2. A Levite ... 2 Chr. 29:12
3. A Jew who divorced his foreign wife ... Ezra 10:26

Abdiel—*servant of God*

A Gadite residing in Gilead ... 1 Chr. 5:15, 16

Abdon—*servile*

1. A minor judge ... Judg. 12:13-15
2. A Benjamite living in Jerusalem ... 1 Chr. 8:23, 28
3. A son of Jeiel ... 1 Chr. 8:30
4. A courtier of King Josiah ... 2 Chr. 34:20
5. A Levitical city ... Josh. 21:30; 1 Chr. 6:74

SUBJECT REFERENCE

Abed-nego—*servant of Nego*

Name given to Azariah, a Hebrew captive ... Dan. 1:7
Appointed by Nebuchadnezzar ... Dan. 2:49
Accused of disobedience ... Dan. 3:12
Cast into furnace but delivered ... Dan. 3:13-27
Promoted by Nebuchadnezzar ... Dan. 3:28-30

Abel—*breath*

Adam's second son ... Gen. 4:2
The first shepherd ... Gen. 4:2
Offering of, accepted ... Gen. 4:4
Hated and slain by Cain ... Gen. 4:8
Christ's blood superior to ... Heb. 12:24
Place of, filled by Seth ... Gen. 4:25

Abel—*meadow*

1. A city involved in Sheba's rebellion ... 2 Sam. 20:14-18
2. Translated as "great stone of Abel" in ... 1 Sam. 6:18
   First martyr ... Matt. 23:35
   Righteous ... Matt. 23:35
   Sacrificed to God by faith ... Heb. 11:4
3. Elsewhere in place names (see below)

Abel-beth-maachah—*meadow of the house of oppression*

Captured by Tiglath-pileser ... 2 Kin. 15:29
A town in North Palestine ... 2 Sam. 20:14, 15
Refuge of Sheba; saved from destruction ... 2 Sam. 20:14-22
Seized by Ben-hadad ... 1 Kin. 15:20

Abel-maim—*meadow of waters*

Another name for Abel-beth-maacah ... 2 Chr. 16:4

Abel-meholah—*meadow of dancing*

Midianites flee to ... Judg. 7:22
A few miles east of Jabesh-gilead ... 1 Kin. 4:12
Elisha's native city ... 1 Kin. 19:16

Abel-mizraim—*meadow of Egypt*

A place, east of Jordan, where Israelites mourned for Jacob ... Gen. 50:10, 11

Abel-shittim—*meadow of acacias*

A place in Moab ... Num. 33:49

Abez—*whiteness*

A town of Issachar ... Josh. 19:20

Abhor—*to detest; loathe; hate*

A. *Descriptive of:*

Disliking God's laws ... Lev. 26:15
Prejudice toward non-Israelites ... Deut. 23:7
Right attitude toward idolatry ... Deut. 7:25, 26
Self-rejection ... Job 42:6
Israel abhorred by Rezon ... 1 Kin. 11:25
Israel's rejection by God ... Ps. 89:38, 39
Rejection by former friends ... Job 19:19
Loss of appetite ... Job 33:20
Rejecting false description ... Prov. 24:24

B. *Expressive of God's loathing of:*

Israel's idolatry ... Deut. 32:17-19
Customs of other nations ... Lev. 20:23
Men of bloodshed ... Ps. 5:6

C. *Expressive of Israel's rejection of God's:*

Judgments ... Lev. 26:15
Ceremonies ... 1 Sam. 2:17
Promises ... Is. 7:16

D. *Expressive of the believer's hatred of:*

Lying ... Ps. 119:163
Evil ... Rom. 12:9

Abi—(an old form of *"father of"*)

King Hezekiah's mother ... 2 Kin. 18:2
Also called Abijah ... 2 Chr. 29:1

Abi-albon

An Arabathite ... 2 Sam. 23:31

See Abiel

Abiasaph—*the father gathers*

A descendant of Levi through Korah ... Ex. 6:24

SUBJECT REFERENCE

Called Ebiasaph ..... 1 Chr. 6:23, 37
Descendants of, act as doorkeepers ..... 1 Chr. 9:19

Abiathar—*father of pre-eminence*

A priest who escapes Saul at Nob ..... 1 Sam. 22:20-23
Becomes high priest under David ..... 1 Sam. 23:6, 9-12
Shares high priesthood with Zadok ..... 2 Sam. 8:17
Remains faithful to David ..... 2 Sam. 15:24-29
Informs David about Ahithophel ..... 2 Sam. 15:34-36
Supports Adonijah's usurpation ..... 1 Kin. 1:7, 9, 25
Deposed by Solomon ..... 1 Kin. 2:26, 27, 35
Eli's line ends ..... 1 Sam. 2:31-35
Referred by Christ ..... Mark 2:26

Abib—*an ear of corn*

First month in Hebrew year ..... Ex. 12:1, 2
Commemorative of the Passover ..... Ex. 12:1-28
Called Nisan in postexilic times ..... Neh. 2:1

Abida, Abidah—*the father knows*

A son of Midian; grandson of Abraham and Keturah ..... Gen. 25:4

Abidan—*the father is judge*

Represents tribe of Benjamin ..... Num. 1:11
Brings offering ..... Num. 7:60, 65
Lead Benjamites ..... Num. 10:24

Abide, abiding—*continuing in a permanent state*

A. *Applied to:*
Earth's existence ..... Ps. 119:90
Believer's works ..... 1 Cor. 3:14
Three graces ..... 1 Cor. 13:13
God's faithfulness ..... 2 Tim. 2:13
Christ's priesthood ..... Heb. 7:3
God's Word ..... 1 Pet. 1:23
Believer's eternity ..... 1 John 2:17

B. *Sphere of, in the Christian's life:*
Christ ..... John 15:4-6
Christ's words ..... John 15:7
Christ's love ..... John 15:10
Christ's doctrine ..... 2 John 9
The Holy Spirit ..... John 14:16
God's Word ..... 1 John 2:14, 24
One's earthly calling ..... 1 Cor. 7:20, 24
The truth ..... 2 John 2

C. *Descriptive of the believer's:*
Protection ..... Ps. 91:1
Satisfaction ..... Prov. 19:23
Fruitfulness ..... John 15:4, 5
Prayer life ..... John 15:7
Assurance ..... 1 John 2:28

Abiel—*God is father*

1. The grandfather of Saul and Abner ..... 1 Sam. 9:1
2. David's mighty man ..... 1 Chr. 11:32
Also called Abi-albon ..... 2 Sam. 23:31

Abiezer—*the father is help*

1. A descendant of Joseph ..... Josh. 17:1, 2
Called Jeezer ..... Num. 26:30
Family settles at Ophrah ..... Judg. 6:24
Gideon belongs to ..... Judg. 6:11, 12
Family rallies to Gideon's call ..... Judg. 6:34
2. A mighty man and commander in David's army ..... 2 Sam. 23:27

Abiezrite

A member of the family of Abiezer ..... Judg. 6:11; Judg. 6:24, 34

Abigail—*the father is joyful*

1. Nabal's beautiful and wise wife ..... 1 Sam. 25:3
Appeases David's anger ..... 1 Sam. 25:14-35
Becomes David's wife ..... 1 Sam. 25:36-42
Captured and rescued ..... 1 Sam. 30:5, 18
Mother of Chileab ..... 2 Sam. 3:3
2. A stepsister of David ..... 1 Chr. 2:16, 17

Abihail—*the father is might*

1. A Levite head of the house of Merari ..... Num. 3:35
2. Abishur's wife ..... 1 Chr. 2:29
3. A Gadite chief in Bashan ..... 1 Chr. 5:14
4. Wife of King Rehoboam ..... 2 Chr. 11:18
5. Father of Queen Esther ..... Esth. 2:15

Abihu—*he is father*

Second of Aaron's four sons ..... Ex. 6:23
Ascends Mt. Sinai ..... Ex. 24:1, 9
Chosen as priest ..... Ex. 28:1
Offers, with Nadab, strange fire ..... Lev. 10:1-7
Died in the presence of the Lord ..... Num. 3:4
Dies with heirs ..... 1 Chr. 24:2

Abihud—*the father is majesty*

A Benjamite ..... 1 Chr. 8:3

Abijah, Abia, Abiah—*Jehovah is Father*

1. Wife of Hezron ..... 1 Chr. 2:24
2. Son of Becher ..... 1 Chr. 7:8
3. Samuel's second son; follows corrupt ways ..... 1 Sam. 8:2
4. Descendant of Aaron; head of an office of priests ..... 1 Chr. 24:3, 10
Zechariah belongs to ..... Luke 1:5
5. Son of Jeroboam I ..... 1 Kin. 14:1-18
6. Slays 500,000 Israelites ..... 2 Chr. 13:13-20
7. Fathers 38 children by 14 wives ..... 2 Chr. 13:21
8. The mother of Hezekiah ..... 2 Chr. 29:1
Called Abi ..... 2 Kin. 18:2
9. A priest who signs the document ..... Neh. 10:7
10. A priest returning from Babylon with Zerubbabel ..... Neh. 12:1, 4, 17

Abijam—(another form of Abijah)

King of Judah ..... 1 Kin. 14:31
Son and successor of King Rehoboam ..... 1 Kin. 15:1-7
Follows in his father's sins ..... 1 Kin. 15:3, 4
Wars against King Jeroboam ..... 1 Kin. 15:6, 7

Abilene—*grassy place*

A province or tetrarchy of Syria ..... Luke 3:1

Ability—*power to perform*

A. *Descriptive of:*
Material prosperity ..... Deut. 16:17
Emotional strength ..... Num. 11:14
Military power ..... Num. 13:31; 1 Kin. 9:21
Physical strength ..... Ex. 18:18, 23
Mental power ..... Gen. 15:5
Moral power ..... 1 Cor. 3:2
Spiritual power ..... James 3:2
Divine power ..... Rom. 4:21

B. *Of God's power to:*
Deliver ..... 1 Cor. 10:13
Humble men ..... Dan. 4:37
Create life ..... Matt. 3:9
Destroy ..... Matt. 10:28
Preserve believers ..... John 10:28
Keep His promise ..... Rom. 4:21
Make us stand ..... Rom. 16:25
Supply grace ..... 2 Cor. 9:8
Exceed our petitions ..... Eph. 3:20
Service ..... 1 Pet. 4:11
Comfort others ..... 2 Cor. 1:4
Keep what we have entrusted ..... 2 Tim. 1:12
Save from death ..... Heb. 5:7
Resurrect men ..... Heb. 11:19
Keep from falling ..... Jude 24, 25

C. *Of Christ's power to:*
Heal ..... Matt. 9:28
Subdue all things ..... Phil. 3:21
Help His own ..... Heb. 2:18
Have compassion ..... Heb. 4:15, 16
Save completely ..... Heb. 7:25

D. *Of the Christian's power to:*
Speak for the Lord ..... Luke 21:15
Admonish ..... Rom. 15:14
Survive testings ..... 1 Cor. 3:13
Withstand Satan ..... Eph. 6:11, 13
Convince opposition ..... Titus 1:9
Bridle the whole body ..... James 3:2

Abimael—*God is Father*

A son of Joktan ..... Gen. 10:28

Abimelech—*the father is king*

1. A Philistine king of Gerar ..... Gen. 20:1-18
Makes treaty with Abraham ..... Gen. 21:22-34
2. A second king of Gerar ..... Gen. 26:1-12
Tells Isaac to go home ..... Gen. 26:13-16
Makes a treaty with Isaac concerning certain wells ..... Gen. 26:17-33
3. A son of Gideon by a concubine ..... Judg. 8:31
Conspires to become king ..... Judg. 9:1-4
Slays his 70 brothers ..... Judg. 9:5
Made king of Shechem ..... Judg. 9:6
Rebuked by Jotham, lone survivor ..... Judg. 9:7-21
Conspired against by Gaal ..... Judg. 9:22-29
Captures Shechem and Thebez ..... Judg. 9:41-50
Death of ..... Judg. 9:51-57
4. A son of Abiathar the priest ..... 1 Chr. 18:16
Also called Ahimelech ..... 1 Chr. 24:6

Abinadab—*the father is generous*

1. A man of Kirjath-jearim whose house tabernacles the ark of the Lord ..... 1 Sam. 7:1, 2
2. The second of Jesse's eight sons ..... 1 Sam. 16:8
A soldier in Saul's army ..... 1 Sam. 17:13
3. A son of Saul slain at Mt. Gilboa ..... 1 Sam. 31:1-8
Bones of, buried by men of Jabesh ..... 1 Chr. 10:1-12
4. The father of one of Solomon's sons-in-law ..... 1 Kin. 4:11

Abinoam—*the father is pleasantness*

Father of Barak ..... Judg. 4:6

Abiram—*the father is exalted*

1. Reubenite who conspired against Moses ..... Num. 16:1-50
2. The first-born son of Hiel ..... 1 Kin. 16:34; Josh. 6:26

Abishag—*the father wanders*

A Shunammite employed as David's nurse ..... 1 Kin. 1:1-4, 15
Witnessed David's choice of Solomon as successor ..... 1 Kin. 1:15-31
Adonijah slain for desiring to marry her ..... 1 Kin. 2:13-25

Abishai—*father of a gift*

A son of Zeruiah, David's sister ..... 2 Sam. 2:18
Brother of Joab and Asahel ..... 1 Chr. 2:16
Rebuked by David ..... 1 Sam. 26:5-9
Serves under Joab in David's army ..... 2 Sam. 2:17, 18
Joins Joab in blood-revenge against Abner ..... 2 Sam. 2:18-24
Co-commander of David's army ..... 2 Sam. 10:9, 10
Loyal to David during Absalom's uprising ..... 2 Sam. 16:9-12
Sternly rebuked by David ..... 2 Sam. 19:21-23
Loyal to David during Sheba's rebellion ..... 2 Sam. 20:1-6, 10
Slays 300 Philistines ..... 2 Sam. 23:18
Slays 18,000 Edomites ..... 1 Chr. 18:12, 13
Saves David by killing a giant ..... 2 Sam. 21:16, 17

Abishalom—*father of peace*

A variant form of Absalom ..... 1 Kin. 15:2, 10

Abishua—*the father is salvation*

1. A Benjamite ..... 1 Chr. 8:3, 4
2. Phinehas' son ..... 1 Chr. 6:4, 5, 50

Abishur—*the father is a wall*

A Jerahmeelite ..... 1 Chr. 2:28, 29

Abital—*the father is dew*

Wife of David ..... 2 Sam. 3:2, 4

Abitub—*the father is goodness*

A Benjamite ..... 1 Chr. 8:8-11

Abiud—Greek form of Abihud

Ancestor of Jesus ..... Matt. 1:13

Ablution—*ceremonial washing*

Of priests ..... Ex. 30:18-21; Ex. 40:30, 31

SUBJECT	REFERENCE
Of ceremonially unclean	Lev. 14:7-9 Lev. 15:5-10
Of a house	Lev. 14:52
By Pharisees	Mark 7:1-5

Abner—*the father is a lamp*

Commands Saul's army	1 Sam. 14:50, 51
Introduces David to Saul	1 Sam. 17:55-58
Rebuked by David	1 Sam. 26:5, 14-16
Saul's cousin	1 Sam. 14:50, 51
Supports Ish-bosheth as Saul's successor	2 Sam. 2:8-10
Defeated by David's men	2 Sam. 2:12-17
Kills Asahel in self-defense	2 Sam. 2:18-23
Pursued by Joab	2 Sam. 2:24-32
Slain by Joab	2 Sam. 3:8-27
Death of, condemned by David	2 Sam. 3:28-39

Abolish—*to do away with*

A. *Of evil things:*

Idolatry	Is. 2:18
Man-made ordinances	Col. 2:20-22
Death	1 Cor. 15:26
Evil works	Ezek. 6:6
Enmity	Eph. 2:15

B. *Of things good for a while:*

Old covenant	2 Cor. 3:13
Present world	Heb. 1:10-12
Temporal rule	1 Cor. 15:24
The partial	1 Cor. 13:10

C. *Of things not to be abolished:*

God's righteousness	Is. 51:6
God's Word	Matt. 5:18

Abominations—*things utterly repulsive*

A. *Descriptive of:*

Hebrew eating with Egyptians	Gen. 43:32
Undesirable social relations	Ex. 8:26
Spiritist practices	Deut. 18:9-12
Heathen idolatry	Deut. 7:25, 26
Child-sacrifice	Deut. 12:31
Pagan gods	2 Kin. 23:13

B. *Applied to perverse sexual relations:*

Unnatural acts	Lev. 18:19-29
Wrong clothing	Deut. 22:5
Prostitution and sodomy	Deut. 23:17, 18
Reclaiming a defiled woman	Deut. 24:4
Racial inter-marriage	Ezra 9:1-14

C. *In ceremonial matters, applied to:*

Unclean animals	Lev. 11:10-23, 41-43
Deformed animals	Deut. 17:1
Heathen practices in God's house	2 Chr. 36:14

D. *Sinfulness of, seen in:*

Being enticed	1 Kin. 11:5, 7
Delighting in	Is. 66:3
Rejecting admonitions against	Jer. 44:4, 5
Defiling God's house	Jer. 7:30
Being polluted	Ezek. 20:7, 30-32

E. *Judgments upon, manifested in:*

Stoning to death	Deut. 17:2-5
Destroying a city	Deut. 13:13-17
Forfeiting God's mercy	Ezek. 5:11-13
Experiencing God's fury	Ezek. 20:7, 8

F. *Things especially classed as:*

Silver or gold from graven images	Deut. 7:25
Perverse man	Prov. 3:32
Seven sins	Prov. 6:16-19
False balance	Prov. 11:1
Lying lips	Prov. 12:22
Sacrifices of the wicked	Prov. 15:8, 9
Proud in heart	Prov. 16:5
Justifying the wicked	Prov. 17:15
Scorner	Prov. 24:9
Prayer of one who turns away his ear	Prov. 28:9
False worship	Is. 1:13
Scant measures	Mic. 6:10
Self-righteousness	Luke 16:15

Abomination of desolation

Predicted by Daniel	Dan. 9:27
Cited by Christ	Matt. 24:15

SUBJECT	REFERENCE

Abortion—*accidental or planned miscarriage*

Laws concerning	Ex. 21:22-25
Pronounced as a judgment	Hos. 9:14
Sought to relieve misery	Job 3:16
Of animals, by thunder	Ps. 29:9
Figurative of abrupt conversion	1 Cor. 15:8

Abound—*to increase greatly*

A. *Of good things:*

God's truth	Rom. 3:7
God's grace	Rom. 5:15, 20
Hope	Rom. 15:13
God's work	1 Cor. 15:58
Suffering for Christ	2 Cor. 1:5
Joy in suffering	2 Cor. 8:2
Gracious works	2 Cor. 8:7
Good works	2 Cor. 9:8
Wisdom	Eph. 1:8
Love	Phil. 1:9
Fruitfulness	Phil. 4:17, 18
Faith	Col. 2:7
Pleasing God	1 Thess. 4:1
Christian qualities	2 Pet. 1:5-7
Blessings	Prov. 28:20
Charity	2 Thess. 1:3

B. *Source of, in good things:*

From God	2 Cor. 9:8
From Christian generosity	2 Cor. 8:2, 3
Faithfulness	Prov. 28:20
Generosity	Phil. 4:14-17

C. *Of evil things:*

Transgressions	Prov. 29:22
Lawlessness	Matt. 24:12
Increasing sins	Rom. 5:20

Abraham—*the father of a multitude*

A. *Ancestry and family:*

Descendant of Shem	1 Chr. 1:24-27
Son of Terah	Gen. 11:26
First named Abram	Gen. 11:27
A native of Ur	Gen. 11:28, 31
Pagan ancestors	Josh. 24:2
Weds Sarai	Gen. 11:29

B. *Wanderings of:*

Goes to Haran	Gen. 11:31
Receives God's call	Gen. 12:1-3 Acts 7:2-4
Prompted by faith	Heb. 11:8
Enters Canaan	Gen. 12:4-6
Canaan promised to, by God	Gen. 12:1, 7
Pitched his tent at Beth-el	Gen. 12:8
Famine sends him to Egypt	Gen. 12:10-20
Returns to Canaan enriched	Gen. 13:1-5
Chooses Hebron rather than strife	Gen. 13:6-12

C. *Testing and victory of:*

Separates from Lot	Gen. 13:8-12
Rescues captured Lot	Gen. 14:14-16
Receives Melchizedek's blessing	Gen. 14:18-20
Covenant renewed; a son promised to	Gen. 15:1-21
Justified by faith	Gen. 15:6 Rom. 4:3
Takes Hagar as concubine	Gen. 16:1-4
Ishmael born	Gen. 16:5-16
Covenant renewed; named Abraham	Gen. 17:1-8
Household of, circumcised	Gen. 17:9-14, 23-27
Promised a son	Gen. 17:15-19
Covenant in Isaac, not Ishmael	Gen. 17:20-22 Gal. 4:22-31
Receives messengers	Gen. 18:1-15
Intercedes concerning Sodom	Gen. 18:16-33
Witnesses Sodom's doom	Gen. 19:27, 28
His faith saves Lot	Gen. 19:29
Sojourns at Gerar; deceives Abimelech	Gen. 20:1-18
Isaac born to, and circumcised	Gen. 21:1-8
Sends Hagar and Ishmael away	Gen. 21:9-21
Makes covenant with Abimelech	Gen. 21:22-34
Testing of, in offering Isaac	Gen. 22:1-19
Receives news about Nahor	Gen. 22:20-24
Buys burial place for Sarah	Gen. 23:1-20

SUBJECT	REFERENCE
Obtains wife for Isaac	Gen. 24:1-67
Marries Keturah; fathers other children; dies	Gen. 25:1-10

D. *Characteristics of:*

Friend of God	2 Chr. 20:7
Obedient	Gen. 22:1-18
Tither	Gen. 14:20 Heb. 7:1, 2, 4
Generous	Gen. 13:8, 9
Courageous	Gen. 14:13-16
Independent	Gen. 14:21-23
Man of prayer	Gen. 18:23-33
Man of faith	Gen. 15:6
Rich man	Gen. 13:2
Mighty prince	Gen. 23:5, 6
Good provider	Gen. 25:5, 6

E. *References to, in the New Testament:*

In the line of faith	Heb. 11:8-10
Christ the true seed of	Matt. 1:1
Foresees Christ's day	John 8:56
Hears the Gospel preached	Gal. 3:8
Justified by faith	Rom. 4:1-12
Faith of, seen in works	James 2:21-23
Father of true believers	Matt. 8:11 Rom. 4:11-25 Gal. 3:7, 29
Sees the eternal city	Heb. 11:8-10, 13-16
Covenant with, still valid	Luke 1:73 Acts 3:25
Sons of, illustrate covenants	Gal. 4:22-31
Tithing of, has deeper meaning	Heb. 7:9, 10
Headship of, in marriage	1 Pet. 3:6, 7
Eternal home of, in heaven	Luke 16:19-25

Abraham's bosom

Expressive of heavenly status	Luke 16:22, 23

Abram (see Abraham)

Absalom—*the father of peace*

Son of David	2 Sam. 3:3
A handsome man	2 Sam. 14:25
Receives Tamar after her rape by Ammon	2 Sam. 13:20
Slays Ammon for raping Tamar	2 Sam. 13:22-33
Flees from David	2 Sam. 13:34-39
Returns through Joab's intrigue	2 Sam. 14:1-24
Fathers children	2 Sam. 14:27
Reconciled to David	2 Sam. 14:28-33
Alienates the people from David	2 Sam. 15:1-6
Conspires against David	2 Sam. 15:7-12
Takes Jerusalem	2 Sam. 15:13-29
Receives Hushai	2 Sam. 15:31-37
Hears Ahithophel's counsel	2 Sam. 16:20-23
Prefers Hushai's counsel	2 Sam. 17:5-14
Strategy of, revealed to David	2 Sam. 17:15-22
Masses his army against David	2 Sam. 17:24-26
Caught and slain by Joab	2 Sam. 18:9-18
Death of, brings sorrow to David	2 Sam. 18:19-33
Joab rebukes David for mourning over	2 Sam. 19:1-8
Death of, unites Israel again to David	2 Sam. 19:9-15

Absence

A. *Of physical relations:*

A child from its father	Gen. 37:32-35
Israel's ark	1 Sam. 4:21, 22
Israel from her land	2 Chr. 36:17-21
Believers from one another	Phil. 1:25, 26
Believers from Christ	2 Cor. 5:6-9

B. *Of God's Spirit as:*

Judgment on the world	Gen. 6:3
Judgment on an individual	1 Sam. 16:14
Unable to flee	Ps. 139:7-12

C. *Of graces:*

Holy Spirit	Jude 19
Faith	2 Thess. 3:2
Natural love	2 Tim. 3:2
Holiness	Rev. 22:11
Righteousness	Rev. 22:11

Absenteeism—*habitual absence from*

Work, condemned	2 Thess. 3:6-14
Church, rebuked	Heb. 10:25

SUBJECT — REFERENCE

Abstain—*to refrain from*

A. *From moral evil:*
- Vindictiveness .... 2 Sam. 16:5-14
- Idolatry .... Acts 15:20, 29
- Fornication .... Acts 15:20
- Sexual sins .... 1 Thess. 4:3
- Fleshly lusts .... 1 Pet. 2:11
- Evil appearances .... 1 Thess. 5:22

B. *From things:*
- Food .... 2 Sam. 12:16, 23
- Married relations .... Ex. 19:15; 1 Cor. 7:5
- Meats .... Rom. 14:1-23; 1 Cor. 8:1-13

C. *From unauthorized commands:*
- Forbidding to marry .... 1 Tim. 4:3
- Requiring man-made ceremonies .... Col. 2:20-23
- Abstaining from meats .... 1 Tim. 4:3

Abstinence—*to refrain from*
- Blood .... Acts 15:20
- Evil .... 1 Thess. 5:22
- Food .... Acts 27:21
- Fornication .... Acts 15:20; 1 Thess. 4:3
- Idolatry .... Acts 15:20
- Intoxicants .... Prov. 23:31
- Lust .... 1 Pet. 2:11
- Meats .... 1 Tim. 4:3
- Things offered to idols .... Acts 15:29
- Meats contaminated .... Acts 15:20

Abstinence—*to refrain from strong drink*

A. *Required of:*
- Priests .... Lev. 10:9
- Kings .... Prov. 31:4
- Nazarites .... Num. 6:1-4

B. *Failure of, a cause of:*
- Sudden death .... 1 Sam. 25:36-38
- Delirium tremens .... Prov. 23:31-35
- Insensibility to justice .... Is. 5:11, 12, 22, 23
- Error in judgment .... Is. 28:7
- Moral callousness .... Is. 56:12
- Revelry .... Dan. 5:2-4
- Debauchery .... Hab. 2:15, 16
- A weaker brother's stumble .... Rom. 14:20, 21
- Excess .... Eph. 5:18

C. *Examples of:*
- Manoah's wife .... Judg. 13:3, 4, 7
- Samson .... Judg. 16:17
- Hannah .... 1 Sam. 1:15
- Rechabites .... Jer. 35:1-19
- Daniel .... Dan. 1:8
- John the Baptist .... Luke 1:13-15

Abundance—*plentiful supply*

A. *Of material things:*
- Wealth .... 1 Kin. 10:10
- Rain .... 1 Kin. 18:41
- Metals .... 1 Chr. 22:3, 14
- Trees .... 1 Chr. 22:4; Neh. 9:25
- Sacrifices .... 1 Chr. 29:21
- Camels .... 2 Chr. 14:15
- Followers .... 2 Chr. 15:9
- Flocks and herds .... 2 Chr. 18:2; 2 Chr. 32:29
- Money .... 2 Chr. 24:11
- Weapons .... 2 Chr. 32:5
- Riches .... Ps. 52:7
- Milk .... Is. 7:22
- Wine .... Is. 56:12
- Horses .... Ezek. 26:10
- Labors .... 2 Cor. 11:23

B. *Of God's spiritual blessings:*
- Goodness .... Ex. 34:6
- Pardon .... Is. 55:7
- Peace and truth .... Jer. 33:6
- Answers to our prayers .... Eph. 3:20
- Grace .... 1 Tim. 1:14
- Mercy .... 1 Pet. 1:3

C. *Of spiritual things:*
- Predicted for Gospel times .... Is. 35:2
- Realized in the Messiah .... Ps. 72:7
- Given to the meek .... Ps. 37:11
- Through Christ .... Rom. 5:17, 20
- By grace .... 2 Cor. 4:15

D. *Of good things for Christians:*
- Greater usefulness .... Matt. 13:12
- Greater reward .... Matt. 25:29
- Spiritual life .... John 10:10
- Grace .... Rom. 5:17; 2 Cor. 4:15
- Christian service .... 1 Cor. 15:10
- Joy .... 2 Cor. 8:2
- Thanksgiving .... 2 Cor. 9:12
- Rejoicing .... Phil. 1:26
- Spiritual renewal .... Titus 3:5, 6
- Entrance in God's kingdom .... 2 Pet. 1:11

E. *Of undesirable things:*
- Witchcraft .... Is. 47:9
- Idleness .... Ezek. 16:49

F. *Characteristics of:*
- Given to the obedient .... Lev. 26:3-13
- Useful in God's work .... 2 Chr. 24:11
- Cannot satisfy fully .... Eccl. 5:10-12
- Not to be trusted .... Ps. 52:7
- Subject to conditions .... Mal. 3:10-12; Matt. 6:32, 33
- Can be taken away .... Luke 12:13-21
- Not a sign of real worth .... Luke 12:15

G. *Obtained by:*
- Putting away sin .... 2 Chr. 15:9
- Following God's commands .... 2 Chr. 17:5
- Given by God .... Job 36:31
- Through Christ .... John 10:10

Abuse—*application to a wrong purpose*

A. *Of physical things:*
- Sexual perversions .... Gen. 19:5-9, 31-38
- Immoral acts .... 1 Cor. 6:9
- Torture .... Judg. 16:21

B. *Of spiritual things:*
- Misuse of authority .... Num. 20:10-13; 1 Cor. 9:18
- Using the world wrongly .... 1 Cor. 7:31
- Perverting the truth .... 2 Pet. 2:10-22
- Corrupting God's ordinances .... 1 Sam. 2:12-17; 1 Cor. 11:17-22

C. *Manifested by:*
- Unbelieving .... Mark 15:29-32

Abyss

Translated:
- "deep" .... Luke 8:31
- "bottomless pit" .... Rev. 9:1, 2, 11; Rev. 17:8

Accad—*a city in the land of Shinar*
- City in Shinar .... Gen. 10:10

Acceptance—*the reception of one's person or service*

A. *Objects of, before God:*
- Righteousness and justice .... Prov. 21:3
- Our words and meditations .... Ps. 19:14
- Our dedication .... Rom. 12:1, 2
- Service .... Rom. 14:18
- Giving .... Rom. 15:16, 27
- Offerings .... Phil. 4:18
- Intercession .... 1 Tim. 2:1-3
- Helping parents .... 1 Tim. 5:4
- Spiritual sacrifices .... 1 Pet. 2:5
- Suffering because of Christ .... 1 Pet. 2:20

B. *Qualifications of, seen in:*
- Coming at God's time .... Is. 49:8; 2 Cor. 6:2
- Meeting God's requirements .... Job 42:8, 9
- Receiving divine sign .... Judg. 6:9-21
- Noting God's response .... 1 Sam. 7:8-10; John 12:28-30
- Responding to God's renewal .... Ezek. 20:40-44
- Manifesting spiritual rectitude .... Mic. 6:6-8

C. *Persons disqualified for, such as:*
- The wicked .... Ps. 82:2
- Blemished sacrifices .... Mal. 1:8, 10, 13
- Man's person .... Gal. 2:6
- Those who swear deceitfully .... Ps. 24:3-6

Access to God

A. *By means of:*
- Christ .... John 14:6
- Christ's blood .... Eph. 2:13
- Holy Spirit .... Eph. 2:18
- Faith .... Rom. 5:2
- Clean hands .... Ps. 24:3-5
- God's grace .... Eph. 1:6
- Prayer .... Matt. 6:6

B. *Characteristics of:*
- On God's choosing .... Ps. 64:4
- Sinners commanded to seek .... Is. 55:6; James 4:8
- With confidence .... Heb. 4:16
- Boldness .... Eph. 3:12
- Results from reconciliation .... Col. 1:21, 22
- Open to Gentiles .... Acts 14:27
- Experienced in Christ's priesthood .... Heb. 7:19-25
- Sought by God's people .... Ps. 27:4
- Bold in prayer .... Heb. 4:16
- A blessing to be chosen .... Ps. 65:4

Accho—*modern Acre* (a seaport 8 miles north of Mt. Carmel)
- Assigned to Asher .... Judg. 1:31
- Called Ptolemais in the New Testament .... Acts 21:7

Accident—*event not foreseen*

A. *Caused by:*
- An animal .... Num. 22:25
- A fall .... 2 Sam. 4:4

B. *Explanation of:*
- Known to God .... Deut. 29:29; Prov. 16:9, 33
- Misunderstood by men .... Luke 13:4, 5
- Subject to God's providence .... Rom. 8:28

Accommodation—*adaptation caused by human limitations*

A. *Physically, caused by:*
- Age and sex .... Gen. 33:13-15
- Strength and size .... 1 Sam. 17:38-40
- Inability to repay .... Luke 7:41, 42

B. *Spiritually, caused by:*
- Man's blindness .... Matt. 13:10-14
- Absence of the Spirit .... John 16:12, 13
- Carnality .... 1 Cor. 3:1, 2
- Spiritual immaturity .... Rom. 14:1-23
- Man's present limitations .... 1 Cor. 2:7-16
- Degrees of light .... Heb. 9:7-15

Accomplish—*to fulfill*

A. *Of God's Word concerning:*
- Judah's captivity .... 2 Chr. 36:23
- Judah's return .... Dan. 9:2
- God's sovereign plan .... Is. 55:11
- The Messiah's advent .... Dan. 9:24-27
- Christ's suffering .... Luke 18:31
- Christ's death .... John 19:28-30
- Final events .... Dan. 12:7

B. *Of human things:*
- Food .... 1 Kin. 5:9
- Purification rites .... Esth. 2:12
- Priestly ministry .... Luke 1:23
- Time of pregnancy .... Luke 2:6
- Afflictions .... 1 Pet. 5:9

Accord—*united agreement*

A. *Descriptive of:*
- A spontaneous response .... Acts 12:10, 20
- Voluntary action .... 2 Cor. 8:17
- Single-mindedness .... Josh. 9:2
- Spiritual unity .... Acts 1:14

B. *Manifested in:*
- Fellowship .... Acts 2:46
- Prayer .... Acts 4:24
- Opposition .... Acts 7:57
- Response .... Acts 8:6
- Decisions .... Acts 15:25
- Mind .... Phil. 2:2

Accountability—*responsibility for own acts*

A. *Kinds of:*
- Universal .... Rom. 14:12
- Personal .... 2 Sam. 12:1-15
- Personal and family .... Josh. 7:1-26
- Personal and national .... 2 Sam. 24:1-17
- Delayed but exacted .... 2 Sam. 21:1-14
- Final .... Rom. 2:1-12

B. *Determined by:*
- Federal headship .... Gen. 3:1-24; Rom. 5:12-21

SUBJECT REFERENCE

- Personal responsibility ...... Ezek. 18:1-32
- Faithfulness ...... Matt. 25:14-30
- Knowledge ...... Luke 12:47, 48
- Conscience ...... Rom. 2:12-16
- Greater light ...... Rom. 2:17-29
- Maturity of judgment ...... 1 Cor. 8:1-13

Accursed—*under a curse*

A. *Caused by:*

- Hanging on a tree ...... Deut. 21:23
- Sin among God's people ...... Josh. 7:12
- Possessing a banned thing ...... Josh. 6:18
- Preaching contrary to the Gospel ...... Gal. 1:8, 9
- Blaspheming Christ ...... 1 Cor. 12:3

B. *Objects of being:*

- A city ...... Josh. 6:17
- A forbidden thing ...... Josh. 22:20
- An old sinner ...... Is. 65:20
- Christ-haters or non-believers ...... 1 Cor. 16:22
- Paul (for the sake of Israel) ...... Rom. 9:3

Accusations—*charges*

A. *Kinds of:*

- Pagan ...... Dan. 3:8
- Personal ...... Dan. 6:24
- Public ...... John 18:29
- Perverted ...... 1 Pet. 3:16

B. *Sources of, in:*

- The devil ...... Job 1:6-12; Rev. 12:9, 10
- Enemies ...... Ezra 4:6
- Man's conscience ...... John 8:9
- God's Word ...... John 5:45
- Hypocritical ...... John 8:6, 10, 11
- The last days ...... 2 Tim. 3:1, 3
- Apostates ...... 2 Pet. 2:10, 11

C. *Forbidden:*

- Against servants ...... Prov. 30:10
- Falsely ...... Luke 3:14
- Among women ...... Titus 2:3

D. *False, examples of, against:*

- Jacob ...... Gen. 31:26-30
- Joseph ...... Gen. 39:10-21
- Ahimelech ...... 1 Sam. 22:11-16
- David ...... 2 Sam. 10:3
- Job ...... Job 2:4, 5
- Jeremiah ...... Jer. 26:8-11
- Amos ...... Amos 7:10, 11
- Joshua ...... Zech. 3:1-5
- Christ ...... Matt. 26:59-66
- Stephen ...... Acts 6:11-14
- Paul and Silas ...... Acts 16:19-21
- Paul ...... Acts 21:27-29
- Christians ...... 1 Pet. 2:12

Aceldama

- Field called "field of blood" ...... Acts 1:19

Achaia—*a region of Greece*

- Visited by Paul ...... Acts 18:1, 12
- Gallio proconsul ...... Acts 18:12
- Apollos preaches in ...... Acts 18:24-28
- Christians of, very generous ...... Rom. 15:26
- Saints in all of ...... 2 Cor. 1:1
- Paul commends Christians of ...... 2 Cor. 11:10
- Gospel proclaimed throughout ...... 1 Thess. 1:7, 8

Achaicus—*belonging to Achaia*

- A Corinthian Christian who visited Paul ...... 1 Cor. 16:17, 18

Achan, Achar—*trouble*

- A son of Carmi ...... Josh. 7:1
- Sin of, caused Israel's defeat ...... Josh. 7:1-15
- Stoned to death ...... Josh. 7:16-25
- Sin of, recalled ...... Josh. 22:20
- Also called Achar ...... 1 Chr. 2:7

Achaz—*Greek name of Ahaz*

- Ancestor of Jesus ...... Matt. 1:9

Achbor—*mouse*

1. Father of Edomite king ...... Gen. 36:36, 38
2. A courtier under Josiah ...... 2 Kin. 22:12, 14
   Called Abdon ...... 2 Chr. 34:20

Achim—*short form of Jehoiachim*

- Ancestor of Jesus ...... Matt. 1:14

Achish—*serpent-charmer*

- A king of Gath ...... 1 Sam. 21:10-15

SUBJECT REFERENCE

- David seeks refuge ...... 1 Sam. 27:1-12
- Forced to expel David by Philistine lords ...... 1 Sam. 28:1, 2
- Receives Shimei's servants ...... 1 Kin. 2:39, 40

Achmetha—*capital of Media* (same as Ecbatana)

- Site of Persian archives ...... Ezra 6:2

Achor, valley of—*trouble*

- Site of Achan's stoning ...... Josh. 7:24-26
- On Judah's boundary ...... Josh. 15:7
- Promises concerning ...... Is. 65:10

Achsa, Achsah—*anklet*

- A daughter of Caleb ...... 1 Chr. 2:49
- Given to Othniel ...... Josh. 15:16-19
- Given springs of water ...... Judg. 1:12-15

Achshaph—*dedicated*

- A royal city of Canaan ...... Josh. 11:1
- Captured by Joshua ...... Josh. 12:7, 20
- Assigned to Asher ...... Josh. 19:24, 25

Achzib—*a lie*

1. City of Judah ...... Josh. 15:44
   Also called Chezib ...... Gen. 38:5
2. Town of Asher ...... Josh. 19:29

Acknowledge—*to recognize*

A. *Evil objects of:*

- Sin ...... Ps. 32:5
- Transgressions ...... Ps. 51:3
- Iniquity ...... Jer. 3:13
- Wickedness ...... Jer. 14:20

B. *Good objects of:*

- God ...... Prov. 3:6
- God's might ...... Is. 33:13
- God's people ...... Is. 61:9
- God's mystery ...... Col. 2:2
- God's truth ...... 2 Tim. 2:25
- The apostles ...... 1 Cor. 14:37
- Christian leaders ...... 1 Cor. 16:18

Acquaintance—*personal knowledge*

- With God, gives peace ...... Job 22:21
- Deserted by ...... Ps. 31:11
- Made an abomination ...... Ps. 88:8, 18
- Jesus sought among ...... Luke 2:44
- Stand afar off from Christ ...... Luke 23:49
- Come to Paul ...... Acts 24:23
- Of God, with man's ways ...... Ps. 139:3

Acquit—*to declare to be innocent*

- Not possible with the wicked ...... Nah. 1:3
- Sought by the righteous ...... Job 7:21
- Difficulty of obtaining ...... Job 9:28-31

Acre—*a land measurement*

- Plowing of, by a yoke of oxen ...... 1 Sam. 14:14
- Descriptive of barrenness ...... Is. 5:10

Acrostic

- A literary device using the Hebrew alphabet; illustrated best in Hebrew ...... Ps. 119:1-176

Acts of the Apostles—*book of New Testament*

- Written by Luke ...... Luke 1:1-4; Acts 1:1, 2

Adadah—*holiday*

- A city of Judah ...... Josh. 15:22

Adah—*ornament*

1. One of Lamech's wives ...... Gen. 4:19
2. One of Esau's wives ...... Gen. 36:2, 4, 10, 12
   Also called Bashemath ...... Gen. 26:34

Adaiah—*Jehovah has adorned*

1. The maternal grandfather of Josiah ...... 2 Kin. 22:1
2. A Levite ...... 1 Chr. 6:41
3. Son of Shimhi ...... 1 Chr. 8:21
   Called Shema ...... 1 Chr. 8:13
4. Aaronite priest ...... 1 Chr. 9:10-12
5. The father of Maaseiah ...... 2 Chr. 23:1
6. A son of Bani ...... Ezra 10:29
7. Another of a different family of Bani ...... Ezra 10:34, 39
8. A descendant of Judah ...... Neh. 11:4, 5

Adalia

- Haman's son ...... Esth. 9:8, 10

SUBJECT REFERENCE

Adam—*red earth*

A. *Creation of:*

- In God's image ...... Gen. 1:26, 27
- By God's breath ...... Gen. 2:7
- A living soul ...... 1 Cor. 15:45
- From dust ...... Gen. 2:7
- Before Eve ...... 1 Tim. 2:13
- Upright ...... Eccl. 7:29
- Intelligent being ...... Gen. 2:19, 20

B. *Position of, first:*

- Worker ...... Gen. 2:8, 15
- To receive God's law ...... Gen. 2:16, 17
- Husband ...... Gen. 2:18-25
- Man to sin ...... Gen. 3:6-12
- To receive promise of the Messiah ...... Gen. 3:15
- Father ...... Gen. 4:1
- Head of race ...... Rom. 5:12-14

C. *Sin of:*

- Instigated by Satan ...... Gen. 3:1-5
- Prompted by Eve ...... Gen. 3:6
- Done knowingly ...... 1 Tim. 2:14
- Resulted in broken fellowship ...... Gen. 3:8
- Brought God's curse ...... Gen. 3:14-19

D. *Descendants of, are all:*

- Sinners ...... Rom. 5:12
- Subject to death ...... Rom. 5:12-14
- Scattered over the earth ...... Deut. 32:8
- In need of salvation ...... John 3:16

Adam—*a city near Zaretan*

- Site of Jordan's waters rising to let Israel pass over ...... Josh. 3:16

Adam, Last—*an attribution of Christ*

- Prefigured in Adam ...... Rom. 5:14
- Gift of, abound to many ...... Rom. 5:15
- A quickening spirit ...... 1 Cor. 15:45
- Spiritual and heavenly ...... 1 Cor. 15:46-48

Adamah—*red ground*

- City of Naphtali ...... Josh. 19:35, 36

Adami—*earthy*

- In Naphtali ...... Josh. 19:33

Adam, second

- Expressive of Christ ...... 1 Cor. 15:20-24; 1 Cor. 15:45

Adar—*dark or cloudy*

- A town of Judah ...... Josh. 15:1, 3

Adar—*the 12th month of the Hebrew year*

- Date set by Haman for massacre of Jews ...... Esth. 3:7, 13
- Date adopted for Purim ...... Esth. 9:19, 21, 26-28
- Date of completion of Temple ...... Ezra 6:15

Adbeel—*disciplined of God*

- A son of Ishmael ...... Gen. 25:13

Add—*to increase the sum of*

A. *Of material things:*

- Another child ...... Gen. 30:24
- A population ...... 2 Sam. 24:3
- Heavy burdens ...... 1 Kin. 12:11, 14
- Years to life ...... Prov. 3:2
- Kingly majesty ...... Dan. 4:36
- Stature ...... Matt. 6:27

B. *Of good things:*

- No sorrow ...... Prov. 10:22
- Inspired words ...... Jer. 36:32
- Learning ...... Prov. 16:23
- Spiritual blessings ...... Matt. 6:33
- Converts to Christ ...... Acts 2:41, 47
- A covenant ...... Gal. 3:15
- The Law ...... Gal. 3:19

C. *Of evil things:*

- Additions to God's Word ...... Deut. 4:2
- National sins ...... 1 Sam. 12:19
- Iniquity ...... Ps. 69:27
- Sin to sin ...... Is. 30:1
- Grief to sorrow ...... Jer. 45:3
- Personal sin ...... Luke 3:19, 20
- Afflictions ...... Phil. 1:16

Addan—*strong*

- A place in Babylonia whose returnees fail to prove Israelite ancestry ...... Ezra 2:59

SUBJECT	REFERENCE
Addar—*wide, open place*	
A Benjamite	1 Chr. 8:3
Also called Ard	Num. 26:40
Adder—*a venomous serpent*	
Figurative of Dan's treachery	Gen. 49:17
Sting of wine	Prov. 23:31, 32
Wickedness of sinners	Ps. 58:3, 4
Triumph of saints	Ps. 91:13
Addi—*my witness*	
Ancestor of Jesus	Luke 3:23, 28
Addiction—*compulsive or habitual devotion*	
To ministry of the saints	1 Cor. 16:15
Additions to the church	
A. *Manner and number of:*	
"The Lord added"	Acts 2:47
"Believers . . . added to the Lord"	Acts 5:14
"Disciples . . . multiplied"	Acts 6:1
"A great company of priests"	Acts 6:7
"Churches . . . were multiplied"	Acts 9:31
"A great number believed"	Acts 11:21
"Much people added"	Acts 11:24
"Churches . . . increased in number"	Acts 16:5
B. *By means of:*	
Word preached	Acts 2:14-41
The Spirit's convicting power	John 16:7-11
The Gospel as God's power	Rom. 1:16
Responding faith	Acts 14:1
Addon (see Addan)	
Address—*a public message*	
A. *In Old Testament:*	
Moses' expository	Deut. 1:1—4:40
Moses' second	Deut. 4:44—26:19
Moses' third	Deut. 27:1—30:20
Moses' fourth	Deut. 32:1-43
Moses' final	Deut. 33:1-29
Joshua's exhortation	Josh. 23:2-16
Joshua's farewell	Josh. 24:1-25
Solomon's to God	1 Kin. 3:6-9
Ezra's expository	Neh. 8:1-8
Jeremiah's Temple sermon	Jer. 7:1—10:25
B. *Of Paul:*	
First	Acts 9:20-22
Second	Acts 13:16-41
To Peter	Gal. 2:14-21
To women	Acts 16:13
With Silas	Acts 16:29-32
At Athens	Acts 17:22-31
At Troas	Acts 20:6, 7
To elders	Acts 20:17-35
To the crowd	Acts 22:1-21
Before Felix	Acts 24:10-21
Before Agrippa	Acts 26:1-29
On the ship	Acts 27:21-26
Final recorded	Acts 28:25-28
C. *Of Peter:*	
In upper room	Acts 1:13-22
Pentecost	Acts 2:14-40
At Temple	Acts 3:12-26
In house of Cornelius	Acts 10:34-43
At Jerusalem council	Acts 15:7-11
D. *Of Others:*	
Stephen	Acts 7:2-60
Herod	Acts 12:21, 22
James	Acts 15:13-21
Tertullus	Acts 24:1-8
Adiel—*ornament of God*	
1. A Simeonite prince	1 Chr. 4:24, 36
2. Aaronite priest	1 Chr. 9:12, 13
3. Father of Azmaveth	1 Chr. 27:25
Adin—*effeminate*	
1. A man whose descendants return with Zerubbabel	Ezra 2:2, 15
2. A man whose descendants return with Ezra	Ezra 8:1, 6
3. Sealer of the covenant	Neh. 10:1, 16
Adina—*delicate*	
A Reubenite captain under David	1 Chr. 11:42
Adino—*slender*	
A mighty man under David	2 Sam. 23:8
Compare parallel passage in	1 Chr. 11:11
Adithaim—*double ornaments*	
A city of Judah	Josh. 15:21, 36
Adjuration—*placing under oath*	
Joshua's, to Jericho	Josh. 6:26
Saul's, to those breaking a fast	1 Sam. 14:24-28
Ahab's, to the prophet Micaiah	1 Kin. 22:16
Caiaphas', by God	Matt. 26:63
Demon's, by God	Mark 5:7
Exorcists', by Jesus	Acts 19:13
Paul's charge, by the Lord	1 Thess. 5:27
Adlai—*Jehovah is just*	
Father of Shaphat	1 Chr. 27:29
Admah—*red earth*	
A city near Sodom	Gen. 10:19
Joins other cities against Chedorlaomer	Gen. 14:1-4, 8
Destroyed with Sodom and Gomorrah	Gen. 19:24-28
Admatha—*God-given*	
One of Ahasuerus' chamberlains	Esth. 1:14, 15
Administer—*service*	
Applied to:	
Judgment	1 Kin. 3:28
Vengeance	Jer. 21:12
Justice	2 Sam. 8:15
Administration—*the management or disposition of affairs*	
Of gifts to Jerusalem saints	2 Cor. 8:19, 20
Of spiritual gifts	1 Cor. 12:5 2 Cor. 9:12
Of government matters	Rom. 13:3-5
Of new covenant	2 Cor. 3:6
Admiration—*exceptional esteem*	
Reserved for saints	2 Thess. 1:10
Flattering, shown by false teachers	Jude 16
Astounding, manifested by John	Rev. 17:6, 7
Admonition—*wise words spoken against evil acts*	
A. *Performed by:*	
God	Heb. 8:5
Earthly fathers	Eph. 6:4
Leaders	1 Thess. 5:12
Christians	Rom. 15:14
B. *Directed against:*	
A remnant	Jer. 42:19
Elders	Acts 20:28-35
Those who will not work	2 Thess. 3:10, 15
Heretics	Titus 3:10
C. *Sources of in:*	
Scriptures	1 Cor. 10:11
Wise words	Eccl. 12:11, 12
Spiritual knowledge	Col. 3:16
Adna—*pleasure*	
1. Jew who divorced his foreign wife	Ezra 10:18-30
2. Postexilic priest	Neh. 12:12-15
Adnah—*pleasure*	
1. Captain of Saul	1 Chr. 12:20
2. Chief Captain of Jehoshaphat	2 Chr. 17:14
Ado—*activity, tumult, fuss*	
Not to make	Mark 5:39
Adonai—*Lord*	
The Hebrew name for God (translated "Lord") expressing lordship (found in the following five compound words)	
Adoni-bezek—*lord of Bezek*	
A king of Bezek	Judg. 1:3-7
Adonijah—*my Lord is Jehovah*	
1. David's fourth son	2 Sam. 3:2, 4
Attempts to usurp throne	1 Kin. 1:5-53
Desires Abishag as wife	1 Kin. 2:13-18
Executed by Solomon	1 Kin. 2:19-25
2. A teacher	2 Chr. 17:8, 9
3. A Jew who signed the document	Neh. 9:38; 10:16
Probably the same as Adonikam in	Ezra 2:13
Adonikam—*my Lord has risen*	
Descendants of, return from exile	Ezra 2:13
Adoniram, Adoram—*my Lord is exalted*	
A son of Abda	1 Kin. 4:6
Official under David, Solomon, and Rehoboam	2 Sam. 20:24 1 Kin. 5:14 1 Kin. 12:18
Stoned by angry Israelites	1 Kin. 12:18
Called Hadoram	2 Chr. 10:18
Adoni-zedek—*my Lord is righteous*	
An Amorite king of Jerusalem	Josh. 10:1-5
Defeated and slain by Joshua	Josh. 10:6-27
Adoption—*the legal act of investing with sonship*	
A. *Used naturally of:*	
Eliezer under Abraham	Gen. 15:2-4
Joseph's sons under Jacob	Gen. 48:5, 14, 16
Moses under Pharaoh's daughter	Ex. 2:10 Acts 7:21
Esther under Mordecai	Esth. 2:7
B. *Used spiritually of Israel as:*	
Elected by God	Deut. 14:1, 2 Rom. 11:1-32
Blessed by God	Rom. 9:4
Realized in history	Ex. 4:22, 23
C. *Used spiritually of the Gentiles as:*	
Predicted in the prophets	Is. 65:1
Confirmed by faith	Rom. 10:20
Realized in the new covenant	Eph. 2:12 Eph. 3:1-6
D. *The time of:*	
Past, predestined to	Rom. 8:29
Present, regarded as sons	John 1:12, 13 John 3:1-11
Future, glorified as sons	Rom. 8:19, 23 1 John 3:2
E. *The source of:*	
By God's grace	Rom. 4:16, 17
By faith	Gal. 3:7, 26
Through Christ	Gal. 4:4, 5
F. *Assurances of, by:*	
Spirit's witness	Rom. 8:16
Spirit's leading	Rom. 8:14
"Abba, Father"	Rom. 8:15
Changed life	1 John 3:9-17
Father's chastening	Prov. 3:11, 12 Heb. 12:5-11
G. *The blessings of:*	
A new nature	2 Cor. 5:17
A new name	Is. 62:2, 12 Rev. 3:12
Access to God	Eph. 2:18
Fatherly love	1 John 3:1
Help in prayer	Matt. 6:5-15
Spiritual unity	John 17:11, 21 Eph. 2:18-22
A glorious inheritance	John 14:1-3 Rom. 8:17, 18
Adoraim—*double honor*	
A city fortified by Rehoboam	2 Chr. 11:5, 9
Adoram—*the Lord is exalted*	
An official over forced labor	2 Sam. 20:24 1 Kin. 12:18
See Adoniram	
Adoration—*reverential praise*	
A. *Rendered falsely to:*	
Idols	Is. 44:15, 17, 19
An image	Dan. 3:5-7
Heavenly hosts	2 Kin. 17:16
Satan	Luke 4:8
Men	Acts 10:25, 26
Angels	Col. 2:18, 23
B. *Rendered properly to God:*	
Illustrated	Is. 6:1-5

SUBJECT ... REFERENCE

Taught ... Ps. 95—100
Proclaimed ... Rev. 4:8-11

C. *Rendered properly to Christ as God by:*
Wise men ... Matt. 2:1, 11
Leper ... Matt. 8:2
Ruler ... Matt. 9:18
Disciples ... Matt. 14:22, 33
Woman ... Matt. 15:25
Mother ... Matt. 20:20
Blind man ... John 9:1, 38
Every creature ... Phil. 2:10, 11

See also Worship

Adornment

A. *Used literally of:*
A ruler ... Gen. 41:42-44
A harlot ... Gen. 38:14, 15; Rev. 17:3, 4
A woman ... Is. 3:16-24; 1 Tim. 2:9
A building ... Luke 21:5
A bride ... Rev. 21:2

B. *Used spiritually of:*
God ... Ps. 104:1, 2
Messiah ... Ps. 45:7, 8
Believer as justified ... Is. 61:10
Believer as sanctified ... Titus 2:10
Israel restored ... Jer. 31:4
Saintly woman ... 1 Tim. 2:9
Saints in glory ... Rev. 19:14

C. *Guidelines for:*
In modesty ... 1 Tim. 2:9
Not external ... 1 Pet. 3:3-5

Adrammelech—*Adar is king*

1. An Assyrian god worshiped by the Samarians ... 2 Kin. 17:31
2. Killed Sennacherib ... 2 Kin. 19:36, 37; Is. 37:38

Adramyttium—*a seaport of Mysia in Asia Minor*

Travels of Paul ... Acts 27:2-6

Adriatic Sea

A part or the whole of the Adriatic Sea named after Adria, a city of Italy ... Acts 27:27

Adriel—*my help is God*

Marries Saul's eldest daughter ... 1 Sam. 18:19
Sons of, slain to atone Saul's crime ... 2 Sam. 21:8, 9

Adullam—*refuge*

A town of Canaan ... Gen. 38:1, 12, 20
Conquered by Joshua ... Josh. 12:7, 15
Assigned to Judah ... Josh. 15:20, 35
Fortified by Rehoboam ... 2 Chr. 11:5-7
Symbol of Israel's glory ... Mic. 1:15
Reoccupied ... Neh. 11:30
David seeks refuge in caves of ... 1 Sam. 22:1, 2
Exploits of mighty men while there ... 2 Sam. 23:13-17

Adullamite—*a citizen of Adullam*

Judah's friend ... Gen. 38:1, 12, 20

Adulterer—*a man who commits adultery*

Punishment of ... Lev. 20:10
Waits for the twilight ... Job 24:15
Offspring of ... Is. 57:3
Land is full of ... Jer. 23:10
Shall not inherit the kingdom of God ... 1 Cor. 6:9
God will judge ... Heb. 13:4

Adulteress—*a woman guilty of adultery*

A. *Sin of:*
Punished by death ... Lev. 20:10
Ensnares the simple ... Prov. 7:6-23
Brings a man to poverty ... Prov. 6:26
Leads to death ... Prov. 2:16-19
Increases transgressors ... Prov. 23:27, 28
Defined by Christ ... Matt. 5:32
Forgiven by Christ ... John 8:1-11

B. *Examples of:*
Tamar ... Gen. 38:13-24
Potiphar's wife (attempted) ... Gen. 39:7-20
Midianite women ... Num. 25:6-8
Rahab ... Josh. 2:1
Bath-sheba ... 2 Sam. 11:4, 5
Herodias ... Matt. 14:3, 4
Unnamed woman ... John 8:1-11

See Harlot

SUBJECT ... REFERENCE

Adultery—*sexual intercourse outside marriage*

A. *Defined:*
In God's Law ... Ex. 20:14
By Christ ... Matt. 5:28, 32
By Paul ... Rom. 7:3
In mental attitude ... Matt. 5:28
As a work of the flesh ... Gal. 5:19

B. *Sin of:*
Breaks God's Law ... Deut. 5:18
Punishable by death ... Lev. 20:10-12
Brings death ... Prov. 2:18, 19
Makes one poor ... Prov. 29:3
Produces moral insensibility ... Prov. 30:20; 2 Cor. 12:21
Corrupts a land ... Hos. 4:1, 2, 11
Justifies divorce ... Matt. 19:7-9
Excludes from Christian fellowship ... 1 Cor. 5:1-13
Excludes from God's kingdom ... 1 Cor. 6:9, 10
Merits God's judgments ... Heb. 13:4
Ends in hell (Sheol) ... Prov. 7:27; Rev. 21:8

C. *Forgiveness of, by:*
Man ... Judg. 19:1-4
Christ ... John 8:10, 11
Repentance ... 2 Sam. 12:7-14
Regeneration ... 1 Cor. 6:9-11

D. *Examples of:*
Lot ... Gen. 19:31-38
Shechem ... Gen. 34:2
Judah ... Gen. 38:1-24
Eli's sons ... 1 Sam. 2:22
David ... 2 Sam. 11:1-5
Amnon ... 2 Sam. 13:1-20
The Samaritan woman ... John 4:17, 18

Adultery, spiritual

Seen in Israel's idolatry ... Judg. 2:11, 17
Described graphically ... Ezek. 16
Symbolized in Hosea's marriage ... Hos. 1:1-3
Symbolized in final apostasy ... Rev. 17:1-5
Figurative of friendship with the world ... James 4:4
Figurative of false teaching ... Rev. 2:14, 15, 20-22

Adummim—*red spots*

A hill between Jerusalem and Jericho ... Josh. 15:5, 7, 8
The probable site of Good Samaritan parable in ... Luke 10:30-37

Advancement—*progression*

A. *Promotion to a higher office:*
Moses and Aaron, by the Lord ... 1 Sam. 12:6
Promised to Balaam ... Num. 22:16, 17
Joseph, by true interpretation ... Gen. 41:38 46
Levites, for loyalty ... Ex. 32:26-28
Phinehas, by decisive action ... Num. 25:7-13
Haman, by intrigue ... Esth. 3:1, 2
Mordecai, by ability ... Esth. 10:2
Daniel, by fidelity ... Dan. 2:48
Deacons, by faithfulness ... 1 Tim. 3:10, 13

B. *Conditions of, seen in:*
Humility ... Matt. 18:4
Faithfulness ... Matt. 25:14-30
Skilled in work ... Prov. 22:29; Luke 22:24-30

C. *Hindrances to, occasioned by:*
Self-glory ... Is. 14:12-15; 1 Cor. 4:7-9
Pride ... Ezek. 28:11-19; 1 Pet. 5:5, 6

Advantage—*superior circumstance or ability*

A. *In God's kingdom, none by:*
Birth ... Matt. 3:8, 9
Race ... Gal. 2:14-16
Position ... John 3:1-6
Works ... Matt. 5:20
Wealth ... Luke 9:25

B. *In God's kingdom, some by:*
Industry ... 1 Cor. 15:10
Faithfulness ... Matt. 25:14-30
Kindred spirit ... Phil. 2:19-23
Works ... 1 Cor. 3:11-15
Dedication ... Rev. 14:1-5

SUBJECT ... REFERENCE

Advent of Christ, the first

A. *Announced in the Old Testament by:*
Moses ... Deut. 18:18, 19
Samuel ... Acts 3:24
David ... Ps. 40:6-8; Heb. 10:5-8
Prophets ... Luke 24:26, 27

B. *Prophecies fulfilled by his:*
Birth ... Is. 7:14; Matt. 1:23
Forerunner ... Mal. 3:1, 2; Matt. 3:1-3
Incarnation ... Is. 9:6
Time of arrival ... Dan. 9:24; Mark 1:15
Rejection ... Is. 53:1-4; Rom. 10:16-21
Crucifixion ... Ps. 2:1, 2; Acts 4:24-28
Atonement ... Is. 53:1-12; 1 Pet. 1:18-21
Resurrection ... Ps. 16:8-11; Acts 2:25-31
Priesthood ... Ps. 110:4, 5; Heb. 5:5, 6

C. *His first coming:*
Introduces Gospel age ... Acts 3:24
Consummates new covenant ... Jer. 31:31-34; Heb. 8:6-13
Fulfills prophecy ... Luke 24:44, 45
Nullifies the ceremonial system ... Heb. 9
Brings Gentiles in ... Acts 15:13-18

Advent of Christ, the second (see Second coming of Christ)

Advents of Christ, compared

A. *First Advent:*
Prophesied ... Deut. 18:18, 19; Is. 7:14
Came as man ... Phil. 2:5-7
Announced ... Luke 2:10-14
Time predicted ... Dan. 9:25
To save the lost ... Matt. 18:11
Subject to government ... Matt. 17:24-27

B. *Second Advent:*
Prophesied ... John 14:1-3; 1 Thess. 4:16
Come as God ... 1 Thess. 4:16
As a thief ... 1 Thess. 5:2
At a time unknown ... Matt. 24:36
To judge the lost ... Matt. 25:32-36
Source of government ... Rev. 20:4-6; Rev. 22:3-5

Adversaries—*those who actively oppose*

A. *Descriptive of:*
Satan ... 1 Pet. 5:8
Gospel's enemies ... 1 Cor. 16:9
Israel's enemies ... Josh. 5:13
An enemy ... Esth. 7:6
A rival ... 1 Sam. 1:6
God's agent ... 1 Kin. 11:14, 23
God's angel ... Num. 22:22

B. *Believer's attitude toward:*
Pray for ... Ps. 71:13
Use God's weapons against ... Luke 21:15
Not to be terrified by ... Phil. 1:28
Not to give occasion to ... 1 Tim. 5:14
Remember God's judgment on ... Heb. 10:27

Adversity—*adverse circumstances*

A. *Caused by:*
Man's sin ... Gen. 3:16, 17
Disobedience to God's Law ... Lev. 26:14-20

B. *Purposes of, to:*
Punish for sin ... 2 Sam. 12:9-12
Humble us ... 2 Chr. 33:12
Lead us to God's Word ... Deut. 8:2, 3
Chasten and correct ... Heb. 12:5-11
Test our faith ... 1 Pet. 1:5-8
Give us final rest ... Ps. 94:12, 13

C. *Reactions to:*
Rebellious ... Ex. 14:4-8; Job 2:9

A

SUBJECT ... REFERENCE

Distrustful ... Ex. 6:8, 9
Complaining ... Ruth 1:20, 21
Questioning ... Jer. 20:7-9
Fainting ... Prov. 24:10
Arrogant ... Ps. 10:6
Hopeful ... Lam. 3:31-40
Submissive ... Job 5:17-22
Joyful ... James 1:2-4

D. *God's relation to, He:*
Troubles nations with ... 2 Chr. 15:5, 6
Knows the soul in ... Ps. 31:7
Saves out of ... 1 Sam. 10:19
Redeems out of ... 2 Sam. 4:9

E. *Helps under:*
By prayer ... Jon. 2:1-7
By understanding God's purpose ... Lam. 3:31-39; Rom. 5:3

Advertise—*to make known publicly*
Messiah's advent ... Num. 24:14-19
A piece of property ... Ruth 4:4

Advice—*one's best judgment*

A. *Sought by:*
A king ... Esth. 1:13-15
Another ruler ... Acts 25:13-27
A usurper ... 2 Sam. 16:20-23
Five men ... 2 Kin. 22:12-20

B. *Sought from:*
The ephod ... 1 Sam. 23:9-12
A prophet ... Jer. 42:1-6
A dead prophet ... 1 Sam. 28:7-20
A council ... Acts 15:1-22
A grieving husband ... Judg. 20:4-7

C. *Kinds of:*
Helpful ... Ex. 18:12-25
Rejected ... 1 Kin. 12:6-8
Timely ... 1 Sam. 25:32-34
Good ... 2 Kin. 5:13, 14
God-inspired ... 2 Sam. 17:6-14
Foolish ... Job 2:9
Humiliating ... Esth. 6:6-11
Fatal ... Esth. 5:14
Ominous ... Matt. 27:19
Accepted ... Acts 5:34-41

D. *Sought from:*
Congregation of Israel ... Judg. 20:7

Advocate, Christ our

A. *His interest in believers, by right of:*
Election ... John 15:16
Redemption ... Rev. 1:5
Regeneration ... Col. 1:27
Imputed righteousness ... 2 Cor. 5:21; Phil. 3:9

B. *His defense of believers by:*
Prayer ... Luke 22:31-34
Protection ... Heb. 13:6
Provision ... Ps. 23:1; John 10:28
Perseverance ... 2 Tim. 4:17, 18

C. *His blessings upon believers:*
Another Comforter ... John 14:16, 17
New commandment ... John 13:34, 35
New nature ... 2 Cor. 5:17
New name ... Rev. 2:17
New life ... John 4:14
New relationship ... John 15:15

D. *Our duties prescribed by Him:*
Our mission—world evangelization ... Matt. 28:16-20
Our means—the Holy Spirit ... Acts 1:8
Our might—the Gospel ... Rom. 1:16
Our motivation—the love of Christ ... 2 Cor. 5:14, 15

Aeneas—*praise*
A paralytic healed by Peter ... Acts 9:32-35

Aenon—*springs*
A place near Salim where John the Baptist baptized ... John 3:22, 23

Afar off—*at a far distance*

A. *Applied physically to:*
Distance ... Gen. 22:4
A journey ... Num. 9:10
Sound of joy ... Ezra 3:13
Ostracism ... Luke 17:12

SUBJECT ... REFERENCE

B. *Applied spiritually to:*
God's knowledge ... Ps. 139:2
Unworthiness ... Luke 18:13
Eternal separation ... Luke 16:23
Backsliding ... Luke 22:54
Gentiles ... Acts 2:39
God's promises ... Heb. 11:13
Consignment to doom ... Rev. 17:10-17

Affability—*a personality overflowing with benign sociability*

A. *Manifested in:*
Cordiality ... Gen. 18:1-8
Compassion ... Luke 10:33-37
Generosity ... Phil. 4:10, 14-18
Unantagonizing speech ... 1 Sam. 25:23-31

B. *Examples of:*
Jonathan ... 1 Sam. 18:1-4
Titus ... 2 Cor. 8:16-18
Timothy ... Phil. 2:17-20
Gaius ... 3 John 1-6
Demetrius ... 3 John 12

Affectation—*a studied pretense*
Parade of egotism ... Esth. 6:6-9
Boast of the power ... Dan. 4:29, 30
Sign of hypocrisy ... Matt. 6:1, 2, 16
Outbreak of false teachers ... 2 Pet. 2:18, 19
Sign of antichrist ... 2 Thess. 2:4, 9
Proof of spiritual decay ... 1 Cor. 4:6-8

Affection—*an inner feeling or emotion*

A. *Kinds of:*
Natural ... Rom. 1:31
Paternal ... Luke 15:20
Maternal ... 1 Kin. 3:16-27
Fraternal ... Gen. 43:30-34
Filial ... Gen. 49:29, 30
National ... Ps. 137:1-6
Racial ... Rom. 9:1-3
For wife ... Eph. 5:25-33
For husband ... Titus 2:4
Christian ... Rom. 12:10
Heavenly ... Col. 3:1, 2

B. *Good, characteristics of:*
Loyal, intense ... Ruth 1:14-18
Memorable ... 2 Sam. 1:17-27
Natural, normal ... 2 Sam. 13:37-39
Tested, tried ... Gen. 22:1-19
Emotional ... John 11:33-36
Grateful ... Luke 7:36-50
Joyous ... Ps. 126:1-6
Christ-centered ... Matt. 10:37-42

C. *Evil, characteristics of:*
Unnatural ... Rom. 1:18-32
Pretended ... Matt. 26:47-49
Abnormal ... 2 Tim. 3:3
Fleshly ... Rom. 13:13, 14
Worldly ... 2 Tim. 4:10
Defiling, degrading ... 2 Pet. 2:10-12
Agonizing, in hell ... Luke 16:23-28

Afflictions—*hardships and trials*

A. *Visited upon:*
Israel in Egypt ... Gen. 15:13
Samson by Philistines ... Judg. 16:5, 6, 19
David by God ... Ps. 88:7
Judah by God ... Lam. 3:33
Israel by the world ... Ps. 129:1, 2
The just by the wicked ... Amos 5:12; Heb. 11:37
Christians by the world ... 2 Cor. 1:6

B. *Design of, to:*
Show God's mercy ... Is. 63:9
Make us seek God ... Hos. 5:15
Bring us back to God ... Ps. 119:67
Humble us ... 2 Chr. 33:12
Test us ... Is. 48:10

C. *In the Christian's life:*
A means of testing ... Mark 4:17
A part of life ... Matt. 24:9
To be endured ... 2 Tim. 4:5
Part of Gospel ... 1 Thess. 1:6
Must not be disturbed by ... 1 Thess. 3:3
Commendable examples of ... 2 Tim. 3:11
Momentary ... 2 Cor. 4:17
Sometimes intense ... 2 Cor. 1:8-10
Must be shared ... Phil. 4:14
Cannot separate from God ... Rom. 8:35-39
Deliverance from, promised ... Ps. 34:19
Need prayer in ... James 5:13

SUBJECT ... REFERENCE

Terminated at Christ's return ... 2 Thess. 1:4-7

See also Trials

Afraid—*overcome with fear*

A. *Caused by:*
Nakedness ... Gen. 3:10
Unusual dream ... Gen. 28:16, 17
God's presence ... Ex. 3:6
Moses' approach ... Ex. 34:30
A burning mountain ... Deut. 5:5
Giant's raging ... 1 Sam. 17:11, 24
A prophet's words ... 1 Sam. 28:20
Angel's sword ... 1 Chr. 21:30
God's judgments ... Ps. 65:8
Gabriel's presence ... Dan. 8:17
A terrifying storm ... Jon. 1:5, 10
Peter's sinking ... Matt. 14:30
Changed person ... Mark 5:15
Heavenly hosts ... Luke 2:9

B. *Overcome by:*
The Lord's presence ... Ps. 3:5, 6
Trusting God ... Ps. 27:1-3
God's protection ... Ps. 91:4, 5
Stability of heart ... Ps. 112:7, 8
God's coming judgment ... Is. 10:24-26
The Messiah's advent ... Is. 40:9-11
God's sovereign power ... Is. 51:12, 13
Christ's comforting words ... Matt. 14:27

Afternoon—*part of the day following noon*
Called cool of the day ... Gen. 3:8

Afterthought—*a later reflection*
Of Esau ... Heb. 12:16, 17
Of the Israelites ... Num. 14:40-45
Of one of two sons ... Matt. 21:28-30
Of the prodigal son ... Luke 15:17
Of the unjust steward ... Luke 16:1-8
Of the rich man in hell ... Luke 16:23-31
Of Judas ... Matt. 27:3-5

Afterward(s)
Your hands will be ... Judg. 7:11
Those who are invited ... 1 Sam. 9:13
David's conscience bothered him ... 1 Sam. 24:5
His mouth shall ... Prov. 20:17
Jesus findeth him ... John 5:14

Agabus—*he loved*
A Christian prophet who foretells a famine and warns Paul ... Acts 11:27, 28; Acts 21:10, 11

Agag—*flaming or violent*

1. A King of Amalek in Balaam's prophecy ... Num. 24:7
2. Amalekite king spared by Saul, but slain by Samuel ... 1 Sam. 15:8, 9, 20-24, 32, 33

Agagite—*descendant of Agag*
A title applied to Haman, enemy of the Jews ... Esth. 3:1, 10

Agape—Greek word rendered both as *"love"* and *"charity"*
Descriptive of God ... 1 John 4:8
Demanded toward God ... Matt. 22:37
Demanded toward neighbors ... Matt. 22:39
Fulfills Law ... Matt. 22:40
Activity of described ... 1 Cor. 13:1-13

Agate—*a stone of translucent quartz*
Worn by the high priest ... Ex. 28:19
Sold by Syrians ... Ezek. 27:16
Figurative of the new Israel ... Is. 54:11, 12

Age—*time counted by years*

A. *Handicaps of, seen in:*
Physical infirmities ... Gen. 48:10
Unwillingness to adventure ... 2 Sam. 19:31-39
Declining strength ... Ps. 71:9
Deterioration of body ... Eccl. 12:2-7

B. *Glories of, manifested in:*
Wisdom ... Job 12:12
Maturity ... Job 5:26
Spiritual beauty ... Prov. 16:31
Fruitfulness ... Ps. 92:12-15
Judgment ... 1 Kin. 12:6-8
Strong faith ... Josh. 24:15

SUBJECT ... REFERENCE

C. *Attitude of others toward:*

- Respect ... Lev. 19:32
- Disrespect ... 2 Chr. 36:17
- Insolence ... Is. 3:5

D. *Unusual things connected with:*

- Retaining physical vigor ... Deut. 34:7
- Becoming a father ... Gen. 18:9-15; Luke 1:18, 36
- Living to see Christ ... Luke 2:25-32
- Knowing kind of death in ... John 21:19

E. *Attaining unto, by:*

- Honoring parents ... Ex. 20:12; Eph. 6:2, 3
- Keeping God's law ... Prov. 3:1, 2
- Following wisdom ... Prov. 3:13, 16
- The fear of the Lord ... Ps. 128:1, 6
- Keeping from evil ... Ps. 34:11-14
- God's promise ... Gen. 15:15

F. *Those of Bible times who lived beyond age of 100.*

- Methuselah ... Gen. 5:27
- Jared ... Gen. 5:20
- Noah ... Gen. 9:29
- Adam ... Gen. 5:5
- Seth ... Gen. 5:8
- Cainan ... Gen. 5:14
- Enos ... Gen. 5:11
- Mahalaleel ... Gen. 5:17
- Lamech ... Gen. 5:31
- Enoch ... Gen. 5:23
- Terah ... Gen. 11:32
- Isaac ... Gen. 35:28
- Abraham ... Gen. 25:7
- Jacob ... Gen. 47:28
- Ishmael ... Gen. 25:17
- Jehoiada ... 2 Chr. 24:15
- Sarah ... Gen. 23:1
- Aaron ... Num. 33:39
- Moses ... Deut. 34:7
- Joseph ... Gen. 50:26
- Joshua ... Josh. 24:29

Agee—*fugitive*

- Shammah's father ... 2 Sam. 23:11

Ages—*extended periods of time*

- Descriptive of the Old Testament period ... Eph. 3:5
- Descriptive of eternity ... Eph. 2:7

Agitation—*a disturbance*

A. *Physically of:*

- Mountain ... Ex. 19:16-18
- The earth ... Matt. 27:51-53
- The world ... Ps. 46:2-6
- End-time events ... Luke 21:25-27
- World's end ... 2 Pet. 3:7-12

B. *Emotionally of:*

- Extreme grief ... 2 Sam. 19:1-4
- Remorse ... Matt. 27:3, 4
- Fear ... Matt. 28:1-4

C. *Figuratively of:*

- Messiah's advent ... Hag. 2:6, 7
- Enraged people ... Acts 4:25-28
- The wicked ... Is. 57:20
- The drunkard ... Prov. 23:29-35

Agony—*extreme suffering*

A. *Used literally of:*

- Christ in Gethsemane ... Luke 22:44
- Christ on the cross ... Mark 15:34-37
- Paul's sufferings ... 2 Cor. 1:8, 9

B. *Used figuratively of:*

- Spiritual mastery ... 1 Cor. 9:25
- Spiritual striving ... Col. 1:29
- Laborious prayer ... Col. 4:12
- Faithful conflict ... 1 Tim. 6:12

Agree, agreement

A. *Forbidden between:*

- Israel and pagans ... Ex. 34:12-16
- God and Baal ... 1 Kin. 18:21-40
- Believers, unbelievers ... 1 Cor. 10:21
- Truth, error ... 1 John 4:1-6

B. *Necessary between:*

- Prophecy, fulfillment ... Acts 15:15
- Doctrine, life ... James 2:14-21
- Words, performance ... 2 Cor. 10:9-11
- Believers in prayer ... Matt. 18:19
- Christian brothers ... Matt. 5:24, 25
- Christian workers ... Gal. 2:7-9

SUBJECT ... REFERENCE

C. *Examples of:*

- Laban and Jacob ... Gen. 31:43-53
- God and Israel ... Ex. 19:3-8
- David and Jonathan ... 1 Sam. 18:1-4
- The wicked and Sheol ... Is. 28:15, 18
- Employer and employees ... Matt. 20:10-13
- Judas and the Sanhedrin ... Matt. 26:14-16
- Witnesses ... Mark 14:56, 59
- Husband and wife ... Acts 5:9
- The Jews and Gamaliel ... Acts 5:34-40
- Conspiring Jews ... Acts 23:20
- The people of antichrist ... Rev. 17:17

Agriculture—*the cultivation of the soil*

A. *Terms and implements involved:*

- Binding ... Gen. 37:7
- Cultivating ... Luke 13:6-9
- Fertilizing ... Is. 25:10
- Gleaning ... Ruth 2:3
- Grafting ... Rom. 11:17-19
- Harrowing ... Is. 28:24
- Harvesting ... Matt. 13:23
- Mowing ... Amos 7:1
- Planting ... Prov. 31:16
- Plowing ... Job 1:14
- Pruning ... Is. 5:6
- Reaping ... Is. 17:5
- Removing stones ... Is. 5:2
- Rooting ... Matt. 13:28, 29
- Sowing ... Matt. 13:3
- Stacking ... Ex. 22:6
- Threshing ... Judg. 6:11
- Treading ... Neh. 13:15
- Watering ... 1 Cor. 3:6-8
- Winnowing ... Ruth 3:2

B. *Virtues required in:*

- Wisdom ... Is. 28:24-29
- Diligence ... Prov. 27:23-27
- Labor ... 2 Tim. 2:6
- Patience ... James 5:7
- Industry ... Prov. 28:19
- Faith ... Hab. 3:17-19
- Bountifulness ... 2 Cor. 9:6, 7
- Hopefulness ... 1 Cor. 9:10

C. *Enemies of:*

- War ... Jer. 50:16
- Pestilence ... Joel 1:9-12
- Fire ... Joel 1:19
- Animals ... Song 2:15
- Dry seasons ... Jer. 14:1, 4

D. *Restrictions involving:*

- Coveting another's field ... Deut. 5:21
- Removing boundaries ... Deut. 19:14
- Roaming cattle ... Ex. 22:5
- Spreading fire ... Ex. 22:6
- Military service ... Deut. 20:5, 6
- Working on the Sabbath ... Ex. 34:21
- Complete harvest ... Lev. 19:9, 10

E. *God's part in:*

- Began in Eden ... Gen. 2:15
- Sin's penalty ... Gen. 3:17
- Providence of, impartial ... Matt. 5:45
- Goodness of, recognized ... Acts 14:16, 17
- Judgments against, cited ... Hag. 1:10, 11

F. *Figurative of:*

- Gospel seed ... Matt. 13:1-9
- Gospel dispensation ... Matt. 13:24-30, 36-43
- God's workers ... John 4:36-38
- God's Word ... Is. 55:10, 11
- Spiritual barrenness ... Heb. 6:7, 8
- Spiritual bountifulness ... 2 Cor. 9:9, 10
- Final harvest ... Mark 4:28, 29

Aground—*stranded in shallow water*

- Ship carrying Paul ... Acts 27:41

Ague—*a malarial fever; jaundice*

- A divine punishment ... Lev. 26:16

Agur—*collector*

- Writer of proverbs ... Prov. 30:1-33

Ahab—*father's brother*

1. A wicked king of Israel ... 1 Kin. 16:29
   - Marries Jezebel ... 1 Kin. 16:31
   - Introduces Baal worship ... 1 Kin. 16:31-33
   - Denounced by Elijah ... 1 Kin. 17:1
   - Gathers prophets of Baal ... 1 Kin. 18:17-46
   - Wars against Ben-hadad ... 1 Kin. 20:1-43
   - Covets Naboth's vineyard ... 1 Kin. 21:1-16
   - Death of, predicted ... 1 Kin. 21:17-26

SUBJECT ... REFERENCE

   - Repentance of, delays judgment ... 1 Kin. 21:27-29
   - Joins Jehoshaphat against Syrians ... 1 Kin. 22:1-4
   - Rejects Micaiah's warning ... 1 Kin. 22:5-33
   - Slain in battle ... 1 Kin. 22:34-38
   - Seventy sons of, slain ... 2 Kin. 10:1-11
   - Prophecies concerning, fulfilled ... 1 Kin. 20:42
2. Lying prophet ... Jer. 29:21-23

Aharah—*after his brother*

- Son of Benjamin ... 1 Chr. 8:1
- Called Ahiram ... Num. 26:38
- Called Ehi ... Gen. 46:21

Aharhel—*brother of Rachel*

- A descendant of Judah ... 1 Chr. 4:8

Ahasai—*Jehovah has grasped*

- A postexilic priest ... Neh. 11:13
- Also called Jahzerah ... 1 Chr. 9:12

Ahasbai—*blooming, shining*

- The father of Eliphelet ... 2 Sam. 23:34

Ahasuerus—*king*

1. The father of Darius the Mede ... Dan. 9:1
2. Persian king ... Esth. 1:1
   - Makes Esther queen ... Esth. 2:16, 17
   - Follows Haman's intrigue ... Esth. 3:1, 8-12
   - Orders Jews annihilated ... Esth. 3:13-15
   - Responds to Esther's plea ... Esth. 7:1-8
   - Orders Haman hanged ... Esth. 7:9, 10
   - Promotes Mordecai ... Esth. 8:1, 2
   - Reverses Haman's plot ... Esth. 8:3-17
   - Exalts Mordecai ... Esth. 10:1-3
3. A king of Persia; probably Xerxes, 486-465 B.C. ... Ezra 4:6

Ahava—*a town in Babylonia*

- Jewish exiles gather here ... Ezra 8:15-31

Ahaz—*he has grasped*

1. A king of Judah; son of Jotham ... 2 Kin. 16:1, 2
   - Pursues evil ways ... 2 Kin. 16:3, 4
   - Defends Jerusalem against Rezin and Pekah ... 2 Kin. 16:5, 6
   - Refuses a divine sign ... Is. 7:1-16
   - Defeated with great loss ... 2 Chr. 28:5-15
   - Becomes subject to Assyria ... 2 Kin. 16:7-9
   - Makes Damascus a pagan city ... 2 Kin. 16:10-18
   - Erects sundial ... 2 Kin. 20:11
   - Death of ... 2 Kin. 16:19, 20
2. A descendant of Jonathan ... 1 Chr. 8:35, 36; 1 Chr. 9:40-42
3. Ancestor of Jesus ... Matt. 1:9

Ahaziah—*Jehovah has grasped*

1. A king of Israel; son of Ahab and Jezebel ... 1 Kin. 22:40, 51
   - Worships Baal ... 1 Kin. 22:52, 53
   - Seeks alliance with Jehoshaphat ... 1 Kin. 22:48, 49
   - Falls through lattice; sends to Baal-zebub, the god of Ekron for help ... 2 Kin. 1:2-16
   - Dies according to Elijah's word ... 2 Kin. 1:17, 18
2. A king of Judah; son of Jehoram and Athaliah ... 2 Kin. 8:25, 26
   - Made king by Jerusalem inhabitants ... 2 Chr. 22:1, 2
   - Taught evil by his mother ... 2 Chr. 22:2, 3
   - Follows Ahab's wickedness ... 2 Chr. 22:4
   - Joins Joram against the Syrians ... 2 Kin. 8:28
   - Visits wounded Joram ... 2 Kin. 9:16
   - Slain by Jehu ... 2 Kin. 9:27, 28
   - Called Jehoahaz ... 2 Chr. 21:17
   - Called Azariah ... 2 Chr. 22:6

Ahban—*brother of intelligence*

- A son of Abishur ... 1 Chr. 2:29

Aher—*another*

- A Benjamite ... 1 Chr. 7:12

Ahi—*brother*

1. Gadite chief ... 1 Chr. 5:15
2. Asherite chief ... 1 Chr. 7:34

SUBJECT REFERENCE

Ahiah—*brother of Jehovah*
1. A priest during Saul's reign . . 1 Sam. 14:3, 18
2. A secretary of Solomon . . . . . 1 Kin. 4:3
3. A Benjamite . . . . 1 Chr. 8:7

Ahiam—*mother's brother*
One of David's mighty men . . . . . 2 Sam. 23:33

Ahian—*fraternal*
A Manassite . . . . 1 Chr. 7:19

Ahiezer—*brother is help*
1. Head of the tribe of Dan . . . . Num. 1:12
2. Benjamite chief, joined David at Ziklag . . . . 1 Chr. 12:3

Ahihud—*brother is majesty*
1. Asherite leader, helped Moses divide Canaan . . . . Num. 34:27
2. A Benjamite . . . . 1 Chr. 8:6, 7

Ahijah—*brother of Jehovah*
1. A great-grandson of Judah . . . 1 Chr. 2:25
2. One of David's warriors . . . . . 1 Chr. 11:36
3. A Levite treasurer in David's reign . . . . 1 Chr. 26:20
4. A prophet of Shiloh who foretells division of Solomon's kingdom . . . . 1 Kin. 11:29-39
Foretells elimination of Jeroboam's line . . . . 1 Kin. 14:1-18
A writer of prophecy . . . . 2 Chr. 9:29
5. The father of Baasha . . . . 1 Kin. 15:27, 33
6. A Jew who seals Nehemiah's covenant . . . . Neh. 10:26

See Ahiah

Ahikam—*my brother has arisen*
A son of Shaphan the scribe . . . . 2 Kin. 22:12
Sent in Josiah's mission to Huldah . . . . 2 Kin. 22:12-14
Protects Jeremiah . . . . Jer. 26:24
The father of Gedaliah, governor under Nebuchadnezzar . . . . 2 Kin. 25:22
Jer. 39:14

Ahilud—*a child's brother*
1. The father of Jehoshaphat, the recorder under David and Solomon . . . . 2 Sam. 8:16
2. The father of Baana, a commissionary official . . . . 1 Kin. 4:7, 12

Ahimaaz—*brother of anger*
1. The father of Ahinoam, wife of King Saul . . . . 1 Sam. 14:50
2. A son of Zadok the high priest . . . . 1 Chr. 6:8, 9
Warns David of Absalom's plans . . . . 2 Sam. 15:27, 36
Good man . . . . 2 Sam. 18:27
First to tell David of Absalom's defeat . . . . 2 Sam. 18:19-30
3. Solomon's son-in-law and commissioner in Naphtali . . . . 1 Kin. 4:15
May be the same as 2.

Ahiman—*my brother is a gift*
1. A giant son of Anak seen by Israelite spies . . . . Num. 13:22, 33
Driven out of Hebron by Caleb . . . . Josh. 15:13, 14
Slain by tribe of Judah . . . . . . Judg. 1:10
2. A Levite gatekeeper . . . . 1 Chr. 9:17

Ahimelech—*my brother is king*
1. The high priest at Nob during Saul's reign . . . . 1 Sam. 21:1
Feeds David the showbread . . . . 1 Sam. 21:2-6
Gives Goliath's sword to David . . . . 1 Sam. 21:8, 9
Betrayed by Doeg . . . . 1 Sam. 22:9-16
Slain by Doeg at Saul's command . . . . 1 Sam. 22:17-19
Abiathar, son of, escapes . . . . 1 Sam. 22:20
David wrote concerning . . . . . Ps. 52 (title)
2. Abiathar's son . . . . 2 Sam. 8:17
Co-priest with Zadok . . . . 1 Chr. 24:3, 6, 31
3. David's Hittite warrior . . . . . . 1 Sam. 26:6

Ahimoth—*my brother is death*
A Kohathite Levite . . . . 1 Chr. 6:25

SUBJECT REFERENCE

Ahinadab—*my brother is noble*
One of Solomon's officers . . . . 1 Kin. 4:14

Ahinoam—*my brother is delight*
1. Wife of Saul . . . . 1 Sam. 14:50
2. David's wife . . . . 1 Sam. 25:43
Lived with David at Gath . . . 1 Sam. 27:3
Captured by Amalekites at Ziklag . . . . 1 Sam. 30:5
Rescued by David . . . . 1 Sam. 30:18
Lives with David in Hebron . . . . 2 Sam. 2:1, 2
Mother of Amnon . . . . 2 Sam. 3:2

Ahio—*brotherly*
1. Abinadab's son . . . . 2 Sam. 6:3
2. A Benjamite . . . . 1 Chr. 8:14
3. A son of Jehiel . . . . 1 Chr. 8:31
1 Chr. 9:37

Ahira—*my brother is evil*
A tribal leader . . . . Num. 1:15

Ahisamach—*my brother supports*
A Danite . . . . Ex. 31:6

Ahishahar—*brother of dawn*
A Benjamite . . . . 1 Chr. 7:10

Ahishar—*my brother has sung*
A manager of Solomon's household . . . . 1 Kin. 4:6

Ahithophel—*brother of folly*
David's counselor . . . . 2 Sam. 15:12
Joins Absalom's insurrection . . . . 2 Sam. 15:31
Plans of, prepared against by David . . . . 2 Sam. 15:31-34
Counsels Absalom . . . . 2 Sam. 16:20-22
Reputed wise . . . . 2 Sam. 16:23
Counsel of, rejected by Absalom . . . . 2 Sam. 17:1-22
Commits suicide . . . . 2 Sam. 17:23

Ahitub—*my brother is goodness*
1. Phinehas' son . . . . 1 Sam. 14:3
2. The father of Zadok the priest . . . . 2 Sam. 8:17
3. The father of another Zadok . . . . 1 Chr. 6:11, 12

Ahlab—*fruitful*
A city of Asher . . . . Judg. 1:31

Ahlai—*O would that!*
1. David's warrior . . . . 1 Chr. 11:41
2. Marries an Egyptian servant . . . . 1 Chr. 2:31-35

Ahoah—*brotherly*
A son of Bela . . . . 1 Chr. 8:4

Ahohite—*a descendant of Ahoah*
Applied to Dodo, Zalmon, and Ilai . . . . 2 Sam. 23:9, 28

Aholah—*tent-woman*
Symbolic name of Samaria and Israel . . . . Ezek. 23:4, 5, 36

Aholiab—*a father's tent*
Son of Ahisamach . . . . Ex. 31:6

Ahumai—*heated by Jehovah*
A descendant of Judah . . . . 1 Chr. 4:2

Ahuzzam—*possessor*
A man of Judah . . . . 1 Chr. 4:6

Ahuzzath—*possession*
A friend of Abimelech . . . . Gen. 26:26

Ai—*ruin*
1. A city east of Beth-el in central Palestine . . . . Josh. 7:2
Abraham camps near . . . . Gen. 12:8
A royal city of Canaan . . . . . . Josh. 10:1
Israel defeated at . . . . Josh. 7:2-5
Israel destroys completely . . . Josh. 8:1-28
Occupied after exile . . . . Ezra 2:28
2. An Ammonite city near Heshbon . . . . Jer. 49:3

Aiah—*falcon*
1. A Horite . . . . Gen. 36:24

SUBJECT REFERENCE

2. The father of Rizpah, Saul's concubine . . . . 2 Sam. 3:7

Aijalon—*place of gazelles*
1. A town assigned to Dan . . . . . Josh. 19:42
Amorites not driven from . . . . Judg. 1:35
Miracle there . . . . Josh. 10:12
Assigned to Kohathite Levites . . . . Josh. 21:24
City of refuge . . . . 1 Chr. 6:66-69
Included in Benjamin's territory . . . . 1 Chr. 8:13
Fortified by Rehoboam . . . . 2 Chr. 11:10
Captured by Philistines . . . . . . 2 Chr. 28:18
2. The burial place of Elon, a judge . . . . Judg. 12:12

Ain—*spring*
1. A town near Riblah . . . . Num. 34:11
2. Town of Judah . . . . Josh. 15:32
Transferred to Simeon . . . . . Josh. 19:7
Later assigned to the priests . . . . Josh. 21:16
Called Ashan . . . . 1 Chr. 6:59
3. Letter of the Hebrew alphabet . . . . Ps. 119:121-136

Air—*the atmosphere around the earth*
Man given dominion over . . . . . . Gen. 1:26-30
Man names birds of . . . . Gen. 2:19, 20
God destroys birds of . . . . Gen. 6:7
Mystery of eagle in . . . . Prov. 30:19
Satan, prince of . . . . Eph. 2:2
Believers meet Jesus in . . . . 1 Thess. 4:17
God's wrath poured out in . . . . . . Rev. 9:2
Figurative of emptiness . . . . 1 Cor. 9:26

Akkub—*cunning*
1. Elioenai's son . . . . 1 Chr. 3:24
2. A Levite head of a family of porters . . . . 1 Chr. 9:17
3. A family of Nethinim . . . . Ezra 2:45
4. A Levite interpreter . . . . Neh. 8:7

Akrabbim—*scorpions*
An "ascent" on the south of the Dead Sea . . . . Num. 34:4
One border of Judah—Acrabbim . . . . Josh. 15:3

Alabaster—*a container for perfumes and ointments*
Used by woman anointing Jesus . . . . Matt. 26:7

Alameth (see Alemeth)

Alammelech—*oak of a king*
Village of Asher . . . . Josh. 19:26

Alamoth—*virgins*
A musical term probably indicating a women's choir . . . . 1 Chr. 15:20

Alarm—*sudden and fearful surprise*
A. *Caused physically by:*
Sudden attack . . . . Judg. 7:20-23
Death plague . . . . Ex. 12:29-33
A mysterious manifestation . . 1 Sam. 28:11-14
Prodigies of nature . . . . Matt. 27:50-54
B. *Caused spiritually by:*
Sin . . . . 1 Sam. 12:17-19
Remorse . . . . Gen. 27:34-40
Conscience . . . . Acts 24:24, 25
Hopelessness in hell . . . . Luke 16:22-31
C. *Shout of jubilee or warning:*
Instruction to Israel . . . . Num. 10:5, 6
Causes anguish . . . . Jer. 4:19
Prophecy of judgment . . . . Jer. 49:2

See Agitation

Alas—*an intense emotional outcry*
A. *Emotional outcry caused by:*
Israel's defeat . . . . Josh. 7:7-9
An angel's appearance . . . . . . Judg. 6:22
A vow's realization . . . . Judg. 11:34, 35
Army without water . . . . 2 Kin. 3:9, 10
Loss of an ax . . . . 2 Kin. 6:5
Servant's fear . . . . 2 Kin. 6:14, 15
B. *Prophetic outcry caused by:*
Israel's future . . . . Num. 24:23, 24
Israel's punishment . . . . Amos 5:16-20

SUBJECT REFERENCE

Jacob's trouble ... Jer. 30:7-9
Babylon's fall ... Rev. 18:10-19

Alemeth, Alameth—*hidden*

1. A Benjamite ... 1 Chr. 7:8
2. A descendant of Saul ... 1 Chr. 8:36
3. A Levitical city ... 1 Chr. 6:60

Aleph

The first letter in the Hebrew alphabet ... Ps. 119:1-8

Alert—*watchful*

In battle ... Judg. 7:15-22
In personal safety ... 1 Sam. 19:9, 10
In readiness for attack ... Neh. 4:9-23
In prayer ... Matt. 26:41
In spiritual combat ... Eph. 6:18
In waiting for Christ's return ... Matt. 24:42-51
Daily living ... 1 Cor. 16:13
Times of testing ... Luke 21:34-36
Against false teachers ... Acts 20:29-31

Alexander—*man-defending*

1. A son of Simon of Cyrene ... Mark 15:21
2. A member of the high-priestly family ... Acts 4:6
3. A Jew in Ephesus ... Acts 19:33, 34
4. An apostate condemned by Paul ... 1 Tim. 1:19, 20

Alexander the Great—*Alexander III of Macedonia* (356-323 B.C.)

A. *Not named in the Bible, but referred to as:*

The four-headed leopard ... Dan. 7:6
The goat with a great horn ... Dan. 8:5-9, 21
A mighty king ... Dan. 11:3

B. *Rule of, described:*

His invasion of Palestine ... Zech. 9:1-8
His kingdom being divided ... Dan. 7:6

Alexandria—*a city of Egypt founded by Alexander the Great* (332 B.C.)

Men of, persecute Stephen ... Acts 6:9
Apollos, native of ... Acts 18:24
Paul sails in ship ... Acts 27:6

Algum, almug—*a tree* (probably the red sandalwood)

Imported from Ophir by Hiram's navy ... 1 Kin. 10:11, 12
Used in constructing the temple ... 2 Chr. 9:10, 11
Also imported from Lebanon ... 2 Chr. 2:8

Aliens—*citizens of a foreign country*

A. *Descriptive, naturally, of:*

Israel in the Egyptian bondage ... Gen. 15:13
Abraham in Canaan ... Gen. 23:4
Moses in Egypt ... Ex. 18:3
Israel in Babylon ... Ps. 137:4

B. *Descriptive, spiritually, of:*

Estrangement from friends ... Job 19:15
Israel's apostasy ... Ezek. 23:17, 18, 22, 28
The condition of the Gentiles ... Eph. 2:12
Spiritual deadness ... Eph. 4:18

Alive—*the opposite of being dead*

A. *Descriptive of:*

Natural life ... Gen. 43:7, 27, 28
Spiritual life ... Luke 15:24, 32
Restored physical life ... Acts 9:41
Christ's resurrected life ... Acts 1:3
The believer's glorified life ... 1 Cor. 15:22
The unbeliever's life in hell ... Num. 16:33

B. *The power of keeping:*

Belongs to God ... Deut. 32:39
Not in man's power ... Ps. 22:29
Promised to the godly ... Ps. 33:19
Gratefully acknowledged ... Josh. 14:10
Transformed by Christ's return ... 1 Thess. 4:15, 16

Allegory—*an extended figure of speech using symbols*

A. *Of natural things:*

A king's doom ... Judg. 9:8-15
Old age ... Eccl. 12:3-7

SUBJECT REFERENCE

Israel as a transplanted vine ... Ps. 80:8-19

B. *Of spiritual things:*

Christian as sheep ... John 10:1-16
Two covenants ... Gal. 4:21-31
Israel and the Gentiles ... Rom. 11:15-24
Christ and His Church ... Eph. 5:22-33
The Christian's armor ... Eph. 6:11-17

Alleluia—*praise ye the Lord*

The Greek form of the Hebrew Hallelujah ... Rev. 19:1-6

Alliances—*treaties between nations or individuals*

A. *In the time of the patriarchs:*

Abraham with Canaanite chiefs ... Gen. 14:13
Abraham with Abimelech ... Gen. 21:22-34
Isaac with Abimelech ... Gen. 26:26-33
Jacob with Laban ... Gen. 31:44-54

B. *In the time of the wilderness:*

Israel with Moab ... Num. 25:1-3

C. *In the time of the conquest:*

Israel with Gibeonites ... Judg. 9:3-27

D. *In the time of David:*

David with Achish ... 1 Sam. 27:2-12

E. *In the time of Solomon:*

Solomon with Hiram ... 1 Kin. 5:12-18
Solomon with Egypt ... 1 Kin. 3:1

F. *In the time of the divided kingdom:*

Asa with Ben-hadad ... 1 Kin. 15:18-20
Ahab with Ben-hadad ... 1 Kin. 20:31-34
Israel with Syria ... 2 Kin. 16:5-9
Hoshea with Egypt ... 2 Kin. 17:1-6

G. *In the time of Judah's sole kingdom:*

Hezekiah with Egypt ... 2 Kin. 18:19-24
Josiah with Assyria ... 2 Kin. 23:29
Jehoiakim with Egypt ... 2 Kin. 23:31-35

Alliance with evil

A. *Forbidden to:*

Israel ... Ex. 34:11-16
Christians ... Rom. 13:12
Christ ... Matt. 4:1-11

B. *Forbidden because:*

Leads to idolatry ... Ex. 23:32, 33
Deceives ... Num. 25:1-3, 18
Enslaves ... 2 Pet. 2:18, 19
Defiles ... Ezra 9:1, 2
Brings God's anger ... Ezra 9:13-15
Corrupts ... 1 Cor. 15:33
Incompatible with Christ ... 2 Cor. 6:14-16
Pollutes ... Jude 23

C. *The believer should:*

Avoid ... Prov. 1:10-15
Hate ... Ps. 26:4, 5
Confess ... Ezra 10:9-11
Separate from ... 2 Cor. 6:17

D. *Examples of:*

Solomon ... 1 Kin. 11:1-11
Rehoboam ... 1 Kin. 12:25-33
Jehoshaphat ... 2 Chr. 20:35-37
Judas Iscariot ... Matt. 26:14-16
Heretics ... Rev. 2:14-15, 20

See Association

All in all—*complete*

Descriptive of:

God ... 1 Cor. 15:28
Christ ... Eph. 1:23

Allon—*oak*

1. A Simeonite prince ... 1 Chr. 4:37
2. A town in south Naphtali ... Josh. 19:33

Allon-bachuth—*oak of weeping*

A tree marking Deborah's grave ... Gen. 35:8

Allowance—*a stipulated amount*

Daily to Jehoiachin ... 2 Kin. 25:27-30
Also called a diet ... Jer. 52:34

Almighty—*a title of God*

Applied to God ... Gen. 17:1
2 Cor. 6:18
Applied to Christ ... Rev. 1:8

SUBJECT REFERENCE

Almodad—*the beloved*

Eldest son of Joktan ... Gen. 10:26

Almond—*a small tree bearing fruit*

Sent as a present to Pharaoh ... Gen. 43:11
Used in the tabernacle ... Ex. 25:33, 34
Aaron's rod produces ... Num. 17:2, 3, 8
Used figuratively of old age ... Eccl. 12:5
Translated "hazel" in ... Gen. 30:37

Almon-diblathaim—*Almon of the double cake of figs*

An Israelite encampment ... Num. 33:46, 47

Alms, almsgiving—*gifts prompted by love to help the needy*

A. *Design of, to:*

Help the poor ... Lev. 25:35
Receive a blessing ... Deut. 15:10, 11

B. *Manner of bestowing with:*

A willing spirit ... Deut. 15:7-11
Simplicity ... Matt. 6:1-4
Cheerfulness ... 2 Cor. 9:7
True love ... 1 Cor. 13:3
Fairness to all ... Acts 4:32-35
Regularity ... Acts 11:29, 30
Law of reciprocity ... Rom. 15:25-27

C. *Cautions concerning:*

Not for man's honor ... Matt. 6:1-4
Not for lazy ... 2 Thess. 3:10
Needful for the rich ... 1 Tim. 6:17, 18

D. *Rewarded:*

Now ... Deut. 14:28, 29
2 Cor. 9:9, 10
In heaven ... Matt. 19:21

E. *Examples of:*

Zacchaeus ... Luke 19:8
Dorcas ... Acts 9:36
Cornelius ... Acts 10:2
The early Christians ... Acts 4:34-37

Aloes—*a perfume-bearing tree*

A. *Used on:*

Beds ... Prov. 7:17
The dead ... John 19:39

B. *Figurative of:*

Israel ... Num. 24:5, 6
The Church ... Ps. 45:8

Aloth—*ascents, steeps*

A town in Asher ... 1 Kin. 4:16

Alpha and Omega—*first and last letters of the Greek alphabet* ("A to Z")

Expressive of God and Christ's eternity ... Rev. 1:8, 17, 18; Rev. 21:6, 7

Alphabet—*the letters of a language*

The Hebrew, seen in ... Ps. 119

Alphaeus—*leader, chief*

1. The father of Levi (Matthew) ... Mark 2:14
2. The father of James ... Matt. 10:3

Altar—*an elevated structure*

A. *Uses of:*

Sacrifice ... Gen. 8:20
Incense ... Ex. 30:1, 7, 8
Luke 1:10, 11
National unity ... Deut. 12:5, 6
A memorial ... Ex. 17:15, 16
Protection ... Ex 21:13, 14

B. *Made of:*

Earth ... Ex. 20:24
Unhewn stone ... Ex. 20:25
Stones ... Deut. 27:5, 6
Natural rock ... Judg. 6:19-21
Bronze ... Ex. 27:1-6

C. *Built worthily by:*

Noah ... Gen. 8:20
Abraham ... Gen. 12:7, 8
Isaac ... Gen. 26:25
Jacob ... Gen. 33:18, 20
Moses ... Ex. 17:15
Joshua ... Deut. 27:4-7
Eastern tribes ... Josh. 22:10, 34
Gideon ... Judg. 6:26, 27
Manoah ... Judg. 13:19, 20
Israelites ... Judg. 21:4

SUBJECT — REFERENCE

Samuel ... 1 Sam. 7:17
Saul ... 1 Sam. 14:35
David ... 2 Sam. 24:18-25
Elijah ... 1 Kin. 18:31, 32

D. *Built unworthily* (for idolatry) *by:*
Gideon's father ... Judg. 6:25-32
King Jeroboam ... 1 Kin. 12:32, 33
King Ahab ... 1 Kin. 18:25, 26
King Ahaz ... 2 Chr. 28:1, 3, 5
Israelite people ... Is. 65:3
Athenians ... Acts 17:23

E. *Pagan altars destroyed by:*
Gideon ... Judg. 6:25-29
King Asa ... 2 Chr. 14:2, 3
Jehoiada ... 2 Kin. 11:17, 18
King Hezekiah ... 2 Kin. 18:22
King Josiah ... 2 Kin. 23:12

F. *Burnt offering:*
1. *Of the tabernacle, features concerning:*
Specifications ... Ex. 27:1-9
Bezaleel, builder of ... Ex. 37:1
Place of, outside tabernacle ... Ex. 40:6, 29
Only priests allowed at ... Num. 18:3, 7
The defective not acceptable on ... Lev. 22:22
The putting on of blood ... Ex. 29:12
2. *Of Solomon's Temple:*
Described ... 1 Kin. 8:63, 64
Renewed by King Asa ... 2 Chr. 15:8
Cleansed by King Hezekiah ... 2 Chr. 29:18-24
Repaired by King Manasseh ... 2 Chr. 33:16
Vessels of, carried to Babylon ... 2 Kin. 25:14
3. *Of the postexilic* (Zerubbabel's) *temple:*
Described ... Ezra 3:1-6
Polluted ... Mal. 1:7, 8
4. *Of Ezekiel's vision:*
Described ... Ezek. 43:13-27

G. *Incense:*
In the tabernacle, described ... Ex. 30:1-10
Location of ... Ex. 30:6
Anointed with oil ... Ex. 30:26, 27
Annual atonement made at ... Ex. 30:10
In Solomon's Temple ... 1 Kin. 7:48
In John's vision ... Rev. 8:3

H. *New covenant:*
A place of spiritual sacrifices ... Rom. 12:1, 2
Christ, our pattern ... Heb. 13:10-16

Al-taschith—*destroy not*
A term found in the title of ... Ps. 57; 59; 75

Altruism—*living for the good of others*
A. *Manifested in:*
Service ... Matt. 20:26-28
Doing good ... Acts 10:38
Seeking the welfare of others ... Gal. 6:1, 2, 10
Helping the weak ... Acts 20:35
B. *Examples of:*
Moses ... Ex. 32:30-32
Samuel ... 1 Sam. 12:1-5
Jonathan ... 1 Sam. 18:1-4
Christ ... John 13:4-17
Paul ... 1 Cor. 9:19-22

Alush—*wild place*
An Israelite encampment ... Num. 33:13, 14

Alvah—*high, tall*
An Edomite chief ... Gen. 36:40
Also called Aliah ... 1 Chr. 1:51

Alvan—*tall*
A son of Shobal the Horite ... Gen. 36:23
Also called Alian ... 1 Chr. 1:40

Always—*continually, forever*
A. *Of God's:*
Care ... Deut. 11:12
Covenant ... 1 Chr. 16:15
Chide ... Ps. 103:9
B. *Of Christ's:*
Determination ... Ps. 16:8-11; Acts 2:25

SUBJECT — REFERENCE

Delight ... Prov. 8:30-31
Presence ... Matt. 28:20
Desire ... John 8:29
Prayer ... John 11:42

C. *Of the believer's:*
Prayer ... Luke 21:36
Peace ... 2 Thess. 3:16
Obedience ... Phil. 2:12
Work ... 1 Cor. 15:58
Defense ... 1 Pet. 3:15
Rejoicing ... Phil. 4:4
Thanksgiving ... 1 Thess. 1:2
Victory ... 2 Cor. 2:14
Conscience ... Acts 24:16
Confidence ... 2 Cor. 5:6
Sufficiency ... 2 Cor. 9:8

D. *Of the unbeliever's:*
Probation ... Gen. 6:3
Turmoil ... Mark 5:5
Rebellion ... Acts 7:51
Lying ... Titus 1:12

Amad—*people of duration*
A city of Asher ... Josh. 19:26

Amal—*toil*
Asher's descendant ... 1 Chr. 7:35

Amalek—*warlike*
A son of Eliphaz ... 1 Chr. 1:36
Grandson of Esau ... Gen. 36:11, 12
A duke of Edom ... Gen. 36:16
Founder of first nation ... Num. 24:20

Amalekites—*a nation hostile to Israel*
A. *Defeated by:*
Chedorlaomer ... Gen. 14:5-7
Joshua ... Ex. 17:8, 13
Gideon ... Judg. 7:12-25
Saul ... 1 Sam. 14:47, 48
David ... 1 Sam. 27:8, 9
Simeonites ... 1 Chr. 4:42, 43
B. *Overcame Israel during:*
Wilderness ... Num. 14:39-45
Judges ... Judg. 3:13
C. *Destruction of:*
Predicted ... Ex. 17:14
Reaffirmed ... Deut. 25:17-19
Fulfilled in part by David ... 1 Sam. 27:8, 9; 2 Sam. 1:1-16
Fulfilled by the Simeonites ... 1 Chr. 4:42, 43

Amam—*gathering place*
A city of Judah ... Josh. 15:26

Amana—*permanent*
A summit in the Anti-Lebanon mountain range ... Song 4:8

Amaranthine—*like the amaranth flower: unfading, perennial*
This Greek word is used to describe our inheritance and our glory ... 1 Pet. 1:4; 1 Pet. 5:4

Amariah—*Jehovah said*
1. The grandfather of Zadok the priest ... 1 Chr. 6:7-8, 52
2. A priest ... 1 Chr. 6:11
3. Levite in David's time ... 1 Chr. 23:19
4. A high priest ... 2 Chr. 19:11
5. A Levite in Hezekiah's reign ... 2 Chr. 31:14, 15
6. Son of King Hezekiah ... Zeph. 1:1
7. One who divorced his foreign wife ... Ezra 10:42, 44
8. A signer of Nehemiah's document ... Neh. 10:3
9. A postexilic chief priest ... Neh. 12:1, 2, 7

Amasa—*burden-bearer*
1. The son of Ithra; David's nephew ... 2 Sam. 17:25
Commands Absalom's rebels ... 2 Sam. 17:25
Made David's commander ... 2 Sam. 19:13
Treacherously killed by Joab ... 2 Sam. 20:9-12
Death avenged ... 1 Kin. 2:28-34
2. An Ephraimite leader ... 2 Chr. 28:9-12

SUBJECT — REFERENCE

Amasai—*Jehovah has borne*
1. A Kohathite Levite ... 1 Chr. 6:25, 35
2. David's officer ... 1 Chr. 12:18
3. A priestly trumpeter in David's time ... 1 Chr. 15:24
4. A Kohathite Levite ... 2 Chr. 29:12

Amashai—*carrying spoil*
A priest ... Neh. 11:13

Amasiah—*Jehovah bears*
One of Jehoshaphat's commanders ... 2 Chr. 17:16

Amazement—*an intense emotional shock*
A. *Caused by:*
Christ's miracles ... Matt. 12:22, 23; Luke 5:25, 26
Christ's teaching ... Matt. 19:25
God's power ... Luke 9:43
Apostolic miracle ... Acts 3:7-10
B. *Manifested by:*
Christ's parents ... Luke 2:48
Christ's disciples ... Matt. 19:25
The Jews ... Mark 9:15
Jesus ... Mark 14:33
The early Christians ... Acts 9:19-21

Amaziah—*Jehovah is strong*
1. King of Judah ... 2 Kin. 14:1-4
Kills his father's assassinators ... 2 Kin. 14:5, 6
Raises a large army ... 2 Chr. 25:5
Employs troops from Israel ... 2 Chr. 25:6
Rebuked by a man of God ... 2 Chr. 25:7-10
Defeats Edomites ... 2 Kin. 14:7
Worships Edomite gods ... 2 Chr. 25:14
Rebuked by a prophet ... 2 Chr. 25:15, 16
Defeated by Israel ... 2 Kin. 14:8-14
Killed by conspirators ... 2 Chr. 25:25-28
2. A priest of Bethel ... Amos 7:10-17
3. A Simeonite ... 1 Chr. 4:34, 42-44
4. A Merarite Levite ... 1 Chr. 6:45

Ambassador—*an official sent to deal with a foreign government*
A. *Some purposes of, to:*
Grant safe passage ... Num. 20:14-21
Settle disputes ... Judg. 11:12-28
Arrange business ... 1 Kin. 5:1-12
Stir up trouble ... 1 Kin. 20:1-12
Issue an ultimatum ... 2 Kin. 19:9-14
Spy ... 2 Kin. 20:12-19
Learn God's will ... Jer. 37:6-10
B. *Some examples of:*
Judah to Fgypt ... Is. 30:1-4
Babylonians to Judah ... 2 Chr. 32:31
Necho to Josiah ... 2 Chr. 35:20, 21
C. *Used figuratively of:*
Christ's ministers ... 2 Cor. 5:20
Paul in particular ... Eph. 5:20

Ambassage—*an official commission*
Coming to seek peace ... Luke 14:32

Amber—*a yellow, fossilized resin*
Descriptive of the divine glory ... Ezek. 1:4, 27

Ambidextrous—*equally skilled with either hand*
True of some of David's warriors ... 1 Chr. 12:1, 2

Ambition, Christian
A. *Good, if for:*
The best gifts ... 1 Cor. 12:31
Spiritual growth ... Phil. 3:12-14
The Gospel's extension ... Rom. 15:17-20
Acceptance before God ... 2 Cor. 5:7
Quietness ... 1 Thess. 4:11
B. *Evil, if it leads to:*
Strife ... Matt. 20:20-28
Sinful superiority ... Matt. 18:1-6
A Pharisaical spirit ... Mark 12:38-40
Contention about gifts ... 1 Cor. 3:3-8
Selfish ambition ... Phil. 1:14-17

Ambition, worldly
A. *Inspired by:*
Satan ... Gen. 3:1-6; Luke 4:5-8

SUBJECT ... REFERENCE

Pride ... Is. 14:12-15
1 Tim. 3:6
Jealousy ... Num. 12:2

B. *Leads to:*
Sin ... Acts 8:18-24
Strife ... James 4:1, 2
Suicide ... 2 Sam. 17:23
Self-glory ... Hab. 2:4, 5

C. *Examples of:*
Builders of Babel ... Gen. 11:4
Korah's company ... Num. 16:3-35
Abimelech ... Judg. 9:1-6
Absalom ... 2 Sam. 15:1-13
Adonijah ... 1 Kin. 1:5-7
Haman ... Esth. 5:9-13
Nebuchadnezzar ... Dan. 3:1-7
James and John ... Mark 10:35-37
The antichrist ... 2 Thess. 2:4
Diotrephes ... 3 John 9, 10

Ambush—*strategic concealment for surprise attack*
Joshua at Ai ... Josh. 8:2-22
Abimelech against Shechem ... Judg. 9:31-40
Israel at Gibeah ... Judg. 20:29-41
David against the Philistines ... 2 Sam. 5:23-25
Jehoshaphat against the Ammonites ... 2 Chr. 20:22

Amen—*a strong assent to a prayer* (also translated *"verily"*)

A. *Used in the Old Testament to:*
Confirm a statement ... Num. 5:22
Close a doxology ... 1 Chr. 16:36
Confirm an oath ... Neh. 5:13
Give assent to laws ... Deut. 27:15-26

B. *Used in the New Testament to:*
Close a doxology ... Rom. 9:5
Close epistle ... Rom. 16:27
Personalize Christ ... 2 Cor. 1:20
Close prayer ... 1 Cor. 14:16
Give assent ... Rev. 1:7
Emphasize a truth (translated "verily") ... John 3:3, 5, 11

Amerce—*to inflict a penalty*
For false charges ... Deut. 22:19

Amethyst—*a form of quartz purple to blue-violet*
Worn by the high priest ... Ex. 28:19
Ex. 39:12
In the New Jerusalem ... Rev. 21:20

Ami
Head of a family of Solomon's servants ... Ezra 2:57
Called Amon ... Neh. 7:59

Amiable—*pleasing, lovable*
God's tabernacles ... Ps. 84:1

Amittai—*true*
The father of Jonah the prophet ... Jon. 1:1

Ammah—*mother or beginning*
A hill near Giah ... 2 Sam. 2:24

Ammi—*my people*
A symbolic name of Israel ... Hos. 2:1

Ammiel—*my kinsman is God*
1. A spy representing the tribe of Dan ... Num. 13:12
2. The father of Machir ... 2 Sam. 9:4, 5
3. The father of Bath-shua (Bath-sheba), one of David's wives ... 1 Chr. 3:5
Called Eliam ... 2 Sam. 11:3
4. A son of Obed-edom ... 1 Chr. 26:4-5

Ammihud—*my kinsman is glorious*
1. An Ephraimite ... Num. 1:10
2. A Simeonite, father of Shemuel ... Num. 34:20
3. A Naphtalite ... Num. 34:28
4. The father of the king of Geshur ... 2 Sam. 13:37
5. A Judahite ... 1 Chr. 9:4

Amminadab—*my kinsman is noble*
1. Man of Judah ... 1 Chr. 2:10
The father of Nashon ... Num. 1:7
Aaron's father-in-law ... Ex. 6:23
An ancestor of David ... Ruth 4:19, 20
An ancestor of Christ ... Matt. 1:4
2. Chief of a Levitical house ... 1 Chr. 15:10, 11
3. Son of Kohath ... 1 Chr. 6:22

Amminadib—*my people is liberal*
Should probably be translated "my princely (or willing) people" ... Song 6:12

Ammishaddai—*my kinsman is the Almighty*
A captain representing the Danites ... Num. 1:12

Ammizabad—*my kinsman has endowed*
A son of Benaiah ... 1 Chr. 27:6

Ammon—*a people*
A son of Lot by his youngest daughter ... Gen. 19:38

Ammonites—*descendants of Ammon*

A. *Characterized by:*
Cruelty ... Amos 1:13
Pride ... Zeph. 2:9, 10
Callousness ... Ezek. 25:3, 6
Idolatry ... 1 Kin. 11:7, 33

B. *Hostility toward Israel, seen in:*
Aiding the Moabites ... Deut. 23:3, 4
Helping the Amalekites ... Judg. 3:13
Proposing a cruel treaty ... 1 Sam. 11:1-3
Abusing David's ambassadors ... 2 Sam. 10:1-4
Hiring Syrians against David ... 2 Sam. 10:6
Assisting the Chaldeans ... 2 Kin. 24:2
Harassing postexilic Jews ... Neh. 4:3, 7, 8

C. *Defeated by:*
Jephthah ... Judg. 11:4-33
Saul ... 1 Sam. 11:11
David ... 2 Sam. 10:7-14
Jehoshaphat ... 2 Chr. 20:1-25
Jotham ... 2 Chr. 27:5

D. *Prohibitions concerning:*
Exclusion from worship ... Deut. 23:3-6
No intermarriage with ... Ezra 9:1-3

E. *Prophecies concerning their:*
Captivity ... Amos 1:13-15
Subjection ... Jer. 25:9-21
Destruction ... Ps. 83:1-18

Ammonitess—*a female Ammonite*
Naamah ... 1 Kin. 14:21, 31
Shimeath ... 2 Chr. 24:26

Amnesty—*a pardon granted to political offenders*
To Shimei ... 2 Sam. 19:16-23
To Amasa ... 2 Sam. 17:25
2 Sam. 19:13

Amnon—*faithful*
1. A son of David ... 2 Sam. 3:2
Rapes his half sister ... 2 Sam. 13:1-18
Killed by Absalom ... 2 Sam. 13:19-29
2. Son of Shimon ... 1 Chr. 4:20

Amok—*deep, inscrutable*
A chief priest ... Neh. 12:7, 20

Amon—*master workman*
1. King of Judah ... 2 Kin. 21:18, 19
Follows evil ... 2 Chr. 33:22, 23
Killed by conspiracy ... 2 Kin. 21:23, 24
2. A governor of Samaria ... 1 Kin. 22:10, 26

Amorites—*mountain dwellers*

A. *Described as:*
Descendants of Canaan ... Gen. 10:15, 16
Original inhabitants of Palestine ... Ezek. 16:3
One of seven nations ... Gen. 15:19-21
A confederation ... Josh. 10:1-5
Ruled by great kings ... Ps. 136:18, 19
Of great size ... Amos 2:9
Very wicked ... Gen. 15:16
Worshipers of idols ... Judg. 6:10

B. *Contacts of, with Israel:*
Their defeat by Joshua ... Josh. 10:1-43
Their not being destroyed ... Judg. 1:34-36
Peace with ... 1 Sam. 7:14
Their being taxed by Solomon ... 1 Kin. 9:20, 21
Intermarriage with ... Judg. 3:5, 6

Amos—*burden-bearer*
1. A prophet of Israel ... Amos 1:1
Pronounces judgment against nations ... Amos 1:1-3, 15
Denounces Israel's sins ... Amos 4:1—7:9
Condemns Amaziah, the priest of Beth-el ... Amos 7:10-17
Predicts Israel's downfall ... Amos 9:1-10
Foretells great blessings ... Amos 9:11-15
2. An ancestor of Christ ... Luke 3:25

Amoz—*strong*
The father of Isaiah the prophet ... Is. 1:1

Amphipolis—*a city in Macedonia*
Visited by Paul ... Acts 17:1

Amplias
Christian at Rome ... Rom. 16:8

Amram—*a people exalted*
1. Son of Kohath ... Num. 3:17-19
The father of Aaron, Moses and Miriam ... Ex. 6:18-20; 1 Chr. 6:3
2. Jew who divorced his foreign wife ... Ezra 10:34

Amramites—*descendants of Amram*
A subdivision of the Levites ... Num. 3:27

Amraphel—*powerful people*
A king of Shinar who invaded Canaan during Abraham's time; identified by some as the Hammurabi of the monuments ... Gen. 14:1, 9

Amulet—*charm worn to protect against evil*
Condemned ... Is. 3:18-23

Amusements—*entertainment*

A. *Found in:*
Dancing ... Ex. 32:18, 19, 25
Music ... 1 Sam. 18:6, 7
Earthly pleasures ... Eccl. 2:1-8
Drunkenness ... Amos 6:1-6
1 Pet. 4:3
Feasting ... Mark 6:21, 22
Games ... Luke 7:32
Gossip ... Acts 17:21

B. *Productive of:*
Sorrow ... Prov. 14:13
Poverty ... Prov. 21:17
Vanity ... Eccl. 2:1-11
Immorality ... 1 Cor. 10:6-8
Spiritual deadness ... 1 Tim. 5:6

C. *Prevalence of:*
In the last days ... 2 Tim. 3:1, 4
In Babylon ... Rev. 18:21-24
At Christ's return ... Matt. 24:38, 39

Amzi—*strong one*
1. A Merarite Levite ... 1 Chr. 6:46
2. A priest ... Neh. 11:12

Anab—*grapes*
A town of Judah ... Josh. 11:21

Anah—*answer*
1. Father of Esau's wife ... Gen. 36:2, 14, 18
2. A Horite chief ... Gen. 36:20, 29
3. Son of Zibeon ... Gen. 36:24

Anaharath—*narrow way*
A city in the valley of Jezreel ... Josh. 19:19

Anaiah—*Jehovah has answered*
1. A Levite assistant ... Neh. 8:4
2. One who sealed the new covenant ... Neh. 10:22

Anak—*long-necked*
Descendant of Arba ... Josh. 15:13
Father of three sons ... Num. 13:22

Anakim—*descendants of Anak: a race of giants*

A. *Described as:*
Giants ... Num. 13:28-33
Very strong ... Deut. 2:10-11, 21

B. *Defeated by:*
Joshua ... Josh. 10:36-39
Caleb ... Josh. 14:6-15

SUBJECT — REFERENCE

C. *A remnant left:*
- Among the Philistines ... Josh. 11:22
- Possibly in Gath ... 1 Sam. 17:4-7

Anamim—*rockmen*

A tribe or people listed among Mizraim's (Egypt's) descendants ... Gen. 10:13

Anammelech—*Anu is king*

A god worshiped at Samaria ... 2 Kin. 17:24, 31

Anan—*cloud*

A signer of Nehemiah's document ... Neh. 10:26

Anani—*my cloud*

Son of Elioenai ... 1 Chr. 3:24

Ananiah—*Jehovah has covered*

1. The father of Maaseiah ... Neh. 3:23
2. A town inhabited by Benjamite returnees ... Neh. 11:32

Ananias—*Jehovah has been gracious*

1. Disciple at Jerusalem slain for lying to God ... Acts 5:1-11
2. A Christian disciple at Damascus ... Acts 9:10-19; Acts 22:12-16
3. A Jewish high priest ... Acts 23:1-5

Anarchy—*a reign of lawlessness in society*

A. *Manifested in:*
- Moral looseness ... Ex. 32:1-8, 25
- Idolatry ... Judg. 17:1-13
- Religious syncretism ... 2 Kin. 17:27-41
- A reign of terror ... Jer. 40:13-16
- Perversion of justice ... Hab. 1:1-4

B. *Instances of:*
- At Kadesh ... Num. 14:1-10
- During the judges ... Judg. 18:1-31
- In the northern kingdom ... 1 Kin. 12:26-33
- At the crucifixion ... Matt. 27:15-31
- At Stephen's death ... Acts 7:54, 57-58
- At Ephesus ... Acts 19:28-34
- In the time of Antichrist ... 2 Thess. 2:3-12

Anath—*answer*

Father of Shamgar ... Judg. 3:31

Anathema—*curse, accursed*

- Applied to non-believers or Christ haters ... 1 Cor. 16:22; Gal. 1:8, 9
- Translated "accursed" ... Rom. 9:3; 1 Cor. 12:3

See Accursed

Anathoth—*answers*

1. A Benjamite, son of Becher ... 1 Chr. 7:8
2. A leader who signed the document ... Neh. 10:19
3. A Levitical city in Benjamin ... Josh. 21:18
   - Birthplace of Jeremiah ... Jer. 1:1
   - Citizens of, hate Jeremiah ... Jer. 11:21, 23
   - Jeremiah bought property there ... Jer. 32:6-15
   - Home of famous mighty man ... 2 Sam. 23:27
   - Home of Abiathar, the high priest ... 1 Kin. 2:26
   - Reoccupied after exile ... Ezra 2:1, 23
   - Go to, to die ... 1 Kin. 2:26
   - Wretched place ... Is. 10:30
   - Reproved Jeremiah of ... Jer. 29:27

Anchor—*a weight used to hold a ship in place*

- Literally, of Paul's ship ... Acts 27:29-30, 40
- Figuratively of the believer's hope ... Heb. 6:19

Ancient—*that which is old*

- Applied to the beginning (eternity) ... Is. 45:21
- Applied to something very old ... 1 Sam. 24:13; Prov. 22:28
- Applied to old men (elders) ... Ps. 119:100; Jer. 19:1

Ancient of days

Title applied to God ... Dan. 7:9, 13, 22

Andrew—*manly*

- A fisherman ... Matt. 4:18
- A disciple of John the Baptist ... John 1:40
- Brought Peter to Christ ... John 1:40-42
- Called to Christ's discipleship ... Matt. 4:18, 19
- Enrolled among the Twelve ... Matt. 10:2
- Told Jesus about a lad's lunch ... John 6:8, 9
- Carried a request to Jesus ... John 12:20-22
- Sought further light on Jesus' words ... Mark 13:3, 4
- Met in the upper room ... Acts 1:13

Andronicus—*conqueror of men*

A notable Christian at Rome ... Rom. 16:7

Anem—*double fountain*

Levitical city ... 1 Chr. 6:73

Aner—*waterfall*

1. Amorite chief ... Gen. 14:13, 24
2. A Levitical city ... 1 Chr. 6:70

Anethothite—*a native of Anathoth*

Abiezer thus called ... 2 Sam. 23:27

Angels—*heavenly beings created by God*

A. *Described as:*
- Created ... Ps. 148:2, 5; Col. 1:16
- Spiritual beings ... Heb. 1:14
- Immortal ... Luke 20:36
- Holy ... Matt. 25:31
- Innumerable ... Heb. 12:22
- Wise ... 2 Sam. 14:17, 20
- Powerful ... Ps. 103:20
- Elect ... 1 Tim. 5:21
- Meek ... Jude 9
- Sexless ... Matt. 22:30
- Invisible ... Num. 22:22-31
- Obedient ... Ps. 103:20
- Possessing emotions ... Luke 15:10
- Concerned in human things ... 1 Pet. 1:12
- Incarnate in human form at times ... Gen. 18:2-8
- Not perfect ... Job 4:18
- Organized in ranks or orders ... Is. 6:2; 1 Thess. 4:16

B. *Ministry of, toward believers:*
- Guide ... Gen. 24:7, 40
- Provide for ... 1 Kin. 19:5-8
- Protect ... Ps. 34:7
- Deliver ... Dan. 6:22; Acts 12:7-10
- Gather ... Matt. 24:31
- Direct activities ... Acts 8:26
- Comfort ... Acts 27:23, 24
- Minister to ... Heb. 1:14

C. *Ministry of, toward unbelievers:*
- A destruction ... Gen. 19:13
- A curse ... Judg. 5:23
- A pestilence ... 2 Sam. 24:15-17
- Sudden death ... Acts 12:23
- Persecution ... Ps. 35:5, 6

D. *Ministry of, in Christ's life, to:*
- Announce His conception ... Matt. 1:20, 21
- Herald His birth ... Luke 2:10-12
- Sustain Him ... Matt. 4:11
- Witness His resurrection ... 1 Tim. 3:16
- Proclaim His resurrection ... Matt. 28:5-7
- Accompany Him to heaven ... Acts 1:9-11

E. *Ministry of, on special occasions, at:*
- The world's creation ... Job 38:7
- Sinai ... Acts 7:38, 53
- Satan's binding ... Rev. 20:1-3
- Christ's return ... Matt. 13:41, 49; 1 Thess. 4:16

F. *Appearance of, during the Old Testament, to:*
- Abraham ... Gen. 18:2-15
- Hagar ... Gen. 16:7-14
- Lot ... Gen. 19:1-22
- Jacob ... Gen. 28:12
- Moses ... Ex. 3:2
- Balaam ... Num. 22:31-35
- Joshua ... Josh. 5:13-15
- All Israel ... Judg. 2:1-4
- Gideon ... Judg. 6:11-24
- Manoah ... Judg. 13:6-21
- David ... 2 Sam. 24:16, 17
- Elijah ... 1 Kin. 19:5-7
- Daniel ... Dan. 6:22
- Zechariah ... Zech. 2:3

G. *Appearances of, during the New Testament, to:*
- Zechariah ... Luke 1:11-20
- The virgin Mary ... Luke 1:26-38
- Joseph ... Matt. 1:20-25
- Shepherds ... Luke 2:9-14
- Certain women ... Matt. 28:1-7
- Mary Magdalene ... John 20:12, 13
- The apostles ... Acts 1:10, 11
- Peter ... Acts 5:19, 20
- Philip ... Acts 8:26
- Cornelius ... Acts 10:3-32
- Paul ... Acts 27:23, 24
- John ... Rev. 1:1
- Seven churches ... Rev. 1:20

Angels, fallen

- Fall of, by pride ... Is. 14:12-15; Jude 6
- Seen by Christ ... Luke 10:18
- Make war on saints ... Rev. 12:7-17
- Imprisoned ... 2 Pet. 2:4
- Everlasting fire prepared for ... Matt. 25:41

Angel of God, the—*distinct manifestation of God*

A. *Names of:*
- Angel of God ... Gen. 21:17
- Angel of the Lord ... Gen. 22:11
- Captain of host of the Lord ... Josh. 5:14

B. *Appearances of, to:*
- Hagar ... Gen. 16:7, 8; Gen. 21:17
- Abraham ... Gen. 22:11, 15; Gen. 18:1-33
- Eliezer ... Gen. 24:7, 40
- Jacob ... Gen. 31:11-13; Gen. 32:24-30
- Moses ... Ex. 3:2
- Children of Israel ... Ex. 13:21, 22; Ex. 14:19
- Balaam ... Num. 22:22-35
- Joshua ... Judg. 2:1
- David ... 1 Chr. 21:16-18

C. *Divine characteristics:*
- Deliver Israel ... Judg. 2:1-3
- Extend blessings ... Gen. 16:7-12
- Pardon sin ... Ex. 23:20-22

Angels' food

- Eaten by men ... Ps. 78:25
- Eaten by Elijah ... 1 Kin. 19:5-8

Anger of God

A. *Caused by man's:*
- Sin ... Num. 32:10-15
- Unbelief ... Ps. 78:21, 22
- Error ... 2 Sam. 6:7
- Disobedience ... Josh. 7:1, 11, 12
- Idolatry ... Judg. 2:11-14

B. *Described as:*
- Sometimes delayed ... 2 Kin. 23:25-27
- Slow ... Neh. 9:17
- Brief ... Ps. 30:5
- Restrained ... Ps. 78:38
- Fierceness ... Ps. 78:49, 50
- Consuming ... Ps. 90:7
- Powerful ... Ps. 90:11
- Not forever ... Mic. 7:18
- To be feared ... Ps. 76:7

C. *Visitation of, upon:*
- Miriam and Aaron ... Num. 12:9-15
- Israelites ... Num. 11:4-10
- Balaam ... Num. 22:21, 22
- Moses ... Deut. 4:21, 22
- Israel ... Deut. 9:8
- Aaron ... Deut. 9:20
- Wicked cities ... Deut. 29:23
- A land ... Deut. 29:24-28
- A king ... 2 Chr. 25:15, 16

D. *Deliverance from, by:*
- Intercessory prayer ... Num. 11:1, 2; Deut. 9:19, 20
- Decisive action ... Num. 25:3-12
- Obedience ... Deut. 13:16-18
- Executing the guilty ... Josh. 7:1, 10-26
- Atonement ... Is. 63:1-6

See Wrath of God

Anger of Jesus

- Provoked by unbelievers ... Mark 3:5
- In the Temple ... Matt. 21:12; Mark 11:15

SUBJECT	REFERENCE
Anger of man	
A. *Caused by:*	
A brother's deception	Gen. 27:45
A wife's complaint	Gen. 30:1,2
Rape	Gen. 34:1, 7
Inhuman crimes	Gen. 49:6, 7
A leader's indignation	Ex. 11:8
A people's idolatry	Ex. 32:19, 22
Disobedience	Num. 31:14-18
The Spirit's arousal	1 Sam. 11:6
A brother's jealousy	1 Sam. 17:28
	Luke 15:28
A king's jealousy	1 Sam. 20:30
Righteous indignation	1 Sam. 20:34
Priestly rebuke	2 Chr. 26:19
Unrighteous dealings	Neh. 5:6, 7
Wife's disobedience	Esth. 1:12
Lack of respect	Esth. 3:5
Failure of astrologers	Dan. 2:12
Flesh	Gal. 5:19, 20
Harsh treatment	Eph. 6:4
B. *Justifiable, seen in:*	
Jacob	Gen. 31:36
Moses	Ex. 32:19
Samson	Judg. 14:1, 19
Saul	1 Sam. 11:6
Samuel	1 Sam. 15:16-31
Jonathan	1 Sam. 20:34
Christ	Mark 3:5
C. *Unjustifiable, seen in:*	
Cain	Gen. 4:5, 6
Simeon and Levi	Gen. 49:5-7
Potiphar	Gen. 39:1, 19
Moses	Num. 20:10-12
Balaam	Num. 22:27, 28
Saul	1 Sam. 20:30
Naaman	2 Kin. 5:11, 12
Asa	2 Chr. 16:10
Uzziah	2 Chr. 26:19
Ahasuerus	Esth. 1:9, 12
Haman	Esth. 3:5
Nebuchadnezzar	Dan. 3:13
Jonah	Jon. 4:1-9
Herod	Matt. 2:16
The Jews	Luke 4:28
Jewish officialdom	Acts 5:17
D. *The Christian attitude toward:*	
To be slow in	Prov. 14:17
Not to sin in	Eph. 4:26
To put away	Eph. 4:31
E. *Effects of, seen in:*	
Attempted assassination	Esth. 2:21
Punishment	Prov. 19:19
Mob action	Acts 19:28, 29
F. *Pacified by:*	
Kindly suggestion	2 Kin. 5:10-14
Righteous execution	Esth. 7:10
Gentle answer	Prov. 15:1
Angle—*a fishing instrument*	
Of Egyptian fishermen	Is. 19:8
Anguish—*extreme pain*	
A. *Caused by:*	
Physical hardships	Gen. 6:9
Physical pain	2 Sam. 1:9
Impending destruction	Deut. 2:25
Conflict of soul	Job 7:11
National distress	Is. 8:21, 22
Childbirth	John 16:21
A spiritual problem	2 Cor. 2:4
B. *Reserved for:*	
People who refuse wisdom	Prov. 1:20-27
The wicked	Job 15:20, 24
Those in Hell	Luke 16:23, 24
Aniam—*lament of the people*	
A Manassite	1 Chr. 7:19
Anim—*springs*	
A city in south Judah	Josh. 15:50
Animals	
A. *Described as:*	
Domesticated and wild	2 Sam. 12:3
Clean and unclean	Lev. 11:1-31
	Deut. 14:1-20
For sacrifices	Ex. 12:3-14
	Lev. 16:3, 5

SUBJECT	REFERENCE
B. *List of, in the Bible:*	
Antelope	Deut. 14:5
Ape	1 Kin. 10:22
Asp	Is. 11:8
Ass	Gen. 22:3
Badger	Ex. 25:5
Bats	Deut. 14:18
Bear	1 Sam. 17:34
Bittern	Is. 14:23
Boar	Ps. 80:13
Bulls	Jer. 52:20
Calf	Gen. 18:7
Camel	Gen. 12:16
Cattle	Gen. 1:25
Chameleon	Lev. 11:30
Chamois	Deut. 14:5
Cockatrice (adder)	Is. 11:8
Colt	Zech. 9:9
Coney	Lev. 11:5
Crocodile (Leviathan)	Job 41:1
Deer	Deut. 14:5
Dog	Deut. 23:18
Dragon	Is. 51:9
Elephant ("ivory")	1 Kin. 10:22
Ewe lambs	Gen. 21:30
Ferret	Lev. 11:30
Fox	Judg. 15:4
Frogs	Ex. 8:2-14
Goat	Gen. 27:9
Greyhound	Prov. 30:31
Hare	Deut. 14:7
Hart	Ps. 42:1
Heifer	Gen. 15:9
Hind	Hab. 3:19
Hippopotamus (Behemoth)	Job 40:15
Horse	Gen. 47:17
Jackal ("Dragons")	Is. 13:22
Kine	Gen. 32:15
Lamb	Ex. 29:39
Leopard	Rev. 13:2
Lion	1 Sam. 17:34
Lizard	Lev. 11:30
Mole	Is. 2:20
Mouse	Lev. 11:29
Mule	2 Sam. 13:29
Ox	Ex. 21:28
Pygarg	Deut. 14:5
Ram	Gen. 15:9
Roebuck	Deut. 14:5
Satyr	Is. 13:21
Scorpion	Deut. 8:15
Serpents	Matt. 10:16
Sheep	Gen. 4:2
Snail	Lev. 11:30
Spider	Prov. 30:28
Swine	Is. 65:2-4
Tortoise	Lev. 11:29
Unicorn	Num. 23:22
Weasel	Lev. 11:29
Whale (sea monster)	Gen. 1:21
Wolf	Is. 11:6
C. *Used figuratively of:*	
Human traits	Gen. 49:9 14, 21
Universal peace	Is. 11:6-9
Man's innate nature	Jer. 13:23
World empires	Dan. 7:2-8
Satanic powers	Rev. 12:4, 9
Christ's sacrifice	1 Pet. 1:18-20
Anise—*a plant for seasoning; the dill*	
Tithed by the Jews	Matt. 23:23
Ankle—*joint connecting foot and leg*	
Lame man's healed	Acts 3:7
Anklet—*an ornament worn by women on the ankles*	
Included in Isaiah's denunciation	Is. 3:16, 18
Anna—*grace*	
Aged prophetess	Luke 2:36-38
Annas—*gracious*	
A Jewish high priest	Luke 3:2
Christ appeared before	John 18:12-24
Peter and John appeared before	Acts 4:6
Anointing—*pouring oil upon*	
A. *Performed upon:*	
The patriarchs	1 Chr. 16:22
Priest	Ex. 29:7
Prophets	1 Kin. 19:16
Israel's kings	1 Sam. 10:1
Foreign kings	1 Kin. 19:15
The Messianic King	Ps. 2:2
Sacred objects	Ex. 30:26-28

SUBJECT	REFERENCE
B. *Ordinary, purposes of, for:*	
Adornment	Ruth 3:3
Invigoration	2 Sam. 12:20
Hospitality	Luke 7:38, 46
Purification	Esth. 2:12
Battle	Is. 21:5
Burial	Matt. 26:12
Sanctifying	Ex. 30:29
C. *Medicinal, purposes of, for:*	
Wound	Luke 10:34
Healing	Mark 6:13
	James 5:14
D. *Sacred, purposes of, to:*	
Memorialize an event	Gen. 28:18
Confirm a covenant	Gen. 35:14
Set apart	Ex. 30:22-29
Institute into office	1 Sam. 16:12, 13
E. *Absence of:*	
Sign of judgment	Deut. 28:40
Fasting	2 Sam. 12:16, 20
Mourning	2 Sam. 14:2
F. *Of Christ the Messiah "the Anointed One," as:*	
Predicted	Ps. 45:7
	Is. 61:1
Fulfilled	Luke 4:18
	Heb. 1:9
Interpreted	Acts 4:27
Symbolized in His name ("the Christ")	Matt. 16:16, 20 Acts 9:22
Typical of the believer's anointing	1 John 2:27
G. *Significance of, as indicating:*	
Divine appointment	2 Chr. 22:7
Special honor	1 Sam. 24:6, 10
Special privilege	Ps. 105:15
God's blessing	Ps. 23:5
Anointing of the Holy Spirit	
A. *Of Christ:*	
Predicted	Is. 61:1
Fulfilled	John 1:32-34
Explained	Luke 4:18
B. *Of Christians:*	
Predicted	Ezek. 47:1-12
Foretold by Christ	John 7:38, 39
Fulfilled at Pentecost	Acts 2:1-41
Fulfilled at conversion	2 Cor. 1:21
	1 John 2:20, 27
Answer—*a reply*	
A. *Good:*	
Soft	Prov. 15:1
Confident	Dan. 3:16-18
Convicting	Dan. 5:17-28
Astonished	Luke 2:47
Unanswerable	Luke 20:3-8
Spontaneous	Luke 21:14, 15
Spirit-directed	Luke 12:11, 12
Ready	1 Pet. 3:15
B. *Evil:*	
Unwise	1 Kin. 12:12-15
Incriminating	2 Sam. 1:5-16
Insolent	2 Kin. 18:27-36
Humiliating	Esth. 6:6-11
Satanic	Job 1:8-11
Ant—*a small insect*	
An example of industry	Prov. 6:6-8
	Prov. 30:24
Antagonism—*unceasing opposition*	
A. *Of men, against:*	
God's people	Ex. 5:1-19
	Deut. 2:26-33
The prophets	Amos 7:10-17
	Zech. 1:2-6
The light	John 3:19, 20
The truth	John 8:12-47
	Acts 7:54-60
Christians	Acts 16:16-24
B. *Of Satan, against:*	
Job	Job 2:9-12
Christ	Luke 4:1-13
Peter	Luke 22:31-34
Paul	1 Thess. 2:18
Christians	Eph. 6:11-18

SUBJECT REFERENCE

Antediluvians—*those who lived before the flood*

A. *Described as:*
Long-lived . . . . . Gen. 5:3-32
Very wicked . . . . . Gen. 6:5
A mixed race . . . . . Gen. 6:1-4
Jude 6, 7
Of great size . . . . . Gen. 6:4

B. *Warnings against, made by:*
Enoch . . . . . Jude 14, 15
Noah . . . . . 2 Pet. 2:5
Christ . . . . . 1 Pet. 3:19, 20

C. *Destruction of:*
Only Noah's family escaped . . . . . Gen. 7:21-23
Predicted . . . . . Gen. 6:5-7
Comparable to Christ's return . . . . . Matt. 24:37-39; Luke 17:26, 27
Comparable to the world's end . . . . . 2 Pet. 3:3-7

Anthropomorphisms—*applying human attributes to God*

A. *Physical likenesses, such as:*
Feet . . . . . Ex. 24:10
Hands . . . . . Ex. 24:11
Mouth . . . . . Num. 12:8
Eyes . . . . . Hab. 1:13
Arms . . . . . Ex. 6:6

B. *Non-physical characteristics, such as:*
Memory . . . . . Gen. 9:16
Anger . . . . . Ex. 22:24
Jealousy . . . . . Ps. 78:58
Repentance . . . . . Jon. 3:10

Antichrist—*Satan's final opponent of Christ and Christians*

A. *Called:*
Man of sin . . . . . 2 Thess. 2:3
Son of perdition . . . . . 2 Thess. 2:3
Wicked one . . . . . 2 Thess. 2:8
Antichrist . . . . . 1 John 2:18, 22
Beast . . . . . Rev. 11:7

B. *Described as:*
Lawless . . . . . 2 Thess. 2:3-12
Opposing Christ . . . . . 2 Thess. 2:4
Working wonders . . . . . 2 Thess. 2:9
Deceiving the world . . . . . 2 John 7
Rev. 19:20
Persecuting Christians . . . . . Rev. 13:7
Satan-inspired . . . . . 2 Thess. 2:9
Denying Christ's incarnation . . . . . 1 John 4:3; 2 John 7
One and many . . . . . 1 John 2:18-22
A person and a system . . . . . 2 Thess. 2:3, 7
Seeking man's worship . . . . . 2 Thess. 2:4

C. *Coming of:*
Foretold . . . . . 2 Thess. 2:5
In the last time . . . . . 1 John 2:18
Now restrained . . . . . 2 Thess. 2:6
Follows removal of hindrance . . . . . 2 Thess. 2:7, 8
Before Christ's return . . . . . 2 Thess. 2:8
By Satan's deception . . . . . 2 Thess. 2:9, 10

D. *Destruction of:*
At Christ's return . . . . . 2 Thess. 2:8
Rev. 19:20
Eternal in lake of fire . . . . . Rev. 20:10

Antidote—*a remedy given to counteract poison*

A. *Literal:*
A tree . . . . . Ex. 15:23-25
Meal . . . . . 2 Kin. 4:38-41

B. *Figurative and spiritual, for:*
Sin, Christ . . . . . Num. 21:8,9
John 3:14, 15
Christ's absence, the Holy Spirit . . . . . John 14:16-18
Sorrow, joy . . . . . John 16:20-22
Satan's lies, God's truth&2:5
In the last time . . . . .
Earth's trials, faith . . . . . 1 Pet. 1:6-8
Testings, God's grace . . . . . 1 Cor. 10:13
2 Cor. 12:7-9
Suffering, heaven's glory . . . . . Rom. 8:18
2 Cor. 5:1-10

Antinomianism—*the idea that Christian liberty exempts one from the moral law*

A. *Prevalence of, among:*
Christians . . . . . Rom. 6:1-23
False Teachers . . . . . 2 Pet. 2:19
Jude 4

B. *Based on error, that:*
Grace allows sin . . . . . Rom. 6:1, 2
Moral law is abolished . . . . . Rom. 7:1-14
Liberty has no bounds . . . . . 1 Cor. 10:23-33

C. *Corrected by remembering that liberty is:*
Not a license to sin . . . . . Rom. 6:1-23
Limited by moral law . . . . . Rom. 8:1-4
Controlled by Holy Spirit . . . . . Rom. 8:5-14
Not to be a stumbling block . . . . . Rom. 14:1-23; 1 Cor. 8:1-13
Motivated by love . . . . . Gal. 5:13-15

Antioch—*a city of Syria*

Home of Nicolas . . . . . Acts 6:5
Haven of persecuted Christians . . . . . Acts 11:19
Home of first Gentile church . . . . . Acts 11:20, 21
Name "Christian" originated in . . . . . Acts 11:26
Barnabas ministered here . . . . . Acts 11:22-24
Barnabas and Paul minister in church of . . . . . Acts 11:25-30
Paul commissioned by church of . . . . . Acts 13:1-4; Acts 15:35-41
Paul reports to . . . . . Acts 14:26-28
Church of, troubled by Judaizers . . . . . Acts 15:1-4; Gal. 2:11-21

Antioch—*a city of Pisidia*

Jewish synagogue . . . . . Acts 13:14
Paul visits . . . . . Acts 13:14, 42
Jews of, reject the Gospel . . . . . Acts 13:45-51
Paul revisits . . . . . Acts 14:21
Paul recalls persecution at . . . . . 2 Tim. 3:11

Antipas

A Christian martyr of Pergamum . . . . . Rev. 2:13

Antipatris—*belonging to Antipater*

A city between Jerusalem and Caesarea . . . . . Acts 23:31

Antitype—*the fulfillment of a type*

The Greek word translated "figure" in . . . . . Heb. 9:24; 1 Pet. 3:21
Generally, a fulfillment of an Old Testament type . . . . . Matt. 12:39, 40; John 1:29

Antonia, Tower of—(fortress built by Herod the Great, not mentioned by name in Scripture)

Called "castle" . . . . . Acts 21:30-40
Possible site of Jesus' trial, called "the Pavement" . . . . . John 19:13

Antothijah—*answers of Jehovah*

A Benjamite . . . . . 1 Chr. 8:24

Antothite—*a native of Anathoth*

Home of famous soldiers . . . . . 1 Chr. 11:28
1 Chr. 12:3

Anub—*strong*

A man of Judah . . . . . 1 Chr. 4:8

Anvil—*a block for forging hot metals*

Used figuratively in . . . . . Is. 41:7

Anxiety—*A disturbed state of mind produced by real or imaginary fears*

A. *Caused by:*
Brother's hatred . . . . . Gen. 32:6-12
Son's rebellion . . . . . 2 Sam. 18:24-33
King's decree . . . . . Esth. 4:1-17
Child's absence . . . . . Luke 2:48
Son's sickness . . . . . John 4:46-49
Friend's delay . . . . . 2 Cor. 2:12, 13

B. *Overcome by:*
Trust . . . . . Ps. 37:1-5
Reliance upon the Holy Spirit . . . . . Mark 13:11
God's provision . . . . . Luke 12:22-30
Upward look . . . . . Luke 21:25-28
Assurance of God's sovereignty . . . . . Rom. 8:28
Angel's word . . . . . Acts 27:21-25
Prayer . . . . . Phil. 4:6
God's care . . . . . 1 Pet. 5:6, 7

See Cares, worldly

Ape—*a monkey*

Article of trade . . . . . 1 Kin. 10:22

Apelles

A Christian in Rome . . . . . Rom. 16:10

Apharsites

Assyrian colonists in Samaria opposing Zerubbabel's work . . . . . Ezra 4:9

Aphek—*strength, fortress*

1. A town in Plain of Sharon . . . . . Josh. 12:18
Site of Philistine camp . . . . . 1 Sam. 4:1
1 Sam. 29:1
2. A city assigned to Asher . . . . . Josh. 19:30
3. Border city . . . . . Josh. 13:4
4. A city in Jezreel . . . . . 1 Kin. 20:26-30
Syria's defeat prophesied here . . . . . 2 Kin. 13:14-19

Aphekah—*fortress*

A city of Judah . . . . . Josh. 15:53

Aphiah—*striving*

An ancestor of King Saul . . . . . 1 Sam. 9:1

Aphik—*strength, fortress*

Spared by Asher . . . . . Judg. 1:31
See Aphek 2

Aphrah—*house of dust*

A Philistine city; symbolic of doom . . . . . Mic. 1:10

Aphses—*shattering*

Chief of a priestly course . . . . . 1 Chr. 24:15

Apocalypse—*an unveiling of something unknown*

The Greek word usually translated "revelation" . . . . . Rom. 16:25; Gal. 1:12

Apocrypha—*hidden things*

Writings in Greek written during the period between the Testaments; rejected by Protestants as uninspired

Apollonia—*pertaining to Apollo*

A town between Amphipolis and Thessalonica . . . . . Acts 17:1

Apollos—*a short or pet name for Apollonios*

An Alexandrian Jew mighty in the Scriptures . . . . . Acts 18:24, 25
Receives further instruction . . . . . Acts 18:26
Sent to preach in Achaia . . . . . Acts 18:27, 28
A minister in Corinth . . . . . 1 Cor. 1:12
1 Cor. 3:4, 22
Cited by Paul . . . . . 1 Cor. 4:6
Urged to revisit Corinth . . . . . 1 Cor. 16:12
Journey of, noted by Paul . . . . . Titus 3:13

Apollyon—*the destroyer*

Angel of the bottomless pit . . . . . Rev. 9:11

Apostasy—*a falling away from God's truth*

A. *Kinds of:*
National . . . . . 1 Kin. 12:26-33
Individual . . . . . 2 Kin. 21:1-9
Heb. 3:12
Satanic . . . . . Rev. 12:7-9
Angelic . . . . . 2 Pet. 2:4
General . . . . . 2 Tim. 3:1-5
Imputed . . . . . Acts 21:21
Final . . . . . 2 Thess. 2:3
Irremedial . . . . . Heb. 6:1-8

B. *Caused by:*
Satan . . . . . Luke 22:31
False teachers . . . . . Acts 20:29, 30
Perversion of Scripture . . . . . 2 Tim. 4:3, 4
Persecution . . . . . Matt. 13:21
Unbelief . . . . . Heb. 4:9-11
Love of world . . . . . 2 Tim. 4:10
Hardened heart . . . . . Acts 7:54, 57
Spiritual blindness . . . . . Acts 28:25-27

C. *Manifested in:*
Resisting truth . . . . . 2 Tim. 3:7, 8
Resorting to deception . . . . . 2 Cor. 11:13-15
Reverting to immorality . . . . . 2 Pet. 2:14, 19-22

D. *Safeguards against, found in:*
God's Word . . . . . 2 Tim. 3:13-17
Spiritual growth . . . . . 2 Pet. 1:5-11
Indoctrination . . . . . Acts 20:29-31
Faithfulness . . . . . Matt. 24:42-51
Spiritual perception . . . . . 1 John 4:1-6
Being grounded in the truth . . . . . Eph. 4:13-16

SUBJECT ... REFERENCE

Using God's armor ... Eph. 6:10-20
Preaching the Word ... 2 Tim. 4:2, 5

E. *Examples of, seen in:*

Israelites ... Ex. 32:1-35
Saul ... 1 Sam. 15:11
Solomon ... 1 Kin. 11:1-10
Amaziah ... 2 Chr. 25:14-16
Judas ... Matt. 26:14-16
Hymenaeus and Philetus ... 2 Tim. 2:17, 18
Demas ... 2 Tim. 4:10
Certain men ... Jude 4

Apostles—*men divinely commissioned to represent Christ*

A. *Descriptive of:*

Christ ... Heb. 3:1
The twelve ... Matt. 10:2
Others (Barnabas, James, etc.) ... Acts 14:4; Gal. 1:19
Messengers ... 2 Cor. 8:23
False teachers ... 2 Cor. 11:13
Simon Peter ... Matt. 10:2
Andrew ... Matt. 10:2
James, son of Zebedee ... Matt. 10:2
John ... Matt. 10:2
Philip ... Matt. 10:3
Bartholomew (Nathanael) ... Matt. 10:3; John 1:45
Thomas ... Matt. 10:3
Matthew (Levi) ... Matt. 10:3; Luke 5:27
James, son of Alphaeus ... Matt. 10:3
Thaddaeus (Judas) ... Matt. 10:3; John 14:22
Simon the Zealot ... Luke 6:15
Judas Iscariot ... Matt. 10:4
Matthias ... Acts 1:26
Paul ... 2 Cor. 1:1
Barnabas ... Acts 14:14
James, the Lord's brother ... Gal. 1:19
Silvanus and Timothy ... 1 Thess. 1:1; 1 Thess. 2:9
Andronicus and Junias ... Rom. 16:7

B. *Mission of, to:*

Perform miracles ... Matt. 10:1, 8
Preach Gospel ... Matt. 28:19, 20
Witness Christ's resurrection ... Acts 1:22; Acts 10:40-42
Write Scripture ... Eph. 3:5
Establish the Church ... Eph. 2:20

C. *Limitations of, before Pentecost:*

Lowly in position ... Matt. 4:18
Unlearned ... Acts 4:13
Subject to disputes ... Matt. 20:20-28
Faith often obscure ... Matt. 16:21-23
Need of instruction ... Matt. 17:4, 9-13

D. *Position of, after Pentecost:*

Interpreted prophecy ... Acts 2:14-36
Defended truth ... Phil. 1:7, 17
Exposed heretics ... Gal. 1:6-9
Upheld discipline ... 2 Cor. 13:1-6
Established churches ... Rom. 15:17-20

Apothecary—*"pharmacist", "perfumer"*

Used in tabernacle ... Ex. 30:25, 35
Used in embalming ... 2 Chr. 16:14
A maker of ointment ... Eccl. 10:1
Among returnees ... Neh. 3:8

Appaim—*nostrils*

A man of Judah ... 1 Chr. 2:30, 31

Apparel—*clothing*

A. *Kinds of:*

Harlot's ... Gen. 38:14
Virgin's ... 2 Sam. 13:18
Mourner's ... 2 Sam. 12:20
Splendid ... Luke 7:25
Rich ... Ezek. 27:24
Worldly ... 1 Pet. 3:3
Showy ... Luke 16:19
Official ... 1 Kin. 10:5
Royal ... Esth. 6:8
Priestly ... Ezra 3:10
Angelic ... Acts 1:10
Heavenly ... Rev. 19:8

B. *Attitude toward:*

Not to covet ... Acts 20:33
Without show ... 1 Pet. 3:3
Be modest in ... 1 Tim. 2:9

C. *Figurative of:*

Christ's blood ... Is. 63:1-3

SUBJECT ... REFERENCE

Christ's righteousness ... Zech. 3:1-5
The Church's purity ... Ps. 45:13, 14

Apparition—*appearance of ghost or disembodied spirit*

Samuel ... 1 Sam. 28:12-14
Christ mistaken for ... Matt. 14:26; Luke 24:37, 39

Appeal—*petition for higher judgment*

To Christ ... Luke 12:13, 14
Of Paul, to Caesar ... Acts 25:11, 25-28; Acts 26:32

Appearance, outward

A. *Can conceal:*

Deception ... Josh. 9:3-16
Hypocrisy ... Matt. 23:25-28
Rottenness ... Acts 12:21-23
Rebellion ... 2 Sam. 15:7-13
False apostles ... 2 Cor. 11:13-15
Inner glory ... Is. 53:1-3; Matt. 17:1, 2

B. *Can be:*

Misunderstood ... Josh. 22:10-31
Mistaken ... 1 Sam. 1:12-18
Misleading ... 2 Cor. 10:7-11
Misjudged ... John 7:24
Misinterpreted ... Matt. 11:16-19

Appearances, divine

A. *Of the Lord in the Old Testament:*

To Abraham ... Gen. 12:7
To Isaac ... Gen. 26:2, 24
To Jacob ... Gen. 35:1, 9
To Moses ... Ex. 3:2, 16
To Israel ... Ex. 16:10
In mercy seat ... Lev. 16:2
In tabernacle ... Num. 14:10
To Gideon ... Judg. 6:11, 12
To Manoah ... Judg. 13:3, 10, 21
To Samuel ... 1 Sam. 3:21
To David ... 2 Chr. 3:1
To Solomon ... 1 Kin. 3:5

B. *Of Christ's first advent, in:*

Nativity ... 2 Tim. 1:10
Transfiguration ... Luke 9:30, 31
Resurrected form ... Luke 24:34
Priestly intercession ... Heb. 9:24
Return ... Col. 3:4

C. *Of Christ resurrected, to, at:*

Mary Magdalene ... John 20:11-18
Other women ... Matt. 28:9-10
Disciples on road to Emmaus ... Luke 24:13-35
Ten disciples ... John 20:19-25
Thomas ... John 20:26-31
Sea of Galilee ... John 21:1-25
Give great commission ... Matt. 28:16-20
Five hundred brethren ... 1 Cor. 15:6
His ascension ... Acts 1:4-11
Paul ... Acts 9:3-6
John ... Rev. 1:10-18

D. *Of Christ's second advent, a time of:*

Salvation ... Heb. 9:28
Confidence ... 1 John 2:28
Judgment ... 2 Tim. 4:1
Reward ... 2 Tim. 4:8
Blessedness ... Titus 2:13
Joy ... 1 Pet. 1:7, 8
Rulership ... 1 Tim. 6:14, 15

See Theophany

Appeasement—*means used to reconcile two parties*

A. *Kinds of, between:*

Brothers ... Gen. 32:20
Nations ... 1 Kin. 20:31-34
Tribes ... Josh. 22:10-34
Jews and Gentiles ... Eph. 2:11-17

B. *Means of, by:*

Gifts ... Gen. 43:11-16
Special pleading ... 1 Sam. 25:17-35
Correcting an abuse ... Acts 6:1-6
Slowness to anger ... Prov. 15:18
Wisdom ... Prov. 16:14

C. *None allowed between:*

Righteousness, evil ... 2 Cor. 6:14-17
Truth, error ... Gal. 1:7-9
Faith, works ... Gal. 5:1-10
Flesh, Spirit ... Gal. 5:16-26

SUBJECT ... REFERENCE

Christ, Satan ... Matt. 4:1-11
Heaven, Sheol ... Is. 28:18

D. *Of God's wrath, by:*

Righteous action ... Num. 16:44-50
Repentance ... 2 Sam. 12:10-14
Atoning for an evil ... 2 Sam. 21:1-14
Christ's death ... Is. 63:1-7
Christ's righteousness ... Zech. 3:1-5; 2 Cor. 5:18-21

Appetite—*desire to fulfill some basic need*

A. *Kinds of:*

Physical ... 1 Sam. 14:31-33
Sexual ... 1 Cor. 7:1-9
Lustful ... Matt. 5:28
Insatiable ... Prov. 27:20
Spiritual ... Ps. 119:20, 131

B. *Perversion of, by:*

Gluttony ... Prov. 23:1, 2
Wine ... Prov. 23:29-35
Adultery ... Prov. 6:24-29; Ezek. 23:1-49
Impurity ... Rom. 1:24-32

C. *Loss of, by:*

Age ... 2 Sam. 19:35
Trouble ... 1 Sam. 28:22, 23
Visions ... Dan. 10:3-16
Deep concern ... John 4:31-34

D. *Spiritual, characteristics of:*

Satisfying ... Is. 55:1, 2
Sufficient ... Matt. 5:6
Spontaneous ... John 7:38, 39
Sanctifying ... 1 Pet. 2:2
Sublime ... Col. 3:1-3

See Gluttony; Hunger; Temperance

Apphia

Christian lady of Colossae ... Philem. 2

Appii forum—*a town about 40 miles south of Rome*

Paul meets Christians here ... Acts 28:15

Applause—*a visible expression of public approval*

Men seek after ... Matt. 6:1-5

"Apple of the eye"—*a figurative expression for something very valuable*

A. *Translated as:*

"The pupil of his eye" ... Deut. 32:10
"The apple of his eye" ... Zech. 2:8

B. *Figurative of:*

God's care ... Deut. 32:10
God's Law ... Prov. 7:2
The saint's security ... Ps. 17:8
Abundance of sorrow ... Lam. 2:18

Apples of gold—*something of great value*

A word fitly spoken ... Prov. 25:11

Appoint—*to set in an official position or relationship*

A. *Descriptive of ordination, to:*

Priesthood ... Num. 3:10
Prophetic office ... Heb. 3:2
Ruler ... 2 Sam. 6:21
Apostleship ... Luke 10:1
Deacon's office ... Acts 6:3

B. *Descriptive of God's rule, over:*

Earth ... Ps. 104:20
World history ... Acts 17:26
Israel's history ... 2 Chr. 33:8
Nations ... Jer. 47:7
Man's plans ... 2 Sam. 17:14
Man's life ... Job 14:5
Death ... Heb. 9:27
Final judgment ... Acts 17:31
Man's destiny ... Matt. 24:51

C. *Descriptive of the believer's life:*

Trials ... 1 Thess. 3:3
Service ... Acts 22:10
Salvation ... 1 Thess. 5:9

Appreciation—*favorable recognition of blessings*

Sought for among men ... Ps. 107:8-21
Of favors, rebuffed ... 2 Sam. 10:1-5
Of blessings, unnoticed ... Acts 14:15-18

Apprehension—*the ability to understand*

God ... Job 11:7

SUBJECT ... REFERENCE

God's Word ... Acts 17:11
Prophecy ... 1 Pet. 1:10-12
Parables ... Matt. 13:10-17
Spiritual truths ... 1 Cor. 2:7-16
Christ ... Phil. 3:12-14

Appropriation—*possessing for one's use*
God's promises ... Heb. 11:8-16
God's Word ... Ps. 119:11
Salvation ... Acts 16:30-34

Approval—*favorable acceptance*
A. *Means of, by:*
God ... Acts 2:22
The Lord ... 2 Cor. 10:18
The Jews ... Rom. 2:18
A church ... 1 Cor. 16:3
Men ... Rom. 14:18
B. *Obtained by:*
Endurance ... 2 Cor. 6:4
Innocence ... 2 Cor. 7:11
Spiritual examination ... 2 Cor. 13:5-8
Spiritual judgment ... Phil. 1:9, 10
Diligence ... 2 Tim. 2:15

Aprons—*articles of clothing*
Item of miraculous healing ... Acts 19:12

Aquila—*eagle*
Jewish tentmaker ... Acts 18:2, 3
Paul stays with ... Acts 18:3
Visits Syria ... Acts 18:18
Resides in Ephesus ... Acts 18:19
Instructs Apollos ... Acts 18:24-26
Esteemed by Paul ... Rom. 16:3, 4

Ar—*city*
A chief Moabite city ... Num. 21:15
On Israel's route ... Deut. 2:18
Destroyed by Sihon ... Num. 21:28
Destroyed by God ... Is. 15:1

Ara—*strong*
A descendant of Asher ... 1 Chr. 7:38

Arab—*a court*
A mountain city of Judah ... Josh. 15:52

Arabah—*desert plain, steppe*
A district east of Jordan ... 2 Sam. 2:29
A major natural division of Palestine ... Josh. 11:16; Josh. 12:8
Opposite Gigal ... Deut. 11:30
Restoration of, predicted ... Ezek. 47:1-12
Referred by "desert" in ... Is. 35:1

Arabia—*steppe*
A. *Place of:*
Mt. Sinai ... Gal. 4:25
Gold mines ... 2 Chr. 9:14
Paul visited ... Gal. 1:17
B. *People of:*
Lustful ... Is. 13:20
Paid tribute to Solomon ... 1 Kin. 10:14, 15
Plundered Jerusalem ... 2 Chr. 21:16, 17
Defeated by Uzziah ... 2 Chr. 26:7
Sold sheep and goats to Tyre ... Ezek. 27:21
Opposed Nehemiah ... Neh. 2:19
Denounced by prophets ... Is. 21:13-17
Visited Jerusalem at Pentecost ... Acts 2:11

Arad—*fugitive*
1. A Benjamite ... 1 Chr. 8:15
2. A city south of Hebron ... Num. 21:1-3
Defeated by Joshua ... Josh. 12:14
Kenites settled near ... Judg. 1:16

Arah—*wayfarer*
1. A descendant of Asher ... 1 Chr. 7:39
2. A family of returnees ... Ezra 2:5

Aram—*high, exalted*
1. A son of Shem ... Gen. 10:22, 23
2. A grandson of Nahor ... Gen. 22:21
3. A descendant of Asher ... 1 Chr. 7:34
4. A district in Gilead ... 1 Chr. 2:23
5. An ancestor of Christ ... Matt. 1:3, 4

Aramaic—*a Semitic language*
Used by the Syrians ... 2 Kin. 18:26
The language of the postexilic period ... Ezra 4:7; Dan. 2:4
Portions of the Bible written in, include ... Dan. 2:4—7:28; Ezra 4:8—6:18; Ezra 7:12-26
The same as "Hebrew" in ... John 19:20
Words and phrases of, found in ... Matt. 27:46; Mark 5:41; Mark 7:34

Aran—*wild goat*
Esau's descendant ... Gen. 36:28

Ararat—*a high mountain range in eastern Armenia*
Site of ark's landing ... Gen. 8:4
Assassins flee to ... 2 Kin. 19:37; Is. 37:38

Aratus—*a Greek poet living about 270 B.C.*
Paul quotes from his *Phaenomena* ... Acts 17:28

Araunah—*Jehovah is firm*
A Jebusite ... 2 Sam. 24:15-25
His threshing floor bought by David ... 2 Sam. 24:18-25
Became site of Temple ... 2 Chr. 3:1
Also called Ornan ... 1 Chr. 21:18-28

Arba—*four*
The father of the Anakim ... Josh. 14:15

Arbathite—*a native of Beth-arabah*
Two of David's mighty men ... 2 Sam. 23:31

Arbite—*a native of Arab*
In Judah ... 2 Sam. 23:35

Arbitrator—*one authorized to settle disputes*
A. *Exercised by:*
Judges ... Ex. 18:18-27
Priests ... Deut. 17:8-13
Kings ... 1 Kin. 3:9, 16-28
Christ ... Matt. 22:17-33
Apostles ... Acts 6:1-6
Church ... Acts 15:1-29
B. *Purposes of:*
Determine the Lord's will ... Lev. 24:11-16, 23; Num. 15:32-36
Settle disputes ... Josh. 22:9-34
Settle labor disputes ... Matt. 18:23-35; Matt. 20:1-16

Archaeology—*the science of digging up ancient civilizations*
Truth springs out of the earth ... Ps. 85:11
The stones cry out ... Luke 19:40
See article on Greatest Archaeological Discoveries

Archangel—*a chief angel*
Contends with Satan ... Jude 9
Will herald the Lord's return ... 1 Thess. 4:16

Archelaus—*leader of the people*
Son of Herod the Great ... Matt. 2:22

Archers—*experts with the bow and arrow*
A. *Descriptive of:*
Ishmael ... Gen. 21:20
Jonathan ... 1 Sam. 20:34-39
Sons of Ulam ... 1 Chr. 8:40
B. *Instrumental in the death of:*
Saul ... 1 Sam. 31:3
Uriah the Hittite ... 2 Sam. 11:24
Josiah ... 2 Chr. 35:23, 24
C. *Figurative of:*
Invincibility ... Gen. 49:23
The Lord's chastisements ... Job 16:13
Loss of glory ... Is. 21:17
Divine judgment ... Jer. 50:29

Archevites—*people settled in Samaria during exile*
Opposed rebuilding of Jerusalem ... Ezra 4:9-16

Archippus—*master of the horse*
A church worker ... Col. 4:17

Archite—*the long*
Canaanite tribe ... Josh. 16:2
David's friend ... 2 Sam. 15:32

Architect—*one who draws plans for a building*
Plan of, given to Noah ... Gen. 6:14-16
Plan of, shown to Moses ... Ex. 25:8, 9, 40
Bezaleel, an inspired ... Ex. 35:30-35
Plan of, given to Solomon ... 1 Chr. 28:11-21
Seen in Ezekiel's vision ... Ezek. 40—42

Archives—*storage place for public and historical documents*
The book of the law found in ... 2 Kin. 22:8
Jeremiah's roll placed in ... Jer. 36:20, 21
Record book kept in ... Ezra 4:15
Genealogies kept in ... Neh. 7:5, 64

Arcturus—*a constellation called the Great Bear*
Cited as evidence of God's sovereignty ... Job 9:9

Ard—*humpbacked*
A son of Benjamin ... Gen. 46:21
Progenitor of the Ardites ... Num. 26:40
Also called Addar ... 1 Chr. 8:3

Ardon—*descendant*
A son of Caleb ... 1 Chr. 2:18

Areli—*valiant, heroic*
A son of Gad ... Gen. 46:16

Areopagite—*a member of the court*
A convert ... Acts 17:34

Areopagus—*a rocky hill at Athens: also the name of a court*
Paul preached ... Acts 17:18-34
Called "Mars' Hill" ... Acts 17:22

Aretas—*pleasing*
The title borne by four Nabataean rulers, the last of whom Paul mentions (Aretas IV, Philopatris, 9 B.C.-A.D. 40) ... 2 Cor. 11:32, 33

Argob—*mound or region of clods*
1. District of Bashan with 60 fortified cities ... Deut. 3:4; 1 Kin. 4:13
2. Guard killed by Pekah ... 2 Kin. 15:25

Aridai
A son of Haman ... Esth. 9:9

Aridatha
A son of Haman ... Esth. 9:8

Arieh—*lion*
Guard killed by Pekah ... 2 Kin. 15:25

Ariel—*lion of God*
1. Ezra's friend ... Ezra 8:15-17
2. Name applied to Jerusalem ... Is. 29:1, 2, 7

Arimathea—*a height*
Joseph's native city ... John 19:38

Arioch—*lion-like*
1. King of Ellasar ... Gen. 14:1, 9
2. Captain of Nebuchadnezzar ... Dan. 2:14, 15

Arisai
A son of Haman ... Esth. 9:9

Arise—*to stand up*
A. *Descriptive of:*
Natural events ... Eccl. 1:5
Standing up ... 1 Sam. 28:23
Regeneration ... Luke 15:18, 20
Resurrection ... Matt. 9:25
A miracle ... Luke 4:39
B. *Descriptive of prophetic events:*
World kingdoms ... Dan. 2:39
The Messiah's advent ... Is. 60:1-3
Persecution ... Mark 4:17
False Christs ... Matt. 24:24

Aristarchus—*the best ruler*
A Macedonian Christian ... Acts 19:29
Accompanied Paul ... Acts 20:4
Imprisoned with Paul ... Col. 4:10

Aristobulus—*the best counselor*
A Christian at Rome ... Rom. 16:10

SUBJECT REFERENCE

Ark of bulrushes—*a basket made of reeds (papyrus)*
- Moses placed in ... Ex. 2:3-6
- Made by faith ... Heb. 11:23

Ark of Noah
- Construction ... Gen. 6:14-16
- Cargo ... Gen. 6:19-21
- Ready for the flood ... Matt. 24:38, 39
- Rested on Mt. Ararat ... Gen. 8:1-16
- A type of baptism ... 1 Pet. 3:20, 21

Ark of the Covenant—*a small box containing the tablets of the Law*

A. *Called:*
- Ark of the covenant ... Num. 10:33
- Ark of the testimony ... Ex. 30:6
- Ark of the Lord ... Josh. 4:11
- Ark of God ... 1 Sam. 3:3
- Ark of God's strength ... 2 Chr. 6:41

B. *Construction of:*
- Described ... Ex. 25:10-22
- Executed ... Ex. 37:1-5

C. *Contained:*
- The Ten Commandments ... Deut. 10:4
- Aaron's rod ... Num. 17:10; Heb. 9:4
- Pot of manna ... Ex. 16:33, 34

D. *Conveyed:*
- By Levites ... Num. 3:30, 31
- Before Israel ... Josh. 3:3-17
- Into battle ... 1 Sam. 4:4, 5
- On a cart ... 1 Sam. 6:7-15

E. *Purposes of:*
- Symbol of God's Law ... Ex. 25:16, 21
- Memorial of God's provision ... Ex. 16:33, 34
- Place to know God's will ... Ex. 25:22; Ex. 30:6, 36
- Place of entreaty ... Josh. 7:6-15
- Symbol of God's holiness ... 1 Sam. 6:19; 2 Sam. 6:6, 7
- Place of atonement ... Lev. 16:2, 14-17
- Type of Christ ... Rom. 3:25-31
- Symbol of heaven ... Rev. 11:19

F. *History of:*
- Carried across Jordan ... Josh. 3:16, 14-17
- Caused Jordan's stoppage ... Josh. 4:5-11, 18
- Carried around Jericho ... Josh. 6:6-20
- At Mt. Ebal ceremony ... Josh. 8:30-33
- Set up at Shiloh ... Josh. 18:1
- Moved to house of God ... Judg. 20:26, 27
- Returned to Shiloh ... 1 Sam. 1:3
- Carried into battle ... 1 Sam. 4:3-22
- Captured ... 1 Sam. 4:10-21
- Caused Dagon's fall ... 1 Sam. 5:1-4
- Brought a plague ... 1 Sam. 5:6-12
- Returned to Israel ... 1 Sam. 6:1-21
- Set in Abinadab's house ... 1 Sam. 7:1, 2
- In Obed-edom's house ... 2 Sam. 6:10-12
- Established in Jerusalem ... 2 Sam. 6:12-17
- During Absalom's rebellion ... 2 Sam. 15:24-29
- Placed in Temple ... 1 Kin. 8:1-11
- Restored by Josiah ... 2 Chr. 35:3
- Carried to Babylon ... 2 Chr. 36:6, 18
- Prophetic fulfillment ... Jer. 3:16, 17; Acts 15:13-18

Arkite—*belonging to Arka*
- Canaan's descendants ... Gen. 10:17; 1 Chr. 1:15

Arm of God

A. *Described as:*
- Stretched out ... Deut. 4:34
- Everlasting ... Deut. 33:27
- Strong, mighty ... Ps. 89:10, 13
- Holy ... Ps. 98:1
- Glorious ... Is. 63:12

B. *Descriptive of, God's:*
- Redeeming ... Ex. 6:6
- Saving ... Ps. 44:3
- Victorious ... Ps. 98:1
- Ruling ... Is. 40:10
- Strengthening ... Ps. 89:21
- Protecting ... Deut. 7:19
- Destroying ... Is. 30:30

Arm of the wicked—*expression for molestation*
- Shall be broken ... Ps. 10:15

SUBJECT REFERENCE

Armageddon—*Mount Megiddo; site of*
- Historic wars ... Judg. 5:19
- Notable deaths ... 1 Sam. 31:8
- Final battle ... Rev. 16:16

Armenia—*land southeast of Black Sea*
- Assassins flee to ... 2 Kin. 19:37
- See Ararat

Armholes
- Armpits, protected with rags ... Jer. 38:12
- Articles of alluring dress ... Ezek. 13:18

Armoni—*belonging to the palace*
- A son of Saul ... 2 Sam. 21:8-11

Armor—*a protective article of warfare*

A. *As a protective weapon:*
- Shield ... 1 Sam. 17:7, 41
- Helmet ... 1 Sam. 17:38
- Scale-armor ... 1 Sam. 17:5, 38; 1 Kin. 22:34
- Greaves ... 1 Sam. 17:6
- Girdle ... 1 Sam. 18:4
- Body armor ... 2 Chr. 26:14

B. *As an aggressive weapon:*
- Rod ... Ps. 2:9
- Sling ... 1 Sam. 17:40
- Bow and arrow ... 2 Sam. 1:18
- Spear ... Is. 2:4
- Sword ... 1 Sam. 17:51

Armor bearer—*man who bears the arms of another*
- Assists kings in battle ... Judg. 9:54
- David serves Saul as ... 1 Sam. 16:21
- Jonathan's, a man of courage ... 1 Sam. 14:7, 12
- Saul's, dies with him ... 1 Sam. 31:4-6
- Goliath's, precedes him ... 1 Sam. 17:7, 41

Armor, spiritual
- The Christian's, complete ... Eph. 6:11-17; 1 Thess. 5:8
- Of light ... Rom. 13:12
- Of righteousness ... 2 Cor. 6:7
- The Bible, the sword ... Eph. 6:17
- Not of flesh ... 2 Cor. 10:4, 5

Armory—*an arsenal*
- Armor stored in ... Neh. 3:19
- God's, opened for war ... Jer. 50:25
- David's, well stocked ... Song 4:4

Army—*men organized and disciplined for battle*

A. *Consisted of:*
- Men over 20 ... Num. 1:3
- Infantrymen ... 2 Chr. 25:5
- Archers ... 1 Chr. 5:18
- Sling stones ... 2 Chr. 26:14
- Chariots ... 1 Kin. 4:26
- Foreigners ... 2 Sam. 15:18
- Choice men ... 2 Sam. 10:7-9

B. *Commanded by:*
- God ... Josh. 5:14
- Judges ... Judg. 11:1, 6, 32
- Captain ... 2 Sam. 2:8
- Kings ... 2 Sam. 12:28, 29

C. *Commands regarding:*
- Use of chariots ... Deut. 17:16
- Deferred certain classes ... Num. 2:33; Deut. 20:1-9
- Division of spoil ... 1 Sam. 30:21-25
- Fearfulness ... Deut. 20:1

D. *Units of:*
- Fifties ... 2 Kin. 1:9
- Hundreds ... Num. 31:14, 48
- Legions ... Matt. 26:53
- Bands ... Acts 21:31
- Guards ... Acts 28:16
- Quaternions ... Acts 12:4
- Thousands ... Num. 31:14, 48

E. *Of Israel, conquered:*
- Egyptians ... Ex. 14:19-31
- Jericho ... Josh. 6:1-25
- Midianites ... Judg. 7:1-23
- Philistines ... 1 Sam. 14:14-23
- Syrians ... 2 Kin. 7:1-15
- Assyrians ... 2 Kin. 19:35, 36

Army, Christian

A. *Warfare against:*
- The world ... James 4:4; 1 John 2:15-17
- The flesh ... Gal. 5:17-21
- Satan ... 1 Pet. 5:8, 9
- Evil men ... 2 Tim. 3:8
- False teachers ... Jude 3, 4
- Spiritual wickedness ... Eph. 6:12
- Worldly "vain babblings" ... 1 Tim. 6:20

B. *Equipment for:*
- Sufficient for total war ... Eph. 6:12-17; 1 Thess. 5:8
- Spiritual in nature ... 2 Cor. 10:3, 4
- Sharper than any sword ... Heb. 4:12

C. *The soldier in, must:*
- Enlist ... Matt. 28:18-20
- Obey ... 2 Cor. 10:5, 6
- Please captain ... 2 Tim. 2:4
- Use self-control ... 1 Cor. 9:25-27
- Stand firm ... Eph. 6:13-17
- Endure hardship ... 2 Tim. 2:3
- Show courage ... 2 Tim. 4:7-18
- Fight hard ... 1 Tim. 6:12
- Be pure ... 1 Pet. 2:11, 12
- Be alert ... 1 Pet. 5:8
- Be faithful ... 1 Tim. 1:18-20

D. *Jesus Christ, the Captain of, is:*
- Perfect ... Heb. 2:10
- Undefiled ... Heb. 7:26
- Powerful ... 2 Thess. 2:8

Arnan—*strong*
- A descendant of David ... 1 Chr 3:21

Arnon—*a river*
- Boundary between Moab and Ammon ... Num. 21:13, 26
- Border of Reuben ... Deut. 3:12, 16
- Ammonites reminded of ... Judg. 11:18-26

Arod—*hunchbacked*
- A son of Gad ... Num. 26:17
- Called Arodi ... Gen. 46:16

Aroer—*naked*

1. A town in east Jordan ... Deut. 2:36
   - An Amorite boundary city ... Josh. 13:9, 10, 16
   - Sihon ruled ... Josh. 12:2
   - Assigned to Reuben ... Deut. 3:12
   - Rebuilt by Gadites ... Num. 32:34
   - Beginning of David's census ... 2 Sam. 24:5
   - Taken by Hazael ... 2 Kin. 10:32
   - Possessed by Moab ... Jer. 48:19
2. A city of Judah ... 1 Sam. 30:28
3. A city of Gad ... Josh. 13:25

Aroma—*a pleasant smell*
- Of sacrifices ... Lev. 26:31
- Figurative of gifts ... Phil. 4:18

Arpad—*a couch, resting place*
- A town in Samaria ... 2 Kin. 18:34
- End of, predicted ... Jer. 49:23

Arphaxad
- A son of Shem ... Gen. 10:22, 24
- Born two years after the flood ... Gen. 11:10-13
- An ancestor of Christ ... Luke 3:36

Arrogance—*overbearing pride*
- Mentioned with other evils ... Prov. 8:13
- To be punished by God ... Is. 13:11
- Seen in haughtiness ... Jer. 48:29

Arrows—*sharp instruments hurled by a bow*

A. *Uses of:*
- Hunting ... Gen. 27:3
- Send message ... 1 Sam. 20:20-22
- Divination ... Ezek. 21:21
- Prophecy ... 2 Kin. 13:14-19
- War ... 2 Kin. 19:32

B. *Described as:*
- Deadly ... Prov. 26:18
- Sharp ... Ps. 120:4
- Bright ... Jer. 51:11
- Like lightning ... Zech. 9:14

C. *Figurative of:*
- God's judgments ... Deut. 32:23, 42
- Intense affliction ... Job 6:4
- Wicked intentions ... Ps. 11:2
- Messiah's mission ... Ps. 45:5
- Bitter words ... Ps. 64:3

SUBJECT — REFERENCE

God's power ... Ps. 76:3
Daily hazards ... Ps. 91:5
Children ... Ps. 127:4
A false witness ... Prov. 25:18
A deceitful tongue ... Jer. 9:8

Arson—*setting fire to property maliciously*

A. *Features concerning:*
A law forbidding ... Ex. 22:6
A means of revenge ... Judg. 12:1

B. *Instances of, by:*
Samson ... Judg. 15:4, 5
Danites ... Judg. 18:27
Absalom ... 2 Sam. 14:30
Enemies ... Ps. 74:7, 8

Art

Ointment after the ... Ex. 30:25
Spices prepared by ... 2 Chr. 16:14
Stones graven by ... Acts 17:29

Artaxerxes—*great king*

Artaxerxes I, king of Persia (465-425 B.C.), authorizes Ezra's mission to Jerusalem ... Ezra 7:1-28
Temporarily halts rebuilding program at Jerusalem ... Ezra 4:7-23
Commissions Nehemiah's mission ... Neh. 2:1-10
Permits Nehemiah to return ... Neh. 13:6

Artemas—*gift of Artemis*

Paul's companion at Nicopolis .. Titus 3:12

Artemis—*the mother-goddess of Asia Minor* (known as Cybele)

Worship of, at Ephesus, creates uproar ... Acts 19:23-41

Artificers—*skilled workmen*

Tubal-cain, the earliest ... Gen. 4:22
Employed in temple construction ... 1 Chr. 29:5
Removed in judgment ... Is. 3:1-3

Arts and crafts in the Bible

Apothecary ... Ex. 30:25, 35
Armorer ... 1 Sam. 8:12
Artificer ... Gen. 4:22
Baker ... Gen. 40:1
Barber ... Ezek. 5:1
Brickmaker ... Ex. 5:7
Calker ... Ezek. 27:9
Carpenter ... Mark 6:3
Carver ... Ex. 31:5
Confectioner ... 1 Sam. 8:13
Cook ... 1 Sam. 8:13
Coppersmith ... 2 Tim. 4:14
Draftsman ... Ezek. 4:1
Dyer ... Ex. 25:5
Embalmer ... Gen. 50:2, 3
Embroiderer ... Ex. 35:35
Engraver ... Ex. 28:11
Fisherman ... Matt. 4:18
Fuller ... Mark 9:3
Gardener ... John 20:15
Goldsmith ... Is. 40:19
Husbandman ... Gen. 4:2
Jeweler ... Ex. 28:17-21
Lapidary ... Ex. 35:33
Mariner ... Ezek. 27:8, 9
Mason ... 2 Sam. 5:11
Moulder ... Ex. 32:4
Musician ... 2 Sam. 6:5
Needleworker ... Ex. 26:36
Painting ... Jer. 22:14
Potter ... Jer. 18:3
Porter ... 2 Sam. 18:26
Refiner ... Mal. 3:2, 3
Ropemaker ... Judg. 16:11
Sewing ... Ezek. 13:18
Ship building ... 1 Kin. 9:26
Silversmith ... Acts 19:24
Smelter ... Job 28:1, 2
Smith ... 1 Sam. 13:19
Spinner ... Prov. 31:19
Stonecutter ... Ex. 31:5
Tailor ... Ex. 28:3, 4
Tanner ... Acts 10:6
Tentmaking ... Acts 18:3
Watchman ... 2 Sam. 18:26
Weaver ... Ex. 35:35
Winemaker ... Neh. 13:15
Worker in metal ... Ex. 31:3, 4
Writer ... Judg. 5:14

Aruboth—*the lattices*

A town in one of Solomon's districts ... 1 Kin. 4:10

Arumah—*height*

A village near Shechem; Abimelech's refuge ... Judg. 9:41

Arvad—*wandering*

A Phoenician city built on an island north of Tyre ... Ezek. 27:8, 11

Arvadites—*inhabitants of Arvad*

Of Canaanite ancestry ... Gen. 10:18; 1 Chr. 1:16

Arza—*earth*

King Elah's steward in Tirzah ... 1 Kin. 16:9

Asa—*physician*

1. Third king of Judah ... 1 Kin. 15:8-10
Reigns 10 years in peace ... 2 Chr. 14:1
Overthrows idolatry ... 2 Chr. 14:2-5
Removes his mother ... 1 Kin. 15:13
Fortifies Judah ... 2 Chr. 14:6-8
Defeats the Ethiopians ... 2 Chr. 14:9-15
Leads in national revival ... 2 Chr. 15:1-15
Hires Ben-hadad against Baasha ... 2 Chr. 16:1-6
Reproved by a prophet ... 2 Chr. 16:7-10
Diseased, seeks physicians rather than the Lord ... 2 Chr. 16:12
Buried in Jerusalem ... 2 Chr. 16:13, 14
An ancestor of Christ ... Matt. 1:7
2. A Levite among returnees ... 1 Chr. 9:16

Asahel—*God has made*

1. A son of Zeruiah, David's sister ... 1 Chr. 2:16
Noted for valor ... 2 Sam. 2:18; 2 Sam. 23:24
Pursues Abner ... 2 Sam. 2:19
Killed by Abner ... 2 Sam. 2:23
Avenged by Joab ... 2 Sam. 3:27, 30
Made a commander in David's army ... 1 Chr. 27:7
2. A Levite teacher ... 2 Chr. 17:8
3. A collector of tithes ... 2 Chr. 31:13
4. A priest who opposes Ezra's reforms ... Ezra 10:15

Asaiah—*Jehovah has made*

1. A Simeonite chief ... 1 Chr. 4:36
2. A Levite during David's reign ... 1 Chr. 6:30
Helps restore ark to Jerusalem ... 1 Chr. 15:6, 11
3. An officer sent to Huldah ... 2 Chr. 34:20-22; 2 Kin. 22:12-14
4. The first-born of the Shilonites ... 1 Chr. 9:5
Probably called Maaseiah ... Neh. 11:5

Asaph—*collector*

1. A Gershonite Levite choir leader in the time of David and Solomon ... 1 Chr. 15:16-19; 1 Chr. 16:4-7; 2 Chr. 5:12
Called a seer ... 2 Chr. 29:30
Sons of, made musicians ... 1 Chr. 25:1-9
Twelve Psalms assigned to ... Ps. 50—83; 2 Chr. 29:30
Descendants of, among returnees ... Ezra 2:41; Neh. 7:44
In dedication ceremony ... Ezra 3:10
2. The father of Hezekiah's recorder ... 2 Kin. 18:18, 37
3. A chief forester whom Artaxerxes commands to supply timber to Nehemiah ... Neh. 2:8
4. A Korhite Levite ... 1 Chr. 26:1
Also called Ebiasaph ... 1 Chr. 9:19

Asareel—*God has bound*

A son of Jehaleleel ... 1 Chr. 4:16

Asarelah—*Jehovah is joined*

A son of Asaph in David's time ... 1 Chr. 25:2
Called Jesharelah ... 1 Chr. 25:14

Ascension—*rising to a higher place*

A. *Descriptive of:*
Physical rising of smoke ... Ex. 19:18; Josh. 8:20, 21
Going uphill ... Luke 19:28
Rising to heaven ... Ps. 139:8
Christ's ascension ... John 6:62
Sinful ambition ... Is. 14:13, 14

B. *Of saints:*
Enoch, translation of ... Gen. 5:24; Heb. 11:5
Elijah, translation of ... 2 Kin. 2:11; Matt. 17:1-9
Christians, at Christ's return ... 1 Thess. 4:13-18; 1 Cor. 15:51, 52

C. *Of Christ:*
Foretold in the Old Testament ... Ps. 68:18; Eph. 4:8-10
Announced by Christ ... Luke 9:51; John 20:17
Forty days after His resurrection ... Luke 24:48-51; Acts 1:1-12
Necessary for the Spirit's coming ... John 16:7
Enters heaven by redemption ... Heb. 6:19, 20; Heb. 9:12, 24
Crowned with glory and honor ... Heb. 2:9
Rules from David's throne ... Acts 2:29-36
Sits at the Father's side ... Eph. 1:20; Heb. 1:3
Intercedes for the saints ... Rom. 8:34
Preparing place for His people ... John 14:2
Highly exalted ... Acts 5:31; Phil. 2:9
Reigns triumphantly ... 1 Cor. 15:24-28; Heb. 10:12, 13
Exercises priestly ministry ... Heb. 4:14-16; Heb. 8:1, 2

Asceticism—*stern restraint upon bodily appetites*

A. *Forms of, seen in:*
Nazarite vow ... Num. 6:1-21
Manoah's wife ... Judg. 13:3-14
Samson ... Judg. 16:16, 17
Elijah's life ... 1 Kin. 19:4-9
The Rechabites ... Jer. 35:1-19
John the Baptist ... Matt. 3:4; Matt. 11:18
Jesus Christ ... Matt. 4:2
Paul ... 1 Cor. 9:27

B. *Teaching concerning:*
Extreme, repudiated ... Luke 7:33-36
False, rejected ... Col. 2:20-23; 1 Tim. 4:3, 4
Some, necessary ... 1 Cor. 9:26, 27; 2 Tim. 2:3, 4
Temporary helpful ... Ezra 8:21-23; 1 Cor. 7:3-9
Figurative of complete consecration ... Matt. 19:12; Rev. 14:1-5

Asenath—*belonging to the goddess Neith*

Daughter of Potiphera and wife of Joseph ... Gen. 41:45
Mother of Manasseh and Ephraim ... Gen. 41:50-52; Gen. 46:20

Ash—*a tree*

Idols made from ... Is. 44:14

Ashamed—*shame instilled by evil doing*

A. *Caused by:*
Mistreatment ... 2 Sam. 10:4, 5
Sad tidings ... 2 Kin. 8:11-13
Transgression ... Ps. 25:3
Inconsistent action ... Ezra 8:22
Idolatry ... Is. 44:9-17
Rebellion against God ... Is. 45:24
Lewdness ... Ezek. 16:27
False prophecy ... Zech. 13:3, 4
Rejecting God's mercy ... Is. 65:13
Unbelief ... Mark 8:38
Unpreparedness ... 2 Cor. 9:4

B. *Avoidance of, by:*
Waiting for the Lord ... Ps. 34:5; Is. 49:23
Regarding God's commands ... Ps. 119:6
Sound in statutes ... Ps. 119:80
Trusting God ... Ps. 25:20
Believing in Christ ... Rom. 9:33; Rom. 10:11
Christian diligence ... 2 Tim. 2:15

SUBJECT — REFERENCE

- Assurance of faith ... 2 Tim. 1:12
- Abiding in Christ ... 1 John 2:28

C. *Possible objects of, in the Christian's life:*

- Life's plans ... Phil. 1:20
- God's message ... 2 Tim. 1:8
- The Gospel ... Rom. 1:16
- The old life ... Rom. 6:21
- One's faith ... 1 Pet. 4:16

Ashan—*smoke*

- A city of Judah ... Josh. 15:42
- Later allotted to Judah ... Josh. 19:7
- Assigned to the Levites ... 1 Chr. 6:59

Ashbea—*let me call as witness*

- A descendant of Shelah ... 1 Chr. 4:21

Ashbel—*having a long upper lip*

- A son of Benjamin ... Gen. 46:21; 1 Chr. 8:1
- Progenitor of the Ashbelites ... Num. 26:38

Ashdod—*stronghold, fortress*

- One of five Philistine cities ... Josh. 13:3
- Anakim refuge ... Josh. 11:22
- Assigned to Judah ... Josh. 15:46, 47
- Seat of Dagon worship ... 1 Sam. 5:1-8
- Captured by Tartan ... Is. 20:1
- Opposed Nehemiah ... Neh. 4:7
- Women of, marry Jews ... Neh. 13:23, 24
- Called a mingled people ... Jer. 25:20
- Called Azotus ... Acts 8:40

Ashdoth-pisgah—*springs of Pisgah*

- The slopes of Mt. Pisgah ... Deut. 3:17; Josh. 12:3
- Translated "springs" in ... Deut. 4:49

Asher, Aser—*happy*

1. Jacob's second son by Zilpah ... Gen. 30:12, 13
   - Goes to Egypt with Jacob ... Gen. 46:17
   - Father of five children ... Gen. 46:17
   - Blessed by Jacob ... Gen. 49:20
2. The tribe fathered by Asher, Jacob's son ... Deut. 33:24
   - Census of ... Num. 1:41; Num. 26:47
   - Tolerant of Canaanites ... Judg. 1:31, 32
   - Failure of, in national crisis ... Judg. 5:17
   - Among Gideon's army ... Judg. 6:35; Judg. 7:23
   - A godly remnant among ... 2 Chr. 30:11
   - Anna, descendant of ... Luke 2:36-38
3. A town in Manasseh ... Josh. 17:7

Asherah—*a goddess of the Phoenicians and Arameans*

1. Translated "groves," the female counterpart of Baal ... Judg. 3:7; 1 Kin. 18:19
   - Translated "Ashtaroth" (plural) in ... Judg. 2:13
   - Asa's mother worships ... 1 Kin. 15:13
   - Curtains for, made by women ... 2 Kin. 23:7
   - Vessels of, destroyed by Josiah ... 2 Kin. 23:4
2. Translated "groves," the images (idols) made to Asherah ... 2 Kin. 23:6
   - Erected by Manasseh in the temple ... 2 Kin. 21:7
   - Set up by Ahab in Samaria ... 1 Kin. 16:32, 33
3. Translated "groves," the trees or poles symbolizing the worship of Asherah ... Ex. 34:13; Deut. 12:3; Deut. 16:21

Ashes—*the powdery residue of burned material*

A. *Used for:*

- A miracle ... Ex. 9:8-10
- Purification ... Num. 19:1-10; Heb. 9:13
- A disguise ... 1 Kin. 20:38, 41

B. *Symbolic of:*

- Mourning ... 2 Sam. 13:19; Esth. 4:1, 3
- Dejection ... Job 2:8
- Repentance ... Job 42:6; Matt. 11:21
- Fasting ... Dan. 9:3

C. *Figurative of:*

- Frailty ... Gen. 18:27
- Destruction ... Ezek. 28:18
- Victory ... Mal. 4:3
- Worthlessness ... Job 13:12
- Transformation ... Is. 61:3
- Deceit ... Is. 44:20
- Afflictions ... Ps. 102:9
- Destruction ... Jer. 6:26

Ashima—*heaven*

- A god or idol worshiped by Assyrian colonists at Samaria ... 2 Kin. 17:30

Ashkelon—*holm-oak*

- One of five Philistine cities ... Josh. 13:3; Jer. 47:5, 7
- Captured by Judah ... Judg. 1:18
- Men of, killed by Samson ... Judg. 14:19
- Repossessed by Philistines ... 1 Sam. 6:17; 2 Sam. 1:20
- Doom of, pronounced by the prophets ... Jer. 47:5, 7; Amos 1:8; Zeph. 2:4, 7; Zech. 9:5

Ashkenaz

1. A descendant of Noah through Japheth ... Gen. 10:3; 1 Chr. 1:6
2. A nation (probably descendants of 1) associated with Ararat, Minni ... Jer. 51:27

Ashnah—*hard, firm*

1. A village of Judah near Zorah ... Josh. 15:33
2. Another village of Judah ... Josh. 15:43

Ashpenaz

- The chief of Nebuchadnezzar's eunuchs ... Dan. 1:3

Ashtaroth, Astaroth—(plural of "Ashtoreth")

- A city in Bashan; residence of King Og ... Deut. 1:4; Josh. 12:4
- Captured by Israel ... Josh. 9:10
- Assigned to Manasseh ... Josh. 13:31
- Made a Levitical city ("Be-eshterah") ... Josh. 21:27
- Uzzia, a native of ... 1 Chr. 11:44

Ashteroth-karnaim—*twin peaks near Ashtaroth*

- A fortified city in Gilead occupied by the Rephaims ... Gen. 14:5

Ashtoreth—the name given by Hebrews to the goddess Ashtart (*Astarte*)

A. *A mother goddess of love, fertility and war worshiped by:*

- Philistines ... 1 Sam. 31:10
- Sidonians ... 1 Kin. 11:5, 33
- Hebrews (see below)

B. *Israel's relation to:*

- Ensnared by ... Judg. 2:13; Judg. 10:6
- Repent of, in Samuel's time ... 1 Sam. 7:3, 4
- Worship of, by Solomon ... 1 Kin. 11:5, 33
- Destroyed by Josiah ... 2 Kin. 23:13

Ashur—*blackness*

- A descendant of Judah ... 1 Chr. 2:24; 1 Chr. 4:5-7

Ashurites

- A people belonging to Ish-bosheth's kingdom ... 2 Sam. 2:8, 9

Ashvath—*made*

- An Asherite ... 1 Chr. 7:33

Asia—*in New Testament times, the Roman province of proconsular Asia*

- People from, at Pentecost ... Acts 2:9, 10
- Paul forbidden to preach in ... Acts 16:6
- Paul's later ministry in ... Acts 19:1-26
- Paul plans to pass by ... Acts 20:16, 17
- Converts in, greeted by Paul ... Rom. 16:5
- Paul's great conflict in ... 2 Cor. 1:8
- Paul writes to saints of ... 1 Pet. 1:1
- Seven churches of ... Rev. 1:4, 11

Asiel—*God has made*

- A Simeonite ... 1 Chr. 4:35

Asking in prayer

A. *Based upon:*

- God's foreknowledge ... Matt. 6:8
- God's willingness ... Luke 11:11-13
- God's love ... John 16:23-27
- Abiding in Christ ... John 15:7

B. *Receiving of answer, based upon:*

- Having faith ... James 1:5, 6
- Keeping God's commands ... 1 John 3:22
- Regarding God's will ... 1 John 5:14, 15
- Believing trust ... Matt. 21:22
- Unselfishness ... James 4:2, 3
- In Christ's name ... John 14:13, 14; John 15:16

Asnah—*thornbush*

- The head of a family of Nethinims ... Ezra 2:50

Asnapper—(probably the Aramaean name for "*Ashurbanipal*", an Assyrian king)

- Called "the great and noble" ... Ezra 4:10

Asp—*a deadly snake*

- Figurative of man's evil nature ... Deut. 32:33; Rom. 3:13
- Figurative of man's changed nature ... Is. 11:8

Aspatha—*horse-given*

- A son of Haman ... Esth. 9:7

Aspiration—*exalted desire combined with holy zeal*

A. *Centered in:*

- God Himself ... Ps. 42:1, 2
- God's kingdom ... Matt. 6:33
- The high calling ... Phil. 3:10-14
- Heaven ... Col. 3:1, 2
- Acceptableness with Christ ... 2 Tim. 2:4

B. *Inspired by:*

- Christ's love ... 2 Cor. 5:14-16
- Work yet to be done ... Rom. 15:18-20; 2 Cor. 10:13-18
- Christ's grace ... 2 Cor. 12:9-15
- The reward ... 2 Tim. 4:7, 8
- The Lord's return ... Matt. 24:42-47; 1 John 3:1-3
- World's end ... 2 Pet. 3:11-14

Asriel, Ashriel—*God has filled with joy*

- A descendant of Manasseh and progenitor of the Asrielites ... Num. 26:31; Josh. 17:2; 1 Chr. 7:14

Ass—*donkey*

A. *Used for:*

- Riding ... Gen. 22:3
- Carrying burdens ... Gen. 42:26
- Food ... 2 Kin. 6:25
- Royalty ... Judg. 5:10

B. *Regulations concerning:*

- Not to be yoked with an ox ... Deut. 22:10
- To be rested on Sabbath ... Ex. 23:12; Luke 13:15
- To be redeemed with a lamb ... Ex. 34:20

C. *Special features regarding:*

- Spoke to Balaam ... Num. 22:28-31
- Knowing his owner ... Is. 1:3
- Jawbone kills many ... Judg. 15:15-17
- Jesus rides upon one ... Zech. 9:9; Matt. 21:2, 5
- All cared for by God ... Ps. 104:11

D. *Figurative of:*

- Wildness (in Hebrew, "wild ass") ... Gen. 16:12
- Stubbornness ... Hos. 8:9
- Promiscuity ... Jer. 2:24

Assassination—*killing by secret and sudden assault*

A. *Actual cases of:*

- Eglon by Ehud ... Judg. 3:21
- Sisera by Jael ... Judg. 4:17-21
- Abner by Joab ... 2 Sam. 3:27
- Ish-bosheth by sons of Rimmon ... 2 Sam. 4:5-8
- Amnon by Absalom ... 2 Sam. 13:28, 29
- Absalom by Joab ... 2 Sam. 18:14
- Amasa by Joab ... 2 Sam. 20:10
- Elah by Zimri ... 1 Kin. 16:10
- Ben-hadad by Hazael ... 2 Kin. 8:7, 15

SUBJECT REFERENCE

Jehoram by Jehu .... 2 Kin. 9:24
Ahaziah by Jehu .... 2 Kin. 9:27
Jezebel by Jehu .... 2 Kin. 9:30-37
Joash by servants .... 2 Kin. 12:20, 21
Zechariah by Shallum .... 2 Kin. 15:10
Shallum by Menahem .... 2 Kin. 15:14
Pekahiah by Pekah .... 2 Kin. 15:25
Pekah by Hoshea .... 2 Kin. 15:30
Amon by servants .... 2 Kin. 21:23
Gedaliah by Ishmael .... 2 Kin. 25:25
Sennacherib by his sons ..... 2 Kin. 19:37

B. *Attempted cases of:*

Jacob by Esau .... Gen. 27:41-45
Joseph by his brothers ...... Gen. 37:18-22
David by Saul .... 1 Sam. 19:10-18
David by Absalom .... 2 Sam. 15:10-14
Joash by Athaliah .... 2 Kin. 11:1-3
Ahasuerus by servants ...... Esth. 2:21-23
Jesus by the Jews .... Luke 4:28-30; John 7:1
Paul by the Jews .... Acts 9:23-25; Acts 23:12-31

C. *Crime of:*

Against God's image in man .... Gen. 9:6
Punishable by death .... Ex. 21:12-15; Num. 35:33
Not to be condoned .... Deut. 19:11-13
Puts the guilty under a curse .... Deut. 27:24
Abhorred by the righteous ... 2 Sam. 4:4-12

Assembly—*a large gathering for official business*

A. *Descriptive of:*

Israel as a people .... Num. 10:2-8
Israel as a nation .... Judg. 20:2; 2 Chr. 30:23
God's elect people .... Ps. 111:1
A civil court .... Acts 19:32-41
A church gathering .... James 2:2

B. *Purposes of:*

Proclaim war .... Judg. 10:17, 18; 1 Sam. 14:20
Establish the ark in Zion .... 1 Kin. 8:1-6
Institute reforms .... Ezra 9:4-15; Neh. 9:1, 2
Celebrate victory .... Esth. 9:17, 18
Condemn Christ .... Matt. 26:3, 4, 57
Worship God .... Acts 4:31; Heb. 10:25

C. *Significant ones, at:*

Sinai .... Ex. 19:1-19
Joshua's farewell .... Josh. 23:1-16; Josh. 24:1-28
David's coronation .... 2 Sam. 5:1-3
The Temple's dedication ..... 2 Chr. 5:1-14
Josiah's reformation .... 2 Kin. 23:1-3, 21, 22
Ezra's reading the Law ...... Neh. 8:1-18
Jesus' trial .... Matt. 27:11-26
Pentecost .... Acts 2:1-21
The Jerusalem Council ...... Acts 15:5-21

Assent—*agreeing to the truth of a statement or fact*

A. *Concerning good things:*

Accepting God's covenant ... Ex. 19:7, 8
Agreeing to reforms .... 1 Sam. 7:3, 4; Ezra 10:1-12, 19
Accepting a Scriptural decision .... Acts 15:13-22
Receiving Christ as Savior ... Rom. 10:9, 10

B. *Concerning evil things:*

Tolerating idolatry .... Jer. 44:15-19
Condemning Christ to death .... Matt. 27:17-25
Putting Stephen to death .... Acts 7:51-60
Refusing to hear the Gospel .... Acts 13:44-51

Asshur—*level plain*

1. One of the sons of Shem; progenitor of the Assyrians .... Gen. 10:22; 1 Chr. 1:17
2. The chief god of the Assyrians; seen in names like Ashurbanipal (Asnapper) ... Ezra 4:10
3. A city in Assyria or the nation of Assyria ..... Num. 24:22, 24; Ps. 83:8; Ezek. 27:23; Ezek. 32:22

SUBJECT REFERENCE

Asshurim—*mighty ones*

Descendants of Abraham by Keturah .... Gen. 25:3

Assir—*prisoner*

1. A son of Korah .... Ex. 6:24; 1 Chr. 6:22
2. A son of Ebiasaph .... 1 Chr. 6:23, 37
3. A son of King Jeconiah ..... 1 Chr. 3:17

Assistance, divine

A. *Offered, in:*

Battle .... 2 Chr. 20:5-15
Trouble .... Ps. 50:15
Crises .... Luke 21:14, 15
Prayer .... Rom. 8:16-27
Testimony .... 2 Tim. 4:17
Guidance .... James 1:5-8

B. *Given:*

Internally .... Phil. 2:13; Heb. 13:21
By God .... 2 Cor. 8:9
By Christ .... Phil. 4:13
By the Spirit .... Zech. 4:6
By God's Word .... 1 Thess. 2:13
By grace .... 1 Cor. 15:10
By prayer .... James 5:15-18
By trusting God .... Ps. 37:3-7
By God's providence .... Rom. 8:28

Association—*joining together for mutually beneficial purposes*

A. *Among believers, hindered by:*

Sin .... Acts 5:1-11
Friction .... Acts 6:1-6
Inconsistency .... Gal. 2:11-14
Disagreement .... Acts 15:36-40
Selfishness .... 3 John 9-11
Ambition .... Matt. 20:20-24
Error .... 2 John 7-11
Partiality .... James 2:1-5

B. *Among believers, helped by:*

Common faith .... Acts 2:42-47
Mutual helpfulness .... Gal. 6:1-5
United prayer .... Matt. 18:19, 20
Impending dangers .... Neh. 4:1-23
Grateful praise .... Acts 4:23-33

See Alliance with evil; Fellowship

Assos—*a seaport of Mysia in Asia Minor*

Paul walks to, from Troas ..... Acts 20:13, 14

Assurance—*the security of knowing that one's name is written in heaven*

A. *Objects of, one's:*

Election .... 1 Thess. 1:4
Adoption .... Eph. 1:4, 5
Union with Christ .... 1 Cor. 6:15
Possession of eternal life ..... John 5:24; 1 John 5:13
Peace .... Rom. 5:1

B. *Steps in:*

Believing God's Word .... 1 Thess. 2:13
Accepting Christ as Savior ... Rom. 10:9, 10
Standing upon the promises .... John 10:28-30
Desiring spiritual things ..... 1 Pet. 2:2
Growing in grace .... 2 Pet. 1:5-11
Knowing life is changed ..... 2 Cor. 5:17; 1 John 3:14-22
Having inner peace and joy .... Rom. 15:12, 13; Phil. 4:7
Victorious living .... 1 John 5:4, 5
The Spirit's testimony .... Rom. 8:15, 16
Absolute assurance .... Rom. 8:33-39; 2 Tim. 1:12

C. *Compatible with:*

A nature still subject to sin .. 1 John 1:8-10; 1 John 2:1
Imperfection of life .... Gal. 6:1
Limited knowledge .... 1 Cor. 13:9-12
Fatherly chastisement .... Heb. 12:5-11

Assyria—*the nation ruled from Asshur* (first) *and Nineveh* (later)

A. *Significant facts regarding:*

Of remote antiquity .... Gen. 2:14
Of Shem's ancestry .... Gen. 10:22
Founded by Nimrod .... Gen. 10:8-12; Mic. 5:6
Nineveh, chief city of .... Gen. 10:11

SUBJECT REFERENCE

Tigris river flows through .... Gen. 2:14
Proud nation .... Is. 10:5-15
A cruel military power ...... Nah. 3:1-19
Agent of God's purposes .... Is. 7:17-20; Is. 10:5, 6

B. *Contacts of, with Israel:*

Pul (Tiglath-pileser III, 745–727 B.C.) captures Damascus .... Is. 8:4
Puts Menahem under tribute .... 2 Kin. 15:19, 20
Occasions Isaiah's prophesy .... Is. 7–8
Puts Pekah under tribute .... 2 Kin. 15:29
Shalmaneser (727-722 B.C.) besieges Samaria .... 2 Kin. 17:3-5
Sargon II (722-705 B.C.) captures Israel .... 2 Kin. 17:6-41

C. *Contacts of, with Judah:*

Sargon's general takes Ashdod (in Philistia) .... Is. 20:1-6
Sennacherib (704-681 B.C.) invades Judah .... 2 Kin. 18:13
Puts Hezekiah under tribute .... 2 Kin. 18:14-16
Threatens Hezekiah through Rabshakeh .... 2 Kin. 18:17-37
Army of, miraculously slain .... 2 Kin. 19:35
Assassination of, by his sons .... 2 Kin. 19:37

D. *Prophecies concerning:*

Destruction of, anciently foretold .... Num. 24:22-24
Israel captive in land of ..... Hos. 10:6; Hos. 11:5
Doom of, mentioned .... Is. 10:12, 19; Is. 14:24, 25
End eulogized .... Nah. 3:1-19
Shares, figuratively, in Gospel blessings .... Is. 19:23-25

Astonishment—*an emotion of perplexed amazement*

A. *Caused by:*

God's judgments .... 1 Kin. 9:8, 9; Jer. 18:16
Racial intermarriage .... Ezra 9:2-4
Utter desolation .... Jer. 50:13
Urgent message .... Ezek. 3:15
A miracle .... Dan. 3:24
King's dream .... Dan. 4:19
An unexplained vision ...... Dan. 8:27
Christ's knowledge .... Luke 2:47
Christ's teaching .... Luke 4:32
Christ's miracles .... Mark 5:42; Luke 5:9
Gentile conversions .... Acts 10:45
Miracles .... Acts 12:16; Acts 13:6-12

B. *Applied figuratively to:*

God .... Jer. 14:9
Babylon .... Jer. 51:37, 41
Jerusalem .... Ezek. 4:16, 17; Ezek. 5:5, 15
Priests .... Jer. 4:9

Astrologers—*those who search the heavens for supposed revelations*

Cannot save Babylon .... Is. 47:1, 12-15
Cannot interpret dreams .... Dan. 2:2, 10-13; Dan. 4:7
Cannot decipher handwriting ... Dan. 5:7, 8
Daniel surpasses .... Dan. 1:20
Daniel made master of .... Dan. 5:11
God does not speak through ... Dan. 2:27, 28

Asuppim—*collectors*

Should be rendered as "storehouse" in .... 1 Chr. 26:15, 17
Same word translated "thresholds" in .... Neh. 12:25

Asylum—*protection, refuge*

Afforded by altar .... 1 Kin. 1:50-53; 1 Kin. 2:28
Cities of refuge .... Ex. 21:12-14; Deut. 19:1-13

Asyncritus—*incomparable*

A Christian at Rome .... Rom. 16:14

Atad—*thorn*

A mourning site east of Jordan .... Gen. 50:9-13

SUBJECT — REFERENCE

Atarah—*crown*
- A wife of Jerahmeel .... 1 Chr. 2:26

Ataroth—*crowns*
1. Town of Gad .... Num. 32:3, 34
2. A town of Ephraim .... Josh. 16:7
3. A town between Ephraim and Benjamin .... Josh. 16:2
   Probably the same as Atarothaddar .... Josh. 16:5; Josh. 18:13
4. A village near Bethlehem .... 1 Chr. 2:54

Ataroth-addar—*crowns of Addar*
- A frontier town of Ephraim .... Josh. 16:5
- See Ataroth 3

Ater—*crippled one*
1. The ancestors of a family of returnees .... Ezra 2:16; Neh. 7:21
2. The ancestor of a family of porters .... Ezra 2:42; Neh. 7:45
3. A signer of Nehemiah's document .... Neh. 10:17

Athach—*lodging, inn*
- A town in south Judah .... 1 Sam. 30:30

Athaiah—*Jehovah is helper*
- A Judahite in Nehemiah's time .... Neh. 11:4

Athaliah—*Jehovah is exalted*
1. The daughter of Ahab and Jezebel .... 2 Kin. 8:18, 26; 2 Chr. 22:2, 3
   Destroys all the royal seed except Joash .... 2 Kin. 11:1, 2; 2 Chr. 22:10, 11
   Usurps throne for six years .... 2 Kin. 11:3
   Killed by priestly uprising .... 2 Kin. 11:4-16; 2 Chr. 23:1-21
   Called wicked .... 2 Chr. 24:7
2. A Benjamite .... 1 Chr. 8:26, 27
3. The father of Jeshaiah .... Ezra 8:7

Atharim—*spys*
- Israel attacked there .... Num. 21:1

Atheism—*the denial of God's existence*

A. *Defined as:*
- The fool's philosophy .... Ps. 14:1; Ps. 53:1
- Living without God .... Rom. 1:20-32; Eph. 2:12

B. *Manifestations of, seen in:*
- Defiance of God .... Ex. 5:2; 2 Kin. 18:19-35
- Irreligion .... Titus 1:16
- Corrupt morals .... Rom. 13:12, 13; 1 Pet. 4:3

C. *Evidences against, seen in:*
- Man's inner conscience .... Rom. 2:14, 15
- Design in nature .... Job 38:1-41; Job 39:1-30
- God's works .... Ps. 19:1-6
- God's providence .... Ps. 104:1-35; Acts 14:17
- Clear evidence .... Rom. 1:19, 20
- The testimony of pagans .... Dan. 4:24-37
- Fulfillment of prophecy .... Is. 41:20-23; Is. 46:8-11

Athens—*a Greek city named after the goddess Athena*
- Paul preaches in .... Acts 17:15-34
- Paul resides in .... 1 Thess. 3:1

Athlai—*Jehovah is strong*
- A Jew who divorced his foreign wife .... Ezra 10:28

Athletes
- Discipline .... 1 Cor. 9:24-27
- Removal of weights .... Heb. 12:1
- Prize .... Phil. 3:14

Atonement—*reconciliation of the guilty by divine sacrifice*

A. *Elements involved in, seen in:*
- Man's sin .... Ex. 32:30; Ps. 51:3, 4
- The blood sacrificed .... Lev. 16:11, 14-20; Heb. 9:13-22

SUBJECT — REFERENCE

- Guilt transferred .... Lev. 1:3, 4; 2 Cor. 5:21
- Guilt removed .... Lev. 16:21; 1 Cor. 6:11
- Forgiveness granted .... Lev. 5:10, 11; Rom. 4:6, 7
- Righteousness given .... Rom. 10:3, 4; Phil. 3:9

B. *Fulfilled by Christ:*
- Predicted .... Is. 53:10-12; Dan. 9:24-26
- Symbolized .... Is. 63:1-9; Zech. 3:1-9
- Realized .... Rom. 3:23-26; 1 Pet. 1:18-21

Atonement, Day of

A. *Features regarding:*
- Time specified .... Lev. 23:26, 27
- The ritual involved in .... Lev. 16:3, 5-15
- A time of humiliation .... Lev. 16:29, 31
- Exclusive ministry of the high priest in .... Lev. 16:2, 3; Heb. 9:7

B. *Benefits of, for:*
- The holy place .... Lev. 16:15, 16
- The people .... Lev. 16:17, 24
- The high priest .... Lev. 16:11; Heb. 9:7

C. *Result of, seen in:*
- Atonement for sin .... Rom. 3:25
- Removal of sin .... Heb. 9:8-28; Heb. 13:10-13

Atonement of Christ

A. *Typified by:*
- The paschal lamb .... Ex. 12:5, 11, 14; John 1:29; 1 Cor. 5:7
- The Day of Atonement .... Lev. 16:30, 34; Heb. 9:8-28

B. *What man is:*
- A sinner .... Rom. 5:8
- Alienated in mind .... Col. 1:21
- Strangers .... Eph. 2:12

C. *What God does:*
- Loves us .... John 3:16
- Commends His love to us .... Rom. 5:8
- Sends Christ to save us .... Gal. 4:4
- Spared not His own Son .... Rom. 8:32

D. *What Christ does:*
- Takes our nature .... Heb. 2:14
- Becomes our ransom .... Matt. 20:28
- Dies in our place .... 1 Pet. 3:18
- Dies for our sins .... 1 Pet. 2:24
- Dies as a sacrifice .... Eph. 5:2
- Dies willingly .... John 10:18
- Reconciles us to God .... Rom. 5:10
- Brings us to God .... 1 Pet. 3:18
- Restores our fellowship .... 1 Thess. 5:10

See Blood of Christ

E. *What the believer receives:*
- Forgiveness .... Eph. 1:7
- Peace .... Rom. 5:1
- Reconciliation .... 2 Cor. 5:19
- Righteousness .... 2 Cor. 5:21
- Justification .... Rom. 3:24-26
- Access to God .... Eph. 2:18
- Cleansing .... 1 John 1:7
- Liberty .... Gal. 5:1
- Freedom from the devil's power .... Heb. 2:14
- Christ's intercession .... Heb. 2:17, 18

Atroth-shophan
- A city built by the Gadites .... Num. 32:35

Attai—*timely*
1. A half-Egyptian Judahite .... 1 Chr. 2:35, 36
2. A Gadite in David's army .... 1 Chr. 12:11
3. Rehoboam's son .... 2 Chr. 11:20

Attalia—*a seaport town of Pamphylia named after Attalus II*
- Paul sails from, to Antioch .... Acts 14:25, 26

Attend
- To care for .... Esth. 4:5

SUBJECT — REFERENCE

Attendance, church
- Taught by example .... Acts 11:25-26; Acts 14:27
- Not to be neglected .... Heb. 10:25

Attitude—*the state of mind toward something*

A. *Of Christians toward Christ, must:*
- Confess .... Rom. 10:9, 10
- Obey .... John 14:15, 23
- Follow .... Matt. 16:24
- Imitate .... 1 Pet. 2:21

B. *Of Christians toward the world, not to:*
- Conform to .... Rom. 12:2
- Abuse .... 1 Cor. 7:31
- Love .... 1 John 2:15
- Be friend of .... James 4:4
- Be entangled with .... 2 Tim. 2:4
- Be polluted with .... Jude 23

C. *Of Christians toward sinners:*
- Seek their salvation .... 1 Cor. 9:22
- Pray for .... Rom. 9:1-3
- Plead with .... Acts 17:22-31
- Rebuke .... Titus 1:10-13
- Persuade .... 2 Cor. 5:11

Audience—*an assembly of hearers*
- Disturbed .... Neh. 13:1-3
- Attentive .... Luke 7:1
- Hostile .... Luke 4:28-30
- Receptive .... Acts 2:1-40
- Menacing .... Acts 7:54-60
- Rejecting .... Acts 13:44-51
- Critical .... Acts 17:22-34
- Sympathetic .... Acts 20:17-38
- Vast .... Rev. 5:9; Rev. 7:9, 10

See Assembly

Auditorium—*a room for assembly*
- Hearing .... Acts 25:23

Augustus' band—*a battalion of Roman soldiers*
- Paul placed in custody of .... Acts 27:1

Author—*creator; originator; writer*
- God of peace .... 1 Cor. 14:33
- Christ of salvation .... Heb. 5:9
- Christ of faith .... Heb. 12:2
- Solomon of many writings .... 1 Kin. 4:32

Authority—*the lawful right to enforce obedience*

A. *As rulers:*
- Governor .... Acts 23:24, 26; Matt. 10:18

B. *Delegated to, man as:*
- Created .... Gen. 1:26-31
- A legal state .... Esth. 9:29; Luke 22:25
- Agent of the state .... Matt. 8:9; Rom. 13:1-6
- Husband .... 1 Cor. 14:35
- Agent of religious leaders .... Acts 26:10, 12

C. *Christ's, seen in His power:*
- Over demons .... Mark 1:27
- In teaching .... Matt. 7:29
- To forgive .... Luke 5:24
- To judge .... John 5:22, 27
- To rule .... Matt. 2:6; 1 Cor. 15:24; 1 Pet. 3:22
- To commission .... Matt. 28:18-20

D. *Purpose:*
- Protection .... Heb. 13:17
- Instruction .... 1 Pet. 5:2, 3
- Example of Christ's power .... Matt. 8:5-13
- Testimony to unbelievers .... 1 Tim. 6:1; 1 Pet. 3:13-15

E. *Of Christians, given to:*
- Apostles .... 2 Cor. 10:8
- Ministers .... Titus 2:15
- The righteous .... Prov. 29:2

Ava—*a region or city in Assyria*
- Colonists from, brought to Samaria by Sargon .... 2 Kin. 17:24
- Worshipers of Nibhaz and Tartak .... 2 Kin. 17:31

Avarice—*covetousness; greed*

A. *Productive of:*
- Defeat .... Josh. 7:11, 21

SUBJECT REFERENCE

Death ... 1 Kin. 21:5-16
Discontent ... James 4:1-4

B. *Examples of:*

Balaam ... 2 Pet. 2:15
Achan ... Josh. 7:20, 21
Ahab ... 1 Kin. 21:1-4
Judas Iscariot ... Matt. 26:15, 16
Ananias and Sapphira ... Acts 5:1-10
Rich men ... Luke 12:16-21; James 5:1-6

Aven—*wickedness*

1. The city of On in Egypt near Cairo; known as Heliopolis ... Gen. 41:45; Ezek. 30:17
2. A name contemptuously applied to Bethel ... Hos. 10:5, 8
3. Valley in Syria ... Amos 1:5

Avenge—*to retaliate for an evil done*

A. *Kinds of:*

Commanded by God ... Num. 31:1, 2
Given strength for ... Judg. 16:28-30
Sought maliciously ... 1 Sam. 18:25
Possible but not done ... 1 Sam. 24:12
Attempted but hindered ... 1 Sam. 25:26-33
Obtained in self-defense ... Esth. 8:12, 13

B. *Sought because of:*

A murdered neighbor ... Num. 35:12; Josh. 20:5
A wife's mistreatment ... Judg. 15:6-8
Judah's sins ... Jer. 5:9
Mistreatment ... Acts 7:24, 25
Impurity ... 1 Thess. 4:5-7

C. *Performed by:*

God Himself ... Lev. 26:25; Luke 18:7, 8
Wicked men ... 2 Sam. 4:8-12
Impetuous general ... 2 Sam. 18:18, 19, 31
An anointed king ... 2 Kin. 9:6, 7
A judge ... Luke 18:3, 5
Jesus Christ ... Rev. 19:2

D. *Restrictions on:*

Personal, prohibited ... Lev. 19:17, 18
Christians prohibited ... Rev. 12:9

Avenger of blood—(literally, "*redeemer of blood*")

An ancient practice ... Gen. 4:14
Seen in kinsman as "redeemer" of enslaved relative ... Lev. 25:25, 47-49; Ruth 4:1-10
Seen also in kinsman as "avenger" of a murdered relative ... Num. 35:11-34
Avenger alone must kill murderer ... Deut. 19:6, 11-13
Practice, of, set aside by David ... 2 Sam. 14:4-11
Same word translated "kinsman" and "redeemer" ... Ruth 4:1; Job 19:25
Figurative of a violent person ... Ps. 8:2

Avim, Avims, Avites—*villagers*

1. A tribe of early Canaanites living near Gaza; absorbed by the Caphtorim (Philistines) ... Deut. 2:23
2. A city of Benjamin near Beth-el ... Josh. 18:23
3. Colonists brought from Ava in Assyria ... 2 Kin. 17:24, 31

Avith—*ruin*

An Edomite city ... Gen. 36:35

Awakening, spiritual

A. *Produced by:*

Returning to Beth-el ... Gen. 35:1-7
Discovering God's Word ... 2 Kin. 22:8-11
Reading God's Word ... Neh. 8:2-18
Confessing sin ... Ezra 10:1-17
Receiving the Spirit ... John 7:38, 39; Acts 2:1-47

B. *Old Testament examples of, under:*

Joshua ... Josh. 24:1-31
Samuel ... 1 Sam. 7:3-6
Elijah ... 1 Kin. 18:21-40
Hezekiah ... 2 Chr. 30:1-27
Josiah ... 2 Kin. 23:1-3
Ezra ... Ezra 10:1-17

C. *New Testament examples of:*

John the Baptist ... Luke 3:2-14
Jesus in Samaria ... John 4:28-42
Philip in Samaria ... Acts 8:5-12
Peter at Lydda ... Acts 9:32-35
Peter with Cornelius ... Acts 10:34-48
Paul at Antioch in Pisidia ... Acts 13:14-52
Paul at Thessalonica ... Acts 17:11, 12; 1 Thess. 1:1-10
Paul at Corinth ... 2 Cor. 7:1-16

Awe—*fear mingled with reverence*

A restraint on sin ... Ps. 4:4
Proper attitude toward God ... Ps. 33:8
Also toward God's Word ... Ps. 119:161

Awl—*a sharp tool for piercing*

Used on the ear as a symbol of perpetual obedience ... Ex. 21:6; Deut. 15:17

Axe—*a sharp instrument for cutting wood*

A. *Used in:*

Cutting timber ... Judg. 9:48
War ... 1 Chr. 20:3
Malicious destruction ... Ps. 74:5-7
A miracle; floated in water ... 2 Kin. 6:5, 6

B. *As a figure of:*

Judgment ... Matt. 3:10
Wrath ... Jer. 51:20-24
God's sovereignty ... Is. 10:15

Axletree—*a shaft on which a wheel is mounted*

Used in the temple ... 1 Kin. 7:32, 33

Azal, Azel

1. A descendant of Jonathan ... 1 Chr. 8:37, 38
2. A place near Jerusalem ... Zech. 14:5

Azaliah—*Jehovah has set aside*

Father of Shaphan ... 2 Kin. 22:3

Azaniah—*Jehovah has heard*

A Levite who signs the document ... Neh. 10:9

Azarael, Azareel—*God has helped*

1. A Levite in David's army at Ziklag ... 1 Chr. 12:6
2. A musician in David's time ... 1 Chr. 25:18
3. A prince of Dan under David ... 1 Chr. 27:22
4. A Jew who divorced his foreign wife ... Ezra 10:41
5. A postexilic priest ... Neh. 11:13
6. A musician in dedication service ... Neh. 12:36

Azariah—*Jehovah has helped*

1. Man of Judah ... 1 Chr. 2:8
2. A Kohathite Levite ... 1 Chr. 6:36
3. A son of Zadok the high priest ... 1 Kin. 4:2
4. A son of Ahimaaz ... 1 Chr. 6:9
5. A great-grandson of Ahimaaz ... 1 Chr. 6:9-10
6. Son of Nathan ... 1 Kin. 4:5
7. A son of Jehu, with Egyptian ancestry ... 1 Chr. 2:34-38
8. A prophet who encourages King Asa ... 2 Chr. 15:1-8
9. Son of King Jehoshaphat ... 2 Chr. 21:2
10. A captain under Jehoiada ... 2 Chr. 23:1
11. Another under Jehoiada ... 2 Chr. 23:1
12. A head of Ephraim ... 2 Chr. 28:12
13. King of Judah ... 2 Kin. 15:1
14. A high priest who rebukes King Uzziah ... 2 Chr. 26:16-20
15. Kohathite, father of Joel ... 2 Chr. 29:12
16. A reforming Levite ... 2 Chr. 29:12
17. Chief priest in time of Hezekiah ... 2 Chr. 31:9, 10
18. A high priest, son of Hilkiah ... 1 Chr. 6:13, 14
19. Ancestor of Ezra ... Ezra 7:1-3
20. An opponent of Jeremiah ... Jer. 43:2
21. The Hebrew name of Abed-nego ... Dan. 1:7
22. Postexilic Jew ... Neh. 7:6, 7
23. A workman under Nehemiah ... Neh. 3:23, 24
24. A prince of Judah ... Neh. 12:32, 33
25. An expounder of the law ... Neh. 8:7
26. A signer of the covenant ... Neh. 10:1, 2
27. A descendant of Hilkiah ... 1 Chr. 9:11

Azaz—*strong*

A Reubenite ... 1 Chr. 5:8

Azaziah—*Jehovah is strong*

1. A musician ... 1 Chr. 15:21
2. Father of Hoshea ... 1 Chr. 27:20
3. A temple overseer ... 2 Chr. 31:13

Azbuk—*pardon*

Father of a certain Nehemiah; but not the celebrated one ... Neh. 3:16

Azekah—*tilled*

Great stones cast upon ... Josh. 10:11
Camp of Goliath ... 1 Sam. 17:1, 4, 17
Fortified by Rehoboam ... 2 Chr. 11:9
Reoccupied after exile ... Neh. 11:30
Besieged by Nebuchadnezzar ... Jer. 34:7

Azem, Ezem—*bone*

A town of Judah ... Josh. 15:29
Allotted to Simeon ... Josh. 19:3
Also called Ezem ... 1 Chr. 4:29

Azgad—*fate is hard*

Head of exile family ... Ezra 2:12; Ezra 8:12
Among document signers ... Neh. 10:15

Aziel—*God strengthens*

A Levite musician ... 1 Chr. 15:20
Called Jaaziel ... 1 Chr. 15:18

Aziza—*strong*

Divorced foreign wife ... Ezra 10:27

Azmaveth—*death is strong*

1. One of David's mighty men ... 2 Sam. 23:31
2. A Benjamite ... 2 Chr. 12:3
3. David's treasurer ... 1 Chr. 27:25
4. A son of Jehoaddah ... 1 Chr. 8:36
5. A village near Jerusalem ... Neh. 12:29
Also called Beth-azmaveth ... Neh. 7:28

Azmon—*strong*

A place in south Canaan ... Num. 34:4, 5

Aznoth-tabor—*peaks of Tabor*

Place in Naphtali ... Josh. 19:34

Azor—*helper*

Ancestor of Christ ... Matt. 1:13, 14

Azotus—*fortress*

Philip went there ... Acts 8:40
Same as Ashdod ... 1 Sam. 6:17

Azriel—*God is a help*

1. A chief of Manasseh ... 1 Chr. 5:24
2. Father of Jerimoth ... 1 Chr. 27:19
3. Father of Seraiah ... Jer. 36:26

Azrikam—*my help has arisen*

1. Son of Neariah ... 1 Chr. 3:23
2. A son of Aziel ... 1 Chr. 8:38
3. A Merarite Levite ... 1 Chr. 9:14
4. Governor under King Ahaz ... 2 Chr. 28:7

Azubah—*forsaken*

1. Wife of Caleb ... 1 Chr. 2:18, 19
2. Mother of Jehoshaphat ... 1 Kin. 22:42

Azur, Azzur—*helpful*

1. Father of Hananiah ... Jer. 28:1
2. Father of Jaazaniah ... Ezek. 11:1
3. A covenant signer ... Neh. 10:17

Azzan—*strong*

Father of Paltiel ... Num. 34:26

SUBJECT REFERENCE

B

Baal—*lord, possessor, husband*

A. *The nature of:*

The male god of the Phoenicians and Canaanites; the counterpart of the female Ashtaroth .... Judg. 10:6; 1 Sam. 7:4
Connected with immorality .. Num. 25:3, 5; Hos. 9:10
Incense burned to .... Jer. 7:9
Kissing the image of .... 1 Kin. 19:18; Hos. 13:1, 2
Dervish rites by priests of ... 1 Kin. 18:26, 28
Children burned in fire of ... Jer. 19:5
Eating sacrifices .... Ps. 106:28

B. *History of:*

Among Moabites in Moses' time .... Num. 22:41
Altars built to, during time of judges .... Judg. 2:11-14; Judg. 6:28-32
Jezebel introduces into Israel .... 1 Kin. 16:31, 32
Elijah's overthrow of, on Mt. Carmel .... 1 Kin. 18:17-40
Athaliah introduces it into Judah .... 2 Kin. 11:17-20; 2 Chr. 22:2-4
Revived again in Israel and Judah .... Hos. 2:8; Amos 5:26
Ahaz makes images to .... 2 Chr. 28:2-4
Manasseh worships .... 2 Kin. 21:3
Altars everywhere .... Jer. 11:13
Overthrown by Josiah .... 2 Kin. 23:4, 5
Denounced by prophets ..... Jer. 19:4, 5; Ezek. 16:20, 21
Historic retrospect .... Rom. 11:4

Baal—*master, possessor*

1. A Benjamite, from Gibeon ... 1 Chr. 8:30
2. A descendant of Reuben .... 1 Chr. 5:5, 6
3. A village of Simeon .... 1 Chr. 4:33
Also called Baalath-beer ..... Josh. 19:8

Baalah—*mistress*

1. A town also known as Kirjath-jearim .... Josh. 15:9, 10
2. A hill in Judah .... Josh. 15:11
3. A town in South Judah ...... Josh. 15:29
Probably the same as Bilhah .... 1 Chr. 4:29
May be the same as Balah ... Josh. 19:3

Baalath—*mistress*

A village of Dan .... Josh. 19:44
Fortified by Solomon .... 1 Kin. 9:18

Baalath-beer—*mistress of the well*

A border town of Simeon ...... Josh. 19:8
Called Ramath of the south ..... Josh. 19:8
Also called Baal .... 1 Chr. 4:33

Baal-berith—*lord of covenant*

A god (Baal) of Shechem .... Judg. 8:33; Judg. 9:4
Also called El-berith .... Judg. 9:46

Baale—*judah*

A town of Judah .... 2 Sam. 6:2
Also called Baalah and Kirjath-jearim .... Josh. 15:9, 10

Baal-gad—*lord of good fortune*

A place in the valley of Lebanon .... Josh. 11:17

Baal-hamon—*lord of a multitude*

Site of Solomon's vineyard ...... Song 8:11

Baal-hanan—*lord of grace*

1. Edomite king .... Gen. 36:38
2. David's gardener .... 1 Chr. 27:28

Baal-hazor—*lord of a village*

A place near Ephraim .... 2 Sam. 13:23

Baal-hermon—*lord of Hermon*

A mountain east of Jordan ...... Judg. 3:3

Baali—*my master* (lord)

A title rejected by Jehovah ..... Hos. 2:16

Baalim—*lords* (plural of Baal)

Deities of Canaanite polytheism .... Judg. 10:10-14

Ensnared Israelites .... Judg. 2:11; Judg. 3:7
Rejected in Samuel's time ...... 1 Sam. 7:4
Historic reminder .... 1 Sam. 12:10

Baalis

An Ammonite king .... Jer. 40:14

Baal-meon—*lord of Meon* (habitation)

An Amorite city on the Moabite boundary .... Ezek. 25:9
Rebuilt by Reubenites .... Num. 32:38; Josh. 13:17

Baal-peor, Baal of Peor—*lord of Peor*

A Moabite god .... Num. 25:1-5
Infected Israel; 24,000 died ..... Num. 25:1-9
Vengeance taken on .... Num. 31:1-18
Sin long remembered .... Deut. 4:3, 4; Josh. 22:17; Ps. 106:28, 29
Historic reminder .... 1 Cor. 10:8

Baal-perazim—*lord of breaking through*

Where David defeated the Philistines .... 2 Sam. 5:18-20
Same as Perazim .... Is. 28:21

Baal-shalisha—*lord of Shalisha* (a third)

A place from which Elisha received food .... 2 Kin. 4:42-44

Baal-tamar—*lord of the palm*

A place in Benjamin .... Judg. 20:33

Baal-zebub—*lord of flies*

A Philistine god at Ekron ..... 2 Kin. 1:2
Ahaziah inquired of .... 2 Kin. 1:2, 6, 16
Also called Beelzebub .... Matt. 10:25; Matt. 12:24

Baal-zephon—*lord of darkness*

Israelite camp site .... Ex. 14:2, 9; Num. 33:7

Baana—*affliction*

1. Supply officer .... 1 Kin. 4:12
2. Zadok's father .... Neh. 3:4

Baanah—*affliction*

1. A murderer of Ish-bosheth ... 2 Sam. 4:1-12
2. Heled's father .... 1 Chr. 11:30
3. A returning exile .... Ezra 2:2; Neh. 7:7
Signs document .... Neh. 10:27
4. Supply officer .... 1 Kin. 4:16

Baara—*foolish*

Shaharaim's wife .... 1 Chr. 8:8

Baaseiah—*work of Jehovah*

A Levite ancestor of Asaph ..... 1 Chr. 6:40

Baasha—*boldness*

Gains throne by murder .... 1 Kin. 15:27, 28
Kills Jeroboam's household ..... 1 Kin. 15:29, 30
Wars against Asa .... 1 Kin. 15:16, 32
Restricts access to Judah .... 1 Kin. 15:17
Contravened by Asa's league with Ben-hadad .... 1 Kin. 15:18-22
Evil reign .... 1 Kin. 15:33, 34

Babbler—*an inane talker*

The mumblings of drunkards ... Prov. 23:29-35
Like a serpent .... Eccl. 10:11
Paul called such .... Acts 17:18
Paul's warnings against .... 1 Tim. 6:20; 2 Tim. 2:16

Babe—*an infant child*

A. *Natural:*

Moses .... Ex. 2:6
John Baptist .... Luke 1:41, 44
Christ .... Luke 2:12, 16
Timothy .... 2 Tim. 3:15
Offspring .... Ps. 17:14

B. *Figurative of:*

Unenlightened .... Rom. 2:20
True believers .... Matt. 11:25; Matt. 21:16
New Christians .... 1 Pet. 2:2
Carnal Christians .... 1 Cor. 3:1; Heb. 5:13

Babel—*confusion*

A city built by Nimrod in the plain of Shinar .... Gen. 10:10

Babel, Tower of

A huge brick structure intended to magnify man and preserve the unity of the race .. Gen. 11:1-4
Objectives thwarted by God .... Gen. 11:5-9

Babylon, city of

A. *History of:*

Built by Nimrod .... Gen. 10:9, 10
Tower built there .... Gen. 11:1-9
Amraphel's capital .... Gen. 14:1
Once the capital of Assyria .. 2 Chr. 33:11
Greatest power under Nebuchadnezzar .... Dan. 4:30
A magnificent city .... Is. 13:19; Is. 14:4
Wide walls of .... Jer. 51:44
Gates of .... Is. 45:1, 2
Bel, god of .... Is. 46:1
Jews carried captive to ...... 2 Kin. 25:1-21; 2 Chr. 36:5-21

B. *Inhabitants, described as:*

Idolatrous .... Jer. 50:35, 38; Dan. 3:18
Enslaved by magic .... Is. 47:1, 9-13
Sacrilegious .... Dan. 5:1-3

C. *Prophecies concerning:*

Babylon, God's agent .... Jer. 25:9; Jer. 27:5-8
God fights with .... Jer. 21:1-7
Jews, 70 years in .... Jer. 25:12; Jer. 29:10
First of great empires .... Dan. 2:31-38; Dan. 7:2-4
Downfall of .... Is. 13:1-22; Jer. 50:1-46
Cyrus, God's agent .... Is. 45:1-4
Perpetual desolation of ...... Is. 13:19-22; Jer. 50:13, 39

Babylon in the New Testament

A. *The city on the Euphrates*

Listed as a point of reference .... Matt. 1:11, 12, 17
As the place of Israel's exile .... Acts 7:43
As the place of Peter's residence .... 1 Pet. 5:13

B. *The prophetic city*

Fall predicted .... Rev. 14:8
Wrath taken on .... Rev. 16:19
Called "the Mother of Harlots" .... Rev. 17:1-18
Fall described .... Rev. 18:1-24

Babylonians—*sons of Babel*

Inhabitants of Babylonia .... Ezra 4:9; Ezek. 23:15-23

Babylonish garment—*a valuable robe worn in Babylon*

Coveted by Achan .... Josh. 7:21

Baca—*weeping*

Figurative of sorrow .... Ps. 84:6

Bachelor—*unmarried man*

Described literally .... 1 Cor. 7:26-33
Described figuratively .... Is. 56:3, 4; Matt. 19:12; Rev. 14:1-5
Not for elders .... Titus 1:5, 6

Bachrites

Family of Becher .... Num. 26:35

Backbiting—*reviling another in secret; slander*

A fruit of sin .... Rom. 1:30
Expressed by the mouth .... Ps. 50:20
An offspring of anger .... Prov. 25:23
Merits punishment .... Ps. 101:5
Keeps from God .... Ps. 15:1, 3
To be laid aside .... 1 Pet. 2:1
Unworthy of Christians .... 2 Cor. 12:20

Backsliding—*to turn away from God after conversion*

A. *Described as:*

Turning from God .... 1 Kin. 11:9
Turning to evil .... Ps. 125:5

SUBJECT | REFERENCE

Turning to Satan ... 1 Tim. 5:15
Turning back to the world ... 2 Tim. 4:10
Tempting Christ ... 1 Cor. 10:9
Turning from first love ... Rev. 2:4
Turning from the Gospel ... Gal. 3:1-5

B. *Prompted by:*
Haughty spirit ... Prov. 16:18
Spiritual blindness ... 2 Pet. 1:9; Rev. 3:17
Murmuring ... Ex. 17:3
Lusting after evil ... Ps. 106:14
Material things ... Mark 4:18, 19; 1 Tim. 6:10
Prosperity ... Deut. 8:11-14
Tribulation ... Matt. 13:20, 21

C. *Results:*
Displeases God ... Ps. 78:56-59
Punishment ... Num. 14:43-45; Jer. 8:5-13
Blessings withheld ... Is. 59:2
Unworthiness ... Luke 9:62

D. *Examples of Israel's:*
At Meribah ... Ex. 17:1-7
At Sinai ... Ex. 32:1-35
In wilderness ... Ps. 106:14-33
After Joshua's death ... Judg. 2:8-23; Ps. 106:34-43
In Solomon's life ... 1 Kin. 11:4-40; Neh. 13:26
During Asa's reign ... 2 Chr. 15:3, 4
During Manasseh's reign ... 2 Chr. 33:1-10

E. *Examples of, among believers:*
Lot ... Gen. 19:1-22
David ... 2 Sam. 11:1-5; Ps. 51:1-19
Peter ... Matt. 26:69-75; Luke 22:31, 32
Galatians ... Gal. 1:6; Gal. 4:9-11
Corinthians ... 1 Cor. 5:1-13
Churches of Asia ... 2 Tim. 1:15; Rev. 2, 3

See Apostasy

Badger—*a specie of dolphin or porpoise*
Skins of, used in tabernacle coverings ... Ex. 26:14; Ex. 35:7
Used for sandals ... Ezek. 16:10

Bag—*a purse or pouch*
A. *Used for:*
Money ... 2 Kin. 12:10; John 12:6
Stones ... 1 Sam. 17:40, 49
Weights ... Deut. 25:13; Prov. 16:11
Food ("vessels") ... 1 Sam. 9:7
B. *Figurative of:*
Forgiveness ... Job 14:17
True righteousness ... Prov. 16:11
True riches ... Luke 17:33
Insecure riches ... Hag. 1:6

Barhumite—*a native of Baharum*
Applied to Azmaveth ... 2 Sam. 23:31

Bahurim—*young men*
A village near Jerusalem ... 2 Sam. 3:16
Where Shimei cursed David ... 2 Sam. 16:5
Where two men hid in a well ... 2 Sam. 17:18

Bajith—*house*
A derisive reference to the temple of Moabite gods ... Is. 15:2

Bakbakkar—*investigator*
A Levite ... 1 Chr. 9:15

Bakbuk—*a flask*
Head of postexilic family ... Ezra 2:51; Neh. 7:53

Bakbukiah—*Jehovah has poured out*
1. A Levite of high position ... Neh. 11:17
2. Levite porter ... Neh. 12:25

Baker—*one who cooks food* (bread)
A. *Kinds of:*
Household ... Gen. 18:6
Public ... Jer. 37:21
Royal ... Gen. 40:1, 2

SUBJECT | REFERENCE

B. *Features of:*
Usually a woman's job ... Lev. 26:26
Considered menial ... 1 Sam. 8:13

Balaam—*destroyer of the people*
A. *Information concerning:*
A son of Beor ... Num. 22:5
From Mesopotamia ... Deut. 23:4
A soothsayer ... Josh. 13:22
A prophet ... 2 Pet. 2:15
A Midianite ... Num. 31:8
Killed because of his sin ... Num. 31:1-8
B. *Mission of:*
Balak sent to curse Israel ... Num. 22:5-7; Josh. 24:9
Hindered by speaking ass ... Num. 22:22-35; 2 Pet. 2:16
Curse becomes a blessing ... Deut. 23:4, 5; Josh. 24:10
C. *Prophecies of:*
Under divine control ... Num. 22:18, 38; Num. 23:16, 20, 26
By the Spirit's prompting ... Num. 24:2
Blessed Israel three times ... Num. 24:10
Spoke of the Messiah in final message ... Num. 24:14-19
D. *Nature of:*
"Unrighteousness"—greed ... 2 Pet. 2:14, 15
"Error"—rebellion ... Jude 11

Baladan—(Marduk) *has given a son*
Father of Merodach-baladan (*also spelled* Berodach-baladan) ... 2 Kin. 20:12

Balak, Balac—*empty*
A Moabite king ... Num. 22:4
Hired Balaam to curse Israel ... Num. 22-24

Balances—*an instrument for weighing; scales*
A. *Used for weighing:*
Things ... Lev. 19:36
Money ... Jer. 32:10
B. *Laws concerning:*
Must be just ... Lev. 19:36
False, an abomination ... Prov. 11:1
Deceit, condemned ... Amos 8:5
C. *Figurative of:*
God's justice ... Job 31:6
Man's smallness ... Ps. 62:9; Is. 40:12, 15
God's judgment ... Dan. 5:27
Man's tribulation ... Rev. 6:5

Bald Locust (see Locust)
A specie of edible locust ... Lev. 11:22

Baldness—*a head without hair*
A. *Natural:*
Not a sign of leprosy ... Lev. 13:40, 41
Elijah mocked for ... 2 Kin. 2:23, 24
B. *Artificial:*
A sign of mourning ... Is. 22:12
An idolatrous practice ... Lev. 21:5; Deut. 14:1
Inflicted upon captives ... Deut. 21:12
Forbidden to priests ... Ezek. 44:20
A part of Nazarite vow ... Num. 6:9, 18
C. *Figurative of judgment, upon:*
Israel ... Is. 3:24; Amos 8:10
Moab ... Is. 15:2
Philistia ... Jer. 47:5
Tyre ... Ezek. 27:31

Ball—*spherical object*
Prophetic ... Is. 22:18

Ballad singers
Rendered "they that speak proverbs" ... Num. 21:27

Balm—*an aromatic resin or gum*
A product of Gilead ... Jer. 8:22
Sent to Joseph ... Gen. 43:11
Exported to Tyre ... Ezek. 27:17
Healing qualities of ... Jer. 46:11; Jer. 51:8

Bamah—*high place*
A place of idolatry ... Ezek. 20:29

SUBJECT | REFERENCE

Bamoth—*high places*
Encampment site ... Num. 21:19, 20
Also called Bamoth-baal ... Josh. 13:17

Bamoth-baal—*high places of Baal*
Assigned to Reuben ... Josh. 13:17

Ban (see Excommunication)

Bandage
Used as disguise ... 1 Kin. 20:37-41
In prophecy against Egypt ... Ezek. 30:20-22

Bani—*built*
1. Gadite warrior ... 2 Sam. 23:36
2. A Judahite ... 1 Chr. 9:4
3. A postexilic family ... Ezra 2:10; Neh. 10:14
4. A Merarite Levite ... 1 Chr. 6:46
5. A Levite; father of Rehum ... Neh. 3:17
6. Signed document ... Neh. 10:13
7. Head of Levitical family ... Ezra 10:34
8. A postexilic Levite ... Ezra 10:38
9. A descendant of Asaph ... Neh. 11:22

Banishment—*forceful expulsion from one's place*
A. *Political, of:*
Absalom by David ... 2 Sam. 14:13, 14
The Jews into exile ... 2 Chr. 36:20, 21
The Jews from Rome ... Acts 18:2
B. *Moral and spiritual, of:*
Adam from Eden ... Gen. 3:22-24
Cain from others ... Gen. 4:12, 14
Lawbreaker ... Ezra 7:26
John to Patmos ... Rev. 1:9
Satan from heaven ... Rev. 12:7-9
The wicked to lake of fire ... Rev. 20:15; Rev. 21:8

Bank
A. *A mound:*
Raised against a besieged city ... 2 Sam. 20:15; Is. 37:33
B. *A place for money:*
Exchange charges ... John 2:15
Interest paid on deposits ... Matt. 25:27; Luke 19:23

Bankruptcy—*inability to pay one's debts*
A. *Literal:*
Condition of David's men ... 1 Sam. 22:2
Unjust steward ... Matt. 18:25
B. *Moral and spiritual:*
Israel's condition ... Hos. 4:1-5
Mankind's condition ... Rom. 1:20-32; Rom. 3:9-19
Individual's condition ... Phil. 3:4-8; 1 Tim. 1:13

Banner—*a flag or standard*
A. *Literal:*
Used by armies ... Num. 2:2, 3
Signal for blowing trumpet ... Is. 18:3
B. *Figurative of:*
Jehovah's name ("Jehovah is my banner") ... Ex. 17:15
God's salvation ... Ps. 20:5; Ps. 60:4
God's protection ... Song 2:4
God's power ... Song 6:4, 10

Banquet—*a sumptuous feast*
A. *Reasons for:*
Birthday ... Gen. 40:20
Marriage ... Gen. 29:22
Reunion ... Luke 15:22-25
State affairs ... Esth. 1:3, 5; Dan. 5:1
B. *Features of:*
Invitations sent ... Esth. 5:8, 9; Luke 14:16, 17
Non-acceptance merits censure ... Luke 14:18-24
Courtesies to guests ... Luke 7:40-46
Special garment ... Matt. 22:11; Rev. 3:4, 5
A presiding governor ... John 2:8
Protocol of seating ... Gen. 43:33; Prov. 25:6, 7

B

SUBJECT REFERENCE

Anointing oil ... Ps. 45:7
Honor guest noted ... 1 Sam. 9:22-24

Baptism, Christian

A. *Commanded by:*
Christ ... Matt. 28:19, 20; Mark 16:15, 16
Peter ... Acts 10:46-48
Christian ministers ... Acts 22:12-16

B. *Administered by:*
The apostles ... Acts 2:1, 41
Ananias ... Acts 9:17, 18
Philip ... Acts 8:12; Acts 8:36-38
Peter ... Acts 10:44-48
Paul ... Acts 18:8; 1 Cor. 1:14-17

C. *Places:*
Jordan ... Matt. 3:13-16; Mark 1:5-10
Jerusalem ... Acts 2:5, 41
Samaria ... Acts 8:12
A house ... Acts 10:44-48
A jail ... Acts 16:25-33

D. *Subjects of:*
Believing Jews ... Acts 2:41
Believing Gentiles ... Acts 10:44-48; Acts 18:8
Households ... Acts 16:15, 33; 1 Cor. 1:16

E. *Characteristics of:*
By water ... Acts 10:47
Only one ... Eph. 4:5
Necessary ... Acts 2:38, 41
Source of power ... Acts 1:5
Follows faith ... Acts 2:41; Acts 18:8

F. *Symbolism of:*
Forecast in prophecy ... Joel 2:28, 29; Acts 2:16-21
Prefigured in types ... 1 Cor. 10:2; 1 Pet. 3:20, 21
Visualized by the Spirit's descent ... John 1:32, 33; Acts 2:3, 4, 41; Acts 10:44-48
Expressive of spiritual unity ... 1 Cor. 12:13; Gal. 3:27, 28
Figurative of regeneration ... John 3:3, 5, 6; Rom. 6:3, 4, 11
Illustrative of cleansing ... Acts 22:16; Titus 3:5

Baptism, John's

Administrator—John ... Matt. 3:7
Place—at Jordan ... Matt. 3:6, 13, 16
in Aenon ... John 3:23
Persons—people and Jesus ... Mark 1:5, 9; Acts 13:24
Character—repentance ... Luke 3:3
Reception—rejected by some ... Luke 7:29, 30
Nature—of God ... Matt. 21:25, 27
Insufficiency—rebaptism ... Acts 19:1-7
Intent—to prepare ... Matt. 3:11, 12; Acts 11:16; Acts 19:4
Jesus' submission to—fulfilling all righteousness ... Matt. 3:13-17

Barabbas—*son of Abba* (father)
A murderer released in place of Jesus ... Matt. 27:16-26; Acts 3:14, 15

Barachel—*God has blessed*
Father of Elihu ... Job 32:2, 6

Barachias—*Jehovah has blessed*
Father of Zechariah ... Matt. 23:35

Barak—*lightning*
Defeats Jabin ... Judg. 4:1-24
A man of faith ... Heb. 11:32

Barbarian—*rude*
Primitive people ... Acts 28:2, 4
Unintelligible language ... 1 Cor. 14:11
Those included in the Gospel ... Rom. 1:14; Col. 3:11

Barber—*one who cuts hair*
Expressive of divine judgment ... Is. 7:20; Ezek. 5:1

Bare—*uncovered, naked*
Figurative of:
Destitution ... Ezek. 16:22, 39
Uncleanness ... Lev. 13:45
Undeveloped state, immaturity ... Ezek. 16:7; 1 Cor. 15:37
Power revealed ... Is. 52:10
Destruction ... Joel 1:7
Mourning ... Is. 32:9-11

Barefoot—*bare feet*
Expression of great distress ... 2 Sam. 15:30
Forewarning of judgement ... Is. 20:2-4
Indicative of reverence ... Ex. 3:5

Bargain—*an agreement between persons*
A disastrous ... Gen. 25:29-34
A blessed ... Gen. 28:20-22
Involving a wife ... Gen. 29:15-20
Deception of ... Prov. 20:14
Resulting in death ... Matt. 14:7-10
History's most notorious ... Matt. 26:14-16

Barhumite (another form of Baharumite)
One of David's mighty men ... 2 Sam. 23:31

Bariah—*fugitive*
A decendant of David ... 1 Chr. 3:22

Bar-jesus (Elymas)
A Jewish imposter ... Acts 13:6-12

Bar-jona—*son of Jonah*
Surname of Peter ... Matt. 16:17

Barkos—*party-colored*
Postexilic family ... Ezra 2:53

Barley—*a bearded cereal grass*
A product of Palestine ... Deut. 8:8; Ruth 1:22
Food for animals ... 1 Kin. 4:28
Used by the poor ... Ruth 2:17
Used in trade ... 2 Chr. 2:10
In a miracle ... John 6:9, 13

Barn—*a storehouse*

A. *Literal:*
A place of storage ... Deut. 28:8; Joel 1:17

B. *Spiritual, of:*
God's blessings ... Prov. 3:10; Mal. 3:10
Man's vanity ... Luke 12:16-19
Heaven itself ... Matt. 13:30, 43

Barnabas—*son of exhortation*
Gives property ... Acts 4:36, 37
Supports Paul ... Acts 9:27
Assists in Antioch ... Acts 11:22-24
Brings Paul from Tarsus ... Acts 11:25, 26
Carries relief to Jerusalem ... Acts 11:27-30
Travels with Paul ... Acts 13:2
Called Jupiter by the multitudes ... Acts 14:12
Speaks before Jerusalem Council ... Acts 15:1, 2, 12
With Paul, takes decree to churches ... Acts 15:22-31
Breaks with Paul over John Mark ... Acts 15:36-39
Highly regarded by Paul ... 1 Cor. 9:6; Gal. 2:1, 9
Not always steady ... Gal. 2:13

Barrel
For food storage ... 1 Kin. 17:12-16
For water ... 1 Kin. 18:33

Barren—*unable to reproduce*

A. *Physically, of:*
Unproductive soil ... Ps. 107:34; Joel 2:20
Trees ... Luke 13:6-9
Females ... Prov. 30:16

B. *Significance of:*
A reproach ... Gen. 16:2
A judgment ... 2 Sam. 6:23
Absence of God's blessing ... Ex. 23:26; Deut. 7:14
Removal of, from the Lord ... Ps. 113:9

C. *Spiritually:*
Removal of, in new Israel ... Is. 54:1; Gal. 4:27
Remedy against ... 2 Pet. 1:8

SUBJECT REFERENCE

D. *Examples of:*
Sarah ... Gen. 21:2
Rebekah ... Gen. 25:21
Rachel ... Gen. 30:22
Manoah's wife ... Judg. 13:2, 3, 24
Hannah ... 1 Sam. 1:18-20
The Shunammite woman ... 2 Kin. 4:14-17
Elizabeth ... Luke 1:7, 13, 57

Barsabas—*son of Saba*
1. Nominated to replace Judas ... Acts 1:23
2. Sent to Antioch ... Acts 15:22

Barter—*to exchange for something*
Between Joseph and the Egyptians ... Gen. 47:17
Between Solomon and Hiram ... 1 Kin. 5:10, 11

Bartholomew—*son of Talmai*
One of Christ's apostles ... Matt. 10:3; Acts 1:13
Called Nathanael ... John 1:45, 46

Bartimaeus—*son of Timaeus*
Blind beggar healed by Jesus ... Mark 10:46-52

Baruch—*blessed*
1. Son of Neriah ... Jer. 32:12, 13
Jeremiah's faithful friend ... Jer. 36:4-32
The Jewish remnant takes him to Egypt ... Jer. 43:1-7
2. Son of Zabbai ... Neh. 3:20
Signs document ... Neh. 10:6
3. A Shilonite of Judah ... Neh. 11:5

Barzillai—*of iron*
1. Helps David with food ... 2 Sam. 17:27-29
Age restrains him from following David ... 2 Sam. 19:31-39
2. Father of Adriel ... 2 Sam. 21:8
3. A postexilic priest ... Ezra 2:61

Base
As a foundation ... 1 Kin. 7:27-43
Of lowly estate ... 2 Sam. 6:22
Of evil character ... 1 Cor. 1:28
Of humble nature ... 2 Cor. 10:1

Bashemath—*fragrance*
1. Wife of Esau ... Gen. 26:34
Called Adah ... Gen. 36:2, 3
2. Wife of Esau ... Gen. 36:3, 4, 13
Called Mahalath ... Gen. 28:9
3. A daughter of Solomon ... 1 Kin. 4:15

Bashan—*smooth soil*
A vast highland east of the Sea of Chinnereth (Galilee) ... Num. 21:33-35
Ruled by Og ... Deut. 29:7
Conquered by Israel ... Neh. 9:22
Assigned to Manasseh ... Deut. 3:13
Smitten by Hazael ... 2 Kin. 10:32, 33
Fine cattle ... Ezek. 39:18
Typical of cruelty ... Ps. 22:12; Amos 4:1

Bashan Havoth-jair
A district named after Jair ... Deut. 3:14

Basin—*cup or bowl for containing liquids*
Moses used ... Ex. 24:6
Made for the altar ... Ex. 38:3; Ex. 27:3
Brought for David ... 2 Sam. 17:28, 29
Hiram made ... 1 Kin. 7:40

Baskets—*something made to hold objects*

A. *Used for carrying:*
Produce ... Deut. 26:2
Food ... Matt. 14:20
Ceremonial offerings ... Ex. 29:3, 23
Paul ... Acts 9:24, 25
Other objects (heads) ... 2 Kin. 10:7

B. *Symbolic of:*
Approaching death ... Gen. 40:16-19
Israel's judgment ... Amos 8:1-3
Judah's judgment ... Jer. 24:1-3

Bastard—*an illegitimate child*
A. *Penalty attached to* ... Deut. 23:2

SUBJECT — REFERENCE

B. *Examples of:*
- Ishmael ... Gen. 16:3, 15; Gal. 4:22
- Moab and Ammon ... Gen. 19:36, 37
- Sons of Tamar by Judah ... Gen. 38:12-30
- Jephthah ... Judg. 11:1

C. *Figurative of:*
- A mixed race ... Zech. 9:6
- The unregenerate state ... Heb. 12:8

Bat—*a flying mammal*
- Listed among unclean birds ... Lev. 11:19; Deut. 14:18
- Lives in dark places ... Is. 2:19, 20

Bath—*a liquid measure* (about 9 gallons)
- A tenth of a homer ... Ezek. 45:10, 11
- For measuring oil and wine ... 2 Chr. 2:10; Is. 5:10

Bathing

A. *For pleasure:*
- Pharaoh's daughter ... Ex. 2:5
- Bath-sheba ... 2 Sam. 11:2, 3

B. *For purification:*
- Cleansing the feet ... Gen. 24:32; John 13:10
- Ceremonial cleansing ... Lev. 14:8; 2 Kin. 5:10-14
- Before performing priestly duties ... Ex. 30:19-21; Lev. 16:4, 24
- Jewish rituals ... Mark 7:2

Bath-rabbim—*daughter of multitudes*
- Gate of Heshbon ... Song 7:4

Bath-sheba—*daughter of an oath*
- Wife of Uriah ... 2 Sam. 11:2, 3
- Commits adultery with David ... 2 Sam. 11:4, 5
- Husband's death contrived by David ... 2 Sam. 11:6-25
- Mourns husband's death ... 2 Sam. 11:26
- Becomes David's wife ... 2 Sam. 11:27
- Her first child dies ... 2 Sam. 12:14-19
- Solomon's mother ... 2 Sam. 12:24
- Secures throne for Solomon ... 1 Kin. 1:15-31
- Deceived by Adonijah ... 1 Kin. 2:13-25

Bath-shua—*daughter of prosperity*
- Same as Bath-sheba ... 1 Chr. 3:5

Battering ram (see Armor)
- Used in destroying walls ... Ezek. 4:2; Ezek. 21:22

Battle (See War)

Battle-axe—*an instrument of war*
- Applied to Israel ... Jer. 51:19, 20

Battlement—*a lodge on roofs*
- A protective ... Deut. 22:8
- Figurative of partial destruction ... Jer. 5:10

Bavai—*wisher*
- Postexilic worker ... Neh. 3:18

Bay—*inlet*
1. Dead Sea's cove at Jordan's mouth ... Josh. 15:5
   Used also of the Nile ... Is. 11:15
2. Color of a horse ... Zech. 6:2
3. Name of a tree; figurative of pride ... Ps. 37:35

Bazluth—*stripping*
- Head of a family ... Ezra 2:52
- Called Bazlith in ... Neh. 7:54

Bdellium—*an oily gum, or a white pearl*
- A valuable mineral of Havilah ... Gen. 2:12
- Manna colored like ... Num. 11:7

Beach—*coast*

Place of:
- Jesus' preaching ... Matt. 13:2
- Fisherman's task ... Matt. 13:48
- Jesus' meal with disciples ... John 21:9
- A prayer meeting ... Acts 21:5
- A notable shipwreck ... Acts 27:39-44
- A miracle ... Acts 28:1-6

Beacon—*a signal*
- Figurative, a warning to others ... Is. 30:17

Bealiah—*Jehovah is Lord*
- A warrior ... 1 Chr. 12:5

Bealoth—*mistresses*
- Village of Judah ... Josh. 15:24

Beam

A. *Physical:*
- Wood undergirding floors ... 1 Kin. 7:2
- Part of weaver's frame ... 1 Sam. 17:7

B. *Figurative of:*
- The cry for vengeance ... Hab. 2:11
- God's power ... Ps. 104:3
- Notorious faults ... Matt. 7:3-5

Bean—*a food*
- Brought to David by friends ... 2 Sam. 17:27, 28
- Mixed with grain for bread ... Ezek. 4:9

Bear—*a wild animal*

A. *Natural:*
- Killed by David ... 1 Sam. 17:34, 35
- Two tore up forty-two lads ... 2 Kin. 2:23, 24

B. *Figurative of:*
- Fierce revenge ... 2 Sam. 17:8
- Fool's folly ... Prov. 17:12
- Wicked rulers ... Prov. 28:15
- World empire ... Dan. 7:5
- Final antichrist ... Rev. 13:2
- Messianic times ... Is. 11:7

Bear—*to carry, yield*

A. *Used literally of:*
- Giving birth ... Gen. 17:19
- Carrying a load ... Josh. 3:13; Jer. 17:21
- Cross ... Matt. 27:32

B. *Used figuratively of:*
- Excessive punishment ... Gen. 4:13
- Divine deliverance ... Ex. 19:4
- Responsibility for sin ... Lev. 5:17; Lev. 24:15
- Burden of leadership ... Deut. 1:9, 12
- Personal shame ... Ezek. 16:54
- Evangelism ... Acts 9:15
- Spiritual help ... Gal. 6:1, 2
- Spiritual productivity ... John 15:2, 4, 8

Beard—*hair grown on the face*

A. *Long, worn by:*
- Aaron ... Ps. 133:2
- Samson ... Judg. 16:17
- David ... 1 Sam. 21:13

B. *In mourning:*
- Left untrimmed ... 2 Sam. 19:24
- Plucked ... Ezra 9:3
- Cut ... Jer. 48:37, 38

C. *Features regarding:*
- Leper's must be shaven ... Lev. 13:29-33
- Half-shaven, an indignity ... 2 Sam. 10:4, 5
- Marring of, forbidden ... Lev. 19:27
- Shaven, by Egyptians ... Gen. 41:14
- Spittle on, sign of lunacy ... 1 Sam. 21:13
- Holding to, a token of respect ... 2 Sam. 20:9

Beasts—*four-footed animals; mammals*

A. *Characteristics of:*
- God-created ... Gen. 1:21
- Of their own order ... 1 Cor. 15:39
- Named by Adam ... Gen. 2:20
- Suffer in man's sin ... Rom. 8:20-22
- Perish at death ... Ps. 49:12-15
- Follow instincts ... Is. 1:3; Jude 10
- Under God's control ... 1 Sam. 6:7-14
- Wild ... Mark 1:13
- For man's food ... Gen. 9:3; Acts 10:12, 13
- Eat people ... 1 Sam. 17:46; 1 Cor. 15:32
- Used in sacrifices ... Lev. 27:26-29
- Spiritual lessons from ... 1 Kin. 4:33; Job 12:7

B. *Treatment of:*
- No sexual relation with ... Lev. 20:15, 16
- Proper care of, sign of a righteous man ... Gen. 33:13, 14; Prov. 12:10
- Abuse of, rebuked ... Num. 22:28-32
- Extra food for, while working ... Deut. 25:4; 1 Tim. 5:18

C. *Typical of:*
- Man's folly ... Ps. 73:22
- Unregenerate men ... Titus 1:12
- False prophets ... 2 Pet. 2:12
- Antichrist ... Rev. 13:1-4

See Animals

Beaten gold—*gold shaped by hammering*
- Ornamental shields ... 1 Kin. 10:16, 17; 2 Chr. 9:15, 16

Beaten oil—*highest quality of olive oil*
- In sacrifices ... Ex. 29:39, 40
- In tent of meeting lamp ... Lev. 24:2

Beaten silver—*silver shaped by hammering*
- Overlaid idols ... Is. 30:22; Hab. 2:19
- In trade ... Jer. 10:9

Beatings—*striking the body with blows; floggings*

A. *Inflicted on:*
- The wicked ... Deut. 25:3
- The guilty ... Lev. 19:20
- Children ... Prov. 22:15
- The disobedient ... Prov. 26:3; Luke 12:47, 48

B. *Victims of unjust beatings:*
- A servant ... Luke 20:10, 11
- Christ ... Is. 50:6; Mark 15:19
- The apostles ... Acts 5:40
- Paul ... Acts 16:19-24

Beatitudes—*pronouncements of blessings*
- Jesus begins His sermon with ... Matt. 5:3-12; Luke 6:20-22

Beautiful gate—*gate at East of Temple area*
- Lame man healed there ... Acts 3:1-10

Beauty, physical

A. *Temporal:*
- Seen in nature ... Hos. 14:6; Matt. 6:28, 29
- Consumed in dissipation ... Is. 28:1
- Contest Abishag, winner of ... 1 Kin. 1:1-4
- Esther, winner of ... Esth. 2:1-17
- Destroyed by sin ... Ps. 39:11
- Ends in grave ... Ps. 49:14

B. *In Women:*
- Vain ... Prov. 31:30
- Without discretion ... Prov. 11:22
- Enticements of ... Prov. 6:25
- Source of temptation ... Gen. 6:2; 2 Sam. 11:2-5
- Leads to marriage ... Deut. 21:11
- A bride's ... Ps. 45:11
- Sarah's ... Gen. 12:11
- Rebekah's ... Gen. 24:15, 16
- Rachel's ... Gen. 29:17
- Daughters of Job ... Job 42:15
- Abigail's ... 1 Sam. 25:3
- Bath-sheba's ... 2 Sam. 11:2, 3
- Tamar's ... 2 Sam. 13:1
- Abishag's ... 1 Kin. 1:3, 4
- Vashti's ... Esth. 1:11
- Esther's ... Esth. 2:7

C. *In Men:*
- Of Man ... Is. 44:13
- Of the aged ... Prov. 20:29
- Joseph's ... Gen. 39:6
- David's ... 1 Sam. 16:12, 13
- Absalom's ... 2 Sam. 14:25

Beauty, spiritual
- The Messiah ... Ps. 110:3; Is. 52:7
- The true Israel ... Ps. 45:8-11; Song 1:8
- The meek ... Ps. 149:4
- Spiritual worship ... 2 Chr. 20:21
- Christian ministers ... Rom. 10:15
- Holy garments ... Is. 52:1
- Christ's rejection by Israel ... Zech. 11:7-14

Bebai—*fatherly*
1. Family head ... Ezra 2:11
2. One who signs document ... Neh. 10:15

SUBJECT REFERENCE

Becher—*young camel*
1. Benjamin's son .... Gen. 46:21
2. Son of Ephraim .... Num. 26:35
Called Bered .... 1 Chr. 7:20

Bechorath—*the first birth*
Ancestor of Saul .... 1 Sam. 9:1

Bed
A. *Made of:*
The ground .... Gen. 28:11
Iron, 13½ feet long .... Deut. 3:11
Ivory .... Amos 6:4
Gold and silver .... Esth. 1:6
B. *Used for:*
Sleep .... Luke 11:7
Rest .... 2 Sam. 4:5-7
Sickness .... Gen. 49:33
Meals .... Amos 6:4
Prostitution .... Prov. 7:16, 17
Evil .... Ps. 36:4
Marriage .... Song 3:1
Heb. 13:4
Singing .... Ps. 149:5
C. *Figurative of:*
The grave .... Job 17:13-16
Divine support .... Ps. 41:3
Worldly security .... Is. 57:7

Bed—*a garden plot*
Used literally .... Song 6:2
Used figuratively .... Song 5:13

Bedad—*separation*
Father of Hadad .... Gen. 36:35

Bedan—*son of judgment*
1. Judge of Israel .... 1 Sam. 12:11
2. Descendant of Manasseh .... 1 Chr. 7:17

Bedchamber—*a bedroom*
A place of sleep .... 2 Sam. 4:7
Elijah's special .... 2 Kin. 4:8, 10
Secrets of .... 2 Kin. 6:12
Joash hidden in .... 2 Kin. 11:2

Bedeiah—*servant of Jehovah*
Son of Bani .... Ezra 10:34, 35

Bedfellows
Provide mutual warmth .... Eccl. 4:11

Bee—*insect*
Abundant in Canaan .... Judg. 14:8
Amorites compared to .... Deut. 1:44
David's enemies compared to .... Ps. 118:12
Assyria compared to .... Is. 7:18
See Honey

Beef, boiled
Elisha gives people .... 1 Kin. 19:21

Beeliada—*the Lord knows*
Son of David .... 1 Chr. 14:7
Called Eliada .... 2 Sam. 5:14-16

Beelzebub
Prince of demons .... Matt. 12:24
Identified as Satan .... Matt. 12:26
Jesus thus called .... Matt. 10:25

Beer—*a well*
1. Moab station .... Num. 21:16-18
2. Jotham's place of refuge .... Judg. 9:21

Beera—*a well*
An Asherite .... 1 Chr. 7:37

Beerah—*a well*
Reubenite prince .... 1 Chr. 5:6

Beeri—*expounder*
1. Esau's father-in-law .... Gen. 26:34
2. Hosea's father .... Hos. 1:1
3. Well dug by leaders of Israel .... Is. 15:8
(also spelled Beer-elim)

Beer-lahai-roi—*the well of The Living One who sees me*
Angel met Hagar there .... Gen. 16:7-14
Isaac dwelt in .... Gen. 24:62

SUBJECT REFERENCE

Beeroth—*wells*
1. Edom station .... Deut. 10:6
2. Gibeonite city .... Josh. 9:17

Beerothite, Berothite
An inhabitant of Beeroth .... 2 Sam. 4:2
1 Chr. 11:39

Beer-sheba—*well of the oath*
A. *God appeared to:*
Hagar .... Gen. 21:14, 17-19
Isaac .... Gen. 26:23, 24
Jacob .... Gen. 46:1-5
Elijah .... 1 Kin. 19:3-7
B. *Other features of:*
Named after an oath .... Gen. 21:31-33
Gen. 26:26-33
Isaac's residence at .... Gen. 26:23-25
Jacob's departure from .... Gen. 28:10
Assigned to Judah .... Josh. 15:20, 28
Later assigned to Simeon .... Josh. 19:1, 2, 9
Judgeship of Samuel's sons .... 1 Sam. 8:2
Became seat of idolatry .... Amos 5:5
Amos 8:14
"From Dan even to Beer-sheba" .... 2 Sam. 17:11

Beeshterah—*temple of Ashterah*
A Levitical city .... Josh. 21:27
Same as Ashtaroth .... 1 Chr. 6:71

Beggar—*needy*
A. *Statements concerning:*
Shame of .... Luke 16:3
Seed of righteous, kept from .... Ps. 37:25
Punishment of .... Ps. 109:10
Object of prayer .... 1 Sam. 2:1, 8
B. *Examples of:*
Bartimaeus .... Mark 10:46
Lazarus .... Luke 16:20-22
Blind man .... Luke 18:35
Lame man .... Acts 3:2-6

Beginning—*the starting point; origin of*
Creation .... Gen. 1:1
John 1:1-3
Sin .... Gen. 3:1-6
Rom. 5:12-21
Death .... Gen. 3:3, 22-24
Salvation .... Eph. 1:4
Satan .... John 8:44
The Gospel .... Gen. 3:15
Gal. 3:8
The old covenant .... Ex. 19:5
Heb. 8:9
The new covenant .... Jer. 31:31-34
Matt. 26:28
Heb. 9:14-28

Begotten—*from "beget" meaning to bring into being*
A. *Applied to Christ:*
Predicted .... Ps. 2:7
Acts 13:33
Prefigured .... Heb. 11:17
Proclaimed .... John 1:14
Proffered .... John 3:16
Professed .... Heb. 1:6
B. *Applied to Christians:*
By the Gospel .... 1 Cor. 4:15
In bonds .... Philem. 10
Unto hope .... 1 Pet. 1:3
For safekeeping .... 1 John 5:18

Beguile—*to deceive or mislead*
A. *In Old Testament:*
Eve, by Satan .... Gen. 3:13
Israel, by the Midianites .... Num. 25:18
Joshua, by the Gibeonites .... Josh. 9:22
B. *Of Christians:*
By flattering words .... Rom. 16:18
By false reasoning .... Col. 2:4

Behavior—*one's conduct*
A. *Strange:*
Feigned insanity .... 1 Sam. 21:13
Supposed drunkenness .... 1 Sam. 1:12-16
Pretended grief .... 2 Sam. 14:1-8
Professed loyalty .... Matt. 26:48, 49

SUBJECT REFERENCE

Insipid hypocrisy .... Esth. 6:5-11
Counterfeit religion .... 2 Cor. 11:13-15
B. *True:*
Reverent .... Titus 2:7
Orderly .... 2 Thess. 3:7
Good .... 1 Tim. 3:2
Without blame .... 1 Thess. 2:10

Beheading—*a form of capital punishment*
Ish-bosheth .... 2 Sam. 4:5-7
John the Baptist .... Matt. 14:10
James .... Acts 12:2
Martyrs .... Rev. 20:4

Behemoth—*a colossal beast*
Described .... Job 40:15-24

Bekah—*see Jewish measures*
Half a shekel .... Ex. 38:26

Bel—*lord*
Patron god of Babylon .... Is. 46:1
Jer. 51:44
Merodach title .... Jer. 50:2

Bela, Belah—*destruction*
1. King of Edom .... Gen. 36:32
2. Reubenite chief .... 1 Chr. 5:8
3. Benjamin's son .... Gen. 46:21
4. A city .... Gen. 14:2, 8

Belial—*worthless, wicked*
A. *Applied properly to:*
Seducers .... Deut. 13:13
The profligate .... Judg. 19:22
Eli's sons .... 1 Sam. 2:12
Rebels .... 1 Sam. 10:27
A fool .... 1 Sam. 25:25
The wicked .... 1 Sam. 30:22
Liars .... 1 Kin. 21:10, 13
Satan .... 2 Cor. 6:15
B. *Applied improperly to:*
Hannah .... 1 Sam. 1:16
David .... 2 Sam. 16:7

Believers—*those who have received Christ; Christians*
Applied to converts .... Acts 5:14
1 Tim. 4:12

Bellows—*an instrument used in forcing air at fire*
A figure of affliction .... Jer. 6:29
Descriptive of God's judgment .... Jer. 6:27-30

Bells
On Aaron's garment .... Ex. 28:33, 34
Ex. 39:25, 26
Attention-getters .... Is. 3:16, 18
Symbols of consecration .... Zech. 14:20

Beloved—*a title of endearment*
A. *Applied naturally to:*
A wife .... Deut. 21:15, 16
A husband .... Song 6:1-3
B. *Applied spiritually to:*
Christ .... Matt. 3:17
Spiritual Israel .... Rom. 9:25
Believers .... Col. 3:12
Christian friends .... Rom. 16:8, 9
New Jerusalem .... Rev. 21:9, 10

Belshazzar—*Bel protect the king*
Son of Nebuchadnezzar .... Dan. 5:2
Gives feast .... Dan. 5:1, 4
Disturbed by handwriting .... Dan. 5:5-12
Seeks Daniel's aid .... Dan. 5:13-16
Daniel interprets for him .... Dan. 5:17-29
Last Chaldean king .... Dan. 5:30, 31

Belteshazzar—*protect his life*
Daniel's Babylonian name .... Dan. 1:7

Ben—*son*
Levite porter .... 1 Chr. 15:18

Benaiah—*Jehovah has built*
1. Jehoiada's son .... 2 Sam. 23:20
A mighty man .... 2 Sam. 23:20, 21
David's bodyguard .... 2 Sam. 8:18
Faithful to David .... 2 Sam. 15:18
2 Sam. 20:23
Escorts Solomon to the throne .... 1 Kin. 1:38-40

SUBJECT REFERENCE

Executes Adonijah, Joab and Shimei ... 1 Kin. 2:25, 29-34; 1 Kin. 2:46
Commander-in-chief ... 1 Kin. 2:35

2. One of David's mighty men ... 2 Sam. 23:30
Divisional commander ... 1 Chr. 27:14
3. Levite musician ... 1 Chr. 15:18-20
4. Priestly trumpeter ... 1 Chr. 15:24; 1 Chr. 16:6
5. Levite of Asaph's family ... 2 Chr. 20:14
6. Simeonite ... 1 Chr. 4:36
7. Levite overseer ... 2 Chr. 31:13
8. Father of leader Pelatiah ... Ezek. 11:1, 13
9-12. Four postexilic Jews who divorced their foreign wives ... Ezra 10:25-43

Ben-ammi—*son of my kinsman*

Son of Lot; father of the Ammonites ... Gen. 19:38

Benches—*deck of ship*

Made of ivory ... Ezek. 27:6

Bene-berak—*sons of berak* (lightning)

A town of Dan ... Josh. 19:45

Benediction—*an act of blessing*

A. *Characteristics of:*
Instituted by God ... Gen. 1:22, 28
Divinely approved ... Deut. 10:8
Aaronic form ... Num. 6:23-26
Apostolic form ... 2 Cor. 13:14
Jesus' last words ... Luke 24:50, 51

B. *Pronounced upon:*
Creation ... Gen. 1:22, 28
New world ... Gen. 9:1, 2
Abraham ... Gen. 14:19, 20
Marriage ... Gen. 24:60
Son (Jacob) ... Gen. 27:28, 29
Monarch (Pharaoh) ... Gen. 47:7, 10
Sons (Joseph's) ... Gen. 48:15, 16, 20
Tribes (Israel's) ... Deut. 33:1-29
Foreigner ... Ruth 1:8, 9
People ... 2 Sam. 6:18
Jesus ... Luke 2:34
Song of Zecharias ... Luke 1:68-79
Children's blessing ... Mark 10:16

Benefactor—*one who bestows benefits*

A. *Materially, God as:*
Israel's ... Deut. 7:6-26
Unbeliever's ... Acts 14:15-18
Christian's ... Phil. 4:19

B. *Spiritually:*
By God ... Eph. 1:3-6
Through Christ ... Eph. 2:13-22
For enrichment ... Eph. 1:16-19

C. *Attitudes toward:*
Murmuring ... Num. 11:1-10
Forgetfulness ... Ps. 106:13
Rejection ... Acts 13:44-47
Remembrance ... Luke 7:1-5
Gratefulness ... Acts 13:48

Benefice—*an enriching act or gift*

Manifested by a church ... Phil. 4:15-17
Encouraged in a friend ... Philem. 17-22
Justified in works ... James 2:14-17
Remembered in heaven ... 1 Tim. 6:18, 19

Bene-jaakan—*sons of Jaakan*

A wilderness station ... Num. 33:31

Benevolence—*generosity toward others*

A. *Exercised toward:*
The poor ... Gal. 2:10
The needy ... Eph. 4:28
Enemies ... Prov. 25:21
God's servant ... Phil. 4:14-17

B. *Measured by:*
Ability ... Acts 11:29
Love ... 1 Cor. 13:3
Sacrifice ... Mark 12:41-44
Bountifulness ... 2 Cor. 9:6-15

C. *Blessings of:*
Fulfills a grace ... Rom. 12:6, 13
Performs a spiritual sacrifice ... Heb. 13:16
Makes us "more blessed" ... Acts 20:35

SUBJECT REFERENCE

Enriches the giver ... Prov. 11:25; Is. 58:10, 11
Reward ... 1 Tim. 6:18, 19

Ben-hadad—*son of the god Hadad*

1. Ben-hadad I, king of Damascus. Hired by Asa, king of Judah, to attack Baasha, king of Israel ... 1 Kin. 15:18-21
2. Ben-hadad II, king of Damascus. Makes war on Ahab, king of Israel ... 1 Kin. 20:1-21
Defeated by Israel ... 1 Kin. 20:26-34
Fails in siege against Samaria ... 2 Kin. 6:24-33; 2 Kin. 7:6-20
Killed by Hazael ... 2 Kin. 8:7-15
3. Ben-hadad III, king of Damascus. Loses all Israelite conquests made by Hazael, his father ... 2 Kin. 13:3-25

Ben-hail—*son of strength*

A teacher ... 2 Chr. 17:7

Ben-hanan—*son of the gracious one*

A son of Shimon ... 1 Chr. 4:20

Beninu—*our son*

A Levite document signer ... Neh. 10:13

Benjamin—*son of the right hand*

Jacob's youngest son ... Gen. 35:16-20
Jacob's favorite son ... Gen. 42:4; Gen. 43:1-14
Loved by Joseph ... Gen. 43:29-34
Judah intercedes for ... Gen. 44:18-34
Joseph's gifts to ... Gen. 45:22
Father of five sons ... 1 Chr. 8:1, 2
Head of a tribe ... Num. 26:38-41
Jacob's prophecy concerning ... Gen. 49:27

Benjamin (others bearing this name)

1. A son of Bilhan ... 1 Chr. 7:10
2. Son of Harim ... Ezra 10:18, 31, 32
Same as in ... Neh. 3:23

Benjamin, tribe of

A. *Background features of:*
Descendants of Jacob's youngest son ... Gen. 35:18
Family divisions of ... Num. 26:38-41
Strength of ... Num. 1:36, 37
Bounds of ... Josh. 18:11-28
Prophecies respecting ... Gen. 49:27; Deut. 33:12

B. *Memorable events of:*
Almost destroyed for protecting men of Gibeah ... Judg. 20:12-48
Wives provided for, to preserve the tribe ... Judg. 21:1-23
Furnished Israel her first king ... 1 Sam. 9:1-17
Hailed David's return ... 2 Sam. 19:16, 17

C. *Celebrities belonging to:*
Ehud, a judge ... Judg. 3:15
Saul, Israel's first king ... 1 Sam. 9:1
Abner, David's general ... 1 Sam. 17:55
Mordecai ... Esth. 2:5
The apostle Paul ... Phil. 3:5

Beno—*his son*

A Merarite Levite ... 1 Chr. 24:26, 27

Ben-oni—*son of my sorrow*

Rachel's name for Benjamin ... Gen. 35:16-18

Ben-zoheth—*son of Zoheth*

A man of Judah ... 1 Chr. 4:20

Beon—*house of On*

A locality east of Jordan ... Num. 32:3
Same as Baal-meon ... Num. 32:37, 38

Beor, Bosor—*a burning*

1. Father of Bela ... Gen. 36:32
2. Father of Balaam ... Num. 22:5; 2 Pet. 2:15

Bera—*excellent*

A king of Sodom ... Gen. 14:2

Berachah—*blessing*

1. David's warrior ... 1 Chr. 12:3
2. A valley in Judah near Tekoa ... 2 Chr. 20:26

Beraiah—*Jehovah has created*

A Benjamite chief ... 1 Chr. 8:21

SUBJECT REFERENCE

Berea—*watered*

A city of Macedonia visited by Paul ... Acts 17:10-15

Bereavement—*the emotional state after a loved one's death*

A. *General attitudes in:*
Horror ... Ex. 12:29, 30
Great emotion ... 2 Sam. 18:33
Complaint ... Ruth 1:20, 21
Genuine sorrow ... Gen. 37:33-35
Submission ... Job 1:18-21

B. *Christian attitudes in:*
Unlike world's ... 1 Thess. 4:13-18
Yet sorrow allowed ... John 11:35; Acts 9:39
With hope of reunion ... John 11:20-27

C. *Unusual circumstances of, mourning:*
Forbidden ... Lev. 10:6
Of great length ... Gen. 50:1-11
Turned to joy ... John 11:41-44

Berechiah—*blessed by Jehovah*

1. Asaph's father ... 1 Chr. 6:39
2. Levite doorkeepers ... 1 Chr. 15:23, 24
3. Head man of Ephraim ... 2 Chr. 28:12
4. Son of Zerubbabel ... 1 Chr. 3:20
5. Levite ... 1 Chr. 9:16
6. Postexilic workman ... Neh. 3:4, 30
7. Father of Zechariah ... Zech. 1:1, 7; Matt. 23:35

Bered—*hail*

1. A place in the wilderness of Shur ... Gen. 16:7, 14
2. An Ephraimite ... 1 Chr. 7:20

Beri—*belonging to a well*

An Asherite ... 1 Chr. 7:36

Beriah—*evil*

1. Son of Asher ... Gen. 46:17
2. Ephraim's son ... 1 Chr. 7:22, 23
3. Chief of Benjamin ... 1 Chr. 8:13, 16
4. Levite ... 1 Chr. 23:10, 11

Beriites

Descendants of Beriah (No. 1) ... Num. 26:44

Berites

A people in north Palestine ... 2 Sam. 20:14, 15

Berith—*covenant*

Shechem idol ... Judg. 9:46
Same as Baal-berith ... Judg. 8:33; Judg. 9:4

Bernice—*victorious*

Sister of Herod Agrippa II ... Acts 25:13, 23
Hears Paul's defense ... Acts 26:1-30

Berodach-baladan

A king of Babylon ... 2 Kin. 20:12-19
Also called Merodach-baladan ... Is. 39:1

Berothah, Berothai—*wells*

City of Syria taken by David ... 2 Sam. 8:8
Boundary in the ideal kingdom ... Ezek. 47:16

Beryl—*a precious stone*

In breastplate of high priest ... Ex. 28:20; Ex. 39:13
Ornament of a king ... Ezek. 28:12, 13
Describes a lover ... Song 5:14
Applied to an angel ... Dan. 10:5, 6
Wheels like color of ... Ezek. 1:16
In New Jerusalem ... Rev. 21:20

Besai

A family head ... Ezra 2:49

Besodeiah—*in the counsel of Jehovah*

Father of Meshullam ... Neh. 3:6

Besom—*a broom made of twigs*

Symbol of destruction ... Is. 14:23

Besor—*cold*

A brook south of Ziklag ... 1 Sam. 30:9, 10, 21

B

SUBJECT REFERENCE

Bestial—*beast like*
Condemned .... Ex. 22:19
Punishment of .... Lev. 20:13-21

Betah—*trust, confidence*
Cities of Hadadezer .... 2 Sam. 8:8
Called Tibhath .... 1 Chr. 18:8

Beten—*valley*
City of Asher .... Josh. 19:25

Beth—*house*
Second letter of the Hebrew alphabet .... Ps. 119:9-16

Bethabara—*house of passage*
A place beyond Jordan where John baptized .... John 1:28

Beth-anath—*house of Anath* (the goddess)
A town of Naphtali .... Josh. 19:38, 39
Canaanites remain in .... Judg. 1:33

Beth-anoth—*house of Anath* (the goddess)
A town of Judah .... Josh. 15:59

Bethany—*house of poverty*
A town on Mt. of Olives .... Luke 19:29
Home of Lazarus .... John 11:1
Home of Simon, the leper .... Matt. 26:6
Jesus visits there .... Mark 11:1, 11, 12
Scene, Ascension .... Luke 24:50, 51

Beth-arabah—*house of desert*
A village of Judah .... Josh. 15:6, 61
Assigned to Benjamin .... Josh. 18:21, 22

Beth-aram—*a house of the height*
A town of Gad .... Josh. 13:27
Probably same as Beth-haran .... Num. 32:36

Beth-arbel—*house of God's ambush*
A town destroyed by Shalman .... Hos. 10:14

Beth-aven—*house of nothingness* (vanity)
A town of Benjamin .... Josh. 7:2
Israel defeated Philistines there .... 1 Sam. 13:5

Beth-baal-meon
City of Reuben .... Josh. 13:17

Beth-barah—*house of the ford*
A passage over Jordan .... Judg. 7:24

Beth-bire—*house of my creation*
A town of Simeon .... 1 Chr. 4:31
Probably same as Beth-lebaoth .... Josh. 19:6

Beth-car—*house of a lamb*
Site of Philistines' retreat .... 1 Sam. 7:11

Beth-dagon—*house of Dagon*
1. Village of Judah .... Josh. 15:41
2. Town of Asher .... Josh. 19:27

Beth-diblathaim—*house of fig cakes*
A Moabite town .... Jer. 48:21, 22

Beth-el—*house of God*
1. A town of Benjamin .... Judg. 21:19
   Abraham settles near .... Gen. 12:8
   Site of Abraham's altar .... Gen. 13:3, 4
   Scene of Jacob's ladder .... Gen. 28:10-18
   Luz becomes Bethel .... Gen. 28:19
   Jacob returns to .... Gen. 35:1-15
   On Ephraim's border .... Josh. 16:2
   Samuel judged there .... 1 Sam. 7:15, 16
   Site of worship and sacrifice .... 1 Sam. 10:3
   Center of idolatry .... 1 Kin. 12:28-33
   School of prophets .... 2 Kin. 2:1, 3
   Youths from, mock Elisha .... 2 Kin. 2:23, 24
   Denounced by a man of God .... 1 Kin. 13:1-10
   Denounced by Amos .... Amos 7:10-13
   Josiah destroys altars of .... 2 Kin. 23:4, 15-20
   Denounced by Jeremiah .... Jer. 48:13
   Denounced by Hosea .... Hos. 10:15
2. Simeonite town .... 1 Sam. 30:27
   Called Bethul and Bethuel .... Josh. 19:4; 1 Chr. 4:30

Beth-emek—*house of the valley*
A town of Asher .... Josh. 19:27

SUBJECT REFERENCE

Bether—*separation*
Designates mountains .... Song 2:17

Bethesda—*house of mercy*
Jerusalem pool .... John 5:2-4

Beth-ezel—*a place near*
A town of Judah .... Mic. 1:11

Beth-gader—*house of the wall*
A town of Judah .... 1 Chr. 2:51
Probably same as Geder .... Josh. 12:13

Beth-gamul—*house of recompense*
A Moabite town .... Jer. 48:23

Beth-haccerem—*house of the vineyard*
Town of Judah .... Jer. 6:1

Beth-haram—*mountain house*
A town of Gad .... Josh. 13:27
Same as Beth-haran .... Num. 32:36

Beth-hogla, Beth-hoglah—*house of the partridge*
A village of Benjamin .... Josh. 15:6; Josh. 18:19, 21

Beth-horon—*house of the hollow*
Twin towns of Ephraim .... Josh. 16:3, 5
The nether, built by Sherah, a woman .... 1 Chr. 7:24
Assigned to Kohathite Levites .... Josh. 21:20, 22
Fortified by Solomon .... 2 Chr. 8:5
Prominent in battles .... Josh. 10:10-14; 1 Sam. 13:18

Beth-jeshimoth—*house of the wastes*
A town near Pisgah .... Josh. 12:3
Israel camps near .... Num. 33:49
Assigned to Reubenites .... Josh. 13:20
Later a town of Moab .... Ezek. 25:9

Beth-lebaoth—*house of lionesses*
A town in south Judah; assigned to Simeonites .... Josh. 19:6
Called Lebaoth .... Josh. 15:32

Beth-lehem (of Judah)—*house of bread*
A. *Significant features of:*
   Built by Salma .... 1 Chr. 2:51
   Originally called Ephrath .... Gen. 35:16
   Burial of Rachel .... Gen. 35:19
   Two wandering Levites of .... Judg. 17:1-13; Judg. 19:1-30
   Naomi's home .... Ruth 1:1, 19
   Home of Boaz .... Ruth 4:9-11
   Home of David .... 1 Sam. 16:1-18
   Stronghold of Philistines .... 2 Sam. 23:14, 15
   Fortified by Rehoboam .... 2 Chr. 11:6
   Refuge of Gedaliah's murderers .... Jer. 41:17
B. *Messianic features of:*
   Sought for the tabernacle .... Ps. 132:6
   Predicted place of the Messiah's birth .... Mic. 5:2
   Fulfillment cited .... Matt. 2:1, 5
   Infants of, slain by Herod .... Jer. 31:15; Matt. 2:16-18

Beth-lehem (of Zebulun)
Town assigned to Zebulun .... Josh. 19:15, 16
Home of Judge Ibzan .... Judg. 12:8-11

Beth-maahah—*house of Maacah*
Tribe of Israel .... 2 Sam. 20:14, 15

Beth-marcaboth—*house of the chariots*
Town of Simeon .... Josh. 19:5

Beth-meon—*house of habitation*
Moabite town .... Jer. 48:23

Beth-nimrah—*house of the leopard*
Town of Gad .... Num. 32:3, 36

Beth-pazzez—*house of dispersion*
Town of Issachar .... Josh. 19:21

Beth-palet—*house of escape*
Town of Judah .... Josh. 15:27

Beth-peor—*house of Peor*
Town near Pisgah .... Deut. 3:29
Valley of Moses' burial place .... Deut. 34:6
Assigned to Reubenites .... Josh. 13:15, 20

SUBJECT REFERENCE

Bethphage—*house of unripe figs*
Village near Bethany .... Mark 11:1
Near Mt. of Olives .... Matt. 21:1

Beth-rapha—*house of a giant*
A town or family of Judah .... 1 Chr. 4:12

Beth-rehob—*house of a street*
A town in north Palestine .... Judg. 18:28
Inhabited by Syrians .... 2 Sam. 10:6

Bethsaida—*place of fishing*
A city of Galilee .... Mark 6:45
Home of Andrew, Peter and Philip .... John 1:44; John 12:21
Blind man healed .... Mark 8:22, 23
Near feeding of 5,000 .... Luke 9:10-17
Unbelief of, denounced .... Matt. 11:21; Luke 10:13

Beth-shan, Beth-shean—*house of security*
A town in Issachar .... Josh. 17:11
Assigned to Manasseh .... 1 Chr. 7:29
Tribute paid by .... Josh. 17:12-16
Users of iron chariots .... Josh. 17:16
Saul's corpse hung up at .... 1 Sam. 31:10-13; 2 Sam. 21:12-14

Beth-shemesh—*house of the sun*
1. A border town between Judah and Dan .... Josh. 15:10
   Also called Ir-shemesh .... Josh. 19:41
   Assigned to priests .... Josh. 21:16
   Ark brought to .... 1 Sam. 6:12-19
   Joash defeats Amaziah at .... 2 Kin. 14:11
   Taken by Philistines .... 2 Chr. 28:18
2. A town of Naphtali .... Josh. 19:38
3. A town of Issachar .... Josh. 19:22
4. Egyptian city .... Jer. 43:13

Beth-shittah—*house of the acacia*
A town in the Jordan valley .... Judg. 7:22

Beth-tappuah—*house of apples*
A town of Judah .... Josh. 15:53

Bethuel—*abode of God*
1. Father of Laban and Rebekah .... Gen. 22:20-23; Gen. 24:29
2. Simeonite town .... 1 Chr. 4:30
   Called Bethul .... Josh. 19:4

Beth-zur—*house of a rock*
A town of Judah .... Josh. 15:58
Fortified by Rehoboam .... 2 Chr. 11:7
Help to rebuild .... Neh. 3:16

Betonim—*pistachio nuts*
A town of Gad .... Josh. 13:26

Betrayal—*a breach of trust*
A. *Of Christ:*
   Predicted .... Ps. 41:9
   Frequently mentioned .... Matt. 17:22; John 13:21
   Betrayer identified .... John 13:26
   Sign of, a kiss .... Matt. 26:48, 49
   Guilt of .... Matt. 27:3, 4
   Supper before .... 1 Cor. 11:23
   Jewish nation guilty of .... Matt. 27:9, 10; Acts 7:52, 53
B. *Examples of:*
   Israelites by Gibeonites .... Josh. 9:22
   Samson by Delilah .... Judg. 16:18-20
   The woman of En-dor by Saul .... 1 Sam. 28:9-12
   Jesus by Judas .... Matt. 26:14, 15
   Christians .... Matt. 10:21

Betrothed—*given in marriage*
Treatment of .... Ex. 21:8, 9

Beulah—*married*
A symbol of true Israel .... Is. 62:4, 5

Beverage—*a drink*
A. *Literal:*
   Milk .... Judg. 4:19; Judg. 5:25
   Strong drink .... Prov. 31:6
   Water .... Matt. 10:42
   Wine .... 1 Tim. 5:23

SUBJECT	REFERENCE
B. *Figurative:*	
Christ's blood	John 6:53
Cup of suffering	John 18:11
Living water	John 4:10
Water of life	Rev. 22:17

Beware—*be wary of; guard against*

A. *Of evil things:*	
Strong drink	Judg. 13:4
False prophets	Matt. 7:15
Evil men	Matt. 10:17
Covetousness	Luke 12:15
Dogs (figurative)	Phil. 3:2
B. *Of possibilities:*	
Disobeying God	Ex. 23:20, 21
Forgetting God	Deut. 6:12
Being led away	2 Pet. 3:17

Bewitch—*to charm, captivate, or astound*

Activity of Simon	Acts 8:9-11
Descriptive of legalism	Gal. 3:1

Bezai—*shining, high*

Postexilic family head	Ezra 2:17 Neh. 7:23
Signs document	Neh. 10:18

Bezaleel—*in the shadow* (protection) *of God*

1. Hur's grandson	1 Chr. 2:20
Tabernacle builder	Ex. 31:1-11 Ex. 35:30-35
2. Divorced foreign wife	Ezra 10:18, 30

Bezek—*scattering*

1. Town near Jerusalem	Judg. 1:4, 5
2. Saul's army gathered there	1 Sam. 11:8

Bezer—*fortress*

1. An Asherite	1 Chr. 7:37
2. City of Reuben	Deut. 4:43
Place of refuge	Josh. 20:8

Bible history, outlined

A. *Pre-patriarchal period, the:*	
Creation	Gen. 1:1—2:25
Fall of man	Gen. 3:1-24
Development of wickedness	Gen. 4:1—6:8
Flood	Gen. 6:9—8:22
Establishment of nations	Gen. 9:1—10:32
Confusion of tongues	Gen. 11:1-32
B. *Patriarchal period:*	
Abraham	Gen. 12:1—25:11
Isaac	Gen. 21:1—28:9 Gen. 35:27-29
Jacob	Gen. 25:19—37:36 Gen. 45:21—46:7 Gen. 49:1-33
Joseph	Gen. 37:1—50:26
C. *Egypt and the Exodus:*	
Preparation of Moses	Ex. 1:1—7:7
Plagues and Passover	Ex. 7:8—12:36
From Egypt to Sinai	Ex. 12:37—18:27
The Law and tabernacle	Ex. 19:1—40:38
D. *Wilderness:*	
Spies at Kadesh-Barnea	Num. 13:1—14:38
Fiery serpents	Num. 21:4-9
Balak and Balaam	Num. 22:1—24:25
Appointment of Joshua	Num. 27:18-23
Death of Moses	Deut. 34:1-8
E. *Conquest and settlement:*	
Spies received by Rahab	Josh. 2:1-21
Crossing Jordan	Josh. 3:14-17
Fall of Jericho	Josh. 6:1-27
Southern and central mountains	Josh. 7:1-11
Victory at Merom	Josh. 11:1-14
Division of the land	Josh. 14:1—21:45
F. *Period of the judges:*	
Later conquests	Judg. 1:1—2:23
Othniel	Judg. 3:8-11
Ehud	Judg. 3:12-30
Shamgar	Judg. 3:31
Deborah and Barak	Judg. 4:1—5:31
Gideon	Judg. 6:11—8:35
Abimelech	Judg. 9:1-57
Tola and Jair	Judg. 10:1-5
Jephthah	Judg. 11:1—12:7
Ibzan, Elon, and Abdon	Judg. 12:8-15
Samson	Judg. 13:1—16:31
Tribal wars	Judg. 17:1—21:25
G. *From Samuel to David:*	
Eli and Samuel	1 Sam. 1:1—4:22
Samuel as judge	1 Sam. 5:1—8:22
The first king	1 Sam. 9:1—12:25
Battle of Michmash	1 Sam. 13:1—14:52
Saul and the Amalekites	1 Sam. 15:1-35
David chosen	1 Sam. 16:1-13
David and Goliath	1 Sam. 17:1-58
David in exile	1 Sam. 18:5—31:13
H. *Kingdom united:*	
David's reign at Hebron	2 Sam. 2:1—4:12
David's reign at Jerusalem	2 Sam. 5:1—10:19
David's sin	2 Sam. 11:1-25
Absalom's rebellion	2 Sam. 15:1—18:33
David's death	1 Kin. 2:10-12
Accession of Solomon	1 Kin. 1:32-53 1 Chr. 29:20-25
The Temple	1 Kin. 6:1—9:9 2 Chr. 2:1—7:22
Death of Solomon	1 Kin. 11:41-43 2 Chr. 9:29-31
I. *Kingdom divided:*	
Rebellion of Israel	2 Chr. 10:1-19
Rehoboam and Abijah	2 Chr. 10:1—13:22
Jeroboam and Nadab	1 Kin. 12:25—14:20 1 Kin. 15:25-31
Asa	1 Kin. 15:9-24 1 Chr. 14:1—16:14
Baasha, Elah, Zimri and Omri	1 Kin. 15:32—16:27
J. *Mutual alliance:*	
Ahab and Elijah	1 Kin. 16:28—18:19
Contest on Mount Carmel	1 Kin. 18:20-40
Ahab and Ben-hadad	1 Kin. 20:1-34
Murder of Naboth	1 Kin. 21:1-29
Revival under Jehoshaphat	1 Kin. 22:41-50 2 Chr. 17:1-19
Battle of Ramoth-gilead	1 Kin. 22:1-40 2 Chr. 18:1-34
Wars of Jehoshaphat	2 Chr. 19:1—20:30
Translation of Elijah	2 Kin. 2:1-11
Jehoshaphat and Jehoram	2 Kin. 3:1-27
Ministry of Elisha	2 Kin. 4:1—6:23 2 Kin. 8:1-15
Siege of Samaria	2 Kin. 6:24—7:20
Death of Elisha	2 Kin. 13:14-20
K. *Decline of both kingdoms:*	
Accession of Jehu	2 Kin. 9:1—10:31
Athaliah and Joash	2 Kin. 11:1—12:21
Amaziah and Jeroboam	2 Kin. 14:1-29
Captivity of Israel	2 Kin. 15:1-23
Reign of Hezekiah	2 Kin. 18:1—20:21 2 Chr. 29:1—32:33
Reign of Manasseh	2 Kin. 21:1-18 2 Chr. 33:1-20
Josiah's reforms	2 Kin. 22:1—23:30 2 Chr. 34:1—35:27
Captivity of Judah	2 Kin. 24:1—25:30 2 Chr. 36:5-21
L. *Captivity:*	
Daniel and Nebuchadnezzer	Dan. 1:1—4:37
Belshazzar and Darius	Dan. 5:1—6:28
Rebuilding the Temple	Ezra 1:1—6:15
Rebuilding Jerusalem	Neh. 1:1—6:19
Esther and Mordecai	Esth. 2:1—10:3
M. *Ministry of Christ:*	
Birth	Matt. 1:18-25 Luke 2:1-20
Childhood	Luke 2:40-52
Baptism	Matt. 3:13-17 Luke 3:21-23
Temptation	Matt. 4:1-11 Luke 4:1-13
First miracle	John 2:1-11
With Nicodemus	John 3:1-21
The Samaritan woman	John 4:5-42
Healing	Luke 4:31-41
Controversy on the Sabbath	Luke 6:1-11
Apostles chosen	Mark 3:13-19 Luke 6:12-16
Sermon on the Mount	Matt. 5:1—7:29 Luke 6:20-49
Raises dead son	Luke 7:11-17
Anointed	Luke 7:36-50
Accused of blasphemy	Matt. 12:22-37 Mark 3:19-30
Calms the sea	Matt. 8:23-27 Mark 4:35-41
Demoniac healed	Matt. 8:28-34 Mark 5:1-20
Daughter of Jairus healed	Matt. 9:18-26 Luke 8:41-56
Feeds 5,000	Matt. 14:13-21 Mark 6:30-44
Feeds 4,000	Matt. 15:32-39
Peter confesses Jesus is Christ	Matt. 16:5-16 Mark 8:27-29
Foretells death	Matt. 16:21-26 Luke 9:22-25
Transfiguration	Matt. 17:1-13 Luke 9:28-36
Forgiving of adulteress	John 7:53—8:11
Resurrection of Lazarus	John 11:1-44
Blesses the children	Matt. 19:13-15 Mark 10:13-16
Bartimaeus healed	Matt. 20:29-34 Mark 10:46-52
Meets Zacchaeus	Luke 19:1-10
Triumphant entry	Matt. 21:1-9 Luke 19:29-44
Anointed	Matt. 26:6-13 Mark 14:3-9
The Passover	Matt. 26:17-19 Luke 22:7-13
The Lord's Supper	Matt. 26:26-29 Mark 14:22-25
Gethsemane	Luke 22:39-46
Betrayal and arrest	Matt. 26:47-56 John 18:3-12
Before the Sanhedrin	Matt. 26:57-68 Luke 22:54-65
Denied by Peter	John 18:15-27
Before Pilate	Matt. 27:2-14 Luke 23:1-7
Before Herod	Luke 23:6-12
Returns to Pilate	Matt. 27:15-26 Luke 23:13-25
Crucifixion	Matt. 27:35-56 Luke 23:33-49
Burial	Matt. 27:57-66 Luke 23:50-56
Resurrection	Matt. 28:1-15 John 20:1-18
Appearance to disciples	Luke 24:36-43 John 20:19-25
Appearance to Thomas	John 20:26-31
Great commission	Matt. 28:16-20
Ascension	Luke 24:50-53
N. *The early church:*	
Pentecost	Acts 2:1-42
In Jerusalem	Acts 2:3—6:7
Martyrdom of Stephen	Acts 6:8—7:60
In Judaea and Samaria	Acts 8:1—12:25
Conversion of Saul	Acts 9:1-18
First missionary journey	Acts 13:1—14:28
Jerusalem conference	Acts 15:1-35
Second missionary journey	Acts 15:36—18:22
Third missionary journey	Acts 18:23—21:16
Captivity of Paul	Acts 21:27—28:31

Bichri—*first-born*

Father of Sheba	2 Sam. 20:1

Bidkar—*servant of Kar*

Captain under Jehu	2 Kin. 9:25

Bier—*a frame for carrying a corpse*

Abner's body borne on	2 Sam. 3:31

Bigamist—*having more than one wife*

First, Lamech	Gen. 4:19

Bigamy (See Marriage)

Bigotry—*excessive prejudice; blind fanaticism*

A. *Characteristics of:*	
Name-calling	John 8:48, 49
Spiritual blindness	John 9:39-41
Hatred	Acts 7:54-58
Self-righteousness	Phil. 3:4-6
Ignorance	1 Tim. 1:13
B. *Examples of:*	
Haman	Esth. 3:8-10
The Pharisees	John 8:33-48
The Jews	1 Thess. 2:14-16
Saul (Paul)	Acts 9:1, 2
Peter	Acts 10:14, 28

See Intolerance; Persecution

Bigtha—*gift of God*

An officer of Ahasuerus	Esth. 1:10

Bigthan, Bigthana—*gift of God*

Conspired against Ahasuerus	Esth. 2:21 Esth. 6:2

SUBJECT — REFERENCE

Bigvai—*happy*
1. Zerubbabel's companion ..... Ezra 2:2; Neh. 7:7, 19
2. One who signs covenant ..... Neh. 10:16

Bildad—*Bel has loved*
- One of Job's friends ..... Job 2:11
- Makes three speeches ..... Job 8:1-22; Job 18:1-21; Job 25:1-6

Bileam—*greed*
- A town of Manasseh ..... 1 Chr. 6:70

Bilgah—*brightness, cheerfulness*
1. A descendant of Aaron ..... 1 Chr. 24:1, 6, 14
2. A chief of the priests ..... Neh. 12:5, 7, 18
   - Same as Bilgai; signs document ..... Neh. 10:8
   - Called Bilgai ..... Neh. 10:8

Bilhah—*foolish, simple*
1. Rachel's maid ..... Gen. 29:29
   - The mother of Dan and Naphtali ..... Gen. 30:1-8
   - Commits incest with Reuben ..... Gen. 35:22
2. Simeonite town ..... 1 Chr. 4:29
   - Same as Baalah ..... Josh. 15:29

Bilhan—*foolish, simple*
1. A Horite chief; son of Ezer ..... Gen. 36:27; 1 Chr. 1:42
2. A Benjamite family head ..... 1 Chr. 7:10

Bilshan—*searcher*
- A postexilic leader ..... Ezra 2:2; Neh. 7:7

Bimhal—*with pruning*
- An Asherite ..... 1 Chr. 7:33

Binding—*a restraint; a tying together*

A. *Used literally of:*
- Tying a man ..... Gen. 22:9
- Imprisonment ..... 2 Kin. 17:4; Acts 22:4
- Ocean's shores ..... Prov. 30:4

B. *Used figuratively of:*
- A fixed agreement ..... Num. 30:2
- God's Word ..... Prov. 3:3
- The brokenhearted ..... Is. 61:1
- Satan ..... Luke 13:16
- The wicked ..... Matt. 13:30
- Ceremonialism ..... Matt. 23:4
- The keys ..... Matt. 16:19
- A determined plan ..... Acts 20:22
- Marriage ..... Rom. 7:2

Binea
- A son of Moza ..... 1 Chr. 8:37

Binnui—*built*
1. Head of postexilic family ..... Neh. 7:15
   - Called Bani ..... Ezra 2:10
2. Son of Pahath-moab ..... Ezra 10:30
3. Son of Bani ..... Ezra 10:38
4. Postexilic Levite ..... Neh. 12:8
   - Henadad's son ..... Neh. 10:9
   - Family of, builds wall ..... Neh. 3:24

Bird cage
- Used figuratively ..... Jer. 5:27

Birds—*vertebrates with feathers and wings*

A. *List of:*
- Cock ..... Matt. 26:34, 74; Mark 14:30; John 18:27; Luke 22:61
- Cormorant ..... Lev. 11:17
- Crane ..... Jer. 8:7
- Cuckoo ..... Lev. 11:16
- Dove ..... Gen. 8:8
- Eagle ..... Job 39:27
- Glede ..... Deut. 14:13
- Hawk ..... Job 39:26
- Hen ..... Matt. 23:37
- Heron ..... Lev. 11:19
- Kite ..... Deut. 14:13
- Lapwing ..... Lev. 11:19
- Ossifrage ..... Lev. 11:13
- Ostrich ..... Lev. 11:16
- Owls ..... Job 30:29
  - Desert ..... Ps. 102:6
  - Great ..... Lev. 11:17
  - Little ..... Lev. 11:17
- Partridge ..... 1 Sam. 26:20
- Peacock ..... 1 Kin. 10:22
- Pelican ..... Ps. 102:6
- Pigeon ..... Lev. 12:6
- Quail ..... Num. 11:31, 32
- Raven ..... Job 38:41
- Sparrow ..... Matt. 10:29-31
- Stork ..... Ps. 104:17
- Swallow ..... Ps. 84:3
- Turtledove ..... Song 2:12
- Vulture ..... Lev. 11:13

B. *Features regarding:*
- Created by God ..... Gen. 1:20, 21
- Named by Adam ..... Gen. 2:19, 20
- Clean, unclean ..... Gen. 8:20
- Differ from animals ..... 1 Cor. 15:39
- Under man's dominion ..... Ps. 8:8
- For food ..... Gen. 9:2, 3
- Belong to God ..... Ps. 50:11
- God provides for ..... Ps. 104:10-12; Luke 12:23, 24
- Can be tamed ..... James 3:7
- Differ in singing ..... Song 2:12
- Some migratory ..... Jer. 8:7
- Solomon writes of ..... 1 Kin. 4:33
- Clean, used in sacrifices ..... Lev. 1:14; Luke 2:24
- Worshiped by man ..... Rom. 1:23

C. *Figurative of:*
- Escape from evil ..... Ps. 124:7
- A wanderer ..... Prov. 27:8
- Snares of death ..... Eccl. 9:12
- Cruel kings ..... Is. 46:11
- Hostile nations ..... Jer. 12:9
- Wicked rich ..... Jer. 17:11
- Kingdom of heaven ..... Matt. 13:32
- Maternal love ..... Matt. 23:37

Birsha—*with wickedness*
- A king of Gomorrah ..... Gen. 14:2, 8, 10

Birth—*the act of coming into life*

A. *Kinds of:*
- Natural ..... Eccl. 7:1
- Figurative ..... Is. 37:3
- Supernatural ..... Matt. 1:18-25
- The new ..... John 3:5

See New birth

B. *Natural, features regarding:*
- Pain of, results from sin ..... Gen. 3:16
- Produces a sinful being ..... Ps. 51:5
- Makes ceremonially unclean ..... Lev. 12:2, 5; Luke 2:22
- Affliction from ..... John 9:1
- Twins of, differ ..... Gen. 25:21-23
- Sometimes brings death ..... Gen. 35:16-20
- Pain of, forgotten ..... John 16:21

Birthday—*date of one's birth*
- Job and Jeremiah curse theirs ..... Job 3:1-11; Jer. 20:14, 15

Celebration:
- Pharaoh's ..... Gen. 40:20
- Herod's ..... Mark 6:21

Birthright—*legal rights inherited by birth*

A. *Blessings of:*
- Seniority ..... Gen. 43:33
- Double portion ..... Deut. 21:15-17
- Royal succession ..... 2 Chr. 21:3

B. *Loss of:*
- Esau's—by sale ..... Gen. 25:29-34; Rom. 9:12
- Reuben's—as a punishment ..... Gen. 49:3, 4; 1 Chr. 5:1, 2
- Manasseh's—by Jacob's will ..... Gen. 48:15-20; 1 Chr. 5:1, 2
- David's brother—by divine will ..... 1 Sam. 16:2-22
- Adonijah's—by the Lord ..... 1 Kin. 2:15
- Hosah's son's—by his father's will ..... 1 Chr. 26:10

C. *Transferred to:*
- Jacob ..... Gen. 27:6-46
- Judah ..... Gen. 49:8-10
- Solomon ..... 1 Chr. 28:5-7

See First-born

Births, foretold

A. *Over a short period:*
- Ishmael's ..... Gen. 16:11
- Isaac's ..... Gen. 18:10
- Samson's ..... Judg. 13:3, 24
- Samuel's ..... 1 Sam. 1:11, 20
- Shunammite's son's ..... 2 Kin. 4:16, 17
- John the Baptist's ..... Luke 1:13

B. *Over a longer period:*
- Josiah's ..... 1 Kin. 13:2
- Cyrus' ..... Is. 45:1-4
- Christ's ..... Gen. 3:15; Mic. 5:1-3

Birzavith—*olive well*
- An Asherite ..... 1 Chr. 7:31

Bishlam—*in peace*
- A Persian officer ..... Ezra 4:7

Bishop—*an overseer; elder*

A. *Qualifications of, given by:*
- Paul ..... 1 Tim. 3:1-7
- Peter, called "elder" ..... 1 Pet. 5:1-4

B. *Duties of:*
- Oversee the church ..... Acts 20:17, 28-31
- Feed God's flock ..... 1 Pet. 5:2
- Watch over men's souls ..... Heb. 13:17
- Teach ..... 1 Tim. 5:17

C. *Office of:*
- Same as elder ..... Acts 20:17, 28
- Several in a church ..... Acts 20:17, 28; Phil. 1:1
- Follows ordination ..... Titus 1:5, 7
- Held by Christ ..... 1 Pet. 2:25

Bit—*a part of a horse's bridle*
- Figurative, of man's stubborn nature ..... Ps. 32:9; James 3:3

Bithiah—*daughter of Jehovah*
- Pharaoh's daughter; wife of Mered ..... 1 Chr. 4:18

Bith-ron—*ravine, gorge*
- A district east of Jordan ..... 2 Sam. 2:29

Bithynia—*a province of Asia Minor*
- The Spirit keeps Paul from ..... Acts 16:7
- Peter writes to Christians of ..... 1 Pet. 1:1

Bitter herbs
- Part of Passover meal ..... Ex. 12:8; Num. 9:11
- Descriptive of sorrow ..... Lam. 3:15

"Bitter is sweet"
- Descriptive of man's hunger ..... Prov. 27:7

Bittern—*a nocturnal member of heron family*
- Sings in desolate windows ..... Zeph. 2:14

Bitterness—*extreme enmity; sour temper*

A. *Kinds of:*
- The soul ..... Job 3:20
- The heart ..... Prov. 14:10
- Words ..... Ps. 64:3
- Death ..... 1 Sam. 15:32
- "Water of" ..... Num. 5:24

B. *Causes of:*
- Childlessness ..... 1 Sam. 1:10
- A foolish son ..... Prov. 17:25
- Demanding woman ..... Eccl. 7:26
- Sickness ..... Is. 38:17
- Sin ..... Prov. 5:4
- Death ..... Jer. 31:15
- Apostasy ..... Acts 8:23

C. *Avoidance of:*
- Toward others ..... Eph. 4:31
- Toward a wife ..... Col. 3:19
- As a source of defilement ..... Heb. 12:15
- As contrary to the truth ..... James 3:14

Bitter waters
- Made sweet by a tree ..... Ex. 15:23-25
- Swallowed by suspected wife ..... Num. 5:11-31

Bizjothjah—*contempt of Jehovah*
- A town in south Judah ..... Josh. 15:28

SUBJECT REFERENCE

Biztha—*eunuch*

An officer under Ahasuerus ... Esth. 1:10

Blackness—*destitute of light*

A. *Literally of:*
- Hair ... Song 5:11
- Skin ... Song 1:5
- Horse ... Zech. 6:2
- Sky ... 1 Kin. 18:45
- Mountain ... Heb. 12:18
- Night ... Prov. 7:9

B. *Figuratively of:*
- Affliction ... Job 30:30
- Mourning ... Jer. 8:21
- Foreboding evil ... Joel 2:6; Nah. 2:10
- Hell ... Jude 13

C. *Specifically:*
- Let blackness of the day ... Job 3:5
- Clothe heaven with ... Is. 50:3
- Shall gather ... Joel 2:6

Blains—*blisters full of pus*

The sixth plague on Egypt ... Ex. 9:8-11

Blamelessness—*freedom from fault; innocency*

A. *Used ritualistically of:*
- Priests ... Matt. 12:5
- Proper observance ... Luke 1:6
- Works, righteousness ... Phil. 3:6

B. *Desirable in:*
- Bishops (elders) ... 1 Tim. 3:2; Titus 1:6, 7
- Deacons ... 1 Tim. 3:10
- Widows ... 1 Tim. 5:7

C. *Attainment of:*
- Desirable now ... Phil. 2:15
- At Christ's return ... 1 Cor. 1:8; 1 Thess. 5:23; 2 Pet. 3:14

Blasphemy—*cursing God*

A. *Arises out of:*
- Pride ... Ps. 73:9, 11; Ezek. 35:12, 13
- Hatred ... Ps. 74:18
- Affliction ... Is. 8:21
- Injustice ... Is. 52:5
- Defiance ... Is. 36:15, 18, 20
- Scepticism ... Ezek. 9:8; Mal. 3:13, 14
- Self-deification ... Dan. 11:36, 37; 2 Thess. 2:4
- Unworthy conduct ... 2 Sam. 12:14; Rom. 2:24

B. *Instances of:*
- Job's wife ... Job 2:9
- Shelomith's son ... Lev. 24:11-16, 23
- Sennacherib ... 2 Kin. 19:4, 10, 22
- The beast ... Dan. 7:25; Rev. 13:1, 5, 6
- The Jews ... Luke 22:65
- Saul of Tarsus ... 1 Tim. 1:13
- Ephesians ... Rom. 2:9
- Hymenaeus ... 1 Tim. 1:20

C. *Those falsely accused of:*
- Naboth ... 1 Kin. 21:12, 13
- Jesus ... Matt. 9:3; Matt. 26:65
- Stephen ... Acts 6:11, 13

D. *Guilt of:*
- Punishable by death ... Lev. 24:11, 16
- Christ accused of ... John 10:33, 36

See Revile

Blasphemy against the Holy Spirit

Attributing Christ's miracles to Satan ... Matt. 12:22-32

Never forgivable ... Mark 3:28-30

Blasting—*injure severely*

Shows God's power ... Ex. 15:8

Sent as judgment ... Deut. 28:22; Amos 4:9

Figurative of death ... Job 4:9

Blastus—*sprout*

Herod's chamberlain ... Acts 12:20

SUBJECT REFERENCE

Blemish—*any deformity or injury*

A. *Those without physical:*
- Priests ... Lev. 21:17-24
- Absalom ... 2 Sam. 14:25
- Animals used in sacrifices ... Lev. 22:19-25; Mal. 1:8

B. *Those without moral:*
- Christ ... Heb. 9:14
- The Church ... Eph. 5:27

C. *Those with:*
- Apostates ... 2 Pet. 2:13

Bless—*to bestow blessings upon*

To give divine blessings ... Gen. 1:22; Gen. 9:1-7

To adore God for His blessings ... Gen. 24:48; Ps. 103:1

To invoke blessings upon another ... Gen. 24:60; Gen. 27:4, 27

Blessed—*the objects of God's favors*

A. *Reasons for, they:*
- Are chosen ... Eph. 1:3, 4
- Believe ... Gal. 3:9
- Are forgiven ... Ps. 32:1, 2
- Are justified ... Rom. 4:6-9
- Are chastened ... Ps. 94:12
- Keep God's Word ... Rev. 1:3

B. *Time of:*
- Eternal past ... Eph. 1:3, 4
- Present ... Luke 6:22
- Eternal future ... Matt. 25:34

Blessings—*the gift of God's grace*

A. *Physical and temporal:*
- Prosperity ... Mal. 3:10-12
- Food, clothing ... Matt. 6:26, 30-33
- Sowing, harvest ... Acts 14:17
- Longevity ... Ex. 20:12
- Children ... Ps. 127:3-5

B. *National and Israelitish:*
- General ... Gen. 12:1-3
- Specific ... Rom. 9:4, 5
- Fulfilled ... Rom. 11:1-36
- Perverted ... Rom. 2:17-29
- Rejected ... Acts 13:46-52

C. *Spiritual and eternal:*
- Salvation ... John 3:16
- Election ... Eph. 1:3-5
- Regeneration ... 2 Cor. 5:17
- Forgiveness ... Col. 1:14
- Adoption ... Rom. 8:15-17
- No condemnation ... Rom. 8:1
- Holy Spirit ... Acts 1:8
- Justification ... Acts 13:38, 39
- New covenant ... Heb. 8:6-13
- Fatherly chastisement ... Heb. 12:5-11
- Christ's intercession ... Rom. 8:34
- Sanctification ... Rom. 8:3-14
- Perseverance ... John 10:27-29
- Glorification ... Rom. 8:30

Blindfold—*a covering over the eyes*

A prelude to execution ... Esth. 7:8

Put on Jesus ... Luke 22:63, 64

Blindness—*destitute of vision*

A. *Causes of:*
- Old age ... Gen. 27:1
- Disobedience ... Deut. 28:28, 29
- Miracle ... 2 Kin. 6:18-20
- Judgment ... Gen. 19:11
- Captivity ... Judg. 16:20, 21
- Condition of servitude ... 1 Sam. 11:2
- Defeat in war ... 2 Kin. 25:7
- Unbelief ... Acts 9:8, 9
- God's glory ... John 9:1-3

B. *Disabilities of:*
- Keep from priesthood ... Lev. 21:18
- Offerings unacceptable ... Lev. 22:22; Mal. 1:8
- Make protection ... Lev. 19:14
- Helplessness ... Judg. 16:26
- Occasional derision ... 2 Sam. 5:6-8

C. *Remedies for:*
- Promised in Christ ... Is. 42:7, 16
- Proclaimed in the Gospel ... Luke 4:18-21; Acts 26:18
- Portrayed in a miracle ... John 9:1-41; Acts 9:1-18

SUBJECT REFERENCE

- Perfected in faith ... John 11:37; Eph. 1:18
- Perverted by disobedience ... 1 John 2:11

Blood

A. *Used to designate:*
- Unity of mankind ... Acts 17:26
- Human nature ... John 1:13
- Human depravity ... Ezek. 16:6, 22
- The individual soul ... Ezek. 33:8
- The essence of life ... Gen. 9:4; Lev. 17:11, 14
- The sacredness of life ... Gen. 9:5, 6
- Means of atonement ... Lev. 17:10-14
- Regeneration ... Is. 4:4; Ezek. 16:9; Joel 3:21
- New covenant ... Matt. 26:28
- The new life ... John 6:53-56
- Christ's atonement ... Heb. 9:14
- Redemption ... Zech. 9:11

B. *Miracles connected with:*
- Water turns to ... Ex. 7:20, 21
- Water appears like ... 2 Kin. 3:22, 23
- The moon turns to ... Acts 2:20; Rev. 6:12
- Flow of, stops ... Mark 5:25, 29
- Sea becomes ... Rev. 11:6
- Believers become white in ... Rev. 7:14

C. *Figurative of:*
- Sin ... Is. 59:3
- Cruelty ... Hab. 2:12
- Abominations ... Is. 66:3
- Guilt ... 2 Sam. 1:16; Matt. 27:25
- Inherited guilt ... Matt. 23:35
- Vengeance ... Ezek. 35:6
- Retribution ... Is. 49:25, 26
- Slaughter ... Is. 34:6-8
- Judgment ... Rev. 16:6
- Victory ... Ps. 58:10

Blood of Christ

A. *Described as:*
- Innocent ... Matt. 27:4
- Precious ... 1 Pet. 1:19
- Necessary ... Heb. 9:22, 23
- Sufficient ... Heb. 9:13, 14
- Final ... Heb. 9:24-28
- Cleansing ... 1 John 1:7
- Conquering ... Rev. 12:11

B. *Basis of:*
- Reconciliation ... Eph. 2:13-16
- Redemption ... Rom. 3:24, 25
- Justification ... Rom. 5:9
- Sanctification ... Heb. 10:29
- Communion ... Matt. 26:26-29
- Victory ... Rev. 12:11
- Eternal life ... John 6:53-56

Bloodguiltiness—*guilt incurred by murder*

Incurred by willful murderer ... Ex. 21:14

Not saved by altar ... 1 Kin. 2:29

Provision for innocent ... Ex. 21:13; 1 Kin. 1:50-53

David's prayer concerning ... Ps. 51:14

Judas' guilt in ... Matt. 27:4

The Jews' admission of ... Matt. 27:25

Figurative, of individual responsibility ... Ezek. 37:1-9

Of Christ-rejectors ... Acts 18:6

Blood money

Payment made to Judas ... Matt. 26:14-16

Bloody—*Descriptive of:*

Saul's house ... 2 Sam. 21:1

Crimes ... Ezek. 7:23

Cities ... Ezek. 22:2; Ezek. 24:6, 9

David ... 2 Sam. 16:7

Bloody sweat—(believed to be caused by agony or stress)

Agony in Gethsemane ... Luke 22:44

Blossom—*to open into blossoms; to flower*

Aaron's rod ... Num. 17:5, 8

A fig tree ... Hab. 3:17

A desert ... Is. 35:1, 2

Israel ... Is. 27:6

Blot—*to rub or wipe off*

One's name in God's Book ... Ex. 32:32, 33

SUBJECT	REFERENCE
One's sins	Ps. 51:1, 9 Acts 3:19
Legal ordinances	Col. 2:14
Amalek	Deut. 25:19
Israel as a nation	2 Kin. 14:27

Blue

Often used in tabernacle	Ex. 25:4 Ex. 28:15
Used by royalty	Esth. 8:15
Imported	Ezek. 27:7, 24

Blush—*to redden in the cheeks*

Sin makes impossible	Jer. 6:15 Jer. 8:12
Sin causes saints to	Ezra 9:6

Boanerges—*sons of thunder*

Surname of James and John	Mark 3:17

Boar—*male wild hog*

Descriptive of Israel's enemies	Ps. 80:13

Boasting—*to speak of with pride; to brag*

A. *Excluded because of:*

Man's limited knowledge	Prov. 27:1, 2
Uncertain issues	1 Kin. 20:11
Evil incurred thereby	Luke 12:19-21 James 3:5
Salvation by grace	Eph. 2:9
God's sovereignty	Rom. 11:17-21

B. *Examples of:*

Goliath	1 Sam. 17:44
Ben-hadad	1 Kin. 20:10
Rabshakeh	2 Kin. 18:27, 34
Satan	Is. 14:12-15 Ezek. 28:12-19

See Haughtiness; Pride

Boasting in God

Continual duty	Ps. 34:2
Always in the Lord	2 Cor. 10:13-18
Necessary to refute the wayward	2 Cor. 11:5-33
Of spiritual rather than natural	Phil. 3:3-14

Boats

In Christ's time	John 6:22, 23
In Paul's travel to Rome	Acts 27:16
Lifeboats	Acts 27:30
Ferryboats	2 Sam. 19:18

Boaz—*strength*

1. A wealthy Beth-lehemite	Ruth 2:1, 4-18
Husband of Ruth	Ruth 4:10-13
Ancestor of Christ	Matt. 1:5
2. Pillar of Temple	1 Kin. 7:21

Bocheru—*first-born*

A son of Azel	1 Chr. 8:38

Bochim—*weepers*

A place near Gilgal	Judg. 2:1-5

Body of Christ

A. *Descriptive of His own body:*

Prepared by God	Heb. 10:5
Conceived by the Holy Spirit	Luke 1:34, 35
Subject to growth	Luke 2:40, 52 Heb. 5:8, 9
Part of our nature	Heb. 2:14
Without sin	2 Cor. 5:21
Subject to human emotions	Heb. 5:7
Raised without corruption	Acts 2:31
Glorified by resurrection	Phil. 3:21
Communion with	1 Cor. 11:27

B. *Descriptive of the true church:*

Identified	Col. 1:24
Described	Eph. 2:16
Christ, the head of	Eph. 1:22
Christ dwells in	Eph. 1:23

Body of man

A. *By creation:*

Made by God	Gen. 2:7, 21
Various organs of	1 Cor. 12:12-25
Bears God's image	Gen. 9:6 Col. 3:10
Wonderfully made	Ps. 139:14

B. *By sin:*

Subject to death	Rom. 5:12
Destroyed	Job 19:26
Instrument of evil	Rom. 1:24-32

C. *By salvation:*

A Temple of the Holy Spirit	1 Cor. 6:19
A living sacrifice	Rom. 12:1
Dead to the Law	Rom. 7:4
Dead to sin	Rom. 8:10
Control over	Rom. 6:12-23
Christ, the center of	Rom. 6:8-11 Phil. 1:20
Sins against, forbidden	1 Cor. 6:13, 18
Needful requirements of	1 Cor. 7:4 Col. 2:23

D. *By resurrection, to be:*

Redeemed	Rom. 8:23
Raised	John 5:28, 29
Changed	Phil. 3:21
Glorified	Rom. 8:29, 30
Judged	2 Cor. 5:10-14
Perfected	1 Thess. 5:23

E. *Figurative descriptions of:*

House	2 Cor. 5:1
House of clay	Job 4:19
Earthen vessel	2 Cor. 4:7
Tabernacle	2 Pet. 1:13
Temple of God	1 Cor. 3:16, 17
Members of Christ	1 Cor. 6:15

Bohan—*thumb*

1. Reuben's son	Josh. 15:6
2. Border mark	Josh. 18:17

Boil—*an inflamed ulcer*

Sixth Egyptian plague	Ex. 9:8-11
A symptom of leprosy	Lev. 13:18-20
Satan afflicts Job with	Job 2:7
Hezekiah's life endangered by	2 Kin. 20:7

Boiling—*the state of bubbling*

A part of cooking	1 Kin. 19:21
Of a child, in famine	2 Kin. 6:29
Figurative, of trouble	Job 30:27

Boldness—*courage; bravery; confidence*

A. *Comes from:*

Righteousness	Prov. 28:1
Prayer	Eph. 6:19
Fearless preaching	Acts 9:27-29
Christ	Eph. 3:12 Phil. 1:20
Testimony	Phil. 1:14
Communion with God	Heb. 4:16
Perfect love	1 John 4:17

B. *Examples of:*

Tribe of Levi	Ex. 32:26-28
David	1 Sam. 17:45-49
Three Hebrew men	Dan. 3:8-18
Daniel	Dan. 6:10-23
The apostles	Acts 4:13-31
Paul	Acts 9:27-29
Paul, Barnabas	Acts 13:46

See Courage; Fearlessness

Bolled—*in bud, in seed*

Flax of Egypt	Ex. 9:31

Bondage, literal

Israel in Egypt	Ex. 1:7-22
Gibeonites to Israel	Josh. 9:23
Israel in Assyria	2 Kin. 17:6, 20, 23
Judah in Babylon	2 Kin. 25:1-21
Denied by Jews	John 8:33

Bondage, spiritual

A. *Subjection to:*

The devil	2 Tim. 2:26
Sin	John 8:34
Fear of death	Heb. 2:14, 15
Death	Rom. 7:24
Corruption	2 Pet. 2:19

B. *Deliverance from:*

Promised	Is. 42:6, 7
Proclaimed	Luke 4:18, 21
Through Christ	John 8:36
By obedience	Rom. 6:17-19
By the truth	John 8:32

Bones—*structural parts of the body*

A. *Descriptive of:*

Unity of male and female	Gen. 2:23
Human nature	Luke 24:39
Family unity	Gen. 29:14
Tribal unity	1 Chr. 11:1

B. *Prophecies concerning:*

The paschal lamb's	Ex. 12:46 John 19:36
Jacob's	Gen. 50:25 Heb. 11:22
Valley of dry	Ezek. 37:1-14

C. *Figurative of health, affected by:*

Shameful wife	Prov. 12:4
Good report	Prov. 15:30
Broken spirit	Prov. 17:22

Bonnet—*a headdress*

Used by priests	Ex. 28:40
Worn by women	Is. 3:20
Used by sons of Zadok	Ezek. 44:18

Books—*written compositions*

A. *Features of:*

Old	Job 19:23, 24
Made of paper reeds	Is. 19:7
Made of parchment	2 Tim. 4:13
Made in a roll	Jer. 36:2
Written with ink	3 John 13
Dedicated	Luke 1:3
Sealed	Rev. 5:1
Many	Eccl. 12:12
Quotations in	Matt. 21:4, 5
Written by secretary	Jer. 36:4, 18

B. *Contents of:*

Genealogies	Gen. 5:1
Law of Moses	Deut. 31:9, 24, 26
Geography	Josh. 18:9
Wars	Num. 21:14
Records	Ezra 4:15
Miracles	Josh. 10:13
Legislation	1 Sam. 10:25
Lamentations	2 Chr. 35:25
Proverbs	Prov. 25:1
Prophecies	Jer. 51:60-64
Symbols	Rev. 1:1
The Messiah	Luke 24:27, 44 Heb. 10:7

C. *Mentioned but not preserved:*

Book of wars	Num. 21:14
Book of Jasher	Josh. 10:13
Chronicles of David	1 Chr. 27:24
Book of Gad	1 Chr. 29:29
Story of prophet Iddo	2 Chr. 13:22
Book of Nathan	1 Chr. 29:29
Book of Jehu	2 Chr. 20:34

Book of God's judgment

In visions of Daniel and John	Dan. 7:10 Rev. 20:12

Book of the law

Called "the law of Moses"	Josh. 8:31, 32
Copied	Deut. 17:18
Placed in the ark	Deut. 31:26
Foundation of Israel's religion	Deut. 28:58
Lost and found	2 Kin. 22:8
Produces reformation	2 Kin. 23:2-14
Produces revival	Neh. 8:2, 8-18
Quoted	2 Kin. 14:6
To be remembered	Josh. 1:7, 8 Mal. 4:4
Prophetic of Christ	Luke 24:27, 44

Book of life

A. *Contains:*

The names of the saved	Phil. 4:3
The deed of the righteous	Mal. 3:16-18

B. *Excludes:*

Renegades	Ex. 32:33 Ps. 69:28
Apostates	Rev. 13:8 Rev. 17:8

C. *Affords, basis of:*

Joy	Luke 10:20
Hope	Heb. 12:23
Judgment	Dan. 7:10 Rev. 20:12-15

Booths—*stalls made of branches*

Used for cattle	Gen. 33:17
Required in feast of tabernacle	Lev. 23:40-43 Neh. 8:14-17

Booty—*spoils taken in war*

A. *Stipulations concerning:*

No Canaanites	Deut. 20:14-17

B

SUBJECT	REFERENCE
No cursed thing	Josh. 6:17-19
Destruction of Amalek	1 Sam. 15:2, 3
Destruction of Arad	Num. 21:1-3
The Lord's judgment	Jer. 49:30-32
B. *Division of:*	
On percentage basis	Num. 31:26-47
Rear troops share in	1 Sam. 30:24, 25

Border—*boundary*

A. *Marked by:*	
Natural landmarks	Josh. 18:16
Rivers	Josh. 18:19
Markers	Deut. 19:14
B. *Enlargement of:*	
By God's power	Ex. 34:24
A blessing	1 Chr. 4:10

Born again—*new birth, regeneration*

A. *Necessity of, because of:*	
Inability	John 3:3, 5
The flesh	John 3:6
Deadness	Eph. 2:1
B. *Produced by:*	
The Holy Spirit	John 3:5, 8 Titus 3:5
The Word of God	James 1:18 1 Pet. 1:23
Faith	1 John 5:1
C. *Results of:*	
New creature	2 Cor. 5:17
Changed life	Rom. 6:4-11
Holy life	1 John 3:9
Righteousness	1 John 2:29
Love	1 John 3:10
Victory	1 John 5:4

Borrow—*to get by loan*

A. *Regulations regarding:*	
From other nations, forbidden	Deut. 15:6 Deut. 28:12
Obligation to repay	Ex. 22:14, 15
Non-payment, wicked	Ps. 37:21
Involves servitude	Prov. 22:7
Evils of, corrected	Neh. 5:1-13
Christ's words on	Matt. 5:42
B. *Examples of:*	
Jewels	Ex. 11:2
A widow's vessels	2 Kin. 4:3
A woodsman's axe	2 Kin. 6:5
Christ's transportation	Matt. 21:2, 3

Bosom—*the breast as center of affections*

A. *Expressive of:*	
Procreation	Gen. 16:5
Prostitution	Prov. 6:26, 27
Anger	Eccl. 7:9
Procrastination	Prov. 19:24
Protection	Is. 40:11
Iniquity	Job 31:33
B. *Symbolic of:*	
Man's impatience	Ps. 74:11
Christ's deity	John 1:18
Eternal peace	Luke 16:22, 23

Bosor—*a lamp*

Father of Balaam	2 Pet. 2:15
Same as Beor	Num. 22:5

Botch—*a boil*

A punishment of disobedience	Deut. 28:27

Bottle—*a hollow thing* (vessel)

A. *Used for:*	
Milk	Judg. 4:19
Water	Gen. 21:14
Wine	Hab. 2:15
B. *Made of:*	
Clay	Jer. 19:1, 10, 11
Skins	Matt. 9:17 Mark 2:22
C. *Figurative of:*	
God's remembrance	Ps. 56:8
God's judgments	Jer. 13:12-14
Sorrow	Ps. 119:83
Impatience	Job 32:19
Clouds of rain	Job 38:37
Old and new covenants	Matt. 9:17

SUBJECT	REFERENCE

Bottomless pit

Apollyon, king of	Rev. 9:11
Beast comes from	Rev. 11:7 Rev. 17:8
Devil, cast into	Rev. 20:1-3
A prison	Rev. 20:7

Bough—*branch of a tree*

A. *Used:*	
To make ceremonial booths	Lev. 23:39-43
In siege of Shechem	Judg. 9:45-49
B. *Figurative of:*	
Joseph's offspring	Gen. 49:22
Judgment	Is. 17:1-11
Israel	Ps. 80:8-11
Nebuchadnezzar's kingdom	Dan. 4:10-12

Bow—*an instrument for shooting arrows*

A. *Uses of:*	
For hunting	Gen. 27:3
For war	Is. 7:24
As a token of friendship	1 Sam. 18:4
As a commemorative song	2 Sam. 1:18
B. *Illustrative of:*	
Strength	Job 29:20
The tongue	Ps. 11:2
Defeat	Hos. 1:5
Peace	Hos. 2:18, 19

Bowels

A. *Used literally of:*	
Intestines	Num. 5:22
Source of offspring	Gen. 15:4
Source of descendants	Gen. 25:23
Source of the Messiah	2 Sam. 7:12
Amasa's—shed out	2 Sam. 20:10
Jehoram's—fell out	2 Chr. 21:14-19
Judas'—gushed out	Acts 1:16-18
B. *Used figuratively of:*	
Natural love	Gen. 43:30
Deep emotion	Job 30:27
Intense suffering	Ps. 22:14
Great concern	Jer. 31:20
Spiritual distress	Lam. 1:20

Bowing the knee

A. *Wrong:*	
Before idols	Ex. 20:5
In mockery	Matt. 27:29
Before an angel	Rev. 22:8, 9
B. *True, in:*	
Prayer	1 Kin. 8:54
Homage	2 Kin. 1:13
Repentance	Ezra 9:5, 6
Worship	Ps. 95:6
Submission	Eph. 3:14 Phil. 2:10

Box—*a covered case*

Used for oil or perfume	2 Kin. 9:1 Matt. 26:7

Box tree—*an evergreen tree*

Descriptive of Messianic times	Is. 41:19, 20

Boy—*male child*

Esau and Jacob	Gen. 25:27
Payment for a harlot	Joel 3:3
Play in streets	Zech. 8:5
See Children; Young men	

Bozez—*shining*

Rock of Michmash	1 Sam. 14:4, 5

Bozkath, Boscath—*height*

A town in south Judah	Josh. 15:39
Home of Jedidah	2 Kin. 22:1

Bozrah—*fortress, sheepfold*

1. City of Edom	Gen. 36:33
Destruction of, foretold	Amos 1:12
Figurative, of Messiah's victory	Is. 63:1
2. City of Moab	Jer. 48:24

Bracelet—*ornament*

Worn by both sexes	Ezek. 16:11
Given to Rebekah	Gen. 24:22
In tabernacle offerings	Ex. 35:22
Worn by King Saul	2 Sam. 1:10
A sign of worldliness	Is. 3:19

SUBJECT	REFERENCE

Braided hair

Contrasted to spiritual adornment	1 Tim. 2:9, 10

Bramble—*a thorny bush*

Emblem of a tyrant	Judg. 9:8-15
Used for fuel	Ps. 58:9
Symbol of destruction	Is. 34:13

Branch—*a limb*

A. *Used naturally of:*	
Limbs of tree	Num. 13:23
B. *Used figuratively of:*	
A king	Ezek. 17:3-10
Israel	Rom. 11:16, 21
The Messiah	Is. 11:1
Christians	John 15:5, 6
Prosperity	Prov. 11:28
Adversity	Job 15:32

Brass—*an alloy of copper and zinc* (tin)

A. *Used for:*	
Tabernacle vessels	Ex. 38:2-31
Temple vessels	1 Kin. 7:41-46
Armor	2 Chr. 12:10
Mirrors, etc.	Ex. 38:8 Is. 45:2
Money	Matt. 10:9
B. *Workers in:*	
Tubal-cain	Gen. 4:22
Hiram	1 Kin. 7:14
Alexander	2 Tim. 4:14
C. *Figurative of:*	
Grecian Empire	Dan. 2:39
Obstinate sinners	Is. 48:4
Endurance	Jer. 15:20
God's decrees	Zech. 6:1
Christ's glory	Dan. 10:6 Rev. 1:15

Bravery, moral

Condemning sin	2 Sam. 12:1-14
Denouncing hypocrisy	Matt. 23:1-39
Opposing enemies	Phil. 1:28
Exposing inconsistency	Gal. 2:11-15
Uncovering false teachers	2 Pet. 2:1-22
Rebuking Christians	1 Cor. 6:1-8 James 4:1-11

Brawler—*a wrangler*

Descriptive of certain women	Prov. 21:9
Disqualifies bishops	1 Tim. 3:3

Brazen serpent

Occasion of ruin	2 Kin. 18:4

Breach—*a break*

A. *Used literally of:*	
Jerusalem's walls	Neh. 4:7
B. *Used figuratively of:*	
Sin	Is. 30:13

Bread—*food*

A. *God's provision for;*	
A gift	Ruth 1:6 2 Cor. 9:10
Earned by sweat	Gen. 3:19
Object of prayer	Matt. 6:11
Without work, condemned	2 Thess. 3:8, 12
B. *Uses of unleavened, for:*	
Heavenly visitors	Gen. 19:3
The Passover	Ex. 12:8
Priests	2 Kin. 23:9
Nazarites	Num. 6:13, 15
Lord's Supper	Luke 22:7-19
C. *Special uses of:*	
Provided by ravens	1 Kin. 17:6
Strength	1 Kin. 19:6-8
Satan's	Matt. 4:3
Miracle	Matt. 14:19-21
Insight	Luke 24:35
D. *Figurative of:*	
Adversity	Is. 30:20
Christ	John 6:33-35
Christ's death	1 Cor. 11:23-28
Communion with Christ	Acts 2:46 1 Cor. 10:17
Extreme poverty	Ps. 37:25
Prodigality	Ezek. 16:49
Wickedness	Prov. 4:17
Idleness	Prov. 31:27

SUBJECT — REFERENCE

E. *Bread of life:*
Christ is .... John 6:32-35
Same as manna .... Ex. 16:4, 5
Fulfilled in Lord's Supper ... 1 Cor. 11:23, 24

Breaking of bread—*a meal*
Prayer before .... Matt. 14:19
Insight through .... Luke 24:35
Fellowship thereby .... Acts 2:42
Strength gained by .... Acts 20:11
See Lord's Supper

Breastplate—*protection*
A. *Worn by:*
High priest .... Ex. 28:4, 15-20
Soldiers .... 1 Sam. 17:5, 38
"Locusts" .... Rev. 9:7, 9
B. *Figurative of:*
Christ's righteousness .... Is. 59:17
Faith's righteousness .... Eph. 6:14

Breasts—*the female teats*
A. *Literally of:*
Married love .... Prov. 5:19
Song 1:13
An infant's life .... Job 3:12
Ps. 22:9
Posterity .... Gen. 49:25
B. *Figuratively, of:*
Health .... Job 21:24
Mother Jerusalem .... Is. 66:10, 11

Breath
Comes from God .... Gen. 2:7
Necessary for all .... Eccl. 3:19
Held by God .... Dan. 5:23
Absence of, death .... Ps. 146:4
Taken by God .... Ps. 104:29
Figurative, of new life .... Ezek. 37:5-10

Breath of God
Cause of:
Creation .... 2 Sam. 22:16
Life .... Job 33:4
Destruction .... Is. 11:4
Death .... Job 4:9

Breeches—*garment*
Worn by priests .... Ex. 28:42

Brevity of human life
A. *Compared to:*
Pilgrimage .... Gen. 47:9
A tale .... Ps. 90:9
Sleep .... Ps. 90:5
Flower .... Job 14:2
Grass .... 1 Pet. 1:24
Vapor .... James 4:14
Shadow .... Eccl. 6:12
Moment .... 2 Cor. 4:17
A weaver's shuttle .... Job 7:6
B. *Truths arising from:*
Prayer can prolong .... Is. 38:2-5
Incentive to improvement .... Ps. 90:12
Some kept from old age .... 1 Sam. 2:32, 33
Some know their end .... 2 Pet. 1:13, 14
Hope regarding .... Phil. 1:21-25
Life's completion .... 2 Tim. 4:6-8

Bribery—*gifts to pervert*
A. *The effects of:*
Makes sinners .... Ps. 26:10
Corrupts conscience .... Ex. 23:8
Perverts justice .... Is. 1:23
Brings chaos .... Amos 5:12
Merits punishment .... Amos 2:6
B. *Examples of:*
Balak .... Num. 22:17, 37
Delilah .... Judg. 16:5
Samuel's sons .... 1 Sam. 8:3
Ben-hadad .... 1 Kin. 15:18, 19
Shemaiah .... Neh. 6:10-13
Haman .... Esth. 3:8, 9
Judas and priests .... Matt. 27:3-9
Soldiers .... Matt. 28:12-15
Simon .... Acts 8:18
Felix .... Acts 24:26

Brick—*baked clay*
Babel built of .... Gen. 11:3
Israel forced to make .... Ex. 1:14
Altars made of .... Is. 65:3
Forts made of .... Is. 9:10
Made in kiln .... 2 Sam. 12:31

Brickkiln—*a place for making bricks*
Forced labor in .... 2 Sam. 12:31

Bridal
Gift:
A burned city .... 1 Kin. 9:16
Veil:
Rebekah wears first .... Gen. 24:64-67

Bride—*newly wed woman*
Wears adornments .... Is. 61:10
Receives presents .... Gen. 24:53
Has damsels .... Gen. 24:59, 61
Adorned for husband .... Rev. 19:7, 8
Rejoices husband .... Is. 62:5
Stands near husband .... Ps. 45:9
Receives benediction .... Ruth 4:11, 12
Must forget father's house .... Ruth 1:8-17
Must be chaste .... 2 Cor. 11:2
Figurative of Israel .... Ezek. 16:8-14
Figurative of Church .... Rev. 21:2, 9

Bridegroom—*newly wed man*
Wears special garments .... Is. 61:10
Attended by friends .... John 3:29
Adorned with garlands .... Song 3:11
Rejoices over bride .... Is. 62:5
Returns with bride .... Matt. 25:1-6
Exempted from military service .... Deut. 24:5
Figurative of God .... Ezek. 16:8-14
Figurative of Christ .... John 3:29

Bridle—*a harness*
A. *Used literally of:*
An ass .... Prov. 26:3
B. *Used figuratively of:*
God's control .... Is. 30:28
Self-control .... James 1:26
Imposed control .... Ps. 32:9

Briers—*thorny shrub*
A. *Used literally of:*
Thorns .... Judg. 8:7, 16
B. *Used figuratively of:*
Sinful nature .... Mic. 7:4
Change of nature .... Is. 55:13
Rejection .... Is. 5:6

Brigandine—*a coat of mail*
Used as armor .... Jer. 46:4

Brimstone—*sulphur*
Falls upon Sodom .... Gen. 19:24
Sent as judgment .... Deut. 29:23
State of wicked .... Ps. 11:6
Condition of hell .... Rev. 14:10

Broiled fish
Eaten by Jesus .... Luke 24:42, 43

Broken-handed
Disqualifies for priesthood .... Lev. 21:19

Brokenhearted—*grieving*
Christ's mission to .... Is. 61:1

Brooks—*streams*
A. *Characteristics of:*
Numerous .... Deut. 8:7
Produce grass .... 1 Kin. 18:5
Abound in fish .... Is. 19:8
Afford protection .... Is. 19:6
B. *Names of:*
Arnon .... Num. 21:14, 15
Besor .... 1 Sam. 30:9
Gaash .... 2 Sam. 23:30
Cherith .... 1 Kin. 17:3, 5
Eschol .... Num. 13:23, 24
Kidron .... 2 Sam. 15:23
Kishon .... Ps. 83:9
Zered .... Deut. 2:13
C. *Figurative of:*
Wisdom .... Prov. 18:4
Prosperity .... Job 20:17
Deception .... Job 6:15
Refreshment .... Ps. 110:7

Broth—*thin, watery soup*
Served by Gideon .... Judg. 6:19, 20
Figurative of evil .... Is. 65:4

Brother, brethren
A. *Used naturally of:*
Sons of same parents .... Gen. 42:4
Common ancestry .... Gen. 14:16
Same race .... Deut. 23:7
Same humanity .... Gen. 9:5
B. *Used figuratively of:*
An ally .... Amos 1:9
Christian disciples .... Matt. 23:8
A spiritual companion .... 1 Cor. 1:1
C. *Characteristics of Christian brothers:*
One Father .... Matt. 23:8, 9
Believe .... Luke 8:21
Some weak .... 1 Cor. 8:11-13
In need .... James 2:15
Of low degree .... James 1:9
Disorderly .... 2 Thess. 3:6
Evil .... James 4:11
Falsely judge .... Rom. 14:10-21
Need admonishment .... 2 Thess. 3:15

Brotherhood of man
A. *Based on common:*
Creation .... Gen. 1:27, 28
Blood .... Acts 17:26
Needs .... Prov. 22:2
Mal. 2:10
B. *Disrupted by:*
Sin .... 1 John 3:12
Satan .... John 8:44

Brotherly kindness (love)
A. *Toward Christians:*
Taught by God .... 1 Thess. 4:9
Commanded .... Rom. 12:10
Explained .... 1 John 4:7-21
Fulfills the Law .... Rom. 13:8-10
Badge of new birth .... John 13:34
A Christian grace .... 2 Pet. 1:5-7
Must continue .... Heb. 13:1
B. *Toward others:*
Neighbors .... Matt. 22:39
Enemies .... Matt. 5:44

Brothers (brethren) of Christ
Four: James, Joses, Simon, Judas (Jude) .... {Matt. 13:55 / Mark 6:3}
Born after Christ .... Matt. 1:25
Luke 2:7
Travel with Mary .... Matt. 12:47-50
Disbelieve Christ .... John 7:4, 5
Become believers .... Acts 1:14
Work for Christ .... 1 Cor. 9:5
One (James) becomes prominent .... Acts 12:17
Wrote an epistle .... James 1:1
Another (Jude) wrote an epistle .... Jude

Brothers, Twin
Figureheads on Paul's ship to Rome, called Castor and Pollux .... Acts 28:11

Brought up—*reared*
Ephraim's children—by Joseph .... Gen. 50:23
Esther—by Mordecai .... Esth. 2:5-7, 20
Wisdom (Christ)—by the Lord .. Prov. 8:30
Jesus—at Nazareth .... Luke 4:16
Paul—at Gamaliel's feet .... Acts 22:3

Brow
The forehead .... Is. 48:4
Top of hill .... Luke 4:29

Bruised—*injured*
A. *Used literally of:*
Physical injuries .... Luke 9:39
B. *Used figuratively of:*
Evils .... Is. 1:6
The Messiah's pains .... Is. 53:5
Satan's defeat .... Gen. 3:15
Rom. 16:20

Bucket—*container for water*
Figurative of blessing .... Num. 24:7
Pictures God's magnitude .... Is. 40:15

SUBJECT REFERENCE

Buffet—*to strike with the fist*
- Jesus subjected to .... Matt. 26:67; Mark 14:65
- Descriptive of Paul .... 2 Cor. 12:7
- Figurative of self-discipline ..... 1 Cor. 9:27

Build—*construct or erect*
- A. *Used literally, of:*
  - City .... Gen. 4:17
  - Altar .... Gen. 8:20
  - Tower .... Gen. 11:4
  - House .... Gen. 33:17
  - Sheepfolds .... Num. 32:16
  - Fortifications .... Deut. 20:20; Ezek. 4:2
  - Temple .... 1 Kin. 6:1, 14; Ezra 4:1
  - High place .... 1 Kin. 11:7
  - Walls .... Neh. 4:6
  - Tombs .... Matt. 23:29; Luke 11:47
  - Synagogue .... Luke 7:2-5
- B. *Used figuratively, of:*
  - Obeying Christ .... Matt. 7:24-27
  - Church .... Matt. 16:18
  - Christ's resurrection .... Matt. 26:61; John 2:19
  - Return to legalism .... Gal. 2:16-20
  - Christian unity .... Eph. 2:19-22
  - Spiritual growth .... Acts 20:32; Col. 2:7; 1 Pet. 2:5

See Edification

Bukki
1. Danite chief .... Num. 34:22
2. A descendant of Aaron ...... 1 Chr. 6:5, 51

Bukkiah—*proved of Jehovah*
- A Levite musician .... 1 Chr. 25:4, 13

Bul—*growth*
- Eighth Hebrew month .... 1 Kin. 6:38

Bull—*male of any bovine animal*
- Used in sacrifices .... Heb. 9:13
- Blood of, insufficient .... Heb. 10:4
- Wild, trapped .... Is. 51:20
- Symbol of evil men .... Ps. 22:12
- Symbol of mighty men .... Ps. 68:30
- Restrictions on .... Deut. 15:19, 20
- Sacrifices of, inadequate .... Ps. 69:30, 31
- Blood of, unacceptable .... Is. 1:11
- Figurative of the Lord's sacrifice .... Is. 34:6, 7
- Figurative of strength .... Deut. 33:17

Bullock—*young bull*
- Used in sacrifices .... Ex. 29:1, 10-14
- Restrictions on .... Deut. 15:19, 20
- Sacrifices of, inadequate .... Ps. 69:30, 31
- Blood of, unacceptable .... Is. 1:11
- Figurative of the Lord's sacrifice .... Is. 34:6, 7
- Figurative of strength .... Deut. 33:17

Bulrush—*a reed*
- Used in Moses' ark .... Ex. 2:3
- Found in river banks .... Job 8:11
- Figurative of judgment .... Is. 9:14

Bulwark—*defensive wall*
- Around Jerusalem .... Ps. 48:13
- Used in wars .... Eccl. 9:14
- Made of logs .... Deut. 20:20
- Foundation of weapons .... 2 Chr. 26:15

Bunah—*intelligence*
- A descendant of Judah .... 1 Chr. 2:25

Bunni—*erected*
1. A pre-exilic Levite .... Neh. 11:15
2. A postexilic Levite .... Neh. 9:4
3. Signer of document .... Neh. 10:15

Burden—*load*
- A. *Used physically of:*
  - Load, cargo .... Neh. 4:17
- B. *Used figuratively of:*
  - Care .... Ps. 55:22
  - Prophet's message .... Hab. 1:1
  - Rules, rites .... Luke 11:46
  - Sin .... Ps. 38:4
  - Responsibility .... Gal. 6:2, 5
  - Christ's law .... Matt. 11:30

Burden-bearer
- Christ is the believer's .... Ps. 55:22

Burglarizing—*stealing*
- Severe penalty for .... Ex. 21:16

See Stealing; Theft, thief

Burial
- A. *Features regarding:*
  - Body washed .... Acts 9:37
  - Ointment used .... Matt. 26:12
  - Embalm sometimes .... Gen. 50:26
  - Body wrapped .... John 11:44
  - Placed in coffin .... Gen. 50:26
  - Carried on a bier .... Luke 7:14
  - Mourners attend .... John 11:19
  - Graves provided .... Gen. 23:5-20
  - Tombs erected .... Matt. 23:27-29
- B. *Places of:*
  - Abraham and Sarah .... Gen. 25:7-10
  - Deborah .... Gen. 35:8
  - Rachel .... Gen. 35:19, 20
  - Miriam .... Num. 20:1
  - Moses .... Deut. 34:5, 6
  - Gideon .... Judg. 8:32
  - Samson and Manoah .... Judg. 16:30, 31
  - Saul and his sons .... 1 Sam. 31:12, 13
  - David .... 1 Kin. 2:10
  - Joab .... 1 Kin. 2:33, 34
  - Solomon .... 1 Kin. 11:43
  - Rehoboam .... 1 Kin. 14:31
  - Asa .... 1 Kin. 15:24
  - Manasseh .... 2 Kin. 21:18
  - Amon .... 2 Kin. 21:23-26
  - Josiah .... 2 Chr. 35:23, 24
  - Jesus .... Luke 23:50-53
  - Lazarus .... John 11:14, 38

Buried alive
- Two rebellious families .... Num. 16:27-34
- Desire of some .... Rev. 6:15, 16

Burning bush
- God speaks from .... Ex. 3:2

Bushel—*a measurement*
- Mentioned by Christ .... Matt. 5:15

Business—*one's work*
- A. *Attitudes toward:*
  - See God's hand .... James 4:13
  - Be diligent .... Prov. 22:29
  - Be industrious .... Rom. 12:8, 11
  - Be honest .... 2 Cor. 8:20-22
  - Put God's first .... Matt. 6:33, 34
  - Keep heaven in mind .... Matt. 6:19-21
  - Give portion .... Mal. 3:8-12
  - Avoid anxiety .... Luke 12:22-30
  - Remember the fool .... Luke 12:15-21
- B. *Those diligent in:*
  - Joseph .... Gen. 39:11
  - Moses .... Heb. 3:5
  - Officers in Israel .... 2 Chr. 34:11, 12
  - Daniel .... Dan. 6:4
  - Mordecai .... Esth. 10:2, 3
  - Paul .... Acts 20:17-35

Busybodies—*meddlers*
- Women guilty of .... 1 Tim. 5:13
- Some Christians .... 2 Thess. 3:11, 12
- Admonitions against .... 1 Pet. 4:15

See Slander; Whisperer

Butler—*an officer*
- Imprisonment of Pharaoh's .... Gen. 40:1-13
- Same as "cupbearer" .... 1 Kin. 10:5

Butter—*curdled milk*
- Article of diet .... 2 Sam. 17:29
- Set before visitors .... Gen. 18:8
- Got by churning .... Prov. 30:33
- Fed to infants .... Is. 7:15, 22
- Illustrative of prosperity .... Deut. 32:14
- Figurative of smooth words .... Ps. 55:21

Buz—*contempt*
1. A Gadite .... 1 Chr. 5:14
2. An Aramean tribe descending from Nahor .... Gen. 22:20, 21

Buzi—*descendant of Buz*
- Father of Ezekiel .... Ezek. 1:3

Buzite—*belonging to Buz*
- Of the tribe of Buz .... Job 32:2

By and by—archaic expression meaning immediately or right away
- Quickly offended .... Matt. 13:21
- Rapid granting of a wish .... Mark 6:25
- Servant's duty .... Luke 7:7
- Signs of Christ's return .... Luke 21:9

Byway—*winding or secluded path*
- Used by travelers .... Judg. 5:6
- Figurative of error .... Jer. 18:15

Byword—*saying; remark*
- Predicted as a taunt .... Deut. 28:37
- Job describes himself .... Job 17:6

C

Cab
- A measure for dry things .... 2 Kin. 6:25

Cabbon—*surround*
- Village of Judah .... Josh. 15:40

Cabin—*a dungeon*
- Jeremiah's imprisonment in .... Jer. 37:16

Cabul—*unproductive*
1. Town of Asher .... Josh. 19:27
2. A district of Galilee offered to Hiram .... 1 Kin. 9:12, 13
   - Solomon placed people in .... 2 Chr. 8:2

Caesar—*a title of Roman emperors*
- A. *Used in reference to:*
  1. Augustus Caesar (31 B.C.—A.D. 14) Decree of brings Joseph and Mary to Bethlehem .... Luke 2:1
  2. Tiberius Caesar (A.D. 14-37) Christ's ministry dated by .... Luke 3:1-23
     - Tribute paid to .... Matt. 22:17-21
     - Jews side with .... John 19:12
  3. Claudius Caesar (A.D. 41-54) Famine in time of .... Acts 11:28
     - Banished Jews from Rome .... Acts 18:2
  4. Nero Caesar (A.D. 54—68) Paul appealed to .... Acts 25:8-12
     - Converts in household of .... Phil. 4:22
     - Paul before .... 2 Tim. 4:16-18
     - Called Augustus .... Acts 25:21
- B. *Represented Roman authority*
  - Image on coins .... Matt. 22:19-21; Mark 12:15-16; Luke 20:24
  - Received tax .... Matt. 22:19, 21; Mark 12:14, 17; Luke 20:25
  - Jesus called threat to .... Luke 23:2; John 19:12
  - Pilate's loyalty to, questioned .... John 19:12
  - Chosen over Jesus .... John 19:12

Caesar's household—*the imperial staff*
- Greeted the Philippians .... Phil. 4:22

Caesarea—*pertaining to Caesar*
- Roman capital of Palestine .... Acts 12:19; Acts 23:33
- Home of Philip .... Acts 8:40
- Home of Cornelius .... Acts 10:1
- Peter preached at .... Acts 10:34-43
- Paul preached here three times .... Acts 9:30; Acts 18:22; Acts 21:8
- Paul escorted to .... Acts 23:23, 33
- Paul imprisoned at .... Acts 25:4
- Paul appealed to Caesar at .... Acts 25:8-13

Caesarea Philippi
- A city in north Palestine; scene of Peter's great confession .... Matt. 16:13-20
- Probable place of the transfiguration .... Matt. 17:1-13

Cage—*an enclosure*
- Judah compared to .... Jer. 5:27
- Figurative of captivity .... Ezek. 19:9
- Babylon called .... Rev. 18:2

SUBJECT	REFERENCE
Caiaphas—*depression*	
Son-in-law of Annas; high priest	John 18:13
Makes prophecy	John 11:49-52
Jesus before	John 18:23, 24
Apostles before	Acts 4:1-22
Cain—*smith, spear*	
Adam's son	Gen. 4:1
Offering rejected	Gen. 4:2-7
	Heb. 11:4
Was of the evil one	1 John 3:12
Murders Abel	Gen. 4:8
Becomes a vagabond	Gen. 4:9-15
Builds city	Gen. 4:16, 17
A type of evil	Jude 11
Cainan—*fixed*	
A son of Arphaxad	Luke 3:36, 37
Cake—*a bread*	
A. *Kinds of:*	
Bread	Ex. 29:23
Unleavened	Num. 6:19
Fig	1 Sam. 30:12
Raisin	1 Chr. 16:3
Barley	Ezek. 4:12
Of fine flour	Lev. 2:4
Leavened	Lev. 7:13
Baked with oil	Num. 11:8
B. *Used literally of:*	
Food	2 Sam. 13:6
Idolatry	Jer. 44:19
Food prepared for Elijah	1 Kin. 17:13
C. *Used figuratively of:*	
Defeat	Judg. 7:13
Weak religion	Hos. 7:8
Calah	
A great city of Assyria built by Nimrod	Gen. 10:11, 12
Calamities—*disasters*	
A. *Kinds of:*	
Personal	Job 6:2
Tribal	Judg. 20:34-48
National	Lam. 1:1-22
Punitive	Num. 16:12-35
Judicial	Deut. 32:35
World-wide	Luke 21:25-28
Sudden	Prov. 6:15
	1 Thess. 5:3
B. *Attitudes toward:*	
Unrepentance	Prov. 1:24-26
Repentance	Jer. 18:8
Hardness of heart	Ex. 14:8, 17
Bitterness	Ruth 1:20, 21
Defeat	1 Sam. 4:15-18
Submission	Job 2:9, 10
Prayerfulness	Ps. 141:5
Hopefulness	Ps. 27:1-3
Calamus—*the sweet cane*	
Used in holy oil	Ex. 30:23
Figurative of love	Song 4:14
Rendered "sweet cane"	Jer. 6:20
Calcol, Chalcol	
A son of Zerah	1 Chr. 2:6
Famous for wisdom	1 Kin. 4:31
Caldron—*a large kettle*	
A. *Used literally of:*	
Temple vessels	2 Chr. 35:13
B. *Used figuratively of:*	
Leviathan's smoke	Job 41:20
Safety	Ezek. 11:3, 7, 11
Oppression	Mic. 3:3
Caleb—*dog; also bold*	
1. Son of Jephunneh	Josh. 15:13
Sent as spy	Num. 13:2, 6
Gave good report	Num. 13:27, 30
His life saved	Num. 14:10-12
Told to divide Canaan	Num. 34:17, 19
Entered Canaan	Num. 14:24-38
Eighty-five at end of conquest	Josh. 14:6-13
Given Hebron	Josh. 14:14, 15
	Josh. 15:13-16
Gave daughter to Othniel	Judg. 1:12-15
Descendants of	1 Chr. 4:15

SUBJECT	REFERENCE
2. Son of Hezron	1 Chr. 2:18, 42
3. A son of Hur	1 Chr. 2:50
Caleb-ephratah	
Hezron died at	1 Chr. 2:24
Calendar—*a system of dating*	
Year divided	1 Chr. 27:1-15
Determined by moon	Ps. 104:19
See Jewish calendar	
Calf—*the young of a cow*	
A. *Characteristics of:*	
Playfulness of	Ps. 29:6
Used for food	Amos 6:4
A delicacy	Luke 15:23, 27
In sacrifice	Lev. 9:2, 3
Redeemed, if first-born	Num. 18:17
B. *Figurative of:*	
Praise	Hos. 14:2
Saints sanctified	Mal. 4:2
Patience	Ezek. 1:7
Calf, Calves of Gold	
A. *Making of:*	
Inspired by Moses' delay	Ex. 32:1-4
Repeated by Jeroboam	1 Kin. 12:25-28
To represent God	Ex. 32:4, 5
To replace Temple worship	1 Kin. 12:26, 27
Priests appointed for	1 Kin. 12:31
Sacrifices offered to	Ex. 32:6
	1 Kin. 12:32, 33
B. *Sin of:*	
Immorality	1 Cor. 10:7
Great	Ex. 32:21, 30, 31
An apostasy	Ex. 32:8
Wrathful	Deut. 9:14-20
Brings punishment	Ex. 32:26-29, 35
Repeated by Jeroboam	Hos. 8:5, 6
Calker—*a sealer*	
Used on Tyrian vessels	Ezek. 27:9, 27
Call	
To:	
Name	Gen. 1:5
Pray	Gen. 4:26
Be in reality	Luke 1:35
Set in office	Ex. 31:2
	Is. 22:20
Give privileges	Luke 14:16, 17
Offer salvation	Matt. 9:13
Engage in work	1 Cor. 7:20
Calling—*one's vocation*	
Faith and one's	1 Cor. 7:20-22
Calling, the Christian	
A. *Manifested through:*	
Christ	Matt. 9:13
Holy Spirit	Rev. 22:17
Gospel	2 Thess. 2:14
B. *Described as:*	
Heavenly	Heb. 3:1
Holy	2 Tim. 1:9
High	Phil. 3:14
Unchangeable	Rom. 11:29
By grace	Gal. 1:15
	2 Tim. 1:9
According to God's purpose	2 Tim. 1:9
C. *Goals of:*	
Fellowship with Christ	1 Cor. 1:9
Holiness	1 Thess. 4:7
Liberty	Gal. 5:13
Peace	1 Cor. 7:15
Glory and virtue	2 Pet. 1:3
Eternal glory	2 Thess. 2:14
Eternal life	1 Tim. 6:12
D. *Attitudes toward:*	
Walk worthy of	Eph. 4:1
Make it sure	2 Pet. 1:10
Of Gentiles	Eph. 4:19
Calneh—*fort of Ana*	
1. Nimrod's city	Gen. 10:9, 10
2. A city linked with Hamath and Gath	Amos 6:2
Same as Calno	Is. 10:9

SUBJECT	REFERENCE
Calvary—*from the Latin "calvaria"* (skull)	
Christ was crucified there	Luke 23:33
Same as "Golgotha" in Hebrew	John 19:17
Camel—*humpbacked animal*	
A. *Used for:*	
Riding	Gen. 24:61, 64
Trade	Gen. 37:25
War	Judg. 7:12
Hair of, for clothing	Matt. 3:4
Used for garment worn by John the Baptist	Matt. 3:4
Wealth	Job 42:12
B. *Features of:*	
Swift	Jer. 2:23
Docile	Gen. 24:11
Unclean	Lev. 11:4
Adorned	Judg. 8:21, 26
Prize for booty	Job 1:17
Treated well	Gen. 24:31, 32
Illustrative of the impossible	Matt. 19:24
Camon—*elevation*	
Jair was buried there	Judg. 10:5
Camp—*to pitch a tent*	
A. *The Lord's guidance of, by:*	
An angel	Ex. 14:19
	Ex. 32:34
His presence	Ex. 33:14
A cloud	Ps. 105:39
B. *Israel's:*	
On leaving Egypt	Ex. 13:20
At Sinai	Ex. 18:5
Orderly	Num. 2:2-34
Tabernacle in center of	Num. 2:17
C. *Exclusion of:*	
Unclean	Deut. 23:10-12
Lepers	Lev. 13:46
Dead	Lev. 10:4, 5
Executions outside	Lev. 24:23
Log kept of	Num. 33:1-49
In battle	Josh. 10:5, 31, 34
D. *Spiritual significance of.*	
Christ's crucifixion outside	Heb. 13:13
God's people	Rev. 20:9
Camphire—*henna, a fragrant shrub*	
Illustrative of beauty	Song 1:14
Cana of Galilee	
A village of upper Galilee; home of Nathanael	John 21:2
Christ's first miracle at	John 2:1-11
Healing at	John 4:46-54
Canaan—*low*	
1. A son of Ham	Gen. 10:6
Cursed by Noah	Gen. 9:20-25
2. Promised land	Gen. 12:5
Canaan, Land of	
A. *Specifications regarding:*	
Boundaries	Gen. 10:19
Fertility	Ex. 3:8, 17
Seven nations	Deut. 7:1
Language	Is. 19:18
B. *God's promises concerning, given to:*	
Abraham	Gen. 12:1-3
Isaac	Gen. 26:2, 3
Jacob	Gen. 28:13
Israel	Ex. 3:8
C. *Conquest of:*	
Announced	Gen. 15:7-21
Preceded by spies	Num. 13:1-33
Delayed by unbelief	Num. 14:1-35
Accomplished by the Lord	Josh. 23:1-16
Done only in part	Judg. 1:21, 27-36
Canaan, names of	
Canaan	Gen. 11:31
Land of Hebrews	Gen. 40:15
Palestine	Ex. 15:14
Land of Israel	1 Sam. 13:19
Immanuel's land	Is. 8:8
Beulah	Is. 62:4
Pleasant	Dan. 8:9
The Lord's land	Hos. 9:3
Holy land	Zech. 2:12

C

SUBJECT	REFERENCE
Land of the Jews	Acts 10:39
Land of promise	Heb. 11:9

Canaanites—*original inhabitants of Palestine*

A. *Described as:*

Descendants of Ham	Gen. 10:5, 6
Under a curse	Gen. 9:25, 26
Amorites	Gen. 15:16
Seven nations	Deut. 7:1
Fortified	Num. 13:28
Idolatrous	Deut. 29:17
Defiled	Lev. 18:24-27

B. *Destruction of:*

Commanded by God	Ex. 23:23, 28-33
Caused by wickedness	Deut. 9:4
In God's time	Gen. 15:13-16
Done in degrees	Ex. 23:29, 30

C. *Commands prohibiting:*

Common league with	Deut. 7:2
Intermarriage with	Deut. 7:3
Idolatry of	Ex. 23:24
Customs of	Lev. 18:24-27

Canaanites—*a Jewish sect*

"Simon the Canaanite"	Matt. 10:4
Woman from that region	Matt. 15:22
Called Zelotes	Luke 6:15

Candace—*dynastic title of Ethiopian queens*

Conversion of eunuch of	Acts 8:27-39

Candle—*a light*

A. *Used literally of:*

Household lights	Matt. 5:15

B. *Used figuratively of:*

Conscience	Prov. 20:27
Prosperity	Job 29:3
Industry	Prov. 31:18
Death	Job 18:6
God's justice	Zeph. 1:12

Candlestick, The Golden

A. *Specifications regarding:*

Made of gold	Ex. 25:31
After a divine model	Ex. 25:31-40
Set in holy place	Heb. 9:2
Continual burning of	Ex. 27:20, 21
Carried by Kohathites	Num. 4:4, 15
Temple's ten branches of	1 Kin. 7:49, 50
Taken to Babylon	Jer. 52:19

B. *Used figuratively of:*

Christ	Zech. 4:2, 11
The church	Rev. 1:13, 20

Cane—*a tall sedgy grass*

Used in sacrifices	Is. 43:24 Jer. 6:20
Used in holy oil	Ex. 30:23
Trading city	Ezek. 27:23

Cankerworm—*a caterpillar-like insect*

Sent as judgment	Joel 1:4
Large appetite of	Nah. 3:15

Cannibalism—*using human flesh as food*

Predicted as a judgment	Deut. 28:53-57
Fulfilled in a siege	2 Kin. 6:28, 29

Capacity—*ability to perform*

Hindered by sin	Gal. 5:17
Fulfilled in Christ	Phil. 4:13

Capernaum—*village of Nahum*

A. *Scene of Christ's healing of:*

Centurion's servant	Matt. 8:5-13
Nobleman's son	John 4:46-54
Peter's mother-in-law	Matt. 8:14-17
The demoniac	Mark 1:21-28
The paralytic	Matt. 9:1-8
Various diseases	Matt. 8:16, 17

B. *Other events connected with:*

Jesus' headquarters	Matt. 4:13-17
Simon Peter's home	Mark 1:21, 29
Jesus' sermon on the Bread of Life	John 6:24-71
Other important messages	Mark 9:33-50
Judgment pronounced upon	Matt. 11:23, 24

Caph

Eleventh letter of Hebrew alphabet	Ps. 119:81-88

SUBJECT	REFERENCE

Caphtor—*cup*

The place (probably Crete) from which the Philistines came to Palestine	Jer. 47:4

Caphtorim

Those of Caphtor	Deut. 2:23
Descendants of Mizraim	Gen. 10:13, 14
Conquerors of the Avim	Deut. 2:23

Capital punishment—*the death penalty*

A. *Institution of:*

By God	Gen. 9:5, 6 Ex. 21:12-17

B. *Crimes punished by:*

Murder	Gen. 9:5, 6
Adultery	Lev. 20:10
Incest	Lev. 20:11-14
Sodomy	Lev. 20:13
Rape	Deut. 22:25
Witchcraft	Ex. 22:18
Disobedience to parents	Ex. 21:18-21
Blasphemy	Lev. 24:11-16, 23
False doctrines	Deut. 13:1-10

Cappadocia—*a province of Asia Minor*

Natives of, at Pentecost	Acts 2:1, 9
Christians of, addressed by Peter	1 Pet. 1:1

Captain—*a civil or military officer*

A. *Applied literally to:*

Tribal heads	Num. 2:3, 5
Military leader	Judg. 4:2
King Saul	1 Sam. 9:15, 16
Potiphar	Gen. 37:36
David as leader	1 Sam. 22:2
David as king	2 Sam. 5:2
Temple police head	Luke 22:4
Roman officer	Acts 21:31

B. *Applied spiritually to:*

Angel of the Lord	Josh. 5:14

Captain, chief of the Temple—*priest who kept order*

Conspired with Judas	Luke 22:3, 4
Arrested Jesus	Luke 22:52-54
Arrested apostles	Acts 5:24-26

Captive—*an enslaved person*

A. *Good treatment of:*

Compassion	Ex. 6:4-8
Kindness	2 Chr. 28:15
Mercy	2 Kin. 6:21-23

B. *Bad treatment of:*

Tortured	2 Sam. 12:31
Blinded	Judg. 16:21
Maimed	Judg. 1:6, 7
Ravished	Lam. 5:11-13
Enslaved	2 Kin. 5:2
Killed	1 Sam. 15:32, 33

C. *Applied figuratively to those:*

Under Satan	2 Tim. 2:26
Under sin	2 Tim. 3:6
Liberated by Christ	Luke 4:18

Captivity—*a state of bondage; enslavement*

A. *Foretold regarding:*

Hebrews in Egypt	Gen. 15:13, 14
Israelites	Deut. 28:36-41
Ten tribes (Israel)	Amos 7:11
Judah	Is. 39:6

B. *Fulfilled:*

In Egypt	Ex. 1:11-14
In many captivities	Judg. 2:14-23
In Assyria	2 Kin. 17:6-24
In Babylon	2 Kin. 24:11-16
Under Rome	John 19:15

C. *Causes of:*

Disobedience	Deut. 28:36-68
Idolatry	Amos 5:26, 27
Breaking Sabbatic law	2 Chr. 36:20, 21

Caravan—*a group traveling together*

Ishmaelite traders	Gen. 37:25
Jacob's family	Gen. 46:5, 6
Jacob's funeral	Gen. 50:7-14
Queen of Sheba	1 Kin. 10:1, 2
Returnees from exile	Ezra 8:31

Carbuncle—*a precious gem*

In high priest's garment	Ex. 28:17

SUBJECT	REFERENCE
Figuratively of glory	Is. 54:12
Descriptive of Tyre's beauty	Ezek. 28:12, 13

Carcas—*severe*

Eunuch under Ahasuerus	Esth. 1:10

Carcase—*a dead body*

A. *Used literally of:*

Sacrificial animals	Gen. 15:9, 11
Unclean beasts	Lev. 5:2
Lion	Judg. 14:8
Men	Deut. 28:25, 26
Idols	Jer. 16:18

B. *Aspects of:*

Makes unclean	Lev. 11:39
Food for birds	Jer. 16:4

Carchemish

Eastern capital of Hittites on the Euphrates	2 Chr. 35:20
Conquered by Sargon II	Is. 10:9
Josiah wounded here	2 Chr. 35:20-24

Care, carefulness—*wise and provident concern*

A. *Natural concern for:*

Children	Luke 2:44-49
Duties	Luke 10:40
Mate	1 Cor. 7:32-34
Health	Is. 38:1-22
Life	Mark 4:38
Possessions	Gen. 33:12-17

B. *Spiritual concern for:*

Duties	Phil. 2:20
Office	1 Tim. 3:6-8
A minister's needs	Phil. 4:10-12
The flock of God	John 10:11 1 Pet. 5:2, 3
Churches	2 Cor. 11:28
Christians	1 Cor. 12:25
Spiritual things	Acts 18:17

Care, divine—*God's concern for His creatures*

For the world	Ps. 104:1-10
For animals	Ps. 104:11-30
For pagans	Jon. 4:11
For Christians	Matt. 6:25-34
Babylon	Is. 47:1, 8-11
Ethiopians	Ezek. 30:9
Gallio	Acts 18:17
Inhabitants of coastlands	Ezek. 39:6
Moab	Jer. 48:10-17
Nineveh	Zeph. 2:10-15
Those at ease in Zion	Amos 6:1
Women of Jerusalem	Is. 32:9-11

Careah—*made bold*

Father of Johanan	2 Kin. 25:23
Same as Kareah	Jer. 40:8

Cares, worldly—*overmuch concern for earthly things*

A. *Evils of:*

Chokes the Word	Matt. 13:7, 22
Gluts the soul	Luke 21:34
Obstructs the Gospel	Luke 14:18-20
Hinders Christ's work	2 Tim. 2:4
Manifests unbelief	Matt. 6:25-32

B. *Antidotes for God's:*

Protection	Ps. 37:5-11
Provision	Matt. 6:25-34
Promises	Phil. 4:6, 7

Carelessness—*lack of proper concern*

Babylon	Is. 47:8-11
Ethiopians	Ezek. 30:9
Islanders	Ezek. 39:6
Nineveh	Zeph. 2:15
Women of Jerusalem	Is. 32:9-11

Carmel—*field, park, garden*

1. Rendered as:

"Fruitful field"	Is. 10:18
"Plentiful field"	Is. 16:10
"Plentiful country"	Jer. 2:7

2. City of Judah

City of Judah	Josh. 15:55
Site of Saul's victory	1 Sam. 15:12
Home of David's wife	1 Sam. 27:3

3. A mountain of Palestine

A mountain of Palestine	Josh. 19:26
Joshua defeated king there	Josh. 12:22
Scene of Elijah's triumph	1 Kin. 18:19-45
Elisha visits	2 Kin. 2:25
Place of beauty	Song 7:5
Figurative of strength	Jer. 46:18
Barrenness foretold	Amos 1:2

SUBJECT — REFERENCE

Carmelite, Carmelitess
Nabal ... 1 Sam. 30:5; 2 Sam. 2:2
Hezro ... 2 Sam. 23:35
Abigail ... 1 Sam. 27:3

Carmi—*vinedresser*
1. Son of Reuben ... Gen. 46:9
2. Father of Achan ... Josh. 7:1

Carnal—*fleshly, worldly*
Used literally of:
Sexual relations ... Lev. 19:20
Paul calls himself ... Rom. 7:14
Gentiles ministered in ... Rom. 15:27
Paul calls brethren at Corinth ... 1 Cor. 3:1, 3
Things not spiritual called ... 1 Cor. 9:11

Carob pod—*seedcase of the carob, or locust tree*
Rendered "husk"; fed to swine ... Luke 15:16

Carpenter—*a skilled woodworker*
David's house built by ... 2 Sam. 5:11
Temple repaired by ... 2 Chr. 24:12
Idols made by ... Is. 44:13
Temple restored by ... Ezra 3:7
Joseph works as ... Matt. 13:55

Carpenter tools—*implements for the carpenter trade*
Axe ... Deut. 19:5
Hammer ... Jer. 23:29
Line ... Zech. 2:1
Nail ... Jer. 10:4
Saw ... 1 Kin. 7:9

Carpus—*fruit*
Paul's friend at Troas ... 2 Tim. 4:13

Carriage (outdated word for baggage)
Goods, provisions ... 1 Sam. 17:22
An army's baggage ... Is. 10:28
Heavy goods ... Judg. 18:21
A vehicle ... Is. 46:1

Carrion vulture
Unclean bird ... Lev. 11:18

Carshena—*plowman*
Prince of Persia ... Esth. 1:14

Cart—*a wagon*
Made of wood ... 1 Sam. 6:14
Sometimes covered ... Num. 7:3
Drawn by cows ... 1 Sam. 6:7
Used in threshing ... Is. 28:28
Used for hauling ... Amos 2:13
Ark carried by ... 2 Sam. 6:3
Figurative of sin ... Is. 5:18

Carving—*cutting figures in wood or stone*
Used in worship ... Ex. 31:1-7
Found in homes ... 1 Kin. 6:18
Employed by idolators ... Judg. 18:18
Used in the Temple ... 1 Kin. 6:35

Casement—*lattice, criss-crossed strips of wood or metal*
Looked through ... Prov. 7:6

Casiphia—*silvery*
Home of exiled Levites ... Ezra 8:17

Casluhim
A tribe descended from Mizraim ... Gen. 10:14
Descendant of Ham ... 1 Chr. 1:8, 12

Cassia—*amber*
An ingredient of holy oil ... Ex. 30:24, 25
An article of commerce ... Ezek. 27:19
Noted for fragrance ... Ps. 45:8

Castaway—*worthless; reprobated*
The rejected ... Matt. 25:30; 2 Pet. 2:4
Warning concerning ... 1 Cor. 9:27

Caste—*divisions of society*
Some leaders of low ... Judg. 11:1-11
David aware of ... 1 Sam. 18:18, 23
Jews and Samaritans observe ... John 4:9
Abolished ... Acts 10:28-35

Castle—*fortress, tower*
A. *Used literally of:*
King's residence ... 2 Kin. 15:25
An encampment ... Gen. 25:16
A tower for guards ... 1 Chr. 6:54
Barracks for soldiers ... Acts 21:34
A fortress ... 1 Chr. 11:7
David conquers Jebusite ... 1 Chr. 11:5, 7
B. *Used figuratively of:*
Offended brother ... Prov. 18:19

Castor and Pollux—*sons of Jupiter*
Gods in Greek and Roman mythology; figureheads on Paul's ship to Rome ... Acts 28:11

Castration—*removal of male testicles*
Disqualified for congregation ... Deut. 23:1
Rights restored in new covenant ... Is. 56:3-5
Figurative of absolute devotion ... Matt. 19:12

Caterpillar—*an insect living on vegetation*
Works with locust ... Is. 33:4
Devours land ... Amos 4:9

Cattle—*animals* (collectively)
Created by God ... Gen. 1:24
Adam named ... Gen. 2:20
Entered the ark ... Gen. 7:13, 14
Struck by God ... Ex. 12:29
Firstborn of, belong to God ... Ex. 34:19
Can be unclean ... Lev. 5:2
Taken as plunder ... Josh. 8:2, 27
Belong to God ... Ps. 50:10
Nebuchadnezzar eats like ... Dan. 4:33
Pastureless ... Joel 1:18
East of Jordan good for ... Num. 32:1, 4
Given as ransom ... Num. 3:45

Caul
1. A lining surrounding the stomach ... Ex. 29:13, 22
2. A hair net worn by women ... Is. 3:18

Causeway—*a road or passage*
Steps leading into temple ... 1 Chr. 26:16, 18

Caution—*provident care; alertness*
For safety ... Acts 23:10, 16-24
For defense ... Neh. 4:12-23
For attack ... 1 Sam. 20:1-17
A principle ... Prov. 14:15, 16
Neglect of ... 1 Sam. 26:4-16

Cave—*a cavern*
A. *Used for:*
Habitation ... Gen. 19:30
Refuge ... 1 Kin. 18:4
Burial ... John 11:38
Concealment ... 1 Sam. 22:1
Protection ... Is. 2:19; Rev. 6:15
B. *Mentioned in Scripture:*
Machpelah ... Gen. 23:9
Makkedah ... Josh. 10:16, 17
Adullam ... 1 Sam. 22:1
Engedi ... 1 Sam. 24:1, 3

Cedar—*an evergreen tree*
A. *Used in:*
Ceremonial cleansing ... Lev. 14:4-7
Building Temple ... 1 Kin. 5:5, 6
Building palaces ... 2 Sam. 5:11
Gifts ... 1 Chr. 22:4
Making idols ... Is. 44:14, 17
B. *Figurative of:*
Israel's glory ... Num. 24:6
Christ's glory ... Ezek. 17:22, 23
Growth of saints ... Ps. 92:12
Mighty nations ... Amos 2:9
Arrogant rulers ... Is. 2:13

Cedar chests
Sold by traders ... Ezek. 27:23, 24

Ceiling—*upper surface of a room*
Temple's ... 1 Kin. 6:15

Celebrate—*to commemorate*
Feast of Weeks ... Ex. 34:22
Feast of Ingathering ... Ex. 34:22
The Sabbath ... Lev. 23:32, 41
Passover ... 2 Kin. 23:21
Feast of Unleavened Bread ... 2 Chr. 30:13
Feast of Tabernacles ... Zech. 14:16

Celestial—*heavenly*
Bodies called ... 1 Cor. 15:40

Celibacy—*the unmarried state*
Useful sometimes ... Matt. 19:10, 12
Not for bishops ... 1 Tim. 3:2
Requiring, a sign of apostasy ... 1 Tim. 4:1-3
Figurative of absolute devotion ... Rev. 14:4

Cellars—*depositories*
Wines stored in ... 1 Chr. 27:27

Cemetery—*a burial place*
Bought by Abraham ... Gen. 23:15, 16
Pharisees compared to ... Matt. 23:27
Man dwelt in ... Mark 5:2, 3
A resurrection from ... Matt. 27:52

Cenchrea—*millet*
A harbor of Corinth ... Acts 18:18
A church near ... Rom. 16:1

Censer—*firepan*
Used for incense ... Num. 16:6, 7, 39
Made of bronze ... Num. 16:39
Used in idol worship ... Ezek. 8:11
Typical of Christ's intercession ... Rev. 8:3, 5

Censoriousness—*a critical spirit*
Rebuked by Jesus ... Matt. 7:1-5
Diotrephes ... 3 John 9, 10
Apostates ... Jude 10-16

Census—*counting the population*
At Sinai ... Ex. 38:26
In Moab ... Num. 26:1-64
By David ... 2 Sam. 24:1-9
Provoked by Satan ... 1 Chr. 21:1
Completed by Solomon ... 2 Chr. 2:17
Of exiles ... Ezra 2:1-70
By Rome ... Luke 2:1

Centurion—*a Roman officer*
Servant of, healed ... Matt. 8:5-13
Watches crucifixion ... Matt. 27:54
Is converted ... Acts 10:1-48
Protects Paul ... Acts 22:25-28
Takes Paul to Rome ... Acts 27:1

Cephas—*stone*
Name of Peter ... John 1:42

Ceremonialism—*adherence to forms and rites*
Jews guilty of ... Is. 1:11-15
Christ condemns ... Matt. 15:1-9
Apostles reject ... Acts 15:12-28
Sign of apostasy ... 1 Tim. 4:1-3
Exhortations against ... Col. 2:14-23

Certainties—*absolute truths*
Sin's exposure ... Num. 32:23
The Gospel ... Luke 1:4
Jesus' claims ... Acts 1:3
Apostolic testimony ... 2 Pet. 1:16-21
Death's approach ... Heb. 9:27
Ultimate judgment ... Acts 17:31

Chaff—*the husk of threshed grain*
Describes the ungodly ... Ps. 1:4
Emptiness ... Is. 33:11
False doctrine ... Jer. 23:28
God's judgment ... Is. 17:13
Punishment ... Matt. 3:12

Chain—*a series of connected links*
A. *A badge of office:*
On Joseph's neck ... Gen. 41:42
Promised to Daniel ... Dan. 5:7
B. *An ornament:*
Worn by women ... Is. 3:20
C. *A means of confinement of:*
Prisoners ... Judg. 16:21
Paul ... Eph. 6:20
Manasseh bound ... 2 Chr. 33:12
D. *Used figuratively of:*
Oppression ... Lam. 3:7
Sin's bondage ... Jer. 40:3, 4
Punishment ... Jude 6
Satan's defeat ... Rev. 20:1

C

SUBJECT	REFERENCE
Chalcedony—*from Chalcedon*	
Variegated stone	Rev. 21:19
Chaldea	
Originally, the south portion of Babylonia	Gen. 11:31
Applied later to all Babylonia	Is. 13:19
Abraham came from	Gen. 11:28, 31
Ezekiel prophesies in	Ezek. 1:3
Chaldeans, Chaldees	
Abraham, a native	Gen. 11:31
Ur, a city of	Neh. 9:7
Babylon, "the glory of"	Is. 13:19
Attack Job	Job 1:17
Nebuchadnezzar, king of	2 Kin. 24:1
God's agent	Hab. 1:6
Predicted captivity of Jews among	Jer. 25:1-26
Jerusalem defeated by	2 Kin. 25:1-21
Noted for astrologers	Dan. 2:2, 5, 10
Chalkstone—*limestone*	
Used figuratively	Is. 27:9
Chamber—*inner room; enclosed place*	
A. *Used literally of:*	
Elisha's room	2 Kin. 4:10
Guest room	Mark 14:14
Upper room	Acts 9:37
Place of idolatry	2 Kin. 23:12
B. *Used figuratively of:*	
Heavens	Ps. 104:3, 13
Death	Prov. 7:27
Chamberlain—*a high official; a eunuch*	
Seven, serving Ahasuerus	Esth. 1:10, 15
Blastus, serving Herod	Acts 12:20
Erastus, at Corinth	Rom. 16:23
See Eunuch	
Chamois—*probably the wild sheep*	
Permitted for food	Deut. 14:4, 5
Chameleon—*a lizard-like reptile*	
Unclean	Lev. 11:30
Champion—*a mighty one; a winner*	
Goliath	1 Sam. 17:23, 51
David	1 Sam. 17:45-54
Chancellor	
Persian official	Ezra 4:8
Chance, second	
Not given to:	
Angels	2 Pet. 2:4
Noah's world	2 Pet. 2:5
Esau	Heb. 12:16, 17
Israelites	Num. 14:26-45
Saul	1 Sam. 16:1, 14
Judas	John 13:26-30
Apostates	Heb. 10:26-31
Those in hell	Luke 16:19-31
Change of clothes—*gala, festal garments*	
A gift	Gen. 45:22
A wager	Judg. 14:12-19
From a king	2 Kin. 5:5
Chapiter—*top of a post or column*	
Variegated decorations of	Ex. 36:38
Part of temple	1 Kin. 7:16, 19, 20
Chapman—*a merchant*	
Sells gold to Solomon	2 Chr. 9:14
Same as "merchantmen"	1 Kin. 10:15
Character—*one's total personality*	
A. *Traits of:*	
Described prophetically	Gen. 49:1-28
Indicated before birth	Gen. 25:21-34
Seen in childhood	Prov. 20:11
Fixed in hell	Rev. 22:11, 15
B. *Manifested by:*	
Decisions (Esau)	Gen. 25:29-34
Destiny (Judas)	John 6:70, 71
Desires (Demas)	2 Tim. 4:10
Deeds (Saul)	1 Sam. 15:1-35
Character of God's people	
A. *Their dedication:*	
Hear Christ	John 10:3, 4
Follow Christ	John 10:4, 5, 27
Receive Christ	John 1:12
B. *Their standing before God:*	
Blameless	Phil. 2:15
Faithful	Rev. 17:14
Godly	2 Pet. 2:9
Holy	Col. 3:12
C. *Their graces:*	
Humble	1 Pet. 5:5
Loving	1 Thess. 4:9
Humility	Phil. 2:3, 4
Meek	Matt. 5:5
Merciful	Matt. 5:7
Obedient	Rom. 16:19
Pure	Matt. 5:8
Sincere	2 Cor. 1:12
Zealous	Titus 2:14
Courteous	1 Pet. 3:8
Unity of mind	Rom. 15:5-7
Hospitable	1 Pet. 4:9
Generous	2 Cor. 8:1-7
Peaceable	Heb. 12:14
Patient	James 5:7, 8
Content	Heb. 13:5
Steadfast	1 Cor. 15:58
Character of the wicked	
A. *Their attitude toward God:*	
Hostile	Rom. 8:7
Denial	Ps. 14:1
Disobedience	Titus 1:16
B. *Their spiritual state:*	
Blindness	2 Cor. 4:4
Slavery to sin	2 Pet. 2:14, 19
Deadness	Eph. 2:1
Inability	Rom. 8:8
C. *Their works:*	
Boastful	Ps. 10:3-6
Full of evil	Rom. 1:29-32
Haters of the Gospel	John 3:19, 20
Sensual	2 Pet. 2:12-22
Charashim—*craftsmen*	
Valley near Jerusalem	1 Chr. 4:14
Called a "valley of craftsmen"	Neh. 11:35
Charchemish (see Carchemish)	
Charger—*a dish or platter*	
In tribal offerings	Num. 7:13
Translated "dish"	Ex. 25:29
Used for a dead man's head	Matt. 14:8, 11
Used figuratively ("platter")	Luke 11:39
Chariot—*a vehicle*	
A. *Used for:*	
Travel	Gen. 46:29
War	1 Kin. 20:25
B. *Employed by:*	
Kings	1 Kin. 22:35
Persons of distinction	Gen. 41:43
God	2 Kin. 2:11, 12
C. *Illustrative of:*	
Clouds	Ps. 104:3
God's judgments	Is. 66:15
Angels	2 Kin. 6:16, 17
Chariot, war machine	
A. *Used by:*	
Egyptians	Ex. 14:7
Canaanites	Josh. 17:16
Philistines	1 Sam. 13:5
Syrians	2 Sam. 10:18
Assyrians	2 Kin. 19:23
Jews	2 Kin. 8:21
B. *Numbers employed by:*	
Pharaoh—600	Ex. 14:7
Jabin—900	Judg. 4:3
Philistines—30,000	1 Sam. 13:5
Chariot cities	
Many in Solomon's time	1 Kin. 9:19
Chariot horses	
Hamstrung	1 Chr. 18:4
Chariot of fire	
Used in Elijah's exit from earth	2 Kin. 2:11
Chariots of the sun—*used in sun worship*	
Destroyed	2 Kin. 23:11
Charitableness—*a generous spirit toward others*	
Bearing burdens	Gal. 6:2-4
Showing forgiveness	2 Cor. 2:1-10
Seeking concord	Phil. 4:1-3
Helping the tempted	Gal. 6:1
Encouraging the weak	Rom. 14:1-15
Not finding fault	Matt. 7:1-3
Charity—*alms giving*	
From within	Luke 11:41
Given freely	Luke 12:33
Of Dorcas	Acts 9:36
Charmers—*users of magic*	
Falsified by God	Ps. 58:4, 5
Chastisement—*fatherly correction*	
A. *Sign of:*	
Sonship	Prov. 3:11, 12
God's love	Deut. 8:5
B. *Design of, to:*	
Correct	Jer. 24:5, 6
Prevent sin	2 Cor. 12:7-9
Bless	Ps. 94:12, 13
C. *Response to:*	
Penitence	2 Chr. 6:24-31
Submission	2 Cor. 12:7-10
Chastity—*sexual purity*	
A. *Manifested in:*	
Dress	1 Pet. 3:1-6
Looks	Matt. 5:28, 29
Speech	Eph. 5:4
Intentions	Gen. 39:7-12
B. *Aids to:*	
Shun the unchaste	1 Cor. 5:11
Consider your sainthood	Eph. 5:3, 4
Dangers of unchastity	Prov. 6:24-35
Let marriage suffice	1 Cor. 7:1-7
"Keep thyself pure"	1 Tim. 5:22
C. *Examples of:*	
Job	Job 31:1, 9-12
Joseph	Gen. 39:7-20
Ruth	Ruth 3:10, 11
Boaz	Ruth 3:13, 14
Saints	Rev. 14:4
Cheating—*defrauding by deceitful means*	
The Lord	Mal. 3:8, 9
One's soul	Matt. 16:26
The needy	Amos 8:4, 5
Others	1 Cor. 7:5
See Dishonesty	
Chebar—*joining*	
River in Babylonia	Ezek. 1:3
Site of Ezekiel's visions and Jewish captives	Ezek. 10:15, 20
Chedorlaomer—*servant of the god Lagamar*	
A king of Elam; invaded Canaan	Gen. 14:1-16
Cheek—*side of face*	
Micaiah struck on	1 Kin. 22:24
Slapped on	Job 16:10
Messiah's plucked	Is. 50:6
Description of:	
Beauty	Song 5:13
Patience	Matt. 5:39
Victory	Ps. 3:7
Attack	Mic. 5:1
Cheerfulness—*serene joyfulness*	
A. *Caused by:*	
A merry heart	Prov. 15:13
The Lord's goodness	Zech. 9:16, 17
The Lord's presence	Mark 6:54, 55
Victory	John 16:33
Confidence	Acts 24:10
B. *Manifested in:*	
Giving	2 Cor. 9:7
Christian graces	Rom. 12:8
Times of danger	Acts 27:22-36
Cheese—*a dairy product*	
Used for food	1 Sam. 17:18
Received by David	2 Sam. 17:20
Figurative of trials	Job 10:10

SUBJECT	REFERENCE
Chelal—*completeness, perfection*	
A son of Pahath-moab	Ezra 10:30
Chelluh—*robust*	
A son of Bani	Ezra 10:35
Chelub—*basket; bird's cage*	
1. A brother of Shuah	1 Chr. 4:11
2. Father of Ezri	1 Chr. 27:26
Chelubai	
A son of Hezron	1 Chr. 2:9
Another form of Caleb	1 Chr. 2:18, 42
Chemarim—*servants, priests*	
Denounced	Zeph. 1:4
Translated "idolatrous priests"	2 Kin. 23:5
Translated "priests"	Hos. 10:5
Chemosh—*fire, hearth*	
The god of the Moabites	Num. 21:29
Children sacrificed to	2 Kin. 3:27
Solomon builds altars to	1 Kin. 11:7
Josiah destroys altars of	2 Kin. 23:13
Chenaanah—feminine form of *"Canaan"*	
1. A Benjamite	1 Chr. 7:10
2. Father of Zedekiah	2 Chr. 18:10
Chenani—contraction of *"Chenaniah"*	
A reforming Levite	Neh. 9:4
Chenaniah—*Jehovah has established*	
1. A chief Levite in David's reign	1 Chr. 15:22, 27
2. A reforming Levite; contracted to Chenani	Neh. 9:4
Chephar haammonai—*village of the Ammonite*	
A village of Benjamin	Josh. 18:24
Chephirah—*village*	
A city of the Gibeonites	Josh. 9:17
Assigned to Benjamin	Josh. 18:26
Residence of exiles	Ezra 2:25
Cheran—*lyre*	
A Horite, son of Dishon	1 Chr. 1:41
Cherethites—*Cretans in southwest Palestine*	
Tribes in southwest Canaan	1 Sam. 30:14
Identified with Philistines	Ezek. 25:16
In David's bodyguard	2 Sam. 8:18
Serve Solomon	1 Kin. 1:38
Cherith—*cut, brook*	
Elijah hid there	1 Kin. 17:3-6
Cherub	
A district in Babylonia	Ezra 2:59 Neh. 7:61
Cherubim (plural of cherub)	
A. *Appearances of:*	
Fully described	Ezek. 1:5-14
B. *Functions of:*	
Guard	Gen. 3:22-24
Fulfill God's purposes	Ezek. 10:9-16
Show God's majesty	2 Sam. 22:11
C. *Images of:*	
On the mercy seat	Ex. 25:18-22
On the veil	Ex. 26:31
On curtains	Ex. 36:8
In the Temple	1 Kin. 8:6, 7
Chesalon—*trust*	
A town of Judah	Josh. 15:10
Chesed	
Fourth son of Nahor	Gen. 22:22
Chesil—*a fool*	
A village of Judah	Josh. 15:30
Probably same as Bethul and Bethuel	Josh. 19:4 1 Chr. 4:30
Chest—*case or box*	
For offering	2 Kin. 12:9, 10
For money ("treasuries")	Esth. 3:9
For levy fixed by Moses	2 Chr. 24:8, 9

SUBJECT	REFERENCE
Chestnut tree—*plane tree*	
Used by Jacob	Gen. 30:37
In Eden, God's garden	Ezek. 31:8, 9
Chesulloth—*loins or slopes*	
A border town of Issachar	Josh. 19:18
Cheth	
Eighth letter in Hebrew alphabet	Ps. 119:57-64
Chezib—*deceitful*	
Same as Azib; birthplace of Shelah	Gen. 38:5
Chicken—*domestic fowl*	
Hen and brood	Luke 13:34
Rooster (cock)	Luke 22:34
Chicks—*the young of a hen*	
Figurative of Israel	Matt. 23:37
Chiding—*to reprove or rebuke*	
A. *Between men:*	
Jacob with Laban	Gen. 31:36
Israelites with Moses	Ex. 17:2
Ephraimites with Gideon	Judg. 8:1
Paul with Peter	Gal. 2:11, 14
B. *By Christ, because of:*	
Unbelief	Matt. 11:20-24
Spiritual dullness	Matt. 16:8-12
Censoriousness	Mark 10:13-16
Sluggishness	Matt. 26:40
Chidon—*a javelin*	
Where Uzza was struck dead	1 Chr. 13:9, 10
Called Nahon	2 Sam. 6:6
Chief seats—*seats or places of honor*	
Sought by scribes and Pharisees	Matt. 23:1, 6 Mark 12:38, 39
Not be be sought	Luke 14:7-11
Child-bearing	
Agreeable to God's command	Gen. 1:28
Result of marriage	1 Tim. 5:14
Attended with pain	Gen. 3:16
Productive of joy	John 16:21
Productive of the Messiah	Luke 2:7
Means of salvation	1 Tim. 2:15
Expressed in symbols	Rev. 12:2, 5
Childhood, characteristics of	
Dependence	1 Thess. 2:7
Immaturity	1 Cor. 13:11
Foolishness	Prov. 22:15
Unstableness	Eph. 4:14
Humility	Matt. 18:1-5
Need for instruction	Prov. 22:6
Influence on adults	Is. 49:15
Childishness—*an immature spirit*	
Manifested by Saul	1 Sam. 18:8
Seen in Haman	Esth. 6:6-9
Childlikeness	
Requirement of God's kingdom	Mark 10:15
An element in spiritual growth	1 Pet. 2:2
A model to be followed	1 Cor. 14:20
Children, figurative	
Disciples of a teacher	Mark 10:24
God's own	Rom. 8:16, 17
Christians	Eph. 5:8
Devil's own	1 John 3:10
Those who show such trait	Matt. 11:16-19
Children, illegitimate	
No inheritance	Gal. 4:30
No fatherly care	Heb. 12:8
Not in congregation	Deut. 23:2
Despised	Judg. 11:2
Children, natural	
A. *Right estimate of:*	
God's gifts	Gen. 33:5
God's heritage	Ps. 127:3-5
Crown of age	Prov. 17:6
B. *Characteristics of:*	
Imitate parents	1 Kin. 15:11, 26
Diverse in nature	Gen. 25:27
Playful	Matt. 11:16-19

SUBJECT	REFERENCE
C. *Capacities of:*	
Glorify God	Matt. 21:15, 16
Come to Christ	Mark 10:13-16
Understand Scripture	2 Tim. 3:15
Receive the promises	Acts 2:39
Believe	Matt. 18:6
Receive training	Eph. 6:4
Worship in God's house	1 Sam. 1:24, 28
D. *Parental obligations toward:*	
Nourishment	1 Sam. 1:22
Discipline	Eph. 6:4
Instruction	Gal. 4:1, 2
Employment	1 Sam. 17:15
Inheritance	Luke 12:13, 14
E. *Duties of:*	
Obedience	Eph. 6:1-3
Honor to parents	Heb. 12:9
Respect for age	1 Pet. 5:5
Care for parents	1 Tim. 5:4
Obedience to God	Deut. 30:2
Remembering God	Eccl. 12:1
F. *Description of ungrateful:*	
Stubborn	Deut. 21:18-21
Scorners	Prov. 30:17
Robbers	Prov. 28:24
Strikers	Ex. 21:15
Cursers	Lev. 20:9
G. *Examples of good:*	
Isaac	Gen. 22:6-10
Joseph	Gen. 45:9, 10
Jephthah's daughter	Judg. 11:34-36
Samuel	1 Sam. 2:26
David	1 Sam. 17:20
Josiah	2 Chr. 34:3
Esther	Esth. 2:20
Daniel	Dan. 1:6
John the Baptist	Luke 1:80
Jesus	Luke 2:51
In the Temple	Matt. 21:15, 16
Timothy	2 Tim. 3:15
H. *Examples of bad:*	
Esau	Gen. 26:34, 35
Job's haters	Job 19:18
Sons of Eli	1 Sam. 2:12, 17
Sons of Samuel	1 Sam. 8:3
Absalom	2 Sam. 15:10
Adonijah	1 Kin. 1:5, 6
Elisha's mockers	2 Kin. 2:23
Adrammelech	2 Kin. 19:37
I. *Acts performed upon:*	
Naming	Ruth 4:17
Blessing	Luke 1:67, 76-79
Circumcision	Luke 2:21
J. *Murder of:*	
By Pharaoh	Ex. 1:16
By Herod the Great	Matt. 2:16-18
In war	Num. 31:17
Chileab—*restraint of father*	
A son of David	2 Sam. 3:3
Also called Daniel	1 Chr. 3:1
Chilion—*wasting away*	
Elimelech's son	Ruth 1:2
Orpah's deceased husband	Ruth 1:4, 5
Boaz redeems his estate	Ruth 4:9
Chilmad	
A town or country trading with Tyre	Ezek. 27:23
Chimham—*pining*	
A son of Barzillai	2 Sam. 19:37-40
Inn bearing his name	Jer. 41:17
Chinnereth, Cinneroth—*lyre*	
1. A city of Naphtali	Deut. 3:17
2. The region of Chinneroth	1 Kin. 15:20
Same as plain of Gennesaret	Matt. 14:34
3. The Old Testament name for Sea of Galilee	Num. 34:11
Also called Lake of Gennesaret and Sea of Galilee	Luke 5:1
Chios—*snow*	
An island of the Aegean Sea; on Paul's voyage	Acts 20:15
Chisleu	
Ninth month of Hebrew year	Neh. 1:1

SUBJECT REFERENCE

Chislon—*trust, hope*
Father of Elidad ... Num. 34:21

Chisloth-tabor—*the flanks of Tabor*
A locality near Mt. Tabor ... Josh. 19:12
Probably same as Chesulloth ... Josh. 19:18

Chittim, Kittim
The island of Cyprus; inhabited by descendants of Japheth (through Javan) ... Gen. 10:4
Ships of, in Balaam's prophecy ... Num. 24:24
A haven for Tyre's ships ... Is. 23:1-12
Mentioned in the prophets ... Jer. 2:10

Chiun—*detestable thing*
Astral images made by Israel ... Amos 5:26

Chloe—*verdure*
Woman of Corinth ... 1 Cor. 1:11

Choice, choose
A. *Of human things:*
Wives ... Gen. 6:2
Land ... Gen. 13:11
Soldiers ... Ex. 17:9
King ... 1 Sam. 8:18
Disciples ... Luke 6:13
Church officers ... Acts 6:5
Missionaries ... Acts 15:40
Delegates ... Acts 15:22, 25

B. *Of God's choice:*
Moses as leader ... Num. 16:28
Levites to priesthood ... 1 Sam. 2:28
Kings ... 1 Sam. 10:24
Jerusalem ... Deut. 12:5
Israel as His people ... Deut. 7:6-8
Cyrus as deliverer ... Is. 45:1-4
The Servant (the Messiah) ... Is. 42:1-7
The new Israel (the Church) ... 1 Pet. 2:9
The weak as God's own ... 1 Cor. 1:27, 28
The elect ... Matt. 20:16

C. *Kind of:*
God and the Devil ... Gen. 3:1-11
Life and death ... Deut. 30:19, 20
God and idols ... Josh. 24:15-28
Obedience and disobedience ... 1 Sam. 15:1-35
God and Baal ... 1 Kin. 18:21-40
Wisdom and folly ... Prov. 8:1-21
Obedience and sin ... 2 Pet. 2:4
Christ and antichrist ... 1 John 2:18, 19

D. *Factors determining choice, man's:*
First choice ... Rom. 5:12
Depraved nature ... John 3:19-21
Spiritual deadness ... Eph. 4:17-19
Blindness ... John 9:39-41
Inability ... Rom. 8:7, 8

E. *Bad choice made by:*
Disobeying God ... Num. 14:1-45
Putting the flesh first ... Gen. 25:29-34
Following a false prophet ... Matt. 24:11, 24
Letting the world overcome ... Matt. 19:16-22
Rejecting God's promises ... Acts 13:44-48

F. *Good choice made by:*
Using God's Word ... Ps. 119:9-11
Believing God ... Heb. 11:24-27
Obedience ... Acts 26:19-23
Prayer ... Eph. 1:16-19
Faith ... Heb. 11:8-10

Choir—*musicians trained to sing together*
Appointed by Nehemiah ... Neh. 12:31
In house of God ... Neh. 12:40
Under instructor ... 1 Chr. 15:22, 27

Chor-ashan (see Ashan)

Chorazin
A city denounced for its unbelief ... Matt. 11:21

Chozeba
Town of Judah ... 1 Chr. 4:22

Christ—*the Anointed One*
A. *Pre-existence of:*
Affirmed in Old Testament ... Ps. 2:7
Confirmed by Christ ... John 8:58
Proclaimed by apostles ... Col. 1:15-19

SUBJECT REFERENCE

B. *Birth of:*
Predicted ... Is. 7:14
Fulfilled ... Matt. 1:18-25
In the fullness of time ... Gal. 4:4

C. *Deity of:*
Prophecy ... Is. 9:6
Acknowledged by Christ ... John 20:28, 29
Acclaimed by witnesses ... John 1:14, 18
Affirmed by apostles ... Rom. 9:5
Heb. 1:8

D. *Attributes of:*
All-powerful ... Matt. 28:18
All-knowing ... Col. 2:3
Ever-present ... Matt. 18:20
Eternal ... John 1:1, 2, 15

E. *Humanity of:*
Foretold ... Gen. 3:15
1 Cor. 15:45-47
Took man's nature ... John 1:14
Heb. 2:9-18
Seed of woman ... Gal. 4:4
A son of man ... Luke 3:38
Of David's line ... Matt. 22:45
A man ... 1 Tim. 2:5
Four brothers ... Mark 6:3

F. *Mission of:*
Do God's will ... John 6:38
Save sinners ... Luke 19:10
Bring in everlasting righteousness ... Dan. 9:24
Destroy Satan's works ... Heb. 2:14
1 John 3:8
Fulfill the Old Testament ... Matt. 5:17
Give life ... John 10:10, 28
Abolish ceremonialism ... Dan. 9:27
Complete revelation ... Heb. 1:1

G. *Worship of, by:*
Old Testament saints ... Josh. 5:13-15
Demons ... Mark 5:6
Men ... John 9:38
Angels ... Heb. 1:6
Disciples ... Luke 24:52
Saints in glory ... Rev. 7:9, 10
All ... Phil. 2:10, 11

H. *Character of:*
Holy ... Luke 1:35
Righteous ... Is. 53:11
Just ... Zech. 9:9
Guileless ... 1 Pet. 2:22
Sinless ... 2 Cor. 5:21
Spotless ... 1 Pet. 1:19
Innocent ... Matt. 27:4
Meek ... Matt. 11:29
Merciful ... Heb. 2:17
Humble ... Phil. 2:8
Forgiving ... Luke 23:34

I. *Types of:*
Adam ... Rom. 5:14
Abel ... Heb. 12:24
Moses ... Deut. 18:15
Passover ... 1 Cor. 5:7
Manna ... John 6:32
Brazen serpent ... John 3:14

J. *Other names for:*
Adam, the second ... 1 Cor. 15:45-47
Advocate ... 1 John 2:1
Almighty ... Rev. 19:15
Alpha and Omega ... Rev. 21:6
Amen ... Rev. 3:14
Ancient of Days ... Dan. 7:9
Angel of his presence ... Is. 63:9
Anointed above His fellows ... Ps. 45:7
Anointed of the Lord ... Ps. 2:2
Apostle of our profession ... Heb. 3:1
Arm of the Lord ... Is. 51:9, 10
Author and finisher of our faith ... Heb. 12:2
Babe ... Luke 2:16
Beginning and end ... Rev. 21:6
Beloved ... Eph. 1:6
Beloved of God ... Matt. 12:18
Beloved Son ... Mark 1:11
Blessed and only Potentate ... 1 Tim. 6:15
Born of God ... 1 John 5:18
Branch ... Zech. 3:8
Branch, a righteous ... Jer. 23:5
Branch of righteousness ... Jer. 33:15
Bread ... John 6:41
Bread of Life ... John 6:35
Bridegroom ... John 3:29

SUBJECT REFERENCE

Bright morning star ... Rev. 22:16
Captain of salvation ... Heb. 2:10
Carpenter ... Mark 6:3
Carpenter's son ... Matt. 13:55
Chief corner stone ... Ps. 118:22
Mark 12:10
Chief Shepherd ... 1 Pet. 5:4
Child ... Is. 9:6
Child Jesus ... Luke 2:27
Chosen of God ... 1 Pet. 2:4
Christ, the ... John 1:41
Acts 9:22
Christ a King ... Luke 23:2
Christ, Jesus ... Rom. 8:2
Christ Jesus our Lord ... Rom. 8:39
Christ of God, the ... Luke 9:20
Christ, of God, His Chosen One ... Luke 23:35
Christ, the Lord ... Luke 2:11
Christ, the power of God ... 1 Cor. 1:24
Christ, the Son of the Blessed ... Mark 14:61
Commander ... Is. 55:4
Consolation of Israel ... Luke 2:25
Costly cornerstone ... Is. 28:16
Counselor ... Is. 9:6
Covenant of the people ... Is. 42:6
Dayspring ... Luke 1:78
Day star ... 2 Pet. 1:19
Deity ... Col. 2:9
Deliverer ... Rom. 11:26
Desire of all nations ... Hag. 2:7
Diadem ... Is. 28:5
Door ... John 10:2
Door of the sheep ... John 10:1
Emmanuel ... Matt. 1:23
Ensign of the people ... Is. 11:10
Eternal life ... 1 John 5:20
Everlasting Father ... Is. 9:6
Faithful and True ... Rev. 19:11
Faithful witness ... Rev. 1:5
Firmly placed foundation ... Is. 28:16
First-begotten ... Heb. 1:6
First-born from the dead ... Col. 1:18
First-born of the dead ... Rev. 1:5
First-born of every creature ... Col. 1:15
First-born among many brethren ... Rom. 8:29
First fruits ... 1 Cor. 15:23
First and last ... Rev. 22:13
Forerunner ... Heb. 6:20
Foundation laid in Zion ... Is. 28:16
Friend of publicans and sinners ... Luke 7:34
Glorious Lord ... Is. 33:21
God ... John 20:28
God blessed forever ... Rom. 9:5
God of Israel ... Is. 45:15
God, our Savior ... 1 Tim. 2:3
God with us ... Matt. 1:23
Good Master ... Mark 10:17
Governor ... Matt. 2:6
Great God ... Titus 2:13
Great High Priest ... Heb. 4:14
Great Shepherd ... Heb. 13:20
Guardian of souls ... 1 Pet. 2:25
Head, even Christ ... Eph. 4:15
Head of all ... Col. 2:10
Head of every man ... 1 Cor. 11:3
Head of the body, the church ... Col. 1:18
Head over all things ... Eph. 1:22
Heir of all things ... Heb. 1:2
High Priest ... Heb. 4:14
His beloved Son ... Col. 1:13
Holy One ... 1 John 2:20
Holy and Righteous One ... Acts 3:14
Holy One of God ... Luke 4:34
Holy One of Israel ... Is. 37:23
Holy Child ... Acts 4:27
Hope of glory ... Col. 1:27
Horn of salvation ... Luke 1:69
Husband ... 2 Cor. 11:2
I Am ... John 8:58
Image of God ... 2 Cor. 4:4
Image of the Invisible God ... Col. 1:15
Jesus ... Luke 1:31
Jesus Christ ... Rom. 1:4
Jesus Christ our Lord ... Rom. 6:23
Jesus Christ our Savior ... Titus 3:6
Jesus of Nazareth ... Luke 24:19
Jesus, the Son of God ... Heb. 4:14
Jesus, the (supposed) son of Joseph ... Luke 3:23
Judge of Israel ... Mic. 5:1

SUBJECT	REFERENCE
Judge of the quick and the dead	Acts 10:42
Just man	Matt. 27:19
King	John 12:13
King eternal	1 Tim. 1:17
King of glory	Ps. 24:7
King of Israel	John 12:13
King of kings	1 Tim. 6:15
King of the Jews	Matt. 27:37
King of Zion	Zech. 9:9
King over all the earth	Zech. 14:9
Lamb	Rev. 13:8
Lamb of God	John 1:36
Leader	Is. 55:4
Life	John 14:6
Light	John 1:9
Light of the Gentiles	Acts 13:47
Light of the World	John 9:5
Lily of the valleys	Song 2:1
Lion of the tribe of Judah	Rev. 5:5
Living bread	John 6:51
Living stone	1 Pet. 2:4
Lord	John 21:7
Lord Christ	Col. 3:24
Lord God Almighty	Rev. 4:8
Lord Jesus	Acts 19:17
Lord Jesus Christ	2 Thess. 2:1
Lord and Savior Jesus Christ	2 Pet. 2:20
Lord both of dead and living	Rom. 14:9
Lord of all	Acts 10:36 Rom. 10:12
Lord of glory	1 Cor. 2:8
Lord of hosts	Is. 54:5
Lord of lords	1 Tim. 6:15
Lord of Sabbath	Luke 6:5
Lord our righteousness	Jer. 23:6
Lord, your redeemer	Is. 43:14
Man of peace	Luke 10:6
Man of sorrows	Is. 53:3
Master	Mark 12:14
Mediator	Heb. 12:24
Messenger of the covenant	Mal. 3:1
Messiah	John 4:25, 26
Mighty God	Is. 9:6
Mighty One of Jacob	Is. 60:16
Minister of the circumcision	Rom. 15:8
Minister of the sanctuary	Heb. 8:1, 2
Morning star	Rev. 22:16
Most Mighty	Ps. 45:3
Nazarene	Matt. 2:23
Only begotten of the Father	John 1:14
Only begotten Son	John 1:18
Only wise God	1 Tim. 1:17
Our Passover	1 Cor. 5:7
Our peace	Eph. 2:14
Physician	Luke 4:23
Power of God	1 Cor. 1:24
Precious cornerstone	1 Pet. 2:6
Priest	Heb. 5:6
Prince	Acts 5:31
Prince of life	Acts 3:15
Prince of peace	Is. 9:6
Prince of the kings of the earth	Rev. 1:5
Prophet	Deut. 18:15, 18
Propitiation	Rom. 3:25
Purifier and refiner	Mal. 3:3
Rabbi	John 6:25
Rabboni	John 20:16
Ransom	1 Tim. 2:6
Redeemer	Is. 59:20
Resurrection and the life	John 11:25
Righteous Judge	2 Tim. 4:8
Righteous One	Is. 53:11
Rock	1 Cor. 10:4
Rock of offense	Rom. 9:33
Rod of the stem of Jesse	Is. 11:1
Root of David	Rev. 22:16
Root of Jesse	Is. 11:10
Rose of Sharon	Song 2:1
Ruler in Israel	Mic. 5:2
Salvation	Luke 2:30
Savior	1 Tim. 4:10
Savior, Jesus Christ	2 Pet. 2:20
Savior, God our	Titus 1:3
Savior of the world	1 John 4:14
Scepter out of Israel	Num. 24:17
Second man	1 Cor. 15:47
Seed of David	John 7:42
Seed of the woman	Gen. 3:15
Shepherd	John 10:11
Shepherd of souls	1 Pet. 2:25
Shoot of the stem of Jesse	Is. 11:1
Son of the Blessed	Mark 14:61
Son of David	Matt. 9:27
Son of God	Rom. 1:4
Son of Man	Acts 7:56
Son of Mary	Mark 6:3
Son of the Father	2 John 3
Son of the Most High	Luke 1:32
Source of eternal salvation	Heb. 5:9
Sower	Matt. 13:3, 37
"Star out of Jacob"	Num. 24:17
Stone	Dan. 2:45
Stone rejected	Luke 20:17
Stone of stumbling	Rom. 9:32, 33
Sun of righteousness	Mal. 4:2
Teacher from God	John 3:2
Tried stone	Is. 28:16
True vine	John 15:1
Truth	John 14:6
Unspeakable gift	2 Cor. 9:15
Way	John 14:6
Wonderful	Is. 9:6
Word	1 John 1:1
Word of God	Rev. 19:13
Word of Life	1 John 1:1

Christian attributes

SUBJECT	REFERENCE
A. *Manifested toward God:*	
Belief	Heb. 11:6
Holiness	Heb. 12:10, 14
Godliness	Titus 2:12
Love	Matt. 22:36, 37
Faith	Mark 11:22
Joy	Phil. 4:4
B. *Manifested toward Christ:*	
Faith	2 Tim. 1:12
Worship	Phil. 2:4-11
Obedience	2 Thess. 1:8
Imitation	1 Cor. 11:1
Fellowship	1 John 1:3
C. *Manifested toward the Holy Spirit:*	
Walking in	Gal. 5:16
Filled with	Eph. 5:18
Guided by	John 16:13
Praying in	Jude 20
Quench not	1 Thess. 5:19
Taught by	John 14:26
Living in	Gal. 5:25
Grieve not	Eph. 4:30
D. *Manifested in the world:*	
Chastity	1 Tim. 5:22
Contentment	Heb. 13:5
Diligence	1 Thess. 3:7
Forbearance	Eph. 4:2
Honesty	Rom. 12:17
Industry	1 Thess. 4:11, 12
Love toward enemies	Matt. 5:44
Peacefulness	Rom. 14:17-19
Temperance	1 Cor. 9:25
Tolerance	Rom. 14:1-23
Zealous for good deeds	Titus 2:14
E. *Manifested toward other Christians:*	
Bearing burdens	Gal. 6:2
Helping the needy	Acts 11:14, 30
Fellowship	Acts 2:42
Brotherly kindness	1 Pet. 4:7-11
Mutual edification	1 Thess. 5:11
F. *Manifested as signs of faith:*	
Spiritual growth	2 Pet. 3:18
Fruitfulness	John 15:1-6
Perseverance	1 Cor. 15:58
Persecution	2 Tim. 3:9-12
Obedience	Phil. 2:12
Good works	James 2:14-26
G. *Manifested as internal graces:*	
Kindness	Col. 3:12, 13
Humility	1 Pet. 5:5, 6
Gentleness	James 3:17, 18
Love	1 Cor. 13:1-13
Self-control	Gal. 5:23
Peace	Phil. 4:7

Christianity, a way of life

SUBJECT	REFERENCE
Founded on Christ	1 Cor. 3:10, 12
Based on doctrines	1 Cor. 15:1-4
Designed for all	Matt. 28:18-20
Centers in salvation	Acts 4:12
Produces change	1 Cor. 6:11

Christians—*Believers in Jesus Christ*

SUBJECT	REFERENCE
First applied at Antioch	Acts 11:26
Agrippa almost becomes	Acts 26:28
Proof of, by suffering	1 Pet. 4:16
Sometimes referred to as:	
Believers	Acts 5:14
Brethren	Rom. 7:1
Brethren, beloved	1 Thess. 1:4
Brethren, holy	Heb. 3:1
Children	2 Cor. 6:13
Children of God	Rom. 8:16
Children of Light	Eph. 5:8
Dear children	Eph. 5:1
Disciples	Acts 9:25
Elect, the	Rom. 8:33
Friends	John 15:14
Heirs of God and joint heirs with	Rom. 8:17
Light in the Lord	Eph. 5:8
Light of the world	Matt. 5:14
Little children	1 John 2:1
Members	1 Cor. 12:18, 25
Priests	Rev. 1:6
Saints	Rom. 8:27
Salt of the earth	Matt. 5:13
Servants of God	Acts 16:17
Sheep	John 10:27
Soldier	2 Tim. 2:4
Sons of God	Rom. 8:14
Strangers	1 Pet. 2:11
Vessels of honor	2 Tim. 2:21
Witnesses	Acts 1:8

Christlikeness

SUBJECT	REFERENCE
Model	2 Cor. 3:18
Motivation	2 Cor. 5:14-17
Manifestation	Gal. 5:22, 23
Means	Rom. 8:1-17
Mystery	Phil. 3:20, 21

Chronicles—two books of Old Testament from Heb. meaning *"the words of the days"*

Chrysolite—*gold stone*

SUBJECT	REFERENCE
In New Jerusalem	Rev. 21:20

Chrysoprasus—*golden-green stone*

SUBJECT	REFERENCE
In New Jerusalem	Rev. 21:20

Chub

SUBJECT	REFERENCE
Desolation of, predicted	Ezek. 30:5

Chun—*founding*

SUBJECT	REFERENCE
A town of Syria	1 Chr. 18:8
Called Berothah	Ezek. 47:16

Church—*the called-out ones*

SUBJECT	REFERENCE
A. *Descriptive of:*	
Local church	Acts 8:1
Churches generally	Rom. 16:4
Believers gathered	Rom. 16:5
The body of believers	1 Cor. 12:28
Body of Christ	Eph. 1:22, 23
B. *Title applied to:*	
The Bride of Christ	Eph. 5:22-32
The body	Col. 1:18
One body	1 Cor. 12:18-24
Body of Christ	Eph. 4:12
The Church	Eph. 3:21
Church of the first-born	Heb. 12:23
Church of God	1 Cor. 1:2
Church of the Living God	1 Tim. 3:15
Churches of Christ	Rom. 16:16
Church of the Gentiles	Rom. 16:4
City of God	Heb. 12:22
Flock	Acts 20:28
Flock of God	1 Pet. 5:2
God's building	1 Cor. 3:9
God's husbandry	1 Cor. 3:9
Habitation of God	Eph. 2:22
Household of God	Eph. 2:19
Israel of God	Gal. 6:16
Jerusalem	Gal. 4:26
Kingdom	Heb. 12:28
Kingdom of God's dear Son	Col. 1:13
Lamb's wife	Rev. 19:7
Mount Zion	Heb. 12:22
People of God	1 Pet. 2:10
Spiritual house	1 Pet. 2:5
Temple of God	1 Cor. 3:16
C. *Relation to Christ:*	
Saved by	Eph. 5:25-29
Purchased by	Acts 20:28
Sanctified by	Eph. 5:26, 27
Founded on	Eph. 2:19, 20
Built by	Matt. 16:18
Loved by	Eph. 5:25
Subject to	Rom. 7:4

SUBJECT	REFERENCE
D. *Members of:*	
Added by faith	Acts 2:41
Added by the Lord	Acts 2:47
Baptized into one Spirit	1 Cor. 12:13
Edified by the Word	Eph. 4:15, 16
Persecuted	Acts 8:1-3
Disciplined	Matt. 18:15-17
Worship	Acts 20:7
Fellowship together	Acts 2:42-46
Urged to attend	Heb. 10:25
Subject to pastoral oversight	1 Pet. 5:1-3
Unified in Christ	Gal. 3:28
E. *Organization of:*	
Under bishops	1 Tim. 3:1-7
Function of deacons	Acts 6:3-6
Place of evangelists	Eph. 4:11
Official assemblies	Acts 15:1-31
Function of the presbytery	1 Tim. 4:14
F. *Mission of:*	
Evangelize the world	Matt. 28:18-20
Guard the truth	2 Tim. 2:1, 2
Edify the saints	Eph. 4:11-15
Discipline unruly	2 Cor. 13:1-10
G. *Local, examples of:*	
Antioch	Acts 11:26
Asia	1 Cor. 16:19 Rev. 1:11
Babylon	1 Pet. 5:13
Caesarea	Acts 18:22
Cenchrea	Rom. 16:1
Colossae	Col. 1:2
Corinth	1 Cor. 1:2
Ephesus	Acts 20:17
Galatia	Gal. 1:2
Jerusalem	Acts 8:1
Judea	Gal. 1:22
Laodicea	Col. 4:15
Macedonia	2 Cor. 8:1
Pergamos	Rev. 2:12
Philadelphia	Rev. 3:7
Philippi	Phil. 1:1
Rome	Rom. 1:7
Sardis	Rev. 3:1
Smyrna	Rev. 2:8
Thyatira	Rev. 2:18
Thessalonica	1 Thess. 1:1

Church sleeper

Falls from window during Paul's sermon	Acts 20:7-12

Churl—*a rude, surly person*

Nabal	1 Sam. 25:3
Descriptive of the fraudulent	Is. 32:5, 7

Chushan-rishathaim—*extra wicked*

A Mesopotamian king; oppressed Israel	Judg. 3:8
Othniel delivers Israel from	Judg. 3:9, 10

Chuza

Herod's steward	Luke 8:3

Cilicia—*a province of Asia Minor*

Paul's country	Acts 21:39
Students from, argued with Stephen	Acts 6:9
Paul labors in	Gal. 1:21

Cinnamon—*a laurel-like spicy plant*

Used in holy oil	Ex. 30:23
A perfume	Prov. 7:17
In Babylon's trade	Rev. 18:13
Figurative of a lover	Song 4:12, 14

Circle—*a curved line equally distant from a common center*

Used of the earth	Is. 40:22

Circuit—*circle, regular course*

Judge's itinerary	1 Sam. 7:16
Sun's orbit	Ps. 19:6

Circumcision—*a cutting*

A. *The physical rite:*	
Instituted by God	Gen. 17:10-14
A seal of righteousness	Rom. 2:25-29
Performed on the eighth day	Luke 1:59
Child named when performed	Luke 1:59
Allowed right to Passover	Ex. 12:48
Neglect of, punished	Ex. 4:24
Neglected during wilderness	Josh. 5:7
A sign of covenant relation	Rom. 4:11
B. *Necessity of:*	
Asserted in old dispensation	Gen. 17:10-14
Abolished by the Gospel	Gal. 5:1-4 Eph. 2:11, 15
Avails nothing	Gal. 5:6 Col. 3:11
Avowed by false teachers	Acts 15:1
Acclaimed a yoke	Acts 15:10
Abrogated by apostles	Acts 15:5-29 1 Cor. 7:18, 19
C. *Spiritual significance of:*	
Regeneration	Deut. 10:16 Deut. 30:6 Jer. 4:4
The true Jew (Christian)	Rom. 2:29
The Christian	Phil. 3:3 Col. 2:11

Circumstances

A. *Relationship to Christian:*	
Work for good	Rom. 8:28
Produce perseverance	Rom. 5:3
Not cause for anxiety	Phil. 4:6
Test and purify	1 Pet. 1:5-7
To be met with thanksgiving	Eph. 5:20 Phil. 4:6
Can be overcome	Phil. 4:11-13
B. *Examples, victory over:*	
Moses	Ex. 14:10-31
Joshua	Josh. 6:8-21
Shamgar	Judg. 3:31
Gideon	Judg. 7:19-23
Hannah	1 Sam. 1:9-19
David	1 Sam. 17:40-51
Widow of Zarephath	1 Kin. 17:8-16
Hezekiah	2 Kin. 20:1-11
Peter	Acts 12:5-17
Paul	Acts 14:19-20 Acts 16:19-26

Cistern—*an underground reservoir for water*

A. *Literal uses of:*	
Water	2 Kin. 18:31
Imprisonment (when empty)	Jer. 38:6
B. *Figurative uses of:*	
Wife	Prov. 5:15
Heart	Eccl. 12:6
False religion	Jer. 2:13
C. *Kinds of:*	
Family cisterns	Is. 36:16
Garden ponds	Eccl. 2:6

Cities—*organized population centers*

A. *Features regarding:*	
Earliest	Gen. 4:17
Walled	Lev. 25:29-31 Deut. 3:5
Often built on hills	Matt. 5:14
Gates guarded	Acts 9:24
Guard posted	2 Kin. 7:10 Neh. 13:19
Difficult to attack	Prov. 16:32
Business at gate	Gen. 23:10 Ruth 4:1-11
B. *Descriptions of:*	
Sodom—wicked	Gen. 13:13
Jerusalem—like Sodom	Is. 1:10
Nineveh—repentant	Jon. 3:5-10
Capernaum—arrogant	Matt. 11:23
Athens—idolatrous	Acts 17:16

Cities, Levitical

Forty-eight	Num. 35:7
Six designed for refuge	Deut. 19:1-13

Cities of refuge

Given to Levites	Num. 35:6
For the manslayer	Num. 35:11

Cities of the mountains

Avoided by Israel	Deut. 2:37

Cities of the plain

Admah	Gen. 14:8
Bela	Gen. 14:2
Gomorrah	Gen. 19:28 Jude 7
Sodom	Gen. 19:28-29
Zeboiim	Gen. 14:8
Dibon, Bamoth-baal, Beth-baal-meon	Josh. 13:17

Cities of the valley

Restored	Jer. 32:44
Taken by Israel	Deut. 3:8, 10

Citizen, citizenship

A. *Kinds of:*	
Hebrew	Eph. 2:12
Roman	Acts 21:39
Spiritual	Phil. 3:20
Christian (see below)	
B. *Duties of Christian citizens:*	
Be subject to rulers	Rom. 13:1-7
Pray for rulers	1 Tim. 2:1, 2
Honor rulers	1 Pet. 2:17
Seek peace	Jer. 29:7
Pay taxes	Matt. 22:21
Obey God first	Acts 5:27-29
Love one's nation	Neh. 2:3
Live righteously	1 Pet. 3:8-17

City builder

Cain builds first	Gen. 4:17
Woe to, who uses bloodshed	Hab. 2:12

City, Holy

Applied to Jerusalem	Dan. 9:24 Rev. 11:2
Prophecy concerning	Joel 3:17
Clothed with beautiful garments	Is. 52:1
New Jerusalem	Rev. 21:2

City of David

Applied to the castle of Zion	1 Chr. 11:5
Taken by David from Jebusites	1 Chr. 11:4-8
Ark brought to	1 Chr. 15:1-29
Bethlehem called	Luke 2:4

City of destruction

Prophecy concerning an Egyptian city	Is. 19:18

City of God

Prophetic description of Zion	Ps. 48:1-14
Dwelling place of God	Ps. 46:4, 5
Sought by the saints	Heb. 11:9, 10, 16
Descriptive of the heavenly Jerusalem	Rev. 21:2

City of Moab

Where Balak met Balaam	Num. 22:36

City of palm trees—*Jericho*

Seen by Moses	Deut. 34:1-3
Occupied by Kenites	Judg. 1:16
Captured by Eglon	Judg. 3:12-14

City of Salt

Near the Dead Sea	Josh. 15:62

City of waters

Applied to Rabbah	2 Sam. 12:26, 27

Civil

1. Righteousness	
Principle of	Prov. 14:34
Precepts of	Zech. 8:16, 17
Practice of	Mic. 4:2
Perversion of	Mic. 7:1-4
2. Service	
A. *Characteristics of:*	
Loyalty	Neh. 2:3
Industry	Gen. 41:37-57
Esteem	Esth. 10:3
B. *Examples of:*	
Joseph	Gen. 39:1-6
Daniel	Dan. 1:17-21
Mordecai	Esth. 8:1, 2, 9
Nehemiah	Neh. 2:1-8
3. Authority:	
Obedience to commanded	Eccl. 8:2-7 Rom. 13:1-7
Submit for Christ's sake	1 Pet. 2:13-15

Civility—*good breeding; courtesy*

Shown by Joseph	Gen. 47:1-10
Taught by Christ	Luke 14:8-10
Shown by Timothy	Phil. 2:19-23
Shown by Gaius	3 John 1-6

C

SUBJECT REFERENCE

Class distinction
Egyptians—against Hebrews .... Gen. 43:32
Haman—against Hebrews .... Esth. 3:8, 9
Jews—against Samaritans .... John 4:9
Jews—against Gentiles .... Acts 22:21, 22
Forbidden .... Ex. 12:48, 49

Clauda—*lamentable*
Small island southeast of Crete .... Acts 27:16

Claudia
Disciple at Rome .... 2 Tim. 4:21

Claudius Lysias
Roman commander who protected Paul .... Acts 24:22-24

Clay—*firm, plastic earth*
A. *Uses of:*
Making bricks .... 2 Sam. 12:31
Making pottery .... Is. 41:25
Sealing .... Job 38:14
Miracle .... John 9:6, 15
B. *Figurative of:*
Man's weakness .... Is. 64:8
Unstable kingdom .... Dan. 2:33-35, 42
Trouble .... Ps. 40:2
Wealth .... Hab. 2:6

Clean—*pure, innocent*
A. *Used physically:*
Outward purity .... Matt. 23:26
B. *Used ceremonially of:*
Clean animals .... Gen. 7:2
Freedom from defilement .... Luke 5:14, 15
C. *Used spiritually of:*
Men's nature .... Job 9:30, 31
Repentance .... Gen. 35:2
Regeneration .... Ezek. 36:25
Sanctification .... Ps. 24:4
Glorification .... Rev. 19:8, 14

Cleanliness
Required of priests .... Is. 52:11
Acceptability of worship .... Heb. 10:22
Inner, better than outward .... Matt. 23:25-28

Cleansing, spiritual
Promise of .... Jer. 33:8
Need of .... Ps. 51:2
Extent of .... Ps. 19:12
Command regarding .... 2 Cor. 7:1
Means of .... 1 John 1:7, 9
Perfection of .... Eph. 5:26

Cleanthes—Stoic teacher not mentioned by name in the Bible
Quoted by Paul .... Acts 17:28

Clement—*mild, merciful*
Paul's companions .... Phil. 4:3

Cleopas—*of a renowned father*
Christ appeared to .... Luke 24:18

Cleophas—*of a renowned father*
Husband of Mary .... John 19:25
Called Alphaeus .... Matt. 10:3

Climate—*temperature and weather conditions*
A. *Elements of:*
Cold .... Job 37:9
Acts 28:2
Clouds .... Job 35:5
Thirsty ground .... Deut. 8:15
Heat .... Is. 49:10
Rain .... Ezra 10:13
Snow .... 1 Chr. 11:22
Sunshine .... Ex. 16:21
Wind .... Matt. 14:24
B. *Order of:*
Promised .... Gen. 8:22
Controlled by God .... Job 37:5-13
Used in judgment .... Jer. 50:38
Hag. 1:10-11
Tool of correction .... Jon. 1:3, 4
Shows deity of Christ .... Mark 4:37-39

Cloak—*outer garment*
A. *Used literally of:*
Outer garment .... Matt. 5:40

SUBJECT REFERENCE

B. *Used figuratively of:*
Covering for sin .... John 15:22
Covering for license .... 1 Pet. 2:16

Closet
A place of prayer .... Matt. 6:6

Clothing—*garments*
A. *Need of:*
Cover nakedness .... Gen. 3:10, 11
Maintain modesty .... 1 Pet. 3:1-5
Keep warm .... 2 Tim. 4:13
Remove anguish .... Esth. 4:3, 4
B. *Unusual features regarding:*
Lasted forty years .... Deut. 8:4
Torn into twelve pieces .... 1 Kin. 11:29, 30
Borrowed from enemies .... Ex. 12:35
Some stripped of .... Luke 10:30
C. *Regulations concerning:*
Wearing opposite sex's, forbidden .... Deut. 22:5
Gaudy, denounced .... Is. 3:16-24
Ostentatious, prohibited .... 1 Tim. 2:9
Warnings concerning .... Matt. 7:15
Judgments by, deceptive .... Luke 16:19
Proper sign of Christian sanity .... Mark 5:15

Clothing, tearing of—*symbolic expression of grief*
By Reuben .... Gen. 37:29, 34
By Joshua .... Josh. 7:6
By Tamar .... 2 Sam. 13:19
By Job .... Job 1:20
By Ezra .... Ezra 9:3
By high priest .... Mark 14:63
By Paul and Barnabas .... Acts 14:14
Forbidden to Aaron .... Lev. 10:6

Cloud—*a visible mass of vapor*
A. *Miraculous uses of:*
Israel's guidance .... Ex. 13:21, 22
Manifesting the divine glory .... Ex. 16:10
Manifesting the divine presence .... 2 Chr. 5:13
Jesus' transfiguration .... Luke 9:34, 35
Jesus' ascension .... Acts 1:9-11
Jesus' return .... Matt. 24:30
B. *Figurative of:*
God's unsearchableness .... Ps. 97:2
Sins .... Is. 44:22
Witnesses .... Heb. 12:1
False teachers .... 2 Pet. 2:17
Baptism .... 1 Cor. 10:1, 2
Boasting .... Prov. 25:14

Cloudburst—*a sudden downpour of rain*
Sent as a punishment .... Ezra 10:9-14

Cloud, pillar of
A. *Designed to:*
Regulate Israel's movements .... Ex. 40:36, 37
Guide Israel .... Ex. 13:21
Defend Israel .... Ex. 14:19
Cover the tabernacle .... Ex. 40:34
B. *Special manifestations of, at:*
Time of murmuring .... Ex. 16:9, 10
Giving of Law .... Ex. 19:9, 16
Rebellion of Aaron and Miriam .... Num. 12:5
Korah's rebellion .... Num. 16:19, 42

Clusters—*bunches*
Kinds of:
Grapes .... Num. 13:23
Henna blossoms .... Song 1:14
Raisins .... 1 Sam. 25:18
Dates .... Song 5:11

Cnidus—*age*
City of Asia Minor on Paul's voyage .... Acts 27:7

Coal—*charcoal*
A. *Uses of:*
Heating .... John 18:18
Cooking .... John 21:9
By smiths .... Is. 44:11, 12

SUBJECT REFERENCE

B. *Figurative of:*
Lust .... Prov. 6:25-28
Purification .... Is. 6:6
Good deeds .... Rom. 12:20
Posterity .... 2 Sam. 14:7

Coat—*an outer garment*
A. *Makers of:*
God—for man .... Gen. 3:21
Jacob—for Joseph .... Gen. 37:3
Hannah—for Samuel .... 1 Sam. 2:18, 19
Dorcas—for widows .... Acts 9:39

Cockatrice—*venomous snake*
Figurative of evil deeds .... Is. 11:8
Figurative of man's evil nature .... Deut. 32:33

Cockcrowing
Announced the dawn .... Mark 13:35
Reminded Peter .... Matt. 26:34, 74

Cockle—*stinging weeds*
Obnoxious among barley .... Job 31:40

Coffer—*a strongbox; a chest*
Used to safeguard jewels .... 1 Sam. 6:8-15

Coffin—*a box-like container for a corpse*
In Joseph's burial .... Gen. 50:26
Jesus touched .... Luke 7:14

Coins—*metal mediums of exchange*
Beckah (1/2 shekel) .... Ex. 38:26
Brass .... Matt. 10:9
Dram .... Ezra 2:69
Farthing .... Matt. 10:29
Gerah .... Ex. 30:13
Maneh .... Ezek. 45:12
Mite .... Mark 12:42
Penny .... Matt. 20:2
Piece of gold .... 2 Kin. 5:5
Piece of money .... Matt. 17:27
Piece of silver .... Matt. 26:15

Cold—*absence of heat*
A. *Used literally of:*
Winter .... Gen. 8:22
Cold weather .... John 18:18
B. *Used figuratively of:*
God's power .... Ps. 147:17
Indolence .... Prov. 20:4
Good news .... Prov. 25:25
Apostasy .... Jer. 18:14
Spiritual decay .... Matt. 24:12

Col-hozeh—*all seeing*
A man of Judah .... Neh. 3:15
Neh. 11:5

Collaborators
Delilah .... Judg. 16:4-21
Doeg .... 1 Sam. 21:7
Judas .... Matt. 26:14-16

Collection box
For Temple offerings .... 2 Kin. 12:9

Collection of money
The Temple tax .... 2 Chr. 24:6, 9
For saints .... Rom. 15:25, 26

College
Huldah's dwelling .... 2 Kin. 22:14

Colony—*citizens transported to another land*
A. *Illustrated by:*
Israel in Egypt .... Gen. 46:28
Israel in Assyria .... 2 Kin. 17:6, 24
Judah in Babylon .... 2 Kin. 25:8-12
B. *Applied to:*
Philippi as a Roman colony .... Acts 16:12
Philippian Christians .... Phil. 3:20

Colors
A. *White, descriptive of:*
Glory and majesty .... Dan. 7:9
Rev. 20:11
Purity, glory .... Rev. 1:14
Victory .... Rev. 6:2
Completion .... John 4:35
B. *Black, descriptive of:*
Sorrow, calamity .... Rev. 6-12
Hell .... Jude 13

SUBJECT — REFERENCE

C. *Green, descriptive of:*
- Spiritual privileges ... Jer. 11:16
- Spiritual life ... Ps. 52:8; Ps. 92:12-15

D. *Red* (crimson), *descriptive of:*
- Atonement ... Is. 63:2
- Military might ... Nah. 2:3
- Persecution ... Rev. 12:3
- Drunkenness ... Prov. 23:29
- Sinfulness ... Is. 1:18

E. *Purple, descriptive of:*
- Royalty ... Judg. 8:26
- Wealth ... Luke 16:19
- Luxury ... Rev. 17:4

F. *Blue, descriptive of:*
- Heavenly character ... Ex. 28:31

Colossae—*punishment*
- A city in Asia Minor ... Col. 1:2
- Evangelized by Epaphras ... Col. 1:7
- Not visited by Paul ... Col. 2:1
- Paul writes against errors of ... Col. 2:16-23

Colossians, the epistle to the
- Written by Paul ... Col. 1:1

Colt—*young beast of burden*
- Descriptive of Messiah ... Gen. 49:10, 11
- Christ rides on ... Matt. 21:2, 5, 7
- Of camel, as gift ... Gen. 32:13, 15

Come—*to approach, arrive*
- Of invitation ... Is. 1:18
- Of salvation ... Matt. 18:11
- Of rest ... Matt. 11:28
- Of promise ... John 14:3
- Of prayer ... Heb. 4:16
- The final ... Rev. 22:17, 20

Comfort—*to relieve distress; to console*

A. *Sources of:*
- God ... 2 Cor. 1:3, 4
- Christ ... Matt. 9:22
- Holy Spirit ... Acts 9:31
- The Scriptures ... Rom. 15:4
- Christian friends ... 2 Cor. 7:6

B. *Those in need of:*
- Afflicted ... Is. 40:1, 2
- Sorrowful ... 2 Cor. 2:7
- Weak ... 1 Thess. 5:14
- Discouraged ... 2 Cor. 2:7
- Troubled ... 2 Cor. 7:5-7
- One another ... 1 Thess. 4:18

Comforter—*the Holy Spirit*
- Abides with believers ... John 14:16
- Teaches ... John 14:26
- Testifies of Christ ... John 15:26
- Convicts ... John 16:7-11
- Guides into truth ... John 16:13
- Glorifies Christ ... John 16:14, 15

Coming of Christ (see Second Coming of Christ)

Commander—*a leading official*

Names of:
- Phichol ... Gen. 21:32
- Sisera ... Judg. 4:7
- Abner ... 1 Sam. 17:55
- Shobach ... 2 Sam. 10:16
- Joab ... 2 Sam. 24:2
- Amasa ... 1 Kin. 2:32
- Zimri ... 1 Kin. 16:9
- Omri ... 1 Kin. 16:16
- Shophach ... 1 Chr 19:16
- Adnah ... 2 Chr. 17:14
- Jehohanan ... 2 Chr. 17:15
- Rehum ... Ezra 4:8
- Hananiah ... Neh. 7:2
- Arioch ... Dan. 2:15
- Lysias ... Acts 24:7

Commandment—*a rule imposed by authority*

A. *God's, described as:*
- Faithful ... Ps. 119:86
- Broad ... Ps. 119:96
- A lamp ... Prov. 6:23
- Holy ... Rom. 7:12
- Not burdensome ... 1 John 5:3

B. *Christ's, described as:*
- New ... John 13:34
- Obligatory ... Matt. 5:19, 20
- Promissory ... John 15:10, 12
- Eternal life ... John 12:49, 50

Commandments, divine
- Sought by men ... Phil. 3:6-15
- Not material ... Rom. 14:1-23
- Lives an epistle of ... 2 Cor. 3:1-3
- Revealed at judgment ... Matt. 25:20, 21

Commandment, the new
- Given by Christ ... John 13:34, 35
- Based on old ... 1 John 2:7-11; 2 John 5
- Fulfills the Law ... Matt. 22:34-40

Commandments, The Ten
- Divine origin ... Ex. 20:1
- Written by God ... Ex. 32:16
- Described ... Ex. 20:3-17
- Christ sums up ... Matt. 22:35-40
- Spiritual nature ... Matt. 5:28
- Love fulfills ... Rom. 13:8-10

Commerce—*trade on a large scale*

A. *Engaged in:*
- Locally ... Prov. 31:14-18
- Nationally ... 2 Chr. 9:21
- Internationally ... Rev. 18:10-24

B. *Abuses of:*
- Sabbath trading ... Neh. 13:15-22
- Temple business ... John 2:13-16
- Ignoring the Lord ... James 4:13-17
- Pride ... Ezek. 28:2-18

Commission—*special assignment*

A. *Kinds of:*
- Christ's—to mankind ... John 3:16-18
- Israel's—to the Gentiles ... Acts 13:47
- The Church's—to the world ... Matt. 28:19, 20

B. *Requirements of:*
- Faithfulness ... 2 Tim. 4:1-8
- Diligence ... Rom. 15:15-32
- Willingness ... 1 Sam. 3:9, 10

Common—*public, general*
- Normal, natural ... 1 Cor. 10:13
- Ceremonially unclean ... Acts 10:14
- Ordinary people ... Jer. 26:23
- Shared togetherness ... Acts 2:44
- Things believed alike ... Titus 1:4

Common people
- Burial place of ... Jer. 26:23

Commonwealth—*a nation*
- Descriptive of Israel ... Eph. 2:12

Communion of the Lord's Supper (see Lord's Supper)

Communion of the Saints (see Fellowship)

Communion with Christ

A. *Based on:*
- Redemption ... Heb. 2:10-13
- Regeneration ... 1 Cor. 6:14-17
- Resurrection (Spiritual) ... Col. 3:1-3

B. *Identifies Christians, in:*
- Name ... 1 Pet. 4:12-16
- Character ... John 14:23
- Hope ... 1 John 3:1-3

Communion with God

A. *Prerequisites of:*
- Reconciliation ... 2 Cor. 5:18, 19
- Acceptance of Christ ... John 14:6
- Obedience ... John 14:23
- Holiness ... 2 Cor. 6:14-18

B. *Saints:*
- Desire such ... Heb. 11:10
- Seek it through prayer ... Matt. 6:6-15
- Realized fully in eternity ... Rev. 7:13-17

Communism, Christian

A. *Supposedly found in:*
- Early church ... Acts 2:44, 45

B. *Differs from modern Communism:*
- In being voluntary ... Acts 5:4
- Confined to Christians ... Acts 4:32
- Not under government control ... Acts 4:34-37

Companion—*a fellow worker*
- Wife ... Mal. 2:14
- Companion in tribulation ... Rev. 1:9
- Co-worker ... Ezra 4:7, 9, 11
- Fellow fool ... Prov. 13:20
- Fellow believer ... Ps. 119:63
- Fellow worker ... Phil. 2:23, 25

Companions, evil

A. *Cause:*
- Rebellion ... Num. 16:1-50
- Idolatry ... Ex. 32:1-8
- Violence, death ... Acts 23:12-22
- Persecution ... Acts 17:5-9

B. *Warnings against:*
- Do not consent with them ... Prov. 1:10-19
- Avoid them ... 1 Cor. 5:9-11
- Remember their end ... Rev. 22:11, 15

Comparison—*likeness, similarity*

A. *Worthy comparisons, between:*
- God's greatness and man's littleness ... Is. 46:12, 13
- Christ's glory and humiliation ... Phil. 2:5-11
- Israel's call and responsibility ... Rom. 2:17-29
- Gentile faith and Jewish unbelief ... Matt. 12:41, 42
- Former and present unbelief ... Matt. 11:20-24
- Old and new covenants ... 2 Cor. 3:6-18
- The believer's status now and hereafter ... 1 John 3:1-3

B. *Unworthy comparisons, based on:*
- Position ... Num. 16:3
- Privileges ... 1 Cor. 3:1-9
- Ancestry ... James 2:1-9

Compassion—*suffering with another*

A. *God's, described as:*
- From of old ... Ps. 26:6
- New every morning ... Lam. 3:22, 23
- Great ... Is. 54:7
- Kindled ... Hos. 11:8

B. *God's, expressed:*
- Fully ... Ps. 78:38
- Sovereignly ... Rom. 9:15
- Unfailingly ... Lam. 3:22
- Willingly ... Luke 15:20

C. *Christ's, expressed toward the:*
- Weary ... Matt. 11:28-30
- Tempted ... Heb. 2:18
- Helpless ... Mark 9:20-22
- Ignorant ... Heb. 5:2
- Sorrowful ... Luke 7:13, 14
- Multitude ... Matt. 15:32

D. *Examples of:*
- David in sorrow ... Ps. 51:1-12
- God to Israel ... Hos. 11:8
- Christ to sinners ... Matt. 9:13

E. *Christian's:*
- Commanded ... Zech. 7:9; Col. 3:12; Jude 22
- Expressed ... Heb. 10:34; 1 Pet. 3:8
- Illustrated ... Luke 10:33
- Unified ... Phil. 2:1, 2

Complicity—*partnership in wrongdoing*
- In Adam's sin ... Rom. 5:12
- In the sins of others ... Ps. 50:18
- In national guilt ... Matt. 27:25

Composure—*calmness; tranquility; self-possession*
- Before enemies ... Neh. 4:1-23
- Under great strain ... Acts 27:21-26
- Facing death ... Acts 7:59, 60
- Lack of ... Dan. 6:18-20

Compromise—*agreement by concession*

A. *Forbidden with:*
- Ungodly ... Ps. 1:1
- Evil ... Rom. 12:9
- Unbelievers ... 2 Cor. 6:14-18
- False teachers ... Gal. 1:8-10; 2 John 7-11
- Spiritual darkness ... Eph. 5:11

SUBJECT ... REFERENCE

B. *Examples:*
- Lot ... Gen. 13:12, 13; Gen. 19:1-29
- Samson ... Judg. 16:1-21
- Solomon ... 1 Kin. 11:1-14
- Asa ... 2 Chr. 16:1-9
- Jehoshaphat ... 2 Chr. 18:1-3; 2 Chr. 19:1, 2; 2 Chr. 20:35-37

Concealment—*keeping something secret*
- Of sin, impossible ... Is. 29:15
- Of intrigue, exposed ... Esth. 2:21-23
- Of intentions, revealed ... Acts 23:12-22

Conceit—*self-flattery*

Of persons:
- Goliath ... 1 Sam. 17:42-44
- Sanballat ... Neh. 4:1-3
- Haman ... Esth. 6:6-9
- The wicked ... Prov. 6:12-17
- Christians, deplored ... Rom. 12:16

Characteristic of:
- False teachers ... 1 Tim. 6:3, 4
- New convert ... 1 Tim. 3:6

Conceited—*a self-righteous spirit*
- Christians warned against ... Rom. 11:20
- Rich tempted to ... 1 Tim. 6:17
- To prevail in last days ... 2 Tim. 3:1-5

Conception of children
- In marriage ... Gen. 21:1-3
- In adultery ... 2 Sam. 11:2-5
- In virginity ... Matt. 1:18-21

Concision—*mutilation*
- Used of legalistic circumcision ... Phil. 3:2

Conclude—*to decide*
- The main issue ... Eccl. 12:13

Concubine—*a "wife" who is not legally a wife*

A. *Features regarding:*
- Could be divorced ... Gen. 21:10-14
- Has certain rights ... Deut. 21:10-14
- Children of, legitimate ... Gen. 22:24
- Unfaithfulness of ... Judg. 19:9
- Source of trouble ... Gen. 21:10-14
- Incompatible with Christianity ... Matt. 19:5

B. *Men who had:*
- Abraham ... Gen. 25:6
- Nahor ... Gen. 22:24
- Jacob ... Gen. 30:1, 4
- Eliphaz ... Gen. 36:12
- Gideon ... Judg. 8:30, 31
- Saul ... 2 Sam. 3:7
- David ... 2 Sam. 5:13
- Solomon ... 1 Kin. 11:3
- Caleb ... 1 Chr. 2:46
- Manasseh ... 1 Chr. 7:14
- Rehoboam ... 2 Chr. 11:21
- Abijah ... 2 Chr. 13:21
- Belshazzar ... Dan. 5:2

Concupiscence—*sinful desire*

A. *Causes of:*
- Learning evil ... Rom. 16:19
- Making provision for flesh ... Rom. 13:14
- Not fearing God ... Prov. 8:13; Prov. 9:10
- Not seeing consequences of sin ... Ex. 34:6, 7; Rom. 6:23; Heb. 11:25

B. *Fruits of:*
- Evil inclinations ... Rom. 7:7, 8
- Temptations ... James 1:14
- Unchastity ... 1 Thess. 4:5
- Reprobation ... Rom. 1:21-32

C. *Remedy for:*
- Repentance ... 2 Cor. 7:9, 10; James 4:9, 10
- Submitting to God ... Rom. 12:1, 2; James 4:7
- Resisting the devil ... James 4:7
- Drawing near to God ... James 4:8
- Walking in the Spirit ... Rom. 8:1-8

Condemnation—*the judicial act of declaring one guilty*

A. *Causes of:*
- Adam's sin ... Rom. 5:16-18

SUBJECT ... REFERENCE

- Actual sin ... Matt. 27:3
- Our words ... Matt. 12:37
- Self-judgment ... Rom. 2:1; Titus 3:11
- Legal requirements ... 2 Cor. 3:9
- Rejection of Christ ... John 3:18, 19

B. *Escape from:*
- In Christ ... Rom. 8:1, 3
- By faith ... John 3:18, 19

Condescend—*to humble oneself to the level of others*
- Christ's example ... John 13:3-5
- The believer's practice ... Rom. 12:16
- The divine model ... Phil. 2:3-11

Condolence—*an expression of sympathy*

A. *Received by:*
- Job from friends ... Job 2:11
- Hanun from David ... 2 Sam. 10:2
- Hezekiah from a king ... 2 Kin. 20:12
- Mary from Jesus ... John 11:23-35

B. *Helps in expressing, assurance of:*
- Trust ... Ps. 23:1-6
- Hope ... John 14:1-4
- Resurrection ... 1 Thess. 4:13-18
- Help ... Is. 40:10, 11

Coney—*the Syrian rock hyrax*
- Listed as unclean ... Lev. 11:5
- Lives among rocks ... Ps. 104:18
- Likened to people ... Prov. 30:26

Confectionaries—*perfumers*
- A female occupation ... 1 Sam. 8:13

Confederacy—*an alliance*
- Denounced ... Is. 8:12

Confessing Christ

A. *Necessity of:*
- For salvation ... Rom. 10:9, 10
- A test of faith ... 1 John 2:23
- An evidence of spiritual union ... 1 John 4:15
- His confessing us ... Matt. 10:32

B. *Content of:*
- Christ's incarnation ... 1 John 4:2, 3
- Christ's Lordship ... Phil. 2:11

C. *Prompted by:*
- Holy Spirit ... 1 Cor. 12:3
- Faith ... Rom. 10:9

D. *Hindrances to:*
- Fear of men ... John 7:13
- Persecution ... Mark 8:34, 35
- False teachers ... 2 John 7

Confession of sin

A. *Manifested by:*
- Repentance ... Ps. 51:1-19
- Self-abasement ... Jer. 3:25
- Godly sorrow ... Ps. 38:18
- Turning from sin ... Prov. 28:13
- Restitution ... Num. 5:6, 7

B. *Results in:*
- Forgiveness ... 1 John 1:9, 10
- Pardon ... Ps. 32:1-5
- Renewed fellowship ... Ps. 51:12-19
- Healing ... James 5:16

C. *Instances of:*
- Aaron ... Num. 12:11
- Israelites ... 1 Sam. 12:19
- David ... 2 Sam. 24:10
- Ezra ... Ezra 9:6
- Nehemiah ... Neh. 1:6, 7
- Daniel ... Dan. 9:4
- Peter ... Luke 5:8
- Thief ... Luke 23:41

Confidence—*assurance*

A. *True, based upon:*
- God's Word ... Acts 27:22-25
- Assurance ... 2 Tim. 1:12
- Trust ... Hab. 3:17-19
- Christ's promise ... Phil. 1:6
- Illustrated ... 1 Sam. 17:45-50

B. *False, based upon:*
- Unwarranted use of sacred things ... 1 Sam. 4:5-11
- Presumption ... Num. 14:40-45
- Pride ... 1 Sam. 17:43, 44

SUBJECT ... REFERENCE

C. *The believer's:*
- Source of ... 1 John 3:21, 22
- In prayer ... 1 John 5:14, 15
- In testimony ... Acts 28:31
- In others ... 2 Cor. 2:3; 2 Cor. 7:16
- Of God's will ... Phil. 1:25
- Of faith's finality ... Phil. 1:6
- Of future things ... 2 Cor. 5:6, 8
- Must be held ... Heb. 10:35

C

Confirmation—*making something steadfast and sure*
- Human things ... Ruth 4:7; Esth. 9:31, 32
- A kingdom ... 2 Kin. 14:5
- An oath ... Heb. 6:17
- A covenant ... Gal. 3:17
- Prophecy ... Dan. 9:12, 27
- Promises ... Rom. 15:8
- Defense of faith ... Phil. 1:7
- Establishing faith ... Acts 14:22; Acts 15:32, 41

Conformity—*likeness of one thing to another*
- To the world, forbidden ... Rom. 12:2

Confused—*disorderly; perplexed*

Concerning:
- God's will ... 1 Sam. 23:1-12
- The Messiah ... Matt. 11:3
- A great event ... Acts 2:1-6

Confusion—*bewilderment*

A. *Aspects of:*
- God not author of ... 1 Cor. 14:33
- Typical of evil ... James 3:16
- Prayer concerning ... Ps. 70:2
- Illustrations of ... Acts 19:29

B. *Examples of:*
- Babel ... Gen. 11:9
- Philistines ... 1 Sam. 7:10
- Egyptians ... Ex. 14:24
- City of Shushan ... Esth. 3:15
- Jerusalem ... Acts 21:31

Congratulate—*to express happiness to another*
- Tou to David ... 1 Chr. 18:9,10

Congregation—*an assembly of people*

A. *Used of:*
- The political Israel ... Ex. 12:3, 19, 47
- A religious assembly ... Acts 13:43
- The tent of meeting ... Ex. 27:21

B. *Regulations concerning:*
- Ruled by representatives ... Num. 16:6
- Summoned by trumpets ... Num. 10:3, 4, 7
- Bound by decisions of representatives ... Josh. 9:15-21
- Atonement of sin of ... Lev. 4:13-21
- Exclusion of certain ones from ... Deut. 23:1-8

Coniah—*Jehovah is creating*
- King of Judah ... Jer. 22:24, 28
- Same as Jehoiachin ... 2 Kin. 24:8

Connivance at wrong—*tacit approval of evil*
- Involves guilt ... Ps. 50:18-22
- Aaron's, at Sinai ... Ex. 32:1, 2, 22
- Pilate's, at Jesus' trial ... Matt. 27:17-26
- Saul's (Paul's) at Stephen's death ... Acts 8:1

Cononiah—*Jehovah has established*
1. A Levite ... 2 Chr. 31:11, 12, 13
2. A Levite official ... 2 Chr. 35:9

Conscience—*the inner judge of moral issues*

A. *Described as*
- Good ... Acts 23:1
- Pure ... 1 Tim. 3:9
- Evil ... Heb. 10:22
- Defiled ... 1 Cor. 8:7
- Seared ... 1 Tim. 4:2

B. *Functions of:*
- A witness ... Rom. 2:15
- An accuser ... John 8:9
- An upholder ... 1 Tim. 1:19
- Server of good ... Rom. 13:5
- Source of joy ... 2 Cor. 1:12
- Dead ... Prov. 30:20

SUBJECT — REFERENCE

C. *Limitations of:*
Needs cleansing .... Heb. 9:14
Subject to others' .... 1 Cor. 10:28, 29
Differs .... 1 Cor. 8:7-13
Fallible .... Prov. 16:25

Conscience, clear—*freedom from guilt feelings*

A. *Necessary for:*
Freedom from legalism .... Heb. 9:13, 14
Access to God .... Heb. 10:21, 22
Liberty in witnessing .... 1 Pet. 3:15, 16
Christian love .... 1 Tim. 1:5
Confidence in prayer .... 1 John 3:21, 22
Proud confidence .... 2 Cor. 1:12

B. *Requirements for:*
Doctrinal purity .... {1 Tim. 1:3-5, 18—2:1; 1 Tim. 4:1, 2}
Proper conduct .... Acts 24:10-13, 16; Rom. 13:4-6
Faith in Christ's blood .... Heb. 9:14; Heb. 10:19-22
Knowledge .... 1 Cor. 8:7
Belief .... Titus 1:15
Submissive spirit .... 1 Pet. 2:18, 19
Faith in God's greatness .... 1 John 3:20
Consideration of others .... 1 Cor. 10:28, 29
Seeking forgiveness .... Prov. 28:13; Matt. 5:23, 24

Conscription—*to enroll for compulsory service*
Employed by Solomon .... 1 Kin. 7:13, 14; 1 Kin. 9:20, 21
To build Temple .... 1 Kin. 5:2, 3, 18
To restore cities .... 1 Kin. 9:15-17
Led to revolt .... 1 Kin. 12:3-16
See Levy

Consecration—*dedication to God's service*

A. *Applied to:*
Israel .... Ex. 19:6
Priests .... Lev. 8:1-13
Levites .... Num. 8:5, 6
Individuals .... 1 Sam. 1:11
First-born .... Ex. 13:2, 12
Possessions .... Lev. 27:28, 29
Christ .... Heb. 2:10

B. *The Christian's:*
By Christ .... John 17:23
Complete and entire .... Rom. 12:1, 2
Separation from world .... 2 Cor. 6:14-18
Devotion to Christ .... Rev. 14:1-6
Sacred anointing .... 1 John 2:20, 27
New priesthood .... 1 Pet. 2:5, 9

Conservation—*preserving worthwhile things*
Material things .... John 6:12, 13
Spiritual things .... Rev. 3:2, 3
Good .... Acts 26:22, 23
Unwise .... Luke 5:36, 37

Consolation—*comfort fortified with encouragement*
God, source of .... Rom. 15:5
Simeon waits for .... Luke 2:25
Source of joy .... Acts 15:31
To be shared .... 2 Cor. 1:4-11

Conspiracy—*a plot to overthrow lawful authority*
Against:
Joseph .... Gen. 37:18-20
Moses .... Num. 16:1-35
Samson .... Judg. 16:4-21
Daniel .... Dan. 6:4-17
Jesus .... Matt. 12:14
Paul .... Acts 23:12-15

Constancy—*firmness of purpose*
Ruth's, to Naomi .... Ruth 1:16
Jonathan's, to David .... 1 Sam. 20:17
Virgins, to Christ .... Rev. 14:4, 5

Constellation—*a group of stars*
Arcturus .... Job 9:9; Job 38:32
The Serpent .... Job 26:13
Orion .... Job 38:31; Amos 5:8
Pleiades (seven stars) .... Job 9:9; Job 38:31
Castor and Pollux .... Acts 28:11

SUBJECT — REFERENCE

Judgment on .... Is. 13:10, 11
Incense burned to .... 2 Kin. 23:5

Consultation—*seeking advice from others*
Demonical .... 1 Sam. 28:7-25
Divided .... 1 Kin. 12:6, 8
Determined .... Dan. 6:7
Devilish .... Matt. 26:4; John 12:10, 11

Contempt—*scorn compounded with disrespect*

A. *Forbidden toward:*
Parents .... Prov. 23:22
Weak Christians .... Matt. 18:10; Rom. 14:3
Believing masters .... 1 Tim. 6:2
The poor .... James 2:1-3

B. *Objects of:*
The righteous .... Ps. 80:6
Spiritual things .... Matt. 22:2-6
Christ .... John 9:28, 29

C. *Examples of:*
Nabal .... 1 Sam. 25:10, 11
Michal .... 2 Sam. 6:16
Sanballat .... Neh. 2:19
Jews .... Matt. 26:67, 68
False teachers .... 2 Cor. 10:10
The wicked .... Prov. 18:3

Contention—*a quarrelsome spirit*

A. *Caused by:*
Pride .... Prov. 13:10
Disagreement .... Acts 15:36-41
Divisions .... 1 Cor. 1:11-13
A quarrelsome spirit .... Gal. 5:15

B. *Antidotes:*
Avoid the contentious .... Prov. 21:19
Avoid controversies .... Titus 3:9
Abandon the quarrel .... Prov. 17:14
Follow peace .... Rom. 12:18-21

Contentment—*an uncomplaining acceptance of one's share*

A. *Opposed to:*
Anxiety .... Matt. 6:25, 34
Murmuring .... 1 Cor. 10:10
Greed .... Heb. 13:5
Envy .... James 3:16

B. *Shown by our recognition of:*
Our unworthiness .... Gen. 32:10
Our trust .... Hab. 3:17-19
God's care .... Ps. 145:7-21
God's provisions .... 1 Tim. 6:6-8
God's promises .... Heb. 13:5

Contracts—*covenants legally binding*

A. *Ratified by:*
Giving presents .... Gen. 21:25-30
Public witness .... Ruth 4:1-11
Oaths .... Josh. 9:15, 20
Joining hands .... Prov. 17:18
Pierced ear .... Ex. 21:2-6

B. *Examples of:*
Abraham and Abimelech .... Gen. 21:25-32
Solomon and Hiram .... 1 Kin. 5:8-12

Contrition—*a profound sense of one's sinfulness*
Of the heart .... Ps. 51:17
The publican .... Luke 18:13
Peter's example .... Matt. 26:75

Controversy—*dispute between people*
Between men .... Deut. 25:1
Between God and men .... Hos. 4:1
A public .... Acts 15:1-35
A private .... Gal. 2:11-15

Conversion—*turning to God from sin*

A. *Produced by:*
God .... Acts 21:19
Christ .... Acts 3:26
Holy Spirit .... 1 Cor. 2:13
The Scriptures .... Ps. 19:7
Preaching .... Rom. 10:14

B. *Of Gentiles:*
Foretold .... Is. 60:1-5
Explained .... Rom. 15:8-18; Acts 15:3
Illustrated .... Acts 10:1-48; Acts 16:25-34
Confirmed .... Acts 15:1-31
Defended .... Gal. 3:1-29

SUBJECT — REFERENCE

C. *Results in:*
Repentance .... Acts 26:20
New creation .... 2 Cor. 5:17
Transformation .... 1 Thess. 1:9, 10

D. *Fruits of:*
Faithfulness .... Matt. 24:45-47
Gentleness .... 1 Thess. 2:7
Patience .... Col. 1:10-12
Love .... 1 John 3:14
Obedience .... Rom. 15:18
Peacefulness .... James 3:17, 18
Self-control .... 2 Pet. 1:6
Self-denial .... John 12:25

Conviction—*making one conscious of his guilt*

A. *Produced by:*
Holy Spirit .... John 16:7-11
The Gospel .... Acts 2:37
Conscience .... Rom. 2:15
The Law .... James 2:9

B. *Instances of:*
Adam .... Gen. 3:8-10
Joseph's brothers .... Gen. 42:21, 22
Israel .... Ex. 33:4
David .... Ps. 51:1-17
Isaiah .... Is. 6:5
Men of Nineveh .... Matt. 12:41
Peter .... Luke 5:8
Saul of Tarsus .... Acts 9:4-18
Philippian jailer .... Acts 16:29, 30

Convocation—*a gathering for worship*

A. *Applied to:*
Sabbaths .... Lev. 23:2, 3
Passover .... Ex. 12:16
Pentecost .... Lev. 23:21
Feast of Trumpets .... Num. 29:1
Feast of Weeks .... Num. 28:26
Feast of Tabernacles .... Lev. 23:34-36
Day of Atonement .... Lev. 23:27

B. *Designed to:*
Gather the people .... Josh. 23:1-16
Worship God .... 2 Kin. 23:21, 22

Cooking—*making food palatable*
Done by women .... Gen. 18:2-6
Carefully performed .... Gen. 27:3-10
Savory dish .... Gen. 27:4
Vegetables .... Gen. 25:29
Forbidden on the Sabbath .... Ex. 35:3
Fish .... Luke 24:42

Co-operation—*working together*

A. *Kinds of:*
Man with man .... Ex. 17:12
God with man .... Phil. 2:12, 13

B. *Needed to:*
Complete job .... Neh. 4:16, 17
Secure results .... Matt. 18:19
Win converts .... John 1:40-51
Maintain peace .... Mark 9:50

C. *Basis:*
Obedience to God .... Ps. 119:63
Faith .... Rom. 14:1

Coos
An island between Rhodes and Miletus .... Acts 21:1

Coral—*a rocklike substance formed from skeletons of sea creatures*
Wisdom more valuable than .... Job 28:18
Bought by traders .... Ezek. 27:16

Corban—*an offering*
Money dedicated .... Mark 7:11

Cordiality—*sincere affection and kindness*
Abraham's .... Gen. 18:1-8
Seen in Jonathan .... 1 Sam. 20:11-23
Lacking in Nabal .... 1 Sam. 25:9-13

Coriander
A plant whose seed is compared to manna .... Ex. 16:31

Corinth—*a city of Greece*
Paul labors at .... Acts 18:1-18
Site of church .... 1 Cor. 1:2
Visited by Apollos .... Acts 19:1
Abode of Erastus .... 2 Tim. 4:20

SUBJECT — REFERENCE

Corinthians, epistles to the—*two books of the New Testament*

Written by Paul .... 1 Cor. 1:1
2 Cor. 1:1

Cormorant

An unclean bird .... Lev. 11:17

Corn—*the generic term for cereal grasses*

A. *Features regarding:*

Grown in Palestine .... 2 Kin. 18:32
Chaff blown from .... Matt. 3:12
Article of food .... Gen. 42:1, 2, 19
Eaten with oil .... Lev. 2:14, 15
Parched .... Ruth 2:14

B. *Figurative of:*

Blessings .... Ezek. 36:29
Heavenly food .... Ps. 78:24
Christ .... John 12:24
Life's maturity .... Job 5:26

Cornelius—*a horn*

A religious Gentile .... Acts 10:1-48

Cornerstone, corner stone—*a stone placed to bind two walls together*

Laid in Zion .... Is. 28:16
Rejected .... Ps. 118:22
Christ is .... 1 Pet. 2:6, 8
Christ promised as .... Zech. 4:7
Christ fulfills .... Acts 4:11
1 Pet. 2:7

Cornet—*a musical instrument*

Used on occasions .... 1 Chr. 15:28
A part of worship .... 2 Sam. 6:5
Used in Babylon .... Dan. 3:7, 10

Corpse—*a dead body*

A. *Laws regarding:*

Dwelling made unclean by .... Num. 19:11-22
Contact with, makes unclean .... Lev. 11:39
Food made unclean .... Lev. 11:40

B. *Used figuratively of:*

Those in hell .... Is. 66:24
Idolatrous kings .... Ezek. 43:7, 9
Attraction .... Matt. 24:28

Correction—*punishment designed to restore*

A. *Means of:*

God's judgments .... Jer. 46:28
The rod .... Prov. 22:15
Wickedness .... Jer. 2:19
Prayer .... Jer. 10:24
Scriptures .... 2 Tim. 3:16

B. *Benefits of:*

Needed for children .... Prov. 23:13
Sign of sonship .... Prov. 3:12
Brings rest .... Prov. 29:17
Makes happy .... Job 5:17

Corruption—*rottenness; depravity*

A. *Descriptive of:*

Physical blemishes .... Mal. 1:14
Physical decay .... Matt. 6:19, 20
Moral decay .... Gen. 6:12
Eternal ruin .... Gal. 6:8

B. *Characteristics of:*

Unregenerate men .... Luke 6:43, 44
Apostates .... 2 Cor. 2:7
2 Pet. 2:12, 19

C. *Deliverance from:*

By Christ .... Acts 2:27, 31
Promised .... Rom. 8:21
Through conversion .... 1 Pet. 1:18, 23
Perfected in heaven .... 1 Cor. 15:42, 50

Corruption, mount of

Site of pagan altars .... 1 Kin. 11:7
Altars of, destroyed .... 2 Kin. 23:13

Corruption of body

Results from Adam's sin .... Rom. 8:21
Begins in this life .... 2 Cor. 5:4
Consummated by death .... John 11:39
Freedom from, promised .... Rom. 8:21
Freedom from, accomplished .... 1 Cor. 15:42

Cosam—*a diviner*

Father of Addi .... Luke 3:28

Cosmetics

Used by Jezebel .... 2 Kin. 9:30
Futility of .... Jer. 4:30

Cosmic conflagration—*to destroy by fire*

Day of judgment .... 2 Pet. 3:7-10

Council—*Jewish Sanhedrin*

A judicial court .... Matt. 5:22
Christ's trial .... Matt. 26:57-59
Powers of, limited .... John 18:31
Apostles before .... Acts 4:5-30
Stephen before .... Acts 6:12-15
Paul before .... Acts 23:1-5

Counsel, God's

A. *Called:*

Immutable .... Heb. 6:17
Faithful .... Is. 25:1
Wonderful .... Is. 28:29
Great .... Jer. 32:19
Sovereign .... Dan. 4:35
Eternal .... Eph. 3:11

B. *Events determined by:*

History .... Is. 46:10, 11
Christ's death .... Acts 2:23
Salvation .... Rom. 8:28-30
Union in Christ .... Eph. 1:9, 10

C. *Attitudes toward:*

Christians declare .... Acts 20:27
Proper reserve .... Acts 1:7
Wicked despise .... Is. 5:19
They reject .... Luke 7:30

Counsel, man's

Jethro's, accepted .... Ex. 18:13-27
Hushai's followed .... 2 Sam. 17:14
Of a woman, brings peace .... 2 Sam. 20:16-20
David's dying .... 1 Kin. 2:1-10
Of old men, rejected .... 1 Kin. 12:8, 13
Of friends, avenged .... Esth. 5:14

Counselor—*an advisor*

Christ is .... Is. 9:6
Thy testimonies are .... Ps. 119:24
Safety in many .... Prov. 11:14
Brings security .... Prov. 15:22
Jonathan, a .... 1 Chr. 27:32
Gamaliel .... Acts 5:33-40

Count—*to number*

Things counted:

Stars .... Gen. 15:5
Days .... Lev. 15:13
Years .... Lev. 25:8
Booty .... Num. 31:26
Weeks .... Deut. 16:9
Money .... 2 Kin. 22:4
People .... 1 Chr. 21:17
Bones .... Ps. 22:17
Towers .... Ps. 48:12
Houses .... Is. 22:10

Countenance—*facial expression*

A. *Kinds of:*

Unfriendly .... Gen. 31:1, 2
Fierce .... Deut. 28:50
Terrible .... Judg. 13:6
Sad .... Neh. 2:2, 3
Beautiful .... 1 Sam. 16:12
Cheerful .... Prov. 15:13
Angry .... Prov. 25:23
Hatred .... Prov. 10:18

B. *Transfigured:*

Moses' .... 2 Cor. 3:7
Christ's .... Matt. 17:2
The believer's .... 2 Cor. 3:18

Counterfeit—*a spurious imitation of the real thing*

A. *Applied to persons:*

Christ .... Matt. 24:4, 5, 24
Apostles .... 2 Cor. 11:13
Ministers .... 2 Cor. 11:14, 15
Christians .... Gal. 2:3, 4
Teachers .... 2 Pet. 2:1
Prophets .... John 4:1
The antichrist .... Rev. 19:20

B. *Applied to things:*

Worship .... Matt. 15:8, 9
Gospel .... Gal. 1:6-12
Miracles .... 2 Thess. 2:7-12
Science .... 1 Tim. 6:20
Commandments .... Titus 1:13, 14
Doctrines .... Heb. 13:9
Religion .... James 1:26
Prayers .... James 4:3

Country—*the land of a nation*

Commanded to leave .... Gen. 12:1-4
Love of native .... Gen. 30:25
Exiled from .... Ps. 137:1-6
A prophet in his own .... Luke 4:24
A heavenly .... Heb. 11:16

Courage—*fearlessness in the face of danger*

A. *Manifested:*

Among enemies .... Ezra 5:11
In battle .... 1 Sam. 17:46
Against great foes .... Judg. 7:7-23
Against great odds .... 1 Sam. 17:32, 50
When threatened .... Dan. 3:16-18
When intimidated .... Dan. 6:10
When facing death .... Judg. 16:28
In youth .... 1 Sam. 14:6-45
In old age .... Josh. 14:10-12
Before a king .... Esth. 4:8, 16
In moral crises .... Neh. 13:1-31
In preaching Christ .... Acts 3:12-26
In rebuking .... Gal. 2:11-15

B. *Men encouraged to:*

Leaders .... Deut. 31:7
Joshua .... Josh. 1:5-7
Gideon .... Judg. 7:11
Philistines .... 1 Sam. 4:9
Zerubbabel .... Hag. 2:4
Solomon .... 1 Chr. 28:20

Course—*onward movement; advance*

A ship's direction .... Acts 16:11
A prescribed path .... Judg. 5:20
One's life .... 2 Tim. 4:7
The age .... Eph. 2:2
The cycle of life .... James 3:6
Orderly arrangement .... 1 Chr. 27:1-15

Courtesy—*visible signs of respect*

A. *Shown in:*

Manner of address .... Gen. 18:3
Gestures of bowing .... Gen. 19:1
Rising before superiors .... Lev. 19:32
Well-wishing remarks .... Gen. 43:29
Expressions of blessing .... Ruth 2:4

B. *Among Christians:*

Taught .... Rom. 12:9-21
Illustrated .... 3 John 1-6, 12

Courts—*institution designed for justice*

A. *Kinds of:*

Circuit .... 1 Sam. 7:15-17
Superior and inferior .... Ex. 18:21-26
Ecclesiastical .... Matt. 18:15-18

B. *Places held:*

At the tabernacle .... Num. 27:2
Outside the camp .... Lev. 24:14
At the city's gates .... Ruth 4:1, 2
Under a tree .... Judg. 4:5

C. *Features of:*

Witness examined .... Deut. 19:15-21
Accused speaks .... Mark 15:3-5
Sentence of, final .... Deut. 17:8-13
Contempt of, forbidden .... Acts 23:1-5
Corruption of, deplored .... Matt. 26:59-62

Courtship—*the period leading to marriage*

Isaac and Rebekah .... Gen. 24:1-67
Jacob and Rachel .... Gen. 29:9-30
Samson .... Judg. 14:1-7
Boaz and Ruth .... Ruth 3:4-13
Ahasuerus and Esther .... Esth. 2:17

Courtyard—*an enclosed area*

Tabernacle .... Ex. 27:9
Temple .... 1 Kin. 6:36
Prison .... Jer. 32:2
House .... 2 Sam. 17:18
Garden place .... Esth. 1:5

Covenant—*agreement between men*

A. *Designed for:*

Mutual protection .... Gen. 31:50-52
Securing peace .... Josh. 9:15, 21
Friendship .... 1 Sam. 18:3
Promoting commerce .... 1 Kin. 5:6-11

SUBJECT REFERENCE

B. *Requirements of:*

Witnessed .... Gen. 23:16-18
Confirmed by an oath .... Gen. 21:23, 31
Specified .... 1 Sam. 11:1, 2
Written and sealed .... Neh. 9:38

C. *Examples of:*

Abraham and Abimelech .... Gen. 21:27-32
Laban and Jacob .... Gen. 31:43-55
David and elders .... 2 Sam. 5:1-3
Ahab and Ben-hadad .... 1 Kin. 20:34
New covenant .... Matt. 26:28
New Testament dispensation .... 2 Cor. 3:6
Superiority of the new .... Heb. 8:6-13
Descriptive of a person's will .... Heb. 9:15-17

Covenant—*spiritual agreement*

A. *Between a leader and people:*

Joshua's .... Josh. 24:1-28
Jehoiada's .... 2 Kin. 11:17
Hezekiah's .... 2 Chr. 29:10
Josiah's .... 2 Kin. 23:3
Ezra's .... Ezra 10:3

B. *Between God and man:*

Adam .... Gen. 2:16, 17
Noah .... Gen. 9:1-17
Abraham .... Gen. 15:18
Isaac .... Gen. 26:3-5
Jacob .... Gen. 28:13-22
Israel .... Ex. 19:5
Levi .... Mal. 2:4-10
Phinehas .... Num. 25:11-13
David .... Ps. 89:3, 28, 34

C. *The old* (Sinaitic):

Instituted at Sinai .... Ex. 19:5
Ratified by sacrifice .... Ex. 24:6-8
Heb. 9:16
Does not annul the Abrahamic .... Gal. 3:16-18
Designed to lead to Christ .... Gal. 3:17-25
Consists of outward rites .... Heb. 9:1-13
Sealed by circumcision .... Gen. 17:9-14
Prefigures the Gospel .... Heb. 9:8-28

D. *The new* (evangelical):

Promised in Eden .... Gen. 3:15
Proclaimed to Abraham .... Gen. 12:3
Dated in prophecy .... Dan. 9:24-27
Fulfilled in Christ .... Luke 1:68-79
Ratified by His blood .... Heb. 9:11-23
Remembered in the Lord's Supper .... 1 Cor. 11:25
Called everlasting .... Heb. 13:20

Covenant-breakers

Under God's judgment .... Is. 24:5
By abominations .... Ezek. 44:7

Covenant-keepers

God's blessing upon .... Ex. 19:5

Covenant of salt—*of perpetual purity*

Descriptive of Levites .... Num. 18:19
Descriptive of David .... 2 Chr. 13:5
Used figuratively .... Mark 9:50

Covered carts

Used as offerings .... Num. 7:3

Coverings

Symbolic of:

Immorality .... Prov. 7:16
Diligence .... Prov. 31:22

Covert—*hiding place*

Used by Abigail .... 1 Sam. 25:20
Destroyed by Ahaz .... 2 Kin. 16:18
Figurative of protection .... Is. 32:2

Covetousness—*an insatiable desire for worldly gain*

A. *Described as:*

Idolatry .... Col. 3:5
Root of evil .... 1 Tim. 6:9-11
Never satisfied .... Hab. 2:9
Vanity .... Ps. 39:6

B. *Productive of:*

Theft .... Josh. 7:21
Lying .... 2 Kin. 5:20-27
Murder .... Prov. 1:18, 19
Falsehood .... Acts 5:1-10

SUBJECT REFERENCE

Hurtful lusts .... 1 Tim. 6:9
Apostasy .... 1 Tim. 6:10

C. *Excludes from:*

God's kingdom .... 1 Cor. 6:10
Eph. 5:5
Sacred offices .... 1 Tim. 3:3
Heaven .... Eph. 5:5

D. *Examples of:*

Achan .... Josh. 7:21
Saul .... 1 Sam. 15:9, 19
Judas .... Matt. 26:14, 15
Ananias .... Acts 5:1-11

See Avarice

Cowardice, spiritual

A. *Causes of:*

Fear of life .... Gen. 12:11-13
Fear of others .... Ex. 32:22-24
Unbelief .... Num. 13:28-33
Fear of rulers .... John 9:22

B. *Results in:*

Defeat .... Num. 14:40-45
Escape .... 2 Sam. 15:13-17
Compromise .... John 19:12-16
Denial .... Matt. 26:69-74

C. *Guilty conscience makes:*

Joseph's brothers .... Gen. 42:21-28
David .... 2 Sam. 12:1-14
Pharisees .... John 8:1-11

Cows

Jacob's possessions .... Gen. 32:15
Found in Egypt .... Gen. 41:2
Use of milk .... 2 Sam. 17:29
Used in rituals .... Lev. 3:1

Coz—*thorn*

Father of Anub .... 1 Chr. 4:8

Cozbi—*false*

Slain by Phinehas .... Num. 25:6-18

Craft

Ships of Tarshish .... Is. 2:16
A trade .... Rev. 18:22

Craftiness—*cunning deception*

Man's, known by God .... 1 Cor. 3:19
Enemies', perceived by Christ .... Luke 20:23
Use of, rejected .... 2 Cor. 4:2
Warning against .... Eph. 4:14

Craftsmen—*men who work at a trade*

Makers of idols .... Deut. 27:15
Destroyed in Babylon .... Rev. 18:21, 22

Crane—*a migratory bird*

Chatters .... Is. 38:14

Creation—*causing what did not exist to exist*

A. *Author of:*

God .... Heb. 11:3
Jesus Christ .... Col. 1:16, 17
Holy Spirit .... Ps. 104:30

B. *Objects of:*

Heaven, earth .... Gen. 1:1-13
Vegetation .... Gen. 1:11, 12
Animals .... Gen. 1:21
Man .... Gen. 1:26-28
Stars .... Is. 40:26

C. *Expressive of God's:*

Deity .... Rom. 1:20
Power .... Is. 40:26, 28
Glory .... Ps. 19:1
Goodness .... Ps. 33:5-6
Wisdom .... Ps. 104:24
Sovereignty .... Rev. 4:11

D. *Illustrative of:*

The new birth .... 2 Cor. 5:17
Renewal of believers .... Ps. 51:10
The eternal world .... Is. 65:17
2 Pet. 3:11, 13

Creator—*the Supreme Being*

A title of God .... Is. 40:28
Man's disrespect of .... Rom. 1:25
To be remembered .... Eccl. 12:1

Creature—*a being with life*

Subject to vanity .... Rom. 8:19, 20
Will be delivered .... Rom. 8:21
Believer, a new .... 2 Cor. 5:17

SUBJECT REFERENCE

Creditor—*one to whom a debt is payable*

Interest, forbidden .... Ex. 22:25
Debts remitted .... Neh. 5:10-12
Some very cruel .... Matt. 18:28-30
Christian principle .... Rom. 13:8

Cremation—*burning a body*

Two hundred fifty were consumed .... Num. 16:35
Zimri's end .... 1 Kin. 16:15-19

Crescens—*growing*

Paul's assistant .... 2 Tim. 4:10

Crete—*an island in the Mediterranean Sea*

Some from, at Pentecost .... Acts 2:11
Paul visits .... Acts 27:7-21
Titus dispatched to .... Titus 1:5
Inhabitants of, evil and lazy .... Titus 1:12

Crib

Animals feed from .... Is. 1:3
A stall .... Prov. 14:4

Criminal—*a lawbreaker*

Paul considered a .... Acts 25:16, 27
Christ accused of .... John 18:30
Christ crucified between .... Luke 23:32, 33
One unrepentant; one repentant .... Luke 23:39-43

Cripple—*one physically impaired*

Mephibosheth, by a fall .... 2 Sam. 4:4
Paul's healing of .... Acts 14:8-10
Jesus heals .... Matt. 15:30, 31

Crisis—*the crest of human endurance*

Bad advice in .... Job 2:9, 10
God's advice in .... Luke 21:25-28

Crispus—*curled*

Chief ruler of synagogue at Corinth .... Acts 18:8
Baptized by Paul .... 1 Cor. 1:14

Crookback

Barred from priesthood .... Lev. 21:20, 21

Crop—*the craw of a bird*

Removed by priest .... Lev. 1:16

Cross—*a method of execution*

A. *Used literally of:*

Christ's death .... Matt. 27:32

B. *Used figuratively of:*

Duty .... Matt. 10:38
Christ's sufferings .... 1 Cor. 1:17
The Christian faith .... 1 Cor. 1:18
Reconciliation .... Eph. 2:16

Crown—*an emblem of glory*

A. *Worn by:*

High priest .... Lev. 8:9
Kings .... 2 Sam. 12:30
Queens .... Esth. 2:17
Ministers of state .... Esth. 8:15

B. *Applied figuratively to:*

A good wife .... Prov. 12:4
Old age .... Prov. 16:31
Grandchildren .... Prov. 17:6
Honor .... Prov. 27:24
Material blessings .... Ps. 65:11

C. *Applied spiritually to:*

Christ .... Ps. 132:18
Christ at His return .... Rev. 19:12
Christ glorified .... Heb. 2:7-9
The church .... Is. 62:3
The Christian's reward .... 2 Tim. 2:5
The minister's reward .... Phil. 4:1
Soul winners .... 1 Thess. 2:19
The Christian's incorruptible prize .... 1 Cor. 9:25

Crown of thorns

Placed on Christ .... Matt. 27:29
John 19:2

Crowns of Christians

Joy .... 1 Thess. 2:19
Righteousness .... 2 Tim. 4:8
Life .... James 1:12
Glory .... 1 Pet. 5:4
Incorruptible .... 1 Cor. 9:25

SUBJECT	REFERENCE
Crucifixion—*death on a cross*	
A. *Jesus' death by:*	
Predicted	Matt. 20:19
Demanded	Mark 15:13, 14
Gentiles	Matt. 20:19
Jews	Acts 2:23, 36
Between thieves	Matt. 27:38
Nature of, unrecognized	1 Cor. 2:8
B. *Figurative of:*	
Utter rejection	Heb. 6:6
Apostasy	Rev. 11:8
Union with Christ	Gal. 2:20
Separation	Gal. 6:14
Sanctification	Rom. 6:6
Dedication	1 Cor. 2:2
Cruelty—*violence*	
Descriptive of the wicked	Ps. 74:20
To animals, forbidden	Num. 22:27-35
Crumbs—*fragments of bread*	
Dogs eat of	Matt. 15:27
Lazarus begs for	Luke 16:20, 21
Cruse—*a small earthen vessel*	
For water	1 Sam. 26:11, 12
For oil	1 Kin. 17:12, 14
Crying—*an emotional upheaval*	
Accusation	Gen. 4:10
Remorse	Heb. 12:17
Pretense	Judg. 14:15-18
Sorrow	2 Sam. 18:33
Others' sins	Ps. 119:136
Pain	Heb. 5:7
None in heaven	Rev. 21:4
Crystal—*rock crystal*	
Wisdom surpasses	Job 28:17-20
Gates of Zion	Is. 54:12
Descriptive of heaven	Rev. 4:6
Cubs—*offspring of beasts*	
Figurative of:	
Babylonians	Jer. 51:38
Assyrians	Nah. 2:11, 12
Princes of Israel	Ezek. 19:2-9
Cucumber—*an edible fruit grown on a vine*	
Lusted after	Num. 11:5
Grown in gardens	Is. 1:8
Cud—*partly digested food*	
Animals chew again	Lev. 11:3-8
Cuckow—*an unclean bird*	
Probably refers to sea gull	Lev. 11:16
Cummin—*an annual of the parsley family*	
Seeds threshed by a rod	Is. 28:25, 27
A trifle of tithing	Matt. 23:23
Cunning—*sly, clever*	
A. *Used in a good sense:*	
David	1 Sam. 23:19-22
Jehu	2 Kin. 10:19
B. *Used in a bad sense:*	
Thwarted by God	Job 5:13
Of harlot's heart	Prov. 7:10
Cup	
A. *Literal use of:*	
For drinking	2 Sam. 12:3
B. *Figurative uses of:*	
One's portion	Ps. 11:6
Blessings	Ps. 23:5
Suffering	Matt. 20:23
Hypocrisy	Matt. 23:25, 26
New covenant	1 Cor. 10:16
Cupbearer—*a high court official*	
Many under Solomon	1 Kin. 10:5
Nehemiah, a faithful	Neh. 1:11
Cure—*to restore to health*	
Of the body	Matt. 17:16
Of the mind	Mark 5:15
Of the demonized	Matt. 12:22
With means	Is. 38:21
By faith	Num. 21:8, 9
By prayer	James 5:14, 15

SUBJECT	REFERENCE
By God's mercy	Phil. 2:27
Hindered	2 Kin. 8:7-15
Curiosity—*seeking to know things forbidden or private*	
Into God's secrets, forbidden	John 21:21, 22
Leads 50,070 to death	1 Sam. 6:19
Curiosity seekers	
Eve	Gen. 3:6
Israelites	Ex. 19:21, 24
Babylonians	2 Kin. 20:13
Herod	Matt 2:4-8
Zacchaeus	Luke 19:1-6
Certain Greeks	John 12:20, 21
Lazarus' visitors	John 12:9
Peter	Matt. 26:58
At the crucifixion	Matt. 27:46-49
Athenians	Acts 17:21
Curse, cursing—*a violent expression of evil upon others*	
A. *Pronounced upon:*	
The earth	Gen. 3:17
Cain	Gen. 4:11
Canaan	Gen. 9:25
Two sons	Gen. 49:7
Disobedient	Deut. 28:15-45
Meroz	Judg. 5:23
Jericho's rebuilders	Josh. 6:26
B. *Forbidden upon:*	
Parents	Ex. 21:17
Ruler	Ex. 22:28
Deaf	Lev. 19:14
Enemies	Luke 6:28
God	Job 2:9
God's people	Gen. 12:3
C. *Instances of:*	
Goliath's	1 Sam. 17:43
Balaam's attempted	Num. 22:1-12
The fig tree	Mark 11:21
Peter's	Matt. 26:74
The crucified	Gal. 3:10, 13
D. *Manifested by:*	
Rebellious	2 Sam. 16:5-8
Curtains—*an awning like screen*	
Ten, in tabernacle	Ex. 26:1-13
Figurative of the heavens	Ps. 104:2
Cush—*black*	
1. Ham's oldest son	1 Chr. 1:8-10
2. Means Ethiopia	Is. 18:1
3. A Benjamite	Ps. 7 (Title)
Cushan—*blackness*	
Probably same as Cush	Hab. 3:7
Cushan-rishathaim—*extra wicked*	
A. *Mesopotamian King*	
Oppressed Israel	Judg. 3:8
Othniel delivers Israel from	Judg. 3:9, 10
Cushi—*an Ethiopian*	
1. Ancestor of Jehudi	Jer. 36:14
2. Father of Zephaniah	Zeph. 1:1
Cushite—*an Ethiopian*	
1. David's servant	2 Sam. 18:21-32
2. Moses' wife	Num. 12:1
Custom—*tax; usage*	
A. *As a tax:*	
Matthew collected	Matt. 9:9
Kings require	Matt. 17:25
Christians give	Rom. 13:6, 7
B. *As a common practice:*	
Abominable	Lev. 18:30
Vain	Jer. 10:3
Worthy	Luke 4:16
Traditional	Acts 21:21
Cuth, Cuthah—*burning*	
People from, brought to Samaria	2 Kin. 17:24, 30
Cymbal—*hollow of a vessel*	
A musical instrument	1 Chr. 13:8
Figurative of pretense	1 Cor. 13:1
Cypress—*a hardwood tree*	
Used by idol-makers	Is. 44:14-17

SUBJECT	REFERENCE
Cyprus—*fairness*	
A large Mediterranean island; home of Barnabas	Acts 4:36
Christians reach	Acts 11:19, 20
Paul visits	Acts 13:4-13
Barnabas visits	Acts 15:39
Paul twice sails past	Acts 21:3
Cyrene—*wall*	
A Greek colonial city in North Africa; home of Simon	Matt. 27:32
People from, at Pentecost	Acts 2:10
Synagogue of	Acts 6:9
Some from, become missionaries	Acts 11:20
Cyrenius—*of Cyrene*	
Roman governor of Syria	Luke 2:1-4
Cyrus—*sun, throne*	
Prophecies concerning, God's:	
"Anointed"	Is. 45:1
Liberator	Is. 45:1
Rebuilder	Is. 44:28

C

D

SUBJECT	REFERENCE
Dabbasheth—*hump*	
Town of Zebulun	Josh. 19:10, 11
Daberath—*pasture*	
Correct rendering of Dabareh	Josh. 21:28
Assigned to Gershomites	1 Chr. 6:71, 72
Dagon—*fish*	
The national god of the Philistines	Judg. 16:23
Falls before ark	1 Sam. 5:1-5
Dainties—*savory food, delicacies*	
Used as a warning	Prov. 23:3-6
Unrighteous fellowship	Ps. 141:4
Dale, the King's	
A valley near Jerusalem	Gen. 14:17-20
Site of Absalom's monument	2 Sam. 18:18
Daleth	
The fourth letter in the Hebrew alphabet	Ps. 119:25-32
Dalmanutha	
A place near the Sea of Galilee	Mark 8:10
Dalmatia—*deceitful*	
A region east of the Adriatic Sea; Titus departs to	2 Tim. 4:10
Dalphon—*crafty*	
A son of Haman	Esth. 9:7-10
Dam—*mother*	
Laws concerning:	
Animals	Ex. 22:30
Birds	Deut. 22:6, 7
Damages and Remuneration	
A. *In law for:*	
Personal injury	Ex. 21:18, 19
Causing miscarriage	Ex. 21:22
Injuries by animals	Ex. 21:28-32
Injuries to animals	Ex. 21:33-35
Losses	Ex. 22:1-15
Stealing	Lev. 6:1-7
Defaming a wife	Deut. 22:13-19
Rape	Deut. 22:28, 29
B. *In practice:*	
Jacob's	Gen. 31:38-42
Samson's	Judg. 16:28-30
Tamar's	2 Sam. 13:22-32
Zacchaeus'	Luke 19:8
Paul's	Acts 16:35-39
Philemon's	Philem. 10-18
Damaris—*gentle*	
An Athenian woman converted by Paul	Acts 17:33, 34

SUBJECT REFERENCE

Damascus—*chief city of Aram*

A. *In the Old Testament:*

Abram passed through ...... Gen. 14:15
Abram heir from .... Gen. 15:2
Captured by David .... 2 Sam. 8:5, 6
Rezon, king of .... 1 Kin. 11:23, 24
Ben-hadad, king of .... 1 Kin. 15:18
Rivers of, mentioned .... 2 Kin. 5:12
Elisha's prophecy in .... 2 Kin. 8:7-15
Taken by Assyrians .... 2 Kin. 16:9
Prophecies concerning .... Is. 8:4

B. *In the New Testament, Paul:*

Journeys to .... Acts 9:1-9
Is converted near .... Acts 9:3-19
First preaches at .... Acts 9:20-22
Escapes from .... 2 Cor. 11:32, 33
Revisits .... Gal. 1:17

Damnation—*condemnatory judgment*

A. *Described as:*

Having degrees .... Matt. 23:14
Just .... Rom. 3:8
Justified .... Rom. 13:2
Self-inflicted .... 1 Cor. 11:29
Merited .... 1 Tim. 5:12

B. *Inflicted:*

Now .... Rom. 14:23
In eternity .... Matt. 23:33

Damsel—*a young woman*

Rebekah .... Gen. 24:57
Ruth .... Ruth 2:5, 6
Raised by Jesus .... Mark 5:39-42
Demands John's head .... Matt. 14:10, 11
Questions Peter .... John 18:17
Is disbelieved .... Acts 12:13-17
Healed by Paul .... Acts 16:16-18

Dan—*judge*

1. Jacob's son by Bilhah .... Gen. 30:6
Prophecy concerning .... Gen. 49:16, 17

2. *Tribe of:*

Census of .... Num. 1:38, 39
Position of .... Num. 2:25, 31
Blessing of .... Deut. 33:22
Inheritance of .... Josh. 19:40-47
Conquest by .... Josh. 19:47
Failure of .... Judg. 1:34, 35
Idolatry of .... Judg. 18:1-31

3. *Town of:*

Called Leshem .... Josh. 19:47
Captured by Danites .... Josh. 19:47
Northern boundary of Israel .... Judg. 20:1
Center of idolatry .... 1 Kin. 12:28-30
Destroyed by Ben-hadad .... 1 Kin. 15:20
Later references to .... Jer. 4:15

Dance—*an emotional movement of the body*

A. *Kinds of:*

Joyful .... Ps. 30:11
Evil .... Ex. 32:19

B. *Designed to:*

Express joy in victory .... 1 Sam. 18:6, 7
Greet a returning son .... Luke 15:23-25
Rejoice in the Lord .... 2 Sam. 6:14-16
Inflame lust .... Matt. 14:6

C. *Performed by:*

Children .... Matt. 11:16, 17
Women .... Judg. 11:34
David .... 2 Sam. 6:14, 16
Worshipers .... Ps. 149:3

Dancing

David only .... 2 Sam. 6:14-16
Greeting a prodigal .... Luke 15:20, 23-25
Lustful exhibition .... Mark 6:22
Religious exercise .... 1 Chr. 15:25-29
Time of rejoicing .... 1 Sam. 18:6, 7
Time to dance .... Eccl. 3:4
Young women alone .... Judg. 21:20, 21

Danger—*risk, peril*

Physical .... Acts 27:9-44
Spiritual .... Heb. 2:1-3
Comfort in .... Acts 27:22-25
Jesus sought in .... Luke 8:22-24
Of many kinds .... 2 Cor. 11:23-33
Paul's escape from .... Acts 9:22-25

SUBJECT REFERENCE

Daniel—*God is my judge*

1. Son of David .... 1 Chr. 3:1
Called Chileab .... 2 Sam. 3:2, 3

2. Postexilic priest .... Ezra 8:1, 2
Signs covenant .... Neh. 10:6

3. Taken to Babylon .... Dan. 1:1-7
Refuses king's choice foods .. Dan. 1:8
Interprets dreams .... Dan. 2:1-45
Honored by Nebuchadnezzar .... Dan. 2:46-49
Interprets handwriting ...... Dan. 5:10-29
Made a high official .... Dan. 6:1-3
Conspired against .... Dan. 6:4-15
Cast into lion's den .... Dan. 6:16-22
Honored by Belshazzar ...... Dan. 5:29
Vision of beasts .... Dan. 7:1-28
Vision of ram and goat ...... Dan. 8:1-27
Great confession of .... Dan. 9:1-19
Vision of the seventy weeks .... Dan. 9:20-27
Vision by the great river ..... Dan. 10:1-21
Vision of the kings .... Dan. 11:1-45
Vision of the two men .... Dan. 12:1-13

Daniel—*book of Bible*

History in Babylon .... Dan. 1—6
Prophecy of nations .... Dan. 2:4-45
Visions .... Dan. 7, 8
Kingdom .... Dan. 9—12

Danites

Descendants of Dan .... Judg. 13:2

Dan-jaan

Town near Zidon .... 2 Sam. 24:6

Dannah—*low ground*

A city of Judah .... Josh. 15:49

Darda—*pearl of wisdom*

Famed for wisdom .... 1 Kin. 4:31
Also called Dara .... 1 Chr. 2:6

Darius—*possessing the good*

1. *Darius the Mede:*

Son of Ahasuerus .... Dan. 9:1
Succeeds Belshazzar .... Dan. 5:30, 31
Co-ruler with Cyrus .... Dan. 6:28
Made king of the Chaldeans .... Dan. 9:1

2. *Darius Hystaspis* (521–486 B.C.)

King of all Persia .... Ezra 4:5
Confirms Cyrus' royal edict .... Ezra 6:1-14
Temple work dated by his reign .... Ezra 4:24
Prophets during his reign .... Hag. 1:1

3. *Darius the Persian* (424–404 B.C.)

Priestly records to reign ..... Neh. 12:22

Dark sayings

Speaks openly .... Num. 12:8
Utter of old .... Ps. 78:2

Darkness—*absence of light*

A. *Kinds of:*

Pre-creational .... Gen. 1:2-4
Natural .... Gen. 15:17
Miraculous .... Ex. 10:21, 22
Supernatural .... Matt. 27:45
Spiritual .... Acts 13:8-11
Eternal .... Matt. 8:12

B. *Illustrative of:*

God's unsearchableness ..... Ps. 97:2
The way of sin .... Eph. 5:11
Afflictions .... Ps. 112:4
Moral depravity .... Rom. 13:12
Ignorance .... 1 John 2:8-11
Death .... Job 10:21, 22
Hell .... Matt. 22:13

Darkon—*scatterer*

Founder of a family .... Neh. 7:58

Darling—*"only one"*

Used poetically of the soul ..... Ps. 35:17

Dart—*a pointed weapon*

Absalom slain by .... 2 Sam. 18:14
Figurative of sin's penalty ...... Prov. 7:23
Figurative of Satan's weapons ... Eph. 6:16

SUBJECT REFERENCE

Dathan—*fount*

A Reubenite .... Num. 26:7-11
Joins Korah's rebellion .... Num. 16:1-35
Swallowed up by the earth ...... Ps. 106:17

Daughter—*a female descendant*

A. *Applied to:*

Female child .... Gen. 20:12
Female inhabitants of a city .... Judg. 21:1
Female worshipers of God ... Is. 43:6
Citizens of a town .... Ps. 9:14

B. *Described as:*

Licentious .... Gen. 19:30-38
Dutiful .... Judg. 11:36-39
Ideal .... Prov. 31:29
Beautiful .... Ps. 45:9-13
Careless .... Is. 32:9-11
Prophesy .... Joel 2:28

C. *Daughter-in-law:*

Bride, son's wife
Ruth, a loyal .... Ruth 1:11-18
Strife against .... Matt. 10:35

Daughter of Zion—*a name referring to Jerusalem and the inhabitants therein*

Show praise to .... Ps. 9:14
Gaze on Solomon .... Song 3:11
Left desolate .... Is. 1:8
The King comes to .... Matt. 21:5

David—*well-beloved*

A. *Early life of:*

Born at Bethlehem .... 1 Sam. 17:12
Son of Jesse .... Ruth 4:17, 22
Genealogy of .... 1 Chr. 2:3-15
Of tribe of Judah .... 1 Chr. 28:4
Youngest son .... 1 Sam. 16:10-13
Handsome .... 1 Sam. 17:42
A shepherd .... 1 Sam. 16:11
Strong .... 1 Sam. 17:34-36
Chosen by God .... 1 Sam. 16:1, 13

B. *His life under King Saul:*

Royal harpist .... 1 Sam. 16:14-23
Armor bearer .... 1 Sam. 16:21
Kills Goliath .... 1 Sam. 17:4-49
Subdues Philistines .... 1 Sam. 17:32-54
Loved by Jonathan .... 1 Sam. 18:1-4
Wise behavior of .... 1 Sam. 18:5-30
Writes a Psalm .... Ps. 59 (Title)

C. *The fugitive hero:*

Flees from Saul .... 1 Sam. 19:1-18
Takes refuge with Samuel .... 1 Sam. 19:20-24
Makes covenant with Jonathan .... 1 Sam. 20:1-42
Eats showbread .... Matt. 12:3, 4
Feigns insanity in Gath ..... 1 Sam. 21:10-15
Dwells in cave .... 1 Sam. 22:1-8
Saves Keilah .... 1 Sam. 23:1-13
God delivers .... 1 Sam. 23:14, 15
Second covenant with Jonathan .... 1 Sam. 23:16-18
Betrayed but saved .... 1 Sam. 23:19-29
Writes a Psalm .... Ps. 54 (Title)
Spares Saul's life .... 1 Sam. 24:1-22
Scorned by Nabal .... 1 Sam. 25:1-38
Marries Nabal's widow ...... 1 Sam. 25:39-42
Again spares Saul's life ..... 1 Sam. 26:1-25
Dwells in Ziklag .... 1 Sam. 27:5-7
Rejected by Philistines ...... 1 Sam. 29:1-11
Smites the Amalekites .... 1 Sam. 30:1-31
Kills Saul's murderer .... 2 Sam. 1:1-16
Laments Saul's death .... 2 Sam. 1:17-27

D. *King over Judah:*

Anointed at Hebron .... 2 Sam. 2:1-4, 11
List of supporters .... 1 Chr. 12:23-40
Long war with Saul's house .... 2 Sam. 3:1
Abner, rebuffed, makes covenant with David .... 2 Sam. 3:6-21
Mourns Abner's death .... 2 Sam. 3:28-39
Punishes Ish-bosheth's murderers .... 2 Sam. 4:1-12

E. *King over all Israel:*

Recognized as king .... 2 Sam. 5:1-5
Takes Zion from Jebusites ... 2 Sam. 5:6-10
Builds a house .... 2 Sam. 5:11
Strengthens kingdom .... 2 Sam. 5:11-16
Strikes down the Philistines .... 2 Sam. 5:17-25
Escorts ark to Jerusalem ..... 2 Sam. 6:1-16

SUBJECT ... REFERENCE

Organizes worship ... 1 Chr. 15:1-29
Organizes musicians ... 1 Chr. 25:1-31
Blesses the people ... 2 Sam. 6:17-19
Upbraided by Michal ... 2 Sam. 6:20-23
Receives eternal covenant ... 2 Sam. 7:1-29
Subdues many nations ... 2 Sam. 8:1-18
2 Sam. 10:1-19
Commits adultery ... 2 Sam. 11:1-27
Rebuked by Nathan ... 2 Sam. 12:1-14
Repents ... Ps. 32:1-11
Ps. 51:1-19
Afflictions follow ... 2 Sam. 12:15-23
Family strife ... 2 Sam. 13:1-39
Absalom's rebellion ... 2 Sam. 15:1-31
Flees from Jerusalem ... 2 Sam. 15:13-37
Mourns Absalom's death ... 2 Sam. 19:1-10
Returns to Jerusalem ... 2 Sam. 19:15-43
Sheba's conspiracy ... 2 Sam. 20:1-26
Atones for Saul's crime ... 2 Sam. 21:1-14
Further conflicts ... 2 Sam. 21:15-22
Song of deliverance ... 2 Sam. 22:1-51
Last words of ... 2 Sam. 23:1-7
His mighty men ... 2 Sam. 23:8-39
Sins by numbering people ... 2 Sam. 24:1-17
Buys Araunah's threshing floor ... 2 Sam. 24:18-25
Secures Solomon's succession ... 1 Kin. 1:5-53
Gives dying charge to Solomon ... 1 Kin. 2:1-11
Reign of forty years ... 1 Kin. 2:11

F. *Spiritual significance of:*
Prophet ... Acts 2:30
Musician ... 2 Sam. 23:1
Inspired man ... Matt. 22:43
Type of Christ ... Jer. 23:5, 6
Name designates Christ ... Ezek. 34:23, 24
Christ, son of ... Matt. 1:1
"Kingdom of" ... Mark 11:10
"Throne of" ... Luke 1:32
"Tabernacle of" ... Acts 15:16
"Key of" ... Is. 22:22
Faith ... Heb. 11:32, 33
Covenant with ... 2 Sam. 7:4-17

David, Root of—*a title of Christ*
Opens sealed book ... Rev. 5:5
Jesus describes Himself as ... Rev. 22:16

David, Tower of—fortress built by David, location now unknown
Symbolic of strength ... Song 4:4

Dawn
Not even one remained ... 2 Sam. 17:22
Worked from ... Neh. 4:21
See the breaking ... Job 3:9
Continually tossing until ... Job 7:4
Murderer arises at ... Job 24:14
Mary came to the grave at ... Matt. 28:1
Luke 24:1

Day—*a division of time*
A. *Natural uses of:*
The daylight ... Gen. 1:5, 16
Twelve hours ... John 11:9
Opposite of night ... Mark 5:5
The civil day (24 hours) ... Luke 13:14
Divisions of ... Neh. 9:3
Security of ... Gen. 8:22

B. *Extended uses of:*
Noah's time ... Matt. 24:37
Gospel age ... John 9:4
Long period ... 2 Pet. 3:8

C. *Descriptive of:*
Believers ... 1 Thess. 5:5, 8
Christ's return ... 1 Thess. 5:2
Prophetic period ... Dan. 12:11
Rev. 2:10
Eternity ... Dan. 7:9, 13
Present age ... Heb. 1:2

Day of the Lord
A. *In Old Testament:*
Punishment of faithless ... Is. 13:6-13
Amos 5:18-20
Day of wrath ... Is. 2:6-22
Restoration of remnant ... Is. 10:20-22
Hos. 2:16-20

B. *In New Testament:*
The last times ... Matt. 24:29
2 Pet. 3:10
The great day ... Rev. 16:14

SUBJECT ... REFERENCE

Day, Joshua's long
Described ... Josh. 10:12-14

Day's Journey
Described as:
A distance ... Gen. 30:36
Gen. 31:23
Traveled to make a sacrifice ... { Ex. 3:18; Ex. 5:3; Ex. 8:27 }

Daysman—*umpire or mediator*
Desired by Job ... Job 9:33

Deaconess—*a female attendant*
Phoebe thus called ("a servant") ... Rom. 16:1

Deacons—*church officers*
Ordained by the apostles ... Acts 6:1-6
Stephen, the first martyr of ... Acts 6:5-15
Named with bishops ... Phil. 1:1
Qualifications of ... 1 Tim. 3:8-13

Dead—*lacking life*
A. *Used literally of:*
Lost physical functions ... Rom. 4:19
Those in the other world ... Rev. 20:12

B. *Used figuratively of:*
Unregenerate ... Eph. 2:1
Unreal faith ... James 2:17, 19
Decadent church ... Rev. 3:1
Legal requirements ... Heb. 9:14
Freedom from sin's power ... Rom. 6:2, 8, 11
Freedom from the Law ... Rom. 7:4

Dead Sea
Called the:
Salt Sea ... Gen. 14:3
Sea of the Plain ... Deut. 3:17

Deaf—*unable to hear*
Protection afforded ... Lev. 19:14
Healing of ... Matt. 11:5
Figurative of spiritual inability ... Is. 42:18, 19
Figurative of patience ... Ps. 38:13

Dearth—*famine*
Visited upon Egypt ... Acts 7:11
Agabus predicts ... Acts 11:28
See Famine

Death, eternal
A. *Described as:*
Everlasting punishment ... Matt. 25:46
Resurrection of damnation ... John 5:29
God's wrath ... 1 Thess. 1:10
Destruction ... 2 Thess. 1:9
2 Pet. 2:12
Second death ... Rev. 20:14

B. *Truths regarding:*
A consequence of man's sin ... Gen. 3:17-19
The punishment of the wicked ... Matt. 25:41, 46
Separates from God ... 2 Thess. 1:9
Christ saves from ... John 3:16
Saints shall escape from ... 1 Cor. 15:54-58
Rev. 2:11
Vividly described ... Luke 16:23-26

Death, natural
A. *Features regarding:*
Consequence of sin ... Rom. 5:12
Lot of all ... Heb. 9:27
Ends earthly life ... Eccl. 9:10
Christ delivers from fear of ... Heb. 2:15
Some escaped from ... Gen. 5:24
Some will escape ... 1 Cor. 15:51, 52
All to be raised from ... Acts 24:15
Illustrates regeneration ... Rom. 6:2

B. *Described as:*
Return to dust ... Gen. 3:19
Removal of breath ... Gen. 25:8
Removal from tabernacle ... 2 Cor. 5:1
Naked ... 2 Cor. 5:3, 4
Sleep ... John 11:11-14
Departure ... Phil. 1:23
Yielded up the ghost ... Acts 5:10

SUBJECT ... REFERENCE

C. *Recognition after:*
Departed saints recognized by the living ... Matt. 17:1-8
Greater knowledge in future world ... 1 Cor. 13:12
The truth illustrated ... Luke 16:19-24

Death of saints
A. *Described as:*
Sleep in Jesus ... 1 Thess. 4:14
Blessed ... Rev. 14:13
A gain ... Phil. 1:21
Peace ... Is. 57:1, 2
Crown of righteousness ... 2 Tim. 4:8

B. *Exemplified in:*
Abraham ... Gen. 25:8
Isaac ... Gen. 35:28, 29
Jacob ... Gen. 49:33
Elisha ... 2 Kin. 13:14, 20
The criminal ... Luke 23:39-43

Death of wicked
Result of sin ... Rom. 5:12
Often punishment ... Ex. 23:25-29
Is. 65:11, 12
Unpleasant for God ... Ezek. 33:11
Without hope ... 1 Thess. 4:13
Rev. 20:10, 14, 15

Death Penalty—*legal execution*
By stoning ... Deut. 13:6-10
Deut. 17:5

Debate—*discussion, contention*
With a neighbor ... Prov. 25:9
Wicked, full of ... Rom. 1:29
Saints must avoid ... 2 Cor. 12:20

Debir—*oracle*
1. King of Eglon ... Josh. 10:3-26
2. City of Judah ... Josh. 15:15
Also called Kirjath-sepher ... Josh. 15:15
Captured by Joshua ... Josh. 10:38, 39
Recaptured by Othniel ... Josh. 15:15-17
Judg. 1:11-13
Assigned to priests ... Josh. 21:13, 15
3. A place east of the Jordan ... Josh. 13:26
4. Town of Judah ... Josh. 15:7

Deborah—*a bee*
1. Rebekah's nurse ... Gen. 35:8
2. A prophetess and judge ... Judg. 4:4-14
Composed song of triumph ... Judg. 5:1-31

Debt, debtor
A. *Safeguards regarding:*
No oppression allowed ... Deut. 23:19, 20
Collateral protected ... Ex. 22:25-27
Time limitation of ... Deut. 15:1-18
Non-payment forbidden ... Neh. 5:5
Debts to be honored ... Rom. 13:6
Interest (usury) forbidden ... Ezek. 18:8-17
Love, the unpayable ... Rom. 13:8
Parable concerning ... Matt. 18:23-35

B. *Evils of:*
Brings slavery ... Lev. 25:39, 47
Causes complaint ... 2 Kin. 4:1-7
Produces strife ... Jer. 15:10
Makes outlaws ... 1 Sam. 22:2
Endangers property ... Prov. 6:1-5

C. *Figurative of:*
Sins ... Matt. 6:12
Works ... Rom. 4:4
Moral obligation ... Rom. 1:14
God's mercy ... Ps. 37:26

Decalogue (see Ten Commandments)

Decapolis—*league of ten cities*
Multitudes from, follow Jesus ... Matt. 4:25
Healed demon-possessed, preaches in ... Mark 5:20

Deceit, deceivers, deception
A. *The wicked:*
Devise ... Ps. 35:20
Speaks ... Jer. 9:8
Are full of ... Rom. 1:29
Increase in ... 2 Tim. 3:13

B. *Agents of:*
Satan ... 2 Cor. 11:14
Sin ... Rom. 7:11

SUBJECT REFERENCE

Self .... 1 Cor. 3:18
James 1:22
Others .... 2 Thess. 2:3

C. *Warnings against:*
Among religious workers .... 2 Cor. 11:3-15
As a sign of apostasy .... 2 Thess. 2:10
As a sign of the antichrist ... 1 John 4:1-6

D. *Examples of:*
Eve .... 1 Tim. 2:14
Abram .... Gen. 12:11-13
Isaac .... Gen. 26:6, 7
Jacob .... Gen. 27:18-27
Joseph's brothers .... Gen. 37:31, 32
Pharaoh .... Ex. 8:29
David .... 1 Sam. 21:12, 13
Amnon .... 2 Sam. 13:6-14
Gehazi .... 2 Kin. 5:20-27
Elisha .... 2 Kin. 6:19-23
Herod .... Matt. 2:7, 8
Pharisees .... Matt. 22:15, 16
Peter .... Mark 14:70, 71
Ananias .... Acts 5:1-11
The earth .... Rev. 13:14

Deceive—*to delude or mislead*

A. *In Old Testament:*
Eve, by Satan .... Gen. 3:13
Israel, by the Midianites ..... Num. 25:18
Joshua, by the Gibeonites ... Josh. 9:22

B. *Of Christians:*
By flattering words .... Rom. 16:18
By false report .... 2 Thess. 2:3
By false reasoning .... Col. 2:4

Decision—*determination to follow a course of action*

A. *Sources of:*
Loyalty .... Ruth 1:16
Prayer .... 1 Sam. 23:1-13
The Lord .... 1 Kin. 12:15
Satan .... 1 Chr. 21:1
The world .... Luke 14:16-24
Human need .... Acts 11:27-30
Disagreement .... Acts 15:36-41
Faith .... Heb. 11:24-28

B. *Wrong, leading to:*
Spiritual decline .... Gen. 13:7-11
Repentance .... Heb. 12:16, 17
Defeat .... Num. 14:40-45
Rejection .... 1 Sam. 15:6-26
Apostasy .... 1 Kin. 11:1-13
Division .... 1 Kin. 12:12-20
Death .... Acts 1:16-20

C. *Good, manifested in:*
Siding with the Lord .... Ex. 32:26
Following God .... Num. 14:24
Josh. 14:8
Loving God .... Deut. 6:5
Seeking God .... 2 Chr. 15:12
Obeying God .... Neh. 10:28-30

Decision, valley of—*location unknown*
Called 'Valley of Jehoshaphat' .. Joel 3:2, 12, 14
Refers to final judgment .... Joel 3:1-21

Decisiveness—*showing firmness of decision*
In serving God .... Josh. 24:15, 16
Heb. 11:24, 25
Toward family .... Ruth 1:15-18
Toward a leader .... 2 Kin. 2:1-6
To complete a task .... Neh. 4:14-23
In morality .... Gen. 39:10-12
Dan. 1:8
In prayer .... Dan. 6:1-16

Deck—*floor of a ship*
Made of ivory .... Ezek. 27:6

Decree—*a course of action authoritatively determined*

A. *As a human edict:*
Issued by kings .... Dan. 6:7-14
Considered inflexible .... Dan. 6:15-17
Published widely .... Esth. 3:13-15
Providentially nullified ...... Esth. 8:3-17
Sometimes beneficial .... Dan. 4:25-28

B. *As a divine edict, to:*
Govern nature .... Jer. 5:22

Dedan—*low*
1. Raamah's son .... Gen. 10:7
2. Jokshan's son .... Gen. 25:3
3. Descendants of Raamah; a commercial people .... Ezek. 27:15, 20; Ezek. 38:13

Dedication—*setting apart for a sacred use*

A. *Of things:*
Tabernacle .... Ex. 40:34-38
Solomon's Temple .... 1 Kin. 8:12-66
Second temple .... Ezra 6:1-22

B. *Offerings in, must be:*
Voluntary .... Lev. 22:18-25
Without blemish .... Lev. 1:3
Unredeemable .... Lev. 27:28, 29

C. *Examples of:*
Samuel .... 1 Sam. 1:11, 22
The believer .... Rom. 12:1, 2

Dedication, Feast of
Jesus attended .... John 10:22, 23

Deeds—*things done*

A. *Descriptive of one's:*
Past record .... Luke 11:48
Present achievements .... Acts 7:22
Future action .... 2 Cor. 10:11

B. *Expressive of one's:*
Evil nature .... 2 Pet. 2:8
Parentage .... John 8:41
Record .... Luke 24:19
Profession .... 3 John 10
Love .... 1 John 3:18
Judgment .... Rom. 2:6

C. *Toward God:*
Weighed .... 1 Sam. 2:3
Wrong punished .... Luke 23:41

D. *Lord's are:*
Righteous .... Judg. 5:11
1 Sam. 12:7
Mighty .... Ps. 106:2
Beyond description .... Ps. 106:2

E. *Considered positively:*
Example of .... Titus 2:7
Zealous for .... Titus 2:14
Careful to engage in .... Titus 3:8, 14
Stimulate to .... Heb. 10:24
In heaven .... Rev. 14:13

Deeds, the unbeliever's

A. *Described as:*
Evil .... Col. 1:21
Done in dark place .... Is. 29:15
Abominable .... Ps. 14:1
Unfruitful .... Eph. 5:11

B. *God's attitude toward, will:*
Never forget .... Amos 8:7
Render according to .... Prov. 24:12
Bring to judgment .... Rev. 20:12, 13

C. *Believer's relation to:*
Lay aside .... Rom. 13:12
Not participate in .... Eph. 5:11
Be delivered from .... 2 Tim. 4:18

Defense—*protection during attack*
Of a city .... 2 Kin. 19:34
Of Israel .... Judg. 10:1
Of a plot .... 2 Sam. 23:11, 12
Of the upright .... Ps. 7:10
Of one accused .... Acts 22:1
Of the Gospel .... Phil. 1:7, 16

Deference—*respectful yielding to another*
To a woman's entreaty .... Ruth 1:15-18
To an old man's wish .... 2 Sam. 19:31-40
Results in exaltation .... Matt. 23:12
Commanded .... Heb. 13:17

Defilement—*making the pure impure*

A. *Ceremonial causes of:*
Childbirth .... Lev. 12:2-8
Leprosy .... Lev. 13:3, 44-46
Bodily discharge .... Lev. 15:1-15
Copulation .... Lev. 15:17
Menstruation .... Lev. 15:19-33
Touching the dead .... Lev. 21:1-4, 11

B. *Spiritual manifestations of:*
Abominations .... Jer. 32:34

C. *Objects of:*
Conscience .... 1 Cor. 8:7
Fellowship .... Heb. 12:15
Flesh .... Jude 8

Defrauding—*depriving others through deceit*
Forbidden .... Mark 10:19
To be accepted .... 1 Cor. 6:5-8
In marriage .... 1 Cor. 7:3-5
Paul, not guilty of .... 2 Cor. 7:2
Product of sexual immorality .... 1 Thess. 4:3-6

Degrees—*ascents; steps*
The sun dial .... 2 Kin. 20:9-11
Movement toward Jerusalem .... Ps. 120—134 (Titles)
Order of work .... 1 Chr. 15:18
Rank in society .... Luke 1:52
Advancement in service .... 1 Tim. 3:13

Degrees, Songs of
"Songs of Ascent" .... Ps. 120—134

Dehavites—*people who settled in Samaria during exile*
Opposed rebuilding of Jerusalem .... Ezra 4:9-16

Deity of Christ (see Christ)

Dekar—*piercing; mattock*
Father of one of Solomon's officers .... 1 Kin. 4:9

Delaiah—*Jehovah has delivered*
1. Descendant of Aaron .... 1 Chr. 24:18
2. Son of Shemaiah; urges Jehoiakim not to burn Jeremiah's roll .... Jer. 36:12, 25
3. Founder of a family .... Ezra 2:60
4. A son of Elioenai .... 1 Chr. 3:24

Deliberation—*careful consideration of elements involved in a decision*
Necessary in life .... Luke 14:28-32
Illustrated in Jacob .... Gen. 32:1-23

Delight—*great pleasure in something*

A. *Wrong kind of:*
Showy display .... Esth. 6:6-11
Physical strength .... Ps. 147:10
Sacrifices .... Ps. 51:16
Is. 1:11
Abominations .... Is. 66:3

B. *Right kind of:*
God's will .... Ps. 40:8
God's commandments .... Ps. 112:1
God's goodness .... Neh. 9:25
Lord Himself .... Is. 58:14

Delilah—*lustful*
Deceives Samson .... Judg. 16:4-22

Deliver—*to rescue or save from evil*

A. *By Christ, from:*
Trials .... 2 Tim. 3:11
Evil .... 2 Tim. 4:18
2 Pet. 2:9
Death .... 2 Cor. 1:10
Power of darkness .... Col. 1:13
God's wrath .... 1 Thess. 1:10

B. *Examples of, by God:*
Noah .... Gen. 8:1-22
Lot .... Gen. 19:29, 30
Jacob .... Gen. 33:1-16
Israel .... Ex. 12:29-51
David .... 1 Sam. 23:1-29
Jews .... Esth. 9:1-19
Daniel .... Dan. 6:13-27
Jesus .... Matt. 2:13-23
Apostles .... Acts 5:17-26
Paul .... 2 Cor. 1:10

Deluge, the—*the Flood*

A. *Warnings of:*
Believed by Noah .... Heb. 11:7
Disbelieved by the world .... 2 Pet. 2:5

B. *Coming of:*
Announced .... Gen. 6:5-7
Dated .... Gen. 7:11
Sudden .... Matt. 24:38, 39

C. *Purpose of:*
Punish sin .... Gen. 6:1-7
Destroy the world .... 2 Pet. 3:5, 6

D. *Its non-repetition based on God's:*
Promise .... Gen. 8:21, 22

SUBJECT REFERENCE

Covenant .... Gen. 9:9-11
Token (the rainbow) .... Gen. 9:12-17
Pledge .... Is. 54:9, 10

E. *Type of:*
Baptism .... 1 Pet. 3:20, 21
Christ's coming .... Matt. 24:36-39
Destruction .... Is. 28:2, 18
The end .... 2 Pet. 3:5-15

Delusions, common—*self-deception*
Rejecting God's existence .... Ps. 14:1
Supposing God does not see .... Ps. 10:1-11
Trusting in one's heritage .... Matt. 3:9
Living for time alone .... Luke 12:17-19
Presuming on time .... Luke 13:23-30
Believing antichrist .... 2 Thess. 2:1-12
Denying facts .... 2 Pet. 3:5, 16, 17

Demagogue—*one who becomes a leader by mass prejudice*
Absalom .... 2 Sam. 15:2-6
Haman .... Esth. 3:1-11
Judas of Galilee .... Acts 5:37

Demas—*popular*
Follows Paul .... Col. 4:14
Forsakes Paul .... 2 Tim. 4:10

Demetrius
1. A silversmith at Ephesus .... Acts 19:24-31
2. A good Christian .... 3 John 12

Demon—*an evil spirt*
A. *Nature of:*
Evil .... Luke 10:17, 18
Powerful .... Luke 8:29
Numerous .... Mark 5:8, 9
Unclean .... Matt. 10:1
Under Satan .... Matt. 12:24-30

B. *Ability of:*
Recognize Christ .... Mark 1:23, 24
Possess human beings .... Matt. 8:29
Overcome men .... Acts 19:13-16
Know their destiny .... Matt. 8:29-33
Receive sacrifice .... 1 Cor. 10:20
Instigate deceit .... 1 Tim. 4:1

Demon possession
A. *Recognized as:*
Not insanity .... Matt. 4:24
Not disease .... Mark 1:32
Productive harm .... Mark 5:1-5

B. *Instances of:*
Man in the synagogue .... Mark 1:23-26
Blind and dumb man .... Matt. 12:22, 23
Two men of the Gergesenes .... Matt. 8:28-34
Dumb man .... Matt. 9:32, 33
Canaanite woman's daughter .... Matt. 15:22-28
Epileptic child .... Matt. 17:14-21
Mary Magdalene .... Mark 16:9

Den of Lions
Daniel placed in .... Dan. 6:16-24

Denial of Christ
A. *The realm of:*
Doctrine .... Mark 8:38
2 Tim. 1:8
Practice .... Titus 1:16

B. *The agents of:*
Individuals .... Matt. 26:69-75
Jews .... John 18:40
False teachers .... 2 Pet. 2:1
Antichrist .... 1 John 2:22, 23

C. *The consequences of:*
Christ denies them .... Matt. 10:33
They merit destruction .... 2 Pet. 2:1

Deportation—*exile from a nation*
Captives carried into .... 2 Kin. 15:29
To Babylon .... 2 Kin. 24:8-17

Depravity of man
A. *Extent of:*
Universal .... Gen. 6:5
In the heart .... Jer. 17:9
Man's whole being .... Rom. 3:9-19
From birth .... Ps. 51:5

SUBJECT REFERENCE

B. *Effects of:*
Hardness .... Rom. 2:5
Inability to listen .... Jer. 17:23
2 Pet. 2:14, 19
Lovers of evil .... John 3:19
Defilement of conscience .... Titus 1:15, 16

Deputy—*a person empowered to act for another*
King .... 1 Kin. 22:47

Derbe—*a city of Lycaonia*
Paul visits .... Acts 14:6, 20
Paul meets Timothy here .... Acts 16:1
Gaius, native of .... Acts 20:4

Derision—*contempt manifested by laughter*
Heaped on God's people .... Jer. 20:7, 8

Descend
As a dove .... Matt. 3:16
John 1:32
The angels of God .... John 1:51

Desert—*a wilderness place*
Israel journeys through .... Is. 48:21
Place of great temptation .... Ps. 106:14
Rejoicing of, predicted .... Is. 35:1
A highway in .... Is. 40:3
John's home in .... Luke 1:80
Israel received manna in .... John 6:31

Desertion—*forsaking a person or thing*
Jesus, by His disciples .... Matt. 26:56
Jesus, by God .... Matt. 27:46
Paul, by others .... 2 Tim. 4:16
Christ, by professed disciples .... 2 Pet. 2:15

Desire, spiritual
Renewed fellowship .... 1 Thess. 2:17
Church office .... 1 Tim. 3:1
Spiritual knowledge .... 1 Pet. 2:2
Spiritual gifts .... 1 Cor. 14:1

Desire of all nations
A title descriptive of the Messiah .... Hag. 2:6, 7

Despair—*a hopeless state*
A. *Results from:*
Heavy burdens .... Num. 11:10-15
Disobedience .... 1 Sam. 28:16-25
Disappointment .... 2 Sam. 17:23
Impending death .... Esth. 7:7-10
Futility of human things .... Eccl. 6:1-12
Rejection .... Matt. 27:3-5
Rebellion against God .... Rev. 9:6
Hopelessness .... Luke 16:23-31

B. *Remedies against:*
Hope in God .... Ps. 42:5, 11
God's faithfulness .... 1 Cor. 10:13
Accept God's chastening .... Heb. 12:5-11
Cast your care upon the Lord .... 1 Pet. 5:7

Despondency—*depression of spirits*
A. *Causes of:*
Mourning .... Gen. 37:34, 35
Sickness .... Is. 38:9-12
Sorrow .... 2 Sam. 18:32, 33
2 Cor. 2:7
Adversity .... Job 9:16-35
Fears .... 2 Cor. 7:5, 6

B. *Examples of:*
Moses .... Ex. 14:15
Joshua .... Josh. 7:7-9
Elijah .... 1 Kin. 19:2, 4
David .... Ps. 42:6
Jonah .... Jon. 4:3, 8
Two disciples .... Luke 24:13-17

Destitute—*a state of extreme need*
The soul .... Ps. 102:17
The body .... James 2:14-17
Spiritual realities .... Prov. 15:21

Destruction—*a state of ruin*
A. *Past:*
Cities .... Gen. 19:29
People .... 1 Cor. 10:9, 10
Nations .... Jer. 48:42

B. *Present:*
Satan's power of .... 1 Cor. 5:5
Power of lusts .... 1 Tim. 6:9
Wicked on way to .... Rom. 3:16

SUBJECT REFERENCE

C. *Future:*
Men appointed to .... Prov. 31:8
2 Pet. 2:12
Men fitted for .... Rom. 9:22
End of the enemies of Christ .... Phil. 3:19
Sudden .... 1 Thess. 5:3
Swift .... 2 Pet. 2:1
Everlasting .... 2 Thess. 1:9

Determinate counsel
God's fixed purpose .... Acts 2:23

Determination—*resolute persistence*
Against popular opposition .... Num. 13:26-31
Num. 14:1-9
Against great numbers .... 1 Sam. 14:1-5
Beyond human advice .... 2 Kin. 2:1-6
In perilous situation .... Esth. 4:10-16
In spite of persecution .... Acts 6:8—7:60

Deuel—*invocation of God*
Father of Eliasaph .... Num. 1:14

Deuteronomy—*book of the Old Testament containing the farewell speeches of Moses*
Written and spoken by Moses .... Deut. 31:9, 22, 24

Devil—*the chief opponent of God*
A. *Titles of:*
Abaddon .... Rev. 9:11
Accuser .... Rev. 12:10
Adversary .... 1 Pet. 5:8
Angel of the bottomless pit .... Rev. 9:11
Apollyon .... Rev. 9:11
Beelzebub .... Matt. 12:24
Belial .... 2 Cor. 6:15
God of this world .... 2 Cor. 4:4
Murderer .... John 8:44
Old serpent .... Rev. 20:2
Prince of demons .... Matt. 12:24
Prince of the power of the air .... Eph. 2:2
Prince of this world .... John 14:30
Ruler of darkness .... Eph. 6:12
Satan .... Luke 10:18
Serpent .... Gen. 3:4
Wicked one .... Matt. 13:19

B. *Origin of:*
Heart lifted up in pride .... Is. 14:12-20
Perfect until sin came .... Ezek. 28:14-19
Greatest of fallen angels .... Rev. 12:7-9
Tempts man to sin .... Gen. 3:1-7
Father of lies .... John 8:44

C. *Character of:*
Subtle .... Gen. 3:1
2 Cor. 11:3
Slanderous .... Job 1:9
Fierce .... Luke 8:29
Deceitful .... 2 Cor. 11:14
Powerful .... Eph. 2:2
Proud .... 1 Tim. 3:6
Cowardly .... James 4:7
Wicked .... 1 John 2:13

D. *Power of, over the wicked:*
They are his children .... Acts 13:10
1 John 3:10
They do his will .... John 8:44
He possesses .... Luke 22:3
He blinds .... 2 Cor. 4:4
He deceives .... Rev. 20:7, 8
He ensnares .... 1 Tim. 3:7
He troubles .... 1 Sam. 16:14
They are punished with him .... Matt. 25:41

E. *Power of, over God's people:*
Tempt .... 1 Chr. 21:1
Afflict .... Job 2:7
Accuse .... Zech. 3:1
Sift .... Luke 22:31
Beguile .... 2 Cor. 11:3
Disguise .... 2 Cor. 11:14, 15

F. *The believer's power over:*
Watch against .... 2 Cor. 2:11
Fight against .... Eph. 6:11-16
Resist .... James 4:7
1 Pet. 5:9
Overcome .... 1 John 2:13
Rev. 12:10, 11

G. *Christ's triumph over:*
Predicted .... Gen. 3:15
Portrayed .... Matt. 4:1-11

SUBJECT REFERENCE

Proclaimed ... Luke 10:18
Perfected ... Mark 3:27, 28

Devotion to God

A. *How?:*

With our whole selves ... Prov. 3:9; Rom. 12:1; 1 Cor. 6:20

B. *Why? Because of:*

God's goodness ... 1 Sam. 12:24; 1 Thess. 2:12
Christ's death ... 2 Cor. 5:15
Our redemption ... 1 Cor. 6:19, 20

Devotion to the ministry of saints

Household of Stephanas ... 1 Cor. 16:15

Devotions, morning

Jacob's ... Gen. 28:16-18
Samuel's parents' ... 1 Sam. 1:19
Hezekiah's ... 2 Chr. 29:20-31
Job's ... Job 1:5
Jesus' ... Mark 1:35

Devout—*pious, religious, sincere*

Simeon ... Luke 2:25
Cornelius ... Acts 10:1, 2, 7
Ananias ... Acts 22:12
Those who buried Stephen ... Acts 8:2
Converts ... Acts 13:43
Women of Antioch ... Acts 13:50
Greeks in Thessalonica ... Acts 17:4
Gentiles ... Acts 17:17
Men ... Is. 57:1

Dew—*moisture condensed on the earth*

A. *Used literally of:*

Natural dew ... Ex. 16:13, 14
A miraculous test ... Judg. 6:37-40
A curse ... 1 Kin. 17:1; Hag. 1:10

B. *Used figuratively of:*

God's blessings ... Gen. 27:28
God's truth ... Deut. 32:2
The Messiah ... Is. 26:19
Man's fickleness ... Hos. 6:4
Peace and harmony ... Ps. 133:3

Dexterity—*skill in using one's hands or body*

Of 700 men ... Judg. 20:16
David's ... 1 Sam. 17:40-50

Diadem—*a crown*

Removed by judgment ... Ezek. 21:25-27
Reserved for God's people ... Is. 28:5
Restored by grace ... Is. 62:3

Dial—*an instrument for telling time*

Miraculous movement of ... Is. 38:8

Diamond—*crystallized carbon*

Sacred ... Ex. 28:18
Precious ... Ezek. 28:13

Diana

A pagan goddess ... Acts 19:24-34

Diblaim—*twin fig cakes*

Hosea's father-in-law ... Hos. 1:3

Diblath—*rounded cake*

An unidentified place ... Ezek. 6:14

Dibon—*a wasting away*

1. Amorite town ... Num. 21:30
   Taken by Israel ... Num. 32:3
   Rebuilt by Gadites ... Num. 32:34
   Called Dibon-gad ... Num. 33:45, 46
   Later given to Reubenites ... Josh. 13:9, 17
   Destruction of, foretold ... Jer. 48:18, 22
2. A village of Judah ... Neh. 11:25

Dibri—*loquacious; wordy*

A Danite ... Lev. 24:11-14

Dictator—*ruler with absolute authority*

A. *Powers of, to:*

Take life ... 1 Kin. 2:46
Judge ... 1 Kin. 10:9
Tax ... 2 Kin. 15:19
Levy labor ... 1 Kin. 5:13-15
Make war ... 1 Kin. 20:1
Form alliances ... 1 Kin. 15:18, 19

B. *Examples, evil:*

Pharoah ... Ex. 1:8-22
Ahab ... 1 Kin. 16:28-33
Herod ... Matt. 2:16

C. *Examples, benevolent:*

Solomon ... 1 Kin. 8:12-21; 1 Kin. 10:23-24
Cyrus ... Ezra 1:1-4

Didymus—*twin*

Surname of Thomas ... John 11:16

Diet

Of the Hebrews ... Lev. 11:1-47

Differing weights

Prohibited ... Deut. 25:13, 14

Difficulties—*problems hard to solve*

A. *Kinds of:*

Mental ... Ps. 139:6, 14
Moral ... Ps. 38:1-22
Theological ... John 6:48-60

B. *Examples of:*

Birth of a child in old age ... Gen. 18:9-15
Testing of Abraham ... Gen. 22:1-14
Slaughter of Canaanites ... Ex. 23:27-33
God's providence ... Ps. 44:1-26
Prosperity of wicked ... Ps. 73:1-28
Israel's unbelief ... John 12:39-41

C. *Negative attitudes toward:*

Rebellion against ... Num. 21:4, 5
Unbelief under ... Heb. 3:12-19

D. *Positive attitudes toward:*

Submission under ... Num. 14:7-9
Prayer concerning ... Mark 11:23, 24
Admission of ... 2 Pet. 3:16

Diklah—*palm tree*

Son of Joktan ... Gen. 10:27

Dilean—*cucumber*

Town of Judah ... Josh. 15:38

Dilemma—*unpleasant alternatives*

Given to David ... 1 Chr. 21:9-17
Presented to Jews ... Matt. 21:23-27

Diligence—*faithful applications to one's work*

A. *Manifested in:*

A child's education ... Deut. 6:7
Dedicated service ... Rom. 12:11
A minister's task ... 2 Tim. 4:1-5

B. *Special objects of:*

The soul ... Deut. 4:9
God's commandments ... Deut. 6:17
The heart ... Prov. 4:23
Christian qualities ... 2 Pet. 1:5-9
One's calling ... 2 Pet. 1:10

C. *Rewards of:*

Prosperity ... Prov. 10:4
Ruling hand ... Prov. 12:24
Perseverance ... 2 Pet. 1:10

Dimnah—*dung heap*

City of Zebulun ... Josh. 21:35
Same as Rimmon ... 1 Chr. 6:77

Dimon—*river bed*

Place in Moab ... Is. 15:9

Dimonah

Town in Judah ... Josh. 15:22
Same as Dibon ... Neh. 11:25

Dinah—*judgment*

Daughter of Leah ... Gen. 30:21
Defiled by Shechem ... Gen. 34:1-24
Avenged by brothers ... Gen. 34:25-31
Guilt concerning ... Gen. 49:5-7

Dinaites

Foreigners who settled in Samaria ... Ezra 4:9

Dinhabah—*give judgment*

City of Edom ... Gen. 36:32

Dionysius—*of the (god)Dionysos*

Prominent Athenian; converted by Paul ... Acts 17:34

Diotrephes—*nurtured by Zeus*

Unruly church member ... 3 John 9, 10

Diplomacy—*the art of managing affairs of state*

Joseph, an example in ... Gen. 41:33-46
Mordecai's advancement in ... Esth. 10:1-3
Daniel's ability in ... Dan. 2:48, 49
Paul's resort to ... Acts 21:20-25

Disappointment—*the non-fulfillment of one's hopes*

A. *Concerning one's:*

Sons ... 1 Sam. 2:12-17
Mate ... 1 Sam. 25:23-31
Failure ... 2 Sam. 17:23
Wisdom ... Eccl. 1:12-18
Acceptance ... Jer. 20:7-9
Mission ... Jon. 4:1-9
Hopes ... Luke 24:17-24

B. *Antidotes against:*

Let trust prevail ... Hab. 3:17-19
Put God first ... Hag. 1:2-14
Accept God's plan ... Rom. 8:28
Remember God's promises ... Heb. 6:10-12

Disarmament—*abolishing weapons of war*

Imposed upon Israel ... 1 Sam. 13:19-22
Figurative of peace ... Is. 2:4

Discernment, spiritual

Requested by Solomon ... 1 Kin. 3:9-14
Prayed for by David ... Ps. 119:18
Sought by Daniel ... Dan. 7:15, 16
Denied to the unregenerate ... 1 Cor. 2:14
Necessity of ... 1 John 4:1-6

Disciples—*followers of a teacher*

John the Baptist's ... John 1:35
Jesus' ... John 2:2
Moses' ... John 9:28
False teachers' ... Acts 20:30

Discipleship—*adherence to a teacher's faith*

A. *Tests of:*

Obedience ... John 14:15
Faithfulness ... John 15:8
Perseverance ... John 8:31
Love ... John 13:35
Humility ... Matt. 10:24, 25
Surrender of all ... Luke 14:26, 33
Bearing the cross ... Matt. 16:25

B. *Rewards of:*

Acknowledged by Christ ... Matt. 12:49, 50
Enlightened by Christ ... John 8:12
Guided by the Spirit ... John 16:13
Honored by the Father ... John 12:26

Discipline of the church

A. *Needed to:*

Maintain sound faith ... Titus 1:13
Correct disorder ... 2 Thess. 3:6-15
Remove the wicked ... 1 Cor. 5:3-5, 13

B. *How performed:*

In meekness ... Gal. 6:1
In love ... 2 Cor. 2:6-8
In submission ... Heb. 13:17
For edification ... 2 Cor. 10:8

Discipline, parental

A. *Needed to:*

Produce understanding ... Prov. 10:13
Drive out foolishness ... Prov. 22:15
Deliver from Sheol ... Prov. 23:13, 14
Produce obedience ... Prov. 19:18
Develop reverence ... Heb. 12:8-10

B. *How performed:*

Without anger ... Eph. 6:4
In love ... Heb. 12:5-7

Disclosure—*an unfolding of the unknown*

A person's identity ... Gen. 45:1-5
Desirable information ... 1 Sam. 23:10-12
God's plan ... Rom. 16:25-27

Discontentment—*unhappy at the condition of things*

Between Jacob and Laban ... Gen. 31:1-16
Between Moses and Miriam ... Num. 12:1-16
Among soldiers ... Luke 3:14

Discord—*lack of love; disagreement*

Caused by contention ... Prov. 26:20, 21

SUBJECT	REFERENCE
Envy	1 Cor. 3:3
Caused by lies	Prov. 6:16-19
Among Jews	John 6:43

Discouragement—*depression of one's spirits*

A. *Causes of:*

Heavy burden	Num. 11:10-15
Defeat	Josh. 7:7-9
Apparent failure	1 Kin. 19:4
Sickness	Is. 38:9-20

B. *Remedies against:*

"What doest thou here?"	1 Kin. 19:9-18
"Cast thy burden upon the Lord"	Ps. 55:22
"Come ye apart"	Mark 6:31
"Lift up your heads"	Luke 21:28

Discourtesy—*rudeness in manners*

Nabal's	1 Sam. 25:3, 14
Hanun's	2 Sam. 10:1-5
Simon's	Luke 7:44

Discretion—*action based upon caution*

Joseph chosen for	Gen. 41:33, 39
The value of	Prov. 2:11
A woman without	Prov. 11:22
A woman with	Titus 2:5
God teaches	Is. 28:26
Trait of a good man	Ps. 112:5

Discrimination—*making distinctions*

A. *Forbidden, on basis of:*

Wealth	James 2:1-9
Personal righteousness	Rom. 3:10, 23

B. *Between truth and error:*

Test the spirits	1 John 4:1-6
Spirit of truth	John 14:17
Word is truth	Ps. 119:160 John 17:17
Satan, father of lies	John 8:44

C. *Between God's Word and man's:*

Paul preached	1 Thess. 2:13
God's Word inspired	2 Tim. 3:16
By Spirit	1 Cor. 2:10-16

Diseases—*physical impairments of health*

A. *Kinds of:*

Ague	Lev. 26:16
Boil	2 Kin. 20:7
Atrophy	Job 16:8
Blindness	Matt. 9:27
Boils and blains	Ex. 9:10
Consumption	Deut. 28:22
Deafness	Mark 7:32
Weakness	Ps. 102:23
Dropsy	Luke 14:2
Dumbness	Matt. 9:32
Dysentery	2 Chr. 21:12-19
Emerods	1 Sam. 5:6, 12
Epilepsy	Matt. 4:24
Fever	Matt. 8:14, 15
Inflammation	Deut. 28:22
Insanity	Dan. 4:33
Issue of blood	Matt. 9:20
Itch	Deut. 28:27
Leprosy	2 Kin. 5:1
Palsy	Matt. 4:24
Plague	2 Sam. 24:15-25
Scab	Deut. 28:27
Sores	Luke 16:20

B. *Causes of:*

Man's original sin	Gen. 3:16-19
Man's actual sin	2 Kin. 5:27 2 Chr. 21:12-19
Satan's afflictions	Job 2:7 Luke 13:16
God's sovereign will	John 9:1-3 2 Cor. 12:7-10

C. *Cures of:*

From God	2 Chr. 16:12 Ps. 103:3
By Jesus	Matt. 4:23, 24
By prayer	Acts 28:8, 9 James 5:14, 15
By the use of means	Is. 38:21 Luke 10:34

See Sickness

Disfigured face

Disqualifies for service	Lev. 21:18

Disgrace—*shame produced by evil conduct*

Treachery	2 Sam. 10:4, 5
Private	2 Sam. 13:6-20
Public	Esth. 6:6-13
Posthumous	Jer. 8:1-3
Permanent	Matt. 27:21-25
Paramount	Matt. 27:26-44

Disgraceful—*comtemptuous reproach or shame*

Immorality	Gen. 34:7
Transgression	Josh. 7:15
Rape	2 Sam. 13:12

Dish

Tabernacle implement	Ex. 25:29
Figurative of annihilating Jerusalem	2 Kin. 21:13

Dishan—*antelope*

Son of Seir	Gen. 36:21, 28

Dishes—*platters used for food*

In the tabernacle	Ex. 25:29
A common	Matt. 26:23
Man washing	2 Kin. 21:13

Dishon—*antelope*

1. Son of Seir	Gen. 36:21-30
2. Grandson of Seir	Gen. 36:25

Dishonesty—*untruthfulness*

A. *Manifested in:*

Half-truths	Gen. 12:11-20
Trickery	Gen. 27:6-29
Falsifying one's word	Gen. 34:15-31
Wicked devices	Prov. 1:10-19
Theft	John 12:6
Unpaid wages	James 5:4

B. *Consequences of:*

Uncovered by God	1 Kin. 21:17-26
Uncovered by men	Josh. 9:3-22
Condemned by conscience	Matt. 27:3-5

Disobedience—*rebellion against recognized authority*

A. *Sources of:*

Satan's temptations	Gen. 3:1-13
Lust	James 1:13-15
Rebellion	Num. 20:10-24 1 Sam. 15:16-23

B. *Consequences of:*

Death	Rom. 5:12-19
The flood	1 Pet. 3:20
Exclusion from the promised land	Num. 14:26-39
Defeat	Judg. 2:2, 11-15
Doom	1 Pet. 2:7, 8

Disorderly—*unruly and irregular*

Paul not guilty	1 Thess. 5:14
Some guilty	2 Thess. 3:6-11

Dispensation—*a stewardship entrusted to one*

Of divine working	Eph. 1:10
Of the Gospel	1 Cor. 9:17
Paul's special privilege in	Eph. 3:2

Dispersion—*a scattering abroad*

Of Noah's generation	Gen. 11:8
Of Israelites	2 Kin. 17:5, 6
Because of disobedience	Hos. 9:1-12
Of the early Christians	1 Pet. 1:1

Display—*an unusual exhibition*

A. *Of God's:*

Power	Ex. 14:23-31
Glory	Ex. 33:18-23
Wrath	Num. 16:23-35
Universe	Job 38:1-41
Holiness	Is. 6:1-10

B. *Of man's:*

Kingdom	Esth. 1:2-7
Pride	Esth. 5:11
Wealth	Is. 39:2
Hypocrisy	Luke 20:46, 47

Displeasure—*disapproval*

God's, at man	1 Chr. 21:7
Man's, at God	2 Sam. 6:8
Man's, at men	Acts 12:20

Disposition—*natural temperament*

Ambitious Absalom	2 Sam. 15:1-6
Boastful Nebuchadnezzar	Dan. 4:30
Cowardly Peter	Matt. 26:58
Devilish Judas	John 13:20-30
Envious Saul	1 Sam. 18:6-12
Foolish Nabal	1 Sam. 25:10-25
Gullible Haman	Esth. 6:6-11
Humble Job	Job 1:20-22

Ditch—*a trench*

Miraculously filled	2 Kin. 3:16-20
Wicked fall into	Ps. 7:15
Blind leaders fall into	Luke 6:39

Divers—*various kinds*

Colors	Ezek. 17:3
Diseases	Luke 4:40
Doctrines	Heb. 13:9
Flies	Ps. 78:45
Lusts	Titus 3:3
Manners	Heb. 1:1
Measures	Prov. 20:10
Miracles	Heb. 2:4
Seeds	Deut. 22:9
Temptations	James 1:2
Tongues	1 Cor. 12:10
Vanities	Eccl. 5:7
Washings	Heb. 9:10
Weights	Prov. 20:10, 23

Diversity—*variety*

Among hearers	Mark 13:3-8
Of God's gifts	1 Cor. 12:4-11
Of God's times	Heb. 1:1

Divination—*attempt to foretell the unknown by occult means*

A. *Considered as:*

System of fraud	Ezek. 13:6, 7
Lucrative employment	Acts 16:16
Abomination	Deut. 18:11, 12
Punishable by death	Lev. 20:6, 27

B. *Practiced by:*

Astrologers	Is. 47:13
Charmers	Deut. 18:11
Consulters	Deut. 18:14
Enchanter	Deut. 18:10
False prophets	Jer. 14:14
Magicians	Gen. 41:8
Necromancer	Deut. 18:11
Soothsayers	Is. 2:6
Sorcerers	Acts 13:6, 8
Witch	Ex. 22:18
Wizard	Deut. 18:11

Division—*diversity; discord*

A. *Causes of:*

Real faith	Luke 12:51-53
Carnal spirit	1 Cor. 3:3

B. *Opposed to:*

Prayer of Christ	John 17:21-23
Unity of Christ	1 Cor. 1:13
Unity of the church	John 10:16 1 Cor. 12:13-25

Division of Priests—*assignments for service*

Outlined by David	1 Chr. 24:1-19
Determined by casting lots	1 Chr. 24:5, 7
Of Zacharias	Luke 1:5

Divorce—*breaking of the marriage tie*

A. *The Old Testament teaching:*

Permitted	Deut. 24:1-3
Divorced may not return to first husband	Deut. 24.4
Denied to those making false claims	Deut. 22:13-19
Denied to those seducing a virgin	Deut. 22:28, 29
Unjust, reproved	Mal. 2:14-16
Required, foreign wives put away	Ezra 10:1-16
Disobedience, a cause among heathen	Esth. 1:10-22
A prophet's concern with	Hos. 2:1-22

B. *In the New Testament:*

Marriage binding as long as life	Mark 10:2-9 Rom. 7:2, 3
Divorce allowed because of adultery	Matt. 5:27-32
Marriage of the divorced constitutes adultery	Luke 16:18
Reconciliation encouraged	1 Cor. 7:10-17

D

SUBJECT	REFERENCE
Dizahab—*abounding in gold*	
Location of Moses' farewell addresses	Deut. 1:1
Doctors—*teachers*	
Christ questions	Luke 2:46
They hear Christ	Luke 5:17
Gamaliel, a famous doctor	Acts 5:34
Doctrine—*teaching*	
A. *Statements of:*	
Foundational	Heb. 6:1, 2
Traditional	1 Cor. 15:1-4
Creedal	2 Tim. 3:16
B. *Essentials of:*	
The Bible's inspiration	2 Tim. 3:16
Christ's deity	1 Cor. 12:3
Christ's incarnation	1 John 4:1-6
Christ's resurrection	1 Cor. 15:12-20
Christ's return	2 Pet. 3:3-13
Salvation by faith	Acts 2:38
C. *Attitudes toward:*	
Obey	Rom. 6:17
Receive	1 Cor. 15:1-4
Devote	Acts 2:42
Hold fast	2 Tim. 1:13
Adorn	Titus 2:10
Doctrine, false	
A. *What constitutes:*	
Perverting the Gospel	Gal. 1:6, 7 1 John 4:1-6
Satanic deception	2 Cor. 11:13-15
B. *Teachers of:*	
Deceive many	Matt. 24:5, 24
Attract many	2 Pet. 2:2
Speak perverse things	Acts 20:30
Are savage	Acts 20:29
Deceitful	2 Cor. 11:13
Ungodly	Jude 4, 8
Proud	1 Tim. 6:3, 4
Corrupt	2 Tim. 3:8
Love error	2 Tim. 4:3, 4
C. *Christian attitude toward:*	
Avoid	Rom. 16:17, 18
Test	1 John 4:1
Detest	Jude 23
Dodai	
An Ahohite	1 Chr. 27:4
Dodanim	
Descendants of Javan	Gen. 10:4
Dodavah—*beloved of Jehovah*	
Eliezer's father	2 Chr. 20:37
Dodo—*loving*	
1. A descendant of Issachar	Judg. 10:1
2. A mighty man of David's	2 Sam. 23:9
Called Dodai	1 Chr. 27:4
3. Father of Elhanan	2 Sam. 23:24
Doeg—*fearful*	
An Edomite; chief of Saul's herdsmen	1 Sam. 21:7
Betrays David	1 Sam. 22:9, 10
Kills 85 priests	1 Sam. 22:18, 19
Dog—*a domesticated animal*	
A. *Described as:*	
Carnivorous	1 Kin. 14:11
Blood-eating	1 Kin. 21:19
Dangerous	Ps. 22:16
Domesticated	Matt. 15:26, 27
Unclean	Is. 66:3
B. *Figurative of:*	
Promiscuity	Deut. 23:18
Contempt	1 Sam. 17:43
Worthlessness	2 Sam. 9:8
Satan	Ps. 22:20
Hypocrite	Matt. 7:6
Gentiles	Matt. 15:26
False teachers	2 Pet. 2:22
The unsaved	Rev. 22:15
Dominion—*supreme authority to govern*	
A. *Man's:*	
Delegated by God	Gen. 1:26-28
Under God's control	Jer. 25:12-33
Misused	Dan. 5:18-23
B. *Satan's:*	
Secured by rebellion	Is. 14:12-16
Offered to Christ	Luke 4:6
Destroyed by Christ	1 John 3:8
Abolished at Christ's return	2 Thess. 2:8, 9
C. *Christ's:*	
Predicted	Is. 11:1-10
Announced	Luke 1:32, 33
Secured by His resurrection	Acts 2:24-36 Rev. 1:18
Perfected at His return	1 Cor. 15:24-28
Door—*an entrance*	
A. *Used literally of:*	
City gates	Neh. 3:1-6
Prison gates	Acts 5:19
B. *Used figuratively of:*	
Christ	John 10:7, 9
Christ's return	Matt. 24:33
Day of salvation	Matt. 25:10
Inclusion of Gentiles	Acts 14:27
Opportunity	2 Cor. 2:12
Doorkeeper	
Descriptive of:	
Maaseiah	Jer. 35:4
Good shepherd	John 10:3
One who was spoken to by a disciple	John 18:16
Doorpost	
Servant's ears pierced at	Ex. 21:6
Dophkah—*cattle driving*	
A desert encampment	Num. 33:12, 13
Dor—*habitation*	
Jabin's ally	Josh. 11:1, 2
Taken by Joshua	Josh. 12:23
Assigned to Manasseh	Josh. 17:11
Inhabitants unexpelled	Judg. 1:27
Dorcas—*gazelle*	
Good woman	Acts 9:36
Raised to life	Acts 9:37-42
Called Tabitha	Acts 9:36, 40
Dothan—*wells*	
Ancient town	Gen. 37:14-25
Joseph sold there	Gen. 37:17-28
Elisha strikes Syrians at	2 Kin. 6:8-23
Double-mindedness—*inability to hold a fixed belief*	
Makes one unstable	James 1:8
Double-tongued—*two-faced, hypocritical*	
Condemned in deacons	1 Tim. 3:8
Doubt—*uncertainty of mind*	
A. *Objects of, Christ's:*	
Miracles	Matt. 12:24-30
Resurrection	John 20:24-29
Messiahship	Luke 7:19-23
Return	2 Pet. 3:4
B. *Causes of:*	
Satan	Gen. 3:4
Unbelief	Luke 1:18-20
Worldly wisdom	1 Cor. 1:18-25
Spiritual instability	James 1:6, 7
C. *Removal of, by:*	
Putting God to the test	Judg. 6:36-40 John 7:17
Searching the Scriptures	Acts 17:11, 12
Believing God's Word	Luke 16:27-31
Dove—*pigeon*	
A. *Features regarding:*	
Sent from ark	Gen. 8:8, 10, 12
Offered in sacrifice	Gen. 15:9
Habits of, migratory	Jer. 8:7
Sold in Temple	Matt. 21:12
B. *Figurative of:*	
Loveliness	Song 2:14
Desperate mourning	Is. 38:14
Foolish insecurity	Hos. 7:11
Israel's restoration	Hos. 11:11
Holy Spirit	Matt. 3:16
Harmlessness	Matt. 10:16
Dove's dung—*an edible plant bulb*	
Sold in Samaria	2 Kin. 6:25
Dowry—*gifts given to bride's father for the bride*	
A. *Regulations regarding:*	
Sanctioned in the Law	Ex. 22:17
Amount of, specified	Deut. 22:29
Sometimes given by bride's father	Josh. 15:16-19
B. *Instances of:*	
Abraham (Isaac) for Rebekah	Gen. 24:22-53
Jacob for Rachel	Gen. 29:15-20
Shechem for Dinah	Gen. 34:12
David for Michal	1 Sam. 18:20-25
Dragon	
A. *Applied (Heb.,* tan*) to:*	
Some wild asses	Jer. 14:6
Wicked men	Is. 43:19, 20
B. *Applied (Heb.,* tannin*) to:*	
Sea monster	Gen. 1:21
Great serpents	Ex. 7:9, 10, 12
Cruel tyrants	Is. 51:9
C. *Applied (Gr.,* dragon*) to:*	
Satan	Rev. 12:9
Antichrist	Rev. 12:3
Dragon Well	
In Jerusalem	Neh. 2:13
Draught	
Excrement	Matt. 15:17
Catch of fish	Luke 5:9
Drawers of water—*a lowly servant classification*	
Women	Gen. 24:13 1 Sam. 9:11
Defeated enemies	Josh. 9:21
Young men	Ruth 2:9
Included in covenant	Deut. 29:10-13
Dreams—*thoughts visualized in sleep*	
A. *Purposes of:*	
Restrain from evil	Gen. 20:3
Reveal God's will	Gen. 28:11-22
Encourage	Judg. 7:13-15
Reveal future	Gen. 37:5-10
Instruct	Matt. 1:20
B. *The interpretation of:*	
Sought anxiously	Dan. 2:1-3
Belong to God	Gen. 40:8
Revealed by God	Gen. 40:8
Sought for God's will	Num. 12:6
Sometimes delusive	Is. 29:7, 8
False, by false prophets	Deut. 13:1-5
C. *Notable examples of:*	
Abimelech	Gen. 20:3
Jacob	Gen. 28:10, 12
Laban	Gen. 31:24
Joseph	Gen. 37:5
Pharaoh	Gen. 41:1-13
Unnamed person	Judg. 7:13, 14
Solomon	1 Kin. 3:5
Job	Job 7:14
Nebuchadnezzar	Dan. 2:1-13
Joseph	Matt. 1:19, 20
Pilate's wife	Matt. 27:13, 19
Dregs—*the sediments of liquids; grounds*	
Wicked shall drink down	Ps. 75:8
Contains God's fury	Is. 51:17, 22
Dress—*to prepare something to:*	
Cultivate land	Gen. 2:15
Trim lamps	Ex. 30:7
Prepare foods	Heb. 6:7
Become presentable	2 Sam. 19:24
Drink—*to swallow liquids*	
A. *Used literally of:*	
Water	Gen. 24:14
Milk	Judg. 5:25
Wine	Gen. 9:21
B. *Used figuratively of:*	
Famine	2 Kin. 18:27
Misery	Is. 51:22, 23
Married pleasure	Prov. 5:15-19
Unholy alliances	Jer. 2:18
God's blessings	Zech. 9:15-17
Spiritual communion	John 6:53, 54
Holy Spirit	John 7:37-39

SUBJECT — REFERENCE

Drink offerings
Of wine ... Hos. 9:4
Of water ... 1 Sam. 7:6

Dromedary—*a specie of camel; a swift steed*
Used by Solomon ... 1 Kin. 4:28
Used by Ahasuerus ... Esth. 8:10
Noted for speed ... Jer. 2:23
Figurative of Gospel blessings ... Is. 60:6

Dropsy—*an unnatural accumulation of fluid in parts of the body*
Healing of ... Luke 14:2-4

Dross—*impurities separated from metals*
Result of refinement ... Prov. 25:4
Figurative of Israel ... Is. 1:22, 25

Drought—*an extended dry season*
Unbearable in the day ... Gen. 31:40
Seen in the wilderness ... Deut. 8:15
Comes in summer ... Ps. 32:4
Sent as a judgment ... Hag. 1:11
Only God can stop ... Jer. 14:22
Descriptive of spiritual barrenness ... Jer. 14:1-7
The wicked dwell in ... Jer. 17:5, 6
The righteous endure ... Jer. 17:8
Longest ... 1 Kin. 18:1; Luke 4:25

Drown
Of the Egyptians ... Ex. 14:27-30
Jonah saved from ... Jon. 1:15-17
Of severe judgment ... Matt. 18:6
The woman saved from ... Rev. 12:15, 16
Figurative of lusts ... 1 Tim. 6:9

Drowsiness—*the mental state preceding sleep*
Prelude to poverty ... Prov. 23:21
Disciples guilty of ... Matt. 26:43

Drunkenness—*state of intoxication*
A. *Evils of:*
Debases ... Gen. 9:21, 22
Provokes anger ... Prov. 20:1
Poverty ... Prov. 23:21
Perverts justice ... Is. 5:22, 23
Confuses the mind ... Is. 28:7
Licentiousness ... Rom. 13:13
Disorderliness ... Matt. 24:48-51
Hinders watchfulness ... 1 Thess. 5:6, 7
B. *Actual instances of the evil of:*
Defeat in battle ... 1 Kin. 20:16-21
Degradation ... Esth. 1:10, 11
Debauchery ... Dan. 5:1-4
Weakness ... Amos 4:1
Disorder ... 1 Cor. 11:21, 22
C. *Penalties of:*
Death ... Deut. 21:20, 21
Exclusion from fellowship ... 1 Cor. 5:11
Exclusion from heaven ... 1 Cor. 6:9, 10
D. *Figurative of:*
Destruction ... Is. 49:26
Roaring waves ... Ps. 107:27
Giddiness ... Is. 19:14
Error ... Is. 28:7
Spiritual blindness ... Is. 29:9-11
International chaos ... Jer. 25:15-29
Persecution ... Rev. 17:6

Drusilla—feminine of *"Drusus"*
Wife of Felix; hears Paul ... Acts 24:24, 25

Dulcimer—*a bagpipe; musical instrument*
Used in Babylon ... Dan. 3:5-15

Dumah—*silence*
1. Descendants (a tribe) of Ishmael ... Gen. 25:14
2. Town in Judah ... Josh. 15:52

Dumb—*inability to speak*
A. *Used literally of dumbness:*
Natural ... Ex. 4:11
Imposed ... Ezek. 3:26, 27
Demonized ... Mark 9:17, 25
Penalized ... Luke 1:20-22
B. *Used figuratively of:*
External calamity ... Ps. 38:13
Submissiveness ... Is. 53:7

SUBJECT — REFERENCE

Inefficient leaders ... Is. 56:10
Helplessness ... 1 Cor. 12:2
Lamb before shearer is ... Acts 8:32
With silence ... Ps. 39:2

Dung—*excrement*
A. *Used for:*
Fuel ... Ezek. 4:12, 15
Food in famine ... 2 Kin. 6:25
B. *Figurative of:*
Something worthless ... 2 Kin. 9:37

Dungeon—*an underground prison*
Joseph's imprisonment ... Gen. 40:8, 15; Jer. 37:16

Dung Gate—*a gate of Jerusalem*
Wall dedicated near ... Neh. 12:31

Dunghills—*heaps of manure*
Pile of manure ... Luke 14:35
Figurative of a wretched condition ... Ps. 113:7

Dura—*circuit, wall*
Site of Nebuchadnezzar's golden image ... Dan. 3:1

Dust—*powdery earth*
A. *Used literally of:*
Man's body ... Gen. 2:7
Dust of Egypt ... Ex. 8:16, 17
Particles of soil ... Num. 5:17
B. *Used figuratively of:*
Man's mortality ... Gen. 3:19
Descendants ... Gen. 13:16
Judgment ... Deut. 28:24
Act of cursing ... 2 Sam. 16:13
Dejection ... Job 2:12
Subjection ... Is. 49:23
The grave ... Is. 26:19
Rejection ... Matt. 10:14

Duty—*an obligation*
A. *Toward men:*
Husband to wife ... Eph. 5:25-33
Wife to husband ... Eph. 5:22-24
Parents to children ... Eph. 6:4
Children to parents ... Eph. 6:1-3
Subjects to rulers ... 1 Pet. 2:12-20
Rulers to subjects ... Rom. 13:1-7
Men to men ... 1 Pet. 3:8-16
The weak ... 1 Cor. 8:1-13
B. *Toward God:*
Love ... Deut. 11:1
Obey ... Matt. 12:50
Serve ... 1 Thess. 1:9
Worship ... John 4:23

Dwarf—*a diminutive person*
Excluded from priesthood ... Lev. 21:20

Dwelling, God
In the tabernacle ... Ex. 29:45, 46
In the temple ... 1 Kin. 6:12, 13; 2 Chr. 7:1-3
In Zion ... Is. 8:18
In Christ ... Col. 2:9
Among men ... John 1:14
In our hearts ... 1 John 4:12-16
In the Holy Spirit ... 1 Cor. 3:16
In the New Jerusalem ... Rev. 7:15

Dyeing—*coloring*
Leather ... Ex. 25:5

Dysentery
Cured by Paul ... Acts 28:8

E

Eagle—*a bird of prey of the falcon species*
A. *Described as:*
Unclean ... Lev. 11:13
A bird of prey ... Job 9:26
Large ... Ezek. 17:3, 7
Swift ... 2 Sam. 1:23
Keen in vision ... Job 39:27-29
Nesting high ... Jer. 49:16
B. *Figurative of:*
God's care ... Ex. 19:4

SUBJECT — REFERENCE

Swift armies ... Jer. 4:13
Spiritual renewal ... Is. 40:31
Flight of riches ... Prov. 23:5
False security ... Jer. 49:16

Ear—*the organ of hearing*
A. *Ceremonies respecting:*
Priest's, anointed ... Ex. 29:20
Leper's, anointed ... Lev. 14:14, 25
Servant's bored ... Ex. 21:5, 6
B. *The hearing of the unregenerate:*
Deafened ... Deut. 29:4
Stopped ... Ps. 58:4
Dulled ... Matt. 13:15
Disobedient ... Jer. 7:23, 24
Uncircumcised ... Acts 7:51
Itching ... 2 Tim. 4:3, 4
C. *Promises concerning, in:*
Prophecy ... Is. 64:4
Fulfillment ... Matt. 13:16, 17
A miracle ... Mark 7:35
A foretaste ... 2 Cor. 12:4
Final realization ... 1 Cor. 2:9

Early, arose
A. *For spiritual purposes:*
Abraham—looked on Sodom and Gomorrah ... Gen. 19:27-28
Abraham—to offer a burnt offering ... Gen. 22:2, 3
Jacob—to worship the Lord ... Gen. 28:18-22
Moses—to meet God on Sinai ... Ex. 34:4, 5
Elkanah and Hannah—to worship God ... 1 Sam. 1:19-28
Hezekiah—to worship God ... 2 Chr. 29:20-24
Job—to offer sacrifices ... Job 1:5
Jesus—to pray ... Mark 1:35
Jesus—to prepare to teach ... John 8:2
The people—to hear Jesus ... Luke 21:38
B. *For military reasons:*
Joshua—to lead Israel over Jordan ... Josh. 3:1-17
Joshua—to capture Jericho ... Josh. 6:12-27
Joshua—to capture Ai ... Josh. 8:10
People of Jerusalem—to see dead men ... 2 Kin. 19:35
C. *For personal reasons:*
Gideon—to examine the fleece ... Judg. 6:36-38
Samuel—to meet Saul ... 1 Sam. 15:12
David—to obey his father ... 1 Sam. 17:20
The ideal woman—to do her work ... Prov. 31:15
Drunkards—to pursue strong drink ... Is. 5:11
Certain women—to visit Christ's grave ... Mark 16:2

Early rising
Hezekiah to worship God ... 2 Chr. 29:20-24

Earnest—*a pledge of full payment*
The Holy Spirit in the heart ... 2 Cor. 1:22
Given by God ... 2 Cor. 5:5
Guarantee of future redemption ... Eph. 1:13, 14

Earnestness—*a serious and intense spirit*
Warning men ... Gen. 19:15-17; Ezek. 18:1-32
Accepting promises ... Gen. 28:12-22
Admonishing a son ... 1 Chr. 28:9, 10
Public prayer ... 2 Chr. 6:12-42
Asking forgiveness ... Ps. 51:1-19
Calling to repentance ... Acts 2:38-40
Seeking salvation ... Acts 16:30-34
Preaching the Gospel ... Acts 20:18-38
Writing an epistle ... Jude 3-5

Earrings—*ornaments worn on the ear*
Sign of worldliness ... Gen. 35:2-4
Made into a golden calf ... Ex. 32:2-4
Spoils of war ... Judg. 8:24-26
Used figuratively ... Ezek. 16:12

Ears of corn
Seen in Pharaoh's dream ... Gen. 41:5-7
Regulations concerning ... Lev. 2:14
Ruth gleans ... Ruth 2:2
Christ's disciples pluck ... Matt. 12:1

E

SUBJECT REFERENCE

Earth—*our planet*

A. *Described as:*
Inhabitable .... Is. 45:18
God's footstool .... Is. 66:1
A circle .... Is. 40:22
Full of minerals .... Deut. 8:9

B. *Glory of God's:*
Goodness .... Ps. 33:5
Glory .... Is. 6:3
Riches .... Ps. 104:24
Mercy .... Ps. 119:64

C. *History of:*
Created by God .... Gen. 1:1
Given to man .... Gen. 1:27-31
Affected by sin .... Rom. 8:20-23
Destroyed .... Gen. 7:7-24
Final destruction .... 2 Pet. 3:7-12
To be renewed .... Is. 65:17

D. *Unusual events of:*
Swallows several families .... Num. 16:23-35
Reversed in motion .... 2 Kin. 20:8-11
Shaking .... Heb. 12:26
Smiting .... Mal. 4:6
Earthquake .... Matt. 27:51-54

E. *Man's relation to:*
Made of .... 1 Cor. 15:47, 48
Given dominion over .... Gen. 1:26
Brings curse on .... Gen. 3:17
Returns to dust .... Gen. 3:19

F. *Promises respecting:*
Continuance of seasons ...... Gen. 8:21, 22
No more flood .... Gen. 9:11-17
God's knowledge to fill ...... Is. 11:9
The meek shall inherit .... Matt. 5:5
Long life upon .... Eph. 6:2, 3
To be renewed .... Is. 65:17

Earthquake—*a trembling of the earth*

A. *Expressive of God's:*
Power .... Heb. 12:26
Presence .... Ps. 68:7, 8
Anger .... Ps. 18:7
Judgments .... Is. 24:18-21
Overthrowing of kingdoms ... Hag. 2:6, 7
Rev. 16:18-21

B. *Mentioned in the Scriptures:*
Mt. Sinai .... Ex. 19:18
The wilderness .... Num. 16:31, 32
Saul's time .... 1 Sam. 14:15
Ahab's reign .... 1 Kin. 19:11, 12
Uzziah's reign .... Amos 1:1
Christ's death .... Matt. 27:50, 51
Christ's resurrection .... Matt. 28:2
Philippi .... Acts 16:26
This age .... Matt. 24:7

Ease—*contentment of body and mind*

Israel's .... Amos 6:1
Pagan nations' .... Zech. 1:15

East country—*southeastern Palestine, Arabia*

Abraham sent family there ...... Gen. 25:6

East gate—*a gate of Jerusalem*

In Temple area .... Ezek. 10:19
Ezek. 11:1

East wind—*a scorching desert wind, the sirocco*

Destroys vegetation .... Gen. 41:6
Ezek. 17:10
Destroys houses .... Job 1:19
Destroys ships .... Ps. 48:7
Ezek. 27:26
Brings judgment .... Is. 27:8
Jer. 4:11, 12
Dries springs and fountains ..... Hos. 13:15
Afflicts Jonah .... Jon. 4:8
Called Euroclydon .... Acts 27:14

Eat, eating

A. *Restrictions on:*
Forbidden tree .... Gen. 2:16, 17
Blood .... Acts 15:19, 20
Unclean things .... Lev. 11:1-47
Deut. 14:1-29
Excess, condemned .... Eccl. 10:16, 17
Phil. 3:19
Anxiety concerning, prohibited .... Matt. 6:24-34

B. *Spiritual significance of:*
Covenant .... Ex. 24:11
Adoption .... Jer. 52:33, 34
Fellowship .... Luke 22:15-20

C. *Christian attitude toward:*
Tradition rejected .... Mark 7:1-23
Disorderliness condemned ... 1 Cor. 11:20-22
Regard for weaker brother ... Rom. 14:1-23
No work, no eating .... 2 Thess. 3:7-10

Ebal—*to be bare, stony*

1. Son of Shobal .... Gen. 36:23
2. Same as Obal .... Gen. 10:28
3. Mountain in Samaria .... Deut. 27:12, 13
Law to be written upon ..... Deut. 27:1-8
Fulfilled by Joshua .... Josh. 8:30-35

Ebed—*slave*

1. Gaal's father .... Judg. 9:28, 30
2. Son of Jonathan .... Ezra 8:6

Ebed-melech—*slave of the king*

Ethiopian eunuch; rescues Jeremiah .... Jer. 38:7-13
Promised divine protection ..... Jer. 39:15-18

Ebenezer—*stone of help*

Site of Israel's defeat .... 1 Sam. 4:1-10
Ark transferred from .... 1 Sam. 5:1
Site of memorial stone .... 1 Sam. 7:10, 12

Eber—*the region beyond*

1. Great-grandson of Shem ..... Gen. 10:21-24
Progenitor of the: Hebrews ... Gen. 11:16-26
Arabians and Arameans ..... Gen. 10:25-30
2. Gadite leader .... 1 Chr. 5:13
3. Son of Elpaal .... 1 Chr. 8:12
4. Son of Shashak .... 1 Chr. 8:22, 25
5. Postexilic priest .... Neh. 12:20

Ebiasaph—*gatherer*

Forefather of Samuel .... 1 Chr. 6:23
Same as Abiasaph .... Ex. 6:16, 18, 24

Ebony

Black, heavy hardwood; article of trade .... Ezek. 27:15

Ebronah—*passage*

Israelite encampment .... Num. 33:34

Ecclesiastes, Book of—from Gr. word *"assembly"* and Heb. word *"one who assembles"*

Vanity of earthly things .... Eccl. 1:2
Material goods .... Eccl. 5:10-12

Eclipse of the sun

Foretold .... Amos 8:9

Economy—*living thriftily*

The law of .... Prov. 11:24
The wrong kind .... Hag. 1:6, 9-11
Exemplified by Jesus .... John 6:12

Ed—*witness*

The name (not in Heb.) of an altar .... Josh. 22:34

Eden—*delight, pleasantness*

1. First home .... Gen. 2:8-15
Zion becomes like .... Is. 51:3
Called the "garden of God" .... Ezek. 28:13
Terrible contrast .... Joel 2:3
2. Region in Mesopotamia ..... Is. 37:12
3. Gershonite Levite .... 2 Chr. 29:12

Eder—*a flock*

1. Watchtower .... Gen. 35:21
2. Town in Judah .... Josh. 15:21
3. Benjamite .... 1 Chr. 8:15
4. Levite .... 1 Chr. 23:23

Edification—*building up one's faith*

A. *Objects of:*
The church .... 1 Cor. 14:4-12
The body of Christ .... Eph. 4:12
One another .... Rom. 14:19

B. *Accomplished by:*
The ministry .... 2 Cor. 12:19
Christian gifts .... 1 Cor. 14:3-12
Word of God .... Acts 20:32
Love .... 1 Cor. 8:1
Spiritual things .... Rom. 14:19
Seeking another's goods ..... Rom. 15:2
God's authority .... 2 Cor. 10:8

C. *Hindrances of:*
Carnal spirit .... 1 Cor. 3:1-4
Foolish questions .... 1 Tim. 1:3, 4
Spiritual luke-warmness ..... Rev. 3:14-22
Worldly spirit .... James 4:1-6

Edom—*red*

1. Name given to Esau .... Gen. 25:30
2. Edomites .... Num. 20:18-21
3. Land of Esau; called Seir .... Gen. 32:3
Called Edom and Idumea .... Mark 3:8
Mountainous land .... Jer. 49:16, 17
People of, cursed .... Is. 34:5, 6

Edomites—*descendants of Esau*

A. *Character of:*
Warlike .... Gen. 27:40
Idolatrous .... 2 Chr. 25:14, 20
Superstitious .... Jer. 27:3, 9
Proud .... Jer. 49:16
Cruel .... Jer. 49:19
Vindictive .... Ezek. 25:12

B. *Relations with Israel:*
Descendants of Esau .... Gen. 36:9
Refused passage to .... Num. 20:18-20
Enemies of .... Ezek. 35:5, 6
Wars against .... 1 Sam. 14:47
Joined enemies of .... 2 Chr. 20:10
Aided Babylon against .... Ps. 137:7

C. *Prophecies concerning:*
Subjection to Israel .... Gen. 27:37
Punishment for persecuting Israel .... Is. 34:5-8
Utter desolation of .... Is. 34:9-17
Figurative of Gentiles .... Amos 9:11, 12

Edrei—*mighty*

1. Capital of Bashan .... Deut. 3:10
Site of Og's defeat .... Num. 21:33-35
2. City of Naphtali .... Josh. 19:37

Education—*instruction in knowledge*

A. *Performed by:*
Parents .... Eph. 6:4
Tutors .... Gal. 4:1-3
Teachers .... 2 Chr. 17:7-9
Learned men .... Acts 22:3

B. *Method of:*
Sharing .... Gal. 6:6
Recalling God's works ...... Ps. 78:1-8
Learning from nature .... Prov. 6:6-11
Step by step .... Is. 28:10
Asking questions .... Luke 2:46

C. *Examples of:*
Moses .... Acts 7:22
Daniel .... Dan. 1:17
Paul .... Acts 22:3
Timothy .... 2 Tim. 3:15, 16

Effeminate—*a man with female traits*

Curse on Egypt .... Is. 19:16
The weakness of Nineveh .... Nah. 3:13
Rebuked by Paul .... 1 Cor. 16:13
Shall not inherit the kingdom of God .... 1 Cor. 6:9

Effort—*using energy to get something done*

Organized .... Neh. 4:15-23
Diligence in .... Neh. 6:1-4
Inspired to .... Hag. 1:12-14
Ill-considered .... Luke 14:28-30
The highest .... Phil. 3:11-14

Egg

Prohibition concerning that of birds .... Deut. 22:6
Article of food .... Luke 11:12
White of, without taste .... Job 6:6

Eglah—*heifer*

Wife of David .... 2 Sam. 3:2, 5

Eglaim—*two ponds*

Moabite town .... Is. 15:8

Eglon—*heifer-like*

1. Moabite king .... Judg. 3:12-15
2. City of Judah .... Josh. 15:39

SUBJECT — REFERENCE

Egotism—*a sinful exultation of one's self*
Satan ... Is. 14:13-15; Luke 4:5, 6
Goliath ... 1 Sam. 17:4-11
Haman ... Esth. 6:6-12
Simon ... Acts 8:9-11
Herod ... Acts 12:20-23
Diotrephes ... 3 John 9-10
Sign of antichrist ... 2 Thess. 2:4
Sign of the last days ... 2 Tim. 3:1-5

Egypt—*black*
A. *Israel's contact with:*
Abram visits ... Gen. 12:10
Joseph sold into ... Gen. 37:28, 36
Joseph becomes leader in ... Gen. 39:1-4
Hebrews move to ... Gen. 46:5-7
Persecution by ... Ex. 1:15-22
Israel leaves ... Ex. 12:31-33
Army of, perishes ... Ex. 14:26-28
B. *Characteristics of:*
Superstitious ... Is. 19:3
Unprofitable ... Is. 30:1-7
Treacherous ... Is. 36:6
Ambitious ... Jer. 46:8, 9
C. *Prophecies concerning:*
Israel's sojourn in ... Gen. 15:13
Destruction of ... Ezek. 30:24, 25
Ever a lowly kingdom ... Ezek. 29:14, 15
Conversion of ... Is. 19:18-25
Christ, called out of ... Matt. 2:15

Egyptian, the—*an unknown insurrectionist*
Paul mistaken for ... Acts 21:37, 38

Ehi—*brotherly*
Benjamin's son ... Gen. 46:21
Same as Ahiram ... Num. 26:38

Ehud—*union*
1. Great-grandson of Benjamin ... 1 Chr. 7:10
2. Son of Gera ... Judg. 3:15
Slays Eglon ... Judg. 3:16-26

Eker—*offshoot*
Descendant of Judah ... 1 Chr. 2:27

Ekron—*extermination*
Philistine city ... Josh. 13:3
Captured by Judah ... Judg. 1:18
Assigned to Dan ... Josh. 19:43
Ark sent to ... 1 Sam. 5:10
Denounced by the prophets ... Jer. 25:9, 20

El—*ancient word for God, often used as prefix to Hebrew names*
El-beth-el ... Gen. 35:6, 7

Eladah—*God has adorned*
A descendant of Ephraim ... 1 Chr. 7:20

Elah—*an oak*
1. Duke of Edom ... Gen. 36:41
2. Son of Caleb ... 1 Chr. 4:15
3. Benjamite ... 1 Chr. 9:8
4. King of Israel ... 1 Kin. 16:6, 8-10
5. Father of Hoshea ... 2 Kin. 15:30
6. Valley of ... 1 Sam. 17:2, 19
7. Father of Shimei ... 1 Kin. 4:18

Elam—*hidden*
1. Son of Shem ... Gen. 10:22
2. Benjamite ... 1 Chr. 8:24
3. Korahite Levite ... 1 Chr. 26:1, 3
4. Head of postexilic families ... Ezra 2:7
5. Another family head ... Ezra 2:31
6. One who signs covenant ... Neh. 10:1, 14
7. Priest ... Neh. 12:42

Elamites—*descendants of Elam*
A Semite (Shem) people ... Gen. 10:22
An ancient nation ... Gen. 14:1
Connected with Media ... Is. 21:2
Destruction of ... Jer. 49:34-39
In Persian empire ... Ezra 4:9
Jews from, at Pentecost ... Acts 2:9

Elasah—*God has made*
1. Shaphan's son ... Jer. 29:3
2. Son of Pashur ... Ezra 10:22

SUBJECT — REFERENCE

Elath, Eloth—*a grove*
Seaport on Red Sea ... 1 Kin. 9:26
Edomite dukedom ... Gen. 31:41
Conquered by David ... 2 Sam. 8:14
Built by Azariah ... 2 Kin. 14:21, 22
Captured by Syrians ... 2 Kin. 16:6

El-beth-el—*God of Bethel*
Site of Jacob's altar ... Gen. 35:6, 7

Eldaah—*God has called*
Son of Midian ... Gen. 25:4

Eldad—*God has loved*
Elder of Moses ... Num. 11:26-29

Elderly
A. *Contributions of:*
Counsel ... 1 Kin. 12:6-16; Job 12:12
Spiritual service ... Luke 2:36-38
Fruitfulness ... Ps. 92:13, 14
Leadership ... Josh. 24:2, 14, 15, 29
B. *Attitude toward:*
Minister to needs ... 1 Kin. 1:15
Respect ... Ps. 71:18, 19
As cared for by God ... Is. 46:4
Honor ... Lev. 19:32; Prov. 16:31

Elders of Israel
A. *Functions of, in Mosaic period:*
Rule the people ... Judg. 2:7
Represent the nation ... Ex. 3:16, 18
Share in national guilt ... Josh. 7:6
Assist in government ... Num. 11:16-25
Perform religious acts ... Ex. 12:21, 22
B. *Functions of, in later periods:*
Choose a king ... 2 Sam. 3:17-21
Ratify a covenant ... 2 Sam. 5:3
Assist at a dedication ... 1 Kin. 8:1-3
Counsel kings ... 1 Kin. 12:6-8, 13
Legislate reforms ... Ezra 10:8-14
Try civil cases ... Matt. 26:3-68

Elders in the church
A. *Qualifications of, stated by:*
Paul ... Titus 1:5-14
Peter ... 1 Pet. 5:1-4
B. *Duties of:*
Administer relief ... Acts 11:29, 30
Correct error ... Acts 15:4, 6, 23
Hold fast the faithful Word ... Titus 1:5, 9
Rule well ... 1 Tim. 5:17
Minister to the sick ... James 5:14, 15
C. *Honors bestowed on:*
Ordination ... Acts 14:19, 23
Obedience ... Heb. 13:7, 17
Due respect ... 1 Tim. 5:1, 19
See Bishop

Elead—*God has testified*
Ephraimite ... 1 Chr. 7:21

Elealeh—*God has ascended*
Moabite town ... Is. 15:1, 4
Rebuilt by Reubenites ... Num. 32:37

Eleasah—*God has made*
1. Descendant of Judah ... 1 Chr. 2:2-39
2. Descendant of Saul ... 1 Chr. 8:33-37

Eleazar—*God has helped*
1. Son of Aaron ... Ex. 6:23
Father of Phinehas ... Ex. 6:25
Consecrated a priest ... Ex. 28:1
Ministers in priest's position ... Lev. 10:6, 7
Made chief Levite ... Num. 3:32
Succeeds Aaron ... Num. 20:25-28
Aids Joshua ... Josh. 14:1
Buried at Ephraim ... Josh. 24:33
2. Merarite Levite ... 1 Chr. 23:21, 22
3. Son of Abinadab; custodian of the ark ... 1 Sam. 7:1
4. One of David's mighty men ... 2 Sam. 23:9
5. Priest ... Ezra 8:33
6. Son of Parosh ... Ezra 10:25

SUBJECT — REFERENCE

7. Musician priest ... Neh. 12:27-42
8. Ancestor of Jesus ... Matt. 1:15

Elect, Election
A. *Descriptive of:*
The Messiah ... Is. 42:1
Israel ... Is. 45:4
Good angels ... 1 Tim. 5:21
Christians ... Matt. 24:22, 31
Christian ministers ... Acts 9:15
Lady or church ... 2 John 1, 13
B. *Characteristics of:*
Eternal ... Eph. 1:4
Personal ... Acts 9:15
Sovereign ... Rom. 9:11-16
Unmerited ... Rom. 9:11
God's foreknowledge ... 2 Pet. 1:3, 4
Of grace ... Rom. 11:5, 6
Through faith ... 2 Thess. 2:13
Recorded in heaven ... Luke 10:20
Knowable ... 1 Thess. 1:4
Of high esteem ... 2 Tim. 2:4
C. *Results in:*
Adoption ... Eph. 1:5
Salvation ... 2 Thess. 2:13
Conformity to Christ ... Rom. 8:29
Good works ... Eph. 2:10
Eternal glory ... Rom. 9:23
Inheritance ... 1 Pet. 1:2, 4, 5
D. *Proof of:*
Faith ... 2 Pet. 1:10
Holiness ... Eph. 1:4, 5
Divine protection ... Mark 13:20
Manifest it in life ... Col. 3:12

El-elohe-Israel—*God, the God of Israel*
Name of Jacob's altar ... Gen. 33:20

Elements—*basic parts of anything*
A. *Used literally of:*
Basic forces of nature ... 2 Pet. 3:10, 12
B. *Used figuratively of:*
"Rudiments" of religion ... Gal. 4:3, 9
"Rudiments" of tradition ... Col. 2:8, 20
"First principles" of religion ... Heb. 5:12

Eleph—*ox*
Town of Benjamin ... Josh. 18:28

Eleven, the—*the disciples without Judas*
Were told of resurrection ... Luke 24:9, 33
Met Jesus ... Matt. 28:16
At Pentecost ... Acts 2:1, 14

Elhanan—*God has been gracious*
1. Son of Dodo ... 2 Sam. 23:24
Brave man ... 1 Chr. 11:26
2. Son of Jair ... 1 Chr. 20:5
Slays a giant ... 2 Sam. 21:19

Eli—*my God*
Jesus' cry on the cross ... Matt. 27:46
Same as "Eloi" ... Mark 15:34

Eli—*high* (that is, God is high)
Officiates in Shiloh ... 1 Sam. 1:3
Blesses Hannah ... 1 Sam. 1:12-19
Becomes Samuel's guardian ... 1 Sam. 1:20-28
Samuel ministers before ... 1 Sam. 2:11
Sons of ... 1 Sam. 2:12-17
Rebukes sons ... 1 Sam. 2:22-25
Rebuked by a man of God ... 1 Sam. 2:27-36
Instructs Samuel ... 1 Sam. 3:1-18
Death of ... 1 Sam. 4:15-18

Eliab—*God is father*
1. Son of Helon ... Num. 1:9
Leader of Zebulun ... Num. 7:24, 29
2. Father of Dathan and Abiram ... Num. 16:1, 12
3. Ancestor of Samuel ... 1 Chr. 6:27, 28
4. Brother of David ... 1 Sam. 16:5-13
Fights in Saul's army ... 1 Sam. 17:13
Discounts David's worth ... 1 Sam. 17:28, 29
5. Gadite warrior ... 1 Chr. 12:1-9
6. Levite musician ... 1 Chr. 15:12-20

Eliada—*God has known*
1. Son of David ... 2 Sam. 5:16
Also called Beeliada ... 1 Chr. 14:7

SUBJECT	REFERENCE
2. Father of Rezon	1 Kin. 11:23
3. Benjamite warrior	2 Chr. 17:17

Eliah—*my God is Jehovah*

Son of Jeroham	1 Chr. 8:27

Eliahba—*God conceals*

One of David's mighty men	2 Sam. 23:32

Eliakim—*God will establish*

1. Son of Hilkiah	2 Kin. 18:18
Confers with Rabshakeh	Is. 36:3, 11-22
Sent to Isaiah	Is. 37:2-5
Becomes type of the Messiah	Is. 22:20-25
2. Son of King Josiah	2 Kin. 23:34
Name changed to Jehoiakim	2 Chr. 36:4
3. Postexilic priest	Neh. 12:41
4. Ancestor of Christ	Matt. 1:13
	Luke 3:30

Eliam—*God of the people*

1. Father of Bathsheba	2 Sam. 11:3
Called Ammiel	1 Chr. 3:5
2. Son of Ahithophel	2 Sam. 23:34

Eliasaph—*God has added*

1. Gadite prince	Num. 1:4, 14
Presents offering	Num. 7:41, 42
2. Levite	Num. 3:24

Eliashib—*God will restore*

1. Davidic priest	1 Chr. 24:1, 12
2. Divorced foreign wife	Ezra 10:24
	Ezra 10:27
3. High priest	Neh. 12:10
Rebuilds Sheep Gate	Neh. 3:1, 20, 21
Allies with foreigners	Neh. 13:4, 5, 28
4. Descendant of Zerubbabel	1 Chr. 3:19-24

Eliathah—*God has come*

Son of Heman	1 Chr. 25:1-27

Elidad—*God has loved*

Benjamite leader	Num. 34:17, 21

Eliel—*God is God*

1. Ancestor of Samuel	1 Chr. 6:33, 34
2. One of David's mighty men	1 Chr. 11:26, 46
3. Another of David's mighty men	1 Chr. 11:47
4. Gadite warrior	1 Chr. 12:1-11
5. Levite	1 Chr. 15:9, 11
6. Benjamite	1 Chr. 8:1-21
7. Benjamite, son of Shashak	1 Chr. 8:22, 25
8. Manassite chief	1 Chr. 5:24
9. Overseer of tithes	2 Chr. 31:12, 13

Elienai—*toward God are my eyes*

Benjamite chief	1 Chr. 8:1, 20

Eliezer—*God of help*

1. Abraham's servant	Gen. 15:2
2. Son of Moses	Ex. 18:4
3. Son of Zichri	1 Chr. 27:16
4. Son of Becher	1 Chr. 7:8
5. Priest of David	1 Chr. 15:24
6. Prophet	2 Chr. 20:37
7. Ezra's delegate	Ezra 8:16
8, 9, 10. Three men who divorced their foreign wives	Ezra 10:18-31
11. An ancestor of Christ	Luke 3:29

Elihoenai—*toward God are my eyes*

Son of Zerahiah	Ezra 8:4
Korahite gatekeeper	1 Chr. 26:1-3

Elihoreph—*God of autumn*

One of Solomon's scribes	1 Kin. 4:3

Elihu—*He is my God*

1. Ancestor of Samuel	1 Sam. 1:1
Also called Eliab and Eliel	1 Chr. 6:27, 34
2. David's brother	1 Chr. 27:18
Called Eliab	1 Sam. 16:6
3. Manassite captain	1 Chr. 12:20
4. Temple servant	1 Chr. 26:1, 7
5. One who reproved Job and his friends	Job 32:2, 4-6

Elijah—*Jehovah is God*

A. *Life of the prophet:*

Denounces Ahab	1 Kin. 17:1
Hides by the brook Cherith	1 Kin. 17:3
Fed by ravens	1 Kin. 17:4-7
Fed by widow	1 Kin. 17:8-16
Restores widow's son	1 Kin. 17:17-24
Sends message to Ahab	1 Kin. 18:1-16
Overthrows Baal prophets	1 Kin. 18:17-46
Flees from Jezebel	1 Kin. 19:1-3
Fed by angels	1 Kin. 19:4-8
Hears God	1 Kin. 19:9-14
Sent on a mission	1 Kin. 19:15-21
Condemns Ahab	1 Kin. 21:15-29
Condemns Ahaziah	2 Kin. 1:1-16
Taken up to heaven	2 Kin. 2:1-15

B. *Miracles of:*

Widow's oil	1 Kin. 17:14-16
Dead child raised	1 Kin. 17:17-24
Causes rain	1 Kin. 18:41-45
Causes fire to consume sacrifices	1 Kin. 18:24-38
Causes fire to consume soldiers	2 Kin. 1:10-12

C. *Prophecies of:*

Drought	1 Kin. 17:1
Ahab's destruction	1 Kin. 21:17-29
Ahaziah's death	2 Kin. 1:2-17
Plague	2 Chr. 21:12-15

D. *Significance of:*

Prophecy of his coming	Mal. 4:5, 6
Appears with Christ	Matt. 17:1-4
Type of John the Baptist	Luke 1:17

Elijah—*Jehovah is God*

1. Priest who divorced his foreign wife	Ezra 10:21
2. Divorced foreign wife	Ezra 10:18, 26

Elika—*God has spewed out*

David's warrior	2 Sam. 23:25

Elim—*large trees*

Israel's encampment	Ex. 15:27
Place of palm trees	Num. 33:9, 10

Elimelech—*God is king*

Man of Judah	Ruth 1:1, 2
Dies in Moab	Ruth 1:3
Kinsman of Boaz	Ruth 2:1, 3
Boaz buys his land	Ruth 4:3-9

Elioenai—*toward God are my eyes*

1. Descendant of Benjamin	1 Chr. 7:8
2. Simeonite head	1 Chr. 4:36
3. Son of Neariah	1 Chr. 3:23, 24
4. Postexilic priest	Neh. 12:41
Divorced his foreign wife	Ezra 10:19, 22
5. Son of Zattu; divorced his foreign wife	Ezra 10:27

Eliphal—*God has judged*

David's warrior	1 Chr. 11:26, 35
Called Eliphelet	2 Sam. 23:34

Eliphaz—*God is fine gold*

1. Son of Esau	Gen. 36:2, 4
2. One of Job's friends	Job 2:11
Rebukes Job	Job 4:1, 5
Is forgiven	Job 42:7-9

Elipheleh—*whom God makes distinguished*

Levite singer	1 Chr. 15:18, 21

Eliphelet—*God is deliverance*

1. Son of David	1 Chr. 3:5, 6
2. Another son of David	2 Sam. 5:16
3. Descendant of Jonathan	1 Chr. 8:33, 39
4. David's warrior	2 Sam. 23:34
5. Returnee from Babylon	Ezra 8:13
6. Son of Hashum; divorced his foreign wife	Ezra 10:33

Elisabeth—*God is an oath*

Wife of Zacharias	Luke 1:5
Barren	Luke 1:7, 13
Conceives a son	Luke 1:24, 25
Cousin of Mary	Luke 1:36
Salutation to Mary	Luke 1:39-45
Mother of John the Baptist	Luke 1:57-60

Elisha—*God is salvation*

A. *Life of:*

Succeeds Elijah	1 Kin. 19:16
Follows Elijah	1 Kin. 19:19-21
Sees Elijah translated	2 Kin. 2:1-12
Is recognized as a prophet	2 Kin. 2:13-22
Mocked	2 Kin. 2:23-25
Deals with kings	2 Kin. 3:11-20
Helps two women	2 Kin. 4:1-17

B. *Miracles of:*

Divides Jordan	2 Kin. 2:14
Purifies water	2 Kin. 2:19-22
Increases widow's oil	2 Kin. 4:1-7
Raises Shunammite's son	2 Kin. 4:18-37
Neutralizes poison	2 Kin. 4:38-41
Multiplies bread	2 Kin. 4:42-44
Heals Naaman the leper	2 Kin. 5:1-19
Inflicts Gehazi with leprosy	2 Kin. 5:26, 27
Causes iron to float	2 Kin. 6:6
Reveals secret counsels	2 Kin. 6:8-12
Opens servant's eyes	2 Kin. 6:13-17
Strikes Syrian army with blindness	2 Kin. 6:18-23

C. *Prophecies of:*

Birth of a child	2 Kin. 4:16
Abundance	2 Kin. 7:1
King's death	2 Kin. 7:2
Great famine	2 Kin. 8:1-3
Ben-hadad's death	2 Kin. 8:7-15
Joash's victories	2 Kin. 13:14-19

Elishah—*God is salvation*

Son of Javan	Gen. 10:4

Elishama—*God has heard*

1. Son of Ammihud	Num. 1:10
Ancestor of Joshua	1 Chr. 7:26
2. Man of Judah	1 Chr. 2:41
3. Son of David	1 Chr. 3:1, 5, 6
Also called Elishua	2 Sam. 5:15
4. Another son of David	2 Sam. 5:16
5. Teaching priest	2 Chr. 17:7, 8
6. Scribe	Jer. 36:12, 20, 21

Elishaphat—*God has judged*

Captain	2 Chr. 23:1

Elisheba—*God is an oath*

Wife of Aaron	Ex. 6:23

Elishua—*God is salvation*

Son of David	2 Sam. 5:15
Called Elishama	1 Chr. 3:6

Eliud—*God is mighty*

Father of Eleazar	Matt. 1:14, 15

Elizaphan—*God has concealed*

1. Chief of Kohathites	Num. 3:30
Heads family	1 Chr. 15:5, 8
Family consecrated	2 Chr. 29:12-16
2. Son of Parnach	Num. 34:25

Elizur—*God is a rock*

Reubenite warrior	Num. 1:5

Elkanah—*God has possessed*

1. Father of Samuel	1 Sam. 1:1-23
2. Son of Korah	Ex. 6:24
Escapes judgment	Num. 26:11
3. Levite	1 Chr. 6:23-36
4. Descendant of Korah	1 Chr. 6:22, 23
5. Levite	1 Chr. 9:16
6. Korahite warrior	1 Chr. 12:1, 6
7. Officer under Ahaz	2 Chr. 28:7
8. Doorkeeper of the ark	1 Chr. 15:23

Elkoshite—*an inhabitant of Elkosh*

Descriptive of Nahum	Nah. 1:1

Ellasar

Place in Babylon	Gen. 14:1, 9

Elmodam

Ancestor of Christ	Luke 3:28

SUBJECT — REFERENCE

Elnaam—*God is pleasantness*
Father of two warriors ... 1 Chr. 11:26, 46

Elnathan—*God has given*
1. Father of Nehushta ... 2 Kin. 24:8
Goes to Egypt ... Jer. 26:22
Entreats with king ... Jer. 36:25
2, 3, 4. Three Levites ... Ezra 8:16

Eloi (same as Eli)
Jesus' cry ... Mark 15:34

Elon—*oak*
1. Hittite ... Gen. 26:34
2. Son of Zebulun ... Gen. 46:14
3. Judge in Israel ... Judg. 12:11, 12
4. Town of Dan ... Josh. 19:43

Elon-beth-hanan—*oak of house of grace*
Town of Dan ... 1 Kin. 4:9

Elonites—*belonging to Elon*
Descendants of Elon ... Num. 26:26

Eloquent—*fluent and persuasive in speech*
Moses is not ... Ex. 4:10
Paul rejects ... 1 Cor. 2:1, 4, 5
Apollos is ... Acts 18:24
False prophets boast of ... 2 Pet. 2:18

Elpaal—*God has wrought*
Benjamite ... 1 Chr. 8:11-18

Elpalet—*God of deliverance*
Son of David ... 1 Chr. 14:3, 5
Same as Eliphelet ... 1 Chr. 3:6

El-paran—*oak of Paran*
Place in Canaan ... Gen. 14:6

Eltekeh—*God is dread*
City of Dan ... Josh. 19:44
Assigned to Levites ... Josh. 21:23

Eltekon—*founded by God*
Village in Judah ... Josh. 15:59

Eltolad—*kindred of God*
Town in Judah ... Josh. 15:21, 30
Assigned to Simeonites ... Josh. 19:4
Called Tolad ... 1 Chr. 4:29

Elul—*vine*
Sixth month of Hebrew year ... Neh. 6:15

Eluzai—*God is my defense*
Ambidextrous warrior of David ... 1 Chr. 12:1, 5

Elymas—*a wise man*
Arabic name of Bar-jesus, a false prophet ... Acts 13:6-12

Elzabad—*God has bestowed*
1. Gadite warrior ... 1 Chr. 12:8, 12
2. Korahite Levite ... 1 Chr. 26:7, 8

Elzaphan (contraction of Elizaphan)
Son of Uzziel ... Ex. 6:22
Given instructions by Moses ... Lev. 10:4

Emancipation—*a setting free from slavery*
Of Hebrew nation ... Ex. 12:29-42
Of Hebrew slaves ... Ex. 21:2
In the year of jubilee ... Lev. 25:8-41
Proclaimed by Zedekiah ... Jer. 34:8-11
By Cyrus ... 2 Chr. 36:23; Ezra 1:1-4

Emasculation—*castration*
Penalty of ... Deut. 23:1

Embalming—*preserving a corpse from decay*
Unknown to Abraham ... Gen. 23:4
Practiced in Egypt ... Gen. 50:2, 3, 26
Manner of, among Jews ... 2 Chr. 16:14
Limitation of ... John 11:39, 44
Forbidden by Law ... Num. 5:1-4; Num. 19:11-22

Embroider—*to decorate by needlework*
In tabernacle curtains ... Ex. 26:1, 36
Bezaleel and Aholiab inspired in ... Ex. 35:30-35
On Sisera's garments ... Judg. 5:30
Worn by women ... Ps. 45:14

SUBJECT — REFERENCE

Emerald—*a precious stone of the beryl variety*
In Tyre's trade ... Ezek. 27:16
Used for ornamentation ... Ezek. 28:13
Foundation stone ... Rev. 21:19

Emerods—*hemorrhoids; boils; tumors*
Threatened as a curse ... Deut. 28:27
Inflicted upon Philistines ... 1 Sam. 5:6-12

Emims—*terrors*
Giant race of Anakim east of the Dead Sea ... Gen. 14:5

Emmaus—*hot spring*
Town near Jerusalem ... Luke 24:13-18

Emmor
Father of Shechem ... Acts 7:16

Emotion—*a person's response to living situations*
A. *Objects of:*
Self ... Job 3:1-26
Nation ... Ps. 137:1-6
Family ... Gen. 49:1-28
Mate ... 1 Sam. 25:24, 25
Foreigners ... Ruth 1:16-18
B. *Kinds of:*
Conviction ... Acts 2:37
Contempt ... 1 Sam. 17:42-44
Despondency ... 1 Kin. 19:4-10
Disappointment ... Luke 18:23
Disgust ... Neh. 4:1-3
Envy ... 1 Sam. 17:28
Fear ... 1 Kin. 19:1-3
Flattery ... 1 Sam. 25:23-31
Hate ... Acts 7:54, 57
Joy ... Luke 15:22-24
Love ... Ex. 32:26-29
Loyalty ... 2 Sam. 18:32, 33
Regret ... Luke 16:27-31
Revenge ... Gen. 27:41-45
Sorrow ... 2 Sam. 12:13-19
C. *Control of:*
Unsuppressed ... 1 Sam. 20:30-33
Suppressed ... Is. 36:21
Uncontrollable ... Mark 5:4, 5
Controlled ... Mark 5:19

Employees—*those who work for others*
A. *Types of:*
Diligent ... Gen. 30:27-31
Discontented ... Matt. 20:1-15
Lazy ... Job 7:1-3
Unworthy ... Matt. 21:33-41
B. *Duties of:*
Contentment ... Luke 3:14
Fulfilling terms ... Matt. 20:1-15
Respect ... 1 Tim. 6:1
Diligence ... Prov. 22:29
C. *Rights of:*
Equal wage ... Matt. 10:10
Prompt payment ... Lev. 19:13
Good treatment ... Ruth 2:4
D. *Oppression of, by:*
Arbitrary changes ... Gen. 31:38-42
Unscrupulous landowners ... James 5:4-6

Employers—*those who hire others to work for them*
Must not oppress ... Deut. 24:14
Must be considerate ... Job 31:31
Must be just and fair ... Col. 4:1

Employment—*the state of one who has regular work*
A. *Usefulness of:*
Manifest graces ... Prov. 31:10-31
Provided food ... 2 Thess. 3:7-12
B. *Examples of:*
Adam ... Gen. 2:15
Workmen after the exile ... Neh. 4:15-23
Paul ... 1 Thess. 2:9-11

Enam—*two springs*
Village of Judah ... Josh. 15:20, 34

Enan—*having fountains*
Father of Ahira ... Num. 1:15

SUBJECT — REFERENCE

Encampment—*a resting place on a march or journey*
Israel's, on leaving Egypt ... Ex. 13:20
At Sinai ... Ex. 18:5
List of ... Num. 33:10-46
In battle ... Josh. 10:5, 31, 34

Enchantment—*the practice of magical arts*
A. *Practiced in:*
Egypt ... Ex. 7:11
Judah ... 2 Kin. 17:17
Babylon ... Ezek. 21:21
Chaldea ... Dan. 5:11
Greece ... Acts 16:16
Asia Minor ... Acts 19:13, 19
B. *Futility of:*
Vanity of ... Is. 47:9-15
Inability of ... Ex. 7:11, 12
Abomination of ... Deut. 18:9-12
C. *Examples of:*
Simon ... Acts 8:9
Bar-jesus ... Acts 13:6-12
Slave-girl ... Acts 16:16
Vagabond Jews ... Acts 19:13
Jannes and Jambres ... 2 Tim. 3:8

Encouragement—*inspiration to hope and service*
A. *Needed by:*
Prophets ... 1 Kin. 19:1-19
People ... Neh. 4:17-23
Servants ... 2 Kin. 6:15-17
Kings ... 2 Kin. 11:10-21
Heathen ... Dan. 6:18-23
B. *Agents of:*
Angels ... Gen. 32:1, 2
A dream ... Gen. 28:11-22
God's promises ... Josh. 1:1-9
A friend ... 1 Sam. 23:16-18
A relative ... Esth. 4:13-16
Paul ... Acts 27:21-26
C. *Reasons for, Christ is:*
Risen ... 1 Cor. 15:11-58
Present ... Matt. 28:19, 20
Coming ... Luke 21:25-28

Encumbrance—*that which hinders freedom of action*
Universal ... Gen. 3:16-19
Imposed ... Gen. 32:31, 32
Perpetual ... Matt. 27:25
Moral ... Titus 1:12, 13
Spiritual ... Heb. 12:1

End of the world
A. *Events connected with:*
Day of salvation ended ... Matt. 24:3, 14
Harvest of souls ... Matt. 13:36-43
Defeat of man of sin ... 2 Thess. 2:1-12
Judgment ... Matt. 25:31-46
Destruction of world ... 2 Thess. 1:6-10
B. *Coming of:*
Denied by scoffers ... 2 Pet. 3:3-5
Preceded by lawlessness ... Matt. 24:12
Preceded by apostasy ... Luke 18:8
Without warning ... Matt. 24:37-42
With fire ... 2 Thess. 1:7-10
C. *Attitude toward:*
Watchfulness ... Matt. 25:1-13
Industry ... Matt. 25:14-30
Hopefulness ... Luke 21:25-28
Holy living ... Rom. 13:12-14; 2 Pet. 3:11, 14
Seeking the lost ... 2 Pet. 3:9, 15
Waiting for eternity ... 2 Pet. 3:13; Rev. 21:1

En-dor—*fountain of habitation*
Town of Manasseh ... Josh. 17:11
Site of memorable defeat ... Ps. 83:9, 10
Home of notorious witch ... 1 Sam. 28:1-10

Endow—*to purchase*
Required to wed ... Ex. 22:16

Endurance, blessedness of
Commanded ... Matt. 10:22; 2 Tim. 2:3
Exemplified ... 2 Tim. 2:10; Heb. 10:32, 33
Rewarded ... 2 Tim. 3:11; James 1:12

SUBJECT	REFERENCE
Enduring things	
God's faithfulness	Ps. 89:33
God's mercies	Ps. 103:17
God's Word	Matt. 24:35
Spiritual nourishment	John 6:27
Spiritual rewards	1 Cor. 3:14
Graces	1 Cor. 13:13
The real things	2 Cor. 4:18
God's kingdom	Heb. 12:27, 28
En-eglaim—*fountain of calf*	
Place near the Dead Sea	Ezek. 47:10
Enemies—*foes; adversaries; opponents*	
A. *Applied to:*	
Foreign nations	Gen. 14:20
Israel	Mic. 2:8
Gentiles	Col. 1:21
Unregenerate men	Rom. 5:10
The world	Matt. 22:44
Satan	Matt. 13:39
Death	1 Cor. 15:26
B. *Characteristics of, hate for:*	
God	Rom. 1:30
The Gospel	1 Thess. 2:14-18
The light	John 3:19-21
C. *Examples of:*	
Amalek against Israel	Ex. 17:8-16
Saul against David	1 Sam. 18:29
Jezebel against Elijah	1 Kin. 19:1, 2
Ahab against Elijah	1 Kin. 21:20
Haman against the Jews	Esth. 3:10
Jews against Gentiles	Acts 22:21, 22
Jews against Christians	Acts 7:54-60
D. *Christian attitude toward:*	
Overcome by kindness	1 Sam. 26:18-21
Do not curse	Job 31:29, 30
Feed	Rom. 12:20
Love	Luke 6:27, 35
Forgive	Matt. 6:12-15
Pray for	Luke 23:34
Energy—*effective force to perform work*	
A. *God's, in nature:*	
Creative	Job 38:4-11
Beyond natural law	Job 26:12
Maintains matter	Heb. 1:3
B. *God's, in man:*	
To be witnesses	Acts 1:8
For abundant living	Rom. 15:13
For miracles	Rom. 15:14
To raise dead	1 Cor. 6:14 2 Cor. 13:4
En-gannim—*fountains of gardens*	
1. Village of Judah	Josh. 15:34
2. Border town of Issachar	Josh. 19:21
Assigned to Levites	Josh. 21:29
En-gedi—*fountain of a kid*	
May have been originally called Hazazon-tamar	2 Chr. 20:2
Occupied by the Amorites	Gen. 14:7
Assigned to Judah	Josh. 15:62
David's hiding place	1 Sam. 23:29
Noted for vineyards	Song 1:14
Engine—*a machine designed for a distinct purpose*	
Shooting arrows	2 Chr. 26:15
Engraving—*cutting or carving on some hard substance*	
Stone set in priest's breastplate	Ex. 28:9-11, 21
Bezaleel, inspired in	Ex. 35:30-33
Of a seal	Ex. 28:21
Of a signet	Ex. 39:6
Of cherubim	1 Kin. 6:29
En-haddah—*swift fountain*	
Frontier village of Issachar	Josh. 19:17, 21
En-hakkore—*fountain of him who called*	
Miraculous spring	Judg. 15:14-19
En-hazor—*fountain of a village*	
City of Naphtali	Josh. 19:32, 37
Enjoyment—*satisfaction in something*	
A. *Of material things:*	
Depends upon obedience	Deut. 7:9-15
Withheld for disobedience	Hag. 1:3-11
Must not trust in	Luke 12:16-21
Cannot fully satisfy	Eccl. 2:1-11
B. *Of spiritual things:*	
Abundant	1 Tim. 6:17
Never-ending	Is. 58:11
Satisfying	Is. 55:1, 2
Internal	John 7:37-39
For God's people only	Is. 65:22-24
Complete in heaven	Ps. 16:11
Enlargement—*extension in quantity or quality*	
Japheth's territory	Gen. 9:27
Israel's prosperity	Ex. 34:24
Solomon's kingdom	1 Kin. 4:20-25
Solomon's wisdom	1 Kin. 4:29-34
Pharisaical hypocrisy	Matt. 23:5
Spiritual: Relationship	2 Cor. 6:11, 13
Knowledge	Eph. 1:15-19
Opportunity	Is. 54:1-3
Enlightenment, spiritual	
A. *Source of:*	
From God	Ps. 18:28
Through God's Word	Ps. 19:8
By prayer	Eph. 1:18
By God's ministers	Acts 26:18
B. *Degrees of:*	
Partial now	1 Cor. 13:9-12
Hindered by sin	1 Cor. 2:14
Complete in heaven	Is. 60:19
Enoch—*dedicated*	
1. Son of Cain	Gen. 4:17
2. City built by Cain	Gen. 4:17
3. Father of Methuselah	Gen. 5:21
Walks with God	Gen. 5:22
Taken up to heaven	Gen. 5:24
Prophecy of, cited	Jude 14, 15
Enos, Enosh—*mortal*	
Grandson of Adam	Gen. 4:25, 26
Son of Seth	Gen. 5:6-11
Ancestor of Christ	Luke 3:38
Genealogy of	1 Chr. 1:1
En-rimmon—*fount of pomegranates*	
Reinhabited after the exile	Neh. 11:29
Same as Rimmon	Zech. 14:10
En-rogel—*the fuller's fountain*	
Fountain outside Jerusalem	2 Sam. 17:17
On Benjamin's boundary	Josh. 18:11, 16
Seat of Adonijah's plot	1 Kin. 1:5-9
En-shemesh—*fountain of the sun*	
Spring and town near Jericho	Josh. 15:7
Ensign—*a banner or standard*	
A. *Used literally of:*	
Hosts	Num. 1:52
Enemy	Ps. 74:4, 5
B. *Used figuratively of:*	
Enemy force	Is. 5:26
God's uplifted hand	Is. 31:9
Christ	Is. 11:10, 12
En-tappuah—*fountain of the apple tree*	
Town of Ephraim	Josh. 17:7, 8
Entertainment—*affording an enjoyable occasion*	
A. *Occasions of:*	
Child's weaning	Gen. 21:8
Ratifying covenants	Gen. 31:54
King's coronation	1 Kin. 1:9, 18, 19
National deliverance	Esth. 9:17-19
Marriage	Matt. 22:2
Return of loved ones	Luke 15:23-25
B. *Features of:*	
Invitations sent	Luke 14:16
Preparations made	Matt. 22:4
Helped by servants	John 2:5
Under a leader	John 2:8, 9
Often with music	Luke 15:25
Sometimes out of control	1 Sam. 25:36
Unusual	Heb. 13:2
Enthusiasm—*a spirit of intense zeal*	
Caleb's	Num. 13:30-33
Phinehas'	Num. 25:7-13
David's	2 Sam. 6:12-22
Saul's (Paul's)	Acts 9:1, 2
Paul's	Phil. 3:7-14
Enticers—*those who allure to evil*	
A. *Means of:*	
Man	Ex. 22:16
Spirit	2 Chr. 18:20
Sinners	Prov. 1:10
Lusts	James 1:14
Human wisdom	1 Cor. 2:4
B. *Reasons proposed:*	
Turn from God	Deut. 13:6-8
Obtain secrets	Judg. 16:5
Defeat a king	2 Chr. 18:4-34
Commit a sin	James 1:14
Envy—*resentment against another's success*	
A. *Characterized as:*	
Powerful	Prov. 27:4
Dominant in unregenerate nature	Rom. 1:29
Of the flesh	Gal. 5:21
Source of evil	1 Tim. 6:4
B. *The evil of, among Christians:*	
Hinders growth	1 Pet. 2:1, 2
C. *Examples of:*	
Philistines	Gen. 26:14
Joseph's brothers	Gen. 37:5, 11
Aaron and Miriam	Num. 12:2
Korah	Num. 16:3
David	Ps. 73:3, 17-20
Haman	Esth. 5:13
Chief priests	Mark 15:10
The Jews	Acts 13:45
Epaenetus	
Addressed by Paul	Rom. 16:5
Epaphras	
Leader of the Colossian church	Col. 1:7, 8
Suffers as a prisoner in Rome	Philem. 23
Epaphroditus—*lovely, charming*	
Messenger from Philippi	Phil. 2:25-27
Brings a gift to Paul	Phil. 4:18
Ephah (I)—*dark one*	
1. Son of Midian	Gen. 25:4
2. Concubine of Caleb	1 Chr. 2:46
3. Son of Jahdai	1 Chr. 2:47
Ephah (II)—*a measure*	
Dry measure	Ex. 16:36
Used for measuring barley	Ruth 2:17
Ephai—*bird-like*	
Netophathite	Jer. 40:8
Epher—*young deer*	
1. Son of Midian	Gen. 25:4
2. Man of Judah	1 Chr. 4:17
3. Chief in Manasseh	1 Chr. 5:23, 24
Ephes-dammim—*end of bloods*	
Philistine encampment	1 Sam. 17:1
Called Pasdammin	1 Chr. 11:13
Ephesians, the Epistle to the—*a book of the New Testament*	
Written by Paul	Eph. 1:1
Election	Eph. 1:4-6
Salvation by grace	Eph. 1:7, 8 Eph. 2:8
Headship of Christ	Eph. 4:15, 16
Ephesus—*a city of Asia Minor*	
Site of Jewish synagogue	Acts 18:19
Paul visits	Acts 18:19-21
Miracles done here	Acts 19:11-23
Demetrius stirs up riot in	Acts 19:24-29
Elders of, addressed by Paul at Miletus	Acts 20:17-38
Letter sent to	Eph. 1:1
Paul sends Tychicus	Eph. 6:21
Paul leaves Timothy	1 Tim. 1:3
One of seven churches	Rev. 1:11
Ephlal—*judgment*	
A descendant of Judah	1 Chr. 2:37
Ephod—*a vest*	
1. Worn by:	
The high priest	Ex. 28:4-35

SUBJECT ... REFERENCE

Samuel ... 1 Sam. 2:18
David ... 2 Sam. 6:14
Used in asking counsel of God ... 1 Sam. 23:9-12
Used in idolatry ... Judg. 8:27
2. Father of Hanniel ... Num. 34:23

Ephphatha—*be opened*
Christ's command ... Mark 7:34

Ephraim—*doubly fruitful*
1. Joseph's younger son ... Gen. 41:52
Obtains Jacob's blessing ... Gen. 48:8-20
2. Tribe of Ephraim ... Josh. 16:4, 10
Predictions concerning ... Gen. 48:20
Large number of ... Num. 1:33
Joshua, an Ephraimite ... Josh. 19:50
Territory assigned to ... Josh. 16:1-10
Make Canaanites slaves ... Judg. 1:29
Assist Deborah ... Judg. 5:14, 15
Assist Gideon ... Judg. 7:24, 25
Quarrel with Gideon ... Judg. 8:1-3
Quarrel with Jephthah ... Judg. 12:1-4
Attend David's coronation ... 1 Chr. 12:30
Leading tribe of kingdom of Israel ... Is. 7:2-17
Provoke God by sin ... Hos. 12:7-14
Many of, join Judah ... 2 Chr. 15:9
Beth-el, idolatrous city of ... 1 Kin. 12:29
Captivity of, predicted ... Hos. 9:3-17
Mercy promised to ... Jer. 31:9, 20
Messiah promised to ... Zech. 9:9-13
3. Hill country in Palestine ... 1 Sam. 1:1
4. Forest where Absalom was killed ... 2 Sam. 18:6-18
5. Gate in Jerusalem ... 2 Kin. 14:13
6. Town to which Jesus withdrew ... John 11:54
7. Ten tribes considered as a unit ... Hos. 4:16, 17

Ephratah, Ephrath—*fruitfulness*
1. Ancient name of Bethlehem ... Ruth 4:11
Prophecy concerning ... Mic. 5:2
2. Land of Palestine ... Ps. 132:6
3. Wife of Caleb ... 1 Chr. 2:19, 50

Ephrathite
1. Inhabitant of Beth-lehem (Ephrath) ... Ruth 1:2
2. David was the son of ... 1 Sam. 17:12
Also called Ephraimites ... Judg. 12:5, 6

Ephron—*fawn-like*
1. Hittite who sold Machpelah to Abraham ... Gen. 23:8-20
2. Landmarks of Judah ... Josh. 15:9

Epicureans—*followers of Epicurus*
Sect of pleasure-loving philosophers ... Acts 17:18

Equality of man
A. *Seen in same:*
Creation ... Acts 17:26
Guilt ... Rom. 5:12-21
Sinfulness ... Rom. 3:10-19
Salvation ... John 3:16
Judgment ... 2 Cor. 5:10
B. *Consistent with:*
God's plan ... Rom. 9:6-33
Different talents ... Matt. 25:14-30
Different gifts ... 1 Cor. 12:4-31
Different functions ... Eph. 5:22-33; Eph. 6:1-9
Rule ... Ps. 9:8

Equity—*justice*
Jehovah judges with ... Ps. 98:9

Er—*watching*
1. Son of Judah ... Gen. 38:1-7; Gen. 46:12
2. Descendant of Judah ... 1 Chr. 4:21
3. Ancestor of Christ ... Luke 3:28

Eran—*watchful*
Founder of the Eranites ... Num. 26:36

Erastus—*beloved*
1. Paul's friend at Ephesus ... Acts 19:22; 2 Tim. 4:20
2. Treasurer of Corinth ... Rom. 16:23
May be same person as 1.

Erech—*size*
City of Shinar ... Gen. 10:10

Eri—*watching*
Son of Gad ... Gen. 46:16
Founder of the Erites ... Num. 26:16

Error—*a departure from the truth*
Deceptive ... 2 Tim. 3:13
False ... Matt. 24:4, 11
Produces misunderstanding ... Matt. 22:29
Against Christ ... 1 John 4:1-6
Sign of the end ... 1 Tim. 4:1

Esar-haddon—*Ashur has given a brother*
Son of Sennacherib; king of Assyria (681–669 B.C.) ... 2 Kin. 19:37

Esau—*hairy*
Son of Isaac ... Rom. 9:11-13
Hairy ... Gen. 25:25
Hunter ... Gen. 25:27
Isaac's favorite son ... Gen. 25:28
Sells his birthright ... Gen. 25:29-34
Unable to repent ... Heb. 12:16, 17
Marries two women ... Gen. 26:34
Deprived of blessing ... Gen. 27:1-40
Hates his brother Jacob ... Gen. 27:41-45
Reconciled to Jacob ... Gen. 33:1-17
With Jacob, buries his father ... Gen. 35:29
Descendants of ... Gen. 36:1-43
Ancestor of Edomites ... Jer. 49:7, 8
Prophecy concerning ... Obad. 18

Escape—*to flee from*
A. *Physical things:*
Flood ... Gen. 7:7, 8
City of destruction ... Gen. 19:15-30
Mob ... Luke 4:28-30
Insane king ... 1 Sam. 19:9-18
Wicked queen ... 1 Kin. 11:1-3
Assassination ... Esth. 2:21-23
Hanging ... Esth. 5:14
Prison ... Acts 5:18-20
Sinking ship ... Acts 27:30-44
B. *Spiritual things:*
Sin ... Gen. 39:10-12
Destruction ... Luke 21:36
Corruption ... 2 Pet. 1:4
God's wrath ... 1 Thess. 1:9, 10
The great tribulation ... Rev. 7:13-17

Eschatology—*teaching dealing with final destiny*
A. *In Old Testament:*
Judgment ... Is. 2:12-22
Messianic kingdom ... Jer. 23:4-18; Jer. 33:14-17
B. *In New Testament:*
Coming of Christ ... Matt. 24; Luke 21:5-36
Resurrection of dead ... 1 Cor. 15:51-58; 1 Thess. 4:13-18
Destruction of earth ... 2 Pet. 3:10-13
Reign of Christ ... Rev. 20:4, 6

Esek—*strife*
A well in Gerar ... Gen. 26:20

Esh-baal—*man of Baal*
Son of Saul ... 1 Chr. 8:33

Eshban—*wise man*
Son of Dishon ... Gen. 36:26

Eshcol—*cluster of grapes*
1. Brother of Aner and Mamre ... Gen. 14:13, 24
2. Valley near Hebron ... Num. 13:22-27; Deut. 1:24

Eshean—*support*
City of Judah ... Josh. 15:52

Eshek—*oppression*
Descendant of Saul ... 1 Chr. 8:39

Eshkalonites
Natives of Ashkelon ... Josh. 13:3

Eshtaol—*a way*
Town of Judah ... Josh. 15:20, 33
Assigned to Danites ... Josh. 19:40, 41
Near Samson's home and burial site ... Judg. 16:31

Eshtaulites
Inhabitants of Eshtaol ... 1 Chr. 2:53

Eshtemoa, Eshtemoh—*obedience*
Town of Judah ... Josh. 15:20, 50
Assigned to Levites ... Josh. 21:14
David sends spoils to ... 1 Sam. 30:26, 28

Eshton—*restful*
Man of Judah ... 1 Chr. 4:1-12

Esli—*reserved*
Ancestor of Christ ... Luke 3:25

Establish—*a permanent condition*
A. *Of earthly things:*
Kingdom ... 2 Chr. 17:5
Festival ... Esth. 9:21
B. *Of spiritual things:*
Messiah's kingdom ... 2 Sam. 7:13
God's Word ... Ps. 119:38
Our:
Hearts ... 1 Thess. 3:13
Faith ... Col. 2:7
Works ... 2 Thess. 2:17
Lives ... 1 Pet. 5:10
C. *Accomplished by:*
God ... 2 Cor. 1:21, 22

Esther—*star*
Daughter of Abihail ... Esth. 2:15
Mordecai's cousin ... Esth. 2:7, 15
Selected for harem ... Esth. 2:7-16
Chosen queen ... Esth. 2:17, 18
Seeks to help Mordecai ... Esth. 4:4-6
Told of Haman's plot ... Esth. 4:7-9
Sends message to Mordecai ... Esth. 4:10-12
Told to act ... Esth. 4:13, 14
Seeks Mordecai's aid ... Esth. 4:15-17
Appears before Ahasuerus ... Esth. 5:1-5
Invites Ahasuerus to banquet ... Esth. 5:4-8
Reveals Haman's plot ... Esth. 7:1-7
Given Haman's house ... Esth. 8:1, 2
Secures change of edict ... Esth. 8:3-6
Makes further request ... Esth. 9:12, 13
With Mordecai, institutes Purim ... Esth. 9:29-32

Estrangement from God
Caused by:
Natural status ... Esth. 2:11, 12
Adam's sin ... Gen. 3:8-11, 24
Personal sin ... Ps. 51:9-12
National sin ... Jer. 2:14-16

Etam—*Wild beasts' lair*
1. Village of Simeon ... 1 Chr. 4:32
2. Rock where Samson took refuge ... Judg. 15:8-19
3. Town of Judah ... 2 Chr. 11:6

Eternal, everlasting—*without end*
A. *Applied to Trinity:*
God ... Ps. 90:2
Christ ... Prov. 8:23
Holy Spirit ... Heb. 9:14
B. *Applied to God's attributes:*
Home ... Eccl. 12:5
Power ... Rom. 1:20
Covenant ... Is. 55:3
Gospel ... Rev. 14:6
Counsels ... Eph. 3:10, 11
Righteousness ... Ps. 119:142, 144
Kingdom ... Ps. 145:13
Lovingkindness ... Ps. 100:5
Love ... Jer. 31:3
Father ... Is. 9:6
C. *Applied to the believer:*
Comfort ... 2 Thess. 2:16
Life ... John 3:15
Redemption ... Heb. 9:12
Salvation ... Heb. 5:9
Inheritance ... Heb. 9:15
Glory ... 1 Pet. 5:10
Kingdom ... 2 Pet. 1:11
Reward ... John 4:36

SUBJECT ... REFERENCE

Name ... Is. 56:5
Glory ... 2 Tim. 2:10
Light ... Is. 60:19, 20
Joy ... Is. 51:11
Dwellings ... Luke 16:9
Purpose ... Eph. 3:11

D. *Applied to the wicked:*
Damnation ... Mark 3:29
Judgment ... Heb. 6:2
Punishment ... Matt. 25:46
Destruction ... 2 Thess. 1:9
Contempt ... Dan. 12:2
Bonds ... Jude 6
Fire ... Matt. 25:41
Sin ... Mark 3:29

Eternity—*time without end mentioned once*
God's habitation ... Is. 57:15

Etham—*sea bound*
Israel's encampment ... Ex. 13:20

Ethan—*perpetuity*
1. One noted for wisdom ... 1 Kin. 4:31
2. Levite ... 1 Chr. 6:44
3. Ancestor of Asaph ... 1 Chr. 6:42, 43

Ethanim—*incessant rains*
Seventh month in the Hebrew year ... 1 Kin. 8:2

Ethbaal—*with Baal*
Father of Jezebel ... 1 Kin. 16:31

Ether—*plenty*
Town of Judah ... Josh. 15:42

Ethics—*a system setting forth standards of right conduct*
Perversion of ... Rom. 1:19-32
Law of ... Rom. 2:14-16
Summary of Christian ... Rom. 12:1-21

Ethiopia (Cush)—*burnt face*
Country south of Egypt ... Ezek. 29:10
Home of the Sons of Ham ... Gen. 10:6
Famous for minerals ... Job 28:19
Merchandise of ... Is. 45:14
Wealth of ... Is. 43:3
Militarily strong ... 2 Chr. 12:3
Anguished people ... Ezek. 30:4-9
Defeated by Asa ... 2 Chr. 14:9-15
Subdued ... Dan. 11:43
Prophecies against ... Is. 20:1-6
God's love for ... Amos 9:7
Hopeful promise ... Ps. 68:31

Ethiopians—*descendants of Cush*
Skin of, unchangeable ... Jer. 13:23
Moses' marriage to ... Num. 12:1
Ebed-melech saves Jeremiah ... Jer. 38:7
Eunuch converted ... Acts 8:26-40

Ethnan—*hire*
Judahite ... 1 Chr. 4:5-7

Ethni—*liberal*
Levite ... 1 Chr. 6:41

Eubulus—*prudent*
Christian at Rome ... 2 Tim. 4:21

Eucharist (see Lord's Supper)

Eunice—*blessed with victory*
Mother of Timothy ... 2 Tim. 1:5

Eunuch—*an officer or official, emasculated*
A. *Rules concerning:*
Excluded from congregation ... Deut. 23:1
Given promise ... Is. 56:3-5

B. *Duties of:*
Guard ... Gen. 37:36
Servant ... Gen. 40:2, 7
Attendant ... Dan. 1:3, 7, 10, 11
Keeper of harem ... Esth. 2:3, 14
Treasurer ... Acts 8:27

Euodias—*good journey*
Christian woman at Philippi ... Phil. 4:2

Euphrates—*that which makes fruitful*
River of Eden ... Gen. 2:14
Assyria bounded by ... 2 Kin. 23:29
Babylon on ... Jer. 51:13, 36
Boundary of God's promise ... Gen. 15:18; 1 Kin. 4:21, 24
Persian boundary ... Ezek. 4:10, 11
Scene of battle ... Jer. 46:2, 6, 10
Exiled Jews weep there ... Ps. 137:1
Angels bound there ... Rev. 9:14

Euroclydon—*east wind*
Violent wind ... Acts 27:14

Eutychus—*fortunate*
Sleeps during Paul's sermon ... Acts 20:9
Restored to life ... Acts 20:12

Evangelism—*declaring Gospel to the unregenerate*
A. *Scope:*
To all nations ... Matt. 28:19, 20; Mark 16:15
House to house ... Acts 5:42
Always ... 1 Pet. 3:15
As ambassadors ... 2 Cor. 5:18-20

B. *Source:*
Jesus Christ ... Gal. 1:6-12
The Father ... John 6:44, 65
The Spirit ... Acts 1:8

Evangelist—*one who proclaims good news*
Distinct ministry ... Eph. 4:11
Applied to Philip ... Acts 21:8
Timothy works as ... 2 Tim. 4:5

Eve—*life*
Made from Adam's rib ... Gen. 2:18-22
Named by Adam ... Gen. 3:20
Deceived by Satan ... Gen. 3:1-24
Leads Adam to sin ... 1 Tim. 2:13, 14

Evening—*last hours of sunlight*
Labor ceases ... Judg. 19:16; Ruth 2:17
Workers paid ... Deut. 24:15
Ritual impurity ends ... Lev. 11:24-28; Num. 19:19
Meditation ... Gen. 24:63
Prayer ... Matt. 14:15, 23
Eating ... Luke 24:29, 30
Sacrifice ... Ex. 29:38-42; Num. 28:3-8

Evening sacrifice—*part of Israelite worship*
Ritual described ... Ex. 29:38-42
Part of continual offering ... Num. 28:3-8

Events, Biblical, classified
A. *Orginating, originating other events:*
Creation ... Gen. 1
Fall of man ... Rom. 5:12

B. *Epochal, introducing new period:*
Flood ... Gen. 6—8
The death of Christ ... Matt. 27:50, 51; Heb. 9

C. *Typical, foreshadowing some New Testament event:*
The Passover—Christ as Lamb ... Ex. 12; John 1:35-37; 1 Cor. 5:7, 8
Jonah and great fish—Christ's death and resurrection ... Jon. 1, 2; Matt. 12:38-41

D. *Prophetic, prophesying future events:*
Return from exile ... 2 Chr. 36:22, 23; Jer. 29:10
Destruction of Jerusalem ... Luke 19:41-44; Luke 21:20-24

E. *Redemptive, connected with man's salvation:*
Advent of Christ ... Luke 2:11; Gal. 4:4, 5
Death of Christ ... Matt. 20:28; Luke 24:44-47; 1 Tim. 1:15

F. *Unique, those without parallel:*
Creation ... Gen. 1
Virgin birth ... Matt. 1:18-25; Luke 1:30-37

G. *Miraculous, those produced by supernatural means:*
Plagues on Egypt ... Ex. 7—12
Crossing Red Sea ... Ex. 14—15
Fall of Jericho ... Josh. 6
Sun's standing still ... Josh. 10:12-14

H. *Judgmental, those judging people for sins:*
Flood ... 2 Pet. 2:5
Sodom and Gomorrah ... Gen. 19; 2 Pet. 2:6
Killing of Israelites ... Ex. 32:25-35; Num. 25:1-9

I. *Transforming, those producing a change:*
Christ's transformation ... Matt. 17:1-8
Conversion of Paul ... Acts 9; 1 Tim. 1:12-14
Believer's regeneration ... John 3:1-8; 2 Cor. 5:17

J. *Providential, those manifesting God's providence:*
Baby's cry ... Ex. 2:5-10
Joseph's being sold into Egypt ... Gen. 37:26-28; Gen. 45:1-8
King's sleepless night ... Esth. 6:1-10

K. *Confirmatory, those confirming some promise:*
Worship at Sinai ... Ex. 3:12
Aaron's rod ... Num. 17:1-11
Thunder and rain ... 1 Sam. 12:16-18
Sun's shadow moved backward ... 2 Kin. 20:8-11; Is. 38:1-8

L. *Promissory, those fulfilling some promise:*
Pentecost ... Joel 2:28-32; Acts 2
Spirit's coming ... Luke 24:49; Acts 1:4, 5, 8; Acts 2:1-4
Possession of land ... Gen. 15:18-21; Josh. 24:3, 11-19

M. *Eschatological, those connected with Christ's return:*
Doom of antichrist ... 2 Thess. 2:1-12
Resurrection and translation ... 1 Cor. 15:35-38; 1 Thess. 4:13-18
Resurrection and judgment ... Matt. 25:31-46; Acts 17:31; Rev. 20:11-15
Destruction of the world ... 2 Pet. 3:7-15

Evi—*desirous*
King of Midian ... Num. 31:8
Land of, assigned to Reuben ... Josh. 13:15, 21

Evidence—*ground for belief*
A. *Based upon:*
Testimony of witnesses ... Matt. 18:16
Personal testimony ... Acts 26:1-27
Fulfilled prophecy ... Matt. 1:22, 23
Supernatural testimony ... Matt. 3:17
New life ... 1 John 3:14

B. *Kinds of:*
Circumstantial ... Gen. 39:7-19
False ... Matt. 26:59-61
Fabricated ... Gen. 37:29-33
Confirmed ... Heb. 2:3, 4
Satanic ... 2 Thess. 2:9, 10
Indisputable ... 1 Cor. 15:1-19

C. *Need of:*
Confirm weak faith ... Luke 7:19, 22
Remove doubt ... John 20:24-29
Refute mockers ... 2 Pet. 3:3-7
Attest a messenger of God ... Ex. 8:18, 19
Produce faith ... John 20:30, 31

Evil—*that which is morally injurious*
A. *Origin of:*
Begins with Satan ... Is. 14:12-14
Enters world ... Rom. 5:12
Comes from man ... Matt. 15:18, 19
Inflamed by lust ... James 1:14

B. *Applied to:*
Men ... Matt. 12:35
Heart ... Jer. 17:9
Imaginations ... Gen. 6:5
Generation ... Matt. 12:39
Age ... Gal. 1:4
Our days ... Eph. 5:16
Conscience ... Heb. 10:22
Spirits ... Matt. 12:45

C. *Satan as "the evil one":*
Unregenerate belong to ... Matt. 13:38
Snatches away the good seed ... Matt. 13:19
World lies in ... 1 John 5:19
Lord safeguards against ... John 17:15
Christians can overcome ... 1 John 2:13

SUBJECT — REFERENCE

D. *The Christian should guard against, evil:*
- Heart of unbelief .... Heb. 3:12
- Thoughts .... James 2:4
- Boastings .... James 4:16
- Things .... Rom. 12:9
- Deeds .... 2 John 9-11
- Person .... 1 Cor. 5:13
- Appearance .... 1 Thess. 5:22
- One (Satan) .... Eph. 6:16

Evil—*that which is physically harmful: floods, earthquakes, etc.*
- Created by God .... Is. 45:7
- Part of man's curse .... Gen. 3:17-19
- Men cry out against .... Rev. 9:18-21
- Can be misinterpreted .... Luke 13:1-3
- Foreseen by prudent .... Prov. 22:3
- Will continue to the end .... Matt. 24:6-8, 14
- Believers share in .... 2 Cor. 12:7-10
- To be borne patiently .... Job 2:7-10; James 5:11
- Prospects of relief from .... Rom. 8:18-39
- Relieved now by faith .... Heb. 3:17-19
- None in heaven .... Rev. 7:14-17

Evil companions (see Association)

Evil day
- Time of judgment .... Eccl. 12:1

Evildoers—*workers of evil*
- Christians wrongly called .... 1 Pet. 2:12
- Christians should not be .... 1 Pet. 4:15
- Christians cry against .... Ps. 119:115
- Punished by magistrates .... Rom. 13:1-4
- End of, certain .... Ps. 34:16

Evil eye
- Descriptive of a man's inner being .... Mark 7:21, 22
- Shown in attitudes .... Matt. 20:15

Evil-merodach—*man of Marduk*
- Babylonian king (562-560 B.C.); follows Nebuchadnezzar .... 2 Kin. 25:27-30

Evil speaking

A. *The evil of:*
- Sign of unregeneracy .... Ps. 10:7
- Aimed at righteous .... Ps. 64:2-5
- Defiles the whole body .... James 3:5-10
- Disrupts fellowship .... 3 John 9-11
- Severely condemned .... James 4:11
- Punished .... 1 Cor. 6:9, 10

B. *Not to be confused with:*
- Denunciation of vice .... Titus 1:12, 13
- Description of sinners .... Acts 13:9, 10
- Defense of the faith .... Jude 4, 8-16

Evil spirits—*demons*
- Sent upon King Saul .... 1 Sam. 16:14
- Ahab prompted to evil by .... 1 Kin. 22:1-23
- Cast out by Jesus .... Luke 7:21
- Cast out by Paul .... Acts 19:11, 12

Evolution—*development of life from lower to higher forms*

A. *Conflicts with:*
- God's description .... Gen. 1:26, 27; Gen. 2:21-25
- Moses' record .... Ex. 20:11; Deut. 4:32

B. *Not accepted by:*
- Jesus .... Matt. 19:4-6; Rom. 5:12-19
- Paul .... 1 Cor. 15:22, 45; 1 Tim. 2:13, 14

Exaltation—*the state of being raised up*

A. *Of evil man:*
- Originates in Satan .... Luke 4:5, 6
- Defies God .... 2 Kin. 18:28-35
- Perverts religion .... Dan. 11:36, 37
- Brings downfall .... Esth. 6:6-14
- Merits punishment .... 1 Kin. 16:1-4
- Displayed by Herod .... Acts 12:21-23
- Seen in antichrist .... 2 Thess. 2:4, 9

B. *Of good men:*
- Principle of .... Matt. 23:12
- Follows humility .... 1 Pet. 5:6
- Restrictions upon .... 2 Cor. 10:5
- Brings glory .... James 1:9
- False, brings sorrow .... 1 Cor. 4:6-14
- Final, in heaven .... Rev. 22:5

C. *Of Christ:*
- Promised .... Ps. 2:8, 9
- Predicted by Christ .... Matt. 26:64
- The ascension .... Acts 2:33, 34
- Seen by Stephen .... Acts 7:55, 56
- Taught by the apostles .... Eph. 1:20-22
- Set forth as a reward .... Phil. 2:9-11
- Introduces priestly intercession .... Heb. 1:3

Examination of others
- Of Jesus .... Luke 23:13, 14
- Of Peter .... Acts 4:8, 9
- Of Paul .... Acts 22:24

Examination of self
- Sought by David .... Ps. 26:2
- Must precede Lord's Supper .... 1 Cor. 11:28
- Necessary for real faith .... 2 Cor. 13:5

Example—*a pattern to follow*

A. *Purposes of:*
- Set forth sin's punishment .... 2 Pet. 2:6
- Show unbelief's consequences .... Heb. 4:11
- Restrain from evil .... 1 Cor. 10:6, 11
- Illustrate humility .... John 13:15; 1 Pet. 3:5
- Exemplify patience .... James 5:10, 11; 1 Pet. 2:20-22
- Portray Christian conduct .... Phil. 3:17

B. *Of evil men:*
- Covetousness—Achan .... Josh. 7:20, 21
- Immorality—Eli's sons .... 1 Sam. 2:22-25
- Rebellion—Saul .... 1 Sam. 15:17-23
- Folly—Nabal .... 1 Sam. 25:25-37
- Idolatry—Jeroboam .... 1 Kin. 12:26-33

C. *Of good men:*
- Holy zeal—Phinehas .... Num. 25:7-13
- Faith—Caleb .... Josh. 14:6-15
- Fidelity—Joshua .... Josh. 24:15 25
- Courage—David .... 1 Sam. 17:32-37
- Holy life—Daniel .... Ezek. 14:14, 20
- Patience—Job .... James 5:10, 11
- Christian living—Paul .... Phil. 3:17

Example of Christ, the

A. *Virtues illustrated by:*
- Meekness .... Matt. 11:29
- Self-denial .... Matt. 16:24
- Love .... John 13:34
- Obedience .... John 15:10
- Benevolence .... 2 Cor. 8:7, 9
- Humility .... Phil. 2:5, 7
- Forgiveness .... Col. 3:13
- Suffering wrongfully .... 1 Pet. 2:21-23
- Purity .... 1 John 3:3

B. *The Christian approach to:*
- Progressive .... 2 Cor. 3:18
- Instructive .... Eph. 4:20-24
- Imitative .... 1 Pet. 2:21-23
- Perfective .... Rom. 8:29

Excitement—*something that stirs us emotionally*

A. *Causes of:*
- Great sin .... Ex. 32:17-20
- Great victory .... 1 Sam. 17:52
- God's power .... 1 Kin. 18:22-41
- King's coronation .... 2 Kin. 11:12-16
- Human destruction .... Esth. 9:1-11
- Handwriting on the wall .... Dan. 5:5-9
- Miracle .... Acts 19:13-29

B. *Time of:*
- The giving of the Law .... Heb. 12:18-21
- Christ's death .... Matt. 27:51-54
- Pentecost .... Acts 2:1-47
- Christ's return .... Luke 21:25-28

Exclusiveness—*setting boundaries against others*

A. *Christianity's, only one:*
- Door .... John 10:1, 7, 9
- Way .... John 14:6
- Salvation .... Acts 4:12

B. *The Bible's, only book:*
- Inspired .... 1 Tim. 3:16
- Revealing God .... Heb. 1:1
- Written to save men .... John 20:30, 31
- Containing true prophecies .... John 5:45-47

Excommunication—*expulsion from membership in a body*

A. *Separation from:*
- Kingship .... 1 Sam. 16:1
- Foreigners .... Neh. 13:1-3
- Priesthood .... Neh. 13:27, 28

B. *Practice of:*
- To intimidate people .... John 9:19-23
- Against true Christians .... John 16:1, 2
- Against false teachers .... 2 John 10, 11

C. *Method of:*
- Described .... Matt. 18:15-17
- Illustrated .... 1 Cor. 5:1-13
- Perverted .... 3 John 9, 10

Excuse—*an invalid reason for neglect of duty*

A. *Nature of, blaming:*
- Wife .... Gen. 3:12
- The people .... 1 Sam. 15:20, 21
- God's mercy .... Jon. 4:1-4
- God's providence .... Num. 14:1-23

B. *Invalidity of:*
- Shown to Moses .... Ex. 3:10-12
- Proved to Gideon .... Judg. 6:36-40
- Made plain to Esther .... Esth. 4:13-17
- Illustrated by Christ .... Luke 14:16-24
- Relayed to Hell's inhabitants .... Luke 16:27-31
- Made evident to Thomas .... John 20:24-28

Exhortation—*encouraging others to commendable conduct*

A. *Objects of:*
- Call to repentance .... Luke 3:17, 18
- Continue in the faith .... Acts 14:22
- Convict gainsayers .... Titus 1:9
- Warn the unruly .... 1 Thess. 5:14
- Encourage soberness .... Titus 3:1
- Strengthen godliness .... 1 Thess. 4:1-6
- Stir up liberality .... 2 Cor. 9:5-7

B. *Office of:*
- Commended .... Rom. 12:8
- Part of the ministry .... Titus 2:15
- Needed in times .... 2 Tim. 4:2-5

C. *Nature of:*
- Daily duty .... Heb. 3:13
- For holiness .... 1 Thess. 2:3, 4
- Worthy of reception .... Heb. 13:22
- Belongs to all .... Heb. 10:25
- Special need of .... Jude 3, 4

Exile—*banished from one's native land*
- David .... 1 Sam. 21:10-15
- Jeroboam .... 1 Kin. 11:40
- Jeremiah .... Jer. 43:4-7
- Christ .... Matt. 2:13-15
- John .... Rev. 1:9
- Jehoiachin .... 2 Kin. 24:15
- Judah .... 2 Kin. 25:21
- Jeconiah .... Jer. 27:20
- Nebuchadnezzar .... Jer. 29:1
- Chemosh .... Jer. 48:7
- Syrians .... Amos 1:5
- See Captivity

Exodus—*a departure*
- Israel's, from Egypt .... Ex. 12:41

Exodus, Book of—*a book of the Old Testament*
- Escape from Egypt .... Ex. 12:31-42
- The Law .... Ex. 20:1-17
- The tabernacle and priesthood .... Ex. 24:12—31:18

Exorcists—*those who use oaths to dispel evil spirits*
- Paul encounters .... Acts 19:13, 19

Expanse—*firmament, vault*
- Created by God .... Gen. 1:8
- Stars placed in .... Gen. 1:14, 17
- Compared to a tent curtain .... Ps. 104:2
- Expressive of God's glory .... Ps. 19:1
- Saints compared to .... Dan. 12:3

Expectation—*looking forward*
- Conquest .... Num. 14:1-24
- Victory .... Josh. 7:4-13
- Relief .... 1 Kin. 12:4-15
- Impending doom .... 2 Kin. 23:25-27
- Elevation .... Esth. 6:6-14
- The wicked .... Prov. 10:28

E

SUBJECT — REFERENCE

- Righteous ... Ps. 62:5
- Destruction ... John 4:1-11
- Death ... Acts 28:3-6

Expediency—*a method of justifying an act*
- To fulfill God's plan ... John 11:50
- To avoid offense ... 1 Cor. 8:8-13
- To save men ... 1 Cor. 9:19-23
- To accomplish a task ... 2 Cor. 8:10-12
- Illustrations ... Acts 16:3

Expense—*the cost involved*
- Royalty, foretold ... 1 Sam. 8:11-18
- Royalty, realized ... 1 Kin. 4:22, 23

Experiment—*a test designed to prove something*
- Jacob ... Gen. 30:37-43
- Aaron's sons ... Lev. 10:1-3
- Philistines ... 1 Sam. 6:1-18
- Daniel ... Dan. 1:11-16
- God's goodness ... Mal. 3:10-12

Expiation—*atonement*
- Under Law ... Lev. 14:11-20; Lev. 16:11-28
- Prophecy of Isaiah ... Is. 53:1-12
- Fulfilled in Christ ... Acts 8:27-39; 1 Pet. 2:21-25

Explanation—*making simple and plain*
- Of a condition ... Luke 16:25-31
- Of a phenomenon ... Acts 2:1-21
- Of a decision ... Acts 15:15-31

Expulsion—*driving out by force from*
- Eden ... Gen. 3:22-24
- The priesthood ... Neh. 13:27, 28
- A city ... Luke 4:16-29
- By persecution ... Acts 13:50, 51

Extortion—*money obtained by force or threat*
- Innocency from, pretended ... Matt. 23:25
- Fellowship with, forbidden ... 1 Cor. 5:10, 11
- Sin of, proscribed ... Luke 3:13, 14
- Examples of ... Gen. 47:13-26

Extremity—*the greatest degree of something*
- Human faith ... Gen. 22:1-3
- Grief ... 2 Sam. 18:33
- Pride ... Is. 14:13, 14
- Pain ... Matt. 27:46-50
- Degradation ... Luke 15:13-16
- Torments ... Luke 16:23, 24
- Human endurance ... 2 Cor. 1:8-10

Eye—*the organ of sight*

A. *Affected by:*
- Age ... Gen. 27:1
- Wine ... Gen. 49:12
- Sorrow ... Job 17:7
- Disease ... Lev. 26:16
- Grief ... Ps. 6:7
- Light ... Acts 22:11

B. *Of God, figurative of:*
- Omniscience ... 2 Chr. 16:9
- Justice ... Amos 9:8
- Holiness ... Hab. 1:13
- Guidance ... Ps. 32:8
- Protection ... Ps. 33:18

C. *Of man, figurative of:*
- Revealed knowledge ... Num. 24:3
- Lawlessness ... Judg. 17:6
- Jealousy ... 1 Sam. 18:9
- Understanding ... Ps. 19:8
- Agreement ... Is. 52:8
- Great sorrow ... Jer. 9:1
- Retaliation ... Matt. 5:38
- The essential nature ... Matt. 6:22, 23
- Moral state ... Matt. 7:3-5
- Spiritual inability ... Matt. 13:15
- Spiritual dullness ... Mark 8:17, 18
- Future glory ... 1 Cor. 2:9
- Illumination ... Eph. 1:18
- Unworthy service ... Eph. 6:6
- Worldliness ... 1 John 2:16
- Evil desires ... 2 Pet. 2:14

D. *Prophecies concerning:*
- Shall see the Redeemer ... Job 19:25-27
- Gentiles shall see ... Is. 42:6, 7
- Blind shall see ... Is. 29:18
- Will see the King ... Is. 33:17
- Will see Jesus ... Rev. 1:7
- Tears of, shall be wiped away ... Rev. 7:17

Eyebrows—*the arch of hair over the eyes*
- Of lepers, shaved off ... Lev. 14:2, 9

Eyesalve—*an ointment*
- Christ mentions ... Rev. 3:18

Eyeservice—*service performed only when watched by another*
- Highly obnoxious ... Eph. 6:6

Eyewitness—*a firsthand observer*
- Consulted by Luke ... Luke 1:1, 2
- Of Christ's majesty ... 2 Pet. 1:16

Ezbai—*shining*
- Naarai's father ... 1 Chr. 11:37

Ezbon—*bright*
1. Son of Gad ... Gen. 46:16
2. Benjamite ... 1 Chr. 7:7

Ezekiel—*God strengthens*

A. *Life of:*
- Hebrew prophet; son of Buzi ... Ezek. 1:3
- Carried captive to Babylon ... Ezek. 1:1-3
- Lived among exiles ... Ezek. 3:15-17
- His wife died ... Ezek. 24:18
- Persecuted ... Ezek. 3:25
- Often consulted ... Ezek. 8:1
- Prophetic minister ... Ezek. 3:17-21

B. *Visions of:*
- God's glory ... Ezek. 1:4-28
- Abominations ... Ezek. 8:5-18
- Valley of dry bones ... Ezek. 37:1-14
- Messianic times ... Ezek. 40:48
- River of life ... Ezek. 47:1-5

C. *Methods employed by:*
- Threatens dumbness ... Ezek. 3:26
- Symbolizes siege of Jerusalem ... Ezek. 4:1-3
- Shaves himself ... Ezek. 5:1-4
- Removes baggage ... Ezek. 12:3-16
- Uses boiling pot ... Ezek. 24:1-14
- Does not mourn for wife ... Ezek. 24:16-27
- Uses parables ... Ezek. 17:2-10

Ezekiel, Book of—*a Book of the Old Testament*
- Prophecies against Israel ... Ezek. 1:1—24:27
- Prophecies against the nations ... Ezek. 25:1—32:32
- Prophecies of restoration ... Ezek. 33:1—39:29
- The Messianic kingdom ... Ezek. 40:1—48:35

Ezel—*departure*
- David's hiding place ... 1 Sam. 20:19

Ezem—*bone*
- Village of Judah ... Josh. 15:29
- Assigned to Simeon ... Josh. 19:3

Ezer—*help*
1. Horite tribe ... 1 Chr. 1:38
   Son of Seir ... Gen. 36:21
2. Ephraimite ... 1 Chr. 7:21
3. Judahite ... 1 Chr. 4:1, 4
4. Gadite warrior ... 1 Chr. 12:9
5. Son of Jeshua ... Neh. 3:19
6. Postexilic priest ... Neh. 12:42

Ezion-geber—*backbone of a giant*
- Town on the Red Sea ... 1 Kin. 9:26
- Israelite encampment ... Num. 33:35
- Seaport of Israel's navy ... 1 Kin. 22:48

Eznite—*spear; to be sharp*
- Warrior of David ... 2 Sam. 23:8
- Called Tachmonite ... 2 Sam. 23:8
- Called Hachmonite ... 1 Chr. 11:11

Ezra, Ezrah—*help*
1. Postexilic priest ... Neh. 12:1, 7
   Called Azariah ... Neh. 10:2
2. Scribe, priest and reformer of postexilic times ... Ezra 7:1-6
   - Commissioned by Artaxerxes ... Ezra 7:6-28
   - Takes exiles with him ... Ezra 8:1-20
   - Proclaims a fast ... Ezra 8:21-23
   - Commits treasures to the priests ... Ezra 8:24-30
   - Comes to Jerusalem ... Ezra 8:31, 32
   - Institutes reforms ... Ezra 9:1-15
   - Reads the Law ... Neh. 8:1-18
   - Helps in dedication ... Neh. 12:27-43

Ezra, Book of—*a book of the Old Testament*
- Return from exile ... Ezra 1:1—2:70
- Rebuilding the Temple ... Ezra 3:1—6:22
- Reformation ... Ezra 9:1—10:44

Ezrahite—*belonging to Ezrach*
- Family name of Ethan and Heman ... 1 Kin. 4:31

Ezri—*my help*
- David's farm overseer ... 1 Chr. 27:26

F

Fable—*a fictitious story*

A. *Form of allegory:*
- The trees ... Judg. 9:7-15
- The thistle ... 2 Kin. 14:9

B. *Form of fiction, contrary to:*
- Edification ... 1 Tim. 1:4
- Godliness ... 1 Tim. 4:6, 7
- Truth ... 2 Tim. 4:4
- Facts ... 2 Pet. 1:16

Face—*front part of head*

A. *Acts performed on:*
- Spitting on ... Deut. 25:9
- Disfiguring of ... Matt. 6:16
- Painting of ... 2 Kin. 9:30
- Hitting ... 2 Cor. 11:20

B. *Acts indicated by:*
- Falling on—worship ... Gen. 17:3
- Covering of—mourning ... 2 Sam. 19:4
- Hiding of—disapproval ... Deut. 31:17, 18
- Turning away of—rejection ... 2 Chr. 30:9
- Setting of—determination ... 2 Kin. 12:17

Face of the Lord

A. *Toward the righteous:*
- Shine on ... Num. 6:25
- Do not hide ... Ps. 102:2
- Hide from our sins ... Ps. 51:9
- Shall see ... Rev. 22:4

B. *Toward the wicked:*
- Is against ... Ps. 34:16
- Set against ... Jer. 21:10
- They hide from ... Rev. 6:16

Failure

A. *Causes of:*
- Contrary to God's will ... Gen. 11:3-8
- Disobedience ... Num. 14:40-45
- Sin ... Josh. 7:3-12
- Lack of prayer ... Matt. 17:15-20; Mark 9:24-29
- Not counting the cost ... Luke 14:28-32
- Unbelief ... Heb. 4:6

B. *Examples of:*
- Esau ... Gen. 25:29-34
- Eli's sons ... 1 Sam. 2:12-17
- King Saul ... 1 Sam. 16:1
- Absalom ... 2 Sam. 18:6-17
- Hananiah ... Jer. 28:1-17
- Haman ... Esth. 7:1-10

Fainting, faintheartedness—*a loss of vital powers*

A. *Causes of:*
- Physical fatigue ... Gen. 25:29, 30
- Famine ... Gen. 47:13
- Unbelief ... Gen. 45:26
- Fear ... Josh. 2:24
- Sin ... Lev. 26:31
- Sickness ... Job 4:5
- Human weakness ... Is. 40:29-31
- Ecstasy of visions ... Dan. 8:27
- Disappointment ... Jon. 4:8
- God's reproving ... Heb. 12:5

B. *Antidotes against:*
- Removal of the fearful ... Deut. 20:8

Fair—English rendering of numerous Hebrew and Greek words
- Beautiful ... Gen. 6:2; Song 1:15, 16
- Unspotted ... Zech. 3:5
- Persuasive ... Prov. 7:21; Gal. 6:12
- Good ... Matt. 16:2

SUBJECT REFERENCE

Fair Havens
Harbor of Crete . . . . . Acts 27:8

Faith—*confidence in the testimony of another*

A. *Nature of:*
Fruit of the Spirit . . . . . Gal. 5:22
Work of God . . . . . John 6:29
God's gift . . . . . Eph. 2:8
Comes from the heart . . . . . Rom. 10:9, 10
Substance of unseen things . . Heb. 11:1

B. *Results from:*
Scriptures . . . . . John 20:30, 31
Preaching . . . . . John 17:20
Gospel . . . . . Acts 15:7

C. *Objects of:*
God . . . . . John 14:1
Christ . . . . . John 20:31
Moses' writings . . . . . John 5:46
Writings of the prophets . . . . . Acts 26:27
Gospel . . . . . Mark 1:15
God's promises . . . . . Rom. 4:21

D. *Kinds of:*
Saving . . . . . Rom. 10:9, 10
Temporary . . . . . Luke 8:13
Intellectual . . . . . James 2:19
Dead . . . . . James 2:17, 20

E. *Described as:*
Boundless . . . . . John 11:21-27
Common . . . . . Titus 1:4
Great . . . . . Matt. 8:10
Holy . . . . . Jude 20
Humble . . . . . Luke 7:6, 7
Little . . . . . Matt. 8:26
Mutual . . . . . Rom. 1:12
Perfect . . . . . James 2:22
Precious . . . . . 2 Pet. 1:1
Rootless . . . . . Luke 8:13
Small . . . . . Matt. 17:20
Unfeigned . . . . . 1 Tim. 1:5
United . . . . . Mark 2:5
Vain . . . . . 1 Cor. 15:14, 17
Venturing . . . . . Matt. 14:28, 29

F. *The fruits of:*
Remission of sins . . . . . Acts 10:43
Justification . . . . . Acts 13:39
Freedom from condemnation . . . . . John 3:18
Salvation . . . . . Mark 16:16
Sanctification . . . . . Acts 15:9
Freedom from spiritual death . . . . . John 11:25, 26
Spiritual light . . . . . John 12:36, 46
Spiritual life . . . . . John 20:31
Eternal life . . . . . John 3:15, 16
Adoption . . . . . John 1:12
Access to God . . . . . Eph. 3:12
Edification . . . . . 1 Tim. 1:4
Preservation . . . . . John 10:26-29
Inheritance . . . . . Acts 26:18
Peace and rest . . . . . Rom. 5:1

G. *Place of, in Christian life:*
Live by . . . . . Rom. 1:17
Walk by . . . . . Rom. 4:12
Pray by . . . . . Matt. 21:22
Resist evil by . . . . . Eph. 6:16
Overcome world by . . . . . 1 John 2:13-17
Die in . . . . . Heb. 11:13

H. *Growth of, in Christian life:*
Stand fast in . . . . . 1 Cor. 16:13
Continue in . . . . . Acts 14:22
Be strong in . . . . . Rom. 4:20-24
Abound in . . . . . 2 Cor. 8:7
Be grounded in . . . . . Col. 1:23
Hold fast . . . . . 1 Tim. 1:19
Pray for increase of . . . . . Luke 17:5
Have assurance of . . . . . 2 Tim. 1:12

I. *Examples of, in Old Testament:*
Abel . . . . . Heb. 11:4
Enoch . . . . . Heb. 11:5
Noah . . . . . Heb. 11:7
Abraham . . . . . Rom. 4:16-20
Sarah . . . . . Heb. 11:11
Jacob . . . . . Heb. 11:21
Joseph . . . . . Heb. 11:22
Moses . . . . . Heb. 11:23-29
Caleb . . . . . Josh. 14:6, 12
Rahab . . . . . Heb. 11:31
Jonathan . . . . . 1 Sam. 14:6
David . . . . . 1 Sam. 17:37
Jehoshaphat . . . . . 2 Chr. 20:5, 12
Three Hebrew captives . . . . . Dan. 3:16, 17
Job . . . . . Job 19:25
Others . . . . . Heb. 11:32-39

J. *Examples of, in New Testament:*
Centurion . . . . . Matt. 8:5-10
Jairus . . . . . Mark 5:22, 23
Sick woman . . . . . Mark 5:25-34
Syrophoenician woman . . . . . Mark 7:24-30
Bartimaeus . . . . . Mark 10:46-52
Sinful woman . . . . . Luke 7:36-50
Ten lepers . . . . . Luke 17:11-19
Certain nobleman . . . . . John 4:46-54
Mary and Martha . . . . . John 11:1-32
Thomas . . . . . John 20:24-29
Multitudes . . . . . Acts 5:14
Stephen . . . . . Acts 6:8
Samaritans . . . . . Acts 8:5-12
Ethiopian eunuch . . . . . Acts 8:26-39
Barnabas . . . . . Acts 11:22-24
Lydia . . . . . Acts 16:14, 15
Philippian jailer . . . . . Acts 16:25-34
Paul . . . . . Acts 27:23-25

Faith as a body of belief
Priest obedient to . . . . . Acts 6:7
Churches established in . . . . . Acts 16:5
Stand fast in . . . . . 1 Cor. 16:13
Paul preaches . . . . . Gal. 1:23
Now revealed . . . . . Gal. 3:23
Household of . . . . . Gal. 6:10
Contending for . . . . . Phil. 1:27
Hold purely . . . . . 1 Tim. 3:9
Denial of . . . . . 1 Tim. 5:8
Some erred from . . . . . 1 Tim. 6:10, 21
Reprobate . . . . . 2 Tim. 3:8
Paul keeps . . . . . 2 Tim. 4:7
Chosen of God . . . . . Titus 1:1
Common among redeemed . . . . . Titus 1:4
To be sound in . . . . . Titus 1:13

Faithfulness—*making faith a living reality in one's life*

A. *Manifested in:*
God's service . . . . . Matt. 24:45
Declaring God's Word . . . . . Jer. 23:38
Bearing witness . . . . . Prov. 14:5
Keeping secrets . . . . . Prov. 11:13
Helping others . . . . . 3 John 5
Doing work . . . . . 2 Chr. 34.12
Positions of trust . . . . . Neh. 13:13
Reproving others . . . . . Prov. 27:6
Conveying messages . . . . . Prov. 25:13
Smallest things . . . . . Luke 16:10-12

B. *Illustrated in lives of:*
Abraham . . . . . Gal. 3:9
Abraham's servant . . . . . Gen. 24:33
Joseph . . . . . Gen. 39:22, 23
Moses . . . . . Num. 12:7
David . . . . . 2 Sam. 22:22-25
Elijah . . . . . 1 Kin. 19:10, 14
Josiah . . . . . 2 Kin. 22:1, 2
Abijah . . . . . 2 Chr. 13:4-12
Micaiah . . . . . 2 Chr. 18:12, 13
Jehoshaphat . . . . . 2 Chr. 20:1-30
Azariah . . . . . 2 Chr. 26:16-20
Hanani and Hananiah . . . . . Neh. 7:1, 2
Isaiah . . . . . Is. 39:3-7
Jeremiah . . . . . Jer. 26:1-15
Daniel . . . . . Dan. 6:10
John the Baptist . . . . . Luke 3:7-19
Jesus . . . . . Heb. 3:2
Peter . . . . . Acts 4:8-12
Paul . . . . . Acts 17:16, 17

Faithfulness of God

A. *Described as:*
Everlasting . . . . . Ps. 119:90
Established . . . . . Ps. 89:2
Unfailing . . . . . Ps. 89:33
Infinite . . . . . Ps. 36:5
Great . . . . . Lam. 3:23
Incomparable . . . . . Ps. 89:8

B. *Manifested in:*
Counsels . . . . . Is. 25:1
Covenant-keeping . . . . . Deut. 7:9
Forgiving sins . . . . . 1 John 1:9
Testimonies . . . . . Ps. 119:138
Judgments . . . . . Jer. 51:29
Promises . . . . . 1 Kin. 8:20

Fall of man

A. *Occasion of:*
Satan's temptation . . . . . Gen. 3:1-5
Eve's yielding . . . . . 2 Cor. 11:3
Adam's disobedience . . . . . Rom. 5:12-19

B. *Temporal consequences of:*
Driven from Paradise . . . . . Gen. 3:24
Condemned to hard labor . . . Gen. 3:16, 19
Condemned to die . . . . . 1 Cor. 15:22

C. *Spiritual consequences of:*
Separated from God . . . . . Eph. 4:18
Born in sin . . . . . John 3:6
Evil in heart . . . . . Matt. 15:19
Corrupt and perverse . . . . . Rom. 3:12-16
In bondage to sin . . . . . Rom. 6:19
In bondage to Satan . . . . . Heb. 2:14, 15
Dead in sin . . . . . Col. 2:13
Spiritually blind . . . . . Eph. 4:18
Utterly depraved . . . . . Titus 1:15
Change from, not in man . . . . Jer. 2:22
Only God can change . . . . . John 3:16

Fallow deer—*roebuck*
Among clean animals . . . . . Deut. 14:5
In Solomon's diet . . . . . 1 Kin. 4:22, 23

Fallow ground—*a field plowed and left for seeding*
Used figuratively . . . . . Jer. 4:3
Hos. 10:12

False accusations

A. *Against men:*
Joseph . . . . . Gen. 39:7-20
Moses . . . . . Num. 16:1-3, 13
Ahimelech . . . . . 1 Sam. 22:11-16
David . . . . . Ps. 41:5-9
Elijah . . . . . 1 Kin. 18:17, 18
Naboth . . . . . 1 Kin. 21:1-14
Jeremiah . . . . . Jer. 26:8-11
Amos . . . . . Amos 7:10, 11
Stephen . . . . . Acts 6:11, 13
Paul . . . . . Acts 21:27-29

B. *Against Christ:*
Gluttony . . . . . Matt. 11:19
Blasphemy . . . . . Matt. 26:64, 65
Insanity . . . . . Mark 3:21
Demon possession . . . . . John 7:20
Sabbath desecration . . . . . John 9:16
Treason . . . . . John 19:12

False apostles
Opposed Paul . . . . . 2 Cor. 11:1-15

False Christs
Christ foretells their coming . . . . Matt. 24:24
Christ warns against . . . . . Mark 13:21-23
See Antichrist

False confidence

A. *Characteristics of:*
Self-righteous . . . . . Rom. 2:3
Spiritually blind . . . . . Is. 28:15, 19
Sensualist . . . . . Gal. 6:7, 8
Worldly secure . . . . . 1 Thess. 5:3

B. *Causes of trusting in:*
Riches . . . . . 1 Tim. 6:17
Worldly success . . . . . Luke 12:19, 20
Men . . . . . Is. 30:1-5
Oneself . . . . . Matt. 26:33-35
Ignoring God's providence . . . James 4:13-15

C. *Warnings against:*
Curse on . . . . . Jer. 17:5
Do not glory in men . . . . . 1 Cor. 3:21
Man's limitation . . . . . 2 Cor. 1:9
Mighty will fail . . . . . Ps. 33:16, 17
Boasting . . . . . 1 Kin. 20:11

D. *Instances of:*
Babel's men . . . . . Gen. 11:4
Sennacherib . . . . . 2 Kin. 19:20-37
Asa . . . . . 2 Chr. 16:7-12
Peter . . . . . Luke 22:33, 34

Falsehood—*turning truth into a lie*

A. *Manifested by false:*
Witnesses . . . . . Ps. 27:12
Balances . . . . . Prov. 11:1
Tongue . . . . . Ps. 120:3
Report . . . . . Ex. 23:1
Prophets . . . . . Jer. 5:2, 31
Science . . . . . 1 Tim. 6:20

B. *God's people:*
Must avoid . . . . . Ex. 23:7
Must hate . . . . . Ps. 119:104, 128
Must endure . . . . . Acts 6:13
Are falsely charged with . . . . . Jer. 37:14
Matt. 5:11

SUBJECT — REFERENCE

False professions

A. *Pretending to be:*

Harmless .... Josh. 9:3-16
Innocent .... Matt. 27:24
Divine .... Acts 12:21-23
Sincere .... Matt. 26:48, 49
True prophets .... 1 Kin. 22:6-12

B. *Exposed by:*

Prophets .... Jer. 28:1-17
Christ .... John 13:21-30
Apostles .... Acts 5:1-11

False prophets

A. *Tests of:*

Doctrine .... Is. 8:20
Prophecies .... 1 Kin. 13:1-32
Lives .... Matt. 7:15, 16

B. *Characteristics of:*

Prophesy peace .... Jer. 23:17
Teach a lie .... Jer. 28:15
Pretend to be true .... Matt. 7:22, 23
Teach corruption .... 2 Pet. 2:10-22

C. *Examples of:*

Zedekiah .... 1 Kin. 22:11, 12
Hananiah .... Jer. 28:1-17
In the last days .... Matt. 24:11

False teachers

A. *Characteristics of:*

Grace-perverters .... Gal. 1:6-8
Money-lovers .... Luke 16:14
Christ-deniers .... 2 Pet. 2:1
Truth-resisters .... 2 Tim. 3:8
Fable-lovers .... 2 Tim. 4:3, 4
Destitute of the truth .... 1 Tim. 6:3-5
Bound by traditions .... Matt. 15:9
Unstable .... 1 Tim. 1:6, 7
Deceitful .... Eph. 4:14
Lustful .... 2 Pet. 2:12-19

B. *Prevalence of:*

In Paul's time .... 2 Tim. 1:14, 15
During this age .... 1 Tim. 4:1-3
At Christ's return .... 2 Tim. 4:3, 4

C. *Examples of:*

Balaam .... Rev. 2:14
Bar-jesus .... Acts 13:6
Ephesian elders .... Acts 20:30; Rev. 2:2
Epicureans .... Acts 17:18
False apostles .... 2 Cor. 11:5, 13; 2 Cor. 12:11
Herodians .... Mark 3:6; Mark 12:13
Hymenaeus .... 2 Tim. 2:17
Libertines .... Acts 6:9
Nicolaitanes .... Rev. 2:15
Pharisees .... Matt. 23:26
Philetus .... 2 Tim. 2:17
Sadducees .... Matt. 16:12
Scribes .... Matt. 12:38, 39
Serpent (Satan) .... Gen. 3:4
Stoic philosophers .... Acts 17:18

False weights

Prohibited .... Deut. 25:13, 14

False witnesses

A. *Features regarding:*

Deceptive .... Prov. 12:17
Cruel .... Prov. 25:18
Utter lies .... Prov. 6:19; Prov. 14:5
Shall perish .... Prov. 21:28
Hated by God .... Zech. 8:17
Forbidden .... Ex. 20:16

B. *Sin of:*

Comes from corrupt heart .... Matt. 15:19
Causes suffering .... Ps. 27:12
Merits punishment .... Prov. 19:5, 9

C. *Punishment of:*

Specified .... Lev. 6:1-5
Described .... Deut. 19:16-20
Visualized .... Zech. 5:3, 4

D. *Examples of, against:*

Ahimelech .... 1 Sam. 22:8-18
Naboth .... 1 Kin. 21:13
Jeremiah .... Jer. 37:12-14
Jesus .... Matt. 26:59-61
Stephen .... Acts 6:11, 13
Paul .... Acts 16:20, 21

Fame—*report; renown; news*

A. *As report or news of:*

Joseph's brothers .... Gen. 45:16
Israel's departure .... Num. 14:15
Jesus' ministry .... Matt. 4:24

B. *As reputation or renown of:*

Nation .... Ezek. 16:14, 15
Joshua's exploits .... Josh. 6:27
God's works .... Josh. 9:9
Solomon's wisdom .... 1 Kin. 4:31
David's power .... 1 Chr. 14:17
The Temple's greatness .... 1 Chr. 22:5
God's glory .... Is. 66:19
Mordecai's fame .... Esth. 9:4
Jesus' works .... Matt. 9:31

Familiar spirits

A. *Described as:*

Source of defilement .... Lev. 19:31
Abominable .... Deut. 18:10-12
Vain .... Is. 8:19

B. *The practicers of, to be:*

Cut off .... Lev. 20:6
Put to death .... Lev. 20:27

C. *Consulted by:*

Saul .... 1 Sam. 28:3-25
Manasseh .... 2 Kin. 21:6

Family

A. *Founded on:*

Divine creation .... Gen. 1:27, 28
Marriage .... Matt. 19:6
Monogamy .... Ex. 20:14
Unity of parents .... Ex. 20:12
Headship of husband .... 1 Cor. 11:3-7
Subordination of children .... Eph. 6:1-4
Common concern .... Luke 16:27, 28

B. *Disturbed by:*

Polygamy .... Gen. 4:19-24
Jealousy .... Gen. 37:3, 4, 18-27
Hatred .... Gen. 4:5, 8
Deceit .... Gen. 37:31-35
Ambition .... 2 Sam. 15:1-16
Waywardness .... Luke 15:11-18
Insubordination .... Gen. 34:6-31
Unbelief .... John 7:3-10
Lust .... Gen. 34:1-31

C. *Unity of:*

Husband and wife .... 1 Cor. 7:3
Parents and children .... Jer. 35:1-19
Worship .... 1 Cor. 16:19
Faith .... 2 Tim. 1:5
Baptism .... Acts 16:14, 15

D. *Worship in:*

Led by the father .... Gen. 18:19
Instructed in the Scriptures .... Eph. 6:4
Observing religious rites .... Acts 10:2, 47, 48
Common consecration .... Josh. 24:15

Famine—*deficiency of food*

A. *Kinds of:*

Physical .... Gen. 12:10
Prophetic .... Matt. 24:7; Rev. 6:5-8
Spiritual .... 2 Chr. 15:3; Amos 8:11

B. *Causes of:*

Hail storms .... Ex. 9:23
Insects .... Joel 1:4
Enemies .... Deut. 28:49-51
Siege .... 2 Kin. 6:25
Sin .... Ezek. 14:12, 13
Punishment .... 2 Kin. 8:1

C. *Characteristics of:*

Often long .... Gen. 41:27
Often severe .... Deut. 28:49-53
Suffering intense .... Jer. 14:1, 5, 6
Destructive .... Jer. 14:12, 15

D. *Instances of, in:*

Abram's time .... Gen. 12:10
Isaac's time .... Gen. 26:1
Joseph's time .... Gen. 41:53-56
Time of judges .... Ruth 1:1
David's reign .... 2 Sam. 21:1
Elisha's time .... 2 Kin. 4:38
Samaria's siege .... 2 Kin. 6:25
Reign of Claudius Caesar .... Acts 11:28
Jeremiah's time .... Jer. 14:1
Ahab's reign .... 1 Kin. 17:1

Fan—*to toss about*

A. *Used literally of:*

Fork for winnowing grain .... Is. 30:24

B. *Used figuratively of judgments:*

God's .... Is. 30:24
Nation's .... Jer. 51:2
Christ's .... Matt. 3:12

Fanaticism—*unbridled obsession*

A. *Kinds of:*

Personal .... Acts 9:1, 2
Group .... 1 Kin. 18:22-29
Civic .... Acts 19:24-41
National .... John 19:15

B. *Characteristics of:*

Intolerance .... Acts 7:57
Persecution .... 1 Thess. 2:14-16
Inhumanity .... Rev. 11:7-10
Insanity .... 1 Sam. 18:9-12

Farewell message

Joshua's .... Josh. 24:1-28
David's .... 1 Kin. 2:1-9
Christ's .... Matt. 28:18-20
Paul's .... 2 Tim. 4:1-8

Farewells—*expressions at departing*

Naomi's, to Orpah .... Ruth 1:11-14
Paul's, to Ephesians .... Acts 18:18-21
Paul's, to elders .... Acts 20:17-38
Paul's, to Tyrians .... Acts 21:3-6
Paul's, to Jews .... Acts 28:23-29

Farm—*a cultivated field*

Preferred more than a wedding .... Matt. 22:1-5

Farmer—*one who farms*

Cain, the first .... Gen. 4:2
Elisha .... 1 Kin. 19:19, 20
Uzziah .... 2 Chr. 26:9, 10
Diligence required in .... Prov. 24:30-34
Reward of .... 2 Cor. 9:6-11
Unwise .... Luke 12:16-21

Farming—*the art of agriculture*

Rechabites forbidden to engage in .... Jer. 35:5-10

Farthing—See Jewish Measures

Utmost payment .... Matt. 5:26
Price of two sparrows .... Matt. 10:29

Fashion—*the outward form*

A. *Used physically of:*

Outward form of a building .... Acts 7:44
One's appearance .... Luke 9:29

B. *Used figuratively of:*

World's life ("conformed") .... Rom. 12:2
World's lusts .... 1 Pet. 1:14
World's riches .... James 1:11
World's exit .... 1 Cor. 7:31
Believer's conformity to Christ .... Phil. 3:21

Fasting—*abstaining from physical nourishment*

A. *Occasions of:*

Public disasters .... 1 Sam. 31:11-13
Private emotions .... 1 Sam. 1:7
Grief .... 2 Sam. 12:16
Anxiety .... Dan. 6:18-20
Approaching danger .... Esth. 4:16
National repentance .... 1 Sam. 7:5, 6
Sad news .... Neh. 1:4
Sacred ordination .... Acts 13:3

B. *Accompaniments of:*

Prayer .... Luke 2:37
Confession .... Neh. 9:1, 2
Mourning .... Joel 2:12
Humiliation .... Neh. 9:1

C. *Safeguards concerning:*

Avoid display .... Matt. 6:16-18
Remember God .... Zech. 7:5-7
Chasten the soul .... Ps. 69:10

SUBJECT — REFERENCE

Humble the soul ... Ps. 35:13
Consider the true meaning of ... Is. 58:1-14

D. *Results of:*
Divine guidance ... Judg. 20:26
Victory over temptation ... Matt. 4:1-11

E. *Instances of:*
Moses ... Ex. 34:27, 28
Israelites ... Judg. 20:26
Samuel ... 1 Sam. 7:5, 6
David ... 2 Sam. 12:16
Elijah ... 1 Kin. 19:8
Ninevites ... Jon. 3:5-8
Nehemiah ... Neh. 1:4
Darius ... Dan. 6:9, 18
Daniel ... Dan. 9:3
Anna ... Luke 2:36, 37
Jesus ... Matt. 4:1, 2
John's disciples and the Pharisees ... Mark 2:18
Early Christians ... Acts 13:2
Apostles ... 2 Cor. 6:4, 5
Paul ... 2 Cor. 11:27

Fat
Figurative of best ... Gen. 45:18
Of sacrifices, burned ... Ex. 29:13
Lev. 4:26
Figurative of pride ... Ps. 119:69, 70
Sacrificed by Abel ... Gen. 4:4
Offered to God ... Ex. 23:18
Lev. 3:14-16

Father—*male parent*

A. *Kinds of:*
Natural ... Gen. 28:13
Ancestors ... Jer. 35:6
Natural leaders ... Rom. 9:5
Head of households ... Ex. 6:14

B. *Figurative of:*
Source ... Job 38:28
Original inventor ... Gen. 4:20
Creator ... James 1:17
Spiritual likeness ... John 8:44
Counselor ... Gen. 45:8
Superior ... 2 Kin. 2:12
Praise-seeking ... Matt. 23:9

C. *Powers of in Old Testament times:*
Arrange son's marriage ... Gen. 24:1-9
Sell children ... Ex. 21:7

D. *Duties of, toward his children:*
Love ... Gen. 37:4
Command ... Gen. 50:16
Instruct ... Prov. 1:8
Guide and warn ... 1 Thess. 2:11
Train ... Hos. 11:3
Rebuke ... Gen. 34:30
Restrain ... 1 Sam. 3:13
Punish ... Deut. 21:18-21
Chasten ... Heb. 12:7
Nourish ... Is. 1:2
Supply needs ... Matt. 7:8-11
Do not provoke ... Eph. 6:4

E. *Examples of devout:*
Abraham ... Gen. 18:18, 19
Isaac ... Gen. 26:12, 13
Joshua ... Josh. 24:15
Job ... Job 1:5

F. *Christ's command about:*
"Call no man your father" ... Matt. 23:9

Fatherhood of God
Of all men ... Mal. 2:10
Of Israel ... Jer. 31:9
Of Gentiles ... Rom. 3:29
Of Christians ... John 1:12, 13

Fatherless—*orphans*

A. *Proper attitude toward:*
Share blessings with ... Deut. 14:28, 29
Leave gleanings for ... Deut. 24:19-22
Do not defraud ... Prov. 23:10
Defend ... Ps. 82:3
Visit ... James 1:27
Oppress not ... Zech. 7:10
Do no violence to ... Jer. 22:3

B. *God's help toward:*
Father of ... Ps. 68:5
Helper of ... Ps. 10:14
Hears cry of ... Ex. 22:23
Executes judgment of ... Deut. 10:18

SUBJECT — REFERENCE

Father's house
The family home ... Gen. 12:1
1 Sam. 18:2
A household ... Ex. 12:3
Tribal divisions ... Num. 3:15, 20
Num. 17:2, 3
Temple ... John 2:14-16
Heaven ... John 14:2

Fathom—*a sea measure; about six feet*
Mentioned in Paul's shipwreck ... Acts 27:28

Fatigue—*physical or mental exhaustion*

From:
Marching ... 1 Sam. 30:9, 10
Fighting ... 2 Sam. 23:10, 15
Much study ... Eccl. 12:12
Fasting ... Acts 27:21

In:
Sleeping ... Matt. 26:45

Fault—*an imperfection*

A. *Examples of:*
A promise forgotten ... Gen. 41:9
Unworthy conduct ... 1 Sam. 29:3
Guilt ... John 18:38
Deficient behavior ... Matt. 18:15
Human weakness ... James 5:16

B. *Absence of:*
Flawless devotion ... Rev. 14:5
Ultimate sinlessness ... Jude 24

Faultfinders—*carping critics*

A. *Motives behind:*
Supposed injustice ... Matt. 20:9-12
Supposed defilement ... Luke 5:29, 30
Greed and avarice ... John 12:3-6

B. *Against God's:*
Choice ... Num. 12:1, 2
Leading ... Num. 14:1-4
Mercy ... Jon. 4:1-11
Government ... Rom. 9:19-23

C. *Guilt of:*
Punishable ... Num. 12:2, 8-13
Productive of evil ... 3 John 10

Faultless—*without blame*
David ... 1 Sam. 29:3, 6
Daniel ... Dan. 6:4
Christ ... Luke 23:4, 14

Favoritism—*being unfairly partial*

A. *Forbidden to:*
Parents ... Deut. 21:15-17
Judges ... Deut. 25:1-3
Ministers ... 1 Tim. 5:21

B. *Results in:*
Family friction ... Gen. 27:6-46
Jealousy ... Gen. 37:3-35

Fear—*anxiety caused by approaching danger*

A. *Causes of:*
Disobedience ... Gen. 3:10
Impending judgment ... Heb. 11:7
Persecution ... John 20:19
Events of nature ... Acts 27:17, 29
Suspicion ... Acts 9:26
Uncertainty ... 2 Cor. 11:3
Final events ... Luke 21:26
Death ... Heb. 2:15

B. *Effects of:*
Demoralization ... 1 Sam. 13:5-8
Paralysis ... Matt. 28:4
Silent testimony ... John 9:22

C. *Instances of:*
Abraham ... Gen. 20:11
Jacob ... Gen. 32:11
Soldiers ... Matt. 27:54

Fear, godly

A. *Defined as:*
Hating evil ... Prov. 8:13
Satisfying ... Prov. 14:27
Sanctifying ... Ps. 19:9
Beginning of wisdom ... Prov. 1:7

B. *Motives to, God's:*
Majesty ... Jer. 10:7
Holiness ... Rev. 15:4
Forgiveness ... Ps. 130:4

SUBJECT — REFERENCE

Power ... Josh. 4:23, 24
Goodness ... 1 Sam. 12:24
Judgment ... Rev. 14:7

C. *Examples of:*
Noah ... Heb. 11:7
Abraham ... Gen. 22:12
Jacob ... Gen. 28:16, 17
Joseph ... Gen. 42:18
David ... Ps. 5:7
Obadiah ... 1 Kin. 18:12
Job ... Job 1:8
Nehemiah ... Neh. 5:15
Early Christians ... Acts 9:31

Fearlessness—*without fear*

A. *Source of:*
Believing God's promises ... Num. 13:30
Challenge of duty ... Ex. 32:26-29
Regard for God's holiness ... Num. 25:1-9
Believing God ... Acts 27:22-26

B. *Exemplified by:*
Abram ... Gen. 14:14-16
Jonathan ... 1 Sam. 14:6-14
David ... 1 Sam. 17:34-37
Nehemiah ... Neh. 4:1-23
Hebrew men ... Dan. 3:16-30
Peter and John ... Acts 4:13
Paul ... Acts 21:10-14

Feasts, Hebrew

A. *Three annual:*
Passover ... Lev. 23:5-8
Weeks (Pentecost) ... Ex. 23:16
Tabernacle ... Lev. 23:34-44

B. *Purposes of:*
Unify the nation ... Deut. 12:5-14
Worship God ... Ex. 5:1
Illustrate spiritual truths ... John 7:37-39
Foretell the Messiah ... 1 Cor. 11:23-26

C. *Brief history of:*
Pre-Sinaitic observance ... Ex. 12:1-27
Three instituted at Sinai ... Ex. 23:14-17
Celebrated in the wilderness ... Num. 9:3-5
Again at beginning of conquest ... Josh. 5:10, 11
At dedication of Temple ... 1 Kin. 8:2, 65
"Dedication" introduced by Solomon ... 2 Chr. 7:9-11
Idolatrous counterfeits introduced by Jeroboam ... 1 Kin. 12:27-33
Observed in Hezekiah's reign ... 2 Chr. 30:1
Perversion of, by Jews ... Is. 1:13, 14
Restored in Josiah's reformation ... 2 Kin. 23:22, 23
Failure in, cause of exile ... 2 Chr. 36:20, 21
Restored after the exile ... Ezra 3:4
Purim instituted by Mordecai ... Esth. 9:17-32
Christ attends ... John 2:23
John 13:1
Christ fulfills the Passover ... 1 Cor. 5:8
Christianity begins with Pentecost ... Acts 2:1-41
All fulfilled in Christ ... 2 Cor. 3:3-18

Feasts, social

A. *Worldly, occasions of:*
Idolatry ... Ex. 32:6
Drunkenness ... 1 Sam. 25:36
Proud display ... Esth. 1:1-8
Profane carousals ... Dan. 5:1-16
Licentiousness ... Mark 6:21, 22

B. *Proper, occasions of:*
Refreshment ... Gen. 19:1-3
Reconciliation ... Gen. 31:54, 55
Reunion ... Gen. 43:16-34
Restoration ... Luke 15:22-24

See Entertainment

Feed—*to supply food to*

A. *Used naturally of:*
Food for men ... 2 Sam. 19:33
Food for animals ... Gen. 30:36
God's provision ... Matt. 6:26

B. *Used figuratively of:*
Instruction and care ... 2 Sam. 5:2
Messiah ... Ezek. 34:23
Good deeds ... Matt. 25:35
Supernatural supply ... Rev. 12:6

F

SUBJECT REFERENCE

Elemental teaching ... 1 Cor. 3:2
Change of nature ... Is. 11:7
Corruption ... Ps. 49:14
Vanity ... Hos. 12:1

Feet—*the lower parts of the body*

A. *Acts performed by or on, indicating:*
Subjection ... Josh. 10:24
Conquest ... 2 Sam. 22:39
Humiliation ... Judg. 5:27
Submission and entreaty ... 1 Sam. 25:24, 41
Great love ... Luke 7:38, 44-46
Worship ... Rev. 19:10
Learner's position ... Luke 10:39
Humility ... John 13:5-14
Changed nature ... Luke 8:35
Rejection ... Matt. 10:14

B. *Figurative of:*
God's holiness ... Ex. 3:5
God's nature ... Ex. 24:10
Clouds ... Nah. 1:3
God's messengers ... Rom. 10:15
Final conquest ... Rom. 16:20

C. *Unusual features concerning:*
No swelling ... Neh. 9:21
Lameness ... 2 Sam. 9:3, 13
Neglected ... 2 Sam. 19:24
Impotent ... Acts 14:8-10
Binding ... Acts 21:11

See Foot

Feet washing
Performed on guests ... Gen. 18:4
Proffered by Abigail ... 1 Sam. 25:40, 41
On Jesus, with tears ... Luke 7:44
Performed by Jesus ... John 13:5
Duty of saints ... 1 Tim. 5:10

Felix—*happy*
Governor of Judaea ... Acts 23:24, 26
Letter addressed to ... Acts 23:25-30
Paul's defense before ... Acts 24:1-21
Convicted, but unchanged ... Acts 24:22-25
Subject to bribery ... Acts 24:26, 27

Felloes—*obsolete word meaning rims*
Of wheels ... 1 Kin. 7:33

Fellow citizens
With the saints ... Eph. 2:19

Fellow countryman
Shall not hate ... Lev. 19:17
Becomes poor ... Lev. 25:25
Judge righteously ... Deut. 1:16
Lord gives rest ... Deut. 3:20
Save some ... Rom. 11:14

Fellow servant
Were to be killed ... Rev. 6:11
Who hold fast the testimony of Jesus ... Rev. 19:10
Who heed the words ... Rev. 22:9

Fellowship—*sharing together*

A. *Based upon common:*
Purpose ... Ps. 133:1-3
Belief ... Acts 2:42
Conviction ... 1 Pet. 3:8
Work ... Neh. 4:1-23
Hope ... Heb. 11:39, 40
Faith ... 1 Sam. 20:30-42
Suffering ... Dan. 3:16-30
Need ... 2 Cor. 8:1-15

B. *Persons sharing together:*
Father, the Son, and Christians ... 1 John 1:3
Christ and Christians ... 1 Cor. 1:9
Holy Spirit and Christians ... Phil. 2:1
Apostles ... Acts 2:42
Believers ... 1 John 1:7

C. *Things shared together:*
Material things ... 2 Cor. 8:4
Suffering ... Phil. 3:10
The Gospel ministry ... Gal. 2:9
Gospel privileges ... Phil. 1:5
Gospel mystery ... Eph. 3:9

Fellow slave
Who owed a hundred denarii ... Matt. 18:28-33
Evil slave beats ... Matt. 24:48, 49

SUBJECT REFERENCE

Fellow workers
In the truth ... 3 John 8
In the kingdom ... Col. 4:11
Prisca and Aquila described as ... Rom 16:3
Urbanas ... Rom. 16:9
Timothy ... Rom. 16:21
Paul ... 1 Cor. 3:1-9
Titus ... 2 Cor. 8:23
Epaphroditus ... Phil. 2:25
Philemon ... Philem. 1
Marcus, Aristarchus, Demas, Lucas ... Philem. 24

Fenced cities
Means of protection ... 2 Sam. 20:6
Mighty and strong ... Deut. 9:1
Conquerable ... Deut. 3:5
Utterly destroyed ... 2 Kin. 3:19, 25
No substitute for God ... Hos. 8:14

Ferret—*an unclean animal*
Either the gecho (wall lizard) or the field mouse ... Lev. 11:30

Ferryboats
David's use of ... 2 Sam. 19:16-18

Festus—*feastful, joyful*
Governor of Judaea ... Acts 24:27
Paul's defense made to ... Acts 25:1-22

Fetters—*shackle for binding the feet*

A. *Used literally of:*
Imprisonment ... Ps. 105:18
Bondage ... Luke 8:29

B. *Used figuratively of:*
Trouble ... Job 36:8
Subjection ... Ps. 149:8

Fetus—*unborn child*
Protected by law ... Ex. 21:22
Possesses sin nature ... Ps. 51:5
Fashioned by God ... Ps. 139:13-16
Called by God ... Is. 49:1; Jer. 1:5
Active ... Luke 1:41

Fever—*abnormal body temperature*
Sent as a judgment ... Deut. 28:22
Rebuked by Christ ... Luke 4:38, 39
Healed by Paul ... Acts 28:8

Few—*the opposite of many*
Days ... Gen. 47:9
Do not determine God's power ... 1 Sam. 14:6
Words in prayer ... Eccl. 5:2
The saved ... Matt. 7:14
Gospel messengers ... Matt. 9:37
The chosen ... Matt. 22:14

Fidelity—*faithfulness in the performance of duty*
In finances ... 2 Kin. 12:15
In industry ... 2 Chr. 34:11, 12
Seen in Joseph ... Gen. 39:6
Seen in Daniel ... Dan. 6:1-3, 28

Field—*open or cleared land*

A. *Used literally of:*
Cultivated land ... Gen. 47:20
A city ... Ps. 78:12, 43

B. *Laws regarding:*
Fires ... Ex. 22:6
Mixed seed ... Lev. 19:19
Coveting others' ... Deut. 5:21
Destruction of trees ... Deut. 20:19, 20
Total harvest of ... Deut. 24:19-22
Sabbath rest ... Lev. 25:3-12
Redemption of ... Lev. 27:16-24
Title of ... Ruth 4:5-11

C. *Figurative of:*
World ... Matt. 13:38, 44
Harvest of souls ... John 4:35

Field of Blood
A field, predicted in the Old Testament, bought as a cemetery for Judas' burial ... Zech. 11:12, 13; Matt. 27:1-10

Fiery serpents
Attack Israelites ... Num. 21:6, 8

Fig—*pear-shaped fruit of fig tree*
Destruction foretold ... Hos. 2:12

SUBJECT REFERENCE

Fig cakes
Prescribed for boils ... Is. 38:21

Fig tree

A. *The leaves of, used for:*
Covering nakedness ... Gen. 3:7
Shade ... John 1:48, 50

B. *Fruit of:*
Used for food ... 1 Sam. 30:12
Sent as present ... 1 Sam. 25:18
Sold in markets ... Neh. 13:15
Used for healing ... Is. 38:21
Sometimes fails ... Hab. 3:17

C. *Figurative of:*
Prosperity and peace ... 1 Kin. 4:25
Righteous and the wicked ... Jer. 24:1-10
Fathers of Israel ... Hos. 9:10
Barren religion ... Matt. 21:19
Jewish nation ... Luke 13:6-9
Christ's return ... Matt. 24:32, 33
Final judgment ... Rev. 6:13

Fight—*a conflict*

A. *Used literally of:*
War ... Ex. 17:8, 10
Individual combat ... 1 Sam. 17:10, 32

B. *Used figuratively of:*
Determined resolve ... 1 Cor. 9:26
Opposition of evil men ... 1 Cor. 15:32
Christian life ... 1 Tim. 6:12
Dissension ... James 4:1, 2
Spiritual conflict ... Rev. 12:7

Fighting against God

A. *Manifested by:*
Pharaoh ... Ex. 5:1, 2
Rabshakeh ... 2 Kin. 18:28-36
Jeroboam ... 2 Chr. 13:8-19

B. *Futility of:*
Seen by Gamaliel ... Acts 5:34, 39
Admitted by Pharisees ... Acts 23:9
Experienced by Satan ... Rev. 12:7-17
Blasphemy of unregenerate ... Rev. 16:9-21

Figurehead—*symbol on ship's prow*
Twin Brothers ... Acts 28:11

Figures of speech
Allegory ... Gal. 4:24
Fable ... Judg. 9:8-15; 1 Tim. 4:7
Hyperbole ... 1 Sam. 13:5; John 21:25
Interrogation ... 1 Cor. 12:29, 30
Irony ... Luke 15:7-10
Metaphor ... Luke 13:32
Parable ... Matt. 13:10
Parallelism ... Gen. 4:23, 24
Personification ... Is. 55:12
Proverb ... 1 Kin. 4:32
Sarcasm ... Matt. 27:29
Simile ... Is. 1:8, 9
Similitude ... Ps. 90:4-6

Filial devotion

A. *Duty of:*
Commanded ... Ex. 20:12
Corrupted ... Matt. 15:4-6
Confirmed ... Eph. 6:1-3

B. *Examples of:*
Joseph ... Gen. 47:12
David ... 1 Sam. 22:3
Solomon ... 1 Kin. 2:19
Elisha ... 1 Kin. 19:19, 20
Young man ... Matt. 19:16-20

C. *Obedience:*
Continual ... Prov. 6:20-22
Total ... Col. 3:20
Lack of, severely punished ... Deut. 21:18-21
Lack of, cursed ... Prov. 20:20

Filth—*uncleanness, defilement, corruption*
Men ... Job 15:16; Ps. 14:2, 3
Garments and furniture ... Is. 4:1-4; Is. 28:8
Ceremonial uncleanness ... Ezek. 22:15
Unrighteousness ... Is. 64:6; Ezek. 16:6

SUBJECT — REFERENCE

Filthy lucre—*money*
- Bishop (elders) forbidden to seek — 1 Tim. 3:3

Fine—*penalty payment*
- Paid by guilty — Ex. 21:23-30; Deut. 22:19
- Restitution — Ex. 22:5-15; Num. 5:7

Finger

A. *Used literally of:*
- Man's fingers — John 20:25, 27
- Deformity — 2 Sam. 21:20
- Measurement — Jer. 52:21
- Mysterious hand — Dan. 5:5

B. *Used figuratively of:*
- God's power — Ex. 8:19
- Inspiration — Ex. 31:18
- Suggestiveness — Prov. 6:13
- Contrast of burdens — 1 Kin. 12:10
- Lord's authority — Luke 11:20

Fins
- Signs of a clean fish — Lev. 11:9

Fir—*a tree of the pine family*
- Tree of Lebanon — 1 Kin. 5:8, 10
- Used in Solomon's temple — 1 Kin. 6:15, 34
- Used in ships — Ezek. 27:5
- Used for musical instruments — 2 Sam. 6:5

Fire

A. *Physical uses of:*
- Warmth — John 18:18
- Cooking — Ex. 16:23
- Signs — Judg. 20:38, 40
- Sacrifices — Gen. 8:20, 21
- Refining — Ps. 12:6
- Torture — Dan. 3:6
- Sacrifice of children — 2 Kin. 16:3

B. *Supernatural uses of:*
- Manifest God — Ex. 3:2
- Indicate God's power — Ex. 9:24
- Express God's approval — Lev. 9:24
- Vindicate God's wrath — 2 Kin. 1:9-12
- Guide Israel — Ex. 13:21, 22
- Transport a saint to heaven — 2 Kin. 2:11

C. *Used figuratively of:*
- God's protection — Zech. 2:5
- God's vengeance — Heb. 12:29
- God's Word — Jer. 5:14
- Christ — Mal. 3:2
- Holy Spirit — Acts 2:3
- Angels — Heb. 1:7
- Tongue — James 3:6
- Persecution — Luke 12:49-53
- Affliction — Is. 43:2
- Purification — Is. 6:5-7
- Love — Song 8:6
- Lust — Prov. 6:27, 28

D. *Final uses of:*
- Destroy world — 2 Pet. 3:10-12
- Punish wicked — Matt. 25:41

Fire, Lake of—*place of eternal punishment*
- The beast — Rev. 19:20
- The false prophet — Rev. 19:20
- The devil — Rev. 20:10
- Death and hell — Rev. 20:14
- Sinners — Rev. 21:8

Firebrand—*torch*
- Figurative of enemies — Is. 7:4
- Thrown by a madman — Prov. 26:18
- Have no fear of — Is. 7:4
- All who encircle — Is. 50:11
- Snatched from a blaze — Amos 4:11

Firepan—*a shovel used for carrying fire*
- Part of the altar — Ex. 27:3

Firmament—*expanse*
- Created by God — Gen. 1:8
- Stars placed in — Gen. 1:14, 17
- Compared to a tent — Ps. 104:2
- Expressive of God's glory — Ps. 19:1
- Saints compared to — Dan. 12:3

First
- Came out red — Gen. 25:25
- This came out — Gen. 38:28
- These should set forth — Num. 2:9
- Amalek, of nations — Num. 24:20
- Hands of witness shall be — Deut. 17:7
- Altar Solomon built — 1 Sam. 14:35
- Case pleaded — Prov. 18:17
- Seek — Matt. 6:33
- Cast out beam — Matt. 7:5; Luke 6:42
- Last state worse than — Luke 11:26
- The blade, then the head — Mark 4:28
- Let the children — Mark 7:27
- Desire to be — Mark 9:35
- Commandment — Mark 12:28
- Gospel must, be preached — Mark 13:10
- Appeared to Mary Magdalene — Mark 16:9
- Not sit down — Luke 14:28
- Stepped in, made whole — John 5:4
- Gave themselves — 2 Cor. 8:5
- Trusted in Christ — Eph. 1:12
- A falling away — 2 Thess. 2:3
- Let these also — 1 Tim. 3:10
- Dwelt, in — 2 Tim. 1:5
- He takes away — Heb. 10:9

First (things mentioned)
- Altar — Gen. 8:20
- Archer — Gen. 21:20
- Artificer — Gen. 4:22
- Bigamist — Gen. 4:19
- Birthday celebration — Gen. 40:20
- Book — Gen. 5:1
- Bottle — Gen. 21:14
- Bridal veil — Gen. 24:64-67
- Cave dwellers — Gen. 19:30
- Christian martyr — Acts 22:19, 20
- City builder — Gen. 4:17
- Coffin — Gen. 50:26
- Command — Gen. 1:3
- Commanded by Christ — Matt. 6:33
- Commissioners — Dan. 6:2
- Cremation — 1 Sam. 31:12
- Curse — Gen. 3:14
- Death — Gen. 4:8
- Diet — Jer. 52:31-34
- Doubt — Gen. 3:1
- Dream — Gen. 20:3
- Drunkenness — Gen. 9:21
- Emancipator — Ex. 3:7-22
- Embalming — Gen. 50:2, 3
- European convert — Acts 16:14, 15
- Execution — Gen. 40:20-22
- Family — Gen. 4:1, 2
- Famine — Gen. 12:10
- Farewell address — Josh. 23:1-16
- Farmer — Gen. 4:2
- Female government — Judg. 4:4, 5
- Ferry boat — 2 Sam. 19:18
- Food control — Gen. 41:25-27
- Frying pan — Lev. 2:7
- Gardener — Gen. 2:15
- Gold — Gen. 2:11
- Harp — Gen. 4:21
- Hebrew (Jew) — Gen. 14:13
- High priest — Ex. 28:1
- Hunter — Gen. 10:8, 9
- Idolatry — Josh. 24:2
- "In-law" trouble — Gen. 26:34, 35
- Iron bedstead — Deut. 3:11
- Judge — 1 Sam. 7:15
- Kiss — Gen. 27:26, 27
- Left-handed man — Judg. 3:15
- Letter — 2 Sam. 11:14
- Liar — Gen. 3:1-5
- Man to hang himself — 2 Sam. 17:23
- Man to shave — Gen. 41:14
- Man to wear a ring — Gen. 41:42
- Miracles of Christ — John 2:1-11
- Mother of twins — Gen. 25:21-28
- Murderer — Gen. 4:8
- Musician — Gen. 4:21
- Navy — 1 Kin. 9:26
- Oath — Gen. 21:24
- Orchestra — 2 Sam. 6:5
- Organ — Gen. 4:21
- Pilgrim — Gen. 12:1-8
- Prayer — Gen. 4:26
- Prison — Gen. 39:20
- Prophecy — Gen. 3:15
- Prophetess — Ex. 15:20
- Proposal of adultery — Gen. 39:7-12
- Pulpit — Neh. 8:4
- Purchase of land — Gen. 23:3-20
- Question — Gen. 3:1
- Rainbow — Gen. 9:13, 14
- Rape — Judg. 19:24, 25
- Riddle — Judg. 14:12-18
- Sabbath — Gen. 2:2, 3
- Sacrifice — Gen. 8:20
- Saddle — Gen. 22:3
- Scribe — Ex. 24:4
- Selective Service — Num. 31:3-6
- Shepherd — Gen. 4:2
- Shepherdess — Gen. 29:9
- Sheriffs — Dan. 3:2
- Shipbuilder — Gen. 6:14
- Sin — Gen. 3:1-24
- Singing school — 1 Chr. 25:5-7
- Sunstroke — 2 Kin. 4:18-20
- Surveying of land — Josh. 18:8, 9
- Temptation — Gen. 3:1-6
- Theater — Acts 19:29-31
- To be named before birth — Gen. 16:11
- To confess Christ — John 1:49
- Tombstone — Gen. 35:20
- Tower — Gen. 11:4, 5
- Vagabond — Gen. 4:9-12
- Voluntary fasting — Judg. 20:26
- Wage contract — Gen. 29:15-20
- War — Gen. 14:2-12
- Warships — Num. 24:24
- Well — Gen. 16:14
- Whirlwind — 2 Kin. 2:1
- Wife — Gen. 3:20
- Winding stairs — 1 Kin. 6:8
- Woman thief — Gen. 31:19
- Woman to curse — Judg. 17:1, 2
- Woman to use cosmetics — 2 Kin. 9:30
- Words spoken to man — Gen. 1:28
- Worship — Gen. 4:3-5

First-born
- Said to the younger — Gen. 19:31; Gen. 19:34
- Bore a son — Gen. 19:37
- Give younger before — Gen. 29:26
- According to birthright — Gen. 43:33
- Israel is My — Ex. 4:22
- Will slay your — Ex. 4:23
- All in the land of Egypt — Ex. 11:5
- Will smite all — Ex. 12:12
- Killed all the — Ex. 13:15; Ps. 105:36
- Sanctify to me all — Ex. 13:2
- Of Israel are Mine — Num. 3:13
- Lay foundation in — Josh. 6:26
- Of death shall — Job 18:13
- Gave birth — Luke 2:7
- Of all creation — Col. 1:15
- So that he who destroyed — Heb. 11:28

A. *Privileges of:*
- First in family — Gen. 48:13, 14
- Delegated authority of — Gen. 27:1-29
- Received father's special blessing — Gen. 27:4, 35
- Bears father's title — 2 Chr. 21:1, 3
- Given double portion of inheritance — Deut. 21:17
- Object of special love — Jer. 31:9, 20
- Precious and valuable — Mic. 6:7

B. *Laws concerning:*
- Dedicated to God — Ex. 22:29-31
- To be redeemed — Ex. 34:20
- Redemption price of — Num. 3:46-51
- Tribe of Levi substituted for — Num. 3:11-45
- Death of, next brother substituted — Matt. 22:24-28
- Change of, forbidden — Deut. 21:15-17
- Forfeited by evil deeds — Gen. 49:3, 4, 8
- Forfeited by sale — Heb. 12:16, 17
- Changed sovereignty — 1 Sam. 16:6-12
- Christ subject to — Luke 2:22-24

C. *Figurative of, Christ in:*
- Authority — Ps. 89:27
- Honor — Heb. 1:6
- Resurrection — Col. 1:18
- Church — Rom. 8:29
- Glory — Heb. 12:22, 23

First day of the week—*Sunday*
- Day of Christ's resurrection — Mark 16:9; John 20:1, 19
- Day after the Sabbath — Matt. 28:1; Mark 16:1, 2
- Day of Christian worship — Acts 20:7; 1 Cor. 16:1, 2
- Called "the Lord's day" — Rev. 1:10

First fruits

A. *Regulations concerning:*
- Law specified — Lev. 23:9-14

F

SUBJECT — REFERENCE

Brought to God's house ... Ex. 34:26
Ritual of, described ... Deut. 26:3-10
Considered holy ... Ezek. 48:14
God honored by ... Prov. 3:9

B. *Figurative of:*
Israel's position ... Rom. 11:16
Christ's place in resurrection ... 1 Cor. 15:20, 23
Christians ... James 1:18
First converts ... Rom. 16:5

Firstlings
Abel brought ... Gen. 4:4
Set apart every ... Ex. 13:12; Ex. 34:19
Of an ass thou shall redeem ... Ex. 13:13; Ex. 34:20
Lords, no man shall sanctify ... Lev. 27:26
Of unclean beasts ... Num. 18:15
Ye shall bring, of your herd ... Deut. 12:6
Males sanctify ... Deut. 15:19
Glory is like ... Deut. 33:17

Fish
A. *Features regarding:*
Created by God ... Gen. 1:20, 21
Worship of forbidden ... Deut. 4:15-18
Caught by net ... Matt. 4:18
Worshiped by pagans ... 1 Sam. 5:4
Some disciples called as fishermen ... Matt. 4:18-21

B. *Miracles concerning:*
Jonah's life in ... Jon. 1:17
Multiplied by Christ ... Matt. 14:17-21
Bearing a coin ... Matt. 17:27

C. *Figurative of:*
Men in the sea of life ... Ezek. 47:9, 10
Ministers as fishermen ... Matt. 4:19
Ignorant men ... Eccl. 9:12

Fish Gate—*a gate of Jerusalem*
Manasseh built wall there ... 2 Chr. 33:13, 14
Built by sons of Hassenaah ... Neh. 3:3
Two choirs took their stand ... Neh. 12:38-40
A cry there prophesied ... Zeph. 1:10

Fish hook—*hook for catching fish*
Cannot catch Leviathan ... Job 41:1
Fishing in the brooks ... Is. 19:8

Fist fighting
Punishment of ... Ex. 21:18, 19

Fitches—*vetches*
Annual plant for forage ... Is. 28:25, 27
Same as rye in ... Ezek. 4:9

Flag—*fluttering*
Name of many water plants ... Ex. 2:3-5
Rendered as "weeds" in ... Jon. 2:5

Flagellation—*punishment by whipping, flogging*
For immorality ... Lev. 19:20
For defamation ... Deut. 22:16-18
Forty blows ... Deut. 25:3
Of Christ ... Matt. 27:26; Mark 15:15
Thirty-nine lashes ... 2 Cor. 11:24
Of apostles ... Acts 5:40

Flagon—*flask*
Small vessels for liquids ... Is. 22:24

Flat nose
Disqualifies for service ... Lev. 21:18

Flattery—*unjustified praise*
A. *Used by:*
False prophets ... Rom. 16:18
Hypocrites ... Ps. 78:36
Wicked ... Ps. 36:1-4
Prostitutes ... Prov. 2:16

B. *Attitude of saints toward:*
Should avoid users of ... Prov. 20:19
Pray against ... Ps. 5:8, 9
Should not use ... 1 Thess. 2:5

C. *Dangers of:*
Leads to ruin ... Prov. 26:28
Brings deception ... Prov. 29:5
Corrupts ... Dan. 11:21, 25, 27
Brings death ... Acts 12:21-23

SUBJECT — REFERENCE

Flax—*the flax plant*
Grown in Egypt and Palestine ... Ex. 9:31
Used for:
Cords ... Judg. 15:14
Spinning ... Is. 19:9
Garments ("linen") ... Deut. 22:11

Flea—*a parasitic, blood-sucking insect*
Figurative of insignificance ... 1 Sam. 24:14

Fleece—*freshly sheared wool*
Given to priests ... Deut. 18:3, 4
Sign to Gideon ... Judg. 6:36-40
Warm ... Job 31:20

Flesh
A. *Used to designate:*
All created life ... Gen. 6:13, 17, 19
Kinsmen (of same nature) ... Rom. 9:3, 5, 8
The body ... Job 33:25
Marriage ... Matt. 19:5
Human nature ... John 1:14
Christ's mystical nature ... John 6:51, 53-63
Human weakness ... Matt. 16:17
Outward appearance ... 2 Cor. 5:16
The evil principle in man ... Rom. 7:18
Food ... Ex. 16:12

B. *In a bad sense, described as:*
Having passions ... Gal. 5:24
Producing evil works ... Gal. 5:19-21
Dominating the mind ... Eph. 2:3
Absorbing the affections ... Rom. 13:14
Seeking outward display ... Gal. 6:12, 13
Antagonizing the Spirit ... Gal. 5:17
Fighting against God's Law ... Rom. 8:7
Reaping corruption ... Gal. 6:8
Producing death ... Rom. 7:5

C. *Christian's attitude toward:*
Still confronts ... Rom. 7:18-23
Source of opposition ... Gal. 5:17
Make no provision for ... Rom. 13:14
Do not love ... 1 John 2:15-17
Do not walk in ... Rom. 8:1, 4
Do not live in ... Rom. 8:12, 13
Crucified ... Gal. 5:24

Flesh hook—*fork*
In tabernacle ... Ex. 27:3; Num. 4:14
By priests ... 1 Sam. 2:12-14
In Temple ... 1 Chr. 28:11, 17; 2 Chr. 4:16

Flies—*small winged insects*
Cause of evil odor ... Eccl. 10:1
Figurative of Egypt ... Is. 7:18
Plague upon the Egyptians ... Ex. 8:21-31; Ps. 78:45

Flint—*a very hard stone*
Water from ... Deut. 8:15
Oil from ... Deut. 32:13
Turning into fountain of water ... Ps. 114:8
Hoofs shall seem like ... Is. 5:28
Figurative of a fixed course ... Is. 50:7; Ezek. 3:9

Flock—*a group of domesticated animals*
Sheep and goats ... Gen. 27:9
Nations ... Jer. 51:23
National leaders ... Jer. 25:34, 35
Jewish people ... Jer. 13:17, 20
True church ... Is. 40:11; Acts 20:28

Flood—*overflowing of water*
A. *Used literally of:*
Earth's flood ... Gen. 6:17

B. *Used figuratively of:*
Great trouble ... Ps. 32:6
Hostile world powers ... Ps. 93:3
An invading army ... Jer. 46:7, 8
Great destruction ... Dan. 9:26
Testing ... Matt. 7:25, 27
Persecution ... Rev. 12:15, 16

Floodgates
Descriptive of judgment ... Gen. 7:11

Floor
For threshing wheat ... Judg. 6:37; 1 Kin. 22:10
Of a building ... 1 Kin. 6:15

SUBJECT — REFERENCE

Flour—*finely ground wheat*
Offered in sacrifices ... Lev. 5:11, 13

Flowers
A. *Described as:*
Wild ... Ps. 103:15, 16
Beautiful ... Matt. 6:28, 29
Sweet ... Song 5:13
Fading ... Is. 40:7, 8

B. *Figurative of:*
Shortness of life ... Job 14:2
Israel ... Is. 28:1
Man's glory ... James 1:10, 11

Flute—*a hollow musical instrument*
In Babylon ... Dan. 3:5
Used in God's worship ... Ps. 150:4

Foal—*a colt, young donkey*
Given to Esau ... Gen. 32:13-15
Ridden by Christ ... Zech. 9:9; Matt. 21:5

Fodder—*food for domestic animals*
Given to oxen and wild ass ... Job 6:5; Is. 30:24

Following
A. *In Old Testament:*
Commanded ... Deut. 8:6
Brought reward ... Deut. 19:9
Covenant ... 2 Kin. 23:3

B. *In New Testament:*
Multitudes ... Matt. 4:25; Matt. 12:15
Disciples ... Matt. 8:19; Luke 5:11-27
Left all ... Matt. 4:18-22
In light ... John 8:12
After Christ's example ... John 13:15; 1 John 2:6
Example of Godly men ... Phil. 3:17; Heb. 6:12; James 5:10

Folly—*contemptuous disregard of holy things*
A. *Described as:*
Unnatural sin ... Judg. 19:22-24

B. *Associated with:*
Deception ... Prov. 14:8
Hasty spirit ... Prov. 14:29
Gullibility ... Prov. 13:16
Ferociousness ... Prov. 17:12
Disgust ... Prov. 26:11

C. *Warnings against:*
Saints not to return to ... Ps. 85:8
Prophets guilty of ... Jer. 23:13
Angels charged with ... Job 4:18
Apostles subject to ... 2 Cor. 11:1

Food
A. *Features regarding;*
Given by God ... Ps. 104:21, 27
Necessary for man ... Gen. 1:29, 30
Gives physical strength ... Acts 9:19
Revives the spirit ... 1 Sam. 30:12
Object of daily prayer ... Matt. 6:11
Object of thanksgiving ... 1 Sam. 9:13
Sanctified by prayer ... 1 Tim. 4:4, 5
Scruples recognized ... Rom. 14:2-23

B. *Lack of:*
Testing of faith ... Hab. 3:17

C. *Provided by:*
God ... Ps. 145:15
Christ ... John 21:5, 6

D. *Prohibitions concerning:*
Dead animals ... Ex. 22:31
Eating blood ... Deut. 12:16
Clean and unclean ... Deut. 14:4-20
Wine ... Prov. 23:29-35
Strangled animals ... Acts 21:25
Not in itself commendable ... 1 Cor. 8:8
Not to be a stumbling block ... 1 Cor. 8:13
Life more important than ... Matt. 6:25

E. *Miracles connected with:*
Destruction of ... Ps. 105:29-35
Provision for ... Ps. 105:40, 41

SUBJECT .... REFERENCE

Supply of .... 1 Kin. 17:4-6
Multiplication of .... John 6:5-13
Refused .... Matt. 4:1-4

F. *Figurative of:*

God's will .... John 4:32, 34
Christ .... John 6:27, 55
Strong doctrines .... 1 Cor. 3:2

Food control

First .... Gen. 41:25-27
Final .... Rev. 13:11-17

Food, spiritual

A. *Elements of:*

The Word .... Ps. 19:10
Christ .... John 6:48-51

B. *Need of, by:*

The naive .... Prov. 9:1-5
The immature .... 1 Cor. 3:1, 2
The mature .... Heb. 5:14
All .... Matt. 22:4

C. *Characteristics of:*

Abundant .... Is. 55:1-3
Satisfying .... Ps. 22:26
Enduring .... John 6:48-51
Life-giving .... John 6:53-63

Foods of Bible times

A. *Obtaining; storing; use:*

Shall be for .... Gen. 6:21
Let them gather .... Gen. 41:35
But to buy .... Gen. 42:10
Go again, buy .... Gen. 43:2
Buy .... Gen. 43:4
Much .... Prov. 13:23
Of the offering .... Lev. 3:11
Of Holy things .... Lev. 22:7
In giving him .... Deut. 10:18
Seeking in wilderness .... Job 24:5
Man did eat that of angels' .. Ps. 78:25
Bring forth .... Ps. 104:14

B. *Specific kinds:*

Almonds .... Gen. 43:11
Barley .... Judg. 7:13
Beans .... Ezek. 4:9
Beef .... 1 Kin. 4:22, 23
Beef stew .... 1 Kin. 19:21
Bread .... 1 Sam. 17:17
Broth .... Judg. 6:19
Cakes .... 2 Sam. 13:8
Cheese .... Job 10:10
Cucumbers .... Num. 11:5
Curds of cows .... Deut. 32:14
Eggs .... Deut. 22:6
Figs .... Num. 13:23
Fish .... Matt. 7:10
Fowl .... 1 Kin. 4:23
Fruit .... 2 Sam. 16:2
Garlic .... Num. 11:5
Goat's milk .... Prov. 27:27
Grain .... Ruth 2:14
Grapes .... Deut. 23:24
Grasshoppers .... Lev. 11:22
Herbs .... Ex. 12:8
Honey .... Is. 7:15
Leeks .... Num. 11:5
Lentils .... Gen. 25:34
Locusts .... Matt. 3:4
Meal .... Matt. 13:33
Melons .... Num. 11:5
Nuts .... Gen. 43:11
Oil .... Prov. 21:17
Olives .... Deut. 28:40
Onions .... Num. 11:5
Pomegranates .... Num. 13:23
Pottage .... Gen. 25:30
Pulse .... 2 Sam. 17:28
Quail .... Num. 11:32, 33
Raisins .... 2 Sam. 16:1
Salt .... Job 6:6
Sheep .... Deut. 14:4
Sheep's milk .... Deut. 32:14
Spices .... Gen. 43:11
Veal .... Gen. 18:7, 8
Vegetables .... Prov. 15:17
Vinegar .... Num. 6:3
Venison .... Gen. 25:28
Wild honey .... Ps. 19:10
Wine .... John 2:3, 10

Foolish—*those who misuse wisdom*

A. *Those described as:*

Clamorous woman .... Prov. 9:13

SUBJECT .... REFERENCE

Builder on sand .... Matt. 7:26
Five virgins .... Matt. 25:1-13
Galatians .... Gal. 3:1, 3
Gentiles .... Titus 3:3

B. *Things described as:*

The Heart .... Rom. 1:21
Things .... 1 Cor. 1:27
Lusts .... 1 Tim. 6:9
Questions .... 2 Tim. 2:23

C. *Characteristics of:*

Destructive .... Prov. 10:14
Despicable .... Prov. 15:20
Disappointing .... Prov. 19:13

Foolishness—*a disregard of final issues*

A. *Characteristics of:*

Form of sin .... Prov. 24:9
Originates in the heart .... Mark 7:21-23
Sign of wickedness .... Eccl. 7:25
Known by God .... Ps. 69:5

B. *Consequences of:*

Brings sorrow .... Ps. 38:4-10
Perverts man's way .... Prov. 19:3
Spiritual blindness .... 1 Cor. 1:18

Fools—*those who misuse true wisdom*

A. *Described as:*

Atheistic .... Ps. 14:1
Blasphemous .... Ps. 74:18
Contentious .... Prov. 18:6
Hypocritical .... Luke 11:39, 40
Idle .... Eccl. 4:5
Vexation .... Prov. 12:16
Materialistic .... Luke 12:16-21
Meddling .... Prov. 20:3
Mischievous .... Prov. 10:23
Mocking .... Prov. 14:9
Raging .... Prov. 14:16
Self-confident .... Prov. 28:26
Self-righteous .... Prov. 12:15
Self-sufficient .... Rom. 1:22
Slandering .... Prov. 10:18
Wasteful .... Prov 21:20
Wordy .... Eccl. 10:12-14

B. *Further characteristics of:*

Hate knowledge .... Prov. 1:22
Come to shame .... Prov. 3:35
Mock at sin .... Prov. 14:9
Cannot attain to wisdom .... Prov. 24:7
Trust in their hearts .... Prov. 28:26
Walk in darkness .... Eccl. 2:14

C. *Examples of:*

Nabal .... 1 Sam. 25:3, 25
Rehoboam .... 1 Kin. 12:8
Pharisees .... Matt. 23:17, 19
The rich man .... Luke 12:16-21

Foot

A. *To sit at, figurative of:*

Teachableness .... Luke 10:39

B. *To be under, figurative of:*

God's sovereignty .... Ps. 8:6
Christ's victory .... Ps. 110:1
Conquest .... Josh. 10:24

C. *Examples, figurative of:*

Prosperity .... Deut. 33:24
Possession .... Josh. 1:3
Reverence .... Josh. 5:15
Whole person .... Prov. 1:15

See Feet

Footman—*the infantry force*

10,000 in Samaria .... 2 Kin. 13:6, 7

Footstool

A. *Used literally of:*

In the Temple .... 2 Chr. 9:18
Prominent seat .... James 2:3

B. *Used figuratively of:*

Earth .... Matt. 5:35
Ark .... 1 Chr. 28:2
Temple worship .... Ps. 99:5
Subjection .... Acts 2:35

Forbearance of God

A. *God's withholding of judgment, upon:*

The Amorites .... Gen. 15:16
Sodom .... Gen. 18:23-32
Israel .... Neh. 9:30, 31

SUBJECT .... REFERENCE

Nineveh .... Jon. 4:10, 11
The world .... Rom. 3:25

B. *Attitudes toward:*

Not to be despised .... Rom. 2:4
To be remembered .... 2 Pet. 3:8-10
Means of preparation .... Mal. 3:1-6

Forbearance toward others

Expression of love .... 1 Cor. 13:7
Christian grace .... Eph. 4:2

Forced labor—*conscripted workers or slaves*

Prisoners of war .... Deut. 20:10, 11
As slaves .... Ex. 13:3
By Solomon .... 1 Kin. 9:20, 21

Forces—*military power*

False worship of .... Dan. 11:10, 38
Weakness of .... Zech. 4:6
Destruction of great .... Rev. 20:7-10

Forcible—*powerful*

Power of right words .... Job 6:25

Ford—*a shallow crossing of a body of water*

Of the Jabbok .... Gen. 32:22
Of the Jordan .... Judg. 3:28

Forehead—*the upper part of the face*

A. *Used literally of:*

Aaron's .... Ex. 28:38
Philistines' .... 1 Sam. 17:49
Uzziah's .... 2 Chr. 26:19, 20

B. *Used figuratively of:*

Shamelessness .... Rev. 17:5
Stronger power .... Ezek. 3:8, 9
Devotion to God .... Ezek. 9:4
Christ's true servants .... Rev. 7:3

Foreign affairs—*dealings with other countries*

War .... Gen. 14:1-16
Josh. 8:1-29
Treaties .... Josh. 9:1-27
Trade agreement .... 1 Kin. 5:1-18
Alliances .... 1 Kin. 15:16-22
1 Kin. 22:1-6
Conquest .... 2 Kin. 25:1-11

Foreigners—*sojourners in Israel*

Kept from feast .... Ex. 12:43-45
Taxable .... Deut. 15:2, 3
Figurative of Gentiles .... Eph. 2:19

See Strangers

Foreign missionaries

Jonah as .... Jon. 1:1, 2
Came from Antioch church .... Acts 13:1-3
Report of .... Acts 15:7-12

Foreknowledge of Christ

Concerning:

Men's nature .... John 1:47, 48
Men's acts .... John 6:64
His death and resurrection .... Matt. 20:18, 19
John 13:1
Jerusalem's destruction .... Luke 19:41-44
Prophetic events .... Matt. 24:1-51

Foreknowledge of God

A. *Manifested in:*

Naming a place .... 1 Kin. 13:2, 3
Matt. 2:5, 6
Setting a time .... Mark 1:15
Determining the boundaries of nations .... Acts 17:26
Indicating successive nations .... Dan. 2:26-47
Announcing Israel's captivity .... Dan. 9:2, 24
Foretelling Christ's death .... Acts 2:23

B. *Based upon God's:*

Infinite knowledge .... Is. 41:22, 23
Eternal being .... Is. 43:9-13
Foredetermination of events .... Rom. 8:29

C. *Plan of Salvation:*

Planned in eternity .... Eph. 1:3-12
Announces from beginning .. Gen. 3:15
Expanded to include Gentiles .... Gal. 3:8
Elaborated in details .... Is. 53:1-12
Visualized in prophecy .... Zech. 3:1-10

F

SUBJECT	REFERENCE
Consummated in Christ's death	John 19:30

Foresee—*to see something before it takes place*

Approaching evil	Prov. 22:3
Resurrection of Christ	Acts 2:31
Salvation of Gentiles	Gal. 3:8

Foreskin (see Circumcision)

A. *Used literally of:*

Circumcision	Gen. 17:9-17
Death	1 Sam. 18:25

B. *Figuratively of:*

Regeneration	Jer. 4:4

Forest

A. *Descriptive of wooded areas in:*

Hareth	1 Sam. 22:5
Lebanon	1 Kin. 7:2
Beth-el	2 Kin. 2:23, 24
Arabia	Is. 21:13

B. *Used figuratively of:*

Army	Is. 10:18, 19
Kingdom	Jer. 21:14
Unfruitfulness	Jer. 26:18
	Hos. 2:12

Forethought—*thinking ahead*

In meeting a danger	Gen. 32:3-23
In anticipating evil	Prov. 22:3
Concerning physical needs	Phil. 4:10-19
Neglect of, dangerous	Matt. 25:8-13
Examples of ant, in	Prov. 6:6-8
For eternal riches	Luke 12:23-34

Foretold—*made known beforehand*

Destruction of Jerusalem	Mark 13:1, 2
Gospel blessings	Acts 3:24
Paul's trip to Corinth	2 Cor. 13:2

Forewarn—*to warn beforehand*

God's judgment	Luke 12:5
God's vengeance	1 Thess. 4:6

Forfeit—*loss incurred by one's failure*

Leadership	1 Sam. 15:16-28
Possessions	Ezra 10:8
Salvation	Matt. 16:26

Forfeiting spiritual rights

Birthright	Gen. 25:34
Headship	Gen. 49:3, 4
Apostleship	Matt. 26:14-16
Spiritual heritage	Acts 13:45-48

Forger—*a counterfeiter*

Applied to David's enemies	Ps. 119:69

Forget—*be unable to remember*

God does not	Is. 49:15
Our sinful past	Phil. 3:13

Forgetful—*unable to remember*

Concerning our hearing	James 1:25

Forgetting of God

A. *Seen in forgetting God's:*

Covenant	Deut. 4:23
Works	Ps. 78:7, 11
Blessings	Ps. 103:2
Law	Ps. 119:153, 176
Word	James 1:25

B. *Characteristics of:*

Wicked	Is. 65:11
Form of backsliding	Jer. 3:21, 22
Instigated by false teachers	Jer. 23:26, 27

Forgiveness—*an act of pardon*

A. *Synonyms of:*

"Blotteth out"	Is. 43:25
"Remission"	Matt. 26:28
"Pardon"	Is. 55:7
"Remember no more"	Jer. 31:34
"Healed"	2 Chr. 30:18-20

B. *Basis of:*

God's nature	Ps. 86:5
God's grace	Luke 7:42
Shedding of blood	Heb. 9:22
Christ's death	Col. 1:14
Son's power	Luke 5:21-24
Man's repentance	Acts 2:38
Our forgiveness	Matt. 6:12-14
Faith in Christ	Acts 10:43

SUBJECT	REFERENCE

C. *Significance of:*

Shows God's righteousness	Rom. 3:25
Makes salvation real	Luke 1:77
Must be preached	Luke 24:47

Forgiving one another

A. *The measure of:*

Seventy times seven	Matt. 18:21, 22
Unlimited	Luke 17:3, 4
As God forgave us	Eph. 4:32

B. *Benefits of:*

Means of our forgiveness	Mark 11:25, 26
Restored Christian fellowship	2 Cor. 2:7-10
Spiritual cleansing	James 5:15, 16

C. *Examples of:*

Esau and Jacob	Gen. 33:4-15
Joseph	Gen. 45:8-15
Moses	Num. 12:1-13
David	2 Sam. 19:18-23
Solomon	1 Kin. 1:53
Jesus	Luke 23:34
Stephen	Acts 7:60
Paul	2 Tim. 4:16

Fork

Rendered:

"Three-pronged fork"	1 Sam. 2:13, 14
"Fork"	Is. 30:24

Form—*the outward appearance*

A. *Of physical things:*

Earth without	Gen. 1:2
Man in the womb	Is. 44:24
Sexes	1 Tim. 2:13
Idols	Is. 44:10

B. *Of spiritual realities:*

Incarnate Christ	Is. 53:2
	Rom. 9:20
Molder	Rom. 9:20
Christian truth	Rom. 6:17
New birth	Gal. 4:19

Formalism—*forms performed mechanically*

A. *Characterized by:*

Outward forms of religion	Is. 1:10-15
Lifelessness	Is. 58:1-14
Coldness	Rev. 3:14-18

B. *Sign of:*

Hypocrisy	Luke 18:10-12
Deadness	Phil. 3:4-8
Last days	2 Tim. 3:1, 5

Formula—*a prescribed method*

Success	Prov. 22:29
Prosperity	Matt. 6:32, 33
Peace	Is. 26:3
Making friends	Prov. 18:24

Fornication—*sex relations among the unmarried*

Evil of:

Comes from evil heart	Matt. 15:19
Sins against the body	1 Cor. 6:18
Excludes from God's kingdom	1 Cor. 6:9
Disrupts Christian fellowship	1 Cor. 5:9-11

Forsaken—*left deserted*

God's house	Neh. 13:11
God's children	Ps. 37:25
Messiah	Is. 53:3
God's Son	Matt. 27:46

Forsaking Christ

Disciples left	Matt. 26:56
Cause of separation	John 6:66-70

Forsaking God

A. *Manifested in:*

Going after idols	1 Kin. 11:33
Going backward	Jer. 15:6
Following human forms	Jer. 2:13

B. *Evil of:*

Manifests ingratitude	Jer. 2:5-12
Brings confusion	Jer. 17:13
Merits God's wrath	Ezra 8:22

C. *Examples of:*

Israel	2 Kin. 17:7-18
Judah	2 Chr. 12:1, 5

SUBJECT	REFERENCE

Fort—*stronghold*

In Jerusalem	2 Sam. 5:9

Fortifications—*walls or towers for protection*

Cities	1 Kin. 9:15
	2 Chr. 11:5-11
City of David	2 Sam. 5:7-9

Fortified cities

Means of protection	2 Sam. 20:6
Mighty and strong	Deut. 9:1
Conquerable	Deut. 3:5
Utterly destroyed	2 Kin. 3:19, 25
No substitute for God	Hos. 8:14

Fortress—*center of military strength*

Nation's security	2 Chr. 26:9
Illustrative of God's protection	Ps. 18:2
Typical of Christ	Is. 33:16, 17
Applied to God's prophet	Jer. 6:27

Fortunatus—*fortunate*

Christian at Corinth	1 Cor. 16:17

Forty days

Length of flood	Gen. 7:17
Israel's embalming	Gen. 50:2, 3
Moses on Mt. Sinai	Ex. 24:18
Spies in Canaan	Num. 13:25
Moses' prayer	Deut. 9:25-29
The Philistine's arrogance	1 Sam. 17:16
Elijah's fast	1 Kin. 19:2, 8
Nineveh's probation	Jon. 3:4
Christ's temptation	Luke 4:1, 2
Christ's ministry after His resurrection	Acts 1:3

Forty stripes

Limit for scourging	Deut. 25:3
Paul's, one less	2 Cor. 11:24

Forty years

Isaac's age at marriage	Gen. 25:20
Israel's diet	Ex. 16:35
Israel's wanderings	Num. 32:13
Same shoes for	Deut. 29:5
Period of rest	Judg. 3:11
Egypt's desolation	Ezek. 29:11-13
Saul's reign	Acts 13:21
David's reign	1 Kin. 2:11
Solomon's reign	1 Kin. 11:42

Forwardness—*haste; overboldness*

Peter's faltering	Matt. 14:28, 29
Paul's desire for the Corinthians	2 Cor. 8:8, 10

Foundation

A. *Used literally of:*

Cities	Josh. 6:26
Walls	Ezra 4:12
Houses	Luke 6:48
Prison house	Acts 16:26
House of the Lord	1 Kin. 6:37
Towers	Luke 14:28, 29

B. *Used figuratively of:*

Christ	Is. 28:16
	Matt. 16:18
Christian truth	Eph. 2:20
God decrees	2 Tim. 2:19
Security of parents	1 Tim. 6:19
Eternal city	Heb. 11:10

C. *Importance of:*

Must be on a rock	Matt. 7:24
	Matt. 16:18
Must be firm	Luke 6:48
Must be Christ	1 Cor. 3:11
Without, hopeless	Ps. 11:3

Foundation, Gate of the—*a gate of Jerusalem*

Levites stationed there	2 Chr. 23:2-5
Possibly the Horse Gate	2 Kin. 11:16
	2 Chr. 23:15

Fountain—*a flow of water from the earth*

Figurative of:

Mouth of the righteous	Prov. 10:11
Understanding	Prov. 16:22
Rich blessings	Jer. 2:13

Fountain Gate—*a gate of Jerusalem*

Viewed by Nehemiah	Neh. 2:13, 14
Repaired	Neh. 3:15

SUBJECT — REFERENCE

Foursquare
Altar ... Ex. 27:1
Breastplate ... Ex. 39:8, 9
City of God ... Rev. 21:16

Fowl
Bird ... Gen. 1:20, 21
Clean, edible ... Deut. 14:20
Solomon's knowledge of ... 1 Kin. 4:33

Fowler—*one who catches birds*
Law restricting ... Deut. 22:6, 7
Figurative of false prophets ... Hos. 9:8
Figurative of temptations ... Ps. 91:3
Ps. 124:7

Fox—*a dog-like animal*
A. *Described as:*
Plentiful ... Judg. 15:4
Destructive ... Neh. 4:3
Crafty ... Luke 13:32
Carnivorous ... Ps. 63:10
Living in holes ... Matt. 8:20
Loves grapes ... Song 2:15
B. *Figurative of:*
False prophets ... Ezek. 13:4
Enemies ... Song 2:15
Deceivers ... Luke 13:32

Fragment—*a part of a larger whole*
Of food ... Mark 6:43

Fragrance—*a sweet odor*
Of perfume ... John 12:3
Figurative of restoration ... Hos. 14:6

Frankincense—*a fragrant gum of a tree*
Used in holy oil ... Ex. 30:34-38
Used in meal offerings ... Lev. 2:1, 2, 15
Excluded from certain offerings ... Lev. 5:11
Used in the showbread ... Lev. 24:7
Product of Arabia ... Is. 60:6
Presented to Jesus ... Matt. 2:11
Figurative of worship ... Ps. 141:2

Fratricide—*murder of a brother*
Abel, by Cain ... Gen. 4:8
70, by Abimelech ... Judg. 9:1, 5
Amnon, by Absalom ... 2 Sam. 13:28
Adonijah, by Solomon ... 1 Kin. 2:23-25
Six, by Jehoram ... 2 Chr. 21:4
Predicted ... Matt. 10:21

Fraud—*something designed to deceive*
A. *Examples of:*
Rebekah's, on Isaac ... Gen. 27:5-36
Laban's, on Jacob ... Gen. 29:21-25
Gibeonites', on Israelites ... Josh. 9:3-9
Jonathan's, on Saul ... 1 Sam. 20:11-17
B. *Discovery of, by:*
A miracle ... Ex. 7:9-12
Events ... Matt. 28:11-15
Character ... Matt. 26:47-50

Free moral agency of man—*ability to choose*
Resulted in sin ... Gen. 2:16, 17
Recognized by God ... Gen. 4:6-10
John 7:17
Appealed to ... Is. 1:18-20
Jer. 36:3, 7

Freedom—*unrestricted action*
A. *Of the unregenerate, limited by:*
Sin ... John 8:34
Inability ... John 8:43
Satan ... John 8:41, 44
Bondage ... Rom. 6:20
Deadness ... Eph. 2:1
B. *Of the regenerate:*
Made free by Christ ... John 8:36
Freed from bondage ... Rom. 6:18, 22
Not of license ... 1 Pet. 2:16
Not of bondage again ... Gal. 5:1
Not of the flesh ... Gal. 5:13

Freewill offerings
Obligatory ... Deut. 12:6
Must be perfect ... Lev. 22:17-25
Eaten in tabernacle by the priests ... Lev. 7:16, 17
First fruits ... Prov. 3:9
According to one's ability ... Deut. 16:17

SUBJECT — REFERENCE

Willing mind ... 2 Cor. 8:10-12
Cheerful heart ... 2 Cor. 9:6, 7

Fretting—*a peevish state of mind*
Of the saints, forbidden ... Ps. 37:1, 7, 8

Friend
A. *Nature of, common:*
Interest ... 1 Sam. 18:1
Love ... 1 Sam. 20:17
Sympathy ... Job 2:11
Sacrifice ... John 15:13
B. *Value of:*
Constructive criticism ... Prov. 27:6
Helpful advice ... Prov. 27:7
Valuable in time of need ... Prov. 27:10
Always faithful ... Prov. 17:17
C. *Dangers of:*
May entice to sin ... Deut. 13:6
Some are necessary ... Prov. 14:20
Some are untrustworthy ... Ps. 41:9
D. *Examples of:*
God and Abraham ... Is. 41:8
David and Jonathan ... 1 Sam. 18:1
David and Hushai ... 2 Sam. 15:37
Elijah and Elisha ... 2 Kin. 2:1-14
Christ and His disciples ... John 15:13-15
Paul and Timothy ... 2 Tim. 1:2

Friendless—*lacking friends*
David's plight ... Ps. 142:4
Prodigal son ... Luke 15:16

Friendship
A. *Kinds of:*
True ... 1 Sam. 18:1-3
Close ... Prov. 18:24
Ardent ... 2 Cor. 2:12, 13
Treacherous ... Matt. 26:48-50
Dangerous ... Deut. 13:6-9
Unfaithful ... Job 19:14-19
False ... 2 Sam. 16:16-23
Worldly ... James 4:4
B. *Tests of:*
Continued loyalty ... 2 Sam. 1:23
Willingness to sacrifice ... John 15:13
Obedient spirit ... John 15:14, 15
Likemindedness ... Phil. 2:19-23

Frog—*a small, leaping creature*
Plague on Egypt ... Ps. 78:45
Of unclean spirits ... Rev. 16:13

Frontlets—*ornaments worn on the forehead*
Of God's Word ... Deut. 6:6-9

Frost
Figurative of God's power ... Job 37:10
Figurative of God's creative ability ... Job 38:29

Frowardness—*perverseness*
Comes from the heart ... Prov. 6:14
Issues from the mouth ... Prov. 2:12
Causes strife ... Prov. 16:28
Abomination to God ... Prov. 11:20
Hard way ... Prov. 22:5
Shall be cut off ... Prov. 10:31

Frugality—*thrift*
Manifested by Jesus ... John 6:11-13
Wrong kind ... Prov. 11:24, 25

Fruit—*product of life*
A. *Used literally of:*
Produce of trees ... Gen. 1:29
Produce of the earth ... Gen. 4:3
Progeny of livestock ... Deut. 28:51
B. *Factors destructive of:*
Blight ... Joel 1:12
Locusts ... Joel 1:4
Enemies ... Ezek. 25:4
Drought ... Hag. 1:10
God's anger ... Jer. 7:20
C. *Used figuratively of:*
Repentance ... Matt. 3:8
Industry ... Prov. 31:16, 31
Christian graces ... Gal. 5:22, 23
Holy life ... Prov. 11:30
Christian converts ... John 4:36
Christ ... Ps. 132:11
Sinful life ... Matt. 7:16
Reward of righteousness ... Phil. 1:11

SUBJECT — REFERENCE

Fruit-bearing—*productiveness of*
Old age ... Ps. 92:14
Good hearers ... Matt. 13:23
Christian converts ... Col. 1:6, 10
Abiding ... John 15:2-8

Fruitfulness
A. *Literally, dependent upon:*
Right soil ... Matt. 13:8
Rain ... James 5:18
Sunshine ... Deut. 33:14
Seasons ... Matt. 21:34
Cultivation ... Luke 13:8
God's blessing ... Acts 14:17
B. *Spiritually, dependent upon:*
Death ... John 12:24
New life ... Rom. 7:4
Abiding in Christ ... John 15:2-8
Yielding to God ... Rom. 6:13-23
Christian effort ... 2 Pet. 1:5-11
Absence of, reprobated ... Matt. 21:19

Fruitless discussion—*self-conceited talk against God*
Characteristic of false teachers ... 1 Tim. 1:6, 7

Fruit trees
Protected by Law ... Lev. 19:23-25

Frying pan
Mentioned in ... Lev. 2:7

Fulfill—*to bring to its designed end*
A. *Spoken of God's:*
Word ... Ps. 148:8
Prophecy ... 1 Kin. 2:27
Threat ... 2 Chr. 36:20, 21
Promise ... Acts 13:32, 33
Righteousness ... Matt. 3:15
Good pleasure ... 2 Thess. 1:11
Will ... Acts 13:22
B. *Spoken of the believer's:*
Love ... Rom. 13:8
Righteousness ... Rom. 8:4
Burden-bearing ... Gal. 6:2
Mission ... Col. 1:25
Ministry ... Col. 4:17

Full—*complete*
A. *Of natural things:*
Years ... Gen. 25:8
Breasts ... Job 21:24
Children ... Ps. 127:5
Wagon ... Amos 2:13
Leprosy ... Luke 5:12
B. *Of miraculous things:*
Guidance ... Judg. 6:38
Supply ... 2 Kin. 4:4, 6
Protection ... 2 Kin. 6:17
C. *Of evil emotions:*
Evil ... Eccl. 9:3
Fury ... Dan. 3:19
Wrath ... Acts 19:28
Envy ... Rom. 1:29
Cursing ... Rom. 3:14
Deadly poison ... James 3:8
Adultery ... 2 Pet. 2:14
D. *Of good things:*
Power ... Mic. 3:8
Grace, truth ... John 1:14
Joy ... John 15:11
Faith ... Acts 6:5, 8
Good works ... Acts 9:36
Holy Spirit ... Acts 11:24

Fuller—*one who treats or dyes cloth*
Outside city ... 2 Kin. 18:17
Is. 7:3
God is like ... Mal. 3:2
Makes white ... Mark 9:3

Fullness—*completion*
A. *Of time:*
Christ's advent ... Gal. 4:4
Gentile age ... Rom. 11:25
Age of grace ... Eph. 1:10
B. *Of Christ:*
Eternal Christ ... Col. 2:9
Incarnate Christ ... John 1:16
Glorified Christ ... Eph. 1:22, 23

F

SUBJECT — REFERENCE

Funeral—*burial rites*
Sad ... 1 Kin. 13:29, 30
Joyful ... Luke 7:11-17

Furlong—*a Greek measure of length* (660 linear feet)
Measure on land or sea ... Luke 24:13

Furnace—*fire made very hot*
A. *Used literally of:*
Smelting ovens ... Gen. 19:28
Baker's oven ... Hos. 7:4
B. *Used figuratively of:*
Egyptian bondage ... Deut. 4:20
Spiritual refinement ... Ps. 12:6
Lust ... Hos. 7:4
Hell ... Matt. 13:42, 50
Punishment ... Ezek. 22:18-22

Furnace, fiery
Deliverance from ... Dan. 3:8-26

Furniture
Tabernacle ... Ex. 31:7
Room ... 2 Kin. 4:8-10

Future—*that which is beyond the present*
Only God knows ... Is. 41:21-23
Revealed by:
Christ ... John 13:19
The Spirit ... John 16:13
Man's ignorance of ... Luke 19:41-44
No provision for, dangerous ... Luke 12:16-21
Proper provision for ... Matt. 6:19-34

G

Gaal—*loathing*
Son of Ebed; vilifies Abimelech ... Judg. 9:26-41

Gaash—*quaking*
Hill of Ephraim ... Judg. 2:9
Joshua's burial near ... Josh. 24:30

Gaba—*a hill*
City of Benjamin ... Josh. 18:21, 24

Gabbai—*tax gatherer*
Postexilic Benjamite ... Neh. 11:8

Gabbatha—*pavement*
Place of Pilate's court ... John 19:13

Gabriel—*man of God*
Interprets Daniel's vision ... Dan. 8:16-27
Reveals the prophecy of 70 weeks ... Dan. 9:21-27
Announces John's birth ... Luke 1:11-22
Announces Christ's birth ... Luke 1:26-38
Stands in God's presence ... Luke 1:19

Gad—*good fortune*
1. Son of Jacob by Zilpah ... Gen. 30:10, 11
Father of seven sons who founded tribal families ... Gen. 46:16
2. Descendants of the tribe of Gad ... Deut. 27:13
Census of ... Num. 1:24, 25
Territory of ... Num. 32:20-36
Captivity of ... 1 Chr. 5:26
Later references to ... Rev. 7:5
3. Seer of David ... 1 Sam. 22:5
Message of, to David ... 2 Sam. 24:10-16

Gadarenes, Gergesenes
People east of the Sea of Galilee ... Mark 5:1
Healing of demon-possessed here ... Matt. 8:28-34

Gaddi—*fortunate*
Manassite spy ... Num. 13:11

Gaddiel—*Gad* (fortune) *is God*
Zebulunite spy ... Num. 13:10

Gadi—*a Gadite*
Father of King Menahem ... 2 Kin. 15:14

Gaham—*burning*
Son of Nahor ... Gen. 22:23, 24

Gahar—*hiding place*
Head of a family of Temple servants ... Ezra 2:47

Gain through loss
A. *Elements of:*
Death first ... John 12:24
Servant status ... Mark 9:35
Discount all temporal gains ... Matt. 19:29
Loss of "life" ... Mark 8:35
B. *Examples of:*
Abraham ... Heb. 11:8-19
Moses ... Heb. 11:24-27
Ruth ... Ruth 1:16-18
Abigail ... 1 Sam. 25:18-42
Esther ... Esth. 2:1-17
Christ ... Phil. 2:5-11

Gains unjustly gotten
By:
Deceit ... Josh. 7:15-26
Violence ... Prov. 1:19
Oppression ... Prov. 22:16
Divination ... Acts 16:16, 19
Unjust wages ... James 5:4

Gaius—*commended*
1. Companion of Paul ... Acts 19:29
2. Convert at Derbe ... Acts 20:4
3. Paul's host at Corinth ... Rom. 16:23
Corinthian convert ... 1 Cor. 1:14
4. One addressed by John ... 3 John 1-5

Galal—*a rolling*
1. Levite ... 1 Chr. 9:15
2. Another Levite ... 1 Chr. 9:16

Galatia—*a province of Asia Minor*
Paul's first visit to ... Acts 16:6
Paul's second visit to ... Acts 18:23
Churches of ... 1 Cor. 16:1
Peter writes to Christians in ... 1 Pet. 1:1

Galatians—*people of Galatia*
Paul's:
Rebuke of their instability ... Gal. 1:6, 7
Defense of the Gospel among them ... Gal. 1:8-24
Concern for them ... Gal. 4:9-31
Confidence in them ... Gal. 5:7-13

Galatians, the Epistle to—*a book of the New Testament*
True gospel ... Gal. 1:6-12
Freedom from the Law ... Gal. 2:15—4:31
Fruits of the Holy Spirit ... Gal. 5:22, 23

Galbanum—*a yellowish-brown aromatic resin*
Used in the holy oil ... Ex. 30:34

Galeed—*heap of witness*
Memorial site ... Gen. 31:48

Galilean—*an inhabitant of Galilee*
Speech of ... Mark 14:70
Slaughter of ... Luke 13:1
Faith of ... John 4:45
Pilate's cruelty toward ... Luke 13:1, 2

Galilee—*circle, circuit*
A. *History of:*
Moses' prophecy concerning ... Deut. 33:18-23
Conquered by Syrians ... 1 Kin. 15:18, 20
Conquered by Assyrians ... 2 Kin. 15:29
Dialect of, distinctive ... Matt. 26:73
Herod's jurisdiction over ... Luke 3:1
Christian churches in ... Acts 9:31
B. *Christ's contacts with:*
Resided in ... Matt. 2:22
Chooses disciples from ... Matt. 4:18, 21
Fulfills prophecy concerning ... Matt. 4:14, 15
Performs many miracles in ... Matt. 4:23
People of, receive Him ... Matt. 4:25
Seeks refuge in ... John 4:1, 3
Women of, minister to Him ... Matt. 27:55
Seen in, after His resurrection ... Matt. 26:32

Galilee, Sea of
Scene of many events in Christ's life ... Mark 7:31
Called Chinnereth ... Num. 34:11
Later called Gennesaret ... Luke 5:1

Gall—*bile*
A. *Used literally of:*
Liver secretion ... Job 16:13
Poisonous herb ... Matt. 27:34
B. *Used figuratively of:*
State of sin ... Acts 8:23

Gallantry—*a chivalrous act of bravery*
Example of ... Ex. 2:16-21

Gallim—*heaps*
Village north of Jerusalem ... Is. 10:29, 30
Home of Phalti ... 1 Sam. 25:44

Gallio—*who lives on milk*
Roman proconsul of Achaia; dismisses charges against Paul ... Acts 18:12-17

Gallows—*a structure used for hanging*
Haman had made ... Esth. 5:14
Haman hanged on ... Esth. 7:9, 10
Haman's sons hanged on ... Esth. 9:13, 25

Gamaliel—*God has rewarded*
1. Leader of Manasseh ... Num. 2:20
2. Famous Jewish teacher ... Acts 22:3
Respected by people ... Acts 5:34-39

Game—*the flesh of wild animals*
Isaac's favorite dish ... Gen. 27:1-33

Games—*various kinds of contests*
Figurative examples of, (as of a race):
Requiring discipline ... 1 Cor. 9:25-27
Requiring obedience to rules ... 2 Tim. 2:5
Testing the course ... Gal. 2:2
Press on to the goal ... Phil. 3:13, 14

Gammadim—*warriors*
Manned Tyre's towers ... Ezek. 27:11

Gamul—*rewarded*
Descendant of Aaron ... 1 Chr. 24:17

Garden—*a protected and cultivated place*
A. *Notable examples of:*
In Eden ... Gen. 2:15
In Egypt ... Deut. 11:10
In Shushan ... Esth. 1:5
In Gethsemane ... Mark 14:32
A royal ... 2 Kin. 25:4
B. *Used for:*
Festivities ... Esth. 1:5
Idolatry ... Is. 65:3
Meditations ... Matt. 26:36
Burial ... John 19:41
C. *Figurative of:*
Desolation ... Amos 4:9
Fruitfulness ... Is. 51:3
Prosperity ... Is. 58:11
Righteousness ... Is. 61:11

Gardener—*one whose work is gardening*
Adam, the first ... Gen. 2:15
Christ, mistaken for ... John 20:15, 16

Gareb—*scab*
1. One of David's warriors ... 2 Sam. 23:38
2. Hill near Jerusalem ... Jer. 31:39

Garland—*ceremonial headdress or wreath*
Brought by priests of Jupiter ... Acts 14:13
Of grace ... Prov. 4:9
Granted to those who mourn ... Is. 61:3
Worn by bridegrooms ... Is. 61:10

Garlic—*an onion-like plant*
Egyptian food ... Num. 11:5

Garments (see Clothing)

Garmite—*bony*
Gentile name applied to Keilah ... 1 Chr. 4:19

SUBJECT — REFERENCE

Garner—*a place for storing grain*
Full, prayed for ... Ps. 144:13
Desolate, lamented ... Joel 1:17
Figurative of heaven ... Matt. 3:12
Translated "barn" ... Matt. 6:26

Garnish—*to adorn; to decorate*
Literally, of buildings ... Luke 11:24, 25
Figuratively, of the heavens ... Job 26:13
Of the new Jerusalem ... Rev. 21:19

Garrison—*a military post*
Smitten by Jonathan ... 1 Sam. 13:3, 4
Attacked by Jonathan ... 1 Sam. 14:1-15

Gashmu—*shower*
Opposes Nehemiah ... Neh. 6:6

Gatam—*puny*
Esau's grandson; chief of Edomite clan ... Gen. 36:11-16

Gate—*an entrance*
A. *Made of:*
Wood ... Neh. 2:3, 17
Iron ... Acts 12:10
Brass ... Ps. 107:16
Stones ... Rev. 21:12
B. *Opening for:*
Camps ... Ex. 32:26, 27
Cities ... Judg. 16:3
Palaces ... Neh. 2:8
Sanctuary ... Ezek. 44:1, 2
Tombs ... Matt. 27:60
Prisons ... Acts 12:5, 10
C. *Used for:*
Business transactions ... 1 Kin. 22:10
Legal business ... Ruth 4:1-11
Criminal cases ... Deut. 25:7-9
Proclamations ... Jer. 17:19, 20
Festivities ... Ps. 24:7
Protection ... 2 Sam. 18:24, 33
D. *Figurative of:*
Satanic power ... Matt. 16:18
Death ... Is. 38:10
Righteousness ... Ps. 118:19, 20
Salvation ... Matt. 7:13
Heaven ... Rev. 21:25

Gates of Jerusalem
1. Corner Gate ... 2 Chr. 26:9
2. Dung Gate ... Neh. 12:31
3. Of Ephraim ... Neh. 8:16
4. Fish Gate ... Zeph. 1:10
5. Fountain Gate ... Neh. 12:37
6. Horse Gate ... Jer. 31:40
7. Benjamin's Gate ... Zech. 14:10
8. Prison gate ... Neh. 12:39
9. Sheep Gate ... Neh. 3:1
10. Upper Benjamin Gate ... Jer. 20:2
11. Valley Gate ... Neh. 2:13
12. Water Gate ... Neh. 8:16

Gatekeeper
Duty of:
Zechariah ... 1 Chr. 9:21
Shallum ... 1 Chr. 9:17
Akkub ... 1 Chr. 9:17
Talmon ... 1 Chr. 9:17
Ahiman ... 1 Chr. 9:17
Ben ... 1 Chr. 15:18
Jaaziel ... 1 Chr. 15:18
Shemiramoth ... 1 Chr. 15:18
Jehiel ... 1 Chr. 15:18
Unni ... 1 Chr. 15:18
Eliab ... 1 Chr. 15:18
Benaiah ... 1 Chr. 15:18
Maaseiah ... 1 Chr. 15:18
Mattithiah ... 1 Chr. 15:18
Eliphelehu ... 1 Chr. 15:18
Mikneiah ... 1 Chr. 15:18
Obed-edom ... 1 Chr. 15:18
Jeiel ... 1 Chr. 15:18
Heman ... 1 Chr. 15:17
Asaph ... 1 Chr. 15:17
Ethan ... 1 Chr. 15:17
Berechiah ... 1 Chr. 15:23
Elkanah ... 1 Chr. 15:23
Jehiah ... 1 Chr. 15:24
Jeduthun ... 1 Chr. 16:38
Hosah ... 1 Chr. 16:38

SUBJECT — REFERENCE

Gath—*wine press*
Philistine city ... 1 Sam. 6:17
Last of Anakim here ... Josh. 11:22
Ark carried to ... 1 Sam. 5:8
Home of Goliath ... 1 Sam. 17:4
David takes refuge in ... 1 Sam. 21:10-15
David's second flight to ... 1 Sam. 27:3-12
Captured by David ... 1 Chr. 18:1
Captured by Hazael ... 2 Kin. 12:17
Rebuilt by Rehoboam ... 2 Chr. 11:5, 8
Uzziah broke down walls of ... 2 Chr. 26:6
Destruction of, prophetic ... Amos 6:1-3
Name becomes proverbial ... Mic. 1:10

Gath-hepher—*wine press of the pit*
Birthplace of Jonah ... 2 Kin. 14:25
Boundary of Zebulun ... Josh. 19:13

Gath-rimmon—*pomegranate press*
1. City of Dan ... Josh. 19:40-45
Assigned to Levites ... Josh. 21:24
2. Town in Manasseh ... Josh. 21:25

Gaza—*strong place*
1. Philistine city ... Josh. 13:3
Conquered by Joshua ... Josh. 10:41
Refuge of Anakim ... Josh. 11:22
Assigned to Judah ... Josh. 15:47
Gates of, removed by Samson ... Judg. 16:1-3
Samson deceived by Delilah here ... Judg. 16:4-20
Samson blinded here ... Judg. 16:21
Ruled by Solomon ... 1 Kin. 4:22, 24
Sin of, condemned ... Amos 1:6, 7
Judgment pronounced upon ... Jer. 25:20
Philip journeys to ... Acts 8:26
2. Ephraimite town ... 1 Chr. 7:28

Gazelle—*medium-sized antelope; translated "roe"; "roebuck"*
Used for food ... Deut. 12:15
Figurative of speed ... Prov. 6.5

Gazez—*shearer*
1. Son of Caleb ... 1 Chr. 2:46
2. Grandson of Caleb ... 1 Chr. 2:46

Gazingstock—*an object of contempt*
Ignominy of ... Nah. 3:6
Lot of Christians ... Heb. 10:33

Gazites
Inhabitants of Gaza ... Judg. 16:2

Gazzam—*consuming*
Head of family of Temple servants ... Ezra 2:48

Geba—*a hill*
City of Benjamin ... Josh. 18:24
Assigned to Levites ... Josh. 21:17
Crag rose opposite ... 1 Sam. 14:4, 5
Rebuilt by Asa ... 1 Kin. 15:22
Repossessed after the exile ... Neh. 11:31

Gebal—*mountain*
1. Phoenician maritime town ... Ezek. 27:9
Translated "stonesquarers" ... 1 Kin. 5:18
Inhabitants called Giblites ... Josh. 13:5
2. Mountainous region in Edom ... Ps. 83:7

Geber—*strong one; hero*
Solomon's purveyors ... 1 Kin. 4:13, 19

Gebim—*ditches*
Place north of Jerusalem ... Is. 10:31

Gedaliah—*Jehovah has made great*
1. Jeduthun's son ... 1 Chr. 25:3, 9
2. Pashur's son ... Jer. 38:1
3. Grandfather of Zephaniah ... Zeph. 1:1
4. Ahikam's son ... Jer. 39:14
Made governor of Judea ... 2 Kin. 25:22-26
Befriends Jeremiah ... Jer. 40:5, 6
Murdered by Ishmael ... Jer. 41:2, 18
Postexilic priest ... Ezra 10:18

Geder—*wall*
Town of Judah ... Josh. 12:13

SUBJECT — REFERENCE

Gederah—*sheepfold*
Town in Judah ... Josh. 15:36

Gederathite
Native of Gederah ... 1 Chr. 12:4

Gederite
Native of Geder ... 1 Chr. 27:28

Gederoth—*sheepfolds*
Town of Judah ... Josh. 15:41
Captured by Philistines ... 2 Chr. 28:18

Gederothaim—*two sheepfolds*
Town of Judah ... Josh. 15:36

Gedor—*wall*
1. Town of Judah ... Josh. 15:58
2. Simeonite town ... 1 Chr. 4:39
3. Town of Benjamin ... 1 Chr. 12:7
4. Family in Judah ... 1 Chr. 4:4, 18

Gehazi—*valley of vision*
Elisha's servant ... 2 Kin. 5:25
Seeks reward from Naaman ... 2 Kin. 5:20-24
Afflicted with leprosy ... 2 Kin. 5:25-27
Relates Elisha's deeds to Jehoram ... 2 Kin. 8:4-6

Gehenna (see Hell)

Geliloth—*circles*
Probably Gilgal, in the land of Benjamin ... Josh. 18:17

Gemalli—*camel driver*
Father of Ammiel ... Num. 13:12

Gemariah—*Jehovah has perfected*
1. Hilkiah's son ... Jer. 29:3
2. Shaphan's son ... Jer. 36:10-25

Gems—*precious stones*
On breastplate ... Ex. 28:15-21
Figurative of value ... Prov. 3:15; Prov. 31:10
In commerce ... Ezek. 27:16
In New Jerusalem ... Rev. 21:19-21

Genealogies—*ancestral lineage*
A. *Importance:*
Chronology ... Matt. 1:17
Priesthood claims ... Ezra 2:61, 62; Neh. 7:63, 64
Messiahship ... Matt. 1:1-17
B. *Lists of:*
Patriarchs' ... Gen. 5:1-32
Noah's ... Gen. 10:1-32
Shem's ... Gen. 10:21-32
Abraham's ... 1 Chr. 1:28-34
Jacob's ... Gen. 46:8-27
Esau's ... Gen. 36:1-43
Israel's ... 1 Chr. 9:1-44
David's ... 1 Chr. 3:1-16
Levites' ... 1 Chr. 6:1-81

Genealogy of Jesus
Seed of Abraham ... Gal. 3:16
Through Joseph ... Matt. 1:2-17
Through Mary ... Luke 3:23-38

General—*chief military authority*
Commander ... 1 Chr. 27:34; Rev. 6:15
Also rendered "princes" ... Gen. 12:15

Generation
Descriptive of:
Period of time ... Gen. 9:12
Living people or race ... Matt. 24:34
Descendants ... Matt. 12:34
Eternity ... Eph. 3:21

Genesis, Book of—*first book of the Old Testament*
Creation ... Gen. 1:1—2:25
The fall ... Gen. 3:1-24
The flood ... Gen. 6:8—7:24
Abraham ... Gen. 12:1—25:18
Isaac ... Gen. 25:19—26:35
Jacob ... Gen. 27:1—36:43
Joseph ... Gen. 37:1—50:26

SUBJECT — REFERENCE

Genius—*unusual mental ability*
Applicable to Solomon ... 1 Kin. 4:29-34

Gentiles—*non-Jews*
A. *Described as:*
Superstitious ... Deut. 18:14
Ignorant of God ... Rom. 1:21
Without the Law ... Rom. 2:14
Wicked ... Rom. 1:23-32
Idolatrous ... 1 Cor. 12:2
Uncircumcised ... Eph. 2:11
Without Christ ... Eph. 2:12
Dead in sins ... Eph. 2:1
B. *Blessings promised to:*
Included in God's covenant ... Gen. 12:3; Gal. 3:8
Given to Christ ... Ps. 2:8
Conversion predicted ... Is. 11:10; Rom. 15:9-16
Christ their light ... Is. 49:6
Included in "all flesh" ... Joel 2:28-32
Called "other sheep" ... John 10:16
C. *Conversion of:*
Predicted ... Is. 60:1-14
Proclaimed ... Matt. 4:12-17
Anticipated ... John 10:16
Questioned ... Acts 10:9-29
Realized ... Acts 10:34-48
Explained ... Acts 11:1-18
Hindered ... Acts 13:45-51
Debated ... Acts 15:1-22
Confirmed ... Acts 15:23-31
Vindicated ... Acts 28:25-29
D. *Present position:*
Barrier removed ... Eph. 2:11-22
Brought near ... Eph. 2:13
Fellow citizens ... Eph. 2:19
Fellow heirs ... Eph. 3:6
In body ... Eph. 3:6

Gentleness—*mildness combined with tenderness*
A. *Examples of:*
God's ... 2 Sam. 22:36
Christ's ... Matt. 11:29
Paul's ... 1 Thess. 2:7
Holy Spirit ... Gal. 5:22
B. *A Christian essential in:*
Living in the world ... Titus 3:1, 2
Instruction ... 2 Tim. 2:24, 25
Restoring a brother ... Gal. 6:1
Calling ... Eph. 4:1, 2
Marriage ... 1 Pet. 3:1-4
C. *Commandments concerning:*
Put it on ... Col. 3:12
Follow after ... 1 Tim. 6:11

Genubath—*theft*
Edomite ... 1 Kin. 11:20

Geology—*study of the earth*
Allusions to ... Gen. 1:9, 10

Gera—*grain*
1. Son of Bela ... Gen. 46:21
2. A descendant of Bela ... 1 Chr. 8:3-8
3. Father of Ehud ... Judg. 3:15
4. Father of Shimei ... 2 Sam. 16:5

Gerah—*smallest coin and weight among the Jews*
Twentieth part of a shekel ... Ex. 30:13; Lev. 27:25

Gerar—*region*
Town of Philistia ... Gen. 10:19
Visited by Abraham ... Gen. 20:1-18
Visited by Isaac ... Gen. 26:1-17
Abimelech, king of ... Gen. 26:1, 26

Gerizim—*cutters*
Mountain of blessing in Ephraim ... Deut. 11:29
Jotham's parable ... Judg. 9:7
Samaritans' sacred mountain ... John 4:20, 21

Gershom—*exile*
1. Son of Levi ... 1 Chr. 6:16-20
Called Gershon ... Gen. 46:11
Founder of Gershonites ... Num. 3:17-26
2. Son of Moses ... Ex. 2:21, 22
Circumcised ... Ex. 4:25
Founder of Levite family ... 1 Chr. 23:14-16
3. Descendant of Phinehas ... Ezra 8:2
4. Father of Jonathan ... Judg. 18:30

Gershon—*exile*
Eldest son of Levi ... Ex. 6:16
Father of Libni and Shimei ... Ex. 6:17

Gershonites
Descendants of Gershon (Gershom) ... Num. 3:21, 22
Tabernacle servants ... Num. 3:25, 26
Achievements of ... 1 Chr. 15:7-19

Geshan—*firm*
Descendant of Caleb ... 1 Chr. 2:47

Geshur—*bridge*
Not expelled ... Josh. 13:13
Talmai, king of ... 2 Sam. 3:3
Absalom flees to ... 2 Sam. 13:37, 38

Geshurites
1. People of Geshur ... Deut. 3:14
2. People living south of Philistia ... 1 Sam. 27:8

Gether—*fear*
Son of Aram ... Gen. 10:23

Gethsemane—*oil press*
Garden near Jerusalem ... Matt. 26:30, 36
Scene of Christ's agony and betrayal ... Matt. 26:36-56; John 18:1-12
Often visited by Christ ... Luke 22:39

Geuel—*majesty of God*
Gadite spy ... Num. 13:15, 16

Gezer—*portion*
Canaanite city ... Josh. 10:33
Not expelled ... Josh. 16:10
Assigned to Kohathites ... Josh. 21:21
Scene of warfare ... 1 Chr. 14:16
Burned by Egyptian king ... 1 Kin. 9:16
Rebuilt by Solomon ... 1 Kin. 9:17

Ghost
Christ thought to be ... Matt. 14:26; Mark 6:49
Worshiped by Egyptians ... Is. 19:3

Giah—*waterfall*
Place near Ammah ... 2 Sam. 2:24

Giants—*men of unusual size*
A. *Names of:*
Nephilim ... Gen. 6:4
Rephaim ... Gen. 14:5
Anakim ... Num. 13:28-33
Emim ... Gen. 14:5
Zamzummim ... Deut. 2:20
Goliath ... 1 Sam. 17:4-7
Og ... Deut. 3:11, 13
Others ... 2 Sam. 21:16-22
B. *Destroyed by:*
Moses ... Deut. 3:3-11
Joshua ... Josh. 11:21
David ... 1 Sam. 17:48-51
David and his men ... 2 Sam. 21:16-22

Gibbar—*huge*
Family head ... Ezra 2:20

Gibbethon—*mound*
Town of Dan ... Josh. 19:44
Assigned to Levites ... Josh. 21:20-23
Nadab's assassination at ... 1 Kin. 15:27, 28
Besieged by Omri ... 1 Kin. 16:17

Gibea—*hill*
Caleb's grandson ... 1 Chr. 2:49

Gibeah—*hill*
1. Village of Judah ... Josh. 15:57
2. Town of Benjamin ... Judg. 19:14-16
Known for wickedness ... Judg. 19:12-30
Destruction ... Judg. 20:1-48
Saul's birthplace ... 1 Sam. 10:26
Saul's political capital ... 1 Sam. 15:34
Saul's sons executed ... 2 Sam. 21:6-10
Wickedness of, long remembered ... Hos. 9:9
3. Hill or town where Eleazar was buried ... Josh. 24:33

Gibeathites
Inhabitants of Gibeah ... 1 Chr. 12:3

Gibeon—*hill town*
Hivite town ... Josh. 9:3, 7
Mighty, royal city ... Josh. 10:2
Sun stands still at ... Josh. 10:12
Assigned to Benjamin ... Josh. 18:25
Given to Levites ... Josh. 21:17
Location of tabernacle ... 1 Chr. 16:39
Joab struck Amasa ... 2 Sam. 20:8-10
Joab killed here ... 1 Kin. 2:28-34
Site of Solomon's sacrifice and dream ... 1 Kin. 3:5-15
Natives of, return from exile ... Neh. 3:7

Gibeonites—*inhabitants of Gibeon*
Deceive Joshua ... Josh. 9:3-15
Deception discovered ... Josh. 9:16-20
Made hewers of wood ... Josh. 9:21-27
Rescued by Joshua ... Josh. 10:1-43
Massacred by Saul ... 2 Sam. 21:1
Avenged by David ... 2 Sam. 21:2-9

Giddalti—*I have made great*
Son of Heman ... 1 Chr. 25:4

Giddel—*very great*
1. Head of family of Temple servants ... Ezra 2:47
2. Children of Solomon's servants ... Ezra 2:56; Neh. 7:58

Gideon—*cutter of trees*
Son of Joash ... Judg. 6:11
Called by an angel ... Judg. 6:11-24
Destroys Baal's altar ... Judg. 6:25-32
Fleece confirms call from God ... Judg. 6:36-40
His army reduced ... Judg. 7:2-8
Encouraged by a dream ... Judg. 7:9-15
Employs successful strategy ... Judg. 7:16-25
Soothes angry Ephraimites ... Judg. 8:1-3
Takes revenge on Succoth and Penuel ... Judg. 8:4-22
Refuses kingship ... Judg. 8:22, 23
Unwisely makes an ephod ... Judg. 8:24-27
Judgeship of forty years ... Judg. 8:28, 29
Father of 71 sons ... Judg. 8:30, 31
His death brings apostasy ... Judg. 8:32-35
Called Jerubbaal ... Judg. 8:35
Man of faith ... Heb. 11:32

Gideoni—*a cutting down*
Benjamite ... Num. 1:11
Father of Abidan ... Num. 1:11
Brought offering for the tribe of Benjamin ... Num. 7:60-65
Over tribal army of Benjamin ... Num. 10:24

Gidom—*a cutting off*
Village of Benjamin ... Judg. 20:45

Gier-eagle
Unclean bird ... Lev. 11:18

Gifts
A. *Of God:*
1. *Material:*
Food ... Matt. 6:25, 26
Rain ... Matt. 5:45
Health ... Phil. 2:25-30
Sleep ... Prov. 3:24
Rest ... Deut. 12:10
All things ... 1 Tim. 6:17
All needs ... Phil. 4:19
2. *Spiritual:*
Christ ... John 3:16
Holy Spirit ... Luke 11:13
Grace ... James 4:6
Wisdom ... James 1:5
Repentance ... Acts 11:18
Faith ... Eph. 2:8
New heart ... Ezek. 11:19
Peace ... Phil. 4:7
Rest ... Heb. 4:1, 9
Glory ... 1 Pet. 5:10
Eternal life ... John 10:28
B. *Of man:*
1. *Purposes of:*
Confirm covenants ... Gen. 21:27-32
Appease anger ... 1 Sam. 25:27-35
Show respect ... Judg. 6:18-21
Manifest friendship ... 1 Sam. 30:26-31
Reward ... 2 Sam. 18:11, 12

SUBJECT REFERENCE

Memorialize an event .... Esth. 9:20-22
Render worship .... Matt. 2:11
Give help .... Phil. 4:10-18
Seal friendship .... 1 Sam. 18:3, 4

2. *Times given:*
Betrothals .... Gen. 24:50-53
Weddings .... Ps. 45:12
Departures .... Gen. 45:21-24
Returns home .... Luke 15:22, 23
Times of recovery .... Job 42:10, 11
Trials, forbidden .... Ex. 23:8

C. *Spiritual:*
Listed and explained .... Rom. 12:6-8
1 Cor. 12:4-30
Came from God .... James 1:17
Assigned sovereignty .... 1 Cor. 12:28
Cannot be bought .... Acts 8:18-20
Always for edification .... Rom. 1:11
Counterfeited by Satan .... 2 Cor. 11:13-15
Spiritually discerned .... 1 Cor. 12:2, 3
Love, the supreme .... 1 Cor. 13:1-13

Gihon—*bursting forth*
1. River of Eden .... Gen. 2:13
2. Spring outside Jerusalem .... 1 Kin. 1:33-45
3. Source of water supply .... 2 Chr. 32:30

Gilalai—*weighty*
Levite musician .... Neh. 12:36

Gilboa—*bubbling fountain*
Range of limestone hills in Issachar .... 1 Sam. 28:4
Scene of Saul's death .... 1 Sam. 31:1-7
Philistines desecrate Saul's body .... 1 Sam. 31:8, 9
Under David's curse .... 2 Sam. 1:21

Gilead—*rocky or strong*
1. Grandson of Manasseh .... Num. 26:29, 30
2. Father of Jephthah .... Judg. 11:1
3. Gadite .... 1 Chr. 5:14
4. Condemned city .... Hos. 6:8
5. Mountain .... Judg. 7:3
6. Tableland east of the Jordan between the Arnon and Jabbok rivers .... Judg. 20:1
Possessed by Israel .... Num. 21:21-31
Assigned to Reuben, Gad, and Manasseh .... Deut. 3:12-17
Rebuked by Deborah .... Judg. 5:17
Hebrews flee to .... 1 Sam. 13:7
Ish-bosheth's rule over .... 2 Sam. 2:8, 9
David takes refuge in .... 2 Sam. 17:26, 27
2 Sam. 19:31
In David's census .... 2 Sam. 24:1, 6
Elijah's birthplace .... 1 Kin. 17:1
Smitten by Hazael .... 2 Kin. 10:32, 33
Mentioned by Amos .... Amos 1:3, 13

Gilead, Balm of—*an aromatic gum for medicinal purposes; figurative of:*
National healing .... Jer. 8:22
Jer. 51:8

Gilgal—*a circle, a wheel*
1. Memorial site between Jordan and Jericho .... Josh. 4:19-24
Israel circumcised .... Josh. 5:2-9
Passover observed .... Josh. 5:10
Site of Gibeonite covenant .... Josh. 9:3-15
On Samuel's circuit .... 1 Sam. 7:16
Saul made king .... 1 Sam. 11:15
Saul rejected .... 1 Sam. 13:4-15
Denounced for idolatry .... Hos. 9:15
2. Town near Bethel .... 2 Kin. 2:1
Home of Elisha .... 2 Kin. 4:38

Giloh—*exile*
Town of Judah .... Josh. 15:51

Gilonite—*Giloh native*
Ahithophel called .... 2 Sam. 15:12

Gimel
Third letter in Hebrew alphabet .... Ps. 119:17-24

Gimzo—*producing sycamores*
Village of Judah .... 2 Chr. 28:18

Gin—*a trap*
Used for catching beasts or birds .... Amos 3:5
Used figuratively .... Ps. 141:9

SUBJECT REFERENCE

Ginath—*protection*
Father of Tibni .... 1 Kin. 16:21, 22

Ginnetho—*gardener*
Postexilic priest .... Neh. 12:4

Ginnethon—*gardener*
Family head and signer of document .... Neh. 10:6
Probably same as Ginnethoi

Gird—*to put on, as a belt*
A. *Purposes of:*
Strengthening .... Prov. 31:17
Supporting clothing .... 2 Kin. 4:29

B. *Figurative of:*
Gladness .... Ps. 30:11
Truth .... Eph. 6:14
Readiness .... 1 Pet. 1:13

C. *Those girding:*
Priests .... Ex. 28:4, 39
Warriors .... 1 Sam. 18:4
Jesus .... John 13:3, 4

Girdle—*waistcloth; sash; belt*
Priestly garment .... Ex. 28:4, 39
Worn by warriors .... 1 Sam. 18:4

Girgashites—*an original tribe of Canaan*
Descendants of Canaan .... Gen. 10:15, 16
Land of, given to Abraham's descendants .... Gen. 15:18, 21
Delivered to Israel .... Josh. 24:11

Girl—*a female child*
Sold for wine .... Joel 3:3
Prophecy concerning .... Zech. 8:4, 5

Girzites—*inhabitants of Gezer*
Raided by David .... 1 Sam. 27:8

Gispa—*fondle*
Overseer .... Neh. 11:21

Gittaim—*two winepresses*
Village of Benjamin .... Neh. 11:31, 33
Refuge of the Beerothites .... 2 Sam. 4:2, 3

Gittites—*natives of Gath*
600 follow David .... 2 Sam. 15:18-23

Gittith—*belonging to Gath*
Musical instrument or tune .... Ps. 8; 81; 84 (Titles)

Giving to God
A. *Manner of:*
Without show .... Matt. 6:1-4
According to ability .... 1 Cor. 16:1, 2
Willingly .... 1 Chr. 29:3-9
Liberally .... 2 Cor. 9:6-15
Cheerfully .... 2 Cor. 9:7
Proportionately .... Mal. 3:10

B. *Examples of:*
Israelites .... Ex. 35:21-29
Princes of Israel .... Num. 7:2-28
Poor widow .... Luke 21:2-4
Macedonian churches .... 2 Cor. 8:1-5

Gizonite
Hashem thus described .... 1 Chr. 11:34

Gladness—*cheerfulness*
A. *Causes of:*
Forgiveness .... Ps. 51:8
Salvation .... Is. 51:3, 11
John 8:56
Recovery of a son .... Luke 15:32
Restoration of hope .... John 20:20
Temporal blessings .... Acts 14:17
Christ's coming .... 1 Pet. 4:13

B. *Wrong kinds of:*
At an enemy's downfall .... Prov. 24:17
At wickedness .... Hos. 7:3

Glass
A. *Used literally of:*
Crystal .... Job 28:17, 18

B. *Used figuratively of:*
Christ's glory .... 2 Cor. 3:18
God's nature .... Rev. 4:6
New Jerusalem .... Rev. 21:18, 21

SUBJECT REFERENCE

Gleaning—*gathering grain left by reapers*
Laws providing for .... Lev. 19:9, 10
Illustrated by Ruth .... Ruth 2:2-23
Gideon's reference to .... Judg. 8:2

Glede
Unclean bird of prey .... Deut. 14:12, 13

Glorification of Christ
A. *Nature of:*
Predicted .... Is. 55:5
Prayed for .... John 12:28
Not of Himself .... Heb. 5:5
Predetermined .... John 17:1

B. *Accomplished by:*
Father .... John 13:31, 32
Holy Spirit .... John 16:13, 14
Miracles .... John 11:4
His resurrection .... Acts 3:13
Believers .... Acts 21:20

Glorifying God
A. *By means of:*
Praise .... Ps. 50:23
Fruitfulness .... John 15:8
Service .... 1 Pet. 4:11
Suffering .... 1 Pet. 4:14, 16

B. *Reason for:*
Deliverance .... Ps. 50:15
Mercy shown .... Rom. 15:9
Subjection .... 2 Cor. 9:13

C. *Extent of:*
Universal .... Ps. 86:9
In body and soul .... 1 Cor. 6:20

Glory—*honor; renown*
A. *Of temporal things:*
Granted by God .... Dan. 2:37
Used to entrap .... Matt. 4:8
Not to be sought .... 1 Thess. 2:6
Quickly passes .... 1 Pet. 1:24

B. *Of believers:*
Given by God .... John 17:22
Transformed by the Spirit .... 2 Cor. 3:18
Through Christ's death .... Heb. 2:9, 10
Follows salvation .... 2 Tim. 2:10
In suffering .... Rom. 5:3
In the cross .... Gal. 6:14
Greater than present suffering .... Rom. 8:18
Hope of .... Col. 1:27
At Christ's advent .... Col. 3:4

Glory of Christ
A. *Aspects of:*
Manifested to men .... John 2:11
Not selfish .... John 8:50
Given by God .... John 17:22
Crowned with .... Heb. 2:9
Ascribed to forever .... Heb. 13:21

B. *Stages of:*
Before creation .... John 17:5
Revealed in Old Testament .... John 12:41
In His incarnation .... John 1:14
In His transfiguration .... Luke 9:28-36
In His resurrection .... Luke 24:26
In His exaltation .... 1 Tim. 3:16
At His return .... Matt. 25:31
In heaven .... Rev. 5:12

Glory of God
A. *Manifested to:*
Moses .... Ex. 24:9-17
Stephen .... Acts 7:55

B. *Reflected in:*
Christ .... John 1:14
Man .... 1 Cor. 11:7

C. *Appearances of:*
The tabernacle .... Ex. 40:34
The Temple .... 1 Kin. 8:11
At Jesus' birth .... Luke 2:8-11

D. *The believer's relation to:*
Does all for .... 1 Cor. 10:31
Illuminated by .... 2 Cor. 4:6
Will stand in presence of .... Jude 24

E. *Man's relation to:*
Corrupts .... Rom. 1:23

SUBJECT — REFERENCE

Falls short of ... Rom. 3:23
Refuse to give to God ... Acts 12:23

Glory of man

Prefigured in creation ... Heb. 2:6-8
Lost by sin ... Rom. 3:23
Soon passes away ... 1 Pet. 1:24
Removed by death ... Ps. 49:17
Restored by Christ ... 2 Cor. 5:17

Gluttony—*excessive appetite*

Sternly forbidden ... Prov. 23:1-3
Characteristic of the wicked ... Phil. 3:19
Leads to poverty ... Prov. 23:21
Christ accused of ... Matt. 11:19

Gnat—*small insect*

Third plague on Egypt, produced from dust ... Ex. 8:16-18
Used as illustration ... Matt. 23:24

Gnosticism—*early heresy based on knowledge instead of faith*

Warned against ... Col. 2:8, 18
Arrogant ... 1 Cor. 8:1
False ... 1 Tim. 6:20
Surpassed by Christ ... Eph. 3:19

Goad—*a pointed rod*

Used as a weapon ... Judg. 3:31
Figurative of pointed morals ... Eccl. 12:11
Figurative of conscience ... Acts 26:14
Sharpened by files ... 1 Sam. 13:21

Goals, spiritual

Provide motivation ... Phil. 3:12-14
Promise reward ... 1 Cor. 9:24, 25

Goat—*a domesticated animal*

A. *Literal uses of:*
Clothing ... Num. 31:20; Heb. 11:37
Milk of, food ... Prov. 27:27
Curtains ... Ex. 26:7
Bottles ... Josh. 9:4
Sacrifices ... Ex. 12:5

B. *Figurative uses of:*
Great leaders ... Jer. 50:8
Kingdom of Greece ... Dan. 8:5, 21
Wicked ... Matt. 25:32, 33

Goath—*constance*

Place near Jerusalem ... Jer. 31:39

Gob—*a pit*

Plain where Hebrews and Philistines fought ... 2 Sam. 21:18, 19
Also called Gezer ... 1 Chr. 20:4

Goblet—*a bowl or basin*

Used as a comparison ... Song 7:2
Same word translated "basins" and "cups" ... Ex. 24:6; Is. 22:24

God—*the Supreme Being*

A. *Names of:*
God ... Gen. 1:1
LORD God ... Gen. 2:4
Most high God ... Gen. 14:18-22
Lord God ... Gen. 15:2, 8
Almighty God ... Gen. 17:1
Everlasting God ... Gen. 21:33
God Almighty ... Gen. 28:3
I Am ... Ex. 3:14
Jehovah ... Ex. 6:3
Jealous ... Ex. 34:14
Eternal God ... Deut. 33:27
Living God ... Josh. 3:10
God of hosts ... Ps. 80:7
Lord of hosts ... Is. 1:24
Holy One of Israel ... Is. 43:3, 14, 15
Mighty God ... Jer. 32:18
God of heaven ... Jon. 1:9
Heavenly Father ... Matt. 6:26
King eternal ... 1 Tim. 1:17
Only Potentate ... 1 Tim. 6:15
Father of lights ... James 1:17

B. *Manifestations of:*
Face of ... Gen. 32:30
Voice of ... Deut. 5:22-26
Glory of ... Ex. 40:34, 35
Angel of ... Gen. 16:7-13
Name of ... Ex. 34:5-7
Form of ... Num. 12:6-8
Comes from Teman ... Hab. 3:3

C. *Nature of:*
Spirit ... John 4:24
One ... Deut. 6:4
Personal ... John 17:1-3
Trinitarian ... 2 Cor. 13:14
Omnipotent ... Rev. 19:6

D. *Natural attributes of:*
Incomparable ... 2 Sam. 7:22
Invisible ... John 1:18
Inscrutable ... Is. 40:28
Unchangeable ... Num. 23:19
Unequaled ... Is. 40:13-25
Unsearchable ... Rom. 11:33, 34
Infinite ... 1 Kin. 8:27
Eternal ... Is. 57:15
Omnipotence (All-powerful) ... Jer. 32:17, 27
Omnipresence (Ever-present) ... Ps. 139:7-12
Omniscience (All-knowing) ... 1 John 3:20
Foreknowledge ... Is. 48:3, 5
Wise ... Acts 15:18

E. *Moral attributes of:*
Goodness (see Goodness of God)
Hatred ... Ps. 5:5, 6
Holiness ... Rev. 4:8
Impartiality ... 1 Pet. 1:17
Justice ... Ps. 89:14
Long-suffering ... Ex. 34:6, 7
Love ... 1 John 4:8, 16
Mercy ... Lam. 3:22, 23
Truth ... Ps. 117:2
Vengeance ... Deut. 32:34-41
Wrath ... Deut. 32:22

F. *Human expressions applied to:*
Fear ... Deut. 32:26, 27
Grief ... Gen. 6:6
Repentance ... Gen. 6:7
Jealousy ... Ex. 34:14
Swearing ... Jer. 44:26
Laughing ... Ps. 2:4
Sleeping ... Ps. 78:65
Human parts ... Ex. 33:21-23

G. *Titles given to:*
Creator ... Is. 40:12, 22, 26
Judge ... Ps. 96:10, 13
King ... Ps. 47:2, 7, 8
Defender ... Ps. 18:35
Preserver ... Ps. 121:3-8
Shepherd ... Gen. 49:24

H. *Works of, described as:*
Terrible ... Ps. 66:3
Incomparable ... Ps. 86:8
Great ... Ps. 92:5
Manifold ... Ps. 104:24
Marvelous ... Ps. 139:14

I. *Ways of, described as:*
Perfect ... Ps. 18:30
Knowledgeable ... Ps. 86:11
Made known ... Ps. 103:7
Righteous ... Ps. 145:17
Not like man's ... Is. 55:8, 9
Everlasting ... Hab. 3:6
Inscrutable ... Rom. 11:33
Just and true ... Rev. 15:3

See Goodness of God; Love of God; Power of God

Godhead—*the Deity*

Revealed to mankind ... Rom. 1:20
Corrupted by mankind ... Acts 17:29
Incarnated in Jesus Christ ... Col. 2:9

Godliness—*holy living*

Profitable ... 1 Tim. 4:7, 8
Perverted ... 1 Tim. 6:5
Pursuit ... 1 Tim. 6:11
Duty ... Titus 2:12

See Holiness of Christians

Gods, false

A. *Names of:*
Adrammelech (Syria) ... 2 Kin. 17:31
Anammelech (Babylon) ... 2 Kin. 17:31
Ashtoreth (Canaan) ... 1 Kin. 11:5
Baal (Canaan) ... 1 Kin. 18:19
Baal-peor (Moab) ... Num. 25:1-9
Beelzebub (Philistine) ... Luke 11:19-23
Bel (Babylon) ... Jer. 51:44
Calf worship (Egypt) ... Ex. 32:1-6
Chemosh (Moab) ... 1 Kin. 11:7
Dagon (Philistine) ... 1 Sam. 5:1-7
Diana (Greek) ... Acts 19:35
Jupiter (Roman) ... Acts 14:12, 13
Milcom (Ammon) ... 1 Kin. 11:5
Molech (Ammon) ... 1 Kin. 11:7
Nebo (Babylon) ... Is. 46:1
Nisroch (Assyria) ... 2 Kin. 19:37
Rimmon (Syria) ... 2 Kin. 5:18
Tammuz (Babylon) ... Ezek. 8:14

B. *Evils connected with:*
Immorality ... Num. 25:1-9
Prostitution ... 2 Kin. 23:7
Divination ... Lev. 20:1-6
Sacrilege ... Dan. 5:4
Pride ... 2 Kin. 18:28-35
Persecution ... 1 Kin. 19:1-3
Child sacrifice ... Jer. 7:29-34

Gog—*mountain*

1. Reubenite ... 1 Chr. 5:4
2. Prince of Rosh, Meshech and Tubal ... Ezek. 38:2, 3
3. Leader of the final battle ... Rev. 20:8-15

Golan—*circuit*

City of Bashan ... Deut. 4:43
Assigned to Levites ... Josh. 21:27
City of refuge ... Josh. 20:8

Gold

A. *Found in:*
Havilah ... Gen. 2:11, 12
Ophir ... 1 Kin. 9:28
Sheba ... 1 Kin. 10:2, 10
Arabia ... 2 Chr. 9:14

B. *Used for:*
Money ... Matt. 10:9
Offerings ... Ex. 35:22
Presents ... Matt. 2:11
Holy adornment ... Ex. 28:4-6
Jewelry ... Gen. 24:22
Physical adornment ... Ex. 36:34, 38
Idols ... Ex. 32:31

C. *Figurative of:*
Saints refined ... Job 23:10
Babylonian empire ... Dan. 2:38
Redeemed ... 2 Tim. 2:20
Faith purified ... 1 Pet. 1:7
Christ's doctrine ... Rev. 3:18

Golden apples

Appropriate word ... Prov. 25:11

Golden city

Babylon called ... Is. 14:4

Golden rule

For Christian conduct ... Matt. 7:12; Luke 6:31

Golden wedge

Figurative term ... Is. 13:12

Goldsmiths

In the tabernacle ... Ex. 31:1-4
Refiners ... Mal. 3:3
Shapers of objects ... Ex. 25:11, 18
Makers of idols ... Num. 33:52
Guilds ... Neh. 3:8, 32

Golgotha—*place of a skull*

Where Jesus died ... Matt. 27:33-35

Goliath—*exile*

1. Giant of Gath ... 1 Sam. 17:4
Killed by David ... 1 Sam. 17:50
2. Another giant; killed by Elhanan ... 2 Sam. 21:19

See Giant

Gomer—*completion*

1. Son of Japheth ... Gen. 10:2, 3; 1 Chr. 1:5, 6
Northern nation ... Ezek. 38:6
2. Wife of Hosea ... Hos. 1:2, 3

Gomorrah—*submersion*

In a fruitful valley ... Gen. 13:10
Defeated by Chedorlaomer ... Gen. 14:8-11
Destroyed by God ... Gen. 19:23-29
Symbol of evil ... Is. 1:10
Symbol of destruction ... Amos 4:11
Punishment of ... Matt. 10:15

SUBJECT ... REFERENCE

Good for evil
- Illustrated by Joseph ... Gen. 45:5-15
- Christian duty ... Luke 6:27, 35

Goodness of God

A. *Described as:*
- Abundant ... Ex. 34:6
- Great ... Ps. 31:19
- Enduring ... Ps. 52:1
- Satisfying ... Ps. 65:4
- Universal ... Ps. 145:9

B. *Manifested in:*
- Material blessings ... Matt. 5:45; Acts 14:17
- Spiritual blessings ... Ps. 31:19
- Forgiving sin ... Ps. 86:5

C. *Saints' attitude toward:*
- Rejoice in ... Ex. 18:9
- Remember ... Ps. 145:7
- Be satisfied with ... Jer. 31:14

Gopher wood
- Used in Noah's ark ... Gen. 6:14

Gore—*to push or thrust*
- By an ox ... Ex. 21:28-32
- Rendered "push" ... Deut. 33:17
- Rendered "thrust" ... Ezek. 34:21

Goshen
1. District of Egypt where Israel lived ... Gen. 45:10
   - Land of pastures ... Gen. 47:1-6
   - Called the land of Rameses ... Gen. 47:6-11
2. Region in south Judah ... Josh. 10:41
3. City of Judah ... Josh. 15:51

Gospel—*good news*

A. *Described as, of:*
- God ... Rom. 1:1
- Christ ... 2 Cor. 2:12
- The kingdom ... Matt. 24:14
- Grace of God ... Acts 20:24
- Peace ... Eph. 6:15
- Salvation ... Eph. 1:13
- Glory of Christ ... 2 Cor. 4:4

B. *Defined as:*
- Of supernatural origin ... Gal. 1:10-12
- God's power ... Rom. 1:16
- Mystery ... Eph. 6:19
- Revelation ... Eph. 3:1-6
- Deposit of truth ... 1 Cor. 15:1-4

C. *Source of:*
- Hope ... Col. 1:23
- Salvation ... 2 Thess. 2:13, 14
- Faith ... Acts 15:7
- Life ... 1 Cor. 4:15
- Immortality ... 2 Tim. 1:10
- Afflictions ... Phil. 1:16
- Peace ... Eph. 6:15

D. *Proclaimed by or in:*
- Old Testament ... Gal. 3:8
- Prophets ... Rom. 1:1, 2
- John ... Mark 1:1-4
- Jesus Christ ... Mark 1:14, 15
- Chosen men ... 1 Pet. 1:12

E. *Should be proclaimed:*
- To all people ... Mark 16:15, 16
- Everywhere ... Rom. 15:19, 20
- At all times ... Rev. 14:6
- With great urgency ... 1 Cor. 9:16
- With boldness ... Eph. 6:19
- As a testimony ... Matt. 24:14

F. *Proclaimers of, are:*
- Separated ... Rom. 1:1
- Called ... Acts 16:10
- Entrusted with it ... 1 Thess. 3:2
- Set apart for its defense ... Phil. 1:7, 16, 27
- Under divine orders ... 1 Cor. 9:16

G. *Negative reactions to, some:*
- Disobey ... 2 Thess. 1:8
- Are blinded to ... 2 Cor. 4:3, 4
- Hinder ... 1 Cor. 9:12
- Pervert ... Gal. 1:7

H. *Believer's reaction to:*
- Believing ... Eph. 1:13
- Submitting to ... 2 Cor. 9:13
- Being established by ... Rom. 16:25
- Living by ... Phil. 1:27
- Defending ... Phil. 1:7, 16, 27

Gossip—*idle talk or rumors about others*
- Forbidden ... Lev. 19:16
- Cause of friction ... Prov. 16:28
- Warns against associating with ... Prov. 20:19
- Called "talebearer" ... Prov. 11:13; Prov. 20:19
- Called "infamy" ... Ezek. 36:3
- Called "whisperers" ... Rom. 1:29
- Called "whisperings" ... 2 Cor. 12:20
- Called "tattlers" ... 1 Tim. 5:13

Gourd—*a running plant with large leaves*
- One variety: Shade ... Jon. 4:6-10
- Poison variety ... 2 Kin. 4:39-41

Government—*recognized rulership*

A. *Types of:*
- Patriarchal, in families ... Gen. 27:29-39
- Theocratic, under God ... Ex. 18:13-26
- Monarchial, under kings ... 1 Sam. 8:5-22
- Antichristian, under antichrist ... 2 Thess. 2:3-12
- Absolute and final, under Christ ... Is. 9:6, 7

B. *Characteristics of:*
- Ruled by God ... Is. 45:1-13
- Successions of, determined by God ... Dan. 2:28-45
- Ignorant of spiritual things ... 1 Cor. 2:8
- Providentially used ... Acts 26:32

C. *Christian attitude toward:*
- Occupy positions in ... Gen. 42:6
- Pay taxes to ... Matt. 22:18-21
- Pray for ... 1 Tim. 2:1-3
- Obey rules of ... Rom. 13:1-7
- But obey God first ... Acts 5:29

Governor—*a ruler*
- Title used of Zerubbabel ... Ezra 2:63
- Applied to Nehemiah ... Neh. 8:9
- Prime minister ... Gen. 42:6
- Provincial ruler ... Acts 23:24, 26
- Chief of ceremonies ... John 2:8, 9
- Household teachers ... Gal. 4:2
- Magistrates ... Matt. 10:18
- Christ ... Matt. 2:6

Gozan—*quarry*
- Town and district in Mesopotamia ... 2 Kin. 17:6
- Israelites deported to ... 2 Kin. 18:11

Grace—*unmerited favor*

A. *Descriptive of:*
- God's favor ... Gen. 6:8
- God's forgiving mercy ... Rom. 11:6
- Gospel ... John 1:17
- Gifts (miracles, etc.) ... 1 Pet. 4:10
- Eternal life ... 1 Pet. 1:13

B. *Is the source of:*
- Salvation ... Acts 15:11
- Call of God ... Gal. 1:15
- Faith ... Acts 18:27
- Justification ... Rom. 3:24
- Forgiveness ... Eph. 1:7
- Consolation ... 2 Thess. 2:16

C. *Described as:*
- All-abundant ... Rom. 5:15-20
- All-sufficient ... 2 Cor. 12:9
- Glorious ... Eph. 1:6
- Great ... Acts 4:33
- Manifold ... 1 Pet. 4:10
- Rich ... Eph. 2:4, 5
- Undeserved ... 1 Tim. 1:12-16

D. *Believers:*
- Are under ... Rom. 6:14
- Receive ... John 1:16
- Stand in ... Rom. 5:2
- Abound in ... 2 Cor. 9:8
- Be strong in ... 2 Tim. 2:1
- Grow in ... 2 Pet. 3:18
- Speak with ... Eph. 4:29
- Inherit ... 1 Pet. 3:7

E. *Dangers of, can:*
- Be abused ... Jude 4
- Be frustrated ... Gal. 2:21
- Be turned from ... Gal. 5:3, 4

Graces, Christian
- Growth in, commanded ... 2 Pet. 1:5-8

Grafting—*uniting a portion of one plant to another*
- Gentiles, on Israel's stock ... Rom. 11:17, 24

Grain—*the generic term for cereal grasses*

A. *Features regarding:*
- Grown in Palestine ... 2 Kin. 18:32
- Article of food ... Gen. 42:1, 2, 19
- Offered mixed with oil ... Lev. 2:14, 15
- Roasted ... Ruth 2:14

B. *Figurative of:*
- Blessings ... Ezek. 36:29
- Christ ... John 12:24
- Life's maturity ... Job 5:26

Grandchildren
- Lot becomes father of, through incest ... Gen. 19:30-38
- Abdon's ... Judg. 12:13, 14
- Widow's ... 1 Tim. 5:4
- Iniquity visited on ... Ex. 34:7
- Served idols ... 2 Kin. 17:41
- Crown of old men ... Prov. 17:6
- Practice piety toward family ... 1 Tim. 5:4

Grandmother
- Lois thus called ... 2 Tim. 1:5

Grapes
- Grown in Palestine ... Num. 13:23
- Used for wine ... Num. 6:3
- "Sour grapes" ... Ezek. 18:2
- Figurative of judgment ... Rev. 14:18
- See Vine, vineyard

Grass

A. *Features:*
- Created by God ... Gen. 1:11, 12
- Produced by rain ... Deut. 32:2
- Adorns earth ... Matt. 6:30
- Failure of, a calamity ... Jer. 14:5, 6
- Nebuchadnezzar eats ... Dan. 4:1, 33
- Disappears ... Prov. 27:25
- Withered away ... Is. 15:6

B. *Figurative of:*
- Life's shortness ... Ps. 90:5, 6
- Prosperous wicked ... Ps. 92:7
- God's grace ... Ps. 72:6

Grasshopper—*locust*
- Used as food ... Lev. 11:22
- Inferiority ... Num. 13:33
- Insignificance ... Is. 40:22
- Burden ... Eccl. 12:5
- Destroys crops ... Ps. 78:46
- See Locust

Gratitude (see Thankfulness)

Gratitude to man

A. *Reasons for:*
- Deliverance from an enemy ... Judg. 8:22, 23
- Deliverance from death ... 1 Sam. 26:21-25
- Interpretation of a dream ... Dan. 2:46-48
- Rescue from murderers ... Esth. 6:1-6

B. *Examples of:*
- Ruth to Boaz ... Ruth 2:8-17
- Israelites to Jonathan ... 1 Sam. 14:45
- Abigail to David ... 1 Sam. 25:40-42
- David to Jonathan ... 2 Sam. 9:1
- David to Hanum ... 2 Sam. 10:1, 2
- Pagans to Paul ... Acts 28:1-10

Grave—*a place of burial*

A. *Features regarding:*
- Dug in ground ... Gen. 50:5
- Some in caves ... Gen. 23:9
- Marker set on ... Gen. 35:20
- Touching of, makes unclean ... Num. 19:16, 18

B. *Resurrection from:*
- Symbolized ... Ezek. 37:1-14

Graveclothes—*clothes for the dead*
- Lazarus attired in ... John 11:43, 44
- Jesus lays His aside ... Luke 24:12

G

SUBJECT — REFERENCE

Gravel—*small pebbles*

Figurative of:

- Distress … Prov. 20:17
- Numerous offspring; rendered "grains" … Is. 48:19
- Suffering … Lam. 3:16

Graven image—*an idol*

- Of Canaanites, to be destroyed … Deut. 7:1-5, 25; Deut. 12:2, 3
- Cause of God's anger … Ps. 78:58; Jer. 8:19

See Idols, idolatry

Great

A. *Descriptive of:*

- Sun and moon … Gen. 1:16
- Euphrates … Gen. 15:18
- Mediterranean … Josh. 1:4
- Nineveh … Jon. 3:2, 3
- Babylon … Rev. 14:8

B. *Applied to God's:*

- Nature … Deut. 10:17
- Signs and miracles … Deut. 29:3
- Works … Judg. 2:7
- Victory … 2 Sam. 23:10, 12
- Mercy … 2 Chr. 1:8
- Wrath … 2 Chr. 34:21
- Glory … Ps. 21:5
- Power … Ps. 147:5

C. *Descriptive of Christ as:*

- God … Titus 2:13
- Prophet … Luke 7:16
- Priest … Heb. 4:14
- King … Luke 1:32, 33; Rev. 11:17
- Shepherd … Heb. 13:20

D. *Applied to the believer's:*

- Reward … Matt. 5:12
- Faith … Matt. 15:28
- Joy … Acts 8:8
- Zeal … Col. 4:13
- Affliction … 2 Cor. 8:2
- Boldness … 1 Tim. 3:13
- Promises … 2 Pet. 1:4

E. *Applied to final things:*

- Gulf fixed … Luke 16:26
- Wrath … Rev. 6:17
- Tribulation … Rev. 7:14
- White throne judgment … Rev. 20:11

Great fish

- Swallows Jonah … Jon. 1:17

Greatness, true

Hinges on:

- God's gentleness … Ps. 18:35
- Great work … Neh. 6:3
- Unselfishness … Jer. 45:5
- Servanthood … Matt. 23:11
- God's estimate … Matt. 5:19

Grecians

1. The people of Greece … Joel 3:6
2. Greek-speaking Jews … Acts 6:1
   - Hostile to Paul … Acts 9:29
   - Gospel preached unto … Acts 11:20

Greece—*the southern extremity of the Balkan peninsula*

- Prophecy concerning … Dan. 8:21
- Paul preaches in … Acts 17:16-31
- Called Javan … Is. 66:19

Greed—*excessive desire for things*

A. *Productive of:*

- Defeat … Josh. 7:11-26
- Murder … 1 Kin. 21:1-16
- Betrayal … Luke 22:1-6

B. *Examples of:*

- Samuel's sons … 1 Sam. 8:1, 3
- False prophets … Is. 56:10,11
- False teachers … 2 Pet. 2:14, 15

See Avarice; Covetousness

Greek

1. Native of Greece … Acts 16:1
   - Spiritual state of … Rom. 10:12
   - Some believe … Acts 14:1
2. Foreigners speaking Greek … John 12:20
3. Language of Greece … Acts 21:37

SUBJECT — REFERENCE

Greyhound—*a tall, slender hound*

- Poetically described … Prov. 30:29, 31

Grief

A. *Causes of:*

- Son's marriage … Gen. 26:34, 35
- Barrenness … 1 Sam. 1:11, 16
- Death … 2 Sam. 19:1, 2
- Disease … Job 2:11-13
- Sinners … Ps. 119:158
- Foolish son … Prov. 17:25

B. *Descriptive of:*

- Messiah … Is. 53:3, 4, 10
- God … Ps. 95:10
- Holy Spirit … Eph. 4:30
- God's saints … Ps. 139:21

See Sorrow

Groves

1. Tamarisk tree … Gen. 21:33; 1 Sam. 22:6
2. Idolatrous shrine (Asherah) … Deut. 12:3; 2 Kin. 21:7
   - Destruction of, commanded … Ex. 34:13
   - Israel's fondness for … Jer. 17:2
   - Punishment … Is. 27:9

Grow—*to increase*

A. *Of material things:*

- Power … 2 Sam. 3:1
- Age … Josh. 23:1
- Sound … Ex. 19:19

B. *Of immaterial things:*

- Spirituality … Luke 2:40
- God's hand … Num. 11:23
- Old covenant … Heb. 8:13
- God's kingdom … Luke 13:18, 19

Growth, spiritual

A. *Expressed by words indicating:*

- Fruitfulness … John 15:2, 5
- Increase … 2 Cor. 9:10
- Addition … 2 Pet. 1:5-10
- Growth … 1 Pet. 2:2
- Building up … Jude 20

B. *Hindrances to:*

- Lack of knowledge … Acts 18:24-28
- Carnality … 1 Cor. 3:1-3
- Instability … Eph. 4:14, 15
- Dullness … Heb. 5:11-14

Grudge—*to harbor resentment*

- Forbidden … Lev. 19:18

Guard

A. *Aspects of:*

- Called mighty … 2 Sam. 23:8-23
- Often foreigners … 2 Sam. 20:7
- Respected … Jer. 40:1-5

B. *Duties of:*

- Run before chariots … 2 Sam. 15:1
- Form a military guard … 1 Sam. 22:17
- Keep watch … 2 Kin. 11:6
- Carry out commandments … Jer. 39:11-14
- Execute criminals … Dan. 2:14

Guardian—*a custodian*

- Christ, of our souls … 2 Tim. 1:12

Guardian angels

- Helpers … Gen. 24:7; Heb. 1:1-14
- Protectors … Ps. 91:11; Matt. 18:10
- Aided apostles … Acts 5:17-19; Acts 8:26

Gudgodah—*cutting; cleft*

- Israelite encampment … Deut. 10:7
- Also called Hor-hagidgad … Num. 33:32

Guest

Kinds of:

- Terrified … 1 Kin. 1:41, 49
- Dead … Prov. 9:18
- Unwelcomed … Prov. 25:17
- Unprepared … Matt. 22:11
- Criticized … Luke 7:39-50
- Congenial … Acts 18:1-3
- Courteous … 1 Cor. 10:27
- Angelic … Heb. 13:2

SUBJECT — REFERENCE

Guidance, divine

- To the meek … Ps. 25:9
- To the wise … Prov. 23:19
- To the good man … Ps. 112:5
- In God's strength … Ex. 15:13
- On every side … 2 Chr. 32:22
- With God's eye … Ps. 32:8
- With counsel … Ps. 73:24
- Like a flock … Ps. 78:52
- By skillfulness … Ps. 78:72
- Continually … Is. 58:11

Guide—*a leader*

A. *Kinds of:*

- Human … Num. 10:29-32
- Supernatural … Ex. 13:20-22
- Blind … Matt. 23:16, 24

B. *Goals of:*

- Peace … Luke 1:79
- Truth … John 16:13
- God's word … Acts 8:30, 31

Guilt, universality of

Described as:

- Filthy rags … Is. 64:6
- Fall short … Rom. 3:23
- All declared … Rom. 5:12-14; Gal. 3:22

Guni—*colored*

1. One of Naphtali's sons … Gen. 46:24; 1 Chr. 7:13
   - Descendants called Gunites … Num. 26:48
2. Gadite … 1 Chr. 5:15

Gur—*lion's cub*

- Site of Ahaziah's death … 2 Kin. 9:27

Gur-baal—*sojourn of Baal*

- Place in Arabia … 2 Chr. 26:7

H

Haahashtari—*runner*

- Son of Ashur … 1 Chr. 4:5, 6

Habaiah—*Jehovah has hidden*

- Father of excommunicated Jewish priests … Ezra 2:61, 62
- Also spelled Hobaiah … Neh. 7:63, 64

Habakkuk—*embrace*

A. *Complaints of:*

- God's silence … Hab. 1:2-4
- God's response … Hab. 1:5-11
- Chaldean cruelty … Hab. 1:12-17
- God's response … Hab. 2:1-20

B. *Prayer of:*

- Praise of God … Hab. 3:1-19

Habakkuk, the Book of—*a book of the Old Testament*

- Author … Hab. 1:1
- Setting … Hab. 1:2-4
- Historical reference … Hab. 1:6
- The life of the just … Hab. 2:4

Habaziniah

- Grandfather of Jaazaniah … Jer. 35:3

Habergeon—*a coat of mail*

- Worn by priests … Ex. 28:32; Ex. 39:23

Habit—*a custom*

Kinds of:

- Doing evil … Jer. 13:23
- Doing good … Acts 10:38
- Of animals, instinctive … 2 Pet. 2:22

Habitation—*a place of residence*

A. *Used literally of:*

- Canaan … Num. 15:2
- A tree … Dan. 4:20, 21
- Nation … Acts 17:26

B. *Used figuratively of:*

- Eternity … Is. 57:15

SUBJECT — REFERENCE

God's throne ... Is. 63:15
Sky ... Hab. 3:11
Heaven ... Luke 16:9
New Jerusalem ... Is. 33:20

Habor—*joined together*
On the river of Gozan ... 2 Kin. 17:6

Hachaliah—*darkness of Jehovah*
Father of Nehemiah ... Neh. 1:1

Hachilah—*dark, gloomy*
Hill in the wilderness of Ziph where David hid ... 1 Sam. 23:19-26

Hachmoni
Tutor to king's son ... 1 Chr. 27:32

Hadad—*fierceness*
1. Ishmael's son ... Gen. 25:13, 15; 1 Chr. 1:30
2. King of Edom ... Gen. 36:35, 36
3. Another king of Edom ... 1 Chr. 1:50
   Called Hadar ... Gen. 36:39
4. Edomite leader ... 1 Kin. 11:14-25

Hadadezer—*Hadad is a help*
King of Zobah ... 2 Sam. 8:3-13
Defeated by David ... 2 Sam. 10:6-19

Hadadrimmon—*Hadad and Rimmon*
Name of the two Aramean deities; a place in Jezreel ... Zech. 12:11

Hadashah—*new*
Village of Judah ... Josh. 15:37

Hadassah—*myrtle*
Esther's Jewish name ... Esth. 2:7

Hadattah—*new*
Town in south Judah; probably should be read as Hazorhadattah ... Josh. 15:25

Hadid—*sharp*
Town of Benjamin ... Neh. 11:31, 34

Hadlai—*restful*
Ephraimite ... 2 Chr. 28:12

Hadoram—*Hadar is exalted*
1. Son of Joktan ... Gen. 10:26, 27
2. Son of Tou ... 1 Chr. 18:9, 10
3. Rehoboam's tribute officer ... 2 Chr. 10:18
   Called Adoram ... 1 Kin. 12:18
   Probably same as Adoniram ... 1 Kin. 4:6

Hadrach—*periodical return*
Place in Syria ... Zech. 9:1

Hagab—*locust*
Head of a family of Temple servants ... Ezra 2:46

Hagaba—*locust*
Head of a family of Temple servants ... Neh. 7:46, 48

Hagabah—*locust*
Head of a family of Temple servants ... Ezra 2:43, 45

Hagar, Agar—*flight*
Sarah's Egyptian handmaid ... Gen. 16:1
Flees from Sarah ... Gen. 16:5-8
Returns; becomes mother of Ishmael ... Gen. 16:3-16
Abraham sends her away ... Gen. 21:14
Paul's allegory of ... Gal. 4:22-26

Hagarites
Nomad people east of Gilead ... 1 Chr. 5:10-22
Called Hagarenes ... Ps. 83:6

Hagerite—*a descendant of Hagar*
Jaziz, keeper of David's flocks ... 1 Chr. 27:31

Haggai—*festive*
Postexilic prophet ... Ezra 5:1, 2
Contemporary of Zechariah ... Ezra 6:14
Prophecies of, dated in reign of Darius Hystaspes (520 B.C.) ... Hag. 1:1, 15; Hag. 2:1, 10, 20

SUBJECT — REFERENCE

Haggai, the Book of—*a book of the Old Testament*
Purpose ... Hag. 1:1-15
The coming glory ... Hag. 2:4-9
On Levitical cleanliness ... Hag. 2:10-14

Haggedolim
Father of Zabdiel ... Neh. 11:14

Haggeri—*a Hagerite*
A mighty man of David's guard ... 1 Chr. 11:38
Called "Bani the Gadite" in ... 2 Sam. 23:36

Haggi—*festal*
Son of Gad ... Gen. 46:16
Head of tribal family ... Num. 26:15

Haggiah—*festival of Jehovah*
Merarite Levite ... 1 Chr. 6:30

Haggith—*festal*
One of David's wives ... 2 Sam. 3:4
Mother of Adonijah ... 1 Kin. 1:5

Hail—*frozen rain*
Illustrative of God's:
Wonders ... Job 38:22
Glory ... Ps. 18:12
Chastening ... Is. 28:2, 17
Wrath ... Rev. 8:7

Hail—*a salutation* ("Hale be thou")
Gabriel to Mary ... Luke 1:26-28
Judas to Christ ... Matt. 26:47-49
Soldiers to Christ ... Matt. 27:27-29

Hair
A. *Of women:*
   Covering ... 1 Cor. 11:15
   Uses of ... Luke 7:38
   Prohibitions concerning ... 1 Tim. 2:9; 1 Pet. 3:3
B. *Of men:*
   Not to be worn long ... 1 Cor. 11:14
   Rules for cutting ... Lev. 19:27
   Long, during Nazarite vow ... Num. 6:5
   Gray, sign of age ... 1 Sam. 12:2
   Absalom's beautiful ... 2 Sam. 14:25, 26
   Numbered ... Matt. 10:30
C. *Figurative of:*
   Minuteness ... Judg. 20:16
   Complete safety ... 1 Sam. 14:45
   Fear ... Job 4:14, 15
   Great numbers ... Ps. 40:12
   Grief ... Ezra 9:3
   Respect ... Prov. 16:31
   Attractiveness ... Song 5:2, 11
   Affliction ... Is. 3:17, 24
   Entire destruction ... Is. 7:20
   Decline and fall ... Hos. 7:9

Hakkatan—*the smallest*
Johanan's father ... Ezra 8:12

Hakkoz—*the thorn*
Descendant of Aaron ... 1 Chr. 24:1, 10
Descendants of, kept from priesthood ... Ezra 2:61, 62

Hakupha—*crooked*
Ancestor of certain Temple servants ... Ezra 2:43, 51

Halah—*a district of Assyria*
Israelite captives carried to ... 2 Kin. 17:6

Halak—*smooth*
Mountain near Seir ... Josh. 11:17

Half-shekel tax—*a temple tax*
Commanded ... Ex. 30:13, 14
Also called "two-drachma tax" ... Matt. 17:24-27

Half-tribe of Manasseh—*the part of Manasseh east of the Jordan*
Clans of:
Machir ... Josh. 17:1
Hezron ... 1 Chr. 2:21-23

Halhul—*contorted*
A city in Judah ... Josh. 15:20, 21, 58

SUBJECT — REFERENCE

Hali—*necklace*
Town of Asher ... Josh. 19:25

Hallohesh—*enchanter*
Repairs walls and signs covenant ... Neh. 3:12; Neh. 10:24

Ham—*hot*
1. Noah's youngest son ... Gen. 5:32
   Enters ark ... Gen. 7:7
   His immoral behavior merits Noah's curse ... Gen. 9:22-25
   Father of descendants of repopulated earth ... Gen. 10:6-20
2. Poetical name of Egypt ... Ps. 105:23, 27
3. Hamites at Gedor ... 1 Chr. 4:39, 40
4. Place where Chedorlaomer defeated the Zuzim ... Gen. 14:5

Haman
Plots to destroy Jews ... Esth. 3:3-15
Invited to Esther's banquet ... Esth. 5:1-14
Forced to honor Mordecai ... Esth. 6:5-14
Hanged on his own gallows ... Esth. 7:1-10

Hamath—*fortification*
Hittite city north of Damascus ... Josh. 13:5
Spies visit ... Num. 13:21
Israel's northern limit ... Num. 34:8
Solomon's boundary ... 1 Kin. 8:65
Storage cities built ... 2 Chr. 8:3, 4
Captured by the Assyrians ... 2 Kin. 18:34
People of, deported to Samaria ... 2 Kin. 17:24, 30
Israelites exiled ... Is. 11:11
Mentioned by Jeremiah ... Jer. 49:23
Limit of Ezekiel's prophecy ... Ezek. 47:16-20

Hamathites
People of Hamath ... Gen. 10:18

Hamath-zobah—*fortress of Zobah*
Captured by Solomon ... 2 Chr. 8:3

Hammath—*hot springs*
1. City of Naphtali ... Josh. 19:35
   Probably the same as Hammon and Hammothdor ... 1 Chr. 6:76
2. Founder of the Rechabites ... 1 Chr. 2:55

Hammedatha—*given by Ham*
Father of Haman ... Esth. 3:1

Hammelech—*the king*
Father of Jerahmeel ... Jer. 36:26

Hammer—*a workman's tool*
A. *Literal uses of:*
   Drive tent pegs ... Judg. 4:21
   Not used in Temple ... 1 Kin. 6:7
   Straighten metal ... Is. 41:7
B. *Figurative uses of:*
   God's Word ... Jer. 23:29
   Babylon ... Jer. 50:23

Hammoleketh—*the queen*
Sister of Gilead ... 1 Chr. 7:17, 18

Hammon—*glowing*
1. Village of Asher ... Josh. 19:28
2. Town of Naphtali ... 1 Chr. 6:76
See Hammath 1

Hammoth-dor—*hot springs of Dor*
City of refuge ... Josh. 21:32
See Hammath 1

Hamonah—*multitude*
Site of Gog's defeat ... Ezek. 39:11-16

Hamon-gog—*multitude of Gog*
Memorial name of Gog's burial ... Ezek. 39:11

Hamor—*ass*
Sells land to Jacob ... Gen. 33:18-20
Killed by Jacob's sons ... Gen. 34:1-31

Hamuel—*anger of God*
Son of Mishma ... 1 Chr. 4:26

Hamul—*spared*
Son of Pharez ... Gen. 46:12
Founder of tribal family ... Num. 26:21

SUBJECT REFERENCE

Hamutal—*kinsman of dew*

Wife of King Josiah ... 2 Kin. 23:30, 31
Mother of Jehoahaz and Zedekiah ... 2 Kin. 24:18
Daughter of Jeremiah of Libnah ... Jer. 52:1

Hanameel—*God has pitied*

Cousin of Jeremiah the prophet ... Jer. 32:7

Hanan—*merciful*

1. One of David's mighty men ... 1 Chr. 11:26, 43
2. Benjamite ... 1 Chr. 8:23, 25
3. Descendant of Jonathan ... 1 Chr. 8:38
4. Prophet ... Jer. 35:4
5. Head of Temple servants ... Ezra 2:46
6. Explained Law ... Neh. 8:7
7. Nehemiah's assistant treasurer ... Neh. 13:13

8, 9. Signers of the covenant ... Neh. 10:22, 26

Hananeel—*God has been gracious*

Tower at Jerusalem ... Jer. 31:38

Hanani—*gracious*

1. Father of Jehu the prophet ... 1 Kin. 16:1, 7
   Rebukes Asa; confined to prison ... 2 Chr. 16:7-10
2. Son of Heman; head of Levitical course ... 1 Chr. 25:4, 25
3. Priest who divorced his foreign wife ... Ezra 10:20
4. Nehemiah's brother; brings news concerning the Jews ... Neh. 1:2
   Becomes a governor of Jerusalem ... Neh. 7:2
5. Levite musician ... Neh. 12:35, 36

Hananiah—*Jehovah has been gracious*

1. Benjamite chief ... 1 Chr. 8:24, 25
2. Son of Heman; head of Levitical division ... 1 Chr. 25:4, 23
3. One of King Uzziah's captains ... 2 Chr. 26:11
4. Father of Zedekiah ... Jer. 36:12
5. False prophet who contradicts Jeremiah ... Jer. 28:1-17
6. Ancestor of Irijah ... Jer. 37:13-15
7. Hebrew name of Shadrach ... Dan. 1:6, 7, 11
8. Son of Zerubbabel ... 1 Chr. 3:19-21
   Probably same as Joanna ... Luke 3:27
9. Son of Bebai; divorced his foreign wife ... Ezra 10:28
10. Postexilic workman ... Neh. 3:8, 30
11. Postexilic priest ... Neh. 12:41
12. Postexilic chief; signs document ... Neh. 10:23
13. Postexilic ruler ... Neh. 7:2
14. Priest of Joiakim's time ... Neh. 12:12

Hand

Mysterious ... Dan. 5:1-6
Healing withered ... Mark 3:1-3
Offending, to be cut off ... Matt. 18:8

Handbreadth—*a linear measurement*

Border of ... Ex. 37:12
Figurative of human life ... Ps. 39:5

Handful

Of fine flour ... Lev. 2:2—5:12
Of grain offering ... Num. 5:26
Of barley ... Ezek. 13:19

Handkerchief

Touch of, brings healing ... Acts 19:12
Rendered "napkin" ... John 11:44
John 20:7

Handle—*to manage with the hands*

Used literally for:

Hold ... 2 Chr. 25:5
Touch ... Luke 24:39
Feel ... Ps. 115:7

Used figuratively for:

Give attention ... Prov. 16:20
Treat ... Mark 12:4

SUBJECT REFERENCE

Handmaid—*female servant*

Examples of:

Hagar ... Gen. 16:1
Zilpah ... Gen. 29:24
Bilhah ... Gen. 30:4

Expressive of humility:

Ruth ... Ruth 2:13
Woman of Endor ... 1 Sam. 28:7, 21, 22
Mary ... Luke 1:38

Hand of God

Expressive of:

Judgment ... Ex. 9:3
Chastening ... Job 19:21
Security ... John 10:29
Miracles ... Ex. 3:20
Providence ... Ps. 31:15
Provision ... Ps. 145:16
Protection ... Ps. 139:10
Punishment ... Ps. 75:8
Pleading ... Is. 65:2

Hands

Clapping—in joy ... 2 Kin. 11:12
Washing—in innocency ... Matt. 27:24
Joining—in agreement ... 2 Kin. 10:15
Striking—in suretyship ... Prov. 17:16-18
Striking—in anger ... Num. 24:10
Under thigh—in oaths ... Gen. 47:29, 31

Right hand, expressive of:

Honor ... Ps. 45:9
Power ... Ps. 110:1
Love ... Song 2:6
Oath ... Is. 62:8
Accusation ... Zech. 3:1
Self-denial ... Matt. 5:30
Fellowship ... Gal. 2:9

Hands, laying on of

A. *In the Old Testament:*

Blessing a person ... Gen. 48:14, 20
Transferring one's guilt ... Lev. 4:14, 15
Setting apart for service ... Num. 8:10, 11
Inaugurating a successor ... Num. 27:18-23

B. *In the New Testament:*

Blessing ... Matt. 19:13-15
Healing ... Matt. 9:18
Ordaining deacons ... Acts 6:6
Sending out missionaries ... Acts 13:2, 3
Ordaining officers ... 1 Tim. 4:14
In bestowing the Holy Spirit ... Acts 8:17, 18

Handwriting

Of a king, changeable ... Dan. 6:8-27
Of God, unchangeable ... Dan. 5:5-31

Hanes—*mercury*

Probably an Egyptian city ... Is. 30:4

Hanging—*a form of punishment*

Absalom ... 2 Sam. 18:9-17
Ahithophel ... 2 Sam. 17:23
Judas ... Matt. 27:5
Chief baker ... Gen. 40:19, 22
King of Ai ... Josh. 8:29
Five Canaanite kings ... Josh. 10:26, 27
Ish-bosheth's murderers ... 2 Sam. 4:12
Bodies of Saul and Jonathan ... 2 Sam. 21:12
Law of ... Ezra 6:11
Haman ... Esth. 7:10
Haman's sons ... Esth. 9:14
Curse of ... Gal. 3:13
Saul's descendants ... 2 Sam. 21:9
Jesus Christ ... John 19:31

Hannah—*graciousness*

Favored wife of Elkanah ... 1 Sam. 1:5
Childless ... 1 Sam. 1:5, 6
Provoked by Peninnah ... 1 Sam. 1:6, 7
Wrongly accused by Eli ... 1 Sam. 1:14
Prayerful ... 1 Sam. 1:10
Attentive to her child ... 1 Sam. 1:22
Fulfills her vows ... 1 Sam. 1:11-28
Magnifies God ... 1 Sam. 2:1-10
Recognizes the Messiah ("his anointed") ... 1 Sam. 2:10
Model of Mary's song ... Luke 1:46-54

Hannathon—*regarded with favor*

Town of Zebulun ... Josh. 19:14

SUBJECT REFERENCE

Hanniel—*God has been gracious*

1. Manassite prince ... Num. 34:23
2. Asherite ... 1 Chr. 7:30, 39

Hanoch—*dedicated*

1. Descendant of Abraham ... Gen. 25:4
   1 Chr. 1:33
2. Son of Reuben ... Gen. 46:9
3. Head of tribal family ... Num. 26:5

Hanun—*favored*

1. King of Ammon ... 2 Sam. 10:1
   Disgraces David's ambassadors ... 2 Sam. 10:2-5
   Is defeated by David ... 2 Sam. 10:6-14

2, 3. Postexilic workmen ... Neh. 3:13, 30

Hapharaim—*double pit*

Town of Issachar ... Josh. 19:19

Happiness of the saints

A. *Is derived from:*

Fear of God ... Ps. 128:1, 2
Trust in God ... Prov. 16:20
Obedience to God ... John 13:15, 17
Wisdom's ways ... Prov. 3:13-18

B. *Examples of:*

Israel ... Deut. 33:29
Job ... James 5:11
Mary ... Luke 1:46-55
Paul ... Acts 26:2

C. *In spite of:*

Discipline ... Job 5:17
Suffering ... 1 Pet. 4:12-14
Persecution ... Matt. 5:10-12
Lack ... Phil. 4:6, 7
Trouble ... 2 Cor. 4:7-18

D. *Described as:*

Blessed ... Matt. 5:3-12
Filled ... Ps. 36:8
In God alone ... Ps. 73:25, 26

See Gladness; Joy

Happiness of the wicked

A. *Described as:*

Short ... Job 20:5
Uncertain ... Luke 12:20
Vain ... Eccl. 2:1, 2
Limited to this life ... Luke 16:24, 25
Under God's judgment ... Job 15:21
Ps. 73:18-20

B. *Derived from:*

Prominence ... Job 21:7
Ps. 37:35
Prosperity ... Ps. 17:14
Ps. 37:7
Sensuality ... Is. 22:13

C. *Saints:*

Sometimes stumble at ... Ps. 73:2, 3
Should not envy ... Ps. 37:1, 7
Will see end ... Ps. 73:17-20

Hara—*hill*

Place in Assyria where captive Israelites settled ... 1 Chr. 5:26

Haradah—*fear*

Israelite encampment ... Num. 33:24

Haran—*mountainous*

1. Abraham's younger brother ... Gen. 11:26-31
2. Gershonite Levite ... 1 Chr. 23:9
3. Son of Caleb ... 1 Chr. 2:46
4. City of Mesopotamia ... Gen. 11:31
   Abraham lives in ... Acts 7:2, 4
   Abraham leaves ... Gen. 12:4, 5
   Jacob flees to ... Gen. 27:43
   Jacob dwells at ... Gen. 29:4-35
   Center of idolatry ... Gen. 35:2
   2 Kin. 19:12

Hararite—*mountaineer*

Applied to David's mighty men ... 2 Sam. 23:11, 33
1 Chr. 11:34, 35

Harbona—*bald man*

Chamberlain of Ahasuerus ... Esth. 1:10
Same as Harbonah ... Esth. 7:9

SUBJECT ... REFERENCE

Harbor—*a sheltered bay*
Unacceptable ... Acts 27:12

Hard labor
A. *Spiritual:*
Subduing flesh ... 1 Cor. 9:24-27
Striving against sin ... Heb. 12:4
Reaching goal ... Phil. 3:11-14
B. *Physical:*
Jacob ... Gen. 31:40-42
Israelites ... Ex. 1:11-14
Gibeonites ... Josh. 9:3-27
Samson ... Judg. 16:20, 21

Hardness of heart
A. *Causes of:*
God ... Rom. 9:18
Man ... Job 9:4
Unbelief ... John 12:40
Sin ... Heb. 3:13
B. *Examples of:*
Pharaoh ... Ex. 4:21
Zedekiah ... 2 Chr. 36:11-13
Israel ... Ezek. 3:7
Nebuchadnezzar ... Dan. 5:20
Jews ... Mark 3:5
Believers ... Mark 6:52
C. *Warnings against:*
Recognized by Egyptians ... 1 Sam. 6:6
Unheeded by Israel ... Jer. 5:3
Lamented by the prophets ... Is. 63:17
Addressed to Christians ... Heb. 3:8-15
Heb. 4:7

Harem—*group of females associated with one man*
Esther a member of King Ahasuerus' ... Esth. 2:8-14

Hareph—*plucking*
Son of Caleb ... 1 Chr. 2:50, 51

Hareth
Forest in Judah ... 1 Sam. 22:5

Harhaiah—*Jehovah is protecting*
Father of Uzziel ... Neh. 3:8

Harhas—*splendor*
Grandfather of Shallum ... 2 Kin. 22:14

Harhur—*fever*
Ancestor of returning Temple servants ... Ezra 2:43, 51

Harim—*consecrated to God*
1. Descendant of Aaron ... 1 Chr. 24:1, 6, 8
2. Postexilic leader ... Ezra 2:32, 39
3. Father of Malchijah ... Neh. 3:11
4. Signer of the covenant ... Neh. 10:1, 5
5. Signer of the covenant ... Neh. 10:1, 27
6. Family house of priests ... Neh. 12:12, 15
7. Descendants of, divorced foreign wives ... Ezra 10:19, 21

Hariph—*autumn rain*
Family of returnees ... Neh. 7:24
Signers of covenant ... Neh. 10:19
Same as Jorah ... Ezra 2:18

Harlot—*a prostitute*
A. *Characteristics of:*
Shameless ... Jer. 3:3
Painted ... Ezra 23:40
Enticing ... Prov. 9;14-18
Roaming streets ... Prov. 7:12
Expensive ... Prov. 29:3
B. *Evils of:*
Profanes God's name ... Amos 2:7
Connected with idolatry ... Ex. 34:15, 16
Brings spiritual error ... Hos. 4:10-19
Cause of divorce ... Jer. 3:8, 14
C. *Prohibitions concerning:*
Forbidden in Israel ... Lev. 19:29
Priests not to marry ... Lev. 21:1, 7, 14
To be shamed ... Prov. 5:3-20
Punishment ... Lev. 21:9
D. *Examples of:*
Tamar ... Gen. 38:13-20

SUBJECT ... REFERENCE

Rahab ... Josh. 2:1-21
Jephthah's mother ... Judg. 11:1
Samson's ... Judg. 16:1
Hosea's wife ... Hos. 1:2
The great ... Rev. 17:1-18
E. *Figurative of:*
Tyre ... Is. 23:15, 17
Israel ... Is. 1:21
Spiritual adultery ... Is. 57:7-9
Rev. 17:1-18
See Adultery

Harmony—*agreement, co-operation*
Husband and wife ... 1 Cor. 7:3-6; Eph. 5:22-23; Col. 3:18, 19
Christians ... John 13:34, 35
Rom. 15:5-7
Christians and unbelievers ... Rom. 12:16-18
Heb. 12:14

Harnepher
Asherite ... 1 Chr. 7:36

Harness—*to equip*
Horses ... Jer. 46:4

Harod—*fountain of trembling*
Well near Gideon's camp ... Judg. 7:1

Harodite
Inhabitant of Harod ... 2 Sam. 23:25
Same as Harorite ... 1 Chr. 11:27

Haroeh—*the seer*
Judahite ... 1 Chr. 2:50, 52
Called Reaiah ... 1 Chr. 4:2

Harosheth—*carving of the nations*
Residence of Sisera ... Judg. 4:2, 13, 16

Harp—*a stringed musical instrument*
Used by:
The wicked ... Is. 5:11, 12
David ... 1 Sam. 16:16, 23
Prophets ... 1 Sam. 10:5
Temple orchestra ... 1 Chr. 16:5
Temple worshipers ... Ps. 33:2
Celebrators ... 2 Chr. 20:27, 28
Jewish captives ... Ps. 137:2
Worshipers in heaven ... Rev. 5:8

Harpoon—*a barbed spear for hunting large fish*
Used against Leviathan ... Job 41:7

Harrow
Instrument for breaking clods ... Job 39:10
Figurative of affliction ... Is. 28:24

Harsha—*enchanter*
Head of Temple servants ... Ezra 2:43, 52
Neh. 7:46, 54

Hart—*a male deer*
A. *Described as:*
Clean animal ... Deut. 12:15
Hunted animal ... Lam. 1:6
B. *Figurative of:*
Christ ... Song 2:9, 17
Afflicted saints ... Ps. 42:1-3
Converted sinners ... Is. 35:6

Harum—*exalted*
Judahite ... 1 Chr. 4:8

Harumaph—*flat-nosed*
Father of Jedaiah ... Neh. 3:10

Haruphite
Designation of Shephatiah ... 1 Chr. 12:5
Member of Hariph's family ... Neh. 7:24

Haruz—*active*
Father-in-law of King Manasseh ... 2 Kin. 21:19

Harvest—*the time when the crops are ripe*
A. *Occasion of:*
Great joy ... Is. 9:3
Bringing the first fruits ... Lev. 23:10
Remembering the poor ... Lev. 19:9, 10
B. *Figuratively of:*
Seasons of grace ... Jer. 8:20

SUBJECT ... REFERENCE

Judgment ... Jer. 51:33
God's wrath ... Rev. 14:15
Gospel opportunities ... Matt. 9:37, 38
World's end ... Matt. 13:30, 39
Measure of fruitfulness ... 2 Cor. 9:6
C. *Promises concerning:*
To continue ... Gen. 8:22
Rain ... Jer. 5:24
Patience ... James 5:7
D. *Failure caused by:*
Drought ... Amos 4:7
Locusts ... Joel 1:4
Sin ... Jo. 17:1 12

Hasadiah—*Jehovah has been gracious*
Son of Zerubbabel ... 1 Chr. 3:20

Hasenuah—*thorny*
Benjamite family ... 1 Chr. 9:7
Neh. 11:7-9

Hashabiah—*Jehovah has imputed*
1. Merarite Levite ... 1 Chr. 6:44, 45
Perhaps the same as in ... 1 Chr. 9:14
2. Levite musician ... 1 Chr. 25:3, 19
3. Kohathite Levite ... 1 Chr. 26:30
4. Levite ruler ... 1 Chr. 27:17
5. Chief Levite during Josiah's reign ... 2 Chr. 35:9
6. Postexilic Levite ... Ezra 8:19, 24
Probably the same in ... Neh. 10:11
7. Postexilic ruler ... Neh. 3:17
8. Descendant of Asaph ... Neh. 11:22
9. Priest in the time of Joiakim ... Neh. 12:21

Hashabnah—*covenant sealer*
Signed covenant ... Neh. 10:25

Hashabniah—*Jehovah has regarded me*
1. Father of Hattush ... Neh. 3:10
2. Postexilic Levite ... Neh. 9:5
Probably the same as Hashabiah 6.

Hashbadana—*thoughtful judge*
Assistant to Ezra ... Neh. 8:4

Hashem—*shining*
Father of David's warriors ... 1 Chr. 11:34
Also called Jashen ... 2 Sam. 23:32

Hashmonah—*fertility*
Israelite encampment ... Num. 33:29

Hashub—*thoughtful*
1. Postexilic workman ... Neh. 3:11
2. Signer of the covenant ... Neh. 10:23
3. Levite chief ... Neh. 11:15

Hashubah—*esteemed*
Son of Zerubbabel ... 1 Chr. 3:19, 20

Hashum—*opulent*
Founder of postexilic family ... Ezra 2:19
Assists Ezra and signs document ... Neh. 8:4; Neh. 10:18

Hasrah—*want*
Grandfather of Shallum ... 2 Chr. 34:22
Called Harhas ... 2 Kin. 22:14

Hassenaah—*thorny*
Father of postexilic workmen ... Neh. 3:3
Same as Senaah ... Ezra 2:35
Neh. 7:38

Haste—*to do something quickly*
Prompted by good ... 2 Chr. 35:21
Luke 19:5, 6
Prompted by evil ... Prov. 14:29
Prov. 28:20

Hasupha—*naked*
Head of Temple servants ... Ezra 2:43
Same as Hashupha ... Neh. 7:46

Hat
Better rendered as mantle ... Dan. 3:21

Hate—*to dislike something with strong feeling*
A. *Meanings of:*
React as God does ... Rev. 2:6

H

SUBJECT ... REFERENCE

Twist moral judgments ... Prov. 8:36
Esteem of less value ... John 12:25
Make a vital distinction ... Luke 14:26
Despise ... Is. 1:14

B. *Causes of:*
Parental favoritism ... Gen. 37:4, 5
Rape ... 2 Sam. 13:15, 22
Failure to please ... 1 Kin. 22:8
God's purpose ... Ps. 105:25
Belonging to Christ ... Matt. 24:9, 10
Evil nature ... John 3:20

C. *Objects of:*
God's people ... Gen. 26:27
God ... Ex. 20:5
Christ ... John 15:25
Light ... John 3:20
Evil men ... Ps. 26:5
Wickedness ... Ps. 45:7

D. *Toward Christians, sign of their:*
Discipleship ... Matt. 24:9
Election ... John 15:19
Regeneration ... 1 John 3:13-15

Hatach—*chamberlain*
Esther's attendant ... Esth. 4:5-10

Hathath—*terror*
Son of Othniel ... 1 Chr. 4:13

Hatipha—*captive*
Head of Temple servants ... Ezra 2:43, 54

Hatita—*dug up*
Father of porters ... Ezra 2:42
Neh. 7:45

Hattil—*vacillating*
Ancestor of Solomon's servants ... Ezra 2:55, 57; Neh. 7:57-59

Hattush—*assembled*
1. Descendant of David ... Ezra 8:2
2. Man of Judah ... 1 Chr. 3:22
Probably the same as 1
3. Priest returning with Zerubbabel ... Neh. 12:1, 2
4. Postexilic workman ... Neh. 3:10
5. Priest who signs covenant ... Neh. 10:1, 4

Haughtiness—*an arrogant spirit*
Precedes a fall ... Prov. 16:18
To be brought low ... Is. 2:11, 17
Guilt of Jerusalem for ... Ezek. 16:50
Zeph. 3:11

Haunt—*to frequent a place*
Place of abode ... 1 Sam. 23:22

Hauran—*hollow land*
District southeast of Mt. Hermon ... Ezek. 47:16

Haven—*a sheltered area*
Zebulun's assets ... Gen. 49:13
Desired ... Ps. 107:30
Near Lasea ... Acts 27:8

Havilah—*circle*
1. Son of Cush ... Gen. 10:7
2. Son of Joktan ... Gen. 10:29
3. District of Arabia ... Gen. 2:11
Limit of Ishmaelite territory ... Gen. 25:18
Saul defeated Amalekites ... 1 Sam. 15:7

Havoth-jair—*tent villages of Jair*
Villages of Jordan in Gilead ... Num. 32:40, 41
Or in Bashan ... Deut. 3:13, 14
Taken by Jair ... Num. 32:41

Hawk—*a plundering bird*
Ceremonially unclean ... Lev. 11:16
Migratory ... Job 39:26

Hay—*food for cattle*
Build with ... 1 Cor. 3:12
Rendered "leeks" ... Num. 11:5

Hazael—*God has seen*
King over Syria ... 1 Kin. 19:15-17
Defeats Joram of Israel ... 2 Kin. 8:25-29
Defeats Jehu ... 2 Kin. 10:31, 32
Oppresses Israel ... 2 Kin. 13:3-7, 22
His son defeated ... 2 Kin. 13:24, 25

SUBJECT ... REFERENCE

Hazaiah—*Jehovah has seen*
Man of Judah ... Neh. 11:5

Hazar-addar—*village of Addar*
Place in Canaan ... Num. 34:4

Hazar-enan—*village of springs*
Village of north Palestine ... Num. 34:9, 10

Hazar-gaddah—*village of good fortune*
Town on the border of Judah ... Josh. 15:21, 27

Hazar-hatticon—*the middle village*
Town on the border of Hauran ... Ezek. 47:16

Hazar-maveth—*village of death*
Descendants of Joktan ... Gen. 10:26

Hazar-shual—*fox village*
Town in south Judah ... Josh. 15:21, 28
Assigned to Simeon ... Josh. 19:1, 3
Reoccupied after exile ... Neh. 11:27

Hazar-susah—*village of a mare*
Simeonite village ... Josh. 19:5

Hazel—*almond*
Jacob peeled ... Gen. 30:37

Hazelelponi—*give shade, thou who turnest toward me*
Female descendant of Judah ... 1 Chr. 4:3

Hazerim—*villages*
Habitations of the Avim ... Deut. 2:23

Hazeroth—*courts*
Israelite camp ... Num. 33:17
Scene of sedition of Miriam and Aaron ... Num. 12:1-16

Hazezon-tamar—*pruning of the palm*
Dwelling of Amorites ... Gen. 14:7
Also called Engedi ... 2 Chr. 20:2

Haziel—*God sees*
Gershonite Levite ... 1 Chr. 23:9

Hazo—*seer*
Son of Nahor ... Gen. 22:22, 23

Hazor—*enclosure*
1. Royal Canaanite city destroyed by Joshua ... Josh. 11:1-13
Rebuilt and assigned to Naphtali ... Josh. 19:32, 36
Army of, defeated by Deborah and Barak ... Judg. 4:1-24
Fortified by Solomon ... 1 Kin. 9:15
Captured by Tiglathpileser ... 2 Kin. 15:29
2. Town in south Judah ... Josh. 15:21, 25
3. Another town of south Judah ... Josh. 15:21, 23
4. Town of Benjamin ... Neh. 11:31, 33
5. Region in the Arabian desert ... Jer. 49:28-33

Hazor-hadattah—*new Hazor*
Town in south Judah ... Josh. 15:25

He
Fifth letter of Hebrew alphabet ... Ps. 119:33-40

Head
A. *Attitudes expressed by:*
Covered, in grief ... 2 Sam. 15:30
Covered, in subjection ... 1 Cor. 11:5
Hand upon, in sorrow ... 2 Sam. 13:19
Ashes upon, in dismay ... Josh. 7:6
Uncovered, in leprosy ... Lev. 13:45
Wagging, in derision ... Matt. 27:39
Anointed, in dedication ... Matt. 6:17

B. *Figurative of:*
God ... 1 Cor. 11:3
Christ ... Eph. 1:22
Husband ... 1 Cor. 11:3, 7
Protection ... Ps. 140:7
Judgment ... Is. 15:2
Confidence ... Luke 21:28
Pride ... Ps. 83:2
Exaltation ... Ps. 27:6
Joy and prosperity ... Ps. 23:5

SUBJECT ... REFERENCE

See Hands, laying on of

Head of the Church—*position of pre-eminence in the Church*
Christ ... Eph. 1:22; Eph. 5:23; Col. 1:18
Prophesied ... Dan. 7:13, 14

Headband
Part of feminine attire ... Is. 3:20

Headstone—*the cornerstone*
Christ promised as ... Zech. 4:7
Christ fulfills ... Acts 4:11
1 Pet. 2:7

Headship—*office of authority, responsibility*
A. *Of Christ:*
Over all things ... Eph. 4:15
Over man ... 1 Cor. 11:3
Of Church ... Eph. 5:23
Col. 1:18
Of the Corner Stone ... Acts 4:11
1 Pet. 2:7, 8

B. *Of the Father:*
Over Christ ... 1 Cor. 11:3
Gives authority ... John 5:26, 27
1 Cor. 15:25-28

C. *Of Man:*
Of human race ... Rom. 5:12
Over woman ... 1 Cor. 11:3
Eph. 5:23

Healing—*restoration of health*
A. *Resulting from:*
Intercession ... Num. 12:10-15
Repentance ... 1 Kin. 13:1-6
Prayer ... James 5:14, 15
Faith ... Num. 21:8, 9
John 4:46-53
God's Word ... Ps. 107:20

B. *Power of:*
Belongs to God ... Gen. 20:17, 18
Possessed by Jesus ... Matt. 4:24
Matt. 8:16
Given to apostles ... Matt. 10:1-8
Given as a gift ... 1 Cor. 12:9
Eternal in heaven ... Rev. 22:2

See Diseases; Sickness

Healing, spiritual
A. *Source of:*
Only in God ... Jer. 17:14
Through Christ ... Is. 53:5
Through the Gospel ... Ezek. 47:8-11

B. *Provided for:*
Heartbroken ... Ps. 147:3
Repentant ... 2 Chr. 7:14
Egyptians ... Is. 19:22-25
Faithful ... Mal. 4:2

C. *Necessary because of man's:*
Sin ... Ps. 41:4
Backsliding ... Jer. 3:22
Spiritual sickness ... Is. 6:10

Health—*the body freed from disease*
A. *Factors conducive to:*
Exercise ... 1 Tim. 4:8
Food ... Acts 27:34
Temperance ... Jer. 35:5-8
Obedience ... Prov. 4:20-22
Cheerfulness ... Prov. 17:22
God's will ... John 9:1-3

B. *Factors destructive of:*
Moral looseness ... Prov. 7:22-27
Wickedness ... Ps. 55:23
Disease ... 1 Sam. 5:6-12
Injury ... Luke 10:30
Debauchery ... Titus 1:12

Heap of stones—*a monument of stones*
Symbolic of:
Shameful acts ... Josh. 7:26
Covenant ... Gen. 31:46-52
Judgment ... Jer. 9:11

Hearers—*those who hear*
A. *Element necessary in:*
Attentiveness ... Neh. 8:1-3

SUBJECT	REFERENCE
Belief	Rom. 10:14
Conviction	Acts 2:37
Discrimination	Luke 8:18

B. *Reactions of:*

Responsiveness	2 Sam. 7:17-29
Repentance	2 Sam. 12:12, 13
Rebellion	Ezek. 33:30-33
Retreat	John 6:60-66
Resistance	Acts 7:51-54
Rejoicing	Acts 13:48
Rejection	Acts 28:23-29
Research	Acts 17:11

Heart

A. *Seat of:*

Adultery	Matt. 5:28
Desire	Rom. 10:1
Doubt	Mark 11:23
Fear	Is. 35:4
Hatred	Lev. 19:17
Gladness	Acts 2:26
Love	Mark 12:30, 33
Lust	Rom. 1:24
Meditation	Ps. 19:14
Mischief	Ps. 28:3
Obedience	Rom. 6:17
Pride	Prov. 16:5
Purpose	2 Cor. 9:7
Reason	Mark 2:8
Rebellion	Jer. 5:23
Sorrow	John 14:1
Thought	Matt. 9:4

B. *Of the wicked, described as:*

Blind	Eph. 4:18
Darkened	Rom. 1:21
Covetous	2 Pet. 2:14
Full of evil	Gen. 6:5
Unrepentant	Rom. 2:5
Lustful	Prov. 6:25
Proud	Jer. 49:16
Rebellious	Jer. 5:23
Uncircumcised	Acts 7:51

C. *God's action upon:*

Knows	Ps. 44:21
Searches	1 Chr. 28:9
Enlightens	2 Cor. 4:6
Opens	Acts 16:14
Recreates	Ezek. 11:19
Examines	Jer. 12:3
Strengthens	Ps. 27:14
Establishes	1 Thess. 3:13

D. *Regenerate's, described as:*

Circumcised	Rom. 2:29
Clean	Ps. 73:1
Contrite	Ps. 51:17
Enlarged	Ps. 119:32
Enlightened	2 Cor. 4:6
Fixed	Ps. 57:7
Joyful in God	1 Sam. 2:1
Meditative	Ps. 4:4
Perfect	Ps. 101:2
Prayerful	1 Sam. 1:12, 13
Pure	Matt. 5:8
Glad and sincere	Acts 2:46
Tender	2 Kin. 22:19
Treasury of good	Matt. 12:35
Wise	Prov. 10:8

E. *Regenerate's, responses of:*

Believe with	Rom. 10:10
Keep with diligence	Prov. 4:23
Love God with all	Matt. 22:37
Sanctify God in	1 Pet. 3:15
Serve God with all	Deut. 26:16
Walk before God with all	1 Kin. 2:4
Trust the Lord with all	Prov. 3:5
Regard not iniquity in	Ps. 66:18
Do God's will from	Eph. 6:6

Hearth—*a place for fire*

Bed of live coals	Is. 30:14 Ps. 102:3

Heartlessness—*without moral feeling; cruelty*

A. *Among unbelievers:*

Philistines, toward Samson	Judg. 16:21
Saul, toward David	1 Sam. 18:25
Nabal, toward David	1 Sam. 25:4-12
Haman, toward Jews	Esth. 3:8, 9
Priest, toward a certain man	Luke 10:30-32

B. *Among professing believers:*

Laban, toward Jacob	Gen. 31:7, 36-42
Jacob's sons, toward Joseph	Gen. 37:18-35
David, toward Uriah	2 Sam. 11:9-27

Heath—*a desert plant*

Figurative of:

Self-sufficient man	Jer. 17:6
Devastation	Jer. 48:6

Heat, hot

Figurative of:

God's wrath	Deut. 9:19
Man's anger	Deut. 19:6
Determination	Gen. 31:36
Zeal	Ps. 39:3
Persecution	Matt. 13:6, 21
Heavy toil	Matt. 20:12
Real faith	Rev. 3:15

Heathen (see Gentiles)

Heave offering

A. *Consisted of:*

First fruits	Num. 5:19-21
Tenth of all tithes	Num. 18:21-28

B. *Part of:*

All gifts	Num. 18:29
Spoils	Num. 31:26-47
Offerings	Ex. 29:27 Lev. 7:14, 32

C. *Requirements concerning:*

To be the best	Num. 18:29
Brought to God's house	Deut. 12:6
Given to priests	Ex. 29:27, 28
Sanctified the whole offering	Num. 18:27-32
Eaten in a clean place	Lev. 10:12-15

Heaven—*the place of everlasting bliss*

A. *Inhabitants of:*

God	1 Kin. 8:30
Christ	Heb. 9:12, 24
Holy Spirit	Ps. 139:7, 8
Angels	Matt. 18:10
Just men	Heb. 12:22, 23

B. *Things lacking in:*

Marriage	Matt. 22:30
Death	Luke 20:36
Flesh and blood	1 Cor. 15:50
Imperishable	1 Cor. 15:42, 50
Sorrow	Rev. 7:17
Pain	Rev. 21:4
Curse	Rev. 22:3
Night	Rev. 22:5
Wicked people	Rev. 22:15
End	Matt. 25:46 Rev. 22:5

C. *Positive characteristics of:*

Joy	Luke 15:7, 10
Rest	Rev. 14:13
Peace	Luke 16:25
Righteousness	2 Pet. 3:13
Service	Rev. 7:15
Reward	Matt. 5:11, 12
Inheritance	1 Pet. 1:4
Glory	Rom. 8:17, 18

D. *Entrance into, for:*

Righteous	Matt. 23:34, 37
Changed	1 Cor. 15:51
Saved	John 3:5, 18, 21
Called	2 Pet. 1:10, 11
Overcomers	Rev. 2:7, 10, 11
Those recorded	Luke 10:20
Obedient	Rev. 22:14
Holy	Rev. 19:8

E. *Believer's present attitude toward:*

Given foretaste of	Acts 7:55, 56
Earnestly desires	2 Cor. 5:2, 8
Looks for	2 Pet. 3:12
Considers "far better" than now	Phil. 1:23
Puts treasure there	Luke 12:33

F. *Described as:*

House	John 14:2
Kingdom	Matt. 25:34
Abraham's bosom	Luke 16:22, 23
Paradise	2 Cor. 12:2, 4
Better country	Heb. 11:10, 16
Holy city	Rev. 21:2, 10-27 Rev. 22:1-5

Heavens, natural

A. *Facts regarding:*

Created by God	Gen. 1:1
Stretched out	Is. 42:5 Jer. 10:12
Will be destroyed	Heb. 1:10-12 2 Pet. 3:10
New heavens to follow	Is. 65:17 2 Pet. 3:13

B. *Purposes of:*

To declare God's glory	Ps. 19:1
To declare God's righteousness	Ps. 50:6
To manifest God's wisdom	Prov. 8:27

Heaviness—*a spirit of grief or anxiety*

Unrelieved by mirth	Prov. 14:13
God's children experience	Phil. 2:26
Needed exchange	James 4:9
Experienced by Christ	Ps. 69:20, 21
Remedy for	Prov. 12:25

Heavy—*oppressive*

A. *Used literally of:*

Eli's weight	1 Sam. 4:18
Absalom's hair	2 Sam. 14:26
Stone	Prov. 27:3

B. *Used figuratively of:*

Fatigue	Matt. 26:43
Burdens	2 Chr. 10:11, 14
Sins	Is. 24:20
Sullenness	1 Kin. 21:4
God's judgments	1 Sam. 5:6, 11

Heber, Eber—*associate*

1. Son of Beriah	Gen. 46:17
Descendants called Heberites	Num. 26:45
2. Husband of Jael, the slayer of Sisera	Judg. 4:11-24
3. Descendant of Ezra	1 Chr. 4:17, 18
4. Gadite chief	1 Chr. 5:11, 13
5. Benjamite	1 Chr. 8:17
6. Benjamite chief	1 Chr. 8:22
7. In Christ's genealogy	Luke 3:35
Same as Eber in	Gen. 10:24 1 Chr. 1:25

Hebrew—*one from the other side*

Applied to:

Abram	Gen. 14:13
Israelites	1 Sam. 4:6, 9
Jews	Acts 6:1
Paul, a sincere	Phil. 3:5

Hebrew language

Called "the Jews' language"	2 Kin. 18:26, 28
Alphabet of, in divisions	Ps. 119
Language of Christ's time	John 19:13, 20 Acts 21:40

See Aramaic

Hebrews, Epistle of the—*a book of the New Testament*

Christ greater than the angels	Heb. 1:3, 4
Christ of the order of Melchizedek	Heb. 4:14—5:10
The new covenant	Heb. 8:1—10:18
The life of faith	Heb. 10:19—13:17

Hebron—*alliance*

1. Ancient town in Judah	Num. 13:22
Originally called Kirjath-arba	Gen. 23:2
Abram dwells here	Gen. 13:18
Abraham buys cave here	Gen. 23:2-20
Isaac and Jacob sojourn here	Gen. 35:27
Visited by spies	Num. 13:22
Defeated by Joshua	Josh. 10:1-37
Caleb expels Anakim from	Josh. 14:12-15
Assigned to Levites	Josh. 21:10-13
City of refuge	Josh. 20:7
David's original capital	2 Sam. 2:1-3, 11
Birthplace of David's sons	2 Sam. 3:2
Abner's death here	2 Sam. 4:1
Absalom's rebellion here	2 Sam. 15:7-10
Fortified by Rehoboam	2 Chr. 11:10
2. Town of Asher	Josh. 19:28

SUBJECT — REFERENCE

3. Son of Kohath ... Ex. 6:18
Descendants called Hebronites ... Num. 3:19, 27
4. Descendant of Caleb ... 1 Chr. 2:42, 43

Hebronites (see Hebron 3)

Hedge—*a fence or barrier*

Illustrative of:
God's protection ... Job 1:10
Afflictions ... Job 19:8
Slothfulness ... Prov. 15:19
Removal of protection ... Ps. 80:12

Hedgehog—*porcupine*

Rendered "bittern" ... Is. 14:23; Zeph. 2:14

Heedfulness—*giving proper attention to something important*

A. *Objects of:*
God's commandments ... Josh. 22:5
Our ways ... Ps. 39:1
False teachers ... Matt. 16:6
God's Word ... 2 Pet. 1:19

B. *Admonitions to Christians, concerning:*
Deception ... Matt. 24:4
Outward display ... Matt. 6:1
Worldliness ... Luke 21:34
Duty ... Acts 20:28-31
Foundation ... 1 Cor. 3:10
Liberty ... 1 Cor. 8:9
Security ... 1 Cor. 10:12
Effectiveness ... Gal. 5:15
Ministry ... Col. 4:17
Fables ... 1 Tim. 1:4
Unbelief ... Heb. 3:12

See Caution

Heel—*the back part of the human foot*

Used literally of:
Esau's ... Gen. 25:26

Used figuratively of:
Seed of the woman ... Gen. 3:15
Enemy of Dan ... Gen. 49:17
The wicked ... Job 18:5, 9
Friend of David ... Ps. 41:9

Hegai

Eunuch under King Ahasuerus ... Esth. 2:3, 8, 15

Heifer—*a young cow*

A. *Ceremonial uses of:*
In a covenant ... Gen. 15:9
In purification ... Num. 19:1-22

B. *Red heifer, ceremony concerning:*
Without spot ... Num. 19:2
Never yoked ... Num. 19:2
Slaughtered and burned outside the camp ... Num. 19:3-8
Ashes kept ... Num. 19:9, 10
Ashes, with water, used to purify ... Num. 19:11-22
Significance of ... Heb. 9:13, 14

C. *Figurative of:*
Improper advantage ... Judg. 14:18
Contentment ... Jer. 50:11
Stubborn ... Hos. 4:16

Heirs, natural

A. *Persons and property involved:*
First-born ... Deut. 21:15-17
Sons of concubines ... Gen. 21:10
Daughters ... Num. 27:1-11
Widows ... Ruth 3:12, 13
Order of succession ... Num. 27:8-11

B. *Exceptions:*
Father could make concubines' sons heirs ... Gen. 49:12-27
Daughters receive marriage portion ... Gen. 29:24, 29
Daughters sometimes share with sons ... Job 42:15
Daughters receive, if no sons ... Num. 27:8

C. *Examples of heirship changes by divine election:*
Ishmael to Isaac ... Gen. 21:10, 11
Esau to Jacob ... Gen. 27:37; Rom. 9:13
Reuben to Joseph ... Gen. 49:24-26
Adonijah to Solomon ... 1 Kin. 1:11-14

See Birthright; Inheritance, earthly

Heirs, spiritual

A. *Of Christ:*
Recognized ... Matt. 21:38
Appointed ... Heb. 1:2

B. *Of Christians, means of:*
By promise ... Gal. 3:29
Through Christ ... Gal. 4:7
Through faith ... Rom. 4:13, 14
By grace ... Gal. 4:28-31

C. *Of Christians, receiving:*
Grace ... 1 Pet. 3:7
Promise ... Heb. 11:9
Kingdom ... James 2:5
Salvation ... Heb. 1:14
Righteousness ... Heb. 11:7
Eternal life ... Titus 3:7

See Inheritance, spiritual

Helah—*ornament*

One of Asher's wives ... 1 Chr. 4:5, 7

Helam—*fortress*

Place between Damascus and Hamath where David defeated Syrians ... 2 Sam. 10:16-19

Helbah—*fertility*

City of Asher ... Judg. 1:31

Helbon—*fertile*

City north of Damascus ... Ezek. 27:18

Heldai—*worldly*

1. One of David's captains ... 1 Chr. 27:15
Probably same as Heled and Heleb ... 1 Chr. 11:30
2. Exile from Babylon bearing gifts ... Zech. 6:10, 11
Called Helem ... Zech. 6:14

Helek—*portion*

Son of Gilead ... Num. 26:30
Founder of a family ... Josh. 17:2

Helem—*strength*

1. Asherite ... 1 Chr. 7:34, 35
2. Same as Heldai ... Zech. 6:11
Called Hotham ... 1 Chr. 7:32

Heleph—*strong*

Frontier town of Naphtali ... Josh. 19:32, 33

Helez—*strong*

1. One of David's captains ... 2 Sam. 23:26
2. Judahite ... 1 Chr. 2:39

Heli—*climbing*

Father of Joseph, husband of Mary ... Luke 3:23

Helkai—*portion*

Postexilic priest ... Neh. 12:15

Helkath—*portion, field*

Frontier town of Asher ... Josh. 19:24, 25
Assigned to Levites ... Josh. 21:31
Same as Hukok ... 1 Chr. 6:75

Helkath-hazzurim—*field of sharp flints*

Scene of bloody combat ... 2 Sam. 2:16

Hell—*the place of eternal torment*

A. *Described as:*
Everlasting fire ... Matt. 25:41
Everlasting punishment ... Matt. 25:46
Outer darkness ... Matt. 8:12
Everlasting destruction ... 2 Thess. 1:9
Lake of fire ... Rev. 19:20

B. *Prepared for:*
Devil and his angels ... Matt. 25:41
Wicked ... Rev. 21:8
Disobedient ... Rom. 2:8, 9
Fallen angels ... 2 Pet. 2:4
Beast and the false prophet ... Rev. 19:20
Worshipers of the beast ... Rev. 14:11
Rejectors of the Gospel ... Matt. 10:15

C. *Punishment of, described as:*
Bodily ... Matt. 5:29, 30
In the soul ... Matt. 10:28
With degrees ... Matt. 23:14

Helmet—*armor for the head*

Used figuratively of salvation:
Prepared ... Is. 59:17
Provided ... Eph. 6:17
Promised ... 1 Thess. 5:8

Helon—*strong*

Father of Eliab ... Num. 1:9

Helper—*one who assists another*

A. *Used of:*
God ... Heb. 13:6
Christ ... Heb. 4:15, 16
Holy Spirit ... Rom. 8:26
Angels ... Dan. 10:13
Woman ... Gen. 2:18, 20
Levites ... 2 Chr. 29:3, 4
Christians ... Acts 16:9; 2 Cor. 1:24

B. *As the Holy Spirit:*
With believers forever ... John 14:16
Teaches ... John 14:26
Testifies of Christ ... John 15:26
Convicts ... John 16:7-11

Helps—*the acts of bearing another's burden*

A gift to the Church ... 1 Cor. 12:28
Christians admonished to ... 1 Thess. 5:14
Elders admonished to ... Acts 20:28, 35

Hemam—*raging*

Son of Lotan ... Gen. 36:22
Same as Homam ... 1 Chr. 1:39

Heman—*faithful*

1. Famous wise man ... 1 Kin. 4:31
Judahite ... 1 Chr. 2:6
Composer of a Psalm ... Ps. 88 (Title)
2. Musician under David; grandson of Samuel ... 1 Chr. 6:33
Appointed as chief singer ... 1 Chr. 15:16, 17
Man of spiritual insight ... 1 Chr. 25:5

Hemdan—*pleasant*

Descendant of Seir ... Gen. 36:26
Same as Amram ... 1 Chr. 1:41

Hemlock—*a bitter poisonous substance*

Properly means "gall" ... Amos 6:12

Hemorrhage—*a flow of blood*

Healed ... Luke 8:43, 44
Woman suffered from, for 12 years ... Matt. 9:20; Mark 5:25

Hen—*favor*

1. Son of Zephaniah ... Zech. 6:14
2. Domestic fowl ... Matt. 23:37

Hena—*low land*

City captured by the Assyrians ... 2 Kin. 18:34

Henadad—*favor of Hadad*

Postexilic Levite ... Ezra 3:9
Sons of, help Nehemiah ... Neh. 3:18, 24

Henoch

1. Same as Enoch ... 1 Chr. 1:3
2. Same as Hanoch 1 ... 1 Chr. 1:33

Hepher—*pit, well*

1. Town west of the Jordan ... Josh. 12:17
Name applied to a district ... 1 Kin. 4:10
2. Founder of Hepherites ... Num. 26:30, 32
3. Son of Ashur ... 1 Chr. 4:5, 6
4. One of David's guards ... 1 Chr. 11:26, 36

Hephzibah—*my delight is in her*

Mother of King Manasseh ... 2 Kin. 21:1

Herald—*a representative of a government official*

Of Nebuchadnezzar ... Dan. 3:3, 4
Of Pharaoh ... Gen. 41:42, 43
Zion ... Is. 40:9

Herbs—*grass or leafy vegetables*

Bitter, used at Passover ... Ex. 12:8
Poisonous, not fit ... 2 Kin. 4:39, 40

Herdsman—*one who tends cattle*

Conflict among ... Gen. 13:7, 8

SUBJECT REFERENCE

Heredity—*transmission of physical and mental traits*

A. *Factors involved:*
- Likeness of nature ... Gen. 5:3
- Common transgression ... Rom. 5:12
- Sinful nature ... John 3:6, 7
- Family and national traits ... Titus 1:12
- Physical traits ... Jer. 13:26
- God's purpose of plan ... Gen. 9:22-27

B. *Consistent with:*
- Individual responsibility ... Jer. 31:29, 30
- God's sovereign plan ... Rom. 9:6-16
- Need of a new nature ... Matt. 3:9; John 3:1-12
- Family differences ... 1 John 3:12
- Child different from his parents ... 1 Sam. 8:1-5

Heres—*sun*

1. Mountain in Dan ... Judg. 1:35, 36
   Probably connected with Beth-shemesh or Ir-shemesh ... 1 Kin. 4:9; Josh. 19:40, 41
2. Egyptian city; probably is the "city of destruction" referred to ... Is. 19:18

Heresh—*silent*
- Levite ... 1 Chr. 9:15

Heresy—*a teaching contrary to the truth*

A. *Applied to:*
- Religious sect ... Acts 5:17
- Pharisees ... Acts 26:5
- Christians (derisively) ... Acts 24:5, 14

B. *Characteristics of:*
- Damnable ... 2 Pet. 2:1
- Contagious ... 2 Pet. 2:2
- Subversive ... Gal. 1:7

C. *Attitude toward:*
- Recognize purpose ... 1 John 2:18, 19
- Withdraw ... 1 Tim. 6:4, 5, 11
- Do not receive ... 2 John 9-11

Heritage, earthly

A. *Of believers:*
- Children ... Ps. 127:3
- Long life ... Ps. 91:16

B. *Of Israel:*
- Promised land ... Ex. 6:8
- Forsaken of God ... Jer. 12:7-9
- Discontinue ... Jer. 17:4
- Return to ... Jer. 12:15

Heritage, spiritual

A. *Described as:*
- laid up ... Ps. 31:19; Col. 1:5
- Reserved ... 1 Pet. 1:4
- Prepared ... 1 Cor. 2:9

B. *Consists of:*
- Protection ... Is. 54:17
- Provision ... Is. 58:14
- Unseen things ... Matt. 25:34
- Kingdom ... 1 Cor. 2:9-12
- All things ... Rom. 8:32

Hermas
- Christian at Rome ... Rom. 16:14

Hermes
- Christian at Rome ... Rom. 16:14

Hermogenes—*sprung from Hermes*
- Turns from Paul ... 2 Tim. 1:15

Hermon—*sacred mountain*
- Highest mountain (9,166 ft.) in Syria; also called Sirion, Shenir ... Deut. 3:8, 9
- Northern limit of conquest ... Josh. 11:3, 17
- Joined with Tabor, Zion and Lebanon in Hebrew poetry ... Ps. 89:12

Hero—*a person acclaimed for unusual deeds*
- Caleb, a rejected ... Num. 13:30-33
- Phinehas, a rewarded ... Num. 25:7-13
- Deborah, a militant ... Judg. 4:4-16
- Jonathan, a rescued ... 1 Sam. 14:6-17, 38-45
- David, a popular ... 1 Sam. 18:5-8
- Esther, a hesitant ... Esth. 4:10-17

Herod—*family name of Idumaean rulers of Palestine*

1. Herod the Great, procurator of Judea (37—4 B.C.) ... Luke 1:5
   Inquires of Jesus' birth ... Matt. 2:3-8
   Slays Bethlehem infants ... Matt. 2:12-18
2. Archelaus (4 B.C.—A.D. 6) succeeds Herod the Great ... Matt. 2:22
3. Herod Antipas, the tetrarch, ruler of Galilee and Peraea (4 B.C.—A.D. 39) ... Luke 3:1
   Imprisons John the Baptist ... Luke 3:18-21
   Has John the Baptist beheaded ... Matt. 14:1-12
   Disturbed about Jesus ... Luke 9:7-9
   Jesus sent to him ... Luke 23:7-11
   Becomes Pilate's friend ... Luke 23:12
   Opposes Jesus ... Acts 4:27
4. Philip, tetrarch of Ituraea and Trachonitis (4 B.C.—A.D. 34) ... Luke 3:1; Acts 13:1
5. Herod Philip, disinherited son of Herod the Great ... Matt. 14:3
6. Herod Agrippa I (A.D. 37-44) ... Acts 12:1, 19
   Kills James ... Acts 12:1, 2
   Imprisons Peter ... Acts 12:3-11, 19
   Slain by an angel ... Acts 12:20-23
7. Herod Agrippa II (A.D. 53-70), called Agrippa and King Agrippa ... Acts 25:22, 23; Acts 25:24, 26
   Festus tells him about Paul ... Acts 25:13-27
   Paul makes a defense before ... Acts 26:1-23
   Rejects the Gospel ... Acts 26:24-30
   Recognizes Paul's innocency ... Acts 26:31, 32
8. Aristobulus; identified by some as son of Herod the Great ... Rom. 16:10

Herodians—*an influential Jewish party*
- Join Pharisees against Jesus ... Mark 3:6
- Seek to trap Jesus ... Matt. 22:15-22
- Jesus warns against ... Mark 8:15

Herodias—*feminine form of Herod*
- Granddaughter of Herod the Great; plots John's death ... Matt. 14:3-12
- Married her uncle ... Mark 6:17

Herodion
- Christian at Rome ... Rom. 16:11

Heron
- Unclean bird ... Lev. 11:19; Deut. 14:18

Hesed—*mercy*
- Father of one of Solomon's officers ... 1 Kin. 4:7, 10

Heshbon—*intelligence*
- Ancient Moabite city; taken by Sihon, king of the Amorites ... Num. 21:25-34
- Taken by Moses ... Num. 21:23-26
- Assigned to Reubenites ... Num. 32:1-37
- Built by Reuben ... Num. 32:37
- On Gad's southern boundary ... Josh. 13:26
- Levitical city ... Josh. 21:39
- Later held by Moabites ... Is. 15:1-4
- Judgment of, announced ... Is. 16:8-14
- Fall of, predicted ... Jer. 48:2, 34, 35
- Fishpools in ... Song 7:4

Heshmon—*fatness*
- Town of Judah ... Josh. 15:21, 27

Hesitation—*delay prompted by indecision*

Causes of:
- Uncertain about God's will ... 1 Sam. 23:1-13
- Fear of man ... John 9:18-23
- Selfish unconcern ... 2 Cor. 8:10-14
- Unbelief ... John 20:24-28

Heth—*terror*
- Son of Canaan ... Gen. 10:15
- Ancestor of the Hittites ... Gen. 23:10
- Abraham buys field from sons of ... Gen. 23:3-20
- Esau marries daughters of ... Gen. 27:46
- See Hittites

Hethlon—*hiding place*
- Place indicating Israel's ideal northern boundary ... Ezek. 47:15

Hewers of wood

A slave classification:
- Gibeonites ... Josh. 9:17-27
- Classed with "drawers of water" ... Josh. 9:21, 23

Hezeki—*my strength*
- Benjamite ... 1 Chr. 8:17

Hezekiah—*Jehovah strengthens*

1. King of Judah ... 2 Chr. 29:1-3
   Reforms Temple services ... 2 Chr. 29:3-36
   Restores pure worship ... 2 Chr. 31:1-19
   Military exploits of ... 2 Kin. 18:7-12
   Defeated by Sennacherib ... 2 Kin. 18:13
   Sends messengers to Isaiah ... 2 Kin. 19:1-5
   Rabshakeh's further taunts ... 2 Kin. 19:8-13
   Prays earnestly ... 2 Kin. 19:14-19
   Encouraged by Isaiah ... 2 Kin. 19:20-37
   Healed; his life prolonged 15 years ... 2 Kin. 20:1-11
   His thanks ... Is. 38:9-22
   Rebuked for his pride ... 2 Kin. 20:12-19
   Death of ... 2 Kin. 20:20, 21
   Ancestor of Christ ... Matt. 1:9
2. Ancestor of returning exiles ... Ezra 2:1, 16
3. Ancestor of Zephaniah, spelled Hizkiah ... Zeph. 1:1
4. Postexilic workman who returned with Zerubbabel ... Ezra 2:16

Hezion—*vision*
- Grandfather of Ben-hadad ... 1 Kin. 15:18

Hezir—*swine*

1. Descendant of Aaron ... 1 Chr. 24:1, 15
2. One who signs document ... Neh. 10:1, 20

Hezro
- One of David's mighty men ... 1 Chr. 11:37

Hezron—*enclosure*

1. Place in south Judah ... Josh. 15:1, 3
   Same as Hazaraddar ... Num. 34:4
2. Son of Reuben ... Gen. 46:9
   Founder of the Hezronites ... Num. 26:6
3. Son of Pharez ... Gen. 46:12
   Head of tribal family ... Num. 26:21
   Ancestor of David ... Ruth 4:18-22
   Ancestor of Christ ... Matt. 1:3

Hiddai—*joyful*
- One of David's warriors ... 2 Sam. 23:30
- Same as Hurai ... 1 Chr. 11:32

Hiddekel—*rapid*
- Hebrew name of the river Tigris ... Gen. 2:14; Dan. 10:4

Hide—*to conceal*

A. *Used literally of:*
- Man in Eden ... Gen. 3:10
- Baby Moses ... Ex. 2:2, 3
- Spies ... Josh. 6:17, 25

B. *Used figuratively of:*
- God's face ... Deut. 31:17, 18
- Protection ... Is. 49:2
- Darkness ... Ps. 139:12
- The Gospel ... 2 Cor. 4:3
- Believer's life ... Col. 3:3

Hiel—*God lives*
- Native of Beth-el; rebuilds Jericho ... 1 Kin. 16:34
- Fulfills Joshua's curse ... Josh. 6:26

Hierapolis—*sacred city*
- City of Asia Minor; center of Christian activity ... Col. 4:13

Higgaion—*a deep sound*
- Used as a musical term ... Ps. 9:16
- Translated "meditation" in ... Ps. 19:14
- Translated "solemn sound" in ... Ps. 92:3

High—*exalted, lofty*

Descriptive of:
- Rich ... Ps. 49:2
- Eminent people ... 1 Chr. 17:17
- God's mercy ... Ps. 103:11

SUBJECT | REFERENCE

High-mindedness—*a self-righteous spirit*

Christians warned against ... Rom. 11:20
Rich tempted to ... 1 Tim. 6:17
To prevail in last days ... 2 Tim. 3:1-5

High places—*places of idolatrous worship*

A. *Evils of:*

Contrary to one sanctuary ... Deut. 12:1-14
Source of idolatry ... 2 Kin. 12:3
Place of child sacrifices ... Jer. 7:31
Cause of God's wrath ... 1 Kin. 14:22, 23; Ps. 78:58
Denounced by the prophets ... Ezek. 6:1-6; Hos. 4:11-14
Cause of exile ... Lev. 26:29-34

B. *Built by:*

Solomon ... 1 Kin. 11:7-11
Jeroboam ... 1 Kin. 12:26-31
Jehoram ... 2 Chr. 21:9, 11
Ahaz ... 2 Chr. 28:24, 25
Manasseh ... 2 Kin. 21:1, 3
People of Judah ... 1 Kin. 14:22, 23
People of Israel ... 2 Kin. 17:9
Sepharvites ... 2 Kin. 17:32

C. *Destroyed by:*

Asa ... 2 Chr. 14:3, 5
Jehoshaphat ... 2 Chr. 17:6
Hezekiah ... 2 Kin. 18:4, 22
Josiah ... 2 Kin. 23:5, 8, 13

High priest

A. *Duties of:*

Offer gifts and sacrifices ... Heb. 5:1
Make atonement ... Lev. 16:1-34
Inquire of God ... 1 Sam. 23:9-12
Consecrate Levites ... Num. 8:11-21
Anoint kings ... 1 Kin. 1:34
Bless the people ... Num. 6:22-27
Preside over courts ... Matt. 26:3, 57-62

B. *Typical of Christ's priesthood:*

Called of God ... Heb. 5:4, 5
Making atonement ... Lev. 16:33
Subject to temptation ... Heb. 2:18
Exercise of compassion ... Heb. 4:15, 16
Holiness of position ... Lev. 21:15
Marrying a virgin ... 2 Cor. 11:2
Alone entering Holy of Holies ... Heb. 9:7, 12, 24
Ministry of intercession ... Num. 16:43-48; Heb. 7:25
Blessing people ... Acts 3:26

Highway—*a main thoroughfare*

A. *Characteristics of:*

Roads for public use ... Num. 20:19
Straight and broad ... Is. 40:3
Made to cities of refuge ... Deut. 19:2, 3
Robbers use ... Luke 10:30-33
Animals infest ... Is. 35:8, 9
Beggars sit by ... Matt. 20:30
Byways sometimes better ... Judg. 5:6

B. *Figurative of:*

Holy way ... Prov. 16:17
Israel's restoration ... Is. 11:16
Gospel's call ... Is. 40:3
Way of salvation ... Is. 35:8-10
Two destinies ... Matt. 7:13, 14
Christ ... John 14:6

Hilen—*strong place*

Town of Judah ... 1 Chr. 6:57, 58
Also called Holon ... Josh. 15:51

Hilkiah—*Jehovah is my portion*

1. Levite, son of Amzi ... 1 Chr. 6:45, 46
2. Levite, son of Hosah ... 1 Chr. 26:11
3. Father of Eliakim ... Is. 22:20
4. Priest, father of Jeremiah ... Jer. 1:1
5. Father of Gemariah ... Jer. 29:3
6. Shallum's son ... 1 Chr. 6:13
   High priest in Josiah's reign ... 2 Chr. 34:9-22
   Oversees Temple work ... 2 Kin. 22:4-7
   Finds the book of the Law ... 2 Kin. 22:8-14
   Aids in reformation ... 2 Kin. 23:4
7. Chief of postexilic priest ... Neh. 12:1, 7
   Later descendants of ... Neh. 12:12, 21
8. One of Ezra's assistants ... Neh. 8:4

Hill, hill country—*an elevation of the earth's surface*

Rendered "Gibeah" ... 1 Sam. 11:4
Rendered "hills" ... Luke 23:30

Hillel—*he has praised*

Father of Abdon the judge ... Judg. 12:13, 15

Hind—*a doe* (female deer)

Figurative of:

Spiritual vivacity ... 2 Sam. 22:34
Buoyancy of faith ... Hab. 3:19
Peaceful quietude ... Song 2:7

Hinder parts

God smites enemies in ... Ps. 78:66

Hindrances—*things which obstruct one's way*

A. *Physical:*

Heavy armor ... 1 Sam. 17:38, 39
Ship's cargo ... Acts 27:18-38

B. *Spiritual:*

Satanic temptations ... Matt. 4:8-10
Riches ... Matt. 19:24
Unbelief ... Matt. 11:21-24
Ceremonialism ... Matt. 15:1-9
Love of world ... 2 Tim. 4:10
Sin ... Heb. 12:1

C. *Removal of, by:*

Faith ... Matt. 17:20, 21
God's armor ... Eph. 6:11-18
Walking in the Spirit ... Gal. 5:16, 17
Self-control ... 1 Cor. 9:25-27

Hinge—*a pivot of a door*

Of gold ... 1 Kin. 7:50

Hinnom, valley of (Ben-Hinnom)

A. *Location of:*

Near Jerusalem ... Jer. 19:2
Boundary line ... Josh. 15:8
Topheth ... Jer. 19:6, 11-14

B. *Uses of:*

For idol worship ... 1 Kin. 11:7
For sacrificing children ... 2 Chr. 28:3
Defiled by Josiah ... 2 Kin. 23:10-14
Jeremiah addresses people here ... Jer. 19:1-5
Will become "valley of the slaughter" ... Jer. 7:31, 32
Make holy ... Jer. 31:40

Hirah—*nobility*

Adullamite, a friend of Judah ... Gen. 38:1, 12

Hiram—*highborn*

1. King of Tyre ... 2 Sam. 5:11
   Provides men and material for David's palace ... 1 Chr. 14:1
   David's friend ... 1 Kin. 5:1
   Provides men and material for Solomon's Temple ... 1 Kin. 5:1-12
   Refuses gifts of cities from Solomon ... 1 Kin. 9:10-13
   Helps Solomon with money and seamen ... 1 Kin. 9:14, 26-28; 1 Kin. 10:11
2. Craftsman; a son of a Tyrian and a widow of Naphtali ... 1 Kin. 7:13, 14
   Sent by King Solomon to work on Temple ... 1 Kin. 7:14-40, 45
   Called Huram ... 2 Chr. 2:11

Hire—*wages*

A. *Used literally of payments to:*

Prostitute ... Deut. 23:18
Priests ... Judg. 18:4
Pay the poor ... James 5:4
Mercenary soldiers ... 2 Sam. 10:6
Mercenary prophets ... Deut. 23:4
Gospel messengers ... Luke 10:7

B. *Used figuratively of:*

Spiritual adultery ... Ezek. 16:33
Sexual relations ... Gen. 30:16
Reward ("wages") ... John 4:36

See Wages, hire

Hireling—*a common laborer*

Anxious for the day to close ... Job 7:1, 2
Figurative of man's life ... Job 14:6
Subject to oppression ... Mal. 3:5
Guilty of neglect ... John 10:12, 13

Hiss—*meaning to call, allure, or entice*

Applied to:

Nations ... Is. 5:26
Egypt and Assyria ... Is. 7:18
Israel ... Zech. 10:8

History, Biblical

A. *Characteristics of:*

Dated with human events ... Hag. 1:1, 15; Luke 3:1
Inspired ... 2 Tim. 3:16
Free of myths ... 2 Pet. 1:16

B. *Valuable for:*

Outline of ancient history ... Acts 7:1-53
Spiritual lessons ... 1 Cor. 10:1-11
Prophecy and fulfillment ... Acts 4:24-28

Hittites—*an ancient nation*

A. *Facts concerning:*

Descendants of Canaan ... Gen. 10:15
One of seven Canaanite nations ... Deut. 7:1
Original inhabitants of Palestine ... Ezek. 16:3, 45
Ruled by kings ... 1 Kin. 10:29
Great nation ... 2 Kin. 7:6
Their land promised to Israel ... Gen. 15:18, 20
Destruction of, commanded ... Deut. 7:1, 2, 24
Destruction of, incomplete ... Judg. 3:5

B. *Intermarriage with:*

By Esau ... Gen. 36:2
By Israelites after the conquest ... Judg. 3:5, 6
By Solomon ... 1 Kin. 11:1
By Israelites after the exile ... Ezra 9:1, 2

C. *Notable persons of:*

Ephron ... Gen. 49:30
Ahimelech ... 1 Sam. 26:6
Uriah ... 2 Sam. 11:6, 21

Hivites

Descendants of Canaan ... Gen. 10:15, 17
One of seven Canaanite nations ... Deut. 7:1
Esau intermarries with ... Gen. 36:2
Gibeonites belong to ... Josh. 9:3, 7
Land of, promised to Israel ... Ex. 3:8; Ex. 23:23
Destruction of:
Commanded ... Deut. 7:1, 2, 24
Incomplete ... Judg. 3:3

Hizkiah—*Jehovah strengthens*

Son of Neariah ... 1 Chr. 3:23

Hizkijah—*Jehovah strengthens*

Ancestor of returning exiles ... Neh. 10:17

Hoar—*white*

Applied to frost ... Ex. 16:14
Applied to gray hair ... Lev. 19:32

Hobah—*hiding place*

Town north of Damascus ... Gen. 14:15

Hod—*majesty*

Asherite ... 1 Chr. 7:30, 37

Hodaviah—*praise ye Jehovah*

1. Son of Elioenai ... 1 Chr. 3:24
2. Chief of Manasseh ... 1 Chr. 5:23, 24
3. Benjamite ... 1 Chr. 9:7
4. Levite, founder of a family ... Ezra 2:40
   Called Judah ... Ezra 3:9

Hodesh—*new moon*

Wife of Shaharaim ... 1 Chr. 8:8, 9

Hodiah—*splendor of Jehovah*

1. Judahite ... 1 Chr. 4:1, 19
2. Levite interpreter ... Neh. 8:7
   Leads in prayer ... Neh. 9:5
   Probably the same as one of the signers of the covenant ... Neh. 10:10, 13
3. Signer of the covenant ... Neh. 10:18

Hoglah—*partridge*

Daughter of Zelophehad ... Num. 26:33

SUBJECT — REFERENCE

Hoham—*Jehovah protests*
- Amorite king defeated by Joshua ... Josh. 10:3-27

Hold fast
- Good thing ... 1 Thess. 5:21
- Faithful word ... Titus 1:9
- Our confidence ... Heb. 3:6
- Our profession ... Heb. 4:14
- What we have ... Rev. 2:25; Rev. 3:11

Holiness of Christ

A. *Announced in:*
- Psalms ... Ps. 16:10
- Prophets ... Is. 11:4, 5

B. *Proclaimed by:*
- Gabriel ... Luke 1:35
- Demons ... Mark 1:24
- Centurion ... Luke 23:47
- Peter ... Acts 4:27, 30
- Paul ... 2 Cor. 5:21
- John ... 1 John 2:1, 29

C. *Manifested negatively in freedom from:*
- Sin ... 1 John 3:5
- Guilt ... John 8:46
- Defilement ... Heb. 7:26, 27

D. *Manifested as "the Holy One" applied by:*
- Demons ... Mark 1:24
- Peter ... Acts 2:27
- Paul ... Acts 13:35
- John ... 1 John 2:20
- Christ Himself ... Rev. 3:7

Holiness of Christians

A. *In their calling:*
- Elected to ... Rom. 8:29
- Called to ... 1 Thess. 4:7
- Created in ... Eph. 4:24
- Possessed by ... 1 Cor. 3:16, 17

B. *In their lives:*
- Bodies ... Rom. 6:13, 19
- Manner of life ... 1 Pet. 1:15
- Fruitfulness ... John 15:8

C. *Reasons for:*
- God's holiness ... 1 Pet. 1:15, 16
- God's mercies ... Rom. 12:1, 2
- Christ's love ... 2 Cor. 5:14, 15
- World's end ... 2 Pet. 3:11
- Inheritance in kingdom ... Eph. 5:5

D. *God's means of:*
- Word ... John 17:17
- Chastisement ... Heb. 12:10
- Grace ... Titus 2:3, 11, 12

See Godliness; Sanctification

Holiness to the Lord
- Breastplate insignia ... Ex. 28:36

Holon—*strong place*
1. City of Judah ... Josh. 15:51
2. City of Moab ... Jer. 48:21

Holy Day, holy-day—*any of the Jewish high holidays*
- Sabbath ... Ex. 35:2
- "Holyday" ... Col. 2:16
- Rendered "Feast" ... Luke 2:41

Holy Land (see Canaan, Land of)

Holy of Holies

A. *Described as:*
- Sanctuary ... Lev. 4:6
- Holy sanctuary ... Lev. 16:33
- Holy place ... Ex. 28:29
- Holy of Holies ... Ex. 26:33; Heb. 9:3
- Inner sanctuary ... 1 Kin. 6:5-20

B. *Contents of:*
- Ark of the testimony ... Ex. 26:33
- Mercy seat ... Ex. 26:34
- Cherubim ... Ex. 25:18-22
- Altar of incense ... Heb. 9:4
- Pot of manna ... Ex. 16:33
- Aaron's rod ... Num. 17:10
- Written copy of the Law ... Deut. 31:26; 2 Kin. 22:8

C. *Entrance to, by the high priest:*
- Not at all times ... Lev. 16:2
- Alone, once a year ... Heb. 9:7
- With blood ... Lev. 16:14, 15
- To make atonement ... Lev. 16:15-17, 33, 34

D. *Significance of:*
- Abolished by Christ's death ... Matt. 27:51
- Typical of heaven ... Ps. 102:19
- Believers now enter boldly ... Heb. 10:19

See Tabernacle

Holy Spirit

A. *Titles applied to:*
- Spirit of:
  - God ... Gen. 1:2
  - The Lord God ... Is. 61:1
  - The Father ... Matt. 10:20
  - Grace ... Zech. 12:10
  - Truth ... John 14:17
  - Holiness ... Rom. 1:4
  - Life ... Rom. 8:2
  - Christ ... Rom. 8:9
  - Adoption ... Rom. 8:15
  - The Son ... Gal. 4:6
  - Glory ... 1 Pet. 4:14
  - Prophecy ... Rev. 19:10
- My Spirit ... Gen. 6:3
- Holy Spirit ... Ps. 51:11
- The Comforter ... John 14:16, 26
- Eternal Spirit ... Heb. 9:14

B. *Deity of:*
- Called God ... Acts 5:3, 4
- Joined with the Father and Son ... Matt. 28:19; 2 Cor. 13:14
- Eternal ... Heb. 9:14
- Omnipotent ... Luke 1:35
- Omniscient ... 1 Cor. 2:10, 11
- Omnipresent ... Ps. 139:7-13
- Creator ... Gen. 1:2
- Sovereign ... 1 Cor. 12:6, 11
- New creation ... John 3:3, 8
- Sin against, eternal ... Matt. 12:31, 32

C. *Personality of:*
- Speaks ... Acts 28:25
- Teaches ... John 14.26
- Strives with sinners ... Gen. 6:3
- Comforts ... Acts 9:31
- Helps our infirmities ... Rom. 8:26
- Is grieved ... Eph. 4:30
- Is resisted ... Acts 7:51

D. *Work in the world:*
- Creates ... Job 33:4
- Renews ... Is. 32:15
- Convicts men ... John 16:8-11
- Stirs up pagan king ... 2 Chr. 36:22

E. *Work of, in Christ's ministry:*
- Christ conceived by ... Luke 1:35
- Miracles performed by ... Matt. 12:28
- Anointed by ... Matt. 3:16
- Supported by ... Luke 4:1, 17
- Filled by ... Luke 4:1
- Offered to God by ... Heb. 9:14
- Raised by ... Rom. 1:4
- Justified by ... 1 Tim. 3:16

F. *Work of, in the Scriptures:*
- Speaks in:
  - Prophets ... Acts 28:25
  - Psalms ... Acts 1:16
  - All Scripture ... 2 Tim. 3:16
- His sword ... Eph. 6:17

G. *Ministry of, among believers:*
- Regenerates ... John 3:3, 5
- Indwells ... Rom. 8:11
- Anoints ... 1 John 2:20, 27
- Baptizes ... Acts 2:17-41
- Guides ... John 16:13
- Empowers ... Mic. 3:8
- Sanctifies ... Rom. 15:16; 2 Thess. 2:13
- Bears witness ... Rom. 8:16; Heb. 10:15
- Comforts ... John 14:16-26
- Gives joy ... Rom. 14:17
- Gives discernment ... 1 Cor. 2:10-16; 1 John 4:1-6
- Bears fruit ... Gal. 5:22, 23
- Give gifts ... 1 Cor. 12:3-11

H. *Ministry of, in the Church:*
- Fills ... Acts 2:4
- Baptizes ... 1 Cor. 12:13
- Appoints officers ... Acts 20:17, 18
- Sends out missionaries ... Acts 13:2, 4
- Directs missionaries ... Acts 8:29
- Comforts the Church ... Acts 9:31
- Sanctifies the Church ... Rom. 15:16

I. *Reception of:*
- Promised ... Joel 2:28-32
- Awaits Christ's glorification ... John 7:38, 39
- Realized at Pentecost ... Acts 2:1-21
- Realized by Gentiles ... Acts 10:45
- Contingent ... Acts 2:38; Acts 5:32
- Can be sinned against ... Matt. 12:31, 32

J. *Filling of:*
- Bezaleel ... Ex. 31:2
- Jesus ... Luke 4:1
- John the Baptist ... Luke 1:15, 60
- Elizabeth ... Luke 1:41
- Zechariah ... Luke 1:67
- Pentecost Christians ... Acts 2:1-4
- Peter ... Acts 4:8
- Seven men ... Acts 6:3-5
- Stephen ... Acts 7:55
- Barnabas ... Acts 11:22, 24
- Paul ... Acts 13:9
- Certain disciples ... Acts 13:52

K. *As teacher:*
- Illuminates the mind ... 1 Cor. 2:12, 13; Eph. 1:16, 17
- Reveals things of God ... Is. 40:13, 14; 1 Cor. 2:10, 13

H

Home—*center of family life*

Things associated with:
- Eating ... 1 Cor. 11:34
- Keeping house ... Titus 2:5
- Religious training ... 1 Tim. 5:4
- Entertainment ... Luke 15:6
- Domestic:
  - Counsel ... 1 Cor. 14:35
  - Discord ... 2 Sam. 14:13-24
- Land ... Ruth 1:22
- Friends ... Mark 5:19
- Present life ... 2 Cor. 5:6

See House

Homeless
- Christ's condition ... Luke 9:58
- True of apostles also ... 1 Cor. 4:11

Homer—*a heap*
- Measure; equal to about 11 bushels ... Ezek. 45:11, 14

Homesickness
- Jacob ... Gen. 30:25
- Edomite Hadad ... 1 Kin. 11:21, 22
- Exiles ... Ps. 137:1-6
- Prodigal son ... Luke 15:11-19
- Epaphroditus ... Phil. 2:25, 26

Homestead—*the family dwelling*
- Redeemable ... Lev. 25:25-30

Homicide

Provisions provided:
- Distinction between guilty and innocent ... Ex. 21:12-14; Num. 35:16-23
- Determination of guilt ... Num. 35:24, 30
- Detention in cities of refuge ... Num. 35:11, 15, 25-29
- Defilement of land by slack justice ... Num. 35:31-34

See Murder

Homosexuality
- Forbidden ... Lev. 18:22
- Considered an abomination ... 1 Kin. 14:24
- Punishment ... Lev. 20:13
- Unclean ... Rom. 1:24, 26, 27

Honest, honesty—*uprightness*

A. *Necessity of:*
- Signs of a righteous man ... Ps. 1:1-3; Luke 8:15
- Means of testimony ... 1 Pet. 2:12
- Obligatory upon Christians ... 2 Cor. 13:7

B. *Blessings of:*
- Brings advancement ... Is. 33:15-17
- Makes acceptable with God ... Ps. 15:1, 2

SUBJECT REFERENCE

C. *Examples of:*
Samuel ..... 1 Sam. 12:1-5
David ..... 1 Sam. 25:7, 15
Workmen ..... 2 Kin. 12:15
Zacchaeus ..... Luke 19:8
Paul ..... 2 Cor. 8:20, 21

Honey—*a sweet substance*

A. *Characteristics of:*
Product of bees ..... Judg. 14:8, 9
Not acceptable in offerings ..... Lev. 2:11
Offered as part of first fruits ..... 2 Chr. 31:5

B. *Figurative of:*
God's Word ..... Ps. 19:10
God's blessings ..... Ex. 3:8, 17
Wisdom ..... Prov. 24:13, 14
Pleasant words ..... Prov. 16:24
Prostitute's enticements ..... Prov. 5:3
Immanuel's diet ..... Is. 7:14, 15

Honor—*to esteem or regard highly*

A. *Those worthy of:*
God ..... 1 Tim. 1:17
Christ ..... John 5:23
Parents ..... Eph. 6:2
Aged ..... 1 Tim. 5:1, 3
Church officers ..... Phil. 2:25, 29

B. *Obtainable by:*
Wisdom ..... Prov. 3:16
Graciousness ..... Prov. 11:16
Discipline ..... Prov. 13:18
Humility ..... Prov. 15:33
Peaceableness ..... Prov. 20:3
Righteousness and mercy ..... Prov. 21:21
Honoring God ..... 1 Sam. 2:30
Serving Christ ..... John 12:26

C. *Those advanced to:*
Joseph ..... Gen. 41:41-43
Phinehas ..... Num. 25:7-13
Joshua ..... Num. 27:18-20
Solomon ..... 1 Kin. 3:13
Abishai ..... 1 Chr. 11:20, 21
Daniel ..... Dan. 2:48
Mordecai ..... Esth. 8:15
Apostles ..... Matt. 19:27-29

Hoof—*the horny covering of the extremities of certain animals*

Test of clean animals ..... Lev. 11:3-8
All must leave with Israel ..... Ex. 10:26
Break because of prancings ..... Judg. 5:22
Like flint ..... Is. 5:28
Cause noise ..... Jer. 47:3

Hook

Used:
For curtains ..... Ex. 26:32, 37
In fishing ..... Job 41:1, 2
For pruning ..... Is. 2:4
Expressive of God's sovereignty ..... 2 Kin. 19:28

Hope—*the expectation of future good*

A. *Kinds of:*
Natural expectation ..... Acts 27:20
Sinful expectation ..... Acts 24:26
Impossible ..... Rom. 4:18
Spiritual assurance ..... 2 Cor. 1:7

B. *Described as:*
Living ..... 1 Pet. 1:3
Blessed ..... Titus 2:13
Good ..... 2 Thess. 2:16
Better ..... Heb. 7:19
Sure and steadfast ..... Heb. 6:19
One of the great virtures ..... 1 Cor. 13:13

C. *Productive of:*
Purity ..... 1 John 3:3
Patience ..... Rom. 8:25
Courage ..... Rom. 5:4, 5
Joy ..... Rom. 12:12
Salvation ..... Rom. 8:23
Assurance ..... Heb. 6:18, 19
Stability ..... Col. 1:23

D. *Grounds of:*
God's Word ..... Ps. 119:42-81; Rom. 15:4
God's promises ..... Acts 26:6, 7; Titus 1:2

E. *Objects of:*
God ..... Ps. 39:7
Christ ..... 1 Cor. 15:19
Salvation ..... Rom. 5:1-5
Resurrection ..... Acts 23:6
Eternal life ..... Titus 1:2
Glory ..... Rom. 5:2
Christ's return ..... Rom. 8:22-25

Hopelessness—*without hope*

Condition of the wicked ..... Eph. 2:12
Their unchangeable condition ..... Luke 16:23-31

Hophni—*fighter*

Son of Eli; brother of Phinehas ..... 1 Sam. 1:3
Called "sons of Belial" ..... 1 Sam. 2:12
Guilty of unlawful practices ..... 1 Sam. 2:13-17
Immoral ..... 1 Sam. 2:22
Eli's warning rejected by ..... 1 Sam. 2:23-25
Cursed by a man of God ..... 1 Sam. 2:27-36
Warned by Samuel ..... 1 Sam. 3:11-18
Ark taken to battle by ..... 1 Sam. 4:1-8
Slain in battle ..... 1 Sam. 4:11
News of, causes Eli's death ..... 1 Sam. 4:12-18

Hor—*mountain*

1. Mountain of Edom ..... Num. 20:23
   Scene of Aaron's death ..... Num. 20:22-29; Num. 33:37-39
2. Prominent peak of the Lebanon range ..... Num. 34:7, 8

Horam—*elevated*

King of Gezer ..... Josh. 10:33

Horeb—*desert*

God appears to Moses ..... Ex. 3:1-22
Water flows from ..... Ex. 17:6
Law given here ..... Mal. 4:4
Site of Israel's great sin ..... Deut. 9:8, 9; Ps. 106:19
Covenant made ..... Deut. 29:1
Elijah lodged here 40 days ..... 1 Kin. 19:8, 9
See Sinai

Horem—*consecrated*

City of Naphtali ..... Josh. 19:32, 38

Hor-hagidgad—*cavern of Gidgah*

Israelite encampment ..... Num. 33:32
See Gudgodah

Hori—*cave dweller*

1. Son of Lotan ..... Gen. 36:22; 1 Chr. 1:39
2. Horites ..... Gen. 36:21-30
3. Father of Shaphat the spy ..... Num. 13:5

Horim, Horites—*cave dwellers*

Inhabitants of Mt. Seir ..... Gen. 36:20
Defeated by Chedorlaomer ..... Gen. 14:5, 6
Ruled by chieftains ..... Gen. 36:29, 30
Driven out by Esau's descendants ..... Gen. 36:20-29; Deut. 2:12, 22

Hormah—*devoted to destruction*

Originally called Zephath ..... Judg. 1:17
Scene of Israel's defeat ..... Num. 14:45
Destroyed by Israel ..... Num. 21:1-3
Assigned to Judah ..... Josh. 15:30
Transferred to Simeon ..... Josh. 19:4
David sends spoils to ..... 1 Sam. 30:26, 30

Horn—*bone-like protrusion from an animal's head*

A. *Descriptive of:*
Ram's ..... Gen. 22:13
Ox's ..... Ex. 21:29
Unicorn ..... Ps. 92:10
Goat's ..... Dan. 8:5
Altar's ..... 1 Kin. 1:50

B. *Uses of:*
For trumpets ..... Josh. 6:4, 13
For vessels ..... 1 Sam. 16:1-13

C. *Figurative of:*
God's power ..... Hab. 3:4
Christ's power ..... Rev. 5:6
Power of the wicked ..... Ps. 22:21
Power of earthly kingdoms ..... Dan. 7:7, 8, 24
Power of the antichrist ..... Rev. 13:1
Arrogance ..... 1 Kin. 22:11
Conquests ..... Deut. 33:17
Exaltation ..... 1 Sam. 2:1, 10
Degradation ..... Job 16:15
Destruction ..... Jer. 48:25
Salvation ..... Luke 1:69

D. *As musical instrument:*
Heard at Sinai ..... Ex. 19:16
Sounded in jubilee year ..... Lev. 25:9
Used on occasions ..... 1 Chr. 15:28
A part of worship ..... 2 Chr. 15:14
Used in Babylon ..... Dan. 3:7, 10

Hornets—*a large, strong wasp*

God's agents ..... Ex. 23:28; Deut. 7:20
Kings driven out by ..... Josh. 24:12

Horns of the altar—*the protruding points at the four corners of an altar*

Description ..... Ex. 27:2
Provides sanctuary ..... 1 Kin. 1:50

Horonaim—*two caverns*

Moabite city ..... Is. 15:5

Horonite

Native of Horonaim ..... Neh. 2:10, 19

Horoscope—*fortune-telling by astrology*

Forbidden ..... Jer. 10:2
Unprofitable ..... Deut. 17:2-5
Punishment ..... Is. 47:13, 14

Horse

A. *Used for:*
Travel ..... Deut. 17:16
War ..... Ex. 14:9
Bearing burdens ..... Neh. 7:68
Sending messages ..... Esth. 8:10
Idolatry ..... 2 Kin. 23:11

B. *Figurative of:*
Human trust ..... Hos. 14:3
Obstinacy ..... Ps. 32:9; James 3:3
Impetuosity in sin ..... Jer. 8:6
God's protection ..... 2 Kin. 2:11

Horseleech—*a large leech*

Figurative of insatiable appetite ..... Prov. 30:15, 16

Horse traders

Tyre famous for ..... Ezek. 27:2, 14

Horse gate—*a gate of Jerusalem*

Restored by Nehemiah ..... Neh. 3:28

Hosah—*seeking refuge*

1. Village of Asher ..... Josh. 19:29
2. Temple porter ..... 1 Chr. 16:38

Hosanna—*save, now, we beseech thee*

Triumphal acclaim ..... Matt. 21:9, 15; Mark 11:9

Hosea—*salvation*

Son of Beeri, prophet of the northern kingdom ..... Hos. 1:1
Reproved idolatory ..... Hos. 1—2
Threatens God's judgment; calls to repentance ..... Hos. 3—6
Foretells impending judgment ..... Hos. 7—10
Calls an ungrateful people to repentance; promises God's blessings ..... Hos. 11—14

Hosen—*trousers*

Bound in ..... Dan. 3:21

Hoshaiah—*Jehovah has saved*

1. Father of Jezaniah and Azariah ..... Jer. 42:1
2. Participant in a dedication ..... Neh. 12:31, 32

Hoshama—*Jehovah has heard*

Son of King Jeconiah ..... 1 Chr. 3:17, 18

Hoshea—*save*

1. Original name of Joshua, the son of Nun ..... Deut. 32:44

   See Joshua, Jehoshua
2. Ephraimite chieftain ..... 1 Chr. 27:20
3. One who signs covenant ..... Neh. 10:1, 23
4. Israel's last king; usurps throne ..... 2 Kin. 15:30

SUBJECT — REFERENCE

5. Reigns wickedly; Israel taken to Assyria during reign ... 2 Kin. 17:1-23

Hospitality—*reception and entertainment of strangers*

A. *Kinds of:*
- Treacherous ... Judg. 4:17-21
- Rewarded ... Josh. 6:17-25
- Unwise ... 2 Kin. 20:12-19
- Critical ... Luke 7:36-50
- Unwelcomed ... Luke 9:51-53
- Joyful ... Luke 19:5, 6
- Turbulent ... Acts 17:5-9
- Forbidden ... 3 John 1, 9, 10

B. *Act of:*
- Commanded ... Rom. 12:13
- Required of church leaders ... 1 Tim. 3:2
- Discipleship ... Matt. 25:35

C. *Courtesies of:*
- Protection provided ... Gen. 19:6-8
- Shelter and food ... Luke 11:5-8
- Washing of feet ... Luke 7:44
- Kissing ... Luke 7:45
- Denied with indignities ... Judg. 19:15-28; Luke 10:10-16

D. *Examples of:*
- Abraham to angels ... Gen. 18:1-8
- Lot to an angel ... Gen. 19:1-11
- Laban to Abraham's servant ... Gen. 24:31-33
- Joseph to his brothers ... Gen. 43:31-34
- Pharaoh to Jacob ... Gen. 45:16-20
- Rahab to the spies ... Josh. 2:1-16
- David to Mephibosheth ... 2 Sam. 9:6-13
- Martha to Jesus ... Luke 10:38-42
- Lydia to Paul and Silas ... Acts 16:14, 15
- Barbarians to Paul ... Acts 28:2, 7

Host—*one who entertains*
- One who entertains hospitably ... Rom. 16:23

Hostage—*a person held as security*
- Captive for pledge ... 2 Kin. 14:14; 2 Chr. 25:24

Host of Heaven

A. *Used of stars as objects of worship:*
- Objects of idolatry ... Deut. 4:19
- Practiced in Israel ... 2 Kin. 17:16
- Introduced by Manasseh ... 2 Kin. 21:5
- Abolished by Josiah ... 2 Kin. 23:4-12
- Worship of, on roofs ... Jer. 19:13

B. *Used of stars as created things:*
- Created by God ... Is. 45:12
- Cannot be numbered ... Jer. 33:22
- Named by God ... Is. 40:26
- To be dissolved ... Is. 34:4

C. *Used of angels:*
- Created by God ... Neh. 9:6
- Around the throne ... 1 Kin. 22:19

Hosts, Lord of—*a title of God*
- Commander of: Israel's armies ... 1 Sam. 17:45; Is. 31:4
- Armies (angels) of heaven ... Gen. 28:12, 13; Hos. 12:4, 5; Ps. 89:6-8
- Same as Sabaoth ... Rom. 9:29

Hotham, Hothan—*determination*
1. Asherite ... 1 Chr. 7:30, 32
2. Father of two of David's valiant men ... 1 Chr. 11:26, 44

Hothir—*abundance*
- Son of Heman; a musician ... 1 Chr. 25:4, 28

Hough—*to cut the tendons of the leg*
- To render captured animals useless ... Josh. 11:6, 9; 2 Sam. 8:4

Hour—*a division of time*

A. *Used literally of:*
- One-twelfth of daylight ... Matt. 20:1-12
- One-twelfth of night ... Luke 12:39

B. *Jewish reckoning (from 6 P.M. and from 6 A.M.):*
- Third (9 A.M.) ... Matt. 20:3
- Sixth and ninth (12 noon; 3 P.M.) ... Matt. 20:5
- Ninth (3 P.M.) ... Acts 3:1
- Eleventh (5 P.M.) ... Matt. 20:6, 9, 12
- Third (9 P.M.) ... Acts 23:23

C. *Used literally and descriptively of Christ's:*
- Death ... Mark 14:35
- Betrayal ... Matt. 26:45
- Glorification ... John 13:1
- Set time ... John 7:30
- Predestined time ... John 12:27

D. *Used prophetically of:*
- Gospel age ... John 4:21
- Great tribulation ... Rev. 3:10
- God's judgment ... Rev. 14:7, 15
- Christ's return ... Matt. 24:42, 44, 50

Hours of prayer

A. *Characteristics of:*
- Jewish custom ... Luke 1:10
- Centered in the Temple ... Luke 18:10
- Directed toward Jerusalem ... 1 Kin. 8:48

B. *Times of:*
- Three times daily ... Dan. 6:10
- First, at third hour (9 A.M.) ... Acts 2:15
- Second, at sixth hour (12 noon) ... Acts 10:9
- Third, at ninth hour (3 P.M.) ... Acts 3:1

House

A. *Descriptive of:*
- Family dwelling ... Judg. 11:34; Acts 16:34
- Family ... Gen. 14:14; Acts 16:31
- Descendants ... Gen. 18:19; Luke 2:4
- Racial or religious group ... Is. 7:13; Jer. 31:31
- Tabernacle or Temple ... Ex. 34:26; 1 Kin. 6:1

B. *Figurative of:*
- Grave ... Job 30:23
- Body ... 2 Cor. 5:1
- Visible Church ... Gal. 6:10
- True Church ... Heb. 10:21
- Earthly life ... Ps. 119:54
- Heaven ... John 14:2
- Security and insecurity ... Matt. 7:24-27
- Division ... Mark 3:25

See Home

Household idols
- Laban's stolen by Rachel ... Gen. 31:19-35
- Used in idolatry ... Hos. 3:4

Householder—*master of a house*
- Parable of ... Matt. 13:27; Matt. 21:33

Housekeeper
- Sarah ... Gen. 18:6
- Rebekah ... Gen. 27:6-9
- Abigail ... 1 Sam. 25:41, 42
- Happy ... Ps. 113:9
- Ideal woman ... Prov. 31:10-31
- Martha ... Luke 10:40, 41

House of God
- Tabernacle called ... Luke 6:4
- Temple described ... Ezra 5:2, 8
- Church named ... 1 Tim. 3:15
- Center of God's worship ... Ps. 42:4

House of prayer
- Corrupted into a den of thieves ... Matt. 21:13; Mark 11:17

Houses—*dwellings made for habitations*
- Rechabites refuse to dwell in ... Jer. 35:5-10

Hukkok—*decreed*
- Border town of Naphtali ... Josh. 19:32, 34

Hukok
- Land given as place of refuge ... 1 Chr. 6:75

Hul—*circle*
- Aram's second son ... Gen. 10:23

Huldah—*weasel, mole*
- Wife of Shallum ... 2 Kin. 22:14
- Foretells Jerusalem's ruin ... 2 Kin. 22:15-17; 2 Chr. 34:22-25
- Exempts Josiah from trouble ... 2 Kin. 22:18-20

Human dignity

Based on:
- God's image ... Gen. 1:26
- Elevated by God ... Ps. 8:3-8
- Loved ... John 3:16
- Chosen ... John 15:16

Humaneness—*a kind spirit*
- Toward animals ... Ex. 23:5
- Not shown by Balaam ... Num. 22:27-30

Humanitarianism—*promoting the welfare of humanity*
- Illustrated by Jesus ... Luke 10:30-37
- Enjoined on Christians ... 1 Thess. 5:15

Human nature of Christ

A. *Predicted as seed of:*
- Woman ... Gen. 3:15
- Abraham ... Gal. 3:8, 16
- David ... Luke 1:31, 32

B. *Proved by:*
- Virgin's conception ... Matt. 1:18
- Birth ... Matt. 1:16, 25
- Incarnation ... John 1:14
- Circumcision ... Luke 2:21
- Growth ... Luke 2:52
- Genealogy ... Matt. 1:1-17

C. *Manifested in:*
- Hunger ... Matt. 4:2
- Thirst ... John 19:28
- Weariness ... John 4:6
- Sleep ... Matt. 8:24
- Suffering ... Luke 22:44
- Death ... John 19:30
- Burial ... Matt. 27:59, 60
- Resurrection ... Luke 24:39; 1 John 1:1, 2

D. *Importance of, necessary for:*
- Sinlessness ... John 8:46
- His death ... Heb. 2:14, 17
- His resurrection ... 2 Tim. 2:8
- His exaltation ... Phil. 2:9-11
- His priestly intercession ... Heb. 7:26, 28
- His return ... Heb. 9:24-28
- Faith ... 2 John 7-11

See Incarnation of Christ

Human sacrifice

A. *Practiced by:*
- Canaanites ... Deut. 12:31
- Ammonites ... Lev. 20:2, 3
- Moabites ... 2 Kin. 3:26, 27
- Phoenicians ... Jer. 19:5
- Israel ... 2 Kin. 16:3, 4
- Judah ... 2 Chr. 28:3

B. *Sin of:*
- Condemned ... Lev. 18:21
- Source of defilement ... Ezek. 20:31
- Source of demonism ... Ps. 106:37, 38
- Cause of captivity ... 2 Kin. 17:17, 18

Humiliation—*state of deflated pride*

A. *Causes of:*
- Pride ... Esth. 6:6-13
- Arrogance ... Dan. 4:29-33
- Boastfulness ... 1 Sam. 17:42-50
- National sins ... Dan. 9:1-21
- Self-will ... Luke 15:11-19

B. *Remedies against:*
- Be humble ... Luke 14:8-11
- Avoid sinners ... Judg. 16:16-21
- Obey God ... Josh. 7:11-16
- Avoid self-sufficiency ... Luke 22:31-34
- Rely upon God's grace ... 2 Cor. 12:6-10

Humiliation of Christ—*the state that He took while on earth*

A. *Exhibited in His:*
- Taking our nature ... Phil. 2:7
- Birth ... Matt. 1:18-25
- Obedience ... Luke 2:51
- Submission to ordinances ... Matt. 3:13-15
- Becoming a servant ... Matt. 20:28
- Menial acts ... John 13:4-15
- Suffering ... Matt. 26:67, 68
- Death ... John 10:15-18

B. *Rewards of:*
- Exalted by God ... Acts 2:22-36
- Crowned king ... Heb. 1:1, 2

SUBJECT REFERENCE

Perfected forever .... Heb. 2:10
Acceptable high priest .... Heb. 2:17

Humility

A. *Factors involved in sense of:*

One's sinfulness .... Luke 18:13, 14
One's unworthiness .... Luke 15:17-21
One's limitations .... 1 Kin. 3:6-14
God's holiness .... Is. 6:1-8
God's righteousness .... Phil. 3:4-7

B. *Factors producing:*

Affliction .... Deut. 8:3
Impending doom .... 2 Chr. 12:5-12
Submissiveness .... Luke 10:39
Christ's example .... Matt. 11:29

C. *Rewards of:*

Road to honor .... 1 Kin. 3:11-14
Leads to riches .... Prov. 22:4
Brings blessings .... 2 Chr. 7:14, 15
Guarantees exaltation .... James 4:10
Insures God's presence ...... Is. 57:15
Makes truly great .... Matt. 18:4
Unlocks more grace .... Prov. 3:34
James 4:6

D. *Christians exhorted to:*

Put on .... Col. 3:12
Be clothed with .... 1 Pet. 5:5
Walk with .... Eph. 4:1, 2
Avoid false .... Col. 2:18-23

E. *Examples of:*

Abraham .... Gen. 18:27, 32
Jacob .... Gen. 32:10
Moses .... Ex. 3:11
Joshua .... Josh. 7:6
David .... 1 Sam. 18:18-23
Job .... Job 42:2-6
Jeremiah .... Jer. 1:6
Daniel .... Dan. 2:30
Elizabeth .... Luke 1:43
John the Baptist .... John 3:29, 30
Jesus .... Matt. 11:29
Paul .... Acts 20:19

Humtah—*a place of lizards*

Town of Judah .... Josh. 15:54

Hunger, physical

A. *Causes of:*

Fasting .... Matt. 4:1-3
Fatigue .... Gen. 25:30
Famine .... Luke 15:14-17
God's judgment .... Is. 9:19-21

B. *Some results of:*

Selling birthright .... Gen. 25:30-34
Murmuring .... Ex. 16:2, 3
Breaking God's Law .... 1 Sam. 14:31-34
Cannibalism .... 2 Kin. 6:28, 29
Cursing God .... Is. 8:21

C. *Satisfaction of:*

Supplied:
By friends .... 1 Sam. 17:27-29
Supernaturally .... Ex. 16:4-21
Sent as a judgment .... Ps. 106:14, 15
Provided by God .... Matt. 6:11
Christian duty .... 1 Sam. 30:11, 12
Complete in heaven .... Rev. 7:14-17

D. *Examples of:*

David .... 1 Sam. 21:3-6
Elijah .... 1 Kin. 17:11-13
Jeremiah .... Jer. 38:9
Peter .... Acts 10:10
Paul .... 1 Cor. 4:11

E. *Strike:*

By forty men .... Acts 23:11-16

Hunger, spiritual

More important than physical ... Deut. 8:3
Sent as a judgment .... Amos 4:11-13
Will be satisfied .... Is. 55:1, 2
Blessing of .... Matt. 5:6
Satisfied by Christ .... John 6:33-35

Hunter, hunting

A. *Purposes of:*

Kill harmful beasts .... 1 Sam. 17:34-36

B. *Methods of:*

Decoys .... Job 18:10
Nets .... Amos 3:5
Pits .... 2 Sam. 23:20

SUBJECT REFERENCE

Bows and quiver .... Gen. 27:3
Sword, etc. .... Job 41:26-30

C. *Examples of:*

Nimrod .... Gen. 10:8, 9
Ishmael .... Gen. 21:20
Esau .... Gen. 27:3, 5, 30

Hupham—*protected*

Son of Benjamin; founder of
Huphamites .... Num. 26:39
Called Huppim .... Gen. 46:21

Huppah—*covering*

Descendant of Aaron .... 1 Chr. 24:1, 13

Huppim—*protection*

1. Son of Benjamin .... Gen. 46:21
2. Son of Ir .... 1 Chr. 7:12

See Hupham

Hur—*splendor*

1. Man of Judah; of Caleb's house .... 1 Chr. 2:18-20
Grandfather of Bezaleel .... Ex. 31:1, 2
Supports Moses' hands ...... Ex. 17:10-12
Aids Aaron .... Ex. 24:14
2. King of Midian .... Josh. 13:21
3. Father of Rephaiah .... Neh. 3:9

Hurai—*free, noble*

One of David's mighty men ..... 1 Chr. 11:32

Huram—*noble, free*

1. Son of Bela .... 1 Chr. 8:5
2. King of Tyre .... 2 Chr. 2:11

Huri—*linen worker*

Gadite .... 1 Chr. 5:14

Husband—*married man*

A. *Regulations concerning:*

One flesh .... Matt. 19:5, 6
Until death .... Rom. 7:2, 3
Rights of .... 1 Cor. 7:1-5
Sanctified by wife .... 1 Cor. 7:14-16

B. *Duties of, toward wife:*

Love .... Eph. 5:25-33
Live with for life .... Matt. 19:3-9
Be faithful to .... Mal. 2:14, 15
Be satisfied with .... Prov. 5:18, 19
Instruct .... 1 Cor. 14:34, 35
Honor .... 1 Pet. 3:7
Confer with .... Gen. 31:4-16
Provide for .... 1 Tim. 5:8
Rule over .... Gen. 3:16

C. *Kinds of:*

Adam, blaming .... Gen. 3:9-12
Isaac, loving .... Gen. 24:67
Elkanah, sympathetic .... 1 Sam. 1:8-23
Nabal, evil .... 1 Sam. 25:3
Ahab, weak .... 1 Kin. 21:5-16
David, ridiculed .... 2 Sam. 6:20
Job, strong .... Job 2:7-10

Husbandman—*a man of the soil*

Farmer .... Gen. 9:20
2 Kin. 25:12
Tenant farmer .... Matt. 21:33-42
Takes share of crops .... 2 Tim. 2:6

Hushah—*haste*

Judahite .... 1 Chr. 4:4

Hushai—*hasty*

Archite; David's friend .... 2 Sam. 15:32-37
Feigns sympathy with
Absalom .... 2 Sam. 16:16-19
Defeats Ahithophel's advice ..... 2 Sam. 17:5-23

Husham—*hastily*

Temanite king of Edom .... Gen. 36:34, 35

Hushathite

Inhabitant of Hushah .... 2 Sam. 21:18

Hushim—*hasters*

1. Head of a Danite family ..... Gen. 46:23
Called Shuham .... Num. 26:42
2. Sons of Aher .... 1 Chr. 7:12
3. Wife of Shaharaim .... 1 Chr. 8:8, 11

SUBJECT REFERENCE

Husks—*the pods of the carob or locust tree*

Fed to swine .... Luke 15:15, 16

Huzzab—*uncertain meaning*

May refer to Assyrian queen or to Nineveh; or may be rendered "it is decreed" .... Nah. 2:7

Hymenaeus—*belonging to Hymen*

False teacher excommunicated by
Paul .... 1 Tim. 1:19, 20
Teaches error .... 2 Tim. 2:17, 18

Hymn—*a spiritual song*

A. *Occasions producing:*

Great deliverance .... Ex. 15:1-19
Great victory .... Judg. 5:1-31
Prayer answered .... 1 Sam. 2:1-10
Mary's "Magnificat" .... Luke 1:46-55
Father's ecstasy .... Luke 1:68-79
Angel's delight .... Luke 2:14
Old man's faith .... Luke 2:29-32
Heaven's eternal praise ...... Rev. 5:9-14

B. *Purposes of:*

Worship God .... 2 Chr. 23:18
Express joy .... Matt. 26:30
Edify .... 1 Cor. 14:15
Testify to others .... Acts 16:25

Hypocrisy, hypocrite—*showy, empty display of religion*

A. *Kinds of:*

Worldly .... Matt. 23:5-7
Legalistic .... Rom. 10:3
Evangelical .... 2 Pet. 2:10-22
Satanic .... 2 Cor. 11:13-15

B. *Described as:*

Self-righteous .... Luke 18:11, 12
"Holier than thou" .... Is. 65:5
Blind .... Matt. 23:17-26
Covetous .... 2 Pet. 2:3
Showy .... Matt. 6:2, 5, 16
Highly critical .... Matt. 7:3-5
Indignant .... Luke 13:14-16
Bound by traditions .... Matt. 15:1-9
Neglectful of major duties ... Matt. 23:23, 24
Pretended but unpracticed ... Ezek. 33:31, 32
Interested in the externals ... Luke 20:46, 47
Fond of titles .... Matt. 23:6, 7
Inwardly unregenerate ...... Luke 11:39

C. *Examples of:*

Jacob .... Gen. 27:6-35
Jacob's sins .... Gen. 37:29-35
Delilah .... Judg. 16:4-20
Ishmael .... Jer. 41:6, 7
Herod .... Matt. 2:7, 8
Pharisees .... John 8:4-9
Judas .... Matt. 26:25-49
Ananias .... Acts 5:1-10
Peter .... Gal. 2:11-14

Hyssop—*a small plant*

Grows from walls .... 1 Kin. 4:33
Used in sprinkling blood .... Ex. 12:22
Used to offer Jesus vinegar ..... John 19:28, 29
Typical of spiritual cleansing .... Ps. 51:7

I

I AM—*a title indicating self-existence*

Revealed to Moses .... Ex. 3:14
Said by Christ .... John 8:57, 58

Christ expressing, refers to:

Bread of Life .... John 6:35, 41 48, 51
Light of the world .... John 8:12
John 9:5
Door of the sheep .... John 10:7, 9
Good Shepherd .... John 10:11, 14
Resurrection and the Life ...... John 11:25
True and living Way .... John 14:6
True Vine .... John 15:1, 5

Ibleam—*he destroys the people*

City assigned to Manasseh ...... Josh. 17:11, 12
Canaanites remain in .... Judg. 1:27
Called Bileam .... 1 Chr. 6:70
Ahaziah slain near .... 2 Kin. 9:27

Ibneiah—*Jehovah builds up*

Head of a Benjamite family ..... 1 Chr. 9:8

SUBJECT — REFERENCE

Ibnijah—*Jehovah builds up*
Father of Reuel ... 1 Chr. 9:8

Ibri—*a Hebrew*
Son of Jaaziah ... 1 Chr. 24:27

Ibsam—*fragrant*
Descendant of Issachar ... 1 Chr. 7:2

Ibzan—*active*
Judge of Israel ... Judg. 12:8
Father of 60 children ... Judg. 12:8, 9

Ice
Figurative of:
God casts forth ... Ps. 147:17
By reason of ... Job 6:16

Ichabod—*inglorious*
Son of Phinehas ... 1 Sam. 4:19-22

Iconium—*image-like*
City of Asia Minor; visited by Paul ... Acts 13:51
Many converts in ... Acts 14:1-6
Paul visits again ... Acts 14:21
Timothy's ministry ... Acts 16:1, 2
Paul persecuted ... 2 Tim. 3:11

Iconoclast—*a breaker of images*
Moses, an angry ... Ex. 32:19, 20
Gideon, an inspired ... Judg. 6:25-32
Jehu, a subtle ... 2 Kin. 10:18-31
Josiah, a reforming ... 2 Kin. 23:12-25

Idalah—*memorial of God*
Border town of Zebulun ... Josh. 19:15

Idbash—*honey-sweet*
Man of Judah ... 1 Chr. 4:3

Iddo—*festal*
1. Chief officer under David ... 1 Chr. 27:21
2. Father of Abinadab ... 1 Kin. 4:14
3. Leader of Jews at Casiphia ... Ezra 8:17-20
4. Gershonite Levite ... 1 Chr. 6:20, 21
   Called Adaiah ... 1 Chr. 6:41
5. Seer whose writings are cited ... 2 Chr. 9:29
6. Grandfather of Zechariah the prophet ... Zech. 1:1, 7
7. Postexilic priest ... Neh. 12:4, 16

Identification—*proving something or somebody to be what it or he really is*
A. *Among men:*
At birth ... Gen. 25:22-26
By the life ... Luke 6:43-45
By speech ... Judg. 12:6
By a search ... 2 Kin. 10:23
By a kiss ... Matt. 26:48, 49
B. *Of Christ the Messiah, by:*
A divine sign ... John 1:31-34
A divine voice ... Matt. 17:5
Divine works ... Matt. 11:2-6
Human testimony ... John 3:26-36
Scriptures ... John 5:39-47
C. *Of spiritual things:*
New birth ... 2 Cor. 5:17
Apostates ... Matt. 7:22, 23
Antichrist ... 2 Thess. 2:1-12
Believers and unbelievers ... Matt. 25:31-46

Identifying with Christ
A. *Proper time, when tempted:*
To harm ... Prov. 1:10-19
To violate convictions ... Dan. 1:8
To conform to world ... Rom. 12:2
To rebellion ... Rom. 13:1-5
To learn evil ... Rom. 16:19
Prov. 19:27
With improper associations ... 2 Cor. 6:14-17
B. *Results:*
Hatred ... John 17:14
Separation ... Luke 6:22, 23
Suffering ... 1 Pet. 2:20, 21
Witness ... 1 Pet. 3:15
Good conscience ... 1 Pet. 3:16
C. *Basis:*
Future glory ... Rom. 8:18
Life of Christ ... Gal. 2:20
Reward ... 2 Tim. 2:12

SUBJECT — REFERENCE

Idleness—*inactivity; slothfulness*
A. *Consequences of:*
Poverty ... Prov. 20:13
Begging ... Prov. 20:4
Hunger ... Prov. 19:15
Bondage ... Prov. 12:24
Ruin ... Prov. 24:30-34
B. *Admonitions against, consider:*
Ant ... Prov. 6:6-11
Ideal woman ... Prov. 31:10-31
Lord ... John 9:4
Apostles ... 2 Thess. 3:7-9
Judgment ... 1 Cor. 3:8-15
See Laziness; slothfulness

Idol makers
Maacah ... 1 Kin. 15:13
Foreign peoples ... Is. 45:16
Men of Judah ... Is. 2:20
People of Jerusalem ... Ezek. 22:3

Idol making
Described by Isaiah ... Is. 44:9-18

Idols, idolatry—*worship of idols*
A. *Described as:*
Irrational ... Acts 17:29
Degrading ... Rom. 1:22, 23
Demonical ... 1 Cor. 10:20, 21
Defiling ... 2 Cor. 6:15-18
Enslaving ... Gal. 4:8, 9
Abominable ... 1 Pet. 4:3
B. *Brief history of:*
Begins in man's apostasy ... Rom. 1:21-25
Prevails in Ur ... Josh. 24:2, 14
In Laban's household ... Gen. 31:19-35
Judgments on Egyptian ... Num. 33:4
Brought from Egypt by Israel ... Josh. 24:14
Forbidden in Law at Sinai ... Ex. 20:1-5
Warnings against, at Sinai ... Ex. 34:13-16
Israel yields to, at Sinai ... Ex. 32:1-8
Moabites entice Israel to ... Num. 25:1-18
Early zeal against ... Josh. 22:10-34
Gideon destroys ... Judg. 6:25-32
Gideon becomes an occasion of ... Judg. 8:24-27
Enticements to Baalism ... Judg. 10:6-16
Levite corrupted by ... Judg. 17:1-13
Danites establish, at Shiloh ... Judg. 18:30, 31
Overthrow of Philistines ... 1 Sam. 5:1-12
Revival against, under Samuel ... 1 Sam. 7:3-6
Solomon yields to ... 1 Kin. 11:1-8
Jeroboam establishes in Jerusalem ... {1 Kin. 12:26-33, 2 Chr. 11:15}
Rehoboam tolerates in Judah ... 1 Kin. 14:22-24
Conflict—Elijah and Ahab ... 1 Kin. 18:1-46
Wicked kings of Israel ... 1 Kin. 21:25, 26
2 Kin. 16:3
Prophet denounces in Israel ... Hos. 4:12-19
Cause of Israel's exile ... 2 Kin. 17:5-23
Judah follows Israel's example ... 2 Chr. 28:1-4
Manasseh climaxes Judah's apostasy in ... {2 Kin. 21:1-18, 2 Chr. 33:1-11}
Reformation against, under Asa ... 2 Chr. 14:3-5
Under Hezekiah ... 2 Chr. 29:15-19
Under Josiah ... 2 Kin. 23:1-20
Prophets denounce in Judah ... Jer. 16:11-21
Cause of Judah's exile ... 2 Kin. 23:26, 27
C. *Christians warned against:*
No company with ... 1 Cor. 5:11
Flee from ... 1 Cor. 10:14
No fellowship with ... 1 Cor. 10:19, 20
Keep from ... 1 John 5:21
Testify against ... Acts 14:15
Turn from ... 1 Thess. 1:9
D. *Enticements to, due to:*
Heathen background ... Josh. 24:2
Ezek. 16:44, 45
Contact with idolaters ... Num. 25:1-6
Intermarriage ... 1 Kin. 11:1-13
Imagined good ... Jer. 44:15-19
Corrupt heart ... Rom. 1:21-23

SUBJECT — REFERENCE

E. *Removed through:*
Punishment ... Deut. 17:2-5
Display of powerlessness ... 1 Sam. 5:1-5
1 Kin. 18:25-29
Logic ... Is. 44:6-20
Display of God's power ... 2 Kin. 19:10-37
Denunciation ... Mic. 1:5-7
Exile ... Zeph. 1:4-6
Hos. 8:5-14
New birth ... Amos 5:26, 27
Hos. 14:1-9

Idumea—*pertaining to Edom*
Name used by Greek and Romans to designate Edom ... Mark 3:8
See Edom

Igal—*He* (God) *redeems*
1. Issachar's spy ... Num. 13:2, 7
2. One of David's mighty men ... 2 Sam. 23:36
3. Shemaiah's son ... 1 Chr. 3:22

Igdaliah—*great is Jehovah*
Father of Hanan the prophet ... Jer. 35:4

Ignorance—*lack of knowledge*
A. *Kinds of:*
Pardonable ... Luke 23:34
Pretended ... Luke 22:57-60
Innocent ... Acts 19:2-5
Excusable ... Acts 17:30
Judicial ... Rom. 1:28
Guilty ... Rom. 1:19-25
Partial ... 1 Cor. 13:12
Confident ... Heb. 11:8
B. *Causes of:*
Unregeneracy ... Eph. 4:18
Unbelief ... 1 Tim. 1:13
Spiritual:
Darkness ... 1 John 2:11
Immaturity ... 1 Cor. 8:7-13
C. *Productive of:*
Unbelief ... John 8:19-43
Error ... Matt. 22:29
D. *Objects of:*
God ... John 8:55
Scriptures ... Matt. 22:29
Christ's return ... 1 Thess. 4:13, 14

Iim—*ruins*
Town of Judah ... Josh. 15:29

Ije-abarim—*ruins of the Abarim* (regions beyond)
Wilderness camp ... Num. 21:11
Same as Iim ... Num. 33:44, 45

Ijon—*heap*
Town of Naphtali; captured by Ben-hadad ... 1 Kin. 15:20
Captured by Tiglath-pileser ... 2 Kin. 15:29

Ikkesh—*crooked*
Father of Ira ... 2 Sam. 23:26
Commander of 24,000 ... 1 Chr. 27:9

Ilai—*supreme*
One of David's mighty men ... 1 Chr. 11:26, 29
Called Zalmon ... 2 Sam. 23:28

Illumination—*enlightenment, understanding*
Of Daniel ... Dan. 5:11, 14

Illumination, spiritual
By the Gospel ... John 1:9
At conversion ... Heb. 6:4
In Christian truth ... Eph. 1:18
By Holy Spirit ... John 16:13-16
By God ... 1 Cor. 4:5

Illustration—*something used to explain something else*
From:
Ancient history ... 1 Cor. 10:1-14
Current history ... Mark 12:1-11
Nature ... Prov. 6:6-11

Illyricum—*a province of Europe*
Paul preaches ... Rom. 15:19

Image (see Idols; idolatry)

Image of God
A. *In man:*
Created in ... Gen. 1:26, 27

SUBJECT REFERENCE

Reason for sanctity of life ... Gen. 9:6
Reason for man's headship ... 1 Cor. 11:7
Restored by grace ... Col. 3:10
Transformed of ... 2 Cor. 3:18

B. *In Christ:*

In essential nature ... Col. 1:15
Manifested on earth ... John 1:14, 18
Believers conformed ... Rom. 8:29

Imagination—*creating mental picture of*

A. *Described as:*

Evil ... Gen. 6:5
Willful ... Jer. 18:12
Deceitful ... Prov. 12:20
Vain ... Rom. 1:21

B. *Cleansing of:*

Promised ... Jer. 3:17
By the power of God ... 2 Cor. 10:5

Imitation—*attempting to duplicate*

Of the good:

God ... Eph. 5:1
Paul's conduct ... 2 Thess. 3:7, 9
Apostles ... 1 Thess. 1:6
Heroes of the faith ... Heb. 6:12
Good ... 3 John 11
Other churches ... 1 Thess. 2:14

See Example of Christ, the

Imla—*fullness*

Father of Micaiah the prophet ... 2 Chr. 18:7, 8
As Imlah ... 1 Kin. 22:8, 9

Immanuel—*God* (is) *with us*

Name given to the child born of the virgin ... {Is. 7:14 / Matt. 1:23}
Emmanuel in ... Matt. 1:23

Immer—*eloquent*

1. Descendant of Aaron ... 1 Chr. 24:1-14
2. Father of Pashur ... Jer. 20:1
3. Founder of a postexilic family ... Ezra 2:37
   The same as the father of Meshillemith ... 1 Chr. 9:12
   Also the ancestor of priests marrying foreigners ... Ezra 10:19, 20
4. Person or place in Babylonia ... Neh. 7:61
5. Zadok's father ... Neh. 3:29

Immorality—*state of a wrongful act or relationship*

Attitude toward:

Consider sanctity of the body ... 1 Cor. 6:13-20
Flee from it ... 1 Cor. 6:18
Get married ... 1 Cor. 7:2
Abstain from it ... 1 Thess. 4:3
Mention it not ... Eph. 5:3
Corrupts the earth ... Rev. 19:2

Immortality—*eternal existence*

A. *Proof of, based upon:*

God's image in man ... Gen. 1:26, 27
Translation of Enoch and Elijah ... {Gen. 5:24 / 2 Kin. 2:11, 12}
Promises of Christ ... John 11:25, 26; John 14:2, 3
Appearance of Moses and Elijah ... Matt. 17:2-9
Eternal rewards and punishments ... {Matt. 25:31-46 / Luke 16:19-31}
Resurrection of Christ ... Rom. 8:11; 1 Cor. 15:12-58
Resurrection of men ... Dan. 12:2, 3; John 5:28, 29

B. *Expression indicative of:*

"I am" ... Matt. 22:32
"Today" ... Luke 23:43
"Shall never die" ... John 11:25, 26
"The redemption of our body" ... Rom. 8:22, 23
"Neither death" ... Rom. 8:38, 39
"We know" ... 2 Cor. 5:1-10
"A lively hope" ... 1 Pet. 1:3-8
"We shall be like him" ... 1 John 3:2

See Eternal, everlasting; Life, eternal

SUBJECT REFERENCE

Immunity—*exemption from something*

From:

Egyptian plagues ... Ex. 8:22, 23
Disease ... Deut. 7:15
Corruption ... Ps. 16:10, 11
Harm ... Luke 10:19
Second death ... Rev. 20:6

Immutability—*unchangeableness*

A. *Of God, expressed by:*

"I AM" ... Ex. 3:14
"Thou art the same" ... Ps. 102:25-27
"I change not" ... Mal. 3:6
"Are without repentance" ... Rom. 11:29
"Who cannot lie" ... Titus 1:2
"The immutability" ... Heb. 6:17, 18
"No variableness" ... James 1:17

B. *Of Christ, expressed by:*

"I am" ... John 8:58
"Thou art the same" ... Heb. 1:12
"Unchangeable" ... Heb. 7:22-24
"The same" ... Heb. 13:8
"I am Alpha and Omega" ... Rev. 1:8-18

C. *Of God, characteristics of:*

Unique ... Is. 43:10
Purposive ... Ps. 138:8
Active ... Phil. 1:6

Imna—*he keeps back*

Asherite chief ... 1 Chr. 7:35

Imnah—*prosperity*

1. Eldest son of Asher ... 1 Chr. 7:30
   Called Jimna and Jimnah ... Num. 26:44; Gen. 46:17
2. Levite in Hezekiah's reign ... 2 Chr. 31:14

Impartiality—*that which is equitable, just, and fair*

In God's:

Material blessings ... Matt. 5:45
Spiritual blessings ... Acts 10:34, 35
Judgments ... Rom. 2:3-12

Impatience—*inability to control one's desire for action*

A. *Causes of:*

Lust ... Gen. 19:4-9
Revenge ... Gen. 34:25-27
Irritability ... Num. 20:10

B. *Consequences of:*

Kept from promised land ... Num. 20:10-12
Great sin ... Ex. 32:1, 21, 30
Foolish statements ... Job 2:7-9
Loss of birthright ... Gen. 25:29-34
Shipwreck ... Acts 27:29-34

Impeccability (see Holiness of Christ)

Impediment—*something that hinders one's activity*

In speech, cured ... Mark 7:32-35
Avoided by obedience ... Prov. 4:10, 12

Impenitence—*without a change of mind*

A. *Expressed by:*

Willful disobedience ... Jer. 44:15-19
Hardness of heart ... John 12:37-40
Refusing to hear ... Luke 16:31
Rebellion against the truth ... 1 Thess. 2:15, 16

B. *Consequences of:*

Spiritual bondage ... John 8:33-44
Judicial blindness ... John 9:39-41
Eternal destruction ... 2 Thess. 1:8, 9

Imperfection of man

A. *Manifested in:*

Falling short of God's glory ... Rom. 3:23
Total corruption ... Is. 1:5, 6

B. *Remedy for:*

New creature ... 2 Cor. 5:17
Conformity to Christ ... 1 John 3:2, 3

Imperishable—*enduring, lasting forever*

Resurrected body ... 1 Cor. 15:42, 52, 53
Christian's inheritance ... 1 Pet. 1:4
Seed of Christian life ... 1 Pet. 1:23

Impertinence—*an action or remark inappropriate for the occasion*

Christ rebukes Peter's ... Mark 8:31-33

SUBJECT REFERENCE

Impetuousness—*acting suddenly with little thought*

Characterized by:

Ill-considered judgment ... Esth. 1:10-22
Enraged disposition ... Gen. 34:25-31
Hasty action ... Josh. 22:10-34

Import—*to receive from other countries*

Things imported:

Horses ... 1 Kin. 10:28
Chariots ... 2 Chr. 1:17
Fish ... Neh. 13:16

Importunity in prayer

Need involved ... Luke 11:5-13
Christ's example ... Luke 22:44
Great intensity of ... Acts 12:5
Results of ... Mark 7:24-30

See Prayer

Impossibilities—*powerless, weak*

A. *Natural:*

Change one's color ... Jer. 13:23
Hide from God ... Ps. 139:7-12
Change one's size ... Matt. 6:27
Control the tongue ... James 3:7, 8

B. *Spiritual:*

God to sin ... Hab. 1:13
God to fail His promises ... Titus 1:2
Believers to be lost ... John 10:27-29

Imposter—*a pretender*

A. *Characteristics of:*

Not believed as ... Jer. 40:14-16
Speaks falsely ... Josh. 9:3-14
Poses as real ... 2 Cor. 11:13-15
Much like the real ... Matt. 7:21-23
Deception of, revealed to prophets ... Acts 13:8-12

B. *Examples of:*

Jannes and Jambres ... 2 Tim. 3:8
Judas ... John 13:18-30
Antichrist ... 2 Thess. 2:1-4

Impotent—*powerless*

Moab ... Is. 16:14

Imprecation—*pronouncing a curse*

God's enemies ... Ps. 55:5-15
One's enemies ... Ps. 35:4-8, 26
Heretics ... Gal. 1:9
Persecutors ... Jer. 11:18-20
Forbidden ... Luke 9:54-56

See Curse, cursing

Imprisonment—*physical confinement in jail*

A. *Of Old Testament persons:*

Joseph ... Gen. 39:20
Simeon ... Gen. 42:19, 24
Samson ... Judg. 16:21, 25
Jehoiachin ... 2 Kin. 25:27-29
Micaiah ... 2 Chr. 18:26
Jeremiah ... Jer. 32:2, 8, 12

B. *Of New Testament persons:*

John the Baptist ... Mark 6:17-27
Apostles ... Acts 5:18
Peter ... Acts 12:4
Paul and Silas ... Acts 16:24
Paul ... Acts 23:10, 18
John ... Rev. 1:9

See Prisoners

Improvement—*a betterment*

Expressed by:

Growth ... 1 Pet. 2:2
Addition ... 2 Pet. 1:5-11
Press on ... Phil. 3:13-15

Improvidence—*wasting present possession*

Material things ... Luke 15:11-13
Spiritual things ... Luke 12:16-23
Eternal things ... Luke 16:19-31

Impure—*ritually unclean; mixed with foreign elements*

Things impure:

Discharge ... Lev. 15:30
Hands ... Mark 7:2
Person ... Eph. 5:5
Sons of Israel ... Lev. 16:16
Nations ... Ezra 6:21

SUBJECT REFERENCE

Impurity (see Unclean)

Imputation—*counting or crediting something to another*

A. *Described as charging:*
- Evil to an innocent person ... Philem. 18
- Evil to an evil person ... Lev. 17:4
- Good to a good person ... Ps. 106:30, 31

B. *Of Adam's sin to the race:*
- Based on the fall ... Gen. 3:1-19
- Explained fully ... Rom. 5:12-21
- The wider implications of ... Rom. 8:20-23

C. *Of the believer's sin to Christ:*
- Our iniquity laid on Him ... Is. 53:5, 6
- Made to be sin for us ... 2 Cor. 5:21
- Became a curse for us ... Gal. 3:13
- Takes away our sins ... John 1:29; Heb. 9:28

D. *Of Christ's righteousness to the believer:*
- Negatively stated ... Rom. 4:6-8
- Positively affirmed ... Rom. 10:4-10
- Explained graphically ... Luke 15:22-24
- God justifies the ungodly ... Rom. 5:18, 19
- Christ becomes our righteousness ... 1 Cor. 1:30
- We become the righteousness of God in Him ... 2 Cor. 5:21
- Illustrated by Abraham's faith ... Rom. 4:3

See Justification

Imrah—*He* (God) *resists*
- Son of Zophah ... 1 Chr. 7:36

Imri—*eloquent*
1. Son of Bani ... 1 Chr. 9:4
2. Father of Zaccur ... Neh. 3:2
3. May be Amariah in ... Neh. 11:4

Inability (see Impossibilities)

Incarnation of Christ

A. *Foreshadowed by:*
- Angel ... Josh. 5:13-15
- Prophecies ... Is. 7:14

B. *Described as:*
- Becoming flesh ... John 1:14
- Born of woman ... Gal. 4:4
- Coming in flesh ... 1 John 4:2
- Appearing in flesh ... 1 Tim. 3:16
- Our likeness ... Rom. 8:3; Heb. 2:14
- Body ... Heb. 10:5, 10; 1 John 1:1-3
- Dying in flesh ... 1 Pet. 3:18; 1 Pet. 4:1

C. *Purposes of:*
- Reveal the Father ... John 14:8-11
- Do God's will ... Heb. 10:5-9
- Fulfill prophecy ... Luke 4:17-21
- Die for our sins ... 1 Pet. 3:18
- Fulfill all righteousness ... Matt. 3:15
- Reconcile the world ... 2 Cor. 5:18-21
- Become our high priest ... Heb. 7:24-28
- Become our example ... 1 Pet. 2:21-23

D. *Importance of:*
- Evidence Christ's deity ... Rom. 9:3-5
- Confirm Christ's resurrection ... Acts 2:24-32
- Mark of believers ... 1 John 4:1-6

See Human nature of Christ

Incense—*sweet perfume*

A. *Offered:*
- By priests ... Lev. 16:12, 13
- On the altar ... Ex. 30:1-8
- On day of atonement ... Lev. 16:12, 13
- According to strict formula ... Ex. 30:34-36

B. *Illegal offering of:*
- Forbidden ... Ex. 30:37, 38
- Excluded from certain offerings ... Lev. 5:11
- Punished severely ... Lev. 10:1, 2; 2 Chr. 26:16-21
- Among idolaters ... Is. 65:3

C. *Typical of:*
- Worship ... Ps. 141:2
- Prayer ... Rev. 5:8; Rev. 8:3, 4
- Praise ... Mal. 1:11
- Approved service ... Eph. 5:2

D. *Purposes of:*
- Used in holy oil ... Ex. 30:34-38
- Used in meal offerings ... Lev. 2:1, 2, 15
- Excluded from certain offerings ... Lev. 5:11
- Used in the showbread ... Lev. 24:7
- Product of Arabia ... Is. 60:6
- Presented to Jesus ... Matt. 2:11
- Figurative of worship ... Ps. 141:2

Incentives to good works
- Reap kindness ... Hos. 10:12
- Remain ... John 15:16
- Reap ... Gal. 6:7-10

Incest—*sexual relations between persons related*

A. *Relations prohibited:*
- Same family ... Lev. 18:6-12
- Grandchildren ... Lev. 18:10
- Aunts and uncles ... Lev. 18:12-14
- In-laws ... Lev. 18:15, 16
- Near kin ... Lev. 18:17, 18

B. *Punishment for:*
- Death ... Lev. 20:11-17
- Childlessness ... Lev. 20:19-21
- A curse ... Deut. 27:20-23

C. *Examples of:*
- Lot—with his daughters ... Gen. 19:30-38
- Reuben—with his father's concubine ... Gen. 35:22

Inconsistency—*the non-agreement of two things*

Between:
- Criticism of ourselves and others ... Matt. 7:3
- Legalism and human mercy ... John 7:23
- Profession and reality ... Luke 22:31-62
- Preaching and practice ... Rom. 2:21-23
- Private and public convictions ... Gal. 2:11-14
- Faith and works ... James 2:14 26
- Profession and works ... Titus 1:16

Inconstancy—*inability to stand firm in crisis*

A. *Causes of:*
- Little faith ... Matt. 13:19-22
- Satan ... Luke 22:31-34
- False teachers ... Gal. 1:6-10
- Doubt ... James 1:6-8
- Immaturity ... 2 Pet. 1:5-10

B. *Remedies against:*
- Firm foundation ... Matt. 7:24-27
- Strong faith ... Hab. 3:16-19
- Full armor ... Eph. 6:10-20

Incontinency—*uncontrolled indulgence of the passions*

A. *Expressed in:*
- Unbridled sexual morals ... Ex. 32:6, 18, 25
- Abnormal sexual desires ... 2 Sam. 13:1-15
- Unnatural sexual appetites ... Gen. 19:5-9; Rom. 1:26, 27

B. *Sources of:*
- Lust ... 1 Pet. 4:2, 3
- Satan ... 1 Cor. 7:5
- Apostasy ... 2 Tim. 3:3

Increase—*to become more abundant*

A. *Used literally of:*
- Descendants ... 1 Sam. 2:33
- Knowledge ... Dan. 12:4

B. *Used spiritually of:*
- Messiah's kingdom ... Is. 9:7
- Wisdom ... Luke 2:52
- Faith ... Luke 17:5
- Esteem ... John 3:30
- God's Word ... Acts 6:7
- Spiritual fruit ... 2 Cor. 9:10
- Knowledge of God ... Col. 1:10
- Love ... 1 Thess. 4:9, 10
- Ungodliness ... 2 Tim. 2:16

Incredulity—*an unwillingness to believe*

Characterized by:
- Exaggerated demand for evidence ... John 20:24, 25
- Desire for more signs ... Judg. 6:37-40
- Attempts to nullify plain evidence ... John 9:13-41
- Blindness of mind ... Acts 28:22-29

Indecency
- Noah guilty of ... Gen. 9:21-23
- Israelites sin in ... Ex. 32:25
- Forbidden, to priests ... Ex. 20:26
- Michal rebukes David for ... 2 Sam. 6:20-23
- Men committing ... Rom. 1:27

Indecision—*inability to decide between vital issues*

A. *Manifested in, mixing:*
- Truth and idolatry ... 1 Kin. 18:21
- Duty and compromise ... John 19:12-16
- Holiness and sin ... Gal. 5:1-7
- Faith and works ... Gal. 3:1-5

B. *Results in:*
- Spiritual unfitness ... Luke 9:59-62
- Instability ... James 1:6-8
- Sinful compromise ... 2 Cor. 6:14-18
- Spiritual defeat ... Rom. 6:16-22
- Spiritual deadness ... Rev. 3:15-17

C. *Examples of:*
- Israel at Kadesh ... Num. 13:26-33
- Joshua at Ai ... Josh. 7:6-10
- David at Keilah ... 1 Sam. 23:1-5
- Pilate ... Matt. 27:11-24
- Felix ... Acts 24:25, 26

See Inconstancy

Independence—*control of one's affairs apart from outside influences*

A. *Virtues of:*
- Freedom of action ... Gen. 14:22-24
- Responsibility ... John 9:21, 23

B. *Evils of:*
- Arbitrary use of authority ... 1 Sam. 14:24-45
- Selfishness ... 1 Sam. 25:1-11
- Mismanagement ... Luke 15:12-16
- Arrogance ... 3 John 9, 10

India
- Eastern limit of Persian Empire ... Esth. 1:1

Indictment—*formal accusation for a crime*

A. *For real crimes:*
- Korah's company ... Num. 16:1-50
- Achan ... Josh. 7:1-26
- Baal worshipers ... 1 Kin. 18:19-42
- David ... 2 Sam. 12:1-14
- Ananias ... Acts 5:1-10

B. *For supposed crimes:*
- Certain tribes ... Josh. 22:10-34
- Naboth ... 1 Kin. 21:1-16
- Three Hebrew men ... Dan. 3:1-28
- Jews ... Ezra 5:3-17; Esth. 3:8, 9
- Christ ... Matt. 26:61-65
- Stephen ... Acts 6:11, 13
- Paul ... Acts 17:7; Acts 16:20, 21

Indifference—*not concerned for or against something*

A. *Characteristic of:*
- Unbelievers ... Luke 17:26-30
- Backsliders ... Rev. 3:15, 16

B. *As a good feature concerning, worldly:*
- Comforts ... Phil. 4:11-13
- Applause ... Gal. 1:10
- Traditions ... Col. 2:16-23

C. *As a bad feature:*
- Inhumanitarianism ... Luke 10:30-32
- In the use of one's talents ... Luke 19:20-26
- Moral callousness ... Matt. 27:3, 4
- Religious unconcern ... Acts 18:12-16

Indignation—*boiling wrath against something sinful*

A. *God's:*
- Irresistible ... Nah. 1:6
- Victorious ... Hab. 3:12
- Poured out ... Zeph. 3:8
- Toward His enemies ... Is. 66:14
- On Israel ... Deut. 29:28
- Against Edom forever ... Mal. 1:4
- Angels, instruments of ... Ps. 78:49
- On believers ... Job 10:17
- Will hide His own from ... Is. 26:20

SUBJECT — REFERENCE

Entreated, on the wicked .... Ps. 69:24
As punishment .... Rom. 2:8

B. *Man's against:*

Others .... Esth. 5:9
Jews .... Neh. 4:1
Christ .... Luke 13:14
Christians .... Acts 5:17

Indignities suffered by Christ

A. *Against His body:*

Spit on .... Matt. 26:67
Struck .... John 18:22, 23
Crowned with thorns .... Matt. 27:29
Crucified .... Matt. 27:31-35

B. *Against His person:*

Called guilty without a trial .... John 18:30, 31
Mocked and derided .... Matt. 27:29, 31, 39-44
Rejected in favor of a murderer .... Matt. 27:16-21
Crucified between two men .... John 19:18

Indiscrimination—*showing lack of distinction in*

Devastation .... Is. 24:1-4
Judgment .... Ezek. 18:1-32
God's providences .... Matt. 5:45

Indulge—*to yield to desires*

Fleshly desires .... Eph. 2:3
Corrupt desires .... 2 Pet. 2:10
Gross immorality .... Jude 7

Indulgence—*a kindness often misused*

Parental .... 1 Sam. 3:11-14
Kingly .... 2 Sam. 13:21-39
Priestly .... Judg. 17:1-13

Industry—*diligence in one's work*

A. *Characteristics of:*

Established .... Gen. 2:15
Commanded .... 1 Thess. 4:11
Commendable .... Prov. 27:23-27
Done willingly .... Prov. 31:13
Mark of wisdom .... Prov. 10:5
Suspended on Sabbath .... Ex. 20:10
Neglect of, rebuked .... 2 Thess. 3:10-12

B. *Necessity of:*

Our needs .... 1 Thess. 2:9
Needs of others .... Acts 20:35
Faithful witness .... 1 Tim. 5:8

C. *Blessings of:*

Wealth .... Prov. 10:4, 5
Praise .... Prov. 31:28, 31
Food sufficient .... Prov. 12:11
Will rule .... Prov. 12:24

Indwelling, of believers

A. *By Christ:*

Through faith .... Eph. 3:14-19
Mystery .... Col. 1:27

B. *Spirit:*

Every believer .... Rom. 8:9-11
Body, a temple of God .... 1 Cor. 3:16

Infant salvation

Suggested by scripture .... Matt. 18:3-5, 10; Matt. 19:14

Infants

A. *Acts performed upon:*

Naming .... Ruth 4:17
Blessing .... Luke 1:67, 76-79
Circumcision .... Luke 2:21

B. *Capacity to:*

Believe .... Matt. 18:6
Know the Scriptures .... 2 Tim. 3:15
Receive training .... Eph. 6:4
Worship in God's house .... 1 Sam. 1:24, 28

C. *Murder of:*

By Pharaoh .... Ex. 1:16
By Herod the Great .... Matt. 2:16-18
In war .... Num. 31:17

Infidelity—*unbelief in God's revelation*

A. *Causes of:*

Unregenerate heart .... Rom. 2:5
Hatred of the light .... John 3:19-21
Spiritual blindness .... 1 Cor. 2:8, 14
Self-trust .... Is. 47:10, 11
Unbelief .... Acts 6:10-15
Inveterate prejudice .... Acts 7:54, 57
Worldly wisdom .... 1 Cor. 1:18-22

B. *Manifested in:*

Rejecting God's Word .... 2 Pet. 3:3-5
Scoffing at God's servants .... 2 Chr. 30:6, 10
Hiding under lies .... Is. 28:15
Living without God .... Job 22:13-17
Using derisive words .... Matt. 12:24
Doubting God's righteousness .... Ps. 10:11, 13
Calling religion worthless .... Mal. 3:14

C. *Punishment of:*

Eternal separation from God .... 2 Thess. 1:8, 9
God's wrath .... 1 Thess. 2:14-16
Hell .... Luke 16:23-31
Severe punishment .... Heb. 10:28, 29

D. *Remedies against:*

Remember the end .... Ps. 73:16-28
Trust when you can't explain .... Job 2:9, 10
Stand upon the Word .... Matt. 4:3-11
Use God's armor .... Eph. 6:10-19
Grow spiritually .... 2 Pet. 1:4-11

Infinite—*extending immeasurably*

God's understanding .... Ps. 147:5

Infirmities—*weaknesses of our human nature*

A. *Kinds of:*

Sickness or disease .... Matt. 8:17
Imperfections of the body .... 2 Cor. 11:30
Moral defects .... Rom. 8:26

B. *Our duties with reference to:*

Rejoice in .... 2 Cor. 12:10
Help those afflicted with .... Rom. 15:1; Gal. 6:1
Not to despise in others .... Gal. 4:13, 14
Be sympathetic concerning .... Heb. 5:2, 3; Heb. 7:27, 28
Make us humble .... Rom. 6:19
Come to Jesus with .... Heb. 4:15, 16
Serve God more, if without .... Josh. 14:10-14

Influence—*that invisible force in one's personality that causes others to act*

Christians, should be:

As salt .... Matt. 5:13
As light .... Matt. 5:14-16; Phil. 2:15
As examples .... 1 Thess. 1:7, 8
Beneficial to spouse .... 1 Pet. 3:1, 2; 1 Cor. 7:14, 16
Above criticism .... 1 Cor. 8:10-13
Honorable .... 1 Tim. 6:1
Permanent .... Heb. 11:4
Beneficial to others .... 1 Pet. 2:11, 12
Without reproach .... Phil. 2:15, 16

Ingenuity—*skill shown in unusual contrivances*

Of God .... Job 38:4-41; Ps. 139:13-16
Of man .... Ex. 35:30-33; Ex. 2:1-9; Gen. 27:7-29

Ingratitude—*unthankfulness for blessings received*

A. *Characteristics of:*

Inconsiderate .... Deut. 32:6, 7
Unreasonable .... Jer. 2:5-7
Unnatural .... Is. 1:2, 3
Ungrateful .... Jer. 5:7-9, 24

B. *Causes of:*

Prosperity .... Deut. 6:10-12
Self-sufficiency .... Deut. 8:12-18
Forgetfulness .... Luke 17:12-18
Fear .... 1 Sam. 23:5, 12
Greed .... 1 Sam. 25:4-11
Pride .... Dan. 5:18-20

C. *Attitudes toward:*

Acknowledged .... 1 Sam. 24:17-19
Abused .... 2 Chr. 24:22
Revealed .... 1 Sam. 23:5-12
Forgiven by kindness .... 1 Sam. 25:14-35
Long remembered .... Deut. 25:17-19
Overcome by faithfulness .... Gen. 31:38-42

D. *Examples of:*

Moses by Israel .... Ex. 17:1-3
Gideon by Israel .... Judg. 8:33-35
God by Saul .... 1 Sam. 15:16-23
God by David .... 2 Sam. 12:7-14
Jeremiah by Judah .... Jer. 18:19, 20
God by the world .... Rom. 1:21

Inheritance, earthly

A. *Among Israelites:*

God the owner .... Lev. 25:23, 28
Possessed by families .... Num. 27:4, 7
Law of transmission .... Num. 27:8-11
If sold, restored in year of jubilee .... Lev. 25:25-34
Must remain in tribe .... Num. 36:6-10
Repossessed by kinsman .... Ruth 4:3-5, 10

B. *General characteristics of:*

From fathers .... Prov. 19:14
Uncertain use .... Eccl. 2:18, 19
Object of seizure .... 1 Kin. 21:3, 4; Matt. 21:38
Squandered .... Luke 15:11-13
Foolish not blessed .... Prov. 11:29
Descendants blessed .... Ps. 25:12, 13

See Heirs, natural

Inheritance of Israel

A. *Basic features of:*

Lord, Israel's .... Deut. 9:26, 29
Land promised to Abraham's seed .... Gen. 15:7-18
Limits defined .... Gen. 15:18-21
Limits fulfilled .... 1 Kin. 4:21, 24
Possession of, based on obedience .... 2 Kin. 21:12-15
Blessed by the Lord .... Deut. 15:4
Tribes destroyed from .... Deut. 20:16-18
Possessed by degrees .... Ex. 23:29-31
Apportioned .... Josh. 13:7-33
Tribes encouraged to possess .... Josh. 18:1-10
Levites excluded from .... Num. 18:20-24
Lost by sin .... Ps. 79:1
Restored after the captivity .... Neh. 11:20

B. *Figurative of:*

Messianic blessings .... Ps. 2:8
Call of the Gentiles .... Is. 54:3
Elect remnant .... Is. 65:8, 9
Eternal possessions .... Is. 60:21

Inheritance, spiritual

A. *Objects of:*

Kingdom .... Matt. 25:34
Eternal life .... Matt. 19:29
Promises .... Heb. 6:12
Blessing .... 1 Pet. 3:9
All things .... Rev. 21:7
Glory .... Prov. 3:35

B. *Nature of:*

Sealed by the Spirit .... Eph. 1:13, 14
Received from the Lord .... Col. 3:24
Results from Christ's death .... Heb. 9:15
Depends on belief .... Gal. 3:18, 22
Incorruptible .... 1 Pet. 1:4
Final, in heaven .... 1 Pet. 1:4

C. *Restrictions upon, only:*

For the righteous .... 1 Cor. 6:9, 10
For the sanctified .... Acts 20:32
In Christ .... Eph. 1:11, 12
For the transformed .... 1 Cor. 15:50-53

See Heirs, spiritual

Inhospitality—*unwillingness to entertain strangers*

Edomites .... Num. 20:17-21
Sihon .... Num. 21:22, 23
Gibeah .... Judg. 19:15
Nabal .... 1 Sam. 25:10-17
Samaritans .... Luke 9:53
Diotrephes .... 3 John 10
Penalty for .... Deut. 23:3, 4; Luke 10:10-16

Iniquity—*the depth of sin*

A. *Sources of:*

Heart .... Ps. 41:6; Matt. 23:28

B. *Effects upon man:*

Insatiable appetite for .... Ezek. 7:16, 19
Perversion .... Ezek. 9:9

C. *God's attitude toward:*

Cannot look on .... Hab. 1:13
Does not do .... Zeph. 3:5
Remembers and punishes .... Jer. 14:10
Visits on children .... Ex. 34:7

SUBJECT — REFERENCE

- Pardons and subdues ... Mic. 7:18, 19
- Takes away from us ... Zech. 3:4
- Lays upon the Messiah ... Is. 53:5, 6, 11
- Remembers no more ... Heb. 8:12

D. *Christ's relation to:*

- Bears our ... Is. 53:5, 6, 11
- Makes reconciliation for ... Dan. 9:24
- Redeems us ... Titus 2:14

E. *Believer's relation to:*

- Will declare it ... Ps. 38:18
- Confesses ... Neh. 9:2
- Prays for pardon of ... Ps. 25:11
- Forgiven of ... Ps. 32:5
- Must depart from ... 2 Tim. 2:19
- Protection from ... Ps. 125:3
- Separation from God ... Is. 59:2
- Prays for freedom from ... Ps. 119:133
- Hindrance to prayer ... Ps. 66:18

F. *Punishment for:*

- Wanderings ... Num. 14:34
- Loss of strength ... Ps. 31:10
- Destruction ... Gen. 19:15
- Captivity ... Ezra 9:7
- Death ... Ezek. 18:24, 26
- Less than deserved ... Ezra 9:13
- Remembered forever ... 1 Sam. 3:13, 14
- In hell ... Ezek. 32:27

Injustice—*that which violates another's rights*

A. *Examples of, among men:*

- Laban's treatment of Jacob ... Gen. 31:36-42
- Saul's treatment of:
  - Priests ... 1 Sam. 22:15-23
  - David ... 1 Sam. 24:8-22; 1 Sam. 26:14-25
- David's treatment of Uriah ... 2 Sam. 12:1-12
- Irijah's treatment of Jeremiah ... Jer. 37:11-21

B. *Charges made against God for His:*

- Choice ... Num. 16:1-14
- Inequality ... Ezek. 18:25
- Partiality ... Rom. 9:14
- Delay ... Rev. 6:10

C. *Punishment on executed:*

- Severely ... 1 Sam. 15:32, 33
- Swiftly ... Esth. 7:9, 10
- According to prophecy ... 1 Kin. 22:34-38

See Just, justice

Ink—*a writing fluid*

- Used for writing a book ... Jer. 36:18
- Used in letter writing ... 2 John 12; 3 John 13

Inkhorn—*a case for pens and ink*

- Writer's tool ... Ezek. 9:2, 3

Inn—*a shelter providing lodging for travelers*

- Lodging place ... Jer. 9:2
- Place for rest ... Luke 2:7

Inner group

- At girl's bedside ... Mark 5:35-40
- At Christ's transfiguration ... Mark 9:2
- In Gethsemane ... Matt. 26:36, 37

Inner man—*man's genuine identity*

- Often hidden ... Matt. 23:27, 28
- Seen by God ... 1 Sam. 16:7
- Strengthened ... Eph. 3:16

Inner natures, conflict of

A. *Sin nature:*

- Called flesh ... Rom. 8:5
- Called old self ... Col. 3:9
- Corrupt and deceitful ... Eph. 4:22
- Works of ... Gal. 5:19-21
- Cannot please God ... Rom. 8:8
- To be mortified ... Col. 3:5

B. *New nature:*

- By Spirit's indwelling ... 1 Cor. 3:16
- Strengthened by Spirit ... Eph. 3:16
- Called inward man ... 2 Cor. 4:16
- Called new man ... Col. 3:10
- Fruits of ... Gal. 5:22, 23

C. *Conflict:*

- Called warfare ... Rom. 7:19-23; Gal. 5:17

D. *Victory:*

- Recognize source ... James 1:14-16

SUBJECT — REFERENCE

- Realize former condition ... Eph. 2:1-7
- Put off former conversation ... Eph. 4:22
- Make no provision ... Rom. 13:14
- Complete surrender to God ... Rom. 12:1, 2
- Spiritual food ... 1 Pet. 2:1, 2

Innocence—*freedom from guilt or sin*

A. *Loss of, by:*

- Disobedience ... Rom. 5:12
- Idolatry ... Ps. 106:34-39

B. *Kinds of:*

- Absolute ... 2 Cor. 5:21
- Legal ... Luke 23:4
- Moral ... Josh. 22:10-34
- Spiritual ... 2 Pet. 3:14

C. *Of Christ:*

- In prophecy ... Is. 53:7-9
- In type ... 1 Pet. 1:19
- In reality ... 1 Pet. 3:18
- By examination ... Luke 23:13-22
- By testimony ... Acts 13:28

Innocents, massacre of:

- Mourning foretold ... Jer. 31:15
- After Jesus' birth ... Matt. 2:16-18

Innumerable—*uncounted multitude*

- Evils ... Ps. 40:12
- Animal life ... Ps. 104:25
- Descendants ... Heb. 11:12
- People ... Luke 12:1
- Angels ... Heb. 12:22

Inquiry—*a consulting or seeking for counsel*

- By Israel ... Ex. 18:15
- With ephod ... 1 Sam. 23:9, 11
- Unlawful method ... 1 Sam. 28:6, 7
- Through prayer ... James 1:5; 2 Cor. 12:7-9

Insanity—*mental derangement*

A. *Characteristics of:*

- Abnormal behavior ... Dan. 4:32-34
- Self-destruction ... Matt. 17:14-18
- Distinct from demon possession ... Matt. 4:24

B. *Figurative of:*

- Moral instability ... Jer. 25:15-17; Jer. 51:7
- God's judgment ... Zech. 12:4

Inscription—*a statement written or engraved*

- On Christ's cross ... John 19:19-22
- On an altar ... Acts 17:23
- Roman coin ... Mark 12:16

Insects of the Bible

A. *Characteristics of:*

- Created by God ... Gen. 1:24, 25
- Some clean ... Lev. 11:21, 22
- Some unclean ... Lev. 11:23, 24
- Fed by God ... Ps. 104:25, 27

B. *List of:*

- Ant ... Prov. 6:6
- Bee ... Judg. 14:8
- Beetle ... Lev. 11:22
- Cankerworm ... Joel 1:4
- Caterpillar ... Ps. 78:46
- Flea ... 1 Sam. 24:14
- Fly ... Eccl. 10:1
- Gnat ... Matt. 23:24
- Grasshopper ... Lev. 11:22
- Hornet ... Deut. 7:20
- Horseleech ... Prov. 30:15
- Locust ... Ex. 10:4
- Moth ... Is. 50:9
- Spider ... Prov. 30:28
- Worms ... Ex. 16:20

C. *Illustrative of:*

- Design in nature ... Prov. 30:24-28
- Troubles ... Ps. 118:12
- Insignificance ... 1 Sam. 24:14
- Desolation ... Joel 1:4
- Appetite ... Prov. 30:15
- Transitoriness ... Is. 51:8; Matt. 6:20
- Vast numbers ... Judg. 6:5

Insecurity—*a state of anxiety about earthly needs*

A. *Descriptive of:*

- Wicked ... Ps. 37:1, 2, 10

SUBJECT — REFERENCE

- Riches ... 1 Tim. 6:17
- Those trusting in themselves ... Luke 12:16-21

B. *Cure of:*

- Steadfast of mind ... Is. 26:3
- Rely upon God's promises ... Ps. 37:1-26
- Remember God's provision ... Phil. 4:9-19
- Put God first ... Matt. 6:25-34

Insensibility—*deadness of spiritual life*

A. *Kinds of:*

- Physical ... Judg. 19:26-29
- Spiritual ... Jer. 5:3, 21
- Judicial ... Acts 28:25-28

B. *Causes of:*

- Seared conscience ... 1 Tim. 4:2
- Spiritual ignorance ... Eph. 4:18, 19
- Wanton pleasure ... 1 Tim. 5:6

Insincerity—*hypocritical deceitfulness*

A. *Manifested in:*

- Mock ceremonies ... Is. 58:3-6
- Unwilling preaching ... Jon. 4:1-11
- Trumped-up questions ... Matt. 22:15-22
- Boastful pretentions ... Luke 22:33

B. *Those guilty of:*

- Hypocrites ... Luke 11:42-47
- False teachers ... Gal. 6:12, 13
- Immature Christians ... 1 Cor. 4:17-21

See Hypocrisy

Insomnia—*inability to sleep*

A. *Causes of:*

- Excessive work ... Gen. 31:40
- Worry ... Esth. 6:1
- Dreams ... Dan. 2:1
- Conscience ... Dan. 6:9, 18

B. *Cure of:*

- Trust ... Ps. 3:5, 6
- Peacefulness ... Ps. 4:8
- Confidence ... Ps. 127:1, 2
- Obedience ... Prov. 6:20-22

Inspiration of the Scriptures

A. *Expressed by:*

- "Thus saith the Lord" ... Jer. 13:1
- "The word of the Lord came" ... 1 Kin. 16:1
- "It is written" ... Rom. 10:15
- "As the Holy Spirit saith" ... Heb. 3:7
- "According to the Scripture" ... James 2:8
- "My words in thy mouth" ... Jer. 1:9

B. *Described as:*

- Inspired by God ... 2 Tim. 3:16
- Moved by the Holy Spirit ... 2 Pet. 1:21
- Christ-centered ... Luke 24:27; 2 Cor. 13:3

C. *Modes of:*

- Various ... Heb. 1:1
- Inner impulse ... Judg. 13:25; Jer. 20:9
- A voice ... Rev. 1:10
- Dreams ... Dan. 7:1
- Visions ... Ezek. 11:24, 25

D. *Proofs of:*

- Fulfilled prophecy ... Jer. 28:15-17; Luke 24:27-45
- Miracles attesting ... Ex. 4:1-9; 2 Kin. 1:10-14
- Teachings supporting ... Deut. 4:8; Ps. 19:7-11

E. *Design of:*

- Reveal God's mysteries ... Amos 3:7; 1 Cor. 2:10
- Reveal the future ... Acts 1:16; 1 Pet. 1:10-12
- Instruct and edify ... Mic. 3:8; Acts 1:8
- Counteract distortion ... 2 Cor. 13:1-3; Gal. 1:6-11

F. *Results of Scriptures:*

- Unbreakable ... John 10:34-36
- Eternal ... Matt. 24:35
- Authoritative ... Matt. 4:4, 7, 10
- Trustworthy ... Ps. 119:160
- Verbally accurate ... Matt. 22:32, 43-46; Gal. 3:16

SUBJECT ... REFERENCE

Sanctifying ... 2 Tim. 3:16, 17
Effective ... Jer. 23:29
2 Tim. 2:15

See Word of God

Instability—*lack of firmness of convictions*

A. *Causes of:*
Deception ... Gal. 3:1
Col. 2:4-8
Immaturity ... 1 Tim. 3:6
False teaching ... Gal. 1:6-11
2 Cor. 11:3, 4
Lack of depth ... Heb. 5:11-14
Unsettled mind ... Eph. 4:14
James 1:6-8

B. *Examples of:*
Pharaoh ... Ex. 10:8-20
Israel ... Judg. 2:17
Solomon ... 1 Kin. 11:1-8
Disciples ... John 6:66
John Mark ... Acts 15:38
Galatians ... Gal. 1:6

Instinct—*inbred characteristic of*
Animals ... Is. 1:3
Birds ... Jer. 8:7

Instruction—*imparting knowledge to others*

A. *Given by:*
Parents ... Deut. 6:6-25
Priests ... Deut. 24:8
God ... Jer. 32:33
Pastors ... Eph. 4:11
Pedagogues ... Neh. 8:7, 8
Paraclete (the Holy Spirit) ... John 14:26

B. *Means of:*
Nature ... Prov. 6:6-11
Human nature ... Prov. 24:30-34
Law ... Rom. 2:18
Proverbs ... Prov. 1:1-30
Songs ... Deut. 32:1-44
History ... 1 Cor. 10:1-11
God's Word ... 2 Tim. 3:15, 16

See Education; Teaching, teachers

Instrument—*a tool or implement*
Tabernacle furniture ... Num. 3:8
For threshing ... 2 Sam. 24:22
For sacrifices ... Ezek. 40:42
Of iron ... 2 Sam. 12:31
Figurative of Jesus ... Acts 9:15
Body members, used as ... Rom. 6:13

Insult—*to treat insolently*
Ignored by King Saul ... 1 Sam. 10:26, 27
Job treated with ... Job 30:1, 9, 10
Children slain because of ... 2 Kin. 2:23, 24
Pharisees treat Jesus with ... Matt. 12:24, 25
Paul's reaction to ... Acts 23:1-5
Forbidden ... 1 Pet. 3:8, 9

Insurrection—*rebellion against constituted authority*
In Jerusalem ... Ezra 4:19
Absalom's miserable ... 2 Sam. 18:33
Attempted by Jews ... Mark 15:7
Acts 18:12

Integrity—*moral uprightness*

A. *Manifested in:*
Moral uprightness ... Gen. 20:3-10
Unselfish service ... Num. 16:15
Performing vows ... Jer. 35:12-19
Rejecting bribes ... Acts 8:18-23
Honest behavior ... 2 Cor. 7:2

B. *Illustrated in:*
Job's life ... Job 2:3, 9, 10
David's kingship ... Ps. 7:8
Nehemiah's service ... Neh. 5:14-19
Daniel's rule ... Dan. 6:1-4
Paul's ministry ... 2 Cor. 4:2

Intemperance—*not restraining the appetites*

A. *Manifested in:*
Drunkenness ... Prov. 23:19-35
Gluttony ... Titus 1:12
Immorality ... Rom. 1:26, 27

B. *Evils of:*
Puts the flesh first ... Phil. 3:19
Brings about death ... 1 Sam. 25:36-38

See Drunkenness

SUBJECT ... REFERENCE

Intention—*a fixed determination to do a specified thing*

A. *Good:*
Commended but not allowed ... 1 Kin. 8:17-19
Planned but delayed ... Rom. 15:24-28

B. *Evil:*
Restrained by God ... Gen. 31:22-31
Turned to good by God ... Gen. 45:4-8
Overruled by God's providence ... Esth. 9:23-25

C. *Of Christ:*
Predicted ... Ps. 40:6-8
Announced ... Matt. 20:18-28
Misunderstood ... Matt. 16:21-23
Fulfilled ... John 19:28-30
Explained ... Luke 24:25-47

Interbreeding—*crossbreed*
Forbidden:
In animals, vegetables, cloth ... Lev. 19:19

Intercession—*prayer offered in behalf of others*

A. *Purposes of:*
Secure healing ... James 5:14-16
Avert judgment ... Num. 14:11-21
Insure deliverance ... 1 Sam. 7:5-9
Give blessings ... Num. 6:23-27
Obtain restoration ... Job 42:8-10
Encourage repentance ... Rom. 10:1-4

B. *Characteristics of:*
Pleading ... Gen. 18:23-33
Specific ... Gen. 24:12-15
Victorious ... Ex. 17:9-12
Very intense ... Ex. 32:31, 32
Quickly answered ... Num. 27:15-23
Confessing ... 2 Sam. 24:17
Personal ... 1 Chr. 29:19
Covenant pleading ... Neh. 1:4-11
Unselfish ... Acts 7:60

C. *Examples of:*
Moses ... Ex. 32:11-13
Joshua ... Josh. 7:6-9
Jehoshaphat ... 2 Chr. 20:5-13
Isaiah ... 2 Chr. 32:20
Daniel ... Dan. 9:3-19
Christ ... John 17:1-26
Paul ... Col. 1:9-12

Intercourse—*copulation*
Kinds of, forbidden:
With neighbor's wife ... Lev. 18:20
With animal ... Lev. 18:23

Interest—*money charged on borrowed money*
From poor man, forbidden ... Ex. 22:25
From a stranger, permitted ... Deut. 23:19, 20
Exaction of, unprofitable ... Prov. 28:8
Condemned as a sin ... Ezek. 18:8-17
Exaction of, rebuked ... Neh. 5:1-13
Reward for non-exaction of ... Ps. 15:5
Used to illustrate ... Luke 19:23

Intermediate state—*the state of the believer between death and the resurrection*

A. *Described as:*
Like sleep ... John 11:11-14
"Far better" ... Phil. 1:21, 23
"Present with the Lord" ... 2 Cor. 5:6, 8

B. *Characteristics of:*
Persons identifiable ... Matt. 17:3
Conscious and enjoyable ... Ps. 17:15
Luke 16:25
Unchangeable ... Luke 16:26
Without the body ... 2 Cor. 5:1-4
Rev. 6:9
Awaiting the resurrection ... Phil. 3:20, 21
1 Thess. 4:13-18

See Immortality

Interpretation—*making the unknown known*

A. *Things in need of:*
Dreams ... Gen. 41:15-36
Languages ... Gen. 42:23
Writings ... Dan. 5:7-31
Scripture ... Acts 8:30-35
Tongues ... 1 Cor. 12:10

B. *Agents of:*
Jesus Christ ... Luke 24:25-47

SUBJECT ... REFERENCE

Holy Spirit ... 1 Cor. 2:11-16
Angels ... Luke 1:26-37
Prophets and apostles ... Eph. 3:2-11

Intimidation—*suggesting possible harm if one acts contrary to another's wishes*
Attitudes toward:
Discovers its deceit ... Neh. 6:5-13
Do not yield ... Jer. 26:8-16
Go steadfastly on ... Dan. 6:6-10
Answer boldly ... Amos 7:12-17

Intolerance—*active opposition to the views of others*

A. *Of the state against:*
Jews ... Esth. 3:12, 13
Rival religions ... Dan. 3:13-15
Christian faith ... Rev. 13:1-18

B. *Of the Jews against:*
Their prophets ... Matt. 23:31-35
Christ ... Luke 4:28-30
Christians ... Acts 5:40, 41
Christianity ... Acts 17:1-8

C. *Of the Church against:*
Evil ... 2 Cor. 6:14-18
False teaching ... 2 John 10, 11
False religions ... Gal. 1:6-9

D. *Manifestations of:*
Prejudice ... Acts 21:27-32
Persecution ... Acts 13:50
Passion ... Acts 9:1, 2, 21

Intrigue—*using hidden methods to cause another's downfall*

A. *Characteristics of:*
Deceit ... Gen. 27:6-23
Plausible arguments ... Judg. 9:1-6
Subtle maneuvers ... 2 Sam. 15:1-13
False front ... 2 Kin. 10:18-28
Political trickery ... Esth. 3:5-10

B. *Against Christ by:*
Herod ... Matt. 2:8, 12-16
Satan ... Matt. 4:3-11
Jews ... Luke 11:53, 54

Invention—*something new made by man*
Product of wisdom ... Prov. 8:12
Products made by ... Gen. 4:21, 22
Skill required in ... 2 Chr. 26:15
Many made ... Eccl. 7:29
Of evil things ... Ps. 106:39
God provoked by ... Ps. 106:29
God takes vengeance on ... Ps. 99:8

Investigation—*close examination*

A. *Characteristics of:*
Involves research ... Ezra 6:1-13
Causes sought out ... Eccl. 1:13, 17
Claims checked ... Num. 13:1-25
Suspicions followed through ... Josh. 22:10-30
Historic parallels cited ... Jer. 26:17-24

B. *Lack of:*
Cause of later trouble ... Josh. 9:3-23
Productive of evil ... Dan. 5:22, 23

Investments, spiritual
In heavenly riches ... Matt. 6:20
Dividends later paid ... 1 Tim. 6:19

Invisible—*the unseeable*
God is ... 1 Tim. 1:17
Faith sees ... Heb. 11:27

Invitations of the Bible
Come:
And reason ... Is. 1:18
My people ... Is. 26:20
Buy wine and milk ... Is. 55:1
"Unto Me" ... Is. 55:3
And see ... John 1:46
And rest ... Matt. 11:28
After Me ... Mark 1:17
Take up the cross ... Mark 10:21
To the marriage ... Matt. 22:4
Everything is ready ... Luke 14:17
The blessed ... Matt. 25:34
Threefold ... Rev. 22:17

Iphedeiah—*the Lord redeems*
A descendant of Benjamin ... 1 Chr. 8:1, 25

SUBJECT — REFERENCE

Ira—*watchful*
1. Priest to David — 2 Sam. 20:26
2. One of David's mighty men — 2 Sam. 23:26; 1 Chr. 11:28
3. Ithrite — 2 Sam. 23:38; 1 Chr. 11:40

Irad—*fugitive*
Son of Enoch; grandson of Cain — Gen. 4:18

Iram—*aroused*
Edomite chief — Gen. 36:43; 1 Chr. 1:54

Iri—*urbane*
Benjamite — 1 Chr. 7:7

Irijah—*Jehovah sees*
Accuses Jeremiah of desertion — Jer. 37:13, 14

Irnahash—*serpent city*
City of Judah — 1 Chr. 4:1, 12

Iron—*a useful metal*
A. *Features concerning:*
Used very early — Gen. 4:22
Used in weapons — Job 20:24
B. *Items made of:*
Armor — 2 Sam. 23:7
Axe — 2 Kin. 6:5
Bedstead — Deut. 3:11
Chariot — Josh. 17:16, 18
Gate — Acts 12:10
Gods — Dan. 5:4, 23
Tools — 1 Kin. 6:7; 2 Sam. 12:31
Vessels — Josh. 6:24
Weapons — Job 20:24
Yokes — Deut. 28:48
Implements — Gen. 4:22
Stylus — Job 19:24
C. *Figurative of:*
Affliction — Deut. 4:20
Barrenness — Deut. 28:23
Authority — Ps. 2:9
Stubbornness — Is. 48:4
Slavery — Jer. 28:13, 14
Strength — Dan. 2:33-41
Insensibility — 1 Tim. 4:2

Iron—*conspicuous*
City of Naphtali — Josh. 19:38

Irony—*a pretense of ignorance*
Show contempt — 2 Sam. 6:20
Mockery — 1 Kin. 18:27
Rebuke distrust — 1 Kin. 22:15
Multiply transgression — Amos 4:4
Mocked honor — Matt. 27:29
Deflate the wise — 2 Cor. 11:19, 20

Irpeel—*God heals*
Town of Benjamin — Josh. 18:21, 27

Irreconcilable—*violators of agreements opposing compromise*
Characteristic of the last days — 2 Tim. 3:1, 3

Irrigation—*supply with water*
Not usually needed — Deut. 11:11, 14
Source of — Eccl. 2:5, 6
Figurative of spiritual life — Is. 43:19, 20; Is. 58:11

Irritability—*the quality of easily being provoked to anger*
A. *Characteristics of:*
Quick temper — 1 Sam. 20:30-33
Morose disposition — 1 Sam. 25:3, 36-39
Hotheaded — Gen. 49:6
Complaining — Ex. 14:10-14
B. *Cure by God's:*
Love — 1 Cor. 13:4-7
Peace — Phil. 4:7, 8
Spirit — Gal. 5:22-26

Irritate—*anger of displeasure*
Of Hannah — 1 Sam. 1:6

Ir-shemesh—*city of the sun*
Danite city — Josh. 19:41
Same as Beth-shemesh — 1 Kin. 4:9

SUBJECT — REFERENCE

Iru—*watchful*
Son of Caleb — 1 Chr. 4:15

Isaac—*laughter*
A. *Life of:*
Son of Abraham and Sarah — Gen. 21:1-3
His birth promised — Gen. 17:16-18
Heir of the covenant — Gen. 17:19, 21
Born and circumcised — Gen. 21:1-8
Offered up as a sacrifice — Gen. 22:1-19
Secures Rebekah as wife — Gen. 24:1-67
Covenant confirmed to — Gen. 26:2-5
Buries his father — Gen. 25:8, 9
Father of Esau and Jacob — Gen. 25:19-26
Prefers Esau — Gen. 25:27, 28
Lives in Gerar — Gen. 26:1, 6
Covenant reaffirmed with — Gen. 26:2-5
Calls Rebekah his sister — Gen. 26:7-11
Becomes prosperous — Gen. 26:12-14
Trouble over wells — Gen. 26:14-22
Covenant with Abimelech — Gen. 26:23-33
Grieves over Esau — Gen. 26:34, 35
Deceived by Jacob — Gen. 27:1-25
Blesses his sons — Gen. 27:26-40
Dies in his old age — Gen. 35:28, 29
B. *Character of:*
Obedient — Gen. 22:9
Peaceable — Gen. 26:14-22
Thoughtful — Gen. 24:63
Prayerful — Gen. 25:21; Gen. 26:25
C. *Significance of:*
Child of promise — Gal. 4:22, 23
Man of faith — Heb. 11:9, 20
Type of believers — Gal. 4:28-31
Ancestor of Christ — Luke 3:34
Patriarch of Israel — Ex. 32:13

Isaiah—*Jehovah is salvation*
A. *Life of:*
Son of Amoz — Is. 1:1
Prophesies during reigns of Uzziah, Jotham, Ahaz and Hezekiah — Is. 1:1
Contemporary of Amos and Hosea — Amos 1:1; Hos. 1:1
Responds to prophetic call — Is. 6:1-13
Protests against policy of Ahaz — Is. 7:1-25; Is. 8:1-22
Gives symbolic names to his sons — Is. 8:1-4, 18
Walks naked and barefoot — Is. 20:2, 3
Encourages Hezekiah — 2 Kin. 19:1-34
Warns Hezekiah of death — 2 Kin. 20:1
Instructs Hezekiah concerning his recovery — 2 Kin. 20:4-11
Upbraids Hezekiah for his acts — 2 Kin. 20:12-19
Writes Uzziah's biography — 2 Chr. 26:22
Writes Hezekiah's biography — 2 Chr. 32:32
B. *Messianic prophecies of:*
Christ's birth — Is. 7:14; Is. 11:1-9; Matt. 1:22, 23
John's coming — Is. 40:3; Matt. 3:3
Christ's mission — Is. 61:1, 2; Luke 4:17-19
Christ's death — Is. 53:1-12; Matt. 8:17; 1 Pet. 2:21-25
Christ as Servant — Is. 42:1-4; Matt. 12:17-21
Gospel invitation — Is. 55:1-13; Acts 13:34
Conversion of Gentiles — Is. 11:10; Rom. 15:8-12
C. *Other prophecies of:*
Assyrian invasion — Is. 8:1-4
Babylon's fall — Is. 13:1-22
Devastation of Moab — Is. 16:1-14
Tyre and Sidon condemned — Is. 23:1-18
Destruction of Sennacherib — Is. 37:14-38
Babylonian captivity — Is. 39:3-7
D. *Other features concerning:*
Calls Christ Immanuel — Is. 7:14
Names Cyrus — Is. 45:1-3
Eunuch reads from — Acts 8:27, 28, 30
Quoted in New Testament — Rom. 9:27, 29; Rom. 10:16, 20, 21; Rom. 11:26, 27

SUBJECT — REFERENCE

Isaiah, the Book of—*a book of the Old Testament*
Call of Isaiah — Is. 6
Promise of Immanuel — Is. 7:10-25
Prophecies against nations — Is. 13—23
Historical section — Is. 36—39
Songs of the servant — Is. 42, 49—53
Future hope of Zion — Is. 66

Iscah—*watchful*
Daughter of Haran — Gen. 11:29

Iscariot, Judas—*man of Kerioth*
A. *Life of:*
Listed among the Twelve — Mark 3:14, 19
Called Iscariot and a traitor — Luke 6:16
Criticizes Mary — John 12:3-5
Treasurer — John 13:29
Identified as betrayer — John 13:21-26
Sells out Christ — Matt. 26:14-16
Betrays Christ with a kiss — Mark 14:10, 11, 43-45
Returns betrayal money — Matt. 27:3-10
Commits suicide — Matt. 27:5
Goes to his own place — Acts 1:16-20, 25
Better not to have been born — Matt. 26:24
B. *Described as:*
Thief — John 12:6
Callous — John 12:4-6
Deceitful — Matt. 26:14-16
Possessed by Satan — John 13:27
Son of perdition — John 17:12
Devil — John 6:70, 71

Ishbah—*he praises*
Man of Judah — 1 Chr. 4:17

Ishbak—*leaving*
Son of Abraham and Keturah — Gen. 25:2

Ishbi-benob—*my dwelling is at Nob*
Philistine giant — 2 Sam. 21:16, 17

Ish-bosheth—*man of shame*
One of Saul's sons — 2 Sam. 2:8
Made king — 2 Sam. 2:8-10
Offends Abner — 2 Sam. 3:7-11
Slain; but assassins executed — 2 Sam. 4:1-12

Ishhod—*man of majesty*
Manassite — 1 Chr. 7:18

Ishi, (I)—*salutary*
1. Son of Appaim — 1 Chr. 2:31
2. Descendant of Judah — 1 Chr. 4:20
3. Simeonite whose sons destroyed Amalekites — 1 Chr. 4:42
4. Manassite leader — 1 Chr. 5:23, 24

Ishi, (II)—*my husband*
Symbolic name of God — Hos. 2:16, 17

Ishiah—*Jehovah will lend*
Son of Izrahiah — 1 Chr. 7:3

Ishijah—*Jehovah will lend*
Son of Harim — Ezra 10:31

Ishma—*desolate*
Man of Judah — 1 Chr. 4:1, 3

Ishmael—*God hears*
1. Abram's son by Hagar — Gen. 16:3, 4, 15
Angel foretells his name and character — Gen. 16:11-16
Circumcised at 13 — Gen. 17:25
Mocks at Isaac's feast — Gen. 21:8, 9
Evidence of fleshly origin — Gal. 4:22-31
Becomes an archer — Gen. 21:20
Dwells in wilderness — Gen. 21:21
Marries an Egyptian — Gen. 21:21
Buries his father — Gen. 25:9
Dies at age 137 — Gen. 25:17
His generations — Gen. 25:12-19
His descendants — 1 Chr. 1:29-31
2. Descendant of Jonathan — 1 Chr. 8:38
3. Father of Zebadiah — 2 Chr. 19:11
4. Military officer under Joash — 2 Chr. 23:1-3, 11
5. Son of Nethaniah; instigates murder of Gedaliah — 2 Kin. 25:22-25
6. Priest who divorced his foreign wife — Ezra 10:22

I

SUBJECT — REFERENCE

Ishmaelites—*descendants of Ishmael*

- Settle at Havilah ... Gen. 25:17, 18
- Joseph sold to ... Gen. 37:25-28
- Sell Joseph to Potiphar ... Gen. 39:1
- Wear golden earrings ... Judg. 8:22, 24
- Become known as Arabians ... 2 Chr. 17:11

Ishmaiah—*Jehovah hears*

1. Gibeonite ... 1 Chr. 12:4
2. Tribal chief in Zebulun ... 1 Chr. 27:19

Ishmerai—*Jehovah keeps*

- Benjamite ... 1 Chr. 8:18

Ishod—*man of majesty*

- Manassite ... 1 Chr. 7:18

Ishpah—*firm, strong*

- A Benjamite ... 1 Chr. 8:16

Ishpan—*he will hide*

- Son of Shashak ... 1 Chr. 8:22, 25

Ish-tob—*man of Tob*

- Small kingdom of Aram ... 2 Sam. 10:6, 8
- Jephthah seeks asylum in ... Judg. 11:3, 5

Ishuah—*he is equal*

- Son of Asher ... Gen. 46:17

Ishuai—*man of Jehovah*

1. Son of Asher and chief ... 1 Chr. 7:30
2. Son of Saul ... 1 Sam. 14:49

Island—*surrounded by water*

A. *Descriptive of:*

- Coastal land of Palestine ... Is. 20:6
- Land surrounded by water ... Is. 23:2
- Remote regions ... Is. 42:10

B. *List of:*

- Caphtor (Crete?) ... Jer. 47:4
- Clauda ... Acts 27:16
- Chios ... Acts 20:15
- Coos ... Acts 21:1
- Crete ... Acts 27:12
- Cyprus ... Acts 11:19
- Elishah ... Ezek. 27:7
- Kittim (Cyprus) ... Jer. 2:10
- Melita ... Acts 28:1, 7, 9
- Patmos ... Rev. 1:9
- Rhodes ... Acts 21:1
- Samos ... Acts 20:15
- Samothrace ... Acts 16:11
- Syracuse ... Acts 28:12
- Tyre ... Is. 23:1, 2

Ismachiah—*Jehovah will sustain*

- Temple overseer ... 2 Chr. 31:13

Ispah—*to lay bear*

- Benjamite ... 1 Chr. 8:16

Israel—*God strives*

A. *Used literally of:*

- Jacob ... Gen. 32:28
- Descendants of Jacob ... Gen. 49:16, 28
- Ten northern tribes (in contrast to Judah) ... 1 Sam. 11:8
- Restored nation after exile ... Ezra 9:1

B. *Used spiritually of:*

- Messiah ... Is. 49:3
- God's redeemed ones ... Rom. 9:6-13
- True church ... Gal. 6:16

Israelites—*descendants of Israel* (Jacob)

A. *Brief history of:*

- Begin as a nation in Egypt ... Ex. 1:12, 20
- Afflicted in Egypt ... Ex. 1:12-22
- Moses becomes their leader ... Ex. 3:1-22
- Saved from plagues ... Ex. 9:4, 6, 26
- Expelled from Egypt ... Ex. 12:29-36
- Pass through Red Sea ... Ex. 14:1-31
- Receive Law at Sinai ... Ex. 19:1-25
- Sin at Sinai ... Ex. 32:1-35
- Rebel at Kadesh ... Num. 13:1-33
- Wander 40 years ... Num. 14:26-39
- Cross Jordan ... Josh. 4:1-24
- Conquer Canaan ... Josh. 12:1-24
- Ruled by judges ... Judg. 2:1-23
- Samuel becomes leader ... 1 Sam. 7:1-17
- Seek to have a king ... 1 Sam. 8:1-22
- Saul chosen king ... 1 Sam. 10:18-27
- David becomes king ... 2 Sam. 2:1-4
- Solomon becomes king ... 1 Kin. 1:28-40
- Kingdom divided ... 1 Kin. 12:1-33
- Israel (northern kingdom) carried captive ... 2 Kin. 17:5-23
- Judah (southern kingdom) carried captive ... 2 Kin. 24:1-20
- 70 years in exile ... 2 Chr. 36:20, 21
- Return after exile ... Ezra 1:1-5
- Nation rejects Christ ... Matt. 27:20-27
- Nation destroyed ... Luke 21:20-24; 1 Thess. 2:14-16

B. *Blessed with:*

- Great leaders ... Heb. 11:8-40
- Inspired prophets ... 1 Pet. 1:10-12
- God's oracles ... Rom. 3:2
- Priesthood ... Rom. 9:3-5
- The Law ... Gal. 3:16-25
- Messianic promises ... Acts 3:18-26
- Temple ... Heb. 9:1-10
- Messiah ... Dan. 9:24-27
- God's covenant ... Jer. 31:31-33
- Regathering ... Is. 27:12; Jer. 16:15, 16

C. *Sins of:*

- Idolatry ... Hos. 13:1-4
- Hypocrisy ... Is. 1:11-14
- Disobedience ... Jer. 7:22-28
- Externalism ... Matt. 23:1-33
- Unbelief ... Rom. 11:1-31
- Works—righteousness ... Phil. 3:4-9

D. *Punishments upon:*

- Defeat ... Lev. 26:36-38
- Curses upon ... Deut. 28:15-46
- Captivity ... Judg. 2:13-23
- Destruction ... Luke 19:42-44
- Dispersion ... Deut. 4:26-28
- Blindness ... Rom. 11:25
- Forfeiture of blessings ... Acts 13:42-49
- Replaced by Gentiles ... Rom. 11:11-20

See Jews

Israel, the religion of

A. *History of:*

- Call of Abraham ... Gen. 12:1-3
- Canaan promised ... Gen. 15:18-21
- Covenant at Sinai ... Ex. 20
- Covenant at Shechem ... Josh. 24:1-28
- Ark brought to Jerusalem ... 2 Sam. 6
- Dedication of the Temple ... 1 Kin. 8:1-66
- Reform movements ... 2 Kin. 23:4-14; 2 Chr. 29:3-36
- Destruction of Jerusalem ... Jer. 6
- Restoration of the Law ... Neh. 8, 9

B. *Beliefs about God:*

- Creator ... Gen. 1:1; Ps. 104:24
- Sustainer of creation ... Ps. 104:27-30
- Active in human affairs ... Deut. 26:5-15
- Omniscient ... Ps. 139:1-6
- Omnipresent ... Jer. 23:23, 24
- Everlasting ... Ps. 90:2
- Moral ... Ex. 34:6, 7

Issachar—*man of hire*

1. Jacob's fifth son ... Gen. 30:17, 18
2. Tribe of, descendants of Jacob's fifth son ... Num. 26:23, 24
   - Prophecy concerning ... Gen. 49:14, 15
   - Census at Sinai ... Num. 1:28, 29
   - On Gerizim ... Deut. 27:12
   - Inheritance of ... Josh. 19:17-23
   - Assists Deborah ... Judg. 5:15
   - At David's coronation ... 1 Chr. 12:32
   - Census in David's time ... 1 Chr. 7:1-5
   - Attended Hezekiah's Passover ... 2 Chr. 30:18
   - Prominent person of ... Judg. 10:1
3. Doorkeeper ... 1 Chr. 26:1, 5

Isshiah—*Jehovah exists*

1. Descendant of Issachar ... 1 Chr. 7:1, 3
   - Son of Izrahiah ... 1 Chr. 7:3
2. Mighty man of David ... 1 Chr. 12:1, 6
3. Kohathite Levite ... 1 Chr. 23:20; 1 Chr. 24:25
4. Levite and family head ... 1 Chr. 24:21

Italy—*a peninsula of southern Europe*

- Soldiers of, in Caesarea ... Acts 10:1
- Jews expelled from ... Acts 18:2
- Paul sails for ... Acts 27:1, 6
- Christians in ... Acts 28:14

Itching ears—*descriptive of desire for something exciting*

- Characteristic of the last days ... 2 Tim. 4:2, 3

Ithai—*with me* (is Jehovah)

- Son of Ribai ... 1 Chr. 11:31
- Also called Ittai ... 2 Sam. 23:29

Ithamar—*island of palms*

- Youngest son of Aaron ... Ex. 6:23
- Consecrated as priest ... Ex. 28:1
- Duty entrusted to ... Ex. 38:21
- Jurisdiction over Gershonites and Merarites ... Num. 4:21-33
- Founder of Levitical family ... 1 Chr. 24:4-6

Ithiel—*God is with me*

1. Man addressed by Agur ... Prov. 30:1
2. Benjamite ... Neh. 11:7

Ithmah—*bereavement*

- Moabite of David's mighty men ... 1 Chr. 11:46

Ithnan—*perennial*

- Town in south Judah ... Josh. 15:23

Ithra—*excellence*

- Israelite (or Ishmaelite); father of Amasa ... 2 Sam. 17:25
- Called Jether ... 1 Kin. 2:5, 32

Ithran—*excellent*

1. Son of Dishon ... Gen. 36:26
2. Son of Zophah ... 1 Chr. 7:37
   - Same as Jether ... 1 Chr. 7:38

Ithream—*residue of the people*

- Son of David ... 2 Sam. 3:2-5

Ithrite—*pre-eminence*

- Family dwelling at Kirjath-jearim ... 1 Chr. 2:53
- One of David's guard ... 2 Sam. 23:38

Itinerary, Israelites in Wilderness

- Leave Egypt ... Ex. 12:29-36
- Cross Red Sea ... Ex. 14:1-31
- Bitter water sweetened ... Ex. 15:22-26
- Manna in wilderness ... Ex. 16:1-36
- Water from a rock ... Ex. 17:1-7
- Defeat of Amalek ... Ex. 17:8-16
- At Sinai ... Ex. 19:1-25
- Depart Sinai ... Num. 10:33, 34
- Lord sends quails ... Num. 11:1-35
- Twelve spies ... Num. 13:1-33
- Rebellion at Kadesh ... Num. 14:1-45
- Korah's rebellion ... Num. 16:1-34
- Aaron's rod ... Num. 17:1-13
- Moses' sin ... Num. 20:2-13
- Fiery serpents ... Num. 21:4-9
- Balak and Balaam ... Num. 22:1—24:25
- Midianites conquered ... Num. 31:1-24
- Death of Moses ... Deut. 34:1-8
- Accession of Joshua ... Deut. 34:9

Ittah-kazin—*time of a judge*

- On border of Zebulun ... Josh. 19:13, 16

Ittai—*with me* (is Jehovah)

1. One of David's guard ... 2 Sam. 23:23-29
2. Native of Gath; one of David's commanders ... 2 Sam. 15:18-22

Ituraea—*pertaining to Jetur*

- Ruled by Philip ... Luke 3:1

Ivah—*sky*

- City conquered by the Assyrians ... Is. 37:13

Ivory—*the tusks of certain mammals*

- Imported from Tharshish ... 1 Kin. 10:22
- Imported from Chittim ... Ezek. 27:6, 15
- Ahab's palace made of ... 1 Kin. 22:39
- Thrones made of ... 1 Kin. 10:18
- Beds made of ... Amos 6:4
- Sign of luxury ... Amos 3:15
- Figuratively used ... Song 5:14
- Descriptive of wealth ... Ps. 45:8
- Among Babylon's trade ... Rev. 18:12

SUBJECT — REFERENCE

Izhar—*shining*
Son of Kohath ... Ex. 6:18, 21; Num. 3:19
Ancestor of the Izharites ... Num. 3:27; 1 Chr. 6:38

Izliah—*Jehovah delivers*
Son of Elpaal ... 1 Chr. 8:18

Izrahiah—*Jehovah will shine*
Chief of Issachar ... 1 Chr. 7:1, 3

Izrahite—*descendant of Zerah*
Applied to Shamhuth ... 1 Chr. 27:8

Izri—*fashioner*
Leader of Levitical choir ... 1 Chr. 25:11
Also called Zeri ... 1 Chr. 25:3

Izziah—*Jehovah sprinkles*
One who divorced his foreign wife ... Ezra 10:25

J

Jaakan, Jakan, Akan
Son of Ezer ... 1 Chr. 1:42
Also called Akan ... Gen. 36:27
Of Horite origin ... Gen. 36:20-27
Tribe of, at Beeroth ... Deut. 10:6
Dispossessed by Edomites ... Deut. 2:12
Same as Benejaakan ... Num. 33:31, 32

Jaakobah—*heel catcher*
Simeonite ... 1 Chr. 4:36

Jaala, Jaalah—*wild she-goat*
Family head of exile returnees ... Ezra 2:56
Descendants of Solomon's servants ... Neh. 7:57, 58

Jaalam
Son of Esau ... Gen. 36:5, 18

Jaanai—*answerer*
Gadite chief ... 1 Chr. 5:12

Jaare-oregim—*forests of weavers*
Father of Elhanan ... 2 Sam. 21:19
Also called Jair ... 1 Chr. 20:5

Jaasiel—*God makes*
1. One of David's mighty men ... 1 Chr. 11:47
2. Son of Abner ... 1 Chr. 27:21

Jaasu—*Jehovah makes*
Son of Bani; divorced foreign wife ... Ezra 10:37

Jaazaniah—*Jehovah hearkens*
1. Military commander supporting Gedaliah ... 2 Kin. 25:23
2. Rechabite leader ... Jer. 35:3
3. Idolatrous Israelite elder ... Ezek. 8:11
4. Son of Azur; seen in Ezekiel's vision ... Ezek. 11:1

Jaaziah—*Jehovah strengthens*
Merarite Levite ... 1 Chr. 24:26, 27

Jaaziel—*God strengthens*
Levite musician ... 1 Chr. 15:18, 20

Jabal—*moving*
Son of Lamech; father of herdsmen ... Gen. 4:20

Jabbok—*luxuriant river*
River entering the Jordan about 20 miles north of the Dead Sea ... Num. 21:24
Scene of Jacob's conflict ... Gen. 32:22-32
Boundary marker ... Deut. 3:16

Jabesh—*dry*
1. Father of Shallum ... 2 Kin. 15:10, 13, 14
2. Abbreviated name of Jabesh-gilead ... 1 Sam. 11:1-10

Jabesh-gilead—*Jabesh of Gilead*
Consigned to destruction ... Judg. 21:8-15
Saul struck the Ammonites here ... 1 Sam. 11:1-11
Citizens of, rescue Saul's body ... 1 Sam. 31:11-13
David thanks citizens of ... 2 Sam. 2:4-7

Jabez—*he makes sorrowful*
1. City of Judah ... 1 Chr. 2:55
2. Man of Judah noted for his prayer ... 1 Chr. 4:9, 10

Jabin—*He (God) perceives*
1. Canaanite king of Hazor; leads confederacy against Joshua ... Josh. 11:1-14
2. Another king of Hazor; oppresses Israelites ... Judg. 4:2
Defeated by Deborah and Barak ... Judg. 4:3-24
Immortalized in poetry ... Judg. 5:1-31

Jabneel—*built of God*
1. Town in north Judah ... Josh. 15:11
Probably same as Jabneh ... 2 Chr. 26:6
2. Town of Naphtali ... Josh. 19:33

Jachan—*troubled*
Gadite chief ... 1 Chr. 5:13

Jachin—*He (God) establishes*
1. Son of Simeon ... Gen. 46:10
Family head ... Num. 26:12
Called Jarib ... 1 Chr. 4:24
2. Descendant of Aaron ... 1 Chr. 24:1, 17
Representatives of ... Neh. 11:10
3. One of two pillars in front of Solomon's Temple ... 1 Kin. 7:21, 22

Jacinth—*a sapphire stone*
In high priest's breastplate ... Ex. 28:19
Foundation stone ... Rev. 21:20
Breastplates the color of ... Rev. 9:17

Jacob—*supplanter*
Son of Isaac and Rebekah ... Gen. 25:20-26; Hos. 12:3
Born in answer to prayer ... Gen. 25:21
Rebekah's favorite ... Gen. 25:27, 28
Obtains Esau's birthright ... Gen. 25:29-34; Heb. 12:16
Obtains Isaac's blessing ... Gen. 27:1-38
Hated by Esau ... Gen. 27:41-46
Departs for Haran ... Gen. 28:1-5
See heavenly ladder ... Gen. 28:10-19
Makes a vow ... Gen. 28:20-22
Meets Rachel and Laban ... Gen. 29:1-14
Serves for Laban's daughters ... Gen. 29:15-30
His children ... Gen. 29:31-35
Requests departure from Laban ... Gen. 30:25-43
Flees from Laban ... Gen. 31:1-21
Overtaken by Laban ... Gen. 31:22-43
Covenant with Laban ... Gen. 31:44-55
Meets angels ... Gen. 32:1, 2
Sends message to Esau ... Gen. 32:3-8
Prays earnestly ... Gen. 32:9-12
Sends gifts to Esau ... Gen. 32:13-21
Wrestles with an angel ... Gen. 32:22-32; Hos. 12:3, 4
Name becomes Israel ... Gen. 32:32
Reconciled to Esau ... Gen. 33:1-16
Erects altar at Shechem ... Gen. 33:17-20
Trouble over Dinah ... Gen. 34:1-31
Renewal at Bethel ... Gen. 35:1-15
Buries Rachel ... Gen. 35:16-20
List of 12 sons ... Gen. 35:22-26
Buries Isaac ... Gen. 35:27-29
His favoritism toward Joseph ... Gen. 37:1-31
Mourns over Joseph ... Gen. 37:32-35
Sends sons to Egypt for food ... Gen. 42:1-5
Allows Benjamin to go ... Gen. 43:1-15
Revived by good news ... Gen. 45:25-28
Goes with family to Egypt ... Gen. 46:1-27
Meets Joseph ... Gen. 46:28-34
Meets Pharaoh ... Gen. 47:7-12
Makes Joseph swear ... Gen. 47:28-31
Blesses Joseph's sons ... Gen. 48:1-22
Blesses his own sons ... Gen. 49:1-28
Dies in Egypt ... Gen. 49:29-33
Burial in Canaan ... Gen. 50:1-14

Jacob
Father of Joseph, Mary's husband ... Matt. 1:15, 16

Jacob's oracles—*blessings and curses on twelve tribes*
Recorded ... Gen. 49:1-27

Jacob's well
Christ teaches a Samaritan woman ... John 4:5-26

Jada—*knowing*
Grandson of Jerahmeel ... 1 Chr. 2:26, 28, 32

Jadau—*praised*
Son of Nebo ... Ezra 10:43

Jaddua—*known*
1. Chief layman who signs the document ... Neh. 10:21
2. Levite who returns with Zerubbabel ... Neh. 12:8, 11

Jadon—*he judges*
Meronothite worker ... Neh. 3:7

Jael—*mountain goat*
Wife of Heber the Kenite ... Judg. 4:17
Slays Sisera ... Judg. 4:17-22
Praised by Deborah ... Judg. 5:24-27

Jagur—*lodging place*
Town in south Judah ... Josh. 15:21

Jah—*a poetic form of Jehovah*
Found only in poetry and in proper names ... Ps. 68:4

Jahath—*comfort, revival*
1. Grandson of Judah ... 1 Chr. 4:2
2. Great-grandson of Levi ... 1 Chr. 6:20, 43
3. Son of Shimei ... 1 Chr. 23:10
4. Son of Shelemoth ... 1 Chr. 24:22
5. Merarite Levite ... 2 Chr. 34:12

Jahaz—*a place trodden under foot*
Town in Moab at which Sihon was defeated ... Num. 21:23
Assigned to Reubenites ... Josh. 13:18
Levitical city ... Josh. 21:36
Regained by Moabites ... Is. 15:4
Same as Jahzah ... 1 Chr. 6:78

Jahaziah—*Jehovah sees*
Postexilic returnee ... Ezra 10:15

Jahaziel—*God sees*
1. Kohathite Levite ... 1 Chr. 23:19
2. Benjamite warrior ... 1 Chr. 12:4
3. Priest ... 1 Chr. 16:6
4. Inspired Levite ... 2 Chr. 20:14

Jahdai—*Jehovah leads*
Judahite ... 1 Chr. 2:47

Jahdiel—*God makes glad*
Manassite chief ... 1 Chr. 5:24

Jahdo—*union*
Gadite ... 1 Chr. 5:14

Jahleel—*wait for God*
Son of Zebulun ... Gen. 46:14
Family head ... Num. 26:26

Jahleelites
Descendants of Jahleel ... Num. 26:26

Jahmai—*may God protect*
Descendant of Issachar ... 1 Chr. 7:1, 2

Jahzeel—*God divides*
Son of Naphtali ... Gen. 46:24
Same as Jahziel ... 1 Chr. 7:13

Jahzeelites
Descendants of Jahzeel ... Num. 26:48

Jahzerah—*prudent*
Priest ... 1 Chr. 9:12
Called Ahasai ... Neh. 11:13

Jahziel—*God divides*
Son of Naphtali ... 1 Chr. 7:13

Jailer—*one who guards a prison*
At Philippi, converted by Paul ... Acts 16:19-34

Jair—*he enlightens*
1. Manassite warrior ... Num. 32:41; Deut. 3:14
Conquers towns in Gilead ... Num. 32:41

SUBJECT REFERENCE

2. Eighth judge of Israel ....Judg. 10:3-5
3. Father of Mordecai, Esther's uncle ....Esth. 2:5
4. Father of Elhanan ....1 Chr. 20:5
   Called Jaare-oregim.........2 Sam. 21:19

Jairite

Descendant of Jair, the Manassite...................2 Sam. 20:26

Jairus—Greek form of "*Jair*"

Ruler of the synagogue; Jesus raises his daughter....................Mark 5:22-24, 35-43

Jakeh—*pious*

Father of Agur................Prov. 30:1

Jakim—*He* (God) *raises up*

1. Descendant of Aaron ....1 Chr. 24:1, 12
2. Benjamite ....1 Chr. 8:19

Jalon—*passing the night*

Calebite, son of Ezra..........1 Chr. 4:17

Jambres—*opposer*

Egyptian magician..............2 Tim. 3:8
See Jannes and Jambres

James—*a form of Jacob*

1. Son of Zebedee ....Matt. 4:21
   Fisherman.................Matt. 4:21
   One of the Twelve..........Matt. 10:2
   In business with Peter.......Luke 5:10
   Called Boanerges...........Mark 3:17
   Of fiery disposition ....Luke 9:52-55
   Makes a contention.........Mark 10:35-45
   One of inner circle..........Matt. 17:1
   Sees the risen Lord ....John 21:1, 2
   Awaits the Holy Spirit ......Acts 1:13
   Slain by Herod Agrippa .....Acts 12:2
2. Son of Alphaeus; one of the Twelve.................Matt. 10:3, 4
   Identified usually as "the less"...................Mark 15:40
   Brother of Joses ....Matt. 27:56
3. Son of Joseph and Mary.....Matt. 13:55, 56
   Lord's brother ....Gal. 1:19
   Rejects Christ's claim ......Mark 3:21
   Becomes a believer ....Acts 1:13, 14
   Sees the risen Lord ....1 Cor. 15:7
   Becomes moderator of Jerusalem Council................Acts 15:13-23
   Paul confers with him ....Gal. 2:9, 12
   Wrote an epistle............James 1:1
   Brother of Jude ....Jude 1

James, the Epistle of—*a book of the New Testament*

Trials........................James 1:2-8
Temptation....................James 1:12-18
Doing the word ....James 1:19-25
Faith and works ....James 2:14-26
Patience ....James 5:7-11
Converting the sinner ....James 5:19, 20

Jamin—*the right hand*

1. Son of Simeon ....Gen. 46:10
   Family head ....Ex. 6:14, 15
2. Man of Judah...............1 Chr. 2:27
3. Postexilic Levite; interprets the law......................Neh. 8:7, 8

Jaminites

Descendants of Jamin..........Num. 26:12

Jamlech—*whom He* (God) *makes king*

Simeonite chief ....1 Chr. 4:34

Janai—*answerer*

Gadite chief ....1 Chr. 5:12

Jangling—*self-conceited talk against God*

Characteristic of false teachers ..1 Tim. 1:6, 7
Translated also "babblings".....1 Tim. 6:20

Jannai—*a form of John*

Ancestor of Christ.............Luke 3:23, 24

Jannes and Jambres

Two Egyptian magicians; oppose Moses ....2 Tim. 3:8
Compare account ....Ex. 7:11-22

SUBJECT REFERENCE

Janoah—*rest, quiet*

1. Town of Naphtali ....2 Kin. 15:29
2. Border town of Ephraim.....Josh. 16:6,7

Janum—*sleep*

Town near Hebron ....Josh. 15:53

Japheth—*widespreading*

One of Noah's three sons.......Gen. 5:32
Saved in the ark...............1 Pet. 3:20
Receives Messianic blessing ......Gen. 9:20-27
His descendants occupy Asia Minor and Europe ....Gen. 10:2-5

Japhia—*may He* (God) *cause to shine forth*

1. King of Lachish; slain by Joshua ....Josh. 10:3-27
2. One of David's sons ....2 Sam. 5:13-15
3. Border town of Zebulun .....Josh. 19:10, 12

Japhlet—*He* (God) *will deliver*

Asherite family ....1 Chr. 7:32, 33

Japhleti

Unidentified tribe on Joseph's boundary ....Josh. 16:1, 3

Japho—*beautiful*

Hebrew form of Joppa ....Josh. 19:46

Jarah—*honeycomb*

Descendant of King Saul ....1 Chr. 9:42
Called Jehoaddah ....1 Chr. 8:36

Jareb—*he will contend*

Figurative description of Assyrian king.........................Hos. 5:13

Jared—*descent*

Father of Enoch ....Gen. 5:15-20
Ancestor of Noah ....1 Chr. 1:2
Ancestor of Christ.............Luke 3:37

Jaresiah—*Jehovah nourishes*

Benjamite head ....1 Chr. 8:27

Jarha

Egyptian slave; marries master's daughter ....1 Chr. 2:34-41

Jarib—*he contends*

1. Head of a Simeonite family ....1 Chr. 4:24
   Called Jachin ....Gen. 46:10
2. Man sent to search for Levites....................Ezra 8:16, 17
3. Priest who divorced his foreign wife ....Ezra 10:18

Jarmuth—*height*

1. Royal city of Canaan ....Josh. 10:3
   King of, slain by Joshua ....Josh. 10:3-27
   Assigned to Judah ....Josh. 15:20, 35
   Inhabited after exile ....Neh. 11:29
2. Town in Issachar assigned to the Levites...................Josh. 21:28, 29
   Called Ramoth ....1 Chr. 6:73
   Called Remeth ....Josh. 19:21

Jaroah—*new moon*

Gadite chief ....1 Chr. 5:14

Jashen—*sleeping*

Sons of, in David's bodyguard ..2 Sam. 23:32
Called Hashem ....1 Chr. 11:34

Jasher—*upright*

Book of, quoted ....Josh. 10:13

Jashobeam—*let the people return*

1. Chief of David's mighty men ....1 Chr. 11:11
   Becomes military captain ....1 Chr. 27:2, 3
2. Benjamite warrior ....1 Chr. 12:1, 2, 6

Jashub—*he returns*

1. Issachar's son ....1 Chr. 7:1
   Head of family.............Num. 26:24
   Called Job.................Gen. 46:13
2. Son of Bani; divorced his foreign wife ....Ezra 10:29

Jashubi-lehem—*bread returns*

A man of Judah...............1 Chr. 4:22

SUBJECT REFERENCE

Jashubites

Descendants of Jashub ....Num. 26:24

Jason—Greek equivalent for "*Joshua*" or "*Jesus*"

Welcomes Paul at Thessalonica.................Acts 17:5-9
Described as Paul's kinsman ....Rom. 16:21

Jasper—*a precious stone (quartz)*

Set in high priest's breastplate...Ex. 28:20

Descriptive of:

Tyre's adornments.............Ezek. 28:12, 13
Heavenly vision ....Rev. 4:3

Jathniel—*God bestows*

Korahite porters ....1 Chr. 26:1, 2

Jattir—*pre-eminence*

Town of Judah................Josh. 15:48
Assigned to Aaron's children....Josh. 21:13, 14
David sends spoil to ....1 Sam. 30:26, 27

Javan—*Greece* (Ionia)

Son of Japheth................Gen. 10:2, 4
Descendants of, to receive good news ....Is. 66:19, 20
Trade with Tyre...............Ezek. 27:13, 19
King of, in Daniel's visions .....Dan. 8:21
Conflict with ....Zech. 9:13

Javelin—*a light, short spear*

Used by Saul ....1 Sam. 18:10

Jaw—*jawbone*

Used figuratively of:

Power over the wicked ....Job 29:17
Prov. 30:14
God's sovereignty ....Is. 30:28
Human trial ....Hos. 11:4

Jawbone—*cheek bone*

Weapon used by Samson ....Judg. 15:15-19

Jazer—*helpful*

Town east of Jordan near Gilead ....2 Sam. 24:5
Amorites driven from ....Num. 21:32
Assigned to Gad ....Josh. 13:24, 25
Becomes Levitical city ....Josh. 21:34, 39
Taken by Moabites ....Is. 16:8, 9
Desired by sons of Reuben and Gad ....Num. 32:1-5

Jaziz—*shining*

Shepherd over David's flocks....1 Chr. 27:31

Jealous, jealousy

A. *Kinds of:*
   Divine ....Ex. 20:5
   Marital ....Num. 5:12-31
   Motherly ....Gen. 30:1
   Brotherly..................Gen. 37:4-28
   Sectional ....2 Sam. 19:41-43
   National ....Judg. 8:1-3
B. *Good causes of:*
   Zeal for the Lord ....Num. 25:11
   Concern over Christians ....2 Cor. 11:2
C. *Evil causes of:*
   Favoritism.................Gen. 37:3-11
   Regard for names ....1 Cor. 3:3-5
   Carnality ....2 Cor. 12:20
   Amos 3:14-16
D. *Described as:*
   Implacable ....Prov. 6:34, 35
   Cruel ....Song 8:6
   Burning ....Deut. 29:20
   Godly ....2 Cor. 11:2

Jearim—*forests*

Mountain 10 miles west of Jerusalem ....Josh. 15:10

Jeaterai—*steadfast*

Descendant of Levi ....1 Chr. 6:21
Also called Ethni ....1 Chr. 6:41

Jeberechiah—*Jehovah blesses*

Father of Zechariah (not the prophet) ....Is. 8:2

Jebus—*trodden under foot*

Same as Jerusalem.............1 Chr. 11:4
Entry denied to David ....1 Chr. 11:5

SUBJECT REFERENCE

Levite came near ....Judg. 19:1, 11
See Zion; Sion

Jebusi, Jebusite—*trodden under foot*
Assigned to Benjamin ....Josh. 18:28
Same as Jerusalem..............Josh. 18:28
On the border of Judah ....Josh. 15:8

Jebusites
Descendants of Canaan ....Gen. 10:15, 16
Mountain tribe..................Num. 13:29
Land of, promised to Israel .....Gen. 15:18-21
Adoni-zedek, their king, raises confederacy ....Josh. 10:1-5
Their king killed by Joshua .....Josh. 10:23-26
Join fight against Joshua ....Josh. 11:1-5
Assigned to Benjamin ....Josh. 18:28
Royal city not taken ....Judg. 1:21
Taken by David ....2 Sam. 5:6-8
Old inhabitants remain ....2 Sam. 24:16-25
Become slaves ....1 Kin. 9:20, 21

Jecoliah—*Jehovah is able*
Mother of King Azariah ....2 Kin. 15:2
Called Jechiliah ....2 Chr. 26:3

Jeconiah—*Jehovah establishes*
Variant form of Jehoiachin .....1 Chr. 3:16, 17
Abbreviated to Coniah ....Jer. 22:24, 28
Son of Josiah ....Matt. 1:11
See Jehoiachin

Jedaiah—*Jehovah has been kind*
1. Priestly family ....1 Chr. 24:7
2. Head of the priests ....Neh. 12:6
3. Another head priest ....Neh. 12:7, 21
4. Simeonite ....1 Chr. 4:37
5. Postexilic worker ....Neh. 3:10
6. One who brings gifts for the Temple ....Zech. 6:10, 14

Jediael—*known of God*
1. Son of Benjamin and family head ....1 Chr. 7:6, 10, 11
2. Manassite; joins David ....1 Chr. 12:20
3. One of David's mighty men ....1 Chr. 11:45
4. Korahite porter ....1 Chr. 26:1, 2

Jedidah—*beloved*
Mother of King Josiah ....2 Kin. 22:1

Jedidiah—*beloved of Jehovah*
Name given to Solomon by Nathan ....2 Sam. 12:24, 25

Jeduthun—*praising*
1. Levite musician appointed by David ....1 Chr. 16:41, 42
Heads a family of musicians ....2 Chr. 5:12
Name appears in Psalm titles ....Ps. 39; 62; 77
Family officiates after Exile ..Neh. 11:17
Possibly same as Ethan ....1 Chr. 15:17, 19
2. Father of Obed-edom ....1 Chr. 16:38

Jegar-sahadutha—*heap of testimony*
Name given by Laban to memorial stones ....Gen. 31:46, 47

Jehaleleel—*God will flash light*
1. Man of Judah and family head ....1 Chr. 4:16
2. Merarite Levite ....2 Chr. 29:12

Jehdeiah—*Jehovah will make glad*
1. Kohathite Levite ....1 Chr. 24:20
2. Meronothite in charge of David's asses ....1 Chr. 27:30

Jehezekel—*God will strengthen*
Descendant of Aaron ....1 Chr. 24:1, 16

Jehiah—*Jehovah lives*
Doorkeeper......................1 Chr. 15:24

Jehiel—*God lives*
1. Levite musician ....1 Chr. 15:18, 20
2. Gershonite and family head ....1 Chr. 23:8
3. Son of Hachmoni............1 Chr. 27:32

SUBJECT REFERENCE

4. Son of King Jehoshaphat .....2 Chr. 21:2, 4
5. Hemanite Levite ....2 Chr. 29:14
6. Overseer in Hezekiah's reign ....2 Chr. 31:13
7. Official of the Temple ....2 Chr. 35:8
8. Father of Obadiah, a returned exile.......................Ezra 8:9
9. Father of Shechaniah ....Ezra 10:2
10. Postexilic priest ....Ezra 10:21
11. Postexilic priest ....Ezra 10:26

Jehieli
A Levite family ....1 Chr. 26:21, 22

Jehizkiah—*Jehovah strengthens*
Ephraimite chief ....2 Chr. 28:12

Jehoadah—*whom Jehovah adorns*
Descendant of Saul ....1 Chr. 8:36
Also called Jarah ....1 Chr. 9:42

Jehoaddan—*Jehovah delights*
Mother of Amaziah.............2 Kin. 14:2

Jehoahaz—*Jehovah has taken hold of*
1. Son and successor of Jehu, king of Israel ....2 Kin. 10:35
Seeks the Lord in defeat .....2 Kin. 13:2-9
2. Son and successor of Josiah, king of Judah......................2 Kin. 23:30-34
Called Shallum...............1 Chr. 3:15
3. Another form of Ahaziah, youngest son of King Joram ....2 Chr. 21:17

Jehoash (see Joash)

Jehohanan, Johanan—*Jehovah is gracious*
1. Korahite Levite ....1 Chr. 26:3
2. Captain under Jehoshaphat ..2 Chr. 17:10, 15
3. Father of Ishmael, Jehoiada's supporter ....2 Chr. 23:1
4. Priestly family head ....Neh. 12:13
5. Priest who divorced his wife ....Ezra 10:28
6. Son of Tobiah the Ammonite....................Neh. 6:17, 18
7. Postexilic singer ....Neh. 12:42

Jehoiachin—*Jehovah establishes*
Son of Jehoiakim; next to the last king of Judah ....2 Kin. 24:8
Deported to Babylon ....2 Kin. 24:8-16
Liberated by Evil-merodach....Jer. 52:31-34
See Jeconiah

Jehoiada—*Jehovah knows*
1. Aaronite supporter of David ....1 Chr. 12:27
2. Father of Benaiah, one of David's officers.....................2 Sam. 8:18
3. Son of Benaiah; one of David's counselors.....................1 Chr. 27:34
4. High priest ....2 Kin. 11:9
Proclaims Joash king ....2 Kin. 11:4-16
Institutes a covenant ....2 Kin. 11:17-21
Instructs Joash ....2 Kin. 12:2
Commanded to repair the Temple ....2 Kin. 12:3-16
Receives honorable burial ...2 Chr. 24:15, 16
5. Deposed priest ....Jer. 29:26
6. Postexilic returnee ....Neh. 3:6

Jehoiakim—*Jehovah raises up*
Son of King Josiah ....2 Kin. 23:34, 35
Made Pharaoh's official ....2 Kin. 23:34,36
Wicked king ....2 Chr. 36:5, 8
Burns Jeremiah's roll ....Jer. 36:1-32
Becomes Nebuchadnezzar's servant ....2 Kin. 24:1
Punished by the Lord ....2 Kin. 24:2-4
Taken by Nebuchadnezzar......2 Chr. 36:5, 6
Returns to idolatry ....2 Chr. 36:5, 8
Treats Jeremiah with contempt ....Jer. 36:21-28
Kills a true prophet.............Jer. 26:20-23
Bound in fetters ....2 Chr. 36:6
Buried as an ass...............Jer. 22:18, 19
Curse on ....Jer. 36:30, 31

Jehoiarib—*Jehovah contends*
Descendant of Aaron ....1 Chr. 24:1, 6, 7
Founder of an order of priests ..1 Chr. 9:10, 13

SUBJECT REFERENCE

Jehonadab—*Jehovah is liberal*
A Rechabite ....2 Kin. 10:15
See Jonadab

Jehonathan—*Jehovah has given*
1. Levite teacher...............2 Chr. 17:8
2. Postexilic priest ....Neh. 12:1, 18

Jehoram—*Jehovah is high*
1. King of Judah; son and successor of Jehoshaphat ....1 Kin. 22:50
Called Joram ....2 Kin. 8:21, 23, 24
Reigns eight years ....2 Kin. 8:16, 17
Marries Athaliah, who leads him astray......................2 Kin. 8:18, 19
Killed his brothers............2 Chr. 21:2, 4, 13
Edom revolts from............2 Kin. 8:20-22
Elijah predicts his terrible end.........................2 Chr. 21:12-15
Nations fight against ....2 Chr. 21:16, 17
Smitten by the Lord; dies in disgrace.....................2 Chr. 21:18-20
2. King of Israel; son of Ahab ....2 Kin. 1:17
Called Joram ....2 Kin. 8:16, 25, 28
Reigns 12 years ....2 Kin. 3:1
Puts away Baal...............2 Kin. 3:2
Joins Jehoshaphat against Moabites.....................2 Kin. 3:1-27
Naaman sent to, for cure ....2 Kin. 5:1-27
Informed by Elijah of Syria's plans ....2 Kin. 6:8-23
Wounded in war with Syria ....2 Kin. 8:28, 29
3. Levite teacher................2 Chr. 17:8

Jehoshabeath—*Jehovah is an oath*
Safeguards Joash from Athaliah ....2 Chr. 22:11

Jehoshaphat—*Jehovah has judged*
1. King of Judah; son and successor of Asa ....1 Kin. 15:24
Reigns 25 years ....1 Kin. 22:42
Fortifies his kingdom ....2 Chr. 17:2
Institutes reforms............2 Chr. 17:3
Inaugurates public instruction ....2 Chr. 17:7-9
Honored and respected.......2 Chr. 17:10-19
Joins Ahab against Ramoth-gilead.....................1 Kin. 22:1-36
Rebuked by a prophet ......2 Chr. 19:2, 3
Develops legal system ....2 Chr. 19:4-11
By faith defeats invading forces....................2 Chr. 20:1-30
Navy of, destroyed ....2 Chr. 20:35-37
Provision for his children ....2 Chr. 21:2, 3
Death of ....2 Chr. 21:1
Ancestor of Christ ....Matt. 1:8
2. Son of Ahilud ....2 Sam. 8:16
Recorder under David and Solomon ....2 Sam. 20:24
3. Father of King Jehu ....2 Kin. 9:2

Jehoshaphat, valley of
Described as a place of judgment ....Joel 3:2, 12

Jehosheba—*Jehovah is an oath*
King Joram's daughter ....2 Kin. 11:2

Jehovah—*title of God*
Defined ....Ex. 6:3-5
Early known ....Gen. 4:26
Usually rendered LORD in Old Testament...................Ex. 17:14
Used in certain combinations ...Gen. 22:14
Often found in names (e.g., Jehoshaphat, Elijah) ....1 Kin. 15:24
Applied to Christ as Lord ......Is. 40:3
Matt. 3:3

Jehovah-jireh—*Jehovah will provide*
Names used by Abraham ....Gen. 22:14

Jehovah-nissi—*Jehovah is my banner*
Name used by Moses for memorial ....Ex. 17:15, 16

Jehovah-shalom—*Jehovah is peace*
Name used by Gideon for significant visit ....Judg. 6:23, 24

J

SUBJECT REFERENCE

Jehozabad—*Jehovah has bestowed*

1. Son of Obed-edom ....1 Chr. 26:4
2. Son of a Moabitess; assassinates Joash ....2 Kin. 12:20, 21
   Put to death ....2 Chr. 25:3
3. Military captain under King Jehoshaphat ....2 Chr. 17:18

Jehozadak—*Jehovah has justified*

Son of Seriah, the high priest ...1 Chr. 6:14
His father killed...............2 Kin. 25:18-21
Carried captive to Babylon .....1 Chr. 6:15
Father of Joshua the high priest.......................Hag. 1:1, 12, 14

Jehu—*Jehovah is He*

1. Benjamite warrior ....1 Chr. 12:3
2. Prophet and son of Hanani ..1 Kin. 16:1
   Denounces Baasha..........1 Kin. 16:2-4, 7
   Rebukes Jehoshaphat ....2 Chr. 19:2, 3
   Writes Jehoshaphat's biography ....2 Chr. 20:34
3. Descendant of Judah........1 Chr. 2:38
4. Simeonite ....1 Chr. 4:35
5. Grandson of Nimshi ....2 Kin. 9:2
   Commander under Ahab ....2 Kin. 9:25
   Divinely commissioned to destroy Ahab's house.....................1 Kin. 19:16, 17
   Carries out orders with zeal ....2 Kin. 9:11-37
   Killed Ahab's sons..........2 Kin. 10:1-17
   Destroys worshipers of Baal ....2 Kin. 10:18-28
   Serves the Lord outwardly ...2 Kin. 10:29-31

Jehubbah—*he hides*

Asherite......................1 Chr. 7:34

Jehucal—*Jehovah is able*

Son of Shelemiah; sent by Zedekiah to Jeremiah ....Jer. 37:3
Also called Jucal ....Jer. 38:1

Jehud—*praise*

Town of Dan ....Josh. 19:40, 45

Jehudi—*a man of Judah; a Jew*

Reads Jeremiah's roll ....Jer. 36:14, 21, 23

Jehudijah—*a Jewess*

One of Mered's two wives; should be rendered "the Jewess" ....1 Chr. 4:18

Jeiel—*God snatches away*

1. Ancestor of Saul ....1 Chr. 9:35-39
2. One of David's mighty men ....1 Chr. 11:44
   Reubenite prince ....1 Chr. 5:6, 7
3. Levite musician ....1 Chr. 16:5
4. Porter ....1 Chr. 15:18, 21
   May be the same as 3 ....1 Chr. 16:5
   Called Jehiah ....1 Chr. 15:24
5. Inspired Levite.............2 Chr. 20:14
6. Levite chief ....2 Chr. 35:9
7. Scribe.....................2 Chr. 26:11
8. Temple Levite ....2 Chr. 29:13
9. One who divorced his foreign wife ....Ezra 10:19, 43

Jekabzeel—*God will gather*

Town in Judah ....Neh. 11:25
Called Kabzeel................Josh. 15:21
Home of Benaiah, David's friend ....2 Sam. 23:20

Jekameam—*people will rise*

Kohathite Levite ....1 Chr. 23:19

Jekamiah—*Jehovah will rise*

1. Son of Shallum............1 Chr. 2:41
2. Son of Jeconiah ....1 Chr. 3:17, 18

Jekuthiel—*God will support*

Man of Judah ....1 Chr. 4:18

Jemima—*dove*

Job's daughter ....Job 42:14

Jemuel—*day of God*

Son of Simeon ....Gen. 46:10
Called Nemuel ....Num. 26:12

SUBJECT REFERENCE

Jephthah—*he will open*

Gilead's son by a harlot........Judg. 11:1
Flees to Tob; becomes a leader ....Judg. 11:2-11
Cites historical precedents against invading Ammonites.................Judg. 11:12-27
Makes a vow before battle......Judg. 11:28-31
Smites Ammonites.............Judg. 11:32, 33
Fulfills vow...................Judg. 11:34-40
Defeats quarrelsome Ephraimites ....Judg. 12:1-7
Cited by Samuel ....1 Sam. 12:11
In faith's chapter ....Heb. 11:32

Jephunneh—*it will be prepared*

1. Caleb's father ....Num. 13:6
2. Asherite...................1 Chr. 7:38

Jerah—*moon*

Son of Joktan; probably an Arabian tribe ....{Gen. 10:26; 1 Chr. 1:20}

Jerahmeel—*may God have compassion*

1. Great-grandson of Judah ....1 Chr. 2:9, 25-41
2. Son of Kish, not Saul's father.....................1 Chr. 24:29
3. King Jehoiakim's officer .....Jer. 36:26

Jerahmeelites

Raided by David..............1 Sam. 27:10

Jered—*descent*

A descendant of Judah ....1 Chr. 4:18
See Jared

Jeremai—*high*

One who divorced his foreign wife ....Ezra 10:19, 33

Jeremiah (I)—*Jehovah establishes*

A. *Life of:*

Son of Hilkiah; a Benjamite ....Jer. 1:1
Native of Anathoth ....Jer. 1:1
Called before birth ....Jer. 1:4-10
Prophet under kings Josiah, Jehoiakim, and Zedekiah ....Jer. 1:2, 3
Imprisoned by Pashur ....Jer. 20:1-6
Writes his prophecy; Jehoiakim burns it ....Jer. 36:1-26
Prophecy rewritten ....Jer. 36:27-32
Accused of desertion ....Jer. 37:1-16
Released by Zedekiah ....Jer. 37:17-21
Cast into a dungeon ....Jer. 38:1-6
Saved by an Ethiopian ......Jer. 38:7-28
Set free by Nebuchadnezzar ....Jer. 39:11-14
Given liberty of choice by Nebuzaradan ....Jer. 40:1-6
Forced to flee to Egypt.....Jer. 43:5-7
Last prophecies at Tahpanhes, Egypt..................Jer. 43:8-13

B. *Characteristics of:*

Forbidden to marry..........Jer. 16:1-13
Has internal conflicts ....Jer. 20:7-18
Has incurable pain ....Jer. 15:18
Motives misunderstood ......Jer. 37:12-14
Tells captives to build in Babylon ....Jer. 29:4-9
Denounces false prophets in Babylon....................Jer. 29:20-32
Rebukes idolatry ....Jer. 7:9-21

C. *Prophecies of, foretell:*

Egypt's fall ....Jer. 43:8-13
70 years of captivity ....2 Chr. 36:21
Restoration to land ....Jer. 16:14-18
New covenant ....Jer. 31:31-34
Herod's massacre ....Jer. 31:15

D. *Teachings of:*

God's sovereignty ....Jer. 18:5-10
God's knowledge ....Jer. 17:5-10
Shame of idolatry ....Jer. 10:14, 15
Spirituality of worship, etc. ..Jer. 3:16, 17
Need of regeneration........Jer. 9:26
Man's sinful nature ....Jer. 2:22
Gospel salvation ....Jer. 23:5, 6
Call of the Gentiles ....Jer. 3:17-19

Jeremiah (II)

1. Benjamite warrior ....1 Chr. 12:4
2. Gadite warrior ....1 Chr. 12:10
3. Another Gadite warrior .....1 Chr. 12:13

SUBJECT REFERENCE

4. Manassite head ....1 Chr. 5:23, 24
5. Father of Hamutal, a wife of Josiah ....2 Kin. 23:31
6. Father of Jaazaniah.........Jer. 35:3
7. Postexilic priest ....Neh. 12:1, 7
   Head of a priestly line ......Neh. 12:12
8. Priest who signs the covenant ....Neh. 10:2

Jeremiah, the Book of—*a book of the Old Testament*

Jeremiah's call ....Jer. 1:1-19
Jeremiah's life ....Jer. 26:1—45:5
Israel's sin against God ....Jer. 2:1—10:25
Against false prophets ....Jer. 23:9-40
Against foreign nations.........Jer. 46:1—51:64
The Messianic king ....Jer. 23:1-8

Jeremoth—*elevation*

1. Son of Becher..............1 Chr. 7:8
2. Benjamite ....1 Chr. 8:14
3. Merarite Levite ....1 Chr. 23:23
4. Musician of David..........1 Chr. 25:22
5. Ruler of Napthali ....1 Chr. 27:19
6. One who divorced his foreign wife ....Ezra 10:26
7. Another who divorced his foreign wife ....Ezra 10:27
8. Spelled Jerimoth ....1 Chr. 24:30

Jeriah, Jerijah—*Jehovah sees*

Kohathite Levite ....1 Chr. 23:19, 23
Hebronite chief ....1 Chr. 26:31

Jeribai—*Jehovah contends*

One of David's warriors ....1 Chr. 11:46

Jericho—*place of fragrance*

City near the Jordan ....Num. 22:1
Viewed by Moses.............Deut. 34:1-3
Called the city of palm trees ....Deut. 34:3
Viewed by spies ....Josh. 2:1
Home of Rahab the harlot......Heb. 11:31
Scene of Joshua's vision ....Josh. 5:13-15
Destroyed by Joshua...........Heb. 11:30
Curse of rebuilding of ....Josh. 6:26
Assigned to Benjamin ....Josh. 16:1, 7
Moabites retake ....Judg. 3:12, 13
David's envoys tarry here.......2 Sam. 10:4, 5
Rebuilt by Hiel ....1 Kin. 16:34
Visited by Elijah and Elisha ....2 Kin. 2:4-22
Zedekiah captured here ....2 Kin. 25:5
Reinhabited after exile ....Ezra 2:34
People of, help rebuild Jerusalem ....Neh. 3:2
Blind men of, healed by Jesus ...Matt. 20:29-34
Home of Zacchaeus............Luke 19:1-10

Jeriel—*God sees*

Son of Tola ....1 Chr. 7:2

Jerimoth

1. Son of Bela ....1 Chr. 7:7
2. Warrior of David...........1 Chr. 12:5
3. Musician of David..........1 Chr. 25:4
4. Son of David ....2 Chr. 11:18
5. Levite overseer ....2 Chr. 31:13
6. Spelled Jeremoth ....1 Chr. 23:23

See Jeremoth

Jerioth—*tent curtains*

One of Caleb's wives...........1 Chr. 2:18

Jeroboam—*may the people increase*

1. Son of Nebat ....1 Kin. 11:26
   Rebels against Solomon .....1 Kin. 11:26-28
   Ahijah's prophecy concerning ....1 Kin. 11:29-39
   Flees to Egypt ....1 Kin. 11:40
   Recalled, made king ....1 Kin. 12:1-3, 12, 20
   Perverts the true religion ....1 Kin. 12:25-33
   Casts Levites out ....2 Chr. 11:14
   Rebuked by a man of God ..1 Kin. 13:1-10
   Leads people astray.........1 Kin. 13:33, 34
   His wife consults Ahijah.....1 Kin. 14:1-18
   War with Abijam ....1 Kin. 15:7
   Reigns 22 years ....1 Kin. 14:20
   Struck by the Lord ....2 Chr. 13:20
2. Jeroboam II; king of Israel ..2 Kin. 13:13
   Successor of Joash (Jehoash).................2 Kin. 14:16, 23

SUBJECT — REFERENCE

Conquers Hamath and Damascus .... 2 Kin. 14:25-28
Reigns wickedly 41 years .... 2 Kin. 14:23, 24
Denounced by Amos .... Amos 7:7-13
Death of .... 2 Kin. 14:29

Jeroham—*he is pitied*
1. Grandfather of Samuel .... 1 Sam. 1:1
2. Benjamite .... 1 Chr. 9:8
3. Father of Benjamite chief men .... 1 Chr. 8:27
4. Benjamite of Gedor .... 1 Chr. 12:7
5. Father of Adaiah .... 1 Chr. 9:12
6. Danite chief's father .... 1 Chr. 27:22
7. Military captain .... 2 Chr. 23:1

Jerubbaal—*Baal contends*
Name given to Gideon for destroying Baal's altar .... Judg. 6:32

Jerubbesheth—*let shame contend*
Father of Abimelech .... 2 Sam. 11:21

Jeruel—*founded by God*
Wilderness west of the Dead Sea .... 2 Chr. 20:16

Jerusalem—*possession of peace*
A. *Names applied to:*
City of God .... Ps. 46:4
City of David .... 2 Sam. 5:6, 7
City of Judah .... 2 Chr. 25:28
Zion .... Ps. 48:12
Jebusi .... Josh. 18:28
Holy city .... Matt. 4:5
Faithful city .... Is. 1:21, 26
City of righteousness .... Is. 1:26
City of truth .... Zech. 8:3,
City of the great King .... Ps. 48:2
Salem .... Gen. 14:18

B. *History of:*
Originally Salem .... Gen. 14:18
Occupied by Jebusite .... Josh. 15:8
King of, defeated by Joshua .... Josh. 10:5-23
Assigned to Benjamin .... Josh. 18:28
Attacked by Judah .... Judg. 1:8
Jebusites remain in .... Judg. 1:21
David brings Goliath's head to .... 1 Sam. 17:54
Conquered by David .... 2 Sam. 5:6-8
Name changed .... 2 Sam. 5:7-9
Ark brought to .... 2 Sam. 6:12-17
Saved from destruction .... 2 Sam. 24:16
Solomon builds Temple here .... 1 Kin. 5:5-8
Suffers in war .... 1 Kin. 14:25-27
Plundered by Israel .... 2 Kin. 14:13, 14
Besieged by Syrians .... Is. 7:1
Earthquake damages .... Amos 1:1
Miraculously saved .... 2 Kin. 19:31-36
Ruled by Egypt .... 2 Kin. 23:33-35
Besieged by Babylon .... 2 Kin. 24:10, 11
Captured by Babylon .... Jer. 39:1-8
Desolate 70 years .... Jer. 25:11, 12
Temple rebuilt in .... Ezra 1:1-4
Exiles return to .... Ezra 2:1-70
Work on, hindered .... Ezra 5:1-17
Walls of, dedicated .... Neh. 12:27-47
Christ: Enters as King .... Matt. 21:9, 10
Laments for .... Matt. 23:37
Crucified at .... Luke 9:31
Weeps over .... Luke 19:41, 42
Predicts destruction .... Luke 19:43, 44
Gospel preached at .... Luke 24:47
Many miracles performed in .... John 4:45
Church begins here .... Acts 2:1-47
Christians of, persecuted .... Acts 4:1-30
Stephen martyred at .... Acts 7:1-60
First Christian council held here .... Acts 15:1-29
Paul:
Visits .... Acts 20:16
Arrested in .... Acts 21:30-36
Taken from .... Acts 23:12-33

C. *Prophecies concerning:*
Destruction by Babylon .... Jer. 20:5
Utter ruin .... Jer. 26:18
Rebuilding by Cyrus .... Is. 44:26-28
Christ's entry into .... Zech. 9:9
Gospel proclaimed from .... Is. 2:3
Perilous times .... Matt. 24:1-22
Being under Gentiles .... Luke 21:24

D. *Described:*
Physically—strong .... Ps. 48:12, 13
Ps. 125:2
Morally—corrupt .... Is. 1:1-16
Jer. 5:1-5
Spiritually—the redeemed .... Gal. 4:26-30
Prophetically—New Jerusalem .... Rev. 21:1-27
See Zion; Sion

Jerusha—*possessed* (married)
Wife of King Uzziah .... 2 Kin. 15:33
Called Jerushah .... 2 Chr. 27:1

Jeshaiah—*Jehovah saves*
1. Musician of David .... 1 Chr. 25:3
2. Grandson of Zerubbabel .... 1 Chr. 3:21
3. Levite in David's reign .... 1 Chr. 26:25
4. Son of Athaliah; returns from Babylon .... Ezra 8:7
5. Levite who returns with Ezra .... Ezra 8:19
6. Benjamite .... Neh. 11:7

Jeshanah—*old*
City of Ephraim taken by Abijah .... 2 Chr. 13:19

Jesharelah—*upright toward God*
Levite musician .... 1 Chr. 25:14
Called Asarelah .... 1 Chr. 25:2

Jeshebeab—*may the father tarry* (live)
Descendant of Aaron .... 1 Chr. 24:13

Jesher—*uprightness*
Caleb's son .... 1 Chr. 2:18

Jeshimon—*waste*
Wilderness west of the Dead Sea .... 1 Sam. 23:19, 24

Jeshishai—*aged*
Gadite .... 1 Chr. 5:14

Jeshohaiah—*humbled by Jehovah*
Leader in Simeon .... 1 Chr. 4:36

Jeshua—*Jehovah is salvation*
1. Joshua, the military leader after Moses .... Neh. 8:17
2. Descendant of Aaron .... Ezra 2:36
3. Levite treasurer .... 2 Chr. 31:14, 15
4. Postexilic high priest .... Zech. 3:8
Returns with Zerubbabel .... Ezra 2:2
Aids in Temple rebuilding .... Ezra 3:2-8
Withstands opponents .... Ezra 4:1-3
Figurative act performed on .... Zech. 3:1-10
5. Levite assistant .... Ezra 2:40
Explains the Law .... Neh. 8:7
Leads in worship .... Neh. 9:4, 5
Seals the covenant .... Neh. 10:1, 9
6. Repairer of the wall .... Neh. 3:19
7. Man of the house of Pahath-moab .... Ezra 2:6
8. Village in south Judah .... Neh. 11:26

Jeshurun—*upright one*
Poetic name of endearment for Israel .... Deut. 32:15

Jesimiel—*God sets up*
Simeonite leader .... 1 Chr. 4:36

Jesse—*Jehovah exists*
Grandson of Ruth and Boaz .... Ruth 4:17-22
Father of:
David .... 1 Sam. 16:18, 19
Eight sons .... 1 Sam. 16:10, 11
Two daughters .... 1 Chr. 2:15, 16
Citizen of Bethlehem .... 1 Sam. 16:1, 18
Protected by David .... 1 Sam. 22:1-4
Of humble origin .... 1 Sam. 18:18, 23
Mentioned in prophecy .... Is. 11:1, 10
Ancestor of Christ .... Matt. 1:5, 6

Jesting—*giving an immoral turn to something*
Condemned .... Eph. 5:4
Lot appeared to be .... Gen. 19:14
Of godless men .... Ps. 35:16

Jesus (see Christ)

Jether—*abundance*
1. Gideon's oldest son .... Judg. 8:20, 21
2. Descendant of Judah .... 1 Chr. 2:32
3. Son of Ezra .... 1 Chr. 4:17
4. Asherite; probably same as Ithran .... 1 Chr. 7:30-38
5. Amasa's father .... 1 Kin. 2:5, 32

Jetheth—*subjection*
Chief of Edom .... Gen. 36:40

Jethlah—*an overhanging place*
Danite town .... Josh. 19:42

Jethro—*excellent*
Priest of Midian; Moses' father-in-law .... Num. 10:29
Also called Reuel .... Num. 10:29
Moses marries his daughter Zipporah .... Ex. 2:16-22
Moses departs from .... Ex. 4:18-26
Visits and counsels Moses .... Ex. 18:1-27

Jetur
Son of Ishmael .... Gen. 25:15
Conflict with Israel .... 1 Chr. 5:18, 19
Tribal descendants of; the Ituraeans .... Luke 3:1

Jeuel—*snatching away*
Son of Zerah .... 1 Chr. 9:6

Jeush—*may he aid*
1. Son of Esau and Edomite chief .... Gen. 36:5, 18
2. Benjamite head .... 1 Chr. 7:10
3. Gershonite Levite .... 1 Chr. 23:10, 11
4. Descendant of Jonathan .... 1 Chr. 8:39
5. Rehoboam's son .... 2 Chr. 11:19

J

Jeuz—*counseling*
Benjamite .... 1 Chr. 8:8, 10

Jewels—*ornaments used on the body*
A. *Used for:*
Ornaments .... Is. 3:18-24
Evil offering .... Ex. 32:1-5
Good offering .... Ex. 35:22
Spoils of war .... 2 Chr. 20:25
Farewell gifts .... Ex. 11:2

B. *Significance of:*
Betrothal present .... Gen. 24:22, 53
Sign of wealth .... James 2:2
Standard of value .... Prov. 3:15
Tokens of repentance .... Gen. 35:4
Tokens of love .... Ezek. 16:11-13
Indications of worldliness .... 1 Tim. 2:9
Figurative of God's own .... Matt. 13:45, 46

Jewess—*a female Jew*
Woman of the Hebrew race .... Acts 24:24

Jewish alphabet
Given topically .... Ps. 119

Jewish calendar
A. *List of months of:*
Abib, or Nisan (March—April) .... Ex. 13:4
Zif or Iyyar (April—May) .... 1 Kin. 6:1, 37
Sivan (May—June) .... Esth. 8:9
Tammuz (June—July) .... Jer. 39:2
Ab (July—August) .... Num. 33:38
Elul (August—September) .... Neh. 6:15
Ethanim or Tishri (September—October) .... 1 Kin. 8:2
Bul or Heshvan (October—November) .... 1 Kin. 6:38
Chisleu or Kislev (November—December) .... Neh. 1:1
Tebeth (December—January) .... Esth. 2:16
Shebat or Sebat (January—February) .... Zech. 1:7
Adar (February—March) .... Esth. 3:7

B. *Feasts of:*
Abib (14)—Passover .... Ex. 12:18

SUBJECT — REFERENCE

Abib (15-21)—
Unleavened Bread .... Lev. 23:5, 6
Abib (16)—
First fruits .... Lev. 23:10, 11
Zif (14)—Later
Passover .... Num. 9:10, 11
Sivan (6)—
Pentecost, Feast of Weeks,
Harvest .... Lev. 23:15-21
Ethanim (1)—
Trumpets .... Lev. 23:24
Ethanim (10)—
Day of Atonement .... Lev. 16:29-34
Ethanim (15-21)—
Tabernacles .... Lev. 23:34, 35
Ethanim (22)—
Holy Convocation .... Lev. 23:36
Chisleu (25)—
Dedication .... John 10:22

Jewish measures (Metrology)

A. *Long Measures:*
Finger (3/4 inch) .... Jer. 52:21
Handbreadth
(3 to 4 inches) .... Ex. 25:25
Span (about 9 inches) .... Ex. 28:16
Cubit of man (about 18
inches) .... Gen. 6:15
Pace (about 3 feet) .... 2 Sam. 6:13
Fathom (about 6 feet) .... Acts 27:28
Reed (about 11 feet) .... Ezek. 40:5
Line .... Ezek. 40:3

B. *Land measures:*
Cubit of God (1 3/4 feet) .... Josh. 3:4
Mile (1760 yds.) .... Matt. 5:41
Sabbath day's journey
(3/5 mile) .... Acts 1:12
Day's journey (24 miles) .... Gen. 30:36
Furlong (660 feet) .... Luke 24:13

C. *Weights and dry measures:*
Cab (about 2 quarts) .... 2 Kin. 6:25
Omer (about 7 pints) .... Ex. 16:16-18, 36
Ephah (about 4 1/2 pecks) .... Ex. 16:36
Homer (about 11 bushels) .... Num. 11:32
Hos. 3:2
Talent (about 93 pounds) .... Ex. 25:39

D. *Liquid measures:*
Log (about 1 pint) .... Lev. 14:10, 15
Hin (about 1 1/2 gallons) .... Num. 15:4-10
Bath (about 9 gallons) .... Is. 5:10
Homer or Cor
(c. 85 gallons) .... Ezek. 45:11, 14

Jews—*the Hebrew people*

A. *Descriptive of:*
Hebrew race .... Esth. 3:6, 13
Postexilic Hebrew nation .... Ezra 5:1, 5
Believers .... Rom. 2:28, 29

B. *Kinds of:*
Hypocritical .... Matt. 23:1-31
Persecuting .... 1 Thess. 2:14, 15
Prejudiced .... John 4:9
Penitent .... John 12:10, 11

C. *Their sins:*
Self-righteousness .... Rom. 10:1-3
Hypocrisy .... Rom. 2:17-25
Persecution .... 1 Thess. 2:14, 15
Rejection of Christ .... Matt. 27:21-25
Rejection of the Gospel .... Acts 13:42-46
Embitter Gentiles .... Acts 14:2-6
Spiritual blindness .... John 3:1-4
Ignorance .... Luke 19:41, 42

D. *Their punishment:*
Blinded .... Rom. 11:25
Cast out .... Matt. 8:11, 12
Desolation as a nation .... Luke 21:20-24
Scattered .... Deut. 28:48-64

Jezaniah—*Jehovah answers*
Judahite military officer .... Jer. 40:7, 8
Seeks advice from Jeremiah .... Jer. 42:1-3
Called Jaazaniah .... 2 Kin. 25:23

Jezebel—*unmarried, chaste*
1. Daughter of Ethbaal;
Ahab's wife .... 1 Kin. 16:31
Follows her idolatry .... 1 Kin. 16:32, 33
Destroyed Jehovah's
prophets .... 1 Kin. 18:4-13
Plans Elijah's death .... 1 Kin. 19:1, 2
Secures Naboth's death .... 1 Kin. 21:1-15

SUBJECT — REFERENCE

Sentence:
Pronounced upon .... 1 Kin. 21:23
Fulfilled by Jehu .... 2 Kin. 9:7, 30-37
2. Type of paganism in the
church .... Rev. 2:20

Jezer—*form, purpose*
Son of Naphtali .... Gen. 46:24
Family head of the Jezerites .... Num. 26:49

Jeziah—*Jehovah sprinkles*
One who divorced his foreign
wife .... Ezra 10:25

Jeziel—*God sprinkles*
Benjamite warrior .... 1 Chr. 12:2, 3

Jezliah—*Jehovah delivers*
Son of Elpaal .... 1 Chr. 8:18

Jezoar—*he will shine*
Descendant of Judah .... 1 Chr. 4:7

Jezrahiah—*Jehovah shines*
Leads singing at dedication
service .... Neh. 12:42

Jezreel—*God sows*
1. Fortified city of Issachar .... Josh. 19:17, 18
Gideon fights Midianites in valley
of .... Judg. 6:33
Israelites camp here .... 1 Sam. 29:1, 11
Center of Ish-bosheth's
rule .... 2 Sam. 2:8, 9
Capital city .... 1 Kin. 18:45
Home of Naboth .... 1 Kin. 21:1, 13
Site of Jezebel's tragic end .... 1 Kin. 21:23
Heads of Ahab's sons piled
here .... 2 Kin. 10:1-10
City of bloodshed .... Hos. 1:4
Judgment in valley of .... Hos. 1:5
2. Town of Judah .... Josh. 15:56
David's wife from .... 1 Sam. 25:43
3. Judahite .... 1 Chr. 4:3
4. Symbolic name of Hosea's
son .... Hos. 1:4
5. Symbolic name of the new
Israel .... Hos. 2:22, 23

Jezreelite—*a person from Jezreel*
Naboth .... 1 Kin. 21:1

Jezreelitess—*a female from Jezreel*
Ahinoam .... 1 Sam. 30:5

Jibsam—*fragrant*
Descendant of Issachar .... 1 Chr. 7:2

Jimnah—*prosperity*
Son of Asher .... Gen. 46:18

Jidlaph—*he weeps*
Son of Nahor .... Gen. 22:22

Jiphthah-el—*God will open*
Valley between Asher and
Naphtali .... Josh. 19:10-27

Jiphtah—*he will open*
City of Judah .... Josh. 15:43

Joab—*Jehovah is father*
1. Son of Zeruiah, David's half-
sister .... 2 Sam. 8:16
Leads David's army to victory over Ish-
bosheth .... 2 Sam. 2:10-32
Assassinates Abner
deceptively .... 2 Sam. 3:26, 27
David rebukes him .... 2 Sam. 3:28-39
Commands David's army against
Edomites .... 1 Kin. 11:14-17
Defeats Syrians and
Ammonites .... 2 Sam. 10:1-14
Obeys David's orders concerning
Uriah .... 2 Sam. 11:6-27
Allows David to beseige
Rabbah .... 2 Sam. 11:1
Makes David favorable toward
Absalom .... 2 Sam. 14:1-33
Remains loyal to David .... 2 Sam. 18:1-5
Killed Absalom .... 2 Sam. 18:9-17
Rebukes David's grief .... 2 Sam. 19:1-8
Demoted by David .... 2 Sam. 19:13
Puts down Sheba's revolt .... 2 Sam. 20:1-22
Killed Amasa .... 2 Sam. 20:8-10
Regains command .... 2 Sam. 20:23

SUBJECT — REFERENCE

Opposes David's numbering
of the people .... 2 Sam. 24:1-9; 1 Chr. 21:1-6
Supports Adonijah .... 1 Kin. 1:7
David's dying words
against .... 1 Kin. 2:1-6
His crimes punished by
Solomon .... 1 Kin. 2:28-34
2. Son of Seraiah .... 1 Chr. 4:13, 14
3. Family head of exiles .... Ezra 2:6

Joah—*Jehovah is brother*
1. Son of Obed-edom .... 1 Chr. 26:4
2. Gershonite Levite .... 1 Chr. 6:21
Hezekiah's assistant .... 2 Chr. 29:12
3. Son of Aspah; a recorder under
Hezekiah .... Is. 36:3, 11, 22
4. Son of Joahaz .... 2 Chr. 34:8

Joahaz—*Jehovah has laid hold of*
Father of Joah, a recorder .... 2 Chr. 34:8

Joanna—*Jehovah has been gracious*
1. Ancestor of Christ .... Luke 3:27
2. Wife of Chuza, Herod's
steward .... Luke 8:1-3
With others, heralds Christ's
resurrection .... Luke 23:55, 56

Joash, Jehoash (I)—*Jehovah has given*
1. Father of Gideon .... Judg. 6:11-32
2. Judahite .... 1 Chr. 4:21, 22
3. Benjamite warrior .... 1 Chr. 12:3
4. Son of Ahab .... 1 Kin. 22:26
5. Son and successor of Ahaziah, king of
Judah .... 2 Kin. 11:1-20
Rescued and hid by
Jehosheba .... 2 Kin. 11:1-3
Proclaimed king by
Jehoiada .... 2 Kin. 11:4-12
Instructed by Jehoiada .... 2 Kin. 12:1, 2
Repairs the Temple .... 2 Kin. 12:4-16
Turns to idols after Jehoiada's
death .... 2 Chr. 24:17-19
Murdered Zechariah, Jehoiada's
son .... Matt. 23:35
Killed, not buried with
kings .... 2 Chr. 25:23-28
6. Son and successor of Jehoahaz, king of
Israel .... 2 Kin. 13:10-13
Follows idolatry .... 2 Kin. 13:11
Laments Elijah's sickness .... 2 Kin. 13:14-19
Defeats:
Syria .... 2 Kin. 13:24, 25
Amaziah .... 2 Kin. 13:12

Joash (II)—*Jehovah has come to help*
1. Benjamite .... 1 Chr. 7:8
2. Officer of David .... 1 Chr. 27:28

Job—*returning*

A. *Life of:*
Lives in Uz .... Job 1:1
Afflicted by Satan .... Job 1:6-19
Debate between Job and his three
friends .... Job 3—33
Elihu intervenes .... Job 34—37
Lord answers Job .... Job 38—41
His final reply .... Job 42:1-6
The Lord rebukes Job's three
friends .... Job 42:7-9
Restored to prosperity .... Job 42:10-15
Dies "old and full of days" .... Job 42:16, 17

B. *Strength of his:*
Faith .... Job 19:23-27
Patience .... James 5:11
Integrity .... Job 31:1-40

C. *Sufferings of:*
Lost property .... Job 1:13-17
Lost children .... Job 1:18, 19
Lost health .... Job 2:4-8
Misunderstood by friends .... Job 4:1-8; Job 8:1-6; Job 11:1-20

D. *Restoration of:*
After repentance .... Job 42:1-6
After prayer .... Job 42:8-10
To greater prosperity .... Job 42:11-17

Job, the Book of—*a book of the Old Testament*
Wisdom described .... Job 1:1-5
Wisdom tested .... Job 1:6—2:10

SUBJECT REFERENCE

Wisdom sought .... Job 3—37
God challenges Job .... Job 38—41
Wisdom in humility .... Job 42:1-6

Jobab—*to call shrilly*

1. Son of Joktan .... Gen. 10:29
   Tribal head .... 1 Chr. 1:23
2. King of Edom .... Gen. 36:31, 33
3. Canaanite king defeated by Joshua .... Josh. 11:1, 7-12
4. Benjamite .... 1 Chr. 8:9
5. Another Benjamite .... 1 Chr. 8:18

Jochebed—*Jehovah is glory*

Daughter of Levi; mother of Miriam, Aaron, and Moses .... Ex. 6:20

Jod

Tenth letter of the Hebrew alphabet .... Ps. 119:73-80

Joed—*Jehovah is witness*

Benjamite .... Neh. 11:7

Joel—*Jehovah is God*

1. Son of Samuel .... 1 Sam. 8:1, 2; 1 Chr. 6:28, 33
   Father of Heman the singer .... 1 Chr. 15:17
2. Kohathite Levite .... 1 Chr. 6:36
3. Leader of Simeon .... 1 Chr. 4:35
4. Reubenite chief .... 1 Chr. 5:4, 8, 9
5. Gadite chief .... 1 Chr. 5:12
6. Chief man of Issachar .... 1 Chr. 7:3
7. One of David's mighty men .... 1 Chr. 11:38
8. Gershonite Levite .... 1 Chr. 15:7, 11, 17
   Probably the same as in .... 1 Chr. 23:8
9. Manassite chief officer .... 1 Chr. 27:20
10. Kohathite Levite during Hezekiah's reign .... 2 Chr. 29:12
11. Son of Nebo; divorced his foreign wife .... Ezra 10:43
12. Benjamite overseer under Nehemiah .... Neh. 11:9
13. Prophet .... Joel 1:1

Joel, Book of

Prophecies of:

Predict Pentecost .... Joel 2:28-32
Proclaim salvation in Christ .... Joel 2:32
Portray the universal judgment .... Joel 3:1-16
Picture the eternal age .... Joel 3:17-21

Joelah—*let him help*

David's recruit at Ziklag .... 1 Chr. 12:7

Joezer—*Jehovah is help*

One of David's supporters at Ziklag .... 1 Chr. 12:6

Jogbehah—*lofty*

Town in Gilead .... Judg. 8:11

Jogli—*exiled*

Father of Bukki, a Danite prince .... Num. 34:22

Joha—*Jehovah is living*

1. Benjamite .... 1 Chr. 8:16
2. One of David's mighty men .... 1 Chr. 11:45

Johanan—*Jehovah is gracious*

1. One of David's mighty men .... 1 Chr. 12:2, 4
2. Gadite captain of David .... 1 Chr. 12:12, 14
3. Father of Azariah the priest .... 1 Chr. 6:10
4. Ephraimite leader .... 2 Chr. 28:12
5. Son of King Josiah .... 1 Chr. 3:15
6. Son of Kareah .... 2 Kin. 25:22, 23
   Supports Gedaliah .... Jer. 40:8, 9
   Warns Gedaliah of assassination plot .... Jer. 40:13, 14
   Avenges Gedaliah's murder .... Jer. 41:11-15
   Removes Jewish remnant to Egypt against Jeremiah's warning .... Jer. 41:16-18
7. Elioenai's son .... 1 Chr. 3:24

SUBJECT REFERENCE

8. Returned exile .... Ezra 8:12
9. Son of Tobiah .... Neh. 6:17, 18
10. Postexilic high priest .... Neh. 12:22

John—*Jehovah has been gracious*

1. Father of Simon Peter .... John 1:42
   Called Barjona .... Matt. 16:17
2. Jewish official .... Acts 4:6
3. Also called Mark .... Acts 12:12, 25
4. John the Baptist .... Matt. 3:1
5. John the Apostle .... Matt. 4:21

John the Apostle

A. *Life of:*

Son of Zebedee .... Matt. 4:21
Fisherman .... Luke 5:1-11
Leaves his business for Christ .... Matt. 4:21, 22
Called to be an apostle .... Matt. 10:2
Rebuked by Christ .... Luke 9:54, 55; Mark 13:3
Sent to prepare Passover .... Luke 22:8-13
Close to Jesus at Last Supper .... John 13:23-25
Christ commits His mother to .... John 19:26, 27
Witnesses Christ's ascension .... Acts 1:9-13
With Peter, heals a man .... Acts 3:1-11
Imprisoned with Peter .... Acts 4:1-21
With Peter, becomes a missionary .... Acts 8:14-25
Encourages Paul .... Gal. 2:9
Exiled on Patmos .... Rev. 1:9
Wrote a Gospel .... John 21:23-25
Wrote three epistles .... 1 John; 2 John; 3 John
Wrote the Revelation .... Rev. 1:1, 4, 9

B. *Described as:*

Uneducated .... Acts 4:13
Intolerant .... Mark 9:38
Ambitious .... Mark 10:35-37
Trustworthy .... John 19:26, 27
Humble .... Rev. 19:10
Beloved by Jesus .... John 21:20

John the Baptist

A. *Life of:*

Prophecies:
  Concerning .... Is. 40:3-5
  Fulfilled by .... Matt. 3:3
Angel anounces birth of .... Luke 1:11-20
Set apart as Nazarite .... Num. 6:2, 3; Luke 1:15
Lives in deserts .... Luke 1:63, 80
Ministry of, dated .... Luke 3:1-3
Public confusion .... Luke 3:15
Identifies Jesus as the Messiah .... John 1:29-36
Bears witness to Christ .... John 5:33
Exalts Christ .... John 3:25-36
Baptizes Christ .... Matt. 3:13-16
Doubts .... Matt. 11:2-6
Identified with Elijah .... Matt. 11:13, 14
Public reaction to .... Matt. 11:16-18
Christ's testimony concerning .... Matt. 11:9-13
Reproves Herod for adultery .... Mark 6:17, 18
Imprisoned by Herod .... Matt. 4:12
Beheaded by Herod .... Matt. 14:3-12

B. *Described as:*

Fearless .... Matt. 14:3, 4
Righteous .... Mark 6:20
Humble .... John 3:25-31
Faithful .... Acts 13:24, 25
Resourceful .... Matt. 3:4
Baptism of, insufficient .... Acts 18:24-26; Acts 19:1-5
Preaching a baptism of repentance .... Luke 3:2-18

John, the Epistles of—*books of the New Testament*

A. *1 John:*

God is light .... 1 John 1:5-7
True knowledge .... 1 John 2:3, 4
Love one another .... 1 John 3:11-24
God is love .... 1 John 4:7-21
Eternal life .... 1 John 5:13-21

SUBJECT REFERENCE

B. *2 John:*

Commandment to love .... 2 John 4-6
Warning against deceit .... 2 John 7-11

C. *3 John:*

Walking in truth .... 3 John 3, 4
Service to the brethren .... 3 John 5-8
Rebuke to Diotrephes .... 3 John 9, 10
Do good .... 3 John 11, 12

John, the Gospel of—*a book of the New Testament*

Deity of Christ .... John 1:1-18
Testimony of the Baptist .... John 1:19-34
Wedding at Cana .... John 2:1-11
Samarian mission .... John 4:1-42
Feast of Tabernacles .... John 7:1-53
The Good Shepherd .... John 10:1-42
Lazarus raised .... John 11:1-57
Priestly prayer .... John 17:1-26
Sufferings and glory .... John 18:1—20:31
Purpose of .... John 20:30, 31

Joiada—*Jehovah knows*

1. Son of Meshullam .... Neh. 3:6
2. Postexilic high priest .... Neh. 12:10, 11, 22
   Son banished from priesthood .... Neh. 13:28

Joiakim—*Jehovah establishes*

Postexilic high priest; son of Jeshua .... Neh. 12:10-26

Joiarib—*Jehovah contends*

1. Teacher sent by Ezra .... Ezra 8:16, 17
2. Postexilic Judahite chief .... Neh. 11:5
3. Founder of an order of priests .... Neh. 11:10
4. Postexilic priest .... Neh. 12:6
   Father of Joiakim .... Neh. 12:19

Jokdeam—*anger of the people*

City of Judah .... Josh. 15:56

Jokim—*Jehovah raises up*

Judahite .... 1 Chr. 4:22

Jokmeam—*let the people arise*

Town of Ephraim .... 1 Chr. 6:68
Home of Kohathite Levites .... 1 Chr. 6:66, 68
Same as Kibzaim in .... Josh. 21:22
Called Jokneam .... 1 Kin. 4:12

Jokneam—*let the people inquire*

1. Town near Mt. Carmel .... Josh. 12:22
   In tribe of Zebulun .... Josh. 19:11
   Assigned to Levites .... Josh. 21:34
2. Town of Ephraim .... 1 Kin. 4:12

See Jokmeam

Jokshan—*fowler*

Son of Abraham and Keturah .... Gen. 25:1, 2

Joktan—*he will be made small*

A descendant of Shem .... Gen. 10:21, 25

Joktheel—*God's reward of victory*

1. Village of Judah .... Josh. 15:20, 38
2. Name given by King Amaziah to Selah .... 2 Kin. 14:7

Jona—*Greek form of Jonah*

Father of Peter .... John 1:42

Jonadab—*Jehovah is bounteous*

1. Son of Shimeah; David's nephew .... 2 Sam. 13:3
   Very subtle man .... 2 Sam. 13:3-6, 32-36
2. Son of Rechab .... Jer. 35:6
   Makes Rechabites primitive and temperate .... Jer. 35:5-17
   Blessing upon .... Jer. 35:18, 19
   Opposes idolatry .... 2 Kin. 10:15, 16, 23
   Called Jehonadab .... 2 Kin. 10:15, 23

Jonah—*dove*

Son of Amittai .... Jon. 1:1
Ordered to go to Nineveh .... Jon. 1:2
Flees to Tarshish .... Jon. 1:3
Cause of storm; cast into sea .... Jon. 1:4-16
Swallowed by a great fish .... Jon. 1:17
Prays in fish's belly .... Jon. 2:1-9
Vomited upon land .... Jon. 2:10
Obeys second order to go to Nineveh .... Jon. 3:1-10

J

SUBJECT	REFERENCE
Grieved at Nineveh's repentance	Jon. 4:1-3
Taught God's mercy	Jon. 4:4-11
Type of Christ's resurrection	Matt. 12:39, 40

Jonam

Found in the genealogy of Jesus	Luke 3:30

Jonan—*Jehovah has been gracious*

Ancestor of Christ	Luke 3:30

Jonathan—*Jehovah has given*

1. Levite; becomes Micah's priest	Judg. 17:1-13
Follows Danites to idolatrous Dan	Judg. 18:3-31
Grandson of Moses (Manasseh)	Judg. 18:30
2. King Saul's eldest son	1 Sam. 14:49
Smites Philistine garrison	1 Sam. 13:2, 3
Attacks Michmash	1 Sam. 14:1-14
Saved from his father's vow	1 Sam. 14:24-45
Makes covenant with David	1 Sam. 18:1-4
Pleads for David's life	1 Sam. 19:1-7
Warns David of Saul's wrath	1 Sam. 20:1-42
Makes second covenant with David	1 Sam. 23:15-18
Killed by Philistines	1 Sam. 31:2, 8
Mourned by David	2 Sam. 1:17-27
David provides for his son	2 Sam. 9:1-8
3. Uncle of King David	1 Chr. 27:32
4. Son of the high priest Abiathar	2 Sam. 15:27
Remains faithful to David	2 Sam. 15:26-36
Brings David Absalom's plans	2 Sam. 17:15-22
Informs Adonijah of David's choice	1 Kin. 1:41-49
5. Son of Shimeah	2 Sam. 21:21, 22
6. One of David's mighty men	2 Sam. 23:32
7. Judahite	1 Chr. 2:32, 33
8. Son of Kareah	Jer. 40:8, 9
9. Scribe	Jer. 37:15, 20
10. Opponents of Ezra's reforms	Ezra 10:15
11. Descendant of Adin	Ezra 8:6
12. Levite of Asaph's line	Neh. 12:35
13. Head of a priestly house	Neh. 12:14
14. Postexilic high priest	Neh. 12:11

Jonath-elem-rechokim—*the silent dove of the far ones*

Musical tune	Ps. 56 (Title)

Joppa, Japho—*beauty*

Allotted to Dan	Josh. 19:40, 46
Seaport city	2 Chr. 2:16
Center of commerce	Ezra 3:7
Scene of Peter's vision	Acts 10:5-23, 32

Jorah—*rain*

Family of returnees	Ezra 2:18
Called Hariph	Neh. 7:24

Jorai—*rainy*

Gadite chief	1 Chr. 5:13

Joram, Jehoram—*Jehovah is exalted*

1. Son of Toi, king of Hamath	2 Sam. 8:10
Called Hadoram	1 Chr. 18:10
2. Levite	1 Chr. 26:25
3. Son of Ahab, king of Israel	2 Kin. 3:1
Institutes some reforms	2 Kin. 3:2, 3
Joins Judah against Moab	2 Kin. 3:1-27
Slain by Jehu	2 Kin. 9:14-26
Called Jehoram	2 Kin. 1:17
4. Priest sent to teach the people	2 Chr. 17:8
5. Son and successor of Jehoshaphat, king of Judah	2 Kin. 8:16
Murders his brothers	2 Chr. 21:1-4
His wife, Ahab's daughter, leads him astray	2 Kin. 8:17, 18
Edomites revolt against	2 Chr. 21:8-10
Unable to withstand invaders	2 Chr. 21:16, 17
Elijah's prophecy against	2 Chr. 21:12-15
Dies horribly without mourners	2 Chr. 21:18-20
Called Jehoram	2 Chr. 21:1, 5

Jordan—*the descender; a river in Palestine*

Canaan's eastern boundary	Num. 34:12
Despised by foreigners	2 Kin. 5:10, 12
Lot dwells near	Gen. 13:8-13
Jacob crosses	Gen. 32:10
Moses forbidden to cross	Deut. 3:27
Israel crosses miraculously	Josh. 3:1-17
Stones commemorate crossing of	Josh. 4:1-24
David crosses in flight	2 Sam. 17:22, 24
Divided by Elijah	2 Kin. 2:5-8
Divided by Elisha	2 Kin. 2:13, 14
Naaman healed in	2 Kin. 5:10, 14
John's baptism in	Matt. 3:6
Christ baptized in	Matt. 3:13-17

Jorim—*Jehovah is exalted*

Ancestor of Christ	Luke 3:29

Jorkoam

Judahite family name	1 Chr. 2:44
May be same as Jokdeam in	Josh. 15:56

Josabad—*Jehovah endowed*

One of David's mighty men	1 Chr. 12:4

Jose

Ancestor of Christ	Luke 3:29

Josedech—*Jehovah is just*

Father of the high priest Joshua	Hag. 1:1, 12, 14

Joseph—*may He* (Jehovah) *add*

1. Son of Jacob by Rachel	Gen. 30:22-24
2. Father of one of the spies	Num. 13:7
3. Son of Asaph	1 Chr. 25:2, 9
4. One who divorced his foreign wife	Ezra 10:32, 42
5. Pre-exilic ancestor of Christ	Luke 3:30
6. Priest in the days of Joiakim	Neh. 12:14
7. Postexilic ancestor of Christ	Luke 3:26
8. Son of Mattathias, in Christ's ancestry	Luke 3:24, 25
9. Husband of Mary, Jesus' mother	Matt. 1:16
Of Davidic lineage	Matt. 1:20
Angel explains Mary's condition to	Matt. 1:19-25
With Mary at Jesus' birth	Luke 2:16
Obeys Old Testament ordinances	Luke 2:21-24
Takes Jesus and Mary to Egypt	Matt. 2:13-15
Returns to Nazareth with family	Matt. 2:19-23
Jesus subject to	Luke 2:51
10. Man of Arimathea	John 19:38
Devout man	Luke 23:50, 51
Secret disciple	John 19:38
Obtains Christ's body; prepares it	Mark 15:43, 46
Receives Nicodemus' help	John 19:39, 40
Puts Christ's body in his new tomb	Luke 23:53
11. Called Barsabas; one of two chosen to occupy Judas' place	Acts 1:22-26
12. Also called Barnabas	Acts 4:36

Joseph—*increaser*

A. *Life of:*

Jacob's son by Rachel	Gen. 30:22-25
Jacob's favorite	Gen. 37:3
Aroused his brothers' hatred	Gen. 37:4
Sold into Egypt	Gen. 37:25-30
Wins esteem in Egypt	Gen. 39:1-23
Interprets Pharaoh's dream	Gen. 41:1-37
Made Pharaoh's Prime Minister	Gen. 41:38-46
Recognizes his brothers	Gen. 42:1-8
Reveals his identity	Gen. 45:1-16
Invites Jacob to Egypt	Gen. 45:17-28
Enslaves Egypt	Gen. 47:13-26
Put under oath by Jacob	Gen. 47:28-31
His sons blessed by Jacob	Gen. 48:1-22
Blessed by Jacob	Gen. 49:22-26
Mourns his father's death	Gen. 50:1-14
Deals kindly with his brothers	Gen. 50:15-21
His death at 110	Gen. 50:22-26
Descendants of	Num. 26:28-37

B. *Character of:*

Spiritually sensitive	Gen. 37:2
Wise and prudent	Gen. 41:38-49
Of strong emotions	Gen. 43:29-31
Sees God's hand in human events	Gen. 45:7, 8
Forgiving	Gen. 50:19-21
Man of faith	Heb. 11:22

Joses—*increaser*

One of Christ's brothers	Matt. 13:55

Joshah—*Jehovah's gift*

Simeonite leader	1 Chr. 4:34, 38

Joshaphat—*Jehovah has judged*

1. Mighty man of David	1 Chr. 11:43
2. Priestly trumpeter	1 Chr. 15:24

Joshaviah—*Jehovah is equality*

One of David's mighty men	1 Chr. 11:46

Joshbekashah—*he returns a hard fate*

Head of musical order	1 Chr. 25:4, 24

Josheb-basshebeth—*one who sat on the seat*

Chief of David's mighty men	2 Sam. 23:8
Called Jashobeam	1 Chr. 11:11

Joshibiah—*Jehovah causes to dwell* (in peace)

Simeonite	1 Chr. 4:35

Joshua, Jeshua—*Jehovah is salvation*

1. Native of Beth-shemesh	1 Sam. 6:14, 18
2. Governor of Jerusalem during Josiah's reign	2 Kin. 23:8
3. High priest during Zerubbabel's time	Hag. 1:1, 12, 14
Called Jeshua in Ezra and Nehemiah	Ezra 2:2
Type of Christ	Zech. 6:11-13
4. Son of Nun	Num. 13:8, 16

Joshua, Jehoshua—*Jehovah saves*

A. *Life of:*

Son of Nun; an Ephraimite	Num. 13:8, 16
Defeats Amalek	Ex. 17:8-16
Minister under Moses	Ex. 24:13
One of the spies	Num. 13:1-3, 8, 16
Reports favorably	Num. 14:6-10
Moses' successor	Num. 27:18-23
Inspired by God	Num. 27:18
Unifies the people	Josh. 1:10-18
Sends spies out	Josh. 2:1-24
Crosses Jordan	Josh. 3:1-17
Destroys Jericho	Josh. 6:1-27
Conquers Canaan	Josh. 10—12
Divides the land	Josh. 13—19
Orders Israel's leaders	Josh. 23:1-16
Final address to the nation	Josh. 24:1-28
Dies at 110	Josh. 24:29, 30
Called: Jehoshua	Num. 13:16

B. *Character of:*

Courageous	Num. 14:6-10
Emotional	Josh. 7:6-10
Wise military man	Josh. 8:3-29
Easily beguiled	Josh. 9:3-27
Prophetic	Josh. 6:26, 27
Strong religious leader	Judg. 2:7

Joshua, the Book of—*a book of the Old Testament*

Entering promised land	Josh. 1:1—5:12
The divine captain	Josh. 5:13—6:5
Capture of Jericho	Josh. 6:6-27
Capture of Ai	Josh. 8:1-29
Apportionment of the land	Josh. 13:1—22:34
Covenant at Shechem	Josh. 24:1-28
Death of Joshua	Josh. 24:29-33

Josiah—*Jehovah heals*

1. Son and successor of Amon, king of Judah	2 Kin. 21:25, 26
Crowned at 8; reigns righteously 31 years	2 Kin. 22:1
Named before birth	1 Kin. 13:1, 2

SUBJECT	REFERENCE
Repairs the Temple	2 Kin. 22:3-9
Receives the Book of Law	2 Kin. 22:10-17
Saved from predicted doom	2 Kin. 22:18-20
Reads the Law	2 Kin. 23:1, 2
Makes a covenant	2 Kin. 23:3
Destroys idolatry	2 Kin. 23:4, 20, 24
Observes the Passover	2 Kin. 23:21-23
Exceptional king	2 Kin. 23:25
Slain in battle	2 Chr. 35:20-24
Lamented by Jeremiah	2 Chr. 35:25-27
Commended by Jeremiah	Jer. 22:15-18
Ancestor (Josias) of Christ	Matt. 1:10, 11
2. Son of Zephaniah	Zech. 6:10

Josibiah—*Jehovah causes to dwell* (in peace)

Simeonite	1 Chr. 4:35

Josiphiah—*Jehovah will increase*

Father of a postexilic Jew	Ezra 8:10

Jot—*Greek iota* (i); *Hebrew yodh* (y)

Figurative of the smallest detail	Matt. 5:18

Jotbah—*pleasantness*

City of Haruz, the father of Meshullemeth	2 Kin. 21:19

Jotbathah—*pleasantness*

Israelite encampment	Num. 33:33
Called Jotbath	Deut. 10:7

Jotham—*Jehovah is perfect*

1. Gideon's youngest son	Judg. 9:5
Escapes Abimelech's massacre	Judg. 9:5, 21
Utters a prophetic parable	Judg. 9:7-21
Sees his prophecy fulfilled	Judg. 9:22-57
2. Son and successor of Azariah (Uzziah), king of Judah	2 Kin. 15:5, 7
Reign of, partly good	2 Kin. 15:32-38
Conquers Ammonites	2 Chr. 27:5-9
Contemporary of Isaiah and Hosea	Is. 1:1
Ancestor (Joatham) of Christ	Matt. 1:9
3. Son of Jahdai	1 Chr. 2:47

Journey—*an extended trip*

Preparation for, by:

Prayer	Rom. 1.10
God's providence acknowledged	James 4:13-17

Joy—*gladness of heart*

A. *Kinds of:*

Foolish	Prov. 15:21
Temporary	Matt. 13:20
Motherly	Ps. 113:9
Figurative	Is. 52:9
Future	Matt. 25:21, 23

B. *Described as:*

Everlasting	Is. 51:11
Great	Acts 8:8
Full	1 John 1:4
Abundant	2 Cor. 8:2
Unspeakable	1 Pet. 1:8

C. *Causes of:*

Victory	1 Sam. 18:6
Christ's birth	Luke 2:10, 11
Christ's resurrection	Matt. 28:7, 8
Sinner's repentance	Luke 15:5, 10
Miracles among the Gentiles	Acts 8:7, 8
Forgiveness	Ps. 51:8, 12
God's Word	Jer. 15:16
Spiritual discovery	Matt. 13:44
Names written in heaven	Luke 10:17, 20
True faith	1 Pet. 1:8

D. *Place of, in:*

Prayer	Is. 56:7
Christian:	
Fellowship	Phil. 1:25
Tribulation	2 Cor. 7:4-7
Giving	2 Cor. 8:2

E. *Contrasted with:*

Weeping	Ezra 3:12, 13 Ps. 30:5
Tears	Ps. 126:5
Sorrow	Is. 35:10
Mourning	Jer. 31:13
Pain	John 16:20, 21
Loss	Heb. 13:17 Heb. 10:34
Adversity	Eccl. 7:14
Discipline	Ps. 51:8 Heb. 12:11
Persecution	Luke 6:22, 23

F. *Of angels:*

At creation	Job 38:4, 7
At Christ's birth	Luke 2:10, 13, 14
At sinner's conversion	Luke 15:10

G. *Expressed by:*

Songs	Gen. 31:27
Musical instruments	1 Sam. 18:6
Sounds	1 Chr. 15:16
Praises	2 Chr. 29:30
Shouting	Ezra 3:12, 13
Heart	1 Kin. 21:7

See Gladness; Happiness of the Saints

Jozabad—*Jehovah has bestowed*

1, 2, 3. Three of David's mighty men	1 Chr. 12:4, 20
4. Levite overseer in Hezekiah's reign	2 Chr. 31:13
5. Chief Levite in Josiah's reign	2 Chr. 35:9
6. Levite, son of Jeshua	Ezra 8:33
Probably the same as in	Ezra 10:23
7. Expounder of the Law	Neh. 8:7
8. Levitical chief	Neh. 11:16
Some consider 6, 7, 8 the same person	
9. Priest who divorced his foreign wife	Ezra 10:22

Jozachar—*Jehovah has remembered*

Assassin of Joash	2 Kin. 12:19-21
Called Zabad	2 Chr. 24:26

Jozadak—*Jehovah is righteous*

Postexilic priest	Ezra 3:2

Jubal—*playing*

Son of Lamech	Gen. 4:21

Jubilee, Year of

A. *Regulations concerning:*

Introduced by trumpet	Lev. 25:9
After 49 years	Lev. 25:8
Rules for fixing prices	Lev. 25:15, 16, 25-28

B. *Purposes of:*

Restore liberty (to the enslaved)	Lev. 25:38-43
Restore property (to the original owner)	Lev. 25:23-28
Remit debt (to the indebted)	Lev. 25:47-55
Restore rest (to the land)	Lev. 25:11, 12, 18-22

C. *Figurative of:*

Christ's mission	Is. 61:1-3
Earth's jubilee	Rom. 8:19-24

Judaea—*a district in southern Palestine*

District under a governor	Luke 3:1
All Palestine	Luke 23:5
All the land of the Jews	Acts 10:37
Rural people outside Jerusalem	Matt. 4:25
Wilderness country near Dead Sea	Matt. 3:1
Christ born in	Matt. 2:1, 5, 6
Hostile toward Christ	John 7:1
Gospel preached in	Acts 8:1, 4
Churches established in	Acts 9:31

Judah—*let Him* (God) *be praised*

1. Son of Jacob and Leah	Gen. 29:15-35
Intercedes for Joseph	Gen. 37:26, 27
Marries a Canaanite	Gen. 38:1-10
Fathers Perez and Zerah by Tamar	Gen. 38:11-30
Through Tamar, an ancestor of David	Ruth 4:18-22
Ancestor of Christ	Matt. 1:3-16
Offers himself as Benjamin's ransom	Gen. 44:33, 34
Leads Jacob to Goshen	Gen. 46:28
Jacob bestows birthright on	Gen. 49:3-10
Messiah promised through	Gen. 49:10
2. Judah, Tribe of See separate article	
3. Postexilic Levite	Ezra 3:9
4. Levite returning with Zerubbabel	Neh. 12:8
5. Levite divorced his foreign wife	Ezra 10:23
6. Postexilic overseer	Neh. 11:9
7. Priest and musician	Neh. 12:36
Probably same as 4 and 5	
8. Postexilic prince	Neh. 12:32-34

Judah, Tribe of

Descendants of Judah	Gen. 29:35
Prophecy concerning	Gen. 49:8-12
Five families of	Num. 26:19-22
Leads in wilderness journey	Num. 2:3, 9
Numbering of, at Sinai	Num. 1:26, 27
Numbering of, in Moab	Num. 26:22
Leads in conquest of Canaan	Judg. 1:1-19
Territory assigned to	Josh. 15:1-63
Fights against Gibeah	Judg. 20:18
Makes David king	2 Sam. 2:1-11
Elders of, upbraided by David	2 Sam. 19:11, 15
Conflict with other tribes	2 Sam. 19:41-43
Loyal to David during Sheba's rebellion	2 Sam. 20:1, 2
Loyal to Davidic house at Jeroboam's rebellion	1 Kin. 12:20
Becomes leader of southern kingdom (Judah)	1 Kin. 14:21, 22
Taken to Babylon	2 Kin. 24:1-16
Returns after exile	2 Chr. 36:20-23
Christ comes of	Luke 3:23-33

Judas—*Greek form of Judah*

1. Judah, Jacob's son	Matt. 1:2, 3
See Judah 1	
2. Judas Lebbaeus, surnamed Thaddaeus	Matt. 10:3
One of Christ's apostles	Luke 6:13, 16
Offers a question	John 14:22
3. Betrayer of Christ (see Iscariot)	Luke 6:13, 16
4. Brother of Christ (see Brethren of Christ)	Matt. 13:55
See Jude	
5. Leader of an insurrection	Acts 5:37
6. Jew of Damascus	Acts 9:11
7. Judas Barsabbas, a chief deputy	Acts 15:22-32
Probably related to the disciple Joseph	Acts 1:23

Jude, Judas

Brother of Christ	Matt. 13:55
Does not believe in Christ	John 7:5
Becomes Christ's disciple	Acts 1:14
Writes an Epistle	Jude 1

See Judas 5

Jude, the Epistle of—*a book of the New Testament*

Author	Jude 1
Against false teachers	Jude 3-5
Against the ungodly	Jude 6-16
Exhortation	Jude 17-23 Acts 9:31

Judge—*an official authorized to hear and decide cases of law*

A. *History of, in scripture:*

Family head	Gen. 38:24
Established by Moses	Ex. 18:13-26 Deut. 1:9-17
Rules for	Deut. 16:18-20 Deut. 17:2-13
Circuit	1 Sam. 7:6, 15-17
King acts as	2 Sam. 15:2 1 Kin. 3:9, 28
Levites assigned	1 Chr. 23:1-4
Jehoshaphat established court	2 Chr. 19:5-11
Restored after exile	Ezra 7:25

B. *Procedure before:*

Public trial	Ex. 18:13
Case presented	Deut. 1:16 Deut. 25:1
Position of parties	Zech. 3:1
Accused heard	John 7:51

SUBJECT REFERENCE

Witness .... Deut. 19:15-19
Priests .... Deut. 17:8-13
Oath .... Ex. 22:11
Heb. 6:16
Casting of lots sometimes used .... Prov. 18:18
Divine will sought .... Lev. 24:12-14

C. *Office of:*
Divinely instituted .... 2 Sam. 7:11
Limits to human affairs .... 1 Sam. 2:25
Restricted by righteousness .... Deut. 16:18-20
Needful of great wisdom .... 1 Kin. 3:9
Easily corrupted .... Mic. 7:3
Unjustly used .... Acts 23:3
Acts 25:9-11
Fulfilled perfectly in the Messiah .... Is. 2:4
Is. 11:3, 4
Acts 17:31

Judge, God as
Manner of:
According to righteousness .... 1 Pet. 2:23
According to one's works .... 1 Pet. 1:17
Openly .... Rom. 2:16
By Christ .... John 5:22, 30
In a final way .... Joel 3:12-14

Judges of Israel
A. *Characteristics of era:*
No central authority .... Judg. 17.6
Judg. 21:25
Spiritual decline .... Judg. 2:18
Judg. 18:1-31

B. *List of:*
Othniel .... Judg. 3:9-11
Ehud .... Judg. 3:15-30
Shamgar .... Judg. 3:31
Deborah and Barak .... Judg. 4:4-9
Gideon .... Judg. 6:11-40
Abimelech .... Judg. 9:1-54
Tola .... Judg. 10:1, 2
Jair .... Judg. 10:3-5
Jephthah .... Judg. 12:1-7
Ibzan .... Judg. 12:8-10
Elon .... Judg. 12:11, 12
Abdon .... Judg. 12:13-15
Samson .... Judg. 15:20
Eli .... 1 Sam. 4:15, 18
Samuel .... 1 Sam. 7:15
Samuel's sons .... 1 Sam. 8:1-3

Judges, the Book of—*a book of the Old Testament*
The death of Joshua .... Judg. 2:6-10
Deborah and Barak .... Judg. 4:1—5:31
Gideon .... Judg. 6:1—8:32
Jephthah .... Judg. 10:6—11:40
Samson .... Judg. 13:1—16:31
Micah and the Danites .... Judg. 18
The war against Benjamin .... Judg. 19:1—21:25

Judgment, divine
A. *Design of:*
Punish evil .... Ex. 20:5
Chasten .... 2 Sam. 7:14, 15
Manifest God's righteousness .... Ex. 9:14-16
Correct .... Hab. 1:12
Warn others .... Luke 13:3, 5

B. *Causes of:*
Disobedience .... 2 Chr. 7:19-22
Rejecting God's warnings .... 2 Chr. 36:16, 17
Idolatry .... Jer. 7:30-34
Sins of rulers .... 2 Chr. 21:1-17
Loving evil .... Rom. 1:18-32

C. *Kinds of:*
Physical destruction .... Deut. 28:15-68
Material loss .... Mal. 3:11
Spiritual blindness .... Is. 6:9, 10
Eternal destruction .... Luke 12:16-21
Luke 16:19-31

D. *Avoidance of, by:*
Turning to God .... Deut. 30:1-3
Turning from sin .... Jer. 7:3-7
Humiliation .... Jon. 1:1-17
Prayer .... 2 Kin. 19:14-36
2 Chr. 20:5-30

Judgment Hall
Of Solomon .... 1 Kin. 7:1, 7
Pilate's .... John 18:28
Herod's .... Acts 23:35

SUBJECT REFERENCE

Judgment, human
A. *Weaknesses of:*
Often circumstantial .... Josh. 22:10-34
Sometimes wrong .... Gen. 39:10-20
Hasty and revengeful .... 1 Sam. 25:20-35
Full of conceit .... Esth. 5:11-14
Prejudicial .... Luke 7:38-50

B. *Rules regarding:*
Begin with self-judgment .... Matt. 7:1-5
Become spiritually minded .... 1 Cor. 2:12-15
Abound in love .... Phil. 1:9, 10
Await the final judgment .... Rom. 14:10

C. *Basis of:*
Circumstance .... Gen. 39:10-20
Opinion .... Acts 28:22
Moral Law .... Rom. 2:14-16
Conscience .... 1 Cor. 10:27-29
Nature .... 1 Cor. 11:13, 14
Apostolic authority .... 1 Cor. 5:3, 4
Law of Christ .... Gal. 6:2-4
Divine illumination .... Josh. 7:10-15

Judgment, the last
A. *Described as:*
Day of wrath .... Rom. 2:5
Day of judgment .... 2 Pet. 3:7
Judgment seat of Christ .... Matt. 25:31

B. *Time of:*
After death .... Heb. 9:27
At Christ's return .... Matt. 25:31
Appointed day .... Acts 17:31
After the world's destruction .... 2 Pet. 3:7-15

C. *Grounds of:*
One's works .... 1 Cor. 3:11-15
One's faith .... Matt. 7:22, 23
Conscience .... Rom. 2:12, 14-16
Law .... Rom. 2:12
Gospel .... James 2:12
Christ's Word .... John 12:48
Book of Life .... Rev. 20:12, 15

D. *Results of:*
Separation of righteous from the wicked .... Matt. 13:36-43
Retribution for disobedience .... 2 Thess. 1:6-10
Crown of righteousness .... 2 Tim. 4:8

E. *Attitudes toward:*
Be prepared for .... 1 Thess. 5:1-9
Beware of deception .... Matt. 7:21-27
Warn the wicked concerning .... 2 Cor. 5:10, 11

Judith—*Jewess*
Hittite wife of Esau .... Gen. 26:34
Called Aholibamah .... Gen. 36:2

Julia—*feminine form of Julius*
Christian woman at Rome .... Rom. 16:15

Julius—*the family name of the Caesars*
Roman centurion assigned to guard Paul .... Acts 27:1, 3
Disregards Paul's warning .... Acts 27:11
Accepts Paul's warning .... Acts 27:31
Saves Paul's life .... Acts 27:42:44

Junia—*a kinsman of Paul*
Jewish Christian at Rome .... Rom. 16:7

Juniper—*a shrub of the broom family*
Roots produce charcoal .... Ps. 120:4
Leaves provide little shade .... 1 Kin. 19:4, 5
Roots eaten in desperation .... Job 30:3, 4

Jupiter—*chief god of Roman mythology*
Barnabas called .... Acts 14:12

Jushab-hesed—*kindness returned*
Son of Zerubbabel .... 1 Chr. 3:20

Just, justice—*integrity of character*
A. *Descriptive of:*
Righteous man .... Gen. 6:9
Upright Gentile .... Acts 10:22
God's nature .... Deut. 32:4
Promised Messiah .... Zech. 9:9
Christ .... Acts 3:14
Saved .... Heb. 12:23

SUBJECT REFERENCE

B. *Produced by:*
True wisdom .... Prov. 8:15
Parental instruction .... Gen. 18:19
True faith .... Heb. 10:38
See Injustice

Justification—*accounting the guilty just before God*
A. *Negatively considered, not by:*
The Law .... Rom. 3:20, 28
Men's righteousness .... Rom. 10:1-5
Human works .... Rom. 4:1-5
Faith mixed with works .... Acts 15:1-29
Gal. 2:16
A dead faith .... James 2:14-26

B. *Positively considered, by:*
Grace .... Rom. 5:17-21
Christ:
Blood .... Rom. 5:9
Resurrection .... Rom. 4:25
Righteousness .... Rom. 10:4
Faith .... Rom. 3:26, 27

C. *Fruits of:*
Forgiveness of sins .... Acts 13:38, 39
Peace .... Rom. 5:1
Holiness .... Rom. 6:22
Imputed righteousness .... 2 Cor. 5:21
Outward righteousness .... Rom. 8:4
Eternal life .... Titus 3:7

D. *Evidence of:*
Works (by faith) .... James 2:18
Wisdom .... James 3:17
Patience .... James 5:7, 8
Suffering .... James 5:10, 11
See Imputation

Justus—*righteous*
1. Surname of Joseph .... Acts 1:23
2. Man of Corinth; befriends Paul .... Acts 18:7
3. Converted Jew .... Col. 4:11

Juttah—*extended*
Town of Judah .... Josh. 15:55
Assigned to the priests .... Josh. 21:13, 16

Juvenile delinquents
A. *Examples of:*
Eli's sons .... 1 Sam. 2:12-17
Samuel's sons .... 1 Sam. 8:1-5
Elisha's mockers .... 2 Kin. 2:22-24

B. *Safeguards against:*
Praying mother .... 1 Sam. 1:9-28
Strict discipline .... Prov. 13:24
Early training .... Prov. 22:6

K

Kab—*a hollow vessel*
Jewish measure; about 2 quarts .... 2 Kin. 6:25

Kabzeel—*God's gathering*
Town in south Judah .... Josh. 15:21
Benaiah's home town .... 2 Sam. 23:20
Called Jekabzeel .... Neh. 11:25

Kadesh—*holy*
Location of .... Num. 27:14
Captured by Chedorlaomer .... Gen. 14:5-7
Hagar flees near .... Gen. 16:7, 14
Abraham dwells here .... Gen. 20:1
Spies sent from .... Num. 13:3, 26
Miriam buried here .... Num. 20:1
Moses strikes rock there .... Num. 20:1-13
Request passage through Edom here .... Num. 20:14-22
Figurative of God's power .... Ps. 29:8
Boundary in the new Israel .... Ezek. 47:19

Kadesh-barnea—*another name for Kadesh*
Boundary of promised land .... Num. 34:1-4
Extent of Joshua's military campaign .... Josh. 10:41

Kadmiel—*God is the Ancient One*
1. Levite family head; returns from Babylon .... Ezra 2:40

SUBJECT REFERENCE

2. Takes part in rebuilding ..... Ezra 3:9
Participates in national repentance .... Neh. 9:4, 5

Kadmonites—*easterners*

Tribe whose land Abraham is to inherit .... Gen. 15:18, 19

Kallai—*smith*

Postexilic priest .... Neh. 12:1, 20

Kanah—*place of reeds*

1. Brook between Ephraim and Manasseh .... Josh. 16:8
2. Border town of Asher .... Josh. 19:28

Karka—*floor, ground*

Place in south Judah .... Josh. 15:3

Karkor—*even ground*

Place in east Jordan .... Judg. 8:10

Karnaim—*two peaks*

Conquered .... Amos 6:13

Kartah—*city*

Levitical town in Zebulun ...... Josh. 21:34

Kartan—*town*

Town in Naphtali assigned to Levites .... Josh. 21:32
Called Kirjathaim .... 1 Chr. 6:76

Kattath—*little*

Town of Zebulun.............. Josh. 19:15, 16
Same as Kitron .... Judg. 1:30

Kedar—*dark*

Son of Ishmael................ Gen. 25:12, 13
Skilled archers .... Is. 21:17
Prophecy against .... Jer. 49:28, 29
Inhabit villages .... Is. 42:11
Famous for flocks .... Is. 60:7
Tents of, called black .... Song 1:5
Type of barbarous people ...... Ps. 120:5

Kedemah—*toward the east*

Ishmaelite tribe .... Gen. 25:15

Kedemoth—*ancient places*

City east of the Jordan assigned to the tribe of Reuben .... Josh. 13:15, 18
Assigned to Merarite Levites .... Josh. 21:34, 37
Messengers sent from .... Deut. 2:26

Kedesh—*sacred place*

1. Town in south Judah .... Josh. 15:23
2. City of Issachar assigned to Gershonite Levites.................. 1 Chr. 6:72
Called Kishion .... Josh. 19:20
3. Canaanite town taken by Joshua and assigned to Naphtali .... Josh. 12:22
Called Kedesh in Galilee .... Josh. 20:7
Called Kedeshnaphtali ..... Judg. 4:6
City of refuge .... Josh. 21:27, 32
Home of Barak .... Judg. 4:6
People of, carried captive ... 2 Kin. 15:29

Keeper—*one who watches over, or guards*

Guardian of:

Sheep....................... Gen. 4:2
Brother .... Gen. 4:9
Wardrobe .... 2 Kin. 22:14
Gate .... Neh. 3:29
1 Chr. 9:21
Women .... Esth. 2:3, 8
Prison .... Acts 16:27

Keeping—*holding or observing something firmly*

A. *Christian objects of:*

Christ's commandments ..... John 14:15-23
God's commandments....... 1 John 5:2
God's Word .... Rev. 22:7, 9
Unity of the Spirit.......... Eph. 4:3
Faith .... 2 Tim. 4:7
Purity..................... 1 Tim. 5:22
Oneself .... 1 John 5:18
In God's love .... Jude 21

B. *Manner of, by God's:*

Power .... John 10:28, 29
Name..................... John 17:11, 12

C. *Promises respecting:*

Provision .... Ps. 121:3-8
Preservation .... John 17:11, 12

SUBJECT REFERENCE

Power .... Rev. 2:26
Purity...................... Rev. 16:15
See Heart

Kehelathah—*assembly*

Israelite camp................ Num. 33:22, 23

Keilah—*enclosed*

Town of Judah................ Josh. 15:21, 44
Rescued from Philistines by David .... 1 Sam. 23:1-5
Betrays David .... 1 Sam. 23:6-12
David escapes from .... 1 Sam. 23:13
Reoccupied after the exile ...... Neh. 3:17

Kelaiah—*Jehovah is light*

Levite who divorced foreign wife .... Ezra 10:18, 19, 23
See Kelita

Kelita—*dwarf*

Levite who divorced foreign wife .... Ezra 10:23
Explains the Law............. Neh. 8:7
Called Kelaiah .... Ezra 10:23

Kemuel—*congregation of God*

1. Son of Nahor; father of six sons .... Gen. 22:20, 21
2. Ephraimite prince .... Num. 34:24
3. Levite in David's time....... 1 Chr. 27:17

Kenan—*fixed*

Descendant of Adam .... 1 Chr. 1:2
See Cainan

Kenath—*possession*

City of Gilead near Bozrah taken by Nobah .... Num. 32:40, 42
Reconquered by Geshur and Aram...................... 1 Chr. 2:23

Kenaz—*side, flank*

1. Descendant of Esau......... Gen. 36:10, 11
2. Edomite duke.............. Gen. 36:42
3. Caleb's brother; father of Othniel .... Josh. 15:17
Family called Kenezites ..... Num. 32:12
4. Grandson of Caleb .... 1 Chr. 4:15

Kenezite, Kenizzite

1. Canaanite tribe whose land is promised to Abraham's seed .... Gen. 15:19
2. Title applied to Caleb .... Num. 32:12
Probably related to Kenaz, the Edomite .... Gen. 36:11-42

Kenites—*pertaining to coppersmiths*

Canaanite tribe whose land is promised to Abraham's seed .... Gen. 15:19
Subjects of Balaam's prophecy .. Num. 24:20-22
Mix with Midianites .... Num. 10:29
Member of, becomes Israel's guide .... Num. 10:29-32
Settle with Judahites .... Judg. 1:16
Heber separates from Kenites ... Judg. 4:11
Heber's wife (Jael) slays Sisera .. Judg. 4:17-22
Spared by Saul in war with Amalekites .... 1 Sam. 15:6
David shows friendship to ...... 1 Sam. 30:29
Recorded among Judahites; ancestors of Rechabites .... 1 Chr. 2:55

Kerchief—*a covering for the head*

Worn by idolatrous women of Israel...................... Ezek. 13:18, 21

Keren-happuch—*horn of eye paint*

Daughter of Job............... Job 42:14

Kerioth—*cities*

1. Town in south Judah .... Josh. 15:25
2. City of Moab .... Amos 2:2

Keros—*bent*

Head of a Nethinim family returning from exile...................... Ezra 2:44

Kettle—*pot*

Large cooking vessel .... 1 Sam. 2:14
Same word rendered "pots"..... Ps. 81:6

Keturah—*incense*

Abraham's second wife......... Gen. 25:1

SUBJECT REFERENCE

Sons of:
Listed .... Gen. 25:1, 2
Given gifts and sent away ..... Gen. 25:6

Key—*a small instrument for unlocking doors*

Used literally for:

Doors .... Judg. 3:25

Used figuratively of:

Prophetic authority of Christ.... Is. 22:22
Present authority of Christ...... Rev. 1:18
Plenary authority of Christ's apostles .... Matt. 16:19
Teachers .... Luke 11:52

Kezia—*cassia*

Daughter of Job............... Job 42:14

Keziz—*cut off*

City of Benjamin .... Josh. 18:21

Kibroth-hattaavah—*graves of lust*

Burial site of Israelites slain by God....................... Num. 11:33-35

Kibzaim—*double heap*

Ephramite city assigned to Kohathite Levites .... Josh. 21:22
Called Jokmeam .... 1 Chr. 6:68
See Jokmeam

Kid—*a young goat*

A. *Used for:*

Food .... Gen. 27:9
Payment .... Gen. 38:17-23
Sacrifices .... Lev. 4:23
Offerings .... Judg. 13:15, 19
Festive occasions .... Luke 15:29

B. *Figurative of:*

Weakness .... Judg. 14:6
Peacefulness .... Is. 11:6

See Goat

Kidnapping

A. *Punishment for:*

Death..................... Ex. 21:16

B. *Examples of:*

Joseph .... Gen. 37:23-28
Daughters of Shiloh .... Judg. 21:20-23
Joash .... 2 Kin. 11:1-12
Jeremiah .... Jer. 43:1-8

Kidneys

Select internal organs of an animal...................... Ex. 29:13, 22
Translated "wheat" .... Deut. 32:14

Kidron—*dark, turbid*

Valley (dry except for winter torrents) near Jerusalem .... John 18:1
East boundary of Jerusalem..... Jer. 31:40
Crossed by David and Christ ... John 18:1
Used for burials............... Jer. 26:23
Site of dumping of idols........ 2 Chr. 29:16

Killing—*causing life to cease*

A. *Reasons for:*

Take another's wife .... Gen. 12:12
Take another's property ..... 1 Kin. 21:19
Take revenge .... Gen. 27:42
Satisfy anger............... Num. 22:29
Hate...................... John 5:18
Execute God's wrath .... Num. 31:2, 16-19
Destroy people .... Ex. 1:16
Seize a throne.............. 2 Kin. 15:25
Put down rebellion .... 1 Kin. 12:27
Fulfill prophecy .... 1 Kin. 16:1-11
Fear of punishment .... Acts 16:27
Get rid of an unwanted person .... Matt. 21:38

B. *Reasons against:*

God's Law .... Ex. 20:13
Regard for:
Life .... Gen. 37:21
One's position .... 1 Sam. 24:10
1 Sam. 11

C. *Of Christians:*

In God's hand .... Luke 12:4, 5
Result of persecution .... Matt. 24:9
Time will come............. John 16:2
Under antichrist............ Rev. 11:7
Rev. 13:15

SUBJECT REFERENCE

Kinah—*lamentation*
Village in south Judah .... Josh. 15:22

Kindness—*a friendly attitude toward others*
A. *Kinds of:*
Extraordinary .... Acts 28:2
Acquired .... Col. 3:12
Developed .... Prov. 31:26
Commended .... 2 Cor. 6:6
Divine .... Neh. 9:17
B. *Of God, described as:*
Great .... Neh. 9:17
Everlasting .... Is. 54:8
Not removable .... Is. 54:10
Manifested .... Ps. 31:21
Through Christ .... Eph. 2:7
Cause of man's salvation .... Titus 3:4-7
C. *Manifestation of:*
Rewarded .... 1 Sam. 15:6
Recalled .... 2 Sam. 2:5, 6
Rebuffed .... 2 Sam. 3:8
Remembered .... 2 Sam. 9:1-7
Refused .... 2 Sam. 10:1-6

Kindred—*one's family connections*
Manifestation of:
Felt with great emotion .... Esth. 8:6
Through faith .... Josh. 6:23
By gospel .... Acts 3:25
Rev. 14:6

Kine—*archaic for cow, ox, steer*
Used for:
Ox .... Deut. 7:13
Cattle .... Deut. 32:14
Cow .... Gen. 32:15
1 Sam. 6:7

King, Christ as
A. *In Old Testament prophecy:*
Judah's tribe .... Gen. 49:10
With a scepter .... Num. 24:15-17
David's lineage .... 2 Sam. 7:1-29
Divine origin .... Is. 9:6, 7
In righteousness .... Is. 11:1-5
At God's appointed time ..... Ezek. 21:27
Will endure forever .... Dan. 2:44
Born in Bethlehem .... Mic. 5:2, 3
As Priest-king .... Zech. 6:9-15
Having salvation .... Zech. 9:9
He is coming .... Mal. 3:1-5
B. *Christ's right to rule, determined by:*
Divine decree .... Ps. 2:6, 7
Prophecy .... Ps. 45:6, 7
Birth .... Is. 9:6, 7
Being seated at God's right hand .... Ps. 16:8-11; Ps. 110:1, 2; Acts 2:34-36
Crowning .... Zech. 6:11-15
C. *Described as:*
Eternal .... Rev. 11:15
Spiritual .... John 18:36, 37
Not for immoral or impure person .... Eph. 5:5
For redeemed .... Col. 1:13

Kingdom of God
A. *Described as, of:*
God .... Mark 1:15
Heaven .... Matt. 3:2
Christ and God .... Eph. 5:5
Their Father .... Matt. 13:43
My Father's .... Matt. 26:29
His dear Son .... Col. 1:13
B. *Special features of:*
Gospel of .... Matt. 24:14
Word of .... Matt. 13:19
Mysteries of .... Mark 4:10-13
Key of David .... Rev. 3:7
C. *Entrance into, by:*
New birth .... John 3:1-8
Granted .... Luke 22:29
Divine call .... 1 Thess. 2:12
Repentance .... Matt. 3:2
D. *Members of:*
Seek it first .... Matt. 6:33
Suffer tribulation .... Acts 14:22
Preach it .... Acts 8:12
Pray for it .... Matt. 6:10
Work in .... Col. 4:11

SUBJECT REFERENCE

E. *Nature of:*
Spiritual .... Rom. 14:17
Eternal .... 2 Pet. 1:11

Kings, earthly
A. *Some characteristics of:*
Arose over Egypt .... Ex. 1:8
Desired by people .... 1 Sam. 8:5, 6
Under God's control .... Dan. 4:25, 37
Rule by God's permission ... Dan. 2:20, 21
Subject to temptations ...... 2 Sam. 11:1-5
Prov. 31:5
Good .... 2 Kin. 22:1, 2
Evil .... 2 Kin. 21:1-9
B. *Position of before God, by God:*
Chosen .... 1 Chr. 28:4-6
Anointed .... 1 Sam. 16:12
Removed and established .... Dan. 2:21
Rejected .... 1 Sam. 15:10-26
C. *Duties of:*
Make covenants .... Gen. 21:22-32
Read Scriptures .... Deut. 17:19
Make war .... 1 Sam. 11:5-11
Pardon .... 2 Sam. 14:1-11
2 Sam. 19:18-23
Judge .... 2 Sam. 15:2
Govern righteously .... 2 Sam. 23:3, 4
Keep Law .... 1 Kin. 2:3
Make decrees .... Dan. 3:1-6, 29

King's Garden—*a garden of Jerusalem*
Near a gate .... 2 Kin. 25:4
By the pool of Siloah .... Neh. 3:15

King's Highway—*an important passageway connecting Damascus and Egypt*
Use of, requested .... Num. 20:17

Kings of ancient Israel
A. *Over the United Kingdom:*
Saul .... 1 Sam. 11:15—31:13
David .... 2 Sam. 2:4—1 Kin. 2:11
Solomon .... 1 Kin. 1:39—11:43
B. *Over Israel* (the northern kingdom):
Jeroboam (22 yrs.) .... 1 Kin. 12:20—14:20
Nadab (2 yrs.) .... 1 Kin. 15:25-27, 31
Baasha (24 yrs.) .... 1 Kin. 15:28-34
1 Kin. 16:1-7
Elah (2 yrs.) .... 1 Kin. 16:8-14
Zimri (7 days) .... 1 Kin. 16:15
Omri (12 yrs.) .... 1 Kin. 16:23-28
Ahab (22 yrs.) .... 1 Kin. 16:29—22:40
Ahaziah (2 yrs.) .... 1 Kin. 22:51-53
Jehoram (Joram)(12 yrs.) .... 2 Kin. 3:1—9:26
Jehu (28 yrs.) .... 2 Kin. 9:2—10:36
Jehoahaz (17 yrs.) .... 2 Kin. 13:1-9
Jehoash (Joash) (16 yrs.) ..... 2 Kin. 13:10-25
Jeroboam II (41 yrs.) .... 2 Kin. 14:23-29
Zechariah (6 mos.) .... 2 Kin. 15:8-12
Shallum (1 mo.) .... 2 Kin. 15:13-15
Menahem (10 yrs.) .... 2 Kin. 15:16-22
Pekahiah (2 yrs.) .... 2 Kin. 15:23-26
Pekah (20 yrs.) .... 2 Kin. 15:27-31
Hoshea (9 yrs.) .... 2 Kin. 17:1-6
C. *Over Judah* (the southern kingdom):
Rehoboam (17 yrs.) .... 1 Kin. 12:21-24
Abijam (Abijah) (3 yrs.) ...... 1 Kin. 15:1-8
Asa (41 yrs.) .... 1 Kin. 15:9-24
Jehoshaphat (25 yrs.) .... 1 Kin. 22:41-50
Jehoram (Joram) (8 yrs.) ..... 2 Kin. 8:16-24
Ahaziah (1 yr.) .... 2 Kin. 8:25-29
Athaliah (Queen) (usurper) (6 yrs.) .... 2 Kin. 11:1-3
Joash (Jehoash) (40 yrs.) ..... 2 Kin. 12:1, 21
Amaziah (29 yrs.) .... 2 Kin. 14:1-20
Azariah (Uzziah) (52 yrs.) ... 2 Kin. 15:1, 2
Jotham (16 yrs.) .... 2 Kin. 15:32-38
Ahaz (16 yrs.) .... 2 Kin. 16:1-20
Hezekiah (29 yrs.) .... 2 Kin. 18:1—20:21
Manasseh (55 yrs.) .... 2 Kin. 21:1-18
Amon (2 yrs.) .... 2 Kin. 21:19-26
Josiah (31 yrs.) .... 2 Kin. 22:1—23:30
Jehoahaz (Shallum) (3 mos.) .... 2 Kin. 23:31-33
Jehoiakim (11 yrs.) .... 2 Kin. 23:34—24:6
Jehoiachin (Jeconiah) (3 mos.) .... 2 Kin. 24:8-16
Zedekiah (Mattaniah) (11 yrs.) .... 2 Kin. 24:17—25:7

SUBJECT REFERENCE

Kings, the Books of—*books of the Old Testament*
A. *1 Kings*
Solomon ascends to the throne .... 1 Kin. 1:1—2:46
The kingdom of Solomon .... 1 Kin. 3:1—10:13
The fall of Solomon .... 1 Kin. 11:1-40
Rehoboam against Jeroboam .... 1 Kin. 12:1-33
Ahab and Jezebel .... 1 Kin. 16:29-34
Ministry of Elijah .... 1 Kin. 17:1—19:21
Syria against Samaria .... 1 Kin. 20:1-34
Ahab and Naboth .... 1 Kin. 21:1-29
B. *2 Kings*
Ministry of Elijah and Elisha .... 2 Kin. 1:1—9:1
Reign of Jehu .... 2 Kin. 9:11—10:36
Fall of Israel .... 2 Kin. 17:1-41
Reign of Hezekiah .... 2 Kin. 18:1—20:21
Reform of Judah .... 2 Kin. 22:1—23:30
Fall of Jerusalem .... 2 Kin. 25:1-21

Kingship of God—*the position of God as sovereign ruler of the universe*
Over Jerusalem .... Matt. 5:35
Over all .... Ps. 103:19
Of all kingdoms .... 2 Kin. 19:15

Kir—*wall*
1. Place mentioned by Amos to which Syrians were taken .... Amos 1:5
Tiglath-pileser carries people of Damascus here .... 2 Kin. 16:9
Inhabitants of, against Judah .... Is. 22:6
2. Fortified city of Moab ...... Is. 15:1
Same as Kir-hareseth .... Is. 16:7, 11
Strong place .... 2 Kin. 3:25

Kiriathaim, Kirjathaim—*twin cities*
1. Assigned to Reuben .... Num. 32:37
Repossessed by Moabites .... Jer. 48:1-23
2. Town in Naphtali .... 1 Chr. 6:76
Same as Kartan .... Josh. 21:32

Kirjath—*city*
Town of Benjamin .... Josh. 18:21, 28

Kirjath-arba—*city of Arba, or four-fold city*
Ancient name of Hebron .... Gen. 23:2
Named after Arba the Anakite .. Josh. 15:54
City of refuge .... Josh. 20:7
Possessed by Judah .... Judg. 1:10

Kirjath-jearim—*city of forests*
Gibeonite town .... Josh. 9:17
Assigned to Judah .... Josh. 15:60
Reassigned to Benjamin .... Josh. 18:28
Ark taken from .... 1 Chr. 13:5
Home of Urijah .... Jer. 26:20
Called:
Baalah .... Josh. 15:9, 10
Kirjath-baal .... Josh. 15:60
Baale of Judah .... 2 Sam. 6:2
Shortened to Kirjath-arim .... Ezra 2:25

Kirjath-sannah—*city of destruction*
City of Judah; also called Debir .... Josh. 15:49

Kirjath-sepher—*city of books*
Same as Debir .... Judg. 1:11-13
Taken by Othniel .... Josh. 15:15-17

Kish—*bow*
1. Benjamite of Gibeah; father of King Saul .... 1 Sam. 9:1-3; Acts 13:21
2. Benjamite of Jerusalem ...... 1 Chr. 8:30
3. Merarite Levite in David's time .... 1 Chr. 23:21, 22
4. Another Merarite Levite in Hezekiah's time .... 2 Chr. 29:12
5. Benjamite and great-grandfather of Mordecai .... Esth. 2:5

Kishi—*snarer*
One of David's singers .... 1 Chr. 6:31, 44
Called Kushaiah .... 1 Chr. 15:17

Kishion—*hardness*
Border town of Issachar .... Josh. 19:17, 20
Called Kishon .... Josh. 21:28
See Kedesh 2

SUBJECT REFERENCE

Kishon—*bending*
River of north Palestine; Sisera's army swept away by .... Judg. 4:7, 13
Elijah slew Baal prophets here .. 1 Kin. 18:40; Ps. 83:9

Kiss—*a physical sign of affection*
A. *Times employed, at:*
Departure .... Gen. 31:28, 55
Separation .... Acts 20:37
Reunions .... Luke 15:20
Great joy .... Luke 7:38, 45
Blessing .... Gen. 48:10-16
Anointings .... 1 Sam. 10:1
Reconciliation .... Gen. 33:4
Death .... Gen. 50:1
B. *Figurative of:*
Complete:
Submission to evil .... Hos. 13:2
Submission to God .... Ps. 2:12
Reconciliation .... Ps. 85:10
Utmost affection .... Song 1:2
C. *Kinds of:*
Deceitful .... 2 Sam. 20:9, 10; Luke 22:48
Insincere .... 2 Sam. 15:5
Fatherly .... Gen. 27:26, 27
Friendship .... Ex. 18:7; 1 Sam. 20:41
Esteem .... 2 Sam. 19:32, 39
Sexual love .... Gen. 29:11; Song 1:2
Illicit love .... Prov. 7:13
False religion .... 1 Kin. 19:18; Hos. 13:2
Holy love .... Rom. 16:16; 1 Cor. 16:20

Kite—*a bird of the falcon family*
Ceremonially unclean .... Lev. 11:14

Kith-lish—*a man's wall*
Town of Judah .... Josh. 15:1, 40

Kitron—*shortened, little*
Town in Zebulun .... Judg. 1:30

Kittim
Sons of Javan .... Gen. 10:4

Kneading—*mixing elements together*
Part of food process .... Gen. 18:6
Done by women .... Jer. 7:18

Kneading trough—*a bowl for kneading dough*
Overcome by frogs .... Ex. 8:3
Carried out of Egypt .... Ex. 12:33-34

Knee
A. *Place of weakness, due to:*
Terror .... Dan. 5:6
Fasting .... Ps. 109:24
Disease .... Deut. 28:35
Lack of faith .... Is. 35:3
B. *Lying upon:*
Sign of true parentage or adoption .... Gen. 30:3
Place of fondling .... Is. 66:12
Place of sleep .... Judg. 16:19
C. *Bowing of:*
Act of:
Respect .... 2 Kin. 1:13
False worship .... 1 Kin. 19:18
True worship .... Rom. 14:11
D. *Bowing of, in prayer:*
Solomon .... 2 Chr. 6:13, 14
Daniel .... Dan. 6:10
Christ .... Luke 22:41
Stephen .... Acts 7:59, 60
Peter .... Acts 9:40
Paul .... Acts 20:36
Christians .... Acts 21:5

Knife—*a sharp instrument for cutting*
A. *Used for:*
Slaying animals .... Gen. 22:6-10
Circumcision .... Josh. 5:2, 3
Dismembering a body .... Judg. 19:29
Sharpening pens .... Jer. 36:23
B. *Figurative of:*
Inordinate appetite .... Prov. 23:2
Cruel oppressors .... Prov. 30:14

SUBJECT REFERENCE

Knob—*an ornament*
Round protrusions on lampstand .... Ex. 25:31-34
Ornaments carved on the walls of the temple .... 1 Kin. 6:18; 1 Kin. 7:24

Knock—*to rap on a door*
Rewarded .... Luke 11:9, 10
Expectant .... Luke 12:36
Disappointed .... Luke 13:25-27
Unexpected .... Acts 12:13, 16
Invitation .... Rev. 3:20

Knowledge
A. *Kinds of:*
Natural .... Matt. 24:32
Deceptive .... Gen. 3:5
Sinful .... Gen. 3:7
Personal .... Josh. 24:31
Practical .... Ex. 36:1
Experimental .... Ex. 14:4, 18
Friendly .... Ex. 1:8
Intuitive .... 1 Sam. 22:22
Intellectual .... John 7:15, 28
Saving .... John 17:3
Spiritual .... 1 Cor. 2:14
Revealed .... Luke 10:22
B. *Sources of:*
God .... Ps. 94:10
Nature .... Ps. 19:2
Scriptures .... 2 Tim. 3:15
Doing God's will .... John 7:17
C. *Believer's attitude toward:*
Not to be puffed up .... 1 Cor. 8:1
Should grow in .... 2 Pet. 3:18
Should add to .... 2 Pet. 1:5
Not to be forgetful of .... 2 Pet. 3:17
Accept our limitations of .... 1 Cor. 13:8-12
Be filled with .... Phil. 1:9
D. *Christ's, of:*
God .... Luke 10:22
Man's nature .... John 2:24, 25
Man's thoughts .... Matt. 9:4
Believers .... John 10:14, 27
Things future .... 2 Pet. 1:14
All things .... Col. 2:3
E. *Attitude of sinful men toward:*
Turn from .... Rom. 1:21
Ignorant of .... 1 Cor. 1:21
Raised up against .... 2 Cor. 10:5
Did not acknowledge God .... Rom. 1:28
Never able to come to .... 2 Tim. 3:7
F. *Value of:*
Superior to gold .... Prov. 8:10
Increases strength .... Prov. 24:5
Keeps from destruction .... Is. 5:13
Insures stability .... Is. 33:6

Koa
People described as enemies of Jerusalem .... Ezek. 23:23

Kohath—*assembly*
Second son of Levi .... Gen. 46:8, 11
Goes with Levi to Egypt .... Gen. 46:11
Brother of Jochebed, mother of Aaron and Moses .... Ex. 6:16-20
Dies at age 133 .... Ex. 6:18

Kohathites—*descendants of Kohath*
A. *History of:*
Originate in Levi's son (Kohath) .... Gen. 46:11
Divided into 4 groups (Amram, Izhar, Hebron, Uzziel) .... Num. 3:19, 27
Numbering of .... Num. 3:27, 28
Duties assigned to .... Num. 4:15-20
Cities assigned to .... Josh. 21:4-11
B. *Privileges of:*
Aaron and Moses .... Ex. 6:20
Special charge of sacred instruments .... Num. 4:15-20
Temple music by Heman the Kohathite .... 1 Chr. 6:31-38
Under Jehoshaphat, lead in praise .... 2 Chr. 20:19
Under Hezekiah, help to cleanse Temple .... 2 Chr. 29:12, 15

SUBJECT REFERENCE

C. *Sins of:*
Korah (of Izhar) leads rebellion .... Num. 16:1-35; Jude 11

Kolaiah—*voice of Jehovah*
1. Father of the false prophet Ahab .... Jer. 29:21-23
2. Postexilic Benjamite family .. Neh. 11:7

Koph
Letter of the Hebrew alphabet .. Ps. 119:145-152

Korah—*baldness*
1. Son of Esau .... Gen. 36:5, 14, 18
2. Son of Eliphaz and grandson of Esau .... Gen. 36:16
3. Calebite .... 1 Chr. 2:42, 43
4. Son of Izhar the Kohathite .. Ex. 6:21, 24
Leads a rebellion against Moses and Aaron .... Num. 16:1-3
Warned by Moses .... Num. 16:4-27
Supernaturally destroyed .... Num. 16:28-35
Sons of, not destroyed .... Num. 26:9-11
Sons of, porters .... 1 Chr. 26:19

Korahites
Descendants of Korah .... Ex. 6:24
Some become:
David's warriors .... 1 Chr. 12:6
Servants .... 1 Chr. 9:19-31
Musicians .... 1 Chr. 6:22-32
A maschil for .... Ps. 42 (Title)

Kore—*a partridge*
1. Korahite Levite .... 1 Chr. 9:19
2. Porter of the eastern gate .... 2 Chr. 31:14

Koz—*thorn*
Father of Anub .... 1 Chr. 4:8

Kushaiah—*bow of Jehovah* (that is, rainbow)
Merarite Levite musician .... 1 Chr. 15:17
Called Kishi .... 1 Chr. 6:44

L

Laadah—*festival*
Judahite .... 1 Chr. 4:21

Laadan
1. Son of Gershon, the son of Levi .... 1 Chr. 23:7-9
Called Libni .... 1 Chr. 6:17
2. Ephraimite .... 1 Chr. 7:26

Laban—*white*
1. Son of Bethuel .... Gen. 24:24, 29
Brother of Rebekah .... Gen. 24:15, 29
Father of Leah and Rachel .. Gen. 29:16
Chooses Rebekah for Isaac .. Gen. 24:29-60
Entertains Jacob .... Gen. 29:1-14
Deceives Jacob in marriage arrangement .... Gen. 29:15-30
Agrees to Jacob's business arrangement .... Gen. 30:25-43
Changes attitude toward Jacob .... Gen. 31:1-9
Pursues after fleeing Jacob ... Gen. 31:21-25
Rebukes Jacob .... Gen. 31:26-30
Rebuked by Jacob .... Gen. 31:31-42
Makes covenant with Jacob .... Gen. 31:43-55
2. City in the wilderness .... Deut. 1:1

Labor—*physical or mental effort*
A. *Physical:*
Nature of:
As old as creation .... Gen. 2:5, 15
Ordained by God .... Gen. 3:17-19
One of the commandments ... Ex. 20:9
From morning until night ... Ps. 104:23
With the hands .... 1 Thess. 4:11
To life's end .... Ps. 90:10
Without God, vanity .... Eccl. 2:11
Shrinking from, denounced .. 2 Thess. 3:10
Benefits of:
Profit .... Prov. 14:23
Happiness .... Ps. 128:2
Proclaim gospel .... 1 Thess. 2:9
Supply of other's needs .... Acts 20:35; Eph. 4:28
Restful sleep .... Eccl. 5:12
Double honor .... 1 Tim. 5:17

SUBJECT REFERENCE

Eternal life ... John 6:27
Not in vain ... 1 Cor. 15:58; Phil. 2:16

B. *Spiritual:*

Characteristics of:

Commissioned by Christ ... John 4:38
Accepted by few ... Matt. 9:37, 38
Working with God ... 1 Cor. 3:9
By God's grace ... 1 Cor. 15:10
Result of faith ... 1 Tim. 4:10
Characterized by love ... 1 Thess. 1:3
Done in prayer ... Col. 4:12
Subject to discouragement ... Is. 49:4; Gal. 4:11
Interrupted by Satan ... 1 Thess. 3:5

See Work, the Christian's

C. *Problems:*

Inspired by opposition ... Ezra 4:1-6
Complaint over wages ... Matt. 20:1-16
Mistreatment of employees ... Matt. 21:33-35
Characteristics of last days ... James 5:1-6

Labor, (childbirth)

A. *Of a woman's, described as:*

Fearful ... Ps. 48:6
Painful ... Is. 13:8
Hazardous ... Gen. 35:16-19
Joyful afterwards ... John 16:21

B. *Figurative of:*

New Israel ... Is. 66:7, 8
Messiah's birth ... Mic. 4:9, 10
Redemption ... Mic. 5:3
New birth ... Gal. 4:19
Creation's rebirth ... Rom. 8:22

Lace—*a cord or heavy thread*

Of priest's garments ... Ex. 28:28; Ex. 39:21

Lachish

Town in south Judah ... Josh. 15:1, 39
Joins coalition against Gibeonites ... Josh. 10:3-5
Defeated by Joshua ... Josh. 10:6-33
Fortified by Rehoboam ... 2 Chr. 11:5, 9
City of sin ... Mic. 1:13
Amaziah murdered here ... 2 Kin. 14:19; 2 Chr. 25:27
Taken by Sennacherib ... 2 Kin. 18:13-17
Military headquarters ... Is. 36:1, 2; Is. 37:8
Fights against Nebuchadnezzar ... Jer. 34:1, 7
Reoccupied after exile ... Neh. 11:30

Lack—*something still needed*

A. *How to avoid:*

Remember God's promises ... Deut. 2:7
Work diligently ... 1 Thess. 4:11, 12
Live chastely ... Prov. 6:32
Share in common ... Acts 4:34

B. *Things subject to:*

Food ... 2 Sam. 3:29
Physical needs ... 2 Cor. 11:9
Possessions ... 1 Sam. 30:19
Service to others ... Phil. 2:30
Entire commitment ... Luke 18:22
Wisdom ... James 1:5
Graces ... 2 Pet. 1:9

Lad—*a young boy*

Heard by God ... Gen. 21:17-20
Saved by God ... Gen. 22:12
Loved by his father ... Gen. 44:22-34
Slain with Samson ... Judg. 16:26-30
Unsuspecting ... 1 Sam. 20:21-41
Tattling ... 2 Sam. 17:18
Providing ... John 6:9

Ladder

Jacob's ... Gen. 28:10-12

Lady

Applied to females of high rank ... Judg. 5:29
Among royalty ... Esth. 1:18
Elect ... 2 John 1, 5
Figurative of Babylon ... Is. 47:5-7

Lael—*belonging to God*

Gershonite Levite ... Num. 3:24

SUBJECT REFERENCE

Lahad—*oppression*

Judahite ... 1 Chr. 4:2

Lahai-roi—*of the Living One who sees me*

Name of a well ... Gen. 24:62
Same as Beer-lahairoi ... Gen. 6:7, 14

Lahmam—*place of light*

City of Judah ... Josh. 15:1, 40

Lahmi—*Beth-lehemite*

Brother of Goliath slain by Elhanan ... 1 Chr. 20:5

Laish—*lion*

1. Benjamite ... 1 Sam. 25:44
2. City in north Palestine at the head of the Jordan ... Judg. 18:7, 14
   Called Leshem ... Josh. 19:47
3. Village in Benjamin between Anathoth and Gallim ... Is. 10:30

Lake

Sea of Galilee is called ... Luke 5:1, 2; Luke 8:22-33
Bottomless pit described as ... Rev. 19:20

Lake of fire—*the place of final punishment*

A. *Those consigned to:*

The beast and false prophet ... Rev. 19:20
The devil ... Rev. 20:10
Death and hell ... Rev. 20:14
Those whose names are not in book of life ... Rev. 20:15

B. *Described as:*

Burning brimstone ... Rev. 19:20
Second death ... Rev. 20:14

Lakum—*obstruction*

Town of Naphtali ... Josh. 19:32, 33

Lama—*the Aramaic for why*

Spoken by Christ on the cross ... Matt. 27:46

Lamb—*a young sheep*

A. *Used for:*

Food ... 2 Sam. 12:4
Clothing ... Prov. 27:26
Trade ... Ezra 7:17
Tribute ... 2 Kin. 3:4
Covenants ... Gen. 21:28-32
Sacrifices ... Ex. 12:5

B. *Figurative of:*

God's people ... Is. 5:17
Weak believers ... Is. 40:11
God's ministers ... Luke 10:3
God's dealing with the wicked ... Ps. 37:20
Messiah's reign ... Is. 11:6

Lamb of God, the (Christ)

A. *Descriptive of Christ as:*

Predicted ... Is. 53:7
Presented to Israel ... John 1:29
Preached to world ... Acts 8:32-35
Praised throughout eternity ... Rev. 5:6, 13

B. *Descriptive of Christ as:*

Sacrifice ... 1 Pet. 1:19; Rev. 7:13, 14
Redeemer ... Rev. 5:9
King ... Rev. 15:3

Lame, lameness—*inability to walk properly*

A. *Healing of, by:*

Christ ... Matt. 11:5
Peter ... Acts 3:2-7
Philip ... Acts 8:5-7

B. *Figurative of:*

Extreme weakness ... 2 Sam. 5:6, 8
Inconsistency ... Prov. 26:7
Weak believers ... Jer. 31:8
Healed ... Is. 35:6

C. *Causes of:*

Birth defect ... Acts 3:2
Accident ... 2 Sam. 4:4

D. *Renders unfit for:*

Priesthood ... Lev. 21:17, 18
Sacrifice ... Deut. 15:21
Active life ... 2 Sam. 9:13; 2 Sam. 19:24-26

SUBJECT REFERENCE

Lamech—*wild man*

1. Son of Methusael, of Cain's race ... Gen. 4:17, 18
   Had two wives ... Gen. 4:19
2. Son of Methuselah; father of Noah ... Gen. 5:25-31
   Man of faith ... Gen. 5:29
   In Christ's ancestry ... Luke 3:36

Lamed

Letter of the Hebrew alphabet ... Ps. 119:89-96

Lamentation—*mournful speeches; elegies; dirges*

A. *Historical of:*

Jeremiah over Josiah ... 2 Chr. 35:25
David over Saul ... 2 Sam. 1:17-27
David over Abner ... 2 Sam. 3:33, 34
Jeremiah over Jerusalem ... Lam. 1:1

B. *Prophetic of:*

Isaiah over Babylon ... Is. 14:1-32
Jeremiah over Jerusalem ... Jer. 7:28-34
Ezekiel over Tyre ... Ezek. 27:2-36
Christ over Jerusalem ... Luke 19:41-44
John over Babylon ... Rev. 18:1-24

Lamentations, the Book of—*a book of the Old Testament*

The suffering of Zion ... Lam. 1:1—2:22
Individual prayer ... Lam. 3:1-66
Collective prayer ... Lam. 5:1-22

Lamp

A. *Used in:*

Tabernacle ... Ex. 37:23
Temple ... 1 Chr. 28:15
Processions ... Matt. 25:1-8

B. *Figurative of:*

God ... 2 Sam. 22:29
God's Word ... Prov. 6:23; Ps. 119:105
God's justice ... Zeph. 1:12
Conscience ... Prov. 20:27
Prosperity ... Job 29:3
Industry ... Prov. 31:18
Death ... Job 18:6
Churches ... Rev. 1:20
Christ ... Dan. 10:6; Rev. 1:14

Lance—*a spear*

Used in war ... Jer. 50:42

Lancet—*a javelin or light spear*

Used by Baal's priests ... 1 Kin. 18:28

Landmark—*a boundary marker*

Removal of, forbidden ... Deut. 19:14

Land of promise (Canaan)

A. *Described as:*

The land of promise ... Heb. 11:9
The land of Canaan ... Ezek. 16:3, 29
The land of the Jews ... Acts 10:39
The holy land ... Zech. 2:12
"Beulah" ... Is. 62:4

B. *Conquest of, by:*

Divine command ... Ex. 23:24
God's angel ... Ex. 23:20, 23
Hornets ... Ex. 23:28
Degrees ... Ex. 23:29, 30

C. *Inheritance of:*

Promised to Abraham's seed ... Gen. 12:1-7
Awaits God's time ... Gen. 15:7-16
Boundaries of, specified ... Gen. 15:18-21
Some kept from ... Deut. 1:34-40
For the obedient ... Deut. 5:16
Sin separates from ... Deut. 28:49-68

D. *Laws concerning:*

Land allotted to 12 tribes ... Num. 26:52-55
None for priests ... Num. 18:20, 24
Sale and redemption of ... Lev. 25:15-33
Transfer of title ... Ruth 4:3-8
Witness of sale ... Ruth 4:9-11
Relieved of debt on ... Neh. 5:3-13
Leased to others ... Matt. 21:33-41
Widow's right in ... Ruth 4:3-9
Rights of unmarried women in ... Num. 27:1-11
Rest of, on the seventh years ... Ex. 23:11

SUBJECT — REFERENCE

E. *Original inhabitants of:*
- Seven Gentile nations .... Deut. 7:1; Josh. 24:11
- Mighty .... Deut. 4:38
- Tall .... Deut. 9:1, 2
- Idolatrous .... Ex. 23:23, 24; Deut. 12:29-31
- Corrupt .... Lev. 18:1-30; Ezek. 16:47
- Mingled with Israel .... Ps. 106:34-38

Language—*man's means of communication*

A. *Kinds of:*
- Jews' .... 2 Kin. 18:28
- Chaldean .... Dan. 1:4
- Syrian .... 2 Kin. 18:26
- Egyptian .... Ps. 114:1
- Arabic .... Acts 2:11
- Greek .... Acts 21:37
- Latin .... John 19:19, 20
- Lycaonian .... Acts 14:11
- Medes and Persians .... Esth. 3:12

B. *Varieties of:*
- Result of confusion (Babel) .. Gen. 11:1-9
- Result of division of Noah's three sons .... Gen. 10:5, 20, 31
- Seen in one empire .... Esth. 1:22; Dan. 3:4, 7, 29
- Seen in Christ's inscription .. John 19:19, 20
- Witnessed at Pentecost .... Acts 2:6-12
- Evident in heaven .... Rev. 5:9

See Tongue

Lantern—*an enclosed lamp*
- Used by soldiers arresting Jesus .... John 18:3

Laodicea—*a chief city of Asia Minor*
- Church of, sharply rebuked .... Rev. 1:11
- Epaphras labors here .... Col. 4:12, 13
- Paul writes letter to .... Col. 4:16
- Not visited by Paul .... Col. 2:1; Col. 4:15

Lap

A. *As a loose skirt of a garment*
- For carrying objects .... 2 Kin. 4:39
- Lots cast into .... Prov. 16:33

B. *As an act of dogs:*
- For selecting Gideon's army .... Judg. 7:5, 6, 7

Lapidoth—*torches*
- Husband of Deborah the prophetess .... Judg. 4:4

Lapwing—*a bird of the plover family* (hoopoe)
- Unclean bird .... Lev. 11:19

Lasciviousness—*unbridled lust*
- Flows from the heart .... Mark 7:20-23
- Seen in the flesh .... Gal. 5:19
- Characterizes the old life .... 1 Pet. 4:3
- Found among Gentiles .... Eph. 4:19, 20
- Sign of apostasy .... Jude 4
- Among Christians, lamentable ... 2 Cor. 12:21
- To be cast away ("wantonness") .... Rom. 13:13

Lasea
- Seaport of Crete .... Acts 27:8

Lash—*a punishment imposed with a whip or scourge*
- Rendered "stripes" .... Deut. 25:3
- Imposed on Paul .... 2 Cor. 11:24

Lasha—*bursting forth*
- Boundary town of southeast Palestine .... Gen. 10:19

Lasharon—*to Sharon*
- Town possessed by Joshua .... Josh. 12:1, 18

Last—*the terminal point*

A. *Senses of:*
- Final consequence .... Prov. 23:32
- God .... Is. 44:6

B. *Of events, last:*
- Day (resurrection) .... John 6:39, 40
- Day (judgment) .... John 12:48
- Days (present age) .... Acts 2:17
- Time (present age) .... 1 John 2:18
- Times (present age) .... 1 Pet. 1:20
- Days (time before Christ's return) .... 2 Tim. 3:1; 2 Pet. 3:3
- Enemy (death) .... 1 Cor. 15:26
- Time (Christ's return) .... 1 Pet. 1:5
- Trump (Christ's return) .... 1 Cor. 15:52

Last Supper
- At Feast of Unleavened Bread .. Matt. 26:17; Mark 14:12
- Fulfills Passover .... Luke 22:15-18

Latchet—*the thong binding the sandal to the foot*

Descriptive of:
- Something insignificant .... Gen. 14:23
- Menial task .... Luke 3:16

Latin—*the Roman language*
- Used in writing Christ's inscription .... John 19:19, 20

Lattice—*a framework of crossed wood or metal strips*
- Window of Sisera's mother .... Judg. 5:28
- Ahaziah fell through .... 2 Kin. 1:2

Laughter—*an emotion expressive of joy, mirth or ridicule*

A. *Kinds of:*
- Divine .... Ps. 59:8
- Natural .... Job 8:21
- Derisive .... Neh. 2:19
- Fake .... Prov. 14:13
- Scornful .... 2 Chr. 30:10
- Confident .... Job 5:22
- Joyful .... Ps. 126:2

B. *Causes of:*
- Man's folly .... Ps. 2:4
- Something unusual .... Gen. 18:12-15
- Something untrue .... Matt. 9:24
- Ridicule .... 2 Chr. 30:10
- Highly contradictory .... Ps. 22:7, 8

Laver—*a basin for washing*
- Made for the tabernacle .... Ex. 30:18

Law—*an authoritative rule of conduct*
- Law of man .... Luke 20:22
- Natural Law written upon the heart .... Rom. 2:14, 15
- Law of Moses .... Gal. 3:17-21
- Entire Old Testament .... John 10:34
- Expression of God's will .... Rom. 7:2-9
- Operating principle .... Rom. 3:27

Law of Moses

A. *History of:*
- Given at Sinai .... Ex. 20:1-26
- Called a covenant .... Deut. 4:13, 23
- Dedicated with blood .... Heb. 9:18-22
- Called the Law of Moses .... Josh. 8:30-35
- Restated in Deuteronomy .... Deut. 4:44-46
- Written on stone .... Deut. 4:4:13
- Plaster-coated stone .... Deut. 27:3-8
- Placed with the ark .... Deut. 31:9, 26
- Given to Joshua .... Josh. 1:1-9
- Repeated by Joshua .... Josh. 23:6-16
- Disobeyed by:
  - Israel .... Judg. 2:10-20
  - Israel's kings .... 2 Kin. 10:31
  - The Jews .... Is. 1:10-18
- Finding of book of .... 2 Chr. 34:14-33
- Disobedience to, cause of exile .... 2 Kin. 17:3-41
- Read to postexilic assembly .... Neh. 8:1-18
- Recalled at close of Old Testament .... Mal. 4:4
- Meaning of, fulfilled by Christ .... Matt. 5:17-48
- Pharisees insist on observance of .... Acts 15:1-29

B. *Purposes of:*
- Knowledge of sin .... Rom. 3:20
- Manifest God's righteousness .... Rom. 7:12
- Lead to Christ .... Gal. 3:24, 25

C. *Christ's relation to:*
- Born under .... Gal. 4:4
- Explains proper meaning to .... Matt. 5:17-48; Matt. 12:1-14
- Redeems sinners from curse of .... Gal. 3:13
- Shows fulfillment of, in Himself .... Luke 24:27, 44

D. *Christian's relation to:*
- Freed from .... Acts 15:1-29
- Spirit of, fulfilled in love .... Rom. 13:8-10
- Now written on the heart .... 2 Cor. 3:3-1

E. *Inadequacies of, cannot:*
- Make worshiper perfect .... Heb. 9:9-15
- Justify .... Acts 13:38, 39

Lawgiver—*a lawmaker*
- Only one .... James 4:12
- The LORD is .... Is. 33:22

Lawlessness—*living outside or contrary to law*

A. *Described as:*
- Wickedness .... Acts 2:23
- Iniquity .... Matt. 13:41
- Unrighteousness .... 2 Cor. 6:14

B. *Features concerning:*
- Called sin .... 1 John 3:4
- Incompatible with righteousness .... 2 Cor. 6:14
- Torments the righteous .... Matt. 24:12; 2 Pet. 2:8
- Led to crucifixion .... Acts 2:22, 23
- Descriptive of antichrist .... 2 Thess. 2:7, 8
- Scribes and Pharisees full of .... Matt. 23:27, 28
- Basis for condemnation .... Matt. 7:23
- Law made for .... 1 Tim. 1:9
- Forgiven .... Rom. 4:7; Titus 2:14
- Forgotten .... Heb. 8:12; Heb. 10:17

Lawsuits—*suing another for damages*
- Between Christians, forbidden ... Matt. 5:25, 40; 1 Cor. 6:1-8

Lawyers—*interpreters of the law*
- Test Jesus .... Matt. 22:34-40
- Jesus answers one .... Luke 10:25-37
- Condemned by Jesus .... Luke 11:45-52
- Zenas, a Christian .... Titus 3:13

Lazarus—*God has helped*
1. Beggar described in a parable .... Luke 16:20-25
2. Brother of Mary and Martha; raised from the dead .... John 11:1-44
   - Attends a supper .... John 12:1, 2
   - Jews seek to kill .... John 12:9-11

Laziness

A. *Leads to:*
- Poverty .... Prov. 6:9-11
- Waste .... Prov. 18:9
- Loss of all .... Matt. 25:26-30

B. *Admonitions against:*
- Make the most of time .... Eph. 5:16
- Have a great work .... Neh. 6:3
- Work day and night .... 1 Thess. 2:9
- Consider the ant .... Prov. 6:6-8
- No work, no eat .... 2 Thess. 3:10-12

Lead—*a heavy metal*
- Purified by fire .... Num. 31:22, 23
- Engraved with .... Job 19:23, 24
- Very heavy .... Ex. 15:10
- Object of trade .... Ezek. 27:12

Leader—*a guide*

A. *Kinds of:*
- False .... Is. 3:12
- Blind .... Luke 6:39
- Young .... Is. 11:6
- Safe .... Ps. 78:53
- Gentle .... Is. 40:11
- Faithful .... Deut. 8:2, 15

B. *Names of:*
- The LORD .... Ex. 13:21
- Christ .... John 10:3
- The Lamb .... Rev. 7:17
- The Spirit .... Luke 4:1; Gal. 5:18

L

SUBJECT REFERENCE

C. *Course of, in:*
God's truth .... Ps. 25:5
Righteousness .... Ps. 5:8
Way you should go .... Is. 48:17
Unknown ways .... Is. 42:16
Plain path .... Ps. 27:11
Everlasting way .... Ps. 139:24

Leaf, leaves
Trees .... Matt. 21:19
Doors .... 1 Kin. 6:34
Book .... Jer. 36:23

League—*an agreement between two or more parties*
Fraudulent .... Josh. 9:3-6
Forbidden .... Judg. 2:2
Secret .... 1 Sam. 22:8
Conditional .... 2 Sam. 3:12, 13
Acceptable .... 2 Sam. 3:21
Unifying .... 2 Sam. 5:1-3
International .... 1 Kin. 5:12
Purchased .... 1 Kin. 15:18-21
Deceitful .... Dan. 11:23

Leah—*a wild cow*
Laban's eldest daughter .... Gen. 29:16, 17
By Laban's deceit, becomes Jacob's wife .... Gen. 29:19-27
Hated by Jacob .... Gen. 29:30-33
Mother of seven children .... Gen. 30:19-21
Buried in Machpelah's cave .... Gen. 49:31
Builder of house of Israel .... Ruth 4:11

Leaping—*to spring or bound forward suddenly*
A. *Used physically of:*
Insects .... Joel 2:5
Men .... 1 Kin. 18:26
Unborn child .... Luke 1:41, 44
Lame man .... Acts 3:8
B. *Expressive of:*
Great joy .... 2 Sam. 6:16
Renewed life .... Is. 35:6
Victory in persecution .... Luke 6:22, 23

Learning—*knowledge acquired through experience or instructions*
A. *Aspects of:*
God's statutes .... Ps. 119:71, 73
Righteousness .... Is. 26:9, 10
Good works .... Titus 3:14
Obedience .... Heb. 5:8
B. *Objects of:*
Abominable things .... Deut. 18:9
Heathen ways .... Ps. 106:35
Deut. 18:9
Fear of the LORD .... Deut. 14:23; Deut. 17:19; Deut. 31:13
C. *Sources of:*
Experience .... Gen. 30:27
Worldly knowledge .... John 7:15
Christian experience .... Phil. 4:11
Scriptures .... Rom. 15:4

Leasing—*an old word for "lie" or sin*
Translated "leasing" in .... Ps. 4:2
Same Hebrew word elsewhere translated "lies" .... Ps. 40:4
Illustrated by Joab's conduct .... 2 Sam. 3:27

Leather—*an animal's dried skin*
Worn by John the Baptist .... Matt. 3:4

Leaven—*dough in a state of fermentation*
A. *Forbidden in:*
Passover .... Ex. 12:8-20
Meat offerings .... Lev. 2:11
B. *Permitted in:*
Peace offerings .... Lev. 7:13
First fruits of grain .... Lev. 23:17
Num. 15:20, 21
C. *Figurative of:*
Kingdom of heaven .... Matt. 13:33
Corrupt teaching .... Matt. 16:6, 12
Infectious sin .... 1 Cor. 5:5-7
False doctrine .... Gal. 5:1-9

Lebanah—*white*
Founder of a family of returning exiles .... Ezra 2:43, 45; Neh. 7:48
Called Lebana .... Neh. 7:48

SUBJECT REFERENCE

Lebanon—*mountain range* (10,000 ft.) *in north Canaan*
A. *Source of:*
Wood for Solomon's Temple .... 1 Kin. 5:5, 6
Stones for Solomon's Temple .... 1 Kin. 5:14, 18
Wood for the second Temple .... Ezra 3:7
B. *Significant as:*
A sight desired by Moses .... Deut. 3:25
Israel's northern boundary .... Deut. 1:7
Captured by Joshua .... Josh. 11:16, 17
Josh. 12:7
Assigned to Israelites .... Josh. 13:5-7
Not completely conquered .... Judg. 3:1-3
Possessed by Assyria .... Is. 37:24
C. *Figurative of:*
Great kingdoms .... Is. 10:24, 34
Spiritual transformation .... Is. 29:17
Jerusalem and the Temple .... Ezek. 17:3
Spiritual growth .... Hos. 14:5-7
Messiah's glory .... Is. 35:2
D. *Noted for:*
Blossoms .... Nah. 1:4
Wine .... Hos. 14:6, 7
Wild beast .... 2 Kin. 14:9
Snow .... Jer. 5:15
Cedars .... Song 5:15
Is. 14:8

Lebaoth—*lionesses*
Town of south Judah .... Josh. 15:32
Also called Beth-labaoth .... Josh. 19:6

Lebbaeus (see Judas 3)
Surname of Judas (Jude) .... Matt. 10:3

Lebonah—*incense*
Town north of Shiloh .... Judg. 21:19

Lecah—*journey*
Descendant of Judah .... 1 Chr. 4:21

Ledge—*a protrusion around an altar*
Part of altars rendered "compass" .... Ex. 27:5

Leek—*an onion-like plant*
Desired by Israelites .... Num. 11:5

Lees—*sediment in wine jars*
Figurative of:
Negligence and ease .... Jer. 48:11

Left—*opposite of right*
A. *Of direction:*
Location .... Gen. 14:15
Making a choice .... Gen. 13:9
Position .... Matt. 20:21-23
B. *Of the hand:*
Unusual capacity of 700 men .... Judg. 20:15, 16
Lesser importance of .... Gen. 48:13-20
C. *Figurative of:*
Weakness .... Eccl. 10:2
Shame .... Matt. 25:33, 41
Bride's choice .... Song 2:6
Singleness of purpose .... Matt. 6:3
Riches .... Prov. 3:16
Ministry of God .... 2 Cor. 6:7

Left—*that which remains over*
A. *Descriptive of:*
Aloneness .... Gen. 32:24
Entire destruction .... Josh. 11:11, 12
Entire separation .... Ex. 10:26
Survival .... Num. 26:65
Remnant .... Is. 11:11, 16
Heir .... 2 Sam. 14:7
B. *Blessings upon:*
Equal booty .... 1 Sam. 30:9-25
Greater heritage .... Is. 49:21-23
Holiness .... Is. 4:3
Lord's protection .... Rom. 11:3-5
Not wasted .... Matt. 15:37

Legacy—*that which is bequeathed to heirs*
Left by:
Abraham .... Gen. 25:5, 6

SUBJECT REFERENCE

David .... 1 Kin. 2:1-7
Christ .... John 14:15-27

Legal—*lawful*
Kingship, determined by David .... 1 Kin. 1:5-48
Priests' rights, divinely enforced .... 2 Chr. 26:16-21
Priesthood, rejected .... Neh. 7:63-65
Right to rebuild, confirmed .... Ezra 5:3-17
Mixed marriages, condemned .... Ezra 10:1-44
David's act, justified .... Matt. 12:3-8
Christ's trial, exposed .... Matt. 27:4-31
Paul's right of appeal, recognized .... Acts 26:31, 32

Legion—*a great number or multitude*
Demons .... Mark 5:9, 15
Christ's angels .... Matt. 26:53

Legs—*lower parts of human or animal body*
A. *Used literally of:*
Animal's .... Ex. 12:9
Man's .... 1 Sam. 17:6
Christ's .... John 19:31, 33
B. *Used figuratively of:*
Fool .... Prov. 26:7
Man's weakness .... Ps. 147:10
Children of Israel .... Amos 3:12
Strength .... Dan. 2:33, 40
Christ's appearance .... Song 5:15

Lehabim—*flaming*
Nation (probably the Libyans) related to the Egyptians .... Gen. 10:13

Lehi—*cheek, jawbone*
Place in Judah; Samson kills Philistines .... Judg. 15:9-19

Leisure—*spare time*
None found .... Mark 6:31

Lemuel—*devoted to God*
King taught by his mother .... Prov. 31:1-31

Lending—*to give to another for temporary use*
A. *As a gift:*
Expecting no return .... Luke 6:34, 35
To the LORD .... 1 Sam. 1:28
1 Sam. 2:20
B. *As a blessing:*
Recognized by God .... Deut. 28:12, 44
Remembered by God .... Ps. 112:5, 6
Rewarded by God .... Ps. 37:25, 26

See Borrow

Length of life
A. *Factors prolonging:*
Keeping commandments .... 1 Kin. 3:14
Wisdom .... Prov. 3:13, 16
Prayer .... 2 Kin. 20:1-11
Honor to parents .... Eph. 6:3
Fear of the LORD .... Prov. 10:27
B. *Factors decreasing:*
Killing .... 2 Sam. 3:27
God's judgment .... Job 22:15, 16
Suicide .... Matt. 27:5

Lentil—*plant of the legume family*
Prepared as Esau's pottage .... Gen. 25:29-34
Bread made of .... Ezek. 4:9

Leopard—*a wild, spotted animal*
A. *Characteristics of:*
Swift .... Hab. 1:8
Watches .... Jer. 5:6
Lies in wait .... Hos. 13:7
Lives in mountains .... Song 4:8
B. *Figurative of:*
Man's inability to change .... Jer. 13:23
Transformation .... Is. 11:6
Greek empire .... Dan. 7:6
Antichrist .... Rev. 13:2

Leprosy—*scourge; a cancer-like disease*
A. *Characteristics of:*
Many diseased with .... Luke 4:27
Unclean .... Lev. 13:44, 45
Outcast .... 2 Kin. 15:5
Considered incurable .... 2 Kin. 5:7

SUBJECT — REFERENCE

Often hereditary ... 2 Sam. 3:29
Excluded from the priesthood ... Lev. 22:2-4

B. *Kinds of, in:*
Man ... Luke 17:12
House ... Lev. 14:33-57
Clothing ... Lev. 13:47-59

C. *Treatment of:*
Symptoms described ... Lev. 13:1-46
Cleansing prescribed ... Lev. 14:1-32
Healing by a miracle ... Ex. 4:6, 7

D. *Used as a sign:*
Miriam ... Num. 12:1-10
Gehazi ... 2 Kin. 5:25, 27
Uzziah ... 2 Chr. 26:16-21
Moses ... Ex. 4:6, 7

Letters—*written communications*

A. *Kinds of:*
Forged ... 1 Kin. 21:7, 8
Rebellious ... Jer. 29:24-32
Authoritative ... Acts 22:5
Instructive ... Acts 15:23-29
Weighty ... 2 Cor. 10:10
Causing sorrow ... 2 Cor. 7:8

B. *Descriptive of:*
One's writing ... Gal. 6:11
Learning ... John 7:15
External ... Rom. 2:27, 29
Legalism ... Rom. 7:6
Christians ... 2 Cor. 3:1, 2

"Let us"
"Arise, go hence" ... John 14:31
"Cast off the works of darkness" ... Rom. 13:12
"Walk honestly" ... Rom. 13:13
"Be sober" ... 1 Thess. 5:8
"Fear" ... Heb. 4:1
"Labor to enter into that rest" ... Heb. 4:11
"Come boldly" ... Heb. 4:16
"Go on unto perfection" ... Heb. 6:1
"Draw near" ... Heb. 10:22
"Hold fast" ... Heb. 10:23
"Consider one another" ... Heb. 10:24
"Run with patience" ... Heb 12:1
"Go forth" ... Heb. 13:13
"Offer sacrifice" ... Heb. 13:15

Letushim—*sharpened*
Tribe descending from Dedan ... Gen. 25:3

Leummim—*peoples*
Tribe descending from Dedan ... Gen. 25:3

Levi—*joined*
1. Third son of Jacob and Leah ... Gen. 29:34
Participates in revenge ... Gen. 34:25-31
Father of Gershon, Kohath, Merari ... Gen. 46:11
Descendants of, to be scattered ... Gen. 49:5-7
Dies in Egypt at age 137 ... Ex. 6:16
2. Ancestor of Christ ... Luke 3:24
3. Another ancestor of Christ ... Luke 3:29
4. Apostle called Matthew ... Luke 5:27, 29
5. Tribe descending from Levi ... Ex. 32:26, 28

Leviathan—*twisted, coiled*
Great beast created by God ... Ps. 104:26
Habit of, graphically described (crocodile) ... Job 41:1-34
God's power over ... Ps. 74:14

Levites—*descendants of Levi*

A. *History of:*
Descendants of Levi, Jacob's son ... Gen. 29:34
Jacob's prophecy concerning ... Gen. 49:5-7
Divided into three families ... Ex. 6:16-24
Aaron, great-grandson of Levi, chosen for priesthood ... Ex. 28:1
Tribe of Levi rewarded for dedication ... Ex. 32:26-29
Chosen by God for holy service ... Deut. 10:8
Not numbered among Israel ... Num. 1:47-49
Substituted for Israel's first-born ... Num. 3:12-45
Given as gifts to Aaron's sons ... Num. 8:6-21
Rebellion among, led by Korah ... Num. 16:1-50
Choice of, confirmed by the Lord ... Num. 17:1-13
Bear ark of the covenant across the Jordan ... Josh. 3:2-17
Hear Law read ... Josh. 8:31-35
Cities (48) assigned to ... Num. 35:2-8; Josh. 14:3, 4
One of, becomes Micah's idolatrous priest ... Judg. 17:5-13; Judg. 18:18-31
Perform priestly functions ... 1 Sam. 6:15
Appointed over service of song ... 1 Chr. 6:31-48
Service of heads of households ... 1 Chr. 9:26-34
Excluded by Jeroboam ... 2 Chr. 11:13-17
Help repair the Temple ... 1 Chr. 23:2-4
Carried to Babylon ... 2 Chr. 36:19, 20
Return from exile ... Ezra 2:40-63
Tithes withheld from ... Neh. 13:10-13
Intermarry with foreigners ... Ezra 10:2-24
Seal the covenant ... Neh. 10:1, 9-28
Present defiled offerings will be purified ... Mal. 1:6-14; Mal. 3:1-4

B. *Duties of:*
Serve the LORD ... Deut. 10:8
Serve the priesthood ... Num. 3:5-9
Attend to sanctuary duties ... Num. 18:3
Distribute the tithe ... 2 Chr. 31:11-19
Prepare sacrifices for priests ... 2 Chr. 35:10-14
Teach the people ... 2 Chr. 17:9-11
Declare verdicts of Law ... Deut. 17:9-11
Protect the king ... 2 Chr. 23:2-10
Perform music ... 1 Chr. 25:1-7
Precede the army ... 2 Chr. 20:20, 21, 28

C. *Spiritual truths illustrated by:*
Representation—duties of the congregation ... Num. 3:6-9
Substitution—place of the first-born ... Num. 3:12, 13, 41, 45
Subordination—service to the Temple ... Num. 3:5-10
Consecration—separated for God's work ... Num. 8:9-14
Holiness—cleansed ... Num. 8:6, 7, 21
Election—God's choice ... Num. 17:7-13
Inheritance—in the Lord ... Num. 18:20

See Priest

Leviticus, the Book of—*a book of the Old Testament*
Laws of sacrifice ... Lev. 1:1—7:38
Laws of purity ... Lev. 11:1—15:33
Day of atonement ... Lev. 16:1-34
Laws of holiness ... Lev. 17:1—25:55
Blessings and curses ... Lev. 26:1-46

Levy—*forced labor imposed upon a people*
Israelites ... 1 Kin. 5:13-15
Canaanites ... 1 Kin. 9:15, 21

Lewd, lewdness—*wickedness*

A. *Characteristics of:*
Shameful ... Ezek. 16:27
Sexual ... Ezek. 22:11
Youthful ... Ezek. 23:21
Adulterous ... Jer. 13:27
Filthiness ... Ezek. 24:13
Folly ... Judg. 20:6

B. *Committed by:*
Men of Gibeah ... Judg. 20:5
Israel ... Hos. 2:10
Jerusalem ... Ezek. 16:27, 43

Liars, lies, lying—*manifestation of untruth*

A. *Defined as:*
Nature of the devil ... John 8:44
Denial that Jesus is Christ ... 1 John 2:22
Not keeping Christ's commandments ... 1 John 2:4
Hating one's brother ... 1 John 4:20
All that is not of the truth ... 1 John 2:21, 27

B. *Those who speak:*
Wicked ... Ps. 58:3
False witnesses ... Prov. 14:5, 25
Astrologers ... Dan. 2:9
Israel ... Hos. 7:3, 13
Judah ... Jer. 9:1-5

C. *Attitude of the wicked toward:*
Are always ... Titus 1:12
Forge against the righteous ... Ps. 119:69
Change God's truth into ... Rom. 1:25

D. *Attitude of the righteous toward:*
Keep far from ... Prov. 30:8
Shall not speak ... Zeph. 3:13
Pray for deliverance from ... Ps. 120:2
"Put away" ... Eph. 4:25

E. *Attitude of God toward:*
Will not ... Num. 23:19
Is an abomination ... Prov. 6:16-19
Will discover man's ... Is. 28:15, 17
Is against ... Ezek. 13:8

F. *Punishment of, shall:*
Not escape ... Prov. 19:5
Be stopped ... Ps. 63:11
Be silenced ... Ps. 31:18
Be short-lived ... Prov. 12:19
End in lake of fire ... Rev. 21:8, 27

G. *The evils of:*
Produces error ... Amos 2:4
Increases wickedness ... Prov. 29:12
Destruction ... Hos. 10:13-15
Death ... Prov. 21:6; Zech. 13:3

Liberality—*a generous spirit in helping the needy*

A. *Object of:*
Poor ... Deut. 15:11
Strangers ... Lev. 25:35
Afflicted ... Luke 10:30-35
Servants (slaves) ... Deut. 15:12-18
All men ... Gal. 6:10
God's children ... 2 Cor. 8:1-9, 12

B. *Reasons for:*
Make our faith real ... James 2:14-16
Secure true riches ... Luke 12:33; 1 Tim. 6:17-19
Follow Christ's example ... 2 Cor. 8:9
Help God's kingdom ... Phil. 4:14-18
Relieve distress ... 2 Cor. 9:12

C. *Blessings of:*
God remembers ... Prov. 3:9, 10
Will return abundantly ... Prov. 11:24-27
Brings deliverance in time of need ... Is. 58:10, 11
Insures sufficiency ... Ps. 37:25, 26
Brings reward ... Ps. 112:5-9; Matt. 25:40
Provokes others to ... 2 Cor. 9:2

Libertines freedmen
Jews opposing Stephen ... Acts 6:9

Liberty, civil
Obtained by:
Purchase ... Acts 22:28
Birth ... Acts 22:28
Release ... Deut. 15:12-15
Victory ... Ex. 14:30, 31

Liberty, spiritual

A. *Described as:*
Predicted ... Is. 61:1
Where the spirit is ... 2 Cor. 3:17

B. *Relation of Christians toward, they:*
Are called to ... Gal. 5:13
Abide by ... James 1:25
Should walk at ... Ps. 119:45
Have in Jesus Christ ... Gal. 2:4, 5

See Freedom

Libnah—*whiteness*
1. Israelite camp ... Num. 33:20, 21
2. Canaanite city near Lachish ... Josh. 10:29-32
Captured by Joshua ... Josh. 10:30, 39
In Judah's territory ... Josh. 15:42
Given to Aaron's descendants ... Josh. 21:13
Fought against by Assyria ... 2 Kin. 19:8, 9
Home of Hamutal ... 2 Kin. 23:31

Libni—*white, pure*
1. Son of Gershon ... Num. 3:18, 21
Family of, called Libnites ... Num. 3:21
Called Laadan ... 1 Chr. 23:7
2. Descendant of Merari ... 1 Chr. 6:29

L

SUBJECT — REFERENCE

Libya, Libyans—*the land and people west of Egypt*

- Called Lubim ... Nah. 3:9
- Will fall by the sword ... Ezek. 30:5
- Will be controlled ... Dan. 11:43
- Some from, at Pentecost ... Acts 2:1-10

Lice—*some small, harmful insects*

- Third plague upon Egypt, produced from dust ... Ex. 8:16-18

License—*authority to do something*

- Granted to Paul ... Acts 21:40

Life, eternal

A. *Defined as:*

- Knowing the true God ... John 17:3
- God's commandment ... John 12:50
- Jesus Christ ... 1 John 1:2
- He gives ... John 10:28, 29
- God's gift ... Rom. 6:23

B. *Christ's relation to:*

- It is in Him ... 2 Tim. 1:1
- Manifested through Him ... 2 Tim. 1:10
- He has the words of ... John 6:68
- It comes through Him ... Rom. 5:21

C. *Means of securing, by:*

- God's gift ... Rom. 6:22, 23
- Having the Son ... 1 John 5:11, 12
- Knowing the true God ... John 17:3
- Knowing the Scriptures ... John 20:31
- Believing the Son ... John 3:15-36
- Drinking the water of life ... John 4:14
- Eating the bread of life ... John 6:50-58
- Reaping ... John 4:36
- Fight the good fight of faith ... 1 Tim. 6:12, 19

D. *Present aspect of, for Christians, they:*

- Believe in the Son ... John 3:36
- Have assurance of ... John 5:24
- Have promise of ... Titus 1:2
- Have hope of ... Titus 3:7
- Take hold of ... 1 Tim. 6:12, 19
- Hates his life in this world ... John 12:25

E. *Future aspect of, for Christians, they shall:*

- Inherit ... Matt. 19:29
- In the world to come ... Luke 18:30
- In them you think you have ... John 5:39
- Reap ... Gal. 6:8

Life, natural

A. *Origin of, by:*

- God's creation ... Acts 17:28, 29
- Natural birth ... Gen. 4:1, 2
- Supernatural conception ... Luke 1:31-35

B. *Shortness of, described as:*

- Dream ... Job 20:8
- Shadow ... 1 Chr. 29:15
- Cloud ... Job 7:9
- Flower ... Job 14:1, 2
- Vapor ... James 4:14
- Sleep ... Ps. 90:5
- Tale told ... Ps. 90:9
- Pilgrimage ... Gen. 47:9
- Grass ... 1 Pet. 1:24

C. *God's concern for, its:*

- Preservation ... Gen. 7:1-3
- Protection ... Ps. 34:7, 17, 19
- Perpetuity (continuance) ... Gen. 1:28
- Provisions ... Ps. 104:27, 28
- Punishment ... Gen. 3:14-19
- Perfection in glory ... Col. 3:4

D. *Believer's attitude toward:*

- Seeks to preserve it ... Acts 27:10-31
- Attends to needs of ... Acts 27:34
- Accepts suffering of ... Job 2:4-10
- Makes God's kingdom first in ... Matt. 6:25-33
- Gives it up for Christ ... Matt. 10:39
- Lays it down for others ... Acts 15:26
- Prizes it not too highly ... Acts 20:24
- Puts Jesus first in ... 2 Cor. 4:10-12
- Regards God's will in ... James 4:13-15
- Puts away the evil of ... Col. 3:5-9
- Does not run with ... 1 Pet. 4:1-4
- Praises God all the days of ... Ps. 63:3, 4
- Doesn't fear enemies of ... Luke 12:4

E. *Cares of:*

- Stunt spiritual growth ... Luke 8:14
- Divide loyalty ... Luke 16:13
- Delay preparedness ... Luke 17:26-30; Luke 21:34
- Hinder service ... 2 Tim. 2:4

Life, spiritual

A. *Source of:*

- God ... Ps. 36:9
- Christ ... John 14:6
- Holy Spirit ... Ezek. 37:14
- God's Word ... James 1:18

B. *Described as:*

- New birth ... John 3:3-8
- Resurrection ... John 5:24
- Translation ... Acts 26:18
- New creation ... 2 Cor. 5:17
- Seed ... 1 John 3:9
- Crucifixion ... Gal. 2:20

C. *Evidences of:*

- Growth ... 1 Pet. 2:2
- Love ... 1 John 3:14
- Obedience ... Rom. 6:16-22
- Victory ... Rom. 6:1-15
- Spiritual-mindedness ... Rom. 8:6
- Possession of the Spirit ... Rom. 8:9-13
- Spirit's testimony ... Rom. 8:15-17
- Walking in the Spirit ... Gal. 5:16, 25
- Bearing the fruit of the Spirit ... Gal. 5:22
- Name in the book of life ... Phil. 4:3; Rev. 17:8

D. *Growth of:*

- Begins in birth ... John 3:3-8
- Feeds on milk in infancy ... 1 Pet. 2:2
- Must not remain in infancy ... Heb. 5:11-14
- Comes to adulthood ... 1 John 2:13, 14
- Arrives at maturity ... Eph. 4:14-16

E. *Characteristics of:*

- Imperishable ... John 11:25, 26
- Transforming ... Rom. 12:1, 2
- Invisible ... Col. 3:3, 4
- Abides forever ... 1 John 2:17

F. *Enemies of:*

- Devil ... Eph. 6:11-17
- World ... 1 John 2:15-17
- Flesh ... Gal. 5:16-21

Life, triumphant Christian

A. *Over:*

- Sorrow ... John 16:22-24; 1 Thess. 4:13-18
- The world ... John 16:33; 1 John 5:4, 5
- Transgressions ... Rom. 6:6, 7, 11-18; 1 John 5:4, 5; Rom. 8:1-4; Eph. 2:5, 6
- Circumstances ... Rom. 8:37; Phil. 4:11-13
- Death ... 1 Cor. 15:54-57; Rom. 6:6-9

B. *Through:*

- Prayer ... John 16:22-24
- Christ's death ... Rom. 6:6, 7
- Doctrine ... Rom. 6:17
- Holy Spirit ... Rom. 8:1, 2
- Christ ... Phil. 4:13
- Grace ... Eph. 2:7; Rom. 6:14
- Exaltation with Christ ... Eph. 2:5, 6
- God's will ... Phil. 2:13
- Hope of resurrection ... 1 Thess. 4:16
- Return of Christ ... 1 Thess. 4:16, 17
- Faith ... 1 John 5:4, 5

C. *When?*

- Forever ... 1 Cor. 15:54
- Always ... 2 Cor. 2:14

D. *By whom? Those who:*

- Are in Christ ... Rom. 8:1
- Were dead in transgressions ... Eph. 2:5
- Are born of God ... 1 John 5:4
- Believe ... 1 John 5:5

E. *Goal:*

- To demonstrate God's grace ... Eph. 3:7-10
- To glorify Christ ... 1 Pet. 4:11; Rom. 8:16-18

Light—*the absence of darkness*

A. *Kinds of:*

- Cosmic ... Gen. 1:3-5
- Natural ... Judg. 19:26
- Miraculous ... Acts 12:7
- Artificial ... Acts 16:29

B. *Descriptive of God's:*

- Nature ... 1 John 1:5
- Word ... Ps. 119:105
- Wisdom ... Dan. 2:21, 22
- Guidance ... Ps. 78:14; Ps. 89:15
- Favor ... Ps. 4:6

C. *Descriptive of Christ's:*

- Preincarnation ... John 1:4-9
- Person ... 2 Cor. 4:6
- Prediction ... Is. 42:6
- Presentation to the world ... Luke 2:32
- Proclamation ... John 8:12
- Perfection in glory ... Rev. 21:23, 24

D. *Descriptive of Christians as:*

- Forerunners ... John 5:35
- Examples ... Matt. 5:14, 16
- Missionaries ... Matt. 10:27
- Transformed people ... Eph. 5:8-14
- Heirs of glory ... Rev. 21:23

Lightning—*electrical discharges between the clouds and the earth*

A. *Used literally of God's:*

- Visitation at Sinai ... Ex. 19:16
- A power in storms ... Job 38:35

B. *Descriptive of:*

- Swiftness ... Nah. 2:4
- Brightness ... Matt. 28:3
- God's judgments ... Rev. 11:19
- Christ's coming ... Luke 17:24
- Satan's fall ... Luke 10:18

Ligure—*gem*

- Worn by the high priest ... Ex. 28:19

Likeness—*similarity of features*

Between:

- Spiritual and the moral ... 2 Cor. 3:6
- Spiritual and the physical ... Jer. 23:29
- Two events ... 2 Chr. 35:18
- God and idols ... Is. 46:5, 6, 9
- Believers and unbelievers ... Ps. 73:5
- Now and the future ... 1 John 3:2

Likhi—*Jehovah is doctrine*

- Manassite ... 1 Chr. 7:19

Lilith—*an evil female demon in Babylonian mythology*

- Rendered "screech owl," suggesting desolation ... Is. 34:14

Lily—*a bulbous plant*

Descriptive of:

- Beauty ... Song 5:13
- Spiritual growth ... Hos. 14:4, 5
- Christ ... Song 2:1

Lily work—*decorations upon the capitals of columns*

- In Solomon's Temple ... 1 Kin. 7:19, 22

Lime—*containing limestone*

Descriptive of:

- Cruel treatment ... Amos 2:1
- Devastating judgment ... Is. 33:12

Line

A. *Literal uses of:*

- As a measurement ... Jer. 31:39
- Rahab's cord ... Josh. 2:18, 21

B. *Figurative uses of:*

- God's providences ... Ps. 16:6
- God's judgments ... Is. 28:17

Linen—*cloth made from flax*

A. *Used for:*

- Priestly garments ... Ex. 28:1, 39
- Tabernacle curtains ... Ex. 26:1
- Sacred veil ... Ex. 26:31, 36
- Garments for royalty ... Esth. 8:15
- Levitical singers ... 2 Chr. 5:12

SUBJECT REFERENCE

Gifts to a woman..........Ezek. 16:10, 13
Clothing of the rich........Luke 16:19
Embalming...............Matt. 27:59

B. *Figurative of:*

Righteousness.............Rev. 19:8
Purity...................Rev. 19:14
Babylon's pride............Rev. 18:2, 16

Lintel—*a beam of wood overhanging the door*

Sprinkled with blood..........Ex. 12:22, 23
Command to smite............Amos 9:1
Descriptive of Nineveh's fall....Zeph. 2:14

Linus

Christian at Rome.............2 Tim. 4:21

Lions

A. *Described as:*

Strongest among beasts......Prov. 30:30
Destructive................Amos 3:12
Strong....................Judg. 14:18
Fierce....................Job 10:16
Stealthy..................Ps. 10:9
Majestic..................Prov. 30:29, 30
Provoking fear.............Amos 3:8

B. *God's use of:*

Slay the disobedient.........1 Kin. 13:24, 26
Punish idolaters............2 Kin. 17:25, 26
Show His power over.........Dan. 6:16-24

C. *Figurative of:*

Tribe of Judah.............Gen. 49:9
Christ...................Rev. 5:5
Devil....................1 Pet. 5:8
Transformation............Is. 11:6-8
Victory..................Ps. 91:13
Boldness.................Prov. 28:1
Persecutors...............Ps. 22:13
World empire..............Dan. 7:1-4
Antichrist................Rev. 13:2

Lips

A. *Described as:*

Uncircumcised.............Ex. 6:12, 30
Unclean..................Is. 6:5, 7
Stammering................Is. 28:11
Flattering................Ps. 12:2, 3
Perverse.................Prov. 4:24
Righteous................Prov. 16:13
False....................Prov. 17:4
Burning..................Prov. 26:23

B. *Of the righteous, used for:*

Knowledge................Job 33:3
Prayer...................Ps. 17:1
Silent prayer..............1 Sam. 1:13
Righteousness.............Ps. 40:9
Grace....................Ps. 45:2
Praise...................Ps. 51:15
Vows....................Ps. 66:13, 14
Singing..................Ps. 71:23
God's judgments...........Ps. 119:13
Feeding many..............Prov. 10:21
Spiritual fruitfulness........Hos. 14:2
Heb. 13:15

C. *Of the wicked, used for:*

Flattery..................Prov. 7:21
Mocking..................Ps. 22:7
Defiance.................Ps. 12:4
Lying....................Is. 59:3
Poison...................Ps. 140:3, 9
Mischief.................Prov. 24:2
Evil.....................Prov. 16:27, 30
Deception................Prov. 24:28

D. *Warnings:*

Put away perverse...........Prov. 4:24
Refrain use...............Prov. 17:28
1 Pet. 3:10
Of an adulteress, avoid......Prov. 5:3-13
Hypocrites................Mark 7:6

Litigation—*a lawsuit*

Christ's warning concerning.....Matt. 5:25, 40
Paul's warning concerning......1 Cor. 6:1, 2

Litter—*a covered framework for carrying a single passenger*

Of nations..................Is. 66:20

Liver—*body organ that secretes bile*

A. *Used literally of:*

Animals:
In sacrifice...............Ex. 29:13, 22
For divination.............Ezek. 21:21

SUBJECT REFERENCE

B. *Used figuratively of:*

Extreme pain or death......Prov. 7:23

Living, Christian

Source—Christ...............John 14:19
Length—forever..............John 11:25, 26
Means—faith in Christ.........Rom. 1:17
Kind—resurrected.............2 Cor. 5:15
End—to God.................Rom. 14:7, 8
Purpose—for Christ...........1 Thess. 5:10
Motivation—Christ............Gal. 2:20
Atmosphere—in the Spirit......Gal. 5:25
Manner—righteously...........Titus 2:12
Enemies—flesh and sin.........Rom. 8:12, 13
Price—persecution............2 Tim. 3:12

Living creatures—*a phrase referring to animals or living beings*

Aquatic animals..............Gen. 1:21
Land animals................Gen. 1:24
Angelic beings...............Ezek. 1:5

Lizard—*a small, swift reptile with legs*

Ceremonially unclean..........Lev. 11:29, 30

Lo-ammi—*not my people*

Symbolic name of Hosea's son..Hos. 1:8, 9

Loan (see Borrow; Lending)

Lock

Doors......................Judg. 3:23, 24
Hair.......................Judg. 16:13, 19
City gates...................Neh. 3:6, 13, 14

Locust—*devastating, migratory insects*

A. *Types, or stages, of:*

Eating....................Joel 1:4
Devastating................Lev. 11:22

B. *Used literally of insects:*

Miraculously brought forth....Ex. 10:12-19
Sent as a judgment.........Deut. 28:38
1 Kin. 8:37
Used for food..............Matt. 3:4

C. *Used figuratively of:*

Weakness.................Ps. 109:23, 24
Running men...............Is. 33:4
Nineveh's departing glory....Nah. 3:15, 17
Final plagues..............Rev. 9:3, 7

See Grasshopper

Lod

Benjamite town..............1 Chr. 8:1, 12
Mentioned in postexilic books...Ezra 2:33
Aeneas healed here, called
Lydda......................Acts 9:32-35

Lo-debar

City in Manasseh
(in Gilead).................2 Sam. 9:4, 5
David flees to................2 Sam. 17:27

Lodge—*to pass the night*

Travelers—in a house..........Judg. 19:4-20
Spies—in a house.............Josh. 2:1
Animals—in ruins.............Zeph. 2:14
Birds—in trees...............Matt. 13:32
Righteousness—in a city.......Is. 1:21
Thoughts—in Jerusalem........Jer. 4:14

Loft—*a room upstairs*

Dead child taken to...........1 Kin. 17:19-24
Young man falls from..........Acts 20:9

Loins

A. *Used literally of:*

Hips......................Gen. 37:34
Ex. 28:42
Waist.....................2 Sam. 20:8

B. *Used figuratively of:*

Physical strength...........Ps. 66:11
Source of knowledge.........Eph. 6:14
Source of hope.............1 Pet. 1:13

Lois

Timothy's grandmother........2 Tim. 1:5

Loneliness

Jacob—in prayer..............Gen. 32:23-30
Joseph—in weeping............Gen. 43:30, 31

SUBJECT REFERENCE

Elijah—in discouragement......1 Kin. 19:3-14
Jeremiah—in witnessing........Jer. 15:17
Nehemiah—in a night vigil.....Neh. 2:12-16
Christ—in agony..............Matt. 26:36-45
Paul—in prison...............2 Tim. 4:16

Longevity—*a great span of life*

Allotted years, 70............Ps. 90:10
See Length of life

Long-suffering—*forbearance*

A. *Manifested in God's:*

Description of His nature....Ex. 34:6
Delay in executing wrath....Rom. 9:22
Dealing with sinful men.....Rom. 2:4
Desire for man's salvation...2 Pet. 3:9, 15

B. *As a Christian grace:*

Exemplified by the prophets
("patience")...............James 5:10
Manifested by Old Testament saints
("patience")...............Heb. 6:12
Produced by the Spirit......Gal. 5:22
Witnessed in Paul's life.....2 Cor. 6:6
Taught as a virtue..........Eph. 4:1
Given power for............Col. 1:11
Set for imitation...........2 Tim. 3:10
Needed by preachers........2 Tim. 4:2

Look—*focusing the eyes toward something*

Promise....................Gen. 15:5
Warning...................Gen. 19:17, 26
Astonishment...............Ex. 3:2-6
Disdain...................1 Sam. 17:42
Lust......................2 Sam. 11:2-4
Encouragement..............Ps. 34:5
Disappointment..............Is. 5:2, 4
Salvation..................Is. 45:22
Glory.....................Acts 7:55

Lord—*title of majesty and kingship*

A. *Applied to:*

God.....................Gen. 3:1-23
Christ....................Luke 6:46
Masters..................Gen. 24:14, 27
Men ("sir")...............Matt. 21:29
Husbands.................Gen. 18:12
1 Pet. 3:6

B. *As applied to Christ, "kyrios" indicates:*

Identity with Jehovah.......Joel 2:32
Confession of Christ's Lordship ("Jesus as
Lord")...................Rom. 10:9
Absolute Lordship..........Phil. 2:11

Lord's Day (see First day of week)

Lord's Prayer

Taught by Jesus to His
disciples...................Matt. 6:9-13

Lord's Supper

A. *Described as:*

Sharing of communion.......1 Cor. 10:16
Breaking of bread..........Acts 2:42, 46
Lord's supper.............1 Cor. 11:20
Eucharist "Giving of
thanks"..................Luke 22:17, 19

B. *Features concerning:*

Instituted by Christ........Matt. 26:26-29
Commemorative of Christ's
death....................Luke 22:19, 20
Introductory to the new
covenant.................Matt. 26:28
Means of Christian
fellowship................Acts 2:42, 46
Memorial feast.............1 Cor. 11:23-26
Inconsistent with demon
fellowship................1 Cor. 10:19-22
Preparation for, required....1 Cor. 11:27-34
Spiritually explained........John 6:26-58

Lordship—*supreme authority*

Human kings................Mark 10:42
Divine King.................Phil. 2:9-11

Lo-ruhamah—*not pitied*

Symbolic name of Hosea's
daughter...................Hos. 1:6

Loss, spiritual

A. *Kinds of:*

One's soul................Luke 9:24, 25
Reward...................1 Cor. 3:13-15
Heaven...................Luke 16:19-31

L

SUBJECT — REFERENCE

B. *Causes of:*
- Love of this life .... Luke 17:33
- Sin .... Ps. 107:17, 34

Lost—*not found*

Descriptive of men as:
- Separated from God .... Luke 15:24, 32
- Unregenerated .... Matt. 15:24
- Objects of Christ's mission .... Luke 15:4-6
- Blinded by Satan .... 2 Cor. 4:3, 4
- Defiled .... Titus 1:15, 16

Lot—*covering*

A. *Life of:*
- Abraham's nephew .... Gen. 11:27-31
- Goes with Abraham to Canaan .... Gen. 12:5
- Accompanies Abraham to Egypt .... Gen. 13:1
- Settles in Sodom .... Gen. 13:5-13
- Rescued by Abraham .... Gen. 14:12-16
- Befriends angels .... Gen. 19:1-14
- Saved from Sodom's destruction .... Gen. 19:15, 26
- His wife, disobedient, becomes pillar of salt .... Gen. 19:15, 26
- His daughters commit incest with .... Gen. 19:30-38
- Unwilling father of Moabites and Ammonites .... Gen. 19:37, 38

B. *Character of:*
- Makes selfish choice .... Gen. 13:5-13
- Lacks moral stability .... Gen. 19:6-10
- Loses moral influence .... Gen. 19:14, 20
- Still "vexed" by Sodomites .... 2 Pet. 2:7, 8

Lotan—*a covering*
- Tribe of Horites in Mt. Seir .... Gen. 36:20, 29; 1 Chr. 1:38, 39

Lot(s)—*a means of deciding doubtful matters*

A. *Characteristic of:*
- Preceded by prayer .... Acts 1:23-26
- With divine sanction .... Num. 26:55
- Considered final .... Num. 26:56
- Used also by the ungodly .... Matt. 27:35

B. *Used for:*
- Selection of scapegoat .... Lev. 16:8
- Detection of a criminal .... Josh. 7:14-18
- Selection of warriors .... Judg. 20:9, 10
- Choice of a king .... 1 Sam. 10:19-21
- Deciding priestly rotation .... Luke 1:9

Lot's wife
- Disobedient, becomes pillar of salt .... Gen. 19:26
- Event to be remembered .... Luke 17:32

Love, Christian

A. *Toward God:*
- First commandment .... Matt. 22:37, 38
- With all the heart .... Matt. 22:37
- More important than ritual .... Mark 12:31-33
- Gives boldness .... 1 John 4:17-19

B. *Toward Christ:*
- Sign of true faith .... John 8:42
- Manifested in obedience .... John 14:15, 21, 23
- Leads to service .... 2 Cor. 5:14

C. *Toward others:*
- Second command .... Matt. 22:37-39
- Commanded by Christ .... John 13:34
- Described in detail .... 1 Cor. 13:1-13

Love of Christ, the

A. *Objects of:*
- Father .... John 14:31
- Believers .... Gal. 2:20
- Church .... Eph. 5:2, 25

B. *Described as:*
- Knowing .... Eph. 3:19
- Personal .... Gal. 2:20
- Conquering .... Rom. 8:37
- Unbreakable .... Rom. 8:35
- Intimate .... John 14:21
- Imitative .... 1 John 3:16
- Like the Father's .... John 15:9
- Sacrificial .... Gal. 2:20

C. *Expressions of:*
- In taking our nature .... Heb. 2:16-18
- In dying for us .... John 15:13

SUBJECT — REFERENCE

Love of God, the

A. *Objects of:*
- Christ .... John 3:35
- Christians .... 2 Thess. 2:16
- Mankind .... Titus 3:4
- Cheerful giver .... 2 Cor. 9:7

B. *Described as:*
- Great .... Eph. 2:4
- Everlasting .... Jer. 31:3
- Sacrificial .... Rom. 5:8

C. *As seen in believers':*
- Hearts .... Rom. 5:5
- Regeneration .... Eph. 2:4, 5
- Love .... 1 John 4:7-12
- Faith .... 1 John 4:16
- Security .... 2 Thess. 3:5
- Daily life .... 1 John 2:15-17
- Obedience .... 1 John 2:5
- Without fear .... 1 John 4:18-21
- Glorification .... 1 John 3:1, 2

Love, physical
- Isaac and Rebekah .... Gen. 24:67
- Jacob and Rachel .... Gen. 29:11-30
- Boaz and Ruth .... Ruth 2:4-15
- Samson and Delilah .... Judg. 16:4, 15

Lovingkindness—*gentle and steadfast mercy*

Attitude of believers, to:
- Expect .... Ps. 17:7; Ps. 36:10
- Rejoice in .... Ps. 63:3; Ps. 69:16

Loyalty—*fidelity to a person or cause*

A. *Kinds of:*
- People .... Acts 25:7-11
- Relatives .... Esth. 2:21-23
- King .... 1 Sam. 24:6-10
- Cause .... 2 Sam. 11:9-11
- Oath .... 2 Sam. 21:7

B. *Signs of:*
- General obedience .... Rom. 13:1, 2
- Prayer for rulers .... Ezra 6:10
- Hatred of disloyalty .... Josh. 22:9-20

Lucifer—*light-bearer*
- Name applied to Satan .... Is. 14:12
- Allusion to elsewhere .... Luke 10:18

Lucius—*of light*
1. Prophet and teacher at Antioch .... Acts 13:1
2. Paul's companion in Corinth .... Rom. 16:21

Lucre—*gain; money*
- Priests guilty of .... 1 Sam. 8:3
- Elders must avoid .... 1 Tim. 3:2, 3
- Deacons must shun .... 1 Tim. 3:8
- Sign of false teachers .... Titus 1:11

Lud, Ludim (plural)
1. Lud, a people descending from Shem .... 1 Chr. 1:17
2. Ludim, a people descending from Mizraim (Egypt) .... Gen. 10:13
   Mentioned as men of war .... Ezek. 27:10

Luhith—*of tablets or planks*
- Moabite town .... Is. 15:5

Luke—*another name for Lucius*
- "The beloved physician" .... Col. 4:14
- Paul's last companion .... 2 Tim. 4:11

Luke, the Gospel of—*a book of the New Testament*
- The annunication .... Luke 1:26-56
- John the Baptist .... Luke 3:1-22
- The temptation .... Luke 4:1-13
- Public ministry begins .... Luke 4:15
- The disciples chosen .... Luke 6:12-19
- The disciple's instructions .... Luke 10:25—13:21
- The Jerusalem ministry .... Luke 19:28—21:38
- The Last Supper .... Luke 22:1-38
- The Crucifixion .... Luke 22:39—23:56
- The Resurrection .... Luke 24:1-53

Lukewarm—*neither hot nor cold*
- Descriptive of Laodicea .... Rev. 3:14-16

SUBJECT — REFERENCE

Lunatic—*an insane person*
- David acts as .... 1 Sam. 21:13-15
- Nebuchadnezzar inflicted as .... Dan. 4:31-36
- Christ heals .... Matt. 4:24
- Christ declared .... John 10:20
- Paul called .... Acts 26:24

See Madness

Lust—*evil desire*

A. *Origin of, in:*
- Satan .... 1 John 3:8-12
- Heart .... Matt. 15:19
- Flesh .... James 1:14, 15
- World .... 2 Pet. 1:4

B. *Described as:*
- Deceitful .... Eph. 4:22
- Enticing .... James 1:14, 15
- Hurtful .... 1 Tim. 6:9
- Numerous .... 2 Tim. 3:6

C. *Among the unregenerate, they:*
- Live and walk in .... Eph. 2:3
- Are punished with .... Rom. 1:24-32

D. *Among false teachers, they:*
- Walk after .... 2 Pet. 2:10-22
- Will prevail in the last days .... 2 Pet. 3:3
- Are received because of .... 2 Tim. 4:3, 4

E. *Among Christians:*
- Once lived in .... Eph. 2:3
- Consider it dead .... Col. 3:5
- Deny .... Titus 2:12
- Flee from .... 2 Tim. 2:22
- Not carry out .... Gal. 5:16

Luxuries

A. *Characteristic of:*
- Egypt .... Heb. 11:24-27
- Tyre .... Ezek. 27:1-27
- Ancient Babylon .... Dan. 4:30
- Israel .... Amos 6:1-7
- Persia .... Esth. 1:3-11
- Harlot Babylon .... Rev. 18:10-13

B. *Productive of:*
- Temptation .... Josh. 7:20, 21
- Physical weakness .... Dan. 1:8, 10-16
- Moral decay .... Nah. 3:1-19
- Spiritual decay .... Rev. 3:14-17

Luz—*almond tree*
1. Ancient Canaanite town .... Gen. 28:19
   Called Bethel .... Gen. 35:6
2. Hittite town .... Judg. 1:23-26

Lycaonia—*a rugged, inland district of Asia Minor*
- Paul preaches in three of its cities .... Acts 14:6, 11

Lycia—*a province of Asia Minor*

Paul:
- Visits Patara, a city of .... Acts 21:1, 2
- Lands at Myra, a city of .... Acts 27:5, 6

Lydia—*from Lud*
1. Woman of Thyatira; Paul's first European convert .... Acts 16:14, 15, 40
2. District of Asia Minor containing Ephesus, Smyrna, Thyatira, and Sardis .... Rev. 1:11

Lying (see Liars)

Lysanias—*ending sadness*
- Tetrarch of Abilene .... Luke 3:1

Lysias, Claudius
- Roman captain who rescues Paul .... Acts 23:10
- Listens to Paul's nephew .... Acts 23:16-22
- Sends Paul to Felix .... Acts 23:23-31
- Felix awaits arrival of .... Acts 24:22

Lystra—*a city of Lycaonia*
- Visited by Paul .... Acts 14:6, 21
- Lame man healed here .... Acts 14:8-10
- People of, attempt to worship Paul and Barnabas .... Acts 14:11-18
- Paul stoned here .... 2 Tim. 3:11
- Home of Timothy .... Acts 16:1, 2

SUBJECT REFERENCE

M

Maacah, Maachah—*oppression*
1. Daughter of Nahor .... Gen. 22:24
2. Small Syrian kingdom near Mt. Hermon .... Deut. 3:14
   Not possessed by Israel ..... Josh. 13:13
   Called Syria-maachah .... 1 Chr. 19:6, 7
3. Machir's wife .... 1 Chr. 7:15, 16
4. One of Caleb's concubines ... 1 Chr. 2:48
5. Father of Shephatiah .... 1 Chr. 27:16
6. Ancestress of King Saul ..... 1 Chr. 8:29
   1 Chr. 9:35
7. One of David's warriors ..... 1 Chr. 11:43
8. Father of Achish, king of Gath .... 1 Kin. 2:39
9. David's wife and mother of Absalom .... 2 Sam. 3:3
10. Wife of Rehoboam; mother of King Abijah .... 2 Chr. 11:18-21
    Makes idol, is deposed as queenmother.............. 1 Kin. 15:13

Maachathites—*inhabitants of Maachah*
Not conquered by Israel........ Josh. 13:13
Among Israel's warriors .... 2 Sam. 23:34
See Maacah, Maacath 2

Maadai—*ornament of Jehovah*
Postexilic Jew; divorced his foreign wife .... Ezra 10:34

Maadiah
Priest who returns from Babylon with Zerubbabel .... Neh. 12:5, 7
Same as Moadiah in .... Neh. 12:17

Maai—*compassionate*
Postexilic trumpeter .... Neh. 12:35, 36

Maaleh-acrabbim—*steep*
Ascent south of the Dead Sea ... Josh. 15:3

Maarath—*barren place*
Town of Judah................ Josh. 15:1, 59

Maaseiah—*work of Jehovah*
1. Levite musician during David's reign .... 1 Chr. 15:16, 18
2. Levite captain under Jehoiada .... 2 Chr. 23:1
3. Official during King Uzziah's reign .... 2 Chr. 26:11
4. Son of Ahaz, slain by Zichri.................... 2 Chr. 28:7
5. Governor of Jerusalem during King Josiah's reign .... 2 Chr. 34:1, 8
6. Ancestor of Baruch .... Jer. 32:12
7. Father of the false prophet Zedekiah .... Jer. 29:21
8. Father of Zephaniah the priest .... Jer. 21:1
9. Temple doorkeeper .... Jer. 35:4
10. Judahite postexilic Jew ...... Neh. 11:5
11. Benjamite ancestor of a postexilic Jew .... Neh. 11:7
12, 13, 14. Three priests who divorced their foreign wives .... Ezra 10:18, 21, 22
15. Layman who divorced his foreign wife .... Ezra 10:30
16. Representative who signs the covenant .... Neh. 10:1, 25
17. One who stood by Ezra ..... Neh. 8:4
18. Levite who explains the Law .... Neh. 8:7
19. Priest who takes part in dedication services .... Neh. 12:41
20. Another participating priest .... Neh. 12:42
21. Father or ancestor of Azariah .... Neh. 3:23

Maasiai—*work of Jehovah*
Priest of Immer's family .... 1 Chr. 9:12

Maath—*to be small*
Ancestor of Christ .... Luke 3:26

SUBJECT REFERENCE

Maaz—*anger*
Judahite .... 1 Chr. 2:27

Maaziah—*Jehovah is a refuge*
1. Descendant of Aaron; heads a course of priests .... 1 Chr. 24:1-18
2. One who signs the covenant .... Neh. 10:1, 8

Macedonia—*Greece* (northern)
A. *In Old Testament prophecy:*
   Called the kingdom of Grecia .... Dan. 11:2
   Brazen part of Nebuchadnezzar's image .... Dan. 2:32, 39
   Described as a leopard with four heads .... Dan. 7:6, 17
   Described as a "he" goat .... Dan. 8:5, 21
   Dan. 11:4
B. *In New Testament missions:*
   Man of, appeals to .... Acts 16:9, 10
   Paul preaches in, at Philippi, etc. .... Acts 16:10—17:14
   Paul's troubles in .... 2 Cor. 7:5
   Churches of, very generous .. Rom. 15:26
   2 Cor. 8:1-5

Machbanai—*clad with a cloak*
One of David's mighty men ..... 1 Chr. 12:13

Machbenah—*lump*
Son of Sheva .... 1 Chr. 2:49

Machi
Father of the Gadite spy .... Num. 13:15

Machir—*sold*
1. Manasseh's only son .... Gen. 50:23
   Founder of the family of Machirites................ Num. 26:29
   Conqueror of Gilead .... Num. 32:39, 40
   Name used of Manasseh tribe.................... Judg. 5:14
2. Son of Ammiel .... 2 Sam. 9:4, 5
   Provides food for David ..... 2 Sam. 17:27-29

Machnadebai—*gift of the noble one*
Son of Bani; divorced foreign wife .... Ezra 10:34, 40

Machpelah—*double*
Field containing a cave; bought by Abraham .... Gen. 23:9-18
Sarah and Abraham buried here .... Gen. 23:19
Isaac, Rebekah, Leah, and Jacob buried here .... Gen. 49:29-31

Madai—*middle*
Third son of Japheth; ancestor of the Medes .... Gen. 10:2

Made—*something brought into being*
A. *Why Christ was made for us:*
   Sin .... 2 Cor. 5:21
   In our likeness .... Phil. 2:7
   High priest .... Heb. 6:20
B. *What Christians are made by Him:*
   Righteous .... 2 Cor. 5:21
   Heirs .... Titus 3:7

Madmannah—*dunghill*
Town in south Judah .... Josh. 15:20, 31
Son of Shaaph .... 1 Chr. 2:49

Madmen—*dunghill*
Moabite town................. Jer. 48:2

Madmenah—*dunghill, or dungheap*
Town near Jerusalem .... Is. 10:31

Madness—*emotional or mental derangement*
A. *Kinds of:*
   Extreme jealousy .... 1 Sam. 18:8-10
   Extreme rage .... Luke 6:11
B. *Causes of:*
   Disobedience to God's Laws .... Deut. 28:28
   Judgment sent by God ...... Dan. 4:31-33
C. *Manifestations of:*
   Irrational behavior.......... 1 Sam. 21:12-15
   Uncontrollable emotions .... Mark 5:1-5

SUBJECT REFERENCE

   Moral decay .... Jer. 50:38
See Insanity; Lunatic

Madon—*contention*
Canaanite town .... Josh. 12:19
Joins confederacy against Joshua...................... Josh. 11:1-12

Magbish—*strong*
Town of Judah................ Ezra 2:30

Magdala—*tower*
City of Galilee .... Matt. 15:39

Magdalene—*of Magdala*
Descriptive of one of the Marys .... Matt. 27:56
See Mary 3

Magdiel—*God is glory*
Edomite duke................. Gen. 36:43

Magi—*a priestly sect in Persia*
Brings gifts to the infant Jesus .. Matt. 2:1, 2

Magic, magician—*the art of doing superhuman things by "supernatural" means*
A. *Special manifestations of:*
   At the exodus .... Ex. 7:11
   During apostolic Christianity.............. Acts 8:9, 18-24
B. *Modified power of:*
   Acknowledged in history .... Ex. 7:11, 22
   Recognized in prophecy ..... 2 Thess. 2:9-12
   Fulfilled in antichrist........ Rev. 13:13-18
C. *Failure of, to:*
   Perform miracles .... Ex. 8:18, 19
   Overcome demons .... Acts 19:13-19
D. *Condemnation of, by:*
   Explicit Law .... Lev. 20:27
   Their inability .... Ex. 8:18
   Final judgment............ Rev. 21:8
See Divination

Magistrates *civil rulers*
A. *Descriptive of:*
   Ruler .... Judg. 18:7
   Authorities .... Luke 12:11
B. *Office of:*
   Ordained by God........... Rom. 13:1, 2
   Due proper respect .... Acts 23:5
C. *Duties of:*
   To judge:
   Impartially .... Deut. 1:17
   Righteously............... Deut. 25:1
D. *Christian's attitude toward:*
   Pray for.................. 1 Tim. 2:1, 2
   Honor .... Ex. 22:28
   Submit to .... 1 Pet. 2:13, 14

Magnanimity—*loftiness*
A. *Expressions of, toward men:*
   Abram's offer to Lot .... Gen. 13:7-12
   Jacob's offer to Esau .... Gen. 33:8-11
B. *Expression of, toward God:*
   Moses' plea for Israel .... Ex. 32:31-33
   Paul's prayer for Israel ...... Rom. 9:1-3

Magnificat—*he magnifies*
Poem of the Virgin Mary .... Luke 1:46-55

Magnify—*to make or declare great*
A. *Concerning God's:*
   Name..................... 2 Sam. 7:26
   Word .... Ps. 138:2
   Law .... Is. 42:21
   Christ's name .... Acts 19:17
B. *Duty of, toward God:*
   With others .... Ps. 34:3
   With thanksgiving .... Ps. 69:30
   In the body .... Phil. 1:20

Magog—*region of Gog*
People among Japheth's descendants .... Gen. 10:2
Associated with Gog .... Ezek. 38:2
Representatives of final enemies .... Rev. 20:8

M

SUBJECT REFERENCE

Magor-missabib—*terror on every side*
Name indicating Pashur's end ... Jer. 20:3

Magpiash—*collector of a cluster of stars*
Signer of the covenant .... Neh. 10:20

Mahalah—*disease*
Manassite .... 1 Chr. 7:14, 18

Mahalaleel—*praise of God*
1. Descendant of Seth .... Gen. 5:12
2. Postexilic Judahite .... Neh. 11:4

Mahalath—*sickness*
1. One of Esau's wives .... Gen. 28:9
Called Bashemath .... Gen. 36:3, 4, 13
2. One of Rehoboam's wives ... 2 Chr. 11:18
3. Musical term .... Ps. 53 (Title)

Mahanaim—*two camps*
Name given by Jacob to a sacred site .... Gen. 32:2
On boundary between Gad and Manasseh .... Josh. 13:26, 30
Assigned to Merarite Levites .... Josh. 21:38
Becomes Ish-bosheth's capital ... 2 Sam. 2:8-29
David flees to, during Absalom's rebellion .... 2 Sam. 17:24, 27
Solomon places Ahinadab over .... 1 Kin. 4:14

Mahaneh-dan—*camp of Dan*
Place between Zorah and Eshtaol .... Judg. 13:25

Maharai—*swift, hasty*
One of David's mighty men ..... 2 Sam. 23:28
Becomes an army captain ...... 1 Chr. 27:13

Mahath—*grasping*
1. Kohathite Levite .... 1 Chr. 6:35
2. Levite in Hezekiah's reign ... 2 Chr. 29:12
Appointed an overseer of tithes .... 2 Chr. 31:13

Mahavite
Applied to Eliel .... 1 Chr. 11:46

Mahazioth—*visions*
Levite musician .... 1 Chr. 25:4, 30

Maher-shalal-hash-baz—*spoil speeds, prey hastes*
Symbolic name of Isaiah's second son; prophetic of the fall of Damascus and Samaria .... Is. 8:1-4

Mahlah—*disease*
1. Zelophehad's daughter ...... Num. 26:33
2. Child of Hammoleketh ...... 1 Chr. 7:18

Mahli—*weak, silly*
1. Eldest son of Merari .... Num. 3:20
Father of three sons .... 1 Chr. 6:29
Father of tribal family ...... Num. 3:33
Called Mahali .... Ex. 6:19
2. Another Merarite Levite; nephew of 1 .... 1 Chr. 6:47; 1 Chr. 23:23; 1 Chr. 24:30

Mahlon—*sickly*
Husband of Ruth; without child .... Ruth 1:2-5

Mahol—*dance*
Father of certain wise men ..... 1 Kin. 4:31

Maid—*a young woman*
A. *Characteristics of:*
Obedient .... Ps. 123:2
B. *Provision for:*
Physical needs of .... Prov. 27:27
Accepted as wives .... Gen. 30:3

Mail
Letters were sent .... Esth. 3:13

Mainsail—*the lowest sail on the foremast, providing directional control*
Hoisted .... Acts 27:40

Maintenance—*provision for support*
Household supply .... Prov. 27:27
King's service .... Ezra 4:14
Solomon's supply .... 1 Kin. 4:22, 23

Majesty—*the dignity and power of a ruler*
A. *Of God:*
Splendor of .... Is. 2:2, 19, 21
Voice of .... Ps. 29:4
Clothed with .... Ps. 93:1
B. *Of Christ:*
Promised to .... Mic. 5:2-4
Laid upon .... Ps. 21:5
Eyewitness .... 2 Pet. 1:16
C. *Of kings:*
Solomon .... 1 Chr. 29:25
Nebuchadnezzar .... Dan. 4:28, 30, 36; Dan. 5:18-21

Makaz—*end, boundary*
Town in Judah .... 1 Kin. 4:9

Makheloth—*assemblies*
Israelite camp .... Num. 33:25, 26

Makkedah—*place of shepherds*
Canaanite town assigned to Judah .... Josh. 15:20, 41

Maktesh—*mortar*
Valley in Jerusalem .... Zeph. 1:11

Malachi—*my messenger*
Prophet and writer .... Mal. 1:1

Malachi, the Book of—*a book of the Old Testament*
God's love for Jacob .... Mal. 1:1-5
The priesthood rebuked .... Mal. 1:6—2:17
The messenger of the LORD .... Mal. 3:1-5
The Day of the LORD .... Mal. 4:1-6

Malcham—*their king*
Benjamite leader .... 1 Chr. 8:9

Malchiel—*God is king*
Grandson of Asher; founder of Malchielites .... Gen. 46:17

Malchijah—*Jehovah is king*
1. Gershonite Levite .... 1 Chr. 6:40
2. The father of Pashur .... 1 Chr. 9:12; Jer. 21:1
3. Head of a priestly division ... 1 Chr. 24:1, 6, 9
4. Royal prince .... Jer. 38:6
5, 6. Two sons of Parosh; divorced their foreign wives .... Ezra 10:25
7. Son of Harim; divorced his foreign wife .... Ezra 10:31
Helps rebuild walls .... Neh. 3:11
8. Son of Rechab; repairs gates .... Neh. 3:14
9. Postexilic goldsmith .... Neh. 3:31
10. Ezra's assistant .... Neh. 8:4
11. Signer of the covenant ...... Neh. 10:1, 3
12. Choir member .... Neh. 12:42
13. Called Melchiah .... Jer. 21:1

Malchiram—*the king is exalted*
Son of King Jeconiah .... 1 Chr. 3:17, 18

Malchi-shua—*the king is salvation*
Son of King Saul .... 1 Sam. 14:49
Killed at Gilboa .... 1 Sam. 31:2

Malchus—*king*
Servant of the high priest .... John 18:10

Malefactor—*rebel; criminal*
Christ accused of .... John 18:30
Christ crucified between .... Luke 23:32, 33
One unrepentant; one repentant .... Luke 23:39-43

Maleleel—*Greek form of Mahalaleel*
Ancestor of Christ .... Luke 3:37

Malformation—*irregular features*
Of a giant .... 2 Sam. 21:20

Malice—*active intent to harm others*
A. *Causes of:*
Unregenerate heart .... Prov. 6:14-16, 18, 19
Satanic hatred .... 1 John 3:12
Jealousy .... 1 Sam. 18:8-29
Racial prejudice .... Esth. 3:5-15

B. *Christian's attitude toward:*
Pray for those guilty of ...... Matt. 5:44
Clean out .... 1 Cor. 5:7, 8
Put away .... Eph. 4:31
Put aside .... Col. 3:8
Putting aside .... 1 Pet. 2:1
Avoid manifestations .... 1 Pet. 2:16
C. *Characteristics:*
Unregenerate .... Rom. 1:29; Titus 3:3
God's wrath .... Rom. 1:18, 29
Brings own punishment ...... Ps. 7:15, 16

Malignity
Full of envy .... Rom. 1:29

Mallothi—*I have talked*
Son of Heman .... 1 Chr. 25:4, 26

Mallows—*saltiness*
Perennial shrub that grows in salty marshes .... Job 30:4

Malluch—*reigning*
1. Merarite Levite .... 1 Chr. 6:44
2. Chief of postexilic priests .... Neh. 12:2, 7
3. Son of Bani; divorced his foreign wife .... Ezra 10:29
4. Son of Harim; divorced his foreign wife .... Ezra 10:32
5, 6. Two who sign the covenant .... Neh. 10:4, 27

Mammon—*wealth*
Served as a master other than God .... Matt. 6:24

Mamre—*firmness*
1. Town or district near Hebron .... Gen. 23:19
West of Machpelah .... Gen. 23:17, 19
Abraham dwelt by the oaks of .... Gen. 13:18
2. Amorite, brother of Eschol ... Gen. 14:13

Man—*human being, male or female*
A. *Original state of:*
Created for God's pleasure and glory .... Is. 43:7; Rev. 4:11
Created by God .... Gen. 1:26, 27
Made in God's image .... Gen. 9:6
Formed of dust .... Gen. 2:7
Made upright .... Eccl. 7:29
Endowed with intelligence ... Gen. 2:19, 20; Col. 3:10
Wonderfully made .... Ps. 139:14-16
Given wide dominion .... Gen. 1:28
From one .... Acts 17:26-28
Male and female .... Gen. 1:27
Superior to animals .... Matt. 10:31
Living being (soul) .... Gen. 2:7
B. *Sinful state of:*
Result of Adam's disobedience .... Gen. 2:16, 17; Gen. 3:1-6
Makes all sinners .... Rom. 5:12
Brings physical death .... Gen. 2:16, 17, 19; Rom. 5:12-14
Makes spiritually dead ...... Eph. 2:1
C. *Redeemed state of:*
Originates in God's love ..... John 3:16
Provides salvation for .... Titus 2:11
Accomplished by Christ's death .... 1 Pet. 1:18-21
Fulfills the new covenant .... Heb. 8:8-13
Entered by new birth .... John 3:1-12
D. *Final state of:*
Continues eternally .... Matt. 25:46
Cannot be changed .... Luke 16:26
Determined by faith or by unbelief .... John 3:36; 2 Thess. 1:6-10
E. *Christ's relation to:*
Gives light to .... John 1:9
Knows nature of .... John 2:25
Took nature of .... Heb. 2:14-16
In the likeness .... Rom. 8:3
Only Mediator for .... 1 Tim. 2:5
Died for .... Heb. 9:26,28; 1 Pet. 1:18-21

SUBJECT — REFERENCE

F. *Certain aspects of:*
- First—Adam .... 1 Cor. 15:45, 47
- Last—Christ .... 1 Cor. 15:45
- Natural—unregenerate .... 1 Cor. 2:14
- Outward—physical .... 2 Cor. 4:16
- Inner—spiritual .... Rom. 7:22
- New—regenerate .... Eph. 2:15

Man of sin (see Antichrist)

Manaen—*comforter*
- Prophet and teacher in church at Antioch .... Acts 13:1

Manahath—*resting place*
1. Son of Shobal .... Gen. 36:23
2. City of exile for sons of Ehud .... 1 Chr. 8:6
   - Citizens of, called Manahethites .... 1 Chr. 2:54

Manasseh—*making to forget*
1. Joseph's first-born son .... Gen. 41:50, 51
   - Adopted by Jacob .... Gen. 48:5, 6
   - Loses his birthright to Ephraim .... Gen. 48:13-20
   - Ancestor of a tribe .... Num. 1:34, 35
2. Sons of .... Num. 26:28-34
   - Census of .... Num. 1:34, 35
   - One half of, desire region in east Jordan .... Num. 32:33-42
   - Help Joshua against Canaanites .... Josh. 1:12-18
   - Division of, into eastern and western .... Josh. 22:7
   - Region assigned to eastern half .... Deut. 3:12-15
   - Land assigned to western half .... Josh. 17:1-13
   - Zelophehad's daughters included in .... Josh. 17:3, 4
   - Question concerning altar .... Josh. 22:9-34
   - Joshua's challenge to .... Josh. 17:14-18
   - City (Golan) of refuge in .... Josh. 20:8
   - Did not drive out Canaanites .... Judg. 1:27, 28
   - Gideon, a member of .... Judg. 6:15
   - Some of, help David .... 1 Chr. 12:19-31
   - Many support Asa .... 2 Chr. 15:9
   - Attend Passovers .... 2 Chr. 30:1-18
   - Idols destroyed in .... 2 Chr. 31:1
3. Intentional change of Moses' name to .... Judg. 18:30
4. Son and successor of Hezekiah, king of Judah .... 2 Kin. 21:1
   - Reigns wickedly; restores idolatry .... 2 Kin. 21:1-16; 2 Chr. 33:1-9
   - Captured and taken to Babylon .... 2 Chr. 33:10, 11
   - Repents and is restored .... 2 Chr. 33:12, 13
   - Removes idols and altars .... 2 Chr. 33:14-20

5, 6. Two men who divorce their foreign wives .... Ezra 10:30, 33

Mandrake—*a rhubarb-like herb, having narcotic qualities*
- Supposed to induce human fertility .... Gen. 30:14-16; Song 7:13

Manger—*a feeding place for cattle*
- Place of Jesus' birth .... Luke 2:7, 12
- Called "crib" .... Is. 1:3
- Same as "stall" in .... Luke 13:15

Manifest—*to make something clear or evident*

A. *Applied to God's:*
- Nature .... Rom. 1:19
- Revelation .... Col. 1:26
- Knowledge .... 2 Cor. 2:14
- Love .... 1 John 4:9

B. *Applied to Christ's:*
- Nature .... 1 Tim. 3:16
- Presence .... John 1:31
- Life .... 1 John 1:2

C. *Applied to evil:*
- Works of the flesh .... Gal. 5:19
- Man's:
  - Deeds .... John 3:21
  - Folly .... 2 Tim. 3:9

Manliness—*masculine characteristics at their best*

A. *Qualities of:*
- Self-control .... 1 Cor. 9:25-27
- Mature understanding .... 1 Cor. 14:20
- Courage in danger .... 2 Sam. 10:11, 12
- Endure hardship .... 2 Tim. 2:3-5

B. *Examples of:*
- Caleb .... Num. 13:30
- Joshua .... Josh. 1:1-11
- Jonathan .... 1 Sam. 14:1, 6-14
- Daniel .... Dan. 6:1-28

Manna—*what is it?*

A. *Features regarding:*
- Description of .... Num. 11:7-9
- Bread given by God .... Ex. 16:4, 15; John 6:30-32
- Previously unknown .... Deut. 8:3, 16
- Fell at evening .... Num. 11:9
- Despised by people .... Num. 11:4-6
- Ceased at conquest .... Josh. 5:12

B. *Illustrative of:*
- God's glory .... Ex. 16:7
- Christ as the true bread .... John 6:32-35

Manners—*a way of life*

A. *Evil kinds:*
- Sexual immorality .... Gen. 19:31-36
- Customs of other nations .... Lev. 20:23
- Careless living .... Judg. 18:7

B. *Good kinds:*
- Prayer .... Matt. 6:9
- Faithfulness .... Acts 20:18

Manoah—*rest, quiet*
- Danite; father of Samson .... Judg. 13:1-25

Mantle—*a garment*
- Sheet or rug .... Judg. 4:18
- Female garment .... Is. 3:22
- Upper garment (coat) .... 1 Sam. 15:27
- Outer garment (robe) .... 1 Kin. 19:13, 19; 2 Kin. 2:8, 13, 14

Maoch—*oppression*
- Father of Achish, king of Gath .... 1 Sam. 27:2

Maon—*abode*
1. Village in Judah .... Josh. 15:55
   - David stayed at .... 1 Sam. 23:24, 25
   - House of Nabal .... 1 Sam. 25:2
2. Shammai's son .... 1 Chr. 2:45
3. People called Maonites among Israel's oppressors .... Judg. 10:12
   - Called Mehunim .... 2 Chr. 26:7
   - Listed among returnees .... Ezra 2:50; Neh. 7:52

Mara—*bitter*
- Name chosen by Naomi .... Ruth 1:20

Marah—*bitterness*
- First Israelite camp after passing through the Red Sea .... Num. 33:8, 9

Maralah—*downward slope*
- Village in Zebulun .... Josh. 19:11

Maranatha—*our Lord, come*
- Aramaic phrase expressive of Christ's return .... 1 Cor. 16:22
- Compare the same thought in .... Phil. 4:5

Marble—*crystalline limestone*
- In columns .... Esth. 1:6
- In Babylon's trade .... Rev. 18:12

Marduk—*bold*
- Supreme deity of the Babylonians .... Jer. 50:2
- Otherwise called Bel .... Is. 46:1

Mareshah—*summit*
1. Father of Hebron .... 1 Chr. 2:42
2. Judahite .... 1 Chr. 4:21
3. Town of Judah .... Josh. 15:44
   - City built for defense by Rehoboam .... 2 Chr. 11:5, 8
   - Great battle here between Asa and Zerah .... 2 Chr. 14:9-12

Mariners—*sailors*
- Skilled .... 1 Kin. 9:27
- Fearful .... Jon. 1:5
- Weeping .... Ezek. 27:8-36
- Storm-tossed .... Acts 27:27-31

Mark

A. *As object, thing:*
- Sign for preservation .... Ezek. 9:4-6
- Sign of those following antichrist .... Rev. 13:16, 17; Rev. 14:9, 11; Rev. 20:4

Mark (John)—*a large hammer*
- Son of Mary, a believer .... Acts 12:12
- Cousin of Barnabas .... Col. 4:10
- Returns with Barnabas to Antioch .... Acts 12:25
- Leaves Paul and Barnabas at Perga .... Acts 13:13
- Paul refuses to take him again .... Acts 15:37-39
- Paul's approval of .... 2 Tim. 4:11
- Peter's companion .... 1 Pet. 5:13
- The author of the second Gospel .... Mark 1:1 (Title)

Mark, the Gospel of—*a book of the New Testament*
- John the Baptist .... Mark 1:1-11
- Choosing of the disciples .... Mark 3:13-19
- Parables .... Mark 4:1-34
- Galilean tours .... Mark 1:21-45; Mark 6:1-44
- Peter's confession .... Mark 8:27-30
- The transfiguration .... Mark 9:1-13
- Foretelling of Jesus' death .... Mark 10:32-34
- Entry into Jerusalem .... Mark 11:1-11
- Controversy with Jews .... Mark 11:27—12:40
- Events of the crucifixion .... Mark 14:43—15:47
- The resurrection .... Mark 16:1-20

Market
- Greetings in the .... Mark 11:16

Market of Appius
- Called Forum .... Acts 28:15

Market place

Place of:
- Greetings .... Matt. 23:7
- Public trial .... Acts 16:19, 20
- Evangelism .... Acts 17:17

Maroth—*bitter fountains*
- Town of Judah .... Mic. 1:12

Marriage

A. *Described as:*
- Instituted by God .... Gen. 2:18-24
- Honorable in all .... Heb. 13:4
- Permanent bond .... Matt. 19:6
- Intimate bond .... Matt. 19:5
- Blessed of God for having children .... Gen. 1:27, 28
- Dissolved by death .... Rom. 7:2, 3
- Means of sexual love .... Prov. 5:15-19
- Centered in love and obedience .... Eph. 5:21-33
- Worthy of Jesus' presence .... John 2:1-11

B. *Prohibitions concerning:*
- Near of kin .... Lev. 18:6-18
- Fornication excludes remarriage .... Matt. 5:32
- Polygamy forbidden .... Lev. 18:18
- Idol worshipers .... Ex. 34:16

C. *Arrangements for* (among Hebrews):
- Arranged by parents .... Gen. 21:21
- Parties consenting .... Gen. 24:8
- Parental concern in .... Gen. 26:34, 35
- Romance involved in .... Gen. 29:10, 11
- Commitment considered binding .... Gen. 24:58, 60
- Unfaithfulness in, brings God's judgment .... Heb. 13:4

D. *Ceremonies of* (among Hebrews):
- Time of joy .... Jer. 7:34
- Bride richly attired .... Ps. 45:13-15
- Bride veiled .... Gen. 24:65
- Bridegroom decks himself .... Is. 61:10
- Wedding feast in bridegroom's house .... Matt. 22:1-10
- Distinctive clothing of guests .... Matt. 22:11, 12
- Christ attends .... John 2:1-11
- Festivities following .... John 2:8-10
- Gifts bestowed at .... Ps. 45:12
- Parental blessing on .... Gen. 24:60
- Change of name .... Ps. 45:10, 16
- Consummation of .... Gen. 29:23
- Proof of virginity .... Deut. 22:13-21

SUBJECT REFERENCE

E. *Purposes of:*
Man's happiness ....Gen. 2:18
Continuance of the race .....Gen. 1:28
Godly seed ....Mal. 2:14, 15
Prevention of fornication ....1 Cor. 7:2, 9
Complete satisfaction ....Prov. 5:19
1 Tim. 5:14

F. *Denial of:*
As a prophetic sign ....Jer. 16:2
For a specific purpose.......Matt. 19:10-12
As a sign of apostasy ....1 Tim. 4:1-3
To those in heaven ....Matt. 22:30

G. *Figurative of:*
God's union with Israel .....Is. 54:5
Christ's union with His Church ....Eph. 5:23-32

Marrow—*the vascular tissue which occupies the cavities of bones*

A. *Used literally of:*
Healthy man..............Job 21:23, 24
Inner being................Heb. 4:12

B. *Used figuratively of:*
Spiritual sustenance.........Ps. 63:5

Marsena—*forgetful man*
Persian prince ....Esth. 1:14

Mars Hill (see Areopagus)

Marsh—*an area of grassy, soft, wet land*
Spelled "marish" ....Ezek. 47:11

Mart—*market*
Tyre, to all nations ....Is. 23:1-4

Martha—*lady, mistress*
Sister of Mary and Lazarus .....John 11:1, 2
Welcomes Jesus into her home ..Luke 10:38
Rebuked by Christ ....Luke 10:38-42
Affirms her faith ....John 11:21-32
Serves supper ....John 12:1-3

Martyrdom—*death for the sake of one's faith*

A. *Causes of:*
Evil deeds ....1 John 3:12
Antichrist's persecution......Rev. 13:15
Harlot Babylon's hatred .....Rev. 17:5, 6
Our Christian faith ....Rev. 6:9

B. *Believer's attitude toward:*
Remember Christ's warning ....Matt. 10:21, 22
Do not fear................Matt. 10:28
Be prepared ....Matt. 16:24, 25
Be ready to, if necessary.....Acts 21:13

C. *Examples of:*
Prophets and apostles ....Luke 11:50, 51
John the Baptist.............Mark 6:18-29
Stephen ....Acts 7:58-60
Early disciples of the Lord...Acts 9:1, 2

Marvel—*to express astonishment*

A. *Expressed by Christ because of:*
Centurion's faith ....Matt. 8:10

B. *Expressed by men because of Christ's:*
Power ....Matt. 8:27
Knowledge ....John 7:15

Mary—*same as Miriam*

1. Jesus' mother ....Matt. 1:16
Prophecies concerning.......Is. 7:14
Engaged to Joseph..........Luke 1:26, 27
Told of virginal conception ..Luke 1:28-38
Visits Elizabeth ....Luke 1:39-41
Offers praise ....Luke 1:46-55
Gives birth to Jesus........Luke 2:6-20
Flees with Joseph to Egypt ..Matt. 2:13-18
Mother of other children ....Mark 6:3
Visits Jerusalem with Jesus...Luke 2:41-52
Intrusted to John's care .....John 19:25-27

2. Wife of Cleophas ....John 19:25
Mother of James and Joses ..Matt. 27:56
Looking on the crucified Savior ....Matt. 27:55, 56
Follows Jesus' body to the tomb ....Matt. 27:61
Sees the risen Lord ....Matt. 28:1, 9, 10
Tells His disciples of resurrection ....{Matt. 28:7-9; Luke 24:9-11}

3. Mary Magdalene ....Matt. 27:56, 61
Delivered from seven demons ....Luke 8:2
Contributes to support of Christ ....Luke 8:2, 3
Looks on the crucified Savior ....Matt. 27:55, 56
Follows Jesus' body to the tomb ....Matt. 27:61
Visits Jesus' tomb with Mary, mother of James..................Mark 16:1-8
Tells the disciples..........John 20:2
First to see the risen Lord ...Mark 16:9
John 20:11-18

4. Mary, the sister of Martha and Lazarus ....John 11:1, 2
Commended by Jesus ......Luke 10:38-42
Grieves for Lazarus.........John 11:19, 20, 28-33
Anoints Jesus ....John 12:1-3, 7
Commended again by Jesus ....Matt. 26:7-13

5. Mark's mother ....Acts 12:12-17

6. Christian disciple at Rome...Rom. 16:6

Maschil—*attentive*
Hebrew word in the title of 13 Psalms.........................Ps. 32, 42, 44, etc.

Mash
Division of the Arameans ......Gen. 10:23
Called Meshech ....1 Chr. 1:17

Mashal
Refuge city given to the Levites ....1 Chr. 6:74
Called Mishal...............Josh. 19:26
Josh. 21:30

Mason—*one who lays stones or bricks*
Sent by Hiram to help:
David ....2 Sam. 5:11
Solomon ....1 Kin. 5:18
Used in Temple:
Repairs ....2 Chr. 24:12
Rebuilding ....Ezra 3:7

Masrekah—*vineyard*
City of Edom ....Gen. 36:36

Massa—*burden*
Son of Ishmael..............Gen. 25:12, 14

Massah and Meribah—*testing and strife*
Named together.............Ex. 17:7
Named separately ....Deut. 33:8
First, at Rephidim, Israel just out of Egypt ....Ex. 17:1-7
Levites proved ....Deut. 33:8
Second, at Kadesh-barnea, 40 years later.......................Num. 20:1-13
Moses and Aaron rebel here ....Num. 20:24
Tragic events recalled by Moses.....................Deut. 6:16
Events later recalled ....Ps. 81:7
Used as a boundary of the land......................Ezek. 47:17, 19
Used for spiritual lesson.......Heb. 3:7-12

Mast—*a vertical support for sails and rigging on a sailing ship*

A. *Used literally of:*
Cedars of Lebanon ....Ezek. 27:5

B. *Used figuratively of:*
Strength of enemies ....Is. 33:23

Master

A. *Descriptive of:*
Owner of slaves ....Ex. 21:4-6
King.......................1 Chr. 12:19
Prophet ....2 Kin. 2:3, 5
Teacher ....Matt. 23:8

B. *Kinds of:*
Unmerciful ....1 Sam. 30:13-15
Angry ....Luke 14:21
Good ....Gen. 24:9-35
Believing ....1 Tim. 6:2
Heavenly ....Col. 4:1

Master builder
Paul describes himself as ....1 Cor. 3:10

Master workmen—*craftsmen*
Bezaleel.....................Ex. 31:1-5
Hiram of Tyre ....1 Kin. 7:13-50
Aquila and Priscilla............Acts 18:2, 3
Demetrius ....Acts 19:24

Mate—*the male or female of a pair*
God provides for..............Is. 34:15, 16

Materialistic—*concerned for worldly goods only*
Christ condemns ....Luke 12:16-21
Sadducees described ....Acts 23:8
Christians forbidden to live as...1 Cor. 15:30-34

Mathematics, spiritual

A. *General:*

Addition:
God's Word ....Deut. 4:2
Knowledge will increase .....Dan. 12:4
Increased riches ....Ps. 62:10

Subtraction:
God's commandments.......Deut. 12:32

Multiplication:
Human family ....Gen. 1:28

B. *Unrighteous:*

Addition:
Wealth....................Ps. 73:12
Guilt ....2 Chr. 28:13
Sin ....Is. 30:1

Subtraction:
Wealth obtained by fraud....Prov. 13:11
Life shortened ....Ps. 55:23
Prov. 10:27

Multiplication:
Sorrow by idolatry..........Ps. 16:4
Transgression ....Prov. 29:16

C. *Righteous:*

Addition:
Years ....Prov. 3:1, 2
Prov. 4:10
Blessing without sorrow .....Prov. 10:22
By putting God first ....Matt. 6:33
Graces ....2 Pet. 1:5-7
In latter years..............Job 42:12

Subtraction:
Disease ....Ex. 15:26
Taken from evil ....Is. 57:1

Multiplication:
Prosperity ....Deut. 8:1, 11-13
Length of days ....Deut. 11:18-21
Prov. 9:11
Mercy, peace, love ....Jude 2
Church ....Acts 9:31

Matred—*expulsion*
Mother-in-law of Hadar (Hadad), an Edomite king.........................Gen. 36:39

Matri—*rainy*
Saul's Benjamite family ....1 Sam. 10:21

Mattan—*gift*

1. Priest of Baal ....2 Kin. 11:18
Killed by the people ....2 Chr. 23:16, 17

2. Father of Shephatiah........Jer. 38:1

Mattanah—*gift*
Israelite camp...............Num. 21:18, 19

Mattaniah—*gift of Jehovah*

1. King Zedekiah's original name ....2 Kin. 24:17

2. Son of Mica, a Levite and Asaphite ....1 Chr. 9:15

3. Musician, son of Heman.....1 Chr. 25:4, 16

4. Spirit of the LORD came upon ....2 Chr. 20:14

5. Levite under King Hezekiah..................2 Chr. 29:13

6. Postexilic Levite and singer ..Neh. 11:17

7. Levite gatekeeper ....Neh. 12:25

8. Postexilic Levite...........Neh. 12:35

9. Levite in charge of treasuries................Neh. 13:13

10, 11, 12, 13. Four postexilic Jews who divorced foreign wives ....Ezra 10:26-37

SUBJECT REFERENCE

Mattatha—*gift (of God)*
Son of Nathan; ancestor of Christ .... Luke 3:31

Mattathias—*Greek form of Mattathiah*
1. Postexilic ancestor of Christ .... Luke 3:25
2. Another postexilic ancestor of Christ .... Luke 3:26

Mattathah—*gift of Jehovah*
Jew who put away his foreign wife .... Ezra 10:33

Mattenai—*gift of Jehovah*
1. Priest in the time of Joiakim .... Neh. 12:19
2, 3. Two postexilic Jews who put away their foreign wives .... Ezra 10:33, 37

Matter—*something*
A. *Descriptive of:*
Lawsuit .... 1 Cor. 6:1
Sum of something .... Eccl. 12:13
Love affair .... Ruth 3:18
News .... Mark 1:45
Speech .... 1 Sam. 16:18
B. *Kinds of:*
Good .... Ps. 45:1
Evil .... Ps. 64:5
Unknown .... Dan. 2:5, 10
Revealed .... Dan. 2:23

Matthan—*gift*
Ancestor of Joseph .... Matt. 1:15, 16

Matthat—*gift*
1. Ancestor of Christ .... Luke 3:24
2. Another ancestor of Christ .... Luke 3:29

Matthew—*gift of Jehovah*
Tax gatherer .... Matt. 9:9
Becomes Christ's follower .... Matt. 9:9
Appointed an apostle .... Matt. 10:2, 3
Called Levi, the son of Alphaeus .... Mark 2:14
Entertains Jesus with a great feast .... Mark 2:14, 15
In the upper room .... Acts 1:13
Author of the first Gospel .... Matt. 1:1 (Title)

Matthew, the Gospel of—*a book of the New Testament*
Events of Jesus' birth .... Matt. 1:18—2:23
John the Baptist .... Matt. 3:1-17
The temptation .... Matt. 4:1-11
Jesus begins His ministry .... Matt. 4:12-17
The Great Sermon .... Matt. 5:1—7:29
Christ, about John the Baptist .... Matt. 11:1-19
Conflict with the Pharisees and Sadducees .... Matt. 15:39—16:6
Peter's confession .... Matt. 16:13-20
Prophecy of death and resurrection .... Matt. 20:17-19
Jerusalem entry .... Matt. 21:1-11
Authority of Jesus .... Matt. 21:23—22:14
Woes to the Pharisees .... Matt. 23:1-36
Garden of Gethsemane .... Matt. 26:36-56
Crucifixion and burial .... Matt. 27:27-66
Resurrection of Christ .... Matt. 28:1-20

Matthias—*gift of Jehovah*
Chosen by lot to replace Judas .... Acts 1:15-26

Mattithiah—*gift of Jehovah*
1. Korahite Levite .... 1 Chr. 9:31
2. Levite, son of Jeduthun, and Temple musician .... 1 Chr. 15:18, 21
3. Jew who put away his foreign wife .... Ezra 10:43
4. Levite attendant to Ezra .... Neh. 8:4

Mattock—*an agricultural instrument for digging and hoeing*
Sharpened for battle .... 1 Sam. 13:20-22

Maturity, spiritual
Do away with childish things .... 1 Cor. 13:11
Be mature in your thinking .... 1 Cor. 14:20
Solid food is for .... Heb. 5:11-14
Overcoming the evil one .... 1 John 2:14

Maul—*a stick or a club*
Used against neighbor .... Prov. 25:18

SUBJECT REFERENCE

Maw—*the fourth stomach of ruminants* (divided-hoof animals)
Given to the priests .... Deut. 18:3

Mazzaroth—*the signs of the Zodiac or a constellation*
Descriptive of God's power .... Job 38:32
Objects of idolatrous worship .... 2 Kin. 23:5

Meadow—*sown fields*
1. Reed grass or papyrus thickets .... Is. 19:6, 7
Translated "flag" in .... Job 8:11
2. Place near Gibeah .... Judg. 20:33

Meah, tower of the
Restored by Eliashib .... Neh. 3:1

Meal—*ground grain used for food*
One tenth of an ephah of .... Num. 5:15
Used in offerings .... 1 Kin. 4:22
"Then bring" .... 2 Kin. 4:41
Millstones and grind .... Is. 47:2
Three pecks of .... Matt. 13:33

Meals—*times of eating*
A. *Times of:*
Early morning .... John 21:4-12
At noon (for laborers) .... Ruth 2:14
In the evening .... Gen. 19:1-3
B. *Extraordinary and festive:*
Guests invited .... Matt. 22:3, 4
Received with a kiss .... Luke 7:45
Feet washed .... Luke 7:44
Anointed with ointment .... Luke 7:38
Proper dress .... Matt. 22:11, 12
Seated according to rank .... Matt. 23:6
Special guest honored .... 1 Sam. 9:22-24
Entertainment provided .... Luke 15:25
Temperate habits taught .... Prov. 23:1-3
Intemperance condemned .... Amos 6:1-6

See Entertainment; Feasts

Means of grace
A. *Agents of:*
Holy Spirit .... Gal. 5:16-26
God's Word .... 1 Thess. 2:13
Prayer .... Rom. 8:15-27
Christian fellowship .... Mal. 3:16-18
Public worship .... 1 Thess. 5:6
Christian witnessing .... Acts 8:4
B. *Words expressive of:*
Stir up the gift .... 1 Tim. 1:6
Neglect not the spiritual gift .... 1 Tim. 4:14
Take heed to the ministry .... Col. 4:17
Grow in grace .... 2 Pet. 3:18
C. *Use of, brings:*
Assurance .... 2 Pet. 1:5-12
Stability .... Eph. 4:11-16
D. *Enemies of:*
Devil .... 1 Thess. 3:5
World .... 1 John 2:15-17
Coldness .... Rev. 3:14-18

Mearah—*cave*
Unconquered by Joshua .... Josh. 13:1, 4

Measure—*a standard of size, quantity or values*
A. *Objectionable:*
Differing (different) .... Deut. 25:14, 15
Scant .... Mic. 6:10
Using themselves as a gauge .... 2 Cor. 10:12
B. *As indicative of:*
Earth's weight .... Is. 40:12
Punishment inflicted .... Matt. 7:2
C. *Figurative of:*
Great size .... Hos. 1:10
Sin's ripeness .... Matt. 23:32
The Spirit's infilling .... John 3:34
Man's ability .... 2 Cor. 10:13
Perfection of faith .... Eph. 4:13, 16

Measuring line—*a cord of specified length for measuring*
Signifies hope .... Jer. 31:38-40
Zech. 2:1

SUBJECT REFERENCE

Meat—*food in general* (not just flesh)
A. *Characteristics of:*
Given by God .... Ps. 104:21, 27
Necessary for man .... Gen. 1:29, 30
B. *Lack of:*
Testing of faith .... Hab. 3:17
Provided by:
God .... Ps. 145:15
Christ .... John 21:5, 6
C. *Prohibitions concerning:*
Not in itself commendable .... 1 Cor. 8:8
Not to be a stumbling block .... 1 Cor. 8:13
Life more important than .... Matt. 6:25
D. *Figurative of:*
God's will .... John 4:32, 34
Christ .... John 6:27, 55
Strong doctrines .... 1 Cor. 3:2

Mebunnai—*built*
One of David's mighty men .... 2 Sam. 23:27
Called Sibbecai .... 1 Chr. 11:29

Mecherathite—*a dweller in Mecharah*
Descriptive of Hepher, one of David's mighty men .... 1 Chr. 11:36

Medad—*beloved*
One of the seventy elders receiving the Spirit .... Num. 11:26-29

Medan—*judgment*
Son of Abraham by Keturah .... Gen. 25:1, 2

Meddling—*interfering with the affairs of others*
Brings a king's death .... 2 Chr. 35:21-24
Christians .... 1 Pet. 4:15
Such called "busybodies" .... 2 Thess. 3:11

Medeba—*full waters*
Old Moabite town .... Num. 21:29, 30
Assigned to Reuben .... Josh. 13:9, 16
Syrians defeated here .... 1 Chr. 19:6, 7
Reverts to Moab .... Is. 15:2

Medes, Media—*the people and country of the Medes*
A. *Characteristics of:*
Descendants of Japheth .... Gen. 10:2
Part of Medo-Persian empire .... Esth. 1:19
Inflexible laws of .... Dan. 6:8, 12, 15
Among those at Pentecost .... Acts 2:9
B. *Kings of, mentioned in the Bible:*
Cyrus .... Ezra 1:1
Ahasuerus .... Ezra 4:6
Artaxerxes I .... Ezra 4:7
Darius .... Ezra 6:1
Xerxes .... Dan. 11:2
Artaxerxes .... Ezra 6:14
C. *Place of, in Bible hisory:*
Israel deported to .... 2 Kin. 17:6
Babylon falls to .... Dan. 5:30, 31
"Darius the Mede," new ruler of Babylon .... Dan. 5:31
Daniel rises high in the kingdom of .... Dan. 6:1-28
Cyrus, king of Persia, allows Jews to return .... 2 Chr. 36:22, 23
Esther and Mordecai live under Ahasuerus, king of .... Esth. 1:3, 19
D. *Prophecies concerning:*
Agents in Babylon's fall .... Is. 13:17-19
Cyrus, king of, God's servant .... Is. 44:28
"Inferior" kingdom .... Dan. 2:39
Compared to a bear .... Dan. 7:5
Kings of .... Dan. 11:2
War with Greece .... Dan. 11:2

Mediation—*a friendly intervention designed to render assistance*
A. *Purposes of:*
Save a life .... Gen. 37:21, 22
Save a people .... Ex. 32:11-13
Obtain a wife .... 1 Kin. 2:13-25
Obtain justice .... Job 9:33
B. *Motives prompting:*
People's fear .... Deut. 5:5
Regard for human life .... Jer. 38:7-13

SUBJECT REFERENCE

Sympathy for a sick man ....2 Kin. 5:6-8
Matt. 17:15

C. *Methods used:*
Intense prayer ....Deut. 9:20-29
Flattery ....1 Sam. 25:23-35
Appeal to self-preservation...Esth. 4:12-17

Mediator, Christ our

A. *His qualifications:*
Bears God's image, man's likeness ....Phil. 2:6-8; Heb. 2:14-17
Is both sinless and sin-bearer...................Is. 53:6-10; Eph. 2:13-18
Endures God's wrath, brings God's righteousness ....Rom. 5:6-19
Is sacrifice and the priest ....Heb. 7:27
Heb. 10:5-22

B. *How He performs the function:*
Took our nature............1 John 1:1-3
Died as our substitute.......1 Pet. 1:18, 19
Reconciled us to God ....Eph. 2:16

Medicine—*something prescribed to cure an illness*

A. *General prescriptions:*
Merry heart ....Prov. 15:13
Rest ....Ps. 37:7-11
Sleep ....John 11:12, 13
Quarantine ....Lev. 12:1-4
Sanitation ....Deut. 23:10-14

B. *Specific prescriptions:*
Figs ....Is. 38:21
Roots and leaves ....Ezek. 47:12
Wine ....1 Tim. 5:23

C. *Used figuratively of:*
Salvation ....Jer. 8:22
Incurableness ....Jer. 46:11
Spiritual stubbornness.......Jer. 51:8, 9

See Diseases

Meditation—*quiet contemplation of spiritual truths*

A. *Objects of, God's:*
Word ....Ps. 119:148
Law ....Josh. 1:8
Instruction ....1 Tim. 4:15

B. *Value of, for:*
Understanding ....Ps. 49:3
Spiritual satisfaction ....Ps. 63:5, 6
Superior knowledge ....Ps. 119:99

C. *Extent of:*
All the day ....Ps. 119:97
At evening ....Gen. 24:63
In night watches ....Ps. 119:148

Mediterranean Sea

Described as:
Sea........................Gen. 49:13
Great Sea ....Josh. 1:4
Josh. 9:1
Sea of the Philistines.........Ex. 23:31
Uttermost Sea ....Deut. 11:24; Joel 2:20; Zech. 14:8

Mediums

A. *Described as:*
Source of defilement ....Lev. 19:31
Abomination ....Deut. 18:10-12
Whisperers ....Is. 8:19

B. *The practicers, to be:*
Cut off....................Lev. 20:6
Put to death ....Lev. 20:27

C. *Consulted by:*
Saul ....1 Sam. 28:3-25
Manasseh ....2 Kin. 21:6

D. *Condemned by:*
Josiah ....2 Kin. 23:24

Meek

A. *Blessings upon:*
Gospel ....Is. 61:1
Spiritual satisfaction ....Ps. 22:26
Guidance and instruction ....Ps. 25:9
Salvation ....Ps. 76:9

B. *A Christian essential in:*
Living in the Spirit ....Gal. 5:22, 23
Receiving the Word.........James 1:21
Stating our assurance ....James 3:13

SUBJECT REFERENCE

Megiddo—*place of troops*
City conquered by Joshua ......Josh. 12:21
Assigned to Manasseh ....Josh. 17:11
Inhabitants of, made slaves .....Judg. 1:27, 28
Canaanites defeated here ....Judg. 5:19-21
Site of Baana's headquarters ....1 Kin. 4:12
Fortified by Solomon ....1 Kin. 9:15-19
King Ahaziah dies here ....2 Kin. 9:27
King Josiah killed here.........2 Kin. 23:29, 30
Mentioned in prophecy ....Zech. 12:11
Site of Armageddon ....Rev. 16:16

Mehetabel—*God benefits*
1. King Hadar's wife ....Gen. 36:39
2. Father of Delaiah ....Neh. 6:10

Mehida—*renowned*
Ancestor of a family of returning Temple servants.....................Ezra 2:52

Mehir—*price*
Judahite ....1 Chr. 4:11

Meholathite—*a native of Meholah*
Descriptive of Adriel...........1 Sam. 18:19

Mehujael—*smitten of God*
Cainite; father of Methusael ....Gen. 4:18

Mehuman—*faithful*
Eunuch under King Ahasuerus..................Esth. 1:10

Mehunim
Arabian tribe near Mt. Seir .....2 Chr. 26:7
Smitten by Simeonites ....1 Chr. 4:39-42
Descendants of, serve as Nethinim ....Ezra 2:50

Me-jarkon—*waters of yellow color*
Territory of Dan near Joppa ....Josh. 19:40, 46

Mekonah—*foundation*
Town of Judah................Neh. 11:25, 28

Melatiah—*Jehovah has set free*
Postexilic workman ....Neh. 3:7

Melchi—*my king*
Two ancestors of Jesus ....Luke 3:24, 28

Melchizedek—*king of righteousness*

A. *Described as:*
King of Salem ....Gen. 14:18
Priest of God ....Gen. 14:18
Receiver of a tenth of Abram's goods.....................Gen. 14:18-20
King of righteousness ....Heb. 7:2
Without parentage..........Heb. 7:3
Great man ....Heb. 7:4

B. *Typical of Christ's:*
Eternity ....Heb. 7:3
Priesthood.................Ps. 110:4
Kingship ....Heb. 8:1

Melea
Ancestor of Jesus..............Luke 3:31

Melech—*king*
Son of Micah, grandson of Jonathan....................1 Chr. 8:35

Melicu—*reigning*
Head of a household...........Neh. 12:14

Melita—*an island in the Mediterranean Sea*
Paul's shipwreck ....Acts 28:1-8

Melon—*the watermelon*
Desired by Israelites in wilderness...................Num. 11:5

Melting—*making a solid a liquid*
Used figuratively of:
Complete destruction ....Ex. 15:15
Discouragement ....Josh. 7:5
Defeatism ....Josh. 5:1
National discouragement ....Is. 19:1
Destruction of the wicked ......Ps. 68:2
God's presence...............Mic. 1:4
Testings.....................Jer. 9:7
Troubled sea ....Ps. 107:26
Christ's pain on the cross.......Ps. 22:14

SUBJECT REFERENCE

Melzar—*sentry*
Steward placed over Daniel .....Dan. 1:11, 16

Mem
Letter of the Hebrew alphabet ..Ps. 119:97-104

Member—*a part of a larger whole*

A. *Descriptive of:*
Parts of the body ....Matt. 5:29, 30
Union with Christ ....1 Cor. 6:15
True Church ....1 Cor. 12:27

B. *Of the body:*
Effect of sin in ....Rom. 7:5
Struggle in ....Rom. 7:23

C. *Illustrative of:*
Variety of Christian gifts ....Rom. 12:4, 5
God's design in ....1 Cor. 12:18, 24

Memorials—*things established to commemorate an event or a truth*

A. *Established by men:*
Jacob's stone ....Gen. 28:18-22
Altar at Jordan.............Josh. 22:9-16
Feast of Purim ....Esth. 9:28

B. *Established by God:*
Passover ....Ex. 12:14
Pot of manna ....Ex. 16:32-34
Lord's Supper..............Luke 22:19

Memories—*the ability to revive past experiences*

A. *Uses of, to recall:*
Past blessings ....Ezra 9:5-15
Past sins ....Josh. 22:12-20
God's blessings.............Neh. 9:1-38
God's promises ....Neh. 1:8-11
Christian truths ....2 Pet. 1:15-21
Prophecies.................John 2:19-22
Lost opportunities ....Ps. 137:1-3

B. *Aids to:*
Reminder ....2 Sam. 12:1-13
Prick of conscience ....Gen. 41:9
Holy Spirit ....John 14:26

Memphis—*haven of good*
Ancient capital of Egypt ....Hos. 9:6
Prophesied against by Isaiah ....Is. 19:13
Jews flee to...................Jer. 44:1
Denounced by the prophets.....Jer. 46:19

Memucan
Persian prince ....Esth. 1:14-21

Menahem—*comforter*
Cruel king of Israel ....2 Kin. 15:14-18

Menan
Ancestor of Jesus..............Luke 3:31

Mending—*restoring something*
Of nets ....Matt. 4:21
Used figuratively ....Luke 5:36

Mene—*numbered*
Sentence of doom ....Dan. 5:25, 26

Mene, Tekel, Upharsin
Written by God ....Dan. 5:5, 25
Interpreted by Daniel ....Dan. 5:24-29

Menstealers—*Those who seize another by unlawful force*
Condemned by law ....1 Tim. 1:10

Menstruation—*a woman's monthly flow*
Intercourse during, prohibited ...Lev. 18:19
End of, in old age ....Gen. 18:11
Called:
"Sickness"...................Lev. 20:18
"The custom of women" ....Gen. 31:35

Meonenim—*augurs*
Tree or place where soothsayers performed ....Judg. 9:37

Meonenim, plain of—*plain of clouds*
Abimelech's route ....Judg. 9:35, 37

Meonothai—*my habitations*
Judahite ....1 Chr. 4:14

Mephaath—*splendor*
Reubenite town ....Josh. 13:18

SUBJECT REFERENCE

Assigned to Merarite Levites....Josh. 21:34, 37
Repossessed by Moabites.......Jer. 48:21

Mephibosheth—*one who destroys shame*

1. Son of King Saul...........2 Sam. 21:8
2. Grandson of King Saul; crippled son of Jonathan...............2 Sam. 4:4-6
Reared by Machir..........2 Sam. 9:6
Sought out and honored by David...............2 Sam. 9:1-13
Accused by Ziba...........2 Sam. 16:1-4
Later explains his side to David...............2 Sam. 19:24-30
Spared by David...........2 Sam. 21:7
Father of Micha...........2 Sam. 9:12
Called Merib-baal..........1 Chr. 8:34

Merab—*increase*

King Saul's eldest daughter.....1 Sam. 14:49
Saul promises her to David, but gives her to Adriel.....................1 Sam. 18:17-19
Five sons of, hanged...........2 Sam. 21:8, 9

Meraiah—*rebellious*

Postexilic priest...............Neh. 12:12

Meraioth—*rebellious*

1. Levite....................1 Chr. 6:6, 7
2. Son of Ahitub and father of Zadok.................1 Chr. 9:11
3. Priestly household in Joiakim's time.................Neh. 12:15
Called Meremoth...........Neh. 12:3

Merari—*bitter*

1. Third son of Levi; brother of Gershon and Kohath..................Gen. 46:11
Goes with Jacob to Egypt...Gen. 46:8, 11
2. Descendants of Merari; called Merarites................Num. 26:57
Divided into two groups.......Ex. 6:19
Duties assigned to.........Num. 3:35-37
Follow Judah in march......Num. 10:14, 17
Twelve cities assigned to.....Josh. 21:7, 34-40
Superintend Temple music...1 Chr. 6:31-47
Help David bring up the ark...................1 Chr. 15:1-6
Divided into courses........1 Chr. 23:6-23
Their duties described.......1 Chr. 26:10-19
Participate in cleansing the house of the LORD.................2 Chr. 29:12-19
After exile, help Ezra.......Ezra 8:18, 19

Merarites (see Merari 2)

Merathaim—*double rebellion*

Name applied to Babylon......Jer. 50:21

Merchandise—*things for sale in trade*

A. *Characteristics of:*
Countries employed in......Is. 45:14
Men occupied with..........Matt. 22:5
Not mixed with spiritual things....................John 2:16
To be abolished.............Rev. 18:11, 12

B. *Figurative of:*
Wisdom's profit............Prov. 3:13, 14
Gospel transformation.......Is. 23:18

Merchants—*traders*

Characteristics of:
Crossed the sea................Is. 23:2
Lamentation over..............Ezek. 27:2-36
Some do not observe the Sabbath....................Neh. 13:19-21
Burden people with debts.......Neh. 5:1-13
Peddle goods...................Neh. 13:16
Trade with farmers............Prov. 31:24
Form guilds...................Neh. 3:8-32
Destroyed with Babylon........Rev. 18:3-19
Sailors, in Solomon's service...1 Kin. 9:27, 28
Bring Solomon..................2 Chr. 9:14
Bring Solomon..................2 Chr. 9:28

Mercurius

Paul acclaimed as.............Acts 14:12

Mercy

A. *Described as:*
Great.....................Is. 54:7
Sure......................Is. 55:3
Abundant..................1 Pet. 1:3
Tender....................Ps. 25:6
New every morning.........Lam. 3:22, 23

SUBJECT REFERENCE

B. *Of God, seen in:*
Regeneration..............1 Pet. 1:3
Salvation.................Titus 3:5
Christ's mission..........Luke 1:72, 78
Forgiveness...............Ps. 51:1

C. *In the Christian life:*
Received in salvation.......1 Cor. 7:25
Taught as a principle of life.....................Matt. 5:7
Practiced as a gift..........Rom. 12:8
Evidenced in God's provinces.................Phil. 2.27
Obtained in prayer.........Heb. 4:16
Reason of consecration......Rom. 12:1
Reason for hope............Jude 21

D. *Special injunctions concerning:*
Put on.....................Col. 3:12

E. *Examples of:*
David to Saul..............1 Sam. 24:10-17
Christ to sinners...........Matt. 9:13

F. *Attitude of believers, to:*
Cast themselves on.........2 Sam. 24:14
Look for...................Jude 21

Mercy seat—*the covering of the ark*

Made of pure gold............Ex. 25:17
Blood sprinkled upon.........Lev. 16:14, 15
God manifested over..........Lev. 16:2
Figurative of Christ..........Heb. 9:5-12

Mered—*rebellion*

Judahite....................1 Chr. 4:17
Had two wives...............1 Chr. 4:17, 18

Meremoth—*elevations*

1. Signer of the covenant......Neh. 10:5
Called Meraioth............Neh. 12:15
2. One who divorced his foreign wife....................Ezra 10:34, 36
3. Priest, son of Uriah; weighs silver and gold...................Ezra 8:33
Repairs wall of Jerusalem....Neh. 3:4, 21

Meres—*the forgetful one*

Persian prince................Esth. 1:13, 14

Merib-baal—*Baal contends*

Another name for Mephibosheth...............1 Chr. 8:34

Merit—*reward given for something done additionally*

A. *Of man, impossible because:*
None is good..............Rom. 3:12
None is righteous..........Rom. 3:10
We are all sinful...........Is. 6:5
Our good comes from God...1 Cor. 15:9, 10
Our righteousness:
Is unavailing..............Matt. 5:20
Is Christ's................2 Cor. 5:21
Cannot save...............Rom. 10:1-4

B. *Of Christ:*
Secured by obedience.......Rom. 5:17-21
Secured by his death........Is. 53:10-12
Obtained by faith..........Phil. 3:8, 9

Merodach—*bold*

Supreme deity of the Babylonians..............Jer. 50:2
Otherwise called Bel..........Is. 46:1

Merodach-baladan—*Merodach has given a son*

Sends ambassadors to Hezekiah...................Is. 39:1-8
Also called Berodach-baladan...2 Kin. 20:12

Merom—*high place*

Lake on Jordan north of the Sea of Galilee.....................Josh. 11:5, 7

Meronothite

Citizen of Meronoth..........1 Chr. 27:30

Meroz—*refuge*

Town cursed for failing to help the Lord.....................Judg. 5:23

Merry—*a spirit of gaiety*

A. *Good, comes from:*
Heart.....................Prov. 15:13, 15
Restoration...............Jer. 30:18, 19
Christian joy..............James 5:13

SUBJECT REFERENCE

B. *Evil, results from:*
Careless unconcern..........Judg. 9:27
Gluttony...................1 Sam. 25:36
False optimism..............1 Kin. 21:7
Sinful glee.................Rev. 11:10

Mesha—*retreat*

1. Border of Joktan's descendants..............Gen. 10:30
2. Benjamite.................1 Chr. 8:8, 9
3. Son of Caleb...............1 Chr. 2:42
4. King of Moab..............2 Kin. 3:4

Meshach—*the shadow of the prince*

Name given to Mishael.........Dan. 1:7
Advanced to high position......Dan. 2:49
Remains faithful in testing......Dan. 3:13-30

Meshech—*tall*

1. Son of Japheth.............Gen. 10:2
Called Mesech.............Ps. 120:5
Famous traders............Ezek. 27:13
Confederates with Gog......Ezek. 38:2, 3
Inhabitants of the nether world....................Ezek. 32:18, 26
2. Son of Shem...............1 Chr. 1:17
Same as Mash.............Gen. 10:23

Meshelemiah—*Jehovah repays*

Father of Zechariah............1 Chr. 9:21
Porter in the Temple..........1 Chr. 26:1
Called Shelemiah..............1 Chr. 26:14

Meshezabeel—*God delivers*

1. Postexilic wall repairer......Neh. 3:4
2. One who signs covenant.....Neh. 10:21
3. Judahite....................Neh. 11:24

Meshillemith—*recompense*

Postexilic priest...............1 Chr. 9:10-12
Called Meshillemoth...........Neh. 11:13

Meshillemoth—*acts of recompense*

Ephraimite leader.............2 Chr. 28:12

Meshobab—*restored*

Descendant of Simeon.........1 Chr. 4:34-38

Meshullam—*recompensed; rewarded*

1,2,3. Three Benjamites.........1 Chr. 8:17
4. Gadite leader...............1 Chr. 5:11, 13
5. Shaphan's grandfather......2 Kin. 22:3
6. Hilkiah's father............1 Chr. 9:11
7. Son of Zerubbabel..........1 Chr. 3:19
8. Priest.....................1 Chr. 9:10-12
9. Kohathite overseer..........2 Chr. 34:12
10. Man commissioned to secure Levites....................Ezra 8:16
11. Levite who supports Ezra's reforms..................Ezra 10:15
12. One who divorced his foreign wife....................Ezra 10:29
13. Postexilic workman.........Neh. 3:4, 30
His daughter married Tobiah's son....................Neh. 6:18
14. Postexilic workman.........Neh. 3:6
15. One of Ezra's attendants....Neh. 8:4
16, 17. Two priests who sign covenant...................Neh. 10:7, 20
18, 19. Two priests in Joiakim's time....................Neh. 12:13, 16
20. Porter.....................Neh. 12:25
21. Participant in dedication services..................Neh. 12:33

Meshullemeth—*feminine form of Meshullam*

Wife of King Manasseh........2 Kin. 21:18, 19

Mesobaite—*found of Jehovah*

Title given Jasiel..............1 Chr. 11:47

Mesopotamia—*the country between two rivers*

Abraham's native home.......Acts 7:2
Place of Laban's household.....Gen. 24:4, 10, 29
Called:
Padan-aram...................Gen. 25:20
Syria.........................Gen. 31:20, 24
Balaam came from............Deut. 23:4
Israel enslaved to.............Judg. 3:8, 10

M

SUBJECT — REFERENCE

Chariots and horsemen hired from .... 1 Chr. 19:6
Called Haran; conquered by Sennacherib .... 2 Kin. 19:12, 16
People from, at Pentecost .... Acts 2:9

Mess—*a portion of food*

Set before Joseph's brothers .... Gen. 43:30, 34
Provided for Uriah .... 2 Sam. 11:8

Messenger—*one sent on a mission*

A. *Mission of, to:*

Appease wrath .... Gen. 32:3-6
Ask for favors .... Num. 20:14-17
Spy out .... Josh. 6:17, 25
Assemble a nation .... Judg. 6:35
Secure provisions .... 1 Sam. 25:4-14
Relay news .... 1 Sam. 11:3-9
Stir up war .... Judg. 11:12-28
Sue for peace .... 2 Sam. 3:12, 13
Offer sympathy .... 1 Chr. 19:2
Call for help .... 2 Kin. 17:4
Issue an ultimatum .... 1 Kin. 20:2-9
Deliver the LORD's message .... Hag. 1:13

B. *Reception of:*

Rejected .... Deut. 2:26-30
Humiliated .... 1 Chr. 19:2-4
Rebuked .... 2 Kin. 1:2-5, 16

C. *Significant examples of:*

John the Baptist .... Mal. 3:1
Paul's thorn .... 2 Cor. 12:7
Gospel workers .... 2 Cor. 8:23; Phil. 2:25

Messiah, the

A. *Described as:*

Seed of woman .... Gen. 3:15
Promised seed .... Gen. 12:1-3; Gal. 3:16
Star out of Jacob .... Num. 24:17; Luke 3:34
Of Judah's tribe .... Gen. 49:10; Heb. 7:14
Son of David .... Is. 11:1-10; Matt. 1:1
Prophet .... Deut. 18:15-19; Acts 3:22, 23
Priest after Melchizedek's order .... Ps. 110:4; Heb. 6:20
King of David's line .... Jer. 23:5; Luke 1:32, 33
Son of God .... Ps. 2:7, 8; Acts 13:33
Son of Man .... Dan. 7:13; Mark 8:38
Immanuel .... Is. 7:14; Matt. 1:22, 23
Branch .... Jer. 23:5; Zech. 3:8
Headstone .... Ps. 118:22; 1 Pet. 2:4, 7
Servant .... Is. 42:1-4; Matt. 12:18, 21

B. *Mission of, to:*

Introduce the new covenant .... Jer. 31:31-34; Matt. 26:26-30
Preach the Gospel .... Is. 61:1-3; Luke 4:17-19
Bring peace .... Is. 9:6, 7; Heb. 2:14-16
Die for man's sin .... Is. 53:4-6; 1 Pet. 1:18-20
Unite God's people .... Is. 19:23-25; Eph. 2:11-22
Call the Gentiles .... Is. 11:10; Rom. 15:9-12
Be a priest .... Zech. 6:12, 13; Heb. 1:3; Heb. 8:1
Rule from David's throne .... Ps. 45:5-7; Acts 2:30-36
Destroy Satan .... Rom. 16:20; 1 John 3:8
Bring in everlasting righteousness .... Dan. 9:24; Matt. 3:15; 2 Cor. 5:21

C. *Christ the true Messiah, proved by:*

Birth at Bethlehem .... Mic. 5:2; Luke 2:4-7
Born of a virgin .... Is. 7:14; Matt. 1:18-25
Appearing in the second Temple .... Hag. 2:7, 9; John 18:20
Working miracles .... Is. 35:5, 6; Matt. 11:4, 5
Rejection by the Jews .... John 1:11
Vicarious death .... Is. 53:1-12; 1 Pet. 3:18
Coming at the appointed time .... Dan. 9:24-27; Mark 1:15

D. *Other prophecies concerning:*

Worship .... Ps. 72:10-15; Matt. 2:1-11
Flight to Egypt .... Hos. 11:1; Matt. 2:13-15
Forerunner .... Mal. 3:1; Mark 1:1-8
Zeal .... Ps. 69:9; John 2:17
Triumphal entry .... Zech. 9:9, 10; Matt. 21:1-11
Betrayal .... Ps. 41:9; Mark 14:10
Being sold .... Zech. 11:12; Matt. 26:15
Silent defense .... Is. 53:7; Matt. 26:62, 63
Being spit on .... Is. 50:6; Mark 14:65
Being crucified with sinners .... Is. 53:12; Matt. 27:38
Piercing of hands and feet .... Ps. 22:16; John 19:36, 37
Being mocked .... Ps. 22:6-8; Matt. 27:39-44
Dying drink .... Ps. 69:21; John 19:29
Prayer for the enemies .... Ps. 109:4; Luke 23:34
Side pierced .... Zech. 12:10; John 19:34
Garments gambled for .... Ps. 22:18; Mark 15:24
Death without broken bones .... Ps. 34:20; John 19:33
Separation from God .... Ps. 22:1; Matt. 27:46
Burial with the rich .... Is. 53:9; Matt. 27:57-60
Preservation from decay .... Ps. 16:8-10; Acts 2:31
Ascension .... Ps. 68:18; Eph. 4:8-10
Exaltation .... Ps. 2:6-12; Phil. 2:9, 10

See Christ

Metallurgy—*mining and processing of metal*

Mining and refining .... Job 28:1, 2
Heat needed .... Jer. 6:29

Metaphors—*graphic comparisons*

A. *Concerning God, as:*

Rock .... Deut. 32:4
Sun and shield .... Ps. 84:11
Consuming fire .... Heb. 12:29
Husbandman .... John 15:1

B. *Concerning Christ, as:*

Bread of life .... John 6:35
Light of the world .... John 8:12
Door .... John 10:9
Good Shepherd .... John 10:14
Way, Truth, Life .... John 14:6
True vine .... John 15:1

C. *Concerning Christians, as:*

Light .... Matt. 5:14
Salt .... Matt. 5:13
Epistles .... 2 Cor. 3:3
Living stones .... 1 Pet. 2:5

D. *Concerning the Bible, as:*

Fire .... Jer. 5:14
Hammer .... Jer. 23:29
Light; lamp .... Ps. 119:105
Sword .... Eph. 6:17

Mete—*to measure*

Dry measure .... Ex. 16:18
Linear measure .... Is. 40:12
Figurative measure .... Matt. 7:2

Metheg-ammah—*power of the metropolis*

Probably a figurative name for Gath .... 2 Sam. 8:1

Methuselah—*man of a javelin*

Son of Enoch .... Gen. 5:21
Oldest man on record .... Gen. 5:27
Ancestor of Christ .... Luke 3:37

Methusael—*man of God*

Cainite, father of Lamech .... Gen. 4:18
See Maon

Mezahab—*waters of gold*

Grandfather of Mehetabel, wife of King Hadar .... Gen. 36:39

Mibhar—*choice*

One of David's mighty men .... 1 Chr. 11:38

Mibsam—*sweet odor*

1. Son of Ishmael .... Gen. 25:13
2. Simeonite .... 1 Chr. 4:25

Mibzar—*stronghold*

Edomite duke .... Gen. 36:42

Mica, Micah—*who is like Jehovah?*

1. Ephraimite who hires a traveling Levite .... Judg. 17:1-13
2. Reubenite .... 1 Chr. 5:1, 5
3. Son of Mephibosheth .... 2 Sam. 9:12
4. Descendant of Asaph .... 1 Chr. 9:15; Called Michaiah .... Neh. 12:35
5. Kohathite Levite .... 1 Chr. 23:20
6. Father of Abdon .... 2 Chr. 34:20
7. Prophet, contemporary of Isaiah .... Is. 1:1; Mic. 1:1
8. One who signs the covenant .... Neh. 10:11

Micah, the Book of—*a book of the Old Testament*

Judgment of Israel and Judah .... Mic. 1:2-16
Promise to the remnant .... Mic. 2:12, 13
Judgment on those in authority .... Mic. 3:1-12
The coming peace .... Mic. 4:1-8
The Redeemer from Bethlehem .... Mic. 5:1-4
Hope in God .... Mic. 7:8-20

Micaiah, Michaiah—*who is like Jehovah?*

1. Wife of King Rehoboam .... 2 Chr. 13:2
2. Prophet who predicts Ahab's death .... 1 Kin. 22:8-28
3. Teaching official .... 2 Chr. 17:7
4. Father of Achbor .... 2 Kin. 22:12; Called Micah .... 2 Chr. 34:20
5. Contemporary of Jeremiah .... Jer. 36:11-13
6. Descendant of Asaph .... Neh. 12:35
7. Priest in dedication service .... Neh. 12:41

Michael—*who is like God?*

1. Father of an Asherite spy .... Num. 13:13
2, 3. Two Gadites .... 1 Chr. 5:13, 14
4. Levite ancestor of Asaph .... 1 Chr. 6:40
5. Issacharian chief .... 1 Chr. 7:3
6. Benjamite .... 1 Chr. 8:16
7. Manassite chief under David .... 1 Chr. 12:20
8. Father of Omri .... 1 Chr. 27:18
9. Son of King Jehoshaphat .... 2 Chr. 21:2
10. Father of Zebadiah .... Ezra 8:8
11. Chief prince .... Dan. 10:13, 21; Stands against forces .... Dan. 10:21; Disputes with Satan .... Jude 9; Fights the dragon .... Rev. 12:7-9

Michal—*who is like God?*

Daughter of King Saul .... 1 Sam. 14:49
Loves and marries David .... 1 Sam. 18:20-28
Saves David from Saul .... 1 Sam. 19:9-17
Given to Phalti .... 1 Sam. 25:44
David demands her from Abner .... 2 Sam. 3:13-16
Ridicules David; becomes barren .... 2 Sam. 6:16-23

Michmash, Michmas—*hidden place*

Town occupied by Saul's army .... 1 Sam. 13:2
Site of battle with Philistines .... 1 Sam. 13:5, 11, 16, 23
Scene of Jonathan's victory .... 1 Sam. 14:1-18

SUBJECT — REFERENCE

Mentioned in prophecy ... Is. 10:28
Exiles return ... Ezra 2:1, 27

Michmethah—*lurking place*
Place on the border of Ephraim and Manasseh ... Josh. 16:5, 6

Michri—*purchase price*
Benjamite ... 1 Chr. 9:8

Michtam
Word of unknown meaning used in titles of ... Ps. 16; 56-60

Middin—*extensions*
In the wilderness ... Josh. 15:61

Midian—*place of judgment*
1. Son of Abraham by Keturah ... Gen. 25:1-4
2. Region in the Arabian desert occupied by the Midianites ... Gen. 25:6

Midianites—*descendants of Midian*
A. *Characteristics of:*
Descendants of Abraham by Keturah ... Gen. 25:1, 2
Moses fled to ... Ex. 2:15
Retain worship of Jehovah ... Ex. 2:16
Ruled by kings ... Num. 31:8
Immoral people ... Num. 25:18
B. *Contacts with Israel:*
Joining Moab in cursing ... Num. 22:4-7
Seduction of ... Num. 25:1-18
Defeat because of ... Num. 31:1-18
Being sent as punishment ... Judg. 6:1-10

Midnight
A. *Significant happenings at:*
Death in Egypt ... Ex. 11:4
Prayer meeting ... Acts 16:25
Possible time of Christ's return ... Matt. 25:6
B. *Other happenings at:*
Quick departure ... Judg. 16:2, 3
Friend's need ... Luke 11:5
Great fear ... Job 34:20

Midwife—*one who assists at childbirth*
Helps in the birth of a child ... Gen. 35:17

Migdal-el—*tower of God*
City of Naphtali ... Josh. 19:38

Migdal-gad—*a tower of Gad* (fortune)
Town of Judah ... Josh. 15:37

Migdol—*tower*
1. Israelite encampment ... Ex. 14:2
2. Place in Egypt to which Jews flee ... Jer. 44:1

Might—*effective power*
A. *God's:*
Irresistible ... 2 Chr. 20:6
God's hand is ... 1 Chr. 29:12
Unutterable ... Ps. 106:2
B. *Man's physical:*
Boasted in, brings destruction ... Dan. 4:30-33
Not to be gloried in ... Deut. 8:17
Will fail ... Jer. 51:30
Exhortation concerning ... Eccl. 9:10
C. *Man's intellectual and moral:*
Invites self-glory ... Jer. 9:23
Makes salvation difficult ... 1 Cor. 1:26
D. *Man's spiritual, comes from:*
God ... Eph. 1:19
Christ ... Col. 1:28, 29
The Spirit ... Mic. 3:8

Mighty
Literally of:
Hunter ... Gen. 10:9
Nation ... Gen. 18:18
Prince ... Gen. 23:6
Waters ... Ex. 15:10
Hand ... Ex. 32:11
Acts ... Deut. 3:24
Deeds ... 2 Sam. 23:20
Men of valor ... 1 Chr. 7:9-11
Warrior ... 2 Chr. 32:21
Kings ... Ezra 4:20
Wind ... Job 8:2
Strength ... Job 9:4
Thunder ... Job 26:14
Fear ... Job 41:25

Mighty man—*a powerful man; a valiant warrior*
Men of renown ... Gen. 6:4
Gideon ... Judg. 6:11, 12
Warriors of David ... 2 Sam. 10:7

Migron—*precipitous* (very steep)
1. Place where Saul stayed ... 1 Sam. 14:2
2. Village north of Michmash ... Is. 10:28

Mijamin—*from the right side*
1. Descendant of Aaron ... 1 Chr. 24:1, 6, 9
2. Chief priest; returns with Zerubbabel ... Neh. 12:5, 7
Probably same as 1
3. Divorced his foreign wife ... Ezra 10:25
4. Priest who signs the covenant ... Neh. 10:7
Same as Miniamin in ... Neh. 12:17, 41

Mikhtam
Possible meaning is "Atonement Psalm," used in titles of ... Ps. 16—56, 60

Mikloth—*rods*
1. Ruler under David ... 1 Chr. 27:4
2. Benjamite ... 1 Chr. 8:32

Mikneiah—*possession of Jehovah*
Porter and musician in David's time ... 1 Chr. 15:18, 21

Milalai—*eloquent*
Levite musician in dedication service ... Neh. 12:36

Milcah—*counsel*
1. Wife of Nahor ... Gen. 11:29
Mother of eight children ... Gen. 22:20-22
Grandmother of Rebekah ... Gen. 22:23
2. Daughter of Zelophehad ... Num. 26:33

Milcom—*an Ammonite god*
Solomon went after ... 1 Kin. 11:5
Altar destroyed by Josiah ... 2 Kin. 23:12, 13

Mildew—*a disease of grain due to dampness*
Threatened as a punishment ... Deut. 28:22
Sent upon Israel ... Amos 4:9
Removed by repentance ... 1 Kin. 8:37-39

Mile—*a thousand paces* (about 12/13 of an English mile)
Used illustratively ... Matt. 5:41
See Jewish measures

Miletus—*a city of Asia Minor*
Paul meets Ephesian elders here ... Acts 20:15-38
Paul leaves Trophimus here ... 2 Tim. 4:20

Milk—*a white liquid secreted by mammary glands*
A. *Produced by:*
Goats ... Prov. 27:27
Sheep ... Deut. 32:14
Camels ... Gen. 32:15
Cows ... 1 Sam. 6:7, 10
Humans ... Is. 28:9
B. *Figurative of:*
Abundance ... Deut. 32:14
Egypt's supposed blessings ... Num. 16:13
Elementary teaching ... 1 Cor. 3:2
Pure doctrine ... 1 Pet. 2:2

Mill, millstone
A. *Uses of:*
Grinding grain ... Num. 11:8
Weapon ... Judg. 9:53
Pledge, forbidden ... Deut. 24:6
Weight ... Matt. 18:6
B. *Operated by:*
Women ... Matt. 24:41
Maidservant ... Ex. 11:5
Prisoners ... Judg. 16:21
C. *Figurative of:*
Courage ... Job 41:24
Old age ... Eccl. 12:4
Desolation ... Jer. 25:10

Millennium—*thousand years*
Latin for a thousand years ... Rev. 20:1-10

Millet—*a cereal*
Ezekiel makes bread of ... Ezek. 4:9

Millo—*terrace, elevation*
1. House or stronghold at Shechem, called Beth-millo ... Judg. 9:6, 20
2. Fort at Jerusalem ... 2 Sam. 5:9
Prepared by Solomon ... 1 Kin. 9:15
Strengthened by Hezekiah ... 2 Chr. 32:5
Scene of Joash's death ... 2 Kin. 12:20, 21

Mincing—*affected elegance in walking*
Denounced ... Is. 3:16

Mind—*the reasoning faculty*
A. *Faculties of:*
Perception ... Luke 9:47
Remembrance ... Titus 3:1
Reasoning ... Rom. 7:23, 25
Feelings ... 2 Sam. 17:8
Desire ... Neh. 4:6
Imagination ... Gen. 6:5
Purpose ... 2 Cor. 1:15, 17
B. *Of the unregenerate, described as:*
Alienated ... Ezek. 23:17-22
Despiteful ... Ezek. 36:5
Reprobate ... Rom. 1:28
Blinded ... 2 Cor. 3:14
Hostile ... Col. 1:21
Defiled ... Titus 1:15
C. *Of the regenerate, described as:*
Willing ... 1 Chr. 28:9
In peace ... Rom. 8:6
Right ... Luke 8:35
Renewed ... Rom. 12:2
Having Christ's ... 1 Cor. 2:16
Obedient ... Heb. 8:10
D. *Dangers of, to the Christian:*
Worry ... Luke 12:29
Doubt ... Rom. 14:5
Disunity ... Rom. 12:16
Phil. 4:2
Mental disturbance ... 2 Thess. 2:2
Spiritual disturbance ... Rom. 7:23, 25
Grow weary ... Heb. 12:3
E. *Exhortations concerning, to Christians:*
Love God with all ... Matt. 22:37

Minerals of the Bible
A. *Features concerning:*
Mined ... Job 28:1-11
Plentiful in Canaan ... Deut. 8:9
Refined by fire ... Ezek. 22:18, 20
Trade in ... Ezek. 27:12
B. *List of:*
Asphalt (bitumen) ... Gen. 11:3
Brass ... Num. 21:9
Brimstone (sulphur) ... Deut. 29:23
Chalk ... Is. 27:9
Clay ... Is. 41:25
Copper (brass) ... Deut. 8:9
Coral ... Job 28:18
Flint ... Deut. 32:13
Gold ... Gen. 2:11, 12
Iron ... Gen. 4:22
Lead ... Job 19:24
Lime ... Amos 2:1
Nitre ... Jer. 2:22
Salt ... Gen. 14:3
Sand ... Prov. 27:3
Silver ... Gen. 44:2
Slime (asphalt) ... Gen. 6:14
Tin ... Num. 31:22

Mingle, mix—*to put different elements together*
A. *Instances of:*
Offerings ... Lev. 2:4, 5
Garment ... Lev. 19:19
Judgments ... Rev. 8:7
Human sacrifice ... Luke 13:1
Intermarriage ... Ezra 9:2
B. *Figurative of:*
Sorrow ... Ps. 102:9
Wisdom ... Prov. 9:2, 5
Instability ... Is. 19:14

SUBJECT REFERENCE

Severity ....Ps. 75:8
Impurity ....Is. 1:22
Intoxication ....Is. 5:22
Worldliness....................Hos. 7:8

Miniamin—*fortunate*

1. Levite assistant ....2 Chr. 31:14, 15
2. Postexilic priest ....Neh. 12:17
3. Priestly participant in dedication ....Neh. 12:41

Minish—*obsolete for diminish*

To make something less ....Ex. 5:19

Minister—*one who serves*

A. *Descriptive of:*

Proclaiming the Word.......Acts 13:5
Court attendants ....1 Kin. 10:5
Angels ....Ps. 103:20
Priests and Levites.........Joel 1:9, 13
Servant ....Matt. 20:22-27
Ruler ....Rom. 13:4, 6
Christ....................Rom. 15:8
Christ's messengers ....1 Cor. 3:5
False teachers..............2 Cor. 11:15

B. *Christian, qualifications of:*

Able to teach ....1 Tim. 3:2
Courageous................Acts 20:22-24
Diligent ....1 Cor. 15:10
Faithful ....Rom. 15:17-19
Impartial ....1 Tim. 5:21
Industrious ....2 Cor. 10:12-16
Meek ....2 Tim. 2:25
Obedient ....Acts 16:9, 10
Persevering ....2 Cor. 11:23-33
Prayerful ....Acts 6:4
Sincere....................2 Cor. 4:1, 2
Spirit-filled ....Acts 1:8
Studious ....1 Tim. 4:13, 15
Sympathetic ....Heb. 5:2
Temperate....................1 Cor. 9:25-27
Willing....................1 Pet. 5:2
Worthy of imitation ....1 Tim. 4:12

C. *Sins to avoid:*

Arrogance ....1 Pet. 5:3
Contentiousness ....Titus 1:7
Discouragement ....2 Cor. 4:8, 9
Insincerity....................Phil. 1:15, 16
Perverting the truth ....2 Cor. 11:3-15
Unfaithfulness ....Matt. 24:48-51

D. *Duties of:*

Preach:

Gospel....................1 Cor. 1:17
Christ crucified ....1 Cor. 1:23
Christ's riches..............Eph. 3:8-12
Feed the Church ....John 21:15-17
Edify the Church ....Eph. 4:12
Pray for people ....Col. 1:9
Teach....................2 Tim. 2:2
Exhort ....Titus 1:9
Rebuke ....Titus 2:15
Warn of apostasy ....2 Tim. 4:2-5
Comfort ....2 Cor. 1:4-6
Win souls ....1 Cor. 9:19-23

E. *Attitude of believers toward:*

Pray for....................Eph. 6:18-20
Follow the example of ....1 Cor. 11:1
Obey ....1 Cor. 4:1, 2
Esteem highly ....1 Thess. 5:12, 13
Provide for ....1 Cor. 9:6-18

Minni—*a people* (Manneans) *of Armenia*

Summoned to destroy Babylon ....Jer. 51:27

Minnith—*distribution*

Wheat-growing Ammonite town ....Ezek. 27:17

Minority—*the lesser number*

On God's side ....Num. 14:1-10
To be preferred ....Ex. 23:2
Saved are ....Matt. 7:13-23

Minstrel—*a player of an instrument*

Used by Elisha..............2 Kin. 3:15
Among funeral attendants ......Matt. 9:23

Mint—*a fragrant herb*

Tithed by Pharisees............Matt. 23:23

SUBJECT REFERENCE

Miphkad—*appointed place*

Gate of Jerusalem rebuilt by Nehemiah ....Neh. 3:31

Miracle

A. *Described:*

Signs ....Acts 4:30
Wonders ....Acts 6:8
Works ....John 10:25-38

B. *Kinds of, over:*

Nature....................Josh. 10:12-14
Animals....................Num. 22:28
Human beings ....Gen. 19:26
Nations ....Ex. 10:1, 2
Sickness and disease ....2 Kin. 5:10-14
Natural laws ....2 Kin. 6:5-7
Future events ....2 Kin. 8:8-13
Death....................John 11:41-44

C. *Produced by:*

God's power ....Acts 15:12
Christ's power ....Matt. 10:1
Spirit's power ....Matt. 12:28

D. *Design of:*

Manifest:

God's glory..................John 11:40-42
Christ's glory ....John 2:11
God's presence..............Judg. 6:11-24
Proof of God's messengers ....Ex. 4:2-9
Produce obedience.........Ex. 16:4
Vindicate God ....Ex. 17:4-7
Produce faith ....John 20:30, 31
Proof of Jesus as the Messiah....................Matt. 11:2-5
Signs of a true apostle .....2 Cor. 12:12
Authenticate the Gospel....Rom. 15:18, 19
Fulfill prophecy ....John 12:37-41

E. *Effect of, upon people:*

Forced acknowledgment .....John 11:47
Acts 4:16
Amazement..................Mark 6:49-51
Faith ....John 2:23
John 11:42
God glorified ....Matt. 9:1-8

F. *False:*

Not to be followed ....Deut. 13:1-3
Sign of antichrist ....2 Thess. 2:3, 9
Rev. 13:13
Predicted by Christ ....Matt. 24:24

G. *Evidence of:*

Logic ....John 9:16
Sufficient to convince ....John 3:2
John 6:14
Insufficient to convince ......Luke 16:31
John 12:37
Sought by Jews ....John 2:18
Demanded unreasonably ....Matt. 27:42, 43
Incurs guilt ....Matt. 11:20-24
John 15:24

Miracles of the Bible—*Old Testament*

Creation ....Gen. 1:1-27
Enoch's translation ....Gen. 5:24
The Flood....................Gen. 7:17-24
Confusion of tongues at Babel ..Gen. 11:3-9
Sodom and Gomorrah destroyed ....Gen. 19:24
Lot's wife turned to a pillar of salt....................Gen. 19:26
Ass speaking ....Num. 22:21-35

Those associated with Moses and Aaron:

Burning bush ....Ex. 3:3
Moses' rod changed into a serpent ....Ex. 4:3, 4, 30
Moses' hand made leprous......Ex. 4:6, 7, 30
Aaron's rod changed into a serpent ....Ex. 7:8-10

Ten plagues:

River turned to blood.........Ex. 7:20-25
Frogs....................Ex. 8:1-15
Lice ....Ex. 8:16-19
Flies ....Ex. 8:20-24
Murrain ....Ex. 9:1-7
Boils ....Ex. 9:8-12
Hail....................Ex. 9:18-24
Locusts ....Ex. 10:1-20
Darkness....................Ex. 10:21-23
First-born destroyed ....Ex. 12:29-30

Pillar of cloud and fire ....Ex. 13:21-22
Ex. 14:19-20

SUBJECT REFERENCE

Crossing the sea...............Ex. 14:21, 23
Bitter waters sweetened ....Ex. 15:25
Manna sent ....Ex. 16:13-36
Water from the rock at Rephidim ....Ex. 17:5-8
Amalek defeated ....Ex. 17:9-13
Fire on Aaron's sacrifice ....Lev. 9:24
Nadab and Abihu devoured .....Lev. 10:1, 2
Israel's judgment by fire........Num. 11:1-3
Miriam's leprosy ....Num. 12:10-15
Destruction of Korah ....Num. 16:31-35
Aaron's rod blossoms ....Num. 17:8
Water from the rock in Kadesh ....Num. 20:8-11
Brass serpent ....Num. 21:9

Those associated with Joshua:

Jordan divided ....Josh. 3:14-17
Fall of Jericho ....Josh. 6:6-20
Sun and moon stand still ....Josh. 10:12-14

Those associated with Samson:

Lion killed ....Judg. 14:5, 6
Thirty Philistines killed.........Judg. 14:19
Water from the hollow place in Lehi....................Judg. 15:19
Gates of the city carried away...Judg. 16:3
Dagon's house pulled down .....Judg. 16:29, 30

Those associated with Elijah:

Drought ....1 Kin. 17:1
James 5:17
Fed by ravens ....1 Kin. 17:4-6
Widow's oil and meal increased....................1 Kin. 17:12-16
Widow's son raised from dead ..1 Kin. 17:17-23
Sacrifice consumed by fire ......1 Kin. 18:38
Rain in answer to prayer ....1 Kin. 18:41
Captains consumed by fire......2 Kin. 1:9-12
Jordan divided ....2 Kin. 2:8
Translated to heaven in a chariot of fire....................2 Kin. 2:11

Those associated with Elisha:

Jordan divided ....2 Kin. 2:14
Waters of Jericho healed ....2 Kin. 2:20-22
Mocking young men destroyed by bears....................2 Kin. 2:24
Water supplied for Jehoshaphat ....2 Kin. 3:16-20
Widow's oil multiplied ....2 Kin. 4:1-7
Shunammite's child raised from dead ....2 Kin. 4:19-37
Poisoned pottage made harmless ....2 Kin. 4:38-41
Hundred fed with twenty loaves ....2 Kin. 4:42-44
Naaman cured of leprosy.......2 Kin. 5:10-14
Gehazi struck with leprosy......2 Kin. 5:27
Axe head caused to float ....2 Kin. 6:5-7
Ben-hadad's plans revealed .....2 Kin. 6:8-13
Syrian army defeated ....2 Kin. 6:18-20
Revival of a man by touch with Elisha's bones....................2 Kin. 13:21

Those associated with Isaiah:

Hezekiah healed...............2 Kin. 20:7
Shadow turns backward on sun dial ....2 Kin. 20:11

Other miracles of the Old Testament:

Dew on Gideon's fleece ....Judg. 6:37-40
Dagon's fall before the ark .....1 Sam. 5:1-12
Men of Beth-shemesh destroyed ....1 Sam. 6:19, 20
Thunder and rain in harvest ....1 Sam. 12:18
Uzzah's death..................2 Sam. 6:6, 7
Jeroboam's hand withered and restored ....1 Kin. 13:4-6
Rending of the altar ....1 Kin. 13:5
Sennacherib's army destroyed ...2 Kin. 19:35
Uzziah afflicted with leprosy ....2 Chr. 26:16-21
Three men protected from the fiery furnace ....Dan. 3:19-27
Daniel delivered from the lion's den ....Dan. 6:16-23
Preservation of Jonah in stomach of fish three days....................Jon. 2:1-10

Miracles of the Bible—*New Testament*

Of Christ (listed chronologically):

Water made wine (Cana) ....John 2:1-11
Son of nobleman healed (Cana)....................John 4:46-54
Passed unseen through crowd (Nazareth) ....Luke 4:28-30

SUBJECT	REFERENCE
Man with unclean spirit in synagogue cured (Capernaum)	Mark 1:23-26 Luke 4:33-35
Peter's mother-in-law healed (Capernaum)	Matt. 8:14-17 Mark 1:29-31 Luke 4:38-39
Net full of fishes (Lower Galilee)	Luke 5:1-11
Leper cleansed (Capernaum)	Matt. 8:1-4 Mark 1:40-45 Luke 5:12-15
Paralytic cured (Capernaum)	Matt. 9:1-8 Mark 2:3-12 Luke 5:18-26
Man healed (Jerusalem)	John 5:1-9
Withered hand restored (Galilee)	Matt. 12:10-13 Mark 3:1-5 Luke 6:6-11
Centurion's servant cured of palsy (Capernaum)	Matt. 8:5-13 Luke 7:1-10
Widow's son raised from dead (Nain)	Luke 7:11-17
Demon-possessed man healed (Galilee)	Matt. 12:22, 23 Luke 11:14
Tempest stilled (Lower Galilee)	Matt. 8:23-27 Mark 4:37-41 Luke 8:22-25
Two demon-possessed men cured (Gadara)	Matt. 8:28-34 Mark 5:1-20 Luke 8:26-39
Raised Jairus' daughter (Capernaum)	Matt. 9:23 Mark 5:23 Luke 8:41
Woman with issue of blood healed (Capernaum)	Matt. 9:20-22 Mark 5:25-34 Luke 8:43-48
Blind men cured (Capernaum)	Matt. 9:27-31
Dumb spirit cast out (Capernaum)	Matt. 9:32, 33
Five thousand fed (Lower Galilee)	Matt. 14:15-21 Mark 6:35-44 Luke 9:10-17 John 6:1-14
Walking on the sea (Lower Galilee)	Matt. 14:25-33 Mark 6:48-52 John 6:15-21
Syrophoenician's daughter healed (District of Tyre)	Matt. 15:21-28 Mark 7:24-30
Four thousand fed (Lower Galilee)	Matt. 15:32-39 Mark 8:1-9
Deaf and dumb man cured (Lower Galilee)	Mark 7:31-37
Blind man healed (Bethsaida)	Mark 8:22-26
Demon cast out of boy (near Caesarea)	Matt. 17:14-18 Mark 9:14-29 Luke 9:37-43
Tribute money provided (Capernaum)	Matt. 17:24-27
Passed unseen through crowd (in Temple)	John 8:59
Ten lepers cleansed (Samaria)	Luke 17:11-19
Man born blind, healed (Jerusalem)	John 9:1-7
Lazarus raised from dead (Bethany)	John 11:38-44
Woman with sickness cured (Peraea)	Luke 13:11-17
Man with dropsy cured (Peraea)	Luke 14:1-6
Two blind men cured (Jericho)	Matt. 20:29-34 Mark 10:46-52 Luke 18:35-43
Fig tree withered (Mt. Olivet)	Matt. 21:18-22 Mark 11:12-14
Malchus' ear healed (Gethsemane)	Luke 22:50, 51
Second net full of fishes (Lower Galilee)	John 21:1-14
Resurrection of Christ	Luke 24:6 John 10:18
Appearances of Christ after his resurrection, to:	
Mary Magdalene (Jerusalem)	Mark 16:9
Other women (Jerusalem)	Matt. 28:9
Two disciples (Emmaus)	Luke 24:15-31
Peter (Jerusalem)	1 Cor. 15:5
Ten apostles, Thomas absent (Jerusalem)	John 20:19, 24
Eleven apostles, Thomas present (Jerusalem)	John 20:26-28
Seven disciples fishing (Lower Galilee)	John 21:1-24
Eleven apostles (Galilee)	Matt. 28:16, 17
Five hundred brethren	1 Cor. 15:6
James	1 Cor. 15:7
Eleven apostles on day of His ascension (Bethany)	Acts 1:2-9

SUBJECT	REFERENCE
Paul at his conversion	Acts 9:1-5 1 Cor. 15:8
Those associated with Peter:	
Lame man cured	Acts 3:6
Death of Ananias and Sapphira	Acts 5:5, 10
Sick healed	Acts 5:15
Aeneas healed of palsy	Acts 9:34
Dorcas restored to life	Acts 9:40
His release from prison	Acts 12:7-11
Those associated with Paul:	
His sight restored	Acts 9:17-18 Acts 22:12-13
Elymas blinded	Acts 13:11
Lame man cured	Acts 14:10
Damsel freed of evil spirits	Acts 16:18 Acts 19:11, 12
Earthquake at Philippi	Acts 16:25, 26
Evil spirits overcame Sceva's seven sons	Acts 19:13-16
Eutychus restored to life	Acts 20:10
Unharmed by viper's bite	Acts 28:5
Publius' father healed	Acts 28:8
Other miracles of the New Testament:	
Outpouring of the Holy Spirit	Acts 2:1-14
Gift of tongues	Acts 2:3, 4, 11 Acts 10:46 Acts 19:6
Apostles freed from prison	Acts 5:19 Acts 12:7-11
Agabus' prophesies	Acts 11:28 Acts 21:11
Visions:	
Three apostles'	Matt. 17:2 Luke 9:32
Of Christ, by dying:	
Stephen	Acts 7:55, 56
Ananias'	Acts 9:10
Peter's	Acts 10:1-48 Acts 11:1-30
Cornelius'	Acts 10:3, 4, 30-32
Paul's	Acts 16:9 2 Cor. 12:1-5
John's on Patmos	Rev. 1:10 Rev. 4—22
Miracles by the seventy	Luke 10:17
Stephen performed great miracles	Acts 6:8
Philip cast out unclean spirits	Acts 8:6-13

Miracles pretended, or false

SUBJECT	REFERENCE
Egyptian magicians	Ex. 7:11-22 Ex. 8:18, 19
In support of false religions	Deut. 13:1-3
Witch of Endor	1 Sam. 28:9-12
False prophets	Matt. 7:22, 23 Matt. 24:24
False christs	Matt. 24:24
Deceive the ungodly	Rev. 13:13 Rev. 19:20
Sign of apostasy	2 Thess. 2:3, 9 Rev. 13:13

Mire—*deep mud*

SUBJECT	REFERENCE
A. *Places of:*	
Dungeon	Jer. 38:22
Streets	Is. 10:6
B. *Figurative of:*	
Affliction	Job 30:19
External prosperity	Job 8:11
Insecurity	Is. 57:20
Subjection	2 Sam. 22:43
Plentifulness	Zech. 9:3

Miriam—*obstinacy* (stubbornness)

SUBJECT	REFERENCE
1. Sister of Aaron and Moses	Num. 26:59
Chosen by God; called a prophetess	Ex. 15:20
Leads in victory song	Ex. 15:20, 21
Punished for rebellion	Num. 12:1-16
Buried at Kadesh	Num. 20:1
2. Judahite	1 Chr. 4:17

Mirma—*deceit*

SUBJECT	REFERENCE
Benjamite	1 Chr. 8:10

Mirror

SUBJECT	REFERENCE
In the tabernacle	Ex. 38:8
Of molten brass	Job 37:18
Used figuratively	1 Cor. 13:12 2 Cor. 3:18 James 1:23, 25

Mirth—*a spirit of gaiety*

SUBJECT	REFERENCE
Occasions of	Gen. 31:27 Neh. 8:10-12
Absence of	Jer. 25:10, 11 Hos. 2:11
Inadequacy of	Prov. 14:13 Eccl. 2:1, 2

Miscarriage—*premature ejection of a fetus from the mother's womb, resulting in the death of the fetus.*

SUBJECT	REFERENCE
Wished for	Job 3:16 Eccl. 6:3
Against the wicked	Ps. 58:8

Miscegenation—*intermarriage of different races*

SUBJECT	REFERENCE
A. Restrictions in Law of Moses	Ex. 34:12-16
B. *Notable examples:*	
Moses	Num. 12:1-10
Ruth	Matt. 1:5
C. *Unity of all races:*	
Descended from Adam	Gen. 3:20 Rom. 5:12
From one	Acts 17:26
D. *Christian marriage:*	
Spiritual basis	Matt. 19:6
In the Lord	1 Cor. 7:39 2 Cor. 6:14

Mischief—*harm; evil*

SUBJECT	REFERENCE
A. *Descriptive of:*	
Moral evil	Ps. 36:4
Physical harm	Ex. 21:22, 23
Trouble	1 Kin. 11:25
B. *Of the wicked, they:*	
Boast	Ps. 52:1
Devise	Ps. 62:3 Prov. 6:14
Practice	1 Sam. 23:9 Prov. 10:23
Run to	Prov. 6:18
Think to do	Neh. 6:2
Seek	1 Kin. 20:7

Miser—*a covetous man*

SUBJECT	REFERENCE
A. *Characteristics of:*	
Selfish	Eccl. 4:8
Covetous	Luke 12:15
Divided loyalty	Matt. 6:24
B. *Punishment of:*	
Dissatisfaction	Eccl. 5:10
Loss	Matt. 6:19
Sorrows	1 Tim. 6:10
Destruction	Ps. 52:5, 7
C. *Examples of:*	
Rich fool	Luke 12:16-21
Rich ruler	Luke 18:18-23
Ananias and Sapphira	Acts 5:1-11

Miserable—*the wretched*

SUBJECT	REFERENCE
A. *State of:*	
Wicked	Rom. 3:12-16
Trapped	Rom. 7:24
Lost	Luke 13:25-28
B. *Caused by:*	
Forgetfulness of God	Is. 22:12-14
Ignorance	Luke 19:42-44

Misfortune—*an unexpected adversity*

SUBJECT	REFERENCE
Explained by the nations	Deut. 29:24-28
Misunderstood by Gideon	Judg. 6:13
Understood by David	2 Sam. 16:5-13
Caused by sin	Is. 59:1, 2

Misgab—*high place*

SUBJECT	REFERENCE
Moabite city	Jer. 48:1
Capital of Moab	Is. 15:1
Translated "high fort"	Is. 25:12

Mishael—*who is like God?*

SUBJECT	REFERENCE
1. Kohathite Levite	Ex. 6:22
Removes dead bodies	Lev. 10:4, 5
2. Hebrew name of Meshach	Dan. 1:6-19
3. One of Ezra's assistants	Neh. 8:4

Mishal, Misheal

SUBJECT	REFERENCE
Town in Asher	Josh. 19:24, 26
Assigned to Levites	Josh. 21:30
Called Mashal	1 Chr. 6:74

SUBJECT REFERENCE

Misham—*swift*
Son of Elpaal . . . . . 1 Chr. 8:12

Mishma—*hearing*
1. Son of Ishmael . . . . . Gen. 25:13, 14; 1 Chr. 1:30
2. Descendant of Simeon . . . . . 1 Chr. 4:25

Mishmannah—*fatness*
One of David's Gadite warriors . . . . . 1 Chr. 12:10

Mishraites
Family living in Kirjath-jearim . . 1 Chr. 2:53

Mispar—*writing*
Exile returnee . . . . . Ezra 2:2
Called Mispereth . . . . . Neh. 7:7

Misrephoth-maim—*burning of waters*
Haven of fleeing Canaanites . . . . Josh. 11:8
Near the Sidonians . . . . . Josh. 13:6

Missionaries—*those sent out to spread the Gospel*
Jonah . . . . . Jon. 3:2, 3
The early church . . . . . Acts 8:4
Philip . . . . . Acts 8:5
Some from Cyrene become missionaries . . . . . Acts 11:20
Paul and Barnabas . . . . . Acts 13:1-4
Peter . . . . . Acts 15:7
Apollos . . . . . Acts 18:24
Noah . . . . . 2 Pet. 2:5

Mission of Christ
Do God's will . . . . . John 6:38
Save sinners . . . . . Luke 19:10
Bring in everlasting righteousness . . . . . Dan. 9:24
Destroy Satan's works . . . . . Heb. 2:14; 1 John 3:8
Fulfill the Old Testament . . . . . Matt. 5:17
Give life . . . . . John 10:10, 28
Stop sacrifices . . . . . Dan. 9:27
Complete revelation . . . . . Heb. 1:3

Missions
A. *Commands concerning:*
"Shall be" . . . . . Matt. 24:14
"Go" . . . . . Matt. 28:18-20
"Tarry" . . . . . Luke 24:49
"Come" . . . . . Acts 16:9
B. *Motives prompting:*
God's love . . . . . John 3:16
Christ's love . . . . . 2 Cor. 5:14, 15
Mankind's need . . . . . Rom. 3:9-31
C. *Equipment for:*
Word . . . . . Rom. 10:14, 15
Spirit . . . . . Acts 1:8
Prayer . . . . . Acts 13:1-4

Mist—*a vapor* (physical and spiritual)
Physical (vapor) . . . . . Gen. 2:6
Spiritual (blindness) . . . . . Acts 13:11
Eternal (darkness) . . . . . 2 Pet. 2:17

Mistake—*an error arising from human weakness*
Causes of:
Motives misunderstood . . . . . Josh. 22:9-29
Appearance misjudged . . . . . 1 Sam. 1:13-15
Trust misplaced . . . . . Josh. 9:3-27

Mistress—*a married woman*
Over a maid . . . . . Gen. 16:4, 8, 9
Figurative of Nineveh . . . . . Nah. 3:4

Misunderstandings—*disagreements among*
Israelites . . . . . Josh. 22:9-29
Christ's disciples . . . . . Matt. 20:20-27
Apostles . . . . . Gal. 2:11-15
Christians . . . . . Acts 6:1

Misused—*putting to a wrong use*
Guilt of, brings wrath . . . . . 2 Chr. 36:16

Mite—*Jews' smallest coin*
Widow's . . . . . Mark 12:42

Mithcah—*sweetness*
Israelite encampment . . . . . Num. 33:28, 29

Mithnite
Descriptive of Joshaphat, David's officer . . . . . 1 Chr. 11:43

Mithredath—*consecrated to Mithra*
1. Treasurer of Cyrus . . . . . Ezra 1:8
2. Persian official . . . . . Ezra 4:7

Mitre, miter—*headdress or turban*
Worn by the high priest . . . . . Ex. 28:36-39
Inscription "Holiness to the Lord" worn on . . . . . Ex. 39:28-31
Worn by Aaron for anointing and on Day of Atonement . . . . . Lev. 8:9; Lev. 16:4
Uncovering of upper lip a sign of uncleanness and mourning . . . . . Lev. 13:45
Uncovering of, forbidden . . . . . Lev. 21:10-12
Removal of, because of sin . . . . . Ezek. 21:26
Symbolic restoration of . . . . . Zech. 3:5

Mitylene—*a city on the island of Lesbos*
Visited by Paul . . . . . Acts 20:13-15

Mix (see Mingle; Miscegenation)

Mizar—*small*
Hill east of Jordan . . . . . Ps. 42:6

Mizpah, Mizpeh—*watchtower*
1. Site of covenant between Jacob and Laban . . . . . Gen. 31:44-53
2. Town in Gilead; probably same as 1 . . . . . Judg. 10:17
Jephthah's home . . . . . Judg. 11:11, 29, 34
Probably same as Ramathmizpeh . . . . . Josh. 13:26
3. Region near Mt. Hermon . . . . Josh. 11:3, 8
4. Town in Judah . . . . . Josh. 15:1, 38
5. Place in Moab; David brings his parents to . . . . . 1 Sam. 22:3, 4
6. Town of Benjamin . . . . . Josh. 18:21, 26
Outraged Israelites gather here . . . . . Judg. 20:1, 3
Samuel gathers Israel . . . . . 1 Sam. 7:5-16; 1 Sam. 10:17-25
Built by Asa . . . . . 1 Sam. 15:22
Residence of Gedaliah . . . . . 2 Kin. 25:23, 25
Home of exile returnees . . . . . Neh. 3:7, 15, 19

Mizraim—*Egypt*
1. Son of Ham; ancestor of Ludim, Anamim, etc. . . . . . 1 Chr. 1:8, 11
2. Hebrew name for Egypt . . . . . Gen. 50:11
Called the land of Ham . . . . . Ps. 105:23, 27

Mizzah—*fear*
Grandson of Esau; a duke of Edom . . . . . Gen. 36:13, 17

Mnason
Christian of Cyprus and Paul's host . . . . . Acts 21:16

Moab—*seed*
1. Son of Lot . . . . . Gen. 19:33-37
2. Country of the Moabites . . . . Deut. 1:5

Moabites—*inhabitants of Moab*
A. *History of:*
Descendants of Lot . . . . . Gen. 19:36, 37
Became a great nation . . . . . Num. 21:28, 30
Governed by kings . . . . . Num. 23:7; Josh. 24:9
Driven out of their territory by Amorites . . . . . Num. 21:26
Refused to let Israel pass . . . . Judg. 11:17, 18
Joined Midian to curse Israel . . . . . Num. 22:4
Excluded from Israel . . . . . Deut. 23:3-6
Friendly relation with Israel . . . . . Ruth 1:1, 4, 16
Defeated by Saul . . . . . 1 Sam. 14:47
Refuge for David's parents . . . 1 Sam. 22:3, 4
Defeated by David . . . . . 2 Sam. 8:2, 12
Solomon married women of . . . . . 1 Kin. 11:1, 3
Paid tribute to Israel . . . . . 2 Kin. 3:4
Fought Israel and Judah . . . . . 2 Kin. 3:5-7
Conquered by Israel and Judah . . . . . 2 Kin. 3:8-27
Intermarried with Jews . . . . . Ezra 9:1, 2; Neh. 13:23
B. *Characteristics of:*
Idolatrous . . . . . 1 Kin. 11:7
Wealthy . . . . . Jer. 48:1, 7
Superstitious . . . . . Jer. 27:3, 9
Satisfied . . . . . Jer. 48:11
Proud . . . . . Jer. 48:29
C. *Prophecies concerning their:*
Desolation . . . . . Is. 15:1-9
Ruin and destruction . . . . . Jer. 27:3, 8
Punishment . . . . . Amos 2:1-3
Subjection . . . . . Is. 11:14

Mob—*a lawless crowd*
Caused Pilate to pervert justice . . . . . Matt. 27:20-25
Made unjust charges . . . . . Acts 17:5-9
Paul saved from . . . . . Acts 21:27-40

Mocking—*imitating in fun or derision*
A. *Evil agents of:*
Children . . . . . 2 Kin. 2:23
Men of Israel . . . . . 2 Chr. 30:10
Men of Judah . . . . . 2 Chr. 36:16
Fools . . . . . Prov. 14:9
Wine . . . . . Prov. 20:1
Jews . . . . . Matt. 20:19
Roman soldiers . . . . . Luke 23:36
False teachers . . . . . Jude 18
B. *Good agents of:*
Ass . . . . . Num. 22:29
Samson . . . . . Judg. 16:10-15
Elijah . . . . . 1 Kin. 18:27
Wisdom (God) . . . . . Prov. 1:20, 26
The Lord . . . . . Ps. 2:4
C. *Reasons for, to:*
Show unbelief . . . . . 2 Chr. 36:16
Portray scorn . . . . . 2 Chr. 30:10
Ridicule . . . . . Acts 2:13
Insult . . . . . Gen. 39:14, 17
D. *Objects of:*
Christ . . . . . Luke 23:11, 36
Believers . . . . . Heb. 11:36

Modesty in dress
A. *Of women:*
Instructed . . . . . 1 Tim. 2:9
Illustrated in Israel . . . . . 1 Pet. 3:3-5
Lack of, an enticement . . . . . 2 Sam. 11:2-5
B. *Of men:*
Lack of, condemned . . . . . Gen. 9:21-27
Illustrated . . . . . John 21:7
Manifested in conversion . . . . Mark 5:15

Moladah—*birth, origin*
Town of Judah . . . . . Josh. 15:1, 26
Inheritance of Simeon . . . . . Josh. 19:1, 2
Returning Levites inhabit . . . . . Neh. 11:26

Molding—*a decorative ledge of gold*
Around:
Ark . . . . . Ex. 25:11
Incense altar . . . . . Ex. 30:3, 4

Mole—*a small, burrowing mammal*
Among unclean animals . . . . . Is. 2:20

Molech—*king*
A. *Worship of:*
By Ammonites . . . . . 1 Kin. 11:7
By human sacrifice . . . . . 2 Kin. 23:10
Strongly condemned . . . . . Lev. 18:21
Introduced by Solomon . . . . . 1 Kin. 11:7
B. *Prevalence of, among Jews:*
Favored by Solomon . . . . . 1 Kin. 11:7

See Human sacrifice

Molid—*begetter*
Judahite . . . . . 1 Chr. 2:29

Molten—*made of melted metal*
A. *Applied to:*
Great basin in the Temple . . . 1 Kin. 7:16-33
Mirror . . . . . Job 37:18
Images . . . . . Ex. 32:4, 8
B. *Of images:*
Making of forbidden . . . . . Ex. 34:17
Made by Israel . . . . . 2 Kin. 17:16
Worshiped by Israel . . . . . Ps. 106:19
Destroyed by Josiah . . . . . 2 Chr. 34:3, 4
Folly of . . . . . Is. 42:17
Vanity . . . . . Is. 41:29

SUBJECT REFERENCE

See Gods, false

Moment—*a small unit of time*

A. *Descriptive of:*
- Man's life ....Job 34:20
- Lying tongues ....Prov. 12:19
- Satan's temptation ....Luke 4:5

B. *Descriptive of God's:*
- Anger ....Num. 16:21, 45
- Punishment ....Is. 47:9
- Destruction ....Jer. 4:20

C. *Descriptive of the believer's:*
- Problems ....Job 7:18
- Protection ....Is. 26:20, 21
- Perfection in glory ....1 Cor. 15:52

Monarchy—*the rule of one man* (king)

Described by Samuel ....1 Sam. 8:11-18

Money—*an authorized medium of exchange*

A. *Wrong uses of:*
- Misuse ....Gen. 31:15
- Forced tribute ....2 Kin. 15:20
- Make interest on ....Ps. 15:5
- Bribe ....Ps. 15:5
- Miser ....Matt. 25:18
- Buy spiritual gifts ....Acts 8:18, 20

B. *Good uses of:*
- Buy property ....Gen. 23:9, 13
- Buy food ....Deut. 2:6, 28
- Give as an offering ....Deut. 14:22-26
- Repair God's house ....2 Kin. 12:4-15
- Pay taxes ....Matt. 17:27; Matt. 22:19-21
- Use for the Lord ....Matt. 25:27

C. *Evils connected with:*
- Greed ....2 Kin. 5:20-27
- Debts ....Neh. 5:2-11

Moneychangers—*dealers in changing money*

Christ drives them out ....Matt. 21:12

Monogamy—*marriage to one spouse*

- Commanded ....Matt. 19:3-9; 1 Cor. 7:1-16
- Example of Christ and the Church ....Eph. 5:25-33
- Demanded of bishop ....1 Tim. 3:2

Monotheism—*a belief in one god*

Statements of:
- The great commandment ....Deut. 6:4, 5
- Song of Moses ....Deut. 32:36-39
- About eternal life ....John 17:3, 22

Moon—*earth's satellite*

A. *Miraculous use of:*
- Standing still ....Hab. 3:11
- Darkened ....Is. 13:10
- Turned to blood ....Acts 2:20

B. *Worship of:*
- Among Jews ....Jer. 7:18
- Forbidden ....Deut. 4:19
- Punishable ....Jer. 8:1-3

C. *Illustrative of:*
- Eternity ....Ps. 72:5, 7
- Universal praise ....Is. 66:23
- God's faithfulness ....Jer. 31:35-37
- Greater light of Gospel age ....Is. 30:26

D. *Purpose of:*
- Rule the night ....Gen. 1:16
- Marking time ....Gen. 1:14
- Designating seasons ....Ps. 104:19
- Signaling prophetic events ....Matt. 24:29; Luke 21:25

Morality—*principles of right conduct*

A. *Of the unregenerate:*
- Based upon conscience ....Rom. 2:14, 15
- Commanded by law ....John 8:3-5
- Limited to outward appearance ....Is. 1:14, 15
- Object of boasting ....Mark 10:17-20

B. *Of the regenerated:*
- Based upon the new birth ....2 Cor. 5:17
- Prompted by the Spirit ....Gal. 5:22, 23
- Comes from the heart ....Heb. 8:10
- No boasting except in Christ ....1 Cor. 15:10; Phil. 3:7-10

SUBJECT REFERENCE

Morasthite—*a native of Moresheth*

Descriptive of Micah ....Jer. 26:18

Mordecai—*dedicated to Mars*

1. Jew exiled in Persia ....Esth. 2:5, 6
   - Brings up Esther ....Esth. 2:7
   - Directs Esther's movements ....Esth. 2:10-20
   - Reveals plot to kill the king ....Esth. 2:22, 23
   - Refuses homage to Haman ....Esth. 3:1-6
   - Gallows made for ....Esth. 5:14
   - Honored by the king ....Esth. 6:1-12
   - Becomes a third ruler ....Esth. 8:7, 15
   - Becomes famous ....Esth. 9:4
   - Writes to Jews about Feast of Purim ....Esth. 9:20-31
2. Postexilic returnee ....Ezra 2:2

More—*something in addition*

A. *"More than" promises:*
- Repentance ....Matt. 18:13
- Love ....John 21:15

B. *"Much more" promises:*
- Grace ....Rom. 5:9-17
- Witnessing ....Phil. 1:14
- Obedience ....Phil. 2:12

C. *"No more" promises:*
- Christ's death ....Rom. 6:9
- Grace ....Rom. 11:6
- Remember sin ....Heb. 8:12

Moreh—*teacher, soothsayer*

1. Place (oak tree or grove) near Shechem ....Gen. 12:6
   - Probably place of:
     - Idol burying ....Gen. 35:4
     - Covenant-stone ....Josh. 24:26
2. Hill in the valley of Jezreel ....Judg. 7:1

Moresheth-gath—*possession of Gath*

Birthplace of Micah the prophet ....Mic. 1:14

Moriah

- God commands Abraham to sacrifice Isaac here ....Gen. 22:1-13
- Site of Solomon's Temple ....2 Chr. 3:1

Morning—*the first part of the day*

A. *Early risers in:*
- Do the LORD's will ....Gen. 22:3
- Worship ....Ex. 24:4
- Do the LORD's work ....Josh. 6:12
- Fight the LORD's battles ....Josh. 8:10
- Depart on a journey ....Judg. 19:5, 8
- Correct an evil ....Dan. 6:19
- Pray ....Mark 1:35
- Visit the tomb ....Mark 16:2
- Preach ....Acts 5:21

B. *For the righteous, a time for:*
- Joy ....Ps. 30:5
- God's loving-kindness ....Ps. 92:2
- God's mercies ....Lam. 3:23

C. *For the unrighteous, a time of:*
- Dread ....Deut. 28:67
- Destruction ....Is. 17:14

D. *Figurative of:*
- Man's unrighteousness ....Hos. 6:4
- Judgment ....Zeph. 3:5
- God's light ....Amos 5:8
- Christ's return ....Rev. 2:28

Morning sacrifice—*part of Israelite worship*

- Ritual described ....Ex. 29:38-42
- Part of continual offering ....Num. 28:3-8
- Under Ahaz ....2 Kin. 16:15

Morning Star

Figurative of Christ:
- To church at Thyatira ....Rev. 2:24, 28
- Christ, of Himself ....Rev. 22:16
- Applied to Christ ....2 Pet. 1:19

Morsel—*a small piece of food*

- Offered to angels ....Gen. 18:5
- Rejected by a doomed man ....1 Sam. 28:22
- Asked of a dying woman ....1 Kin. 17:11, 12
- Better than strife ....Prov. 17:1
- Exchanged for a birthright ....Heb. 12:16

SUBJECT REFERENCE

Mortar (I)—*a vessel*

- Vessel used for beating grains ....Num. 11:8
- Used figuratively ....Prov. 27:22

Mortar (II)—*a building material*

Made of:
- Clay ....Is. 41:25
- Slime (bitumen) ....Gen. 11:3
- Plaster ....Lev. 14:42, 45

Mortgage—*something given in security for debt*

Postexilic Jews burdened with ....Neh. 5:3

Mortification—*a putting to death*

A. *Objects of:*
- Law ....Rom. 7:4
- Sin ....Rom. 6:6, 11
- Flesh ....Rom. 13:14
- Members of earthly body ....Col. 3:5

B. *Agents of:*
- Holy Spirit ....Rom. 8:13
- Our obedience ....Rom. 6:17-19

Mosera (sing.), **Moseroth** (pl.)—*bond*

- Place of Aaron's death and burial ....Deut. 10:6
- Israelite encampment ....Num. 33:30, 31

Moses—*drawn out*

A. *Early life of* (first 40 years):
- Descendant of Levi ....Ex. 2:1
- Son of Amram and Jochebed ....Ex. 6:16-20
- Brother of Aaron and Miriam ....Ex. 15:20
- Born under slavery ....Ex. 2:1-10
- Hid by mother ....Ex. 2:2, 3
- Educated in Egyptian wisdom ....Acts 7:22
- Refused Egyptian sonship ....Heb. 11:23-27
- Defended his people ....Ex. 2:11-14
- Rejected, flees to Midian ....Ex. 2:15

B. *In Midian* (second 40 years):
- Married Zipporah ....Ex. 2:16-21
- Father of two sons ....Ex. 2:22; Acts 7:29
- Became Jethro's shepherd ....Ex. 3:1

C. *Leader of Israel* (last 40 years; to the end of his life):
- Heard God's voice ....Ex. 3:2-6
- God's plan revealed to him ....Ex. 3:7-10
- Argued with God ....Ex. 4:1-17
- Met Aaron ....Ex. 4:14-28
- Assembled elders of Israelites ....Ex. 4:29-31
- Rejected by Pharaoh and Israel ....Ex. 5:1-23
- Conflict with Pharaoh; ten plagues sent ....Ex. 7—12
- Commanded to institute the Passover ....Ex. 12:1-29; Heb. 11:28

D. *From Egypt to Sinai:*
- Led people from Egypt ....Ex. 12:30-38
- Observed the Passover ....Ex. 12:39-51
- Healed bitter waters ....Ex. 15:22-27
- People hunger; flesh and manna supplied ....Ex. 16:1-36; John 6:31, 32
- Came to Sinai ....Ex. 19:1, 2

E. *At Sinai:*
- Called to God's presence ....Acts 7:38
- Prepared Israel for the Law ....Ex. 19:7-25
- Received the Law ....Ex. 20—23
- Confirmed the covenant with Israel ....Ex. 24:1-11
- Stayed 40 days on Sinai ....Ex. 24:12-16
- Shown the pattern of the tabernacle ....Ex. 25—31
- Israel sins; Moses interceded ....Ex. 32:1-35
- Recommissioned and encouraged ....Ex. 33:1-23
- Instructions received; tabernacle erected ....Ex. 36—40
- Consecrated Aaron ....Lev. 8:1-36
- Numbered the men ....Num. 1:1-54
- Observed the Passover ....Num. 9:1-5

F. *From Sinai to Kadesh-barnea:*
- Resumed journey to Canaan ....Num. 10:11-36

SUBJECT — REFERENCE

- Complained; 70 elders appointed .... Num. 11:1-35
- Spoke against by Miriam and Aaron .... Num. 12:1-6

G. *At Kadesh-barnea:*

- Sent spies to Canaan .... Num. 13:1-33
- Pleaded with rebellious Israel .... Num. 14:1-19
- Announced God's judgment .... Num. 14:20-45

H. *Wanderings:*

- Instructions received .... Num. 15:1-41
- Sinned in anger .... Num. 20:1-13
- Sent messengers to Edom .... Num. 20:14-21
- Made a brass serpent .... Num. 21:4-9; John 3:14
- Traveled toward Canaan .... Num. 21:10-20
- Ordered destruction .... Num. 25:1-18
- Numbered the people .... Num. 26:1-65
- Gave instruction concerning inheritance .... Num. 27:1-11
- Commissioned Joshua as his successor .... Num. 27:12-23
- Received further laws .... Num. 28—30
- Conquered Midianites .... Num. 31:1-54
- Final instruction and records .... Num. 32—36
- Enough .... Deut. 3:24-27
- Reinterpreted the Law .... Deut. 1—31
- Gave farewell messages .... Deut. 32—33
- Committed written Law to the priests .... Deut. 31:9, 26
- Saw the promised land .... Deut. 34:1-4
- Died, in full strength, at 120 .... Deut. 34:5-7
- Israel wept over .... Deut. 34:8

I. *Character of:*

- Believer .... Heb. 11:23-28
- Faithful .... Num. 12:7; Heb. 3:2-5
- Meek .... Num. 12:3
- Respected .... Ex. 33:8-10
- Logical .... Num. 14:12-20
- Impatient .... Ex. 5:22, 23
- Given to anger .... Ex. 32:19

Moses, oracles of—*blessings on tribes of Israel*

- Pronounced .... Deut. 33:6-25
- Song introduces .... Deut. 33:2-5
- Song concludes .... Deut. 33:26-29

Most High—*a name of God*

- Melchizedek, priest of .... Heb. 7:1
- Applied to Jesus by demons .... Mark 5:7, 8
- Paul and Silas called servants of .... Acts 16:17

Mote—*a small particle*

- Used in contrast to a beam .... Matt. 7:3, 5

Moth—*a garment-destroying insect*

Used figuratively of:

- Inner corruption .... Is. 50:9
- God's judgments .... Hos. 5:12
- Man's insecurity .... Job 4:19
- Man's fading glory .... Job 13:28

Mother

A. *Described as:*

- Loving .... Ex. 2:1-25
- Appreciative .... 2 Kin. 4:19-37
- Weeping .... Luke 7:12-15
- Remembering .... Luke 2:51

B. *Kinds of:*

- Idolatrous .... Judg. 17:1-4
- Troubled .... 1 Kin. 17:17-24
- Cruel .... 2 Kin. 11:1, 2
- Joyful .... Ps. 113:9
- Good .... Prov. 31:1
- Scheming .... Matt. 20:20-23
- Prayerful .... Acts 12:12

C. *Duties toward:*

- Honor .... Eph. 6:2
- Obedience .... Deut. 21:18, 19
- Protection .... Gen. 32:11
- Provision .... John 19:25-27

D. *Figurative of:*

- Israel .... Hos. 2:2, 5
- Judah .... Ezek. 19:2, 10
- Heavenly Jerusalem .... Gal. 4:26

E. *Duties performed by:*

- Selecting son's wife .... Gen. 21:21
- Hospitality .... Gen. 24:55
- Nourishment .... Ex. 2:8, 9
- Provision .... 1 Kin. 1:11-21
- Comfort .... Is. 66:12, 13

F. *Dishonor of, punished by:*

- Death .... Lev. 20:9
- Shame .... Prov. 19:26
- Darkness .... Prov. 20:20
- Destruction .... Prov. 28:24

Motherhood

A. *Described as:*

- Painful .... Gen. 3:16
- Sometimes dangerous .... Gen. 35:16-20
- Yet joyful .... John 16:21
- Object of prayer .... Gen. 25:21

B. *Blessings of:*

- Fulfills divine Law .... Gen. 1:28
- Makes joyful .... Ps. 113:9
- Woman's "preserved" .... 1 Tim. 2:15

Mother-in-law

- Judith's—grief .... Gen. 26:34, 35
- Ruth's—loved .... Ruth 1:14-17
- Peter's—healed by Christ .... Matt. 8:14, 15

Motive—*inner impulse producing outward action*

A. *Good:*

- Questioned .... 2 Kin. 5:5-8
- Misapplied .... Esth. 6:6-11
- Misrepresented .... Job 1:9-11
- Misunderstood .... Acts 21:26-31

B. *Evil:*

- Prompted by Satan .... Matt. 16:22, 23
- Designed to deceive .... Acts 5:1-10

Mouldy—*musty or stale*

- Applied to bread .... Josh. 9:5, 12

Mount Baalah—*mistress*

- Part of the territory of Judah .... Josh. 15:11

Mount Baal-hermon—*possessor of Hermon*

- Lived on by nations that tested Israel .... Judg. 3:3, 4

Mount Carmel—*fruitful*

- Prophets gathered together here .... 1 Kin. 18:19, 20
- Elisha journeyed to .... 2 Kin. 2:25
- Shunammite woman comes to Elisha .... 2 Kin. 4:25

Mount Ebal—*bald*

- Cursed by God .... Deut. 11:29
- Joshua built an altar here .... Josh. 8:30

Mount Gaash—*quaking*

- Place of Joshua's burial .... Josh. 24:30

Mount Gerizim—*rocky*

- Place the blessed stood .... Deut. 27:12
- Jotham spoke to people of Shechem here .... Judg. 9:7

Mount Gilboa—*bubbling spring*

- Men of Israel slain .... 1 Sam. 31:1
- Saul and his sons slain here .... 1 Sam. 31:8

Mount Gilead—*heap of witness*

- Gideon divides the people for battle .... Judg. 7:3

Mount Hor—*mountain*

- LORD spoke to Moses and Aaron .... Num. 20:23
- Aaron died there .... Num. 20:25-28

Mount Horeb—*desolate*

- Sons of Israel stripped of ornaments .... Ex. 33:6

Mount of Olives

- Prophecy concerning .... Zech. 14:4
- Jesus sent disciples for donkey .... Matt. 21:1, 2; Mark 11:1, 2
- Jesus speaks of the signs of His coming .... Matt. 24:3; Mark 13:3, 4
- After the Lord's supper went out to .... Matt. 26:30; Mark 14:26
- Called Mount Olivet .... Luke 19:29; Luke 21:37

Mount Seir—*rugged*

- Horites defeated by Chedorlaomer .... Gen. 14:5, 6

Mount Shepher—*beauty*

- Israelites camped at .... Num. 33:23, 24

Mount Sinai

- Lord descended upon, in fire .... Ex. 19:18
- Lord called Moses to the top .... Ex. 19:20
- The glory of the LORD rested on, for six days .... Ex. 24:16

Mount Tabor—*broken*

- Deborah sent Barak there to defeat Canaanites .... Judg. 4:6-14

Mount Zion

- Survivors shall go out from .... 2 Kin. 19:31

Mountain—*a high elevation of earth*

A. *Mentioned in the Bible:*

- Abarim .... Num. 33:47, 48
- Ararat .... Gen. 8:4
- Bashan .... Ps. 68:15
- Carmel .... 1 Kin. 18:19
- Ebal .... Deut. 27:13
- Gaash .... Judg. 2:9
- Gerizim .... Deut. 11:29
- Gilboa .... 2 Sam. 1:6, 21
- Hachilah .... 1 Sam. 23:19
- Hermon .... Josh. 13:11
- Hor .... Num. 34:7, 8
- Horeb (same as Sinai) .... Ex. 3:1
- Lebanon .... Deut. 3:25
- Mizar .... Ps. 42:6
- Moreh .... Judg. 7:1
- Moriah .... Gen. 22:2
- Nebo .... Deut. 34:1
- Olives or Olivet .... Matt. 24:3
- Pisgah .... Num. 21:20
- Sinai .... Ex. 19:2-20
- Sion or Zion .... 2 Sam. 5:7
- Tabor .... Judg. 4:6-14

B. *In Christ's life, place of:*

- Temptation .... Matt. 4:8
- Sermon .... Matt. 5:1
- Prayer .... Matt. 14:23
- Transfiguration .... Matt. 17:1
- Prophecy .... Matt. 24:3
- Agony .... Matt. 26:30, 31
- Ascension .... Luke 24:50

C. *Uses of:*

- Boundaries .... Num. 34:7, 8
- Distant vision .... Deut. 3:27
- Hunting .... 1 Sam. 26:20
- Warfare .... 1 Sam. 17:3
- Protection .... Amos 6:1
- Refuge .... Matt. 24:16
- Idolatrous worship .... Is. 65:7
- Assembly sites .... Josh. 8:30-33

D. *Significant Old Testament events on:*

- Ark rested upon (Ararat) .... Gen. 8:4
- Abraham's testing (Moriah) .... Gen. 22:1-19
- Giving of the Law (Sinai) .... Ex. 19:2-25
- Moses' view of Canaan (Pisgah) .... Deut. 34:1
- Combat with Baalism (Carmel) .... 1 Kin. 18:19-42
- David's city (Zion) .... 2 Sam. 5:7

E. *Figurative of:*

- God's:
  - Protection .... Is. 31:4
  - Dwelling .... Is. 8:18
  - Judgments .... Jer. 13:16
- Gospel age .... Is. 27:13
- Messiah's advent .... Is. 40:9
- Great joy .... Is. 44:23
- Great difficulties .... Matt. 21:21
- Pride of man .... Luke 3:5
- Supposed faith .... 1 Cor. 13:2

Mourning—*expression of sorrow*

A. *Caused by:*

- Death .... Gen. 50:10
- Defection .... 1 Sam. 15:35
- Disobedience .... Ezra 9:4-7
- Desolation .... Joel 1:9, 10
- Defeat .... Rev. 18:11
- Discouragement .... Ps. 42:9
- Disease .... Job 2:5-8

SUBJECT	REFERENCE
B. *Transformed into:*	
Gladness	Is. 51:11
Hope	John 11:23-28
Everlasting joy	Is. 35:10
C. *Signs of:*	
Tearing of clothing	2 Sam. 3:31, 32
Ashes on head	2 Sam. 13:19
Sackcloth	Gen. 37:34
Neglect of appearance	2 Sam. 19:24
Presence of mourners	John 11:19, 31
Apparel	2 Sam. 14:2
Shave head	Jer. 16:6, 7

Mouse, mice—*a small quadruped*

Accounted unclean	Lev. 11:29
Destructive of crops	1 Sam. 6:5
Eaten by idolatrous Israelites	Is. 66:17

Mouth

A. *Descriptive of:*	
Top of a well	Gen. 29:2, 3, 8
Opening of a sack	Gen. 42:27, 28
Man's	Job 3:1
B. *Exhortations concerning:*	
Make all acceptable	Ps. 19:14
Keep with a bridle	Ps. 39:1
Set a watch before	Ps. 141:3
Keep the corrupt from	Eph. 4:29
Keep filthy speech from	Col. 3:8
C. *Of unregenerate, source of:*	
Idolatry	1 Kin. 19:18
Lying	1 Kin. 22:13, 22, 23
Unfaithfulness	Ps. 5:9
Cursing	Ps. 10:7
Pride	Ps. 17:10
Evil	Ps. 50:19
Lies	Ps. 63:11
Vanity	Ps. 144:8, 11
Foolishness	Prov. 15:2, 14
D. *Of regenerate, used for:*	
Prayer	1 Sam. 1:12
God's Law	Josh. 1:8
Praise	Ps. 34:1
Wisdom	Ps. 37:30
Testimony	Eph. 6:9
Confession	Rom. 10:8-10
Righteousness	Ps. 71:15

Move—*to change the position*

A. *Of God's Spirit in:*	
Creation	Gen. 1:2
Man	Judg. 13:25
Prophets	2 Pet. 1:21
B. *Of things immovable:*	
Righteous	Ps. 112:6
City of God	Ps. 46:4, 5
Eternal kingdom	Ps. 96:10

Mowing—*to cut grass*

First growth for taxes	Amos 7:1
Left on the ground	Ps. 72:6

Moza—*a going forth*

1. Descendant of Judah	1 Chr. 2:46
2. Descendant of Saul	1 Chr. 8:36, 37

Mozah—*drained*

A Benjamite town	Josh. 18:21, 26

Mufflers—*an elaborate veil*

Worn by women	Is. 3:16, 19

Mulberry tree

Referred to by Jesus	Luke 17:6

Mule—*a hybrid between a horse and a donkey*

Breeding of, forbidden	Lev. 19:19
Sign of kingship	1 Kin. 1:33
Used in trade	Ezek. 27:14
Considered stubborn	Ps. 32:9

Multiply—*to increase in quantity or quality*

A. *Of good things:*	
Holy seed	Jer. 30:19
Churches	Acts 9:31
Word of God	Acts 12:24
God's wonders	Ex. 7:3
Loaves and fish	Matt. 15:32-39 John 6:1-15
B. *Secret of:*	
God's:	
Promise	Gen. 16:10
Oath	Gen. 26:3, 4
Man's obedience	Deut. 7:12, 13

Multitude—*a large number of people*

A. *Dangers of:*	
Mixed, source of evil	Ex. 12:38
Follow after in doing evil	Ex. 23:2
Sacrifices, vain	Is. 1:11
B. *Christ's compassion upon:*	
Teaching	Matt. 5:1
Healing	Matt. 12:15
Teaching parables to	Matt. 13:1-3, 34
Feeding	Matt. 14:15-21
C. *Their attitude toward Christ:*	
Reaction to	Matt. 9:8, 33
Recognition of	Matt. 14:5 Matt. 21:46
Reception of	Matt. 21:8-11
Running after	John 6:2
Rejection of	Matt. 27:20

Munificence—*generous in giving*

Measure of, on:	
God's part	Mal. 3:10
Israel's part	Ex. 36:3-7
Judah's part	1 Chr. 29:3-9
Christian's part	2 Cor. 8:1-5

Munition

Kept for war	Nah. 2:1

Muppim—*obscurities*

Son of Benjamin	Gen. 46:21
Called Shupham	Num. 26:39
Shuppim and Shephuphan	1 Chr. 7:12, 15

Murder

A. *Defined as:*	
Coming out of the heart	Matt. 15:19
Result from anger	Matt. 5:21, 22
Work of the flesh	Gal. 5:19
Excluding from eternal life	1 John 3:15
B. *Guilt of:*	
Determined by witnesses	Num. 35:30
Not redeemable	Num. 35:30
Not forgiven by flight to the altar	Ex. 21:14
C. *Penalty of:*	
Ordained by God	Gen. 9:6
Executed by avenger of blood	Deut. 19:6

See Homicide

Murmuring—*sullen dissatisfaction with things*

A. *Caused by:*	
Thirst	Ex. 15:24
Hunger	Ex. 16:2, 3, 8
Fear	Num 14:1-4
B. *Against Christ, because of His:*	
Practices	Luke 15:1, 2
Pronouncements	John 6:41-61
C. *Of Christians:*	
Provoked	Acts 6:1
Forbidden	John 6:43
Excluded	Phil. 2:14

Murrain—*pestilence*

Fifth Egyptian plague	Ex. 9:1-6

Mushi—*drawn out*

Son of Merari	Ex. 6:19
Descendants of, called Mushites	Num. 3:33 Num. 26:58

Music

A. *Used in:*	
Farewells	Gen. 31:27
Entertainments	Is. 5:12
Weddings	Jer. 7:34
Funerals	Matt. 9:18, 23
Sacred processions	1 Chr. 13:6-8
Victory celebrations	Ex. 15:20, 21
Coronation services	2 Chr. 23:11, 13
Dedication services	2 Chr. 5:11-13
B. *Influence of, upon:*	
Mental disorders	1 Sam. 16:14-17, 23
Sorrowful	Ps. 137:1-4
C. *List of instruments of:*	
Cornet	Dan. 3:5, 7
Cymbal	1 Cor. 13:1
Dulcimer	Dan. 3:5, 10, 15
Harp	1 Sam. 16:16, 23
Organ	Ps. 150:4
Pipe	Is. 30:29
Psaltery	1 Sam. 10:5
Sackbut	Dan. 3:5, 7, 10
Timbrel	Gen. 31:27 Ex. 15:20
Trumpet	Josh. 6:4
Viol	Is. 5:12
Complete orchestra	2 Sam. 6:5

Music in Christian worship

From heart	Eph. 5:19
Means of teaching	Col. 3:16

Must—*something that is imperative*

A. *Concerning Christ's:*	
Preaching	Luke 4:43
Suffering	Matt. 16:21
Death	John 3:14
Fulfillment of Scripture	Matt. 26:54
Resurrection	John 20:9
Ascension	Acts 3:21
Reign	1 Cor. 15:25
B. *Concerning the believer's:*	
Belief	Heb. 11:6
Regeneration	John 3:7
Salvation	Acts 4:12
Worship	John 4:24
Duty	Acts 9:6
Suffering	Acts 9:16
Mission	Acts 19:21
Moral life	Titus 1:7
Inner life	2 Tim. 2:24
Judgment	2 Cor. 5:10
C. *Concerning prophecy:*	
Gospel's proclamation	Mark 13:10
Gentiles' inclusion	John 10:16
Earth's tribulations	Matt. 24:6
Resurrection	1 Cor. 15:53

Mustard seed—*very small seed*

Kingdom compared to	Matt. 13:31
Faith compared to	Matt. 17:20

Mutability—*capable of change*

A. *Asserted of:*	
Physical world	Matt. 5:18
Earthly world	1 John 2:15-17
Old covenant	Heb. 8:8-13
Present order	2 Cor. 4:18
B. *Denied of:*	
God	Mal. 3:6
Christ	Heb. 1:10, 11 Heb. 13:8

See Immutability; Move

Mutilation—*to maim, to damage, to disfigure*

A. *Object of, forbidden:*	
On the body	Lev. 19:28
For:	
Priesthood	Lev. 21:18
Sacrifice	Lev. 22:22
Mourning	Jer. 41:5-7
B. *Practiced by:*	
Jews	Judg. 19:29, 30
Philistines	Judg. 16:21
Canaanites	Judg. 1:6, 7
Baal prophets	1 Kin. 18:28

Mutiny—*revolt against authority*

By Israelites	Num. 14:1 4

Mutual—*a common interest*

Spoken of faith	Rom. 1:12

Muzzling

Applied:	
To oxen	Deut. 25:4
Figuratively, to Christians	1 Cor. 9:9-11

Myra—*a city of Lycia*

Paul changes ships here	Acts 27:5, 6

Myrrh

A. *Dried gum* (Heb., *mor*) *of a balsam tree, used:*	
In anointing oil	Ex. 30:23
As a perfume	Ps. 45:8
For beauty treatment	Esth. 2:12
Brought as gifts	Matt. 2:11

M

SUBJECT REFERENCE

Given as a sedative ....Mark 15:23
Used for embalming ....John 19:38, 39

B. *Fragrant resin* (Heb., *lot*) *used:*
In commerce ....Gen. 37:25
As presents ....Gen. 43:11

Myrtle—*a shrub*
Found in mountains; booths made of ....Neh. 8:15
Figurative of the Gospel ....Is. 41:19
Used symbolically ....Zech. 1:10, 11

Mysia—*a province of Asia Minor*
Paul and Silas pass through .....Acts 16:7, 8

Mystery—*something unknown except by divine revelation*

A. *Concerning God's:*
Secrets ....Deut. 29:29
Providence ....Rom. 11:33-36
Sovereignty ....Rom. 9:11-23
Prophecies ....1 Pet. 1:10-12
Predestination ....Rom. 8:29, 30

B. *Concerning Christianity:*
Christ's incarnation ....1 Tim. 3:16
Christ's nature ....Col. 2:2
Kingdom of God ....Luke 8:10
Christian faith ....1 Tim. 3:9
Indwelling Christ ....Col. 1:26, 27
Union of all believers ....Eph. 3:4-9
Israel's blindness ....Rom. 11:25
Lawlessness ....2 Thess. 2:7
Harlot Babylon ....Rev. 17:5, 7
Resurrection of saints ....1 Cor. 15:51
God's completed purpose .....Rev. 10:7

Mythology, referred to
Jupiter ....Acts 14:12, 13
Mercurius ....Acts 14:12
Pantheon ....Acts 17:16-23
Diana ....Acts 19:24-41
Castor and Pollox ....Acts 28:11

Myths—*speculative and philosophical fable or allegory*
Condemned ....1 Tim. 1:4
Fables ....1 Tim. 4:7
False ....2 Tim. 4:4

N

Naam—*pleasantness*
Son of Caleb ....1 Chr. 4:15

Naamah—*sweet, pleasant*
1. Daughter of Lamech ....Gen. 4:19-22
2. Ammonite wife of Solomon; mother of King Rehoboam ....1 Kin. 14:21, 31
3. Town of Judah ....Josh. 15:1, 41

Naaman—*pleasant*
1. Son of Benjamin ....Gen. 46:21
2. Captain in the Syrian army ..2 Kin. 5:1-11
Healed of his leprosy ....2 Kin. 5:14-17
Referred to by Christ ....Luke 4:27

Naamathite—*an inhabitant of Naamah*
Applied to Zophar, Job's friend ....Job 2:11

Naamites
Descendants of Naaman ....Num. 26:40

Naarah, Naarath—*girl*
1. Wife of Ashur ....1 Chr. 4:5, 6
2. Town of Ephraim ....Josh. 16:7
Same as Naaran ....1 Chr. 7:28

Naarai—*pleasantness of Jehovah*
One of David's mighty men .....1 Chr. 11:37

Nabal—*fool*
Wealthy sheep owner ....1 Sam. 25:2, 3
Refuses David's request ....1 Sam. 25:4-12
Abigail, wife of, appeases David's wrath against ....1 Sam. 25:13-35
Drunk, dies of a stroke ....1 Sam. 25:36-39
Widow of, becomes David's wife ....1 Sam. 25:39-42

SUBJECT REFERENCE

Naboth—*sprout*
Owner of vineyard coveted by King Ahab ....1 Kin. 21:1-4
Accused falsely of blasphemy and disloyalty ....1 Kin. 21:5-16
Murder of, avenged ....1 Kin. 21:17-25

Nachon—*prepared*
Threshing floor, site of Uzzah's death ....2 Sam. 6:6, 7
Called:
Perez-uzzah ("breach") ....2 Sam. 6:8
Chidon ....1 Chr. 13:9

Nadab—*willing, liberal*
1. Eldest of Aaron's four sons ..Ex. 6:23
Takes part in affirming covenant ....Ex. 24:1, 9-12
Becomes priest ....Ex. 28:1
Consumed by fire ....Lev. 10:1-7
Dies childless ....Num. 3:4
2. Judahite ....1 Chr. 2:28, 30
3. Benjamite ....1 Chr. 8:30
4. King of Israel ....1 Kin. 14:20
Killed by Baasha ....1 Kin. 15:25-31

Naggai
Ancestor of Christ ....Luke 3:25

Nagging woman
Gets Samson's secret ....Judg. 16:13-17
Called brawling ....Prov. 21:9, 19
Undesirable ....Prov. 25:24
Prov. 27:15

Nahalal, Nahalol—*drinking place for flocks*
Village of Zebulun ....Josh. 19:10, 15
Assigned to Merarite Levites ....Josh. 21:35
Canaanites not driven from .....Judg. 1:30

Nahaliel—*valley of God*
Israelite camp ....Num. 21:19

Naham—*consolation*
Father of Keilah ....1 Chr. 4:19

Nahamani—*compassionate*
Returned after the exile ....Neh. 7:7

Naharai—*snorting*
Armor-bearer of Joab ....2 Sam. 23:37
1 Chr. 11:39

Nahash—*serpent*
1. King of Ammon; makes impossible demands ....1 Sam. 11:1-15
2. King of Ammon who treats David kindly ....2 Sam. 10:2
Son of, helps David ....2 Sam. 17:27-29
3. Father of Abigail and Zeruiah, David's half sisters ....2 Sam. 17:25

Nahath—*descent*
1. Edomite chief ....Gen. 36:13
2. Kohathite Levite ....1 Chr. 6:26
Called Tohu ....1 Sam. 1:1
3. Levite in Hezekiah's reign ...2 Chr. 31:13

Nahbi—*concealed*
Spy of Naphtali ....Num. 13:14

Nahor, Nachor—*snorting*
1. Grandfather of Abraham ....Gen. 11:24-26
2. Son of Terah, brother of Abraham ....Gen. 11:27
Marries Milcah, begets eight sons by her and four by concubine .....Gen. 11:29
City of Haran ....Gen. 24:10
God of ....Gen. 31:53

Nahshon
Judahite leader ....Num. 1:4, 7
Aaron's brother-in-law ....Ex. 6:23
Ancestor of David ....Ruth 4:20-22
Ancestor of Christ ....Matt. 1:4

Nahum—*full of comfort*
Inspired prophet to Judah concerning Nineveh ....Nah. 1:1

Nahum, the Book of—*a book of the Old Testament*
The awesomeness of God ....Nah. 1:1-15
The destruction of Nineveh .....Nah. 2—3

SUBJECT REFERENCE

Nail

A. *Significant uses of:*
Killing a man ....Judg. 4:21, 25
Holding idols in place ....Is. 41:7
Fastening Christ to cross ....John 20:25

B. *Figurative uses of:*
Words fixed in the memory ..Eccl. 12:11
Revived nation ....Ezra 9:8
Messiah's kingdom ....Is. 22:23, 24
Messiah's death ....Is. 22:25
Atonement for man's sin ....Col. 2:14

Nain—*pleasant*
Village south of Nazareth; Jesus raises widow's son here ....Luke 7:11-17

Naioth—*habitations*
Prophets' school in Ramah .....1 Sam. 19:18, 19, 22, 23

Naked, nakedness—*nude, nudity*

A. *Used of man's:*
Original state ....Gen. 2:25
Sinful state ....Gen. 3:7, 10, 11
State of grace ....Rom. 8:35
Disembodied state ....2 Cor. 5:3

B. *Evil of:*
Strictly forbidden ....Lev. 18:6-20
Brings a curse ....Gen. 9:21-25
Judged by God ....Ezek. 22:10

C. *Instances of:*
Noah guilty of ....Gen. 9:21-23
Forbidden, to priests ....Ex. 20:26
Michal rebukes David for ....2 Sam. 6:20-23

D. *Putting clothing on:*
Indicates a changed life .....Mark 5:15
Promises a reward ....Matt. 25:34-40
Takes away shame ....Rev. 3:18
Sign of true faith ....James 2:15-17

E. *Figurative of:*
Separation from God ....Is. 20:3
Israel's unworthiness ....Ezek. 16:7-22
Judah's spiritual adultery ....Ezek. 16:36-38
God's judgment ....Ezek. 16:39
Spiritual need ....Hos. 2:9
Wickedness ....Nah. 3:4, 5
Needy ....Matt. 25:36, 38
God's knowledge ....Heb. 4:13
Unpreparedness ....Rev. 16:15

Name—*a word used to identify a person, animal or thing*

A. *Determined by:*
Events of the time ....Gen. 30:8
Prophetic position ....Gen. 25:26
Fondness of hope ....Gen. 29:32-35
Change of character ....John 1:42
Innate character ....1 Sam. 25:25
Coming events ....Is. 8:1-4
Divine mission ....Matt. 1:21

B. *Of God, described as:*
Great ....Josh. 7:9
Secret ....Judg. 13:18
Glorious ....Is. 63:14
Everlasting ....Ps. 135:13
Excellent ....Ps. 148:13
Holy ....Is. 57:15

C. *Of God, evil acts against:*
Taken in vain ....Ex. 20:7
Sworn falsely ....Lev. 19:12
Lies spoken in ....Zech. 13:3
Despised ....Mal. 1:6

D. *Of God, proper attitude toward:*
Exalt ....Ps. 34:3
Praise ....Ps. 54:6
Love ....Ps. 69:36

E. *Of Christ:*
Given before birth ....Matt. 1:21, 23
Hated by the world ....Matt. 10:22
Deeds done in, rewarded ....Matt. 10:42
Believers baptized in ....Acts 2:38
Miracles performed by ......Acts 3:16
Believers suffer for ....Acts 5:41
Speaking in ....Acts 9:27, 29
Gentiles called by ....Acts 15:14, 17
Final subjection to ....Phil. 2:9, 10

F. *Of believers:*
Called everlasting ....Is. 56:5

SUBJECT REFERENCE

Written in heaven . . . Luke 10:20
Called evil by world . . . Luke 6:22
Known by Christ . . . John 10:3
Confessed by Christ . . . Rev. 3:5
"Called by" . . . Is. 62:2; Rev. 3:12

Names of Christ (see Christ, names of)

Naomi—*my delight*
Widow of Elimelech . . . Ruth 1:1-3
Returns to Bethlehem with Ruth . . . Ruth 1:14-19
Arranges Ruth's marriage to Boaz . . . Ruth 3—4
Considers Ruth's child (Obed) her own . . . Ruth 4:16, 17

Naphish—*numerous*
Ishmael's eleventh son . . . Gen. 25:15

Naphtali—*my wrestling*
1. Son of Jacob by Bilhah . . . Gen. 30:1, 8
Sons of, form tribe . . . Gen. 46:24
Receives Jacob's blessing . . . Gen. 49:21, 28
2. Tribe of . . . Num. 1:42
Stationed last . . . Num. 2:29-31
Territory assigned by . . . Josh. 19:32-39
Canaanites not driven out by . . . Judg. 1:33
Barak becomes famous . . . Judg. 4:6, 14-16
Bravery of, praised . . . Judg. 5:18
Warriors of, under Gideon . . . Judg. 7:23
Warriors of, help David . . . 1 Chr. 12:34
Conquered by wars . . . 1 Kin. 15:20
Taken captive . . . 2 Kin. 15:29
Prophecy of a great light in . . . Is. 9:1-7
Fulfilled in Christ's ministry in . . . Matt. 4:12-16

Naphtuhim
Fourth son of Mizraim; probably district around . . . Gen. 10:13

Narcissus
Christian in Rome . . . Rom. 16:11

Nathan—*gift*
1. Son of David . . . 2 Sam. 5:14
Mary's lineage traced through . . . Zech. 12:12
2. Judahite . . . 1 Chr. 2:36
3. Prophet under David and Solomon . . . 1 Chr. 29:29
Reveals God's plan to David . . . 2 Sam. 7:2-29
Rebukes David's sin . . . 2 Sam. 12:1-15
Renames Solomon as Jedidiah . . . 2 Sam. 12:24, 25
Reveals Adonijah's plot . . . 1 Kin. 1:10-46
Sons of, in official positions . . . 1 Kin. 4:1, 2, 5
4. Father of Igal . . . 2 Sam. 23:36
5. A chief among returnees . . . Ezra 8:16
6. One who divorced his foreign wife . . . Ezra 10:34, 39

Nathanael—*God has given*
One of Christ's disciples . . . John 1:45-51

Nathan-melech—*the king has given*
An official in Josiah's reign . . . 2 Kin. 23:11

National duties (see Citizen, citizenship)

Nations—*people under a sovereign government*
A. *Of the world:*
Descendants of Noah's sons . . . Gen. 10:32
Originate in a person . . . Gen. 19:37, 38
Made of one blood . . . Acts 17:26
Separated by God . . . Deut. 32:8
Inherit separate characteristics . . . Gen. 25:23
Laden with iniquity . . . Is. 1:4
Destroyed by corruption . . . Lev. 18:26-28
Exalted by righteousness . . . Prov. 14:34
Father of many nations . . . Gen. 17:4
LORD will set you high above all . . . Deut. 28:1
Subject to repentance . . . Jer. 18:7-10
Judged by God . . . Gen. 15:14
Under God's control . . . Jer. 25:8-14
Future of, revealed . . . Dan. 2:27-45
Gospel to be preached to all . . . Matt. 24:14
Sarah shall be mother of many . . . Gen. 17:16
B. *Of Israel:*
Descendants of Abraham . . . Gen. 12:2; John 8:33, 37
Designated . . . Ex. 19:6
Given blessings . . . Deut. 4:7, 8; Rom. 9:4, 5
Punished by God . . . Jer. 25:1-11
Scattered among nations . . . Neh. 1:8; Luke 21:24
Christ died for . . . John 11:51
C. *Of the true people of God:*
Described as righteous . . . Is. 26:2
Born in a day . . . Is. 66:8
Accounted fruitful . . . Matt. 21:43
Believers are . . . 1 Pet. 2:9

Nations, table of
Record . . . Gen. 10:1-32

Natural—*that which is innate and real; not artificial or man-made*
A. *Described as:*
Physical origin . . . James 1:23
Normal . . . Rom. 1:26
Unregenerate . . . 1 Cor. 2:14
Unnatural . . . 2 Pet. 2:12
Temporal . . . 1 Cor. 15:46
B. *Contrasted with:*
Acquired . . . Rom. 11:21, 24
Perverted . . . Rom. 1:26, 27
Spiritual (life) . . . 1 Cor. 2:14
Spiritual (body) . . . 1 Cor. 15:44-46

Naturalization—*becoming a citizen of an adopted country*
Natural level, rights of . . . Acts 22:25-28
Spiritual level, blessings of . . . Eph. 2:12-19

Natural man
Does not accept things of God . . . 1 Cor. 2:14
Contrasted with spiritual . . . 1 Cor. 15:44-46

Natural religion
A. *Contents of, God's:*
Glory . . . Ps. 19:1-3
Nature . . . Rom. 1:19, 20
Sovereignty . . . Acts 17:23-31
Goodness . . . Acts 14:15-17
B. *Characteristics of:*
Original . . . Rom. 1:19, 20
Universal . . . Rom. 10:18
Inadequate . . . Rom. 2:12-15
Corrupted . . . Rom. 1:21-32
Valuable . . . Dan. 5:18-23

Nature—*the essential elements resident in something*
A. *Descriptive of:*
Right order of things . . . Rom. 1:26
Natural sense of right . . . Rom. 2:14
Physical origin . . . Rom. 2:27
Non-existence . . . Gal. 4:8
Man's natural depravity . . . Eph. 2:3
Divine . . . 2 Pet. 1:4
B. *Of man's unregenerate, described as:*
Under wrath . . . Eph. 2:3
Source of:
Iniquity . . . James 3:6
Corruption . . . 2 Pet. 2:12

Nature, beauties of
Reveal God's glory . . . Ps. 19:1-6
Greater than outward appearance . . . Matt. 6:28-30
Descriptive of spiritual blessings . . . Is. 35:1, 2

Naughty person
Wrongly ascribed . . . 1 Sam. 17:28
Descriptive of the wicked . . . Prov. 6:12
Downfall of . . . Prov. 11:6

Navel—*the point at which the umbilical cord is attached*
A. *Used literally of:*
Lover's appeal . . . Song 7:2
B. *Used figuratively of:*
Inward self . . . Prov. 3:8
Israel's wretched condition . . . Ezek. 16:4

Navy—*ships owned by a country*
Solomon's . . . 1 Kin. 9:26
Jehoshaphat's . . . 1 Kin. 22:48

Nazarene—*a native of Nazareth*
Jesus to be called . . . Matt. 2:23
Descriptive of Jesus' followers . . . Acts 24:5

Nazareth
A. *Town in Galilee:*
Considered obscure . . . John 1:46
City of Jesus' parents . . . Matt. 2:23
Early home of Jesus . . . Luke 2:39-51
Jesus departs from . . . Mark 1:9
Jesus rejected by . . . Luke 4:16-30
B. *As a title of honor descriptive of Jesus:*
Anointed by the Spirit . . . Acts 10:38
Risen Lord . . . Acts 22:8

Nazirite—*one especially consecrated to God*
A. *Methods of becoming, by:*
Birth . . . Judg. 13:5, 7
Vow . . . Num. 6:2
B. *Requirements of:*
Separation . . . Num. 6:4
No:
Strong drink . . . Num. 6:3, 4
Shaving . . . Num. 6:5
Defilement . . . Num. 6:6, 7
Corruption . . . Amos 2:11, 12
Holiness . . . Num. 6:8
C. *Examples of:*
Samson . . . Judg. 16:17
Samuel . . . 1 Sam. 1:11-28
John the Baptist . . . Luke 1:13, 15
Christians . . . 2 Cor. 6:17

Neah—*the settlement*
Town in Zebulun . . . Josh. 19:13

Neapolis—*new city*
Seaport of Philippi . . . Acts 16:11

Near—*close at hand* (in place or time)
A. *Of dangers, from:*
Prostitute . . . Prov. 7:8
Destruction . . . Prov. 10:14
God's judgment . . . Joel 3:14
B. *Of the Messianic salvation, as:*
Promised . . . Is. 50:8
Available . . . Is. 51:5
C. *Of Christ's return, described by:*
Christ . . . Matt. 24:33
Paul . . . Rom 13:11

Neariah—*Jehovah drives away*
1. Descendant of David . . . 1 Chr. 3:22, 23
2. Simeonite captain . . . 1 Chr. 4:42

Nearness of God
A. *Old Testament:*
In sense of time . . . Is. 46:13; Zeph. 1:14
In prayer . . . Is. 55:6
B. *New Testament:*
In sense of time . . . Rev. 1:1-3; Rev. 22:10
In prayer . . . Phil. 4:5-9

Nebai—*projecting*
Leader who signs the sealed covenant . . . Neh. 10:19

Nebaioth
Eldest son of Ishmael . . . Gen. 25:13
Descendants of, form Arabian tribe . . . Is. 60:7

Neballat—*hard, firm*
Postexilic town of Benjamin . . . Neh. 11:31, 34

Nebat—*look*
Father of Jeroboam . . . 1 Kin. 11:26

Nebo—*height*
1. Babylonian god of literature and science . . . Is. 46:1

N

SUBJECT REFERENCE

2. Mountain peak near Jericho ... Num. 33:47
Name of Pisgah's summit ... Deut. 34:1
3. Moabite town near Mt. Nebo ... Num. 32:3
Restored by Reubenites ... Num. 32:37, 38
Mentioned in the prophecy ... Is. 15:2
4. Town in Judah ... Ezra 2:29

Nebuchadnezzar—*Nebo, defend the boundary*

A. *Life of:*
Monarch of the Neo-Babylonian Empire (605–562 B.C.); defeats Pharaoh Necho at Carchemish ... 2 Chr. 35:20; Jer. 46:2
Besieges Jerusalem; carries captives to Babylon ... Dan. 1:1, 2
Crushes Jehoiachin's revolt (597 B.C.) ... 2 Kin. 24:10-17
Carries sacred vessels to Babylon ... 2 Kin. 24:13
Destroys Jerusalem; captures Zedekiah (587 B.C.) ... Jer. 39:5, 6
Leads attack on Tyre ... Ezek. 26:7

B. *Features concerning:*
Builder of Babylon ... Dan. 4:30
First of four great empires ... Dan. 2:26-48
Instrument of God's judgment ... Jer. 27:8
Called God's servant ... Jer. 25:9
Afflicted with insanity ... Dan. 4:28-37

C. *Prophecies concerning his:*
Conquest of Judah and Jerusalem ... Jer. 21:7, 10
Destruction of Jerusalem ... Jer. 32:28-36
Conquest of other nations ... Jer. 27:7-9
Conquest of Egypt ... Jer. 43:10-13
Destruction of Tyre ... Ezek. 26:7-12
Utter destruction ... Is. 14:4-27

Nebushasban—*Nebo delivers me*
Babylonian officer ... Jer. 39:13

Nebuzar-adan—*Nebo has given seed*
Nebuchadnezzar's captain at siege of Jerusalem ... 2 Kin. 25:8-20
Carries out Nebuchadnezzar's commands ... 2 Kin. 25:8-20
Protects Jeremiah ... Jer. 39:11-14

Necessary, necessity—*something imperative*

A. *As applied to God's plan:*
Preaching to the Jews first ... Acts 13:46
Change of the Law ... Heb. 7:12
Of Christ's sacrifice ... Heb. 8:3

B. *In the Christian's life:*
Wise decisions ... 2 Cor. 9:5
Personal needs ... Acts 20:34

See Must

Neck

A. *Uses of:*
Ornaments ... Ezek. 16:11
Beauty ... Song 4:4
Authority ... Gen. 41:42

B. *Significant acts performed by:*
Emotional salutation ... Gen. 45:14
Subjection of enemies ... Josh. 10:24

C. *Figurative of:*
Servitude ... Gen. 27:40
Severe punishment ... Is. 8:8
Rescue ... Is. 52:2

See Yoke

Necklace—*an ornament worn about the neck*
Signifying rank ... Gen. 41:41, 42
Worn by animals ... Judg. 8:26

Necromancer—*one who inquires of the dead*
Strongly condemned ... Deut. 18:10, 11
Consulted by King Saul ... 1 Sam. 28:7-19
Consultation with, rebuked ... Is. 8:19

Nedabiah—*Jehovah has been gracious*
Son of King Jeconiah ... 1 Chr. 3:18

Need(s)—*an inner or outward lack; a compulsion to something*

A. *Physical necessity, arising from lack of:*
Food ... Deut. 15:8
Provisions ... 2 Chr. 2:16

B. *Moral necessity, arising from:*
Spiritual immaturity ... Heb. 5:12
Order of things ... Matt. 3:14
Spiritual need ... Luke 10:42

C. *Promises concerning supply of:*
Promised ... Matt. 6:8, 32
Provided ... Acts 2:45
Fulfilled ... Rev. 21:23

D. *Caused by:*
Riotous living ... Luke 15:14

E. *Provision against, by:*
Help of others ... 2 Cor. 9:12

F. *Reaction to, shown in:*
Humble submission to God's will ... Phil. 4:11, 12

See Must; Necessary, necessity

Needle—*a sharp instrument used in sewing or embroidering*
Product of, used in tabernacle ... Ex. 26:36
Figurative of something impossible ... Matt. 19:24

Needlework—*embroidered work*
Of the tabernacle ... Ex. 26:36; Ex. 28:39; Ex. 38:18

Needy—*the poor*

A. *Evil treatment of:*
Oppression ... Amos 4:1
Injustice toward ... Is. 10:2

B. *Promise toward:*
God's:
Remembrance of ... Ps. 9:18
Deliverance ... Ps. 35:10
Salvation of ... Ps. 72:4-13
Exaltation of ... Ps. 113:7
Strength of ... Is. 25:4

C. *Right treatment of:*
Recommended ... Deut. 24:14, 15
Remembered ... Jer. 22:16
Rewarded ... Matt. 25:34-40

See Poor, poverty

Negev—*dry, parched; denotes southern Palestine*
Hebron located in ... Num. 13:22

Neglect—*to fail to respond to duties*

A. *Of material things:*
One's appearance ... 2 Sam. 19:24
Needs of the body ... Col. 2:23

B. *Of spiritual things:*
Gospel ... Matt. 22:2-5
Salvation ... Heb. 2:1-3

C. *Consequences of:*
Kept out ... Matt. 25:1-13
Sent to hell ... Matt. 25:24-30
Reward lost ... 1 Cor. 3:10-15

Nehelamite
Term applied to Shemaiah, a false prophet ... Jer. 29:24-32

Nehemiah (I)—*Jehovah has comforted*
1. Leader in the postexilic community ... Ezra 2:2
2. Postexilic workman ... Neh. 3:16

Nehemiah (II)—*Jehovah has comforted*

A. *Life of:*
Son of Hachaliah ... Neh. 1:1
Cupbearer to the Persian King Artaxerxes I (465–424 B.C.) ... Neh. 1:11
Grieves over Jerusalem's desolation ... Neh. 1:4-11
Appointed governor ... Neh. 5:14
Sent to rebuild Jerusalem ... Neh. 2:1-8
Unwelcome by non-Jews ... Neh. 2:9, 10
Views walls at night ... Neh. 2:11-20
Gives list of builders ... Neh. 3:1-32
Continues work in spite of opposition ... Neh. 4:1-23
Makes reforms among Jews ... Neh. 5:1-19
Opposition continues, but work completed ... Neh. 6:1-19
Introduces law and order ... Neh. 7:1-73
Participates with Ezra in restored worship ... Neh. 8—10
Registers inhabitants ... Neh. 11:1-36
Registers priests and Levites ... Neh. 12:1-26
Returns to Artaxerxes; revisits Jerusalem ... Neh. 13:6, 7
Institutes reforms ... Neh. 13:1-31

B. *Character of:*
Patriotic ... Neh. 1:1-4
Prayerful ... Neh. 1:5-11
Perceptive ... Neh. 2:17-20
Persistent ... Neh. 4:1-23
Persuasive ... Neh. 5:1-13
Pure in motives ... Neh. 5:14-19
Persevering ... Neh. 6:1-19

See the next article

Nehemiah, the Book of—*a book of the Old Testament*
Nehemiah's prayer ... Neh. 1:4-11
Inspection of the wall ... Neh. 2:11-16
Rebuilding the wall ... Neh. 3:1-32
The enemies' plot ... Neh. 6:1-14
The reading of the Law ... Neh. 8:1-18
Confession of the priests ... Neh. 9:4-38
Nehemiah's reform ... Neh. 13:7-31

Nehum—*consolation*
Postexilic returnee ... Neh. 7:7
Called Rehum ... Ezra 2:2

Nehushta—*of bronze*
Wife of King Jehoiakim ... 2 Kin. 24:8

Nehushtan—*piece of brass*
Applied to brazen serpent ... 2 Kin. 18:4

Neiel—*dwelling of God*
Town in Asher ... Josh. 19:24, 27

Neigh—*to cry lustfully*
Used of:
Horses ... Jer. 8:16
Lustful desires ... Jer. 5:8
Rendered "bellow" ... Jer. 50:11

Neighbor

A. *Sins against, forbidden:*
False witness ... Ex. 20:16
Coveting ... Ex. 20:17
Lying ... Lev. 6:2-5
Hating ... Deut. 19:11-13
Despising ... Prov. 14:21
Enticing ... Prov. 16:29
Deception ... Prov. 26:19
Flattery ... Prov. 29:5
Failure to pay ... Jer. 22:13
Adultery ... Jer. 29:23

B. *Duties toward, encouraged:*
Love ... Rom. 13:9, 10
Speak truth to ... Eph. 4:25
Teach ... Jer. 31:34
Show mercy to ... Luke 10:29, 37

Nekeb—*a narrow pass*
Village in Naphtali ... Josh. 19:33

Nekoda—*dotted*
Founder of a family of Temple servants ... Ezra 2:48
Genealogy of, rejected ... Ezra 2:59, 60

Nemuel—*God is spreading*
1. Brother of Dathan and Abiram ... Num. 26:9
2. Eldest son of Simeon ... 1 Chr. 4:24
Head of Nemuelites ... Num. 26:12
Called Jemuel ... Gen. 46:10

Nepheg—*sprout*
1. Izhar's son; Korah's brother ... Ex. 6:21
2. David's son born in Jerusalem ... 2 Sam. 5:13-15

Nephew—*old English for grandson*
Applied to:
Abdon's ... Judg. 12:14
Widow's ... 1 Tim. 5:4
Used as a curse ... Is. 14:22

SUBJECT	REFERENCE
Nephtoah—*opening*	
Border town between Judah and Benjamin	Josh. 15:9
Nepotism—*putting relatives in public offices*	
Joseph's	Gen. 47:11, 12
Saul's	1 Sam. 14:50
David's	2 Sam. 8:16-18
Nehemiah's	Neh. 7:2
Ner—*lamp*	
Father of Abner; grandfather of Saul	1 Sam. 14:50, 51
Nereus—*the name of a sea god*	
Christian at Rome	Rom. 16:15
Nergal—*a Babylonian god of war*	
Worshiped by men of Cuth	2 Kin. 17:30
Nergal-sharezer—*Nergal preserve the king*	
Babylonian prince during capture of Jerusalem	Jer. 39:3, 13
Neri	
Ancestor of Christ	Luke 3:27
Neriah—*Jehovah is a lamp*	
Father of Baruch	Jer. 32:12
Nest	
A. *Kinds of:*	
Eagle's	Job 39:27
Swallow's	Ps. 84:3
Great owl's	Is. 34:15
Dove's	Jer. 48:28
B. *Figurative of:*	
False security	Num. 24:21, 22
Lord's resting place	Matt. 8:20
Full maturity	Job 29:18
Something out of place	Prov. 27:8
Helplessness	Is. 10:14
Net	
A. *Kinds of:*	
Design in a structure	Ex. 27:4, 5
Trapping a bird or animal	Prov. 1:17
Catching fish	John 21:6-11
B. *Figurative of:*	
Plots of evil men	Ps. 9:15
Predatory men	Ps. 31:4
God's chastisements	Job 19:6
Flattery	Prov. 29:5
God's soveriegn plan	Ezek. 12:13 Ezek. 17:20
Nethaneel—*God has given*	
1. Leader of Issachar	Num. 1:8
2. Jesse's fourth son	1 Chr. 2:13, 14
3. Levite trumpeter	1 Chr. 15:24
4. Levite scribe	1 Chr. 24:6
5. Obed-edom's fifth son	1 Chr. 26:4
6. Prince sent to teach Judah	2 Chr. 17:7
7. Levite chief	2 Chr. 35:9
8. Priest who married a foreign wife	Ezra 10:18-22
9. Priest in Joiakim's time	Neh. 12:21
10. Levite musician in dedication service	Neh. 12:36
Nethaniah—*Jehovah has given*	
1. Son of Asaph	1 Chr. 25:2, 12
2. Levite teacher in Jehoshaphat's reign	2 Chr. 17:8
3. Father of Jehudi	Jer. 36:14
4. Father of Ishmael, struck down Gedaliah	2 Kin. 25:23, 25
Nethinim—*given*	
A. *Described as:*	
Servants of the Levites	Ezra 8:20
B. *Probable origin of:*	
Midianites	Num. 31:2, 41
Gibeonites	Josh. 9:23, 27
Solomon's slaves	1 Kin. 9:20, 21
C. *Characteristics of:*	
Governed by captains	Neh. 11:21
Assigned certain cities	1 Chr. 9:2
Exempt from taxes	Ezra 7:24

SUBJECT	REFERENCE
Zealous for Israel's covenant	Neh. 10:28, 29
Assigned important jobs	Ezra 8:17
Returned from exile in large numbers	Ezra 2:43-54
Netophathite—*an inhabitant of Netophah*	
Town of Judah near Jerusalem	1 Chr. 2:54
Occupied by returning Levites	1 Chr. 9:16
Applied to two of David's mighty men	2 Sam. 23:28, 29
Loyalty of, demonstrated	2 Kin. 25:23, 24
Nettles—*thorn bushes*	
Sign of:	
Indolence	Prov. 24:31
Desolation	Is. 34:13
Retreat for cowards	Job 30:7
Network—*artistic handwork in*	
Tabernacle	Ex. 27:4
Temple	2 Kin. 7:18-41
Neutrality	
Impossibility of, taught	Matt. 6:24 Matt. 12:30
Invitation to, rejected	Josh. 24:15, 16
Never—*not ever*	
A. *Concerning God's spiritual promises:*	
Satisfaction	John 4:14
Stability	Ps. 55:22
Security	John 10:28
B. *Concerning God's threats:*	
Chastisement	2 Sam. 12:10
Desolation	Is. 13:20
Forgiveness	Mark 3:29
New—*something recent or fresh*	
Commandment	John 13:34
Covenant	Jer. 31:31
Creature	2 Cor. 5:17
Fruit	Ezek. 47:12
Earth	Is. 65:17
Spirit	Ezek. 11:19
Heaven	Is. 66:22
Jerusalem	Rev. 21:2
Name	Is. 62:2
Man	Eph. 2:15
Song	Is. 42:10
New thing (Christ's birth)	Jer. 31:22
All things new	Rev. 21:5
New birth—*regeneration*	
A. *Described as:*	
One heart	Ezek. 11:19
Resurrection	Rom. 6:4-10
New creature	2 Cor. 5:17
Circumcision	Deut. 30:6
Holy seed	1 John 3:9
Begotten	1 Pet. 1:3
Name written in heaven	Luke 10:20
B. *Productive of:*	
Growth	1 Pet. 2:1, 2
Knowledge	1 Cor. 2:12-16
Change	2 Cor. 3:18
Fruitfulness	John 15:1-8
Victory	1 John 5:4
Discipline	Heb. 12:3-11
See Born again	
New covenant	
A. *Described as:*	
Everlasting	Is. 55:3
Of peace	Ezek. 34:25
Of life	Mal. 2:5
B. *Elements of:*	
Author—God	Eph. 2:4
Cause—God's love	John 3:16
Mediator—Christ	1 Tim. 2:5
Time originated—in eternity	Rom. 8:29, 30
Time instituted—at man's sin	Gen. 3:15
Time realized—at Christ's death	Eph. 2:13-22
Time consummated—in eternity	Eph. 2:7
Duties—faith and repentance	Mark 1:15
C. *Ratification of, by:*	
God's promise	Gen. 3:15
God's oath	Is. 54:9, 10

SUBJECT	REFERENCE
Christ's blood	Heb. 9:12-26
Spirit's sealing	2 Cor. 1:22
D. *Superiority of, to the old:*	
Hope	Heb. 7:19
Priesthood	Heb. 7:20-28
Covenant	Heb. 8:6
Sacrifice	Heb. 9:23
New Gate—*a Temple gate*	
Princes meet at	Jer. 26:10
New Jerusalem	
Vision, seen by Abraham	Heb. 11:10, 16
Reality of, experienced by believers	Gal. 4:26, 31
Consummation of, awaits eternity	Heb. 13:14
New man (see New birth)	
New moon	
A festival day	Ps. 81:3 Col. 2:16
A point of reference	Is. 66:23
News	
A. *Kinds of:*	
Distressing	Gen. 32:6-8
Disturbing	Josh. 22:11-20
Alarming	1 Sam. 4:13-22
Agonizing	2 Sam. 18:31-33
Sorrowful	Neh. 1:2-11
Joyful	Luke 2:8-18
Good	1 Kin. 1:42
Fatal	1 Sam. 4:19
B. *Of salvation:*	
Out of Zion	Is. 40:9
By a person	Is. 41:27
Bringer of peace	Is. 52:7
By Christ	Is. 61:1-3
New Year	
Erection of the tabernacle on	Ex. 40:17, 18
Neziah—*pre-eminent*	
Head of a Nethinim family	Ezra 2:43, 54
Nezib—*garrison*	
Town of Judah	Josh. 15:1, 43
Nibhaz	
Idol of Avites	2 Kin. 17:31
Nibshan—*the furnace*	
Town of Judah	Josh. 15:1, 62
Nicanor—*victorious*	
One of the seven men chosen as deacons	Acts 6:1-5
Nicodemus—*conqueror of the people*	
Pharisee; converses with Jews	John 3:1-12
Protests unfairness of Christ's trial	John 7:50-52
Brings gifts to anoint Christ's body	John 19:39, 40
Nicolaitanes—*early Christian sect*	
Group teaching moral looseness	Rev. 2:6-15
Nicolas—*victor over the people*	
Non-Jewish proselyte deacon	Acts 6:5
Nicopolis—*city of victory*	
Town in Epirus (near Actium)	Titus 3:12
Niger—*black*	
Latin surname of Simeon, a teacher in Antioch	Acts 13:1
Night—*the time of darkness*	
A. *Important facts concerning:*	
Made by God	Ps. 104:20
Named at creation	Gen. 1:5
Begins at sunset	Gen. 28:11
Established by God's covenant	Gen. 8:22
Displays God's glory	Ps. 19:2
Designed for rest	Ps. 104:23
Wild beasts creep in	Ps. 104:20-22
None in heaven	Zech. 14:7
Divided into "watches" and hours	Mark 13:35

SUBJECT REFERENCE

B. *Special events in:*
Jacob's wrestling ... Gen. 32:22-31
Egypt's greatest plague ... Ex. 12:12-31
Ordinance of the Passover ... Ex. 12:42
King's sleeplessness ... Esth. 6:1
Nehemiah's vigil ... Neh. 2:11-16
Belshazzar slain ... Dan. 5:30
Angelic revelation ... Luke 2:8-15
Nicodemus' talk ... John 3:2
Release from prison ... Acts 5:19
Paul's escape ... Acts 9:24, 25
Wonderful conversion ... Acts 16:25-33
Lord's return ... Mark 13:35

C. *Good acts in:*
Toil ... Luke 5:5
Prayer ... 1 Sam. 15:11; Luke 6:12
Song ... Job 35:10; Ps. 42:8
Flight from evil ... 1 Sam. 19:10; Matt. 2:14
Dreams ... Matt. 2:12, 13, 19

D. *Evil acts in:*
Drunkenness ... Is. 5:11
Thievery ... Obad. 5; Matt. 27:64
Debauchery ... 1 Thess. 5:2-7
Betrayal ... Matt. 26:31, 34, 46-50
Death ... Luke 12:20

F. *Figurative of:*
Present age ... Rom. 13:11, 12
Death ... John 9:4
Unregenerate state ... 1 Thess. 5:5, 7
Judgment ... Mic. 3:6

Nighthawk
Unclean bird ... Lev. 11:16

Night monster—*a nocturnal creature*
Dwells in ruins ... Is. 34:14

Nile—*Egypt's main river*

A. *Called:*
Sihor ... Is. 23:3
Stream of Egypt ... Is. 27:12
Sea ... Nah. 3:8

B. *Characteristics of:*
Has seven streams ... Is. 11:15
Overflows annually ... Jer. 46:8
Source of Egyptian wealth ... Is. 19:5-8

C. *Events connected with:*
Drowning of male children ... Ex. 1:22
Moses placed in ... Ex. 2:3
Water of, turned to blood ... Ex. 7:15, 20

D. *Figurative of:*
Judgment ... Ezek. 30:12; Amos 9:5
Army ... Jer. 46:7-9

Nimrah—*an abbreviation of Beth-nimrah*
Town in Gilead ... Num. 32:3, 36

Nimrim—*wholesome waters*
Place in south Moab ... Is. 15:6

Nimrod—*strong*
Ham's grandson ... Gen. 10:6-8
Becomes a mighty hunter ... Gen. 10:8, 9
Establishes cities ... Gen. 10:10-12
Land of Assyria, thus described ... Mic. 5:6

Nimshi—*Jehovah reveals*
Grandfather of King Jehu ... 2 Kin. 9:2, 14
Called Jehu's father ... 2 Kin. 9:20

Nineveh—*the capital of ancient Assyria*

A. *History of:*
Built by Asshur ... Gen. 10:11, 12
Capital of Assyria ... 2 Kin. 19:36
Jonah preaches to ... Jon. 1:1, 2
Citizens of:
Repent ... Jon. 3:5-9
At the judgment seat ... Matt. 12:41

B. *Prophecies concerning its:*
Destruction by Babylon ... Nah. 2:1-4
Internal weakness ... Nah. 3:11-17
Utter desolation ... Nah. 3:18, 19

C. *Described as:*
Great city ... Jon. 3:2, 3
Wealthy ... Nah. 2:9
Fortified ... Nah. 3:8, 12
Wicked ... Jon. 1:2
Idolatrous ... Nah. 1:14
Careless ... Zeph. 2:15
Full of lies ... Nah. 3:1

Ninth hour—*that is, 3 P.M.*
Time of Christ's death ... Matt. 27:46
Customary hour of prayer ... Acts 3:1
Time of Cornelius' vision ... Acts 10:1, 3

Nisan—*beginning*
Name of Abib (first month of Jewish year) after the exile ... Neh. 2:1
See Jewish calendar

Nisroch—*eagle, hawk*
Sennacherib's god ... 2 Kin. 19:37

Nitre—*carbonate of soda* (in the Bible)
Figurative of agitation ... Prov. 25:20
As a cleansing agent ... Jer. 2:22

No-amon—*the Egyptian city Thebes*
Nineveh compared to ... Nah. 3:8

Noadiah—*Jehovah has met by appointment*
1. Levite in Ezra's time ... Ezra 8:33
2. Prophetess who tries to frighten Nehemiah ... Neh. 6:14

Noah (I)—*rest*

A. *Life of:*
Son of Lamech ... Gen. 5:28, 29
Father of Shem, Ham and Japheth ... Gen. 5:32
Finds favor with God ... Gen. 6:8
Lives in the midst of corruption ... Gen. 6:1-13
Instructed to build the ark ... Gen. 6:13-22
Preacher of righteousness ... 2 Pet. 2:5
Enters ark with family and animals ... Gen. 7:1-24
Preserved during flood ... Gen. 8:1-17
Builds an altar ... Gen. 8:18-22
Covenant established with ... Gen. 9:1-19
Plants a vineyard; becomes drunk ... Gen. 9:20, 21
Pronounces curse and blessings ... Gen. 9:22-27
Dies at 950 ... Gen. 9:28, 29

B. *Character of:*
Righteous ... Gen. 6:9
Obedient ... Heb. 11:7
In fellowship with God ... Gen. 6:9
Notable in history ... Ezek. 14:14, 20

Noah (II)—*trembling*
Daughter of Zelophehad ... Num. 26:33

Nob—*height*
City of priests; David flees to ... 1 Sam. 21:1-9
Priests of, killed by Saul ... 1 Sam. 22:9-23
Near Jerusalem ... Is. 10:32
Reinhabited after the exile ... Neh. 11:32

Nobah—*barking*
1. Manassite leader ... Num. 32:42
2. Town in Gad ... Judg. 8:11

Nobleman—*one who belongs to the upper class*
Jesus:
Heals son of ... John 4:46-54
Cites in parable ... Luke 19:12-27

Nod—*wandering exile*
Place (east of Eden) of Cain's abode ... Gen. 4:16, 17

Nodab—*nobility*
Arabian tribe ... 1 Chr. 5:19

Nogah—*brilliance*
One of David's sons ... 1 Chr. 3:1, 7

Nohah—*rest*
Benjamin's fourth son ... 1 Chr. 8:1, 2

Noise—*a sound of something*

A. *Kinds of:*
Sea ... Ps. 65:7
Battle ... Is. 13:4; Jer. 47:3
Songs ... Ezek. 26:13; Amos 5:23
Mourners ... Matt. 9:23
Crying ... 1 Sam. 4:13, 14
Revelry ... Ex. 32:17, 18
Dog ... Ps. 59:6
God's glory ... Ezek. 43:2

B. *Figurative of:*
Strong opposition ... Is. 31:4
Worthlessness ... Jer. 46:17

Noisome—*something evil or deadly*
Hurtful beasts ... Ezek. 14:15, 21
Deadly pestilence ... Ps. 91:3
Foul sore ... Rev. 16:2

Nomad—*wanderer*
Life style of patriarchs ... Gen. 12:1-9; Gen. 13:1-18
Israel's history ... Deut. 26:5

Noon—*midday*

A. *Time of:*
Eating ... Gen. 43:16, 25
Resting ... 2 Sam. 4:5
Praying ... Ps. 55:17
Complain and murmer ... Ps. 55:17
Drunkenness ... 1 Kin. 20:16
Destruction ... Ps. 91:6
Death ... 2 Kin. 4:20

B. *Figurative of:*
Blindness ... Deut. 28:29
Cleansing ... Job 11:17

Nophah—*windy place*
Moabite town ... Num. 21:29, 30

North
Refers to:
A geographical direction ... Gen. 28:14; Ps. 107:3
Invading forces ... Is. 14:31; Jer. 6:1

Nose, nostrils—*the organ of breathing*

A. *Used literally for:*
Breathing ... Gen. 2:7
Smelling ... Amos 4:10
Ornamentation ... Is. 3:21
Bondage ... Is. 37:29
Blood (forced) ... Prov. 30:33
Behemoth ... Job 40:15-24
Idols ... Ps. 115:6
Nosebleeding produced by wringing ... Prov. 30:33

B. *Used figuratively of:*
Man's life ... Job 27:3
God's:
Power ... Ex. 15:8
Sovereign control ... 2 Kin. 19:28
Overindulgence ... Num. 11:20
National hope (Zedekiah) ... Lam. 4:20
Something very offensive ... Is. 65:5

Nose ring
Worn by women ... Is. 3:21
Put in swine's snout ... Prov. 11:22

Nothing—*not a thing*
Things classified as:
Service without:
Christ ... John 15:5
Love ... 1 Cor. 13:3
Circumcision ... 1 Cor. 7:19
Flesh ... John 6:63

Not my people, Not loved—*symbolic names of Hosea's children*
Lo-ammi ... Hos. 1:9
Lo-ruhamah ... Hos. 1:6

Nought

A. *Descriptive of:*
Something:
Fruitless ... Is. 49:24
Without payment ... Gen. 29:15
Vain ... Mal. 1:10
Nothing ... Is. 41:24

B. *Time of:*
Past ... Neh. 4:15
Present ... Amos 6:13
Future ... Ps. 33:10

SUBJECT ... REFERENCE

C. *Things that will come to:*
Wicked ... Job 8:22
Wicked counsel ... Is. 8:10
Babylon ... Rev. 18:17

Nourish—*provide means of growth*

A. *Descriptive of the growth or care of:*
Children ... Acts 7:20, 21
Animals ... 2 Sam. 12:3
Plants ... Is. 44:14
Family ... Gen. 45:11
Country ... Acts 12:20

B. *Figurative of:*
Protection ... Is. 1:2
Provision ... Ruth 4:15
Pampering ... James 5:5
Preparedness ... 1 Tim. 4:6

Novice—*one who is inexperienced. A recent Christian convert*
Bishops, not to be ... 1 Tim. 3:1, 6

Now—*the present time*

A. *As contrasted with:*
Old Testament ... John 4:23
Past ... John 9:25
Future ... John 13:7, 19
Two conditions ... Luke 16:25

B. *In Christ's life, descriptive of His:*
Atonement ... Rom. 5:11
Humiliation ... Heb. 2:8
Resurrection ... 1 Cor. 15:20
Glorification ... John 13:31
Intercession ... Heb. 9:24
Return ... 1 John 2:28

C. *In the Christian's life, descriptive of:*
Salvation ... Rom. 13:11
Regeneration ... John 5:25
Reconciliation ... Col. 1:21, 22
Justification ... Rom. 5:9
Victory ... Gal. 2:20
Worship ... John 4:23
Suffering ... 1 Pet. 1:6-8
Hope ... Rev. 12:10
Glorification ... Rom. 8:21, 22; 1 John 3:2

D. *Descriptive of the present age as:*
Time of:
Opportunity ... 2 Cor. 6:2
Evil ... 1 Thess. 2:6
God's:
Greater revelation ... Eph. 3:5
Completed redemption ... Col. 1:26, 27
Final dealing with mankind ... Heb. 12:26

Nuisance—*something very irritating*
Descriptive of:
Widow ... Luke 18:2-5

Numbers
Symbolic of:
One—unity ... Deut. 6:4; Matt. 19:6
Two—unity ... Gen. 1:27
Two—division ... 1 Kin. 18:21; Matt. 7:13, 14
Three—the Trinity ... Matt. 28:19; 2 Cor. 13:14
Three—resurrection ... Hos. 6:1, 2; Matt. 12:40; Luke 13:32
Three—completion ... 1 Cor. 13:13
Three—testing ... Judg. 7:16
Four—completion ... Matt. 13:4-8; Matt. 25:2; John 4:35
Five—incompletion ... Matt. 25:15-20
Six—man's testing ... Gen. 1:27, 31; Rev. 13:18
Seven—completion ... Ex. 20:10
Seven—fulfillment ... Josh. 6:4
Seven—perfection ... Rev. 1:4
Eighth—new beginning ... Ezek. 43:27; 1 Pet. 3:20
Ten—completion ... 1 Cor. 6:9, 10
Tenth—God's part ... Gen. 14:20; Mal. 3:10
Twelve—God's purpose ... John 11:9; Rev. 21:12-17
Forty—testing ... Jon. 3:4; Matt. 4:2
Forty—judgment ... Num. 14:33; Ps. 95:10
Seventy—God's completed purpose ... Jer. 25:11; Dan. 9:24

Numbers, the Book of—*a book of the Old Testament*
The census ... Num. 1:1—4:49
Cleansing of Levites ... Num. 8:5-22
The cloud and the tabernacle ... Num. 9:15-23
The provision of manna ... Num. 11:4-9
The spies ... Num. 13:1—14:45
The rebellion of Korah ... Num. 16:1-35
The sin of Moses ... Num. 20:1-13
Aaron's death ... Num. 20:22-29
Balaam and Balak ... Num. 22:2—24:25
Offerings and feasts ... Num. 28:1—29:40
Settlements in Gilead ... Num. 32:1-42
Preparation for Canaan ... Num. 33:50—35:34

Nun—*fish*
1. Father of Joshua, Israel's military leader ... Josh. 1:1
Called Non ... 1 Chr. 7:27
2. Letter in the Hebrew alphabet ... Ps. 119:105-112

Nurse—*nourishment and protection to the young*

A. *Duties of:*
Provide nourishment ... Gen. 21:7
Protect ... 2 Kin. 11:2
Called "guardian" ... 2 Kin. 10:1, 5

B. *Figurative of:*
Judgment ... Lam. 4:4
Provision ... Num. 11:12
Gentleness ... 1 Thess. 2:7

Nuts
Provided as gifts ... Gen. 43:11
Grown in gardens ... Song 6:11

Nympha—*sacred to the nymphs*
Christian of Laodicea ... Col. 4:15

O

Oak—*a large and strong tree*

A. *Uses of:*
Landmarks ... Judg. 6:11, 19
Burial place ... Gen. 35:8
Place of rest ... 1 Kin. 13:14
Place of idolatry ... Is. 44:14
For oars ... Ezek. 27:6

B. *Figurative of:*
Strength ... Amos 2:9
Judgment ... Is. 1:29, 30
Haughtiness ... Is. 2:11, 13

Oars—*wooden blades used for rowing*
Made of oak ... Ezek. 27:6, 29
Used on galleys ... Is. 33:21

Oaths—*solemn promises*

A. *Expressions descriptive of:*
"As the LORD liveth" ... 1 Sam. 19:6
"God is witness" ... Gen. 31:50
"The LORD . . . be witness" ... Jer. 42:5
"God judge between us" ... Gen. 31:53
"The LORD make thee like" ... Jer. 29:22
"I adjure thee" ... Matt. 26:63
"I call God for a record" ... 2 Cor. 1:23

B. *Purposes of:*
Confirm covenant ... Gen. 26:28
Insure protection ... Gen. 31:44-53
Establish truth ... Ex. 22:11
Confirm fidelity ... Num. 5:19-22
Guarantee duties ... Gen. 24:3, 4
Sign a covenant ... 2 Chr. 15:12-15
Fulfill promises ... Neh. 5:12, 13

C. *Sacredness of:*
Obligatory ... Num. 30:2-16
Maintained even in deception ... Josh. 9:20
Upheld by Christ ... Matt. 26:63, 64
Rewarded ... 2 Chr. 15:12-15
Maintained in fear ... 1 Sam. 14:24, 26

D. *Prohibitions concerning, not:*
In idol's name ... Josh. 23:7
In creature's name ... Matt. 5:34-36
Falsely ... Lev. 19:12
Among Christians ... Matt. 5:34

Oaths of God

A. *Made in Old Testament concerning:*
Promise to Abraham ... Gen. 50:24
Davidic covenant ... 2 Sam. 7:10-16
Messianic priesthood ... Ps. 110:4, 5

B. *Fulfilled in New Testament in Christ's:*
Birth ... Luke 1:68-73
Kingship on David's throne ... Luke 1:32, 33
Priesthood ... Heb. 7:20-28

See Swearing

Obadiah—*servant of Jehovah*
1. King Ahab's steward ... 1 Kin. 18:3-16
2. Descendant of David ... 1 Chr. 3:21
3. Chief of Issachar ... 1 Chr. 7:3
4. Descendant of Saul ... 1 Chr. 8:38
5. Gadite captain ... 1 Chr. 12:8, 9
6. Man of Zebulun ... 1 Chr. 27:19
7. Prince sent by Jehoshaphat to teach ... 2 Chr. 17:7
8. Levite overseer ... 2 Chr. 34:12
9. Leader in the postexilic community ... Ezra 8:9
10. Priest who signs the covenant ... Neh. 10:5
11. Levite ... 1 Chr. 9:16
Called Abda ... Neh. 11:17
12. Postexilic porter ... Neh. 12:25
13. Prophet of Judah ... Obad. 1

Obadiah, the Book of—*a book of the Old Testament*
Against Edom ... Obad. 1-9
Edom against Judah ... Obad. 10-14
The day of the LORD ... Obad. 15, 16
Zion's victory ... Obad. 17-21

Obal—*to be bare*
Descendants of Joktan ... Gen. 10:28

Obduracy—*resistance to pleadings of mercy*
Expressed by:
"Stiffnecked" ... Ex. 33:3, 5
"Uncircumcised" ... Lev. 26:41
"Impenitent" ... Rom. 2:5
"Harden your hearts" ... 1 Sam. 6:6
"Neither will I let" ... Ex. 5:1, 2
"I will not hear" ... Jer. 22:21
"Seek not" ... John 5:44
"He trespass yet more" ... 2 Chr. 28:22-25
"Being past feeling" ... Eph. 4:18, 19
"God gave them up" ... Rom. 1:24-28
"Therefore they could not believe" ... John 12:39
"That cannot cease from sin" ... 2 Pet. 2:14
"They were appointed" ... 1 Pet. 2:8
"Let him be unjust still" ... Rev. 22:11

See Hardness of heart; Impenitence

Obed—*servant*
1. Son of Ephlal ... 1 Chr. 2:37, 38
2. Son of Boaz and Ruth ... Ruth 4:17-22
3. One of David's mighty men ... 1 Chr. 11:47
4. Korhite porter ... 1 Chr. 26:7
5. Father of Azariah ... 2 Chr. 23:1

Obed-edom—*servant of Edom*
1. Philistine from Gath; ark of the Lord left in his house ... 2 Sam. 6:10-12; 1 Chr. 13:13, 14
2. Overseer of the storehouse ... 1 Chr. 26:4-8, 15
3. Levitical musician ... 1 Chr. 16:5
4. Guardian of the sacred vessels ... 2 Chr. 25:24

Obedience—*submission to authority*

A. *Relationship involved:*
God—man ... Acts 5:29
Parent—child ... Gen. 28:7; Eph. 6:1
Husband—wife ... 1 Cor. 14:34, 35
Master—slave ... Eph. 6:5
Ruler—subject ... Titus 1:1

SUBJECT	REFERENCE
Leader—follower	Acts 5:36, 37
Pastor—people	Heb. 13:17
Man—nature	James 3:3
God—nature	Matt. 8:27
God—demons	Mark 1:27
B. *Spiritual objects of:*	
God	Acts 5:29
Christ	Heb. 5:9
Truth	Gal. 5:7
Faith	Acts 6:7
C. *In the Christian's life:*	
Comes from the heart	Rom. 6:17
Needs testing	2 Cor. 2:4
Aided by the Spirit	1 Pet. 1:22
Manifested in Gentiles	Rom. 15:18
In pastoral relations	2 Cor. 7:15
D. *Lack of, brings:*	
Rejection	1 Sam. 15:20-26
Captivity	2 Kin. 18:11, 12
Death	1 Kin. 20:36
Retribution	2 Thess. 1:8
E. *Examples of:*	
Noah	Gen. 6:22
Abram	Gen. 12:1-4
Israelites	Ex. 12:28
Caleb and Joshua	Num. 32:12
David	Ps. 119:106
Asa	1 Kin. 15:11, 14
Elijah	1 Kin. 17:5
Hezekiah	2 Kin. 18:6
Josiah	2 Kin. 22:2
Zerubbabel	Hag. 1:12
Christ	Rom. 5:19
Paul	Acts 26:19
Christians	Phil. 2:12
Obedience of Christ, our example	
To death	Phil. 2:5-11
Learned	Heb. 5:7-10
Submissive	Matt. 26:39, 42
Obedience to civil government	
Meet obligation	Mark 12:13-17
Of God	Rom. 13:1-7
Duty	Titus 3:1
For Lord's sake	1 Pet. 2:13-17
Obeisance—*bending or bowing*	
As an act of:	
Respect	Ex. 18:7
Reverence	Matt. 2:11
Flaunting fidelity	2 Sam. 1:2-16
Fawning favor	2 Sam. 14:2-4
Feigned flattery	2 Sam. 15:5, 6
Obil—*camel driver*	
Ishmaelite in charge of camels	1 Chr. 27:30
Obituary—*an account of a person's life; a death notice*	
Written of Moses	Deut. 34:1-12
Objectors—*those who oppose something*	
A. *Argue against God's:*	
Power	Ex. 14:10-15
Provision	Ex. 16:2-17
Promises	Num. 14:1-10
B. *Overcome by:*	
Prophecies cited	Jer. 26:8-19
Promises claimed	Acts 4:23-31
Oblivion—*the state of being forgotten*	
God's punishment on the wicked	Ps. 34:16
Oboth—*water skins*	
Israelite camp	Num. 21:10, 11 Num. 33:43, 44
Observe—*to keep; to remember*	
A. *Descriptive of:*	
Remembrance	Gen. 37:11
Laws	Ex. 31:16
Obedience	Matt. 28:20
Watchfulness	Jer. 8:7 Mark 6:20
False rituals	Gal. 4:10
B. *Blessings of proper:*	
Material prosperity	Deut. 6:3
Righteousness	Deut. 6:25
Elevation	Deut. 28:1, 13
Loving-kindness	Ps. 107:43

SUBJECT	REFERENCE
C. *Manner of proper:*	
Carefully	Deut. 12:28
Without change	Deut. 12:32
Diligently	Deut. 24:8
Forever	2 Kin. 17:37
Without preference	1 Tim. 5:21
Obstacles—*obstructions*	
Eliminated by:	
God's help	Is. 45:2
Christ's help	Is. 49:9-11
Spirit's help	Zech. 4:6, 7
Obstacles to faith	
Men's honor	John 5:44
Highmindedness	Rom. 11:20
Obstinacy—*stubbornness*	
Continuing in sin	2 Chr. 28:22, 23
Rejecting counsel	1 Kin. 12:12-15
Refusing to change	Jer. 44:15-27
Obstruct—*to hamper progress*	
Attempted	Ezra 4:1-5
Condemned	3 John 9, 10
Obtain—*to bring into one's possession*	
A. *Of material things:*	
Advancement	Esth. 2:9-17
B. *Of spiritual things:*	
Favor	Prov. 8:35
Joy and gladness	Is. 35:10
Heaven	Luke 20:35-38
Divine help	Acts 26:22
Salvation	Rom. 11:7
Better resurrection	Heb. 11:35
Faith	2 Pet. 1:1
Occultism—*pertaining to supernatural, especially evil, influences*	
A. *Forms of:*	
Astrology	Is. 47:13
Charming	Deut. 18:11
Consulting with spirits	Deut. 18:11
Divination	Deut. 18:14
Magic	Gen. 41:8
Necromancy	Deut. 18:11
Soothsaying	Is. 2:6
Sorcery	Ex. 22:8
Witchcraft	Deut. 18:10
Wizardry	Deut. 18:11
B. *Attitude toward:*	
Forbidden	Deut. 18:10, 11 Jer. 27:9
Punished by death	Ex. 22:18 Lev. 20:6, 27
Forsaken	Acts 19:18-20
Ocran—*troubled*	
Man of Asher	Num. 1:13 Num. 2:27
Oded	
1. Father of Azariah the prophet	2 Chr. 15:1
2. Prophet of Samaria	2 Chr. 28:9-15
Odors, sweet	
A. *Used literally of:*	
Sacrificial incense	Lev. 26:31
Ointment fragrance	John 12:3
B. *Used figuratively of:*	
New life	Hos. 14:7
Prayers	Rev. 5:8
Christian service	Phil. 4:18
Offend, offense	
A. *Causes of:*	
Christ	Matt. 11:6
Persecution	Matt. 13:21 Matt. 24:10
The cross	1 Cor. 1:23
Physical parts	Matt. 18:8, 9
B. *Causes of, in Christ's:*	
Lowly position	Matt. 13:54-57
Teaching	Matt. 18:8, 9
Being the Rock	Is. 8:14
Being the Bread	John 6:58-66
Being crucified	1 Cor. 1:23
Being the righteousness of God	Rom. 9:31-33

SUBJECT	REFERENCE
C. *Christians forbidden to give:*	
In anything	2 Cor. 6:3
By their liberty	1 Cor. 8:9, 13
At any time	Phil. 1:10
See Stumble	
Offering of Christ	
Of Himself:	
Predicted	Ps. 40:6-8
Prepared	Heb. 5:1-10
Proclaimed	Heb. 10:5-9
Purified	Heb. 9:14
Personalized	Heb. 7:27
Perfected	Heb. 10:11-14
Praised	Eph. 5:2
Offerings	
A. *Characteristics of:*	
Made to God alone	Ex. 22:20
Limitation of	Heb. 9:9
Prescribed under the Law	Mark 1:44
B. *Thing offered must be:*	
Perfect	Lev. 22:21
Ceremonially clean	Lev. 27:11, 27
Best	Mal. 1:14
C. *Offerer must:*	
Not delay	Ex. 22:29, 30
Offer in righteousness	Mal. 3:3
Offer with thanksgiving	Ps. 27:6
D. *Classification of:*	
Private and public	Lev. 4:1-12
Physical and spiritual	Lev. 5:1-13
Voluntary and required	Lev. 1:3
Accepted and rejected	Judg. 6:17-24
Purified and perverted	Mal. 3:3, 4
Passing and permanent	Jer. 7:21-23
Jew and Gentile	Ps. 96:8
Typical and fulfilled	Gen. 22:2, 13
Offerings of the leaders—*by heads, of twelve tribes*	
1. Six wagons and twelve oxen to transport tabernacle	Num. 7:1-89
2. Dedication gift	Num. 7:1-89
Office—*a position of trust*	
Holders of:	
Butler	Gen. 40:13
Judge	Deut. 17:9
Priest	Deut. 26:3
Ministers of song	1 Chr. 6:32
Porters	1 Chr. 9:22
Publican	Matt. 9:9
Bishop	1 Tim. 3:1
Officers—*men appointed to rule over others*	
A. *Descriptive of:*	
Magistrate	Luke 12:58
Principal officer	1 Kin. 4:5, 7
B. *Functions of:*	
Administer justice	Num. 11:16
Offices of Christ	
As Prophet	Deut. 18:18, 19 Is. 61:1-3
As Priest	Ps. 110:4 Is. 53:1-12
As King	2 Sam. 7:12-17 Luke 1:32, 33
Offscouring—*something vile or worthless*	
Jews thus described	Lam. 3:45
Offspring—*issue* (physical or spiritual)	
A. *Used literally of:*	
Set-apart firstlings	Ex. 13:12 Ex. 34:19
Of a donkey you shall redeem	Ex. 13:13 Ex. 34:20
Man's issue (children)	Job 5:25
Man as created by God	Acts 17:28, 29
Christ as a descendant of David	Rev. 22:16
B. *Used figuratively of:*	
True believer	Is. 22:24
New Israel	Is. 44:3-5
Gentile church	Is. 61:9
True Church	Is. 65:23

SUBJECT — REFERENCE

Og—*giant*
- Amorite king of Bashan ... Deut. 3:1, 8
- Extent of rule ... Deut. 3:8, 10
- Residences at Ashtaroth and Edrei ... Josh. 12:4
- Man of great size ... Deut. 3:11
- Defeated and killed by Israel ... Num. 21:32-35
- Territory of, assigned to Manasseh ... Deut. 3:13
- Memory of, long remembered ... Ps. 135:11

Ohad—*powerful*
- Son of Simeon ... Gen. 46:10

Ohel—*family*
- Son of Zerubbabel ... 1 Chr. 3:19, 20

Oil—*a liquid extracted from olives*

A. *Features concerning:*
- Given by God ... Ps. 104:14, 15
- Subject to tithing ... Deut. 12:17

B. *Uses of:*
- Food ... Num. 11:8
- Anointing ... 1 Sam. 10:1
- Beautification ... Ruth 3:3
- Perfume ... Eccl. 10:1
- Illumination ... Ex. 25:6; Ex. 30:26-32; Matt. 25:3-8

C. *Types of oil:*
- Anointing ... Ex. 25:6
- Pure ... Ex. 27:20
- Baking ... Ex. 29:23
- Beaten ... Ex. 29:40
- Olive ... Ex. 30:24
- Precious ... 2 Kin. 20:13
- Golden ... Zech. 4:12

D. *Figurative of:*
- Prosperity ... Deut. 32:13
- Joy and gladness ... Is. 61:3
- Wastefulness ... Prov. 21:17
- Brotherly love ... Ps. 133:2
- Real grace ... Matt. 25:4
- Holy Spirit ... 1 John 2:20, 27

Oil tree
- Signifies restoration ... Is. 41:17-20

Ointment—*a salve made of olive oil and spices*

A. By special prescription for tabernacle ... Ex. 30:23-25
- Misuse of, forbidden ... Ex. 30:37, 38
- Ingredients stirred together ... Job 41:31

B. *Features concerning:*
- Considered very valuable ... 2 Kin. 20:13
- Carried or stored in containers ... Matt. 26:7
- Can be polluted ... Eccl. 10:1

C. *Uses of:*
- Cosmetic ... Eccl. 9:8
- Sign of hospitality ... Luke 7:46
- Embalming agent ... Luke 23:55, 56
- Sexual attraction ... Is. 57:9

Old—*mature; ancient*

A. *Descriptive of:*
- Age ... Gen. 25:8
- Mature person ... 1 Kin. 12:6-13
- Experienced ... Ezek. 23:43
- Ancient times ... Mal. 3:4
- Old Testament age ... Matt. 5:21-33
- Old Testament ... 2 Cor. 3:14
- Unregenerate nature ... Rom. 6:6

B. *Of man's age, infirmities of:*
- Waning sexual desire ... Luke 1:18
- Physical handicaps ... 1 Kin. 1:1, 15
- Failing strength ... Ps. 71:9

C. *Of man's age, dangers of:*
- Spiritual decline ... 1 Kin. 11:4
- Not receiving instruction ... Eccl. 4:13
- Disrespect toward ... Deut. 28:50

D. *Of man's age, blessing of:*
- God's care ... Is. 46:4
- Continued fruitfulness ... Ps. 92:14
- Security of faith ... Prov. 22:6
- Fulfillment of life's goals ... Is. 65:20
- Honor ... Lev. 19:32
- Grandchildren ... Prov. 17:6
- Men dream dreams ... Acts 2:17

See Length of life

Old Testament

A. *Characteristics of:*
- Inspired ... 2 Tim. 3:16
- Authoritative ... John 10:34, 35
- Written by the Holy Spirit ... Heb. 3:7
- Uses many figurative expressions ... Is. 55:1, 12, 13
- Written for our admonition ... 1 Cor. 10:1-11
- Israel now blinded to ... 2 Cor. 3:14-16
- Foreshadows the New ... Heb. 9:1-28

B. *With the New Testament, unified in:*
- Authorship ... Heb. 1:1
- Plan of salvation ... 1 Pet. 1:9-12
- Presenting Christ (see Messiah, the) ... Luke 24:25-44

Olive tree

A. *Used for:*
- Oil of, many uses (see Oil) ... Ex. 27:20
- Temple furniture ... 1 Kin. 6:23
- Temple construction ... 1 Kin. 6:31-33
- Booths ... Neh. 8:15

B. *Cultivation of:*
- By grafting ... Rom. 11:24
- Hindered by disease ... Deut. 28:40
- Failure of, a great calamity ... Hab. 3:17, 18
- Poor provided for ... Deut. 24:20
- Palestine suitable for ... Deut. 6:11

C. *Figuratively of:*
- Peace ... Gen. 8:11
- Kingship ... Judg. 9:8, 9
- Israel ... Jer. 11:16
- The righteous ... Ps. 52:8
- Faithful remnant ... Is. 17:6
- Gentile believers ... Rom. 11:17, 24
- True Church ... Rom. 11:17, 24
- Prophetic symbols ... Zech. 4:3, 11, 12

Olives, Mount of

A. *Described as:*
- "The mount of Olives" ... Zech. 14:4
- "The hill that is before Jerusalem" ... 1 Kin. 11:7
- "The mount of corruption" ... 2 Kin. 23:13
- "The mount" ... Neh. 8:15

B. *Scene of:*
- David's flight ... 2 Sam. 15:30
- Solomon's idolatry ... 2 Kin. 23:13
- Ezekiel's vision ... Ezek. 11:23
- Postexilic festivities ... Neh. 8:15
- Zechariah's prophecy ... Zech. 14:4
- Triumphal entry ... Matt. 21:1
- Weeping ... Luke 19:37, 41
- Great prophetic discourse ... Matt. 24:3
- Ascension ... Acts 1:12

Oliveyard
- Freely given ... Josh. 24:13
- Taken in greed ... 2 Kin. 5:20, 26

Olympas
- Christian in Rome ... Rom. 16:15

Omar—*eloquent*
- Grandson of Esau ... Gen. 36:11, 15; 1 Chr. 1:36

Omega—*the last letter in the Greek alphabet*
- Descriptive of Christ's infinity ... Rev. 1:8, 11; Rev. 21:6; Rev. 22:13

Omen—*a portent*
- Forbidden ... Deut. 18:10
- The LORD causes to fail ... Is. 44:25

Omission, sins of

A. *Concerning ordinances:*
- Moses' neglect of circumcision ... Ex. 4:24-26
- Israel's neglect of the tithe ... Mal. 3:7-12
- Christians neglecting to assemble ... Heb. 10:25

B. *Concerning moral duties:*
- Witnessing ... Ezek. 33:1-6
- Warning ... Jer. 42:1-22
- Watchfulness ... Matt. 24:42-51; Matt. 26:36-46

Omnipotence—*infinite power*

A. *Of God, expressed by His:*
- Names ("Almighty," etc.) ... Gen. 17:1
- Creative word ... Gen. 1:3
- Control of:
  - Nature ... Amos 4:13
  - Nations ... Amos 1:1—2:3
  - All things ... Ps. 115:3
- Power ... Rom. 4:17-24
- Unweariness ... Is. 40:28

B. *Of Christ, expressed by His power over:*
- Disease ... Matt. 8:3
- Unclean spirit ... Mark 1:23-27
- Devil ... Matt. 4:1-11
- Death ... John 10:17, 18
- Destiny ... Matt. 25:31-33

C. *Of the Holy Spirit, expressed by:*
- Christ's anointing ... Is. 11:2
- Confirmation of the Gospel ... Rom. 15:19

Omnipresence—*universal presence of*
- God ... Jer. 23:23, 24
- Christ ... Matt. 18:20
- Holy Spirit ... Ps. 139:7-12

Omniscience—*infinite knowledge of*
- God ... Is. 40:14
- Christ ... Col. 2:2, 3
- Holy Spirit ... 1 Cor. 2:10-13

Omri—*Jehovah apportions*
1. Descendant of Benjamin ... 1 Chr. 7:8
2. Judahite ... 1 Chr. 9:4
3. Chief officer of Issachar ... 1 Chr. 27:18
4. King of Israel; made king by Israel's army ... 1 Kin. 16:15, 16
   - Prevails over Zimri and Tibni ... 1 Kin. 16:17-23
   - Builds Samaria ... 1 Kin. 16:24
   - Reigns wickedly ... 1 Kin. 16:25-28

On—*stone*
1. Reubenite leader; joins Korah's rebellion ... Num. 16:1
2. City of Lower Egypt; center of sun-worship ... Gen. 41:45, 50
   - Called Bethshemesh ... Jer. 43:13

See Heres

Onam—*vigorous*
1. Horite chief ... Gen. 36:23
2. Man of Judah ... 1 Chr. 2:26, 28

Onan—*strong*
- Second son of Judah; slain for failure to consummate union ... Gen. 38:8-10

O

Oneness—*unity*

A. *Of Christ, with:*
- The Father ... John 10:30
- Christians ... Heb. 2:11

B. *Among Christians of:*
- Baptized ... 1 Cor. 12:13
- Union ... Ezek. 37:16-24
- Headship ... Ezek. 34:23
- Faith ... Eph. 4:4-6
- Mind ... Phil. 2:2
- Heart ... Acts 4:32

See Unity of believers

Onesimus—*useful*
- Slave of Philemon converted by Paul in Rome ... Philem. 10-17
- With Tychicus, carries Paul's letters to Colossae and to Philemon ... Col. 4:7-9

Onesiphorus—*profit-bearing*
- Ephesian Christian commended for his service ... 2 Tim. 1:16-18

Onion—*a bulbous plant used for food*
- Lusted after by Israelites ... Num. 11:5

Only begotten

Of Christ's:
- Incarnation ... John 1:14
- Godhead ... John 1:18
- Mission ... John 3:16, 18; 1 John 4:9

SUBJECT REFERENCE

Ono—*strong*

Town of Benjamin rebuilt by Shamed . . . . . 1 Chr. 8:12
Reinhabited by returnees . . . . . Ezra 2:1, 33

Onycha—*nail, claw, husk*

Ingredient of holy incense . . . . . Ex. 30:34

Onyx—*fingernail* (Greek)

Translation of a Hebrew word indicating a precious stone . . . . Job 28:16; Ezek. 28:13
Found in Havilah . . . . . Gen. 2:11-12
Placed in high priest's ephod . . . . Ex. 28:9-20
Gathered by David . . . . . 1 Chr. 29:2

Open—*to unfasten; to unlock; to expose*

A. *Descriptive of miracles on:*
Earth . . . . . Num. 16:30, 32
Eyes . . . . . John 9:10-32
Ears . . . . . Mark 7:34, 35
Mouth . . . . . Luke 1:64
Prison doors . . . . . Acts 5:19, 23
Death . . . . . 2 Kin. 4:35
Graves . . . . . Matt. 27:52

B. *Descriptive of spiritual things:*
God's provision . . . . . Ps. 104:28
God's bounty . . . . . Mal. 3:10
Christ's blood . . . . . Zech. 13:1
Man's corruption . . . . . Rom. 3:13
Spiritual eyesight . . . . . Luke 24:31, 32
Door of faith . . . . . Acts 14:27
Opportunity . . . . . 1 Cor. 16:9

Ophel—*bulge, hill*

South extremity of Jerusalem's eastern hill . . . . . Neh. 3:15-27
Fortified by Jotham and Manasseh . . . . . 2 Chr. 27:3
Residence of Nethinim . . . . . Neh. 3:26

Ophir—*rich*

1. Son of Joktan . . . . . Gen. 10:26, 29
2. Land, probably in southeast Arabia, inhabited by descendants of 1 . . . . . Gen. 10:29, 30
Famous for its gold . . . . . 1 Chr. 29:4

Ophni—*the high place*

Village of Benjamin . . . . . Josh. 18:24

Ophrah—*hind*

1. Judahite . . . . . 1 Chr. 4:14
2. Town in Benjamin near Michmash . . . . . Josh. 18:21, 23
3. Town in Manasseh; home of Gideon . . . . . Judg. 6:11, 15
Site of Gideon's burial . . . . . Judg. 8:32

Opportunity—*the best time for something*

A. *Kinds of:*
Rejected . . . . . Matt. 23:37
Spurned . . . . . Luke 14:16-24
Prepared . . . . . Acts 8:35-39
Providential . . . . . 1 Cor. 16:9
Good . . . . . Gal. 6:10

B. *Loss of, due to:*
Unbelief . . . . . Num. 14:40-43
Neglect . . . . . Jer. 8:20
Unpreparedness . . . . . Matt. 24:50, 51
Blindness . . . . . Luke 19:41, 42

Opposed—*stand against*

A. *Of evil things:*
Proud . . . . . James 4:6

B. *Of good things:*
Truth . . . . . 2 Tim. 3:8

Oppression—*subjection to unjust hardships*

A. *Kinds of:*
Personal . . . . . Is. 38:14
National . . . . . Ex. 3:9
Economic . . . . . Mic. 2:1, 2
Messianic . . . . . Is. 53:7
Spiritual . . . . . Acts 10:38

B. *Those subject to:*
Widows . . . . . Zech. 7:10
Hired servant . . . . . Deut. 24:14
Poor . . . . . Ps. 12:5
People . . . . . Is. 3:5
Soul . . . . . Ps. 54:3

C. *Evils of, bring:*
Guilt . . . . . Is. 59:12, 13
Reproach . . . . . Prov. 14:31
Poverty . . . . . Prov. 22:16
Judgment . . . . . Ezek. 18:12, 13

D. *Punishment of:*
God's judgment . . . . . Is. 49:26
Captivity . . . . . Is. 14:2, 4
Destruction of . . . . . Ps. 72:4

E. *Protection against:*
Sought in prayer . . . . . Deut. 26:7
Given by the LORD . . . . . Ps. 103:6
Secured in refuge . . . . . Ps. 9:9

F. *Agents of:*
Nations . . . . . Judg. 10:12
Enemy . . . . . Ps. 42:9; Ps. 106:42
Wicked . . . . . Ps. 55:3
Man . . . . . Ps. 119:134
Leaders . . . . . Prov. 28:16
Sword . . . . . Jer. 46:16; Jer. 50:16
Devil . . . . . Acts 10:38
Rich . . . . . James 2:6

Oracle—*a revelation; a wise saying*

A. *Descriptive of the Holy of Holies:*
Place in temple . . . . . 1 Kin. 6:16
Direction of prayer . . . . . Ps. 28:2
Source of truth . . . . . 1 Sam. 23:9-12

B. *Descriptive of God's Word:*
Received by Israel . . . . . Acts 7:38
Test of truth . . . . . 1 Pet. 4:11

Oration, orator

Character of:
Egotistical . . . . . Acts 12:21-23
Prejudiced . . . . . Acts 24:1-9
Inspired . . . . . Acts 26:1-29

Orchard—*a cultivated garden or park*

Source of fruits . . . . . Song 4:13
Source of nuts . . . . . Song 6:11

Orchestra—*group of musicians playing together*

Instituted by David . . . . . 2 Sam. 6:5

Ordain, ordained—*to establish, appoint, set, decree*

A. *As appointment to office:*
Idolatrous priests . . . . . 1 Kin. 13:33
Priesthood . . . . . Lev. 8:1-36
Prophet . . . . . Jer. 1:5
Royal officer . . . . . Dan. 2:24
Apostles . . . . . Mark 3:14
Christ as judge . . . . . Acts 10:42
Elders . . . . . Titus 1:5
Paul as a preacher . . . . . 1 Tim. 2:7
Christ as high priest . . . . . Heb. 5:1

B. *As appointment of temporal things:*
World order . . . . . Ps. 8:3
Institution of:
Passover . . . . . Ps. 81:5
Government . . . . . Rom. 13:1
Life . . . . . Num. 24:23; Ps. 139:16
Man's steps . . . . . Prov. 20:24
Offering . . . . . Num. 28:6
Law . . . . . Acts 7:53; Gal. 3:19

C. *As appointment of eternal things:*
Covenant . . . . . Ps. 111:9
Salvation . . . . . Acts 13:48
Hidden wisdom . . . . . 1 Cor. 2:7
Good works . . . . . Eph. 2:10
Apostles . . . . . Jude 4

Order—*harmony; symmetry; in proper places*

A. *As an arrangement in rows:*
Wood for sacrifices . . . . . Gen. 22:9
Lamps set orderly . . . . . Ex. 27:21
Battle formation . . . . . 1 Chr. 12:38
Words logically developed . . . Job 33:5
Consecutive narrative . . . . . Luke 1:3
Logical defense . . . . . Job 13:18
Absence of . . . . . Job 10:22

B. *As a classification according to work:*
Priestly service . . . . . 2 Kin. 23:4
Christ's priesthood . . . . . Ps. 110:4
Church services . . . . . 1 Cor. 11:34
Church officers . . . . . Titus 1:5

C. *Of something prescribed:*
Rules and regulations . . . . . Judg. 13:12
Ritual regulations . . . . . 1 Chr. 15:13
Church regulations . . . . . 1 Cor. 14:40
Subjection to . . . . . 1 Chr. 25:2, 6

D. *Of preparation for death:*
Ahithophel's . . . . . 2 Sam. 17:23
Hezekiah's . . . . . 2 Kin. 20:1

E. *Figurative of:*
God's covenant . . . . . 2 Sam. 23:5
Believer's life . . . . . Ps. 37:23
Man's sins . . . . . Ps. 50:21

Ordinances—*regulations established for proper procedure*

A. *Descriptive of:*
Ritual observance . . . . . Heb. 9:1, 10
God's laws . . . . . Is. 24:5
God's laws in nature . . . . . Jer. 31:35
Man's regulations . . . . . Neh. 10:32
Man's laws . . . . . 1 Pet. 2:13
Apostolic messages . . . . . 1 Cor. 11:2
Jewish legalism . . . . . Eph. 2:15

B. *Of the Gospel:*
Baptism . . . . . Matt. 28:19
Lord's Supper . . . . . 1 Cor. 11:23-29
Preaching the Word . . . . . Rom. 10:15

Oreb—*a raven*

1. Midianite prince slain by Gideon . . . . . Judg. 7:25
2. Rock on which Oreb was slain . . . . . Judg. 7:25

Oren—*a fir or cedar tree*

Judahite . . . . . 1 Chr. 2:25

Organ—*a wind instrument*

Of ancient origin . . . . . Gen. 4:21
Used in:
Entertainments . . . . . Job 21:12
God's worship . . . . . Ps. 150:4

Orion—*strong*

Brilliant constellation . . . . . Job 9:9

Ornaments—*outward adornments of the body*

Figurative of:
Wisdom's instruction . . . . . Prov. 1:9
Reproof received . . . . . Prov. 25:12
God's provisions . . . . . Ezek. 16:7-14
Apostasy from God . . . . . Jer. 4:30
See Clothing; Jewels

Orpah—*neck*

Ruth's sister-in-law . . . . . Ruth 1:4, 14

Orphans—*children deprived of parents*

Description of . . . . . Lam. 5:3
Provision for . . . . . Deut. 24:17, 21
Job helps . . . . . Job 29:12
Vistation of, commended . . . . . James 1:27
Christians not left "orphans" . . . . . John 14:18

Osee—*Greek name for the prophet Hosea*

Quoted by Paul . . . . . Rom. 9:25

Oshea—*God saves*

Same as Joshua . . . . . Num. 13:8, 16

Osprey—*a dark brown eagle*

Unclean bird . . . . . Lev. 11:13

Ossifrage—*Latin for bone breaker*

Unclean bird (eagle) . . . . . Lev. 11:13

Ostentatious—*vain, ambitious*

Manifested in:
Boastfulness . . . . . Luke 18:10-14
Hypocrisy . . . . . Matt. 6:1-7, 16
Conceit . . . . . 2 Sam. 15:1-6
Egotism . . . . . Acts 12:20-23

Ostracism—*exclusion of a person from society*

Accepted . . . . . Luke 6:22
See Excommunication

Ostrich—*a two-toed, swift and flightless bird*

Figurative of cruelty . . . . . Lam. 4:3

Othni—*abbreviation of Othniel*

Son of Shemaiah . . . . . 1 Chr. 26:7

SUBJECT — REFERENCE

Othniel—*God is force*
- Son of Kenaz, Caleb's youngest brother ... Judg. 1:13
- Captures Kirjath-sepher; receives Caleb's daughter as wife ... Josh. 15:15-17
- First judge of Israel ... Judg. 3:9-11

Ouches—*woven together* (Heb.)
- Setting for precious stones worn by the high priest ... Ex. 28:11
- Fastener or clasp for cords ... Ex. 28:13, 14
- Same Hebrew word translated "wrought" ... Ps. 45:13

Ought—*something morally imperative*

A. *Of duties not properly done:*
- Use of talents ... Matt. 25:27
- Accusation ... Acts 24:19
- Growth ... Heb. 5:12

B. *Of acts wrongly done:*
- Worship ... John 4:20, 21
- Death ... John 19:7
- Wrong behavior ... 2 Cor. 2:3
- Inconsistent speaking ... James 3:10

C. *Of moral duties among Christians:*
- Witnessing ... Luke 12:12
- Prayer ... Luke 18:1
- Service ... John 13:14
- Obedience ... 1 Thess. 4:1
- Helping the weak ... Rom. 15:1
- Love toward wife ... Eph. 5:28
- Proper behavior ... 2 Thess. 3:7
- Holy conduct ... 2 Pet. 3:11
- Willingness to sacrifice ... 1 John 3:16
- Love of one another ... 1 John 4:11

See Must; Necessary, necessity

Outcasts—*dispossessed people*
- Israel among the nations ... Ps. 147:2
- Israel as objects of mercy ... Is. 16:3, 4
- New Israel ... Jer. 30:17-22

Outrageous—*extremely bad; going beyond bounds of decency*
- Descriptive of anger ... Prov. 27:4

Oven—*a place for baking or cooking*

A. *Characteristics of:*
- Used for cooking ... Ex. 8:3
- Fuel for, grass ... Matt. 6:30
- Made on ground ... Gen. 18:6

B. *Figurative of:*
- Scarcity in famine ... Lev. 26:26
- Lust ... Hos. 7:4, 6, 7
- God's judgments ... Ps. 21:9
- Effects of famine ... Lam. 5:10

Overcome—*to conquer*

A. *Means of, by:*
- Wine ... Jer. 23:9
- Fleshly desire ... 2 Pet. 2:19, 20
- God ... Rom. 8:37

B. *Objects of:*
- World ... John 16:33
- Evil ... Rom. 12:21
- Satan ... 1 John 2:13, 14
- Evil spirits ... 1 John 4:4
- Two witnesses ... Rev. 11:7
- Evil powers ... Rev. 17:13, 14

C. *Promises concerning, for Christians:*
- Eating of the tree of life ... Rev. 2:7
- Exemption from the second death ... Rev. 2:11
- Power over the nations ... Rev. 2:26
- Clothed in white raiment ... Rev. 3:5
- Made a pillar in God's Temple ... Rev. 3:12
- Rulership with Christ ... Rev. 3:21

Overlay—*to spread or place over*

Materials used:
- Gold ... Ex. 26:32
- Bronze ... Ex. 38:2
- Silver ... Ex. 38:17

Objects overlaid:
- Pillar—with gold ... Ex. 26:32
- Board—with gold ... Ex. 36:34
- Altar—with cedar ... 1 Kin. 6:20
- Sanctuary—with gold ... 1 Kin. 6:21
- Cherubim—with gold ... 1 Kin. 6:28
- Earthen vessel—with silver dross ... Prov. 26:23
- Images—with silver ... Is. 30:22

Overplus—*excess*
- Restoration of, required ... Lev. 25:27

Overseer—*a leader or supervisor*

Kinds of:
- Prime minister ... Gen. 39:4, 5
- Managers ... Gen. 41:34
- Elders ... Acts 20:17, 28

Overthrow—*to throw down; destroy*

Agents of:
- God ... Prov. 21:12
- Evil ... Ps. 140:11
- Wickedness ... Prov. 11:11
- Evil ruler ... Dan. 11:41
- Christ ... John 2:15

Overwork—*too much work*
- Complaint of Israelites ... Ex. 5:6-21
- Solution of, for Moses ... Ex. 18:14-26

Owe—*an obligation of*
- Financial debt ... Matt. 18:24, 28
- Moral debt ... Philem. 18, 19
- Spiritual debt ... Rom. 13:8

Owl—*a large-eyed bird of prey*
- Varieties of, all unclean ... Lev. 11:13-17
- Solitary in habit ... Ps. 102:6

Ownership—*title of possession*

A. *By men, acquired by:*
- Purchase ... Gen. 23:16-18
- Inheritance ... Luke 15:12
- Covenant ... Gen. 26:25-33

B. *By God, of:*
- World ... Ps. 24:1
- Souls of men ... Ezek. 18:4
- Redeemed ... 1 Cor. 6:19, 20

Ox

A. *Uses of:*
- Pulling covered wagons ... Num. 7:3
- Plowing ... 1 Kin. 19:19
- Food ... Deut. 14:4
- Sacrifice ... Ex. 20:24
- Means of existence ... Job 24:3
- Designs in Temple ... 1 Kin. 7:25

B. *Laws concerning:*
- To rest on Sabbath ... Ex. 23:12
- Not to be:
  - Yoked with an ass ... Deut. 22:10
  - Muzzled while treading ... Deut. 25:4
- To be restored ... Ex. 22:4, 9-13

C. *Figurative of:*
- Easy victory ... Num. 22:4
- Youthful rashness ... Prov. 7:22
- Sumptuous living ... Prov. 15:17
- Preach the Gospel ... Is. 32:20
- Minister's support ... 1 Cor. 9:9, 10

D. *Descriptive of:*
- Of great strength ... Num. 23:22
- Very wild and ferocious ... Job 39:9-12
- Frisky in youth ... Ps. 29:6

Ox goad—*spike used to drive oxen*
- As a weapon ... Judg. 3:31

Ozem—*anger*
1. Son of Jesse ... 1 Chr. 2:13, 15
2. Descendant of Judah ... 1 Chr. 2:25

Ozni—*gives ear*
- Son of Gad and head of a family ... Num. 26:15, 16
- Called Ezbon ... Gen. 46:16

P

Paarai—*devotee of Peor*
- One of David's mighty men ... 2 Sam. 23:35
- Called Naarai ... 1 Chr. 11:37

Pacification—*causing anger to rest*

A. *Means of:*
- Gift ... Prov. 21:14
- Wise man ... Prov. 16:14
- Yielding ... Eccl. 10:4

B. *Examples of:*
- Esau, by Jacob ... Gen. 32:11-19
- Lord, toward His people ... Ezek. 16:63
- Ahasuerus, by Haman's death ... Esth. 7:10

Pack animals
- Used by Israelites ... 1 Chr. 12:40

Padan-aram—*the plain of Aram* (Mesopotamia)
- Home of Isaac's wife ... Gen. 25:20
- Jacob flees to ... Gen. 28:2-7
- Jacob returns from ... Gen. 31:17, 18
- Same as Mesopotamia ... Gen. 24:10
- People of, called Syrians ... Gen. 31:24
- Language of, called Syrian ... 2 Kin. 18:26

See Aramaic

Paddle—*a spadelike digging instrument*
- Part of a soldier's equipment ... Deut. 23:13
- Translated "nail" in ... Judg. 4:21

Padon—*ransom*
- Head of Nethinim family ... Ezra 2:44; Neh. 7:47

Pagan gods

A. *Mentioned:*
- Molech ... Lev. 18:21
- Chemosh ... Judg. 11:24
- Dagon ... Judg. 16:23
- Baal ... 2 Kin. 17:16
- Nergal ... 2 Kin. 17:30
- Succoth-benoth ... 2 Kin. 17:30
- Ashima ... 2 Kin. 17:30
- Nibhaz ... 2 Kin. 17:31
- Tartak ... 2 Kin. 17:31
- Adrammelech ... 2 Kin. 17:31
- Anammelech ... 2 Kin. 17:31
- Nisroch ... Is. 37:38
- Jupiter ... Acts 14:12
- Mercurius ... Acts 14:12
- Greek Pantheon ... Acts 17:16-23
- Diana ... Acts 19:23 37

B. *Worship of condemned:*
- By apostolic command ... 1 Cor. 10:14
- By Law ... Ex. 20:3, 4; Deut. 5:7

Pagiel—*God meets*
- Son of Ocran, chief of Asher's tribe ... Num. 1:13

Pahath-moab—*governor of Moab*
- Family of postexilic returnees ... Ezra 2:6
- Members of, divorced foreign wives ... Ezra 10:19, 30
- One of, signs covenant ... Neh. 10:1, 14
- Hashub, one of, helps Nehemiah ... Neh. 3:11

Pain—*physical or mental suffering*

A. *Kinds of:*
- Childbirth ... Rev. 12:2
- Physical fatigue ... 2 Cor. 11:27
- Physical afflictions ... Job 33:19
- Mental disturbance ... Ps. 55:4

B. *Characteristics of:*
- Affects face ... Joel 2:6
- Means of chastening ... Job 15:20
- Affects the whole person ... Jer. 4:19
- Common to all men ... Rom. 8:22

C. *Remedies for:*
- Balm ... Jer. 51:8
- Prayer ... Ps. 25:17, 18
- God's deliverance ... Acts 2:24
- Heaven ... Rev. 21:4

D. *Figurative of:*
- Mental anguish ... Ps. 48:6
- Impending trouble ... Jer. 22:23
- Distressing news ... Is. 21:2, 3
- Israel's captivity ... Is. 26:17, 18

Paint—*to apply liquid colors*
- Applied to a wide house ... Jer. 22:14
- Used by women ... 2 Kin. 9:30
- Used especially by prostitutes ... Jer. 4:30; Ezek. 23:40

SUBJECT REFERENCE

Paintings
Of Chaldeans (bas-reliefs) ...... Ezek. 23:14
Of animals and idols (on a secret wall) ...... Ezek. 8:7-12

Pair—*two*
Sandals ...... Amos 2:6
Turtledoves ...... Luke 2:24
Balances ...... Rev. 6:5

Palace—*a royal building*
A. *Descriptive of:*
King's residence ...... 2 Chr. 9:11
Foreign city ...... Is. 25:2
Dwellings in Zion ...... Ps. 48:3
Heathen king's residence ...... Ezra 6:2
Residence of the high priest ...... Matt. 26:3, 58
Fortified place ...... Neh. 7:2
B. *Characteristics of:*
Place of luxury ...... Luke 7:25
Subject to destruction ...... Is. 13:22
C. *Figurative of:*
Messiah's Temple ...... Ps. 45:8, 15
Divine workmanship ...... Ps. 144:12
Eternal city ...... Jer. 30:18

Palal—*judge*
Postexilic laborer ...... Neh. 3:25

Pale—*deficient in color*
Figurative of:
Shame ...... Is. 29:22

Palestine (see Canaan, Land of)

Palliation of sin—*excusing sin*
A. *Manifested by:*
Calling bad men good ...... Mal. 2:17
Describing sin as good ...... Is. 5:20
Justifying the wicked ...... Is. 5:23
Encouraging the wicked ...... Ezek. 13:22
Calling the proud happy ...... Mal. 3:13-15
Envying the wicked ...... Ps. 73:3-15
Supposing God cannot see sin ...... Ps. 10:11-13
Ignoring reproof ...... Job 34:5-36
Sinning defiantly ...... Is. 5:18, 19
Considering God indifferent to evil ...... Zeph. 1:12
Misjudging people ...... Matt. 11:18, 19
Questioning God's Word ...... Ezek. 20:49
B. *Caused by:*
Moral darkness ...... Matt. 6:23
Man-made concepts ...... Matt. 16:3-6
Hypocrisy ...... Matt. 23:15-23
Evil heart ...... Luke 16:15
False teaching ...... 2 Pet. 2:1-19

Pallu, Phallu—*distinguished*
Son of Reuben; head of tribal family ...... Gen. 46:9; Ex. 6:14; Num. 26:5, 8

Palm of the hand
Used literally of:
Priest's hand ...... Lev. 14:15, 26
Idol's hand ...... 1 Sam. 5:4
Daniel's hand ...... Dan. 10:10
Soldier's hand ...... Matt. 26:67

Palm tree
A. *Uses of:*
Fruit of, for food ...... Joel 1:12
Figures of, carved on Temple ...... 1 Kin. 6:29-35
Branches of, for booths ...... Lev. 23:40-42
Places of, at Elim and Jericho ...... Ex. 15:27
Site of, for judgeship ...... Judg. 4:5
B. *Figurative of:*
Righteous ...... Ps. 92:12
Beauty ...... Song 7:7
Victory ...... John 12:13

Palmerworm—*caterpillar*
Name probably designates the locust ...... Amos 4:9

Palms, city of
Moabites conquer ...... Judg. 3:12, 13

SUBJECT REFERENCE

Palsy, paralysis—*loss of bodily motion*
Healed by:
Christ ...... Matt. 4:24
Christians ...... Acts 8:7

Palti, Phalti—*abbreviation of Pelatiah*
1. Benjamite spy ...... Num. 13:9
2. Man to whom Saul gives Michal, David's wife-to-be, in marriage ...... 1 Sam. 25:44

Paltiel, Phaltiel—*God has delivered*
1. Prince of Issachar ...... Num. 34:26
2. Same as Palti 2 ...... 2 Sam. 3:15

Paltite, the
Native of Beth-palet ...... Josh. 15:27
Home of one of David's mighty men ...... 2 Sam. 23:26
Same referred to as the Pelonite ...... 1 Chr. 11:27

Pamphylia—*coastal region in South Asia Minor*
People from, at Pentecost ...... Acts 2:10
Paul visits ...... Acts 13:13
John Mark returns home from ...... Acts 13:13; Acts 15:38
Paul preaches in cities of ...... Acts 14:24, 25
Paul sails past ...... Acts 27:5

Pan—*thin plate*
Offering in ...... Lev. 2:5
Cooking ...... Lev. 6:21
Pouring ...... 2 Sam. 13:9

Panic—*fright*
A. *Among Israelites:*
At the Red Sea ...... Ex. 14:10-12
Before the Philistines ...... 1 Sam. 4:10
Of Judah before Israel ...... 2 Kin. 14:12
B. *Among nations:*
Egyptians ...... Ex. 14:27
Philistines ...... 1 Sam. 14:22
Syrians ...... 2 Kin. 7:6, 7
Ammonites and Moabites ...... 2 Chr. 20:22-25

Pannag—*sweet*
Product of Palestine sold in Tyre ...... Ezek. 27:17

Paper—*sheet*
Writing material ...... 2 John 12
See Papyrus

Paphos—*capital of Cyprus*
Paul blinds Elymas ...... Acts 13:6-13

Paps—*the breasts of*
Prostitute ...... Ezek. 23:21
Mary the virgin ...... Luke 11:27
Women ...... Luke 23:29
Son of man (chest) ...... Rev. 1:13

Papyrus—*a tall marsh plant growing in the Nile river region*
Referred to as bulrush in ...... Ex. 2:3
See Paper

Parables—*an earthly story with a heavenly meaning*
A. *Descriptive of:*
Prophecy ...... Num. 23:7, 18
Discourse ...... Job 27:1
Wise saying ...... Prov. 26:7, 9
Prophetic message ...... Ezek. 17:1-10
Illustration (especially true of Christ's) ...... Matt. 13:18
B. *Of Christ, characteristics of:*
Numerous ...... Mark 4:33, 34
Illustrative ...... Luke 12:16-21
Meaning of:
Self-evident ...... Mark 12:1-12
Unknown ...... Matt. 13:36
Explained ...... Luke 8:9-15
Prophetic ...... Luke 21:29-36
C. *Design of:*
Bring under conviction ...... 2 Sam. 12:1-6
Teach a spiritual truth ...... Is. 5:1-6
Illustrate a point ...... Luke 10:25-37
Fulfill prophecy ...... Matt. 13:34, 35
Conceal truth from the unbelieving ...... Matt. 13:10-16

SUBJECT REFERENCE

D. *Of Christ, classification of:*
Concerning God's love in Christ:
Lost sheep ...... Luke 15:4-7
Lost money ...... Luke 15:8-10
Prodigal son ...... Luke 15:11-32
Hidden treasure ...... Matt. 13:44
Pearl of great price ...... Matt. 13:45, 46
Concerning Israel:
Barren fig tree ...... Luke 13:6-9
Two sons ...... Matt. 21:28-32
Wicked husbandman ...... Matt. 21:33-46
Concerning Christianity (the Gospel) in this age:
New cloth ...... Matt. 9:16
New wine ...... Matt. 9:17
Sower ...... Matt. 13:3-8
Tares ...... Matt. 13:24-30
Mustard seed ...... Matt. 13:31, 32
Leaven ...... Matt. 13:33
Net ...... Matt. 13:47-50
Great supper ...... Luke 14:16-24
Seed growing secretly ...... Mark 4:26-29
Concerning salvation:
House built on the rock ...... Matt. 7:24-27
Pharisee and publican ...... Luke 18:9-14
Two debtors ...... Luke 7:36-50
Marriage of the king's Son ...... Matt. 22:1-14
Concerning Christian life:
Candle under a bushel ...... Matt. 5:15, 16
Unmerciful servant ...... Matt. 18:23-35
Friend at midnight ...... Luke 11:5-13
Importunate widow ...... Luke 18:1-8
Tower ...... Luke 14:28-35
Good Samaritan ...... Luke 10:25-37
Unjust steward ...... Luke 16:1-13
Laborers in the vineyard ...... Matt. 20:1-17
Concerning rewards and punishments:
Ten virgins ...... Matt. 25:1-13
Talents ...... Matt. 25:14-30
Pounds ...... Luke 19:12-27
Sheep and goats ...... Matt. 25:31-46
Master and servant ...... Luke 17:7-10
Servants watching ...... Mark 13:33-37; Luke 12:36-40
Rich fool ...... Luke 12:16-21
Rich man and Lazarus ...... Luke 16:19-31

Paraclete—*called to one's side*
Greek word translated "Comforter" and "Advocate" ...... John 14:16-18; John 15:26; 1 John 2:1

Paradise—*an enclosed park similar to the Garden of Eden*
Applied in the New Testament to heaven ...... Luke 23:43; 2 Cor. 12:4; Rev. 2:7

Paradox—*a statement appearing to be untrue or contradictory*
Getting rich by poverty ...... Prov. 13:7
Dead burying the dead ...... Matt. 8:22
Finding life by losing it ...... Matt. 10:39
Not peace, but a sword ...... Matt. 10:34-38
Wise as serpents; harmless as doves ...... Matt. 10:16
Hating and loving ...... Luke 14:26
Becoming great by serving ...... Mark 10:43
Dying in order to live ...... John 12:24, 25
Becoming a fool to be wise ...... 1 Cor. 3:18

Parah—*young cow*
City in Benjamin ...... Josh. 18:23

Paralytic—*one affected with incapacitation*
Brought to Jesus ...... Matt. 9:2; Mark 2:3
Healed by Jesus ...... Matt. 4:24; Luke 5:24
Healed by Jesus, through Peter ...... Acts 9:33

Paramours—*illegal lovers*
Applied to the male lover ...... Ezek. 23:20

Paran—*a wilderness region in the Sinaitic Peninsula*
Mountainous country ...... Hab. 3:3
Residence of exiled Ishmael ...... Gen. 21:21
Israelites camp in ...... Num. 10:12
Headquarters of spies ...... Num. 13:3, 26
Site of David's refuge ...... 1 Sam. 25:1

SUBJECT REFERENCE

Parbar—*suburb*
Precinct or colonnade west of the Temple ..... 1 Chr. 26:18
Same word translated "suburbs" in ..... 2 Kin. 23:11

Parched—*roasted, dry*
Corn ..... Josh. 5:11
Pulse ..... 2 Sam. 17:28

Parchments—*writing material made from animal skin*
Paul sends request ..... 2 Tim. 4:13

Pardon—*to forgive*
A. *Objects of our:*
Transgressions ..... Ex. 23:21
Iniquities ..... Ex. 34:9
Backslidings ..... Jer. 5:6, 7
B. *God's, described as:*
Not granted ..... 2 Kin. 24:4
Requested ..... Num. 14:19, 20
Abundant ..... Is. 55:7
Covering all sins ..... Jer. 33:8
Belonging to the faithful remnant ..... Is. 40:2
C. *Basis of:*
LORD's name ..... Ps. 25:11
Repentance ..... Is. 55:7
Seeking the faith ..... Jer. 5:1
See Forgiveness

Parents—*fathers and mothers*
A. *Kinds of:*
Faithful (Abraham) ..... Gen. 18:18, 19
Neglectful (Moses) ..... Ex. 4:24-26
Presumptuous (Jephthah) ..... Judg. 11:30-39
Holy (Hannah) ..... 1 Sam. 1:11
Indulgent (Eli) ..... 1 Sam. 2:22-29
Distressed (David) ..... 2 Sam. 18:32, 33
Honored (Jonadab) ..... Jer. 35:5-10
Arrogant (Haman) ..... Esth. 3:1-10
Forgiving (prodigal son's father) ..... Luke 15:17-24
B. *Duties toward:*
Obedience ..... Eph. 6:1
Honor ..... Ex. 20:12
Fear ..... Lev. 19:3
C. *Duties of, toward children:*
Protection ..... Heb. 11:23
Training ..... Deut. 6:6, 7
Education ..... Gen. 18:19
Deut. 4:9
Correction ..... Deut. 21:18-21
Provision ..... 2 Cor. 12:14
D. *Sins of:*
Favoritism ..... Gen. 25:28
Not restraining children ..... 1 Sam. 2:27-36
Bad example ..... 1 Kin. 15:26
Anger ..... Eph. 6:4
E. *Sins against, by children:*
Disobedience ..... Rom. 1:30
Cursing ..... Ex. 21:17
Mocking ..... Prov. 30:17
Disrespect ..... Gen. 9:21-27

Parlor
Upper room in Eglon's home ..... Judg. 3:20-25
Room or hall for sacrificial meals ..... 1 Sam. 9:22
Inside room of the temple ..... 1 Chr. 28:11

Parmashta—*the very first*
Haman's son ..... Esth. 9:9

Parmenas
One of the seven deacons ..... Acts 6:5

Parnach
Zebulunite ..... Num. 34:25

Parosh—*flea*
1. Head of a postexilic family ..... Ezra 2:3
Called Pharoush ..... Ezra 8:3
Members of, divorced foreign wives ..... Ezra 10:25
One of, Pedaiah, helps rebuild ..... Neh. 3:25
2. Chief who seals the covenant ..... Neh. 10:1, 14

Patricide—*murder of one's father and/or mother*
Sennacherib's sons guilty of ..... 2 Kin. 19:36, 37

Parshandatha—*inquisitive*
Haman's son ..... Esth. 9:7

Parsimony—*stinginess; living like a miser*
A. *Characteristics of:*
Choosing selfishly ..... Gen. 13:5-11
Living luxuriantly ..... Amos 6:4-6
Showing greediness ..... John 12:5, 6
Withholding God's tithe ..... Mal. 3:8
Unmerciful toward the needy ..... Zech. 7:10-12
B. *Punishment of:*
Brings:
Poverty ..... Prov. 11:24, 25
A curse ..... Prov. 11:26
Revenge ..... Prov. 21:13
The closing of God's kingdom ..... Luke 18:22-25

Part—*a portion of the whole*
Mary chooses the good ..... Luke 10:42
Israel's blindness ..... Rom. 11:25
Our knowledge ..... 1 Cor. 13:9-12

Partake—*to share in*
A. *Of physical things:*
Sacrifices ..... 1 Cor. 10:18
Suffering ..... 2 Cor. 1:7
Benefit ..... 1 Tim. 6:2
Human nature ..... Heb. 2:14
Discipline ..... Heb. 12:8
Bread ..... 1 Cor. 10:17
B. *Of evil things:*
Evil ..... Eph. 5:3-7
Demonism ..... 1 Cor. 10:21
C. *Of spiritual things:*
Divine nature ..... 2 Pet. 1:4
Christ ..... Heb. 3:14
Holy Spirit ..... Heb. 6:4
Heavenly calling ..... Heb. 3:1
Grace ..... Phil. 1:7
Gospel ..... 1 Cor. 9:23
Spiritual blessings ..... Rom. 11:17
Future glory ..... 1 Pet. 5:1
Promise of salvation ..... Eph. 3:6

Partakers
A. *Of physical things:*
Sacrifices ..... 1 Cor. 10:18
Suffering ..... 2 Cor. 1:7
B. *Of evil things:*
Sins ..... 1 Tim. 5:22
C. *Of spiritual things:*
Holiness ..... Heb. 12:10
Communion ..... 1 Cor. 10:16, 17
Spiritual things ..... Rom. 15:27
Inheritance ..... Col. 1:12

Parthians—*inhabitants of Parthia*
Some present at Pentecost ..... Acts 2:1, 9

Partiality—*favoritism*
A. *Manifested:*
In marriages ..... Gen. 29:30
Among brothers ..... Gen. 43:30, 34
Between parents and children ..... Gen. 25:28
In social life ..... James 2:1-4
B. *Inconsistent with:*
Household harmony ..... Gen. 37:4-35
Justice in law ..... Lev. 19:15
Favoritism in:
Ministry ..... 1 Tim. 5:21
Spiritual things ..... 2 Cor. 5:16
Restriction of salvation ..... Acts 10:28-35
C. *Consistent with:*
Choice of workers ..... Acts 15:36-40
Estimate of friends ..... Phil. 2:19-22
God's predestination ..... Rom. 9:6-24
See Favoritism

Partition—*a dividing wall*
In the sanctuary ..... 1 Kin. 6:21
Between people ..... Eph. 2:11-14

Partner—*an associate in*
Crime ..... Prov. 29:24
Business ..... Luke 5:7, 10
Christian work ..... 2 Cor. 8:23
Philem. 17

Partridge—*a wild bird meaning "the caller"* (in Heb.)
Hunted in mountains ..... 1 Sam. 26:20
Figurative of ill-gotten riches ..... Jer. 17:11

Paruah—*sprouting*
Father of Jehoshaphat, an officer of Solomon ..... 1 Kin. 4:17

Parvaim
Unidentified place providing gold for Solomon's Temple ..... 2 Chr. 3:6

Pasach—*divider*
Asherite ..... 1 Chr. 7:33

Pas-dammin—*boundary of bloodshed*
Philistines gathered here ..... 1 Chr. 11:13

Paseah—*lame*
1. Judahite ..... 1 Chr. 4:12
2. Head of a family of Nethinim ..... Ezra 2:43, 49
One of, repairs walls ..... Neh. 3:6
3. A family of Temple servants ..... Neh. 7:46, 51

Pashur—*free*
1. Official opposing Jeremiah ..... Jer. 21:1
Jer. 38:1-13
Descendants of, returnees ..... Neh. 11:12
2. Priest who put Jeremiah in jail ..... Jer. 20:1-6
3. Father of Gedaliah, Jeremiah's opponent ..... Jer. 38:1
4. Priestly family of returnees ..... Ezra 2:38
Members of, divorced foreign wives ..... Ezra 10:22
5. Priest who signs the covenant ..... Neh. 10:3
Blocked by burial ground ..... Ezek. 39:11
Stripped ..... Mic. 2:8
Simon of Cyrene ..... Mark 15:21

Passing away—*ceasing to exist*
A. *Things subject to:*
Our days ..... Ps. 90:9
Old things ..... 2 Cor. 5:17
World's fashion ..... 1 Cor. 7:31
World's lust ..... 1 John 2:17
Heaven and earth ..... 2 Pet. 3:10
B. *Things not subject to:*
Christ's words ..... Luke 21:33
Christ's dominion ..... Dan. 7:14

Passion—*suffering*
A. *Descriptive of:*
Christ's sufferings ..... Acts 1:3
Man's nature ..... James 5:17
Lusts ..... Rom. 1:26
B. *As applied* (theologically) *to Christ's sufferings:*
Predicted ..... Is. 53:1-12
Portrayed visibly ..... Mark 14:3-8
Preached ..... Acts 3:12-18
1 Pet. 1:10-12

Passover—*a Jewish festival commemorative of the exodus from Egypt*
A. *Features concerning:*
Commemorative of the tenth plague ..... Ex. 12:3-28
Necessity of blood applied ..... Ex. 12:7
To be repeated annually ..... Ex. 12:24-27
B. *Observances of:*
At Sinai ..... Num. 9:1-14
At the conquest ..... Josh. 5:10-12
By Christ ..... Matt. 26:18, 19
C. *Typical of the Lord's death* (the Lord's Supper):
Lamb without blemish ..... 1 Pet. 1:19
One of their own ..... Ex. 12:5
Heb. 2:14, 17

P

SUBJECT	REFERENCE
Lamb chosen	Ex. 12:3 1 Pet. 2:4
Slain at God's appointed time	Ex. 12:6 Acts 2:23
Christ is	1 Cor. 5:7
See Lamb of God, the	

Password—*a secret word used to identify friends*

Used by Gileadites	Judg. 12:5, 6

Pastor—*shepherd*

To perfect the saints	Eph. 4:11, 12
Appointed by God	Jer. 3:15
Some rebellious	Jer. 2:8
Unfaithful ones are punished	Jer. 22:22
See Shepherd	

Pasture—*a place for grazing animals*

A. *Used literally of:*

Places for:	
Cattle to feed	Gen. 47:4
Wild animals to feed	Is. 32:14
God's material blessings	Ps. 65:11-13

B. *Used figuratively of:*

Restoration and peace	Ezek. 34:13-15
True Israel	Ps. 95:7
Kingdom of God	Is. 49:9, 10
Kingdom of Israel	Jer. 25:36
Gospel	Is. 30:23
Abundant provision for salvation	Ezek. 45:15

C. *Of the true Israel* (the Church), *described as:*

God's people	Ps. 100:3
Provided for	John 10:9
Purchased	Ps. 74:1, 2
Thankful	Ps. 79:13
Scattered by false pastors	Jer. 23:1
See Shepherd	

Patara—*a port of Lycia in Asia Minor*

Paul changes ships here	Acts 21:1, 2

Pate—*the top of the head*

Figurative of retribution	Ps. 7:16

Path—*a walk; manner of life*

A. *Of the wicked:*

Brought to nothing	Job 6:18
Becomes dark	Job 24:13
Is crooked	Is. 59:8
Leads to death	Prov. 2:18
Filled with wickedness	Prov. 1:15, 16
Is destructive	Is. 59:7
Followed by wicked rulers	Is. 3:12
Made difficult by God	Hos. 2:6

B. *Of believers:*

Beset with difficulties	Job 19:8
Under God's control	Job 13:27
Hindered by the wicked	Job 30:13
Enriched by the LORD	Ps. 23:3
Upheld by God	Ps. 17:5
Provided with light	Ps. 119:105
Known by God	Ps. 139:3
Like a shining light	Prov. 4:18
Directed by God	Is. 26:7
To be pondered	Prov. 4:26
No death at the end	Prov. 12:28
Sometimes unknown	Is. 42:16
Sometimes seems crooked	Lam. 3:9
To be made straight	Heb. 12:13

C. *Of righteousness:*

Taught by father	Prov. 4:1, 11
Kept	Prov. 2:20
Shown to Messiah	Ps. 16:11 Acts 2:28
Taught to believers	Ps. 25:4, 5
Sought by believers	Ps. 119:35 Is. 2:3
Rejected by unbelieving	Jer. 6:16 Jer. 18:15

D. *Of the Lord:*

True	Ps. 25:10
Plain	Ps. 27:11
Rich	Ps. 65:11
Guarded	Prov. 2:8
Upright	Prov. 2:13
Living	Prov. 2:19
Peaceful	Prov. 3:17

Pathros—*the Southland*

Name applied to south (Upper) Egypt	Ezek. 29:10-14
Described as a lowly kingdom	Ezek. 29:14-16
Refuge for dispersed Jews	Jer. 44:1-15
Jews to be regathered from	Is. 11:11

Pathrusim—*the inhabitants of Pathros*

Hamitic people descending from Mizraim and living in Pathros	Gen. 10:14

Patience—*the ability to bear trials without grumbling*

A. *Of the Trinity:*

God, the author of	Rom. 15:5
Christ, the example of	2 Thess. 3:5
Spirit, the source of	Gal. 5:22

B. *Described as:*

Rewarded	Rom. 2:7
Endured with joy	Col. 1:11

C. *Product of:*

Good heart	Luke 8:15
Tribulation	Rom. 5:3, 4
Testing of faith	James 1:3
Hope	Rom. 8:25
Scriptures	Rom. 15:4

D. *Necessary grace, in:*

Times of crises	Luke 21:15-19
Dealing with a church	2 Cor. 12:12
Opposing evil	Rev. 2:2
Soundness of faith	Titus 2:2
Waiting for Christ's return	James 5:7, 8

Patmos—*an Aegan island off the southwestern coast of Asia Minor*

John, banished here, receives the Revelation	Rev. 1:9

Patriarchal age—*the time of Abraham, Isaac, Jacob* (between 1900 and 1600 B.C.)

A. *Rulers of:*

Kings	Gen. 12:15-20
Chiefs	Gen. 26:1
Family heads (fathers)	Gen. 18:18, 19

B. *Business of:*

Cattle, etc.	Gen. 12:16
Caravans	Gen. 37:28-36
Selling, etc.	Gen. 23:1-20
Contracts	Gen. 21:27-30
Business agreements	Gen. 30:28-34

C. *Customs of:*

Prevalence of polygamy	Gen. 16:4
Existence of slavery	Gen. 12:16
Son's wife, selected by his father	Gen. 24:1-4
Children given significant names	Gen. 29:31-35

D. *Religion of:*

Existence of idolatry	Gen. 35:1, 2
Worship of God Almighty	Gen. 14:19-22
God's covenant recognized	Gen. 12:1-3
Circumcision observed	Gen. 17:10-14
Headship of father	Gen. 35:2
Obedience primary	Gen. 18:18, 19
Prayers and sacrifices offered	Gen. 12:8
Blessings and curses pronounced by father	Gen. 27:27-40
True faith believed	Matt. 15:28 Heb. 11:8-22

Patriarchs—*ancient family, or tribal heads*

Applied, in New Testament, to Abraham, to Jacob's sons, and to David	Heb. 7:4

Patrimony—*inherited possessions*

Applied to Levites' portion	Deut. 18:8
Same idea found in	Luke 12:13
See Inheritance, earthly	

Patriotism—*love of one's country*

Manifested in:

Willingness to fight for one's country	1 Sam. 17:26-51
Concern for national survival	Esth. 4:13-17
Desire for national revival	Neh. 1:2-11
Loyalty to national leader	2 Sam. 2:10
Respect for national leaders	2 Sam. 1:18-27

Patrobas

Christian at Rome	Rom. 16:14

Pattern—*a copy; an example*

A. *Of physical things:*

Tabernacle	Heb. 8:5
Temple	1 Chr. 28:11-19

B. *Of spiritual things:*

Good works	Titus 2:7
Heavenly originals	Heb. 9:23
See Example; Example of Christ, the	

Pau, Pai—*groaning, bleating*

Edomite town, residence of King Hadar (Hadad)	Gen. 36:39 1 Chr. 1:50

Paul—*little*

A. *Life of:*

From birth to conversion:

Born at Tarsus in Cilicia	Acts 22:3
Born a Roman citizen	Acts 22:25-28
Called Saul until changed to Paul	Acts 9:11 Acts 13:9
Benjamite Jew	Phil. 3:5
Citizen of Tarsus	Acts 21:39
By trade a tentmaker	Acts 18:1, 3
Zealot for Judaism	Gal. 1:14 Phil. 3:5
Very strict Pharisee	Acts 23:6 Phil. 3:5, 6
Educated under Gamaliel	Acts 22:3
His sister in Jerusalem	Acts 23:16
Apparently unmarried or a widower	1 Cor. 9:5
Member of Jewish council	Acts 26:10
Zealous for the Mosaic Law	Acts 26:4, 5
Consented to Stephen's death	Acts 7:58 Acts 8:1 Acts 22:20
Intensified persecution of Christians	Acts 9:1-3 Acts 22:3-5 Acts 26:10, 11 Gal. 1:13
Conscientious persecutor	Acts 26:9 1 Tim. 1:13

His conversion:

On road to Damascus	Acts 9:1-19
At noon	Acts 26:13
Blinded by supernatural vision	Acts 9:3, 8 2 Cor. 12:1-7
Responded willingly to Jesus' entreaty	Acts 9:4-9
Given a divine commission	Acts 9:6, 10-18 Eph. 3:1-8
Instructed and baptized by Ananias	Acts 9:6, 10-18
Repeated his conversion story	Acts 22:1-16 Acts 26:1-20
Referred to it often	1 Cor. 9:1, 16 1 Cor. 15:8-10 Gal. 1:12-16
Considered himself unworthy	Eph. 3:1-8
Cites details of his change	Phil. 3:4-10
Regretted former life	1 Tim. 1:12-16
Not ashamed of Christ	Rom. 1:16 2 Tim. 1:8-12
Preached Jesus as God's Son and as the Christ (that is, the Messiah)	Acts 9:19-22
Persecuted by Jews; went to Arabia	Acts 9:23-25 2 Cor. 11:32, 33 Gal. 1:17
Returned to Damascus	Gal. 1:17
Visited Jerusalem briefly	Acts 9:26-29 Gal. 1:18, 19
Received vision of his ministry to Gentiles	Acts 22:17-21
Sent by disciples to Tarsus	Acts 9:29, 30 Gal. 1:21
Brought to Antioch (in Syria) by Barnabas	Acts 11:22-26
Sent to Jerusalem with relief	Acts 11:27-30
Returned to Antioch	Acts 12:25

First Missionary Journey:

Divinely chosen and commissioned	Acts 13:1-4 Acts 26:19, 20
Accompanied by Barnabas and John Mark	Acts 13:1, 5
Preached in Cyprus	Acts 13:4-12
Sailed to Perga; Mark left him	Acts 13:13
Preached in Antioch (in Pisidia); rejected by Jews	Acts 13:14-51 2 Tim. 3:11
Rejected in Iconium	Acts 13:51, 52 Acts 14:1-5
Stoned at Lystra	Acts 14:6-20 2 Tim. 3:11

SUBJECT — REFERENCE

Went to Derbe ... Acts 14:20, 21
Returned to Antioch (in Syria) ... Acts 14:21-26
Told Christians about his work ... Acts 14:27, 28
Participated in Jerusalem Council ... Acts 15:2-22; Gal. 2:1-10
Rebuked Peter in Antioch for inconsistency ... Gal. 2:11-21

Second Missionary Journey:

Rejected John Mark as companion; took Silas ... Acts 15:36-40
Strengthened churches in Syria and Cilicia ... Acts 15:41
Revisited Derbe and Lystra ... Acts 16:1
Took Timothy as worker ... Acts 16:1-5
Directed by the Spirit where to preach ... Acts 16:6, 7
Responded to Macedonian vision ... Acts 16:8, 9
Joined by Luke ("we") ... Acts 16:10
Entered Macedonia ... Acts 16:10, 11
Converted Lydia at Philippi ... Acts 16:12-15
Cast into prison; jailer converted ... Acts 16:16-34
Used Roman citizenship ... Acts 16:35-39
Preached at Thessalonica ... Acts 17:1-9; 1 Thess. 1:7; 1 Thess. 2:2-18
Received by the Bereans ... Acts 17:10-13
Left Silas and Timothy; went to Athens ... Acts 17:14-17
Preached on Mars' Hill (the Areopagus) ... Acts 17:18-34
Arrived in Corinth; stayed with Aquila and Priscilla ... Acts 18:1-5
Reunited with Silas and Timothy ... Acts 18:5; 1 Thess. 3:6
Wrote letters to Thessalonians ... 1 Thess. 3:1-6; 2 Thess. 2:2
Established a church at Corinth ... Acts 18:5-18
Stopped briefly at Ephesus ... Acts 18:19-21
Saluted Jerusalem church; returned to Antioch (in Syria) ... Acts 18:22

Third Missionary Journey:

Strengthened churches of Galatia and Phrygia ... Acts 18:23
Gave direction for relief collection ... 1 Cor. 16:1
Ministered three years in Ephesus ... Acts 19:1-12; Acts 20:31
Saved from angry mob ... Acts 19:13-41
Probably wrote *Galatians* here ... Gal. 1:1
Wrote *First Corinthians* here ... 1 Cor. 5:9
Went to Troas; failed to meet Titus ... 2 Cor. 2:12, 13
Reunited with Titus in Macedonia ... Acts 20:1; 2 Cor. 7:5-16
Wrote *Second Corinthians;* sent Titus to Corinth with this letter ... 2 Cor. 8:6-18
Traveled extensively ... Acts 20:2; Rom. 15:19
Visited Greece and Corinth ... Acts 20:2, 3
Wrote *Romans* in Corinth ... Rom. 1:1
Returned through Macedonia ... Acts 20:3
Preached long sermon in Troas ... Acts 20:5-13
Gave farewell talk to Ephesian elders at Miletus ... Acts 20:14-38
Arrived in Caesarea ... Acts 21:1-8
Warned by Agabus ... Acts 21:9-14

In Jerusalem and Caesarea:

Arrived in Jerusalem; welcomed by church ... Acts 21:15-19
Falsely charged; riot follows ... Acts 21:20-40
Defended his action; removed by Roman police ... Acts 22:1-30
Defended his action before Jewish council ... Acts 23:1-10
Saved from Jewish plot; taken to Caesarea ... Acts 23:11-35
Defended himself before Felix ... Acts 24:1-23
Preached to Felix and Drusilla ... Acts 24:24-26
Imprisoned for two years ... Acts 24:27
Accused before Festus by Jews ... Acts 25:1-9
Appealed to Caesar ... Acts 25:10-12
Defended himself before Agrippa ... Acts 25:13-27; Acts 26:1-32

Voyage to Rome:

Sailed from Caesarea to Crete ... Acts 27:1-13
Ship tossed by storm ... Acts 27:14-20
Assured by the Lord ... Acts 27:21-25
Ship wrecked; all saved ... Acts 27:26-44
On island of Melita ... Acts 28:1-10
Continued journey to Rome ... Acts 28:11-16
Rejected by Jews in Rome ... Acts 28:17-29
Dwelt in Rome two years ... Acts 28:30, 31
Wrote *Ephesians, Colossians, Philippians,* and *Philemon* here ... Eph. 3:1; Eph. 6:20; Phil. 1:7, 13; Col. 4:7-18; Philem. 10, 22

Final ministry and death:

Released from first Roman imprisonment ... Phil. 1:25; Phil. 2:17, 24; 2 Tim. 4:16, 17
Wrote *First Timothy* and *Titus* ... 1 Tim. 1:1-3; Titus 1:1-5
Visited Macedonia and other places ... 2 Tim. 4:20
Wrote *Second Timothy* from Roman prison ... 2 Tim. 1:8; 2 Tim. 4:6-8
Sent final news and greetings ... 2 Tim. 4:9-22

B. *Missionary methods of:*

Pay his own way ... Acts 18:3; Acts 20:33-35; 2 Cor. 11:7, 9
Preach to the Jews first ... Acts 13:46; Acts 17:1-5
Establish churches in large cities ... Acts 19:1-10; Rom. 1:7-15
Travel with companions ... Acts 15:40; Acts 20:4; Col. 4:14
Report work to sending church ... Acts 14:26-28; Acts 21:17-20
Use his Roman citizenship when necessary ... Acts 16:36-39; Acts 22:24-29; Acts 25:10-12
Seek to evangelize the world ... Col. 1:23-29; 2 Tim. 4:17

C. *Writings of:*

Inspired by God ... 2 Cor. 13:3; 1 Thess. 2:13; 2 Tim. 3:15, 16
Contain difficult things ... 2 Pet. 3:15, 16
Written by himself ... Gal. 6:11; 2 Thess. 3:17
Sometimes dictated to a scribe ... Rom. 16:22
Considered weighty by some ... 2 Cor. 10:10
His name sometimes forged ... 2 Thess. 2:2
Reveal personal information ... 2 Cor. 11:1-33; 2 Cor. 12:1-11
Convey personal messages ... Phil. 2:19-30; Heb. 13:23, 24
Contain salutation and closing doxology ... 2 Cor. 1:2, 3; 2 Cor. 13:14
Disclose personal plans ... Phil. 2:19-24; Philem. 22
Some complimentary ... Phil. 4:10-19
Some filled with rebuke ... Gal. 1:6-8; Gal. 5:1-10

D. *Characteristics of:*

Consecrated ... 1 Cor. 4:1-15; Phil. 3:7-14
Cheerful ... Acts 16:25; 2 Cor. 4:8-10
Courageous ... Acts 9:29; Acts 20:22-24
Considerate of others ... Phil. 2:25-30; Philem. 7-24
Conscientious ... 2 Cor. 1:12-17; 2 Cor. 6:3, 4
Christ-centered ... 2 Cor. 4:10, 11; Phil. 1:20-23
Conciliatory ... 2 Cor. 2:1-11; Gal. 2:1-15
Composed ... 2 Cor. 12:8-10; 2 Tim. 4:7, 8

Pauline theology

Given by revelation ... Gal. 1:11, 12
Salvation by grace ... Eph. 2:1-10
To Gentiles ... Eph. 3:1-12

Paulus, Sergius

Roman proconsul of Cyprus ... Acts 13:4, 7

Pavement—*a terrace made of bricks or stones*

God's, made of sapphire ... Ex. 24:10
Shushan's, made of precious stones ... Esth. 1:5, 6
Of stone ... 2 Kin. 16:17
Ezekiel's Temple, surrounded by ... Ezek. 40:17, 18
Judgment place of Pilate ... John 19:13
See Gabbatha

Pavilion—*a covered place, tent, booth*

Place of refuge ... Ps. 27:5
Canopy of God's abode ... Job 36:29
Protective covering ("tabernacle") ... Is. 4:6

Paws—*the feet of animals having claws*

Descriptive of certain animals ... Lev. 11:27
Of bears and lions ... 1 Sam. 17:37

Pay—*to give something for something*

Lord's blessing ... Prov. 19:17
Punishment ... Matt. 5:26
Servitude and forgiveness ... Matt. 18:23-35
Sign of righteousness ... Ps. 37:21
See Vow

Pe

Letter in the Hebrew alphabet ... Ps. 119:129-136

Peace

A. *Kinds of:*

International ... 1 Sam. 7:14
National ... 1 Kin. 4:24
Civil ... Rom. 14:19
Domestic ... 1 Cor. 7:15
Individual ... Luke 8:48
False ... 1 Thess. 5:3
Hypocritical ... James 2:16
Spiritual ... Rom. 5:1

B. *Source of:*

God ... Phil. 4:7
Christ ... John 14:27
Holy Spirit ... Gal. 5:22

C. *Of Christ:*

Predicted ... Is. 9:6, 7
Promised ... Hag. 2:9
Announced ... Is. 52:7

D. *Lord's relation to. He:*

Reveals ... Jer. 33:6
Gives ... Ps. 29:11
Ordains ... Is. 26:12

E. *Among the wicked:*

Not known by ... Is. 59:8
None for ... Is. 48:22

F. *Among believers, truths concerning:*

Comes through Christ's atonement ... Is. 53:5
Results from reconciliation ... Col. 1:20
Product of justification ... Rom. 5:1
Obtained by faith ... Is. 26:3

G. *Among believers, exhortations regarding:*

Should live in ... 2 Cor. 13:11
Should pursue ... 2 Tim. 2:22

Peacemakers—*those who work for peace*

Christ the great ... 2 Cor. 5:18-21
Christians become ... Matt. 5:9; Rom. 14:19
Rules regarding ... 1 Pet. 3:8-13

Peacock—*peafowl*

Imported by Solomon from Tarshish ... 1 Kin. 10:22
Trade item ... 2 Chr. 9:21

Pearl—*a precious gem found in oyster shells*

A. *Used literally of:*

Valuable gems ... Rev. 18:12, 16
Woman's attire ... 1 Tim. 2:9

B. *Used figuratively of:*

Spiritual truths ... Matt. 7:6
Kingdom ... Matt. 13:45, 46
Worldly adornment ... Rev. 17:4

SUBJECT REFERENCE

Wonders of heaven's glories ..... Rev. 21:21

Peculiar—*something separated to one's own use*

A. *Applied literally to:*
- Israel (God's own) ..... Ex. 19:5
- Treasure (Solomon's own) ... Eccl. 2:8
- Translated:
  - "Special" ..... Deut. 7:6
  - "Jewels" ..... Mal. 3:17

B. *Applied figuratively to:*
- True Israel ..... Ps. 135:4
- Christian ..... Titus 2:14
- True church ..... 1 Pet. 2:9

Pedahel—*God saves*
- Prince of Naphtali ..... Num. 34:28

Pedahzur—*the Rock* (God) *has redeemed*
- Father of Gamaliel ..... Num. 1:10

Pedaiah—*Jehovah redeems*
1. Father of Joel, ruler in David's reign ..... 1 Chr. 27:20
2. Grandfather of Jehoiakim ... 2 Kin. 23:36
3. Son of Jeconiah ..... 1 Chr. 3:18, 19
4. Postexilic workman ..... Neh. 3:25
5. Ezra's Levite attendant ..... Neh. 8:4
6. Man appointed as treasurer ..... Neh. 13:13
7. Postexilic Benjamite ..... Neh. 11:7

Pekah—*opening* (of the eye)
- Son of Remaliah; usurps Israel's throne ..... 2 Kin. 15:25-28
- Forms alliance with Rezin of Syria against Ahaz ..... Is. 7:1-9
- Alliance defeated; captives returned ..... 2 Kin. 16:5-9
- Territory of, overrun by Tiglath-pileser ..... 2 Kin. 15:29
- Assassinated by Hoshea ..... 2 Kin. 15:30

Pekahiah—*Jehovah hath opened* (the eyes)
- Son of Menahem; king of Israel ..... 2 Kin. 15:22-26
- Assassinated by Pekah ..... 2 Kin. 15:23-25

Pekod—*visitation*
- Aramean tribe during Nebuchadnezzar's reign ..... Jer. 50:21

Pelaiah—*Jehovah is wonderful*
1. Judahite ..... 1 Chr. 3:24
2. Ezra's Levite attendant; reads covenant ..... Neh. 8:7

Pelaliah—*Jehovah has judged*
- Postexilic priest ..... Neh. 11:12

Pelatiah—*Jehovah has freed*
1. Simeonite captain in war with Amalekites ..... 1 Chr. 4:42, 43
2. Prince dying while Ezekiel prophesies ..... Ezek. 11:1-13
3. Descendant of Solomon ..... 1 Chr. 3:21
4. One who signs the covenant ..... Neh. 10:1, 22

Peleg—*division*
- Brother of Joktan ..... Gen. 10:25
- Son of Eber ..... Luke 3:35

Pelet—(God) *has freed*
1. Judahite ..... 1 Chr. 2:47
2. Benjamite warrior under David ..... 1 Chr. 12:3

Peleth—*swiftness*
1. Reubenite, father of On ..... Num. 16:1
2. Judahite ..... 1 Chr. 2:33

Pelethites—*perhaps a contraction of Philistines*
- David's faithful soliders during Absalom's and Sheba's rebellions ..... 2 Sam. 15:18-22

See Cherethites

Pelican—*the vomiter*
- Ceremonially unclean bird ..... Lev. 11:18
- Dwells in wilderness ..... Ps. 102:6
- Lives in ruins ..... Is. 34:11; Zeph. 2:14

Pelonite
- Descriptive of two of David's mighty men ..... 1 Chr. 11:27, 36

Pen
- Figurative of tongue ..... Ps. 45:1
- Lying ..... Jer. 8:8
- Not preferred ..... 3 John 1:13

Penalties—*punishment inflicted for wrongdoing*

A. *For sexual sins:*
- Adultery—death ..... Lev. 20:10
- Incest—death ..... Lev. 20:11-14
- Sodomy—destruction ..... Gen. 19:13, 17, 24

B. *For bodily sins:*
- Drunkenness—exclusion ..... 1 Cor. 5:11; 1 Cor. 6:9, 10
- Murder—death ..... Ex. 21:12-15
- Persecution—God's judgment ..... Matt. 23:34-36

C. *For following heathen ways:*
- Human sacrifice—death ..... Lev. 20:2-5
- Witchcraft—death ..... Ex. 22:18
- Idolatry—death ..... Ex. 22:20

D. *For internal sins:*
- Ingratitude—punished ..... Prov. 17:13
- Pride—abomination ..... Prov. 16:5
- Unbelief—exclusion ..... Num. 20:12
- Swearing—curse ..... Jer. 23:10; Zech. 5:3
- Blasphemy—death ..... Lev. 24:14-16, 23

Peniel—*the face of God*
- Place east of Jordan; site of Jacob's wrestling with angel ..... Gen. 32:24-31

See Penuel 1

Peninnah—*coral, pearl*
- Elkanah's second wife ..... 1 Sam. 1:2, 4

Penitence—*state of being sorry for one's sins*

A. *Results of:*
- Forgiveness ..... Ps. 32:5, 6
- Restoration ..... Job 22:23-29
- Renewed fellowship ..... Ps. 51:12, 13

B. *Examples of:*
- Job ..... Job 42:1-6
- David ..... Ps. 51:1-19
- Josiah ..... 2 Kin. 22:1, 19
- Publican ..... Luke 18:13
- Thief on the cross ..... Luke 23:39-42

C. *Elements:*
- Acknowledgment of sin ..... Job 33:27, 28; Luke 15:18, 21
- Broken heart ..... Ps. 34:18; Ps. 51:17
- Plea for mercy ..... Luke 18:13
- Confession ..... 1 John 1:9

See Repentance

Penknife—*a scribe's knife*
- Used by Jehoiakim on Jeremiah's roll ..... Jer. 36:23-28

Penny, pence—*the Roman denarius*
- Debt of 100 ..... Matt. 18:28
- Day laborer's pay ..... Matt. 20:2-13
- Roman coin ..... Matt. 22:19-21
- Two, the cost of lodging ..... Luke 10:35
- Ointment, worth 300 ..... John 12:5
- Famine prices ..... Rev. 6:6

See Jewish measures

Pentecost—*fiftieth* (day)

A. *In the Old Testament:*
- Called "the Feast of Weeks" ..... Ex. 34:22, 23
- Marks completion of barley harvest ..... Lev. 23:15, 16
- Called "Feast of Harvest" ... Ex. 23:16
- Work during, prohibited ..... Lev. 23:21
- Two loaves presented ..... Lev. 23:17, 20
- Other sacrifices prescribed ... Lev. 23:18
- Offerings given by Levites ... Deut. 16:10-14
- Time of consecration ..... Deut. 16:12, 13
- Observed during Solomon's time ..... 2 Chr. 8:12, 13

See Feasts, Hebrew

B. *In the New Testament:*
- Day of the Spirit's coming; the formation of the Christian Church ..... Acts 2:1-47
- Paul desires to attend ..... Acts 20:16
- Paul plans to stay in Ephesus until ..... 1 Cor. 16:8

Penuel—*the face of God*
1. Inhabitants of, slain by Gideon ..... Judg. 8:8, 9, 17
   - Later refortified by Jeroboam ..... 1 Kin. 12:25
2. Judahite ..... 1 Chr. 4:4
3. Benjamite ..... 1 Chr. 8:25

Penury—*extreme poverty; destitution*
- Widow's gift in, commended ..... Luke 21:1-4

People
- Found among Israel ..... Deut. 7:6
- Not limited to Israel ..... Rom. 2:28, 29
- Called the remnant ..... Is. 11:10, 11, 16
- Gentiles included in ..... Is. 19:25; Is. 65:1; Rom. 15:10, 11
- Became such by covenant ..... Jer. 31:31-34
- Secured through the Messiah ..... Ezek. 34:22-31
- Accomplished by Christ's death ..... Matt. 1:21; Luke 1:68, 77
- Separated from others ..... 2 Cor. 6:16-18; Rev. 18:4
- God's true Church ..... 1 Pet. 2:9, 10
- All nations included in ..... Rev. 5:9; Rev. 7:9
- God's eternal people ..... Rev. 21:3

People of the land—*the conservative element of the population consisting mainly of landholders*
- The influence of ..... 2 Kin. 11:13-15
- Taxed ..... 2 Kin. 23:35

Peor—*opening*
1. Mountain of Moab opposite Jericho ..... Num. 23:28
   - Israel's camp seen from ..... Num. 24:2
2. Moabite god called Baalpeor ..... Num. 25:3, 5, 18
   - Israelites punished for worship of ..... Num. 31:16

Perceive, perception—*knowledge derived through one of the senses*
- Outward circumstances ..... 2 Sam. 12:19; Acts 27:10
- Outward intentions ..... John 6:15; Acts 23:29
- Intuition ..... 1 Sam. 3:8; John 4:19
- Unusual manifestations ..... 1 Sam. 12:17, 18; Acts 10:34
- Spiritual insight ..... Neh. 6:12; Acts 14:9
- God's blessings ..... 2 Sam. 5:12; Neh. 6:16
- Bitter experience ..... Eccl. 1:17; Eccl. 3:22
- Obvious implication ..... Matt. 21:45; Luke 20:19
- God's revelation ..... Gal. 2:9; 1 John 3:16
- Internal consciousness ..... Luke 8:46; Acts 8:23

Perdition—*the state of the damned; destruction*
- Judas Iscariot ..... John 17:12
- Lost ..... Phil 1:28
- Antichrist ..... 2 Thess. 2:3; Rev. 17:8, 11

Peres—*to split into pieces*
- Sentence of doom ..... Dan. 5:28

Peresh—*dung*
- Man of Manasseh ..... 1 Chr. 7:16

Perez—*a breach*
- One of Judah's twin sons by Tamar ..... Gen. 38:24-30
- Numbered among Judah's sons ..... Gen. 46:12
- Founder of a tribal family ..... Num. 26:20, 21
- Descendants of, notable in later times ..... 1 Chr. 27:3
- Ancestor of David and Christ ... Ruth 4:12-18

Perezites
- Descendants of Perez ..... Num. 26:20

SUBJECT — REFERENCE

Perfection—*the extreme degree of excellence*

A. *Applied to natural things:*
- Day .... Prov. 4:18
- Gold .... 2 Chr. 4:21
- Weights .... Deut. 25:15
- Beauty .... Ezek. 28:12
- Offering .... Lev. 22:21

B. *Applied to spiritual graces:*
- Patience .... James 1:4
- Love .... Col. 3:14
- Holiness .... 2 Cor. 7:1
- Praise .... Matt. 21:16
- Faith .... 1 Thess. 3:10
- Good works .... Heb. 13:21
- Unity .... John 17:23
- Strength .... 2 Cor. 12:9

C. *Means of:*
- God .... 1 Pet. 5:10
- Christ .... Heb. 10:14
- Holy Spirit .... Gal. 3:3
- God's Word .... 2 Tim. 3:16, 17
- Ministry .... Eph. 4:11, 12
- Sufferings .... Heb. 2:10

D. *Stages of:*
- Eternally accomplished .... Heb. 10:14
- Objective goal .... Matt. 5:48
- Subjective process .... 2 Cor. 7:1
- Daily activity .... 2 Cor. 13:9
- Present possession .... 1 Cor. 2:6
- Experience not yet reached .... Phil. 3:12
- Descriptive of the completed Church .... Heb. 11:40
- Heaven's eternal standard .... 1 Cor. 13:10-12

Perfume—*a substance producing pleasant scents*

A. *Made by:*
- Apothecary .... Ex. 30:25, 35

Combining:
- Various ingredients .... Job 41:31
- Olive oil with imported aromatics .... 1 Kin. 10:10

B. *Uses of:*
- Incense and ointment for tabernacle .... Ex. 30:22-28
- Personal adornment .... Prov. 27:9
- Seduction .... Prov. 7:17

C. *Figurative of:*

Christ's:
- Glories .... Ps. 45:8
- Righteousness and intercession .... Song 3:6
- Spiritual prostitution .... Is. 57:9

Perfumer—*to mix, compound*
- Great art .... Ex. 30:25; Eccl. 10:1
- Used in tabernacle .... Ex. 30:25, 35
- Used in embalming .... 2 Chr. 16:14
- A maker of ointment .... Eccl. 10:1
- Among returnees .... Neh. 3:8

Perga—*the capital of Pamphylia*
- Visited by Paul .... Acts 13:13, 14; Acts 14:25

Pergamos—*a leading city in Mysia in Asia Minor*
- One of the seven churches here .... Rev. 1:11
- Antipas martyred here .... Rev. 2:12, 13
- Special message to .... Rev. 2:12-17

Perida
- Head of a family of Temple servants .... Neh. 7:46, 57

Perils—*physical or spiritual dangers*

Escape from, by:
- Prayer .... Gen. 32:6-12
- Pacifying gifts .... Gen. 32:13-20
- Quick action .... 1 Sam. 18:10, 11
- Flight .... Matt. 2:12-15
- Love of Christ .... Rom. 8:35
- God .... 2 Cor. 1:10

Perish—*to be destroyed violently*

A. *Applied to:*
- Universe .... Heb. 1:11
- Old world .... 2 Pet. 3:6
- Animals .... Ps. 49:12, 20
- Vegetation .... Jon. 4:10
- Food .... John 6:27
- Gold .... 1 Pet. 1:7
- Human body .... 2 Cor. 4:16
- Soul .... Matt. 10:28

B. *Safeguards against:*

God's:
- Power .... John 10:28
- Will .... Matt. 18:14
- Providence .... Luke 21:18
- Christ's resurrection .... 1 Cor. 15:18, 19
- Repentance .... Luke 13:3, 5

See Lost

Perizzites—*dwellers in the open country*
- One of seven Canaanite nations .... Deut. 7:1
- Possessed Palestine in Abraham's time .... Gen. 13:7
- Land of, promised to Abraham's seed .... Gen. 15:18, 20
- Jacob's fear of .... Gen. 34:30
- Israel commanded to utterly destroy .... Deut. 20:17
- Israel forbidden to intermingle with .... Ex. 23:23-25
- Defeated by Joshua .... Josh. 3:10
- Many of, slain by Judah .... Judg. 1:4, 5
- Israel intermarries with .... Judg. 3:5-7
- Made slaves by Solomon .... 1 Kin. 9:20, 21

See Canaanites

Perjury—*swearing falsely*
- Condemned by the Law .... Lev. 19:12
- Hated by God .... Zech. 8:17
- Requires atonement .... Lev. 6:2-7
- Brings punishment .... Zech. 5:3, 4; Mal. 3:5

See False Witnesses

Permission—*authority to do something*
- Speak by .... 1 Cor. 7:6

Perpetual—*lasting forever*
- Statute .... Ex. 27:21
- Incense .... Ex. 30:8
- Covenant .... Ex. 31:16
- Priesthood .... Ex. 40:15
- Possession .... Lev. 25:34
- Allotment .... Num. 18:8
- Ruins .... Ps. 9:6; Ps. 74:3
- Pain .... Jer. 15:18
- Hissing .... Jer. 18:16
- Sleep .... Jer. 51:39
- Desolation .... Jer. 51:62
- Mountains .... Hab. 3:6

Perplexity—*a state wherein no way out is seen*
- Predicted by Christ .... Luke 21:25

Persecution—*to afflict, oppress, torment*

A. *Caused by:*
- Man's sinful nature .... Gal. 4:29
- Hatred of God .... John 15:20-23
- Ignorance of God .... John 16:1-3
- Hatred of Christ .... 1 Thess. 2:15; Rev. 12:13
- Preaching the cross .... Gal. 5:11; Gal. 6:12
- Godly living .... Matt. 13:21; 2 Tim. 3:12
- Mistaken zeal .... Acts 13:50; Acts 26:9-11

B. *Christian's attitude under:*
- Flee from .... Matt. 10:23
- Rejoice in .... Matt. 5:12
- Be patient under .... 1 Cor. 4:12
- Glorify God in .... 1 Pet. 4:16
- Pray during .... Matt. 5:44

Persecution psalm
- Of David .... Ps. 69

Perseverance—*steadfastness, persistence*

Elements involved in:
- Spiritual growth .... Eph. 4:15
- Fruitfulness .... John 15:4-8
- God's armor .... Eph. 6:11-18
- Chastening .... Heb. 12:5-13
- Assurance .... 2 Tim. 1:12
- Salvation .... Matt. 10:22
- Reward .... Gal. 6:9

Persis—*Persian*
- Christian woman in Rome .... Rom. 16:12

Personal devotions

A. *Prayer:*
- In morning .... Ps. 5:3; Ps. 119:147
- Three times daily .... Ps. 55:17; Dan. 6:10
- Continually .... 1 Thess. 3:10; 1 Tim. 5:5

B. *Study:*
- Daily .... Deut. 17:19
- For learning .... Acts 17:11; Rom. 15:4

Personal work—*seeking to win persons to Christ*
- Need of .... John 4:35-38
- Model of .... John 4:4-30
- Means of .... 1 Thess. 1:5, 6
- Power of .... John 16:7-11
- Methods of .... 1 Cor. 9:19-22

Persuasion—*inclining another's will toward something*

A. *Good, to:*
- Worship .... Acts 18:13
- Steadfastness .... Acts 13:43
- Belief .... Acts 18:4; Acts 19:8
- Turn from idolatry .... Acts 19:26
- Trust Jesus .... Acts 28:23

B. *Evil, to:*
- Unbelief .... 2 Chr. 32:10-19
- Unholy alliance .... 2 Chr. 18:2
- Fatal conflict .... 1 Kin. 22:20-22
- Turmoil .... Acts 14:19
- Error .... Gal. 5:8

C. *Objects of:*
- Hereafter .... Luke 16:31
- One's faith in God .... Rom. 4:21
- Personal assurance .... Rom. 8:38
- Personal liberty .... 2 Tim. 1:12
- Spiritual stability .... Rom. 15:14
- Another's faith .... 2 Tim. 1:5
- God's promises .... Heb. 11:13

Peruda—*separated*
- One of Solomon's servants whose descendants return from exile .... Ezra 2:55; Neh. 7:57

Perverseness—*willfully continuing in sinful ways*

A. *Applied to:*
- Heart .... Prov. 12:8
- Nation .... Phil. 2:15

B. *Source of:*
- False doctrine .... Acts 20:30

Pervert—*to change something from its right use*

A. *Evil of, in dealing with:*
- Man's judgment .... Deut. 24:17
- God's:
  - Judgment .... Job 8:3
  - Word .... Jer. 23:36
  - Ways .... Acts 13:10
- Gospel .... Gal. 1:7

B. *Caused by:*
- Drink .... Prov. 31:5
- Worldly wisdom .... Is. 47:10
- Spiritual blindness .... Luke 23:2, 14

Pestilence
- Fifth Egyptian plague .... Ex. 9:1-16
- Threatened by God .... Deut. 28:21
- Sent because of David's sin .... 2 Sam. 24:13, 15
- Used for man's corrections .... Ezek. 38:22
- Precedes the Lord's coming .... Hab. 3:5

Pestle—*instrument used for pulverizing material*
- Figurative of severe discipline .... Prov. 27:22

Peter

A. *Life of:*

Before his call:
- Simon Barjona .... Matt. 16:17; John 21:15
- Brother of Andrew .... Matt. 4:18
- Married man .... Mark 1:30; 1 Cor. 9:5
- Not highly educated .... Acts 4:13
- Fisherman .... Matt. 4:18

SUBJECT REFERENCE

From his call to Pentecost:

Brought to Jesus by Andrew ..... John 1:40-42
Named Cephas by Christ ..... John 1:42
Called to discipleship by Christ ..... Matt. 4:18-22
Mother-in-law healed ..... Matt. 8:14, 15
Called as apostle ..... Matt. 10:2-4
Walks on water ..... Matt. 14:28-33
Confessed Christ's deity ..... Matt. 16:13-19
Rebuked by Jesus ..... Matt. 16:21-23
Witnesses transfiguration ..... Matt. 17:1-8; 2 Pet. 1:16-18
Asked important questions ..... Matt. 18:21
Refused Christ's menial service ..... John 13:6-10
Cuts off high priest's slave's ear ..... John 18:10, 11
Denied Christ three times ..... Matt. 26:69-75
Wept bitterly ..... Matt. 26:75
Ran to Christ's sepulcher ..... John 20:1-8
Returned to fishing ..... John 21:1-14
Witnessed Christ's ascension ..... Matt. 28:16-20
Returned to Jerusalem ..... Acts 1:12-14
Led disciples ..... Acts 1:15-26

From Pentecost onward:

Explained Spirit's coming at Pentecost ..... Acts 2:1-41
Healed lame man ..... Acts 3:1-11
Pronounces judgment ..... Acts 5:1-11
Heals ..... Acts 5:14-16
Met Paul ..... Acts 9:26; Gal. 1:17, 18
Raises Dorcas ..... Acts 9:36-43
Called to Gentiles ..... Acts 10:1-23
Preached the Gospel to Gentiles ..... Acts 10:24-46
Explained his action to apostles ..... Acts 11:1-18
Imprisoned—delivered ..... Acts 12:3-19
Attends Jerusalem Council ..... Acts 15:7-14
Rebuked by Paul for inconsistency ..... Gal. 2:14
Commended Paul's writings ..... 2 Pet. 3:15, 16

B. *His life contrasted before and after Pentecost, once:*

Coward; now courageous ..... Matt. 26:58, 69-74
Impulsive; now humble ..... John 18:10
Ignorant; now enlightened ..... Matt. 16:21, 22
Deeply inquisitive; now submissive ..... John 21:21, 22
Boastful of self; now boastful of Christ ..... Matt. 26:33, 34
Timid and afraid; now fearless ..... Matt. 14:28-31

C. *Significance of:*

Often the representative for the others ..... Matt. 17:24-27
Only disciple personally restored by the Lord ..... John 21:15-19
Leader in the early church ..... Acts 3:12-26

Peter, the Epistles of—*books of the New Testament*

A. *1 Peter*

God's salvation ..... 1 Pet. 1:3-12
Obedience and holiness ..... 1 Pet. 1:13-23
Christ the corner stone ..... 1 Pet. 2:4-6
A royal priesthood ..... 1 Pet. 2:9
Christ's example ..... 1 Pet. 2:18-25
Husbands and wives ..... 1 Pet. 3:1-7
Partakers of His suffering ..... 1 Pet. 4:12-19
Be humble before God ..... 1 Pet. 5:6-10

B. *2 Peter*

Things pertaining to life ..... 2 Pet. 1:1-4
Diligent growth ..... 2 Pet. 1:5-11
False teachers ..... 2 Pet. 2:1-22
The hope of the day ..... 2 Pet. 3:9, 10

Pethahiah—*Jehovah opens* (the womb)

1. Priest of David's time ..... 1 Chr. 24:16
2. Judahite serving as a Persian official ..... Neh. 11:24
3. Levite who divorced his foreign wife ..... Ezra 10:19, 23
   Prays with the other Levites ..... Neh. 9:4, 5

SUBJECT REFERENCE

Pethor—*a town in North Mesopotamia*

Balaam's home ..... Num. 22:5, 7

Pethuel—*God delivers*

Father of Joel the prophet ..... Joel 1:1

Petitions—*entreaties for favors*

A. *Offered to men:*

Treacherous ..... Dan. 6:7

B. *Offered to God:*

Favored ..... 1 Sam. 1:17
Granted ..... 1 Sam. 1:27

Peulthai—*reward of Jehovah*

Levite doorkeeper ..... 1 Chr. 26:5

Phaltiel—*deliverance of God*

Husband of Michal ..... 2 Sam. 3:14, 15

Phanuel—*face of God*

Father of Anna ..... Luke 2:36

Pharaoh—*great house*

A. *Unnamed ones, contemporary of:*

Abraham ..... Gen. 12:15-20
Joseph ..... Gen. 37:36
Moses (the oppression) ..... Ex. 1:8-11
Moses (the exodus) ..... Ex. 5-14
Solomon ..... 1 Kin. 3:1; 1 Kin. 11:17-20
Hezekiah ..... 2 Kin. 18:21

B. *Named ones:*

Shishak ..... 1 Kin. 14:25, 26
So ..... 2 Kin. 17:4
Tirhakah ..... 2 Kin. 19:9
Nechoh ..... 2 Kin. 23:29
Hophra ..... Jer. 44:30
Probably also referred to in ..... Jer. 37:5, 7, 11

Pharisees—*separated ones*

A. *Characteristics of:*

Jewish sect ..... Acts 15:5
Upholders of traditions ..... Mark 7:3, 5-8; Gal. 1:14
Sticklers for Mosaic Law ..... Acts 26:5; Phil. 3:5
Very careful in outward details ..... Matt. 23:23; Luke 18:11
Rigid in fasting ..... Luke 5:33; Luke 18:12
Zealous for Judaism ..... Matt. 23:15
Lovers of display ..... Matt. 23:5-7
Covetous ..... Luke 16:14
Cruel persecutors ..... Acts 9:1, 2; Phil. 3:5, 6

B. *Chief errors of, their:*

Outward righteousness ..... Luke 7:36-50
Blindness to spiritual things ..... John 3:1-10
Emphasis on the ceremonial Law ..... Matt. 15:1-9
Perversion of Scripture ..... Matt. 15:1, 9
Self-justification before men ..... Luke 16:14, 15
Hindering potential believers ..... John 9:16, 22
Refusal to accept Christ ..... Matt. 12:24-34

C. *Christ's description of:*

Vipers ..... Matt. 12:24, 34
Blind ..... Matt. 15:12-14
Hypocrites ..... Matt. 23:13-19
Serpents ..... Matt. 23:33
Children of the devil ..... John 8:13, 44

D. *Attitude of, toward Christ, sought to:*

Destroy Him ..... Matt. 12:14
Tempt Him ..... Matt. 16:1; Matt. 19:3
Entangle Him ..... Matt. 22:15
Accuse Him ..... Luke 11:53, 54

Pharpar—*haste*

One of the two rivers of Damascus ..... 2 Kin. 5:12

Pharzites

Descendants of Pharez (Perez) ..... Num. 26:20

Phebe—*pure, bright*

Deaconess of the church at Cenchrea ..... Rom. 16:1, 2

SUBJECT REFERENCE

Phi-beseth—*the house of the goddess Bast*

City of Lower Egypt 40 miles north of Memphis ..... Ezek. 30:17

Phichol

Captain of King Abimelech's army ..... Gen. 21:22, 32

Philadelphia—*brotherly love*

City of Lydia in Asia Minor; church established here ..... Rev. 1:11

Philanthropy

A. *Manifested by:*

Ethiopian ..... Jer. 38:6-13
Samaritan ..... Luke 10:30, 33
Roman centurion ..... Luke 7:2-5
Pagans ..... Acts 28:2, 7, 10
Christians ..... Acts 4:34-37

B. *Precepts concerning:*

"Do good unto all" ..... Gal. 6:10
"Love your enemies" ..... Matt. 5:43-48
"Follow that which is good" ..... 1 Thess. 5:15

Philemon—*loving*

Christian at Colossae to whom Paul writes ..... Philem. 1
Paul appeals to him to receive Onesimus ..... Philem. 9-21

Philemon, the Epistle to—*a book of the New Testament*

Thanksgiving ..... Philem. 4-7
Plea for Onesimus ..... Philem. 10-21
Hope through prayer ..... Philem. 22

Philetus—*worthy of love*

False teacher ..... 2 Tim. 2:17, 18

Philip—*lover of horses*

1. Son of Herod the Great ..... Matt. 14:3
2. One of the twelve apostles ..... Matt. 10:3
   Brought Nathanael to Christ ..... John 1:43-48
   Tested by Christ ..... John 6:5-7
   Introduced Greeks to Christ ..... John 12:20-22
   Gently rebuked by Christ ..... John 14:8-12
   In the upper room ..... Acts 1:13
3. One of the seven deacons ..... Acts 6:5
   Called an evangelist ..... Acts 21:8
   Father of four prophetesses ..... Acts 21:8, 9
   Preached in Samaria ..... Acts 8:5-13
   Led the Ethiopian eunuch to Christ ..... Acts 8:26-40
   Visited by Paul ..... Acts 21:8

Philippi—*pertaining to Philip*

City of Macedonia (named after Philip of Macedon); visited by Paul ..... Acts 16:12; Acts 20:6
Paul wrote letter to church of ..... Phil. 1:1

Philippians, the Epistle to the—*a book of the New Testament*

Thanksgiving ..... Phil. 1:3-10
Christ is preached ..... Phil. 1:12-18
To live is Christ ..... Phil. 1:21
The humility of Christ ..... Phil. 2:5-11
Lights in the world ..... Phil. 2:12-16
Perseverance ..... Phil. 3
Rejoicing in the Lord ..... Phil. 4:1-13

Philistia—*the country of the Philistines*

"The land of the Philistines" ..... Gen. 21:32, 34
"The borders of the Philistines" ..... Josh. 13:2
Philistia ..... Ps. 60:8

Philistim—*plural of Philistine*

Race of Canaanites inhabiting Philistia ..... Gen. 10:14

Philistines—*the people of Philistia*

A. *History of:*

Descendants of Mizraim ..... Gen. 10:13, 14
Originally on the island of Caphtor ..... Jer. 47:4
Israel commanded to avoid ..... Ex. 13:17
Not attacked by Joshua ..... Josh. 13:1-3
Left to prove Israel ..... Judg. 3:1-4
Israel sold into ..... Judg. 10:6, 7
Delivered from, by Samson ..... Judg. 13—16

SUBJECT	REFERENCE
Defeat Israel	1 Sam. 4:1-11
Take ark to house of Dagon	1 Sam. 4—5
Defeated at Mizpeh	1 Sam. 7:7-14
Champion, Goliath, killed	1 Sam. 17:1-52
David seeks asylum among	1 Sam. 27:1-7
Gather at Aphek; Saul and sons slain by	1 Sam. 29:1
Often defeated by David	2 Sam. 5:17-25
Besieged by Nadab	1 Kin. 15:27
War against Jehoram	2 Chr. 21:16, 17
Defeated by Uzziah	2 Chr. 26:6, 7
Defeated by Hezekiah	2 Kin. 18:8

B. *Prophecies concerning:*

Union against Israel	Is. 9:11, 12
Punishment pronounced	Jer. 25:15, 20
Hatred against Israel revenged	Ezek. 25:15-17
Destruction by Pharaoh	Jer. 47:1-7
Ultimate decay	Zeph. 2:4-6

Philogus—*lover of words*

Christian at Rome .... Rom. 16:15

Philosophy

Divisions of .... Acts 17:18
Deception of .... Col. 2:8

Phinehas—*oracle*

1. Eleazar's son; Aaron's grandson .... Ex. 6:25
   Slays an Israelite and a Midianite woman .... Num. 25:1-18
   Wonderfully rewarded .... Ps. 106:30, 31
   Fights against Midianites .... Num. 31:6-12
   Settles dispute over memorial altar .... Josh. 22:11-32
   Prays for Israel .... Judg. 20:28
2. Younger son of Eli .... 1 Sam. 1:3
   Worthless man .... 1 Sam. 2:12-25
   Slain by Philistines .... 1 Sam. 4:11, 17
   Wife of, dies in childbirth .... 1 Sam. 4:19-22
3. Father of a postexilic priest .... Ezra 8:33

Phlegon—*scorching*

Christian at Rome .... Rom. 16:14

Phoebe—*pure, bright*

Deaconess of the church at Cenchrea .... Rom. 16:1, 2

Phoenicia—*purple*

Mediterranean coastal region including the cities of Ptolemais, Tyre, Zarephath and Sidon; evangelized by early Christians .... Acts 11:19
Jesus preaches here .... Matt. 15:21

Phoenix—*harbor in southern Crete*

Paul was to winter there .... Acts 27:12

Phrygia—*a large province of Asia Minor*

Jews from, at Pentecost .... Acts 2:1, 10
Visited twice by Paul .... Acts 16:6

Phurah—*branch*

Gideon's servant .... Judg. 7:10, 11

Phut, Put—*foreign bowman*

1. Third son of Ham .... Gen. 10:6
2. Warriors (from Africa) allied with Egypt .... Ezek. 27:10
   Same as Libyans in .... Jer. 46:9

Phuvah, Pua, Puah—*utterance*

1. Issachar's second son .... Gen. 46:13
   Descendants of Punites .... Num. 26:23
2. Father of Tola, Israel's judge .... Judg. 10:1

Phygellus—*fugitive*

Becomes an apostate .... 2 Tim. 1:15

Phylactery—*charm*

Scripture verses placed on the forehead; based upon a literal interpretation of .... Ex. 13:9-16
Condemned by Christ .... Matt. 23:5

Physicians—*trained healers*

God the only true .... Deut. 32:39
Practiced embalming .... Gen. 50:2, 26
Job's friends of no value .... Job 13:4
Consulted by Asa .... 2 Chr. 16:12
For the sick only .... Matt. 9:12
Proverb concerning, quoted .... Luke 4:23
Payment for services of .... Mark 5:26
Luke, "the beloved" .... Col. 4:14

Pi-beseth—*the house of the goddess Bast*

City of Lower Egypt 40 miles north of Memphis .... Ezek. 30:17

Pictures—*drawn or carved representations of life scenes*

Descriptive of idolatrous images .... Num. 33:52
Like a word .... Prov. 25:11
"Pleasant pictures" .... Is. 2:16

Piece—*part of a larger whole*

Land .... Gen. 33:19
Silver .... 1 Sam. 2:36
Fig cake .... 1 Sam. 30:12
Money .... Job 42:11
Fish .... Luke 24:42

Pierce—*to push a pointed instrument through something*

A. *Used literally of:*

Nail in Sisera .... Judg. 5:26
Messiah's predicted death .... Ps. 22:16
Christ's death .... John 19:34, 37

B. *Used figuratively of:*

God's destruction .... Num. 24:8
Egypt's weakness .... 2 Kin. 18:21
Harsh words .... Prov. 12:18
Great conflict of soul .... Job 30:16, 17
God's Word .... Heb. 4:12
Coveted riches .... 1 Tim. 6:10

Piety—*holy living*

A. *Aided by:*

God's Word .... 2 Tim. 3:14-17
Godly parents .... 1 Sam. 1:11
Prayer .... James 5:16-18
Good works .... 1 Tim. 5:10
Hope of Christ's return .... Titus 2:11-14

B. *Hindered by:*

World .... James 4:4
Flesh .... Rom. 8:1-13
Satan .... Luke 22:31
Envying and strife .... 1 Cor. 3:1-7

C. *Value of:*

Profitable now and later .... 1 Tim. 4:8
Safeguard in temptation .... Gen. 39:7-9
Rewarded in heaven .... Rev. 14:13

See Holiness of Christians; Sanctification

Pigeon

As a sin offering .... Lev. 12:6
As a burnt offering .... Lev. 1:14
Offered by Mary .... Luke 2:22, 24
See Dove

Pi-hahiroth—*the place of meadows*

Israelite camp before crossing the Red Sea .... Ex. 14:2, 9; Num. 33:7, 8

Pilate, Pontius

Procurator of Judea (A.D. 26-36) .... Luke 3:1
Destroyed Galileans .... Luke 13:1
Jesus brought before .... Matt. 27:2
Washed hands in mock innocency .... Matt. 27:24
Notorious in history .... Acts 3:13; Acts 4:27

Pildash—*steely*

Son of Nahor and Milcah .... Gen. 22:20-22

Pileha—*plowman*

Signer of the covenant .... Neh. 10:24

Pilgrims—*God's people as*

A. *Elements involved in:*

Forsaking all for Christ .... Luke 14:26, 27, 33
Traveling by faith .... Heb. 11:9
Faces set toward Zion .... Jer. 50:5
Encouraged by God's promises .... Heb. 11:13
Sustained by God .... Is. 35:1-10

B. *Their journey in this world as:*

Pilgrims and strangers .... 1 Pet. 2:11, 12
Lights .... Phil. 2:15
Salt .... Matt. 5:13
God's own .... 1 Pet. 2:9, 10
Chosen out of the world .... John 17:6; 1 Pet. 1:1, 2

See Strangers

Pillar—*a column or support*

A. *Descriptive of:*

Memorial sites .... Gen. 28:18, 22
Woman turned to salt .... Gen. 19:26
Altars of idolatry .... Deut. 12:3
Supports for a building .... Judg. 16:25, 26, 29
Covenant site .... Ex. 24:4-8
Miracles .... Joel 2:30

B. *Figurative of:*

God's presence .... Ex. 33:9, 10
Earth's supports .... Job 9:6
God's sovereignty over nations .... Is. 19:19
Man's legs .... Song 5:15
Important persons .... Gal. 2:9
Church .... 1 Tim. 3:15
True believers .... Rev. 3:12
Angel's feet .... Rev. 10:1

Pillar of cloud and fire

A. *As means of:*

Guiding Israel .... Ex. 13:21, 22
Protecting Israel .... Ex. 14:19, 24
Regulating Israel's journeys .... Num. 9:15-23
Manifesting His glory to Israel .... Ex. 24:16-18
Manifesting His presence .... Ex. 34:5-8
Communicating with Israel .... Ex. 33:9, 10

B. *Effect of:*

Cause of fear .... Ex. 19:9, 16
Repeated in the Temple .... 1 Kin. 8:10, 11
Long remembered .... Ps. 99:7
Recalled with gratitude .... Neh. 9:12, 19
Repeated in Christ's transfiguration .... Matt. 17:5

C. *Figurative of God's:*

Wonders .... Joel 2:30
Departure from Jerusalem .... Ezek. 9:3
Presence among believers .... Matt. 18:20

Pillow—*a cushion*

Stone used as .... Gen. 28:11, 18
Made of goat's hair .... 1 Sam. 19:13, 16
Used on a ship .... Mark 4:38

Pilot—*one who guides*

Of Tyre's ships .... Ezek. 27:8-29
Shipmaster .... Jon. 1:6
Used figuratively .... James 3:4

Piltai—*Jehovah delivers*

Priest of Joiakim's time .... Neh. 12:12, 17

Pin—*a wooden or metal peg*

Used in a weaver's loom .... Judg. 16:13, 14
See Nail

Pine away—*to waste away*

From disobedience .... Lev. 26:14, 16
Egypt .... Is. 19:8
Judah .... Is. 33:9; Jer. 15:9
Jerusalem .... Lam. 4:9

Pine trees—*evergreen trees*

Used in Solomon's Temple .... 2 Chr. 3:5
Product of Lebanon .... Is. 60:13
Used figuratively .... Is. 41:19

Pinnacle—*a summit; highest ledge*

Of the Temple .... Matt. 4:5

Pinon—*darkness*

Edomite chief .... Gen. 36:41; 1 Chr. 1:52

Pipe, piper—*a flute*

A. *Descriptive of:*

Musical instrument .... 1 Sam. 10:5
Player of a flute .... Rev. 18:22
Hollow tube .... Zech. 4:2, 12

B. *Figurative of:*

Joyful deliverance .... Is. 30:29
Mournful lamentation .... Jer. 48:36
Inconsistent reactions .... Matt. 11:17
Spiritual discernment .... 1 Cor. 14:7

P

SUBJECT REFERENCE

Piram—*indomitable*
Amorite king of Jarmuth ....Josh. 10:3

Pirathon—*height*
Town in Ephraim ....Judg. 12:15

Pirathonite—*inhabitant of Pirathon*
Descriptive of:
Abdon ....Judg. 12:13-15
Benaiah ....2 Sam. 23:30

Pisgah—*a mountain peak in the Abarim range in Moab*
Balaam offers sacrifice upon ....Num. 23:14
Moses views promised land from ....Deut. 3:27
Site of Moses' death ....Deut. 34:1-7
Summit of, called Nebo ....Deut. 32:49-52
See Nebo

Pisidia—*a mountainous district in Asia Minor*
Twice visited by Paul ....Acts 13:13, 14; Acts 14:24

Pison—*freely flowing*
One of Eden's four rivers ....Gen. 2:10, 11

Pispah—*dispersion*
Asherite......................1 Chr. 7:38

Pit—*a hole*
Figurative of:
Grave ....Ps. 30:9
Snare ....Ps. 35:7
Harlot ....Prov. 23:27
Mouth of strange woman ....Prov. 22:14
Destruction...................Ps. 55:23
Self-destruction ....Prov. 28:10
Hell ....Ps. 28:1
Devil's abode ....Rev. 9:1, 2, 11
See Abyss

Pitch
Ark covered with ....Gen. 6:14
In Babel's tower..............Gen. 11:3
In Moses' ark ....Ex. 2:3
Kings fall in ....Gen. 14:10

Pitcher—*an earthenware vessel with handles*
A. *Used for:*
Water.....................Gen. 24:16
Protection of a torch ....Judg. 7:16, 19
B. *Figurative of:*
Heart ....Eccl. 12:6

Pithom—*mansion of the god Atum*
Egyptian city built by Hebrew slaves.......................Ex. 1:11

Pithon—*harmless*
Son of Micah ....1 Chr. 8:35

Pitilessness—*showing no mercy*
Examples of:
Rich man ....2 Sam. 12:1-6
Nebuchadnezzar ....2 Kin. 25:6-21
Medes ....Is. 13:18
Edom........................Amos 1:11
Heartless creditor ....Matt. 18:29, 30
Strict religionists ....Luke 10:30-32
Merciless murderers ....Acts 7:54-58

Pity—*to show compassion*
A. *Of God, upon:*
Heathen...................Jon. 4:10, 11
Israel ....Is. 63:9
Faithful remnant ....Is. 54:8-10
Believer ....James 5:11
B. *Of men:*
Pleaded ....Job 19:21
Upon the poor ....Prov. 19:17
Upon children ....Ps. 103:13
Encouraged................1 Pet. 3:8
See Compassion; Mercy

Plague—*a severe epidemic*
A. *Descriptive of:*
Divine judgment ....Ex. 9:14
Leprosy ....Lev. 13:1-59
Disease ....Mark 3:10
Final judgment.............Rev. 9:20
B. *Instances of:*
In Egypt ....Ex. 11:1
At Kibroth-hattaavah ....Num. 11:33, 34
At Kadesh.................Num. 14:37
At Peor ....Josh. 22:17
Among:
Philistines ....1 Sam. 5:7
Israelites ....2 Sam. 24:15
Sennacherib's soldiers .....Is. 37:36
C. *Sent by God:*
Because of sin ....Gen. 12:17
As final judgments..........Rev. 15:1, 8
D. *Remedy against, by:*
Judgment ....Ps. 106:29, 30
Prayer and confession ....1 Kin. 8:37, 38
Separation.................Rev. 18:4
Promise ....Ps. 91:10
Obedience.................Rev. 22:18

Plain—*a geographically flat area;* (usually refers to specific regional areas)
Dry region ....Num. 22:1; Deut. 3:17; Deut. 34:3
Low regions ....Jer. 17:26; Obad. 19

Plait, plaiting—*to intertwine*
Of Christ's crown ....Matt. 27:29
Of woman's hair ....1 Pet. 3:3

Plaited hair
Contrasted to spiritual adornment ....1 Pet. 3:3

Plans—*methods of action*
Acknowledging God in.........Prov. 3:6
Considering all possibilites......Luke 14:31-33
Leaving God out ....Luke 12:16-21
Not trusting God.............Ps. 52:7

Plants
Created by God ....Gen. 1:11, 12
Given as food.................Gen. 1:28, 29

Plants of the Bible
Anise ....Matt. 23:23
Bramble ....Judg. 9:14, 15
Brier ....Judg. 8:7, 16
Broom ("juniper") ....Ps. 120:4
Calamus ....Song 4:14
Camphire (Henna).............Song 1:14
Cummin ....Is. 28:25, 27
Fitch ....Ezek. 4:9
Garlic ....Num. 11:5
Gourd ....2 Kin. 4:39
Grass.......................Ps. 103:15
Hyssop ....Ex. 12:22
Lily ....Song 5:13
Mallows ....Job 30:4
Mandrakes ....Gen. 30:14-16
Mint ....Matt. 23:23
Mustard ....Matt. 13:31
Myrtle ....Is. 55:13
Rose ....Is. 35:1
Rue ....Luke 11:42
Saffron ....Song 4:13, 14
Spikenard ....Song 4:13, 14
Thorn ....Judg. 8:7
Vine of Sodom ....Deut. 32:32
Wormwood ....Deut. 29:18

Plaster
A. *Building material used on:*
Infested walls ....Lev. 14:42, 48
Mt. Ebal ....Deut. 27:2, 4
Babylon's walls ....Dan. 5:5
See Lime; Mortar
B. *Medicinal material:*
Figs applied to Hezekiah's boil ....Is. 38:21

Platter
Deep dish or basin ("charger") ....Matt. 14:8, 11
Side dish for food ....Matt. 23:25, 26
Used figuratively ....Matt. 23:25, 26

Play
Music ....1 Sam. 16:16-23
Immoral acts ....Ex. 32:6
Fighting ....2 Sam. 2:14
Dancing ....2 Sam. 6:5, 21
Fish ....Ps. 104:26
Children ....Is. 11:8

Plead—*to entreat intensely*
A. *Asking for judgment against:*
Idolatry ....Judg. 6:31, 32
Evil king ....1 Sam. 24:15
B. *Asking for protection of:*
Poor......................Prov. 22:23
Widows ....Is. 1:17
Repentant ....Mic. 7:9

Please—*to satisfy*
A. *Applied to God's:*
Sovereignty ....Ps. 115:3
Election ....1 Sam. 12:22
Method ....1 Cor. 1:21
Reactions to man...........1 Kin. 3:10
Purpose ....Col. 1:19
Creative acts ....1 Cor. 12:18
Will ....Matt. 3:17
B. *Applied to the unregenerate's:*
Behavior ....Rom. 8:8
Passions..................Matt. 14:6
Ways ....1 Thess. 2:15
Prejudices ....Acts 12:3
C. *Applied to the regenerate's:*
Faith ....Heb. 11:5, 6
Calling...................2 Tim. 2:4
Concern for others..........Rom. 15:26, 27
Married life................1 Cor. 7:12, 13
Example, Christ ....John 8:29

Pleasure—*satisfying the sensations*
A. *Kinds of:*
Physical..................Eccl. 2:1-10
Sexual ....Gen. 18:12
Worldly ....Luke 8:14
Immoral ....Titus 3:3
Spiritual ....Ps. 36:8
Heavenly ....Ps. 16:11
B. *God's, described as:*
Sovereign.................Eph. 1:5, 9
Creative..................Rev. 4:11
In righteousness ....1 Chr. 29:17
Purpose ....Luke 12:32
Not in evil ....Ps. 5:4
Not in the wicked ....Ezek. 18:23, 32; Ezek. 33:11
C. *Christian's described as:*
Subject to God's will........2 Cor. 12:10
Inspired by God ....Phil. 2:13
Fulfilled by God ....2 Thess. 1:11
D. *The unbeliever's, described as:*
Unsatisfying ....Eccl. 2:1
Enslaving ....Titus 3:3
Deadening.................1 Tim. 5:6
Judged ....2 Thess. 2:12
Defiant ....Rom. 1:32

Pledge—*something given for security of a debt*
A. *Of material things:*
Garments ....Ex. 22:26
Regulations concerning......Deut. 24:10-17
Evil of ....Job 22:6
Restoration of, sign of righteousness ....Ezek. 18:7, 16
Unlawfully held back ....Ezek. 18:12
B. *Of spiritual things:*
The Holy Spirit in the heart ....2 Cor. 1:22
Given by God ....2 Cor. 5:5
Guarantee of future redemption ....Eph. 1:13, 14
See Borrow; Debt; Lending; Surety

Pleiades—*cluster of many stars*
Part of God's creation ....Job 9:9; Amos 5:8

Plenteous, plenty
A. *Of physical things:*
Food ....Gen. 41:29-47
Prosperity ....Deut. 28:11
Productivity ....Jer. 2:7
Rain ....Ps. 68:9
Water.....................Lev. 11:36
B. *Of spiritual things:*
God's loving kindness ....Ps. 86:5, 15
God's redemption ....Ps. 130:7

SUBJECT ... REFERENCE

Recompenses ... Ps. 31:23
Souls in need ... Matt. 9:37

C. *How to obtain, by:*
Industry ... Prov. 28:19
Putting God first ... Prov. 3:9, 10
Lord's blessing ... 2 Chr. 31:10

See Abundance

Plottings

A. *Against:*
Poor ... Ps. 10:7-11
Perfect ... Ps. 64:4-7
Prophets ... Jer. 18:18
Persecuted ... Matt. 5:11, 12

B. *Inspired by:*
Contempt ... Neh. 4:1-8
Hatred ... Gen. 37:8-20
Devil ... John 13:27
Envy ... Matt. 27:18

C. *Examples of:*
Esau against Jacob ... Gen. 27:41-45
Satan against Job ... Job 1:8-22
Ahab against Naboth ... 1 Kin. 21:1-16
Jews against Jeremiah ... Jer. 26:8-15
Haman against the Jews ... Esth. 7:3-6
Chaldeans against Daniel ... Dan. 6:1-8
Jews against Christ ... Matt. 26:1-5
John 11:47-53
Jews against Paul ... Acts 23:12-22

Plow, plowing—*to dig up the earth for sowing seed*

A. *Used literally of:*
Elisha ... 1 Kin. 19:19
Forbidden with mixed animals ... Deut. 22:10
Job's sons ... Job 1:14

B. *Used figuratively of:*
Proper learning ... Is. 28:24, 26
Wrongdoing ... Hos. 10:13
Punishment ... Hos. 10:11
Affliction ... Ps. 129:3
Destruction ... Jer. 26:18
Persistent sin ... Job 4:8
Christian labor ... 1 Cor. 9:10
Information from a wife ... Judg. 14:18
Constancy in decision ... Luke 9:62
Perverse action ... Amos 6:12

Plowman—*a farmer*

Used literally of:
Farming ... Is. 28:24

Used figuratively of:
Prosperity ... Amos 9:13
Christian ministry ... 1 Cor. 9:10

Plowshares—*the hard part of a plow*

Made into swords ... Joel 3:10
Swords made into ... Is. 2:4

Plumbline—*a cord with a weight* (plummet)

Figurative of:
Destruction ... 2 Kin. 21:13
God's judgment ... Amos 7:7, 8
God's building ... Zech. 4:10

Pochereth—*binder*

Descendants of, among Solomon's servants ... Ezra 2:57; Neh. 7:59

Poetry, Hebrew

A. *Classified according to form:*
Synonymous—repetition of same thoughts ... Ps. 19:2
Progressive—advance of thought in second line ... Job 3:17
Synthetic—second line adds something new ... Ps. 104:19
Climactic—the thought climbs to a climax ... Ps. 121:3, 4
Antithetic—the second line contrasted with first ... Prov. 14:1
Comparative—the "as" compared with the "so" ... Prov. 10:26
Acrostic—alphabetic ... Ps. 119:1-176

B. *Classified according to function:*
Didactic (teaching) ... Deut. 32:1-43
Book of Job
Lyrics ... Ex. 15:1-19
Judg. 5:1-31

SUBJECT ... REFERENCE

Elegies ... 2 Sam. 1:17-27
Psalms ... Book of Psalms

Poison

Reptiles ... Deut. 32:24
Dragons ... Deut. 32:33
Adders ... Ps. 140:3
Gourd ... 2 Kin. 4:39
Hemlock ... Hos. 10:4
Waters ... Jer. 8:14
Asps ... Rom. 3:13
Job 20:16

Politeness—*refined manners*

A. *Manifested by:*
Kings ... Gen. 47:2-11
Hebrews ... Gen. 43:26-29
Romans ... Acts 27:3
Pagans ... Acts 28:1, 2
Christians ... Philem. 8-21

B. *Counterfeited by:*
Trickery ... 2 Sam. 20:9, 10
Deceit ... 2 Sam. 15:1-6
Hypocrisy ... Matt. 22:7, 8
Pride ... Luke 14:8-10
Snobbery ... James 2:1-4
Selfishness ... 3 John 9, 10

See Courtesy

Politicians—*governmental officials*

A. *Evils manifested by:*
Ambition ... 2 Sam. 15:1-6
Flattery ... Dan. 6:4-15
Indifference ... Acts 18:12-16
Avarice ... Acts 24:26

B. *Good manifested by:*
Provision ... Gen. 41:33-49
Protection ... Neh. 2:7-11
Piety ... 2 Chr. 34:1-33
Prayer ... 2 Chr. 20:6-12
Praise ... 2 Chr. 20:27-29

Poll

A. *Descriptive of a person:*
In a military census ... Num. 1:2, 18, 20
Num. 3:47

B. *Descriptive of cutting off the hair:*
Absalom ... 2 Sam. 14:26
Priests ... Ezek. 44:20
Mourning (figurative) ... Mic. 1:16

Pollute—*to defile*

A. *Described as something unclean:*
Morally ... Num. 35:33, 34
Spiritually ... Acts 15:20

B. *Means of:*
Blood ... Ps. 106:38
Idolatry ... Ezek. 20:30, 31
Abominations ... Jer. 7:30
Unregenerate service ... Ezek. 44:7
Wickedness ... Jer. 3:1, 2
Contempt of the Lord ... Mal. 1:7, 12
Captivity ... Is. 47:6

See Unclean

Polygamy—*having more than one wife*

A. *Caused by:*
Barrenness of first wife ... Gen. 16:1-6
Desire for large family ... Judg. 8:30
Political ties with other countries ... 1 Kin. 3:1, 2
Sexual desire ... 2 Chr. 11:23
Slavery ... Gen. 16:1, 3

B. *Contrary to:*
God's original Law ... Gen. 2:24
Ideal picture of marriage ... Ps. 128:1-6
God's commandment ... Ex. 20:14
God's equal distribution of the sexes ... Gen. 1:27; 1 Cor. 7:2
Relationship between Christ and the Church ... Eph. 5:22-33

C. *Productive of:*
Dissension ... Gen. 16:1
Discord ... 1 Sam. 1:6
Degeneracy ... 1 Kin. 11:1-4

See Adultery; Family; Fornication; Marriage

Pomegranate—*a small tree bearing an apple-shaped fruit*

Grown in Canaan ... Num. 13:23

SUBJECT ... REFERENCE

Ornaments of:
Worn by priests ... Ex. 28:33
In Temple ... 1 Kin. 7:18
Sign of fruitfulness ... Hag. 2:19
Used figuratively ... Song 4:3

Pommel—*round; a bowl*

Round ornament ... 2 Chr. 4:12, 13
Same as "bowl" ... 1 Kin. 7:41, 42

Pond, pool—*a reservoir of water*

A. *Used for:*
Washing ... 1 Kin. 22:38
Water supply ... 2 Kin. 20:20
Irrigation ... Eccl. 2:6
Healing ... John 5:2-7

B. *Famous ones:*
Gibeon ... 2 Sam. 2:13
Hebron ... 2 Sam. 4:12
Samaria ... 1 Kin. 22:38
Bethesda ... John 5:2
Siloam ... John 9:7
The upper ... Is. 7:3
The lower ... Is. 22:9, 11
The King's ... Neh. 2:14

Pontus—*a coastal strip of north Asia Minor*

Jews from, at Pentecost ... Acts 2:5, 9
Home of Aquila and Priscilla ... Acts 18:2
Christians of, addressed by Peter ... 1 Pet. 1:1

Poor, poverty

A. *Descriptive of:*
Needy ... Luke 21:2
Lower classes ... 2 Kin. 24:14
Rebellious ... Jer. 5:3, 4
Holy remnant ... Zeph. 3:12-14

B. *Causes of:*
God's sovereignty ... 1 Sam. 2:7
Sloth ... Prov. 6:10, 11
Lack of industry ... Prov. 24:30-34
Love of pleasure ... Prov. 21:17
Stubbornness ... Prov. 13:18
Empty pursuits ... Prov. 28:19
Drunkenness ... Prov. 23:21

C. *Wrong treatment of:*
Reproaches God ... Prov. 14:31
Brings punishment ... Prov. 21:13
Brings poverty ... Prov. 22:16
Regarded by God ... Eccl. 5:8
Judged by God ... Is. 3:13-15

D. *Legislation designed for protection of:*
Daily payment of wages ... Lev. 19:13
Sharing of tithes with ... Deut. 14:28, 29
Loans to, without interest ... Lev. 25:35, 37
Right to glean ... Lev. 19:9, 10
Land of, restored in jubilee year ... Lev. 25:25-30
Equal participation in feasts ... Lev. 16:11, 14
Permanent bondage of, forbidden ... Deut. 15:12-15

See Needy; Poverty, spiritual

Poor in spirit—*humble, self-effacing*

Promised blessing ... Matt. 5:3

Poplar tree

Used in deception of Laban ... Gen. 30:37
Pagan rites among ... Hos. 4:13
Probably same as "willows" in ... Lev. 23:40

Popularity—*one's esteem in the world*

Obtained by:
Heroic exploits ... Judg. 8:21, 22
Unusual wisdom ... 1 Kin. 4:29-34
Trickery ... 2 Sam. 15:1-6
Outward display ... Matt. 6:2, 5, 16

Popularity of Jesus

A. *Factors producing His:*
Teaching ... Mark 1:22, 27
Healing ... Mark 5:20
Miracles ... John 12:9-19
Feeding the people ... John 6:15-27

B. *Factors causing decline of His:*
High ethical standards ... Mark 8:34-38
Foretells His death ... Matt. 16:21-28

SUBJECT — REFERENCE

Population—*the total inhabitants of a place*
- Israel's, increased in Egypt — Ex. 1:7, 8
- Nineveh's, great — Jon. 4:11
- Heaven's, vast — Rev. 7:9

Poratha
- One of Haman's sons — Esth. 9:8

Porch
- Central court of a house — Matt. 26:71
- Portico for pedestrians — John 5:2
- Roofed colonnade — John 10:23
- Court of the temple — 1 Kin. 6:3, 6, 7

Porcius Festus—*successor to Felix*
- Paul stands trial before — Acts 25:1-22

Pork—*swine's flesh*
- Classified as unclean — Lev. 11:7, 8

Port—*a harbor*
- At Joppa — Jon. 1:3
- Fair Havens — Acts 27:8
- Phoenix — Acts 27:12
- Syracuse — Acts 28:12
- Rhegium — Acts 28:13
- Puteoli — Acts 28:13

Porter—*gatekeeper or doorkeeper*
- Watchman of a city — 2 Sam. 18:26
- Watchman of a house — Mark 13:34
- Shepherd's attendant — John 10:3
- Official of the temple (see below) — 1 Chr. 23:5
- Origin of, in Moses' time — 1 Chr. 9:17-26
- Belongs to Levites — Neh. 12:47
- Duties of, designed by David — 1 Chr. 26:1-19
- Office of, important — 1 Chr. 9:26

Portico—*porch*
- Solomon's — John 10:23
- Of Bethesda — John 5:2

Portion—*a stipulated part*

A. *Of things material:*
- Inheritance — Gen. 48:22

B. *Of good things:*
- Spirit — 2 Kin. 2:9
- Lord — Ps. 119:57
- Spiritual riches — Is. 61:7

C. *Of evil things:*
- Things of the world — Ps. 17:14
- Fellowship with the wicked — Neh. 2:20

D. *Of things eternal:*
- Punishment of the wicked — Ps. 11:6

See Inheritance

Position—*place of influence*
- Sought after by Pharisees — Matt. 23:5-7
- James and John request — Mark 10:37
- Seeking after, denounced — Luke 14:7-11
- Diotrephes, a seeker after — 3 John 9

Possess—*to acquire*

A. *Objects of:*
- Promised land — Deut. 4:1, 5
- Ruins — Is. 14:21
- Spiritual riches — Is. 57:13
- Christ — Prov. 8:22
- One's:
  - Soul — Luke 21:19
  - Body of wife — 1 Thess. 4:4
  - Sins — Job 13:26

B. *Of Canaan:*
- Promised — Gen. 17:8
- Under oath — Neh. 9:15
- Israel challenged to — Num. 13:20

Possible—*that which can exist*

A. *Things possible:*
- All, with God — Matt. 19:26
- All, to the believer — Mark 9:23
- Peaceful living — Gal. 4:15

B. *Things impossible:*
- Deception of the saints — Matt. 24:24
- Removal of the Cross — Matt. 26:39
- Christ's remaining in the grave — Acts 2:24
- Removal of sins by animal sacrifice — Heb. 10:4

Post
- Private homes — Ex. 12:7
- Tabernacle — 1 Sam. 1:9
- Temple — 1 Kin. 6:31, 33

Posthumous—*after death*
- Mary of Bethany — Matt. 26:13
- Abel — Heb. 11:4
- All believers — Rev. 14:13

Posts—*runners; couriers; postmen*
- Letters sent by — 2 Chr. 30:6, 10
- Sent on swift horses — Esth. 3:13, 15
- Figurative of speed — Job 9:25

Pot—*a rounded, open-mouthed vessel*

A. *Use of:*
- Cooking — Zech. 14:21
- Refining — Prov. 17:3

B. *Figurative of:*
- Egyptian slavery — Ps. 81:6
- Sudden destruction — Ps. 58:9
- Impending national destruction — Jer. 1:13
- Merciless punishment — Mic. 3:2, 3
- Complete sanctification — Zech. 14:20, 21

Potentate—*a mighty one*
- Christ the only absolute — 1 Tim. 6:15

Potiphar—*whom Re* (the sun god) *has given*
- High Egyptian officer — Gen. 39:1
- Puts Joseph in jail — Gen. 39:20

Poti-phera
- Egyptian priest of On (Heliopolis) — Gen. 41:45-50
- Father of Asenath, Joseph's wife — Gen. 46:20

Potsherd—*a fragment of broken pottery*

Figurative of:
- Weakness — Ps. 22:15
- Leviathan's underparts — Job 41:30

Uses of:
- Scraping — Job 2:8
- Scooping water — Is. 30:14

Potsherd gate—*a gate of Jerusalem*
- By valley of Ben-hinnom — Jer. 19:2

Pottage—*a thick vegetable soup*
- Price of Esau's birthright — Gen. 25:29-34
- Eaten by Elisha's disciples — 2 Kin. 4:38-41
- Ordinary food — Hag. 2:12

Potter—*one who makes earthenware vessels*

A. *Art of, involves:*
- Reducing clay to paste — Is. 41:25
- Shaping by revolving wheel — Jer. 18:1-4
- Molding by hands — Jer. 18:6

B. *Figurative of:*
- Complete destruction — Is. 30:14
- God's sovereignty over men — Is. 64:8
- Israel's lack of understanding — Is. 29:16

Potter's Field—*burial place for poor people*
- Judas' money used for purchase of — Matt. 27:7, 8

Pound—*a Greek measure*
- Used in parable — Luke 19:12-27

Pour—*to flow freely from something*

A. *Applied to:*
- Rain from clouds — Amos 9:6
- Oil from vessels — Gen. 35:14
- Blood from animals — Lev. 8:15
- Water from barrels — 1 Kin. 18:33

B. *Used figuratively of:*
- Christ's death — Ps. 22:14
- Spirit's coming — Joel 2:28, 29
- Holy Spirit — Ezek. 39:29
- God's:
  - Wrath — 2 Chr. 34:21, 25
  - Blessings — Mal. 3:10
  - Sovereignty — Job 10:9, 10
- Prayer and repentance — Lam. 2:19
- Extreme emotions — 1 Sam. 1:15

Poverty, spiritual

A. *In a bad sense, of spiritual:*
- Decay — Rev. 2:9
- Immaturity — 1 Cor. 3:1-3

B. *Used in a good sense, of:*
- The contrite — Is. 66:2
- God's people — Is. 14:32

C. *Caused by:*
- Hastiness — Prov. 21:5
- Greed — Prov. 22:16
- Laziness — Prov. 24:30-34

Power of Christ

A. *Described as:*
- Given by God — John 17:2
- Derived from the Spirit — Luke 4:14
- Delegated to others — Luke 9:1
- Determined by Himself — John 10:18

B. *Manifested as power in:*
- Creation — John 1:3, 10
- Upholds all things — Heb. 1:3
- Miracles — Luke 4:36
- Regeneration — John 5:21-26
- Salvation — Heb. 7:25
- Resurrecting believers — John 5:28, 29
- His return — Matt. 24:30

C. *Manifested as authority to:*
- Forgive sins — Matt. 9:6, 8
- Teach — Luke 4:32
- Give sonship — John 1:12
- Lay down His life — John 10:18
- Authority — Matt. 28:18

D. *Benefits from, to believers:*
- Life — John 17:2
- Strength — Phil. 4:13
- Effective service — 1 Tim. 1:12; 2 Tim. 4:17
- Perfected in weakness — 2 Cor. 12:9
- Conquest over temptation — Heb. 2:18
- Glorification — Phil. 3:20, 21

Power of God

A. *Manifested in:*
- Creation — Jer. 51:15
- Keeps watch on the nations — Ps. 66:7
- Christ's:
  - Birth — Luke 1:35
  - Miracles — Luke 11:20
  - Resurrection — 2 Cor. 13:4
  - Exaltation — Eph. 1:19, 20
- Regeneration — Eph. 1:19
- Sanctification — Phil. 2:13
- Believer's resurrection — 1 Cor. 6:14

B. *Believer's attitude toward:*
- Renders praise for — Ps. 21:13
- Sings of — Ps. 59:16
- Talks of — Ps. 145:11

Power of the Holy Spirit

A. *Manifested in Christ's:*
- Conception — Luke 1:35
- Ministry — Luke 4:14
- Miracles — Luke 11:20
- Resurrection — Rom. 1:4

B. *Manifested in the believer's:*
- Regeneration — Ezek. 37:11-14
- Effective ministry — Luke 24:49

Power, spiritual

Sources of:
- Holy Spirit — 1 Cor. 2:4, 5
- Christ — 1 Cor. 1:24
- Gospel — Rom. 1:16
- God's kingdom — Mark 9:1
- God's Word — Heb. 4:12
- New life — Eph. 1:19

Powerlessness—*ineffective testimony*

Produced by:
- Worldliness — Gen. 19:14
- Unbelief — Matt. 17:16-20

Practice—*customary habit*
- Wicked works — Ps. 141:4
- Hypocrisy — Is. 32:6
- Power — Dan. 8:24
- Work evil — Mic. 2:1

SUBJECT — REFERENCE

Praetorium—*the governor's official residence*

1. Pilate's, in Jerusalem ... Mark 15:16
   Translated "common hall" and "judgment hall" ... Matt. 27:27
2. Herod's palace at Caesarea ... Acts 23:35
3. Praetorian guard at Rome ... Phil. 1:13

Praise of God

A. *Objects of:*
- God Himself ... Ps. 139:14
- God's:
  - Name ... 1 Chr. 29:13; Ps. 99:3
  - Power ... Ps. 21:13
  - Wonders ... Ps. 89:5
  - Loving-kindness ... Ps. 138:2
  - Works ... Ps. 145:4

B. *Times of:*
- Daily ... Ps. 72:15
- Continually ... Ps. 71:6
- Seven times daily ... Ps. 119:164
- All the day ... Ps. 35:28
- At midnight ... Ps. 119:62; Acts 16:25
- While I live ... Ps. 146:2

Praise of men

A. *Worthy:*
- From another ... Prov. 27:2
- For:
  - Faithfulness ... Prov. 31:28
  - Obedience ... Rom. 13:3
  - Works ... Prov. 31:31

B. *Unworthy for:*
- Wicked ... Prov. 28:4
- Disorder ... 1 Cor. 11:17, 22
- Self-seeking ... John 12:43

Prating—*foolish babbling*

Descriptive of:
- Fool ... Prov. 10:8, 10
- Diotrephes ... 3 John 10

Prayer—*a request to God*

A. *Kinds of:*
- Secret ... Matt. 6:6
- Family ... Acts 10:2, 30
- Group ... Matt. 18:20
- Public ... 1 Cor. 14:14-17

B. *Parts of:*
- Adoration ... Dan. 4:34, 35
- Confession ... 1 John 1:9
- Supplication ... 1 Tim. 2:1-3
- Intercession ... James 5:15
- Thanksgiving ... Phil. 4:6

C. *Personal requirements of:*
- Purity of heart ... Ps. 66:18, 19
- Believing ... Matt. 21:22
- In Christ's name ... John 14:13
- According to God's will ... 1 John 5:14

D. *General requirements of:*
- Forgiving spirit ... Matt. 6:14
- Simplicity ... Matt. 6:5, 6
- Humility and repentance ... Luke 18:10-14
- Unity of believers ... Matt. 18:19, 20
- Tenacity ... Luke 18:1-8
- Importunity ... Luke 11:5-8
- Intensity ... Matt. 7:7-11
- Confident expectation ... Mark 11:24
- Without many words ... Matt. 6:7
- Unceasingly ... 1 Thess. 5:17

E. *Answers refused, because of:*
- Sin ... Ps. 66:18
- Selfishness ... James 4:3
- Doubt ... James 1:5-7
- Disobedience ... Prov. 28:9
- Inhumanity ... Prov. 21:13
- Pride ... Luke 18:11, 12, 14

F. *Posture for:*
- Standing ... Neh. 9:5
- Kneeling ... Ezra 9:5
- Sitting ... 1 Chr. 17:16-27
- Bowing ... Ex. 34:8
- Hands uplifted ... 1 Tim. 2:8

Prayer meetings
- In the upper room ... Acts 1:13, 14
- In a house ... Acts 12:5-17
- By a river ... Acts 16:13
- On a beach ... Acts 21:5

SUBJECT — REFERENCE

Prayers of Christ

A. *Their nature:*
- Adoration ... Matt. 11:25-27
- Intercession ... John 17:1-26
- Thanksgiving ... John 11:41, 42

B. *Their great occasions:*
- At His baptism ... Luke 3:21, 22
- Before selecting the apostles ... Luke 6:12-16
- At His transfiguration ... Luke 9:28, 29
- In Gethsemane ... Matt. 26:36-42

C. *Their times and places:*
- In secret ... Luke 5:16; Luke 9:18
- Early in morning ... Mark 1:35
- With others ... Luke 11:1
- On mountain ... Matt. 14:23

Preach, preaching—*proclaiming the Gospel*

A. *Of the Gospel:*
- Necessity of ... 1 Cor. 9:16
- Without charge ... 1 Cor. 9:18
- Extent of, to all ... Col. 1:25
- Only one ... Gal. 1:8, 9
- Centers in the Cross ... 1 Cor. 1:23
- Preacher's importance in ... Rom. 10:14, 15

B. *Attitudes toward:*
- Accepted ... Luke 11:32
- Rejected ... 2 Pet. 2:4, 5
- Not perfected by ... Heb. 4:2
- Perverted ... Gal. 1:6-9
- Contentious about ... Phil. 1:15-18
- Counted foolishness ... 1 Cor. 1:18-21
- Ridiculed ... Acts 17:16-18
- Not ashamed of ... Rom. 1:15, 16

Preacher—*one who proclaims publically*
- Author of Ecclesiastes ... Eccl. 1:1, 2
- Causes to hear ... Rom. 10:14
- Paul, speaking of himself ... 1 Tim. 2:7; 2 Tim. 1:11
- Noah, of righteousness ... 2 Pet. 2:5

Precepts—*specific charges*

God's:
- Commanded ... Heb. 9:19
- Corrupted ... Matt. 15:9
- Kept ... Ps. 119:56-69
- Sought ... Ps. 119:40-94
- Not forgotten ... Ps. 119:93, 141
- Loved ... Ps. 119:159
- Source of understanding ... Ps. 119:100, 104

See Traditions

Precious—*something extremely valuable*

A. *Applied to spiritual things:*
- Word of God ... 1 Sam. 3:1
- Wisdom ... Prov. 3:13, 15
- Soul ... 1 Sam. 26:21
- One's life ... 2 Kin. 1:13, 14
- Redemption of a soul ... Ps. 49:8
- God's thoughts toward us ... Ps. 139:17
- Death of God's people ... Ps. 72:14
- Christ ... Is. 28:16
- Christ's blood ... 1 Pet. 1:19
- Faith ... 2 Pet. 1:1
- Promises ... 2 Pet. 1:4
- Trial of faith ... 1 Pet. 1:7

B. *Applied figuratively to:*
- Knowledge ... Prov. 20:15
- Sons of Zion ... Lam. 4:2
- Rewards ... 1 Cor. 3:12-14
- Final harvest ... James 5:7
- Worldly pomp ... Rev. 17:4
- Heaven's glory ... Rev. 21:11, 19

Precious promises

A. *To the troubled by:*
- Doubts ... Ps. 73:1-28
- Afflictions ... Ps. 34:1-22
- Persecution ... Matt. 5:11, 12
- Anxiety ... Phil. 4:6
- Temptation ... 1 Cor. 10:13
- Infirmities ... 2 Cor. 12:7-10
- Discipline ... Heb. 12:3-13

B. *To the sorrowful over:*
- Death ... 1 Thess. 4:13-18
- Sickness ... James 5:13-16
- Their sins ... Ps. 32:1-11
- Disappointment ... Rom. 8:28

SUBJECT — REFERENCE

C. *To those troubled by:*
- World ... 1 John 2:15-17
- Flesh ... Gal. 5:16-18
- Satan ... Luke 22:31, 32
- Anxious ... Matt. 6:31-34
- Sin ... James 1:12-15
- Pride ... 1 Pet. 5:5-7

D. *To the active Christian in his:*
- Giving ... Mal. 3:10
- Zeal ... Phil. 4:13
- Soul winning ... James 5:20
- Fruitfulness ... John 7:38, 39
- Graces ... 2 Pet. 1:5-11
- Prayers ... James 5:16
- Perseverance ... Gal. 6:9
- Watchfulness ... Eph. 6:10-20
- Assurance ... Rom. 8:32-39
- Ministry ... Ps. 138:8

Predestination—*God's eternal plan*

A. *Described as:*
- "Purpose" ... Rom. 8:28
- "Afore prepared" ... Rom. 9:23
- "Foreknowledge" ... Acts 2:23
- "Foreknew" ... Rom. 8:29
- "Ordained" ... Acts 13:48
- "Appointed" ... Acts 22:10
- "Determined" ... Luke 22:22
- "Foreseeing" ... Gal. 3:8
- "Before the world began" ... 2 Tim. 1:9

B. *Determined by God's:*
- Counsel ... Acts 2:23
- Foreknowledge ... Acts 2:23
- Good pleasure ... Luke 12:32; 1 Cor. 1:21
- Will ... Eph. 1:5, 9, 11
- Purpose ... Eph. 3:11
- Power ... Is. 40:10-17; Rom. 9:15-24

C. *Expressed toward the believer in:*
- Election ... Eph. 1:4
- Salvation ... 2 Thess. 2:13, 14
- Justification ... Rom. 8:30
- Sanctification ... 1 Thess. 2:12, 13
- Glorification ... Rom. 8:30
- Eternal destiny ... Matt. 25:34

See Foreknowledge of God; Elect

Predict—*to foretell*
- Astrologers ... Is. 47:13

Preeminence—*being supreme above all*

A. *Of creatures:*
- Sought by the devil ... Is. 14:12-15
- Sought by man ... Gen. 3:5, 6
- Illustrated by Diotrephes ... 3 John 9, 10

B. *Of Christ:*
- Predicted ... Ps. 45:6, 7
- Proclaimed ... Luke 1:31-33
- Visualized ... Matt. 17:4, 5
- Realized ... Col. 1:19
- Acknowledged ... Phil. 2:9, 10

Pregnancy
- Safeguards provided ... Ex. 21:22-25
- Evidences of ... Luke 1:44
- God's call during ... Jer. 1:4, 5; Gal. 1:15

Prejudice—*a biased opinion*

A. *Toward men, based on:*
- Race ... Acts 19:34
- Social position ... James 2:1-4
- Jealousy ... Gen. 37:3-11

B. *Toward Christ, based on His:*
- Lowly origin ... Mark 6:3
- Residence in Galilee ... John 1:46
- Race ... John 4:9
- Teaching ... John 9:16-41

See Bigotry

Premeditation—*deliberate plan to perform an act*

With:
- Evil intent ... Gen. 27:41-45
- Good intent ... Luke 14:28-33
- Heavenly sanctions ... James 4:13-17

Preparation day
- Evening ... Matt. 27:57, 62
- Day before Sabbath ... Mark 15:42; Luke 23:54

SUBJECT	REFERENCE
Prepare—*to make ready*	
A. *Of spiritual things:*	
To build an altar	Josh. 22:26
Lord's way	Matt. 8:3
God	Amos 4:12
God's throne	Ps. 9:7
Heart	Ezra 7:10
Passover	Luke 22:8, 9
Spiritual provision	Ps. 23:5
Service	2 Tim. 2:21
Redeemed people	Rom. 9:23, 24
B. *Of eternal things:*	
Reward	Matt. 20:23
Kingdom	Matt. 25:34
Heaven	John 14:2, 3
Heavenly city	Heb. 11:16
Everlasting fire	Matt. 25:41
Presbytery—*the Christian eldership acting as a body*	
Ordination ascribed to	1 Tim. 4:14
See Elders in the Church	
Presence, divine	
Described as:	
Glory	1 Chr. 16:27
Joyful	Ps. 16:11
Protective	Ps. 31:20
Everywhere	Ps. 139:7
Guide	Ex. 33:14, 15
Present to—*to offer*	
A. *As an introduction of:*	
Joseph's brothers	Gen. 47:2
Joseph to his father	Gen. 46:29
Dorcas to her friends	Acts 9:41
Paul to a governor	Acts 23:33
B. *Descriptive of the Christian's life as:*	
Living and holy sacrifice	Rom. 12:1
Chaste virgin	2 Cor. 11:2
Holy	Col. 1:22
Perfect	Col. 1:28
Without blemish	Eph. 5:27
Resurrected	2 Cor. 4:14
Presents—*gifts*	
A. *Offered to:*	
Brother	Gen. 32:13-20
King	Is. 39:1
Solomon	1 Kin. 4:21
Foreign nation	Hos. 10:6
B. *Purposes of:*	
Conceal a treacherous act	Judg. 3:15-23
Verify a messenger	Judg. 6:18-24
Secure a message	2 Kin. 8:7-10
Pay tribute	2 Kin. 17:3, 4
Show friendship	2 Kin. 20:12, 13
Show obedience	Ps. 72:10
See Gifts of man	
Preservation, God's	
A. *As manifested over:*	
World	Neh. 9:6
King	2 Sam. 8:6, 14
Animals	Ps. 36:6
Nation	Gen. 45:5, 7
Messiah	Is. 49:8
Apostle	2 Tim. 4:18
Believers	1 Thess. 5:23
Faithful	Ps. 31:23
B. *Special objects of:*	
Those who trust Him	Ps. 16:1
Holy	Ps. 86:2
Souls of saints	Ps. 97:10
Simple	Ps. 116:6
Those who love Him	Ps. 145:20
Strangers	Ps. 146:9
C. *Spiritual means of:*	
Integrity	Ps. 25:21
Loving-kindness	Ps. 40:11
Mercy and truth	Ps. 61:7
Wisdom	Prov. 4:5, 6
Losing one's life	Luke 17:33
Prophet	Hos. 12:13
President—*a ruler*	
Daniel acted as	Dan. 6:2

SUBJECT	REFERENCE
Press—*a machine for extracting the juice from grapes*	
Used literally	Neh. 13:15
Figurative of appointed time	Joel 3:13
Pressure—*force exerted*	
A. *As evil:*	
Perversion	Gen. 19:9
Enticement	Judg. 16:16
B. *As a good, to:*	
Hear God's Word	Luke 5:1
Get into the kingdom	Luke 16:16
Attain a goal	Phil. 3:14
Presumption—*to speak or act without warrant*	
A. *Manifested in:*	
Speaking without divine warrant	Deut. 18:20-22
Acting without God's presence	Num. 14:44, 45
Living without God	Luke 12:19-21
Performing functions without authority	Num. 16:3-11
Supposing God will not judge sin	Ps. 73:8, 9
Aspiring to divine titles	Is. 14:12-15
Posing as righteous	Luke 18:11, 12
Making plans without God	James 4:13, 14
B. *Judgment upon:*	
Defeat	Is. 37:23-36
Loss of power	Judg. 16:20
Quick punishment	2 Sam. 6:6, 7
Rejection	1 Sam. 15:3, 9-23
Destruction	Lev. 10:1, 2
Pretense—*a false or counterfeit profession*	
Pharisees condemned for	Matt. 23:14
Prevail—*to get the mastery over*	
A. *Of physical force:*	
Waters	Gen. 7:18-24
Enemies	Num. 22:6
Combat	1 Sam. 17:50
B. *Of supernatural force in:*	
Battle	Ex. 17:11
Combat	1 Sam. 17:9, 50
Accomplish much	1 Sam. 26:25
Conquest	Jer. 20:7
Victory	Rev. 5:5
Prevarication—*evasion of truth*	
Ananias and Sapphira killed for	Acts 5:1-10
Solemn warning against	Col. 3:9
Prey—*that which is taken by attack*	
Used figuratively of:	
Enemies	Gen. 49:9
Innocent victims	Ezek. 22:27
Pride—*a conceited sense of one's superiority*	
A. *Origin of, in:*	
Devil	Is. 14:13-15
Ambition	Dan. 5:20-23
Evil heart	Mark 7:21, 22
World	1 John 2:16
Self-righteousness	Luke 18:11, 12
Worldly power	Ezek. 16:49, 56
B. *Evils of:*	
Hardens the mind	Dan. 5:20
Produces spiritual decay	Hos. 7:9, 10
Keeps from real progress	Prov. 26:12
Hinders coming to God	Ps. 10:4
Issues in self-deception	Jer. 49:16
Makes men reject God's Word	Jer. 43:2
Leads to ruin	Prov. 16:18
C. *Characteristic of:*	
Wicked	Ps. 73:6
World rulers	Hab. 2:4, 5
Last days	2 Tim. 3:2
Priest	
A. *Requirements of:*	
Must be a son of Aaron	Ex. 29:9
Sanctified to office	Ex. 29:44
Statute perpetual	Ex. 27:21
No physical blemish	Lev. 21:17-23
Genealogy of, necessary	Ezra 2:62

SUBJECT	REFERENCE
B. *Duties of:*	
Keeping the sanctuary	Num. 3:38
Keep lamp burning continually	Ex. 27:20, 21
Continuing the sacred fire	Lev. 6:12, 13
Covering furniture when moved	Num. 4:5-15
Burning incense	Ex. 30:7, 8
Offering sacrifices	Lev. 1:1-17
Blessing the people	Num. 6:23-27
Purifying the unclean	Lev. 15:15-31
Diagnosing leprosy	Lev. 13:2-59
Blowing the trumpets	Num. 10:1-10
Carrying the ark of the covenant	Josh. 3:6-17
Teaching the Law	Lev. 10:11
C. *Names of:*	
Aaron	Ex. 31:10
Abiathar	1 Sam. 23:9
Ahimelech	1 Sam. 22:11
Amariah	2 Chr. 19:11
Ananias	Acts 23:2
Caiaphas	Matt. 26:3
Christ	Heb. 3:1
Eleazar	Num. 16:39
Eli	1 Sam. 1:9
Eliashib	Neh. 3:1
Ezekiel	Ezek. 1:3
Ezra	Ezra 7:11, 12
Hilkiah	2 Kin. 22:4
Ira	2 Sam. 20:26
Jehoiada	2 Kin. 11:9
Jehozadak	Hag. 1:1
Joshua	Zech. 3:1
Maaseiah	Jer. 37:3
Mattan (of Baal)	2 Kin. 11:18
Melchizedek	Heb. 7:1
Pashhur	Jer. 20:1
Phinehas	Josh. 22:30
Sceva	Acts 19:14
Seraiah	2 Kin. 25:18
Shelemiah	Neh. 13:13
Urijah	2 Kin. 16:10
Zabud	1 Kin. 4:5
Zacharias	Luke 1:5
Zadok	2 Sam. 15:27
Zephaniah	2 Kin. 25:18
See Levites	
Priesthood of believers	
Typical of Israel	1 Pet. 2:9
Predicted in prophecy	Is. 61:6
Including all believers	Rev. 1:5, 6
Having access to God	Eph. 2:18
Body as a living sacrifice	Rom. 12:1
Spiritual sacrifices	1 Pet. 2:5
Praise and good works	Heb. 13:15, 16
Deeds of kindness	Phil. 4:18
Priesthood of Christ	
A. *Superior to Aaron as:*	
Man; Christ the Son of God	Heb. 7:28
Sinner; Christ, sinless	Heb. 7:26, 27
Typical; Christ's the fulfillment	Heb. 8:1-6
Subject to change; Christ's unchangeable	Heb. 7:23, 24
Imperfect; Christ's perfect	Heb. 7:11, 25
B. *Christ as priest:*	
Satisfies God's justice	Rom. 3:24-28
Pacifies God's wrath	Rom. 5:9
Justifies the sinner	Rom. 5:1
Sanctifies the believer	1 Cor. 1:30
See High priest	
Prince—*a ruler*	
A. *Descriptive of:*	
Ruler	Judg. 5:15
Head or captain	Ex. 2:14
Noble or volunteer	Ps. 47:9
B. *Of the Messiah:*	
Of David's line	Ezek. 34:23, 24
Reign of, forever	Ezek. 37:24, 25
Time of, determined	Dan. 9:25, 26
Reign of, peaceful	Is. 9:6
Author of life	Acts 3:15
Exalted to be Savior	Acts 5:31
Prince of this world	
Satan thus called	John 14:30
To be cast out	John 12:31
Is judged	John 16:11
Source of evil	Eph. 2:2

SUBJECT — REFERENCE

Principalities

- Christians subject to ... Titus 3:1
- Created by Christ ... Col. 1:16
- Subject to Christ ... Eph. 1:20, 21
- Beholders of God's redemption ... Eph. 3:10
- Overcome by Christ ... Col. 2:15
- Fighting against Christians ... Eph. 6:12
- Powerless against Christians ... Rom. 8:38

Principles—*elementary Christian truths*

- To be maintained ... 1 Tim. 5:21
- Christians must go beyond ... Heb. 5:12

Print—*a recognizable sign*

- On the body, forbidden ... Lev. 19:28
- On the hands, desired ... John 20:25
- In a book, longed for ... Job 19:23

Priscilla, Prisca

- Wife of Aquila ... Acts 18:1-3
- An instructed Christian ... Acts 18:26
- One of Paul's helpers ... Rom. 16:3
- Greetings sent from ... 1 Cor. 16:19
- Timothy commanded to greet ... 2 Tim. 4:19

Prison—*place of confinement*

A. *Place of:*

- Hard labor ... Judg. 16:21, 25
- Confinement ... Jer. 52:11
- Guards ... Acts 12:3-6
- Stocks ... Acts 16:23, 24
- Torture ... Acts 22:24, 25
- Execution ... Matt. 14:10

B. *Notable occupants of:*

- Joseph ... Gen. 40:2, 3
- Micaiah ... 1 Kin. 22:26-28
- Jeremiah ... Jer. 32:2, 8, 12
- Hanani ... 2 Chr. 16:7-10
- Zedekiah ... Jer. 52:11
- John the Baptist ... Luke 3:20
- Apostles ... Acts 5:18, 19
- Peter ... Acts 12:1-4
- Paul ... Acts 16:24

See Imprisonment

Prisoners—*those confined to jails*

A. *Used literally of:*

- Criminals ... Matt. 27:15, 16
- Christians ... Eph. 4:1; Col. 4:10

B. *Used figuratively of:*

- Gentiles ... Is. 42:6, 7
- Those in spiritual darkness ... Is. 49:9; Zech. 9:11, 12
- Righteous in their need ... Ps. 69:33; Ps. 79:11; Ps. 146:7, 8

Privileges of believers

- Access to God ... Rom. 5:2
- Christ's intercession ... Heb. 7:25, 26
- Eternal life ... John 17:2, 3
- Growth assured ... 1 Pet. 2:2
- Intercession of the Spirit ... Rom. 8:16, 17
- Kinship with Christ ... Heb. 2:10-14
- Membership in God's kingdom ... 1 Cor. 6:9-11
- Names written in book of life ... Rev. 20:15
- Partakers of the divine nature ... 2 Pet. 1:4
- Reconciled to God ... Rom. 5:10
- Suffering with Christ ... Acts 5:41
- Trials overcome ... 1 Pet. 1:6-8
- Victorious living ... Rom. 8:37-39

Privileges of Israel

A. *Consisted of:*

- Chosen by God ... Deut. 7:6-8
- Entrusted with God's revelation ... Rom. 3:1, 2
- Blessings bestowed upon ... Rom. 9:4, 5
- Messiah (Christ) ... Acts 2:22-39
- Gospel first preached to ... Acts 3:18-26

B. *Lost because of:*

- Unbelief ... Matt. 8:10-12
- Spiritual hardness ... John 12:37-40
- Spiritual blindness ... John 9:39-41

C. *Now given to:*

- Gentiles ... Matt. 21:43
- Faithful remnant ... Rom. 11:1-7
- Church ... 1 Pet. 2:5-10

Prize—*a reward for faithful accomplishment*

A. *Described as crown of:*

- Righteousness ... 2 Tim. 4:8
- Glory ... 1 Pet. 5:4
- Life ... James 1:12

B. *Factors involved in obtaining:*

- Self-control ... 1 Cor. 9:25-27
- Following the rules ... 2 Tim. 2:5
- Pressing toward ... Phil. 3:14
- Enduring temptation ... James 1:12
- Looking to Jesus ... Heb. 12:1, 2
- Loving His appearing ... 2 Tim. 4:8

Probation—*a period of testing*

A. *Factors determining:*

- God's promises ... Matt. 21:33-43
- Specific time ... Dan. 9:24-27
- Faith or unbelief ... Acts 13:32-48; Rom. 10:1-21

B. *None after death:*

- No change permitted ... Luke 16:26
- Judgment final ... Rev. 20:11-15
- Destinies eternally fixed ... Matt. 25:46

Prochorus—*leader in advance*

- One of the seven deacons ... Acts 6:5

Proclaim—*to officially announce*

A. *Physical objects of:*

- Idolatrous feast ... Ex. 32:4, 5
- Holy convocation ... Lev. 23:2, 4, 21
- Year of jubilee ... Lev. 25:10
- Fast ... 2 Chr. 20:3
- Release ... Jer. 34:17

B. *Spiritual objects of:*

- God's name ... Ex. 33:19
- God's Word ... Jer. 3:12
- Salvation ... Is. 62:11

Procrastination—*putting off something*

A. *Manifested in:*

- Delaying a decision ... Matt. 19:22
- Putting minor things first ... Luke 9:59-62
- Presuming on tomorrow ... Prov. 27:1
- Postponing service ... 2 Cor. 8:10-14
- Rejecting reproof ... Prov. 29:1

B. *Evils of, missing:*

- Salvation ... 2 Cor. 6:1
- Life's importance ... Eccl. 12:1
- God's opportunity ... Jer. 13:16

Prodigal son

- Parable concerning ... Luke 15:11-32

Profane—*to act or speak irreverently of holy things*

A. *Manifested in:*

- Breaking God's Law ... Amos 2:7
- Defiling God's house ... Mal. 1:12, 13
- Not observing the Sabbath ... Neh. 13:17, 18
- Committing abominations ... Mal. 2:10, 11
- Idolatry ... Lev. 18:21
- Swearing falsely ... Lev. 19:12
- Illegal marriages ... Lev. 21:14, 15
- Blemished service ... Lev. 21:21-23

B. *Punishment of:*

- Excommunication ... Lev. 19:8
- Death ... Lev. 21:9
- Destruction ... Ezek. 28:16

Profession—*to declare one's faith publicly*

- Best ... Heb. 3:1
- Good ... 1 Tim. 6:12
- Steadfast ... Heb. 3:14
- Commendable ... 2 Cor. 9:13
- Harmful ... 1 Tim. 6:20, 21
- Inconsistent ... Titus 1:16
- Degrading ... Rom. 1:22
- Tragic ... Matt. 7:23

Profit—*gain*

A. *Things empty of:*

- Wickedness ... Prov. 10:2
- Riches ... Prov. 11:4
- Labor without God ... Eccl. 2:11
- Lying words ... Jer. 7:8
- World ... Matt. 16:26
- Flesh ... John 6:63
- Word without faith ... Heb. 4:2
- Mere profession ... James 2:14, 16

B. *Things full of:*

- Spiritual gifts ... 1 Cor. 12:7
- Godliness ... 1 Tim. 4:8
- Inspired Word ... 2 Tim. 3:16
- Youthful service ... 2 Tim. 4:11
- Good works ... Titus 3:8

Prognosticators—*those who profess to know the future*

- Help from, vain ... Is. 47:13-15

Prohibition—*restraint placed against evil tendencies*

A. *Against:*

- Idolatry ... 1 John 5:21
- Drunkenness ... Luke 21:34
- Uncleanness ... Eph. 4:18, 19
- Worldliness ... 1 John 2:15-17

B. *Based upon:*

- Sanctity of the body ... 1 Cor. 6:13-20
- New life in Christ ... Col. 3:1-10
- God's holiness ... 1 Pet. 1:14-16

Promises of God

A. *Described as:*

- Never failing ... Josh. 23:5-15; 1 Kin. 8:56
- Backed by God's oath ... Heb. 6:12-20
- Fulfilled on schedule ... Acts 7:6, 17; Gal. 4:4
- Given to Israel ... Rom. 9:4
- Confirmed by Christ ... Rom. 15:8
- Centered in Christ ... 2 Cor. 1:20; 2 Tim. 1:1
- Kept by faith ... Rom. 4:20, 21; Heb. 11:13-40
- Exceedingly great ... 2 Pet. 1:4
- Not slow ... 2 Pet. 3:4-13

B. *Objects of, for Israel:*

- Land of Palestine ... Acts 7:5; Heb. 11:9
- Davidic kingship ... 2 Chr. 6:10-16
- Messiah ... Acts 13:23-33
- Gospel ... Acts 10:43
- New heart ... Jer. 31:33

C. *Objects of, for Christians:*

- Holy Spirit ... Luke 24:49
- Salvation ... Acts 2:39
- Kingdom ... James 2:5
- Life eternal ... Titus 1:2
- Crown of life ... James 1:12
- New earth ... 2 Pet. 3:13

See Messiah, the

Promises to believers (see Privileges of believers)

Promotion—*advancement in status*

- Deserved ... Gen. 41:38-42
- Desirable ... Prov. 4:8
- Divine ... Ps. 75:6, 7
- Despicable ... Num. 22:17, 37

Pronunciation—*giving the right sound to words*

- Peter's detected ... Matt. 26:73
- Correct, required in church ... 1 Cor. 14:7-16

Property—*material possessions*

Acquired by:

- Industry ... Gen. 31:36-42
- Inheritance ... Eccl. 2:21
- Purchase ... Gen. 23:7-20
- Deception ... 1 Kin. 21:1-16
- Coveting ... Josh. 7:21

See Ownership

Prophecy—*inspired foretelling of events*

A. *Characteristics of:*

- Given by God ... Is. 41:22, 23
- Centered in Christ ... Luke 24:26, 27, 44
- Inspired by the Spirit ... 2 Pet. 1:21
- Not of one's own interpretation ... 2 Pet. 1:20
- Always relevant ... Rev. 22:10
- Must not be changed by man ... Rev. 22:18, 19

B. *True, based on:*

- Inspiration ... Mic. 3:8
- Foreknowledge ... Is. 42:9

C. *False, evidenced by:*

- Nonfulfillment ... Jer. 28:1-17
- Peaceful message ... Jer. 23:17-22

P

SUBJECT — REFERENCE

Apostasy from God .... Deut. 13:1-5
Lying .... Jer. 23:25-34
Scoffing .... 2 Pet. 3:3, 4

D. *Fulfillment of:*
Unconditional .... Ezek. 12:25-28
Sometimes:
Conditional .... Jon. 3:1-10
Dated .... Dan. 9:24-27
Nonliteral .... Matt. 17:10-12
Unrecognized by Jews .... Acts 13:27-29
Interpretation of, needed .... Luke 24:25-44
Often referred to .... Matt. 1:22, 23; Matt. 2:14-23

Prophetess—*a female prophet*

A. *Good:*
Miriam .... Ex. 15:20, 21
Deborah .... Judg. 4:4, 5
Huldah .... 2 Kin. 22:12-20
Isaiah's wife .... Is. 8:1-3
Anna .... Luke 2:36
Daughters of Philip .... Acts 21:8, 9
Prophecy concerning .... Joel 2:28

B. *False:*
Women of Judah .... Ezek. 13:17
Noadiah .... Neh. 6:14
Jezebel .... Rev. 2:20

Prophets—*inspired messengers*

A. *Described as:*
God's servants .... Zech. 1:6
God's messengers .... 2 Chr. 36:15
Holy prophets .... Luke 1:70
Holy men .... 2 Pet. 1:21
Watchmen .... Ezek. 3:17
Prophets of God .... Ezra 5:2

B. *Message of:*
Centered in Christ .... Luke 10:24
Interpreted by Christ .... Luke 24:27, 44
United in testimony .... Acts 3:21, 24
Contains grace and salvation .... 1 Pet. 1:9-12
Abiding revelation .... Matt. 5:17, 18

Prophets, names of

Enoch .... Gen. 5:21, 24
Noah .... Gen. 9:25-27
Abraham .... Gen. 20:1, 7
Jacob .... Gen. 49:1
Aaron .... Ex. 7:1
Moses .... Deut. 18:18
Joshua .... 1 Kin. 16:34
One sent to Israel .... Judg. 6:8-10
One sent to Eli .... 1 Sam. 2:27-36
Samuel .... 1 Sam. 3:20
David .... Acts 2:25, 30
Nathan .... 2 Sam. 7:2
Zadok .... 2 Sam. 15:27
Gad .... 2 Sam. 24:11-14
Ahijah .... 1 Kin. 11:29
One of Judah .... 1 Kin. 13:1
Iddo .... 2 Chr. 9:29; 12:15
Shemaiah .... 2 Chr. 12:5, 7, 15
Azariah .... 2 Chr. 15:1-8
Hanani .... 2 Chr. 16:7-10
Jehu .... 1 Kin. 16:1, 7, 12
Elijah .... 1 Kin. 17:1
Elisha .... 1 Kin. 19:16
Micaiah .... 1 Kin. 22:7, 8
Jonah .... 2 Kin. 14:25
Isaiah .... 2 Kin. 19:2
Hosea .... Hos. 1:1
Amos .... Amos 1:1
Micah .... Mic. 1:1
Oded .... 2 Chr. 28:9
Nahum .... Nah. 1:1
Joel .... Joel 1:1
Zephaniah .... Zeph. 1:1
Jeduthun .... 2 Chr. 35:15
Jeremiah .... 2 Chr. 36:12, 21
Habakkuk .... Hab. 1:1
Obadiah .... Obad. 1
Ezekiel .... Ezek. 1:3
Daniel .... Matt. 24:15
Haggai .... Ezra 5:1
Zechariah .... Ezra 5:1; Zech. 1:1; Luke 1:67
Malachi .... Mal. 1:1
John the Baptist .... Luke 7:26-28
Agabus .... Acts 11:28
Paul .... 1 Tim. 4:1
Peter .... 2 Pet. 2:1, 2
John .... Rev. 1:1

Prophets in the New Testament

A. *Office of, based upon:*
Christ's prophetic office .... Deut. 18:15, 18
Old Testament prediction .... Joel 2:28; Acts 2:18
Holy Spirit's coming .... John 16:7, 13
Divine institution .... 1 Cor. 12:28

B. *Functions of:*
Strengthen .... Acts 15:32
Define God's will .... Acts 13:1-3
Predict the future .... Acts 21:10, 11

Propitiation—*appeasing or conciliating*

Elements in Christ's:
Dying for man's sins .... 1 Pet. 1:18, 19
Satisfying God's justice .... Rom. 3:25, 26
Becoming the mercy seat .... Rom. 3:25
Reconciling God and man .... 2 Cor. 5:18, 19
Offering believing sinner perfect righteousness .... 2 Cor. 5:20, 21

Proselyte—*convert to Judaism*

A. *Regulations imposed upon:*
Circumcision .... Gen. 17:13
Observance of the Law .... Ex. 12:48, 49
Obedience to the covenant .... Deut. 29:10-13
Association with Israel .... Ruth 1:16
Separation from heathenism .... Ezra 6:21
Participation in feasts .... John 12:20; Acts 8:27

B. *Special significance of:*
Typical of Gentile converts .... Is. 56:3-8
Concerned about Christ .... John 12:20
Among early converts .... Acts 6:5
Source of Gentile church .... Acts 13:42-46

Prosperity—*a state of material or spiritual bountifulness*

A. *Kinds of:*
Material .... 1 Cor. 16:2
National .... Ezek. 16:13, 14
Personal .... Dan. 6:28
Deceitful .... 1 Kin. 22:12, 15
Evil .... Ps. 73:12
Spiritual .... 3 John 2
Divine .... Is. 53:10

B. *Of the righteous:*
Promised .... Ps. 1:3
Prayed for .... Neh. 1:11
Perplexed .... Jer. 12:1-3

C. *Of the wicked:*
Lack of understanding over .... Ps. 73:3-12
Righteous must not fret over .... Ps. 37:7
Terrible end of .... Jer. 20:11

D. *Hindrances to:*
Transgression .... 2 Chr. 24:20
Hiding one's sins .... Prov. 28:13
Distrust of the Lord .... Jer. 2:36, 37

E. *True secrets of:*
Lord's blessings .... Ps. 35:27
Keeping God's Law .... Josh. 1:7, 8
God's guidance .... Gen. 24:40-56
Trust in God .... Neh. 2:20
Dedication to God .... 2 Chr. 31:20, 21
Listening to God's prophets .... Ezra 6:14
Belief in God's Word .... 2 Chr. 20:20

F. *Perils of:*
Forgetting God .... Deut. 8:10-12; Prov. 30:7-9
Destruction .... Prov. 1:32
Rebellion .... Jer. 22:21

Prostitute—*one engaged in promiscuous sexual activity*

Forbidden .... Lev. 19:29

Prostitution (see Harlot)

Protection, divine

A. *Characteristics of:*
Continuous .... Ps. 121:3-8
Unfailing .... Josh. 1:5
Assuring .... Is. 41:10
Persevering .... John 10:28-30
Satisfying .... 2 Cor. 12:9, 10
Necessary .... Ps. 124:1-5

B. *Provided against:*
Evil .... 2 Thess. 3:3
Temptation .... 1 Cor. 10:13
Persecution .... Rev. 3:10
Enemies .... Ps. 56:9
Falling .... Jude 24
Dangers .... Ps. 91:3-7
Calamities .... Ps. 57:1

Protector, divine

God as .... Ps. 18:2
Christ as .... 2 Tim. 4:17, 18

Proud—*the defiant and haughty*

A. *Descriptive of:*
Moabites .... Jer. 48:29
Babylonians .... Jer. 50:29-32
Wicked .... Ps. 17:9, 10
Scoffers .... Prov. 21:24

B. *God's attitude toward:*
Does not respect .... Ps. 40:4
Rebukes .... Ps. 119:21
Resists .... James 4:6

See Pride

Prove—*to show something to be true*

A. *Descriptive of:*
Testing physically .... 1 Sam. 17:39; Luke 14:19
Testing morally .... John 6:6
Showing something to be true .... Gen. 42:15, 16

B. *Oojects of, among Christians:*
Love .... 2 Cor. 8:8
Sacrifice .... Rom. 12:2
Faith .... 2 Cor. 13:5
Works .... Gal. 6:4
Abilities .... 1 Tim. 3:10

Provender—*cattle food*

Supplied for animals .... Gen. 24:25, 32; Gen. 42:27

Proverb—*a wise saying*

A. *Descriptive of:*
Wise saying .... 1 Sam. 24:13
Something generally accepted .... Ezek. 12:22, 23
Object of taunt .... Deut. 28:37
Figurative language .... John 16:25, 29

B. *Characteristics of:*
Brief .... 1 Sam. 10:12
Striking statement .... Luke 4:23
Authoritative .... Prov. 1:1-6
Emphasis by repetition .... Prov. 3:17

Proverbs, the Book of—*a book of the Old Testament*

Tribute to wisdom .... Prov. 1—2
Against immorality .... Prov. 5:1-23
Parental counsel .... Prov. 6—7
Miscellaneous proverbs .... Prov. 10—24
Proverbs of Agur and Lemuel .... Prov. 30:1—31:9
The worthy woman .... Prov. 31:10-31

Providence—*divine guidance of men and things*

A. *Described as:*
Universal .... Ps. 103:19
Purposive .... Gen. 45:5-8
Righteous .... Ps. 145:17
Something mysterious .... Job 11:7-9
Irresistible .... Dan. 4:35

B. *Manifested, in the world, in God's:*
Preserving the world .... Neh. 9:6
Providing for His possesions .... Ps. 104:27, 28
Guiding world events .... Acts 17:26, 27
Ruling over the elements .... Is. 50:2, 3
Preserving nature .... Gen. 8:22
Ordering man's life .... Ps. 75:6, 7
Controlling minute details .... Matt. 10:29, 30

C. *Attitude of believers toward:*
Acknowledge in prosperity .... 1 Chr. 29:11, 12; Prov. 3:6
Humble himself before in adversity .... Job 1:21; Ps. 119:75
Remember God's hand .... Ps. 37:1-40; Ps. 139:10

Province—*a governmental district*

A. *Ruled by:*
Governors .... Esth. 3:12
Proconsuls .... Acts 13:4, 7

SUBJECT — REFERENCE

B. *Characteristics of:*
Numerous ... Esth. 1:1
Ruled by one man ... Dan. 2:48, 49
Justice perverted in ... Eccl. 5:8
People, citizens of ... Acts 23:34
News spreads to ... Esth. 9:4

C. *Of the Roman Empire:*
Achaia ... Acts 18:12
Asia ... Acts 19:10
Bithynia ... Acts 16:7
Cappadocia ... Acts 2:9
Cyprus ... Acts 13:4
Egypt ... Matt. 2:13
Galatia ... Acts 16:6
Macedonia ... Acts 16:12
Pamphylia ... Acts 13:13
Lycia ... Acts 27:5
Syria ... Matt. 4:24

Provision
Provide for own house ... 1 Tim. 5:8
Provide for poor ... Is. 58:7

Provoke—*to agitate another's soul*
A. *Between people:*
Two women ... 1 Sam. 1:7
Satan and man ... 1 Chr. 21:1
Peoples (nations) ... Rom. 10:19
Christians ... 2 Cor. 9:2
Father and children ... Eph. 6:4

B. *Causes of, between God and man:*
Evil ... Deut. 4:25
Sins ... 1 Kin. 16:2
Whoredoms ... Ezek. 16:26

Prudence—*wisdom applied to practical matters*
A. *Characteristics of:*
Dwells with wisdom ... Prov. 8:12
Observant ... Prov. 14:15
Foresees evil ... Prov. 22:3
Regards reproof ... Prov. 15:5
Conceals knowledge ... Prov. 12:23
Crowned with knowledge ... Prov. 14:18
Keeps silent ... Amos 5:13

B. *Descriptive of:*
David ... 1 Sam. 16:18
Solomon ... 2 Chr. 2:12
Messiah ... Is. 52:13
Wife ... Prov. 19:14
Believers ... Hos. 14:9
Worldly-wise ... Matt. 11:25

C. *Examples of:*
Jacob ... Gen. 32:3-23
Joseph ... Gen. 41:39-49
Gideon ... Judg. 8:1-3

Prune—*to cut back plants for the purpose of producing more growth*
Vineyards ... Lev. 25:3, 4
Figurative of God's care ... Is. 5:6; John 15:2

Instruments used to:
Hooks ... Is. 2:4
Knives ... Is. 18:5

Psalm—*a spiritual song*
Some written by David ... 2 Sam. 23:1
Prophetic of Christ ... Luke 24:44
Used in worship ... Ps. 95:2
Used in church ... 1 Cor. 14:26

Psalms, the Book of—*a book of the Old Testament*
Book I—The Genesis Book Concerning Man ... Ps. 1—41
Blessed are the righteous ... Ps. 1
The holy hill ... Ps. 15
The creation of God ... Ps. 19
Messianic Psalm ... Ps. 22
Prayer for God's help ... Ps. 28
Book II—The Exodus Book Concerning Israel as a Nation ... Ps. 42—72
Psalm of longing ... Ps. 42
Prayer for cleansing ... Ps. 51
Prayer for deliverance ... Ps. 70
Book III—The Leviticus Book Concerning the Sanctuary ... Ps. 73-89
Prayer for restoration ... Ps. 80
Book IV—The Numbers Book Concerning Israel and the Nation ... Ps. 90—106
The Lord reigns ... Ps. 93
God's wondrous works ... Ps. 105
Book V—The Deuteronomy Book Concerning God and His word ... Ps. 107—150
On God's commandments ... Ps. 119
Psalm of faithfulness ... Ps. 128
God is gracious ... Ps. 145
Psalms of praise ... Ps. 149; Ps. 150

Psaltery—*a musical instrument*
Used in:
Prophecy ... 1 Sam. 10:5
Processions ... 2 Sam. 6:5
Worship ... Ps. 150:3
Government proclamations ... Dan. 3:5, 7

Ptolemais—*a seaport city south of Tyre*
Paul lands at ... Acts 21:7
Same as Accho ... Judg. 1:31

Public opinion
Rescues Jonathan ... 1 Sam. 14:45
Delays John's death ... Matt. 14:1-5
Protects the apostles ... Acts 5:26
Makes Saul sin ... 1 Sam. 15:24
Increases Pilate's guilt ... Matt. 27:21-26
Incites persecution ... Acts 12:1-3

Publicans—*Jews engaged in tax collecting*
A. *Features concerning:*
Collector of taxes ... Luke 5:27
Often guilty of extortion ... Luke 3:12, 13
Classed with lowest sinners ... Matt. 9:10, 11; Matt. 21:31, 32
Do not even, the same ... Matt. 5:46
Thomas and Matthew, the ... Matt. 10:3
Thank thee I am not ... Luke 18:11
As an heathen and a ... Matt. 18:17

B. *Spiritual attitude of:*
Often conscientious ... Luke 19:2, 8
Often hospitable ... Luke 5:29
Received John's baptism ... Matt. 21:32
Listened to Jesus ... Luke 15:1
Conscious of their sins ... Luke 18:13, 14
Many sat with him ... Mark 2:15
Why do ye eat with ... Luke 5:30
A friend of ... Matt. 11:19; Luke 7:34

Publish—*to proclaim publicly*
A. *Descriptive of:*
Victory ... 1 Sam. 31:9
Message of doom ... Jon. 3:7
Royal decree ... Esth. 1:20, 22
Good news ... Mark 1:45

B. *Objects of:*
Peace ... Is. 52:7
Doom ... Jer. 4:5, 15, 16
Gospel ... Mark 13:10
God's Word ... Acts 13:49

Publius—*common*
Roman official; entertains Paul ... Acts 28:7, 8

Pudens—*modest*
Believer at Rome ... 2 Tim. 4:21

Puhites
Family of Kirjath-jearim ... 1 Chr. 2:53

Pul—*strong*
King of Assyria; same as Tiglath-pileser ... 2 Kin. 15:19

Pulpit—*a rostrum*
Ezra reads law from ... Neh. 8:4-8

Pulse—*a vegetable diet*
Preferred by Daniel ... Dan. 1:12, 16

Punishment, everlasting (see Hell; Eternal, everlasting)

Punishments—*penalties inflicted on criminals*
A. *Agents of:*
State ... Rom. 13:1-4
Nation ... Josh. 7:25
Prophet ... 1 Sam. 15:33
Witnesses ... John 8:7
Soldiers ... Matt. 27:27-35

B. *Kinds of* (non-capital):
Imprisonment ... Matt. 5:25
Fine ... Ex. 21:22
Restitution ... Ex. 22:3-6
Retaliation ... Deut. 19:21
Scourging ... Acts 22:25
Bondage ... Matt. 18:25
Banishment ... Rev. 1:9
Torture ... Heb. 11:35
Mutilation ... Judg. 1:5-7

C. *Kinds of* (capital):
Burning ... Gen. 38:24
Hanging ... Esth. 7:9, 10
Crucifying ... Matt. 27:35
Beheading ... Mark 6:16, 27
Stoning ... Lev. 24:14
Cutting in pieces ... Dan. 2:5
Exposing to lions ... Dan. 6:16, 24
Killing with the sword ... Acts 12:2
See Capital punishment

Punites
Descendants of Pua ... Num. 26:23

Punon
Israelite camp ... Num. 33:42, 43

Pur—*a lot*
Cast for Jews' slaughter ... Esth. 3:7
Origin of Purim ... Esth. 9:24-26

Purah—*branch*
Gideon's servant ... Judg. 7:10, 11

Purchase—*to buy*
A. *Used literally of:*
Cave ... Gen. 49:32
Field ... Jer. 32:9-16
Wife ... Ruth 4:10

B. *Used figuratively of:*
Israel's redemption ... Ex. 15:16
God's gifts ... Acts 8:20
Church ... Acts 20:28

Pure, purity—*uncontaminated with dross or evil*
A. *Descriptive of:*
Chastity ... 1 Tim. 5:2
Uncontaminated ... 1 Kin. 5:11
Innocent ... Acts 20:26
Regenerated ... Titus 1:15

B. *Applied figuratively to God's:*
Law ... Ps. 19:8
Word ... Ps. 119:140
Wisdom ... James 3:17

C. *Applied figuratively to the believer's:*
Heart ... Ps. 24:4
Mind ... 2 Pet. 3:1
Conscience ... 1 Tim. 3:9
Language ... Zeph. 3:9
Body ... Heb. 10:22

D. *Applied to the Christian's life:*
Source ... Titus 1:15
Command ... 1 Tim. 4:12
Means ... Phil. 4:8
Outward manifestation ... James 1:27
Inward evidence ... 1 Tim. 1:5
Goal ... 1 John 3:3
Reward ... Matt. 5:8
False ... Prov. 20:9

E. *Applied symbolically to:*
New Jerusalem ... Rev. 21:18, 21

Purge—*to cleanse thoroughly*
A. *Used, in the Old Testament, ceremonially of:*
Cleansing ... Ezek. 20:38
Separation from idolatry ... 2 Chr. 34:3, 8

B. *Used, in the Old Testament, figuratively of:*
Reformation ... Ezek. 24:13
Regeneration ... Is. 4:4
Sanctification ... Is. 1:25
Forgiveness ... Ps. 51:7
Consecration ... Is. 6:7
Atonement ... Mal. 3:3, 4
Judgment ... Is. 22:14

Purification—*ceremonial or spiritual cleansing*
A. *Objects of:*
Israelites at Sinai ... Ex. 19:10
Priests at ordination ... Ex. 29:4
Levites at ordination ... Num. 8:6, 7
Offerings ... 2 Chr. 4:6
High priest ... Lev. 16:4, 24

P

SUBJECT	REFERENCE
People unclean	Lev. 15:2-13
Nazarite after vow	Acts 21:24, 26
B. *Accomplished by:*	
Sprinkling	Num. 19:13-18
Washing parts of the body	Ex. 30:18, 19
Washing the whole body	Lev. 8:6
Running water	Lev. 15:13
C. *Figurative of:*	
Christ's atonement	Mal. 3:3
Regeneration	Acts 15:9
Sanctification	James 4:8
Obedience	1 Pet. 1:22
Purim—*lots*	
Jewish festival celebrating being rescued from Haman's plot	Esth. 9:26-28
Purloining—*stealing*	
Forbidden	Titus 2:10
Purple	
Used in the tabernacle	Ex. 25:4
Sign of riches	Luke 16:19
Worn by royalty	Judg. 8:26
Lydia, seller of	Acts 16:14
Purposes of God	
Characteristics of:	
Centered in Christ	Eph. 3:11
Irresistible	Is. 14:26, 27
Unknown to the wise	Is. 19:11, 12
Made known	Jer. 50:45
Irreversible	Jer. 4:28
Planned	Is. 23:9
Fulfilled	Rom. 9:11
Victorious	2 Chr. 32:2-22
Purposes of man	
A. *Good:*	
Hindered by evil men	Ezra 4:5
Known by others	2 Tim. 3:10
Permitted	Dan. 1:8-16
Accomplished	1 Kin. 5:5
Determine	Ps. 17:3
Delayed	Acts 19:21
Not vacillating	2 Cor. 1:17
B. *Evil:*	
Known by God	Jer. 49:30
Designed against the righteous	Ps. 140:4
Hindered	Dan. 6:17-23
Purse—*a bag*	
One, forbidden	Prov. 1:14
Disciples forbidden to take	Luke 10:4
Pursue—*To go after*	
"Enemy said, I will"	Ex. 15:9
"Shall flee when none"	Lev. 26:17
"I will arise and"	2 Sam. 17:1
"Seek peace, and"	Ps. 34:14
"Blood shall"	Ezek. 35:6
Put	
Country and people in Africa	Is. 66:19
Puteoli—*little wells*	
Seaport of Italy	Acts 28:13
Puthites	
Descendants of Caleb	1 Chr. 2:50, 53
Putiel—*God enlightens*	
Father-in-law of Eleazar	Ex. 6:25
Puah—*utterance*	
Father of Tola	Judg. 10:1
Pygarg—*a white-rumped antelope*	
Clean animal	Deut. 14:5

Q

SUBJECT	REFERENCE
Quail—*a small bird*	
Sent to satisfy hunger	Ex. 16:12, 13
Sent as a judgment	Num. 11:31-34
Quarantine—*restricted in public contacts*	
Required of lepers	Lev. 13:45, 46
Miriam consigned	Num. 12:14-16
Imposed under King Azariah	2 Kin. 15:1-5

SUBJECT	REFERENCE
Quarrel—*a dispute*	
A. *Caused by:*	
Flesh	James 4:1, 2
Hatred	Mark 6:18, 19
B. *Productive of:*	
Friction	Matt. 20:20-24
Separation	Acts 15:37-40
C. *Cured by:*	
Gentleness	2 Tim. 2:24-26
Forgiveness	Col. 3:13
Unity of mind	Phil. 2:3, 4
See Contention; Strife	
Quarry—*a place for mining stone*	
Israelites flee to ("Shebarim")	Josh. 7:5
Some near Gilgal	Judg. 3:19, 26
Same word translated "graven images" in	Deut. 7:5, 25
Quartus—*fourth*	
Christian at Corinth	Rom. 16:23
Quaternion—*a company of four soldiers*	
Peter guarded by four	Acts 12:4
Queen—*a king's wife*	
A. *Applied to:*	
Queen regent	1 Kin. 10:1-13
Queen mother	1 Kin. 15:13
Heathen deity	Jer. 44:15-30
Mystical Babylon	Rev. 18:7
B. *Names of:*	
Of Sheba	1 Kin. 10:1
Vashti	Esth. 1:9
Esther	Esth. 5:3
Of Heaven	Jer. 7:18
Of the South	Matt. 12:42
Quench—*to extinguish*	
A. *Applied literally to:*	
Fire	Num. 11:2
Thirst	Ps. 104:11
B. *Applied figuratively to:*	
Love	Song 8:7
God's wrath	2 Kin. 22:17
Spirit	1 Thess. 5:19
Persecution	Heb. 11:34
Question—*an inquiry*	
Asked by:	
Wicked	Matt. 22:16-40 John 18:33-38
Sincere	Matt. 18:1-6 Acts 1:6
Jesus	Matt. 22:41-45
Quickening—*reviving again*	
A. *Descriptive of:*	
Spiritual revival	Ps. 71:20
Physical resurrection	John 5:21
Spiritual resurrection (regeneration)	Eph. 2:5
B. *Accomplished by:*	
God	1 Tim. 6:13
Christ	1 Cor. 15:45
Holy Spirit	John 6:63
God's Word	Ps. 119:25, 50
God's precepts	Ps. 119:93
Quicksand—*sand which engulfs*	
Endangers Paul's ship	Acts 27:17
Quietness—*noiselessness*	
A. *Descriptive of:*	
Man	Jer. 51:59
People	Judg. 18:7, 27
City	2 Kin. 11:20
Nation	2 Chr. 14:1, 5
Earth	Is. 14:7
B. *Realization of:*	
Predicted	Is. 32:17, 18
Comes from God	1 Chr. 22:9
Preferred	Prov. 17:1
To be sought	1 Thess. 4:11
Undeniable	Acts 19:36
Commanded	2 Thess. 3:12
Obtainable	Ps. 131:2
Very valuable	1 Pet. 3:4
Rewarded	Is. 30:15

SUBJECT	REFERENCE
Quitters, quitting	
Unworthy	Luke 9:62
Believers should not	Gal. 6:9 2 Thess. 3:13
Press on	Phil. 3:12-14
Continue	2 Tim.
Quiver—*a case for carrying arrows*	
Used by:	
Hunters	Gen. 27:3
Soldiers	Job 39:23 Is. 22:6
Figurative of:	
Children	Ps. 127:5
Messiah	Is. 49:2
Quotations	
A. *Introduced by:*	
"The Holy Spirit"	Acts 28:25
"As it is written"	Rom. 15:9
"The Scripture"	Gal. 3:8
Old Testament writer	Rom. 10:5-20
B. *Purposes of:*	
Cite fulfillment	Matt. 1:22, 23
Confirm a truth	Matt. 4:4
Prove a doctrine	Rom. 4:7, 8
Show the true meaning	Acts 2:25-36

R

SUBJECT	REFERENCE
Raamah—*trembling*	
Son of Cush	Gen. 10:6, 7
Father of Sheba and Dedan	Gen. 10:7
Noted traders	Ezek. 27:22
Raamiah—*Jehovah has thundered*	
Postexilic chief	Neh. 7:7
Same as Reelaiah	Ezra 2:2
Raamses—*Ra* (Egyptian sun god) *created him*	
Part of Egypt inhabited by Jacob	Gen. 47:11
Treasure city built by Hebrew slaves	Ex. 1:11
Rabbah, Rabbath—*great*	
1. Town of Judah	Josh. 15:60
2. Capital of Ammon	Amos 1:14
Bedstead of Og here	Deut. 3:11
On Gad's boundary	Josh. 13:25
Besieged by Joab	2 Sam. 12:26
Defeated and enslaved by David	2 Sam. 12:29-31
Destruction of, foretold	Jer. 49:2, 3
Rabbi, Rabboni—*my master*	
A. *Applied to:*	
John the Baptist	John 3:26
Jewish leader	John 3:2
Jesus Christ	John 1:38, 49
B. *Significance of:*	
Coveted title	Matt. 23:6, 7
Forbidden by Christ	Matt. 23:8
Expressive of imperfect faith	{Mark 14:45 {John 20:16
Translated "Master"	Mark 14:45
Rabbith—*multitude*	
Frontier town of Issachar	Josh. 19:20
Rabble, the	
Cause of discord	Num. 11:4-6
Clamors for Jesus' death	Matt. 26:47
Seeks Paul's life	Acts 17:1-8
Rabboni—*Aramaic form of Rabbi*	
Mary addresses Christ as	John 20:16
Rab-mag—*head of the Magi*	
Title applied to Nergal-sharezer	Jer. 39:3, 13
Rab-saris—*head chamberlain*	
A. *Title applied to:*	
Assyrian officials sent by Sennacherib	2 Kin. 18:17
Babylonian Nebushasban	Jer. 39:13
Babylonian prince	Jer. 39:3
B. *Office of:*	
Considered important	Dan. 1:7

SUBJECT REFERENCE

Rab-shakeh—*Head of the cupbearers*
Sent .... 2 Kin. 18:17
King of Assyria sent .... Is. 36:2
And told him the words of .... Is. 36:22
Hear all the words .... 2 Kin. 19:4

Raca—*a term of insult*
Use of, forbidden by Christ .... Matt. 5:21, 22

Race, Christian
Requirements of:
Discipline .... 1 Cor. 9:24-27
Patience .... Eccl. 9:11
Steadfastness .... Gal. 5:7

Race, human
Unity of .... Gen. 3:20
Divisions of .... Gen. 10:1-32
Scattering of .... Gen. 11:1-9
Bounds of .... Acts 17:26
Depravity of .... Rom. 1:18-32
Salvation of .... John 3:16

Rachal—*trader*
City in Judah .... 1 Sam. 30:29

Rachel—*ewe*
Laban's younger daughter; Jacob's favorite wife .... Gen. 29:28-30
Supports her husband's position .... Gen. 31:14-16
Mother of Joseph and Benjamin .... Gen. 30:22-25
Prophecy concerning, quoted .... Jer. 31:15
Matt. 2:18

Rachel, tomb of
At Bethlehem—first mention of in Bible .... Gen. 35:19

Racial relations
Salvation is for all .... Eph. 2:11-22
Eph. 3:7-9
All are same in Christ .... Col. 3:9-11

Raddai—*Jehovah has subdued*
One of David's brothers .... 1 Chr. 2:14

Radiance in life
Caused by:
Wisdom .... Prov. 4:7-9
Soul-winning .... Dan. 12:3
Transfiguration .... Matt. 17:2
Beholding the Lord .... Ps. 34:5
2 Cor. 3:7-18

Rafters—*timbers used to support a roof*
Made of fir .... Song 1:17

Ragau (see Reu)

Rage—*raving and violent madness*
A. *Descriptive of:*
Sea .... Luke 8:24
Strong drink .... Prov. 20:1
Anger .... Dan. 3:13
Heathen .... Ps. 2:1
B. *Caused by:*
Insane madness .... 2 Chr. 16:7-10
Supposed insult .... 2 Kin. 5:11, 12
Jealousy .... Prov. 6:34
Insolence against God .... 2 Kin. 19:27, 28

Rags—*tattered and spoiled clothing*
Used as cushions .... Jer. 38:11-13
Reward of drowsiness .... Prov. 23:21
Man's righteousness like .... Is. 64:6

Rahab (I)—*violence*
Prostitute living in Jericho .... Josh. 2:1
Concealed Joshua's spies .... Josh. 2:1-24
Spared by invading Israelites .... Josh. 6:17-25
Included among the faithful .... Heb. 11:31
Cited as an example .... James 2:25
Ancestress of Christ .... Matt. 1:5

Rahab (II)—*pride, arrogance*
Used figuratively of Egypt .... Ps. 87:4
Translated "the proud" .... Job 9:13

Raham—*pity*
Descendant of Caleb .... 1 Chr. 2:44

Raiment—*clothing*
A. *Indicative of:*
Plenty .... Gen. 24:53
Position .... Judg. 8:26
Provision .... Matt. 6:28
Poverty .... James 2:2
Personality .... Gen. 27:15, 27
B. *Regulations concerning:*
Not to be kept .... Ex. 22:26
To be divided .... Josh. 22:8
To be purified .... Num. 31:20
Not to be multiplied .... 1 Tim. 6:8
C. *Figurative of:*
Redemption .... Is. 63:3
Imputation of righteousness .... Zech. 3:4
Purity .... Rev. 3:5, 18
Honor of position .... Ps. 45:14

Rain—*water falling from clouds*
A. *Features concerning:*
Sent by God .... Jer. 14:22
Sent on all mankind .... Matt. 5:45
Sign of God's goodness .... Deut. 28:12
Controlled by God's decrees .... Job 28:26; Job 37:6
Withheld because of sin .... Deut. 11:17
Sent as a result of judgment .... Gen. 7:4
Former and latter .... Jer. 5:24
To be prayed for .... 1 Kin. 8:35, 36
B. *Figurative of:*
God's Word .... Is. 55:10, 11
Spiritual blessing .... Ps. 72:6
Righteousness .... Hos. 10:12
Final judgment .... Matt. 7:24-27
Hell .... Ps. 11:6
Earth's ingathering .... James 5:7

Rainbow
Appears after the flood .... Gen. 9:12, 13
Sign of God's covenant .... Gen. 9:16, 17
Around angel's head .... Rev. 10:1
Over God's throne .... Rev. 4:3

Raisins—*dried grapes*
Nourishing food .... 1 Sam. 25:18
Provided for David .... 2 Sam. 16:1

Rakem—*variegated*
Manassite .... 1 Chr. 7:16

Rakkath—*bank, shore*
Fortified city of Naphtali .... Josh. 19:32, 35

Rakkon—*shore*
Danite village .... Josh. 19:40, 46

Ram (I)—*high, exalted*
1. Ancestor of David .... Ruth 4:19
Ancestor of Christ .... Matt. 1:3, 4
2. Man of Judah .... 1 Chr. 2:25, 27

Ram (II)—*a male sheep*
Used as food .... Gen. 31:38
Used in offerings .... Gen. 22:13
Appointed for certain offerings .... Lev. 5:15
Skin of, used as coverings .... Ex. 26:14
Horns of, used as trumpets .... Josh. 6:4-13

Ram (III)—*an instrument of war*
Used to destroy gates and walls .... Ezek. 4:2

Ramah
1. Town of Asher .... Josh. 19:24, 29
2. City of Naphtali .... Josh. 19:32, 36
3. Benjamite city near Jerusalem .... Josh. 18:21, 25
Deborah's palm near here .... Judg. 4:5
Fortress built .... 1 Kin. 15:17-22
Gathering of captives .... Jer. 40:1
Reinhabited after exile .... Ezra 2:26
Probable site of Rachel's tomb .... 1 Sam. 10:2
Samuel's headquarters .... 1 Sam. 7:15, 17
David flees to .... 1 Sam. 19:18-23
4. Town called Ramoth-gilead .... 2 Kin. 8:28, 29

Ramathaim-zophim
Home of Elkanah .... 1 Sam. 1:1
Also called "Ramah" .... 1 Sam. 1:19
See Ramah 4

Ramathite—*an inhabitant of Ramah*
Shimei called .... 1 Chr. 27:27

Ramath-mizpeh—*a town in Palestine*
An inheritance of Gad .... Josh. 13:24-26

Ramoth—*high places*
1. Town of Issachar; possibly same as Remeth and Jarmuth .... Josh. 19:21
2. Town of the south; see Ramah
3. Town of Gilead .... Deut. 4:43

Ramoth-gilead
City of refuge east of Jordan .... Deut. 4:43; Josh. 20:8; 1 Chr. 6:80
Site of Ahab's fatal conflict with Syrians .... 1 Kin. 22:1-39

Rampart—*a city's outer fortification*
Around:
Certain cities .... 2 Sam. 20:15
Jerusalem .... Ps. 48:13

Ransom—*to redeem by a payment*
A. *Of man, for:*
Israelites .... Ex. 30:12-16
Murderer, forbidden .... Num. 35:31, 32
Some, unpayable .... Prov. 6:34, 35
Brother, impossible .... Ps. 49:7, 8
B. *Of Christ:*
For all .... Matt. 20:28
From grave .... Hos. 13:14
From Satan .... Jer. 31:11
Cause of joy .... Is. 35:10

Rapacity—*seizing others' goods; covetous*
Descriptive of Satan .... 1 Pet. 5:8
Characteristic of false teachers .... Luke 11:39

Rape—*forced sexual relations*
A *Features concerning:*
Death penalty for .... Deut. 22:25-27
Captives subjected to .... Is. 13:16
B. *Example of:*
Tamar by Amnon .... 2 Sam. 13:6-29, 32, 33

Rapha, Raphah—*he* (God) *has healed*
1. Benjamin's fifth son .... 1 Chr. 8:1, 2
But not listed .... Gen. 46:21
2. Descendant of Jonathan .... 1 Chr. 8:37
Called Rephaiah in .... 1 Chr. 9:43
3. Same word translated "giant" .... 2 Sam. 21:16-20

Raphu—*cured*
Benjamite .... Num. 13:9

Rapture, the—*translation of saved at Christ's return*
Not all will sleep .... 1 Cor. 15:51
1 Thess. 4:15, 17
Dead in Christ will rise .... 1 Cor. 15:52
1 Thess. 4:13, 14, 16
Living to be transformed .... 1 Cor. 15:51-53
Saints caught up .... 1 Thess. 4:16, 17

Rashness—*ill-advised and hasty action*
Examples of:
Moses' killing the Egyptian .... Ex. 2:11, 12
Jephthah's vow .... Judg. 11:30-39
Israel's vow against the Benjamites .... Judg. 21:1-6
Josiah's war against Necho .... 2 Chr. 35:20-24
Peter's cutting off the ear of Malchus .... John 18:10

Rationing—*limits prescribed for necessities*
By Joseph, to save Egypt .... Gen. 41:35-57

Raven—*a flesh-eating bird*
A. *Characteristics of:*
Unclean for food .... Lev. 11:15
Solitary in habit .... Is. 34:11
Flesh-eating .... Prov. 30:17
Black .... Song 5:11
B. *Special features concerning:*
First creature sent from the ark .... Gen. 8:7
Elijah fed by .... 1 Kin. 17:4-7
Fed by God .... Luke 12:24

Q-R

SUBJECT REFERENCE

Razor—*a sharp instrument used for cutting off hair*

Forbidden to:

Nazarites .... Num. 6:1-5
Samson .... Judg. 13:5
Mentioned in Hannah's vow .... 1 Sam. 1:11
Used by barbers .... Ezek. 5:1

See Hair; Knife

Readiness—*being prepared for action*

A. *Descriptive of:*

Being prepared .... Matt. 22:4, 8
Being responsive .... 2 Cor. 8:11, 19

B. *Objects of:*

Willing people .... Luke 1:17
Passover .... Luke 22:12, 13
Lord's return .... Matt. 24:44
Preaching the Gospel .... Rom. 1:15

Reading the Bible

A. *Blessings of:*

Brings repentance .... 2 Kin. 22:8-20
Reminds us of duties .... Neh. 8:12, 13
Produces reformation .... Neh. 13:1-3
Gives knowledge of prophecy .... Rev. 1:3

B. *Reactions to:*

Responsiveness .... Ex. 24:7
Rejection .... Jer. 36:21-28
Rebellion .... Luke 4:16-30
Request for more light .... Acts 8:29-35
Research .... Acts 17:10, 11

Reaiah—*Jehovah has provided for*

1. Reubenite .... 1 Chr. 5:5
2. Founder of Nethinim family .... Ezra 2:47
3. Calebite family .... 1 Chr. 4:2

Real property

A. *Characteristic features of:*

Property desired .... Gen. 23:4
Price stipulated .... Gen. 33:19
Posts erected .... Deut. 19:14
Posterity remembered .... Num. 33:54
Publicity required .... Ruth 4:1-4
Proof documented .... Jer. 32:10-17

B. *Unusual examples of:*

Monopoly of land established .... Gen. 47:20
Sale as a prophetic proof .... Jer. 32:6-44
Mark of beast required .... Rev. 13:16, 17

Reaping

A. *Provisions concerning:*

Areas restricted .... Lev. 19:9, 10
Times restricted .... Lev. 25:1-11
Sin hinders .... Jer. 12:13

B. *Figurative of:*

Harvest of souls .... John 4:35-38
Trust in God .... Matt. 6:26
Gospel age .... Amos 9:13-15
Injustice .... Matt. 25:26
Payment for services .... 1 Cor. 9:11
Blessings .... 2 Cor. 9:6
Reward for righteousness .... Gal. 6:8, 9
Punishment for sin .... Hos. 10:13
Judgment on the world .... Rev. 14:14-16
Final judgment .... Matt. 13:30-43

Reason—*the faculty by which we think*

A. *Faculty of:*

Makes men sane .... Dan. 4:36
Prepares for salvation .... Is. 1:18
Makes men guilty .... Mark 11:31-33

B. *Inadequacy of:*

Biased against the truth .... Mark 2:6-8
Gospel not explained by .... 1 Cor. 1:18-31; 1 Cor. 2:1-14

Reba—*fourth part*

Midianite chief slain by Israelites .... Num. 31:8; Josh. 13:21

Rebekah, Rebecca—*loops of a rope*

Daughter of Bethuel .... Gen. 22:20-23
Becomes Isaac's wife .... Gen. 24:15-67
Mother of Esau and Jacob .... Gen. 25:21-28
Poses as Isaac's sister .... Gen. 26:6-11
Disturbed by Esau's marriages .... Gen. 26:34, 35
Causes Jacob to deceive Isaac .... Gen. 27:1-29
Urges Jacob to leave home .... Gen. 27:42-46
Burial of, in Machpelah .... Gen. 49:31
Mentioned by Paul .... Rom. 9:10

Rebellion—*active opposition to authority*

A. *Against:*

God .... Dan. 9:5, 9
God's word .... Num. 20:24
Davidic kingship .... 1 Kin. 12:19
Constituted priesthood .... Num. 17:1-10
Spirit .... Is. 63:10

B. *Evil of:*

Keeps from blessings .... Num. 20:24
Increases sin .... Job 34:37
Needs to be confessed .... Dan. 9:4-12
Characterizes a people .... Is. 65:2

See Insurrection

Rebuilding Jerusalem

Permitted by proclamation .... Ezra 1:1-4
Opposed .... Ezra 4:1-6; Neh. 4:1-3
Temple .... Ezra 5:1, 2; Ezra 6:14, 15
Walls .... Neh. 6:15, 16

Rebuke—*to reprimand sharply*

Jesus' power to restrain:

Sea .... Matt. 8:26
Demons .... Matt. 17:18
Fever .... Luke 4:39
Peter .... Mark 8:33

Rebuke for sin

A. *Manner of:*

Before all .... 1 Tim. 5:20
With longsuffering .... 2 Tim. 4:2
Sharply .... Titus 2:15
With all authority .... Titus 2:15

B. *Examples of:*

Isaac by Abimelech .... Gen. 26:6-11
Laban by Jacob .... Gen. 31:36-42
Saul by Samuel .... 1 Sam. 13:13
Ahab by Elijah .... 1 Kin. 21:20
Judah by Zechariah .... 2 Chr. 24:20
Israel by Ezra .... Ezra 10:10, 11
David by God .... Ps. 39:11
Peter by Paul .... Gal. 2:11-14

Receive—*to take into one's possession*

A. *Good things:*

Word .... James 1:21
Holy Spirit .... Acts 2:38
Christ Jesus .... Col. 2:6
Forgiveness .... Acts 26:18
Petitions .... 1 John 3:22
Reward .... 1 Cor. 3:8, 14

B. *Evil things:*

Punishment .... Rom. 1:27
Wrong .... Col. 3:25
Beast's mark .... Rev. 13:16
Reward for unrighteousness .... 2 Pet. 2:13

Rechab—*rider*

1. Assassin of Ish-bosheth .... 2 Sam. 4:2, 6
2. Father of Jehonadab, founder of the Rechabites .... 2 Kin. 10:15-23
   Related to the Kenites .... 1 Chr. 2:55
3. Postexilic ruler .... Neh. 3:14

Rechabites—*descendants of Rechab*

Kenite clan fathered by Rechab and believing in the simple life .... Jer. 35:1-19

Rechah—*softness*

Place in Judah .... 1 Chr. 4:12

Reciprocation—*mutual interchange*

Gentiles to Jews .... Rom. 15:27
Students to teachers .... Gal. 6:6

Recompense—*to pay back in kind*

A. *On the righteous:*

Even now .... Prov. 11:31
According to one's righteousness .... Ps. 18:20, 24
Eagerly expected .... Heb. 10:35

B. *On the unrighteous:*

Justly deserved .... Rom. 1:27
Belongs to God only .... Heb. 10:30
Will surely come .... Jer. 51:56
To the next generation .... Jer. 32:18
Fully at the second advent .... 2 Thess. 1:6

Reconciliation—*making peace between enemies*

A. *Effected on men while:*

Helpless .... Rom. 5:6
Sinners .... Rom. 5:8
Enemies of God .... Rom. 5:10
God-haters .... Col. 1:21

B. *Accomplished by:*

God in Christ .... 2 Cor. 5:18
Christ's death .... Rom. 5:10
Christ's blood .... Eph. 2:13

C. *Productive of:*

Peace with God .... Rom. 5:1
Access to God .... Rom. 5:2
Union of Jews and Gentiles .... Eph. 2:14

Recorder—*high court official*

Records events .... 2 Sam. 8:16
Represents the king .... 2 Kin. 18:18
Repairs the Temple .... 2 Chr. 34:8

Recover—*to restore lost things*

A. *Of sickness:*

By remedy .... 2 Kin. 20:7
By a miracle .... 2 Kin. 5:3-14
Sought from idols .... 2 Kin. 1:2-17
Prayed for .... Is. 38:16

B. *Of physical things:*

Defeat in war .... 2 Chr. 13:19, 20
Conquered territory .... 2 Sam. 8:3; 2 Kin. 13:25
Captured people .... Jer. 41:16

Recreation—*relaxation and restoration*

Among children, natural .... Zech. 8:5
Among adults, sometimes boring .... Eccl. 2:1-11
Lord's place in .... Jer. 33:11
Of the wicked, evil .... Judg. 16:25

Rectitude—*uprightness of life*

True way of living .... Prov. 4:23-27

Red—*being red or ruddy*

Blood .... 2 Kin. 3:22
Wine .... Prov. 23:31
Complexion .... Lam. 4:7

Red dragon—*another name for Satan*

Seen in John's vision .... Rev. 12:3-17

Redemption—*salvation by sacrifice*

A. *Defined as deliverance from:*

Curse of the Law .... Gal. 3:13
Bondage of the Law .... Gal. 4:5
Iniquity .... Titus 2:14
Enemies .... Ps. 136:24
Destruction .... Ps. 103:4
Death .... Hos. 13:14
Grave .... Ps. 49:15
Vain conversation .... 1 Pet. 1:18
Present evil world .... Gal. 1:4

B. *Accomplished by:*

God's power .... Deut. 7:8
Christ's blood .... Eph. 1:7
God's grace .... Rom. 3:24, 25

C. *Benefits of:*

Forgiveness .... Col. 1:14
Justification .... Rom. 3:24
Adoption .... Gal. 4:4, 5
God's possession .... 1 Cor. 6:20
God's people .... Titus 2:14
Purification .... Titus 2:14
Sealing .... Eph. 4:30
Inheritance .... Heb. 9:15
Heaven's glory .... Rev. 14:3, 4

Red heifer (see Heifer)

Red horse—*symbol of war*

Seen in John's vision .... Rev. 6:4

Red Sea—*sea of reeds*

Locusts destroyed .... Ex. 10:19
Divided by God .... Ex. 14:21
Crossed by Israel .... Ex. 14:22, 29
Egyptians drowned .... Ex. 15:4, 21

SUBJECT — REFERENCE

- Boundary of promised land ..... Ex. 23:31
- Israelites camp by ..... Num. 33:10, 11
- Ships built on ..... 1 Kin. 9:26

Reed—*tall grass growing in marshes*

Figurative of:

- Weakness ..... Is. 36:6
- Instability ..... Matt. 11:7
- God's measure ..... Ezek. 40:3
- Davidic line ..... Is. 42:3

Refining, spiritual

- By afflictions ..... Is. 48:10
- By fire ..... Zech. 13:9
- For a purpose ..... John 15:2
- More precious than gold ..... 1 Pet. 1:7

Reflection—*contemplation on*

- Past ..... Mark 14:72
- Present ..... Luke 14:31-33
- Future ..... Acts 21:12-14

Reformations, religious

Manifested by or in:

- Recovery of the Law ..... 2 Kin. 22:8-20
- Resolving to follow the Lord ..... Ezra 10:1-17
- Religious zeal for the Lord ..... Neh. 13:11-31
- Restoration of judges ..... 2 Chr. 19:1-11

Refresh—*to renew; to restore*

Spiritual:

- In the spirit ..... 1 Cor. 16:18
- In the heart ..... Philem. 7, 20
- Often needed ..... 2 Tim. 1:16
- Mutual ..... Rom. 15:32
- Special times ..... Acts 3:19
- Refused ..... Is. 28:12

Refuge—*a shelter against harm*

Divine:

- In the Lord ..... Ps. 142:5
- From storms ..... Is. 4:5, 6
- Time of trouble ..... Ps. 9:9
- Place of protection ..... Ps. 91:9, 10
- Always ready ..... Ps. 46:1

Refuge, cities of (see Cities, Levitical)

Refuse—*to reject or decline*

A. *Of things, physical:*

- Marriage ..... Ex. 22:17
- Passage ..... Num. 20:21
- King ..... 1 Sam. 16:7
- Display ..... Esth. 1:12
- Leader ..... Acts 7:35
- Martyrdom ..... Acts 25:11
- Fables ..... 1 Tim. 4:7
- Adoption ..... Heb. 11:24

B. *Of things, spiritual:*

- Hardness of heart ..... Ex. 7:14
- Disobedience ..... Ex. 16:28
- Obedience ..... 1 Sam. 8:19
- Messiah ..... Ps. 118:22
- Salvation ..... Is. 8:6
- Shame ..... Jer. 3:3
- Repentance ..... Hos. 11:5
- Healing ..... Jer. 15:18
- God ..... Heb. 12:25

Refuse Gate—*a gate of Jerusalem*

- Nehemiah viewed city from ..... Neh. 2:13
- Wall dedicated near ..... Neh. 12:31

Regard—*to think highly of*

- Honors God ..... Is. 17:7, 8
- Honors God's Word ..... Ps. 119:6, 15, 117
- Rejects the unbelieving ..... Gen. 4:4, 5

Regem—*friend*

- Calebite ..... 1 Chr. 2:47

Regem-melech—*friend of the king*

- Sent in deputation to Zechariah ..... Zech. 7:2

Regeneration (see Born again; New birth)

Register—*a record of genealogies*

- Priests not recorded in ..... Ezra 2:62
- Excluded from priesthood ..... Neh. 7:63-65
- Those recorded in ..... Neh. 7:5-62

Rehabiah—*Jehovah is wide*

- Grandson of Moses ..... 1 Chr. 23:17

SUBJECT — REFERENCE

Rehob—*open place*

1. Two cities of Asher ..... Josh. 19:24, 28
   - One assigned to Levites ..... Josh. 21:31
   - Delayed conquest of one ..... Judg. 1:31
2. Northern city visited by Joshua's spies ..... Num. 13:21
   - Defeated by David ..... 2 Sam. 10:8
3. Father of Hadadezer ..... 2 Sam. 8:3, 12
4. Signer of the covenant ..... Neh. 10:11

Rehoboam—*the people are enlarged*

- Son and successor of Solomon ..... 1 Kin. 11:43
- Refuses reformatory measures ..... 1 Kin. 12:1-15
- Ten tribes revolt from ..... 1 Kin. 12:16-24
- Temporary prosperity of ..... 2 Chr. 11:5-23
- Lapses into idolatry ..... 1 Kin. 14:21-24
- Kingdom of, invaded by Egypt ..... 1 Kin. 14:25-28
- Reigns 17 years ..... 1 Kin. 14:21
- Death of ..... 1 Kin. 14:29-31
- In Christ's genealogy ..... Matt. 1:7

Rehoboth—*broad places, streets*

1. Name of a well dug by Isaac ..... Gen. 26:22
2. City "by the river" ..... Gen. 36:37
3. Built by Asshur ..... Gen. 10:11

Rehum—*beloved*

1. Persian officer ..... Ezra 4:8-23
2. Postexilic returnee ..... Ezra 2:2
3. Priest who returns with Zerubbabel ..... Neh. 12:3, 7
   - Same as Harim ..... Neh. 12:15
4. Signer of the covenant ..... Neh. 10:25
5. Postexilic Levite ..... Neh. 3:17

Rei—*friendly*

- One of David's faithful officers ..... 1 Kin. 1:8

Reign—*to rule over*

A. *Descriptive of the rule of:*

- Man ..... Gen. 36:31
- God ..... Ps. 47:8
- Christ ..... Rev. 20:4, 6
- Believers ..... Rev. 5:10
- Sin ..... Rom. 5:21
- Death ..... Rom. 5:14, 17
- Grace ..... Rom. 5:21

B. *Of Christ's rule:*

- Predicted ..... Is. 32:1
- Described ..... Jer. 23:5, 6
- Announced ..... Luke 1:31-33
- Rejected ..... Luke 19:14, 27
- Fulfilled ..... Rom. 15:12
- Enthroned ..... 1 Cor. 15:25
- Eternal ..... Rev. 11:15-17

Reject—*to refuse; to disown*

A. *Man's rejection of:*

- God ..... 1 Sam. 8:7
- God's Word ..... 1 Sam. 15:23, 26
- God's knowledge ..... Hos. 4:6
- Christ ..... Mark 8:31

B. *God's rejection of man, as:*

- Unbeliever ..... John 12:48
- Heretic ..... Titus 3:10
- Unfruitful ..... Heb. 6:8
- Reprobate ..... Heb. 12:17

Rejoice—*to be glad*

A. *Kinds of:*

- Gloating ..... Mic. 7:8
- Vindictive ..... Rev. 18:20
- Marital ..... Prov. 5:18
- Defiant ..... Is. 8:6
- Prophetic ..... John 8:56
- Future ..... Phil. 2:16
- Rewarded ..... Ps. 126:6

B. *Caused by:*

- God's blessing ..... Ex. 18:9
- God's Word ..... Jer. 15:16
- Assurance ..... Luke 10:20
- Salvation ..... Luke 15:6-10
- Persecution ..... Acts 5:41
- Reunion of believers ..... Phil. 2:28
- Exaltation ..... James 1:9
- Christ's return ..... 1 Pet. 4:13

SUBJECT — REFERENCE

C. *Sphere of, in:*

- God's salvation ..... Ps. 21:1
- God's protection ..... Ps. 63:7
- God's blessings ..... Ps. 106:5
- Lord Himself ..... Hab. 3:18

D. *Agents of:*

- Heart ..... 1 Chr. 16:10
- Soul ..... Ps. 35:9
- Earth ..... Ps. 97:1
- God's people ..... Ps. 118:24
- Believing spirit ..... Luke 1:47

Rekem—*friendship*

1. Midianite king slain by Moses ..... Num. 31:8
2. Descendant of Caleb ..... 1 Chr. 2:43, 44
3. City of Benjamin ..... Josh. 18:27

Relapse—*to turn back to sin again*

- Danger of, explained ..... Heb. 6:4-6

Relatives—*those of near kin*

A. *Good derived from:*

- Encouragement ..... Esth. 4:12-17
- Salvation ..... John 1:40-42

B. *Evil derived from:*

- Strife ..... Gen. 31:1-42
- Persecution ..... Mark 13:12
- Jealousy ..... Gen. 37:3-11

Relief—*thorough service*

- In early church ..... Acts 4:32-37
- Determined to send ..... Acts 11:29
- Fulfilled at Christ's return ..... 2 Thess. 1:7

Religion, false

Characterized by:

- Apostasy ..... 2 Thess. 2:3, 4
- Backsliding ..... Jer. 5:23-31
- Ceremonialism ..... Mark 7:3-13
- Display ..... Matt. 6:5
- Ease ..... 1 Kin. 12:27-31
- Formalism ..... 2 Tim. 3:5

Remaliah—*whom Jehovah has adored*

- Father of Pekah ..... 2 Kin. 15:25

Remedy—*a cure*

- Without ..... Prov. 6:15
- Right kind ..... 1 John 1:7

Remember—*to call to mind again*

Aids to:

- Rainbow ..... Gen. 9:15, 16
- Covenant ..... Ex. 2:24
- Passover ..... Ex. 13:3
- Sabbath ..... Ex. 20:8
- Offering ..... Num. 5:15
- Son (child) ..... 2 Sam. 18:18
- Prophet's presence ..... 1 Kin. 17:18
- Book ..... Mal. 3:16
- Lord's Supper ..... Luke 22:19
- Epistle ..... 2 Pet. 3:1
- See Memories

Remeth—*a high place*

- Frontier town of Issachar ..... Josh. 19:21

Remission—*forgiveness*

A. *Based upon:*

- Christ's death ..... Matt. 26:28
- Faith in Christ ..... Acts 10:43
- Repentance ..... Mark 1:4

B. *Significance of:*

- Shows God's righteousness ..... Rom. 3:25
- Makes salvation real ..... Luke 1:77
- Must be preached ..... Luke 24:47

Remmon-methoar

- City of Zebulun ..... Josh. 19:10, 13

Remnant—*what is left over*

A. *Used literally of:*

- Cloth left over ..... Ex. 26:12
- Race left remaining ..... Deut. 3:11
- Nation still surviving ..... Amos 1:8

B. *Used spiritually of the faithful Israel:*

- Punished ..... Is. 1:9
- Protected ..... Is. 37:31-33
- Scattered ..... Ezek. 5:10
- Gathered ..... Is. 10:20-22
- Repentant ..... Jer. 31:7-9

SUBJECT ... REFERENCE

Forgiven ... Mic. 7:18
Saved ... Jer. 23:3-8
 Rom. 9:27
Blessing ... Mic. 5:7, 8
Holy ... Zeph. 3:12, 13
Elected ... Rom. 11:5

Remorse—*distress arising from guilt*

Of a renegade ... Matt. 27:3-5
Of a disciple ... Luke 22:62
In flame ... Luke 16:24

Remphan—*a name for Kiyyan*

Worshiped by Israelites ... Acts 7:41-43

Rend—*to tear apart by force*

A. *Used literally of:*
Garments ... Ezra 9:3, 5
Clothing ... Esth. 4:1
Rocks ... Matt. 27:51
Veil ... Matt. 27:51
Flesh ... Matt. 7:6
Body ... Mark 9:26

B. *Figuratively of:*
Repentance ... Joel 2:13
Harlotry ... Jer. 4:30
Destruction ... Hos. 13:8
Dissolution of the old economy ... Mark 15:38
Joy ... 1 Kin. 1:40

Renewal of strength

A. *Sources of:*
Holy Spirit ... Titus 3:5
Wait for the Lord ... Is. 40:31
Cleansing from sin ... Ps. 51:10

B. *Objects of:*
Youthfulness ... Ps. 103:5
Peoples ... Is. 41:1
Inward man ... 2 Cor. 4:16
New man ... Col. 3:10
Mind ... Rom. 12:2

Renown—*of great reputation*

Man ... Gen. 6:4
City ... Ezek. 26:17
God ... Dan. 9:15
Plant ... Ezek. 34:29

Renunciation—*giving up the right to do something*

Blessings of:
True discipleship ... Luke 14:33
True reward ... Mark 10:28-31
Future reward ... Luke 18:28-30

Repentance

A. *Described as:*
"Turned" ... Acts 9:35
"Repent" ... Acts 8:22
"Return" ... 1 Sam. 7:3
"Conversion" ... Acts 15:3

B. *Kinds of:*
National ... Joel 3:5-8
Internal ... Ps. 51:10-13
Unavailing ... Heb. 12:16, 17
True ... Acts 9:1-20
Unreal ... Ex. 9:27-35

C. *Derived from gift of:*
God ... Acts 11:18
Christ ... Acts 5:31
Spirit ... Zech. 12:10

D. *Things leading to:*
God's long-suffering ... 2 Pet. 3:9
God's goodness ... Rom. 2:4
Conviction of sin ... Acts 2:37, 38

E. *Productive of:*
Life ... Acts 11:18
Remission of sins ... Mark 1:4
New spirit ... Ezek. 18:31
New heart ... Ezek. 18:31
Joy ... Luke 15:7, 10

F. *Signs of:*
Reformation of life ... Matt. 3:8
Restitution ... Luke 19:8
Godly sorrow ... 2 Cor. 7:9, 10

See Conversion

Rephael—*God has healed*

Levite porter ... 1 Chr. 26:7

SUBJECT ... REFERENCE

Rephah—*riches*

Ancestor of Joshua ... 1 Chr. 7:25-27

Rephaiah—*Jehovah has healed*

1. Man of Issachar ... 1 Chr. 7:2
2. Descendant of Jonathan ... 1 Chr. 9:43
 Called Rapha ... 1 Chr. 8:37
3. Simeonite prince ... 1 Chr. 4:42, 43
4. Postexilic ruler ... Neh. 3:9
5. Descendant of David ... 1 Chr. 3:21

Rephaim—*giants*

1. Early race of giants in Palestine ... Gen. 14:5
 Among doomed nations ... Gen. 15:20

See Giants

2. Valley near Jerusalem ... 2 Sam. 23:13, 14
 Very fertile ... Is. 17:5
 Scene of Philistine defeats ... 2 Sam. 5:18-22

Rephidim—*rests*

Israelite camp ... Num. 33:12-15
Moses struck rock ... Ex. 17:1-7
Amalek defeated ... Ex. 17:8-16

Report—*a transmitted account of something*

A. *Kinds of:*
True ... 1 Kin. 10:6
Good ... Prov. 15:30
False ... Ex. 23:1
Defaming ... Jer. 20:10
Slanderous ... Rom. 3:8
Evil ... 2 Cor. 6:8

B. *Good, obtained by:*
Fear ... Deut. 2:25
Just life ... Acts 10:22
Devout life ... Acts 22:12
Outsiders ... 1 Tim. 3:7
Faith ... Heb. 11:2, 39
Friends ... 3 John 12

Reproach—*something imputed to the discredit of others*

A. *Objects of:*
God ... 2 Kin. 19:4-23
God's people ... Neh. 6:13
Messiah ... Rom. 15:3
Christians ... Luke 6:22

B. *Agents of:*
Enemies ... Neh. 4:4
Foolish ... Ps. 74:22
Scorner ... Prov. 22:10
Satan ... 1 Tim. 5:14, 15
 1 Tim. 3:7

C. *Evil causes of:*
Unbelief ... Jer. 6:10
Idolatry ... Ezek. 22:4
Breaking God's Law ... Num. 15:30, 31
Sin ... Prov. 14:34

D. *Good causes of:*
Faith in God's promises ... Heb. 11:24-26
Living for Christ ... 1 Pet. 4:14
Suffering for Christ ... Heb. 13:13

E. *Of God's people:*
Permitted by God ... Jer. 15:15

Reprobate—*rejected after testing*

A. *Causes of:*
Not having Christ ... 2 Cor. 13:3-5
Rejecting the faith ... 2 Tim. 3:8
Spiritual barrenness ... Heb. 6:7, 8
Lack of discipline ... 1 Cor. 9:24-27
Rejection by the Lord ... Jer. 6:30

B. *Consequences of, given up to:*
Evil ... Rom. 1:24-32
Delusion ... 2 Thess. 2:11, 12
Blindness ... Matt. 13:13-15
Destruction ... 2 Pet. 2:9-22

Reproof—*a cutting rebuke for misconduct*

A. *Sources of:*
God ... Ps. 50:8, 21
Backslidings ... Jer. 2:19
God's Word ... 2 Tim. 3:16
John the Baptist ... Luke 3:16, 19

B. *Examples of:*
Samuel ... 1 Sam. 13:13
Daniel ... Dan. 5:22, 23

SUBJECT ... REFERENCE

John the Baptist ... Matt. 3:7-12
Stephen ... Acts 7:51
Paul ... Gal. 2:11

Reprove—*to express disapproval of*

Designed for good ... Heb. 12:5
Accomplished in love ... Rev. 3:19

Reptiles of the Bible

A. *Features concerning:*
Created by God ... Gen. 1:24, 25
Made to praise God ... Ps. 148:7, 10
Placed under man's power ... Gen. 1:26
Classified as unclean ... Lev. 11:31-43
Seen in a vision ... Acts 10:11-14
Worshiped by pagans ... Rom. 1:23
Likeness of, forbidden ... Deut. 4:16, 18
Portrayed on walls ... Ezek. 8:10

B. *List of:*
Adder ... Prov. 23:32
Asp ... Rom. 3:13
Chameleon ... Lev. 11:30
Cockatrice ... Is. 11:8
Dragon ... Deut. 32:33
Ferret ... Lev. 11:30
Frog ... Rev. 16:13
Leviathan ... Job 41:1, 2
Lizard ... Lev. 11:30
Scorpion ... Deut. 8:15
Serpents ... Matt. 10:7
Snake ... Matt. 7:10
Snail ... Ps. 58:8
Tortoise ... Lev. 11:29
Viper ... Acts 28:3

Reputation—*public esteem; fame*

A. *Good:*
Wonderful asset ... Prov. 22:1
Based on integrity ... 2 Cor. 8:18-24
Hated by wicked ... Dan. 6:4-8
Required of church officials ... Acts 6:3
Worthy of trust ... Acts 16:2

B. *Dangers of:*
Universal praise ... Luke 6:26
Flattering speech ... Rom. 16:18
Worldly friendship ... James 4:4
Worldly praise ... 1 John 4:5, 6
Undue deference toward ... Gal. 2:6

Resen—*fortress*

City built by Asshur ... Gen. 10:11, 12

Reservoirs—*where water is stored*

Family cisterns ... Is. 36:16
Garden pools ... Eccl. 2:6

Resh

Letter of the Hebrew alphabet ... Ps. 119:153-160

Resheph—*home*

Descendant of Ephraim ... 1 Chr. 7:23-25

Residue—*a remnant*

A. *Used literally of:*
Survivors ... Jer. 8:3

B. *Used spiritually of:*
Faithful remnant ... Is. 28:5
Promised seed ... Zech. 8:11-13

Resignation—*patient submission to*

Disquieting problem ... Josh. 22:9-34
Tragic death ... 2 Sam. 19:1-8
God's chastening ... Job 2:10
Cross ... Mark 14:36
Sufferings ahead ... Acts 21:11-14
Pain ... 2 Cor. 12:7-10
Want ... Phil. 4:11, 12

Resist—*to stand against*

A. *Of evil things:*
Sin ... Heb. 12:4
Adversaries ... Luke 21:15

B. *Of good things:*
God's will ... Rom. 9:19
Holy Spirit ... Acts 7:51
Truth ... 2 Tim. 3:8
Wisdom ... Acts 6:10
Constituted authority ... Rom. 13:2

Respect—*honor manifested toward the worthy*

A. *Wrong kind:*
Favoring the wealthy ... James 2:3, 9

SUBJECT REFERENCE

B. *Right kind:*
Rejects the proud ... Ps. 40:4

C. *On God's part:*
Regards the lowly ... Ps. 138:6
Honors His covenant ... 2 Kin. 13:23
Makes God just ... 1 Pet. 1:17

Responsibility—*accountability for one's actions*

A. *Shifting of, by:*
Blaming another ... Gen. 3:12
Claiming innocency ... Matt. 27:24
Blaming a people ... Ex. 32:21-24

B. *Cannot be excused by:*
Ignorance ... Acts 17:30, 31
Unbelief ... John 3:18-20
Previous good ... Ex. 33:12, 13
One's ancestors ... Matt. 3:9, 10

C. *Is increased by:*
Sight ... John 9:39-41
Privilege ... John 15:22, 24
Opportunity ... Matt. 11:20-24
Continuance in sin ... Matt. 23:31-35
Rejection ... Matt. 10:11-15

Rest—*peace and quiet*

A. *Descriptive of:*
Physical relaxation ... Gen. 18:4
Sinful laziness ... Matt. 26:45
Confidence ... Hab. 3:16-19
Completion of salvation ... Heb. 4:3, 8-11

B. *Need of:*
Recognized in God's Law ... Ex. 20:10, 11
Recognized by Christ ... Mark 6:31
Longed after ... Ps. 55:6
Provided for ... Rev. 6:11
Enjoyed after death ... Job 3:13, 17
Rev. 14:13

C. *Source of, in:*
Christ ... Matt. 11:28, 29
Trust ... Ps. 37:7
Returning to God ... Is. 30:15

D. *Disturbance of, by:*
Sin ... Is. 57:20
Rebellion ... Is. 28:12
Persecution ... Acts 9:23
Anxiety ... 2 Cor. 2:13

See Quietness

Restitution—*restoring*
Time of ... Acts 3:21
Of damaged property ... Ex. 22:3-12

Restoration—*renewal of something to its former state*

A. *Miraculous, from:*
Death ... 2 Kin. 8:1, 5
Dried hand ... 1 Kin. 13:4, 6
Withered hand ... Mark 3:5
Blindness ... Mark 8:25

B. *Natural of:*
Man's wife ... Gen. 20:7, 14
Man's position ... Gen. 40:13, 21
Land ... 2 Sam. 9:7
Visit ... Heb. 13:19

C. *Spiritual:*
Joy ... Ps. 51:11, 12
Recovery ... Jer. 30:17
God's blessings ... Joel 2:25
Christ ... Is. 49:6

Restoration of Israel
Promised in the prophets ... Is. 11:11
Seen in John's ministry ... Matt. 17:11
Anticipated by Caiaphas ... John 11:49-52
Questioned by the disciples ... Acts 1:6
Realized at Pentecost ... Joel 2:28-32
Fulfilled in the Church ... Eph. 2:11-22
Perfected in Heaven ... Heb. 12:22-28

Restraints, divine

On:
Man's wrath ... Ps. 76:10
Man's designs ... Gen. 11:6
Natural forces ... Gen. 8:2
Childbearing ... Gen. 16:2
Wicked ... 2 Kin. 19:28
Antichrist ... 2 Thess. 2:3-7

SUBJECT REFERENCE

Rests—*supporting ledge*
For the beams of the Temple ... 1 Kin. 6:6

Resurrection—*arising from the dead*

A. *Doctrine of:*
Looked for in faith ... Job 19:25-27
Taught in Old Testament ... Is. 26:19
Dan. 12:2, 3, 13
Denied by Sadducees ... Matt. 22:23-28
Acts 23:6, 8
Affirmed by Christ ... John 5:28, 29
John 6:39, 40, 44
Illustrated by Lazarus ... John 11:23-44
Explained away by false teachers ... 2 Tim. 2:18
Questioned by some ... 1 Cor. 15:12
Mocked at by heathen ... Acts 17:32
Proclaimed by Paul ... Acts 24:14, 15

B. *Accomplished by:*
God's power ... Matt. 22:28, 29
Christ ... John 5:28, 29
Holy Spirit ... Rom. 8:11

C. *Proof of, based on:*
God's power ... 1 Cor. 6:14
Union with Christ ... Rom. 8:11
Christ's resurrection ... 1 Cor. 15:12-56

D. *Time of, at:*
Last day ... John 6:39-44
Christ's return ... 1 Thess. 4:13-18
Last trumpet ... 1 Cor. 15:51-55

E. *Nature of:*
Incorruptible ... 1 Cor. 15:42, 54
Glorious ... 1 Cor. 15:43
Spiritual ... 1 Cor. 15:44
Transforming ... 1 Cor. 15:51
Like angels ... Matt. 22:30
Like Christ ... Phil. 3:21

F. *Of the wicked:*
Predicted ... Dan. 12:2
Described ... John 5:28, 29
Simultaneous ... Acts 24:15

Resurrection of Christ

A. *Features concerning:*
Foretold in the Psalms ... Ps. 16:10, 11
Acts 13:34, 35
Presented in prophecy ... Is. 53:10-12
1 Cor. 15:4
Announced by Christ ... Mark 9:9, 10
John 2:19-22
Proclaimed by the apostles ... Acts 2:32
Acts 3:15

B. *Accomplished by:*
God's power ... Acts 2:24
Christ's power ... John 10:18
Spirit's power ... Rom. 8:11

C. *Proven by:*
Empty tomb ... John 20:1-9
Angelic testimony ... Matt. 28:5-7
His enemies ... Matt. 28:11-15
Many infallible proofs ... John 20:20, 27
Acts 1:3
Apostolic preaching ... Acts 1:22
Acts 4:33
LORD's Day (first day of the week) ... John 20:1, 19; 1 Cor. 16:2

D. *Purposes of:*
Fulfill Scripture ... Luke 24:45, 46
Forgive sins ... 1 Cor. 15:17
Justify the sinner ... Rom. 4:25
Rom. 8:34
Give hope ... 1 Cor. 15:18, 19
Make faith real ... 1 Cor. 15:14-17
Prove His Sonship ... Ps. 2:7
Rom. 1:4
Set Him on David's throne ... Acts 2:30-32
Insure His exaltation ... Acts 4:10, 11
Phil. 2:9, 10
Guarantee the coming judgment ... Acts 17:31
Seal the believer's resurrection ... Acts 26:23; 1 Cor. 15:20, 23

E. *Appearances of, to:*
Mary Magdalene ... Mark 16:9
Other women ... Matt. 28:9
Two disciples ... Luke 24:13-15
Simon Peter ... Luke 24:34
Ten apostles ... John 20:19, 24
Eleven apostles ... John 20:26

SUBJECT REFERENCE

Apostles at Sea of Tiberias ... John 21:1
Apostles in Galilee ... Matt. 28:16, 17
500 brethren ... 1 Cor. 15:6
All the apostles ... Luke 24:51
Acts 1:9
Paul ... 1 Cor. 15:8
James ... 1 Cor. 15:7

Resurrections of the Bible
Widow's son ... 1 Kin. 17:17-22
Shunammite's son ... 2 Kin. 4:32-35
Unnamed man ... 2 Kin. 13:20, 21
Jairus' daughter ... Matt. 9:23-25
Widow's only son ... Luke 7:11-15
Lazarus of Bethany ... John 11:43, 44
Many saints ... Matt. 27:52, 53
Dorcas ... Acts 9:36-40
In symbolism ... Rev. 11:8, 11

Resurrection, spiritual

A. *Accomplished by power of:*
God ... Eph. 1:19
Christ ... Eph. 5:14
Holy Spirit ... Ezek. 11:19

B. *Features concerning:*
Takes place now ... John 5:25
Gives eternal life ... John 5:24
Delivers from spiritual death ... Rom. 6:4, 13
Changes life ... Is. 32:15
Issues in immortality ... John 11:25, 26
Delivers from Satan's power ... Acts 26:18
Realized in new life ... Phil. 3:10, 11
Called "first" ... Rev. 20:5, 6

Retaliation—*returning like for like*
Forbidden ... Luke 9:54, 55
Return good, not evil ... Prov. 25:21, 22
God's responsibility ... Prov. 20:22
Christ's teaching on ... Matt. 5:39-44

Retribution—*merited punishment for evil done*

A. *Expressed by:*
God's wrath ... Rom. 1:18
Lamb's wrath ... Rev. 6:16, 17
Vengeance ... Jude 7
Punishment ... 2 Thess. 1:6-9
Corruption ... 2 Pet. 2:9-22

B. *Due to the sinner's:*
Sin ... Rom. 2:1-9
Evil works ... Ex. 32:34
Persecution of the righteous ... 2 Thess. 1:6
Rejection of Christ ... Heb. 10:29, 30

C. *Deliverance from, by:*
Christ ... 1 Thess. 1:10
God's appointment ... 1 Thess. 5:9

Return

Descriptive of:
Going back home ... Gen. 31:3, 13
Repentance ... 2 Chr. 6:24, 38
Vengeance or retribution ... 1 Kin. 2:33, 44
Divine visitation ... Joel 2:14
Christ's advent ... Acts 15:16
Death ... Gen. 3:19

Reu—*friend*
Descendant of Shem ... Gen. 11:10-21
Called Ragau ... Luke 3:35

Reuben—*behold a son*
Jacob's eldest son ... Gen. 29:31, 32
Guilty of misconduct; loses pre-eminence ... Gen. 35:22
Proposes plan to save Joseph's life ... Gen. 37:21-29
Offers sons as pledge ... Gen. 42:37
Father of four sons ... Gen. 46:8, 9
Pronounced unstable ... Gen. 49:3, 4
Descendants of ... Num. 26:5-11

Reubenites—*descendants of Reuben*
Divided into four tribal families ... Num. 26:5-11
Elizur, warrior ... Num. 1:5
Census of, at Sinai ... Num. 1:18-21
Census of, at conquest ... Num. 26:7
Place of, in march ... Num. 2:10
Seek inheritance east of Jordan ... Num. 32:1-42
Join in war against Canaanites ... Josh. 1:12-18

SUBJECT — REFERENCE

Altar erected by, misunderstood — Josh. 22:10-34
Criticized by Deborah — Judg. 5:15, 16
Enslaved by Assyria — 2 Kin. 15:29

Reuel—*friend of God*

1. Son of Esau — Gen. 36:2-4
2. Moses' father-in-law — Ex. 2:18
3. Benjamite — 1 Chr. 9:8
4. Gadite leader — Num. 2:14
   Called Deuel — Num. 7:42, 47

Reumah—*exalted*

Nahor's concubine — Gen. 22:24

Revelation—*an uncovering of something hidden*

A. *Source of:*
God — Dan. 2:28-47
Christ — John 1:18
The Spirit — 1 Cor. 2:10
Not in man — Matt. 16:17

B. *Objects of:*
God — Matt. 11:25, 27
Christ — 2 Thess. 1:7
Man of sin — 2 Thess. 2:3, 6, 8

C. *Instruments of:*
Prophets — 1 Pet. 1:12
Daniel — Dan. 10:1
Christ — Heb. 1:1, 2
Apostles — 1 Cor. 2:10
Paul — Gal. 1:16

D. *Of the first advent:*
Predicted — Is. 40:5
Revealed — Is. 53:1
Rejected — John 12:38-41
Of God's righteousness — Is. 56:1
Of peace and truth — Jer. 33:6-8; Eph. 2:11-17

E. *Time of the second advent:*
Uncovering — Matt. 10:26
Judgment — Luke 17:26-30
Victory — 2 Thess. 2:3, 6, 8
Glory — 1 Pet. 5:1
Resurrection — Rom. 8:18, 19
Reward — 1 Cor. 3:13
Glorification — 1 John 3:2
Grace — 1 Pet. 1:5, 13
Joy — 1 Pet. 4:13

F. *Of divine truth, characteristics of:*
God-originated — Dan. 2:47
Verbal — Heb. 1:1
In the created world — Ps. 19:1, 2
Illuminative — Eph. 1:17
Now revealed — Rom. 16:26
Truth communicating — Eph. 3:3, 4

Revelation, the—*a book of the New Testament*

Vision of the Son of Man — Rev. 1:9-20
Message to the seven churches — Rev. 2:1—3:22
The book of seven seals — Rev. 4:1—6:17
The judgment — Rev. 7:1—9:21
The two beasts — Rev. 13
Babylon doomed — Rev. 17:1—18:24
The marriage supper — Rev. 19:6-10
The judgment of the wicked — Rev. 20:11-15
New heaven and new earth — Rev. 21:1-8
The new Jerusalem — Rev. 21:9—22:5
Christ's coming — Rev. 22:6-21

Revenge—*to take vengeance*

A. *Manifestation of:*
Belongs to God — Rev. 18:20
Performed by rulers — Rom. 13:4
Righteously allowed — 1 Kin. 20:42
Pleaded for — Jer. 11:20
Disallowed among men — Prov. 20:22
Forbidden to disciples — Luke 9:54, 55

B. *Antidotes of:*
Overcome by kindness — 1 Sam. 25:30-34
Exhibit love — Luke 6:35
Bless — Rom. 12:14
Forbear wrath — Rom. 12:19
Manifest forbearance — Matt. 5:38-41
Flee from — Gen. 27:41-45

C. *Examples of:*
Simeon and Levi — Gen. 34:25
Joseph — Gen. 42:9-24
Samson — Judg. 16:28-30
Joab — 2 Sam. 3:27, 30
Jezebel — 1 Kin. 19:2
Ahab — 1 Kin. 22:26, 27
Haman — Esth. 3:8-15
Philistines — Ezek. 25:15-17
Herodias — Mark 6:19-24
Jews — Acts 7:54, 59

Reverence—*a feeling of deep respect, love, awe and esteem*

Manifested toward:
God — Ps. 89:7
God's house — Lev. 19:30
Christ — Matt. 21:37
Kings — 1 Kin. 1:31
Parents — Heb. 12:9
Husbands — Eph. 5:33

Reverend—*worthy of reverence*

Applies only to God in the Scriptures — Ps. 111:9

Revile—*to speak of another abusively*

Christ, object of — Matt. 27:39
Christ, submissive under — 1 Pet. 2:23
Christians, objects of — Matt. 5:11
Right attitude toward — 1 Cor. 4:12
Punishment of — 1 Cor. 6:10
False teachers — 2 Pet. 2:10-12

Revival—*renewed zeal to obey God*

Conditions for:
Humility — 2 Chr. 7:14
Prayer — 2 Chr. 7:14; James 5:16
Broken heart — Ps. 34:18
Confession — Ps. 66:18
Repentance — 2 Cor. 7:10
Turning from sin — 2 Chr. 7:14; 2 Tim. 2:19
Complete surrender — Acts 9:5, 6; Rom. 12:1, 2

Revive—*to live again more vigorously*

A. *Descriptive of:*
Renewed strength — Gen. 45:27
Refreshment — Judg. 15:19
Restoration — Neh. 4:2
Resurrection — 1 Kin. 17:22

B. *Of the Spirit:*
Given to the humble — Is. 57:15
Source of joy — Ps. 85:6
Possible even in trouble — Ps. 138:7
Source of fruitfulness — Hos. 6:2, 3; Hos. 14:7

Reward of the righteous

A. *Described as:*
Sure — Prov. 11:18
Full — Ruth 2:12
Remembered — 2 Chr. 15:7
Great — Matt. 5:12
Open — Matt. 6:4, 6, 18

B. *Obtained by:*
Keeping God's commandments — Ps. 19:11
Sowing righteousness — Prov. 11:18
Fearing God's commandments — Prov. 13:13
Feeding an enemy — Prov. 25:21, 22
Simple service — Matt. 6:1
Grace through faith — Rom. 4:4, 5, 16
Faithful service — Col. 3:23, 24
Seeking God diligently — Heb. 11:6

C. *At Christ's return:*
After the resurrection — Rev. 11:18
Tested by fire — 1 Cor. 3:8-14
According to works — Rev. 22:12

See Crowns of Christians; Hire; Wages

Reward of the wicked

A. *Visited upon:*
Now — Ps. 91:8
At the judgment — 2 Tim. 4:14

B. *Measure of:*
By retribution — Rev. 18:6
According to the wickedness — 2 Sam. 3:39
Plentifully — Ps. 31:23

Rezeph—*glowing stone*

Place destroyed by the Assyrians — 2 Kin. 19:12

Rezia—*delight*

Asherite — 1 Chr. 7:39

Rezin

1. King of Damascus; joins Pekah against Ahaz — 2 Kin. 15:37
   Confederacy of, inspires Isaiah's great Messianic prophecy — Is. 7:1—9:12
2. Head of a Nethinim family — Ezra 2:48

Rezon—*prince*

Son of Eliada; establishes Syrian kingdom — 1 Kin. 11:23-25

Rhegium—*a city of southern Italy*

Paul's ship arrived at — Acts 28:13

Rhesa

Ancestor of Christ — Luke 3:27

Rhoda—*rosebush*

Servant girl — Acts 12:13-16

Rhodes—*an island off the southwest coast of Asia Minor*

Paul's ship passes by — Acts 21:1

Rib

Eve formed of Adam's — Gen. 2:22

Ribai—*Jehovah strives*

One of David's mighty men — 2 Sam. 23:29

Ribband—*a ribbon*

On the fringe of garments — Num. 15:38

Riblah—*fertility*

1. Town on Israel's eastern border — Num. 34:11
2. Town in the land of Hamath — 2 Kin. 23:33
   Headquarters of:
   Pharaoh Nechoh — 2 Kin. 23:31-35
   Nebuchadnezzar — 2 Kin. 25:6, 20, 21
   Zedekiah blinded here — Jer. 39:5-7

Rich—*wealthy*

A. *Spiritual handicaps of:*
Selfishly satisfied — Luke 6:24
Reluctant to leave riches — Luke 18:22-25
Forgetful of God — Luke 12:15-21
Indifferent to others' needs — Luke 16:19-31
Easily tempted — 1 Tim. 6:9
Hindered spiritually — Matt. 19:23, 24
Misplaced trust — Prov. 11:28

B. *Applied, spiritually, to:*
God — Eph. 2:4
Christ — Rom. 10:12
Christians — James 2:5
True riches — 2 Cor. 8:9
Good works — 1 Tim. 6:18
Worldly people — Jer. 5:27, 28
Self-righteous — Hos. 12:8
Synagogue of Satan — Rev. 2:9

Riches, earthly

A. *Described as:*
Spiritually valueless — Ps. 49:6, 7
Inferior — Heb. 11:26
Fleeting — Prov. 23:5
Unsatisfying — Eccl. 4:8
Hurtful — Eccl. 5:13, 14
Deceitful — Matt. 13:22
Choking — Luke 8:14
Uncertain — 1 Tim. 6:17
Corrupted — James 5:2

B. *Proper attitude toward:*
Not to:
Put first — 1 Kin. 3:11, 13
Be trusted — Ps. 52:7
Set heart upon — Ps. 62:10
Be desired — Prov. 30:8
Not forever — Prov. 27:24
Use in giving — 2 Cor. 8:2
Remember God's supply — Phil. 4:19

Riches, management of

Reflects spiritual attitude — Luke 16:10-12
Demands budget — Luke 14:28-30

Riches, spiritual

Source of, in:
God's Law — Ps. 119:14

SUBJECT ... REFERENCE

Divine wisdom ... Prov. 3:13, 14
Unselfish service ... Prov. 13:7
Reverential fear ... Prov. 22:4
Fulfillment ... Rom. 11:12
Christ ... Col. 1:27
Assurance ... Col. 2:2
Christ's Word ... Col. 3:16

Riddle—*a hidden saying solved by guessing*

Samson's famous ... Judg. 14:12-19
Classed as a parable ... Ezek. 17:2
Avoided by God ... Num. 12:8

Ridicule (see Mocking)

Right—*that which is just and fair*

A. *Things that are:*
God's Law ... Ps. 19:8
God's Word ... Ps. 33:4
God's Way ... Ps. 107:7
Thoughts of the righteous ... Prov. 12:5
Work of the pure ... Prov. 21:8
Obedience to God ... Acts 4:19, 20
Obedience to parents ... Eph. 6:1

B. *Things that are not:*
False riches ... Jer. 17:11
Injustice to the poor ... Is. 10:2
Man's way ... Prov. 21:2
Man's heart ... Ps. 78:37

Righteous—*that which is upright*

A. *Applied to:*
God ... John 17:25
Christ ... 1 John 2:1
Messiah ... Is. 53:11
Christians ... Matt. 25:37, 46

B. *Blessings of:*
Prayers of, heard ... Prov. 15:29
Safely guarded ... Prov. 18:10
Bold as a lion ... Prov. 28:1
Shine forth ... Matt. 13:43

Righteousness—*uprightness before God*

A. *Kinds of:*
Created ... Eph. 4:24
Legal ... Phil. 3:6
Personal ... Phil. 3:9
Imputed ... Phil. 3:9
Experimental ... Heb. 5:13
Actual ... Heb. 11:33
Real ... 1 John 2:29

B. *Of Christ, He:*
Is the believer's ... Jer. 33:16
Loves ... Heb. 1:9
Judges with ... Is. 11:4
Is girded with ... Is. 11:5
Brings in ... Is. 46:13
Fulfills all ... Matt. 3:15
Confers upon believers ... Is. 61:10

Rimmon, Remmon—*pomegranate*

1. Benjamite ... 2 Sam. 4:2-9
2. Rock near Gibeah ... Judg. 20:45-47
   Benjamites hide here ... Judg. 21:13-23
3. Town in south Judah ... Josh. 15:1, 32
   Assigned to Simeon ... Josh. 19:7, 8
   Mentioned in prophecy ... Zech. 14:10
   Called En-rimmon ... Neh. 11:29
4. Syrian God (meaning "thunderer") worshiped by Naaman ... 2 Kin. 5:18
5. City of Zebulun ... Josh. 19:13
   Levitical city ... 1 Chr. 6:77
   Called Dimnah ... Josh. 21:35

Rimmon-parez—*pomegranate of breach*

Israelite camp ... Num. 33:19, 20

Ring

A. *Article of furniture, for:*
Staves of the ark ... Ex. 25:12-15
Curtains ... Ex. 26:29
Priest's ephod ... Ex. 28:23-28
Incense altar ... Ex. 30:4
Drapery ... Esth. 1:6

B. *Article of apparel:*
Symbol of authority ... Gen. 41:42
Sealing royal documents ... Esth. 3:12
Gifts ... Ex. 35:22
Feminine adornment ... Is. 3:16, 21
Expressive of position ... Luke 15:22
Sign of social status ... James 2:2

Ringleader—*the leader of a mob*

Paul contemptuously called ... Acts 24:5

Rinnah—*ringing cry*

Son of Shimon ... 1 Chr. 4:20

Riot—*an unruly mob*

Pacified by town clerk ... Acts 19:20-41

Riotous—*living without restraint*

Loose living ... Luke 15:13
Gluttonous eaters ... Prov. 23:20, 21
Sexual promiscuity ... Rom. 13:13

Riphath—*descendants of Gomer*

Son of Gomer ... Gen. 10:3
Called Diphath ... 1 Chr. 1:6

Rise, risen, rising, raised

A. *Of resurrection:*
Christ's ... Mark 8:31
Believers' (spiritually) ... Col. 2:12
Believers' (physically) ... John 11:23, 24

B. *Of Christ's resurrection:*
Predicted ... Mark 14:28
Fulfilled ... Matt. 28:6, 7
Remembered ... John 2:22
Evidenced ... John 21:14
Preached ... 1 Cor. 15:11-15
Misunderstood ... Mark 9:9, 10

Rissah—*ruin; rain*

Israelite camp ... Num. 33:21, 22

Rithmah—*broom plant*

Israelite camp ... Num. 33:18, 19

Rivalry—*competition*

Between man and neighbor ... Eccl. 4:4

River—*a large stream of water*

A. *Uses of:*
Water ... Jer. 2:18
Irrigation ... Gen. 2:10
Bathing ... Ex. 2:5
Baptisms ... Matt. 3:6
Healing ... 2 Kin. 5:10

B. *List of:*
Abana ... 2 Kin. 5:12
Arnon ... Josh. 12:1
Chebar ... Ezek. 10:15, 20
Euphrates ... Gen. 2:14
Gihon ... Gen. 2:13
Gozan ... 2 Kin. 17:6
Hiddekel ... Gen. 2:14
Jabbok ... Deut. 2:37
Jordan ... Josh. 3:8
Kanah ... Josh. 16:8
Kishon ... Judg. 5:21
Nile (Sihor) ... Jer. 2:18
Pharpar ... 2 Kin. 5:12
Pison ... Gen. 2:11
Ulai ... Dan. 8:2, 16

C. *Figurative of:*
Prosperity of saints ... Ps. 1:3
Affliction ... Ps. 124:4
Christ ... Is. 32:1, 2
God's presence ... Is. 33:21
Peace ... Is. 66:12
Holy Spirit ... John 7:38, 39

Rizpah—*glowing coal*

Saul's concubine taken by Abner ... 2 Sam. 3:6-8
Sons of, killed ... 2 Sam. 21:8, 9
Grief-stricken, cares for corpses ... 2 Sam. 21:10-14

Rob, robbery

A. *Used literally of:*
Plundering ... 1 Sam. 23:1
Taking from the poor ... Prov. 22:22
Robbers ... Judg. 9:25

B. *Used figuratively of:*
Dishonest riches ... Ps. 62:10
Holding back from God ... Mal. 3:8, 9
False teachers ... John 10:1, 8
Taking wages ... 2 Cor. 11:8

Rock

A. *Used for:*
Altars ... Judg. 6:20, 26
Idol worship ... Is. 57:5
Protection ... 1 Sam. 13:6
Shade ... Is. 32:2
Inscriptions ... Job 19:24
Executions ... 2 Chr. 25:12
Foundations ... Matt. 7:24, 25
Shelter ... Job 24:8
Tomb ... Matt. 27:60

B. *Miracles connected with:*
Water from ... Ex. 17:6
Fire from ... Judg. 6:21
Broken by wind ... 1 Kin. 19:11
Rent at Christ's death ... Matt. 27:51

C. *Figurative of Christ, as:*
Refuge ... Is. 32:2
Foundation of the Church ... Matt. 16:18
Source of blessings ... 1 Cor. 10:4
Stone of stumbling ... Is. 8:14
Foundation of faith ... Matt. 7:24, 25

Rod—*a staff or stick*

A. *Used for:*
Sign of authority ... Ex. 4:17, 20
Egyptians' staffs ... Ex. 7:12
Punishment ... Ex. 21:20
Club ... 1 Sam. 14:27
Correction of children ... Prov. 13:24

B. *Figurative of:*
Christ ... Is. 11:1
Christ's rule ... Ps. 2:9
Authority ... Is. 14:5, 29
The Gospel ... Ps. 110:2

Roe, roebuck—*the deer, gazelle*

A. *Described as:*
Fit for food ... Deut. 12:15, 22
Cheerful ... Prov. 5:19
Swift ... 1 Chr. 12:8
Wild ... 2 Sam. 2:18
Hunted by men ... Prov. 6:5
In Solomon's provisions ... 1 Kin. 4:23

B. *Figurative of:*
Timidity ... Is. 13:14
Swiftness ... 2 Sam. 2:18
Good wife ... Prov. 5:19
Church ... Song 4:5
Christ ... Song 2:9, 17

See Hart; Hind

Rogelim—*spies*

Town in Gilead ... 2 Sam. 17:27

Rogue—*a mischievous individual*

Descriptive of the fraudulent ... Is. 32:5, 7

Rohgah—*tumult*

Asherite ... 1 Chr. 7:34

Roll

Called a volume ... Ps. 40:7
State documents written on ... Ezra 6:2
Scripture written on ... Is. 8:1

Romamti-ezer—*I have raised up help*

Son of Heman ... 1 Chr. 25:4, 31

Roman

1. Inhabitant of Rome ... Acts 2:10
2. Official agent of the Roman government ... John 11:46
3. Person possessing Roman citizenship ... Acts 16:21-38

Romans, the Epistle to the—*a book of the New Testament*

The power of the Gospel ... Rom. 1:16
The pagans condemned ... Rom. 1:17-32
The Jews condemned ... Rom. 2:1-9
The advantages of the Jews ... Rom. 3:1-8
None righteous ... Rom. 3:9-20
Righteousness through faith ... Rom. 3:21-31
Abraham justified ... Rom. 4
The second Adam ... Rom. 5:12-21
On baptism ... Rom. 6
The pull of sin ... Rom. 7
The spiritual life ... Rom. 8
The destiny of the Jews ... Rom. 9—11
Life as worship ... Rom. 12:1, 2
Serving the body ... Rom. 12:3-21
Bearing with one another ... Rom. 14, 15
Greetings ... Rom. 16:1-24

SUBJECT REFERENCE

Rome—*the chief city of Italy*
Jews expelled from . . . . Acts 18:2
Paul:
Writes to Christians of . . . . Rom. 1:7
Desires to go to . . . . Acts 19:21
Comes to . . . . Acts 28:14
Imprisoned in . . . . Acts 28:16

Root—*the part of a plant underground*
Used figuratively of:
Material foundation . . . . Jer. 12:2
Remnant . . . . Judg. 5:14
National existence . . . . Is. 14:30
National source . . . . Rom. 11:16-18
Source of evil . . . . 1 Tim. 6:10
Judgment and destruction . . . . . . 1 Kin. 14:15
Restoration . . . . 2 Kin. 19:30
Spiritual life . . . . Hos. 14:5
Spiritual foundation . . . . Eph. 3:17
Messiah . . . . Is. 11:1, 10

Rose—*a beautiful flower*
Of Sharon . . . . Song 2:1
Desert shall blossom . . . . Is. 35:1

Rosh—*head, chief*
1. Benjamin's son . . . . Gen. 46:21
2. Northern people connected with Meshech and Tubal . . . . Ezek. 38:2

Rot—*to decay*
A. *Used literally of:*
Sickness . . . . Num. 5:21-27
Hardwood trees . . . . Is. 40:20
B. *Used figuratively of:*
Wicked . . . . Prov. 10:7
Foolish wife . . . . Prov. 12:4

Rowing—*to navigate a boat with oars*
Against odds . . . . Jon. 1:13
With much labor . . . . Mark 6:48

Royal—*belonging to a king*
A. *Used literally of:*
King's children . . . . 2 Kin. 11:1
Robes of royalty . . . . Esth. 6:8
City of a king . . . . 2 Sam. 12:26
B. *Used spiritually of:*
True Israel . . . . Is. 62:3
True Church . . . . 1 Pet. 2:9

Ruby—*a valuable gem* (red pearl)
Very valuable . . . . Prov. 3:15
Wisdom more valuable than . . . . Job 28:18
Good wife above price of . . . . Prov. 31:10
Reddish color . . . . Lam. 4:7

Rudder—*a steering apparatus*
Literally . . . . Acts 27:40
Figuratively . . . . James 3:4

Rudeness—*discourtesy*
Shown toward:
Christ . . . . Matt. 26:67, 68
Paul . . . . Acts 23:2

Rue—*a pungent perennial shrub*
Tithed by Pharisees . . . . Luke 11:42

Rufus—*red-haired*
1. Son of Simeon of Cyrene . . . . Mark 15:21
2. Christian of Rome . . . . Rom. 16:13
Probably the same as 1.

Ruhamah—*pitied*
Symbolic name for Israel . . . . Hos. 2:1

Rule—*to govern*
A. *Of natural things:*
Sun and moon . . . . Gen. 1:16, 18
Sea . . . . Ps. 89:9
B. *Among men:*
Man over woman . . . . Gen. 3:16
King over people . . . . Ezra 4:20
Diligent over the lazy . . . . Prov. 12:24
Servant over a son . . . . Prov. 17:2
Rich over poor . . . . Prov. 22:7
Servants over a people . . . . . . Neh. 5:15
C. *Of the Messiah:*
Predicted . . . . Is. 40:9, 10
Promised . . . . Zech. 6:13
Victorious . . . . Ps. 110:2
Announced . . . . Matt. 2:6
Established . . . . Rev. 12:5
Described . . . . Rev. 2:27

Ruler—*one who governs*
A. *Good characteristics of:*
Upholding the good . . . . Rom. 13:3
Believing . . . . Matt. 9:18, 23
Chosen by God . . . . 2 Sam. 7:8
B. *Bad characteristics of:*
Men-pleasers . . . . John 12:42, 43
Ignorant . . . . Acts 3:17
Hostile . . . . Acts 4:26
Loving bribes . . . . Hos. 4:18
C. *Respect toward:*
Commanded . . . . Ex. 22:28
Illustrated . . . . Acts 23:5

Rumah—*high place*
Residence of Pedaiah . . . . 2 Kin. 23:36

Run—*to move swiftly*
A. *Used literally of:*
Man . . . . Num. 11:27
Water . . . . Ps. 105:41
Fire . . . . Ex. 9:23
Race . . . . 1 Cor. 9:24
B. *Used figuratively of:*
Eagerness in:
Evil . . . . Prov. 1:16
Good . . . . Ps. 119:32
Joy of salvation . . . . Ps. 23:5
Christian life . . . . 1 Cor. 9:26

Rush—*a cylindrical, often hollow marsh plant*
Cut off from Israel; rendered "bulrush" . . . . Is. 9:14
Concerning growth of . . . . Job 8:11
Signifying restoration . . . . Is. 35:7

Rust—*corrosion of metals*
Destruction of earthly treasures . . . . Matt. 6:19, 20
Of gold and silver . . . . James 5:3

Ruth—*female companion*
Moabitess . . . . Ruth 1:4
Follows Naomi . . . . Ruth 1:6-18
Marries Boaz . . . . Ruth 4:9-13
Ancestress of Christ . . . . Ruth 4:13, 21, 22

Ruth, the Book of—*a book of the Old Testament*
Naomi's misfortunes . . . . Ruth 1:1-14
Ruth's loyalty . . . . Ruth 1:14-22
The favor of Boaz . . . . Ruth 2:1-23
Boaz redeems . . . . Ruth 3:8—4:12
The generations of Ruth . . . . Ruth 4:13-22

S

Sabachthani—*hast thou forsaken me?*
Christ's cry on the cross . . . . Matt. 27:46

Sabaoth—*hosts*
God as Lord of . . . . Rom. 9:29
James 5:4

Sabbath—*rest*
A. *History of:*
Instituted at creation . . . . Gen. 2:2, 3
Observed before Sinai . . . . Ex. 16:22-30
Commanded at Sinai . . . . Ex. 20:8-11
Repeated at Canaan's entry . . . . Deut. 5:12-15
References to . . . . 2 Kin. 4:23
Proper observance of, described . . . . Is. 56:2-7
Postexilic Jews encouraged to keep . . . . Neh. 10:31
Perversion of, condemned by Christ . . . . Luke 13:14-17
Christ teaches on . . . . Mark 6:2
Paul preached on . . . . Acts 13:14
First day kept as, by Christians . . . . John 20:19
B. *Features concerning:*
Commemorative of creation . . . . Ex. 20:8-11
Seventh day during the Old Testament . . . . Deut. 5:14
Observance of, a perpetual covenant . . . . Ex. 31:16, 17
Made for man's good . . . . Mark 2:27
Christ's Lordship over . . . . Luke 6:5
C. *Regulations concerning:*
Work prohibited on . . . . Lev. 23:3
Cattle must rest on . . . . Ex. 20:10
Business forbidden on . . . . Jer. 17:21, 22
To last from evening until evening . . . . Lev. 23:32
Worship on . . . . Ezek. 46:3
Works of mercy on . . . . Matt. 12:12
Necessities lawful on . . . . Luke 13:15, 16
See First day of the week

Sabbath day's journey—*about 3,100 feet*
Between Mt. Olivet and Jerusalem . . . . Acts 1:12

Sabbatical year—*a rest every seventh year*
A. *Purpose of:*
Rest the land . . . . Ex. 23:10, 11
Emancipate slaves . . . . Ex. 21:2-6
Remit debts . . . . Deut. 15:1-6
B. *Allusions to, in history, in:*
Time of the judges . . . . Ruth 4:1-10
Pre-exilic times . . . . Jer. 32:6-16
Postexilic times . . . . Neh. 10:31
C. *Spiritual significance of:*
Punishment for nonobservance . . . . Lev. 26:33-35
Illustrative of spiritual release . . . . {Is. 61:1-3 / Luke 4:18-21}
Figurative of spiritual rest . . . Heb. 4:1-11
See Jubilee, Year of

Sabeans—*descendants of Sheba*
Job's property attacked by . . . . . . Job 1:13-15
Subject to Israel . . . . Is. 45:14
See Sheba 4, 5, 6

Sabtah
Son of Cush and grandson of Ham . . . . Gen. 10:7

Sabtecha
Son of Cush and grandson of Ham . . . . Gen. 10:7

Sacar—*hired*
1. Ahiam's father . . . . 1 Chr. 11:35
Called Sharar . . . . 2 Sam. 23:33
2. Family of gatekeepers . . . . 1 Chr. 26:4

Sackbut—*a wind musical instrument*
Mistranslation of a harp in Babylonian orchestra . . . . Dan. 3:5-15

Sackcloth—*a coarse fabric made of goat's hair*
A. *Worn by:*
Kings . . . . 2 Kin. 6:30
Prophets . . . . Is. 20:2
John . . . . Matt. 3:4
People . . . . Luke 10:13
Women . . . . Is. 32:11
B. *Expressive of:*
Sorrow . . . . Gen. 37:34
Repentance . . . . Joel 1:8, 13
Subjection . . . . 1 Kin. 20:31, 32
Fasting . . . . Is. 58:5
Protest . . . . Esth. 4:1-4
C. *Symbolic of:*
Severe judgment . . . . Is. 50:3
God's judgment . . . . Rev. 6:12

Sacrament (see Baptism, Christian; Lord's Supper)

Sacred places
Chosen by God . . . . Deut. 12:11
Not to trust in . . . . John 4:20-24

Sacrifice, sacrifices
A. *Requirements of:*
Upon altar only . . . . Ex. 20:24
Clean animals . . . . Gen. 8:20
To God alone . . . . Ex. 22:20
Perfect animals . . . . Lev. 22:19
At place divinely established . . . . Deut. 12:6
By appointed priests . . . . 1 Sam. 2:28
In faith . . . . Gen. 4:4
In obedience . . . . 1 Sam. 15:22
B. *Perversion of, in offering:*
To demons . . . . 1 Cor. 10:20
To idols . . . . 2 Chr. 34:25
Defective animals . . . . Mal. 1:13, 14
Without respect . . . . 1 Sam. 2:29

SUBJECT REFERENCE

C. *Inadequacy of:*
Could not atone for sins ..... Ps. 40:6
Limited to legal purification .... Heb. 9:13, 22

D. *Figurative of:*
Christ's sacrifice .... 1 Cor. 5:7
Prayer .... Ps. 141:2
Worship .... 1 Pet. 2:5
Righteousness .... Ps. 51:19

E. *Of Christ to:*
Redeem from the curse ...... Gal. 3:13
Secure our redemption ...... Matt. 20:28
Reconcile God and man ..... Rom. 5:10

Sacrilege—*profaning holy things*

A. *Done by:*
Defaming God's name ...... 2 Kin. 18:28-35
Profaning the Sabbath ...... Neh. 13:15-21
Debauching holy things ..... John 2:14-16

B. *Those guilty of:*
People .... 1 Sam. 6:19
Pagans .... Dan. 5:1-4
Priests .... Lev. 10:1-7
Pharisees .... Matt. 23:16-22

Saddle—*cloth or leather seat for a rider*
Balaam's .... Num. 22:21

Sadducees—*followers of Zadok*
Rejected by John .... Matt. 3:7
Tempted Jesus .... Matt. 16:1-12
Silenced by Jesus .... Matt. 22:23-34
Disturbed by teaching of resurrection .... Acts 4:1, 2
Opposed apostles .... Acts 5:17-40

Sadoc—*righteous*
Ancestor of Christ .... Matt. 1:14

Safe, safety—*dwelling without fear or harm*

A. *False means of:*
Wickedness .... Job 21:7-9, 17
Folly .... Job 5:2-4
False hope .... 1 Thess. 5:3

B. *True means of:*
LORD .... Ps. 4:8
LORD's protection .... Deut. 33:12
Apostolic admonition .... Phil. 3:1

Saffron—*a variety of crocus; used as a perfume or medicine*
Figurative of the bride .... Song 4:14

Sail—*an expanse of material used to catch the wind and propel a sailing ship*
Figurative of:
Enemies' weakness .... Is. 33:23
The pride of Tyre .... Ezek. 27:7

Sailors—*mariners*
Skilled .... 1 Kin. 9:27
Fearful .... Jon. 1:5
Cry bitterly .... Ezek. 27:8-36
Storm-tossed .... Acts 27:18-31

Saints—*God's redeemed people*

A. *Descriptive of:*
Old Testament believers ..... Matt. 27:52
Christians .... Acts 9:32, 41
Christian martyrs .... Rev. 16:6
Present with Christ at His return .... 1 Thess. 3:13

B. *Their weaknesses, subject to:*
Needs .... 2 Cor. 9:1, 12; Rom. 12:13
Persecution .... Dan. 7:21, 25

C. *Their duty to:*
Keep God's Word .... Jude 3
Grow spiritually .... Eph. 4:12
Avoid evil .... Eph. 5:3
Judge Christians .... 1 Cor. 6:1, 2
Pray for others .... Eph. 6:18
Minister to others .... Heb. 6:10

D. *God's protection of, He:*
Forsakes them not .... Ps. 37:28
Gathers them .... Ps. 50:5
Keeps them .... 1 Sam. 2:9
Counts them precious .... Ps. 116:15
Intercedes for them .... Rom. 8:27
Will glorify them .... 2 Thess. 1:10

Salamis—*a town of Cyprus*
Paul preaches here .... Acts 13:4, 5

Salchah—*wandering*
City in Bashan .... Deut. 3:10

Salem—*peace*
Jerusalem's original name ...... Gen. 14:18
Used poetically .... Ps. 76:2

Salim—*completeness*
Place near Aenon .... John 3:23

Sallai—*rejecter*
1. Benjamite chief .... Neh. 11:8
2. Priestly family .... Neh. 12:20
Called Sallu .... Neh. 12:7

Sallu—*contempt*
Benjamite family .... 1 Chr. 9:7
See Sallai 2

Salma—*clothing*
Son of Hur .... 1 Chr. 2:50, 51

Salmon
Father of Boaz .... Ruth 4:20, 21
Ancestor of Christ .... Matt. 1:4, 5

Salome—*feminine of Solomon*
1. Among ministering women .. Mark 15:40, 41
Visits empty tomb .... Mark 16:1
2. Herodias' daughter (not named in the Bible) .... Matt. 14:6-11

Salt

A. *Uses of:*
Seasoning:
Food .... Job 6:6
Sacrifice .... Lev. 2:13
Everlasting covenant .... Num. 18:19
Rubbed on infants at birth .. Ezek. 16:4
Making land unproductive ... Judg. 9:45

B. *Miracles connected with:*
Lot's wife becomes pillar of .... Gen. 19:26
Elisha purified water with .... 2 Kin. 2:19-22

C. *Figurative of:*
God's everlasting covenant ... Num. 18:19
Barrenness and desolation ... Deut. 29:23
Good influence .... Matt. 5:13
Peace in the heart .... Mark 9:50
Wise speech .... Col. 4:6
Final judgment .... Mark 9:49
Reprobation .... Ezek. 47:9, 11

Salt, City of
City in the wilderness of Judah .... Josh. 15:62

Salt Sea
Old Testament name for the Dead Sea .... Gen. 14:3; Num. 34:3, 12

Salt, Valley of—*a valley south of the Dead Sea*
Site of:
David's victory .... 2 Sam. 8:13
Amaziah's victory .... 2 Kin. 14:7

Salu—*restored*
Simeonite prince .... Num. 25:14

Salutations—*greetings from one person to another*

A. *Normal:*
Between:
Brothers .... 1 Sam. 17:22
Social ranks .... Gen. 47:7
Strangers .... 1 Sam. 10:3, 4
Christians .... Acts 18:22
On visits .... Rom. 16:21-23

B. *Examples of forms used in:*
"God be gracious" .... Gen. 43:29
"Peace be with thee" .... Judg. 19:20
"The LORD be with you" .... Ruth 2:4
"The LORD bless thee" ...... Ruth 2:4
"Blessed be thou" .... Ruth 3:10
"Hail" .... Luke 1:28
"All hail" .... Matt. 28:9

See Benediction

Salvation

A. *Descriptive of:*
National deliverance .... Ex. 14:13
Deliverance from enemies ... 2 Chr. 20:17
Messiah .... Matt. 1:21

B. *Source of, in:*
God's grace .... Eph. 2:5, 8
God's love .... Rom. 5:8
God's mercy .... Titus 3:5
Christ alone .... Acts 4:12
Cross .... 1 Cor. 1:18

C. *History of:*
Promised to Adam .... Gen. 3:15
Announced to Abram .... Gen. 12:1-3
Revealed to the prophets .... 1 Pet. 1:10-12
Longed for by the saints ..... Ps. 119:81, 174
Promised to Gentiles .... Is. 45:21, 22
To be realized by the Messiah .... Is. 59:16, 17
Seen in Christ's birth .... Luke 1:69, 77
Christ, the author .... Heb. 5:9
Appeared to all men .... Titus 2:11
Proclaimed to Israel .... Zech. 9:9
Accomplished on the cross ... John 3:14, 15
Preached through the Gospel .... Eph. 1:13
Rejected by Israel .... Acts 13:26-46
Extended to Gentiles .... Acts 28:28
This age, day of .... 2 Cor. 6:2
God's long-suffering in ...... 2 Pet. 3:9
Final, nearer each day .... Rom. 13:11
Consummated in the second advent .... Heb. 9:28
Praise for, in heaven .... Rev. 7:10

D. *Requirements of:*
Confession .... Acts 2:21
Repentance .... Mark 1:15
Faith .... John 3:14-18
Regeneration .... John 3:3-8
Holy scripture .... 2 Tim. 3:15

E. *Negative blessings of, deliverance from:*
Sin .... Matt. 1:21
Satan's power .... Heb. 2:14, 15
Wrath .... Rom. 5:9
Eternal death .... John 3:16, 17

F. *Positive blessings of:*
Chosen to .... 2 Thess. 2:13
Appointed to .... 1 Thess. 5:9
Kept unto .... 1 Pet. 1:5
Rejoiced in .... 1 Pet. 4:13
To be worked out .... Phil. 2:12

G. *Temporal aspects of:*
Past .... Eph. 2:8
Present .... 1 Cor. 1:18
Future .... Heb. 9:28

Samaria—*watch tower*
1. Capital of Israel .... 1 Kin. 16:24-29
Israel's "crown of pride" .... Is. 28:1
Besieged twice by Ben-hadad .... 1 Kin. 20:1-22
Miraculously saved .... 2 Kin. 6:8-23
Worshipers of Baal destroyed .... 2 Kin. 10:1-28
Threatened with divine judgment .... Is. 28:1-4; Amos 3:11, 12
Repopulated with foreigners .... 2 Kin. 17:24-41
2. Name of Northern Kingdom .... 1 Kin. 21:1
3. District of Palestine in Christ's time .... Luke 17:11-19
Preaching in, forbidden by Christ .... Matt. 10:5
Gospel preached .... Acts 1:8
Churches established there ... Acts 9:31
Paul preached there .... Acts 15:3

Samaritans—*inhabitants of Samaria*
Made of mixed races .... 2 Kin. 17:24-41
Seek alliance with Jews .... Ezra 4:1-4
Help of, rejected by Nehemiah .. Neh. 4:1, 2
Christ and the woman of .... John 4:5-42
Story of "the good Samaritan" .. Luke 10:30-37
Beliefs of .... John 4:25
Converts among .... Acts 8:5-25

Samech
Letter of the Hebrew alphabet .. Ps. 119:113-120

Samgar-nebo—*be gracious, Nebo*
Prince of Nebuchadnezzar ...... Jer. 39:3

SUBJECT	REFERENCE
Samlah—*a garment*	
Edomite king	Gen. 36:36, 37
Samos—*an island off the coast of Lydia*	
Visited by Paul	Acts 20:15
Samothracia—*an island in the Aegean Sea*	
Visited by Paul	Acts 16:11
Samson—*sunlike*	
A. *Life of:*	
Birth of, predicted	Judg. 13:2-23
God's Spirit moves him	Judg. 13:24, 25
Desired a Philistine wife	Judg. 14:1-9
Propounded a riddle	Judg. 14:10-14
Betrayed, kills 30 men	Judg. 14:15-20
Enticed by Delilah, loses strength	Judg. 16:4-20
Blinded and bound	Judg. 16:21
Destroyed over 3,000 in his death	Judg. 16:22-31 Heb. 11:32
B. *Contrasts of his life:*	
Parents' concern; his unconcern	Judg. 13:8
Obedient, victorious; disobedient, defeated	Judg. 15:14
Seeks revenge; is revenged	Judg. 15:1-8
Spirit-moved; animated by lust	Judg. 15:14
Physically strong; morally weak	Judg. 16:3, 12
Greater victory in death than in life	Judg. 16:29, 30 Heb. 11:32
Samuel—*name of God* (a godly name)	
A. *Life of:*	
Born in answer to Hannah's prayer	1 Sam. 1:5-21
Dedicated to God before his birth	1 Sam. 1:11, 22
Brought to Shiloh	1 Sam. 1:24-28
His mother praised God for	1 Sam. 2:1-10
Received a revelation concerning Eli's house	1 Sam. 3:1-19
Recognized as a prophet	1 Sam. 3:20, 21
Became a circuit judge	1 Sam. 7:15-17
Organized porter service	1 Chr. 9:22 1 Chr. 26:28
Called Israel to repentance	1 Sam. 7:3-6
Anointed Saul as king	1 Sam. 10:1
Lamented in death	1 Sam. 25:1
B. *Character of:*	
Inspired as a writer	1 Chr. 29:29
Inspired as a prophet	Acts 3:24
Diligent as a judge	1 Sam. 7:15-17
Faithful to God	Heb. 11:32-34
Industrious in service	1 Chr. 9:22
Devout in life	Jer. 15:1
Powerful in prayer	Ps. 99:6
Remembered in death	1 Sam. 25:1
Samuel, the Books of—*books of the Old Testament*	
A. *1 Samuel:*	
Birth of Samuel	1 Sam. 1:19-28
Hannah's song	1 Sam. 2:1-10
The ark captured	1 Sam. 4:1-11
The ark returned	1 Sam. 6:1-21
Saul chosen as king	1 Sam. 9:1-27
Saul anointed	1 Sam. 10:1-27
Saul against the Philistines	1 Sam. 13:1-4
Saul is rejected	1 Sam. 15:10-31
David is anointed	1 Sam. 16:1-13
David and Goliath	1 Sam. 17:23-58
Jonathan's love	1 Sam. 19:1-7
Saul against David	1 Sam. 23:6-29
David spares Saul	1 Sam. 24:1-8 1 Sam. 26:1-16
The medium of En-dor	1 Sam. 28:7-25
David against the Amalekites	1 Sam. 30:1-31
Death of Saul	1 Sam. 31:1-13
B. *2 Samuel:*	
David's lament	2 Sam. 1:17-27
David anointed as king	2 Sam. 2:1-7
The ark in Zion	2 Sam. 6:1-19
David plans the Temple	2 Sam. 7:1-29
The kingdom expands	2 Sam. 8:1-18
David and Bath-sheba	2 Sam. 11:1-27
Nathan rebukes David	2 Sam. 12:1-12
David repents	2 Sam. 12:13, 14
David's child dies	2 Sam. 12:15-23

SUBJECT	REFERENCE
Amnon and Tamar	2 Sam. 13:1-19
The mighty men	2 Sam. 23:8-39
David takes a census	2 Sam. 24:1-25
Sanballat—*Sin* (the moon-god) *has given life*	
Influential Samaritan	Neh. 2:10
Opposes Nehemiah's plans	Neh. 4:7, 8
Seeks to assassinate Nehemiah	Neh. 6:1-4
Fails in intimidation	Neh. 6:5-14
His daughter marries Eliashib, the high priest	Neh. 13:4, 28
Sanctification—*growing in holiness*	
Produced by:	
God	1 Thess. 5:23
Christ	Heb. 2:11
Holy Spirit	1 Pet. 1:2
Truth	John 17:17, 19
Christ's blood	Heb. 9:14
Prayer	1 Tim. 4:4, 5
See Godliness; Holiness of Christians; Piety	
Sanctimoniousness—*assumed and pretended holiness*	
Condemned by Christ	Matt. 6:5
Sanctuary (see Holy of Holies; Tabernacle)	
Sand	
Figurative uses of:	
One's posterity	Gen. 22:17
Weight	Job 6:3
Large number of people	Josh. 11:4
God's thoughts toward us	Ps. 139:17, 18
Sandals, Shoe—*leather strapped to the feet*	
A. *Characteristics of:*	
Worn on the feet	1 Kin. 2:5
Tied by a latchet	Gen. 14:23
Some considered worthless	Amos 2:6
Used for dress occasions	Luke 15:22
Worn as adornment	Song 7:1
Worn out after a journey	Josh. 9:5, 13
Preserved supernaturally	Deut. 29:5
Worn by Christ's disciples	Mark 6:9
B. *Symbolism of:*	
Taking on—readiness for a journey	Ex. 12:11
Putting off—reverence before God	Ex. 3:5 Josh. 5:15
Want of—mourning	2 Sam. 15:30
Giving to another—manner of attestation in Israel	Ruth 4:7, 8
To unloose another's—act of homage	Luke 3:16
C. *Figurative of:*	
Preparation for service	Eph. 6:15
Alertness	Is. 5:27
Sanitation and hygiene	
A. *Laws relating to:*	
Dead bodies	Lev. 11:24-40
Contagion	Num. 9:6, 10
Leprosy	Lev. 13:2-59
Menstruation	Lev. 15:19-30
Women in childbirth	Lev. 12:2-8
Man's discharge	Lev. 15:2-18
B. *Provisions for health:*	
Washing	Deut. 23:10, 11
Burning	Num. 31:19-23
Isolation	Lev. 13:2-5, 31-33
Destruction	Lev. 14:39-45
Covering excrement	Deut. 23:12, 13
Sanity, spiritual	
Young men urged to	Titus 2:6
Accomplished by Christ	Luke 8:35
Illustrated by Paul's change	Acts 26:11, 25
Sansannah—*palm branch*	
Town in south Judah	Josh. 15:31
Sap—*the living fluid of woody plants*	
Lord's trees full of	Ps. 104:16
Saph—*basin*	
Philistine giant	2 Sam. 21:18
Called Sippai	1 Chr. 20:4
Saphir—*glittering*	
Town of Judah	Mic. 1:11

SUBJECT	REFERENCE
Sapphira—*beautiful*	
Wife of Ananias	Acts 5:1
Struck dead for lying	Acts 5:1-11
Sapphire—*a precious stone*	
Worn by high priest	Ex. 28:18
John's vision	Rev. 21:19
Sarah, Sarai—*princess*	
Wife of Abram	Gen. 11:29-31
Abraham's half-sister	Gen. 20:11-13
Represented as Abram's sister	Gen. 12:10-20
Barren	Gen. 11:30
Gave Abram her maid	Gen. 16:1-3
Promised a son	Gen. 17:15-21 Rom. 9:9
Gave birth to Isaac	Gen. 21:1-8
Saraph—*burning*	
Descendant of Judah	1 Chr. 4:22
Sarcasm—*a biting taunt, mock*	
A. *Purposes of, to:*	
Recall injustice	Judg. 9:7-19
Remind of duty neglected	1 Sam. 26:15
Mock idolaters	1 Kin. 18:27
Deflate pride	1 Kin. 20:10, 11
Warn of defeat	2 Kin. 14:8-12
B. *Uttered by:*	
Friend	Job 11:2-12
Enemies	Neh. 4:2, 3
Persecutors	Matt. 27:28, 29
Apostle	Acts 23:1-5
God	Jer. 25:27
Sardis—*the chief city of Lydia in Asia Minor*	
One of the seven churches	Rev. 1:11
Sardites	
Descendants of Sered	Num. 26:26
Sardius—*a precious stone*	
Used in "breastplate"	Ex. 28:15-17
In the Garden of Eden	Ezek. 28:13
Worn by Priest	Ex. 28:17
Sardonyx—*a precious stone*	
In John's vision	Rev. 21:19, 20
Sargon—*the constituted king*	
King of Assyria	Is. 20:1
Sarid—*survivor*	
Village of Zebulun	Josh. 19:10, 12
Saron—*same as Sharon*	
Inhabitants turn to the Lord	Acts 9:35
Sarsechim	
Prince of Nebuchadnezzar	Jer. 39:3
Satan—*adversary*	
A. *Names of* (see Devil)	
B. *Designs of, to:*	
Undo God's work	Mark 4:15
Make men turn away from God	Job 2:4, 5
Instigate evil	John 13:2, 27
Secure men's worship	Luke 4:6-8 2 Thess. 2:3, 4
C. *Character of:*	
Deceiver	Rev. 12:9
Father of lies	John 8:44
Adversary	1 Pet. 5:9
D. *Methods of:*	
Disguises himself	2 Cor. 11:14
Insinuates doubt	Gen. 3:1
Misuses Scripture	Matt. 4:6
Uses schemes	2 Cor. 2:11
Afflicts believers	Luke 13:16
E. *Judgment upon:*	
Bound	Mark 3:27
Cast out	John 12:31
Judged	John 16:11
Bruised	Rom. 16:20
Assigned to hell	Matt. 25:41
Satiate(d)—*To be satisfied*	
Scorners and fools shall be	Prov. 1:22, 31
The sword shall be	Jer. 46:10
Satire—*exposing problems to ridicule*	
Jesus' devastating use of	Matt. 23:1-33

SUBJECT REFERENCE

Satisfaction—*that which completely fulfills*

A. *Of physical things:*
- Sexual pleasures ... Prov. 5:19
- Bread of heaven ... Ps. 105:40
- Long life ... Ps. 91:16

B. *Of spiritual things, God's:*
- Mercy ... Ps. 90:14
- Presence ... Ps. 17:15

C. *Of things empty of:*
- Labor ... Is. 55:2
- Sinful ways ... Ezek. 16:28, 29
- Persecution ... Job 19:22

Satrap—*protector of the land*
- Officials appointed over the kingdom ... Dan. 6:1

Satyr—*he-goat, hairy one* (a Greek god)
- Objects of worship ("devils") ... 2 Chr. 11:15

Saul—*asked* (of God)
- Son of Kish; first king of Israel ... 1 Sam. 9:1, 2
- Seeks his father's asses ... 1 Sam. 9:3-14
- Meets Samuel ... 1 Sam. 9:16-27
- Anointed as king ... 1 Sam. 10:1-16
- Victories and family ... 1 Sam. 14:47-52
- Fights against Philistines, becomes jealous of David ... {1 Sam. 17:1-58, 1 Sam. 18:6-13
- Promises his daughter to David ... 1 Sam. 18:14-30
- Seeks to murder David ... 1 Sam. 19:1-24
- Pursues David ... 1 Sam. 23:1-28
- His life spared by David ... 1 Sam. 26:1-25
- Defeated, commits suicide ... 1 Sam. 31:1-6
- Burial of ... 1 Sam. 31:7-13
- David's lament over ... 2 Sam. 1:17-27
- Sin of, exposed ... 2 Sam. 21:1-9

Savior—*one who saves*

Applied to:
- God ... Ps. 106.21
- Christ ... 2 Tim. 1:10

Savior, Jesus as

A. *Characteristics of:*
- Only ... Acts 4:10, 12
- Complete ... Col. 2:10
- Powerful ... Jude 24
- Authoritative ... John 10:18
- Universal ... 1 Tim. 4:10

B. *Announcement of, by:*
- Prophets ... Is. 42:6, 7
- Angels ... Matt. 1:20, 21
- John the Baptist ... John 1:29
- Christ ... John 12:44-50
- Peter ... Acts 5:31
- Paul ... 1 Tim. 1:15
- John ... 1 John 4:14

C. *Office of, involves His:*
- Becoming man ... Heb. 2:14
- Perfect righteousness ... Heb. 5:8, 9
- Perfect obedience ... Rom. 5:19, 20
- Dying for us ... 1 Pet. 1:18-20

D. *Saves us from:*
- Wrath ... Rom. 5:9
- Sin ... John 1:29
- Death ... John 11:25, 26

Saw—*a toothed tool for cutting*
- Stones ... 1 Kin. 7:9
- Wood ... Is. 10:15
- For torture ... 1 Chr. 20:3

Scab
- Disqualifies an offering ... Lev. 22:21, 22
- Priest observes ... Lev. 13:6-8
- Israel threatened with ... Deut. 28:27

Scabbard—*a sheath*
- For God's Word ... Jer. 47:6

Scandal—*something disgraceful in*
- Priesthood ... 1 Sam. 2:22-24
- Family ... 2 Sam. 13:1-22

Scant measure
- Abomination ... Mic. 6:10

Scapegoat—*a goat of departure*
- Bears sin away ... Lev. 16:8-22
- Typical of Christ ... Is. 53:6, 11, 12

Scarlet—*a brilliant crimson*

A. *Literal uses of, for:*
- Tabernacle ... Ex. 26:1, 31, 36
- Identification ... Gen. 38:28, 30

B. *Symbolic uses of:*
- Royalty ... Matt. 27:28
- Prosperity ... 2 Sam. 1:24
- Conquest ... Nah. 2:3
- Deep sin ... Is. 1:18

Scatter—*to disperse abroad*

A. *Applied to:*
- Nations ... Gen. 11:8, 9
- Christians ... Acts 8:1, 4

B. *Caused by:*
- Sin ... 1 Kin. 14:15, 16
- Persecution ... Acts 11:19

Scepter—*a royal staff*
- Sign of authority ... Esth. 4:11
- Of Judah's tribe ... Gen. 49:10
- Promise concerning ... Num. 24:17
- Fulfilled in Christ ... Heb. 1:8

Sceva
- Jewish priest at Ephesus ... Acts 19:14

Schemes of Satan
- Known by Christians ... 2 Cor. 2:11
- Warnings against ... 2 Cor. 11:3, 13-15
- Armor provided against ... Eph. 6:11
- World falls before ... Rev. 13:1-18

Schin
- Letter of the Hebrew alphabet ... Ps. 119:161-168

Schism—*a division within a body*
- Prohibition concerning ... 1 Cor. 12:25
- Translated "rent" and "division" ... Matt. 9:16

Scholars—*men reputed for learning*
- Numbered by David ... 1 Chr. 25:1, 7, 8
- God's judgment against ... Mal. 2:12
- Moses, an expert ... Acts 7:22
- Gamaliel, famous as ... Acts 5:34

School—*an institution of learning*
- Home ... Deut. 6:6-10
- Temple ... 1 Chr. 25:7, 8
- In Ephesus ... Acts 19:1, 9
- Levites, teachers of ... 2 Chr. 17:7-9
- Best subjects of ... Is. 50:4

Schoolmaster—*a tutor*
- Applied to the Mosaic law ... Gal. 3:24, 25

Science—*exact knowledge*

A. *Implied reference to:*
- Architecture ... 2 Chr. 2:1-18
- Astronomy ... Gen. 15:5
- Biology ... Ps. 139:13-16
- Carpentry ... Gen. 6:14-16
- Medicine ... Ps. 103:3
- Meteorology ... Job 38:22-38
- Surveying ... Ezek. 40:5, 6

B. *Significance of, to:*
- Manifest God's existence ... Ps. 19:1-6
- Prove God's prophecies ... Jer. 25:12
- Illustrate heaven's glory ... Rev. 21:9-23
- Point to Christ as source of ... Col. 2:3

Scorners—*arrogant disdainers of others*

A. *Classified among:*
- Fools ... Prov. 1:22
- Wicked ... Prov. 9:7

B. *Described as:*
- Unwilling to take rebuke ... Prov. 9:7, 8
- Incorrigible ... Prov. 15:12
- Abomination ... Prov. 24:9

Scorpion—*an eight-legged creature having a poisonous tail*

A. *Used literally of:*
- Desert creatures ... Deut. 8:15
- Poisonous creatures ... Luke 10:19

B. *Used figuratively of:*
- Heavy burdens ... 1 Kin. 12:11
- Agents of antichrist ... Rev. 9:3, 5, 10

Scourging—*whipping*

A. *Objects of:*
- Christ ... John 19:1
- Christians ... Matt. 10:17
- Paul ... Gal. 6:17

B. *Inflicted by:*
- Roman government ... Acts 22:25-29

Screech owl—*a nocturnal creature*
- Dwells in ruins ... Is. 34:14

Scribe's knife—*a knife used to sharpen reed pens*
- Used by Jehoiakim on Jeremiah's scroll ... Jer. 36:23-28

Scribes—*experts in legal matters*

A. *Employment of:*
- Transcribers of legal contracts ... Jer. 32:12
- Keepers of records ... Jer. 36:25, 26
- Advisers in state affairs ... 1 Chr. 27:32
- Custodians of draft records ... 2 Kin. 25:19
- Collectors of Temple revenue ... 2 Kin. 12:10
- Teacher of the Law ... Ezra 7:6, 10, 12

B. *Characteristics of, in New Testament times, their:*
- Righteousness external ... Matt. 5:20
- Teaching without authority ... Matt. 7:29

C. *Their attitude toward Christ:*
- Accusing Him of blasphemy ... Mark 2:6, 7
- Seeking to accuse ... Luke 6:7
- Questioning His authority ... Luke 20:1, 2

D. *Christ's attitude toward:*
- Exposes them ... Matt. 23:13-36
- Condemns them ... Luke 20:46, 47
- Calls them hypocrites ... Matt. 15:1-9

Scrip—*a traveler's bag, wallet*

Used by:
- Shepherds ... 1 Sam. 17:40
- Travelers ... Luke 9:3

Scriptures—*God's revelation*

A. *Called:*
- Word of God ... Heb. 4:12
- Word of truth ... James 1:18
- Oracles of God ... Rom. 3:2
- Word ... James 1:21-23
- Holy Scriptures ... Rom. 1:2
- Sword of the Spirit ... Eph. 6:17
- Scriptures of the prophets ... Rom. 16:26

B. *Described as:*
- Authoritative ... 1 Pet. 4:11
- Inspired ... 2 Tim. 3:16
- Effectual in life ... 1 Thess. 2:13
- True ... Ps. 119:160
- Perfect ... Ps. 19:7
- Sharp ... Heb. 4:12
- Pure ... Prov. 30:5

C. *Inspiration of, proved by:*
- External evidence ... Heb. 2:1-4
- Internal nature ... 2 Tim. 3:16, 17
- Infallibility ... John 10:35
- Fulfillment of prophecy ... John 5:39, 45-47

D. *Understanding of, by:*
- Spirit's illumination ... 1 Cor. 2:10-14
- Searching ... John 5:39
- Reasoning ... Acts 17:2
- Comparing ... 2 Pet. 1:20, 21
- Human help ... Acts 17:10-12

E. *Proper uses of:*
- Regeneration ... 1 Pet. 1:23
- Salvation ... 2 Tim. 3:15
- Producing life ... John 20:31
- Searching our hearts ... Heb. 4:12
- Spiritual growth ... Acts 20:32
- Sanctification ... John 17:17
- Illumination ... Ps. 119:105
- Keeping from sin ... Ps. 119:9, 11
- Defeating Satan ... Eph. 6:16, 17
- Proving truth ... Acts 18:28

F. *Misuses of, by:*
- Satan ... Matt. 4:6
- Hypocrites ... Matt. 22:23-29
- False teachers ... 2 Cor. 2:17
- Unlearned ... 2 Pet. 3:16

SUBJECT — REFERENCE

G. *Positive attitudes toward:*
- Let dwell in richly ... Col. 3:16
- Search daily ... Acts 17:11
- Hide in the heart ... Ps. 119:11
- Delight in ... Ps. 1:2
- Love ... Ps. 119:97, 113, 167
- Receive with meekness ... James 1:21
- Teach to children ... Deut. 11:19
- Obey ... James 1:22
- Read ... Deut. 17:19

H. *Negative attitudes toward, not to:*
- Add to or subtract from ... Deut. 4:2
- Handle deceitfully ... 2 Cor. 4:2
- Wrest ... 2 Pet. 3:16
- Invalidating by traditions ... Mark 7:9-13

I. *Fulfillment of, cited to show:*
- Christ's:
  - Mission ... Luke 4:16-21
  - Death ... Luke 24:27, 45-47
  - Rejection ... Acts 28:25-29
  - Resurrection ... Acts 2:24-31
- Spirit's descent ... John 14:16-21
- Faith ... Rom. 4:3

J. *Distortion of:*
- Condemned ... Prov. 30:5, 6; Rev. 22:18-20
- Predicted ... 2 Tim. 4:3, 4

K. *Memorization of:*
- Keeps from sin ... Ps. 119:11
- Gives understanding ... Ps. 119:130
- Facilitates prayer ... John 15:7

Scriptures, devotional readings

A. *For personal needs:*
- Comfort ... Ps. 43:1-5; Rom. 8:26-28
- Courage ... Ps. 46:1-11; 2 Cor. 4:7-18
- Direction ... Heb. 4:16; James 1:5, 6
- Peace ... Ps. 4:1-8; Phil. 4:4-7
- Relief ... Ps. 91:1-16; 2 Cor. 12:8-10
- Rest ... Matt. 11:28-30; Rom. 8:31-39
- Temptation ... Ps. 1:1-6; 1 Cor. 10:6-13; James 1:12-16

B. *For Instruction:*
- Sermon on the mount ... Matt. 5:1—7:29
- Prayer ... Matt. 6:5-15; Phil. 4:6, 7
- Golden rule ... Matt. 7:12
- Great commandment ... Matt. 22:36-40
- Salvation ... John 3:1-36
- Good shepherd ... John 10:1-18
- Spiritual fruit ... John 15:1-17; Gal. 5:22, 23
- Guilt ... Rom. 8:1
- Righteousness ... Rom. 3:19-28
- Justification ... Rom. 5:1-21
- Christian service ... Rom. 12:1-21; Rom. 13:1-14
- Love ... 1 Cor. 13:1-13
- Stewardship ... 2 Cor. 8:1-24; 2 Cor. 9:1-15
- Regeneration ... Eph. 2:1-10
- Christ's exaltation ... Phil. 2:5-11
- Resurrection ... 1 Thess. 4:13-18
- Judgment ... Rev. 20:10-15
- New heaven and earth ... Rev. 21:1-27; Rev. 22:1-5

Scriptures, distortion of
- Condemned ... Prov. 30:5, 6
- Turning unto fables ... 2 Tim. 4:3, 4
- By unlearned ... 2 Pet. 3:15-17
- God will punish ... Rev. 22:18-20

Scroll—*a papyrus or leather roll* (book)
- Applied to the heavens ... Is. 34:4
- Sky split apart like a ... Rev. 6:14

Scum—*the residue of dirt*
- Used figuratively ... Ezek. 24:6-12

Scythians—*natives of Scythia*
- In the Christian church ... Col. 3:11

Sea—*a large body of water*

A. *Described as:*
- Created by God ... Acts 4:24
- Deep ... Ps. 68:22
- Turbulent and dangerous ... Ps. 89:9
- All rivers run into ... Eccl. 1:7
- Bound by God's decree ... Jer. 5:22
- Manifesting God's works ... Ps. 104:24, 25

B. *List of, in the Bible:*
- Great Sea (Mediterranean) ... Ezek. 47:10
- Salt or Dead Sea ... Gen. 14:3
- Red Sea ... Ex. 10:19
- Sea of Galilee (Chinnereth) ... Num. 34:11
- Adriatic ... Acts 27:27

C. *Figurative of:*
- Extension of the Gospel ... Is. 11:9
- Righteousness ... Is. 48:18
- False teachers ... Jude 13

Sea, molten
- Vessel in the Temple ... 1 Kin. 7:23

Sea of glass
- Before the throne of God ... Rev. 4:6

Seal—*instrument used to authenticate ownership*

A. *Used literally to:*
- Guarantee business deals ... Jer. 32:11-14
- Ratify covenants ... Neh. 10:1
- Insure a prophecy ... Dan. 9:24
- Protect books ... Rev. 5:2, 5, 9
- Lock doors ... Matt. 27:66

B. *Used figuratively of:*
- Ownership of married love ... Song 4:12; Song 8:6
- Hidden things ... Is. 29:11
- Acceptance of Christ ... John 3:33
- God's witness to Christ ... John 6:27
- Believer's security ... 2 Cor. 1:22
- Assurance ... Eph. 4:30
- God's ownership of His people ... Rev. 7:3-8

Seamstress—*a dressmaker*
- Dorcas known as ... Acts 9:36-42

Search—*to make intensive investigation*

A. *Applied literally to:*
- Land ... Num. 13:2-32
- Lost article ... Gen. 31:34-37
- Records ... Ezra 4:15, 19
- Child ... Matt. 2:8
- Scriptures ... John 5:39
- Enemy ... 1 Sam. 23:23

B. *Applied figuratively to:*
- Man's heart ... Ps. 139:1, 23
- Understanding ... Prov. 2:4
- Conscience ... Prov. 20:27
- Self-examination ... Judg. 5:16

Season—*a period of time*

A. *Descriptive of:*
- Period of the year ... Gen. 1:14
- Revealed times ... 1 Thess. 5:1
- Prophetic period ... Rev. 6:11
- Right time ... Deut. 11:14
- Short period ... Philem. 15
- Appointed time ... Num. 9:2, 3, 7

B. *Of the year:*
- Guaranteed by God ... Gen. 8:22
- Proof of God's providence ... Acts 14:17
- Indicated by the moon ... Ps. 104:19

Seat—*a place of authority*

A. *Descriptive of:*
- Inner court ... Ezek. 8:3
- Assembly ... Matt. 23:6

B. *Figurative of:*
- God's throne ... Job 23:3
- Association with evil ... Ps. 1:1
- Satanic power ... Rev. 13:2

Seba
- Cush's oldest son ... Gen. 10:7
- See Sabeans

Sebat
- Eleventh month of the Hebrew year ... Zech. 1:7

Secacah—*thicket*
- Village of Judah ... Josh. 15:1, 61

Sechu—*observatory*
- Village near Ramah ... 1 Sam. 19:22

Second

A. *Descriptive of:*
- Next in order ... Gen. 1:8
- Repetition ... 1 Kin. 18:34
- Second advent ... Heb. 9:28

B. *Used figuratively and spiritually of:*
- Christ ... 1 Cor. 15:47
- Finality ... Titus 3:10
- New covenant ... Heb. 8:7
- Death ... Rev. 2:11

Second chance
- None in hell ... Luke 16:23-31

Second coming of Christ

A. *Described as:*
- Day of:
  - The Lord ... 1 Thess. 5:2
  - Lord Jesus ... 1 Cor. 5:5
  - God ... 2 Pet. 3:12
- That day ... 2 Thess. 1:10
- Last day ... John 12:48

B. *Purposes of, to:*
- Fulfill His Word ... John 14:3
- Raise the dead ... 1 Thess. 4:13-18
- Destroy death ... 1 Cor. 15:25, 26
- Gather the elect ... Matt. 24:31
- Judge the world ... Matt. 25:32-46
- Glorify believers ... Col. 3:4
- Reward God's people ... Matt. 16:27

C. *Time of:*
- Unknown to us ... Matt. 24:27, 36
- After the Gospel's proclamation to all ... Matt. 24:14
- After the rise of antichrist ... 2 Thess. 2:2, 3
- At the last trump ... 1 Cor. 15:51, 52
- In days like Noah's ... Matt. 24:37-47

D. *Manner of:*
- In the clouds ... Matt. 24:30
- In flaming fire ... 2 Thess. 1:7, 8
- With the angels ... Matt. 25:31
- As a thief ... 1 Thess. 5:2, 3
- In His glory ... Matt. 25:31

E. *Believer's attitude toward, to:*
- Wait for ... 1 Cor. 1:7
- Look for ... Titus 2:13
- Be ready for ... Matt. 24:42-51
- Love ... 2 Tim. 4:8
- Be busy until ... Luke 19:13-18
- Pray for ... Rev. 22:20

Secret disciples
- Among Jewish leaders ... John 12:42
- Fearful of Jewish disfavor ... John 19:38

Secret prayer
- Commended by Christ ... Matt. 6:6
- Practiced by:
  - Christ ... Mark 1:35
  - Peter ... Acts 10:9

Secret things
- Known by God ... Deut. 29:29
- See Mystery

Secrets—*things unknown to others*
- To be kept ... Prov. 25:9
- Sign of faithfulness ... Prov. 11:13
- To those who expose, condemned ... Prov. 20:19

Sects of Christ's time
- Pharisees ... Acts 15:5
- Sadducees ... Acts 5:17
- Herodians ... Matt. 22:16
- Christians described as ... Acts 24:5

Secundus—*second*
- Thessalonian Christian ... Acts 20:4

Security of the saints

A. *Expressed by:*
- "Shall never perish" ... John 10:28
- "None of them is lost" ... John 17:12
- "Protected by the power of God" ... 1 Pet. 1:5

B. *Guaranteed by:*
- Spirit's sealing ... 2 Cor. 1:21, 22

SUBJECT — REFERENCE

Christ's intercession .... Rom. 8:34-39
God's power .... Jude 24

See Assurance

Sedition—*attack upon an established government*

Miriam and Aaron, against Moses .... Num. 12:1-13

Seducers—*those who lead others astray*

A. *Agents of:*

Evil spirits .... 1 Tim. 4:1
False teachers .... Mark 13:22
Evil leaders .... 2 Kin. 21:9

B. *Characteristics of:*

Grow worse .... 2 Tim. 3:13
Self-deceived .... Prov. 12:26
Lead to evil .... Rev. 2:20
Preach false message .... Ezek. 13:9, 10

Seed—*the essential element of transmitting life*

A. *Descriptive of:*

One's ancestry .... Gen. 12:7
Messianic line .... Gen. 21:12
Nation .... 2 Kin. 17:20
Christ .... Gal. 3:16, 19

B. *Figurative of true believers:*

Born of God .... 1 Pet. 1:23
Abraham's true children .... Gal. 3:29
Children of promise .... Rom. 9:7, 8
Including Israel's faithful .... Rom. 9:29

C. *Sowing of, figurative of:*

God's Word .... Matt. 13:3, 32
Spiritual blessings .... 1 Cor. 9:11
Christ's death .... John 12:24
Christian's body .... 1 Cor. 15:36-49

Seeking—*trying to obtain*

A. *Things of the world:*

Worldly things .... Matt. 6:32
One's life .... Luke 17:33
One's selfish interest .... Phil. 2:21

B. *Things of the Spirit:*

True wisdom .... Prov. 2:4
God's kingdom .... Matt. 6:33
Another's benefit .... 2 Cor. 12:14
Peace .... 1 Pet. 3:11
Heavenly country .... Heb. 11:14

Seers—*prophets*

Amos .... Amos 7:12
Asaph .... 2 Chr. 29:30
Gad .... 2 Sam. 24:11
Heman .... 1 Chr. 25:5
Samuel .... 1 Sam. 9:19
Zadok .... 2 Sam. 15:27
Iddo .... 2 Chr. 9:29
Hanani .... 2 Chr. 16:7
Jeduthun .... 2 Chr. 35:15

Segub—*exalted*

1. Son of Hiel .... 1 Kin. 16:34
2. Son of Hezron .... 1 Chr. 2:21, 22

Seir—*hairy; shaggy*

1. Mt. Seir .... Gen. 14:6
   Home of Esau .... Gen. 32:3
   Mountain range of Edom .... Gen. 36:21
   Horites dispossessed by Esau's descendants .... Deut. 2:12
   Refuge of Amalekite remnant .... 1 Chr. 4:42, 43
   Desolation of .... Ezek. 35:15
2. Landmark on Judah's boundary .... Josh. 15:10

Seirath—*rough*

Ehud's refuge .... Judg. 3:26

Seize—*to take or keep fast, hold*

Let darkness .... Job 3:6
Let us kill him and .... Matt. 21:38

Selah

Place in Edom .... 2 Kin. 14:7
Musical term found in Psalms .... Ps. 3:2
Found in .... Hab. 3:3, 9, 13

Sela-hammah-lekoth—*rock of divisions*

Cliff on the Wilderness of Maon .... 1 Sam. 23:28

SUBJECT — REFERENCE

Seled—*exultation*

Judahite .... 1 Chr. 2:30

Seleucia—*a city on the seacoast of Syria*

Paul and Barnabas embark from .... Acts 13:4

Self-abasement

Jacob, before Esau .... Gen. 33:3-10
Moses, before God .... Ex. 3:11
Roman, before Christ .... Luke 7:7-9
Christ, true example of .... Phil. 2:5-8

Self-acceptance—*having the proper attitude toward oneself*

A. *Based on, by Christians:*

Planned before birth by God .... Ps. 139:13-16
Workmanship of God .... Ps. 138:8
 .... Eph. 2:10
Christ has provided life .... John 10:10
God desires man's fellowship .... John 17:3
God's love .... Rom. 5:8
Living epistle of God .... 2 Cor. 3:2
Complete in Christ .... Col. 2:10
Chosen by God .... 1 Pet. 2:9

B. *Hindered by, false attitudes:*

Looking on outward appearance .... 1 Sam. 16:7
Questioning God's direction .... Is. 45:9
Doubting God's grace .... 2 Cor. 12:9, 10

Self-condemnation

Caused by one's:

Heart .... 1 John 3:20
Conscience .... John 8:7-9
Sins .... 2 Sam. 24:17
Mouth .... Job 9:20
Evil works .... Matt. 23:31

Self-control

A. *Origin of:*

Brought about by Christ .... Luke 8:35
Christian grace .... 2 Pet. 1:6

B. *Elements involved in:*

Ruling one's spirit .... Prov. 16:32
Soberness .... Rom. 12:3
Control of the body .... 1 Cor. 9:27

C. *Hindered by:*

Fleshly lusts .... 1 Pet. 2:11
Tongue .... Ps. 39:1, 2
Drink .... Prov. 23:29-35
Sexual sins .... 1 Thess. 4:3, 4
Unclean spirit .... Mark 5:2-16
Self-expressionism .... Prov. 25:28

Self-deception

A. *Factors contributing to:*

Scoffers .... 2 Pet. 3:3, 4
Worldliness .... Matt. 24:48-51
False teaching .... 1 Thess. 5:3
Self-deception .... Prov. 14:12

B. *Examples of:*

Babylon .... Is. 47:7-11
Jewish women .... Jer. 44:16-19
Jewish leaders .... John 8:33, 41

Self-denial

A. *Expressed by:*

"Denying" .... Titus 2:12
"Abstaining" .... 1 Pet. 4:2
"Forsaketh not" .... Luke 14:33
"Taking up the cross" .... Matt. 10:38
"Crucifying the flesh" .... Gal. 5:24
"Put off" .... Eph. 4:22
"Mortify" .... Col. 3:5

B. *Objects of:*

Appetite .... Prov. 23:2
Sinful pleasures .... Heb. 11:25, 26
Worldly ambitions .... Matt. 16:24-26

C. *Willingness to, manifested by:*

Judah .... Gen. 44:33
Moses .... Ex. 32:32
Paul .... Acts 20:22-24

D. *Commended as:*

Christian duty .... Rom. 12:1, 2
Rewardable .... Luke 18:28-30

SUBJECT — REFERENCE

Self-exaltation

A. *Manifested by:*

Satan .... Is. 14:12-15
Antichrist .... 2 Thess. 2:4
Wicked .... Ps. 73:9

B. *Evils of, seen in:*

Self-abasement .... Matt. 23:12
Pride .... Prov. 16:18

C. *Antidotes of:*

Humility .... Prov. 15:33
Christ's example .... Phil. 2:5-8

See Pride

Self-examination

A. *Purposes of, to:*

Test one's faith .... 2 Cor. 13:5
Prepare for the Lord's Supper .... 1 Cor. 11:28-32
Prove one's work .... Gal. 6:4
Prove all things .... 1 Thess. 5:21

B. *Means of:*

God Himself .... Ps. 26:2
God's Word .... Heb. 4:12
Christ's example .... Heb. 12:1, 2

Selfishness—*loving one's self first*

A. *Exemplified in:*

Self-love .... 2 Tim. 3:2
Self-seeking .... Phil. 2:21

B. *Avoidance of, by:*

Seeking the good of others .... 1 Cor. 10:24
Putting Christ first .... Phil. 1:21, 22
Manifesting love .... 1 Cor. 13:5

C. *Examples of:*

Nabal .... 1 Sam. 25:3, 11
Haman .... Esth. 6:6
James and John .... Mark 10:35-37
Jewish people .... John 6:26
Solomon .... Eccl. 2:10, 11
Rich fool .... Luke 12:16-21
Rich man .... Luke 16:19-25

D. *Consequences of:*

Poverty .... Prov. 23:21
Sin .... Rom. 13:13, 14
Loss of spirituality .... Gal. 5:16, 17

Self-righteousness

A. *Described as:*

Objectionable .... Deut. 9:4-6
Self-condemned .... Job 9:20
Unprofitable .... Is. 57:12
Like filthy rags .... Is. 64:6
Offensive .... Is. 65:5
External .... Matt. 23:25-28
One-sided .... Luke 11:42
Boastful .... Luke 18:11, 12
Insufficient .... Phil. 3:4-9

B. *Condemned because it:*

Cannot make pure .... Prov. 30:12
Cannot save .... Matt. 5:20
Rejects God's righteousness .... Rom. 10:3

C. *Examples of:*

Saul .... 1 Sam. 15:13-21
Young man .... Matt. 19:16-20
Lawyer .... Luke 10:25, 29
Pharisees .... Luke 11:39

Self-will—*stubbornness*

A. *Manifested in:*

Presumption .... Num. 14:40-45
Unbelief .... 2 Kin. 17:14
Evil heart .... Jer. 7:24
Disobeying parents .... Deut. 21:18-20
Pride .... Neh. 9:16, 29
Stubbornness .... Is. 48:4-8
Rejecting God's messengers .... Jer. 44:16
Resisting God's Spirit .... Acts 7:51
False teaching .... 2 Pet. 2:10

B. *Sin of, among Christians:*

Illustrated .... Acts 15:36-40
Warned against .... Heb. 3:7-12

C. *Examples of:*

Simeon and Levi .... Gen. 49:5, 6
Israelites .... Ex. 32:9

S

SUBJECT — REFERENCE

Saul ... 1 Sam. 15:19-23
David ... 2 Sam. 24:4
See Pride

Sem—*Greek form of Shem*
In Christ's ancestry ... Luke 3:36

Semachiah—*Jehovah supports*
Levite porter ... 1 Chr. 26:7

Semei—*Greek form of Shimei*
In Christ's ancestry ... Luke 3:26

Senaah—*thorny*
Family of returnees ... Neh. 7:38; Ezra 2:35

Senate—*the Jewish Sanhedrin*
Disturbed by miracle ... Acts 5:18-21

Senators—*old men*
Instructed by Joseph ... Ps. 105:17-23

Seneh—*thorn bush*
Sharp rock between Michmash and Gibeah ... 1 Sam. 14:4, 5

Senir, Shenir—*mount of light*
Amorite name of Mt. Hermon ... Deut. 3:9
Noted for firs ... Ezek. 27:5

Sennacherib—*Sin* (moon-god) *multiplied brothers*
Assyrian king (705-681 B.C.); son and successor of Sargon II ... 2 Kin. 18:13
Death of, by assassination ... 2 Kin. 19:37

Senses—*the faculties of feeling*
Described figuratively ... Eccl. 12:3-6
Used by Isaac ... Gen. 27:21-27
Impaired in Barzillai ... 2 Sam. 19:32-35
Use of, as evidence ... John 20:26-29
Proper use of ... Heb. 5:14

Senses, spiritual
Taste ... Ps. 34:8
Sight ... Eph. 1:18
Hearing ... Gal. 3:2

Sensual—*fleshly*
Descriptive of:
Unregenerate ... Jude 19
Worldly wisdom ... James 3:15
Same as "natural" ... 1 Cor. 2:14
Rebellious against God ... Rom. 8:7

Sensualist—*one who satisfies the physical senses*
Illustrated by:
Nabal ... 1 Sam. 25:36
Rich fool ... Luke 12:16-20

Seorim—*barley*
Name of a priestly course ... 1 Chr. 24:1-8

Separate place—*the Temple yard*
Of Ezekiel's Temple ... Ezek. 41:12

Separation—*setting apart from something*
A. *As a good act from:*
Unclean ... Lev. 15:31
Evil workers ... Num. 16:21
Heathen filthiness ... Ezra 6:21
Pagan intermarriages ... Ezra 9:1, 2
Foreigners ... Neh. 13:3
Strong drink ... Num. 6:2-6
B. *As an evil act by:*
False teachers ... Luke 6:22
Separatists ... Jude 19
Whisperers ... Prov. 16:28
Gossipers ... Prov. 17:9
C. *As descriptive of:*
God's judgment ... Deut. 29:21
God's sovereignty ... Deut. 32:8
Israel's uniqueness ... Lev. 20:24
Choice of the Levites ... Num. 8:14
Nazarite vow ... Num. 6:2-6
Christian obedience ... 2 Cor. 6:17
Union with Christ ... Rom. 8:35, 39
Christ's purity ... Heb. 7:26
Final separation ... Matt. 25:32

Sephar—*numbering*
Place on Joktan's boundary ... Gen. 10:30

Sepharad
Place inhabited by exiles ... Obad. 20

SUBJECT — REFERENCE

Sepharvaim—*an Assyrian city*
People of, sent to Samaria ... 2 Kin. 17:24, 31

Sepulcher—*a place of burial*
A. *Used literally of:*
Place of burial ... Gen. 23:6
Christ's grave ... John 19:41, 42
B. *Used figuratively of:*
Hypocrisy ... Matt. 23:27

Serah—*abundance*
Daughter of Asher ... Gen. 46:17

Seraiah—*Jehovah has prevailed*
Called Sarah ... Num. 26:46
1. David's secretary ... 2 Sam. 8:17
Called Sheva, Shisha, and Shavsha ... 2 Sam. 20:25; 1 Kin. 4:3; 1 Chr. 18:16
2. Son of Tanhumeth ... 2 Kin. 25:23
3. Son of Kenaz ... 1 Chr. 4:13, 14
4. Simeonite ... 1 Chr. 4:35
5. Chief priest ... Jer. 52:24, 27
6. Postexilic leader ... Neh. 12:1, 12
7. Signer of the covenant ... Neh. 10:2
8. Postexilic priest ... Neh. 11:11
9. Officer of King Jehoiakim ... Jer. 36:26
11. Prince of Judah; carries Jeremiah's prophecy to Babylon ... Jer. 51:59, 61

Seraphim—*burning ones*
Type of angels ... Is. 6:1, 2

Sered—*deliverance*
Son of Zebulun; founder of Sardites ... Gen. 46:14

Sergius Paulus
Roman proconsul of Cyprus converted by Paul ... Acts 13:7-12

Sermon—*a discourse on a Bible subject*
A prolonged message ... Acts 20:7

Sermon on the Mount
Preached by Christ ... Matt. 5—7
Those blessed ... Matt. 5:3-12
Salt and light ... Matt. 5:13-16
The law fulfilled ... Matt. 5:17-20
On anger ... Matt. 5:21-26
On adultery and divorce ... Matt. 5:27-32
Oaths ... Matt. 5:33-37
Love your enemies ... Matt. 5:38-48
The religious life ... Matt. 6:1-4; Matt. 6:5-15
How to pray ... Matt. 6:16-18
Undivided devotion ... Matt. 6:19-34
Judging others ... Matt. 7:1-6
Encouragement to pray ... Matt. 7:7-12
Entering the kingdom ... Matt. 7:13-23
Two foundations ... Matt. 7:24-27

Serpents
A. *Characteristics of:*
Created by God ... Job 26:13
Subtle ... Gen. 3:1
Some poisonous ... Num. 21:6
Live on rocks, walls, etc. ... Prov. 30:19
Cursed by God ... Gen. 3:14, 15
B. *Miracles connected with:*
Aaron's rod turned into ... Ex. 7:9, 15
Israelites cured by looking at ... Num. 21:6-9; John 3:14, 15
Power over, given to apostles ... Mark 16:18
Healing from bite of ... Acts 28:5, 6
C. *Figurative of:*
Intoxication ... Prov. 23:31, 32
Wisdom ... Matt. 10:16
Malice ... Ps. 58:4
Unexpected evil ... Eccl. 10:8
Enemies ... Is. 14:29
Christ ... John 3:14-16
Satan ... Rev. 20:2
Dan's treachery ... Gen. 49:17
Sting of wine ... Prov. 23:31, 32
Wickedness of sinners ... Ps. 58:3, 4

Serug—*branch*
Descendant of Shem ... Gen. 11:20-23
In Christ's ancestry ... Luke 3:35

SUBJECT — REFERENCE

Servant—*one who serves others*
A. *Descriptive of:*
Slave ... Gen. 9:25
Social inferior ... Gen. 19:2
Worshiper of God ... 1 Sam. 3:9
Messenger of God ... Josh. 1:2
Messiah ... Is. 42:1
Follower of Christ ... 2 Tim. 2:24
B. *Applied distinctively to:*
Prophets ... Zech. 1:6
Messiah ... Zech. 3:8
Moses ... Mal. 4:4
Christians ... Acts 2:18
Glorified saints ... Rev. 22:3
See Slave

Service to God
A. *Requirements of:*
Fear ... Ps. 2:11
Upright walking ... Ps. 101:6
Absolute loyalty ... Matt. 6:24
Regeneration ... Rom. 7:6
Serve the Lord ... Rom. 12:11
Humility ... Acts 20:19
Love ... Gal. 5:13
B. *Rewards of:*
Divine honor ... John 12:26
Acceptance before God ... Rom. 14:18
Inheritance ... Col. 3:24
Eternal blessedness ... Rev. 7:15; Rev. 22:3

Seth—*appointed*
Third son of Adam ... Gen. 4:25
In Christ's ancestry ... Luke 3:38

Sethur—*hidden*
Asherite spy ... Num. 13:2, 13

Setting—*woven together*
For precious stones worn by the high priest ... Ex. 28:11
Corded chains on filigree ... Ex. 28:13, 14
Same Hebrew word translated "interwoven" ... Ps. 45:13

Seven—*one more than six*
A. *Of social customs:*
Serving for a wife ... Gen. 29:20, 27
Bowing ... Gen. 33:3
Mourning ... Gen. 50:10
Feast ... Judg. 14:12, 17
Fasting ... 1 Sam. 31:13
B. *Of things:*
Days ... Gen. 2:3
Weeks ... Dan. 9:25
Months ... Lev. 23:24-44
Years ... Gen. 41:1-57
Nations ... Deut. 7:1
Ways ... Deut. 28:7
Women ... Is. 4:1
Brethren ... Mark 12:20-22
Spirits ... Matt. 12:45
Men ... Acts 6:3-5
Churches ... Rev. 1:4, 20
C. *Of rituals:*
Victims of sacrifices ... Lev. 23:18
Sprinkling of blood ... Lev. 4:6
Sprinkling of oil ... Lev. 14:16
Passover ... Ex. 12:15
Consecration ... Ex. 29:30, 35
Defilement ... Lev. 12:2
Convocation ... Lev. 23:24-44
Jubilee ... Lev. 25:8
D. *Miracles:*
Plagues ... Ex. 7:25
Jericho's fall ... Josh. 6:4, 8, 13
Naaman's baths ... 2 Kin. 5:10
Loaves ... Matt. 15:34
Baskets ... Matt. 15:37
E. *Of symbols:*
Purification ... Ps. 12:6
Worship ... Ps. 119:164
Gospel light ... Is. 30:26
Spirits ... Rev. 1:4
Seals ... Rev. 5:1
Angels ... Rev. 8:2
Heads and crowns ... Rev. 13:1
Plagues ... Rev. 15:6
Vials ... Rev. 15:7
Kings ... Rev. 17:10

SUBJECT REFERENCE

Seven sayings from the cross
1. "Father, forgive them" ...... Luke 23:34
2. "Today shalt thou be with me in paradise" ...... Luke 23:43
3. "Woman, behold thy son" ... John 19:26
4. "My God, my God" ...... Matt. 27:46
5. "I thirst" ...... John 19:28
6. "It is finished" ...... John 19:30
7. "Father, into thy hands" .... Luke 23:46

Seventy
Elders appointed ...... Ex. 24:1, 9
Years in Babylon ...... Dan. 9:2
Weeks in prophetic vision ...... Dan. 9:24
In forgiveness ...... Matt. 18:22
Disciples sent forth ...... Luke 10:1

Sexes—*male and female*
A. *Creation of:*
By God ...... Gen. 1:27
For:
Union ...... Gen. 2:23-25
Helpfulness ...... Gen. 2:18
Procreation ...... Gen. 4:1
Sexual needs ...... Prov. 5:17-19
B. *Regulations concerning:*
Distinctive clothing for ...... Deut. 22:5
Subordination of ...... 1 Cor. 11:3-16
Equality in Christ ...... Gal. 3:28
Different functions of ...... 1 Tim. 2:8-15
Love between ...... Eph. 5:22-33

Sexual love
Good and holy ...... Gen. 1:27, 28
Gen. 2:24, 25
For procreation ...... Gen. 4:1
In marriage only ...... Prov. 5:15-20
Expression of love ...... Song 1:12-15
Song 3:1-5
Mutual responsibility ...... 1 Cor. 7:3-5

Sexual perversion
A. *Types of:*
Adultery ...... Deut. 22:22-29
Prostitution ...... Deut. 23:17
Incest ...... Lev. 18:6-18
Homosexuality ...... Rom. 1:26, 27
Mankind with beasts ...... Deut. 27:21
B. *Judgment upon:*
Defilement ...... Lev. 18:22-28
Destruction ...... 1 Cor. 5:1-5
Death ...... Lev. 20:13-16

Shaalbim, Shaalabbin—*jackals*
Amorite city assigned to Danites ...... Josh. 19:42
Subdued by house of Joseph .... Judg. 1:35

Shaalbonite—*an inhabitant of Shaalbim*
Eliahba called ...... 2 Sam. 23:32

Shaaph—*friendship*
1. Descendant of Caleb ...... 1 Chr. 2:47
2. Son of Caleb ...... 1 Chr. 2:49

Shaaraim—*double gate*
1. Village in Judah ...... Josh. 15:36
2. City of Simeon ...... 1 Chr. 4:31

Shaashgaz
Persian eunuch ...... Esth. 2:14

Shabbethai—*Sabbath-born*
Postexilic Levite ...... Ezra 10:15
Interprets the law ...... Neh. 8:7, 8

Shachia—*fame of Jehovah*
Benjamite ...... 1 Chr. 8:10

Shadow
A. *Used literally of:*
Man ...... Acts 5:15
Mountain ...... Judg. 9:36
Sundial ...... 2 Kin. 20:9-11
B. *Used figuratively of:*
Protection ...... Ps. 91:1
Brevity ...... Ps. 102:11
Change ...... James 1:17
Death ...... Matt. 4:16
Types ...... Col. 2:17
Old Testament period ...... Heb. 10:1

SUBJECT REFERENCE

Shadrach
Hananiah's Babylonian name ... Dan. 1:3, 7
Cast into the fiery furnace ...... Dan. 3:1-28

Shage—*wandering*
Father of one of David's mighty men ...... 1 Chr. 11:34

Shaharaim—*double dawn*
Benjamite ...... 1 Chr. 8:8-11

Shahazimah—*heights*
Town of Issachar ...... Josh. 19:17, 22

Shake—*to move violently*
A. *Descriptive of:*
Thunder ...... Ps. 77:18
Earthquakes ...... Acts 4:31
Fear ...... Matt. 28:4
B. *Used figuratively of:*
Fear ...... Is. 14:16
Second Advent ...... Heb. 12:26, 27
Rejection ...... Luke 9:5
Acts 18:6

Shalem—*safe*
Town near Shechem; can mean "in peace" ...... Gen. 33:18

Shalim—*district of foxes*
Mentioned in Saul's pursuit ..... 1 Sam. 9:4

Shalisha—*a third part*
Mentioned in Saul's pursuit ..... 1 Sam. 9:4

Shallecheth—*a casting out*
Gate of Solomon's temple ...... 1 Chr. 26:16

Shallum—*recompense*
1. King of Israel ...... 2 Kin. 15:10-15
2. Husband of Huldah ...... 2 Kin. 22:14
3. Judahite ...... 1 Chr. 2:40, 41
4. Simeonite ...... 1 Chr. 4:25
5. Father of Hilkiah ...... 1 Chr. 6:12, 13
6. Naphtali's son ...... 1 Chr. 7:13
7. Family of porters ...... Ezra 2:42
8. Called Shelemiah ...... 1 Chr. 26:14
9. Father of Jehizkiah ...... 2 Chr. 28:12
10. One who divorced his foreign wife ...... Ezra 10:24
11. Another who divorced his foreign wife ...... Ezra 10:42
12. Son of Hallohesh ...... Neh. 3:12
13. Jeremiah's uncle ...... Jer. 32:7
14. Father of Maaseiah ...... Jer. 35:4

Shalmai—*Jehovah is recompenser*
Head of a family of Nethinim ... Ezra 2:46

Shalman
Contraction of Shalmaneser ..... Hos. 10:14

Shalmaneser—*Shulmanu* (a god) *is chief*
Assyrian king ...... 2 Kin. 17:3

Shama—*He* (God) *has heard*
Son of Hotham ...... 1 Chr. 11:44

Shamariah—*Jehovah has kept*
Son of Rehoboam ...... 2 Chr. 11:18, 19

Shamble—*meat market*
Question concerning meat bought in ...... 1 Cor. 10:25

Shame—*a feeling of guilt*
A. *Caused by:*
Rape ...... 2 Sam. 13:13
Defeat ...... 2 Chr. 32:21
Folly ...... Prov. 3:35
Idleness ...... Prov. 10:5
Pride ...... Prov. 11:2
A wicked wife ...... Prov. 12:4
Lying ...... Prov. 13:5
Stubbornness ...... Prov. 13:18
Haste in speech ...... Prov. 18:13
Mistreatment of parents ...... Prov. 19:26
Evil companions ...... Prov. 28:7
Juvenile delinquency ...... Prov. 29:15
Nakedness ...... Is. 47:3
Idolatry ...... Jer. 2:26, 27

SUBJECT REFERENCE

Impropriety ...... 1 Cor. 11:6
Lust ...... Phil. 3:19
B. *Of the unregenerate:*
Hardened in ...... Jer. 8:12
Pleasure in ...... Rom. 1:26, 27, 32
Vessels of ...... Rom. 9:21
Glory in ...... Phil. 3:19
Like foam ...... Jude 13
C. *In the Christian life, of:*
Unregenerate's life ...... Rom. 6:21
Sinful things ...... Eph. 5:12
Improper behavior ...... 1 Cor. 11:14, 22
Christ ...... Rom. 1:16

Shamed—*destruction*
Son of Elpaal ...... 1 Chr. 8:12

Shamer—*guard*
1. Levite ...... 1 Chr. 6:46
2. Asherite ...... 1 Chr. 7:30, 34

Shamgar—*cupbearer*
Judge of Israel; struck down 600 Philistines ...... Judg. 3:31

Shamhuth—*desolation*
Commander in David's army .... 1 Chr. 27:8

Shamir—*a sharp point*
1. Town in Judah ...... Josh. 15:1, 48
2. Town in Ephraim ...... Judg. 10:1
3. Levite ...... 1 Chr. 24:24

Shamma—*astonishment*
Asherite ...... 1 Chr. 7:36, 37

Shammah—*waste*
1. Son of Reuel ...... Gen. 36:13, 17
2. Son of Jesse ...... 1 Sam. 16:9
Called Shimea ...... 1 Chr. 2:13
3. One of David's mighty men ...... 2 Sam. 23:11
Also called Shammoth the Harorite ...... 1 Chr. 11:27

Shammai—*celebrated*
1. Grandson of Jerahmeel ...... 1 Chr. 2:28, 32
2. Descendant of Caleb ...... 1 Chr. 2:44, 45
3. Descendant of Judah ...... 1 Chr. 4:17

Shammoth—*waste*
One of David's mighty men ..... 1 Chr. 11:27

Shammua—*renowned*
1. Reubenite spy ...... Num. 13:2-4
2. Son of David ...... 2 Sam. 5:13, 14
3. Levite ...... Neh. 11:17
4. Postexilic priest ...... Neh. 12:1, 18

Shamsherai—*sunlike*
Son of Jeroham ...... 1 Chr. 8:26

Shapham—*youthful*
Gadite ...... 1 Chr. 5:12

Shaphan—*prudent, shy*
Scribe under Josiah ...... 2 Kin. 22:3
Takes Book of the Law to Josiah ...... 2 Kin. 22:8-10
Is sent to Huldah for interpretation ...... 2 Kin. 22:14
Assists in repairs of temple ...... 2 Chr. 34:8
Father of notable son ...... Jer. 36:10-12, 25

Shaphat—*he has judged*
1. Simeonite spy ...... Num. 13:2-5
2. Son of Shemaiah ...... 1 Chr. 3:22
3. Gadite chief ...... 1 Chr. 5:11, 12
4. One of David's herdsmen .... 1 Chr. 27:29
5. Father of the prophet Elisha ...... 1 Kin. 19:16, 19

Shapher—*beauty*
Israelite encampment ...... Num. 33:23

Sharai—*Jehovah is deliverer*
Divorced his foreign wife ...... Ezra 10:34, 40

Sharar—*firm*
Father of Ahiam ...... 2 Sam. 23:33

SUBJECT REFERENCE

Sharers

A. *Of physical things:*
Sacrifices .... 1 Cor. 10:18
Suffering .... 2 Cor. 1:7
1 Pet. 4:13

B. *Of evil things:*
Sins .... 1 Tim. 5:22

C. *Of spiritual things:*
Holiness .... Heb. 12:10
Communion .... 1 Cor. 10:16, 17
Spiritual things .... Rom. 15:27
Inheritance .... Col. 1:12

Sharezer, Sherezer—*protect the king*
1. Son of Sennacherib .... Is. 37:38
2. Sent to Zechariah concerning fasting .... Zech. 7:1-3

Sharon—*plain*
1. Coastal plain between Joppa and Mt. Carmel .... 1 Chr. 27:29
Famed for roses .... Song 2:1
2. Pasture east of the Jordan ... 1 Chr. 5:16

Sharonite—*an inhabitant of Sharon*
Shitrai .... 1 Chr. 27:29

Sharp—*having a keen edge; biting*

A. *Descriptive of:*
Stone .... Ex. 4:25
Knives .... Josh. 5:2, 3
Share .... 1 Sam. 13:20, 21
Rocks .... 1 Sam. 14:4
Arrows .... Is. 5:28

B. *Used to compare a sword with:*
Tongue .... Ps. 57:4
Adulteress .... Prov. 5:4
Mouth .... Is. 49:2
God's Word .... Heb. 4:12

C. *Figurative of:*
Deceitfulness .... Ps. 52:2
Falsehood .... Prov. 25:18
Contention .... Acts 15:39
Severe rebuke .... 2 Cor. 13:10
Christ's conquest .... Rev. 14:14-18

Sharuhen—*abode of pleasure*
Town of Judah assigned to Simeon .... Josh. 19:1, 6
Called Shaaraim .... Josh. 15:36
1 Chr. 4:31

Shashai—*whitish*
Divorced his foreign wife .... Ezra 10:34, 40

Shashak—*assaulter*
Benjamite .... 1 Chr. 8:14, 25

Shaul—*asked* (of God)
1. King of Edom .... Gen. 36:37
2. Son of Simeon .... Gen. 46:10
Founder of a tribal family ... Num. 26:13
3. Kohathite Levite .... 1 Chr. 6:24

Shave—*to cut off the hair*

A. *Used worthily to express:*
Accommodation .... Gen. 41:14
Cleansing .... Lev. 14:8, 9
Commitment .... Deut. 21:12
Mourning .... Job 1:18-20
Sorrow .... Jer. 41:5

B. *Used unworthily to express:*
Defeat of a Nazarite .... Judg. 16:19
Contempt .... 2 Sam. 10:4
Unnaturalness .... 1 Cor. 11:5, 6

Shaveh—*plain*
Valley near Salem; Abram meets king of Sodom here .... Gen. 14:17, 18

Shaveh-kiriathaim—*plain of Kiriathaim*
Plain near Kiriathaim inhabited by Emim .... Gen. 14:5

Shavsha, Shisha—*nobility*
David's secretary .... 1 Chr. 18:14, 16
Serves under Solomon also ..... 1 Kin. 4:3

Sheal—*asking*
Divorced his foreign wife .... Ezra 10:29

SUBJECT REFERENCE

Shealtiel—*I have asked God*
Son of King Jeconiah and father of Zerubbabel .... 1 Chr. 3:17

Sheariah—*Jehovah has esteemed*
Descendant of Saul .... 1 Chr. 9:44

Shear-jashub—*a remnant shall return*
Symbolic name given to Isaiah's son .... Is. 7:3

Sheba—*seven; an oath*
1. City in territory assigned to Simeon .... Josh. 19:1, 2
2. Benjamite insurrectionist .... 2 Sam. 20:1-22
3. Descendant of Cush through Raamah .... Gen. 10:7
4. Descendant of Shem .... Gen. 10:28
5. Grandson of Abraham and Keturah .... Gen. 25:3
6. Gadite chief .... 1 Chr. 5:13
7. Land of, occupied by Sabeans, famous traders ... Job 1:15; Ps. 72:10
Queen of, visits Solomon; marvels at his wisdom .... 1 Kin. 10:1-13
Mentioned by Christ .... Matt. 12:42

Shebah—*seven; an oath*
Name given to a well and town (Beer-sheba) .... Gen. 26:31-33

Shebaniah—*Jehovah has returned me*
1. Levite trumpeter .... 1 Chr. 15:24
2. Levite; offers prayer and signs covenant .... Neh. 9:4, 5
3. Levite who signs covenant ... Neh. 10:12
4. Priest who signs covenant .... Neh. 10:4

Shebarim—*breakings*
Place near Ai .... Josh. 7:5
See Quarry

Sheber—*breaking*
Son of Caleb .... 1 Chr. 2:48

Shebna—*perhaps an abbreviation of Shebaniah*
Treasurer under Hezekiah ...... Is. 22:15
Demoted to position of scribe ... 2 Kin. 19:2
Man of pride and luxury; replaced by Eliakim .... Is. 22:19-21

Shebuel—*God is renown*
1. Son of Gershom .... 1 Chr. 23:16
2. Son of Heman .... 1 Chr. 25:4

Shecaniah—*Jehovah has dwelt*
1. Descendant of Zerubbabel ... 1 Chr. 3:21, 22
2. Postexilic returnee .... Ezra 8:5
3. Descendant of Aaron .... 1 Chr. 24:11
4. Priest .... 2 Chr. 31:15
5. Divorced his foreign wife .... Ezra 10:2, 3
6. Father of Shemaiah .... Neh. 3:29
(Probably same as 1)
7. Postexilic priest .... Neh. 12:3, 7
8. Father-in-law of Tobiah ..... Neh. 6:18

Shechem—*shoulder*
1. Son of Hamor; seduces Dinah, Jacob's daughter .... Gen. 34:1-31
2. Son of Gilead; founder of a tribal family .... Num. 26:31
3. Son of Shemida .... 1 Chr. 7:19
4. Ancient city of Ephraim ..... Gen. 33:18
Abram camps near .... Gen. 12:6
Jacob buys ground here ..... Gen. 33:18, 19
Hivites, inhabit .... Gen. 34:2
Inhabitants of, slaughtered by Simeon and Levi .... Gen. 34:25-29
Pastures near .... Gen. 37:12, 13
Becomes city of refuge ...... Josh. 20:7
Joseph buried here .... Josh. 24:32
Joshua's farewell address here .... Josh. 24:1, 25
Center of idol-worship ...... Judg. 9:1, 4-7
Town destroyed .... Judg. 9:23, 45
Jeroboam made king here ..... 1 Kin. 12:1-19
Name of, used poetically .... Ps. 108:7

Shed—*to pour out*

A. *Descriptive of:*
Blood .... Gen. 9:6

SUBJECT REFERENCE

Bowels .... 2 Sam. 20:10
Holy Spirit .... Titus 3:6

B. *As applied to blood, indicative of:*
Justifiable execution .... Gen. 9:6
Unjustifiable murder .... Gen. 37:22
Unacceptable sacrifice .... Lev. 17:1-5
Attempted vengeance .... 1 Sam. 25:31, 34
Unpardonable .... 2 Kin. 24:4
Abomination .... Prov. 6:16, 17
Heinous crime .... Is. 59:7
New covenant .... Matt. 26:28

Shedeur—*shedder of light*
Reubenite leader .... Num. 1:5

Sheep—*a domesticated animal*

A. *Characteristics of:*
Domesticated .... 2 Sam. 12:3
Gentle .... Jer. 11:19
Defenseless .... Mic. 5:8
Needful of care .... Ezek. 34:5

B. *Uses of, for:*
Food .... 1 Sam. 25:18
Milk .... 1 Cor. 9:7
Clothing .... Prov. 31:13
Coverings .... Ex. 26:14
Presents .... 2 Sam. 17:29
Tribute .... 2 Kin. 3:4
Sacrifice .... Gen. 4:4

C. *Uses of, in Levitical system as:*
Burnt offering .... Lev. 1:10
Sin offering .... Lev. 4:32
Guilt offering .... Lev. 5:15
Peace offering .... Lev. 22:21

D. *Needs of, for:*
Protection .... Job 30:1
Shepherd .... John 10:4, 27
Fold .... John 10:1
Pastures .... Ex. 3:1
Water .... Gen. 29:8-10
Rest .... Ps. 23:2
Shearing .... 1 Sam. 25:2, 11

E. *Figurative of:*
Innocent .... 2 Sam. 24:17
Wicked .... Ps. 49:14
Jewish people .... Ps. 74:1
Backsliders .... Jer. 50:6
Lost sinners .... Matt. 9:36
Christians .... John 10:1-16
Christ .... John 1:29
Saved .... Matt. 26:31-34
Church .... Acts 20:28

See Lamb; Lamb of God

Sheepcote—*an enclosure for sheep*
David chosen .... 2 Sam. 7:8

Sheepfold—*shelter*
Enclosure for flocks .... Num. 32:16
Entrance to, only by Christ ..... John 10:1

Sheep Gate—*a gate of the restored Jerusalem*
Repaired .... Neh. 3:32
Dedicated .... Neh. 12:38, 39

Sheepmaster
Mesha, king of Moab .... 2 Kin. 3:4

Sheepshearers
Employed by Judah .... Gen. 38:12
Many employed by Nabal ...... 1 Sam. 25:7, 11
Used figuratively .... Is. 53:7

Sheets
Large piece of cloth .... Acts 11:5

Shehariah—*Jehovah is the dawn*
Benjamite .... 1 Chr. 8:26

Shekel—*A Jewish measure (approximately .533 oz.)*

A. *As a weight:*
Standard of, defined .... Ex. 30:13
Used in weighing .... Josh. 7:21

See Weights

B. *As money:*
Used in currency .... 1 Sam. 9:8
Fines paid in .... Deut. 22:19, 29
Revenues of the sanctuary paid in .... Neh. 10:32

SUBJECT REFERENCE

Shekinah—*a word expressing the glory and presence of God*

A. *As indicative of God's presence:*
- In nature ... Ps. 18:7-15
- In the exodus from Egypt ... Ex. 13:21, 22
- At Sinai ... Ex. 24:16-18
- In tabernacle ... Ex. 40:34-38
- Upon the mercy seat ... Ex. 25:22
- In the wilderness ... Num. 9:15-23; Num. 10:11-36
- In the Temple ... 2 Chr. 7:1-3

B. *Illustrated by Christ in His:*
- Divine nature ... Col. 2:9
- Incarnation ... Luke 1:35
- Nativity ... Luke 2:9
- Manifestation to Israel ... Hag. 2:9; Zech. 2:5
- Transfiguration ... 2 Pet. 1:17
- Ascension ... Acts 1:9
- Transforming us by His Spirit ... 2 Cor. 3:18; 2 Cor. 4:6
- Return ... Matt. 24:44
- Eternal habitation with saints ... Rev. 21:3

C. *Accompanied by:*
- Angels ... Is. 6:1-4
- Cloud ... Num. 9:15-23
- Fire ... Heb. 12:18-21
- Earthquake ... Hag. 2:21

Shelah—*sprout; request*
1. Son of Arphaxad ... 1 Chr. 1:18
   Called Salah ... Luke 3:35
2. Son of Judah ... Gen. 38:1-26
   Founder of the Shelanites ... Num. 26:20

Shelemiah—*friend of Jehovah*
1. Father of Hananiah ... Neh. 3:30
2. Postexilic priest ... Neh. 13:13
3. Father of Irijah ... Jer. 37:13
4. Porter ... 1 Chr. 26:14
   Called Meshelemiah ... 1 Chr. 9:21
5. Ancestor of Jehudi ... Jer. 36:14
6. Son of Abdeel ... Jer. 36:26
7. Father of Jehucal ... Jer. 37:3

Sheleph—*drawn out*
Son of Joktan; head of a tribe ... 1 Chr. 1:20

Shelesh—*might*
Asherite ... 1 Chr. 7:35

Shelomi—*at peace*
Father of an Asherite prince ... Num. 34:27

Shelomith, Shelomoth—*peaceful*
1. Daughter of Dibri; her son executed ... Lev. 24:10-23
2. Chief Levite of Moses ... 1 Chr. 23:18
3. Gershonites in David's time ... 1 Chr. 23:9
4. Descendant of Moses, had charge of treasures ... 1 Chr. 26:25
5. Son or daughter of King Rehoboam ... 2 Chr. 11:20
6. Daughter of Zerubbabel ... 1 Chr. 3:19
7. Family who went with Ezra ... Ezra 8:10

Shelumiel—*at peace with God*
Simeonite warrior ... Num. 1:6

Shem—*name; renown*
- Oldest son of Noah ... Gen. 5:32
- Escapes the flood ... Gen. 7:13
- Receives a blessing ... Gen. 9:23, 26
- Ancestor of Semitic people ... Gen. 10:22-32
- Ancestor of:
  - Abram ... Gen. 11:10-26
  - Jesus ... Luke 3:36

Shema—*report; rumor*
1. Reubenite ... 1 Chr. 5:8
2. Benjamite head ... 1 Chr. 8:12, 13
3. Ezra's attendant ... Neh. 8:4
4. City of Judah ... Josh. 15:26
5. Son of Hebron ... 1 Chr. 2:43

SUBJECT REFERENCE

Shemaah—*fame*
Father of two of David's warriors ... 1 Chr. 12:3

Shemaiah—*Jehovah has heard*
1. Father of Shimri ... 1 Chr. 4:37
2. Reubenite ... 1 Chr. 5:4
3. Levite who helped move the ark ... 1 Chr. 15:8, 12
4. Scribe in David's time ... 1 Chr. 24:6
5. Son of Obed-edom ... 1 Chr. 26:4, 6, 7
6. Prophet of Judah ... 1 Kin. 12:22-24
   Explains Shishak's invasion as divine punishment ... 2 Chr. 12:5-8
   Records Rehoboam's reign ... 2 Chr. 12:15
7. Levite teacher under Jehoshaphat ... 2 Chr. 17:8
8. Levite in Hezekiah's reign ... 2 Chr. 29:14, 15
9. Levite treasurer ... 2 Chr. 31:14, 15
10. Officer of Levites in Josiah's reign ... 2 Chr. 35:9
11. Father of Urijah ... Jer. 26:20
12. False prophet ... Jer. 29:24-28
13. Father of Delaiah ... Jer. 36:12
14. Descendant of David ... 1 Chr. 3:22
15. Keeper of the East Gate for Nehemiah ... Neh. 3:29
16. Merarite Levite living in Jerusalem ... 1 Chr. 9:14
17. Son of Adonikam ... Ezra 8:13
18. Leading man under Ezra ... Ezra 8:16
19. Priest who divorced his foreign wife ... Ezra 10:21
20. Man who divorced his foreign wife ... Ezra 10:31
21. Prophet hired by Sanballat ... Neh. 6:10-14
22. Priest who signs covenant ... Neh. 10:1, 8
23. Participant in dedication service ... Neh. 12:34
24. Postexilic priest ... Neh. 12:35
25. Levite musician ... Neh. 12:36

Shemariah—*Jehovah keeps*
1. Mighty man of Benjamin ... 1 Chr. 12:5
2. Son of Rehoboam ... 2 Chr. 11:18, 19
3. Divorced his foreign wife ... Ezra 10:31, 32

Shemeber—*splendor of heroism*
King of Zeboiim ... Gen. 14:2

Shemed—*destruction*
Son of Elpaal ... 1 Chr. 8:12

Shemer—*guard*
1. Sells Omri hill on which Samaria is built ... 1 Kin. 16:23, 24
2. Levite ... 1 Chr. 6:46
3. Asherite ... 1 Chr. 7:30, 34

Shemida, Shemidah—*fame of knowing*
Descendant of Manasseh; founder of the Shemidaites ... Num. 26:29, 32

Sheminith—*eighth*
Musical term ... 1 Chr. 15:21

Shemiramoth—*fame of the highest*
1. Levite musician in David's time ... 1 Chr. 15:18, 20
2. Levite teacher under Jehoshaphat ... 2 Chr. 17:8

Shemuel—*name of God*
1. Grandson of Issachar ... 1 Chr. 7:1, 2
2. Another spelling of Samuel ... 1 Chr. 6:33

Shen—*tooth; a pointed rock*
Rock west of Jerusalem ... 1 Sam. 7:12

Shenir (see Senir)

Shenazar
Son of Jeconiah ... 1 Chr. 3:18

Shepham—*nakedness*
Place near the Sea of Galilee ... Num. 34:11

SUBJECT REFERENCE

Shephatiah—*Jehovah judges*
1. Benjamite warrior ... 1 Chr. 12:5
2. Son of David ... 2 Sam. 3:4
3. Simeonite chief ... 1 Chr. 27:16
4. Son of King Jehoshaphat ... 2 Chr. 21:2
5. Opponent of Jeremiah ... Jer. 38:1
6. Descendant of Judah ... Neh. 11:4
7. Servant of Solomon whose descendants return from exile ... Ezra 2:57

Shepherd—*one who cares for the sheep*

A. *Duties of, toward his flock:*
- Defend ... 1 Sam. 17:34-36
- Water ... Gen. 29:2-10
- Give rest to ... Jer. 33:12
- Know ... John 10:3-5
- Number ... Jer. 33:13
- Secure pasture for ... 1 Chr. 4:39-41
- Search for the lost ... Ezek. 34:12-16; Luke 15:4, 5

B. *Good, described as:*
- Faithful ... Gen. 31:38-40
- Fearless ... 1 Sam. 17:34-36
- Unselfish ... Luke 15:3-6
- Considerate ... Gen. 33:13, 14
- Believing ... Luke 2:8-20

C. *Bad, described as:*
- Unfaithful ... Ezek. 34:1-10
- Cowardly ... John 10:12, 13
- Selfish ... Is. 56:11, 12
- Ruthless ... Ex. 2:17, 19
- Unbelieving ... Jer. 50:6

D. *Descriptive of:*
- God ... Ps. 78:52, 53
- Christ ... Heb. 13:20
- Joshua ... Num. 27:16-23
- David ... 2 Sam. 5:2
- Judges ... 1 Chr. 17:6
- National leaders ... Jer. 49:19
- Cyrus ... Is. 44:28
- Jewish leaders ... Matt. 9:36
- Church elders ... 1 Pet. 5:2

Shepherd, Jesus the good

A. *Described prophetically in His:*
- Prophetic position (teaching) ... Is. 40:10, 11
- Priestly position (sacrifice) ... Zech. 13:7; Matt. 26:31
- Kingly position (ruling) ... Ezek. 37:24; Matt. 2:6

B. *Described typically as:*
- Good ... John 10:11, 14
- Chief ... 1 Pet. 5:4
- Great ... Heb. 13:20
- One ... John 10:16
- Gentle ... Is. 40:11
- One who separates ... Matt. 25:31-46

Shepho—*unconcern*
Son of Shobal ... Gen. 36:23

Sherah—*blood-relationship*
Daughter of Ephraim; builder of cities ... 1 Chr. 7:24

Sherebiah—*Jehovah has sent burning heat*
1. Levite family returning with Ezra ... Ezra 8:18
2. Levite who assists Ezra ... Neh. 8:7

Sheresh—*root*
Grandson of Manasseh ... 1 Chr. 7:16

Sheriffs—*court officials*
Called by Nebuchadnezzar ... Dan. 3:2, 3

Sheshach—*probably a cryptogram*
Symbolic of Babylon ... Jer. 25:26

Sheshai—*whitish*
- Descendant of Anak ... Num. 13:22
- Driven out by Caleb ... Josh. 15:14
- Destroyed by Judah ... Judg. 1:10

Sheshan—*whitish*
Jerahmeelite ... 1 Chr. 2:31-35

Sheshbazzar—*sin* (the moon god) *protect the father*
Prince of Judah ... Ezra 1:8, 11

SUBJECT REFERENCE

Sheth (I)—*compensation*
Son of Adam (same as Seth) 1 Chr. 1:1

Sheth (II)—*tumult*
Name descriptive of the Moabites Num. 24:17

Shethar—*star*
Persian prince Esth. 1:14

Shethar-boznai—*starry splendor*
Official of Persia Ezra 5:3, 6

Sheva—*self-satisfying*
1. Son of Caleb 1 Chr. 2:43, 49
2. David's scribe 2 Sam. 20:25

Shibboleth—*stream or ear of corn*
Password Judg. 12:5, 6

Shicron—*drunkenness*
Town of Judah Josh. 15:11

Shield—*a protective armor*
A. *Uses of:*
Protection 2 Chr. 14:8
Treasures in war 1 Kin. 14:25, 26
Riches 2 Chr. 32:27
Ornamenting public buildings 1 Kin. 10:17
B. *Figurative of:*
God's:
Protection Ps. 33:20
Favor Ps. 5:12
Salvation Ps. 18:35
Truth Ps. 91:4
Faith Eph. 6:16
Rulers Ps. 47:9

Shiggaion—*irregular*
Musical term Ps. 7 (Title)
Plural form:
Shigionoth Hab. 3:1

Shihon—*ruin*
Town of Issachar Josh. 19:19

Shihor-libnath—*turbid stream of Libnath*
Small river in Asher's territory Josh. 19:26

Shilhi—*Jehovah has sent*
Father of Azubah 1 Kin. 22:42

Shilhim—*missiles*
Town in south Judah Josh. 15:1, 32

Shillem—*compensation*
Son of Napthali Gen. 46:24

Shiloah—*sent*
A pool of Jerusalem, figurative of God's protection Is. 8:6
See Siloam

Shiloh
1. Town of Ephraim Judg. 21:19
Center of religious worship Judg. 18:31
Canaan divided here Josh. 18:1, 10
Benjamites seize women here Judg. 21:19-23
Ark of the covenant taken from 1 Sam. 4:3-11
Site of Eli's judgeship 1 Sam. 4:12-18
Home of Ahijah 1 Kin. 14:2, 4
Punishment given to Jer. 7:12-14
2. Messianic title Gen. 49:10

Shiloni—*a Shilonite*
Father of Zechariah Neh. 11:5

Shilonite
Native of Shiloh 1 Kin. 11:29

Shilshah—*might*
Asherite 1 Chr. 7:36, 37

Shimea, Shimeah—*He* (God) *has heard*
1. Gershonite Levite 1 Chr. 6:39
2. Merarite Levite 1 Chr. 6:30
3. Brother of David 2 Sam. 13:3
4. Son of David 1 Chr. 3:1, 5
5. Benjamite 1 Chr. 8:1, 32
Called Shimeam 1 Chr. 9:38

SUBJECT REFERENCE

Shimeath—*report*
Ammonitess 2 Kin. 12:21

Shimeathites
Family of scribes 1 Chr. 2:55

Shimei—*renowned*
1. Son of Gershon Ex. 6:17
2. Son of Merari 1 Chr. 6:29
3. Simeonite 1 Chr. 4:24-27
4. Levite 1 Chr. 6:42
5. Benjamite family head 1 Chr. 8:21
6. Gershonite family head 1 Chr. 23:7, 9
7. Levite musician in David's time 1 Chr. 25:3, 17
8. Overseer of vineyards under David 1 Chr. 27:27
9. Benjamite; insults David 2 Sam. 16:5-13
Pardoned, but confined 2 Sam. 19:16-23
Breaks parole; executed by Solomon 1 Kin. 2:39-46
10. Faithful follower of Solomon 1 Kin. 1:8
11. Levite; assists in purification 2 Chr. 29:14-16
12. Levite treasurer in Hezekiah's reign 2 Chr. 31:12, 13
13. Benjamite ancestor of Mordecai Esth. 2:5
14. Brother of Zerubbabel 1 Chr. 3:19

Shimeon—*hearing*
Divorced his foreign wife Ezra 10:31

Shimon—*trier*
Judahite family 1 Chr. 4:1, 20

Shimrath—*guarding*
Benjamite 1 Chr. 8:21

Shimri—*vigilant*
1. Father of Jediael 1 Chr. 11:45
2. Merarite Levite 1 Chr. 26:10
3. Levite; assists in purification 2 Chr. 29:13

Shimrith—*vigilant*
Moabitess 2 Chr. 24:26

Shimron—*watching*
1. Son of Issachar Gen. 46:13
2. Town of Zebulun Josh. 11:1

Shimron-meron—*guard of lashing*
Town conquered by Joshua Josh. 12:20

Shimshai—*sunny*
Scribe opposing the Jews Ezek. 4:8

Shinab—*king of Admah*
Fought against Chedorlaomer Gen. 14:1, 12

Shinar—*the region around Babylon*
Original home of Noah's sons Gen. 10:10
Tower built here Gen. 11:2-9
Amraphel, king of Gen. 14:1, 9
Home of the remnant Jews Is. 11:11

Shine—*to radiate with light*
A. *Used literally of:*
Sun Job 31:26
Moon Job 25:5
Star Joel 3:15
Earth Ezek. 43:2
Moses' face Ex. 34:29-35
Christ's face Matt. 17:2
Angels Acts 12:7
Glorified Christ Acts 9:3
Christ's return Luke 17:24
B. *Applied figuratively to:*
God's blessing Num. 6:25
God's Word 2 Pet. 1:19
Christ's first Advent Is. 9:2; John 1:5
Gospel 2 Cor. 4:4
Believer's life Matt. 5:16
Regeneration 2 Cor. 4:6
Believer's glory Dan. 12:3; Matt. 13:43

SUBJECT REFERENCE

Shihon—*ruin*
Town of Issachar Josh. 19:19

Shiphi—*abundant*
Simeonite 1 Chr. 4:37

Shiphmite—*a native of Shiphmoth*
Zabdi called 1 Chr. 27:27

Shiphrah—*beauty*
Hebrew midwife Ex. 1:15

Shiphtan—*judicial*
Ephraimite Num. 34:24

Ships—*vessels designed for use on water*
A. *Uses of:*
Fishing John 21:3-8
Travel Jon. 1:3
Cargoes Acts 27:3, 10, 38
War Num. 24:24
Commerce Ps. 107:23
B. *Parts of:*
Sign Acts 28:11
Lifeboats Acts 27:16-32
Anchor Acts 27:29, 40
Rudder Acts 27:40
Cables Acts 27:17
Ropes Acts 27:32
Sails Is. 33:23
Oars Ezek. 27:6
C. *Notable ones:*
Ark Gen. 7:17, 18
Jonah's Jon. 1:3, 4
Of Tarshish Is. 23:1, 14
Christ's Matt. 8:23-27
Paul's Acts 27:1-44

Shipwreck—*a wreck of a seagoing vessel*
Paul in three 2 Cor. 11:25
Figurative of apostasy 1 Tim. 1:19

Shisha—*distinction*
Father of Solomon's scribes 1 Kin. 4:3
Called Shavsha 1 Chr. 18:16

Shitrai—*Jehovah is deciding*
Sharonite overseer of David's herds 1 Chr. 27:29

Shittim—*acacia*
1. Israel's last camp before crossing the Jordan Josh. 3:1
Scene of Balaam's attempted curse Num. 22—24
Sin of Baal-peor here Num. 25:1-18
Site of Joshua's commission Num. 27:12-23
War with Midianites here Num. 31:1-54
Reuben and Gad receive inheritance here Num. 32:1-42
Scene of Moses' final addresses Deut. 1—34
Spies sent from Josh. 2:1
2. Valley blessed by the LORD Joel 3:18

Shittim wood—*wood of the shittah tree*
Used in:
Making the ark Ex. 25:10, 13
Table of showbread Ex. 37:10
Altar of incense Ex. 30:1
Altar of burnt offering Ex. 38:1, 6
Tabernacle boards Ex. 26:15-37

Shiza—*splendor*
Reubenite 1 Chr. 11:42

Shoa—*rich*
Race or tribe against Israel Ezek. 23:23

Shobab—*returning*
1. Son of Caleb 1 Chr. 2:18
2. Son of David 2 Sam. 5:14

Shobach—*expansion*
Commander of the Syrian army 2 Sam. 10:16-18
Spelled Shophach 1 Chr. 19:16, 18

Shobai—*glorious*
Head of a family of porters Ezra 2:42

Shobal—*flowing*
1. Son of Seir; a Horite chief Gen. 36:20-29

SUBJECT — REFERENCE

2. Judahite, son of Caleb and ancestor of the people of Kirjath-jearim ... 1 Chr. 2:50, 52

Shobek—*forsaking*

Signer of Nehemiah's sealed covenant ... Neh. 10:24

Shobi—*Jehovah is glorious*

Ammonite who brings food to David ... 2 Sam. 17:27, 28

Shoe—*footwear*

A. *Characteristics of:*
- Worn on the feet ... 1 Kin. 2:5
- Tied by a latchet ... Gen. 14:23
- Some considered worthless ... Amos 2:6
- Used for dress occasions ... Luke 15:22
- Worn as adornment ... Song 7:1
- Dirty after a trip ... Josh. 9:5, 13
- Preserved supernaturally ... Deut. 29:5

B. *Symbolism of:*
- Putting on—readiness for a journey ... Ex. 12:11
- Putting off—reverence before God ... Ex. 3:5; Josh. 5:15
- Want of—mourning ... 2 Sam. 15:30
- Giving to another—renunciation of Mosaic marriage rights ... Ruth 4:7, 8
- To loose another's—act of homage ... Luke 3:16

C. *Figurative of:*
- Preparation for service ... Eph. 6:15
- Protection and provision ... Deut. 33:25
- Alertness ... Is. 5:27

See Sandals

Shoham—*beryl or onyx*

Merarite Levite ... 1 Chr. 24:27

Shomer—*keeper, watchman*

Asherite ... 1 Chr. 7:30, 32
Called Shamer ... 1 Chr. 7:34

Shophan—*hidden*

Town in Gad ... Num. 32:34, 35

Short—*not long; brief*

A. *Descriptive of:*
- Life ... Ps. 89:47
- Time of the devil on earth ... Rev. 12:12
- Gospel age ... 1 Cor. 7:29

B. *Expressive of God's:*
- Power ... Is. 50:2
- Plan ... Rev. 22:6
- Provision ... Is. 59:1, 2
- Tribulation ... Matt. 24:21, 22

Shoshannim—*lilies*

Musical term ... Ps. 45 (Title)

Shoulder

A. *Of men, used for:*
- Burdens ... Is. 46:7
- Supporting clothes ... Ex. 12:34

B. *Figurative of:*
- Notable persons ... Ezek. 24:4, 5
- Destruction ... Ezek. 29:7
- Servitude ... Is. 10:27
- Rebellion ... Zech. 7:11
- Messianic authority ... Is. 9:6
- Security ... Deut. 33:12

Shout, Shouted

A. *Occasions of, in:*
- Conquest ... Josh. 6:5, 16, 20
- Choosing a king ... 1 Sam. 10:24
- Sound of singing ... Ex. 32:17, 18
- Laying foundation of the Temple ... Ezek. 3:11-13

B. *In spiritual things:*
- At creation ... Job 38:7
- In the Messiah's arrival ... Zech. 9:9

Shovel

1. Used for removing ashes ... Ex. 27:3
2. Winnowing tool ... Is. 30:24

Showbread—*"bread of thy face"*

A. *Provisions concerning:*
- Provided by the people ... Lev. 24:8
- Prepared by the Levites ... 1 Chr. 9:32
- Placed in two rows ... Ex. 25:30
- Perennially supplied ... Num. 4:7
- Presented to the Lord ... Lev. 24:7, 8
- Provided for priests only ... Lev. 24:9; Matt. 12:4, 5

B. *Table of:*
- Placed in Holy Place ... Ex. 26:35; Heb. 9:2
- Made of acacia ... Ex. 25:23-28
- Carried by: Kohathite Levites ... Num. 4:4, 7, 15
- High priest ... Num. 4:7, 8, 16

C. *Symbolic of:*
- Twelve tribes ... Ex. 28:10-12
- Christ ... John 6:48
- Church ... 1 Cor. 10:17

Showers—*sudden outpourings*

A. *Used literally of rain:*
- Withheld ... Jer. 3:3
- Predicted ... Luke 12:54
- Requested ... Zech. 10:1
- Blessing ... Ps. 65:10

B. *Used figuratively of:*
- God's Word ... Deut. 32:2
- God's wrath ... Ezek. 13:11, 13
- Messiah's advent ... Ps. 72:6
- Gospel ... Ezek. 34:25, 26
- Remnant ... Mic. 5:7

Shroud—*to cover or shelter*

Used figuratively ... Ezek. 31:3

Shua, Shuah—*prosperity*

1. Son of Abraham by Keturah ... Gen. 25:1, 2
2. Father of Judah's wife ... Gen. 38:2, 12
3. Descendant of Judah ... 1 Chr. 4:1, 11
4. Daughter of Heber ... 1 Chr. 7:32

Shual—*jackal*

1. Asherite ... 1 Chr. 7:30, 36
2. Region raided by a Philistine company ... 1 Sam. 13:17

Shubael, Shebuel

1. Levite, son of Amram ... 1 Chr. 24:20
2. Levite, son of Heman ... 1 Chr. 25:4

Shuham—*depression*

Son of Dan ... Num. 26:42
Called Hushim ... Gen. 46:23
Head of the Shuhamites ... Num. 26:42, 43

Shuhite—*a descendant of Shua*

Bildad called; a descendant of Abraham by Keturah ... Gen. 38:2, 12; Job 2:11

Shulamite—*a native of Shulam*

Shepherd's sweetheart ... Song 6:13

Shumathites

Family of Kirjath-jearim ... 1 Chr. 2:53

Shunammite—*a native of Shunem*

1. Abishag, David's nurse called ... 1 Kin. 1:3, 15
2. Woman who cared for Elisha ... 2 Kin. 4:8-12

Shunem—*uneven*

Border town of Issachar ... Josh. 19:18

Shuni—*fortunate*

Son of Gad ... Gen. 46:16

Shuppim—*serpent*

Levite porter ... 1 Chr. 26:16

Shur—*fortification*

Wilderness in south Palestine ... Gen. 16:7
Israel went from Red Sea to ... Ex. 15:22
On Egypt's border ... 1 Sam. 15:7
Hagar flees to ... Gen. 16:7

Shushan—*a city of Elam*

Residence of Persian monarchs ... Esth. 1:2
Located on river Ulai ... Dan. 8:2
Court of Ahasuerus here ... Esth. 1:2, 5

Shut—*to close securely*

A. *Applied literally to:*
- Ark ... Gen. 7:16
- Door ... Gen. 19:6, 10
- Leper ... Lev. 13:4-44
- Animals ... Dan. 6:22
- Court ... Jer. 33:1
- Prison ... Acts 26:10

B. *Applied figuratively to:*
- Womb ... 1 Sam. 1:5, 6
- God's mercies ... Ps. 77:9
- Finality of salvation ... Matt. 25:10
- Union with Christ ... Song 4:12
- Spiritual blindness ... Is. 6:10
- Awe ... Is. 52:15
- Heaven's glory ... Is. 60:11
- God's Word ... Jer. 20:9
- Vision ... Dan. 12:4
- Secret prayer ... Matt. 6:6
- Christ's sovereignty ... Rev. 3:7, 8

Shuthelah

1. Son of Ephraim; head of a family ... Num. 26:35, 36
2. Ephraimite ... 1 Chr. 7:20, 21

Shuttle—*a weaving tool*

Our days swifter than ... Job 7:6

Siaha—*assembly*

Family of returning Nethinim ... Ezra 2:43, 44; Neh. 7:47

Sibbecai, Sibbechai

One of David's mighty men ... 1 Chr. 11:29
Slays a Philistine giant ... 2 Sam. 21:18
Commander of a division ... 1 Chr. 27:11

Sibmah—*balsam*

Town of Reuben ... Num. 32:3, 38
Famous for wines ... Is. 16:8, 9

Sibraim—*double hope*

Place in north Palestine ... Ezek. 47:16

Sick, Sickness—*the state of being unwell*

A. *Caused by:*
- Age ... Gen. 48:1, 10
- Accident ... 2 Kin. 1:2
- Wine ... Hos. 7:5
- Sins ... Mic. 6:13
- Despondency ... Prov. 13:12
- Prophetic visions ... Dan. 8:27
- Love ... Song 2:5
- God's judgment ... 2 Chr. 21:14-19
- God's sovereignty ... John 11:4

B. *Healing of, by:*
- Figs ... 2 Kin. 20:7
- Miracle ... 1 Kin. 17:17-23
- Prayer ... James 5:14, 15
- God's mercy ... Phil. 2:25-30

See Diseases; Healing

Sickle—*an instrument for cutting grain*

Literally ... Deut. 16:9
Figuratively ... Mark 4:29; Rev. 14:14-19

Siddim, Vale of

Valley of bitumen pits near the Dead Sea ... Gen. 14:3, 8, 10

Sidon, Zidon—*fishery*

Canaanite city 20 miles north of Tyre ... Gen. 10:15, 19
Israel's northern boundary ... Josh. 19:28
Canaanites not expelled from ... Judg. 1:31
Israelites oppressed by ... Judg. 10:12
Gods of, entice Israelites ... 1 Kin. 11:5, 33
Judgments pronounced on ... Is. 23:12
Israelites sold as slaves by ... Joel 3:4-6
People from, hear Jesus ... Luke 6:17
Visited by Jesus ... Matt. 15:21
Paul visits at ... Acts 27:3

Siege of a city—*a military blockade*

A. *Methods employed in:*
- Supplies cut off ... 2 Kin. 19:24
- Ambushes laid ... Judg. 9:34
- Battering rams used ... Ezek. 4:2
- Arrows shot ... 2 Kin. 19:32

B. *Suffering of:*
- Famine ... 2 Kin. 6:26-29
- Pestilence ... Jer. 21:6

SUBJECT REFERENCE

C. *Examples of:*
Jericho ..... Josh. 6:2-20
Jerusalem ..... 2 Kin. 24:10, 11
See War

Sieve, sift—*screen*
Used figuratively of:
God's judgment ..... Amos 9:9
Satan's temptation ..... Luke 22:31

Sign—*an outward token having spiritual significance*
A. *Descriptive of:*
Heavenly bodies ..... Gen. 1:14
Rainbow ..... Gen. 9:12-17
Circumcision ..... Gen. 17:11
Bloodshed ..... Ex. 12:13
God's wonders ..... Ps. 65:8
Covenant ..... Rom. 4:11
Miracles ..... Deut. 26:8
Memorial ..... Num. 16:38
Symbolic act ..... Is. 8:18
Witness ..... Is. 19:19, 20
Outward display ..... John 4:48
B. *Purposes of, to:*
Authenticate a prophecy ..... Deut. 13:1
1 Sam. 2:31, 34
Strengthen faith ..... Judg. 6:17
Is. 7:11
Recall God's blessings ..... Josh. 24:15-17
Confirm God's Word ..... 2 Kin. 19:28, 29
Heb. 2:4
Insure a promise ..... 2 Kin. 20:5, 9-11
Confirm a prophecy ..... 1 Kin. 13:3-5
C. *Concerning Christ in His:*
Nativity ..... Luke 2:12
Ministry ..... John 20:30
Acts 2:22
Resurrection ..... Matt. 12:38-40
D. *Value of:*
Discounted as such ..... Matt. 16:1-4
Demanded unnecessarily ..... John 6:30
Demonstrated by apostles ..... Acts 5:12
Displayed by Paul ..... Rom. 15:19
E. *In prophecy, concerning:*
Christ's first Advent ..... Is. 7:11, 14
Matt. 1:21-23
Second Advent ..... Matt. 24:3, 30
Antichrist ..... 2 Thess. 2:9
End ..... Rev. 15:1
F. *As assurance of:*
Presence ..... Ex. 3:12
Judgment upon sin ..... Num. 17:10
Goodness ..... Ps. 86:17

Signify—*to make known by signs*
A. *Concerning men:*
Peter's death ..... John 21:19
Ritual performed ..... Acts 21:26
Jewish scheme ..... Acts 23:15
B. *Concerning predicted events:*
New dispensation ..... Heb. 9:8
Christ's: Death ..... John 12:33
Sufferings ..... 1 Pet. 1:11
Gospel age ..... Rev. 1:1
Famine ..... Acts 11:28
World's end ..... Heb. 12:27

Sihon—*bold*
Amorite king residing at Heshbon ..... Num. 21:26-30
Victorious over Moabites ..... Num. 21:26-30
Ruler of five Midianite princes ..... Josh. 13:21
Refused Israel's request for passage ..... Deut. 2:26-28
Defeated by Israel ..... Num. 21:21-32
Territory of, assigned to Reuben and Gad ..... Num. 32:1-38
Victory over, long celebrated ..... Deut. 31:4

Sihor—*black, turbid*
Name given to the Nile ..... Is. 23:3
Israel's southwestern border ..... Josh. 13:3

Silas, Silvanus—*wooded*
Leader in the Jerusalem church ..... Acts 15:22
Christian prophet ..... Acts 15:32
Sent on a mission ..... Acts 15:22-35
Became Paul's companion ..... Acts 15:36-41
Roman citizen ..... Acts 16:25-39

SUBJECT REFERENCE

Paul commended his work at Corinth ..... 2 Cor. 1:19
Called Silvanus ..... 1 Thess. 1:1
Associated in Paul's writings ..... 2 Thess. 1:1
Peter's helper ..... 1 Pet. 5:12

Silence—*the lack of noise*
A. *Kinds of:*
Will of God ..... Rev. 8:1
1 Pet. 2:15
Troubled ..... Jer. 20:9
B. *Virtue of:*
Suitable time for ..... Eccl. 3:7
Commanded ..... 1 Cor. 14:34
Sign of prudence ..... Prov. 21:23
Sign of wisdom ..... Prov. 17:28
C. *Forbidden to God's:*
Watchmen ..... Is. 62:6
Messengers ..... Acts 5:27-42
Praisers ..... Ps. 30:12
D. *Considered as:*
Blessing ..... Zech. 2:13
Curse ..... 1 Sam. 2:9
Judgment ..... Jer. 8:14
Punishment ..... Is. 15:1
E. *Of God:*
Broken in judgment ..... Ps. 50:3
Misunderstood by men ..... Ps. 50:21, 23
F. *Of Christ:*
Predicted ..... Is. 53:7
Before:
Sinners ..... John 8:6
High priest ..... Matt. 26:62, 63
Pilate ..... Matt. 27:14
Herod ..... Luke 23:9

Silk—*a clothing material derived from the silkworm*
Sign of:
Luxury ..... Ezek. 16:10, 13
Wantonness ..... Rev. 18:12

Silla—*twig; basket*
Quarter of suburb of Jerusalem ..... 2 Kin. 12:20

Silly women
Weighed down with sin ..... 2 Tim. 3:6

Siloam, Siloah—*sent*
Pool at Jerusalem ..... Neh. 3:15
Tower of, kills 18 people ..... Luke 13:4
Blind man washes in ..... John 9:1-11

Silver—*a precious metal*
A. *Features concerning:*
Mined from the earth ..... Job 28:1
Melted by fire ..... Ezek. 22:22
Sign of wealth ..... Gen. 13:2
Used as money ..... Gen. 23:15, 16
Article of commerce ..... Ezek. 27:12
Given as presents ..... 1 Kin. 10:25
Used in:
Tabernacle ..... Ex. 38:19
Temple ..... 2 Kin. 12:13
Christ sold for 30 pieces of ..... Zech. 11:12
Matt. 26:15
Peter devoid of ..... Acts 3:6
B. *Figurative of:*
God's Word ..... Ps. 12:6
God's people ..... Zech. 13:9
Understanding ..... Prov. 3:13, 14
Degeneration ..... Is. 1:22
Rejection ..... Jer. 6:30

Silversmith—*a worker in silver*
Demetrius, an Ephesian ..... Acts 19:24-41

Simeon—*hearing*
1. Son of Jacob by Leah ..... Gen. 29:33
Joined Levi in massacre of Shechemites ..... Gen. 34:25-31
Held as hostage by Joseph ..... Gen. 42:24, 36
Denounced by Jacob ..... Gen. 34:30
Sons of ..... Gen. 46:10
2. Tribe of, descendants of Jacob's son ..... Gen. 46:10
Number of, at first census ..... Num. 1:23
Number of, at second census ..... Num. 26:12-14

SUBJECT REFERENCE

Position of, on Mt. Gerizim ..... Deut. 27:12
Inheritance of, within Judah's ..... Josh. 19:1-9
With Judah, fought Canaanites ..... Judg. 1:1, 3, 17
Victory over Ham and Amalekites ..... 1 Chr. 4:24-43
Recognized in Ezekiel's vision ..... Ezek. 48:24-33
3. Ancestor of Christ ..... Luke 3:30
4. Righteous man; blessed the child Jesus ..... Luke 2:25-35
5. Christian prophet at Antioch ..... Acts 13:1
6. Simon Peter ..... Acts 15:14

Similitude—*likeness of two things*
A. *Expressive of:*
Physical ..... 2 Chr. 4:3
Typical ..... Rom. 5:14
Literary (simile) ..... Ps. 144:12
Spiritual ..... James 3:9
B. *Expressed by:*
"Like" ..... James 1:6
"As" ..... 1 Pet. 2:5
"Likeness" ..... Rom. 6:5
"Liken" ..... Matt. 7:24, 26

Simon—*hearing*
1. Simon Peter ..... Matt. 4:18
See Peter
2. One of the Twelve; called "the Canaanite" ..... Matt. 10:4
3. One of Jesus' brothers ..... Matt. 13:55
4. The leper ..... Matt. 26:6
5. Pharisee ..... Luke 7:36-40
6. Man of Cyrene ..... Matt. 27:32
7. Father of Judas Iscariot ..... John 6:71
8. Sorcerer ..... Acts 8:9-24
9. Tanner in Joppa ..... Acts 9:43

Simple, the
Enlightened by God's Word ..... Ps. 119:105
Ps. 19:7
Able to understand ..... Prov. 1:4
Receptive of correction ..... Prov. 19:25
Void of understanding ..... Prov. 7:7
Easily tempted ..... Prov. 9:4, 16
Gullible ..... Prov. 14:15
Inherit folly ..... Prov. 14:18
Unmindful of danger ..... Prov. 22:3
The LORD preserves ..... Ps. 116:6

Simplicity—*that which is in its purest form*
A. *Necessary in:*
Prayer ..... Matt. 6:5-15
Dress ..... 1 Pet. 3:3-5
Conduct ..... 2 Cor. 1:12
Giving ..... Rom. 12:8
Preaching ..... 1 Thess. 2:3-7
B. *Purposes of, to:*
Avoid outward display ..... Matt. 6:1-4
Defeat Satan ..... 2 Cor. 11:3, 4
Remain pure in an evil world ..... Rom. 16:19

Sin—*disobedience of God's Law*
A. *Defined as:*
Transgression ..... 1 John 3:4
Unrighteousness ..... 1 John 5:17
Omission of known duty ..... James 4:17
Not from faith ..... Rom. 14:23
Thought of foolishness ..... Prov. 24:9
B. *Sources of, in:*
Satan ..... John 8:44
Man's heart ..... Matt. 15:19, 20
Lust ..... James 1:15
Adam's transgression ..... Rom. 5:12, 16
Natural birth ..... Ps. 51:5
C. *Kinds of:*
National ..... Prov. 14:34
Personal ..... Josh. 7:20
Secret ..... Ps. 90:8
Presumptuous ..... Ps. 19:13
Open ..... 1 Tim. 5:24
Shameless ..... Is. 3:9
Youthful ..... Ps. 25:7
Public ..... 2 Sam. 24:10, 17

SUBJECT	REFERENCE
Unforgiveable	Matt. 12:21, 32 John 8:24
Of ignorance	Lev. 4:2
Willfully	Heb. 10:26
D. *Consequences of, among the unregenerate:*	
Blindness	John 9:41 2 Cor. 4:3, 4
Servitude	John 8:34
Irreconcilable	1 Tim. 3:1-7
Death	Rom. 6:23
E. *God's attitude toward:*	
Withholds men from	Gen. 20:6
Punishes for	Ex. 32:34
Provides a fountain for	Zech. 13:1
Blots out	Is. 44:22
Casts away	Mic. 7:19
Forgives	Ex. 34:7
Remembers no more	Jer. 31:34
F. *Christ's relationship to:*	
Free of	1 John 3:5
Knew no	2 Cor. 5:21
Makes men conscious of	John 15:22, 24
Died for our	1 Cor. 15:3
As an offering for	Is. 53:10 Heb. 9:28
Substitutionary	Is. 53:5, 6 Matt. 26:28
Takes it away	John 1:29
Saves His people from	Matt. 1:21
Has power to forgive	Matt. 9:6
Makes reconciliation for	Heb. 2:17
Purges our	Heb. 1:3
Cleanses us from	1 John 1:7, 9
Washes us from	Rev. 1:5
G. *Regenerate must:*	
Acknowledge	Ps. 32:5
Confess	Ps. 51:3, 4
Be sorry for	Ps. 38:18
Not serve	Rom. 6:6
Not obey	Rom. 6:6, 12
Subdue	Rom. 6:14-22
Lay aside	Heb. 12:1
Resist	Heb. 12:4
Keep from	Ps. 19:13
H. *Helps against:*	
Use God's Word	Ps. 119:11
Guard the tongue	Ps. 39:1
Walk in the Spirit	Rom. 8:1-14
Avoid evil companions	1 Tim. 5:22
Confess to the Lord	1 John 1:8, 9
Exercise love	1 Pet. 4:8
Go to the Advocate	1 John 2:1

Sin—*wrongdoing; transgression*

1. Wilderness between the Red Sea and Sinai	Ex. 16:1
2. City of Egypt	Ezek. 30:15, 16

Sinai, Sina

Mountain (same as Horeb) where the Law was given	Ex. 19:1-25
Used allegorically by Paul	Gal. 4:24, 25
See Horeb	

Sincerity—*freedom from deceit; genuineness*

A. *Descriptive of:*	
God's Word	1 Pet. 2:2
Faith	1 Tim. 1:5
Believer's love	2 Cor. 8:8, 24
B. *Should characterize:*	
Young men	Titus 2:6, 7
Worship	John 4:23, 24
Preaching	2 Cor. 2:17
Believer's life	2 Cor. 1:12
Public relationships	Judg. 9:16, 19
C. *Examples of:*	
Nathanael	John 1:47
Christ	1 Pet. 2:22
Paul	1 Thess. 2:3-5

Singed—*burnt hair*

Miraculously saved from being	Dan. 3:27

Singers—*those who make music with voice*

Leaders of	1 Chr. 25:2-6
Under teachers	1 Chr. 15:22, 27
Mixed	2 Chr. 35:15, 25

Singing—*uttering words in musical tones*

SUBJECT	REFERENCE
A. *Descriptive of:*	
Birds	Ps. 104:12
Trees	1 Chr. 16:33
Believers	Eph. 5:19
Redeemed	Rev. 5:9
Morning stars	Job 38:7
B. *Occasions of:*	
Times of:	
Victory	Ex. 15:1, 21
Revelry	Ex. 32:18
Imprisonment	Acts 16:25
Joy	James 5:13
Lord's Supper	Matt. 26:30
C. *Manner of, with:*	
Thanksgiving	Ps. 147:7
Joy	Ps. 27:6
Gladness	Jer. 31:7
Spirit	1 Cor. 14:15
Grace	Col. 3:16
D. *Objects of:*	
God's:	
Power	Ps. 59:16
Mercies	Ps. 89:1
Righteousness	Ps. 51:14
New song	Rev. 14:3

Singular—*something special*

Descriptive of a vow	Lev. 27:2

Sinim, Sinites—*people in the far east*

1. Canaanite people	Gen. 10:15-18
2. Distant land from which people will return	Is. 49:7-12

Sink—*to go down under something soft*

Used literally of:	
Stone	1 Sam. 17:49
Army	Ex. 15:4, 5, 10
Boat	Luke 5:7
Man	Matt. 14:30

Sinlessness (see Holiness of Christ; Perfection)

Sinners—*those who are unregenerate*

A. *Descriptive of:*	
Wicked city	Gen. 13:13
Race	1 Sam. 15:18
Wicked Israelites	Amos 9:8, 10
Jewish people	Matt. 26:45, 47
Man under conviction	Luke 5:8 Luke 18:13
Human race	Rom. 5:8, 19
B. *Characteristics of:*	
Hostile to God	Jude 15
Scheme wickedly	Ps. 26:9, 10
Easily ensnared	Eccl. 7:26
Righteous enticed by	Prov. 1:10
Law made for	1 Tim. 1:9
Conscious of sin	Luke 18:13
Able to repent	Luke 15:7, 10
Conversion of	James 5:20
In need of cleansing	James 4:8
C. *Punishment of:*	
Pursued by evil	Prov. 13:21
Overthrown by evil	Prov. 13:6
Wealth of, acquired by the just	Prov. 13:22
Sorrow given to	Ezek. 18:20
Will be punished	Prov. 11:31
Will be consumed	Ps. 104:35
D. *Christ's relationship to:*	
Came to call	Luke 5:32
Friend of	Luke 7:34
Receives such	Luke 15:1, 2
Endures hostility from	Heb. 12:3
Separate from	Heb. 7:26

Sion—*elevated*

Name given to all or part of Mt. Hermon	Deut. 4:48
See Zion	

Siphmoth—*fruitful*

David shares spoils with	1 Sam. 30:26-28

Sippai—*Jehovah is preserver*

Philistine giant	1 Chr. 20:4
Called Saph	2 Sam. 21:18

Sirah—*turning aside*

Well near Hebron	2 Sam. 3:26

SUBJECT	REFERENCE

Siron—*coat of mail*

Sidonian name for Mt. Hermon	Deut. 3:9

Sisamai—*Jehovah is distinguished*

Judahite	1 Chr. 2:40

Sisera—*meditation*

1. Canaanite commander of Jabin's army; slain by Jael	Judg. 4:2-22
2. Ancestor of postexilic Nethinim	Ezra 2:43, 53

Sister

A. *Descriptive of:*	
Female relative	Gen. 24:30-60
Women of the same tribe	Num. 25:18
B. *Features concerning:*	
Protected by:	
Brothers	Gen. 34:13-31
Laws	Lev. 18:9-13, 18
Friction between	Luke 10:39, 40
Loved by Jesus	John 11:5
C. *Figurative of:*	
Samaria and Jerusalem	Ezek. 23:1-49
Christian	Matt. 12:50
Christian woman	Rom. 16:1
Church	2 John 13

Sit

A. *Descriptive of:*	
Partridge	Jer. 17:11
Man	Gen. 18:1
Judge	Ex. 18:13, 14
Priest	Zech. 6:13
King	Deut. 17:15, 18
God	Ps. 2:4
Messiah	Ps. 110:1
B. *Purposes of, to:*	
Eat	Matt. 26:20, 21
Rest	John 4:6
Mourn	Neh. 1:4
Teach	Matt. 26:55
Transact business	Matt. 9:9
Beg	Luke 18:35
Learn	Mark 5:15
Ride	Matt. 21:5
Worship	Acts 2:2
C. *Figurative of Christ's:*	
Session	Heb. 1:3
Rule	Matt. 19:28
Judgment	Matt. 25:31

Sitnah—*enmity*

Well dug by Isaac near Gerar	Gen. 26:21

Sivan

Third month of the Jewish and Babylonian year	Esth. 8:9

Skeptical—*characterized by doubts*

Thomas, the doubter	John 20:24-28

Skilled—*those possessing special abilities*

A. *Required of:*	
Soldiers	1 Chr. 5:18
Craftsmen	2 Chr. 2:7, 14
Musicians	2 Chr. 34:12
B. *Obtained by:*	
Spirit's help	Ex. 31:2-5
God's Word	Ps. 119:98-100
LORD's help	Ps. 144:1

Skins—*the outer covering of a body*

A. *Of animals, used for:*	
Clothing	Gen. 3:21
Deception	Gen. 27:16
Coverings	Ex. 26:14
Bottles	Josh. 9:4
B. *Of man:*	
Diseased	Lev. 13:1-46
Sign of race	Jer. 13:23
Seal of death	Job 19:26

Skull—*skeleton of the head*

Abimelech's crushed by a woman	Judg. 9:53
Jezebel's left by dogs	2 Kin. 9:30-37
They brought Him to a place called	Mark 15:22
Another name for Golgotha	Matt. 27:33
See Golgotha	

SUBJECT	REFERENCE

Sky—*the expanse of the heaven*

A. *Place of:*
- Stars .... Heb. 11:12
- Expansion .... Job 37:18
- Weather changes .... Matt. 16:2, 3
- Thunder .... Ps. 77:17

B. *Figurative of:*
- God's abode .... Ps. 18:11
- Righteousness .... Is. 45:8
- Ultimate judgment .... Jer. 51:9

Slander—*a malicious statement*

A. *Described as:*
- Destructive .... Prov. 11:9
- Deceitful .... Ps. 52:2
- Deluding .... Prov. 10:18
- Devouring .... Prov. 16:27-30

B. *Hurled against:*
- Joseph .... Gen. 39:14-19
- David .... 2 Sam. 10:3
- Jews .... Ezra 4:7-16
- Christ .... Matt. 26:59-61
- Paul .... Acts 24:5, 6
- Stephen .... Acts 6:11
- Christians .... 1 Pet. 2:12

C. *Hurled against the righteous by:*
- Devil .... Job 1:9-11
- Revilers .... 1 Pet. 3:16
- Hypocrites .... Prov. 11:9
- False leaders .... 3 John 9, 10

D. *Charged against Christ as:*
- Winebibber .... Matt. 11:19
- Blasphemer .... Matt. 9:3
- Demonized .... John 8:48, 52
- Rebel .... Luke 23:5
- Insurrectionist .... Luke 23:2

E. *Christians:*
- Warned against .... Titus 3:1, 2
- Must endure .... Matt. 5:11, 12
- Must lay aside .... Eph. 4:31

Slave, slavery—*a state of bondage*

A. *Acquired by:*
- Purchase .... Gen. 17:12
- Voluntary service .... Ex. 21:5-6
- Birth .... Ex. 21:2-4
- Capture .... Deut. 20:11-14
- Debt .... 2 Kin. 4:1
- Arrest .... Ex. 22:2, 3
- Inheritance .... Lev. 25:46
- Gift .... Gen. 29:24, 29

B. *Rights of:*
- Sabbath rest .... Ex. 20:10
- Share in religious feasts .... Deut. 12:12, 18
- Membership in covenant .... Gen. 17:10-14
- Refuge for fugitive .... Deut. 23:15, 16
- Murder of, punishable .... Ex. 21:12
- Freedom of, if maimed .... Ex. 21:26, 27
- Entitled to justice .... Job 31:13-15

C. *Privileges of:*
- Entrusted with missions .... Gen. 24:1-14
- Advice of, heeded .... 1 Sam. 9:5-10
- Marriage in master's house .... 1 Chr. 2:34, 35
- Rule over sons .... Prov. 17:2
- May become heir .... Gen. 15:1-4
- May secure freedom .... Ex. 21:2-6

D. *State of, under Christianity:*
- Union "in Christ" .... Gal. 3:28
- Treatment of with justice .... Eph. 6:9
- Duties of, as pleasing God .... Eph. 6:5-8

Sleep—*a state of complete or partial unconsciousness*

A. *Descriptive of:*
- Slumber .... Prov. 6:4, 10
- Desolation .... Jer. 51:39, 57
- Unregeneracy .... 1 Thess. 5:6, 7
- Death .... John 11:11-14
- Spiritual indifference .... Matt. 25:5
- Prophetic vision .... Dan. 8:18

B. *Beneficial:*
- When given by God .... Ps. 3:5; Ps. 127:2
- While trusting God .... Ps. 4:8
- While obeying parents .... Prov. 6:20-22
- When following wisdom .... Prov. 3:21-24
- To the working man .... Eccl. 5:12
- After duty is done .... Ps. 132:1-5
- During a pleasant dream .... Jer. 31:23-26

C. *Condemned:*
- When excessive .... Prov. 6:9-11
- During harvest .... Prov. 10:5
- In times of danger .... Matt. 26:45-47

D. *Inability to:*
- Caused by worry .... Dan. 2:1
- Produced by insomnia .... Esth. 6:1
- Brought on by overwork .... Gen. 31:40

Sleight—*cunning; artifice*
- Christians, beware of .... Eph. 4:14

Slime
- Used in Babel's tower .... Gen. 11:3

Sling—*an instrument for throwing stones*

A. *Used by:*
- Warriors .... Judg. 20:16
- David .... 1 Sam. 17:40-50

B. *Figurative of:*
- God's punishment .... 1 Sam. 25:29
- Captivity .... Jer. 10:18
- Foolishness .... Prov. 26:8

Slothfulness, sluggard—*laziness*

A. *Sources of, in:*
- Excessive sleep .... Prov. 6:9-11
- Laziness .... Prov. 19:15, 24
- Indifference .... Judg. 18:9
- Desires .... Prov. 21:25
- Fearful imaginations .... Prov. 22:13

B. *Way of:*
- Brings hunger .... Prov. 19:15
- Leads to poverty .... Prov. 20:4
- Produces waste .... Prov. 18:9
- Causes decay .... Eccl. 10:18
- Results in forced labor .... Prov. 12:24

C. *Antidotes of, in:*
- Faithfulness .... Matt. 25:26-30
- Fervent spirit .... Rom. 12:11
- Following the faithful .... Heb. 6:12

Slow bellies
- Paul calls Cretians such .... Titus 1:12

Small—*little in size; few in number*

A. *Applied to God's:*
- Choice .... Num. 16:5, 9
- Faithful remnant .... Is. 1:9

B. *Applied to man's:*
- Sin .... Ezek. 16:20
- Unconcern .... Zech. 4:10

Smite, smitten—*to clobber; plague*

A. *Descriptive of:*
- Curse .... Gen. 8:21
- Plagues .... Ex. 3:20
- Miracle .... Ex. 17:5, 6
- God's punishments .... Deut. 28:22-28
- Defeat .... 1 Sam. 4:2, 10
- Death .... 2 Sam. 4:6, 7
- Fear .... Dan. 5:6
- Slapping .... Matt. 5:39

B. *Expressive of God's judgment on:*
- Philistines .... 1 Sam. 5:6, 9
- Pagan nation .... 2 Chr. 14:12
- King's house .... 2 Chr. 21:5-19
- Jews .... Jer. 14:19

C. *Used Messianically of Christ's:*
- Scourging .... Is. 50:6
- Bearing our sins .... Is. 53:4
- Death .... Zech. 13:7
- Judgment .... Is. 11:4

Smith—*a metal worker*
- Blacksmith .... 1 Sam. 13:19, 20
- Worker in iron .... Is. 44:12
- Tubal-cain, first .... Gen. 4:22
- Demetrius, silversmith .... Acts 19:24-27
- Alexander, coppersmith .... 2 Tim. 4:14

Smoke

A. *Resulting from:*
- Destruction .... Gen. 19:28
- God's presence .... Is. 6:4
- God's vengeance .... Is. 34:8-10
- Babylon's end .... Rev. 14:8-11
- World's end .... Is. 51:6

B. *Figurative of:*
- God's anger .... Deut. 29:20
- Our life .... Ps. 102:3
- Spiritual distress .... Ps. 119:83
- Something offensive .... Is. 65:5
- Spirit's advent .... Joel 2:29, 30

Smyrna—*a city of Iona in Asia Minor*
- One of the seven churches .... Rev. 1:11

Snail
- Creature with a spiral tail .... Ps. 58:8

Snake charmer
- Alluded to .... Ps. 58:4, 5

Snares—*traps*

A. *Uses of:*
- Catch birds .... Prov. 7:23

B. *Figurative of:*
- Pagan nations .... Josh. 23:12, 13
- Idols .... Judg. 2:3
- God's representative .... Ex. 10:7
- Words .... Prov. 6:2
- Wicked works .... Ps. 9:16
- Fear of man .... Prov. 29:25
- Immoral woman .... Eccl. 7:26
- Christ .... Is. 8:14, 15
- Sudden destruction .... Luke 21:34, 35
- Riches .... 1 Tim. 6:9, 10
- Devil's trap .... 2 Tim. 2:26

Sneezed
- Seven times .... 2 Kin. 4:35

Snow—*frozen crystallized flakes of water*

A. *Characteristics of:*
- Comes in winter .... Prov. 26:1
- Sent by God .... Job 37:6
- Waters the earth .... Is. 55:10
- Melts with heat .... Job 6:16, 17
- Notable event during .... 2 Sam. 23:20

B. *Whiteness illustrative of:*
- Leprosy .... Ex. 4:6
- Converted sinner .... Ps. 51:7; Is. 1:18
- Nazarite's purity .... Lam. 4:7
- Angel .... Matt. 28:3
- Risen Christ .... Rev. 1:14

Snuffers, snuff dishes
- Used for trimming wicks in lamps .... Ex. 37:23
- Dishes used to catch snuff of lamps .... Ex. 25:38

So
- Egyptian king .... 2 Kin. 17:4

Soap
- Figuratively in .... Mal. 3:2

Sober, sobriety

A. *Described as:*
- Sanity .... 2 Cor. 5:13
- Soberness (not drunk) .... 1 Tim. 3:2, 11
- Temperate nature .... Titus 1:8
- Humble mind .... Rom. 12:3
- Moral rectitude .... Titus 2:12
- Self-control .... Gal. 5:23; 1 Cor. 7:9

B. *Incentives to, found in:*
- Lord's return .... 1 Thess. 5:1-7
- Nearness of the end .... 1 Pet. 4:7
- Satan's attacks .... 1 Cor. 7:5

C. *Required of:*
- Christians .... 1 Thess. 5:6, 8
- Church officers .... 1 Tim. 3:2, 3
- Wives of church officers .... 1 Tim. 3:11
- Aged men .... Titus 2:2
- Young women .... Titus 2:4
- Young men .... Titus 2:6
- Women .... 1 Tim. 2:9
- Children .... 1 Tim. 2:15
- Evangelists .... 2 Tim. 4:5

See Temperance

Sociability—*friendly relations in social gatherings*

A. *Manifested in:*
- Family life .... John 12:1-9
- National life .... Neh. 8:9-18
- Church life .... Acts 2:46

SUBJECT	REFERENCE
B. *Christian's kind, governed by:*	
No fellowship with evil	2 Cor. 6:14-18
Righteous living	Titus 2:12
Honesty in all things	Col. 3:9-14

Socialism (see Communism, Christian)

Socoh, Sochoh—*thorn*

1. Town in south Judah	Josh. 15:1, 35
Where David killed Goliath	1 Sam. 17:1, 49
2. Town in Judah's hill country	Josh. 15:1, 48

Sodi—*an acquaintance*

Father of the Zebulunite spy	Num. 13:10

Sodom—*burnt*

A. *History of:*	
Located in Jordan plain	Gen. 13:10
Became Lot's residence	Gen. 13:11-13
Wickedness of, notorious	Gen. 13:13
Plundered by Chedorlaomer	Gen. 14:9-24
Abraham interceded for	Gen. 18:16-33
Destroyed by God	Gen. 19:1-28
Lot sent out of	Gen. 19:29, 30
B. *Destruction of, illustrative of:*	
God's wrath	Deut. 29:23
Sudden destruction	Lam. 4:6
Total destruction	Jer. 49:18
Future judgment	Matt. 11:23, 24
Example to the ungodly	2 Pet. 2:6
C. *Sin of, illustrative of:*	
Shamelessness	Is. 3:9
Obduracy	Jer. 23:14
Unnaturalness	Jude 7
D. *Figurative of:*	
Wickedness	Deut. 32:32
Jerusalem	Is. 1:9, 10
Judah	Ezek. 16:46-63

Sodomite—*a male cult prostitute*

Prohibition of	Deut. 23:17, 18
Prevalence of, under Rehoboam	1 Kin. 14:24
Asa's removal of	1 Kin. 15:11, 12
Jehoshaphat's riddance of	1 Kin. 22:46
Josiah's reforms against	2 Kin. 23:7
Result of unbelief	Rom. 1:27

Soil—*dirt*

It was planted in good	Ezek. 17:8
Uzziah loved it	2 Chr. 26:10

Sojourn, sojourner

A. *Descriptive of:*	
Abram in Egypt	Gen. 12:10
Jacob with Laban	Gen. 32:4
Israel in Egypt	Gen. 47:4
Stranger	Ex. 12:48, 49
Wandering Levite	Deut. 18:6
Naomi in Moab	Ruth 1:1
Remnant in Egypt	Jer. 42:15-23
Jews in captivity	Ezra 1:4
B. *Characterized by:*	
Simplicity of living	Heb. 11:9
Being among enemies	2 Kin. 8:1, 2
LORD's blessing	Gen. 26:2, 3
C. *Figurative of:*	
Righteous in the world	1 Chr. 29:15
Christian in the world	1 Pet. 1:17

See Foreigners; Strangers

Sold

Descriptive of:	
Purchase	Matt. 26:9
Slavery	Ps. 105:17
Bondage to sin	Rom. 7:14

Soldiers—*military agents of a nation*

A. *Good characteristics of:*	
Obedience	Matt. 8:9
Devotion	Acts 10:7
Subduing riots	Acts 21:31-35
Guarding prisoners	Acts 12:4-6
B. *Bad charcteristics of:*	
Cowardice	Deut. 20:8
Discontent and violence	Luke 3:14
Rashness	Acts 27:42
Bribery	Matt. 28:12
Irreligion	John 19:2, 3, 23
C. *Figurative of:*	
Christians	2 Tim. 2:4
Christian workers	Phil. 2:25
Spiritual armor	Eph. 6:10-18

Solitude—*aloneness*

For:	
Adam, not good	Gen. 2:18
Prayer, good	Matt. 6:6 Matt. 14:23
Rest, necessary	Mark 6:30, 31

Solomon—*peace*

A. *Life of:*	
David's son by Bathsheba	2 Sam. 12:24
Name of, significant	1 Chr. 22:9
Anointed over opposition	1 Kin. 1:5-48
Spared Adonijah	1 Kin. 1:49-53
Received dying instruction from David	1 Kin. 2:1-10
Purged his kingdom of corrupt leaders	1 Kin. 2:11-46
Prayer of, for wisdom	1 Kin. 3:1-15
Organized his kingdom	1 Kin. 4:1-28
Fame of, world wide	1 Kin. 4:29-34
Built the Temple	1 Kin. 5—6
Dedicated the Temple	1 Kin. 8:22-66
Built personal palace	1 Kin. 7:1-12
LORD reappeared to	1 Kin. 9:1-9
Strengthened his kingdom	1 Kin. 9:10-28
Received queen of Sheba	1 Kin. 10:1-13
Encouraged commerce	1 Kin. 10:14-29
Falls into polygamy and idolatry	1 Kin. 11:1-8
God warned him	1 Kin. 11:9-13
Adversaries arise against him	1 Kin. 11:14-40
Reign and death	1 Kin. 11:41-43
B. *Good features of:*	
Chooses an understanding heart	1 Kin. 3:5-9
Exhibited sound judgment	1 Kin. 3:16-28
Excels in wisdom	1 Kin. 4:29-34
Great writer	1 Kin. 4:32
Writer of Psalms	Ps. 72 (Title)
C. *Bad features of:*	
Loves luxury	Eccl. 2:1-11
Marries pagans	1 Kin. 11:1-3
Turns to idolatry	1 Kin. 11:4-8
Enslaves Israel	1 Kin. 12:1-4

Son

A. *Descriptive of:*	
Male child	Gen. 4:25, 26
Half-brothers	Gen. 25:9
Grandson	Gen. 29:5
Disciple	Prov. 7:1
One possessing a certain character	1 Sam. 2:12
One destined to a certain end	John 17:12
Messiah	Is. 7:14
Christian	John 1:12
Angels	Job 1:6
B. *Characteristics of, sometimes:*	
Jealous	Judg. 9:2, 18
Quite different	Gen. 9:18-27
Disloyal	Luke 15:25-30
Unlike their father	2 Sam. 13:30-39
Spiritually different	Gen. 25:22-34
C. *Admonitions addressed to, concerning:*	
Instruction	Prov. 1:8
Sinners	Prov. 1:10-19
Wisdom	Prov. 3:13-35
Correction	Prov. 3:11, 12
Immorality	Prov. 5:1-23
Life's dangers	Prov. 6:1-35

Son-in-law—*a daughter's husband*

Sinful	Gen. 19:14
Believing	Mark 1:29, 30

Son of God—*a title indicating Christ's deity*

A. *Descriptive of Christ as:*	
Eternally begotten	Ps. 2:7 Heb. 1:5
Messianic King	Ps. 89:26, 27
Virgin-born	Luke 1:31-35
Trinity-member	Matt. 28:19
Priest-king	Heb. 1:8 Heb. 5:5, 6
B. *Witnesses of, by:*	
Father	Matt. 17:5
Angels	John 1:51
Demons	Mark 5:7
Satan	Matt. 4:3, 6
Men	Matt. 16:16
Christ Himself	John 9:35-37
His resurrection	Rom. 1:1-4
Christians	Acts 2:36
Scriptures	John 20:31
Inner witness	1 John 5:10-13
C. *Significance of, as indicating:*	
Cost of man's reconciliation	Rom. 5:6-11
Greatness of God's love	John 3:16
Sin of unbelief	Heb. 10:28, 29
Worship due Christ	Rev. 4:11
Dignity of human nature	Rom. 8:3 Heb. 2:14
Humanity of Christ	Gal. 4:4
Pattern of glorification	Rom. 8:29 Phil. 3:21
Destruction of Satan	1 John 3:8
Uniqueness of Christ	Heb. 1:5-9
D. *Belief in Christ as:*	
Derived from the Scriptures	John 20:31
Necessary for eternal life	John 3:18, 36
Source of eternal life	John 6:40
Foundation of the faith	Acts 9:20
Affirmation of deity	1 John 2:23, 24
Illustrated	John 11:14-44
E. *Powers of Christ as, to:*	
Have life in Himself	John 5:26
Reveal the Father	Matt. 11:27
Glorify the Father	John 17:1
Do the Father's works	John 5:19, 20
Redeem men	Gal. 4:4, 5
Give freedom	John 8:36
Raise the dead	John 5:21, 25
Judge men	John 5:22

Son of Man—*a self-designation of Christ*

A. *Title of, applied to:*	
Ezekiel	Ezek. 2:1, 3, 6
Daniel	Dan. 8:17
Messiah	Dan. 7:13
Christ:	
By Himself	Matt. 8:20
By only Stephen elsewhere	Acts 7:56
In John's vision	Rev. 1:13
B. *As indicative of Christ's:*	
Self-designation	Matt. 16:13
Humanity	Matt. 11:19
Messiahship	Luke 18:31
Lordship	Matt. 12:8
Sovereignty	Matt. 13:41
Obedience	Phil. 2:8
Suffering	Mark 9:12
Death	Matt. 12:40
Resurrection	Matt. 17:9-23
Regal power	Matt. 16:28
Return	Matt. 24:27-37
Glorification	Heb. 2:6-10
C. *Christ's powers as, to:*	
Forgive sins	Matt. 9:6
Save men	Luke 19:10
Redeem men	Matt. 20:28
Reward men	Matt. 16:27
Reward men	Matt. 19:28
Rule His Church	Col. 1:17, 18

Song of Solomon—*a book of the Old Testament*

The bride and the bridegroom	Song 1
Song of the bride	Song 2:8—3:5
Song of the bridegroom	Song 4:1-15
The bride meditates	Song 4:16—6:3
The bridegroom appeals	Song 6:4—7:9
Lovers united	Song 7:10—8:14

Songs

A. *Described as:*	
New	Rev. 5:9
Spiritual	Eph. 5:19
B. *Uses of, as:*	
Witness	Deut. 31:19-22
Torment	Ps. 137:3
March	Num. 21:17, 18
Processional	1 Chr. 13:7, 8

S

SUBJECT REFERENCE

C. *Expressive of:*

Triumph ... Judg. 5:12
Physical joy ... Gen. 31:27
Spiritual joy ... Ps. 119:54
Deliverance ... Ps. 32:7
Hypocrisy ... Amos 5:23
Derision ... Ps. 69:12

D. *Figurative of:*

Passover (the Lord's Supper) ... Is. 30:29; Matt. 26:26-30
Messiah's advent ... Is. 42:10
Gospel age ... Is. 26:1, 2

Song writer

Solomon, famous as ... 1 Kin. 4:32

Sonship of believers

A. *Evidences of, seen in:*

New nature ... 1 John 3:9-12
Possession of the Spirit ... Rom. 8:15-17
Chastisement ... Heb. 12:5-8

B. *Blessedness of, manifested in:*

Regeneration ... John 1:12
Adoption ... Gal. 4:5, 6
Glorification ... Rom. 8:19-21

Soothsayer—*a diviner, fortune teller*

Among Philistines ... Is. 2:6
At Babylon ... Dan. 2:27
At Philippi ... Acts 16:12, 16
Unable to interpret ... Dan. 4:7
Forbidden in Israel ... Mic. 5:12
See Divination

Sop—*a small portion of food*

Christ gives to Judas ... John 13:26-30

Sopater—*of sound parentage*

One of Paul's companions ... Acts 20:4

Sophereth—*writer, scribe*

Descendants of Solomon's servants ... Neh. 7:57

Sorcerers—*supposed possessors of supernatural powers*

A. *Prevalence of, in:*

Assyria ... Nah. 3:4, 5
Egypt ... Ex. 7:11
Babylon ... Is. 47:9-13
Palestine ... Acts 8:9-24
Last days ... Rev. 9:21

B. *Punishment of, described:*

Legally ... Deut. 18:10-12
Prophetically ... Mal. 3:5
Symbolically ... Rev. 21:8

See Divination; Magic, magician

Sorcery—*the practice of magic*

Forbidden in Israel ... Deut. 18:10
Condemned by the prophets ... Mic. 5:12
Practiced by Manasseh ... 2 Chr. 33:6
Work of the flesh ... Gal. 5:20

Sore

Intense feeling ... 2 Sam. 13:36
Crisis ... Gen. 41:56, 57
Plague ... Lev. 13:42, 43

Sorek—*a choice vine*

Valley, home of Delilah ... Judg. 16:4

Sorrow—*grief*

A. *Kinds of:*

Hypocritical ... Matt. 14:9
Unfruitful ... Matt. 19:22
Temporary ... John 16:6, 20-22
Continual ... Rom. 9:2
Fruitful ... 2 Cor. 7:8-11
Christian ... 1 Thess. 4:13

B. *Caused by:*

Sin ... Gen. 3:16, 17
Death ... John 11:33-35
Drunkenness ... Prov. 23:29-35
Love of money ... 1 Tim. 6:10
Apostasy ... Ps. 16:4
Persecution ... Esth. 9:22
Hardship of life ... Ps. 90:10
Knowledge ... Eccl. 1:18
Distressing news ... Acts 20:37, 38

SUBJECT REFERENCE

C. *Of the righteous:*

Not like the world's ... 1 Thess. 4:13
Sometimes intense ... Ps. 18:4, 5
Seen in the face ... Neh. 2:2-4
None in God's blessings ... Prov. 10:22
Shown in repentance ... 2 Cor. 7:10
To be removed ... Is. 25:8
None in heaven ... Rev. 21:4
Shall flee away ... Is. 51:11

See Grief

Sosipater—*saving a father*

Kinsman of Paul ... Rom. 16:21

Sosthenes—*of sound strength*

1. Ruler of the synagogue at Corinth ... Acts 18:17
2. Paul's Christian brother ... 1 Cor. 1:1

Sotai—*Jehovah is turning aside*

Head of a family of servants ... Ezra 2:55

Sottish—*thick-headed*

Judah thus called ... Jer. 4:22

Soul—*the immaterial part of man*

A. *Descriptive of:*

Man's life ... 1 Sam. 24:11
People ... Acts 2:41, 43
Sinner ... James 5:20
Emotional life ... 1 Sam. 18:1, 3
Spiritual life ... Ps. 42:1, 2, 4
Disembodied state ... Rev. 6:9; Rev. 20:4

B. *Characteristics of:*

Made by God ... Gen. 2:7
Belongs to God ... Ezek. 18:3, 4
Possesses immortality ... Matt. 10:28
Most vital asset ... Matt. 16:26
Leaves body at death ... Gen. 35:18

C. *Abilities of, able to:*

Believe ... Heb. 10:39
Love God ... Luke 10:27
Sin ... Mic. 6:7
Prosper ... 3 John 2
Survive death ... Matt. 10:28

D. *Duties of, to:*

Keep itself ... Deut. 4:9
Seek the LORD ... Deut. 4:29
Love the LORD ... Deut. 6:5
Serve the LORD ... Deut. 10:12
Store God's Word ... Deut. 11:18
Keep God's Law ... Deut. 26:16
Obey God ... Deut. 30:2, 6, 10
Get wisdom ... Prov. 19:8

E. *Enemies of, seen in:*

Fleshly lusts ... 1 Pet. 2:11
Evil environment ... 2 Pet. 2:8
Sin ... Lev. 5:4, 15, 17
Adultery ... Prov. 6:32
Evil men ... Prov. 22:24, 25
Ignorance ... Prov. 8:36
Hell ... Prov. 23:14

F. *Of the righteous:*

Kept by God ... Ps. 121:7
Vexed by sin ... 2 Pet. 2:8
Subject to authorities ... Rom. 13:1
Purified by obedience ... 1 Pet. 1:22
Not allowed to famish ... Prov. 10:3
Restored ... Ps. 23:1, 3
Enriched ... Prov. 11:25
Satisfied ... Prov. 13:25
Reign with Christ ... Rev. 20:4

G. *Of the wicked:*

Desires evil ... Prov. 21:10
Delights in abominations ... Is. 66:3
Has nothing ... Prov. 13:4
Required ... Luke 12:19, 20
To be punished ... Rom. 2:9

Soul winning

Importance of ... James 5:20
Christ's command ... Matt. 4:19
Our reward ... Dan. 12:3

Sound doctrine

A. *Manifested in:*

Heart's prayer ... Ps. 119:80
Speech ... 2 Tim. 1:13
Righteous living ... 1 Tim. 1:10

SUBJECT REFERENCE

B. *Need of:*

For exhortation ... Titus 1:9
For the faith ... Titus 1:13
Denied by some ... 2 Tim. 4:3

Sour grapes—*not yet mature*

Used proverbially ... Jer. 31:29, 30

Sowing—*scattering seed*

A. *Restrictions upon, regarding:*

Sabbath year ... Lev. 25:3-22
Mingled seed ... Lev. 19:19
Weather ... Eccl. 11:4, 6

B. *Figurative of evil things:*

Iniquity ... Job 4:8
Wind ... Hos. 8:7
Discord ... Prov. 6:14, 19
Strife ... Prov. 16:28
False teaching ... Matt. 13:25, 39
Sin ... Gal. 6:7, 8

C. *Figurative of good things:*

God's Word ... Is. 55:10
Reward ... 2 Cor. 9:6, 10
Gospel ... Matt. 13:3, 4, 37
Gospel messengers ... John 4:36, 37
Resurrection ... 1 Cor. 15:36-44
Eternal life ... Gal. 6:7-9

Spain—*a country in southwest Europe*

Paul desires to visit ... Rom. 15:24, 28

Sparrow—*a small bird*

Value of ... Matt. 10:29, 31

Spearmen—*infantry men with spears*

One of, pierces Christ's side ... John 19:34
Paul's military escort ... Acts 23:23, 24

Speckled

Spotted (of goats) ... Gen. 30:32-39
Colored (of birds) ... Jer. 12:9

Speech—*the intelligible utterance of the mouth*

A. *Of the wicked, consisting of:*

Lies ... Ps. 58:3
Cursing ... Ps. 59:12
Enticements ... Prov. 7:21
Blasphemies ... Dan. 7:25
Earthly things ... John 3:31
Deception ... Rom. 16:18

B. *Of the righteous, consisting of:*

God's righteousness ... Ps. 35:28
Wisdom ... 1 Cor. 2:6, 7
God's Word ... Ps. 119:172
Truth ... Eph. 4:25
Mystery of Christ ... Col. 4:3, 4
Sound doctrine ... Titus 2:1, 8

Speed—*to hasten*

"Let him make" ... Is. 5:19
"They will come with" ... Is. 5:26

Spending—*paying out money or service for things*

A. *Wastefully, on:*

Harlots ... Luke 15:30
Physicians ... Mark 5:26

B. *Wisely:*

In Christ's service ... 2 Cor. 12:15

Spices—*aromatic vegetable compounds*

A. *Uses of:*

Food ... Song 8:2
Incense ... Ex. 30:34-38
Fragrance ... Song 4:10

B. *Features concerning:*

Used as presents ... Gen. 43:11
Objects of commerce ... Gen. 37:25
Tokens of royal favor ... 1 Kin. 10:2
Stored in the temple ... 1 Chr. 9:29
Sign of wealth ... 2 Kin. 20:13

Spider

Web of, figurative of:

Insecurity ... Is. 59:5
Godless ... Job 8:14

Spies—*secret agents of a foreign government*

A. *Purpose of, to:*

Search out Canaan ... Num. 13:1-33
Prepare for invasion ... Josh. 2:1-21
Search out new land ... Judg. 18:2-17
Make false charges ... Luke 20:20

SUBJECT REFERENCE

B. *Men accused of, falsely:*
- Jacob's sons ... Gen. 42:9-34
- David's servants ... 2 Sam. 10:3

Spikenard
- Used as a perfume ... Song 1:12
- Mary uses it in anointing Jesus ... Mark 14:3; John 12:3

Spill—*to flow forth*
- Water ... 2 Sam. 14:14
- Wine ... Luke 5:37

Spinning—*twisting fibers together to form cloth*
- Work done by women ... Ex. 35:25
- Sign of industry ... Prov. 31:19
- As an illustration ... Matt. 6:28

Spirit—*an immaterial being*

A. *Descriptive of:*
- Holy Spirit ... Gen. 1:2
- Angels ... Heb. 1:7, 14
- Man's immaterial nature ... 1 Cor. 2:11
- Evil ... 1 Sam. 16:14-23
- Believer's immaterial nature ... 1 Cor. 5:3, 5
- Controlling influence ... Is. 29:10
- Inward reality ... Rom. 2:29
- Disembodied state ... Heb. 12:23; 1 Pet. 3:19

B. *Characteristics of, in man:*
- Center of emotions ... 1 Kin. 21:5
- Source of passions ... Ezek. 3:14
- Cause of volitions (will) ... Prov. 16:32
- Subject to divine influence ... Deut. 2:30; Is. 19:14
- Leaves body at death ... Eccl. 12:7; James 2:26

See Soul

Spirit, Holy (see Holy Spirit)

Spirit of Christ

A. *Descriptive of the Holy Spirit as:*
- Dwelling in Old Testament prophets ... 1 Pet. 1:10-11
- Sent by God ... Gal. 4:6
- Given to believers ... Rom. 8:9
- Supplying believers ... Phil. 1:19
- Produces boldness ... Acts 4:29-31
- Commanded ... Eph. 5:18

B. *Christ's human spirit (consciousness), of His:*
- Perception ... Mark 2:8
- Emotions ... Mark 8:12
- Life ... Luke 23:46

Spirits, distinguishing of

A. *Described as:*
- Spiritual gift ... 1 Cor. 12:10
- Necessary ... 1 Thess. 5:19-21

B. *Tests of:*
- Christ's:
  - Deity ... 1 Cor. 12:3
  - Humanity ... 1 John 4:1-6
- Christian fellowship ... 1 John 2:18, 19

Spiritual—*the holy or immaterial*

A. *Applied to:*
- Gifts ... 1 Cor. 12:1
- Law ... Rom. 7:14
- Things ... Rom. 15:27
- Christians ... 1 Cor. 3:1
- Resurrected body ... 1 Cor. 15:44-46
- Evil forces ... Eph. 6:12

B. *Designating, Christians:*
- Ideal state ... 1 Cor. 3:1
- Discernment ... 1 Cor. 2:13-15
- Duty ... Gal. 6:1
- Manner of life ... Col. 3:16

Spiritual gifts (see Gifts, spiritual)

Spiritually—*a holy frame of mind*
- Source of ... Gal. 5:22-26
- Expression of ... 1 Cor. 13:1-13
- Growth in ... 2 Pet. 1:4-11
- Enemies of ... 1 John 2:15-17

Spite—*an injury prompted by contempt*
- Of vexation of grief ... Ps. 10:14
- Inflicted upon Christ ... Matt. 22:6

SUBJECT REFERENCE

Spitting, spittle

A. *Symbolic of:*
- Contempt ... Num. 12:14
- Rejection ... Matt. 26:67
- Uncleanness ... Lev. 15:8

B. *Miraculous uses of, to heal:*
- Dumb man ... Mark 7:33-35
- Blind man ... Mark 8:23-25
- Man born blind ... John 9:6, 7

Spoil—*loot or plunder*
- Clothing ... Ex. 3:22
- Cattle ... Josh. 8:2
- Sheep ... Num. 31:32
- House ... Mark 3:27
- Silver and gold ... Nah. 2:9
- Camp ... 1 Sam. 17:53

Spokesman—*one who speaks for others*
- Aaron deputed to be ... Ex. 4:14-16

Sponge—*a very absorbent sea fossil*
- Full of vinegar, offered to Christ ... Matt. 27:48

Spot, spotless

A. *Descriptive of:*
- Blemish on the face ... Job 11:15
- Imperfection of the body ... Song 4:7
- Mixed colors ... Gen. 30:32-39
- Leopard's spots ... Jer. 13:23

B. *Figuratively* ("spotless") *of:*
- Sin ... Jude 23
- False teachers ... 2 Pet. 2:13
- Christ's death ... 1 Pet. 1:19
- Believer's perfection ... 2 Pet. 3:14
- Glorified Church ... Eph. 5:27
- Perfect offering ... Num. 19:2
- Obedience ... 1 Tim. 6:14

Springtime—*the season of nature's rebirth*
- Symbolically described ... Song 2:11-13

Sprinkle

A. *Used literally of:*
- Water ... Num. 8:7
- Oil ... Lev. 14:16
- Human blood ... 2 Kin. 9:33

B. *Of blood, used in:*
- Passover ... Ex. 12:21, 22
- Sinaitic covenant ... Ex. 24:8; Heb. 9:19, 21
- Sin offering ... Lev. 4:6
- New covenant ... Heb. 12:24

C. *Used figuratively of:*
- Regeneration ... Heb. 10:22
- Purification ... 1 Pet. 1:2

Square—*having four equal sides*
- Altar ... Ex. 27:1
- Breastplate ... Ex. 39:8, 9
- City of God ... Rev. 21:16

Stab—*to pierce with a knife*
- Asahel by Abner ... 2 Sam. 2:22, 23
- Abner by Joab ... 2 Sam. 3:27
- Amasa by Joab ... 2 Sam. 20:10

Stachys—*head of grain*
- One whom Paul loved ... Rom. 16:9

Staff—*a long stick or rod*
- A traveler's support ... Gen. 32:10
- Denotes food support ... Lev. 26:26
- A military weapon ... Is. 10:24

Stairs, winding
- Part of Solomon's Temple ... 1 Kin. 6:8

Stalls—*quarters for animals*
- 40,000 in Solomon's time ... 1 Kin. 4:26

Stammerer—*one who stutters*
- Used of judicial punishment ... Is. 28:11
- Of the Gospel age ... Is. 32:1, 4

Stars

A. *Features concerning:*
- Created by God ... Gen. 1:16
- Ordained by God ... Ps. 8:3
- Set in the expanse ... Gen. 1:17
- Follow fixed ordinances ... Jer. 31:35, 36

SUBJECT REFERENCE

- Named by God ... Ps. 147:4
- Established forever ... Ps. 148:3, 6
- Of vast numbers ... Gen. 15:5
- Manifest God's power ... Is. 40:26
- Of different proportions ... 1 Cor. 15:41
- Very high ... Job 22:12

B. *Worship of:*
- Forbidden ... Deut. 4:19
- Punished ... Deut. 17:3-7
- Introduced by Manasseh ... 2 Kin. 21:3
- Condemned by the prophets ... Jer. 8:2; Zeph. 1:4, 5

C. *List of, in Bible:*
- Arcturus ... Job 9:9
- Mazzaroth ... Job 38:32
- Orion ... Job 9:9
- Pleiades ... Job 9:9
- Chambers of the south ... Job 9:9
- Of Bethlehem ... Matt. 2:2, 9, 10

D. *Figurative of:*
- Christ's:
  - First Advent ... Num. 24:17
  - Second Advent ... Rev. 22:16
- Angels ... Rev. 1:16, 20
- Judgment ... Ezek. 32:7
- False security ... Obad. 4
- Glorified saints ... Dan. 12:3
- Apostates ... Jude 13

State—*established government*

A. *Agents of:*
- Under God's control ... Dan. 4:17, 25; Jon. 19:10, 11
- Sometimes evil ... Mark 6:14-29
- Sometimes good ... Neh. 2:1-9
- Protectors of the Law ... Rom. 13:1-4

B. *Duties of Christians to:*
- Pray for ... 1 Tim. 2:1, 2
- Pay taxes to ... Matt. 22:17-21
- Be subject to ... Rom. 13:5, 6
- Resist (when evil) ... Acts 4:17-21

Stature—*the natural height of the body*

A. *Used physically of:*
- Giants ... Num. 13:32
- Sabeans ... Is. 45:14

B. *Significance of:*
- Normal, in human growth ... Luke 2:52
- Cannot be changed ... Matt. 6:27
- Not indicative of greatness ... 1 Sam. 16:7
- In spiritual things ... Eph. 4:13

Statute of limitation
- Recognized in the Law ... Deut. 15:1-5, 9

Steadfastness—*firm, persistent and determined in one's endeavors*

A. *In human things, following:*
- Person ... Ruth 1:18
- Leader ... Jer. 35:1-19
- Principle ... Dan. 1:8

B. *In spiritual things:*
- Enduring chastisement ... Heb. 12:7
- Bearing persecution ... Rom. 8:35-37
- Maintaining perseverance ... Heb. 3:6, 14
- Stability of faith ... Col. 2:5
- Persevering in service ... 1 Cor. 15:58
- Resisting Satan ... 1 Pet. 5:9
- Defending Christian liberty ... Gal. 5:1

C. *Elements of, seen in:*
- Having a goal ... Phil. 3:12-14
- Discipline ... 1 Cor. 9:25-27
- Run the race ... Heb. 12:1, 2
- Never give up ... Rev. 3:10, 21

Stealing—*taking another's property*
- Common on earth ... Matt. 6:19
- Forbidden in:
  - Law ... Ex. 20:15
  - Gospel ... Rom. 13:9
- Christians not to do ... Eph. 4:28
- Excludes from heaven ... 1 Cor. 6:9, 10
- None in heaven ... Matt. 6:20

Stephanas—*crowned*
- Corinthian Christian ... 1 Cor. 1:16
- First convert of Achaia ... 1 Cor. 16:15
- Visits Paul ... 1 Cor. 16:17

Stephen—*wreath or crown*
- One of the seven deacons ... Acts 6:1-8

SUBJECT ... REFERENCE

Stray animals

Must be returned ... Ex. 23:4
Saul's pursuit of ... 1 Sam. 9:3-5

Streets—*principal thoroughfares*

A. *Uses of:*

Display ... Matt. 6:5
Teaching ... Luke 13:26
Parades ... Esth. 6:9, 11
Proclamations ... Neh. 8:3-5
Healing ... Mark 6:56

B. *Dangers of, from:*

Fighting ... Josh. 2:19
Prostitutes ... Prov. 7:6-23
Wicked ... Ps. 55:11
Assault ... Judg. 19:15-26

Strength, strengthen—*resident power*

A. *Kinds of:*

Physical ... Prov. 20:29
Constitutional ... Ps. 90:10
Hereditary ... Gen. 49:3
Angelic ... Ps. 103:20
Military ... Dan. 2:37
Spiritual ... Ps. 138:3
Superhuman ... Judg. 16:5, 6, 19
Divine ... Is. 63:1

B. *Dissipation of, by:*

Iniquity ... Ps. 31:10
Hunger ... 1 Sam. 28:20, 22
Sexual looseness ... Prov. 31:3
Age ... Ps. 71:9
Visions ... Dan. 10:8, 16, 17

C. *Increase of:*

From:
God ... Is. 41:10
Christ ... 2 Tim. 4:17
Spirit ... Eph. 3:16
Brothers ... Luke 22:32

By:
Wisdom ... Eccl. 7:19
Waiting on the LORD ... Is. 40:31
Lord's grace ... 2 Cor. 12:9

Strife—*conflicts between people*

A. *Sources of, in:*

Hatred ... Prov. 10:12
Perverseness ... Prov. 16:28
Transgression ... Prov. 17:19
Scorner ... Prov. 22:10
Anger ... Prov. 29:22
Flesh ... Gal. 5:19, 20

B. *Actual causes of, seen in:*

Self-seeking ... Luke 22:24
Dispute between men ... Gen. 13:7-11
Contentious man ... Prov. 26:21
Being carnal ... 1 Cor. 3:3
Disputes ... 1 Tim. 6:4

C. *Avoidance of, by:*

Being slow to anger ... Prov. 15:18
Simplicity of life ... Prov. 17:1

See Contention; Quarrel

Strike—*afflict; attack*

A. *Descriptive of:*

Smeared blood ... Ex. 12:7, 22
Advance in age ... Luke 1:7, 18
Slapping ... John 18:22
God's judgment ... Ps. 39:10

B. *Of divine punishment, upon:*

Christ ... Is. 53:4, 8
Sinners ... Prov. 7:23
World ... Ps. 110:5
Rebellious ... Is. 14:6
Israel ... Is. 30:26

Striker—*a contentious person*

Disqualifies for church office ... 1 Tim. 3:3

Stripes—*used in scourging*

Limit of ... Deut. 25:1-4
Because of sin ... Ps. 89:32
Upon the Messiah, healing ... Is. 53:5; 1 Pet. 2:24
Uselessness of, on a fool ... Prov. 17:10
Paul's experience with ... Acts 16:23, 33; 2 Cor. 11:23

Striving, spiritual

To enter the strait gate ... Luke 13:24

SUBJECT ... REFERENCE

Against sin ... Heb. 12:4
With divine help ... Col. 1:29
In prayer ... Rom. 15:30
For the faith of the Gospel ... Phil. 1:27

Stroke—*a blow*

With an ax ... Deut. 19:5
With a sword ... Esth. 9:5

Strong drink (see Drunkenness)

Stronghold—*fortress*

David captured ... 2 Sam. 5:7
The LORD is ... Nah. 1:7

Studs—*ornaments*

Of silver ... Song 1:11

Study—*intensive intellectual effort*

Of the Scriptures ... Acts 17:10, 11; 2 Tim. 3:16, 17

Stumble—*to trip on some obstacle*

A. *Occasions of, found in:*

Strong drink ... Is. 28:7
God's Word ... 1 Pet. 2:8
Christ ... Rom. 9:32, 33
Christ crucified ... 1 Cor. 1:23
Christian liberty ... 1 Cor. 8:9

B. *Avoidance of, by:*

Following wisdom ... Prov. 3:21, 23

See Offend, offense

Suah—*sweepings*

Asherite ... 1 Chr. 7:36

Subjection—*the state of being under another's control*

A. *Of domestic and civil relationships:*

Servants to masters ... 1 Pet. 2:18
Citizens to government ... Rom. 13:1-6
Children to parents ... 1 Tim. 3:4
Wives to husbands ... Eph. 5:24
Younger to elder ... 1 Pet. 5:5

B. *Of spiritual relationships:*

Creation to sin ... Rom. 8:20, 21
Demons to the disciples ... Luke 10:17, 20
Believers to the Gospel ... 2 Cor. 9:13
Christians to one another ... 1 Pet. 5:5
Christians to God ... Heb. 12:9
Creation to Christ ... Heb. 2:5, 8
Church to Christ ... Eph. 5:24
Christ to God ... 1 Cor. 15:28

Subjugation—*the state of being subdued by force*

Physical force ... 1 Sam. 13:19-23
Spiritual power ... Mark 5:1-15

Submission—*humble obedience to another's will*

Each other ... Eph. 5:21
Husbands ... Eph. 5:22
Rulers ... 1 Pet. 2:13
Elders ... 1 Pet. 5:5
Christian leaders ... Heb. 13:17
God ... James 4:7

Substitution—*replacing one person or thing for another*

Ram for the man ... Gen. 22:13
Offering for the offerer ... Lev. 16:21, 22
Levites for the first-born ... Num. 3:12-45
Christ for the sinner ... Is. 53:4-6; 1 Pet. 2:24

Subtlety—*craftiness of*

Satan ... Gen. 3:1
Wicked ... Acts 13:10
Jewish leaders ... Matt. 26:3, 4
Jacob ... Gen. 27:35

Success—*accomplishment of goals in life*

A. *Rules of:*

Put God first ... Matt. 6:32-34
Follow the Book ... Josh. 1:7-9
Seek the goal ... Phil. 3:13, 14
Never give up ... Gal. 6:9
Do all for Christ ... Phil. 1:20, 21

B. *Hindrances of, seen in:*

Unbelief ... Heb. 4:6, 11
Enemies ... Neh. 4:1-23
Sluggishness ... Prov. 24:30-34
Love of the world ... Matt. 16:26

SUBJECT ... REFERENCE

Succoth—*booths*

1. Place east of the Jordan ... Judg. 8:4, 5
Jacob's residence here ... Gen. 33:17
2. Israel's first camp ... Ex. 12:37

Succoth-benoth—*tabernacles of girls*

Idol set up in Samaria by Babylonians ... 2 Kin. 17:30

Suchathites

Descendants of Caleb ... 1 Chr. 2:42, 55

Suck—*to give milk to offspring*

Characteristics of:

True among animals ... 1 Sam. 7:9
Normal for human mothers ... Job 3:12
Figurative of Israel's restoration ... Is. 60:16
Figurative of wicked ... Job 20:16

Suffering for Christ

Necessary in Christian living ... 1 Cor. 12:26; Phil. 1:29
Blessed privilege ... Acts 5:41
Never in vain ... Gal. 3:4
After Christ's example ... Phil. 3:10; 1 Pet. 2:20, 21
Of short duration ... 1 Pet. 5:10
Not comparable to heaven's glory ... Rom. 8:18; 1 Pet. 4:13

Sufferings of Christ

A. *Features concerning:*

Predicted ... 1 Pet. 1:11
Announced ... Mark 9:12
Explained ... Luke 24:26, 46
Fulfilled ... Acts 3:18
Witnessed ... 1 Pet. 5:1
Proclaimed ... Acts 17:2, 3

B. *Benefits of, to Christ:*

Preparation for priesthood ... Heb. 2:17, 18
Learned obedience ... Heb. 5:8
Way to glory ... Heb. 2:9, 10

C. *Benefits of, to Christians:*

Brought to God ... 1 Pet. 3:18

Our:
Sins atoned ... Heb. 9:26-28
Example ... 1 Pet. 2:21-23
Fellowship ... Phil. 3:10
Comfort ... 2 Cor. 1:5-7

Suicide—*self-murder*

A. *Thought of, induced by:*

Life's weariness ... Job 3:20-23
Life's vanity ... Eccl. 2:17
Anger ... Jon. 4:3, 8, 9

B. *Brought on by:*

Hopelessness ... Judg. 16:29, 30
Sin ... 1 Kin. 16:18, 19
Disappointment ... 2 Sam. 17:23
Betrayal of Christ ... Matt. 27:3-5

C. *Other features concerning:*

Desired by some ... Rev. 9:6
Attempted but prevented ... Acts 16:27, 28
Imputed to Christ ... John 8:22
Satan tempts Christ to ... Luke 4:9

D. *Principles prohibiting, found in:*

Body's sacredness ... 1 Cor. 6:19
Prohibition against murder ... Ex. 20:13
Faith's expectancy ... 2 Tim. 4:6-8, 18

Sakkiim

African people in Shishak's army ... 2 Chr. 12:3

Summer

Made by God ... Ps. 74:17
Sign of God's covenant ... Gen. 8:22

Time of:
Fruit harvest ... 2 Sam. 16:1, 2
Sowing and harvest ... Prov. 6:6-8

Figurative of: Industry ... Prov. 10:5
Opportunity ... Jer. 8:20

Preceded by spring ... Matt. 24:32

Sun

A. *Characteristics of:*

Created by God ... Gen. 1:14, 16
Under God's control ... Ps. 104:19; Matt. 5:45
Made to rule ... Gen. 1:16

SUBJECT	REFERENCE
Necessary for fruit	Deut. 33:14
Given for light	Jer. 31:35
Made for God's glory	Ps. 148:3
Causes: Scorching	Jon. 4:8
Sunstroke	2 Kin. 4:18, 19
B. *Miracles connected with:*	
Stands still	Josh. 10:12, 13
Shadows of, turned back	2 Kin. 20:9-11
Darkening of, at crucifixion	Luke 23:44-49
Going down at noon	Amos 8:9
C. *Worship of:*	
Forbidden	Deut. 4:19
By Manasseh	2 Kin. 21:3, 5
By Jews	Jer. 8:2
D. *Figurative of:*	
God's presence	Ps. 84:11
Earth's sphere of action	Eccl. 1:3, 9, 14
God's Law	Ps. 19:4-7
Future glory	Matt. 13:43
Christ's glory	Matt. 17:2

Sunday (see First day of week)

Sundial—*an instrument for telling time*

Miracle of	Is. 38:8

Sundry—*in many parts*

Applied to God's revelation	Heb. 1:1

Sunstroke—*stricken by sun's heat*

Child dies of	2 Kin. 4:18-20

Superscription—*something inscribed on*

Roman coin	Mark 12:16
Cross of Christ	Luke 23:38

Superstition—*gullible ideas based on fancy or fear*

A. *Causes of, in wrong views of:*	
God	1 Kin. 20:23
Holy objects	1 Sam. 4:3
God's providence	Jer. 44:15-19
B. *Manifestations of, in:*	
Seeking illogical causes	Acts 28:4
Ignorance of the true God	Acts 17:22
Perverting true religion	Mark 7:1-16

Supper (see Lord's Supper)

Sur—*turning aside, entrance*

Name given to a gate	2 Kin. 11:6
Called "Gate of the Foundation"	2 Chr. 23:5

Sure—*something trustworthy*

A. *Descriptive of divine things:*	
God's law	Ps. 19:7
Messianic line	2 Sam. 23:5
Messiah	Is. 22:23, 25
New covenant	Acts 13:34
God's: Prophecies	2 Pet. 1:19
Promises	Rom. 4:16
Purposes	2 Tim. 2:19
B. *Applied to the believer's:*	
Calling and election	2 Pet. 1:10
Faith	John 6:69
Dedication	Neh. 9:38
Life of faith	Is. 32:18
Confidence in God's Word	Luke 1:1
Reward	Prov. 11:18

Surety—*one who guarantees another's debt*

A. *Descriptive of:*	
Certainty	Gen. 15:13
Guarantee	Gen. 43:9
Our Lord	Heb. 7:22
B. *Features concerning:*	
Risks involved in	Prov. 11:15
Warning against	Prov. 6:1-5

Surfeiting—*gluttonous indulgence*

Christ warns against	Luke 21:34

Surname—*a family name*

A. *Descriptive of:*	
Simon Peter	Acts 10:5, 32
John Mark	Acts 12:12, 25
Judas Iscariot	Luke 22:3
Judas Barsabas	Acts 15:22
Joses Barnabas	Acts 4:36
James and John Boanerges	Mark 3:17

SUBJECT	REFERENCE
B. *Figurative of God's:*	
Call of Gentiles	Is. 44:5
Sovereignty over kings	Is. 45:4

Susanna—*lily*

Believing woman ministering to Christ	Luke 8:2, 3

Susi—*horseman*

Mannassite spy	Num. 13:11

Suspicion—*doubt of another's intent*

A. *Kinds of:*	
Unjustified	Josh. 22:9-31
Pretended	Gen. 42:7-12
Unsuspected	John 13:21-28
B. *Objects of:*	
Esau by Jacob	Gen. 32:3-12
Jeremiah by officials	Jer. 37:12-15
Jews by Haman	Esth. 3:8, 9
Mary by Joseph	Matt. 1:18-25
Peter by a damsel	Matt. 26:69-74

Sustenance—*means of sustaining life*

Israel by the Lord	Neh. 9:21
Elijah by ravens and a widow	1 Kin. 17:1-9
Believer by the LORD	Ps. 3:5

Swaddling—*bandages, wrappings*

Figurative of Jerusalem	Ezek. 16:3, 4
Jesus wrapped in	Luke 2:7

Swallow—*a long-winged, migratory bird*

Nesting in the sanctuary	Ps. 84:3
Noted for chattering	Is. 38:14

Swallow—*to engulf; to overwhelm*

A. *Applied miraculously to:*	
Aaron's rod	Ex. 7:12
Red Sea	Ex. 15:12
Earth	Num. 16:30-34
Great fish	Jon. 1:17
B. *Applied figuratively to:*	
God's judgments	Ps. 21:9
Conquest	Jer. 51:34, 44
Captivity	Hos. 8:7, 8
Sorrow	2 Cor. 2:7
Resurrection	Is. 25:8

Swan

Should be translated "horned owl"	Lev. 11:18

Swearing—*taking an oath*

A. *Kinds of:*	
Proclamatory	Ex. 17:16
Protective	Gen. 21:23
Personal	1 Sam. 20:17
Purificatory	Neh. 13:25-30
Promissory	Luke 1:73
Prohibited	James 5:12
B. *Of God, objects of:*	
God's purpose	Is. 14:24, 25
God's covenant	Is. 54:9, 10
Messianic priesthood	Heb. 7:21

See Oaths

Sweat—*perspiration*

Penalty of man's sin	Gen. 3:18, 19
Cause of, avoided	Ezek. 44:18
Of Jesus, in prayer	Luke 22:44

Sweet—*that which is pleasing to the taste*

A. *Descriptive, literally, of:*	
Water	Ex. 15:25
Honey	Judg. 14:18
Incense	Ex. 25:6
Perfumes	Esth. 2:12
B. *Descriptive, figuratively, of:*	
God's Law	Ps. 19:10
God's Word	Ps. 119:103
Spiritual fellowship	Ps. 55:14
Meditation	Ps. 104:34
Pleasant words	Prov. 16:24
Sleep	Prov. 3:24
Christians	2 Cor. 2:15
Christian service	Eph. 5:2

Swim—*to propel oneself in water by natural means*

Miraculously, of iron	2 Kin. 6:6
Naturally, of people	Acts 27:42, 43
Figuratively, of tears	Ps. 6:6

SUBJECT	REFERENCE

Swine—*hogs*

A. *Features concerning:*	
Classed as unclean	Lev. 11:7, 8
Eating of, abominable	Is. 65:4
Caring of, a degradation	Luke 15:16
Herd of, drowned	Matt. 8:30-32
B. *Figurative of:*	
Abominable things	Is. 65:4
False teachers	2 Pet. 2:22
Indiscrete woman	Prov. 11:22
Reprobate	Matt. 7:6

Sword—*a weapon of war*

A. *Described as:*	
Having haft and blade	Judg. 3:22
Worn in a sheath	1 Sam. 17:15
Fastened at the waist	2 Sam. 20:8
B. *Used for:*	
Defense	Luke 22:36, 38
Fighting in war	Josh. 6:21
Executing criminals	1 Sam. 15:33
Suicide	Acts 16:27
C. *Figurative of:*	
Divine retribution	Deut. 32:41
Divine victory	Josh. 5:13
God's judgment	1 Chr. 21:12
An adulteress	Prov. 5:3, 4
Anguish of soul	Luke 2:35
State	Rom. 13:4
God's Word	Eph. 6:17

Sycamine—*the black mulberry*

Referred to by Jesus	Luke 17:6

Sycamore—*a fig-bearing tree* (not the same as the American sycamore)

Overseers appointed to care for	1 Chr. 27:28
Abundant in Palestine	1 Kin. 10:27
Amos, a gatherer of	Amos 7:14
Zacchaeus climbs up	Luke 19:4

Sychar

City of Samaria; Jesus talks to woman near	John 4:5-39

Syene—*seven*

An Egyptian city	Ezek. 29:10 Ezek. 30:6

Symbols—*a thing or act representing something spiritual*

A. *Of things:*	
Names	Is. 7:3, 14
Numbers	Rev. 13:18
Garments	Zech. 3:3-9
Metals	1 Cor. 3:12
Animals	Dan. 7:1-8
B. *Of acts* (gestures):	
Tearing:	
Mantle	1 Sam. 15:27, 28
Garment	1 Kin. 11:30-32
Veil	Matt. 27:51
Wearing a yoke	Jer. 27:2-12
Buying a field	Jer. 32:6-15
Boring the ear	Ex. 21:6
Surrendering the shoe	Ruth 4:7
Going naked	Is. 20:2, 3
C. *Of spiritual truths:*	
Bow—God's covenant	Gen. 9:12, 13
Circumcision—God's covenant	Gen. 17:1-14 Rom. 4:11
Passover—Christ	Ex. 12:3-28 1 Cor. 5:7
Mercy seat—Christ	Ex. 25:17-22 Rom. 3:25
Rock—Christ	1 Cor. 10:4
Blood sprinkled—Christ's blood	Ex. 12:21, 22 1 Pet. 1:18, 19
Bronze serpent—Christ	Num. 21:8, 9 John 3:14
Lamb—Christ	John 1:29
Bread and wine—the new covenant	Matt. 26:26-28 1 Cor. 11:23-29

Sympathy—*a fellow-feeling for another person*

A. *Manifested in:*	
Bearing others' burdens	Gal. 6:2 Heb. 13:3
Expressing sorrow	John 11:19-33

SUBJECT ... REFERENCE

Offering help in need ... Luke 10:33-35
Helping the weak ... Acts 20:35

B. *Expressed by:*

Servant for a prophet ... Jer. 38:7-13
King for a king ... 2 Sam. 10:2
A maid for a general ... 2 Kin. 5:1-4
Old man for a king ... 2 Sam. 19:31-39
Pagan for a Jew ... Dan. 6:18-23

Synagogue—*a Jewish assembly*

A. *Organization of:*

Under elders ... Luke 7:3-5
Ruler in charge ... Mark 5:22
Attendant ... Luke 4:17, 20
Chief seats of, coveted ... Matt. 23:6
Expulsion from ... John 9:22, 34

B. *Purposes of, for:*

Prayer ... Matt. 6:5
Reading Scripture ... Acts 13:15
Hearing expositions ... Acts 13:14, 15
Discipline ... Acts 9:2

C. *Christ's relation to:*

Teaches often in ... John 18:20
Worships in ... Luke 4:16-21
Performs miracles in ... Matt. 12:9, 10
Expelled from ... Luke 4:22-30

Syntyche—*fortunate*

Philippian woman exhorted by Paul ... Phil. 4:2

Syracuse—*a city of Sicily*

Visited by Paul ... Acts 28:12

Syria—*the high land*

News of Jesus went into ... Matt. 4:24
Governed by Romans ... Luke 2:2
Gospel preached to ... Acts 15:23, 41

Syria, Syrians—*the Aramaeans*

Descendants of Aram, Shem's son ... Gen. 10:22
Related to the Hebrews ... Deut. 26:5
Intermarriage of, with Hebrews ... Gen. 24:4, 10-67
Called Syrians ... 2 Sam. 10:11
Speak Syriac (Aramaic) ... Dan. 2:4
Idolatrous ... 2 Kin. 5:18
Subdued by David ... 2 Sam. 8:11-13
Elijah anointed king over ... 1 Kin. 19:15
Army of, routed ... 2 Kin. 7:5-7
Joined Israel against Jerusalem ... 2 Kin. 16:5
Taken captive by Assyria ... 2 Kin. 16:9
Destruction of, foretold ... Is. 17:1-3
Governed by Romans ... Luke 2:2
Gospel preached to ... Acts 15:23, 41

Syrophoenician—*an inhabitant of Phoenicia*

Daughter of, freed of demon ... Mark 7:25-31

System—*an orderly method of procedure in*

Orderly writing ... Luke 1:3
Governing people ... Ex. 18:13-27
Church government ... Acts 6:1-7
Priestly ministry ... Luke 1:8, 9
Giving ... 1 Cor. 16:1, 2

T

Taanach—*sandy*

Canaanite city conquered by Joshua ... Josh. 12:21
Assigned to Manasseh ... Josh. 17:11
Assigned to Kohathite Levites ... Josh. 21:25
Canaanites not expelled from ... Josh. 17:12, 13
Site of Canaanite defeat ... Judg. 5:19-22

Taanath-shiloh—*approach to Shiloh*

City of Ephraim ... Josh. 16:5, 6

Tabbaoth—*rings*

Ancestor of a Nethinim family ... Ezra 2:43

Tabbath—*extension*

Refuge of Midianites ... Judg. 7:22

Tabeel—*God is good*

Persian official ... Ezra 4:7
Father of a puppet king put forth by Rezin and Pekah ... Is. 7:1, 6

SUBJECT ... REFERENCE

Taberah—*burning*

Israelite camp; fire destroys many here ... Num. 11:1-3

Tabering—*drumming* (tabret)

Beating the breasts in sorrow ... Nah. 2:7

Tabernacle

A. *Descriptive of:*

Moses' administrative office ... Ex. 33:7-11
Structure erected at Sinai ... Ex. 40:2, 35-38
Portable shrine containing an idol ... Acts 7:43
Tent prepared for the ark by David ... 1 Chr. 16:1-43
Lord's incarnate Word ... John 1:14
Heavenly prototype ... Heb. 8:2, 5; Heb. 9:11, 24
Holy city ... Rev. 21:3

B. *Sinaitic, constructed:*

By divine revelation ... Ex. 25:27; Heb. 8:5
By craftsmen inspired by the Spirit ... Ex. 31:1-11
Out of contributions willingly supplied ... Ex. 25:1-9
For the manifestation of God's glory ... Ex. 25:8; Ex. 29:42, 43
In two parts—holy place and Holiest of all ... Ex. 26:33, 34; Heb. 9:2-7
With surrounding court ... Ex. 40:8
Within a year's time ... Ex. 40:2, 17

C. *History of:*

Set up at Sinai ... Ex. 40:1-38
Sanctified and dedicated ... Ex. 40:9-16
Moved by priests and Levites ... Num. 4:1-49
Camped at Gilgal ... Josh. 5:10, 11
Set up at Shiloh ... Josh. 18:1
Israel's center of worship ... Judg. 18:31; 1 Sam. 1:3, 9, 24
Ark of, taken by Philistines ... 1 Sam. 4:1-22
Worship not confined to ... 1 Sam. 7:1, 2, 15-17
Located at Nob during Saul's reign ... 1 Sam. 21:1-6
Moved to Gibeon ... 1 Kin. 3:4
Ark of, brought to Jerusalem by David ... 2 Sam. 6:17
Brought to the Temple by Solomon ... 1 Kin. 8:1, 4, 5

D. *Typology of, seen in:*

Christ ... John 1:14
God's household ... Eph. 2:19
Believer ... 1 Cor. 6:19
Heaven ... Heb. 9:23, 24

E. *Typology of, seen in Christ:*

Candlestick—His enlightening us ... Rev. 1:13
Sacred bread—His sustaining us ... John 6:27-59
Altar of incense—His intercession for us ... John 17:1-26; Heb. 7:25
Veil—His flesh ... Heb. 10:20
Ark (wood and gold)—His humanity and deity ... John 1:14

Tabernacle, Feast of (see Feasts, Hebrew)

Table

A. *Descriptive of:*

Article of furniture ... Matt. 15:27
For showbread ... Heb. 9:2
Small writing tablet ... Luke 1:63
Tablet of wood or stone ... Ex. 24:12

B. *Figurative of:*

Human heart ... Prov. 3:3
Christian's heart ... 2 Cor. 3:3
God's provision ... Ps. 23:5
Intimate fellowship ... Luke 22:30
Lord's Supper ... 1 Cor. 10:21

Tabor—*mountain height*

1. Mountain on borders of Zebulun and Issachar ... Josh. 19:12, 22
Great among mountains ... Jer. 46:18
Scene of rally against Sisera ... Judg. 4:6, 12, 14
2. Town of Zebulun ... 1 Chr. 6:77
3. Oak of, near Ramah ... 1 Sam. 10:3

SUBJECT ... REFERENCE

Tabret—*a musical instrument* (timbrel)

Used by:

Prophets ... 1 Sam. 10:5
People ... Gen. 31:27

Tabrimmon,—*Rimmon is good*

Father of Ben-hadad ... 1 Kin. 15:18

Taches—*hooks or clasps*

Couplings for curtains ... Ex. 26:6, 11, 33

Tachmonite—*wise*

Descriptive of one of David's heroes ... 2 Sam. 23:8
Same as Hachmonite in ... 1 Chr. 11:11

Tackling—*ropes, cord, line*

Ship's ropes ... Is. 33:23
All of a ship's removable gear ... Acts 27:19

Tactfulness—*the knack of knowing the right thing to do or say*

A. *Manifested in:*

Appeasing hatred ... Gen. 32:4, 5, 13-21
Settling disputes ... 1 Kin. 3:24-28
Obtaining one's wishes ... Esth. 5:1-8; Esth. 7:1-6

B. *Illustrated by Christ, in:*

Rebuking a Pharisee ... Luke 7:39-50
Teaching humility ... Mark 10:35-44
Forgiving a sinner ... John 8:1-11
Rebuking His disciples ... John 21:15-23

Tadmor—*palm tree*

Trading center near Damascus ... 2 Chr. 8:4
A desert town ... 1 Kin. 9:18

Tahan—*encampment*

Ephraimite; founder of the Tahanites ... Num. 26:35; 1 Chr. 7:25

Tahath—*station*

1. Kohathite Levite ... 1 Chr. 6:24
2, 3. Two descendants of Ephraim ... 1 Chr. 7:20
4. Israelite encampment ... Num. 33:26, 27

Tahpanhes, Tehaphnehes

City of Egypt; refuge of fleeing Jews ... Jer. 2:16; Jer. 44:1; Ezek. 30:18

Tahpenes—*royal wife*

Egyptian queen ... 1 Kin. 11:19, 20

Tahrea—*flight*

Descendant of Saul ... 1 Chr. 9:41
Called Tarea ... 1 Chr. 8:33, 35

Tahtim-hodshi

Place visited by census-taking Joab ... 2 Sam. 24:6

Tailoring—*the art of making clothes*

For Aaron's garments ... Ex. 39:1

Tale

Stipulated quantity ... Ex. 5:8, 18
Brief meditation ... Ps. 90:9
Nonsensical talk ... Luke 24:11

Talebearer—*one who gossips*

Reveals secrets ... Prov. 11:13
Injures character ... Prov. 18:8
Creates strife ... Prov. 26:20

Talent—*see Jewish measures*

Of gold ... Ex. 37:24
Of silver ... 2 Kin. 5:5, 22, 23
Of bronze ... Ex. 38:29
Of iron ... 1 Chr. 29:7
Of brass ... 1 Chr. 29:7
Parable of ... Matt. 25:14-30

Talitha-cumi—*"Damsel, arise"*

Jairus' daughter thus addressed ... Mark 5:41

Talk—*verbal communication between persons*

A. *Described as:*

Divine ... Ex. 33:9
Deceitful ... Job 13:7
Proud ... 1 Sam. 2:3
Mischievous ... Prov. 24:2

T

SUBJECT REFERENCE

Vain ..... Titus 1:10
Foolish ..... Eph. 5:4

B. *Of good things, God's:*
Law ..... Deut. 6:7
Judgment ..... Ps. 37:30, 31
Righteousness ..... Ps. 71:24
Power ..... Ps. 145:11

Talmai—*plowman*
1. Son of Anak driven out by Caleb ..... Josh. 15:14
2. King of Geshur whose daughter, Maacah, becomes David's wife ..... 2 Sam. 3:3

Talmon—*oppressor, violent*
Levite porter ..... 1 Chr. 9:17
Descendants of, return from exile ..... Ezra 2:42
Members of, become Temple porters ..... Neh. 11:19

Tamar, Thamar—*palm tree*
1. Wife of Er and mother of Perez and Zerah ..... Gen. 38:6-30
Ancestress of tribal families ..... Num. 26:20, 21
2. Absalom's sister ..... 2 Sam. 13:1-32
3. Absalom's daughter ..... 2 Sam. 14:27
4. Place south of the Dead Sea ..... Ezek. 47:19

Tammuz—*a Babylonian god*
Mourned by women of Jerusalem ..... Ezek. 8:14

Tanhumeth—*consolation*
Father of Seraiah ..... 2 Kin. 25:23

Tanner (Simon, the)—*dresser of hides*
Peter lodges with ..... Acts 10:5, 6, 32

Tapestry—*hand-woven coverings*
Symbolic of:
Licentiousness ..... Prov. 7:16
Diligence ..... Prov. 31:22

Taphath—*a drop*
Daughter of Solomon ..... 1 Kin. 4:11

Tappuah—*apple*
1. Town of Judah ..... Josh. 15:1, 34
2. Town of Ephraim ..... Josh. 16:8, 9
3. Son of Hebron ..... 1 Chr. 2:43

Tarah—*wandering*
Israelite encampment ..... Num. 33:1, 27

Taralah—*power of God*
City of Benjamin ..... Josh. 18:21, 27

Tares—*the bearded darnel*
Sown among wheat ..... Matt 13:24-40

Tarpelites
People transported to Samaria by the Assyrians ..... Ezra 4:9

Tarry—*to delay*
A. *Of human things:*
Prolonged visit ..... Acts 9:43
Unnecessary delay ..... 1 Sam. 1:23
Sinful delay ..... 2 Sam. 11:1, 2
Embarrassed delay ..... 2 Sam. 10:5
Indulgence in wine ..... Prov. 23:30

B. *Of divine things:*
Heavenly visitation ..... Judg. 6:18
God's salvation ..... Is. 46:13
Divine visitation ..... Hab. 2:3
Spirit's coming ..... Luke 24:49
Christ's return ..... Heb. 10:37

Tarshish, Tharshish
1. Son of Javan and great grandson of Noah ..... Gen. 10:4
2. City at a great distance from Palestine ..... Jon. 1:3
Minerals imported from, by Phoenicians ..... 1 Kin. 10:22
Ships of, noted in commerce ..... Ps. 48:7
Ships of, sent by Jehoshaphat ..... 1 Kin. 22:48

SUBJECT REFERENCE

3. Benjamite ..... 1 Chr. 7:10
4. Persian prince ..... Esth. 1:14

Tarsus—*the capital of the Roman province of Cilicia*
Paul's birthplace ..... Acts 21:39
Saul sent to ..... Acts 9:30
Visited by Barnabas ..... Acts 11:25

Tartak—*hero of darkness*
Deity worshiped by the Avites ..... 2 Kin. 17:31

Tartan—*the title of Assyria's commander*
Sent to fight against Jerusalem ..... 2 Kin. 18:17

Taskmaster—*a foreman*
Over sons of Israel ..... Ex. 1:11

Taste
A. *Of divine things:*
God's Word ..... Ps. 119:103
Lord ..... Ps. 34:8
Heavenly gift ..... Heb. 6:4

B. *Of material things:*
Honey ..... 1 Sam. 14:29, 43
Manna ..... Ex. 16:31
Food ..... 1 Sam. 14:24
Wine ..... John 2:9
Vinegar ..... Matt. 27:34
Death ..... Heb. 2:9

Tatnai
Persian governor opposing the Jews ..... Ezra 5:3, 6

Tattooing—*marking the skin indelibly*
Forbidden by God ..... Lev. 19:28

Tau
Letter in the Hebrew alphabet ..... Ps. 119:169-176

Taunt—*a scornful glee*
Goliath against David ..... 1 Sam. 17:43, 44
David against Abner ..... 1 Sam. 26:14-16
Rabshakeh against the Jews ..... 2 Kin. 18:28-35
Soldiers and people against Christ ..... Matt. 27:28-41

Taverns, The Three
Place about 30 miles south of Rome ..... Acts 28:15

Taxes—*money, goods or labor paid to a government*
A. *Derived from:*
People's possessions ..... 1 Sam. 8:10-18
Poor ..... Amos 5:11

B. *Paid by:*
Forced labor ..... Deut. 20:11
Foreigners ..... 1 Chr. 22:2
Captured people ..... 2 Sam. 8:6, 14
Forced labor ..... 1 Kin. 5:13-17
All except Levites ..... Ezra 7:24

C. *Used for:*
Sanctuary ..... Ex. 30:11-16
King's household ..... 1 Kin. 4:7-19
Tribute to foreign nations ..... 2 Kin. 15:17-22
Authorities ..... Rom. 13:6, 7

D. *Abuses of:*
Lead to rebellion ..... 1 Kin. 12:1-19
Burden people with debts ..... Neh. 5:1-13
Bring enslavement ..... Neh. 9:36, 37

Tax-gatherers—*Jews engaged in tax collecting*
A. *Features concerning:*
Collector of taxes ..... Luke 5:27
Often guilty of extortion ..... Luke 3:12, 13
Classed with lowest sinners ..... Matt. 9:10, 11; Matt. 21:31, 32
Do not even, do the same ..... Matt. 5:46
Thomas and Matthew, the ..... Matt. 10:3
"Thank thee that I am not" ..... Luke 18:11
As a heathen and a ..... Matt. 18:17

B. *Spiritual attitude of:*
Often conscientious ..... Luke 19:2, 8
Often hospitable ..... Luke 5:29
Received John's beliefs ..... Matt. 21:32
Listened to Jesus ..... Luke 15:1
Conscious of their sins ..... Luke 18:13, 14
Many sat with Him ..... Mark 2:15
Why do ye eat with ..... Luke 5:30
A friend of ..... Matt. 11:19; Luke 7:34

SUBJECT REFERENCE

Teacher—*the Greek equivalent of the Hebrew word "rabbi"* (meaning "my master")
Instructed in song ..... 1 Chr. 25:1
Come from God ..... John 3:2
To the Gentiles ..... 2 Tim. 1:11

Teaching, teachers
A. *Those capable of:*
Parents ..... Deut. 11:19
Levites ..... Lev. 10:11
Ancestors ..... Jer. 9:14
Disciples ..... Matt. 28:19, 20
Older women ..... Titus 2:3
Nature ..... 1 Cor. 11:14

B. *Significance of:*
Combined with preaching ..... Matt. 4:23
Divine calling ..... Eph. 4:11
Necessary for bishops ..... 1 Tim. 3:2
Necessary for the Lord's bond-servants ..... 2 Tim. 2:24-26
From house to house ..... Acts 20:20
By sharing ..... Gal. 6:6
Not granted to women ..... 1 Tim. 2:12

C. *Authority of, in divine things:*
Derived from Christ ..... Matt. 28:19, 20
Empowered by the Spirit ..... John 14:26
Taught by the LORD ..... Is. 54:13
Originates in revelation ..... Gal. 1:12

D. *Objects of, in divine things, concerning:*
God's way ..... Ps. 27:11
God's path ..... Ps. 25:4, 5
God's Law ..... Ps. 119:12, 26, 66
God's will ..... Ps. 143:10
Holiness ..... Titus 2:12
Spiritual truths ..... Heb. 8:11, 12

E. *Perversion of, by:*
False prophets ..... Is. 9:15
False priests ..... Mic. 3:11
Traditionalists ..... Matt. 15:9
False teachers ..... 1 Tim. 4:1-3
Judaizers ..... Acts 15:1
False believers ..... 2 Tim. 4:3, 4

Tears
A. *Kinds of:*
Agonizing ..... Ps. 6:6
Rewarded ..... Ps. 126:5
Repentant ..... Luke 7:38, 44
Insincere ..... Heb. 12:17
Intense ..... Heb. 5:6-8
Woman's ..... Esth. 8:3

B. *Caused by:*
Remorse ..... Gen. 27:34
Approaching death ..... 2 Kin. 20:1-5
Oppression ..... Eccl. 4:1
Defeat ..... Is. 16:9
Affliction and anguish ..... 2 Cor. 2:4
Christian service ..... Acts 20:19, 31

Tebah—*slaughter*
Son of Nahor ..... Gen. 22:24

Tebaliah—*Jehovah has immersed*
Merarite Korahite ..... 1 Chr. 26:11

Tebeth—*the name of the Hebrew tenth month*
Esther becomes queen in ..... Esth. 2:16, 17

Teeth, tooth
A. *Used for:*
Eating ..... Num. 11:33
Showing hatred ..... Acts 7:54

B. *Figurative of:*
Destruction ..... Job 4:10
Holding on to life ..... Job 13:14
God's chastening ..... Job 16:9
Escaped with the "skin of my teeth" ..... Job 19:20
Judgment ..... Ps. 3:7
Hatred ..... Ps. 35:16
Persecution ..... Ps. 57:4
Corporate guilt ..... Jer. 31:29, 30
Greediness ..... Dan. 7:5, 7, 19
Starvation ..... Amos 4:6
Hired prophets ..... Mic. 3:5
Remorse ..... Matt. 13:42, 50

SUBJECT REFERENCE

Tehinnah—*grace*
- Judahite .... 1 Chr. 4:12

Tekel—*weighed*
- Descriptive of Babylon's judgment .... Dan. 5:25

Tekoa, Tekoah—*firm, settlement*
- Ashur the father of .... 1 Chr. 2:24; 1 Chr. 4:5
- Fortress city of Judah .... 2 Chr. 20:20
- Home of a wise woman .... 2 Sam. 14:2, 4, 9
- Fortified by Rehoboam .... 2 Chr. 11:6
- Home of Amos .... Amos 1:1

Tekoite—*an inhabitant of Tekoa*
- Ikkesh thus called .... 2 Sam. 23:26
- Among postexilic workmen .... Neh. 3:5, 27

Tel-abib—*hill of grain*
- Place in Babylonia .... Ezek. 3:15

Telah—*fracture*
- Ephraimite .... 1 Chr. 7:25

Telaim—*little lambs*
- Saul assembles his army here .... 1 Sam. 15:4

Telassar, Thelasar—*hill of Assur*
- City of Mesopotamia .... 2 Kin. 19:12
- Children of Eden in .... Is. 37:12

Telem—*a lamb*
1. Town in south Judah .... Josh. 15:24
2. Divorced his foreign wife .... Ezra 10:24

Tel-haresha—*mound of the craftman's work*
- Babylonian town .... Neh. 7:61

Tel-melah—*hill of salt*
- Place in Babylonia .... Ezra 2:59

Tema—*sunburnt*
- Son of Ishmael .... Gen. 25:15
- Descendants of Abraham .... 1 Chr. 1:30
- Troops of .... Job 6:19
- Remote from Palestine .... Jer. 25:23
- On trade route through Arabia .... Is. 21:13, 14

Teman—*the south*
1. Grandson of Esau; duke of Edom .... Gen. 36:11, 15
2. Another duke of Edom .... Gen. 36:42
3. Tribe in northeast Edom .... Gen. 36:34
   - Judgment pronounced against .... Amos 1:12
   - God appears from .... Hab. 3:3

Temanite—*an inhabitant of Teman*
- Job's friend, Eliphaz .... Job 42:7, 9

Temeni—*fortunate*
- Son of Ashur .... 1 Chr. 4:5, 6

Temperance

A. *Needed in:*
- Eating .... Prov. 23:1-3
- Sexual appetites .... 1 Cor. 7:1-9
- All things .... 1 Cor. 9:25-27

B. *Helped by:*
- Self-control .... Prov. 16:32
- God's Spirit .... Gal. 5:23
- Spiritual growth .... 2 Pet. 1:6

C. *In the use of wine, total recommended by:*
- Solomon .... Prov. 23:31-35
- Angel .... Judg. 13:3-5
- Nazarite vow .... Num. 6:2, 3
- First, among Rechabites .... Jer. 35:1-10

See Self-control; Sober, sobriety

Tempests—*terrible storms*

A. *Literal uses of:*
- At Sinai .... Heb. 12:18-21
- Jonah's ship tossed by .... Jon. 1:4-15
- Calmed by Christ .... Matt. 8:23-27
- Paul's ship destroyed by .... Acts 27:14-20

B. *Figurative of:*
- Destructiveness .... Is. 28:2
- God's wrath .... Jer. 30:23
- God's chastening .... Job 9:17
- Furious troubles .... Ps. 55:8
- God's judgments .... Ps. 83:15

SUBJECT REFERENCE

- Hell's torments .... Ps. 11:6
- Raging destructiveness .... 2 Pet. 2:17
- Destruction by war .... Amos 1:14

Temple, Herod's
- Zechariah received vision in .... Luke 1:5-22
- Infant Jesus greeted here by Simeon and Anna .... Luke 2:22-39
- Jesus visited at 12 .... Luke 2:42-52
- Jesus visited and cleansed .... John 2:15-17
- Construction of, specified .... John 2:19, 20
- Jesus taught in .... John 8:20
- Jesus cleansed again .... Matt. 21:12-16
- Jesus spoke parables in .... Matt. 21:23-46
- Jesus exposes Pharisees in .... Matt. 23:1-39
- Destruction of, foretold .... Matt. 24:1, 2
- Veil of, rent at Christ's death .... Matt. 27:51; Heb. 10:20
- Christians worshiped here .... Acts 2:46
- Apostles taught here .... Acts 3:1-26
- Stephen's teaching on the true .... Acts 7:46-50
- Apostles understand prophecy concerning .... Acts 15:14-18
- Paul accused of profaning .... Acts 21:20-30

Temple, Solomon's

A. *Features regarding:*
- Site of, on Mt. Moriah .... 2 Sam. 24:18-25
- Conceived by David .... 2 Sam. 7:1-3
- Building of, forbidden to David .... 1 Chr. 22:5-16
- David promised a greater house .... 2 Sam. 7:4-29
- Pattern of, given to Solomon by David .... 1 Chr. 28:1-21
- Provisions for, given to Solomon .... 1 Chr. 29:1-19
- Supplies furnished by Hiram .... 1 Kin. 5:1-18
- Construction of, by Solomon .... 2 Chr. 3-4
- Dedication of, by Solomon .... 2 Chr. 6
- Seven years in building .... 1 Kin. 6:38
- No noise in building .... 1 Kin. 6:7
- Date of building .... 1 Kin. 6:1, 37, 38
- Workmen employed in .... 1 Kin. 5:15-17

B. *History of:*
- Ark brought into .... 1 Kin. 8:1-9
- Filled with God's glory .... 1 Kin. 8:10, 11
- Treasures taken away .... 1 Kin. 14:25, 26
- Repaired by Jehoash .... 2 Kin. 12:4-14
- Treasures of, given to Arameans by Jehoash .... 2 Kin. 12:17, 18
- Treasures of, given to Assyrians by Ahaz .... 2 Kin. 16:14, 18
- Worship of, restored by Hezekiah .... 2 Chr. 29:3-35
- Treasures of, given by Hezekiah to Assyrians .... 2 Kin. 18:13-16
- Desecrated by Manasseh's idolatry .... 2 Kin. 21:4-7
- Repaired and purified by Josiah .... 2 Kin. 23:4-12
- Plundered and burned by Babylonians .... 2 Kin. 25:9-17

Temple, spiritual

A. *Descriptive of:*
- Christ's body .... John 2:19, 21
- Believer's body .... 1 Cor. 6:19
- True Church .... 1 Cor. 3:16, 17
- Apostate church .... 2 Thess. 2:4

B. *Believers as, described as:*
- Indwelt by God .... 2 Cor. 6:16
- Indwelt by Christ .... Eph. 3:17, 18
- Indwelt by the Spirit .... Eph. 2:21, 22
- Priests .... 1 Pet. 2:5
- Offering spiritual sacrifices .... Heb. 13:15, 16

Temple, Zerubbabel's
- By the order of Cyrus .... Ezra 1:1-4
- Temple vessels restored for .... Ezra 1:7-11
- Worship of, restored .... Ezra 3:3-13
- Work of rebuilding hindered .... Ezra 4:1-24
- Building of, completed .... Ezra 6:13-18
- Inferiority of .... Ezra 3:12

Temporal—*for a short time*
- Things that are seen .... 2 Cor. 4:18

Temporal blessings

A. *Consisting of:*
- Rain .... Matt. 5:45
- Seedtime and harvest .... Gen. 8:22

SUBJECT REFERENCE

- Food and raiment .... Luke 12:22-31
- Prosperity .... Deut. 8:7-18
- Children .... Ps. 127:3-5
- Preservation of life .... 2 Tim. 4:16-18
- Providential guidance .... Gen. 24:12-14, 42-44

B. *God's supply of:*
- Promised .... Prov. 3:9, 10
- Provided .... Neh. 9:15
- Prayed for .... Matt. 6:11
- Acknowledged .... Ps. 23:1-5
- Explained .... Deut. 8:2, 3
- Contingent upon obedience .... Mal. 3:7-11; Matt. 6:25-34
- Object of praise .... Ps. 103:1-5

Temptation—*a testing designed to strengthen or corrupt*

A. *Of God:*
- Forbidden .... Matt. 4:7
- By Israel .... Ps. 78:18-56; Heb. 3:9
- Not possible .... James 1:13

B. *Of Christ:*
- By:
  - The devil .... Matt. 4:1-10
  - Jewish leaders .... Matt. 16:1
  - His disciples .... Matt. 16:23
- Like us, but without sin .... Heb. 4:15
- Design of .... Heb. 2:18

C. *Of Satan, against:*
- Job .... Job 1:6-12
- David .... 1 Chr. 21:1
- Joshua .... Zech. 3:1-5
- Jesus .... Luke 4:1-13
- Ananias and Sapphira .... Acts 5:1-3
- Christians .... 1 Cor. 7:5

D. *Of Christians:*
- By:
  - Lust .... James 1:13-15
  - Riches .... 1 Tim. 6:9
- Liability to .... Gal. 6:1
- Warnings against .... Matt. 26:41
- Prayer against .... Matt. 6:13
- Limitation of .... 1 Cor. 10:13
- Deliverance from .... 2 Pet. 2:9

Temptress—*female tempter*
- Eve .... Gen. 3:6
- Potiphar's wife .... Gen. 39:1-19
- Delilah .... Judg. 16:6-20
- Jezebel .... 1 Kin. 21:7
- Job's wife .... Job 2:9
- Adulteress .... Prov. 7:5-27
- Herodias' daughter (Salome) .... Mark 6:22-29

Ten Commandments

A. *Features concerning:*
- Given at Sinai .... Ex. 20:1-17
- Written on stone .... Ex. 24:12
- Written by God .... Ex. 31:18
- First stones broken .... Ex. 32:19
- Another copy given .... Ex. 34:1
- Put in the ark .... Deut. 10:1-5
- Called a covenant .... Ex. 34:28
- Given in a different form .... Deut. 5:6-21
- The greatest of these .... Matt. 22:35-40; Rom. 13:8-10

B. *Allusions to, in Scripture:*
- First .... Acts 17:23
- Second .... 1 Kin. 18:17-40
- Third .... Matt. 5:33-37
- Fourth .... Jer. 17:21-27
- Fifth .... Deut. 21:18-21; Eph. 6:1-3
- Sixth .... Num. 35:16-21
- Seventh .... Num. 5:12-31; Matt. 5:27-32
- Eighth .... Matt. 19:18
- Ninth .... Deut. 19:16-21
- Tenth .... Rom. 7:7

Tender—*soft; compassionate*

A. *Used of physical things:*
- Animal .... Gen. 18:7
- Grass .... 2 Sam. 23:4
- Son .... Prov. 4:3
- Weak eyes .... Gen. 29:17
- Small children .... Gen. 33:13
- Women .... Deut. 28:56
- Instability .... Deut. 28:54

T

SUBJECT REFERENCE

B. *Used of spiritual things:*
- Messiah ... Is. 53:2
- Compassion ... Eph. 4:32
- God's mercy ... Luke 1:78
- Man's heart ... 2 Kin. 22:19
- Christ's return ... Matt. 24:32
- Babylon's destruction ... Is. 47:1

Tenderness—*expressing a feeling or sympathy*
- Shown toward the young ... Gen. 33:13
- Expressed toward an enemy ... 1 Sam. 30:11-15
- Illustrated by a Samaritan ... Luke 10:33-36
- Manifested by a father ... Luke 15:11-24

Tens of the Bible

A. *Descriptive of:*
- Brothers ... Gen. 42:3
- Cubits ... Ex. 26:16
- Pillars and sockets ... Ex. 27:12
- Commandments ... Ex. 34:28
- Shekels ... Num. 7:14
- Years ... Ruth 1:4
- Loaves ... 1 Sam. 17:17
- Tribes ... 1 Kin. 11:31, 35
- Degrees ... 2 Kin. 20:9-11
- Virgins ... Matt. 25:1-13
- Talents ... Matt. 25:28
- Lepers ... Luke 17:11-19
- Pieces of money ... Luke 19:12-27
- Horns ... Rev. 12:3

B. *Expressive of:*
- Representation ... Ruth 4:2
- Intensity ... Num. 14:22
- Sufficiency ... Neh. 4:12
- Magnitude ... Dan. 1:20
- Remnant ... Amos 5:3
- Completion ... Dan. 7:7, 20, 24
- Perfection ... Luke 19:16-24

Tentmaking

The occupation of:
- Aquila and Priscilla ... Acts 18:2, 3
- Paul ... Acts 18:2, 3

Tents—*movable habitations*

A. *Used by:*
- People ... 1 Chr. 17:5
- Shepherds ... Is. 38:12
- Armies ... 1 Sam. 13:2
- Rechabites ... Jer. 35:7, 10
- Women ... Gen. 24:67
- Maidservants ... Gen. 31:33

B. *Features concerning:*
- Fastened by cords ... Is. 54:2
- Door provided ... Gen. 18:1
- Used for the ark ... 2 Sam. 7:1-6

C. *Figurative of:*
- Shortness of life ... Is. 38:12; 2 Cor. 5:1
- Heavens ... Is. 40:22
- Enlarge ... Is. 54:2

Terah—*duration, wandering*
- Father of Abram ... Gen. 11:26
- Idolater ... Josh. 24:2
- Dies in Haran ... Gen. 11:25-32

Teraphim
- Laban's, stolen by Rachel ... Gen. 31:19-35
- Used in idolatry ... Hos. 3:4

Teresh—*dry*
- King's official ... Esth. 2:21

Terrestrial—*belonging to the earth*
- Spoken of bodies ... 1 Cor. 15:40

Terror—*extreme fear*

A. *Caused by:*
- Lord's presence ... Heb. 12:21
- Fear ... Job 9:34
- Death ... Job 24:17
- Arrogance and pride ... Jer. 49:16
- War ... Ezek. 21:12
- Fright ... Luke 24:37
- Persecutors ... 1 Pet. 3:14

B. *Sent as means of:*
- Protection ... Gen. 35:5
- Punishment ... Lev. 26:16

C. *Safeguards against, found in:*
- God's promise ... Ps. 91:5
- God's plan ... Luke 21:9

SUBJECT REFERENCE

Tertius—*third*
- Paul's scribe ... Rom. 16:22

Tertullus—*diminutive of Tertius*
- Orator who accuses Paul ... Acts 24:1-8

Test—*something that manifests a person's real character*

A. *Kinds of:*
- Given to Solomon ... 1 Kin. 10:1-3
- Physical ... 1 Sam. 17:38, 39
- Supernatural ... Ex. 7—11
- Spiritual ... Dan. 6:1-28
- National ... Ex. 32:1-35

B. *Purposes of, to:*
- Test obedience ... Gen. 3:1-8; Gen. 22:1-18
- Learn God's will ... Judg. 6:36-40
- Accept good diet ... Dan. 1:12-16
- Refute Satan's claims ... Job 1:6-22
- Destroy idolatry ... 1 Kin. 18:22-24

C. *Descriptive of:*
- Testing physically ... 1 Sam. 17:39
- Testing morally ... John 6:6
- Showing something to be true ... Gen. 42:15, 16

D. *Objects of, among Christians:*
- Faith ... 2 Cor. 13:5
- Abilities ... 1 Tim. 3:10

Testament—*a will or covenant*
- Descriptive of a person's will ... Heb. 9:15-17
- New covenant ... Matt. 26:28
- New Testament dispensation ... 2 Cor. 3:6
- Superiority of the new ... Heb. 8:6-13

Testimony—*witness borne in behalf of something*

A. *Necessary elements of, seen in:*
- Verbal expression ... 2 Sam. 1:16
- Witnesses ... Neh. 13:15; John 8:17

B. *Means of:*
- Prophets ... Acts 10:42, 43
- Messengers ... Acts 20:21, 24
- Song ... Deut. 31:21
- Our sins ... Is. 59:12

C. *Reaction to:*
- Believed ... 2 Thess. 1:10
- Confirmed ... 1 Cor. 1:6

D. *Purpose of, to:*
- Establish the Gospel ... Acts 10:42
- Prove Jesus was the Christ ... Acts 18:5
- Lead to repentance ... Acts 20:21

Tests of Faith

By:
- Difficult demands ... Gen. 12:1, 2
- Severe trials ... Job 1:6-22
- Prosperity of the wicked ... Ps. 73:1-28
- Hardships ... 2 Cor. 11:21-33

Teth
- Letter in the Hebrew alphabet ... Ps. 119:65-72

Tetrarch—*a ruler over a fourth part of a kingdom*
- Applied to Herod Antipas ... Matt. 14:1

Thaddaeus—*breast*
- One of the twelve disciples ... Mark 3:18

Thahash—*porpoise, dolphin*
- Son of Nahor ... Gen. 22:24

Thamah—*combat*
- Family of Nethinim ... Ezra 2:15

Thankfulness—*gratitude for blessings*

A. *Described as:*
- Spiritual sacrifice ... Ps. 116:17
- Duty ... 2 Thess. 2:13
- Unceasing ... Eph. 1:16
- Spontaneous ... Phil. 1:3
- In Christ's name ... Eph. 5:20
- God's will ... 1 Thess. 5:18
- Heaven's theme ... Rev. 7:12

B. *Expressed for:*
- Food ... John 6:11, 23
- Wisdom ... Dan. 2:23
- Converts ... 1 Thess. 1:2
- Prayer answered ... John 11:41

SUBJECT REFERENCE

- Victory ... 1 Cor. 15:57
- Salvation ... 2 Cor. 9:15
- Lord's Supper ... 1 Cor. 11:24
- Changed lives ... 1 Thess. 2:13

C. *Expressed by:*
- Healed Samaritan ... Luke 17:12-19
- Righteous ... Ps. 140:13

Theater—*a place of public assembly*
- Paul kept from entering ... Acts 19:29-31

Thebez—*brightness*
- Fortified city near Shechem ... Judg. 9:50-55

Theft, thief—*the act and agent of stealing*

A. *Kinds of:*
- Imputed ... Gen. 44:1-17
- Improbable ... Matt. 28:11-13
- Real ... Acts 5:1-3

B. *Characteristics of:*
- Done often at night ... Jer. 49:9
- Comes unexpectedly ... Luke 12:39
- Purpose of, to steal ... John 10:10
- Window used by ... John 10:1

C. *Objects of:*
- Idol ... Gen. 31:19-35
- Food ... Prov. 6:30
- Traveler ... Luke 10:30, 36
- Money ... John 12:6

D. *Evil of:*
- Condemned ... Ex. 22:1-12
- Punished ... Josh. 7:21-26
- Inconsistent with truth ... Jer. 7:9, 10
- Defiles a man ... Matt. 15:19, 20
- Excludes from heaven ... 1 Cor. 6:10
- Not to be among Christians ... Eph. 4:28

See Stealing

Theocracy—*government by God*
- Evident under Moses ... Ex. 19:3-6
- Continued under Joshua ... Josh. 1:1-8
- Rejected by Israel ... 1 Sam. 8:4-9
- To be restored ... Is. 2:2-4; Is. 9:6, 7

Theophany—*an appearance of God*

A. *Of God:*
- At Sinai ... Ex. 24:9-12
- In the tabernacle ... Ex. 40:34-38
- In the Temple ... 1 Kin. 8:10, 11
- To Isaiah ... Is. 6:1-9

B. *Of Christ as "the angel," to:*
- Abraham ... Gen. 18:1-8
- Jacob ... Gen. 31:11, 13
- Moses ... Ex. 3:1-11
- Joshua ... Josh. 5:13-15
- Israel ... Judg. 2:1-5
- Gideon ... Judg. 6:11-24
- Manoah ... Judg. 13:2-25
- Paul ... Acts 27:23, 24

C. *Of Christ, as incarnate, in:*
- Old Testament ... 1 Cor. 10:4, 9
- Nativity ... John 1:14, 18
- His:
  - Resurrected form ... John 20:26-29
  - Ascended form ... Acts 7:55, 56
  - Return in glory ... Rev. 1:7, 8
  - Glorified form ... Matt. 17:1-15

Theophilus—*beloved of God*
- Luke addresses his writings to ... Luke 1:3; Acts 1:1

Thessalonians, the Epistles to the—*books of the New Testament*

A. *1 Thessalonians:*
- Commendation ... 1 Thess. 1:2-10
- Paul's apostolic ministry ... 1 Thess. 2:1-20
- Timothy as envoy ... 1 Thess. 3:1-10
- The quiet life ... 1 Thess. 4:11, 12
- The second coming ... 1 Thess. 4:13-18
- Sons of light, not darkness ... 1 Thess. 5:4-7
- Christian conduct ... 1 Thess. 5:12-24

B. *2 Thessalonians:*
- Encouragement in suffering ... 2 Thess. 1:3-12
- The man of sin ... 2 Thess. 2:3-10
- Steadfastness ... 2 Thess. 2:15-17
- Maintaining order ... 2 Thess. 3:1-15

SUBJECT REFERENCE

Thessalonica—*an important city of Macedonia (modern Salonika)*

Paul preaches in ... Acts 17:1-13
Paul writes letters to churches of ... 1 Thess. 1:1

Theudas—*God-giving*

Leader of an unsuccessful revolt ... Acts 5:36

Thirst—*a craving for water*

A. *Caused by:*
- Wilderness drought ... Ex. 17:3
- Unbelief ... Deut. 28:47, 48
- Siege ... 2 Chr. 32:11
- Travels ... 2 Cor. 11:27
- Extreme pain ... John 19:28
- Flame ... Luke 16:24

B. *Figurative of:*
- Salvation ... Is. 55:1
- Righteousness ... Matt. 5:6
- Holy Spirit ... John 7:37-39
- Serving Christ ... Matt. 25:35-42

C. *Satisfaction of:*
- By a miracle ... Neh. 9:15, 20
- Longed for ... Ps. 63:1
- In Christ alone ... John 6:35
- Final invitation ... Rev. 22:17
- Perfectly fulfilled ... Is. 49:10; Rev. 7:16

Thirty heroes, the

Served David ... 1 Chr. 12:1-40

Thirty pieces of silver—*bribe of Judas*

Price of slave ... Ex. 21:32
Given to Judas ... Matt. 26:14-16
Buys field ... Matt. 27:3-10

Thomas—*twin*

Apostle of Christ ... Matt. 10:3
Ready to die with Christ ... John 11:16
In need of instruction ... John 14:1-6
Not present when Christ appears ... John 20:19-24
States terms of belief ... John 20:25
Christ appears again and convinces him ... John 20:26-29; John 21:1, 2
In the upper room ... Acts 1:13

Thongs—*leather straps*

Used to bind Paul ... Acts 22:25

Thorn—*a plant with sharp projections on its stems*

A. *Used literally of:*
- Earth's produce ... Gen. 3:18
- Land under judgment ... Is. 34:13
- Christ's crown ... John 19:2

B. *Used figuratively of:*
- Unbelief ... Is. 32:13-15
- Judgments ... Hos. 2:6
- Pain ... Prov. 26:9
- False prophets ... Matt. 7:15, 16
- Agent of Satan ... 2 Cor. 12:7
- Barrenness ... Matt. 13:7, 22

Thought—*the reasoning of the mind*

A. *Of the wicked, described as:*
- Evil ... Gen. 6:5
- Abominable ... Prov. 15:26
- Sinful ... Is. 59:7
- Devoid of God ... Ps. 10:4
- Known by God ... 1 Cor. 3:20
- In need of repentance ... Acts 8:22
- Sinful ... Is. 59:7
- Devoid of God ... Ps. 10:4

B. *Of the believer:*
- Comprehended by God ... 1 Chr. 28:9; Ps. 139:2
- Captivated by Christ ... 2 Cor. 10:5
- Criticized by God's Word ... Heb. 4:12
- In need of examination ... Ps. 139:23

C. *Of God:*
- Not like man's ... Is. 55:8, 9
- To believer, good ... Ps. 139:17

Thousand years

As one day ... 2 Pet. 3:8
Millennial reign ... Rev. 20:1-7

SUBJECT REFERENCE

Thread

Refused by Abram ... Gen. 14:23
Tied to hand ... Gen. 38:28
Tied in window ... Judg. 2:18
Lips like scarlet ... Song 4:3

Threatenings—*menacing actions or words against another*

A. *Purposes of, to:*
- Silence a prophet ... 1 Kin. 19:1, 2
- Hinder a work ... Neh. 6:1-14
- Hinder the Gospel ... Acts 4:17, 21

B. *Exemplified by:*
- Jehoram against Elisha ... 2 Kin. 6:31
- Jews against Christians ... Acts 4:29
- Saul against Christians ... Acts 9:1

Threshing—*separating kernels of grain by force*

A. *Characteristics of:*
- Done by a stick ... Is. 28:27
- By cart wheels also ... Is. 28:27, 28
- By the feet of oxen ... Hos. 10:11
- Large and roomy place ... Gen. 50:10

B. *Figurative of:*
- God's judgments ... Jer. 51:33
- Minister's labor ... 1 Cor. 9:9, 10

Thrice—*three times*

Males of Israel assemble ... Ex. 34:23, 24
Peter's denial ... Luke 22:34, 61
Vessel's appearance ... Acts 10:16
Paul's shipwrecks ... 2 Cor. 11:25
Paul's petitions ... 2 Cor. 12:8

Throat—*the front part of the neck*

Glutton's warning ... Prov. 23:2
Thirsty one ... Ps. 69:3
Source of evil ... Ps. 5:9

Throne—*the seat and symbol of regal authority*

A. *Of men:*
- Under God's sovereignty ... Dan. 5:18-21
- Established on righteousness ... Prov. 16:12
- Upheld by mercy ... Prov. 20:28
- Subject to:
  - Succession ... 2 Chr. 6:10, 16
  - Termination ... Jer. 22:4-30

B. *Of God:*
- Resplendent in glory ... Is. 6:1-3
- Relentless in power ... Dan. 2:44
- Ruling over all ... Dan. 4:25, 34, 35
- Righteous in execution ... Ps. 9:4, 7, 8
- Regal throughout eternity ... Rev. 22:1, 3

C. *Of Christ:*
- Based upon the Davidic covenant ... 2 Sam. 7:12-16
- Of eternal duration ... Ps. 89:4, 29, 36; Dan. 7:13, 14
- Explained in its nature ... Is. 9:6, 7
- Symbolized in its functions ... Zech. 6:12, 13
- Promised to Christ ... Luke 1:31-33
- Christ rises to possess ... Heb. 8:1
- Christ now rules from ... Eph. 1:20-22; 1 Pet. 3:20-22
- Shares with the Godhead ... Rev. 5:12-14
- Shares with believers ... Luke 22:30; Rev. 3:21
- Judges men from ... Matt. 25:31

Thumb—*first of man's fingers*

Anointing of, as an act of consecration ... Lev. 8:23, 24
As an act of purification ... Lev. 14:14, 17, 25, 28
Cutting off of, an act of subjugation ... Judg. 1:6, 7

Thunder—*the sound produced by lightning*

A. *Supernaturally brought:*
- Upon the Egyptians ... Ex. 9:22-34
- At Sinai ... Ex. 19:16
- Against the Philistines ... 1 Sam. 7:10
- At David's deliverance ... 2 Sam. 22:14, 15

B. *Figurative of:*
- God's:
  - Power ... Job 26:14
  - Control ... Ps. 104:7
  - Majesty ... Rev. 4:5
- Visitations of judgment ... Rev. 11:19

SUBJECT REFERENCE

Thyatira—*an important town in the Roman province of Asia*

Residence of Lydia ... Acts 16:14
One of the seven churches ... Rev. 2:18-24
Sea of Galilee called ... John 6:1, 23

Thyine—*a small cone-bearing tree*

Wood of, used for furniture ... Rev. 18:12

Tibhath—*slaughter*

Town in the kingdom of Zobah ... 1 Chr. 18:8

Tibni—*intelligent*

Son of Ginath ... 1 Kin. 16:21, 22

Tidal—*splendor*

King allied with Chedorlaomer ... Gen. 14:1, 9

Tidings

A. *Descriptive of:*
- Joyful ... Gen. 29:13
- Good ... 1 Kin. 1:42
- Bad ... 1 Sam. 11:4-6
- Foreboding ... Jer. 37:5
- Distressing ... 2 Sam. 4:4
- Fatal ... 1 Sam. 4:19

B. *Of salvation:*
- Out of Zion ... Is. 40:9
- By a person ... Is. 41:27
- Bringer of peace ... Is. 52:7
- By Christ ... Is. 61:1-3

Tiglath-pileser—*my trust is in the god Ninib*

Powerful Assyrian king who invades Samaria ... 2 Kin. 15:29

Tikvah—*hope*

1. Father-in-law of Huldah ... 2 Kin. 22:14
   Called Tikvath ... 2 Chr. 34:22
2. Father-in-law of Jahaziah ... Ezra 10:15

Tile

Large brick of soft clay ... Ezek. 4:1
Earthen roof ... Luke 5:19

Tiller—*a farmer*

Man's first job ... Gen. 2:5
Sin's handicap on ... Gen. 4:12
Industry in, commended ... Prov. 12:11

Tilon—*scorn*

Son of Shimon ... 1 Chr. 4:20

Timaeus—*highly prized*

Father of Bartimaeus ... Mark 10:46

Timbrel—*a small hand drum*

Used in:
- Entertainment ... Gen. 31:27
- Worship ... Ps. 81:1-4

Time—*the period between two eternities*

A. *Computation of, by:*
- Years ... Gen. 15:13
- Months ... 1 Chr. 27:1
- Weeks ... Dan. 10:2
- Days ... Gen. 8:3
- Moments ... Ex. 33:5
- Sundial ... 2 Kin. 20:9-11

B. *Events of, dated by:*
- Succession of families ... Gen. 5:1-32
- Lives of great men ... Gen. 7:6, 11
- Succession of kings ... 1 Kin. 11:42, 43
- Earthquakes ... Amos 1:1
- Important events (the exodus) ... 1 Kin. 6:1
- Important emperors ... Luke 3:1

C. *Periods of, stated in years:*
- Bondage in Egypt ... Acts 7:6
- Wilderness wanderings ... Deut. 1:3
- Judges ... Judg. 11:26
- Captivity ... Dan. 9:2
- Seventy weeks (490 years) ... Dan. 9:24-27

D. *Sequence of prophetic events in, indicated by:*
- "The time is fulfilled" (Christ's Advent) ... Mark 1:15
- "The fullness of the time" (Christ's Advent) ... Gal. 4:4
- "The times of the Gentiles" (the Gospel age) ... Luke 21:24

SUBJECT	REFERENCE
"The day of salvation" (the Gospel age)	2 Cor. 6:2
"In the last days" (the Gospel age)	Acts 2:17
"In the last days" (the time before Christ's return)	2 Tim. 3:1; 2 Pet. 3:3
"The last day" (Christ's return)	John 6:39, 54; John 12:48
"New heavens" (eternity)	2 Pet. 3:13
E. *Importance of, indicated by:*	
Shortness of life	Ps. 89:47
Making the most of it	Eph. 5:16
Purpose of, for salvation	2 Pet. 3:9, 15
Uncertainty of	Luke 12:16-23
Our goal, eternity	Heb. 11:10, 13-16
God's plan in	Acts 14:15-17
F. *For everything:*	
To give birth, to die	Eccl. 3:1-8, 17

Timidity—*lack of courage*

Nicodemus	John 3:1, 2
Joseph of Arimathea	John 19:38
Certain people	John 9:18-23

Timna—*restraint*

1. Concubine of Eliphaz	Gen. 36:12, 22
2. Duke of Edom	Gen. 36:40

Timnah, Timnath, Thimnathah—*allotted portion*

1. Town of Judah	Josh. 15:10
Assigned to Dan	Josh. 19:40, 43
Captured by Philistines	2 Chr. 28:18
2. Town in Judah's hill country	Josh. 15:57

Timnath-serah—*extra portion*

Village in Ephraim's hill country	Josh. 19:50
Place of Joshua's burial	Josh. 24:29, 30
Called Timnath-heres	Judg. 2:9

Timnite—*an inhabitant of Timnah*

Samson thus called	Judg. 15:6

Timon—*deeming worthy*

One of the seven deacons	Acts 6:1-5

Timothy, the Epistles to—*books of the New Testament*

A. *1 Timothy:*	
Toward true doctrine	1 Tim. 1:3-7
Paul's ministry	1 Tim. 1:12-17
Christ, the Mediator	1 Tim. 2:5, 6
Instructions to women	1 Tim. 2:9 15
Church officials	1 Tim. 3:1-13
The good minister	1 Tim. 4:6-16
Fight the good fight	1 Tim. 6:11-21
B. *2 Timothy:*	
Call to responsibility	2 Tim. 1:6-18
Call for strength	2 Tim. 2:1-13
Against apostasy	2 Tim. 3:1-9
The Scriptures called inspired	2 Tim. 3:14-17
Charge to Timothy	2 Tim. 4:1-8
Paul's personal concerns	2 Tim. 4:9-18

Timothy—*revere God*

A. *Life of:*	
Of mixed parentage	Acts 16:1, 3
Faith of, from childhood	2 Tim. 1:5; 2 Tim. 3:15
Becomes Paul's companion	Acts 16:1-3
Ordained by the presbytery	1 Tim. 4:14
Left behind at Troas	Acts 17:14
Sent by Paul to Thessalonica	1 Thess. 3:1, 2, 6
Rejoined Paul at Corinth	Acts 18:1-5
Preached Christ to Corinthians	2 Cor. 1:19
Sent by Paul into Macedonia	Acts 19:22
Sent by Paul to Corinth	1 Cor. 4:17
Returned with Paul to Jerusalem	Acts 20:1-5
With Paul in Rome	Phil. 1:1; Phil. 2:19, 23
Set free	Heb. 13:23
Left at Ephesus by Paul	1 Tim. 1:3
Paul summoned him to Rome	2 Tim. 4:9, 11, 21
B. *Character of:*	
Devout from childhood	2 Tim. 3:15
Faithful in service	Phil. 2:22
Beloved by Paul	1 Tim. 1:2, 18
Follows Paul's way	1 Cor. 4:17
In need of instruction	1 Tim. 4:12-16
Of sickly nature	1 Tim. 5:23
Urged to remain faithful	1 Tim. 6:20, 21
Emotional	2 Tim. 1:4

Tin—*a metal obtained by smelting*

Used in early times	Num. 31:22
Brought from Tarshish	Ezek. 27:12
Figurative of degeneracy	Is. 1:25

Tiphsah—*passage; crossing*

1. Place designating Solomon's northern boundary	1 Kin. 4:24
2. Unidentified town attacked by Menahem	2 Kin. 15:16

Tiras

Son of Japheth	Gen. 10:2

Tirathites

Family of scribes	1 Chr. 2:55

Tire—*an ornamental headdress*

Worn by:	
Ezekiel	Ezek. 24:17, 23
Daughters of Zion	Is. 3:18
Jezebel	2 Kin. 9:30

Tirhakah—*the king of Cush (Nubia)*

Opposes Sennacherib	2 Kin. 19:9

Tirhanah—*kindness*

Son of Caleb	1 Chr. 2:42, 48

Tiria—*foundation*

Son of Jehaleleel	1 Chr. 4:16

Tirshatha—*governor*

Persian title used of Zerubbabel	Ezra 2:63
Applied to Nehemiah	Neh. 8:9

Tirzah—*delight*

1. Zelophehad's youngest daughter	Num. 26:33
2. Town near Samaria	Josh. 12:24
Seat of Jeroboam's rule	1 Kin. 14:17
Israel's kings rule here down to Omri	1 Kin. 16:6-23
Famous for its beauty	Song 6:4

Tishbite—*an inhabitant of Tishbeh*

Elijah thus called	1 Kin. 17:1

Tithes—*the tenth of one's income*

Given by Abraham to Melchizedek	Heb. 7:1, 2, 6
Promised by Jacob	Gen. 28:22
Belongs to the LORD	Lev. 27:30-33
Given to Levites	Num. 18:21-24
Given by Levites to priests	Num. 18:25, 26
Taken to Temple	Deut. 12:5-19
Rules regarding	Deut. 14:22-29
Honesty in, required	Deut. 26:13-15
Of animals, every tenth	Lev. 27:32, 33
Recognition of, by Jews	Neh. 13:5, 12
Promise regarding	Mal. 3:7-12
Pharisaic legalism on, condemned	Luke 18:9-14

Titles—*appellations of honor*

Condemned by Christ	Matt. 23:1-8

Tittle—*a mark distinguishing similar letters*

Figurative of minute requirements	Matt. 5:18

See Jot

Titus

Greek Christian and Paul's companion	Titus 1:4
Sent by Paul to Corinth	2 Cor. 7:13, 14
Organized Corinthian relief fund	2 Cor. 8:6-23
Met Paul in Macedonia	2 Cor. 7:6, 7
Accompanied Paul to Crete	Titus 1:5
Sent by Paul to Dalmatia	2 Tim. 4:10

Titus, the Epistle to—*a book of the New Testament*

Qualifications of an elder	Titus 1:5-9
Against false teachings	Titus 1:10-16
Domestic life	Titus 2:1-10
Godly living	Titus 3:3-8

Tizite

Description of Joha, David's mighty man	1 Chr. 11:45

Tob—*good*

Jephthah's refuge east of the Jordan	Judg. 11:3, 5

Tobadonijah—*good is Lord Jehovah*

Levite teacher	2 Chr. 17:7, 8

Tobiah—*Jehovah is good*

1. Founder of a postexilic family	Ezra 2:60
2. Ammonite servant; ridiculed the Jews	Neh. 2:10

Tobijah—*Jehovah is good*

1. Levite teacher	2 Chr. 17:7, 8
2. Came from Babylon	Zech. 6:10, 14

Tochen—*a measure*

Town of Simeon	1 Chr. 4:32

Toe—*the terminal part of the foot*

Aaron's, anointed	Ex. 29:20
Of captives, amputated	Judg. 1:6, 7
Of an image	Dan. 2:41, 42

Togarmah

Northern country inhabited by descendants of Gomer	Gen. 10:3

Toi

King of Hamath; sends embassy to salute David	2 Sam. 8:9-12

Token—*a visible sign*

A. *Descriptive of:*	
Rainbow	Gen. 9:12-17
Circumcision	Gen. 17:11
Bloodshed	Ex. 12:13
God's wonders	Ps. 65:8
B. *As assurance of:*	
God's: Presence	Ex. 3:12
Judgment upon sin	Num. 17:10
Goodness	Ps. 86:17
Guarantee	Josh. 2:12, 18, 21
Identification	Mark 14:44
Genuineness	2 Thess. 3:17
Coming judgment	2 Thess. 1:5

Tola—*worm; scarlet*

1. Son of Issachar and family head	Gen. 46:13
2. Son of Puah; a judge of Israel	Judg. 10:1

Tolad—*begetter*

Simeonite town	1 Chr. 4:29
Called Eltolad	Josh. 19:4

Tolerance—*an attitude of patience toward opposing views*

A. *Approved in dealing with:*	
Disputes among brothers	Mark 9:38-40
Weaker brother	Rom. 14:1-23
Repentant brother	2 Cor. 2:4-11
B. *Condemned in dealing with:*	
Sin	1 Cor. 5:1-13
Evil	2 Cor. 6:14-18
Sin in ourselves	Mark 9:43-48
Error	2 John 10, 11

Toll—*taxes*

Imposed by Jews	Ezra 4:20
Imposed upon Jews	Ezra 4:13
Levites excluded from	Ezra 7:24

Tomb—*a place of burial*

John's body placed in	Mark 6:25-29
Christ's body placed in Joseph's	Matt. 25:57-60

Tongue—*the organ of speech*

A. *Descriptive of:*	
Language	Gen. 10:5, 20, 21
Speech	Ex. 4:10
The physical organ	Judg. 7:5
Externalism	1 John 3:18
People or race	Is. 66:18
Spiritual gift	1 Cor. 12:10-30
Submission	Is. 45:23

SUBJECT | REFERENCE

B. *Kinds of:*
Backbiting ... Prov. 25:23
As of fire ... Acts 2:3
Deceitful ... Mic. 6:12
Double ... 1 Tim. 3:8
False ... Ps. 120:3
Flattering ... Prov. 6:24
Just ... Prov. 10:20
Lying ... Prov. 21:6
Muttering ... Is. 59:3
New ... Mark 16:17
Perverse ... Prov. 17:20
Sharpened ... Ps. 140:3
Slow ... Ex. 4:10
Soft ... Prov. 25:15
Stammering ... Is. 33:19
Wholesome ... Prov. 15:4
Wise ... Prov. 15:2

C. *Characteristics of:*
Small but important ... James 3:5
Untameable ... James 3:6
Source of trouble ... Prov. 21:23
Means of sin ... Ps. 39:1
Known by God ... Ps. 139:4

D. *Proper employment of, in:*
Speaking:
God's righteousness ... Ps. 35:28
Wisdom ... Ps. 37:30
God's Word ... Ps. 119:172
Singing praises ... Ps. 126:2
Kindness ... Prov. 31:26
Confessing Christ ... Phil. 2:11

See Slander

Tongues, speaking in

A. *At Pentecost:*
Opposite of Babel ... Gen. 11:6-9
Sign of the Spirit's coming ... Acts 2:3, 4
External manifestation ... Acts 2:4, 5
Meaning of, interpreted by Peter ... Acts 2:14-40

B. *At Corinth:*
Spiritual gift (last rank) ... 1 Cor. 12:8-10, 28-30
Interpreter of, required ... 1 Cor. 14:27, 28
Love superior to ... 1 Cor. 13:1-13
Subject to abuse ... 1 Cor. 14:22-26

Tools of the Bible
Anvil ... Is. 41:7
Awl ... Deut. 15:17
Axe ... 1 Chr. 20:3
Bellows ... Jer. 6:29
Brickkiln ... 2 Sam. 12:31
Compass ... Is. 44:13
Fining pot ... Prov. 17:3
Fleshhook ... Ex. 27:3
Fork ... 1 Sam. 2:13
Furnace ... Prov. 17:3
Goad ... 1 Sam. 13:21
Graving tool ... Ex. 32:4
Hammer ... Ps. 74:6
Inkhorn ... Ezek. 9:2
Knife ... Gen. 22:6
Mattock ... 1 Sam. 13:21
Ox-goad ... Judg. 3:31
Pan ... Ex. 27:3
Plane ... Is. 44:13
Plowshare ... Is. 2:4
Plumb line ... Amos 7:8
Pruning hook ... Is. 2:4
Razor ... Num. 6:5
Saw ... 2 Sam. 12:31
Shovel ... Ex. 27:3
Sickle ... Deut. 16:9
Wheel ... Eccl. 12:6

Topaz—*a precious stone*
Used in breastplate ... Ex. 39:10
Of great value ... Job 28:19
In Eden ... Ezek. 28:13
In New Jerusalem ... Rev. 21:2, 20

Tophel—*lime; cement*
Israelite camp ... Deut. 1:1

Tophet—*altar*
Place of human sacrifice in the valley of Hinnom ... Jer. 7:31, 32

Torment—*to suffer unbearable pain*

A. *Kinds of:*
Physical ... Matt. 8:6
Eternal ... Rev. 20:10

SUBJECT | REFERENCE

B. *Means of:*
Official ... Matt. 18:34
Persecutors ... Heb. 11:35
Fear ... 1 John 4:18
Flame ... Luke 16:23-25
God ... Rev. 14:9-11

Tortoise—*the great lizard*
Classed as unclean ... Lev. 11:29

Touch—*contact between two things*

A. *Kinds of:*
Unclean ... Lev. 5:2, 3
Angelic ... 1 Kin. 19:5, 7
Queenly ... Esth. 5:2
Divine ... Job 19:21
Cleansing ... Is. 6:7
Healing ... Matt. 8:3
Sexual ... 1 Cor. 7:1
Satanic ... 1 John 5:18

B. *Purposes of, to:*
Purify ... Is. 6:7
Strengthen ... Dan. 10:10-18
Harm ... Zech. 2:8
Heal ... Mark 5:27-31
Receive a blessing ... Mark 10:13
Restore to life ... Luke 7:14
Manifest faith ... Luke 7:39-50

Towel—*a cloth used in drying*
Used by Christ ... John 13:4, 5

Tower of Furnaces—*a tower of Jerusalem*
Rebuilt by Nehemiah ... Neh. 3:11

Towers

A. *Purposes of, for:*
Protection ... Matt. 21:33
Watchmen ... 2 Kin. 9:17
Safeguarding people ... 2 Chr. 26:10, 15

B. *Partial list of:*
Babel ... Gen. 11:4, 9
David ... Song 4:4
Lebanon ... Song 7:4
Penuel ... Judg. 8:17
Shechem ... Judg. 9:40, 47, 49
Siloam ... Luke 13:4

To wit—*namely; that is to say*
Used by Paul twice ... 2 Cor. 5:19

Town clerk—*a keeper of court records*
Appeases the people ... Acts 19:35

Trachonitis—*hilly land*
Volcanic region southeast of Damascus ... Luke 3:1

Trade and transportation

A. *Objects of, such as:*
Gold ... 1 Kin. 9:28
Timber ... 1 Kin. 5:6, 8, 9
Hardwood ... 1 Kin. 10:11, 12
Spices ... 1 Kin. 10:10, 15
Property ... Ruth 4:3, 4
Slaves ... Joel 3:6

B. *Means of, by:*
Wagons ... Gen. 46:5, 6
Kines ... 1 Sam. 6:7, 8
Floats ... 1 Kin. 5:7-9
Camels ... 1 Kin. 10:1, 2
Asses ... Num. 22:21-33
Horses ... 1 Kin. 20:20
Caravans ... Gen. 37:25-36

C. *Centers of, in:*
Tyre ... Ezek. 27:1-36
Jerusalem ... Neh. 13:15-21

Trades and crafts
Baker ... Gen. 40:1
Brick makers ... Ex. 5:7
Carpenter ... Is. 41:7
Engineers ... Gen. 11:3, 4
Farmers ... Ps. 104:13-15
Fishermen ... Matt. 4:18-22
Lawyers ... Luke 5:17
Millers ... Ex. 11:5
Physician ... Col. 4:14
Smiths ... Is. 44:12

SUBJECT | REFERENCE

Traditions—*precepts passed down from past generations*

A. *Jewish, described as:*
Commandments of men ... Matt. 15:9
Rejection of God's Word ... Mark 7:8, 9
Productive of hypocrisy ... Mark 7:6, 7
Inconsistent with Christ ... Col. 2:8

B. *Christian described as:*
Inspired by the Spirit ... John 15:26, 27
Handed down by apostles ... 2 Thess. 3:6, 7
Based on eyewitnesses ... 2 Pet. 1:16, 19
Classed as Scripture ... 1 Tim. 5:18; 2 Pet. 3:16
Once for all delivered ... Jude 3
Consisting of fundamental truths ... 1 Cor. 15:1-3
Originating with Christ ... Matt. 28:20; 1 Cor. 11:1-23

Traffic, spiritual
Buying the truth ... Prov. 23:23
Value of wisdom ... Prov. 2:2-4
Above gold in value ... Ps. 119:72, 127
Without price ... Is. 55:1
True gold, from Christ ... Rev. 3:18

Train
Monarch's retinue ... 1 Kin. 10:2
Trailing robe ... Is. 6:1

Traitor—*one who betrays a trust*

Descriptive of:
Judas ... Luke 6:16
End-time people ... 2 Tim. 3:4

Trance—*a somnolent state*
Peter's on a housetop ... Acts 10:10

Transfiguration—*a radical change in appearance of:*
Moses ... Ex. 34:29-35
Christ, on a high mountain ... Matt. 17:1-17
Christ, remembered ... 2 Pet. 1:16-18
Stephen ... Acts 6:15

Transgression—*a violation of God's Law*

A. *Described as:*
Personal ... 1 Tim. 2:14
Public ... Rom. 5:14
Political ... Esth. 3:3
Premeditated ... Josh. 7:11-25

B. *Caused by:*
Law ... Rom. 4:15
Sin ... 1 John 3:4
Wine ... Hab. 2:5
Idolatry ... 1 Chr. 5:25
Intermarriage ... Ezra 10:10, 13
Fear of the people ... 1 Sam. 15:24

C. *Productive of:*
Powerlessness ... Judg. 2:20-23
Unfaithfulness ... 1 Chr. 9:1
Death ... 1 Chr. 10:13
Destruction ... Ps. 37:38
Curse ... Is. 24:5, 6

D. *Punishment of, by:*
Defeat ... 2 Chr. 12:1-5
Disease ... 2 Chr. 26:16-21
Captivity ... Neh. 1:8
Affliction ... Ps. 107:17
Death in hell ... Is. 66:24

E. *Reaction to, by:*
Further disobedience ... Num. 14:41-45
Covering up ... Job 31:33
Repentance ... Ezra 9:4-7

F. *Forgiveness of:*
Difficult ... Josh. 24:19
Out of God's mercy ... Ex. 34:7
By:
Confession ... Ps. 32:1, 5
Removal ... Ps. 103:12
Blotting out ... Is. 44:22

G. *Christ's relation to:*
Wounded for our ... Is. 53:5
Stricken for our ... Is. 53:8
Make intercession for ... Is. 53:12
Provided a Redeemer for ... Rom. 11:26, 27
Died for our ... Heb. 9:15

See Sin

T

SUBJECT — REFERENCE

Transitory—*passing quickly away*

A. *Descriptive of man's:*
- Life ... Ps. 39:4, 5
- Pleasures ... Is. 47:8, 9
- Plans ... Luke 12:16-21

B. *Caused by:*
- World's passing away ... 1 John 2:15-17
- Our mortality ... Ps. 90:3-12
- Impending future world ... 2 Cor. 4:17, 18

Translations—*physical transportation to heaven*
- Enoch ... Heb. 11:5
- Elijah ... 2 Kin. 2:1-11
- Christians ... 1 Thess. 4:16, 17

Travail—*the labor pains of childbirth*

A. *Descriptive of:*
- Childbirth pains ... Gen. 38:27
- Anguish ... Is. 53:11

B. *Of a woman's, described as:*
- Fearful ... Ps. 48:6
- Painful ... Is. 13:8
- Hazardous ... Gen. 35:16-19
- Joyful afterwards ... John 16:21

C. *Figurative of:*
- New Israel ... Is. 66:7, 8
- Messiah's birth ... Mic. 4:9, 10
- Redemption ... Mic. 5:3
- New birth ... Gal. 4:19
- Creation's rebirth ... Rom. 8:22

Treachery—*pretending friendship in order to betray*

A. *Manifested by:*
- Woman ... Judg. 4:18-21
- People ... Josh. 9:3-15
- King ... 2 Sam. 11:14, 15
- Son ... 2 Sam. 13:28, 29
- Enemy ... Esth. 3:8-15
- Disciple ... Matt. 26:47-50

B. *Accompanied by:*
- Deceit ... Gen. 34:13-31
- Soothing words ... Judg. 9:1-5
- Professed favor ... 1 Sam. 18:17-19
- Pretense ... Dan. 6:1-8

Treason—*betrayal of one's country*

A. *Instances of:*
- Rahab against Jericho ... Josh. 2:1-24
- Israelites against Rehoboam ... 1 Kin. 12:16-19
- Absalom against David ... 2 Sam. 15:1-14
- Sheba against David ... 2 Sam. 20:1-22
- Athaliah against Judah ... 2 Kin. 11; 2 Chr. 22:10-12

B. *Characterized by:*
- Conspiracy ... 1 Kin. 16:9-11, 20
- Giving secrets ... 1 Sam. 30:15, 16
- Falling out ... 2 Sam. 3:6-21
- Jealousy ... Num. 12:1-11

See Conspiracy; Treachery

Treasure—*something valuable stored away*

A. *Descriptive of:*
- Storage cities ... Ex. 1:11
- Storehouses ... 1 Kin. 7:51
- Places for storing archives ... Ezra 5:17
- Offering boxes ... Luke 21:1

B. *Figurative of:*
- Earth's productive capacity ... Ps. 17:14
- Wisdom ... Prov. 2:4
- People of God ... Ex. 19:5
- Man's spiritual possibilities ... Matt. 12:35
- New life in Christ ... 2 Cor. 4:6, 7
- Christ as the divine depository ... Col. 2:3, 9
- Future rewards ... Matt. 6:19, 20

Treasurer—*a custodian of public funds*

Under:
- David, Ahijah ... 1 Chr. 26:20
- Solomon, Jehiel ... 1 Chr. 29:7, 8
- Hezekiah, Shebna ... Is. 22:15
- Cyrus, Mithredath ... Ezra 1:8
- Candace, the Ethiopian eunuch ... Acts 8:27
- At Corinth, Erastus ... Rom. 16:23

SUBJECT — REFERENCE

Tree

A. *Characteristics of:*
- Created by God ... Gen. 1:11, 12
- Of fixed varieties ... Gen. 1:12, 29
- Can be grafted ... Rom. 11:24
- Subject to God's judgments ... Hag. 2:17, 19

B. *Used for:*
- Shade ... Gen. 18:4
- Burial sites ... Gen. 35:8
- Food ... Deut. 20:19, 20
- Cross ... Acts 5:30
- Buildings ... 1 Kin. 5:10
- Idolatry ... Is. 44:14, 17
- Fuel ... Is. 44:15, 16, 19

C. *List of, in Bible:*
- Aloe ... Ps. 45:8
- Ash ... Is. 44:14
- Bay ... Ps. 37:35
- Cedar ... 1 Kin. 10:27
- Chestnut ... Ezek. 31:8
- Cypress ... Is. 44:14
- Elm ... Hos. 4:13
- Fig ... Deut. 8:8
- Fir ... 2 Sam. 6:5
- Hazel ... Gen. 30:37
- Juniper ... 1 Kin. 19:4, 5
- Mulberry ... 2 Sam. 5:23
- Myrtle ... Is. 41:19
- Oak ... Is. 1:30
- Olive ... Judg. 9:9
- Palm ... Ex. 15:27
- Pomegranate ... Deut. 8:8
- Poplar ... Hos. 4:13
- Shittim ... Ex. 36:20
- Sycamore ... Amos 7:14
- Willow ... Is. 44:4

D. *Figurative of:*
- Righteous ... Ps. 1:1-3
- Believer's life ... Prov. 11:30
- Wisdom ... Prov. 3:18
- Basic character ... Matt. 7:17-19
- Continued prosperity ... Is. 65:22
- Judgment ... Luke 23:31
- Eternal life ... Rev. 22:14
- Covenant ... Rom. 11:24

Tree of life
- In Eden ... Gen. 2:9
- In New Jerusalem ... Rev. 22:1, 2

Tremble—*to shake with fear*

A. *Expressive of:*
- Deep concern ... Gen. 27:33
- Fear ... Mark 16:8
- Filial trust ... Is. 66:2, 5
- Apprehension ... 1 Sam. 16:4
- Infirmity ... Eccl. 12:3
- Obedience ... Phil. 2:12

B. *Applied to:*
- People ... Dan. 6:26
- Earth ... Ps. 97:4
- Nations ... Is. 64:2
- Heart ... Deut. 28:65
- Flesh ... Ps. 119:120
- Servants ... Eph. 6:5
- Christians ... 1 Cor. 2:3

C. *Caused by:*
- Physical change ... Luke 8:47
- Earthquake ... Acts 16:29

Trials—*hardships that try our faith*

A. *Characteristics of:*
- Some very severe ... 2 Cor. 1:8-10
- Cause of, sometimes unknown ... Job 1:7-22
- Sometimes physical ... 2 Cor. 12:7-10
- Endurable ... 1 Cor. 10:13
- Rewardable ... Matt. 5:10-12

B. *Design of, to:*
- Test faith ... Gen. 22:1-18
- Purify faith ... Mal. 3:3, 4; 1 Pet. 1:6-9
- Increase patience ... James 1:3, 4, 12
- Bring us to a better place ... Ps. 66:10-12
- Chasten us ... Is. 48:10
- Glorify God ... 1 Pet. 4:12-16

Tribes of Israel
- Twelve in number ... Gen. 49:28
- Descended from Jacob's sons ... Gen. 35:22-26

SUBJECT — REFERENCE

- Jacob forecasted future of ... Gen. 49:3-27
- Moses foretold future of ... Deut. 33:6-35
- Numbered ... Num. 1:44-46
- Camped by standards ... Num. 2:2-31
- Canaan divided among ... Josh. 15-17
- Names of, engraven ... Ex. 39:14
- United until Rehoboam's rebellion ... 1 Kin. 12:16-20
- Returned after exile ... Ezra 8:35
- Typical of Christians ... James 1:1

Tribulation—*a state or time of great affliction*

A. *Descriptive of:*
- National distress ... Deut. 4:30
- Afflictions ... 1 Sam. 10:19
- Persecutions ... 1 Thess. 3:4
- Severe testings ... Rev. 2:10, 22

B. *Christian's attitude toward:*
- Must expect ... Acts 14:22
- Glory in ... Rom. 5:3
- Overcome ... Rom. 8:35-37
- Patient in ... Rom. 12:12
- Joyful in ... 2 Cor. 7:4
- Faint not at ... Eph. 3:13

Tribute—*a tax imposed upon a subjugated nation*
- Israelites ... 2 Kin. 23:33
- Christ settles question concerning ... Matt. 22:17-21
- Paul's admonition concerning ... Rom. 13:6, 7

Tribute money—*Temple tax*
- Levied yearly upon all Jews ... Matt. 17:24-27; Matt. 22:17-21

Trickery—*use of guile or deceit*
- By Gibeonites ... Josh. 9:3-6
- By Saul ... 1 Sam. 28:7-10
- By Amnon ... 2 Sam. 13:1-15
- Christians, beware of ... Eph. 4:14

Trifles—*things of slight importance*
- Pharisees obsessed by ... Matt. 23:23-25
- Avoidance of, by Christians ... Titus 3:9

Trinity, the

A. *Revealed in the Old Testament:*
- At Creation ... Gen. 1:1-3, 26
- In the personality of the Spirit ... Is. 40:13; Is. 48:16
- By:
  - Divine angel ... Judg. 13:8-23
  - Personification of Wisdom ... Prov. 8:22-31
  - Threefold "Holy" ... Is. 6:3
  - Aaronic benediction ... Num. 6:24-27

B. *Revealed in the New Testament:*
- At Christ's baptism ... Matt. 3:16, 17
- In:
  - Christ's teaching ... John 14:26; John 15:26
  - Baptismal formula ... Matt. 28:19
  - Apostolic benediction ... 2 Cor. 13:14
  - Apostolic teaching ... Gal. 4:4-6

Triumphal entrance—*Jesus' entry into Jerusalem on the last week of his earthly ministry*
- Prophesied ... Zech. 9:9
- Fulfilled ... Matt. 21:2-11

Troas—*a seaport city near Troy*
- Paul received vision here ... Acts 16:8-11

Trogyllium—*a seaport city of Asia Minor*
- Paul's ship tarried here ... Acts 20:15

Troops—*a group of soldiers*
- Place in fortified cities ... 2 Chr. 17:2
- Come together and camp ... Job 19:12
- "Daughter of troops" ... Mic. 5:1

Trophimus—*nourishing*
- One of Paul's companions ... Acts 20:4

Trouble—*that which causes concern or distress*

A. *Kinds Of:*
- Physical, of nature ... Ps. 46:3
- Mental ... Dan. 5:9
- Spiritual, of the wicked ... Is. 57:20
- Spiritual, of the righteous ... Ps. 77:3
- National ... Jer. 30:7
- Domestic ... Prov. 11:29

B. *Caused by:*
- Misdeeds of sons ... Gen. 34:30

SUBJECT — REFERENCE

Mysterious dream ... Dan. 2:1, 3
Unexpected news ... 1 Sam. 28:21
Sin ... Josh. 7:25
Evil spirits ... 1 Sam. 16:14, 15
Enemies ... Ezra 4:4
Physical malady ... Job 4:5
God's:
  Presence ... Job 23:15
  Withdrawal ... Ps. 30:7
  Wrath ... Ps. 78:49
Our sins ... Ps. 38:4-6
Mouth ... Prov. 21:23
Angel visitant ... Luke 1:12, 29
Wars, etc ... Mark 13:7
Trials ... 2 Cor. 7:5
Afflicted ... 2 Thess. 1:7

C. *God's help to His saints in, to:*
Hide ... Ps. 27:5
Deliver ... Ps. 50:15
Help ... Ps. 46:1
Attend ... Ps. 91:15
Revive ... Ps. 138:7

Truce—*a temporary cessation of warfare*
With good results ... 2 Sam. 2:25-31

Trucebreakers—*violators of agreements*
Characteristic of the last days ... 2 Tim. 3:1, 3

True—*that which agrees with the facts*

A. *Applied to:*
God ... John 17:3
Christ ... Rev. 3:7, 14
God's:
  Word ... John 21:24
  Judgments ... Rev. 16:7
Believer's heart ... 2 Cor. 6:8
Worshipers ... John 4:23

B. *Proof of:*
Given by men ... John 5:32
Based upon testimony ... John 8:13-18
Recognized by men ... John 10:41

See Truth

Trumpet—*a wind musical instrument*

A. *Features concerning:*
Instrument of music ... 1 Chr. 13:8
Made of ram's horn ... Josh. 6:4

B. *Uses of, in Israel, to:*
Signal God's presence ... Ex. 19:16, 19
Regulate marchings ... Num. 10:2, 5, 6
Call assemblies ... Num. 10:2, 3, 7
Announce a feast ... Lev. 23:23-25
Gather the nation ... Judg. 3:27
Alert against an enemy ... Neh. 4:18, 20
Herald a new king ... 1 Kin. 1:34-41
Hail a religious event ... 1 Chr. 13:8
Assist in worship ... Neh. 12:35-41

C. *Uses of, at Christ's return, to:*
Herald Christ's coming ... Matt. 24:31
Signal prophetic events ... Rev. 8:2, 6, 13; Rev. 9:14
Raise the dead ... 1 Thess. 4:16

Trust—*to put one's confidence in*

A. *Not to be placed in:*
Weapons ... Ps. 44:6
Wealth ... Ps. 49:6, 7
Leaders ... Ps. 146:3
Man ... Jer. 17:5
Works ... Jer. 48:7
One's own righteousness ... Ezek. 33:13

B. *To be placed in:*
God's:
  Name ... Ps. 33:21
  Word ... Ps. 119:42
Christ ... Matt. 12:17-21

C. *Benefits of:*
Joy ... Ps. 5:11
Deliverance ... Ps. 22:4, 5
Triumph ... Ps. 25:2, 3
God's goodness ... Ps. 31:19
Mercy ... Ps. 32:10
Provision ... Ps. 37:3, 5
Blessedness ... Ps. 40:4
Safety ... Ps. 56:4, 11
Usefulness ... Ps. 73:28
Guidance ... Prov. 3:5, 6
Inheritance ... Is. 57:13

SUBJECT — REFERENCE

Truth—*that which agrees with final reality*

A. *Ascribed to:*
God's Law ... Ps. 119:142-160
Christ ... John 14:6
Holy Spirit ... John 14:17
God's Word ... John 17:17, 19
Gospel ... Gal. 2:5, 14

B. *Effects of, to:*
Make free ... John 8:31, 32
Sanctify ... John 17:17-19
Purify ... 1 Pet. 1:22
Establish ... Eph. 4:15

C. *Wrong attitudes toward, to:*
Change into a lie ... Rom. 1:25
Disobey ... Rom. 2:8
Walk contrary to ... Gal. 2:14
Love not ... 2 Thess. 2:10
Believe not ... 2 Thess. 2:12
Be destitute of ... 1 Tim. 6:5
Never come to ... 2 Tim. 3:7
Resist ... 2 Tim. 3:8
Turn from ... 2 Tim. 4:4

D. *Right attitudes toward, to:*
Speak ... Eph. 4:25
Walk in ... 3 John 3, 4
Declare ... Acts 26:25
Worship in ... John 4:23, 24
Come to ... 1 Tim. 2:4
Believe and know ... 1 Tim. 4:3
Handle accurately ... 2 Tim. 2:15
Obey ... 1 Pet. 1:22
Be established ... 2 Pet. 1:12

Truthfulness—*abiding by the truth*
Commanded ... Ps. 15:2
Exemplified by Levi ... Mal. 2:6
Should characterize Christians ... Eph. 4:25

Tryphaena—*delicate*
Woman at Rome commended by Paul ... Rom. 16:12

Tryphosa—*dainty*
Woman at Rome commended by Paul ... Rom. 16:12

Tubal
1. Son of Japheth ... Gen. 10:2
2. Tribe associated with Javan and Meshech ... Is. 66:19
  In Gog's army ... Ezek. 38:2, 3
  Punishment of ... Ezek. 32:26, 27

Tubal-cain—*Tubal, the smith*
Son of Lamech ... Gen. 4:19-22

Tumult—*a confused uproar*
Against:
God ... Is. 37:29
Christ ... Matt. 27:24
Paul ... Acts 19:29, 40
Paul pleads innocent of ... Acts 24:18

Turtledove—*a dove or pigeon*
Migratory bird ... Song 2:12
Term of affection ... Ps. 74:19
Offering of the poor ... Lev. 12:2, 6-8; Luke 2:24

Tutors, guardians—*instructors of children*
Referred to by Paul ... Gal. 4:2

Twelve
Angels ... Rev. 21:12
Apostles ... Rev. 21:14
Baskets ... John 6:13
Brazen bulls ... Jer. 52:20
Brethren ... Gen. 42:32
Cakes ... Lev. 24:5
Cities ... 1 Chr. 6:63
Cubits ... 1 Kin. 7:15
Foundations ... Rev. 21:14
Fountains ... Num. 33:9
Fruits ... Rev. 22:2
Gates ... Rev. 21:12
Golden spoons ... Num. 7:86
He goats ... Ezra 8:35
Hours ... John 11:9
Legions of angels ... Matt. 26:53
Lions ... 1 Kin. 10:20
Men ... Josh. 3:12
Months ... Dan. 4:29
Officers ... 1 Kin. 4:7
Oxen ... 2 Chr. 4:15

SUBJECT — REFERENCE

Patriarchs ... Acts 7:8
Pieces ... 1 Kin. 11:30
Pillars ... Ex. 24:4
Princes ... Gen. 17:20
Rods ... Num. 17:2
Silver bowls ... Num. 7:84
Sons of Jacob ... Gen. 35:22
Spoons ... Num. 7:86
Stars ... Rev. 12:1
Stones ... 1 Kin. 18:31
Thousand ... 2 Sam. 17:1
Thrones ... Matt. 19:28
Tribes ... Luke 22:30
Wells ... Ex. 15:27
Years of age ... Luke 2:42

Twins of the Bible
Esau and Jacob ... Gen. 25:21-26
Pharez and Zarah ... Gen. 38:27-30

Two
Lights ... Gen. 1:16
Tables of stone ... Ex. 34:1, 4
Goats ... Lev. 16:7, 8
Spies ... Josh. 2:1, 4
Wives ... 1 Sam. 1:2
Evils ... Jer. 2:13
Masters ... Matt. 6:24
Witnesses ... Matt. 18:16
People agreeing ... Matt. 18:19, 20
Commandments ... Matt. 22:40
Thieves ... Matt. 27:38
Covenants ... Gal. 4:24
Become one ... Eph. 5:31
Hard pressed from both directions ... Phil. 1:23

Tychicus—*chance happening*
Asian Christian and companion ... Acts 20:4
Carried Paul's letter to Colossians ... Col. 4:7
Carried letter to Ephesians ... Eph. 6:21, 22
Accompanied Onesimus to his master ... Col. 4:7
Later sent to Ephesus by Paul ... 2 Tim. 4:12

Types, typology—*divine illustration of truth*
May be:
Ceremony—Passover ... 1 Cor. 5:7
Event—wilderness journeys ... 1 Cor. 10:1-11
Institution—priesthood ... Heb. 9:11
Person—Adam ... Rom. 5:14
Thing—veil ... Heb. 10:20

Tyrannus—*tyrant*
Paul teaches in his school ... Acts 19:9

Tyre—*a seaport city 25 miles south of Sidon*
Ancient city ... Josh. 19:29
Noted for commerce ... Ezek. 27:1-36
King of, helped Solomon ... 1 Kin. 5:1-10
Denounced by prophets ... Joel 3:4-6
Fall of, predicted ... Ezek. 26:1-21
Jesus visited ... Matt. 15:21-28

Tzaddi
Letter of the Hebrew alphabet ... Ps. 119:137-144

U

Ucal—*I am strong*
Proverbs addressed to ... Prov. 30:1

Uel—*will of God*
Divorced his foreign wife ... Ezra 10:34

Ulai—*a river of Elam near Shushan*
Scene of Daniel's visions ... Dan. 8:2-16

Ulam—*first; leader*
Manassite ... 1 Chr. 7:16, 17

Ulla—*burden*
Descendant of Asher ... 1 Chr. 7:30, 39

Ummah—*association*
Asherite town ... Josh. 19:24, 30

Unbelief

A. *Caused by:*
Sin ... John 16:9
Satan ... John 8:43-47
Evil heart ... Heb. 3:12
Honor from one another ... John 5:44

SUBJECT REFERENCE

Not belonging to Christ ..... John 10:26
Judicial blindness .... John 12:37-40

B. *Manifested in:*

Questioning God's Word .... Gen. 3:1-6; 2 Pet. 3:4, 5
Turning from God .... Heb. 3:12
Questioning God's power .... Ps. 78:19, 20
Hating God's messengers .... Acts 7:54, 57
Resisting the Spirit .... Acts 7:51, 52
Discounting evidence .... John 12:37
Opposing the Gospel .... 1 Thess. 2:14-16
Rejecting Christ .... John 12:48; John 16:9

C. *Consequences of, seen in:*

Hindering miracles .... Matt. 13:58
Exclusion from blessings .... Heb. 3:15-19
Condemnation .... John 3:18, 19
Rejection .... Rom. 11:20
Judgment .... John 12:48
Death .... John 8:24, 25
Destruction .... 2 Thess. 1:8, 9
God's wrath .... John 3:36

D. *Those guilty, described as:*

Stiff-necked .... Acts 7:51
Uncircumcised .... Jer. 6:10
Blinded .... Eph. 4:18
Rebels .... Num. 17:10

Unbelievers—*those who reject Christ*

Condemnation of .... Mark 16:16
Intermarriage with Christians, forbidden .... 2 Cor. 6:14, 15

Uncertainties—*things which may or may not happen*

A. *Caused by:*

Unknown future .... Prov. 27:1
Divine Providence .... James 4:13-17
Our lack of knowledge ...... John 21:18-23

B. *Need not affect our:*

Assurance .... 1 Cor. 9:26
Trust in God .... Rom. 4:19-21
Plans .... Acts 21:11-15

Uncharitableness—*a critical spirit*

Condemning others .... Matt. 7:1-4; James 4:11, 12
Passing false judgments .... Luke 7:39
Assuming superior holiness ..... John 8:1-11
Not forgiving readily .... Luke 15:25-32; 2 Cor. 2:6-11
Imputing evil to others .... 1 Sam. 1:14-17

Uncircumcised—*not circumcised*

A. *Descriptive of:*

Gentiles .... Gal. 2:7
Unregenerate state .... Col. 2:13
Unregenerate Jews and Gentiles .... Jer. 9:25, 26

B. *State of, in the Old Testament, excludes from:*

Covenant .... Ex. 17:14
Passover .... Ex. 12:48
Land .... Josh. 5:7
Sanctuary .... Ezek. 44:7, 9
Holy city .... Is. 52:1

C. *State of, in the New Testament:*

Has no spiritual value .... Gal. 5:6
Need not be changed .... 1 Cor. 7:18, 19
Explained .... Rom. 2:25-29

Unclean—*that which is defiled*

A. *Descriptive of:*

Men and women .... Deut. 23:10; Lev. 15:1-33
Not of the Lord .... Is. 52:1

B. *Transformation of, by:*

Purification .... Is. 6:5-7
Separation .... 2 Cor. 6:17
Knowledge in Jesus .... Rom. 14:14
Prayer .... 1 Tim. 4:3-5

See Clean; Pollute; Sanitation and hygiene

Unconditional surrender

Required by Christ .... Luke 14:26, 27
As sacrifice .... Rom. 12:1

Unction—*an anointing*

With the Holy Spirit .... 1 John 2:20, 27

SUBJECT REFERENCE

Undefiled—*untainted*

Such persons are blessed .... Ps. 119:1
Christ is .... Heb. 7:26
Describes marriage act .... Heb. 13:4
Applied to true religion .... James 1:27
Our inheritance thus called ..... 1 Pet. 1:4

Undersetters—*shoulders*

Supports placed under the laver .... 1 Kin. 7:30, 34

Understanding—*knowing things in their right relationship*

A. *Means of, by:*

God's:
Gift .... 1 Kin. 3:9-12
Revelation .... Rom. 1:20
Word .... Ps. 119:104, 130
Books .... Dan. 9:2, 23
Holy Spirit .... Ex. 31:3
Christ .... 1 John 5:20
Prayer .... Ps. 119:34-125
Faith .... Heb. 11:3
Enlightening .... Eph. 1:18
Interpretation .... Neh. 8:2-13
Explanation .... Luke 24:45
Reproof .... Prov. 15:32
Later event .... Ps. 73:17

B. *Limitations on, by:*

Unbelief .... John 8:43
Unregeneracy .... Eph. 4:18
Spiritual blindness .... Is. 6:9, 10
Judicial punishment .... Is. 44:18, 19
Difficulties .... 2 Pet. 3:16

Unfruitfulness—*not producing good fruit*

A. *Caused by:*

Unfaithfulness .... Is. 5:1-7
Worldliness .... James 4:1-4
Negligence .... Luke 19:20-27

B. *Punished by:*

God's judgments .... Matt. 3:10
Rejection:
Now .... John 15:2, 4, 6
Hereafter .... Heb. 6:8

Ungodliness, ungodly—*the morally corrupt*

A. *Described as:*

Prospering in the world ..... Ps. 73:12
Growing worse .... 2 Tim. 2:16
Perverting God's grace ...... Jude 4
Abounding in the last days .. Jude 18
Christ died for .... Rom. 5:6

B. *Judgments upon, by:*

Flood .... 2 Pet. 2:5, 6
Law .... 1 Tim. 1:9
God's decree .... Jude 4
God's revelation .... Rom. 1:18
Christ's return .... Jude 14, 15
World's end .... 2 Pet. 3:7
Final judgment .... Ps. 1:4-6

Unicorn—*the wild ox*

Of great strength .... Num. 23:22
Very wild and ferocious .... Job 39:9-12
Frisky in youth .... Ps. 29:6

Unintentionally—*without premeditation*

Concerning an innocent killer ... Josh. 20:3-5

Union

Of:

Godhead .... John 17:21, 22
Christ and believers .... John 15:1-7
God and man .... Acts 17:28, 29
Mankind .... Acts 17:26
Satan and the unsaved .... John 8:44
Believers in prayer .... Matt. 18:19, 20

See Oneness

Union with Christ

A. *Compared to:*

Head and the body .... Eph. 4:15, 16
Marriage bond .... Eph. 5:23, 30
Building .... Eph. 2:21, 22
Parts of the body .... 1 Cor. 12:12, 27
Vine and branches .... John 15:4, 5
Food and the body .... John 6:56, 57

B. *Illustrated in the "togethers":*

Crucified .... Rom. 6:6
Buried .... Rom. 6:4

SUBJECT REFERENCE

Made alive .... Eph. 2:5
Sitting .... Eph. 2:6
Suffering .... Rom. 8:17
Reigning .... 2 Tim. 2:12
Glorified .... Rom. 8:17

C. *Manifested in, oneness:*

Of mind .... 1 Cor. 2:16
Of spirit .... 1 Cor. 6:17
In suffering .... Phil. 3:10
In worship .... 1 Cor. 10:16, 17
In ministry .... 2 Cor. 5:18-21

Unity of believers

A. *Based upon:*

Indwelling Spirit .... 1 Cor. 3:16, 17; 1 Cor. 6:19
New birth .... 2 Cor. 5:17
Union with Christ .... 2 Cor. 13:5

B. *Expressed by oneness of:*

Mind .... 1 Pet. 3:8
Unity of Spirit .... Ps. 133:1-3
Faith .... Eph. 4:4-6
Fellowship .... Acts 2:42-47
Concern .... 1 Cor. 12:25, 26

C. *Consistent with such differences as:*

Physical .... 1 Pet. 3:1-7
Social .... Eph. 6:5-9
Mental .... 1 Cor. 1:26-29

Unjust

Described as:

Abomination .... Prov. 29:27
Recipient of God's blessings .... Matt. 5:45
Christ died for .... 1 Pet. 3:18

Unknown god

Altar to .... Acts 17:22, 23

Unleavened bread

Used in the passover .... Ex. 12:8-20; Mark 14:1, 12
Typical of Christians .... 1 Cor. 5:7, 8

Unmercifulness—*lacking mercy*

Shown by Simeon and Levi ..... Gen. 34:25-31
By Pharaoh .... Ex. 5:4-19
By creditor .... Matt. 18:28-30

Unni—*answering is with Jehovah*

Levite musician .... 1 Chr. 15:18

Unpardonable sin

Sin not forgivable .... Matt. 12:31, 32; Luke 12:10

Unrest—*a state of agitation*

Of the nations .... Luke 21:25, 26
Of the wicked .... Is. 57:20
Remedy given by Christ .... Matt. 11:28
Available to Christians .... Phil. 4:7

Unrighteousness—*wickedness*

A. *Attitude toward, by the wicked, they:*

Suppress the truth in .... Rom. 1:18
Are filled with .... Rom. 1:29
Obey it .... Rom. 2:8
Love the wages of .... 2 Pet. 2:15
Take pleasure in .... 2 Thess. 2:12
Receive the reward of .... 2 Pet. 2:13
Shall not inherit the kingdom .... 1 Cor. 6:9

B. *Relation of believers toward:*

They are cleansed from ...... 1 John 1:9
God is merciful toward their .... Heb. 8:12
Must not fellowship with .... 2 Cor. 6:14
All the world guilty .... Rom. 3:1-20

Unselfishness—*not putting self first*

A. *Christ, an example of, in His:*

Mission .... John 6:38
Suffering .... Matt. 26:39, 42
Concern .... John 19:26, 27
Death .... Phil. 2:5-8

B. *In the believer, prompted by:*

Christ's example .... Phil. 2:3-8
Love .... 1 Cor. 13:4, 5
Concern .... 1 Cor. 10:23-33
Christian service .... Phil. 2:25-30
Sacrifice .... Rev. 12:11

C. *Examples of:*

Abram .... Gen. 13:8-12

SUBJECT	REFERENCE
Moses	Num. 14:12-29
Gideon	Judg. 8:22, 23
Jonathan	1 Sam. 18:4
David	1 Chr. 21:17
Nehemiah	Neh. 5:14-19
Daniel	Dan. 5:17
Christians	Acts 4:34, 35
Paul	1 Cor. 9:19-23
Onesiphorus	2 Tim. 1:16-18

Unspeakable

God's Gift .... 2 Cor. 9:15

Untempered mortar—*whitewash*

Figurative of false prophets ..... Ezek. 13:10, 14

Unwittingly—*without premeditation*

Concerning an innocent killer ... Josh. 20:3-5

Unworldliness—*a heavenly frame of mind*

A. *Negatively expressed in, not:*

Loving the world .... 1 John 2:15-17
Fellowshiping with evil ..... 2 Cor. 6:14-18
Mixing in worldly affairs .... 2 Tim. 2:4

B. *Positively expressed in:*

Seeking God's kingdom first .... Matt. 6:33, 34
Living for Jesus .... Gal. 2:20
Becoming a living sacrifice ... Rom. 12:1, 2
Having a heavenly mind ..... Col. 3:1, 2
Looking for Jesus .... Titus 2:11-15
Looking to Jesus .... Heb. 12:1, 2

Unworthiness—*not being fit; lacking merit*

A. *Caused by a sense of:*

Failure .... Gen. 32:10
Social difference .... 1 Sam. 18:18, 23
Sin .... Luke 15:19, 21
Inferiority .... John 1:27

B. *Examples of:*

Moses .... Ex. 4:10
Centurion .... Matt. 8:8
Peter .... Luke 5:8
Paul .... 1 Cor. 15:9

Upharsin—*and divided*

Interpreted by Daniel .... Dan. 5:5, 25, 28

Uphaz

Unidentified place of fine gold .. Jer. 10:9

Upper room—*chamber, usually built on a roof*

Ahaziah fell from .... 2 Kin. 1:2
Ahaz's .... 2 Kin. 23:12
Disciples prepared for Christ.... Mark 14:14-16
Dorcas placed in .... Acts 9:36, 37
Paul preached in .... Acts 20:7, 8

Uprightness—*character approved by God*

A. *Descriptive of:*

God's nature .... Is. 26:7
Man's state .... Eccl. 7:29
Devout .... Job 1:1, 8

B. *Of God, manifested in His:*

Works .... Ps. 111:8
Judgments .... Ps. 119:137
Delights .... 1 Chr. 29:17

C. *Blessings of, for saints:*

Temporal blessings .... Ps. 84:11
Lord's blessings .... Ps. 11:7
Prosperity .... Prov. 14:11
Deliverance .... Prov. 11:3, 6, 11
Salvation .... Ps. 7:10
God's presence .... Ps. 140:13
Light in darkness .... Ps. 112:4
Answered prayer .... Prov. 15:8
Righteousness .... Ps. 36:10
Joy .... Ps. 32:11
Glory .... Ps. 64:10
Final dominion .... Ps. 49:14

D. *Attitude of wicked toward, they:*

Are devoid of .... Hab. 2:4
Leave the path of .... Prov. 2:13
Hate .... Prov. 29:10
Persecute .... Ps. 37:14
Laugh to scorn .... Job 12:4

Ur—*flame*

Father of Eliphal .... 1 Chr. 11:35
Called Ahasbai .... 2 Sam. 23:34

Ur of the Chaldees

City of Abram's early life .... Gen. 11:28-31; Gen. 15:7
Located in Mesopotamia by Stephen .... Acts 7:2, 4

Urbane—*polite*

Christian .... Rom. 16:9

Uri—*an abbreviation of Urijah*

1. Father of Bezaleel .... 1 Chr. 2:20
2. Father of Geber .... 1 Kin. 4:19
3. Divorced his foreign wife .... Ezra 10:24

Uriah—*Jehovah is light*

1. Hittite and one of David's warriors .... 2 Sam. 23:39
   Condemned to death by David .... 2 Sam. 11:1-27
2. Priest .... Ezra 8:33
3. Prophet in Jeremiah's time ... Jer. 26:20-23
4. Stands with Ezra .... Neh. 8:4

Uriel—*God is light*

1. Kohathite Levite .... 1 Chr. 6:22, 24
2. Man of Gibeah .... 2 Chr. 13:2

Urijah—*Jehovah is light*

1. High priest in Ahaz' time .... 2 Kin. 16:10-16
2. Postexilic priest .... 2 Kin. 16:10-16
3. Prophet in Jeremiah's time ... Jer. 26:20
4. Stands with Ezra .... Neh. 8:4

Urim and Thummim—*lights and perfections*

Placed in the breastplate of the high priest .... Ex. 28:30
Method of consulting God .... Num. 27:21; 1 Sam. 14:3-37
Use of, confined to priests ...... Deut. 33:8
Answer by, refused .... 1 Sam. 28:6

Usurpation—*seizing authority illegally*

A. *Methods of, by:*

Intrigue .... 2 Sam. 15:1-12
Defying God's Law .... 1 Sam. 13:8-14
Changing God's worship .... 2 Kin. 16:10-17
Conspiracy .... 1 Kin. 15:27, 28
Assuming dictatorial rights ... 3 John 9, 10

B. *Consequences of, seen in:*

Defeat and death .... 2 Kin. 11:1-6
Another conspiracy .... 2 Kin. 15:10-15
Defeat and conditional forgiveness .... 1 Kin. 1:5-53

C. *Spirit of, manifested in:*

Man's transgression .... Gen. 3:1-7
Satan's fall .... Is. 14:12-14
Woman's weakness .... 1 Tim. 2:12
Antichrist's desire .... 2 Thess. 2:3, 4; Rev. 13:1-18

Utensils, kitchen

Bowls .... Amos 6:6
Charger .... Matt. 14:11
Cruse .... 1 Kin. 17:12
Cup and platter .... Matt. 23:25
Fork (tongs) .... 1 Sam. 2:13, 14
Iron pan .... Ezek. 4:3
Kettle (pot) .... 1 Sam. 2:14
Kneading trough .... Ex. 8:3
Millstones .... Is. 47:2
Pan .... Lev. 2:5

Uthai—*Jehovah is help*

1. Judahite .... 1 Chr. 9:4
2. Postexilic returnee .... Ezra 8:14

Uz—*firmness*

1. Descendant of Shem .... Gen. 10:23
2. Descendant of Seir .... Gen. 36:28
3. Son of Nahor .... Gen. 22:20, 21
4. Place in south Edom; residence of Job .... Job 1:1

Uzai—*hoped for*

Father of Palal .... Neh. 3:25

Uzal

Son of Joktan .... Gen. 10:27

Uzza, Uzzah—*strength*

1. Son of Shimei .... 1 Chr. 6:29
2. Descendant of Ehud .... 1 Chr. 8:7
3. Head of a returning Temple servant family .... Ezra 2:49
4. Name of a garden .... 2 Kin. 21:18, 26
5. Son of Abinadab struck down for touching the ark of the covenant .... 2 Sam. 6:3-11

Uzzen-sherah—*top of Sherah*

Town built by Sherah, Ephraim's daughter .... 1 Chr. 7:24

Uzzi—*my strength*

1. Descendant of Aaron .... 1 Chr. 6:5, 51
2. Descendant of Issachar .... 1 Chr. 7:1-3
3. Son of Bela .... 1 Chr. 7:7
4. Levite overseer .... Neh. 11:22
5. Postexilic priest .... Neh. 12:19, 42

Uzzia—*my strength is Jehovah*

One of David's mighty men ..... 1 Chr. 11:44

Uzziah—*my strength is Jehovah*

1. Kohathite Levite .... 1 Chr. 6:24
2. Father of Jehonathan .... 1 Chr. 27:25
3. King of Judah, called Azariah .... 2 Kin. 14:21; 2 Kin. 15:1-7
   Reigned 52 years .... 2 Kin. 15:1, 2
   Reigned righteously .... 2 Chr. 26:4, 5
   Conquered the Philistines .... 2 Chr. 26:6-8
   Strengthened Jerusalem .... 2 Chr. 26:9
   Developed agriculture .... 2 Chr. 26:10
   Usurped priestly function; stricken with leprosy .... 2 Chr. 26:16-21
   Life of, written by Isaiah .... 2 Chr. 26:22, 23
   Earthquake in the days of ... Amos 1:1
   Death of, time of Isaiah's vision .... Is. 6:1
4. Priest who divorced his foreign wife .... Ezra 10:19, 21
5. Judahite .... Neh. 11:4

Uzziel—*God is my strength*

1. Levite, son of Kohath and family head .... Ex. 6:18, 22
2. Son of Bela .... 1 Chr. 7:7
3. Simeonite captain .... 1 Chr. 4:41-43
4. Levite musician .... 1 Chr. 25:3, 4
5. Levite assisting in Hezekiah's reforms .... 2 Chr. 29:14-19
6. Goldsmith working on Jerusalem's wall .... Neh. 3:8

V

Vagabond—*an aimless wanderer*

Curse on Cain .... Gen. 4:12, 14
Curse upon the wicked .... Ps. 109:10
Professional exorcists thus called .... Acts 19:13

Vail (see Veil, the sacred; Veil, woman's)

Vain—*empty; useless*

A. *Applied to physical things:*

Beauty .... Prov. 31:30
Life .... Eccl. 6:12
Customs .... Jer. 10:3
Men .... Job 11:12
Adornment .... Jer. 4:30
Healing .... Jer. 46:11
Sacrifice .... Is. 1:13
Protection .... 1 Sam. 25:21
Safety .... Ps. 33:17
World's creation .... Is. 45:18, 19

B. *Applied to spiritual things:*

Obedience .... Deut. 32:46, 47
Chastisement .... Jer. 2:30
Visions .... Ezek. 13:7
Serving God .... Mal. 3:14
Faith .... 1 Cor. 15:17
Words .... Eph. 5:6
Imaginations .... Rom. 1:21
Babblings .... 2 Tim. 2:16

C. *Applied to possibilities:*

God's grace .... 1 Cor. 15:10
Christ's death .... Gal. 2:21
Scriptures .... James 4:5
Faith .... 1 Cor. 15:2-17
Religion .... James 1:26

SUBJECT	REFERENCE
Worship	Is. 45:19
Labor	1 Thess. 3:5
Reception	1 Thess. 2:1, 2
Sufferings	Gal. 3:4

Vainglory—*conceit*

- Very offensive in the Christian's life — Gal. 5:26; Phil. 2:3

Vajezatha—*son of the atmosphere*

- One of Haman's sons — Esth. 9:9

Valley Gate

- Entrance into Jerusalem — Neh. 2:13

Valley of Dry Bones

- Vision of Ezekiel — Ezek. 37:1-14

Vaniah—*Jehovah is praise*

- Divorced his foreign wife — Ezra 10:36

Vanity—*emptiness, futility*

A. *Descriptive of:*
- Man's life — Ps. 144:4
- Sin's end — Prov. 22:8
- Man's thoughts — Ps. 94:11
- Idolatry — Acts 14:15

B. *Manifested in the wicked's:*
- Words — Ps. 12:2
- Thoughts — Ps. 94:11
- Trust — Is. 59:4
- Worship — Jer. 51:17, 18

C. *Believer's attitude toward:*
- Request for removal from — Prov. 30:8
- "Turn away mine eyes" — Ps. 119:37
- Should not walk in — Eph. 4:17

Vashni—*weak*

- Son of Samuel — 1 Chr. 6:28

Vashti—*beautiful woman*

- Queen of Ahasuerus, deposed and divorced — Esth. 1:9-22

Vau

- Letter in the Hebrew alphabet — Ps. 119:41-48

Veal

- Prepared for King Saul — 1 Sam. 28:21-25

Vegetables—*plants grown for food*

- Part of God's creation — Gen. 1:11, 12
- Controversy regarding — Rom. 14:1-23
- Preferred by Daniel — Dan. 1:12, 16

Veil, the sacred

A. *Features regarding:*
- Made by divine command — Ex. 26:31, 32
- Used to separate the holy and most holy — Ex. 26:33
- Means of concealing the divine person — Ex. 40:3
- In the Temple also — 2 Chr. 3:14
- Rent at Christ's death — Matt. 27:51

B. *Entrance through:*
- By the high priest alone — Heb. 9:6, 7
- On Day of Atonement only — Heb. 9:7
- Taking blood — Heb. 9:7

C. *Figurative of:*
- Old Testament dispensation — Heb. 9:8
- Christ's flesh — Heb. 10:20
- Access now into God's presence — Heb. 10:19-22

Veil, woman's

A. *Literal uses of:*
- For modesty — Gen. 24:65
- For adornment — Is. 3:23
- To conceal identity — Gen. 38:14
- To soften the divine glory of God — Ex. 34:33-35

B. *Figurative of:*
- Coming of the Lord — Is. 25:7
- Turning to the Lord — 2 Cor. 3:14-16

Vengeance—*retribution as a punishment*

A. *Belonging to God, as:*
- Judgment upon sin — Jer. 11:20-23
- Right not to be taken by man — Ezek. 25:12-17; Heb. 10:30
- Set time — Jer. 46:9, 10

B. *Visitation of, by God, at:*
- Nation's fall — Jer. 51:6, 11, 36
- Christ's first coming — Is. 35:4-10
- Jerusalem's destruction — Luke 21:22
- Sodom's destruction — Jude 7
- Christ's return — 2 Thess. 1:8

See Revenge

Venison—*the flesh of deer*

- Isaac's favorite dish — Gen. 27:1-33

Ventriloquism—*appearing to speak from another source*

- From the dust — Is. 29:4

Verdict—*a judicial decision*

- Unjustly rendered — Luke 23:13-26
- Pronounced by hypocrites — John 8:1-11

Verily, verily—*a strong affirmation*

A. *Concerning Christ's:*
- Glory — John 1:51
- Eternity — John 8:58
- Uniqueness — John 10:1, 7
- Mission — John 6:32
- Betrayal — John 13:21
- Death — John 12:24

B. *Concerning man's:*
- Spiritual bondage — John 8:34
- Spiritual darkness — John 6:26
- Need of regeneration — John 3:3, 5
- Need of salvation — John 5:24, 25
- Means of salvation — John 6:47, 53
- Life eternal — John 8:51

C. *Concerning the believer's:*
- Fickleness — John 13:38
- Work — John 14:12
- Mission — John 13:16, 20
- Prayer — John 16:23
- Life — John 21:18

Vermilion—*a brilliant red color*

- Ceiling painted with — Jer. 22:14

Vessels—*hollow utensils for holding things*

A. *Made of:*
- Wood or stone — Ex. 7:19
- Gold and silver — Dan. 5:2
- Clay — Rom. 9:21
- Copper — Ezra 8:27

B. *Of the tabernacle:*
- Under care of Levites — Num. 3:31, 32
- Carried away into Babylon — 2 Chr. 36:18
- Belshazzar uses in feast — Dan. 5:1-4
- Returned to Jerusalem — Ezra 1:7-11

C. *Figurative of:*
- Mankind — Rom. 9:21-23
- Human weakness — 2 Cor. 4:7
- Believers — 2 Tim. 2:20, 21
- Person's body or wife — 1 Thess. 4:4
- Chosen person — Acts 9:15

Vex—*to irritate the soul*

A. *Caused by:*
- Nagging — Judg. 16:16
- Lust — 2 Sam. 13:2
- Evil environment — 2 Pet. 2:7, 8
- Temptations — Num. 25:18
- Evil men — Num. 20:15
- Demons — Matt. 15:22

B. *Agents of:*
- God — Ps. 2:5
- People — Ex. 22:21
- King — Acts 12:1
- Enemies — Judg. 10:8

C. *Objects of:*
- Human soul — Job 19:2
- Righteous soul — 2 Pet. 2:8
- Holy Spirit — Is. 63:10

Vial—*a small flask or vessel*

- Used for anointing — 1 Sam. 10:1
- Full of incense — Rev. 5:8
- Filled with God's wrath — Rev. 16:1-17

Vicarious suffering of Christ

A. *Expressed in Old Testament, by:*
- Types — Gen. 22:7, 8, 13
- Explicit prophecies — Is. 53:1-12; Acts 8:32-35

B. *Expressed in the New Testament, by:*
- John the Baptist — John 1:29
- Christ Himself — Mark 10:45
- Peter — 1 Pet. 1:18, 19
- John — 1 John 3:16
- Paul — Gal. 2:20
- Hebrews — Heb. 2:9, 17

Victory—*attaining the mastery over*

A. *Of Christ:*
- Promised — Ps. 110:1-7
- Accompanied by suffering — Is. 53:10-12
- By resurrection — Acts 2:29-36
- By His return — Rev. 19:11-21

B. *Of Christians:*
- Through Christ — Phil. 4:13
- By the Holy Spirit — Gal. 5:16, 17, 22, 25
- Over:
  - Flesh — Gal. 5:16-21
  - World — 1 John 5:4
  - Satan — James 4:7

Vigor in old age

- Moses at 120 — Deut. 34:7
- Caleb at 85 — Josh. 14:10-13
- Jehoiada at 130 — 2 Chr. 24:15, 16

Vileness—*the state of physical or moral corruption*

A. *Described as:*
- Worthless — 1 Sam. 15:9
- Dirty and filthy — James 2:2
- Frail and weak — Phil. 3:21
- Something insignificant — Job 40:4

B. *Caused by:*
- God's judgment — Jer. 29:17
- Human corruption — Judg. 19:24

Village—*a settlement*

- Of the Samaritans — Luke 9:52

Vine, vineyard

A. *Features regarding:*
- Grown by Noah — Gen. 9:20
- Native of Palestine — Deut. 6:11
- Reaping of, by poor — 2 Kin. 25:12
- Fruit of, God's gift — Ps. 107:37
- Pruning of, necessary — Lev. 25:3, 4
- Dead branches burned — John 15:6

B. *Enemies of:*
- Hail and frost — Ps. 78:47
- Foxes — Song 2:15
- Boars — Ps. 80:13
- Thieves — Jer. 49:9
- Stones — Is. 5:2
- Sloth — Prov. 24:30, 31

C. *Laws concerning:*
- Care of, exempts from military service — Deut. 20:6
- Diverse seed forbidden in — Deut. 22:9
- Neighbors may eat — Deut. 23:24
- No cultivation of, during Sabbatical year — Ex. 23:11
- Second gathering of, forbidden — Lev. 19:10
- New, five years' waiting — Lev. 19:23-25
- Nazirites forbidden to eat of — Num. 6:3, 4
- Rechabites forbidden to plant — Jer. 35:7-9
- Not to be mortgaged — Neh. 5:3, 4

D. *Figurative of:*
- Jewish nation — Is. 5:1-7
- Growth in grace — Hos. 14:7
- Purifying afflictions — John 15:2
- Peacefulness — 1 Kin. 4:25
- Worthlessness — John 15:2, 6
- Fruitful wife — Ps. 128:3
- God's kingdom — Matt. 20:1-16

Vinedresser

- Poor made to be — 2 Kin. 25:12

Vinegar—*wine or strong drink fermented*

- Hard on teeth — Prov. 10:26
- Forbidden to Nazarites — Num. 6:3
- Offered to Christ in mockery — Ps. 69:21

Viol—*a six-stringed musical instrument*

- Used in merrymaking — Is. 5:12
- Destruction of — Is. 14:11

SUBJECT — REFERENCE

Viper—*a deadly snake*
Figurative of spiritual transformation .... Is. 11:8
Jewish leaders compared to .... Matt. 3:7
Paul bit by .... Acts 28:3-5

Virgin—*a woman untouched sexually*
Penalty for seduction of .... Deut. 22:28, 29
Parable of ten .... Matt. 25:1-13
Specifications regarding .... 1 Cor. 7:28-38
Christ born of .... Luke 1:26-35
Figurative of Christians .... Rev. 14:4

Virgin conception
Prophesied .... Is. 7:14
Christ conceived of Holy Spirit .... {Matt. 1:18; Luke 1:26-35}
Born of virgin .... Matt. 1:19-25

Virtuous woman
Graphically described .... Prov. 31:10-31
Illustrated by Sarah .... 1 Pet. 3:1-7
Adornment of .... 1 Tim. 2:9, 10

Visions—*divine revelations*
A. *Characteristics of:*
Understandable .... Dan. 7:15-19
Authenticated by divine glory .... Ezek. 8:1-4
Personal and phenomenal .... Dan. 10:7-9
Prophetic .... Dan. 9:23-27
Dated and localized .... Ezek. 1:1-3
Causes trembling and dread .... Dan. 10:7-17
Meaning of, interpreted .... Dan. 9:21-24
Absence of, tragic .... Prov. 29:18
Performances of, sure .... Ezek. 12:21-28
Proof of Messianic times .... Joel 2:28; Acts 2:17
Imitated by false prophets .... Jer. 14:14
B. *Productive of:*
Guidance .... Gen. 46:2-5
Direction .... Acts 16:9, 10
Encouragement .... Acts 18:9, 10
Warning .... Is. 21:2-6
Judgment .... 1 Sam. 3:15-18
Action for the Lord .... Acts 26:19, 20
C. *Objects of, revealed in:*
Israel's future .... Gen. 15:1-21
Succession of world empires .... Dan. 7:1-8
Ram .... Dan. 8:1-7, 20
Expanding river .... Ezek. 47:1-12
Throne of God .... Rev. 4:1-11

Visit, visitation—*to go to see a person*
Descriptive of:
Going to a person .... Acts 15:36
God's care .... Ps. 65:9
God's purposed time .... Luke 19:44

Visitors
Moses and Elijah .... Matt. 17:3

Vocation—*a calling*
We must walk worthy of .... Eph. 4:1

Voice of God, the
A. *Importance of:*
Must be obeyed .... Gen. 3:1-19
Disobedience to, judged .... Jer. 42:5-22
Obedience to, the essence of true religion .... 1 Sam. 15:19-24
Obedience to, rewarded .... Gen. 22:6-18
Sign of the covenant .... Josh. 24:24, 25
B. *Heard by:*
Adam .... Gen. 3:9, 10
Moses .... Ex. 19:19
Israel .... Deut. 5:22-26
Samuel .... 1 Sam. 3:1-14
Elijah .... 1 Kin. 19:12, 13
Isaiah .... Is. 6:8-10
Ezekiel .... Ezek. 1:24, 25
Christ .... Mark 1:11
Peter, James and John .... Matt. 17:1, 5
Paul .... Acts 9:4, 7
John .... Rev. 1:10-15

Vomit—*to throw up*
A. *Used literally of:*
Dog .... Prov. 26:11
One who eats in excess .... Prov. 25:16
Drunken man .... Is. 19:14
Great fish .... Jon. 2:10
B. *Used figuratively of:*
False teaching .... 2 Pet. 2:22
Judgment .... Jer. 48:25, 26
Riches .... Job 20:15

Vophsi—*rich*
Naphtalite spy .... Num. 13:14

Vow—*a voluntary pledge to fulfill an agreement*
A. *Objects of one's:*
Life .... Num. 6:1-21
Children .... 1 Sam. 1:11-28
Possessions .... Gen. 28:22
Gifts .... Ps. 76:11
B. *Features concerning:*
Must be voluntary .... Deut. 23:21, 22
Must be uttered .... Deut. 23:23
Once made, binding .... Eccl. 5:4, 5
Benefits of, sometimes included .... Gen. 28:20-22
Invalidity of, specified .... Num. 30:1-16
Abuse of, condemned .... Matt. 15:4-6
Rashness in, condemned .... Prov. 20:25
Perfection in, required .... Lev. 22:18-25
Wickedness of some .... Jer. 44:25

Voyage—*an extended trip*
Paul's to Rome .... Acts 27:10

Vulture—*a carrion-eating bird of prey*
Classed as unclean .... Lev. 11:13, 14

W

Wafers—*thin cakes of flour*
Often made with honey .... Ex. 16:31
Used in various offerings .... Ex. 29:2; Lev. 2:4

Wages, hire—*payments for work performed*
A. *Principles governing payment of:*
Must be paid promptly .... Deut. 24:14, 15
Withholding of, forbidden .... James 5:4
Laborer worthy of .... Matt. 10:10
B. *Paid to such classes as:*
Soldiers .... 2 Sam. 10:6
Fishermen .... Mark 1:20
Shepherds .... John 10:12, 13
Masons and carpenters .... 2 Chr. 24:12
Farm laborers .... Matt. 20:1-16
Male prostitutes .... Deut. 23:18
Nurses .... Ex. 2:9
Ministers .... 1 Cor. 9:4-14
Teachers .... Gal. 6:6, 7
C. *Figurative of:*
Spiritual death .... Rom. 6:23
Unrighteousness .... 2 Pet. 2:15

Wagon—*a vehicle with wheels*
Used to move Jacob to Egypt .... Gen. 45:19, 21
Used in moving objects .... Num. 7:3-9

Wailing—*crying out in constant mourning*
A. *Caused by:*
King's decree .... Esth. 4:3
City's destruction .... Ezek. 27:31, 32
God's judgment .... Amos 5:16, 17
Girl's death .... Mark 5:38-42
Christ's return .... Rev. 1:7
Hell's torments .... Matt. 13:42, 50
B. *Performed by:*
Women .... Jer. 9:17-20
Prophets .... Mic. 1:8
Merchants .... Rev. 18:15, 19
See Mourning

Waiting on the Lord
A. *Agents of:*
Creatures .... Ps. 145:15
Creation .... Rom. 8:19, 23
Gentiles .... Is. 51:5
Christians .... 1 Cor. 1:7
B. *Manner of:*
With the soul .... Ps. 62:1, 5
With quietness .... Lam. 3:25, 26
With patience .... Ps. 40:1
With courage .... Ps. 27:14
All the day .... Ps. 25:5
Continually .... Hos. 12:6
With great hope .... Ps. 130:5, 6
With crying .... Ps. 69:3
C. *Objects of God's:*
Salvation .... Is. 25:9
Law .... Is. 42:4
Protection .... Ps. 33:20
Pardon .... Ps. 39:7, 8
Food .... Ps. 104:27
Kingdom .... Mark 15:43
Holy Spirit .... Acts 1:4
Son .... 1 Thess. 1:10
D. *Blessings attending, described as:*
Spiritual renewal .... Is. 40:31
Not be ashamed .... Ps. 69:6
Inherit the land .... Ps. 37:9, 34
Something unusual .... Is. 64:4
Unusual blessing .... Luke 12:36, 37

Walk of believers
A. *Stated negatively, not:*
In darkness .... John 8:12
After the flesh .... Rom. 8:1, 4
As Gentiles .... Eph. 4:17
In craftiness .... 2 Cor. 4:2
In sin .... Col. 3:5-7
In disorder .... 2 Thess. 3:6, 11
B. *Stated positively:*
In the light .... 1 John 1:7
In the truth .... 3 John 3, 4
In Christ .... Col. 2:6
In the Spirit .... Gal. 5:16, 25
In love .... Eph. 5:2
As children of light .... Eph. 5:8
As Christ walked .... 1 John 2:6
After His commandments .... 2 John 6
By faith .... 2 Cor. 5:7
In good works .... Eph. 2:10
Worthy .... Eph. 4:1
Worthy of the Lord .... Col. 1:10
Worthy of God .... 1 Thess. 2:12
Circumspectly .... Eph. 5:15
In wisdom .... Col. 4:5
Pleasing God .... 1 Thess. 4:1

Wall—*a rampart or partition*
A. *Used for:*
Shooting arrows from .... 2 Sam. 11:24
Observation .... 2 Sam. 18:24
B. *Unusual events connected with:*
Woman lives on .... Josh. 2:15
Jericho's, falls by faith .... Josh. 6:5, 20
Saul's body fastened to .... 1 Sam. 31:10, 11
Woman throws stone from .... 2 Sam. 11:20, 21
27,000 killed by .... 1 Kin. 20:30
Son sacrificed on .... 2 Kin. 3:27
Warning inscribed on .... Dan. 5:5, 25-28
Paul escapes through .... Acts 9:25
C. *Figurative of:*
Defense .... 1 Sam. 25:16
Protection .... Ezra 9:9
Great power .... Ps. 18:29
Peacefulness .... Ps. 122:7
Self-sufficiency .... Prov. 18:11
Powerless .... Prov. 25:28
Salvation .... Is. 26:1
God's kingdom .... Is. 56:5
Heaven .... Is. 60:18-21
Spiritual leaders .... Is. 62:6
God's messengers .... Jer. 1:18, 19
Protection .... Zech. 2:5
Hypocrisy .... Acts 23:3
Ceremonial law .... Eph. 2:14
New Jerusalem .... Rev. 21:12-19
D. *Of Jerusalem:*
Built by Solomon .... 1 Kin. 3:1
Broken down by Jehoash .... 2 Kin. 14:13
Destroyed by Babylonians .... 2 Chr. 36:19
Seen at night by Nehemiah .... Neh. 2:12-18
Rebuilt by returnees .... Neh. 6:1, 6, 15
Dedication of .... Neh. 12:27-47

Wallow—*to roll about in an ungainly manner*
Blood .... 2 Sam. 20:12
Vomit .... Jer. 48:26
Ashes .... Jer. 6:26
On the ground .... Mark 9:20
Mire .... 2 Pet. 2:22

SUBJECT REFERENCE

Wandering—*roaming about*

A. *Descriptive of:*
- Hagar's travels ..... Gen. 21:14
- Israel's wilderness travels ..... Num. 32:13
- God's pilgrims ..... Heb. 11:37, 38
- Captivity ..... Hos. 9:17
- Joseph in the field ..... Gen. 37:15
- Syrian ..... Deut. 26:5
- Early Saints ..... Heb. 11:38

B. *Figurative of:*
- Apostasy ..... Ps. 119:10
- Dissatisfaction ..... Prov. 27:8
- Hopelessness ..... Jude 13

Wanderer—*one who moves about aimlessly*
- Curse on Cain ..... Gen. 4:12, 14
- Curse on the wicked ..... Ps. 109:10
- Professional exorcists called ..... Acts 19:13

Want—*to lack*

A. *Caused by:*
- Hastiness ..... Prov. 21:5
- Greed ..... Prov. 22:16
- Sloth ..... Prov. 24:30-34
- Debauchery ..... Dan. 5:27
- God's judgments ..... Amos 4:6
- Physical need ..... 2 Cor. 8:14

B. *Provision against, by:*
- Trusting the LORD ..... Ps. 23:1
- God's plan ..... Jer. 33:17, 18

Wantonness—*lustful behavior*
- In suggestive movements ..... Is. 3:16
- Characteristic of doctrinal laxity ..... 2 Pet. 2:18
- Unbecoming to a Christian ..... Rom. 13:13

War—*armed conflicts between nations*

A. *Caused by:*
- Sin ..... James 4:1, 2
- God's judgments ..... 2 Sam. 12:10
- God's decree ..... Ex. 17:16

B. *Regulations concerning:*
- Consultation of:
  - Urim ..... 1 Sam. 28:6
  - Ephod ..... 1 Sam. 30:7, 8
  - Prophets ..... 1 Kin. 22:7-28
- Troops mustered ..... Judg. 3:27
- Some dismissed ..... Deut. 20:5-8
- Spies dispatched ..... Num. 13:17
- Ark brought in ..... 1 Sam. 4:4-6
- Sacrifice offered ..... 1 Sam. 7:9
- Speech delivered ..... 2 Chr. 20:20-22
- Demand made for surrender ..... Deut. 20:10
- Trumpet sounded ..... Num. 10:9

C. *Methods of attack, by:*
- Ambush ..... Josh. 8:3-26
- Surprise attack ..... Judg. 7:16-22
- Personal combat of champions ..... 1 Sam. 17:1-51
- Divided tactics ..... 2 Sam. 10:9-14
- Massed formation ..... 1 Kin. 22:31-33
- Battle cry ..... Jer. 4:19

D. *Captives of:*
- Sometimes eliminated ..... Josh. 6:21
- Made servants ..... 2 Sam. 8:2
- Ruled over ..... 2 Sam. 5:2
- Deported ..... 2 Kin. 17:6

See Siege of a city

Wardrobe—*one's clothing*
- Woman's ..... Is. 3:18-23
- Directions concerning ..... 1 Pet. 3:3-5
- Keeper of ..... 2 Kin. 22:14

Wares
- Sold in Tyrus ..... Ezek. 27:1-27

Warfare, spiritual

A. *Enemies combatted:*
- World ..... James 4:1-4
- Flesh ..... 1 Pet. 4:1-4
- Devil ..... 1 Pet. 5:8
- Invisible foes ..... Eph. 6:12

B. *Conquest over, by:*
- God's Word ..... Eph. 6:17
- God's armor ..... Eph. 6:10-17
- Faith ..... 1 John 5:4, 5
- Christ's promise ..... John 16:33

SUBJECT REFERENCE

C. *Soldiers of, must:*
- Avoid worldly entanglements ..... 2 Tim. 2:4
- Pray ..... Eph. 6:18
- Deny self ..... 1 Cor. 9:25-27
- Endure hardness ..... 2 Tim. 2:3, 10
- Be self-controlled ..... 1 Thess. 5:6
- Be alert ..... 1 Cor. 16:13
- Wear armor ..... Eph. 6:11

Warning—*to caution one concerning his action*

A. *Means of, by:*
- God's Word ..... Ps. 19:9-11
- Prophet ..... Ezek. 3:17-27
- Messenger ..... Acts 20:31
- Dream ..... Matt. 2:12, 22
- Angel ..... Acts 10:22
- God ..... Heb. 11:7

B. *Reactions to:*
- Obeyed ..... Jon. 3:1-10
- Accepted ..... Heb. 11:7
- Ignored ..... 2 Sam. 2:20-23
- Rejected ..... Gen. 2:16, 17
- Scoffed at ..... Gen. 19:14
- Disobeyed ..... Num. 14:40-45

C. *Disobedience to, brings:*
- Judgment ..... Jude 6, 7
- Torments ..... Luke 16:23-28
- Destruction ..... Prov. 29:1

Wash—*to cleanse something with a liquid*

A. *Kinds of:*
- Ceremonial ..... Ex. 30:18-20
- Miraculous ..... John 9:7, 11, 15
- Demonstrative ..... John 13:5-14
- Symbolic ..... Matt. 27:24
- Typical ..... Ps. 51:2, 7
- Spiritual ..... Acts 22:16
- Regenerative ..... Titus 3:5

B. *Materials used:*
- Water ..... Gen. 24:32
- Tears ..... Luke 7:38, 44
- Snow ..... Job 9:30
- Wine ..... Gen. 49:11
- Blood ..... Ps. 58:10

C. *Objects of:*
- Hands ..... Matt. 27:24
- Face ..... Gen. 43:31
- Feet ..... Gen. 18:4
- Body ..... 2 Sam. 11:2
- Clothes ..... 2 Sam. 19:24

See Purification

Washpot
- Moab described as God's ..... Ps. 60:6-8

Waste—*a state of ruin*

A. *Objects of:*
- Cities ..... Ezek. 19:7
- Nations ..... Nah. 3:7
- Captives ..... Ps. 137:3
- Possessions ..... Luke 15:13
- Temple ..... Is. 64:11
- Church ..... Gal. 1:13
- Parents ..... Prov. 19:26
- Body ..... Job 14:10

B. *Caused by:*
- God's judgments ..... Amos 7:9
- Unbelief ..... Num. 14:33
- Failure to serve God ..... Is. 60:12
- God's hatred ..... Mal. 1:3
- Squandering ..... Luke 15:11-32

C. *State of:*
- Lamented ..... Neh. 2:3, 17
- To be corrected ..... Is. 61:4

Watch—*to attend to, guard*
- The LORD ..... Gen. 31:49
- As guards ..... 2 Kin. 11:4-7

Watches of day, night—*period of time*
- Jesus walks on water ..... Matt. 14:25
- Time of coming ..... Matt. 24:43; Luke 12:37, 38

Watchmen, spiritual
- Set by God ..... Is. 62:6
- Message to ..... Is. 21:11, 12
- Responsibility of ..... Ezek. 33:1-9
- Some are faithful ..... Ezek. 3:17-21
- Some are faithless ..... Is. 56:10

SUBJECT REFERENCE

- In vain without the LORD ..... Ps. 127:1
- Leaders in the church ..... Heb. 13:17

Water

A. *Described as:*
- Living ..... Jer. 2:13
- Cold ..... Jer. 18:14
- Still ..... Ps. 23:2
- Deep ..... Ps. 69:2, 14
- Standing ..... Ps. 107:35
- Mighty ..... Is. 28:2

B. *God's control over, He:*
- Creates ..... Gen. 1:2, 6, 7
- Gives ..... Ps. 104:13
- Blesses the earth with ..... Is. 55:10
- Withholds ..... Is. 50:2
- Reveals His wonders in ..... Ps. 107:23-32
- Sets bounds to ..... Ps. 104:5-9

C. *Miracles connected with:*
- Changed into blood ..... Ex. 7:17-25
- Divided ..... Ex. 14:21-29
- Bitter made sweet ..... Ex. 15:22-25
- From a rock ..... Ex. 17:1-7
- Jordan divided ..... Josh. 3:14-17
- From a jawbone ..... Judg. 15:17-19
- Consumed by fire ..... 1 Kin. 18:38
- Valley, full of ..... 2 Kin. 3:16-24
- Axe floats on ..... 2 Kin. 6:5-7
- Christ walks on ..... Mark 6:49-52
- Changed into wine ..... John 2:1-11
- Healing of ..... 2 Kin. 2:19-22

D. *Normal uses of, for:*
- Drinking ..... Gen. 24:43
- Washing ..... Gen. 18:4
- Animals ..... Ps. 42:1
- Vegetation ..... Deut. 11:10, 11
- Sea creatures ..... Ps. 104:25, 26

E. *Special uses of, for:*
- Ordination ..... Ex. 30:18-20
- Cleansing ..... Ex. 40:7-32
- Purification ..... Ex. 19:10
- Baptism ..... Acts 8:36-39
- Sanctification ..... Eph. 5:26
- Business ..... Ps. 107:23

F. *Figurative of:*
- Instability ..... Gen. 49:4
- Cowardice ..... Josh. 7:5
- Spiritual growth ..... Ps. 1:3
- Peace ..... Ps. 23:2
- Afflictions ..... Is. 43:2
- Persecution ..... Ps. 124:4, 5
- Adultery ..... Prov. 9:17
- Universal Gospel ..... Is. 11:9
- Salvation ..... Is. 55:1
- Gospel age ..... Is. 41:17-20
- Holy Spirit ..... Ezek. 47:1-12
- Eternal life ..... Rev. 22:17
- Christ ..... John 4:10-15
- Regeneration ..... John 7:37, 38

G. *Cure for:*
- Doubting captain ..... 2 Kin. 5:1-15
- Afflicted ..... John 5:1-7
- Blind man ..... John 9:6-11

H. *Used for a test:*
- By Gideon ..... Judg. 7:4-7

I. *Conduit:*
- Hezekiah builds ..... 2 Kin. 20:20

Water and blood
- From Christ ..... John 19:34

Water Gate—*a gate of Jerusalem*
- Law is read ..... Neh. 8:1, 2

Waterproofing—*making vessels watertight*

By means of:
- Pitch ..... Gen. 6:14
- Slime and pitch ..... Ex. 2:3

Wax (I)—*beeswax*
- Figurative of persecution ..... Ps. 22:14
- Of the wicked before God ..... Ps. 68:2
- Of the mountains ..... Ps. 97:5

Wax (II)—*to grow, increase*

A. *Of material things:*
- Power ..... 2 Sam. 3:1
- Prestige ..... Esth. 9:4
- Age ..... Josh. 23:1
- Sound ..... Ex. 19:19

SUBJECT — REFERENCE

B. *Of immaterial things:*
- Courage ... Heb. 11:34
- Spirituality ... Luke 2:40
- God's hand ... Num. 11:23
- Old covenant ... Heb. 8:13
- God's kingdom ... Luke 13:18, 19

Way (see Highway; Path)

Way, Christ as
- Leading to Father ... John 14:6

Way, God's
- Right ... Hos. 14:9
- Just ... Dan. 4:37
- True ... Rev. 15:3
- Higher than man's ... Is. 55:8, 9
- Unsearchable ... Rom. 11:33

Waymarks—*roadmarkings*
- Give direction ... Jer. 31:21

Ways of God's people

A. *With reference to God's way, to:*
- Understand ... Ps. 119:27
- Pray for direction in ... Ex. 33:13
- Walk in ... Deut. 8:6
- Remember ... Deut. 8:2
- Known ... Ps. 67:2
- Teach to transgressors ... Ps. 51:13
- Rejoice in ... Ps. 119:14

B. *God's attitude toward, He:*
- Knows ... Ps. 1:6
- Is acquainted with ... Ps. 139:3
- Delights in ... Ps. 37:23
- Leads us in ... Ps. 139:24
- Teaches ... Ps. 25:9, 12
- Makes known ... Ps. 103:7
- Makes perfect ... Ps. 18:32
- Blesses ... Prov. 8:32

C. *With reference to our way:*
- Acknowledge Him in ... Prov. 3:6
- Commit to the LORD ... Ps. 37:5
- Makes prosperous ... Josh. 1:8
- All before God ... Ps. 119:168
- Teach me ... Ps. 143:8

Ways of man

Described as:
- Perverse before God ... Num. 22:32
- Hard ... Prov. 13:15
- Abomination ... Prov. 15:9
- Not good ... Prov. 16:29
- Dark ... Prov. 2:13

Weak, weakness

A. *Kinds of:*
- Political ... 2 Sam. 3:1
- Physical ... Judg. 16:7, 17; 2 Cor. 11:30
- Spiritual ... Is. 35:3
- Moral ... 2 Sam. 3:39

B. *Caused by:*
- Fasting ... Ps. 109:24
- Discouragement ... Neh. 6:9
- Sin ... 1 Cor. 11:26-30
- Discouraging preaching ... Jer. 38:4
- Conscientious doubts ... Rom. 14:1-23

C. *Victory over, by:*
- Christ ... 2 Cor. 13:3, 4
- Grace ... 2 Cor. 12:9, 10
- Faith ... Heb. 11:33, 34

D. *Our duty toward, to:*
- Bear ... Rom. 15:1
- Support ... Acts 20:35; 1 Cor. 9:22
- Not become a stumbling block ... 1 Cor. 8:9

E. *Our duties with reference to:*
- Pleasure in ... 2 Cor. 12:10
- Help those afflicted with ... Rom. 15:1

Wealth—*riches*

A. *Descriptive of:*
- Material possessions ... Gen. 34:29

B. *Advantages of:*
- Given by God ... Deut. 8:18, 19
- Source of security ... Prov. 18:11
- Adds friends ... Prov. 19:4

C. *Disadvantages of:*
- Produces self-sufficiency ... Deut. 8:17
- Leads to conceit ... Job 31:25
- Subject to loss ... Prov. 13:11
- Lost by dissipation ... Prov. 5:8-10
- Cannot save ... Ps. 49:6, 7
- Must be left to others ... Ps. 49:10

See Riches, earthly

Wean—*to accustom a child to independance from the mother's milk*
- Celebrated ... Gen. 21:8
- Figurative of spiritual rest ... Ps. 131:2

Weapons, spiritual

Against:
- World—faith ... 1 John 5:4
- Satan—armor of God ... Eph. 6:11-17
- Flesh—the Spirit ... Gal. 5:16-25

Weary—*to become tired*

A. *Caused by:*
- Journeys ... John 4:6
- Ritualism ... Is. 1:14
- Study ... Eccl. 12:12
- Anxiety ... Gen. 27:46
- Words ... Mal. 2:17
- Not speaking ... Jer. 20:9
- Too frequent visits ... Prov. 25:17

B. *Overcome by:*
- Waiting on the LORD ... Is. 40:30, 31
- Appropriate word ... Is. 50:4
- God's promise ... Is. 28:12
- Persevering faith ... Gal. 6:9
- Promised ruler ... Is. 32:1, 2
- Looking to Jesus ... Heb. 12:2, 3

Weather
- Proverb concerning ... Job 37:9-11
- Under divine control ... 1 Sam. 12:16-19
- Signs of ... Luke 12:54-57

Weaving—*uniting threads to produce cloth*
- Men endowed in art of ... Ex. 35:35
- Performed by worthy women ... Prov. 31:13, 19
- Figurative of life's shortness ... Job 7:6

See Spinning

Wedding (See Marriage)

Wedge of gold
- Stolen by Achan ... Josh. 7:20, 21

Weeds
- Wrapped around Jonah's head ... Jon. 2:5

Week—*seven days*
- Origin of, early ... Gen. 2:1-3
- Used in dating events ... Gen. 7:4, 10
- One, length of mourning ... Gen. 50:10
- Part of ceremonial Law ... Ex. 13:6, 7
- Seventy, prophecy of ... Dan. 9:24
- Christ arose on first day of ... Matt. 28:1
- Christians worship on first day of ... Acts 20:7; 1 Cor. 16:2

See Pentecost

Weeks of years
- Seven ... Lev. 25:8
- Seventy ... Dan. 9:2; Jer. 25:11

Weeping—*intense crying*

A. *Kinds of:*
- Rebellious ... Num. 11:4-20
- Hypocritical ... Judg. 14:16, 17
- Sincere ... 1 Sam. 20:41
- Exhausting ... 1 Sam. 30:4
- Secret ... Jer. 13:17
- Permanent ... Matt. 8:12
- Bitterly ... Matt. 26:75
- Divine ... John 11:35
- Sympathetic ... Rom. 12:15

B. *Caused by:*
- Despair ... Gen. 21:16
- Death ... Gen. 50:1
- Loss of blessing ... Gen. 27:34, 38
- Love ... Gen. 29:11
- Joy of reunion ... Gen. 33:4
- Loss of child ... Gen. 37:35
- Restraint of joy ... Gen. 42:24
- Hearing God's Word ... Neh. 8:9

C. *Passing away of:*
- After a child's death ... 2 Sam. 12:21-23
- In the morning ... Ps. 30:5
- In eternity ... Is. 65:19
- After seeing the Lord ... John 20:11-18

Weights and measures

A. *Monies of the Bible:*
- Beka ... Ex. 38:26
- Gerahs ... Ex. 30:13
- Mite ... Mark 12:42
- Pence ... Matt. 18:28
- Pieces of silver ... Matt. 26:15
- Shekel ... Ex. 30:24
- Shekels of Brass ... 2 Sam. 21:16
- Shekels of gold ... 1 Chr. 21:25
- Shekels of silver ... 2 Sam. 24:24
- Silver ... 2 Chr. 21:3
- Talents ... Matt. 18:24
- Talents of brass ... 1 Chr. 29:7
- Talents of gold ... 1 Chr. 29:4
- Talents of iron ... 1 Chr. 29:7
- Talents of silver ... 1 Chr. 29:4

B. *Distance or length measurements:*
- Acre ... 1 Sam. 14:14
- Cubit ... Gen. 6:15
- Fathom ... Acts 27:28
- Finger ... Jer. 52:21
- Furlong ... Luke 24:13
- Handbreadth ... Ex. 25:25
- Measuring reed ... Ezek. 40:3
- Pace ... 2 Sam. 6:13
- Span ... Ex. 28:16
- Sabbath day's journey ... Acts 1:12

C. *Liquid measures:*
- Bath ... 1 Kin. 7:26
- Cor ... Ezek. 45:14
- Firkin ... John 2:6
- Hin ... Ex. 29:40
- Homer ... Ezek. 45:11
- Kab ... 2 Kin. 6:25
- Log ... Lev. 14:10

D. *Dry measures:*
- Cab ... 2 Kin. 6:25
- Ephah ... Ex. 16:36
- Homer ... Lev. 27:16
- Log ... Lev. 14:10
- Omer ... Ex. 16:16
- Gerah ... Ex. 30:13
- Pound ... 1 Kin. 10:17

E. *Weight measures:*
- Beka ... Ex. 38:26
- Shekel ... 2 Sam. 14:26
- Talents ... Ex. 38:27

Welcome—*to receive with gladness*

A. *Extended to:*
- Returning brother ... Gen. 33:1-11
- Father ... Gen. 46:29-34
- Hero ... 1 Sam. 18:6, 7
- Prodigal son ... Luke 15:20-32
- Messiah ... Matt. 21:6-10

B. *Circumstances attending:*
- Courtesies offered ... Gen. 18:1-8
- Discourtesies shown ... 2 Sam. 10:1-5
- Fear expressed ... 1 Sam. 16:4, 5
- Fellowship denied ... 2 John 10, 11

Wells—*pits dug for water*

A. *Features concerning:*
- Women come to, for water ... Gen. 24:13, 14; John 4:7
- Surrounded by trees ... Gen. 49:22
- Often very deep ... John 4:11
- Covered with large stone ... Gen. 29:2, 3
- Sometimes cause strife ... Gen. 21:25

B. *Names of:*
- Beer ... Num. 21:16-18
- Beer-lahai-roi ... Gen. 16:14
- Beer-sheba ... Gen. 21:30, 31
- Beeroth ... Deut. 10:6
- Esek ... Gen. 26:20
- Jacob ... John 4:6
- Rehoboth ... Gen. 26:22
- Sitnah ... Gen. 26:21

C. *Figurative of:*
- Salvation ... Is. 12:3
- False teaching ... 2 Pet. 2:17
- One's wife ... Prov. 5:15
- The Holy Spirit ... John 4:10

Wen—*a running sore*
- Makes an animal unacceptable ... Lev. 22:22

SUBJECT REFERENCE

Wench—*a maid or servant*
Informant . . . . . 2 Sam. 17:17

Whale
Jonah swallowed by . . . . . Matt. 12:40
Created by God . . . . . Gen. 1:21

Wheat—*a cereal grass used for food*
A. *Features concerning:*
Grown in Egypt . . . . . Ex. 9:32
Grown in Palestine . . . . . 1 Kin. 5:11
Made into bread . . . . . Ex. 29:2
Used in trade . . . . . Ezek. 27:17
Harvested . . . . . Ruth 2:23
Threshed . . . . . Judg. 6:11
Gathered . . . . . Matt. 3:12
Harvesting of, celebrated . . . . Ex. 34:22
B. *Figurative of:*
Spiritual blessings . . . . . Ps. 81:16
Christians . . . . . Matt. 3:12
Christ's death . . . . . John 12:24
Resurrection . . . . . 1 Cor. 15:37

Wheel—*a circular frame*
A. *Used on:*
Carts . . . . . Is. 28:27, 28
Threshing instrument . . . . . Prov. 20:26
Chariots . . . . . Nah. 3:2
Jehovah's throne . . . . . Ezek. 10:1-22
B. *Figurative of:*
Future things . . . . . Ezek. 1:15-28
Punishment . . . . . Prov. 20:26
Cycle of nature ("course") . . . James 3:6
God's sovereignty . . . . . Ezek. 10:9-19

Whelp—*offspring of certain animals*
Figurative of:
Judah . . . . . Gen. 49:9
Dan . . . . . Deut. 33:22
Babylonians . . . . . Jer. 51:38
Assyrians . . . . . Nah. 2:11, 12
Princes of Israel . . . . . Ezek. 19:2-9

Whirlwind—*a great storm or tempest*
A. *Used literally of:*
Elijah's translation . . . . . 2 Kin. 2:1
Its fury . . . . . Is. 17:13
B. *Used figuratively of:*
Sudden destruction . . . . . Prov. 1:27
Suddenness . . . . . Is. 5:28
God's anger . . . . . Jer. 23:19
God's might . . . . . Nah. 1:3

Whisperer—*a gossiper*
Separates chief friends . . . . . Prov. 16:28

White (see Colors)

Whole, wholesome
A. *Means of making, by:*
Normal healing . . . . . Josh. 5:8
Touch . . . . . Matt. 9:21
Faith . . . . . Mark 10:52
Risen Christ . . . . . Acts 4:9, 10
B. *Effects of, seen in:*
Perfect restoration . . . . . Matt. 14:36
Instantaneous healing . . . . . John 5:9
Complete obedience . . . . . John 5:11-15

Whore, Whoredom (see Adultery; Harlot)

Wicked, the
A. *Descriptive of:*
Sodomites . . . . . Gen. 13:13
Egyptians . . . . . Ex. 9:27
Athaliah . . . . . 2 Chr. 24:7
Haman . . . . . Esth. 7:6
Jews . . . . . Matt. 12:38, 45
B. *State of, described as:*
Desiring evil . . . . . Prov. 21:10
Have no peace . . . . . Is. 48:22
Pours out evil . . . . . Prov. 15:28
Refusing judgment . . . . . Prov. 21:7
Cruel in their mercies . . . . . Prov. 12:10
Like the troubled sea . . . . . Is. 57:20
Far from God . . . . . Prov. 15:29
Offering abominable sacrifice . . . . . Prov. 15:8
Way is like darkness . . . . . Prov. 4:19
C. *God's attitude toward:*
Will not justify . . . . . Ex. 23:7
Will punish . . . . . Ps. 75:8
Will overthrow . . . . . Prov. 21:12
Their thoughts abominable to . . . . . Prov. 15:26
God tries them . . . . . Ps. 11:5
Made for the day of evil . . . . . Prov. 16:4
D. *Punishment of:*
Shortened life . . . . . Prov. 10:27
Soon destroyed . . . . . Ps. 37:35, 36
Driven away . . . . . Prov. 14:32
Slain by evil . . . . . Ps. 34:21
His candle put out . . . . . Job 21:17
His triumph short . . . . . Ps. 37:10
His name put out forever . . . . . Ps. 9:5
Silent in the grave . . . . . Ps. 31:17
God rains fire on . . . . . Ps. 11:6
Cast into hell . . . . . Ps. 9:17
Consumed . . . . . Ps. 37:20
Will die . . . . . Prov. 11:7
In the resurrection, judgment . . . . . Acts 24:15
E. *Attitude of believers toward:*
Wonder about their prosperity . . . . . Ps. 73:3
Concerned about their triumph . . . . . Ps. 94:3, 4
Will not sit with . . . . . Ps. 26:5
Must not envy . . . . . Prov. 24:19
Will triumph over . . . . . Ps. 58:10

Wickedness—*all forms of evil*
A. *Man's relationship to:*
Not profited by . . . . . Prov. 10:2
Not established by . . . . . Prov. 12:3
Sells himself to . . . . . 1 Kin. 21:25
Strengthens himself in . . . . . Ps. 52:7
Refuses to turn from . . . . . Jer. 44:5
Inside mankind . . . . . Luke 11:39
Among all . . . . . Jer. 44:9
Will fall by . . . . . Prov. 11:5
Driven away . . . . . Prov. 14:32
B. *God's punishment of, seen in:*
Driving out other nations . . . . Deut. 9:4, 5
Shiloh's destruction . . . . . Jer. 7:12
Judah's punishment . . . . . Jer. 1:16
Destruction of food supply . . Ps. 107:33, 34
Causing the flood . . . . . Gen. 6:5-7
Death of men . . . . . Judg. 9:56
Destroying men . . . . . Ps. 94:23
C. *Attitude of the righteous toward:*
Wash heart of . . . . . Jer. 4:14
Struggle against . . . . . Eph. 6:12
Fear to commit . . . . . Gen. 39:9
Not to dwell in . . . . . Ps. 84:10
Pray for end of . . . . . Ps. 7:9
Confession of . . . . . 1 Kin. 8:47

Widow—*a woman who has outlived her husband*
A. *Provision of, for:*
Remarriage . . . . . Rom. 7:3
Food . . . . . Deut. 24:19-21
Protection . . . . . Is. 1:17, 23
Vows of . . . . . Num. 30:9
Raiment . . . . . Deut. 24:17
B. *Mistreatment of, by:*
Children . . . . . 1 Tim. 5:4
Neglect . . . . . Acts 6:1
Scribes . . . . . Mark 12:40
Creditors . . . . . 2 Kin. 4:1
Princes . . . . . Is. 1:23
Judges . . . . . Is. 10:1, 2
C. *Protection of, by:*
God . . . . . Ex. 22:22-24
Law . . . . . Deut. 24:17
Pure religion . . . . . James 1:27
Honor . . . . . 1 Tim. 5:3
D. *Examples of:*
Naomi . . . . . Ruth 1:20, 21
Woman of Tekoa . . . . . 2 Sam. 14:4, 5
Woman of Zarephath . . . . . 1 Kin. 17:9, 10
Anna . . . . . Luke 2:36, 37
"A certain poor widow" . . . . . Luke 21:2, 3

Wife—*a married woman*
A. *Described as:*
"A helpmeet" . . . . . Gen. 2:18, 20
"A crown to her husband" . . . Prov. 12:4
"A good thing" . . . . . Prov. 18:22
"The weaker vessel" . . . . . 1 Pet. 3:7
"The wife of his youth" . . . . . Mal. 2:14, 15
"Thy companion" . . . . . Mal. 2:14
B. *Duties of, to:*
Submit to husband . . . . . 1 Pet. 3:5, 6
Reverence her husband . . . . . Eph. 5:33
Love her husband . . . . . Titus 2:4
Learn from her husband . . . . . 1 Cor. 14:34, 35
Be trustworthy . . . . . Prov. 31:11, 12
Love her children . . . . . Titus 2:4
Be chaste . . . . . Titus 2:5
Be keepers at home . . . . . Titus 2:5
C. *Duties of husband toward, to:*
Love . . . . . Eph. 5:25, 28
Honor . . . . . 1 Pet. 3:7
Provide for . . . . . 1 Tim. 5:8
Instruct . . . . . 1 Cor. 14:35
Protect . . . . . 1 Sam. 30:1-19
Not divorce . . . . . 1 Cor. 7:11
D. *Relationship with her husband, to be:*
Exclusive . . . . . Prov. 5:15-17, 20
Satisfying . . . . . Prov. 5:18, 19
Mutually agreeable . . . . . 1 Cor. 7:1-5
Undefiled . . . . . Heb. 13:4
E. *Special temptations of:*
Disobedience . . . . . Gen. 3:1-19
Unfaithfulness . . . . . John 4:17, 18
Contentiousness . . . . . Prov. 19:13
Assertion of authority . . . . . 1 Tim. 2:11-15
F. *Types of:*
Disobedient—Eve . . . . . Gen. 3:1-8
Obedient—Sarah . . . . . 1 Pet. 3:5, 6
Worldly—Lot's . . . . . Gen. 19:26
Humble—Manoah's . . . . . Judg. 13:22, 23
Prayerful—Hannah . . . . . 1 Sam. 1:1-15
Prudent—Abigail . . . . . 1 Sam. 25:3, 14-35
Criticizing—Michal . . . . . 2 Sam. 6:15, 16
Unscrupulous—Jezebel . . . . . 1 Kin. 21:5-15
Modest—Vashti . . . . . Esth. 1:11, 12
Foolish—Job's wife . . . . . Job 2:7-10
Cruel—Herodias . . . . . Matt. 14:3-12
Righteous—Elisabeth . . . . . Luke 1:5, 6
Lying—Sapphira . . . . . Acts 5:1-10

Wilderness—*a desolate place*
A. *Descriptive of:*
Israel's wanderings . . . . . Ex. 16:1
Desolate place . . . . . Matt. 3:1, 3
Desolation . . . . . Jer. 22:6
B. *Characterized by:*
Wild creatures . . . . . Deut. 8:15
No water . . . . . Deut. 8:15
"Great and terrible" things . . Deut. 1:19
Uninhabited . . . . . Ps. 107:4, 5
C. *Israel's journey in, characterized by:*
God's provision . . . . . Deut. 2:7
God's guidance . . . . . Ps. 78:52
God's mighty acts . . . . . Ps. 78:15, 16
Israel's provoking God . . . . . Ps. 78:17-19, 40
Israel's sin . . . . . Heb. 3:7-19
Testings . . . . . Deut. 8:2
D. *Significant events in:*
Hagar's flight . . . . . Gen. 16:6-8
Israel's journeys . . . . . Ps. 136:16
John's preaching . . . . . Matt. 3:1-12
Jesus' temptation . . . . . Matt. 4:1
Jesus' miracle . . . . . Matt. 15:33-38
Moses' serpent . . . . . John 3:14

Willingness
A. *On God's part, to:*
Exercise mercy . . . . . 2 Kin. 8:18, 19
Rule sovereignly . . . . . Dan. 4:17
Save men . . . . . 1 Tim. 2:4
2 Pet. 3:9
B. *On Christ's part, to:*
Do God's will . . . . . Heb. 10:7, 9
Submit to the Father . . . . . John 8:28, 29
Reveal the Father . . . . . Matt. 11:27
Heal people . . . . . Matt. 8:2, 3
Die . . . . . Mark 14:36
C. *On man's part, to:*
Do Satan's will . . . . . John 8:44
Refuse salvation . . . . . John 5:40
Pervert the truth . . . . . 2 Pet. 3:5
Follow evil . . . . . Mark 15:15
Persecute the righteous . . . . . Matt. 2:13
D. *On the believer's part, to:*
Be saved . . . . . Rev. 22:17
Follow Christ . . . . . Matt. 16:24
Live godly . . . . . 2 Tim. 3:12
Give . . . . . 2 Cor. 8:3-12
Die . . . . . 2 Cor. 5:8

SUBJECT	REFERENCE
Will of God	
A. *Defined in terms of:*	
Salvation	2 Pet. 3:9
Salvation of children	Matt. 18:14
Belief in Christ	Matt. 12:50
Everlasting life	John 6:39, 40
Thanksgiving	1 Thess. 5:18
Sanctification	1 Thess. 4:3
B. *Characteristics of:*	
Can be:	
Known	Rom. 2:18
Proved	Rom. 12:2
Done	Matt. 6:10
Sovereign over:	
Nations	Dan. 4:35
Individuals	Acts 21:14
C. *God's power in doing, seen in:*	
Predestination	Rom. 9:18-23
Sovereignty	Dan. 4:35
Man's salvation	1 Tim. 2:4
Believer's salvation	James 1:18
Redemption	Gal. 1:4
D. *Believer's relationship to, seen in his:*	
Calling	1 Cor. 1:1
Regeneration	James 1:18
Sanctification	Heb. 10:10
Transformation	Rom. 12:2
Instruction	Ps. 143:10
Prayers	1 John 5:14
Submission	Acts 21:14
Whole life	1 Pet. 4:2
Daily work	Eph. 6:6
Travels	Rom. 1:10
Plans	James 4:13-15
Suffering	1 Pet. 3:17
Perfection	Col. 4:12
Will of man (see Freedom; Liberty, spiritual)	
Willow—*a tree*	
Booths made of	Lev. 23:40, 42
Grows beside brooks	Job 40:22
Harps hung on	Ps. 137:2
See Poplar tree	
Wimple—*a shawl*	
Worn by women	Is. 3:22
Wind—*movement of the air*	
A. *Characteristics of:*	
Movement of, significant	Luke 12:54, 55
Cannot be seen	John 3:8
Sometimes destructive	Job 1:19
Dries the earth	Gen. 8:1
Often accompanies rain	1 Kin. 18:44, 45
Makes sea rough	Ps. 107:25
Drives ships	Acts 27:7, 13-18
Drives chaff away	Ps. 1:4
Possesses weight	Job 28:25
B. *God's relation to, He:*	
Creates	Amos 4:13
Sends	Ps. 147:18
Brings out of His treasuries	Ps. 135:7
Gathers	Prov. 30:4
Controls	Ps. 107:25
C. *Directions of, from:*	
East	Jer. 18:17
West	Ex. 10:19
North	Prov. 25:23
South	Acts 27:13
All directions	Ezek. 37:9
D. *Miracles connected with:*	
Flood subsided by	Gen. 8:1
Locusts brought and taken by	Ex. 10:13, 19
Red Sea divided by	Ex. 14:21
Quail brought by	Num. 11:31
Rain brought by	1 Kin. 18:44, 45
Mountains broken by	1 Kin. 19:11
Jonah's ship tossed by	Jon. 1:4
Christ calms	Matt. 8:26
E. *Figurative of:*	
Empty speech	Job 8:2
Empty boasting	Prov. 25:14
Vanity	Eccl. 5:16
Calamity	Is. 32:2
God's discipline	Hos. 13:15
God's judgment	Jer. 22:22
Dispersion	Ezek. 5:10

SUBJECT	REFERENCE
Ruin	Hos. 8:7
Holy Spirit	Acts 2:2
False teaching	Eph. 4:14
Windows of Heaven	
Descriptive of:	
Judgment rendered "opened"	Gen. 7:11
Unbelief	2 Kin. 7:2, 19
Blessings	Mal. 3:10
Wine	
A. *Kinds of:*	
New	Luke 5:37-39
Old	Luke 5:39
Fermented	Num. 6:3
Refined	Is. 25:6
B. *Features concerning:*	
Made from grapes	Gen. 40:11
Mixed	Prov. 23:30
Kept in bottles	Jer. 13:12
Kept in wineskins	Matt. 9:17
C. *Used by:*	
Noah	Gen. 9:20, 21
Melchizedek	Gen. 14:18
Isaac	Gen. 27:25
Esther	Esth. 5:6
Jesus	John 2:1-11
Timothy	1 Tim. 5:23
D. *Uses of, as:*	
Offering	Lev. 23:13
Drink	Gen. 27:25
Festive drink	Esth. 1:7
Disinfectant	Luke 10:34
Drug	Mark 15:23
Medicine	1 Tim. 5:23
E. *Evil effects of:*	
Leads to violence	Prov. 4:17
Mocks a man	Prov. 20:1
Make poor	Prov. 23:20, 21
Bites like a serpent	Prov. 23:31, 32
Impairs the judgment	Prov. 31:4, 5
Inflames the passions	Is. 5:11
Takes away the heart	Hos. 4:11
F. *Intoxication from, falsely charged to:*	
Hannah	1 Sam. 1:12-16
Jesus	Matt. 11:19
Apostles	Acts 2:13
G. *Uses of, in:*	
Offering	Num. 15:4-10
Miracle	John 2:1-9
Lord's Supper	Matt. 26:27-29
H. *Figurative of:*	
God's wrath	Ps. 75:8
Wisdom's blessings	Prov. 9:2, 5
Gospel	Is. 55:1
Christ's blood	Matt. 26:27-29
Fornication	Rev. 17:2
See Drunkenness; Temperance	
Wings—*the locomotive appendages on flying creatures*	
A. *Used literally of:*	
Flying creatures	Gen. 1:21
Cherubim	Ex. 25:20
B. *Used figuratively of:*	
God's mercy	Ps. 57:1
Protection	Luke 13:34
Winking the eye	
Hate	Ps. 35:19
Evil	Prov. 6:12, 13
Winnow—*to toss about*	
A. *Used literally of:*	
Fork for winnowing grain	Is. 30:24
B. *Used figuratively of judgments:*	
God's	Is. 30:24
Nation's	Jer. 51:2
Christ's	Matt. 3:12
Winter—*the cold season of the year*	
Made by God	Ps. 74:17
Continuance of, guaranteed	Gen. 8:22
Time of snow	2 Sam. 23:20
Hazards of travel during	2 Tim. 4:21
Wipe—*to clean or dry*	
A. *Used literally of:*	
Dust removal	Luke 10:11
Feet dried	John 13:5

SUBJECT	REFERENCE
B. *Used figuratively of:*	
Jerusalem's destruction	2 Kin. 21:13
Tears removed	Rev. 7:17
Wire—*threads*	
Used in ephod	Ex. 39:3
Wisdom—*knowledge guided by understanding*	
A. *Sources of, in:*	
Spirit	Ex. 31:3
Lord	Ex. 36:1, 2
God's Law	Deut. 4:6
Fear of the LORD	Prov. 9:10
Righteous	Prov. 10:31
B. *Ascribed to:*	
Workmen	Ex. 36:2
Women	Prov. 31:26
Bezaleel	Ex. 31:2-5
Joseph	Acts 7:9, 10
Moses	Acts 7:22
Joshua	Deut. 34:9
Hiram	1 Kin. 7:13, 14
Solomon	1 Kin. 3:12, 16-28
Children of Issachar	1 Chr. 12:32
Ezra	Ezra 7:25
Daniel	Dan. 1:17
Magi	Matt. 2:1-12
Stephen	Acts 6:3, 10
Paul	2 Pet. 3:15
C. *Described as:*	
Discreet	Gen. 41:33
Technical skill	Ex. 28:3
Common sense	2 Sam. 20:14-22
Mechanical skill	1 Kin. 7:14
Understanding	Prov. 10:13, 23
Military ability	Is. 10:13
Commercial industry	Ezek. 28:3-5
D. *Value of:*	
Gives happiness	Prov. 3:13
Benefits of, many	Prov. 4:5 10
Keeps from evil	Prov. 5:1-6
Better than rubies	Prov. 8:11
Above gold in value	Prov. 16:16
Should be acquired	Prov. 23:23
Excels folly	Eccl. 2:13
Gives life	Eccl. 7:12
Makes strong	Eccl. 7:19
Better than weapons	Eccl. 9:18
Insures stability	Is. 33:6
Produces good fruit	James 3:17
E. *Limitations of:*	
Cannot save us	1 Cor. 1:19-21
Cause of self-glory	Jer. 9:23
Can pervert	Is. 47:10
Nothing, without God	Jer. 8:9
Can corrupt	Ezek. 28:17
Of this world, foolishness	1 Cor. 3:19
Earthly, sensual	James 3:15
Gospel not preached in	1 Cor. 2:1-5
F. *Of believers:*	
Given by Christ	Luke 21:15
Gift of the Spirit	1 Cor. 12:8
Given by God	Eph. 1:17
Prayed for	Col. 1:9
Means of instruction	Col. 1:28
Lack of, ask for	James 1:5
Wisdom of Christ	
Predicted	Is. 11:1, 2
Incarnated	1 Cor. 1:24
Realized	Luke 2:52
Displayed	Matt. 13:54
Perfected	Col. 2:3
Imputed	1 Cor. 1:30
Wisdom of God	
A. *Described as:*	
Universal	Dan. 2:20
Infinite	Ps. 147:5
Unsearchable	Is. 40:28
Mighty	Job 36:5
Perfect	Job 37:16
B. *Manifested in:*	
Creation	Ps. 104:24
Nature	Job 38:34-41
Sovereignty	Dan. 2:20, 21
The Church	Eph. 3:10

SUBJECT	REFERENCE
Wist, wit—*obsolete for "to know"*	
Of things:	
Unknown	Ex. 2:4
Known by others	Ex. 34:29
That should be known	Luke 2:49
Witch—*one adept at magic*	
Saul consults one	1 Sam. 28:7-25
Witchcraft—*the practice of sorcery*	
Forbidden in Israel	Deut. 18:9-14
Used by Jezebel	2 Kin. 9:22
Condemned by the prophets	Mic. 5:12
Practiced by Manasseh	2 Chr. 33:6
Suppressed by Saul	1 Sam. 28:3, 9
Work of the flesh	Gal. 5:20
See Divination	
Wither—*to dry up*	
A. *Caused by:*	
God's judgment	Is. 40:7, 24
Christ's judgment	Matt. 21:19, 20
No root	Matt. 13:6
Heat	James 1:11
B. *Applied literally to:*	
Ear of grain	Gen. 41:23
Gourd	Jon. 4:7
Man's hand	Luke 6:6, 8
Witnessing—*bearing testimony to something*	
A. *Elements of, seen in:*	
Public transaction	Ruth 4:1-11
Signing a document	Jer. 32:10-12
Calling witnesses	Lev. 5:1
Requiring two witnesses	1 Tim. 5:19
Rejection of false witnesses	Prov. 24:28
B. *Material means of, by:*	
Heap stones	Gen. 31:44-52
Song	Deut. 31:19-21
Altar	Josh. 22:26-34
Works	John 10:25
Sign (miracles)	Heb. 2:4
C. *Spiritual means of, by:*	
God's Law	Deut. 31:26
Gospel	Matt. 24:14
Father	John 5:37
Conscience	Rom. 2:15
Holy Spirit	Rom. 8:16
D. *To Christ as object, by:*	
John the Baptist	John 1:7, 8, 15
His works	John 5:36
Father	John 8:18
Himself	John 8:18
Holy Spirit	John 15:26, 27
His disciples	John 15:27
Prophets	Acts 10:43
E. *Of Christians to Christ:*	
Chosen	Acts 10:41
Commissioned	Acts 1:8
Empowered	Acts 4:33
Confirmed	Heb. 2:3, 4
F. *Objects of Christ's:*	
Resurrection	Acts 2:32
Saviorhood	Acts 5:31, 32
Life	Acts 1:21, 22
Mission	Acts 10:41-43
Sufferings	1 Pet. 5:1
See Testimony	
Witty—*obsolete for "intelligent"*	
Applied to inventions	Prov. 8:12
Wizard (see Witchcraft)	
Wolf—*a dog-like animal*	
A. *Characteristics of:*	
Ravenous	Gen. 49:27
Nocturnal	Jer. 5:6
Sheep-eating	John 10:12
B. *Figurative of:*	
False prophets	Matt. 7:15
Gospel transformation	Is. 11:6
Woman—*the female sex*	
A. *Described as:*	
Beautiful	2 Sam. 11:2
Wise	2 Sam. 20:16
Widow	1 Kin. 17:9, 10
Evil	Prov. 6:24
Foolish	Job 2:10
Gracious	Prov. 11:16
Virtuous	Prov. 12:4
Contentious	Prov. 21:19
Adulterous	Prov. 30:20
Honorable	Acts 17:12
Silly	2 Tim. 3:6
Holy	1 Pet. 3:5
B. *Work of:*	
Kneading meal	Gen. 18:6
Drawing water	Gen. 24:11, 13, 15
Tending sheep	Gen. 29:6
Making cloth	Prov. 31:13, 19
Caring for the household	Prov. 31:27 1 Tim. 5:14
C. *Rights of, to:*	
Marry	1 Cor. 7:36
Hold property	Num. 27:6-11
Make vows	Num. 30:3-9
D. *Position of, in relation to man:*	
Created from man	Gen. 2:21-25
Made to help man	Gen. 2:18, 20
Glory of man	1 Cor. 11:7-9
Becomes subject to man	Gen. 3:16
Weaker than man	1 Pet. 3:7
E. *Position of, in spiritual things:*	
Insight of, noted	Judg. 13:23
Prayer of, answered	1 Sam. 1:9-28
Understanding of, rewarded	1 Sam. 25:3-42
Faith of, brings salvation	Luke 7:37-50
Made equal in Christ	Gal. 3:28
Labor of, commended	Phil. 4:2, 3
Faith of, transmitted	2 Tim. 1:5
F. *Good traits of:*	
Obedience	1 Pet. 3:5-7
Concern for children	Ex. 2:2-10
Loyalty	Ruth 1:14-18
Desire for children	1 Sam. 1:9-28
Modesty	Esth. 1:10-12
Industry	Prov. 31:10-31
Complete devotion	Luke 7:38-50
Tenderness	John 11:20-35
G. *Bad traits of:*	
Inciting to evil	Gen. 3:6, 7
Subtle	Prov. 7:10
Fond of adornments	Is. 3:16-24
Self-indulgent	Is. 32:9, 11
Easily led into idolatry	Jer. 7:18
Led away	2 Tim. 3:6
H. *Prohibitions concerning, not to:*	
Wear man's clothing	Deut. 22:5
Have head shaved	1 Cor. 11:5-15
Usurp authority	1 Tim. 2:11-15
Be unchaste	1 Pet. 3:1-7
Womb—*the uterus*	
A. *God's control over, to:*	
Close	Gen. 20:18
Open	Gen. 29:31
Fashion us in	Job 31:15
Separate and call	Gal. 1:15
Cause to conceive	Luke 1:31
Make alive	Rom. 4:19-21
B. *Babe inside:*	
Grows mysteriously	Eccl. 11:5
Known by God	Ps. 139:13-16
Deformed	Acts 3:2
Leaps	Luke 1:41, 44
C. *Man coming from:*	
Different	Gen. 25:23, 24
Consecrated	Judg. 13:5, 7
Naked	Job 1:21
Helpless	Ps. 22:9, 10
Sustained	Ps. 71:6
Estranged	Ps. 58:3
Women of the Bible, named	
Abi, wife of Ahaz	2 Kin. 18:1, 2
Abiah, wife of Hezron	1 Chr. 2:24
Abigail	
(1) wife of Nabal	1 Sam. 25:3
(2) sister of David	1 Chr. 2:15, 16
Abihail, wife of Abishur	1 Chr. 2:29
Abishag, nurse of David	1 Kin. 1:1-3
Abital, David's wife	2 Sam. 3:1, 4
Achsah, daughter of Caleb	Josh. 15:16
Adah	
(1) a wife of Lamech	Gen. 4:19
(2) Canaanite wife of Esau	Gen. 36:2
Ahinoam	
(1) wife of Saul	1 Sam. 14:50
(2) a Jezreelitess	1 Sam. 25:43
Aholah	Ezek. 23:4
Aholibah	Ezek. 23:4
Aholibamah	Gen. 36:2
Anah, daughter of Zibeon	Gen. 36:2
Anna, an aged widow	Luke 2:36, 37
Apphia, a Christian of Colossae	Philem. 2
Asenath, wife of Joseph	Gen. 41:45
Atarah, wife of Jerahmeel	1 Chr. 2:26
Athaliah, mother of Ahaziah	2 Kin. 8:26
Azubah	
(1) first wife of Caleb	1 Chr. 2:18
(2) daughter of Shilhi	1 Kin. 22:42
Baara, wife of Shaharaim	1 Chr. 8:8
Basemath	
(1) daughter of Elon	Gen. 26:34
(2) a third wife of Esau	Gen. 36:2-3
Bath-sheba, wife of David	2 Sam. 11:3, 27
Bernice, sister of Agrippa	Acts 25:13
Bilhah, Rachel's handmaid	Gen. 29:29
Bithiah, daughter of a Pharoah	1 Chr. 4:17
Candace, a queen	Acts 8:27
Chloe, woman of Corinth	1 Cor. 1:11
Claudia, Christian of Rome	2 Tim. 4:21
Cozbi, Midianite slain	Num. 25:15-18
Damaris, woman of Athens	Acts 17:34
Deborah	
(1) Rebekah's nurse	Gen. 35:8
(2) judge	Judg. 4:4
Delilah, Philistine woman	Judg. 16:4, 5
Dinah, daughter of Jacob	Gen. 30:19, 21
Dorcas, called Tabitha	Acts 9:36
Drusilla, wife of Felix	Acts 24:24
Eglah, one of David's wives	2 Sam. 3:5
Elisabeth, mother of John the Baptist	Luke 1:5, 13
Elisheba, wife of Aaron	Ex. 6:23
Ephah, concubine of Caleb	1 Chr. 2:46
Ephrath, mother of Hur	1 Chr. 2:19
Esther, a Jewess who became queen of Persia	Esth. 2:16, 17
Eunice, mother of Timothy	2 Tim. 1:5
Euodias, a deaconess	Phil. 4:2
Eve, first woman	Gen. 3:20
Gomer, wife of Hosea	Hos. 1:2, 3
Hagar, Sarai's maid	Gen. 16:1
Haggith, wife of David	2 Sam. 3:2, 4
Hammoleketh, mother of Ishod	1 Chr. 7:18
Hamutal, daughter of Jeremiah	2 Kin. 23:31
Hannah, mother of Samuel	1 Sam. 1:20
Hazelelponi, in genealogies of Judah	1 Chr. 4:1-3
Helah, one of the wives of Ashur	1 Chr. 4:5
Hephzibah, mother of Manasseh	2 Kin. 21:1
Herodias, sister-in-law of Herod	Matt. 14:3-6
Hodesh, wife of Shaharaim	1 Chr. 8:8, 9
Hoglah, a daughter of Zelophehad	Num. 26:33
Huldah, a prophetess	2 Kin. 22:14
Hushim, a Moabitess	1 Chr. 8:8-11
Iscah, daughter of Haran	Gen. 11:29
Jael, wife of Heber	Judg. 4:17
Jecholiah, wife of Amaziah	2 Kin. 15:1, 2
Jedidah, mother of Josiah	2 Kin. 22:1
Jehoaddin, wife of Joash	2 Kin. 14:1, 2
Jehosheba, daughter of Joram	2 Kin. 11:2
Jemima, Job's daughter	Job 42:12, 14
Jerioth, wife of Caleb	1 Chr. 2:18
Jerusha, daughter of Zadok	2 Kin. 15:33
Jezebel, wife of Ahab	1 Kin. 16:30, 31
Joanna, wife of Chuza	Luke 8:3
Jochebed, mother of Moses	Ex. 6:20
Judith, daughter of Beeri	Gen. 26:34
Julia, Christian woman of Rome	Rom. 16:15
Keren-happuch, Job's daughter	Job 42:14
Keturah, second wife of Abraham	Gen. 25:1
Kezia, daughter of Job	Job 42:14
Leah, wife of Jacob	Gen. 29:21-25
Lois, grandmother of Timothy	2 Tim. 1:5
Lo-ruhamah, daughter of Gomer	Hos. 1:3-6
Lydia, first Christian convert in Europe	Acts 16:14
Maachah	
(1) daughter of Nahor	Gen. 22:23, 24

SUBJECT REFERENCE

(2) daughter of Talmai........2 Sam. 3:3
(3) daughter of Abishalom....1 Kin. 15:2
(4) mother of Asa...........1 Kin. 15:9, 10
(5) concubine of Caleb.......1 Chr. 2:48
(6) wife of Machir..........1 Chr. 7:16
(7) wife of Jehiel...........1 Chr. 8:29
Mahalath
(1) wife of Esau.............Gen. 28:9
(2) granddaughter of David...2 Chr. 11:18
Mahlah, daughter of Zelophehad................Num. 26:33
Mara, another name for Naomi..................Ruth 1:20
Martha, friend of Christ........Luke 10:38-41
Mary
(1) mother of Jesus..........Matt. 1:16
(2) Mary Magdalene.........Matt. 27:56-61
(3) Mary, sister of Martha.....Luke 10:38, 39
(4) Mary, wife of Cleophas.....John 19:25
(5) Mary, mother of Mark.....Acts 12:12
(6) a Christian at Rome.......Rom. 16:6
Matred, mother-in-law of Hadar....................Gen. 36:39
Mehetabeel, daughter of Matred....................Gen. 36:39
Merab, King Saul's eldest daughter...................1 Sam. 14:49
Meshullemeth, wife of Manasseh.................2 Kin. 21:18, 19
Michal, daughter of King Saul..1 Sam. 14:49
Milcah
(1) daughter of Haran........Gen. 11:29
(2) daughter of Zelophehad....Num. 26:33
Miriam
(1) sister of Moses...........Ex. 15:20
(2) disputed daughter of Ezra.....................1 Chr. 4:17
Naamah
(1) daughter of Lamech.......Gen. 4:19-22
(2) wife of Solomon..........1 Kin. 14:21
Naarah, one of the wives of Ashur......................1 Chr. 4:5
Naomi, wife of Elimelech.......Ruth 1:2
Nehushta, daughter of Elnathan...................2 Kin. 24:8
Noadiah, a false prophetess.....Neh. 6:14
Noah, daughter of Zelophehad..Num. 26:33
Orpah, sister-in-law of Ruth....Ruth 1:4
Peninnah, one of the wives of Elkanah.....................1 Sam. 1:1, 2
Persis, convert of early Church..Rom. 16:12
Phebe, a deaconess...........Rom. 16:1-2
Priscilla, wife of Aquila........Acts 18:2
Puah, a midwife..............Ex. 1:15
Rachel, wife of Jacob.........Gen. 29:28
Rahab, aid to Israel's spies.....Josh. 2:1-3
Reumah, mother of Tebah......Gen. 22:24
Rhoda, a damsel.............Acts 12:13
Rizpah, concubine of Saul......2 Sam. 3:7
Ruth, daughter-in-law of Naomi......................Ruth 1:3, 4
Salome, wife of Zebedee.........Matt. 27:56
Mark 15:40
Sapphira, wife of Ananias......Acts 5:1
Sarah, (Sarai) wife of Abraham (Abram)..................Gen. 11:29
Serah, daughter of Asher.......Gen. 46:17
Shelomith
(1) daughter of Dibri.........Lev. 24:11
(2) daughter of Zerubbabel....1 Chr. 3:19
Sherah, daughter of Beriah.....1 Chr. 7:23, 24
Shimeath, mother of Zabad.....2 Chr. 24:26
Shimrith, mother of Jehozabad..2 Chr. 24:26
Shiphrah, a midwife...........Ex. 1:15
Shua, daughter of Heber.......1 Chr. 7:32
Susanna, ministered to Jesus....Luke 8:3
Syntyche, convert of Church at Philippi......................Phil. 4:2
Tabitha, same as Dorcas.......Acts 9:36
Tahpenes, queen of Egypt......1 Kin. 11:19
Tamar
(1) daughter-in-law of Judah...Gen. 38:6
(2) a daughter of David.......2 Sam. 13:1
(3) daughter of Absalom......2 Sam. 14:27
Taphath, one of Solomon's daughters...................1 Kin. 4:11
Timna, concubine of Eliphaz....Gen. 36:12
Tirzah, one of daughters of Zelophehad................Num. 26:33
Tryphaena, convert at Rome....Rom. 16:12
Tryphosa, convert at Rome.....Rom. 16:12
Vashti, wife of Ahasuerus.......Esth. 1:9
Zebudah, mother of Jehoiakim..2 Kin. 23:36
Zeresh, wife of Haman.........Esth. 5:10
Zeruah, a widow.............1 Kin. 11:26
Zeruiah, mother of Joab.......2 Sam. 17:25
Zibiah, mother of Jehoash......2 Kin. 12:1

SUBJECT REFERENCE

Zillah, wife of Lamech.........Gen. 4:19
Zilpah, Leah's handmaid.......Gen. 29:24
Zipporah, wife of Moses........Ex. 2:21

Wonderful—*full of wonder*

A. *Ascribed to:*
Human love...............2 Sam. 1:26
LORD's works..............Ps. 78:4
Mysterious things..........Prov. 30:18
Lord's Law...............Ps. 119:18
Lord's testimonies..........Ps. 119:129
Lord's knowledge...........Ps. 139:6
Our being.................Ps. 139:14
Messiah's name.............Is. 9:6

B. *Descriptive of the Lord's work, as:*
Numerous.................Ps. 40:5
Transmitted...............Ps. 78:4
Remembered..............Ps. 111:4
Praised...................Is. 25:1

Wonders—*miraculous works*

A. *Performed by:*
God.....................Heb. 2:4
Moses and Aaron...........Ex. 11:10
Christ....................Acts 2:22
Apostles..................Acts 2:43
Jesus' name...............Acts 4:30
Stephen..................Acts 6:8
Paul and Barnabas..........Acts 14:3
Paul.....................2 Cor. 12:12

B. *Places of:*
Egypt....................Acts 7:36
Land of Ham...............Ps. 105:27
Canaan...................Josh. 3:5
Deeps....................Ps. 107:24
Heaven...................Dan. 6:27
Among the peoples..........Ps. 77:14

C. *Described as:*
Numerous.................Ex. 11:9
Great....................Acts 6:8
Mighty...................Dan. 4:3

D. *Man's reactions to:*
Did not remember..........Neh. 9:17
Forgetful of...............Ps. 78:11, 12
Not understanding..........Ps. 106:7
Not believing..............Ps. 78:32
Inquiring about............Jer. 21:2

E. *Believer's attitude toward, to:*
Remember................1 Chr. 16:9, 12
Declare..................Ps. 71:17
Give thanks for............Ps. 136:1, 4
Consider.................Job 37:14

Wood

A. *Descriptive of:*
Part of a tree.............Num. 19:6
Forest...................Josh. 17:15, 18

B. *Place of:*
Animals..................2 Kin. 2:24
Fortresses................2 Chr. 27:4

C. *Used for:*
Fire.....................1 Kin. 18:23-38
Carts....................1 Sam. 6:14
Weapons..................Num. 35:18
Ships....................Gen. 6:14
Chariots..................Song 3:9
Musical instruments........1 Kin. 10:12
Buildings.................1 Kin. 6:15-33
Tabernacle furniture........Ex. 25:9-28
Pulpit....................Neh. 8:4
Gods.....................Is. 37:19

Wood, hewers of

Gibeonites made, because of deception..................Josh. 9:21-27

Woodsmen

Provided with food...........2 Chr. 2:3, 10

Woof—*the threads crossing the warp of a woven garment*

Inspection of, for leprosy.....Lev. 13:48-59

Wool—*the soft hair of sheep*

Inspection of, for leprosy.......Lev. 13:47-59
Mixture of, forbidden..........Deut. 22:11
Used as a test................Judg. 6:37
Valuable article of trade.......Ezek. 27:18
Figurative of whiteness.........Is. 1:18

SUBJECT REFERENCE

Word of God

A. *Called:*
Book of the Law...........Neh. 8:3
Law of the LORD...........Ps. 1:2
Scriptures................John 5:39
Holy Scriptures............Rom. 1:2
Word of God..............Heb. 4:12
Word....................James 1:21-23
Word of life...............Phil. 2:16
Book....................Rev. 22:19

B. *Descriptive of:*
Old Testament Law.........Mark 7:13
God's revealed plan.........Rom. 9:6
God's completed revelation..Col. 1:25-27
Christ's message...........Luke 5:1
Christian Gospel...........Acts 4:31

C. *Described as:*
Pure.....................Ps. 19:8
Restraining...............Ps. 119:11
Perfect...................Ps. 19:7
Sure.....................Ps. 111:7, 8
Truth....................Ps. 119:142, 151, 160
Enduring.................Is. 40:8
Effectual.................Is. 55:11
Sanctifying...............Eph. 5:26
Harmonious...............Acts 15:15
Inspired..................2 Pet. 1:21
Living and active..........Heb. 4:12

D. *Compared to:*
Lamp....................Ps. 119:105
Fire.....................Jer. 5:14
Hammer..................Jer. 23:29
Seed....................Matt. 13:18-23
Sword...................Eph. 6:17

E. *Agency of, to:*
Heal....................Ps. 107:20
Make free................John 8:32
Illuminate................Ps. 119:130
Bear witness..............John 20:31
Produce faith.............Rom. 10:17
Make wise................2 Tim. 3:15-17
Exhort...................2 Tim. 4:2
Rejoice the heart..........Jer. 15:16
Create the world...........Heb. 11:3
Regenerate...............James 1:18
Destroy the world..........2 Pet. 3:5-7

F. *Proper attitude toward, to:*
Stand in awe of............Ps. 119:161
Tremble at................Is. 66:2, 5
Speak faithfully............Jer. 23:28
Search...................Acts 17:11
Speak boldly..............Acts 4:29, 31
Preach...................Acts 8:25
Receive..................Acts 11:1
Glorify...................Acts 13:48
Teach....................Acts 18:11
Obey....................1 Pet. 3:1
Handle accurately..........2 Tim. 2:15
Do......................James 1:22, 23
Suffer for.................Rev. 1:9

G. *In the believer's life, as:*
Restraint.................Ps. 119:9, 11
Guide....................Ps. 119:133
Source of joy..............Ps. 119:47, 97, 162
Standard of conduct........Titus 2:5
Source of new life..........1 Pet. 1:23
Spiritual food..............1 Pet. 2:2

H. *Prohibitions concerning, not to be:*
Preached in man's wisdom...1 Cor. 2:4, 13
Used deceitfully............2 Cor. 4:2
Altered..................Rev. 22:18, 19

Words—*intelligible sounds or signs*

A. *Described as:*
Acceptable...............Eccl. 12:10
Lying and corrupt..........Dan. 2:9
Enticing..................1 Cor. 2:4
Easy.....................1 Cor. 14:9, 19
Unspeakable...............2 Cor. 12:4
Vain.....................Eph. 5:6
Flattering.................1 Thess. 2:5
Wholesome...............1 Tim. 6:3

B. *Power of, to:*
Stir up wrath..............Prov. 15:1
Wound...................Prov. 26:22
Sustain..................Is. 50:4
Determine destiny..........Matt. 12:36, 37

W

SUBJECT — REFERENCE

Work, Christ's

A. *Defined as:*
- Doing God's will — John 4:34
- Limited in time — John 9:4
- Incomparable — John 15:24
- Initiated by God — John 14:10
- Finished in the cross — John 17:4

B. *Design of, to:*
- Attest His mission — John 5:36
- Encourage faith — John 14:11, 12
- Judge men — John 15:24

Work, the Christian's

A. *Agency of, by:*
- God — Phil. 2:13
- Spirit — 1 Cor. 12:11
- God's Word — 1 Thess. 2:13
- Faith — Gal. 5:6

B. *Characteristics of:*
- Designed for God's glory — Matt. 5:16
- Divinely called — Acts 13:2
- Produces eventual glory — 2 Cor. 4:17
- Subject to examination — Gal. 6:4
- Final perfection in — Heb. 13:21

C. *God's regard for, will:*
- Reward — Jer. 31:16
- Perfect — Phil. 1:6
- Not forget — Heb. 6:10

See Labor, spiritual

Work, physical
- Part of the curse — Gen. 3:19
- Required of Christians — 2 Thess. 3:7-14
- Nehemiah's zeal — Neh. 6:1-4
- Paul's example — Acts 18:1-3

See Labor, physical

Works, God's

A. *Described as:*
- Perfect — Deut. 32:4
- Terrible — Ps. 66:3
- Incomparable — Ps. 86:8
- Honorable and glorious — Ps. 111:3
- Marvelous — Ps. 139:14
- Holy — Ps. 145:17
- Strange — Is. 28:21
- Great and marvelous — Rev. 15:3

B. *Manifested in:*
- Creation — Gen. 1:1-3
- Heavens — Ps. 8:3
- Deeps — Ps. 107:24
- Regenerate people — Is. 19:25

C. *God's attitude toward:*
- Rejoice in — Ps. 104:31
- Made known to His people — Ps. 111:6
- His mercies over — Ps. 145:9
- Glorified in — Is. 60:21

D. *Believer's attitude toward, to:*
- Consider — Ps. 8:3
- Behold — Ps. 46:8
- Meditate — Ps. 77:12
- Meditate upon — Ps. 143:5
- Triumph in — Ps. 92:4
- Declare — Ps. 107:22
- Praise God for — Ps. 145:4, 10
- Pray for revival of — Hab. 3:2

E. *Unbeliever's attitude toward:*
- Not regarding — Ps. 28:5
- Forgetting — Ps. 78:11
- Not believed — Acts 13:41

Works, good

A. *Considered negatively, they cannot:*
- Justify — Rom. 4:2-6
- Determine God's election — Rom. 9:11
- Secure righteousness — Rom. 9:31, 32
- Substitute for grace — Rom. 11:6

B. *Considered positively:*
- Reward for — 1 Cor. 3:13-15
- Created for — Eph. 2:10
- Prepared for — 2 Tim. 2:21
- Furnished for — 2 Tim. 3:17

Works, Satan's (see Satan)

Works, the unbeliever's

A. *Described as:*
- Wicked — Col. 1:21
- Done in darkness — Is. 29:15
- Abominable — Ps. 14:1
- Deceitful — Prov. 11:18
- Evil — John 7:7
- Unfruitful — Eph. 5:11

B. *God's attitude toward, will:*
- Never forget — Amos 8:7
- Reward — Prov. 24:12
- Bring to judgment — Rev. 20:12, 13

C. *Believer's relation to:*
- Cast off — Rom. 13:12
- Have no fellowship with — Eph. 5:11
- Be delivered from — 2 Tim. 4:18

World

A. *God's relation to, as:*
- Maker — Jer. 10:12
- Possessor — Ps. 24:1
- Redeemer — John 3:16
- Judge — Ps. 96:13

B. *Christ's relation to, as:*
- Maker — John 1:10
- Sin-bearer — John 1:29
- Savior — John 12:47
- Life — John 6:33, 51
- Light — John 8:12
- Judge — Acts 17:31
- Overcomer — John 16:33
- Reconciler — 2 Cor. 5:19

C. *Christian's relation to:*
- Light of — Matt. 5:14
- Not of — John 17:14, 16
- Chosen out of — John 15:19
- Tribulation in — John 16:33
- Sent into by Christ — John 17:18
- Not conformed to — Rom. 12:2
- Crucified to — Gal. 6:14
- To live soberly — Titus 2:12
- Unspotted from — James 1:27
- Overcomers of — 1 John 5:4, 5
- Denying desires of — Titus 2:12

D. *Dangers of, arising from:*
- Wisdom — 1 Cor. 3:19
- Love of — 2 Tim. 4:10
- Friendship — James 4:4
- Corruptions — 2 Pet. 1:4
- Lusts — 1 John 2:15-17
- False prophets — 1 John 4:1
- Deceivers — 2 John 7

E. *In the plan of redemption:*
- Elect chosen before — Eph. 1:4
- Revelation made before — Matt. 13:35
- Sin's entrance into — Rom. 5:12
- Its guilt before God — Rom. 3:19
- Original revelation to — Rom. 1:20
- God's love for — John 3:16
- Christ's mission to — John 12:47
- Spirit's conviction of — John 16:8
- Gospel preached in — Matt. 24:14
- Reconciliation of — 2 Cor. 5:19
- Destruction of — 2 Pet. 3:7
- Final judgment of — Acts 17:31
- Satan deceives — Rev. 12:9

Worm—*a soft-bodied, slender, creeping animal*

A. *Ravages of:*
- On bread — Ex. 16:15, 20
- On plants — Jon. 4:7
- On the body — Acts 12:23
- In the grave — Job 24:19, 20
- In hell — Mark 9:44-48

B. *Figurative of:*
- Insignificance — Job 25:6
- Messiah — Ps. 22:6

Wormwood—*a bitter-tasting plant*
- Figurative of idolatry — Deut. 29:18
- Of adultery — Prov. 5:4
- Of God's judgments — Jer. 9:15
- Symbol of doom — Rev. 8:11

Worry (see Cares, worldly)

Worship—*an act of reverence*

A. *Of God:*
- Defined — John 4:20-24
- Commanded — 1 Chr. 16:29
- Corrupted — Rom. 1:25
- Perverted — 2 Kin. 21:3, 21
- Debated — 1 Kin. 18:21-39

B. *Of Christ, by:*
- Angels — Heb. 1:6
- Magi — Matt. 2:1-2, 11
- Men — John 9:30-38
- Women — Matt. 15:25
- Disciples — Matt. 28:17
- Heavenly choir — Rev. 4:10, 11

C. *Of wrong objects, such as:*
- Heavenly host — Deut. 17:3
- Other gods — Ex. 34:14
- Demons — Deut. 32:17
- Creatures — Rom. 1:25
- Images — Dan. 3:5-18
- Man — Acts 10:25, 26
- Antichrist — Rev. 13:4-13

D. *Of wrong objects, by:*
- Israel — 2 Kin. 21:3, 21
- Pagans — Rom. 1:25
- Professing Christians — Col. 2:18
- World — 2 Thess. 2:3-12

Worthiness—*acceptableness for some benefit*

A. *Of Christ:*
- For more glory — Heb. 3:3
- To open the book — Rev. 5:2, 4
- To receive worship — Rev. 5:9-14

B. *Of believers, for:*
- Provisions — Matt. 10:10
- Discipleship — Matt. 10:37
- Their calling — Eph. 4:1
- Suffering — Acts 5:41
- Their walk — Col. 1:10
- Honor — 1 Tim. 6:1
- Kingdom — 2 Thess. 1:5

Worthless—*useless, despicable*
- Applied to Job's friends — Job 13:4
- Sacrifice — Is. 1:13
- Faith — 1 Cor. 15:17
- Religion — James 1:26
- Worship — Jer. 51:17, 18

Wound—*to injure*

A. *Of physical injury, by:*
- God — Deut. 32:39
- Battle — 1 Sam. 31:3
- Adultery — Prov. 6:32, 33
- Robbers — Luke 10:30, 34
- Evil spirit — Acts 19:16

B. *Of spiritual injury, by:*
- Discouragement — Prov. 18:14
- God's punishment — Jer. 30:14
- Drunkenness — Prov. 23:29, 30
- Adultery — Prov. 6:32, 33
- Sin — Is. 1:6

Wrappings—*clothes for the dead*
- Lazarus attired in — John 11:43, 44
- Jesus lays His aside — Luke 24:12

Wrath of God

A. *Described as:*
- Anger — Num. 32:10-13
- Fury — Ps. 90:9
- Great — Zech. 7:12
- Willing — Rom. 9:22
- Revealed — Rom. 1:18
- Stored up — Rom. 2:5-8
- Abiding — John 3:36
- Accomplished — Rev. 6:16, 17

B. *Caused by:*
- Apostasy — 2 Chr. 34:24, 25
- Sympathy with evil — Lev. 10:1-6
- Unfaithfulness — Josh. 22:20
- Provocations — 2 Kin. 23:26
- Fellowship with evil — 2 Chr. 19:2
- Mockery — 2 Chr. 36:16
- Idolatry — Ps. 78:58, 59
- Intermarriage — Ezra 10:10-14
- Profaning the Sabbath — Neh. 13:18
- Speaking against God — Ps. 78:19-21

C. *Effects of, seen in:*
- Egypt's destruction — Ex. 15:4, 7
- Great plague — Num. 11:33
- Israel's wanderings — Num. 32:10-13
- Withholding of rain — Deut. 11:17
- Destruction of a people — 1 Sam. 28:18
- Trouble — Ps. 90:7
- Man's death — Ps. 90:9
- Jerusalem's destruction — Luke 21:23, 24
- Punishments of hell — Rev. 14:10
- Final judgments — Rev. 19:15
- Israel's captivity — 2 Chr. 36:16, 17

SUBJECT REFERENCE

D. *Deliverance from, by:*
Atonement ... Num. 16:46
Keeping an oath ... Josh. 9:19, 20
Humbling oneself ... 2 Chr. 32:26
Intercession ... Ps. 106:23
Christ ... Rom. 5:8, 9
God's appointment ... 1 Thess. 5:9

Wrestling
Sisters ... Gen. 30:8
Jacob ... Gen. 32:24-30
Christians ... Eph. 6:12

Write, writing, written
A. *Purposes of, to:*
Record God's Word ... Ex. 24:4, 12
Record history ... Luke 1:3
Record dictation ... Jer. 36:2, 27, 28
Make legal ... Deut. 24:1-4
Issue orders ... Esth. 8:5, 8, 10
Insure a covenant ... Neh. 9:38
Indicate name ... Luke 1:63
Indicate the saved ... Rev. 20:15
Establish inspiration ... Rev. 22:18, 19

B. *Unusual:*
By God's finger ... Ex. 31:18
Destroyed and restored ... Jer. 36:21-32
On a wall ... Dan. 5:5-29
On the sand ... John 8:6, 8
On the cross ... John 19:19-22
In hearts ... Rom. 2:15

C. *Of the Bible as written, involving its:*
Authority ... Acts 24:14
Determination of events ... Heb. 10:7
Fulfillment ... Luke 21:22
Messianic character ... Luke 24:44, 46
Saving purpose ... John 20:31
Harmony ... Acts 15:15
Spiritual aim ... Rom. 15:4
Finality ... Rev. 22:18, 19

D. *Figurative of:*
God's real people ... Rev. 20:12, 15
Indelible character ... 2 Cor. 3:2, 3
Innate knowledge ... Rom. 2:15

Y

Yarn—*thread used in weaving*
Of linen ... 1 Kin. 10:28

Years, thousand
In God's sight, one day ... 2 Pet. 3:8
Time of Satan's bondage ... Rev. 20:2-7

Yield—*to produce; to surrender*
A. *Used literally of:*
Plants ... Gen. 1:11-29
Earth ... Ps. 67:6
Standing grain ... Hos. 8:7
Death ... Acts 5:10
Fountain ... James 3:12
God's servants ... Dan. 3:28

B. *Used figuratively of:*
Discipline ... Heb. 12:11
Spiritual fruit ... Mark 4:8
Surrender ... Rom. 6:13, 16

Yoke—*a frame uniting animals for work*
A. *Used literally on:*
Animals ... Deut. 21:3
Captives ... Jer. 28:10-14
Slaves ... 1 Tim. 6:1

B. *Used figuratively of:*
Oppression ... Deut. 28:48
Hard service ... 1 Kin. 12:4-14
Submission ... Jer. 27:8
Bondage to sin ... Lam. 1:14
Discipleship ... Matt. 11:29, 30
Legalistic ordinances ... Gal. 5:1
Marriage ... 2 Cor. 6:14

Young men
A. *Characteristics of, seen in:*
Unwise counsel ... 1 Kin. 12:8-14
Godly fervor ... 1 John 2:13, 14
Passion ... Prov. 7:7-23
Strength ... Prov. 20:29
Impatience ... Luke 15:12, 13

SUBJECT REFERENCE

B. *Special needs of:*
God's Word ... Ps. 119:9
Knowledge and discretion ... Prov. 1:4
Encouragement ... Is. 40:30, 31
Full surrender ... Matt. 19:20-22
Soberness ... Titus 2:6
Counsel ... 1 John 2:13, 14

Youth—*the early age of life*
A. *Evils of, seen in:*
Sin ... Ps. 25:7
Lusts ... 2 Tim. 2:22
Enticements ... Prov. 1:10-16
Self-will ... Luke 15:12, 13

B. *Good of, seen in:*
Enthusiasm ... 1 Sam. 17:26-51
Children ... Ps. 127:3, 4
Hardships ... Lam. 3:27
Godly example ... 1 Tim. 4:12

Z

Zaanan—*rich in flocks*
Town in west Judah ... Mic. 1:11

Zaanannim
Border point of Naphtali ... Josh. 19:32, 33

Zaavan—*unquiet*
Son of Ezer ... Gen. 36:27

Zabad—*gift*
1. Descendant of Judah ... 1 Chr. 2:3, 36
2. Ephraimite ... 1 Chr. 7:20, 21
3. One of Joash's murderers ... 2 Chr. 24:26
Called Jozacar ... 2 Kin. 12:21
4. Son of Zattu ... Ezra 10:27
5. Son of Hashum ... Ezra 10:33
6. Son of Nebo ... Ezra 10:43

Zabbai—(God) *has given*
1. Man who divorced his foreign wife ... Ezra 10:28
2. Father of Baruch ... Neh. 3:20

Zabbud—*given* (by God)
Postexilic returnee ... Ezra 8:14

Zabdi—(God) *has given*
1. Achan's grandfather ... Josh. 7:1, 17, 18
2. Benjamite ... 1 Chr. 8:1, 19
3. One of David's officers ... 1 Chr. 27:27

Zabdiel—*God has given*
1. Father of Jashobeam ... 1 Chr. 27:2
2. Postexilic official ... Neh. 11:14

Zabud—*bestowed*
Son of Nathan ... 1 Kin. 4:5

Zaccai—probably a contraction of *"Zechariah"*
Head of a postexilic family ... Ezra 2:9

Zaccheus—*pure*
Wealthy tax gatherer converted to Christ ... Luke 19:1-10

Zaccur—*remembered*
1. Father of the Reubenite spy ... Num. 13:2, 4
2. Simeonite ... 1 Chr. 4:24, 26
3. Merarite Levite ... 1 Chr. 24:27
4. Asaphite Levite ... 1 Chr. 25:2, 10
5. Signer of the covenant ... Neh. 10:1, 12
6. A treasurer under Nehemiah ... Neh. 13:13

Zachariah—*Jehovah has remembered*
1. Son and successor of King Jeroboam II ... {2 Kin. 14:29; 2 Kin. 15:8-10}
2. Grandfather of Hezekiah ... 2 Kin. 18:1, 2

Zacharias
Father of John the Baptist ... Luke 1:5-17

Zacher—*memorial*
Benjamite ... 1 Chr. 8:31

Zadok—*righteous*
1. Descendant of Aaron ... 1 Chr. 24:1-3
Co-priest with Abiathar ... 2 Sam. 20:25

SUBJECT REFERENCE

Loyal to David ... 2 Sam. 15:24-29
Gently rebuked by David ... 2 Sam. 19:11-14
Remained aloof from Adonijah's usurpation ... 1 Kin. 1:8-26
Commanded by David to anoint Solomon ... 1 Kin. 1:32-45
Replaces Abiathar ... 1 Kin. 2:35
Sons of, faithful ... Ezek. 48:11
2. Priest, the son or grandson of Ahitub ... 1 Chr. 6:12
3. Jotham's maternal grandfather ... 2 Kin. 15:33
4. Postexilic workman, son of Baana ... Neh. 3:4
5. Postexilic workman, son of Immer ... Neh. 3:29
6. Ancestor of Christ ... Matt. 1:14

Zaham—*foul*
Son of Rehoboam ... 2 Chr. 11:18, 19

Zain
Letter of the Hebrew alphabet ... Ps. 119:49-56

Zair—*little*
Battle camp in Edom ... 2 Kin. 8:21

Zalaph—*caper-plant*
Father of Hanum ... Neh. 3:30

Zalmon—*dark*
1. One of David's mighty men ... 2 Sam. 23:28
2. Mount near Shechem ... Judg. 9:48

Zalmonah—*shady*
Israelite camp ... Num. 33:41, 42

Zalmunna—*deprived of shade*
Midianite king ... Judg. 8:4-21

Zamzummims—*murmurers*
Race of giants ... Deut. 2:20, 21
Same as the Zuzim ... Gen. 14:5

Zanoah—*rejected*
1. Town in south Judah ... Josh. 15:1, 34
2. Town of Judah ... Josh. 15:56

Zaphnath-paaneah—*revealer of secrets*
Name given to Joseph by Pharaoh ... Gen. 41:45

Zaphon—*concealed*
Town of Gad east of the Jordan ... Josh. 13:24, 27

Zared—*willow bush*
Brook and valley crossed by Israel ... Num. 21:12

Zarephath
Town of Sidon where Elijah restores widow's son ... {1 Kin. 17:8-24; Luke 4:26}

Zaretan, Zartanah, Zarthan—*cooling*
Town near Jezreel ... Josh. 3:16; 1 Kin. 4:12
Hiram worked near ... 1 Kin. 7:46

Zareth-shahar—*the splendor of dawn*
City of Reuben ... Josh. 13:19

Zattu, Zatthu—*lovely*
Founder of a postexilic family ... Ezra 2:2, 8
Members of, divorced foreign wives ... Ezra 10:18, 19, 27
Signs covenant ... Neh. 10:1, 14

Zayin
Letter of the Hebrew alphabet ... Ps. 119:49-56

Zaza—*projection*
Jerahmeelite ... 1 Chr. 2:33

Zeal—*intense enthusiasm for something*
A. *Kinds of:*
Divine ... Is. 9:7
Glorious ... Is. 63:15
Wrathful ... Ezek. 5:13
Stirring ... 2 Cor. 9:2
Intense ... 2 Cor. 7:11
Boastful ... Phil. 3:4, 6
Ignorant ... Rom. 10:2, 3
Righteous ... John 2:15-17
Sinful ... 2 Sam. 21:1, 2

SUBJECT — REFERENCE

B. *Manifested in concern for:*
Lord's sake .... Num. 25:11, 13
Others' salvation .... Rom. 10:1
Missionary work .... Rom. 15:18-25
Reformation of character .... 2 Cor. 7:11
Desire for spiritual gifts .... 1 Cor. 14:12
Doing good works .... Titus 2:14

C. *Illustrated in Paul's life by his:*
Desire to reach the Jews .... Rom. 9:1-3; Rom. 10:1
Determination to evangelize all .... 1 Cor. 9:19-23
Willingness to lose all things for Christ .... Phil. 3:4-16
Plan to minister to unreached places .... Rom. 1:14, 15
Support of himself .... 2 Cor. 11:7-12

D. *Examples of:*
Moses .... Ex. 32:19-32
Phinehas .... Num. 25:7-13
Joshua .... Josh. 24:14-16
Gideon .... Judg. 6:11-32
David .... 1 Sam. 17:26-51
Elijah .... 1 Kin. 19:10
Jehu .... 2 Kin. 9:1-37
Josiah .... 2 Kin. 22:1-20
Ezra .... Ezra 7:10
Nehemiah .... Neh. 4:1-23
Peter and John .... Acts 4:8-20
Timothy .... Phil. 2:19-22
Epaphroditus .... Phil. 2:25-30
Epaphras .... Col. 4:12, 13

Zealot—*zealous one*
Applied to Simon, the Canaanite; a party of fanatical Jews .... Luke 6:15

Zebadiah—*Jehovah has bestowed*
1, 2. Two Benjamites .... 1 Chr. 8:1, 15, 17
3. Benjamite warrior among David's mighty men .... 1 Chr. 12:1-7
4. One of David's commanders .... 1 Chr. 27:7
5. Korahite Levite .... 1 Chr. 26:1, 2
6. Levite teacher under Jehoshaphat .... 2 Chr. 17:8
7. Officer of Jehoshaphat .... 2 Chr. 19:11
8. Postexilic returnee .... Ezra 8:8
9. Priest who put away his foreign wife .... Ezra 10:20

Zebah—*victim; sacrifice*
King of Midian killed by Gideon .... Judg. 8:4-28

Zebaim—*gazelles*
Native place of Solomon's slaves .... Ezra 2:55, 57

Zebedee—*Jehovah is gift*
Galilean fisherman; father of James and John .... Matt. 4:21, 22

Zebina—*purchased*
Priest who put away his foreign wife .... Ezra 10:43

Zeboim—*hyenas*
1. One of five cities destroyed with Sodom and Gomorrah .... Gen. 10:19
2. Valley in Benjamin .... 1 Sam. 13:16-18
3. City of Judah .... Neh. 11:34

Zebudah—*given*
Mother of Jehoiakim .... 2 Kin. 23:36

Zebul—*hesitation*
Ruler of Shechem; exposes Gaal's revolt .... Judg. 9:26-41

Zebulun—*dwelling*
1. Sixth son of Leah and Jacob .... Gen. 30:19, 20
2. Descendants of 1; a tribe of Israel .... Num. 2:7
Predictions concerning .... Gen. 49:13
First numbering of .... Num. 1:30, 31
Second numbering of .... Num. 26:27
Representatives of .... Num. 1:9
Territory of .... Josh. 19:10-16
Warriors of, fight with Deborah .... Judg. 5:14, 18
Warriors of, aid Gideon .... Judg. 6:34, 35
Judge Elon, member of .... Judg. 12:11, 12
Warriors of, in David's army .... 1 Chr. 12:33, 40
Some of, respond to Hezekiah's reforms .... 2 Chr. 30:10-18
Christ visits land of .... Is. 9:1; Matt. 4:13-15
Those sealed of .... Rev. 7:8

Zebulunites—*natives of Zebulun*
Descendants of Jacob's son .... Num. 26:27
Elon thus called .... Judg. 12:11, 12

Zechariah—*Jehovah remembers*
1. Benjamite .... 1 Chr. 9:35, 37
2. Levite porter and counselor .... 1 Chr. 9:21, 22
3. Levite musician in David's reign .... 1 Chr. 15:18, 20
4. Priestly trumpeter .... 1 Chr. 15:24
5. Kohathite Levite .... 1 Chr. 24:25
6. Merarite Levite in David's reign .... 1 Chr. 26:10, 11
7. Manassite .... 1 Chr. 27:21
8. Teaching prince under Jehoshaphat .... 2 Chr. 17:7
9. Asaphite Levite .... 2 Chr. 20:14
10. Son of King Jehoshaphat .... 2 Chr. 21:2-4
11. Son of Jehoiada killed in the Temple .... 2 Chr. 24:20-22; Matt. 23:35
12. Prophet in Uzziah's reign .... 2 Chr. 26:5
13. King of Israel; last ruler of Jehu's dynasty .... 2 Kin. 15:8-12
14. Reubenite chief .... 1 Chr. 5:7
15. Faithful man in Isaiah's time .... Is. 8:2
16. Hezekiah's maternal grandfather .... 2 Chr. 29:1
17. Levite during Hezekiah's reign .... 2 Chr. 29:13
18. Kohathite Levite employed as overseer .... 2 Chr. 34:12
19. Temple ruler during Josiah's reign .... 2 Chr. 35:8
20. Postexilic returnee .... Ezra 8:3
21. Son of Bebai .... Ezra 8:11
22. Man sent by Ezra to secure Levites .... Ezra 8:15, 16
23. One of Ezra's assistants .... Neh. 8:4
24. Jew who divorced his foreign wife .... Ezra 10:26
25. Levite trumpeter .... Neh. 12:35, 36
26. Priest in dedication ceremony .... Neh. 12:41
27. Man of Judah, family of Perez .... Neh. 11:4
28. Man of Judah, son of a Shilonite .... Neh. 11:5
29. Postexilic priest .... Neh. 11:2
30. Postexilic prophet and priest .... Ezra 5:1; Zech. 1:1, 7

Zechariah, the Book of—*a book of the Old Testament*
Call to repentance .... Zech. 1:2-6
The visions .... Zech. 1:7—6:15
Against insincerity and disobedience .... Zech. 7:1-14
Restoration of Jerusalem .... Zech. 8:1-23
Against nations .... Zech. 9:1-8
The King comes .... Zech. 9:9-17
Parable of shepherds .... Zech. 11:4-17
Jerusalem spoiled .... Zech. 14:1-6
Jerusalem restored .... Zech. 14:7-21

Zedad—*siding*
Place on Palestine's north boundary .... Num. 34:8; Ezek. 47:15

Zedekiah, Zidkijah—*Jehovah is righteousness*
1. False prophet who counsels Ahab unwisely .... 1 Kin. 22:6-24
2. Immoral prophet killed by Nebuchadnezzar .... Jer. 29:21-23
3. Prince under King Jehoiakim .... Jer. 36:12
4. Son of Jeconiah .... 1 Chr. 3:16
5. Last king of Judah; uncle and successor of Jehoiachin .... 2 Kin. 24:17, 18
Reigns wickedly for 11 years .... 2 Chr. 36:11-13
Rebels against Jeremiah .... 2 Chr. 36:12
Rebels against Nebuchadnezzar .... Jer. 52:3
Makes alliance with Egypt .... Ezek. 17:11-21
Rebellion of, denounced by Jeremiah .... Jer. 34:1-22
Consults with Jeremiah .... Jer. 37:15-21; Jer. 38:14-28
Imprisons Jeremiah .... Jer. 38:1-13
Captured, blinded, taken to Babylon .... Jer. 39:1-14; 2 Kin. 25:1-7
6. High official who signs the covenant .... Neh. 10:1

Zeeb—*wolf*
Midianite prince slain by Gideon's men .... Judg. 7:25

Zelah—*rib*
Towns assigned to Benjamin .... Josh. 18:28
Burial place of Kish, Saul, and Jonathan .... 2 Sam. 21:14

Zelek—*cleft*
One of David's mighty men .... 2 Sam. 23:37

Zelophehad—*shadow of the fear*
Manassite whose five daughters secure female rights .... Num. 27:1-7

Zelzah—*sun protection*
Town in south Benjamin near Rachel's tomb .... Gen. 48:7

Zemaraim—*double mount forest*
1. Town of Benjamin near Jericho .... Josh. 18:22
2. Mountain in Ephraim .... 2 Chr. 13:4

Zemarites
Tribe of Canaanites .... Gen. 10:18

Zemira—*song*
Grandson of Benjamin .... 1 Chr. 7:6, 8

Zenan—*place of flocks*
Town in Judah .... Josh. 15:21, 37

Zenas—*gift of Zeus*
Christian lawyer .... Titus 3:13

Zephaniah—*hidden of Jehovah*
1. Ancestor of Samuel .... 1 Chr. 6:33, 36
2. Author of Zephaniah .... Zeph. 1:1
3. Priest and friend of Jeremiah during Zedekiah's reign .... Jer. 21:1
4. Father of a certain Josiah in Zechariah's time .... Zech. 6:10

Zephaniah, the Book of—*a book of the Old Testament*
Coming judgment .... Zeph. 1:2-18
Call to repentance .... Zeph. 2:1-3
The nations judged .... Zeph. 2:4-15
Jerusalem is blessed .... Zeph. 3:9-20

Zephath—*watchtower*
Canaanite town destroyed by Simeon and Judah .... Judg. 1:17
See Hormah

Zephathah
Valley near Mareshah .... 2 Chr. 14:10

Zepho—*watch*
Grandson of Esau and a duke of Edom .... Gen. 36:15, 19; 1 Chr. 1:36

Zephon—*watching*
Son of Gad and tribal head .... Num. 26:15
Called Ziphion .... Gen. 46:16

Zer—*rock*
City assigned to Naphtali .... Josh. 19:32, 35

SUBJECT REFERENCE

Zerah—*dawning*
1. Son of Reuel and duke of Edom ... Gen. 36:17, 19; 1 Chr. 1:44
2. Son of Judah ... Num. 26:20
   Ancestor of Achan ... Josh. 7:1-18
3. Son of Simeon and tribal head ... Num. 26:12, 13
   Called Zohar ... Gen. 46:10
4. Gershomite Levite ... 1 Chr. 6:20, 21, 41
5. Ethiopian general defeated by King Asa ... 2 Chr. 14:8-15

Zerahiah—*Jehovah is appearing*
1. Ancestor of Ezra ... Ezra 7:1, 4, 5
2. Son of Pahath-moab ... Ezra 8:4

Zereda, Zeredathah—*the fortress*
1. City of Ephraim; birthplace of Jeroboam ... 1 Kin. 11:26
2. City in the Jordan valley ... 2 Chr. 4:17
   Same as Zarethan in ... 1 Kin. 7:46

Zererath
Town in the Jordan valley ... Judg. 7:22
Same as Zarthan ... 1 Kin. 7:46

Zeresh—*golden*
Wife of Haman ... Esth. 5:10, 14

Zereth—*splendor*
Judahite ... 1 Chr. 4:5-7

Zereth-shahar—*the splendor of dawn*
City of Reuben ... Josh. 13:19

Zeror—*bundle*
Benjamite ... 1 Sam. 9:1

Zeruah—*smitten; leprous*
Mother of King Jeroboam I ... 1 Kin. 11:26

Zerubbabel, Zorobabel—*seed of Babel*
Descendant of David ... 1 Chr. 3:19
Leader of Jewish exiles ... Neh. 7:6, 7
Restores worship in Jerusalem ... Ezra 3:1-8
Rebuilds the Temple ... Zech. 4:1-14
Prophecy concerning ... Hag. 2:23
Ancestor of Christ ... Matt. 1:12, 13; Luke 3:27

Zeruiah—*balm*
Mother of Joab ... 2 Sam. 17:25

Zetham—*olive tree*
Gershonite Levite ... 1 Chr. 23:7, 8

Zethan—*olive tree*
Benjamite ... 1 Chr. 7:6, 10

Zethar—*sacrifice*
One of the seven chamberlains of King Ahasuerus ... Esth. 1:10

Zia—*the trembler*
Gadite ... 1 Chr. 5:11, 13

Ziba—*plant*
Saul's servant ... 2 Sam. 9:9
Befriends David ... 2 Sam. 16:1-4
Accused of deception by Mephibosheth ... 2 Sam. 19:17-30

Zibeon—*hyena*
Son of Seir and a clan chief ... Gen. 36:20, 21

Zibia—*gazelle*
Benjamite and household head ... 1 Chr. 8:8, 9

Zibiah—*gazelle*
Mother of King Jehoash ... 2 Kin. 12:1

Zichri—*famous*
1. Kohathite Levite ... Ex. 6:21
2, 3, 4. Three Benjamites ... 1 Chr. 8:19, 23, 27
5. Son of Asaph ... 1 Chr. 9:15
6. Descendant of Moses ... 1 Chr. 26:25
7. Reubenite ... 1 Chr. 27:16
8. Judahite ... 2 Chr. 17:16
9. Mighty man in Pekah's army ... 2 Chr. 28:7
10. Benjamite ... Neh. 11:9
11. Postexilic priest ... Neh. 12:17

SUBJECT REFERENCE

Ziddim—*sides*
City of Naphtali ... Josh. 19:35

Zif—*splendor, bloom*
Second month of the Jewish year ... 1 Kin. 6:1

Ziha
Head of a Nethinim family ... Ezra 2:43

Ziklag—*winding*
City on the border of Judah ... Josh. 15:1, 31
Assigned to Simeon ... Josh. 19:1, 5
Held by David ... 1 Sam. 27:6
Overthrown by Amalekites ... 1 Sam. 30:1-31
Occupied by returnees ... Neh. 11:28

Zillah—*shadow*
One of Lamech's wives ... Gen. 4:19-23

Zilpah—*a drop*
Leah's maid ... Gen. 29:24
Mother of Gad and Asher ... Gen. 30:9-13

Zilthai—*shadow of Jehovah*
1. Benjamite ... 1 Chr. 8:20
2. Manassite captain ... 1 Chr. 12:20

Zimmah—*counsel*
Gershonite Levite ... 1 Chr. 6:20, 42, 43

Zimran—*antelope*
Son of Abraham and Keturah ... Gen. 25:1, 2

Zimri—*pertaining to an antelope*
1. Grandson of Judah ... 1 Chr. 2:3-6
   Called Zabdi ... Josh. 7:1-18
2. Simeonite prince slain by Phinehas ... Num. 25:6-14
3. Benjamite ... 1 Chr. 8:1, 36
4. King of Israel for seven days ... 1 Kin. 16:8-20
5. Place or people otherwise unknown ... Jer. 25:25

Zin—*low land*
Wilderness through which the Israelites passed ... Num. 20:1
Border of Judah and Edom ... Josh. 15:1-3

Zina—*abundance*
Son of Shimei ... 1 Chr. 23:10

Zion—*fortress*
A. *Used literally of:*
   Jebusite fortress captured by David ... 2 Sam. 5:6-9
   Place from which Solomon brings the ark ... 2 Chr. 5:2
   Area occupied by the Temple ... Is. 8:18
B. *Used figuratively of:*
   Israel as a people of God ... 2 Kin. 19:21
   God's spiritual kingdom ... Ps. 125:1
   Eternal city ... Heb. 12:22, 28
   Heaven ... Rev. 14:1

Zior—*smallness*
Town of Judah ... Josh. 15:54

Ziph—*refining place*
1. Town in south Judah ... Josh. 15:24
2. City in the hill country of Judah ... Josh. 15:55
   David hides from Saul in wilderness here ... 1 Sam. 23:14, 15
3. Son of Jehaleleel ... 1 Chr. 4:16

Ziphah—*lent*
Son of Jehaleleel ... 1 Chr. 4:16

Ziphites—*inhabitants of Ziph*
Betray David ... 1 Sam. 23:19-24

Ziphron—*beautiful top*
Place in north Palestine ... Num. 34:9

Zippor—*sparrow*
Father of Balak ... Num. 22:4, 10

Zipporah—*bird*
Daughter of Jethro; wife of Moses ... Ex. 18:1, 2

SUBJECT REFERENCE

Zithri—*my protection*
Grandson of Kohath ... Ex. 6:18, 22

Ziz—*brightness*
Pass leading from Dead Sea to Jerusalem ... 2 Chr. 20:16

Ziza—*brightness*
1. Simeonite leader ... 1 Chr. 4:24, 37, 38
2. Son of Rehoboam ... 2 Chr. 11:18-20

Zizah
Gershonite Levite ... 1 Chr. 23:7, 10, 11
See Zina

Zoan
City in Lower Egypt ... Num. 13:22
Places of God's miracles ... Ps. 78:12, 43
Princes resided at ... Is. 30:2, 4
Object of God's wrath ... Ezek. 30:14

Zoar—*little*
Ancient city of Canaan originally named Bela ... Gen. 14:2, 8
Spared destruction at Lot's request ... Gen. 19:20-23
Seen by Moses from Mt. Pisgah ... Deut. 34:1-3
Object of prophetic doom ... Is. 15:5

Zobah
Syrian kingdom; wars against Saul ... 1 Sam. 14:47

Zobebah—*the affable*
Judahite ... 1 Chr. 4:1, 8

Zohar—*gray*
1. Father of Ephron the Hittite ... Gen. 23:8
2. Son of Simeon ... Gen. 46:10

Zoheleth—*serpent*
Stone near En-rogel ... 1 Kin. 1:9

Zoheth—*proud*
Descendant of Judah ... 1 Chr. 4:1, 20

Zophah—*pot-bellied jug*
Asherite ... 1 Chr. 7:30, 35, 36

Zophar—*chirper*
Naamathite and friend of Job ... Job 2:11

Zophim—*watchers*
Field on the top of Mt. Pisgah ... Num. 23:14

Zorah, Zareah, Zoreah—*hornet*
Town of Judah ... Josh. 15:1, 33
Inhabited by Danites ... Josh. 19:40, 41
Place of Samson's birth and burial ... Judg. 13:24, 25; Judg. 16:30, 31
Inhabited by returnees ... Neh. 11:25, 29

Zorathite
Native of Zorah ... 1 Chr. 4:2
Descendants of Caleb ... 1 Chr. 2:50, 53

Zorite
Same as Zorathite ... 1 Chr. 2:54

Zuar—*small, little*
Father of Nethaneel ... Num. 1:8

Zuph—*honeycomb*
1. Ancestor of Samuel ... 1 Chr. 6:33, 35
2. Region in Judah ... 1 Sam. 9:4-6

Zur—*rock*
1. A Midianite leader ... Num. 25:15, 18
2. Son of Jehiel ... 1 Chr. 8:30

Zuriel—*God is a rock*
Merarite Levite ... Num. 3:35

Zurishaddai—*the Almighty is a rock*
Father of Shelumiel ... Num. 7:36, 41

Zuzim—*prominent; giant*
Tribe east of the Jordan ... Gen. 14:5
Probably same as Zamzummims ... Deut. 2:20

Harmony of the Gospels

Date	Event	Location	Matthew	Mark	Luke	John	Related References
	Luke's Introduction				1:1–4		Acts 1:1
	Pre-fleshly state of Christ					1:1–18	Heb. 1:1–14
	Genealogy of Jesus Christ		1:1–17		3:23–38		Ruth 4:18–22 1 Chr. 1:1–4

BIRTH, INFANCY, AND ADOLESCENCE OF JESUS AND JOHN THE BAPTIST IN 17 EVENTS

Date	Event	Location	Matthew	Mark	Luke	John	Related References
7 B.C.	(1) Announcement of Birth of John	Jerusalem (Temple)			1:5–25		Num. 6:3
7 or 6 B.C.	(2) Announcement of Birth of Jesus to the Virgin	Nazareth			1:26–38		Is. 7:14
c. 5 B.C.	(3) Song of Elizabeth to Mary	Hill Country of Judea			1:39–45		
	(4) Mary's Song of Praise				1:46–56		Ps. 103:17
5 B.C.	(5) Birth, Infancy, and Purpose for Future of John the Baptist	Judea			1:57–80		Mal. 3:1
	(6) Announcement of Jesus' Birth to Joseph	Nazareth	1:18–25				Is. 9:6, 7
5–4 B.C.	(7) Birth of Jesus Christ	Bethlehem	1:24, 25		2:1–7		Is. 7:14
	(8) Proclamation by the Angels	Near Bethlehem			2:8–14		1 Tim. 3:16
	(9) The Visit of Homage by Shepherds	Bethlehem			2:15–20		
	(10) Jesus' Circumcision	Bethlehem			2:21		Lev. 12:3
4 B.C.	(11) First Temple Visit with Acknowledgments by Simeon and Anna	Jerusalem			2:22–38		Ex. 13:2 Lev. 12
	(12) Visit of the Wise Men	Jerusalem & Bethlehem	2:1–12				Num. 24:17
	(13) Flight into Egypt and Massacre of Innocents	Bethlehem, Jerusalem & Egypt	2:13–18				Jer. 31:15
	(14) From Egypt to Nazareth with Jesus		2:19–23		2:39		
Afterward	(15) Childhood of Jesus	Nazareth			2:40, 51		
A.D. 7–8	(16) Jesus, 12 Years Old, Visits the Temple	Jerusalem			2:41–50		Deut. 16:1–8
Afterward	(17) 18-Year Account of Jesus' Adolescence and Adulthood	Nazareth			2:51, 52		1 Sam. 2:26

TRUTHS ABOUT JOHN THE BAPTIST

Date	Event	Location	Matthew	Mark	Luke	John	Related References
c. A.D. 25–27	John's Ministry Begins	Judean Wilderness	3:1	1:1–4	3:1, 2	1:19–28	Mal. 3:1
	Man and Message		3:2–12	1:2–8	3:3–14		Is. 40:3
	His Picture of Jesus		3:11, 12	1:7, 8	3:15–18	1:26, 27	Acts 2:38
	His Courage		14:4–12		3:19, 20		

BEGINNING OF JESUS' MINISTRY IN 12 EVENTS

Date	Event	Location	Matthew	Mark	Luke	John	Related References
c. A.D. 27	(1) Jesus Baptized	Jordan River	3:13–17	1:9–11	3:21–23	1:29–34	Ps. 2:7
	(2) Jesus Tempted	Wilderness	4:1–11	1:12, 13	4:1–13		Ps. 91:11
	(3) Calls First Disciples	Beyond Jordan				1:35–51	
	(4) The First Miracle	Cana in Galilee				2:1–11	
	(5) First Stay in Capernaum	(Capernaum is "His" city)				2:12	
A.D. 27	(6) First Cleansing of the Temple	Jerusalem				2:13–22	Ps. 69:9
	(7) Received at Jerusalem	Judea				2:23–25	
	(8) Teaches Nicodemus about Second Birth	Judea				3:1–21	Num. 21:8, 9
	(9) Co-Ministry with John	Judea				3:22–30	

Date	Event	Location	Matthew	Mark	Luke	John	Related References
A.D. 27	(10) Leaves for Galilee	Judea	4:12	1:14	4:14	4:1–4	
	(11) Samaritan Woman at Jacob's Well	Samaria				4:5–42	Josh. 24:32
	(12) Returns to Galilee			1:15	4:15	4:43–45	
A.D. 27–29	**THE GALILEAN MINISTRY OF JESUS IN 55 EVENTS**						
A.D. 27	(1) Healing of the Nobleman's Son	Cana				4:46–54	
	(2) Rejected at Nazareth	Nazareth			4:16–30		Is. 61:1, 2
	(3) Moved to Capernaum	Capernaum	4:13–17				Is. 9:1, 2
	(4) Four Become Fishers of Men	Sea of Galilee	4:18–22	1:16–20	5:1–11		Ps. 33:9
	(5) Demoniac Healed on the Sabbath Day	Capernaum		1:21–28	4:31–37		
	(6) Peter's Mother-in-Law Cured, Plus Others	Capernaum	8:14–17	1:29–34	4:38–41		Is. 53:4
c. A.D. 27	(7) First Preaching Tour of Galilee	Galilee	4:23–25	1:35–39	4:42–44		
	(8) Leper Healed and Response Recorded	Galilee	8:1–4	1:40–45	5:12–16		Lev. 13:49
	(9) Paralytic Healed	Capernaum	9:1–8	2:1–12	5:17–26		Rom. 3:23
	(10) Matthew's Call and Reception Held	Capernaum	9:9–13	2:13–17	5:27–32		Hos. 6:6
	(11) Disciples Defended via a Parable	Capernaum	9:14–17	2:18–22	5:33–39		
A.D. 28	(12) Goes to Jerusalem for Second Passover; Heals Lame Man	Jerusalem				5:1–47	Ex. 20:10
	(13) Plucked Grain Precipitates Sabbath Controversy	En Route to Galilee	12:1–8	2:23–28	6:1–5		Deut. 5:14
	(14) Withered Hand Healed Causes Another Sabbath Controversy	Galilee	12:9–14	3:1–6	6:6–11		
	(15) Multitudes Healed	Sea of Galilee	12:15–21	3:7–12	6:17–19		
	(16) Twelve Apostles Selected After a Night of Prayer	Near Capernaum		3:13–19	6:12–16		
	(17) Sermon on the Mt.	Near Capernaum	5:1—7:29		6:20–49		
	(18) Centurion's Servant Healed	Capernaum	8:5–13		7:1–10		Is. 49:12, 13
	(19) Raises Widow's Son from Dead	Nain			7:11–17		Job 19:25
	(20) Jesus Allays John's Doubts	Galilee	11:2–19		7:18–35		Mal. 3:1
	(21) Woes Upon the Privileged		11:20–30				Gen. 19:24
	(22) A Sinful Woman Anoints Jesus	Simon's House, Capernaum			7:36–50		
	(23) Another Tour of Galilee	Galilee			8:1–3		
	(24) Jesus Accused of Blasphemy	Capernaum	12:22–37	3:20–30	11:14–23		
	(25) Jesus' Answer to a Demand for a Sign	Capernaum	12:38–45		11:24–26, 29–36		
	(26) Mother, Brothers Seek Audience	Capernaum	12:46–50	3:31–35	8:19–21		
	(27) Famous Parables of Sower, Seed, Tares, Mustard Seed, Leaven, Treasure, Pearl, Dragnet, Lamp Told	By Sea of Galilee	13:1–52	4:1–34	8:4–18		Joel 3:13
	(28) Sea Made Serene	Sea of Galilee	8:23–27	4:35–41	8:22–25		
	(29) Gadarene Demoniac Healed	E. Shore of Galilee	8:28–34	5:1–20	8:26–39		
	(30) Jairus' Daughter Raised and Woman with Hemorrhage Healed		9:18–26	5:21–43	8:40–56		
	(31) Two Blind Men's Sight Restored		9:27–31				

Date	Event	Location	Matthew	Mark	Luke	John	Related References
A.D. 28	(32) Mute Demoniac Healed		9:32–34				
	(33) Nazareth's Second Rejection of Christ	Nazareth	13:53–58	6:1–6			
	(34) Twelve Sent Out		9:35—11:1	6:6–13	9:1–6		1 Cor. 9:14
	(35) Fearful Herod Beheads John	Galilee	14:1–12	6:14–29	9:7–9		
Spring A.D. 29	(36) Return of 12, Jesus Withdraws, 5000 Fed	Near Bethsaida	14:13–21	6:30–44	9:10–17	6:1–14	
	(37) Walks on the Water	Sea of Galilee	14:22–33	6:45–52		6:15–21	
	(38) Sick of Gennesaret Healed	Gennesaret	14:34–36	6:53–56			
	(39) Peak of Popularity Passes in Galilee	Capernaum				6:22–71 7:1	Is. 54:13
A.D. 29	(40) Traditions Attacked		15:1–20	7:1–23			Ex. 21:17
	(41) Aborted Retirement in Phoenicia: Syro-Phoenician Healed	Phoenicia	15:21–28	7:24–30			
	(42) Afflicted Healed	Decapolis	15:29–31	7:31–37			
	(43) 4000 Fed	Decapolis	15:32–39	8:1–9			
	(44) Pharisees Increase Attack	Magdala	16:1–4	8:10–13			
	(45) Disciples' Carelessness Condemned; Blind Man Healed		16:5–12	8:14–26			Jer. 5:21
	(46) Peter Confesses Jesus Is the Christ	Near Caesarea Philippi	16:13–20	8:27–30	9:18–21		
	(47) Jesus Foretells His Death	Caesarea Philippi	16:21–26	8:31–37	9:22–25		
	(48) Kingdom Promised		16:27, 28	9:1	9:26, 27		Prov. 24:12
	(49) The Transfiguration	Mountain Unnamed	17:1–13	9:2–13	9:28–36		Is. 42:1
	(50) Epileptic Healed	Mt. of Transfiguration	17:14–21	9:14–29	9:37–42		
	(51) Again Tells of Death, Resurrection	Galilee	17:22, 23	9:30–32	9:43–45		
	(52) Taxes Paid	Capernaum	17:24–27				Ex. 30:11–15
	(53) Disciples Contend About Greatness; Jesus Defines; also Patience, Loyalty, Forgiveness	Capernaum	18:1–35	9:33–50	9:46–62		
	(54) Jesus Rejects Brothers' Advice	Galilee				7:2–9	
c. Sept. A.D. 29	(55) Galilee Departure and Samaritan Rejection		19:1		9:51–56	7:10	

A.D. 29–30 LAST JUDEAN AND PEREAN MINISTRY OF JESUS IN 42 EVENTS

Date	Event	Location	Matthew	Mark	Luke	John	Related References
Oct. A.D. 29	(1) Feast of Tabernacles	Jerusalem				7:2, 11–52	
	(2) Forgiveness of Adulteress	Jerusalem				7:53—8:11	Lev. 20:10
A.D. 29	(3) Christ—the Light of the World	Jerusalem				8:12–20	
	(4) Pharisees Can't Meet the Prophecy Thus Try to Destroy the Prophet	Jerusalem—Temple				8:12–59	Is. 6:9
	(5) Man Born Blind Healed; Following Consequences	Jerusalem				9:1–41	
	(6) Parable of the Good Shepherd	Jerusalem				10:1–21	
	(7) The Service of the Seventy	Probably Judea			10:1–24		
	(8) Lawyer Hears the Story of the Good Samaritan	Judea (?)			10:25–37		
	(9) The Hospitality of Martha and Mary	Bethany			10:38–42		
	(10) Another Lesson on Prayer	Judea (?)			11:1–13		

Date	Event	Location	Matthew	Mark	Luke	John	Related References
A.D. 29	(11) Accused of Connection with Beelzebub				11:14–36		
	(12) Judgment Against Lawyers and Pharisees				11:37–54		Mic. 6:8
	(13) Jesus Deals with Hypocrisy, Covetousness, Worry, and Alertness				12:1–59		Mic. 7:6
	(14) Repent or Perish				13:1–5		
	(15) Barren Fig Tree				13:6–9		
	(16) Crippled Woman Healed on Sabbath				13:10–17		Deut. 5:12–15
	(17) Parables of Mustard Seed and Leaven	Probably Perea			13:18–21		
Winter A.D. 29	(18) Feast of Dedication	Jerusalem				10:22–39	Ps. 82:6
	(19) Withdrawal Beyond Jordan					10:40–42	
	(20) Begins Teaching Return to Jerusalem with Special Words About Herod	Perea			13:22–35		Ps. 6:8
	(21) Meal with a Pharisee Ruler Occasions Healing Man with Dropsy; Parables of Ox, Best Places, and Great Supper				14:1–24		
	(22) Demands of Discipleship	Perea			14:25–35		
	(23) Parables of Lost Sheep, Coin, Son				15:1–32		1 Pet. 2:25
	(24) Parables of Unjust Steward, Rich Man and Lazarus				16:1–31		
	(25) Lessons on Service, Faith, Influence				17:1–10		
	(26) Resurrection of Lazarus	Perea to Bethany				11:1–44	
	(27) Reaction to It: Withdrawal of Jesus					11:45–54	
A.D. 30	(28) Begins Last Journey to Jerusalem via Samaria & Galilee	Samaria, Galilee			17:11		
	(29) Heals Ten Lepers				17:12–19		Lev. 13:45, 46
	(30) Lessons on the Coming Kingdom				17:20–37		Gen. 6—7
	(31) Parables: Persistent Widow, Pharisee and Tax Collector				18:1–14		
	(32) Doctrine on Divorce		19:1–12	10:1–12			Deut. 24:1–4 Gen. 2:23–25
	(33) Jesus Blesses Children: Objections	Perea	19:13–15	10:13–16	18:15–17		Ps. 131:2
	(34) Rich Young Ruler	Perea	19:16–30	10:17–31	18:18–30		Ex. 20:1–17
	(35) Laborers of the 11th Hour		20:1–16				
	(36) Foretells Death and Resurrection	Near Jordan	20:17–19	10:32–34	18:31–34		Ps. 22
	(37) Ambition of James and John		20:20–28	10:35–45			
	(38) Blind Bartimaeus Healed	Jericho		10:46–52	18:35–43		
	(39) Interview with Zacchaeus	Jericho			19:1–10		
	(40) Parable: the Minas	Jericho			19:11–27		
	(41) Returns to Home of Mary and Martha	Bethany				11:55—12:1	
	(42) Plot to Kill Lazarus	Bethany				12:9–11	
Spring A.D. 30	**JESUS' FINAL WEEK OF WORK AT JERUSALEM IN 41 EVENTS**						
Sunday	(1) Triumphal Entry	Bethany, Jerusalem, Bethany	21:1–9	11:1–11	19:28–44	12:12–19	Zech. 9:9

HARMONY OF THE GOSPELS

Date	Event	Location	Matthew	Mark	Luke	John	Related References
Monday	(2) Fig Tree Cursed and Temple Cleansed	Bethany to Jerusalem	21:10–19	11:12–18	19:45–48		Jer. 7:11
	(3) The Attraction of Sacrifice	Jerusalem				12:20–50	Is. 6:10
Tuesday	(4) Withered Fig Tree Testifies	Bethany to Jerusalem	21:20–22	11:19–26			
	(5) Sanhedrin Challenges Jesus. Answered by Parables: Two Sons, Wicked Vinedressers and Marriage Feast	Jerusalem	21:23—22:14	11:27—12:12	20:1–19		Is. 5:1, 2
	(6) Tribute to Caesar	Jerusalem	22:15–22	12:13–17	20:20–26		
	(7) Sadducees Question the Resurrection	Jerusalem	22:23–33	12:18–27	20:27–40		Ex. 3:6
	(8) Pharisees Question Commandments	Jerusalem	22:34–40	12:28–34			
	(9) Jesus and David	Jerusalem	22:41–46	12:35–37	20:41–44		Ps. 110:1
	(10) Jesus' Last Sermon	Jerusalem	23:1–39	12:38–40	20:45–47		
	(11) Widow's Mite	Jerusalem		12:41–44	21:1–4		Lev. 27:30
	(12) Jesus Tells of the Future	Mt. Olives	24:1–51	13:1–37	21:5–36		Dan. 12:1
	(13) Parables: Ten Virgins, Talents. The Day of Judgment	Mt. Olives	25:1–46				Zech. 14:5
	(14) Jesus Tells Date of Crucifixion		26:1–5	14:1, 2	22:1, 2		
	(15) Anointing by Mary at Simon's Feast	Bethany	26:6–13	14:3–9		12:2–8	
	(16) Judas Contracts the Betrayal		26:14–16	14:10, 11	22:3–6		Zech. 11:12
Thursday	(17) Preparation for the Passover	Jerusalem	26:17–19	14:12–16	22:7–13		Ex. 12:14–28
Thursday P.M.	(18) Passover Eaten, Jealousy Rebuked	Jerusalem	26:20	14:17	22:14–16, 24–30		
	(19) Feet Washed	Upper Room				13:1–20	
	(20) Judas Revealed, Defects	Upper Room	26:21–25	14:18–21	22:21–23	13:21–30	Ps. 41:9
	(21) Jesus Warns About Further Desertion; Cries of Loyalty	Upper Room	26:31–35	14:27–31	22:31–38	13:31–38	Zech. 13:7
	(22) Institution of the Lord's Supper	Upper Room	26:26–29	14:22–25	22:17–20		1 Cor. 11:23–34
	(23) Last Speech to the Apostles and Intercessory Prayer	Jerusalem				14:1—17:26	Ps. 35:19
Thursday-Friday	(24) The Grief of Gethsemane	Mt. Olives	26:30, 36–46	14:26, 32–42	22:39–46	18:1	Ps. 42:6
Friday	(25) Betrayal, Arrest, Desertion	Gethsemane	26:47–56	14:43–52	22:47–53	18:2–12	
	(26) First Examined by Annas	Jerusalem				18:12–14, 19–23	
	(27) Trial by Caiaphas and Council; Following Indignities	Jerusalem	26:57, 59–68	14:53, 55–65	22:54, 63–65	18:24	Lev. 24:16
	(28) Peter's Triple Denial	Jerusalem	26:58, 69–75	14:54, 66–72	22:54–62	18:15–18, 25–27	
	(29) Condemnation by the Council	Jerusalem	27:1	15:1	22:66–71		Ps. 110:1
	(30) Suicide of Judas	Jerusalem	27:3–10				Acts 1:18, 19
	(31) First Appearance Before Pilate	Jerusalem	27:2, 11–14	15:1–5	23:1–7	18:28–38	
	(32) Jesus Before Herod	Jerusalem			23:6–12		
	(33) Second Appearance Before Pilate	Jerusalem	27:15–26	15:6–15	23:13–25	18:39—19:16	Deut. 21:6–9
	(34) Mockery by Roman Soldiers	Jerusalem	27:27–30	15:16–19			
	(35) Led to Golgotha	Jerusalem	27:31–34	15:20–23	23:26–33	19:16, 17	Ps. 69:21
	(36) 6 Events of First 3 Hours on Cross	Calvary	27:35–44	15:24–32	23:33–43	19:18–27	Ps. 22:18
	(37) Last 3 Hours on Cross	Calvary	27:45–50	15:33–37	23:44–46	19:28–30	Ps. 22:1
	(38) Events Attending Jesus' Death		27:51–56	15:38–41	23:45, 47–49		
	(39) Burial of Jesus	Jerusalem	27:57–60	15:42–46	23:50–54	19:31–37	Ex. 12:46
Friday-Saturday	(40) Tomb Sealed	Jerusalem	27:61–66		23:55, 56		Ex. 20:8–11
	(41) Women Watch	Jerusalem		15:47			

Date	Event	Location	Matthew	Mark	Luke	John	Related References
A.D. 30	**THE RESURRECTION THROUGH THE ASCENSION IN 12 EVENTS**						
Dawn of First Day (Sunday, "Lord's Day")	(1) Women Visit the Tomb	Near Jerusalem	28:1–10	16:1–8	24:1–11		
	(2) Peter and John See the Empty Tomb				24:12	20:1–10	
	(3) Jesus' Appearance to Mary Magdalene	Jerusalem		16:9–11		20:11–18	
	(4) Jesus' Appearance to the Other Women	Jerusalem	28:9, 10				
	(5) Guards' Report of the Resurrection		28:11–15				
Sunday Afternoon	(6) Jesus' Appearance to Two Disciples on Way to Emmaus			16:12, 13	24:13–35		1 Cor. 15:5
Late Sunday	(7) Jesus' Appearance to Ten Disciples Without Thomas	Jerusalem		16:14	24:36–43	20:19–25	
One Week Later	(8) Appearance to Disciples with Thomas	Jerusalem				20:26–31	
During 40 Days until Ascension	(9) Jesus' Appearance to Seven Disciples by Sea of Galilee	Galilee				21:1–25	
	(10) Appearance to 500	Mt. in Galilee					1 Cor. 15:6
	(11) Great Commission		28:16–20	16:15–18	24:44–49		
	(12) The Ascension	Mt. Olivet		16:19, 20	24:50–53		Acts 1:4–11

TEACHINGS AND ILLUSTRATIONS OF CHRIST

Subject	Reference
Abiding in Christ	John 15:4–10
Ability	Matt. 25:14, 15
Ablution	Matt. 6:17, 18
Abode	John 14:23
Abraham	John 8:37, 56
Abstinence	Luke 21:34
Abundant life	John 10:10
Access to God	John 10:7, 9
Accountability	Luke 12:47, 48
Accusation, false	Matt. 5:11
Adultery	Matt. 5:27, 28
Adversity	Luke 24:46
Affliction	Matt. 24:7–12
Agreement	Matt. 18:19
Altar	Matt. 23:18, 19
Ambition	Luke 22:25–30
Angels	Matt. 13:39, 41
Anger	Matt. 5:22
Anxiety	Luke 12:22–31
Apostasy	Matt. 13:18–22
	Luke 8:13
Apostles	Luke 11:49
Appearance	Matt. 6:16
Appearance, outward	Matt. 23:27, 28
Authority	Matt. 21:24
	Luke 10:19
Avarice	Luke 12:16–21
Backsliding	Luke 9:62
Baptism	Acts 1:5
	Matt. 28:19
Beatitudes	Matt. 5:3–11
Beelzebub	Matt. 10:25
Begging	Luke 16:3
Beneficence	Matt. 5:42
Betrayal	Matt. 26:21
Bigotry	Luke 18:9–14
Birds	Matt. 8:20
Blasphemy	Matt. 12:31, 32
Blessings	Matt. 5:3–11
Blind guides	Matt. 15:14
Borrowing	Matt. 5:42
Bread of life	John 6:32–35
Brothers	Matt. 23:8
Builders	Luke 6:47–49
	Matt. 7:24
Burdens	Luke 11:46
Burial	Matt. 8:22
Caesar	Matt. 22:21
Call of God	Matt. 20:16
Called ones	Matt. 22:14
Capital and labor	Matt. 20:1–15
Capital punishment	Matt. 26:52
Care of God	Matt. 6:30, 33
Caution	Mark 4:24
Celibacy	Matt. 19:11, 12
Character	John 1:47
Charity	Luke 12:33
Cheating	Mark 10:19
Chosen	Matt. 22:14
Church	Matt. 18:17
Circumcision	John 7:22, 23
Cleansing	John 15:3
Coin	Matt. 22:19–21
Coldness	Matt. 24:12
Communication	Luke 24:17
Compassion	Matt. 15:32
	Luke 10:33
Compromise	Matt. 5:25, 26
Conceit	Luke 18:10–12
Conduct, Christian	Matt. 5:16
Confessing Christ	Matt. 10:32, 33
Confession of sin	Luke 18:13, 14
Confidence	Mark 10:24
Conflict	Matt. 10:34–36
Conscience	John 8:7–9
Contention	Matt. 18:15–17
Contentment	John 6:43
Conversion	Matt. 13:15
Convict	John 16:8
Corruption, moral	Luke 11:39
Courage	Matt. 9:22
Covenant	Mark 14:24
Coveting	Mark 7:21, 22
Cross-bearing	Matt. 10:38
Crucifixion	Luke 9:22
Cup of water	Matt. 10:42
Dancing	Luke 15:25–27
Daniel	Matt. 24:15
Darkness	Luke 11:35
David	Matt. 12:3
Day	John 11:9
Deaf	Matt. 13:13–15
Death	Luke 9:22
	John 8:51
Debts	Matt. 18:24
Deceivers	Matt. 24:4, 5
Decision	Matt. 6:24
Defilement	Matt. 15:11, 18, 19
Devil	Matt. 13:38, 39
Diligence	John 9:4
Disbelief	John 5:38
Discernment	Matt. 16:2, 3
Discipleship	Luke 14:33
Disputes	Mark 9:33, 34
Distress	Luke 21:23, 25
Divorce	Matt. 5:31, 32
Doctrine	Mark 7:7
Doubt	Matt. 21:21
Drunkard	Luke 7:34
Drunkenness	Luke 21:34
Dullness	Matt. 13:13
Duty	Luke 17:10
Dwelling places	John 14:2, 3
Earth	Matt. 5:18
Earthquakes	Mark 13:8
Economy	Matt. 15:37
	John 6:12
Elect	Matt. 24:24, 31
Election	Matt. 25:34
Elijah	Matt. 17:11, 12
Employer	Matt. 20:1–16
Encouragement	Matt. 9:2
Endowments	Matt. 25:14, 15
Endurance	Matt. 10:22
	Luke 21:19
Enemies	Matt. 5:43, 44
Eternal life	Matt. 19:29
Eternal sin	Mark 3:29
Etiquette	Luke 10:8
Evil	Matt. 15:19
Exaltation	Matt. 23:12
Example	John 13:15

Subject	*Reference*
Excuses	Luke 14:18–20
Extravagance	Luke 15:11–14
Fainting	Mark 8:2, 3
Faith	Matt. 6:25
	Mark 11:22
	Luke 7:50
Faithfulness	Matt. 25:21
Faithlessness	Matt. 25:24–30
False prophets	Matt. 24:11
False witness	Matt. 19:18
Farm	Matt. 22:2–6
Fasting	Matt. 6:16–18
Faultfinding	Matt. 7:3–5
Faults	Matt. 18:15
Fear of God	Matt. 10:28
Feast	Luke 14:8
Feet washing	John 13:12–15
Fellowship	Matt. 8:11
Flattery	Luke 6:26
Flesh	John 6:53
Flock	Matt. 26:31
Following Christ	Matt. 10:37, 38
Food	Matt. 6:11
	Matt. 6:25
	John 6:27
Fool	Matt. 5:22
Formalism	Matt. 23:23–28
Forsaking all	Luke 14:33
Foxes	Luke 9:58
Friends	Luke 11:5–8
Frugality	John 6:12
Fruitfulness	Matt. 13:23
Fruitlessness	Luke 13:6–9
Generosity	Matt. 25:34–40
Gentiles	Matt. 10:5–7
Gentleness	Matt. 5:5
Giving	Luke 6:38
Gladness	Luke 15:32
Glorifying God	Matt. 5:16
Gluttony	Luke 21:34
God	Matt. 19:17, 26
Godlessness	John 5:42, 44
Golden Rule	Matt. 7:12
Gospel	Luke 4:18
Grace	2 Cor. 12:9
Greatness	Matt. 5:19
Grumble	John 6:43
Guidance	John 16:13
Hairs numbered	Matt. 10:30
Hand of God	John 10:27–29
Happiness	Matt. 5:12
	John 13:16, 17
Harlots	Matt. 21:31
Harvest	Matt. 9:37, 38
Hatred	John 15:18, 19
Healing	Matt. 10:7, 8
	Mark 2:17
Heart	Matt. 13:19
Heaven	Luke 16:17
	John 3:13
Hell	Matt. 5:22
	Matt. 10:28
Helper	John 14:16
	John 15:26
Helpless	John 6:44
Hireling	John 10:11–13
Holy Spirit	John 14:26
Home	Mark 5:19
Honesty	Luke 8:15
	Mark 10:19
Honor of men	Matt. 6:2
Honor of parents	Matt. 15:3–6
Hospitality	Luke 14:12–14
Humility	John 13:14
	Matt. 11:29
Hunger, spiritual	Luke 6:21
	Matt. 5:6
Hypocrisy	Matt. 6:5
	Luke 6:42
Ignorance	Matt. 22:29
Immortality	Matt. 25:46
	John 11:25, 26
Impartiality of God	Matt. 5:45
Inconsistency	Matt. 7:3–5
	Luke 6:41, 42
Indecision	Luke 9:62
Indifference	Matt. 24:12
Industry	John 4:36
Infidelity	John 3:18
Influence	Matt. 5:13
Ingratitude	Luke 17:17, 18
Innocence	Matt. 10:16
Insincerity	Luke 16:15
Inspiration	Luke 12:12
Instability	Matt. 7:26, 27
Instruction	John 6:45
Insufficiency	Mark 10:21
Integrity	Luke 16:10
Intercession	John 17:9
Investment	Matt. 6:19, 20
Jealousy	Luke 15:25–30
John the Baptist	Luke 7:24–28
Jonah	Matt. 12:39–41
Joy	Matt. 25:21
	Luke 15:7, 10
Judge not	Matt. 7:1, 2
Judgment	Matt. 11:24
Judgment day	Matt. 25:31–46
Justice	John 5:30
Justification, self	Luke 16:15
Killing	Matt. 5:21, 22
Kindness	Luke 10:30–35
Kingdom	Luke 7:28
	John 18:36
Kiss	Luke 7:45
Knowledge	John 8:31, 32
Labor	Matt. 20:1–14
Laughter	Luke 6:21
Law	Luke 16:16
Lawsuit	Matt. 5:25, 40
Lawyers	Luke 11:46
Leaven	Matt. 16:6
	Luke 13:20, 21
Lending	Luke 6:34, 35
Lepers	Matt. 10:7, 8
Levite	Luke 10:30–32
Liars	John 8:44, 45
Liberality	Luke 6:30, 38
Liberty	Luke 4:18
Life	Matt. 6:25
	John 5:40
Light	Luke 11:33
	John 8:12
Living water	John 4:10
Log	Luke 6:41, 42
Loneliness	John 16:32
Lord's Supper	Matt. 26:26–29
Loss of soul	Matt. 16:25, 26
Lost opportunity	Matt. 25:7–12
Love	Matt. 22:37–40
Lukewarmness	Matt. 26:40, 41
Lunatic	Matt. 17:14, 15
Lust	Mark 4:18, 19
Magistrates	Luke 12:11, 58
Mammon	Matt. 6:24
Marriage	Matt. 19:4–6
	Mark 12:25
Martyrdom	John 16:1–3
Mary's choice	Luke 10:41, 42
Memorial	Matt. 26:13
Mercy	Matt. 5:7
	Luke 16:24
Minister	Luke 10:2

TEACHINGS OF CHRIST

Subject	*Reference*
Miracles	Matt. 12:28
Money lender, creditor	Luke 7:41, 42
Moses	Matt. 19:8
Moses' Law	John 7:19
Mother	Matt. 10:37
Mourn	Matt. 5:4
Murder	Matt. 15:19
Mysteries of Heaven	Matt. 13:11
Narrow way	Matt. 7:13, 14
Neglect	Luke 12:47
Neighbor	Matt. 19:19
Neutrality	Matt. 12:30
New birth	John 3:3, 5–8
Noah	Luke 17:26, 27
Oath	Matt. 5:33–37
Obedience	Matt. 12:50
Offering	Matt. 5:25
Offerings	Luke 21:3, 4
Opportunity	Matt. 5:25
Parables	Mark 4:11, 12
Paradise	Luke 23:43
Pardoning	Luke 6:37
Parents	Matt. 10:21
Patriotism	Matt. 22:21
Peace	Mark 9:50
Peacemakers	Matt. 5:9
Penitence	Luke 18:13
Perception	John 8:43
Perfection	Matt. 5:48
Persecution	Matt. 24:9
Perseverance	Matt. 10:22
Pharisaism	Matt. 23:2–33
Pharisee and tax collector	Luke 18:10–14
Pharisees	Matt. 5:20
Philanthropy	Luke 11:41
Physician	Matt. 9:12
Piety	John 1:47
Pleasing God	John 8:29
Pleasures	Luke 8:14
Poison	Mark 16:17, 18
Poll tax	Matt. 22:19–21
Polygamy	Matt. 19:8, 9
Poor	Mark 14:7
Power	Matt. 6:13
Prayer	Matt. 7:7–11
	Matt. 6:9–13
Preaching	Mark 16:15, 16
Procrastination	Matt. 25:3
Profit and loss	Matt. 16:26
Prophets	Matt. 10:41
	Matt. 7:15
Proselyte	Luke 23:15
Protection	Luke 18:3
Providence	Matt. 6:25–33
Prudence	Matt. 10:16–20
Punishment	Matt. 21:41
Purity	Matt. 5:8
Ransom	Matt. 20:28
Reaping	John 4:35–38
Receiving Christ	Mark 9:37
Reconciliation	Matt. 5:23, 24
Regeneration	Matt. 19:28
Rejecting Christ	John 3:18
Rejoicing	Luke 10:20
Release	Luke 4:18
Religion	Mark 7:6–8
	Matt. 25:34–36
Repentance	Matt. 11:21
	Luke 13:28
Reproof	Matt. 11:21–23
Resignation	Matt. 26:39
Responsibility	Luke 12:47, 48
Rest	Matt. 26:45
	Matt. 11:28–30
Resurrection	John 6:40
Retaliation	Matt. 5:39–44
Retribution	Matt. 23:34, 35
Reward	Matt. 10:42
Riches	Mark 4:19
Righteousness	Matt. 5:6, 20
	John 16:10
Robbers	Luke 10:30
	John 10:1
Robbery	Matt. 23:25
Sabbath	Matt. 12:5–8
Sackcloth	Matt. 11:21
Sacrifice	Matt. 12:7
Sacrilege	Matt. 21:13
Sadducees	Matt. 16:6
Salt	Matt. 5:13
	Mark 9:50
Salvation	Luke 19:19
	John 4:22
Samaritan	Luke 10:30–35
Sanctification	John 17:17
Satan	Matt. 4:10
	Mark 4:15
Scripture	Matt. 21:42
	Luke 4:21
Secrecy	Luke 12:2, 3
Security	Luke 6:47, 48
Seduction	Mark 13:22
Seeking the kingdom	Matt. 6:19, 20
Self-condemnation	Matt. 23:29–32
	Luke 19:20–24
Self-control	Matt. 5:21
Self-deception	Luke 12:16–21
Self-denial	Matt. 16:24–26
Self-exaltation	Matt. 23:12
Self-examination	Matt. 7:3–5
Selfishness	Luke 6:32–35
Self-righteousness	Matt. 23:23–27
Self-sacrifice	Matt. 16:25
Serpents	Matt. 23:33
	John 3:14
Service	Luke 22:27
Sheep	Luke 15:4–7
Shepherd	John 10:1–18
Sickness	Matt. 10:8
Signs	John 4:48
	Luke 11:16
Silence	Matt. 17:9
Sin	John 8:34
	Matt. 26:28
Sincerity	Matt. 5:13–16
Skepticism	John 20:27, 29
Slaves	Matt. 18:23
	John 15:15
Sleep	Mark 4:26, 27
	Mark 13:35, 36
Slothfulness	Matt. 25:26–30
Son of Man	Luke 9:22
Sorrow	Matt. 19:22
	John 16:6
Soul	Matt. 10:28
	Luke 12:19, 20
Soul winners	Matt. 4:19
Sowing	Mark 4:14
Speech	John 8:43
Spirit	Matt. 26:41
	Mark 5:8
Statement	Matt. 5:37
Steadfastness	Matt. 10:22
Stealing	Matt. 19:18
Steward	Luke 12:42, 43
	Luke 16:1–8
Stewardship	Luke 19:13–27
Stomach	Matt. 15:17
Strife	Luke 22:24

Subject	*Reference*
Stubbornness	John 5:40
Stumbling block	Matt. 23:13
Submission	Matt. 26:39, 42
Suffering	Matt. 26:38
Supper, The Lord's	Luke 22:14–20
Swearing	Matt. 23:16–22
Talents	Matt. 18:24
Taxes	Matt. 22:19–21
Tax collectors	Matt. 5:46, 47
Teaching	Matt. 28:19, 20
	John 13:13–15
Temperance	Luke 21:34
Temptations	Matt. 4:1–11
	Luke 8:13
Thieves	Matt. 6:19
	John 10:1, 8
Timidness	Mark 4:40
Tithes	Luke 18:11, 12
Traditions	Mark 7:9, 13
Transgressions	Matt. 15:2
Treasures	Matt. 6:19–21
Tribulation	Matt. 24:9
	John 16:33
Truth	John 14:6
Unbelievers	Luke 12:46
Uncharitableness	John 7:24
Unchastity	Matt. 5:31, 32
Uncleanness	Matt. 23:27
Unity	John 17:20, 21
Unpardonable sin	Matt. 12:31, 32
Vengeance	Matt. 5:39, 40
Vine	John 15:1, 4, 5
Visions	Matt. 17:9
Walks of Life	John 12:35
	John 8:12
War	Matt. 24:26
Watchfulness	Matt. 24:42, 44
	Luke 12:37–40
Wedding	Luke 14:8–10
Widow	Mark 12:43, 44
Wine	Luke 5:37–39
Wisdom	Luke 21:15
Witness	John 8:14
Witness, false	Matt. 19:18
Witnessing	Acts 1:8
Wives	Luke 14:20, 26
Worker	Matt. 10:10
Worldliness	Luke 21:34
Worm	Mark 9:43–48
Worries of the world	Matt. 13:22
Worship	Matt. 4:10
Yoke	Matt. 11:28, 29
Zacchaeus	Luke 19:5
Zeal	John 2:17

THE PARABLES OF JESUS CHRIST

Parable	*Matthew*	*Mark*	*Luke*
1. Lamp Under a Basket	5:14–16	4:21, 22	8:16, 17 11:33–36
2. A Wise Man Builds on Rock and a Foolish Man Builds on Sand	7:24–27		6:47–49
3. Unshrunk (New) Cloth on an Old Garment	9:16	2:21	5:36
4. New Wine in Old Wineskins	9:17	2:22	5:37, 38
5. The Sower	13:3–23	4:2–20	8:4–15
6. The Tares (Weeds)	13:24–30		
7. The Mustard Seed	13:31, 32	4:30–32	13:18, 19
8. The Leaven	13:33		13:20, 21
9. The Hidden Treasure	13:44		
10. The Pearl of Great Price	13:45, 46		
11. The Dragnet	13:47–50		
12. The Lost Sheep	18:12–14		15:3–7
13. The Unforgiving Servant	18:23–35		
14. The Workers in the Vineyard	20:1–16		
15. The Two Sons	21:28–32		
16. The Wicked Vinedressers	21:33–45	12:1–12	20:9–19
17. The Wedding Feast	22:2–14		
18. The Fig Tree	24:32–44	13:28–32	21:29–33
19. The Wise and Foolish Virgins	25:1–13		
20. The Talents	25:14–30		
21. The Growing Seed		4:26–29	
22. The Absent Householder		13:33–37	
23. The Creditor and Two Debtors			7:41–43
24. The Good Samaritan			10:30–37
25. A Friend in Need			11:5–13
26. The Rich Fool			12:16–21
27. The Faithful Servant and the Evil Servant			12:35–40
28. Faithful and Wise Steward			12:42–48
29. The Barren Fig Tree			13:6–9
30. The Great Supper			14:16–24
31. Building a Tower and a King Making War			14:25–35
32. The Lost Coin			15:8–10
33. The Lost Son			15:11–32
34. The Unjust Steward			16:1–13
35. The Rich Man and Lazarus			16:19–31
36. Unprofitable Servants			17:7–10
37. The Persistent Widow			18:1–8
38. The Pharisee and the Tax Collector			18:9–14
39. The Minas (Pounds)			19:11–27

THE MIRACLES OF JESUS CHRIST

Miracle	*Matthew*	*Mark*	*Luke*	*John*
1. Cleansing a Leper	8:2	1:40	5:12	
2. Healing a Centurion's Servant (of paralysis)	8:5		7:1	
3. Healing Peter's Mother-in-law	8:14	1:30	4:38	
4. Healing the Sick at Evening	8:16	1:32	4:40	
5. Stilling the Storm	8:23	4:35	8:22	
6. Demons Entering a Herd of Swine	8:28	5:1	8:26	
7. Healing a Paralytic	9:2	2:3	5:18	
8. Raising the Ruler's Daughter	9:18, 23	5:22, 35	8:40, 49	
9. Healing the Hemorrhaging Woman	9:20	5:25	8:43	
10. Healing Two Blind Men	9:27			
11. Curing a Demon-possessed, Mute Man	9:32			
12. Healing a Man's Withered Hand	12:9	3:1	6:6	
13. Curing a Demon-possessed, Blind and Mute Man	12:22		11:14	
14. Feeding the Five Thousand	14:13	6:30	9:10	6:1
15. Walking on the Sea	14:25	6:48		6:19
16. Healing the Gentile Woman's Daughter	15:21	7:24		
17. Feeding the Four Thousand	15:32	8:1		
18. Healing the Epileptic Boy	17:14	9:17	9:38	
19. Temple Tax in the Fish's Mouth	17:24			
20. Healing Two Blind Men	20:30	10:46	18:35	
21. Withering the Fig Tree	21:18	11:12		
22. Casting Out an Unclean Spirit		1:23	4:33	
23. Healing a Deaf Mute		7:31		
24. Healing a Blind Paralytic at Bethsaida		8:22		
25. Escape from the Hostile Multitude			4:30	
26. Draught of Fish			5:1	
27. Raising of a Widow's Son at Nain			7:11	
28. Healing the Infirm, Bent Woman			13:11	
29. Healing the Man with Dropsy			14:1	
30. Cleansing the Ten Lepers			17:11	
31. Restoring a Servant's Ear			22:51	
32. Turning Water into Wine				2:1
33. Healing the Nobleman's Son (of fever)				4:46
34. Healing an Infirm Man at Bethesda				5:1
35. Healing the Man Born Blind				9:1
36. Raising of Lazarus				11:43
37. Second Draught of Fish				21:1

PROPHECIES OF THE MESSIAH FULFILLED IN JESUS CHRIST

Presented Here in Their Order of Fulfillment

PROPHETIC SCRIPTURE	SUBJECT	FULFILLED
Gen. 3:15 "And I will put enmity between you and the woman, and between your seed and her Seed; He shall bruise your head, and you shall bruise His heel."	**seed of a woman**	***Gal. 4:4*** "But when the fullness of the time had come, God sent forth His Son, born of a woman, born under the law,"
Gen. 12:3 "I will bless those who bless you, and I will curse him who curses you; And in you all the families of the earth shall be blessed."	**descendant of Abraham**	***Matt. 1:1*** "The book of the genealogy of Jesus Christ, the Son of David, the Son of Abraham:"
Gen. 17:19 "Then God said, 'No, Sarah your wife shall bear you a son, and you shall call his name Isaac; I will establish My covenant with him for an everlasting covenant, *and* with his descendants after him.'"	**descendant of Isaac**	***Luke 3:34*** "*the son* of Jacob, *the son* of Isaac, *the son* of Abraham, *the son* of Terah, *the son* of Nahor,"
Num. 24:17 "I see Him, but not now; I behold Him, but not near; a Star shall come out of Jacob; a Scepter shall rise out of Israel, and batter the brow of Moab, and destroy all the sons of tumult."	**descendant of Jacob**	***Matt. 1:2*** "Abraham begot Isaac, Isaac begot Jacob, and Jacob begot Judah and his brothers."
Gen. 49:10 "The scepter shall not depart from Judah, nor a lawgiver from between his feet, until Shiloh comes; and to Him *shall be* the obedience of the people."	**from the tribe of Judah**	***Luke 3:33*** "*the son* of Amminadab, *the son* of Ram, *the son* of Hezron, *the son* of Perez, *the son* of Judah."
Is. 9:7 "Of the increase of *His* government and peace *there will be* no end, upon the throne of David and over His kingdom, to order it and establish it with judgment and justice from that time forward, even forever. The zeal of the LORD of hosts will perform this."	**heir to the throne of David**	***Luke 1:32, 33*** "He will be great, and will be called the Son of the Highest; and the Lord God will give Him the throne of His father David. And He will reign over the house of Jacob forever, and of His kingdom there will be no end."
Ps. 45:6, 7; 102:25–27 "Your throne, O God, *is* forever and ever; a scepter of righteousness *is* the scepter of Your kingdom. You love righteousness and hate wickedness; therefore God, Your God, has anointed You with the oil of gladness more than Your companions." "Of old You laid the foundation of the earth, and the heavens *are* the work of Your hands. They will perish, but You will endure; yes, all of them will grow old like a garment; like a cloak You will change them, and they will be changed. But You *are* the same, and Your years will have no end."	**anointed and eternal**	***Heb. 1:8–12*** "But to the Son *He says*: '*Your throne, O God, is forever and ever; a scepter of righteousness is the scepter of Your kingdom. You have loved righteousness and hated lawlessness; therefore God, Your God, has anointed You with the oil of gladness more than Your companions*.' And: '*You*, LORD, *in the beginning laid the foundation of the earth, and the heavens are the work of Your hands; they will perish, but You remain; and they will all grow old like a garment; like a cloak You will fold them up, and they will be changed. But You are the same, and Your years will not fail*.'"

PROPHECIES OF THE MESSIAH

PROPHETIC SCRIPTURE	SUBJECT	FULFILLED
Mic. 5:2, "But you, Bethlehem, Ephrathah, *though* you are little among the thousands of Judah, *yet* out of you shall come forth to Me the One to be ruler in Israel, whose goings forth *have been* from of old, from everlasting."	**born in Bethlehem**	***Luke 2:4, 5, 7,*** "And Joseph also went up from Galilee, out of the city of Nazareth, into Judea, to the city of David, which is called Bethlehem, because he was of the house and lineage of David, to be registered with Mary, his betrothed wife, who was with child. . . . And she brought forth her firstborn Son, and wrapped Him in swaddling cloths, and laid Him in a manger, because there was no room for them in the inn."
Dan. 9:25, "Know therefore and understand, *that* from the going forth of the command to restore and build Jerusalem until Messiah the Prince, *there shall be* seven weeks and sixty-two weeks; the street shall be built again, and the wall, even in troublesome times."	**time for His birth**	***Luke 2:1, 2,*** "And it came to pass in those days *that* a decree went out from Caesar Augustus that all the world should be registered. This census first took place while Quirinius was governing Syria."
Is. 7:14, "Therefore the Lord Himself will give you a sign: Behold, the virgin shall conceive and bear a Son, and shall call His name Immanuel."	**to be born of a virgin**	***Luke 1:26, 27, 30, 31,*** "Now in the sixth month the angel Gabriel was sent by God to a city of Galilee named Nazareth, to a virgin betrothed to a man whose name was Joseph, of the house of David. The virgin's name *was* Mary. . . . Then the angel said to her, 'Do not be afraid, Mary, for you have found favor with God. And behold, you will conceive in your womb and bring forth a Son, and shall call His name JESUS.'"
Jer. 31:15, "Thus says the LORD: 'A voice was heard in Ramah, lamentation *and* bitter weeping, Rachel weeping for her children, refusing to be comforted for her children, because they *are* no more.'"	**slaughter of children**	***Matt. 2:16–18,*** "Then Herod, when he saw that he was deceived by the wise men, was exceedingly angry; and he sent forth and put to death all the male children who were in Bethlehem and in all its districts, from two years old and under, according to the time which he had determined from the wise men. Then was fulfilled what was spoken by Jeremiah the prophet, saying: *'A voice was heard in Ramah, lamentation, weeping, and great mourning, Rachel weeping for her children, refusing to be comforted, because they were no more.'*"
Hos. 11:1, "When Israel *was* a child, I loved him, and out of Egypt I called My son."	**flight to Egypt**	***Matt. 2:14, 15,*** "When he arose, he took the young Child and His mother by night and departed for Egypt, and was there until the death of Herod, that it might be fulfilled which was spoken by the Lord through the prophet, saying, *'Out of Egypt I called My Son.'*"
Is. 40:3–5, "The voice of one crying in the wilderness: 'Prepare the way of the LORD; make straight in the desert a highway for our God. Every valley shall be exalted, and every mountain and hill shall be made low; the crooked places shall be made straight, and the rough places smooth; the glory of the LORD shall be revealed, and all flesh shall see *it* together; for the mouth of the LORD has spoken.'"	**the way prepared**	***Luke 3:3–6, p.*** "And he went into all the region around the Jordan, preaching a baptism of repentance for the remission of sins, as it is written in the book of the words of Isaiah the prophet, saying: *'The voice of one crying in the wilderness: "Prepare the way of the LORD, make His paths straight. Every valley shall be filled and every mountain and hill brought low; and the crooked places shall be made straight and the rough ways made smooth; and all flesh shall see the salvation of God."'*"

PROPHETIC SCRIPTURE	SUBJECT	FULFILLED
Mal. 3:1, "'Behold, I send My messenger, and he will prepare the way before Me. And the Lord, whom you seek, will suddenly come to His temple, even the messenger of the covenant, in whom you delight. Behold, He is coming,' says the LORD of hosts."	**preceded by a forerunner**	***Luke 7:24, 27,*** "When the messengers of John had departed, He began to speak to the multitudes concerning John: 'What did you go out into the wilderness to see? A reed shaken by the wind? . . . This is *he* of whom it is written: *"Behold, I send My messenger before Your face, who will prepare Your way before You."'"*
Mal. 4:5, 6, "Behold I will send you Elijah the prophet before the coming of the great and dreadful day of the LORD. And he will turn the hearts of the fathers to the children, and the hearts of the children to their fathers, lest I come and strike the earth with a curse."	**preceded by Elijah**	***Matt. 11:13, 14,*** "For all the prophets and the law prophesied until John. And if you are willing to receive *it,* he is Elijah who is to come."
Ps. 2:7, "I will declare the decree: the LORD has said to Me, "You *are* My Son, today I have begotten You."	**declared the Son of God**	***Matt. 3:17,*** "And suddenly a voice *came* from heaven, saying, 'This is My beloved Son, in whom I am well pleased.'"
Is. 9:1, 2, "Nevertheless the gloom *will* not *be* upon her who *is* distressed, as when at first He lightly esteemed the land of Zebulun and the land of Naphtali, and afterward more heavily oppressed *her, by* the way of the sea, beyond the Jordan, in Galilee of the Gentiles. The people who walked in darkness have seen a great light; those who dwelt in the land of the shadow of death, upon them a light has shined."	**Galilean ministry**	***Matt. 4:13–16,*** "And leaving Nazareth, He came and dwelt in Capernaum, which is by the sea, in the regions of Zebulun and Naphtali, that it might be fulfilled which was spoken by Isaiah the prophet, saying: *'The land of Zebulun and the land of Naphtali, the way of the sea, beyond the Jordan, Galilee of the Gentiles: The people who sat in darkness saw a great light, and upon those who sat in the region and shadow of death light has dawned.'"*
Ps. 78:2–4, "I will open my mouth in a parable; I will utter dark sayings of old, which we have heard and known, and our fathers have told us. We will not hide *them* from their children, telling to the generation to come the praises of the LORD, and His strength and His wonderful works that He has done."	**speaks in parables**	***Matt. 13:34, 35,*** "All these things Jesus spoke to the multitude in parables; and without a parable He did not speak to them that it might be fulfilled which was spoken by the prophet, saying: *'I will open My mouth in parables; I will utter things which have been kept secret from the foundation of the world.'"*
Deut. 18:15, "The LORD your God will raise up for you a Prophet like me from your midst, from your brethren. Him you shall hear."	**a prophet**	***Acts 3:20, 22,*** "And that He may send Jesus Christ, who was preached to you before, . . . For Moses truly said to the fathers, *'The LORD your God will raise up for you a Prophet like me from your brethren. Him you shall hear in all things, whatever He says to you.'"*
Is. 61:1, 2, "The Spirit of the Lord GOD *is* upon Me, because the LORD has anointed Me to preach good tidings to the poor; He has sent Me to heal the brokenhearted, to proclaim liberty to the captives, and the opening of the prison to *those who are* bound; to proclaim the acceptable year of the LORD, and the day of vengeance of our God; to comfort all who mourn."	**to bind up the brokenhearted**	***Luke 4:18, 19,*** *"The Spirit of the LORD is upon Me, because He has anointed Me to preach the gospel to the poor. He has sent Me to heal the brokenhearted, to preach deliverance to the captives and recovery of sight to the blind, to set at liberty those who are oppressed, to preach the acceptable year of the LORD."*
Is. 53:3, "He is despised and rejected by men, a man of sorrows and acquainted with grief. And we hid, as it were, *our* faces from Him; He was despised, and we did not esteem Him."	**rejected by His own people, the Jews**	***John 1:11,*** "He came to His own, and His own did not receive Him." ***Luke 23:18,*** "And they all cried out at once, saying, 'Away with this *Man,* and release to us Barabbas'"—

PROPHETIC SCRIPTURE	SUBJECT	FULFILLED
Ps. 110:4, "The LORD has sworn and will not relent, 'You *are* a priest forever according to the order of Melchizedek.'"	**priest after order of Melchizedek**	***Heb. 5:5, 6,*** "So also Christ did not glorify Himself to become High Priest, *but it* was He who said to Him: *'You are My Son, today I have begotten You.'* As *He* also *says* in another *place: 'You are a priest forever according to the order of Melchizedek.'"*;
Zech. 9:9, "Rejoice greatly, O daughter of Zion! Shout, O daughter of Jerusalem! Behold, your King is coming to you; He *is* just and having salvation, lowly and riding on a donkey, a colt, the foal of a donkey."	**triumphal entry**	***Mark 11:7, 9, 11,*** "Then they brought the colt to Jesus and threw their garments on it, and He sat on it. . . . Then those who went before and those who followed cried out, saying: 'Hosanna! *Blessed is He who comes in the name of the LORD!'* . . . And Jesus went into Jerusalem and into the temple. So when He had looked around at all things, as the hour was already late, He went out to Bethany with the twelve."
Ps. 8:2, "Out of the mouth of babes and infants You have ordained strength, because of Your enemies, that You may silence the enemy and the avenger."	**adored by infants**	***Matt. 21:15, 16,*** "But when the chief priests and scribes saw the wonderful things that He did, and the children crying out in the temple and saying, 'Hosanna to the Son of David!' they were indignant and said to Him, 'Do You hear what these are saying?' And Jesus said to them, 'Yes. Have you never read, *"Out of the mouth of babes and nursing infants You have perfected praise"?'"*
Is. 53:1, "Who has believed our report? And to whom has the arm of the LORD been revealed?"	**not believed**	***John 12:37, 38,*** "But although He had done so many signs before them, they did not believe in Him, that the word of Isaiah the prophet might be fulfilled, which he spoke: *'Lord, who has believed our report? And to whom has the arm of the LORD been revealed?'"*
Ps. 41:9, "Even my own familiar friend in whom I trusted, who ate my bread, has lifted up *his* heel against me."	**betrayed by a close friend**	***Luke 22:47, 48,*** "And while He was still speaking, behold, a multitude; and he who was called Judas, one of the twelve, went before them and drew near to Jesus to kiss Him. But Jesus said to him, 'Judas, are you betraying the Son of Man with a kiss?'"
Zech. 11:12, "Then I said to them, 'If it is agreeable to you, give *me* my wages; and if not, refrain.' So they weighed out for my wages thirty *pieces* of silver."	**betrayed for thirty pieces of silver**	***Matt. 26:14, 15,*** "Then one of the twelve, called Judas Iscariot, went to the chief priests and said, 'What are you willing to give me if I deliver Him to you?' And they counted out to him thirty pieces of silver."
Ps. 35:11, "Fierce witnesses rise up; they ask me *things* that I do not know."	**accused by false witnesses**	***Mark 14:57, 58,*** "And some rose up and bore false witness against Him, saying, 'We heard Him say, "I will destroy this temple that *is* made with hands, and within three days I will build another made without hands."'"
Is. 53:7, "He was oppressed and He was afflicted, yet He opened not His mouth; He was led as a lamb to the slaughter, and as a sheep before its shearers is silent, so He opened not His mouth."	**silent to accusations**	***Mark 15:4, 5,*** "Then Pilate asked Him again, saying, 'Do You answer nothing? See how many things they testify against You!' But Jesus still answered nothing, so that Pilate marveled."

PROPHETIC SCRIPTURE	SUBJECT	FULFILLED
Is. 50:6, "I gave My back to those who struck *Me,* and My cheeks to those who plucked out the beard; I did not hide My face from shame and spitting."	**spat on and struck**	***Matt. 26:67,*** "Then they spat in His face and beat Him; and others struck *Him* with the palms of their hands,"
Ps. 35:19, "Let them not rejoice over me who are wrongfully my enemies; nor let them wink with the eye who hate me without a cause."	**hated without reason**	***John 15:24, 25,*** "If I had not done among them the works which no one else did, they would have no sin; but now they have seen and also hated both Me and My Father. But *this happened* that the word might be fulfilled which is written in their law, *'They hated Me without a cause.'*"
Is. 53:5, "But He *was* wounded for our transgressions, *He was* bruised for our iniquities; the chastisement for our peace *was* upon Him, and by His stripes we are healed."	**vicarious sacrifice**	***Rom. 5:6, 8,*** "For when we were still without strength, in due time Christ died for the ungodly. . . . But God demonstrates His own love toward us, in that while we were still sinners, Christ died for us."
Is. 53:12, "Therefore I will divide Him a portion with the great, and He shall divide the spoil with the strong, because He poured out His soul unto death, and He was numbered with the transgressors, and He bore the sin of many, and made intercession for the transgressors."	**crucified with malefactors**	***Mark 15:27, 28,*** "With Him they also crucified two robbers, one on His right and the other on His left. So the Scripture was fulfilled which says, *'And He was numbered with the transgressors.'*"
Zech. 12:10, "And I will pour on the house of David and on the inhabitants of Jerusalem the Spirit of grace and supplication; then they will look on Me whom they have pierced; they will mourn for Him as one mourns for *his* only *son,* and grieve for Him as one grieves for a firstborn."	**pierced through hands and feet**	***John 20:27,*** "Then He said to Thomas, 'Reach your finger here, and look at My hands; and reach your hand *here,* and put *it* into My side. Do not be unbelieving, but believing.'"
Ps. 22:7, 8, "All those who see Me laugh Me to scorn; they shoot out the lip, they shake the head, *saying,* 'He trusted in the LORD, let Him rescue Him; let Him deliver Him, since He delights in Him!'"	**sneered and mocked**	***Luke 23:35,*** "And the people stood looking on. But even the rulers with them sneered, saying, 'He saved others; let Him save Himself if He is the Christ, the chosen of God.'"
Ps. 69:9, "Because zeal for Your house has eaten me up, and the reproaches of those who reproach You have fallen on me."	**was reproached**	***Rom. 15:3,*** "For even Christ did not please Himself; but as it is written, *'The reproaches of those who reproached You fell on Me.'*"
Ps. 109:4, "In return for my love they are my accusers, but I *give myself to* prayer."	**prayer for His enemies**	***Luke 23:34,*** "Then Jesus said, 'Father, forgive them, for they do not know what they do.' And they divided His garments and cast lots."
Ps. 22:17, 18, "I can count all My bones. They look *and* stare at Me. They divide My garments among them, and for My clothing they cast lots."	**soldiers gambled for His clothing**	***Matt. 27:35, 36,*** "Then they crucified Him, and divided His garments, casting lots, that it might be fulfilled which was spoken by the prophet: *'They divided My garments among them, and for My clothing they cast lots.'* Sitting down, they kept watch over Him there."
Ps. 22:1, "My God, My God, why have You forsaken Me? *Why are You so* far from helping Me, *and from* the words of My groaning?"	**forsaken by God**	***Matt. 27:46,*** "And about the ninth hour Jesus cried out with a loud voice, saying, 'Eli, Eli, lama sabachthani?' that is, *'My God, My God, why have You forsaken Me?'*"

PROPHETIC SCRIPTURE	SUBJECT	FULFILLED
Ps. 34:20, "He guards all his bones; not one of them is broken."	**no bones broken**	***John 19:32, 33, 36,*** "Then the soldiers came and broke the legs of the first and of the other who was crucified with Him. But when they came to Jesus and saw that He was already dead, they did not break His legs. . . . For these things were done that the Scripture should be fulfilled, *'Not one of His bones shall be broken.'*"
Zech. 12:10, "And I will pour on the house of David and on the inhabitants of Jerusalem the Spirit of grace and supplication; then they will look on Me whom they have pierced; they will mourn for Him as one mourns for *his* only *son,* and grieve for Him as one grieves for a firstborn."	**His side pierced**	***John 19:34,*** "But one of the soldiers pierced His side with a spear, and immediately blood and water came out."
Is. 53:9, "And they made His grave with the wicked—but with the rich at His death, because He had done no violence, nor *was any* deceit in His mouth."	**buried with the rich**	***Matt. 27:57–60,*** "Now when evening had come, there came a rich man from Arimathea, named Joseph, who himself had also become a disciple of Jesus. This man went to Pilate and asked for the body of Jesus. Then Pilate commanded the body to be given to him. And when Joseph had taken the body, he wrapped it in a clean linen cloth, and laid it in his new tomb which he had hewn out of the rock; and he rolled a large stone against the door of the tomb, and departed."
Ps. 16:10, "For You will not leave my soul in Sheol, nor will You allow Your Holy One to see corruption." ***Ps. 49:15,*** "But God will redeem my soul from the power of the grave, for He shall receive me. Selah"	**to be resurrected**	***Mark 16:6, 7,*** "But he said to them, 'Do not be alarmed. You seek Jesus of Nazareth, who was crucified. He is risen! He is not here. See the place where they laid Him. But go *and* tell His disciples—and Peter—that He is going before you into Galilee; there you will see Him, as He said to you.'"
Ps. 68:18, "You have ascended on high, You have led captivity captive; You have received gifts among men; even *among* the rebellious, that the LORD God might dwell *there.*"	**His ascension to God's right hand**	***Mark 16:19,*** "So then after the Lord had spoken to them, He was received up into heaven, and sat down at the right hand of God." ***1 Cor. 15:4,*** "And that He was buried, and that He rose again the third day according to the Scriptures." ***Eph. 4:8,*** "Therefore He says: *'When He ascended on high, He led captivity captive, and gave gifts to men.'*"

THE LAWS OF THE BIBLE

I. FORMS OF GOVERNMENT

A. *Patriarchal.* The family being the unit of life, the father as head of the family was the authoritative ruler . . . . Judg. 11:29–40
Job 1:5

B. *Theocracy.* God was the direct ruler of His people . . . . Ex. 19:3–8

C. *Government by judges.* The people forgot God. God chastised them by selling them into slavery to their enemies. Upon repentance God raised up military chieftains as deliverers . . . . Judg. 2:13–18

D. *Monarchy.* This was begun by the coronation of Saul, reached its height in David and Solomon, and ended with the Babylonian captivity . . . . 1 Sam. 10:24

II. CITIZENSHIP UNDER THE THEOCRACY

A. *Israelites.* Those of Israel who ratified the covenant of Sinai, and later their children, were entitled to the rights of citizenship . . . . Ex. 19:5–8
Deut. 6:1–9

B. ***Moabites and Ammonites excluded*** . . . . Deut. 23:3

C. ***Edomites and Egyptians in the third generation were eligible*** . . . . Deut. 23:7, 8

III. LAWS OF THE THEOCRACY

A. *Pertaining to citizenship*

1. Law applied equally to strangers as to natives . . . . Lev. 24:22
Num. 15:22–30
2. Jew not to marry a stranger . . . . Gen. 34:14
3. Strangers could own slaves . . . . Lev. 25:47–55

B. *Pertaining to slavery*

1. Slaves obtained
   a. Captured in war . . . . Num. 31:7–11
   b. Inherited . . . . Lev. 25:46
   c. Bought . . . . Ex. 21:2
   d. Sold for debt or theft . . Ex. 22:3
   Deut. 15:12
2. How to treat slaves
   a. Israelites could be redeemed from slavery . . . . Lev. 25:47–55
   b. Jewish slaves to be set free in Year of Jubilee . . . . . . Lev. 25:39–41
   c. Regarded as part of owner's household and possession . . . . Gen. 12:16
   Ex. 20:17
   d. Could be struck by master . . . . Ex. 21:20, 21
   e. Fugitive not to be returned . . . . Deut. 23:15, 16
   1 Sam. 30:15
   f. Freed if ill-treated . . . Ex. 21:26, 27
   g. To enjoy the Sabbath . . . . Ex. 20:10

C. *Pertaining to taxation*

1. Census taken . . . . Luke 2:1–3
2. Purpose of taxes
   a. Valuation of persons . . Lev. 27:1–13
   b. Temple service . . . . Ex. 30:11–16
   2 Chr. 24:6, 9
   c. Taxes . . . . Matt. 22:15–21
   Rom. 13:6, 7
3. Amount of taxes . . . . . . 1 Sam. 8:10–18
4. Priests and attendants exempt . . . . Ezra 7:24

D. *Military laws*

1. Age of soldiers . . . . Num. 1:2, 3; 26:2
2. Selective draft . . . . Num. 31:3–7
3. Exemption from service
   a. Levites . . . . Num. 1:49
   b. Certain individuals . . . Deut. 20:5–7
   c. Fainthearted . . . . Deut. 20:8
4. Cleanliness in camp . . Num. 31:19, 20
Deut. 23:9–14
5. Regulations in battle
   a. Notice to be given Deut. 20:10, 11
   b. Fruit trees spared Deut. 20:19, 20
   c. Treatment of captives . . . . Num. 21:2, 3, 35; 31:17, 18
   Deut. 20:14–18
   Josh. 11:14
   d. Plunder . . . . Deut. 20:14
   e. Indemnity . . . . 2 Kin. 3:4

IV. CRIMINAL LAWS

A. *Crimes against the public*

1. Bribery .... Ex. 23:8; Deut. 16:19; Prov. 17:23
2. Contempt for the law — Num. 15:30; Deut. 6:16, 17
   Penalty .... Deut. 17:12, 13
3. Perjury .... Ex. 20:16; Lev. 19:12
   Penalty .... Deut. 19:16–20
4. Perverting or obstructing justice .... Ex. 23:1, 2, 6; Lev. 19:15; Ps. 82:2
   Penalty .... Deut. 16:19, 20
5. Conspiracy .... 2 Sam. 15:10–12

B. *Crimes of immoral acts*

1. Adultery .... Ex. 20:14; Deut. 5:18
   Penalty .... Lev. 20:10; Deut. 22:22–25
2. Rape .... Deut. 22:25, 26
   Penalty .... Deut. 22:25–29
3. Prostitution .... Deut. 23:17
   Penalty .... Lev. 19:29; 21:9
4. Seduction .... Ex. 22:16, 17
   Penalty .... Deut. 22:28, 29
5. Incest .... Lev. 18:6–18; Deut. 22:30
   Penalty .... Lev. 20:11–21
6. Sodomy .... Lev. 18:22, 23; Deut. 23:17
   Penalty .... Ex. 22:19; Lev. 20:13, 15, 16

C. *Crimes against persons*

1. Murder .... Ex. 20:13
   Penalty .... Gen. 9:6; Ex. 21:12
2. Manslaughter .... Ex. 21:12–14; Josh. 20:3–6
   Penalty .... Num. 35:11, 22–28
3. Assault .... Ex. 21:18–26
   Penalty .... Ex. 21:19–27; Lev. 24:19, 20
4. Kidnapping .... Ex. 21:16; Deut. 24:7
5. Slander .... Lev. 19:16

D. *Crimes against property*

1. Stealing .... Ex. 20:15; 22:1–12; Deut. 23:24, 25
2. Arson .... Ex. 22:6
3. Moving a landmark ...... Deut. 19:14

V. LAWS PERTAINING TO DOMESTIC RELATIONS

A. *Marriage*

1. Ordained by God ...... Gen. 1:27, 28; 2:18, 24
2. Within the tribe .... Num. 36:6
3. Polygamy forbidden .... 1 Cor. 7:2; 1 Tim. 3:2
4. Marriage forbidden with:
   a. Stepmother .... Lev. 18:8; 20:11
   b. Aliens .... Ex. 34:13–17; Deut. 7:1–3
   c. Sister .... Lev. 20:17
   d. Aunt .... Lev. 20:19
   e. Grandchild .... Lev. 18:10
   f. Daughter-in-law .... Lev. 18:15
5. Divorce .... Lev. 21:7; 22:13; Is. 50:1; 1 Cor. 7:10, 11
   a. Not to remarry woman divorced by another man ...... Deut. 24:1–4
   b. For committing adultery .... Jer. 3:8; Matt. 19:3–9; Mark 10:2–12; Luke 16:8

B. *Parent and child*

1. Father has authority over child .... Num. 30:3–5
2. Father to arrange marriage .... Gen. 24:2–4
3. Parents to educate .... Deut. 21:18–21; Prov. 22:6; Eph. 6:4
4. Parents to discipline .. Deut. 21:18–21; Prov. 22:15
5. Children to honor parents .. Ex. 20:12; 21:15
6. Children to be regarded as gift of God .... Gen. 33:5; 48:9; Josh. 24:3
7. Penalty for children who dishonor parents .... Lev. 20:9; Deut. 21:18–21

VI. ESTATES—DESCENT AND DISTRIBUTION LAWS

A. *Inheritance*

1. Sons inherit father's estate .... Gen. 21:10–13; 1 Chr. 5:1
2. Double portion to firstborn .... Deut. 21:15–17
3. Wife not heir, but descends with property to next of kin ... Ruth 4:1–12
4. Daughters heirs when no sons .... Num. 27:8, 9
5. When no sons or daughters, inheritance to nearest relative Num. 27:9–11

B. *Real property—titles*

1. Real estate
   - a. Land divided among tribes .... Num. 26:52–56; Josh. 14:5
   - b. Not transferable ..... Num. 36:6–9
   - c. Not permanently sold .... Lev. 25:23–28
   - d. Value of land according to years after Jubilee .... Lev. 25:15, 16
   - e. Release of land .... Lev. 25:8–34
   - f. Mode of transfer
     - (1) Deed made .... Jer. 32:9–14
     - (2) Taking off sandal ... Ruth 4:3–11
     - (3) Deed delivered in presence of witnesses ...... Jer. 32:10, 12
     - (4) Deed recorded ...... Jer. 32:14
2. Personal property (All property which is moveable, as against real property such as houses and lands)
   - a. Sale recognized .... Lev. 25:14
   - b. Pledges of:
     - (1) Children given as .. 2 Kin. 4:1–7
     - (2) Upper and lower millstone prohibited .... Deut. 24:6
     - (3) Not retained overnight .... Ex. 22:26, 27; Deut. 24:13
     - (4) Voluntary ...... Deut. 24:10, 11

VII. SOCIAL SECURITY AND WELFARE LAWS

A. *Widows and orphans* .... Ex. 22:22, 23; Deut. 14:28, 29; Acts 6:1–4; 1 Tim. 5:3–16

1. Widow to marry nearest relative .... Deut. 25:5–10
2. Widow and orphans not to be oppressed .... Zech. 7:9–12; Mal. 3:5

B. *Neighbors* .... Lev. 19:13

C. *The poor* .... Ex. 22:25–27; Lev. 19:9, 10; Deut. 15:7–11; Luke 3:11; 14:13, 14

D. *Strangers or aliens* ...... Lev. 19:33, 34; Deut. 24:19–22; Zech. 7:9–12

E. *Poor and needy* .... Deut. 24:14, 15

F. *Servants* .... Deut. 24:14, 15

G. *Handicapped*

1. Blind .... Lev. 19:14; Deut. 27:18; Luke 14:13, 14
2. Deaf .... Lev. 19:14
3. Lame .... Luke 14:12–14

VIII. LAWS PERTAINING TO CONTRACTS

A. *Debts* .... Ex. 22:25; Deut. 15:1–3; Neh. 5:10, 11

B. *With neighbors* .... Deut. 15:1–3

C. *With foreigners* .... Deut. 15:1–3

D. *Interest* .... Ex. 22:25; Lev. 25:35–37; Deut. 23:19, 20; Ezek. 18:10–13

E. *Loans* .... Ex. 22:25; Deut. 23:19, 20; 2 Kin. 4:1–7; Neh. 5:2–5

F. *Mortgages* .... Neh. 5:2–5

G. *Pledges* (See VI. B. 2)

H. *Sales* .... Lev. 25:14

I. *Sales of land* .... Lev. 25:23–28; Ruth 4:3–11; Jer. 32:9–14

J. *Of servitude* .... Ex. 21:2–4; Deut. 15:12

K. *Sureties* .... Prov. 6:1, 2; 17:18

IX. RELIGIOUS LAWS

A. *Clean and unclean meat* . . . Lev. 11:2–31
Deut. 14:3–21

B. *Forbidden foods*
1. Fat and blood . . . . Lev. 17:10–14
2. Flesh torn by beasts . . . . Ex. 22:31
3. Fruit of young trees . . . . Lev. 19:23–25

C. *Sacred obligations*
1. Firstborn . . . . Ex. 34:19, 20
2. Firstfruits . . . . Ex. 34:26
Deut. 18:4
3. Tithes . . . . Gen. 14:19, 20
Lev. 27:30–33
2 Chr. 31:4–12
Mal. 3:8–11
Matt. 23:23
4. Atonement money . . . . . . Ex. 30:12–16
5. Freewill offering . . . . Lev. 22:17–20
Num. 15:1–4

D. *Sacred calendar*
1. Sabbath . . . . Gen. 2:1–3
Ex. 16:23
Lev. 23:3
Num. 28:9, 10
Deut. 5:12–15
Neh. 10:31
Ezek. 46:3
   a. Punishment for not keeping . . . . Num. 15:32–36
   b. Made for man . . . . Mark 2:23–28
   c. Healing on the Sabbath . . . . Luke 13:14–17; 14:3–5
John 5:8–16
2. Passover . . . . Ex. 12:1–14
Deut. 16:1–8
Ezek. 45:21, 24
Luke 22:7–18
3. Feast of Unleavened Bread . . Ex. 34:18
4. Feast of Weeks . . . . Deut. 16:9–11
5. Feast of Tabernacles . . Lev. 23:33–44
Num. 29:12–40
Deut. 16:13–17
6. Sabbatical (seventh) Year . . . . Ex. 21:2–6; 23:10, 11
Lev. 25:1–7
Deut. 15:1–14
2 Chr. 36:21
Neh. 10:31
7. Day of Atonement . . . . . Lev. 23:26–32

E. *Crimes against God*
1. Worship of false gods . . . . . . Ex. 20:1–5
Penalty . . . . Ex. 22:20
2. Spiritualism . . . . Lev. 20:27
Penalty . . . . Ex. 22:18
3. Blasphemy . . . . Lev. 24:16
Deut. 5:11
Penalty . . . . Lev. 24:16

X. LAWS PERTAINING TO LEGAL PROCEDURE

A. *Judges appointed* . . . . Ex. 18:13–26
2 Chr. 19:4–11
1. Moses, first judge . . . . . . Ex. 18:13–27
2. Priests judge in small matters . . . . Ex. 18:22
3. King as judge . . . . 1 Kin. 7:1–7

B. *Submission of cases*
1. Ordinary cases submitted to judges . . . . Deut. 25:1, 2
2. Exceptional cases taken to Levitical priest for verdict . . . . . . Deut. 17:8–11
3. Extreme cases submitted to the LORD for decision . . . . . Num. 5:11–31
Deut. 21:1–9
4. Judges must not pervert justice . . . . Ex. 23:6–8
5. Bribery forbidden . . . . . Deut. 16:18–20

C. *Where courts were held*
1. At gate of city . . . . Deut. 21:19
2. In Hall of Judgment . . . . 1 Kin. 7:7

D. *Judgments*
1. Regarded as from God . . . . Deut. 1:17
2. Righteous to be justified and wicked condemned . . . . Deut. 25:1
3. Sentence to be executed Deut. 25:2, 3

E. *Appeals*
1. To Moses . . . . Ex. 18:26
2. To priests . . . . Deut. 17:8–11
3. To the king . . . . 1 Kin. 3:16–27

F. *Damages*
1. For disfiguring a person Lev. 24:19, 20
2. For stealing . . . . Ex. 22:4, 5
3. Kindling a fire which destroys property . . . . Ex. 22:6
4. Breach of trust . . . . Lev. 6:1–5
5. Killing an animal . . . . . . Ex. 21:35, 36
Lev. 24:18, 21

6. Loss of animal falling into pit . . . . Ex. 21:33, 34
7. Loss of borrowed property . . Ex. 22:14

G. *Methods of punishment*

1. Infliction in kind . . . . Gen. 9:6 Lev. 24:19, 20
2. Burning . . . . Lev. 20:14
3. Mutilation . . . . Deut. 25:11, 12
4. Hanging . . . . Deut. 21:22, 23
5. Stoning . . . . Lev. 24:16
6. Beating . . . . Deut. 25:2, 3
7. Excommunication . . . . Ezra 10:8
8. Imprisonment . . . . Ezra 7:26
9. Compensation for damages . . . . Ex. 21:19, 32, 36
10. Restitution for stolen or borrowed property . . . . Ex. 22:12, 14, 15

H. *Method of protection*

1. Cities of refuge appointed . . . . Num. 35:6–15
2. Protection till trial could be held . . . . Num. 35:12
3. Murderer unprotected Num. 35:30, 31
4. Unintentional manslayer remained in city of refuge till death of high priest . . . . Josh. 20:1–6

XI. TORT LAWS

A. *Assault* . . . . Ex. 21:18, 19
B. *Compensation* . . . . Ex. 21:18, 19, 32
C. *Damage by animals* . . . . Ex. 21:32
D. *Damage by fire* . . . . Ex. 22:6
E. *Injury to animals* . . . . Ex. 21:33–36 Lev. 24:18, 21
F. *Loss of borrowed property* Ex. 22:14, 15
G. *Personal injury* . . . . Lev. 24:19, 20
H. *Rights of strangers* . . . . Lev. 24:22

XII. LAWS OF SANITATION AND CLEANLINESS

A. *Cleansing of the woman after childbirth* . . . . Lev. 12:1–8
B. *Test for leprosy* . . . . Lev. 13:1–59
C. *Cleansing of the leper's house* . . . . Lev. 14:33–57
D. *Cleansing of males with discharge* . . . . Lev. 15:1–15
E. *Laws concerning the woman during menstruation* . . . . Lev. 15:24–33

XIII. LAWS PERTAINING TO ANIMALS

A. *Beasts of burden* . . . . Ex. 23:12 Deut. 25:4
B. *Beasts of the field* . . . . Ex. 23:11
C. *Mother and young* . . . . Lev. 22:28 Deut. 22:6, 7
D. *Enemy's animals* . . . . Ex. 23:4, 5 Deut. 22:4

XIV. LAWS CONCERNING INTEREST AND LOANS

Interest on money was called usury in biblical times. (Now usury means excess interest.)

A. *Taking of interest forbidden among Jews* . . . . Ex. 22:25 Deut. 23:19, 20

The money was borrowed for relief of distress.

B. *Allowed to be taken from foreigners* . . . . Deut. 23:20

Money was borrowed by foreigner to develop trade.

C. *Property returned without interest* . . . . Neh. 5:11–13
D. *Differing weights and measures forbidden* . . . . Deut. 25:13–16

Old Testament Chronology

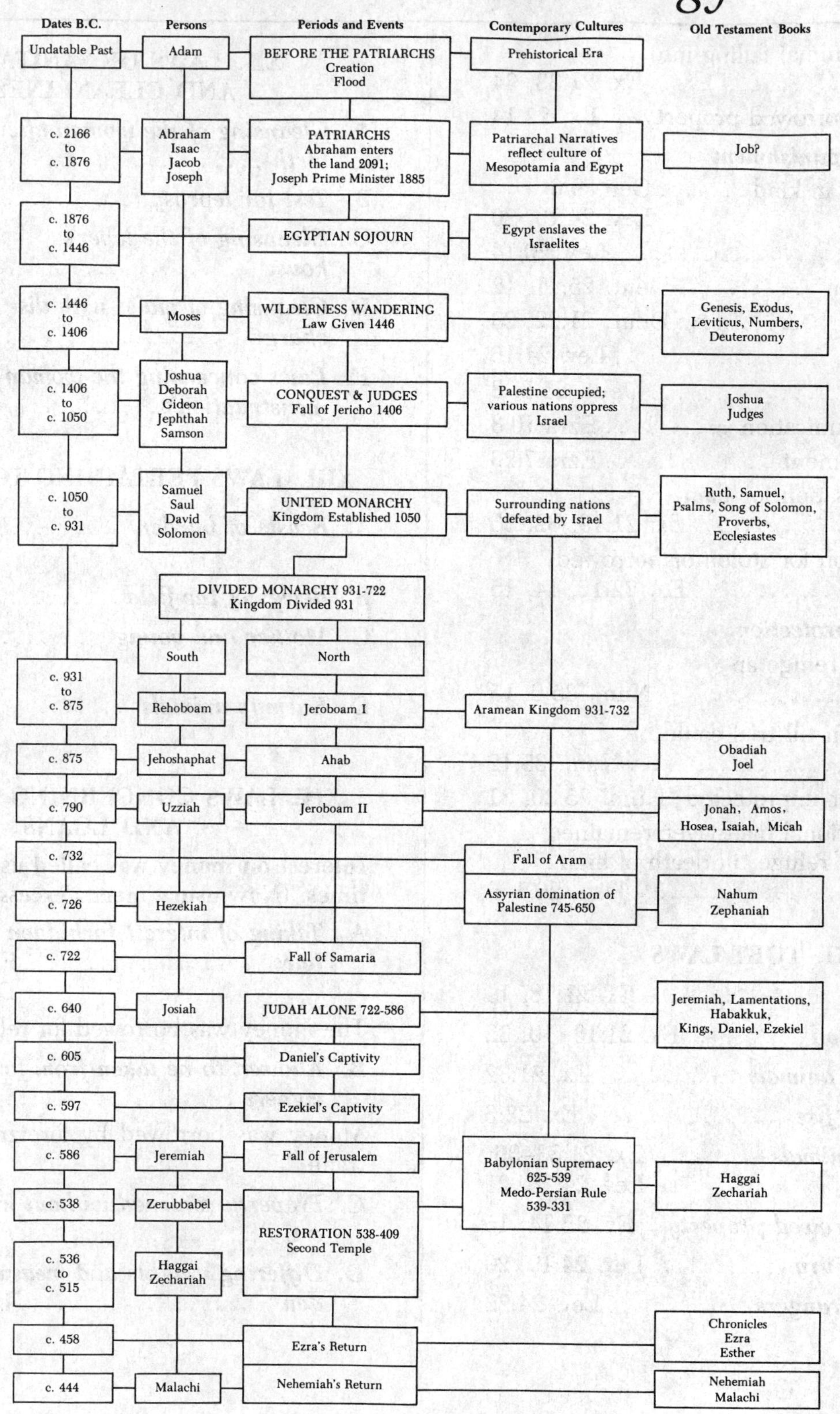

Dates B.C.
Persons
Periods and Events
Contemporary Cultures
Old Testament Books
Undatable Past
Adam
BEFORE THE PATRIARCHS
Creation
Flood
Prehistorical Era
c. 2166
to
c. 1876
Abraham
Isaac
Jacob
Joseph
PATRIARCHS
Abraham enters
the land 2091;
Joseph Prime Minister 1885
Patriarchal Narratives
reflect culture of
Mesopotamia and Egypt
Job?
c. 1876
to
c. 1446
EGYPTIAN SOJOURN
Egypt enslaves the
Israelites
c. 1446
to
c. 1406
Moses
WILDERNESS WANDERING
Law Given 1446
Genesis, Exodus,
Leviticus, Numbers,
Deuteronomy
c. 1406
to
c. 1050
Joshua
Deborah
Gideon
Jephthah
Samson
CONQUEST & JUDGES
Fall of Jericho 1406
Palestine occupied;
various nations oppress
Israel
Joshua
Judges
c. 1050
to
c. 931
Samuel
Saul
David
Solomon
UNITED MONARCHY
Kingdom Established 1050
Surrounding nations
defeated by Israel
Ruth, Samuel,
Psalms, Song of Solomon,
Proverbs,
Ecclesiastes
DIVIDED MONARCHY 931-722
Kingdom Divided 931
South
North
c. 931
to
c. 875
Rehoboam
Jeroboam I
Aramean Kingdom 931-732
c. 875
Jehoshaphat
Ahab
Obadiah
Joel
c. 790
Uzziah
Jeroboam II
Jonah, Amos,
Hosea, Isaiah, Micah
c. 732
Fall of Aram
c. 726
Hezekiah
Assyrian domination of
Palestine 745-650
Nahum
Zephaniah
c. 722
Fall of Samaria
c. 640
Josiah
JUDAH ALONE 722-586
Jeremiah, Lamentations,
Habakkuk,
Kings, Daniel, Ezekiel
c. 605
Daniel's Captivity
c. 597
Ezekiel's Captivity
c. 586
Jeremiah
Fall of Jerusalem
Babylonian Supremacy
625-539
Medo-Persian Rule
539-331
Haggai
Zechariah
c. 538
Zerubbabel
RESTORATION 538-409
Second Temple
c. 536
to
c. 515
Haggai
Zechariah
c. 458
Ezra's Return
Chronicles
Ezra
Esther
c. 444
Malachi
Nehemiah's Return
Nehemiah
Malachi

PRAYERS OF THE BIBLE

Subject	Reference
Abijah's army—for victory	2 Chr. 13:14
Abraham—for a son	Gen. 15:1–6
Abraham—for Ishmael	Gen. 17:18–21
Abraham—for Sodom	Gen. 18:20–32
Abraham—for Abimelech	Gen. 20:17
Abraham's servant—for guidance	Gen. 24:12–52
Asa—for victory	2 Chr. 14:11
Cain—for mercy	Gen. 4:13–15
Centurion—for his servant	Matt. 8:5–13
Christians—for Peter	Acts 12:5–12
Christians—for kings in authority	1 Tim. 2:1, 2
Corinthians—for Paul	2 Cor. 1:9–11
Cornelius—for enlightenment	Acts 10:1–33
Criminal—for salvation	Luke 23:42, 43
Daniel—for the Jews	Dan. 9:3–19
Daniel—for knowledge	Dan. 2:17–23
David—for blessing	2 Sam. 7:18–29
David—for help	1 Sam. 23:10–13
David—for guidance	2 Sam. 2:1
David—for grace	Ps. 25:16
David—for justice	Ps. 9:17–20
Disciples—for boldness	Acts 4:24–31
Elijah—for drought and rain	James 5:17, 18
Elijah—for the raising to life of the widow's son	1 Kin. 17:20–23
Elijah—for triumph over Baal	1 Kin. 18:36–38
Elijah—for death	1 Kin. 19:4
Elisha—for blindness and sight	2 Kin. 6:17–23
Ezekiel—for undefilement	Ezek. 4:12–15
Ezra—for the sins of the people	Ezra 9:6–15
Gideon—for proof of his call	Judg. 6:36–40
Habakkuk—for deliverance	Hab. 3:1–19
Habakkuk—for justice	Hab. 1:1–4
Hagar—for consolation	Gen. 21:14–20
Hannah—for a son	1 Sam. 1:10–17
Hezekiah—for deliverance	2 Kin. 19:15–19
Hezekiah—for health	2 Kin. 20:1–11
Holy Spirit—for Christians	Rom. 8:26, 27
Isaac—for children	Gen. 25:21, 24–26
Israelites—for deliverance	Ex. 2:23–25 Ex. 3:7–10
Jabez—for prosperity	1 Chr. 4:10
Jacob—all night	Gen. 32:24–30
Jacob—for deliverance from Esau	Gen. 32:9–12
Jehoahaz—for victory	2 Kin. 13:1–5
Jehoshaphat—for protection	2 Chr. 20:5–12, 27
Jehoshaphat—for victory	2 Chr. 18:31
Jeremiah—for Judah	Jer. 42:1–6
Jeremiah—for mercy	Jer. 14:7–10
Jesus—Lord's Prayer	Matt. 6:9–13
Jesus—praise for revelation to babes	Matt. 11:25, 26
Jesus—at Lazarus' tomb	John 11:41, 42
Jesus—for the Father's glory	John 12:28
Jesus—for the Church	John 17:1–26
Jesus—for deliverance	Matt. 26:39, 42, 44 Matt. 27:46
Jesus—for forgiveness for others	Luke 23:34
Jesus—in submission	Luke 23:46
Jews—for safe journey	Ezra 8:21, 23
Jonah—for deliverance from the fish	Jon. 2:1–10
Joshua—for help and mercy	Josh. 7:6–9
Leper—for healing	Matt. 8:2, 3
Manasseh—for deliverance	2 Chr. 33:12, 13
Manoah—for guidance	Judg. 13:8–15
Moses—for Pharaoh	Ex. 8:9–13
Moses—for water	Ex. 15:24, 25
Moses—for Israel	Ex. 32:31–35
Moses—for Miriam	Num. 12:11–14
Moses—that he might see the Promised Land	Deut. 3:23–25 Deut. 34:1–4
Moses—for a successor	Num. 27:15–17
Nehemiah—for the Jews	Neh. 1:4–11
Paul—for the healing of Publius' father	Acts 28:8
Paul—for the Ephesians	Eph. 3:14–21
Paul—for grace	2 Cor. 12:8, 9
People of Judah—for a covenant	2 Chr. 15:12–15
Peter—for the raising of Dorcas	Acts 9:40
Priests—for blessing	2 Chr. 30:27
Rebekah—for understanding	Gen. 25:22, 23
Reubenites—for victory	1 Chr. 5:18–20
Samson—for water	Judg. 15:18, 19
Samson—for strength	Judg. 16:29, 30
Samuel—for Israel	1 Sam. 7:5–12
Solomon—for wisdom	1 Kin. 3:6–14
Tax collector—for mercy	Luke 18:13
Zechariah—for a son	Luke 1:13

The Jewish Calendar

The Jews used two kinds of calendars:
Civil Calendar—official calendar of kings, childbirth, and contracts.
Sacred Calendar—from which festivals were computed.

NAMES OF MONTHS	CORRESPONDS WITH	NO. OF DAYS	MONTH OF CIVIL YEAR	MONTH OF SACRED YEAR
TISHRI	Sept.–Oct.	30 days	1st	7th
HESHVAN	Oct.–Nov.	29 or 30	2nd	8th
CHISLEV	Nov.–Dec.	29 or 30	3rd	9th
TEBETH	Dec.–Jan.	29	4th	10th
SHEBAT	Jan.–Feb.	30	5th	11th
ADAR	Feb.–Mar.	29 or 30	6th	12th
NISAN	Mar.–Apr.	30	7th	1st
IYAR	Apr.–May	29	8th	2nd
SIVAN	May–June	30	9th	3rd
TAMMUZ	June–July	29	10th	4th
AB	July–Aug.	30	11th	5th
***ELUL**	Aug.–Sept.	29	12th	6th

The Jewish day was from sunset to sunset, in 8 equal parts:

FIRST WATCH ..... SUNSET TO 9 P.M.
SECOND WATCH ... 9 P.M. TO MIDNIGHT
THIRD WATCH ..... MIDNIGHT TO 3 A.M.
FOURTH WATCH ... 3 A.M. TO SUNRISE

FIRST WATCH ..... SUNRISE TO 9 A.M.
SECOND WATCH ... 9 A.M. TO NOON
THIRD WATCH ..... NOON TO 3 P.M.
FOURTH WATCH ... 3 P.M. TO SUNSET

*Hebrew months were alternately 30 and 29 days long. Their year, shorter than ours, had 354 days. Therefore, about every 3 years (7 times in 19 years) an extra 29-day-month, VEADAR, was added between ADAR and NISAN.

Jewish Feasts

Feast of	Month on Jewish Calendar	Day	Corresponding Month	References
*Passover (Unleavened Bread)	Nisan	14–21	Mar.–Apr.	Ex. 12:43—13:10; Matt. 26:17–20
*Pentecost (Firstfruits or Weeks)	Sivan	6 (50 days after Passover)	May–June	Deut. 16:9–12; Acts 2:1
Trumpets, *Rosh Hashanah*	Tishri	1, 2	Sept.–Oct.	Num. 29:1–6
Day of Atonement, *Yom Kippur*	Tishri	10	Sept.–Oct.	Lev. 23:26–32; Heb. 9:7
*Tabernacles (Booths or Ingathering)	Tishri	15–22	Sept.–Oct.	Neh. 8:13–18; John 7:2
Dedication (Lights), *Hanukkah*	Chislev	25 (8 days)	Nov.–Dec.	John 10:22
Purim (Lots)	Adar	14, 15	Feb.–Mar.	Esth. 9:18–32

*The three major feasts for which all males of Israel were required to travel to the Temple in Jerusalem (Ex. 23:14–19).

Monies and Weights

All values are approximate and are based upon a standard of $1,000 per troy ounce of gold and $20 per troy ounce of silver.

	Talent	*Mina*	*Shekel*	*Gerah*
Talent	91 lb. (troy) silver $21,840 gold $1,092,000			
Mina	60 minas	18.2 oz. (troy) silver $364 gold $18,200		
Shekel	3,000 shekels	50 shekels	.364 oz. (troy) silver $7.28 gold $364	
Gerah	60,000 gerahs	1,000 gerahs	20 gerahs	.0182 oz. (troy) silver $.36 gold $18.20

Drachma—.27 oz. (troy) gold $270; Bekah—.182 oz. (troy) silver $3.64

Conversion to current value—divide 1000 and 20 respectively into the current values of gold and silver. Multiply these factors with the corresponding values found in this chart and in the text.

New Testament Monies

	Denarius	*Copper Coin*	*Quadrans (penny)*	*Mite*
Denarius	1 day's wages			
Copper Coin	16 copper coins	1/16 day's wages		
Quadrans (penny)	64 pennies	4 pennies	1/64 day's wages	
Mite	128 mites	8 mites	2 mites	1/128 day's wages

Temple tax—2 days' wages

Measures of Length

	Rod (reed)	*Pace*	*Cubit*	*Span*	*Handbreadth*	*Finger*
Rod (reed)	9 ft. (Ezek. 10.5 ft.)					
Pace	3 paces	3 ft.				
Cubit	6 cubits	2 cubits	1.5 ft. (Ezek. 18 in.)			
Span	12 spans	4 spans	2 spans	9 in.		
Hand-breadth	36 hand-breadths	12 hand-breadths	6 hand-breadths	3 hand-breadths	3 in.	
Finger	144 fingers	48 fingers	24 fingers	12 fingers	4 fingers	.75 in.

A day's journey—20 mi.; a sabbath day's journey—3,637 ft.; some distance (a little way)—5 mi.; mile (Roman)—4,854 ft.; stadion (furlong)—606 ft.; fathom—6 ft.

Dry Measures

	Homer	*Seah*	*Ephah*	*Omer*
Homer (kor, measure)	6.524 bu.			
Seah (measure)	3 seahs	2.175 bu.		
Ephah	10 ephahs	3.33 ephahs	.652 bu.	
Omer (sheaf)	100 omers	33.33 omers	10 omers	2.087 qt.

Basket—1 peck

Liquid Measures

	Kor	*Bath*	*Hin*	*Kab*	*Log*
Kor	60 gal.				
Bath (measure)	10 baths	6 gal.			
Hin	60 hins	6 hins	1 gal.		
Kab	120 kabs	12 kabs	2 kabs	2 qt.	
Log	480 logs	48 logs	8 logs	4 logs	1 pt.

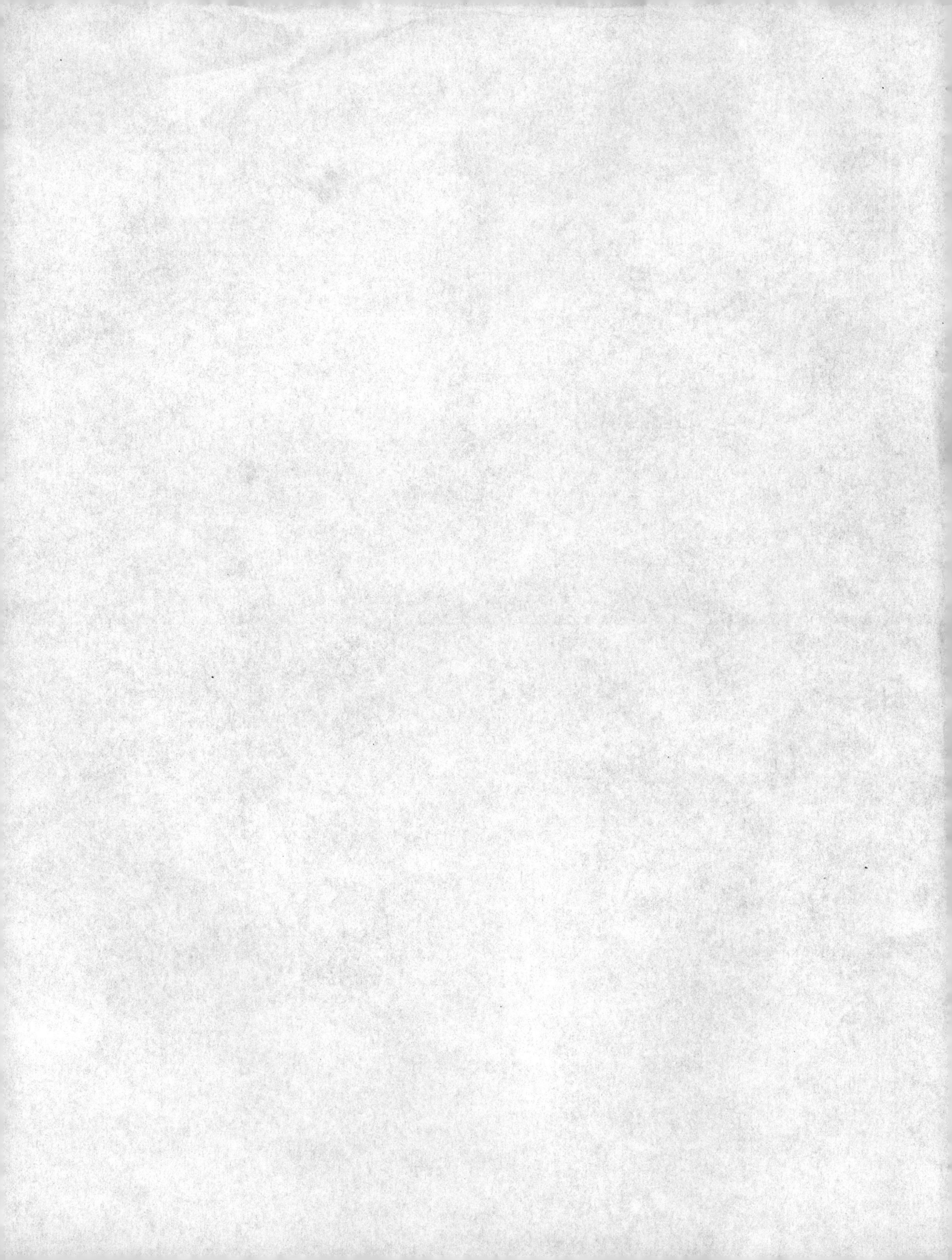